INTERNATIONAL
FINANCIAL
STATISTICS
YEARBOOK

Other Statistical Publications of the International Monetary Fund

Balance of Payments Statistics Yearbook (BOPSY)
Issued in three parts, this annual publication contains balance of payments and international investment position data. Part 1 provides detailed tables on balance of payments statistics for approximately 160 countries and international investment position data for 48 countries. Part 2 presents tables of regional and world totals of major balance of payments components. Part 3 contains descriptions of methodologies, compilation practices, and data sources used by reporting countries *Price:* US$78.

Direction of Trade Statistics (DOTS)
Quarterly issues of this publication provide, for about 154 countries, tables with current data (or estimates) on the value of imports from and exports to their most important trading partners. In addition, similar summary tables for the world, industrial countries, and developing countries are included. The yearbook provides, for the most recent seven years, detailed trade data by country for approximately 184 countries, the world, and major areas. *Price:* Subscription price is US$128 a year (US$89 to university faculty and students) for the quarterly issues and the yearbook. Price for a quarterly issue only is US$25, the yearbook only is US$45, and a guide only is US$12.50.

Government Finance Statistics Yearbook (GFSY)
This annual publication provides detailed data on revenue, grants, expenditure, lending minus repayments, financing, and debt of central governments and indicates the amounts represented by social security funds and extrabudgetary operations. Also provided are data for state and local governments, and information on the institutional units of government. *Price:* US$65.

A Manual on Government Finance Statistics
Issued in 1986, this manual covers concepts, definitions, and procedures for the compilation of government finance statistics. Emphasis is placed on summarizing and organizing statistics appropriately for analysis, planning, and policy formulation. The text focuses on transactions (taxes, expenditures, borrowing, and lending) and on debt. *Price:* US$10.

Balance of Payments Manual
Revised in 1993, the fifth edition of the manual addresses significant changes that have occurred in international transactions since the fourth edition was published in 1977 and presents salient revisions in the structure and classification of international accounts. The new edition also reflects a major shift in orientation that accords prominence to stocks of external financial assets and liabilities (the international investment position) as well as to balance of payments transactions. *Price:* US$27.50.

IFS and *BOPS* CD-ROM Subscriptions

International Financial Statistics (IFS) and *Balance of Payments Statistics (BOPS)* are available on Windows-based CD-ROMs. *Price:* US$1,000 a year for single users (US$350 for university faculty and students); multiple user options are available.

Databases on CD-ROM

The databases for *IFS, BOPS, DOTS,* and *GFS* are available to subscribers on CD-ROM. *Price of each subscription:* US$1,950 a year for single users (US$1,000 for university faculty and students). Redistribution licenses are negotiated on a case-by-case basis; please contact Publication Services.

Subscription Packages

Combined Subscription Package
The combined subscription package includes all issues of *IFS, DOTS, BOPSY, GFSY,* and *Staff Papers,* the Fund's economic journal. *Combined subscription price:* US$446 a year. Airspeed delivery available at additional cost; please inquire.

Combined Statistical Yearbook Subscription
This subscription comprises the *BOPSY,* the *GFSY,* and the yearbooks to *IFS* and *DOTS* at a combined rate of US$195. Because of different publication dates of the four yearbooks, it may take up to one year to service an order. Airspeed delivery available at additional cost; please inquire.

Address orders to
Publication Services, IMF, Washington, DC 20431, USA
Telephone: (202) 623-7430   Telefax: (202) 623-7201   E-mail: publications@imf.org
Internet: http://www.imf.org

Note: Prices include the cost of delivery by surface mail. Enhanced delivery is available for an additional charge.

INTERNATIONAL

FINANCIAL

STATISTICS

YEARBOOK

2000

INTERNATIONAL MONETARY FUND

INTERNATIONAL FINANCIAL STATISTICS
Vol. LIII, 2000
Prepared by the IMF Statistics Department
Carol S. Carson, Director

For information related to this publication, please:
>   fax the Statistics Department at (202) 623-6460,
>   or write Statistics Department
>>   International Monetary Fund
>>   Washington, D.C. 20431
>   or telephone (202) 623-6180.

For copyright inquiries, please fax the Editorial Division at (202) 623-6579.
For purchases only, please contact Publication Services (see information below).

International Financial Statistics (IFS) is a standard source of statistics on
all aspects of international and domestic finance. *IFS* publishes, for most
countries of the world, current data on exchange rates, international
liquidity, international banking, money and banking, interest rates, prices,
production, international transactions (including balance of payments and
international investment position), government finance, and national
accounts. Information is presented in tables for specific countries and in
tables for area and world aggregates. *IFS* is published monthly and
annually in English, French, and Spanish.

Cutoff Date: July 30, 2000

Price: Subscription price is US$289 a year (US$199 to university faculty
and students), which includes the cost of delivery by surface mail, for
twelve monthly issues and the yearbook. Single copy price is US$40 for a
monthly issue and US$72 for a yearbook issue. Enhanced delivery is
available for an additional charge.

Address orders to:
International Monetary Fund
Attention: Publication Services
Washington, D.C. 20431
U.S.A.
Telephone: (202) 623-7430
Telefax: (202) 623-7201
E-mail: publications@imf.org

ISSN 0250-7463
ISBN 1-55775-928-6

POSTMASTER: Send address changes to International Financial
Statistics, Publication Services, 700 19th St., N.W., Washington, D.C.
20431. Postage for periodicals paid at Washington, D.C. USPS 049-610

Recycled paper

TABLE OF CONTENTS

	Page
IMF: Members and Governors, Board of Executive Directors, Management & Senior Officers	vi
Guides to *IFS* Coverage	viii
Introduction	ix

CHARTS

International Reserves	2
Interest Rates	3
Exchange Rates	4
Prices	5
Unit Values and Commodity Prices	6
Trade	7
National Accounts	8

WORLD TABLES

Article VIII Acceptances	13
Exchange Rates Arrangements	14
Exchange Rates..	16
Fund Accounts	21
International Reserves	48
Measures of Money	86
Interest Rates	106
Real Effective Exchange Rate Indices	116
Prices, Wages, Production, Employment	118
International Trade	128
Balance of Payments	146
National Accounts	164
Commodity Prices	180

COUNTRY TABLES

Albania to Zimbabwe	190-1025

COUNTRY NOTES

	1029

The term "country," as used in this publication, does not in all cases refer to a territorial entity that is a state as understood by international law and practice; the term also covers some nonsovereign territorial entities, for which statistical data are maintained and provided internationally on a separate and independent basis.

IMF MEMBERS AND GOVERNORS

Member	Governor*	Alternate*
AFGHANISTAN, ISLAMIC STATE OF	Vacant	Vacant
ALBANIA	Shkelqim Cani	Gramoz Pashko
ALGERIA	Abdelouahab Keramane	Mohammed Laksaci
ANGOLA	Joaquim D. Da Costa David	Aguinaldo Jaime
ANTIGUA AND BARBUDA	John E. St. Luce	Dwight Venner
ARGENTINA	José Luis Machinea	Pedro Pou
ARMENIA	Levon Barkudaryan	Tigran Sargissian
AUSTRALIA	Peter Costello	E. A. Evans
AUSTRIA	Klaus Liebscher	Gertrude Tumpel-Gugerell
AZERBAIJAN	Avaz Alekperov	Elman Siradjogly Rustamov
BAHAMAS, THE	William Allen	Julian W. Francis
BAHRAIN	Adbulla Hassan Saif	Abdulla Khliffa Al-Khalifa
BANGLADESH	Akbar Ali Khan	Mohammed Farashuddin
BARBADOS	Owen S. Arthur	Marion Williams
BELARUS	Petr Petrovich Prokopovich	Nikolay Petrovich Korbut
BELGIUM	Guy Quaden	Gregoire Brouhns
BELIZE	Ralph Fonseca	Keith A. Arnold
BENIN	Abdoulaye Bio Tchane	Idriss L. Daouda
BHUTAN	Sonam Wangchuk	Vacant
BOLIVIA	Herbert Müller Costas	Juan Antonio Morales
BOSNIA AND HERZEGOVINA	Novak Kondic	Jadranko Prlic
BOTSWANA	Linah K. Mohohlo	Freddy Modise
BRAZIL	Pedro Sampaio Malan	Arminio Fraga Neto
BRUNEI DARUSSALAM	Haji Hassanal Bolkiah	Haji Selamat Haji Munap
BULGARIA	Svetoslav Veleslavov Gavriiski	Dimitar Borisov Radev
BURKINA FASO	Tertius Zongo	Lucien Marie Noel Bembamba
BURUNDI	Grégoire Banyiyezako	Cyprien Sinzobahamvya
CAMBODIA	CHEA Chan To	ENG Thaysan
CAMEROON	Edouard Akame Mfoumou	Sadou Hayatou
CANADA	Paul Martin	Gordon G. Thiessen
CAPE VERDE	Antonio Gualberto Do Rosario	Olavo Avelino Garcia Correia
CENTRAL AFRICAN REP.	Anicet-Georges Dologuele	Vacant
CHAD	Mahamat Ali Hassan	Mahamad Amine Ben Barka
CHILE	Carlos A. Massad	Jorge Marshall Rivera
CHINA	Dai Xianglong	LI Ruogu
COLOMBIA	Miguel Urrutia Montoya	Juan Manuel Santos Calderón
COMOROS	Assoumany Aboudou	Said Ahmed Said Ali
CONGO, DEM. REP. OF	Vacant	Vacant
CONGO, REPUBLIC OF	Mathias Dzon	Pacifique Essoïbeka
COSTA RICA	Eduardo Lizano Fait	Leonel Baruch G.
CÔTE D'IVOIRE	Seydou Diarra	N'Golo Coulibaly
CROATIA	Željko Rohatinski	Boris Vujčić
CYPRUS	A. C. Afxentiou	H. G. Akhniotis
CZECH REPUBLIC	Josef Tošovský	Jan Mládek
DENMARK	Bodil Nyboe Andersen	Michael Dithmer
DJIBOUTI	Djama Mahamoud Haid	Houmed Abdou Daoud
DOMINICA	Ambrose George	Ambrose M.J. Sylvester
DOMINICAN REPUBLIC	Héctor Valdez Albizu	Luis Manuel Piantini
ECUADOR	Modesto Correa	Miguel Dávila
EGYPT	Youssef Boutros-Ghali	Ismail Hassan Mohamed
EL SALVADOR	Rafael Barraza	Juan José Daboub
EQUATORIAL GUINEA	Miguel Abia Biteo Boriko	Martin-Crisantos Ebe Mba
ERITREA	Tekie Beyene	Ghebriel Fassil
ESTONIA	Vahur Kraft	Aare Järvan
ETHIOPIA	Teklewold Atnafu	Alemseged Assefa
FIJI	Mahendra Pal Chaudhry	Savenaca Narube
FINLAND	Matti Vanhala	Esko Ollila
FRANCE	Laurent Fabius	Jean-Claude Trichet
GABON	Emile Doumba	Jean-Paul Leyimangoye
GAMBIA, THE	Famara L. Jatta	Momodou Clarke Bajo
GEORGIA	Irakli Managadze	Temur Basilia
GERMANY	Ernst Welteke	Hans Eichel
GHANA	Kwabena D. Duffuor	Victor Selormey
GREECE	Lucas D. Papademos	Nikolaos C. Garganas
GRENADA	Anthony Boatswain	Timothy Antoine
GUATEMALA	Lizardo Arturo Sosa López	Manuel Hirám Maza Castellanos
GUINEA	Ibrahima Kassory Fofana	Ibrahima Cherif Bah
GUINEA-BISSAU	Rui Duarte Barros	Boaventura Eutequio Silva
GUYANA	Bharrat Jagdeo	Dolly Sursattie Singh
HAITI	Fritz Jean	Fred Joseph
HONDURAS	Victoria Asfura de Diaz	Gabriela Nuñez de Reyes
HUNGARY	Gyorgy Suranyi	Péter Adamecz
ICELAND	Birgir Isl. Gunnarsson	Thordur Fridjonsson
INDIA	Yashwant Sinha	Bimal Jalan
INDONESIA	Syahril Sabirin	Noor Fuad
IRAN, ISLAMIC REP. OF	Mohsen Nourbakhsh	Mohammad Jafar Mojarrad
IRAQ	Hikmet M. Al Azawi	Abdul Ahad P. Toma
IRELAND	Charlie McCreevy	Maurice O'Connell
ISRAEL	Avraham B. Shochat	Meir Sokoler
ITALY	Vincenzo Visco	Vincenzo Desario
JAMAICA	Omar Lloyd Davies	Derick Milton Latibeaudiere
JAPAN	Kiichi Miyazawa	Masaru Hayami
JORDAN	Michel Marto	Ziad Fariz
KAZAKHSTAN	Grigori Marchenko	Mazhit Essenbayev
KENYA	Chrysanthus Barnabas Okemo	Micah Kiprono Cheserem
KIRIBATI	Beniamina Tinga	Taneti Maamau

Member	Governor*	Alternate*
KOREA	Hun-Jai Lee	Chol-Hwan Chon
KUWAIT	Ahmed Abdullah Al-Ahmed Al-Sabah	Salem Abdulaziz Al-Sabah
KYRGYZ REPUBLIC	Ulan Sarbanov	Jienbekov Sadriddin
LAO PEOPLE'S DEM. REPUBLIC	Soukanh Mahalath	Yao Phonevantha
LATVIA	Gundars Berzins	Einārs Repše
LEBANON	Riad Toufic Salāmeh	Nasser Saidi
LESOTHO	M.C. Mphutlane	Stephen Mustapha Swaray
LIBERIA	M. Nathaniel Barnes	Elie E. Saleeby
LIBYA	Taher E. Jehaimi	Abdallah Ali Khalifa
LITHUANIA	Reinoldijus Šarkinas	Dalia Grybauskaite
LUXEMBOURG	Jean-Claude Juncker	Yves Mersch
MACEDONIA, FORMER YUGOSLAV REP. OF	Ljube Trpeski	Vacant
MADAGASCAR	Tantely R. G. Andrianarivo	Gaston Edouard Ravelojaona
MALAWI	Elias É. Ngalande	R.P. Dzanjalimodzi
MALAYSIA	Daim Zainuddin	Zeti Akhtar Aziz
MALDIVES	Mohamed Jaleel	Ibrahim Naeem
MALI	Bacari Koné	Bangaly N'ko Traore
MALTA	Michael C. Bonello	David A. Pullicino
MARSHALL ISLANDS	Ruben R. Zackhras	Michael Konelios
MAURITANIA	Mahfoudh Ould Mohamed Ali	Sidi Mohamed Ould Biya
MAURITIUS	Vasant Kumar Bunwaree	Rameswurlall Basant Roi
MEXICO	José Angel Gurria Treviño	Guillermo Ortiz Martinez
MICRONESIA, FEDERATED STATES OF	John Ehsa	Lorin Robert
MOLDOVA	Leonid Talmaci	Valeriu Chiţan
MONGOLIA	Yansanjav Ochirsukh	Jigjid Unenbat
MOROCCO	Mohamed Seqat	Vacant
MOZAMBIQUE	Luísa Dias Diogo	Adriano Afonso Maleiane
MYANMAR	Khin Maung Thein	Kyaw Kyaw Maung
NAMIBIA	Nangolo Mbumba	Tom K. Alweendo
NEPAL	Tilak Rawal	Madhab Prasad Ghimire
NETHERLANDS	A.H.E.M. Wellink	Kees van Dijkhuizen
NEW ZEALAND	Michael Cullen	Donald T. Brash
NICARAGUA	Noel Ramirez	Noel Sacasa
NIGER	Ali Badjo Gamatie	Maliki Barhouni
NIGERIA	Mallam Adamu Ciroma	Joseph Sanusi
NORWAY	Svein Ingvar Gjedrem	Tore Eriksen
OMAN	Ali bin Mohammed bin Moosa	Hamood Sangour Al-Zadjali
PAKISTAN	Ishrat Hussain	Mueen Afzal
PALAU	Tommy E. Remengesau, Jr.	Elbuchel Sadang
PANAMA	Víctor Juliao	Bolívar Pariente
PAPUA NEW GUINEA	Mekere Morauta	Leonard Wilson Kamit
PARAGUAY	Washington Ashwell	Vacant
PERU	Germán Suárez Chávez	Victor Joy Way
PHILIPPINES	Rafael B. Buenaventura	Jose Trinidad Pardo
POLAND	Jaroslaw Bauc	Krzysztof J. Ners
PORTUGAL	Vitor Manuel Riberio Constâncio	António Manuel Pereira Marta
QATAR	Yousef Hussain Kamal	Abdullah Khalid Al-Attiyah
ROMANIA	Emil Iota Ghizari	Mircea Ionut Costea
RUSSIA	Viktor Gerashchenko	Mikhail Zadornov
RWANDA	Donald Kaberuka	François Mutemberezi
ST. KITTS AND NEVIS	Halva Hendrickson	Wendell Lawrence
ST. LUCIA	Kenny D. Anthony	Claire Zenith James
ST. VINCENT AND THE GRENADINES	Arnhim Eustace	Maurice Edwards
SAMOA	Tuilaepa S. Malielegaoi	Hinauri Petana
SAN MARINO	Clelio Galassi	Fausta Morganti
SÃO TOMÉ AND PRÍNCIPE	Maria do Carmo Pires de Carvalho Silveira	Eugénio Lourenço Soares
SAUDI ARABIA	Ibrahim A. Al-Assaf	Hamad Al-Sayyari
SENEGAL	Makhtar Diop	Abdoulaye Diop
SEYCHELLES	James Michel	Norman J.D. Weber
SIERRA LEONE	James O.C. Jonah	James S. Koroma
SINGAPORE	Lee Hsien Loong	Lee Ek Tieng
SLOVAK REPUBLIC	Marián Jusko	Brigita Schmögnerová
SLOVENIA	France Arhar	Samo Nučič
SOLOMON ISLANDS	Rick Nelson Houenipwela	George Kiriau
SOMALIA	Vacant	Vacant
SOUTH AFRICA	Tito Titus Mboweni	Maria Ramos
SPAIN	Rodrigo de Rato Figaredo	Luis Angel Rojo Duque
SRI LANKA	Chandrika Bandaranaika Kumaratunga	Amarananda S. Jayawardena
SUDAN	Vacant	Vacant
SURINAME	L.A.E. Alibux	Henk O. Goedschalk
SWAZILAND	John P. Carmichael	Martin Dlamini
SWEDEN	Urban Bäckström	Sven Hegelund
SWITZERLAND	Hans Meyer	Kaspar Villiger
SYRIAN ARAB REP.	Mohammed Imady	Mohammad Bachar Kabbarah
TAJIKISTAN	Gudomzhon Dzhuraevich Babayev	Murotali M. Alimardonov
TANZANIA	Daniel A.N. Yona	Daudi T.S. Ballali
THAILAND	CHATU MONGOL Sonakul	Pakorn Malakul Na Ayudhya
TOGO	A-H. S.B. Tidjani-Dourodjaye	Mongo Aharh-Kpessou
TONGA	Kinikinilau Tutoatasi Fakafanua	S.T.T. 'Utoikamanu

*According to the latest appointments.

As of August 14, 2000

Member	Governor*	Alternate*	Member	Governor*	Alternate*
Trinidad and Tobago	Brian Kuei Tung	Winston C. Dookeran	Uruguay	César Rodríguez Batlle	Marcelo Brasca
Tunisia	Mohamed El Beji Hamda	Mohamed Daoues	Uzbekistan	MULLAJONOV Faizulla Makhsudjanovich	Tatyana N. Guskova
Turkey	Recep Önal	Gazi Erçel	Vanuatu	Stevens Morking Iatika	Andrew Kausiama
Turkmenistan	Seitbay Kandymov	Khydirkuli M. Achilov	Venezuela, República Bolivariana de	Diego L. Castellanos	Maritza Izaguirre Porras
Uganda	Gerald M. Ssendaula	Charles N. Kikonyogo			
Ukraine	Victor Youshchenko	Ihor Mityukov	Vietnam	Le Duc Thuy	Duong Thu Huong
United Arab Emirates	Sultan Bin Nasser Al-Suwaidi	Mohammed Khalfan Bin Khirbash	Yemen, Republic of	Alawi Saleh Al-Salami	Ahmed Abdul-Rahman Al-Samawi
United Kingdom	Gordon Brown	Edward A. J. George	Zambia	Katele Kalumba	Jacob Mumbi Mwanza
United States	Lawrence H. Summers	Alan Greenspan	Zimbabwe	Simba Herbert Stanley Makoni	Leonard Ladislus Tsumba

*According to the latest appointments.

182 member countries

Board of Executive Directors

Executive Director	From	Alternate	From	Casting Votes of
Karin Lissakers	United States	Vacant		United States
Yukio Yoshimura	Japan	Haruyuki Toyama	Japan	Japan
Bernd Esdar	Germany	Wolf-Dieter Donecker	Germany	Germany
Jean-Claude Milleron	France	Gilles Bauche	France	France
Stephen Pickford	United Kingdom	Stephen Collins	United Kingdom	United Kingdom
Willy Kiekens	Belgium	Johann Prader	Austria	Austria, Belarus, Belgium, Czech Republic, Hungary, Kazakhstan, Luxembourg, Slovak Republic, Slovenia, Turkey
J. de Beaufort Wijnholds	Netherlands	Yuriy G. Yakusha	Ukraine	Armenia, Bosnia and Herzegovina, Bulgaria, Croatia, Cyprus, Georgia, Israel, former Yugoslav Republic of Macedonia, Moldova, Netherlands, Romania, Ukraine
Agustín Carstens	Mexico	Hernán Oyarzábal	Venezuela, República. Bolivariana de	Costa Rica, El Salvador, Guatemala, Honduras, Mexico, Nicaragua, Spain, República Bolivariana de Venezuela,
Riccardo Faini	Italy	Harilaos Vittas	Greece	Albania, Greece, Italy, Malta, Portugal, San Marino
Thomas A. Bernes	Canada	Peter Charleton	Ireland	Antigua and Barbuda, The Bahamas, Barbados, Belize, Canada, Dominica, Grenada, Ireland, Jamaica, St. Kitts and Nevis, St. Lucia, St. Vincent and the Grenadines
Olli-Pekka Lehmussaari	Finland	Åke Törnqvist	Sweden	Denmark, Estonia, Finland, Iceland, Latvia, Lithuania, Norway, Sweden
Gregory F. Taylor	Australia	Jong Nam Oh	Korea	Australia, Kiribati, Korea, Marshall Islands, Federated States of Micronesia, Mongolia, New Zealand, Palau, Papua New Guinea, Philippines, Samoa, Seychelles, Solomon Islands, Vanuatu
Sulaiman M. Al-Turki	Saudi Arabia	Ahmed Alosaimi	Saudi Arabia	Saudi Arabia
Kleo-Thong Hetrakul	Thailand	Cyrillus Harinowo	Indonesia	Brunei Darussalam, Cambodia, Fiji, Indonesia, Lao People's Democratic Republic, Malaysia, Myanmar, Nepal, Singapore, Thailand, Tonga, Vietnam
José Pedro de Morais, Jr.	Angola	Cyrus Rustomjee	South Africa	Angola, Botswana, Burundi, Eritrea, Ethiopia, The Gambia, Kenya, Lesotho, Liberia, Malawi, Mozambique, Namibia, Nigeria, Sierra Leone, South Africa, Swaziland, Tanzania, Uganda, Zambia, Zimbabwe
A. Shakour Shaalan	Egypt	Abdelrazaq F. Al-Faris	United Arab Emirates	Bahrain, Egypt, Iraq, Jordan, Kuwait, Lebanon, Libya, Maldives, Oman, Qatar, Syrian Arab Republic, United Arab Emirates, Republic of Yemen
Aleksei V. Mozhin	Russia	Andrei Lushin	Russia	Russian Federation
Roberto F. Cippa	Switzerland	Wieslaw Szczuka	Poland	Azerbaijan, Kyrgyz Republic, Poland, Switzerland, Tajikistan, Turkmenistan, Uzbekistan
Murilo Portugal	Brazil	Roberto Junguito	Colombia	Brazil, Colombia, Dominican Republic, Ecuador, Guyana, Haiti, Panama, Suriname, Trinidad and Tobago
Vijay L. Kelkar	India	A. G. Karunasena	Sri Lanka	Bangladesh, Bhutan, India, Sri Lanka
Abbas Mirakhor	Islamic Republic of Iran	Mohammed Daïri	Morocco	Algeria, Ghana, Islamic Republic of Iran, Morocco, Pakistan, Tunisia
WEI Benhua	China	Jin Qi	China	China
Ana Maria Jul	Chile	A. Guillermo Zoccali	Argentina	Argentina, Bolivia, Chile, Paraguay, Peru, Uruguay
Alexandre Barro Chambrier	Gabon	Damian Ondo Mañe	Equatorial Guinea	Benin, Burkina Faso, Cameroon, Cape Verde, Central African Republic, Chad, Comoros, Republic of Congo, Côte d'Ivoire, Djibouti, Equatorial Guinea, Gabon, Guinea, Guinea-Bissau, Madagascar, Mali, Mauritania, Mauritius, Niger, Rwanda, São Tomé and Príncipe, Senegal, Togo

Management and Senior Officers

Managing Director	Horst Köhler	Research Department	Michael Mussa, Director
First Deputy Managing Director	Stanley Fischer	Secretary's Department	Shailendra J. Anjaria, Secretary
Deputy Managing Director	Eduardo Aninat	Statistics Department	Carol S. Carson, Director
Deputy Managing Director	Shigemitsu Sugisaki	Technology and General Services Dept.	Brian C. Stuart, Director
Economic Counsellor	Michael Mussa		Warren N. Minami, Associate Director
Human Resources Department	Margaret Kelly, Director	Treasurer's Department	Eduard Brau, Treasurer
African Department	G.E. Gondwe, Director	Western Hemisphere Department	Claudio M. Loser, Director
	Ernesto Hernández-Catá, Associate Director	Office of Budget and Planning	Ernst-Albrecht Conrad, Director
Asia and Pacific Department	Yusuke Horiguchi, Director	Office of Internal Audit and Inspection	Rafael Muñoz, Director
European I Department	Michael C. Deppler, Director	Regional Office for Asia and the Pacific	Kunio Saito, Director
European II Department	John Odling-Smee, Director	Office in Europe (Paris)	Flemming Larsen, Director
External Relations Department	Thomas C. Dawson, II, Director	Office in Geneva	Grant B. Taplin, Assistant Director and Special Trade Representative
Fiscal Affairs Department	Vito Tanzi, Director		
IMF Institute	Mohsin S. Khan, Director	Office at the United Nations	Reinhard Munzberg, Special Represen... to the UN (also supervising th... Office in his personal ca...
Legal Department	François P. Gianviti, General Counsel		
Middle Eastern Department	Paul Chabrier, Director		
Monetary and Exchange Affairs Dept.	Stefan Ingves, Director		
Policy Development and Review Dept.	Jack Boorman, Director		

Guide to the Country Coverage of *IFS* World Tables

Country Codes		Reserves	Money	Consumer Prices	Exports, Imports	Export Unit Values	Import Unit Values	Country Page
001	WORLD							
010	ALL COUNTRIES							
110	*Industrial Countries*							
111	United States	x	x	x	x	w	w	x
156	Canada	x	x	x	x	x	x	x
193	Australia	x	x	x	x	w	w	x
158	Japan	x	x	x	x	x	x	x
196	New Zealand	x	x	x	x	x	x	x
122	Austria	x	x	x	x	x	x	x
124	Belgium	x	x	x	x			x
126	Belgium-Luxembourg				x	x	x	
128	Denmark	x	x	x	x	x	x	x
163	Euro Area	x	x	x	x	x	x	x
172	Finland	x	x	x	x	x	x	x
132	France	x	x	x	x	x	x	x
134	Germany	x	x	x	x	x	x	x
174	Greece	x	x	x	x	x	x	x
176	Iceland	x	x	x	x	x	x	x
178	Ireland	x	x	x	x	x	x	x
136	Italy	x	x	x	x	x	x	x
137	Luxembourg	x		x	x			x
138	Netherlands	x	x	x	x	x	x	x
142	Norway	x	x	x	x	x	x	x
182	Portugal	x	x	x	x	w	w	x
135	San Marino							
184	Spain	x	x	x	x	x	x	x
144	Sweden	x	x	x	x	x	x	x
146	Switzerland	x	x	x	x	x	x	x
112	United Kingdom	x	x	x	x	x	x	x
200	*Developing Countries*							
605	*Africa*							
612	Algeria[2]	x	x	x	x			x
614	Angola		x		x			x
638	Benin	x	x		x			x
616	Botswana[1]	x	x	x	x			x
748	Burkina Faso	x	x	x	x	x	x	x
618	Burundi	x	x	x	x			x
622	Cameroon	x	x	x	x			x
624	Cape Verde	x	x	x	x			x
626	C. African Rep.	x	x	x	x			x
628	Chad	x	x	x	x			x
632	Comoros	x	x	x	x			x
636	Congo, Dem. Rep. of	x	x	x	x			x
634	Congo, Rep. of	x	x	x	x			x
662	Côte d'Ivoire	x	x	x	x	x	x	x
611	Djibouti		x		x			x
642	Equatorial Guinea	x	x	x				x
643	Eritrea							
644	Ethiopia	x	x	x	x			x
646	Gabon	x	x	x	x			x
648	Gambia, The	x	x	x	x			x
652	Ghana	x	x	x	x			x
656	Guinea	x	x		x			x
654	Guinea-Bissau	x	x	x	x			x
664	Kenya	x	x	x	x	x	x	x
666	Lesotho[1]	x		x	x			x
668	Liberia	x	x	x	x	x	x	x
674	Madagascar	x	x	x	x			x
676	Malawi	x	x	x	x	x	x	x
678	Mali	x	x	x	x			x
682	Mauritania	x	x	x	x			x
684	Mauritius	x	x	x	x			x
686	Morocco	x	x	x	x		x	x
688	Mozambique	x		x	x			x
728	Namibia	x	x	x	x			x
692	Niger	x	x	x	x			x
694	Nigeria[2]	x	x	x	x	x		x
696	Réunion				x			
714	Rwanda	x	x	x	x	w		x
856	St. Helena				x			
716	São Tomé & Príncipe		x		x			x
722	Senegal	x	x	x	x	x	x	x
718	Seychelles	x	x	x	x			x
724	Sierra Leone	x	x	x	x			x
726	Somalia							
199	South Africa[1]	x	x	x	x	x	x	x
732	Sudan	x	x	x	x	w		x
734	Swaziland[1]	x	x	x	x			x
738	Tanzania	x	x	x	x			x
742	Togo	x	x	x	x	w	x	x
744	Tunisia	x	x	x	x	x	w	x
746	Uganda	x	x	x	x			x
754	Zambia	x	x	x	x			x
698	Zimbabwe	x	x	x	x	x	x	x
505	*Asia*							
512	Afghanistan, I.S. of	x	x	x	x			
859	American Samoa				x			
513	Bangladesh	x	x	x	x			x
514	Bhutan	x	x	x	x			x
516	Brunei Darussalam				x			
522	Cambodia		x	x				x
924	China, P.R.: Mainland	x	x	x	x			x
532	China, P.R.: Hong Kong	x	x	x	x	x	x	x
546	China, P.R.: Macao				x			
815	Cook Island				x			
819	Fiji	x	x	x	x	x		x
887	French Polynesia				x			
829	Guam				x			
534	India	x	x	x	x	x	x	x
536	Indonesia[2]	x	x	x	x	x		x
826	Kiribati				x			
542	Korea	x	x	x	x	x	x	x
544	Lao P. D. Rep.	x	x	x	x			x
548	Malaysia	x	x	x	x	x	x	x
556	Maldives	x	x	x	x			x
867	Marshall Islands							
868	Micronesia, Fed. States of							
948	Mongolia	x	x	x	x			x
518	Myanmar	x	x	x	x	x		x
836	Nauru				x			
558	Nepal	x	x	x	x			x
839	New Caledonia				x			
564	Pakistan	x	x	x	x	x	x	x
565	Palau							
853	Papua New Guinea	x	x	x	x	x		x
566	Philippines	x	x	x	x	x	x	x
862	Samoa	x	x	x	x			x
576	Singapore	x	x	x	x	w	w	x
813	Solomon Islands	x	x	x	x	x		x
524	Sri Lanka	x	x	x	x	x	x	x
578	Thailand	x	x	x	x	w	x	x
866	Tonga		x	x	x			x
846	Vanuatu	x	x	x	x			x
582	Vietnam	x						
170	*Europe*							
914	Albania	x	x	x	x			x
911	Armenia	x	x	x	x			x
912	Azerbaijan		x	x	x			x
913	Belarus		x	x	x			x
963	Bosnia & Herzegovina							
918	Bulgaria	x	x	x				x
960	Croatia	x	x	x	x			x
423	Cyprus	x	x	x	x	x	x	x
935	Czech Republic	x	x	x	x			x
934	Czechoslovakia	x			x	x	x	
939	Estonia	x	x	x	x			x
816	Faeroe Islands				x			
915	Georgia	x	x	x	x			x
823	Gibraltar				x			
944	Hungary	x	x	x	x	w	w	x
916	Kazakhstan	x		x	x			x
917	Kyrgyz Rep.		x	x				x
941	Latvia	x	x	x	x			x
946	Lithuania	x	x	x	x			x
962	Macedonia, former Yugoslav Rep. of	x	x	x				x
181	Malta	x	x	x	x	x	x	x
921	Moldova	x	x	x	x			x
964	Poland	x	x	x	x	w	w	x
968	Romania	x	x	x	x			x
922	Russia	x	x	x	x			x
936	Slovak Republic	x	x	x	x			x
961	Slovenia	x	x	x	x			x
923	Tajikistan							
186	Turkey	x	x	x	x	x	x	x
925	Turkmenistan							
926	Ukraine	x	x	x	x			x
927	Uzbekistan							
188	Yugoslavia, Socialist Federal Rep. of	x	x	x	x			
405	*Middle East*							
419	Bahrain	x	x	x	x			x
469	Egypt	x	x	x	x			x
429	Iran, I.R. of[2]	x	x	x	x	w		x
433	Iraq[2]	x	x	x	x	w		x
436	Israel	x	x	x	x	x	x	x
439	Jordan	x	x	x	x	x	x	x
443	Kuwait[2]	x	x	x	x	w		x
446	Lebanon	x	x		x			x
672	Libya[2]	x	x	x	x	w		x
449	Oman[2]	x	x		x	w		x
453	Qatar[2]	x	x	x	x	w		x
456	Saudi Arabia[2]	x	x	x	x	w		x
463	Syrian Arab Rep.	x	x	x	x	x	x	x
466	United Arab Emirates[2]	x	x		x	w		x
473	Yemen Arab Rep.	x	x	x	x			
459	Yemen, P. D. Rep.	x	x	x	x			
474	Yemen, Republic of	x	x					x
205	*Western Hemisphere*							
311	Antigua & Barbuda	x	x	x	x			x
213	Argentina	x	x	x	x			x
314	Aruba	x	x					x
313	Bahamas, The	x	x	x	x			x
316	Barbados	x	x	x	x			x
339	Belize	x	x		x			x
319	Bermuda				x			
218	Bolivia	x	x	x	x	x		x
223	Brazil	x	x	x	x	x	x	x
377	Cayman Islands							
228	Chile	x	x	x	x			x
233	Colombia	x	x	x	x	w	w	x
238	Costa Rica	x	x	x	x			x
928	Cuba	x						
321	Dominica	x	x	x	x			x
243	Dominican Rep.	x	x	x	x	x		x
248	Ecuador	x	x	x	x	x		x
253	El Salvador	x	x	x	x			x
323	Falkland Islands				x			
326	Greenland				x			
328	Grenada	x	x	x	x	x		x
329	Guadeloupe				x			
258	Guatemala	x	x	x	x			x
333	Guiana, French				x			
336	Guyana	x	x	x	x			x
263	Haiti	x	x	x	x			x
268	Honduras	x	x	x	x	x		x
343	Jamaica	x	x	x	x			x
349	Martinique				x			
273	Mexico	x	x	x	x			x
351	Montserrat				x			
353	Netherlands Ant.	x	x	x	x			x
278	Nicaragua	x	x	x	x			x
283	Panama	x	x	x	x	x		x
288	Paraguay	x	x	x	x	x		x
293	Peru	x	x	x	x	x		x
361	St. Kitts & Nevis	x	x	x	x			x
362	St. Lucia	x	x	x	x			x
363	St. Pierre & Miquelon		x			x		
364	St. Vincent and the Grenadines	x	x	x	x			x
366	Suriname	x	x	x	x	x		x
369	Trinidad & Tobago	x	x	x	x	x	x	x
298	Uruguay	x	x	x	x			x
299	Venezuela, República Bolivariana de[2]	x	x	x	x	w	w	x
999	*Oil Exporting Countries*							
201	*Non-Oil Developing Countries*							

Country pages for 172 countries

[1] South African trade data refer to the South African Common Customs Area and include data for Botswana, Lesotho and Swaziland.
[2] These countries comprise Oil Exporting Countries grouping shown as a memorandum item to the world tables. The memorandum item for Non-Oil Developing Countries shown in the world tables comprises the remaining Developing Countries.
Country indices compiled from specific prices are marked "w."

Guide to the Commodity Coverage of *IFS* Country Pages

dr	Aluminum	156
u	Bananas	248
k	Beef	111 193 213
fl	Butter	196
vr	Coal	193
r	Cocoa beans	223 652
ai	Coconut oil	566
e	Coffee	223 233 386 799
c	Copper	111 112 156 228
ag	Copra	566 813
j	Corn (Maize)	111 578
f	Cotton	111 469
al	Fish	176 556 813
	Fishmeal	176 293
kr	Gold	112 156 199 233
bf	Groundnuts	694
p	Hides, Skins	111
g	Iron ore	223
x	Jute	513
pf	Lamb	196
v	Lead	111 112
vx	Logs	548
w	Manganese	534
ul	Newsprint	111 172
pt	Nickel	156
df	Palm kernels	694
dg	Palm oil	548
a	Petroleum	001 111 112 124 142
a	Petroleum (cont.)	156 218 233 248 273 299 369 419 429 433 443 449 453 456 466 536 612 634 672 694 744 968
aw	Phosphates	686
wx	Plywood	566
qr	Potash	156
n	Rice	111 518 578
l	Rubber	111 548 578
rm	Sawnwood	548
bl	Shrimp	111
y	Silver	111
ml	Sisal	639
jf	Soybeans	111
jj	Soybean meal	111
ji	Soybean oil	111
rr	Steel	137
i	Sugar	111 112 223 566
as	Superphosphate	111
s	Tea	112 524
q	Tin	112 218 548 578
m	Tobacco	111
ur	Urea	170
d	Wheat	111 193 213
sl	Wood pulp	144
h	Wool	112 193 196
t	Zinc	111 112 156 218

INTRODUCTION

The yearbook and the monthly issues of *International Financial Statistics (IFS)* consist of country pages and world tables. The country pages normally include data on a country's exchange rates, international liquidity, money and banking accounts, interest rates, production, prices, international transactions, government accounts, and national accounts. Selected series are drawn from the country pages and published in the form of area and world tables in the first part of the yearbook and in monthly issues of *IFS*.

This yearbook reports annual data for the years 1970 through 1999; the available data from 1948 are maintained in the Fund's Economic Information System (EIS). These earlier data can be consulted in previous issues of the yearbook and are available on CD-ROM as described in section 14.

"Country" in this publication refers to a territorial entity that is a state as understood by international law and practice; the term also covers the Euro Area and some nonsovereign territorial entities, for which statistical data are provided internationally on a separate and independent basis.

The following sections describe conceptual and technical aspects of various data published in the *IFS*. Sections 1 through 9 provide general information on the methodologies used in compiling categories of statistics. Sections 10 through 15 discuss the calculation of area and world aggregates, the presentation of charts, the standardization of country and line codes, the use of symbols, conventions, and abbreviations, the production of the *IFS* CD-ROM, and country page notes.

More detailed notes relating to coverage, deviations from the standard methodologies, and discontinuities in the data are published on the individual country pages and world tables of the monthly issues.

1. Exchange Rates and Exchange Rate Arrangements

The country pages carry time series of exchange rates expressed in U.S. dollars per national currency unit or vice versa and an exchange rate expressed in national currency units per SDR (the unit of account for the Fund). The exchange rates are classified into three broad categories, reflecting the role of the authorities in the determination of the exchange rates and/or the multiplicity of exchange rates in a country. **Market rate** is used to describe exchange rates determined largely by market forces; **official rate** is used to describe an exchange rate determined by the authorities, sometimes in a flexible manner. For countries maintaining multiple exchange arrangements, the rates are labeled **principal rate, secondary rate**, and **tertiary rate**.

The SDR values are classified and coded as follows:

Series **aa** denotes the end-of-period national currency value of the SDR, and series **ac** denotes the end-of-period SDR value of the national currency unit. The SDR rates in terms of U.S. dollars—series **sa, sb, sc**, and **sd**—are also given on the country page for the United States. Series **sa** and **sc** refer to end-of-period values of U.S. dollars per SDR and SDRs per U.S. dollar, respectively; series **sb** and **sd** are the geometric averages of values within the period.

The exchange rates in U.S. dollar terms are classified and coded as follows:

Series **ae** refers to end of period, and series **rf** refers to period averages, of market exchange rates and official exchange rates for countries quoting rates in units of national currency per U.S. dollar. Correspondingly, series **ag** denotes end of period, and series **rh** denotes period averages, of market exchange rates and official rates for countries quoting rates in U.S. dollars per unit of national currency. For the period average rates **rf** and **rh**, the data are the monthly average of market rates or official rates of the reporting country, or, if those are not available, monthly average rates in New York. If the latter are not available, estimates based on simple averages of the end-of-month market rates quoted in the reporting country are used.

The end-of-period rates (**sa** and **sc**, **aa** and **ac**, **ae** and **ag**) are reciprocals of each other. Also, the period average SDR rates in terms of the U.S. dollar (**sb** and **sd**) are reciprocals of each other because they are calculated as geometric averages. Other period average rates (**rf** and **rh**) are calculated as arithmetic averages and are not reciprocals.

The country pages carry two U.S. dollar series—either **ae** and **rf** or **ag** and **rh**—depending on the form in which the exchange rate is quoted.

All trade figures in *IFS* are converted from national currency values to U.S. dollars and from U.S. dollar values to national currency, using series **rf**. Conversions are based on the data available for the shortest period, and these data are summed to obtain data for longer periods. Conversion is based on longer period rates of only the difference, if any, between the longer period data and the sum of the shorter period data.

The country page notes in the monthly issues of *IFS* identify the exchange rates used.

Lines **w, x**, and **y** are presented for members maintaining dual or multiple exchange rate systems, which often reflect wide ranges of exchange rates in effect in a particular country. Notes on the relevant country pages in the monthly issues describe current exchange rate systems and identify the exchange rates shown.

Euro and European Currency Unit (ECU)

The country pages of the member countries of the European Union (EU) (Austria, Belgium, Denmark, Finland, France, Germany, Greece, Ireland, Italy, Luxembourg, the Netherlands, Portugal, Spain, Sweden, and the United Kingdom), Norway, and the United States contain a time series for periods prior to January 1999 on the value of the European currency unit (ECU). The European Monetary Institute

(EMI), which assumed the functions of the European Monetary Cooperation Fund on January 1, 1994, issued the ECU against gold and foreign-exchange deposits by the central bank of the EU member states. The ECU was defined as a basket of currencies of the EU member countries. The share of each currency in the basket was based on the gross national product and foreign trade of the country issuing that currency. Representative market exchange rates for the U.S. dollar, as reported by member countries, were used to calculate an ECU equivalent, first in U.S. dollars and then in the currencies of the member countries. Series **ea** and **ec** refer to end-of-period values of national currency units per ECU and ECUs per unit of national currency, respectively; series **eb** and **ed** are the arithmetic averages of values within the period.

On January 1, 1999, the euro replaced the ECU, and irrevocable conversion factors for the euro–which fixed the central rates between the euro and the currencies participating in the exchange rate mechanism–were adopted for the eleven countries in the Euro Area. The irrevocable fixed factors for converting the national currencies into euros (legally mandated to have six significant digits) are Austria (S 13.7603), Belgium (BF 40.3399), Finland (Fmk 5.94573), France (F 6.55957), Germany (DM 1.95583), Ireland (IR£0.787564), Italy (Lit 1936.27), Luxembourg (Lux F 40.3399), the Netherlands (f. 2.20371), Portugal (Esc 200.482), and Spain (Pta 166.386). An accord established compulsory intervention rates for the Danish krone (± 2.25 percent around the euro central rate) and the Greek drachma (± 15 percent around the euro central rate) from January 1, 1999 onwards. In addition, the member countries of the Bank of Central African States and the Central Bank of West African States changed the peg of their currencies from the French franc to the euro, at a rate of CFAF 655.957 per euro from January 1, 1999 onwards. A few other countries also have pegged their currencies to the euro.

Effective Exchange Rates

Measures of effective exchange rates, compiled by the IMF Research Department, the Policy and Review Department, the Statistics Department, and the area departments, are provided in the country pages, the Euro Area pages, and the world tables. (For a description of the latter, see section 10 of this introduction.) A **nominal effective exchange rate** index represents the ratio (expressed on the base 1995=100) of an index of the period average exchange rate of the currency in question to a weighted geometric average of exchange rates for the currencies of selected countries and the Euro Area. A **real effective exchange rate** index is defined as a nominal effective exchange rate index adjusted for relative movements in national price or cost indicators of the home country and selected countries and the Euro Area. The Fund's calculated effective exchange rates data are published only for countries that have given their approval. It should be noted that similar indices that are calculated by country authorities could generate different results.

In both cases an increase in the index reflects an appreciation. In view of certain conceptual and data-related limitations, particularly where Fund estimates have been utilized, movements in nominal and real effective exchange rates need to be interpreted with considerable caution. For ease of comparison, the average exchange rate expressed in terms of U.S. dollars per unit of each of the national currencies (*line* **ah**) is also given in an index form on the basis of 1995=100 (*line* **ahx**).

A Fund working paper entitled "A Primer on the IMF's Information Notice System" (WP/97/71), distributed in May 1997, provides background on the concepts and methodology underlying the effective exchange rates.

Lines **neu** *and* **reu**

The pages for 18 industrial countries and the Euro Area, for which data are available for normalized unit labor costs in manufacturing, include a nominal effective exchange rate index (*line* **neu**) with weights derived from trade in manufactured goods among industrial countries over the period 1989–91. Also published for these countries (excluding Australia and New Zealand) and the Euro Area (excluding Ireland and Portugal) is a real effective exchange rate index (*line* **reu**), which is compiled from the nominal effective exchange rate index (*line* neu) and from a cost indicator of relative normalized unit labor costs in manufacturing. These indices (*lines* reu and **neu**) are discussed more fully in the world tables section of this introduction. A selection of other measures of real effective exchange rates for these countries and the Euro Area, using alternative measures of costs and prices, is shown in the world table *Real Effective Exchange Rates Indices*.

Lines **nec** *and* **rec**

The country pages for selected other countries include a nominal effective exchange rate index (*line* nec) based on a methodology that takes account of each country's trade in both manufactured goods and primary products with its partner—or competitor—countries. From 1990 onwards, the index is weighted by a set of weights based on disaggregated trade data for manufactured goods and primary products covering the three-year period 1988–90. Prior to that, the weights are for the three-year span 1980–82. The series based on the old weights and the new weights are linked by splicing at December 1989, and the reference base is shifted to 1995=100.

For manufactured goods, trade by type of good and market is distinguished in the database, so it is possible to make some allowance at a disaggregated level for competition among various exporters in a foreign market (i.e., third-market competition) as well as that arising from bilateral trade links. For primary products the weights assigned depend principally on a country's role as a global supplier or purchaser of the product. Trade in crude petroleum, petroleum, and other energy products is excluded. For some countries that depend heavily on tourism, bilateral exports of tourism services averaged over 1988–90 are also included in the calculation of the competitiveness weights.

The real effective exchange rate index (*line* **rec**) is derived from the nominal effective exchange rate index, adjusted for relative changes in consumer prices. The use of consumer price indices as a measure of domestic costs and prices for these countries typically reflects the use of consumer prices by the reference and partner–or competitor–countries in the compilation of these indices. Consumer price indices are frequently available on a monthly basis.

Line **ahx**

The notes to the country pages in the monthly issues provide information on exceptions in the choice of the period average exchange rate index (generally *line* **ahx**) and the consumer price index (generally *line 64*). For countries where multiple exchange rates are in effect, Fund staff estimates of a weighted average exchange rate, constructed as an average of the various exchange rates with weights reflecting the share of trade transacted at each rate, are utilized in many cases.

For countries where a weighted average exchange rate cannot be calculated, the principal rate, generally *line* **ahx**, is used. For a relatively small number of countries, notes on the country pages in the monthly issues indicate where alternative price indices, such as the wholesale/producer price index or a weighted average of several price indices, are used, where data constraints have made it necessary to use weighting schemes based on aggregate bilateral non-oil trade data, and where trade in services (such as tourism) has been taken into account.

SDR Value

Prior to July 1974, the value of the SDR was fixed in terms of U.S. dollars as follows: SDR 1=U.S. dollar 1 through November 1971, SDR 1=U.S. dollar 1.08571 from December 1971 through January 1973, and SDR 1=U.S. dollar 1.20635 from February 1973 through June 1974.

Beginning in July 1974, the value of the SDR is determined daily by the Fund on the basis of a basket of currencies, with each currency assigned a weight in the determination of that value. In the derivation of the SDR value, the currencies of the basket are valued at their market exchange rates for the U.S. dollar, and the U.S. dollar equivalents of each of the currencies are summed to yield the rate of the SDR in terms of the U.S. dollar. The method of calculating the U.S. dollar/SDR exchange rate remains the same, although the number and weights of currencies in the SDR basket have changed over time. The currencies that determine the value of the SDR and the amount of each of these currencies in the SDR basket are reviewed every five years. The rates for the SDR in terms of other currencies are derived from the market exchange rates of these currencies for the U.S. dollar and the U.S. dollar rate for the SDR.

From July 1974 through June 1978, the currencies included in the basket were those of the countries whose share in world exports of goods and services averaged more than 1 percent in the period 1968–72. This established a basket of 16 currencies with the relative weight for each currency broadly proportionate to the country's exports but modified for the U.S. dollar to reflect its real weight in the world economy. In order to preserve the continuity of valuation, the amount of each of the 16 currencies in the basket used in the calculation was such that on June 28, 1974 the value of SDR 1=U.S. dollar 1.20635.

From July 1978 through December 1980, the composition of the basket was changed on the basis of updated data. The revised basket of 16 currencies was based on statistics for the period 1972–76. The weights of some currencies were also changed. The amounts of each of the 16 currencies in the revised basket used in the calculation were such as to ensure that the value of the SDR in terms of any currency on June 30, 1978 was exactly the same in the revised valuation as in the previous valuation.

From January 1981 through December 1985, the SDR valuation basket consisted of the currencies of the five members having the largest exports of goods and services during the period 1975–79, that is, the U.S. dollar, deutsche mark, French franc, Japanese yen, and pound sterling. The weights for the five currencies (U.S. dollar, 42 percent; deutsche mark, 19 percent; French franc, Japanese yen, and pound sterling, 13 percent each) broadly reflected the relative importance of these currencies in international trade and finance, based on the value of the exports of goods and services of the members issuing these currencies and the balances of their currencies officially held by members of the Fund over the five-year period 1975–79.

From January 1986 through December 1990, the SDR valuation basket consisted of the currencies of the five members having the largest exports of goods and services during the period 1980–84, that is, the U.S. dollar, deutsche mark, French franc, Japanese yen, and pound sterling. The weights for the five currencies were as follows: U.S. dollar, 42 percent; deutsche mark, 19 percent; Japanese yen, 15 percent; French franc and pound sterling, 12 percent each.

From January 1991 through December 1995, the SDR valuation basket consisted of the currencies of the five members having the largest exports of goods and services during the period 1985–89, that is, the U.S. dollar, deutsche mark, French franc, Japanese yen, and pound sterling. The weights for the five currencies were as follows: U.S. dollar, 40 percent; deutsche mark, 21 percent; Japanese yen, 17 percent; French franc and pound sterling, 11 percent each.

Beginning on January 1, 1996, the SDR valuation basket weights were 39 percent for the U.S. dollar, 21 percent for the deutsche mark, 18 percent for the Japanese yen, and 11 percent each for the French franc and pound sterling.

On January 1, 1999, the currency amount of deutsche mark and French francs were replaced with equivalent amounts of euros, based on the fixed conversion rates between the euro and the deutsche mark and French franc announced on December 31, 1998 by the European Council. The currencies' weights in the valuation basket reflect their relative importance in international trade and reserves, as measured by the value of exports of goods and services of the countries issuing the currency and the balance of the currencies held as reserve members of the Fund. As of January 1, 1999, the SDR valuation basket weights are the sum of the values of the amounts of each currency in the following amounts: 39 percent for the U.S. dollar, 32 percent for the euro (in replacement of the 21 percent for the deutsche mark and 11 percent for the French franc), 18 percent for the Japanese yen, and 11 percent for the pound sterling.

Exchange Rate Tables

The table on exchange rate arrangements is based mainly on information supplied to the Fund on the exchange rate arrangements that individual member countries apply; such notification is required under Article IV, Section 2(a) of the amended Articles of Agreement of the Fund, which entered into force on April 1, 1978. The classification in the table reflects judgments by the Fund staff on the basis of the information obtained from member countries.

The table on market, official, and principal rates provides, in terms of national currency units per SDR, end-of-period rates for the currencies of Fund members, Hong Kong (Special Administrative Region as of 1997), and Netherlands Antilles. The exchange rate table on SDR rates gives the monthly, quarterly, and annual SDR rates in terms of U.S. dollars and the reciprocal of these rates.

Method of Deriving IFS Exchange Rates

For countries that have introduced new currencies, the rates shown in *IFS* for the period prior to the introduction of the most recent currency represent factors that may be used to convert national currency data in *IFS* to U.S. dollar or SDR data. In such cases, the conversion factors are constructed by chain-linking the exchange rates of the old and the new currencies, using as a basis the value of the new currency relative to the old currency as established by the issuing agency at the time that the new currency was introduced. Notes on the introduction of new currencies are found on individual country pages in the monthly issues of *IFS*.

For countries that are members of the Euro Area, the exchange rates shown on individual country pages are expressed in national currency units per SDR or per U.S. dollar through 1998, and in euros per SDR or per U.S. dollar thereafter.

A detailed description of the derivation of the exchange rates in *IFS*, as well as conceptual and technical issues associated with these rates, is contained in the *IFS Supplement on Exchange Rates*, No. 9 (1985).

2. Fund Accounts (Fund Position)

Details of members' positions in the Fund are presented in the Fund Position section of the country pages and in 12 world tables.

The world table *Fund Accounts: Arrangements* reports the current status of stand-by, extended, and poverty reduction and growth (previously, the enhanced structural adjustment) arrangements. The table *Fund Accounts: Position to*

Date reports latest monthly data on members' Fund positions, including quota, reserve position in the Fund, total Fund credit and loans outstanding, Fund holdings of currencies, and positions in the SDR Department. The table *Financing Components of Members' Outstanding Obligations to the Fund* reports latest monthly data on the sources of financing of Fund credit and loans outstanding.

The tables *Purchases (.2kk.)* and *Repurchases (.2lk.)* relate to transactions within the General Resources Account (GRA). The tables *Loan Disbursements (.2kl.)* and *Repayments of Loans (.2ll.)* relate to the Structural Adjustment Facility (SAF), Poverty Reduction and Growth Facility (PRGF: which is previously named Enhanced Structural Adjustment Facility–ESAF), and Trust Fund loans. The table *Total Fund Credit and Loans Outstanding (.2tl.)* relates to the outstanding use of Fund resources under the GRA and to outstanding loans under the SAF, PRGF, and Trust Fund. The table *Use of Fund Credit: GRA (.2egs)* relates to the outstanding use of Fund resources under the GRA.

The world table *SDRs (.1b.s)* shows holdings of SDRs by members and includes a foot table showing SDR holdings by all participants, the IMF, other holders, and the world. The table *Fund Accounts: Borrowing Agreements* reports the current status of the Fund's borrowing activities. The table *Reserve Position in the Fund (.1c.s)* relates to members' claims on the Fund.

Monthly issues of *IFS* give a description in the introduction of members' positions and the underlying transactions. A more detailed description of Fund accounts is contained in the IMF's *Financial Organization and Operations of the IMF*, Pamphlet No. 45, fifth edition, 1998.

3. International Liquidity

The international liquidity sections on the country pages include the U.S. dollar value of monetary authorities' holdings of SDRs, reserve position in the Fund, foreign exchange, and the sum of these items—*Total Reserves minus Gold (line 11.d)*. (Monetary authorities comprise central banks and, to the extent that they perform monetary authorities' functions, currency boards, exchange stabilization funds, and treasuries.) The country pages also show official gold holdings expressed in millions of fine troy ounces and valued, according to national practice, in U.S. dollars.

The international liquidity section of the Euro Area page covers assets of the European Central Bank and the eleven national central banks of the countries that adopted the euro in January 1999.

Beginning in January 1999, total reserves for the Euro Area and individual Euro Area countries are based on the statistical definition of international reserves adopted by the European Central Bank's Statistics Committee in December 1998. They are defined on a Euro Area-wide residency basis and include reserve assets denominated only in currencies of non-Euro Area countries. All positions with residents of other Euro Area countries and with the ECB are excluded from reserve assets.

Foreign Exchange

Foreign Exchange (line 1d.d) includes monetary authorities' claims on nonresidents in the form of foreign banknotes, bank deposits, treasury bills, short- and long-term government securities, ECUs (for periods prior to January 1999), and other claims usable in the event of balance of payments need.

Before December 1971, when the U.S. dollar was at par with the SDR, foreign exchange data were compiled and expressed in terms of U.S. dollars at official par values. Conversions from national currencies to U.S. dollars from December 1971 through January 1973 were calculated at the cross rates reflecting the parities and central rates agreed to in December 1971. From February 1973 through June 1974, foreign exchange was valued at the cross rates of parities or central rates for countries having effective parities or central rates, and at market rates for the Canadian dollar, Irish pound, Italian lira, Japanese yen, and pound sterling. Beginning in July 1974, foreign exchange is valued at end-of-month market rates or, in the absence of market rate quotations, at other prevailing official rates.

Until December 31, 1998, the member countries of the European Union (Austria, Belgium, Denmark, Finland, France, Germany, Greece, Ireland, Italy, Luxembourg, the Netherlands, Portugal, Spain, Sweden, and the United Kingdom) held ECU deposits with the European Monetary Cooperation Fund (EMCF) and/or its successor, the European Monetary Institute (EMI). In the reserves data for each country, deposits of gold and foreign exchange with the EMCF were excluded from gold and foreign exchange holdings, but equivalent amounts of ECU deposits were included in foreign exchange reserves. These deposits were transferred from the EMCF to the EMI upon its creation on January 1, 1994 and to the European Central Bank (ECB) when it became the successor to the EMI on June 1, 1998.

On January 1, 1999, the Eurosystem—the ECB and the national central banks (NCBs) of the eleven member states in the Euro Area—assumed the task of conducting the single monetary policy for the Euro Area. Each NCB deposited gold and foreign exchange with the ECB. Also on January 1, 1999, the euro replaced the ECU at a rate of one euro per one ECU.

For the Euro Area countries, *Total Reserves minus Gold (line 1l.d)* is defined, in broad accordance with the fifth edition of the *Balance of Payments Manual*, to include the monetary authorities' holdings of SDRs, reserve position in the Fund, and foreign exchange, including financial derivative claims on non-Euro Area countries. Claims among Euro Area countries and all euro-denominated claims on non-Euro Area countries are excluded from reserves. Total reserves of the Euro Area comprise the reserve holdings of the NCBs and ECB. Definitions of reserves at the national and Euro Area levels are harmonized.

Other Foreign Assets, Foreign Liabilities

Time series, where significant, are also provided on other foreign assets and foreign liabilities of the monetary authorities. *Other Assets (line 3..d)* usually comprise claims on nonresidents that are of limited usability in the event of balance of payments need, such as balances under bilateral payments agreements and holdings of inconvertible currencies. (Claims on nonresidents under *Other Assets (line 3..d)* are included in *line 11.*) *Other Liabilities (line 4..d)* comprise foreign liabilities of the monetary authorities other than use of Fund credit (GRA), SAF, PRGF , and Trust Fund loans outstanding; positions with the Fund are reported separately, in terms of SDRs, in the Fund position section of the country pages.

Foreign Accounts of Other Financial Institutions

Where significant, foreign accounts of financial institutions other than the monetary authorities are also reported in the international liquidity section of the country pages. The measures provided are sometimes reported directly in U.S. dollars and may differ slightly in coverage, but they are normally U.S. dollar equivalents of time series reported in the appropriate money and banking sections as follows: *line 7a.d* is derived from *line 21*; *line 7b.d* is derived from *line 26c* plus *line 26cl*; *line 7e.d* is derived from *line 41*; and *line 7f.d* is derived from *line 46c* plus *line 46cl*.

In addition, the international liquidity section for some countries provides summary data on the foreign accounts of special or international license banks that operate locally but are not presently covered in the money and banking section. Their foreign assets are reported as *line 7k.d* and their foreign liabilities as *line 7m.d*, when available (although *7m.d* is not shown separately if it is equal to *line 7k.d*).

World Tables on Reserves

World tables on reserves report all country page time series on reserves, other than gold at national valuation, and present totals for countries, country groups, and the world. There is also a world table on total reserves, with gold valued at SDR 35 per ounce. A foot table to that table reports total reserves of all countries, including gold valued both at SDR 35 per ounce and at market prices. Also included is a world table on the ratio of nongold reserves (*line 1l.d*) to imports (*line 71..d*) expressed in terms of the number of weeks of imports covered by the stock of nongold reserves.

Apart from that table and the world table on gold holdings in physical terms (see next paragraph), world tables on reserves are expressed in SDRs. Foreign exchange holdings are expressed in terms of SDRs by converting the U.S. dollar values shown on the country pages on the basis of the end-period U.S. dollar/SDR rate.

Similarly, a foot table to the world table on gold indicates gold holdings valued at SDR 35 per ounce and at market prices for all countries, the IMF, the ECB , the Bank for International Settlements (BIS), and the world. A simple addition of the gold held by all of these holders would involve double-counting, because most of the gold deposited with the BIS is also included in countries' official gold reserves. *IFS* therefore reports BIS gold holdings net of gold deposits; negative figures for BIS gold holdings are balanced by forward operations.

The same foot table also provides data on (1) the U.S. dollar price of gold on the London market, (2) the U.S. dollar/SDR rate, (3) gold transactions that refer to gold sold by the Fund at auction in connection with the Trust Fund, which derived its resources from the profits of the auctions, from income earned from the investment of those profits, and from voluntary contributions or loans, and (4) the end-period derived market price of gold in terms of SDRs.

4. Money and Banking

Statistics on the accounts of monetary and other financial institutions are given in sections 10 through 50 on the country pages.

Monetary Authorities

Data on monetary authorities (section 10) measure the stock of reserve money comprising currency in circulation, deposits of the deposit money banks, and deposits of other residents, apart from the central government, with the monetary authorities.

Major aggregates of the accounts on the asset side are foreign assets (*line 11*) and domestic assets (*line 12**). Domestic assets are broken down into *Claims on Central Government (line 12a)*, *Claims on Deposit Money Banks (line 12e)*, and, if sizable, *Claims on State and Local Governments (line 12b)*; *Claims on Nonfinancial Public Enterprises (line 12c)*; *Claims on the Private Sector (line 12d)*; *Claims on Other Banking Institutions (line 12f)*; and *Claims on Nonbank Financial Institutions (line 12g)*.

In some countries, where insufficient data are available to provide disaggregations of claims on governmental bodies other than the central government, a classification of *Claims on Official Entities (line 12bx)* is used. In addition, in countries where insufficient data are available to provide disaggregations of claims on other banking institutions and nonbank financial institutions, a classification of *Claims on Other Financial Institutions (line 12f)* is used.

The principal liabilities of monetary authorities consist of *Reserve Money (line 14)*, *Foreign Liabilities (line 16c)*, and *Central Government Deposits (line 16d)*.

Monetary authorities' data in *IFS* generally consolidate the accounts of the central bank with the accounts arising from monetary functions undertaken by other institutions. These functions include the issuance of currency, the holding of international reserves, and the conducting of Fund account transactions.

Deposit Money Banks

Deposit money banks' data (section 20) measure the stock of deposit money. Major aggregates of the accounts on the assets side are *Reserves (line 20)*, comprising domestic currency holdings and deposits with the monetary authorities, *Foreign Assets (line 21)*, and *Claims on Other Resident Sectors (lines 22*)*, as described in the preceding section on monetary authorities (*lines 12**).

The principal liabilities consist of *Demand Deposits (line 24)*, *Time, Savings, and Foreign Currency Deposits (line 25)*, *Foreign Liabilities (line 26c)*, and *Central Government Deposits (line 26d)*.

Deposit money banks comprise commercial banks and other financial institutions that accept transferable deposits, such as demand deposits.

Monetary Survey

Monetary authorities' and deposit money banks' data, consolidated into a monetary survey (section 30), measure the stock of narrow *Money (line 34)*, which comprises transferable deposits and currency outside deposit money banks, and the *Quasi-Money (line 35)* liabilities of these institutions, which comprise time, savings, and foreign currency deposits. Standard relationships between the monetary survey lines and the component lines in sections 10 and 20 are as follows:

Foreign Assets (Net) (line 31n) equals the sum of foreign asset *lines 11* and *21*, less the sum of foreign liability *lines 16c* and *26c*.

Claims on Central Government (Net) (line 32an) equals claims on central government (the sum of *lines 12a* and *22a*), less central government deposits (the sum of *lines 16d* and *26d*), plus, where applicable, the counterpart entries of *lines 24..i* and *24..r* (private sector demand deposits with the postal checking system and with the Treasury).

Claims on State and Local Governments (line 32b) equals the sum of *lines 12b* and *22b*. Note that, for some countries, lack of sufficient data to perform the standard classifications of claims has resulted in the use of the alternative classification "claims on official entities" (*line 32bx*), which is the sum of *lines 12bx* and *22bx*. These series may therefore include state and local governments, public financial institutions, and nonfinancial public enterprises.

Claims on Nonfinancial Public Enterprises (line 32c) equals the sum of *lines 12c* and *22c*.

Claims on Private Sector (line 32d) equals the sum of *lines 12d* and *22d*.

Claims on Other Banking Institutions (line 32f) equals the sum of *lines 12f* and *22f*.

Claims on Nonbank Financial Institutions (line 32g) equals the sum of *lines 12g* and *22g*.

Domestic Credit (line 32) is the sum of *lines 32an, 32b, 32c, 32d, 32f*, and *32g* even when, owing to their small size, data for *lines 32b, 32c, 32f*, and *32g* are not published separately. Thus, the data for *line 32* may be larger than the sum of its published components.

Money (line 34) equals the sum of currency outside deposit money banks (*line 14a*) and demand deposits other than those of the central government (*lines 14d, 14e, 14f, 14g, and 24*) plus, where applicable, *lines 24..i* and *24..r*.

Quasi-Money (line 35) equals the sum of *lines 15* and *25*, comprising time, savings, and foreign currency deposits of resident sectors other than central government.

The data in *line 34* are frequently referred to as M1, while the sum of *lines 34* and *35* gives a broader measure of money similar to that which is frequently called M2. The yearbook publishes this time series *(line 35l)* immediately following the monetary survey.

Money Market Instruments (line 36aa) equals the sum of *lines 16aa* and *26aa*.

Bonds (line 36ab) equals the sum of *lines 16ab* and *26ab*.

Liabilities of Central Bank: Securities (line 36ac) equals the outstanding stock of securities issued by the monetary authorities *(line 16ac)* less the holdings of these securities by deposit money banks *(line 20c)*.

Restricted Deposits (line 36b) equals the sum of *lines 16b* and *26b*.

Long-Term Foreign Liabilities (line 36cl) equals the sum of *lines 16cl* and *26cl*.

Counterpart Funds (line 36e) equals the sum of *lines 16e* and *26e*.

Central Government Lending Funds (line 36f) equals the sum of *lines 16f* and *26f*.

Capital Accounts (line 37a) equals the sum of lines *17a* and *27a*.

The monetary survey lines listed above give the full range of *IFS* standard lines. Some of these are not applicable to every country, while others may not be published separately in sections 10 and 20 because the data are small. Unpublished lines are included in *Other Items (Net) (lines 17r* and *27r)* but are classified in the appropriate monetary survey aggregates in section 30.

Exceptions to the standard calculations of monetary survey aggregates are indicated in the notes to the country pages in the monthly issues of *IFS*.

Exceptions also exist in the standard presentation of the consolidation of financial institutions, e.g., for Japan, Nicaragua, the United Kingdom, and the United States.

Other Banking Institutions

Section 40 contains data on the accounts of other banking institutions. This subsector comprises institutions that do not accept transferable deposits but engage in financial intermediation by accepting other types of deposits or by issuing securities or other liabilities that are close substitutes for deposits. This subsector covers such institutions as savings and mortgage loan institutions, post-office savings institutions, building and loan associations, finance companies that accept deposits or deposit substitutes, development banks, and offshore banking institutions.

The major aggregates in section 40 are claims on the various sectors of the economy *(lines 42*)*, as described in the preceding subsections, and quasi-monetary liabilities *(line 45)*, largely in the form of time and savings deposits.

Banking Survey

Where reasonably complete data are available for other banking institutions, a banking survey (section 50) is published, consolidating data for other banking institutions with the monetary survey. The banking survey thus provides a broader measure of monetary liabilities. The sectoral classification of assets in the banking survey follows that used in the monetary survey, as outlined in the description of the monetary survey.

Nonbank Financial Institutions

For a few countries, data are shown on the accounts of nonbank financial institutions, such as insurance companies, pension funds, and superannuation funds. Given the nature of their liabilities, these institutions generally exert minimal impact on the liquidity of a given economy; however, they can play a significant role in the distribution of credit from the financial sector to the rest of the economy.

European Economic and Monetary Union (EMU)

Stage Three of the EMU, which began in January 1999, resulted in new definitions of statistical aggregates and created a substantial break in data series for all Euro Area countries. The main features of the Euro Area monetary statistics are described below.

Creation of the Eurosystem: In Stage Three of EMU, the "Eurosystem" (the ECB and the NCBs of the eleven member states) executes a single monetary policy for the Euro Area. The euro was created as a new common currency unit, while national currency will circulate until 2002, and national authorities were permitted to denominate various types of transactions in either euros or national currency. The monetary statistics standards for the Euro Area countries underwent comprehensive revisions that would permit compilation of consolidated monetary accounts for the Euro Area and would provide the data needed to execute the single monetary policy. Statistical standards are based on the *European System of Accounts 1995 (1995 ESA)* and additional standards prescribed by ECB regulation. Statistics are collected under a "layered approach," whereby monetary statistics compiled at the country level are forwarded to the ECB for consolidation into Euro Area totals. NCBs are required to compile monetary statistics according to a single set of standards and a common format for submission of data to the ECB.

Denomination in euros: Beginning in 1999, monetary data for all Euro Area countries and the ECB are denominated in euros.

Residency principles: Statistics are compiled on the basis of both national residency criteria, as described in the fifth edition of the *Balance of Payments Manual*, and Euro Area-wide residency criteria. In applying the latter criteria, all institutional units located in Euro Area countries are treated as resident, and all units outside the Euro Area are nonresident. For example, claims on government under the national criteria include only claims on the government of the country, whereas under the Euro Area-wide residency criteria, claims on government include claims on the governments of all eleven Euro Area countries. Under the Euro Area-wide residency criteria, the ECB is a resident unit, whereas under the national residency criteria, it is a foreign unit for all countries except Germany where it is a resident unit.

The monetary statistics in the pages for each Euro Area country are presented on both national and Euro Area-wide residency bases.

Monetary Authorities

Monetary authorities refer to the national central bank and other institutional units that perform monetary authorities' functions and are included in the central bank subsector (currency boards, exchange stabilization funds, etc). At the Euro Area level, monetary authorities refers to the European System of the Central Bank.

For purposes of comparison with pre-Euro Area data, "of which" lines show positions with residents of the country.

Beginning in January 1999, *Foreign Assets (line 11)* and *Foreign Liabilities (line 16c)* include only positions with non-Euro Area countries. All positions with residents of other Euro Area countries, including the ECB, are classified as domestic positions in the data based on Euro Area residency.

Claims on General Government (line 12a.u) includes claims on the central government and other levels of government, including the social security system. It also includes claims on general government in other Euro Area countries.

Claims on Banking Institutions (NCBs and Other MFIs) (line 12e.u) and *Liabilities to Banking Institutions (NCBs and Other MFIs) (line 14c.u)* include all positions with NCBs and Other MFIs in all Euro Area countries. Prior to January 1999, positions with NCBs and Other MFIs in other Euro Area countries were in *Foreign Assets and Foreign Liabilities*.

Claims on Other Resident Sectors (line 12d) comprises claims on nonbank financial institutions, public nonfinancial corporations, and the private sector.

Claims on the ECB (line 12u) and *Liabilities to the ECB (line 16u)* consist of the NCB's capital contribution to the ECB, claims resulting from transfer of international reserves to the ECB, and other claims. These lines also include contra-entries to the NCB's holdings of assets acquired in conjunction with open-market or intervention operations. Prior to January 1999, positions with the EMI or ECB were included in *Foreign Assets and Foreign Liabilities*.

Currency in Circulation (line14a) comprises all banknotes and coins issued by the NCB and by central government in some Euro Area countries.

Capital Accounts (line 17a) includes general provisions.

Banking Institutions

For comparison with pre-Euro Area data, "of which" lines show positions with residents of the country.

Beginning in January 1999, this section covers the accounts of other MFIs—monetary institutions other than the NCB and ECB. Other MFIs were previously called deposit money banks (DMBs) and other banking institutions (OBIs). Beginning in January 1999, it also includes money market funds.

Claims on Monetary Authorities (line 20) comprises banking institutions' holdings of banknotes and coins issued by the NCB and by central government in some Euro Area countries, deposits with the NCB, and loans to the NCB.

Claims on Banking Institutions (including ECB) in Other Euro Area Countries (line 20b.u) and *Liabilities to Banking Institutions (including ECB) in Other Euro Area Countries (line 26h.u)* comprise all positions with the ECB, NCBs, and Other MFIs in other Euro Area countries. These positions are classified as domestic under the Euro Area residency criteria. Prior to January 1999, these accounts were classified under *Foreign Assets* and *Foreign Liabilities*. Claims include holdings of currencies issued in other Euro Area countries.

Beginning in January 1999, *Foreign Assets (line 21)* and *Foreign Liabilities (line 26c)* include only positions with non-Euro Area countries. All positions with residents of other Euro Area countries, including the ECB, are classified as domestic positions.

Claims on General Government (line 22a.u) includes claims on central government and other levels of government in all Euro Area countries.

Claims on Other Resident Sectors (line 22d.u) comprises claims on nonbank financial institutions, public nonfinancial corporations, and the private sectors in all Euro Area countries.

Demand Deposits (line 24.u) includes demand deposits in all currencies by other resident sectors in all Euro Area countries.

Other Deposits (line 25.u) includes deposits with fixed maturity, deposits redeemable at notice, securities repurchase agreements, and subordinated debt in the form of deposits. It also includes deposits of all Euro Area countries. Prior to January 1999, subordinated debt was included in *Other Items (Net) (line 27r)*.

Money Market Instruments (line 26m.u) includes money market fund shares and money market paper.

Bonds (Debt Securities) (line 26n.u) includes subordinated debt in the form of securities.

Credit from Monetary Authorities (line 26g) comprises banking institutions' borrowing from the NCBs.

Other Items (Net) (line 27r) includes holdings of shares issued by other MFIs.

Banking Survey (Based on National Residency) consolidates the accounts of the monetary authorities and banking institutions based on national residency criteria.

Foreign Assets (Net) (line 31n) includes positions with nonresidents of the country. Positions with the ECB for all Euro Area countries except Germany are classified in Foreign Assets under the national residency criteria.

Claims on General Government (Net) (line 32an) includes claims on general government minus deposits of central government. Deposits of other levels of government are included in liabilities to other resident sectors.

Currency in Circulation (line 34a.n) equals the issuance of notes and coins issued by the NCBs and, in some countries, coins issued by central government.

Other Items (Net) (line 37r) includes other MFIs' holdings of shares issued by other MFIs.

Banking Survey (Based on Euro Area-Wide Residency) consolidates the accounts of the monetary authorities and banking institutions based on Euro Area-wide residency criteria.

Foreign Assets (Net) (line 31n.u) includes all positions with nonresidents of the Euro Area. Positions with residents of all Euro Area countries, including the ECB, are classified as domestic positions.

Claims on General Government (Net) (line 32anu) includes claims on central government and all other levels of government of all Euro Area countries minus deposits of central government of all Euro Area countries. Deposits of other levels of government are included in liabilities to other resident sectors.

Currency in Circulation (line 34a.u) equals the NCB's notes and coins issued by central government, as well as any currency issued by the ECB.

Other Items (Net) (line 37r.u) includes other MFIs' holdings of shares issued by other MFIs.

5. Interest Rates

Discount Rate/Bank Rate (line 60) is the rate at which the central banks lend or discount eligible paper for deposit money banks, typically shown on an end-of-period basis. *The Eurosystem Marginal Lending Facility Rate (line 60)* is the interest rate at which other MFIs obtain overnight liquidity from NCBs, against eligible assets. The terms and conditions of the lending are identical throughout the Euro Area. The *Eurosystem Refinancing Rate (line 60r)* and *Interbank Rate (Overnight) (line 60a)* are also provided on the Euro Area page.

Money Market Rate (line 60b) is the rate on short-term lending between financial institutions. *Interbank Rate (Three-Month) (line 60b)* is shown on the Euro Area page.

Treasury Bill Rate (line 60c) is the rate at which short-term securities are issued or traded in the market.

Deposit Rate (line 60l) usually refers to rates offered to resident customers for demand, time, or savings deposits. Frequently, rates for time and savings deposits are classified according to maturity and amounts deposited; in addition, deposit money banks and similar deposit-taking institutions may offer short- and medium-term instruments at specified rates for specific amounts and maturities; these are frequently termed "certificates of deposit."

Lending Rate (line 60p) is the bank rate that usually meets the short- and medium-term financing needs of the private sector. This rate is normally differentiated according to creditworthiness of borrowers and objectives of financing.

Government Bond Yield (line 61*) refers to one or more series representing yields to maturity of government bonds or other bonds that would indicate longer term rates.

Interest rates for foreign-currency-denominated instruments are also published for countries where such instruments are important.

Annual interest rate data are arithmetic averages of monthly interest rates reported by the countries.

The country notes in the monthly issues carry a brief description of the nature and characteristics of the rates reported and of the financial instrument to which they relate. A typical series from each of these groups is included in the world table on national interest rates.

World Table on International Interest Rates

The world table on international interest rates reports data for the years 1985–99 and reports London interbank offer rates on deposits denominated in SDRs, U.S. dollars, French francs, deutsche mark, Japanese yen, and Swiss francs and Paris interbank offer rates on deposits denominated in pounds sterling. The table includes the premium or discount on three-month forward rates of currencies of the major industrial countries against the U.S. dollar.

The world table on international interest rates also reports the SDR interest rate and the rate of remuneration. Interest is paid on holdings of SDRs, and charges are levied on participants' cumulative allocations. Interest and charges accrue daily at the same rate and are settled quarterly in SDRs. As a result, participants who have SDR holdings above their net cumulative allocations receive net interest, and those with holdings below their net cumulative allocations pay net charges; other official holders of SDRs—including the Fund's General Resources Account—receive interest on their holdings and pay no charges because they receive no allocations.

The Fund also pays quarterly remuneration to members on their creditor positions arising from the use of their currencies in Fund transactions and operations, which is determined by the positive difference between the remuneration norm and the average daily balances of the member's currency in the General Resources Account.

Effective August 1, 1983, the weekly SDR interest rate has been based on the combined market interest rate, calculated by applying to the specific amounts of the five currencies included in the SDR valuation basket, converted into SDR equivalents, the market rates on specified short-term money market instruments quoted in the five countries. As of January 1, 1991, the interest rates used in this calculation are market yield for three-month U.S. treasury bills, three-month interbank deposit rate *(line 60bs)* in Germany, three-month rate for treasury bills *(line 60cs)* in France, three-month rate on certificates of deposit *(line 60bs)* in Japan, and market yield for three-month U.K. treasury bills *(line 60cs)*. These series are shown in the table.

The combined market rate is calculated each Friday and enters into effect each Monday. The interest rate on the SDR is 100 percent of the combined market rate, rounded to two nearest decimal places. The rate of remuneration, effective February 2, 1987, is 100 percent of the rate of interest on the SDR.

6. Prices, Production, and Labor

This section *(lines 62* through *67)* covers domestic prices, production, and labor market indicators. A more detailed discussion of major price indicators is provided in the *IFS Supplement on Price Statistics*, No. 12 (1986).

The index series are compiled from reported versions of national indices and, for some production and labor series, from absolute data. There is a wide variation between countries and over time in the selection of base years, depending upon the availability of comprehensive benchmark data that permit an adequate review of weighting patterns. The series are linked by using ratio splicing at the first annual overlap, and the linked series are shifted to a common base period 1995=100.

Share Prices

Indices shown for *Share Prices (line 62)* generally relate to common shares of companies traded on national or foreign stock exchanges. All reported indices are adjusted for changes in quoted nominal capital of companies. Indices are in general base-weighted arithmetic averages with market value of outstanding shares as weights.

Producer Price Index (PPI) or Wholesale Price Index (WPI)

Indices shown for *Producer* or *Wholesale Prices (line 63)* are designed to monitor changes in prices of items at the first important commercial transaction. Where a choice is available, preference is given to the PPI because the concept, weighting pattern, and coverage are likely to be more consistent with national accounts and industrial production statistics. In principle, the PPI should include service industries, but in practice it is limited to the domestic agricultural and industrial sectors. The prices should be farm-gate prices for the agricultural sector and ex-factory prices for the industrial sector.

The WPI, when used, covers a mixture of prices of agricultural and industrial goods at various stages of production and distribution, inclusive of imports and import duties. Preference is given to indices that provide broad coverage of the economy, and the indices are computed using the Laspeyres formula, unless otherwise indicated in the country notes in the monthly issues of *IFS*. Subindices are occasionally included for the PPI or the WPI.

Consumer Price Index (CPI)

Indices shown for *Consumer Prices (line 64)* are the most frequently used indicators of inflation and reflect changes in the cost of acquiring a fixed basket of goods and services by the average consumer. Preference is given to series having wider geographical coverage and relating to all income groups, provided they are no less current than more narrowly defined series.

As the weights are usually derived from household expenditure surveys, which may be conducted infrequently, information on the year to which the weights refer is provided in the country page notes in the monthly issues of *IFS*, together with information on any limitations in the coverage of commodities for pricing, income groups, or their expenditures in the chosen index. The Laspeyres formula is used unless otherwise indicated in the country notes in the monthly issues.

For the 15 European Union (EU) countries, a harmonized CPI *(line 64h)* is likewise shown. The harmonized index of consumer prices (HICP) is compiled according to methodological and sampling standards set by the European Commission. Owing to institutional differences between the EU member countries, the HICP excludes expenditure on certain types of goods and services. Examples are medical care and services of owner-occupied dwellings.

Wage Rates or Earnings

Indices shown for *Wages Rates, Cost of Labor,* or *Earnings (line 65)* represent wage rates or earnings per worker employed per specified time period and frequently have the same coverage as the *Industrial Production* index *(line 66)* and the *Industrial Employment* index *(line 67)*. This is more likely where establishment surveys are the source. Preference is given to data for earnings that include payments in kind and family allowances and that cover salaried employees as well as wage earners. The indices either are computed from absolute wage data or are as reported directly to the Fund.

Industrial Production

Indices shown for *Industrial Production (line 66)* are included as indicators of current economic activity and for some countries are supplemented by indicators (such as data on tourism) relevant to a particular country. Generally, the coverage of industrial production indices comprises mining and quarrying, manufacturing and electricity, and gas and water according to the UN International Standard Industrial Classification (ISIC), and the indices are compiled using the Laspeyres formula; for many developing countries the indices refer to the production of a major primary commodity such as crude petroleum (see commodity codes on page viii).

Labor

Labor market indicators refer to the levels of the *Labor Force (line 67d)*, *Employment (line 67e)*, and *Unemployment (line 67c)*, and the *Unemployment Rate (line 67r)*. Data on labor market statistics cover the economically active civilian population and are provided by the International Labor Organization (ILO), which publishes these data in its *Yearbook of Labour Statistics* and its quarterly *Bulletin of Labour Statistics* and supplements. The concept of employment and unemployment conforms to the recommendations adopted by the ILO: Thirteenth International Conference of Labor Statisticians, Geneva, 1992. In addition, indices of employment in the industrial sector *(line 67)* are provided for 42 countries. For the Euro Area, data are provided by Eurostat.

7. International Transactions

Summary statistics on the international transactions of a country are given in *lines 70* through *79*. There is a section on external trade statistics (*lines 70* through *76*) reporting on the values (*lines 70* and *71*), volumes (*lines 72* and *73*), unit values (*lines 74* and *75*), and prices (*line 76*) for exports and imports. This is followed by a section (*lines 78* through *79*) on balance of payments statistics.

External Trade

Merchandise Exports f.o.b. (line 70) and *Imports c.i.f. (line 71)* are, in general, customs statistics reported under the general trade system according to the recommendations of the UN *International Merchandise Trade Statistics: Concepts and Definitions*, 1998. For some countries, data relate to the special trade system. The difference between general and special trade lies mainly in the treatment of recording the movement of goods through customs-bonded storage areas (warehouses, free areas, etc.).

Many countries use customs data on exports and imports as the primary source for the recording of exports and imports of goods in the balance of payments. However, customs data and the entries for goods in the balance of payments may not be equal, owing to differences in definition. These differences may relate to the coverage of transactions (for example, the goods item in the balance of payments often includes adjustments for certain goods transactions that may not be recorded by customs authorities, e.g., parcel post), the time of recording of transactions (e.g., in the balance of payments, transactions are to be recorded when change of ownership occurs, rather than the moment goods cross the customs border, which generally determines when goods are recorded in customs-based trade statistics), and classification differences (e.g., in the balance of payments, repair on goods is part of goods transactions).

The data for *Merchandise Imports f.o.b. (line 71.v)* are obtained directly from statistical authorities.

Details of commodity exports are presented for commodities that are traded in the international markets and have an impact on world market prices. Data for petroleum exports are presented only for 12 oil exporting countries. For a number of these countries, data estimated by Fund staff are derived from available data for the volume of production and estimates for prices that are, in part, taken from *Petroleum Intelligence Weekly* and other international sources; details of these estimates are provided in the country notes in the monthly version of the *IFS*.

For a number of countries where data are uncurrent or unavailable, additional lines are included showing data, converted from U.S. dollars to national currency, from the *Direction of Trade Statistics* quarterly publication (*DOTS*). Exports and imports data published in *DOTS* include reported data, updated where necessary with estimates for the current periods. A description of the nature of the estimates is given in the introduction of the *DOTS*.

Indices for *Volume of Exports (line 72)* and *Volume of Imports (line 73)* are either Laspeyres or Paasche. For nine countries, as indicated in the country notes in the monthly issues of *IFS*, export volume indices are calculated from reported volume data for individual commodities weighted by reported values.

Indices for *Unit Value of Exports (line 74)* and *Unit Value of Imports (line 75)* are Laspeyres with weights derived from the data for transactions. For about seven countries, also as indicated in the country notes in the monthly issue of *IFS*, export unit values are calculated from reported value and volume data for individual commodities.

Indices for export and import prices, compiled from survey data for prices at the wholesale level or directly from the exporter or importer (called "direct pricing"), are shown in *line 76*, where available. In the absence of national sources, data for wholesale prices are taken from world commodity markets and are converted into national currency at period-average exchange rates. Indices based on direct pricing are generally considered preferable to unit value indices, because problems of unit value bias are reduced.

A more detailed presentation of trade statistics is presented in the *IFS Supplement on Trade Statistics*, No. 15 (1988).

Balance of Payments Statistics

The balance of payments lines are presented on the basis of the methodology and presentation of the fifth edition of the *Balance of Payments Manual (BPM5)*, published by the IMF in September 1993. Prior to 1995, issues of the *IFS* yearbook presented balance of payments data on the basis of the fourth edition of the manual (*BPM4*).

Description of Balance of Payments and International Investment Position Lines in IFS

Current Account, n.i.e. (line 78ald) is the credit lines minus the debit lines of goods, services, income, and current transfers, n.i.e.

Goods: Exports f.o.b. and *Goods: Imports f.o.b. (lines 78aad* and *78abd)* are both measured on the "free-on-board" (f.o.b.) basis–that is, by the value of the goods at the border of the exporting country; in the case of imports, this excludes the cost of freight and insurance incurred beyond the border of the exporting country. The *Trade Balance (line 78acd)* is the difference between exports and imports of goods.

Balance on Goods and Services (line 78afd) and *Balance on Goods, Serv., & Inc.* (i.e., Balance on Goods, Services, and Income) (*78aid*) are the relevant credit items minus the debit items.

Current Transfers, n.i.e.: Credit (line 78ajd) comprise all current transfers received by the reporting country, except those made to the country to finance its "overall balance" (see below); hence, the label "n.i.e." The latter are included in *Exceptional Financing (line 79ded)* (see below). (Note: Some of the capital and financial account lines shown below are also labeled "n.i.e." This is to denote that *Exceptional Financing* items (see below) have been excluded from specific capital and financial account components.)

Capital Account, n.i.e. (line 78bcd) is the credit items *Capital Account, n.i.e.: Credit (line 78bad)* minus the debit items *Capital Account: Debit (line 78bbd)*. *Line 78bad* refers mainly to capital transfers linked to the acquisition of a fixed asset other than transactions relating to debt forgiveness (which are classified under *Exceptional Financing*), plus the disposal of nonproduced, nonfinancial assets. *Line 78bbd* refers mainly to capital transfers linked to the disposal of fixed assets by the donor or to the financing of capital formation by the recipient, plus the acquisition of nonproduced, nonfinancial assets.

Financial Account, n.i.e. (line 78bjd) is the net sum of the balance of direct investment (*line 78bdd* minus *line 78bed*), portfolio investment (*line 78bfd* minus *line 78bgd*), other investment transactions (*line 78bhd* minus *line 78bid*), and financial derivatives (*line 78bwd* minus *line 78bxd*).

Direct Investment Abroad (line 78bdd) and *Direct Investment in Rep. Econ., n.i.e.* (Direct Investment in the Reporting Economy, n.i.e.) *(line 78bed)* represent the flows of direct investment capital out of the reporting economy and those into the reporting economy, respectively. Direct investment includes equity capital, reinvested earnings, other capital, and financial derivatives associated with various intercompany transactions between affiliated enterprises. Excluded are flows of direct investment capital into the reporting economy for exceptional financing, such as debt-for-equity swaps.

Portfolio Investment Assets (line 78bfd) and *Portfolio Investment Liab., n.i.e.* (i.e., Portfolio Investment Liabilities) *(line 78bgd)* include transactions with nonresidents in financial securities of any maturity (such as corporate securities, bonds, notes, and money market instruments) other than those included in direct investment, exceptional financing, and reserve assets.

Equity Securities (lines 78bkd and 78bmd) include shares and stocks, and similar documents, such as American depository receipts.

Debt Securities (lines 78bld and 78bnd) cover bonds, debentures, notes, etc. and money market or negotiable debt instruments.

Other Investment Assets (line 78bhd) and *Other Investment Liabilities, n.i.e. (line 78bid)* reflect all other transactions with nonresidents in financial assets and liabilities, except exceptional financing, and reserve assets. Major categories are transactions in currency and deposits, loans, and trade credits.

Net Errors and Omissions (line 78cad) is a residual category needed to ensure that all debit and credit entries in the balance of payments statement sum to zero and reflects statistical inconsistencies in the recording of the credit and debit entries. In the *IFS* presentation, this is equal to the difference between *Reserves and Related Items (line 79dad)* (described below) and the sum of the balances of the current account, the capital account, and the financial account.

Overall Balance (line 78cbd) is the sum of the balances of the current account, the capital account, the financial account, and net errors and omissions.

Reserves and Related Items (line 79dad) is the sum of transactions in reserve assets, exceptional financing, and use of Fund credit and loans.

Reserve Assets (line 79dbd) consists of external assets readily available to and controlled by monetary authorities primarily for direct financing of payments imbalances and for indirect regulating of the magnitude of such imbalances through exchange market intervention.

Use of Fund Credit and Loans (line 79dcd) includes purchases and repurchases in the credit tranches of the Fund's General Resource Account, and net borrowings under the Structural Adjustment Facility (SAF), the Poverty Reduction and Growth Facility (PRGF), which was previously named the Enhanced Structural Adjustment Facility (ESAF), and the Trust Fund.

Exceptional Financing (line 79ded) includes any other transactions undertaken by the authorities to finance the "overall balance," as an alternative to, or in conjunction with, the use of reserve assets and the use of Fund credit and loans from the Fund.

The international investment position (IIP) data appear under *lines 79aad* through *79ljd*. The IIP of a country is a balance sheet of its external financial assets and liabilities. The coverage of the various components of IIP is similar to that of the corresponding components under the balance of payments. The value of IIP, however, reflects not only balance of payments transactions over time but also price changes, exchange rate changes, and other adjustments.

More extensive data for use in cross-country comparisons are published in the *Balance of Payments Statistics Yearbook.*

8. Government Finance

Summary statistics of government finance are given in section 80. Unless otherwise stated in individual country notes in the monthly issues of IFS, annual data are as reported for *IFS*. Data cover operations of the budgetary central government or of the consolidated central government (that is, operations of budgetary central government, extrabudgetary units, and social security funds). The coverage of consolidated central government may not necessarily include all existing extrabudgetary units and/or social security funds.

More extensive data for use in cross-country comparisons are published in the *Government Finance Statistics Yearbook (GFSY)* and are based on *A Manual on Government Finance Statistics.* When countries do not report data for *IFS* but provide data for the *GFSY*, these data are published in *IFS*.

The data for *lines 80* through *87* are flows and are on a cash basis. The *Deficit or Surplus (line 80)* is calculated as the difference between *Revenue* and, if applicable, *Grants Received (lines 81 and 81z)* on the one hand and *Expenditure* and *Lending Minus Repayments (lines 82 and 83)* on the other. The deficit/surplus is also equal, with the opposite sign, to the sum of the net borrowing by the government plus the net decrease in government cash, deposits, and securities held for liquidity purposes.

Revenue (line 81) comprises all nonrepayable government receipts, whether requited or unrequited, other than grants; revenue is shown net of refunds and other adjustment transactions.

Grants Received (line 81z) comprises all unrequited, non-repayable, noncompulsory receipts from other governments—domestic or foreign—and international institutions. Grants are grouped with revenue because, like revenue, they provide the means whereby expenditure can be made without incurring a debt for future repayment.

Expenditure (line 82) comprises all nonrepayable payments by government, whether requited or unrequited and whether for current or capital purposes.

Lending Minus Repayments (line 83) comprises government acquisition of claims on others—both loans and equities—for public policy purposes and is net of repayments of lending and sales of equities previously purchased. *Line 83* includes both domestic and foreign lending minus repayments. In determining the deficit or surplus, lending minus repayments is grouped with expenditure, because it is presumed to represent a means of pursuing government policy objectives and not to be an action undertaken to manage government liquidity.

The total of the financing items equals the deficit or surplus with a reverse sign. *Total Financing* is classified according to the residence of the lender; where this information is not available, the distinction is based on the currency in which the debt instruments are denominated. For some countries, *Total Financing* is broken down between *Net Borrowing* and *Use of Cash Balances. Net Borrowing* covers the net change in government liabilities to all other sectors, representing mainly their direct loans or advances to government or their holding of government securities acquired from the government itself or in transactions with others. Where possible, data for *Domestic* and *Foreign Net Borrowing* are classified according to the residence of the lender.

Use of Cash Balances (line 87) is intended to measure changes over a period—resulting from transactions but not revaluations—in government holdings of currency and deposits with the monetary system, corresponding to changes in *IFS lines 16d* and *26d*. All currency issues are regarded as liabilities of the monetary authorities, rather than government debt, and any proceeds reaching the government are regarded as coming from the monetary authorities.

Data for outstanding *Debt (lines 88* and *89)* relate to the direct and assumed debt of the central government and exclude loans guaranteed by the government. The distinction between *Domestic* and *Foreign Debt (lines 88a* and *89a)* is based on residence of the lender, where possible, but otherwise on the currency in which the debt instruments are denominated *(lines 88b* and *89b)*.

The Euro Area page and the pages of the individual Euro Area countries also present *Deficit or Surplus (line 80g)* and *Debt (line 88g)* data for the general government, expressed as percent of harmonized Gross Domestic Product. Both indicators are defined according to the convergence criteria on public finance as laid down in the Maastricht Treaty. *Deficit or Surplus* corresponds to net lending/borrowing. The data are not comparable with central government *Deficit or Surplus (line 80)* and *Debt (line 88)*, owing to differences in coverage as well as in definition.

9. National Accounts and Population

The summary data for national accounts are compiled according to the *System of National Accounts (SNA)*.

Gross Domestic Product (GDP) (line 99b) is generally presented in *IFS* as the sum of final expenditures: *Exports of Goods and Services (line 90c), Imports of Goods and Services (line 98c), Private Consumption (line 96f), Government Consumption (line 91f), Gross Fixed Capital Formation (line 93e)*, and *Increase/Decrease(-) in Stocks (line 93i)*. Adding *Net Factor Income/Payments(-) Abroad (line 98.n)* to GDP produces *Gross National Income (GNI) (line 99a)*, formerly known as Gross National Product (GNP). Subtracting Consumption of Fixed Capital (not shown) from GNI produces *Net National Income (line 99e)*, formerly known as National Income Market Prices.

For countries that have implemented the *1993 SNA* as well as the *European System of Accounts 1995 (1995 ESA)*, the national accounts lines shown on the country page are as follows:

Gross Domestic Product (GDP) (line 99b) is generally presented in *IFS* as the sum of final expenditures: *Household Consumption Expenditure, including Nonprofit Institutions Serving Households (NPISHs) (line 96f), Government Consumption Expenditure (line 91f), Gross Fixed Capital Formation (line 93e), Changes in Inventories (line 93i)* (formerly Increase/Decrease (-) in Stocks), *Exports of Goods and Services (line 90c)*, and *Imports of Goods and Services (line 98c). Gross National Income (GNI) (line 99a)* is derived by adding *Net Primary Income from Abroad (line 98.n)* to GDP. *Gross National Disposable Income (GNDI) (line 99i)* is derived by adding *Net Current Transfers from Abroad (line 98t)* to GNI, and *Gross Savings (line 99s)* is derived by deducting final consumption expenditure *(lines 96f* and *91f)* from GNDI.

Statistical discrepancies between aggregate GDP compiled from expenditure flows as against GDP compiled from the production or income accounts (or from a mixture of these accounts) generally are not shown explicitly. Hence, in some cases, the components of GDP that are shown in *IFS* may not add up exactly to the total.

For countries that publish seasonally adjusted data, the data in *IFS* are also on a seasonally adjusted basis (codes ending with *c* or *r*) with the quarterly data shown at annual rates for countries that provide them as such.

Lines 99b.p and *99b.r* are measures of GDP volume at reference year value levels. In the past, these series used a common reference year (e.g., 1990) for publication. With the June 1999 issue, these series are published on the same reference year(s) as reported by the national compilers. The code *p* indicates data that are **not** seasonally adjusted, whereas code *r* indicates data that are seasonally adjusted. *Lines 99bvp* and *99bvr* are GDP volume indices that are presented on a standard 1995 reference year and are derived from the GDP volume series reported by national compilers. For this calculation, the data series provided by national compilers are linked together (if there is more than one series) to form a single time series, using the earliest overlapping year from the different reference year series to calculate the link factors.

The *GDP Deflator* (*line 99bip* or *99bir*) series shown in the *IFS Yearbook* are not direct measurements of prices but are derived implicitly by dividing the GDP series at current prices by constant price GDP series referenced to 1995. The latter series is constructed by multiplying the 1995 current price GDP level by the GDP volume index (1995=100). The deflator is expressed in index form, with 1995=100.

Data on *Population (line 99z)*, which represent midyear estimates, are provided by the UN. These estimates are also published in the UN *Monthly Bulletin of Statistics*.

10. World Tables

World tables presented in the yearbook bring together country data on exchange rates, members' Fund transactions and positions, international reserves, reserve money, various measures of money, money plus quasi-money, interest rates, wholesale and consumer prices, wages, production, employment, values and unit values of countries' exports and imports, balance of payments, GDP volume measures, GDP deflators, and the shares of final consumption expenditure and gross capital formation in GDP.

World tables also present series on wholesale prices and unit values (expressed in U.S. dollars) of principal world trade commodities. Tables showing totals or averages of country series may report data for selected countries only. A full listing of countries whose data are included in the calculation of area and world measures is given on page viii.

Country Groups

Countries whose data are included in **world/all countries'** totals and averages are arrayed into two main groups—**industrial countries** and **developing countries**. Separate data for the Euro Area are shown within the industrial countries' group. The developing countries group is further subdivided into area subgroups for **Africa, Asia, Europe,** the **Middle East,** and the **Western Hemisphere**.

Data for subgroups **oil exporting countries** and **non-oil developing countries** are shown as memorandum items. Oil exporting countries are defined as those countries whose oil exports (net of any imports of crude oil) both represent a minimum of two thirds of their total exports and are at least equivalent to approximately 1 percent of world exports of oil. The calculations presently used to determine which countries meet the above criteria are based on 1976–78 averages.

The country composition of the **world** is all countries for which the topic series are available in the *IFS* files; hence, the country coverage of some areas, mainly Africa and Asia, differs from topic to topic, and area and world totals or averages may be biased to some extent toward the larger reporting countries.

Area and World Indices

Area and world indices are obtained as weighted averages of country indices. Arithmetic means are used for unit

values of exports and imports (and terms of trade), where the country indices are expressed in U.S. dollars. Geometric means are used for producer/wholesale and consumer prices, GDP volume measures, GDP deflator, industrial production, wages, and employment because, unlike arithmetic means, geometric means are not unduly influenced by data for the few countries with extreme growth rates. Geometric means assure that, if all series have constant although different rates of increase, their average will have a constant rate of increase.

The country series included in the calculation of the area averages for producer/wholesale and consumer prices, GDP volume measures, and GDP deflator are weighted by the 1995 purchasing power parity (PPP) value of GDP.[1] The country series used in the industrial production, wages, and employment tables are weighted by value added in industry, as derived from individual countries' national accounts, expressed in U.S. dollars. The country series used in the export unit values and import unit values tables are weighted by the 1995 value of exports and imports (both in U.S. dollars), respectively.

Weights are normally updated at about five-year intervals, in accordance with international practice, in order to reflect changes in the importance of each country's data in relation to the data of all other countries. The standard weight base years used are 1953, 1958, 1963, 1970, 1975, 1980, 1984–86, 1990, and 1995; the corresponding time spans to which the weights are applied are 1948–55, 1955–60, 1960–68, 1968–73, 1973–78, 1978–83, 1983–88, 1988–93, and 1994 onward. Separate averages are calculated for each time span, and the index series are linked by the splicing at overlap years and shifted to the reference base 1995=100.

The calculation of area totals and averages takes account of the problem that data for some countries do not run through the end of the period for which world and area data should be calculable. Area totals and averages for most topics are estimated for current and for earlier periods if country data are known that contribute at least 60 percent of the area total or index aggregate during recent periods for which data of all countries of an area are available. Area totals or averages are estimated by assuming that the rate of change in the unreported country data is the same as the rate of change in the weighted total or average of the reported country data for that area. These estimates are made for the area totals and averages only; separate country estimates are not calculated.

With the exception of import unit values, the world totals and averages are made from the calculated and estimated data for the two main groups—industrial countries and developing countries. A world total or average is calculated only when totals or averages are available for both of these country groups. For import unit values, world data are calculated directly from country data, because the number of countries for which the series are available and current is in-

---

[1]See *World Economic Outlook*, May 1993, Annex IV, for a comparison of PPP-based GDP weights and exchange-rate-based GDP weights.

sufficient to allow calculation or estimation of the area averages and because the variability of import unit value indices among countries is judged to be less than that for other topics. World estimates are made when data are available for countries whose combined weights represent at least 80 percent of the total country weights.

For the terms of trade index numbers, the world and area data for the export unit values are divided by the corresponding series for the import unit values, where possible. Thus terms of trade averages are available only for areas with both export and import unit values. The country coverage within the areas for the export and import unit values is not identical, leading to a small degree of assymetry in the terms of trade calculation.

World Table Calculations

International Reserves: Country series on international reserves begin generally with their appropriate dates and are complete monthly time series; hence, earlier period estimates are not required. When current data of a few countries of an area are not reported, the area total is estimated by carrying forward the last reported country figure.

Reserve Money, Money, and *Money plus Quasi-Money:* Percent changes are based on end-of-year data. When there is more than one version or definition of money over time, different time series are chained through a ratio splicing technique. When actual stock data needed for the growth rate calculation are missing, no percent change is shown in the world table.

Ratio of Reserve Money to Money plus Quasi-Money: The measures of money used in calculating this ratio are end-of-year data.

Income Velocity of Money plus Quasi-Money: The measure of income in this table is *IFS* data on GDP. The data for money plus quasi-money are annual averages of the highest frequency data available. The ratio is then converted into an index number with a base year of 1995.

Real Effective Exchange Rate Indices: This table shows a variety of real effective exchange rate indices for industrial countries. Five of these comprise alternative measures of costs and prices that have been applied to the weighting scheme described next. These alternative measures of costs and prices are derived from *Relative Unit Labor Costs (line 65um), Relative Normalized Unit Labor Costs (line reu), Relative Value-Added Deflators (line 99by), Relative Wholesale Prices (line 63ey),* and *Relative Export Unit Values (line 74ey).*

The weighting scheme is based on aggregated data for trade in manufactured goods, averaged over the period 1989–91, with the weights reflecting both the relative importance of a country's trading partners in its direct bilateral trade relations and that resulting from competition in third markets. The measure is expressed as an index 1995=100 in accordance with all indices published in *IFS.*

A discussion of the data sources used to derive the cost and price indicators for the real effective exchange rates shown in the world table is provided in the footnotes to that table. The real effective exchange rate index *Based on Relative Normalized Unit Labor Costs (line* reu) is also shown on the country pages (with the exception of Ireland) together with the *Nominal Effective Exchange Rate Index (line* neu) from which all five measures are drawn.

Beginning with the October 1992 issue of *IFS,* the data published are from a revised database, based on a comprehensive review and update of the underlying data sources and a change in the method of normalization of output per hour; this uses the Hodrick-Prescott filter, which smoothes a time series by removing short-run fluctuations while retaining changes of a larger amplitude.

In addition, there is a real effective exchange rate index, *Based on Relative Consumer Prices (line rec),* as a measure of domestic cost and price developments. It covers trade in manufactured goods and primary products for a range of trading partners—and competitors—by using the same methodology that is used to compile nominal and real effective exchange rates for nonindustrial countries, as discussed in the exchange rate and exchange rate arrangements section of this introduction.

Industrial Production: This table presents seasonally adjusted indices on industrial production for 22 industrial countries together with an aggregate index for the group. The data are those shown on the country pages as either *Industrial Production (lines 66..*)* or *Manufacturing Production (lines 66ey*),* the asterisk representing a wildcard.

Wages: This table presents indices computed either from absolute wage data or from the wage indices reported to the Fund for the industrial sector for 22 industrial countries. The data are those shown in the country pages as *Wage Rates, Cost of Labor,* or *Earnings (line 65).*

Employment: This table presents indices computed from indices of employment or number of persons employed as reported by the countries for the industrial sector for 20 industrial countries. The data are those shown in the country pages as *Employment (lines 67* or *67ey).*

Producer/Wholesale Prices and *Consumer Prices*: Data are those prices reported in *lines 63** and *64** on the country pages. The percent changes are calculated from the index number series.

Exports and Imports: Data are published in U.S. dollars, as reported by the countries, if available. Otherwise, annual data are the national currency value series reported on the country pages (*lines 70...* and *71...*) converted to U.S. dollars at rate **rf**. Conversions are made using the trade-weighted averages of the monthly exchange rates.

Export Unit Values/Export Prices and Import Unit Values/Import Prices: Data are the index numbers reported on the country pages expressed in U.S. dollars at rate **rf**. The country indices are typically unit value data (*lines 74* and *75*); however, for some countries they are components of wholesale price indices or are derived from specific price quotations (*lines 76, 76.x,* and *76aa*). The exceptions are coded "w" in the tabulation of country coverage on page viii.

Terms of Trade: Data are index numbers computed from the export and import unit value indices and shown in the appropriate world table. The percent changes are calculated from the index number series.

Balance of Payments: For a precise definition of the concepts used in these tables, and for an explanation of changes in definition that are related to the introduction of the fifth edition of the *Balance of Payments Manual*, the reader is referred to section 7, International Transactions.

Trade Balance is the series reported in *line 78acd* of the country pages; Current Account Balance, Excluding Exceptional Financing is the series reported in *line 78ald* of the country pages; Capital and Financial Account, Including New Errors and Omissions but Excluding Reserve Assets, Use of Fund Credit and Loans, and Exceptional Financing are the sum of the series reported in *lines 78bcd, 78bjd,* and *78cad* of the country pages.

Overall Balance Excluding Reserve Assets, Use of Fund Credit and Loans, and Exceptional Financing is the series reported in *line 78cbd* (which equals *lines 78ald, 78bcd, 78bjd,* and *78cad*) of the country pages.

Exports/Imports of Goods and Services as Percent of GDP: The data relate to the percent share of exports and imports of goods and services (calculated as the sums of *lines 78aad* and *78add* and *lines 78abd* and *78aed,* respectively) in *Gross Domestic Product (line 99b). Current Account Balance Excluding Exceptional Financing as Percent of GDP:* The data relate to the percent share of the *Current Account n.i.e. (line 78ald)* in *Gross Domestic Product.*

GDP Volume Measures: Data are derived from those series reported in *lines 99bvp* and *99bvr* on the country pages. The percent changes are calculated from index numbers.

GDP Deflator: Data are derived from those series reported in *lines 99bip* on the country pages. The percent changes are calculated from index numbers.

Gross Capital Formation as Percent of GDP: Data are the percent share of gross capital formation in GDP at current market prices. Gross capital formation comprises *Gross Fixed Capital Formation* and *Increase/Decrease (-) in Stocks (lines 93e* and *93i,* respectively).

Final Consumption Expenditure as a Percentage of GDP: Data are the percent share of final consumption expenditure in GDP at current market prices, which comprises *Government Consumption* and *Private Consumption (91f* and *96f,* respectively).

Commodity Prices: Data are obtained primarily from the Commodities and Special Issues Division of the IMF's Research Department, from *Commodity Price Data* of the World Bank, from *Monthly Commodity Price Bulletin* of the UNCTAD, and from a number of countries that produce commodities that are significantly traded in the international markets. Data derived from the last source are reported on the country pages. The market price series *(lines 76)* are expressed in U.S. dollars per quantity units and refer to values frequently used in the respective commodity markets. For comparison purposes, indices of unit values *(lines 74)* at base 1995=100 are provided. The notes to the table in the monthly issues provide information specific to each commodity series, including data sources, grades, and quotation frequency.

11. Charts

The charts following this introduction show the trends over recent years in some key economic time series published in the statistical tables in *IFS*. The underlying data in general relate to the world, area, and regional totals of the time series.

12. Country Codes and IFS Line Numbers

Each *IFS* time series carries a unique identification code, which for publication purposes has been truncated to a three-digit **country code** and to a five-digit **subject code** referred to as the *IFS* line number.

Country (and area) codes are listed on page viii. They appear also in the upper right-hand corner of the appropriate country pages and as part of the descriptor stub on most of the world tables.

Line numbers apply uniformly across countries, that is, a given line number measures the same economic variable for each country, subject to data availability. The line numbers take the form of two numerics followed by three alphabetic codes (NN*aaa*); the two numerics are the **section** and **subsection** codes, the first two alphabetic codes are the **classification** codes, and the last alphabetic code is the **qualification** code. Any of these positions may be blank: for publication purposes, blanks in the initial or final positions are omitted whereas embedded blanks are represented by a period. The line numbers are part of the descriptor stub on the country pages and also appear at the top of most of the world tables.

Production data *(lines 66)*, export data *(lines 70, 72, 74,* and *76)*, and import data *(lines 71)* for petroleum carry the commodity codes listed on page viii in the alpha positions of the subject code.

Data expressed in units of money (values or prices) are ordinarily expressed in national currency and in natural form, that is, without seasonal adjustment. For these data the qualification code is blank.

Transformations of these data are denoted by various qualification codes. For data that are **not** seasonally adjusted, qualification codes are *d* for U.S. dollar values, *s* for SDR values, and *p* for constant national currency values. For data that are seasonally adjusted for the monthly issues of *IFS*, qualification codes are *f* for U.S. dollar values, *u* for SDR values, and *b* for national currency values. For data that are seasonally adjusted by national compilers, qualification codes are *c* for national currency values and *r* for constant national currency values.

The qualification codes are also used to distinguish separate groups of deposit money banks or other financial institutions when data for separate classes are given.

13. Symbols, Conventions, and Abbreviations

Italic midheadings in the middle of the pages identify the units in which data are expressed and whether data are stocks (end of period), flows (transactions during a period), or averages (for a period).

(—) Indicates that a figure is zero or less than half of a significant digit or that data do not exist.

(....) Indicates a lack of statistical data that can be reported or calculated from underlying observations.

(**⟊**) Marks a break in the comparability of data, if explained in the relevant notes. In these instances, data after the symbol do not form a consistent series with those for earlier dates. The break symbols not otherwise explained in the country pages can indicate a point of splice where series having different base years are linked, as is the case of those series described in section 6 of this introduction.

(e) In superscript position after the figure marks an observation that is an estimate.

(f) In superscript position after the figure marks an observation that is forecast.

(p) In superscript position after the figure indicates that data are in whole or in part provisional or preliminary.

(n.i.e.) Indicates not included elsewhere.

Because of space limitations in the phototypesetting of descriptor stubs on the country pages and table headings of world tables, abbreviations are sometimes necessary. While most are self-explanatory, the following abbreviation in the table headings of the world tables should be noted:

Use of Fund Credit (GRA) = Use of Fund Credit (General Resources Account).

The following descriptor stub on the country pages should be noted:

Of which: Currency Outside DMBs = Of which: Currency Outside Deposit Money Banks.

Data relating to fiscal years are allocated to calendar years to which most of their months refer. Fiscal years ending June 30 are allocated to that calendar year; for instance, the fiscal year from July 1, 1997 to June 30, 1998 is shown as calendar year 1998.

14. IFS Electronic Subscriptions

The *IFS* is available on CD-ROM. It contains:

(1) all time series appearing on *IFS* country pages;
(2) all series published in the IFS world tables, except for the daily exchange rates appearing in the Exchange Rates tables;
(3) the following exchange rate series as available: *aa, ac, ae, af, ag, ah, b, c, de, dg, ea, eb, ec, ed, g, rb, rd, rf,*

rh, sa, sb, sc, sd, wa, wc, we, wf, wg, wh, xe, xf, ye, yf, nec, rec, aat, aet, rbt, rft, neu, reu, and *ahx* (for an explanation of series *af, ah, de, dg, rb,* and *rd,* see *IFS Supplement on Exchange Rates,* No. 9 (1985));
(4) Fund accounts time series, all in SDR terms (*2eb, 2eu, 2ey, 2eg, 2en, 2tl, 1b.s, 1c.s, 2dus, 2ees, 2egs, 2ehs, 2eqs, 2ers, 2ets, 2f.s, 2h.s, 2krs,* and *2kxs*; and the following series which contain the source code T—*1bd, 1bf, 1ch, 1cj, 2af, 2al, 2ap, 2aq, 2as, 2at, 2ej, 2ek, 2en, 2eo, 2fz, 2kk, 2kl, 2lk, 2ll,* and *2tl*);
(5) producer/wholesale price index series (*63*) and consumer price index series (*64*);
(6) export and import series (*70* and *71*); and
(7) balance of payments series (*78aad* to *79ded*).

The series referred to in item 3 are on the CD-ROM for all IMF members, plus Aruba, Hong Kong (Special Administrative Region as of 1997), and the Netherlands Antilles. The series referred to in items 4 through 7 correspond to all countries for which data are available, though some series are not published in the *IFS* book. All series on the *IFS* CD-ROM contain publication code F except for the previously mentioned Fund accounts series that contain the code T and the euro data lines that contain the code W.

A partner country code may in some cases be included in the control field. When it exists, it usually is shown in *IFS* either in the italic midheading (see *Real Effective Exchange Rate Indices* table) or in the notes (see *Commodity Prices* table notes). It should be noted that in some instances the partner country code attached to a commodity price refers to a market (e.g., the London Metals Exchange) rather than the country of origin.

In the book, data expressed in national currency for countries that have undergone periods of high inflation (e.g., Argentina, Brazil, and Peru) are presented in different magnitudes on the same printed line. Users may refer to midheaders on country pages for an indication of the magnitude changes. The practice of expressing different magnitudes on the same line was adopted to prevent early-period data from disappearing from the printed tables.

On the CD-ROM the data are stored in a scientific notation with six significant digits for all time periods. Therefore, historical as well as current data may be viewed when using the display options available on the CD-ROM.

15. Country Page Notes

The country page notes in this yearbook describe discontinuities in time series, each of which are identified by a break symbol (**⟊**). More extensive country and world table notes are carried in the monthly issues of *IFS*.

CHARTS

International Reserves

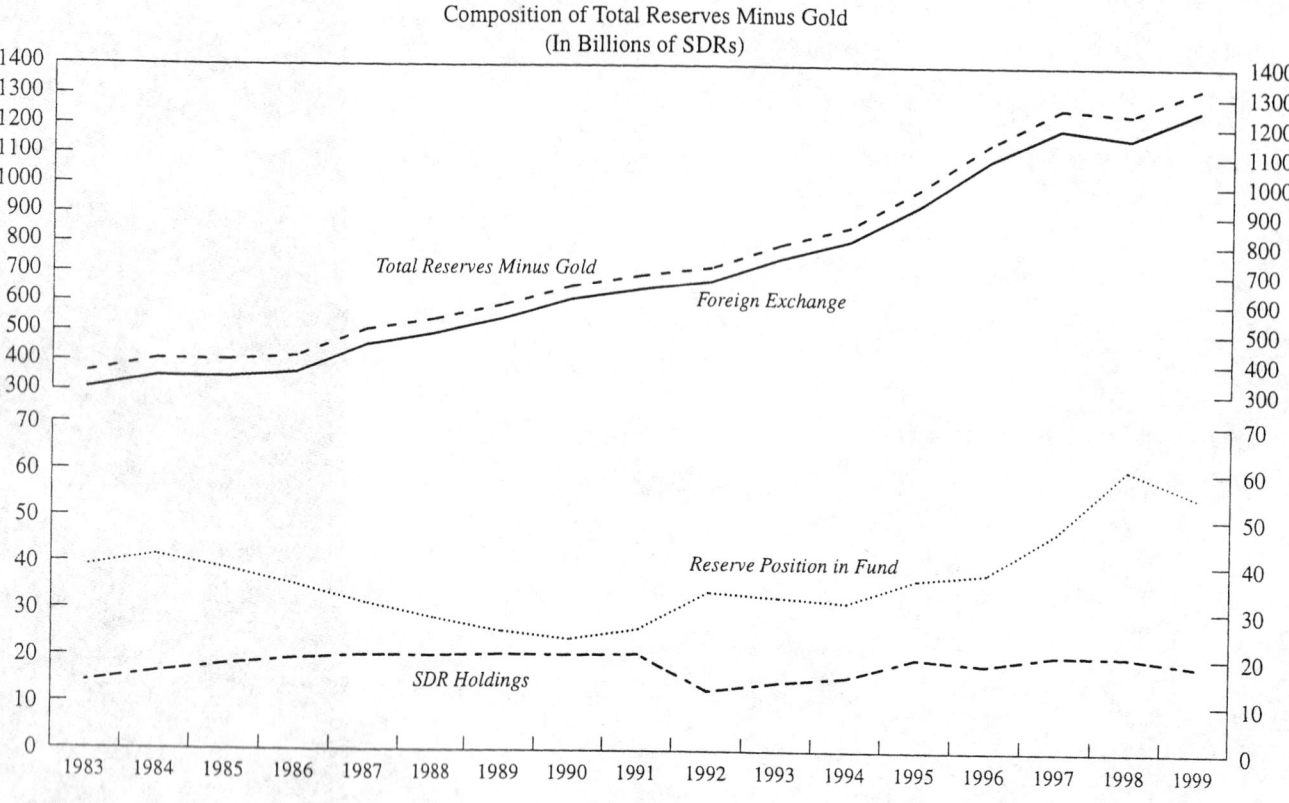

Composition of Total Reserves Minus Gold
(In Billions of SDRs)

Total Reserves Minus Gold

Foreign Exchange

Reserve Position in Fund

SDR Holdings

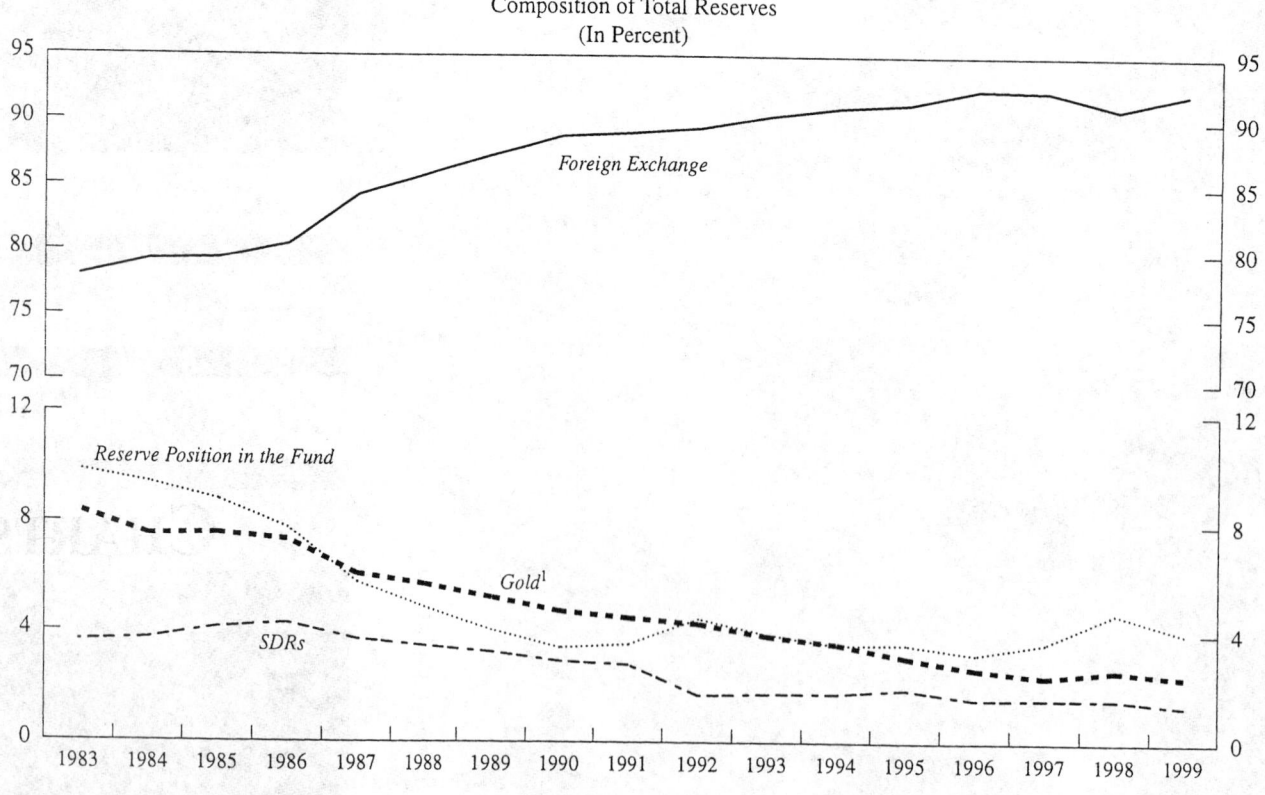

Composition of Total Reserves
(In Percent)

Foreign Exchange

Reserve Position in the Fund

Gold[1]

SDRs

[1]Values at SDR 35 per ounce.

Short-Term Interest Rates[1]
(Period Averages in Percent per Annum)

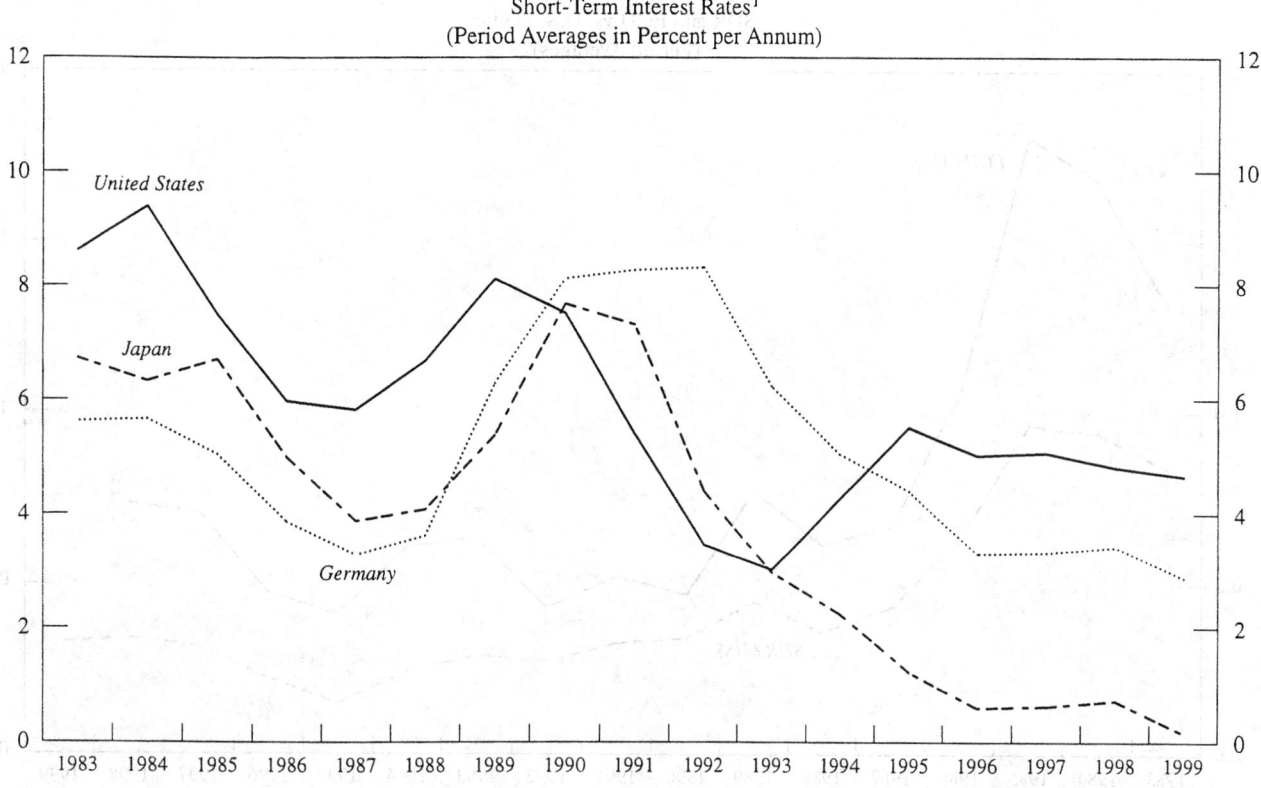

Long-Term Interest Rates[2]
(Period Averages in Percent per Annum)

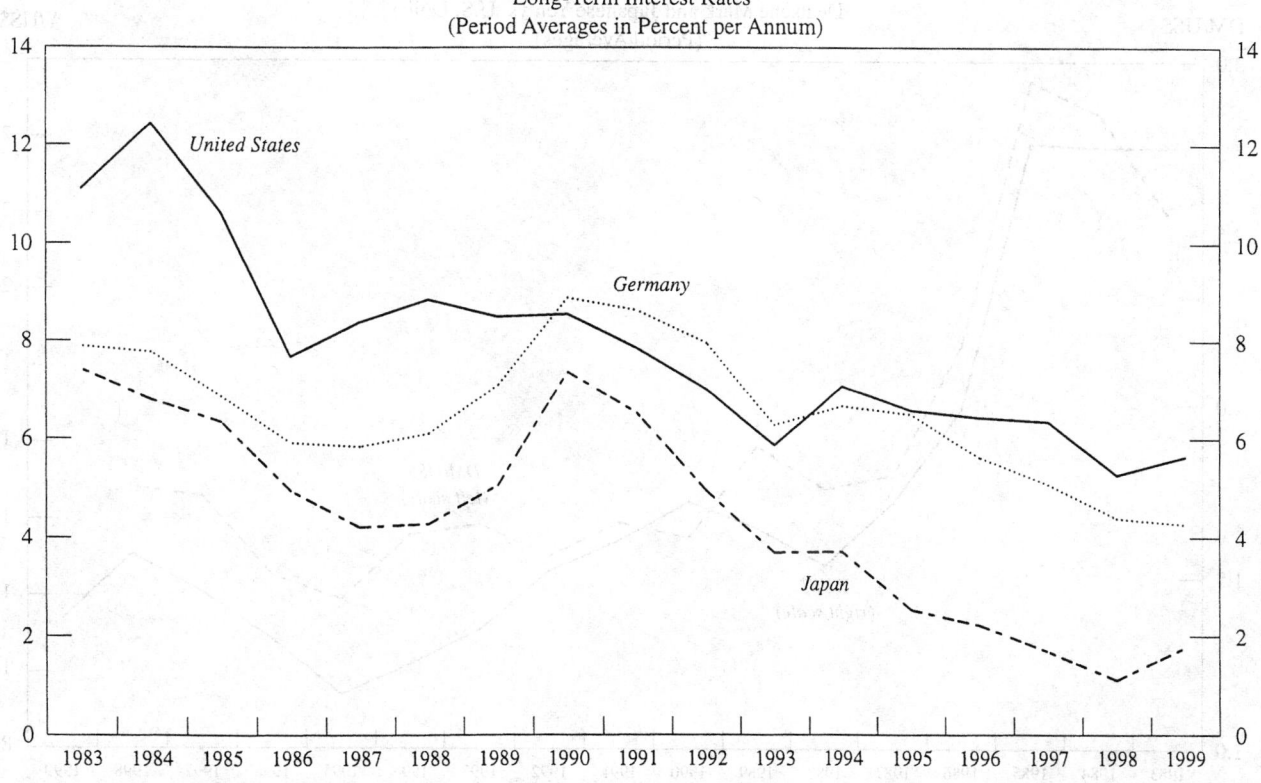

[1]Three-month T-bill rates for U.S. and Germany; private bill rate for Japan.
[2]Long-term government bond yield. (For definitions of the series used, see country notes in the monthly issues of *IFS*.)

Exchange Rates

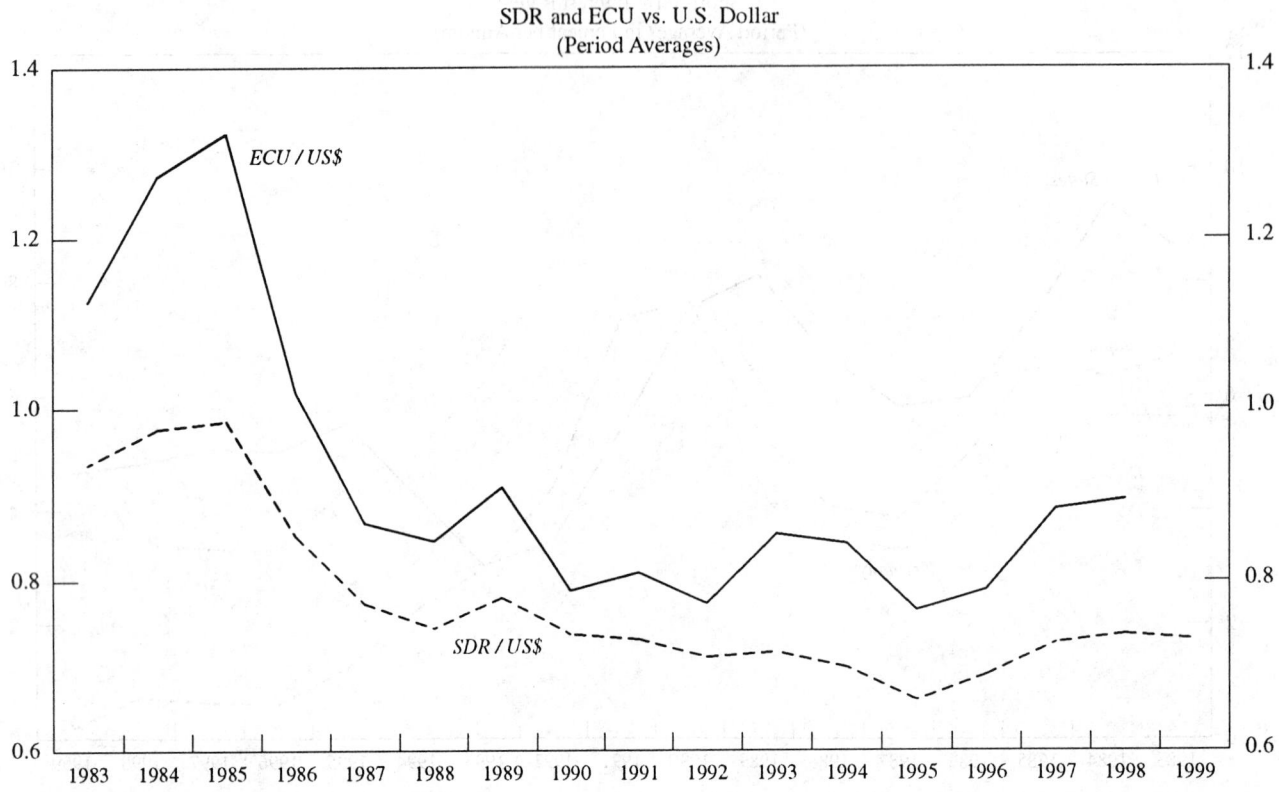

SDR and ECU vs. U.S. Dollar
(Period Averages)

ECU / US$

SDR / US$

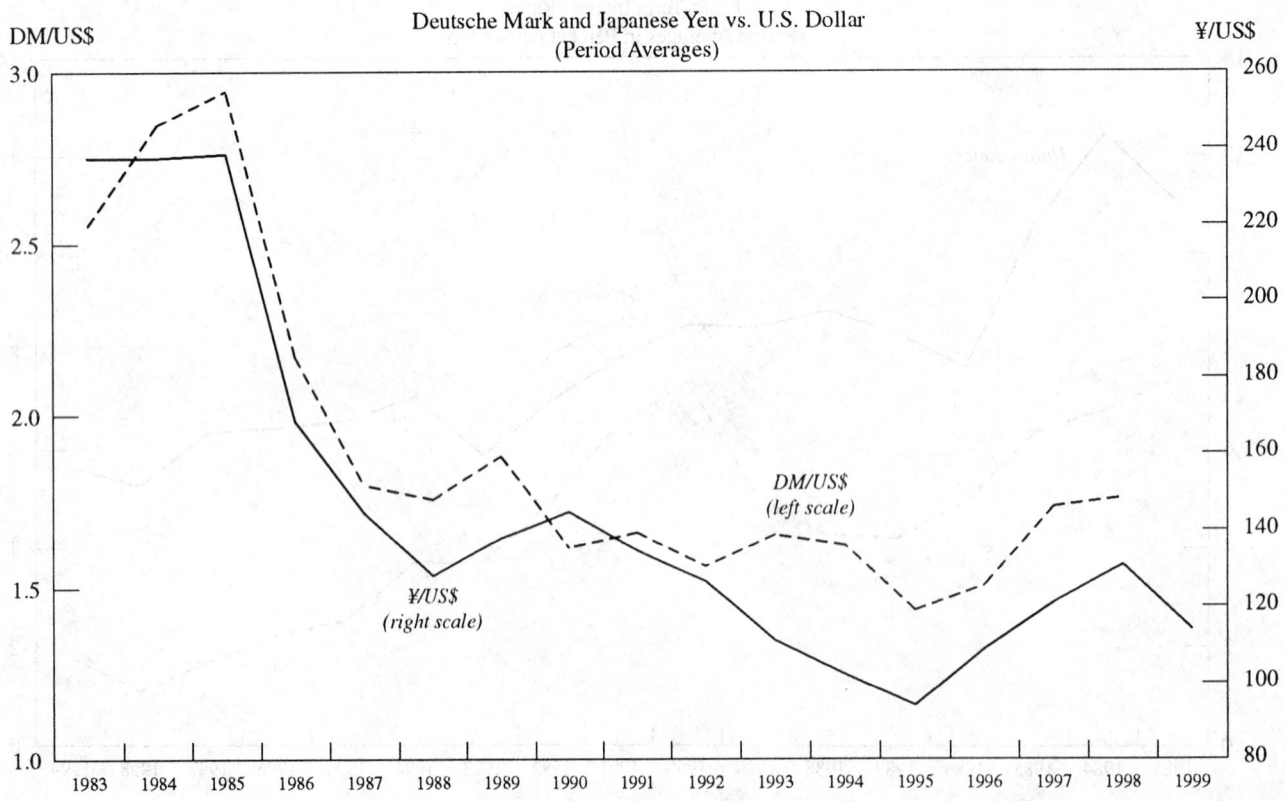

Deutsche Mark and Japanese Yen vs. U.S. Dollar
(Period Averages)

DM/US$

¥/US$

DM/US$
(left scale)

¥/US$
(right scale)

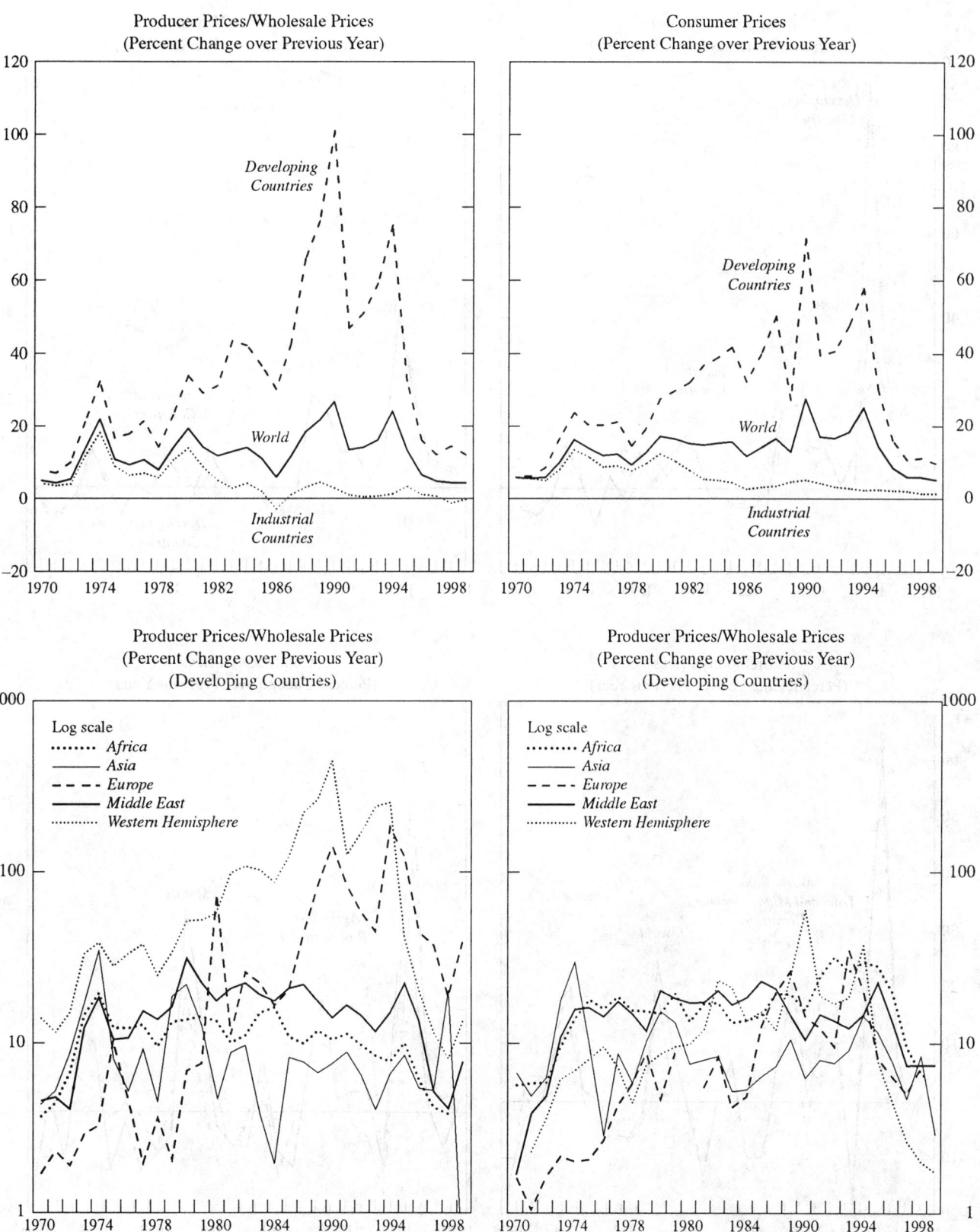

Producer Prices/Wholesale Prices
(Percent Change over Previous Year)

Consumer Prices
(Percent Change over Previous Year)

Producer Prices/Wholesale Prices
(Percent Change over Previous Year)
(Developing Countries)

Producer Prices/Wholesale Prices
(Percent Change over Previous Year)
(Developing Countries)

Unit Values and Commodity Prices

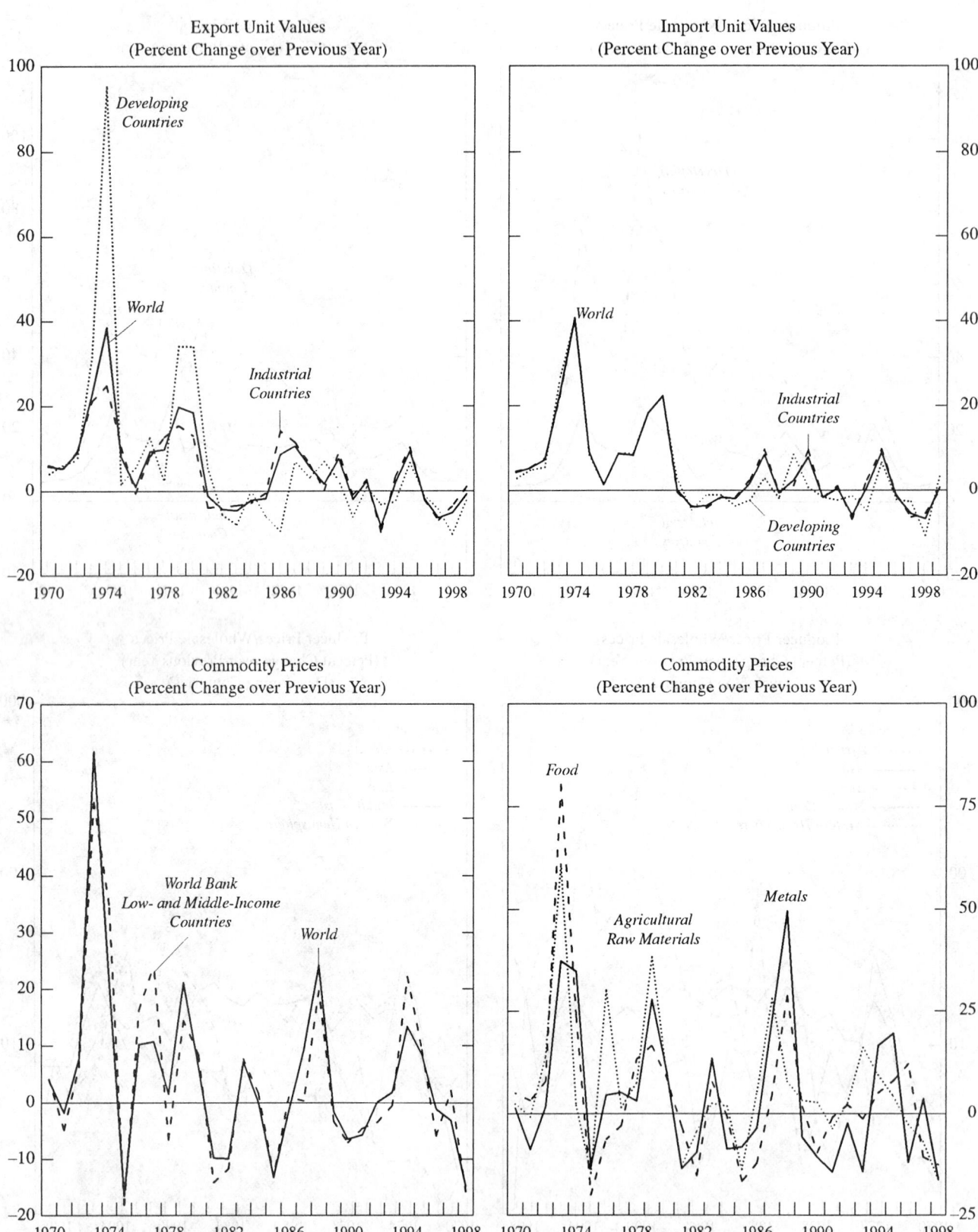

Export Unit Values
(Percent Change over Previous Year)

Developing Countries

World

Industrial Countries

Import Unit Values
(Percent Change over Previous Year)

World

Industrial Countries

Developing Countries

Commodity Prices
(Percent Change over Previous Year)

World Bank
Low- and Middle-Income
Countries

World

Commodity Prices
(Percent Change over Previous Year)

Food

Agricultural
Raw Materials

Metals

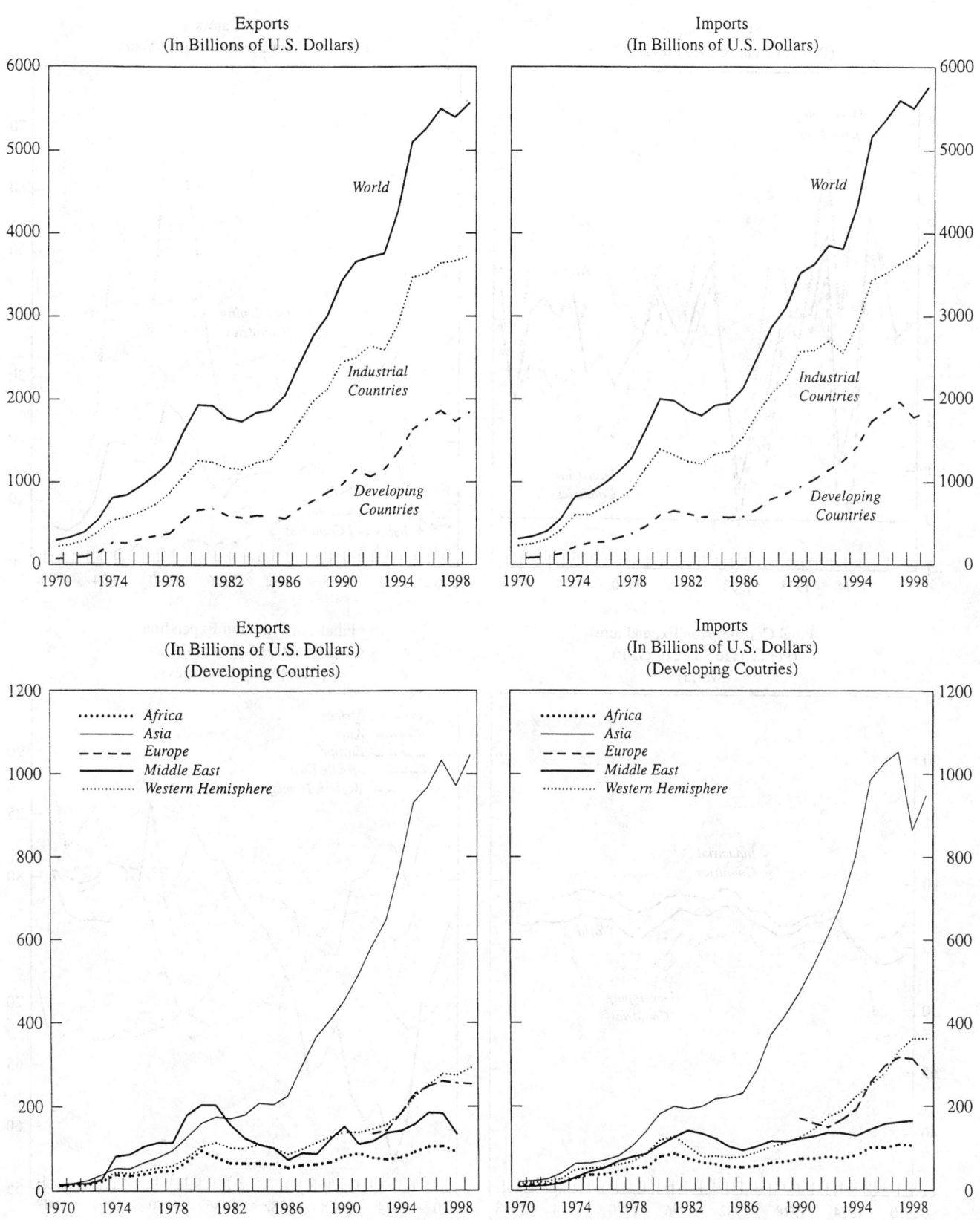

Exports
(In Billions of U.S. Dollars)

Imports
(In Billions of U.S. Dollars)

Exports
(In Billions of U.S. Dollars)
(Developing Coutries)

Imports
(In Billions of U.S. Dollars)
(Developing Coutries)

National Accounts

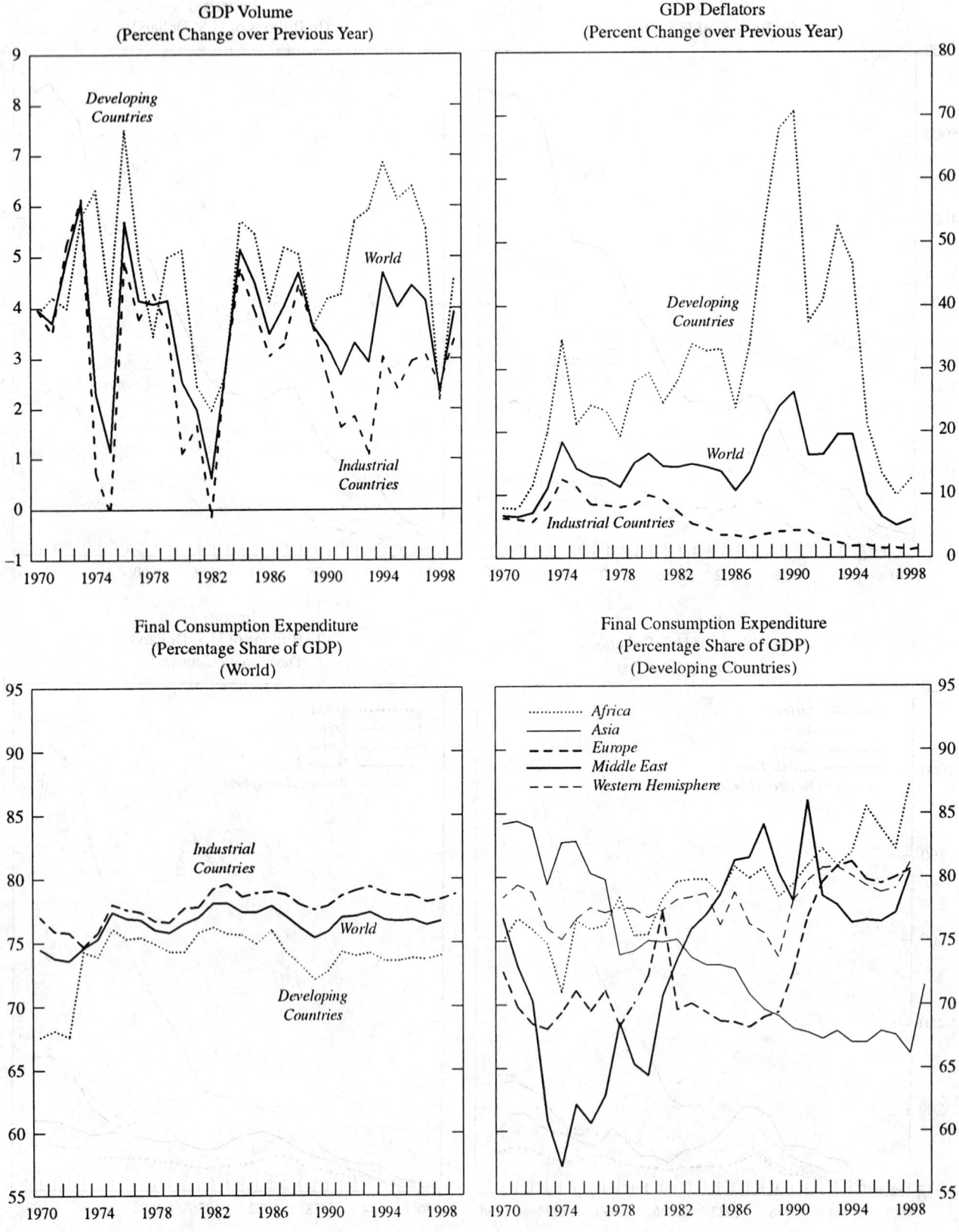

GDP Volume
(Percent Change over Previous Year)

Developing
Countries

World

Industrial
Countries

GDP Deflators
(Percent Change over Previous Year)

Developing
Countries

World

Industrial Countries

Final Consumption Expenditure
(Percentage Share of GDP)
(World)

Industrial
Countries

World

Developing
Countries

Final Consumption Expenditure
(Percentage Share of GDP)
(Developing Countries)

.... Africa
———— Asia
– – – – Europe
———— Middle East
– – – – Western Hemisphere

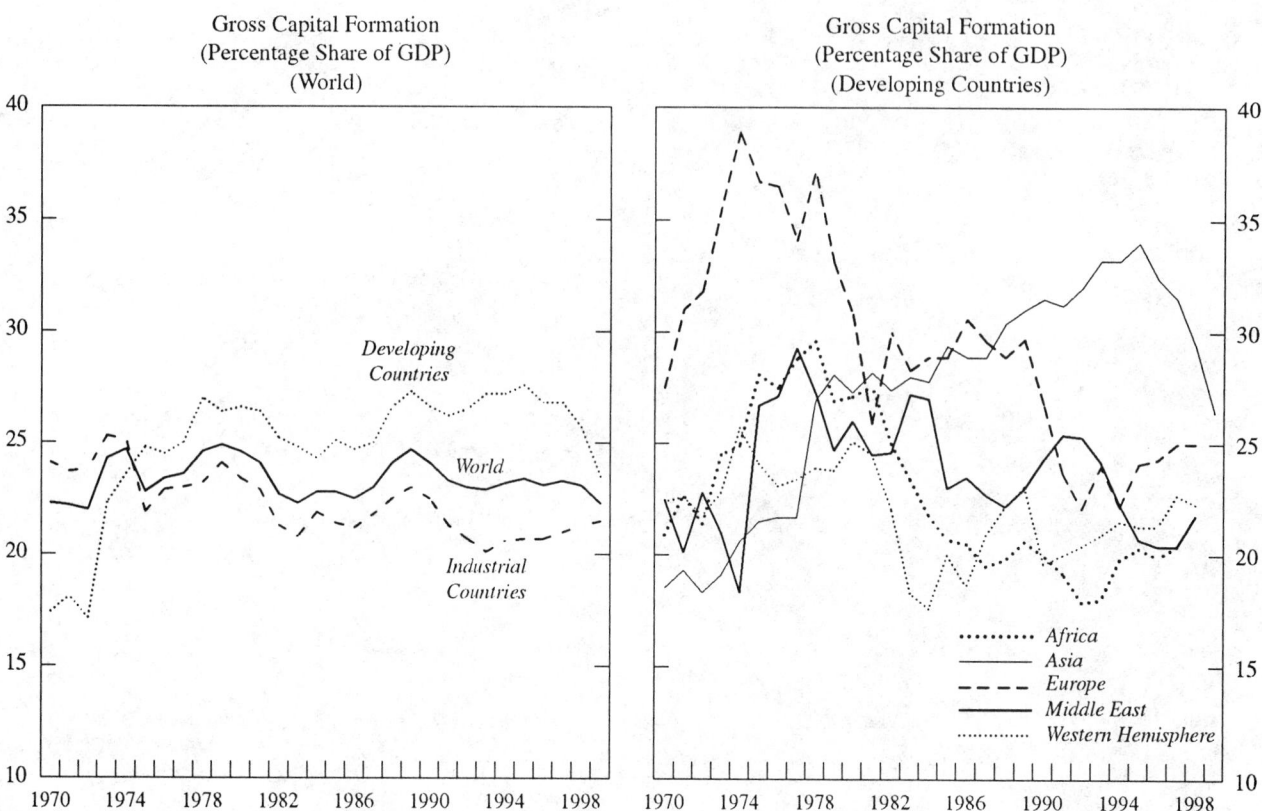

Gross Capital Formation
(Percentage Share of GDP)
(World)

Gross Capital Formation
(Percentage Share of GDP)
(Developing Countries)

WORLD AND AREA TABLES

Acceptances of Article VIII, Sections 2, 3, and 4

Fund Members That Have Accepted the Obligations of Article VIII, Sections 2, 3, and 4 of the IMF's Articles of Agreement and Effective Date of Acceptance

Article VIII of the Fund's Articles imposes certain obligations on member countries of the Fund. In particular Article VIII, Sections 2 (a) and 3 prohibit members, except with the approval of the Fund, from imposing restrictions on the making of payments and transfers for current international transactions or from engaging in multiple currency practices or discriminatory currency arrangements. Moreover, Article VIII, Section 4 requires Fund members, subject to certain conditions, to purchase balances of their currency from other Fund members, which represent that the balances have been recently acquired as a result of current international transactions or that the conversion is necessary for the purpose of making payments for current transactions.

Article XIV, Section 2 of the Fund's Articles establishes a limited exception to Article VIII, Sections 2, 3, and 4. Thus, member countries that avail themselves of Article XIV, Section 2 may, without seeking Fund approval, maintain and adapt to changing circumstances the restrictions on payments and transfers for current international transactions that were in effect on their date of membership in the Fund; however, if such restrictions are terminated and subsequently reintroduce restrictions are introduced by these members after their date of membership, they are subject to Fund approval under Article VIII. Moreover, members availing themselves of Article XIV are required to consult annually with the Fund with respect to the retention of Article XIV measures.

Members may accept the obligations of Article VIII, Sections 2, 3, and 4 at any time. When a member country accepts these obligations, it may no longer avail itself of the transitional arrangements of Article XIV, Section 2 and may not maintain any exchange measures inconsistent with Article VIII, Sections 2, 3, and 4.

As of November 30, 1999 there were 149 members that had accepted the obligations of Article VIII, Sections 2, 3, and 4.

Member	Effective Date of Acceptance	Member	Effective Date of Acceptance	Member	Effective Date of Acceptance
Algeria	September 15, 1997	Guinea-Bissau	January 1, 1997	Papua New Guinea	December 4, 1975
Antigua and Barbuda	November 22, 1983	Guyana	December 27, 1966	Paraguay	August 22, 1994
Argentina	May 14, 1968	Haiti	December 22, 1953	Peru	February 15, 1961
Armenia	May 29, 1997				
Australia	July 1, 1965	Honduras	July 1, 1950	Philippines	September 8, 1995
		Hungary	January 1, 1996	Poland	June 1, 1995
Austria	August 1, 1962	Iceland	September 19, 1983	Portugal	September 12, 1988
Bahamas, The	December 5, 1973	India	August 20, 1994	Qatar	June 4, 1973
Bahrain	March 20, 1973	Indonesia	May 7, 1988	Romania	March 25, 1998
Bangladesh	April 11, 1994				
Barbados	November 3, 1993	Ireland	February 15, 1961	Russia	June 1, 1996
		Israel	September 21, 1993	Rwanda	December 10, 1998
Belgium	February 15, 1961	Italy	February 15, 1961	St. Kitts and Nevis	December 3, 1984
Belize	June 14, 1983	Jamaica	February 22, 1963	St. Lucia	May 30, 1980
Benin	June 1, 1996	Japan	April 1, 1964	St. Vincent and the	
Bolivia	June 5, 1967			Grenadines	August 24, 1981
Botswana	November 17, 1995	Jordan	February 20, 1995		
		Kazakhstan	July 16, 1996	Samoa	October 6, 1994
Brazil	November 30, 1999	Kenya	June 30, 1994	San Marino	September 23, 1992
Brunei Darussalam	October 10, 1995	Kiribati	August 22, 1986	Saudia Arabia	March 22, 1961
Bulgaria	September 24, 1998	Korea	November 1, 1988	Senegal	June 1, 1996
Burkina Faso	June 1, 1996			Seychelles	January 3, 1978
Cameroon	June 1, 1996	Kuwait	April 5, 1963		
		Kyrgyz Republic	March 29, 1995	Sierra Leone	December 14, 1995
Canada	March 25, 1952	Latvia	June 10, 1994	Singapore	November 9, 1968
Central African Rep.	June 1, 1996	Lebanon	July 1, 1993	Slovak Republic	October 1, 1995
Chad	June 1, 1996	Lesotho	March 5, 1997	Slovenia	September 1, 1995
Chile	July 27, 1977			Solomon Islands	July 24, 1979
China, People's Rep.	December 1, 1996	Lithuania	May 3, 1994		
		Luxembourg	February 15, 1961	South Africa	September 15, 1973
Comoros	June 1, 1996	Macedonia, FYR	June 19, 1998	Spain	July 15, 1986
Congo, Rep. of	June 1, 1996	Madagascar	September 18, 1996	Sri Lanka	March 15, 1994
Costa Rica	February 1, 1965	Malawi	December 7, 1995	Suriname	June 29, 1978
Côte d'Ivoire	June 1, 1996			Swaziland	December 11, 1989
Croatia	May 29, 1995	Malaysia	November 11, 1968		
		Mali	June 1, 1996	Sweden	February 15, 1961
Cyprus	January 9, 1991	Malta	November 30, 1994	Switzerland	May 29, 1992
Czech Republic	October 1, 1995	Marshall Islands	May 21, 1992	Tanzania	July 15, 1996
Denmark	May 1, 1967	Mauritius	September 29, 1993	Thailand	May 4, 1990
Djibouti	September 19, 1980			Togo	June 1, 1996
Dominica	December 13, 1979	Mauritania	July 19, 1999		
		Mexico	November 12, 1946	Tonga	March 22, 1991
Dominican Republic	August 1, 1953	Micronesia, Fed.		Trinidad and Tobago	December 13, 1993
Ecuador	August 31, 1970	States of	June 24, 1993	Tunisia	January 6, 1993
El Salvador	November 6, 1946	Moldova	June 30, 1995	Turkey	March 22, 1990
Equatorial Guinea	June 1, 1996	Mongolia	February 1, 1996	Uganda	April 5, 1994
Estonia	August 15, 1994				
		Morocco	January 21, 1993	Ukraine	September 24, 1996
Fiji	August 4, 1972	Namibia	September 20, 1996	United Arab Emirates	February 13, 1974
Finland	September 25, 1979	Nepal	May 30, 1994	United Kingdom	February 15, 1961
France	February 15, 1961	Netherlands	February 15, 1961	United States	December 10, 1946
Gabon	June 1, 1996	New Zealand	August 5, 1982	Uruguay	May 2, 1980
Gambia, The	January 21, 1993				
		Nicaragua	July 20, 1964	Vanuatu	December 1, 1982
Georgia	December 20, 1996	Niger	June 1, 1996	Venezuela, Rep. Bol.	July 1, 1976
Germany	February 15, 1961	Norway	May 11, 1967	Yemen, Rep. of	December 10, 1996
Ghana	February 21, 1994	Oman	June 19, 1974	Zimbabwe	February 3, 1995
Greece	July 7, 1992	Pakistan	July 1, 1994		
Grenada	January 24, 1994				
		Palau	December 1, 1997		
Guatemala	January 27, 1947	Panama	November 26, 1946		
Guinea	November 17, 1995				

Exchange Rate Arrangements

Exchange Rate Arrangements and Anchors of Monetary Policy

(As of March 31, 2000)[1]

Exchange Rate Regime (Number of countries)	Monetary Policy Framework					
	Exchange rate anchor			Monetary aggregate target	Inflation targeting framework	Fund-supported or other monetary program	Other
Exchange arrangements with no separate legal tender (38)	**Another currency as legal tender** Ecuador* Kiribati Marshall Islands Micronesia Palau Panama San Marino **ECCM[2]** Antigua & Barbuda Dominica Grenada St. Kitts & Nevis St. Lucia St. Vincent & the Grenadines	**CFA Franc Zone** **WAEMU** Benin* Burkina Faso* Côte d'Ivoire* Guinea-Bissau Mali* Niger* Senegal* Togo	**CAEMC** Cameroon* C. African Rep.* Chad Congo, Rep.of Equatorial Guinea Gabon			Benin* Burkina Faso* Cameroon* Central African Rep.* Chad* Côte d'Ivoire* Guinea-Bissau* Mali* Senegal*	**Euro Area[3,4]** Austria Belgium Finland France Germany Ireland Italy Luxembourg Netherlands Portugal Spain
Currency board arrangements (8)	Argentina* Bosnia and Herzegovina * Brunei Darussalam Bulgaria* China, P.R. Hong Kong Djibouti* Estonia* Lithuania*					Argentina* Bosnia and Herzegovina* Bulgaria * Djibouti* Estonia* Lithuania*	
Other conventional fixed peg arrangements (including de facto peg arrangements under managed floating) (45)	**Against a single currency (32)** Aruba Bahamas, The[5] Bahrain[6,7] Barbados Belize Bhutan Cape Verde* China, P.R. Mainland*[6] Comoros[8] Egypt[5,6] El Salvador*[6] Iran[5,6] Iraq Jordan*[6] Lebanon[6] Lesotho Macedonia, FYR*[6] Malaysia	Maldives[6] Namibia Nepal Netherlands Antilles Oman Pakistan*[6] Qatar[6,7] Saudi Arabia[6,7] Swaziland Syrian Arab Republic[5] Trinidad & Tobago* Turkmenistan[6] United Arab Emirates[6,7] Zimbabwe*[6]	**Against a composite (13)** Bangladesh* Tonga Botswana[5] Vanuatu Fiji Kuwait Latvia* Malta Morocco Myanmar[5] Samoa Seychelles Solomon Islands	China, P.R.: Mainland*[6]		Bangladesh* Cape Verde* Jordan*[6] Latvia* Macedonia, FYR*[6] Pakistan*[6] Trinidad & Tobago* Zimbabwe*[6]	
Pegged exchange rates within horizontal bands (6)[9]	**Within a cooperative arrangement ERM II (2)** Denmark Greece	**Other band arrangements (5)** Cyprus Iceland Libyan A.J. Vietnam[6]					
Crawling pegs (5)[6]	Costa Rica Nicaragua* Turkey*			Tunisia		Bolivia Nicaragua* Turkey*	
Exchange rates within crawling bands (7)[6,10]	Israel* Honduras* Hungary* Poland*	Sri Lanka* Uruguay* Venezuela, Rep. Bolivariana		Sri Lanka*	Israel* Poland*	Honduras* Uruguay*	

** ECCM: East Caribbean Common Market; WAEMU: West African Economic and Monetary Union; CAEMC: Central African Economic and Monetary Community

Exchange Rate Arrangements

Exchange Rate Arrangements and Anchors of Monetary Policy
(As of March 31, 2000)[1]

Exchange Rate Regime (Number of countries)	Monetary Policy Framework				
	Exchange rate anchor	Monetary aggregate target	Inflation targeting framework	Fund-supported or other monetary program	Other
Managed floating with no preannounced path for exchange rate (27)		Jamaica[6] Kenya Malawi Slovenia	Czech Republic	Azerbaijan Cambodia* Croatia Kyrgyz Republic Mauritania Romania Tajikistan Ukraine	Algeria[3] Belarus[3,5] Burundi[3,5] Dominican Rep.[3,5] Ethiopia[3] Guatemala[3] Lao PDR[3,5] Nigeria[3] Norway[3] Paraguay[3] Singapore Slovak Republic[3] Suriname[3] Uzbekistan[3,5]
Independently floating (49)		Colombia Gambia, The* Ghana* Guinea* Guyana* Mauritius[6] Mongolia* Peru* Philippines* São Tomé and Príncipe* Sierra Leone* Yemen*	Australia Brazil[12] Canada Chile[5] New Zealand South Africa Sweden United Kingdom	Albania Armenia Colombia* Gambia, The* Georgia Ghana* Guinea* Guyana* Haiti Indonesia Kazakhstan Korea Madagascar Mexico Moldova Mongolia* Mozambique Papua New Guinea Peru* Philippines* Russian Federation Rwanda São Tomé and Príncipe* Sierra Leone* Sudan Tanzania Thailand Uganda Yemen* Zambia[5]	Afghanistan[5,11] Angola Congo, Dem. Rep. of[3] Eritrea[3] India[3] Japan[3] Liberia[3] Somalia[5,11] Switzerland[3] United States[3]

Source: Staff Reports

Exchange Arrangements with No Separate Legal Tender: The currency of another country circulates as the sole legal tender or the member belongs to a monetary or currency union in which the same legal tender is shared by the members of the union.

Currency Board Arrangements: A monetary regime based on an implicit legislative commitment to exchange domestic currency for a specified foreign currency at a fixed exchange rate, combined with restrictions on the issuing authority to ensure the fulfillment of its legal obligation.

Other Conventional Fixed Peg Arrangements: The country pegs its currency (formally or de facto) at a fixed rate to a major currency or a basket of currencies where the exchange rate fluctuates within a narrow margin of at most ±1 percent around a central rate.

Pegged Exchange Rates Within Horizontal Bands: The value of the currency is maintained within margins of fluctuation around a formal or de facto fixed peg that are wider than ±1 percent around a central rate.

Crawling Pegs: The currency is adjusted periodically in small amounts at a fixed, preannounced rate or in response to changes in selective quantitative indicators.

Exchange Rates Within Crawling Bands: The currency is maintained within certain fluctuation margins around a central rate that is adjusted periodically at a fixed preannounced rate or in response to changes in selective quantitative indicators.

Managed Floating with No Preannounced Path for the Exchange Rate: The monetary authority influences the movements of the exchange rate through active intervention in the foreign exchange market without specifying, or precommitting to, a preannounced path for the exchange rate.

Independent Floating: The exchange rate is market determined, with any foreign exchange intervention aimed at moderating the rate of change and preventing undue fluctuations in the exchange rate, rather than at establishing a level for it.

Note: The term "country," as used in this publication, does not in all cases refer to a territorial entity that is a state as understood by international law and practice; the term also covers some territorial entities that are not states but for which statistical data are maintained and provided internationally on a separate and independent basis.

[1]A country with * indicates that the country adopts more than one nominal anchor in conducting monetary policy. It should be noted, however, that it would not be possible, for practical reasons, to infer from this table which nominal anchor plays the principal role in conducting monetary policy.
[2]These countries also have a currency board arrangement.
[3]The country has no explicitly stated nominal anchor, but rather monitors various indicators in conducting monetary policy.
[4]Until they are withdrawn in the first half of 2002, national currencies will retain their status as legal tender within their home territories.
[5]Member maintained exchange arrangements involving more than one market. The arrangement shown is that maintained in the major market.
[6]The indicated country has a de facto arrangement under a formally announced policy of managed or independent floating. In the case of Jordan, it indicates that the country has a de jure peg to the SDR but a de facto peg to the U.S. dollar. In the case of Mauritius, the authorities have a de facto policy of independent floating, with only infrequent intervention by the central bank.
[7]Exchange rates are determined on the basis of a fixed relationship to the SDR, within margins of up to ±7.25%. However, because of the maintenance of a relatively stable relationship with the U.S. dollar, these margins are not always observed.
[8]Comoros has the same arrangement with the French Treasury as do the CFA Franc Zone countries.
[9]The band width for these countries is: Cyprus (±2.25%), Denmark (±2.25%), Greece (±15%), Iceland (±9%), Libya (±77.5%), and Vietnam (0.1% daily movement, one-sided).
[10]The band for these countries is: Honduras (±7%), Hungary (±2.25%), Israel (symmetric band of 44%), Poland (±15%), Sri Lanka (±1%), Uruguay (±3%), and República Bolivariana de Venezuela (±7.5%).
[11]There is no relevant information available for the country.
[12]Brazil maintains a Fund-supported program.

Exchange Rates

Market, Official, or Principal Rate

National Currency Units per SDR: End of Period (aa)

	1970	1971	1972	1973	1974	1975	1976	1977	1978	1979	1980	1981	1982	1983	1984
Industrial Countries															
US dollar	1.0000	1.0857	1.0857	1.2064	1.2244	1.1707	1.1618	1.2147	1.3028	1.3173	1.2754	1.1640	1.1031	1.0470	.9802
Canadian dollar	1.0112	1.0881	1.0809	1.2013	1.2136	1.1899	1.1725	1.3294	1.5451	1.5388	1.5237	1.3803	1.3562	1.3028	1.2952
Australian dollar	.8969	.9116	.8515	.8107	.9226	.9312	1.0694	1.0642	1.1324	1.1916	1.0802	1.0320	1.1249	1.1607	1.1841
Japanese yen	357.65	341.78	327.88	337.78	368.47	357.23	340.18	291.53	253.52	315.76	258.91	255.95	259.23	243.10	246.13
New Zealand dollar	.8960	.9084	.9084	.8445	.9307	1.1216	1.2230	1.1912	1.2214	1.3358	1.3254	1.4119	1.5060	1.5994	2.0524
Austrian schilling	25.880	25.742	I25.123	23.946	20.973	21.669	19.481	18.385	17.415	16.376	17.612	18.490	18.408	20.249	21.614
Belgian franc	49.675	48.591	47.839	49.846	44.227	46.273	41.806	40.013	37.520	36.948	40.205	44.766	51.758	58.252	61.832
Danish krone	7.489	7.667	7.434	I7.588	6.918	7.232	6.724	7.018	6.631	7.067	7.672	8.526	9.248	10.339	11.037
Finnish markka	4.1800	4.5057	4.5383	I4.6384	4.3477	4.5070	4.3766	4.8807	5.1148	4.8886	4.8976	5.0714	5.8366	6.0828	6.4008
French franc	5.5542	5.5542	5.5542	5.6801	5.4416	5.2510	5.7740	5.7152	5.4457	5.2957	5.7598	6.6904	7.4184	8.7394	9.4022
Deutsche mark	3.6480	3.5486	3.4759	3.2608	2.9501	3.0698	2.7448	2.5570	2.3815	2.2810	2.4985	2.6245	2.6215	2.8517	3.0857
Greek drachma	30.00	32.57	32.57	35.83	36.73	41.73	43.02	43.13	46.91	50.43	59.35	67.08	77.85	103.30	125.94
Icelandic krona	.881	.949	1.063	1.013	I1.451	1.999	2.204	2.589	4.144	5.202	7.957	I9.513	18.339	30.016	39.743
Irish pound	.41776	.42535	.46238	.51926	.52133	.57853	.68247	.63731	.64035	.61414	.67215	.73668	.78991	.92242	.98861
Italian lira	623.0	644.9	632.4	733.4	795.1	800.2	1,016.6	1,058.7	1,081.0	1,059.1	1,186.8	1,396.8	1,511.3	1,737.4	1,897.6
Luxembourg franc	49.675	48.591	47.839	49.846	44.227	46.273	41.806	40.013	37.520	36.948	40.205	44.766	51.758	58.252	61.832
Netherlands guilder	3.5970	3.5374	3.5030	3.4073	3.0688	3.1473	2.8546	2.7695	2.5652	2.5102	2.7160	2.8732	2.8951	3.2084	3.4793
Norwegian krone	7.1400	7.2851	I7.2091	6.9094	6.3727	6.5381	6.0241	6.2430	6.5433	6.4892	6.6066	6.7597	7.7813	8.0847	8.9072
Portuguese escudo	28.75	29.92	29.31	31.18	30.11	32.16	36.65	48.41	59.94	65.58	67.65	75.95	98.25	137.62	165.93
Spanish peseta	69.72	71.68	69.02	68.70	I68.70	69.98	79.34	98.28	91.34	87.14	101.08	113.43	138.55	164.06	169.97
Swedish krona	5.1700	5.2820	I5.1495	5.5341	4.9960	5.1339	4.7943	5.6721	5.5961	5.4623	5.5771	6.4844	8.0466	8.3766	8.8116
Swiss franc	4.3160	4.2506	4.0975	3.9134	3.1098	3.0671	2.8459	2.4294	2.1105	2.0814	2.2492	2.0934	2.2002	2.2818	2.5338
Pound sterling	.41776	.42535	I.46238	.51926	.52133	.57853	.68247	.63731	.64035	.59232	.53476	.61004	.68325	.72174	.84757
Developing Countries															
Africa															
Algerian dinar	4.9371	I5.0420	4.9465	5.0486	4.8937	4.8290	5.0644	4.9014	4.9955	4.9472	5.0653	5.0958	5.1135	5.1473	5.0213
Benin,CFA franc	276.02	283.61	278.00	284.00	272.08	262.55	288.70	285.76	272.28	264.78	287.99	334.52	370.92	436.97	470.11
Botswana pula	.7172	.8308	.8499	.8097	.8444	1.0180	1.0103	1.0060	1.0789	1.0390	.9461	1.0244	1.1704	1.2098	1.5292
Burkina Faso, CFA franc	276.02	283.61	278.00	284.00	272.08	262.55	288.70	285.76	272.28	264.78	287.99	334.52	370.92	436.97	470.11
Burundi franc	87.50	95.00	95.00	95.00	96.42	92.19	104.56	109.32	117.25	118.56	114.79	104.76	99.28	122.70	122.70
Cameroon, CFA franc	276.02	283.61	278.00	284.00	272.08	262.55	288.70	285.76	272.28	264.78	287.99	334.52	370.92	436.97	470.11
Cape Verde escudo	28.75	29.92	29.31	31.18	30.11	32.16	36.65	41.18	46.82	50.47	54.19	59.20	69.54	83.73	91.17
Cent.African Rep.,CFA franc	276.02	283.61	278.00	284.00	272.08	262.55	288.70	285.76	272.28	264.78	287.99	334.52	370.92	436.97	470.11
Chad, CFA franc	276.02	283.61	278.00	284.00	272.08	262.55	288.70	285.76	272.28	264.78	287.99	334.52	370.92	436.97	470.11
Comorian franc	276.02	283.61	277.99	284.00	272.08	262.55	288.70	285.76	272.28	264.78	287.98	334.52	370.92	436.97	470.10
Congo, Dem.Rep., new zaïre	—	—	—	—	—	—	—	—	—	—	—	—	—	—	—
Congo, Rep. of, CFA franc	276.02	283.61	278.00	284.00	272.08	262.55	288.70	285.76	272.28	264.78	287.99	334.52	370.92	436.97	470.11
Côte d'Ivoire,CFA franc	276.02	283.61	278.00	284.00	272.08	262.55	288.70	285.76	272.28	264.78	287.99	334.52	370.92	436.97	470.11
Djibouti franc	214.39	214.39	214.39	214.39	217.59	208.05	206.48	215.88	231.53	234.12	226.67	206.86	196.05	186.07	174.20
Eq. Guinea, CFA franc	276.02	283.61	278.00	284.00	272.08	262.55	288.70	285.76	272.28	264.78	287.99	334.52	370.92	436.97	470.11
Ethiopian birr	2.5000	2.4971	2.4971	2.4971	2.5344	2.4233	2.4050	2.5144	2.6968	2.7269	2.6401	2.4094	2.2834	2.1672	2.0290
Gabon, CFA franc	276.02	283.61	278.00	284.00	272.08	262.55	288.70	285.76	272.28	264.78	287.99	334.52	370.92	436.97	470.11
Gambian dalasi	2.089	I2.127	2.312	2.077	2.085	2.314	2.730	2.549	2.561	2.369	2.139	2.440	2.733	2.887	4.238
Ghanaian cedi	1.02	1.97	1.39	1.39	1.41	1.35	1.34	1.40	3.58	3.62	3.51	3.20	3.03	31.41	49.01
Guinean franc	24.69	24.68	24.68	24.91	25.28	24.69	24.69	24.69	24.69	24.69	24.69	24.69	24.69	24.69	24.69
Guinea-Bissau, CFA franc	.4	.5	.5	.5	.5	.5	.6	.6	.7	.7	.7	.7	.7	1.4	1.9
Kenya shilling	7.143	7.755	7.755	8.324	8.745	9.660	9.660	9.660	9.660	9.660	9.660	11.950	14.060	14.417	15.187
Lesotho loti	.7172	.8308	.8500	.8097	.8444	1.0180	1.0103	1.0563	1.1329	1.0892	.9507	1.1134	1.1873	1.2793	1.9456
Liberian dollar	1.0000	1.0857	1.0857	1.2064	1.2244	1.1707	1.1618	1.2147	1.3028	1.3173	1.2754	1.1640	1.1031	1.0470	.9802
Malagasy franc	276.0	283.6	278.0	284.0	272.1	262.5	288.7	285.8	272.3	264.8	288.0	334.5	405.6	515.3	645.0
Malawi kwacha	.8333	.8334	.9280	1.0224	1.0291	1.0541	1.0541	1.0541	1.0541	1.0541	1.0541	1.0541	1.2122	1.3577	1.5339
Mali, CFA franc	276.02	283.61	278.00	284.00	272.08	262.55	288.70	285.76	272.28	264.78	287.99	334.52	370.92	436.97	470.11
Mauritanian ouguiya	55.21	56.72	55.60	I56.80	53.01	52.86	50.70	55.94	60.13	60.39	58.71	56.96	58.42	59.71	65.96
Mauritian rupee	5.570	5.671	6.165	6.923	6.951	7.714	7.714	7.714	7.714	I10.000	10.000	12.000	12.000	13.321	15.295
Moroccan dirham	5.029	5.168	5.066	5.175	5.087	4.898	5.210	5.256	5.063	4.925	5.528	6.208	6.914	8.439	9.362
Mozambique, metical	28.7	29.9	29.3	31.2	30.1	32.2	36.7	39.5	42.2	42.5	41.8	41.6	42.1	43.1	42.7
Namibia dollar	.71723	.83085	.85000	.80966	.84435	1.01797	1.01029	1.05627	1.13286	1.08924	.95066	1.11341	1.18729	1.27926	1.94563
Niger, CFA franc	276.02	283.61	278.00	284.00	272.08	262.55	288.70	285.76	272.28	264.78	287.99	334.52	370.92	436.97	470.11
Nigerian naira	.714	.714	.714	.794	.754	.734	.733	.791	.844	.738	.694	.741	.739	.784	.792
Rwanda franc	100.00	100.00	100.00	100.00	113.67	108.68	107.86	112.77	120.95	122.30	118.41	108.06	102.41	102.71	102.71
São Tomé & Príncipe dobra	28.75	29.92	29.31	31.18	30.11	32.16	36.65	45.25	45.25	45.25	45.25	45.25	45.25	45.25	45.25
Senegal, CFA franc	276.02	283.61	278.00	284.00	272.08	262.55	288.70	285.76	272.28	264.78	287.99	334.52	370.92	436.97	470.11
Seychelles rupee	5.5702	5.6713	I6.1650	6.9235	6.9511	7.7137	9.0995	8.4974	8.5380	8.3197	8.3197	7.2345	7.2345	7.2345	7.2345
Sierra Leonean leone	.84	.85	.92	1.04	1.04	1.16	1.36	1.27	1.37	1.37	1.37	1.37	1.36	2.63	2.46
South African rand	.7172	.8308	.8500	.8097	.8444	1.0180	1.0103	1.0563	1.1329	1.0892	.9507	1.1134	1.1873	1.2793	1.9456
Sudanese pound	.0348	.0378	.0378	.0420	.0426	.0408	.0405	.0423	.0521	.0659	.0638	.1049	.1434	.1361	.1274
Swaziland lilangeni	.7172	.8308	.8500	.8097	.8444	1.0180	1.0103	1.0563	1.1329	1.0892	.9507	1.1134	1.1873	1.2793	1.9456
Tanzanian shilling	7.14	7.76	7.76	8.32	8.75	9.66	9.66	9.66	9.66	10.83	10.44	9.69	10.55	13.04	17.75
Togo, CFA franc	276.02	283.61	278.00	284.00	272.08	262.55	288.70	285.76	272.28	264.78	287.99	334.52	370.92	436.97	470.11
Tunisian dinar	.5200	.5211	I.5255	.5369	.4978	.4979	.5007	.5005	.5255	.5215	.5340	.6002	.6792	.7612	.8495
Uganda shilling	.1	.1	.1	.1	.1	.1	.1	.1	.1	.1	1.0	1.2	2.5	5.1	
Zambian kwacha	.714	.776	.776	.776	.788	.753	.922	.922	I1.024	1.024	1.024	1.024	1.024	1.280	2.157
Zimbabwe dollar	.7162	.7287	.7079	.7311	.6718	.7314	.7192	.7857	.8796	.8882	.8043	.8347	1.0143	1.1574	1.4727
Asia															
Afghanistan,afghani	45.000	48.857	48.857	54.286	55.096	52.680	52.282	54.662	58.626	55.657	58.478	58.896	55.817	52.976	49.599
Bangladesh taka		8.068	8.770	9.849	9.888	17.356	17.373	17.486	19.456	20.607	20.726	23.101	26.556	26.174	25.485
Bhutan,ngultrum	7.576	7.903	8.773	9.896	9.978	10.462	10.318	9.971	10.668	10.416	10.114	10.591	10.627	10.986	12.205
Cambodian riel	55.5	141.1	203.0	331.7	....	....									
Chinese yuan	2.4618	2.6728	2.4321	2.4371	2.2524	2.3019	2.1846	2.1014	2.0546	1.9710	1.9518	2.0317	2.1209	2.0739	2.7404
Fiji dollar	.8731	.8890	.9155	.9762	.9795	1.0104	1.0939	1.0575	1.0679	1.1077	1.0089	1.0205	1.0450	1.0954	1.1204
Hong Kong dollar	6.0766	6.1870	I6.1820	6.1403	6.0116	5.8919	5.4292	5.6059	6.2573	6.5181	6.5429	6.6055	7.1647	8.1453	7.6682
Indian rupee	7.576	7.903	8.773	9.896	I9.978	10.462	10.318	9.971	10.668	10.416	10.114	10.591	10.627	10.986	12.205
Indonesian rupiah	378.0	450.6	450.6	500.6	508.1	485.8	482.2	504.1	814.2	826.0	799.4	749.6	763.9	1,040.7	1,052.7
Kiribati, Aust.dollar	.8969	.9116	.8515	.8107	.9226	.9312	1.0694	1.0642	1.1324	1.1916	1.0802	1.0320	1.1249	1.1607	1.1841
Korean won	316.6	405.3	433.1	479.5	592.6	566.6	562.3	587.9	630.6	637.6	841.6	815.4	826.0	832.8	811.0
Lao P.D. Rep., kip	240.00	260.57	651.43	723.81	734.61	I877.99	232.37	242.94	521.12	I13.17	12.75	34.92	38.61	36.64	34.31
Malaysian ringgit	3.07750	3.13336	3.05845	2.95797	2.83168	3.03002	2.94524	2.87340	2.87395	2.88364	2.83447	2.60995	2.56065	2.44808	2.37701
Maldivian rufiyaa	4.750	4.750	4.750	4.741	4.812	7.170	10.021	10.841	11.237	9.946	9.629	8.788	7.777	7.381	6.910

I **See country notes in the monthly *IFS***

Exchange Rates

Market, Official, or Principal Rate

National Currency Units per SDR: End of Period (aa)

1985	1986	1987	1988	1989	1990	1991	1992	1993	1994	1995	1996	1997	1998	1999	
															Industrial Countries
1.0984	1.2232	1.4187	1.3457	1.3142	1.4227	1.4304	1.3750	1.3736	1.4599	1.4865	1.4380	1.3493	1.4080	1.3725	US dollar
1.5350	1.6886	1.8440	1.6050	1.5215	1.6507	1.6530	1.7478	1.8186	2.0479	2.0294	1.9694	1.9282	2.1550	1.9809	Canadian dollar
1.6132	1.8399	1.9635	1.5730	1.6578	1.8397	1.8826	1.9968	2.0286	1.8793	1.9953	1.8053	2.0672	2.2936	2.0993	Australian dollar
220.23	194.61	175.20	169.36	188.52	191.21	179.09	171.53	153.63	145.61	152.86	166.80	175.34	162.77	140.27	Japanese yen
2.2035	2.3366	2.1577	2.1418	2.2005	2.4203	2.6436	2.6735	2.4581	2.2721	2.2754	2.0368	2.3195	2.6723	2.6364	New Zealand dollar
18.981	16.770	15.960	16.909	15.527	15.190	15.290	15.612	16.679	16.013	14.996	15.751	17.045	16.540	....	Austrian schilling
55.316	49.429	47.032	50.255	46.994	44.078	44.730	45.623	49.599	46.478	43.725	46.022	49.814	48.682	....	Belgian franc
9.852	8.981	8.649	9.250	8.683	8.217	8.459	8.601	9.302	8.880	8.244	8.548	9.210	8.992	10.155	Danish krone
5.9501	5.8640	5.5980	5.6102	5.3342	5.1699	5.9120	7.2119	7.9454	6.9244	6.4790	6.6777	7.3139	7.1753	....	Finnish markka
8.3052	7.8957	7.5756	8.1536	7.6064	7.2968	7.4096	7.5714	8.0978	7.8044	7.2838	7.5306	8.0794	7.9161	....	French franc
2.7035	2.3740	2.2436	2.3957	2.2312	2.1255	2.1685	2.2193	2.3712	2.2610	2.1309	2.2357	2.4180	2.3556	....	Deutsche mark
162.30	169.73	178.64	199.30	207.36	224.25	250.73	295.05	342.32	350.51	352.36	355.20	381.31	397.87	450.79	Greek drachma
46.200	49.221	50.589	62.198	80.387	78.801	79.561	87.890	99.899	99.708	96.964	96.185	97.389	97.605	99.576	Icelandic krona
.88333	.87402	.84671	.89267	.84441	.80127	.81748	.84387	.97360	.94360	.92587	.85537	.94327	.94670	....	Irish pound
1,843.7	1,661.3	1,658.8	1,757.2	1,669.6	1,607.8	1,646.5	2,022.4	2,340.5	2,379.2	2,355.7	2,200.9	2,373.6	2,327.6	....	Italian lira
55.316	49.429	47.032	50.255	46.994	44.078	44.730	45.623	49.599	46.478	43.725	46.022	49.814	48.682	....	Luxembourg franc
3.0448	2.6812	2.5217	2.6907	2.5173	2.4043	2.4466	2.4944	2.6659	2.5330	2.3849	2.5072	2.7217	2.6595	....	Netherlands guilder
8.3288	9.0516	8.8418	8.8412	8.6932	8.4044	8.5440	9.5212	10.3264	9.8715	9.3931	9.2641	9.8707	10.7010	11.0343	Norwegian krone
172.99	178.73	184.23	196.97	196.92	190.07	191.94	201.79	242.86	232.25	222.10	224.88	247.35	241.94	....	Portuguese escudo
169.32	161.94	154.63	152.67	144.19	137.87	138.31	157.61	195.34	192.32	180.47	188.77	204.68	200.79	....	Spanish peseta
8.3650	8.3409	8.2963	8.2855	8.1833	8.1063	7.9096	9.6841	11.4054	10.8927	9.8973	9.8802	10.6280	11.3501	11.7006	Swedish krona
2.2809	1.9858	1.8130	2.0239	2.0323	1.8431	1.9389	2.0020	2.0322	1.9146	1.7102	1.9361	1.9636	1.9382	2.1955	Swiss franc
.76042	.82956	.75803	.74369	.81854	.73789	.76465	.90939	.92733	.93430	.95903	.84686	.81585	.84643	.84912	Pound sterling
															Developing Countries
															Africa
5.2425	5.9001	7.0029	9.0576	10.5559	17.3434	30.5996	31.3244	33.1344	62.6166	77.5576	80.7931	78.8150	84.9790	95.1346	Algerian dinar
415.26	394.78	378.78	407.68	380.32	364.84	370.48	378.57	404.89	I780.44	728.38	753.06	807.94	791.61	I896.19	Benin,CFA franc
2.3076	2.2477	2.2212	2.6049	2.4605	2.6622	2.9646	3.1031	3.5229	3.9670	4.1944	5.2404	5.1400	6.2774	6.3572	Botswana pula
415.26	394.78	378.78	407.68	380.32	364.84	370.48	378.57	404.89	I780.44	728.38	753.06	807.94	791.61	I896.19	Burkina Faso, CFA franc
122.70	151.50	161.00	201.00	232.14	232.14	273.07	322.90	362.99	360.78	413.37	462.63	551.56	710.64	860.83	Burundi franc
415.26	394.78	378.78	407.68	380.32	364.84	370.48	378.57	404.89	I780.44	728.38	753.06	807.94	791.61	I896.19	Cameroon, CFA franc
93.78	93.65	93.31	99.13	95.99	94.02	95.08	100.50	118.12	118.45	115.14	122.46	129.85	132.71	147.65	Cape Verde escudo
415.26	394.78	378.78	407.68	380.32	364.84	370.48	378.57	404.89	I780.44	728.38	753.06	807.94	791.61	I896.19	Cent.African Rep.,CFA franc
415.26	394.78	378.78	407.68	380.32	364.84	370.48	378.57	404.89	I780.44	728.38	753.06	807.94	791.61	I896.19	Chad, CFA franc
415.25	394.78	378.78	407.68	380.31	364.84	370.48	378.57	404.89	I585.32	546.28	564.79	605.95	593.70	I672.14	Comorian franc
—	—	—	—	—	—	—	.9	48.1	4,744.5	22,046.1	....	143,020.5	....	....	Congo, Dem.Rep., new zaïre
415.26	394.78	378.78	407.68	380.32	364.84	370.48	378.57	404.89	I780.44	728.38	753.06	807.94	791.61	I896.19	Congo, Rep. of, CFA franc
415.26	394.78	378.78	407.68	380.32	364.84	370.48	378.57	404.89	I780.44	728.38	753.06	807.94	791.61	I896.19	Côte d'Ivoire,CFA franc
195.21	217.39	252.13	239.16	233.55	252.84	254.22	244.37	244.11	259.45	264.18	255.56	239.79	250.24	243.92	Djibouti franc
415.26	394.78	378.78	407.68	380.32	364.84	370.48	378.57	404.89	I780.44	728.38	753.06	807.94	791.61	I896.19	Eq. Guinea, CFA franc
2.2737	2.5320	2.9366	2.7856	2.7203	2.9449	2.9610	6.8750	6.8678	8.6861	9.3946	9.2403	9.2613	10.5644	11.1640	Ethiopian birr
415.26	394.78	378.78	407.68	380.32	364.84	370.48	378.57	404.89	I780.44	728.38	753.06	807.94	791.61	I896.19	Gabon, CFA franc
3.802	9.084	9.134	8.961	10.928	10.662	12.813	12.673	13.096	13.983	14.330	14.225	14.207	15.476	15.849	Gambian dalasi
65.89	110.10	249.76	309.36	398.23	490.57	558.76	716.15[p]	1,125.87	1,536.68	2,154.33	2,522.74	3,066.48	3,274.49	4,732.79	Ghanaian cedi
24.69	288.22	624.21	740.14	814.78	967.41	1,148.56	1,268.31	1,335.67	1,432.15	1,483.49	1,494.23	1,544.82	1,827.67	2,382.68	Guinean franc
3.0	4.5	18.6	28.2	40.2	54.9	109.1	183.1	242.2	345.2	501.5	772.9	807.9	791.6	I896.2	Guinea-Bissau, CFA franc
17.738	19.135	23.429	25.029	28.387	34.263	40.158	49.797	93.626	65.458	83.153	79.118	84.568	87.165	100.098	Kenya shilling
2.8093	2.6707	2.7379	3.1997	3.3327	3.6456	3.9237	4.1979	4.6667	5.1730	5.4220	6.7332	6.5675	8.2511	8.4471	Lesotho loti
1.0984	1.2232	1.4187	1.3457	1.3142	1.4227	1.4304	1.3750	1.3736	1.4599	1.4865	1.4380	1.3493	I60.8973	54.2141	Liberian dollar
698.4	941.6	1,751.0	2,054.1	2,014.0	2,085.4	2,621.5	2,626.5	2,695.8	5,651.2	5,088.2	6,224.2	7,130.3	7,606.5	8,980.6	Malagasy franc
1.8445	2.3882	2.9136	3.4120	3.5204	3.7656	3.8104	6.0442	6.1733	22.3337	22.7479	22.0340	28.6416	61.7894	63.7362	Malawi kwacha
415.26	394.78	378.78	407.68	380.32	364.84	370.48	378.57	404.89	I780.44	728.38	753.06	807.94	791.61	I896.19	Mali, CFA franc
84.66	90.61	101.58	101.91	109.80	110.74	111.32	158.26	170.54	187.40	203.81	204.84	227.15	289.74	308.81	Mauritanian ouguiya
15.718	16.069	17.272	18.616	19.707	20.375	21.162	23.372	25.625	26.077	26.258	25.842	30.041	34.896	34.955	Mauritian rupee
10.568	10.656	11.066	11.049	10.673	11.442	11.658	12.442	13.257	13.080	12.589	12.653	13.107	13.031	13.845	Moroccan dirham
45.2	48.1	573.1	842.7	1,077.2	1,476.9	2,639.7	I4,058.2	7,339.2	9,709.5	16,187.9	16,359.7	15,574.4	17,411.7	18,254.4	Mozambique, metical
2.80926	2.67072	2.73793	3.19971	3.33272	3.64557	3.92371	4.19788	4.66667	5.17298	5.42197	6.73325	6.56747	8.25106	8.44711	Namibia dollar
415.26	394.78	378.78	407.68	380.32	364.84	370.48	378.57	404.89	I780.44	728.38	753.06	807.94	791.61	I896.19	Niger, CFA franc
1.098	4.057	5.874	7.204	10.055	12.805	14.107	27.014	30.056	32.113	32.534	31.471	29.530	30.816	134.437	Nigerian naira
102.71	102.71	102.71	102.71	102.71	171.18	171.18	201.39	201.39	201.94	445.67	437.37	411.31	450.75	479.24	Rwanda franc
45.25	45.25	103.32	132.12	184.46	200.57	400.55	516.37	709.72	1,730.37	2,611.58	4,074.04	9,403.91	9,694.29	10,019.32	São Tomé & Príncipe dobra
415.26	394.78	378.78	407.68	380.32	364.84	370.48	378.57	404.89	I780.44	728.38	753.06	807.94	791.61	I896.19	Senegal, CFA franc
7.2345	7.2345	7.2345	7.2345	7.2345	7.2345	7.2345	7.2345	7.2345	7.2345	7.2345	7.2345	6.9218	7.6699	7.3671	Seychelles rupee
5.74	43.53	32.69	52.57	85.89	268.43	621.93	723.68	793.41	894.90	1,402.35	1,307.24	1,799.00	2,239.84	3,123.90	Sierra Leonean leone
2.8093	2.6707	2.7379	3.1997	3.3327	3.6456	3.9237	4.1979	4.6667	5.1730	5.4220	6.7332	6.5675	8.2511	8.4471	South African rand
.2746	.3058	.6385	.6056	.5914	.6403	2.1446	18.5811	29.8600	58.3940	78.2363	208.4000	232.3409	334.8295	353.6958	Sudanese pound
2.8093	2.6707	2.7379	3.1997	3.3327	3.6456	3.9237	4.1979	4.6667	5.1730	5.4220	6.7332	6.5675	8.2511	8.4471	Swaziland lilangeni
18.12	63.26	118.77	168.21	252.71	279.69	334.58	460.63	659.13	764.16	818.10	856.51	842.70	958.87	1,094.34	Tanzanian shilling
415.26	394.78	378.78	407.68	380.32	364.84	370.48	378.57	404.89	I780.44	728.38	753.06	807.94	791.61	I896.19	Togo, CFA franc
.8314	1.0277	1.1035	1.2090	1.1888	1.1904	1.2366	1.3071	1.4376	1.4470	1.4134	1.4358	1.5483	1.5502	1.7191	Tunisian dinar
15.4	17.1	I85.1	222.0	486.2	768.2	1,308.8	1,673.6	1,552.3	1,352.9	1,500.5	1,480.5	1,538.3	1,918.7	2,067.1	Uganda shilling
6.261	15.546	11.349	13.462	28.451	60.823	127.262	494.604	686.780	993.095	1,421.278	1,844.457	1,908.973	3,236.948	3,612.707	Zambian kwacha
1.8028	2.0527	2.3593	2.6145	2.9833	3.7508	7.2244	7.5384	9.5256	12.2440	13.8407	15.5860	25.1070	52.6170	52.3459	Zimbabwe dollar
															Asia
55.580	61.893	71.784	68.092	66.496	71.987	72.380	69.575	69.502	729.925	1,486.490	I4,313.880	4,047.750	4,224.090	4,117.530	Afghanistan,afghani
34.051	37.674	44.262	43.426	42.408	50.917	55.186	53.625	54.736	58.759	60.574	61.041	61.323	68.289	69.998	Bangladesh taka
13.363	16.051	18.268	20.117	22.387	25.712	36.953	36.025	43.102	45.810	52.295	51.666	52.999	59.813	59.690	Bhutan,ngultrum
....	....	....	....	283.9	853.6	743.8	2,750.0	3,166.1	3,759.1	3,754.9	3,901.2	4,657.6	5,308.3	5,174.4	Cambodian riel
3.5166	4.5528	5.2804	5.0088	6.2056	7.4293	7.7732	7.9087	7.9666	I12.3302	12.3637	11.9325	11.1715	11.6567	11.3637	Chinese yuan
1.2307	1.4010	2.0436	1.8906	1.9632	2.0760	2.1067	2.1511	2.1164	2.0570	2.1248	1.9900	2.0902	2.7965	2.6981	Fiji dollar
8.5798	9.5348	11.0088	10.5072	10.2596	11.0982	11.1302	10.6466	10.6121	11.2963	11.4935	11.1241	10.4513	10.9066	10.6658	Hong Kong dollar
13.363	16.051	18.268	20.117	22.387	25.712	36.953	36.025	43.102	45.810	52.295	51.666	52.999	59.813	59.690	Indian rupee
1,235.7	2,007.3	2,340.8	2,329.4	2,361.5	2,704.5	2,849.4	2,835.3	2,898.2	3,211.7	3,430.8	3,426.7	6,274.0	11,299.4	9,724.2	Indonesian rupiah
1.6132	1.8399	1.9635	1.5730	1.6578	1.8397	1.8826	1.9968	2.0286	1.8793	1.9953	1.8053	2.0672	2.2936	2.0993	Kiribati, Aust.dollar
977.8	1,053.7	1,124.0	920.6	893.1	1,019.2	1,088.3	1,084.1	1,110.0	1,151.4	1,151.6	1,213.9	2,287.0	1,695.3	1,561.9	Korean won
104.35	116.20	549.73	608.93	937.65	989.46	1,017.75	985.88	986.22	1,049.63	I1,372.03	1,344.49	3,554.60	6,017.92	10,431.08	Lao P.D. Rep., kip
2.66532	3.18396	3.53644	3.65398	3.55257	3.84332	3.89649	3.59150	3.71067	3.73722	3.77866	3.63660	5.25115	5.35051	5.21554	Malaysian ringgit
7.830	8.861	13.328	11.472	12.097	13.686	14.762	14.486	15.253	17.182	17.496	16.925	15.881	16.573	16.154	Maldivian rufiyaa

I See country notes in the monthly *IFS*

Exchange Rates

Market, Official, or Principal Rate

National Currency Units per SDR: End of Period (aa)

	1970	1971	1972	1973	1974	1975	1976	1977	1978	1979	1980	1981	1982	1983	1984
Asia (cont.)															
Mongolian togrog	....														
Myanmar kyat	4.8020	5.9377	5.8650	5.8653	5.8891	7.7429	7.7429	8.5085	8.5085	8.5085	8.5085	8.5085	8.5085	8.5085	8.5085
Nepalese rupee	10.125	10.993	10.993	12.739	12.929	14.633	14.523	15.184	15.633	15.808	15.305	15.364	15.774	15.914	17.644
Pakistan rupee	4.791	5.191	11.947	11.913	12.091	11.561	11.473	11.996	12.865	13.009	12.595	11.494	14.129	14.099	15.018
Papua New Guinea kina	.8969	.9116	.8515	.8107	.9226	.9312	.9435	.9202	.8966	.9093	.8212	.7921	.8250	.9166	.9227
Philippine peso I	6.435	6.987	7.362	8.119	8.650	8.778	8.630	8.952	9.608	9.768	9.693	9.544	10.117	14.659	19.369
Samoa tala	.7211	.7336	.7313	.7317	.7427	.8982	.9295	.9093	.9308	1.2002	1.1851	1.2794	1.3647	1.6964	2.1397
Singapore dollar	3.0800	3.1486	3.0617	I2.9991	2.8307	2.9144	2.8529	2.8406	2.8186	2.8441	2.6701	2.3836	2.3259	2.2269	2.1349
Solomon Islands dollar	.8969	.9116	.8515	.8107	.9226	.9312	1.0694	1.0642	1.1324	1.1306	1.0172	1.0346	1.1527	1.2788	1.3170
Sri Lanka rupee	5.958	6.469	7.272	8.140	8.195	9.029	10.257	18.901	20.200	20.346	22.957	23.919	23.518	26.174	25.760
Thai baht	20.928	I22.721	22.721	24.579	24.946	23.881	23.701	24.780	26.564	26.906	26.312	26.771	25.372	24.080	26.613
Tongan pa'anga	.8969	.9116	.8515	.8107	.9226	.9312	1.0694	1.0642	1.1324	1.1916	1.0802	1.0320	1.1249	1.1607	1.1841
Vanuatu,vatu	84.44	91.67	89.86	91.80	87.95	84.86	93.32	92.37	88.01	85.59	93.09	106.19	106.06	106.55	100.55
Vietnamese dong	—	—	.1	.2	.2	.2	.2	.2	.3	.3	I.3	1.3	1.3	1.3 P	1.3 P
Europe															
Albanian lek	....														
Armenian dram	....														
Azerbaijan manat	....														
Belarussian rubel	....														
Bulgarian lev	....														
Croatian kuna															
Cyprus pound	.41667	.42510	.41622	.43511	.43782	.46044	.47822	.46443	.45760	.45527	.46522	.50355	.53850	.58245	.63138
Czech Republic koruna	....														
Czechoslovak koruna			26.56	26.31	25.46	24.84	18.03	18.81	18.32	18.93	15.32	15.49	15.32	16.79	
Estonian kroon															
Hungarian forint	60.000	59.996	59.996	56.400	57.241	50.934	47.984	49.317	46.351	46.868	41.084	40.075	43.694	47.315	50.186
Kazakh tenge	....														
Kyrgyz som	....														
Latvian lats	....														
Lithuanian litas	....														
Macedonian denar	....														
Maltese lira	.41667	.41477	.43067	.46649	.45968	.47257	.49566	.47929	.47383	.45297	.45168	.45075	.45827	.46641	.48208
Moldovan leu	....														
Polish zloty	.0004	.0004	.0004	.0004	.0004	.0004	.0004	.0004	.0043	.0051	.0059	.0065	.0095	.0103	.0124
Romanian leu	6.000	6.004	6.004	24.127	24.487	23.413	23.237	24.294	23.450	23.712	22.957	17.459	16.547	19.191	17.438
Russian ruble	....														
Slovak koruna	....														
Slovenian tolar	....														
Turkish lira	14.9	15.4	15.4	17.1	17.1	17.7	19.4	23.6	32.9	46.6	115.0	155.5	206.0	296.1	435.9
Ukrainian hryvnia	....														
Middle East															
Bahrain dinar	.47619	.47619	.47619	.47620	.48330	.46300	.45968	.48060	.50007	.49664	.47955	.43764	.41477	.39365	.36856
Egyptian pound	.4348	.4720	.4720	.5245	.4791	.4581	.4546	.4753	.5098	.9221	.8928	.8148	.7722	.7329	.6861
Iranian rial	76.38	82.93	82.93	81.58	82.80	81.10	82.05	85.61	91.81	92.84	92.30	92.30	92.30	92.30	92.30
Iraqi dinar	.35908	.36621	.36443	.35625	.36157	.34572	.34311	.35872	.38474	.38903	.37665	.34374	.34291	.32545	.30471
Israeli new sheqel	.0003	.0005	.0005	.0005	.0007	.0008	.0010	.0019	.0025	.0047	I.0096	.0182	.0371	.1128	.6261
Jordan dinar	.35714	.38775	.38775	.39696	.38567	.38775	.38775	.38775	.38775	.38775	.38775	.38775	.38775	.38775	.38775
Kuwaiti dinar	.35714	.35714	.35584	.35791	.35462	.34435	.33339	.34023	.35410	.35978	.34601	.32755	.31847	.30630	.29844
Lebanese pound	3.3	3.4	3.3	3.0	2.8	2.8	3.4	3.6	3.9	4.3	4.7	5.4	4.2	5.7	8.7
Libyan dinar	.35714	.35714	.35714	.35714	.36247	.34657	.34396	.35962	.38569	.39000	.37759	.34459	.32658	.30995	.29019
Rial Omani	.41667	.41666	.41666	.41667	.42289	.40435	.40130	.41956	.44998	.45501	.44053	.40203	.38101	.36162	.33856
Qatar riyal	4.7619	4.7619	4.7619	4.7619	4.8330	4.6679	4.5989	4.8100	5.0008	4.8807	4.6425	4.2368	4.0153	3.8109	3.5680
Saudi Arabian riyal	4.5000	4.5057	4.5057	4.2825	4.3464	4.1324	4.1013	4.2576	4.3187	4.4328	4.2407	3.9749	3.7892	3.6591	3.5043
Syrian pound	3.820	4.147	4.147	4.584	4.530	4.331	4.560	4.768	5.113	5.171	5.006	4.569	4.330	4.109	3.847
U.A.Emirates dirham	4.7619	4.7619	4.7619	4.8344	4.8735	4.6791	4.6206	4.7349	5.0001	4.9611	4.6820	4.2729	4.0495	3.8434	3.5984
Yemen,Rep.,Yemeni rial	....														
Western Hemisphere															
Antigua & Barbuda,E.Car.$	2.0053	2.0417	2.2194	2.4925	2.5024	2.7770	3.1369	3.2797	3.5175	3.5568	3.4436	3.1427	2.9784	2.8268	2.6466
Argentine peso															
Bahamian dollar	1.0000	1.0857	1.0857	1.2064	1.2244	1.1707	1.1618	1.2147	1.3028	1.3173	1.2754	1.1640	1.1031	1.0470	.9802
Barbados dollar	2.0053	2.0417	2.2194	2.4925	2.5024	2.3458	2.3281	2.4431	2.6203	2.6495	2.5652	2.3411	2.2187	2.1057	1.9715
Belize dollar	1.6711	1.7014	I1.8495	2.0770	2.0853	2.3141	2.7299	2.4294	2.6056	2.6347	2.5508	2.3279	2.2062	2.0939	1.9604
Bolivia, boliviano													.0002	.0005	.0086
Brazilian real	—	—	—	—	—	I—	—	—	—	—	—	—	—	—	—
Chilean peso	.01	.03	.05	.90	2.45	9.95	20.24	33.96	44.23	51.38	49.74	45.39	64.50	76.23	87.26
Colombian peso	19.09	22.70	24.74	29.91	35.05	38.58	42.20	46.11	53.41	57.96	64.94	68.76	77.54	92.94	111.64
Costa Rican colon	6.64	7.20	7.20	8.02	10.49	10.03	9.96	10.41	11.16	11.29	10.93	42.01	44.40	45.44	46.81
Dominica, E.Caribbean dollar	2.0053	2.0417	2.2194	2.4925	2.5024	2.7770	3.1369	3.2797	3.5175	3.5568	3.4436	3.1427	2.9784	2.8268	2.6466
Dominican peso	1.000	1.086	1.086	1.206	1.224	1.171	1.162	1.215	1.303	1.317	1.275	1.164	1.103	1.047	.980
Ecuadoran sucre	25.0	27.1	27.1	30.2	30.6	29.3	29.0	30.4	32.6	32.9	31.9	29.1	36.6	56.6	65.8
Salvadoran colon	2.5000	2.7143	2.7143	3.0159	3.0609	2.9267	2.9046	3.0368	3.2570	3.2933	3.1885	2.9099	2.7578	2.6174	2.4505
Grenada, E.Caribbean dollar	2.0053	2.0417	2.2194	2.4925	2.5024	2.7770	3.1369	3.2797	3.5175	3.5568	3.4436	3.1427	2.9784	2.8268	2.6466
Guatemalan quetzal	1.0000	1.0857	1.0857	1.2064	1.2244	1.1707	1.1618	1.2147	1.3028	1.3173	1.2754	1.1640	1.1031	1.0470	.9802
Guyana dollar	2.005	2.217	2.410	2.706	2.717	2.985	2.963	3.098	3.322	3.359	3.252	3.492	3.309	3.141	4.068
Haitian gourde	4.9991	5.4276	5.4276	6.0307	6.1207	5.8523	5.8081	6.0725	6.5128	6.5855	6.3759	5.8188	5.5146	5.2338	4.9002
Honduras lempira	2.0000	2.1714	2.1714	2.4127	2.4487	2.3413	2.3237	2.4294	2.6056	2.6347	2.5508	2.3279	2.2062	2.0939	1.9604
Jamaica dollar	.8355	.8507	.9248	I1.0967	1.1130	1.0642	1.0562	1.1043	2.2082	2.3467	2.2720	2.0735	1.9651	3.4317	4.8324
Mexican peso	—	—	—	—	—	—	—	—	—	—	—	—	.1	.2	.2
Netherlands Antilles guilder	1.8739	1.9543	1.9543	2.1714	2.2038	2.1072	2.0913	2.1865	2.3450	2.3712	2.2957	2.0951	1.9856	1.8845	1.7644
Nicaraguan gold córdoba											I—				
Panamanian balboa	1.0000	1.0857	1.0857	1.2064	1.2244	1.1707	1.1618	1.2147	1.3028	1.3173	1.2754	1.1640	1.1031	1.0470	.9802
Paraguayan guarani	126.0	136.8	136.8	152.0	154.3	147.5	146.4	153.1	164.2	166.0	160.7	146.7	139.0	131.9	235.3
Peruvian new sol															
St.Kitts & Nevis, E.C.dollar	2.0053	2.0417	2.2194	2.4925	2.5024	2.7770	3.1369	3.2797	3.5175	3.5568	3.4436	3.1427	2.9784	2.8268	2.6466
St.Lucia, E.Car. dollar	2.0053	2.0417	2.2194	2.4925	2.5024	2.7770	3.1369	3.2797	3.5175	3.5568	3.4436	3.1427	2.9784	2.8268	2.6466
St. Vinc. & Grens.,E.Car.$	2.0053	2.0417	2.2194	2.4925	2.5024	2.7770	3.1369	3.2797	3.5175	3.5568	3.4436	3.1427	2.9784	2.8268	2.6466
Suriname guilder	1.885	1.938	1.938	2.153	2.185	2.090	2.074	2.168	2.325	2.351	2.277	2.078	1.969	1.869	1.750
Trinidad & Tobago dollar	2.0053	2.0417	2.2194	2.4924	2.5024	2.7769	2.7884	2.9153	3.1267	3.1616	3.0610	2.7935	2.6475	2.5127	2.3525
Uruguayan peso	—	—	—	—	—	I—	—	—	—	—	—	—	—	—	.1
Venezuelan bolivar	4.450	4.723	4.723	5.169	5.246	5.016	4.987	5.214	5.592	5.655	5.475	4.996	4.735	4.502	7.352

I See country notes in the monthly *IFS*

Market, Official, or Principal Rate

National Currency Units per SDR: End of Period (aa)

1985	1986	1987	1988	1989	1990	1991	1992	1993	1994	1995	1996	1997	1998	1999	
															Asia (cont.)
....	....	....	....	....	19.917	56.359	144.467	I544.630	604.509	704.031	997.240	1,097.156	1,270.043	1,471.839	Mongolian togrog
8.5085	8.5085	8.5085	8.5085	8.5085	8.5085	8.5085	8.5085	8.5085	8.5085	8.5085	8.5085	8.5085	8.5085	8.5085	Myanmar kyat
22.737	26.910	30.643	33.912	37.585	43.249	61.079	59.400	67.634	72.817	83.243	82.007	85.408	95.288	94.326	Nepalese rupee
17.509	21.047	24.694	25.035	28.079	31.079	35.272	35.249	41.268	44.851	50.785	57.547	59.286	64.608	I71.075	Pakistan rupee
1.1121	1.1757	1.2462	1.1121	1.1297	1.3558	1.3626	1.3578	1.3479	1.7205	1.9846	1.9366	2.3630	2.9518	3.6995	Papua New Guinea kina
20.905	25.112	29.508	28.711	29.490	39.834	38.121	34.507	38.046	35.647	38.967	37.801	53.936	54.996	55.330	Philippine peso
2.5333	2.6883	2.8527	2.8909	3.0093	3.3193	3.5025	3.5166	3.5816	3.5789	3.7566	3.5004	3.7324	4.2385	4.1428	Samoa tala
2.3122	2.6604	2.8352	2.6190	2.4895	2.4818	2.3323	2.2617	2.2087	2.1324	2.1023	2.0129	2.2607	2.3380	2.2866	Singapore dollar
1.7714	2.4299	2.8009	2.8505	3.1500	3.7184	3.9978	4.2622	4.4611	4.8597	5.1668	5.2081	6.4067	6.8417	6.9671	Solomon Islands dollar
30.105	34.885	43.642	44.453	52.566	57.248	60.908	63.250	68.076	72.963	80.341	81.540	82.689	95.436	98.979	Sri Lanka rupee
29.273	31.962	35.566	33.965	33.761	35.979	36.161	35.090	35.081	36.628	37.445	36.826	I63.748	51.662	51.428	Thai baht
1.6132	1.8399	1.9635	1.5748	1.6539	1.8435	1.9050	1.9116	1.8946	1.8371	1.8883	1.7438	1.8377	2.2749	2.2107	Tongan pa'anga
110.12	142.18	142.00	141.37	145.48	155.43	158.48	163.63	165.93	163.62	169.07	159.28	167.73	182.73	176.90	Vanuatu,vatu
I24.7	27.5	399.0	1,513.9	7,063.6	11,559.1	16,449.9	I14,526.9	14,892.8	16,131.3	16,372.2	15,889.5	16,585.0	19,561.8	....	Vietnamese dong
															Europe
....	....	....	....	....	....	....	141.488	135.570	139.547	140.087	148.211	201.227	197.941	185.454	Albanian lek
....	....	....	....	....	....	....	2.85	103.02	591.98	597.57	625.61	667.85	735.03	718.88	Armenian dram
....	....	....	....	....	....	....	21	960	15,474	17,095	22,288	41,476	309,767	439,203	Belarussian rubel
—	—	—	—	—	—	.03	.03	.04	.10	.11	.70	2.40	2.36	2.67	Bulgarian lev
....	....	....	....	....	....	....	1.09753	9.01316	8.21706	7.90233	7.96572	8.50446	8.79667	10.49648	Croatian kuna
.59681	.62583	.62263	.62751	.62924	.61828	.62802	.66419	.71398	.69523	.67867	.67567	.70935	.70152	.78862	Cyprus pound
....	....	....	....	....	....	....	....	41.14499	40.94733	39.54361	39.30232	46.73262	42.03674	49.38154	Czech Republic koruna
17.57	17.59	18.44	19.26	18.78	39.83	39.82	39.74	....	....	....	....	....	....	....	Czechoslovak koruna
....	....	....	....	....	....	....	17.754	19.062	18.088	17.038	17.888	19.343	18.882	21.359	Estonian kroon
52.007	56.177	65.807	70.699	82.192	87.421	108.169	115.459	138.317	161.591	207.321	237.163	274.572	308.401	346.586	Hungarian forint
....	....	....	....	....	....	....	....	8.67	79.21	95.06	105.40	101.94	117.99	189.68	Kazakh tenge
....	....	....	....	....	....	....	....	11.030	15.547	16.649	24.014	23.443	41.362	62.352	Kyrgyz som
....	....	....	....	....	....	....	1.14813	.81727	.80000	.79825	.79951	.79606	.80117	.80017	Latvian lats
....	....	....	....	....	....	....	5.21125	5.35688	5.83940	5.94596	5.75184	5.39700	5.63212	5.49004	Lithuanian litas
....	....	....	....	....	....	....	....	61.062	59.264	56.456	59.547	74.776	72.987	82.816	Macedonian denar
.46557	.45153	.44221	.44697	.44269	.42788	.43712	.51450	.54272	.53738	.52384	.51712	.52717	.53141	.56558	Maltese lira
....	....	....	....	....	....	.0024	.5698	I4.9998	6.2336	6.6877	6.7215	6.2882	11.7185	15.9077	Moldovan leu
.0162	.0242	.0448	.0676	.8542	1.3515	1.5673	2.1680	2.9317	3.5579	3.6687	4.1349	4.7467	4.9337	5.6936	Polish zloty
17.278	18.690	19.492	19.338	18.976	49.381	I270.351	632.500	1,752.663	2,579.555	3,832.171	5,802.169	—	—	—	Romanian leu
....	....	....	....	....	....	....	.5706	1.7128	5.1825	6.8973	7.9951	8.0415	I29.0758	37.0578	Russian ruble
....	....	....	....	....	....	....	....	45.605	45.660	43.954	45.864	46.930	51.975	58.011	Slovak koruna
....	....	....	....	....	....	81.095	135.713	181.093	184.609	187.283	203.443	228.266	226.974	270.069	Slovenian tolar
633.6	926.9	1,448.3	2,442.2	3,040.6	4,168.5	7,266.5	11,776.1	19,878.9	56,534.2	88,669.1	154,976.1	277,412.5	442,774.7	743,076.9	Turkish lira
....	....	....	....	....	....	....	.0088	.1732	1.5212	2.6668	I2.7163	2.5622	4.8253	7.1594	Ukrainian hryvnia
															Middle East
.41300	.45992	.53341	.50598	.49412	.53492	.53784	.51700	.51646	.54890	.55892	.54067	.50732	.52942	.51606	Bahrain dinar
.7689	.8562	.9931	.9420	1.4456	2.8453	4.7665	4.5906	4.6314	4.9504	5.0392	4.8718	4.5713	4.7704	4.6734	Egyptian pound
92.30	92.30	92.30	92.30	92.30	92.30	92.30	92.30	2,415.49	2,534.26	2,597.64	2,515.19	2,366.94	2,465.36	2,405.04	Iranian rial
.34145	.38024	.44100	.41832	.40852	.44225	.44466	.42743	.42698	.45381	.46209	.44700	.41942	.43770	.42665	Iraqi dinar
I1.6471	1.8181	2.1828	2.2675	2.5797	2.9136	3.2657	3.8005	4.1015	4.4058	4.6601	4.6748	4.7709	5.8588	5.7000	Israeli new sheqel
.38775	.38775	.38775	.64191	.85158	.94604	.96553	.95011	.96699	1.02336	1.05392	1.01951	.95662	.99829	.97311	Jordan dinar
.31745	.35760	.38289	.38031	.38370	....	.40663	.41621	.40990	.43813	.44436	.43123	.41139	.42461	.41749	Kuwaiti dinar
19.9	106.4	645.5	713.2	663.7	1,197.9	1,257.3	2,527.3	2,350.2	2,404.4	2,372.4	2,231.7	2,060.3	2,123.3	2,069.1	Lebanese pound
.32519	.38393	.38393	.38393	.38393	.38393	.38393	.41428 p	.44643	.52500	.52500	.52500	.52500	.53292	.63360	Libyan dinar
.37939	.47032	.54547	.51742	.50529	.54701	.55000	.52869	.52813	.56131	.57156	.55290	.51879	.54139	.52773	Rial Omani
3.9982	4.4524	5.1639	4.8983	4.7835	5.1785	5.2068	5.0050	4.9998	5.3139	5.4108	5.2342	4.9113	5.1252	4.9959	Qatar riyal
4.0037	4.5808	5.3129	5.0396	4.9215	5.3279	5.3570	5.1494	5.1440	5.4671	5.5669	5.3852	5.0529	5.2731	5.1401	Saudi Arabian riyal
4.311	4.801	5.568	15.105	14.751	15.969	16.057	15.434	15.418	16.387	16.686	16.141	15.145	15.805	15.406	Syrian pound
4.0323	4.4903	5.2079	4.9401	4.8243	5.2226	5.2511	5.0476	5.0423	5.3591	5.4569	5.2788	4.9551	5.1710	5.0405	U.A.Emirates dirham
....	....	....	....	....	17.086	17.179	16.514	16.496	17.533	I74.384	182.492	176.023	199.447	....	Yemen,Rep.,Yemeni rial
															Western Hemisphere
2.9657	3.3026	3.8304	3.6334	3.5482	3.8412	3.8622	3.7125	3.7086	3.9416	4.0135	3.8825	3.6430	3.8017	3.7058	Antigua & Barbuda,E. Car.$
—	—	—	—	.2	.8	1.4	1.4	1.4	1.5	1.5	1.4	1.3	1.4	1.4	Argentine peso
1.0984	1.2232	1.4187	1.3457	1.3142	1.4227	1.4304	1.3750	1.3736	1.4599	1.4865	1.4380	1.3493	1.4080	1.3725	Bahamian dollar
2.2093	2.4464	2.8373	2.6914	2.6283	2.8453	2.8609	2.7500	2.7471	2.9197	2.9730	2.8759	2.6985	2.8161	2.7450	Barbados dollar
2.1968	2.4464	2.8373	2.6914	2.6283	2.8453	2.8609	2.7500	2.7471	2.9197	2.9730	2.8759	2.6985	2.8161	2.7450	Belize dollar
I1.8585	2.3522	I3.1352	3.3239	3.9162	4.8370	5.3570	5.6306	6.1467	6.8540	7.3358	7.4558	7.2387	7.9483	8.2213	Bolivia, boliviano
I—	—	—	I—	—	—	—	I.01	.16	I1.24	1.45	1.49	1.51	1.70	2.46	Brazilian real
201.74	250.75	337.80	333.05	389.75	479.24	536.23	525.70	592.06	589.91	605.19	611.09	593.41	667.08	727.53	Chilean peso
189.15	267.88	374.10	451.97	570.24	809.11	1,011.11	1,116.18	1,260.01	1,213.53	1,468.13	1,445.62	1,745.36	2,122.63	2,571.77	Colombian peso
58.99	72.02	98.24	106.98	110.85	147.32	193.72	188.97	208.01	240.98	289.72	316.51	329.61	382.17	409.27	Costa Rican colon
2.9657	3.3026	3.8304	3.6334	3.5482	3.8412	3.8622	3.7125	3.7086	3.9416	4.0135	3.8825	3.6430	3.8017	3.7058	Dominica, E.Caribbean dollar
3.229	3.763	7.037	8.532	8.332	16.147	18.109	17.291	17.536	19.071	20.015	20.220	19.383	22.230	22.014	Dominican peso
105.2	179.2	314.2	582.0	852.1	1,249.4	1,817.5	2,535.8	2,807.3	3,312.4	4,345.8	5,227.0	5,974.5	9,609.8	27,783.7	Ecuadoran sucre
2.7461	6.1160	7.0933	6.7285	6.5708	11.4240	11.5579	12.6088	11.9088	12.7737	13.0142	12.5893	11.8127	12.3273	12.0163	Salvadoran colon
2.9657	3.3026	3.8304	3.6334	3.5482	3.8412	3.8622	3.7125	3.7086	3.9416	4.0135	3.8825	3.6430	3.8017	3.7058	Grenada, E.Caribbean dollar
1.0984	3.0580	3.5467	3.6401	4.4681	7.1341	7.2142	7.2522	7.9876	8.2460	8.8910	8.5782	8.3342	9.6425	10.7342	Guatemalan quetzal
4.558	5.382	14.187	13.457	43.367	64.020	174.512	173.250	179.593	208.029	208.852	203.112	194.292	228.453	247.738	Guyana dollar
5.4911	6.1149	7.0920	6.7273	6.5696	7.1120	I11.7867	15.0604	17.5884	18.9001	24.0215	21.7028	23.3569	23.2390	24.6577	Haitian gourde
2.1968	2.4464	2.8373	2.6914	2.6283	7.6212	7.7243	8.0163	9.9720	13.7227	15.3751	18.5057	17.6673	19.4415	19.9067	Honduran lempira
6.0193	6.7031	7.8026	7.3744	8.5158	11.4348	30.7435	30.5038	44.6057	48.4692	58.8894	50.1351	49.0326	52.1744	56.6719	Jamaica dollar
.4	1.1	3.1	3.1	3.5	4.2	4.4	4.3	4.3	7.8	11.4	11.3	10.9	13.9	13.1	Mexican peso
1.9772	2.2017	2.5536	2.4223	2.3523	2.5466	2.5605	2.4613	2.4587	2.6131	2.6608	2.5739	2.4152	2.5204	2.4568	Netherlands Antilles guilder
—	—	—	I.0002	.0100	.8536	7.1520	6.8750	8.7217	10.3820	11.8399	12.8324	13.4858	15.7615	16.9066	Nicaraguan gold córdoba
1.0984	1.2232	1.4187	1.3457	1.3142	1.4227	1.4304	1.3750	1.3736	1.4599	1.4865	1.4380	1.3493	1.4080	1.3725	Panamanian balboa
351.5	672.8	780.3	740.1	1,600.6	1,789.7	1,974.0	2,241.3	2,582.3	2,809.8	2,942.7	3,033.6	3,184.2	3,999.1	4,568.9	Paraguayan guarani
I—	—	—	.0007	.0069	.7354	1.3732	2.2413	2.9669	3.1825	3.4338	3.7387	3.6835	4.4494	4.8175	Peruvian new sol
2.9657	3.3026	3.8304	3.6334	3.5482	3.8412	3.8622	3.7125	3.7086	3.9416	4.0135	3.8825	3.6430	3.8017	3.7058	St.Kitts & Nevis, E.C. dollar
2.9657	3.3026	3.8304	3.6334	3.5482	3.8412	3.8622	3.7125	3.7086	3.9416	4.0135	3.8825	3.6430	3.8017	3.7058	St.Lucia, E.Car. dollar
2.9657	3.3026	3.8304	3.6334	3.5482	3.8412	3.8622	3.7125	3.7086	3.9416	4.0135	3.8825	3.6430	3.8017	3.7058	St. Vinc. & Grens.,E. Car.$
1.961	2.183	2.532	2.402	2.346	2.539	2.553	2.454	2.452	I597.809	605.001	576.622	541.049	564.620	1,355.354	Suriname guilder
3.9543	4.4035	5.1072	5.7192	5.5852	6.0463	6.0793	5.8438	7.9860	8.6616	8.9146	8.9074	8.5001	9.2881	8.6467	Trinidad & Tobago dollar
.1	.2	.4	.6	1.1	2.3	3.6	4.8	I6.1	8.2	10.6	12.5	13.5	15.2	15.9	Uruguayan peso
8.238	17.736	20.571	19.513	56.612	71.673	88.048	109.244	145.102	I248.175	431.082	685.188	680.359	794.833	889.730	Venezuelan bolivar

I See country notes in the monthly *IFS*

Exchange Rates

SDR Rates: *1980-2000*

sa US Dollars per SDR (*End of Period*)

	Jan.	Feb.	Mar.	April	May	June	July	Aug.	Sept.	Oct.	Nov.	Dec.	I	II	III	IV	Year
1980	1.31574	1.30377	1.25118	1.29474	1.31135	1.32438	1.31200	1.31529	1.31244	1.29004	1.27672	1.27541	1.25118	1.32438	1.31244	1.27541	1.27541
1981	1.24418	1.22328	1.22852	1.19858	1.17015	1.15060	1.12723	1.13271	1.14460	1.15118	1.18072	1.16396	1.22852	1.15060	1.14460	1.16396	1.16396
1982	1.14784	1.12689	1.11309	1.12967	1.12410	1.09224	1.09208	1.08309	1.07234	1.06237	1.07953	1.10311	1.11309	1.09224	1.07234	1.10311	1.10311
1983	1.08645	1.08995	1.07867	1.08163	1.07734	1.06835	1.05563	1.04461	1.05684	1.05928	1.05058	1.04695	1.07867	1.06835	1.05684	1.04695	1.04695
1984	1.03409	1.06013	1.06420	1.04712	1.04140	1.03121	1.01333	1.01663	.99901	.99623	.98935	.98021	1.06420	1.03121	.99901	.98021	.98021
1985	.97499	.95942	.99127	.99117	.99295	.99828	1.03737	1.03536	1.05940	1.07165	1.09319	1.09842	.99127	.99828	1.05940	1.09842	1.09842
1986	1.11115	1.15584	1.13827	1.17596	1.14314	1.17757	1.20371	1.20689	1.21342	1.18661	1.21030	1.22319	1.13827	1.17757	1.21342	1.22319	1.22319
1987	1.26759	1.26419	1.28563	1.30626	1.28658	1.27802	1.26723	1.29313	1.27964	1.32109	1.37379	1.41866	1.28563	1.27802	1.27964	1.41866	1.41866
1988	1.36642	1.36101	1.38729	1.38417	1.36483	1.31061	1.29648	1.28818	1.29039	1.34592	1.36637	1.34570	1.38729	1.31061	1.29039	1.34570	1.34570
1989	1.31093	1.32150	1.29271	1.29566	1.24362	1.24639	1.28749	1.24652	1.27981	1.27782	1.28771	1.31416	1.29271	1.24639	1.27981	1.31416	1.31416
1990	1.32559	1.31681	1.30083	1.30247	1.31200	1.32388	1.36564	1.38595	1.39256	1.43078	1.42677	1.42266	1.30083	1.32388	1.39256	1.42266	1.42266
1991	1.43476	1.42053	1.34632	1.34081	1.34084	1.31452	1.33400	1.33698	1.36800	1.36652	1.38072	1.43043	1.34632	1.31452	1.36800	1.43043	1.43043
1992	1.39733	1.38091	1.37174	1.36976	1.39632	1.43117	1.44416	1.48286	1.47284	1.40595	1.37896	1.37500	1.37174	1.43117	1.47284	1.37500	1.37500
1993	1.38188	1.37610	1.39773	1.42339	1.42847	1.40360	1.39072	1.40758	1.41840	1.39293	1.38389	1.37356	1.39773	1.40360	1.41840	1.37356	1.37356
1994	1.38067	1.39930	1.41260	1.42138	1.41733	1.44837	1.44327	1.44770	1.46738	1.48454	1.45674	1.45985	1.41260	1.44837	1.46738	1.45985	1.45985
1995	1.47670	1.49440	1.56050	1.57303	1.57591	1.56876	1.55954	1.49249	1.50632	1.49455	1.48615	1.48649	1.56050	1.56876	1.50632	1.48649	1.48649
1996	1.45169	1.46868	1.46121	1.45006	1.44219	1.44334	1.46554	1.45766	1.43937	1.44623	1.44462	1.43796	1.46121	1.44334	1.43937	1.43796	1.43796
1997	1.39466	1.38494	1.38689	1.36553	1.39179	1.38814	1.35862	1.36358	1.36521	1.38362	1.36184	1.34925	1.38689	1.38814	1.36521	1.34925	1.34925
1998	1.34536	1.35023	1.33589	1.34666	1.33536	1.33154	1.32949	1.34222	1.37132	1.40835	1.38017	1.40803	1.33589	1.33154	1.37132	1.40803	1.40803
1999	1.38977	1.36556	1.35784	1.35123	1.34196	1.33587	1.36421	1.36986	1.38769	1.38072	1.36963	1.37251	1.35784	1.33587	1.38769	1.37251	1.37251
2000	1.35288	1.33928	1.34687	1.31921	1.32002	1.33728							1.34687	1.33728			

sb US Dollars per SDR (*Period Average, geometric*)

	Jan.	Feb.	Mar.	April	May	June	July	Aug.	Sept.	Oct.	Nov.	Dec.	I	II	III	IV	Year
1980	1.32035	1.31306	1.27713	1.26728	1.30451	1.32050	1.32753	1.31317	1.31836	1.30825	1.28298	1.26726	1.30338	1.29724	1.31967	1.28605	1.30153
1981	1.26792	1.23225	1.22834	1.21023	1.17871	1.15636	1.13570	1.12234	1.14342	1.15398	1.16596	1.16388	1.24271	1.18156	1.13379	1.16126	1.17916
1982	1.15329	1.13288	1.12347	1.11507	1.13472	1.10209	1.09149	1.08656	1.07979	1.07131	1.06707	1.09407	1.13648	1.11721	1.08594	1.07742	1.10401
1983	1.10004	1.09004	1.08544	1.08220	1.08262	1.06890	1.06292	1.04994	1.05087	1.06228	1.05178	1.04272	1.09182	1.07789	1.05456	1.05223	1.06900
1984	1.03579	1.04674	1.06398	1.05716	1.04100	1.03967	1.02009	1.01633	1.00006	.99278	1.00259	.98749	1.04877	1.04591	1.01212	.99427	1.02501
1985	.97558	.96174	.96366	.99036	.98956	.99703	1.01993	1.03341	1.02830	1.06516	1.08003	1.08972	.96697	.99231	1.02720	1.07826	1.01534
1986	1.09786	1.12904	1.14834	1.15007	1.16859	1.16461	1.18935	1.20849	1.21051	1.21175	1.19840	1.20746	1.12489	1.16106	1.20275	1.20586	1.17317
1987	1.25112	1.26216	1.26933	1.29153	1.30442	1.28656	1.26932	1.26927	1.29137	1.29530	1.34938	1.38310	1.26085	1.29415	1.27661	1.34210	1.29307
1988	1.37723	1.35556	1.37141	1.38197	1.37595	1.34654	1.30514	1.29206	1.29368	1.31949	1.35659	1.35588	1.36804	1.36807	1.29695	1.34387	1.34392
1989	1.32525	1.31652	1.30486	1.29975	1.26560	1.24062	1.27158	1.26166	1.24703	1.27221	1.27724	1.30191	1.31552	1.26843	1.26005	1.28372	1.28176
1990	1.31850	1.32659	1.30170	1.30135	1.31832	1.31442	1.34402	1.37719	1.39049	1.42846	1.44481	1.42654	1.31556	1.31134	1.37042	1.43325	1.35675
1991	1.42291	1.44058	1.38077	1.35123	1.34351	1.31934	1.32155	1.33571	1.35355	1.36201	1.38487	1.40799	1.41453	1.33796	1.33687	1.38483	1.36816
1992	1.40925	1.39042	1.36599	1.37060	1.38810	1.41173	1.44375	1.45645	1.45767	1.43476	1.38701	1.38883	1.38844	1.39004	1.45261	1.40336	1.40838
1993	1.37705	1.37168	1.38045	1.41266	1.41561	1.40969	1.39025	1.40151	1.41756	1.40746	1.38903	1.38404	1.37639	1.41265	1.40306	1.39347	1.39633
1994	1.37343	1.38750	1.40197	1.40425	1.41500	1.42736	1.45706	1.45439	1.46377	1.47720	1.47121	1.45201	1.38759	1.41550	1.45840	1.46676	1.43170
1995	1.46580	1.47826	1.53602	1.57620	1.55819	1.56369	1.55763	1.51069	1.48396	1.49828	1.49474	1.48532	1.49305	1.56601	1.51712	1.49277	1.51695
1996	1.46779	1.46625	1.46181	1.45086	1.44464	1.44290	1.45003	1.45830	1.44811	1.43968	1.45295	1.43817	1.46528	1.44613	1.45214	1.44359	1.45176
1997	1.41537	1.38421	1.37811	1.37150	1.38518	1.39032	1.37726	1.35396	1.35939	1.36989	1.37399	1.35418	1.39256	1.38231	1.36350	1.36599	1.37602
1998	1.34310	1.35002	1.34421	1.34312	1.34373	1.33354	1.33092	1.32668	1.36482	1.40747	1.39199	1.40211	1.34577	1.34013	1.34070	1.40051	1.35654
1999	1.40441	1.38073	1.36265	1.35485	1.34869	1.34004	1.33924	1.36415	1.37613	1.38943	1.37626	1.37280	1.38249	1.34785	1.35975	1.37948	1.36732
2000	1.37068	1.34485	1.34286	1.33915	1.31082	1.33062							1.35274	1.32681			

sc SDRs per US Dollar (*End of Period*)

	Jan.	Feb.	Mar.	April	May	June	July	Aug.	Sept.	Oct.	Nov.	Dec.	I	II	III	IV	Year
1980	.76003	.76700	.79924	.77235	.76258	.75507	.76220	.76029	.76194	.77517	.78326	.78406	.79924	.75507	.76194	.78406	.78406
1981	.80375	.81747	.81399	.83432	.85459	.86911	.88713	.88284	.87367	.86868	.84694	.85914	.81399	.86911	.87367	.85914	.85914
1982	.87120	.88740	.89840	.88521	.88960	.91555	.91568	.92328	.93254	.94129	.92633	.90653	.89840	.91555	.93254	.90653	.90653
1983	.92043	.91748	.92707	.92453	.92822	.93602	.94730	.95730	.94622	.94404	.95186	.95515	.92707	.93602	.94622	.95515	.95515
1984	.96703	.94328	.93967	.95500	.96025	.96973	.98685	.98364	1.00100	1.00378	1.01077	1.02019	.93967	.96973	1.00100	1.02019	1.02019
1985	1.02565	1.04230	1.00880	1.00891	1.00710	1.00172	.96398	.96584	.94393	.93314	.91476	.91040	1.00880	1.00172	.94393	.91040	.91040
1986	.89997	.86517	.87853	.85037	.87478	.84921	.83077	.82858	.82412	.84273	.82624	.81753	.87853	.84921	.82412	.81753	.81753
1987	.78890	.79102	.77783	.76554	.77725	.78246	.78913	.77332	.78147	.75695	.72791	.70489	.77783	.78246	.78147	.70489	.70489
1988	.73184	.73475	.72083	.72245	.73269	.76300	.77132	.77629	.77496	.74299	.73187	.74311	.72083	.76300	.77496	.74311	.74311
1989	.76282	.75672	.77357	.77181	.80410	.80232	.77670	.80223	.78137	.78258	.77657	.76094	.77357	.80232	.78137	.76094	.76094
1990	.75438	.75941	.76874	.76777	.76219	.75536	.73226	.72153	.71810	.69892	.70089	.70291	.76874	.75536	.71810	.70291	.70291
1991	.69698	.70396	.74277	.74582	.74580	.76074	.74962	.74795	.73100	.73179	.72426	.69909	.74277	.76074	.73100	.69909	.69909
1992	.71565	.72416	.72900	.73006	.71617	.69873	.69244	.67437	.67896	.71127	.72518	.72727	.72900	.69873	.67896	.72727	.72727
1993	.72365	.72669	.71545	.70255	.70005	.71245	.71905	.71044	.70502	.71791	.72260	.72804	.71545	.71245	.70502	.72804	.72804
1994	.72429	.71465	.70792	.70354	.70555	.69043	.69287	.69075	.68149	.67361	.68646	.68500	.70792	.69043	.68149	.68500	.68500
1995	.67719	.66916	.64082	.63572	.63455	.63745	.64121	.67002	.66387	.66910	.67288	.67273	.64082	.63745	.66387	.67273	.67273
1996	.68885	.68088	.68436	.68963	.69339	.69284	.68234	.68603	.69475	.69145	.69222	.69543	.68436	.69284	.69475	.69543	.69543
1997	.71702	.72205	.72104	.73232	.71850	.72039	.73604	.73336	.73249	.72274	.73430	.74115	.72104	.72039	.73249	.74115	.74115
1998	.74330	.74061	.74856	.74258	.74886	.75101	.75217	.74503	.72922	.71005	.72455	.71021	.74856	.75101	.72922	.71021	.71021
1999	.71954	.73230	.73646	.74007	.74518	.74857	.73303	.73000	.72062	.72426	.73013	.72859	.73646	.74857	72062	72859	72859
2000	.73017	.74667	.74246	.75803	.75757								74246				

sd SDRs per US Dollar (*Period Average, geometric*)

	Jan.	Feb.	Mar.	April	May	June	July	Aug.	Sept.	Oct.	Nov.	Dec.	I	II	III	IV	Year
1980	.75738	.76158	.78300	.78909	.76657	.75729	.75328	.76151	.75852	.76438	.77943	.78910	.76724	.77087	.75776	.77757	.76833
1981	.78869	.81152	.81411	.82629	.84839	.86478	.88051	.89099	.87457	.86656	.85767	.85919	.80469	.84634	.88200	.86113	.84806
1982	.86709	.88270	.89010	.89680	.88128	.90736	.91618	.92034	.92610	.93344	.93714	.91402	.87991	.89509	.92086	.92814	.90579
1983	.90906	.91740	.92128	.92404	.92368	.93554	.94081	.95243	.95160	.94138	.95077	.95903	.91590	.92774	.94826	.95036	.93545
1984	.96545	.95535	.93987	.94593	.96061	.96184	.98031	.98394	.99994	1.00727	.99741	1.01267	.95350	.95611	.98803	1.00577	.97560
1985	1.02503	1.03979	1.03771	1.00974	1.01055	1.00298	.98046	.96767	.97248	.93882	.92590	.91767	1.03416	1.00775	.97352	.92743	.98489
1986	.91086	.88571	.87082	.86951	.85574	.85866	.84080	.82748	.82610	.82526	.83445	.82819	.88898	.86128	.83143	.82929	.85239
1987	.79928	.79229	.78781	.77427	.76662	.77727	.78782	.78785	.77437	.77202	.74108	.72301	.79312	.77271	.78332	.74510	.77335
1988	.72609	.73770	.72918	.72361	.72677	.74264	.76620	.77396	.77299	.75787	.73714	.73753	.73098	.73096	.77104	.74412	.74409
1989	.75458	.75958	.76637	.76938	.79014	.80605	.78642	.79261	.80191	.78603	.78294	.76810	.76016	.78838	.79362	.77899	.78018
1990	.75844	.75381	.76823	.76843	.75854	.76079	.74404	.72612	.71917	.70006	.69213	.70100	.76014	.76258	.72970	.69772	.73706
1991	.70279	.69417	.72423	.74007	.74432	.75795	.75669	.74867	.73880	.73421	.72209	.71023	.70694	.74741	.74802	.72211	.73091
1992	.70960	.71921	.73207	.72961	.72041	.70835	.69264	.68660	.68603	.69698	.72098	.72003	.72024	.71940	.68842	.71258	.71004
1993	.72619	.72903	.72440	.70788	.70641	.70938	.71930	.71352	.70544	.71050	.71993	.72252	.72654	.70789	.71273	.71763	.71616
1994	.72810	.72072	.71328	.71213	.70671	.70059	.68631	.68757	.68317	.67696	.67971	.68870	.72068	.70646	.68568	.68177	.69847
1995	.68222	.67647	.65103	.63444	.64177	.63951	.64200	.66195	.67387	.66743	.66901	.67326	.66977	.63857	.65914	.66990	.65922
1996	.68130	.68201	.68408	.68925	.69221	.69305	.68964	.68573	.69056	.69460	.68825	.69533	.68246	.69150	.68864	.69272	.68882
1997	.70653	.72243	.72563	.72913	.72193	.71926	.72608	.73857	.73562	.72999	.72781	.73845	.71810	.72344	.73341	.73207	.72673
1998	.74455	.74073	.74393	.74453	.74420	.74988	.75136	.75376	.73269	.71114	.71840	.71321	.74307	.74620	.74588	.71424	.73722
1999	.71204	.72425	.73387	.73809	.74146	.74624	.74669	.73306	.72668	.71972	.72661	.72844	.72333	.74192	.73543	.72491	.73136
2000	.72957	.74358	.74468	.74674	.76288	.75153							.73924	.75369			

(As of July 31, 2000 and Amounts Expressed in Millions of SDRs)

Member	Date of Arrangement	Date of Expiration	Amount Agreed	Undrawn Balance
Stand-By Arrangements				
Argentina	March 10, 2000	March 9, 2003	5,398.61	5,398.61
Bosnia & Herzegovina	May 29, 1998	March 31, 2001	94.42	30.15
Brazil	December 2, 1998	December 1, 2001	10,419.84	2,550.69
Ecuador	April 19, 2000	April 18, 2001	226.73	141.73
Estonia	March 1, 2000	August 31, 2001	29.34	29.34
Korea	December 4, 1997	December 3, 2000	15,500.00	1,087.50
Latvia	December 10, 1999	April 9, 2001	33.00	33.00
Lithuania	March 8, 2000	June 7, 2001	61.80	61.80
Mexico	July 7, 1999	November 30, 2000	3,103.00	1,163.50
Panama	June 30, 2000	March 29, 2002	64.00	64.00
Papua New Guinea	March 29, 2000	May 28, 2001	85.54	75.54
Philippines	April 1, 1998	July 31, 2000	1,020.79	475.00
Romania	August 5, 1999	February 28, 2001	400.00	260.25
Russia	July 28, 1999	December 27, 2000	3,300.00	2,828.57
Turkey	December 22, 1999	December 21, 2002	2,892.00	2,226.84
Uruguay	May 31, 2000	March 31, 2002	150.00	150.00
Zimbabwe	August 2, 1999	October 1, 2000	141.36	116.62
Total			42,920.43	16,913.14
Extended Arrangements				
Bulgaria	September 25, 1998	September 24, 2001	627.62	209.22
Colombia	December 20, 1999	December 19, 2002	1,957.00	1,957.00
Indonesia	February 4, 2000	December 31, 2002	3,638.00	3,096.50
Jordan	April 15, 1999	April 14, 2002	127.88	91.34
Kazakhstan	December 13, 1999	December 12, 2002	329.10	329.10
Pakistan	October 20, 1997	October 19, 2000	454.92	341.18
Peru	June 24, 1999	May 31, 2002	383.00	383.00
Ukraine	September 4, 1998	September 3, 2001	1,919.95	1,207.80
Yemen, Republic of	October 29, 1997	March 1, 2001	105.90	65.90
Total			9,543.37	7,681.04
Total (Stand-By and Extended Arrangements)			**52,463.80**	**24,374.18**
Poverty Reduction and Growth Arrangements				
Albania	May 13, 1998	July 31, 2001	45.04	9.65
Benin	July 18, 2000	July 17, 2003	27.00	20.20
Bolivia	September 18, 1998	September 17, 2001	100.96	56.10
Burkina Faso	September 10, 1999	September 9, 2002	39.12	27.94
Cambodia	October 22, 1999	October 21, 2002	58.50	50.14
Cameroon	August 20, 1997	December 20, 2000	162.12	18.02
Central African Republic	July 20, 1998	July 19, 2001	49.44	32.96
Chad	January 7, 2000	January 6, 2003	36.40	26.00
Côte d'Ivoire	March 17, 1998	March 16, 2001	285.84	161.98
Djibouti	October 18, 1999	October 17, 2002	19.08	13.63
Gambia, The	June 29, 1998	June 28, 2001	20.61	10.31
Ghana	May 3, 1999	May 2, 2002	155.00	110.70
Guinea	January 13, 1997	January 12, 2001	70.80	15.73
Guyana	July 15, 1998	July 14, 2001	53.76	35.84
Honduras	March 26, 1999	March 25, 2002	156.75	64.60
Kyrgyz Republic	June 26, 1998	June 25, 2001	73.38	38.23
Madagascar	November 27, 1996	November 30, 2000	105.76	33.88
Mali	August 6, 1999	August 5, 2002	46.65	39.90
Mauritania	July 21, 1999	July 20, 2002	42.49	30.35
Mozambique	June 28, 1999	June 27, 2002	87.20	42.00
Nicaragua	March 18, 1998	March 17, 2001	148.96	53.82
Pakistan	October 20, 1997	October 19, 2000	682.38	417.01
Rwanda	June 24, 1998	June 23, 2001	71.40	38.08
São Tomé and Principe	April 28, 2000	April 27, 2003	6.66	5.71
Senegal	April 20, 1998	April 19, 2001	107.01	42.80
Tajikistan	June 24, 1998	June 23, 2001	100.30	40.02
Tanzania	April 4, 2000	April 3, 2003	135.00	115.00
Uganda	November 10, 1997	November 9, 2000	100.43	17.85
Yemen, Republic of	October 29, 1997	October 28, 2000	264.75	114.75
Zambia	March 25, 1999	March 28, 2003	254.45	244.45
Total			3,507.23	1,927.64
Total (Stand-by, Extended, and Poverty Reduction and Growth Arrangements)			**55,971.03**	**26,301.82**

Fund Accounts: Position to Date

(As of June 30, 2000 and Expressed in Millions of SDRs)

| | Quota | Reserve Position in the Fund | Total Fund Credit and Loans Outstanding | | | | Fund Holdings of Currency | | SDR Department | Holdings of SDRs | |
| | | | Total Amount | Percent of Quota | Outstanding Purchases (GRA) | Outstanding Loans | Amount | Percent of Quota | Net Cumulative Allocation | Amount | Percent of Allocation |
	(1)	(2)	(3)	(4)	(5)	(6)	(7)	(8)	(9)	(10)	(11)
All Countries	210,251.4	47,766.4	49,533.8	23.6	43,201.6	6,332.2	205,631.9	97.8	21,433.3	18,365.5	85.7
Industrial Countries	130,566.6	40,119.7	—	—	—	—	90,445.8	69.3	14,595.3	14,553.7	99.7
United States	37,149.3	11,536.6	—	—	—	—	25,611.0	68.9	4,899.5	7,810.2	159.4
Canada	6,369.2	1,978.5	—	—	—	—	4,390.7	68.9	779.3	413.2	53.0
Australia	3,236.4	997.1	—	—	—	—	2,239.4	69.2	470.6	63.1	13.4
Japan	13,312.8	4,053.6	—	—	—	—	9,259.4	69.6	891.7	1,869.4	209.6
New Zealand	894.6	265.5	—	—	—	—	629.1	70.3	141.3	8.4	5.9
Austria	1,872.3	572.6	—	—	—	—	1,299.7	69.4	179.1	112.5	62.8
Belgium	4,605.2	1,401.7	—	—	—	—	3,203.5	69.6	485.3	219.1	45.1
Denmark	1,642.8	503.3	—	—	—	—	1,139.5	69.4	178.9	193.9	108.4
Finland	1,263.8	391.2	—	—	—	—	872.6	69.0	142.7	174.4	122.2
France	10,738.5	3,327.7	—	—	—	—	7,410.9	69.0	1,079.9	262.8	24.3
Germany	13,008.2	4,070.3	—	—	—	—	8,937.9	68.7	1,210.8	1,354.1	111.8
Greece	823.0	256.2	—	—	—	—	566.8	68.9	103.5	6.6	6.4
Iceland	117.6	18.6	—	—	—	—	99.0	84.2	16.4	.1	.8
Ireland	838.4	262.3	—	—	—	—	576.1	68.7	87.3	33.2	38.0
Italy	7,055.5	2,150.8	—	—	—	—	4,904.7	69.5	702.4	153.1	21.8
Luxembourg	279.1	55.5	—	—	—	—	223.6	80.1	17.0	2.4	14.4
Netherlands	5,162.4	1,531.2	—	—	—	—	3,631.2	70.3	530.3	619.8	116.9
Norway	1,671.7	528.9	—	—	—	—	1,142.9	68.4	167.8	251.5	149.9
Portugal	867.4	264.0	—	—	—	—	603.4	69.6	53.3	36.5	68.4
San Marino	17.0	4.1	—	—	—	—	12.9	75.9	—	.1	. . . .
Spain	3,048.9	949.3	—	—	—	—	2,099.6	68.9	298.8	206.3	69.0
Sweden	2,395.5	730.8	—	—	—	—	1,664.7	69.5	246.5	243.2	98.7
Switzerland	3,458.5	1,032.7	—	—	—	—	2,425.8	70.1	—	215.9	. . . .
United Kingdom	10,738.5	3,237.3	—	—	—	—	7,501.2	69.9	1,913.1	303.9	15.9
Developing Countries	79,684.8	7,646.6	49,533.8	62.2	43,201.6	6,332.2	115,186.2	144.6	6,838.1	3,811.8	55.7
Africa	11,256.1	291.2	6,491.0	57.7	2,561.2	3,929.8	13,526.6	120.2	1,382.5	406.4	29.4
Algeria	1,254.7	85.1	1,359.7	108.4	1,359.7	—	2,529.3	201.6	128.6	.6	.4
Angola	286.3	—	—	—	—	—	286.4	100.1	—	.1	—
Benin	61.9	2.2	62.8	101.5	—	62.8	59.7	96.5	9.4	.1	.7
Botswana	63.0	19.1	—	—	—	—	43.9	69.7	4.4	28.9	663.8
Burkina Faso	60.2	7.2	84.6	140.6	—	84.6	53.0	88.0	9.4	.4	4.6
Burundi	77.0	5.9	7.9	10.3	—	7.9	71.1	92.4	13.7	—	.2
Cameroon	185.7	.5	152.6	82.1	8.5	144.1	193.6	104.3	24.5	—	.1
Cape Verde	9.6	—	—	—	—	—	9.6	100.0	.6	—	.2
Central African Rep.	55.7	.1	16.5	29.6	—	16.5	55.6	99.8	9.3	—	.1
Chad	56.0	.3	54.8	97.8	—	54.8	55.7	99.5	9.4	—	.1
Comoros	8.9	.5	1.4	15.2	—	1.4	8.4	93.9	.7	.1	17.2
Congo, Dem. Rep. of	291.0	—	300.0	103.1	157.1	142.9	448.1	154.0	86.3	—	—
Congo, Republic of	84.6	.5	21.1	25.0	7.2	13.9	91.3	107.9	9.7	—	.1
Côte d'Ivoire	325.2	.2	439.5	135.1	—	439.5	325.0	99.9	37.8	1.8	4.8
Djibouti	15.9	1.1	8.6	53.8	5.8	2.7	20.6	129.8	1.2	.1	7.3
Equatorial Guinea	32.6	—	4.8	14.7	—	4.8	32.6	100.0	5.8	.2	3.8
Eritrea	15.9	—	—	—	—	—	15.9	100.0	—	—	. . . .
Ethiopia	133.7	7.1	64.1	47.9	—	64.1	126.6	94.7	11.2	—	.3
Gabon	154.3	.1	58.8	38.1	58.8	—	213.0	138.0	14.1	—	.2
Gambia, The	31.1	1.5	8.2	26.5	—	8.2	29.6	95.2	5.1	.3	6.8
Ghana	369.0	—	209.4	56.7	—	209.4	369.0	100.0	63.0	40.8	64.7
Guinea	107.1	.1	90.1	84.1	—	90.1	107.0	99.9	17.6	.3	1.6
Guinea-Bissau	14.2	—	14.1	98.9	3.6	10.5	17.8	125.0	1.2	.1	4.5
Kenya	271.4	12.5	77.7	28.6	—	77.7	258.9	95.4	37.0	.6	1.7
Lesotho	34.9	3.5	10.3	29.6	—	10.3	31.4	89.9	3.7	.5	14.2
Liberia	71.3	—	224.6	315.0	201.5	23.1	272.7	382.5	21.0	—	—
Madagascar	122.2	—	43.2	35.4	—	43.2	122.2	100.0	19.3	.1	.4
Malawi	69.4	2.2	59.9	86.3	—	59.9	67.2	96.8	11.0	—	.2
Mali	93.3	8.8	134.4	144.1	—	134.4	84.5	90.6	15.9	.2	1.1
Mauritania	64.4	—	79.5	123.4	—	79.5	64.4	100.0	9.7	.2	2.1
Mauritius	101.6	14.5	—	—	—	—	87.1	85.8	15.7	16.2	103.2
Morocco	588.2	70.4	—	—	—	—	517.8	88.0	85.7	57.7	67.3
Mozambique	113.6	—	170.7	150.3	—	170.7	113.6	100.0	—	—	. . . .
Namibia	136.5	—	—	—	—	—	136.5	100.0	—	—	. . . .
Niger	65.8	8.6	49.0	74.4	—	49.0	57.2	87.0	9.4	.1	1.2
Nigeria	1,753.2	.1	—	—	—	—	1,753.1	100.0	157.2	.1	.1
Rwanda	80.1	—	52.2	65.1	17.1	35.1	97.2	121.4	13.7	6.9	50.4
São Tomé & Príncipe	7.4	—	—	—	—	—	7.4	100.0	.6	—	.2
Senegal	161.8	1.4	204.4	126.3	—	204.4	160.4	99.1	24.5	.1	.3

(As of June 30, 2000 and Expressed in Millions of SDRs)

		Total Fund Credit and Loans Outstanding				Fund Holdings of Currency		SDR Department			
Quota	Reserve Position in the Fund	Total Amount	Percent of Quota	Outstanding Purchases (GRA)	Outstanding Loans	Amount	Percent of Quota	Net Cumulative Allocation	Holdings of SDRs		
									Amount	Percent of Allocation	
(1)	(2)	(3)	(4)	(5)	(6)	(7)	(8)	(9)	(10)	(11)	
											Africa (cont.)
8.8	—	—	—	—	—	8.8	100.0	.4	—	4.5	Seychelles
103.7	—	132.4	127.7	27.1	105.3	130.8	126.2	17.5	4.6	26.4	Sierra Leone
44.2	—	112.0	253.4	96.7	15.3	140.9	318.8	13.7	—	—	Somalia
1,868.5	.2	—	—	—	—	1,868.3	100.0	220.4	216.4	98.2	South Africa
169.7	—	499.3	294.2	440.1	59.2	609.8	359.3	52.2	—	—	Sudan
50.7	6.6	—	—	—	—	44.2	87.1	6.4	2.4	37.8	Swaziland
198.9	10.0	236.9	119.1	—	236.9	188.9	95.0	31.4	.1	.4	Tanzania
73.4	.3	57.1	77.7	—	57.1	73.1	99.7	11.0	.1	.5	Togo
286.5	20.2	40.0	13.9	40.0	—	306.3	106.9	34.2	24.0	70.2	Tunisia
180.5	—	251.5	139.3	—	251.5	180.5	100.0	29.4	2.0	6.8	Uganda
489.1	—	853.4	174.5	—	853.4	489.1	100.0	68.3	—	—	Zambia
353.4	.3	243.8	69.0	138.1	105.7	491.2	139.0	10.2	—	.3	Zimbabwe
20,235.1	**3,375.6**	**18,221.5**	**90.0**	**17,118.3**	**1,103.2**	**33,978.0**	**167.9**	**2,043.7**	**1,017.7**	**49.8**	**Asia**
120.4	4.9	—	—	—	—	115.5	95.9	26.7	—	—	Afghanistan, I.S. of
533.3	.2	204.6	38.4	98.1	106.4	631.2	118.4	47.1	1.7	3.7	Bangladesh
6.3	1.0	—	—	—	—	5.3	83.8	—	.2	....	Bhutan
150.0	35.3	—	—	—	—	114.7	76.5	—	4.3	....	Brunei Darussalam
87.5	—	51.2	58.5	3.6	47.6	91.1	104.2	15.4	1.4	9.1	Cambodia
4,687.2	1,456.2	—	—	—	—	3,231.0	68.9	236.8	575.6	243.1	China,P.R.: Mainland
—	—	—	—	—	—	—	—	—	—	....	China,P.R.:Hong Kong
70.3	14.9	—	—	—	—	55.4	78.7	7.0	4.3	61.4	Fiji
4,158.2	488.6	—	—	—	—	3,669.6	88.2	681.2	6.3	.9	India
2,079.3	145.5	8,008.3	385.1	8,008.3	—	9,942.1	478.1	239.0	103.0	43.1	Indonesia
5.6	—	—	—	—	—	5.6	100.0	—	—	....	Kiribati
1,633.6	208.6	4,462.5	273.2	4,462.5	—	5,887.5	360.4	72.9	3.4	4.6	Korea
39.1	—	35.8	91.5	—	35.8	39.1	100.0	9.4	.3	3.1	Lao People's Dem.Rep
1,486.6	608.2	—	—	—	—	878.4	59.1	139.1	70.0	50.3	Malaysia
8.2	1.6	—	—	—	—	6.6	81.1	.3	.2	61.1	Maldives
2.5	—	—	—	—	—	2.5	100.0	—	—	....	Marshall Islands
5.1	—	—	—	—	—	5.1	100.0	—	1.1	....	Micronesia, Fed.Sts.
51.1	—	41.0	80.2	—	41.0	51.1	100.0	—	.1	....	Mongolia
258.4	—	—	—	—	—	258.4	100.0	43.5	.1	.2	Myanmar
71.3	5.7	11.2	15.7	—	11.2	65.6	92.0	8.1	.1	1.5	Nepal
1,033.7	.1	1,159.1	112.1	689.1	470.0	1,722.7	166.7	170.0	.4	.2	Pakistan
3.1	—	—	—	—	—	3.1	100.0	—	—	....	Palau
131.6	.1	16.8	12.8	16.8	—	148.4	112.8	9.3	9.8	105.8	Papua New Guinea
879.9	87.1	1,324.7	150.6	1,324.7	—	2,117.5	240.7	116.6	2.8	2.4	Philippines
11.6	.7	—	—	—	—	10.9	94.2	1.1	2.3	198.2	Samoa
862.5	264.4	—	—	—	—	598.1	69.3	16.5	97.2	589.8	Singapore
10.4	.5	—	—	—	—	9.9	94.9	.7	—	.1	Solomon Islands
413.4	47.7	155.7	37.7	—	155.7	365.7	88.5	70.9	.9	1.3	Sri Lanka
1,081.9	—	2,500.0	231.1	2,500.0	—	3,581.9	331.1	84.7	131.3	155.1	Thailand
6.9	1.7	—	—	—	—	5.2	75.4	—	.1	....	Tonga
17.0	2.5	—	—	—	—	14.5	85.3	—	.6	....	Vanuatu
329.1	—	250.7	76.2	15.1	235.6	344.2	104.6	47.7	.4	.8	Vietnam
16,802.4	**646.6**	**15,667.8**	**93.2**	**15,021.9**	**645.9**	**31,122.3**	**185.2**	**374.1**	**363.8**	**97.2**	**Europe**
48.7	3.4	68.2	140.1	8.8	59.4	54.2	111.2	—	60.0	....	Albania
92.0	—	140.4	152.6	31.1	109.4	123.1	133.8	—	22.9	....	Armenia
160.9	—	277.2	172.3	195.3	81.9	356.2	221.4	—	5.4	....	Azerbaijan
386.4	—	105.6	27.3	105.6	—	492.0	127.3	—	—	....	Belarus
169.1	—	75.6	44.7	71.8	—	240.9	142.5	20.5	1.5	7.2	Bosnia & Herzegovina
640.2	32.7	981.8	153.4	981.8	—	1,589.3	248.2	—	58.0	....	Bulgaria
365.1	.2	132.3	36.2	132.3	—	497.3	136.2	44.2	125.7	284.3	Croatia
139.6	35.4	—	—	—	—	104.2	74.7	19.4	.6	2.9	Cyprus
819.3	—	—	—	—	—	819.3	100.0	—	.2	....	Czech Republic
65.2	—	16.5	25.3	16.5	—	81.7	125.3	—	—	....	Estonia
150.3	—	223.2	148.5	51.1	172.1	201.4	134.0	—	6.2	....	Georgia
1,038.4	176.8	—	—	—	—	861.6	83.0	—	5.9	....	Hungary
365.7	—	—	—	—	—	365.7	100.0	—	—	....	Kazakhstan
88.8	—	139.8	157.5	17.5	122.4	106.3	119.7	—	.4	....	Kyrgyz Republic
126.8	—	30.5	24.1	30.5	—	157.3	124.0	—	—	....	Latvia
144.2	—	158.3	109.8	158.3	—	302.5	209.7	—	1.0	....	Lithuania
68.9	—	66.5	96.5	39.2	27.3	108.1	156.9	8.4	.9	10.8	Macedonia, FYR
102.0	40.3	—	—	—	—	61.7	60.5	11.3	23.4	207.4	Malta
123.2	—	115.4	93.7	115.4	—	238.6	193.7	—	.3	....	Moldova
1,369.0	172.3	—	—	—	—	1,196.7	87.4	—	10.6	....	Poland
1,030.2	—	395.5	38.4	395.5	—	1,425.7	138.4	76.0	5.9	7.8	Romania

Fund Accounts: Position to Date

(As of June 30, 2000 and Expressed in Millions of SDRs)

	Quota	Reserve Position in the Fund	Total Fund Credit and Loans Outstanding				Fund Holdings of Currency		SDR Department		
			Total Amount	Percent of Quota	Outstanding Purchases (GRA)	Outstanding Loans	Amount	Percent of Quota	Net Cumulative Allocation	Holdings of SDRs	
										Amount	Percent of Allocation
	(1)	(2)	(3)	(4)	(5)	(6)	(7)	(8)	(9)	(10)	(11)
Europe (cont.)											
Russia	5,945.4	.9	9,844.3	165.6	9,844.3	—	15,788.8	265.6	—	1.3	....
Slovak Republic	357.5	—	85.8	24.0	85.8	—	443.3	124.0	—	.1	....
Slovenia	231.7	71.8	—	—	—	—	159.9	69.0	25.4	2.0	7.9
Tajikistan	87.0	—	96.1	110.5	22.5	73.6	109.5	125.9	—	2.0	....
Turkey	964.0	112.8	814.3	84.5	814.3	—	1,665.5	172.8	112.3	.4	.4
Turkmenistan	75.2	—	—	—	—	—	75.2	100.0	—	—	....
Ukraine	1,372.0	—	1,726.6	125.8	1,726.6	—	3,098.6	225.8	—	28.9	....
Uzbekistan	275.6	—	122.2	44.3	122.2	—	397.8	144.3	—	.1	....
Middle East	**15,478.5**	**2,312.1**	**628.6**	**4.1**	**478.6**	**150.0**	**13,645.2**	**88.2**	**986.4**	**965.0**	**97.8**
Bahrain	135.0	63.5	—	—	—	—	71.5	53.0	6.2	1.1	18.4
Egypt	943.7	120.1	—	—	—	—	823.6	87.3	135.9	27.3	20.1
Iran, I.R. of	1,497.2	—	—	—	—	—	1,497.2	100.0	244.1	217.8	89.2
Iraq	504.0	—	—	—	—	—	504.0	100.0	68.5	—	—
Israel	928.2	65.5	—	—	—	—	862.7	92.9	106.4	.2	.2
Jordan	170.5	.1	352.0	206.5	352.0	—	522.5	306.4	16.9	.2	1.0
Kuwait	1,381.1	377.3	—	—	—	—	1,003.8	72.7	26.7	61.0	228.1
Lebanon	203.0	18.8	—	—	—	—	184.2	90.7	4.4	17.5	399.2
Libya	1,123.7	395.5	—	—	—	—	728.2	64.8	58.8	396.4	674.4
Oman	194.0	49.8	—	—	—	—	144.3	74.4	6.3	2.2	34.4
Qatar	263.8	44.7	—	—	—	—	219.1	83.0	12.8	14.9	116.3
Saudi Arabia	6,985.5	987.5	—	—	—	—	5,998.0	85.9	195.5	127.0	65.0
Syrian Arab Republic	293.6	—	—	—	—	—	293.6	100.0	36.6	—	—
United Arab Emirates	611.7	189.3	—	—	—	—	422.4	69.1	38.7	3.9	10.0
Yemen, Republic of	243.5	—	276.6	113.6	126.6	150.0	370.1	152.0	28.7	95.5	332.3
Western Hemisphere	**15,912.7**	**1,021.3**	**8,524.8**	**53.6**	**8,021.6**	**503.2**	**22,914.0**	**144.0**	**2,051.3**	**1,058.9**	**51.6**
Antigua and Barbuda	13.5	—	—	—	—	—	13.5	100.0	—	—	....
Argentina	2,117.1	—	2,810.0	132.7	2,810.0	—	4,927.1	232.7	318.4	22.4	7.0
Bahamas, The	130.3	6.2	—	—	—	—	124.1	95.2	10.2	.1	.9
Barbados	67.5	4.7	—	—	—	—	62.8	93.1	8.0	—	.2
Belize	18.8	4.2	—	—	—	—	14.6	77.5	—	1.1	....
Bolivia	171.5	8.9	180.0	104.9	—	180.0	162.6	94.8	26.7	27.3	102.2
Brazil	3,036.1	—	1,356.8	44.7	1,356.8	—	4,393.6	144.7	358.7	21.7	6.1
Chile	856.1	267.7	—	—	—	—	588.4	68.7	121.9	16.3	13.4
Colombia	774.0	285.8	—	—	—	—	488.2	63.1	114.3	100.7	88.1
Costa Rica	164.1	20.0	—	—	—	—	144.1	87.8	23.7	.6	2.5
Dominica	8.2	—	—	—	—	—	8.2	99.9	.6	—	.1
Dominican Republic	218.9	—	39.7	18.1	39.7	—	258.6	118.1	31.6	.3	.9
Ecuador	302.3	17.2	85.0	28.1	85.0	—	370.1	122.4	32.9	.5	1.4
El Salvador	171.3	—	—	—	—	—	171.3	100.0	25.0	25.0	100.0
Grenada	11.7	—	—	—	—	—	11.7	100.0	.9	—	—
Guatemala	210.2	—	—	—	—	—	210.2	100.0	27.7	8.0	28.8
Guyana	90.9	—	93.1	102.4	—	93.1	90.9	100.0	14.5	.7	4.9
Haiti	60.7	—	30.4	50.0	15.2	15.2	75.8	124.9	13.7	.4	3.1
Honduras	129.5	8.6	151.3	116.8	47.5	103.8	168.4	130.0	19.1	.1	.3
Jamaica	273.5	—	53.6	19.6	53.6	—	327.1	119.6	40.6	.2	.4
Mexico	2,585.8	.3	2,592.5	100.3	2,592.5	—	5,178.0	200.2	290.0	747.7	257.8
Nicaragua	130.0	—	111.2	85.5	—	111.2	130.0	100.0	19.5	—	.1
Panama	206.6	11.9	90.2	43.6	90.2	—	284.9	137.9	26.3	.1	.4
Paraguay	99.9	21.5	—	—	—	—	78.4	78.5	13.7	76.7	559.7
Peru	638.4	—	481.8	75.5	481.8	—	1,120.3	175.5	91.3	.3	.3
St. Kitts and Nevis	8.9	.1	1.6	18.3	1.6	—	10.5	117.5	—	—	....
St. Lucia	15.3	—	—	—	—	—	15.3	100.0	.7	1.5	204.5
St. Vincent & Grens.	8.3	.5	—	—	—	—	7.8	94.0	.4	.1	17.6
Suriname	92.1	6.1	—	—	—	—	86.0	93.4	7.8	1.9	24.5
Trinidad and Tobago	335.6	—	—	—	—	—	335.6	100.0	46.2	.1	.3
Uruguay	306.5	35.7	114.2	37.3	114.2	—	385.0	125.6	50.0	.2	.4
Venezuela, Rep. Bol.	2,659.1	321.9	333.7	12.5	333.7	—	2,670.9	100.4	316.9	5.0	1.6
Memorandum Items											
Oil Exporting Ctys	20,307.3	2,596.7	9,701.7	47.8	9,701.7	—	27,412.4	135.0	1,493.0	931.7	62.4
Non-Oil Develop.Ctys	59,377.5	5,049.9	39,832.1	67.1	33,500.0	6,332.2	87,773.7	147.8	5,345.1	2,880.0	53.9

Column 6 is comprised of outstanding SAF, PRGF (previously, ESAF), and Trust Fund loans.

Column 10 does not report separately data on the SDR positions of the Fund's General Resources Account and of Other Holders. Data on the SDR Holdings of the Fund's General Resources Account and of Other Holders are reported in the foot-table to the table on SDRs.

Totals for **All Countries, Developing Countries,** and **Europe** also include positions in the Fund of the one successor state to Yugoslavia not shown separately (the Federal Republic of Yugoslavia [Serbia/Montenegro]).

Financing Components of Members' Outstanding Obligations to the Fund

(As of June 30, 2000 and Expressed in Millions of SDRs)

Total Fund Credit and Loans Outstanding	Total Amount	Outstanding Purchases (GRA) — Ordinary Resources				Outstanding Purchases (GRA) — Borrowed Resources				Outstanding Loans — SAF Arrangements	Outstanding Loans — PRGF Arrangements		Trust Fund	
		CCFF	STF	Stand-by/ Credit Tranche	Extended Fund Facility	SFF	EAR	GAB	NAB	SDA Resources	SDA Resources	PRGF Trust Resources	Administered Accounts	
(1)	(2)	(3)	(4)	(5)	(6)	(7)	(8)	(9)	(10)	(11)	(12)	(13)	(14)	
49,533.8	43,201.6	3,031.4	2,607.7	20,391.2	15,925.0	129.2	348.7	768.4	—	439.9	45.6	5,757.8	88.8	**All Countries**
—	—	—	—	—	—	—	—	—	—	—	—	—	—	**Industrial Countries**
—	—	—	—	—	—	—	—	—	—	—	—	—	—	United States
—	—	—	—	—	—	—	—	—	—	—	—	—	—	Canada
—	—	—	—	—	—	—	—	—	—	—	—	—	—	Australia
—	—	—	—	—	—	—	—	—	—	—	—	—	—	Japan
—	—	—	—	—	—	—	—	—	—	—	—	—	—	New Zealand
—	—	—	—	—	—	—	—	—	—	—	—	—	—	Austria
—	—	—	—	—	—	—	—	—	—	—	—	—	—	Belgium
—	—	—	—	—	—	—	—	—	—	—	—	—	—	Denmark
—	—	—	—	—	—	—	—	—	—	—	—	—	—	Finland
—	—	—	—	—	—	—	—	—	—	—	—	—	—	France
—	—	—	—	—	—	—	—	—	—	—	—	—	—	Germany
—	—	—	—	—	—	—	—	—	—	—	—	—	—	Greece
—	—	—	—	—	—	—	—	—	—	—	—	—	—	Iceland
—	—	—	—	—	—	—	—	—	—	—	—	—	—	Ireland
—	—	—	—	—	—	—	—	—	—	—	—	—	—	Italy
—	—	—	—	—	—	—	—	—	—	—	—	—	—	Luxembourg
—	—	—	—	—	—	—	—	—	—	—	—	—	—	Netherlands
—	—	—	—	—	—	—	—	—	—	—	—	—	—	Norway
—	—	—	—	—	—	—	—	—	—	—	—	—	—	Portugal
—	—	—	—	—	—	—	—	—	—	—	—	—	—	San Marino
—	—	—	—	—	—	—	—	—	—	—	—	—	—	Spain
—	—	—	—	—	—	—	—	—	—	—	—	—	—	Sweden
—	—	—	—	—	—	—	—	—	—	—	—	—	—	Switzerland
—	—	—	—	—	—	—	—	—	—	—	—	—	—	United Kingdom
49,533.8	43,201.6	3,031.4	2,607.7	20,391.2	15,925.0	129.2	348.7	768.4	—	439.9	45.6	5,757.8	88.8	**Developing Countries**
6,491.0	2,561.2	353.9	—	335.5	1,416.3	129.2	326.3	—	—	398.5	32.2	3,410.3	88.8	**Africa**
1,359.7	1,359.7	223.5	—	—	1,136.2	—	—	—	—	—	—	—	—	Algeria
—	—	—	—	—	—	—	—	—	—	—	—	—	—	Angola
62.8	—	—	—	—	—	—	—	—	—	2.8	4.6	55.5	—	Benin
—	—	—	—	—	—	—	—	—	—	—	—	—	—	Botswana
84.6	—	—	—	—	—	—	—	—	—	1.3	12.6	70.7	—	Burkina Faso
7.9	—	—	—	—	—	—	—	—	—	—	—	7.9	—	Burundi
152.6	8.5	—	—	8.5	—	—	—	—	—	—	—	144.1	—	Cameroon
—	—	—	—	—	—	—	—	—	—	—	—	—	—	Cape Verde
16.5	—	—	—	—	—	—	—	—	—	—	—	16.5	—	Central African Rep.
54.8	—	—	—	—	—	—	—	—	—	—	—	54.8	—	Chad
1.4	—	—	—	—	—	—	—	—	—	1.4	—	—	—	Comoros
300.0	157.1	22.7	—	85.2	7.6	—	41.7	—	—	142.9	—	—	—	Congo, Dem. Rep. of
21.1	7.2	—	—	7.2	—	—	—	—	—	—	—	13.9	—	Congo, Republic of
439.5	—	—	—	—	—	—	—	—	—	—	—	439.5	—	Côte d'Ivoire
8.6	5.8	—	—	5.8	—	—	—	—	—	—	—	2.7	—	Djibouti
4.8	—	—	—	—	—	—	—	—	—	1.7	2.1	1.1	—	Equatorial Guinea
—	—	—	—	—	—	—	—	—	—	—	—	—	—	Eritrea
64.1	—	—	—	—	—	—	—	—	—	34.6	—	29.5	—	Ethiopia
58.8	58.8	—	—	—	58.8	—	—	—	—	—	—	—	—	Gabon
8.2	—	—	—	—	—	—	—	—	—	—	—	8.2	—	Gambia, The
209.4	—	—	—	—	—	—	—	—	—	—	—	209.4	—	Ghana
90.1	—	—	—	—	—	—	—	—	—	—	—	90.1	—	Guinea
14.1	3.6	—	—	3.6	—	—	—	—	—	—	—	10.5	—	Guinea-Bissau
77.7	—	—	—	—	—	—	—	—	—	—	1.4	76.3	—	Kenya
10.3	—	—	—	—	—	—	—	—	—	—	—	10.3	—	Lesotho
224.6	201.5	34.7	—	45.8	—	36.7	84.3	—	—	—	—	—	23.1	Liberia
43.2	—	—	—	—	—	—	—	—	—	—	1.3	41.9	—	Madagascar
59.9	—	—	—	—	—	—	—	—	—	—	1.1	58.8	—	Malawi
134.4	—	—	—	—	—	—	—	—	—	—	5.6	128.8	—	Mali
79.5	—	—	—	—	—	—	—	—	—	—	1.7	77.8	—	Mauritania
—	—	—	—	—	—	—	—	—	—	—	—	—	—	Mauritius
—	—	—	—	—	—	—	—	—	—	—	—	—	—	Morocco
170.7	—	—	—	—	—	—	—	—	—	—	—	170.7	—	Mozambique
—	—	—	—	—	—	—	—	—	—	—	—	—	—	Namibia
49.0	—	—	—	—	—	—	—	—	—	—	—	49.0	—	Niger
—	—	—	—	—	—	—	—	—	—	—	—	—	—	Nigeria
52.2	17.1	2.2	—	14.9	—	—	—	—	—	1.8	—	33.3	—	Rwanda
—	—	—	—	—	—	—	—	—	—	—	—	—	—	São Tomé & Príncipe

Financing Components of Members' Outstanding Obligations to the Fund

(As of June 30, 2000 and Expressed in Millions of SDRs)

		Outstanding Purchases (GRA)								Outstanding Loans			Trust Fund
		Ordinary Resources				Borrowed Resources				SAF Arrangements	PRGF Arrangements		
Total Fund Credit and Loans Outstanding	Total Amount	CCFF	STF	Stand-by/ Credit Tranche	Extended Fund Facility	SFF	EAR	GAB	NAB	SDA Resources	SDA Resources	PRGF Trust Resources	Administered Accounts
(1)	(2)	(3)	(4)	(5)	(6)	(7)	(8)	(9)	(10)	(11)	(12)	(13)	(14)
Africa (cont.)													
Senegal	204.4	—	—	—	—	—	—	—	—	—	—	1.4	203.0	—
Seychelles	—	—	—	—	—	—	—	—	—	—	—	—	—	—
Sierra Leone	132.4	27.1	—	—	27.1	—	—	—	—	—	21.6	—	83.6	—
Somalia	112.0	96.7	28.5	—	12.6	—	—	55.5	—	—	8.8	—	—	6.5
South Africa	—	—	—	—	—	—	—	—	—	—	—	—	—	—
Sudan	499.3	440.1	42.3	—	60.9	99.6	92.5	144.8	—	—	—	—	—	59.2
Swaziland	—	—	—	—	—	—	—	—	—	—	—	—	—	—
Tanzania	236.9	—	—	—	—	—	—	—	—	—	—	—	236.9	—
Togo	57.1	—	—	—	—	—	—	—	—	—	—	.4	56.7	—
Tunisia	40.0	40.0	—	—	—	40.0	—	—	—	—	—	—	—	—
Uganda	251.5	—	—	—	—	—	—	—	—	—	—	—	251.5	—
Zambia	853.4	—	—	—	—	—	—	—	—	—	181.8	—	671.7	—
Zimbabwe	243.8	138.1	—	—	63.9	74.1	—	—	—	—	—	—	105.7	—
Asia	**18,221.5**	**17,118.3**	**352.7**	**18.7**	**11,429.2**	**5,317.7**	**—**	**—**	**—**	**—**	**41.3**	**—**	**1,061.9**	**—**
Afghanistan, I.S. of	—	—	—	—	—	—	—	—	—	—	—	—	—	—
Bangladesh	204.6	98.1	—	—	98.1	—	—	—	—	—	—	—	106.4	—
Bhutan	—	—	—	—	—	—	—	—	—	—	—	—	—	—
Brunei Darussalam	—	—	—	—	—	—	—	—	—	—	—	—	—	—
Cambodia	51.2	3.6	—	3.6	—	—	—	—	—	—	—	—	47.6	—
China, People's Rep.	—	—	—	—	—	—	—	—	—	—	—	—	—	—
Fiji	—	—	—	—	—	—	—	—	—	—	—	—	—	—
India	—	—	—	—	—	—	—	—	—	—	—	—	—	—
Indonesia	8,008.3	8,008.3	—	—	3,669.1	4,339.2	—	—	—	—	—	—	—	—
Kiribati	—	—	—	—	—	—	—	—	—	—	—	—	—	—
Korea	4,462.5	4,462.5	—	—	4,462.5	—	—	—	—	—	—	—	—	—
Lao People's Dem.Rep	35.8	—	—	—	—	—	—	—	—	—	4.1	—	31.7	—
Malaysia	—	—	—	—	—	—	—	—	—	—	—	—	—	—
Maldives	—	—	—	—	—	—	—	—	—	—	—	—	—	—
Marshall Islands	—	—	—	—	—	—	—	—	—	—	—	—	—	—
Micronesia, Fed.Sts.	—	—	—	—	—	—	—	—	—	—	—	—	—	—
Mongolia	41.0	—	—	—	—	—	—	—	—	—	—	—	41.0	—
Myanmar	—	—	—	—	—	—	—	—	—	—	—	—	—	—
Nepal	11.2	—	—	—	—	—	—	—	—	—	—	—	11.2	—
Pakistan	1,159.1	689.1	352.7	—	136.9	199.4	—	—	—	—	32.8	—	437.2	—
Palau	—	—	—	—	—	—	—	—	—	—	—	—	—	—
Papua New Guinea	16.8	16.8	—	—	16.8	—	—	—	—	—	—	—	—	—
Philippines	1,324.7	1,324.7	—	—	545.7	779.0	—	—	—	—	—	—	—	—
Samoa	—	—	—	—	—	—	—	—	—	—	—	—	—	—
Singapore	—	—	—	—	—	—	—	—	—	—	—	—	—	—
Solomon Islands	—	—	—	—	—	—	—	—	—	—	—	—	—	—
Sri Lanka	155.7	—	—	—	—	—	—	—	—	—	4.5	—	151.2	—
Thailand	2,500.0	2,500.0	—	—	2,500.0	—	—	—	—	—	—	—	—	—
Tonga	—	—	—	—	—	—	—	—	—	—	—	—	—	—
Vanuatu	—	—	—	—	—	—	—	—	—	—	—	—	—	—
Vietnam	250.7	15.1	—	15.1	—	—	—	—	—	—	—	—	235.6	—
Europe	**15,667.8**	**15,021.9**	**2,290.6**	**2,588.9**	**3,589.2**	**5,762.3**	**—**	**22.5**	**768.4**	**—**	**—**	**—**	**645.9**	**—**
Albania	68.2	8.8	—	—	8.8	—	—	—	—	—	—	—	59.4	—
Armenia	140.4	31.1	—	28.1	3.0	—	—	—	—	—	—	—	109.4	—
Azerbaijan	277.2	195.3	56.3	51.2	34.6	53.2	—	—	—	—	—	—	81.9	—
Belarus	105.6	105.6	—	99.3	6.3	—	—	—	—	—	—	—	—	—
Bosnia & Herzegovina	75.6	71.8	—	—	71.8	—	—	—	—	—	—	—	—	—
Bulgaria	981.8	981.8	64.0	77.5	421.9	418.4	—	—	—	—	—	—	—	—
Croatia	132.3	132.3	—	103.6	—	28.8	—	—	—	—	—	—	—	—
Cyprus	—	—	—	—	—	—	—	—	—	—	—	—	—	—
Czech Republic	—	—	—	—	—	—	—	—	—	—	—	—	—	—
Estonia	16.5	16.5	—	16.5	—	—	—	—	—	—	—	—	—	—
Georgia	223.2	51.1	—	46.3	4.9	—	—	—	—	—	—	—	172.1	—
Hungary	—	—	—	—	—	—	—	—	—	—	—	—	—	—
Kazakhstan	—	—	—	—	—	—	—	—	—	—	—	—	—	—
Kyrgyz Republic	139.8	17.5	—	17.5	—	—	—	—	—	—	—	—	122.4	—
Latvia	30.5	30.5	—	30.5	—	—	—	—	—	—	—	—	—	—
Lithuania	158.3	158.3	—	32.3	—	125.9	—	—	—	—	—	—	—	—
Macedonia, FYR	66.5	39.2	13.8	18.6	6.8	—	—	—	—	—	—	—	27.3	—

Column 5 includes Korea's purchases and column 6 includes Russia's purchases, both, under
~ns of the Supplemental Reserve Facility (SRF).

Financing Components of Members' Outstanding Obligations to the Fund

(As of June 30, 2000 and Expressed in Millions of SDRs)

Total Fund Credit and Loans Outstanding	Total Amount	Ordinary Resources CCFF	STF	Stand-by/ Credit Tranche	Extended Fund Facility	Borrowed Resources SFF	EAR	GAB	NAB	SAF Arrangements SDA Resources	PRGF Arrangements SDA Resources	PRGF Trust Resources	Trust Fund Administered Accounts	
(1)	(2)	(3)	(4)	(5)	(6)	(7)	(8)	(9)	(10)	(11)	(12)	(13)	(14)	
														Europe (cont.)
—	—	—	—	—	—	—	—	—	—	—	—	—	—	Malta
115.4	115.4	—	26.3	1.6	87.5	—	—	—	—	—	—	—	—	Moldova
—	—	—	—	—	—	—	—	—	—	—	—	—	—	Poland
395.5	395.5	—	125.7	269.8	—	—	—	—	—	—	—	—	—	Romania
9,844.3	9,844.3	2,156.6	1,347.8	1,235.2	4,336.3	—	—	768.4	—	—	—	—	—	Russia
85.8	85.8	—	85.8	—	—	—	—	—	—	—	—	—	—	Slovak Republic
—	—	—	—	—	—	—	—	—	—	—	—	—	—	Slovenia
96.1	22.5	—	—	22.5	—	—	—	—	—	—	—	73.6	—	Tajikistan
814.3	814.3	—	—	814.3	—	—	—	—	—	—	—	—	—	Turkey
—	—	—	—	—	—	—	—	—	—	—	—	—	—	Turkmenistan
1,726.6	1,726.6	—	394.8	619.7	712.2	—	—	—	—	—	—	—	—	Ukraine
122.2	122.2	—	87.3	34.9	—	—	—	—	—	—	—	—	—	Uzbekistan
628.6	**478.6**	**34.1**	—	**86.6**	**357.9**	—	—	—	—	—	—	**150.0**	—	**Middle East**
—	—	—	—	—	—	—	—	—	—	—	—	—	—	Bahrain
—	—	—	—	—	—	—	—	—	—	—	—	—	—	Egypt
—	—	—	—	—	—	—	—	—	—	—	—	—	—	Iran, I.R. of
—	—	—	—	—	—	—	—	—	—	—	—	—	—	Iraq
—	—	—	—	—	—	—	—	—	—	—	—	—	—	Israel
352.0	352.0	34.1	—	—	317.9	—	—	—	—	—	—	—	—	Jordan
—	—	—	—	—	—	—	—	—	—	—	—	—	—	Kuwait
—	—	—	—	—	—	—	—	—	—	—	—	—	—	Lebanon
—	—	—	—	—	—	—	—	—	—	—	—	—	—	Libya
—	—	—	—	—	—	—	—	—	—	—	—	—	—	Oman
—	—	—	—	—	—	—	—	—	—	—	—	—	—	Qatar
—	—	—	—	—	—	—	—	—	—	—	—	—	—	Saudi Arabia
—	—	—	—	—	—	—	—	—	—	—	—	—	—	Syrian Arab Republic
—	—	—	—	—	—	—	—	—	—	—	—	—	—	United Arab Emirates
276.6	126.6	—	—	86.6	40.0	—	—	—	—	—	—	150.0	—	Yemen, Republic of
8,524.8	**8,021.6**	—	—	**4,950.7**	**3,070.9**	—	—	—	—	—	**13.5**	**489.7**	—	**Western Hemisphere**
—	—	—	—	—	—	—	—	—	—	—	—	—	—	Antigua and Barbuda
2,810.0	2,810.0	—	—	507.1	2,302.9	—	—	—	—	—	—	—	—	Argentina
—	—	—	—	—	—	—	—	—	—	—	—	—	—	Bahamas, The
—	—	—	—	—	—	—	—	—	—	—	—	—	—	Barbados
—	—	—	—	—	—	—	—	—	—	—	—	—	—	Belize
180.0	—	—	—	—	—	—	—	—	—	—	.9	179.1	—	Bolivia
1,356.8	1,356.8	—	—	1,356.8	—	—	—	—	—	—	—	—	—	Brazil
—	—	—	—	—	—	—	—	—	—	—	—	—	—	Chile
—	—	—	—	—	—	—	—	—	—	—	—	—	—	Colombia
—	—	—	—	—	—	—	—	—	—	—	—	—	—	Costa Rica
—	—	—	—	—	—	—	—	—	—	—	—	—	—	Dominica
39.7	39.7	—	—	39.7	—	—	—	—	—	—	—	—	—	Dominican Republic
85.0	85.0	—	—	85.0	—	—	—	—	—	—	—	—	—	Ecuador
—	—	—	—	—	—	—	—	—	—	—	—	—	—	El Salvador
—	—	—	—	—	—	—	—	—	—	—	—	—	—	Grenada
—	—	—	—	—	—	—	—	—	—	—	—	—	—	Guatemala
93.1	—	—	—	—	—	—	—	—	—	—	12.5	80.6	—	Guyana
30.4	15.2	—	—	15.2	—	—	—	—	—	—	—	15.2	—	Haiti
151.3	47.5	—	—	47.5	—	—	—	—	—	—	—	103.8	—	Honduras
53.6	53.6	—	—	—	53.6	—	—	—	—	—	—	—	—	Jamaica
2,592.5	2,592.5	—	—	2,514.8	77.7	—	—	—	—	—	—	—	—	Mexico
111.2	—	—	—	—	—	—	—	—	—	—	—	111.2	—	Nicaragua
90.2	90.2	—	—	50.2	40.0	—	—	—	—	—	—	—	—	Panama
—	—	—	—	—	—	—	—	—	—	—	—	—	—	Paraguay
481.8	481.8	—	—	—	481.9	—	—	—	—	—	—	—	—	Peru
1.6	1.6	—	—	1.6	—	—	—	—	—	—	—	—	—	St. Kitts and Nevis
—	—	—	—	—	—	—	—	—	—	—	—	—	—	St. Lucia
—	—	—	—	—	—	—	—	—	—	—	—	—	—	St. Vincent & Grens.
—	—	—	—	—	—	—	—	—	—	—	—	—	—	Suriname
—	—	—	—	—	—	—	—	—	—	—	—	—	—	Trinidad and Tobago
114.2	114.2	—	—	114.2	—	—	—	—	—	—	—	—	—	Uruguay
333.7	333.7	—	—	218.8	114.9	—	—	—	—	—	—	—	—	Venezuela, Rep. Bol.
														Memorandum Items
9,701.7	9,701.7	223.5	—	3,887.9	5,590.3	—	—	—	—	—	—	—	—	Oil Exporting Ctys
39,832.1	33,500.0	2,807.9	2,607.7	16,503.4	10,334.7	129.2	348.7	768.4	—	439.9	45.6	5,757.8	88.8	Non-Oil Develop.Ctys

Purchases*

	1970	1971	1972	1973	1974	1975	1976	1977	1978	1979	1980	1981	1982	1983	1984
					Expressed in Millions of SDRs										
World	948.9	379.9	649.7	342.0	3,087.6	3,935.5	6,019.1	3,344.5	1,208.8	1,695.7	3,393.5	6,771.3	7,448.0	12,618.8	7,291.2
Industrial Countries	635.0	—	—	—	1,512.5	1,973.6	2,627.8	2,415.7	98.8	23.8	—	—	54.0	354.8	217.2
United States	—	—	—	—	—	—	—	—	—	—	—	—	—	—	—
Canada	—	—	—	—	—	—	—	—	—	—	—	—	—	—	—
Australia	—	—	—	—	—	—	332.5	—	—	—	23.8	—	32.5	—	—
Japan	—	—	—	—	—	—	—	—	—	—	—	—	—	—	—
New Zealand	—	—	—	—	85.7	156.6	147.9	—	—	—	—	—	—	—	—
Belgium	—	—	—	—	—	—	—	—	—	—	—	—	—	—	—
Denmark	—	—	—	—	—	—	—	—	—	—	—	—	—	—	—
Finland	—	—	—	—	—	71.3	115.1	—	—	—	—	—	—	—	—
France	485.0	—	—	—	—	—	—	—	—	—	—	—	—	—	—
Germany	—	—	—	—	—	—	—	—	—	—	—	—	—	—	—
Greece	—	—	—	—	36.2	153.5	58.0	—	—	—	—	—	—	—	—
Iceland	—	—	—	—	15.5	15.9	25.1	—	—	—	—	—	21.5	—	—
Ireland	—	—	—	—	—	—	—	—	—	—	—	—	—	—	—
Italy	—	—	—	—	1,375.1	1,080.2	—	—	90.0	—	—	—	—	—	—
Luxembourg	—	—	—	—	—	—	—	—	—	—	—	—	—	—	—
Netherlands	—	—	—	—	—	—	—	—	—	—	—	—	—	—	—
Norway	—	—	—	—	—	—	—	—	—	—	—	—	—	—	—
Portugal	—	—	—	—	—	—	173.3	75.7	—	—	—	—	—	354.8	217.2
Spain	—	—	—	—	—	496.2	75.9	—	98.8	—	—	—	—	—	—
United Kingdom	150.0	—	—	—	—	—	1,700.0	2,250.0	—	—	—	—	—	—	—
Developing Countries	313.9	379.9	649.7	342.0	1,575.2	1,961.9	3,391.3	928.9	1,110.1	1,671.9	3,393.5	6,771.3	7,394.1	12,264.1	7,074.0
Africa	32.1	44.8	83.3	29.5	166.4	326.6	881.4	303.9	285.8	517.3	821.7	1,859.7	2,118.1	1,702.2	1,188.6
Algeria	—	—	—	—	—	—	—	—	—	—	—	—	—	—	—
Benin	—	—	—	—	—	—	—	—	—	—	—	—	—	—	—
Burkina Faso	—	—	—	—	—	—	—	—	—	—	—	—	—	—	—
Burundi	2.5	1.5	—	—	.1	1.2	—	—	—	9.5	—	—	—	—	—
Cameroon	—	—	—	—	4.6	7.5	21.8	—	—	—	—	—	—	—	—
Cape Verde	—	—	—	—	—	—	—	—	—	—	—	—	—	—	—
Central African Rep.	—	—	—	—	2.7	2.3	6.1	—	—	—	4.0	17.0	2.4	4.5	5.0
Chad	2.4	—	—	—	5.0	—	6.5	—	—	—	—	7.1	—	—	—
Comoros	—	—	—	—	—	—	—	—	—	—	—	—	—	—	—
Congo, Dem. Rep. of	—	—	28.3	—	—	45.0	130.0	33.3	—	20.0	78.4	194.6	106.9	114.5	158.0
Congo, Republic of	—	—	—	—	—	—	—	11.2	3.3	2.0	—	—	—	—	—
Côte d'Ivoire	—	—	—	—	11.2	—	36.4	—	—	—	—	319.2	115.4	154.9	41.4
Djibouti	—	—	—	—	—	—	—	—	—	—	—	—	—	—	—
Equatorial Guinea	—	—	—	—	—	—	—	—	—	—	9.4	7.2	—	—	—
Ethiopia	—	—	—	—	—	—	—	—	—	36.0	62.0	23.5	—	—	—
Gabon	—	—	—	—	—	—	—	—	7.5	7.5	—	—	—	—	—
Gambia, The	—	—	—	—	—	—	—	3.5	7.0	—	1.6	9.0	16.9	—	2.6
Ghana	2.0	—	—	—	—	38.6	—	—	—	—	32.0	—	—	263.6	213.6
Guinea	4.2	—	—	—	9.5	—	—	8.7	—	3.0	—	11.5	—	—	—
Guinea-Bissau	—	—	—	—	—	—	—	—	—	—	1.1	1.9	—	—	1.9
Kenya	—	—	—	—	32.0	48.5	27.1	—	—	86.3	60.0	30.0	150.4	129.8	46.2
Lesotho	—	—	—	—	—	—	—	—	—	—	—	—	—	—	—
Liberia	2.0	1.0	—	1.5	—	—	—	—	—	29.8	18.4	46.6	61.7	58.0	35.5
Madagascar	—	—	—	—	3.5	10.9	—	9.4	—	—	39.2	39.0	52.4	10.2	41.4
Malawi	—	—	—	—	—	2.4	1.4	5.4	—	22.1	24.4	30.0	10.9	34.2	37.8
Mali	1.5	2.5	2.0	—	4.0	1.0	4.0	—	—	—	5.1	—	25.4	15.0	24.0
Mauritania	—	—	—	—	—	—	11.8	4.7	—	—	19.4	10.3	15.5	—	—
Mauritius	—	—	—	—	—	—	—	—	11.0	28.0	35.0	68.0	22.5	28.4	24.8
Morocco	10.0	8.3	—	—	—	—	115.5	—	56.0	—	184.5	192.8	433.3	114.4	180.0
Mozambique	—	—	—	—	—	—	—	—	—	—	—	—	—	—	—
Niger	—	—	—	—	—	—	—	—	—	—	—	—	—	30.8	14.4
Nigeria	—	—	1.5	—	—	—	—	—	—	—	—	—	—	—	—
Rwanda	—	—	—	—	—	—	—	—	—	—	—	—	—	—	—
São Tomé & Príncipe	—	—	—	—	—	—	—	—	—	—	—	—	—	—	—
Senegal	—	—	—	—	—	25.4	—	—	21.0	10.5	43.3	57.7	53.2	31.5	31.5
Seychelles	—	—	—	—	—	—	—	—	—	—	—	—	—	—	—
Sierra Leone	—	—	—	—	4.3	.6	17.5	7.0	—	7.5	9.5	33.5	—	20.7	19.0
Somalia	—	—	—	—	—	—	—	—	—	—	6.0	25.9	32.3	45.0	—
South Africa	—	—	—	—	—	—	390.0	162.0	—	—	—	—	795.0	—	—
Sudan	—	—	32.5	9.0	45.7	48.3	26.7	—	42.3	83.2	142.8	165.6	70.0	183.6	45.5
Swaziland	—	—	—	—	—	—	—	—	—	—	—	—	—	10.0	—
Tanzania	—	—	—	—	38.9	23.8	21.0	4.7	—	34.0	40.0	15.9	—	—	—
Togo	—	—	—	—	—	—	7.5	—	—	—	13.3	7.3	—	19.4	18.0
Tunisia	7.5	2.5	—	—	—	—	—	24.0	—	—	—	—	—	—	—
Uganda	—	10.1	—	—	5.0	14.2	20.0	—	—	5.0	37.5	122.5	85.0	106.5	21.0
Zambia	—	19.0	19.0	19.0	—	56.9	38.3	19.0	148.8	100.0	50.0	359.3	34.0	173.7	147.5
Zimbabwe	—	—	—	—	—	—	—	—	—	—	—	37.5	—	153.6	79.6
Asia	91.0	65.7	217.9	144.6	925.2	719.3	752.8	293.8	302.1	355.7	1,344.8	3,121.2	2,395.4	3,206.3	1,275.9
Afghanistan, I.S. of	4.0	—	—	7.5	2.5	8.5	—	—	—	—	—	—	—	—	—
Bangladesh	—	—	62.5	—	70.3	58.8	97.2	—	—	57.0	142.0	106.0	131.2	68.4	—
Cambodia	—	—	6.3	6.3	—	—	—	—	—	—	—	—	—	—	—
China, People's Rep.	—	—	—	—	—	—	—	—	—	—	—	450.0	—	—	—
Fiji	—	—	—	—	.3	—	—	6.5	—	—	—	—	13.5	—	—
India	—	—	—	—	497.0	201.3	—	—	—	—	266.0	300.0	1,500.0	1,500.0	600.0
Indonesia	38.0	2.9	2.7	—	—	—	—	—	—	—	—	—	—	425.1	—
Kiribati	—	—	—	—	—	—	—	—	—	—	—	—	—	—	—
Korea	—	—	—	—	110.0	107.3	104.4	—	—	—	480.0	576.0	106.2	192.0	567.6
Lao People's Dem.Rep	—	—	—	—	—	3.3	3.3	—	4.0	—	8.0	6.0	—	—	—
Malaysia	—	7.3	—	—	—	—	93.0	—	—	—	—	189.8	58.5	113.0	—
Maldives	—	—	—	—	—	—	—	—	—	—	—	—	—	—	—
Micronesia, Fed.Sts.	—	—	—	—	—	—	—	—	—	—	—	—	—	—	—

*Excludes reserve tranche purchases

Expressed in Millions of SDRs

1985	1986	1987	1988	1989	1990	1991	1992	1993	1994	1995	1996	1997	1998	1999	
4,013.9	3,819.7	3,298.8	2,668.7	3,477.7	4,270.0	7,386.5	4,791.1	5,042.2	4,979.5	16,967.9	5,271.0	16,112.9	20,586.2	10,010.1	**World**
—	—	—	—	—	—	—	—	—	—	—	—	—	—	—	**Industrial Countries**
—	—	—	—	—	—	—	—	—	—	—	—	—	—	—	United States
—	—	—	—	—	—	—	—	—	—	—	—	—	—	—	Canada
—	—	—	—	—	—	—	—	—	—	—	—	—	—	—	Australia
—	—	—	—	—	—	—	—	—	—	—	—	—	—	—	Japan
—	—	—	—	—	—	—	—	—	—	—	—	—	—	—	New Zealand
—	—	—	—	—	—	—	—	—	—	—	—	—	—	—	Belgium
—	—	—	—	—	—	—	—	—	—	—	—	—	—	—	Denmark
—	—	—	—	—	—	—	—	—	—	—	—	—	—	—	Finland
—	—	—	—	—	—	—	—	—	—	—	—	—	—	—	France
—	—	—	—	—	—	—	—	—	—	—	—	—	—	—	Germany
—	—	—	—	—	—	—	—	—	—	—	—	—	—	—	Greece
—	—	—	—	—	—	—	—	—	—	—	—	—	—	—	Iceland
—	—	—	—	—	—	—	—	—	—	—	—	—	—	—	Ireland
—	—	—	—	—	—	—	—	—	—	—	—	—	—	—	Italy
—	—	—	—	—	—	—	—	—	—	—	—	—	—	—	Luxembourg
—	—	—	—	—	—	—	—	—	—	—	—	—	—	—	Netherlands
—	—	—	—	—	—	—	—	—	—	—	—	—	—	—	Norway
—	—	—	—	—	—	—	—	—	—	—	—	—	—	—	Portugal
—	—	—	—	—	—	—	—	—	—	—	—	—	—	—	Spain
—	—	—	—	—	—	—	—	—	—	—	—	—	—	—	United Kingdom
4,013.9	3,819.7	3,298.8	2,668.7	3,477.7	4,270.0	7,386.5	4,791.1	5,042.2	4,979.5	16,967.9	5,271.0	16,112.9	20,586.2	10,010.1	**Developing Countries**
941.8	749.9	479.3	589.7	742.4	176.3	425.6	172.7	678.8	761.5	1,038.5	556.9	370.1	313.6	266.9	**Africa**
—	—	—	—	470.9	—	225.0	—	—	587.5	312.8	512.2	337.6	253.3	223.5	Algeria
—	—	—	—	—	—	—	—	—	—	—	—	—	—	—	Benin
—	—	—	—	—	—	—	—	—	—	—	—	—	—	—	Burkina Faso
—	—	—	—	—	—	—	—	—	—	—	—	—	—	—	Burundi
—	—	—	69.5	15.5	—	8.0	—	—	21.9	8.5	19.7	—	—	—	Cameroon
—	—	—	—	—	—	—	—	—	—	—	—	—	—	—	Cape Verde
11.0	6.5	1.0	—	—	—	—	—	—	10.7	—	—	—	—	—	Central African Rep.
7.0	—	—	—	—	—	—	—	—	10.3	—	—	—	—	—	Chad
—	—	—	—	—	—	—	—	—	—	—	—	—	—	—	Comoros
169.0	80.6	69.8	—	75.0	—	—	—	—	12.5	—	—	—	—	—	Congo, Dem. Rep. of
—	9.5	—	—	—	4.0	—	—	—	—	—	—	—	7.2	—	Congo, Republic of
60.4	50.5	—	89.8	29.3	112.7	33.1	—	—	—	—	—	—	—	—	Côte d'Ivoire
—	—	—	—	—	—	—	—	—	—	—	2.9	1.1	2.3	1.0	Djibouti
5.4	—	—	—	—	—	—	—	—	—	—	—	—	—	—	Equatorial Guinea
—	35.3	—	—	—	—	—	—	—	—	—	—	—	—	—	Ethiopia
—	27.4	15.1	56.2	4.0	6.5	4.0	—	—	44.7	37.5	22.1	16.6	—	—	Gabon
—	5.7	4.1	—	—	—	—	—	—	—	—	—	—	—	—	Gambia, The
120.0	32.7	71.6	75.0	—	—	—	—	47.0	—	—	—	—	—	—	Ghana
—	15.0	6.0	—	—	—	—	—	—	—	—	—	—	—	—	Guinea
—	—	—	—	—	—	—	—	—	—	—	—	—	—	2.1	Guinea-Bissau
123.1	—	—	102.6	—	—	—	—	—	—	—	—	—	—	—	Kenya
—	—	—	—	—	—	—	—	—	—	—	—	—	—	—	Lesotho
—	—	—	—	—	—	—	—	—	—	—	—	—	—	—	Liberia
29.0	44.2	20.0	7.8	—	—	—	—	—	—	—	—	—	—	—	Madagascar
23.0	—	—	9.3	—	—	—	—	—	12.7	—	—	—	—	—	Malawi
13.0	9.8	—	2.5	5.1	5.1	—	—	—	—	—	—	—	—	—	Mali
9.6	11.7	8.7	4.0	—	—	—	—	—	—	—	—	—	—	—	Mauritania
35.5	21.0	—	—	—	—	—	—	—	—	—	—	—	—	—	Mauritius
215.1	30.0	160.0	110.0	140.0	48.0	—	18.4	—	—	—	—	—	—	—	Morocco
—	—	—	—	—	—	—	—	—	—	—	—	—	—	—	Mozambique
15.5	12.8	8.1	—	—	—	—	—	—	11.1	—	—	—	—	—	Niger
—	—	—	—	—	—	—	—	—	—	—	—	—	—	—	Nigeria
—	—	—	—	—	—	—	—	—	—	8.9	—	14.9	—	—	Rwanda
—	—	—	—	—	—	—	—	—	—	—	—	—	—	—	São Tomé & Príncipe
55.6	32.5	30.9	12.9	—	—	—	—	—	30.9	—	—	—	—	—	Senegal
—	—	—	—	—	—	—	—	—	—	—	—	—	—	—	Seychelles
—	8.0	—	—	—	—	—	—	—	—	—	—	—	11.6	15.6	Sierra Leone
34.6	18.1	5.5	—	—	—	—	—	—	—	—	—	—	—	—	Somalia
—	—	—	—	—	—	—	—	614.4	—	—	—	—	—	—	South Africa
—	—	—	—	—	—	—	—	—	—	—	—	—	—	—	Sudan
—	—	—	—	—	—	—	—	—	—	—	—	—	—	—	Swaziland
—	33.0	12.5	—	—	—	—	—	—	—	—	—	—	—	—	Tanzania
15.0	12.0	—	10.4	2.6	—	—	—	—	—	—	—	—	—	—	Togo
—	149.7	41.0	15.0	—	—	155.5	51.8	—	—	—	—	—	—	—	Tunisia
—	—	25.0	24.8	—	—	—	—	—	—	—	—	—	—	—	Uganda
—	103.8	—	—	—	—	—	—	—	—	—	651.7	—	—	—	Zambia
—	—	—	—	—	—	—	102.5	17.4	19.1	19.1	—	—	39.2	24.7	Zimbabwe
896.6	1,156.2	729.1	250.7	430.4	42.8	2,456.3	1,452.0	755.3	220.2	167.3	109.2	12,801.7	11,259.8	2,236.4	**Asia**
—	—	—	—	—	—	—	—	—	—	—	—	—	—	—	Afghanistan, I.S. of
91.0	96.0	136.9	71.9	—	—	—	—	—	—	—	—	—	98.1	—	Bangladesh
—	—	—	—	—	—	—	—	6.3	—	—	—	—	—	—	Cambodia
—	597.7	—	—	—	—	—	—	—	—	—	—	—	—	—	China, People's Rep.
4.8	—	—	—	—	—	—	—	—	—	—	—	—	—	—	Fiji
—	—	—	—	—	—	1,988.9	1,109.0	462.0	—	—	—	—	—	—	India
—	—	462.9	—	—	—	—	—	—	—	—	—	2,201.5	4,254.3	1,011.0	Indonesia
—	—	—	—	—	—	—	—	—	—	—	—	—	—	—	Kiribati
135.9	120.0	—	—	—	—	—	—	—	—	—	—	8,200.0	5,850.0	362.5	Korea
—	—	—	—	—	—	—	—	—	—	—	—	—	—	—	Lao People's Dem.Rep
—	—	—	—	—	—	—	—	—	—	—	—	—	—	—	Malaysia
—	—	—	—	—	—	—	—	—	—	—	—	—	—	—	Maldives
—	—	—	—	—	—	—	—	—	—	—	—	—	—	—	Micronesia, Fed.Sts.

*Excludes reserve tranche purchases

Purchases*

	1970	1971	1972	1973	1974	1975	1976	1977	1978	1979	1980	1981	1982	1983	1984
						Expressed in Millions of SDRs										
Asia (cont.)															
Mongolia	—	—	—	—	—	—	—	—	—	—	—	—	—	—	—
Myanmar	12.0	6.5	—	13.5	29.5	9.5	—	25.0	25.0	15.0	—	27.0	25.6	29.2	—
Nepal	—	—	—	—	—	—	4.5	—	9.5	—	10.5	—	—	—	—
Pakistan	—	—	84.0	60.0	129.9	161.4	107.2	67.0	40.0	21.2	105.0	482.9	455.2	285.0	—
Palau	—	—	—	—	—	—	—	—	—	—	—	—	—	—	—
Papua New Guinea	—	—	—	—	—	—	24.8	—	—	—	—	45.0	—	—	—
Philippines	27.5	35.0	35.0	38.8	38.8	125.9	222.7	108.8	93.1	135.5	303.3	200.0	—	288.6	85.0
Samoa	—	—	—	—	—	1.3	.7	.5	1.3	.7	—	2.8	—	2.8	3.4
Solomon Islands	—	—	—	—	—	—	—	—	—	1.1	—	.8	1.6	1.0	—
Sri Lanka	9.5	14.0	25.3	18.6	46.9	42.1	28.2	55.0	38.0	80.0	30.0	175.6	39.2	35.8	20.0
Thailand	—	—	2.2	—	—	—	—	67.0	—	68.8	45.3	531.0	64.4	265.5	—
Vietnam	—	—	—	—	—	—	—	31.0	22.5	—	—	28.4	—	—	—
Europe	75.0	91.8	31.8	47.5	145.4	265.5	499.7	72.5	203.6	328.9	959.9	1,263.5	1,378.5	1,416.7	1,057.4
Albania	—	—	—	—	—	—	—	—	—	—	—	—	—	—	—
Armenia	—	—	—	—	—	—	—	—	—	—	—	—	—	—	—
Azerbaijan	—	—	—	—	—	—	—	—	—	—	—	—	—	—	—
Belarus	—	—	—	—	—	—	—	—	—	—	—	—	—	—	—
Bosnia & Herzegovina	—	—	—	—	—	—	—	—	—	—	—	—	—	—	—
Bulgaria	—	—	—	—	—	—	—	—	—	—	—	—	—	—	—
Croatia	—	—	—	—	—	—	—	—	—	—	—	—	—	—	—
Cyprus	—	—	—	—	6.4	1.7	35.0	—	—	—	9.9	8.5	—	—	—
Czech Republic	—	—	—	—	—	—	—	—	—	—	—	—	—	—	—
Czechoslovakia	—	—	—	—	—	—	—	—	—	—	—	—	—	—	—
Estonia	—	—	—	—	—	—	—	—	—	—	—	—	—	—	—
Georgia	—	—	—	—	—	—	—	—	—	—	—	—	—	—	—
Hungary	—	—	—	—	—	—	—	—	—	—	—	—	214.5	332.5	425.0
Kazakhstan	—	—	—	—	—	—	—	—	—	—	—	—	—	—	—
Kyrgyz Republic	—	—	—	—	—	—	—	—	—	—	—	—	—	—	—
Latvia	—	—	—	—	—	—	—	—	—	—	—	—	—	—	—
Lithuania	—	—	—	—	—	—	—	—	—	—	—	—	—	—	—
Macedonia, FYR	—	—	—	—	—	—	—	—	—	—	—	—	—	—	—
Moldova	—	—	—	—	—	—	—	—	—	—	—	—	—	—	—
Poland	—	—	—	—	—	—	—	—	—	—	—	—	—	—	—
Romania	—	—	—	47.5	—	40.0	150.0	72.5	39.1	41.3	121.3	309.5	310.0	183.9	183.6
Russia	—	—	—	—	—	—	—	—	—	—	—	—	—	—	—
Slovak Republic	—	—	—	—	—	—	—	—	—	—	—	—	—	—	—
Tajikistan	—	—	—	—	—	—	—	—	—	—	—	—	—	—	—
Turkey	75.0	15.0	—	—	—	207.6	129.2	—	164.5	70.0	491.6	400.0	300.0	346.3	168.8
Ukraine	—	—	—	—	—	—	—	—	—	—	—	—	—	—	—
Uzbekistan	—	—	—	—	—	—	—	—	—	—	—	—	—	—	—
Yugoslavia, SFR	—	76.8	31.8	—	139.0	16.2	185.5	—	—	207.8	338.5	554.0	554.0	554.0	280.0
Middle East	17.5	56.5	25.0	49.9	81.8	190.1	215.9	105.0	147.4	—	—	—	15.4	9.8	—
Bahrain	—	—	—	—	—	—	—	—	—	—	—	—	—	—	—
Egypt	17.5	32.0	—	47.0	40.0	—	125.7	105.0	75.0	—	—	—	—	—	—
Iran, I.R. of	—	—	—	—	—	—	—	—	—	—	—	—	—	—	—
Iraq	—	—	—	—	—	—	—	—	—	—	—	—	—	—	—
Israel	—	20.0	—	—	32.5	175.8	77.0	—	72.4	—	—	—	—	—	—
Jordan	—	4.5	—	2.9	—	—	—	—	—	—	—	—	—	—	—
Syrian Arab Republic	—	—	25.0	—	—	—	—	—	—	—	—	—	—	—	—
Yemen Arab Rep.	—	—	—	—	—	—	—	—	—	—	—	—	—	9.8	—
Yemen, P.D. Rep.	—	—	—	—	9.3	14.3	13.2	—	—	—	—	—	15.4	—	—
Yemen, Republic of	—	—	—	—	—	—	—	—	—	—	—	—	—	—	—
Western Hemisphere	98.2	121.2	291.8	70.5	256.3	460.4	1,041.5	153.7	171.1	470.1	267.2	526.9	1,486.7	5,929.2	3,552.2
Antigua and Barbuda	—	—	—	—	—	—	—	—	—	—	—	—	—	—	—
Argentina	—	—	174.0	—	—	186.1	269.5	—	—	—	—	—	—	1,120.6	—
Barbados	—	—	—	—	—	—	—	6.5	—	—	—	—	22.2	14.5	7.8
Belize	—	—	—	—	—	—	—	—	—	—	—	—	—	3.6	1.2
Bolivia	—	4.5	4.3	18.2	—	4.7	—	—	15.0	—	53.4	—	24.5	17.9	—
Brazil	—	—	—	—	—	—	—	—	—	—	—	—	498.8	2,027.0	1,744.2
Chile	—	39.5	39.5	—	120.5	176.8	124.4	—	—	—	—	—	—	579.0	216.0
Colombia	29.3	30.0	—	—	—	—	—	—	—	—	—	—	—	—	—
Costa Rica	—	—	—	—	18.8	12.0	6.8	—	—	20.5	15.4	52.6	—	110.9	—
Dominica	—	—	—	—	—	—	—	—	—	1.9	—	4.8	2.8	2.4	1.5
Dominican Republic	—	7.5	—	—	—	—	21.5	15.0	—	68.3	—	—	46.6	179.1	—
Ecuador	10.0	—	8.3	8.3	—	—	—	—	—	—	—	—	—	203.5	39.4
El Salvador	—	9.0	8.8	—	17.9	—	—	—	—	—	10.8	32.3	59.8	15.5	—
Grenada	—	—	—	—	—	.8	.4	—	—	.7	—	5.0	—	1.1	—
Guatemala	—	—	—	—	—	—	—	—	—	—	—	95.6	—	38.3	19.1
Guyana	—	2.2	—	3.9	5.0	—	17.3	—	12.9	12.9	41.9	16.1	5.9	—	—
Haiti	—	—	—	—	6.8	4.5	4.9	3.0	—	—	16.6	17.0	12.0	29.5	14.0
Honduras	—	—	—	—	16.8	—	—	—	—	—	16.0	20.7	61.7	45.9	—
Jamaica	—	—	—	13.3	13.3	—	55.7	19.2	57.8	145.8	—	203.6	165.2	112.2	100.6
Mexico	—	—	—	—	—	—	319.1	100.0	—	—	—	—	200.6	1,003.1	1,203.8
Nicaragua	10.0	3.0	4.0	12.0	3.3	12.2	—	—	—	43.1	—	—	—	—	—
Panama	—	—	—	—	7.4	10.2	25.1	—	—	—	—	75.3	—	108.9	100.0
Paraguay	—	—	—	—	—	—	—	—	—	—	—	—	—	—	—
Peru	18.0	16.0	30.8	—	—	—	158.8	10.0	85.5	177.0	111.0	—	299.9	165.0	104.7
St. Kitts and Nevis	—	—	—	—	—	—	—	—	—	—	—	—	—	—	—
St. Lucia	—	—	—	—	—	—	—	—	—	—	—	1.8	2.7	—	—
St. Vincent & Grens.	—	—	—	—	—	—	—	—	—	—	—	.4	1.3	—	—
Suriname	—	—	—	—	—	—	—	—	—	—	—	—	—	—	—
Trinidad and Tobago	—	—	—	—	—	—	—	—	—	—	—	—	—	—	—
Uruguay	31.0	9.5	22.3	15.0	46.6	53.2	38.0	—	—	—	—	—	86.8	151.2	—
Venezuela, Rep. Bol.	—	—	—	—	—	—	—	—	—	—	—	—	—	—	—
Memorandum Items															
Oil Exporting Ctys	38.0	2.9	4.2	—	—	—	—	—	—	—	—	—	—	425.1	—
Non-Oil Develop.Ctys	275.9	377.1	645.4	342.0	1,575.2	1,961.9	3,391.3	928.9	1,110.1	1,671.9	3,393.5	6,771.3	7,394.1	11,839.0	7,074.0

*Excludes reserve
tranche purchases

Purchases*

Expressed in Millions of SDRs

1985	1986	1987	1988	1989	1990	1991	1992	1993	1994	1995	1996	1997	1998	1999	
															Asia (cont.)
—	—	—	—	—	—	11.2	2.5	—	—	—	—	—	—	—	Mongolia
—	—	—	—	—	—	—	—	—	—	—	—	—	—	—	Myanmar
10.3	2.1	6.3	—	—	—	—	—	—	—	—	—	—	—	—	Nepal
—	—	—	—	194.5	—	122.4	189.6	88.0	123.2	134.0	107.2	91.5	19.0	409.6	Pakistan
—	—	—	—	—	—	—	—	—	—	—	—	—	—	—	Palau
—	—	—	—	—	42.8	—	—	—	—	33.3	2.0	—	—	—	Papua New Guinea
318.0	229.1	123.0	70.0	235.9	—	333.7	151.0	126.6	36.5	—	—	508.8	538.3	253.3	Philippines
1.7	—	—	—	—	—	—	—	—	—	—	—	—	—	—	Samoa
—	1.3	—	—	—	—	—	—	—	—	—	—	—	—	—	Solomon Islands
—	—	—	108.8	—	—	—	—	—	—	—	—	—	—	—	Sri Lanka
335.0	110.0	—	—	—	—	—	—	—	—	—	—	1,800.0	500.0	200.0	Thailand
—	—	—	—	—	—	—	—	72.5	60.5	—	—	—	—	—	Vietnam
255.0	135.0	—	287.8	50.0	550.6	2,715.9	1,674.6	1,700.0	3,177.1	5,337.2	3,488.2	2,272.3	5,312.9	1,944.9	**Europe**
—	—	—	—	—	—	—	9.7	3.4	—	—	—	8.8	—	—	Albania
—	—	—	—	—	—	—	—	—	16.9	30.4	—	—	—	—	Armenia
—	—	—	—	—	—	—	—	—	—	67.9	53.8	20.5	15.8	68.6	Azerbaijan
—	—	—	—	—	—	—	—	70.1	—	120.1	—	—	—	—	Belarus
—	—	—	—	—	—	—	—	—	—	30.3	—	—	24.2	29.0	Bosnia & Herzegovina
—	—	—	—	—	—	289.2	200.3	31.0	232.5	—	80.0	355.2	228.9	209.2	Bulgaria
—	—	—	—	—	—	—	—	—	78.5	65.4	—	28.8	—	—	Croatia
—	—	—	—	—	—	—	—	—	—	—	—	—	—	—	Cyprus
—	—	—	—	—	—	—	—	70.0	—	—	—	—	—	—	Czech Republic
—	—	—	—	—	—	917.9	238.6	—	—	—	—	—	—	—	Czechoslovakia
—	—	—	—	—	—	—	7.8	34.1	—	—	20.9	—	—	—	Estonia
—	—	—	—	—	—	—	—	—	—	27.8	50.0	—	—	—	Georgia
—	—	—	165.4	50.0	127.4	703.8	118.4	56.7	—	—	—	—	—	—	Hungary
—	—	—	—	—	—	—	—	61.9	136.1	92.8	92.8	—	154.7	—	Kazakhstan
—	—	—	—	—	—	—	—	43.9	—	—	—	—	—	—	Kyrgyz Republic
—	—	—	—	—	—	—	25.2	52.6	32.0	—	—	—	—	—	Latvia
—	—	—	—	—	—	—	17.3	70.7	46.6	41.4	31.1	41.4	—	—	Lithuania
—	—	—	—	—	—	—	—	—	12.4	24.8	9.9	22.5	—	13.8	Macedonia, FYR
—	—	—	—	—	—	—	—	63.0	49.5	42.4	22.5	15.0	—	50.0	Moldova
—	—	—	—	—	357.5	239.1	—	—	—	640.3	—	—	—	—	Poland
—	—	—	—	—	—	565.8	338.5	—	—	245.1	37.7	120.6	—	53.0	Romania
—	—	—	—	—	—	—	719.0	1,078.3	1,078.3	3,594.3	2,587.9	1,467.3	4,600.0	471.4	Russia
—	—	—	—	—	—	—	—	64.4	96.5	—	—	—	—	—	Slovak Republic
—	—	—	—	—	—	—	—	—	—	—	15.0	7.5	7.5	—	Tajikistan
—	—	—	—	—	—	—	—	—	235.5	225.0	—	—	—	583.2	Turkey
—	—	—	—	—	—	—	—	—	249.3	788.0	536.0	207.3	281.8	466.6	Ukraine
—	—	—	—	—	—	—	—	—	—	106.0	59.3	—	—	—	Uzbekistan
255.0	135.0	—	122.4	—	65.7	—	—	—	—	—	—	—	—	—	Yugoslavia, SFR
57.4	—	116.0	—	66.2	—	60.0	288.0	11.1	65.6	75.8	166.2	154.0	32.7	77.4	**Middle East**
—	—	—	—	—	—	—	—	—	—	—	—	—	—	—	Bahrain
—	—	116.0	—	—	—	60.0	87.2	—	—	—	—	—	—	—	Egypt
—	—	—	—	—	—	—	—	—	—	—	—	—	—	—	Iran, I.R. of
—	—	—	—	—	—	—	—	—	—	—	—	—	—	—	Iraq
—	—	—	—	—	—	—	178.6	—	—	—	—	—	—	—	Israel
57.4	—	—	—	66.2	—	—	22.2	11.1	65.6	75.8	82.2	96.7	23.7	55.4	Jordan
—	—	—	—	—	—	—	—	—	—	—	—	—	—	—	Syrian Arab Republic
—	—	—	—	—	—	—	—	—	—	—	—	—	—	—	Yemen Arab Rep.
—	—	—	—	—	—	—	—	—	—	—	—	—	—	—	Yemen, P.D. Rep.
—	—	—	—	—	—	—	—	—	—	—	84.0	57.4	9.0	22.0	Yemen, Republic of
1,863.2	1,778.6	1,974.4	1,540.5	2,188.7	3,500.3	1,728.7	1,203.7	1,896.9	755.1	10,349.1	950.6	514.7	3,667.2	5,484.5	**Western Hemisphere**
—	—	—	—	—	—	—	—	—	—	—	—	—	—	—	Antigua and Barbuda
984.5	473.0	969.8	398.7	184.0	322.0	292.5	584.6	1,154.8	612.0	1,559.0	548.2	321.0	—	—	Argentina
—	—	—	—	—	—	—	36.8	—	—	—	—	—	—	—	Barbados
4.8	1.2	—	—	—	—	—	—	—	—	—	—	—	—	—	Belize
—	96.8	—	45.3	—	—	—	—	—	—	—	—	—	—	—	Bolivia
—	—	—	365.3	—	—	—	127.5	—	—	—	—	—	3,419.0	4,450.1	Brazil
195.6	250.0	225.0	150.0	139.0	—	—	—	—	—	—	—	—	—	—	Chile
—	—	—	—	—	—	—	—	—	—	—	—	—	—	—	Colombia
34.0	—	—	—	—	—	55.3	4.0	—	—	—	—	—	—	—	Costa Rica
—	—	—	—	—	—	—	—	—	—	—	—	—	—	—	Dominica
76.9	17.1	—	—	—	—	44.8	37.4	53.3	—	—	—	—	39.7	—	Dominican Republic
84.4	75.9	37.7	57.8	15.7	23.6	18.6	—	—	98.9	—	—	—	—	—	Ecuador
—	—	—	—	—	—	—	—	—	—	—	—	—	—	—	El Salvador
—	—	—	—	—	—	—	—	—	—	—	—	—	—	—	Grenada
—	—	—	44.8	—	—	—	—	—	—	—	—	—	—	—	Guatemala
—	—	—	—	39.7	—	9.8	—	—	—	—	16.4	—	15.2	—	Guyana
—	—	—	—	13.0	2.0	—	—	—	—	—	—	—	—	—	Haiti
—	—	—	—	—	21.3	2.3	—	—	—	—	—	—	47.5	—	Honduras
51.0	26.6	95.9	43.7	63.8	41.1	87.0	41.8	36.4	34.4	—	7.0	—	—	—	Jamaica
295.8	741.4	600.0	350.0	943.0	1,608.4	932.4	233.1	—	—	8,758.0	—	—	—	1,034.4	Mexico
—	—	—	—	—	—	17.0	—	—	—	—	—	—	—	—	Nicaragua
35.0	44.0	11.0	—	—	—	—	71.6	9.9	9.9	8.7	52.4	33.2	30.0	—	Panama
—	—	—	—	—	—	—	—	—	—	—	—	—	—	—	Paraguay
—	—	—	—	—	—	—	—	642.7	—	—	—	160.5	—	—	Peru
—	—	—	—	—	—	—	—	—	—	—	—	—	1.6	—	St. Kitts and Nevis
—	—	—	—	—	—	—	—	—	—	—	—	—	—	—	St. Lucia
—	—	—	—	—	—	—	—	—	—	—	—	—	—	—	St. Vincent & Grens.
—	—	—	—	—	—	—	—	—	—	—	—	—	—	—	Suriname
—	—	—	85.1	70.7	75.8	37.5	—	—	—	—	—	—	—	—	Trinidad and Tobago
101.2	52.7	35.1	—	—	—	—	16.0	—	—	—	—	—	114.2	—	Uruguay
—	—	—	—	759.5	1,357.5	231.5	—	—	—	—	350.0	—	—	—	Venezuela, Rep. Bol.
															Memorandum Items
—	—	462.9	—	1,230.4	1,357.5	456.5	—	—	587.5	312.8	862.2	2,539.1	4,507.6	1,234.5	Oil Exporting Ctys
4,013.9	3,819.7	2,835.9	2,668.7	2,247.3	2,912.5	6,930.0	4,791.1	5,042.2	4,392.0	16,655.1	4,408.7	13,573.8	16,078.6	8,775.6	Non-Oil Develop.Ctys

*Excludes reserve tranche purchases

Repurchases

Expressed in Millions of SDRs

	1970	1971	1972	1973	1974	1975	1976	1977	1978	1979	1980	1981	1982	1983	1984
World	1,197.1	2,206.9	656.3	407.5	374.2	238.9	840.6	2,844.9	4,377.2	3,991.5	2,428.8	1,880.6	1,505.6	2,029.5	2,284.6
Industrial Countries	592.0	1,887.8	250.2	—	—	—	—	1,651.7	2,591.4	2,521.8	850.1	609.0	522.9	116.7	—
United States	—	—	—	—	—	—	—	—	—	—	—	—	—	—	—
Canada	—	—	—	—	—	—	—	—	—	—	—	—	—	—	—
Australia	—	—	—	—	—	—	—	—	85.6	—	208.9	61.7	—	32.5	—
Japan	—	—	—	—	—	—	—	—	—	—	—	—	—	—	—
New Zealand	—	—	—	—	—	—	—	—	38.4	92.7	136.2	98.7	30.8	2.9	—
Belgium	—	—	—	—	—	—	—	—	—	—	—	—	—	—	—
Denmark	—	—	—	—	—	—	—	—	—	—	—	—	—	—	—
Finland	—	—	—	—	—	—	—	—	34.3	85.7	—	14.3	37.7	14.4	—
France	246.3	587.2	—	—	—	—	—	—	—	—	—	—	—	—	—
Greece	—	—	—	—	—	—	—	71.3	25.8	37.9	68.8	64.6	13.9	—	—
Iceland	7.5	1.8	—	—	—	—	—	—	9.3	12.4	19.0	9.8	5.1	.9	—
Ireland	—	—	—	—	—	—	—	—	—	—	—	—	—	—	—
Italy	—	—	—	—	—	—	—	966.4	858.9	880.0	—	—	—	—	—
Netherlands	—	—	—	—	—	—	—	—	—	—	—	—	—	—	—
Norway	—	—	—	—	—	—	—	—	—	—	—	—	—	—	—
Portugal	—	—	—	—	—	—	—	4.0	29.3	31.9	76.9	46.2	37.7	9.8	—
Spain	—	—	—	—	—	—	—	—	55.5	410.0	—	63.7	136.9	4.8	—
United Kingdom	338.2	1,298.9	250.2	—	—	—	—	610.0	1,454.3	971.2	340.3	250.0	261.0	51.6	—
Developing Countries	605.2	319.1	406.0	407.5	374.2	238.9	840.6	1,193.2	1,785.8	1,469.8	1,578.5	1,271.6	982.7	1,912.8	2,284.6
Africa	73.9	103.6	44.7	15.0	7.3	64.4	181.1	190.1	217.8	457.0	413.4	317.3	243.8	424.3	551.5
Algeria	—	—	—	—	—	—	—	—	—	—	—	—	—	—	—
Burkina Faso	—	—	—	—	—	—	—	—	—	—	—	—	—	—	—
Burundi	.2	3.7	5.3	—	—	-.1	—	—	1.2	—	—	—	—	4.8	4.8
Cameroon	—	—	—	—	—	—	—	—	2.9	8.0	12.8	8.5	3.0	.5	—
Central African Rep.	—	—	—	—	—	—	1.3	—	.9	2.1	4.4	3.1	.6	.3	6.3
Chad	—	—	—	1.0	2.8	—	—	—	1.9	1.2	2.2	5.4	—	—	2.7
Comoros	—	—	—	—	—	—	—	—	—	—	—	—	—	—	—
Congo, Dem. Rep. of	—	—	—	—	—	—	22.6	5.7	9.7	31.5	65.5	80.3	20.8	10.4	54.0
Congo, Republic of	—	—	—	—	—	—	—	3.3	—	1.1	5.3	4.6	—	—	—
Côte d'Ivoire	—	—	—	—	—	—	24.2	10.0	24.1	—	—	—	—	—	27.7
Djibouti	—	—	—	—	—	—	—	—	—	—	—	—	—	—	—
Equatorial Guinea	—	—	—	—	—	—	—	—	—	—	—	.6	—	—	6.1
Ethiopia	—	—	—	—	—	—	—	—	—	—	—	—	2.3	18.0	25.2
Gabon	—	—	—	—	—	—	—	—	—	—	—	—	2.0	7.5	1.8
Gambia, The	—	—	—	—	—	—	—	—	1.8	3.5	—	—	2.2	2.6	1.9
Ghana	24.9	28.1	15.4	1.0	—	—	—	—	4.8	9.7	9.7	9.7	4.8	15.4	4.0
Guinea	—	.5	—	1.9	1.0	2.4	—	—	5.8	4.4	1.1	3.6	.2	—	.4
Guinea-Bissau	—	—	—	—	—	—	—	—	—	—	—	—	.3	.4	.4
Kenya	—	—	—	—	—	12.0	10.6	36.0	2.4	30.6	7.0	7.2	15.6	41.7	56.7
Lesotho	—	—	—	—	—	—	—	—	—	—	—	—	—	—	—
Liberia	5.2	3.4	1.4	1.0	—	—	—	—	—	—	2.4	1.2	—	10.3	19.6
Madagascar	—	—	—	—	—	—	—	8.1	2.6	3.7	1.5	7.2	.7	3.7	23.5
Malawi	—	—	—	—	—	—	—	—	3.8	.8	.9	2.6	12.6	10.3	20.4
Mali	4.0	4.0	1.0	1.0	1.0	1.0	2.5	2.0	1.2	1.8	2.2	2.3	1.1	1.8	3.2
Mauritania	—	—	—	—	—	—	—	—	—	.9	6.7	6.9	1.5	4.4	9.0
Mauritius	3.7	—	—	—	—	—	—	—	—	—	—	11.0	—	14.5	31.5
Morocco	14.2	35.8	—	—	—	—	—	—	—	23.2	66.4	53.4	32.5	23.3	47.5
Niger	—	—	—	—	—	—	—	—	—	—	—	—	—	—	—
Nigeria	—	—	—	1.5	—	—	—	—	—	—	—	—	—	—	—
Rwanda	1.0	3.0	—	—	—	—	—	—	—	—	—	—	—	—	—
Senegal	—	—	—	—	—	—	—	—	4.7	6.4	6.4	6.4	13.3	10.5	14.5
Sierra Leone	5.4	—	—	—	—	—	—	—	1.2	7.3	9.2	8.0	1.3	2.0	8.3
Somalia	—	—	—	—	—	—	—	—	—	—	—	—	—	—	2.9
South Africa	—	—	—	—	—	—	75.0	85.0	80.0	240.0	72.0	—	—	50.0	—
Sudan	8.1	15.1	19.0	7.5	2.5	6.0	21.0	19.6	22.6	33.7	34.7	19.0	30.2	41.6	31.6
Swaziland	—	—	—	—	—	—	—	—	—	—	—	—	—	—	—
Tanzania	—	—	—	—	—	—	—	1.6	28.7	13.0	25.0	26.3	11.1	25.1	24.4
Togo	—	—	—	—	—	—	—	—	7.5	—	—	—	—	—	5.2
Tunisia	7.4	10.0	2.6	—	—	—	—	—	—	—	24.0	—	—	—	—
Uganda	—	—	—	—	—	5.1	4.9	—	10.0	8.0	10.0	10.3	1.5	11.9	37.7
Zambia	—	—	—	—	—	38.0	19.0	19.0	—	26.3	44.0	39.8	86.2	113.5	71.3
Zimbabwe	—	—	—	—	—	—	—	—	—	—	—	—	—	—	9.4
Asia	241.5	73.7	105.0	224.3	117.6	103.1	458.4	555.9	520.8	370.0	407.7	381.2	294.3	865.0	899.8
Afghanistan, I.S. of	4.6	4.4	4.4	6.0	5.0	4.0	7.5	1.8	—	—	—	—	—	—	—
Bangladesh	—	—	—	—	—	20.5	33.0	41.4	17.7	63.0	69.6	32.6	33.9	21.1	58.0
Cambodia	—	—	—	—	—	—	—	—	—	—	—	—	—	—	—
China, People's Rep.	—	—	—	—	—	—	—	—	—	—	—	—	—	450.0	—
Fiji	—	—	—	—	—	—	—	—	—	—	—	6.5	—	—	—
India	175.9	10.0	—	—	—	—	292.0	281.2	201.3	—	—	—	—	33.3	133.0
Indonesia	3.2	15.0	20.0	87.0	18.2	—	—	—	—	—	—	—	—	—	3.6
Korea	—	—	—	—	—	—	20.0	10.3	89.5	97.4	25.0	40.8	35.2	40.9	261.5
Lao People's Dem.Rep	—	—	—	—	—	—	—	—	—	1.6	6.5	1.6	—	—	4.7
Malaysia	—	—	—	7.3	—	—	—	85.7	—	—	—	—	—	46.2	52.2
Mongolia	—	—	—	—	—	—	—	—	—	—	—	—	—	—	—
Myanmar	—	5.0	10.0	6.5	8.0	5.5	6.0	7.8	16.7	21.9	15.1	7.4	2.9	16.2	6.1
Nepal	—	—	—	—	—	—	—	—	4.1	1.0	—	.2	4.8	4.9	5.2
Pakistan	28.4	1.9	15.0	40.0	20.0	25.0	42.0	68.9	84.3	80.7	107.0	132.6	48.7	24.3	51.6
Papua New Guinea	—	—	—	—	—	—	—	—	10.0	5.0	5.0	4.8	—	—	28.3
Philippines	2.5	14.0	29.5	57.8	47.2	29.1	38.8	38.8	73.7	71.1	111.6	44.6	67.7	144.6	212.5
Samoa	—	—	—	—	—	—	—	.8	.6	.1	.4	.9	.7	.9	.8
Solomon Islands	—	—	—	—	—	—	—	—	—	1.1	—	—	—	—	.2
Sri Lanka	27.0	23.4	24.0	19.8	19.2	18.7	19.2	19.3	22.8	27.1	32.7	39.8	44.6	46.2	22.7
Thailand	—	—	2.1	—	—	—	—	—	—	—	16.8	67.4	34.4	35.2	59.3
Vietnam	—	—	—	—	—	—	—	—	—	—	—	11.5	8.5	21.5	1.3

1985	1986	1987	1988	1989	1990	1991	1992	1993	1994	1995	1996	1997	1998	1999	
							Expressed in Millions of SDRs								
3,625.0	5,664.6	7,881.8	6,670.6	5,912.7	5,853.4	4,744.8	4,201.6	3,814.0	4,572.0	6,650.9	5,072.7	5,681.3	6,694.2	19,398.8	**World**
—	10.8	209.6	373.1	—	—	—	—	—	—	—	—	—	—	—	**Industrial Countries**
—	—	—	—	—	—	—	—	—	—	—	—	—	—	—	United States
—	—	—	—	—	—	—	—	—	—	—	—	—	—	—	Canada
—	—	—	—	—	—	—	—	—	—	—	—	—	—	—	Australia
—	—	—	—	—	—	—	—	—	—	—	—	—	—	—	Japan
—	—	—	—	—	—	—	—	—	—	—	—	—	—	—	New Zealand
—	—	—	—	—	—	—	—	—	—	—	—	—	—	—	Belgium
—	—	—	—	—	—	—	—	—	—	—	—	—	—	—	Denmark
—	—	—	—	—	—	—	—	—	—	—	—	—	—	—	Finland
—	—	—	—	—	—	—	—	—	—	—	—	—	—	—	France
—	—	—	—	—	—	—	—	—	—	—	—	—	—	—	Greece
—	10.8	10.8	—	—	—	—	—	—	—	—	—	—	—	—	Iceland
—	—	—	—	—	—	—	—	—	—	—	—	—	—	—	Ireland
—	—	—	—	—	—	—	—	—	—	—	—	—	—	—	Italy
—	—	—	—	—	—	—	—	—	—	—	—	—	—	—	Netherlands
—	—	—	—	—	—	—	—	—	—	—	—	—	—	—	Norway
—	—	198.8	373.1	—	—	—	—	—	—	—	—	—	—	—	Portugal
—	—	—	—	—	—	—	—	—	—	—	—	—	—	—	Spain
—	—	—	—	—	—	—	—	—	—	—	—	—	—	—	United Kingdom
3,625.0	5,653.8	7,672.2	6,297.5	5,912.7	5,853.4	4,744.8	4,201.6	3,814.0	4,572.0	6,650.9	5,072.7	5,681.3	6,694.2	19,398.8	**Developing Countries**
765.2	1,472.4	1,432.1	952.6	1,122.1	912.0	669.3	601.3	626.5	423.3	1,522.4	269.2	730.0	827.9	407.3	**Africa**
—	—	—	—	—	—	—	117.7	235.4	136.5	112.5	93.8	254.6	320.8	262.8	Algeria
—	—	—	—	—	—	—	—	—	—	—	—	—	—	—	Burkina Faso
—	—	—	—	—	—	—	—	—	—	—	—	—	—	—	Burundi
—	—	—	—	—	—	8.7	38.6	33.8	3.9	4.0	4.0	8.2	12.0	13.3	Cameroon
9.5	5.3	2.1	6.1	9.0	6.4	2.5	1.1	.6	.4	—	—	2.7	5.6	2.4	Central African Rep.
3.5	.9	—	.9	3.5	2.6	—	—	—	—	—	—	3.9	5.2	1.3	Chad
—	—	—	—	—	—	—	—	—	—	—	—	—	—	.6	Comoros
103.8	94.0	125.0	78.3	255.6	108.5	35.5	—	—	3.0	.9	22.7	—	.4	.7	Congo, Dem. Rep. of
—	—	—	—	—	1.2	4.8	3.6	.5	2.0	1.5	—	1.6	7.8	3.1	Congo, Republic of
97.6	107.2	102.7	127.6	120.1	87.7	76.3	65.2	36.5	53.5	56.8	32.8	16.1	—	—	Côte d'Ivoire
6.9	1.8	—	.3	3.0	1.8	.4	—	—	—	—	—	—	—	—	Equatorial Guinea
31.0	26.1	10.1	7.3	14.8	17.6	4.4	—	—	—	—	—	—	—	—	Ethiopia
—	—	—	—	—	—	—	—	—	—	—	—	—	—	.7	Djibouti
—	—	—	—	—	10.7	18.1	25.8	25.7	16.1	34.5	3.8	2.6	16.7	17.9	Gabon
2.8	13.4	5.3	3.2	3.1	3.7	4.4	1.5	—	—	—	—	—	—	—	Gambia, The
—	18.7	134.1	196.2	134.4	83.1	56.4	45.3	39.3	27.1	13.1	16.8	34.5	24.6	—	Ghana
—	5.8	5.8	—	4.1	9.8	6.4	.8	—	—	—	—	—	—	—	Guinea
.9	.9	.2	.9	.7	—	—	—	—	—	—	—	—	—	—	Guinea-Bissau
68.4	89.8	83.9	67.4	98.0	75.2	29.1	58.7	41.5	—	—	—	—	—	—	Kenya
—	—	—	—	—	1.1	—	—	—	—	—	—	—	—	—	Lesotho
6.9	—	—	1.0	2.2	.7	—	—	—	—	.1	—	—	—	—	Liberia
33.0	40.8	26.5	29.5	38.3	34.7	25.0	11.5	7.4	4.5	.6	—	—	—	—	Madagascar
16.0	20.6	23.6	19.9	19.0	13.8	15.2	13.6	4.2	1.2	—	—	—	6.4	6.4	Malawi
4.5	13.9	16.5	14.0	15.6	12.9	6.7	4.4	6.3	4.8	1.0	—	—	—	—	Mali
12.4	9.8	5.0	3.4	7.4	11.2	9.6	4.6	1.0	—	—	—	—	—	—	Mauritania
47.8	37.2	23.4	29.0	28.9	32.1	15.5	—	—	—	—	—	—	—	—	Mauritius
143.2	274.2	243.9	169.1	193.3	164.2	125.0	100.8	112.0	106.1	66.2	32.5	2.3	—	—	Morocco
—	1.5	16.1	21.9	12.9	10.0	8.3	5.4	3.5	2.0	—	—	4.2	5.6	1.4	Niger
—	—	—	—	—	—	—	—	—	—	—	—	—	—	—	Nigeria
—	—	—	—	—	—	—	—	—	—	—	—	—	—	4.5	Rwanda
40.9	50.4	44.4	41.7	43.4	39.7	34.5	28.1	11.0	2.5	—	—	11.6	15.5	3.9	Senegal
4.4	20.8	—	.7	.9	1.6	5.4	1.4	5.9	42.6	—	—	—	—	—	Sierra Leone
8.8	28.8	16.0	.7	8.8	2.1	—	—	—	—	—	—	—	—	—	Somalia
—	347.5	397.5	—	—	—	—	—	—	—	—	—	307.2	307.2	—	South Africa
4.9	—	—	—	—	1.0	—	—	—	—	—	23.0	24.5	25.5	42.2	27.6	Sudan
1.0	3.4	3.4	2.3	—	—	—	—	—	—	—	—	—	—	—	Swaziland
4.8	15.1	4.1	—	2.6	19.6	19.4	3.9	—	—	—	—	—	—	—	Tanzania
8.4	2.9	10.8	17.6	16.8	11.2	5.8	7.1	5.2	2.4	2.0	.2	—	—	—	Togo
—	—	—	—	—	82.0	99.1	20.9	3.8	—	10.2	32.1	36.6	36.6	36.6	Tunisia
64.2	69.7	51.1	55.4	54.3	30.3	24.4	18.7	3.1	—	—	—	—	—	—	Uganda
18.7	122.6	—	—	—	14.7	24.8	26.0	49.8	14.6	1,196.2	—	—	—	—	Zambia
20.9	49.4	80.8	58.1	30.0	17.4	4.8	—	—	—	—	5.9	18.5	21.6	24.8	Zimbabwe
1,608.6	1,589.5	2,422.9	1,824.9	1,427.1	1,695.1	1,350.7	734.3	369.7	1,066.0	1,113.8	1,262.8	831.0	2,514.2	8,330.4	**Asia**
—	—	—	—	—	—	—	—	—	—	—	—	—	—	—	Afghanistan, I.S. of
68.7	104.5	104.1	58.6	81.8	146.4	102.9	56.0	35.9	—	—	—	—	—	—	Bangladesh
—	—	—	—	—	—	—	6.3	6.3	—	—	—	—	1.0	1.0	Cambodia
—	—	—	—	—	298.9	298.9	—	—	—	—	—	—	—	—	China, People's Rep.
5.1	6.8	1.7	1.8	2.4	.6	—	—	—	—	—	—	—	—	—	Fiji
174.8	331.3	637.5	787.5	737.5	531.3	362.5	275.0	137.5	821.7	796.5	881.4	495.5	304.9	246.4	India
264.9	—	—	42.0	—	115.7	231.4	115.7	—	—	—	—	—	—	—	Indonesia
361.8	226.8	896.5	369.8	—	—	—	—	—	—	—	—	—	2,050.0	7,900.0	Korea
6.4	1.9	—	—	—	—	—	—	—	—	—	—	—	—	—	Lao People's Dem.Rep
155.7	107.2	—	—	—	—	—	—	—	—	—	—	—	—	—	Malaysia
—	—	—	—	—	—	—	—	—	—	6.3	6.9	.6	—	—	Mongolia
13.5	26.7	27.4	10.9	—	—	—	—	—	—	—	—	—	—	—	Myanmar
3.9	—	—	—	5.4	8.5	3.9	.8	—	—	—	—	—	—	—	Nepal
149.2	269.5	280.3	196.6	143.1	108.1	71.7	116.1	91.4	34.1	61.2	167.0	138.8	39.7	107.6	Pakistan
6.6	10.1	—	—	—	—	—	—	10.7	21.4	10.7	—	—	3.0	16.7	Papua New Guinea
147.0	213.1	240.2	119.7	137.9	249.7	215.0	109.9	46.0	188.7	239.1	207.5	156.9	58.2	39.5	Philippines
1.4	1.3	2.1	2.6	1.4	.6	.4	.2	—	—	—	—	—	—	—	Samoa
.4	1.2	1.3	.3	.2	.6	.5	—	—	—	—	—	—	—	—	Solomon Islands
35.9	58.5	69.4	64.1	46.0	31.9	63.6	54.4	13.6	—	—	—	—	—	—	Sri Lanka
213.5	230.8	162.5	171.1	271.4	202.9	—	—	—	—	—	—	—	—	—	Thailand
—	—	—	—	—	—	—	—	28.4	—	—	—	39.3	57.4	19.2	Vietnam

Repurchases

Expressed in Millions of SDRs

	1970	1971	1972	1973	1974	1975	1976	1977	1978	1979	1980	1981	1982	1983	1984
Europe															
Albania	—	—	—	—	—	—	—	—	—	—	—	—	—	—	—
Armenia	—	—	—	—	—	—	—	—	—	—	—	—	—	—	—
Belarus	—	—	—	—	—	—	—	—	—	—	—	—	—	—	—
Bosnia & Herzegovina	—	—	—	—	—	—	—	—	—	—	—	—	—	—	—
Bulgaria	—	—	—	—	—	—	—	—	—	—	—	—	—	—	—
Croatia	—	—	—	—	—	—	—	—	—	—	—	—	—	—	—
Cyprus	—	—	—	—	—	—	—	—	10.1	4.8	11.6	9.0	9.3	6.8	2.3
Czech Republic	—	—	—	—	—	—	—	—	—	—	—	—	—	—	—
Czechoslovakia	—	—	—	—	—	—	—	—	—	—	—	—	—	—	—
Estonia	—	—	—	—	—	—	—	—	—	—	—	—	—	—	—
Georgia	—	—	—	—	—	—	—	—	—	—	—	—	—	—	—
Hungary	—	—	—	—	—	—	—	—	—	—	—	—	—	—	—
Kazakhstan	—	—	—	—	—	—	—	—	—	—	—	—	—	—	—
Kyrgyz Republic	—	—	—	—	—	—	—	—	—	—	—	—	—	—	—
Latvia	—	—	—	—	—	—	—	—	—	—	—	—	—	—	—
Lithuania	—	—	—	—	—	—	—	—	—	—	—	—	—	—	—
Macedonia, FYR	—	—	—	—	—	—	—	—	—	—	—	—	—	—	—
Moldova	—	—	—	—	—	—	—	—	—	—	—	—	—	—	—
Poland	—	—	—	—	—	—	—	—	—	—	—	—	—	—	—
Romania	—	—	—	—	—	—	—	40.0	47.5	50.0	80.0	60.3	35.1	60.9	132.5
Russia	—	—	—	—	—	—	—	—	—	—	—	—	—	—	—
Slovak Republic	—	—	—	—	—	—	—	—	—	—	—	—	—	—	—
Slovenia	—	—	—	—	—	—	—	—	—	—	—	—	—	—	—
Tajikistan	—	—	—	—	—	—	—	—	—	—	—	—	—	—	—
Turkey	27.0	27.0	62.1	—	—	—	—	—	24.8	68.5	119.2	91.0	116.4	168.3	210.8
Ukraine	—	—	—	—	—	—	—	—	—	—	—	—	—	—	—
Uzbekistan	—	—	—	—	—	—	—	—	—	—	—	—	—	—	—
Yugoslavia, SFR	45.3	10.0	15.0	61.7	21.8	—	21.8	106.0	75.0	45.8	53.7	74.6	39.2	169.1	269.3
Middle East	**9.0**	**16.3**	**84.6**	**19.5**	**23.1**	**29.9**	**16.0**	**28.0**	**126.4**	**111.5**	**155.2**	**128.8**	**96.4**	**30.8**	**—**
Egypt	9.0	11.5	45.0	9.0	9.0	24.5	16.0	28.0	35.0	51.2	78.9	53.9	33.1	2.7	—
Iran, I.R. of	—	—	—	—	—	—	—	—	—	—	—	—	—	—	—
Iraq	—	—	—	—	—	—	—	—	—	—	—	—	—	—	—
Israel	—	—	32.5	—	—	—	—	—	86.4	47.0	67.8	68.9	60.4	27.2	—
Jordan	—	—	—	5.8	1.6	—	—	—	—	—	—	—	—	—	—
Syrian Arab Republic	—	4.8	7.1	4.8	12.5	5.4	—	—	—	—	—	—	—	—	—
Yemen Arab Rep.	—	—	—	—	—	—	—	—	—	—	—	—	—	—	—
Yemen, P.D. Rep.	—	—	—	—	—	—	—	—	5.0	13.3	8.4	6.0	2.9	.9	—
Yemen, Republic of	—	—	—	—	—	—	—	—	—	—	—	—	—	—	—
Western Hemisphere	**208.5**	**88.6**	**94.5**	**87.0**	**204.5**	**41.5**	**163.4**	**273.2**	**763.5**	**362.0**	**337.7**	**209.6**	**148.3**	**187.6**	**218.5**
Argentina	—	—	—	—	110.0	—	64.0	103.1	340.8	—	—	—	—	—	—
Barbados	—	—	—	—	—	—	—	—	—	—	4.2	1.5	.8	.9	—
Belize	—	—	—	—	—	—	—	—	—	—	—	—	—	—	—
Bolivia	—	4.0	3.0	8.0	3.7	5.1	18.6	—	—	—	—	1.9	7.5	10.7	20.3
Brazil	—	—	—	—	—	—	—	—	—	—	—	—	—	—	—
Chile	47.3	1.5	—	—	39.5	6.0	53.0	101.6	73.6	130.6	39.6	54.5	36.1	5.7	—
Colombia	72.7	31.6	53.3	—	—	—	—	—	—	—	—	—	—	—	—
Costa Rica	—	—	—	—	—	.9	4.5	3.0	13.0	1.0	9.4	9.1	4.0	11.7	24.3
Dominica	—	—	—	—	—	—	—	—	—	—	—	—	—	.7	1.8
Dominican Republic	5.3	3.3	7.0	3.8	—	—	—	—	—	10.8	49.8	18.2	2.3	8.1	9.5
Ecuador	6.5	8.3	5.5	16.5	—	—	—	—	—	—	—	—	—	—	—
El Salvador	5.0	5.3	10.2	8.8	—	—	—	17.9	—	—	—	—	—	—	5.4
Grenada	—	—	—	—	—	—	—	—	—	.9	.5	.1	.8	—	.9
Guatemala	8.4	—	—	—	—	—	—	—	—	—	—	—	—	—	—
Guyana	—	—	2.1	—	3.9	5.6	—	—	—	2.8	11.9	9.5	2.2	4.1	1.0
Haiti	2.8	1.4	.8	—	—	—	3.7	6.3	1.3	1.9	2.2	2.2	1.0	.3	—
Honduras	—	—	—	—	—	—	—	12.5	10.5	—	—	—	—	—	1.6
Jamaica	—	—	—	5.5	13.3	—	—	—	7.7	18.0	14.6	43.6	40.3	41.5	58.3
Mexico	—	—	—	—	—	—	—	—	192.5	126.3	100.3	—	—	—	—
Nicaragua	13.3	—	6.8	8.0	5.5	6.7	6.8	6.7	6.8	—	.6	17.5	3.6	4.3	4.3
Panama	1.7	—	—	—	—	—	—	.5	1.8	8.9	13.4	12.9	4.3	.9	7.5
Paraguay	—	—	—	—	—	—	—	—	—	—	—	—	—	—	—
Peru	26.9	22.6	3.3	17.1	13.6	—	—	—	—	60.9	91.2	38.7	43.9	87.5	82.7
St. Kitts and Nevis	—	—	—	—	—	—	—	—	—	—	—	—	—	—	—
St. Lucia	—	—	—	—	—	—	—	—	—	—	—	—	1.5	—	.5
St. Vincent & Grens.	—	—	—	—	—	—	—	—	—	—	—	—	—	—	.5
Trinidad and Tobago	—	—	—	—	—	—	—	—	—	—	—	—	—	—	—
Uruguay	18.8	10.6	2.7	19.5	15.0	17.3	12.9	21.7	115.5	—	—	—	—	11.2	—
Venezuela, Rep. Bol.	—	—	—	—	—	—	—	—	—	—	—	—	—	—	—
Memorandum Items															
Oil Exporting Ctys	**3.2**	**15.0**	**20.0**	**88.5**	**18.2**	**—**	**—**	**—**	**—**	**—**	**—**	**—**	**—**	**—**	**3.6**
Non-Oil Develop.Ctys	**602.0**	**304.1**	**386.0**	**319.0**	**356.0**	**238.9**	**840.6**	**1,193.2**	**1,785.8**	**1,469.8**	**1,578.5**	**1,271.6**	**982.7**	**1,912.8**	**2,280.9**

Repurchases

Expressed in Millions of SDRs

1985	1986	1987	1988	1989	1990	1991	1992	1993	1994	1995	1996	1997	1998	1999	
															Europe
—	—	—	—	—	—	—	—	—	—	.8	5.7	5.8	.9	—	Albania
—	—	—	—	—	—	—	—	—	—	—	—	—	.4	9.6	Armenia
—	—	—	—	—	—	—	—	—	—	—	—	—	17.9	42.5	Belarus
—	—	—	—	—	—	—	—	—	—	18.4	1.4	.7	—	15.2	Bosnia & Herzegovina
—	—	—	—	—	—	—	60.6	—	48.0	162.3	154.9	64.4	134.7	90.7	Bulgaria
—	—	—	—	—	—	—	—	17.2	6.2	3.9	3.1	1.6	6.5	22.9	Croatia
3.2	—	—	—	—	—	—	—	—	—	—	—	—	—	—	Cyprus
—	—	—	—	—	—	—	—	70.0	780.7	—	—	—	—	—	Czech Republic
—	—	—	—	—	—	35.0	—	—	—	—	—	—	—	—	Czechoslovakia
—	—	—	—	—	—	—	—	—	—	1.0	7.7	14.1	18.7	2.9	Estonia
—	—	—	—	—	—	—	—	—	—	—	—	—	.7	15.7	Georgia
88.3	41.0	272.9	263.9	174.2	242.8	55.3	122.8	36.2	114.7	522.9	140.0	—	118.7	—	Hungary
—	—	—	—	—	—	—	—	—	—	—	—	4.6	70.0	128.5	Kazakhstan
—	—	—	—	—	—	—	—	—	—	—	2.7	7.1	8.5	5.4	Kyrgyz Republic
—	—	—	—	—	—	—	—	—	—	1.9	17.5	26.7	18.3	11.1	Latvia
—	—	—	—	—	—	—	—	—	—	—	16.9	31.1	20.6	12.1	Lithuania
—	—	—	—	—	—	—	—	2.2	1.2	.7	.6	.3	1.7	12.4	Macedonia, FYR
—	—	—	—	—	—	—	—	—	—	—	5.1	14.6	47.2	47.9	Moldova
—	—	—	—	—	—	—	—	98.9	219.4	918.6	—	—	—	—	Poland
172.9	199.3	226.0	250.6	106.9	—	—	153.4	—	89.6	245.8	245.4	98.4	92.3	102.0	Romania
—	—	—	—	—	—	—	—	—	—	—	359.5	359.5	673.9	3,101.1	Russia
—	—	—	—	—	—	—	—	—	61.9	132.3	85.6	37.6	49.8	38.1	Slovak Republic
—	—	—	—	—	—	—	—	9.9	3.6	2.2	1.8	.9	—	—	Slovenia
—	—	—	—	—	—	—	—	—	—	—	—	—	—	3.8	Tajikistan
247.5	320.3	344.2	320.9	185.8	36.3	—	—	—	—	—	—	20.1	164.6	210.2	Turkey
—	—	—	—	—	—	—	—	—	—	—	—	—	77.3	407.0	Ukraine
—	—	—	—	—	—	—	—	—	—	—	—	—	—	18.4	Uzbekistan
322.1	362.5	385.8	454.2	451.5	260.0	113.1	72.4	9.6	—	—	....	....	....	....	Yugoslavia, SFR
13.7	**23.8**	**23.2**	**35.2**	**28.7**	**36.2**	**58.0**	**36.3**	**33.1**	**48.4**	**135.2**	**163.2**	**49.4**	**6.8**	**50.7**	**Middle East**
11.8	12.5	12.5	12.5	—	29.0	58.0	29.0	—	22.5	62.7	58.6	10.9	—	—	Egypt
—	—	—	—	—	—	—	—	—	—	—	—	—	—	—	Iran, I.R. of
—	—	—	—	—	—	—	—	—	—	—	—	—	—	—	Iraq
—	—	—	—	—	—	—	—	—	—	67.0	89.3	22.3	—	—	Israel
—	—	—	21.5	28.7	7.2	—	7.3	33.1	25.9	5.6	15.3	16.2	6.8	26.0	Jordan
—	—	—	—	—	—	—	—	—	—	—	—	—	—	—	Syrian Arab Republic
—	3.6	4.9	1.2	—	—	—	—	—	—	—	—	—	—	—	Yemen Arab Rep.
1.9	7.7	5.8	—	—	—	—	—	—	—	—	—	—	—	—	Yemen, P.D. Rep.
—	—	—	—	—	—	—	—	—	—	—	—	—	—	24.8	Yemen, Republic of
403.4	**1,645.0**	**2,565.2**	**2,195.1**	**2,416.5**	**2,671.1**	**2,498.3**	**2,385.6**	**2,540.5**	**1,709.2**	**1,868.8**	**2,329.0**	**3,383.4**	**1,822.5**	**6,301.3**	**Western Hemisphere**
—	337.3	494.4	381.9	558.2	513.6	723.8	637.7	275.1	289.7	319.3	296.5	347.8	484.2	602.5	Argentina
—	11.2	16.8	7.8	4.5	2.8	.5	—	—	—	—	11.9	18.4	6.5	—	Barbados
—	1.2	1.5	2.3	3.3	2.2	.3	—	—	—	—	—	—	—	—	Belize
18.2	25.3	19.2	36.3	4.9	31.4	36.9	22.6	17.0	—	—	—	—	—	—	Bolivia
64.5	525.5	877.0	691.4	633.5	563.7	414.5	411.3	360.4	93.5	32.3	48.2	23.7	15.5	1,445.9	Brazil
—	152.4	280.9	199.8	155.1	153.6	143.5	144.4	178.5	147.0	199.5	—	—	—	—	Chile
—	—	—	—	—	—	—	—	—	—	—	—	—	—	—	Colombia
21.4	30.7	47.7	40.2	26.1	19.0	5.2	2.8	—	13.8	29.1	15.8	.5	—	—	Costa Rica
1.5	1.3	1.6	2.2	1.9	1.0	.7	.4	.1	—	—	—	—	—	—	Dominica
32.2	38.7	49.0	38.2	68.5	42.8	32.9	10.3	7.2	5.6	22.4	41.0	45.3	21.1	—	Dominican Republic
—	5.5	90.2	102.3	69.2	84.8	77.0	54.9	20.8	14.9	19.0	15.8	2.0	49.5	49.5	Ecuador
26.6	45.8	31.2	3.9	—	—	—	—	—	—	—	—	—	—	—	El Salvador
2.1	1.3	.3	.3	.3	.3	—	—	—	—	—	—	—	—	—	Grenada
47.8	48.0	15.5	21.0	9.9	8.7	2.1	22.4	22.4	—	—	—	—	—	—	Guatemala
1.0	—	—	.8	69.6	1.3	—	—	2.4	15.3	15.6	8.1	6.7	1.4	—	Guyana
11.8	19.7	18.1	14.1	14.3	6.5	1.6	—	—	14.8	.3	—	—	6.0	8.2	Haiti
16.7	41.4	32.4	24.3	.3	22.0	1.3	—	2.1	11.2	28.8	26.1	6.4	—	—	Honduras
61.3	103.3	172.1	163.2	130.8	82.1	64.1	55.7	51.9	60.9	62.9	49.5	25.1	12.5	13.9	Jamaica
—	125.4	280.1	419.0	639.6	877.1	807.4	636.1	841.7	841.0	754.1	1,413.6	2,499.2	783.7	3,726.7	Mexico
9.0	—	—	—	—	—	—	—	—	2.1	8.5	6.4	—	—	—	Nicaragua
28.3	38.7	55.7	.1	.6	51.9	40.6	141.7	7.3	.9	25.6	35.8	18.8	9.9	17.2	Panama
—	—	—	—	—	—	—	—	—	—	—	—	—	—	—	Paraguay
49.3	43.5	.1	—	18.4	46.5	37.1	34.7	458.7	—	—	—	53.6	107.1	107.1	Peru
—	—	—	—	—	—	—	—	—	—	—	—	—	—	—	St. Kitts and Nevis
1.7	.3	—	—	—	—	—	—	—	—	—	—	—	—	—	St. Lucia
.7	.3	—	—	—	—	—	—	—	—	—	—	—	—	—	St. Vincent & Grens.
—	—	—	—	—	—	—	63.7	92.5	50.4	28.7	17.3	13.3	3.1	—	Trinidad and Tobago
9.5	48.2	81.5	47.0	76.3	91.6	30.3	18.3	10.2	7.4	6.5	8.0	6.0	—	—	Uruguay
—	—	—	—	—	—	77.2	128.6	192.0	140.6	304.2	328.5	328.5	328.5	330.3	Venezuela, Rep. Bol.
															Memorandum Items
264.9	**—**	**—**	**42.0**	**—**	**115.7**	**308.6**	**362.0**	**427.5**	**277.1**	**416.7**	**422.3**	**583.2**	**649.3**	**593.1**	**Oil Exporting Ctys**
3,360.1	**5,653.8**	**7,672.2**	**6,255.6**	**5,912.7**	**5,737.7**	**4,436.2**	**3,839.6**	**3,386.5**	**4,295.0**	**6,234.2**	**4,650.4**	**5,098.1**	**6,044.9**	**18,805.7**	**Non-Oil Develop.Ctys**

Loan Disbursements

	1970	1971	1972	1973	1974	1975	1976	1977	1978	1979	1980	1981	1982	1983	1984
						Expressed in Millions of SDRs									
World	—	—	—	—	—	—	—	152.9	688.1	526.6	1,256.0	367.7	—	—	—
Developing Countries	—	—	—	—	—	—	—	152.9	688.1	526.6	1,256.0	367.7	—	—	—
Africa	—	—	—	—	—	—	—	49.9	296.7	264.8	326.6	4.0	—	—	—
Benin	—	—	—	—	—	—	—	—	5.4	—	7.3	.1	—	—	—
Burkina Faso	—	—	—	—	—	—	—	—	5.4	3.9	3.3	.1	—	—	—
Burundi	—	—	—	—	—	—	—	2.0	5.8	5.8	4.9	.1	—	—	—
Cameroon	—	—	—	—	—	—	—	—	14.5	10.6	9.0	.1	—	—	—
Central African Rep.	—	—	—	—	—	—	—	—	5.4	—	7.3	.1	—	—	—
Chad	—	—	—	—	—	—	—	—	5.4	—	—	—	—	—	—
Comoros	—	—	—	—	—	—	—	—	—	—	—	—	—	—	—
Congo, Dem. Rep. of	—	—	—	—	—	—	—	12.1	34.8	34.2	28.9	.4	—	—	—
Congo, Republic of	—	—	—	—	—	—	—	1.4	4.0	3.9	3.3	.1	—	—	—
Côte d'Ivoire	—	—	—	—	—	—	—	—	21.6	—	29.1	.2	—	—	—
Djibouti	—	—	—	—	—	—	—	—	—	—	—	—	—	—	—
Equatorial Guinea	—	—	—	—	—	—	—	—	—	—	4.5	—	—	—	—
Ethiopia	—	—	—	—	—	—	—	—	11.2	8.2	6.9	.1	—	—	—
Gambia, The	—	—	—	—	—	—	—	.8	2.2	2.1	1.8	—	—	—	—
Ghana	—	—	—	—	—	—	—	—	—	26.4	22.3	.3	—	—	—
Guinea	—	—	—	—	—	—	—	2.6	7.4	7.3	6.1	.1	—	—	—
Guinea-Bissau	—	—	—	—	—	—	—	—	—	—	—	—	—	—	—
Kenya	—	—	—	—	—	—	—	5.1	14.8	14.5	12.3	.2	—	—	—
Lesotho	—	—	—	—	—	—	—	.5	1.5	1.5	1.3	—	—	—	—
Liberia	—	—	—	—	—	—	—	3.1	8.9	8.8	7.4	.1	—	—	—
Madagascar	—	—	—	—	—	—	—	—	10.8	—	14.5	.1	—	—	—
Malawi	—	—	—	—	—	—	—	1.6	4.6	4.5	3.8	.1	—	—	—
Mali	—	—	—	—	—	—	—	—	9.1	6.7	5.6	.1	—	—	—
Mauritania	—	—	—	—	—	—	—	1.4	4.0	3.9	3.3	.1	—	—	—
Mauritius	—	—	—	—	—	—	—	—	9.1	—	—	—	—	—	—
Morocco	—	—	—	—	—	—	—	12.1	34.8	34.2	28.9	.4	—	—	—
Mozambique	—	—	—	—	—	—	—	—	—	—	—	—	—	—	—
Niger	—	—	—	—	—	—	—	—	5.4	—	7.3	.1	—	—	—
Rwanda	—	—	—	—	—	—	—	—	—	5.8	4.9	.1	—	—	—
São Tomé & Príncipe	—	—	—	—	—	—	—	—	—	—	—	—	—	—	—
Senegal	—	—	—	—	—	—	—	—	14.1	10.3	8.7	.1	—	—	—
Sierra Leone	—	—	—	—	—	—	—	2.7	7.7	7.6	6.4	.1	—	—	—
Somalia	—	—	—	—	—	—	—	—	—	—	10.6	.1	—	—	—
Sudan	—	—	—	—	—	—	—	—	29.8	21.8	18.4	.3	—	—	—
Swaziland	—	—	—	—	—	—	—	—	—	2.4	2.0	—	—	—	—
Tanzania	—	—	—	—	—	—	—	4.5	12.9	12.7	10.8	.2	—	—	—
Togo	—	—	—	—	—	—	—	—	6.2	4.5	3.8	.1	—	—	—
Uganda	—	—	—	—	—	—	—	—	—	—	22.4	.2	—	—	—
Zambia	—	—	—	—	—	—	—	—	—	23.0	19.5	.3	—	—	—
Zimbabwe	—	—	—	—	—	—	—	—	—	—	—	—	—	—	—
Asia	—	—	—	—	—	—	—	77.6	302.9	182.1	821.8	351.2	—	—	—
Afghanistan, I.S. of	—	—	—	—	—	—	—	—	—	—	—	—	—	—	—
Bangladesh	—	—	—	—	—	—	—	13.4	38.4	37.9	32.0	.5	—	—	—
Cambodia	—	—	—	—	—	—	—	—	—	—	—	—	—	—	—
China, People's Rep.	—	—	—	—	—	—	—	—	—	—	—	309.5	—	—	—
India	—	—	—	—	—	—	—	—	—	—	525.5	3.6	—	—	—
Lao People's Dem.Rep	—	—	—	—	—	—	—	—	5.4	3.9	3.3	.1	—	—	—
Maldives	—	—	—	—	—	—	—	—	—	—	—	—	—	—	—
Mongolia	—	—	—	—	—	—	—	—	—	—	—	—	—	—	—
Myanmar	—	—	—	—	—	—	—	6.4	18.5	18.2	15.4	.2	—	—	—
Nepal	—	—	—	—	—	—	—	1.5	4.3	4.2	3.6	.1	—	—	—
Pakistan	—	—	—	—	—	—	—	25.1	72.3	—	131.4	.9	—	—	—
Papua New Guinea	—	—	—	—	—	—	—	—	8.3	—	11.2	.1	—	—	—
Philippines	—	—	—	—	—	—	—	16.6	47.7	47.0	39.7	.6	—	—	—
Samoa	—	—	—	—	—	—	—	.2	.6	.6	.5	—	—	—	—
Solomon Islands	—	—	—	—	—	—	—	—	—	—	—	—	—	—	—
Sri Lanka	—	—	—	—	—	—	—	—	40.6	29.7	25.1	.4	—	—	—
Thailand	—	—	—	—	—	—	—	14.3	41.2	40.6	34.3	.5	—	—	—
Vietnam	—	—	—	—	—	—	—	—	25.7	—	—	34.9	—	—	—
Europe	—	—	—	—	—	—	—	—	—	—	—	—	—	—	—
Albania	—	—	—	—	—	—	—	—	—	—	—	—	—	—	—
Armenia	—	—	—	—	—	—	—	—	—	—	—	—	—	—	—
Azerbaijan	—	—	—	—	—	—	—	—	—	—	—	—	—	—	—
Georgia	—	—	—	—	—	—	—	—	—	—	—	—	—	—	—
Kyrgyz Republic	—	—	—	—	—	—	—	—	—	—	—	—	—	—	—
Macedonia, FYR	—	—	—	—	—	—	—	—	—	—	—	—	—	—	—
Tajikistan	—	—	—	—	—	—	—	—	—	—	—	—	—	—	—
Middle East	—	—	—	—	—	—	—	23.2	66.7	65.7	55.6	.8	—	—	—
Egypt	—	—	—	—	—	—	—	20.1	57.8	57.0	48.1	.7	—	—	—
Yemen Arab Rep.	—	—	—	—	—	—	—	—	—	—	—	—	—	—	—
Yemen, P.D. Rep.	—	—	—	—	—	—	—	3.1	8.9	8.8	7.4	.1	—	—	—
Yemen, Republic of	—	—	—	—	—	—	—	—	—	—	—	—	—	—	—
Western Hemisphere	—	—	—	—	—	—	—	2.3	21.8	13.9	52.0	11.7	—	—	—
Bolivia	—	—	—	—	—	—	—	—	15.3	—	20.7	.1	—	—	—
Dominica	—	—	—	—	—	—	—	—	—	—	—	—	—	—	—
El Salvador	—	—	—	—	—	—	—	—	—	—	19.6	.1	—	—	—
Grenada	—	—	—	—	—	—	—	.2	.6	.6	.5	—	—	—	—
Guyana	—	—	—	—	—	—	—	—	—	—	—	11.3	—	—	—
Haiti	—	—	—	—	—	—	—	2.0	5.8	5.8	4.9	.1	—	—	—
Honduras	—	—	—	—	—	—	—	—	—	7.6	6.4	.1	—	—	—
Nicaragua	—	—	—	—	—	—	—	—	—	—	—	—	—	—	—
Memorandum Items															
Non-Oil Develop.Ctys	—	—	—	—	—	—	—	152.9	688.1	526.6	1,256.0	367.7	—	—	—

1985	1986	1987	1988	1989	1990	1991	1992	1993	1994	1995	1996	1997	1998	1999	
						Expressed in Millions of SDRs									
—	81.8	403.4	410.2	961.1	507.0	781.9	544.3	271.7	910.4	1,431.4	708.6	730.6	896.0	736.8	**World**
—	81.8	403.4	410.2	961.1	507.0	781.9	544.3	271.7	910.4	1,431.4	708.6	730.6	896.0	736.8	**Developing Countries**
—	54.1	251.0	292.4	543.4	359.3	380.6	273.8	142.1	467.1	1,247.8	404.3	348.3	532.6	334.8	**Africa**
—	—	—	—	6.3	—	9.4	—	15.7	18.1	9.1	13.6	4.5	—	7.2	Benin
—	—	—	—	—	—	6.3	—	8.8	17.7	17.7	6.6	13.3	13.3	12.2	Burkina Faso
—	8.5	—	12.8	8.5	—	4.3	14.9	—	—	—	—	—	—	—	Burundi
—	—	—	—	—	—	—	—	—	—	—	—	27.0	54.0	45.0	Cameroon
—	—	6.1	9.1	—	6.1	—	—	—	—	—	—	—	8.2	8.2	Central African Rep.
—	—	6.1	—	9.2	6.1	—	—	—	—	8.3	16.5	8.3	8.3	8.3	Chad
—	—	—	—	—	—	.9	—	—	1.4	—	—	—	—	—	Comoros
—	—	58.2	—	87.3	—	—	—	—	—	—	—	—	—	—	Congo, Dem. Rep. of
—	—	—	—	—	—	—	—	—	—	—	13.9	—	—	—	Congo, Republic of
—	—	—	—	—	—	—	—	—	119.1	119.1	95.3	—	123.9	—	Côte d'Ivoire
—	—	—	—	—	—	—	—	—	—	—	—	—	—	2.7	Djibouti
—	—	3.7	—	—	5.5	—	—	2.8	1.8	—	—	—	—	—	Equatorial Guinea
—	—	—	—	—	—	14.1	21.2	14.1	—	—	14.7	—	14.7	—	Ethiopia
—	3.4	5.1	3.4	6.8	6.8	3.4	—	—	—	—	—	—	3.4	3.4	Gambia, The
—	—	40.9	86.3	137.8	48.0	116.5	—	—	—	27.4	27.4	—	82.2	44.3	Ghana
—	—	11.6	—	17.4	—	8.7	8.7	—	8.7	20.3	—	23.6	23.6	7.9	Guinea
—	—	1.5	—	2.3	—	—	—	—	—	1.6	2.1	4.5	2.4	—	Guinea-Bissau
—	—	—	28.4	80.5	100.5	35.2	—	22.6	22.6	—	24.9	—	—	—	Kenya
—	—	—	3.0	4.5	3.0	2.3	5.3	6.8	3.8	—	—	—	—	—	Lesotho
—	—	—	—	—	—	—	—	—	—	—	—	—	—	—	Liberia
—	—	13.3	—	25.6	12.8	12.8	—	—	—	—	13.6	13.6	—	13.6	Madagascar
—	—	—	9.3	18.6	—	14.9	—	—	5.6	7.6	15.3	7.6	12.8	7.6	Malawi
—	—	—	10.2	—	15.2	—	10.2	10.2	29.5	29.5	20.7	20.7	10.3	17.1	Mali
—	6.8	10.2	—	8.5	8.5	—	8.5	8.5	17.0	14.3	14.3	14.3	—	6.1	Mauritania
—	—	—	—	—	—	—	—	—	—	—	—	—	—	—	Mauritius
—	—	—	—	—	—	—	—	—	—	—	—	—	—	—	Morocco
—	—	12.2	18.3	12.2	9.2	30.5	45.8	15.3	14.7	—	12.6	25.2	25.2	21.0	Mozambique
—	6.7	10.1	8.4	8.4	6.7	—	—	—	—	—	9.7	19.3	19.3	—	Niger
—	—	—	.8	—	—	8.8	—	—	—	—	—	—	11.9	21.4	Rwanda
—	—	—	—	—	—	—	—	—	—	—	—	—	—	—	São Tomé & Príncipe
—	17.0	25.5	29.8	51.1	21.3	42.6	—	—	16.7	54.7	23.8	35.7	35.7	14.3	Senegal
—	11.6	—	—	—	—	—	—	—	95.6	13.1	10.2	5.1	—	—	Sierra Leone
—	—	8.8	—	—	—	—	—	—	—	—	—	—	—	—	Somalia
—	—	—	—	—	—	—	—	—	—	—	—	—	—	—	Sudan
—	—	—	—	—	—	—	—	—	—	—	—	—	—	—	Swaziland
—	—	21.4	32.1	—	21.4	21.4	64.2	—	—	—	25.7	61.4	35.7	58.8	Tanzania
—	—	—	7.7	15.4	15.4	—	7.7	—	10.9	21.7	—	10.9	10.9	—	Togo
—	—	19.9	29.9	42.3	59.8	57.3	39.8	—	36.7	36.8	43.5	43.5	36.8	25.7	Uganda
—	—	—	—	—	—	—	—	—	—	833.4	—	10.0	—	10.0	Zambia
—	—	—	—	—	—	—	—	54.7	30.4	33.4	33.4	—	—	—	Zimbabwe
—	—	151.2	94.6	372.1	87.7	360.9	209.8	105.5	358.9	100.1	132.2	125.2	113.7	52.2	**Asia**
—	—	—	—	—	—	—	—	—	—	—	—	—	—	—	Afghanistan, I.S. of
—	—	143.8	38.8	18.7	43.1	186.9	86.3	28.8	—	—	—	—	—	—	Bangladesh
—	—	—	—	—	—	—	—	—	14.0	28.0	—	—	—	8.4	Cambodia
—	—	—	—	—	—	—	—	—	—	—	—	—	—	—	China, People's Rep.
—	—	—	—	—	—	—	—	—	—	—	—	—	—	—	India
—	—	—	—	5.9	—	8.8	5.9	5.9	5.9	11.7	5.9	5.9	—	—	Lao People's Dem.Rep
—	—	—	—	—	—	—	—	—	—	—	—	—	—	—	Maldives
—	—	—	—	—	—	—	—	9.3	14.8	—	5.6	5.6	—	5.9	Mongolia
—	—	—	—	—	—	—	—	—	—	—	—	—	—	—	Myanmar
—	—	7.5	11.2	7.5	—	—	5.6	5.6	5.6	—	—	—	—	—	Nepal
—	—	—	273.2	—	109.3	—	—	—	202.2	—	—	113.7	113.7	37.9	Pakistan
—	—	—	—	—	—	—	—	—	—	—	—	—	—	—	Papua New Guinea
—	—	—	—	—	—	—	—	—	—	—	—	—	—	—	Philippines
—	—	—	—	—	—	—	—	—	—	—	—	—	—	—	Samoa
—	—	—	—	—	—	—	—	—	—	—	—	—	—	—	Solomon Islands
—	—	—	44.6	66.9	44.6	56.0	112.0	56.0	56.0	—	—	—	—	—	Sri Lanka
—	—	—	—	—	—	—	—	—	—	—	—	—	—	—	Thailand
—	—	—	—	—	—	—	—	—	60.4	60.4	120.8	—	—	—	Vietnam
—	—	—	—	—	—	—	—	8.5	25.0	37.4	105.4	178.4	146.2	107.7	**Europe**
—	—	—	—	—	—	—	—	8.5	15.5	7.1	—	—	5.9	15.5	Albania
—	—	—	—	—	—	—	—	—	—	—	33.8	16.9	37.8	20.9	Armenia
—	—	—	—	—	—	—	—	—	—	—	—	55.6	14.6	11.7	Azerbaijan
—	—	—	—	—	—	—	—	—	—	—	55.5	55.5	27.8	33.3	Georgia
—	—	—	—	—	—	—	—	—	9.5	30.3	16.1	32.3	10.8	19.6	Kyrgyz Republic
—	—	—	—	—	—	—	—	—	—	—	—	18.2	9.1	—	Macedonia, FYR
—	—	—	—	—	—	—	—	—	—	—	—	—	40.3	6.7	Tajikistan
—	—	—	—	—	—	—	—	—	—	—	—	44.0	44.0	62.0	**Middle East**
—	—	—	—	—	—	—	—	—	—	—	—	—	—	—	Egypt
—	—	—	—	—	—	—	—	—	—	—	—	—	—	—	Yemen Arab Rep.
—	—	—	—	—	—	—	—	—	—	—	—	—	—	—	Yemen, P.D. Rep.
—	—	—	—	—	—	—	—	—	—	—	—	44.0	44.0	62.0	Yemen, Republic of
—	27.8	1.2	23.2	45.6	59.9	40.4	60.8	15.6	59.4	46.1	66.8	34.8	59.4	180.1	**Western Hemisphere**
—	18.1	—	22.7	45.4	22.7	22.7	36.3	—	30.4	16.8	33.7	16.8	33.6	16.8	Bolivia
—	.8	1.2	.5	.3	—	—	—	—	—	—	—	—	—	—	Dominica
—	—	—	—	—	—	—	—	—	—	—	—	—	—	—	El Salvador
—	—	—	—	—	—	—	—	—	—	—	—	—	—	—	Grenada
—	—	—	—	—	37.2	17.7	17.7	8.9	9.0	9.0	17.9	17.9	9.0	9.0	Guyana
—	8.8	—	—	—	—	—	—	—	—	—	15.2	—	—	—	Haiti
—	—	—	—	—	—	—	6.8	6.8	—	20.3	—	—	—	76.0	Honduras
—	—	—	—	—	—	—	—	—	20.0	—	—	—	16.8	78.3	Nicaragua
															Memorandum Items
—	81.8	403.4	410.2	961.1	507.0	781.9	544.3	271.7	910.4	1,431.4	708.6	730.6	896.0	736.8	**Non-Oil Develop.Ctys**

Repayments of Loans

	1970	1971	1972	1973	1974	1975	1976	1977	1978	1979	1980	1981	1982	1983	1984
					Expressed in Millions of SDRs										
World	—	—	—	—	—	—	—	—	—	—	—	—	3.15	45.22	173.07
Developing Countries	—	—	—	—	—	—	—	—	—	—	—	—	3.15	45.22	173.07
Africa	—	—	—	—	—	—	—	—	—	—	—	—	2.00	16.58	70.72
Benin	—	—	—	—	—	—	—	—	—	—	—	—	—	.22	1.08
Burkina Faso	—	—	—	—	—	—	—	—	—	—	—	—	—	.22	1.08
Burundi	—	—	—	—	—	—	—	—	—	—	—	—	.10	.53	1.58
Cameroon	—	—	—	—	—	—	—	—	—	—	—	—	—	.60	2.90
Central African Rep.	—	—	—	—	—	—	—	—	—	—	—	—	—	.22	1.08
Chad	—	—	—	—	—	—	—	—	—	—	—	—	—	.23	1.08
Comoros	—	—	—	—	—	—	—	—	—	—	—	—	—	—	—
Congo, Dem. Rep. of	—	—	—	—	—	—	—	—	—	—	—	—	.60	3.16	9.37
Congo, Republic of	—	—	—	—	—	—	—	—	—	—	—	—	.07	.36	1.15
Côte d'Ivoire	—	—	—	—	—	—	—	—	—	—	—	—	—	—	4.31
Equatorial Guinea	—	—	—	—	—	—	—	—	—	—	—	—	—	—	—
Ethiopia	—	—	—	—	—	—	—	—	—	—	—	—	—	—	2.24
Gambia, The	—	—	—	—	—	—	—	—	—	—	—	—	—	.20	.58
Ghana	—	—	—	—	—	—	—	—	—	—	—	—	—	—	1.11
Guinea	—	—	—	—	—	—	—	—	—	—	—	—	—	.67	1.99
Guinea-Bissau	—	—	—	—	—	—	—	—	—	—	—	—	—	—	—
Kenya	—	—	—	—	—	—	—	—	—	—	—	—	.26	1.34	4.59
Lesotho	—	—	—	—	—	—	—	—	—	—	—	—	—	.14	.42
Liberia	—	—	—	—	—	—	—	—	—	—	—	—	.15	.82	2.40
Madagascar	—	—	—	—	—	—	—	—	—	—	—	—	—	.45	2.16
Malawi	—	—	—	—	—	—	—	—	—	—	—	—	—	.42	1.24
Mali	—	—	—	—	—	—	—	—	—	—	—	—	—	.38	1.83
Mauritania	—	—	—	—	—	—	—	—	—	—	—	—	—	.36	1.24
Mauritius	—	—	—	—	—	—	—	—	—	—	—	—	—	.38	1.83
Morocco	—	—	—	—	—	—	—	—	—	—	—	—	.60	3.16	10.82
Mozambique	—	—	—	—	—	—	—	—	—	—	—	—	—	—	—
Niger	—	—	—	—	—	—	—	—	—	—	—	—	—	—	1.07
Rwanda	—	—	—	—	—	—	—	—	—	—	—	—	—	—	—
São Tomé & Príncipe	—	—	—	—	—	—	—	—	—	—	—	—	—	—	—
Senegal	—	—	—	—	—	—	—	—	—	—	—	—	—	.59	2.82
Sierra Leone	—	—	—	—	—	—	—	—	—	—	—	—	—	.70	2.07
Somalia	—	—	—	—	—	—	—	—	—	—	—	—	—	—	—
Sudan	—	—	—	—	—	—	—	—	—	—	—	—	—	—	2.98
Swaziland	—	—	—	—	—	—	—	—	—	—	—	—	—	—	—
Tanzania	—	—	—	—	—	—	—	—	—	—	—	—	.22	1.17	3.49
Togo	—	—	—	—	—	—	—	—	—	—	—	—	—	.26	1.24
Uganda	—	—	—	—	—	—	—	—	—	—	—	—	—	—	—
Zambia	—	—	—	—	—	—	—	—	—	—	—	—	—	—	.97
Zimbabwe	—	—	—	—	—	—	—	—	—	—	—	—	—	—	—
Asia	—	—	—	—	—	—	—	—	—	—	—	—	.90	21.98	76.90
Afghanistan, I.S. of	—	—	—	—	—	—	—	—	—	—	—	—	—	—	—
Bangladesh	—	—	—	—	—	—	—	—	—	—	—	—	—	3.50	10.37
Cambodia	—	—	—	—	—	—	—	—	—	—	—	—	—	—	—
China, People's Rep.	—	—	—	—	—	—	—	—	—	—	—	—	—	—	—
India	—	—	—	—	—	—	—	—	—	—	—	—	—	—	—
Lao People's Dem.Rep	—	—	—	—	—	—	—	—	—	—	—	—	—	—	1.07
Mongolia	—	—	—	—	—	—	—	—	—	—	—	—	—	—	—
Myanmar	—	—	—	—	—	—	—	—	—	—	—	—	—	1.68	5.75
Nepal	—	—	—	—	—	—	—	—	—	—	—	—	.07	.39	1.35
Pakistan	—	—	—	—	—	—	—	—	—	—	—	—	—	6.58	19.48
Papua New Guinea	—	—	—	—	—	—	—	—	—	—	—	—	—	—	1.66
Philippines	—	—	—	—	—	—	—	—	—	—	—	—	.82	4.34	14.83
Samoa	—	—	—	—	—	—	—	—	—	—	—	—	.01	.05	.19
Solomon Islands	—	—	—	—	—	—	—	—	—	—	—	—	—	—	—
Sri Lanka	—	—	—	—	—	—	—	—	—	—	—	—	—	1.69	9.38
Thailand	—	—	—	—	—	—	—	—	—	—	—	—	—	3.75	12.82
Vietnam	—	—	—	—	—	—	—	—	—	—	—	—	—	—	—
Europe	—	—	—	—	—	—	—	—	—	—	—	—	—	—	—
Albania	—	—	—	—	—	—	—	—	—	—	—	—	—	—	—
Kyrgyz Republic	—	—	—	—	—	—	—	—	—	—	—	—	—	—	—
Middle East	—	—	—	—	—	—	—	—	—	—	—	—	.15	6.08	20.39
Egypt	—	—	—	—	—	—	—	—	—	—	—	—	—	5.26	17.99
Yemen Arab Rep.	—	—	—	—	—	—	—	—	—	—	—	—	—	—	—
Yemen, P.D. Rep.	—	—	—	—	—	—	—	—	—	—	—	—	.15	.82	2.40
Yemen, Republic of	—	—	—	—	—	—	—	—	—	—	—	—	—	—	—
Western Hemisphere	—	—	—	—	—	—	—	—	—	—	—	—	.10	.58	5.06
Bolivia	—	—	—	—	—	—	—	—	—	—	—	—	—	—	3.07
Dominica	—	—	—	—	—	—	—	—	—	—	—	—	—	—	—
El Salvador	—	—	—	—	—	—	—	—	—	—	—	—	—	—	—
Grenada	—	—	—	—	—	—	—	—	—	—	—	—	—	.05	.17
Guyana	—	—	—	—	—	—	—	—	—	—	—	—	—	—	—
Haiti	—	—	—	—	—	—	—	—	—	—	—	—	.10	.53	1.82
Honduras	—	—	—	—	—	—	—	—	—	—	—	—	—	—	—
Nicaragua	—	—	—	—	—	—	—	—	—	—	—	—	—	—	—
Memorandum Items															
Non-Oil Develop.Ctys	—	—	—	—	—	—	—	—	—	—	—	—	3.15	45.22	173.07

Expressed in Millions of SDRs

1985	1986	1987	1988	1989	1990	1991	1992	1993	1994	1995	1996	1997	1998	1999	
299.63	538.96	550.24	502.52	400.28	270.04	50.65	23.57	133.39	223.44	373.76	484.47	606.03	620.90	595.23	**World**
299.63	538.96	550.24	502.52	400.28	269.96	50.65	23.57	133.39	223.44	373.76	484.47	606.03	620.90	595.23	**Developing Countries**
121.63	175.45	156.79	137.31	104.48	38.87	3.53	14.03	51.51	145.22	230.61	299.97	338.38	349.98	324.50	**Africa**
1.07	2.54	2.53	2.30	1.46	1.45	.05	—	—	.63	1.25	1.25	3.13	3.91	6.54	Benin
2.13	2.54	2.53	2.30	1.46	.39	.05	—	—	—	—	.63	1.26	2.15	3.92	Burkina Faso
3.12	3.70	3.60	3.17	2.12	.58	.07	1.71	2.99	4.27	5.98	5.98	5.98	6.83	5.55	Burundi
5.75	6.82	6.81	6.21	3.91	1.07	.13	—	—	—	—	—	—	—	—	Cameroon
1.78	2.53	2.53	2.31	1.45	.79	.05	—	.73	2.92	4.86	4.26	2.75	3.94	1.22	Central African Rep.
1.07	1.08	1.08	.85	—	—	—	—	1.22	1.22	4.59	4.28	4.28	3.06	2.14	Chad
—	—	—	—	—	—	—	—	—	—	—	—	—	—	.60	Comoros
18.56	22.01	21.40	18.84	12.63	3.43	.43	—	—	—	—	2.42	—	.17	—	Congo, Dem. Rep. of
2.13	2.46	2.47	2.16	1.46	.39	.05	—	—	—	—	—	—	—	—	Congo, Republic of
6.97	10.13	10.12	10.12	5.82	3.15	.20	—	—	—	—	—	—	—	5.96	Côte d'Ivoire
—	.89	.90	.89	.90	.89	.03	—	—	.37	.74	.76	2.18	2.12	1.83	Equatorial Guinea
4.44	5.26	5.25	5.26	3.02	.82	.10	—	—	—	—	—	—	2.82	7.06	Ethiopia
.50	2.01	1.36	1.17	.78	.24	—	.68	1.71	2.74	4.10	5.13	5.13	4.10	3.08	Gambia, The
7.08	9.73	9.73	9.72	8.62	2.64	.33	—	8.18	30.52	57.80	69.45	85.89	77.71	55.37	Ghana
3.94	4.67	4.67	4.01	2.68	.73	.09	—	2.32	4.05	5.79	5.79	7.53	6.95	5.21	Guinea
—	—	—	—	—	—	—	—	.30	.30	.75	.75	.75	.45	.45	Guinea-Bissau
8.21	9.03	9.09	8.00	4.75	1.46	.18	—	2.84	9.70	25.80	41.87	48.91	46.07	43.73	Kenya
.82	.97	.98	.83	.56	.15	.02	—	—	1.06	1.81	2.34	3.10	3.62	4.30	Lesotho
—	—	—	—	—	—	—	—	—	.69	—	—	.04	.44	.44	Liberia
2.15	5.06	5.07	4.61	2.91	2.90	.10	—	2.66	3.94	9.06	11.63	12.91	10.25	8.97	Madagascar
2.47	2.92	2.92	2.50	1.68	.45	.06	—	—	2.79	6.51	10.23	12.28	12.28	10.04	Malawi
3.61	4.28	4.29	3.90	2.46	.67	.08	—	—	2.03	3.56	5.08	5.08	8.13	8.58	Mali
2.14	2.53	2.53	2.17	1.29	.39	.05	1.36	3.39	4.24	5.93	6.78	5.42	5.09	6.78	Mauritania
1.82	1.82	1.83	1.44	—	—	—	—	—	—	—	—	—	—	—	Mauritius
18.56	22.00	21.40	18.84	11.19	3.43	.43	—	—	—	—	—	—	—	—	Morocco
—	—	—	—	—	—	—	1.22	4.27	7.32	9.46	22.50	10.98	18.07	22.82	Mozambique
1.08	2.53	2.53	2.53	1.46	1.45	.05	1.35	3.37	5.06	6.74	8.09	6.74	4.72	3.03	Niger
1.54	2.13	2.12	2.13	2.12	.58	.07	—	—	—	—	.88	1.75	1.75	1.75	Rwanda
—	—	—	—	—	—	—	—	—	.08	.16	.16	.16	.16	.08	São Tomé & Príncipe
5.58	6.63	6.62	6.03	3.80	1.03	.13	3.40	8.51	17.45	26.81	30.64	34.04	28.93	20.00	Senegal
1.03	7.95	1.31	—	.33	1.83	.09	2.32	—	13.75	2.32	2.32	—	—	9.05	Sierra Leone
—	2.12	2.03	—	.08	—	—	—	—	—	—	—	—	—	—	Somalia
—	—	—	—	—	—	—	—	—	—	—	2.98	—	5.17	—	Sudan
.65	.90	.90	.89	.90	.23	.03	—	—	—	—	—	—	—	—	Swaziland
2.73	12.34	7.96	7.00	4.69	1.28	.16	—	4.28	10.70	12.84	14.98	22.47	27.82	21.40	Tanzania
2.47	2.92	2.92	2.66	1.68	.45	.06	—	.77	2.30	5.38	7.68	8.45	8.45	6.91	Togo
2.04	4.47	4.48	4.47	4.47	2.43	.15	1.99	3.98	17.09	18.77	34.11	41.83	45.82	37.60	Uganda
6.19	8.48	2.83	—	13.80	3.57	.29	—	—	—	—	6.64	—	—	—	Zambia
—	—	—	—	—	—	—	—	—	—	—	—	—	13.980	20.360	Zimbabwe
131.88	302.72	332.77	311.66	263.75	205.25	44.73	5.75	77.84	61.96	123.58	152.07	230.43	224.94	222.65	**Asia**
—	—	—	—	—	—	—	—	—	—	—	—	—	—	—	Afghanistan, I.S. of
20.53	24.34	24.34	20.83	13.98	3.80	.47	5.75	28.75	38.38	40.25	58.94	86.25	77.63	70.87	Bangladesh
—	—	—	—	—	—	—	—	—	—	—	—	—	—	1.40	Cambodia
—	30.96	61.90	61.91	61.90	61.90	30.95	—	—	—	—	—	—	—	—	China, People's Rep.
—	105.09	105.10	105.09	105.09	105.09	3.55	—	—	—	—	—	—	—	—	India
2.14	2.53	2.53	2.53	1.46	.39	.05	—	—	—	1.17	2.05	3.52	4.69	5.86	Lao People's Dem.Rep
—	—	—	—	—	—	—	—	—	—	—	—	—	.93	2.78	Mongolia
9.85	11.70	11.69	10.00	5.94	1.83	.23	—	—	—	—	—	—	—	—	Myanmar
2.29	2.73	2.65	2.34	1.38	.43	.05	—	1.49	3.73	5.22	5.22	5.22	4.85	4.29	Nepal
31.49	45.75	45.75	39.18	26.27	14.26	.89	—	—	10.93	54.63	54.63	87.41	76.48	64.74	Pakistan
1.66	3.89	3.90	3.89	2.24	2.24	.08	—	—	—	—	—	—	—	—	Papua New Guinea
25.47	30.17	29.36	25.84	15.34	4.71	.59	—	—	—	—	—	—	—	—	Philippines
.33	.39	.38	.33	.20	.06	.01	—	—	—	—	—	—	—	—	Samoa
—	—	—	—	—	—	—	—	—	—	—	—	—	—	—	Solomon Islands
16.10	19.08	19.08	17.39	9.70	2.98	.37	—	4.46	8.92	22.31	31.23	48.03	60.37	72.71	Sri Lanka
22.02	26.09	26.09	22.33	13.27	4.07	.51	—	—	—	—	—	—	—	—	Thailand
—	—	—	—	6.98	3.49	6.98	—	43.14	—	—	—	—	—	—	Vietnam
—	—	—	—	—	—	—	—	—	—	—	—	—	—	2.54	**Europe**
—	—	—	—	—	—	—	—	—	—	—	—	—	—	2.54	Albania
—	—	—	—	—	—	—	—	—	—	—	—	—	—	—	Kyrgyz Republic
35.66	42.24	42.09	36.18	21.85	6.60	.82	—	—	—	—	—	—	—	—	**Middle East**
30.89	36.60	36.60	31.34	18.61	5.72	.71	—	—	—	—	—	—	—	—	Egypt
—	—	—	—	—	—	—	—	—	—	—	—	—	—	—	Yemen Arab Rep.
4.77	5.64	5.49	4.84	3.24	.74	—	—	—	—	—	—	—	—	—	Yemen, P.D. Rep.
—	—	—	—	—	.14	.11	—	—	—	—	—	—	—	—	Yemen, Republic of
10.46	18.55	18.59	17.37	10.20	19.24	1.57	3.79	4.03	16.26	19.56	32.43	37.22	45.98	45.53	**Western Hemisphere**
4.96	7.20	7.21	7.20	4.13	2.25	.14	3.63	3.63	10.43	17.23	21.77	24.94	29.93	24.49	Bolivia
—	—	—	—	—	—	—	.16	.40	.53	.56	.56	.40	.16	.03	Dominica
—	3.92	3.91	3.91	3.91	3.92	.13	—	—	—	—	—	—	—	—	El Salvador
.33	.39	.38	.28	.28	.06	.01	—	—	—	—	—	—	—	—	Grenada
—	.56	.71	—	—	8.87	1.13	—	—	—	—	8.33	11.88	14.53	16.30	Guyana
3.13	3.69	3.60	3.17	1.88	.58	.07	—	—	5.29	1.76	1.76	—	—	—	Haiti
2.04	2.79	2.78	2.81	—	3.56	.09	—	—	—	—	—	—	1.36	2.71	Honduras
—	—	—	—	—	—	—	—	—	—	—	—	—	—	2.00	Nicaragua
															Memorandum Items
299.63	538.96	550.24	502.52	400.28	269.96	50.65	23.57	133.39	223.44	373.76	484.47	606.03	620.90	595.23	**Non-Oil Develop.Ctys**

Total Fund Credit & Loans Outstdg.

	1970	1971	1972	1973	1974	1975	1976	1977	1978	1979	1980	1981	1982	1983	1984
					Expressed in Millions of SDRs										
World	3,232.34	1,346.99	1,089.16	1,027.39	3,740.09	7,435.03	12,607.69	13,230.58	11,118.36	9,343.59	11,109.27	16,358.70	22,297.78	32,841.86	37,675.34
Industrial Countries	2,440.03	497.39	—	—	1,514.47	3,488.08	6,115.85	6,877.62	4,495.37	1,978.58	1,216.11	545.80	138.18	376.25	593.40
United States	—	—	—	—	—	—	—	—	—	—	—	—	—	—	—
Canada	—	—	—	—	—	—	—	—	—	—	—	—	—	—	—
Australia	—	—	—	—	—	—	332.50	332.50	246.86	270.62	61.71	—	32.46	—	—
Japan	—	—	—	—	—	—	—	—	—	—	—	—	—	—	—
New Zealand	—	—	—	—	85.68	242.23	390.17	388.06	361.23	270.00	132.33	33.66	2.90	—	—
Belgium	—	—	—	—	—	—	—	—	—	—	—	—	—	—	—
Denmark	—	—	—	—	—	—	—	—	—	—	—	—	—	—	—
Finland	—	—	—	—	—	71.25	186.36	186.36	152.07	66.38	66.38	52.07	14.39	—	—
France	608.95	—	—	—	—	—	—	—	—	—	—	—	—	—	—
Germany	—	—	—	—	—	—	—	—	—	—	—	—	—	—	—
Greece	—	—	—	—	36.22	189.75	247.75	176.49	185.19	147.27	78.46	13.91	—	—	—
Iceland	1.76	—	—	—	15.50	31.35	56.42	56.42	47.27	34.71	15.71	5.92	22.35	21.50	21.50
Ireland	—	—	—	—	—	—	—	—	—	—	—	—	—	—	—
Italy	—	—	—	—	1,377.07	2,457.30	2,457.30	1,580.89	879.96	—	—	—	—	—	—
Luxembourg	—	—	—	—	—	—	—	—	—	—	—	—	—	—	—
Netherlands	—	—	—	—	—	—	—	—	—	—	—	—	—	—	—
Norway	—	—	—	—	—	—	—	—	—	—	—	—	—	—	—
Portugal	—	—	—	—	—	—	173.26	244.91	202.78	171.74	93.66	47.47	9.78	354.75	571.90
Spain	—	—	—	—	—	496.20	572.13	572.12	615.34	205.36	205.36	141.62	4.75	—	—
United Kingdom	1,829.32	497.39	—	—	—	—	1,699.96	3,339.87	1,804.67	812.50	562.50	312.50	51.55	—	—
Developing Countries	792.31	849.60	1,089.16	1,027.39	2,225.62	3,946.95	6,491.84	6,352.96	6,622.99	7,365.01	9,893.16	15,751.78	22,159.60	32,465.61	37,081.94
Africa	147.20	84.62	119.45	133.66	291.94	553.50	1,247.94	1,410.75	1,818.28	2,149.84	2,728.32	4,274.13	6,146.28	7,407.53	7,973.95
Algeria	—	—	—	—	—	—	—	—	—	—	—	—	—	—	—
Angola	—	—	—	—	—	—	—	—	—	—	—	—	—	—	—
Benin	—	—	—	—	—	—	—	—	5.39	5.39	12.65	12.70	12.70	12.48	11.40
Burkina Faso	—	—	—	—	—	—	—	—	5.39	9.33	12.65	12.70	12.70	12.48	11.40
Burundi	7.67	5.34	—	—	—	1.20	1.21	3.25	7.87	23.13	28.00	28.07	27.97	22.69	16.36
Cameroon	—	—	—	—	4.62	12.13	33.89	33.89	47.27	49.92	46.04	37.68	34.74	33.60	30.70
Cape Verde	—	—	—	—	—	—	—	—	—	—	—	—	—	—	—
Central African Rep.	—	—	—	—	2.66	4.85	9.59	9.59	15.67	13.57	18.43	32.41	34.19	38.15	35.77
Chad	2.47	2.32	2.18	1.02	3.11	2.97	9.47	9.47	13.54	12.99	10.81	12.49	12.49	12.26	8.52
Comoros	—	—	—	—	—	—	—	—	—	—	—	—	—	—	—
Congo, Dem. Rep. of	—	—	28.23	28.23	28.23	73.25	180.64	220.33	247.11	271.57	292.75	407.45	492.93	593.87	688.45
Congo, Republic of	—	—	—	—	—	—	—	9.34	16.68	21.58	17.44	12.70	12.63	12.27	11.12
Côte d'Ivoire	—	—	—	—	11.17	11.17	23.36	13.41	21.55	21.55	50.62	370.02	485.43	640.31	649.68
Djibouti	—	—	—	—	—	—	—	—	—	—	—	—	—	—	—
Equatorial Guinea	—	—	—	—	—	—	—	—	—	—	12.62	19.24	19.24	19.24	13.19
Ethiopia	—	—	—	—	—	—	—	—	11.19	55.77	62.29	124.39	145.64	127.64	100.22
Gabon	—	—	—	—	—	—	—	—	7.61	15.22	11.36	11.34	9.35	1.85	—
Gambia, The	—	—	—	—	—	—	—	4.26	11.70	10.36	12.67	21.70	36.35	33.52	33.65
Ghana	46.07	18.31	1.71	—	—	38.60	38.60	38.60	34.43	82.48	82.51	73.19	68.35	316.55	525.05
Guinea	3.45	2.95	2.95	1.02	9.51	7.11	7.11	18.38	19.98	26.16	27.45	23.67	34.95	34.28	32.29
Guinea-Bissau	—	—	—	—	—	—	—	—	—	—	1.10	1.10	2.95	2.68	2.26	3.73
Kenya	—	—	—	—	32.05	68.55	85.03	52.79	72.19	142.74	199.06	222.22	356.73	443.47	428.28
Lesotho	—	—	—	—	—	—	—	.54	2.08	3.59	4.87	4.89	4.89	4.75	4.33
Liberia	4.35	1.52	—	.06	—	—	—	3.11	12.02	50.98	69.78	115.27	176.82	223.75	237.25
Madagascar	—	—	—	—	3.45	14.30	14.30	15.67	24.19	20.65	68.23	100.23	151.95	158.05	173.79
Malawi	—	—	—	—	—	2.37	3.73	10.77	11.75	37.70	62.49	89.94	88.24	111.76	127.92
Mali	8.58	7.46	8.30	7.33	10.36	10.62	12.73	11.18	19.21	22.07	30.33	28.16	52.47	65.32	84.30
Mauritania	—	—	—	—	—	—	11.82	17.92	22.02	25.08	39.06	42.48	56.42	51.67	41.44
Mauritius	—	—	—	—	—	—	—	11.00	20.29	48.41	79.86	136.86	159.35	172.82	164.23
Morocco	27.54	—	—	—	—	—	115.46	127.56	220.00	231.88	358.35	497.37	897.52	985.48	1,107.19
Mozambique	—	—	—	—	—	—	—	—	—	—	—	—	—	—	—
Namibia	—	—	—	—	—	—	—	—	—	—	—	—	—	—	—
Niger	—	—	—	—	—	—	—	—	5.39	5.39	12.65	12.70	12.70	43.50	56.83
Nigeria	—	—	—	—	—	—	—	—	—	—	—	—	—	—	—
Rwanda	2.93	—	—	—	—	—	—	—	—	5.76	10.62	10.69	10.69	10.69	10.69
São Tomé & Príncipe	—	—	—	—	—	—	—	—	—	—	—	—	—	—	—
Senegal	—	—	—	—	—	25.43	25.43	25.44	57.00	70.51	109.88	160.21	200.04	220.45	234.67
Seychelles	—	—	—	—	—	—	—	—	—	—	—	—	—	—	—
Sierra Leone	—	—	—	—	4.32	4.94	22.42	32.10	35.60	43.76	46.56	72.16	70.87	88.85	97.47
Somalia	—	—	—	—	—	—	—	—	—	.14	14.03	39.98	72.22	117.22	114.34
South Africa	—	—	—	—	—	—	315.00	391.99	314.38	76.77	—	—	795.00	745.00	745.00
Sudan	30.87	15.18	28.10	29.03	71.65	113.39	119.08	99.47	150.64	222.44	337.98	484.77	524.61	666.65	677.60
Swaziland	—	—	—	—	—	—	—	—	—	—	2.43	4.47	4.50	14.48	14.48
Tanzania	—	—	—	—	38.85	62.62	83.63	91.23	81.46	115.47	134.32	125.72	114.38	88.11	60.19
Togo	—	—	—	—	—	—	7.50	7.50	6.22	10.76	25.48	32.78	32.78	51.90	63.49
Tunisia	13.27	2.56	—	—	—	—	—	24.00	24.00	24.00	—	—	—	—	—
Uganda	—	9.99	9.99	9.99	14.97	24.07	32.72	32.72	29.20	26.20	70.11	182.45	265.92	360.55	343.82
Zambia	—	18.99	37.99	56.98	56.99	75.93	95.22	95.24	245.12	342.99	350.80	670.55	618.34	678.51	753.79
Zimbabwe	—	—	—	—	—	—	—	—	—	—	—	37.50	37.50	191.10	261.32
Asia	372.11	364.61	477.37	396.54	1,202.73	1,817.72	2,112.46	1,909.89	2,088.32	2,258.20	3,827.43	6,909.52	9,009.65	11,329.02	11,628.26
Afghanistan, I.S. of	14.53	10.13	5.73	7.23	4.74	9.24	1.75	—	—	—	—	—	—	—	—
Bangladesh	—	—	62.50	62.50	133.31	171.60	235.81	207.76	229.43	262.26	332.58	398.94	496.22	539.99	471.61
Bhutan	—	—	—	—	—	—	—	—	—	—	—	—	—	—	—
Cambodia	—	—	6.25	12.50	12.50	12.50	12.50	12.50	12.50	12.50	12.50	12.50	12.50	12.50	12.50
China, People's Rep.	—	—	—	—	—	—	—	—	—	—	—	759.53	759.53	309.53	309.53
Fiji	—	—	—	—	.34	—	—	6.50	6.50	6.50	—	—	13.50	13.50	13.50
India	10.00	—	—	—	496.99	698.32	406.32	125.10	—	—	791.46	1,095.01	2,595.01	4,061.76	4,528.76
Indonesia	138.46	125.36	107.12	19.16	—	—	—	—	—	—	—	—	—	425.10	421.46
Kiribati	—	—	—	—	—	—	—	—	—	—	—	—	—	—	—
Korea	—	—	—	—	110.00	217.28	301.68	280.37	201.84	104.41	535.43	1,070.64	1,141.68	1,292.83	1,598.85
Lao People's Dem.Rep	—	—	—	—	—	3.25	6.50	6.50	15.89	18.30	21.22	25.64	25.64	25.64	19.88
Malaysia	—	7.28	7.28	—	—	93.00	.36	—	—	—	189.75	248.25	315.08	262.86
Maldives	—	—	—	—	—	—	—	—	—	—	—	—	—	—	—

1985	1986	1987	1988	1989	1990	1991	1992	1993	1994	1995	1996	1997	1998	1999	
							Expressed in Millions of SDRs								
37,650.06	35,348.07	30,618.26	26,523.99	24,649.93	23,303.72	26,681.80	27,791.13	29,159.11	30,260.95	41,636.11	42,058.58	52,614.70	66,781.74	57,534.14	**World**
593.40	582.65	373.05	—	—	—	—	—	—	—	—	—	—	—	—	**Industrial Countries**
—	—	—	—	—	—	—	—	—	—	—	—	—	—	—	United States
—	—	—	—	—	—	—	—	—	—	—	—	—	—	—	Canada
—	—	—	—	—	—	—	—	—	—	—	—	—	—	—	Australia
—	—	—	—	—	—	—	—	—	—	—	—	—	—	—	Japan
—	—	—	—	—	—	—	—	—	—	—	—	—	—	—	New Zealand
—	—	—	—	—	—	—	—	—	—	—	—	—	—	—	Belgium
—	—	—	—	—	—	—	—	—	—	—	—	—	—	—	Denmark
—	—	—	—	—	—	—	—	—	—	—	—	—	—	—	Finland
—	—	—	—	—	—	—	—	—	—	—	—	—	—	—	France
—	—	—	—	—	—	—	—	—	—	—	—	—	—	—	Germany
—	—	—	—	—	—	—	—	—	—	—	—	—	—	—	Greece
21.50	10.75	—	—	—	—	—	—	—	—	—	—	—	—	—	Iceland
—	—	—	—	—	—	—	—	—	—	—	—	—	—	—	Ireland
—	—	—	—	—	—	—	—	—	—	—	—	—	—	—	Italy
—	—	—	—	—	—	—	—	—	—	—	—	—	—	—	Luxembourg
—	—	—	—	—	—	—	—	—	—	—	—	—	—	—	Netherlands
—	—	—	—	—	—	—	—	—	—	—	—	—	—	—	Norway
571.90	571.90	373.05	—	—	—	—	—	—	—	—	—	—	—	—	Portugal
—	—	—	—	—	—	—	—	—	—	—	—	—	—	—	Spain
—	—	—	—	—	—	—	—	—	—	—	—	—	—	—	United Kingdom
37,056.66	34,765.42	30,245.21	26,523.99	24,649.93	23,303.72	26,681.80	27,791.13	29,159.11	30,260.95	41,636.11	42,058.58	52,614.70	66,781.74	57,534.14	**Developing Countries**
8,028.91	7,185.06	6,326.39	6,118.60	6,177.94	5,762.74	5,896.23	5,727.20	5,871.46	6,531.57	7,065.31	7,457.33	7,107.34	6,775.67	6,645.54	**Africa**
—	—	—	—	470.90	470.90	695.90	578.18	342.73	793.77	994.07	1,412.54	1,495.52	1,428.04	1,388.75	Algeria
															Angola
10.33	7.79	5.26	2.96	7.76	6.31	15.65	15.65	31.30	48.79	56.60	68.94	70.34	66.43	67.14	Benin
9.27	6.73	4.20	1.90	.44	.05	6.32	6.32	15.16	32.84	50.52	56.52	68.51	79.63	87.93	Burkina Faso
13.24	18.08	14.48	24.12	30.54	29.96	34.16	47.39	44.40	40.13	34.16	28.18	22.20	15.37	9.82	Burundi
24.95	18.13	11.32	74.64	86.18	85.11	84.28	45.66	11.86	29.91	34.41	50.11	68.91	110.94	142.65	Cameroon
															Cape Verde
35.49	34.13	36.58	37.33	26.88	25.73	23.28	22.09	20.96	28.34	23.48	19.22	13.80	12.47	17.09	Central African Rep.
10.90	8.93	13.97	12.24	17.92	21.42	21.42	21.42	20.20	29.30	32.97	45.20	45.31	45.34	50.17	Chad
						.90	.90	.90	2.25	2.25	2.25	2.07	1.89	1.58	Comoros
735.11	699.67	681.26	584.07	478.19	366.28	330.31	330.31	330.31	327.27	326.37	301.26	301.26	300.71	300.03	Congo, Dem. Rep. of
8.99	16.03	13.56	11.40	8.75	7.61	4.00	4.00	3.50	14.00	12.50	26.40	24.83	24.26	21.14	Congo, Republic of
605.53	538.67	425.81	377.88	281.25	303.14	259.72	194.46	159.13	224.75	287.10	349.57	333.48	457.34	451.39	Côte d'Ivoire
—	—	—	—	—	—	—	—	—	—	—	2.88	3.98	6.30	9.28	Djibouti
11.70	9.01	8.11	10.61	6.72	4.10	9.20	9.20	11.96	13.43	12.70	11.93	9.75	7.64	5.80	Equatorial Guinea
64.76	68.76	53.37	40.84	22.98	4.51	—	14.12	35.30	49.42	49.42	64.17	64.17	76.09	69.03	Ethiopia
—	—	27.41	42.50	98.68	102.69	98.49	84.34	58.55	32.89	61.42	64.95	83.26	97.20	80.52	62.60	Gabon
30.36	24.13	26.65	25.69	28.67	31.55	30.61	28.39	26.68	23.94	19.84	14.71	9.58	8.91	9.26	Gambia, The
637.97	642.26	610.94	566.36	561.16	523.39	583.12	537.83	537.30	479.70	436.24	377.35	256.98	236.91	225.84	Ghana
28.35	32.93	40.09	36.08	46.65	36.17	38.39	46.32	44.00	48.64	63.11	57.32	73.39	90.05	92.71	Guinea
2.80	1.87	3.14	2.20	3.75	3.75	3.75	3.75	3.45	3.15	3.98	5.33	9.04	10.95	12.63	Guinea-Bissau
474.73	375.90	282.89	338.44	316.12	338.88	344.85	286.09	264.34	277.25	251.46	234.52	185.60	139.53	95.80	Kenya
3.51	2.54	1.56	3.75	7.72	10.59	12.84	18.12	24.92	27.63	25.82	23.48	20.39	16.76	12.46	Lesotho
230.40	230.40	230.40	229.36	227.20	226.52	226.52	226.52	226.52	225.83	225.74	225.74	225.70	225.26	224.82	Liberia
167.63	165.96	167.72	141.39	125.79	100.98	88.67	77.14	67.04	58.58	48.89	50.82	51.47	41.22	45.81	Madagascar
132.47	108.96	82.43	78.55	76.45	80.83	80.45	66.86	62.62	76.90	78.02	83.06	78.42	72.57	63.79	Malawi
89.19	80.77	60.04	54.87	41.93	48.71	41.97	47.53	51.44	74.10	99.05	114.64	130.23	132.43	140.93	Mali
36.51	42.73	54.10	52.54	52.30	49.16	39.49	42.02	46.10	58.82	67.13	74.60	83.43	78.35	77.64	Mauritania
150.11	132.14	106.94	76.51	47.58	15.51	—	—	—	—	—	—	—	—	—	Mauritius
1,160.57	894.39	789.09	711.10	646.57	526.93	401.54	319.10	207.15	101.06	34.83	2.30	—	—	—	Morocco
—	—	12.20	30.50	42.70	51.85	82.35	126.88	137.86	145.24	135.79	125.89	140.11	147.24	145.42	Mozambique
															Namibia
71.25	86.76	86.33	70.33	64.37	59.66	51.30	44.58	37.74	41.78	35.04	36.61	45.02	54.07	49.65	Niger
															Nigeria
9.15	7.02	4.90	2.77	.65	.07	8.76	8.76	8.76	8.76	17.69	16.81	29.93	40.08	55.29	Rwanda
—	—	—	—	.80	.80	.80	.80	.80	.72	.56	.40	.24	.08	—	São Tomé & Príncipe
243.74	236.25	241.64	236.55	240.42	220.95	228.90	197.36	177.81	205.42	233.31	226.45	216.49	207.77	198.17	Senegal
															Seychelles
92.02	82.85	81.54	80.81	79.54	76.16	70.70	66.97	61.01	100.21	110.95	118.81	123.87	135.45	141.95	Sierra Leone
140.13	127.30	123.69	123.01	114.09	112.00	112.00	112.00	112.00	112.00	112.00	112.00	112.00	112.00	112.00	Somalia
745.00	397.50	—	—	—	—	—	—	614.43	614.43	614.43	614.43	307.22	—	—	South Africa
672.68	672.68	672.68	672.68	672.68	671.64	671.64	671.64	671.64	671.61	645.67	621.15	590.52	548.37	520.76	Sudan
12.85	8.57	4.30	1.16	.26	.03	—	—	—	—	—	—	—	—	—	Swaziland
52.62	58.15	80.00	105.10	97.82	98.35	100.20	160.50	156.22	145.52	132.68	143.41	182.35	190.24	227.60	Tanzania
67.60	73.82	60.13	57.89	57.38	61.12	55.29	55.82	49.87	56.04	70.43	62.53	64.94	67.36	60.44	Togo
—	149.71	190.71	205.71	205.71	123.73	180.10	211.05	207.30	207.30	197.11	165.00	128.39	91.78	55.16	Tunisia
277.59	203.44	192.76	187.59	171.20	198.22	230.91	250.11	243.02	262.59	280.65	290.05	291.74	282.74	270.81	Uganda
728.94	701.63	698.80	698.80	685.00	666.74	641.62	615.62	565.83	551.20	833.43	833.43	843.43	843.43	853.43	Zambia
240.47	191.06	110.30	52.20	22.24	4.84	—	157.20	205.00	257.50	310.00	304.07	285.53	289.18	268.80	Zimbabwe
10,669.76	9,933.73	8,058.36	6,267.08	5,378.75	3,608.97	5,030.78	5,952.44	6,365.68	5,816.83	4,846.87	3,673.42	15,538.86	24,173.17	17,908.69	**Asia**
															Afghanistan, I.S. of
473.29	440.47	592.66	623.88	546.78	439.69	523.24	547.69	511.75	473.37	433.12	374.18	287.93	308.43	237.56	Bangladesh
															Bhutan
12.50	12.50	12.50	12.50	12.50	12.50	12.50	6.25	6.25	20.25	48.25	48.25	48.25	47.21	53.12	Cambodia
309.53	876.30	814.40	752.49	690.59	329.82	—	—	—	—	—	—	—	—	—	China, People's Rep.
13.19	6.44	4.75	2.97	.59	—	—	—	—	—	—	—	—	—	—	Fiji
4,354.01	3,917.67	3,175.07	2,282.48	1,439.89	803.55	2,426.41	3,260.41	3,584.91	2,763.18	1,966.63	1,085.25	589.79	284.92	38.50	India
41.96	41.96	504.86	462.90	462.90	347.18	115.73	—	—	—	—	—	2,201.47	6,455.82	7,466.82	Indonesia
															Kiribati
1,373.03	1,266.25	369.78	—	—	—	—	—	—	—	—	—	8,200.00	12,000.00	4,462.50	Korea
11.36	6.96	4.43	1.90	6.30	5.91	14.65	20.51	26.38	32.24	42.80	46.61	48.96	44.27	38.41	Lao People's Dem.Rep
107.21	—	—	—	—	—	—	—	—	—	—	—	—	—	—	Malaysia
															Maldives

Total Fund Credit & Loans Outstdg.

	1970	1971	1972	1973	1974	1975	1976	1977	1978	1979	1980	1981	1982	1983	1984
						Expressed in Millions of SDRs									
Asia (cont.)															
Mongolia	—	—	—	—	—	—	—	—	—	—	—	—	—	—	—
Myanmar	16.47	17.97	7.98	14.98	36.48	40.48	34.48	58.10	85.29	97.02	87.71	107.55	130.25	141.52	129.71
Nepal	—	—	—	—	—	—	4.49	5.99	15.31	18.56	32.63	32.48	27.66	22.40	15.80
Pakistan	45.38	42.59	110.70	129.82	238.87	374.41	439.55	462.78	492.46	434.76	528.49	879.65	1,286.16	1,540.25	1,469.20
Palau	—	—	—	—	—	—	—	—	—	—	—	—	—	—	—
Papua New Guinea	—	—	—	—	—	—	24.80	24.80	23.09	18.10	24.28	64.55	64.55	64.55	34.59
Philippines	68.75	89.74	95.25	76.25	67.81	164.68	348.41	435.01	505.53	617.99	819.65	974.50	905.92	1,045.55	903.24
Samoa	....	....	....	....	....	....	....	....	....	....	....	.80	2.40	....	3.16
Solomon Islands														3.36	
Sri Lanka	78.52	71.54	74.56	74.10	101.69	124.70	134.25	169.94	226.50	304.78	306.53	442.63	437.22	425.15	413.04
Thailand	—	—	—	—	—	—	67.00	81.34	191.29	278.14	273.06	737.14	767.16	993.76	921.61
Tonga	—	—	—	—	—	—	—	—	—	—	—	—	—	—	—
Vietnam	—	—	—	—	—	—	—	31.00	79.20	80.13	57.38	111.80	90.30	88.99	88.99
Europe	**74.13**	**128.88**	**83.50**	**69.25**	**192.88**	**458.37**	**936.35**	**862.85**	**948.68**	**1,111.07**	**1,710.74**	**2,739.41**	**3,917.91**	**4,929.39**	**5,371.81**
Albania	—	—	—	—	—	—	—	—	—	—	—	—	—	—	—
Armenia	—	—	—	—	—	—	—	—	—	—	—	—	—	—	—
Azerbaijan	—	—	—	—	—	—	—	—	—	—	—	—	—	—	—
Belarus	—	—	—	—	—	—	—	—	—	—	—	—	—	—	—
Bosnia & Herzegovina	—	—	—	—	—	—	—	—	—	—	—	—	—	—	—
Bulgaria	—	—	—	—	—	—	—	—	—	—	—	—	—	—	—
Croatia	—	—	—	—	—	—	—	—	—	—	—	—	—	—	—
Cyprus	—	—	—	—	6.38	8.10	43.07	43.07	32.92	37.98	30.60	21.62	12.30	5.47	3.17
Czech Republic	—	—	—	—	—	—	—	—	—	—	—	—	—	—	—
Czechoslovakia	—	—	—	—	—	—	—	—	—	—	—	—	—	—	—
Estonia	—	—	—	—	—	—	—	—	—	—	—	—	—	—	—
Georgia	—	—	—	—	—	—	—	—	—	—	—	—	—	—	—
Hungary	—	—	—	—	—	—	—	—	—	—	—	—	214.50	547.00	972.00
Kazakhstan	—	—	—	—	—	—	—	—	—	—	—	—	—	—	—
Kyrgyz Republic	—	—	—	—	—	—	—	—	—	—	—	—	—	—	—
Latvia	—	—	—	—	—	—	—	—	—	—	—	—	—	—	—
Lithuania	—	—	—	—	—	—	—	—	—	—	—	—	—	—	—
Macedonia, FYR	—	—	—	—	—	—	—	—	—	—	—	—	—	—	—
Moldova	—	—	—	—	—	—	—	—	—	—	—	—	—	—	—
Poland	—	—	—	—	—	—	—	—	—	—	—	—	—	—	—
Romania	—	—	—	47.50	47.50	87.50	237.50	270.00	255.55	246.80	257.42	506.66	781.61	904.65	955.74
Russia	—	—	—	—	—	—	—	—	—	—	—	—	—	—	—
Slovak Republic	—	—	—	—	—	—	—	—	—	—	—	—	—	—	—
Slovenia	—	—	—	—	—	—	—	—	—	—	—	—	—	—	—
Tajikistan	—	—	—	—	—	—	—	—	—	—	—	—	—	—	—
Turkey	74.13	62.13	—	—	—	207.57	336.81	336.81	477.68	480.29	826.58	1,135.63	1,319.18	1,497.09	1,455.03
Ukraine	—	—	—	—	—	—	—	—	—	—	—	—	—	—	—
Uzbekistan	—	—	—	—	—	—	—	—	—	—	—	—	—	—	—
Yugoslavia, SFR	—	66.75	83.50	21.75	139.00	155.20	318.97	212.97	182.53	346.00	596.14	1,075.50	1,590.32	1,975.18	1,985.87
Middle East	**71.32**	**111.56**	**51.51**	**81.63**	**140.14**	**300.13**	**499.99**	**600.20**	**689.39**	**645.31**	**516.45**	**388.52**	**307.38**	**280.28**	**259.88**
Bahrain	—	—	—	—	—	—	—	—	—	—	—	—	—	—	—
Egypt	49.34	69.84	24.40	62.17	92.95	68.22	177.90	275.01	374.23	381.37	322.06	268.84	235.73	227.77	209.78
Iran, I.R. of	—	—	—	—	—	—	—	—	—	—	—	—	—	—	—
Iraq	—	—	—	—	—	—	—	—	—	—	—	—	—	.01	—
Israel	12.48	32.48	—	—	32.50	208.25	285.25	285.24	271.26	224.21	156.40	87.54	27.15	—	—
Jordan	—	4.49	4.49	1.59	.01	.01	.01	.01	—	—	—	—	—	—	—
Syrian Arab Republic	9.50	4.75	22.62	17.87	5.37	—	—	—	—	.75	—	—	—	—	—
Yemen Arab Rep.	—	—	—	—	—	—	—	—	—	—	—	—	—	9.75	9.75
Yemen, P.D. Rep.	—	—	—	—	9.31	23.65	36.83	39.94	43.90	38.98	37.99	32.14	44.50	42.75	40.35
Yemen, Republic of	—	—	—	—	—	—	—	—	—	—	—	—	—	—	—
Western Hemisphere	**127.55**	**159.93**	**357.33**	**346.31**	**397.93**	**817.23**	**1,695.10**	**1,569.27**	**1,078.32**	**1,200.59**	**1,110.22**	**1,440.20**	**2,778.38**	**8,519.39**	**11,848.04**
Antigua and Barbuda	—	—	—	—	—	—	—	—	—	—	—	—	—	—	—
Argentina	—	—	174.00	174.00	64.00	250.09	455.59	344.50	—	—	—	—	—	1,120.61	1,120.61
Barbados	—	—	—	—	—	—	—	6.50	6.50	6.50	2.27	.77	22.18	35.79	43.59
Belize	—	—	—	—	—	—	—	—	—	—	—	—	—	3.60	4.80
Bolivia	6.08	6.60	7.88	18.05	14.32	13.93	—	—	30.33	30.33	99.04	97.31	114.25	121.40	98.03
Brazil	—	—	—	—	—	—	—	—	—	—	—	—	498.75	2,525.72	4,269.87
Chile	1.49	39.50	79.00	79.00	159.97	330.79	402.22	300.62	266.49	135.94	96.31	41.80	5.68	579.00	795.00
Colombia	54.85	53.25	—	—	—	—	—	—	—	—	—	—	—	—	—
Costa Rica	—	—	—	18.84	29.96	32.30	29.31	24.32	43.81	44.64	88.16	84.18	183.28	158.98	
Dominica	—	—	—	—	—	—	—	—	—	—	1.90	1.65	6.47	9.32	11.00	10.66
Dominican Republic	6.55	10.75	3.75	—	—	—	21.50	36.50	36.50	94.33	38.02	19.77	64.06	235.15	225.69
Ecuador	13.75	5.50	8.25	—	—	—	—	—	—	—	—	—	—	203.53	242.90
El Salvador	6.49	10.19	8.75	—	17.89	17.89	12.82	—	—	—	24.95	57.33	117.07	132.57	127.20
Grenada	—	—	—	—	—	.81	1.21	1.42	2.03	2.40	2.21	7.10	6.27	7.32	6.30
Guatemala	—	—	—	—	—	—	—	—	—	—	—	95.60	95.60	133.85	152.98
Guyana	—	2.06	—	3.87	5.00	—	17.25	17.25	30.27	40.49	67.40	85.31	89.07	85.01	84.01
Haiti	2.19	.80	—	—	6.64	10.97	12.38	10.47	15.51	19.34	35.65	50.56	61.44	90.09	102.27
Honduras	—	—	—	—	16.78	16.78	16.78	4.29	—	7.58	25.73	46.46	108.16	154.06	152.47
Jamaica	—	—	—	13.25	13.25	13.25	68.94	88.14	138.58	266.76	242.49	403.51	528.41	599.08	641.41
Mexico	—	—	—	—	—	—	319.1	419.1	229.4	103.1	—	—	200.6	1,203.8	2,407.5
Nicaragua	8.00	10.99	8.25	12.24	10.06	15.50	8.74	2.00	2.01	43.51	38.67	21.19	17.54	13.29	9.04
Panama	—	—	—	—	7.37	17.52	42.62	42.16	40.32	31.45	18.09	80.45	76.12	184.13	276.61
Paraguay	—	—	—	—	—	—	—	—	—	—	—	—	—	—	—
Peru	9.90	3.27	30.75	13.64	—	—	158.75	168.75	256.09	373.14	371.55	332.86	588.81	666.31	688.28
St. Kitts and Nevis	—	—	—	—	—	—	—	—	—	—	—	—	—	—	—
St. Lucia	—	—	—	—	—	—	—	—	—	—	—	1.35	4.05	2.55	2.55	2.02
St. Vincent & Grens.	—	—	—	—	—	—	—	—	—	—	.20	1.50	1.50	1.50	1.01
Suriname	—	—	—	—	—	—	—	—	—	—	—	—	—	—	—
Trinidad and Tobago	—	—	—	—	—	—	—	—	—	—	—	—	—	—	—
Uruguay	18.25	17.02	36.70	32.26	63.81	99.74	124.88	98.24	—	—	—	—	86.80	226.80	226.80
Venezuela, Rep. Bol.	—	—	—	—	—	—	—	—	—	—	—	—	—	—	—
Memorandum Items															
Oil Exporting Ctys	138.46	125.36	107.12	19.16	—	—	—	—	—	—	—	—	—	425.11	421.46
Non-Oil Develop.Ctys	653.85	724.24	982.04	1,008.23	2,225.62	3,946.95	6,491.84	6,352.96	6,622.99	7,365.01	9,893.16	15,751.77	22,159.60	32,040.50	36,660.48

Expressed in Millions of SDRs

Asia (cont.)

	1985	1986	1987	1988	1989	1990	1991	1992	1993	1994	1995	1996	1997	1998	1999
Mongolia	—	—	—	—	—	—	11.25	13.75	23.03	37.87	31.62	30.31	35.25	34.32	37.47
Myanmar	106.36	67.97	28.90	7.97	2.03	.20	—	—	—	—	—	—	—	—	—
Nepal	19.83	19.20	30.31	39.16	39.85	30.89	26.90	31.71	35.81	37.67	32.45	27.23	22.01	17.16	12.87
Pakistan	1,288.51	973.24	647.20	411.43	709.66	587.26	746.37	819.86	816.50	1,096.83	1,114.95	1,000.51	979.55	996.03	1,271.18
Palau															
Papua New Guinea	26.33	12.34	8.44	4.55	2.31	42.91	42.84	42.84	32.13	10.71	33.34	35.34	35.34	32.35	15.68
Philippines	1,048.75	1,034.60	888.06	812.55	895.26	640.87	759.02	800.12	880.74	728.56	489.48	281.94	633.82	1,113.96	1,327.73
Samoa	9.95	8.28	5.79	2.85	1.23	.59	.16	—	—	—	—	—	—	—	—
Solomon Islands	2.76	2.83	1.55	1.25	1.09	.47	—	—	—	—	—	—	—	—	—
Sri Lanka	361.09	283.55	195.11	267.10	278.31	288.10	280.17	337.77	375.71	422.78	400.47	369.24	321.21	260.83	188.12
Thailand	1,021.11	874.18	685.56	492.11	207.45	.51	—	—	—	—	—	—	1,800.00	2,300.00	2,500.00
Tonga															
Vietnam	88.99	88.99	88.99	88.99	82.01	78.52	71.54	71.54	72.48	193.36	253.76	374.56	335.29	277.87	258.71
Europe	**4,792.79**	**4,004.67**	**2,775.86**	**1,773.89**	**905.53**	**917.13**	**3,464.62**	**4,695.05**	**6,159.49**	**8,036.38**	**11,400.27**	**13,945.27**	**15,708.50**	**19,644.89**	**17,385.41**
Albania	—	—	—	—	—	—	—	9.69	21.60	37.13	43.40	37.70	40.74	45.77	58.69
Armenia	—	—	—	—	—	—	—	—	16.88	47.25	81.00	97.88	135.25	146.62	
Azerbaijan	—	—	—	—	—	—	—	—	—	67.86	121.68	197.73	228.14	296.73	
Belarus	—	—	—	—	—	—	—	—	70.10	70.10	190.20	190.20	190.20	172.27	129.74
Bosnia & Herzegovina	—	—	—	—	—	—	—	—	—	—	32.47	31.02	30.30	54.54	68.42
Bulgaria	—	—	—	—	—	—	289.23	428.90	459.90	644.41	482.12	407.25	698.02	792.27	910.74
Croatia	—	—	—	—	—	—	—	—	14.82	87.06	148.56	145.44	172.66	166.12	143.23
Cyprus															
Czech Republic	—	—	—	—	—	—	—	—	780.68	—	—	—	—	—	—
Czechoslovakia	—	—	—	—	—	.01	917.94	1,121.50							
Estonia	—	—	—	—	—	—	—	7.75	41.85	41.85	61.81	54.15	40.01	21.31	18.41
Georgia	—	—	—	—	—	—	—	—	27.75	77.70	133.20	188.70	215.76	233.33	
Hungary	883.71	842.73	569.87	471.30	347.11	231.68	880.21	875.84	896.30	781.58	258.72	118.72	118.72	—	—
Kazakhstan	—	—	—	—	—	—	—	—	61.88	198.00	290.82	383.60	378.96	463.66	335.15
Kyrgyz Republic	—	—	—	—	—	—	—	—	43.86	53.32	83.64	97.10	122.20	124.43	138.69
Latvia	—	—	—	—	—	—	25.16	77.78	109.80	107.89	90.36	63.67	45.37	34.31	
Lithuania	—	—	—	—	—	—	17.25	87.98	134.55	175.95	190.11	200.46	179.83	167.76	
Macedonia, FYR	—	—	—	—	—	—	—	2.81	14.03	38.09	47.40	65.29	72.72	74.10	
Moldova	—	—	—	—	—	—	—	63.00	112.45	154.85	172.29	172.73	125.56	127.69	
Poland	—	—	—	—	—	357.50	596.60	596.60	497.69	918.59					
Romania	782.85	583.53	357.55	106.91	—	—	565.80	750.90	750.90	906.41	698.34	452.97	475.15	382.85	333.85
Russia	—	—	—	—	—	—	—	719.00	1,797.28	2,875.55	6,469.80	8,698.16	9,805.91	13,731.99	11,102.28
Slovak Republic	—	—	—	—	—	—	—	—	405.17	439.81	307.54	221.97	184.42	134.64	96.53
Slovenia	—	—	—	—	—	—	—	—	8.53	4.94	2.69	.90			
Tajikistan	—	—	—	—	—	—	—	—	—	—	15.00	22.50	70.30	73.21	
Turkey	1,207.51	887.19	542.97	222.03	36.25	—	—	—	235.50	460.50	460.50	440.44	275.81	648.85	
Ukraine	—	—	—	—	—	—	—	—	249.33	1,037.30	1,573.30	1,780.56	1,985.05	2,044.62	
Uzbekistan	—	—	—	—	—	—	—	—	—	—	105.95	165.20	165.20	146.83	
Yugoslavia, SFR	1,918.72	1,691.22	1,305.47	973.65	522.17	327.94	214.84	142.46	77.36	77.36	56.82	56.06	56.06	56.06	56.65
Middle East	**267.88**	**201.83**	**252.57**	**181.15**	**196.83**	**154.06**	**155.24**	**407.03**	**385.02**	**409.73**	**350.32**	**353.34**	**501.96**	**571.78**	**660.49**
Bahrain															
Egypt	167.08	117.98	184.88	141.04	122.43	87.71	89.00	147.20	147.20	132.20	69.50	10.90	—	—	—
Iran, I.R. of															
Iraq															
Israel	—	.01	—	—	—	—	—	178.64	178.64	178.64	111.65	22.33	—	—	—
Jordan	57.40	57.40	57.40	35.88	73.41	66.24	66.24	81.19	59.18	98.89	169.17	236.11	316.58	333.41	362.86
Syrian Arab Republic															
Yemen Arab Rep.	9.75	6.11	1.22	....			....	....	....	....	....	....	....	....	....
Yemen, P.D. Rep.	33.65	20.33	9.07	4.23	.99	....									
Yemen, Republic of						.11	—	—	—	—	—	84.00	185.38	238.38	297.63
Western Hemisphere	**13,297.32**	**13,440.13**	**12,832.03**	**12,183.28**	**11,990.88**	**12,860.81**	**12,134.92**	**11,009.41**	**10,377.46**	**9,466.44**	**17,973.34**	**16,629.23**	**13,758.05**	**15,616.23**	**14,934.01**
Antigua and Barbuda															
Argentina	2,105.11	2,240.85	2,716.24	2,733.00	2,358.82	2,167.20	1,735.92	1,682.80	2,562.44	2,884.69	4,124.39	4,376.04	4,349.28	3,865.09	3,262.60
Barbados	43.59	32.42	15.60	7.75	3.27	.50	—	36.84	36.84	36.84	24.94	6.52	—	—	—
Belize	9.54	9.54	8.03	5.79	2.52	.30									
Bolivia	74.85	157.25	130.90	155.32	191.61	180.68	171.14	181.15	160.54	180.53	180.13	192.02	183.91	187.63	179.96
Brazil	4,205.40	3,679.86	2,802.88	2,476.82	1,843.36	1,279.68	865.14	581.40	221.02	127.50	95.23	47.02	23.31	3,426.78	6,431.00
Chile	990.60	1,088.25	1,032.38	982.58	966.46	812.90	669.38	525.02	346.50	199.48	—	—	—	—	—
Colombia															
Costa Rica	171.64	140.95	93.27	53.03	26.94	7.94	58.03	59.28	59.28	45.46	16.32	.50	—	—	—
Dominica	9.17	8.63	8.23	6.57	4.99	4.00	3.32	2.78	2.26	1.71	1.15	.59	.19	.03	—
Dominican Republic	270.43	248.83	199.89	161.76	93.25	50.44	62.37	89.44	135.48	129.88	107.46	66.45	21.13	39.70	39.70
Ecuador	327.30	397.68	345.18	300.68	247.23	186.00	127.53	72.61	51.77	135.73	116.69	100.86	98.90	49.45	—
El Salvador	100.62	50.86	15.75	7.96	4.05	.13	—	—	—	—	—	—	—	—	—
Grenada	3.83	2.13	1.47	.91	.35	.01									
Guatemala	105.18	57.19	41.65	65.40	55.51	46.82	44.76	22.38	—	—	—	—	—	—	—
Guyana	83.01	82.45	81.74	81.74	80.91	79.38	104.46	122.17	128.60	122.25	115.60	117.11	116.44	109.50	102.15
Haiti	87.37	72.78	51.05	33.75	30.55	25.45	23.82	23.82	23.82	3.78	18.16	31.58	31.58	40.75	32.55
Honduras	133.72	89.54	54.37	27.29	26.96	22.66	23.55	81.35	86.01	74.81	66.36	40.28	33.90	80.04	153.33
Jamaica	631.10	554.42	478.23	358.77	291.75	250.74	273.64	259.69	244.19	217.64	161.71	112.24	87.13	74.66	60.78
Mexico	2,703.3	3,319.3	3,639.3	3,570.3	3,873.6	4,604.9	4,729.9	4,327.0	3,485.2	2,644.2	10,648.1	9,234.5	6,735.2	5,951.5	3,259.2
Nicaragua	.01	—	—	—	—	—	17.03	17.03	17.03	34.92	26.41	20.02	20.02	36.84	113.15
Panama	283.36	288.63	243.90	243.79	243.19	191.27	150.69	79.80	82.32	91.27	74.36	90.99	105.39	125.53	108.33
Paraguay															
Peru	639.00	595.51	595.44	595.42	576.98	530.46	493.41	458.72	642.69	642.69	642.69	642.69	749.63	642.51	535.40
St. Kitts and Nevis	—	—	—	—	—	—	—	—	—	—	—	—	—	1.63	1.63
St. Lucia	.30	—	—	—	—	—	—	—	—	—	—	—	—	—	—
St. Vincent & Grens.	.33	—	—	—	—	—	—	—	—	—	—	—	—	—	—
Suriname															
Trinidad and Tobago	—	—	—	85.05	155.75	231.55	269.05	205.30	112.80	62.44	33.75	16.46	3.13	—	—
Uruguay	318.55	323.07	276.58	229.65	153.35	70.78	40.43	38.13	27.90	20.48	13.98	5.99	—	114.20	114.20
Venezuela, Rep. Bol.	—	—	—	—	759.47	2,116.98	2,271.33	2,142.75	1,950.74	1,810.16	1,505.96	1,527.42	1,198.89	870.36	540.02
Memorandum Items															
Oil Exporting Ctys	41.96	41.96	504.86	462.90	1,693.27	2,935.06	3,082.96	2,720.93	2,293.47	2,603.93	2,500.03	2,939.96	4,895.88	8,754.21	9,395.59
Non-Oil Develop.Ctys	37,014.70	34,723.46	29,740.35	26,061.09	22,956.66	20,368.66	23,598.84	25,070.20	26,865.64	27,657.02	39,136.08	39,118.62	47,718.82	58,027.53	48,138.55

(See notes in the back of the book.)

	1970	1971	1972	1973	1974	1975	1976	1977	1978	1979	1980	1981	1982	1983	1984
					Expressed in Millions of SDRs										
World	3,232.3	1,347.0	1,089.2	1,027.4	3,740.1	7,435.0	12,607.7	13,077.6	10,277.3	7,976.0	8,485.7	13,367.6	19,309.6	29,898.9	34,905.5
Industrial Countries	2,440.0	497.4	—	—	1,514.5	3,488.1	6,115.9	6,877.6	4,495.4	1,978.6	1,216.1	607.2	138.2	376.3	593.4
United States	—	—	—	—	—	—	—	—	—	—	—	—	—	—	—
Canada	—	—	—	—	—	—	—	—	—	—	—	—	—	—	—
Australia	—	—	—	—	—	—	332.50	332.50	246.86	270.62	61.71	—	32.46	—	—
Japan	—	—	—	—	—	—	—	—	—	—	—	—	—	—	—
New Zealand	—	—	—	—	85.68	242.23	390.17	388.06	361.23	270.00	132.33	33.66	2.90	—	—
Belgium	—	—	—	—	—	—	—	—	—	—	—	—	—	—	—
Denmark	—	—	—	—	—	—	—	—	—	—	—	—	—	—	—
Finland	—	—	—	—	—	71.25	186.36	186.36	152.07	66.38	66.38	52.07	14.39	—	—
France	608.95	—	—	—	—	—	—	—	—	—	—	—	—	—	—
Greece	—	—	—	—	36.22	189.75	247.75	176.49	185.19	147.27	78.46	13.91	—	—	—
Iceland	1.76	—	—	—	15.50	31.35	56.42	56.42	47.27	34.71	15.71	5.92	22.35	21.50	21.50
Ireland	—	—	—	—	—	—	—	—	—	—	—	—	—	—	—
Italy	—	—	—	—	1,377.07	2,457.30	2,457.30	1,580.89	879.96	—	—	—	—	—	—
Netherlands	—	—	—	—	—	—	—	—	—	—	—	—	—	—	—
Norway	—	—	—	—	—	—	—	—	—	—	—	—	—	—	—
Portugal	—	—	—	—	—	—	173.26	244.91	202.78	171.74	93.66	47.47	9.78	354.75	571.90
Spain	—	—	—	—	—	496.20	572.13	572.12	615.34	205.36	205.36	141.62	4.75	—	—
United Kingdom	1,829.32	497.39	—	—	—	—	1,699.96	3,339.87	1,804.67	812.50	562.50	312.50	51.55	—	—
Developing Countries	792.3	849.6	1,089.2	1,027.4	2,225.6	3,947.0	6,491.8	6,200.0	5,782.0	5,997.4	7,269.6	12,760.5	19,171.4	29,522.7	34,312.1
Africa	147.2	84.6	119.5	133.7	291.9	553.5	1,247.9	1,360.9	1,471.7	1,538.5	1,790.4	3,332.2	5,206.4	6,484.2	7,121.4
Algeria	—	—	—	—	—	—	—	—	—	—	—	—	—	—	—
Burkina Faso	—	—	—	—	—	—	—	—	—	—	—	—	—	—	—
Burundi	7.67	5.34	—	—	—	1.20	1.21	1.22	—	9.50	9.50	9.50	9.50	4.75	—
Cameroon	—	—	—	—	4.62	12.13	33.89	33.89	32.76	24.81	11.97	3.48	.54	—	—
Central African Rep.	—	—	—	—	2.66	4.85	9.59	9.59	10.28	8.18	5.78	19.71	21.49	25.67	24.37
Chad	2.47	2.32	2.18	1.02	3.11	2.97	9.47	9.47	8.15	7.60	5.42	7.10	7.10	7.10	4.44
Comoros	—	—	—	—	—	—	—	—	—	—	—	—	—	—	—
Congo, Dem. Rep. of	—	—	28.23	28.23	28.23	73.25	180.64	208.24	200.27	190.49	182.75	297.02	383.10	487.20	591.15
Congo, Republic of	—	—	—	—	—	—	—	7.95	11.29	12.25	4.79	—	—	—	—
Côte d'Ivoire	—	—	—	—	11.17	11.17	23.36	13.41	—	—	—	319.20	434.61	589.49	603.17
Djibouti	—	—	—	—	—	—	—	—	—	—	—	—	—	—	—
Equatorial Guinea	—	—	—	—	—	—	—	—	—	—	8.15	14.74	14.74	14.74	8.69
Ethiopia	—	—	—	—	—	—	—	—	—	36.40	36.00	98.00	119.25	101.25	76.07
Gabon	—	—	—	—	—	—	—	—	7.61	15.22	11.36	11.34	9.35	1.85	—
Gambia, The	—	—	—	—	—	—	—	3.51	8.80	5.34	5.86	14.86	29.51	25.68	27.59
Ghana	46.07	18.31	1.71	—	—	38.60	38.60	38.60	34.43	56.12	33.88	24.23	19.39	267.59	477.20
Guinea	3.45	2.95	2.95	1.02	9.51	7.11	7.11	15.81	10.03	8.94	4.09	.22	11.50	11.50	11.50
Guinea-Bissau	—	—	—	—	—	—	—	—	—	1.10	1.10	2.95	2.68	2.26	3.73
Kenya	—	—	—	—	32.05	68.55	85.03	47.65	52.29	108.30	152.33	175.31	310.08	398.16	387.56
Lesotho	—	—	—	—	—	—	—	—	—	—	—	—	—	—	—
Liberia	4.35	1.52	—	.06	—	—	—	—	—	30.18	41.55	86.93	148.63	196.38	212.14
Madagascar	—	—	—	—	3.45	14.30	14.30	15.67	13.41	9.87	42.92	74.82	126.54	133.09	150.99
Malawi	—	—	—	—	—	2.37	3.73	9.16	5.53	26.94	47.89	75.28	73.58	97.52	114.92
Mali	8.58	7.46	8.30	7.33	10.36	10.62	12.73	11.18	10.09	6.29	8.91	6.66	30.97	44.20	65.01
Mauritania	—	—	—	—	—	—	—	11.82	16.53	16.63	15.75	26.41	29.78	39.33	30.34
Mauritius	—	—	—	—	—	—	—	11.00	11.17	39.29	70.74	127.74	150.23	164.08	157.32
Morocco	27.54	—	—	—	—	—	115.46	115.47	173.16	150.80	248.35	386.94	787.69	878.81	1,011.34
Nigeria	—	—	—	—	—	—	—	—	—	—	—	—	—	—	—
Niger	—	—	—	—	—	—	—	—	—	—	—	—	—	30.80	45.20
Rwanda	2.93	—	—	—	—	—	—	—	—	—	—	—	—	—	—
Senegal	—	—	—	—	—	25.43	25.43	25.44	42.91	46.11	76.78	126.98	166.81	187.81	204.85
Sierra Leone	—	—	—	—	4.32	4.94	22.42	29.42	25.23	25.82	22.22	47.73	46.44	65.12	75.81
Somalia	—	—	—	—	—	—	—	—	.14	.14	3.41	29.29	61.53	106.53	103.65
South Africa	—	—	—	—	—	—	315.00	391.99	314.38	76.77	—	—	795.00	745.00	745.00
Sudan	30.87	15.18	28.10	29.03	71.65	113.39	119.08	99.47	120.80	170.79	267.89	414.41	454.25	596.29	610.22
Swaziland	—	—	—	—	—	—	—	—	—	—	—	—	9.98	—	9.98
Tanzania	—	—	—	—	38.85	62.62	83.63	86.74	64.06	85.35	93.44	84.68	73.56	48.46	24.03
Togo	—	—	—	—	—	—	—	7.50	7.50	—	—	10.88	18.12	18.12	37.50	50.33
Tunisia	13.27	2.56	—	—	—	—	24.00	24.00	24.00	—	—	—	—	—	—
Uganda	—	9.99	9.99	9.99	14.97	24.07	32.72	32.72	29.20	26.20	47.75	159.94	243.41	338.04	321.31
Zambia	—	18.99	37.99	56.98	56.99	75.93	95.22	95.24	245.12	319.96	308.31	627.78	575.57	635.74	711.99
Zimbabwe	—	—	—	—	—	—	—	—	—	—	—	37.50	191.10	261.32
Asia	372.1	364.6	477.4	396.5	1,202.7	1,817.7	2,112.5	1,832.3	1,707.8	1,695.6	2,443.0	5,173.9	7,274.9	9,616.3	9,992.4
Afghanistan, I.S. of	14.53	10.13	5.73	7.23	4.74	9.24	1.75	—	—	—	—	—	—	—	—
Bangladesh	—	—	62.50	62.50	133.31	171.60	235.81	194.38	177.62	172.57	210.89	276.78	374.06	421.33	363.32
Bhutan	—	—	—	—	—	—	—	—	—	—	—	—	—	—	—
Cambodia	—	—	6.25	12.50	12.50	12.50	12.50	12.50	12.50	12.50	12.50	12.50	12.50	12.50	12.50
China, People's Rep.	—	—	—	—	—	—	—	—	—	—	—	450.00	450.00	—	—
Fiji	—	—	—	—	.34	—	—	6.50	6.50	6.50	—	13.50	13.50	13.50
India	10.00	—	—	—	496.99	698.32	406.32	125.10	—	—	266.00	566.00	2,066.00	3,532.75	3,999.75
Indonesia	138.46	125.36	107.12	19.16	—	—	—	—	—	—	—	—	425.10	421.46
Korea	—	—	—	—	110.00	217.28	301.68	280.37	201.84	104.41	535.43	1,070.64	1,141.68	1,292.83	1,598.85
Lao People's Dem.Rep	—	—	—	—	—	3.25	6.50	6.50	10.50	8.97	8.57	12.94	12.94	12.94	8.25
Malaysia	—	7.28	7.28	—	—	—	93.00	.36	—	—	—	189.75	248.25	315.08	262.86
Mongolia	—	—	—	—	—	—	—	—	—	—	—	—	—	—	—
Myanmar	16.47	17.97	7.98	14.98	36.48	40.48	34.48	51.68	60.42	53.97	29.30	48.91	71.61	84.56	78.50
Nepal	—	—	—	—	—	—	4.49	4.49	9.50	8.51	19.00	18.80	14.05	9.18	3.93
Pakistan	45.38	42.59	110.70	129.82	238.87	374.41	439.55	437.64	395.06	337.36	299.73	650.00	1,056.51	1,317.18	1,265.61
Palau	—	—	—	—	—	—	—	—	—	—	—	—	—	—	—

Expressed in Millions of SDRs

1985	1986	1987	1988	1989	1990	1991	1992	1993	1994	1995	1996	1997	1998	1999	
35,179.8	33,334.9	28,752.0	24,750.1	22,315.1	20,731.9	23,378.6	23,967.2	25,196.8	25,611.7	35,929.2	36,127.5	46,559.0	60,451.0	51,061.9	**World**
—	—	—	—	—	—	—	—	—	—	—	—	—	—	—	**Industrial Countries**
593.4	582.7	373.1	—	—	—	—	—	—	—	—	—	—	—	—	United States
—	—	—	—	—	—	—	—	—	—	—	—	—	—	—	Canada
—	—	—	—	—	—	—	—	—	—	—	—	—	—	—	Australia
—	—	—	—	—	—	—	—	—	—	—	—	—	—	—	Japan
—	—	—	—	—	—	—	—	—	—	—	—	—	—	—	New Zealand
—	—	—	—	—	—	—	—	—	—	—	—	—	—	—	Belgium
—	—	—	—	—	—	—	—	—	—	—	—	—	—	—	Denmark
—	—	—	—	—	—	—	—	—	—	—	—	—	—	—	Finland
—	—	—	—	—	—	—	—	—	—	—	—	—	—	—	France
—	—	—	—	—	—	—	—	—	—	—	—	—	—	—	Greece
21.50	10.75	—	—	—	—	—	—	—	—	—	—	—	—	—	Iceland
—	—	—	—	—	—	—	—	—	—	—	—	—	—	—	Ireland
—	—	—	—	—	—	—	—	—	—	—	—	—	—	—	Italy
—	—	—	—	—	—	—	—	—	—	—	—	—	—	—	Netherlands
—	—	—	—	—	—	—	—	—	—	—	—	—	—	—	Norway
571.90	571.90	373.05	—	—	—	—	—	—	—	—	—	—	—	—	Portugal
—	—	—	—	—	—	—	—	—	—	—	—	—	—	—	Spain
—	—	—	—	—	—	—	—	—	—	—	—	—	—	—	United Kingdom
34,586.4	32,752.3	28,379.0	24,750.1	22,315.1	20,731.9	23,378.6	23,967.2	25,196.8	25,611.7	35,929.2	36,127.5	46,559.0	60,451.0	51,061.9	**Developing Countries**
7,298.0	6,575.5	5,622.6	5,259.8	4,880.1	4,144.5	3,900.9	3,472.0	3,525.7	3,863.9	3,380.4	3,668.1	3,308.2	2,793.9	2,653.5	**Africa**
—	—	—	—	470.90	470.90	695.90	578.18	342.73	793.77	994.07	1,412.54	1,495.52	1,428.04	1,388.75	Algeria
—	—	—	—	—	—	—	—	—	—	—	—	—	—	—	Burkina Faso
—	—	—	—	—	—	—	—	—	—	—	—	—	—	—	Burundi
—	—	—	69.53	84.98	84.98	84.28	45.66	11.86	29.91	34.41	50.11	41.89	29.88	16.56	Cameroon
25.87	27.04	25.94	19.88	10.84	4.44	2.00	.81	.41	10.71	10.71	10.71	8.03	2.41	—	Central African Rep.
7.89	7.00	7.00	6.12	2.62	—	—	—	—	10.33	10.33	10.33	6.45	1.29	—	Chad
—	—	—	—	—	—	—	—	—	—	—	—	—	—	—	Comoros
656.37	642.94	587.73	509.38	328.83	220.35	184.81	184.81	184.81	181.77	180.87	158.18	158.18	157.81	157.12	Congo, Dem. Rep. of
—	9.50	9.50	9.50	8.31	7.56	4.00	4.00	3.50	14.00	12.50	12.50	10.94	10.37	7.24	Congo, Republic of
565.99	509.26	406.52	368.71	277.90	302.94	259.72	194.46	159.13	105.65	48.90	16.09	—	—	—	Côte d'Ivoire
—	—	—	—	—	—	—	—	—	—	—	2.88	3.98	6.30	6.55	Djibouti
7.20	5.40	5.40	5.11	2.12	.39	—	—	—	—	—	—	—	—	—	Equatorial Guinea
45.05	54.31	44.17	36.90	22.06	4.41	—	—	—	—	—	—	—	—	—	Ethiopia
—	27.41	42.50	98.68	102.69	98.49	84.34	58.55	32.89	61.42	64.95	83.26	97.20	80.52	62.60	Gabon
24.80	17.16	15.91	12.70	9.62	5.90	1.54	—	—	—	—	—	—	—	—	Gambia, The
597.20	611.22	548.73	427.57	293.19	210.06	153.67	108.38	116.03	88.95	75.89	59.04	24.57	—	—	Ghana
11.50	20.75	21.00	21.00	16.88	7.13	.75	—	—	—	—	—	—	—	—	Guinea
2.80	1.87	1.64	.70	—	—	—	—	—	—	—	—	—	—	2.13	Guinea-Bissau
442.22	352.42	268.50	303.65	205.61	129.37	100.28	41.52	—	—	—	—	—	—	—	Kenya
—	—	—	—	—	—	—	—	—	—	—	—	—	—	—	Lesotho
205.43	205.43	205.43	204.39	202.23	201.55	201.55	201.55	201.55	201.55	201.46	201.46	201.46	201.46	201.46	Liberia
146.98	150.37	143.92	122.20	83.88	49.15	24.12	12.59	5.15	.63	—	—	—	—	—	Madagascar
121.94	101.35	77.74	67.06	48.04	34.27	19.07	5.48	1.24	12.73	12.73	12.73	12.73	6.36	—	Malawi
73.51	69.37	52.93	41.50	31.02	23.23	16.57	11.97	5.72	.95	—	—	—	—	—	Mali
27.55	29.52	33.25	33.86	26.43	15.21	5.59	1.00	—	—	—	—	—	—	—	Mauritania
145.02	128.87	105.50	76.51	47.58	15.51	—	—	—	—	—	—	—	—	—	Mauritius
1,083.28	839.10	755.20	696.05	642.71	526.50	401.54	319.10	207.15	101.06	34.83	2.30	—	—	—	Morocco
—	—	—	—	—	—	—	—	—	—	—	—	—	—	—	Nigeria
60.70	72.00	63.99	42.09	29.17	19.17	10.86	5.49	2.02	11.11	11.11	11.11	6.94	1.39	—	Niger
—	—	—	—	—	—	—	—	—	8.93	8.93	23.80	23.80	—	19.34	Rwanda
219.50	201.62	188.10	159.25	115.86	76.15	41.68	13.54	2.50	30.91	30.91	30.91	19.32	3.86	—	Senegal
71.39	58.59	58.59	57.86	56.92	55.37	50.00	48.59	42.63	—	—	—	—	11.58	27.14	Sierra Leone
129.44	118.73	108.31	107.63	98.79	96.70	96.70	96.70	96.70	96.70	96.70	96.70	96.70	96.70	96.70	Somalia
745.00	397.50	—	—	—	—	—	—	614.43	614.43	614.43	614.43	307.22	—	—	South Africa
605.30	605.30	605.30	605.30	605.30	604.26	604.26	604.26	604.26	604.23	581.28	556.76	531.29	489.14	461.53	Sudan
9.00	5.62	2.25	—	—	—	—	—	—	—	—	—	—	—	—	Swaziland
19.19	37.06	45.47	45.47	42.88	23.29	3.90	—	—	—	—	—	—	—	—	Tanzania
56.91	66.05	55.28	48.02	33.83	22.66	16.89	9.74	4.56	2.17	.22	—	—	—	—	Togo
—	149.71	190.71	205.71	205.71	123.73	180.10	211.05	207.30	207.30	197.11	165.00	128.39	91.78	55.16	Tunisia
257.12	187.44	161.32	130.74	76.49	46.18	21.75	3.10	—	—	—	—	—	—	—	Uganda
693.33	674.50	674.50	674.50	674.50	659.81	634.98	—	608.98	559.19	544.57	—	—	—	—	Zambia
240.47	191.06	110.30	52.20	22.24	4.84	—	102.50	119.90	139.00	158.10	152.17	133.63	151.26	151.24	Zimbabwe
9,165.8	8,732.5	7,038.7	5,464.4	4,467.7	2,815.5	3,921.1	4,638.8	5,024.4	4,178.6	3,232.1	2,078.5	14,049.2	22,794.7	16,700.7	**Asia**
—	—	—	—	—	—	—	—	—	—	—	—	—	—	—	Afghanistan, I.S. of
385.53	377.05	409.83	423.07	341.26	194.85	91.99	35.94	—	—	—	—	—	98.13	98.13	Bangladesh
—	—	—	—	—	—	—	—	—	—	—	—	—	—	—	Bhutan
12.50	12.50	12.50	12.50	12.50	12.50	12.50	6.25	6.25	6.25	6.25	6.25	6.25	5.21	4.17	Cambodia
—	597.73	597.73	597.73	597.73	298.86	—	—	—	—	—	—	—	—	—	China, People's Rep.
13.19	6.44	4.75	2.97	.59	—	—	—	—	—	—	—	—	—	—	Fiji
3,825.00	3,493.75	2,856.25	2,068.75	1,331.25	800.00	2,426.41	3,260.41	3,584.91	2,763.18	1,966.63	1,085.25	589.79	284.92	38.50	India
41.96	41.96	504.86	462.90	462.90	347.18	115.73	—	—	—	—	—	2,201.47	6,455.82	7,466.82	Indonesia
1,373.03	1,266.25	369.78	—	—	—	—	—	—	—	—	—	8,200.00	12,000.00	4,462.50	Korea
1.87	—	—	—	—	—	—	—	—	—	—	—	—	—	—	Lao People's Dem.Rep
107.21	—	—	—	—	—	—	—	—	—	—	—	—	—	—	Malaysia
—	—	—	—	—	—	11.25	13.75	13.75	13.75	7.50	.63	—	—	—	Mongolia
65.00	38.31	10.93	—	—	—	—	—	—	—	—	—	—	—	—	Myanmar
10.25	12.35	18.65	18.65	13.26	4.73	.79	—	—	—	—	—	—	—	—	Nepal
1,116.41	846.89	566.60	370.01	421.36	313.22	363.96	437.45	434.09	523.15	595.90	536.09	488.80	468.04	770.02	Pakistan
—	—	—	—	—	—	—	—	—	—	—	—	—	—	—	Palau

Use of Fund Credit (GRA)

	1970	1971	1972	1973	1974	1975	1976	1977	1978	1979	1980	1981	1982	1983	1984
					Expressed in Millions of SDRs										
Asia (cont.)															
Papua New Guinea	—	—	—	—	—	—	24.80	24.80	14.80	9.81	4.81	45.00	45.00	45.00	16.70
Philippines	68.75	89.74	95.25	76.25	67.81	164.68	348.41	418.42	441.28	506.78	668.76	823.03	755.27	899.24	771.76
Samoa	—	—	—	—	—	1.26	1.92	1.63	2.67	3.32	2.57	4.46	3.76	5.67	8.27
Solomon Islands	—	—	—	—	—	—	—	—	—	—	—	.80	2.40	3.36	3.16
Sri Lanka	78.52	71.54	74.56	74.10	101.69	124.70	134.25	169.94	185.88	234.47	211.13	346.86	341.45	331.07	328.34
Thailand	—	—	—	—	—	—	67.00	67.00	135.75	182.00	142.62	606.19	636.21	866.56	807.23
Vietnam	—	—	—	—	—	—	—	31.00	53.50	54.43	31.68	51.21	29.71	28.40	28.40
Europe	**74.1**	**128.9**	**83.5**	**69.3**	**192.9**	**458.4**	**936.4**	**862.9**	**948.7**	**1,111.1**	**1,710.7**	**2,739.4**	**3,917.9**	**4,929.4**	**5,371.8**
Albania	—	—	—	—	—	—	—	—	—	—	—	—	—	—	—
Armenia	—	—	—	—	—	—	—	—	—	—	—	—	—	—	—
Azerbaijan	—	—	—	—	—	—	—	—	—	—	—	—	—	—	—
Belarus	—	—	—	—	—	—	—	—	—	—	—	—	—	—	—
Bosnia & Herzegovina	—	—	—	—	—	—	—	—	—	—	—	—	—	—	—
Bulgaria	—	—	—	—	—	—	—	—	—	—	—	—	—	—	—
Croatia	—	—	—	—	—	—	—	—	—	—	—	—	—	—	—
Cyprus	—	—	—	—	6.38	8.10	43.07	43.07	32.92	37.98	30.60	21.62	12.30	5.47	3.17
Czech Republic	—	—	—	—	—	—	—	—	—	—	—	—	—	—	—
Czechoslovakia	—	—	—	—	—	—	—	—	—	—	—	—	—	—	—
Estonia	—	—	—	—	—	—	—	—	—	—	—	—	—	—	—
Georgia	—	—	—	—	—	—	—	—	—	—	—	—	—	—	—
Hungary	—	—	—	—	—	—	—	—	—	—	—	—	214.50	547.00	972.00
Kazakhstan	—	—	—	—	—	—	—	—	—	—	—	—	—	—	—
Kyrgyz Republic	—	—	—	—	—	—	—	—	—	—	—	—	—	—	—
Latvia	—	—	—	—	—	—	—	—	—	—	—	—	—	—	—
Lithuania	—	—	—	—	—	—	—	—	—	—	—	—	—	—	—
Macedonia, FYR	—	—	—	—	—	—	—	—	—	—	—	—	—	—	—
Moldova	—	—	—	—	—	—	—	—	—	—	—	—	—	—	—
Poland	—	—	—	—	—	—	—	—	—	—	—	—	—	—	—
Romania	—	—	—	47.50	47.50	87.50	237.50	270.00	255.55	246.80	257.42	506.66	781.61	904.65	955.74
Russia	—	—	—	—	—	—	—	—	—	—	—	—	—	—	—
Slovak Republic	—	—	—	—	—	—	—	—	—	—	—	—	—	—	—
Slovenia	—	—	—	—	—	—	—	—	—	—	—	—	—	—	—
Tajikistan	—	—	—	—	—	—	—	—	—	—	—	—	—	—	—
Turkey	74.13	62.13	—	—	—	207.57	336.81	336.81	477.68	480.29	826.58	1,135.63	1,319.18	1,497.09	1,455.03
Ukraine	—	—	—	—	—	—	—	—	—	—	—	—	—	—	—
Uzbekistan	—	—	—	—	—	—	—	—	—	—	—	—	—	—	—
Yugoslavia, SFR	—	66.75	83.50	21.75	139.00	155.20	318.97	212.97	182.53	346.00	596.14	1,075.50	1,590.32	1,975.18	1,985.87
Middle East	**71.3**	**111.6**	**51.5**	**81.6**	**140.1**	**300.1**	**500.0**	**577.0**	**599.4**	**489.6**	**305.2**	**176.5**	**95.5**	**74.5**	**74.4**
Egypt	49.34	69.84	24.40	62.17	92.95	68.22	177.90	254.89	296.30	246.48	139.05	85.12	52.01	49.31	49.31
Iran, I.R. of	—	—	—	—	—	—	—	—	—	—	—	—	—	—	—
Iraq	—	—	—	—	—	—	—	—	—	—	—	—	—	.01	—
Israel	12.48	32.48	—	—	32.50	208.25	285.25	285.24	271.26	224.21	156.40	87.54	27.15	—	—
Jordan	—	4.49	4.49	1.59	.01	.01	.01	.01	—	—	—	—	—	—	—
Syrian Arab Republic	9.50	4.75	22.62	17.87	5.37	—	—	—	—	.75	—	—	—	—	—
Yemen Arab Rep.	—	—	—	—	—	—	—	—	—	—	—	—	—	—	—
Yemen, P.D. Rep.	—	—	—	—	9.31	23.65	36.83	36.83	31.88	18.18	9.76	3.80	16.31	9.75	9.75
Yemen, Republic of	—	—	—	—	—	—	—	—	—	—	—	—	—	15.38	15.38
Western Hemisphere	**127.6**	**159.9**	**357.3**	**346.3**	**397.9**	**817.2**	**1,695.1**	**1,567.0**	**1,054.3**	**1,162.6**	**1,020.2**	**1,338.5**	**2,676.8**	**8,418.4**	**11,752.1**
Argentina	—	—	174.00	174.00	64.00	250.09	455.59	344.50	—	—	—	—	—	1,120.61	1,120.61
Barbados	—	—	—	—	—	—	—	6.50	6.50	6.50	2.27	.77	22.18	35.79	43.59
Belize	—	—	—	—	—	—	—	—	—	—	—	—	—	3.60	4.80
Bolivia	6.08	6.60	7.88	18.05	14.32	13.93	—	—	15.00	15.00	63.02	61.15	78.09	85.24	64.94
Brazil	—	—	—	—	—	—	—	—	—	—	—	—	498.75	2,525.72	4,269.87
Chile	1.49	39.50	79.00	79.00	159.97	330.79	402.22	300.62	266.49	135.94	96.31	41.80	5.68	579.00	795.00
Colombia	54.85	53.25	—	—	—	—	—	—	—	—	—	—	—	—	—
Costa Rica	—	—	—	—	18.84	29.96	32.30	29.31	24.32	43.81	44.64	88.16	84.18	183.28	158.98
Dominica	—	—	—	—	—	—	—	—	—	1.90	1.65	6.47	9.32	11.00	10.66
Dominican Republic	6.55	10.75	3.75	—	—	—	21.50	36.50	36.50	94.33	38.02	19.77	64.06	235.15	225.69
Ecuador	13.75	5.50	8.25	—	—	—	—	—	—	—	—	—	—	203.53	242.90
El Salvador	6.49	10.19	8.75	—	17.89	17.89	12.82	—	—	—	5.38	37.63	97.37	112.87	107.50
Grenada	—	—	—	—	—	.81	1.21	1.21	1.21	.97	.27	5.15	4.32	5.42	4.57
Guatemala	—	—	—	—	—	—	—	—	—	—	—	95.60	95.60	133.85	152.98
Guyana	—	2.06	—	3.87	5.00	—	17.25	17.25	30.27	40.49	67.40	74.05	77.81	73.75	72.75
Haiti	2.19	.80	—	—	6.64	10.97	12.38	8.43	7.63	5.71	17.15	31.99	42.97	72.15	86.15
Honduras	—	—	—	—	16.78	16.78	16.78	4.29	—	—	11.75	32.39	94.09	139.99	138.40
Jamaica	—	—	—	13.25	13.25	13.25	68.94	88.14	138.58	266.76	242.49	403.51	528.41	599.08	641.41
Mexico	—	—	—	—	—	—	—	—	—	—	—	—	200.62	1,203.75	2,407.51
Nicaragua	8.00	10.99	8.25	12.24	10.06	15.50	8.74	2.00	2.01	43.51	38.67	21.19	17.54	13.29	9.04
Panama	—	—	—	—	7.37	17.52	42.62	42.16	40.32	31.45	18.09	80.45	76.12	184.13	276.61
Paraguay	—	—	—	—	—	—	—	—	—	—	—	—	—	—	—
Peru	9.90	3.27	30.75	13.64	—	—	158.75	168.75	256.09	373.14	371.55	332.86	588.81	666.31	688.28
St. Kitts and Nevis	—	—	—	—	—	—	—	—	—	—	—	—	—	—	—
St. Lucia	—	—	—	—	—	—	—	—	—	—	—	1.35	4.05	2.55	2.02
St. Vincent & Grens.	—	—	—	—	—	—	—	—	—	—	—	.20	1.50	1.50	1.01
Trinidad and Tobago	—	—	—	—	—	—	—	—	—	—	—	—	—	—	—
Uruguay	18.25	17.02	36.70	32.26	63.81	99.74	124.88	98.24	—	—	—	—	86.80	226.80	226.80
Venezuela, Rep. Bol.	—	—	—	—	—	—	—	—	—	—	—	—	—	—	—
Memorandum Items															
Oil Exporting Ctys	138.46	125.36	107.12	19.16	—	—	—	—	—	—	—	—	—	425.11	421.46
Non-Oil Develop.Ctys	653.9	724.2	982.0	1,008.2	2,225.6	3,947.0	6,491.8	6,200.0	5,782.0	5,997.4	7,269.6	12,760.5	19,171.4	29,097.6	33,890.6

Expressed in Millions of SDRs

1985	1986	1987	1988	1989	1990	1991	1992	1993	1994	1995	1996	1997	1998	1999	
															Asia (cont.)
10.10	—	—	—	—	42.84	42.84	42.84	32.13	10.71	33.34	35.34	35.34	32.35	15.68	Papua New Guinea
942.74	958.76	841.58	791.91	889.96	640.28	759.02	800.12	880.74	728.56	489.48	281.94	633.82	1,113.96	1,327.73	Philippines
8.58	7.30	5.19	2.58	1.16	—	.16	—	—	—	—	—	—	—	—	Samoa
2.76	2.83	1.55	1.25	1.09	.47	—	—	—	—	—	—	—	—	—	Solomon Islands
292.49	234.03	164.67	209.43	163.41	131.56	68.00	13.60	—	—	—	—	—	—	—	Sri Lanka
928.75	807.91	645.38	474.26	202.87	—	—	—	—	—	—	—	1,800.00	2,300.00	2,500.00	Thailand
28.40	28.40	28.40	28.40	28.40	28.40	28.40	28.40	72.48	132.96	132.96	132.96	93.69	36.27	17.11	Vietnam
4,792.8	**4,004.7**	**2,775.9**	**1,773.9**	**905.5**	**917.1**	**3,464.6**	**4,695.1**	**6,151.0**	**8,002.9**	**11,329.4**	**13,769.1**	**15,353.9**	**19,144.1**	**16,779.5**	**Europe**
—	—	—	—	—	—	—	9.69	13.13	13.13	12.34	6.64	9.68	8.83	8.83	Albania
—	—	—	—	—	—	—	—	—	16.88	47.25	47.25	47.25	46.83	37.27	Armenia
—	—	—	—	—	—	—	—	—	—	67.86	121.68	142.15	157.94	214.83	Azerbaijan
—	—	—	—	—	—	—	—	70.10	70.10	190.20	190.20	190.20	172.27	129.74	Belarus
—	—	—	—	—	—	—	—	—	—	32.47	31.02	30.30	54.54	68.42	Bosnia & Herzegovina
—	—	—	—	—	—	289.23	428.90	459.90	644.41	482.12	407.25	698.02	792.27	910.74	Bulgaria
—	—	—	—	—	—	—	—	14.82	87.06	148.56	145.44	172.66	166.12	143.23	Croatia
—	—	—	—	—	—	—	—	—	—	—	—	—	—	—	Cyprus
—	—	—	—	—	—	—	—	780.68	—	—	—	—	—	—	Czech Republic
—	—	—	—	—	.01	917.94	1,121.50	....	—	—	—	—	—	—	Czechoslovakia
—	—	—	—	—	—	—	7.75	41.85	41.85	61.81	54.15	40.01	21.31	18.41	Estonia
—	—	—	—	—	—	—	—	—	27.75	77.70	77.70	77.70	77.01	61.28	Georgia
883.71	842.73	569.87	471.30	347.11	231.68	880.21	875.84	896.30	781.58	258.72	118.72	118.72	—	—	Hungary
—	—	—	—	—	—	—	—	61.88	198.00	290.82	383.60	378.96	463.66	335.15	Kazakhstan
—	—	—	—	—	—	—	—	43.86	43.86	43.86	41.20	34.05	25.53	20.16	Kyrgyz Republic
—	—	—	—	—	—	—	25.16	77.78	109.80	107.89	90.36	63.67	45.37	34.31	Latvia
—	—	—	—	—	—	—	17.25	87.98	134.55	175.95	190.11	200.46	179.83	167.76	Lithuania
—	—	—	—	—	—	—	—	2.81	14.03	38.09	47.40	47.10	45.44	46.82	Macedonia, FYR
—	—	—	—	—	—	—	—	63.00	112.45	154.85	172.29	172.73	125.56	127.69	Moldova
—	—	—	—	—	357.50	596.60	596.60	497.69	918.59	—	—	—	—	—	Poland
782.85	583.53	357.55	106.91	—	—	565.80	750.90	750.90	906.41	698.34	452.97	475.15	382.85	333.85	Romania
—	—	—	—	—	—	—	719.00	1,797.28	2,875.55	6,469.80	8,698.16	9,805.91	13,731.99	11,102.28	Russia
—	—	—	—	—	—	—	—	405.17	439.81	307.54	221.97	184.42	134.64	96.53	Slovak Republic
—	—	—	—	—	—	—	—	8.53	4.94	2.69	.90	—	—	—	Slovenia
—	—	—	—	—	—	—	—	—	—	—	15.00	22.50	30.00	26.25	Tajikistan
1,207.51	887.19	542.97	222.03	36.25	—	—	—	—	235.50	460.50	460.50	440.44	275.81	648.85	Turkey
—	—	—	—	—	—	—	—	—	249.33	1,037.30	1,573.30	1,780.56	1,985.05	2,044.62	Ukraine
—	—	—	—	—	—	—	—	—	—	105.95	165.20	165.20	165.20	146.83	Uzbekistan
1,918.72	1,691.22	1,305.47	973.65	522.17	327.94	214.84	142.46	77.36	77.36	56.82	56.06	56.06	56.06	55.65	Yugoslavia, SFR
118.1	**94.3**	**187.1**	**151.9**	**189.4**	**153.2**	**155.2**	**407.0**	**385.0**	**409.7**	**350.3**	**353.3**	**458.0**	**483.8**	**510.5**	**Middle East**
37.50	25.00	128.50	116.00	116.00	87.00	89.00	147.20	147.20	132.20	69.50	10.90	—	—	—	Egypt
—	—	—	—	—	—	—	—	—	—	—	—	—	—	—	Iran, I.R. of
—	—	—	—	—	—	—	—	—	—	—	—	—	—	—	Iraq
—	.01	—	—	—	—	—	178.64	178.64	178.64	111.65	22.33	—	—	—	Israel
57.40	57.40	57.40	35.88	73.41	66.24	66.24	81.19	59.18	98.89	169.17	236.11	316.58	333.41	362.86	Jordan
—	—	—	—	—	—	—	—	—	—	—	—	—	—	—	Syrian Arab Republic
9.75	6.11	1.22	—	—	....	....	....	....	....	....	....	....	....	....	Yemen Arab Rep.
13.45	5.77	—	—	—	....	....	....	....	....	....	....	....	....	....	Yemen, P.D. Rep.
....	....	....	....	....	....	....	....	....	....	....	84.00	141.38	150.38	147.63	Yemen, Republic of
13,211.8	**13,345.4**	**12,754.7**	**12,100.1**	**11,872.3**	**12,701.6**	**11,936.8**	**10,754.3**	**10,110.8**	**9,156.6**	**17,636.9**	**16,258.5**	**13,389.8**	**15,234.5**	**14,417.7**	**Western Hemisphere**
2,105.11	2,240.85	2,716.24	2,733.00	2,358.82	2,167.20	1,735.92	1,682.80	2,562.44	2,884.69	4,124.39	4,376.04	4,349.28	3,865.09	3,262.60	Argentina
43.59	32.42	15.60	7.75	3.27	.50	—	36.84	36.84	36.84	24.94	6.52	—	—	—	Barbados
9.54	9.54	8.03	5.79	2.52	.30	—	—	—	—	—	—	—	—	—	Belize
46.72	118.18	99.04	107.98	103.05	71.70	39.62	16.98	—	—	—	—	—	—	—	Bolivia
4,205.40	3,679.86	2,802.88	2,476.82	1,843.36	1,279.68	865.14	581.40	221.02	127.50	95.23	47.02	23.31	3,426.78	6,431.00	Brazil
990.60	1,088.25	1,032.38	982.58	966.46	812.90	669.38	525.02	346.50	199.48	—	—	—	—	—	Chile
—	—	—	—	—	—	—	—	—	—	—	—	—	—	—	Colombia
171.64	140.90	93.27	53.03	26.94	7.94	58.03	59.28	59.28	45.46	16.32	.50	—	—	—	Costa Rica
9.17	7.83	6.23	4.03	2.19	1.20	.52	.14	.02	—	—	—	—	—	—	Dominica
270.43	248.83	199.89	161.76	93.25	50.44	62.37	89.44	135.48	129.88	107.46	66.45	21.13	39.70	39.70	Dominican Republic
327.30	397.68	345.18	300.68	247.23	186.00	127.53	72.61	51.77	135.73	116.69	100.86	98.90	49.45	—	Ecuador
80.92	35.08	3.88	—	—	—	—	—	—	—	—	—	—	—	—	El Salvador
2.43	1.12	.84	.56	.28	—	—	—	—	—	—	—	—	—	—	Grenada
105.18	57.19	41.65	65.40	55.51	46.82	44.76	22.38	—	—	—	—	—	—	—	Guatemala
71.75	71.75	71.75	71.75	70.92	41.02	49.50	49.50	47.08	31.77	16.15	8.08	1.36	—	—	Guyana
74.38	54.66	36.53	22.40	21.08	16.56	15.00	15.00	15.00	.25	16.40	16.40	16.40	25.58	17.38	Haiti
121.69	80.30	47.91	23.64	23.31	22.57	23.55	74.57	72.45	61.25	32.46	6.38	—	47.50	47.50	Honduras
631.10	554.42	478.23	358.77	291.75	250.74	273.64	259.69	244.19	217.64	161.71	112.24	87.13	74.66	60.78	Jamaica
2,703.31	3,319.29	3,639.25	3,570.25	3,873.62	4,604.94	4,729.93	4,326.95	3,485.23	2,644.19	10,648.07	9,234.46	6,735.24	5,951.54	3,259.21	Mexico
.01	—	—	—	—	—	17.03	17.03	17.03	14.90	6.39	—	—	—	—	Nicaragua
283.36	288.63	243.90	243.79	243.19	191.27	150.69	79.80	82.32	91.27	74.36	90.99	105.39	125.53	108.33	Panama
—	—	—	—	—	—	—	—	—	—	—	—	—	—	—	Paraguay
639.00	595.51	595.44	595.42	576.98	530.46	493.41	458.72	642.69	642.69	642.69	642.69	749.63	642.51	535.40	Peru
—	—	—	—	—	—	—	—	—	—	—	—	—	1.63	1.63	St. Kitts and Nevis
.30	—	—	—	—	—	—	—	—	—	—	—	—	—	—	St. Lucia
.33	—	—	—	—	—	—	—	—	—	—	—	—	—	—	St. Vincent & Grens.
—	—	—	85.05	155.75	231.55	269.05	205.30	112.80	62.44	33.75	16.46	3.13	—	—	Trinidad and Tobago
318.55	323.07	276.58	229.65	153.35	70.78	40.43	38.13	27.90	20.48	13.98	5.99	—	114.20	114.20	Uruguay
—	—	—	—	759.47	2,116.98	2,271.33	2,142.75	1,950.74	1,810.16	1,505.96	1,527.42	1,198.89	870.36	540.02	Venezuela, Rep. Bol.
															Memorandum Items
41.96	41.96	504.86	462.90	1,693.27	2,935.06	3,082.96	2,720.93	2,293.47	2,603.93	2,500.03	2,939.96	4,895.88	8,754.21	9,395.59	**Oil Exporting Ctys**
34,544.5	32,710.3	27,874.1	24,287.2	20,621.8	17,796.8	20,295.6	21,246.2	22,903.4	23,007.7	33,429.1	33,187.5	41,663.2	51,696.8	41,666.3	**Non-Oil Develop.Ctys**

Total Reserves Minus Gold

		1970	1971	1972	1973	1974	1975	1976	1977	1978	1979	1980	1981	1982	1983	1984
																Millions of SDRs:
All Countries	010	56,154	87,056	110,904	116,836	144,001	158,697	186,628	228,473	245,487	272,872	321,274	329,677	327,926	362,323	407,128
Industrial Countries	110	39,647	66,994	81,699	79,948	79,841	84,762	93,575	120,053	144,811	154,907	186,037	186,502	185,560	206,185	226,023
United States	111	3,415	1,942	2,453	2,260	3,456	3,952	6,153	6,250	5,357	5,909	12,228	16,258	20,677	21,612	24,319
Canada	156	3,888	4,457	4,804	4,013	3,990	3,781	4,273	3,023	2,730	2,174	2,425	3,039	2,730	3,311	2,542
Australia	193	1,454	2,794	5,397	4,465	3,229	2,524	2,470	1,694	1,582	1,081	1,325	1,436	5,776	8,560	7,592
Japan	158	4,308	13,468	16,177	9,412	10,303	10,208	13,553	18,392	24,875	14,819	19,316	24,235	21,153	23,498	26,963
New Zealand	196	257	453	766	866	522	365	422	364	346	342	276	579	576	743	1,823
Euro Area																
Austria	122	1,044	1,424	1,775	1,652	2,070	3,060	3,065	2,758	3,874	3,094	4,140	4,540	4,805	4,313	4,330
Belgium	124	1,377	1,655	2,056	2,751	2,890	3,476	3,004	3,257	3,044	4,132	6,133	4,254	3,560	4,502	4,656
Finland	172	425	574	615	476	487	370	398	437	939	1,169	1,466	1,275	1,376	1,182	2,810
France	132	1,428	4,078	5,700	3,538	3,697	7,224	4,837	4,834	7,122	13,345	21,436	19,126	14,985	18,961	21,362
Germany	134	9,630	13,108	17,800	23,381	22,346	22,394	25,838	28,573	37,208	39,891	38,099	37,560	40,578	40,760	40,951
Ireland	178	681	901	1,022	835	1,019	1,292	1,565	1,936	2,048	1,679	2,243	2,278	2,377	2,521	2,400
Italy	136	2,465	3,398	2,721	2,448	2,782	1,116	2,774	6,672	8,527	13,814	18,132	17,298	12,774	19,203	21,214
Luxembourg	137	....	....	....	....	....	....	....	....	....	....	....	....	....	....	29
Netherlands	138	1,454	1,588	2,511	3,525	3,782	4,172	4,457	4,727	3,905	5,762	9,131	8,024	9,185	9,715	9,423
Portugal	182	602	870	1,189	1,390	948	340	151	301	669	707	624	459	405	368	527
Spain	184	1,319	2,512	4,120	5,114	4,798	4,703	4,049	4,920	7,762	10,039	9,302	9,283	6,939	7,070	12,197
Denmark	128	419	601	724	1,034	700	686	724	1,308	2,402	2,456	2,655	2,189	2,054	3,458	3,070
Greece	174	194	380	828	745	638	ı823	758	863	1,002	1,019	1,055	878	781	860	973
Iceland	176	53	63	76	82	39	39	68	81	104	123	136	197	132	143	130
Norway	142	788	1,030	1,186	1,271	1,541	1,876	1,884	1,808	2,196	3,200	4,742	5,372	6,231	6,332	9,554
Sweden	144	561	822	1,251	1,894	1,215	2,425	1,941	2,811	3,165	2,667	2,680	3,094	3,184	3,853	3,923
Switzerland	146	2,401	3,507	4,052	4,151	4,448	5,996	8,268	8,471	13,634	12,476	12,276	12,010	14,015	14,360	15,605
United Kingdom	112	1,479	7,358	4,463	4,633	4,931	3,928	2,905	16,557	12,301	14,986	16,192	13,091	11,238	10,831	9,631
Developing Countries	200	16,506	20,062	29,205	36,889	64,159	73,934	93,053	108,420	100,677	117,967	135,237	143,176	142,366	156,138	181,105
Africa	605	2,565	2,435	3,006	3,776	8,491	8,545	9,059	8,369	6,476	10,133	14,956	10,349	7,151	6,842	6,689
Algeria	612	148	275	263	756	1,188	964	1,519	1,386	1,520	2,018	2,958	3,175	2,196	1,796	1,494
Benin	638	16	23	26	27	28	13	17	17	12	11	6	50	4	4	3
Botswana	616	....	....	....	....	....	....	64	82	116	203	269	218	266	378	484
Burkina Faso	748	36	40	44	52	68	65	61	46	28	47	53	61	56	81	108
Burundi	618	15	16	17	18	12	26	42	78	62	68	74	53	27	26	20
Cameroon	622	81	68	40	42	64	25	38	35	40	95	148	73	61	152	55
Cape Verde	624	....	....	....	....	....	....	28	35	30	32	33	33	39	44	42
Central African Rep.	626	1	—	2	1	1	3	16	21	19	33	43	60	42	45	54
Chad	628	2	10	9	1	12	3	20	15	9	9	4	6	11	27	45
Comoros	632	....	....	....	....	....	....	....	....	....	....	5	7	13	14	5
Congo, Dem. Rep. of	636	136	84	113	143	97	41	43	110	97	157	160	130	35	97	140
Congo, Rep. of	634	9	10	10	7	20	12	10	11	7	32	67	106	34	7	4
Côte d'Ivoire	662	119	82	80	73	54	88	66	152	344	112	15	15	2	19	5
Djibouti	611	....	....	....	....	....	....	....	....	....	....	....	....	....	....	46
Equatorial Guinea	642	....	....	....	....	....	....	....	....	....	....	....	....	3	1	1
Ethiopia	644	63	55	77	138	215	236	254	176	117	131	63	229	165	120	45
Gabon	646	15	23	21	40	84	125	100	8	17	15	84	171	283	179	203
Gambia, The	648	8	10	10	13	23	24	18	20	20	1	4	3	8	3	2
Ghana	652	37	33	86	146	58	107	79	122	213	219	141	125	126	138	308
Guinea	656	....	....	....	....	....	....	....	....	....	....	....	....	....	....	....
Guinea-Bissau	654	....	....	....	....	....	....	....	....	....	....	....	....	....	....	....
Kenya	664	220	157	186	193	158	148	237	430	271	477	386	199	192	359	398
Lesotho	666	....	....	....	....	....	....	....	....	....	....	39	37	43	64	50
Liberia	668	....	....	....	....	15	16	15	23	14	42	4	7	6	19	4
Madagascar	674	37	43	48	56	40	30	36	57	45	4	7	23	18	28	60
Malawi	676	29	29	33	55	67	52	23	72	57	53	54	42	21	15	58
Mali	678	1	2	3	4	5	4	6	4	6	5	11	15	15	16	27
Mauritania	682	3	7	12	35	85	41	71	41	61	86	110	139	126	101	79
Mauritius	684	46	48	65	55	107	142	77	55	35	22	71	30	34	17	24
Morocco	686	119	139	197	199	319	301	402	416	475	423	313	197	197	102	50
Mozambique	688	....	....	....	....	....	....	....	....	....	....	....	....	....	....	56
Namibia	728	....	....	....	....	....	....	....	....	....	....	....	....	....	....	....
Niger	692	19	31	38	42	37	43	71	83	99	100	99	91	27	51	90
Nigeria	694	202	376	327	463	4,576	4,771	4,458	3,484	1,448	4,211	8,025	3,347	1,462	946	1,492
Rwanda	714	8	5	6	13	11	22	55	68	67	116	146	149	116	106	109
São Tomé & Príncipe	716	....	....	....	....	....	....	....	....	....	....	....	....	....	....	....
Senegal	722	22	23	35	10	5	27	22	28	14	15	6	7	10	12	4
Seychelles	718	....	....	....	4	4	5	6	9	7	9	14	12	12	10	6
Sierra Leone	724	39	35	43	43	45	24	22	27	27	35	24	14	8	15	8
Somalia	726	21	25	29	29	35	58	73	99	97	33	11	26	6	9	1
South Africa	199	346	245	561	372	308	418	366	342	325	330	569	572	440	786	247
Sudan	732	22	26	33	51	102	31	20	19	22	51	38	15	19	16	18
Swaziland	734	....	....	....	....	11	39	63	78	87	86	124	83	69	88	82
Tanzania	738	65	55	110	120	41	56	97	232	77	52	16	16	4	19	27
Togo	742	35	37	34	31	44	35	57	38	54	50	61	130	152	165	207
Tunisia	744	55	132	201	250	337	325	315	289	340	440	463	461	550	542	415
Uganda	746	57	25	33	24	14	27	38	39	40	17	2	26	71	102	ı69
Zambia	754	508	255	146	154	134	121	80	55	39	61	61	48	53	52	55
Zimbabwe	698	20	6	56	103	58	68	66	60	114	227	167	146	127	72	46

ll s

	1985	1986	1987	1988	1989	1990	1991	1992	1993	1994	1995	1996	1997	1998	1999		
End of Period																	
All Countries	404,882	418,672	507,642	542,845	591,139	655,445	692,686	720,317	797,882	858,989	988,433	1,142,277	1,261,184	1,242,709	1,330,067		010
Industrial Countries	229,440	251,303	324,321	353,065	382,214	414,092	400,659	396,746	413,444	433,819	487,693	548,794	577,696	545,592	551,942		110
United States	29,220	30,619	24,474	27,305	48,358	50,791	46,602	43,831	45,395	43,350	50,307	44,536	43,659	50,211	44,080		111
Canada	2,278	2,658	5,130	11,437	12,217	12,544	11,362	8,314	9,087	8,416	10,124	14,202	13,209	16,553	20,493		156
Australia	5,251	5,924	6,163	10,105	10,486	11,432	11,559	8,152	8,083	7,730	8,003	10,073	12,485	10,398	15,455		193
Japan	24,325	34,546	57,077	71,879	63,887	55,179	50,376	52,089	71,729	86,214	123,277	150,663	162,793	153,030	209,045		158
New Zealand	1,453	3,083	2,298	2,107	2,303	2,902	2,062	2,239	2,430	2,540	2,967	4,140	3,299	2,986	3,246		196
Euro Area																	
Austria	4,340	5,038	5,309	5,475	6,543	6,591	7,223	9,005	10,637	11,523	12,600	15,901	14,628	22,324	†11,017		122
Belgium	4,414	4,527	6,781	6,935	8,192	8,541	8,515	10,037	8,310	9,505	10,883	11,789	11,999	12,977	†7,969		124
Finland	3,414	1,461	4,524	4,733	3,889	6,779	5,319	3,792	3,939	7,303	6,753	4,810	6,238	6,885	†5,980		172
France	24,206	25,715	23,296	18,849	18,728	25,851	21,870	19,657	16,489	17,986	18,065	18,635	22,922	31,471	†28,926		132
Germany	40,403	42,294	55,515	43,492	46,196	47,729	44,043	66,158	56,525	52,994	57,185	57,844	57,504	52,573	†44,472		134
Ireland	2,676	2,646	3,381	3,780	3,087	3,672	4,013	2,502	4,314	4,189	5,806	5,706	4,837	6,674	†3,895		178
Italy	14,198	16,340	21,297	25,797	35,551	44,232	34,031	20,104	20,054	22,102	23,482	31,954	41,311	21,227	†16,339		136
Luxembourg	30	30	30	31	57	57	56	54	49	52	50	51	47	....	†56		137
Netherlands	9,816	9,149	11,280	11,945	12,562	12,289	12,442	15,954	22,819	23,655	22,680	18,615	18,429	15,211	†7,357		138
Portugal	1,270	1,191	2,345	3,810	7,573	10,182	14,421	13,912	11,532	10,627	10,663	11,070	11,606	11,239	†6,447		182
Spain	10,174	12,062	21,618	27,550	31,554	36,008	46,016	33,094	29,882	28,459	23,199	40,284	50,694	39,245	†24,127		184
Denmark	4,942	4,059	7,096	8,000	4,868	7,445	5,176	8,032	7,499	6,203	7,411	9,834	14,174	10,841	16,238		128
Greece	790	†1,242	1,890	2,690	2,453	2,398	3,628	3,486	5,672	9,924	9,943	12,171	9,335	12,399	13,204		174
Iceland	187	253	219	216	257	307	314	362	310	201	207	316	284	303	349		176
Norway	12,670	10,239	10,063	9,859	10,489	10,777	9,250	8,684	14,286	13,033	15,148	18,441	17,343	13,215	14,864		142
Sweden	5,274	5,355	5,762	6,310	7,274	12,644	12,815	16,454	13,869	15,929	16,180	13,288	8,023	10,013	10,943		144
Switzerland	16,402	17,811	19,368	17,985	19,234	20,541	20,277	24,185	23,760	23,790	24,496	26,727	28,926	29,254	26,463		146
United Kingdom	11,707	15,061	29,405	32,773	26,457	25,202	29,286	26,648	26,775	28,094	28,265	27,745	23,952	22,877	21,737		112
Developing Countries	175,443	167,369	183,321	189,780	208,925	241,352	292,027	323,571	384,439	425,170	500,740	593,483	683,489	697,118	778,125		200
Africa	8,295	7,022	7,099	7,547	9,202	11,805	14,288	12,511	13,564	16,242	17,182	21,286	31,018	28,314	32,209		605
Algeria	2,566	1,357	1,156	669	645	509	1,039	1,060	1,074	1,832	1,349	2,945	5,964	4,862	3,297		612
Benin	4	3	3	3		46	134	178	178	177	133	182	188	186	291		638
Botswana	713	979	1,450	1,678	2,162	2,380	2,637	2,796	3,024	3,057	3,205	3,545	4,255	4,279	4,589		616
Burkina Faso	127	191	227	238	202	211	242	248	278	163	234	235	256	265	215		748
Burundi	27	56	43	52	76	74	99	127	119	140	141	97	84	47	35		618
Cameroon	121	48	45	131	61	18	30	15	2	2	3	2	1	1	3		622
Cape Verde	50	46	57	60	57	54	46	55	42	29	39	36	31	26	44		624
Central African Rep.	45	53	68	81	86	83	72	73	82	144	157	162	132	103	99		626
Chad	30	13	37	47	85	90	84	59	28	52	96	114	101	85	69		628
Comoros	14	19	22	17	23	21	20	20	28	30	30	35	30	28	27		632
Congo, Dem. Rep. of	173	220	127	139	148	154	128	114	34	83	99	57	....	....	....		636
Congo, Rep. of	4	6	2	3	5	4	3	3	1	34	40	63	44	1	29		634
Côte d'Ivoire	4	16	6	8	11	3	9	5	2	140	356	421	458	608	459		662
Djibouti	46	44	45	48	45	66	70	61	55	51	49	54	49	47	51		611
Equatorial Guinea	3	2	—	4	5	....	7	10									642
Ethiopia	135	205	86	48	35	14	38	169	332	373	519	509	371	363	334		644
Gabon	175	103	8	50	26	192	229	52	1	120	100	173	209	11	13		646
Gambia, The	2	11	18	14	16	39	47	68	....	67	71	71	71	76	81		648
Ghana	436	419	138	164	264	154	385	233	298	400	469	576	....	268	331		652
Guinea							56	63	96	60	58	61	90	....	....		656
Guinea-Bissau	....	25	7	12	16	13	10	13	10	13	14	8	25	25	26		654
Kenya	356	338	180	196	217	144	82	39[e]	295	382	238	519	584	556	577		664
Lesotho	40	49	48	42	37	51	80	115	184	255	307	320	424	408	364		666
Liberia	1	2	—	—	6	....	1	1	2	3	19	—	—	—	—		668
Madagascar	44	94	131	166	187	65	62	....	....	49	73	168	209	122	166		674
Malawi	41	20	37	108	76	96	107	29	41	29	74	157	120	192	183		676
Mali	20	19	11	27	88	134	223	224	242	152	217	300	308	286	255		678
Mauritania	54	39	51	41	63	38	47	44	32	27	57	98	149	144	163		682
Mauritius	27	111	242	328	394	518	624	596	551	512	581	623	514	397	533		684
Morocco	105	173	290	407	372	1,453	2,167	2,607	2,661	2,981	2,423	2,638	2,959	3,150	4,145		686
Mozambique	42	46	83	129	155	163	168	170	136	122	131	239	383	432	477		688
Namibia								36	97	139	149	135	186	185	223		728
Niger	124	155	175	172	162	156	142	164	140	76	64	55	39	38	29		692
Nigeria	1,518	884	821	484	1,344	2,716	3,101	703	999	949	971	2,834	....	....	....		694
Rwanda	103	133	116	88	54	31	77	57	35	35	67	74	114	120	127		714
São Tomé & Príncipe											3	3	9	7	8		716
Senegal	5	8	6	8	14	8	9	9	2	123	183	200	286	306	294		722
Seychelles	8	6	10	6	9	12	19	23	26	21	18	15	20	15	22		718
Sierra Leone	10	11	4	6	3	4	7	14	21	28	23	18	29	31	29		724
Somalia	2	10	5	11	12	....	....	....	....	....	....	....	....	....	....		726
South Africa	286	303	452	580	730	709	628	721	742	1,154	1,897	655	3,557	3,094	4,629		199
Sudan	11	48	8	9	12	8	5	20	27	54	110	74	60	64	138		732
Swaziland	76	79	90	104	137	152	120	225	192	203	201	177	219	255	274		734
Tanzania	15	50	22	58	41	136	143	238	148	227	182	306	461	426	565		738
Togo	270	280	250	172	217	248	255	198	114	65	88	62	88	84	89		742
Tunisia	212	250	370	668	732	559	552	620	622	1,001	1,080	1,320	1,466	1,314	1,648		744
Uganda	25	24	38	37	11	31	41	69	107	220	309	367	470	515	556		746
Zambia	182	57	77	100	88	136	129	....	140	184	150	155	177	49	33		754
Zimbabwe	85	87	117	133	72	105	105	162	315	278	401	416	119	93	195		698

Total Reserves Minus Gold

		1970	1971	1972	1973	1974	1975	1976	1977	1978	1979	1980	1981	1982	1983	1984
															Millions of SDRs:	
Asia *	505	**5,090**	**5,450**	**7,270**	**8,585**	**10,291**	**10,442**	**15,960**	**21,459**	**22,600**	**26,216**	**29,702**	**36,628**	**43,117**	**54,593**	**67,374**
Afghanistan, Islamic State of	512	13	25	19	18	23	74	113	227	300	335	291	236	234	205	233
Bangladesh	513	....	....	249	119	113	127	249	192	242	293	235	119	166	501	398
Bhutan	514													27	32	46
Cambodia	522															
China, P.R.: Mainland Ɪ	924	....	....	....	....	....	....	....	1,931	1,195	1,635	1,996	4,346	10,288	14,315	Ɪ17,717
China, P.R.: Hong Kong	532															
Fiji	819	27	36	64	61	89	127	100	121	103	104	131	116	115	111	120
India	534	763	868	844	704	839	930	2,403	4,011	4,933	5,642	5,444	4,032	3,912	4,716	5,960
Indonesia	536	156	Ɪ171	527	667	1,217	499	1,288	2,065	2,016	3,083	4,227	4,308	2,851	3,552	4,869
Korea	542	606	399	482	733	226	667	1,696	2,443	2,122	2,246	2,293	2,304	2,545	2,241	2,809
Lao People's Democratic Rep.	544															
Malaysia	548	616	695	836	1,057	1,264	1,244	2,069	2,292	2,490	2,972	3,440	3,521	3,416	3,614	3,798
Maldives	556	....	....	....	....	....	....	—	—	—	1	1	1	8	4	5
Micronesia, Fed. States of	868															
Mongolia	948															
Myanmar	518	Ɪ31	45	37	76	149	113	102	85	74	154	204	197	95	85	63
Nepal	558	89	89	91	97	99	82	Ɪ110	115	111	121	143	173	181	127	84
Pakistan	564	136	119	203	342	320	291	401	370	313	162	389	620	878	1,884	1,056
Papua New Guinea	853	....	....	....	26	27	153	221	351	311	382	332	340	411	420	444
Philippines	566	195	285	442	823	1,192	1,123	1,374	1,218	1,353	1,708	2,232	1,775	805	713	614
Samoa	862	5	6	4	4	5	5	5	8	4	2	2	3	3	7	11
Singapore	576	1,012	1,338	1,610	1,895	2,297	2,568	2,895	3,176	4,070	4,417	5,149	6,486	7,687	8,849	10,626
Solomon Islands	813	....	....	....	....	....	....	....	2	22	28	23	19	34	45	46ᵉ
Sri Lanka	524	43	46	55	72	63	49	79	241	305	392	192	281	319	284	521
Thailand	578	824	726	887	1,000	1,436	1,434	1,547	1,492	1,542	1,399	1,223	1,488	1,394	1,535	1,959
Tonga	866	....	....	....	....	....	....	7	8	10	11	12	14	20	27	
Vanuatu	846												7	5	6	8
Vietnam	582															
of which:																
Taiwan Province of China	528	540	568	877	850	892	917	1,305	1,107	1,079	1,114	1,729	6,216	7,734	11,327	15,980
Europe	170	**735**	**1,144**	**2,352**	**3,379**	**2,878**	**2,544**	**3,808**	**3,270**	**3,712**	**3,318**	**4,790**	**4,865**	**4,839**	**6,897**	**8,469**
Albania	914															
Armenia	911															
Azerbaijan	912															
Belarus	913															
Bulgaria	918															
Croatia	960															
Cyprus	423	194	247	279	239	204	169	236	258	265	268	289	366	474	496	551
Czech Republic	935															
Czechoslovakia Ɪ	934												1,442	821	703	767	986
Estonia	939															
Hungary	944														1,176	1,592
Kazakhstan	916															
Kyrgyz Republic	917															
Latvia	941															
Lithuania	946															
Macedonia, FYR	962															
Malta	181	148	170	241	257	316	415	523	592	710	769	776	923	982	1,062	1,010
Moldova	921															
Poland	964											429	100	239	586	731	1,128
Romania	968	....	....	....	178	196	461	483	211	289	398	253	347	408	502	724
Russia	922															
Slovak Republic	936															
Slovenia	961															
Turkey	186	304	582	1,162	1,646	1,276	806	853	525	615	500	844	797	979	1,230	1,296
Ukraine	926															
Yugoslavia, SFR	188	89	145	622	1,058	886	693	1,713	1,683	1,833	954	1,085	1,372	703	933	1,181
Middle East	405	**3,556**	**5,948**	**8,362**	**10,140**	**28,344**	**37,332**	**44,716**	**52,886**	**41,648**	**46,967**	**55,317**	**58,506**	**62,777**	**60,933**	**58,394**
Bahrain	419	63	79	77	53	107	247	376	415	379	466	748	1,327	1,391	1,362	1,329
Egypt	469	74	53	47	215	206	166	206	355	377	402	820	615	633	737	751
Iran, I.R. of	429	77	441	754	894	6,716	7,469	7,472	9,966	9,194	11,546	8,015	1,379	5,168	....	....
Iraq	433	319	409	576	1,144	2,530	2,186	3,816	5,614							
Israel	436	405	635	1,086	1,466	942	971	1,143	1,253	2,015	2,326	2,628	3,004	3,480	3,487	3,122
Jordan	439	228	205	222	224	255	392	406	529	680	885	896	934	801	787	525
Kuwait	443	117	178	248	316	1,020	1,274	1,465	2,374	1,919	2,179	3,080	3,495	5,360	4,959	4,683
Lebanon	446	98	181	299	392	1,044	1,026	1,121	1,291	1,408	1,163	1,245	1,303	2,364	1,817	685
Libya	672	1,505	2,370	2,609	1,678	2,868	1,790	2,674	3,940	3,151	4,816	10,264	7,735	6,400	4,985	3,708
Oman	449	10	23	34	39	76	138	189	238	195	315	456	639	791	728	918
Qatar	453	30	35	49	56	52	83	111	133	162	219	269	314	350	367	388
Saudi Arabia	456	543	1,223	2,195	3,106	11,559	19,812	23,153	24,617	Ɪ14,737	14,631	18,376	27,695	26,787	26,064	25,248
Syrian Arab Rep.	463	27	53	97	314	381	600	253	398	293	441	264	250	180	50	274
United Arab Emirates	466	....	....	....	76	370	844	1,641	659	623	1,087	1,580	2,751	2,008	1,979	2,333
Yemen Arab Rep.	473	....	....	....	105	162	288	620	1,021	1,120	1,084	1,006	826	502	350	325
Yemen, P.D. Rep.	459	59	59	61	62	55	46	70	82	144	159	183	219	259	269	254
Yemen, Republic of	474															

Ɪ See country notes in the monthly _IFS_

End of Period

1985	1986	1987	1988	1989	1990	1991	1992	1993	1994	1995	1996	1997	1998	1999	Country	Code
66,273	79,811	98,145	110,392	119,928	144,275	175,841	188,497	220,522	261,842	289,589	342,252	382,411	411,618	479,294	Asia *	505
269	211	197	194	185	187	164	....	....	....	....	....	....	....	....	Afghanistan, Islamic State of	512
306	334	594	777	382	442	894	1,327	1,755	2,150	1,574	1,276	1,172	1,353	1,168	Bangladesh	513
46	50	53	70	75	60	69	57	....	79	84	128	134	177	200	Bhutan	514
....	....	....	....	....	....	....	....	18	81	129	185	221	230	286	Cambodia	522
11,588	9,363	11,493	13,778	13,666	20,796	30,532	I 14,997	16,298	36,246	50,708	74,438	105,809	105,955	114,919	China, P.R.: Mainland I	924
....	....	....	....	....	17,269	20,139	25,581	31,295	33,737	37,268	44,374	68,782	63,667	70,117	China, P.R.: Hong Kong	532
119	140	93	173	161	183	190	230	196	187	235	297	267	274	312	Fiji	819
5,845	5,229	4,549	3,641	2,936	1,069	2,535	4,187	7,425	13,493	12,056	14,027	18,298	19,418	23,801	India	534
4,529	3,312	3,942	3,751	4,150	5,243	6,472	7,599	8,200	8,311	9,222	12,692	12,293	16,131	19,268	Indonesia	536
2,612	2,714	2,526	9,175	11,577	10,398	9,578	12,451	14,727	17,563	21,983	23,670	15,096	36,913	53,907	Korea	542
....	....	....	....	1	1	20e	29e	46e	42e	62	115	83	83	74	Lao People's Democratic Rep.	544
4,472	4,928	5,241	4,850	5,922	6,856	7,610	12,529	19,838	17,415	15,994	18,783	15,407	18,153	22,286	Malaysia	548
4	6	6	16	19	17	16	21	19	21	32	53	73	84	93	Maldives	556
....	....	....	....	....	....	....	....	....	....	47	62	71	....	68	Micronesia, Fed. States of	868
....	....	....	....	....	....	....	12	43	56	79	75	130	67	99	Mongolia	948
31	27	19	58	200	220	181	204	221	289	377	159	185	224	193	Myanmar	518
51	71	126	164	161	208	278	340	466	475	395	397	464	537	614	Nepal	558
735	580	354	293	396	208	368	618	871	2,007	1,166	381	886	730	1,101	Pakistan	564
403	348	308	292	292	283	226	174	103	66	176	406	269	137	149	Papua New Guinea	853
560	1,413	683	746	1,078	650	2,269	3,202	3,404	4,122	4,287	6,975	5,385	6,552	9,639	Philippines	566
13	19	26	37	42	49	47	44	37	35	37	42	48	44	50	Samoa	862
11,695	10,578	10,733	12,687	15,481	19,505	23,862	29,007	35,208	39,851	46,213	53,442	52,836	53,215	55,987	Singapore	576
32e	24	26	29	20	12	6	17	15	12	11	23	27	35	37	Solomon Islands	813
411	288	197	165	186	297	479	674	1,186	1,401	1,404	1,364	1,500	1,406	1,192	Sri Lanka	524
1,994	2,293	2,825	4,530	7,241	9,352	12,246	14,806	17,817	20,093	24,206	26,239	19,403	20,472	24,818	Thailand	578
25	18	20	23	19	22	23	23	27	24	19	21	20	20	19	Tonga	866
10	18	28	30	27	26	28	31	33	30	32	31	28	32	30	Vanuatu	846
....	....	....	....	....	....	....	312	264	571	890	1,218	1,472	1,422	....	Vietnam	582

*of which:

1985	1986	1987	1988	1989	1990	1991	1992	1993	1994	1995	1996	1997	1998	1999	Country	Code
20,535	37,860	54,099	54,913	55,719	50,919	57,609	59,859	60,844	63,331	60,754	61,224	61,888	64,161	77,376	Taiwan Province of China	528
7,110	7,739	7,524	9,527	14,436	15,217	15,676	15,583	25,334	30,528	57,515	61,537	71,735	71,647	78,013	Europe	170
....	....	....	....	....	....	....	....	107	140	162	195	229	248	269	Albania	914
....	....	....	....	....	....	....	1	10	22	67	108	170	224	232	Armenia	911
....	....	....	....	....	....	....	....	—	1	81	147	345	318	490	Azerbaijan	912
....	....	....	....	....	....	....	....	....	69	254	326	292	241	218	Belarus	913
....	....	....	....	....	....	217	656	477	686	832	336	1,666	2,010	2,247	Bulgaria	918
....	....	....	....	....	....	....	121	449	962	1,275	1,609	1,882	2,000	2,204	Croatia	960
542	615	616	690	855	1,059	972	748	798	1,003	751	1,072	1,031	980	1,335	Cyprus	423
....	....	....	....	....	....	....	....	2,759	4,209	9,312	8,590	7,214	8,908	9,330	Czech Republic	935
778	912	974	1,176	1,641	775	2,230	I 815	....	....	....	....	....	....	....	Czechoslovakia I	934
....	....	....	....	....	....	....	124	281	304	390	443	562	576	622	Estonia	939
1,960	1,882	1,152	1,090	948	751	2,750	3,218	4,878	4,614	8,055	6,760	6,232	6,618	7,981	Hungary	944
....	....	....	....	....	....	....	....	332	574	764	900	1,258	1,038	1,078	Kazakhstan	916
....	....	....	....	....	....	....	....	35	18	54	66	126	116	167	Kyrgyz Republic	917
....	....	....	....	....	....	....	....	314	373	340	455	522	517	612	Latvia	941
....	....	....	....	....	....	....	33	255	360	509	537	749	1,001	871	Lithuania	946
....	....	....	....	....	....	....	....	76	102	173	167	190	217	313	Macedonia, FYR	962
899	936	997	1,014	1,031	1,006	932	922	992	1,267	1,079	1,126	....	1,181	1,370	Malta	181
....	....	....	....	....	....	—	2	56	123	173	217	271	102	135	Moldova	921
792	570	1,054	1,527	1,761	3,158	2,540	2,981	2,979	4,002	9,939	12,409	15,125	18,773	17,876	Poland	964
181	476	988	580	1,414	368	486	601	725	1,429	1,062	1,462	2,819	2,036	1,958	Romania	968
....	....	....	....	....	....	....	....	4,248	2,727	9,676	7,842	9,557	5,541	6,162	Russia	922
....	....	....	....	....	....	....	....	303	1,158	2,263	2,378	2,394	2,037	2,456	Slovak Republic	936
....	....	....	....	....	....	78	520	574	1,027	1,225	1,598	2,457	2,584	2,308	Slovenia	961
961	1,154	1,252	1,742	3,638	4,252	3,596	4,480	4,566	4,911	8,370	11,430	13,829	13,841	17,005	Turkey	186
....	....	....	....	....	....	....	341	118	446	707	1,363	1,735	541	762	Ukraine	926
997	1,193	492	1,708	3,147	3,848	1,875	....	....	....	....	....	....	....	....	Yugoslavia, SFR	188
57,307	46,597	44,586	40,341	40,983	36,715	40,549	42,936	46,105	45,129	49,558	60,157	72,818	71,568	76,784	Middle East	405
1,511	1,218	810	930	799	868	1,059	1,017	948	801	861	917	956	766	997	Bahrain	419
721	678	972	939	1,157	1,886	3,723	7,862	9,395	9,234	10,886	12,099	13,833	12,872	10,553	Egypt	469
....	....	....	....	....	....	....	....	....	....	....	....	....	....	....	Iran, I.R. of	429
....	....	....	....	....	....	....	....	....	....	....	....	....	....	....	Iraq	433
3,350	3,809	4,142	2,984	4,015	4,411	4,390	3,729	4,647	4,653	5,462	7,938	15,069	16,104	16,470	Israel	436
385	357	299	81	358	597	577	558	1,192	1,159	1,327	1,223	1,631	1,243	1,916	Jordan	439
4,981	4,497	2,919	1,429	2,360	1,372	2,383	3,743	3,068	2,398	2,395	2,444	2,558	2,803	3,515	Kuwait	443
978	399	259	727	714	464	892	1,088	1,646	2,661	3,050	4,125	4,429	4,656	5,665	Lebanon	446
5,375	4,867	4,115	3,211	3,297	4,104	3,981	4,496	....	....	....	....	....	5,163	5,096	Libya	672
993	791	988	783	1,031	1,176	1,163	1,443	661	671	766	966	1,148	756	1,161	Oman	449
406	468	436	353	406	444	467	497	505	451	....	....	....	....	....	Qatar	453
22,764	14,980	15,990	15,273	12,744	8,201	8,161	4,316	5,408	5,054	5,800	I 10,415	11,391	10,536	12,793	Saudi Arabia	456
76	118	157	143	....	....	....	....	....	....	....	....	....	....	....	Syrian Arab Rep.	463
2,917	2,755	3,331	3,295	3,391	3,222	3,751	4,154	4,444	4,561	5,026	5,602	6,205	6,447	7,778	United Arab Emirates	466
270	353	380	212	212	....	....	....	....	....	....	....	....	....	....	Yemen Arab Rep.	473
170	113	68	59	58	....	....	....	....	....	....	....	....	....	....	Yemen, P.D. Rep.	459
....	....	....	....	....	297	475	233	106	175	416	707	892	707	....	Yemen, Republic of	474

I See country notes in the monthly IFS

Total Reserves Minus Gold

11 *s*		1970	1971	1972	1973	1974	1975	1976	1977	1978	1979	1980	1981	1982	1983	1984
															Millions of SDRs:	
Western Hemisphere	205	4,363	4,886	8,021	10,903	14,011	15,071	19,510	22,436	26,241	31,333	30,482	32,825	24,475	26,868	40,102
Antigua and Barbuda	311	....	....	....	....	....	6	8	4	5	9	6	6	8	9	16
Argentina	213	533	177	289	952	935	246	1,244	2,596	3,812	7,127	5,268	2,808	2,272	1,120	1,268
Aruba	314	....	....	....	....	....	....	....	....	....	....	....	....	....	....	....
Bahamas, The	313	22	27	34	36	41	46	41	I 55	45	59	72	86	103	117	164
Barbados	316	17	17	26	27	32	34	24	30	46	50	62	86	110	118	135
Belize	339			....	....	....	....	5	7	11	8	10	9	9	9	6
Bolivia	218	33	37	41	46	144	119	130	174	130	135	83	86	141	153	257
Brazil	223	1,142	1,562	3,806	5,272	4,260	3,400	5,584	5,921	9,078	6,806	4,524	5,673	3,561	4,160	11,740
Chile	228	342	157	89	101	34	48	349	351	837	1,471	2,449	2,761	1,645	1,945	2,350
Colombia	233	189	173	285	428	352	405	947	1,438	1,816	2,918	3,788	4,073	3,500	1,816	1,392
Costa Rica	238	14	25	37	40	34	42	82	157	149	90	114	113	205	297	413
Dominica	321	....	....	....	....	....	—	1	2	1	7	4	3	4	1	5
Dominican Republic	243	29	49	51	70	71	96	106	148	118	181	158	193	117	164	259
Ecuador	248	55	34	112	174	260	216	411	513	488	548	794	543	276	616	624
El Salvador	253	45	43	59	34	63	91	160	174	206	108	61	62	98	153	169
Grenada	328	5	5	5	4	4	I 4	7	6	7	9	10	14	8	14	15
Guatemala	258	61	69	107	159	148	242	423	551	569	529	349	129	102	201	280
Guyana	336	20	24	34	12	51	86	23	19	45	13	10	6	10	6	6
Haiti	263	4	10	16	14	16	11	24	28	30	42	13	21	4	9	13
Honduras	268	20	20	32	35	36	83	113	148	142	159	117	87	102	109	131
Jamaica	343	139	165	147	106	156	107	28	39	45	48	82	73	99	60	99
Mexico	273	568	693	899	962	1,011	1,182	1,023	1,357	1,414	1,573	2,321	3,500	756	3,737	7,419
Netherlands Antilles	353	25	34	46	41	50	61	80	83	51	55	74	116	170	157	120
Nicaragua	278	49	54	74	96	85	104	126	122	39	111	51	96	155	167	....
Panama	283	16	19	40	35	32	29	68	58	115	90	92	103	92	197	220
Paraguay	288	18	19	29	47	71	98	136	221	344	462	597	692	670	650	680
Peru	293	I 296	351	408	436	756	363	249	294	299	1,154	1,552	1,031	1,223	1,304	1,663
St. Kitts and Nevis	361	....	....	....	....	....	....						3	3	3	6
St. Lucia	362	....	....	....	....	....	3	4	5	5	6	6	7	7	8	13
St. Vincent & Grenadines	364	....	....	....	....	....		4	4	4	7	6	8	4	5	13
Suriname	366	28	30	35	47	55	78	95	77	102	129	148	178	159	56	25
Trinidad and Tobago	369	43	64	54	39	319	641	872	1,220	1,385	1,625	2,180	2,876	2,793	2,010	1,384
Uruguay	298	14	19	64	83	66	50	152	265	271	I 245	301	369	105	198	137
Venezuela, Rep. Bol.	299	637	1,010	1,204	1,608	4,928	7,178	6,992	6,368	4,632	5,557	5,178	7,014	5,964	7,300	9,081

Memorandum Items

		1970	1971	1972	1973	1974	1975	1976	1977	1978	1979	1980	1981	1982	1983	1984
Oil Exporting Countries	999	3,744	6,511	8,789	10,803	37,100	47,007	54,779	60,845	44,847	54,913	67,915	67,872	65,637	65,667	68,065
Non-Oil Developing Countries	201	12,763	13,551	20,416	26,085	27,059	26,927	38,274	47,575	55,830	63,054	67,321	75,303	76,729	90,471	113,040

1985	1986	1987	1988	1989	1990	1991	1992	1993	1994	1995	1996	1997	1998	1999		
End of Period																
36,409	26,155	25,883	21,974	24,376	33,339	45,673	64,045	78,913	71,429	86,895	108,251	125,506	113,970	111,825	Western Hemisphere	205
15	23	18	21	21	19	23	37	28	31	40	33	38	42	51	Antigua and Barbuda	311
12,980	2,222	1,140	2,499	1,113	3,228	4,198	7,265	10,040	9,814	9,612	12,590	16,542	17,579	19,127	Argentina..	213
....	60	55	68	66	69	84	103	132	122	146	130	128	158	160	Aruba...	314
166	189	120	128	112	111	127	113	125	121	121	119	168	246	299	Bahamas, The....................................	313
127	124	102	101	83	83	61	102	110	134	147	201	196	180	....	Barbados..	316
13	22	26	38	46	49	37	39	28	24	25	41	44	31	52	Belize	339
182	134	69	79	156	117	74	132	163	309	444	664	805	628	668	Bolivia	218
9,654	14,744	4,440	5,181	5,734	5,230	5,616	16,379	22,281	25,393	33,440	40,560	37,670	30,241	25,352	Brazil	223
2,230	1,922	1,765	2,349	2,761	4,266	4,922	6,667	7,018	8,965	9,512	10,315	12,826	11,124	10,497	Chile	228
1,452	2,204	2,175	2,413	2,752	3,253	4,567	5,634	5,774	5,550	5,686	6,911	7,342	6,217	5,904	Colombia	233
461	428	345	496	565	366	643	741	746	612	704	696	935	755	1,064	Costa Rica	238
3	8	13	10	9	10	12	15	14	11	15	16	18	20	23	Dominica	321
310	308	128	189	125	43	309	363	474	173	246	244	290	356	502	Dominican Republic	243
654	527	346	295	411	589	646	631	1,005	1,263	1,095	1,292	1,551	1,150	1,197	Ecuador..	248
164	139	131	120	202	292	201	307	390	445	510	652	969	1,146	1,460	El Salvador	253
19	17	16	13	12	12	12	19	20	21	25	25	32	33	37	Grenada	328
274	296	203	149	233	198	564	557	632	591	472	605	824	948	866	Guatemala	258
6	7	6	3	10	20	87	137	180	169	181	229	234	196	195	Guyana	336
6	13	12	10	10	2	12	....	....	21	71	75	57	....	....	Haiti	263
96	91	75	37	16	28	73	144	71	117	176	173	430	581	916	Honduras	268
147	80	123	109	82	118^e	74	236	304	504	458	612	506	504	404	Jamaica	343
4,467	4,635	8,786	3,923	4,816	6,933	12,392	13,776	18,281	4,301	11,333	13,514	21,343	22,584	23,156	Mexico	273
160	195	153	195	158	151	124	160	170	123	137	131	159	176	193	Netherlands Antilles	353
....	....	12	28	88	75	94	95	40	97	92	137	280	249	371	Nicaragua	278
89	139	55	54	91	241	349	367	435	482	526	603	851	....	....	Panama	283
486	365	350	241	329	465	673	408	460	706	735	730	619	614	719	Paraguay	288
1,677	1,150	455	380	615	731	1,708	2,072	2,481	4,790	5,531	7,356	8,140	6,794	6,361	Peru	293
7	8	7	8	12	11	12	19	21	22	23	23	27	33	36	St. Kitts and Nevis	361
12	21	22	24	29	31	34	40	44	40	42	39	45	50	54	St. Lucia	362
13	21	14	16	17	19	16	24	23	21	20	21	23	28	31	St. Vincent & Grenadines	364
21	17	11	9	7	15	1	13	13	27	89	67	81	75	....	Suriname..	366
1,027	388	132	94	188	346	237	125	150	241	241	378	524	556	689	Trinidad and Tobago	369
159	394	374	395	381	368	235	370	552	663	774	870	1,154	1,472	1,515	Uruguay...	298
9,332	5,263	4,203	2,297	3,125	5,849	7,457	6,954	6,709	5,526	4,227	8,198	10,656	8,466	8,945	Venezuela, Rep. Bol........................	299
															Memorandum Items	
67,791	50,368	47,621	41,467	42,837	42,421	47,414	44,674	45,062	42,977	43,240	59,729	70,445	69,195	78,008	Oil Exporting Countries	999
107,652	117,001	135,699	148,314	166,089	198,931	244,613	278,897	339,376	382,193	457,500	533,755	613,044	627,923	700,117	Non-Oil Developing Countries	201

Nongold Reserves/Imports

1rl s		1970	1971	1972	1973	1974	1975	1976	1977	1978	1979	1980	1981	1982	1983	1984
															Weeks of Imports	
World	001	9.3	14.3	15.5	13.1	11.2	11.1	11.6	13.0	13.0	11.5	10.8	10.2	10.2	11.1	10.9
Industrial Countries	110	8.9	14.7	15.0	11.9	8.4	8.5	8.1	9.6	10.8	9.1	8.8	8.5	8.5	9.2	8.6
United States	111	4.2	2.3	2.4	1.9	2.0	2.3	2.8	2.5	2.0	1.8	3.2	3.6	4.7	4.4	3.6
Canada	156	14.2	15.3	13.5	10.2	7.4	6.4	6.4	4.5	4.0	2.6	2.6	2.6	2.7	2.8	1.7
Australia	193	14.9	30.2	60.6	37.9	17.2	14.4	12.2	7.9	6.9	4.1	3.9	3.3	12.4	21.7	14.9
Japan	158	11.9	38.6	38.3	15.4	10.6	10.7	12.6	16.3	21.1	9.2	9.1	10.3	9.2	10.1	10.1
New Zealand	196	10.7	19.0	28.4	25.0	9.1	7.0	7.8	6.8	6.7	5.1	3.3	6.1	5.7	7.6	15.0
Euro Area																
Austria	122	15.3	19.2	19.2	14.6	14.6	19.8	16.1	12.2	16.4	10.5	11.2	13.1	14.1	12.1	11.2
Belgium	124															
Finlande	172	8.4	11.5	11.0	6.9	4.5	3.0	3.3	3.6	8.1	7.0	6.2	5.4	5.9	5.0	11.5
France	132	3.9	10.8	11.9	5.9	4.4	8.2	4.6	4.3	5.9	8.5	10.5	9.6	7.4	9.7	10.4
Allemagne	134	16.7	21.6	24.9	26.7	20.4	18.2	17.7	17.8	20.7	17.1	13.4	13.9	14.0	14.5	13.6
Irlande	178	21.8	27.7	27.4	18.8	17.0	20.8	22.5	22.7	19.5	11.6	13.3	13.0	14.0	15.0	12.6
Italie	136	8.6	12.0	8.0	5.5	4.3	1.8	3.8	8.8	10.2	12.1	11.9	11.1	8.4	13.1	12.7
Luxembourg	137															.5
Pays-Bas	138	4.8	5.0	6.9	7.7	6.2	6.2	5.8	5.6	4.3	5.1	6.8	6.4	7.3	7.8	6.9
Portugal	182	20.1	27.2	30.5	28.9	13.4	5.4	2.2	4.0	8.6	7.4	4.4	2.8	2.4	2.4	3.4
Espagne	184	14.5	28.3	34.1	33.2	19.8	17.6	14.0	17.4	28.1	27.0	18.1	17.5	12.7	13.2	12.6
Danemark	128	4.9	7.4	8.0	8.3	4.5	4.0	3.5	6.2	11.0	9.1	9.1	7.5	7.1	11.6	9.4
Grèce	174	5.1	10.2	19.9	13.4	9.3	9.4	7.6	8.0	8.7	7.3	6.6	6.0	4.5	4.9	5.3
Islande	176	17.4	17.1	18.7	14.3	4.7	4.9	8.8	8.4	10.5	10.3	9.4	11.7	8.0	9.5	7.9
Norvège	142	11.1	14.3	15.3	12.7	11.7	11.8	10.2	8.9	12.9	16.0	18.6	20.8	23.1	25.5	35.1
Sweden	144	4.2	6.6	8.7	10.9	4.6	8.5	6.0	8.8	10.4	6.4	5.3	6.5	6.6	8.0	7.6
Switzerland	146	19.6	27.5	27.0	22.4	19.6	27.4	33.8	29.8	38.8	29.1	22.4	23.7	28.0	26.8	26.9
United Kingdom	112	3.5	17.4	9.1	7.5	5.8	4.5	3.1	16.6	11.0	10.3	9.3	7.7	6.5	5.9	4.7
Developing Countries	200	10.5	12.8	16.7	16.9	18.6	16.9	20.1	20.9	18.0	17.6	14.9	13.3	13.2	14.7	15.8
Africa	605	10.4	9.4	11.3	12.0	18.2	13.9	14.4	11.7	8.3	12.7	12.3	7.2	5.4	5.6	5.5
Algeria	612	6.1	12.7	9.9	21.2	18.7	10.7	18.1	12.3	12.0	16.5	18.6	17.0	11.7	9.4	7.4
Benin	638	12.6	16.6	16.1	15.4	12.2	4.2	4.6	4.0	2.6	2.3	1.3	5.5	.6	.6	.4
Botswana	616							18.7	18.2	21.1	25.8	25.8	15.9	21.1	27.4	34.6
Burkina Faso	748	38.1	39.4	36.0	33.2	30.1	26.3	25.8	14.0	8.3	10.6	9.9	10.9	9.3	15.2	21.9
Burundi	618	35.7	30.8	30.4	35.7	17.1	25.9	44.0	66.2	43.0	30.7	29.3	19.8	7.2	7.7	5.5
Cameroon	622	17.3	15.2	7.5	8.0	9.4	2.5	3.7	3.0	2.6	5.1	6.1	3.1	2.9	6.8	2.5
Cape Verde	624							56.5	58.0	38.3	41.5	32.5	27.8	25.3	25.2	21.9
Central African Rep.	626	2.1	.3	2.6	1.8	2.0	2.9	17.8	20.8	22.2	32.9	35.2	38.0	19.5	36.0	31.5
Chad	628	1.9	9.3	8.4	.9	9.1	1.2	10.5	5.2	2.8	6.9	3.6	3.5	5.9	9.3	12.7
Comoros	632											11.4	13.5	17.3	16.3	4.2
Congo, Dem. Rep. of	636	39.6	23.3	30.7	35.7	17.7	8.3	11.6	34.3	33.3	54.0	38.1	35.4	12.6	33.7	10.4
Congo, Rep. of	634	7.8	6.9	5.2	3.2	9.8	4.2	3.7	3.4	1.9	7.5	7.7	14.4	2.5	.6	.3
Côte d'Ivoire	662	15.9	11.6	10.0	6.5	3.5	4.7	3.1	5.5	10.0	3.1	.3	.4	.1	.6	.2
Djibouti	611															10.5
Equatorial Guinea	642													4.7	3.6	4.1
Ethiopia	644	19.2	16.4	22.8	40.3	48.4	46.0	43.5	31.5	17.5	15.8	5.8	18.8	12.0	7.5	2.5
Gabon	646	9.5	14.4	8.7	13.1	16.2	16.2	12.0	.7	1.9	2.0	8.3	12.3	18.7	14.2	14.3
Gambia, The	648	23.5	26.7	23.9	27.1	31.4	24.9	14.5	16.3	13.5	.7	1.8	1.6	4.2	1.3	1.2
Ghana	652	4.6	4.4	16.7	20.3	4.5	8.2	5.5	7.4	14.3	17.6	8.3	6.8	10.2	3.0	25.8
Guinea-Bissau	654															
Kenya	664	25.8	15.9	19.6	19.7	9.8	9.5	14.8	21.1	10.7	19.9	12.0	6.2	6.7	14.7	13.8
Lesotho	666											6.1	4.9	5.4	7.2	5.8
Liberia	668					3.4	3.0	2.2	3.1	1.9	5.6	.5	1.0	.8	2.6	.5
Madagascar	674	11.3	11.3	13.2	17.4	9.1	5.1	7.7	10.3	6.9	.4	.8	2.5	2.5	3.9	8.4
Malawi	676	15.3	15.0	14.4	21.5	18.8	11.3	7.1	17.5	10.1	8.4	8.2	7.4	3.7	2.6	10.2
Mali	678	1.4	1.8	2.5	1.7	1.8	1.2	2.3	1.8	1.5	.9	1.7	2.4	2.6	2.4	5.0
Mauritania	682	3.0	6.8	10.1	17.2	44.9	15.4	23.9	12.6	22.8	22.9	25.5	31.8	26.2	24.3	19.4
Mauritius	684	31.8	32.0	30.6	20.6	22.0	26.0	12.9	7.7	4.8	2.6	7.7	3.2	4.2	2.1	2.6
Morocco	686	9.1	11.2	14.3	10.9	10.7	7.1	9.3	8.2	10.8	7.9	4.9	2.7	2.6	1.5	.6
Namibia	728															
Niger	692	16.6	32.1	32.7	30.8	24.5	25.9	34.0	26.7	21.9	14.9	11.0	10.7	3.3	8.5	16.0
Nigeria	694	9.9	14.0	12.3	15.6	105.1	48.1	32.8	19.8	7.7	28.2	31.9	9.7	5.2	4.2	8.1
Rwanda	714	13.8	9.1	9.6	23.5	11.6	13.5	31.5	35.1	24.2	41.2	39.9	35.1	24.2	21.4	20.0
Senegal	722	5.9	5.8	7.2	1.7	.7	2.8	2.1	2.3	1.3	1.1	.4	.4	.6	.6	.2
Seychelles	718				8.9	9.3	10.4	8.6	13.1	8.3	7.4	9.7	7.7	6.9	5.9	3.2
Sierra Leone	724	17.6	17.6	20.3	17.3	12.8	8.0	8.6	9.6	6.5	7.7	3.7	2.5	1.5	5.3	2.6
South Africa	199	4.7	3.2	8.0	4.5	2.5	3.1	3.0	3.5	2.9	2.5	1.9	1.5	1.4	2.7	1.8
Sudan	732	3.9	4.4	5.8	7.3	10.1	2.1	1.3	1.1	1.2	3.2	1.6	.6	.8	.6	.8
Swaziland	734						5.1	13.3	19.1	27.0	19.0	13.6	13.2	8.5	7.6	8.7	9.4
Tanzania	738	10.6	8.2	15.4	15.2	3.5	4.4	9.1	19.7	4.5	3.2	.8	.8	.2	1.3	2.1
Togo	742	28.3	29.8	22.3	19.6	23.7	12.3	18.7	8.4	8.1	6.6	7.3	18.2	22.2	31.9	39.0
Tunisia	744	9.4	21.5	24.3	23.0	19.0	13.9	12.4	10.0	10.8	10.6	8.7	7.4	9.2	9.5	6.6
Uganda	746	17.1	5.6	11.5	9.3	4.1	7.8	13.4	10.2	10.8	6.0	.5	4.5	10.8	14.7	10.3
Zambia	754	55.4	25.9	14.6	18.1	10.9	7.9	7.2	5.1	4.3	5.6	3.7	2.7	3.0	5.2	4.7
Zimbabwe	698	2.8	.7	6.7	10.7	4.3	4.5	5.7	5.3	11.2	16.7	7.7	5.2	4.4	3.2	2.1
Asia	505	12.3	13.1	14.9	13.2	10.4	9.7	13.7	16.6	14.6	13.1	11.0	11.2	12.8	14.9	15.8
Afghanistan, Islamic State of	512	5.7	9.9	6.6	6.5	5.9	12.9	26.1	43.7	51.4	53.9	23.0	16.1	13.9	10.5	8.6
Bangladesh	513			20.6	7.5	6.7	5.8	15.8	10.4	10.8	10.5	6.0	2.7	3.9	12.6	7.2
China, P.R.: Mainland	924								17.1	7.3	7.2	6.6	11.9	30.6	36.4	32.9
China, P.R.: Hong Kong	532															
Fiji	819	13.7	15.9	22.6	17.3	20.8	28.8	22.9	24.9	19.7	15.1	15.5	11.1	13.0	12.4	13.6
India	534	18.7	20.2	21.4	13.7	10.4	8.9	25.6	38.1	42.5	39.3	24.3	13.8	15.2	18.3	19.9
Indonesia	536	8.1	8.7	19.1	15.3	20.2	6.4	13.7	20.9	20.4	29.3	25.9	19.6	9.7	11.8	17.9
Korea	542	15.9	9.4	10.8	10.9	2.1	5.6	11.7	14.3	9.6	7.6	6.8	5.3	6.0	4.7	4.7
Lao People's Democratic Rep.	544															
Malaysia	548	22.9	27.1	29.3	27.1	19.6	21.2	32.7	31.9	28.5	25.9	21.2	18.4	15.8	14.8	13.8
Maldives	556							.1	.4	2.1	1.7	1.7	1.9	10.1	4.2	5.0
Mongolia	948															
Myanmar	518	10.5	15.0	15.8	45.1	53.8	35.1	34.7	22.3	16.3	33.2	38.3	31.9	13.3	17.4	13.5

Weeks of Imports

1985	1986	1987	1988	1989	1990	1991	1992	1993	1994	1995	1996	1997	1998	1999		1rl s
11.9	12.6	15.0	13.3	13.1	13.8	14.2	13.5	15.1	15.2	14.8	15.9	15.8	16.5	17.0	World	001
9.5	10.3	13.1	11.9	11.7	11.9	11.5	10.5	11.5	11.3	11.0	11.7	11.2	10.7	10.1	Industrial Countries	110
4.7	5.1	4.3	4.2	6.7	7.3	6.8	5.7	5.4	4.8	5.0	4.1	3.4	3.9	3.0	United States	111
1.6	2.0	4.1	7.1	7.0	7.5	6.8	4.6	4.7	4.1	4.7	6.1	4.6	5.9	6.6	Canada	156
11.6	14.4	15.5	19.6	15.9	20.1	20.6	13.3	12.7	11.0	10.1	11.5	13.3	11.8	16.0	Australia	193
10.6	17.2	27.9	26.8	20.8	17.3	15.8	16.0	21.2	23.8	28.4	32.3	33.7	39.9	47.9	Japan	158
13.8	32.3	23.3	20.1	17.9	22.6	18.3	17.4	18.0	16.2	16.4	21.0	15.9	17.5	16.2	New Zealand	196
															Euro Area	
11.8	11.9	12.0	10.5	11.5	9.9	10.6	11.9	15.6	15.8	14.7	17.7	15.8	17.1	11.4	Austria	122
....	....	....	....	....	....	....	....	5.2	5.5	5.3	5.4	5.4	5.9	3.5	Belgium	124
14.7	6.1	17.0	15.7	10.9	18.6	18.1	12.8	15.6	23.9	18.6	12.3	14.7	15.6	13.9	Finlande	172
12.8	12.6	10.8	7.4	6.6	8.2	7.0	5.9	5.8	5.8	5.0	5.9	5.9	7.9	7.1	France	132
14.6	14.1	17.9	12.2	11.7	10.2	8.4	11.8	11.7	10.4	9.5	9.4	9.1	8.2	6.7	Allemagne	134
15.3	14.5	18.3	17.0	12.1	13.1	14.4	8.0	14.0	12.3	13.6	11.9	8.6	11.0	6.0	Irlande	178
9.2	10.5	12.5	13.0	15.9	18.0	13.9	7.6	9.7	9.9	8.8	11.5	13.8	7.1	5.4	Italie	136
.5	.4	.4	.4	.6	.6	.5	.5	.5	.5	.4	.4	.4	....	.4	Luxembourg	137
7.7	7.7	9.1	8.4	8.2	7.2	7.3	8.5	13.1	12.7	9.9	7.7	7.3	5.9	2.8	Pays-Bas	138
9.5	7.8	12.4	14.9	27.1	29.8	40.6	32.8	33.9	29.5	23.7	23.5	23.2	21.4	12.0	Portugal	182
19.4	21.9	32.5	31.9	30.4	30.4	36.8	23.7	26.8	23.4	15.8	24.7	29.0	21.6	11.9	Espagne	184
15.5	11.3	20.5	21.6	12.5	17.1	11.9	16.3	17.5	13.5	12.7	16.5	22.6	17.5	26.4	Danemark	128
4.5	7.0	10.6	15.3	10.4	9.0	12.5	10.7	18.4	40.2	33.5	37.7	27.7	39.1	....	Grèce	174
11.8	14.4	10.2	9.5	12.5	13.5	13.3	15.4	16.5	10.3	9.1	11.6	10.0	8.9	9.9	Islande	176
46.5	32.1	32.8	29.7	30.3	29.3	26.9	24.0	42.6	36.2	35.5	38.7	34.1	26.7	31.2	Norvège	142
10.6	10.4	10.4	9.7	10.1	17.2	19.1	23.5	23.2	23.4	19.3	13.6	8.6	10.7	11.4	Sweden	144
30.5	27.6	28.2	22.3	22.6	21.8	22.7	28.0	29.9	28.2	24.6	26.8	28.6	29.0	25.0	Switzerland	146
6.1	7.6	14.1	12.1	9.1	8.3	10.4	8.6	9.3	9.4	8.2	7.2	5.5	5.3	4.9	United Kingdom	112
17.3	18.2	20.2	16.7	16.6	19.0	21.0	20.2	22.0	22.7	22.4	23.9	24.5	28.5	30.4	Developing Countries	200
8.4	8.1	9.1	8.0	9.2	11.6	14.1	11.2	12.7	14.8	13.1	15.8	20.1	19.5	....	Africa	605
14.9	9.4	12.1	6.1	4.7	3.9	9.9	8.9	9.9	14.8	10.2	24.9	47.0	....	....	Algeria	612
.6	.5	.5	.7	.9	12.7	41.3	22.1	22.2	31.1	13.8	20.8	19.3	20.2	32.4	Benin	638
60.6	72.6	96.7	80.8	76.5	90.4	101.1	105.9	122.3	141.5	129.6	153.8	132.2	131.2	....	Botswana	616
21.9	30.0	38.6	36.8	35.3	29.2	33.8	38.1	39.1	35.4	39.7	27.2	30.5	24.8	22.1	Burkina Faso	748
8.2	17.8	14.9	17.7	27.7	23.7	28.8	40.9	43.2	47.4	46.5	57.1	48.4	21.6	21.1	Burundi	618
6.0	1.8	1.9	7.2	3.3	.9	1.9	.9	.1	.2	.2	.1	—	....	....	Cameroon	622
33.4	20.5	41.8	39.8	34.8	29.5	23.1	21.9	19.5	10.5	11.8	....	....	....	....	Cape Verde	624
22.9	20.3	24.6	40.0	39.1	39.9	57.7	35.8	46.4	78.4	69.8	85.4	64.2	....	....	Central African Rep.	626
10.5	3.9	12.0	14.4	24.7	23.3	24.9	17.2	10.1	22.3	33.5	33.5	28.7	23.6	....	Chad	628
16.7	24.6	30.8	23.3	37.6	29.9	26.1	20.6	33.8	43.5	37.0	....	....	....	....	Comoros	632
12.5	16.0	12.4	12.7	11.9	12.8	13.4	19.4	6.5	16.4	19.2	10.1	....	....	....	Congo, Dem. Rep. of	636
.3	.6	.2	.2	.3	.5	.4	.5	.1	4.1	4.6	3.1	....	....	....	Congo, Rep. of	634
.1	.5	.2	.3	.4	.1	.3	.2	.1	5.5	9.4	10.9	11.6	13.9	10.0	Côte d'Ivoire	662
13.2	15.1	16.1	16.6	15.7	22.7	24.3	19.8	....	....	....	....	....	....	....	Djibouti	611
9.1	2.7	.5	4.7	5.7	.6	4.2	7.5	.7	.8	.1	.2	3.2	1.3	....	Equatorial Guinea	642
7.7	11.8	6.0	3.0	2.5	1.0	6.0	14.4	30.1	27.4	35.0	27.2	....	....	18.1	Ethiopia	644
11.7	7.6	.9	4.4	2.3	15.5	20.4	5.3	—	12.0	8.7	13.5	13.3	....	....	Gabon	646
1.0	6.8	10.5	7.2	6.6	15.3	17.4	22.4	....	24.0	30.3	20.6	28.7	22.6	30.1	Gambia, The	648
28.7	25.5	8.8	12.7	14.2	....	27.1	7.7	5.4	14.4	19.0	20.4	....	7.6	6.7	Ghana	652
....	-.5	....	12.5	14.0	11.1	10.0	9.6	12.0	5.9	7.9	6.9	19.7	29.5	19.4	Guinea-Bissau	654
14.1	13.3	7.7	6.9	6.8	4.8	3.1	1.5	11.9	13.9	6.1	13.2	12.5	12.7	....	Kenya	664
6.7	8.9	7.5	5.0	4.3	5.6	7.4	9.1	15.1	22.8	24.1	24.0	29.0	34.6	....	Lesotho	666
.3	.5	.1	.1	....	....	....	....	....	....	....	....	....	....	....	Liberia	668
6.3	16.9	31.9	30.7	34.3	7.4	10.6	....	....	8.5	10.4	24.7	31.2	17.3	....	Madagascar	674
6.9	5.3	7.4	14.2	9.7	11.1	9.6	2.4	5.9	5.0	16.6	28.3	10.8	36.7	....	Malawi	676
3.9	1.4	2.2	3.7	17.7	16.4	36.1	26.4	27.3	19.5	21.2	26.6	28.4	27.5	24.2	Mali	678
13.2	11.3	15.9	12.1	19.3	12.8	5.9	....	....	5.1	....	....	....	....	....	Mauritania	682
2.9	10.3	17.6	17.8	20.3	23.7	29.8	26.3	22.9	20.1	22.7	20.4	16.5	14.0	....	Mauritius	684
1.6	2.9	5.1	6.0	4.6	15.5	23.5	25.4	28.2	27.4	18.7	20.3	21.8	22.4	29.8	Morocco	686
....	....	....	....	....	....	....	2.0	5.9	8.8	....	....	....	....	....	Namibia	728
19.2	26.7	41.6	31.2	30.4	29.7	29.7	24.4	26.6	17.5	13.2	9.1	7.1	6.7	5.1	Niger	692
9.8	13.9	15.5	7.2	21.9	35.7	25.7	6.1	12.9	9.7	9.5	30.6	38.2	33.7	....	Nigeria	694
19.7	24.2	24.3	16.6	11.0	8.0	18.7	14.2	7.4	26.0	21.7	21.6	26.8	30.8	35.8	Rwanda	714
.3	.5	.5	.5	.8	.5	.6	.6	.2	9.1	10.0	10.4	15.0	15.6	....	Senegal	722
4.5	3.8	6.3	2.8	3.8	4.6	8.3	8.5	7.8	7.6	6.1	4.1	4.0	2.8	....	Seychelles	718
3.7	5.4	2.4	2.5	1.1	1.9	3.1	6.8	10.2	14.0	13.5	6.6	21.6	24.2	25.4	Sierra Leone	724
1.4	1.5	2.2	2.2	2.7	2.8	2.5	2.6	2.7	3.8	4.8	1.6	7.6	7.7	12.4	South Africa	199
.8	3.2	.7	.6	....	1.0	.4	1.7	2.1	3.3	7.0	3.6	2.7	2.5	....	Sudan	732
13.7	14.2	15.1	14.3	16.1	17.0	12.5	18.6	15.8	16.7	14.1	11.2	12.9	....	....	Swaziland	734
1.0	3.4	1.8	4.9	2.8	7.4	6.9	11.3	7.1	11.5	8.4	16.5	24.2	21.4	24.7	Tanzania	738
53.5	57.0	43.6	24.8	31.4	31.6	42.7	35.9	45.3	22.1	11.4	6.9	9.6	9.7	....	Togo	742
4.4	5.5	9.0	12.7	11.4	7.5	7.9	6.9	7.1	11.5	10.6	12.8	13.0	11.5	13.9	Tunisia	744
4.3	4.9	3.3	2.9	1.7	8.0	15.6	9.7	....	19.1	22.6	23.1	25.0	26.7	29.6	Uganda	746
14.4	6.1	7.7	8.3	6.7	8.2	11.7	....	12.4	23.5	16.5	13.9	15.2	....	....	Zambia	754
5.4	5.6	8.2	8.2	3.0	4.2	3.8	5.2	12.4	9.4	11.6	11.1	....	....	....	Zimbabwe	698
17.0	22.0	25.7	21.2	19.8	22.9	24.3	22.3	23.2	25.0	22.9	24.9	25.6	34.5	36.5	Asia	505
12.9	9.6	14.6	15.1	15.4	14.8	19.3	....	....	....	....	....	....	....	....	Afghanistan, Islamic State of	512
6.9	8.4	16.1	17.9	7.1	9.0	19.5	25.4	31.4	35.5	18.7	14.4	11.9	14.2	10.8	Bangladesh	513
15.7	13.9	19.6	17.4	15.8	28.8	35.6	13.3	11.3	23.8	30.4	40.1	52.2	55.3	49.5	China, P.R.: Mainland	924
....	....	....	....	....	15.5	14.9	14.8	16.1	15.8	14.9	16.7	23.1	25.3	27.9	China, P.R.: Hong Kong	532
15.4	20.5	18.1	26.3	19.0	18.0	21.7	26.1	19.5	16.9	20.4	22.5	19.4	27.8	....	Fiji	819
21.0	21.6	20.1	13.3	9.8	3.4	9.2	12.7	23.3	38.2	26.9	27.6	31.0	33.1	37.8	India	534
25.2	19.7	23.5	19.8	17.3	17.8	18.6	19.9	20.7	19.7	17.5	22.1	20.7	43.2	57.3	Indonesia	536
4.8	5.5	4.5	12.4	12.9	11.0	8.7	10.9	12.6	13.0	12.6	11.8	7.3	29.0	32.1	Korea	542
....	....	....	....	.4	.5	8.8	7.8	7.6	5.6	8.1	12.4	8.3	11.0	10.0	Lao People's Democratic Rep.	544
20.8	29.0	30.5	20.6	18.0	17.3	15.4	22.5	31.0	22.2	15.9	17.9	13.7	22.8	24.5	Malaysia	548
4.5	8.0	5.3	12.5	11.4	9.2	7.6	7.7	7.1	7.3	9.3	13.1	14.7	17.4	16.4	Maldives	556
....	....	....	....	....	....	....	2.0	8.2	16.4	14.7	12.4	19.5	9.7	7.0	Mongolia	948
6.2	5.7	5.3	16.5	71.7	60.2	20.8	22.4	19.4	24.8	21.9	8.8	6.4	6.1	6.0	Myanmar	518

1rl *s*

		1970	1971	1972	1973	1974	1975	1976	1977	1978	1979	1980	1981	1982	1983	1984
																Weeks of Imports
Asia (cont.)																
Nepal	558	61.1	59.1	60.1	59.0	47.0	29.0	40.7	43.1	34.1	32.5	27.8	28.4	26.2	14.9	10.2
Pakistan	564	9.7	9.9	10.6	23.1	11.7	8.2	11.1	9.5	6.4	2.7	4.8	6.6	8.2	18.6	8.8
Papua New Guinea	853				4.6	3.3	15.8	26.6	34.5	27.3	29.0	18.7	16.3	20.1	20.4	20.4
Philippines	566	8.2	12.8	18.2	34.4	28.6	18.3	21.5	18.9	20.0	20.0	20.0	12.6	5.4	4.9	4.4
Samoa	862	20.0	24.9	12.2	11.2	11.8	9.0	9.2	11.5	4.7	3.5	2.3	3.0	3.6	7.8	10.9
Singapore	576	21.4	26.6	26.8	23.2	17.4	19.2	19.3	19.2	21.1	17.1	14.2	14.2	15.7	17.1	18.9
Solomon Islands	813								4.5	35.8	27.5	17.2	12.4	27.3	33.5	29.6
Sri Lanka	524	5.8	7.4	8.4	10.5	5.6	3.9	8.2	21.7	21.4	18.5	6.2	8.9	9.1	8.0	14.2
Thailand	578	33.0	31.8	33.7	30.6	29.1	26.6	26.2	20.4	19.5	13.4	8.8	9.0	9.4	8.1	9.6
Tonga	866								23.8	20.6	22.3	19.0	18.1	19.5	29.0	33.4
Vanuatu	846	....	....	....	....	....	....	....	....	....	....	....	7.6	4.9	5.4	6.1
Europe	170	....	....	....	....	....	....	....	....	....	....	....	....	....	....	....
Albania	914	....	....	....	....	....	....	....	....	....	....	....	....	....	....	....
Cyprus	423	42.8	53.7	49.8	33.3	32.0	33.4	33.0	26.2	23.7	18.2	15.9	19.0	22.4	22.1	20.6
Czech Republic	935															
Czechoslovakia	934	....	....	....	....	....	....	....	....	....	....	....	7.5	4.2	3.3	3.4	4.2
Estonia	939															
Hungary	944															
Kazakhstan	916														7.5	10.0
Malta	181	47.8	59.8	77.4	67.5	55.7	67.3	74.7	72.6	83.6	69.3	54.9	64.9	71.4	79.0	71.8
Moldova	921															
Poland	964	....	....	....	....	....	....	....	....	....	....	1.8	.4	1.1	3.2	3.6	5.2
Romania	968	....	....	....	3.0	2.3	4.9	4.4	1.8	2.0	2.3	1.2	1.6	2.2	2.6	3.3
Russia	922															
Slovak Republic	936															
Turkey	186	16.7	28.0	42.0	49.5	21.5	10.4	10.0	5.7	9.1	6.8	7.1	5.4	6.4	7.3	6.1
Ukraine	926															
Yugoslavia, SFR	188	1.6	2.5	10.9	14.7	7.5	5.5	14.0	11.0	12.4	5.1	4.8	5.3	3.0	4.2	5.0
Middle East	405	**20.4**	**31.9**	**37.2**	**34.0**	**57.4**	**50.0**	**50.3**	**47.8**	**35.2**	**37.0**	**33.8**	**27.9**	**25.4**	**24.6**	**24.2**
Bahrain	419	13.2	14.3	11.5	6.5	6.1	12.7	13.6	12.9	12.5	12.9	14.2	19.5	22.1	22.7	19.5
Egypt	469	4.9	3.2	3.0	14.8	5.6	2.6	3.3	4.7	3.8	7.2	11.2	4.2	4.0	3.9	3.6
Iran, I.R. of	429	2.4	13.3	17.7	16.5	78.7	44.0	35.0	44.7	46.0	81.2	43.4	5.7	24.8	....	....
Iraq	433	32.6	32.9	46.1	80.2	67.9	31.6	59.2	79.1	....	....	....	....	....	....	....
Israel	436	10.1	15.2	24.8	21.7	11.0	9.9	12.2	13.7	18.4	18.6	17.8	17.8	20.7	19.8	16.2
Jordan	439	64.2	54.0	45.8	42.7	33.3	32.6	24.4	24.2	30.6	30.9	24.7	17.9	14.2	14.1	9.6
Kuwait	443	9.7	15.4	17.5	18.9	41.8	32.3	26.6	30.9	28.3	28.7	31.3	30.3	37.1	36.6	34.6
Lebanon	446	7.7	14.0	18.3	19.1	28.2	30.5	110.6	53.0	49.6	29.5	22.6	22.5	40.0	27.0	11.8
Libya	672	141.1	190.3	141.2	58.3	66.1	30.8	50.3	66.0	46.4	62.1	100.5	55.9	51.2	45.0	30.4
Oman	449	29.2	38.3	38.8	21.1	12.3	11.0	15.7	17.2	13.9	17.3	17.5	16.9	16.9	15.9	17.0
Qatar	453	24.7	18.3	19.8	18.0	12.2	12.2	8.2	6.9	9.2	10.5	12.5	12.5	10.3	13.7	17.0
Saudi Arabia	456	40.7	85.4	109.1	98.8	257.3	286.3	160.9	106.1	48.9	41.0	40.4	47.6	37.8	36.2	38.2
Syrian Arab Rep.	463	3.9	6.9	10.1	32.1	19.7	21.7	6.4	9.3	8.1	9.1	4.2	2.9	2.6	.6	3.4
United Arab Emirates	466	....	....	....	5.8	13.8	19.1	29.7	8.2	7.9	10.7	12.0	17.3	12.2	13.0	17.1
Yemen Arab Rep.	473				53.7	54.3	59.7	90.8	62.0	59.1	49.8	36.0	28.4	18.9	11.8	10.6
Yemen, P.D. Rep.	459	15.3	21.2	23.2	22.9	8.3	8.7	10.3	9.5	17.0	11.8	8.0	9.3	9.3	9.9	8.4
Yemen, Republic of	474															
Western Hemisphere	205	**13.0**	**14.1**	**20.8**	**23.9**	**17.8**	**17.2**	**21.1**	**23.0**	**25.6**	**24.9**	**16.9**	**15.4**	**13.5**	**18.3**	**24.9**
Antigua and Barbuda	311	....	....	....	....	....	5.7	14.3	7.7	7.6	9.3	4.6	3.4	3.2	4.7	6.1
Argentina	213	16.3	5.4	8.6	26.8	16.4	3.8	24.8	39.4	67.4	72.9	33.1	18.0	24.4	13.5	14.1
Aruba	314															
Bahamas, The	313	3.3	3.0	4.0	2.9	1.4	1.0	.8	1.0	1.0	1.1	.6	.7	.9	1.4	2.1
Barbados	316	7.3	7.9	10.3	10.0	10.0	9.5	6.1	7.1	9.9	8.1	7.8	9.1	11.4	10.3	10.4
Belize	339							3.9	4.6	6.8	4.1	4.4	3.3	4.0	4.3	2.4
Bolivia	218	10.7	12.2	12.4	12.4	23.5	13.0	14.2	17.8	10.9	10.4	8.3	5.7	14.6	14.4	26.8
Brazil	223	20.8	23.8	44.9	47.3	19.1	15.2	24.6	28.2	40.9	23.5	12.0	14.3	9.7	13.5	39.3
Chile	228	16.7	8.0	4.6	4.9	1.0	1.9	11.3	8.7	16.6	21.0	28.0	23.3	23.7	34.3	33.5
Colombia	233	11.7	10.5	18.7	25.3	14.0	16.5	34.4	48.3	41.4	59.4	53.0	47.4	36.6	19.9	15.8
Costa Rica	238	2.3	4.0	5.7	5.5	3.0	3.7	6.4	9.7	8.6	4.4	4.9	5.7	13.2	16.4	19.3
Dominica	321						.9	3.2	5.3	3.5	23.0	5.5	3.2	4.7	1.7	4.7
Dominican Republic	243	5.0	7.7	7.4	9.0	5.6	6.6	7.3	9.6	8.1	10.2	6.4	7.0	4.6	6.1	9.1
Ecuador	248	10.5	5.7	19.8	27.5	24.4	13.3	25.9	27.3	22.0	23.5	23.4	14.6	7.3	22.5	19.7
El Salvador	253	11.0	9.6	12.2	5.7	7.2	9.1	13.1	11.8	13.6	7.1	4.2	3.8	6.6	9.3	8.8
Grenada	328	12.4	13.0	13.1	12.0	15.3	10.9	16.7	12.3	14.1	14.5	13.4	15.4	8.5	12.9	13.2
Guatemala	258	11.1	13.1	18.7	23.1	13.5	20.1	30.4	33.0	30.0	24.1	14.5	4.6	4.2	9.7	11.2
Guyana	336	7.9	10.1	13.4	4.1	12.8	15.2	3.9	3.8	10.9	2.9	1.7	.8	2.0	1.4	1.4
Haiti	263	4.1	8.9	13.5	10.6	8.2	4.3	7.0	8.3	8.6	10.5	2.2	2.7	.6	1.1	1.5
Honduras	268	4.7	5.8	9.4	8.3	6.0	12.6	14.9	16.3	13.8	13.2	7.7	5.5	8.3	7.4	7.5
Jamaica	343	13.8	16.9	13.0	9.8	10.6	5.8	1.8	2.9	3.4	3.3	4.7	3.0	4.1	2.2	4.4
Mexico	273	12.0	16.2	18.7	15.8	10.6	10.9	10.2	15.6	11.8	8.9	7.0	7.4	2.4	16.3	22.7
Netherlands Antilles	353	1.6	2.1	3.0	1.6	.9	1.3	1.3	1.7	1.0	.9	.9	1.2	1.9	1.9	1.5
Nicaragua	278	12.7	14.4	19.1	18.5	9.7	12.2	14.3	10.1	4.4	21.2	3.8	5.8	11.5	11.0	....
Panama	283	2.3	2.8	5.1	4.3	2.5	2.0	4.8	4.3	8.3	5.2	4.2	4.0	3.3	7.6	....
Paraguay	288	12.0	13.1	19.8	24.2	22.8	29.1	37.2	45.2	60.9	60.8	64.4	69.9	57.2	64.8	59.1
Peru	293	24.7	26.0	28.9	26.9	31.4	8.7	7.4	9.7	17.3	43.4	41.2	17.9	19.5	27.9	38.3
St. Kitts and Nevis	361	....	....	....	....	....	....	....	....	....	....	....	4.4	4.0	3.2	5.7
St. Lucia	362	....	....	....	....	....	3.6	5.6	5.0	4.2	4.2	3.5	3.1	3.6	3.2	5.4
St. Vincent & Grenadines	364							10.2	8.2	7.6	9.9	6.6	8.0	3.8	4.2	8.7
Suriname	366	12.5	13.6	13.5	18.7	15.3	18.9	19.5	12.3	17.0	21.5	19.5	19.0	17.9	6.8	3.7
Trinidad and Tobago	369	4.1	5.4	4.0	3.1	11.0	26.6	26.2	42.4	47.7	52.9	45.5	55.7	43.3	42.4	36.8
Uruguay	298	3.1	4.6	17.0	18.4	8.6	5.5	15.6	23.0	24.2	13.9	11.9	13.6	5.4	13.7	9.0
Venezuela, Rep. Bol.	299	17.7	27.1	27.6	35.9	75.6	72.8	55.1	36.8	26.7	35.7	29.0	32.4	26.4	61.9	59.5
Memorandum Items																
Oil Exporting Countries	999	**20.3**	**33.0**	**36.0**	**34.1**	**73.5**	**56.2**	**52.1**	**45.6**	**32.1**	**38.9**	**36.0**	**28.3**	**23.5**	**25.4**	**27.7**
Non-Oil Developing Countries	201	**9.2**	**9.9**	**13.6**	**14.0**	**9.2**	**7.7**	**10.8**	**12.5**	**13.5**	**12.0**	**9.4**	**9.0**	**9.8**	**11.4**	**12.6**

1rl s

Weeks of Imports

Asia (cont.)

1985	1986	1987	1988	1989	1990	1991	1992	1993	1994	1995	1996	1997	1998	1999		
6.4	9.8	16.2	16.9	18.9	22.8	28.0	31.3	37.4	31.2	22.9	21.2	19.2	31.6	....	Nepal	558
6.8	6.6	4.4	3.0	3.5	2.0	3.0	4.6	6.1	16.8	7.6	2.2	5.1	5.5	7.2	Pakistan	564
22.8	20.5	19.5	14.7	13.1	17.6	10.4	8.4	5.7	3.3	9.4	17.4	11.1	8.1	9.0	Papua New Guinea	853
5.3	17.1	8.5	6.5	7.4	4.0	12.8	16.7	14.4	14.9	13.3	16.3	10.5	13.2	22.1	Philippines	566
14.2	26.3	31.2	33.8	38.0	44.5	37.5	28.9	25.2	32.4	30.3	31.5	34.5	33.0	30.7	Samoa	862
25.4	26.4	24.3	20.2	21.3	23.7	26.9	28.7	29.5	29.5	28.7	30.4	28.0	37.2	36.0	Singapore	576
22.3	21.3	23.6	21.1	12.0	10.0	4.0	10.9	7.6	6.5	5.4	11.2	....	....	....	Solomon Islands	813
11.8	9.4	7.1	5.2	5.7	8.2	11.7	13.8	21.2	22.3	20.5	18.7	18.0	17.5	14.4	Sri Lanka	524
12.3	15.9	16.0	15.6	19.2	20.9	24.2	26.0	27.6	28.0	26.4	27.1	21.7	34.9	42.7	Thailand	578
34.8	28.8	31.2	28.6	24.0	26.3	28.3	26.4	31.4	26.7	19.3	21.4	....	....	....	Tonga	866
7.9	19.5	30.0	30.0	25.8	20.4	25.1	27.0	30.1	25.3	26.4	23.4	20.7	26.4	....	Vanuatu	846
....	....	....	....	....	6.6	7.3	7.4	10.8	12.1	17.3	15.5	15.9	16.7	20.2	**Europe**	170
								13.4	17.6	17.6	17.4	24.9	21.9	....	Albania	914
24.8	30.8	30.6	26.0	24.3	28.0	25.4	14.5	21.6	25.2	15.7	20.1	19.6	19.5	26.3	Cyprus	423
....	....	....	....	....	....	....	....	12.9	17.4	27.1	22.1	17.7	21.6	....	Czech Republic	935
3.7	4.0	4.4	5.4	7.5	4.2	15.8	4.4	....	....	....	....	....	....	....	Czechoslovakia	934
								22.5	13.8	11.8	10.3	8.9	9.1	10.8	Estonia	939
13.6	12.5	8.6	8.2	7.4	6.4	17.9	20.7	27.8	24.3	41.4	31.9	21.2	18.9	20.4	Hungary	944
								6.1	12.2	15.5	15.9	20.5	17.5	20.9	Kazakhstan	916
67.6	67.1	64.6	52.5	47.6	38.0	32.8	28.1	32.6	39.4	28.3	30.1	29.7	32.2	34.2	Malta	181
....	....	....	....	....	....	....	.2	6.3	13.3	15.9	15.0	15.9	7.3	....	Moldova	921
3.8	3.1	6.9	8.4	11.3	27.8	12.0	13.6	11.3	14.2	26.4	25.0	25.1	29.6	27.8	Poland	964
.9	2.6	8.1	4.9	10.6	2.8	6.2	6.9	7.9	15.3	8.0	9.6	17.5	12.6	13.4	Romania	968
								9.2	4.1	12.3	8.5	9.1	6.7	10.9	Russia	922
								3.3	12.9	19.0	15.6	15.6	11.0	....	Slovak Republic	936
4.8	6.6	6.5	8.5	15.7	14.1	12.7	14.0	11.1	16.0	18.1	19.6	20.0	22.1	29.8	Turkey	186
							3.4	.9	3.1	3.4	5.5	7.1	2.7	4.6	Ukraine	926
4.7	6.5	2.9	9.1	14.5	15.1	9.5	....	....	....	....	....	....	....	....	Yugoslavia, SFR	188
31.4	**31.2**	**31.4**	**24.1**	**24.3**	**22.2**	**23.5**	**22.4**	**24.3**	**26.5**	**26.4**	**28.6**	**33.0**	**32.9**	....	**Middle East**	405
27.8	32.2	22.0	25.1	17.4	17.3	19.1	17.1	17.6	16.2	17.9	16.0	16.7	15.7	19.8	Bahrain	419
3.7	3.7	4.4	2.8	4.2	8.3	34.4	67.5	81.7	68.6	71.6	69.4	73.5	58.3	47.0	Egypt	469
....	....	....	....	....	....	....	....	....	....	....	....	....	....	....	Iran, I.R. of	429
															Iraq	433
19.4	22.4	21.3	13.9	19.1	19.4	17.5	17.2	14.7	14.0	14.3	18.8	34.3	40.2	35.4	Israel	436
8.0	9.3	8.2	2.1	11.5	17.0	17.1	12.3	24.1	26.0	27.7	21.3	27.9	23.8	36.7	Jordan	439
47.4	50.0	39.2	16.3	25.6	25.6	37.2	36.9	31.1	27.2	23.8	21.8	21.8	23.8	32.9	Kuwait	443
25.3	11.5	10.2	20.7	21.8	13.6	17.7	18.5	53.1	77.7	43.0	40.9	41.6	48.2	65.1	Lebanon	446
74.9	69.6	70.1	38.3	45.8	56.9	55.2	62.2	56.8	55.9	58.1	53.3	50.9	69.2	....	Libya	672
18.0	21.0	40.0	24.9	31.2	32.4	27.1	27.4	11.5	13.0	13.9	15.8	16.0	9.7	17.7	Oman	449
20.4	27.1	28.4	19.5	20.9	19.4	20.2	17.6	19.1	17.7	....	....	....	....	....	Qatar	453
55.0	49.9	58.7	49.1	41.2	25.2	20.9	9.3	13.7	16.4	16.0	26.8	27.1	24.6	....	Saudi Arabia	456
1.1	2.7	1.6	4.5	....	....	....	....	....	....	....	....	....	....	....	Syrian Arab Rep.	463
25.4	27.3	34.0	27.1	23.2	21.3	20.3	17.1	16.3	16.5	18.5	18.5	14.5	19.1	....	United Arab Emirates	466
11.8	19.4	31.8	10.7	....	....	....	....	....	....	....	....	....	....	....	Yemen Arab Rep.	473
6.7	14.9	....	....	....	....	....	....	....	....	....	....	....	....	....	Yemen, P.D. Rep.	459
						17.4	6.4	2.7	6.3	20.4	26.0	31.1	23.9	....	Yemen, Republic of	474
26.7	**20.7**	**21.1**	**14.9**	**14.8**	**19.7**	**23.5**	**26.4**	**29.7**	**24.4**	**26.7**	**29.1**	**26.5**	**23.1**	**22.1**	**Western Hemisphere**	205
5.2	7.1	5.4	5.8	7.6	5.6	5.9	8.2	7.0	7.1	9.0	6.9	7.2	7.9	....	Antigua and Barbuda	311
44.6	29.9	14.5	32.9	18.1	58.6	37.7	34.9	42.7	34.6	36.9	39.6	38.1	41.0	53.5	Argentina	213
....	20.0	17.3	14.1	11.7	9.5	12.9	....	....	....	....	....	....	....	....	Aruba	314
3.1	3.7	3.0	3.9	2.4	7.7	8.6	7.8	9.4	8.7	7.5	6.6	7.3	8.8	11.8	Bahamas, The	313
11.9	13.4	14.6	12.1	8.4	8.7	6.5	13.9	13.6	16.6	14.8	18.1	13.8	13.0	....	Barbados	316
6.0	11.5	13.2	14.8	14.4	17.2	10.8	10.0	7.2	6.9	7.6	11.9	10.8	7.1	10.1	Belize	339
15.1	12.6	6.6	9.3	17.4	12.6	5.7	8.7	9.6	19.4	24.1	30.4	30.5	23.2	38.8	Bolivia	218
38.5	19.4	19.4	22.6	19.7	17.2	18.2	50.8	57.4	53.5	48.1	53.3	40.7	....	....	Brazil	223
41.5	35.6	29.6	31.1	26.1	40.8	44.6	46.8	45.0	57.6	46.2	43.3	45.8	43.4	49.5	Chile	228
20.0	36.3	37.1	33.8	37.6	43.1	69.2	61.8	41.9	35.5	31.7	37.8	33.5	31.1	39.5	Colombia	233
24.0	23.7	18.4	24.6	22.5	13.6	25.5	21.7	15.1	12.3	13.5	12.1	13.3	8.9	12.0	Costa Rica	238
3.1	8.9	14.4	8.4	5.7	6.4	8.4	10.1	11.1	8.3	9.8	9.2	10.0	10.6	11.7	Dominica	321
11.9	13.7	5.2	7.1	3.8	1.6	11.6	10.4	13.9	3.8	5.2	4.4	4.2	4.6	....	Dominican Republic	243
21.1	18.5	11.3	12.1	15.2	23.4	20.0	18.6	28.0	26.5	20.4	24.6	22.0	15.1	28.3	Ecuador	248
9.7	9.4	9.7	8.3	11.9	17.1	10.6	12.9	14.6	15.0	13.8	18.2	22.9	27.0	33.3	El Salvador	253
15.6	12.8	13.3	9.5	8.1	8.7	7.5	12.6	9.7	13.6	14.7	12.2	....	....	....	Grenada	328
13.3	19.6	10.3	6.7	9.6	8.9	22.7	15.7	17.4	16.1	11.1	14.4	15.0	14.9	14.1	Guatemala	258
1.5	1.9	1.7	1.0	2.7	4.8	21.1	22.1	26.6	25.4	26.5	28.7	26.0	....	....	Guyana	336
.8	2.3	2.2	2.0	2.3	.5	2.2	....	....	6.4	8.4	8.4	8.4	6.2	....	Haiti	263
6.2	6.6	6.7	2.8	1.1	2.2	5.7	9.9	4.5	8.4	8.3	7.0	14.0	17.0	24.0	Honduras	268
7.5	5.3	7.3	5.3	3.0	4.5	3.0	10.1	10.2	17.2	12.6	15.4	11.3	12.3	11.2	Jamaica	343
13.3	16.8	32.9	9.3	9.0	11.8	17.6	15.1	19.1	3.9	11.5	10.8	13.0	12.6	11.1	Mexico	273
6.6	11.2	7.5	9.7	6.7	5.2	4.3	6.1	6.2	5.3	....	....	....	....	....	Netherlands Antilles	353
		1.1	2.5	9.8	8.7	9.3	7.9	3.8	8.4	7.4	9.0	12.8	12.2	14.4	Nicaragua	278
3.7	7.2	3.1	5.0	6.3	11.6	15.3	13.0	14.2	15.2	16.2	16.2	19.9	16.1	12.2	Panama	283
55.3	40.2	43.4	29.3	29.6	25.4	34.3	20.5	19.4	22.6	18.1	17.0	12.8	....	....	Paraguay	288
52.2	25.2	9.4	7.9	15.3	15.6	30.3	30.5	36.5	54.3	46.3	58.1	55.6	....	....	Peru	293
7.5	8.5	6.9	5.8	8.3	7.7	7.9	14.3	13.0	13.0	13.1	11.4	....	....	....	St. Kitts and Nevis	361
5.3	8.4	8.9	7.7	7.3	8.6	8.6	9.2	10.4	10.0	10.7	9.6	9.5	11.0	....	St. Lucia	362
9.1	15.4	10.7	9.3	9.3	10.1	8.4	13.1	12.2	12.5	11.4	11.9	8.6	10.5	11.0	St. Vincent & Grenadines	364
4.1	3.3	2.7	1.9	1.1	2.3	.1	1.7	.9	4.9	11.8	10.0	8.6	10.0	....	Suriname	366
38.2	18.3	8.0	5.9	10.5	23.1	10.6	8.1	7.3	16.2	10.9	13.2	12.3	13.6	....	Trinidad and Tobago	369
12.8	28.8	24.1	23.9	21.7	20.3	10.7	13.0	17.0	18.1	20.9	19.6	21.7	28.3	32.2	Uruguay	298
65.8	39.4	32.1	12.6	27.4	59.0	49.8	35.4	38.3	45.7	25.8	62.0	51.2	39.2	43.2	Venezuela, Rep. Bol.	299

Memorandum Items

1985	1986	1987	1988	1989	1990	1991	1992	1993	1994	1995	1996	1997	1998	1999		
37.3	34.7	39.0	27.9	27.0	26.1	25.2	20.8	22.6	24.2	21.4	28.3	30.0	33.2	....	**Oil Exporting Countries**	999
13.0	15.1	17.3	15.0	15.1	17.9	20.4	20.1	22.0	22.6	22.5	23.5	24.0	28.0	29.8	**Non-Oil Developing Countries**	201

		1970	1971	1972	1973	1974	1975	1976	1977	1978	1979	1980	1981	1982	1983	1984
															Millions of SDRs:	
All Countries	010	3,124.0	5,874.5	8,686.1	8,807.1	8,857.9	8,763.8	8,655.4	8,132.7	8,110.0	12,478.9	11,808.5	16,411.2	17,744.6	14,418.2	16,469.5
Industrial Countries	110	2,595.0	4,944.9	7,135.0	7,161.3	7,178.3	7,250.3	7,231.4	6,687.0	6,405.1	9,324.7	8,888.8	11,940.3	14,093.5	11,521.6	13,374.8
United States	111	850.7	1,099.7	1,803.1	1,795.6	1,939.3	1,994.6	2,061.2	2,163.9	1,196.3	2,068.1	2,046.0	3,518.5	4,759.1	4,800.0	5,754.6
Canada	156	182.1	371.9	465.3	467.3	469.1	474.4	480.1	416.0	401.0	444.8	355.4	149.5	64.2	20.1	73.7
Australia	193	90.5	164.0	234.6	234.7	99.9	95.7	36.3	21.8	98.7	31.9	—	44.8	77.7	77.0	213.4
Japan	158	146.3	282.8	424.5	425.1	431.8	443.9	460.2	494.2	1,053.5	1,281.3	1,362.7	1,661.7	1,895.4	1,848.2	1,966.0
New Zealand	196	.4	27.7	58.3	58.1	.5	.8	8.4	34.2	46.1	8.9	—	19.6	1.7	2.7	6.8
Euro Area																
Austria	122	38.2	57.0	85.8	85.9	87.0	87.4	95.9	96.6	104.6	155.8	173.4	185.7	226.5	154.0	224.4
Belgium	124	204.9	405.4	523.1	626.4	584.2	615.5	397.4	407.1	414.1	475.8	496.7	627.9	672.0	399.0	454.2
Finland	172	23.3	47.0	67.5	67.8	68.1	66.2	56.1	41.8	61.8	88.1	81.3	124.2	104.3	37.0	145.7
France	132	171.4	347.9	580.6	72.8	202.2	244.4	226.7	233.5	286.3	644.4	733.4	1,080.1	887.3	421.9	583.7
Germany	134	257.6	454.5	822.4	1,387.5	1,439.8	1,450.9	1,747.3	1,176.5	1,378.9	1,576.2	1,442.9	1,382.5	1,862.1	1,540.9	1,389.7
Ireland	178	13.4	26.4	39.3	39.4	40.6	40.9	45.3	45.6	48.1	70.9	71.1	90.9	96.4	65.4	89.4
Italy	136	76.7	227.9	341.5	342.9	180.8	83.0	78.4	118.8	225.7	449.3	521.0	672.8	711.4	564.9	645.3
Luxembourg	137	3.2	5.2	7.3	7.3	7.3	7.3	7.3	7.4	7.6	11.6	11.3	14.9	15.4	16.0	16.6
Netherlands	138	144.1	570.0	649.6	475.4	485.8	520.5	531.4	564.1	243.9	393.9	439.5	591.7	771.7	501.8	525.0
Portugal	182	—	—	—	—	—	7.0	8.4	3.8	—	.6	—	8.7	2.3	.9	12.5
Spain	184	43.5	86.8	128.7	128.8	133.9	121.4	90.8	48.2	102.7	206.3	230.6	318.6	185.8	65.4	154.5
Denmark	128	17.4	44.8	72.2	119.3	91.5	81.9	81.9	97.1	97.9	137.6	137.6	172.6	176.4	118.7	158.1
Greece	174	—	4.5	25.6	25.2	26.7	17.6	16.9	13.4	13.4	.8	—	.1	—	.6	1.1
Iceland	176	.5	3.0	6.4	6.3	6.3	4.8	1.8	2.7	1.8	.2	1.8	3.4	2.0	.2	.4
Norway	142	27.2	54.9	87.9	88.0	88.2	89.0	89.5	92.8	96.3	139.7	157.6	195.3	284.3	257.3	262.2
San Marino	135															
Sweden	144	37.8	72.6	107.1	107.0	107.0	107.0	107.0	107.1	112.0	173.0	174.2	224.5	233.3	123.0	181.4
Switzerland	146											5.1	.1	3.7	12.9	9.3
United Kingdom	112	265.7	590.9	604.4	600.4	688.2	696.3	603.3	500.6	414.5	965.5	447.2	852.0	1,060.7	494.0	506.9
Developing Countries	200	529.0	929.6	1,551.2	1,645.8	1,679.6	1,513.5	1,424.0	1,445.7	1,704.8	3,097.0	2,919.7	4,470.9	3,651.1	2,896.7	3,094.8
Africa	605	140.8	196.8	320.8	291.0	311.8	322.4	316.5	298.0	312.8	463.1	328.3	627.5	410.8	268.2	191.3
Algeria	612	14.1	28.0	41.8	41.9	42.9	43.0	43.1	46.2	46.4	76.3	75.9	118.9	140.0	102.1	113.2
Angola	614	....	....	....	....	....	....	....	....	....	....	....	....	....	....	....
Benin	638	1.7	3.1	4.5	4.5	4.5	4.5	4.5	4.4	4.4	6.1	1.7	2.9	2.0	1.1	.2
Botswana	616	.5	1.0	1.6	1.6	1.6	1.6	1.6	1.6	1.6	2.5	2.5	5.3	6.2	7.3	8.5
Burkina Faso	748	1.7	3.1	4.4	4.4	4.4	4.4	4.4	4.4	4.4	6.1	5.8	7.5	7.5	7.5	5.6
Burundi	618	2.2	1.8	3.7	3.6	3.6	3.2	3.0	2.8	2.8	5.3	4.1	5.5	4.2	1.0	.1
Cameroon	622	3.1	6.8	10.5	10.5	10.5	10.1	8.8	6.8	3.2	—	—	.2	1.6	.6	6.2
Cape Verde	624										—	—	.2	.2	.1	.1
Central African Rep.	626	—	—	1.2	1.0	.8	2.3	1.6	1.6	1.3	1.4	—	.1	.2	.7	2.6
Chad	628	—	—	1.1	.4	2.4	.2	1.9	1.7	1.5	1.6	—	—	.3	1.5	.4
Comoros	632										.2	—	—	—	—	.2
Congo, Dem. Rep. of	636	15.6	15.7	7.4	6.9	6.4	20.0	27.1	—	4.4	.1	—	.6	—	21.0	—
Congo, Rep. of	634	—	1.3	2.6	2.3	2.3	2.2	2.1	1.5	1.3	1.2	—	.9	1.0	.2	2.1
Côte d'Ivoire	662	3.2	9.8	15.3	15.3	15.2	14.5	11.8	8.6	7.4	17.9	2.7	10.6	.1	15.5	.2
Djibouti	611	....	....	....	....	....	....	....	—	.1	.1	.5	.5	.4	.4
Equatorial Guinea	642	1.0	1.9	1.9	1.9	1.9	1.8	1.8	1.7	1.7	.7	—	—	—	—	.4
Ethiopia	644	—	—	—	—	—	—	—	—	—	.4	—	10.4	3.2	2.3	3.0
Gabon	646	1.6	3.2	4.7	4.7	4.7	4.6	4.6	4.6	4.6	7.2	5.6	7.0	.7	.4	5.8
Gambia, The	648	.8	1.6	2.2	2.1	2.0	2.0	2.0	1.9	1.1	.7	—	.1	.1	.1	—
Ghana	652	—	3.1	10.0	9.7	9.6	7.5	6.7	10.1	9.5	13.7	—	.6	.2	2.1	.1
Guinea	656	.2	.1	2.9	1.4	3.4	3.1	2.9	2.2	—	—	—	—	.2	—	—
Guinea-Bissau	654	....	....	....	....	....	....	....	....	....	—	—	.1	—	—	.1
Kenya	664	5.8	12.0	17.1	17.1	1.9	3.8	2.8	14.4	11.0	82.1	20.2	9.4	14.0	16.6	2.2
Lesotho	666	—	.4	.9	.7	.6	.5	.5	.5	.4	1.1	.9	1.4	1.1	1.0	1.0
Liberia	668	1.0	.1	1.6	3.3	3.2	2.9	3.5	3.3	3.3	6.5	—	1.1	—	—	—
Madagascar	674	3.2	6.0	8.7	8.7	.2	.9	1.9	6.9	8.7	—	—	.3	1.1	.1	1.5
Malawi	676	1.9	3.5	4.6	4.6	4.6	4.6	4.3	3.9	3.3	3.1	—	5.7	3.6	.8	2.9
Mali	678	—	1.3	2.4	2.3	3.0	2.7	2.8	2.7	2.6	1.3	—	.2	.5	.1	1.7
Mauritania	682	1.7	.9	2.2	2.1	2.0	1.7	1.2	.6	.7	1.3	—	1.1	—	.7	—
Mauritius	684	2.6	5.0	7.3	7.3	2.8	2.6	2.7	2.3	1.6	.6	—	5.6	1.7	.1	.1
Morocco	686	.3	2.4	16.6	16.2	15.8	14.8	10.4	8.5	12.6	15.2	.5	1.4	.5	.6	.7
Mozambique	688	....	....	....	....	....	....	....	....	....	....	....	....	....	....	....
Namibia	728	....	....	....	....	....	....	....	....	....	....	....	....	....	....	....
Niger	692	1.7	3.1	4.4	4.4	4.4	4.4	4.4	4.4	4.4	6.0	5.8	7.5	7.5	4.6	2.2
Nigeria	694	16.8	31.2	45.5	45.5	47.5	57.4	61.2	65.8	66.8	107.8	132.5	239.0	40.4	25.7	10.5
Rwanda	714	.5	1.4	.4	2.4	2.5	2.4	2.4	2.4	2.4	4.6	7.7	9.8	10.8	8.4	8.3
São Tomé & Príncipe	716	....	....	....	....	....	....	....	....	—	.2	.2	.4	.4	.4	.1
Senegal	722	1.2	2.5	5.7	5.3	4.6	3.3	1.2	1.7	9.7	11.5	—	3.7	4.9	3.8	.1
Seychelles	718	....	....	....	....	....	....	—	—	—	.1	—	.2	.2	.1	—
Sierra Leone	724	.5	3.1	5.7	5.7	4.4	3.9	2.9	1.4	.2	—	—	.1	.5	.1	—
Somalia	726	.6	2.6	4.6	4.5	4.4	4.4	4.3	4.2	4.1	6.4	5.5	4.2	.7	.4	.1
South Africa	199	39.1	.5	38.2	1.4	39.6	43.4	41.5	39.5	39.3	25.4	37.1	115.5	99.1	27.3	2.3
Sudan	732	.1	—	4.9	13.6	21.5	7.3	—	—	6.0	10.0	—	.5	—	.1	—
Swaziland	734	—	—	.8	.8	.9	1.0	.9	.9	1.0	2.2	1.8	5.9	5.0	1.5	2.3
Tanzania	738	1.9	6.3	6.7	6.6	1.7	1.2	5.1	5.6	6.1	2.8	—	.3	—	.1	.1
Togo	742	1.9	3.5	5.1	5.1	5.1	5.1	5.0	4.8	4.4	6.3	5.8	6.4	3.9	1.2	2.1
Tunisia	744	—	2.0	7.9	7.6	8.5	8.2	10.0	9.6	8.5	14.6	11.8	17.4	16.0	3.6	1.9
Uganda	746	5.4	9.6	13.7	13.4	5.0	3.2	.9	4.5	8.1	8.4	—	2.6	10.1	.9	.2
Zambia	754	8.9	18.9	.2	—	11.7	15.7	19.2	11.4	12.1	4.2	—	7.7	14.5	—	—
Zimbabwe	698	....	....	....	....	....	....	....	....	....	....	—	8.8	6.3	6.1	2.3

1985	1986	1987	1988	1989	1990	1991	1992	1993	1994	1995	1996	1997	1998	1999		
End of Period																
18,212.8	19,494.1	20,212.5	20,172.9	20,484.8	20,354.4	20,551.3	12,867.2	14,614.3	15,761.5	19,773.2	18,521.4	20,532.2	20,379.7	18,456.7	All Countries	010
14,902.3	16,135.0	16,476.0	17,559.2	17,663.4	17,615.4	17,455.3	10,468.2	11,454.4	12,485.9	14,998.5	14,521.1	15,511.5	15,844.0	14,726.0	Industrial Countries	110
6,639.4	6,862.9	7,248.3	7,161.0	7,572.0	7,724.3	7,857.6	6,184.2	6,569.4	6,876.4	7,424.8	7,171.5	7,431.5	7,530.2	7,539.0	United States	111
198.4	202.2	281.2	1,017.4	1,048.1	1,072.5	1,105.7	755.5	773.5	786.4	791.8	812.4	834.3	779.5	383.7	Canada	156
282.5	271.0	260.1	248.3	234.0	218.3	202.4	69.6	59.7	49.9	36.8	25.4	13.8	12.6	52.6	Australia	193
1,926.2	1,813.0	1,736.3	2,182.0	1,862.3	2,138.4	1,803.0	795.5	1,123.4	1,427.0	1,821.1	1,837.3	1,955.1	1,891.0	1,935.5	Japan	158
6.0	9.0	1.0	.7	.4	.4	.3	—	—	.2	.6	.3	.2	1.2	5.0	New Zealand	196
															Euro Area	
191.2	151.8	205.8	199.5	227.1	195.7	197.5	247.6	160.5	193.8	121.7	135.7	124.8	105.9	105.9	Austria	122
328.4	279.8	493.7	418.0	423.2	398.0	411.0	124.1	124.7	123.4	331.1	346.5	362.7	433.3	197.1	Belgium	124
156.4	167.3	160.5	199.8	182.0	152.5	157.7	78.4	83.8	222.7	241.6	201.6	241.7	247.5	211.3	Finland	172
819.4	1,054.4	1,058.6	1,032.9	1,011.0	901.8	926.8	118.3	240.8	248.3	642.8	682.1	719.9	786.2	252.7	France	132
1,408.0	1,651.2	1,384.2	1,380.3	1,372.7	1,321.2	1,340.0	611.4	700.1	763.3	1,346.2	1,326.2	1,324.9	1,326.6	1,427.3	Germany	134
99.0	113.3	126.5	134.3	145.4	158.3	170.0	90.4	96.6	101.3	107.2	114.9	123.1	137.1	29.2	Ireland	178
296.9	480.2	668.2	705.1	759.5	729.2	650.0	173.2	175.4	85.8	—	20.4	49.6	78.7	122.5	Italy	136
17.1	17.5	18.0	18.4	19.1	19.9	20.6	6.6	7.0	7.2	7.5	7.7	8.0	8.7	1.8	Luxembourg	137
569.3	597.8	636.8	576.5	590.4	504.4	529.9	402.6	424.4	441.9	616.4	566.2	586.5	643.8	742.4	Netherlands	138
15.5	54.0	56.1	2.8	1.4	40.3	68.3	33.5	41.9	48.3	57.0	68.2	79.4	95.9	32.1	Portugal	182
254.5	353.2	420.4	456.8	523.0	489.4	319.0	134.0	157.4	174.5	276.8	313.9	351.3	408.1	189.8	Spain	184
178.7	207.2	214.5	167.0	213.1	151.6	169.0	66.7	62.4	124.6	106.8	116.7	248.7	246.0	249.9	Denmark	128
		.2	.3	.2	.3	—	.1	.1	.2	—	.4	.2	.3	3.8	Greece	174
.4	.2	1.9	1.0		.3	.1	—				—			.1	Iceland	176
258.0	318.2	311.2	362.3	345.2	315.5	315.9	139.1	288.4	266.7	311.5	247.2	257.9	294.1	298.0	Norway	142
									.1	.2	.3	.3	.4	.1	San Marino	135
224.3	261.3	208.5	299.1	259.5	204.0	289.6	32.6	42.2	46.4	296.8	198.9	276.7	292.4	227.8	Sweden	144
3.0	—	10.1	15.2	3.6	1.3	1.6	11.7	112.8	162.0	181.3	87.8	170.5	192.3	344.7	Switzerland	146
1,029.8	1,269.6	974.3	980.5	870.1	878.0	919.2	393.2	209.9	335.2	278.7	239.5	350.4	332.2	373.9	United Kingdom	112
3,310.5	3,359.2	3,736.5	2,613.7	2,821.4	2,739.0	3,095.9	2,398.9	3,159.9	3,275.6	4,774.7	4,000.4	5,020.7	4,535.7	3,730.7	Developing Countries	200
206.7	263.2	300.4	88.7	100.7	83.6	239.3	148.6	116.3	119.0	134.0	117.1	122.2	280.2	394.4	Africa	605
125.6	136.6	142.7	1.6	3.0	1.9	1.3	.8	4.9	15.7	.8	3.5	.5	1.1	1.4	Algeria	612
....	....				.1	.1	.1	.1	.1	.1	.1			.1	Angola	614
—	—	.1	.1	—	.1	.2	.1	.2			.2				Benin	638
9.7	14.0	15.4	16.8	18.9	21.7	24.1	22.5	24.0	25.4	27.1	28.7	30.4	32.4	28.1	Botswana	616
5.6	5.6	5.7	5.6	5.6	5.7	5.6	5.6	5.6	5.6	5.5	1.8	1.6	.5	.5	Burkina Faso	748
.1	.5		.1			2.6	1.1	.5	.1		.1		.1	.1	Burundi	618
4.2	2.8	.2	—	.2	.5	3.9	.2	.1			.1		—	1.9	Cameroon	622
.1	.1	.1					.1								Cape Verde	624
1.5	.4	4.9	9.2		3.4	.5					.2				Central African Rep.	626
3.5	1.7	6.4	5.7	1.3	.1	.1			.1		.1			.1	Chad	628
.2	.2	.1	.1	.1	.1			.1		.1		.1			Comoros	632
.2		.1	—	3.7											Congo, Dem. Rep. of	636
1.5	3.8	1.9	.8	1.2	1.2									.1	Congo, Rep. of	634
.1	7.0	.2	.5	3.9	.8	1.4	.2	.8	.1	1.2	.8	—	.1	2.5	Côte d'Ivoire	662
.4	.4	.3	.3	.3	.2	.2	.2	.2	.1	.1	.1	.6	.3	.1	Djibouti	611
3.1	.6	—		.1	.1	5.6	5.5	.3							Equatorial Guinea	642
.2		1.2		—	.2	.1	.1	.2	.3	.2		.1	.1	—	Ethiopia	644
2.1	10.1	8.2	6.5	.2	.2	4.4	.1		.2						Gabon	646
—	.6	3.2	1.0	1.0	1.2	.5	.5	.2	.2	.1	.2	.1	.3	.5	Gambia, The	648
17.2	1.6	11.2	.2	22.8	3.1	8.8	3.2	.4	2.9	1.6	1.6	2.5	42.4	13.3	Ghana	652
	.3	.2	.2		.2	9.4	7.9	8.5	3.8	5.0	.5	2.0	1.0	.9	Guinea	656
		.1												.1	Guinea-Bissau	654
.8	9.9	11.4	.4	8.7	2.8	1.0	.6	.8	.5	.2	.5	.5	.4	1.7	Kenya	664
1.0	.8	.6	1.0	.7	.5	.2	.5	.4	.3	.2	.9	.9	.9	.9	Lesotho	666
															Liberia	668
—	—	.1	.1	.1	.1		.1							.1	Madagascar	674
	.4	—	2.4	.3	2.2	.2	.1	.2	4.2	.6	.9	.1	4.8	.3	Malawi	676
1.7		.2	.2	.1	.3	.3	.1	.1	.1	.3	.2		.1	.4	Mali	678
3.9	2.6	12.1	.1	.1	.6	.1	.1	.1			1.0	.3			Mauritania	682
	.5	4.1	3.7	5.0	10.3	18.0	17.6	21.0	21.3	21.7	22.2	22.5	22.8	16.1	Mauritius	684
.1	15.8	2.9	.3	.4	1.0	102.9	56.3	25.1	18.0	17.3	5.2	.9	2.3	62.1	Morocco	686
															Mozambique	688
....	....														Namibia	728
	1.0	.2	.1	.9			.3		.4	.3	.2	1.3	.1	.1	Niger	692
1.0	.2	.1	—	.4	.8		.2		.4	.4	.4	.5	.1		Nigeria	694
8.2	8.1	8.0	7.9	7.5	7.2	6.7	2.4	2.1	1.7	13.7	12.7	19.6	17.4	10.5	Rwanda	714
															São Tomé & Príncipe	716
.1	2.5	—	—	3.6	.2	.3		.3	.7	2.6	1.2	.3	.4	1.8	Senegal	722
	.3														Seychelles	718
							1.2	2.8	6.2	11.5	5.3	8.3	7.4	15.2	Sierra Leone	724
															Somalia	726
.5	—	1.2	.8	1.3	1.6	1.2	.1	8.8	.8	3.3	.8	6.8	131.7	209.6	South Africa	199
															Sudan	732
.3	2.2	2.8	1.2	.8	8.5	8.7	5.8	5.9	5.9	5.9	5.9	5.9	6.0	2.4	Swaziland	734
	4.6	.1	—							.1	.1	.1	.3	.2	Tanzania	738
.1	.5	.1	.1	1.3	.1	.3	.2	.1		.3	.2	.1		.2	Togo	742
.5	22.6	38.1	21.0	6.4	1.7	23.0	8.8	1.3	1.8	4.7	11.1	12.1	2.1	19.3	Tunisia	744
					4.8	7.2	6.6	—	2.1	.3	.7	4.0	3.5	1.7	Uganda	746
										8.2	1.4	.8	.6	.1	Zambia	754
13.2	5.0	16.3	.5	.5	.2	.1	.3	.6	—	.5	6.8	.2	.3	.8	Zimbabwe	698

SDRs

Millions of SDRs:

		1970	1971	1972	1973	1974	1975	1976	1977	1978	1979	1980	1981	1982	1983	1984
Asia	505	**98.7**	**256.8**	**489.8**	**507.0**	**490.0**	**426.6**	**388.5**	**331.7**	**448.3**	**785.6**	**763.3**	**1,325.0**	**1,174.8**	**713.5**	**1,026.7**
Afghanistan, Islamic State of	512	1.9	3.2	1.2	4.3	4.5	5.3	5.1	5.7	5.4	13.4	12.1	16.3	15.6	10.0	13.5
Bangladesh	513	....	....	—	—	—	15.4	16.1	3.9	.1	9.2	.4	.1	.8	12.9	.3
Bhutan	514	....	....												—	.1
Brunei Darussalam	516															.1
Cambodia	522	1.6	1.7	4.2	.5	1.1	.6	.3	—	—	1.9	3.8	4.5	3.1	1.6	—
China, P.R.: Mainland	924	—									—	72.0	236.3	193.9	320.0	413.8
Fiji	819	—	—	1.4	1.4	1.4	1.3	1.3	1.3	1.3	3.1	2.7	4.5	3.7	.3	6.3
India	534	44.2	148.1	246.5	245.3	239.9	212.0	189.1	149.0	225.8	371.0	376.7	468.3	339.4	104.6	337.6
Indonesia	536	—	—	35.8	43.3	55.7	6.3	4.1	21.7	57.4	129.2	137.2	227.2	281.9	3.9	.5
Kiribati	826															
Korea	542	10.3	17.6	26.1	26.1	1.4	3.4	6.8	10.0	11.4	18.9	9.9	54.1	57.8	60.2	30.9
Lao, People's Democratic Rep.	544	.5	.9	1.3	1.3	1.3	1.6	1.5	1.5	1.0	.8	—	.6	—	.1	—
Malaysia	548	23.4	43.3	63.1	60.6	61.6	61.7	65.1	26.6	38.8	87.3	97.8	125.8	118.1	103.1	99.0
Maldives	556	....	....	—	—	—	—	—	—	—	.1	.1	.2	.2	—	—
Marshall Islands	867															
Micronesia, Fed. States of	868	—	—	—	—	—	—	—	—	—	—	—	—	—	—	—
Mongolia	948															
Myanmar	518	—	—	5.6	9.7	9.5	8.0	7.6	7.5	2.9	4.7	5.4	2.4	1.1	.2	.1
Nepal	558	—	1.1	2.2	2.2	2.2	2.2	2.1	1.9	1.2	1.7	.1	—	.8	.2	.1
Pakistan	564	10.2	13.3	19.1	26.6	19.9	25.0	32.0	28.7	30.5	34.2	22.6	48.5	45.9	.8	37.4
Palau	565															
Papua New Guinea	853							1.7	.2	.4	.8	—	33.1	31.0	17.0	5.0
Philippines	566	—	—	21.9	23.9	27.7	23.5	13.6	19.2	13.1	25.6	.1	1.7	2.5	.9	19.8
Samoa	862	....	—	.2	.2	.2	—	—	—	—	—	.1	—	—	.4	.2
Singapore	576	—	—	—	—	—	—	—	—	—	12.2	15.1	27.5	49.4	59.7	58.0
Solomon Islands	813											1.0	1.2	1.2	1.7	1.3
Sri Lanka	524	—	—	12.8	13.4	14.5	10.8	12.4	19.8	26.3	22.2	—	19.9	6.3	.8	.2
Thailand	578	—	14.3	28.5	28.5	29.5	29.6	28.9	30.5	26.6	37.1	6.4	52.3	22.2	15.2	2.4
Tonga	866															
Vanuatu	846															.1
Vietnam	582	6.6	13.2	19.8	19.8	19.8	19.8	.7	4.2	6.2	12.2	—	.5	—	—	—
Europe	170	**11.8**	**17.8**	**60.5**	**88.1**	**95.7**	**79.9**	**52.4**	**28.5**	**22.9**	**60.7**	**28.0**	**90.5**	**35.5**	**77.0**	**36.2**
Albania	914															
Armenia	911															
Azerbaijan	912															
Belarus	913															
Bosnia and Herzegovina	963	—														
Bulgaria	918															
Croatia	960															
Cyprus	423	3.9	7.7	10.4	10.5	10.4	10.0	7.9	5.1	1.7	9.9	6.5	3.4	.2	.2	.1
Czech Republic	935															
Czechoslovakia	934	—														
Estonia	939															
Georgia	915															
Hungary	944	—												2.3	44.4	—
Kazakhstan	916															
Kyrgyz Republic	917															
Latvia	941	—														
Lithuania	946															
Macedonia, FYR	962															
Malta	181	1.7	3.4	5.1	5.1	5.1	5.1	5.2	5.5	5.8	9.4	11.3	14.6	21.2	31.0	35.7
Moldova	921															
Poland	964															
Romania	968	....	....	—	6.0	5.4	8.1	12.6	6.9	—	.6	—	.4	11.8	.2	.3
Russia	922															
Slovak Republic	936															
Slovenia	961															
Tajikistan	923															
Turkey	186	.1	5.0	38.3	28.5	34.7	27.2	18.5	—	.2	.2	—	.2	.1	1.3	.1
Turkmenistan	925															
Ukraine	926															
Uzbekistan	927															
Yugoslavia, SFR	188	6.1	1.7	6.7	38.1	40.2	29.5	8.3	11.0	15.2	40.7	10.1	71.9	—	—	.1
Middle East	405	**5.5**	**44.4**	**114.1**	**142.3**	**123.2**	**115.9**	**141.3**	**169.8**	**191.3**	**494.2**	**644.9**	**855.3**	**1,288.8**	**1,144.9**	**1,270.5**
Bahrain	419	....								.1	2.2	1.8	5.2	14.0	12.2	13.1
Egypt	469	.1	7.5	5.1	31.2	30.9	14.5	20.3	23.7	8.2	.4	—	.2	.1	.3	.2
Iran, I.R. of	429	1.0	1.2	34.4	36.9	44.5	55.7	64.3	69.6	96.3	167.3	240.5	291.2	299.8	309.2	320.3
Iraq	433	—	11.7	23.2	20.1	23.0	23.0	28.0	34.2	45.5	82.2	87.2	113.7	74.2	8.6	.1
Israel	436	—	13.1	29.2	27.9	2.5	2.0	8.7	22.2	21.0	4.8	8.8	.6	.5	1.6	.1
Jordan	439	2.7	5.1	7.6	7.5	7.4	7.4	7.4	7.4	7.4	11.0	11.7	15.5	16.5	17.4	15.8
Kuwait	443	—	—	—	—	—	—	—	—	—	—	—	35.4	62.3	35.6	76.0
Lebanon	446	—	—	—	—	—	—	—	—	—	1.3	—	1.9	2.0	—	.8
Libya	672	—	—	—	—	—	—	—	—	—	30.7	46.6	104.1	129.4	157.7	132.6
Oman	449	....	—	.7	.7	.7	.7	.7	.7	.7	2.8	5.1	5.2	7.9	11.1	9.4
Qatar	453	....	....	—	—	—	—	—	—	—	4.2	2.7	8.6	14.0	8.7	16.2
Saudi Arabia	456	—	—	—	—	—	—	—	—	—	149.1	212.6	212.7	578.7	486.8	586.0
Syrian Arab Rep.	463	—	—	4.0	8.0	8.3	7.3	6.8	6.4	6.0	12.0	9.8	14.7	11.9	8.8	5.3
United Arab Emirates	466	—	—	—	—	—	—	—	—	—	15.4	8.0	29.5	50.3	61.5	66.0
Yemen Arab Rep.	473	—	1.1	2.1	2.1	2.1	2.1	2.1	2.1	3.2	7.5	10.3	12.9	14.1	8.6	8.8
Yemen, P.D. Rep.	459	1.7	4.8	7.8	7.8	3.7	3.2	3.0	3.6	3.0	3.5	—	4.0	13.1	17.0	19.8
Yemen, Republic of	474	—	—	—	—	—	—	—	—	—	—					

	1985	1986	1987	1988	1989	1990	1991	1992	1993	1994	1995	1996	1997	1998	1999		
End of Period																	
	1,101.8	1,063.8	892.7	832.7	761.3	903.6	768.6	523.0	683.4	647.5	875.4	925.4	1,530.8	1,298.9	906.1	Asia	505
	12.4	11.4	10.5	9.5	8.1	6.3	4.7	3.2	2.0	1.0	—	—	—	—	—	Afghanistan, Islamic State of	512
	11.9	8.4	37.6	40.1	2.3	18.1	49.9	30.1	16.6	24.6	107.3	76.2	21.6	9.1	.7	Bangladesh	513
	.1	.1	.1	.2	.2	.3	.3	.3	.4	.4	.4	.5	.5	.5	.1	Bhutan	514
												.5	1.6	2.7	3.8	Brunei Darussalam	516
									11.4	10.9	10.2	9.5	8.8	6.9	3.8	Cambodia	522
	439.5	465.1	450.9	435.6	411.1	394.8	403.7	305.1	352.0	369.1	391.6	427.1	446.5	480.1	539.6	China, P.R.: Mainland	924
	5.1	5.8	9.9	15.1	15.9	16.5	9.3	6.0	6.3	7.4	7.7	8.0	8.3	8.6	4.1	Fiji	819
	306.2	290.9	112.4	71.1	86.2	222.1	32.3	2.8	72.9	1.4	93.3	85.1	57.4	59.0	3.0	India	534
	51.2	35.6	4.4	2.0	.7	2.3	2.6	.1	.3	.3	.9	1.5	370.0	221.5	.3	Indonesia	536
															—	Kiribati	826
	36.2	14.4	11.6	4.2	1.2	10.1	20.9	30.6	42.3	52.3	65.7	82.3	43.6	8.1	.5	Korea	542
	—	.2						.3	.6	1.9	7.5	9.5	7.2	9.3	4.3	.1	Lao, People's Democratic Rep.	544
	105.4	110.7	115.1	119.7	127.1	136.3	145.0	82.3	87.8	92.7	101.6	115.3	129.9	145.8	60.8	Malaysia	548
	—	—	—	—	—	—	—	—	—	—	—	.1	.1	.1	.1	Maldives	556
	—	—	—	—	—	—	—								—	Marshall Islands	867
	—	—	—	—	—	—	—	.8	.9	.9	.9	1.0	1.0	1.1		Micronesia, Fed. States of	868
										2.0	1.7	.3	.5	.3	.1	Mongolia	948
	....		.1	.1	.4	.6	.1		.2	.1	.1	.1	.1	.2	.1	Myanmar	518
	—	.1	.1	.1	.1	.1	.1	.1		.1			.1		.2	Nepal	558
	24.1	10.7	11.1	4.9	1.1	.6	5.2	.1	.5	.2	9.9	9.2	8.0	.6	.2	Pakistan	564
																Palau	565
	5.9	2.6	3.3	3.0	2.7	—	—	.1	—	.1	.5	—	.1	—	.5	Papua New Guinea	853
	35.3	4.7	.1	.1	.7	.8	3.1	.4	7.3	16.7	5.4	1.7	1.3	1.4	5.1	Philippines	566
	—	.8	1.3	2.4	.7	2.9	2.6	1.9	2.0	2.0	2.0	2.1	2.1	2.2	2.2	Samoa	862
	66.0	73.8	81.2	79.0	79.4	81.4	81.3	49.4	56.9	24.1	33.1	42.5	52.2	64.9	89.2	Singapore	576
	.8	1.3	.2		.1	.3	.1		—	—	—	—	—	—	—	Solomon Islands	813
	.1	.1	.1	.1	10.3	.3	.2	.1	.3	.2	.6	1.3	.3	.9	.7	Sri Lanka	524
	1.3	27.1	42.5	45.2	12.5	9.0	5.7	8.8	15.9	21.8	30.5	41.5	357.6	277.9	188.1	Thailand	578
			.1	.1	.1	.2	.7	.4	.4	.5	—	.1	.1	.2	—	Tonga	866
	.2	.2	.3	.3	.4	.5	.6	.7	.2	.2	.3	.4	.4	.5	.6	Vanuatu	846
	—	—	—	—	—	—	—	—	4.9	11.0	2.2	11.9	9.4	1.8	1.1	Vietnam	582
	40.5	43.5	47.2	50.6	129.7	70.2	214.7	103.4	270.1	373.6	636.8	511.5	784.2	730.0	568.0	Europe	170
										.2	.1	.5	.5	43.4	56.1	Albania	914
										.2	29.8	28.9	27.6	19.9	29.6	Armenia	911
	....		....		....		....		—	—	.8	14.5	4.1	.1	5.2	Azerbaijan	912
									3.2		3.1	.1	—	.3	.3	Belarus	913
									—	—	5.0	1.8	—	3.7	5.6	Bosnia and Herzegovina	963
						—	5.9	.3	.8	10.4	20.1	8.3	8.4	21.4	59.5	Bulgaria	918
									.8	3.1	94.4	87.3	109.0	164.2	138.1	Croatia	960
	.1		.3	.1	.1	.1	.1	.1	.1	.1	—		.2	.2	.4	Cyprus	423
									6.0		.1	—	—	—	—	Czech Republic	935
	—	—	—	—	—	—	97.6	30.8	....	....	....		....	....	....	Czechoslovakia	934
								7.7	41.6	1.1	.2	.1	—	—	1.0	Estonia	939
										1.6	1.1	—	.1	3.7	6.1	Georgia	915
	.1	—	.2	.2	—	.7	.9	1.9	2.1	1.1	.6	3.1	.1	.5	3.2	Hungary	944
									14.0	69.5	154.9	240.2	327.2	275.1	164.2	Kazakhstan	916
								—	9.4	.7	9.6	5.1	.7	.2	3.7	Kyrgyz Republic	917
								19.3	71.1	.2	1.5	1.6	1.5	.2	2.2	Latvia	941
								.9	54.7	10.4	12.2	7.1	8.0	11.5	3.2	Lithuania	946
										—	.2	—	.3	.8	.9	Macedonia, FYR	962
	39.6	43.1	46.6	50.1	53.6	59.1	64.2	33.1	35.3	35.6	37.6	39.7	41.9	44.4	22.5	Malta	181
	....		....		....		....		25.1	14.6	8.8	5.5	.9	.5	.2	Moldova	921
	—	.1	.1	.1	.1	.6	5.4	.8	.5	1.0	1.5	3.1	4.0	5.0	8.1	Poland	964
	—	.1	—	—	76.0	.1	40.3	7.9	1.4	38.1	37.7	2.8	76.9	.8	7.3	Romania	968
									.6	3.7	2.1	78.5	3.1	90.7	.4	Russia	922
									.3	58.9	39.0	11.2	19.6	1.2	.6	Slovak Republic	936
									—	—	—	.1	.2	1.2	Slovenia	961
										—	—	2.2	9.1	2.1	—	Tajikistan	923
	.4	.1	—	—	.4	—	—	—	.1	.8	1.9	1.0	.6	1.0	.1	Turkey	186
																Turkmenistan	925
									—	123.7	97.1	46.7	52.7	129.5	47.9	Ukraine	926
											.8	—	.1	.2	.4	Uzbekistan	927
	.2			.1		9.2	.2		....		....		....			Yugoslavia, SFR	188
	1,281.2	1,149.2	1,224.2	1,072.9	1,292.2	951.5	913.4	765.4	1,014.4	1,090.4	1,165.0	1,397.5	1,556.0	1,424.9	829.9	Middle East	405
	13.6	14.1	14.6	15.1	15.9	16.9	17.8	18.7	10.8	11.0	11.3	11.7	11.9	12.1	—	Bahrain	419
	.1	—	.2	.3	.1	.4	.9	42.8	50.4	59.2	69.5	85.6	83.9	113.8	30.1	Egypt	469
	328.2	335.5	342.3	115.7	304.7	310.4	215.8	7.4	104.8	97.9	89.9	239.8	244.6	1.1	101.3	Iran, I.R. of	429
			5.1													Iraq	433
	.1	—	.1	.1	.1	.2	.3	.2	.4	.2	.4	1.0	—	.2	.1	Israel	436
	21.9	19.6	8.5	—	8.4	.7	.8	.4	4.0	.5	.8	.6	.1	.6	.2	Jordan	439
	104.3	128.4	148.8	166.8	97.8	113.9	128.3	130.4	49.1	55.0	61.3	68.2	74.1	82.5	53.7	Kuwait	443
	1.8	2.6	3.4	4.2	5.4	6.9	8.3	9.5	10.5	11.4	12.3	13.3	14.3	15.4	16.4	Lebanon	446
	156.2	177.6	197.7	218.8	249.4	287.3	322.6	278.3	303.5	324.7	349.7	373.9	398.5	425.8	372.6	Libya	672
	10.9	11.4	7.2	8.7	10.9	13.4	15.5	3.4	5.0	6.2	7.5	8.8	10.1	11.5	1.3	Oman	449
	18.9	21.1	24.7	26.4	28.7	31.3	33.8	17.1	18.7	19.9	21.2	22.5	23.8	25.1	10.7	Qatar	453
	528.7	335.8	370.8	395.5	467.2	69.9	62.0	202.0	402.7	416.0	448.2	481.3	512.1	545.9	110.5	Saudi Arabia	456
	2.8	.2	—	—	—	.1	.1								.1	Syrian Arab Rep.	463
	68.3	76.5	79.8	82.3	85.9	90.8	95.5	52.4	54.1	55.0	55.9	57.6	58.4	59.2	4.5	United Arab Emirates..............	466
	23.2	23.1	19.0	23.9	15.9	....	....	....	....	....	....	....	....	....	....	Yemen Arab Rep.	473
	2.4	3.4	2.1	14.9	1.8											Yemen, P.D. Rep.	459
						9.4	11.7	2.9	.5	33.5	37.0	33.3	124.1	131.6	128.5	Yemen, Republic of	474

SDRs

Millions of SDRs:

		1970	1971	1972	1973	1974	1975	1976	1977	1978	1979	1980	1981	1982	1983	1984
Western Hemisphere	205	272.2	413.9	566.0	617.4	658.8	568.8	525.3	617.7	729.6	1,293.3	1,155.2	1,572.7	741.2	693.1	570.0
Antigua and Barbuda	311	....	....	....	....	....	....	....	....	....	....	....	....	....	....	....
Argentina	213	59.3	2.8	17.8	66.9	83.8	34.8	78.2	73.9	161.6	247.9	256.6	347.1	—	.3	.6
Bahamas, The	313	—									3.4	2.7	6.1	5.8	1.1	.7
Barbados	316	—	1.4	2.8	2.8	2.8	2.8	2.8	2.7	2.5	3.9	1.6	1.4	.8	.3	—
Belize	339	....	....	....	....	....	....	....	....	....	....	....	....	—	—	—
Bolivia	218	2.7	2.4	3.0	2.2	2.6	7.0	6.9	5.7	14.1		.1		—	.1	—
Brazil	223	62.3	110.5	157.0	157.2	162.8	163.3	171.0	173.2	183.8	290.7	300.7	388.1	.3	.1	.9
Chile	228	21.8	38.3	2.0	.3	13.8	20.9	48.3	54.7	20.7	22.0	3.0	16.4	17.7	5.2	11.7
Colombia	233	.1	8.3	17.5	23.1	24.5	20.3	24.3	25.6	37.8	71.9	85.3	119.4	162.4	188.7	.1
Costa Rica	238	.2	.1	4.0	3.9	2.0	3.8	1.2	5.5	3.0	4.5			.1	2.9	.1
Dominica	321	....	....	....	....	....	....	....	....	....	....	....	.7	.3	.4	—
Dominican Republic	243	—	—	6.9	6.8	7.2	6.5	6.0	5.2	4.7	7.2	—	1.6	.5	.2	.4
Ecuador	248	.1	3.4	6.7	5.6	6.5	6.3	6.3	8.2	10.6	19.2	19.0	28.9	—	.1	.5
El Salvador	253	—	2.2	3.7	3.8	3.6	3.9	4.0	7.8	7.6	13.2	—	.1	1.7	.1	—
Grenada	328	....	....	....	....	....	.1	.1	....	....	....	....	....	....	.1	....
Guatemala	258	2.1	7.8	7.6	11.5	11.5	11.5	11.4	11.5	11.6	18.4	17.7	2.2	—	.6	2.0
Guyana	336	.1	2.2	4.1	4.0	3.9	3.8	3.5	2.7	2.8	2.8	—	1.0	2.6	—	—
Haiti	263	—	1.1	3.1	1.7	2.5	2.0	1.2	1.6	3.8	5.5	—	—	1.0	1.0	—
Honduras	268	.2	2.9	5.5	5.4	5.3	4.0	2.7	3.6	3.0	7.7	—	1.4	1.6	2.1	.2
Jamaica	343	6.4	12.8	6.9	6.4	5.1	4.3	.8	14.3	4.5	.4	—	1.1	.1	—	—
Mexico	273	47.8	88.3	127.7	127.8	129.0	86.3	.9	46.8	42.6	152.4	112.9	152.9	5.3	21.9	3.1
Nicaragua	278	1.0	3.7	6.2	5.7	5.8	4.6	3.5	3.8	4.3	—	—	.1	.9	—	—
Panama	283	3.2	2.6	2.7	2.6	2.3	6.4	5.2	4.5	4.0	3.9	1.1	2.8	3.8	.4	—
Paraguay	288	2.5	4.6	6.6	6.6	6.6	6.6	6.6	6.6	6.6	9.4	11.1	15.1	23.7	30.4	35.0
Peru	293	14.3	28.4	41.0	37.3	37.2	37.1	3.3	2.7	4.8	81.3	9.7	9.8	29.9	.6	22.9
St. Kitts and Nevis	361	....	....	....	....	....	....	....	....	....	....	....	....	....	....	—
St. Lucia	362	....	....	....	....	....	....	....	....	....	....	.1	.2			
St. Vincent & Grenadines	364	....	....	....	....	....	....	....	....	....	—	.1	.2	—	—	—
Suriname	366	....	....	....	....	....	....	....	....	....	2.6	2.1	5.4	8.5	1.7	1.3
Trinidad and Tobago	369	.5	7.2	7.3	7.1	7.9	7.6	7.6	12.2	16.9	31.2	35.8	51.3	73.5	94.4	103.1
Uruguay	298	.1	—	7.8	10.8	12.1	1.6	3.7	8.5	11.4	26.2	26.0	37.2	1.7	3.7	5.1
Venezuela, Rep. Bol.	299	47.5	83.1	118.1	118.2	120.3	123.6	126.0	136.5	167.0	267.7	269.9	382.1	399.3	336.8	382.1
Memorandum Items																
Oil Exporting Countries	999	79.4	155.2	299.7	306.6	334.6	309.7	327.3	374.5	480.1	1,032.6	1,218.0	1,767.5	2,078.1	1,547.5	1,712.9
Non-Oil Developing Countries	201	449.6	774.5	1,251.5	1,339.2	1,345.0	1,203.9	1,096.7	1,071.2	1,224.8	2,064.4	1,701.7	2,703.5	1,573.0	1,349.2	1,381.8
World	001	3,414.1	6,363.3	9,314.9	9,314.9	9,314.9	9,314.8	9,314.9	9,314.8	9,315.1	13,348.0	17,385.9	21,433.5	21,437.0	21,446.5	21,450.2
All Participants	969	3,124.0	5,874.5	8,686.1	8,807.1	8,857.9	8,763.8	8,655.4	8,132.7	8,110.0	12,478.9	11,808.5	16,411.2	17,744.6	14,418.2	16,469.5
IMF	992	290.2	488.9	628.7	507.7	457.0	551.0	659.5	1,182.1	1,205.1	868.7	5,571.9	5,018.9	3,686.2	6,998.8	4,957.5
Other Holders	970	—	—	—	—	—	—	—	—	—	—	5.6	3.3	6.2	29.4	23.3

1985	1986	1987	1988	1989	1990	1991	1992	1993	1994	1995	1996	1997	1998	1999		
End of Period																
680.4	839.5	1,272.0	568.9	537.5	730.2	960.0	858.6	1,075.7	1,045.1	1,963.5	1,049.0	1,027.6	801.7	1,032.3	Western Hemisphere	205
....	....	....	....	—	—	—	—	—	—	—	—	—	—	—	Antigua and Barbuda	311
			.3	.2	209.0	134.9	272.8	329.5	385.7	362.7	277.4	123.6	187.7	100.3	Argentina	213
.4	—	.3	.4	.1	.4	.1	—	—	—	—	—	—	—	—	Bahamas, The..............................	313
—	—	.6	.5	—	—	.5	.1	.1	—	—	—	—	—	—	Barbados	316
—	—	.1	—	—	.7	.1	.2	.3	.4	.5	.6	.7	.8	1.0	Belize	339
—	2.0	—	—	—	—	.1	.1	10.2	17.0	26.9	26.8	26.8	26.8	27.3	Bolivia	218
.5	—	.1	.3	—	7.7	8.9	.8	1.7	.3	.7	.7	.4	1.2	7.3	Brazil	223
.3	.2	28.8	32.9	18.5	.7	.5	.5	.9	.5	2.1	1.3	1.0	5.9	13.5	Chile	228
—	114.3	114.3	114.3	114.3	114.2	114.2	42.5	114.9	116.4	118.8	122.8	127.6	139.3	95.2	Colombia	233
—	—	—	—	—	1.1	.2	.2	.1	.1	—	—	—	—	.6	Costa Rica	238
—	—	—	—	—	.2	—	.1	—	—	—	—	—	—	—	Dominica	321
—	.8	.7	.6	.3	—	—	—	—	—	—	—	—	—	—	Dominican Republic	243
28.8	—	—	—	—	—	—	.1	10.3	2.5	.3	.3	.2	.2	.2	Ecuador	248
26.2	45.7	.7	1.0	.7	10.3	28.9	.1	3.2	3.0	2.1	1.9	.4	.2	1.7	El Salvador	253
—	—	—	—	—	—	—	—	—	.1	25.0	25.0	25.0	25.0	25.0	Grenada	328
—	—	1.2	.1	.6	—	—	11.4	11.4	11.4	10.6	10.2	9.4	8.7	8.4	Guatemala	258
—	—	—	—	—	1.5	1.0	.2	—	.1	.1	.1	.1	.2	.9	Guyana	336
—	5.4	—	—	.1	—	—	—	—	—	.4	—	.1	.4	.6	Haiti	263
—	—	—	—	—	—	—	.1	.1	.1	.1	.1	.1	.1	.7	Honduras	268
—	.3	1.0	—	—	.3	—	9.0	9.1	—	.3	—	.2	.5	.5	Jamaica	343
.4	7.2	497.7	292.6	291.5	293.0	409.3	398.8	162.6	121.1	1,074.1	178.7	490.1	239.6	575.5	Mexico	273
—	—	—	—	—	—	—	.1	—	—	—	—	—	—	.2	Nicaragua	278
11.7	1.4	—	—	—	19.4	8.1	3.3	.1	—	.6	—	.4	.1	1.2	Panama	283
38.8	42.1	44.8	47.4	50.8	54.9	58.8	62.1	65.1	67.6	70.6	73.3	76.1	79.1	74.8	Paraguay	288
—	—	—	—	—	—	—	—	.7	.3	.5	.2	.2	1.5	.3	Peru	293
—	—	—	—	—	—	—	—	—	—	—	—	—	—	—	St. Kitts and Nevis........................	361
—	—	—	—	—	1.2	1.3	1.3	1.3	1.4	1.4	1.4	1.4	1.5	1.5	St. Lucia	362
—	—	—	—	—	—	—	—	.1	.1	.1	.1	.1	.1	—	St. Vincent & Grenadines	364
.8	.3	—	—	—	—	—	—	—	—	7.8	8.2	8.2	8.3	2.0	Suriname	366
107.8	112.0	—	—	6.9	.8	1.5	.2	.2	.1	.1	—	.1	.1	—	Trinidad and Tobago	369
13.3	9.7	48.1	22.1	17.5	7.9	3.3	—	.3	—	2.4	2.7	—	.5	.7	Uruguay	298
451.4	498.0	533.6	56.4	36.0	6.7	188.3	54.6	353.6	316.9	255.4	317.0	135.3	73.7	92.9	Venezuela, Rep. Bol.......................	299
															Memorandum Items	
1,844.8	1,756.6	1,857.1	1,074.4	1,284.8	928.7	1,065.6	746.3	1,296.7	1,307.6	1,291.2	1,574.4	1,827.8	1,448.0	749.3	Oil Exporting Countries	999
1,465.8	1,602.6	1,879.4	1,539.3	1,536.7	1,810.3	2,030.3	1,652.6	1,863.1	1,968.0	3,483.5	2,426.0	3,192.9	3,087.7	2,981.4	Non-Oil Developing Countries	201
21,451.9	21,448.1	21,466.5	21,484.2	21,480.9	21,479.4	21,474.2	21,480.1	21,480.9	21,476.9	21,484.5	21,495.2	21,508.2	21,522.1	21,534.8	World	001
18,212.8	19,494.1	20,212.5	20,172.9	20,484.8	20,354.4	20,551.3	12,867.2	14,614.3	15,761.5	19,773.2	18,521.4	20,532.2	20,379.7	18,456.7	All Participants	969
3,068.4	1,937.0	1,207.1	769.5	947.1	995.3	819.6	8,561.2	6,687.3	5,510.1	652.5	1,726.3	634.8	687.3	2,459.3	IMF	992
170.6	17.1	46.8	541.7	49.0	129.6	103.3	51.7	179.4	205.3	1,058.9	1,247.4	341.3	455.1	618.9	Other Holders	970

Fund Accounts

(As of July 31, 2000 and Amounts Expressed in Millions of SDRs)

Amounts Agreed	Amounts Borrowed *	Amounts Repaid	Outstanding Borrowings	Amounts Expired	Amounts Available for Borrowings	
			Borrowing Agreements			
52,500.0	4,319.8	4,319.8	—	—	52,500.0	**General Department**
17,000.0	1,443.5	1,443.5	—	—	17,000.0	General Arrangements to Borrow (GAB)
595.0	50.5	50.5	—	—	595.0	Belgium
892.5	75.8	75.8	—	—	892.5	Canada
1,700.0	144.3	144.3	—	—	1,700.0	France
2,380.0	202.1	202.1	—	—	2,380.0	Germany
1,105.0	93.8	93.8	—	—	1,105.0	Italy
2,125.0	180.4	180.4	—	—	2,125.0	Japan
850.0	72.2	72.2	—	—	850.0	Netherlands
382.5	32.5	32.5	—	—	382.5	Sweden
1,020.0	86.6	86.6	—	—	1,020.0	Switzerland
1,700.0	144.3	144.3	—	—	1,700.0	United Kingdom
4,250.0	360.9	360.9	—	—	4,250.0	United States
1,500.0	—	—	—	—	1,500.0	**Associated Agreement**
1,500.0					1,500.0	Saudi Arabia
34,000.0	2,876.3	2,876.3	—	—	34,000.0	New Arrangements to Borrow (NAB)
810.0	74.7	74.7	—	—	810.0	Australia
412.0	38.0	38.0	—	—	412.0	Austria
967.0	89.1	89.1	—	—	967.0	Belgium
1,396.0	128.7	128.7	—	—	1,396.0	Canada
340.0	31.3	31.3	—	—	340.0	China, P.R.: Hong Kong
371.0	34.2	34.2	—	—	371.0	Denmark
340.0	31.3	31.3	—	—	340.0	Finland
2,577.0	237.6	237.6	—	—	2,577.0	France
3,557.0	327.9	327.9	—	—	3,557.0	Germany
1,772.0	163.4	163.4	—	—	1,772.0	Italy
3,557.0	327.9	327.9	—	—	3,557.0	Japan
340.0					340.0	Korea
345.0	31.8	31.8	—	—	345.0	Kuwait
340.0	31.3	31.3	—	—	340.0	Luxembourg
340.0	—	—	—	—	340.0	Malaysia
1,316.0	121.3	121.3	—	—	1,316.0	Netherlands
383.0	35.3	35.3	—	—	383.0	Norway
1,780.0					1,780.0	Saudi Arabia
340.0	31.3	31.3	—	—	340.0	Singapore
672.0	62.0	62.0	—	—	672.0	Spain
859.0	79.2	79.2	—	—	859.0	Sweden
1,557.0	143.5	143.5	—	—	1,557.0	Switzerland
340.0					340.0	Thailand
2,577.0	237.6	237.6	—	—	2,577.0	United Kingdom
6,712.0	618.8	618.8	—	—	6,712.0	United States

* The maximum combined amount drawn under the GAB and the NAB cannot exceed SDR 34 billion.

			Administered Accounts			
11,218.0	7,597.5	1,641.1	5,956.4	3.6	3,616.9	**PRGF Trust:**
10,974.5	7,359.3	1,641.1	5,718.2	3.6	3,611.6	Loan Account
243.5	238.1	—	238.1	—	5.3	Subsidy Account

Reserve Position in Fund

		1970	1971	1972	1973	1974	1975	1976	1977	1978	1979	1980	1981	1982	1983	1984
															Millions of SDRs:	
All Countries	010	7,696.6	6,351.3	6,324.7	6,168.2	8,844.4	12,624.0	17,736.1	18,088.6	14,838.5	11,759.8	16,835.5	21,322.8	25,455.2	39,112.6	41,569.6
Industrial Countries	110	6,646.6	5,347.1	5,288.0	4,963.1	6,225.4	7,712.6	11,846.8	12,245.8	9,612.6	7,763.9	10,798.2	13,651.8	17,160.8	25,669.7	27,357.2
United States	111	1,935.2	584.5	428.0	457.5	1,513.0	1,889.5	3,816.6	4,071.7	803.5	950.9	2,236.5	4,342.2	6,660.8	10,805.0	11,774.1
Canada	156	669.6	332.6	315.9	280.4	432.6	553.6	812.9	701.5	427.4	296.5	454.0	345.7	331.1	671.9	692.1
Australia	193	267.0	167.4	167.4	166.8	175.8	166.8	166.8	166.3	161.3	156.4	255.2	252.5	.1	108.6	186.7
Japan	158	973.2	489.9	570.8	529.4	603.3	686.4	1,143.5	1,329.3	1,641.7	1,120.9	1,043.9	1,338.8	1,877.5	2,199.3	2,263.8
New Zealand	196	50.5	50.5	50.5	50.6	—	—	—	—	23.0	—	27.5	27.6	—	28.5	—
Euro Area																
Austria	122	156.6	142.4	132.5	125.8	130.7	177.2	343.5	324.5	254.3	231.5	228.5	224.0	258.8	447.1	447.2
Belgium	124	391.7	599.4	516.1	492.4	511.1	591.3	814.2	779.3	605.7	524.0	489.4	390.2	328.1	496.5	521.3
Finland	172	66.8	63.8	63.8	63.8	63.8				46.1	44.7	77.4	77.4	77.5	123.0	133.7
France	132	—	435.9	459.8	377.0	429.0	622.7	843.0	736.4	460.6	478.5	836.5	883.6	868.3	1,291.6	1,290.9
Germany	134	917.1	1,078.2	1,140.2	1,207.0	1,290.4	1,581.4	2,132.7	2,184.8	3,301.9	2,372.2	1,796.0	2,117.4	2,798.9	3,579.9	3,826.1
Ireland	178	30.3	35.3	40.3	40.3	42.1	39.1	68.7	65.7	59.7	60.7	76.6	75.1	75.2	115.7	124.4
Italy	136	275.5	348.5	330.4	297.2					242.5	236.5	645.6	630.6	630.6	945.3	1,095.8
Luxembourg	137	4.0	4.3	5.0	5.0	5.0	5.0	9.0	8.7	9.6	9.4	12.2	12.2	12.2	12.2	12.2
Netherlands	138	539.3	643.7	553.6	309.4	441.6	746.7	899.8	953.5	631.8	457.7	510.3	497.8	561.3	901.0	963.2
Portugal	182	18.8	29.3	29.3	29.3	29.3						34.8	48.8	48.8	29.7	29.7
Spain	184	45.0	103.8	103.8	103.8	121.1				136.3	133.4	205.6	205.6	205.6	321.5	363.0
Denmark	128	26.4	52.3	65.0	119.1	72.9	61.1	67.0	72.8	68.7	76.8	110.9	105.3	99.8	205.0	214.4
Greece	174	34.5	34.5	34.5	34.5					33.5	32.4	55.6	55.6	55.6	86.2	81.4
Iceland	176		5.7	5.8	5.8						5.4	9.0	9.0		4.0	4.0
Norway	142	118.8	61.6	69.0	63.4	68.9	111.8	247.4	234.7	205.7	188.1	201.4	213.8	246.4	411.0	470.4
San Marino	135															
Sweden	144	126.4	83.6	89.9	88.0	89.0	95.1	231.7	225.4	191.0	180.7	193.9	165.6	148.9	240.7	258.3
Switzerland	146	—	—	—	—	—	81.3	250.0	391.2	308.5	207.2	252.4	397.1	467.3	635.8	592.8
United Kingdom	112	—	—	116.5	116.6	205.9	303.7	—	—	—	—	1,045.2	1,236.1	1,408.1	2,010.2	2,011.8
Developing Countries	200	990.1	1,004.2	1,036.7	1,205.1	2,589.0	4,911.4	5,889.2	5,842.9	5,226.0	3,995.9	6,037.3	7,671.0	8,294.5	13,443.0	14,212.4
Africa	605	227.9	252.1	270.6	309.2	258.8	322.1	419.4	414.1	460.8	392.2	699.2	800.2	227.0	376.6	347.3
Algeria	612	32.5	32.5	32.5	32.5	32.5	32.5	33.5	32.5	31.6	30.6	101.8	116.8	125.6	172.4	165.5
Angola	614															
Benin	638	2.1	2.1	2.1	2.1	2.1	2.1	2.1	2.1	2.0	1.9	2.0	2.0	2.0	2.0	2.0
Botswana	616	.6	.6	.6	.6	.6	.6	.6	1.2	1.2	2.2	5.1	9.1	9.2	11.3	12.3
Burkina Faso	748	1.4	2.5	3.1	3.3	3.3	3.3	3.3	4.6	4.6	4.6	5.6	5.6	5.6	5.6	7.5
Burundi	618	—	—	.3	.4	—	—	—	—	4.8	4.5	7.3	7.3	7.4	9.4	9.4
Cameroon	622	6.9	6.9	6.9	6.9	—	—	—	—	3.5	6.4	12.0	12.0	13.9	7.2	.2
Cape Verde	624									—	.3	.6	.6	.6	1.0	1.0
Central African Rep.	626	1.3	.1	.3	.4	—	—	—	—	1.7	1.9			1.2	1.6	.1
Chad	628									1.2	1.8	3.8	3.8	5.1	3.5	.3
Comoros	632									—	—	.3				
Congo, Dem. Rep. of	636	28.3	28.3	28.3	28.3	28.3	—	—	—	—	—	—	23.5	—	—	—
Congo, Rep. of	634	1.6	1.7	1.8	1.8	1.9	2.0	2.0	—	—	—	—	2.1	3.3	3.0	.5
Côte d'Ivoire	662	10.8	10.8	10.8	10.8	—	—	—	—	10.4	12.2	9.5				
Djibouti	611									—	.8	1.2	1.2	1.2	1.2	1.2
Equatorial Guinea	642	1.0	1.0	—	—	—	—	1.8	—	—	.2	—	.2	.5		
Ethiopia	644	6.8	6.8	6.8	6.8	6.8	6.8	6.8	7.3	—	—	4.1	—	—	4.2	—
Gabon	646	2.4	2.4	2.4	2.5	2.5	2.5	2.5	2.5	—	—	—	—	—	7.0	—
Gambia, The	648	.3	.3	.4	.5	.6	1.8	1.7		—	—	—	—	—	—	—
Ghana	652	—	—	—	5.9	10.6				—	—	—	—	—	—	—
Guinea	656									—	—	—	—	.6	1.5	—
Guinea-Bissau	654							.8		—	—	—	.5	—	—	—
Kenya	664	12.0	12.0	12.0	12.3	—	—	—	—	—	—	—	.2	1.5	9.6	10.9
Lesotho	666	—	.1	.2	.4	.6	1.3	1.3	1.3	1.1	1.1	2.0	2.0	.1	1.2	1.3
Liberia	668			.3	—	1.4	1.8			—	—	—	—	—	—	—
Madagascar	674	5.0	5.0	5.0	5.0	—	—	—	—	—	—	—	.3	1.2	—	—
Malawi	676	1.4	1.4	1.9	3.8	3.8	—	—	—	—	—	—	3.8	—	2.2	2.2
Mali	678									—	—	5.4	7.6	8.7	8.7	8.7
Mauritania	682	1.5	.6	.8	.9	—	—	—	—	—	—	—	—	—	—	—
Mauritius	684	1.8	2.5	2.5	2.5	—	5.5	5.5		—	—	—	—	—	—	—
Morocco	686	—	—	28.3	28.2	28.2	28.2			—	—	—	—	—	—	—
Mozambique	688															
Namibia	728															
Niger	692	2.1	2.1	2.1	2.1	2.1	2.1	2.1	3.1	5.0	5.0	6.0	6.0	6.1	8.6	8.6
Nigeria	694	11.4	11.4	12.9	33.0	33.8	212.2	333.8	340.3	365.9	295.2	370.7	446.1	—	—	—
Rwanda	714	—	.1	—	—	—	—	2.1	2.1	2.9	5.5	8.4	7.3	7.3	9.6	9.7
São Tomé & Príncipe	716									.4	.4	.7	.7	.7	.7	—
Senegal	722	3.3	3.6	3.9	4.2	—	—	—	—	2.1	—	—	—	.9	.9	1.0
Seychelles	718								.1	.1	.3	.4	.4	.4		
Sierra Leone	724	4.9	4.9	4.9	4.9	—	—	—	—	—	—	—	1.1	—	—	—
Somalia	726	3.7	3.8	3.9	3.9	3.9	4.2	4.2		—	—	—	—	—	—	—
South Africa	199	50.4	80.5	80.5	80.5	81.4	—	—	—	—	—	128.2	107.2	—	70.0	70.0
Sudan	732	—	—	—	—	—	—	—	—	—	—	—	—	—	—	—
Swaziland	734	.1	.2	.3	.2	.4	1.1	2.0	2.0	2.8	2.7	4.3	4.3	—	1.7	1.7
Tanzania	738	6.9	6.9	6.9	10.5	—	—	—	—	—	—	—	1.7	—	—	—
Togo	742	2.1	2.1	2.1	2.1	2.1	2.1	2.1	2.1	2.0	3.3	—	—	.2	.2	.2
Tunisia	744	—	—	5.9	12.0	12.0	12.0	12.0	12.0	11.7	11.3	19.2	19.2	19.2	30.1	29.4
Uganda	746	6.5	—	—	—	—	—	—	—	5.9	—	—	—	3.5	3.5	3.5
Zambia	754	19.0	19.0	—	—	—	—	—	—	—	—	—	7.5	—	—	—
Zimbabwe	698															
Asia	505	152.6	194.4	196.6	210.8	143.2	118.5	99.9	174.7	230.1	360.7	831.6	742.0	880.1	1,196.8	1,236.2
Afghanistan, Islamic State of	512	—	—	—	—	—	—	—	8.3	9.0	9.4	15.1	15.1	15.1	4.8	4.8
Bangladesh	513			2.0	1.2	—	—	—	—	—	—	—	—	7.5	22.4	22.4
Bhutan	514													.4	.4	.6
Brunei Darussalam	516	—														
Cambodia	522	6.3								—	—	—	—	—	—	—
China, P.R.: Mainland	924									—	—	150.0	—	—	167.7	260.6
China, P.R.: Hong Kong	532															
Fiji	819		2.3	2.3	2.3	—	3.3	3.3	3.3	3.2	3.1	5.3	5.4	5.4	7.8	7.8
India	534	21.1	76.2	76.2	76.2	—	—	—	—	69.2	161.5	329.7	329.7	364.3	486.9	487.0
Indonesia	536	—	—	—	—	28.6	—	—	68.0	69.1	73.7	160.8	196.3	218.4	72.4	72.4
Kiribati	826	—	—	—	—	—	—	—	—	—	—	—	—	—	—	—
Korea	542	12.5	12.5	12.5	20.0	—	—	—	—	10.4	18.8	—	—	—	51.7	—
Lao People's Democratic Rep.	544	2.8	2.8	2.8	2.8	3.3	—	—	—	—	—	—	—	—	—	—
Malaysia	548	50.9	39.2	39.3	46.5	49.5	53.8	53.8	52.3	53.6	67.5	116.5	116.5	116.5	159.3	159.4
Maldives	556									.2	.2	.3	.3	.3	.5	
Marshall Islands	867															
Mongolia	948															
Myanmar	518													9.0	13.0	6.9	6.9
Nepal	558	2.5	2.7	2.9	3.1	3.1	3.1	—	—	2.4	2.3	5.2	5.7	5.7	5.7	5.7

1985	1986	1987	1988	1989	1990	1991	1992	1993	1994	1995	1996	1997	1998	1999		
End of Period																
38,730.8	35,339.3	31,467.1	28,272.9	25,471.0	23,748.9	25,887.7	33,902.8	32,802.2	31,725.6	36,673.2	38,005.3	47,078.0	60,630.9	54,785.6	All Countries....................	010
25,301.1	23,087.8	20,462.9	19,572.2	19,553.6	19,976.5	22,774.1	29,510.6	28,308.8	27,417.0	31,643.8	32,609.8	41,336.5	53,919.2	46,775.8	Industrial Countries....................	110
10,876.2	9,589.5	8,000.1	7,241.7	6,884.8	6,379.7	6,632.8	8,552.3	8,589.0	8,240.8	9,854.7	10,733.8	13,393.4	17,124.1	13,092.9	United States	111
647.1	561.1	465.7	375.2	401.6	363.7	414.1	734.9	689.9	629.2	836.2	852.8	1,167.3	1,632.7	2,308.0	Canada	156
188.7	188.8	188.8	204.6	245.1	245.2	245.3	419.7	400.5	346.9	337.6	334.9	539.0	892.3	1,189.4	Australia	193
2,071.1	1,947.3	2,010.8	2,435.8	2,677.0	4,197.3	5,398.2	6,284.3	6,014.5	5,912.3	5,449.0	4,639.3	6,777.4	6,813.1	4,773.5	Japan	158
.1	.1	.2	8.2	39.8	40.2	54.0	109.1	103.6	100.8	110.3	126.6	131.9	252.8	308.6	New Zealand	196
															Euro Area	
405.2	361.5	330.0	288.9	274.4	241.8	275.8	389.8	381.5	363.9	458.9	562.4	713.7	969.7	698.7	Austria	122
472.4	462.3	392.4	344.8	341.9	326.3	366.6	586.0	560.2	556.3	675.8	747.3	875.8	1,348.4	1,668.4	Belgium	124
130.3	135.0	141.6	167.6	178.9	151.0	192.3	241.0	220.4	196.1	259.5	292.8	414.2	595.0	464.3	Finland	172
1,246.8	1,419.3	1,348.9	1,200.5	1,076.2	1,003.6	1,164.9	1,804.9	1,681.8	1,626.7	1,853.9	1,874.5	2,119.2	3,161.8	3,949.9	France	132
3,467.0	3,146.1	2,748.8	2,486.6	2,315.3	2,147.8	2,493.7	3,083.2	2,876.6	2,760.5	3,505.0	3,802.5	4,406.9	5,698.3	4,676.6	Germany	134
120.8	130.7	130.9	134.3	125.4	104.6	123.9	171.3	155.1	151.9	197.5	226.1	252.1	413.6	302.9	Ireland	178
1,056.1	1,036.6	1,019.7	941.1	1,098.5	1,204.6	1,576.2	1,774.1	1,575.4	1,392.8	1,320.6	1,289.9	1,660.7	3,075.2	2,583.6	Italy	136
12.2	12.2	12.2	12.2	12.3	12.3	12.3	25.9	23.6	23.6	22.9	23.6	21.8	59.4	54.4	Luxembourg	137
898.2	717.0	652.5	562.6	536.9	518.8	559.0	834.0	795.3	802.2	1,169.1	1,275.1	1,625.5	2,112.8	1,879.8	Netherlands	138
29.7	29.7	29.7	29.7	94.9	123.7	188.9	228.3	219.4	230.8	303.0	320.3	313.4	442.1	275.0	Portugal	182
369.0	423.1	553.6	786.0	929.7	796.8	748.8	831.7	750.6	759.5	1,064.9	1,110.3	1,409.5	1,557.8	1,111.2	Spain	184
207.5	127.2	123.2	234.7	254.9	219.8	248.6	345.7	309.1	294.6	400.0	421.8	467.9	827.5	582.1	Denmark	128
75.0	70.1	70.1	71.1	89.2	74.7	74.7	116.9	113.7	113.7	113.7	113.7	113.7	191.5	285.0	Greece	174
4.0	4.0	4.0	4.0	4.0	4.0	4.0	10.5	10.5	10.5	10.5	10.5	10.5	10.5	18.6	Iceland	176
463.7	481.8	498.1	451.3	441.9	407.8	399.0	471.4	425.5	440.9	636.2	643.8	725.5	899.1	621.2	Norway	142
								2.4	2.4	2.4	2.4	2.4	2.4	4.1	San Marino	135
249.6	253.4	277.4	250.8	253.6	233.9	308.4	451.4	451.4	451.4	451.4	451.4	589.1	899.9	862.9	Sweden	144
500.7	369.8	211.5	102.0	31.6			580.9	604.5	643.2	981.2	1,064.9	1,407.5	1,828.0	1,218.1	Switzerland	146
1,809.7	1,621.0	1,252.6	1,238.6	1,245.7	1,179.0	1,292.7	1,463.6	1,354.4	1,366.1	1,629.5	1,689.1	2,198.2	3,111.3	3,846.7	United Kingdom	112
13,429.7	12,251.5	11,004.2	8,700.7	5,917.4	3,772.4	3,113.6	4,392.1	4,493.4	4,308.6	5,029.4	5,395.4	5,741.5	6,711.7	8,009.8	Developing Countries	200
263.1	231.9	188.5	76.3	82.0	76.4	74.7	157.0	157.6	157.6	151.0	152.0	150.5	159.4	335.5	Africa	605
152.9	148.0	107.9	—	—	—	—	—	—	—	—	—	—	—	85.1	Algeria	612
....	....	....													Angola	614
2.0	2.0	2.0	2.0	2.0	2.0	2.0	2.1	2.1	2.1	2.1	2.2	2.2	2.2	2.2	Benin	638
12.9	15.6	15.7	13.6	19.2	16.2	13.5	14.8	16.6	16.3	19.3	19.9	18.1	27.6	22.6	Botswana	616
7.5	7.5	7.5	7.5	7.5	7.2	7.2	7.2	7.2	7.2	7.2	7.2	7.2	7.2	7.2	Burkina Faso	748
9.2	9.2	9.2	9.2	9.2	7.6	7.2	5.9	5.9	5.9	5.9	5.9	5.9	5.9	5.9	Burundi	618
.2	.2	.2	.2	.2	.2	.2	.3	.3	.3	.4	.4	.4	.4	.5	Cameroon	622
1.0															Cape Verde	624
.1	.1	.1	.1	.1	.1	.1	.1	.1	.1	.1	.1	.1	.1	.1	Central African Rep.	626
.3	.3	.3	.3	.3	.3	.3	.3	.3	.3	.3	.3	.3	.3	.3	Chad	628
							.5	.5	.5	.5	.5	.5	.5	.5	Comoros	632
—	—	—	—	—	—	—	—	—	—	—	—	—	—	—	Congo, Dem. Rep. of	636
.5	.5	.5	.5	.5	.5	.5	.5	.5	.5	.5	.5	.5	.5	—	Congo, Rep. of	634
								.1	.1	.1	.1	.2	.2	.2	Côte d'Ivoire	662
1.2	1.2	1.2	1.2	1.2	1.2	1.2	2.1	—	—	—	—	—	—	1.1	Djibouti	611
—	—	—	—	—	—	—	—	—	—	—	—	—	—	—	Equatorial Guinea.........	642
							6.9	7.0	7.0	7.0	7.1	7.1	7.1	7.1	Ethiopia	644
—	—	—	—	—	—	.1	.1	.1	.1	.1	.1	.1	.1	.1	Gabon	646
—	.1	.1	.1	.1	—	—	1.5	1.5	1.5	1.5	1.5	1.5	1.5	1.5	Gambia, The	648
—	—	—	—	—	—	—	17.4	17.4	17.4	17.4	17.4	17.4	17.4	41.1	Ghana	652
—	—	—	—	—	—	—	—	.1	.1	.1	.1	.1	.1	.1	Guinea	656
—	—	—	—	—	—	—	—	—	—	—	—	—	—	—	Guinea-Bissau	654
12.2	12.2	12.2	12.2	12.2	12.2	12.2	12.2	12.2	12.3	12.3	12.3	12.4	12.4	12.4	Kenya	664
1.3	1.3	1.3	1.3	1.3	1.3	1.3	3.5	3.5	3.5	3.5	3.5	3.5	3.5	3.5	Lesotho	666
—	—	—	—	—	—	—	—	—	—	—	—	—	—	—	Liberia	668
....	....	....	....	....											Madagascar	674
2.2	2.2	2.2	2.2	2.2	2.2	2.2	2.2	2.2	2.2	2.2	2.2	2.2	2.2	2.2	Malawi	676
8.7	8.7	8.7	8.7	8.7	8.7	8.7	8.7	8.7	8.7	8.7	8.8	8.8	8.8	8.8	Mali	678
—	—	—	—	—	—	—	—	—	—	—	—	—	—	—	Mauritania	682
—	—	—	—	.1	1.3	6.2	7.3	7.3	7.3	7.4	7.4	7.4	14.5		Mauritius	684
—	—	—	—	—	—	30.3	30.3	30.3	30.3	30.3	30.3	30.3	70.4		Morocco	686
—	—	—	—	—	—	—	—	—	—	—	—	—	—	—	Mozambique	688
....	....	....	....	....											Namibia	728
8.6	8.6	8.6	8.6	8.6	8.6	8.6	8.6	8.6	8.6	8.6	8.6	8.6	8.6	8.6	Niger	692
.1	.1	.1	.1	.1	.1	.1	.1	.1	.1	.1	.1	.1	.1	.1	Nigeria	694
9.3	9.3	9.3	7.1	7.1	6.4	6.5	10.4	9.8	9.8	—	—	—	—	—	Rwanda	714
—	—	—	—	—	—	—	—	—	—	—	—	—	—	—	São Tomé & Príncipe	716
1.0	1.0	1.0	1.0	1.0	1.0	1.0	1.1	1.1	1.1	1.2	1.3	1.3	1.4	1.4	Senegal	722
—	—	—	.1	.1	.1	.8	.8	.8	.8	.8	.8	—	—		Seychelles	718
—	—	—	—	—	—	—	—	—	—	—	—	—	—	—	Sierra Leone	724
—	—	—	—	—	—	.1	—	.1	.1	.1	.1	.1	.1		Somalia	726
—	—	—	—	—	—	—	—	—	—	—	—	—	—	—	South Africa	199
—	—	—	—	—	—	—	—	—	—	—	—	—	—	—	Sudan	732
1.8	—	—	—	—	—	3.0	3.0	3.0	3.0	3.0	3.0	3.0	6.6		Swaziland	734
—	—	—	—	—	—	10.0	10.0	10.0	10.0	10.0	10.0	10.0	10.0		Tanzania	738
.2	.2	.2	.2	.2	.2	.3	.3	—	.2	.3	.3	.3	.3		Togo	742
26.4	—	—	—	—	—	—	—	—	—	—	—	—	20.2		Tunisia	744
3.5	3.5	—	—	—	—	—	—	—	—	—	—	—	—		Uganda	746
—	—	—	—	—	—	—	—	—	—	—	—	—	—		Zambia	754
—	—	—	—	—	.1	.1	.1	.1	.1	.1	.1	.2	.3		Zimbabwe	698
1,210.9	1,220.0	1,213.8	1,231.7	1,409.3	924.3	1,085.5	2,009.0	2,056.7	2,173.8	2,848.4	3,142.2	3,201.8	3,680.0	3,643.0	Asia	505
4.8	4.8	4.8	4.9	4.9	4.9	4.9	4.9	4.9	4.9	4.9	4.9	4.9	4.9	4.9	Afghanistan, Islamic State of	512
22.4	22.4	22.4	22.4	22.4	—	—	—	—	.1	.1	.1	.1	.2	.2	Bangladesh	513
.6	.6	.6	.6	.6	.6	.6	.6	.6	.6	.6	.6	.6	.6	1.0	Bhutan	514
—	—	—	—	—	—	—	—	—	—	—	35.3	35.3	35.3	35.3	Brunei Darussalam.............	516
—	—	—	—	—	—	.9	—	—	—	—	—	—	—	—	Cambodia	522
302.6	302.6	302.6	302.6	302.6	302.6	302.6	551.2	512.8	517.3	817.8	971.0	1,682.4	2,523.3	1,684.7	China, P.R.: Mainland	924
													31.3		China, P.R.: Hong Kong	532
7.8	7.9	7.9	7.9	7.9	7.1	6.8	10.4	10.0	10.0	10.0	10.1	10.1	10.1	14.9	Fiji	819
487.1	487.2	487.2	487.2	487.2	—	.2	212.6	212.6	212.6	212.6	212.6	212.6	212.8	488.6	India	534
72.4	72.4	72.4	72.4	72.4	72.4	72.4	194.4	199.7	214.0	270.0	298.0	—	—	145.5	Indonesia	536
—	.6	—	—	—	—	—	—	—	—	—	—	—	—	—	Kiribati	826
.7	.7	.7	.7	178.2	224.5	255.4	319.1	339.2	363.6	438.5	474.3	443.7	.1	208.6	Korea	542
—	—	—	—	—	—	—	—	—	—	—	—	—	—	—	Lao People's Democratic Rep.	544
159.4	159.4	153.0	172.0	169.7	163.9	179.8	240.3	229.1	273.7	456.3	478.2	444.7	444.7	608.2	Malaysia	548
—	—	—	—	—	—	.9	.9	.9	.9	.9	.9	.9	.9	1.6	Maldives	556
—	—	—	—	—	—	—	—	—	—	—	—	—	—	—	Marshall Islands	867
—	—	—	—	—	—	—	—	—	—	—	—	—	—	—	Mongolia	948
—	—	—	—	—	—	—	—	—	—	—	—	—	—	—	Myanmar	518
5.7	5.7	5.7	5.7	5.7	5.7	5.7	5.7	5.7	5.7	5.7	5.7	5.7	5.7	5.7	Nepal	558

Reserve Position in Fund

		1970	1971	1972	1973	1974	1975	1976	1977	1978	1979	1980	1981	1982	1983	1984
Asia (cont.)															*Millions of SDRs:*	
Pakistan	564	—	—	—	—	—	—	—	—	—	—	—	—	58.8	88.5	88.6
Palau	565	—	—	—	—	—	—	—	—	—	—	—	—	—	—	—
Papua New Guinea	853	. . .	. . .	. . .	—	—	—	—	—	—	2.4	3.8	—	.1	5.3	5.4
Philippines	566	—	—	—	—	—	—	—	—	—	—	—	—	—	—	8.8
Samoa	862	. . .	.4	.4	.4	.4	—	—	—	—	—	—	—	—	—	—
Singapore	576	7.5	9.3	9.3	9.3	9.3	9.3	9.4	9.4	13.1	21.5	44.3	63.4	67.7	68.5	69.1
Solomon Islands	813										.4	.7	—	—	.5	.5
Sri Lanka	524	—	—	—	—	—	—	—	—	—	—	—	.5	5.9	17.1	6.0
Thailand	578	33.5	33.5	33.5	33.5	33.5	33.5	33.5	33.5	—	—	—	—	—	28.8	28.8
Tonga	866															
Vanuatu	846	. . .	. . .	. . .	. . .	. . .	. . .	. . .	. . .	. . .	. . .	. . .	—	1.0	1.6	1.6
Vietnam	582	15.5	15.5	15.5	15.5	15.5	15.5	—	—	—	—	—	—	—	—	—
Europe	170	**14.8**	**10.5**	**86.2**	**48.3**	**41.8**	**7.8**	**13.8**	**12.2**	**81.7**	**19.4**	**15.8**	**23.7**	**29.1**	**157.4**	**67.8**
Albania	914	. . .	. . .	. . .	. . .	. . .	. . .	. . .	. . .	. . .	. . .	. . .	. . .	. . .	. . .	. . .
Armenia	911	. . .	. . .	. . .	. . .	. . .	. . .	. . .	. . .	. . .	. . .	. . .	. . .	. . .	. . .	. . .
Azerbaijan	912	. . .	. . .	. . .	. . .	. . .	. . .	. . .	. . .	. . .	. . .	. . .	. . .	. . .	. . .	. . .
Belarus	913	. . .	. . .	. . .	. . .	. . .	. . .	. . .	. . .	. . .	. . .	. . .	. . .	. . .	. . .	. . .
Bosnia & Herzegovina	963	—	—	—	—	—	—	—	—	—	—	—	—	—	—	—
Bulgaria	918	. . .	. . .	. . .	. . .	. . .	. . .	. . .	. . .	. . .	. . .	. . .	. . .	. . .	. . .	. . .
Croatia	960	. . .	. . .	. . .	. . .	. . .	. . .	. . .	. . .	. . .	. . .	. . .	. . .	. . .	. . .	. . .
Cyprus	423	6.5	6.5	6.5	6.5	—	—	—	—	6.5	6.1	—	—	—	4.7	4.7
Czech Republic	935	. . .	. . .	. . .	. . .	. . .	. . .	. . .	. . .	. . .	. . .	. . .	. . .	. . .	. . .	. . .
Czechoslovakia	934	. . .	. . .	. . .	. . .	. . .	. . .	. . .	. . .	. . .	. . .	. . .	. . .	. . .	. . .	. . .
Estonia	939	. . .	. . .	. . .	. . .	. . .	. . .	. . .	. . .	. . .	. . .	. . .	. . .	. . .	. . .	. . .
Georgia	915	. . .	. . .	. . .	. . .	. . .	. . .	. . .	. . .	. . .	. . .	. . .	. . .	. . .	. . .	. . .
Hungary	944	. . .	. . .	. . .	. . .	. . .	. . .	. . .	. . .	. . .	. . .	. . .	. . .	—	38.9	—
Kazakhstan	916	. . .	. . .	. . .	. . .	. . .	. . .	. . .	. . .	. . .	. . .	. . .	. . .	. . .	. . .	. . .
Kyrgyz Republic	917	. . .	. . .	. . .	. . .	. . .	. . .	. . .	. . .	. . .	. . .	. . .	. . .	. . .	. . .	. . .
Latvia	941	. . .	. . .	. . .	. . .	. . .	. . .	. . .	. . .	. . .	. . .	. . .	. . .	. . .	. . .	. . .
Lithuania	946	. . .	. . .	. . .	. . .	. . .	. . .	. . .	. . .	. . .	. . .	. . .	. . .	. . .	. . .	. . .
Macedonia, FYR	962	. . .	. . .	. . .	. . .	. . .	. . .	. . .	. . .	. . .	. . .	. . .	. . .	. . .	. . .	. . .
Malta	181	4.0	4.0	4.0	4.0	4.0	7.8	13.8	12.2	13.2	13.3	15.8	23.7	25.8	28.8	30.9
Moldova	921	. . .	. . .	. . .	. . .	. . .	. . .	. . .	. . .	. . .	. . .	. . .	. . .	. . .	. . .	. . .
Poland	964	. . .	. . .	. . .	. . .	. . .	. . .	. . .	. . .	. . .	. . .	. . .	. . .	. . .	. . .	. . .
Romania	968	. . .	. . .	47.5	—	—	—	—	—	—	—	—	—	—	—	—
Russia	922	. . .	. . .	. . .	. . .	. . .	. . .	. . .	. . .	. . .	. . .	. . .	. . .	. . .	. . .	. . .
Slovak Republic	936	. . .	. . .	. . .	. . .	. . .	. . .	. . .	. . .	. . .	. . .	. . .	. . .	. . .	. . .	. . .
Slovenia	961	. . .	. . .	. . .	. . .	. . .	. . .	. . .	. . .	. . .	. . .	. . .	. . .	. . .	. . .	. . .
Tajikistan	923	. . .	. . .	. . .	. . .	. . .	. . .	. . .	. . .	. . .	. . .	. . .	. . .	. . .	. . .	. . .
Turkey	186	—	—	28.1	37.8	37.8	—	—	—	—	—	—	—	—	32.3	32.3
Turkmenistan	925	. . .	. . .	. . .	. . .	. . .	. . .	. . .	. . .	. . .	. . .	. . .	. . .	. . .	. . .	. . .
Ukraine	926	. . .	. . .	. . .	. . .	. . .	. . .	. . .	. . .	. . .	. . .	. . .	. . .	. . .	. . .	. . .
Uzbekistan	927	. . .	. . .	. . .	. . .	. . .	. . .	. . .	. . .	. . .	. . .	. . .	. . .	. . .	. . .	. . .
Yugoslavia, SFR	188	4.3	—	—	—	—	—	—	—	62.1	—	—	—	3.3	52.7	—
Middle East	405	**63.1**	**75.2**	**124.0**	**194.3**	**1,412.4**	**3,315.4**	**4,162.9**	**4,105.0**	**3,363.2**	**2,240.2**	**3,011.7**	**4,527.2**	**5,735.9**	**10,264.1**	**11,560.0**
Bahrain	419	. . .	. . .	2.5	2.5	5.5	9.6	4.7	4.8	5.8	5.8	8.5	8.9	12.5	21.4	23.1
Egypt	469	—	—	—	—	—	—	—	—	—	—	—	24.0	—	30.4	—
Iran, I.R. of	429	—	—	19.3	48.0	422.0	958.8	998.0	985.6	725.2	325.1	234.6	141.4	75.7	70.8	70.8
Iraq	433	—	—	17.3	27.3	27.3	27.3	27.3	27.5	27.7	47.8	111.9	111.9	111.9	—	—
Israel	436	—	—	—	32.5	—	—	—	—	—	31.6	25.6	—	—	34.8	—
Jordan	439	5.8	5.8	5.8	5.8	5.8	5.8	5.8	5.8	5.6	10.3	16.6	16.6	16.6	7.2	—
Kuwait	443	21.3	20.7	20.7	19.7	255.8	573.6	742.7	722.2	588.4	389.7	410.5	409.7	461.0	696.7	716.4
Lebanon	446	2.3	2.3	2.3	2.3	2.3	2.3	2.3	2.3	2.3	2.1	6.1	6.1	6.1	18.8	18.8
Libya	672	6.0	6.0	6.0	6.0	6.0	6.0	6.0	6.0	5.9	42.4	148.1	189.2	189.2	189.2	243.5
Oman	449	. . .	1.8	1.8	1.8	15.3	24.4	25.0	19.4	13.9	12.8	14.9	16.5	20.8	30.5	33.2
Qatar	453	. . .	. . .	5.0	5.0	5.0	13.1	16.2	14.5	14.7	13.6	18.1	18.1	19.4	37.2	38.4
Saudi Arabia	456	22.5	33.5	33.5	33.5	595.3	1,570.2	2,205.8	2,215.2	1,895.7	1,289.6	1,896.2	3,428.2	4,621.3	8,902.7	10,187.6
Syrian Arab Rep.	463	—	—	—	—	—	7.1	12.5	—	—	7.1	7.1	—	—	—	—
United Arab Emirates	466	—	—	3.8	3.8	69.6	114.8	114.1	96.5	71.7	62.1	93.1	147.9	201.4	214.6	222.3
Yemen Arab Rep.	473	1.5	1.5	2.5	2.5	2.5	2.5	2.5	5.4	6.3	7.3	10.8	—	—	6.0	6.0
Yemen, P.D. Rep.	459	3.8	3.8	3.8	3.8	—	—	—	—	—	—	9.4	1.6	—	3.9	—
Yemen, Republic of	474	—	—	—	—	—	—	—	—	—	—	—	—	—	—	—
Western Hemisphere	205	**531.7**	**472.0**	**359.3**	**442.4**	**732.9**	**1,147.7**	**1,193.3**	**1,136.8**	**1,090.1**	**983.5**	**1,479.0**	**1,577.9**	**1,422.4**	**1,448.2**	**1,001.0**
Antigua and Barbuda	311	. . .	. . .	. . .	. . .	. . .	. . .	. . .	. . .	. . .	. . .	. . .	. . .	. . .	. . .	. . .
Argentina	213	130.2	110.0	—	—	11.3	—	—	—	130.5	154.4	262.8	239.2	91.0	—	—
Bahamas, The	313	—	—	—	—	5.0	5.0	5.0	5.0	4.9	4.7	8.8	6.6	6.7	10.9	10.9
Barbados	316	2.0	2.0	2.0	2.0	2.0	3.3	3.3	3.3	3.0	2.9	5.0	5.0	—	2.2	2.2
Belize	339	. . .	. . .	. . .	. . .	. . .	. . .	. . .	. . .	. . .	. . .	. . .	. . .	1.3	1.9	1.9
Bolivia	218	—	—	—	—	—	—	6.4	7.4	9.0	—	—	—	—	—	—
Brazil	223	117.4	116.3	116.3	116.3	116.3	116.3	162.2	160.2	138.9	183.2	269.5	226.6	259.8	—	—
Chile	228	—	—	—	—	—	—	—	—	38.3	37.1	64.3	64.3	70.5	—	—
Colombia	233	—	—	—	39.3	39.3	39.3	45.3	76.7	70.1	73.6	114.5	151.7	175.2	262.1	—
Costa Rica	238	6.0	.3	.3	.3	—	—	—	—	7.8	7.5	—	—	—	—	—
Dominica	321	. . .	. . .	. . .	. . .	. . .	. . .	. . .	. . .	. . .	. . .	. . .	. . .	. . .	. . .	. . .
Dominican Republic	243	—	—	—	10.8	—	—	—	—	—	—	—	—	—	7.4	—
Ecuador	248	—	—	—	5.6	9.2	13.2	—	—	8.0	9.4	21.8	24.8	—	11.4	—
El Salvador	253	—	—	—	—	—	—	—	5.1	8.8	8.5	—	—	—	—	—
Grenada	328	. . .	. . .	. . .	. . .	. . .	. . .	. . .	. . .	. . .	. . .	. . .	. . .	. . .	. . .	. . .
Guatemala	258	. . .	3.0	9.0	9.0	9.0	9.0	12.0	12.4	12.9	14.1	21.7	8.4	—	7.9	—
Guyana	336	1.8	—	.6	—	1.8	5.0	—	—	—	—	—	—	—	—	—
Haiti	263	. . .	2.5	2.9	.2	—	—	—	—	2.4	4.4	—	—	.1	.1	.1
Honduras	268	—	—	—	6.3	—	—	—	—	6.3	6.1	—	—	—	4.2	—
Jamaica	343	9.5	13.3	—	—	—	—	—	—	—	—	—	—	2.4	3.8	—
Mexico	273	135.3	97.8	97.8	97.8	97.8	97.8	—	—	—	—	100.3	161.0	—	90.8	—
Nicaragua	278	—	—	—	—	—	—	—	—	—	—	—	—	—	—	—
Panama	283	1.0	4.4	8.0	8.0	—	—	—	—	3.7	2.5	8.1	—	—	8.7	—
Paraguay	288	4.8	4.8	4.8	4.8	4.8	4.8	5.8	6.6	6.5	8.2	14.9	25.2	27.6	32.3	32.3
Peru	293	—	—	—	30.8	30.8	30.8	—	—	—	—	—	—	—	—	—
St. Kitts and Nevis	361	. . .	. . .	. . .	. . .	. . .	. . .	. . .	. . .	. . .	. . .	. . .	. . .	. . .	. . .	. . .
St. Lucia	362	. . .	. . .	. . .	. . .	. . .	. . .	. . .	. . .	. . .	. . .	. . .	. . .	. . .	. . .	. . .
St. Vincent & Grenadines	364	. . .	. . .	. . .	. . .	. . .	. . .	. . .	. . .	. . .	. . .	. . .	. . .	. . .	.4	—
Suriname	366	. . .	. . .	. . .	. . .	. . .	. . .	. . .	. . .	4.8	4.8	7.9	7.9	7.9	3.0	—
Trinidad and Tobago	369	6.6	6.6	6.6	—	4.8	18.7	27.8	27.6	29.8	37.8	63.0	78.3	96.7	118.6	126.8
Uruguay	298	—	—	—	—	—	—	—	—	16.7	16.2	26.7	28.0	—	9.5	—
Venezuela, Rep. Bol.	299	117.1	111.1	111.1	111.5	401.0	804.6	925.6	832.7	588.0	408.1	489.9	548.6	681.8	877.1	827.0
Memorandum Items																
Oil Exporting Countries	999	210.8	216.9	263.8	322.0	1,892.2	4,337.5	5,428.0	5,360.4	4,397.8	2,990.7	4,050.6	5,770.7	6,726.4	11,263.5	12,577.0
Non-Oil Developing Countries	201	779.4	787.3	773.0	883.1	696.8	573.9	461.2	482.5	828.2	1,005.2	1,986.7	1,900.3	1,568.1	2,179.4	1,635.4

End of Period

1985	1986	1987	1988	1989	1990	1991	1992	1993	1994	1995	1996	1997	1998	1999		
															Asia (cont.)	
—	—	.1	.1	.1	.1	.1	.1	.1	.1	.1	.1	.1	.1	.1	Pakistan	564
														—	Palau	565
5.4	5.4	6.9	7.0	7.0	—	—	—	.1	.1	.1	.1	.1	.1	.1	Papua New Guinea	853
23.8	38.8	38.8	38.8	38.8	38.8	38.8	87.1	87.1	87.1	87.1	87.1	87.1	87.1	87.1	Philippines	566
							.7	.7	.7	.7	.7	.7	.7	.7	Samoa	862
80.6	79.9	79.1	77.9	80.1	68.9	60.1	113.4	157.4	172.8	199.8	204.7	248.4	297.6	303.4	Singapore	576
.5	.5	.5	.5	.5	.5	.5	.5	.5	.5	.5	.5	.5	.5	.5	Solomon Islands	813
6.0	—	—	—	—	.1	.1	20.2	20.2	20.2	20.2	20.2	20.2	20.2	47.7	Sri Lanka	524
28.8	28.8	28.8	28.8	28.8	31.8	155.2	243.3	271.5	285.2	318.7	333.5	—	—		Thailand	578
.7	.7	.7	.7	.7	.7	.7	1.2	1.2	1.2	1.2	1.2	1.2	1.2	1.7	Tonga	866
1.6	1.6	1.6	1.6	1.6	1.6	1.6	1.6	2.5	2.5	2.5	2.5	2.5	2.5	2.5	Vanuatu	846
															Vietnam	582
66.6	69.3	68.2	71.3	73.9	67.0	71.0	255.7	262.9	262.8	264.6	268.2	269.2	302.8	653.1	**Europe**	170
…	…	…	…	…	…	…	—	—	—	—	—	—	—	3.4	Albania	914
…	…	…	…	…	…	…	—	—	—	—	—	—	—	—	Armenia	911
…	…	…	…	…	…	…	—	—	—	—	—	—	—	—	Azerbaijan	912
…	…	…	…	…	…	…	—	—	—	—	—	—	—	—	Belarus	913
—	—	—	—	—	—	—	—	—	—	—	—	—	—	—	Bosnia & Herzegovina	963
…	…	…	…	…	…	…	38.7	32.6	32.6	32.6	32.6	32.6	32.6	32.7	Bulgaria	918
…	…	…	…	…	…	…	—	—	—	—	—	.1	.1	.1	Croatia	960
4.7	4.7	4.7	11.7	18.1	15.1	17.9	25.5	25.5	25.5	25.5	25.5	25.5	25.5	35.4	Cyprus	423
—	—	—	—	—	—	—	—	—	—	—	—	—	—	—	Czech Republic	935
—	—	—	—	—	—	—	…	…	…	…	…	…	…	…	Czechoslovakia	934
…	…	…	…	…	…	…	—	—	—	—	—	—	—	—	Estonia	939
…	…	…	…	…	…	…	—	—	—	—	—	—	—	—	Georgia	915
…	…	…	…	…	…	…	56.1	56.1	56.1	56.1	56.1	56.1	56.1	176.8	Hungary	944
…	…	…	…	…	…	…	—	—	—	—	—	—	—	—	Kazakhstan	916
…	…	…	…	…	…	…	—	—	—	—	—	—	—	—	Kyrgyz Republic	917
—	—	—	—	—	—	—	—	—	—	—	—	—	—	—	Latvia	941
…	…	…	…	…	…	…	—	—	—	—	—	—	—	—	Lithuania	946
…	…	…	…	…	…	…	—	—	—	—	—	—	—	—	Macedonia, FYR	962
29.7	32.4	31.2	27.3	23.5	19.6	20.8	25.3	25.3	25.4	27.3	30.7	31.6	31.6	40.3	Malta	181
…	…	…	…	…	…	…	—	—	—	—	—	—	—	—	Moldova	921
—	—	—	—	—	—	—	77.1	77.1	77.1	77.1	77.1	77.1	77.1	172.3	Poland	964
—	—	—	—	—	—	—	—	—	—	—	—	—	—	—	Romania	968
…	…	…	…	…	…	…	.5	1.0	.8	.8	.9	.9	.9	.9	Russia	922
—	—	—	—	—	—	—	…	…	…	…	…	…	…	…	Slovak Republic	936
…	…	…	…	…	…	…	—	12.9	12.9	12.9	12.9	12.9	46.5	78.4	Slovenia	961
…	…	…	…	…	…	…	—	—	—	—	—	—	—	—	Tajikistan	923
32.3	32.3	32.3	32.3	32.3	32.3	32.3	32.3	32.3	32.3	32.3	32.3	32.3	32.3	112.8	Turkey	186
…	…	…	…	…	…	…	—	—	—	—	—	—	—	—	Turkmenistan	925
…	…	…	…	…	…	…	—	—	—	—	—	—	—	—	Ukraine	926
…	…	…	…	…	…	…	—	—	—	—	—	—	—	—	Uzbekistan	927
…	…	…	…	…	…	…	…	…	…	…	…	…	…		Yugoslavia, SFR	188
10,973.4	9,957.2	8,973.5	7,263.0	4,323.8	2,681.7	1,862.3	1,667.2	1,703.3	1,396.5	1,399.0	1,401.7	1,393.2	1,500.1	2,325.2	**Middle East**	405
24.6	26.0	27.3	27.7	29.6	28.0	29.6	31.1	40.9	42.2	43.7	45.1	46.7	48.5	62.4	Bahrain	419
							53.8	53.8	53.8	53.8	53.8	53.8	53.8	120.1	Egypt	469
70.8	70.8	70.8	—	—	—	—	104.6	—	—	—	—	—	—	—	Iran, I.R. of	429
—	—	—	—	—	—	—	—	—	—	—	—	—	—	—	Iraq	433
—	—	—	—	—	—	—	—	—	—	—	—	—	—	65.5	Israel	436
							12.0	—	—	—	—	—	—	—	Jordan	439
639.4	515.8	378.0	247.3	158.2	123.5	111.1	96.7	167.8	142.6	139.0	136.5	167.5	244.8	368.3	Kuwait	443
18.8	18.8	18.8	18.8	18.8	18.8	18.8	18.8	18.8	18.8	18.8	18.8	18.8	18.8	18.8	Lebanon	446
243.5	243.5	243.5	243.5	243.5	243.5	243.5	319.0	319.0	319.0	319.0	319.0	319.0	319.0	395.5	Libya	672
32.1	32.1	32.1	28.7	27.7	25.2	22.7	39.4	37.8	36.0	34.5	34.0	31.1	31.1	49.8	Oman	449
35.8	30.7	27.8	21.1	19.5	17.3	18.7	36.4	33.8	30.7	29.7	29.2	26.4	26.4	44.7	Qatar	453
9,706.8	8,838.4	8,016.2	6,540.4	3,688.0	2,099.1	1,291.6	797.3	868.6	604.3	574.7	560.9	532.5	523.8	987.5	Saudi Arabia	456
—	—	—	—	—	—	—	—	—	—	—	—	—	—	—	Syrian Arab Rep.	463
201.7	181.0	159.1	135.3	138.4	126.3	126.1	158.3	162.8	149.1	185.8	204.4	197.4	233.9	212.6	United Arab Emirates	466
…	…	…	…	…	…	…	…	…	…	…	…	…	…	…	Yemen Arab Rep.	473
…	…	…	…	…	…	…	…	…	…	…	…	…	…	…	Yemen, P.D. Rep.	459
—	—	—	—	—	—	—	—	—	—	—	—	—	—	—	Yemen, Republic of	474
915.6	773.0	560.2	58.4	28.4	23.1	20.2	303.3	313.0	318.0	366.5	431.4	726.8	1,069.3	1,053.0	**Western Hemisphere**	205
—	—	—	—	—	—	—	—	—	—	—	—	—	—	—	Antigua and Barbuda	311
—	—	—	—	—	—	—	—	—	—	—	—	—	—	—	Argentina	213
10.9	10.9	10.7	9.0	8.6	7.9	7.2	6.8	6.2	6.2	6.2	6.2	6.2	6.2	6.2	Bahamas, The	313
2.2	2.2	2.2	2.2	2.2	2.2	—	—	—	—	—	—	—	—	4.7	Barbados	316
1.9	1.9	1.9	1.9	1.9	1.9	1.9	2.9	2.9	2.9	2.9	2.9	2.9	2.9	4.2	Belize	339
							8.9	8.9	8.9	8.9	8.9	8.9	8.9	8.9	Bolivia	218
—	—	—	—	—	—	—	—	—	—	—	—	—	—	—	Brazil	223
							—	—	—	—	35.0	232.0	429.6	299.4	Chile	228
							69.0	79.8	86.7	135.3	165.1	263.4	408.3	285.8	Colombia	233
							8.7	8.7	8.7	8.7	8.7	8.7	8.7	20.0	Costa Rica	238
—	—	—	—	—	—	—	—	—	—	—	—	—	—	—	Dominica	321
—	—	—	—	—	—	—	—	—	—	—	—	—	—	—	Dominican Republic	243
							17.1	17.1	17.1	17.2	17.2	17.2	17.2	17.2	Ecuador	248
—	—	—	—	—	—	—	—	—	—	—	—	—	—	—	El Salvador	253
—	—	—	—	—	—	—	—	—	—	—	—	—	—	—	Grenada	328
—	—	—	—	—	—	—	—	—	—	—	—	—	—	—	Guatemala	258
—	—	—	—	—	—	—	—	—	—	—	—	—	—	—	Guyana	336
.1	.1	.1	.1	.1	.1	.1	.1	—	—	—	—	—	—	—	Haiti	263
—	—	—	—	—	—	—	—	—	—	—	—	—	—	8.6	Honduras	268
—	—	—	—	—	—	—	—	—	—	—	—	—	—	—	Jamaica	343
—	—	—	—	—	—	—	—	—	—	—	.1	.1	.2	.3	Mexico	273
—	—	—	—	—	—	—	—	—	—	—	—	—	—	—	Nicaragua	278
							11.9	11.9	11.9	11.9	11.9	11.9	11.9	11.9	Panama	283
31.6	24.9	19.6	15.0	12.5	11.0	11.0	16.9	16.5	14.5	14.5	14.5	14.5	14.5	21.5	Paraguay	288
—	—	—	—	—	—	—	—	—	—	—	—	—	—	—	Peru	293
—	—	—	—	—	—	—	—	—	—	—	—	—	—	.1	St. Kitts and Nevis	361
—	—	—	—	—	—	—	—	—	—	—	—	—	—	—	St. Lucia	362
							.5	.5	.5	.5	.5	.5	.5	.5	St. Vincent & Grenadines	364
—	—	—	—	—	—	—	—	—	—	—	—	—	—	6.1	Suriname	366
124.4	77.2	53.0	—	—	—	—	15.4	15.4	15.4	15.4	15.4	15.4	15.4	35.7	Trinidad and Tobago	369
744.6	655.9	472.8	30.2	3.1	—	—	145.0	145.0	145.0	145.0	145.0	145.0	145.0	321.9	Uruguay	298
															Venezuela, Rep. Bol.	299

Memorandum Items

1985	1986	1987	1988	1989	1990	1991	1992	1993	1994	1995	1996	1997	1998	1999		
11,900.0	10,788.8	9,580.5	7,319.1	4,351.0	2,707.3	1,886.3	1,891.0	1,934.5	1,640.7	1,697.7	1,727.0	1,418.9	1,524.0	2,610.9	Oil Exporting Countries	999
1,529.7	1,462.8	1,423.7	1,381.6	1,566.5	1,065.0	1,227.3	2,501.1	2,558.9	2,667.9	3,331.8	3,668.4	4,322.6	5,187.6	5,398.9	Non-Oil Developing Countries	201

1d s		1970	1971	1972	1973	1974	1975	1976	1977	1978	1979	1980	1981	1982	1983	1984
															Millions of SDRs:	
All Countries	010	45,135	74,631	95,700	101,755	126,154	137,309	160,236	202,252	222,539	248,633	292,630	291,943	284,726	308,792	349,089
Industrial Countries	110	30,406	56,702	69,276	67,823	66,437	69,800	74,497	101,121	128,793	137,817	166,350	160,909	154,306	168,994	185,291
United States	111	629	258	222	7	4	68	275	15	3,357	2,890	7,946	8,397	9,257	6,007	6,790
Canada	156	3,037	3,753	4,023	3,266	3,088	2,753	2,980	1,905	1,902	1,433	1,616	2,544	2,334	2,619	1,776
Australia	193	1,096	2,463	4,995	4,063	2,953	2,262	2,267	1,506	1,322	893	1,070	1,138	5,698	8,375	7,192
Japan	158	3,188	12,695	15,182	8,458	9,268	9,078	11,949	16,569	22,180	12,417	16,910	21,234	17,380	19,451	22,733
New Zealand	196	206	375	658	758	521	364	414	330	277	333	249	532	575	712	1,816
Euro Area																
Austria	122	849	1,225	1,557	1,440	1,852	2,796	2,625	2,337	3,515	2,706	3,738	4,131	4,320	3,712	3,658
Belgium	124	780	650	1,017	1,632	1,794	2,269	1,793	2,070	2,024	3,132	5,147	3,236	2,560	3,607	3,681
Finland	172	335	463	484	345	355	304	342	395	831	1,036	1,308	1,073	1,194	1,022	2,530
France	132	1,257	3,295	4,660	3,088	3,065	6,357	3,767	3,864	6,375	12,222	19,867	17,162	13,230	17,247	19,488
Germany	134	8,455	11,575	15,838	20,787	19,615	19,362	21,958	25,212	32,527	35,942	34,860	34,060	35,917	35,640	35,735
Ireland	178	637	839	942	755	936	1,212	1,451	1,824	1,940	1,548	2,095	2,112	2,205	2,340	2,186
Italy	136	2,113	2,821	2,049	1,808	2,601	1,033	2,696	6,553	8,059	13,128	16,966	15,995	11,432	17,693	19,473
Luxembourg	137	....	....	....	....	....	....	....	....	....	....	....	....	....	....	....
Netherlands	138	771	374	1,308	2,740	2,855	2,905	3,025	3,210	3,030	4,911	8,181	6,934	7,852	8,312	7,935
Portugal	182	583	841	1,160	1,360	919	333	143	297	669	706	589	401	354	337	485
Spain	184	1,231	2,321	3,888	4,882	4,543	4,582	3,958	4,872	7,523	9,699	8,865	8,759	6,548	6,683	11,679
Denmark	128	375	504	587	796	536	543	575	1,138	2,235	2,242	2,407	1,911	1,778	3,135	2,697
Greece	174	159	341	768	685	612	806	741	850	955	986	1,000	822	725	773	891
Iceland	176	52	55	64	69	32	34	67	78	102	117	125	185	130	138	126
Norway	142	642	914	1,029	1,120	1,384	1,675	1,548	1,480	1,894	2,872	4,383	4,963	5,700	5,664	8,822
Sweden	144	397	666	1,054	1,699	1,018	2,223	1,603	2,479	2,862	2,314	2,312	2,704	2,802	3,489	3,483
Switzerland	146	2,401	3,507	4,052	4,151	4,448	5,915	8,018	8,079	13,326	12,269	12,018	11,613	13,544	13,711	15,003
United Kingdom	112	1,213	6,767	3,742	3,916	4,037	2,928	2,302	16,057	11,887	14,021	14,700	11,003	8,770	8,327	7,112
Developing Countries	200	14,730	17,929	26,424	33,932	59,717	67,509	85,739	101,131	93,746	110,817	126,280	131,034	130,420	139,798	163,798
Africa	605	2,196	1,986	2,415	3,176	7,921	7,901	8,323	7,657	5,702	9,278	13,929	8,921	6,510	6,194	6,206
Algeria	612	101	215	188	682	1,112	888	1,443	1,307	1,442	1,911	2,780	2,939	1,930	1,522	1,215
Benin	638	12	17	20	21	22	6	10	10	5	3	3	45	—	—	—
Botswana	616	....	....	....	....	....	....	62	80	113	198	262	203	250	359	463
Burkina Faso	748	33	34	36	44	61	58	54	37	19	36	42	48	43	68	95
Burundi	618	13	14	13	14	8	23	39	75	55	59	63	40	15	15	11
Cameroon	622	71	54	23	25	54	15	29	28	33	89	136	61	45	144	49
Cape Verde	624	....	....	....	....	....	....	28	35	30	32	33	32	38	43	41
Central African Rep.	626	—	—	—	—	1	1	15	19	16	30	43	59	41	42	51
Chad	628	2	10	8	1	10	—	18	14	6	5	—	2	6	22	44
Comoros	632	....	....	....	....	....	....	....	....	....	....	5	7	10	10	3
Congo, Dem. Rep. of	636	92	40	78	108	62	21	16	110	92	157	160	106	35	76	140
Congo, Rep. of	634	7	7	5	2	15	8	6	10	6	31	67	103	29	4	2
Côte d'Ivoire	662	105	62	54	47	38	73	54	144	326	81	3	5	2	3	5
Djibouti	611	....	....	....	....	....	....	....	....	....	....	....	....	....	....	44
Equatorial Guinea	642	....	....	....	....	....	....	....	....	....	....	....	....	2	1	1
Ethiopia	644	57	48	70	131	208	230	247	168	117	131	59	219	162	114	42
Gabon	646	11	18	14	33	77	118	93	1	13	8	79	164	282	171	198
Gambia, The	648	7	8	8	11	20	21	14	19	19	1	4	3	7	3	2
Ghana	652	37	30	76	130	38	99	72	112	203	206	141	124	126	136	308
Guinea	656	....	....	....	....	....	....	....	....	....	....	....	....	....	....	....
Guinea-Bissau	654	....	....	....	....	....	....	....	....	....	....	....	....	....	....	....
Kenya	664	202	133	157	164	156	144	234	416	260	394	365	189	176	333	385
Lesotho	666	....	....	....	....	....	....	....	....	....	....	37	34	42	61	47
Liberia	668	....	....	....	....	11	12	11	19	10	35	4	6	6	19	4
Madagascar	674	29	32	34	43	40	29	34	50	37	4	7	22	16	28	59
Malawi	676	26	25	27	47	58	48	18	68	54	50	54	33	17	12	53
Mali	678	1	1	1	1	2	1	3	2	4	3	6	7	6	7	17
Mauritania	682	—	5	9	32	83	39	69	41	60	85	110	138	126	100	79
Mauritius	684	42	40	55	46	104	134	69	52	34	22	71	25	33	17	24
Morocco	686	119	136	152	155	275	258	392	408	462	408	312	196	197	101	49
Mozambique	688	....	....	....	....	....	....	....	....	....	....	....	....	....	....	56
Namibia	728	....	....	....	....	....	....	....	....	....	....	....	....	....	....	....
Niger	692	15	26	32	36	31	36	64	76	89	89	87	77	13	38	80
Nigeria	694	174	333	269	385	4,495	4,502	4,063	3,078	1,016	3,808	7,522	2,662	1,421	920	1,481
Rwanda	714	7	4	5	10	8	19	51	64	62	106	130	132	98	88	91
São Tomé & Príncipe	716	....	....	....	....	....	....	....	....	....	....	....	....	....	....	....
Senegal	722	18	17	26	1	1	23	21	26	3	3	6	4	4	7	3
Seychelles	718	....	....	....	4	4	5	6	9	7	9	14	11	11	9	5
Sierra Leone	724	34	27	32	32	40	20	19	26	26	35	24	13	7	15	8
Somalia	726	17	18	20	21	26	50	65	95	93	27	6	22	5	8	1
South Africa	199	256	164	442	290	187	374	324	303	286	304	404	350	341	689	174
Sudan	732	22	26	28	37	80	24	20	19	16	41	38	14	19	16	18
Swaziland	734	....	....	....	....	10	37	60	75	83	81	118	73	64	85	78
Tanzania	738	56	42	97	103	39	55	92	226	71	49	16	14	4	18	27
Togo	742	31	32	26	24	37	28	50	31	47	40	55	124	148	164	205
Tunisia	744	55	130	187	231	317	304	293	268	320	414	432	424	515	508	383
Uganda	746	45	15	19	11	9	23	37	34	26	9	2	23	57	97	166
Zambia	754	480	217	146	154	123	106	61	43	27	56	61	33	38	52	55
Zimbabwe	698	20	6	56	103	58	68	66	60	114	227	167	137	121	66	44

End of Period

1985	1986	1987	1988	1989	1990	1991	1992	1993	1994	1995	1996	1997	1998	1999		
347,939	363,839	455,963	494,399	545,184	611,341	646,247	673,547	750,468	811,506	931,996	1,085,793	1,193,623	1,161,780	1,256,869	All Countries	010
189,236	212,080	287,383	315,933	344,997	376,501	360,429	356,767	373,683	393,918	441,053	501,666	520,851	475,831	490,445	Industrial Countries	110
11,704	14,166	9,226	12,903	33,901	36,687	32,112	29,095	30,237	28,233	33,028	26,631	22,834	25,568	23,448	United States	111
1,433	1,895	4,383	10,044	10,767	11,108	9,842	6,823	7,623	7,000	8,496	12,537	11,208	14,141	17,801	Canada	156
4,780	5,464	5,714	9,652	10,007	10,969	11,112	7,662	7,623	7,334	7,628	9,713	11,932	9,493	14,213	Australia	193
20,327	30,786	53,330	67,262	59,347	48,843	43,174	45,009	64,591	78,875	116,007	144,187	154,060	144,326	202,336	Japan	158
1,447	3,074	2,297	2,099	2,263	2,862	2,008	2,130	2,326	2,439	2,856	4,013	3,167	2,731	2,933	New Zealand	196
															Euro Area	
3,744	4,524	4,774	4,987	6,041	6,153	6,750	8,368	10,095	10,966	12,020	15,203	13,789	14,856	10,212	Austria	122
3,613	3,785	5,895	6,172	7,427	7,817	7,738	9,327	7,625	8,826	9,876	10,696	10,761	11,195	6,103	Belgium	124
3,127	1,159	4,222	4,366	6,475	4,969	3,472	3,635	6,885	6,252	4,315	5,582	6,043	4,916		Finland	172
22,140	23,241	20,889	16,615	16,640	23,946	19,779	17,734	14,567	16,111	15,568	16,078	20,083	27,523	24,723	France	132
35,528	37,497	51,382	39,625	42,508	44,260	40,210	62,463	52,948	49,470	52,334	52,716	51,772	45,548	38,368	Germany	134
2,456	2,402	3,123	3,511	2,817	3,409	3,719	2,240	4,062	3,935	5,501	5,365	4,462	6,123	3,563	Ireland	178
12,845	14,824	19,609	24,151	33,693	42,298	31,805	18,157	18,303	20,623	22,161	30,643	39,601	18,073	13,571	Italy	136
			—	26	24	23	21	18	21	20	20	18	....		Luxembourg	137
8,348	7,834	9,991	10,806	11,435	11,266	11,353	14,718	21,600	22,411	20,895	16,773	16,217	12,455	4,735	Netherlands	138
1,224	1,107	2,259	3,777	7,477	10,018	14,164	13,650	11,271	10,348	10,303	10,681	11,214	10,701	5,833	Portugal	182
9,550	11,286	20,644	26,307	30,101	34,722	44,948	32,128	28,974	27,525	21,857	38,860	48,933	37,279	22,826	Spain	184
4,556	3,724	6,758	7,598	4,400	7,073	4,759	7,619	7,128	5,784	6,904	9,295	13,457	9,767	15,406	Denmark	128
715	1,171	1,820	2,618	2,363	2,323	3,552	3,369	5,558	9,810	9,829	12,057	9,221	12,207	12,915	Greece	174
183	249	214	211	253	302	310	352	300	190	197	305	274	292	330	Iceland	176
11,948	9,439	9,254	9,046	9,702	10,054	8,535	8,073	13,572	12,325	14,201	17,550	16,360	12,022	13,944	Norway	142
4,801	4,841	5,276	5,761	6,761	12,206	12,217	15,970	13,375	15,431	15,432	12,637	7,157	8,820	9,852	Sweden	144
15,898	17,441	19,146	17,868	19,199	20,540	20,275	23,593	23,042	22,985	23,333	25,574	27,348	27,234	24,900	Switzerland	146
8,867	12,171	27,178	30,554	24,341	23,145	27,074	24,791	25,210	26,392	26,357	25,816	21,403	19,434	17,516	United Kingdom	112
158,703	151,758	168,580	178,466	200,186	234,840	285,818	316,780	376,785	417,587	490,943	584,127	672,773	685,949	766,424	Developing Countries	200
7,863	6,559	6,693	7,382	9,020	11,646	13,974	12,205	13,290	15,965	16,898	21,017	30,746	27,875	31,479	Africa	605
2,288	1,073	906	667	641	508	1,037	1,059	1,069	1,816	1,348	2,942	5,963	4,861	3,211	Algeria	612
2	1	—	1	1	44	132	176	175	171	131	180	185	183	289	Benin	638
690	950	1,419	1,648	2,124	2,342	2,600	2,759	2,983	3,015	3,159	3,496	4,206	4,219	4,539	Botswana	616
114	178	214	225	189	198	229	235	266	150	221	226	247	257	207	Burkina Faso	748
18	47	34	42	67	66	89	120	112	134	135	91	78	41	29	Burundi	618
116	45	45	130	60	17	26	14	1	1	2	1	—	—	1	Cameroon	622
49	46	57	60	57	54	45	55	42	29	39	36	31	26	44	Cape Verde	624
44	53	63	71	86	80	71	73	81	144	157	161	132	103	99	Central African Rep.	626
27	11	30	41	83	89	83	58	28	52	96	114	100	85	69	Chad	628
10	14	21	17	23	21	20	19	28	30	29	35	29	27	26	Comoros	632
173	220	127	139	145	154	128	114	34	83	99	57	....	....	....	Congo, Dem. Rep. of	636
2	1	—	2	3	3	3	2	—	34	39	63	44	—	28	Congo, Rep. of	634
4	9	6	7	7	2	8	5	1	140	355	420	458	607	457	Côte d'Ivoire	662
45	42	43	46	44	64	68	58	55	50	48	53	49	47	50	Djibouti	611
—	2	—	4	4	....	1	4	....	....	....	....	4	1	2	Equatorial Guinea	642
135	205	85	48	35	14	38	162	325	366	512	502	364	356	327	Ethiopia	644
173	93	—	44	26	192	224	52	—	120	100	173	209	11	13	Gabon	646
2	10	15	13	15	38	47	66	....	65	70	69	70	74	79	Gambia, The	648
418	418	126	164	242	151	376	212	280	380	450	557	....	208	276	Ghana	652
....	....	....	....	....	....	47	55	88	56	53	60	88	....	....	Guinea	656
....	−1	7	12	16	13	10	13	10	13	14	8	25	25	26	Guinea-Bissau	654
343	316	157	183	196	129	69	26[e]	282	369	225	506	571	543	563	Kenya	664
37	47	46	40	35	49	79	111	180	251	304	316	419	404	360	Lesotho	666
1	2	—	—	6	....	1	1	2	3	19	....	....	....	....	Liberia	668
44	94	130	166	187	65	62	....	....	49	73	167	209	122	165	Madagascar	674
39	18	34	104	74	92	105	27	39	23	71	154	118	184	180	Malawi	676
10	1	2	18	79	125	214	215	233	143	208	291	299	277	246	Mali	678
50	37	38	41	63	37	47	44	32	27	57	97	149	144	163	Mauritania	682
27	111	238	325	389	508	605	573	523	483	552	594	484	367	502	Mauritius	684
105	157	287	406	371	1,452	2,064	2,520	2,605	2,933	2,375	2,603	2,928	3,117	4,013	Morocco	686
42	46	83	129	155	163	168	170	136	122	131	239	383	432	476	Mozambique	688
....	....	....	....	....	....	....	36	97	139	149	135	186	185	223	Namibia	728
116	145	166	164	152	148	133	155	131	67	55	45	31	29	19	Niger	692
1,517	884	821	484	1,343	2,715	3,100	703	999	949	971	2,834	....	....	....	Nigeria	694
86	115	98	73	39	18	64	44	23	24	53	62	94	102	116	Rwanda	714
....	....	....	....	....	....	....	....	....	....	3	3	9	7	8	São Tomé & Príncipe	716
4	4	5	7	10	7	8	8	1	121	179	198	285	304	290	Senegal	722
8	6	10	6	9	12	19	22	25	20	17	14	19	15	22	Seychelles	718
10	11	4	5	3	4	7	13	18	22	12	13	20	24	14	Sierra Leone	724
2	10	5	11	12	....	....	....	....	....	....	....	....	....	....	Somalia	726
286	302	450	579	729	707	627	721	734	1,153	1,894	654	3,550	2,963	4,419	South Africa	199
11	48	8	9	12	8	5	20	27	54	110	74	60	64	138	Sudan	732
74	77	87	103	137	144	112	216	184	195	192	168	210	246	265	Swaziland	734
15	45	22	58	41	136	143	228	138	217	172	296	451	415	555	Tanzania	738
270	279	250	172	216	248	255	198	113	64	87	61	88	83	88	Togo	742
185	227	332	647	725	557	529	611	620	999	1,075	1,309	1,454	1,312	1,608	Tunisia	744
21	20	38	37	11	26	34	62	107	218	308	367	466	512	554	Uganda	746
182	57	77	100	88	136	129	....	140	184	142	153	176	49	33	Zambia	754
72	82	101	132	71	105	104	161	314	277	400	410	118	92	194	Zimbabwe	698

		1970	1971	1972	1973	1974	1975	1976	1977	1978	1979	1980	1981	1982	1983	1984
															Millions of SDRs:	
Asia	**505**	**4,778**	**4,999**	**6,584**	**7,867**	**9,627**	**9,897**	**15,471**	**20,952**	**21,922**	**25,013**	**28,097**	**34,564**	**41,072**	**52,691**	**65,133**
Afghanistan, Islamic State of	512	11	22	18	14	18	69	108	213	285	312	264	204	203	190	215
Bangladesh	513	....	....	247	117	113	111	233	188	242	284	235	119	157	465	375
Bhutan	514	....	....	....	....	....	....	....	....	....	....	....	27	32	38	45
Cambodia	522	....	....	....	....	....	....	....	....	....	....	....	....	....	....	....
China, P.R.: Mainland I	924	....	....	....	....	....	....	....	1,931	1,195	1,635	1,774	4,109	10,094	13,827	I 17,042
China, P.R.: Hong Kong	532	....	....	....	....	....	....	....	....	....	....	....	....	....	....	....
Fiji	819	27	34	60	58	88	122	96	117	99	97	123	106	106	103	106
India	534	698	644	521	382	600	718	2,214	3,862	4,638	5,110	4,738	3,234	3,208	4,124	5,136
Indonesia	536	156	I 171	491	624	1,132	493	1,284	1,976	1,889	2,881	3,929	3,884	2,350	3,475	4,796
Korea	542	584	369	443	687	225	664	1,689	2,433	2,100	2,209	2,283	2,250	2,487	2,130	2,778
Lao People's Democratic Rep.	544	....	....	....	....	....	....	....	....	....	....	....	....	....	....	....
Malaysia	548	542	613	733	950	1,152	1,128	1,950	2,213	2,397	2,817	3,226	3,278	3,181	3,352	3,540
Maldives	556	....	....	....	....	....	....	—	—	—	—	—	1	7	4	5
Micronesia, Fed. States of	868	....	....	....	....	....	....	....	....	....	....	....	....	....	....	....
Mongolia	948	....	....	....	....	....	....	....	....	....	....	....	....	....	....	....
Myanmar	518	I 31	45	31	66	139	105	94	78	71	150	199	185	80	78	56
Nepal	558	86	85	85	92	94	76	I 108	113	108	117	138	168	174	121	78
Pakistan	564	126	106	184	315	301	266	369	341	282	128	366	571	773	1,795	930
Papua New Guinea	853	....	....	....	26	27	153	220	351	310	379	328	307	379	398	434
Philippines	566	195	285	420	799	1,164	1,099	1,361	1,199	1,340	1,682	2,231	1,773	802	713	586
Samoa	862	5	6	4	4	4	5	5	7	4	4	2	3	3	6	11
Singapore	576	1,005	1,328	1,601	1,885	2,287	2,559	2,886	3,166	4,057	4,383	5,089	6,395	7,570	8,721	10,499
Solomon Islands	813	....	....	....	....	....	....	....	2	22	28	22	17	32	43	44ᵉ
Sri Lanka	524	43	46	42	58	49	38	67	221	279	370	192	261	306	266	515
Thailand	578	790	678	825	938	1,373	1,371	1,485	1,428	1,515	1,362	1,217	1,436	1,372	1,491	1,928
Tonga	866	....	....	....	....	....	....	....	7	8	10	11	12	14	20	27
Vanuatu	846	....	....	....	....	....	....	....	....	....	....	....	7	4	5	7
Vietnam	582	....	....	....	....	....	....	....	....	....	....	....	....	....	....	....
Europe	**170**	**708**	**1,116**	**2,206**	**3,242**	**2,741**	**2,456**	**3,742**	**3,229**	**3,608**	**3,238**	**4,746**	**4,751**	**4,774**	**6,662**	**8,365**
Albania	914	....	....	....	....	....	....	....	....	....	....	....	....	....	....	....
Armenia	911	....	....	....	....	....	....	....	....	....	....	....	....	....	....	....
Azerbaijan	912	....	....	....	....	....	....	....	....	....	....	....	....	....	....	....
Belarus	913	....	....	....	....	....	....	....	....	....	....	....	....	....	....	....
Bulgaria	918	....	....	....	....	....	....	....	....	....	....	....	....	....	....	....
Croatia	960	....	....	....	....	....	....	....	....	....	....	....	....	....	....	....
Cyprus	423	184	233	262	222	194	159	228	253	257	252	282	363	474	491	547
Czech Republic	935	....	....	....	....	....	....	....	....	....	....	....	....	....	....	....
Czechoslovakia I	934	....	....	....	....	....	....	....	....	....	....	1,442	821	703	767	986
Estonia	939	....	....	....	....	....	....	....	....	....	....	....	....	....	....	....
Hungary	944	....	....	....	....	....	....	....	....	....	....	....	....	....	1,093	1,591
Kazakhstan	916	....	....	....	....	....	....	....	....	....	....	....	....	....	....	....
Kyrgyz Republic	917	....	....	....	....	....	....	....	....	....	....	....	....	....	....	....
Latvia	941	....	....	....	....	....	....	....	....	....	....	....	....	....	....	....
Lithuania	946	....	....	....	....	....	....	....	....	....	....	....	....	....	....	....
Macedonia, FYR	962	....	....	....	....	....	....	....	....	....	....	....	....	....	....	....
Malta	181	143	163	232	248	307	402	504	575	691	746	749	884	935	1,003	944
Moldova	921	....	....	....	....	....	....	....	....	....	....	....	....	....	....	....
Poland	964	....	....	....	....	....	....	....	....	....	429	100	239	586	731	1,128
Romania	968	....	....	....	172	191	453	471	204	289	398	253	346	396	501	723
Russia	922	....	....	....	....	....	....	....	....	....	....	....	....	....	....	....
Slovak Republic	936	....	....	....	....	....	....	....	....	....	....	....	....	....	....	....
Slovenia	961	....	....	....	....	....	....	....	....	....	....	....	....	....	....	....
Turkey	186	304	577	1,096	1,580	1,203	779	834	525	615	499	844	797	979	1,197	1,264
Ukraine	926	....	....	....	....	....	....	....	....	....	....	....	....	....	....	....
Yugoslavia, SFR	188	78	143	615	1,019	846	664	1,704	1,672	1,756	913	1,075	1,300	699	880	1,181
Middle East	**405**	**3,487**	**5,828**	**8,124**	**9,804**	**26,808**	**33,901**	**40,411**	**48,611**	**38,093**	**44,233**	**51,660**	**53,124**	**55,753**	**49,524**	**45,564**
Bahrain	419	63	79	74	51	102	238	371	410	373	458	737	1,313	1,365	1,329	1,293
Egypt	469	74	45	42	184	175	151	186	331	369	402	820	591	633	706	751
Iran, I.R. of	429	76	440	700	809	6,250	6,454	6,410	8,911	8,372	11,053	7,540	947	4,793	....	....
Iraq	433	319	398	536	1,097	2,480	2,136	3,761	5,553	....	....	....	....	....	....	....
Israel	436	405	622	1,057	1,405	940	969	1,135	1,230	1,994	2,289	2,593	3,004	3,480	3,451	3,122
Jordan	439	219	194	209	211	242	379	393	516	667	864	868	902	768	763	510
Kuwait	443	96	158	227	296	764	700	722	1,651	1,331	1,789	2,670	3,049	4,837	4,227	3,890
Lebanon	446	96	179	297	389	1,042	1,024	1,119	1,289	1,406	1,159	1,239	1,295	2,356	1,798	665
Libya	672	1,499	2,364	2,603	1,672	2,862	1,784	2,668	3,934	3,145	4,743	10,069	7,441	6,081	4,638	3,331
Oman	449	10	21	31	37	60	113	163	218	180	300	436	618	762	687	876
Qatar	453	30	35	44	51	47	70	95	119	147	201	248	288	317	321	333
Saudi Arabia	456	520	1,189	2,162	3,073	10,964	18,242	20,947	22,402	I 12,842	13,192	16,267	24,054	21,587	16,674	14,474
Syrian Arab Rep.	463	27	53	93	306	372	585	233	392	287	429	247	229	168	41	268
United Arab Emirates	466	....	....	....	72	300	729	1,527	562	551	1,010	1,479	2,574	1,757	1,703	2,045
Yemen Arab Rep.	473	....	....	....	101	158	284	615	1,013	1,111	1,069	985	813	488	335	310
Yemen, P.D. Rep.	459	53	50	50	51	51	43	67	78	141	156	174	213	246	248	234
Yemen, Republic of	474	....	....	....	....	....	....	....	....	....	....	....	....	....	....	....

I See country notes in the
monthly *IFS*

Foreign Exchange

End of Period

1985	1986	1987	1988	1989	1990	1991	1992	1993	1994	1995	1996	1997	1998	1999		
63,971	77,540	96,038	108,327	117,757	142,447	173,987	185,965	217,782	259,021	285,865	338,221	377,715	406,709	474,784	**Asia**	505
252	195	182	180	172	176	155	....	....	....	....	....	....	....	....	Afghanistan, Islamic State of	512
272	304	534	715	357	424	844	1,297	1,738	2,125	1,467	1,200	1,150	1,344	1,168	Bangladesh	513
45	49	52	69	74	60	68	56	....	78	83	127	133	176	199	Bhutan	514
....	....	....	....	....	....	....	....	6	70	119	175	212	223	283	Cambodia	522
10,846	8,596	10,740	13,040	12,953	20,099	29,826	ɪ14,140	15,434	35,360	49,498	73,040	103,680	102,952	112,695	China, P.R.: Mainland ɪ	924
....	....	....	....	....	17,269	20,139	25,581	31,295	33,737	37,268	44,374	68,782	63,636	70,117	China, P.R.: Hong Kong	532
106	126	75	150	137	160	174	214	180	170	217	279	249	255	293	Fiji	819
5,052	4,451	3,950	3,082	2,363	847	2,503	3,972	7,140	13,279	11,750	13,729	18,028	19,146	23,309	India	534
4,405	3,204	3,865	3,677	4,077	5,168	6,397	7,405	8,000	8,097	8,951	12,393	11,923	15,910	19,122	Indonesia	536
2,575	2,699	2,514	9,170	11,397	10,163	9,302	12,102	14,345	17,147	21,479	23,114	14,608	36,905	53,697	Korea	542
....	....	....	....	1	1	20ᵉ	29ᵉ	44ᵉ	34ᵉ	52	108	74	74	74	Lao People's Democratic Rep.	544
4,207	4,657	4,973	4,558	5,626	6,556	7,285	12,207	19,522	17,048	15,436	18,190	14,833	17,562	21,617	Malaysia	548
4	6	6	16	19	17	16	20	18	20	31	52	72	83	91	Maldives	556
....	....	....	....	....	....	....	....	....	....	46	61	70	....	66	Micronesia, Fed. States of	868
....	....	....	....	....	....	....	12	43	54	77	74	130	66	99	Mongolia	948
31	27	19	57	200	219	181	204	220	289	377	159	185	223	193	Myanmar	518
45	65	120	158	155	202	272	334	460	469	389	392	458	531	608	Nepal	558
711	569	343	288	395	207	363	618	871	2,006	1,156	372	878	729	1,101	Pakistan	564
392	340	298	282	283	283	226	173	103	66	175	406	269	137	149	Papua New Guinea	853
501	1,369	644	707	1,039	610	2,227	3,115	3,310	4,018	4,194	6,886	5,297	6,464	9,547	Philippines	566
13	19	25	34	41	46	45	42	34	32	34	40	45	41	47	Samoa	862
11,549ᵉ	10,424	10,573	12,530	15,322	19,354	23,721	28,845	34,994	39,654	45,980	53,194	52,535	52,852	55,595	Singapore	576
31ᵉ	22	25	29	19	12	5	17	14	11	10	22	26	34	37	Solomon Islands	813
405	288	197	165	176	297	479	654	1,166	1,381	1,384	1,343	1,480	1,385	1,143	Sri Lanka	524
1,964	2,237	2,753	4,456	7,199	9,311	12,085	14,554	17,530	19,786	23,857	25,864	19,045	20,194	24,630	Thailand	578
24	18	20	22	18	21	21	22	25	23	18	20	19	19	17	Tonga	866
8	16	26	28	25	24	26	29	31	27	30	28	25	29	27	Vanuatu	846
....	....	....	....	....	....	....	312	259	560	888	1,206	1,462	1,420	....	Vietnam	582
7,003	7,626	7,409	9,405	14,232	15,080	15,391	15,224	24,801	29,893	56,621	60,761	70,691	70,624	76,792	**Europe**	170
....	....	....	....	....	....	....	....	107	140	162	195	228	204	209	Albania	914
....	....	....	....	....	....	....	1	10	22	37	79	142	204	202	Armenia	911
....	....	....	....	....	....	....	....	—	1	80	132	341	318	485	Azerbaijan	912
....	....	....	....	....	....	....	....	....	69	251	326	292	240	218	Belarus	913
....	....	....	....	....	....	211	617	444	643	779	295	1,625	1,956	2,154	Bulgaria	918
....	....	....	....	....	....	....	121	448	959	1,181	1,522	1,773	1,835	2,066	Croatia	960
537	611	611	678	837	1,044	954	722	773	978	726	1,047	1,006	954	1,300	Cyprus	423
....	....	....	....	....	....	....	....	2,753	4,209	9,312	8,590	7,214	8,908	9,330	Czech Republic	935
778	912	974	1,176	1,641	775	2,132	ɪ784	....	....	....	....	....	....	....	Czechoslovakia ɪ	934
....	....	....	....	....	....	....	116	240	303	390	443	562	576	621	Estonia	939
1,960	1,882	1,152	1,090	948	751	2,750	3,160	4,820	4,557	7,999	6,703	6,175	6,562	7,801	Hungary	944
....	....	....	....	....	....	....	....	318	504	609	660	931	763	914	Kazakhstan	916
....	....	....	....	....	....	....	....	26	17	45	61	125	116	164	Kyrgyz Republic	917
....	....	....	....	....	....	....	....	243	373	339	453	520	517	610	Latvia	941
....	....	....	....	....	....	....	32	200	350	497	530	741	989	867	Lithuania	946
....	....	....	....	....	....	....	....	76	102	173	167	190	217	312	Macedonia, FYR	962
829	861	919	937	954	928	847	864	931	1,206	1,014	1,056	....	1,105	1,307	Malta	181
....	....	....	....	....	....	—	2	31	109	164	211	270	101	135	Moldova	921
792	570	1,054	1,527	1,761	3,157	2,534	2,903	2,901	3,923	9,860	12,329	15,044	18,690	17,695	Poland	964
181	476	988	580	1,338	368	445	593	723	1,391	1,024	1,459	2,742	2,036	1,950	Romania	968
....	....	....	....	....	....	....	....	4,243	2,724	9,596	7,838	9,465	5,540	6,161	Russia	922
....	....	....	....	....	....	....	....	302	1,100	2,224	2,366	2,375	2,036	2,455	Slovak Republic	936
....	....	....	....	....	....	78	520	561	1,014	1,212	1,585	2,444	2,537	2,229	Slovenia	961
929	1,122	1,219	1,710	3,605	4,220	3,564	4,447	4,533	4,878	8,336	11,397	13,796	13,808	16,892	Turkey	186
....	....	....	....	....	....	....	341	118	322	610	1,316	1,682	411	715	Ukraine	926
996	1,193	492	1,708	3,147	3,838	1,875	....	....	....	....	....	....	....	....	Yugoslavia, SFR	188
45,052	35,490	34,389	32,005	35,368	33,082	37,774	40,504	43,388	42,642	46,994	57,358	69,869	68,643	73,629	**Middle East**	405
1,473	1,177	768	887	754	823	1,011	967	896	748	806	860	898	706	935	Bahrain	419
721	678	971	939	1,157	1,886	3,722	7,765	9,290	9,121	10,762	11,960	13,696	12,704	10,403	Egypt	469
....	....	....	....	....	....	....	....	....	....	....	....	....	....	....	Iran, I.R. of	429
....	....	....	....	....	....	....	....	....	....	....	....	....	....	....	Iraq	433
3,350	3,809	4,142	2,984	4,015	4,411	4,389	3,729	4,646	4,653	5,462	7,937	15,069	16,103	16,404	Israel	436
363	338	291	81	350	596	577	546	1,188	1,159	1,326	1,223	1,631	1,243	1,915	Jordan	439
4,237	3,853	2,393	1,015	2,104	1,134	2,144	3,516	2,851	2,200	2,195	2,240	2,317	2,476	3,092	Kuwait	443
957	378	237	704	690	438	865	1,060	1,616	2,630	3,019	4,093	4,396	4,622	5,630	Lebanon	446
4,975	4,446	3,674	2,749	2,804	3,574	3,415	3,899	....	....	....	....	....	4,418	4,328	Libya	672
950	748	949	746	992	1,137	1,125	1,400	618	629	724	923	1,107	713	1,110	Oman	449
352	416	383	305	358	395	414	443	453	400	....	....	....	....	....	Qatar	453
12,528	5,806	7,603	8,337	8,589	6,032	6,807	3,317	4,137	4,033	4,777	ɪ8,917	9,981	9,030	11,286	Saudi Arabia	456
73	118	157	143	....	....	....	....	....	....	....	....	....	....	....	Syrian Arab Rep.	463
2,647	2,497	3,092	3,077	3,167	3,005	3,529	3,943	4,227	4,357	4,784	5,340	5,949	6,154	7,561	United Arab Emirates	466
247	330	361	188	197	....	....	....	....	....	....	....	....	....	....	Yemen Arab Rep.	473
168	109	66	45	57	....	....	....	....	....	....	....	....	....	....	Yemen, P.D. Rep.	459
....	....	....	....	....	287	463	230	105	141	379	674	768	575	....	Yemen, Republic of	474

ɪ See country notes in the monthly *IFS*

Foreign Exchange

		1970	1971	1972	1973	1974	1975	1976	1977	1978	1979	1980	1981	1982	1983	1984
																Millions of SDRs:
Western Hemisphere	205	3,559	4,000	7,095	9,843	12,619	13,354	17,792	20,682	24,421	29,056	27,847	29,674	22,312	24,727	38,531
Antigua and Barbuda	311	....	....	....	....	....	6	8	4	5	9	6	6	8	9	16
Argentina	213	343	64	271	885	840	211	1,165	2,522	3,520	6,724	4,749	2,222	2,181	1,119	1,267
Aruba	314															
Bahamas, The	313	22	27	34	36	36	41	36	150	40	51	61	73	90	104	153
Barbados	316	15	14	21	22	27	28	18	24	40	43	55	80	109	115	133
Belize	339						....	5	7	11	8	10	9	8	7	4
Bolivia	218	30	34	38	43	141	112	117	161	107	135	83	86	141	153	257
Brazil	223	962	1,336	3,533	4,999	3,981	3,120	5,251	5,587	8,755	6,333	3,953	5,059	3,301	4,160	11,739
Chile	228	320	118	87	100	20	27	300	296	778	1,412	2,382	2,680	1,557	1,940	2,338
Colombia	233	189	165	267	366	288	346	878	1,336	1,709	2,772	3,588	3,802	3,163	1,365	1,392
Costa Rica	238	8	25	33	36	32	38	81	151	138	78	114	113	205	294	413
Dominica	321	....	....	....	....	....	—	1	2	1	7	4	2	4	1	5
Dominican Republic	243	29	49	44	52	64	90	100	143	114	174	158	192	116	156	258
Ecuador	248	55	31	105	163	245	197	405	505	469	520	753	490	276	604	623
El Salvador	253	45	40	55	30	60	87	156	161	189	87	61	62	97	153	169
Grenada	328	5	5	5	4	4	14	7	6	7	9	10	14	8	13	15
Guatemala	258	59	58	90	138	128	222	399	527	545	496	309	118	102	192	278
Guyana	336	19	22	29	8	45	77	20	16	42	10	10	5	7	6	6
Haiti	263	4	6	11	12	14	9	23	26	23	32	13	21	3	8	13
Honduras	268	20	17	27	23	31	79	110	144	132	145	117	85	100	102	131
Jamaica	343	123	139	140	99	150	103	27	25	41	48	82	70	95	60	99
Mexico	273	385	507	673	736	784	998	1,022	1,311	1,371	1,420	2,108	3,187	751	3,625	7,416
Netherlands Antilles	353	25	34	46	41	50	61	80	83	51	55	74	116	170	157	120
Nicaragua	278	48	50	68	91	80	99	122	118	35	111	51	96	154	167	....
Panama	283	12	12	29	24	30	23	63	54	108	84	83	100	88	188	220
Paraguay	288	10	10	18	36	60	87	123	207	331	445	571	652	619	587	612
Peru	293	282	322	367	368	688	296	246	291	294	1,073	1,543	1,021	1,194	1,304	1,641
St. Kitts and Nevis	361	....	....	....	....	....	....						3	3	3	6
St. Lucia	362	....	....	....	....	....	3	4	5	5	6	6	6	7	8	13
St. Vincent & Grenadines	364	....	....	....				4	4	4	7	6	8	4	5	13
Suriname	366	28	30	35	47	55	78	95	77	97	121	138	165	143	52	24
Trinidad and Tobago	369	36	50	40	32	306	615	837	1,180	1,339	1,556	2,082	2,746	2,622	1,797	1,154
Uruguay	298	14	19	56	73	54	48	148	257	242	203	248	304	104	185	132
Venezuela, Rep. Bol.	299	472	816	974	1,379	4,407	6,249	5,941	5,399	3,877	4,881	4,418	6,084	4,883	6,086	7,872

Memorandum Items

		1970	1971	1972	1973	1974	1975	1976	1977	1978	1979	1980	1981	1982	1983	1984
Oil Exporting Countries	999	3,453	6,139	8,225	10,175	34,874	42,360	49,023	55,110	39,969	50,889	62,647	60,334	56,833	52,856	53,776
Non-Oil Developing Countries	201	11,276	11,790	18,199	23,757	24,843	25,149	36,716	46,021	53,777	59,927	63,633	70,700	73,588	86,942	110,022

1985	1986	1987	1988	1989	1990	1991	1992	1993	1994	1995	1996	1997	1998	1999		
End of Period																
34,813	24,542	24,051	21,346	23,810	32,586	44,692	62,883	77,524	70,066	84,565	106,770	123,752	112,099	109,740	Western Hemisphere	205
15	23	18	21	21	19	23	37	28	31	40	33	38	42	51	Antigua and Barbuda	311
I 2,980	2,222	1,140	2,499	1,113	3,019	4,063	6,992	9,711	9,428	9,249	12,313	16,419	17,392	19,027	Argentina............................	213
....	60	55	68	66	69	84	103	132	122	146	130	128	158	160	Aruba	314
155	178	109	118	103	103	119	106	119	115	114	113	162	240	293	Bahamas, The......................	313
125	122	100	98	81	80	60	102	109	134	147	201	196	180	....	Barbados...........................	316
12	20	24	36	44	47	35	35	25	20	22	37	40	28	47	Belize	339
182	132	69	79	156	117	74	123	144	283	408	628	770	593	632	Bolivia..............................	218
9,654	I 4,744	4,440	5,181	5,734	5,222	5,607	16,378	22,279	25,392	33,439	40,559	37,670	30,239	25,345	Brazil...............................	223
2,230	1,922	1,736	2,316	2,743	4,265	4,922	6,667	7,018	8,965	9,510	10,279	12,593	10,688	10,184	Chile	228
1,452	2,090	2,061	2,299	2,637	3,138	4,453	5,522	5,579	5,347	5,432	6,623	6,951	5,670	5,523	Colombia............................	233
461	428	345	496	565	365	643	732	737	603	695	687	926	746	1,043	Costa Rica	238
3	7	12	10	9	10	12	15	14	11	15	16	18	20	23	Dominica............................	321
281	308	128	189	125	43	309	363	464	170	246	243	290	356	502	Dominican Republic	243
628	481	346	294	411	579	617	614	984	1,243	1,076	1,273	1,534	1,133	1,178	Ecuador	248
164	139	131	120	202	292	201	307	390	445	485	627	944	1,121	1,435	El Salvador	253
19	17	16	13	12	12	12	19	20	21	25	25	32	33	37	Grenada	328
274	296	202	149	232	198	564	545	620	580	462	595	814	940	858	Guatemala	258
6	7	6	3	10	19	86	137	180	169	181	229	234	196	195	Guyana	336
6	8	12	10	9	2	12	....	....	21	71	75	57	....	....	Haiti	263
96	91	75	37	16	28	73	143	71	117	176	173	430	581	907	Honduras	268
147	80	122	109	82	118ᵉ	74	227	295	504	458	612	505	503	403	Jamaica.............................	343
4,466	4,628	8,288	3,630	4,525	6,640	11,982	13,377	18,118	4,179	10,259	13,335	20,853	22,344	22,581	Mexico	273
160	195	153	195	158	151	124	160	170	123	137	131	159	176	193	Netherlands Antilles	353
....	....	12	28	88	75	94	95	40	97	92	137	280	249	371	Nicaragua	278
77	138	55	54	91	222	341	352	423	471	513	591	838	666	587	Panama	283
415	298	286	178	266	399	603	329	378	624	650	642	529	520	623	Paraguay............................	288
1,677	1,150	455	380	615	731	1,708	2,072	2,480	4,790	5,530	7,356	8,139	6,792	6,361	Peru	293
7	8	7	8	12	11	12	19	21	22	23	23	27	33	36	St. Kitts and Nevis..................	361
12	21	22	24	29	30	33	39	42	38	41	38	44	49	53	St. Lucia	362
13	21	14	16	17	19	16	24	22	21	19	20	23	27	30	St. Vincent & Grenadines	364
21	17	11	9	7	15	1	13	13	27	82	59	73	67	....	Suriname............................	366
795	198	79	94	181	345	235	125	150	241	241	378	523	556	689	Trinidad and Tobago	369
145	384	326	373	364	360	231	355	536	648	756	852	1,138	1,457	1,479	Uruguay.............................	298
8,136	4,109	3,197	2,211	3,086	5,842	7,268	6,755	6,211	5,064	3,826	7,736	10,376	8,247	8,530	Venezuela, Rep. Bol.................	299
															Memorandum Items	
54,046	37,823	36,184	33,073	37,201	38,785	44,462	42,037	41,831	40,029	40,251	56,427	67,198	66,223	74,648	Oil Exporting Countries	999
104,656	113,936	132,396	145,393	162,986	196,055	241,356	274,743	334,954	377,558	450,691	527,700	605,574	619,727	691,776	Non-Oil Developing Countries	201

Gold (Million Ounces)

		1970	1971	1972	1973	1974	1975	1976	1977	1978	1979	1980	1981	1982	1983	1984
															Millions of Ounces:	
All Countries	010	1,059.74	1,030.28	1,021.52	1,024.09	1,022.08	1,019.87	1,015.38	1,030.35	1,037.98	946.89	955.56	955.19	951.28	950.15	949.02
Industrial Countries	110	941.41	919.66	904.66	904.62	905.11	903.74	903.51	908.40	910.07	815.00	813.88	813.62	813.29	810.92	810.40
United States	111	316.34	291.60	275.97	275.97	275.97	274.71	274.68	277.55	276.41	264.60	264.32	264.11	264.03	263.39	262.79
Canada	156	22.59	22.69	21.95	21.95	21.95	21.95	21.62	22.01	22.13	22.18	20.98	20.46	20.26	20.17	20.14
Australia	193	6.83	7.43	7.40	7.37	7.38	7.38	7.36	7.65	7.79	7.93	7.93	7.93	7.93	7.93	7.93
Japan	158	15.22	19.42	21.10	21.11	21.11	21.11	21.11	21.62	23.97	24.23	24.23	24.23	24.23	24.23	24.23
New Zealand	196	.02	.02	.02	.02	.02	.02	.02	.04	.07	.05	.02	.02	.02	.02	.02
Euro Area																
Austria	122	20.39	20.82	20.85	20.88	20.88	20.88	20.88	21.00	21.05	21.11	21.11	21.11	21.12	21.13	21.13
Belgium	124	42.01	44.12	43.08	42.17	42.17	42.17	42.17	42.45	42.59	34.21	34.18	34.18	34.18	34.18	34.18
Finland	172	.82	1.40	1.40	.82	.82	.82	.82	.90	.95	.99	.99	1.27	1.27	1.27	1.27
France	132	100.91	100.66	100.69	100.91	100.93	100.93	101.02	101.67	101.99	81.92	81.85	81.85	81.85	81.85	81.85
Germany	134	113.70	116.47	117.36	117.61	117.61	117.61	117.61	118.30	118.64	95.25	95.18	95.18	95.18	95.18	95.18
Ireland	178	.46	.46	.46	.44	.43	.45	.45	.47	.45	.38	.36	.36	.36	.36	.36
Italy	136	82.48	82.40	82.37	82.48	82.48	82.48	82.48	82.91	83.12	66.71	66.67	66.67	66.67	66.67	66.67
Luxembourg	137	.44	.44	.44	.44	.44	.44	.44	.45	.46	.46	.46	.46	.46	.46	.43
Netherlands	138	51.06	54.53	54.17	54.33	54.33	54.33	54.33	54.63	54.78	43.97	43.94	43.94	43.94	43.94	43.94
Portugal	182	25.77	26.31	26.88	27.54	27.84	27.72	27.67	24.11	22.13	22.13	22.17	22.14	22.09	20.43	20.30
Spain	184	14.23	14.23	14.23	14.27	14.27	14.27	14.27	14.44	14.52	14.61	14.61	14.61	14.61	14.61	14.63
Denmark	128	1.84	1.81	1.81	1.81	1.81	1.81	1.81	1.93	1.98	1.64	1.63	1.63	1.63	1.63	1.63
Greece	174	3.33	2.81	3.50	3.50	3.61	3.63	3.65	3.73	3.77	3.81	3.84	3.85	3.87	3.88	4.11
Iceland	176	.03	.03	.03	.03	.03	.03	.03	.04	.04	.05	.05	.05	.05	.05	.05
Norway	142	.67	.94	.98	.98	.98	.98	.98	1.08	1.13	1.18	1.18	1.18	1.18	1.18	1.18
Sweden	144	5.72	5.78	5.78	5.79	5.79	5.79	5.79	5.93	6.00	6.07	6.07	6.07	6.07	6.07	6.07
Switzerland	146	78.03	83.11	83.11	83.20	83.20	83.20	83.28	83.28	83.28	83.28	83.28	83.28	83.28	83.28	83.28
United Kingdom	112	38.52	22.18	21.08	21.01	21.03	21.03	21.03	22.23	22.83	18.25	18.84	19.03	19.01	19.01	19.03
Developing Countries	200	118.33	110.62	116.86	119.47	116.97	116.12	111.87	121.94	127.91	131.89	141.68	141.58	137.98	139.22	138.62
Africa	605	28.84	21.32	27.29	28.60	26.64	25.75	20.58	17.87	18.27	18.79	21.13	18.45	16.74	17.18	16.73
Algeria	612	5.47	5.47	5.47	5.47	5.47	5.47	5.47	5.50	5.53	5.58	5.58	5.58	5.58	5.58	5.58
Benin	638	....	....	....	....	....	....	—	.01	.01	.01	.01	.01	.01	.01	.01
Botswana	616	....	....	....	....	....	....									
Burkina Faso	748	....	....	....	....	....	....	—	.01	.01	.01	.01	.01	.01	.01	.01
Burundi	618	—	....	....	....	....	....	—	.01	.01	.01	.02	.02	.02	.02	.02
Cameroon	622	....	....	....	....	....	....		.02	.02	.03	.03	.03	.03	.03	.03
Cape Verde	624	....	....	....	....	....	....						—	—	—	—
Central African Rep.	626	....	....	....	....	....	....	—	.01	.01	.01	.01	.01	.01	.01	.01
Chad	628	....	....	....	....	....	....	—	.01	.01	.01	.01	.01	.01	.01	.01
Comoros	632	....	....	....	....	....	....								—	—
Congo, Dem. Rep. of	636	1.43	1.44	1.45	1.46	.50	.26	.26	.26	.31	.25	.30	.36	.41	.44	.47
Congo, Rep. of	634	....	....	....	....	....	....		.01	.01	.01	.01	.01	.01	.01	.01
Côte d'Ivoire	662	....	....	....	....	....	....	—	.02	.03	.04	.04	.04	.04	.04	.04
Djibouti	611	....	....	....	....	....	....									
Equatorial Guinea	642	....	....	....	....	....	....									
Ethiopia	644	.23	.24	.25	.26	.28	.28	.28	.29	.29	.29	.31	.26	.21	.21	.21
Gabon	646	....	....	....	....	....	....	—	.01	.01	.01	.01	.01	.01	.01	.01
Gambia, The	648	....	....	....	....	....	....									
Ghana	652	.16	.16	.16	.16	.16	.16	.16	.20	.22	.22	.25	.31	.38	.38	.44
Guinea	656	....	....	....	....	....	....									
Guinea-Bissau	654	....	....	....	....	....	....									
Kenya	664	....	....	....	—	—	—		.02	.07	.08	.08	.08	.08	.08	.08
Lesotho	666	....	....	....	....	....	....									
Liberia	668	....	....	....	....	....	....									
Madagascar	674	....	....	....	....	....	....									
Malawi	676	....	....	....	....	....	....		.01	.01	.01	.01	.01	.01	.01	.01
Mali	678	....	....	....	....	....	....		.01	.01	.02	.02	.02	.02	.02	.02
Mauritania	682	....	....	....	....	....	....		.01	.01	.01	.01	.01	.01	.01	.01
Mauritius	684	....	....	....	....	....	....		.01	.03	.04	.04	.04	.04	.04	.04
Morocco	686	.60	.60	.60	.60	.61	.61	.61	.63	.68	.70	.70	.70	.70	.70	.70
Mozambique	688	....	....	....	....	....	....									
Namibia	728	....	....	....	....	....	....									
Niger	692	....	....	....	....	....	....	—	.01	.01	.01	.01	.01	.01	.01	.01
Nigeria	694	.57	.54	.54	.57	.57	.57	.57	.63	.63	.69	.69	.69	.69	.69	.69
Rwanda	714	....	....	....	....	....	....	—	—	—	—	—	—	—	—	—
São Tomé & Príncipe	716	....	....	....	....	....	....									
Senegal	722	....	....	....	....	....	....	—	.01	.02	.03	.03	.03	.03	.03	.03
Seychelles	718	....	....	....	....	....	....									
Sierra Leone	724	....	....	....	....	....	....									
Somalia	726	—	—	—	—	—	—		.01	.01	.01	.02	.02	.02	.02	.02
South Africa	199	19.03	11.72	17.93	18.99	18.25	17.75	12.67	9.72	9.79	10.03	12.15	9.29	7.57	7.79	7.36
Sudan	732	....	....	....	....	....	....									
Swaziland	734	....	....	....	....	....	....									
Tanzania	738	....	....	....	....	....	....									
Togo	742	....	....	....	....	....	....	—	.01	.01	.01	.01	.01	.01	.01	.01
Tunisia	744	.13	.13	.13	.13	.13	.13	.13	.15	.16	.17	.19	.19	.19	.19	.19
Uganda	746	....	....	....	....	....	....									
Zambia	754	.18	.20	.20	.20	.17	.17	.17	.17	.20	.22	.22	.22	.22	.22	—
Zimbabwe	698	1.05	.82	.55	.75	.50	.35	.27	.15	.16	.26	.35	.47	.39	.59	.70

Gold (Million Ounces)

End of Period

1985	1986	1987	1988	1989	1990	1991	1992	1993	1994	1995	1996	1997	1998	1999		
951.50	951.47	945.97	946.68	941.04	939.24	939.26	928.81	919.50	915.42	906.14	903.95	886.69	966.15	940.51	**All Countries**	010
810.84	809.12	804.79	801.12	797.80	795.81	793.68	785.24	770.83	768.05	754.97	748.16	732.47	808.67	786.40	**Industrial Countries**	110
262.65	262.04	262.38	261.87	261.93	261.91	261.91	261.84	261.79	261.73	261.70	261.66	261.64	261.61	261.67	United States	111
20.11	19.72	18.52	17.14	16.10	14.76	12.96	9.94	6.05	3.89	3.41	3.09	3.09	2.49	1.81	Canada	156
7.93	7.93	7.93	7.93	7.93	7.93	7.93	7.93	7.90	7.90	7.90	7.90	2.56	2.56	2.56	Australia	193
24.23	24.23	24.23	24.23	24.23	24.23	24.23	24.23	24.23	24.23	24.23	24.23	24.23	24.23	24.23	Japan	158
.02	.02	.02	.02	—	—	—	—	—	—	—	—	—	—	—	New Zealand	196
															Euro Area	
21.14	21.14	21.15	21.15	20.66	20.39	20.03	19.93	18.60	18.34	11.99	10.75	7.87	9.64	13.10	Austria	122
34.18	34.18	33.63	33.67	30.23	30.23	30.23	25.04	25.04	25.04	20.54	15.32	15.32	9.52	8.30	Belgium	124
1.91	1.91	1.96	1.96	2.00	2.00	2.00	2.00	2.00	2.00	1.60	1.60	1.60	2.00	1.58	Finland	172
81.85	81.85	81.85	81.85	81.85	81.85	81.85	81.85	81.85	81.85	81.85	81.85	81.89	102.37	97.24	France	132
95.18	95.18	95.18	95.18	95.18	95.18	95.18	95.18	95.18	95.18	95.18	95.18	95.18	118.98	111.52	Germany	134
.36	.36	.36	.36	.36	.36	.36	.36	.36	.36	.36	.36	.36	.45	.18	Ireland	178
66.67	66.67	66.67	66.67	66.67	66.67	66.67	66.67	66.67	66.67	66.67	66.67	66.67	83.36	78.83	Italy	136
.43	.43	.43	.43	.34	.34	.34	.34	.31	.31	.31	.31	.31		.08	Luxembourg	137
43.94	43.94	43.94	43.94	43.94	43.94	43.94	43.94	35.05	34.77	34.77	34.77	34.77	27.07	31.57	Netherlands	138
20.23	20.16	20.06	16.07	16.05	15.83	15.87	16.06	16.06	16.07	16.07	16.07	16.07	20.09	19.51	Portugal	182
14.65	14.82	11.92	14.04	15.72	15.61	15.62	15.62	15.62	15.62	15.63	15.63	15.63	19.54	16.83	Spain	184
1.63	1.63	1.63	1.63	1.64	1.65	1.66	1.66	1.64	1.63	1.65	1.66	1.69	2.14	2.14	Denmark	128
4.12	3.31	3.34	3.40	3.40	3.40	3.43	3.43	3.44	3.45	3.46	3.47	3.64	3.62	4.24	Greece	174
.05	.05	.05	.05	.05	.05	.05	.05	.05	.05	.05	.05	.05	.06	.06	Iceland	176
1.18	1.18	1.18	1.18	1.18	1.18	1.18	1.18	1.18	1.18	1.18	1.18	1.18	1.18	1.18	Norway	142
6.07	6.07	6.07	6.07	6.07	6.07	6.07	6.07	6.07	6.07	4.70	4.70	4.72	4.72	5.96	Sweden	144
83.28	83.28	83.28	83.28	83.28	83.28	83.28	83.28	83.28	83.28	83.28	83.28	83.28	83.28	83.28	Switzerland	146
19.03	19.01	19.01	19.00	18.99	18.94	18.89	18.61	18.45	18.44	18.43	18.43	18.42	23.00	20.55	United Kingdom	112
140.66	142.35	141.18	145.56	143.24	143.42	145.57	143.58	148.67	147.38	151.17	155.80	154.22	157.47	154.11	**Developing Countries**	200
14.05	13.87	14.79	12.32	11.75	12.06	14.95	15.24	13.30	12.69	13.03	12.31	12.43	12.51	12.56	**Africa**	605
5.58	5.58	5.58	5.58	5.58	5.14	5.58	5.58	5.58	5.58	5.58	5.58	5.58	5.58	5.58	Algeria	612
.01	.01	.01	.01	.01	.01	.01	.01	.01	.01	.01	.01	.01	.01	.01	Benin	638
															Botswana	616
	.01	.01	.01	.01	.01	.01	.01	.01	.01	.01	.01	.01	.01	.01	Burkina Faso	748
.02	.02	.02	.02	.02	.02	.02	.02	.02	.02	.02	.02	.02	.02	.02	Burundi	618
.03	.03	.03	.03	.03	.03	.03	.03	.03	.03	.03	.03	.03			Cameroon	622
															Cape Verde	624
.01	.01	.01	.01	.01	.01	.01	.01	.01	.01	.01	.01	.01			Central African Rep.	626
.01	.01	.01	.01	.01	.01	.01	.01	.01	.01	.01	.01	.01			Chad	628
															Comoros	632
.45	.47	.49	.45	.22	.11	.03	.03	.02	.03	.03		.05			Congo, Dem. Rep. of	636
.01	.01	.01	.01	.01	.01	.01	.01	.01	.01	.01	.01	.01			Congo, Rep. of	634
.04	.04	.04	.04	.04	.04	.04	.04	.04	.04	.04	.04	.04	.04	.04	Côte d'Ivoire	662
															Djibouti	611
															Equatorial Guinea	642
.21	.21	.21	.21	.19	.09	.15	.11	.11	.11	.11	—	—	.03	.03	Ethiopia	644
.01	.01	.01	.01	.01	.01	.01	.01	.01	.01	.01	.01	.01			Gabon	646
															Gambia, The	648
.23	.28	.28	.22	.22	.24	.27	.28	.27	.28	.28	.28		.28	.28	Ghana	652
															Guinea	656
															Guinea-Bissau	654
.08	.08	.08	.08	.08	.08	.08	.08	.08	.08	.08	.08	.08	—	—	Kenya	664
															Lesotho	666
															Liberia	668
															Madagascar	674
.01	.01	.01	.01	.01	.01	.01	.01	.01	.01	.01	.01	.01	.01	.01	Malawi	676
.02	.02	.02	.02	.02	.02	.02	.02	.02	.02	.02	.02	.02	.02	.02	Mali	678
.01	.01	.01	.01	.01	.01	.01	.01	.01	.01	.01	.01	.01	.01	.01	Mauritania	682
.04	.04	.04	.05	.06	.06	.06	.06	.06	.06	.06	.06	.06	.06	.06	Mauritius	684
.70	.70	.70	.70	.70	.70	.70	.70	.70	.70	.70	.70	.70	.70	.70	Morocco	686
												.07	.07	.06	Mozambique	688
														—	Namibia	728
.01	.01	.01	.01	.01	.01	.01	.01	.01	.01	.01	.01	.01	.01	.01	Niger	692
.69	.69	.69	.69	.69	.69	.69	.69	.69	.69	.69	.69				Nigeria	694
															Rwanda	714
—	—	—	—	—	—	—	—	—	—	—	—	—	—		São Tomé & Príncipe	716
.03	.03	.03	.03	.03	.03	.03	.03	.03	.03	.03	.03	.03	.03	.03	Senegal	722
															Seychelles	718
															Sierra Leone	724
.02	.02	.02	.02	.02											Somalia	726
4.84	4.82	5.83	3.47	3.08	4.09	6.47	6.65	4.76	4.20	4.25	3.79	3.99	4.00	3.94	South Africa	199
															Sudan	732
															Swaziland	734
															Tanzania	738
.01	.01	.01	.01	.01	.01	.01	.01	.01	.01	.01	.01	.01	.01	.01	Togo	742
.19	.19	.19	.19	.19	.19	.22	.22	.22	.22	.22	.22	.22	.22	.22	Tunisia	744
															Uganda	746
—	—	—	.01	.02	.02	.02									Zambia	754
.77	.54	.42	.40	.45	.38	.41	.55	.50	.47	.76	.64	.77	.62	.73	Zimbabwe	698

Gold (Million Ounces)

		1970	1971	1972	1973	1974	1975	1976	1977	1978	1979	1980	1981	1982	1983	1984
																Millions of Ounces:
Asia	505	**19.99**	**19.28**	**19.00**	**18.01**	**18.02**	**17.33**	**17.29**	**31.08**	**33.07**	**34.00**	**37.37**	**38.57**	**39.27**	**38.07**	**39.07**
Afghanistan, Islamic State of	512	.99	.93	.93	.93	.93	.93	.93	.94	.95	.96	.97	.97	.97	.97	.97
Bangladesh	513	...	...	...	...	...	...	...	.05	.03	.05	.05	.05	.06	.06	.06
Bhutan	514															
China, P.R.: Mainland	924	...	...	...	...	...	...	...	12.80	12.80	12.80	12.80	12.70	12.70	12.70	12.70
China, P.R.: Hong Kong	532	...	...	...	...	...	...	...	...	...	...	...	...	...	...	...
Fiji	819								.01	.01	.01	.01	.01	.01	.01	.01
India	534	6.95	6.95	6.95	6.95	6.95	6.95	6.95	7.36	8.36	8.56	8.59	8.59	8.59	8.59	8.74
Indonesia	536	.11	.06	.12	.06	.06	.06	.06	.17	.22	.28	2.39	3.10	3.10	3.10	3.10
Korea	542	.10	.10	.11	.11	.11	.11	.11	.15	.27	.30	.30	.30	.30	.30	.31
Lao People's Democratic Rep.	544															
Malaysia	548	1.37	1.66	1.66	1.66	1.66	1.66	1.66	1.74	1.89	2.13	2.32	2.33	2.33	2.33	2.33
Maldives	556	...	...	...	...	...	...	...	...	...	...	...	—	—	—	—
Micronesia, Fed. States of	868															
Mongolia	948											.04	.05	.04	.04	.04
Myanmar	518	1.79	.62	.32	.20	.20	.20	.20	.23	.24	.25	.25	.25	.25	.25	.25
Nepal	558	.15	.14	.14	.13	.13	.13	.13	.13	.15	.15	.15	.15	.15	.15	.15
Pakistan	564	1.56	1.58	1.59	1.59	1.59	1.59	1.62	1.62	1.72	1.82	1.82	1.85	1.85	1.86	1.86
Papua New Guinea	853								.03	.04	.05	.06	.06	.06	.06	.06
Philippines	566	1.60	1.91	1.86	1.06	1.06	1.06	1.06	1.06	1.51	1.70	1.92	1.66	1.87	.29	.79
Singapore	576															
Solomon Islands	813															
Sri Lanka	524	...	...	...	...	...	...	...	...	.04	.06	.06	.06	.06	.06	.06
Thailand	578	2.34	2.34	2.34	2.34	2.34	2.34	2.34	2.40	2.43	2.46	2.49	2.49	2.49	2.49	2.49
Tonga	866															
Vanuatu	846															
Vietnam	582	.69	.69	.69	.69	.69							.69[e]	.69[e]	.69[e]	.69[e]
Europe	170	**7.64**	**8.96**	**9.36**	**11.75**	**11.44**	**11.21**	**11.73**	**12.13**	**13.27**	**14.76**	**16.11**	**15.43**	**14.87**	**16.05**	**16.76**
Albania	914															
Armenia	911															
Azerbaijan	912															
Bulgaria	918															
Croatia	960															
Cyprus	423	.43	.43	.43	.43	.43	.43	.43	.44	.44	.46	.46	.46	.46	.46	.46
Czech Republic	935															
Czechoslovakia	934	1.85	1.85	1.85	1.85	1.85	1.85	1.85	1.85	1.85	1.85	3.05	3.14	3.65	3.85	3.91
Estonia	939															
Hungary	944	...	1.45	1.67	1.82	1.33	.95	1.32	1.28	1.98	1.78	2.07	1.69	.65	1.53	2.06
Kazakhstan	916															
Kyrgyz Republic	917															
Latvia	941															
Lithuania	946															
Macedonia, FYR	962															
Malta	181	.28	.35	.35	.35	.35	.35	.35	.36	.36	.37	.43	.46	.46	.47	.47
Moldova	921															
Poland	964											1.29	.76	.47	.47	.47	.47
Romania	968	...	...	...	2.28	2.45	2.60	2.75	3.06	3.35	3.54	3.71	3.59	3.55	3.62	3.73
Russia	922															
Slovak Republic	936															
Slovenia	961															
Turkey	186	3.63	3.43	3.57	3.57	3.57	3.57	3.57	3.63	3.67	3.77	3.77	3.77	3.77	3.78	3.80
Ukraine	926															
Yugoslavia, SFR	188	1.46	1.46	1.49	1.46	1.47	1.47	1.47	1.51	1.63	1.72	1.86	1.86	1.86	1.86	1.86
Middle East	405	**30.13**	**30.78**	**30.68**	**31.01**	**31.66**	**32.06**	**34.22**	**31.43**	**33.16**	**33.42**	**34.82**	**35.78**	**36.04**	**36.16**	**36.34**
Bahrain	419	.24	.24	.24	.24	.24	.15	.15	.15	.15	.15	.15	.15	.15	.15	.15
Egypt	469	2.43	2.43	2.43	2.43	2.43	2.43	2.43	2.43	2.47	2.47	2.43	2.43	2.43	2.43	2.43
Iran, I.R. of	429	3.74	3.74	3.74	3.74	3.74	3.74	3.74	3.78	3.82	3.90	4.34	4.34	4.34	4.34	4.34
Iraq	433	4.10	4.10	4.10	4.10	4.10	4.10	4.10	4.14	...	...	...	...	...	...	...
Israel	436	1.24	1.24	1.14	1.10	1.10	1.10	1.10	1.16	1.17	1.23	1.19	1.19	1.08	1.02	1.02
Jordan	439	.80	.80	.80	.80	.80	.80	.80	.81	.81	.82	1.02	1.07	1.08	1.09	1.06
Kuwait	443	2.46	2.48	2.48	2.48	2.85	3.50	3.99	5.58	2.51	2.53	2.54	2.54	2.54	2.54	2.54
Lebanon	446	8.21	9.21	9.21	9.22	9.22	9.22	9.22	9.22	9.22	9.22	9.22	9.22	9.22	9.22	9.22
Libya	672	2.44	2.44	2.44	2.44	2.44	2.44	2.44	2.45	2.45	2.46	3.08	3.58	3.58	3.58	3.65
Oman	449	.06	.01	.01	.01	.03	.03	.05	.10	.19	.19	.21	.27	.28	.29	.29
Qatar	453	.18	.19	.19	.19	.19	.19	.19	.18	.25	.27	.47	.71	.90	1.07	1.21
Saudi Arabia	456	3.40	3.09	3.09	3.09	3.08	3.08	3.08	3.08	4.54	4.57	4.57	4.57	4.60	4.60	4.60
Syrian Arab Rep.	463	.80	.80	.80	.80	.79	.79	.79	.81	.81	.83	.83	.83	.83	.83	.83
United Arab Emirates	466	...	...	...	—	—	—	.55	.57	.58	.58	.58	.68	.82	.82	.82
Yemen Arab Rep.	473	...	...	...	—	—	—	—	—	.01	.01	—	—	—	—	—
Yemen, P.D. Rep.	459	.02	.02	.02	.02	.02	.02	.02	.03	.03	.04	.04	.04	.04	.04	.04
Yemen, Republic of	474	...	...	...	...	...	...	...	...	...	...	...	...	...	...	...

Gold (Million Ounces)

1ad

1985	1986	1987	1988	1989	1990	1991	1992	1993	1994	1995	1996	1997	1998	1999		
End of Period																
41.04	**43.46**	**46.06**	**51.96**	**51.66**	**52.57**	**53.81**	**53.33**	**53.65**	**53.70**	**55.38**	**56.53**	**56.76**	**56.01**	**55.71**	**Asia**	505
.97	.97	.97	.97	.97	.97	.97	....	....	....	....	....	....	....	....	Afghanistan, Islamic State of	512
.06	.07	.07	.07	.08	.08	.08	.09	.09	.09	.09	.09	.10	.11	.11	Bangladesh	513
															Bhutan	514
12.70	12.70	12.70	12.70	12.70	12.70	12.70	12.70	12.70	12.70	12.70	12.70	12.70	12.70	12.70	China, P.R.: Mainland	924
....	....	....	....	....	.23	.23	.23	.07	.07	.07	.07	.07	.07	.07	China, P.R.: Hong Kong	532
.01	.01	—	....	....	....	....	....	....	....	....	....	....	....	....	Fiji	819
9.40	10.45	10.45	10.45	10.45	10.69	11.28	11.35	11.46	11.80	12.78	12.78	12.74	11.49	11.50	India	534
3.10	3.10	3.10	3.10	3.11	3.11	3.11	3.10	3.10	3.10	3.10	3.10	3.10	3.10	3.10	Indonesia	536
.31	.32	.32	.32	.32	.32	.32	.32	.32	.33	.33	.33	.33	.43	.44	Korea	542
....	....	....	....	.02	.02	.02	.02	.02	.02	.02	.02	.02	.02	.12	Lao People's Democratic Rep.	544
2.34	2.34	2.35	2.35	2.37	2.35	2.35	2.39	2.39	2.39	2.39	2.39	2.35	2.35	1.18	Malaysia	548
—	—	—	—	—	—	—	—	—	—	—	—	—	—	—	Maldives	556
															Micronesia, Fed. States of	868
.05	.03	.03	.03	.03	.04	.14	.02	.02	.03	.10	.15	.08	.03	—	Mongolia	948
.25	.25	.25	.25	.25	.25	.25	.25	.25	.25	.23	.23	.23	.23	.23	Myanmar	518
.15	.15	.15	.15	.15	.15	.15	.15	.15	.15	.15	.15	.15	.15	.15	Nepal	558
1.90	1.93	1.94	1.95	1.95	1.95	1.96	2.02	2.04	2.05	2.05	2.06	2.07	2.08	2.09	Pakistan	564
.06	.06	.06	.06	.06	.06	.06	.06	.06	.06	.01	.06	.06	.06	.06	Papua New Guinea	853
1.48	2.26	2.78	2.84	2.45	2.89	3.37	2.80	3.22	2.89	3.58	4.65	4.99	5.43	6.20	Philippines	566
															Singapore	576
															Solomon Islands	813
.06	.06	.06	.06	.06	.06	.11	.16	.06	.06	.06	.06	.06	.06	.06	Sri Lanka	524
2.49	2.49	2.48	2.48	2.48	2.48	2.48	2.47	2.47	2.47	2.47	2.47	2.47	2.47	2.47	Thailand	578
															Tonga	866
															Vanuatu	846
.69e	.69e	....	....	....	....	....	....	....	....	....	....	....	....	....	Vietnam	582
17.07	**16.47**	**13.76**	**13.88**	**14.14**	**12.09**	**13.44**	**12.11**	**22.95**	**21.75**	**23.00**	**27.67**	**30.20**	**30.59**	**29.54**	**Europe**	170
....	....	....	....	....	....	....	....	.05	.05	.06	.12	.12	.12	.12	Albania	914
								—	.01	.03	.03	.04	.04	.04	Armenia	911
															Azerbaijan	912
....	....	....	....	....	....	1.02	1.02	1.02	1.03	1.03	1.03	1.03	1.03	1.03	Bulgaria	918
													—	—	Croatia	960
.46	.46	.46	.46	.46	.46	.46	.46	.46	.46	.46	.44	.46	.46	.46	Cyprus	423
								1.95	2.10	1.99	1.99	1.04	.29	.45	Czech Republic	935
3.81	3.77	3.66	3.73	3.62	2.49	2.79	3.29	....	....	....	....	....	....	....	Czechoslovakia	934
							.08	.01	.01	.01	.01	.01	.01	.01	Estonia	939
2.33	2.35	1.64	1.59	1.50	.30	.26	.10	.11	.11	.11	.10	.10	.10	.10	Hungary	944
								.65	.99	1.36	1.80	1.81	1.75	1.80	Kazakhstan	916
													.08	.08	Kyrgyz Republic	917
							.07	.24	.25	.25	.25	.25	.25	.25	Latvia	941
							.19	.19	.19	.19	.19	.19	.19	.19	Lithuania	946
								.02	.04	.05	.05	.08	.10	.10	Macedonia, FYR	962
.47	.47	.47	.47	.23	.16	.12	.12	.10	.11	.04	.04	.01	.01	.01	Malta	181
															Moldova	921
.47	.47	.47	.47	.47	.47	.47	.47	.47	.47	.47	.47	.90	3.31	3.31	Poland	964
3.82	3.25	1.36	1.45	2.17	2.21	2.25	2.31	2.37	2.63	2.70	2.82	3.02	3.22	3.32	Romania	968
								10.20	8.42	9.41	13.49	16.30	14.74	13.33	Russia	922
								1.29	1.29	1.29	1.29	1.29	1.29	1.29	Slovak Republic	936
												—	—		Slovenia	961
3.86	3.84	3.83	3.82	3.78	4.09	4.16	4.05	4.03	3.82	3.75	3.75	3.75	3.75	3.74	Turkey	186
							—	.01	.04	.05	.03	.06	.11	.16	Ukraine	926
1.86	1.87	1.87	1.89	1.90	1.91	1.92	....	....	....	....	....	....	....	....	Yugoslavia, SFR	188
36.16	**36.05**	**35.86**	**35.65**	**35.61**	**35.42**	**35.03**	**34.65**	**31.48**	**31.41**	**30.96**	**31.55**	**31.35**	**35.97**	**35.20**	**Middle East**	405
.15	.15	.15	.15	.15	.15	.15	.15	.15	.15	.15	.15	.15	.15	.15	Bahrain	419
2.43	2.43	2.43	2.43	2.43	2.43	2.43	2.43	2.43	2.43	2.43	2.43	2.43	2.43	2.43	Egypt	469
4.34	4.34	4.34	4.34	4.34	4.34	4.34	4.34	4.34	4.76	4.74	4.84	....	....	....	Iran, I.R. of	429
															Iraq	433
1.02	1.02	1.02	1.02	1.02	.84	.42	.01	.01	.01	.01	.01	.01	....	....	Israel	436
1.06	1.06	1.00	.74	.75	.75	.79	.79	.79	.79	.79	.80	.81	.83	.49	Jordan	439
2.54	2.54	2.54	2.54	2.54	2.54	2.54	2.54	2.54	2.54	2.54	2.54	2.54	2.54	2.54	Kuwait	443
9.22	9.22	9.22	9.22	9.22	9.22	9.22	9.22	9.22	9.22	9.22	9.22	9.22	9.22	9.22	Lebanon	446
3.60	3.60	3.60	3.60	3.60	3.60	3.60	3.60	....	....	....	....	....	4.62	4.62	Libya	672
.29	.29	.29	.29	.29	.29	.29	.29	.29	.29	.29	.29	.29	.29	.29	Oman	449
1.08	.97	.83	.88	.90	.83	.83	.86	.86	.81	.27	.27	.05	.05	.02	Qatar	453
4.60	4.60	4.60	4.60	4.60	4.60	4.60	4.60	4.60	4.60	4.60	4.60	4.60	4.60	4.60	Saudi Arabia	456
.83	.83	.83	.83	.83	.83	.83	.83	.83	.83	.83	.83	.83	.83	.83	Syrian Arab Rep.	463
.82	.82	.82	.82	.80	.80	.80	.80	.80	.80	.80	.80	.80	.80	.40	United Arab Emirates	466
—	—	—	—	—	....	....	....	....	....	....	....	....	....	....	Yemen Arab Rep.	473
.04	.04	.04	.04	....	....	....	....	....	....	....	....	....	....	....	Yemen, P.D. Rep.	459
....	....	....	....	....	.05	.05	.05	.05	.05	.05	.05	.05	.05	....	Yemen, Republic of	474

Gold (Million Ounces)

		1970	1971	1972	1973	1974	1975	1976	1977	1978	1979	1980	1981	1982	1983	1984
															Millions of Ounces:	
Western Hemisphere	205	**31.73**	**30.29**	**30.54**	**30.10**	**29.21**	**29.77**	**28.04**	**29.43**	**30.13**	**30.93**	**32.26**	**33.35**	**31.07**	**31.77**	**29.73**
Antigua and Barbuda	311	....	....	....	....	....	....	....	....	....	....	....	....	....	....	....
Argentina	213	3.99	2.56	3.99	4.00	4.00	4.00	4.00	4.18	4.28	4.37	4.37	4.37	4.37	4.37	4.37
Aruba	314	....	....	....	....	....	....	....	....	....	....	....	....	....	....	....
Bahamas, The	313	....	....	....	....	....	....	....	.01	.01	.02	—	—	—	—	....
Barbados	316	....	....	....	....	....	....	....	....	....	....	—	.01	.01	.01	.01
Belize	339															
Bolivia	218	.36	.38	.41	.41	.41	.41	.41	.60	.64	.68	.76	.83	.89	.91	.91
Brazil	223	1.29	1.32	1.33	1.33	1.33	1.33	1.33	1.52	1.61	1.70	1.88	2.20	.15	.54	1.47
Chile	228	1.33	1.35	1.36	1.38	1.44	1.30	1.34	1.36	1.39	1.52	1.70	1.70	1.71		
Colombia	233	.49	.40	.43	.43	.43	1.13	1.41	1.73	1.96	2.32	2.79	3.37	3.82	4.22	1.37
Costa Rica	238	.06	.06	.06	.06	.06	.06	.06	.07	.08	.09	.09	.03	.05	.09	.02
Dominica	321	....	....	....	....	....	....	....	....	....	....	....	....	....	....	....
Dominican Republic	243	.09	.09	.09	.09	.09	.09	.09	.10	.10	.11	.13	.14	.09	.08	.02
Ecuador	248	.55	.53	.36	.39	.39	.39	.39	.40	.41	.41	.41	.41	.41	.41	.41
El Salvador	253	.49	.49	.49	.49	.49	.49	.49	.50	.50	.51	.52	.52	.52	.47	.47
Grenada	328	....	....	....	....	....	....	....	....	....	....	....	....	....	....	....
Guatemala	258	.50	.50	.49	.49	.49	.49	.49	.51	.51	.52	.52	.52	.52	.52	.52
Guyana	336	....	....	....	....	....	....	....	....	....	....	....	....	....	....	....
Haiti	263	....	....	....	....	—	—	—	.01	.01	.02	.02	.02	.02	.02	.02
Honduras	268	—	—	—	—	—	—	—	.01	.01	.01	.02	.02	.02	.02	.02
Jamaica	343	....	....	....	....	....	....	....	.01	—	.01	—	—	—	—	—
Mexico	273	5.03	5.26	4.94	4.63	3.66	3.66	1.60	1.75	1.89	1.98	2.06	2.26	2.07	2.31	2.42
Netherlands Antilles	353	.56	.55	.55	.55	.55	.55	.55	.55	.55	.55	.55	.55	.55	.55	.55
Nicaragua	278	.02	.02	.01	.02	.02	.02	.02	.03	.03	.02	.02	.02	.02	.12	....
Panama	283	....	....	....	....	....	....	....	....	....	....	....	....	....	....	....
Paraguay	288	....	....	....	....	....	....	....	.01	.01	.04	.04	.04	.04	.04	.04
Peru	293	1.13	1.13	1.09	1.00	1.00	1.00	1.00	1.00	1.00	1.16	1.40	1.40	1.40	1.40	1.40
St. Kitts and Nevis	361	....	....	....	....	....	....	....	....	....	....	....	....	....	....	....
St. Lucia	362	....	....	....	....	....	....	....	....	....	....	....	....	....	....	....
St. Vincent & Grenadines	364	....	....	....	....	....	....	....	....	....	....	....	....	....	....	....
Suriname	366	.25	.25	.25	.15	.15	.15	.15	.15	.05	.05	.05	.05	.05	.05	.05
Trinidad and Tobago	369	....	....	....	....	....	....	....	....	.04	.05	.05	.05	.05	.05	.05
Uruguay	298	4.61	4.23	3.54	3.54	3.54	3.54	3.54	3.58	3.64	3.31	3.42	3.39	2.86	2.60	2.62
Venezuela, Rep. Bol.	299	10.97	11.17	11.17	11.17	11.18	11.18	11.18	11.32	11.39	11.46	11.46	11.46	11.46	11.46	11.46
Memorandum Items																
Oil Exporting Countries	999	33.51	33.29	33.35	33.68	34.36	34.84	37.00	34.43	36.26	36.66	40.05	41.67	42.03	42.20	42.41
Non-Oil Developing Countries	201	84.81	77.34	83.51	85.79	82.62	81.28	74.88	87.51	91.65	95.23	101.63	99.91	95.96	97.02	96.21

Gold Holdings at SDR 35 per oz.

		1970	1971	1972	1973	1974	1975	1976	1977	1978	1979	1980	1981	1982	1983	1984
															Millions of SDRs:	
World	001	41,192	41,157	41,365	41,408	41,349	41,269	40,932	41,066	40,811	40,166	40,326	40,319	40,170	40,105	40,066
All Countries	010	37,091	36,060	35,753	35,843	35,773	35,695	35,538	36,062	36,329	33,141	33,445	33,432	33,295	33,255	33,216
IMF	992	4,339	4,732	5,370	5,370	5,369	5,370	5,233	4,605	4,137	3,739	3,620	3,620	3,620	3,620	3,620
EPU / EF	994	45	55	41												
EMI	977	—	—	—	—	—	—	—	—	—e	2,985	2,997	2,999	3,000	3,000	3,000
BIS (Net)	993	−282	310	201	195	207	204	160	399	345	301	264	267	255	230	230

Gold Holdings at Market Prices

		1970	1971	1972	1973	1974	1975	1976	1977	1978	1979	1980	1981	1982	1983	1984
															Millions of SDRs:	
World	001	43,982	47,255	70,648	110,085	179,959	141,262	135,636	159,328	202,277	446,031	532,540	393,405	475,370	417,541	360,049
All Countries	010	39,602	41,402	61,063	95,290	155,689	122,184	117,765	139,914	180,063	368,022	441,663	326,205	394,012	346,226	298,489
IMF	992	4,633	5,433	9,171	14,276	23,367	18,381	17,341	17,867	20,505	41,521	47,810	35,325	42,844	37,693	32,534
EPU / EF	994	48	63	70												
EMI	977	—	—	—	—	—	—	—	—	—e	33,147	39,583	29,265	35,500	31,232	26,959
BIS (Net)	993	−301	356	343	518	903	697	531	1,547	1,710	3,342	3,483	2,610	3,014	2,390	2,066

IMF Gold Transactions

		1970	1971	1972	1973	1974	1975	1976	1977	1978	1979	1980	1981	1982	1983	1984
															Millions of SDRs:	
Distribution(at SDR 35 per ounce)	992	—	—	—	—	—	—	—	—	—	—	—	—	—	—	—
Sale (at SDR 35 per ounce)	992	—	—	—	—	—	—	—	—	—	—	—	—	—	—	—
Sale (at auction price)	992	—	—	—	—	—	—	—	—	—	—	—	—	—	—	—

Gold Prices and SDR Rates

		1970	1971	1972	1973	1974	1975	1976	1977	1978	1979	1980	1981	1982	1983	1984
															End of Period	
US Dollars per Ounce(London)	112	37.37	43.63	64.90	112.25	186.50	140.25	134.75	164.95	226.00	512.00	589.50	397.50	456.90	381.50	308.30
US Dollars per SDR	111	1.0000	1.0857	1.0857	1.2064	1.2244	1.1707	1.1618	1.2147	1.3028	1.3173	1.2754	1.1640	1.1031	1.0470	.9802
SDRs per Ounce	112	37.37	40.19	59.78	93.05	152.33	119.80	115.98	135.79	173.47	388.66	462.20	341.51	414.19	364.39	314.52

1985	1986	1987	1988	1989	1990	1991	1992	1993	1994	1995	1996	1997	1998	1999		

End of Period

1985	1986	1987	1988	1989	1990	1991	1992	1993	1994	1995	1996	1997	1998	1999		
32.34	32.50	30.71	31.74	30.07	31.29	28.34	28.24	27.30	27.83	28.81	27.72	23.49	22.38	21.09	Western Hemisphere	205
....	....	....	....	....	....	....	....	....	....	....	....	....	....	....	Antigua and Barbuda	311
4.37	4.37	4.37	4.37	4.37	4.23	4.12	4.37	4.37	4.37	4.37	4.37	.36	.36	.34	Argentina	213
....	—	—	—	.10	.10	.10	.10	.10	.10	.10	.10	.10	.10	.10	Aruba	314
															Bahamas, The	313
.01	.01	.01	.01	.01	—	—	—	—	—	—	—	—	—	....	Barbados	316
															Belize	339
.89	.89	.89	.89	.89	.89	.89	.89	.89	.89	.89	.94	.94	.94	.94	Bolivia	218
3.10	2.43	2.43	2.73	2.98	4.57	2.02	2.23	2.93	3.71	4.58	3.69	3.03	4.60	3.17	Brazil	223
....	1.80	1.81	1.82	1.75	1.86	1.86	1.87	1.87	1.86	1.86	1.86	1.86	1.22	1.22	Chile	228
1.84	2.01	.68	1.10	.61	.63	.86	.48	.30	.29	.27	.25	.36	.36	.33	Colombia	233
.06	.07	.06	.02	.01	.01	.03	.04	.03	.03	.03	—	—	—	—	Costa Rica	238
															Dominica	321
.02	.02	.02	.02	.02	.02	.02	.02	.02	.02	.02	.02	.02	.02	.02	Dominican Republic	243
.41	.41	.41	.41	.41	.44	.44	.44	.41	.41	.41	.41	.41	.41	.41	Ecuador	248
.47	.47	.47	.47	.47	.47	.47	.47	.47	.47	.47	.47	.47	.47	.47	El Salvador	253
															Grenada	328
.52	.52	.52	.52	.54	.21	.21	.12	.21	.21	.21	.21	.21	.22	.22	Guatemala	258
															Guyana	336
.02	.02	.02	.02	.02	.02	.02	.02	.02	.02	.02	.02	.02	.02	—	Haiti	263
.02	.02	.02	.02	.02	.02	.02	.02	.02	.02	.02	.02	.02	.02	.02	Honduras	268
															Jamaica	343
2.36	2.57	2.54	2.55	1.03	.92	.92	.69	.48	.43	.51	.26	.19	.22	.16	Mexico	273
.55	.55	.55	.55	.55	.55	.55	.55	.55	.55	.55	.55	.55	.55	.55	Netherlands Antilles	353
....	....	.20	.31	.12	.15	.10	.48	.01	.01	.02	.02	.02	.02	.02	Nicaragua	278
															Panama	283
.04	.04	.04	.03	.03	.03	.03	.03	.03	.03	.03	.03	.35	.03	.03	Paraguay	288
1.95	2.14	1.50	1.71	1.97	2.21	1.83	1.82	1.30	1.12	1.12	1.11	1.11	1.10	1.10	Peru	293
															St. Kitts and Nevis	361
															St. Lucia	362
															St. Vincent & Grenadines	364
.05	.05	.05	.05	.05	.05	.05	.05	.05	.05	.09	.13	.19	.13	....	Suriname	366
.05	.05	.05	.05	.05	.05	.05	.05	.06	.05	.05	.05	.06	.06	.06	Trinidad and Tobago	369
2.62	2.61	2.61	2.61	2.61	2.40	2.26	2.03	1.70	1.70	1.72	1.74	1.76	1.78	1.80	Uruguay	298
11.46	11.46	11.46	11.46	11.46	11.46	11.46	11.46	11.46	11.46	11.46	11.46	11.46	9.76	9.76	Venezuela, Rep. Bol.	299

Memorandum Items

1985	1986	1987	1988	1989	1990	1991	1992	1993	1994	1995	1996	1997	1998	1999		
42.24	42.13	41.99	42.04	42.05	41.54	41.98	42.00	38.82	38.75	38.31	38.89	38.67	41.59	41.16	Oil Exporting Countries	999
98.42	100.22	99.19	103.52	101.19	101.89	103.60	101.58	109.85	108.63	112.87	116.91	115.55	115.89	112.95	Non-Oil Developing Countries	201

End of Period

Gold Holdings at SDR 35 per oz.

1985	1986	1987	1988	1989	1990	1991	1992	1993	1994	1995	1996	1997	1998	1999		
40,157	40,175	40,074	40,274	40,066	40,040	39,998	39,594	39,240	39,050	38,869	38,708	38,004	37,660	37,608	World	001
33,303	33,302	33,109	33,134	32,936	32,873	32,874	32,509	32,182	32,040	31,715	31,638	31,034	33,815	32,918	All Countries	010
3,620	3,620	3,620	3,620	3,620	3,620	3,620	3,620	3,620	3,620	3,620	3,620	3,620	3,620	3,620	IMF	992
—	—	—	—	—	—	—	—	—	—	....	....	....	....	....	EPU / EF	994
3,000	3,029	3,130	3,289	3,277	3,274	3,273	3,228	3,135	3,146	3,278	3,219	3,131	....	....	EMI	977
234	225	214	231	232	273	230	237	302	244	255	230	218	224	229	BIS (Net)	993

End of Period

Gold Holdings at Market Prices

1985	1986	1987	1988	1989	1990	1991	1992	1993	1994	1995	1996	1997	1998	1999		
341,567	366,829	390,704	350,799	349,304	309,591	282,498	274,175	318,861	292,905	288,935	283,990	233,543	219,931	227,230	World	001
283,262	304,066	322,800	288,603	287,145	254,176	232,183	225,111	261,512	240,324	235,758	232,124	190,712	197,479	198,893	All Countries	010
30,794	33,057	35,298	31,535	31,563	27,993	25,570	25,070	29,419	27,156	26,913	26,562	22,248	21,143	21,875	IMF	992
....	....	....	....	....	....	....	....	....	....	....	....	....	....	....	EPU / EF	994
25,517	27,656	30,520	28,646	28,572	25,314	23,118	22,351	25,478	23,594	24,369	23,618	19,240	....	....	EMI	977
1,993	2,050	2,087	2,015	2,023	2,107	1,627	1,643	2,453	1,831	1,896	1,687	1,343	1,309	1,381	BIS (Net)	993

In Period

IMF Gold Transactions

1985	1986	1987	1988	1989	1990	1991	1992	1993	1994	1995	1996	1997	1998	1999		
....	....	....	....	....	....	....	....	....	....	....	....	....	....	....	Distribution(at SDR 35 per ounce)	992
....	....	....	....	....	....	....	....	....	....	....	....	....	....	....	Sale (at SDR 35 per ounce)	992
....	....	....	....	....	....	....	....	....	....	....	....	....	....	....	Sale (at auction price)	992

End of Period

Gold Prices and SDR Rates

1985	1986	1987	1988	1989	1990	1991	1992	1993	1994	1995	1996	1997	1998	1999		
327.00	390.90	484.10	410.25	401.00	385.00	353.60	333.25	390.65	383.25	386.75	369.25	290.20	287.80	290.25	US Dollars per Ounce(London)	112
1.0984	1.2232	1.4187	1.3457	1.3142	1.4227	1.4304	1.3750	1.3736	1.4599	1.4865	1.4380	1.3493	1.4080	1.3725	US Dollars per SDR	111
297.70	319.57	341.24	304.86	305.14	270.62	247.20	242.36	284.41	262.53	260.18	256.79	215.08	204.40	211.47	SDRs per Ounce	112

Total Reserves

(with Gold at SDR 35 per ounce)

Millions of SDRs:

		1970	1971	1972	1973	1974	1975	1976	1977	1978	1979	1980	1981	1982	1983	1984
All Countries	010	93,244	123,115	146,658	152,679	179,773	194,393	222,166	264,535	281,817	306,013	354,718	363,109	361,221	395,578	440,344
Industrial Countries	110	72,597	99,182	113,362	111,609	111,520	116,393	125,198	151,848	176,663	183,431	214,523	214,978	214,025	234,567	254,387
United States	111	14,487	12,148	12,112	11,919	13,115	13,567	15,767	15,965	15,032	15,170	21,479	25,502	29,918	30,831	33,517
Canada	156	4,679	5,251	5,572	4,782	4,758	4,549	5,029	3,793	3,505	2,951	3,159	3,755	3,439	4,017	3,246
Australia	193	1,693	3,054	5,656	4,723	3,487	2,782	2,728	1,962	1,855	1,359	1,603	1,713	6,053	8,838	7,869
Japan	158	4,840	14,148	16,916	10,151	11,042	10,947	14,292	19,149	25,714	15,667	20,164	25,083	22,001	24,346	27,811
New Zealand	196	258	454	767	867	522	365	423	366	348	344	277	580	577	744	1,824
Euro Area																
Austria	122	1,757	2,153	2,505	2,382	2,801	3,791	3,795	3,493	4,610	3,832	4,879	5,279	5,544	5,052	5,070
Belgium	124	2,847	3,199	3,564	4,227	4,366	4,952	4,480	4,743	4,535	5,329	7,330	5,451	4,757	5,699	5,853
Finland	172	453	623	664	505	515	399	427	469	972	1,204	1,501	1,319	1,420	1,227	2,854
France	132	4,960	7,601	9,224	7,070	7,230	10,757	8,373	8,393	10,691	16,212	24,301	21,991	17,850	21,826	24,227
Germany	134	13,609	17,184	21,908	27,497	26,462	26,510	29,954	32,713	41,360	43,225	41,430	40,892	43,909	44,092	44,282
Ireland	178	697	917	1,038	850	1,034	1,308	1,581	1,952	2,064	1,693	2,255	2,290	2,390	2,534	2,412
Italy	136	5,352	6,281	5,605	5,335	5,669	4,003	5,661	9,574	11,436	16,149	20,466	19,631	15,108	21,537	23,548
Luxembourg	137	....	....	....	....	....	....	....	....	....	....	....	....	....	....	....
Netherlands	138	3,241	3,496	4,407	5,427	5,683	6,074	6,358	6,639	5,823	7,301	10,669	9,562	10,723	11,253	10,961
Portugal	182	1,504	1,791	2,130	2,353	1,923	1,310	1,120	1,145	1,443	1,481	1,399	1,234	1,179	1,083	1,237
Spain	184	1,818	3,010	4,618	5,614	5,297	5,203	4,549	5,425	8,270	10,550	9,813	9,794	7,450	7,581	12,709
Denmark	128	484	665	787	1,097	764	749	788	1,375	2,471	2,514	2,712	2,246	2,111	3,515	3,127
Greece	174	310	478	950	868	765	I 950	886	994	1,134	1,153	1,189	1,013	916	996	1,117
Iceland	176	54	64	77	83	40	40	69	82	106	125	138	199	133	144	132
Norway	142	811	1,063	1,220	1,305	1,575	1,911	1,919	1,845	2,235	3,241	4,783	5,414	6,272	6,373	9,596
Sweden	144	761	1,024	1,453	2,097	1,417	2,627	2,144	3,019	3,375	2,880	2,893	3,306	3,397	4,065	4,135
Switzerland	146	5,132	6,416	6,961	7,063	7,360	8,908	11,183	11,385	16,549	15,391	15,190	14,925	16,930	17,275	18,520
United Kingdom	112	2,827	8,135	5,201	5,368	5,667	4,664	3,641	17,335	13,100	15,625	16,851	13,757	11,904	11,497	10,297
Developing Countries	200	20,648	23,934	33,295	41,070	68,253	77,998	96,968	112,688	105,154	122,583	140,195	148,131	147,195	161,010	185,957
Africa	605	3,575	3,181	3,962	4,777	9,424	9,446	9,780	8,995	7,115	10,791	15,696	10,995	7,737	7,443	7,275
Algeria	612	339	467	454	948	1,379	1,155	1,711	1,578	1,714	2,214	3,153	3,370	2,391	1,991	1,689
Benin	638	16	23	26	27	28	13	17	17	12	11	7	50	5	4	3
Botswana	616	....	....	....	....	....	....	64	82	116	203	269	218	266	378	484
Burkina Faso	748	36	40	44	52	68	65	62	46	28	47	54	61	56	82	109
Burundi	618	15	16	17	18	12	26	42	78	63	69	75	53	27	26	21
Cameroon	622	81	68	40	42	64	25	38	35	41	96	149	74	62	153	56
Cape Verde	624	....	....	....	....	....	....	....	....	....	....	33	33	39	44	42
Central African Rep.	626	1	—	2	1	1	3	16	21	19	34	44	60	42	45	54
Chad	628	2	10	9	1	12	3	20	16	9	9	4	7	12	27	45
Comoros	632														14	5
Congo, Dem. Rep. of	636	186	134	164	194	115	50	52	119	107	166	170	143	50	112	156
Congo, Rep. of	634	9	10	10	7	20	12	10	11	8	32	68	106	34	7	5
Côte d'Ivoire	662	119	82	80	73	54	88	66	153	345	113	17	17	4	20	7
Djibouti	611															46
Equatorial Guinea	642	....	....	....	....	....	....	....	....	....	....	....	....	3	1	1
Ethiopia	644	71	63	85	147	225	246	263	186	127	141	74	238	172	128	53
Gabon	646	15	23	21	40	84	125	100	8	18	16	85	171	283	179	204
Gambia, The	648	8	10	10	13	23	24	18	20	20	1	4	3	8	3	2
Ghana	652	42	39	92	152	64	112	85	129	220	227	150	136	139	152	323
Guinea-Bissau	654	....	....	....	....	....	....	....	....	....	....	....	....	....	....	....
Kenya	664	220	157	186	193	158	148	237	431	273	479	388	201	195	362	400
Lesotho	666	....	....	....	....	....	....	....	....	....	39	37	43	64	50
Liberia	668	....	....	....	....	15	16	15	23	14	42	4	7	6	19	4
Madagascar	674	37	43	48	56	40	30	36	57	4	7	23	18	28	60
Malawi	676	29	29	33	55	67	53	23	72	58	53	54	43	21	15	58
Mali	678	1	2	4	4	5	4	6	5	7	5	12	16	16	16	28
Mauritania	682	3	7	12	35	85	41	71	41	61	87	110	139	126	102	79
Mauritius	684	46	48	65	55	107	142	77	55	36	23	72	31	36	18	25
Morocco	686	140	160	218	220	340	322	423	438	498	447	337	222	222	127	74
Namibia	728	....	....	....	....	....	....	....	....	....	....	....	....	....	....	....
Niger	692	19	31	38	42	37	43	71	83	99	100	99	91	27	51	91
Nigeria	694	222	395	346	483	4,596	4,791	4,478	3,506	1,470	4,236	8,049	3,371	1,486	970	1,516
Rwanda	714	8	5	6	13	11	22	55	68	67	116	146	149	116	106	109
São Tomé & Príncipe	716	....	....	....	....	....	....	....	....	....	....	....	....	....	....	....
Senegal	722	22	27	36	10	5	27	22	28	15	16	7	8	11	13	5
Seychelles	718	....	....	....	4	4	5	6	9	7	9	14	12	12	10	6
Sierra Leone	724	39	35	43	43	45	24	22	27	27	35	24	14	8	15	8
Somalia	726	21	25	29	29	35	58	73	99	97	34	12	27	7	9	2
South Africa	199	1,012	655	1,188	1,037	947	1,039	809	683	667	681	994	898	705	1,059	504
Sudan	732	22	26	33	51	102	31	20	19	22	51	38	15	19	16	18
Swaziland	734	....	....	....	....	11	39	63	78	87	86	124	83	69	88	82
Tanzania	738	65	55	110	120	41	56	97	232	77	52	16	16	4	19	27
Togo	742	35	37	34	31	44	35	57	38	54	50	61	131	152	166	208
Tunisia	744	60	136	205	255	342	329	319	294	346	446	469	467	556	548	421
Uganda	746	57	25	33	24	14	27	38	39	40	17	2	26	71	102	I 69
Zambia	754	514	262	153	161	140	127	86	60	46	68	69	56	60	60	55
Zimbabwe	698	57	34	76	130	75	81	75	65	119	236	180	162	141	93	71

(with Gold at SDR 35 per ounce)

End of Period

1985	1986	1987	1988	1989	1990	1991	1992	1993	1994	1995	1996	1997	1998	1999		
438,185	451,973	540,751	575,979	624,076	688,318	725,560	752,825	830,065	891,029	1,020,148	1,173,916	1,292,219	1,276,524	1,362,985	All Countries.................	010
257,819	279,622	352,489	381,104	410,136	441,946	428,438	424,229	440,423	460,700	514,117	574,980	603,332	573,895	579,466	Industrial Countries................	110
38,412	39,790	33,657	36,471	57,525	59,958	55,769	52,995	54,558	52,510	59,467	53,694	52,817	59,379	53,238	United States.................	111
2,982	3,348	5,778	12,037	12,781	13,060	11,816	8,662	9,299	8,552	10,243	14,310	13,317	16,640	20,556	Canada.................	156
5,528	6,202	6,441	10,383	10,764	11,710	11,837	8,429	8,359	8,007	8,279	10,350	12,575	10,487	15,545	Australia.................	193
25,173	35,394	57,925	72,727	64,735	56,027	51,224	52,937	72,577	87,062	124,125	151,511	163,641	153,878	209,893	Japan.................	158
1,454	3,084	2,298	2,108	2,303	2,902	2,062	2,239	2,430	2,540	2,967	4,140	3,299	2,986	3,246	New Zealand.................	196
															Euro Area	122
5,080	5,778	6,049	6,215	7,266	7,305	7,924	9,703	11,288	12,165	13,020	16,277	14,903	22,661	‡11,475	Austria.................	122
5,611	5,724	7,958	8,113	9,250	9,599	9,573	10,914	9,187	10,382	11,601	12,326	12,535	13,310	‡8,259	Belgium.................	124
3,481	1,528	4,592	4,801	3,959	6,849	5,389	3,862	4,009	7,374	6,809	4,866	6,294	6,955	‡6,035	Finland.................	172
27,071	28,579	26,161	21,713	21,592	28,716	24,735	22,522	19,354	20,851	20,930	21,500	25,788	35,054	‡32,329	France.................	132
43,735	45,626	58,846	46,824	49,527	51,060	47,375	69,489	59,856	56,325	60,517	61,176	60,835	56,737	‡48,375	Germany.................	134
2,689	2,658	3,393	3,793	3,100	3,684	4,026	2,514	4,326	4,201	5,818	5,719	4,849	6,690	‡3,901	Ireland.................	178
16,531	18,674	23,631	28,131	37,884	46,565	36,365	22,438	22,387	24,435	25,815	34,287	43,644	24,144	‡19,098	Italy.................	136
....	....	....	....	....	69	69	68	66	60	63	61	62	58	‡59	Luxembourg.................	137
11,354	10,687	12,818	13,483	14,100	13,827	13,980	17,492	24,046	24,872	23,897	19,832	19,376	16,395	8,462	Netherlands.................	138
1,978	1,896	3,047	4,372	8,135	10,736	14,977	14,474	12,094	11,189	11,225	11,632	12,169	11,942	‡7,130	Portugal.................	182
10,686	12,581	22,035	28,041	32,104	36,555	46,562	33,640	30,429	29,006	23,746	40,831	51,241	39,929	‡24,716	Spain.................	184
4,999	4,116	7,153	8,057	4,925	7,502	5,234	8,090	7,557	6,260	7,468	9,892	14,233	10,916	16,313	Denmark.................	128
935	‡1,357	2,007	2,808	2,572	2,517	3,747	3,606	5,792	10,045	10,064	12,292	9,462	12,526	13,352	Greece.................	174
189	255	221	218	258	308	316	364	312	202	209	317	286	305	351	Iceland.................	176
12,711	10,281	10,105	9,901	10,531	10,819	9,292	8,725	14,327	13,074	15,190	18,482	17,385	13,256	14,905	Norway.................	142
5,487	5,568	5,974	6,523	7,487	12,856	13,028	16,667	14,081	16,141	16,344	13,452	8,188	10,178	11,151	Sweden.................	144
19,317	20,726	22,283	20,900	22,148	23,456	23,191	27,100	26,674	26,704	27,411	29,642	31,840	32,169	29,378	Switzerland.................	146
12,373	15,727	30,070	33,439	27,121	25,865	29,948	27,300	27,420	28,739	28,910	28,390	24,596	23,682	22,456	United Kingdom.................	112
180,366	172,351	188,262	194,875	213,939	246,372	297,122	328,596	389,642	430,328	506,031	598,936	688,886	702,629	783,519	Developing Countries	200
8,787	7,508	7,616	7,978	9,614	12,228	14,811	13,044	14,030	16,686	17,638	21,717	31,453	28,752	32,648	Africa................	605
2,762	1,553	1,352	864	840	689	1,234	1,255	1,269	2,027	1,544	3,141	6,159	5,057	3,493	Algeria.................	612
4	4	3	4	3	46	134	179	178	177	134	182	188	186	292	Benin.................	638
713	979	1,450	1,678	2,162	2,380	2,637	2,796	3,024	3,057	3,205	3,545	4,255	4,279	4,589	Botswana.................	616
127	191	228	239	202	212	242	249	279	163	234	236	256	266	215	Burkina Faso.................	748
27	57	43	52	76	74	99	127	119	141	142	98	84	47	36	Burundi.................	618
122	49	46	132	62	19	31	16	3	3	4	3	2	....	....	Cameroon.................	622
50	46	57	60	....	....	....	....	....	....	....	....	....	....	....	Cape Verde.................	624
46	54	69	81	86	84	72	73	82	144	158	162	133	....	....	Central African Rep.	626
31	13	37	47	85	90	84	59	29	52	96	115	101	....	....	Chad.................	628
14	19	22	18	23	21	20	20	28	30	30	35	....	....	....	Comoros.................	632
188	236	145	155	156	158	129	115	34	84	100	....	....	....	....	Congo, Dem. Rep. of................	636
4	6	3	4	5	5	4	3	1	35	40	....	....	....	....	Congo, Rep. of................	634
6	18	8	9	13	4	11	7	3	141	357	423	460	609	461	Côte d'Ivoire.................	662
46	44	45	48	45	66	70	61	55	51	49	54	49	47	51	Djibouti.................	611
3	2	....	4	5	—	7	10	—	—	—	—	....	1	2	Equatorial Guinea.................	642
142	212	94	55	42	17	43	173	336	377	523	509	371	364	335	Ethiopia.................	644
176	104	9	51	27	193	229	52	1	120	100	173	210	....	....	Gabon.................	646
2	11	18	14	16	39	47	68	....	67	71	71	71	76	81	Gambia, The.................	648
444	429	147	172	272	162	394	242	308	410	479	586	....	277	340	Ghana.................	652
....	25	7	12	16	13	10	13	10	13	14	8	....	....	....	Guinea-Bissau.................	654
358	341	183	199	219	147	85	41[e]	298	385	241	522	587	556	577	Kenya.................	664
40	49	48	42	37	51	80	115	184	255	307	320	424	408	364	Lesotho.................	666
1	2	—	—	6	....	1	1	2	3	19	—	....	....	....	Liberia.................	668
44	94	131	166	187	65	62	....	49	73	168	209	....	122	166	Madagascar.................	674
41	21	37	109	77	97	108	30	42	30	74	157	121	192	183	Malawi.................	676
21	20	12	27	89	135	224	225	243	152	218	301	308	287	255	Mali.................	678
54	40	51	42	63	38	48	45	33	28	58	99	149	144	164	Mauritania.................	684
29	113	243	330	396	521	627	599	553	514	583	625	516	399	535	Mauritius.................	682
129	197	314	431	396	1,477	2,192	2,631	2,686	3,006	2,447	2,663	2,984	3,174	4,170	Morocco.................	686
....	....	....	....	....	....	....	36	97	139	149	135	....	....	....	Namibia.................	728
125	155	176	173	162	157	142	164	140	76	64	55	40	38	29	Niger.................	692
1,542	908	845	508	1,368	2,740	3,125	727	1,023	973	995	2,858	....	....	....	Nigeria.................	694
103	133	116	88	54	31	77	57	35	....	....	74	114	120	127	Rwanda.................	714
....	....	....	....	....	....	....	....	....	....	3	3	9	7	8	São Tomé & Príncipe	716
6	9	8	9	15	9	10	10	4	124	184	202	287	307	295	Senegal.................	722
8	6	10	6	9	12	19	23	26	21	18	15	20	15	22	Seychelles.................	718
10	11	4	6	3	4	7	14	21	28	23	18	29	31	29	Sierra Leone.................	724
3	11	6	12	12	....	....	....	....	....	....	....	....	....	....	Somalia.................	726
456	471	656	701	838	852	855	954	909	1,301	2,046	787	3,697	3,234	4,767	South Africa.................	199
11	48	8	9	12	8	5	20	27	54	110	74	60	64	138	Sudan.................	732
76	79	90	104	137	152	120	225	192	203	201	177	219	255	274	Swaziland.................	734
15	50	22	58	41	136	143	238	148	227	182	306	461	426	565	Tanzania.................	738
270	280	251	173	218	249	256	199	114	65	88	62	88	84	89	Togo.................	742
218	256	377	675	738	565	560	627	629	1,009	1,087	1,327	1,474	1,322	1,655	Tunisia.................	744
25	24	38	37	11	31	41	69	107	220	309	367	470	515	556	Uganda.................	746
182	58	77	100	89	136	130	....	....	....	....	....	....	....	....	Zambia.................	754
112	106	132	147	88	118	119	181	332	294	427	439	146	115	221	Zimbabwe.................	698

Total Reserves

1 *s*

(with Gold at SDR 35 per ounce)

Millions of SDRs:

		1970	1971	1972	1973	1974	1975	1976	1977	1978	1979	1980	1981	1982	1983	1984
Asia *	505	**5,789**	**6,124**	**7,935**	**9,215**	**10,921**	**11,049**	**16,565**	**22,546**	**23,758**	**27,406**	**31,009**	**37,977**	**44,490**	**55,924**	**68,740**
Afghanistan, Islamic State of	512	47	57	52	51	55	107	145	260	333	369	325	269	267	238	267
Bangladesh	513	....	....	249	119	113	127	249	193	243	295	237	121	168	503	400
Bhutan	514	....	....	....	....	....	....	....	....	....	....	....	27	32	38	46
China, P.R.: Mainland ⅼ	924	....	....	....	....	....	....	....	2,379	1,643	2,083	2,444	4,790	10,733	14,759	ⅼ18,161
China, P.R.: Hong Kong	532	....	....	....	....	....	....	....	....	....	....	....	....	....	....	....
Fiji	819	27	36	64	61	89	127	100	121	104	104	132	116	115	111	120
India	534	1,007	1,111	1,087	947	1,083	1,174	2,646	4,268	5,225	5,942	5,745	4,333	4,213	5,017	6,266
Indonesia	536	160	ⅼ173	531	669	1,219	501	1,290	2,071	2,024	3,093	4,311	4,416	2,959	3,660	4,978
Korea	542	610	403	485	737	230	671	1,700	2,448	2,131	2,257	2,304	2,315	2,556	2,252	2,820
Lao People's Democratic Rep.	544	....	....	....	....	....	....	....	....	....	....	....	....	....	....	....
Malaysia	548	664	753	894	1,115	1,322	1,302	2,127	2,353	2,556	3,046	3,521	3,602	3,497	3,696	3,880
Maldives	556	....	....	....	....	....	....	—	—	—	1	1	1	8	4	5
Micronesia, Fed. States of	868	....	....	....	....	....	....	....	....	....	....	....	....	....	....	....
Mongolia	948	....	....	....	....	....	....	....	....	....	....	....	....	....	....	....
Myanmar	518	ⅼ94	67	48	83	156	120	109	93	82	163	213	206	103	94	72
Nepal	558	94	93	95	102	104	86	ⅼ114	119	116	126	149	179	186	133	89
Pakistan	564	191	174	259	397	376	346	458	426	373	225	452	684	943	1,949	1,122
Papua New Guinea	853	....	....	....	26	27	154	221	352	312	384	334	343	413	423	446
Philippines	566	251	352	507	860	1,229	1,160	1,411	1,255	1,406	1,767	2,299	1,833	870	724	642
Samoa	862	5	6	4	4	5	5	5	8	4	4	2	3	3	7	11
Singapore	576	1,012	1,338	1,610	1,895	2,297	2,568	2,895	3,176	4,070	4,417	5,149	6,486	7,687	8,849	10,626
Solomon Islands	813	....	....	....	....	....	....	....	2	22	28	23	19	34	45	46ᵉ
Sri Lanka	524	43	46	55	72	64	50	79	240	307	395	195	283	321	286	523
Thailand	578	905	808	969	1,082	1,518	1,516	1,629	1,576	1,627	1,485	1,310	1,575	1,481	1,622	2,046
Tonga	866	....	....	....	....	....	....	....	7	8	10	11	12	14	20	27
Vanuatu	846	....	....	....	....	....	....	....	....	....	....	....	7	5	6	8
**of which:*																
Taiwan Province of China	528	622	649	957	931	972	998	1,383	1,192	1,164	1,198	1,839	6,330	7,866	11,471	16,136
Europe	170	**1,002**	**1,458**	**2,680**	**3,790**	**3,279**	**2,936**	**4,219**	**3,694**	**4,177**	**3,834**	**5,354**	**5,405**	**5,359**	**7,458**	**9,055**
Albania	914	....	....	....	....	....	....	....	....	....	....	....	....	....	....	....
Armenia	911	....	....	....	....	....	....	....	....	....	....	....	....	....	....	....
Azerbaijan	912	....	....	....	....	....	....	....	....	....	....	....	....	....	....	....
Croatia	960	....	....	....	....	....	....	....	....	....	....	....	....	....	....	....
Cyprus	423	209	262	294	254	219	184	251	273	281	284	305	382	490	512	568
Czech Republic	935	....	....	....	....	....	....	....	....	....	....	....	....	....	....	....
Czechoslovakia ⅼ	934	....	....	....	....	....	....	....	....	....	....	1,549	931	831	902	1,123
Estonia	939	....	....	....	....	....	....	....	....	....	....	....	....	....	....	....
Hungary	944	....	....	....	....	....	....	....	....	....	....	....	....	....	1,230	1,664
Kazakhstan	916	....	....	....	....	....	....	....	....	....	....	....	....	....	....	....
Kyrgyz Republic	917	....	....	....	....	....	....	....	....	....	....	....	....	....	....	....
Latvia	941	....	....	....	....	....	....	....	....	....	....	....	....	....	....	....
Lithuania	946	....	....	....	....	....	....	....	....	....	....	....	....	....	....	....
Macedonia, FYR	962	....	....	....	....	....	....	....	....	....	....	....	....	....	....	....
Malta	181	158	183	253	270	328	427	535	605	723	782	791	939	999	1,079	1,027
Moldova	921	....	....	....	....	....	....	....	....	....	....	....	....	....	....	....
Poland	964	....	....	....	....	....	....	....	....	....	....	474	127	255	603	747	1,145
Romania	968	....	....	....	258	282	552	580	318	406	522	383	472	532	628	854
Russia	922	....	....	....	....	....	....	....	....	....	....	....	....	....	....	....
Slovak Republic	936	....	....	....	....	....	....	....	....	....	....	....	....	....	....	....
Slovenia	961	....	....	....	....	....	....	....	....	....	....	....	....	....	....	....
Turkey	186	431	702	1,287	1,771	1,400	931	977	652	743	631	976	929	1,111	1,362	1,429
Ukraine	926	....	....	....	....	....	....	....	....	....	....	....	....	....	....	....
Yugoslavia, SFR	188	140	196	674	1,109	937	744	1,764	1,736	1,890	1,014	1,150	1,437	768	998	1,247
Middle East	405	**4,610**	**7,025**	**9,436**	**11,226**	**29,452**	**38,454**	**45,913**	**53,986**	**42,809**	**48,137**	**56,536**	**59,758**	**64,039**	**62,198**	**59,666**
Bahrain	419	71	88	85	61	116	253	381	420	384	471	753	1,332	1,397	1,368	1,334
Egypt	469	159	138	133	300	291	251	291	440	464	488	905	700	718	822	836
Iran, I.R. of	429	208	572	885	1,025	6,847	7,600	7,603	10,098	9,327	11,682	8,188	1,591	5,376	....	....
Iraq	433	462	553	720	1,287	2,673	2,330	3,960	5,759	....	....	....	....	....	....	....
Israel	436	449	679	1,126	1,504	980	1,010	1,182	1,293	2,056	2,369	2,670	3,046	3,518	3,523	3,158
Jordan	439	256	233	250	252	283	420	434	558	708	914	932	971	839	825	562
Kuwait	443	203	265	335	415	1,143	1,414	1,660	2,461	2,008	2,268	3,169	3,583	5,449	5,048	4,772
Lebanon	446	385	504	622	714	1,367	1,349	1,444	1,614	1,731	1,485	1,568	1,626	2,687	2,140	1,008
Libya	672	1,590	2,455	2,694	1,763	2,953	1,875	2,759	4,026	3,236	4,902	10,372	7,860	6,525	5,110	3,835
Oman	449	12	23	34	39	77	139	191	242	202	322	463	649	801	738	928
Qatar	453	37	42	56	63	59	89	118	140	171	228	286	339	368	395	414
Saudi Arabia	456	662	1,331	2,303	3,214	11,667	19,920	23,261	24,725	ⅼ14,896	14,790	18,536	27,855	26,948	26,224	25,409
Syrian Arab Rep.	463	55	81	125	342	409	627	280	427	321	470	293	280	209	79	303
United Arab Emirates	466	....	....	....	76	370	844	1,660	679	643	1,107	1,600	2,775	2,037	2,008	2,362
Yemen Arab Rep.	473	....	....	....	105	162	288	620	1,021	1,120	1,084	1,006	826	502	350	325
Yemen, P.D. Rep.	459	59	59	62	63	55	47	71	83	145	161	185	220	261	270	255
Yemen, Republic of	474	....	....	....	....	....	....	....	....	....	....	....	....	....	....	....

ⅼ See country notes in the monthly *IFS*

Total Reserves

(with Gold at SDR 35 per ounce)   1 s

End of Period

1985	1986	1987	1988	1989	1990	1991	1992	1993	1994	1995	1996	1997	1998	1999		
67,708	81,331	99,757	112,210	121,736	146,115	177,725	190,363	222,400	263,722	291,527	344,231	384,397	413,579	481,244	Asia *	505
303	245	231	228	219	221	198									Afghanistan, Islamic State of	512
308	337	597	780	384	445	897	1,330	1,758	2,153	1,577	1,279	1,176	1,357	1,172	Bangladesh	513
46	50	53	70	75	60	69	57		79	84	128	134	177	200	Bhutan	514
12,032	9,808	11,938	14,223	14,111	21,241	30,977	I 15,441	16,743	36,691	51,152	74,883	106,253	106,400	115,364	China, P.R.: Mainland I	924
					17,277	20,147	25,589	31,298	33,739	37,270	44,376	68,784	63,669	70,119	China, P.R.: Hong Kong	532
120	140	93	173	161	183	190	230	196	187	235	297	267	274	312	Fiji	819
6,174	5,594	4,915	4,006	3,302	1,443	2,930	4,584	7,826	13,907	12,504	14,474	18,744	19,820	24,203	India	534
4,637	3,421	4,051	3,860	4,259	5,352	6,581	7,708	8,308	8,419	9,330	12,801	12,402	16,240	19,376	Indonesia	536
2,623	2,725	2,537	9,186	11,588	10,409	9,590	12,463	14,738	17,574	21,995	23,682	15,107	36,928	53,922	Korea	542
					1	20e	29e	46e	42e	62	115	83	83	74	Lao People's Democratic Rep.	544
4,554	5,009	5,323	4,932	6,005	6,938	7,692	12,613	19,922	17,498	16,077	18,867	15,489	18,235	22,328	Malaysia	548
4	6	6	16	19	17	16	21	19	21	32	53	73	84	93	Maldives	556
											62				Micronesia, Fed. States of	868
							13	44	57	82	80	133	68	99	Mongolia	948
40	36	28	66	209	229	189	213	229	298	386	167	193	232	202	Myanmar	518
56	76	131	169	166	213	283	345	471	480	400	403	469	542	620	Nepal	558
802	647	422	361	464	276	437	689	943	2,078	1,238	453	958	803	1,174	Pakistan	564
405	350	310	295	295	286	228	176	105	68	176	408	271	139	152	Papua New Guinea	853
612	1,492	780	845	1,164	751	2,387	3,300	3,517	4,223	4,412	7,138	5,560	6,742	9,856	Philippines	566
13	19	26	37	42	49	47	44	37	35	37	42	48	44	50	Samoa	862
11,695	10,578	10,733	12,687	15,481	19,505	23,862	29,007	35,208	39,851	46,213	53,442	52,836	53,215	55,987	Singapore	576
32e	24	26	29	20	12	6	17	15	12	11	23	27	35	37	Solomon Islands	813
413	290	199	167	188	299	483	679	1,188	1,404	1,407	1,366	1,502	1,408	1,194	Sri Lanka	524
2,081	2,380	2,911	4,617	7,327	9,439	12,333	14,893	17,904	20,179	24,293	26,326	19,490	20,559	24,905	Thailand	578
25	18	20	23	19	22	23	23	27	24	19	21	20	20	19	Tonga	866
10	18	28	30	27	26	28	31	33	30	32	31	28	32	30	Vanuatu	846
															*of which:	
20,710	38,055	54,367	55,385	56,193	51,393	58,082	60,333	61,319	63,806	61,229	61,699	62,362	64,636	77,851	Taiwan Province of China	528
7,707	8,316	8,006	10,013	14,931	15,640	16,147	16,006	26,137	31,289	58,320	62,505	72,792	72,717	79,047	Europe	170
								109	142	164					Albania	914
							1	10	22	68	109	171	225	234	Armenia	911
							—	—	1	81					Azerbaijan	912
							121	449	962	1,275	1,609	1,882	2,000	2,204	Croatia	960
558	631	632	706	871	1,075	988	764	815	1,019	767	1,088	1,048	996	1,352	Cyprus	423
								2,827	4,282	9,382	8,659	7,251	8,918	9,346	Czech Republic	935
911	1,044	1,102	1,307	1,768	862	2,327	I 930								Czechoslovakia I	934
							127	281	304	390	443	562	576	622	Estonia	939
2,042	1,964	1,209	1,146	1,001	762	2,759	3,222	4,882	4,618	8,059	6,763	6,235	6,622	7,985	Hungary	944
								355	608	811	963	1,321	1,099	1,141	Kazakhstan	916
													119	170	Kyrgyz Republic	917
								323	382	349				621	Latvia	941
							39	262	366	516	544	755	1,007	877	Lithuania	946
								78	104	175	169	193	221	317	Macedonia, FYR	962
915	953	1,013	1,030	1,039	1,012	936	927	995	1,271	1,081	1,128		1,181	1,370	Malta	181
									123	173	217	271	102	135	Moldova	921
809	587	1,070	1,544	1,778	3,174	2,556	2,998	2,996	4,018	9,955	12,426	15,156	18,888	17,991	Poland	964
315	590	1,036	630	1,491	446	564	681	808	1,521	1,157	1,561	2,925	2,149	2,074	Romania	968
								4,605	3,021	10,005	8,314	10,127	6,056	6,628	Russia	922
								348	1,204	2,308	2,423	2,439	2,085	2,501	Slovak Republic	936
						78	520	574	1,027	1,225	1,598	2,457	2,584	2,308	Slovenia	961
1,096	1,288	1,386	1,876	3,770	4,396	3,742	4,621	4,707	5,045	8,501	11,561	13,960	13,972	17,136	Turkey	186
							341	118	447	708	1,364	1,737	545	768	Ukraine	926
1,062	1,259	557	1,774	3,214	3,914	1,942									Yugoslavia, SFR	188
58,573	47,859	45,841	41,588	42,230	37,955	41,775	44,149	47,207	46,228	50,642	61,261	73,915	72,827	78,016	Middle East	405
1,516	1,223	815	935	804	873	1,064	1,022	953	806	866	922	962	772	1,003	Bahrain	419
806	763	1,057	1,024	1,242	1,971	3,808	7,947	9,480	9,319	10,971	12,184	13,919	12,957	10,638	Egypt	469
															Iran, I.R. of	429
															Iraq	433
3,386	3,845	4,178	3,020	4,050	4,440	4,404	3,729	4,647	4,653	5,462	7,938	15,069	16,104	16,470	Israel	436
422	395	334	107	384	623	605	586	1,220	1,187	1,355	1,251	1,659	1,272	1,933	Jordan	439
5,069	4,586	3,008	1,518	2,449	1,461	2,472	3,832	3,157	2,487	2,484	2,533	2,647	2,892	3,603	Kuwait	443
1,300	722	582	1,049	1,037	787	1,214	1,411	1,968	2,983	3,372	4,448	4,752	4,979	5,988	Lebanon	446
5,501	4,993	4,241	3,337	3,423	4,230	4,107	4,622						5,325	5,258	Libya	672
1,003	801	998	793	1,041	1,186	1,173	1,453	671	681	776	976	1,158	766	1,171	Oman	449
425	480	440	383	437	473	496	527	535	479						Qatar	453
22,924	15,141	16,151	15,434	12,905	8,362	8,322	4,477	5,569	5,214	5,961	I 10,120	11,187	10,260	12,545	Saudi Arabia	456
105	147	186	173												Syrian Arab Rep.	463
2,946	2,784	3,359	3,323	3,419	3,250	3,779	4,182	4,472	4,589	5,054	5,630	6,233	6,474	7,792	United Arab Emirates	466
270	353	380	212	212											Yemen Arab Rep.	473
171	114	70	61												Yemen, P.D. Rep.	459
					299	477	235	108	176	418	709	893	709		Yemen, Republic of	474

I See country notes in the monthly IFS

Total Reserves

(with Gold at SDR 35 per ounce)		1970	1971	1972	1973	1974	1975	1976	1977	1978	1979	1980	1981	1982	1983	1984
																Millions of SDRs:
Western Hemisphere	205	5,473	5,946	9,089	11,957	15,033	16,113	20,492	23,466	27,296	32,415	31,611	33,992	25,563	27,980	41,142
Antigua and Barbuda	311	....	....	....	....	....	6	8	4	5	9	6	6	8	9	16
Argentina	213	672	267	428	1,092	1,074	386	1,383	2,743	3,962	7,280	5,421	2,961	2,425	1,273	1,421
Aruba	314	....	....	....	....	....									....	....
Bahamas, The	313	22	27	34	36	41	46	41	I 56	45	59	72	86	103	117	164
Barbados	316	17	17	26	27	32	34	24	30	46	50	62	87	110	118	135
Belize	339	....	....	....	....	....		5	7	11	8	10	9	9	9	6
Bolivia	218	46	50	55	60	158	134	145	195	153	159	110	115	172	185	289
Brazil	223	1,187	1,609	3,853	5,318	4,306	3,447	5,631	5,974	9,134	6,866	4,589	5,750	3,566	4,179	11,792
Chile	228	389	204	137	149	84	93	395	399	885	1,525	2,508	2,820	1,705	1,999	2,403
Colombia	233	206	187	300	443	367	445	997	1,499	1,885	2,999	3,885	4,191	3,634	1,963	1,439
Costa Rica	238	16	27	39	42	36	44	84	159	152	93	117	114	207	300	414
Dominica	321	....	....	....	....	....	—	1	2	1	7	4	3	4	1	5
Dominican Republic	243	32	52	54	73	74	99	109	152	122	185	163	198	120	166	259
Ecuador	248	74	53	124	188	274	230	424	527	502	563	809	558	290	630	638
El Salvador	253	63	60	76	51	80	108	177	191	223	126	79	80	116	169	186
Grenada	328	5	5	5	4	4	I 4	7	6	7	9	10	14	8	14	15
Guatemala	258	78	86	124	176	165	260	440	568	587	547	367	147	120	219	298
Guyana	336	20	24	34	12	51	86	23	19	45	13	10	6	10	6	6
Haiti	263	4	10	17	14	16	11	24	28	30	42	13	21	4	9	14
Honduras	268	20	20	32	35	36	83	113	148	142	159	118	87	102	109	131
Jamaica	343	139	165	147	106	156	107	28	40	45	49	82	73	99	60	99
Mexico	273	744	877	1,072	1,124	1,139	1,310	1,079	1,419	1,480	1,642	2,393	3,579	828	3,818	7,504
Netherlands Antilles	353	45	53	65	61	69	80	99	102	71	75	93	135	189	176	140
Nicaragua	278	49	54	74	97	86	104	126	123	40	112	51	96	156	171	....
Panama	283	16	19	40	35	32	29	68	58	115	93	95	103	92	197	220
Paraguay	288	18	19	29	47	71	98	136	221	345	464	599	693	671	651	681
Peru	293	I 336	390	446	471	791	399	284	329	334	1,195	1,601	1,079	1,272	1,353	1,712
St. Kitts and Nevis	361	....	....	....	....	....							3	3	3	6
St. Lucia	362	....	....	....	....	....	3	4	5	5	6	6	7	7	8	13
St. Vincent & Grenadines	364	....	....	....	....	....		4	4	4	7	6	8	4	5	13
Suriname	366	36	39	43	52	60	83	100	83	104	131	150	180	161	58	27
Trinidad and Tobago	369	43	64	54	39	319	642	872	1,221	1,387	1,626	2,182	2,878	2,794	2,012	1,386
Uruguay	298	175	167	187	207	190	174	276	391	398	I 361	421	488	205	289	229
Venezuela, Rep. Bol.	299	1,021	1,401	1,595	1,999	5,320	7,569	7,384	6,764	5,031	5,958	5,579	7,415	6,365	7,701	9,482

Memorandum Items

		1970	1971	1972	1973	1974	1975	1976	1977	1978	1979	1980	1981	1982	1983	1984
Oil Exporting Countries	999	4,917	7,676	9,956	11,982	38,303	48,227	56,074	62,050	46,116	56,196	69,317	69,331	67,108	67,144	69,550
Non-Oil Developing Countries	201	15,731	16,257	23,339	29,088	29,950	29,772	40,895	50,638	59,037	66,387	70,878	78,800	80,087	93,866	116,407

(with Gold at SDR 35 per ounce)																*Millions of SDRs:*
All Countries	010	93	123	147	153	180	194	222	265	282	306	355	363	361	396	440

(with Gold at market prices)																*Millions of SDRs:*
All Countries	010	95,756	128,462	171,967	212,127	299,690	280,844	304,358	368,372	425,540	640,888	763,159	656,411	722,552	709,101	706,500

1985	1986	1987	1988	1989	1990	1991	1992	1993	1994	1995	1996	1997	1998	1999	(with Gold at SDR 35 per ounce)	
End of Period																
37,541	27,292	26,958	23,085	25,428	34,434	46,665	65,033	79,868	72,403	87,903	109,221	126,328	114,753	112,564	Western Hemisphere	205
15	23	18	21	21	19	23	37	28	31	40	33	38	42	51	Antigua and Barbuda	311
I3,133	2,375	1,293	2,652	1,267	3,376	4,342	7,418	10,193	9,967	9,765	12,743	16,555	17,592	19,139	Argentina	213
....	64	59	71	70	72	87	107	135	125	125	134	131	161	164	Aruba	314
166	189	120	128	112	111	127	113	125	121	121	119	168	246	299	Bahamas, The	313
127	124	103	101	84	83	61	102	110	134	147	201	196	180	....	Barbados	316
13	22	26	38	46	49	37	39	28	24	25	41	44	31	52	Belize	339
213	165	100	110	187	149	106	163	194	340	475	697	838	661	701	Bolivia	218
9,763	I4,829	4,525	5,276	5,838	5,390	5,687	16,457	22,383	25,523	33,600	40,689	37,776	30,401	25,463	Brazil	223
2,284	1,985	1,829	2,412	2,822	4,331	4,988	6,733	7,084	9,030	9,577	10,381	12,891	11,167	10,539	Chile	228
1,517	2,274	2,199	2,452	2,773	3,275	4,598	5,651	5,784	5,560	5,695	6,920	7,355	6,230	5,915	Colombia	233
463	430	347	497	565	366	644	742	747	613	705	696	935	755	1,064	Costa Rica	238
3	8	13	10	9	10	12	15	14	11	15	16	18	20	23	Dominica	321
310	308	129	189	125	44	310	364	475	173	247	244	290	357	503	Dominican Republic	243
668	541	361	310	426	605	662	647	1,019	1,278	1,109	1,307	1,566	1,165	1,211	Ecuador	248
180	155	148	137	219	308	217	323	407	461	527	668	986	1,162	1,476	El Salvador	253
19	17	16	13	12	12	12	19	20	21	25	....	....	33	....	Grenada	328
292	314	221	168	252	205	572	561	639	599	480	612	831	956	874	Guatemala	258
6	7	6	3	10	20	87	137	180	169	181	229	234	196	195	Guyana	336
6	14	13	10	10	3	13	....	....	22	72	76	58	....	....	Haiti	263
97	92	75	38	17	29	74	144	71	118	177	174	431	582	917	Honduras	268
147	80	123	109	82	118e	74	236	304	504	458	612	506	504	404	Jamaica	343
4,549	4,725	8,875	4,012	4,852	6,965	12,424	13,800	18,298	4,316	11,351	13,523	21,350	22,592	23,162	Mexico	273
179	215	172	215	177	170	143	179	190	142	156	151	178	195	212	Netherlands Antilles	353
....	....	....	....	....	....	....	....	40	97	92	138	281	249	372	Nicaragua	278
89	139	55	54	91	241	349	367	435	482	526	603	851	678	600	Panama	283
487	366	352	242	330	466	674	410	461	707	736	731	632	615	721	Paraguay	288
1,745	1,225	508	440	684	808	1,772	2,136	2,527	4,829	5,570	7,395	8,179	6,832	6,399	Peru	293
7	8	7	8	12	11	12	19	21	22	23	23	27	33	36	St. Kitts and Nevis	361
12	21	22	24	29	31	34	40	44	40	42	39	45	50	54	St. Lucia	362
13	21	14	16	17	19	16	24	23	21	20	21	23	28	31	St. Vincent & Grenadines	364
23	19	13	11	9	17	3	14	15	29	93	72	88	80	....	Suriname	366
1,029	390	134	96	189	348	239	127	152	243	243	380	526	558	691	Trinidad and Tobago	369
250	485	465	487	473	452	314	441	612	723	834	931	1,215	1,535	1,578	Uruguay	298
9,733	5,664	4,604	2,698	3,526	6,250	7,858	7,356	7,111	5,927	4,628	8,599	11,057	8,807	9,287	Venezuela, Rep. Bol.	299
															Memorandum Items	
69,270	51,843	49,091	42,938	44,308	43,875	48,883	46,144	46,421	44,333	44,581	61,090	71,798	70,650	79,449	Oil Exporting Countries	999
111,096	120,509	139,171	151,937	169,630	202,497	248,239	282,452	343,221	385,995	461,450	537,847	617,088	631,979	704,070	Non-Oil Developing Countries	201
End of Period															(with Gold at SDR 35 per ounce)	
438	452	541	576	624	688	726	753	830	891	1,020	1,174	1,292	1,277	1,363	All Countries	010
End of Period															(with Gold at market prices)	
688,974	723,480	831,014	831,852	878,792	890,382	....	....	....	....	....	....	....	....	....	All Countries	010

		1970	1971	1972	1973	1974	1975	1976	1977	1978	1979	1980	1981	1982	1983	1984
															Percent Change over Previous Year	
Industrial Countries																
United States	111	6.9	9.3	3.8	8.0	6.1	6.6	5.6	9.8	11.4	6.6	6.0	3.5	6.7	5.5	7.4
Canada	156	5.5	15.2	15.5	16.1	14.1	15.4	9.3	12.1	11.8	8.6	10.1	2.3	4.4	1.4	1.9
Australia	193	−.5	18.5	19.9	26.2	−12.2	28.9	12.0	5.1	−1.1	8.9	9.8	11.0	8.8	12.7	10.9
Japan	158	16.6	14.5	29.0	34.3	16.1	4.0	8.6	8.4	14.9	7.5	6.4	2.7	6.2	5.4	8.5
New Zealand	196	13.8	.3	64.8	47.2	4.9	−18.9	5.0	9.0	20.7	8.6	−10.9	14.1	7.8	11.8	7.8
Euro Area																
Austria	122	6.2	12.0	14.9	2.0	10.1	16.9	4.5	4.4	15.4	1.9	7.2	6.4	3.8	6.5	2.2
Belgium	124	2.9	7.2	14.1	12.5	4.3	6.6	6.6	8.8	7.4	3.2	Ⅰ1.1	1.8	—	3.4	.6
Finland	172	3.7	11.1	15.5	11.1	17.3	15.8	1.0	9.8	20.8	60.4	34.6	−2.2	13.8	26.2	40.7
France	132	4.6	10.5	31.7	7.3	13.2	−21.6	7.5	8.9	Ⅰ12.2	7.1	14.9	4.7	18.1	5.7	10.9
Germany	134	21.7	15.1	26.3	7.4	−1.2	2.9	10.2	7.9	13.1	5.2	−3.7	−1.6	5.3	5.6	3.8
Ireland	178	15.6	26.9	12.4	24.7	24.6	16.4	17.1	13.8	25.4	10.2	15.9	−3.2	9.0	11.0	7.8
Italy	136	13.9	17.0	12.1	15.6	17.7	40.3	20.4	19.3	24.7	14.1	12.8	12.3	15.2	16.4	14.4
Luxembourg	137	....	....	....	....	....	....	....	....	....	....	....	....	....	....	....
Netherlands	138	5.5	4.9	9.1	4.8	7.9	12.8	9.1	9.0	7.9	7.8	8.3	1.7	7.6	11.9	5.9
Portugal	182	10.6	14.4	19.2	12.9	34.4	37.8	Ⅰ7.9	5.5	15.1	Ⅰ31.6	20.8	36.5	29.5	13.4	4.5
Denmark	128	−8.4	3.8	5.2	2.2	5.2	38.9	4.2	−12.7	7.7	13.5	4.4	8.8	2.5	7.2	10.1
Greece	174	7.0	20.1	19.8	19.2	21.3	21.9	20.5	21.4	20.7	11.3	27.8	44.9	27.9	9.6	30.5
Iceland	176	19.9	14.8	20.7	46.6	27.6	34.6	36.3	51.7	50.5	52.2	68.0	65.6	55.4	78.4	38.2
Norway	142	3.0	11.6	4.7	6.6	13.8	17.4	Ⅰ12.0	12.0	13.0	9.0	8.6	−.6	6.6	4.1	15.8
Sweden	144	3.4	12.0	9.8	9.6	34.9	−.7	10.7	10.0	13.7	37.3	−9.6	11.7	6.7	2.1	6.5
Switzerland	146	12.7	18.5	7.9	3.8	3.4	2.3	7.7	3.6	17.4	−7.8	1.4	−4.2	6.7	.8	3.9
United Kingdom	112	11.6	−5.1	21.2	31.5	4.1	10.1	19.9	5.3	9.8	9.8	−2.9	3.8	4.3	2.8	−10.9
Developing Countries																
Africa																
Algeria	612	12.9	23.6	20.5	29.8	13.8	28.5	37.0	17.6	31.0	24.7	20.6	12.3	4.1	20.6	14.7
Angola	614	....	....	....	....	....	....	....	....	....	....	....	....	....	....	....
Benin	638	15.0	12.5	17.8	2.8	2.6	30.4	17.7	1.8	−4.4	43.6	24.9	61.8	2.7	−20.2	23.1
Botswana	616	....	....	....	....	....	....		11.0	−2.1	60.4	9.4	−15.3	−12.0	4.5	17.0
Burkina Faso	748	2.5	−1.4	7.5	21.5	18.4	31.1	13.4	17.7	−3.1	30.8	8.9	21.8	8.7	46.8	36.4
Burundi	618	15.1	16.2	5.4	7.5	19.9	−2.4	68.2	38.7	17.3	−4.8	10.7	37.7	−14.1	27.4	7.8
Cameroon	622	6.7	4.6	2.5	17.6	22.0	4.0	18.4	30.3	16.4	18.7	15.7	33.4	5.6	28.8	−1.8
Cape Verde	624	....	....	....	....	....	....	....	41.1	14.4	12.9	26.3	10.9	26.4	22.6	6.2
Central African Rep.	626	7.6	−1.9	12.4	3.6	26.4	3.9	17.9	23.8	19.5	32.3	36.6	30.7	−2.0	11.5	7.1
Chad	628	10.1	12.7	11.8	−1.4	32.2	28.2	18.9	9.5	14.7	35.9	−13.0	9.4	7.9	22.5	53.6
Comoros	632	....	....	....	....	....	....	....	....	....	....	....	....	....	11.0	−12.6
Congo, Dem. Rep. of	636	15.7	−13.0	26.0	17.4	22.2	40.5	82.5	29.0	56.1	−18.2	114.1	59.3	91.5	1,500.1	....
Congo, Rep. of	634	15.7	10.1	17.2	12.9	30.9	23.9	7.3	5.3	1.4	21.2	30.4	19.1	39.2	4.1	−84.2
Côte d'Ivoire	662	20.3	11.5	13.0	10.2	40.0	13.5	21.5	38.8	32.0	4.1	1.1	9.7	−6.1	7.5	−1.1
Djibouti	611	....	....	....	....	....	....	....	....	....	....	....	....	....	....	20.0
Equatorial Guinea	642	....	....	....	....	....	....	....	....	....	....	....	....	....	....	....
Ethiopia	644	1.0	−5.7	11.2	20.1	27.6	38.6	20.2	−.4	9.6	10.2	12.1	14.7	8.8	—	19.9
Gabon	646	20.5	21.2	14.1	29.4	84.6	29.0	64.8	1.7	−12.7	6.1	18.8	7.1	9.0	9.4	18.2
Gambia, The	648	18.8	4.1	9.4	71.9	−1.2	8.1	19.1	−21.0	Ⅰ52.2	18.0	10.7	36.6	17.6	34.8	Ⅰ−2.3
Ghana	652	14.9	3.2	48.0	24.2	35.8	48.0	41.8	61.9	84.5	18.1	30.7	55.4	14.4	43.4	49.1
Guinea	656	....	....	....	....	....	....	....	....	....	....	....	....	....	....	....
Guinea-Bissau	654	....	....	....	....	....	....	....	....	....	....	....	....	....	....	....
Kenya	664	11.3	−8.4	10.6	10.4	28.2	−9.8	24.0	61.6	7.2	24.8	2.2	4.1	25.7	−2.2	11.4
Lesotho	666	....	....	....	....	....	....	....	....	....	....	....	5.9	8.2	57.5	17.6
Liberia	668	....	....	....	....	....	5.9	17.8	19.7	71.6	−4.0	Ⅰ35.6	−3.6	39.6	25.1	20.9
Madagascar	674	19.1	−1.3	15.2	5.6	18.2	6.8	14.1	12.1	33.1	Ⅰ−2.7	35.1	34.2	−1.2	−4.8	9.2
Malawi	676	9.0	12.9	15.9	109.5	30.2	−11.3	−34.1	84.0	−34.5	−7.5	38.3	34.7	18.1	5.7	76.3
Mali	678	18.2	8.5	9.8	7.3	32.7	Ⅰ25.6	20.3	21.8	12.0	24.3	6.4	.7	10.0	11.4	Ⅰ26.8
Mauritania	682	21.8	1.1	37.9	19.1	132.6	−9.8	8.7	13.5	8.4	34.1	6.7	32.1	−1.0	−2.8	.5
Mauritius	684	29.6	.6	49.2	18.9	84.1	37.4	18.5	18.5	17.5	−3.4	10.9	4.2	10.9	6.2	6.7
Morocco	686	8.0	10.8	18.7	14.7	20.8	15.0	21.7	15.5	15.4	16.5	5.2	13.5	6.9	13.3	11.5
Mozambique	688	....	....	....	....	....	....	....	....	....	....	....	....	....	....	....
Namibia	728	....	....	....	....	....	....	....	....	....	....	....	....	....	....	....
Niger	692	2.2	25.7	2.0	15.5	41.5	−4.5	40.6	21.4	53.9	13.2	16.1	18.1	1.4	−8.2	27.2
Nigeria	694	39.5	5.8	7.3	23.5	151.2	53.9	27.8	23.7	−3.4	16.2	68.8	−3.3	8.3	3.7	3.0
Rwanda	714	25.2	−2.5	11.7	29.4	31.5	1.6	30.8	13.6	2.2	43.9	−6.5	−12.7	3.9	11.4	6.1
São Tomé and Príncipe	716	....	....	....	....	....	....	....	....	....	....	....	....	....	....	....
Senegal	722	26.3	5.3	4.8	21.0	49.9	7.5	12.1	15.2	25.1	−8.5	21.4	38.3	24.3	−3.3	−1.0
Seychelles	718	....	....	36.9	12.9	5.0	18.0	33.3	27.4	15.1	32.0	69.1	−9.6	−5.2	6.9	−3.5
Sierra Leone	724	−10.2	8.7	15.4	23.5	12.2	8.3	16.2	16.4	62.5	53.4	−7.5	.8	88.4	25.1	42.2
Somalia	726	40.0	−34.2	40.0	16.0	23.1	27.7	19.5	33.2	40.2	24.3	31.6	27.2	−14.9	2.4	61.6
South Africa	199	8.7	5.0	7.9	19.2	16.4	14.8	5.7	7.2	11.9	14.8	62.7	16.9	−11.4	14.0	15.6
Sudan	732	10.4	8.0	9.8	27.8	37.0	18.7	21.6	62.0	32.0	32.9	12.6	61.3	30.6	Ⅰ10.0	40.4
Swaziland	734	....	....	....	....	....	....	113.1	148.7	38.5	−4.6	4.1	23.9	−14.1	11.7	33.4
Tanzania	738	32.6	21.7	21.9	.7	25.5	15.9	18.7	16.8	21.2	39.0	26.8	28.3	20.9	3.1	30.1
Togo	742	−.2	22.5	−2.7	12.7	40.4	28.1	62.6	5.1	29.9	4.3	17.8	82.5	22.5	10.5	26.4
Tunisia	744	3.1	31.1	13.6	18.4	30.0	14.6	6.8	4.7	17.4	9.7	12.2	26.3	23.1	17.6	10.3
Uganda	746	17.9	.5	12.5	27.2	33.0	57.4	43.3	14.4	48.7	65.0	36.8	28.3	19.1	60.2	116.1
Zambia	754	48.0	−34.9	18.5	31.2	−7.6	42.9	26.6	−1.4	5.2	4.8	13.9	16.5	15.6	14.0	17.7
Zimbabwe	698	....	....	....	....	....	....	23.4	11.6	−5.3	16.4	34.9	32.8	19.4	4.8	10.3
Asia																
Afghanistan, Islamic State of	512	12.3	8.6	8.7	5.3	14.0	17.2	22.1	33.5	16.0	Ⅰ21.6	17.6	14.5	Ⅰ16.4	16.0	9.1
Bangladesh	513	....	....	....	....	25.9	−2.4	2.5	29.5	27.9	16.1	18.7	9.7	Ⅰ10.6	34.1	35.2
Bhutan	514	....	....	....	....	....	....	....	....	....	....	....	....	....	....	117.3
Cambodia	522	....	....	....	....	....	....	....	....	....	....	....	....	....	....	....
China, P.R.: Mainland	924	....	....	....	....	....	....	....	....	....	....	....	....	....	....	....
Fiji	819	10.7	18.2	22.0	51.1	29.0	30.6	−14.1	3.6	13.5	12.4	−8.0	15.3	6.9	6.5	15.7
India	534	10.5	11.2	8.7	22.5	3.5	5.4	16.9	21.1	20.5	21.0	15.2	10.5	18.0	13.0	16.8
Indonesia	536	....	....	....	....	....	....	....	....	....	....	....	....	....	....	....
Korea	542	38.8	−3.8	48.3	46.0	24.2	39.0	33.5	44.1	35.3	23.8	−6.5	−13.6	36.5	7.1	10.9
Lao People's Democratic Rep.	544	....	....	....	....	....	....	....	....	....	....	....	....	....	....	3.7
Malaysia	548	9.4	7.9	30.7	35.6	13.5	2.5	18.7	15.7	15.3	15.6	18.1	10.3	16.7	4.3	3.7
Maldives	556	....	....	....	....	....	....	....	−6.5	−29.8	67.3	58.3	Ⅰ6.9	−9.2	21.5	32.6
Mongolia	948	....	....	....	....	....	....	....	....	....	....	....	....	....	....	....
Myanmar	518	Ⅰ−8.9	3.4	23.9	26.9	22.8	25.3	31.8	−4.5	12.1	19.8	11.6	20.2	−5.2	11.0	14.2
Nepal	558	Ⅰ6.1	8.1	13.7	28.9	4.2	9.3	28.9	8.7	17.5	12.7	10.3	14.4	24.7	15.7	16.0
Pakistan	564	11.4	10.9	17.4	12.0	.7	9.8	19.8	22.7	17.6	26.7	16.7	8.2	17.7	13.8	16.4

Percent Change over Previous Year

1985	1986	1987	1988	1989	1990	1991	1992	1993	1994	1995	1996	1997	1998	1999		
															Industrial Countries	
10.0	15.0	4.6	5.5	4.1	9.0	3.5	8.8	9.1	8.6	4.4	4.7	8.0	6.0	20.0	United States	111
5.7	7.8	8.8	5.0	4.0	2.3	6.4	2.3	5.5	2.3	1.4	4.3	3.3	6.6	24.3	Canada	156
12.3	8.6	11.8	11.4	I.2	7.7	3.0	6.0	6.5	8.1	5.0	61.2	-20.3	5.3	-5.4	Australia	193
3.8	8.1	8.7	13.0	12.9	7.4	-1.4	-3.8	5.8	2.9	7.8	8.5	7.3	3.8	39.1	Japan	158
11.6	-12.9	21.3	I25.2	-2.1	-.5	-2.0	2.2	2.9	11.6	7.1	-2.7	4.9	6.3	76.1	New Zealand	196
															Euro Area	
1.4	7.2	-2.7	1.2	14.1	.1	1.9	10.3	8.1	4.5	-1.0	6.9	-.7	....	....	Austria	122
-1.2	5.0	2.5	1.2	2.9	-2.8	1.6	-.5	2.9	-6.7	9.2	3.7	2.3	56.2	....	Belgium	124
12.3	-2.0	48.4	18.9	23.5	-17.3	11.0	5.1	.6	51.1	1.6	-32.8	-7.7	-1.8	....	Finland	172
15.9	2.1	11.6	-.8	.3	-3.2	-2.6	-12.7	-3.9	.1	8.7	2.2	3.0	22.4	....	France	132
3.3	6.3	9.2	10.7	6.1	12.1	5.3	14.5	-1.3	-1.6	2.0	4.8	-.9	1.1	....	Germany	134
7.8	3.4	10.6	3.1	4.8	10.7	-8.7	-8.2	20.5	4.3	26.6	1.1	18.9	....	....	Ireland	178
17.2	8.0	9.3	8.9	12.0	6.5	6.7	4.0	-8.9	-5.0	-6.3	2.4	7.4	-29.0	....	Italy	136
....	10.6	11.2	6.8	—	18.2	-2.8	-5.3	70.0	—	-11.5	17.1	-.2	....	....	Luxembourg	137
3.9	3.6	9.9	11.3	15.5	3.2	-13.8	30.1	7.4	6.0	-12.3	-4.4	10.2	5.4	....	Netherlands	138
5.5	14.2	25.8	13.1	91.4	8.3	22.5	10.6	9.0	-58.8	-2.5	11.2	-1.3	.6	....	Portugal	182
150.7	-33.7	I-24.2	4.3	-4.1	22.3	-2.8	-12.3	64.2	.7	13.5	33.3	31.1	-22.6	98.8	Denmark	128
6.2	18.6	I23.1	6.4	9.1	23.0	11.5	10.7	8.4	39.6	3.9	14.1	13.4	30.5	21.4	Greece	174
23.5	25.1	6.6	15.8	23.4	-10.4	2.6	3.2	-8.9	3.0	-18.1	26.4	11.4	2.2	....	Iceland	176
7.1	-1.2	7.5	-2.5	5.8	-1.0	7.7	4.9	10.7	3.3	5.2	53.0	-11.5	-11.0	50.2	Norway	142
3.0	25.4	4.7	18.3	10.7	8.2	-7.7	24.2	47.7	22.4	-14.9	-33.1	-25.8	3.8	17.0	Sweden	144
-1.6	4.9	5.8	-18.8	-3.9	2.7	-2.6	10.1	-1.3	.6	-2.4	5.1	-2.3	7.7	17.0	Switzerland	146
6.4	I9.8	7.2	9.8	8.5	1.2	1.0	6.0	6.8	5.3	7.0	3.5	7.1	3.3	17.0	United Kingdom	112
															Developing Countries	
															Africa	
12.5	15.7	12.4	8.9	12.1	10.4	16.2	I22.5	27.6	-5.3	7.6	19.9	16.6	13.1	11.4	Algeria	612
....	....	....	....	....	....	....	....	....	....	....	3,397.1	92.3	49.6	422.6	Angola	614
-18.2	18.6	-17.5	20.1	79.6	59.7	24.6	22.6	-12.9	1.4	-26.1	9.2	19.9	-4.4	75.7	Benin	638
5.3	43.9	20.2	33.4	38.6	33.5	100.3	-17.2	-6.7	-.9	3.5	11.8	26.2	23.6	14.2	Botswana	616
-9.7	41.6	18.1	9.6	-14.7	1.3	20.9	6.1	15.4	-.8	24.0	4.7	23.5	-3.6	-14.1	Burkina Faso	748
24.5	1.7	.1	-3.4	6.1	4.7	15.7	11.1	4.9	26.5	-.8	19.1	1.9	2.7	35.6	Burundi	618
14.7	17.8	-7.1	I-2.6	6.6	-8.8	-.7	-15.3	-23.0	39.3	-21.0	28.3	40.2	10.2	8.2	Cameroon	622
15.3	16.1	1.6	5.7	6.2	8.0	8.8	31.4	43.4	-38.9	I22.7	-6.3	.5	9.3	6.7	Cape Verde	624
.9	12.4	-.3	I-1.1	9.8	.7	—	1.5	19.8	84.2	4.5	7.7	-12.4	-20.2	7.7	Central African Rep.	626
3.1	-.9	10.2	I-10.0	14.4	-7.8	2.9	-5.0	-20.2	23.5	58.2	31.5	-4.2	-10.2	-6.3	Chad	628
11.7	34.1	41.4	-21.6	35.2	-16.6	-8.5	2.2	40.3	14.3	10.0	36.3	-12.4	I-10.8	19.1	Comoros	632
27.7	60.6	100.8	116.9	79.1	186.5	2,331.5	4,342.5	2,608.4	3,264.5	650.3	....	....	....	....	Congo, Dem. Rep. of	636
11.7	1.8	10.4	I-6.8	-1.9	34.8	-19.3	15.8	-4.3	35.4	8.3	8.6	11.6	-20.7	34.2	Congo, Rep. of	634
25.9	4.5	1.7	-13.8	-21.8	6.3	2.9	-11.2	9.1	56.3	11.6	6.7	11.8	19.1	-7.7	Côte d'Ivoire	662
-3.1	10.5	17.2	-.7	-3.7	10.2	.2	23.1	-7.7	5.5	-12.6	-3.7	-2.1	-2.1	....	Djibouti	611
....	57.2	-22.9	I-44.9	70.6	-68.8	10.4	60.7	-20.4	78.0	99.1	14.6	9.8	-19.9	95.3	Equatorial Guinea	642
4.4	24.7	-1.6	18.8	13.9	14.6	27.5	19.1	4.9	10.3	12.6	-16.6	8.8	-12.3	-10.6	Ethiopia	644
-7.8	-11.4	5.6	I8.4	15.8	9.1	28.1	-28.1	-8.2	129.4	-4.2	28.8	1.7	-8.5	-7.9	Gabon	646
80.6	-1.9	19.3	24.2	27.8	6.4	36.0	3.3	11.2	-3.9	25.4	.5	26.8	7.2	14.5	Gambia, The	648
35.5	59.8	41.7	53.8	22.9	2.6	I.4	88.4	4.9	78.9	35.1	44.8	33.4	16.7	12.9	Ghana	652
....	....	....	....	....	....	....	11.8	18.9	-10.0	12.3	-1.4	27.2	....	....	Guinea	656
....	....	94.2	83.9	36.2	22.7	130.6	65.5	32.2	32.3	32.1	38.7	125.8	-13.3	34.5	Guinea-Bissau	654
15.1	39.6	19.4	2.1	19.7	21.8	15.7	53.5	52.5	22.8	31.0	8.2	2.1	-.4	6.0	Kenya	664
29.6	23.9	17.5	46.8	-6.0	-6.1	17.8	-22.0	21.9	6.6	25.2	7.9	13.1	38.5	33.3	Lesotho	666
40.0	39.1	28.4	19.4	30.2	....	....	1.2	27.2	5.4	31.3	17.9	8.0	1.9	4.4	Liberia	668
4.2	70.4	20.7	3.7	37.8	-9.4	55.3	20.8	-6.6	71.9	29.7	48.7	1.1	6.1	25.6	Madagascar	674
5.0	72.6	55.5	11.3	-9.7	-16.3	23.4	17.2	62.6	41.3	89.6	38.5	.2	38.6	32.1	Malawi	676
12.8	12.5	-3.2	10.6	14.5	1.4	31.6	-.2	9.1	-19.4	10.3	18.3	7.7	-5.6	12.7	Mali	678
39.3	-4.4	22.8	13.9	I21.7	-4.2	35.1	21.5	55.1	-3.7	-3.5	-49.5	-13.1	-7.5	4.5	Mauritania	682
18.2	20.5	26.8	24.1	19.7	18.8	133.8	-9.3	-6.8	-7.1	14.5	12.3	-19.8	7.1	7.8	Mauritius	684
7.5	23.7	5.4	15.7	17.7	I21.7	24.8	-8.0	8.6	6.2	5.2	7.6	I8.2	7.1	13.3	Morocco	686
17.5	19.3	59.0	54.5	I30.2	22.7	I34.8	73.3	75.8	66.4	31.7	26.6	16.1	-3.7	17.5	Mozambique	688
....	....	....	....	....	....	7.9	128.4	5.2	60.2	11.2	22.3	19.9	3.6	43.6	Namibia	728
19.7	9.3	2.3	21.9	1.2	3.0	-1.8	2.3	-4.3	-24.0	13.0	-5.9	-21.3	-35.7	32.0	Niger	692
7.1	6.5	18.8	41.9	37.3	28.0	42.0	I90.3	47.2	33.8	20.7	6.9	6.1	17.6	19.9	Nigeria	694
12.0	13.5	10.8	-10.2	-14.4	9.4	44.0	-3.4	27.9	9.3	38.7	22.6	11.4	-8.8	14.8	Rwanda	714
....	....	....	....	....	....	....	....	....	....	....	81.1	144.9	10.1	-10.3	São Tomé and Príncipe	716
5.9	16.3	5.4	-.6	24.7	-3.6	7.0	7.2	-30.3	49.2	4.1	-14.2	3.3	6.8	15.9	Senegal	722
12.1	-1.5	-.5	26.9	4.5	17.1	25.8	51.1	23.1	47.7	20.8	13.7	18.7	-49.3	9.4	Seychelles	718
53.6	105.7	69.0	77.8	74.3	66.4	63.4	18.9	3.7	25.4	12.1	I23.9	109.0	-20.4	39.0	Sierra Leone	724
54.4	65.8	83.0	68.1	192.7	....	....	....	....	....	....	....	....	....	....	Somalia	726
11.6	6.9	17.6	37.8	28.5	I13.0	22.8	.2	-8.5	17.8	29.7	13.7	11.4	5.3	21.0	South Africa	199
61.6	42.2	27.5	31.9	85.4	33.2	48.3	I153.6	64.6	39.9	76.7	81.8	34.3	29.4	35.1	Sudan	732
11.5	59.7	.3	-17.0	30.1	-1.9	-9.4	58.2	-11.3	17.6	2.5	-7.4	5.4	-8.4	11.6	Swaziland	734
21.3	40.6	41.4	31.5	19.4	42.3	13.0	60.3	I35.1	48.7	39.1	6.6	8.7	14.7	21.5	Tanzania	738
17.4	2.1	-3.0	-25.3	9.1	11.1	5.5	-17.9	-32.1	2.4	28.8	-12.6	.8	10.9	14.3	Togo	742
8.8	1.0	7.9	6.4	15.6	13.9	12.0	7.2	4.8	7.2	9.4	35.8	8.1	-11.8	30.5	Tunisia	744
186.9	163.7	....	....	....	....	....	....	23.4	48.1	13.7	11.6	9.1	20.0	15.1	Uganda	746
22.4	170.9	40.7	I58.7	65.0	78.3	101.4	....	....	48.0	-14.6	35.4	48.2	16.8	28.5	Zambia	754
20.5	15.6	6.9	26.0	21.7	25.6	32.2	13.3	52.0	23.6	2.5	65.9	37.8	29.9	60.9	Zimbabwe	698
															Asia	
10.6	13.7	57.1	35.1	39.8	41.1	50.6	....	....	....	....	....	....	....	....	Afghanistan, Islamic State of	512
13.8	7.1	45.8	10.9	11.5	4.5	-1.5	21.2	24.0	29.6	-9.3	8.7	9.4	13.4	12.7	Bangladesh	513
139.1	27.2	66.9	-11.2	79.9	82.2	26.4	-21.1	I53.7	-33.4	67.1	8.3	9.3	55.4	25.7	Bhutan	514
....	....	....	....	....	....	....	....	....	25.4	10.0	43.0	21.2	47.2	15.9	Cambodia	522
....	23.4	12.9	25.2	23.3	30.1	24.2	16.3	I36.2	31.0	20.6	29.5	17.0	2.8	7.6	China, P.R.: Mainland	924
2.5	13.2	-4.4	78.6	-23.7	11.3	11.7	19.7	-2.9	1.7	8.8	1.9	5.0	6.3	56.8	Fiji	819
23.5	16.3	18.2	16.3	18.7	13.7	18.7	8.4	21.7	21.7	12.6	9.5	11.2	12.4	11.2	India	534
17.9	21.6	10.5	-7.2	28.7	16.3	3.3	I19.7	8.3	25.2	17.8	35.8	38.3	59.7	25.3	Indonesia	536
1.7	16.2	48.9	30.2	31.8	7.7	18.2	10.9	27.5	9.2	16.3	-12.2	-12.5	-8.1	37.6	Korea	542
....	....	....	....	....	8.4	18.8	40.6	64.5	22.3	13.4	24.0	43.8	87.7	71.0	Lao People's Democratic Rep.	544
7.6	4.2	5.2	11.5	24.3	22.7	I21.8	11.6	36.2	24.7	I35.2	27.4	-38.6	66.4		Malaysia	548
35.0	14.2	2.5	22.3	19.1	24.4	22.0	34.5	19.0	14.2	1.6	17.7	15.4	10.9	6.9	Maldives	556
....	....	....	....	....	....	....	142.6	184.5	103.8	29.0	36.4	23.1	18.3	50.4	Mongolia	948
-10.7	41.5	-44.2	75.7	176.0	21.5	I-2.0	30.5	20.7	23.1	27.8	32.0	29.5	26.8	18.7	Myanmar	518
13.1	27.1	18.3	15.1	22.4	22.5	28.2	15.6	30.1	11.7	8.6	9.9	14.9	27.2	10.3	Nepal	558
8.6	19.8	19.5	10.8	17.1	15.9	27.3	8.8	14.2	15.7	17.9	-3.6	14.3	13.0	13.0	Pakistan	564

		1970	1971	1972	1973	1974	1975	1976	1977	1978	1979	1980	1981	1982	1983	1984
															Percent Change over Previous Year	

Asia (cont.)

		1970	1971	1972	1973	1974	1975	1976	1977	1978	1979	1980	1981	1982	1983	1984
Papua New Guinea	853	...	...	...	...	27.3	74.2	18.2	21.0	−4.6	21.4	−57.8	−10.7	1.8	52.6	−7.1
Philippines	566	9.8	10.2	25.1	12.7	24.6	13.6	12.5	23.6	24.2	22.6	12.4	10.0	5.5	Ɪ4.1	20.0
Samoa	862	12.8	18.6	11.3	20.3	14.3	118.2	26.0	35.3	2.6	24.7	549.2	35.1	14.4	11.8	16.3
Singapore	576	16.5	11.8	30.1	37.3	4.0	18.8	16.7	13.3	16.0	13.9	13.1	10.8	18.3	9.3	7.0
Solomon Islands	813	...	...	...	...	...	...	...	...	...	11.2	−35.5	−44.2	60.8	33.1	38.9
Sri Lanka	524	−3.4	14.0	17.8	17.5	8.2	−6.6	25.7	45.5	12.6	22.1	19.7	18.0	23.7	26.5	16.8
Thailand	578	9.7	11.0	17.8	17.9	13.1	11.1	12.7	9.2	17.3	17.1	14.0	6.6	12.0	10.5	5.6
Tonga	866	...	...	...	...	...	...	...	...	...	...	...	...	...	32.8	19.8
Vanuatu	846	...	...	...	...	...	...	...	18.2	15.8	24.4	−12.0	−24.4	5.6	17.5	23.2

Europe

		1970	1971	1972	1973	1974	1975	1976	1977	1978	1979	1980	1981	1982	1983	1984
Albania	914	...	...	...	...	...	...	...	...	...	...	...	...	...	...	...
Armenia	911	...	...	...	...	...	...	...	...	...	...	...	...	...	...	...
Azerbaijan	912	...	...	...	...	...	...	...	...	...	...	...	...	...	...	...
Belarus	913	...	...	...	...	...	...	...	...	...	...	...	...	...	...	...
Bulgaria	918	...	...	...	...	...	...	...	...	...	...	...	...	...	...	...
Croatia	960	...	...	...	...	...	...	...	...	...	...	...	...	...	...	...
Cyprus	423	1.7	30.8	19.4	4.9	15.0	1.5	23.3	12.8	16.1	19.7	27.7	22.8	24.0	15.8	17.5
Czech Republic	935	...	...	...	...	...	...	...	...	...	...	...	...	...	...	...
Czechoslovakia	934	...	...	...	...	...	...	...	...	...	...	...	−2.1	−4.7	.5	4.8
Estonia	939	...	...	...	...	...	...	...	...	...	...	...	...	...	...	...
Georgia	915	...	...	...	...	...	...	...	...	...	...	...	...	...	...	...
Hungary	944	...	...	...	...	...	...	...	...	...	...	...	...	...	−10.2	−10.8
Kazakhstan	916	...	...	...	...	...	...	...	...	...	...	...	...	...	...	...
Kyrgyz Republic	917	...	...	...	...	...	...	...	...	...	...	...	...	...	...	...
Latvia	941	...	...	...	...	...	...	...	...	...	...	...	...	...	...	...
Lithuania	946	...	...	...	...	...	...	...	...	...	...	...	...	...	...	...
Macedonia, FYR	962	...	...	...	...	...	...	...	...	...	...	...	...	...	...	...
Malta	181	7.3	16.8	34.6	−3.6	16.0	43.3	27.1	10.5	20.5	11.1	1.8	11.9	2.5	6.5	10.8
Moldova	921	...	...	...	...	...	...	...	...	...	...	...	...	...	...	...
Poland	964	...	...	...	...	...	...	...	...	...	...	30.4	Ɪ18.4	13.4	8.7	5.7
Romania	968	...	...	...	...	49.9	29.6	4.5	−.7	24.1	26.5	37.6	9.6	2.7	−5.2	−11.0
Russia	922	...	...	...	...	...	...	...	...	...	...	...	...	...	...	...
Slovak Republic	936	...	...	...	...	...	...	...	...	...	...	...	...	...	...	...
Slovenia	961	...	...	...	...	...	...	...	...	...	...	...	...	...	...	...
Turkey	186	Ɪ21.0	33.0	36.4	26.4	28.8	31.7	21.0	46.9	45.5	55.6	47.9	56.7	41.0	38.2	50.3
Ukraine	926	...	...	...	...	...	...	...	...	...	...	...	...	...	...	...
Yugoslavia, SFR	188	13.7	19.8	48.5	26.8	6.5	20.8	46.9	Ɪ9.9	83.9	20.5	33.3	34.8	41.5	62.9	56.9

Middle East

		1970	1971	1972	1973	1974	1975	1976	1977	1978	1979	1980	1981	1982	1983	1984
Bahrain	419	7.9	14.0	10.7	−36.2	19.5	154.9	48.0	−4.3	9.0	23.2	−2.6	15.1	19.8	−1.1	−6.1
Egypt	469	14.6	−6.3	14.1	24.6	27.0	13.9	19.7	20.4	27.5	28.1	Ɪ39.4	25.8	31.5	27.9	14.1
Iran, I.R. of	429	21.9	24.0	36.7	37.2	34.0	24.8	39.2	27.8	...	...	27.0	32.0	40.8	12.2	...
Iraq	433	16.2	.1	18.3	33.9	29.0	28.6	27.1	...	...	...	...	...	...	...	...
Israel	436	27.4	50.4	108.8	25.9	20.9	19.1	46.7	221.2	72.4	94.3	115.4	106.4	131.8	271.4	452.4
Jordan	439	13.5	2.3	1.2	16.4	19.9	23.5	24.7	17.9	17.5	26.8	22.9	14.3	11.7	11.3	1.9
Kuwait	443	.6	15.5	20.3	34.9	34.9	31.0	32.9	91.9	−26.1	19.0	33.5	34.2	61.6	−23.4	−11.5
Lebanon	446	2.3	22.0	12.4	14.2	66.8	1.3	33.3	12.4	13.3	−3.3	19.0	15.5	41.8	14.2	13.7
Libya	672	23.5	57.7	10.5	9.1	55.7	10.2	27.6	26.7	29.0	32.3	28.1	−5.7	4.4	−20.4	−4.5
Oman	449	...	84.8	47.3	17.3	95.6	53.6	31.3	24.4	10.6	24.0	32.1	53.1	24.8	−23.9	20.8
Qatar	453	−.5	14.8	32.9	38.5	46.0	58.7	43.8	36.1	32.9	27.6	17.3	3.0	11.0	.8	1.1
Saudi Arabia	456	2.0	20.2	30.9	51.3	35.0	102.3	61.6	62.8	39.4	−10.8	−11.0	13.7	13.9	−2.1	−1.7
Syrian Arab Rep.	463	15.8	8.2	18.5	23.0	30.2	19.6	25.1	24.8	30.4	13.8	33.5	8.5	49.0	26.6	32.4
United Arab Emirates	466	...	...	...	...	155.8	45.1	82.0	36.7	12.2	28.6	−18.7	19.6	13.6	−.9	9.0
Yemen Arab Rep.	473	...	...	...	...	33.0	77.8	125.0	66.3	27.1	23.3	7.6	15.6	25.4	28.0	27.8
Yemen, P.D. Rep.	459	12.7	6.0	20.7	21.1	1.6	10.3	71.2	28.7	29.4	27.6	19.0	14.3	34.6	25.4	17.7
Yemen, Republic of	474	...	...	...	...	...	...	...	...	...	...	...	...	...	...	...

Western Hemisphere

		1970	1971	1972	1973	1974	1975	1976	1977	1978	1979	1980	1981	1982	1983	1984
Antigua and Barbuda	311	...	...	...	...	...	...	62.9	−38.4	14.5	63.4	−16.6	−3.6	18.0	14.7	80.0
Argentina	213	16.5	42.4	34.8	584.2	53.1	175.9	357.9	43.2	97.5	85.5	78.9	117.5	744.0	356.2	435.5
Aruba	314	...	...	...	...	...	...	...	...	...	...	...	...	...	...	...
Bahamas, The	313	−8.5	4.6	38.0	−4.8	17.1	7.2	12.5	—	13.7	15.6	16.5	−.3	13.8	13.3	19.1
Barbados	316	20.0	8.1	14.7	32.5	33.1	35.8	−4.6	21.6	18.1	33.3	12.0	10.2	4.9	19.3	3.5
Belize	339	...	...	...	...	...	...	...	36.1	37.0	−9.9	13.9	20.9	17.6	−5.8	34.7
Bolivia	218	11.6	18.7	17.6	40.2	32.5	18.5	45.2	24.8	12.1	11.3	39.8	17.9	293.5	205.7	1,616.6
Brazil	223	19.0	Ɪ34.3	13.6	48.0	37.8	41.2	51.4	50.5	Ɪ45.1	85.2	57.9	70.1	86.9	105.8	228.0
Chile	228	58.0	177.0	179.8	418.2	222.8	255.6	Ɪ255.6	93.2	71.9	44.3	62.6	−9.9	113.4	129.6	76.6
Colombia	233	15.7	12.1	23.1	31.1	21.3	25.4	41.5	40.1	Ɪ40.1	29.3	29.4	24.3	17.6	18.6	23.5
Costa Rica	238	−.3	28.6	20.9	16.8	14.4	33.1	34.1	46.4	−.4	54.4	18.8	121.6	9.0	33.2	21.1
Dominica	321	...	...	...	...	...	...	57.0	50.4	−8.5	247.0	−36.8	−36.6	39.7	−38.8	226.0
Dominican Republic	243	12.0	16.6	8.7	25.6	46.5	−7.8	.2	28.2	8.4	8.4	−3.6	26.0	2.5	16.3	29.1
Ecuador	248	31.7	10.7	29.5	41.1	41.5	−.5	21.3	21.4	17.0	28.3	13.1	8.0	8.5	20.4	39.2
El Salvador	253	5.7	11.5	26.1	14.5	15.6	27.6	34.8	5.8	−23.4	−7.6	28.1	17.6	169.3	4.0	11.5
Grenada	328	...	1.7	−3.5	8.1	7.7	Ɪ31.7	73.9	−3.9	24.3	24.5	7.1	25.7	−14.9	5.2	36.3
Guatemala	258	12.7	5.9	27.3	18.0	15.7	18.0	53.3	12.8	9.6	4.5	−.2	5.8	16.4	−7.7	4.1
Guyana	336	−4.6	11.6	30.3	3.8	14.3	47.9	12.8	28.5	41.2	3.6	9.3	28.6	55.7	27.4	28.2
Haiti	263	7.7	14.9	21.8	18.9	4.6	24.3	38.3	18.8	10.5	12.1	23.6	16.4	1.1	−1.4	21.2
Honduras	268	11.9	8.1	2.5	21.3	−3.4	14.5	41.1	15.7	21.2	13.5	2.0	6.6	8.0	7.1	−1.6
Jamaica	343	19.3	8.8	13.1	28.5	21.1	19.0	16.0	16.5	10.7	19.9	41.0	−4.2	−11.4	71.6	92.0
Mexico	273	7.1	14.1	72.2	30.6	40.0	33.7	−7.0	Ɪ140.9	28.5	34.7	40.7	44.7	97.9	55.9	51.3
Netherlands Antilles	353	9.9	36.8	15.1	7.4	8.1	27.5	7.7	14.8	−.7	14.2	8.5	1.7	7.2	−8.4	−10.7
Nicaragua	278	11.0	3.8	16.3	41.1	10.6	2.9	26.9	6.1	−9.8	127.5	−6.7	57.1	31.7	Ɪ56.5	87.5
Panama	283	21.8	10.3	84.6	−8.9	−8.2	35.1	39.3	9.9	−19.5	98.0	6.9	32.5	−2.3	−1.2	1.5
Paraguay	288	17.4	12.9	21.9	27.0	17.7	22.9	20.7	31.4	33.1	22.4	27.5	17.7	.6	31.0	17.1
Peru	293	48.5	5.4	31.4	6.6	41.2	5.8	48.4	24.4	55.2	127.2	111.5	55.1	57.0	115.1	142.6
St. Kitts and Nevis	361	...	...	...	...	...	...	...	...	...	...	−52.1	603.6	−28.4	23.2	45.8
St. Lucia	362	...	...	...	...	...	...	54.8	7.0	26.0	28.8	8.0	−3.9	8.2	5.5	58.7
St. Vincent & Grenadines	364	...	...	...	...	...	...	74.3	10.0	7.1	53.8	−14.5	18.7	−10.3	−5.8	86.5
Suriname	366	4.7	10.7	3.8	42.5	−.5	26.0	28.2	23.5	.9	21.5	.2	23.1	9.9	29.2	48.3
Trinidad and Tobago	369	11.2	30.7	9.8	15.5	99.7	57.9	33.5	3.9	4.7	76.2	9.0	22.6	60.7	−5.5	−7.9
Uruguay	298	13.6	53.9	49.6	76.2	61.8	Ɪ68.2	93.5	45.6	84.1	41.8	56.2	16.8	Ɪ30.1	73.9	91.1
Venezuela, Rep. Bol.	299	2.8	23.0	12.3	24.0	42.1	40.7	19.1	22.4	10.6	12.9	6.8	17.0	17.1	28.2	25.6

Percent Change over Previous Year

1985	1986	1987	1988	1989	1990	1991	1992	1993	1994	1995	1996	1997	1998	1999	Country	Code
															Asia (cont.)	
1.8	−3.8	6.8	5.8	7.3	15.6	−6.5	2.6	17.9	11.3	15.3	91.3	−34.3	20.7	73.3	Papua New Guinea	853
14.0	32.0	14.0	16.3	38.9	17.7	20.1	13.0	I18.9	5.1	17.2	14.5	7.9	−11.4	32.7	Philippines	566
129.4	40.1	14.9	3.6	38.7	52.3	−9.7	−20.7	−8.0	3.2	4.4	20.5	19.1	−45.7	21.4	Samoa	862
4.3	5.4	8.1	12.9	15.5	7.2	10.6	10.6	8.4	6.2	9.4	6.7	5.6	−13.3	28.6	Singapore	576
−22.2	2.6	3.7	35.2	−16.2	14.9	35.7	−.1	11.7	30.9	23.0	30.4	−6.2	46.0	−.3	Solomon Islands	813
26.5	3.4	10.3	25.8	I5.9	20.6	27.9	8.5	25.2	19.1	16.1	7.9	−2.1	10.6	5.1	Sri Lanka	524
8.5	10.2	22.4	14.9	16.9	18.6	13.3	17.9	16.1	14.5	22.6	13.5	15.8	−4.5	54.8	Thailand	578
5.5	23.8	15.5	−10.1	−26.2	65.6	2.9	6.8	−62.8	−4.5	−17.7	43.0	12.3	10.3	7.5	Tonga	866
25.1	11.7	−10.0	11.9	32.1	−13.9	27.9	−2.6	53.6	−6.8	30.4	−4.2	−.2	5.2	22.3	Vanuatu	846
															Europe	
....	....	....	....	....	....	....	....	....	....	28.1	14.0	48.1	−1.1	21.6	Albania	914
....	....	....	....	....	....	....	....	1,375.5	842.0	92.0	42.8	24.8	4.9	—	Armenia	911
....	....	....	....	....	....	....	....	1,375.6	642.9	179.8	17.6	41.4	−24.3	15.9	Azerbaijan	912
....	....	....	....	....	....	....	....	....	....	287.9	78.1	107.6	162.9	178.5	Belarus	913
....	....	....	....	....	....	....	50.7	22.8	61.8	73.9	127.8	518.5	9.8	14.0	Bulgaria	918
....	....	....	....	....	....	....	502.8	994.1	109.6	43.1	30.0	18.0	−3.8	3.6	Croatia	960
3.5	8.1	10.8	I14.5	−10.9	37.4	2.5	6.9	1.6	12.5	−4.3	−8.8	−.8	16.2	15.1	Cyprus	423
....	....	....	....	....	....	....	....	....	34.4	53.6	.5	I30.9	22.5	8.9	Czech Republic	935
3.3	2.5	−.3	−.1	6.1	109.8	−58.6	....	....	....	....	....	....	....	....	Czechoslovakia	934
....	....	....	....	....	....	....	154.2	I108.5	11.4	19.0	21.4	37.7	6.4	27.1	Estonia	939
....	....	....	....	....	....	....	....	....	....	....	36.3	32.6	−6.3	18.8	Georgia	915
14.2	6.7	−11.0	−4.5	19.6	46.5	−4.7	21.4	2.9	....	....	....	....	....	....	Hungary	944
....	....	....	....	....	....	....	....	....	623.4	113.5	26.8	I36.8	−29.4	53.7	Kazakhstan	916
....	....	....	....	....	....	....	....	....	....	....	23.9	21.1	7.6	22.4	Kyrgyz Republic	917
....	....	....	....	....	....	....	....	....	19.5	1.6	23.0	31.2	6.7	11.6	Latvia	941
....	....	....	....	....	....	....	....	....	44.2	35.0	2.2	32.4	28.8	−4.0	Lithuania	946
....	....	....	....	....	....	....	....	....	71.7	I30.6	−3.2	22.7	5.6	29.6	Macedonia, FYR	962
.9	.9	2.8	.2	−4.0	−5.6	6.8	6.3	.2	31.7	−12.2	−4.2	1.5	3.0	6.9	Malta	181
....	....	....	....	....	....	....	534.0	391.7	128.9	41.3	I9.5	33.3	−6.6	41.7	Moldova	921
6.4	4.8	.9	131.5	474.5	160.6	I27.3	35.8	7.6	22.6	45.0	20.5	34.0	16.9	−1.3	Poland	964
I−2.3	14.2	6.2	16.5	39.2	I−41.7	22.5	116.3	I191.5	87.5	56.2	51.4	136.5	20.8	92.4	Romania	968
....	....	....	....	....	....	....	....	....	203.5	107.8	27.3	27.6	25.3	66.8	Russia	922
....	....	....	....	....	....	....	....	....	22.9	57.7	8.7	18.8	−4.7	31.8	Slovak Republic	936
....	....	....	....	....	....	....	133.1	38.2	56.9	25.2	15.6	23.0	19.7	21.3	Slovenia	961
38.1	I26.9	47.3	78.8	72.0	38.3	49.9	78.2	67.9	119.5	79.5	91.5	99.9	80.4	97.5	Turkey	186
....	....	....	....	....	....	....	....	1,560.0	407.4	132.8	39.9	49.0	I16.6	41.3	Ukraine	926
62.1	92.4	192.7	255.7	2,273.3	26.7	....	....	....	....	....	....	....	....	....	Yugoslavia, SFR	188
															Middle East	
16.5	−5.5	10.7	−6.2	8.3	9.4	I−4.4	−9.0	−20.1	−4.1	34.5	−11.1	12.6	−21.7	45.5	Bahrain	419
16.8	11.6	6.0	4.1	8.2	28.7	19.2	10.4	19.2	12.5	9.3	4.2	11.1	19.3	1.6	Egypt	469
....	....	24.9	25.2	13.1	3.2	16.2	13.1	18.8	34.2	48.0	27.1	23.0	18.0	17.1	Iran, I.R. of	429
....	....	....	....	....	....	....	....	....	....	....	....	....	....	....	Iraq	433
147.3	4.9	18.5	6.6	9.8	13.8	8.9	6.9	28.1	−6.7	−26.8	34.9	119.3	14.4	23.8	Israel	436
3.8	6.5	4.4	23.0	18.4	12.7	30.2	6.3	I5.2	5.1	6.4	−13.4	−2.8	−4.7	12.4	Jordan	439
−1.9	−8.5	−18.0	−28.0	−1.1	....	−5.8	−6.3	.1	−6.6	.8	−10.1	5.0	30.0		Kuwait	443
41.6	34.8	129.6	239.6	69.4	53.3	57.2	90.2	41.9	76.7	21.2	21.2	50.0	−5.5	5.5	Lebanon	446
29.3	−4.9	6.5	−15.0	24.0	34.4	—	28.5	−2.4	15.9	7.7	9.0	I6.6	−1.0	−5.3	Libya	672
3.8	6.3	−14.6	1.0	22.0	1.8	3.1	−3.5	−4.8	4.1	3.6	6.4	8.5	7.1	−1.1	Oman	449
−3.2	30.0	−.4	−8.9	14.2	8.9	.9	7.9	4.5	−6.9	5.0	6.1	9.7	3.1	12.2	Qatar	453
−2.0	8.8	1.1	−6.3	−3.7	25.5	3.9	−1.2	−.2	4.5	−2.3	−1.4	7.6	−1.2		Saudi Arabia	456
35.8	7.2	9.3	−5.3	20.7	28.5	7.5	22.3	14.6	8.6	4.7	7.6	4.8	5.0		Syrian Arab Rep.	463
15.8	2.6	53.0	−8.1	−11.9	.7	15.8	21.3	−3.3	25.7	13.1	8.1	.5	.2	30.5	United Arab Emirates	466
18.9	20.8	24.1	5.1	4.6	....	....	....	....	....	....	....	....	....	....	Yemen Arab Rep.	473
15.2	13.4	7.4	11.3	4.8	....	....	....	....	....	....	....	....	....	....	Yemen, P.D. Rep.	459
....	....	....	....	....	....	9.2	21.4	29.8	35.5	19.8	6.9	−12.5	11.2	....	Yemen, Republic of	474
															Western Hemisphere	
16.1	38.7	−5.2	11.1	−4.2	3.6	10.1	30.0	−17.2	14.9	17.3	−17.4	4.5	12.9	13.9	Antigua and Barbuda	311
386.9	34.7	94.7	417.8	7,445.6	I588.7	116.3	40.7	36.1	I8.5	−15.4	2.1	13.6	2.6	.8	Argentina	213
....	....	19.3	14.8	−3.6	18.6	25.0	18.3	10.7	−6.4	18.0	−14.3	−4.2	40.5	6.3	Aruba	314
14.3	8.5	3.3	12.4	4.1	6.3	12.8	−2.7	−.4	12.0	2.8	−2.6	14.5	19.7	20.8	Bahamas, The	313
9.5	1.7	20.4	4.5	−3.2	19.4	−14.4	13.3	−11.7	−1.9	15.7	34.2	−9.6	9.0	3.8	Barbados	316
14.7	18.2	11.7	−4.4	24.7	−1.7	3.7	21.4	−.7	−2.0	13.4	2.9	5.2	7.8	21.9	Belize	339
5,909.7	89.1	I25.0	63.8	27.1	27.3	29.3	5.4	32.8	23.3	I15.7	20.1	−20.8	11.3		Bolivia	218
250.9	I196.9	453.7	I306.2	2,415.2	1,835.3	496.6	1,148.2	2,424.4	2,241.7	11.9	22.8	34.2	−11.1	7.8	Brazil	223
108.8	21.4	8.0	2.1	−1.8	54.4	23.7	21.7	13.6	20.7	13.9	15.9	16.0	−3.6	9.4	Chile	228
17.4	20.2	46.0	19.9	I66.5	23.0	27.7	37.6	25.6	28.2	6.8	17.7	16.5	−17.1	39.8	Colombia	233
43.0	29.3	14.6	44.7	16.5	21.0	62.3	17.8	9.5	29.6	16.2	21.9	I16.9	11.2	7.4	Costa Rica	238
−14.5	54.1	47.6	−18.0	−8.6	31.5	9.3	.6	−4.0	−9.4	18.6	−.6	2.7	11.5	12.2	Dominica	321
−1.1	94.6	−6.1	101.8	29.2	31.5	51.1	12.9	28.3	.5	16.4	10.9	18.9	22.4	15.0	Dominican Republic	243
29.6	34.5	39.6	68.1	46.1	I67.9	37.5	63.9	62.9	13.8	16.6	33.0	30.6	I48.1	138.5	Ecuador	248
22.6	.9	25.0	16.0	10.7	29.6	22.5	15.1	43.4	23.3	12.4	10.0	13.3	8.3	10.2	El Salvador	253
28.8	−1.0	8.9	−14.2	3.6	6.6	.8	22.4	−3.9	6.4	8.5	.4	12.4	6.4	6.0	Grenada	328
61.6	20.6	.6	22.4	19.1	33.8	28.1	8.0	23.3	4.5	3.5	12.8	I22.9	−3.9	2.8	Guatemala	258
9.6	23.3	139.7	18.8	−8.0	18.1	156.9	51.7	I−23.1	31.4	19.1	5.9	17.1	11.8	−3.9	Guyana	336
12.3	15.2	20.2	−26.6	64.8	17.2	8.9	29.5	29.2	23.8	14.7	−4.1	I11.1	.3	29.0	Haiti	263
−.9	7.2	24.9	14.7	24.9	24.9	7.8	44.5	6.8	47.0	23.9	43.5	I91.9	15.2	12.4	Honduras	268
34.9	18.7	19.7	37.1	22.7	15.6	28.2	88.6	44.6	34.3	29.7	4.0	15.2	22.1	−4.2	Jamaica	343
17.0	48.0	70.6	44.9	10.2	35.3	27.8	14.4	10.4	21.2	33.4	23.1	I48.4	27.6	43.5	Mexico	273
74.6	21.7	−9.1	2.0	−30.5	17.7	−17.2	29.2	5.5	−6.5	19.9	−14.3	15.6	9.9	−5.9	Netherlands Antilles	353
183.4	238.3	593.9	11,540.2	2,481.9	10,348.1	1,298.3	5.7	7.8	52.5	23.6	I34.6	32.5	19.7	5.7	Nicaragua	278
−3.5	12.5	−34.9	−20.0	−2.3	53.1	35.8	−19.5	4.1	−1.8	2.8	39.8	2.8	3.3	−1.5	Panama	283
18.9	35.3	40.3	I22.7	33.6	27.3	33.9	37.3	20.0	26.8	19.5	3.5	9.7	14.8	12.8	Paraguay	288
214.9	39.5	110.5	568.3	1,436.7	7,782.5	162.2	95.9	59.4	31.0	31.2	37.8	38.7	5.7	15.6	Peru	293
19.4	20.6	5.7	−4.1	24.0	6.6	.8	33.2	11.7	7.3	−1.6	−3.2	6.5	19.7	12.9	St. Kitts and Nevis	361
25.3	41.9	14.4	1.4	12.7	11.0	7.6	−1.1	4.8	−4.7	11.4	−4.4	1.6	13.8	3.2	St. Lucia	362
29.7	46.2	−15.4	−3.6	6.9	14.2	−10.0	30.1	−4.6	−3.2	−5.4	−2.5	9.1	20.8	16.8	St. Vincent & Grenadines	364
52.6	36.1	20.1	21.6	15.3	5.8	26.9	12.6	70.0	207.8	227.0	−10.3	−.4	65.0	42.8	Suriname	366
7.0	−15.6	−21.8	1.9	13.3	10.6	17.1	−9.7	−4.7	56.9	−.7	I8.9	16.1	20.9	3.7	Trinidad and Tobago	369
85.8	77.2	77.4	78.3	93.6	140.5	77.4	45.0	42.6	32.4	30.5	32.5	25.0	I14.4	21.2	Uruguay	298
2.9	−18.1	I27.8	7.3	62.5	129.6	45.3	8.2	9.7	65.1	33.7	155.6	57.5	−1.6	34.3	Venezuela, Rep. Bol.	299

Money

		1970	1971	1972	1973	1974	1975	1976	1977	1978	1979	1980	1981	1982	1983	1984
														Percent Change over Previous Year		

Industrial Countries

		1970	1971	1972	1973	1974	1975	1976	1977	1978	1979	1980	1981	1982	1983	1984
United States	111	5.7	7.0	9.4	6.1	2.4	4.5	6.2	9.8	9.5	9.4	4.9	4.9	7.4	7.7	8.8
Canada	156	.5	14.4	12.4	9.2	1.6	18.9	1.0	10.5	6.8	1.9	10.1	‡ −.5	8.5	10.3	19.6
Australia	193	4.6	5.6	20.0	16.7	−.7	22.7	8.9	6.6	11.6	15.4	17.5	4.9	−.2	15.3	8.2
Japan	158	16.8	29.6	24.7	16.8	11.5	11.1	12.5	8.2	13.4	3.0	−2.0	10.0	5.7	−.1	6.9
New Zealand	196	7.5	10.2	28.5	26.7	3.6	9.3	9.2	1.9	22.3	3.4	3.1	15.4	3.5	13.1	9.8
Euro Area	163	....	....	....	....	....	....	....	....	....	....	....	6.2	8.3	9.8	7.9
Austria	122	6.6	13.6	20.7	8.3	5.8	14.1	8.1	1.3	8.6	−7.9	15.1	−2.5	8.1	10.6	4.2
Belgium	124	7.0	11.2	15.2	7.5	6.2	15.7	7.0	8.3	5.9	2.5	‡ .2	2.2	3.8	8.5	.3
Finland	172	10.2	16.8	23.2	23.3	18.9	34.5	−1.7	2.8	16.5	22.5	6.3	14.7	15.9	7.6	16.4
Germany	134	8.6	12.7	14.2	1.7	10.7	14.3	3.3	12.0	14.5	2.9	3.9	−1.5	7.2	8.4	5.9
Ireland	178	7.1	41.4	21.2	26.1	17.1	18.0	15.8	16.8	33.8	18.8	20.0	20.6	‡ −1.3	12.2	15.6
Italy	136	32.4	19.4	18.2	19.7	‡ 5.6	20.8	21.5	27.8	23.7	13.1	11.1	17.2	12.5	12.3
Luxembourg	137							12.3	6.8	13.8	6.2	6.5	5.0	5.5	2.2	11.4	3.7
Netherlands	138	11.7	14.9	17.6	.3	12.2	19.3	8.1	13.0	4.3	3.0	5.7	−2.4	‡ 13.8	10.0	6.9
Portugal	182	7.0	4.4	16.6	35.4	10.2	24.5	‡ 9.8	11.9	13.9	‡ 26.8	20.5	9.6	16.5	8.1	15.8
Spain	184	6.0	23.8	24.1	23.5	17.3	18.7	21.9	18.5	17.3	8.5	13.5	13.0	11.4	‡ 10.0	8.9
Denmark	128	1.2	7.8	13.6	11.7	4.7	26.7	5.0	7.1	16.0	10.5	7.8	13.6	4.1	23.6	13.0
Greece	174	11.7	16.6	19.2	23.4	19.8	16.4	22.2	16.9	22.3	16.3	16.3	22.2	21.7	14.5	20.0
Iceland	176	22.0	21.9	21.8	38.9	30.1	33.6	24.7	46.9	40.8	46.5	60.4	61.2	27.5	78.2	‡ 142.8
Norway	142	12.6	11.7	16.5	15.3	11.9	16.5	‡ 12.3	14.1	8.6	7.6	5.3	15.0	12.3	12.1	24.4
Sweden	144	4.2	12.4	10.4	8.7	12.6	16.3	10.1	10.1	12.9	12.3	8.5	7.4	6.5	‡ 11.4	11.6
Switzerland	146	10.6	18.0	9.4	3.4	‡ −1.4	4.2	11.4	.9	23.6	−1.9	−.1	−.4	‡ 10.7	6.6	‡ .2
United Kingdom	112	9.3	15.1	14.2	5.1	10.8	‡ 13.2	11.3	20.8	16.3	9.1	4.0	‡ 11.0	17.5	4.4	13.2

Developing Countries

Africa

		1970	1971	1972	1973	1974	1975	1976	1977	1978	1979	1980	1981	1982	1983	1984
Algeria	612	10.6	11.4	29.3	13.0	28.1	31.9	28.5	18.2	28.1	16.1	16.9	16.0	28.0	21.9	18.1
Angola	614															
Benin	638	17.6	19.6	10.3	−3.0	27.6	70.8	−4.6	14.4	5.8	‡ 8.8	32.4	35.3	38.1	−1.7	10.5
Botswana	616								33.7	4.7	34.8	10.3	26.7	11.0	7.8	9.7
Burkina Faso	748	7.4	3.7	4.4	36.5	21.3	37.4	22.5	11.7	11.8	‡ 1.0	19.9	17.2	11.3	11.0	10.2
Burundi	618	22.9	15.7	5.5	15.7	22.4	−6.4	56.4	24.2	28.5	9.5	3.0	24.0	−7.6	21.7	8.1
Cameroon	622	8.2	11.8	7.3	17.4	32.6	4.8	24.6	‡ 33.5	15.7	25.4	13.3	24.4	15.1	26.1	9.7
Cape Verde	624								41.1	14.4	12.9	26.3	10.9	26.4	22.6	6.2
Central African Rep.	626	12.3	1.3	17.5	1.1	33.5	−1.5	39.5	‡ 17.5	13.1	27.0	32.3	22.3	−3.8	11.5	6.5
Chad	628										14.5	−16.1	19.6	4.7	22.9	59.8
Comoros	632														41.5	−15.3
Congo, Dem. Rep. of	636	24.1	−.2	25.0	23.9	34.6	18.1	43.7	55.6	56.7	−2.4	72.6	55.0	76.3	1,272.9	−82.9
Congo, Rep. of	634	17.1	7.9	5.7	15.2	39.7	13.2	15.4	‡ −1.4	7.4	20.0	37.0	38.7	30.3	−6.8	11.7
Côte d'Ivoire	662	19.7	10.2	12.0	14.3	38.0	10.5	44.6	47.3	8.5	‡ 8.0	1.1	5.8	−.9	6.0	17.7
Djibouti	611															
Equatorial Guinea	642															
Ethiopia	644	−.3	−3.6	12.4	26.0	21.9	25.0	1.2	23.7	16.9	14.1	−.2	9.7	10.0	‡ 14.7	7.8
Gabon	646	9.6	16.2	26.3	23.8	65.3	54.7	76.5	‡ −8.8	−8.9	−5.3	10.5	21.8	9.9	13.7	17.3
Gambia, The	648	16.8	−.5	39.2	39.6	3.9	13.0	32.4	−19.5	‡ 48.0	—	6.1	25.6	13.3	15.0	−.7
Ghana	652	5.6	4.9	44.1	21.9	23.7	44.6	41.4	67.9	72.4	13.4	30.1	54.7	19.0	49.2	60.6
Guinea	656															
Guinea-Bissau	654															
Kenya	664	23.6	6.5	18.2	23.0	8.9	10.3	23.6	43.2	7.4	16.5	−8.1	11.6	13.0	7.9	14.1
Lesotho	666												21.0	31.6	9.7	22.0
Liberia	668					7.5		−13.2	52.1	−10.3	36.3	.1	‡ −10.1	−22.5	22.4	15.0	20.0
Madagascar	674	11.2	1.6	13.6	7.5	18.5	2.1	14.9	25.5	12.9	‡ 22.5	21.8	28.1	7.3	−7.4	24.5
Malawi	676	14.8	18.8	4.6	35.7	33.2	.3	−1.1	37.4	−6.3	−3.4	7.3	18.1	14.0	−2.3	20.7
Mali	678	12.2	7.7	10.7	9.7	53.9	18.3	11.5	14.2	19.3	17.1	4.8	1.2	13.4	18.9	‡ 31.8
Mauritania	682	35.0	2.0	26.1	4.6	64.1	19.4	25.8	11.2	1.0	22.9	11.7	34.8	−6.8	13.4	19.2
Mauritius	684	5.6	13.9	43.8	24.0	68.0	26.7	10.6	11.0	18.9	−1.6	20.6	−10.9	13.5	3.6	13.7
Morocco	686	9.0	12.3	18.5	16.8	26.8	18.1	17.6	19.2	15.5	12.3	8.4	14.6	‡ 10.1	13.7	7.6
Mozambique	688															
Namibia	728															
Niger	692	3.4	19.7	7.6	19.7	29.5	14.2	23.1	30.5	43.5	23.4	12.8	15.7	−5.1	−6.2	17.8
Nigeria	694	43.7	4.3	11.5	‡ 23.9	105.5	52.1	51.4	45.4	−5.9	20.5	50.1	5.6	3.1	12.3	8.2
Rwanda	714	18.6	14.2	1.9	41.5	20.3	13.1	34.3	23.3	11.5	25.6	6.9	‡ 4.0	−2.4	7.4	8.4
São Tomé and Príncipe	716															
Senegal	722	23.3	2.0	11.1	13.0	53.3	10.9	26.2	15.0	16.0	‡ −2.0	13.8	18.3	15.8	.1	1.3
Seychelles	718			48.4	6.9	4.0	14.1	41.4	24.0	13.4	20.7	38.4	−.5	−9.2	−8.4	2.6
Sierra Leone	724	−9.1	12.4	19.8	24.1	13.6	9.9	19.6	17.1	27.2	18.7	19.6	−.4	66.7	41.9	35.3
Somalia	726	34.5	−12.4	33.8	15.1	24.0	31.4	20.5	33.2	30.4	35.1	19.2	32.0	9.8	6.9	23.8
South Africa	199	1.6	8.3	14.8	20.4	18.6	6.8	3.5	4.7	10.4	20.7	35.5	34.2	16.4	26.4	41.2
Sudan	732	14.2	7.1	16.7	21.6	35.0	18.6	24.5	41.9	27.5	32.0	31.2	39.5	36.6	11.7	18.3
Swaziland	734						38.3	22.9	18.6	9.0	9.9	21.9	2.5	13.7	4.7	11.5
Tanzania	738	1.4	22.6	13.0	18.1	25.8	23.9	24.5	19.7	7.0	52.9	27.9	15.4	19.0	12.2	.2
Togo	742	4.8	17.0	−.5	−2.2	117.0	−14.0	52.8	10.7	31.9	‡ 11.4	5.1	44.5	12.6	−7.8	9.2
Tunisia	744	6.2	25.2	15.4	16.2	25.1	17.6	8.1	12.1	19.5	14.2	21.0	22.5	24.9	16.8	6.8
Uganda	746	16.1	1.3	35.8	38.0	42.3	8.1	37.3	29.9	20.9	51.1	31.7	101.2	5.1	44.6	123.2
Zambia	754	2.6	‡ 6.8	1.4	28.6	2.6	24.4	21.1	−1.9	1.0	30.2	.5	8.6	22.3	15.3	9.4
Zimbabwe	698							8.6	6.4	10.8	11.6	36.6	7.3	21.8	−9.1	16.3

Asia

		1970	1971	1972	1973	1974	1975	1976	1977	1978	1979	1980	1981	1982	1983	1984
Afghanistan, Islamic State of	512	6.2	11.4	9.3	‡ 7.2	10.6	19.6	22.4	29.6	20.5	19.4	16.4	14.8	16.0	....	....
Bangladesh	513						−1.3	11.3	26.6	25.4	25.4	9.9	12.6	‡ 18.6	35.6	33.6
Bhutan	514															18.4
Cambodia	522															
China, P.R.: Mainland	924									.1	58.8	24.7	17.1	10.6	17.5	40.1
China, P.R.: Hong Kong	532															
Fiji	819	17.5	14.5	22.4	8.1	22.1	21.7	1.6	−1.6	17.1	14.1	−10.4	17.6	4.3	9.1	.9
India	534	12.0	13.0	12.6	17.3	10.1	9.9	24.9	16.8	‡ −11.7	12.2	15.7	13.6	17.7	12.7	18.5
Indonesia	536	33.9	29.9	50.5	42.0	40.5	33.0	28.1	25.3	24.0	35.8	48.3	29.2	10.0	6.4	13.3
Korea	542	22.1	16.4	45.1	40.6	29.5	25.0	30.7	40.7	24.9	20.7	16.3	4.6	45.6	17.0	.6
Lao People's Democratic Rep.	544															
Malaysia	548	8.3	4.9	25.0	37.6	8.6	7.2	20.9	16.6	18.2	17.2	15.0	12.9	13.3	7.7	−.6
Maldives	556								−14.1	−18.8	42.4	51.2	‡ 28.8	−15.2	−4.2	28.3
Mongolia	948															
Myanmar	518	−17.8	4.8	22.8	26.0	27.2	21.6	11.1	3.6	12.6	11.2	12.8	15.3	7.6	12.9	15.5
Nepal	558	‡ 4.8	12.1	7.3	29.5	18.3	3.4	22.7	18.1	13.9	15.2	13.0	11.9	15.6	17.8	13.2
Pakistan	564	11.1	17.6	20.9	11.3	1.5	13.8	32.9	17.4	18.1	20.4	17.3	8.4	20.8	15.1	5.2

Percent Change over Previous Year

1985	1986	1987	1988	1989	1990	1991	1992	1993	1994	1995	1996	1997	1998	1999		
															Industrial Countries	
13.1	17.4	.3	4.8	1.0	5.0	8.6	11.7	9.7	.1	-.9	1.4	3.5	3.5	10.4	United States	111
33.0	14.7	6.2	5.9	5.8	1.2	4.4	7.1	8.3	6.6	10.2	12.7	9.2	5.7	11.3	Canada	156
3.6	11.4	20.3	29.6	I7.5	7.3	7.6	20.0	17.8	10.9	6.5	14.0	13.3	5.9	9.7	Australia	193
3.0	10.4	4.8	8.6	2.4	4.5	9.5	3.9	7.0	4.2	13.1	9.7	8.6	5.0	11.7	Japan	158
9.1	13.7	42.8	I23.5	15.0	1.5	2.0	.8	8.0	4.6	5.0	-4.5	6.5	5.1	18.3	New Zealand	196
6.3	8.0	7.0	9.4	9.2	21.2	2.3	5.2	5.3	4.2	37.0	10.6	11.8	10.0	10.6	Euro Area	163
3.1	6.2	9.6	8.3	3.4	6.1	7.7	6.1	9.2	8.6	14.8	4.7	4.7	....	....	Austria	122
3.0	7.8	4.6	5.5	5.4	.9	1.6	I-1.1	7.5	1.5	4.9	4.2	3.1	....	....	Belgium	124
11.0	.5	9.0	18.4	15.4	7.2	I192.1	3.2	5.1	8.9	14.0	16.4	5.5	4.8	....	Finland	172
I5.2	8.1	7.3	11.4	6.0	28.5	4.3	11.7	8.5	4.5	7.0	12.2	2.0	10.0	....	Germany	134
1.2	3.7	7.0	8.4	8.5	12.9	-1.7	.5	12.9	12.5	64.1	8.8	-17.4	25.2	....	Ireland	178
10.4	11.3	8.1	7.7	I12.6	7.5	11.1	1.4	6.3	3.9	.4	4.9	6.5	11.1	....	Italy	136
-5.5	9.6	10.4	7.9	13.8	9.1	10.4	1.7	....	....	....	....	3.2	....	....	Luxembourg	137
6.9	6.9	7.0	6.9	7.1	4.3	4.2	4.3	10.5	1.7	13.5	12.1	7.8	....	....	Netherlands	138
26.7	37.4	20.4	21.5	13.7	5.3	15.3	18.5	10.7	6.6	10.9	12.1	12.9	17.0	....	Portugal	182
14.7	I15.0	16.2	19.5	14.9	20.1	12.3	-2.0	3.5	7.1	2.9	7.1	14.0	15.8	....	Spain	184
22.2	7.3	I40.1	19.5	.4	8.1	I9.2	-.9	10.5	-1.4	4.6	11.5	5.7	4.8	5.8	Denmark	128
17.8	20.5	I15.1	14.0	23.3	24.3	13.5	13.3	11.3	28.0	13.4	12.9	16.1	10.5	....	Greece	174
27.3	44.3	30.4	16.0	52.2	24.5	19.9	1.3	5.4	10.7	9.6	8.5	16.4	20.3	....	Iceland	176
20.3	3.2	50.0	22.6	16.6	8.9	7.6	26.4	5.2	4.4	1.1	9.5	6.2	19.3	5.6	Norway	142
3.7	8.3	2.3	.9	12.1	....	....	....	....	....	....	....	....	....	....	Sweden	144
-2.5	2.2	13.8	2.3	-2.7	-1.6	-1.7	4.0	5.8	4.0	6.1	I27.4	9.0	6.8	9.5	Switzerland	146
18.0	22.2	I32.7	10.7	14.4	10.1	6.6	I4.3	9.9	.8	16.7	9.3	25.7	9.3	11.1	United Kingdom	112
															Developing Countries	
															Africa	
12.1	1.3	9.3	12.6	-.9	8.2	20.0	I16.2	19.4	7.8	7.1	13.4	14.6	20.9	8.9	Algeria	612
....	....	....	....	....	....	....	....	....	....	....	3,392.6	107.5	39.8	326.2	Angola	614
-3.9	-9.4	-21.6	16.3	17.3	23.9	11.6	9.9	-13.2	67.3	-13.2	17.2	2.0	-4.7	46.9	Benin	638
25.0	29.3	28.2	30.2	24.6	15.7	4.7	-1.1	14.7	11.1	7.2	14.7	9.1	45.8	17.3	Botswana	616
4.6	22.8	6.7	10.6	4.5	-1.7	5.5	.5	11.6	38.9	25.5	7.0	17.5	-2.6	-1.9	Burkina Faso	748
24.3	9.0	-.5	4.8	3.6	9.5	11.3	10.3	12.0	28.3	-3.3	12.5	10.5	1.3	41.9	Burundi	618
4.0	4.0	-13.4	I.4	7.2	-7.5	2.7	-27.6	-14.1	35.1	-11.6	-1.6	34.9	14.5	10.8	Cameroon	622
15.3	16.1	1.6	5.7	6.2	8.0	8.8	31.4	7.0	8.2	I16.6	10.6	21.6	-2.0	17.3	Cape Verde	624
8.5	.2	3.5	I-2.7	3.9	-3.7	-2.8	-3.7	16.4	74.0	7.6	4.9	-8.1	-18.3	12.6	Central African Rep.	626
4.9	1.2	2.1	-12.8	7.9	-.2	3.8	-8.7	-27.7	31.5	42.7	33.5	-4.7	-8.0	-3.1	Chad	628
16.7	-.8	9.3	14.9	13.1	6.0	-7.3	9.4	4.6	9.8	-5.3	8.1	-18.6	I-5.5	16.4	Comoros	632
29.0	59.7	90.8	119.2	75.4	175.8	2,386.7	4,114.5	2,460.6	5,635.4	407.2	....	....	....	....	Congo, Dem. Rep. of	636
10.9	-12.9	4.8	I-6.7	-1.0	25.3	-7.3	6.4	-19.7	40.4	.3	13.6	8.7	-13.6	27.8	Congo, Rep. of	634
7.9	2.8	-6.0	-3.5	-11.5	3.0	-3.1	-4.0	.9	61.7	18.2	2.3	11.7	12.9	-1.7	Côte d'Ivoire	662
3.0	13.4	8.8	6.8	-7.0	8.6	15.7	10.5	4.1	3.3	-1.6	-2.9	-9.6	-10.0	....	Djibouti	611
....	23.3	-9.2	I-37.5	38.8	-57.0	-15.5	35.4	-28.6	135.5	58.4	50.1	-4.3	9.7	89.8	Equatorial Guinea	642
17.0	21.1	2.1	11.4	16.1	22.0	17.6	15.2	4.3	21.2	2.8	-.1	8.8	-7.8	13.1	Ethiopia	644
5.2	-13.5	-12.2	I9.9	5.0	5.7	8.0	-27.2	-3.4	41.9	12.3	26.0	8.1	-5.1	-5.1	Gabon	646
62.8	2.7	18.8	7.9	21.9	13.8	32.9	10.6	6.0	-11.7	15.7	-3.8	38.8	-.5	14.3	Gambia, The	648
42.7	44.0	52.6	45.0	52.7	10.8	I7.7	53.0	27.9	50.3	33.4	31.4	45.4	17.3	2.7	Ghana	652
....	....	....	....	....	....	....	19.7	19.4	-3.2	8.5	-.2	21.3	....	....	Guinea	656
....	....	99.1	84.5	30.5	729.2	-74.8	83.1	27.3	58.1	46.9	51.0	236.3	-12.1	22.4	Guinea-Bissau	654
-1.3	35.6	8.0	1.3	13.0	27.2	15.0	47.1	27.4	12.6	3.8	13.9	15.2	3.4	16.4	Kenya	664
28.9	16.2	1.4	40.2	11.5	7.8	18.4	12.3	23.4	12.3	7.0	21.5	20.5	27.4	-2.8	Lesotho	666
26.1	30.6	18.0	7.3	24.4	....	....	-5.6	59.8	7.6	42.4	6.7	-1.4	128.8	14.9	Liberia	668
-.6	21.4	28.4	22.4	31.5	-4.0	31.0	21.6	11.9	56.5	15.2	17.3	22.9	10.9	....	Madagascar	674
8.2	32.3	35.0	46.3	3.9	6.5	31.5	19.4	34.8	50.5	44.0	24.0	16.7	56.2	33.0	Malawi	676
6.2	3.3	-7.0	4.9	-3.6	-10.8	9.0	.9	8.8	47.9	13.8	21.3	6.5	4.5	-.6	Mali	678
26.3	-6.4	17.6	4.7	I7.3	3.5	10.0	4.3	3.6	-5.4	-8.1	-10.9	8.3	32.9	-15.8	Mauritania	682
-.6	19.3	35.8	15.6	18.1	23.7	19.7	8.0	3.0	19.4	8.0	2.7	7.9	9.2	3.6	Mauritius	684
9.5	18.3	9.1	14.5	10.9	I17.1	14.4	6.1	4.9	11.1	6.0	5.8	I7.3	7.8	11.6	Morocco	686
14.6	18.3	39.4	60.0	I36.8	35.8	I33.2	45.3	52.0	50.5	35.0	20.0	25.1	14.5	24.6	Mozambique	688
....	....	....	....	....	....	33.8	22.0	46.3	14.7	8.3	53.6	3.5	27.0	22.2	Namibia	728
2.8	3.0	-11.9	12.3	7.4	-11.7	2.6	-10.5	11.1	15.4	9.2	-9.5	-19.4	-18.5	15.4	Niger	692
8.4	-4.3	17.7	43.9	24.3	29.5	41.0	I73.2	55.1	45.9	16.3	14.5	18.2	20.4	20.3	Nigeria	694
9.3	18.1	2.7	3.1	-12.5	5.0	7.8	24.9	10.7	15.6	41.1	11.7	22.7	-.8	7.1	Rwanda	714
....	....	....	....	....	....	....	....	....	....	....	66.5	107.8	-3.3	3.9	São Tomé and Príncipe	716
1.0	17.3	-5.5	.2	7.4	-11.5	4.4	2.0	-9.0	54.4	3.7	8.5	-.1	15.7	10.8	Senegal	722
15.3	-.2	.1	21.0	16.9	-1.3	22.8	10.2	14.5	-2.7	2.6	34.4	44.2	20.3	37.2	Seychelles	718
85.1	105.8	56.0	60.5	87.1	64.3	76.1	25.1	11.7	10.0	29.5	I6.6	57.1	7.3	49.4	Sierra Leone	724
83.2	24.3	147.4	51.2	207.7	....	....	....	....	....	....	....	....	....	....	Somalia	726
-8.9	8.8	38.0	24.7	8.5	I15.0	....	....	6.7	25.1	18.3	32.0	17.4	23.2	21.7	South Africa	199
I62.7	41.1	32.8	44.4	68.5	46.4	60.2	I101.3	76.1	54.6	66.7	86.2	32.5	29.3	27.8	Sudan	732
13.4	49.7	8.9	13.8	18.4	14.0	9.8	20.2	14.2	7.3	16.6	16.5	16.2	1.9	32.3	Swaziland	734
23.6	40.6	31.6	37.1	I29.6	35.0	22.8	34.1	I32.9	33.3	29.9	4.9	9.9	10.5	16.0	Tanzania	738
-8.8	8.4	1.5	-29.3	-1.9	19.2	4.3	-27.2	-18.5	104.6	37.7	-7.8	1.9	6.9	9.9	Togo	742
13.5	2.5	.7	17.3	1.2	6.1	.7	7.3	3.6	10.7	16.4	13.0	13.0	7.5	16.0	Tunisia	744
131.1	172.1	....	....	....	....	....	....	25.9	36.5	15.4	10.3	13.7	19.5	13.3	Uganda	746
41.6	87.1	40.0	I62.7	51.5	60.6	77.5	....	....	44.8	61.1	19.4	31.0	I16.8	23.6	Zambia	754
16.8	10.4	11.7	28.5	19.5	27.6	23.0	5.8	94.9	18.2	52.4	23.1	53.7	23.5	34.7	Zimbabwe	698
															Asia	
11.2	11.5	54.4	36.5	39.9	39.8	....	....	....	....	....	....	....	....	....	Afghanistan, Islamic State of	512
8.7	8.8	I2.0	4.2	12.9	9.6	7.7	13.6	16.0	24.3	16.7	4.7	7.7	7.4	12.8	Bangladesh	513
24.7	5.8	14.4	30.1	32.6	-1.2	39.0	12.2	I12.1	27.1	26.6	56.8	4.5	21.2	41.7	Bhutan	514
....	....	....	....	....	....	....	....	-1.1	38.1	18.1	17.0	41.2	-2.1		Cambodia	522
I14.7	27.9	18.5	20.0	6.3	20.1	28.2	30.3	I21.8	28.5	18.8	19.8	25.0	12.7	17.5	China, P.R.: Mainland	924
....	....	....	....	....	....	....	24.9	20.9	.1	.3	15.3	-3.8	-4.6	15.4	China, P.R.: Hong Kong	532
1.3	24.9	-2.2	62.1	-3.4	.7	3.4	14.4	15.8	-5.3	12.0	18.2	-2.4	10.9	40.6	Fiji	819
12.8	16.1	13.5	16.5	18.0	14.3	12.6	7.1	18.7	27.4	11.1	14.1	12.6	11.7	15.9	India	534
18.0	14.9	9.2	13.3	42.9	15.9	12.1	I7.9	22.8	22.9	13.7	9.6	33.2	26.9	31.2	Indonesia	536
10.8	16.6	14.7	20.2	17.9	11.0	36.8	13.0	18.1	11.9	19.6	1.7	-11.4	1.6	24.7	Korea	542
....	....	....	....	....	-.2	12.5	24.5	48.6	17.4	9.5	12.5	5.8	111.4	28.4	Lao People's Democratic Rep.	544
5.8	2.8	12.8	14.4	17.3	15.6	9.9	I27.3	35.3	16.8	13.2	I23.7	11.7	-29.4	29.2	Malaysia	548
43.7	15.3	5.1	11.7	18.7	18.9	28.5	15.4	49.7	22.5	5.7	17.8	12.9	15.8	14.5	Maldives	556
....	....	....	....	....	....	4.5	142.8	78.2	24.9	42.7	25.1	8.5	39.0		Mongolia	948
-9.6	41.4	-42.0	65.4	36.1	43.5	I42.2	34.9	25.2	33.8	28.2	33.4	31.0	28.3	22.6	Myanmar	518
13.6	23.8	24.9	13.2	19.3	21.2	24.0	16.0	23.9	20.6	9.9	5.9	8.6	17.9	21.1	Nepal	558
16.3	18.0	19.1	9.7	14.3	17.3	20.2	21.5	1.7	15.1	12.8	7.5	32.5	4.6	8.6	Pakistan	564

		1970	1971	1972	1973	1974	1975	1976	1977	1978	1979	1980	1981	1982	1983	1984
														Percent Change over Previous Year		
Asia (cont.)																
Papua New Guinea	853	...	...	...	...	41.3	7.4	-10.5	25.4	5.7	9.2	3.1	-3.6	-2.9	9.2	20.9
Philippines	566	7.3	16.3	29.1	12.3	24.0	14.5	17.1	23.7	13.4	11.2	19.6	4.4	—	ɪ 38.8	2.7
Samoa	862	41.7	51.6	19.4	19.5	16.0	8.5	16.3	17.6	9.9	10.4	58.4	54.4	23.5	-2.8	14.4
Singapore	576	15.1	ɪ 13.2	35.5	10.4	8.6	21.5	15.2	10.3	11.7	15.8	7.5	18.0	12.6	5.5	3.0
Solomon Islands	813										40.6	37.7	-6.0	10.9	16.9	53.6
Sri Lanka	524	4.4	9.2	15.7	11.9	6.1	4.8	34.9	29.0	10.6	29.7	22.1	6.6	17.3	25.0	14.1
Thailand	578	8.0	10.2	16.4	20.6	9.3	6.1	ɪ 16.8	9.8	20.0	16.6	12.4	2.6	6.8	4.5	8.5
Tonga	866						16.1	4.6	53.9	19.2	2.0	18.3	9.5	111.6	29.7	4.5
Vanuatu	846	...	...	...	...	...	...	...	8.7	6.7	10.9	-10.1	-22.9	20.3	30.3	33.1
Europe																
Albania	914	...	...	...	...	...	...	...	...	...	...	...	...	...	...	...
Armenia	911	...	...	...	...	...	...	...	...	...	...	...	...	...	...	...
Azerbaijan	912	...	...	...	...	...	...	...	...	...	...	...	...	...	...	...
Belarus	913	...	...	...	...	...	...	...	...	...	...	...	...	...	...	...
Bulgaria	918	...	...	...	...	...	...	...	...	...	...	...	...	...	...	...
Croatia	960	...	...	...	...	...	...	...	...	...	...	...	...	...	...	...
Cyprus	423	12.0	9.7	22.9	5.9	10.1	-7.4	28.9	7.4	17.3	28.5	18.4	22.8	16.0	13.7	4.4
Czech Republic	935	...	...	...	...	...	...	...	...	...	...	...	...	...	...	...
Czechoslovakia	934	...	...	...	...	...	...	...	...	...	...	...	6.7	7.1	3.9	4.8
Estonia	939	...	...	...	...	...	...	...	...	...	...	...	...	...	...	...
Georgia	915	...	...	...	...	...	...	...	...	...	...	...	...	...	...	...
Hungary	944	...	...	...	...	...	...	...	...	...	...	...	...	...	2.5	4.5
Kazakhstan	916	...	...	...	...	...	...	...	...	...	...	...	...	...	...	...
Kyrgyz Republic	917	...	...	...	...	...	...	...	...	...	...	...	...	...	...	...
Latvia	941	...	...	...	...	...	...	...	...	...	...	...	...	...	...	...
Lithuania	946	...	...	...	...	...	...	...	...	...	...	...	...	...	...	...
Macedonia, FYR	962	...	...	...	...	...	...	...	...	...	...	...	...	...	...	...
Malta	181	...	...	...	...	...	...	...	...	...	...	...	...	...	...	...
Moldova	921	...	...	...	...	...	...	...	...	...	...	...	...	...	...	...
Poland	964	...	...	...	...	...	...	...	...	...	...	...	12.7	ɪ 21.1	40.4	9.7	15.5
Romania	968	...	...	...	...	35.8	8.3	15.6	10.9	12.2	7.7	ɪ 12.5	18.4	23.2	-6.4	3.9
Russia	922	...	...	...	...	...	...	...	...	...	...	...	...	...	...	...
Slovak Republic	936	...	...	...	...	...	...	...	...	...	...	...	...	...	...	...
Slovenia	961	...	...	...	...	...	...	...	...	...	...	...	...	...	...	...
Turkey	186	ɪ 18.1	23.5	22.1	32.3	27.6	31.2	27.6	38.6	37.4	58.0	66.1	35.1	38.0	47.9	19.0
Ukraine	926	...	...	...	...	...	...	...	...	...	...	...	...	...	...	...
Yugoslavia, SFR	188	18.2	15.9	41.7	38.4	25.2	32.8	60.2	ɪ 16.8	17.6	17.3	32.5	25.8	27.9	20.2	43.2
Middle East																
Bahrain	419	10.2	28.0	13.7	7.5	3.3	26.8	64.5	19.2	12.4	8.6	3.3	29.4	-10.4	-7.0	.5
Egypt	469	4.9	8.1	16.9	21.8	24.7	23.9	20.2	31.4	20.7	22.6	ɪ 11.6	12.9	24.9	14.5	13.8
Iran, I.R. of	429	14.7	20.7	38.3	29.7	37.2	20.1	45.8	23.0	31.2ᵉ	56.7	33.7	16.8	24.9	19.1	...
Iraq	433	6.0	4.3	14.4	24.2	43.3	35.3	20.7	...	...	...	...	...	...	...	...
Israel	436	13.8	28.7	ɪ 28.0	33.2	17.5	22.0	26.9	38.8	44.0	31.6	96.7	91.3	109.2	140.8	352.3
Jordan	439	9.6	2.4	6.5	21.1	23.5	30.6	23.2	18.9	12.6	25.7	24.7	20.8	12.2	10.4	1.0
Kuwait	443	-8.0	8.8	31.8	21.4	13.5	48.4	35.6	24.6	29.7	5.2	7.7	78.5	-.3	-5.3	-18.3
Lebanon	446	1.2	19.4	13.6	15.1	14.5	27.9	27.9	3.2	21.5	8.7	14.7	17.5	22.9	16.9	6.5
Libya	672	19.4	51.2	13.3	24.5	46.7	15.1	31.3	26.7	16.9	33.2	29.0	21.2	-8.0	-10.8	-6.0
Oman	449	...	...	...	31.6	94.0	48.0	42.5	8.9	2.8	7.7	25.7	37.4	17.0	20.2	-5.1
Qatar	453	9.9	20.0	45.7	19.5	36.6	78.3	56.8	32.4	10.5	8.0	-8.7	49.6	11.5	-4.5	14.1
Saudi Arabia	456	3.4	10.2	42.5	39.9	38.7	93.4	71.1	58.3	28.1	11.2	7.8	23.8	14.8	ɪ 1.4	-2.3
Syrian Arab Rep.	463	12.1	6.9	25.9	20.5	45.9	25.7	22.9	27.6	26.9	16.3	35.6	13.6	18.9	25.3	23.3
United Arab Emirates	466	...	...	...	...	58.4	69.4	81.5	10.4	10.8	8.5	17.3	22.0	8.6	-6.3	-2.6
Yemen Arab Rep.	473	...	...	...	...	31.7	81.1	116.0	60.7	27.6	23.1	7.6	10.1	28.1	23.2	24.7
Yemen, P.D. Rep.	459	8.2	9.4	8.5	16.4	15.0	20.1	47.2	41.4	24.6	28.7	26.9	10.3	14.8	11.7	11.2
Yemen, Republic of	474	...	...	...	...	...	...	...	...	...	...	...	...	...	...	...
Western Hemisphere																
Antigua and Barbuda	311	...	...	...	...	...	...	27.9	27.4	-5.0	18.5	10.8	11.9	-3.4	22.5	14.3
Argentina	213	6.0	13.6	65.0	112.1	57.1	218.2	288.6	134.6	146.4	135.5	95.4	76.6	154.2	362.0	582.3
Aruba	314	...	...	...	...	...	...	...	...	...	...	...	...	...	...	...
Bahamas, The	313	-8.5	-14.5	23.4	-11.4	.4	-3.4	12.5	11.3	16.3	25.7	1.0	6.4	10.1	11.7	12.5
Barbados	316	-1.9	12.2	8.5	9.4	19.4	20.3	6.8	19.3	18.5	38.3	10.2	1.9	.8	24.4	-2.3
Belize	339	...	...	...	...	...	...	15.9	45.9	2.4	12.9	-5.0	-.4	7.6	17.9
Bolivia	218	12.6	15.2	25.2	34.3	43.4	11.8	36.5	20.9	12.4	16.7	42.6	19.7	228.8	207.0	1,798.3
Brazil	223	27.1	ɪ 30.4	37.2	45.8	37.2	42.4	37.5	37.7	ɪ 42.5	74.9	69.7	82.6	68.5	102.7	204.1
Chile	228	65.5	112.2	154.3	322.6	266.0	256.0	ɪ 256.0	72.1	99.1	69.4	51.3	9.5	2.8	15.6	22.8
Colombia	233	15.5	11.9	27.1	30.7	17.8	20.1	34.7	30.4	ɪ 30.4	24.8	28.0	20.7	25.4	23.4	24.1
Costa Rica	238	4.9	30.9	13.9	24.9	14.5	29.1	23.0	32.2	24.9	10.7	16.8	49.0	70.3	38.9	17.6
Dominica	321	...	...	...	...	...	...	9.6	23.2	51.8	72.0	-9.9	-2.5	-3.9	—	27.5
Dominican Republic	243	16.2	12.0	17.5	20.6	38.5	7.2	-1.4	18.6	5.1	27.3	6.3	5.8	10.9	13.7	43.2
Ecuador	248	26.0	12.2	24.6	34.1	48.5	6.7	23.2	30.4	9.7	26.8	23.9	12.1	14.0	31.9	39.6
El Salvador	253	2.5	6.8	23.5	19.6	19.4	16.5	41.4	7.8	10.0	21.5	8.1	.6	ɪ 3.7	-1.3	13.8
Grenada	328	...	9.8	20.6	9.2	1.0	22.8	37.8	10.5	28.9	20.0	6.1	10.1	11.7	-2.5	-12.7
Guatemala	258	7.4	3.5	19.8	23.3	15.6	15.8	39.6	20.3	11.8	10.7	2.4	3.1	1.4	6.0	4.3
Guyana	336	1.2	13.1	19.7	12.0	36.7	56.4	4.2	33.0	5.0	-4.3	11.5	8.7	25.3	17.4	20.2
Haiti	263	8.6	12.6	26.4	22.7	2.9	17.6	36.5	14.5	14.1	11.8	17.8	23.4	-.2	.9	18.2
Honduras	268	7.6	6.6	13.6	24.1	1.3	9.4	39.2	12.7	17.7	11.6	11.5	4.4	13.5	13.6	2.5
Jamaica	343	14.0	26.3	7.9	ɪ 26.4	18.3	24.9	5.0	40.1	20.1	10.4	13.9	8.1	13.1	21.6	23.7
Mexico	273	10.7	7.6	17.9	22.4	20.7	21.4	29.1	ɪ 26.0	27.3	34.3	32.6	33.6	ɪ 62.6	40.3	60.0
Netherlands Antilles	353	16.2	15.9	27.9	.1	14.0	12.8	10.9	25.0	20.7	-1.2	4.6	9.4	12.2	3.8	-5.3
Nicaragua	278	12.7	7.0	21.0	53.1	14.6	-4.4	28.6	5.2	-7.1	96.2	32.4	26.9	25.7	ɪ 67.1	83.5
Panama	283	18.5	4.9	45.7	4.9	21.8	-11.8	9.8	12.2	15.4	22.5	11.3	7.3	5.4	-1.8	2.3
Paraguay	288	11.5	7.4	20.0	32.6	21.0	17.9	21.1	32.3	39.3	24.4	25.9	.1	-3.6	25.6	29.4
Peru	293	57.5	7.6	29.4	25.5	39.4	16.9	25.7	19.4	46.2	70.4	58.4	47.3	40.4	96.5	104.3
St. Kitts and Nevis	361	...	...	...	...	...	...	...	...	...	...	-13.4	229.7	-3.5	8.2	6.1
St. Lucia	362	...	...	...	...	...	...	40.8	13.6	16.3	17.8	16.5	1.6	7.5	1.4	8.0
St. Vincent & Grenadines	364	...	...	...	...	...	...	20.4	3.3	36.2	22.6	1.2	18.6	4.8	16.3	17.8
Suriname	366	7.0	14.1	5.2	28.9	5.2	20.5	17.5	10.8	12.0	11.1	7.6	21.7	17.7	8.0	26.9
Trinidad and Tobago	369	8.5	16.8	19.4	.7	27.0	45.4	45.7	26.8	29.1	22.5	16.6	38.7	37.3	-4.4	-5.8
Uruguay	298	10.9	53.1	55.9	73.2	59.4	ɪ 82.8	65.5	40.4	85.1	71.7	47.4	8.3	ɪ 19.8	6.1	50.4
Venezuela, Rep. Bol.	299	6.5	15.9	18.0	19.0	47.6	51.3	12.5	28.8	-26.1	69.7	17.1	6.9	4.2	25.7	26.7

Percent Change over Previous Year

1985	1986	1987	1988	1989	1990	1991	1992	1993	1994	1995	1996	1997	1998	1999		
															Asia (cont.)	
-1.9	5.1	9.6	14.5	6.9	-.2	21.3	4.9	35.9	3.4	14.0	52.0	-5.5	10.3	21.0	Papua New Guinea	853
6.7	17.4	24.6	13.7	32.8	14.3	15.9	9.1	I22.3	11.3	21.7	19.8	14.2	7.4	38.3	Philippines	566
3.1	8.4	32.6	5.2	9.8	42.6	-9.2	-11.4	14.7	8.1	29.1	-.2	22.5	-10.7	20.7	Samoa	862
-.9	11.8	12.3	8.4	14.9	11.0	7.7	12.7	23.6	2.3	8.3	6.7	1.7	-1.0	14.2	Singapore	576
—	7.2	22.6	31.7	3.8	26.6	23.4	31.9	18.1	31.4	5.0	15.7	7.4	-.2	25.7	Solomon Islands	813
12.1	12.8	18.3	29.1	I9.1	12.8	17.7	7.4	18.6	18.7	6.7	4.0	9.8	12.1	12.8	Sri Lanka	524
-3.3	19.3	29.3	12.2	17.7	11.9	13.8	12.3	18.6	17.0	12.1	9.1	1.5	4.9	64.0	Thailand	578
8.7	21.6	14.3	3.2	9.5	29.8	15.2	-12.7	20.5	1.8	-10.5	-5.7	2.5	6.6	22.0	Tonga	866
-12.7	6.4	50.1	-16.7	24.3	-10.9	12.4	15.5	12.3	.9	10.1	3.5	1.8	14.4	.2	Vanuatu	846
															Europe	
										52.8	52.6	1.4	-8.7	23.0	Albania	914
								1,060.1	907.3	124.3	32.4	10.6	19.6	-.9	Armenia	911
								980.1	468.3	130.5	30.4	36.1	-25.6	19.6	Azerbaijan	912
										273.2	I56.7	115.5	139.1	188.4	Belarus	913
							53.2	32.2	51.3	I41.9	119.3	I867.9	21.6	8.7	Bulgaria	918
									112.2	24.6	37.9	21.0	-1.4	1.7	Croatia	960
10.0	-1.0	11.1	14.3	7.3	11.4	7.8	9.5	8.5	4.9	6.2	6.8	7.8	3.7	41.6	Cyprus	423
									50.2	6.7	4.7	I-7.3	-3.4	2.9	Czech Republic	935
1.1	.4	3.6	14.3	2.7	-8.4	27.6	15.9								Czechoslovakia	934
							291.5	I75.2	20.6	29.1	30.9	22.6	-3.6	32.7	Estonia	939
											36.8	31.0	-10.0	10.0	Georgia	915
19.3	11.2	15.1	-1.5	25.8	36.2	18.2	32.1	11.7	8.0	3.8	22.3	23.5	17.1	18.7	Hungary	944
									576.0	108.2	20.9	I8.2	-21.3	72.3	Kazakhstan	916
											16.6	7.8	2.9	31.0	Kyrgyz Republic	917
									31.1	.8	20.3	33.3	6.0	6.3	Latvia	941
									41.8	40.9	3.5	41.5	9.0	-5.3	Lithuania	946
									78.3	I22.7	-3.6	16.2	9.1	32.4	Macedonia, FYR	962
											-1.9	—	7.2	10.6	Malta	181
							561.3	304.9	116.5	68.8	I12.4	30.6	I-18.0	38.9	Moldova	921
20.4	21.9	25.9	51.3	253.7	401.1	I28.1	38.8	31.3	39.7	36.4	39.8	17.9	16.2	23.1	Poland	964
I7.5	7.6	1.7	16.4	2.5	I8.8	214.3	41.6	95.0	107.8	57.7	58.7	66.9	17.7	34.6	Romania	968
									187.0	120.7	27.2	55.0	14.9	53.7	Russia	922
									6.2	20.9	15.8	-4.4	-11.4	4.2	Slovak Republic	936
							133.7	41.5	35.1	24.8	18.4	18.1	25.2	26.6	Slovenia	961
39.4	I56.6	66.7	30.6	73.2	58.4	46.4	72.5	64.8	81.5	68.3	129.5	69.1	63.1	77.0	Turkey	186
								1,552.5	444.0	151.7	34.9	43.3	I14.1	36.4	Ukraine	926
45.4	110.4	99.6	214.9	2,020.1	147.5										Yugoslavia, SFR	188
															Middle East	
5.2	-3.4	3.5	-1.0	-2.3	22.2	I1.7	15.4	3.7	-5.5	-3.6	.8	3.7	5.1	16.6	Bahrain	419
18.1	8.7	14.2	12.8	9.2	16.6	8.1	8.8	12.1	10.7	8.5	7.2	9.4	20.3	.8	Egypt	469
		17.3	10.2	15.7	18.1	26.1	14.8	30.0	41.6	32.5	33.6	19.9	22.7	21.5	Iran, I.R. of	429
															Iraq	433
245.7	112.8	49.5	11.3	44.4	30.6	13.7	I33.7	27.9	7.7	15.1	20.4	11.3	12.3	20.4	Israel	436
-3.4	5.8	9.2	19.1	11.6	9.4	15.5	4.2	I7.1	1.3	-.2	-11.8	6.1	-.8	10.0	Jordan	439
3.1	.2	5.9	-7.3	-3.6		-7.7	-.5	1.1	5.2	4.9	.4	-8.3	19.3		Kuwait	443
46.2	50.5	127.2	165.4	57.1	56.7	53.2	74.0	-4.7	25.7	8.6	12.4	10.0	6.3	10.2	Lebanon	446
28.8	-12.9	13.1	-12.4	16.9	26.4	-3.6	16.2	4.5	13.0	6.2	1.2	5.2	.4	4.7	Libya	672
15.7	-4.8	7.2	-5.9	9.6	13.1	3.8	6.7	4.3	4.7	-.3	6.8	9.2	-8.0	1.1	Oman	449
-2.8	11.7	6.5	-28.9	.1	19.2	-10.5	10.0	I4.2	-8.1	-4.9	4.4	6.3	2.1	-.9	Qatar	453
-1.4	5.4	4.9	3.2	-2.2	11.6	17.7	I6.4	-1.6	3.4	-.2	6.1	6.1	-.6	11.7	Saudi Arabia	456
20.5	11.3	10.8	17.7	19.1	24.9	14.2	19.1	20.5	8.1	8.4	7.0	6.9	8.1		Syrian Arab Rep.	463
6.9	-3.2	9.7	6.5	2.8	-2.7	20.9	15.1	21.3	5.6	8.6	6.9	13.9	9.5	8.9	United Arab Emirates	466
14.8	25.8	12.5	2.6	6.4											Yemen Arab Rep.	473
9.3	4.2	7.7	4.3	25.3											Yemen, P.D. Rep.	459
						11.5	24.3	31.9	35.1	17.5	-4.5	6.3	8.1		Yemen, Republic of	474
															Western Hemisphere	
17.2	27.6	26.6	15.9	10.1	11.1	7.0	8.9	1.1	19.3	27.1	-8.7	3.6	24.9	-1.3	Antigua and Barbuda	311
584.3	89.7	113.5	351.4	4,168.2	I1,023.2	148.6	49.0	33.0	I15.7	1.6	14.6	12.8	—	-4.1	Argentina	213
		57.3	20.5	28.2	8.5	18.9	5.5	14.1	16.8	.5	.9	5.7	15.6	7.8	Aruba	314
9.4	11.5	11.5	9.1	1.6	14.3	7.0	3.8	.4	9.1	6.8	.5	15.5	14.7	26.1	Bahamas, The	313
15.6	11.8	18.1	12.4	-12.5	14.6	-5.9	1.5	-5.1	8.3	-17.0	46.4	-1.1	23.4	20.5	Barbados	316
17.2	21.2	18.7	-3.0	22.1	6.1	11.6	6.8	7.9	5.7	7.8	5.5	1.3	12.3	33.0	Belize	339
5,784.6	86.1	I36.6	35.3	2.3	39.6	45.1	32.9	30.0	29.3	21.1	I21.7	19.0	7.1	-5.8	Bolivia	218
334.3	I330.1	215.4	I426.9	1,337.0	2,333.6	429.4	981.8	2,017.8	2,195.4	27.1	29.9	22.3	7.5	13.6	Brazil	223
24.2	43.3	21.0	46.5	17.2	23.3	44.7	26.3	21.2	16.2	22.2	16.2	20.2	-13.3	32.8	Chile	228
10.7			25.7			31.9	45.1	28.1	29.0	20.2	23.4	17.4	-7.8	24.3	Colombia	233
7.7	31.0	.3	53.2	-2.0	3.9	20.0	37.2	7.0	37.9	-6.0	16.9	I54.3	17.1	24.3	Costa Rica	238
-3.6	18.6	58.4	-2.5	-1.9	24.7	5.1	17.3	-12.1	-1.8	24.1	5.1	-.3	7.7	24.9	Dominica	321
19.3	55.1	23.2	54.5	26.2	46.8	22.9	17.1	13.9	7.5	17.3	22.3	19.3	6.2	21.8	Dominican Republic	243
25.6	20.1	34.7	52.7	43.8	I59.0	46.7	48.4	63.7	32.5	2.7	28.9	30.0	I32.8	110.6	Ecuador	248
27.0	19.7	-.5	7.9	13.4	22.4	18.1	29.5	17.2	5.2	15.8	12.9	-2.1	3.8	8.1	El Salvador	253
6.7	28.1	7.2	11.7	6.0	3.5	-1.7	23.0	12.7	12.1	4.7	2.0	5.5	13.9	7.1	Grenada	328
54.9	19.5	9.8	14.4	20.7	33.0	18.6	9.1	20.4	40.1	9.9	13.5	I29.9	13.5	13.6	Guatemala	258
20.3	19.4	51.4	54.8	34.0	54.5	65.5	31.5	I26.6	10.4	16.7	14.5	10.0	-1.6	23.0	Guyana	336
14.5	12.7	17.2	-22.1	61.1	-12.6	7.0	27.8	22.7	31.8	31.6	-13.1	I18.7	.3	26.6	Haiti	263
-3.2	8.2	26.6	11.9	20.0	23.6	11.1	22.5	11.9	36.1	21.7	29.4	I41.0	12.7	27.6	Honduras	268
15.3	40.8	5.2	53.0	-8.5	27.4	94.7	71.3	26.2	25.7	38.0	14.4	2.8	6.4	27.6	Jamaica	343
49.6	67.2	118.1	67.8	37.3	63.1	123.9	15.1	17.7	1.1	3.5	36.9	I32.0	15.4	28.3	Mexico	273
13.1	-2.7	10.8	1.6	-1.6	13.0	5.5	8.8	6.5	13.8	7.9	-4.3	—	2.6	3.3	Netherlands Antilles	353
162.8	252.2	637.0	11,673.4	2,368.3	6,286.7	1,336.9	11.4	-4.6	36.2	13.2	I25.9	32.0	16.7	23.5	Nicaragua	278
7.5	9.8	-1.6	-31.3	1.0	41.0	28.7	14.8	10.8	13.5	13.1	3.3	18.3	13.0	1.6	Panama	283
28.0	26.7	53.6	I34.8	31.7	28.3	32.4	22.5	16.5	30.0	28.2	-2.3	10.8	6.3	9.2	Paraguay	288
281.2	87.9	122.0	515.0	1,648.7	6,724.8	127.2	76.9	52.6	28.9	34.2	19.7	69.1	26.3	16.3	Peru	293
12.5	51.4	10.9	-12.3	26.3	-2.0	.6	7.9	9.6	-4.1	14.2	6.8	-1.0	22.6	5.9	St. Kitts and Nevis	361
12.7	37.4	25.6	14.4	12.3	6.3	.4	26.4	6.4	3.5	12.9	-6.9	5.7	6.3	13.5	St. Lucia	362
10.0	20.2	-15.8	17.8	11.5	5.0	-17.5	51.1	-.3	19.2	-.1	6.1	27.2	15.0	22.4	St. Vincent & Grenadines	364
52.5	39.6	27.1	24.5	11.3	4.0	28.2	11.6	87.6	245.6	178.2	-2.0	20.0	34.7	50.2	Suriname	366
-1.5	-7.6	3.9	-13.6	13.7	20.8	13.4	-7.7	16.3	19.5	4.7	I6.1	21.1	5.8	12.3	Trinidad and Tobago	369
108.4	83.7	59.9	57.1	79.2	96.2	96.5	71.2	57.9	40.4	32.3	24.8	16.7	I14.1	3.1	Uruguay	298
8.8	4.4	I39.7	18.7	15.6	58.4	28.4	7.6	11.2	140.1	39.4	I145.0	66.9	-7.3	25.4	Venezuela, Rep. Bol.	299

Money plus Quasi-Money

351 x

		1970	1971	1972	1973	1974	1975	1976	1977	1978	1979	1980	1981	1982	1983	1984
													Percent Change over Previous Year			
Industrial Countries																
United States	111	7.1	13.0	12.7	6.8	5.3	12.1	13.4	10.8	8.2	9.3	8.7	10.7	11.1	10.4	11.0
Canada	156	9.4	9.2	15.0	20.8	19.2	15.4	19.0	14.0	16.9	17.8	9.5	ɪ20.4	5.0	-.9	6.1
Australia	193	5.1	8.7	19.7	21.3	9.2	20.6	12.2	5.9	10.5	11.6	14.0	9.9	10.6	13.2	11.7
Japan	158	16.9	24.3	24.7	16.8	11.5	14.5	13.5	11.1	13.1	8.4	6.8	10.7	7.6	6.9	6.9
New Zealand	196	9.1	16.4	36.1	33.8	6.0	10.7	18.3	14.7	24.7	18.6	9.2	16.4	14.1	6.6	20.4
Euro Area																
Austria	122	12.8	14.7	15.7	13.3	12.5	18.3	16.7	9.0	14.3	8.2	12.7	10.1	10.9	5.2	6.5
Belgium	124	8.1	13.4	16.3	14.0	8.7	15.3	12.6	8.4	7.5	6.2	3.3	6.3	7.2	8.3	4.5
Finland	172	14.6	14.2	18.4	12.7	17.5	22.5	9.2	11.6	15.1	18.0	15.1	15.9	13.4	13.4	15.6
France	132	14.8	18.4	18.9	14.6	17.8	15.7	12.3	ɪ14.3	ɪ12.2	13.6	6.9	11.0	9.6	12.8	10.1
Germany	134	9.5	13.5	14.2	9.5	7.5	11.4	7.8	10.0	10.0	5.5	4.7	3.9	6.6	5.5	5.0
Ireland	178	9.4	8.6	12.9	19.1	19.1	21.7	13.0	20.6	23.5	13.6	20.6	10.8	ɪ16.6	7.1	10.8
Italy	136	15.4	17.8	18.7	20.2	ɪ12.5	24.8	20.5	21.7	23.8	19.6	12.2	11.3	19.7	13.0	12.0
Luxembourg	137	....	....	....	....	....	7.5	16.2	12.0	14.4	14.6	19.4	10.7	-.1	9.1	1.0
Netherlands	138	11.7	13.7	14.0	14.9	14.5	13.1	16.1	13.0	11.6	11.0	5.6	7.7	5.6	4.9	6.6
Portugal	182	14.9	13.5	24.2	28.4	13.6	12.6	ɪ17.0	17.1	20.7	ɪ33.5	34.3	28.7	26.8	20.2	27.7
Spain	184	15.1	24.0	23.1	24.3	19.1	19.0	19.3	18.7	20.3	17.9	16.7	15.8	13.9	ɪ-1.1	5.0
Denmark	128	4.8	8.9	13.4	13.6	8.4	26.9	11.7	9.3	6.4	10.2	11.7	10.8	11.1	27.8	17.2
Greece	174	18.2	22.1	24.2	17.4	20.4	24.1	24.1	22.6	23.8	17.3	21.0	31.3	27.0	21.1	25.8
Iceland	176	23.9	20.8	18.3	32.4	28.6	29.0	32.9	44.1	48.4	57.2	65.3	24.9	70.3	80.1	ɪ34.2
Norway	142	15.0	13.3	12.5	13.5	11.1	15.3	ɪ15.4	17.3	11.9	13.5	10.8	13.3	11.0	10.8	19.2
Sweden	144	5.9	10.2	12.9	13.7	9.7	11.7	5.0	9.1	17.4	17.1	12.2	13.3	8.0	ɪ3.9	8.5
Switzerland	146	10.2	10.5	12.6	7.2	ɪ5.0	7.5	9.0	6.8	11.3	9.5	.5	8.4	ɪ4.8	3.9	ɪ13.8
United Kingdom	112	9.4	13.2	27.9	27.5	12.9	ɪ7.1	11.6	9.5	14.6	12.5	18.5	ɪ25.0	13.7	10.3	11.5
Developing Countries																
Africa																
Algeria	612	12.5	6.5	30.3	12.3	26.6	31.0	29.2	19.1	29.9	18.1	17.4	16.7	26.3	20.3	17.4
Angola	614															
Benin	638	17.2	22.3	13.3	6.4	24.8	72.7	-3.9	14.0	11.7	ɪ14.4	48.9	24.3	30.5	-1.5	15.2
Botswana	616									26.0	11.4	64.5	19.0	-4.4	8.5	28.7	16.6
Burkina Faso	748	7.5	6.0	6.7	36.8	21.0	38.7	29.7	12.7	19.5	ɪ8.7	15.1	19.7	12.0	12.2	15.9
Burundi	618	25.1	14.2	5.4	21.1	17.4	-4.2	51.9	27.9	29.2	7.8	1.1	30.2	-5.1	29.8	3.0
Cameroon	622	11.5	12.9	9.8	22.4	34.9	12.6	25.1	ɪ38.1	15.4	22.5	21.4	28.6	19.0	26.5	20.6
Cape Verde	624	....	....	....	....	....	....		41.0	16.2	17.4	30.6	18.9	26.5	19.3	11.6
Central African Rep.	626	10.3	.9	16.0	4.3	29.5	.6	42.0	ɪ7.0	10.2	20.1	35.0	23.8	-4.2	11.7	7.5
Chad	628	ɪ13.5	7.5	3.4	5.4	41.8	10.4	24.8	13.8	24.1	13.0	-15.3	17.8	4.5	22.3	59.9
Comoros	632													34.9		-16.3
Congo, Dem. Rep. of	636	22.5	7.8	21.5	37.8	32.9	10.0	38.1	59.2	54.3	5.0	62.7	52.0	74.9	1,113.0	-81.7
Congo, Rep. of	634	17.2	8.8	6.3	14.8	39.1	13.4	15.8	ɪ2.4	6.7	21.6	36.6	50.4	26.2	-1.5	7.3
Côte d'Ivoire	662	16.2	10.1	4.4	20.4	50.9	6.4	43.0	50.0	10.9	ɪ6.2	2.8	9.9	3.2	4.8	19.4
Djibouti	611															
Equatorial Guinea	642															
Ethiopia	644	5.8	1.8	16.1	29.9	15.6	9.6	12.8	17.7	12.7	13.2	4.2	11.0	10.3	ɪ15.0	7.8
Gabon	646	8.6	14.2	27.8	32.1	67.1	61.2	86.7	ɪ-2.9	-14.8	8.1	24.6	15.9	13.5	17.9	15.7
Gambia, The	648	15.6	.4	39.2	41.9	9.9	13.4	45.9	-12.1	ɪ47.8	-8.4	10.4	20.9	15.8	26.7	5.5
Ghana	652	10.0	11.1	40.7	18.8	26.7	37.9	37.1	60.3	68.5	15.8	33.8	51.3	23.3	40.2	53.6
Guinea	656															
Guinea-Bissau	654															
Kenya	664	27.6	7.5	13.9	24.7	8.6	17.1	24.1	48.2	13.0	13.1	.8	13.3	16.9	4.9	12.8
Lesotho	666	....	....	....	....	....	....						23.6	28.6	17.1	15.3
Liberia	668	....	....	....	....		-1.5	47.3	12.3	23.5	2.5	ɪ-26.2	-11.5	24.8	10.7	.7
Madagascar	674	15.6	6.1	11.8	3.9	20.8	1.9	16.0	19.9	17.1	ɪ27.6	20.6	23.9	8.9	-9.1	24.0
Malawi	676	15.8	20.3	11.0	34.8	36.6	5.6	-1.1	33.0	4.7	.9	12.6	26.0	14.5	5.9	32.6
Mali	678	11.8	7.6	11.8	8.8	52.0	19.9	11.5	15.4	23.1	ɪ16.7	4.5	3.0	11.7	20.7	34.5
Mauritania	682	32.3	.4	26.3	27.5	55.4	26.5	24.8	5.5	1.9	21.1	14.3	29.3	1.6	5.2	11.8
Mauritius	684	13.9	16.1	26.5	30.0	80.1	22.8	7.1	12.8	21.7	8.8	23.2	4.0	23.4	10.1	14.2
Morocco	686	7.9	12.9	18.2	16.6	29.3	20.1	18.1	19.7	17.7	13.9	10.8	16.4	ɪ21.2	17.7	10.2
Mozambique	688															
Namibia	728															
Niger	692	4.1	26.5	6.3	20.2	31.0	9.8	31.1	28.7	44.0	19.0	20.8	20.7	-11.8	-.3	22.2
Nigeria	694	47.8	6.4	15.6	ɪ25.2	89.2	55.7	41.5	34.5	-2.0	31.0	46.1	5.9	9.5	14.0	11.6
Rwanda	714	21.2	13.7	1.8	35.5	32.8	12.1	34.2	26.0	10.3	26.0	8.1	ɪ9.8	1.4	11.8	10.1
São Tomé and Príncipe	716															
Senegal	722	25.4	2.1	12.6	22.3	47.5	11.4	32.0	15.2	21.3	ɪ3.2	10.3	22.1	20.9	4.1	5.2
Seychelles	718	....	....	43.0	11.1	3.5	29.4	43.5	17.2	13.8	22.3	33.2	-2.2	-7.9	2.8	14.4
Sierra Leone	724	-5.6	11.1	17.6	26.1	18.6	8.3	22.2	21.7	31.6	19.7	21.6	2.6	56.8	31.6	28.3
Somalia	726	42.2	-16.0	32.4	17.5	28.7	28.4	19.4	28.7	32.5	37.4	20.2	30.8	15.7	7.5	26.0
South Africa	199	9.4	8.4	17.6	22.6	16.6	19.4	8.9	10.1	16.0	16.8	22.8	17.2	13.5	13.8	19.8
Sudan	732	12.8	7.8	18.7	23.6	35.3	18.8	24.9	42.9	27.5	30.2	29.4	42.0	41.2	22.7	19.6
Swaziland	734	....	....	....	....	....	51.3	25.4	16.1	28.0	2.6	13.7	5.7	14.2	22.8	20.5
Tanzania	738	12.0	18.2	17.7	17.3	23.1	24.4	25.1	20.2	12.6	47.0	26.9	18.1	19.5	17.8	3.7
Togo	742	10.3	11.3	-1.5	14.5	91.5	-7.2	45.7	16.7	35.1	ɪ13.4	9.1	38.6	16.5	.5	15.6
Tunisia	744	9.1	21.1	16.7	20.2	28.2	22.2	15.6	13.4	19.8	16.8	18.5	22.7	19.9	16.4	11.7
Uganda	746	19.6	-1.2	28.9	35.1	33.9	21.1	32.7	19.4	25.5	47.0	34.8	86.0	11.5	40.0	110.7
Zambia	754	26.3	ɪ4.7	7.1	20.4	7.3	12.0	26.3	12.1	-8.5	30.1	9.0	7.9	33.8	11.1	17.2
Zimbabwe	698	....	....	....	....	....	....						29.6	15.4	24.9	-3.3	9.1
Asia																
Afghanistan, Islamic State of	512	7.2	11.3	13.9	7.6	13.5	12.5	24.2	28.0	16.3	18.6	16.9	17.4	18.3	....	....
Bangladesh	513	....	....	....	....	....	5.3	18.5	23.7	26.3	22.4	20.9	16.8	ɪ14.0	40.0	36.1
Bhutan	514															13.1
Cambodia	522															
China, P.R.: Mainland	924	....	....	....	....	....	....		3.6	49.2	25.9	18.3	14.6	19.7	32.6
China, P.R.: Hong Kong	532															
Fiji	819	18.2	19.1	22.4	13.3	39.2	27.1	1.4	18.7	7.6	20.5	12.3	5.2	8.1	13.4	11.1
India	534	12.0	17.1	15.4	19.5	12.2	14.1	24.5	19.2	21.2	16.9	15.9	17.6	17.0	16.8	18.0
Indonesia	536	39.6	42.7	44.3	49.5	47.3	37.3	31.2	19.5	21.6	37.0	47.8	25.9	14.1	32.5	22.3
Korea	542	27.4	20.8	33.8	36.4	24.0	28.2	33.5	39.7	35.0	24.6	26.9	25.0	27.0	15.2	7.7
Lao People's Democratic Rep.	544															
Malaysia	548	10.9	13.0	23.7	31.2	15.3	14.6	27.7	16.4	17.9	24.1	26.2	17.9	16.3	9.4	11.4
Maldives	556	....	....	....	....	....	....		2.2	5.8	35.4	58.0	ɪ6.7	-10.9	-1.7	32.3
Mongolia	948															
Myanmar	518	ɪ-17.0	4.6	19.3	20.6	22.2	18.7	10.5	4.3	15.7	16.7	17.0	20.4	13.2	15.6	17.7
Nepal	558	ɪ9.2	19.0	16.7	28.6	17.1	11.9	28.9	21.0	19.7	15.8	17.3	19.1	21.4	20.1	13.0
Pakistan	564	11.7	13.8	17.5	13.8	-1.2	21.2	32.2	17.9	19.8	19.1	15.7	11.5	21.8	20.9	4.6

Percent Change over Previous Year

1985	1986	1987	1988	1989	1990	1991	1992	1993	1994	1995	1996	1997	1998	1999		
															Industrial Countries	
9.1	10.6	3.1	6.3	5.8	4.9	3.3	1.7	1.5	.1	5.7	6.1	6.6	10.0	8.2	United States	111
5.8	7.4	8.7	10.6	13.4	7.8	4.8	9.4	11.6	8.0	6.2	5.0	8.6	2.3	5.0	Canada	156
17.9	9.6	16.0	21.3	I−23.2	12.8	1.2	7.4	5.7	10.0	8.5	10.6	7.3	8.4	11.7	Australia	193
8.9	9.3	11.2	9.8	11.8	8.2	2.5	−.1	2.2	3.1	2.7	2.3	3.1	4.1	3.4	Japan	158
32.6	24.9	17.6	I14.9	9.8	12.5	.7	2.6	7.0	7.6	9.3	16.1	5.2	1.8	5.0	New Zealand	196
															Euro Area	
6.0	8.6	7.4	5.8	7.4	9.8	7.5	6.8	5.5	5.4	5.0	2.8	2.2	....	....	Austria	122
5.3	10.5	9.1	5.3	10.1	4.1	5.2	I13.3	12.2	2.8	4.9	6.3	7.1	....	....	Belgium	124
18.1	7.9	12.0	23.0	9.5	5.0	I6.4	−1.0	1.5	1.4	6.0	−2.9	2.5	3.7	....	Finland	172
−.3	7.2	4.7	4.0	6.2	4.1	−4.7	−.1	.7	3.3	8.7	—	6.6	....	....	France	132
I17.8	5.7	5.1	5.3	4.9	17.7	6.3	7.8	10.9	2.5	4.4	7.4	2.4	5.8	....	Germany	134
5.5	−1.3	11.2	6.4	4.5	16.5	4.2	5.4	24.8	10.1	52.8	15.6	19.5	17.8	....	Ireland	178
10.5	8.8	7.5	9.3	I11.7	10.2	9.4	5.4	7.5	1.8	2.3	2.2	−5.8	.6	....	Italy	136
16.1	11.3	15.6	15.8	19.8	16.6	11.4	6.6	....	....	....	....	−4.5	....	....	Luxembourg	137
6.8	5.3	2.0	7.2	10.2	6.9	4.7	4.9	5.7	.3	6.0	5.6	6.7	....	....	Netherlands	138
24.5	17.6	13.7	16.6	12.7	9.2	23.5	17.6	10.7	9.1	8.3	5.6	6.8	5.9	....	Portugal	182
11.8	I19.1	8.4	11.5	11.8	15.3	13.3	4.5	9.8	7.1	6.6	2.6	1.4	7.1	....	Spain	184
18.4	9.4	I4.1	5.5	1.3	6.5	I6.1	−.7	19.7	−10.0	6.2	8.1	6.8	3.3	−.9	Denmark	128
23.1	19.7	I17.6	21.3	22.7	14.3	9.0	7.9	6.9	24.8	12.0	13.3	10.9	6.7	....	Greece	174
54.3	31.7	36.8	30.8	54.4	14.1	15.9	3.9	6.5	2.0	2.5	6.2	9.4	15.2	....	Iceland	176
15.0	2.2	19.2	4.9	8.6	5.6	2.9	8.5	−.7	5.0	3.8	6.9	1.4	15.5	1.7	Norway	142
3.3	13.6	6.0	7.6	11.0	.8	4.2	3.3	4.2	.7	3.1	8.9	1.1	−.4	8.5	Sweden	144
4.2	3.3	10.6	5.4	6.3	.8	2.3	2.6	8.9	4.2	4.6	I9.6	6.6	5.1	13.3	Switzerland	146
11.2	22.6	I24.8	16.7	20.1	10.5	1.7	I6.4	4.5	6.8	13.3	10.7	3.8	7.5	3.8	United Kingdom	112
															Developing Countries	
															Africa	
15.0	1.4	13.6	13.6	5.2	11.4	20.8	I26.1	22.7	13.0	9.2	14.4	18.6	18.9	13.7	Algeria	612
....	....	....	....	....	....	....	....	....	....	....	4,105.6	71.9	57.6	564.8	Angola	614
−.1	−2.2	−11.3	1.1	6.5	28.6	10.7	18.7	−3.1	47.9	−1.8	13.0	4.6	−3.6	34.8	Benin	638
51.1	8.7	67.2	21.2	46.3	−14.0	41.6	13.3	−14.4	12.8	12.3	18.8	28.6	39.4	26.3	Botswana	616
.6	22.4	11.7	16.6	3.7	−.5	4.5	4.0	8.0	29.4	22.3	5.2	17.7	1.0	2.6	Burkina Faso	748
21.8	.1	1.7	15.7	18.9	10.0	18.0	5.7	6.9	33.4	−9.0	21.7	9.2	−3.9	47.6	Burundi	618
17.4	−4.3	−18.3	I2.0	6.1	−1.7	1.8	−21.9	−9.2	26.5	−6.2	−10.1	18.6	7.8	13.3	Cameroon	622
20.0	23.6	8.6	16.9	15.0	14.6	16.2	12.9	18.0	12.2	I18.2	9.7	10.9	2.8	14.9	Cape Verde	624
10.0	2.2	3.6	I−1.1	12.9	−3.7	−4.0	−3.8	12.8	78.5	4.3	4.9	−7.7	−16.1	11.1	Central African Rep.	626
6.1	1.1	3.7	I−12.6	8.1	−2.4	5.6	−8.9	−28.3	31.4	48.7	27.9	−4.1	−7.7	−2.6	Chad	628
15.2	4.3	26.2	15.5	17.7	3.9	3.0	5.3	3.4	7.3	−6.1	9.8	−4.2	I−14.2	18.5	Comoros	632
29.6	58.9	95.9	131.2	67.4	195.4	2,388.6	3,794.3	2,853.1	6,968.9	357.6	....	....	....	....	Congo, Dem. Rep. of	636
21.0	−11.6	6.0	I−2.9	3.7	18.5	−4.2	5.2	−26.6	28.2	−.1	15.7	9.5	−12.8	19.9	Congo, Rep. of	634
13.7	2.7	−3.6	1.5	−8.1	−2.6	.1	−1.2	−1.4	46.8	18.1	3.9	8.2	6.0	−1.7	Côte d'Ivoire	662
18.4	11.3	2.7	7.3	2.4	3.6	4.0	−5.3	.9	3.7	5.3	−7.4	−4.5	−4.1	....	Djibouti	611
....	17.5	−10.5	I−34.5	40.7	−52.0	−11.8	31.0	−25.9	139.5	48.9	42.8	9.3	15.6	68.7	Equatorial Guinea	642
15.8	11.9	6.4	11.3	14.3	18.5	17.0	16.2	9.8	25.3	9.0	9.4	14.6	−2.8	6.8	Ethiopia	644
12.1	−10.1	−13.0	I4.1	6.0	3.3	7.0	−21.6	−1.7	37.4	10.1	17.2	11.3	−1.8	−3.0	Gabon	646
51.3	7.3	24.6	14.7	20.8	8.4	25.7	13.8	12.8	−3.8	14.2	5.8	23.0	10.2	12.1	Gambia, The	648
46.2	47.9	53.3	46.3	54.7	13.3	I16.7	52.2	26.4	45.7	40.4	32.6	45.5	26.1	16.2	Ghana	652
....	....	....	....	....	....	....	23.3	22.8	−3.4	11.3	3.6	18.2	....	....	Guinea	656
....	....	160.9	73.3	37.6	574.6	−67.3	110.9	40.5	48.5	43.0	48.3	119.4	−11.1	21.5	Guinea-Bissau	654
6.3	32.7	11.1	8.0	12.9	20.1	19.6	39.0	28.0	31.5	24.8	25.4	18.7	2.6	6.0	Kenya	664
24.1	13.3	9.9	26.6	13.4	8.4	9.2	9.8	29.4	10.9	8.2	18.1	9.4	20.5	−5.1	Lesotho	666
17.7	18.7	15.0	9.7	21.1	....	....	19.6	65.6	11.7	29.5	−11.9	3.5	106.0	11.6	Liberia	668
13.3	25.6	18.4	22.4	33.7	4.5	31.1	22.3	24.2	52.6	15.9	16.2	20.8	6.2	....	Madagascar	674
−1.0	27.1	36.8	21.5	6.1	11.1	25.4	15.8	39.9	36.5	56.2	39.6	2.1	60.0	26.5	Malawi	676
8.7	6.1	−4.0	8.3	1.0	−4.9	13.1	3.0	8.4	39.2	7.3	24.5	8.9	4.2	1.0	Mali	678
22.2	7.5	18.5	2.0	I13.7	11.5	9.3	7.2	.7	−.5	−5.1	−5.1	8.0	4.1	2.1	Mauritania	682
31.5	29.1	29.8	28.7	15.4	21.2	21.9	15.9	17.0	12.3	18.7	7.6	16.4	11.2	15.2	Mauritius	684
13.2	16.9	9.9	15.2	12.2	I17.4	16.8	9.3	7.9	10.2	7.0	6.6	I8.1	6.0	10.2	Morocco	686
15.1	19.9	47.2	62.7	I44.3	37.2	I40.9	70.8	67.1	50.4	47.5	19.1	23.9	17.9	31.8	Mozambique	688
....	....	....	....	....	....	30.3	23.5	25.7	25.9	24.2	29.0	6.7	11.3	18.4	Namibia	728
7.0	12.0	−5.5	15.2	5.8	−4.1	−8.9	−1.0	.1	6.7	3.8	−6.6	−21.3	−18.5	15.4	Niger	692
9.0	2.0	22.4	32.9	12.9	32.7	37.4	I59.1	52.6	35.9	19.4	16.8	16.9	23.2	31.7	Nigeria	694
17.2	13.6	10.3	7.4	−4.2	5.6	5.5	12.4	2.5	−3.7	69.5	8.6	29.1	3.5	8.1	Rwanda	714
....	....	....	....	....	....	....	....	....	....	....	84.5	116.4	2.8	−2.2	São Tomé and Príncipe	716
4.5	11.2	−.3	.5	10.3	−4.8	5.8	3.6	−12.6	38.7	7.4	11.7	3.7	8.5	13.1	Senegal	722
14.2	11.5	8.8	22.3	17.2	14.5	11.5	13.1	20.9	−.8	10.5	14.8	43.1	20.2	21.7	Seychelles	718
71.1	88.4	64.0	56.9	74.2	74.0	76.2	33.2	21.9	8.8	19.6	I29.7	47.1	11.3	37.8	Sierra Leone	724
81.1	34.1	127.1	57.2	162.8	....	....	....	....	....	....	....	....	....	....	Somalia	726
14.6	8.8	19.5	27.0	20.6	I11.1	....	....	6.3	18.3	16.0	14.3	17.8	13.7	11.0	South Africa	199
I52.8	27.9	36.5	32.8	53.3	48.8	67.5	I139.8	104.0	51.2	73.3	65.3	37.7	29.9	22.4	Sudan	732
22.9	11.1	14.1	37.2	25.7	.6	20.1	21.2	13.6	10.9	3.9	16.3	19.4	12.9	15.6	Swaziland	734
30.3	27.9	32.1	32.8	I32.1	41.9	30.1	40.6	I39.2	35.3	33.0	8.4	12.9	10.8	18.6	Tanzania	738
5.2	15.6	−1.0	−11.9	1.1	9.5	3.1	−18.0	−16.2	44.3	22.3	−6.3	5.3	.1	8.4	Togo	742
14.4	4.9	14.9	17.5	15.5	7.6	5.8	8.3	6.1	8.1	6.6	13.3	16.5	5.4	18.9	Tunisia	744
127.4	174.4	153.4	....	....	....	....	....	57.2	35.8	13.9	19.3	19.4	22.9	14.1	Uganda	746
23.4	93.3	54.3	I61.6	65.2	47.9	97.3	....	....	59.2	55.5	35.0	25.1	I25.6	27.7	Zambia	754
17.7	4.2	27.1	20.8	24.3	15.1	1.4	12.6	71.3	35.1	25.5	33.3	41.2	11.3	35.9	Zimbabwe	698
															Asia	
10.4	12.3	50.6	34.5	37.1	40.6	....	....	....	....	....	....	....	....	....	Afghanistan, Islamic State of	512
13.6	16.2	I18.8	13.6	18.7	10.4	13.7	12.0	10.5	19.3	12.2	10.7	9.8	11.4	15.5	Bangladesh	513
26.4	7.5	10.8	31.0	34.9	10.5	29.6	13.5	I30.0	23.3	35.6	9.0	58.9	13.9	32.0	Bhutan	514
....	....	....	....	....	....	....	....	....	35.6	43.6	40.4	16.6	15.7	17.3	Cambodia	522
I19.9	30.2	25.3	20.7	18.7	28.9	26.7	30.8	I23.7	31.5	29.5	25.3	20.7	14.9	14.7	China, P.R.: Mainland	924
....	....	....	....	....	....	8.5	14.5	11.7	10.6	12.5	8.7	11.1	8.3		China, P.R.: Hong Kong	532
1.9	17.5	4.0	20.6	9.4	25.2	14.3	14.3	6.7	2.7	4.3	.9	−8.7	−.3	14.2	Fiji	819
16.9	18.0	16.3	18.3	15.7	15.1	18.4	16.9	17.2	20.4	11.4	18.3	17.7	18.2	14.0	India	534
29.2	19.1	22.8	24.1	39.1	44.6	17.5	I19.8	20.2	20.0	27.2	27.2	25.2	63.5	12.5	Indonesia	536
15.6	18.4	19.1	21.5	19.8	17.2	21.9	14.9	16.6	18.7	15.6	15.8	14.1	27.0	27.4	Korea	542
....	....	....	....	....	7.8	15.7	49.0	64.6	31.9	16.4	26.7	65.8	113.3	78.5	Lao People's Democratic Rep.	544
6.7	11.0	3.8	6.7	15.2	10.6	16.9	I29.2	26.6	12.8	20.9	I25.5	17.4	−1.4	16.9	Malaysia	548
29.2	25.3	12.0	14.3	19.8	18.7	24.9	13.0	36.3	24.2	15.6	26.0	23.1	22.8	30.9	Maldives	556
....	....	....	....	....	....	....	31.6	227.6	80.0	32.6	17.2	42.2	−1.7	31.6	Mongolia	948
−1.8	31.3	−24.7	29.9	32.2	37.7	I35.7	33.7	26.9	35.6	36.5	38.9	28.8	34.2	29.7	Myanmar	518
20.0	19.4	22.4	22.1	21.0	18.5	22.7	20.7	24.8	18.1	15.6	12.2	15.8	24.0	21.6	Nepal	558
14.7	16.1	16.4	7.7	7.4	11.6	18.9	29.3	18.1	17.4	13.8	20.1	19.9	7.9	4.3	Pakistan	564

Money plus Quasi-Money

351 *x*

Percent Change over Previous Year

		1970	1971	1972	1973	1974	1975	1976	1977	1978	1979	1980	1981	1982	1983	1984
Asia (cont.)																
Papua New Guinea	853	...	...	...	...	63.6	-23.3	13.2	54.2	4.8	27.3	-3.2	.3	2.4	14.5	15.1
Philippines	566	12.6	15.8	14.0	23.5	16.3	13.8	28.1	28.5	24.2	12.4	20.6	17.4	18.5	I19.6	17.3
Samoa	862	10.6	28.9	12.2	25.8	18.2	8.9	21.6	21.6	11.3	43.1	32.6	67.2	35.2	-12.2	11.9
Singapore	576	15.5	I16.0	25.6	15.5	13.5	17.9	12.7	6.6	10.8	18.8	24.5	22.4	15.9	11.9	6.2
Solomon Islands	813	...	...	...	...	...	...	...	...	...	44.9	-1.4	-17.6	23.4	20.0	35.0
Sri Lanka	524	8.4	10.6	15.6	2.8	12.0	3.5	32.5	39.6	31.4	42.8	28.7	19.9	25.4	20.9	16.0
Thailand	578	13.5	16.7	23.8	22.3	20.4	16.3	I21.1	20.0	19.5	14.1	22.4	16.2	24.1	23.3	20.2
Tonga	866	...	...	...	...	...	7.1	31.3	63.6	7.5	12.7	15.8	3.4	39.3	20.2	11.5
Vanuatu	846	...	...	...	...	...	...	...	7.9	.9	3.0	-12.9	1.2	49.1	8.7	27.0
Europe																
Albania	914	...	...	...	...	...	...	...	...	...	...	...	...	...	...	...
Armenia	911	...	...	...	...	...	...	...	...	...	...	...	...	...	...	...
Azerbaijan	912	...	...	...	...	...	...	...	...	...	...	...	...	...	...	...
Belarus	913	...	...	...	...	...	...	...	...	...	...	...	...	...	...	...
Bulgaria	918	...	...	...	...	...	...	...	...	...	...	...	...	...	...	...
Croatia	960	...	...	...	...	...	...	...	...	...	...	...	...	...	...	...
Cyprus	423	10.1	20.5	20.8	12.5	16.0	.5	19.8	14.9	15.0	19.3	15.6	20.0	18.0	11.5	13.7
Czech Republic	935	...	...	...	...	...	...	...	...	...	...	...	...	...	...	...
Czechoslovakia	934	...	...	...	...	...	...	...	...	...	...	...	7.5	8.3	6.4	6.8
Estonia	939	...	...	...	...	...	...	...	...	...	...	...	...	...	...	...
Georgia	915	...	...	...	...	...	...	...	...	...	...	...	...	...	...	...
Hungary	944	...	...	...	...	...	...	...	...	...	...	...	...	...	2.3	5.1
Kazakhstan	916	...	...	...	...	...	...	...	...	...	...	...	...	...	...	...
Kyrgyz Republic	917	...	...	...	...	...	...	...	...	...	...	...	...	...	...	...
Latvia	941	...	...	...	...	...	...	...	...	...	...	...	...	...	...	...
Lithuania	946	...	...	...	...	...	...	...	...	...	...	...	...	...	...	...
Macedonia, FYR	962	...	...	...	...	...	...	...	...	...	...	...	...	...	...	...
Malta	181	...	...	...	...	...	...	...	...	...	...	...	...	...	...	...
Moldova	921	...	...	...	...	...	...	...	...	...	...	...	...	...	...	...
Poland	964	...	...	...	...	...	...	...	...	...	...	13.0	I22.9	37.4	14.3	18.3
Romania	968	...	...	...	...	26.4	11.5	16.5	13.7	17.2	10.2	I12.8	16.0	14.0	-.7	6.3
Russia	922	...	...	...	...	...	...	...	...	...	...	...	...	...	...	...
Slovak Republic	936	...	...	...	...	...	...	...	...	...	...	...	...	...	...	...
Slovenia	961	...	...	...	...	...	...	...	...	...	...	...	...	...	...	...
Turkey	186	I46.8	28.1	26.0	28.4	25.7	28.0	23.4	33.8	36.5	61.7	74.4	88.2	51.1	29.7	58.7
Ukraine	926	...	...	...	...	...	...	...	...	...	...	...	...	...	...	...
Yugoslavia, SFR	188	23.7	21.8	23.3	32.3	23.2	32.7	38.3	I19.8	28.2	22.2	37.7	31.5	32.8	38.9	45.9
Middle East																
Bahrain	419	16.5	29.6	20.2	13.4	46.4	26.3	64.9	19.1	19.5	2.6	26.7	35.5	-41.8	93.7	-3.5
Egypt	469	5.4	3.0	15.7	22.4	30.2	21.5	26.0	34.0	27.0	31.3	I31.7	30.9	31.2	22.6	18.8
Iran, I.R. of	429	18.0	24.0	35.3	30.3	42.8	34.7	43.9	26.1	23.4	35.5	26.3	16.4	25.6	18.7	...
Iraq	433	5.7	7.3	13.4	25.4	42.7	39.0	21.2	...	...	...	...	...	...	...	...
Israel	436	19.9	33.3	I27.4	22.7	41.6	37.1	40.7	63.2	3.9	57.7	142.6	829.3	141.8	206.9	510.2
Jordan	439	8.8	4.6	8.5	20.4	25.0	32.5	32.6	22.3	28.2	26.3	27.8	20.7	18.9	15.0	8.9
Kuwait	443	-3.5	14.5	17.9	8.7	27.7	30.2	36.9	28.6	24.3	16.0	26.3	41.4	12.6	7.6	5.5
Lebanon	446	14.8	23.6	21.0	21.2	23.9	11.2	5.2	28.3	19.9	26.9	31.8	40.1	20.2	27.1	23.6
Libya	672	16.4	20.0	58.4	51.0	88.2	-21.0	24.4	20.8	6.6	48.0	17.2	-8.2	-7.4	28.2	25.1
Oman	449	...	...	...	4.1	82.9	38.4	39.5	25.5	11.6	6.8	32.0	38.7	26.7	23.4	9.9
Qatar	453	4.5	20.4	43.5	17.0	35.0	66.7	54.7	31.9	15.4	9.6	17.0	41.7	14.6	-.9	22.0
Saudi Arabia	456	6.0	14.1	40.6	35.1	43.5	81.9	66.5	53.9	27.4	13.7	17.4	33.0	20.2	I10.7	6.0
Syrian Arab Rep.	463	13.6	8.0	26.2	20.3	45.8	26.0	23.3	28.8	27.2	16.8	34.4	15.8	20.5	26.0	25.3
United Arab Emirates	466	...	...	...	...	167.5	46.1	89.9	-7.2	13.1	3.7	29.1	23.7	15.6	8.0	29.0
Yemen Arab Rep.	473	...	...	...	...	34.0	79.7	124.8	51.3	32.2	19.3	10.6	12.2	25.4	23.6	27.5
Yemen, P.D. Rep.	459	14.6	4.7	9.5	13.2	13.0	28.4	43.7	47.1	I15.5	29.5	31.6	12.3	19.1	16.9	14.1
Yemen, Republic of	474	...	...	...	...	...	...	...	...	...	...	...	...	...	...	...
Western Hemisphere																
Antigua and Barbuda	311	...	...	...	...	...	...	8.6	-3.7	10.4	15.5	11.2	15.9	13.5	23.8	20.8
Argentina	213	20.8	8.7	110.0	74.6	54.5	152.9	353.5	227.2	172.6	187.4	91.8	100.5	139.1	401.2	655.0
Aruba	314	...	...	...	...	...	...	...	...	...	...	...	...	...	...	...
Bahamas, The	313	-8.6	3.1	8.1	1.4	.5	9.6	19.6	2.7	13.4	15.4	14.7	11.0	15.6	13.1	9.3
Barbados	316	15.4	18.4	13.1	-5.4	24.9	14.2	11.9	9.9	22.7	27.8	13.0	13.8	6.4	10.8	7.6
Belize	339	...	...	...	...	...	...	2.6	26.6	3.2	12.8	8.9	6.2	18.5	4.4	
Bolivia	218	14.8	18.1	25.9	32.7	44.3	23.2	47.5	29.4	13.0	14.8	39.0	27.2	230.4	172.7	1,428.9
Brazil	223	28.7	I34.4	25.0	43.1	35.5	42.9	38.9	44.8	I51.1	73.1	61.4	88.1	84.0	135.8	270.1
Chile	228	57.9	102.0	144.6	334.0	297.3	306.7	I318.7	99.4	94.1	66.3	62.1	28.6	34.8	21.5	22.4
Colombia	233	16.7	13.2	29.2	35.0	25.2	23.2	34.0	33.8	I27.9	22.8	45.6	35.7	20.9	25.4	23.9
Costa Rica	238	6.8	41.9	19.6	21.9	30.5	42.3	34.4	31.5	27.7	34.4	15.9	87.2	27.0	37.0	17.1
Dominica	321	...	...	...	...	...	...	12.6	9.5	19.5	43.9	2.4	2.3	18.4	9.8	16.0
Dominican Republic	243	22.3	18.0	25.6	26.9	42.3	16.0	-.2	18.2	1.2	12.4	6.4	8.5	8.9	18.6	28.4
Ecuador	248	22.8	15.0	23.3	30.9	45.1	8.1	41.8	20.8	8.2	30.5	28.6	9.8	25.3	32.6	47.7
El Salvador	253	6.0	10.5	22.6	18.6	16.6	21.2	30.9	13.2	11.9	9.1	4.8	10.6	I10.2	11.3	15.5
Grenada	328	...	6.4	18.7	2.9	-1.8	22.4	18.9	11.1	18.2	18.5	6.1	7.8	3.9	.2	1.0
Guatemala	258	11.2	11.5	24.4	21.6	15.3	21.0	30.1	18.8	14.0	8.0	10.1	12.6	15.0	-1.6	11.3
Guyana	336	6.7	15.6	20.0	17.0	18.4	40.2	7.8	24.7	9.5	8.0	14.8	16.9	26.0	20.3	16.9
Haiti	263	10.8	16.1	31.6	27.7	19.8	25.9	38.2	19.9	17.6	10.0	23.1	12.2	3.3	4.5	13.2
Honduras	268	14.2	11.4	13.9	21.7	3.4	10.4	32.4	18.6	21.0	7.8	8.4	8.7	20.1	17.0	10.5
Jamaica	343	16.7	24.1	12.3	I9.3	18.8	20.6	8.4	16.4	18.2	15.2	20.4	28.3	26.2	27.2	19.0
Mexico	273	10.0	7.7	17.6	26.3	20.9	17.9	48.1	I24.0	33.2	35.8	36.6	49.1	I70.9	61.9	68.5
Netherlands Antilles	353	20.6	17.3	20.8	7.5	23.8	14.0	12.7	13.6	12.3	3.3	12.2	17.9	17.6	5.7	-3.4
Nicaragua	278	14.9	14.5	29.2	41.5	16.3	.7	33.0	5.8	-7.1	67.1	29.7	37.9	24.8	I53.5	73.3
Panama	283	30.4	17.9	30.0	13.1	19.3	3.3	5.5	16.3	23.8	25.3	26.1	18.6	12.1	-.1	6.8
Paraguay	288	13.9	12.8	23.6	29.0	20.9	26.2	23.4	31.5	30.5	24.2	34.6	19.5	5.7	16.7	16.8
Peru	293	36.7	8.2	24.0	23.1	33.6	15.8	24.0	23.6	61.1	92.0	83.5	68.7	72.0	103.3	127.2
St. Kitts and Nevis	361	...	...	...	...	...	...	...	...	...	...	13.5	22.6	12.1	15.1	13.4
St. Lucia	362	...	...	...	...	...	...	22.4	5.9	19.6	17.5	11.8	17.5	9.3	14.5	11.5
St. Vincent & Grenadines	364	...	...	...	...	...	...	18.4	9.9	27.5	23.3	4.8	18.7	12.6	12.5	12.7
Suriname	366	10.6	13.6	13.0	22.6	7.1	18.8	36.5	18.8	16.1	11.7	7.8	19.5	11.1	10.9	20.3
Trinidad and Tobago	369	17.7	24.0	19.3	13.8	30.4	29.4	34.2	26.6	24.6	29.7	12.6	27.8	34.6	7.3	5.1
Uruguay	298	18.4	51.2	68.1	66.9	66.7	I106.8	99.1	81.7	91.5	85.5	73.2	48.9	I76.1	11.5	73.2
Venezuela, Rep. Bol.	299	7.7	16.7	19.7	19.7	35.6	53.3	23.3	25.6	-10.8	39.0	17.3	13.4	8.5	23.6	18.3

Percent Change over Previous Year

Asia (cont.)

1985	1986	1987	1988	1989	1990	1991	1992	1993	1994	1995	1996	1997	1998	1999		
9.6	13.3	1.5	4.4	5.3	4.3	17.6	12.5	17.8	−1.3	13.7	30.7	7.7	2.5	9.2	Papua New Guinea	853
9.7	1.8	13.3	24.6	30.1	22.5	17.3	13.6	I 27.1	24.4	24.2	23.2	26.1	8.5	16.1	Philippines	566
20.4	20.5	27.7	7.8	16.7	19.3	−1.9	.7	1.4	13.9	21.8	4.9	16.5	2.2	12.5	Samoa	862
3.8	10.0	19.8	13.5	22.5	20.0	12.4	8.9	8.5	14.4	8.5	9.8	10.3	30.2	8.5	Singapore	576
2.6	9.3	34.7	32.1	−.4	9.8	23.9	24.5	15.6	25.1	9.2	15.3	6.7	2.5	7.0	Solomon Islands	813
12.8	4.2	15.4	14.9	8.4	21.1	22.4	16.4	23.1	19.2	19.4	10.5	13.8	9.6	12.4	Sri Lanka	524
10.3	13.2	20.4	18.2	26.2	26.7	19.8	15.6	18.4	12.9	17.0	12.6	16.5	9.7	5.4	Thailand	578
25.7	18.9	19.5	−2.4	7.0	20.6	12.0	−4.8	17.4	17.2	−1.5	9.3	6.9	13.9	12.2	Tonga	866
13.1	26.2	−6.6	5.9	47.6	5.6	−.7	−2.6	5.0	2.9	13.4	10.1	−.4	12.6	−9.2	Vanuatu	846

Europe

1985	1986	1987	1988	1989	1990	1991	1992	1993	1994	1995	1996	1997	1998	1999		
....	....	....	....	....	....	....	....	....	....	51.8	43.8	28.5	20.6	22.3	Albania	914
....	....	....	....	....	....	....	....	1,076.8	740.4	64.3	35.1	29.2	38.2	14.4	Armenia	911
....	....	....	....	....	....	....	....	825.8	1,116.5	25.4	17.1	41.4	−17.4	21.5	Azerbaijan	912
....	....	....	....	....	....	....	....	....	....	158.4	I 52.4	111.4	276.0	132.7	Belarus	913
....	....	....	....	....	....	....	53.8	54.6	76.8	I 39.3	117.8	I 362.1	11.6	11.9	Bulgaria	918
....	....	....	....	....	....	....	....	....	74.6	40.4	49.2	38.4	13.0	−1.8	Croatia	960
10.3	10.4	13.0	I 17.6	15.3	16.8	14.9	13.9	16.3	12.5	11.4	10.5	11.0	8.3	15.1	Cyprus	423
....	....	....	....	....	....	....	....	....	20.4	29.3	6.4	I 1.7	3.4	11.5	Czech Republic	935
4.3	3.8	6.0	11.5	4.7	−.7	26.7	20.4	....	....	....	....	....	....	....	Czechoslovakia	934
....	....	....	....	....	....	....	71.1	I 47.1	30.0	30.0	36.4	37.8	6.6	24.7	Estonia	939
....	....	....	....	....	....	....	....	....	....	....	41.0	44.0	−1.1	21.1	Georgia	915
10.9	8.8	9.6	2.2	16.5	29.2	29.4	27.3	16.8	13.0	18.4	21.2	23.6	29.8	15.6	Hungary	944
....	....	....	....	....	....	....	....	....	576.0	108.2	20.9	I 8.2	−14.1	83.4	Kazakhstan	916
....	....	....	....	....	....	....	....	....	....	....	14.9	32.7	17.5	33.8	Kyrgyz Republic	917
....	....	....	....	....	....	....	....	....	50.3	−21.4	19.6	37.0	6.7	8.3	Latvia	941
....	....	....	....	....	....	....	....	....	63.0	28.9	−3.5	34.1	14.5	7.7	Lithuania	946
....	....	....	....	....	....	....	....	....	−57.1	I 11.7	−1.0	23.5	13.0	32.0	Macedonia, FYR	962
....	....	....	....	....	....	....	....	....	....	....	8.6	8.0	7.9	9.8	Malta	181
....	....	....	....	....	....	....	358.0	318.8	115.7	65.3	I 14.8	34.5	I −8.3	42.9	Moldova	921
21.0	26.5	34.2	63.4	527.3	160.1	I 47.4	57.5	36.0	38.2	35.0	31.0	29.1	25.2	19.4	Poland	964
I 8.7	8.4	3.9	10.3	5.3	I 18.6	102.2	75.4	143.3	138.1	70.1	67.4	105.0	48.9	44.9	Romania	968
....	....	....	....	....	....	....	....	....	216.5	112.6	29.6	28.0	37.5	56.7	Russia	922
....	....	....	....	....	....	....	....	....	17.4	18.4	16.2	8.4	14.7	15.0	Slovak Republic	936
....	....	....	....	....	....	....	123.0	62.2	44.7	29.8	23.3	23.3	19.5	15.0	Slovenia	961
55.3	I 43.8	50.5	65.3	68.9	53.2	82.7	78.7	64.4	145.3	103.6	117.3	97.5	89.7	98.3	Turkey	186
....	....	....	....	....	....	....	....	1,809.2	567.9	115.0	35.4	33.9	I 22.3	41.3	Ukraine	926
61.0	82.2	131.5	242.0	2,347.0	39.3	....	....	....	....	....	....	....	....	....	Yugoslavia, SFR	188

Middle East

1985	1986	1987	1988	1989	1990	1991	1992	1993	1994	1995	1996	1997	1998	1999		
9.1	−2.0	9.4	4.0	4.4	−11.6	20.5	4.5	5.9	6.1	7.6	3.2	10.1	16.6	....	Bahrain	419
18.3	21.0	21.0	21.5	17.5	28.7	19.3	19.4	13.2	11.2	9.9	10.8	10.8	10.8	5.7	Egypt	469
....	....	19.3	20.1	22.5	18.0	25.6	24.4	30.3	33.3	30.1	32.5	23.7	20.4	21.5	Iran, I.R. of	429
....	....	....	....	....	....	....	....	....	....	....	....	....	....	....	Iraq	433
168.5	20.8	27.2	22.3	21.1	19.4	17.7	I 25.5	22.0	24.6	21.7	25.0	15.0	19.7	15.6	Israel	436
6.6	10.6	15.7	15.5	16.5	8.3	15.8	3.3	I 9.3	3.3	5.7	−.9	7.6	6.3	14.4	Jordan	439
−1.5	.4	2.5	6.9	4.8	....	....	.7	5.6	5.4	9.4	−.6	3.9	−.8	1.5	Kuwait	443
56.1	171.9	354.3	47.8	13.4	55.1	43.9	114.1	33.1	25.3	16.4	26.4	19.6	16.1	11.7	Lebanon	446
21.7	14.5	−21.6	22.8	−2.9	−3.5	8.8	17.6	11.1	17.3	20.1	.7	−10.4	−6.3	−40.0	Libya	672
21.1	−6.8	5.3	5.9	9.4	10.0	5.5	3.1	3.2	6.7	7.7	8.1	24.5	4.8	6.4	Oman	449
9.2	11.2	8.6	−8.4	13.9	−4.6	2.4	8.0	I 5.8	9.1	1.1	5.6	9.9	8.0	11.4	Qatar	453
1.1	9.2	4.1	6.4	.9	4.6	14.6	I 2.6	3.4	3.0	3.4	7.3	5.2	3.6	6.8	Saudi Arabia	456
20.6	11.8	11.6	22.0	21.4	26.1	23.3	19.6	19.7	9.8	8.5	7.3	7.7	9.4	....	Syrian Arab Rep.	463
6.4	4.4	5.5	5.9	8.7	−8.2	14.5	4.6	−1.6	7.9	10.2	6.9	9.0	4.2	11.5	United Arab Emirates	466
20.0	25.5	10.1	6.2	4.5	....	....	....	....	....	....	....	....	....	....	Yemen Arab Rep.	473
8.0	4.4	7.6	6.1	4.3	....	....	....	....	....	....	....	....	....	....	Yemen, P.D. Rep.	459
....	....	....	....	....	....	11.3	20.9	31.1	32.5	50.7	8.1	11.2	11.8	....	Yemen, Republic of	474

Western Hemisphere

1985	1986	1987	1988	1989	1990	1991	1992	1993	1994	1995	1996	1997	1998	1999		
11.8	18.2	18.9	11.2	13.3	4.8	15.2	5.7	8.6	10.9	21.2	−4.0	7.7	15.7	9.9	Antigua and Barbuda	311
428.2	113.0	163.1	442.8	2,235.2	I 1,098.6	141.3	62.5	46.5	I 17.6	−2.8	18.8	25.5	10.5	2.4	Argentina	213
....	....	40.3	18.7	20.9	17.2	18.6	12.5	5.7	13.9	4.2	4.3	4.0	13.6	10.2	Aruba	314
5.8	9.9	15.7	8.4	7.9	16.8	6.6	5.5	16.1	8.7	8.5	5.6	23.5	16.2	10.6	Bahamas, The	313
9.1	9.3	14.3	11.1	1.1	13.8	−1.1	5.0	2.9	8.9	4.9	19.3	8.8	7.6	12.1	Barbados	316
8.5	18.7	21.4	4.3	13.9	15.2	10.1	13.0	3.3	8.4	18.2	7.6	11.5	5.9	15.8	Belize	339
6,987.9	184.4	I 45.0	28.6	22.2	52.8	50.5	34.5	33.7	24.2	7.7	I 24.2	16.7	12.9	5.7	Bolivia	218
322.5	I 268.7	213.7	I 803.7	1,462.7	1,289.2	633.6	1,606.6	2,936.6	1,211.9	31.9	12.2	18.4	10.0	7.3	Brazil	223
47.3	25.3	35.0	27.1	31.2	23.5	28.1	23.3	23.4	11.3	25.8	19.6	16.3	9.6	14.8	Chile	228
20.2	....	....	21.1	....	....	20.9	45.6	37.6	39.7	21.7	24.4	41.9	20.9	13.8	Colombia	233
15.6	21.3	16.3	40.2	16.4	27.5	33.7	24.5	15.2	22.0	4.8	47.6	I 16.4	26.3	21.7	Costa Rica	238
4.6	14.9	29.6	−3.5	11.9	23.0	15.3	12.1	−2.2	4.4	23.0	6.9	3.6	6.2	9.3	Dominica	321
17.8	78.9	13.1	50.2	31.2	42.5	35.3	27.0	21.1	12.1	17.8	18.4	24.2	16.6	23.7	Dominican Republic	243
21.0	22.9	45.6	55.6	39.3	I 54.1	54.1	52.2	63.0	51.6	36.7	43.7	32.7	I 43.3	99.2	Ecuador	248
29.2	24.4	6.2	12.1	12.8	32.4	23.5	30.6	27.4	25.0	10.9	15.5	18.8	10.5	9.1	El Salvador	253
19.4	28.1	11.7	18.2	7.5	10.0	5.2	7.5	21.9	12.2	9.6	8.7	10.4	11.8	13.4	Grenada	328
33.1	21.4	7.6	19.8	16.1	25.8	48.9	31.1	15.1	12.0	15.8	13.8	I 18.4	19.4	12.5	Guatemala	258
21.8	19.3	46.4	36.6	51.4	52.6	73.4	62.3	I 19.7	12.5	24.4	19.4	10.1	6.7	10.8	Guyana	336
12.9	9.2	12.7	−10.3	37.6	2.5	11.9	30.5	29.2	31.4	27.1	1.1	I 24.8	9.7	23.4	Haiti	263
−2.0	9.4	22.0	14.8	14.5	21.4	17.5	22.4	10.4	30.3	29.2	41.2	I 50.5	23.2	24.4	Honduras	268
24.8	27.7	12.6	32.3	6.6	21.5	51.4	75.8	35.9	40.6	31.8	10.9	13.3	7.7	14.3	Jamaica	343
41.1	72.3	141.3	−19.8	124.7	81.9	48.7	24.0	15.2	19.3	31.7	25.3	I 34.6	19.7	11.8	Mexico	273
2.4	−6.1	8.9	13.1	−.2	10.1	7.9	8.3	9.4	8.7	7.5	−3.5	2.1	4.0	5.6	Netherlands Antilles	353
140.2	234.5	544.2	12,513.1	2,700.2	7,677.8	1,519.6	20.1	25.2	66.0	35.1	I 40.6	54.4	30.5	18.8	Nicaragua	278
4.8	20.9	−3.4	−27.6	−2.9	36.6	31.0	25.0	17.2	15.5	7.9	6.1	15.0	13.0	8.5	Panama	283
20.8	27.4	35.0	I 20.0	60.7	52.5	48.0	36.2	27.7	24.3	21.6	18.2	9.2	9.0	11.7	Paraguay	288
156.5	54.0	106.5	621.0	1,917.3	6,384.9	230.6	88.2	71.8	37.2	29.3	37.2	30.8	17.3	14.5	Peru	293
19.5	13.9	−8.7	8.8	21.2	7.7	5.8	15.2	11.0	1.0	14.9	2.2	14.4	11.1	3.8	St. Kitts and Nevis	361
19.9	25.4	16.3	7.5	16.7	12.5	7.8	4.1	1.9	10.2	9.9	4.3	3.9	10.7	9.0	St. Lucia	362
14.5	15.7	7.4	1.1	13.3	14.0	−1.2	8.4	8.5	5.5	5.4	5.9	12.4	15.4	16.5	St. Vincent & Grenadines	364
32.1	25.3	28.0	23.7	18.2	4.3	23.6	19.4	65.7	204.7	181.5	38.5	19.0	37.8	37.2	Suriname	366
1.2	−2.7	3.5	.6	6.4	6.2	2.5	−6.9	15.3	16.7	4.0	I 5.8	11.3	14.5	4.2	Trinidad and Tobago	369
56.4	94.5	57.4	83.1	104.0	118.5	79.8	50.0	37.4	42.1	39.0	36.6	28.4	I 19.3	13.1	Uruguay	298
9.7	12.9	I 30.9	16.4	45.6	71.2	39.2	16.5	25.3	69.2	37.1	I 69.1	58.5	6.5	20.9	Venezuela, Rep. Bol.	299

Ratio of Reserve Money to Money plus Quasi-Money

		1970	1971	1972	1973	1974	1975	1976	1977	1978	1979	1980	1981	1982	1983	1984
																Percent
Industrial Countries																
United States	111	12.4	12.0	11.0	11.2	11.2	10.7	10.0	9.9	10.1	9.9	9.6	9.0	8.7	8.3	8.0
Canada	156	15.3	16.1	16.2	15.6	14.9	14.9	13.7	13.5	12.9	11.9	12.0	‖10.2	10.1	10.3	9.9
Australia	193	10.4	11.3	11.3	11.8	9.5	10.1	10.1	10.0	9.0	8.8	8.4	8.5	8.4	8.4	8.3
Japan	158	11.4	10.5	10.9	12.5	13.0	11.9	11.3	11.1	11.2	11.1	11.1	10.3	10.2	10.0	10.2
New Zealand	196	12.7	11.0	13.3	14.6	14.5	10.6	9.4	8.9	8.6	7.9	6.5	6.3	6.0	6.3	5.6
Euro Area																
Austria	122	22.7	22.1	22.0	19.8	19.4	19.1	17.1	16.4	16.6	15.6	14.8	14.3	13.4	13.6	13.1
Belgium	124	21.3	20.1	19.8	19.5	18.7	17.3	16.4	16.4	16.4	16.0	‖15.6	15.0	14.0	13.3	12.8
Finland	172	7.7	7.5	7.3	7.2	7.2	6.8	6.3	6.2	6.5	8.8	10.3	8.7	8.8	9.7	11.9
France	132	38.8	36.2	40.1	37.6	36.1	24.5	23.4	‖22.3	‖22.3	21.1	22.6	21.3	23.0	21.6	21.7
Germany	134	19.8	20.1	22.2	21.8	20.1	18.5	18.9	18.6	19.1	19.0	17.5	16.6	16.4	16.4	16.2
Ireland	178	20.8	24.3	24.2	25.3	26.4	25.3	26.2	24.7	25.1	24.3	23.4	20.4	‖19.1	19.8	19.3
Italy	136	21.9	21.8	20.6	19.8	‖20.7	23.3	23.2	22.8	23.0	21.9	22.0	22.2	21.3	22.0	22.5
Luxembourg	137	....	....	....	....	....	....	....	....	....	....	....	....	....	—	—
Netherlands	138	14.7	13.5	12.9	11.8	11.1	11.1	10.4	10.1	9.7	9.5	9.7	9.2	9.3	10.0	9.9
Portugal	182	23.5	23.7	22.8	20.0	23.7	29.0	‖26.7	24.1	23.0	‖22.6	20.4	21.6	22.1	20.8	17.0
Denmark	128	21.4	20.4	18.9	17.0	16.5	18.1	16.8	13.5	13.6	14.0	13.1	12.9	11.9	10.0	9.4
Greece	174	37.6	37.0	35.6	36.2	36.5	35.8	34.8	34.4	33.6	31.9	33.7	37.1	37.4	33.9	35.2
Iceland	176	33.9	32.2	32.9	36.4	36.1	37.7	38.6	40.7	41.2	39.9	40.6	53.8	49.1	48.7	‖50.1
Norway	142	18.9	18.6	17.3	16.2	16.6	16.9	‖16.4	15.7	15.8	15.2	14.9	13.0	12.5	11.8	11.4
Sweden	144	12.3	12.5	12.2	11.7	14.4	12.8	13.5	13.6	13.2	15.5	12.5	12.3	12.1	‖11.9	11.7
Switzerland	146	24.1	25.9	24.8	24.0	‖23.6	22.5	22.2	21.6	22.8	19.2	19.3	17.1	‖17.4	16.9	‖15.4
United Kingdom	112	20.7	17.3	16.4	16.9	15.6	‖16.0	17.2	16.6	15.9	15.5	12.7	‖10.6	9.7	9.0	7.2
Developing Countries																
Africa																
Algeria	612	36.5	42.3	39.2	45.3	40.7	39.9	42.3	41.8	42.2	44.5	45.7	44.0	36.3	36.3	35.5
Angola	614															
Benin	638	47.8	44.0	45.7	44.1	36.3	27.4	33.5	30.0	25.6	‖35.3	29.6	38.5	30.3	24.5	26.2
Botswana	616							38.0	33.5	29.4	28.7	26.4	23.3	18.9	15.4	15.4
Burkina Faso	748	62.7	58.3	58.7	52.2	51.1	48.2	42.2	44.1	35.7	‖43.0	40.6	41.3	40.1	52.5	61.8
Burundi	618	60.6	61.6	61.6	54.7	55.9	56.9	63.0	68.3	62.0	54.8	60.0	·63.4	57.4	56.3	59.0
Cameroon	622	49.5	45.8	42.8	41.1	37.2	34.4	32.5	‖30.7	30.9	30.0	28.6	29.7	26.3	26.8	21.8
Cape Verde	624	....	....	....	....	....	....	102.7	102.7	101.1	97.2	94.0	87.7	87.7	90.1	85.8
Central African Rep.	626	59.8	58.2	56.4	56.0	54.7	56.5	46.9	‖54.3	58.9	64.9	65.7	69.3	70.9	70.7	70.4
Chad	628	‖61.4	64.4	69.6	65.2	60.8	70.5	67.2	64.7	59.8	71.9	73.9	68.7	70.9	71.0	68.2
Comoros	632													56.0	46.1	48.1
Congo, Dem. Rep. of	636	68.6	55.4	57.4	48.9	45.0	57.4	75.9	61.5	62.2	48.5	63.8	66.8	73.2	96.6	83.4
Congo, Rep. of	634	44.7	45.2	49.8	49.0	46.1	50.4	46.7	‖48.0	45.6	45.4	43.4	34.4	37.9	40.1	37.0
Côte d'Ivoire	662	46.0	46.6	50.4	46.1	42.8	44.3	37.6	34.8	41.5	‖40.6	40.0	39.9	36.3	37.2	37.4
Djibouti	611															19.6
Equatorial Guinea	642															
Ethiopia	644	56.7	52.5	50.3	46.5	51.4	64.9	69.2	58.6	57.0	55.4	59.6	61.6	60.8	‖52.9	58.8
Gabon	646	33.2	35.2	31.4	30.8	34.0	27.2	24.0	‖25.1	25.7	25.3	24.1	22.3	21.4	19.9	20.3
Gambia, The	648	36.2	37.5	29.5	35.7	32.1	30.6	25.0	22.5	‖23.1	29.8	29.9	33.8	34.3	36.5	‖33.8
Ghana	652	49.6	46.1	48.4	50.6	54.3	58.2	60.2	60.8	66.6	68.0	66.4	68.1	63.2	64.6	62.7
Guinea	656															
Guinea-Bissau	654															
Kenya	664	35.6	30.3	29.4	26.0	30.7	23.7	23.7	25.8	24.5	27.0	27.4	25.2	27.1	25.2	24.9
Lesotho	666											34.5	29.5	24.8	33.4	34.1
Liberia	668	....	....	....	....	16.4	17.6	14.1	15.0	20.9	19.6	‖35.9	39.1	43.8	49.5	59.4
Madagascar	674	51.2	47.7	49.1	49.9	48.8	51.2	50.4	47.1	53.5	‖40.8	45.7	49.5	44.9	47.0	41.4
Malawi	676	35.1	33.0	34.4	53.6	51.1	42.9	28.6	39.5	24.7	22.7	27.8	29.7	30.7	30.6	40.7
Mali	678	64.4	64.9	63.7	62.8	54.9	‖57.5	62.0	65.5	59.6	‖63.5	64.7	63.2	62.2	57.5	‖54.2
Mauritania	682	38.0	38.3	41.8	39.0	58.4	41.6	36.3	39.0	41.5	45.9	42.9	43.8	42.7	39.5	35.5
Mauritius	684	31.4	27.2	32.1	29.3	30.0	33.6	37.1	39.0	37.7	33.5	30.1	30.1	27.1	26.1	24.4
Morocco	686	43.1	42.3	42.5	41.9	39.1	37.4	38.6	37.2	36.5	37.3	35.4	34.5	‖30.5	29.3	29.7
Mozambique	688															40.8
Namibia	728															
Niger	692	52.4	52.1	50.0	48.0	51.9	45.1	48.4	45.7	48.8	46.4	44.6	43.7	50.3	46.3	48.2
Nigeria	694	50.6	50.3	46.7	‖46.1	61.2	60.5	54.7	50.3	49.5	43.9	50.8	46.4	45.8	41.7	38.5
Rwanda	714	84.6	72.5	79.6	76.0	75.3	68.3	66.6	60.0	55.6	63.5	54.9	‖43.7	44.8	44.7	43.0
São Tomé and Príncipe	716															
Senegal	722	43.9	45.2	42.1	41.7	42.3	40.8	34.7	34.7	35.7	‖31.7	34.9	39.6	40.7	37.8	35.6
Seychelles	718	....	28.7	27.5	27.9	28.3	25.8	24.0	26.1	26.4	28.5	36.2	33.5	34.5	35.8	30.2
Sierra Leone	724	52.4	51.3	50.3	49.3	46.6	46.6	44.3	42.4	52.3	67.1	51.1	50.2	60.3	57.3	63.5
Somalia	726	67.6	53.0	56.0	55.3	52.9	52.6	52.6	54.5	57.6	52.1	57.0	55.5	40.8	38.9	49.8
South Africa	199	11.4	11.0	10.1	9.8	9.8	9.4	9.2	8.9	8.6	8.5	11.2	11.2	8.7	8.7	8.4
Sudan	732	56.1	56.2	52.0	53.8	54.5	54.4	53.0	60.1	62.2	63.5	55.3	62.8	58.1	‖52.1	61.1
Swaziland	734	....	....	....	....	15.6	22.0	43.6	52.0	38.7	39.3	42.8	34.8	34.1	40.1	44.5
Tanzania	738	38.9	40.1	41.5	35.6	36.3	33.8	32.1	31.2	33.6	31.8	31.7	34.5	34.9	30.5	38.3
Togo	742	42.1	46.3	45.8	45.0	33.0	45.6	50.9	45.8	44.1	‖40.5	43.7	57.6	60.6	66.6	72.8
Tunisia	744	31.7	34.3	33.4	32.9	33.4	31.3	28.9	26.7	26.1	24.7	23.4	24.0	24.7	24.9	24.6
Uganda	746	40.6	41.2	36.0	33.9	33.7	43.7	47.2	45.3	53.6	60.2	61.1	42.2	45.0	51.5	52.8
Zambia	754	45.1	‖28.0	31.0	33.8	29.1	37.1	37.2	32.7	37.6	30.3	31.6	34.2	29.5	30.3	30.4
Zimbabwe	698										19.4	20.2	23.3	22.2	24.1	24.4
Asia																
Afghanistan, Islamic State of	512	83.9	81.9	78.1	76.4	76.8	80.0	78.7	82.1	82.0	‖84.1	84.6	82.5	‖81.1	....	80.5
Bangladesh	513	....	....	....	....	37.5	34.8	30.1	31.5	31.9	30.2	29.7	27.9	‖27.1	25.9	25.7
Bhutan	514														12.8	24.7
Cambodia	522															
China, P.R.: Mainland	924															
China, P.R.: Hong Kong	532															
Fiji	819	26.4	26.2	26.1	34.8	32.3	33.1	28.1	24.5	25.9	24.1	19.8	21.7	21.4	20.1	20.9
India	534	46.0	43.6	41.1	42.1	38.9	35.9	33.7	34.3	34.1	35.3	35.1	33.0	33.2	32.2	31.8
Indonesia	536											48.0	44.3	40.6	38.4	34.8
Korea	542	33.4	26.6	29.4	31.5	31.6	34.2	34.2	35.3	35.3	35.1	25.9	17.9	19.2	17.9	17.2
Lao People's Democratic Rep.	544															
Malaysia	548	38.0	36.3	38.4	39.7	39.1	35.0	32.5	32.3	31.6	29.4	27.6	25.8	25.9	24.7	22.9
Maldives	556	....	....	....	....	....	....	89.4	81.8	54.3	67.1	67.2	‖67.4	68.6	84.9	85.0
Mongolia	948															
Myanmar	518	‖72.5	71.6	74.4	78.3	78.7	83.1	99.2	90.8	88.0	90.3	86.2	86.0	72.0	69.2	67.1
Nepal	558	‖69.2	62.8	61.2	61.3	54.6	53.3	53.3	47.9	47.0	45.8	43.1	41.4	42.5	40.9	42.0
Pakistan	564	45.8	44.7	44.6	43.9	44.8	40.5	36.7	38.2	37.5	39.9	40.2	39.0	37.7	35.5	39.4

1985	1986	1987	1988	1989	1990	1991	1992	1993	1994	1995	1996	1997	1998	1999		39ab i

Percent

Industrial Countries

1985	1986	1987	1988	1989	1990	1991	1992	1993	1994	1995	1996	1997	1998	1999	Country	Code
8.1	8.4	8.5	8.5	8.3	8.6	8.7	9.3	10.0	10.8	10.7	10.5	10.7	10.3	11.4	United States	111
9.9	9.9	10.0	9.5	8.7	8.2	8.3	7.8	7.4	7.0	6.7	6.6	6.3	6.6	7.8	Canada	156
7.9	7.8	7.6	6.9	I9.1	8.6	8.8	8.7	8.7	8.6	8.3	12.1	9.0	8.8	7.4	Australia	193
9.7	9.6	9.4	9.6	9.7	9.7	9.3	9.0	9.3	9.3	9.7	10.3	10.7	10.7	14.4	Japan	158
4.7	3.3	3.4	I3.7	3.3	2.9	2.8	2.8	2.7	2.8	2.8	2.3	2.3	2.4	4.0	New Zealand	196
															Euro Area	
12.5	12.3	11.2	10.7	11.3	10.3	9.8	10.1	10.4	10.3	9.7	10.1	9.8	....	....	Austria	122
12.0	11.4	10.8	10.3	9.7	9.0	8.7	I8.4	7.7	7.0	7.3	7.1	6.8	....	....	Belgium	124
11.3	10.3	13.6	13.1	14.8	11.7	I12.2	12.9	12.8	19.1	18.3	12.6	11.4	10.8	....	Finland	172
25.2	24.1	25.7	24.5	23.1	21.5	22.0	19.2	18.3	17.8	17.8	18.1	17.5	....	....	France	132
I14.2	14.3	14.8	15.6	15.8	15.0	14.9	15.8	14.1	13.5	13.2	12.9	12.4	11.9	....	Germany	134
19.7	20.6	20.5	19.9	19.9	18.9	16.6	14.4	13.9	13.2	10.9	9.6	9.5	....	....	Ireland	178
23.8	23.6	24.0	23.9	I24.0	23.2	22.6	22.3	18.9	17.6	16.2	16.2	18.5	13.0	....	Italy	136
1.1	1.1	1.1	1.0	.8	.9	.7	.7	....	1.1	....	1.1	1.1	....	....	Luxembourg	137
9.6	9.5	10.2	10.6	11.1	10.7	8.8	10.9	11.1	11.7	9.7	8.8	9.1	....	....	Netherlands	138
14.4	14.0	15.5	15.1	25.6	25.3	25.1	23.6	23.3	8.8	7.9	8.3	7.7	7.3	....	Portugal	182
19.8	12.0	I8.7	8.6	8.2	9.4	I8.6	7.6	10.4	11.7	12.5	15.4	18.9	14.1	28.4	Denmark	128
30.4	30.1	I31.5	27.6	24.5	26.4	27.0	27.7	28.1	31.5	29.2	29.4	30.1	36.8	....	Greece	174
40.1	38.1	29.7	26.3	21.0	16.5	14.6	14.5	12.4	12.5	10.0	11.9	12.1	10.8	....	Iceland	176
10.6	10.3	9.3	8.6	8.4	7.9	8.2	8.0	8.9	8.7	8.9	12.7	11.1	8.5	12.6	Norway	142
11.7	12.9	12.7	14.0	14.0	15.0	13.3	16.0	22.7	27.6	22.7	14.0	10.3	10.7	11.5	Sweden	144
14.6	14.8	14.1	10.9	9.8	10.0	9.5	10.2	9.3	9.0	8.4	I8.0	7.4	7.5	7.8	Switzerland	146
6.9	I6.2	I5.3	5.0	4.5	4.1	4.1	I4.1	4.2	4.1	3.9	3.6	3.8	3.6	4.1	United Kingdom	112

Developing Countries

Africa

1985	1986	1987	1988	1989	1990	1991	1992	1993	1994	1995	1996	1997	1998	1999	Country	Code
34.8	39.7	39.2	37.6	40.1	39.7	38.2	I37.1	38.6	32.3	31.9	33.4	32.8	31.2	30.6	Algeria	612
....	....	....	....	....	....	....	....	....	46.9	39.0	43.6	41.4	32.6		Angola	614
21.5	26.0	24.2	28.8	48.5	60.3	67.8	70.0	63.0	43.2	32.5	31.4	36.0	35.7	46.5	Benin	638
10.7	14.2	10.2	11.2	10.7	16.5	23.4	17.1	18.6	16.4	15.1	14.2	13.9	12.4	11.2	Botswana	616
55.5	64.2	67.9	63.8	52.5	53.5	61.8	63.1	67.5	51.7	52.4	52.2	54.8	52.3	43.8	Burkina Faso	748
60.3	61.2	60.2	50.3	44.9	42.7	41.9	44.0	43.2	41.0	44.7	43.7	40.8	43.6	40.1	Burundi	618
21.3	26.2	29.8	I28.5	26.6	26.5	25.9	28.0	23.8	26.2	22.0	31.4	37.1	38.0	36.2	Cameroon	622
82.4	77.4	72.4	65.5	60.5	57.0	53.4	62.2	75.5	41.2	I42.7	36.5	33.1	35.2	32.7	Cape Verde	624
64.6	71.1	68.3	I68.4	66.5	69.5	72.5	76.5	81.2	83.8	84.0	86.3	82.0	78.0	75.7	Central African Rep.	626
66.3	64.9	69.1	I71.0	75.2	71.0	69.2	72.1	80.2	75.4	80.2	82.4	82.3	80.1	77.1	Chad	628
46.6	59.9	67.1	45.6	52.3	42.0	37.3	36.2	49.2	52.4	50.1	62.2	56.9	I59.1	59.4	Comoros	632
82.2	83.0	85.1	79.9	85.5	82.9	81.0	92.4	84.7	40.3	66.1	....	....	....	....	Congo, Dem. Rep. of	636
34.1	39.3	41.0	I39.3	37.2	42.3	35.6	39.2	51.1	54.0	58.5	54.9	55.9	50.8	56.9	Congo, Rep. of	634
41.4	42.1	44.4	37.8	32.1	35.1	36.1	32.4	35.9	38.2	36.1	37.1	38.3	43.0	40.4	Côte d'Ivoire	662
16.0	15.9	18.1	16.8	15.8	16.8	16.2	21.0	19.2	19.6	16.2	16.9	17.3	17.7	....	Djibouti	611
60.2	80.6	69.4	I58.5	70.9	46.1	57.7	70.7	75.9	56.4	75.4	60.5	60.8	42.2	48.8	Equatorial Guinea	642
53.0	59.1	54.6	58.3	58.1	56.2	61.2	62.8	60.0	52.8	54.6	41.7	39.5	35.7	29.9	Ethiopia	644
16.7	16.4	20.0	I20.8	22.7	24.0	28.7	26.3	24.6	41.1	35.7	39.3	35.9	33.4	31.7	Gabon	646
40.3	36.9	35.3	38.2	40.4	39.6	42.9	38.9	38.4	38.3	42.1	40.0	41.2	40.1	40.9	Gambia, The	648
58.1	62.8	58.0	61.0	48.5	43.9	I37.8	46.7	38.8	47.6	45.8	50.0	45.9	42.4	41.2	Ghana	652
....	....	....	....	....	....	70.9	64.3	62.2	58.0	58.5	55.7	60.0	....	....	Guinea	656
....	98.9	73.6	78.1	77.3	14.1	99.2	77.9	73.3	65.3	60.3	56.4	58.1	56.7	62.7	Guinea-Bissau	654
27.0	28.4	30.5	28.8	29.8	30.3	29.3	32.3	38.5	36.0	37.8	32.6	28.0	27.2	27.2	Kenya	664
35.6	38.9	41.6	48.3	40.0	34.6	37.3	26.5	25.0	24.0	27.8	25.4	26.3	30.2	42.4	Lesotho	666
70.6	82.8	92.4	100.5	108.1	....	114.5	96.9	74.4	70.2	71.2	95.2	99.3	49.1	46.0	Liberia	668
38.1	51.7	52.7	44.6	46.0	39.9	47.2	46.7	35.1	39.6	44.3	56.6	47.4	47.4	....	Madagascar	674
43.2	58.6	66.6	61.0	51.9	39.1	38.5	39.0	45.3	46.9	56.9	56.5	55.4	48.0	50.1	Malawi	676
56.2	59.6	60.1	61.4	69.6	74.2	86.4	83.8	84.4	48.8	50.2	47.7	42.2	44.7	47.7	Mali	678
40.5	36.0	37.3	41.7	I44.6	38.3	47.4	53.7	82.7	80.1	79.6	42.4	34.1	30.3	31.0	Mauritania	682
21.9	20.5	20.0	19.3	20.0	19.6	37.6	29.4	23.4	19.4	18.7	19.5	13.4	12.9	12.1	Mauritius	684
28.2	29.8	28.6	28.8	30.2	I31.3	33.4	28.1	28.3	27.3	26.8	27.1	I27.1	27.4	28.1	Morocco	686
41.6	41.4	44.7	42.5	I38.3	34.3	I32.8	33.3	35.0	38.7	34.6	36.7	34.4	28.1	25.1	Mozambique	688
....	....	....	....	....	6.1	5.0	9.3	7.8	9.9	8.9	8.4	9.5	8.8	10.7	Namibia	728
53.9	52.6	56.9	60.2	57.6	61.9	66.7	68.9	46.9	46.9	51.1	51.5	51.5	40.6	46.4	Niger	692
37.8	39.5	38.4	41.0	49.8	48.0	49.6	I59.4	57.3	56.4	57.0	52.2	47.3	45.2	41.1	Nigeria	694
41.1	41.1	41.2	34.5	30.8	31.9	43.5	37.4	46.7	53.0	43.4	48.9	42.2	37.2	39.5	Rwanda	714
....	....	....	....	....	....	....	....	....	....	51.4	50.5	57.1	61.2	56.1	São Tomé and Príncipe	716
36.0	37.7	39.8	39.4	44.6	45.1	45.6	47.2	37.6	40.5	39.2	30.1	30.0	29.5	30.3	Senegal	722
29.6	26.2	23.9	24.8	22.1	22.6	25.5	34.1	34.8	51.7	56.6	56.0	46.5	19.6	17.6	Seychelles	718
57.0	62.3	64.2	72.7	72.8	69.6	64.5	57.6	49.0	56.5	53.0	I50.6	71.9	51.4	51.8	Sierra Leone	724
42.5	52.5	42.3	45.3	50.4	....	....	....	....	....	....	....	....	....	....	Somalia	726
8.2	8.1	8.0	8.6	9.2	I9.4	....	I9.6	8.2	8.2	9.2	9.1	8.6	8.0	8.7	South Africa	199
I64.7	71.9	67.1	66.7	80.7	72.2	63.9	I67.6	54.6	50.5	51.5	56.6	55.2	55.0	60.7	Sudan	732
40.4	58.0	51.0	30.8	31.9	31.1	23.5	30.7	24.0	25.4	25.1	20.0	17.6	14.3	13.8	Swaziland	734
35.7	39.2	42.0	41.5	I37.5	37.7	32.7	37.3	I36.2	39.7	41.6	40.9	39.4	40.8	41.8	Tanzania	738
81.2	71.8	70.3	59.6	64.3	65.3	66.8	66.8	54.1	38.4	40.5	37.8	36.1	40.1	42.3	Togo	742
23.4	22.5	21.1	19.1	19.2	20.3	21.5	21.2	21.0	20.8	21.4	25.6	23.8	19.9	21.8	Tunisia	744
66.6	64.0	....	....	....	....	I52.5	....	41.2	44.9	44.8	41.9	38.3	37.4	37.7	Uganda	746
30.2	42.3	38.6	I37.9	37.8	45.6	46.5	....	49.0	45.6	25.0	25.1	29.8	I27.7	27.8	Zambia	754
24.9	27.6	23.2	24.3	23.8	25.9	33.8	34.0	30.2	27.6	22.5	28.1	27.4	32.0	37.9	Zimbabwe	698

Asia

1985	1986	1987	1988	1989	1990	1991	1992	1993	1994	1995	1996	1997	1998	1999	Country	Code
80.7	81.7	85.2	85.6	87.3	87.6	....	....	....	....	....	....	....	....	....	Afghanistan, Islamic State of	512
25.8	23.8	I29.2	28.5	26.8	25.3	22.0	23.8	26.7	29.0	23.4	23.0	22.9	23.3	22.8	Bangladesh	513
46.6	55.2	83.2	56.4	75.2	124.0	121.0	84.1	I99.4	53.7	66.2	65.8	45.2	61.7	58.7	Bhutan	514
....	....	....	....	....	....	....	....	68.4	63.2	48.5	49.3	51.3	65.2	64.5	Cambodia	522
I41.4	39.2	35.3	36.6	38.0	38.4	37.6	33.5	I36.8	36.7	34.2	35.3	34.2	30.6	28.7	China, P.R.: Mainland	924
....	....	....	....	....	....	....	....	....	....	....	....	....	....	8.5	China, P.R.: Hong Kong	532
21.1	20.3	18.7	27.6	19.3	17.1	16.7	17.5	16.0	15.8	16.5	16.7	19.2	20.4	28.1	Fiji	819
33.6	33.1	33.7	33.1	34.0	33.6	33.6	31.2	32.4	32.8	33.1	30.7	29.0	27.5	26.9	India	534
31.8	32.4	29.2	21.8	20.2	16.3	14.3	I14.3	12.9	13.4	12.4	13.3	14.7	14.3	15.9	Indonesia	536
15.1	14.8	18.5	19.9	21.9	20.1	19.5	18.8	20.6	18.9	19.0	14.4	11.1	8.0	8.7	Korea	542
....	....	....	....	49.6	49.8	51.2	48.3	48.2	44.7	43.6	42.6	37.0	32.5	31.2	Lao People's Democratic Rep.	544
23.2	21.7	22.0	23.0	24.8	27.6	27.0	I25.5	22.5	27.1	28.0	I30.1	32.7	20.4	29.0	Malaysia	548
88.9	81.0	74.2	79.4	78.9	82.7	80.8	96.2	84.0	77.2	67.9	63.5	59.5	53.7	55.5	Maldives	556
....	....	....	....	....	....	20.8	38.4	33.4	37.8	36.8	42.8	37.0	44.5	50.9	Mongolia	948
61.1	65.8	48.7	65.9	137.5	121.4	I87.7	85.5	81.3	73.8	69.1	65.6	66.0	62.3	57.0	Myanmar	518
39.6	42.1	40.7	38.4	38.8	40.2	41.9	40.2	41.9	39.6	37.2	36.5	36.2	37.1	33.6	Nepal	558
37.3	38.5	39.6	40.7	44.4	46.1	49.3	41.5	40.1	39.6	41.0	32.9	31.4	32.8	35.6	Pakistan	564

Ratio of Reserve Money to Money plus Quasi-Money

39ab i

		1970	1971	1972	1973	1974	1975	1976	1977	1978	1979	1980	1981	1982	1983	1984
																Percent
Asia (cont.)																
Papua New Guinea	853	....	....	....	32.8	25.5	57.9	60.5	47.5	43.2	41.2	18.0	16.0	15.9	21.2	17.1
Philippines	566	36.5	34.8	38.2	34.8	37.3	37.2	32.7	31.4	31.4	34.3	31.9	29.9	26.6	Ɪ23.2	23.7
Samoa	862	3.6	3.3	3.3	3.2	3.1	6.1	6.3	7.1	6.5	5.7	27.8	22.4	19.0	24.2	25.1
Singapore	576	24.6	Ɪ23.7	24.5	29.2	26.7	26.9	27.9	29.6	31.0	29.8	27.0	24.4	25.0	24.4	24.5
Solomon Islands	813	....	....	....	....	....	....	....	....	88.6	68.0	44.5	30.1	39.3	43.6	44.8
Sri Lanka	524	44.2	45.5	46.4	53.0	51.2	46.2	43.8	45.7	39.1	33.5	31.1	30.6	30.2	31.6	31.8
Thailand	578	36.6	34.8	33.1	31.9	30.0	28.6	Ɪ26.7	24.3	23.8	24.4	22.8	20.9	18.8	16.9	14.8
Tonga	866	....	....	....	....	....	....	....	....	....	....	....	....	109.3	120.7	129.6
Vanuatu	846	....	....	....	....	....	10.5	11.5	13.2	16.0	16.1	12.1	8.5	9.2	9.0	
Europe																
Albania	914	....	....	....	....	....	....	....	....	....	....	....	....	....	....	....
Armenia	911	....	....	....	....	....	....	....	....	....	....	....	....	....	....	....
Azerbaijan	912	....	....	....	....	....	....	....	....	....	....	....	....	....	....	....
Belarus	913	....	....	....	....	....	....	....	....	....	....	....	....	....	....	....
Bulgaria	918	....	....	....	....	....	....	....	....	....	....	....	....	....	....	....
Croatia	960	....	....	....	....	....	....	....	....	....	....	....	....	....	....	....
Cyprus	423	33.9	36.9	36.4	34.0	33.7	34.0	35.0	34.4	34.7	34.8	38.5	39.4	41.4	43.0	44.4
Czech Republic	935	....	....	....	....	....	....	....	....	....	....	....	....	....	....	....
Czechoslovakia	934	14.0	....	....	....	....	17.1	....	....	....	....	30.6	27.8	24.5	23.1	22.7
Estonia	939	....	....	....	....	....	....	....	....	....	....	....	....	....	....	....
Georgia	915	....	....	....	....	....	....	....	....	....	....	....	....	....	....	....
Hungary	944	....	....	....	....	....	....	....	....	....	....	....	....	86.4	75.8	64.4
Kazakhstan	916	....	....	....	....	....	....	....	....	....	....	....	....	....	....	....
Kyrgyz Republic	917	....	....	....	....	....	....	....	....	....	....	....	....	....	....	....
Latvia	941	....	....	....	....	....	....	....	....	....	....	....	....	....	....	....
Lithuania	946	....	....	....	....	....	....	....	....	....	....	....	....	....	....	....
Macedonia, FYR	962	....	....	....	....	....	....	....	....	....	....	....	....	....	....	....
Malta	181	....	....	....	....	....	....	....	....	....	....	....	....	....	....	....
Moldova	921	....	....	....	....	....	....	....	....	....	....	....	....	....	....	....
Poland	964	....	....	....	....	....	....	....	....	....	87.4	100.9	Ɪ97.2	80.2	76.3	68.2
Romania	968	....	....	....	70.1	83.2	96.7	86.8	75.8	80.3	92.2	Ɪ112.5	106.3	95.7	91.3	76.4
Russia	922	....	....	....	....	....	....	....	....	....	....	....	....	....	....	....
Slovak Republic	936	....	....	....	....	....	....	....	....	....	....	....	....	....	....	....
Slovenia	961	....	....	....	....	....	....	....	....	....	....	....	....	....	....	....
Turkey	186	Ɪ47.0	48.7	52.7	51.9	53.2	54.7	53.6	58.9	62.7	60.3	51.2	42.6	39.8	42.4	40.1
Ukraine	926	....	....	....	....	....	....	....	....	....	....	....	....	....	....	....
Yugoslavia, SFR	188	29.3	28.8	34.7	33.3	28.8	26.2	27.8	Ɪ25.5	36.6	36.1	34.9	35.8	38.2	44.7	48.1
Middle East																
Bahrain	419	58.7	51.6	47.5	26.7	21.8	44.1	39.5	31.8	29.0	34.8	26.8	22.8	46.9	23.9	23.3
Egypt	469	73.4	66.8	65.8	67.0	65.3	61.2	58.2	52.3	52.4	51.2	Ɪ54.1	52.0	52.2	54.4	52.2
Iran, I.R. of	429	42.4	42.4	42.9	45.1	42.4	39.2	38.0	38.5	....	45.3	45.6	51.7	57.9	54.7	....
Iraq	433	74.5	69.5	72.5	77.4	70.0	64.8	67.9	....	....	....	....	....	....	....	....
Israel	436	36.6	41.3	Ɪ67.7	69.5	59.3	51.5	53.7	105.8	175.4	216.1	191.9	42.6	40.8	49.4	44.8
Jordan	439	94.4	92.4	86.2	83.3	79.9	74.5	70.1	67.6	61.9	62.2	59.8	56.6	53.2	51.5	48.1
Kuwait	443	14.0	14.1	14.4	17.9	18.9	19.0	18.4	27.5	16.3	16.8	17.7	16.8	24.1	17.2	14.4
Lebanon	446	28.1	27.7	25.7	24.3	32.7	29.8	37.7	33.1	31.3	23.8	21.5	17.7	20.9	18.8	17.3
Libya	672	362.1	476.1	332.0	239.8	198.4	276.6	283.6	297.6	360.1	321.9	351.8	361.5	407.6	252.9	193.1
Oman	449	....	....	31.1	35.0	37.4	41.5	39.1	38.7	38.4	44.6	44.6	49.2	48.5	29.9	32.9
Qatar	453	14.9	14.2	13.2	15.6	16.8	16.0	14.9	15.4	17.7	20.6	20.7	15.0	14.6	14.8	12.3
Saudi Arabia	456	58.2	61.3	57.1	64.0	60.2	66.9	64.9	68.7	75.2	59.0	44.7	38.3	36.2	Ɪ32.1	29.7
Syrian Arab Rep.	463	84.2	84.4	79.3	81.0	72.4	68.7	69.7	67.5	69.2	67.4	67.0	62.8	77.6	78.0	82.5
United Arab Emirates	466	....	....	....	18.2	17.4	17.3	16.6	24.4	24.2	30.0	18.9	18.3	18.0	16.5	13.9
Yemen Arab Rep.	473	....	....	....	77.3	76.8	76.0	76.0	83.6	80.4	83.1	80.8	83.3	83.3	86.2	86.4
Yemen, P.D. Rep.	459	69.5	70.4	77.5	82.9	74.5	64.0	76.3	66.7	Ɪ74.8	73.7	66.7	67.9	76.8	82.4	84.9
Yemen, Republic of	474	....	....	....	....	....	....	....	....	....	....	....	....	....	....	....
Western Hemisphere																
Antigua and Barbuda	311	....	....	....	....	....	19.9	29.8	19.1	19.8	28.0	21.0	17.4	18.1	16.8	25.0
Argentina	213	35.2	46.2	29.6	116.1	115.0	125.4	126.6	55.4	40.2	25.9	24.2	26.2	92.7	84.3	59.8
Aruba	314	....	....	....	....	....	....	....	....	....	....	....	....	....	....	....
Bahamas, The	313	14.1	14.3	18.3	17.2	20.0	19.6	18.4	17.9	18.0	18.0	18.3	16.4	16.2	16.2	17.7
Barbados	316	15.3	14.0	14.2	19.9	21.2	25.2	21.5	23.7	22.9	23.8	23.6	22.9	22.6	24.3	23.3
Belize	339	....	....	....	....	....	....	19.1	25.3	27.4	23.9	24.1	26.8	29.7	23.6	30.5
Bolivia	218	68.1	68.5	64.0	67.6	62.1	59.7	58.8	56.7	56.3	54.5	54.8	50.8	60.5	67.8	76.1
Brazil	223	30.9	Ɪ30.9	28.1	29.1	29.6	29.2	31.8	33.1	Ɪ31.8	34.0	33.3	30.1	30.6	26.7	23.6
Chile	228	49.9	68.5	78.4	93.6	76.0	66.5	Ɪ56.4	54.7	48.4	42.0	42.2	29.5	46.7	88.4	127.5
Colombia	233	53.8	53.2	50.7	49.3	47.8	48.6	51.4	53.8	Ɪ58.9	62.1	55.4	50.7	49.3	46.7	46.5
Costa Rica	238	46.8	42.4	42.9	41.1	36.0	33.7	33.6	37.4	29.2	33.6	34.4	40.7	34.9	33.9	35.1
Dominica	321	....	....	....	....	....	11.2	15.7	21.5	16.5	39.8	24.6	15.2	18.0	10.0	28.1
Dominican Republic	243	62.6	61.8	53.5	52.9	54.5	43.3	43.5	47.2	50.5	48.7	44.1	51.2	48.2	47.3	47.5
Ecuador	248	42.2	40.6	42.6	46.0	44.8	41.2	35.3	35.5	38.4	37.7	33.2	32.6	28.2	25.6	24.2
El Salvador	253	25.6	25.8	26.5	25.6	25.4	26.7	27.5	25.8	17.6	14.9	18.3	19.4	Ɪ47.5	44.3	42.8
Grenada	328	23.7	22.6	18.4	19.3	21.2	Ɪ22.8	33.4	28.9	30.4	31.9	32.2	37.5	30.8	32.3	43.6
Guatemala	258	77.6	73.7	75.4	73.1	73.4	71.6	84.4	80.2	77.1	74.6	67.6	63.6	64.4	60.4	56.5
Guyana	336	31.6	30.6	33.2	29.4	28.4	30.0	31.4	32.4	41.7	40.0	38.1	41.9	51.8	54.9	60.2
Haiti	263	68.0	67.0	62.0	57.7	50.4	49.8	49.9	49.2	46.3	47.2	47.3	49.1	48.0	45.3	48.5
Honduras	268	38.0	36.9	33.2	33.1	30.9	32.1	34.2	33.4	33.4	35.2	33.1	32.4	29.2	26.7	23.8
Jamaica	343	19.7	20.5	20.6	Ɪ24.2	24.7	24.4	26.1	26.1	24.4	25.5	29.8	22.3	15.6	21.1	34.0
Mexico	273	24.3	25.7	37.7	39.0	45.1	51.2	32.1	Ɪ62.4	60.2	59.8	61.5	59.7	Ɪ69.2	66.7	59.9
Netherlands Antilles	353	25.5	29.8	28.3	28.3	24.7	27.6	26.4	26.7	23.6	26.1	25.2	21.8	19.9	17.2	15.9
Nicaragua	278	46.2	41.9	37.7	37.7	35.8	36.6	34.9	35.1	34.0	46.4	33.3	38.0	40.1	Ɪ40.8	44.2
Panama	283	12.9	12.0	17.1	13.8	10.6	13.9	18.3	17.3	11.2	17.7	15.0	16.8	14.7	14.5	13.8
Paraguay	288	72.2	72.3	71.3	70.2	68.3	66.5	65.1	65.0	66.3	65.3	61.9	60.9	58.0	65.1	65.3
Peru	293	42.2	41.1	43.5	37.7	39.8	36.3	43.5	43.8	42.2	49.9	57.5	52.9	48.3	51.1	54.6
St. Kitts and Nevis	361	....	....	....	....	....	....	....	....	....	8.3	3.5	20.2	12.9	13.8	17.8
St. Lucia	362	....	....	....	....	....	14.1	17.8	18.0	18.9	20.8	20.1	16.4	16.2	15.0	21.3
St. Vincent & Grenadines	364	....	....	....	....	....	18.9	27.8	27.8	23.4	29.2	23.8	23.8	18.9	15.8	26.2
Suriname	366	41.7	40.7	37.4	43.4	40.3	42.8	40.1	41.7	36.3	39.4	36.7	37.8	37.4	43.5	53.7
Trinidad and Tobago	369	16.1	17.0	15.6	15.9	24.3	29.6	29.5	24.2	20.3	27.6	26.7	25.6	30.6	26.9	23.6
Uruguay	298	71.1	72.3	64.4	67.9	66.0	Ɪ53.7	52.1	41.8	40.2	30.7	27.7	21.7	Ɪ16.0	25.0	27.6
Venezuela, Rep. Bol.	299	35.7	37.6	35.3	36.5	38.3	35.1	33.9	33.1	41.0	33.3	30.3	31.3	33.7	35.0	37.1

Percent

Asia (cont.)

1985	1986	1987	1988	1989	1990	1991	1992	1993	1994	1995	1996	1997	1998	1999		
15.9	13.5	14.2	14.4	14.7	16.3	12.9	11.8	11.8	13.3	13.5	19.8	12.0	14.2	22.5	Papua New Guinea	853
24.7	32.0	32.2	30.0	32.1	30.8	31.5	31.4	I29.3	24.8	23.4	21.7	18.6	15.2	17.3	Philippines	566
47.9	55.6	50.1	48.1	57.2	73.0	67.2	52.9	48.0	43.5	37.3	42.8	43.8	23.2	25.1	Samoa	862
24.7	23.6	21.3	21.2	20.0	17.9	17.6	17.9	17.9	16.6	16.7	16.2	15.6	10.3	12.3	Singapore	576
34.0	31.9	24.6	25.2	21.2	22.1	24.3	19.5	18.8	19.7	22.2	25.0	22.0	31.3	29.2	Solomon Islands	813
35.7	35.4	33.8	37.1	I36.2	36.1	37.7	35.1	35.7	35.7	34.7	33.9	29.1	29.4	27.5	Sri Lanka	524
14.6	14.2	14.4	14.0	13.0	12.2	11.5	11.7	11.5	11.7	12.2	12.3	12.2	10.7	15.7	Thailand	578
108.8	113.3	109.5	100.8	69.5	95.4	87.7	98.3	31.1	25.4	21.2	27.8	29.2	28.3	27.1	Tonga	866
9.9	8.8	8.4	8.9	8.0	6.5	8.4	8.4	12.3	11.1	12.8	11.1	11.2	10.4	14.0	Vanuatu	846

Europe

1985	1986	1987	1988	1989	1990	1991	1992	1993	1994	1995	1996	1997	1998	1999		
....	....	....	....	....	....	....	43.6	....	59.4	50.1	39.7	45.8	37.5	37.3	Albania	914
								54.6	61.2	71.6	75.7	73.1	55.5	48.5	Armenia	911
							31.9	50.9	31.1	69.3	69.6	69.6	63.8	60.8	Azerbaijan	912
									25.3	38.0	I44.4	43.6	30.5	36.5	Belarus	913
						31.5	30.9	24.6	22.5	I28.0	29.3	I39.3	38.6	39.4	Bulgaria	918
									22.5	27.0	27.5	23.9	20.4	17.4	18.3	Croatia	960
41.7	40.8	40.0	I38.9	30.1	35.4	31.6	29.6	25.9	25.9	22.2	18.4	16.4	17.6	17.6	Cyprus	423
								18.2	20.3	24.1	22.8	I29.3	34.8	33.9	Czech Republic	935
22.5	22.2	20.9	18.7	18.9	40.0	13.1	....	....							Czechoslovakia	934
							29.7	44.2	I62.6	53.7	49.1	43.7	43.7	43.6	44.5	Estonia	939
										83.3	80.6	74.2	70.3	69.0	Georgia	915
66.2	65.0	52.7	49.3	50.6	57.4	42.3	40.3	35.5	30.9	30.7	23.2	24.3	22.6	24.5	Hungary	944
									45.8	49.1	50.3	52.8	I66.7	54.8	45.9	Kazakhstan	916
											73.9	79.7	72.8	66.7	61.0	Kyrgyz Republic	917
								48.6	38.6	49.9	51.3	49.1	49.2	50.7	Latvia	941
								47.0	41.6	43.5	46.1	45.5	51.2	45.6	Lithuania	946
								8.6	34.4	I40.2	39.4	39.1	36.5	35.9	Macedonia, FYR	962
										29.3	25.8	24.3	23.2	22.6	Malta	181
						42.5	58.8	69.0	73.3	62.6	I59.7	59.2	I60.3	59.8	Moldova	921
60.0	49.7	37.3	52.9	48.4	48.5	I41.9	36.1	28.6	25.4	27.3	25.1	26.0	24.3	20.1	Poland	964
I68.7	72.3	73.9	78.1	103.2	I50.7	30.7	37.9	I45.4	35.8	32.9	29.7	34.3	27.8	36.9	Romania	968
								50.1	48.1	47.0	46.2	46.0	41.9	44.6	Russia	922
								12.4	12.9	17.2	16.1	I17.7	14.7	16.8	Slovak Republic	936
						13.3	13.9	11.9	12.9	12.4	11.6	11.6	11.6	12.3	Slovenia	961
35.7	I31.5	30.8	33.3	33.9	30.6	25.1	25.1	25.6	22.9	20.2	17.8	18.0	17.1	17.0	Turkey	186
							71.9	62.5	47.5	51.5	53.1	59.1	I56.4	56.4	Ukraine	926
48.5	51.2	64.7	67.3	65.3	59.4	....	....								Yugoslavia, SFR	188

Middle East

1985	1986	1987	1988	1989	1990	1991	1992	1993	1994	1995	1996	1997	1998	1999		
24.8	24.0	24.2	21.9	22.7	28.0	I22.2	19.4	14.6	13.2	16.5	14.2	14.5	9.8	....	Bahrain	419
51.6	47.6	41.7	35.7	32.9	32.9	32.9	30.4	32.0	32.3	32.2	30.2	30.3	32.7	31.4	Egypt	469
....	58.9	61.6	64.2	59.3	51.9	48.0	43.6	39.8	40.1	45.6	43.8	43.5	42.7	41.1	Iran, I.R. of	429
															Iraq	433
41.2	35.8	33.3	29.1	26.4	25.1	23.2	I19.8	20.8	15.6	9.4	10.1	19.3	18.4	19.7	Israel	436
46.8	45.1	40.7	43.3	44.0	45.8	51.5	53.0	I51.0	51.9	52.2	45.6	41.2	36.9	36.3	Jordan	439
14.3	13.1	10.4	7.0	6.6	....	9.5	8.9	7.9	7.5	6.4	6.5	5.6	5.9	7.6	Kuwait	443
15.7	7.8	3.9	9.0	13.5	13.3	14.5	12.9	13.8	19.4	20.2	19.4	24.3	19.8	18.7	Lebanon	446
205.1	170.4	231.4	160.1	204.4	284.6	261.6	285.7	250.9	247.9	222.5	240.9	I286.5	302.7	477.7	Libya	672
28.2	32.1	26.1	24.8	27.7	25.6	25.1	23.5	21.6	21.1	20.3	20.0	17.4	17.8	16.6	Oman	449
10.9	12.7	11.7	11.6	11.6	13.3	13.1	13.1	I12.9	11.0	11.4	11.5	11.5	11.0	11.0	Qatar	453
28.8	28.7	27.9	24.5	23.4	28.1	25.5	I24.6	23.7	24.1	22.8	20.9	21.4	20.4	....	Saudi Arabia	456
92.9	89.1	87.3	67.8	67.4	68.6	59.9	61.2	58.6	58.0	55.9	56.1	54.6	52.4	....	Syrian Arab Rep.	463
15.2	14.9	21.6	18.7	15.2	16.7	16.8	19.5	19.2	22.4	22.9	23.2	21.4	20.6	24.1	United Arab Emirates	466
85.6	82.5	93.0	92.0	92.1	....	....									Yemen Arab Rep.	473
90.6	98.4	98.2	103.0	103.5	....										Yemen, P.D. Rep.	459
					90.8	89.2	89.5	88.6	90.6	72.0	71.3	56.1	55.8	....	Yemen, Republic of	474

Western Hemisphere

1985	1986	1987	1988	1989	1990	1991	1992	1993	1994	1995	1996	1997	1998	1999		
26.0	30.5	24.3	24.3	20.6	20.3	19.4	23.9	18.2	18.9	18.3	15.7	15.3	14.9	15.4	Antigua and Barbuda	311
55.2	34.9	25.8	24.6	79.5	I45.7	41.0	35.5	33.0	I30.4	26.5	22.8	20.6	19.1	18.8	Argentina	213
....	30.9	26.2	25.4	20.2	20.5	21.6	22.7	23.7	19.5	22.1	18.1	16.7	20.7	19.9	Aruba	314
19.1	18.8	16.8	17.4	16.8	15.3	16.2	14.9	12.8	13.2	12.5	11.5	10.7	11.0	12.0	Bahamas, The	313
23.4	21.8	23.0	21.6	20.7	21.7	18.8	20.3	17.4	15.7	17.3	19.5	16.2	16.4	15.2	Barbados	316
32.2	32.1	29.6	27.1	29.6	25.3	23.8	25.6	24.6	22.3	21.4	20.4	19.3	19.6	20.6	Belize	339
64.5	42.9	I37.0	47.1	49.0	40.8	35.1	27.5	27.3	22.9	26.3	I24.5	25.2	17.7	18.6	Bolivia	218
19.6	I15.8	27.9	I12.5	20.2	28.1	22.9	16.7	13.9	24.8	21.1	23.0	26.1	21.1	21.2	Brazil	223
180.8	175.2	140.2	112.6	84.3	105.3	101.6	100.3	92.4	100.2	90.7	87.9	87.7	77.1	73.5	Chile	228
45.4	....	43.1	42.7	....	I53.4	56.4	53.3	48.7	44.7	39.2	37.0	30.4	20.9	25.6	Colombia	233
43.4	46.3	45.7	47.1	47.2	44.7	54.3	51.4	48.9	51.9	57.5	47.5	I47.7	42.0	37.0	Costa Rica	238
23.0	30.8	35.1	29.8	24.4	26.1	24.7	22.2	21.8	18.9	18.2	16.9	16.8	17.6	18.1	Dominica	321
39.9	43.4	36.0	48.4	47.7	44.0	49.2	43.7	46.3	41.5	41.0	38.4	36.8	38.6	35.9	Dominican Republic	243
25.9	28.3	27.2	29.3	30.8	I33.6	29.9	32.2	32.2	24.2	20.6	19.1	18.8	I19.4	23.3	Ecuador	248
40.7	33.0	38.8	40.2	39.4	38.6	38.3	33.7	38.0	37.5	38.0	36.2	34.5	33.9	34.2	El Salvador	253
47.0	36.4	35.4	25.7	24.8	24.0	23.0	26.2	20.6	19.6	19.4	17.9	18.2	17.3	16.2	Grenada	328
68.6	68.1	63.7	65.1	66.8	71.0	61.1	50.3	53.9	50.3	45.0	44.6	I46.3	37.3	34.1	Guatemala	258
54.2	56.0	91.7	79.8	48.5	37.5	55.6	52.0	I33.4	39.0	37.3	33.1	35.2	36.9	32.0	Guyana	336
48.3	50.9	54.3	44.4	53.2	60.8	59.2	58.8	58.8	55.4	50.0	47.4	I42.2	38.6	40.3	Haiti	263
24.1	23.6	24.1	24.1	26.3	27.1	24.8	29.3	28.4	32.0	30.7	31.2	I39.8	37.2	33.6	Honduras	268
36.8	34.2	36.3	37.7	43.4	41.3	34.9	37.5	39.9	38.1	37.5	35.1	35.7	40.5	33.9	Jamaica	343
49.6	42.6	30.1	54.4	26.7	19.9	17.1	15.8	15.1	15.3	15.5	15.3	I16.8	17.9	23.0	Mexico	273
27.1	35.2	29.3	26.5	18.4	19.7	15.1	18.0	17.4	14.9	16.7	14.8	16.7	17.7	15.8	Netherlands Antilles	353
52.1	52.7	56.8	52.4	48.3	64.9	56.0	49.3	42.5	39.0	35.7	I34.2	29.3	26.9	23.9	Nicaragua	278
12.7	11.8	8.0	8.8	8.9	9.9	10.3	6.6	5.9	5.0	4.8	6.3	5.6	5.1	4.7	Panama	283
64.3	68.2	70.9	I72.5	60.2	50.3	45.5	45.9	43.1	44.0	43.2	37.9	38.0	40.0	40.4	Paraguay	288
67.0	60.7	61.8	57.3	43.7	53.1	42.1	43.8	40.7	38.8	39.4	39.5	41.9	37.8	38.2	Peru	293
17.8	18.8	21.8	19.2	19.7	19.5	18.5	21.4	21.5	22.9	19.6	18.6	17.3	18.7	20.3	St. Kitts and Nevis	361
22.3	25.2	24.8	23.4	22.6	22.3	22.2	21.1	21.7	18.8	19.1	17.5	17.1	17.6	16.6	St. Lucia	362
29.7	37.5	29.5	28.2	26.6	26.6	24.2	29.1	25.5	23.4	21.0	19.3	18.8	19.6	19.7	St. Vincent & Grenadines	364
62.0	67.3	63.2	62.2	60.7	61.6	63.2	59.6	61.2	61.8	71.8	46.5	38.9	46.6	48.5	Suriname	366
25.0	21.7	16.4	16.6	17.7	18.4	21.0	20.4	16.8	22.7	21.6	I22.3	23.2	24.5	24.4	Trinidad and Tobago	369
32.8	29.9	33.7	32.8	31.1	34.2	33.8	32.6	33.9	31.6	29.6	28.8	28.0	I26.9	28.8	Uruguay	298
34.9	25.3	I24.7	22.8	25.4	34.1	35.6	33.1	28.9	28.2	27.5	I41.6	41.3	38.2	42.4	Venezuela, Rep. Bol.	299

Income Velocity of Money plus Quasi-Money

39ad *i*		1970	1971	1972	1973	1974	1975	1976	1977	1978	1979	1980	1981	1982	1983	1984
																Index Numbers:
Industrial Countries																
United States	111	92.9	90.1	88.2	90.2	92.0	91.7	90.8	89.8	93.4	95.9	95.3	97.3	91.8	88.4	90.1
Canada	156	155.6	154.2	150.9	153.7	147.1	144.8	140.9	134.1	130.9	125.6	123.4	127.2	117.4	126.0	134.8
Australia	193	81.3	84.7	82.6	79.1	84.0	85.0	88.0	89.0	90.8	94.2	94.1	95.7	96.7	93.5	94.9
Japan	158	164.5	149.5	139.0	137.6	145.5	142.6	139.0	139.0	136.7	133.3	134.0	132.3	127.3	124.3	124.1
New Zealand	196	222.3	233.5	213.6	176.0	168.1	181.4	186.9	170.3	162.4	158.6	159.0	168.8	169.2	169.2	167.1
Euro Area																
Austria	122	161.9	159.6	158.0	157.0	159.5	146.6	141.8	137.6	130.2	127.9	125.5	120.0	116.1	114.0	115.2
Belgium	124	112.5	110.7	107.4	105.8	111.3	109.9	110.0	109.0	108.3	108.0	111.9	109.7	110.8	111.4	111.1
Finland	172	142.6	139.1	135.5	146.7	161.3	150.0	148.6	146.0	141.0	141.7	142.1	138.6	135.5	132.9	131.4
France	132	80.8	76.1	71.4	71.3	70.0	68.9	68.2	68.8	90.1	72.7	76.0	77.0	79.7	80.5	78.7
Germany	134	136.2	134.7	130.3	130.2	129.6	123.8	121.6	119.7	117.1	117.1	119.3	118.7	115.9	114.4	115.0
Ireland	178	101.4	107.0	116.9	120.3	110.7	117.2	122.2	129.2	127.9	121.3	127.7	129.7	135.2	134.5	136.1
Italy	136	85.0	79.2	73.2	74.6	80.1	77.1	79.3	80.8	77.7	79.1	87.1	93.3	95.9	94.6	96.6
Luxembourg	137	....	....	....	....	140.2	121.8	121.3	111.0	106.3	101.0	92.3	88.4	98.4	107.4	108.5
Netherlands	138	179.7	178.8	176.1	174.1	170.1	164.6	161.9	155.1	150.0	144.6	142.0	137.3	131.8	110.8	109.6
Portugal	182	94.6	92.0	90.1	84.6	85.9	84.1	92.4	102.6	108.5	109.7	102.3	90.5	87.6	88.7	87.7
Spain	184	106.1	99.6	94.6	91.4	92.9	91.8	92.9	98.5	100.6	98.6	96.4	93.9	92.7	ⅈ106.3	115.0
Denmark	128	121.7	127.6	131.5	132.7	136.4	129.1	124.4	126.6	132.8	134.9	134.8	131.5	136.5	125.7	113.2
Greece	174	101.6	93.4	86.2	91.9	92.1	88.7	86.1	81.9	80.9	82.5	83.7	78.6	75.5	74.5	74.5
Iceland	176	105.1	109.0	114.6	126.2	144.7	163.5	174.7	187.1	202.3	193.2	201.8	198.5	239.4	217.7	201.9
Norway	142	110.7	107.5	106.5	107.5	111.9	112.9	111.4	105.0	ⅈ115.9	113.0	119.6	121.0	120.8	121.3	119.7
Sweden	144	73.8	72.9	70.7	69.8	70.1	74.8	77.1	79.2	77.2	75.2	76.8	76.3	73.7	78.5	84.3
Switzerland	146	120.6	119.8	125.7	132.7	135.5	126.0	117.7	111.6	105.9	101.1	108.3	111.6	111.8	110.8	109.4
United Kingdom	112	195.3	195.0	177.3	159.8	151.1	....	183.2	195.5	197.6	208.4	209.8	187.8	172.9	166.9	161.7
Developing Countries																
Africa																
Algeria	612	78.9	76.2	71.1	67.1	98.8	85.6	83.1	75.2	72.7	75.5	79.6	79.9	71.9	66.0	58.9
Benin	638	182.8	156.0	151.6	149.9	151.5	114.0	109.7	106.9	110.3	109.4	97.3	96.1	101.9	103.6	99.0
Botswana	616	....	....	....	....	....	....	79.9	76.4	80.1	71.7	74.4	76.5	79.8	90.8	85.2
Burkina Faso	748	241.8	241.3	243.0	196.5	177.5	147.3	119.6	126.7	126.5	124.4	122.5	118.7	117.2	114.2	99.0
Burundi	618	152.1	150.3	133.0	130.4	131.8	154.2	145.0	135.2	116.8	120.2	146.0	121.4	119.0	115.9	118.1
Cameroon	622	99.6	94.8	94.6	93.2	86.6	83.6	78.8	71.0	69.9	70.4	66.5	72.2	68.7	70.5	69.4
Central African Rep.	626	135.0	137.8	132.8	127.8	136.8	156.5	139.5	122.0	124.5	128.9	121.2	118.7	128.7	125.6	126.1
Chad	628	95.4	96.2	86.9	86.0	89.8	86.1	84.8	67.2	76.9	....	....	....	52.1	79.5	64.0
Comoros	632	....	....	....	....	....	....	....	....	....	....	....	....	....	108.7	110.4
Congo, Dem. Rep. of	636	17.0	16.2	16.0	15.9	13.2	12.9	14.8	13.6	12.3	16.5	47.1	44.0	40.4	20.2	57.6
Congo, Rep. of	634	84.1	82.9	85.2	86.2	86.5	83.6	80.1	78.4	83.1	94.7	97.3	99.5	98.5	97.2	113.2
Côte d'Ivoire	662	119.5	113.2	118.9	122.7	116.8	103.9	114.1	104.7	94.8	94.3	100.4	102.7	104.4	105.1	112.7
Equatorial Guinea	642	....	....	....	....	....	....	....	....	....	....	....	....	....	....	....
Ethiopia	644	285.5	296.0	280.1	238.3	204.3	188.7	172.6	178.9	164.2	162.6	154.6	174.7	ⅈ167.2	161.1	136.7
Gabon	646	90.3	88.2	78.3	86.5	135.0	105.8	97.2	71.0	59.8	76.1	88.5	86.8	83.9	81.1	78.2
Ghana	652	73.9	79.3	64.0	66.0	70.4	59.6	53.0	62.4	69.4	71.3	79.8	99.1	89.0	128.5	141.3
Guinea-Bissau	654	....	....	....	....	....	....	....	....	....	....	....	....	....	....	....
Kenya	664	138.9	131.0	129.6	119.7	122.3	126.8	123.5	109.2	99.2	101.6	103.2	109.4	111.7	115.8	114.9
Lesotho	666	....	....	....	....	....	....	....	....	....	....	78.4	78.3	68.1	58.8	59.8
Madagascar	674	112.8	108.1	100.2	102.5	119.4	111.7	110.4	103.6	88.6	87.2	82.0	79.8	82.5	109.3	139.7
Malawi	676	99.3	106.0	98.0	78.5	75.6	75.0	87.0	85.2	83.0	77.9	85.3	79.9	75.9	80.9	80.4
Mali	678	134.7	129.0	123.3	113.8	98.3	94.6	114.0	113.4	101.5	102.6	119.4	146.6	139.3	134.4	114.9
Mauritania	682	195.1	171.5	172.8	143.5	116.2	101.4	100.5	91.8	91.9	87.0	89.3	79.1	74.9	78.9	81.5
Mauritius	684	187.8	182.8	182.1	182.5	239.1	160.8	151.2	182.6	177.7	187.8	187.5	196.3	193.1	179.0	181.3
Morocco	686	225.6	229.3	209.8	199.3	217.8	191.0	178.2	179.5	173.6	165.2	175.7	168.2	156.6	143.4	144.5
Mozambique	688	....	....	....	....	....	....	....	....	....	....	....	....	....	....	21.6
Namibia	728	....	....	....	....	....	....	....	....	....	....	....	....	....	....	....
Niger	692	214.1	188.6	176.7	152.1	149.7	137.8	148.0	135.2	132.1	126.9	119.1	109.4	121.9	143.7	113.6
Nigeria	694	171.2	162.4	156.3	144.5	153.7	99.5	82.1	70.8	67.7	67.9	60.9	51.3	48.2	46.8	46.0
Rwanda	714	245.5	218.0	212.6	178.5	162.3	141.8	138.3	125.5	120.3	120.9	119.3	120.9	124.1	126.9	126.6
Senegal	722	152.0	142.1	134.9	127.9	113.8	105.3	90.9	81.3	75.8	74.5	76.0	77.0	77.1	75.4	79.0
Seychelles	718	....	....	120.0	131.4	146.7	137.3	148.9	149.9	160.0	181.2	167.5	150.9	158.0	161.6	163.7
Sierra Leone	724	63.1	ⅈ63.0	56.3	49.4	49.7	54.3	51.5	49.5	42.8	41.2	40.1	41.3	40.0	33.3	38.5
South Africa	199	77.9	79.4	77.7	78.1	82.2	77.7	77.7	78.8	79.8	82.3	89.7	87.5	87.5	84.8	86.5
Sudan	732	61.4	61.9	61.2	66.9	63.0	64.2	65.1	57.3	49.3	45.7	45.5	41.8	33.2	34.2	34.8
Swaziland	734	....	....	....	....	....	142.3	115.0	97.5	86.6	77.4	81.5	89.7	96.8	95.2	87.0	78.7
Tanzania	738	101.0	90.5	87.8	86.8	86.3	83.4	84.8	81.8	79.1	65.6	58.7	55.8	58.9	54.7	61.3
Togo	742	175.4	179.3	184.8	181.1	160.8	126.9	125.5	111.0	99.4	90.7	96.5	82.0	66.0	73.2	72.3
Tunisia	744	132.2	134.8	137.0	126.3	136.0	123.4	116.1	115.2	112.4	113.1	117.8	111.3	110.6	111.7	108.3
Uganda	746	62.2	62.8	61.8	54.2	51.0	54.4	49.0	65.4	80.1	88.7	86.6	107.2	116.7	134.9	123.8
Zambia	754	60.7	53.8	58.2	59.8	57.5	51.6	49.1	40.9	47.5	52.3	50.7	53.7	46.5	44.5	46.2
Zimbabwe	698	....	....	....	....	....	....	....	....	....	....	106.1	75.0	99.5	81.9	86.4	88.5
Asia																
Bangladesh	513	....	....	....	....	203.5	349.5	261.2	210.1	235.8	225.7	216.3	205.7	209.8	173.3	151.6
Bhutan	514	....	....	....	....	....	....	....	....	....	....	....	....	....	174.0	181.2
China, P.R.: Mainland	924	....	....	....	....	....	....	....	....	....	3,746.3	3,325.5	3,026.1	2,958.2	2,734.9	2,431.0
China, P.R.: Hong Kong	532	....	....	....	....	....	....	....	....	....	....	....	....	....	....	....
Fiji	819	182.4	161.5	171.2	188.3	197.8	181.7	172.3	167.5	157.7	164.8	161.0	156.1	155.1	142.4	145.9
India	534	194.1	180.3	172.2	176.4	180.1	172.3	157.2	148.0	134.0	121.6	124.7	123.5	121.4	121.0	114.2
Indonesia	536	505.6	388.0	324.8	328.0	349.2	300.1	274.1	269.6	274.5	298.4	289.5	286.4	246.9	252.2	232.4
Korea	542	127.6	124.4	123.2	113.9	126.9	134.4	142.1	132.6	130.3	131.7	127.3	126.3	112.6	110.3	114.4
Lao People's Democratic Rep.	544	....	....	....	....	....	....	....	....	....	....	....	....	....	....	....
Malaysia	548	252.1	239.5	221.4	229.4	226.9	193.4	198.0	187.8	192.5	190.8	172.7	157.5	148.2	144.3	148.4
Maldives	556	....	....	....	....	....	....	....	94.9	134.8	123.3	128.6	125.6	136.7	152.3	137.3
Mongolia	948	....	....	....	....	....	....	....	....	....	....	....	....	....	....	....
Myanmar	518	100.5	109.7	105.3	109.8	ⅈ120.2	116.3	120.2	124.1	122.1	115.3	107.1	99.3	94.3	88.4	81.2
Nepal	558	344.2	308.4	303.4	239.4	245.7	ⅈ287.8	249.6	195.9	189.1	181.5	161.5	159.6	151.6	137.3	138.8
Pakistan	564	100.5	95.2	86.9	91.4	118.7	132.7	124.2	116.4	113.0	103.0	104.5	110.0	111.5	101.5	106.2

1995=100

1985	1986	1987	1988	1989	1990	1991	1992	1993	1994	1995	1996	1997	1998	1999		
															Industrial Countries	
87.4	84.4	84.7	85.6	88.1	88.0	86.9	89.8	93.5	98.0	100.0	99.3	99.3	96.9	94.5	United States	111
137.2	136.8	136.2	136.3	131.4	123.0	115.9	112.0	103.9	100.8	100.0	97.3	95.5	93.1	96.5	Canada	156
90.0	86.8	86.7	85.2	120.0	110.6	106.4	105.4	103.9	102.0	100.0	96.6	92.2	90.5	86.7	Australia	193
122.7	117.8	111.4	107.1	104.1	99.8	102.2	103.9	103.4	101.9	100.0	101.0	100.6	94.7	90.2	Japan	158
150.4	149.5	127.9	131.1	111.2	105.2	99.1	98.5	103.3	103.7	100.0	90.2	86.9	84.3	....	New Zealand	196
															Euro Area	
113.7	111.9	106.8	104.9	105.0	105.7	104.6	102.8	99.4	99.8	I100.0	99.3	99.0	....	....	Austria	122
I115.5	112.0	105.8	105.9	107.1	106.1	105.3	108.7	101.2	97.7	100.0	94.0	94.2	....	....	Belgium	124
123.1	114.9	113.1	112.9	107.2	102.8	95.6	91.8	92.8	95.4	100.0	103.9	111.5	117.1	....	Finland	172
81.9	81.4	82.1	I88.1	90.2	90.4	95.2	99.1	98.1	99.3	I100.0	97.2	96.6	....	....	France	132
113.4	101.9	99.2	99.2	101.0	98.4	I108.1	107.1	101.4	97.7	100.0	95.4	93.2	92.7	....	Germany	134
136.7	148.4	148.7	147.8	158.0	I160.3	151.8	158.8	137.1	134.2	100.0	96.1	91.5	89.2	....	Ireland	178
95.2	97.7	97.3	99.6	100.0	99.8	100.0	97.4	92.8	93.1	100.0	102.1	108.8	116.8	....	Italy	136
114.9	115.7	108.3	105.2	100.0	92.1	88.2	87.1	84.8	91.1	I100.0	104.0	117.5	....	....	Luxembourg	137
109.7	106.8	103.6	104.2	101.5	99.2	98.9	98.1	95.7	97.6	100.0	97.2	96.9	....	....	Netherlands	138
85.9	103.0	105.1	109.9	112.8	121.0	118.2	110.1	110.9	102.8	100.0	101.7	100.6	101.7	....	Portugal	182
116.5	108.7	112.9	113.4	113.5	111.1	106.0	106.2	101.7	99.7	100.0	100.9	105.6	109.1	....	Spain	184
106.0	99.7	99.8	99.6	100.9	99.6	95.1	95.2	90.4	91.6	100.0	95.9	93.3	90.6	93.6	Denmark	128
71.3	71.8	70.3	I83.0	81.1	82.5	94.9	97.5	105.6	102.0	I100.0	97.5	92.8	95.8	....	Greece	174
182.6	171.5	161.8	152.1	138.2	112.0	107.8	98.9	98.0	98.3	100.0	102.2	103.5	100.6	....	Iceland	176
113.8	107.3	97.8	I96.2	97.2	96.2	98.0	96.8	95.9	97.5	100.0	104.6	108.1	105.0	105.3	Norway	142
88.5	87.3	85.7	86.7	88.1	97.1	92.5	93.2	87.8	I92.4	100.0	95.5	94.6	97.7	96.3	Sweden	144
105.0	107.6	101.7	99.4	101.1	107.5	110.2	110.7	107.2	101.4	100.0	92.4	85.7	83.9	79.5	Switzerland	146
157.6	140.4	124.6	120.6	111.4	104.2	101.5	104.2	104.7	103.6	100.0	93.0	91.0	91.9	92.5	United Kingdom	112
															Developing Countries	
															Africa	
59.5	55.7	54.4	I48.1	54.0	72.6	93.5	91.1	81.8	82.1	100.0	100.3	....	....	....	Algeria	612
101.3	102.0	108.0	120.7	118.9	99.9	91.2	86.5	84.9	102.9	100.0	109.4	108.2	111.5	111.8	Benin	638
90.4	89.6	69.2	69.1	82.9	83.2	79.7	74.9	77.4	99.1	100.0	100.1	97.9	86.0	78.2	Botswana	616
168.5	144.5	120.0	114.1	113.6	111.0	113.6	110.2	103.6	110.5	100.0	95.7	90.8	93.2	90.3	Burkina Faso	748
120.9	111.5	110.0	111.2	107.4	103.2	97.0	98.4	96.7	90.1	100.0	101.6	105.5	121.5	113.7	Burundi	618
65.5	70.3	70.4	75.3	69.3	65.3	62.9	62.8	88.4	91.4	100.0	113.1	124.3	121.6	....	Cameroon	622
126.2	123.7	142.8	139.9	132.0	133.0	142.1	140.0	128.5	110.8	100.0	95.6	103.6	125.2	....	Central African Rep.	626
49.2	47.3	46.7	52.1	59.4	56.5	54.5	61.1	62.9	81.4	100.0	70.2	74.3	86.6	82.4	Chad	628
128.9	123.4	106.8	112.3	102.4	97.4	98.4	95.9	97.5	94.7	100.0	....	....	....	....	Comoros	632
53.9	53.1	51.9	50.2	50.6	50.9	84.4	62.1	52.1	....	100.0	....	....	....	....	Congo, Dem. Rep. of	636
100.4	69.4	73.3	73.0	81.8	73.3	67.8	69.5	84.5	98.0	100.0	107.4	102.0	91.9	....	Congo, Rep. of	634
96.3	90.2	88.4	87.4	90.0	94.1	96.5	95.4	100.2	111.6	100.0	104.5	106.3	113.2	....	Côte d'Ivoire	662
72.8	49.0	50.1	49.9	74.5	118.4	149.7	157.6	169.5	128.4	100.0	122.4	194.0	....	....	Equatorial Guinea	642
143.2	130.5	127.0	121.7	115.6	106.6	101.8	I96.0	107.3	99.5	100.0	102.6	103.1	104.9	....	Ethiopia	644
70.3	70.1	61.0	62.6	71.3	75.0	72.2	72.3	89.2	110.0	100.0	104.2	98.3	78.1	....	Gabon	646
124.7	122.4	114.0	111.4	95.8	107.6	115.2	98.9	97.6	98.2	100.0	102.2	95.6	....	....	Ghana	652
....	5,401.5	1,512.9	804.7	752.5	80.3	198.8	161.9	109.8	151.9	100.0	66.6	33.5	....	....	Guinea-Bissau	654
143.6	134.8	127.3	138.5	136.3	136.3	129.9	120.3	116.0	108.4	100.0	84.4	83.6	85.6	84.8	Kenya	664
60.9	59.2	70.7	77.6	80.3	85.4	91.4	107.6	99.0	91.7	100.0	103.8	106.5	96.3	....	Lesotho	666
133.2	118.9	125.7	133.1	122.7	116.0	105.8	100.0	90.7	91.6	100.0	110.5	100.0	101.6	....	Madagascar	674
80.7	84.2	72.9	77.8	80.1	89.7	87.8	84.5	86.3	74.8	100.0	109.7	116.4	108.6	....	Malawi	676
100.0	106.3	102.4	96.3	97.3	106.3	107.4	101.2	97.0	98.8	100.0	92.6	94.6	97.0	....	Mali	678
79.1	80.1	73.5	73.1	77.5	75.6	72.7	69.6	78.6	92.3	100.0	111.7	120.8	....	....	Mauritania	682
169.6	153.8	143.0	130.9	127.5	125.5	116.8	109.2	108.7	104.0	100.0	98.0	99.2	97.3	93.6	Mauritius	684
147.7	148.7	137.0	143.5	133.2	129.2	124.3	111.1	105.8	106.5	100.0	96.5	98.2	98.6	....	Morocco	686
24.8	22.9	53.5	57.9	60.2	56.3	117.2	96.2	87.9	92.2	100.0	122.3	121.1	118.8	109.4	Mozambique	688
....	....	....	....	....	I177.1	153.0	144.3	120.0	110.3	100.0	91.7	82.2	....	....	Namibia	728
97.5	92.4	89.2	86.3	80.8	84.1	85.6	91.4	90.9	93.9	100.0	82.2	144.4	182.6	....	Niger	692
47.4	45.1	62.5	62.7	79.2	75.4	66.5	85.9	85.2	79.0	....	....	....	....	....	Nigeria	694
122.2	106.3	93.6	88.0	93.6	104.6	109.5	114.4	110.0	83.5	100.0	101.2	105.7	111.9	101.4	Rwanda	714
86.6	92.4	88.9	90.6	88.0	89.1	89.8	87.7	92.4	104.2	100.0	95.3	96.6	99.7	....	Senegal	722
155.3	152.7	145.5	140.3	130.1	132.0	118.9	121.4	111.7	102.9	100.0	90.6	79.8	66.0	....	Seychelles	718
39.4	39.9	56.1	59.1	60.2	61.4	69.6	77.1	85.3	87.6	100.0	95.5	67.8	62.7	60.7	Sierra Leone	724
I85.4	88.9	90.9	86.8	85.1	90.0	86.6	93.1	103.2	101.4	100.0	97.5	92.1	85.3	85.7	South Africa	199
29.0	31.2	42.5	42.2	49.7	43.9	48.4	44.4	51.0	54.8	I100.0	118.8	127.4	....	....	Sudan	732
81.1	92.5	90.7	93.8	82.6	86.3	86.0	86.1	88.1	87.7	100.0	110.1	107.1	....	....	Swaziland	734
70.7	72.7	I124.9	147.2	136.3	128.7	128.8	116.4	103.9	102.0	100.0	106.4	116.3	124.8	127.5	Tanzania	738
67.6	65.3	60.7	73.8	76.5	76.2	68.1	79.4	80.6	102.3	100.0	100.1	112.0	....	....	Togo	742
104.8	98.9	101.1	92.9	I87.5	89.5	92.4	96.7	99.8	98.4	100.0	102.8	97.3	96.8	93.2	Tunisia	744
143.2	I140.7	169.2	205.7	212.0	180.2	166.4	163.4	117.3	107.2	100.0	93.0	....	....	....	Uganda	746
56.0	I65.1	57.3	58.3	62.5	83.1	83.6	104.1	123.3	117.1	100.0	89.5	91.8	....	....	Zambia	754
106.5	108.9	102.4	109.2	109.3	114.1	132.9	151.9	135.4	116.0	100.0	105.3	....	....	....	Zimbabwe	698
															Asia	
143.3	138.7	137.3	131.8	124.4	120.7	122.0	116.2	108.8	102.4	100.0	102.0	99.3	99.5	98.8	Bangladesh	513
162.8	177.4	195.9	177.9	148.4	141.6	129.1	125.2	118.4	109.3	100.0	96.0	83.2	....	....	Bhutan	514
175.1	147.3	131.3	130.9	125.8	110.4	99.4	93.8	100.0	104.5	100.0	91.9	82.3	76.0	67.8	China, P.R.: Mainland	924
....	....	....	....	....	....	95.3	102.4	103.0	103.8	100.0	99.0	100.1	88.2	78.9	China, P.R.: Hong Kong	532
138.6	141.4	128.1	122.2	120.5	110.4	99.6	96.6	97.8	97.5	100.0	100.1	112.5	117.1	....	Fiji	819
110.1	105.1	101.8	103.4	101.2	100.7	99.8	95.3	100.9	99.1	100.0	99.6	94.5	93.2	....	India	534
202.9	185.7	179.7	166.3	154.6	123.6	118.0	110.5	I109.2	104.6	100.0	91.7	85.5	105.3	76.1	Indonesia	536
114.0	113.2	112.2	112.9	107.1	106.2	107.5	102.4	98.2	99.4	100.0	95.3	87.0	71.3	60.8	Korea	542
....	....	....	....	170.9	183.4	206.6	162.2	120.9	101.8	100.0	97.5	91.7	84.6	....	Lao People's Democratic Rep.	544
131.9	113.2	I118.7	130.2	134.9	131.6	132.7	115.4	108.3	100.0	100.0	92.0	85.7	81.3	76.6	Malaysia	548
124.8	107.3	112.8	118.2	121.9	121.4	121.1	120.4	116.2	104.8	100.0	91.8	83.2	76.8	68.1	Maldives	556
....	....	....	....	....	....	52.9	100.6	120.5	97.0	100.0	116.9	120.7	120.1	....	Mongolia	948
76.3	72.5	78.6	99.5	120.4	109.5	94.2	95.9	105.2	108.0	100.0	93.5	98.9	110.2	82.4	Myanmar	518
I139.2	136.6	133.5	131.4	124.2	121.0	117.2	118.5	110.9	106.2	100.0	99.1	99.5	87.2	80.3	Nepal	558
105.7	100.4	97.2	102.2	110.2	109.1	113.1	107.7	95.9	96.9	100.0	97.4	94.2	91.6	96.7	Pakistan	564

Income Velocity of Money plus Quasi-Money

39ad *i*		1970	1971	1972	1973	1974	1975	1976	1977	1978	1979	1980	1981	1982	1983	1984
														Index Numbers:		
Asia (cont.)																
Papua New Guinea	853	....	....	....	126.8	103.1	92.6	121.3	‡107.7	102.4	94.2	88.5	92.8	93.3	98.9	84.1
Philippines	566	164.7	165.7	169.6	178.2	200.3	205.6	197.0	177.2	160.6	169.3	163.5	162.2	150.2	148.9	177.7
Samoa	862													106.2	115.2	150.2
Singapore	576	141.9	144.1	143.6	148.3	160.0	145.3	138.7	141.1	142.7	148.2	141.6	135.9	132.4	128.0	127.6
Sri Lanka	524	140.2	129.7	132.1	148.6	163.7	177.1	165.4	147.4	127.9	119.1	118.6	117.0	100.7	106.1	112.2
Thailand	578	281.6	252.4	232.6	243.5	253.1	231.9	223.8	216.3	219.6	217.0	215.6	209.0	192.4	168.1	149.0
Vanuatu	846	....	....	....	....	....	....	....	....	....	....	....	....	139.7	125.0	101.4
Europe																
Armenia	911	....	....	....	....	....	....	....	....	....	....	....	....	....	....	....
Belarus	913	....	....	....	....	....	....	....	....	....	....	....	....	....	....	....
Bulgaria	918	....	....	....	....	....	....	....	....	....	....	....	....	....	....	....
Croatia	960	....	....	....	....	....	....	....	....	....	....	....	....	....	....	....
Cyprus	423	174.4	174.6	164.0	155.5	126.0	102.5	117.5	126.8	132.6	139.3	145.6	141.8	140.0	136.6	141.5
Czech Republic	935	....	....	....	....	....	....	....	....	....	....	....	....	....	....	....
Estonia	939	....	....	....	....	....	....	....	....	....	....	....	....	....	....	....
Hungary	944	....	....	....	....	....	....	....	....	....	....	....	....	79.1	81.8	84.9
Kazakhstan	916	....	....	....	....	....	....	....	....	....	....	....	....	....	....	....
Kyrgyz Republic	917	....	....	....	....	....	....	....	....	....	....	....	....	....	....	....
Latvia	941	....	....	....	....	....	....	....	....	....	....	....	....	....	....	....
Lithuania	946	....	....	....	....	....	....	....	....	....	....	....	....	....	....	....
Macedonia, FYR	962	....	....	....	....	....	....	....	....	....	....	....	....	....	....	....
Malta	181	....	....	....	....	....	....	....	....	....	....	....	....	....	....	....
Moldova	921	....	....	....	....	....	....	....	....	....	....	....	....	....	....	....
Poland	964	....	....	....	....	....	....	....	....	....	....	62.5	55.7	81.7	89.2	93.4
Romania	968	....	....	....	....	....	....	....	....	....	....	67.8	58.3	59.7	59.9	61.7
Russia	922	....	....	....	....	....	....	....	....	....	....	....	....	....	....	....
Slovak Republic	936	....	....	....	....	....	....	....	....	....	....	....	....	....	....	....
Slovenia	961	....	....	....	....	....	....	....	....	....	....	....	....	....	....	....
Turkey	186	....	....	....	....	....	....	....	....	....	....	....	....	....	....	....
Ukraine	926	....	....	....	....	....	....	....	....	....	....	....	....	....	....	....
Middle East																
Bahrain	419	....	....	....	....	....	163.7	156.9	142.2	137.0	142.1	143.7	130.3	115.0	106.7	108.2
Egypt	469	‡191.8	201.0	196.6	175.4	155.7	148.7	149.1	153.7	140.2	135.8	‡130.3	110.7	109.4	101.5	101.4
Iran, I.R. of	429	117.3	125.2	119.1	129.4	176.7	136.3	129.1	124.1	84.0	76.3	64.6	64.2	71.3	74.1	72.5
Israel	436	218.7	212.9	211.1	223.3	263.9	234.2	222.3	214.7	331.4	399.2	‡481.0	117.8	110.3	114.0	109.7
Jordan	439	184.2	180.8	193.4	173.7	161.9	163.0	156.8	154.2	147.8	137.6	137.7	138.4	138.3	‡128.1	124.7
Kuwait	443	266.0	330.3	288.3	286.4	543.8	415.2	327.2	267.9	225.0	304.9	270.5	188.2	127.8	116.2	119.0
Libya	672	538.6	540.5	396.6	378.4	275.6	294.4	365.5	334.7	312.4	344.0	366.0	320.5	370.0	274.6	211.4
Oman	449	....	....	87.1	102.4	214.0	177.3	171.0	137.4	120.5	150.5	189.7	176.1	139.5	128.8	122.4
Qatar	453	224.0	248.1	231.9	206.0	501.8	431.3	347.5	262.1	247.0	314.6	332.3	280.5	205.1	171.4	161.1
Saudi Arabia	456	289.0	420.5	481.9	858.0	861.1	625.0	423.3	303.7	233.0	313.9	361.3	294.4	180.8	139.1	123.2
Syrian Arab Rep.	463	153.4	162.5	161.6	140.4	155.6	158.7	153.7	133.6	125.3	125.1	130.3	130.4	118.3	100.9	82.1
United Arab Emirates	466	....	....	....	322.0	328.4	285.5	218.8	199.6	191.0	244.4	288.4	253.9	192.6	153.3	127.8
Yemen, Republic of	474	....	....	....	....	....	....	....	....	....	....	....	....	....	....	....
Western Hemisphere																
Antigua and Barbuda	311	....	....	....	....	....	91.5	84.4	‡129.6	132.8	141.7	147.8	149.2	144.6	132.7	120.7
Argentina	213	56.1	80.5	110.7	77.3	61.4	105.2	132.1	100.6	82.1	83.7	99.0	118.2	142.4	184.2	199.5
Bahamas, The	313	....	....	....	168.4	166.2	197.2	181.4	203.7	219.9	220.4	194.3	197.4	177.3	152.3	147.3
Barbados	316	105.1	102.4	100.4	107.8	151.5	139.0	143.9	131.6	120.8	135.2	147.8	140.5	134.8	132.4	133.0
Belize	339	....	....	....	....	....	....	109.2	122.9	125.5	124.0	143.3	123.6	112.7	101.1	106.5
Bolivia	218	217.6	207.4	213.8	242.6	286.8	249.4	214.8	177.0	172.4	184.9	189.3	190.2	210.5	271.2	570.9
Brazil	223	86.2	86.0	85.6	96.0	104.6	109.1	118.4	127.3	123.3	128.5	159.3	189.8	197.3	210.5	219.2
Chile	228	236.7	162.3	154.6	210.2	413.7	350.1	254.6	240.2	209.7	199.7	173.7	137.9	108.2	106.7	103.6
Colombia	233	‡85.9	90.1	90.9	88.6	88.5	92.2	94.8	91.6	91.6	97.2	100.0	86.9	83.2	86.2	87.3
Costa Rica	238	162.8	157.5	138.4	141.3	143.6	132.4	120.2	112.4	101.7	90.0	88.2	80.5	95.4	86.8	91.7
Dominica	321	....	....	....	....	....	137.7	141.0	174.6	181.4	123.6	129.1	138.5	146.4	134.5	134.8
Dominican Republic	243	135.9	133.0	131.8	117.3	109.0	102.7	112.7	114.1	107.1	124.4	129.0	139.3	134.1	133.3	141.3
Ecuador	248	105.4	99.6	99.5	102.1	109.3	105.7	103.9	96.1	101.3	103.1	99.9	100.4	99.8	103.9	108.0
El Salvador	253	166.6	163.0	150.1	144.7	140.4	136.1	140.5	134.4	139.8	141.0	137.2	125.4	116.3	120.1	122.0
Grenada	328	....	....	....	116.8	128.9	141.5	137.5	139.2	147.8	154.8	142.0	138.7	150.9	156.5	178.6
Guatemala	258	134.3	133.1	119.1	116.4	120.9	119.2	111.7	114.6	111.2	113.3	119.8	118.4	101.5	101.2	99.0
Guyana	336	181.3	171.5	153.6	141.6	179.6	173.2	136.1	117.5	104.6	106.7	108.9	99.8	74.9	60.4	59.3
Haiti	263	325.3	296.5	248.0	262.4	‡187.8	198.5	181.7	160.0	136.9	136.2	147.6	124.7	123.3	127.4	124.9
Honduras	268	132.6	128.5	126.3	118.1	118.3	122.0	117.7	113.6	111.2	110.0	124.4	126.4	118.5	103.7	95.9
Jamaica	343	143.1	130.4	124.1	‡132.4	154.3	150.8	140.0	132.5	147.9	145.8	135.7	122.3	102.7	96.7	106.6
Mexico	273	109.9	112.6	114.3	113.8	120.7	124.3	114.6	116.0	104.7	103.5	111.0	104.8	101.8	116.8	111.8
Nicaragua	278	169.0	158.4	129.5	113.8	128.9	140.4	128.8	125.9	131.3	124.0	100.9	82.1	80.4	79.5	184.0
Panama	283	287.4	254.9	236.4	210.6	218.0	226.7	223.1	214.8	210.1	193.0	206.0	189.3	181.5	181.8	179.3
Paraguay	288	163.8	153.9	151.3	148.3	163.5	151.8	136.5	125.5	118.4	124.5	128.1	130.2	119.6	119.4	131.0
Peru	293	81.9	75.0	72.2	70.6	69.9	68.7	80.2	90.6	100.3	‡116.3	102.5	107.3	103.2	98.3	101.6
St. Kitts and Nevis	361	....	....	....	....	....	....	....	....	....	94.8	99.9	100.3	88.8	79.5	81.2
St. Lucia	362	....	....	....	....	....	91.0	92.0	125.0	122.3	126.3	139.9	131.5	130.4	128.3	124.0
St. Vincent & Grenadines	364	....	....	....	....	....	91.1	91.5	96.8	95.7	90.2	92.0	98.7	97.7	99.5	96.0
Suriname	366	109.8	105.5	94.9	87.0	93.1	94.0	79.2	80.2	77.9	73.6	67.8	66.8	60.1	51.7	44.3
Trinidad and Tobago	369	140.5	126.9	123.3	127.8	179.5	170.4	146.4	142.5	127.8	131.4	146.4	133.2	116.7	96.9	90.3
Uruguay	298	198.7	177.8	189.9	244.9	246.3	241.2	194.9	164.9	141.2	129.9	124.3	99.4	77.0	72.3	71.1
Venezuela, Rep. Bol.	299	114.2	113.4	101.8	102.0	120.2	86.0	73.9	65.4	75.3	68.9	73.3	73.0	65.4	57.0	64.5

1995=100

1985	1986	1987	1988	1989	1990	1991	1992	1993	1994	1995	1996	1997	1998	1999		
															Asia (cont.)	
79.4	73.7	71.4	89.4	83.9	80.4	86.4	85.2	90.0	90.1	100.0	90.4	72.8	73.2	....	Papua New Guinea	853
176.7	184.9	182.9	176.5	159.9	148.1	142.0	136.3	I125.3	116.4	100.0	92.9	82.8	78.4	79.4	Philippines	566
122.7	111.7	91.1	93.9	84.5	73.1	....	....	....	117.3	100.0	102.8	102.3	....	....	Samoa	862
119.8	112.0	104.5	109.3	102.1	95.7	93.2	90.2	98.8	101.5	100.0	98.9	97.4	85.2	70.9	Singapore	576
103.2	107.7	105.9	103.7	107.8	118.4	115.1	109.0	106.6	102.5	100.0	98.0	101.7	104.0	....	Sri Lanka	524
137.8	132.9	131.3	132.9	128.3	116.7	111.5	106.5	103.5	103.1	100.0	96.6	87.6	82.0	75.5	Thailand	578
91.3	78.3	69.4	77.9	90.1	74.0	84.8	91.5	93.9	98.7	100.0	....	....	....	....	Vanuatu	846
															Europe	
....	....	....	....	....	....	....	....	3,759.5	72.4	100.0	92.2	81.0	73.3	....	Armenia	911
....	....	....	....	....	....	....	....	....	38.4	100.0	92.5	93.0	81.8	91.2	Belarus	913
....	....	....	....	....	....	I97.4	93.7	91.1	90.0	100.0	130.1	235.2	206.4	200.2	Bulgaria	918
....	....	....	....	....	....	....	....	108.4	126.7	100.0	74.2	....	....	....	Croatia	960
141.2	137.8	137.1	132.7	129.3	124.5	113.0	113.8	105.5	102.0	100.0	93.8	88.9	85.9	81.2	Cyprus	423
....	....	....	....	....	....	....	....	112.5	107.1	100.0	96.9	104.0	106.2	100.0	Czech Republic	935
....	....	....	....	....	....	21.9	91.8	106.6	96.9	100.0	93.8	83.0	79.0	....	Estonia	939
80.9	78.3	80.5	92.5	99.9	100.1	I94.8	85.7	84.2	90.2	100.0	102.0	104.6	93.2	....	Hungary	944
....	....	....	....	....	....	....	....	41.0	96.3	100.0	90.3	102.2	98.1	....	Kazakhstan	916
....	....	....	....	....	....	....	....	....	....	100.0	117.0	124.8	107.3	....	Kyrgyz Republic	917
....	....	....	....	....	....	....	....	110.0	99.8	100.0	138.1	120.6	105.8	105.4	Latvia	941
....	....	....	....	....	....	....	....	130.0	100.0	100.0	128.1	126.8	116.7	101.3	Lithuania	946
....	....	....	....	....	....	....	....	16.5	95.5	100.0	98.2	94.7	84.0	....	Macedonia, FYR	962
....	....	....	....	....	....	....	....	....	....	100.0	97.2	96.2	94.4	91.6	Malta	181
....	....	....	....	....	....	48.5	78.4	139.7	127.6	100.0	82.2	76.5	....	....	Moldova	921
I94.0	92.1	89.8	105.1	124.9	I121.3	104.6	99.3	94.4	100.8	100.0	94.8	88.7	82.7	....	Poland	964
57.0	55.4	53.4	49.4	I43.8	39.6	72.2	88.1	128.2	133.8	100.0	88.9	100.4	95.9	89.6	Romania	968
....	....	....	....	....	....	....	....	88.1	99.1	100.0	91.7	82.0	77.1	79.2	Russia	922
....	....	....	....	....	....	....	....	98.6	99.8	100.0	92.8	96.3	90.3	....	Slovak Republic	936
....	....	....	....	....	....	....	....	134.8	117.6	100.0	91.6	85.4	77.3	....	Slovenia	961
....	....	99.3	106.9	107.0	118.3	115.5	108.6	118.9	100.3	100.0	91.6	86.6	76.6	....	Turkey	186
....	....	....	....	....	....	....	47.4	73.1	79.4	100.0	102.1	80.5	....	....	Ukraine	926
															Middle East	
98.7	79.9	87.8	91.5	88.6	96.2	104.8	96.3	98.4	102.0	100.0	100.4	95.4	81.3	....	Bahrain	419
101.3	93.5	96.7	92.1	97.5	99.4	89.8	97.6	95.2	94.8	100.0	101.0	101.4	102.4	101.0	Egypt	469
69.7	63.9	65.9	61.6	62.7	70.0	77.6	82.3	91.0	94.8	100.0	100.0	90.7	90.8	93.7	Iran, I.R. of	429
97.5	103.1	103.6	107.0	105.4	109.2	116.8	139.1	109.7	106.0	I100.0	94.6	89.1	84.0	77.1	Israel	436
118.8	116.4	105.6	94.7	84.3	83.6	84.3	94.6	93.3	98.2	100.0	101.4	101.9	99.9	....	Jordan	439
116.0	95.3	112.0	98.3	113.0	90.0	47.3	91.4	107.6	103.2	100.0	116.9	110.7	94.3	108.4	Kuwait	443
162.3	123.9	109.3	116.5	126.1	141.6	151.4	149.8	119.9	106.8	100.0	100.0	124.3	....	....	Libya	672
111.6	97.8	103.1	96.1	99.1	111.8	I99.2	103.6	99.6	100.1	100.0	102.8	91.6	72.7	77.2	Oman	449
129.9	93.7	91.5	101.9	109.6	114.9	117.4	117.4	102.1	97.5	100.0	109.9	103.3	....	....	Qatar	453
107.5	90.0	85.6	83.4	86.9	106.3	110.5	105.6	94.6	97.4	100.0	106.1	102.5	87.0	91.0	Saudi Arabia	456
76.9	79.3	89.0	111.0	102.8	107.6	94.4	96.4	89.7	100.2	100.0	111.9	113.6	109.6	....	Syrian Arab Rep.	463
111.3	83.1	87.1	82.3	89.2	107.1	105.7	103.2	102.4	101.9	100.0	104.7	106.0	91.9	....	United Arab Emirates	466
....	....	....	....	....	79.4	81.4	89.5	88.7	85.3	100.0	115.0	126.4	109.6	....	Yemen, Republic of	474
															Western Hemisphere	
124.9	129.7	130.6	135.8	132.9	127.8	119.2	114.6	114.5	111.1	100.0	100.2	106.6	....	....	Antigua and Barbuda	311
169.8	137.2	137.5	147.1	175.4	318.8	238.2	167.2	I115.4	97.0	100.0	89.0	78.2	68.4	61.4	Argentina	213
158.9	165.5	162.4	162.9	I172.2	152.8	134.7	125.7	115.0	107.7	100.0	....	....	....	....	Bahamas, The	313
127.8	127.7	128.1	121.5	123.2	117.0	110.1	101.5	97.4	98.4	100.0	95.4	91.4	91.1	....	Barbados	316
98.8	90.6	108.0	108.5	114.5	111.9	104.1	104.9	107.5	104.6	100.0	91.1	83.9	81.1	79.9	Belize	339
977.4	451.7	264.1	253.7	249.3	198.1	161.0	133.9	112.4	98.4	100.0	98.5	91.8	89.7	86.6	Bolivia	218
201.9	115.2	137.8	181.4	171.9	209.8	179.0	125.6	114.8	104.6	100.0	102.1	99.5	88.0	....	Brazil	223
102.0	98.3	100.3	101.1	99.5	98.0	102.8	101.1	97.4	97.8	100.0	89.6	85.5	80.0	73.9	Chile	228
92.5	93.1	89.3	97.0	99.5	108.6	115.9	102.2	96.1	108.1	100.0	101.5	91.7	....	....	Colombia	233
93.9	98.4	96.5	96.1	90.2	86.5	89.2	91.1	91.8	94.5	100.0	89.5	88.9	87.4	81.7	Costa Rica	238
136.9	143.3	126.4	136.7	134.3	123.4	112.8	106.3	108.5	112.6	100.0	97.1	93.6	93.9	....	Dominica	321
163.1	118.6	104.8	119.0	104.8	107.9	133.8	113.6	97.9	96.8	100.0	94.7	94.7	88.2	80.4	Dominican Republic	243
112.4	115.1	113.3	121.7	145.2	161.1	151.7	165.1	139.5	116.0	100.0	93.9	89.8	89.4	....	Ecuador	248
117.9	125.7	130.1	141.0	149.3	134.1	125.4	116.0	112.5	99.5	100.0	95.7	86.9	79.7	78.8	El Salvador	253
186.2	166.5	169.7	157.9	164.1	157.7	160.0	152.6	128.3	120.1	100.0	113.1	109.4	104.5	....	Grenada	328
102.2	109.7	107.6	108.0	107.4	128.2	130.8	101.3	107.5	103.3	100.0	105.2	97.0	96.5	92.4	Guatemala	258
57.9	52.5	60.4	54.7	93.2	92.6	142.3	101.7	90.4	101.2	100.0	91.7	85.6	....	....	Guyana	336
129.4	133.1	114.7	89.2	98.3	116.7	147.7	118.4	106.2	100.5	100.0	102.5	111.6	111.1	107.1	Haiti	263
103.1	102.8	96.6	89.7	89.8	90.8	98.0	95.6	97.5	104.0	100.0	98.2	85.2	68.5	62.8	Honduras	268
106.9	103.8	101.3	100.2	100.9	114.9	128.1	117.4	109.8	102.6	100.0	101.5	95.0	97.9	....	Jamaica	343
122.8	134.6	147.4	181.5	272.4	173.2	126.6	110.7	I102.3	97.7	100.0	105.9	99.5	101.3	103.8	Mexico	273
196.3	221.5	218.4	207.8	196.4	2,016.9	231.1	160.3	161.7	128.5	100.0	83.4	64.8	54.8	49.6	Nicaragua	278
181.7	165.9	150.0	173.9	195.7	172.5	149.5	132.6	118.0	108.4	100.0	96.9	93.3	86.6	....	Panama	283
143.7	160.5	161.0	165.0	167.0	154.0	125.5	109.3	100.9	100.8	100.0	90.4	83.8	84.9	....	Paraguay	288
105.5	110.0	122.1	199.0	220.6	271.8	192.8	147.0	116.6	109.0	100.0	82.5	70.5	63.1	56.0	Peru	293
79.4	80.0	101.3	115.3	105.6	106.1	101.2	99.5	95.9	105.2	100.0	100.7	100.7	....	....	St. Kitts and Nevis	361
118.1	115.0	104.9	113.7	108.0	105.3	101.8	105.7	103.7	104.1	100.0	96.3	93.8	95.7	....	St. Lucia	362
93.9	90.5	93.8	111.8	100.2	99.9	102.3	108.1	103.1	96.7	100.0	100.2	97.4	92.1	....	St. Vincent & Grenadines	364
34.9	27.3	24.1	22.6	21.7	23.3	23.4	26.6	43.2	114.6	100.0	70.1	60.1	58.9	....	Suriname	366
85.9	83.1	81.8	80.2	82.0	92.0	90.9	97.2	97.8	105.6	100.0	105.0	101.3	91.5	....	Trinidad and Tobago	369
82.2	82.4	85.3	82.4	76.6	73.1	76.5	88.0	93.1	108.1	100.0	92.3	86.3	80.5	....	Uruguay	298
63.0	61.0	69.4	74.7	93.8	96.0	81.2	88.5	96.2	94.1	100.0	158.1	141.4	132.1	....	Venezuela, Rep. Bol.	299

International Interest Rates

	1985	1986	1987	1988	1989	1990	1991	1992	1993	1994	1995	1996	1997	1998	1999

London Interbank Offer Rates on SDR Deposits
(99260lsa, 60lsb, 60lsc)
(Period averages in percent per annum)

	1985	1986	1987	1988	1989	1990	1991	1992	1993	1994	1995	1996	1997	1998	1999
Three-Month	8.02	6.65	6.22	6.56	8.40	9.07	7.70	6.27	4.74	3.86	4.60	3.72	3.91	....	....
Six-Month	8.17	6.58	6.31	6.70	8.44	9.17	7.71	6.22	4.64	3.97	4.63	3.79	4.00	....	....
One-Year	8.40	6.58	6.48	6.87	8.46	9.28	7.76	6.34	4.59	4.22	4.72	3.95	4.14	....	....

London Interbank Offer Rates on US Dollar Deposits
(11160lda, 60ldb, 60ldc, 60ldd, 60lde, 60ldf)
(Period averages in percent per annum)

	1985	1986	1987	1988	1989	1990	1991	1992	1993	1994	1995	1996	1997	1998	1999
Overnight	8.04	6.97	6.63	7.56	9.21	8.13	5.78	3.60	3.05	4.24	5.90	5.35	5.54	....	....
Seven-Day	8.20	6.95	6.82	7.68	9.26	8.20	5.87	3.66	3.08	4.31	5.93	5.40	5.58	....	....
One-Month	8.23	6.94	6.99	7.81	9.24	8.29	5.90	3.72	3.16	4.46	5.97	5.44	5.64	5.60	5.25
Three-Month	8.40	6.86	7.18	7.98	9.28	8.31	5.99	3.86	3.29	4.74	6.04	5.51	5.76	5.59	5.41
Six-Month	8.64	6.85	7.30	8.13	9.27	8.35	6.08	3.90	3.41	5.07	6.10	5.59	5.86	5.56	5.53
One-Year	9.11	6.95	7.61	8.41	9.31	8.45	6.29	4.20	3.64	5.59	6.24	5.78	6.08	5.53	5.71

London Interbank Offer Rates on Three-Month Deposits (60ea)
(Pound Sterling Rates Relate to Paris Market)
(Period averages in percent per annum)

	1985	1986	1987	1988	1989	1990	1991	1992	1993	1994	1995	1996	1997	1998	1999
French Franc	10.76	9.46	8.64	8.09	9.35	10.29	9.61	10.37	8.57	5.88	6.68	3.94	3.48	3.64	....
Deutsche Mark	5.37	4.64	4.06	4.33	7.09	8.51	9.31	9.52	7.30	5.36	4.53	3.31	3.37	3.60	2.96
Japanese Yen	6.68	5.12	4.26	4.51	5.46	7.76	7.38	4.46	3.00	2.31	1.27	.63	.63	.71	.22
Netherlands Guilder	6.42	5.66	5.36	4.82	7.40	8.69	9.29	9.37	6.85	5.23	4.47	3.03	3.37	3.55	....
Swiss Franc	5.03	4.33	3.91	3.20	7.07	8.96	8.25	7.88	4.96	4.16	3.09	2.05	1.71	1.60	1.39
Pound Sterling	12.25	10.97	9.80	10.36	13.94	14.79	11.67	9.70	6.05	5.54	6.73	6.09	6.90	7.39	5.54

London Interbank Offer Rates on Six-Month Deposits (60eb)
(Pound Sterling Rates Relate to Paris Market)
(Period averages in percent per annum)

	1985	1986	1987	1988	1989	1990	1991	1992	1993	1994	1995	1996	1997	1998	1999
French Franc	11.11	9.16	8.79	8.32	9.44	10.43	9.64	10.16	7.92	5.95	6.61	4.02	3.54	3.68	....
Deutsche Mark	5.50	4.64	4.16	4.47	7.22	8.77	9.40	9.41	6.95	5.35	4.57	3.31	3.42	3.66	3.05
Japanese Yen	6.56	5.02	4.27	4.56	5.50	7.84	7.16	4.32	2.96	2.36	1.26	.71	.65	.71	.24
Netherlands Guilder	6.44	5.60	5.40	4.93	7.46	8.86	9.35	9.26	6.57	5.25	4.55	3.08	3.46	3.64	....
Swiss Franc	5.09	4.28	3.96	3.42	7.06	8.94	8.18	7.81	4.76	4.23	3.16	2.09	1.78	1.68	1.55
Pound Sterling	11.99	10.82	9.76	10.50	13.89	14.72	11.40	9.65	5.93	5.80	6.91	6.13	7.04	7.32	5.62

Discounts (-) or Premiums (60f) on Three-Month Forward Exchange Rates
(End of period in percent per annum based on end-of-period quotation of
the currencies against the US dollar)

	1985	1986	1987	1988	1989	1990	1991	1992	1993	1994	1995	1996	1997	1998	1999
Canada	−1.49	−2.12	−1.05	−1.51	−3.90	−3.59	−2.98	−3.37	−3.84	−3.99	−.23	22.78	....	....	....
Australia	−12.17	−10.05	−5.79	−7.92	−9.51	−5.93	−4.74	−3.93	....	....	....	....	....	....	....
Japan	.92	−.50	7.97	4.39	1.67	−3.48	−1.50	.03	1.18	3.69	4.86	5.12	5.45	6.25	6.25
Austria	.23	.58	2.84	3.34	−.85	−1.61	−5.65	−5.14	−2.21	−1.13	−1.67	2.34	1.99	2.32	....
Belgium	−1.75	−1.88	.75	1.77	−1.79	−2.29	−5.50	−4.94	−3.54	1.10	1.43	2.44	2.17	1.90	....
Denmark	−.38	−2.86	−2.00	1.30	−3.70	−1.70	−5.80	−11.80	−3.30	.20	.80	1.85	1.74	.99	2.36
Finland	−2.73	−6.76	−1.60	−1.97	−7.13	−6.71	−7.79	−6.61	−2.61	.43	1.14	2.32	2.12	1.85	....
France	−1.01	−2.11	−1.27	.59	.01	1.09[p]	−3.32	−6.71	....	....	....	....	....	....	....
Germany	2.97	1.20	3.67	3.89	−.05	−1.87	−5.54	−5.20	−2.66	1.24	1.81	2.26	2.10	1.89	....
Italy	−10.25	−4.89	−4.28	−5.06	−4.34	−5.36	−7.97	−10.37	−7.10	−.87	−4.64	−1.00	−2.62	.51	....
Netherlands	2.31	.36	2.81	3.50	−14.93	−1.89	−5.52	−4.77	....	....	....	....	....	....	....
Norway	−.58	−11.30	−11.71	−3.07	−3.14	−.51	−7.17	−9.91	−2.47	.09	−1.08	.89	1.98	1.12	.32
Spain	−7.95	−12.62	−11.20	−3.46	−16.33	.48	−23.09	−5.51	−.32	−3.67	−7.31	.79	4.81	3.50	....
Sweden	−4.44	−3.50	−1.64	.45	−3.91	−2.56	−10.63	−54.41	−1.83	−1.66	−.36	−.37	−.58	.84	−9.91
Switzerland	4.91	2.34	4.69	2.93	−1.16	−1.39	−3.10	−2.47	−.95	1.98	3.30	2.50	4.21	3.34	4.65
United Kingdom	−3.57	−4.56	−1.36	−3.56	−6.30	−5.99	−6.66	−3.53	−1.91	−.12	−.86	−.89	−1.77	....	....

SDR Interest Rate (99260s) and Rate of Remuneration (99260r)
(Period averages in percent per annum)

	1985	1986	1987	1988	1989	1990	1991	1992	1993	1994	1995	1996	1997	1998	1999
SDR Interest Rate	7.8064	6.3941	5.8679	6.2544	8.2685	9.0912	7.7229	6.2599	4.6394	4.2858	4.5847	3.8998	4.0719	4.1052	3.4759
Rate of Remuneration	7.1421	6.1074	5.8546	6.2544	8.2685	9.0912	7.7229	6.2599	4.6394	4.2858	4.5847	3.8998	4.0719	4.1052	3.4759

National Interest Rates

Central Bank Discount Rates (60)
(End of period in percent per annum)

1983	1984	1985	1986	1987	1988	1989	1990	1991	1992	1993	1994	1995	1996	1997	1998	1999	
																	Industrial Countries
8.50	8.00	7.50	5.50	6.00	6.50	7.00	6.50	3.50	3.00	3.00	4.75	5.25	5.00	5.00	4.50	5.00	United States
10.04	10.16	9.49	8.49	8.66	11.17	12.47	11.78	7.67	7.36	4.11	7.43	5.79	3.25	4.50	5.25	5.00	Canada
5.00	5.00	5.00	3.00	2.50	2.50	4.25	6.00	4.50	3.25	1.75	1.75	.50	.50	.50	.50	.50	Japan
7.50	13.50	19.80	24.60	18.55	15.10	15.00	13.25	8.30	9.15	5.70	9.75	9.80	8.80	9.70	5.60	5.00	New Zealand
12.14	12.03	15.98	16.93	14.95	13.20	17.23	15.24	10.99	6.96	5.83	5.75	5.75	....	....	....	....	Australia
....	....	....	....	....	....	....	....	....	....	....	....	....	....	....	....	4.00	Euro Area
3.75	4.50	4.00	4.00	3.00	4.00	6.50	6.50	8.00	8.00	5.25	4.50	3.00	2.50	2.50	2.50	....	Austria
10.00	11.00	9.75	8.00	7.00	7.75	10.25	10.50	8.50	7.75	5.25	4.50	3.00	2.50	2.75	2.75	....	Belgium
9.50	9.50	9.00	7.00	7.00	8.00	8.50	8.50	8.50	9.50	5.50	5.25	4.88	4.00	4.00	3.50	....	Finland
4.00	4.50	4.00	3.50	2.50	3.50	6.00	6.00	8.00	8.25	5.75	4.50	3.00	2.50	2.50	2.50	....	Germany
12.25	14.00	10.25	13.25	9.25	8.00	12.00	11.25	10.75	....	7.00	6.25	6.50	6.25	6.75	4.06	....	Ireland
17.00	16.50	15.00	12.00	12.00	12.50	13.50	12.50	12.00	12.00	8.00	7.50	9.00	7.50	5.50	3.00	....	Italy
5.00	5.00	5.00	4.50	3.75	4.50	7.00	7.25	8.50	7.75	5.00	....	....	....	....	....	....	Netherlands
25.00	25.00	19.00	16.00	14.50	13.50	14.50	14.50	I20.00	21.96	11.00	8.88	8.50	6.70	5.31	3.00	....	Portugal
21.40	12.50	10.50	11.84	13.50	12.40	14.52	14.71	12.50	13.25	9.00	7.38	9.00	6.25	4.75	3.00	....	Spain
7.00	7.00	7.00	7.00	7.00	7.00	7.00	8.50	9.50	9.50	6.25	5.00	4.25	3.25	3.50	3.50	3.00	Denmark
20.50	20.50	20.50	20.50	20.50	19.00	19.00	19.00	19.00	19.00	21.50	20.50	18.00	16.50	14.50	....	I11.81	Greece
22.00	16.50	30.00	21.00	49.20	24.10	38.40	21.00	21.00	I16.63	....	4.70	5.93	5.70	6.55	....	....	Iceland
10.00	10.20	10.70	14.80	13.80	12.00	11.00	10.50	10.00	11.00	7.00	6.75	6.75	6.00	5.50	10.00	7.50	Norway
8.50	9.50	10.50	7.50	7.50	8.50	10.50	11.50	8.00	I10.00	5.00	7.00	7.00	3.50	2.50	2.00	1.50	Sweden
4.00	4.00	4.00	4.00	2.50	3.50	6.00	6.00	7.00	6.00	4.00	3.50	1.50	1.00	1.00	1.00	.50	Switzerland
																	Developing Countries
																	Africa
2.75	2.75	2.75	5.00	5.00	5.00	7.00	10.50	11.50	11.50	11.50	21.00	....	13.00	11.00	9.50	8.50	Algeria
....	....	....	....	....	....	....	....	....	....	....	....	160.00	2.00	48.00	58.00	120.00	Angola
10.50	10.50	10.50	8.50	8.50	9.50	11.00	11.00	11.00	12.50	10.50	10.00	7.50	6.50	6.00	6.25	5.75	Benin
10.50	9.00	9.00	9.00	8.50	6.50	6.50	8.50	12.00	14.25	14.25	13.50	13.00	13.00	12.50	12.50	13.25	Botswana
10.50	10.50	10.50	8.50	8.50	9.50	11.00	11.00	11.00	12.50	10.50	10.00	7.50	6.50	6.00	6.25	5.75	Burkina Faso
7.00	7.00	7.00	5.00	7.00	7.00	7.00	8.00	10.70	9.80	9.80	9.40	9.90	....	....	12.40	12.09	Burundi
8.50	8.50	9.00	8.00	8.00	9.50	10.00	11.00	10.75	12.00	11.50	I7.75	8.60	7.75	7.50	7.00	7.30	Cameroon
8.50	8.50	9.00	8.00	8.00	9.50	10.00	11.00	10.75	12.00	11.50	I7.75	8.60	7.75	7.50	7.00	7.60	Central African Rep.
9.00	9.00	9.00	8.00	8.00	9.50	10.00	11.00	10.75	12.00	11.50	I7.75	8.60	7.75	7.50	7.00	7.60	Chad
10.00	10.00	10.00	10.00	8.50	8.50	....	....	....	....	....	....	....	....	....	....	....	Comoros
20.00	20.00	26.00	26.00	29.00	37.00	50.00	45.00	55.00	55.00	95.00	145.00	125.00	238.00	....	....	....	Congo, Dem. Rep. of
8.50	8.50	9.00	8.00	8.00	9.50	10.00	11.00	10.75	12.00	11.50	I7.75	8.60	7.75	7.50	7.00	7.60	Congo, Republic of
10.50	10.50	10.50	8.50	8.50	9.50	11.00	11.00	11.00	12.50	10.50	10.00	7.50	6.50	6.00	6.25	5.75	Côte d'Ivoire
....	....	9.00	8.00	8.00	9.50	10.00	11.00	10.75	12.00	11.50	I7.75	8.60	7.75	7.50	7.00	7.60	Equatorial Guinea
....	....	6.00	6.00	3.00	3.00	3.00	3.00	3.00	5.25	12.00	12.00	12.00	....	....	....	....	Ethiopia
8.50	8.50	9.00	8.00	8.00	9.50	10.00	11.00	10.75	12.00	11.50	I7.75	8.60	7.75	7.50	7.00	7.60	Gabon
9.50	9.50	15.00	20.00	21.00	19.00	15.00	16.50	15.50	17.50	13.50	13.50	14.00	14.00	14.00	12.00	10.50	Gambia, The
14.50	18.00	18.50	20.50	23.50	26.00	26.00	33.00	20.00	30.00	35.00	33.00	45.00	45.00	45.00	37.00	27.00	Ghana
....	....	....	9.00	10.00	10.00	13.00	15.00	19.00	19.00	17.00	17.00	18.00	18.00	15.00	....	....	Guinea
....	....	....	....	....	....	....	42.00	42.00	45.50	41.00	26.00	39.00	54.00	6.00	6.25	5.75	Guinea-Bissau
15.00	12.50	12.50	12.50	12.50	16.02	16.50	19.43	20.27	20.46	45.50	21.50	24.50	26.88	32.27	17.07	26.46	Kenya
12.00	15.00	12.00	9.50	9.00	15.50	17.00	15.75	18.00	15.00	13.50	13.50	15.50	17.00	15.60	19.50	19.00	Lesotho
13.00	13.00	11.50	11.50	11.50	11.50	....	....	....	....	....	....	....	....	....	....	....	Madagascar
10.00	10.00	11.00	11.00	14.00	11.00	11.00	14.00	13.00	20.00	25.00	40.00	50.00	27.00	23.00	43.00	47.00	Malawi
10.50	10.50	10.50	8.50	8.50	9.50	11.00	11.00	11.00	12.50	10.50	10.00	7.50	6.50	6.00	6.25	5.75	Mali
6.00	6.00	6.50	6.50	6.50	6.50	7.00	7.00	7.00	7.00	....	....	....	....	....	....	....	Mauritania
11.00	11.00	11.00	11.00	10.00	10.00	12.00	12.00	11.30	8.30	8.30	13.80	11.40	11.82	10.46	17.19	....	Mauritius
7.00	7.00	8.13	8.50	8.50	8.50	....	....	....	....	....	7.17	....	....	....	6.04	5.42	Morocco
....	....	....	....	....	....	....	....	20.50	16.50	14.50	15.50	17.50	17.75	16.00	18.75	11.50	Namibia
10.50	10.50	10.50	8.50	8.50	8.50	11.00	11.00	11.00	12.50	10.50	10.00	7.50	6.50	6.00	6.25	5.75	Niger
8.00	10.00	10.00	10.00	12.75	12.75	18.50	18.50	15.50	17.50	26.00	13.50	13.50	13.50	13.50	13.50	18.00	Nigeria
9.00	9.00	9.00	9.00	9.00	9.00	9.00	14.00	14.00	11.00	11.00	11.00	16.00	16.00	10.75	11.38	11.19	Rwanda
....	....	....	....	....	....	25.00	25.00	45.00	45.00	30.00	32.00	50.00	35.00	55.00	29.50	17.00	São Tomé & Príncipe
10.50	10.50	10.50	8.50	8.50	9.50	11.00	11.00	11.00	12.50	10.50	10.00	7.50	6.50	6.00	6.25	5.75	Senegal
6.00	6.00	6.00	6.00	6.00	6.00	6.00	I1.00	1.00	1.00	1.00	1.00	1.00	1.00	1.00	1.00	1.00	Seychelles
....	....	....	....	....	....	....	....	....	....	....	....	....	....	....	....	....	Somalia
17.75	20.75	13.00	9.50	9.50	14.50	18.00	18.00	17.00	14.00	12.00	13.00	15.00	17.00	16.00	I19.32	12.00	South Africa
13.50	19.00	12.50	9.50	9.00	11.00	12.00	12.00	13.00	12.00	11.00	12.00	15.00	16.75	15.75	18.00	12.00	Swaziland
4.00	4.00	5.00	8.00	12.50	14.50	15.50	....	....	14.50	14.50	67.50	47.90	19.00	16.20	17.60	20.20	Tanzania
10.50	10.50	10.50	8.50	8.50	9.50	11.00	11.00	11.00	12.50	10.50	10.00	7.50	6.50	6.00	6.25	5.75	Togo
7.00	7.00	9.25	9.25	9.25	9.25	11.37	11.88	11.88	11.38	8.88	8.88	8.88	7.88	....	....	....	Tunisia
15.50	24.00	24.00	36.00	31.00	45.00	55.00	50.00	46.00	41.00	24.00	15.00	13.30	15.85	14.08	9.10	15.75	Uganda
10.00	14.50	25.00	30.00	15.00	15.00	....	....	....	47.00	72.50	20.50	40.20	47.00	17.70	....	....	Zambia
9.00	9.00	9.00	9.00	9.00	9.00	9.00	10.25	20.00	29.50	28.50	29.50	29.50	27.00	31.50	I39.50	74.41	Zimbabwe
																	Asia
10.50	10.50	11.25	10.75	10.75	10.75	10.75	9.75	9.25	8.50	6.00	5.50	6.00	7.00	8.00	8.00	7.00	Bangladesh
....	....	....	....	....	....	....	7.92	7.20	7.20	10.08	10.08	10.44	9.00	8.55	4.59	3.24	China,P.R.: Mainland
....	....	....	....	....	....	....	....	....	4.00	4.00	5.75	6.25	6.00	7.00	6.25	7.00	China,P.R.:Hong Kong
10.17	11.00	11.00	8.00	11.00	11.00	8.00	8.00	8.00	6.00	6.00	6.00	6.00	6.00	1.88	2.50	2.50	Fiji
10.00	10.00	10.00	10.00	10.00	10.00	10.00	10.00	12.00	12.00	12.00	12.00	12.00	12.00	9.00	9.00	8.00	India
....	....	....	....	....	....	....	18.83	18.47	13.50	8.82	12.44	13.99	12.80	20.00	38.44	12.51	Indonesia
5.00	5.00	5.00	7.00	7.00	8.00	7.00	7.00	7.00	7.00	5.00	5.00	5.00	5.00	5.00	3.00	3.00	Korea
....	....	....	....	....	....	....	....	....	23.67	25.00	30.00	32.08	35.00	....	35.00	34.89	Lao People's Dem.Rep
5.20	5.06	4.13	3.89	3.20	4.12	4.89	7.23	7.70	7.10	5.24	4.51	6.47	7.28	....	....	....	Malaysia
....	....	....	....	....	....	....	....	....	....	628.80	180.00	150.00	109.00	45.50	23.30	11.40	Mongolia
....	....	....	....	....	....	....	....	11.00	11.00	11.00	11.00	12.50	15.00	15.00	15.00	12.00	Myanmar
15.00	15.00	15.00	11.00	11.00	11.00	11.00	11.00	13.00	13.00	11.00	11.00	11.00	11.00	9.00	9.00	9.00	Nepal
10.00	10.00	10.00	10.00	10.00	10.00	10.00	10.00	10.00	10.00	10.00	I15.00	17.00	20.00	18.00	16.50	13.00	Pakistan
8.75	8.75	9.75	11.40	8.80	10.80	9.55	9.30	9.30	7.12	I6.39	....	....	....	....	....	....	Papua New Guinea
8.05	12.11	I12.75	10.00	10.00	10.00	12.00	14.00	14.00	14.30	9.40	8.30	10.83	11.70	14.64	12.40	7.89	Philippines
13.00	13.00	11.00	11.00	10.00	10.00	14.00	15.00	17.00	17.00	17.00	17.00	17.00	17.00	17.00	17.00	16.00	Sri Lanka
13.00	12.00	11.00	8.00	8.00	8.00	8.00	12.00	11.00	11.00	9.00	9.50	10.50	10.50	12.50	12.50	4.00	Thailand

National Interest Rates

Central Bank Discount Rates (60) (cont.)
(End of period in percent per annum)

	1983	1984	1985	1986	1987	1988	1989	1990	1991	1992	1993	1994	1995	1996	1997	1998	1999
Europe																	
Albania	....	....	....	....	....	....	....	....	....	40.00	34.00	25.00	20.50	24.00	32.00	23.44	18.00
Armenia	....	....	....	....	....	....	....	....	....	30.00	210.00	210.00	77.80	26.00	65.10	....	....
Azerbaijan	....	....	....	....	....	....	....	....	....	12.00	100.00	200.00	80.00	20.00	12.00	14.00	10.00
Belarus	....	....	....	....	....	....	....	....	....	30.00	210.00	480.00	66.00	8.30	8.90	9.60	23.40
Bulgaria	....	....	....	....	....	....	....	....	54.00	41.00	52.00	78.50	37.31	192.00	....	....	....
Croatia	....	....	....	....	....	....	....	....	....	1,889.39	34.49	8.50	8.50	6.50	5.90	5.90	7.90
Cyprus	6.00	6.00	6.00	6.00	6.00	6.00	6.50	6.50	6.50	6.50	6.50	6.50	6.50	17.50	7.00	7.00	7.00
Czech Republic	....	....	....	....	....	....	....	....	....	....	8.00	8.50	9.50	10.50	13.00	7.50	5.00
Hungary	....	....	11.50	10.50	10.50	14.00	17.00	22.00	22.00	21.00	22.00	25.00	28.00	23.00	20.50	17.00	14.50
Kazakhstan	....	....	....	....	....	....	....	....	....	....	170.00	230.00	152.50	35.00	18.50	25.00	18.00
Kyrgyz Republic	....	....	....	....	....	....	....	....	....	....	....	....	....	....	....	....	....
Latvia	....	....	....	....	....	....	....	....	....	....	27.00	25.00	24.00	9.50	4.00	4.00	4.00
Macedonia, FYR	....	....	....	....	....	....	....	....	....	....	295.00	33.00	15.00	9.20	8.90	8.90	8.90
Malta	6.50	6.50	6.00	6.00	5.50	5.50	5.50	5.50	5.50	5.50	5.50	5.50	5.50	5.50	5.50	5.50	4.75
Poland	3.00	4.00	4.00	4.00	4.00	6.00	104.00	48.00	36.00	32.00	29.00	28.00	25.00	22.00	24.50	18.25	19.00
Russia	....	....	....	....	....	....	....	....	....	....	....	....	160.00	48.00	28.00	60.00	55.00
Slovak Republic	....	....	....	....	....	....	....	....	....	....	12.00	12.00	9.75	8.80	8.80	8.80	8.80
Slovenia	....	....	....	....	....	....	....	....	....	....	....	....	14.62	11.42	13.78	8.55	8.35
Turkey	48.50	52.00	52.00	48.00	45.00	54.00	54.00	45.00	48.00	48.00	48.00	55.00	50.00	....	....	....	....
Ukraine	....	....	....	....	....	....	....	....	....	80.00	240.00	252.00	110.00	40.00	35.00	60.00	45.00
Yugoslavia, SFR	....	....	....	....	....	....	....	....	....	....	....	....	....	....	....	....	....
Middle East																	
Egypt	13.00	13.00	13.00	13.00	13.00	13.00	14.00	14.00	20.00	18.40	16.50	14.00	13.50	13.00	12.25	12.00	12.00
Israel	I 311.00	690.30	79.60	31.40	26.80	30.90	15.00	13.00	14.23	10.39	9.78	17.01	14.19	....	....	....	....
Jordan	6.25	6.25	6.25	6.25	6.25	6.25	8.00	8.50	8.50	8.50	8.50	8.50	8.50	8.50	7.75	9.00	8.00
Kuwait	6.00	6.00	6.00	6.00	6.00	7.50	7.50	....	7.50	7.50	5.75	7.00	7.25	7.25	7.50	7.00	6.75
Lebanon	12.00	12.00	19.70	21.85	21.85	21.84	21.84	21.84	18.04	16.00	20.22	16.49	19.01	25.00	30.00	30.00	25.00
Libya	5.00	5.00	5.00	5.00	5.00	5.00	5.00	5.00	5.00	5.00	5.00	5.00	....	....	....	3.00	5.00
Syrian Arab Republic	5.00	5.00	5.00	5.00	5.00	5.00	5.00	5.00	5.00	5.00	5.00	5.00	....	....	....	....	....
Western Hemisphere																	
Aruba	....	....	....	9.50	9.50	9.50	9.50	9.50	9.50	9.50	9.50	9.50	9.50	9.50	9.50	9.50	6.50
Bahamas, The	9.00	9.50	8.50	7.50	7.50	9.00	9.00	9.00	9.00	7.50	7.00	6.50	6.50	6.50	6.50	6.50	5.75
Barbados	16.00	16.00	13.00	8.00	8.00	8.00	13.50	13.50	18.00	12.00	8.00	9.50	12.50	12.50	9.00	9.00	10.00
Belize	11.50	12.00	20.00	12.00	12.00	10.00	12.00	12.00	12.00	12.00	12.00	12.00	12.00	12.00	12.00	12.00	12.00
Bolivia	61.00	149.00	....	....	....	....	....	....	....	....	....	....	....	16.50	13.25	14.10	12.50
Brazil	....	....	....	....	....	....	....	....	....	....	....	....	....	25.34	45.09	39.41	21.37
Colombia	27.00	27.00	27.00	133.83	34.82	34.25	36.94	146.45	44.98	34.42	33.49	44.90	40.42	35.05	31.32	42.28	23.05
Costa Rica	30.00	28.00	28.00	27.50	31.38	31.50	31.61	37.80	42.50	29.00	35.00	37.75	38.50	35.00	31.00	37.00	34.00
Ecuador	19.00	23.00	23.00	23.00	23.00	23.00	32.00	35.00	49.00	49.00	33.57	44.88	59.41	46.38	37.46	61.84	64.40
Guatemala	9.00	9.00	9.00	9.00	9.00	9.00	13.00	18.50	16.50	....	....	....	....	....	....	....	....
Guyana	14.00	14.00	14.00	14.00	14.00	14.00	35.00	30.00	32.50	24.30	17.00	20.25	17.25	12.00	11.00	11.25	13.25
Honduras	24.00	24.00	24.00	24.00	24.00	24.00	24.00	28.15	30.09	26.10	....	....	....	....	....	....	....
Jamaica	11.00	16.00	21.00	21.00	21.00	21.00	21.00	21.00	....	....	....	....	....	....	....	....	....
Netherlands Antilles	8.00	8.00	8.00	8.00	6.00	6.00	6.00	6.00	6.00	6.00	5.00	5.00	6.00	6.00	6.00	6.00	6.00
Nicaragua	....	....	....	....	....	12,874.63	310.99	10.00	15.00	15.00	11.75	10.50	....	....	....	....	....
Paraguay	....	....	....	....	....	10.00	21.00	133.00	19.75	24.00	27.17	19.15	20.50	15.00	20.00	20.00	20.00
Peru	60.00	60.00	42.58	36.07	29.84	748.04	865.61	289.60	67.65	48.50	28.63	16.08	18.44	18.16	15.94	18.72	17.80
Trinidad and Tobago	7.50	7.50	7.50	5.97	7.50	9.50	9.50	9.50	11.50	13.00	13.00	13.00	13.00	13.00	13.00	13.00	13.00
Uruguay	112.70	133.20	145.10	138.40	143.40	154.50	219.60	251.60	219.00	162.40	164.30	182.30	178.70	160.30	95.50	73.70	66.39
Venezuela, Rep. Bol.	11.00	11.00	8.00	8.00	8.00	8.00	45.00	43.00	43.00	52.20	71.25	48.00	49.00	45.00	45.00	60.00	38.00

National Interest Rates

Money Market Rates (60b)
(Period averages in percent per annum)

1983	1984	1985	1986	1987	1988	1989	1990	1991	1992	1993	1994	1995	1996	1997	1998	1999	
																	Industrial Countries
9.09	10.23	8.10	6.81	6.66	7.57	9.22	8.10	5.69	3.52	3.02	4.20	5.84	5.30	5.46	5.35	4.97	United States
9.07	10.05	9.84	8.16	8.50	10.35	12.06	11.62	7.40	6.79	3.79	5.54	5.71	3.01	4.34	5.11	4.76	Canada
9.50	10.84	14.70	15.75	13.06	11.90	16.75	14.81	10.47	6.44	5.11	5.18	I7.50	7.20	5.50	4.99	I4.78	Australia
6.39	6.10	6.46	4.79	3.51	3.62	4.87	I7.24	7.46	4.58	I3.06	2.20	1.21	.47	.48	.37	.06	Japan
											6.33	6.58	4.92	4.25	3.83	2.97	Euro Area
5.36	6.57	6.11	5.19	4.35	4.59	7.46	8.53	9.10	9.35	7.22	5.03	4.36	3.19	3.27	3.36	....	Austria
8.18	9.47	8.27	6.64	5.67	5.04	7.00	8.29	I9.38	9.38	8.21	5.72	4.80	3.24	3.46	3.58	....	Belgium
14.67	16.50	13.46	11.90	10.03	9.97	12.56	14.00	13.08	13.25	7.77	5.35	5.75	3.63	3.23	3.57	2.97	Finland
12.53	11.74	9.93	7.74	7.98	7.52	9.07	9.85	9.49	10.35	8.75	5.69	6.35	3.73	3.24	3.39	....	France
5.36	5.55	5.19	4.57	3.72	4.01	6.59	7.92	8.84	9.42	7.49	5.35	4.50	3.27	3.18	3.41	2.73	Germany
14.45	12.93	11.87	12.28	10.84	7.84	9.55	11.10	10.45	15.12	10.49	I5.75	5.45	5.74	6.43	4.99	3.14	Ireland
18.44	17.27	15.25	13.41	11.51	11.29	12.69	12.38	I12.21	14.02	10.20	8.51	10.46	8.82	6.88	4.99	2.95	Italy
10.56	10.70	9.26	7.30	6.71	7.16	10.02	9.67	9.10	8.93	8.09	5.16	4.26	3.29	3.36	3.48	....	Luxembourg
5.28	5.78	6.30	5.83	5.16	4.48	6.99	8.29	9.01	9.27	7.10	5.14	4.22	2.89	3.07	3.21	....	Netherlands
18.24	21.27	20.17	I14.52	13.69	12.31	12.68	13.12	15.50	I17.48	13.25	10.62	8.91	7.38	5.78	4.34	2.71	Portugal
19.45	12.60	11.61	11.49	16.06	11.29	14.39	14.76	13.20	13.01	12.33	7.81	8.98	7.65	5.49	4.34	2.72	Spain
12.81	11.77	10.33	9.22	10.20	8.52	9.66	10.97	9.78	11.35	I11.49	6.30	6.19	3.98	3.71	4.27	3.37	Denmark
....	36.90	....	....	31.52	34.49	21.58	12.73	14.85	12.38	8.61	4.96	6.58	6.96	7.38	8.12	9.24	Iceland
12.27	11.84	12.29	14.15	14.66	13.29	11.31	11.45	10.56	13.71	7.64	5.70	5.54	4.97	3.77	6.03	6.87	Norway
10.85	11.77	13.85	10.15	9.16	10.08	11.52	13.45	11.81	18.42	9.08	7.36	8.54	6.28	4.21	4.24	3.14	Sweden
1.84	I57.81	....	40.63	25.42	3.56	9.69	8.75	7.56	6.38	4.13	3.50	1.75	1.50	1.00	.88	1.09	Switzerland
10.01	9.51	12.41	10.80	9.47	9.72	13.62	14.64	11.77	9.39	5.46	4.76	5.98	5.89	6.56	7.09	5.11	United Kingdom
																	Developing Countries
																	Africa
										....	19.80	....	18.50	11.80	10.40	10.40	Algeria
12.23	11.84	10.66	8.58	8.37	8.72	10.07	10.98	10.94	11.44	....	....	....	....	....	4.81	4.95	Benin
12.23	11.84	10.67	8.58	8.37	8.72	10.07	10.98	10.94	11.44	....	....	....	....	....	4.81	4.95	Burkina Faso
12.23	11.84	10.66	8.58	8.37	8.72	10.07	10.98	10.94	11.44	....	....	....	....	....	4.81	4.95	Côte d'Ivoire
12.23	11.92	10.66	8.58	8.37	8.72	10.07	10.98	10.94	11.45	....	....	....	....	....	4.81	4.95	Guinea-Bissau
							15.00	15.00	15.00	....	—	29.00	10.00	....	11.24	....	Madagascar
12.23	11.84	10.66	8.58	8.37	8.72	10.07	10.98	10.94	11.44	....	....	....	....	....	4.81	4.95	Mali
10.82	11.00	11.17	11.05	10.29	10.71	11.98	13.26	12.24	9.05	7.73	10.23	10.35	9.96	9.43	8.99	10.01	Mauritius
....	....	9.41	9.44	....	....	....	....	....	....	....	12.29	10.06	8.42	7.89	6.30	5.64	Morocco
12.23	11.84	10.66	8.58	8.37	8.72	10.07	10.98	10.94	11.44	....	....	....	....	....	4.81	4.95	Niger
12.23	11.84	10.66	8.58	8.37	8.72	10.07	10.98	10.94	11.44	....	....	....	....	....	4.81	4.95	Senegal
13.98	20.31	18.21	10.92	9.50	13.90	18.77	19.46	17.02	14.11	10.83	10.24	13.07	15.54	15.59	17.11	13.06	South Africa
						8.39	10.50	10.61	10.25	9.73	7.01	8.52	9.77	10.35	10.63	8.86	Swaziland
12.23	11.84	10.66	8.58	8.37	8.72	10.07	10.98	10.94	11.44	....	....	....	....	....	4.81	4.95	Togo
8.38	8.89	10.28	9.95	10.00	9.15	9.40	11.53	11.79	11.73	10.48	8.81	8.81	8.64	6.88	6.89	5.99	Tunisia
9.09	8.90	8.80	9.10	9.30	9.08	8.73	8.68	17.49	34.77	34.18	30.90	29.64	26.18	25.15	37.22	53.13	Zimbabwe
																	Asia
							11.50	4.63	3.81	4.00	5.44	6.00	5.13	4.50	5.50	5.75	China,P.R.:Hong Kong
6.20	8.74	6.61	6.55	9.02	1.49	2.34	2.92	4.28	3.06	2.91	4.10	3.95	2.43	1.91	1.27	1.27	Fiji
8.30	9.95	10.00	9.97	9.83	9.73	11.39	15.57	19.35	15.23	8.64	7.14	15.57	11.04	5.29	....	....	India
13.17	18.63	10.33	....	14.52	15.00	12.57	13.97	14.91	11.99	8.66	9.74	13.64	13.96	27.82	62.79	23.58	Indonesia
13.00	11.39	9.35	9.70	8.93	9.62	13.28	14.03	17.03	14.32	12.12	12.45	12.57	12.44	13.24	14.98	5.01	Korea
8.97	8.96	6.76	4.19	3.12	4.11	4.72	6.81	7.83	8.01	6.53	4.65	5.78	I6.98	7.61	8.46	3.38	Malaysia
....	11.00	9.00	9.00	8.67	8.50	7.33	7.00	7.00	7.00	5.00	5.00	6.80	6.80	6.80	6.80	6.80	Maldives
8.15	8.97	8.13	6.59	6.25	6.32	6.30	7.29	7.64	7.51	11.00	8.36	11.52	11.40	12.10	10.76	9.04	Pakistan
7.11	7.67	5.38	4.27	3.89	4.30	5.34	6.61	4.76	2.74	2.50	3.68	2.56	2.93	4.35	5.00	2.04	Singapore
23.88	21.42	14.56	12.95	13.14	18.65	22.19	21.56	25.42	21.63	25.65	18.54	41.87	24.33	18.42	15.74	16.69	Sri Lanka
12.15	13.58	13.48	8.07	5.91	8.66	I10.60	12.87	11.15	6.93	6.54	7.25	10.96	9.23	14.59	13.02	1.77	Thailand
....	....	7.00	6.96	6.50	7.50	7.08	7.00	7.00	5.92	6.00	6.00	6.00	6.00	6.00	8.65	6.99	Vanuatu
																	Europe
													48.56	36.41	27.84	23.65	Armenia
								48.67	52.39	48.07	66.43	53.09	119.88	66.43	2.48	2.93	Bulgaria
									951.20	1,370.50	26.93	21.13	19.26	10.18	14.48	13.72	Croatia
											5.67	4.94	3.53	6.45	11.66	4.92	Estonia
												43.39	26.58		34.61		Georgia
															43.98	43.71	Kyrgyz Republic
											37.18	22.39	13.08	3.76	4.42	4.72	Latvia
											69.48	26.73	20.26	....	9.55	6.12	Lithuania
														28.10	30.91	32.60	Moldova
								49.93	I29.49	24.51	23.32	25.82	20.63	22.43	20.59	13.58	Poland
												190.43	47.65	20.97	50.56	14.79	Russia
									67.58	39.15	29.08	12.18	13.98	9.71	7.45	6.87	Slovenia
				39.82	60.62	40.66	51.91	72.75	65.35	62.83	136.47	72.30	76.24	70.32	74.60	73.53	Turkey
														22.05	40.41	44.98	Ukraine
																	Middle East
			7.20	7.07	7.95	9.18	8.54	6.31	3.99	3.53	5.18	6.24	5.69	....	5.69	5.58	Bahrain
6.78	8.91	7.59	7.52	6.08	6.12	8.70	....	....	....	7.43	6.31	7.43	6.98	7.05	7.24	6.32	Kuwait
4.00	4.00	4.00	4.00	4.00	4.00	4.00	4.00	4.00	4.00	4.00	....	....	....	....	4.00	4.00	Libya
																	Western Hemisphere
739	1,182	1,161	135	253	524	1,387,179	9,695,422	71	15	6	8	9	6	7	7	7	Argentina
												22.42	20.27	13.97	12.57	13.49	Bolivia
203.23	257.32	281.65	105.22	424.38	1,192.87	6,404.97	15,778.57	847.54	1,574.28	3,284.44	4,820.64	53.37	27.45	25.00	29.50	26.26	Brazil
												22.40	28.37	23.83	35.00	18.81	Colombia
													14.70	13.01	16.68	15.30	Dominican Republic
														10.43	9.43	10.68	El Salvador
														7.77	6.62	9.23	Guatemala
57.51	49.94	62.44	88.01	95.59	69.01	I47.43	37.36	23.58	18.87	17.39	16.47	I60.92	33.61	21.91	26.89	24.10	Mexico
								12.39	21.59	22.55	18.64	20.18	16.35	12.48	20.74	17.26	Paraguay
																	Suriname
											39.82	36.81	28.47	23.43	20.48	13.96	Uruguay
														16.70	12.47	18.58	7.48	Venezuela, Rep. Bol.

National Interest Rates

	1983	1984	1985	1986	1987	1988	1989	1990	1991	1992	1993	1994	1995	1996	1997	1998	1999
								Deposit Rates (60l) except for United States (60lc) (Period averages in percent per annum)									
Industrial Countries																	
United States	9.07	10.37	8.05	6.52	6.86	7.73	9.09	8.15	5.84	3.68	3.17	4.63	5.92	5.39	5.62	5.47	5.33
Canada	7.91	10.06	8.40	8.25	7.67	9.54	12.09	12.81	8.62	6.67	4.92	5.59	7.15	4.33	3.59	5.03	4.91
Australia	10.81	9.75	10.46	13.96	13.77	11.92	15.29	13.70	I10.44	6.32	4.76	5.05	7.33	6.86	5.12	4.67	4.59
Japan	3.75	3.50	3.50	2.32	1.76	1.76	1.97	3.56	I4.14	I3.35	2.14	1.70	.90	.30	.30	.27	.12
New Zealand	9.75	10.46	14.71	16.32	....	I13.41	10.92	I11.65	8.93	6.58	6.24	6.38	8.49	8.49	7.26	6.78	4.56
Euro Area	....	....	....	....	....	....	....	....	....	....	....	....	....	4.08	3.41	3.20	2.44
Austria	4.21	4.00	3.94	3.63	3.03	2.73	2.98	3.41	3.75	3.69	2.98	2.31	2.19	1.71	1.50	I2.65	2.21
Belgium	6.67	7.44	6.69	5.33	5.00	4.54	5.13	6.13	6.25	6.25	I7.11	4.86	4.04	2.66	2.88	3.01	2.42
Finland	8.75	9.25	8.75	7.33	7.00	7.75	5.75	7.50	7.50	7.50	4.75	3.27	3.19	2.35	2.00	....	1.22
France	8.08	7.08	6.25	5.00	4.50	4.50	4.50	4.50	4.50	4.50	4.50	4.50	4.50	3.67	3.50	3.21	2.69
Germany	4.56	4.86	4.44	3.71	3.20	3.29	5.50	7.07	7.62	8.01	6.27	4.47	3.85	2.83	2.69	2.88	2.43
Ireland	9.27	7.83	6.98	6.50	6.21	3.63	4.54	6.29	5.21	5.42	2.27	.33	.44	.29	.46	.43	.10
Italy	12.91	11.75	11.00	8.89	7.01	6.69	6.93	6.80	6.64	7.11	I7.79	6.20	6.45	6.49	4.83	3.16	1.61
Luxembourg	7.17	7.00	6.50	5.50	4.94	4.46	5.04	6.00	6.00	6.00	5.33	5.00	5.00	3.54	3.46	3.31	....
Netherlands	4.03	4.10	4.10	3.93	3.55	3.48	3.49	3.31	3.18	3.20	3.11	I4.70	4.40	3.54	3.18	3.10	2.74
Portugal	26.08	28.00	25.08	17.13	14.46	13.21	13.00	13.99	14.80	14.59	11.06	8.37	8.38	6.32	4.56	3.37	2.40
Spain	12.31	12.30	10.53	9.05	8.97	9.06	9.55	10.65	10.47	10.43	9.63	6.70	7.68	6.12	3.96	2.92	1.85
Denmark	9.98	9.00	8.21	6.58	7.07	7.75	8.27	I7.93	7.15	7.50	6.52	I3.53	3.85	2.80	2.65	3.08	2.43
Greece	14.50	15.42	15.50	15.50	15.33	I17.33	17.14	19.52	20.67	19.92	19.33	18.92	15.75	13.51	10.11	10.70	8.69
Iceland	39.46	18.09	24.69	12.21	15.51	17.42	12.30	4.31	4.88	1.43	....	....	I3.40	3.27	3.26	....	....
Norway	5.30	5.30	10.06	10.97	12.03	11.49	9.63	9.68	9.60	10.69	5.51	5.21	4.95	4.15	3.63	7.24	5.38
Sweden	9.75	10.75	12.00	9.00	8.75	9.50	I9.16	9.93	7.96	I7.80	5.10	4.91	6.16	2.47	2.50	1.91	1.65
Switzerland	3.31	3.77	4.36	3.51	3.08	4.50	8.08	8.28	7.63	5.50	3.50	3.63	1.28	1.34	1.00	.69	1.24
United Kingdom	11.19	7.27	11.79	9.85	8.57	8.55	11.51	12.54	10.28	7.46	3.97	3.66	4.11	3.05	3.63	4.48	....
Developing Countries																	
Africa																	
Algeria	3.00	3.00	3.00	4.00	4.00	4.00	8.00	8.00	8.00	8.00	8.00	12.00	....	17.00	9.50	8.50	8.50
Angola	....	....	....	....	....	....	....	....	....	....	....	....	125.92	147.13	29.25	36.88	37.50
Benin	7.50	7.25	7.25	6.08	5.25	5.25	6.42	7.00	7.00	7.75	....	....	....	....	....	3.50	3.50
Botswana	11.88	10.00	9.00	8.67	7.50	5.00	5.58	6.11	11.40	12.50	13.49	10.39	9.98	10.43	9.25	8.72	9.46
Burkina Faso	7.50	7.25	7.25	6.08	5.25	5.25	6.42	7.00	7.00	7.75	....	....	....	....	....	3.50	3.50
Burundi	4.50	4.50	4.50	5.96	5.33	4.00	....	....	....	....	....	....	....	....	....	....	....
Cameroon	7.50	7.50	7.50	7.35	7.15	7.21	7.50	I7.50	7.50	7.50	7.75	8.08	5.50	5.38	5.04	5.00	5.00
Cape Verde	....	....	4.00	4.00	4.00	4.00	4.00	4.00	4.00	4.00	4.00	4.00	I5.00	5.00	5.04	5.27	4.76
Central African Rep.	7.50	7.50	7.50	7.35	7.19	7.44	7.50	I7.50	7.50	7.50	7.75	8.08	5.50	5.46	5.00	5.00	5.00
Chad	5.50	5.50	5.50	5.50	5.33	4.31	4.25	I7.50	7.50	7.50	7.75	8.08	5.50	5.46	5.00	5.00	5.00
Comoros	7.50	7.50	7.50	7.50	6.50	6.50	....	....	....	....	....	....	....	....	....	....	....
Congo, Republic of	7.50	7.50	8.25	8.10	7.79	7.81	8.00	I7.50	7.50	7.50	7.75	8.08	5.50	5.46	5.00	5.00	5.00
Côte d'Ivoire	7.50	7.25	7.25	6.08	5.25	5.25	6.42	7.00	7.00	7.75	....	....	....	....	....	3.50	3.50
Equatorial Guinea	....	....	7.50	8.25	7.88	6.33	6.50	I7.50	7.50	7.50	7.75	8.08	5.50	5.46	5.00	5.00	5.00
Ethiopia	....	....	6.00	6.35	6.70	6.70	6.70	2.43	5.00	3.63	11.50	11.50	11.46	9.42	7.00	6.00	6.32
Gabon	7.50	7.50	7.67	8.00	7.94	8.17	8.75	I7.50	7.50	7.50	7.75	8.08	5.50	5.46	5.00	5.00	5.00
Gambia, The	8.50	9.00	9.75	16.13	15.75	15.00	12.92	11.33	12.71	13.83	13.00	12.58	12.50	12.50	12.50	12.50	12.50
Ghana	11.50	15.00	15.75	17.00	17.58	16.50	....	....	21.32	16.32	23.63	23.15	28.73	34.50	35.76	32.05	23.56
Guinea	....	....	....	....	15.00	16.83	19.50	21.00	22.00	23.00	19.75	18.00	17.50	....	....	....	....
Guinea-Bissau	....	....	....	....	....	23.00	28.00	32.67	36.00	39.33	53.92	28.67	26.50	47.25	4.63	3.50	3.50
Kenya	13.27	11.77	11.25	11.25	10.31	10.33	12.00	13.67	....	....	....	....	13.60	17.59	16.72	18.40	9.55
Lesotho	9.38	9.90	10.42	10.04	7.00	9.58	12.82	13.00	13.00	10.63	8.06	8.43	13.34	12.73	11.81	10.73	7.45
Liberia	10.25	9.81	9.34	7.25	5.88	5.43	6.77	....	....	....	....	6.34	6.37	....	6.43	6.22	6.25
Madagascar	....	....	....	....	....	....	17.75	20.50	20.50	20.50	19.50	19.50	18.50	19.00	14.38	8.00	....
Malawi	9.92	11.75	12.50	12.75	14.25	13.50	12.75	12.10	12.50	16.50	21.75	25.00	37.27	26.33	10.21	19.06	33.21
Mali	7.50	7.25	7.25	6.08	5.25	5.25	6.42	7.00	7.00	7.75	....	....	....	....	....	3.50	3.50
Mauritania	5.50	5.50	7.17	6.58	6.00	6.00	5.00	5.00	5.00	5.00	....	....	....	....	....	....	....
Mauritius	12.06	10.29	9.46	9.50	9.38	10.00	11.06	12.56	12.31	10.07	8.40	11.04	12.23	10.77	9.08	9.28	10.92
Morocco	6.50	6.50	8.00	8.50	8.50	8.50	8.50	8.50	8.50	....	....	....	....	....	....	7.26	6.39
Namibia	....	....	....	....	....	....	....	....	12.77	11.36	9.61	9.18	10.84	12.56	12.70	12.94	10.82
Niger	7.50	7.25	7.25	6.08	5.25	5.25	6.42	7.00	7.00	7.75	....	....	....	....	....	3.50	3.50
Nigeria	7.41	8.25	9.12	9.24	13.09	12.95	14.68	19.78	14.92	18.04	23.24	13.09	13.53	13.06	7.17	10.11	12.81
Rwanda	6.25	6.25	6.25	6.25	6.25	6.25	6.31	6.88	8.75	7.73	5.00	....	....	10.92	9.46	8.50	7.95
São Tomé & Príncipe	....	....	....	....	....	....	16.00	16.00	35.00	35.00	35.00	35.00	35.00	31.00	36.75	38.29	27.00
Senegal	7.50	7.25	7.25	6.08	5.25	5.25	6.42	7.00	7.00	7.75	....	....	....	....	....	3.50	3.50
Seychelles	9.08	9.50	9.60	10.00	10.00	10.00	9.59	9.53	9.55	9.60	9.51	8.92	9.22	9.90	9.20	7.53	5.13
Sierra Leone	11.00	12.00	11.33	14.17	12.67	16.33	20.00	40.50	47.80	54.67	27.00	11.63	7.03	13.96	9.91	7.12	9.50
Somalia	....	....	....	....	....	....	....	....	....	....	....	....	....	....	....	....	....
South Africa	13.71	18.29	17.02	10.98	8.70	13.54	18.13	18.86	17.30	13.78	11.50	11.11	13.54	14.91	15.38	16.50	12.24
Sudan	13.50	13.50	....	....	....	....	....	....	....	....	....	....	....	....	....	....	....
Swaziland	12.50	16.50	10.19	5.75	4.81	9.23	8.92	8.85	10.85	9.00	7.38	8.00	10.25	12.25	11.25	13.43	7.53
Tanzania	4.00	4.00	4.50	8.50	15.75	17.46	17.00	....	....	....	....	....	24.63	13.59	7.83	7.75	7.75
Togo	7.50	7.25	7.25	6.08	5.25	5.25	6.42	7.00	7.00	7.75	....	....	....	....	....	3.50	3.50
Tunisia	4.50	4.50	5.35	6.75	7.22	7.37	....	....	....	....	....	....	....	....	....	....	....
Uganda	10.67	16.00	I20.00	23.33	20.00	21.50	32.17	31.25	31.17	35.83	16.26	9.99	7.61	10.62	11.84	11.36	8.73
Zambia	7.00	7.71	15.33	17.74	13.23	11.44	11.44	25.65	....	48.50	....	46.14	30.24	42.13	34.48	13.08	20.27
Zimbabwe	12.80	10.30	10.04	10.28	9.58	9.68	8.85	8.80	14.20	28.63	29.45	26.75	25.92	21.58	18.60	29.06	38.51
Asia																	
Bangladesh	12.00	12.00	12.00	12.00	12.00	12.00	12.00	12.04	12.05	10.47	8.18	6.40	6.04	7.28	8.11	8.42	8.74
Bhutan	5.50	5.50	6.08	6.50	6.50	6.50	6.50	6.50	6.50	8.00	8.00	8.00	8.00	....	....	....	....
Cambodia	....	....	....	....	....	....	....	....	....	....	....	....	8.71	8.80	8.03	7.80	7.33
China,P.R.: Mainland	5.76	5.76	7.20	7.20	7.20	8.64	11.34	8.64	7.56	7.56	10.98	10.98	10.98	7.47	5.67	3.78	2.25
China,P.R.:Hong Kong	....	....	....	....	....	....	....	6.67	5.46	3.07	2.25	3.54	5.63	4.64	5.98	6.62	4.50
Fiji	6.00	6.00	6.00	6.00	6.00	4.88	4.00	4.00	4.06	4.10	3.69	3.15	3.18	3.38	3.08	2.17	1.24
Indonesia	6.00	16.00	18.00	15.39	16.78	17.72	18.63	I17.53	23.32	19.60	14.55	12.53	16.72	17.26	20.01	39.07	25.74
Korea	8.00	9.17	10.00	10.00	10.00	10.00	10.00	10.00	10.00	10.00	8.58	8.50	8.83	7.50	I10.81	13.29	7.95
Lao People's Dem.Rep	....	....	....	....	....	....	30.00	30.00	I23.50	15.00	13.33	12.00	14.00	16.00	....	17.79	13.42
Malaysia	8.02	9.54	8.81	7.17	3.00	3.19	4.60	5.90	7.18	7.97	7.04	4.94	5.93	I7.09	7.78	8.51	4.12

Deposit Rates (60l) (cont.)
except for United States (60lc)
(Period averages in percent per annum)

Asia (cont.)

Country	1983	1984	1985	1986	1987	1988	1989	1990	1991	1992	1993	1994	1995	1996	1997	1998	1999
Mongolia	...	...	...	300.00	300.00	300.00	300.00	300.00	400.00	500.00	125.20	101.10	60.10	36.40	37.90	24.29	19.80
Myanmar	1.50	1.50	1.50	1.50	1.50	1.50	1.50	5.88	9.00	9.00	9.00	9.00	9.75	12.50	12.50	12.50	11.00
Nepal	12.50	12.50	12.50	12.50	12.50	12.50	12.50	11.92	...	...	...	8.75	...	9.63	9.79	8.92	7.31
Papua New Guinea	9.54	8.13	9.49	11.49	9.60	9.28	8.23	8.67	9.06	7.85	5.03	5.09	12.18	12.19	7.31	13.73	15.46
Philippines	13.58	21.17	18.91	11.25	8.20	11.32	14.13	19.54	18.80	14.27	9.61	10.54	8.39	9.68	10.19	12.11	8.17
Samoa	11.75	12.00	12.00	13.50	12.00	12.00	12.00	8.25	8.25	6.38	5.50	5.50	5.50	5.50	5.50	6.50	6.50
Singapore	6.31	6.98	4.99	3.91	2.89	2.74	3.21	4.67	4.63	2.86	2.30	3.00	3.50	3.41	3.47	4.60	1.68
Solomon Islands	8.38	8.00	8.73	10.50	10.67	10.23	10.46	10.50	10.50	12.00	9.77	9.00	8.38	6.46	2.42	2.33	2.88
Sri Lanka	18.25	19.79	17.33	12.21	11.50	13.23	16.43	19.42	18.54	18.33	18.42	15.33	16.13	16.03	14.17	13.00	11.75
Thailand	13.00	13.00	13.00	9.75	9.50	9.50	9.50	12.25	13.67	8.88	8.63	8.46	11.58	10.33	10.52	10.65	4.73
Tonga	6.25	6.25	6.25	6.25	6.25	6.25	7.25	7.25	7.25	4.25	4.25	4.67	4.75	5.58	5.50	5.50	5.42
Vanuatu	9.44	8.75	7.34	6.81	5.48	6.94	6.58	7.00	7.00	4.69	5.00	5.06	3.00	4.50	3.73	3.29	1.60

Europe

Country	1983	1984	1985	1986	1987	1988	1989	1990	1991	1992	1993	1994	1995	1996	1997	1998	1999
Albania	...	...	...	...	...	...	...	...	...	18.50	[1]27.33	19.83	[1]15.30	16.78	...	...	12.95
Armenia	...	...	...	...	...	...	...	...	...	...	...	...	63.18	32.19	26.08	24.94	27.35
Belarus	...	...	...	...	...	...	...	...	...	...	65.08	89.60	100.82	32.36	15.64	14.33	23.80
Bulgaria	...	...	...	...	...	...	...	...	39.49	45.01	42.56	51.14	35.94	74.68	46.83	3.00	3.21
Croatia	...	...	...	...	...	...	...	...	...	658.51	379.31	6.52	5.53	5.59	4.30	4.62	4.31
Cyprus	5.75	5.75	5.75	5.75	5.75	5.75	5.75	5.75	5.75	5.75	5.75	5.75	5.75	5.75	...	...	...
Czech Republic	...	...	...	...	...	...	...	...	...	...	7.03	7.07	6.96	6.79	7.71	8.08	4.48
Estonia	...	...	...	...	...	...	...	...	...	...	...	11.51	8.74	6.05	6.19	8.07	4.19
Georgia	...	...	...	...	...	...	...	...	...	...	...	...	31.05	13.73	17.00	14.58	...
Hungary	5.00	5.00	5.00	4.50	4.00	5.25	9.42	[1]24.68	30.41	24.41	15.65	20.31	26.10	22.21	18.54	16.16	13.27
Kyrgyz Republic	...	...	...	...	...	...	...	...	...	...	...	...	...	36.73	39.59	35.76	35.58
Latvia	...	...	...	...	...	...	...	...	...	...	34.78	31.68	14.79	11.71	5.90	5.33	5.04
Lithuania	...	...	...	...	...	...	...	...	...	...	88.29	48.43	20.05	13.95	7.89	5.98	4.94
Macedonia, FYR	...	...	...	...	...	...	...	...	...	...	...	117.56	24.07	12.75	11.64	11.68	11.40
Malta	5.00	5.00	4.96	4.50	4.50	4.50	4.50	4.50	4.50	4.50	4.50	4.50	4.50	4.50	4.56	4.64	4.66
Moldova	...	...	...	...	...	...	...	...	...	...	...	...	...	25.43	23.47	21.68	27.54
Poland	...	...	...	...	...	...	100.00	41.67	[1]53.50	37.75	34.00	[1]33.40	26.78	20.02	19.36	18.19	11.23
Russia	...	...	...	...	...	...	...	...	...	...	...	...	101.96	55.05	[1]16.77	17.05	13.68
Slovak Republic	...	...	...	...	...	...	...	...	...	...	8.02	9.32	9.01	9.30	9.34	16.25	14.37
Slovenia	...	...	...	...	...	...	...	...	682.53	153.02	33.04	28.10	15.38	15.08	13.19	10.54	7.24
Turkey	45.33	51.42	49.25	40.58	35.00	49.08	53.45	47.50	62.67	68.74	64.58	87.79	76.02	80.74	79.49	80.11	78.43
Ukraine	...	...	...	...	...	...	...	...	...	...	148.63	208.63	70.29	33.63	18.21	22.25	20.70

Middle East

Country	1983	1984	1985	1986	1987	1988	1989	1990	1991	1992	1993	1994	1995	1996	1997	1998	1999
Bahrain	7.00	7.00	6.71	5.58	5.00	5.50	7.33	7.50	...	[1]3.63	3.03	4.00	5.70	5.18	5.28	4.74	4.80
Egypt	11.00	11.00	11.00	11.00	11.00	11.00	11.67	12.00	12.00	12.00	12.00	11.83	10.92	10.54	9.84	9.36	9.22
Israel	132.90	438.36	178.79	18.59	19.39	14.53	14.10	14.40	13.89	11.29	10.44	12.19	14.08	14.48	13.07	11.00	11.35
Jordan	...	...	...	...	...	...	...	8.15	...	8.13	7.20	6.88	7.09	7.68	8.50	9.10	...
Kuwait	7.13	7.73	7.25	6.80	5.73	5.30	7.40	...	...	7.59	7.07	5.70	6.53	6.05	5.93	6.32	5.76
Lebanon	10.01	11.53	13.24	16.42	21.18	21.96	17.54	16.86	16.76	17.09	15.56	14.80	16.30	15.54	13.37	13.61	12.50
Libya	5.50	5.50	5.50	5.50	5.50	5.50	5.50	5.50	5.50	5.50	5.50	...	...	...	...	...	3.21
Oman	...	9.03	9.04	8.33	7.48	7.57	8.66	8.32	7.06	6.29	4.17	4.34	6.53	6.85	7.30	8.46	8.12
Qatar	6.00	6.00	6.00	6.00	6.00	6.00	6.00	6.00	6.00	4.75	4.08	4.84	6.19	6.50	6.63	6.56	6.50
Saudi Arabia	...	...	...	...	6.68	8.03	9.04	8.01	5.83	3.65	3.52	5.10	6.18	5.47	5.79	6.21	6.14

Western Hemisphere

Country	1983	1984	1985	1986	1987	1988	1989	1990	1991	1992	1993	1994	1995	1996	1997	1998	1999
Antigua and Barbuda	11.00	11.00	9.88	7.71	6.50	6.50	6.50	8.44	8.21	7.44	6.71	6.50	5.92	5.50	5.50	5.50	5.50
Argentina	281.31	396.85	630.03	94.69	175.95	371.85	17,235.81	1,517.88	61.68	16.78	11.34	8.08	11.90	7.36	6.97	7.56	8.05
Aruba	...	...	...	6.40	6.70	6.70	6.70	6.70	6.30	5.70	4.20	4.40	4.30	4.20	4.40	...	...
Bahamas, The	7.47	7.44	6.40	5.57	5.50	5.97	6.48	6.57	6.92	6.13	5.19	4.30	4.20	5.14	5.23	5.36	4.57
Barbados	6.73	6.07	5.49	4.28	3.61	4.26	4.78	6.28	6.53	6.68	4.39	4.32	5.11	5.20	4.58	4.20	4.27
Belize	11.30	9.40	11.63	11.83	9.58	8.42	7.86	8.14	8.42	8.15	8.13	8.55	9.37	9.08	9.09	8.76	8.12
Bolivia	39.83	108.33	68.75	[1]33.39	30.35	27.74	23.67	23.83	23.78	23.22	22.18	18.43	18.87	19.16	14.73	12.82	12.26
Brazil	154.6	267.6	295.4	109.5	401.0	859.4	[1]5,845.0	9,394.3	913.5	1,560.2	3,293.5	5,175.2	52.2	26.4	24.4	28.0	26.0
Chile	28.01	27.63	31.97	18.99	25.22	15.11	27.72	40.27	22.22	18.26	18.24	15.08	13.73	13.46	12.02	14.91	8.55
Colombia	...	...	...	31.36	30.79	33.46	33.73	36.44	37.23	26.67	25.84	29.42	32.34	31.15	24.13	32.58	21.33
Costa Rica	19.50	14.50	16.50	16.67	14.06	15.18	15.62	21.16	27.32	15.80	16.90	17.72	23.88	17.29	13.03	12.76	14.31
Dominica	5.00	5.00	5.00	4.92	5.04	5.00	4.54	4.21	4.38	4.08	4.00	4.00	4.00	4.00	4.00	4.00	4.92
Dominican Republic	...	...	...	...	...	...	...	...	20.02	16.70	14.04	13.70	14.94	13.91	13.40	17.65	16.07
Ecuador	16.00	18.17	21.00	21.39	25.34	34.00	40.24	43.55	41.54	46.81	31.97	33.65	43.31	41.50	28.09	39.39	48.93
El Salvador	12.50	12.50	12.50	15.00	15.00	15.00	16.25	18.00	16.11	11.51	15.27	13.57	14.37	13.98	11.77	10.32	10.75
Grenada	5.88	6.98	7.04	6.50	6.08	5.50	5.04	6.50	6.17	5.46	5.00	4.17	4.00	4.13	4.50	4.58	5.19
Guatemala	9.00	9.00	9.00	10.17	11.00	12.17	13.00	18.21	24.41	10.44	12.63	9.69	7.87	7.65	[1]5.83	5.44	7.96
Guyana	12.00	12.00	12.00	12.00	11.08	12.00	15.81	29.18	29.53	22.51	12.26	11.42	12.90	10.49	8.56	8.10	9.09
Haiti	...	...	...	...	...	...	...	...	...	...	...	...	...	...	10.74	13.06	7.39
Honduras	11.30	10.30	9.93	9.70	9.62	8.63	8.58	8.78	11.45	12.34	11.60	11.56	11.97	16.70	21.28	18.58	19.97
Jamaica	13.60	15.86	19.58	18.76	15.64	15.80	15.95	23.88	24.67	33.63	27.59	36.41	23.21	25.16	13.95	15.61	13.48
Mexico	57.36	48.84	55.23	75.91	92.44	52.70	30.85	27.88	16.57	14.48	15.06	13.32	38.12	24.70	14.66	13.75	9.61
Netherlands Antilles	5.10	5.20	5.20	5.19	4.82	4.63	4.71	4.97	...	...	4.33	4.05	3.75	3.67	3.66	3.58	3.59
Nicaragua	...	...	...	...	...	—	1,585.90	9.50	11.63	12.01	11.61	11.70	11.15	12.35	12.41	10.77	10.28
Panama	...	...	...	6.50	6.59	7.54	8.49	8.40	7.73	[1]5.67	5.90	6.11	7.18	7.20	7.03	6.76	6.92
Paraguay	...	...	...	...	...	...	...	22.92	22.53	20.15	22.10	23.12	21.16	17.16	13.00	15.95	[1]19.75
Peru	...	...	...	...	...	161.78	1,135.59	2,439.56	170.54	59.65	44.14	22.35	15.70	14.90	15.01	15.11	16.27
St. Kitts and Nevis	6.00	6.00	6.33	6.00	5.33	7.00	7.00	7.00	7.00	7.00	5.50	5.50	5.50	5.50	5.46	5.50	5.50
St. Lucia	8.00	8.58	9.13	7.50	5.04	5.00	5.00	5.58	6.06	5.52	4.96	4.50	6.25	7.00	6.25	7.08	9.25
St. Vincent & Grens.	5.50	5.75	5.92	5.96	5.32	4.82	4.29	4.33	4.44	5.00	4.25	4.04	5.00	4.50	5.33	5.50	5.50
Suriname	...	...	...	...	...	...	...	...	4.60	4.50	4.75	7.45	21.00	17.83	...	18.00	16.25
Trinidad and Tobago	6.40	6.76	5.31	6.04	6.03	6.01	6.28	5.96	5.79	6.99	7.06	6.91	...	...	6.91	7.95	8.51
Uruguay	71.40	68.39	81.90	61.70	60.83	67.82	84.70	97.83	75.23	54.47	39.38	36.98	38.24	28.13	19.61	15.09	14.25
Venezuela, Rep. Bol.	...	12.29	10.52	8.93	8.94	8.95	28.91	27.82	31.10	35.43	53.75	39.02	24.72	27.58	14.70	34.84	21.28

National Interest Rates

	1983	1984	1985	1986	1987	1988	1989	1990	1991	1992	1993	1994	1995	1996	1997	1998	1999
	Lending Rates (60p) *(Period averages in percent per annum)*																
Industrial Countries																	
United States	10.79	12.04	9.93	8.33	8.20	9.32	10.87	10.01	8.46	6.25	6.00	7.14	8.83	8.27	8.44	8.35	7.99
Canada	11.17	12.06	10.58	10.52	9.52	10.83	13.33	14.06	9.94	7.48	5.94	6.88	8.65	6.06	4.96	6.60	6.44
Australia	13.63	13.58	15.24	18.09	16.56	15.10	19.58	18.17	14.28	11.06	9.72	9.55	11.12	11.00	9.31	8.04	7.51
Japan	7.13	6.75	6.60	6.02	5.21	5.03	5.29	6.95	7.53	6.15	I4.41	4.13	3.40	2.66	2.45	2.32	2.16
New Zealand	13.83	12.53	....	....	I20.84	17.17	15.78	16.01	14.01	11.39	10.34	9.69	12.16	12.27	11.35	11.22	8.49
Euro Area	....	....	....	....	....	....	....	....	....	....	....	....	....	8.85	7.58	6.74	5.66
Austria	....	....	....	....	....	....	....	....	....	....	....	....	....	....	....	6.42	5.64
Belgium	13.75	14.00	12.54	10.44	9.33	8.92	11.08	13.00	12.88	13.00	11.81	9.42	8.42	7.17	7.06	7.25	6.71
Finland	9.56	10.49	10.41	9.08	8.91	9.72	10.31	11.62	11.80	12.14	9.92	7.91	7.75	6.16	5.29	5.35	4.71
France	12.25	12.15	11.09	9.89	9.60	9.43	10.00	10.57	10.22	10.00	8.90	7.89	8.12	6.77	6.34	6.55	6.36
Germany	10.05	9.82	9.53	8.75	8.36	8.33	9.94	11.59	12.46	13.59	12.85	11.48	10.94	10.02	9.13	9.02	8.81
Ireland	14.13	12.92	12.44	12.23	11.15	8.29	9.42	11.29	10.63	I12.66	9.93	6.13	6.56	5.85	6.57	6.22	3.34
Italy	22.27	21.97	18.06	15.93	13.58	13.57	14.21	I14.09	13.90	15.76	13.87	11.22	12.47	12.06	9.75	7.88	5.58
Luxembourg	9.38	9.25	8.75	7.75	7.19	6.71	7.25	8.23	8.25	8.75	7.65	6.58	6.50	5.50	5.50	5.27	....
Netherlands	8.46	8.88	9.25	8.63	8.15	7.77	10.75	11.75	12.40	12.75	10.40	8.29	7.21	5.90	6.13	6.50	I3.46
Portugal	27.88	29.42	27.29	19.63	I18.92	I17.53	19.59	21.78	I25.02	20.43	16.48	15.01	13.80	11.73	9.15	7.24	5.19
Spain	15.00	16.58	13.52	12.19	16.36	12.43	15.84	16.01	14.38	14.23	12.78	8.95	10.05	8.50	6.08	5.01	3.95
Denmark	14.49	13.38	14.65	12.98	13.62	12.59	13.44	I14.10	11.38	11.78	10.46	I9.95	10.33	8.70	7.73	7.90	7.13
Greece	20.50	20.50	20.50	20.50	21.82	22.89	23.26	27.62	29.45	28.71	28.56	27.44	23.05	20.96	18.92	18.56	15.00
Iceland	42.75	22.83	32.60	18.78	26.61	30.28	27.97	16.18	17.52	13.05	14.11	10.57	11.58	12.43	12.89	12.78	13.30
Norway	14.35	13.69	13.46	14.37	16.31	16.60	14.88	14.26	14.31	14.16	10.97	8.40	7.78	7.10	5.95	7.91	8.16
Sweden	14.91	16.00	16.89	I12.57	12.65	13.29	14.81	16.69	16.05	I15.20	11.40	10.64	11.11	7.38	7.01	5.94	5.53
Switzerland	5.49	5.49	5.43	5.46	5.24	5.07	5.85	7.42	7.83	7.80	6.40	5.51	5.48	4.97	4.47	4.07	3.90
United Kingdom	9.85	9.75	12.33	10.83	9.64	10.29	13.92	14.75	11.54	9.42	5.92	5.48	6.69	5.96	6.58	7.21	5.33
Developing Countries																	
Africa																	
Algeria	....	....	....	....	....	....	....	....	....	....	....	16.00	....	21.00	12.50	12.00	11.00
Angola	....	....	....	....	....	....	....	....	....	....	....	....	206.25	217.88	37.75	45.00	45.00
Benin	14.50	14.50	14.50	13.50	13.50	13.58	15.08	16.00	16.00	16.75	....	....	....	....	....	....	....
Botswana	13.38	12.00	11.50	11.00	10.00	7.83	7.67	7.88	11.83	14.00	14.92	13.88	14.29	14.50	14.08	13.53	14.63
Burkina Faso	14.50	14.50	14.50	13.50	13.50	13.58	15.13	16.00	16.00	16.75	....	....	....	....	....	....	....
Burundi	12.00	12.00	12.00	12.00	12.00	12.00	12.00	12.34	12.78	13.66	13.77	14.20	15.26	....	....	....	15.24
Cameroon	14.50	14.50	14.50	13.50	13.00	13.46	15.00	I18.50	18.15	17.77	17.46	17.50	16.00	22.00	22.00	22.00	22.00
Cape Verde	6.50	6.50	10.00	10.00	10.00	10.00	10.00	10.00	10.00	10.00	10.00	10.67	12.00	12.00	12.06	12.51	12.04
Central African Rep.	12.50	12.50	12.50	12.00	11.42	12.25	13.00	I18.50	18.15	17.77	17.46	17.50	16.00	22.00	22.00	22.00	22.00
Chad	11.50	11.50	11.50	11.00	10.50	10.79	11.50	I18.50	18.15	17.77	17.46	17.50	16.00	22.00	22.00	22.00	22.00
Comoros	15.00	15.00	15.00	15.00	13.00	13.00	....	....	....	....	....	....	....	....	....	....	....
Congo, Republic of	12.00	12.00	12.00	11.50	11.13	11.79	12.50	I18.50	18.15	17.77	17.46	17.50	16.00	22.00	22.00	22.00	22.00
Côte d'Ivoire	14.50	14.50	14.50	13.50	13.50	13.58	15.08	16.00	16.00	16.75	....	....	....	....	....	....	....
Equatorial Guinea	....	....	15.00	14.50	14.13	14.79	15.50	I18.50	18.15	17.77	17.46	17.50	16.00	22.00	22.00	22.00	22.00
Ethiopia	....	....	8.50	7.25	6.00	6.00	6.00	6.00	6.00	8.00	14.00	14.33	15.08	13.92	10.50	10.50	10.50
Gabon	13.00	13.00	12.67	11.50	11.13	11.79	12.50	I18.50	18.15	17.77	17.46	17.50	16.00	22.00	22.00	22.00	22.00
Gambia, The	18.00	18.00	14.48	28.00	27.92	29.54	26.83	26.50	26.50	26.75	26.08	25.00	25.04	25.50	25.50	25.38	24.00
Ghana	19.00	21.17	21.17	20.00	25.50	25.58	....	....	....	....	....	....	....	....	....	....	....
Guinea	....	....	....	....	15.00	15.00	17.25	21.17	24.50	27.00	24.50	22.00	21.50	....	....	....	....
Guinea-Bissau	....	....	....	18.00	18.00	30.00	38.33	45.75	47.00	50.33	63.58	36.33	32.92	51.75	....	....	....
Kenya	15.83	14.42	14.00	14.00	14.00	15.00	17.25	18.75	19.00	21.07	29.99	36.24	28.80	33.79	30.25	29.49	22.38
Lesotho	15.42	17.58	19.67	13.42	11.13	13.67	18.75	20.42	20.00	18.25	15.83	14.25	16.38	17.71	18.03	20.06	19.06
Liberia	20.69	20.63	19.34	14.45	13.63	13.36	13.82	....	....	....	....	14.53	15.57	....	16.83	I21.74	16.72
Madagascar	....	....	....	....	....	....	22.25	25.80	24.50	25.00	26.00	30.50	37.50	32.75	30.00	27.00	....
Malawi	18.33	16.50	18.38	19.00	19.50	22.25	23.00	21.00	20.00	22.00	29.50	31.00	47.33	45.33	28.25	37.67	53.58
Mali	14.50	14.50	14.50	13.50	13.50	13.58	15.08	16.00	16.00	16.75	....	....	....	....	....	....	....
Mauritania	12.00	12.00	12.00	12.00	12.00	12.00	10.00	10.00	10.00	10.00	....	....	....	....	....	....	....
Mauritius	15.08	13.25	13.83	14.33	14.13	14.96	16.13	18.00	17.75	17.13	16.58	18.92	20.81	20.81	18.92	19.92	21.63
Morocco	7.00	7.00	7.75	8.75	9.00	9.00	9.00	9.00	9.00	....	....	10.00	....	....	....	13.50	13.50
Namibia	....	....	....	....	....	....	....	....	23.36	20.21	18.02	17.05	18.51	19.16	20.18	20.72	18.48
Niger	14.50	14.50	14.50	13.50	13.50	13.58	15.13	16.00	16.00	16.75	....	....	....	....	....	....	....
Nigeria	9.98	10.24	9.43	9.96	13.96	16.62	20.44	25.30	20.04	24.76	31.65	20.48	20.23	19.84	17.80	18.18	20.29
Rwanda	13.50	13.50	13.88	14.00	13.00	12.00	12.00	13.17	19.00	16.67	15.00	....	....	....	....	....	....
São Tomé & Príncipe	....	....	....	....	....	....	20.00	20.00	37.00	37.00	37.00	30.00	52.00	38.00	51.50	55.58	40.33
Senegal	14.50	14.50	14.50	13.50	13.50	13.58	15.13	16.00	16.00	16.75	....	....	....	....	....	....	....
Seychelles	....	....	....	....	....	....	15.52	15.65	15.57	15.58	15.66	15.70	15.76	16.22	14.88	14.39	12.01
Sierra Leone	17.25	18.00	17.00	17.19	28.54	28.00	29.67	52.50	56.25	62.83	50.46	27.33	28.83	32.12	23.87	23.83	26.83
Somalia	....	....	....	....	....	....	....	....	....	....	....	....	....	....	....	....	....
South Africa	16.67	22.33	21.50	14.33	12.50	15.33	19.83	21.00	20.31	18.91	16.16	15.58	17.90	19.52	20.00	21.79	18.00
Swaziland	18.00	22.00	17.00	12.50	11.88	15.00	14.50	14.50	16.25	15.00	14.00	15.00	18.00	19.75	18.75	21.00	15.00
Tanzania	13.00	13.00	12.29	18.50	27.50	29.63	31.00	....	....	....	31.00	39.00	42.83	37.21	29.23	26.67	29.83
Togo	14.50	14.50	14.50	13.50	13.50	14.50	16.00	16.00	16.00	17.50	....	....	....	....	....	....	....
Tunisia	8.50	8.50	9.63	9.17	11.08	9.87	4.82	....	....	....	....	....	....	....	....	....	....
Uganda	16.17	21.92	24.00	33.33	34.67	35.00	40.00	38.67	34.42	....	....	....	20.16	20.29	21.37	20.86	21.55
Zambia	13.00	14.54	18.60	27.40	21.20	18.39	18.39	35.10	....	54.57	113.31	70.56	45.53	53.78	46.69	31.80	40.52
Zimbabwe	23.08	23.00	17.17	13.00	13.00	13.00	13.00	11.71	15.50	19.77	36.33	34.86	34.73	34.23	32.55	42.06	55.39
Asia																	
Bangladesh	12.00	12.00	12.00	14.00	16.00	16.00	16.00	16.00	15.92	15.00	15.00	14.50	14.00	14.00	14.00	14.00	14.13
Bhutan	15.00	15.00	15.00	15.00	15.00	15.00	15.00	15.00	15.00	17.00	17.00	16.58	16.00	....	....	....	....
Cambodia	....	....	....	....	....	....	....	....	....	....	....	....	18.70	18.80	18.40	18.33	17.56
China,P.R.: Mainland	7.20	7.20	7.92	7.92	7.92	9.00	I11.34	9.36	8.64	8.64	10.98	10.98	12.06	10.08	8.64	6.39	5.85
China,P.R.:Hong Kong	....	....	....	....	....	....	....	10.00	8.50	6.50	6.50	8.50	8.75	8.50	9.50	9.00	8.50
Fiji	13.50	13.50	13.50	13.50	13.50	20.46	11.64	11.86	12.25	12.35	11.74	11.28	11.06	11.33	11.03	9.66	8.77
India	16.50	16.50	16.50	16.50	16.50	16.50	16.50	16.50	17.88	18.92	16.25	14.75	15.46	15.96	13.83	13.54	12.54
Indonesia	....	....	....	21.49	21.67	22.10	21.70	20.83	25.53	24.03	20.59	17.76	18.85	19.22	21.82	32.15	27.66
Korea	10.00	10.00	10.00	10.00	10.00	10.13	11.25	10.00	10.00	10.00	8.58	8.50	9.00	8.84	I11.88	15.28	9.40
Lao People's Dem.Rep	....	....	....	....	....	....	....	....	26.00	26.00	I25.33	24.00	I25.67	27.00	....	29.28	32.00
Malaysia	11.08	11.35	11.54	10.69	8.19	7.25	7.00	7.17	8.13	9.31	9.05	7.61	7.63	I8.89	9.53	10.61	7.29

Lending Rates (60p) (cont.)
(Period averages in percent per annum)

1983	1984	1985	1986	1987	1988	1989	1990	1991	1992	1993	1994	1995	1996	1997	1998	1999	
																	Asia (cont.)
....	....	....	....	....	....	....	....	....	....	300.00	233.56	114.90	91.87	74.83	40.00	37.65	Mongolia
8.00	8.00	8.00	8.00	8.00	8.00	8.00	8.00	....	8.00	....	16.50	16.50	16.50	16.50	16.50	16.13	Myanmar
17.00	17.00	17.00	15.67	15.00	15.00	15.00	14.42	....	....	....	....	....	12.88	14.54	14.00	11.33	Nepal
11.58	10.64	11.54	12.33	11.94	12.68	14.62	15.52	14.17	14.53	11.29	9.16	13.14	13.30	10.45	17.70	18.90	Papua New Guinea
19.24	28.20	28.61	17.53	13.34	15.92	19.27	24.12	23.07	19.48	14.68	15.06	14.68	14.84	16.28	16.78	11.78	Philippines
20.00	20.00	19.00	18.83	17.50	17.50	17.00	13.25	14.75	12.88	12.00	12.00	12.00	12.00	12.00	11.50	11.50	Samoa
9.05	9.72	7.93	6.82	6.10	5.96	6.21	7.36	7.58	5.95	5.39	5.88	6.37	6.26	6.32	7.44	5.80	Singapore
11.50	12.00	12.83	15.13	17.33	18.00	18.00	18.00	19.46	19.75	17.80	15.72	16.59	17.78	15.71	14.84	14.50	Solomon Islands
13.25	13.15	13.40	11.57	9.80	12.42	13.17	13.00	13.83	13.00	16.43	12.96	14.68	16.27	12.00	6.00	7.00	Sri Lanka
15.21	16.79	16.08	13.38	10.71	11.58	12.25	14.42	15.40	12.17	11.17	10.90	13.25	13.40	13.65	14.42	8.98	Thailand
10.00	10.00	10.00	10.00	10.00	10.00	13.50	13.50	13.50	13.50	19.94	9.39	9.71	10.49	10.10	10.46	10.32	Tonga
17.50	16.83	15.75	16.00	15.42	17.04	17.00	17.33	18.00	16.25	16.00	16.00	10.50	10.50	10.50	10.96	10.29	Vanuatu
																	Europe
....	....	....	....	....	....	....	....	....	20.58	29.58	23.67	119.65	23.96	....	....	21.62	Albania
....	....	....	....	....	....	....	....	....	....	....	....	111.86	66.36	54.23	48.49	38.85	Armenia
....	....	....	....	....	....	....	....	....	....	....	147.50	162.50	....	....	....	....	Azerbaijan
....	....	....	....	....	....	....	....	....	....	71.63	148.50	175.00	62.33	31.80	26.99	51.04	Belarus
....	....	....	....	....	....	....	....	48.37	56.67	58.30	72.58	58.98	123.48	83.96	13.30	12.79	Bulgaria
....	....	....	....	....	....	....	....	....	1,157.79	1,443.61	22.91	20.24	22.52	15.47	15.75	14.94	Croatia
9.00	9.00	9.00	9.00	9.00	9.00	9.00	9.00	9.00	9.00	9.00	8.83	8.50	8.50	....	....	8.68	Cyprus
....	....	....	....	....	....	....	....	....	....	14.07	13.12	12.80	12.54	13.20	12.81	8.68	Czech Republic
....	....	....	....	....	....	....	....	....	30.50	27.30	23.08	15.95	13.67	19.82	16.67	8.70	Estonia
....	....	....	....	....	....	....	....	....	....	....	....	....	58.24	50.64	46.00	33.42	Georgia
....	....	....	....	....	....	20.33	28.78	35.09	33.05	25.43	27.40	32.61	27.31	21.77	19.28	16.34	Hungary
....	....	....	....	....	....	....	....	....	....	....	....	....	65.02	49.38	73.44	60.86	Kyrgyz Republic
....	....	....	....	....	....	....	....	....	....	86.36	55.86	34.56	25.78	15.25	14.29	14.20	Latvia
....	....	....	....	....	....	....	....	....	....	91.84	62.30	27.08	21.56	14.39	12.21	13.09	Lithuania
....	....	....	....	....	....	....	....	....	....	....	159.82	45.95	21.58	21.42	21.03	20.45	Macedonia, FYR
8.00	8.00	8.00	8.00	8.00	8.46	8.50	8.50	8.50	8.50	8.50	8.50	17.38	7.77	7.99	8.09	7.70	Malta
....	....	....	....	....	....	....	....	....	....	....	....	....	36.67	33.33	30.83	35.54	Moldova
9.00	9.00	12.00	12.00	12.00	16.67	64.00	504.17	54.58	39.00	35.25	32.83	133.45	26.08	24.96	24.49	16.98	Poland
....	....	....	....	....	....	....	....	....	....	....	....	320.31	146.81	132.04	41.79	39.72	Russia
....	....	....	....	....	....	....	....	....	....	14.41	14.56	16.85	13.92	18.65	21.17	21.07	Slovak Republic
....	....	....	....	....	....	....	824.56	195.11	....	48.61	38.87	23.36	22.60	20.02	16.09	12.38	Slovenia
....	....	....	....	....	....	....	....	....	....	184.25	250.28	122.70	79.88	49.12	54.50	54.95	Ukraine
																	Middle East
....	....	....	8.96	7.50	7.80	18.50	8.50	9.48	11.85	10.95	10.83	11.83	12.45	12.33	11.92	11.86	Bahrain
15.00	15.00	15.00	15.00	16.33	17.00	18.33	19.00	....	20.33	18.30	16.51	16.47	15.58	13.79	13.02	12.97	Egypt
186.18	823.03	503.42	60.27	61.43	41.68	31.63	26.45	26.43	19.94	16.44	17.45	20.22	20.68	18.71	16.18	16.36	Israel
....	....	....	....	....	....	....	10.31	10.37	10.16	10.23	10.45	10.66	11.25	12.25	....	....	Jordan
8.35	8.58	8.75	8.63	7.86	6.72	8.38	....	....	8.00	7.95	7.61	8.37	8.77	8.80	8.93	8.56	Kuwait
14.53	15.58	17.29	22.21	36.54	44.46	39.86	39.94	38.01	40.21	28.53	23.88	24.69	25.21	20.29	....	19.48	Lebanon
7.00	7.00	7.00	7.00	7.00	7.00	7.00	7.00	7.00	7.00	7.00	....	....	....	....	....	7.00	Libya
....	10.35	10.24	9.65	9.10	9.40	10.01	9.68	9.50	9.24	8.49	8.57	9.38	9.23	9.30	10.09	10.32	Oman
9.50	9.50	9.50	9.50	9.50	9.50	9.50	9.50	9.50	8.13	7.20	8.86	....	....	....	....	....	Qatar
																	Western Hemisphere
14.00	13.63	13.00	14.25	12.38	11.50	12.17	12.38	15.50	13.00	13.00	12.50	11.88	11.38	12.00	12.38	12.13	Antigua and Barbuda
....	....	....	....	....	....	....	....	....	....	....	10.06	17.85	10.51	9.24	10.64	11.04	Argentina
....	....	....	11.00	10.30	10.30	10.60	10.60	10.60	10.60	10.60	10.60	10.30	10.00	....	....	....	Aruba
11.00	11.00	10.33	9.25	9.00	9.00	9.00	9.00	9.00	9.00	8.08	7.46	6.88	6.75	6.75	6.75	6.38	Bahamas, The
11.79	11.50	10.56	9.06	8.75	9.44	9.92	11.42	12.42	13.54	8.92	9.08	10.00	10.00	9.83	9.75	9.40	Barbados
....	....	....	14.69	14.14	13.56	13.77	14.04	14.24	14.32	14.37	14.78	15.69	16.30	16.29	16.50	16.27	Belize
56.83	120.67	172.15	165.78	49.41	39.79	37.27	41.81	41.15	45.51	53.88	55.57	51.02	55.97	50.05	39.41	35.37	Bolivia
42.82	38.33	40.81	26.27	32.80	21.17	35.92	48.83	28.55	23.92	24.30	20.34	18.16	17.37	15.67	20.17	12.62	Chile
....	....	....	40.83	41.10	42.69	43.04	45.25	47.13	37.28	35.81	40.47	42.72	41.99	34.22	42.24	30.41	Colombia
23.25	18.00	20.92	21.80	23.82	28.69	29.17	32.56	38.88	28.46	30.02	33.03	36.70	26.27	22.48	22.47	25.74	Costa Rica
9.50	10.42	10.04	10.25	10.50	10.50	10.50	10.50	10.29	10.00	10.00	9.58	10.33	10.50	10.50	10.50	10.50	Dominica
....	....	....	....	....	....	....	....	35.26	28.34	29.89	28.68	30.68	23.73	21.01	25.64	25.05	Dominican Republic
12.33	16.17	18.00	18.00	18.42	23.00	30.08	37.50	46.67	60.17	47.83	43.99	55.67	54.50	43.02	49.55	64.02	Ecuador
15.00	14.00	14.00	17.00	17.00	17.00	18.50	21.17	19.67	16.43	19.42	19.03	19.08	18.57	16.05	14.98	15.46	El Salvador
10.50	10.50	11.67	11.50	11.42	10.50	10.67	10.50	10.63	10.50	10.50	10.50	10.50	10.50	10.50	10.50	10.50	Grenada
12.00	12.00	12.00	13.17	14.00	15.17	16.00	23.27	34.08	19.49	24.73	22.93	21.16	22.72	118.64	16.56	19.51	Guatemala
15.00	15.00	15.00	15.00	15.00	15.07	18.94	32.75	33.55	28.69	19.36	18.36	19.22	17.79	17.04	16.77	17.11	Guyana
....	....	....	....	....	....	....	....	....	....	....	....	....	....	21.01	23.62	22.88	Haiti
16.10	16.20	16.30	16.12	15.54	15.38	15.43	17.05	21.88	21.68	22.06	24.68	26.95	29.74	32.07	30.69	30.15	Honduras
16.97	18.53	24.92	27.34	25.45	25.19	25.22	30.50	31.51	44.81	43.71	49.46	43.58	39.83	32.86	31.59	27.01	Jamaica
....	....	....	....	....	....	....	....	....	....	22.04	20.38	58.59	36.89	24.55	28.70	25.87	Mexico
11.00	11.20	11.46	11.59	11.37	11.24	11.23	9.25	....	....	12.59	12.73	12.93	13.21	13.29	13.58	13.60	Netherlands Antilles
....	....	....	....	....	....	558.01	22.00	17.92	19.32	20.23	20.14	19.89	20.72	21.02	21.63	22.15	Nicaragua
....	....	....	12.36	12.60	12.47	12.92	11.98	11.79	10.61	10.06	10.15	11.10	10.62	10.63	10.82	10.05	Panama
....	....	....	....	....	....	....	31.00	34.94	27.96	30.78	135.47	33.94	31.88	27.79	30.49	30.21	Paraguay
....	....	....	40.52	35.74	174.28	1,515.86	4,774.53	751.52	173.80	97.37	53.56	27.16	26.07	29.96	30.80	30.79	Peru
9.00	10.00	10.21	10.21	12.00	12.00	12.00	12.00	12.00	12.67	13.00	13.00	12.58	12.25	13.00	13.00	11.50	St. Kitts and Nevis
13.00	13.33	14.00	14.00	11.58	10.58	10.00	10.54	10.50	10.50	10.17	10.13	10.00	10.33	10.54	10.50	10.50	St. Lucia
10.67	12.00	12.13	12.46	12.46	12.08	12.36	12.50	13.50	11.38	11.21	11.00	11.00	11.00	12.00	12.50	12.50	St. Vincent & Grens.
....	....	....	....	....	....	....	....	8.90	8.93	9.35	15.38	40.18	35.78	....	29.00	27.75	Suriname
11.71	12.75	12.69	12.00	11.50	12.58	13.31	12.87	13.17	15.33	15.50	15.98	15.17	15.79	15.33	17.33	17.04	Trinidad and Tobago
93.64	83.23	94.58	94.73	95.80	101.52	127.58	174.45	152.88	117.77	97.33	95.08	99.10	91.52	71.55	57.93	53.28	Uruguay
....	9.57	9.33	8.49	8.47	8.50	22.50	135.53	37.16	41.33	59.90	54.66	39.74	39.41	23.69	46.35	32.13	Venezuela, Rep. Bol.

National Interest Rates

Treasury Bill Rates (60c)
(Period averages in percent per annum)

	1983	1984	1985	1986	1987	1988	1989	1990	1991	1992	1993	1994	1995	1996	1997	1998	1999
Industrial Countries																	
United States	8.62	9.39	7.49	5.97	5.83	6.67	8.12	7.51	5.41	3.46	3.02	4.27	5.51	5.02	5.07	4.82	4.66
Canada	9.31	11.06	9.43	8.97	8.15	9.48	12.05	12.81	8.73	6.59	4.84	5.54	6.89	4.21	3.26	4.73	4.72
Australia	11.06	10.99	15.42	15.39	12.80	12.14	16.80	14.15	9.96	6.27	5.00	5.69	Ɪ7.64	7.02	5.29	4.84	4.76
New Zealand	10.13	9.23	....	19.97	20.50	14.72	13.51	13.78	9.74	6.72	6.21	6.69	8.82	9.09	7.53	7.10	4.58
Euro Area																	
Belgium	10.38	11.60	9.44	8.09	7.00	6.61	8.45	9.62	9.24	9.36	8.52	5.57	4.67	3.19	3.38	3.51	2.72
France	12.63	11.88	10.08	7.79	8.22	7.88	9.34	Ɪ10.18	9.69	10.49	8.41	5.79	6.58	3.84	3.35	3.45	2.72
Germany	5.63	5.66	5.04	3.86	3.28	3.62	6.28	8.13	8.27	8.32	6.22	5.05	4.40	3.30	3.32	3.42	2.88
Ireland	13.26	13.13	11.78	11.85	10.70	7.81	9.70	10.90	10.12	....	Ɪ9.06	5.87	6.19	5.36	6.03	5.37	....
Italy	17.89	15.37	13.71	11.40	10.73	11.19	12.58	12.38	12.54	14.32	10.58	9.17	10.85	8.46	6.33	4.59	2.92
Portugal	18.14	21.15	20.90	Ɪ15.56	13.89	12.97	....	13.51	14.20	12.88	....	....	7.75	5.75	4.43	....	....
Spain	19.80	13.43	10.90	8.63	Ɪ11.38	10.79	13.57	14.17	12.45	12.44	10.53	8.11	9.79	7.23	5.02	3.79	3.01
Greece	....	....	....	17.00	17.29	16.25	16.46	18.50	18.79	17.69	18.23	18.23	14.29	11.92	9.51	11.98	9.54
Iceland	....	....	....	....	....	26.39	23.00	12.92	14.25	Ɪ11.30	8.35	4.95	7.22	6.97	7.04	7.40	8.61
Sweden	12.34	11.93	14.17	9.83	9.39	10.08	11.50	13.66	11.59	12.85	8.35	7.40	8.75	5.79	4.11	4.19	3.12
Switzerland	3.04	3.58	4.15	3.54	3.18	3.01	6.60	8.32	7.74	7.76	4.75	3.97	2.78	1.72	1.45	1.32	1.17
United Kingdom	9.60	9.30	11.55	10.34	9.25	9.87	13.28	14.09	10.85	8.94	5.25	5.15	6.33	5.77	6.48	6.82	5.04
Developing Countries																	
Africa																	
Algeria	3.25	3.25	3.25	3.25	3.25	3.25	3.25	3.25	9.50	9.50	9.50	16.50	....	....	....	9.96	10.05
Ethiopia	3.00	3.00	3.00	3.00	3.00	3.00	3.00	3.00	3.00	5.25	12.00	12.00	12.00	7.22	3.97	3.48	3.65
Ghana	13.00	14.16	17.13	18.47	21.71	19.76	19.84	21.78	29.23	19.38	30.95	27.72	35.38	41.64	42.77	34.33	26.37
Kenya	14.15	13.24	13.90	13.23	12.86	13.48	13.86	14.78	16.59	16.53	49.80	23.32	18.29	22.25	22.87	22.83	13.87
Lesotho	18.00	18.42	17.60	11.21	10.75	11.42	15.75	16.33	15.75	14.20	13.10	Ɪ9.44	12.40	13.89	14.83	15.47	12.45
Malawi	11.00	11.00	12.31	12.75	14.25	15.75	15.75	12.92	11.50	15.62	23.54	27.68	46.30	30.83	18.31	32.98	42.85
Morocco	....	....	....	....	....	....	....	....	....	....	....	....	....	....	....	....	....
Namibia	....	....	....	....	....	....	....	....	....	13.88	12.16	11.35	13.91	15.25	15.69	17.24	13.28
Nigeria	....	....	....	....	....	....	....	....	....	17.89	24.50	12.87	12.50	12.25	12.00	12.26	17.82
Seychelles	12.07	12.61	12.48	12.90	15.15	13.90	13.41	13.00	13.00	13.00	12.91	12.36	12.15	11.47	10.50	7.96	4.50
Sierra Leone	11.00	12.00	12.00	14.50	16.50	18.00	22.00	47.50	50.67	78.63	28.64	12.19	14.73	29.25	12.71	22.10	32.42
South Africa	13.45	19.33	17.56	10.43	8.71	12.03	16.84	17.80	16.68	13.77	11.31	10.93	13.53	15.04	15.26	16.53	12.85
Swaziland	13.04	17.74	16.47	9.76	5.96	7.28	10.16	11.14	12.67	12.34	8.25	8.35	10.87	13.68	14.37	13.09	11.19
Tanzania	....	....	....	....	....	....	....	....	....	....	34.00	35.09	40.33	15.30	9.59	11.83	10.05
Uganda	11.17	18.00	22.00	30.67	30.50	33.00	42.17	41.00	34.17	....	Ɪ21.30	12.52	8.75	11.71	10.59	7.77	7.43
Zambia	7.50	7.67	13.21	24.25	16.50	15.17	18.50	25.92	....	....	124.03	74.21	39.81	52.78	29.48	24.94	36.19
Zimbabwe	8.52	8.49	8.48	8.71	8.73	8.38	8.35	8.39	14.44	26.16	33.04	29.22	27.98	24.53	22.07	32.78	50.48
Asia																	
China,P.R.:Hong Kong	....	....	....	....	....	....	....	....	....	3.83	3.17	5.66	5.55	4.45	7.50	5.04	4.94
Fiji	6.17	7.09	7.03	6.36	9.76	1.78	2.75	4.40	5.61	3.65	2.91	2.69	3.15	2.98	2.60	2.00	2.00
Lao People's Dem.Rep	....	....	....	....	....	....	....	....	....	....	....	....	20.46	....	....	23.66	30.00
Malaysia	5.12	5.10	4.74	4.12	2.68	3.49	5.29	6.12	7.27	7.66	6.48	3.68	5.50	6.41	6.41	6.86	3.53
Nepal	5.00	5.00	5.00	5.00	5.00	5.00	5.62	7.93	8.80	9.00	4.50	6.50	9.90	11.51	2.52	3.70	4.30
Pakistan	....	....	....	....	....	....	....	....	....	12.47	13.03	11.26	12.49	13.61	Ɪ15.74	....	....
Papua New Guinea	10.92	9.28	10.40	12.32	10.44	10.12	10.50	11.40	10.33	8.88	6.25	6.85	17.40	14.44	9.94	21.18	22.70
Philippines	14.23	28.53	26.72	16.08	11.51	14.67	18.65	23.67	21.48	16.02	12.45	12.71	11.76	12.34	12.89	15.00	10.00
Solomon Islands	8.92	9.00	9.58	12.00	11.33	11.00	11.00	11.00	13.71	13.50	12.15	11.25	12.50	12.75	12.88	6.00	6.00
Sri Lanka	12.38	13.08	13.39	10.48	7.30	13.59	14.81	14.08	13.75	16.19	16.52	12.68	16.81	Ɪ17.40	....	12.59	12.51
Thailand	9.35	10.00	11.02	6.76	3.63	5.08	....	....	....	....	....	....	....	....	....	....	....
Europe																	
Albania	....	....	....	....	....	....	....	....	....	....	....	....	13.79	17.67	32.50	....	....
Armenia	....	....	....	....	....	....	....	....	....	....	....	....	37.81	41.40	55.84	45.84	53.28
Bulgaria	....	....	....	....	....	....	....	....	....	48.11	45.45	57.72	48.27	114.31	78.35	6.02	5.43
Hungary	....	....	....	....	....	18.00	20.49	30.13	34.48	22.65	17.22	26.93	32.04	23.96	20.13	17.83	14.68
Kazakhstan	....	....	....	....	....	....	....	....	....	....	....	214.34	48.98	28.91	15.15	23.59	15.63
Kyrgyz Republic	....	....	....	....	....	....	....	....	....	....	....	143.13	34.90	40.10	35.83	43.67	47.19
Latvia	....	....	....	....	....	....	....	....	....	....	....	....	28.24	16.27	4.73	5.27	6.23
Lithuania	....	....	....	....	....	....	....	....	....	....	....	....	26.82	20.95	8.64	10.69	11.14
Malta	....	....	....	....	4.50	4.24	4.24	4.25	4.46	4.58	4.60	4.29	4.65	4.99	5.08	5.41	5.15
Moldova	....	....	....	....	....	....	....	....	....	....	....	....	52.90	39.01	23.63	30.54	28.49
Poland	....	....	....	....	....	....	....	....	....	44.03	33.16	28.81	25.62	20.32	21.58	19.09	13.14
Romania	....	....	....	....	....	....	....	....	....	....	....	....	....	51.09	85.72	63.99	74.21
Russia	....	....	....	....	....	....	....	....	....	....	....	....	168.04	86.07	23.43	....	....
Slovenia	....	....	....	....	....	....	....	....	....	....	....	....	....	....	....	....	8.63
Turkey	....	....	....	....	41.92	54.56	48.01	43.46	67.01	72.17	....	....	....	....	....	....	....
Middle East																	
Bahrain	....	....	....	....	6.40	7.39	9.08	....	5.90	3.78	3.33	4.81	6.07	5.49	5.68	5.53	5.46
Egypt	....	....	....	....	....	....	....	....	....	....	....	....	....	....	8.80	8.80	9.00
Israel	....	217.30	210.11	19.86	19.97	16.01	12.90	15.08	14.50	11.79	10.54	11.77	14.37	15.54	13.88	12.17	....
Kuwait	5.69	5.69	5.69	5.69	5.48	6.01	8.28	....	....	....	....	6.32	7.35	6.93	6.98	....	....
Lebanon	9.52	13.08	14.96	Ɪ18.67	26.91	25.17	18.84	18.84	17.47	22.40	18.27	15.09	19.40	15.19	13.42	12.70	11.57
Western Hemisphere																	
Antigua and Barbuda	7.00	7.00	7.00	7.00	7.00	7.00	7.00	7.00	7.00	7.00	7.00	7.00	7.00	7.00	7.00	7.00	7.00
Bahamas, The	9.11	6.88	5.90	3.47	2.40	4.46	5.21	5.85	6.49	5.32	3.96	1.88	3.01	4.45	4.35	3.84	1.97
Barbados	7.45	6.92	5.53	4.42	4.84	4.75	4.90	7.07	9.34	10.88	5.44	7.26	8.01	6.85	3.61	5.61	5.83
Belize	10.51	9.55	12.76	10.81	8.80	8.32	7.36	7.37	6.71	5.38	4.59	4.27	4.10	3.78	3.51	3.83	5.91
Bolivia	....	....	....	....	....	....	....	....	....	....	....	17.89	24.51	19.93	13.65	12.33	14.07
Brazil	....	....	....	....	....	....	....	....	....	....	....	....	49.93	25.73	24.79	28.57	26.23
Dominica	6.50	6.50	6.50	6.50	6.50	6.50	6.50	6.50	6.50	6.48	6.40	6.40	6.40	6.40	6.40	6.40	6.40
Grenada	6.50	6.50	6.50	6.50	6.50	6.50	6.50	6.50	6.50	6.50	6.50	6.50	6.50	6.50	6.50	6.50	6.50
Guyana	12.75	12.75	12.75	12.75	11.33	11.03	15.19	30.00	30.94	25.75	16.83	17.66	17.51	11.35	8.91	8.33	11.31
Haiti	....	....	....	....	....	....	....	....	....	....	....	....	....	....	14.13	16.21	7.71
Jamaica	12.38	13.29	19.03	20.88	18.16	18.50	19.10	26.21	25.56	34.36	28.85	42.98	27.65	37.95	21.14	25.65	20.75
Mexico	59.07	49.32	63.20	....	103.07	Ɪ69.15	44.99	34.76	19.28	15.62	14.99	14.10	48.44	31.39	19.80	24.76	21.41
Netherlands Antilles	7.25	7.35	7.21	7.34	6.36	5.79	5.96	6.10	....	....	4.83	4.48	5.46	5.66	5.77	5.82	6.15
St. Kitts and Nevis	6.50	6.50	6.50	6.50	6.50	6.50	6.50	6.50	6.50	6.50	6.50	6.50	6.50	6.50	6.50	6.50	6.50
St. Lucia	6.50	6.50	7.00	7.00	7.00	7.00	7.00	7.00	7.00	7.00	7.00	7.00	7.00	7.00	7.00	7.00	7.00
St. Vincent & Grens.	6.50	6.50	6.50	6.50	6.50	6.50	6.50	6.50	6.50	6.50	6.50	6.50	6.50	6.50	6.50	6.50	6.50
Trinidad and Tobago	3.08	3.39	3.47	3.99	4.63	4.88	7.13	7.50	7.67	9.26	9.45	10.00	8.41	10.44	9.83	11.93	10.40
Uruguay	....	....	....	....	....	....	....	....	....	....	....	44.60	39.40	29.20	23.18	....	....

Government Bond Yields (61)
(Average yields to maturity in percent per annum)

1983	1984	1985	1986	1987	1988	1989	1990	1991	1992	1993	1994	1995	1996	1997	1998	1999	
																	Industrial Countries
11.11	12.44	10.62	7.68	8.38	8.85	8.50	8.55	7.86	7.01	5.87	7.08	6.58	6.44	6.35	5.26	5.64	United States
11.79	12.75	11.04	9.52	9.95	10.22	9.92	10.85	9.76	8.77	7.85	8.63	8.28	7.50	6.42	5.47	5.69	Canada
13.89	13.53	13.95	13.42	13.19	12.10	13.41	13.18	10.69	9.22	7.28	9.04	9.17	8.17	6.89	5.50	6.08	Australia
7.42	6.81	6.34	4.94	4.21	4.27	5.05	7.36	6.53	4.94	3.69	3.71	2.53	2.23	1.69	1.10	‖1.77	Japan
12.18	12.57	17.71	16.52	‖16.35	13.45	12.78	12.46	10.00	7.87	6.69	7.48	7.94	8.04	7.21	6.47	6.13	New Zealand
....	....	....	....	....	....	....	....	....	....	....	8.18	8.73	7.23	5.96	4.70	4.66	Euro Area
8.17	8.02	7.77	7.33	6.91	6.67	7.14	8.74	8.62	8.27	6.64	6.69	6.47	5.30	4.79	4.29	4.09	Austria
11.86	11.98	10.61	7.93	7.83	7.85	8.64	10.09	9.26	8.64	7.19	7.82	7.45	6.45	5.74	4.72	4.81	Belgium
....	....	....	....	....	....	....	....	....	....	8.84	9.03	8.78	....	....	....	4.72	Finland
13.63	12.54	10.94	8.44	9.43	9.06	8.79	9.94	9.05	8.60	6.91	7.35	7.59	6.39	5.63	4.72	4.69	France
7.89	7.78	6.87	5.92	5.84	6.10	7.09	8.88	8.63	7.96	6.28	6.67	6.50	5.63	5.08	4.39	4.26	Germany
13.90	14.62	12.64	11.07	11.27	9.49	8.95	10.08	9.17	9.11	7.72	8.19	8.30	7.48	6.49	4.99	....	Ireland
18.02	14.95	13.00	10.52	9.68	10.16	10.72	11.51	‖13.18	13.27	11.31	10.56	12.21	9.40	6.86	4.90	4.73	Italy
9.83	10.22	9.53	8.67	7.96	7.13	7.68	8.51	8.15	7.90	6.93	6.38	6.05	5.21	5.39	5.29	....	Luxembourg
8.61	8.33	7.34	6.32	6.40	6.42	7.22	8.92	8.74	8.10	6.51	7.20	7.20	6.49	5.81	4.87	4.92	Netherlands
19.22	21.50	20.75	15.54	15.02	13.87	15.63	18.55	18.27	15.38	12.45	10.83	10.34	7.25	5.48	4.09	....	Portugal
16.91	16.52	13.37	11.36	12.81	11.74	13.70	14.68	12.43	12.17	10.16	9.69	11.04	8.18	5.84	4.55	4.30	Spain
14.46	‖13.96	11.31	9.91	11.06	9.78	9.75	10.74	9.59	9.47	7.08	7.41	7.58	6.04	5.08	4.59	4.30	Denmark
....	18.46	15.77	15.78	....	16.56	....	....	....	....	....	....	....	....	....	8.48	6.30	Greece
....	....	....	....	....	....	....	....	....	7.75	6.80	5.02	7.18	5.61	5.49	4.73	4.28	Iceland
12.86	12.16	12.58	13.47	13.56	12.97	10.84	10.72	9.87	9.78	6.52	7.13	6.82	5.94	5.13	5.35	5.38	Norway
12.30	12.28	13.09	10.26	‖11.68	11.35	11.18	13.08	10.69	10.02	8.54	‖9.41	....	....	....	....	....	Sweden
4.52	4.70	4.78	4.29	4.12	4.15	5.20	‖6.68	6.35	5.48	4.05	5.23	3.73	3.63	3.08	2.39	‖3.51	Switzerland
10.81	10.42	10.50	9.86	9.47	9.36	9.58	11.08	9.92	9.12	7.87	8.05	8.26	8.10	7.09	5.45	4.70	United Kingdom
																	Developing Countries
																	Africa
....	....	....	6.00	5.00	5.00	5.00	5.00	5.00	7.00	13.00	13.00	13.00	13.00	....	....	....	Ethiopia
10.27	10.58	11.50	11.50	11.50	11.50	11.50	11.50	11.50	....	....	23.50	38.58	42.67	39.25	....	....	Malawi
....	....	....	....	....	....	....	....	15.44	....	13.94	14.63	16.11	15.48	14.70	15.10	14.96	Namibia
12.67	15.23	16.79	16.37	15.30	16.37	16.90	16.15	16.34	15.44	13.97	14.83	16.11	15.48	14.70	15.12	14.90	South Africa
12.63	18.00	24.00	38.33	40.00	38.50	45.33	44.50	42.00	43.50	....	....	....	....	....	....	....	Uganda
13.08	13.29	13.26	13.20	13.87	14.00	14.00	15.24	17.27	17.40	....	....	....	....	....	....	....	Zimbabwe
																	Asia
7.99	8.65	8.99	....	....	....	....	....	....	....	....	....	....	....	....	....	....	India
13.08	14.32	13.58	11.57	12.43	13.04	14.74	15.03	16.46	15.08	12.08	12.30	12.40	10.90	11.70	12.80	8.72	Korea
....	....	....	....	....	....	....	....	....	....	....	10.50	10.50	13.13	14.00	14.00	....	Myanmar
10.50	10.50	‖13.00	13.00	13.00	13.00	13.17	13.54	....	13.33	....	9.00	....	9.00	9.00	9.00	8.75	Nepal
9.31	9.25	9.19	8.77	8.26	8.32	8.18	8.05	7.88	7.67	7.40	7.07	6.63	6.06	5.43	4.79	4.16	Pakistan
14.90	17.50	15.00	14.17	13.50	13.50	13.50	13.50	13.50	13.50	13.50	13.50	13.50	13.50	13.50	13.50	13.50	Samoa
11.00	11.00	12.00	13.00	12.33	12.00	12.44	12.75	12.92	13.00	13.00	13.00	13.00	11.50	11.75	12.50	12.88	Solomon Islands
....	14.67	15.33	12.00	12.00	11.49	11.71	12.20	15.68	16.00	16.25	....	....	....	....	....	....	Sri Lanka
11.13	12.41	12.11	9.11	7.48	7.50	8.09	10.60	10.75	10.75	10.75	10.75	10.75	10.75	10.75	10.25	6.69	Thailand
....	....	9.50	9.50	9.50	9.50	‖8.00	8.00	8.00	8.00	8.00	8.00	8.00	8.00	8.00	8.00	8.00	Vanuatu
																	Europe
....	....	....	....	....	....	....	....	....	....	....	56.86	49.76	....	....	10.10	10.05	Bulgaria
																	Western Hemisphere
9.40	10.30	10.40	10.40	10.40	10.40	10.40	10.40	10.40	10.40	10.40	23.11	27.24	35.55	29.59	20.34	16.04	Honduras
15.16	17.14	22.48	22.62	20.83	20.40	20.17	25.46	26.33	30.50	24.82	26.82	26.85	26.87	26.85	....	....	Jamaica
....	....	....	....	....	....	....	....	....	....	....	....	51.74	32.81	21.44	....	....	Mexico
10.65	10.63	9.46	9.29	10.36	10.74	10.63	10.74	....	....	8.14	7.48	8.02	8.25	8.67	8.60	8.75	Netherlands Antilles
9.88	9.89	9.89	9.62	9.54	9.76	10.77	10.73	10.85	13.30	....	....	....	....	....	....	....	Trinidad and Tobago
....	13.15	12.55	12.07	13.49	14.86	17.32	20.06	27.14	31.66	41.03	54.73	53.38	49.09	25.41	47.88	37.05	Venezuela, Rep. Bol.

Real Effective Exchange Rate Indices

(1995=100)

Based on Relative Unit Labor Costs (65um.110)

		1985	1986	1987	1988	1989	1990	1991	1992	1993	1994	1995	1996	1997	1998	1999
United States	111	179.9	140.2	122.2	115.9	121.6	113.9	110.8	104.9	107.3	106.8	100.0	103.7	111.5	115.6	....
Canada	156	101.5	98.3	101.6	110.4	118.0	121.4	126.8	120.1	109.0	99.9	100.0	103.9	105.5	102.6	....
Japan	158	53.8	71.2	73.5	78.1	73.1	64.2	68.1	73.2	90.3	99.2	100.0	83.1	78.2	74.0	....
Euro Area	163	81.0	90.4	97.3	92.1	90.8	99.0	96.0	101.7	100.6	96.3	100.0	101.7	90.0	87.0	....
Austria	122	117.7	121.1	121.0	112.6	110.1	109.9	107.3	105.6	105.4	104.6	100.0	96.4	91.1	89.6	....
Belgium	124	90.4	93.1	94.6	92.0	90.1	94.8	95.8	96.2	97.1	97.3	100.0	97.9	92.4	93.6	....
Finland	172	133.3	127.7	123.4	126.1	130.2	135.4	132.4	102.7	83.3	87.9	100.0	94.8	90.5	90.5	....
France	132	111.1	113.2	111.1	104.7	101.1	103.9	99.5	99.4	102.3	99.9	100.0	99.3	92.7	92.0	....
Germany	134	66.8	72.6	79.5	79.2	77.9	79.6	77.6	83.9	90.3	91.8	100.0	97.8	90.8	88.2	....
Ireland	178	155.3	163.6	151.0	140.7	128.9	131.9	127.7	123.3	116.3	110.2	100.0	99.9	96.2	95.7	....
Italy	136	129.4	131.6	129.7	127.9	134.8	140.5	144.0	139.1	117.4	110.9	100.0	114.7	120.3	117.5	....
Netherlands	138	98.6	104.5	108.1	104.7	98.8	99.0	97.5	101.0	103.4	98.8	100.0	96.0	91.2	90.7	....
Spain	184	91.1	88.3	88.2	94.4	102.9	112.0	115.1	117.8	107.2	100.9	100.0	104.2	103.4	107.4	....
Denmark	128	85.2	92.7	100.7	97.5	92.8	99.5	96.5	99.6	102.7	96.3	100.0	96.0	97.5	98.7	....
Norway	142	90.6	90.4	95.2	99.5	95.8	94.9	90.5	88.1	86.5	93.1	100.0	102.8	108.7	103.2	....
Sweden	144	123.8	124.1	122.8	129.4	138.3	139.0	142.0	140.8	105.3	101.4	100.0	112.9	106.7	102.8	....
Switzerland	146	74.1	79.7	82.8	84.5	81.0	87.3	88.7	87.0	88.9	94.7	100.0	98.6	95.7	100.2	....
United Kingdom	112	112.0	103.5	104.6	111.5	109.0	110.9	115.0	109.8	98.6	101.2	100.0	103.1	126.7	138.5	....

Based on Relative Normalized Unit Labor Costs (..reu)

		1985	1986	1987	1988	1989	1990	1991	1992	1993	1994	1995	1996	1997	1998	1999
United States	111	174.8	141.5	123.3	116.5	119.0	110.9	108.0	104.9	108.0	106.9	100.0	106.0	115.4	123.2	....
Canada	156	104.4	97.7	101.4	108.5	117.6	122.3	125.1	119.3	108.9	100.5	100.0	99.7	101.0	96.0	....
Japan	158	55.5	70.2	73.7	78.1	74.4	66.9	71.5	74.4	90.3	96.1	100.0	84.9	78.8	71.8	....
Euro Area	163	81.4	90.2	95.0	91.8	91.3	99.7	96.8	99.9	97.7	95.6	100.0	100.0	89.0	85.5	....
Austria	122	114.8	118.4	119.2	114.6	110.6	108.3	104.6	105.2	105.9	103.6	100.0	95.4	90.4	88.6	....
Belgium	124	90.2	92.2	93.8	91.1	91.2	94.0	95.4	95.0	96.8	96.5	100.0	97.3	93.1	92.1	....
Finland	172	130.6	126.2	124.5	127.9	132.3	134.0	123.2	100.4	85.2	89.7	100.0	93.8	89.3	89.2	....
France	132	109.4	111.0	108.2	104.6	101.6	103.0	98.9	99.3	100.2	99.0	100.0	96.9	92.3	90.9	....
Germany	134	69.0	74.7	79.1	79.2	78.3	82.6	81.6	84.5	90.2	93.1	100.0	98.7	92.1	89.5	....
Ireland	178	153.4	157.1	145.4	138.1	129.7	129.5	120.9	118.2	110.1	103.9	100.0	99.1	96.1	89.3	....
Italy	136	126.4	127.9	128.9	127.6	133.1	137.1	138.3	136.5	115.0	108.1	100.0	111.9	115.1	115.6	....
Netherlands	138	99.1	104.8	107.8	103.6	98.6	98.6	96.1	97.8	99.3	99.1	100.0	96.4	90.9	88.3	....
Spain	184	90.5	88.0	89.4	93.8	102.0	108.4	112.5	116.3	108.0	101.4	100.0	103.4	101.8	105.2	....
Denmark	128	85.3	88.7	96.8	96.0	94.5	99.0	94.5	95.2	98.8	97.5	100.0	97.7	95.6	95.9	....
Norway	142	94.8	92.7	96.5	98.5	97.0	95.6	94.0	93.2	92.4	93.4	100.0	103.9	108.2	107.2	....
Sweden	144	122.5	124.0	123.5	128.1	137.5	137.5	136.8	137.2	104.7	101.7	100.0	110.7	104.8	101.7	....
Switzerland	146	72.5	80.5	84.1	85.7	82.1	87.3	89.6	85.6	86.8	94.3	100.0	99.7	95.4	99.7	....
United Kingdom	112	111.6	103.5	107.4	112.4	109.4	109.3	113.6	113.7	104.4	105.2	100.0	102.4	124.5	137.2	....

Based on Relative Value-Added Deflators (99by.110)

		1985	1986	1987	1988	1989	1990	1991	1992	1993	1994	1995	1996	1997	1998	1999
United States	111	159.6	130.0	111.7	104.0	111.8	108.3	109.0	108.2	111.8	109.3	100.0	104.4	112.3	....	....
Canada	156	101.5	95.9	102.9	113.3	115.9	112.7	111.6	101.2	95.0	94.2	100.0	102.4	103.0	....	....
Japan	158	64.6	80.9	85.5	91.6	84.6	74.5	79.2	81.8	95.5	99.4	100.0	86.1	81.6	....	....
Euro Area	163	....	....	....	....	....	....	....	....	....	....	....	....	....	....	....
Austria	122	93.3	94.9	98.2	94.6	92.7	93.9	93.3	94.2	96.2	98.1	100.0	97.4	95.3	....	....
Belgium	124	84.6	87.5	88.3	88.6	87.8	91.4	87.7	89.5	91.2	94.4	100.0	96.6	93.1	....	....
Finland	172	117.2	110.6	114.2	118.8	125.4	123.0	109.9	94.4	84.3	88.8	100.0	91.5	90.2	....	....
France	132	91.0	95.9	97.2	95.4	93.1	97.4	95.9	98.2	101.1	99.0	100.0	97.8	93.6	....	....
Germany	134	77.0	84.3	89.6	87.4	85.6	88.9	88.8	93.3	96.4	96.3	100.0	98.1	92.7	....	....
Ireland	178	110.4	112.5	105.8	100.5	96.5	101.2	99.2	101.5	99.2	99.0	100.0	101.4	100.4	....	....
Italy	136	125.3	128.3	129.5	127.4	131.6	134.1	133.0	129.0	111.0	107.4	100.0	114.0	115.8	....	....
Netherlands	138	90.3	95.8	98.4	99.0	95.9	97.6	96.1	95.7	98.0	96.7	100.0	97.2	94.6	....	....
Spain	184	102.0	96.0	96.1	99.8	107.5	111.7	114.4	110.6	98.1	95.5	100.0	101.1	97.4	....	....
Denmark	128	72.8	76.9	81.7	80.5	77.7	85.0	84.5	89.9	93.1	95.8	100.0	98.0	94.8	....	....
Norway	142	92.4	88.1	89.7	96.8	97.0	92.3	91.7	91.3	91.9	91.6	100.0	99.5	102.1	....	....
Sweden	144	100.3	99.2	99.2	103.8	109.5	111.8	117.7	119.7	99.2	99.6	100.0	107.1	105.1	....	....
Switzerland	146	93.6	94.3	95.5	94.4	90.0	94.2	91.9	88.4	89.9	95.0	100.0	95.7	89.2	....	....
United Kingdom	112	113.9	104.7	105.0	112.7	111.1	109.9	109.4	105.8	99.0	101.5	100.0	104.9	122.8	....	....

Industrial Countries

(1995=100)

Based on Relative Wholesale Prices (63ey.110)

1985	1986	1987	1988	1989	1990	1991	1992	1993	1994	1995	1996	1997	1998	1999		
152.6	124.5	112.9	107.7	114.2	110.3	108.1	105.3	108.9	106.7	100.0	107.4	115.4	....	....	United States	111
101.4	98.1	100.9	107.8	110.6	107.7	108.2	102.5	99.2	97.5	100.0	100.2	100.8	....	....	Canada	156
67.7	81.6	84.4	89.6	84.1	74.9	80.3	82.8	95.2	99.1	100.0	85.4	80.9	....	....	Japan	158
														....	Euro Area	163
99.6	100.0	101.4	98.8	96.4	98.7	97.7	98.1	99.4	99.7	100.0	98.2	95.7	....	....	Austria	122
100.2	95.9	96.1	94.0	95.7	97.3	94.8	95.7	94.4	96.6	100.0	98.2	95.3	....	....	Belgium	124
110.3	105.6	106.6	109.8	115.6	117.0	110.6	97.0	86.2	92.7	100.0	95.5	93.5	....	....	Finland	172
90.8	96.6	98.4	97.0	95.5	97.9	95.9	97.4	99.0	99.0	100.0	97.6	93.3	....	....	France	132
83.6	90.1	92.1	90.1	88.2	90.8	91.4	94.8	97.3	96.7	100.0	96.0	91.9	....	....	Germany	134
100.1	104.8	103.0	102.2	101.5	102.2	99.4	102.9	101.1	100.2	100.0	101.5	100.4	....	....	Ireland	178
112.2	114.5	117.2	115.8	119.7	127.7	121.3	119.0	104.7	103.0	100.0	113.2	113.5	....	....	Italy	136
86.1	91.8	94.9	92.5	91.0	92.7	92.8	96.6	99.5	97.5	100.0	99.1	96.0	....	....	Netherlands	138
103.2	103.4	103.4	107.5	112.8	114.6	115.1	112.9	101.1	97.3	100.0	101.5	97.7	....	....	Spain	184
90.1	91.9	95.1	94.4	93.1	96.9	95.3	96.2	98.0	96.9	100.0	100.1	98.2	....	....	Denmark	128
99.3	100.6	101.9	103.1	101.8	100.2	99.0	100.4	100.3	99.1	100.0	100.4	101.1	....	....	Norway	142
100.5	101.5	102.4	105.7	110.3	109.3	109.4	108.4	92.4	94.2	100.0	106.3	102.3	....	....	Sweden	144
85.6	92.6	95.9	94.7	89.1	93.2	91.9	90.0	92.4	96.8	100.0	96.2	89.3	....	....	Switzerland	146
103.0	97.1	98.1	105.1	102.6	104.1	109.7	108.2	102.3	104.1	100.0	103.9	121.4	....	....	United Kingdom	112

Based on Relative Export Unit Values (74ey.110)

1985	1986	1987	1988	1989	1990	1991	1992	1993	1994	1995	1996	1997	1998	1999		
138.2	118.6	110.8	108.3	111.1	107.1	107.4	105.6	108.7	105.5	100.0	103.1	113.4	....	....	United States	111
115.2	110.8	112.3	115.5	117.9	113.1	110.3	104.6	102.8	101.5	100.0	101.4	98.6	....	....	Canada	156
70.3	76.6	76.4	79.0	78.0	72.8	78.4	82.1	93.2	98.7	100.0	92.9	88.0	....	....	Japan	158
														....	Euro Area	163
97.7	100.5	101.8	101.6	98.8	101.0	100.0	101.5	105.2	105.8	100.0	101.2	100.3	....	....	Austria	122
94.0	96.6	96.5	95.3	97.1	98.5	96.3	97.3	97.9	98.5	100.0	100.0	100.5	....	....	Belgium	124
97.5	93.9	95.5	99.4	103.8	104.3	98.4	89.8	82.3	88.2	100.0	97.8	93.7	....	....	Finland	172
97.5	100.3	100.7	99.0	97.2	99.0	96.5	96.9	98.0	99.6	100.0	99.1	96.5	....	....	France	132
92.0	99.3	102.8	99.1	97.9	100.7	98.8	100.8	97.7	95.7	100.0	94.4	88.4	....	....	Germany	134
														....	Ireland	178
106.0	112.1	114.8	112.2	114.0	118.9	119.9	119.2	106.6	104.8	100.0	112.1	112.4	....	....	Italy	136
92.9	86.3	83.6	89.6	98.7	101.2	98.2	97.8	98.0	97.1	100.0	98.6	98.5	....	....	Netherlands	138
91.1	97.3	99.0	102.2	103.0	107.5	112.4	113.9	107.6	101.6	100.0	101.8	100.4	....	....	Spain	184
86.9	92.8	95.4	92.1	89.9	94.4	93.3	95.2	96.8	98.0	100.0	100.2	99.8	....	....	Denmark	128
101.4	96.6	97.6	112.7	117.2	105.7	100.7	95.2	92.3	90.8	100.0	96.3	95.8	....	....	Norway	142
95.4	96.0	97.7	99.1	101.9	102.9	103.4	102.3	90.7	93.4	100.0	104.4	100.9	....	....	Sweden	144
76.0	85.0	88.3	87.4	83.4	89.5	90.9	90.1	94.1	99.7	100.0	100.5	98.1	....	....	Switzerland	146
98.0	93.4	95.3	100.7	94.8	94.4	96.4	95.1	98.2	100.5	100.0	102.1	111.3	....	....	United Kingdom	112

Based on Relative Consumer Prices (..rec)

1985	1986	1987	1988	1989	1990	1991	1992	1993	1994	1995	1996	1997	1998	1999		
148.6	124.8	112.4	105.9	109.3	104.7	103.5	101.2	104.7	103.4	100.0	104.3	112.1	120.0	119.3	United States	111
126.6	114.6	114.7	121.0	129.5	128.1	131.9	121.1	113.6	103.4	100.0	101.7	103.2	98.6	97.6	Canada	156
61.1	78.4	82.5	88.1	80.6	71.6	76.8	79.2	93.6	98.3	100.0	84.4	80.2	78.9	89.3	Japan	158
79.1	92.7	99.2	95.1	90.8	99.3	96.1	100.8	95.7	95.2	100.0	99.9	90.8	93.0	88.5	Euro Area	163
86.3	90.2	92.6	92.1	90.8	92.5	91.6	93.3	95.7	96.4	100.0	98.0	94.6	94.6	92.8	Austria	122
88.2	91.9	94.8	92.2	90.9	94.8	94.1	95.0	95.0	96.5	100.0	98.1	93.6	93.4	91.8	Belgium	124
108.0	108.0	110.3	112.8	119.3	122.4	116.9	101.1	86.2	91.7	100.0	96.0	93.0	93.1	90.7	Finland	172
94.5	97.9	99.1	96.9	94.8	98.2	95.2	96.6	97.7	97.4	100.0	99.9	95.6	96.0	93.2	France	132
84.7	89.5	92.5	90.1	88.1	90.8	87.2	91.5	95.4	95.7	100.0	96.8	92.0	92.5	89.5	Germany	134
102.5	109.9	108.4	104.7	102.4	107.1	104.1	106.9	99.1	99.4	100.0	101.9	101.6	97.0	94.1	Ireland	178
112.5	120.5	124.0	122.9	125.6	131.5	132.5	130.6	110.5	107.2	100.0	111.6	112.3	113.1	110.9	Italy	136
90.9	96.2	97.9	95.6	91.8	93.7	92.1	93.7	95.3	96.0	100.0	98.2	93.6	94.4	93.7	Netherlands	138
88.0	93.7	97.5	102.1	108.1	114.8	116.2	115.7	103.1	98.3	100.0	102.2	97.4	97.4	96.7	Spain	184
86.5	92.0	96.2	95.8	93.9	98.1	94.9	96.0	96.4	95.9	100.0	99.3	96.5	98.3	97.6	Denmark	128
105.2	103.6	105.7	108.3	107.6	106.5	103.2	103.5	99.3	97.2	100.0	99.8	101.1	98.2	97.8	Norway	142
109.1	108.4	108.2	110.9	113.7	118.2	123.9	123.9	101.7	100.2	100.0	108.4	103.0	100.1	97.0	Sweden	144
81.2	86.7	90.0	88.4	83.2	89.2	89.2	87.7	89.7	93.9	100.0	97.3	90.0	91.1	89.4	Switzerland	146
112.4	104.6	104.5	112.9	113.2	117.1	119.8	115.6	103.5	103.7	100.0	102.4	120.5	128.1	127.6	United Kingdom	112

(See notes in the back of the book.)

Production and Labor Indices

Industrial Production

		1970	1971	1972	1973	1974	1975	1976	1977	1978	1979	1980	1981	1982	1983	1984
													Index Numbers (1995=100):			
Industrial Countries	110	55.9	57.0	61.1	66.8	66.6	61.2	66.2	69.2	72.0	75.5	75.4	75.3	73.3	74.9	79.8
United States	111	51.3	52.0	57.1	61.7	60.8	55.5	60.6	65.5	69.3	71.6	69.7	70.8	67.0	69.5	75.7
Canada	156	51.6	I 54.4	58.5	64.3	66.5	62.5	65.9	67.4	70.2	I 74.3	71.8	73.3	66.1	70.4	78.9
Australia	193	57.2	59.4	60.2	66.3	68.4	63.2	66.4	I 65.3	66.3	69.8	70.2	72.3	71.9	69.8	74.6
Japan	158	47.7	49.0	52.5	60.4	58.1	51.6	57.3	59.7	63.5	68.2	71.4	72.1	72.4	74.5	81.5
New Zealand	196	....	....	....	....	....	....	....	76.9	75.3	80.2	79.9	83.6	87.6	85.6	97.3
Euro Area																
Austria	122	47.7	50.6	54.6	57.5	60.2	56.4	60.0	62.4	64.0	68.7	70.6	69.8	69.3	69.3	73.4
Belgium	124	65.6	67.3	71.5	75.9	78.7	71.2	77.4	77.4	79.0	82.6	81.6	79.4	79.6	81.1	83.2
Finland	172	42.0	42.6	47.8	51.2	53.6	51.6	52.1	52.4	55.1	60.9	I 65.9	67.7	68.2	70.4	73.7
France	132	66.4	70.3	74.3	79.6	81.6	76.3	82.3	83.6	85.6	88.9	I 89.6	88.7	88.1	87.5	87.7
Germany	134	72.9	74.0	76.7	80.9	79.1	73.7	79.1	81.0	82.5	86.6	86.8	84.7	82.0	82.4	84.7
Ireland	178	20.6	21.4	22.3	24.5	25.2	24.2	26.3	28.5	30.7	33.1	I 32.7	34.5	34.2	36.9	40.5
Italy	136	58.1	58.1	60.6	66.5	69.5	63.1	70.9	71.7	73.1	77.9	82.2	80.9	78.4	75.9	78.5
Luxembourg	137	64.4	63.5	66.2	74.1	76.6	59.8	61.2	61.5	64.5	66.6	64.4	60.8	61.3	64.6	73.2
Netherlands	138	57.7	61.6	64.0	69.5	72.7	71.9	76.6	76.6	76.6	79.8	I 79.0	77.3	74.0	76.7	79.8
Portugal	182	48.0	52.1	59.1	66.0	67.6	64.1	67.2	74.9	80.3	111.7	118.1	64.3	69.3	71.5	73.6
Spain	184	49.6	52.9	61.3	68.2	73.3	I 70.0	73.4	77.4	79.2	80.5	80.5	79.9	79.8	81.1	81.8
Denmark	128	I 52.5	53.6	57.4	59.5	I 57.4	54.3	59.8	60.5	62.2	64.6	64.8	64.9	66.3	68.6	76.0
Greece	174	51.2	56.2	65.1	75.3	73.8	77.1	85.2	86.5	93.1	98.8	99.7	....	98.3	96.9	98.2
Norway	142	31.8	I 33.2	35.7	37.7	39.4	41.5	43.9	43.5	48.1	51.8	I 55.1	56.7	56.4	61.6	66.4
Sweden	144	68.3	I 68.9	70.4	75.5	79.0	77.7	75.7	71.5	70.5	75.4	74.5	73.7	72.4	75.4	80.8
Switzerland	146	71.6	72.7	74.5	78.6	79.4	69.4	69.7	73.8	74.0	75.3	79.5	79.1	76.1	75.6	77.5
United Kingdom	112	69.2	68.8	70.0	76.3	74.8	70.7	73.0	76.8	79.0	82.1	76.7	74.2	75.7	78.4	78.5

Wages

		1970	1971	1972	1973	1974	1975	1976	1977	1978	1979	1980	1981	1982	1983	1984
													Index Numbers (1995=100):			
Industrial Countries	110	14.7	16.1	17.7	18.8	21.2	24.1	26.6	29.2	33.5	36.1	39.8	43.6	47.1	53.3	55.3
United States	111	27.1	28.9	30.9	33.0	35.8	39.0	42.2	45.9	49.9	54.1	58.8	64.6	68.7	71.4	74.3
Canada	156	17.9	19.5	21.0	22.9	26.0	30.0	34.2	37.9	40.6	44.2	48.6	54.5	60.9	I 65.1	69.0
Australia	193	11.5	12.8	13.9	15.7	19.2	22.7	25.9	28.7	31.2	33.9	37.9	42.3	I 47.3	50.6	55.4
Japan	158	I 18.4	21.1	24.4	29.0	36.2	42.7	48.0	52.5	56.2	59.4	62.9	66.1	69.4	71.6	74.0
New Zealand	196	....	....	....	....	....	....	....	....	....	....	....	....	....	....	....
Euro Area																
Austria	122	18.0	20.5	22.9	25.8	29.9	33.9	36.9	40.1	42.4	44.8	48.4	51.3	54.5	57.0	59.8
Belgium (1990=100)	124	19.6	22.0	25.1	29.2	35.3	42.4	47.1	51.4	55.0	I 59.3	64.8	71.3	75.7	79.0	82.9
Finland	172	9.7	11.1	12.7	14.8	17.7	I 21.2	24.7	27.1	29.1	32.2	36.2	40.9	45.3	49.7	54.2
France	132	9.7	10.9	12.2	I 13.8	16.5	19.8	23.1	26.4	30.1	34.7	40.3	46.1	55.4	62.5	67.8
Germany (1990=100)	134	24.5	27.7	30.6	34.6	39.6	44.1	46.7	50.7	54.1	57.9	62.8	67.4	70.9	73.8	76.2
Ireland	178	6.7	7.8	9.0	10.8	12.7	16.6	19.9	23.5	27.0	30.9	36.5	42.6	48.0	53.7	60.2
Italy	136	4.7	5.2	5.7	7.0	8.4	10.8	13.0	16.6	19.4	23.0	28.1	34.8	40.9	47.0	52.3
Netherlands	138	26.1	29.2	I 32.9	37.2	43.6	49.5	53.9	57.7	61.0	63.7	66.5	68.7	73.4	75.3	76.2
Spain	184	I 3.3	3.8	4.4	5.3	6.7	8.6	11.2	14.6	18.4	I 22.6	26.8	I 30.2	35.1	40.3	45.1
Denmark (1990=100)	128	15.1	17.4	19.5	22.4	26.9	32.0	35.6	39.2	43.2	48.1	53.6	58.3	64.4	68.7	72.0
Greece	174	1.3	1.4	1.5	1.8	2.2	2.8	3.6	4.3	5.4	6.5	8.2	10.5	14.0	16.7	21.1
Iceland	176	.3	.3	.4	.5	.7	.9	I 1.2	1.6	2.5	3.6	5.6	8.6	13.4	20.3	22.6
Norway	142	12.3	13.8	15.1	16.6	19.5	I 23.4	27.0	30.0	32.4	33.4	36.5	40.3	44.3	48.0	52.1
Sweden	144	14.9	14.7	16.4	17.7	19.9	23.4	26.6	28.4	30.9	33.2	36.0	40.4	43.0	45.7	50.3
Switzerland (1990=100)	146	I 35.6	I 39.0	I 42.5	46.3	I 51.1	54.8	55.5	I 58.2	59.7	61.8	65.1	69.2	74.2	77.1	79.1
United Kingdom	112	8.1	9.0	10.1	11.5	13.5	17.1	19.9	21.7	24.5	28.3	34.1	38.5	42.1	45.6	48.4

Employment

		1970	1971	1972	1973	1974	1975	1976	1977	1978	1979	1980	1981	1982	1983	1984
													Index Numbers (1995=100):			
Industrial Countries	110	92.2	92.6	93.3	95.5	96.2	93.2	93.5	94.4	95.8	97.3	97.4	96.7	94.6	93.7	94.9
United States	111	60.5	60.8	62.9	65.5	66.8	65.7	67.7	70.4	74.0	76.7	77.2	77.8	76.4	76.9	80.6
Canada	156	109.0	108.0	109.9	115.3	118.8	112.2	113.7	112.2	113.3	116.7	114.5	115.3	104.5	101.5	98.4
Australia	193	118.4	122.4	119.3	124.0	123.2	113.2	114.8	114.5	109.4	109.5	111.8	112.3	108.8	102.5	102.6
Japan	158	104.1	104.8	102.8	103.1	102.7	97.3	95.3	94.5	92.4	91.9	92.9	93.8	94.3	94.0	95.1
New Zealand	196	....	82.3	81.9	85.6	89.3	87.9	89.3	90.4	86.7	89.4	89.8	88.0	89.9	85.3	88.0
Euro Area																
Austria	122	77.9	80.0	81.9	85.0	86.6	86.6	87.5	89.2	89.9	90.4	90.9	91.2	90.2	89.1	89.5
Finland	172	....	....	....	....	....	....	131.8	130.4	126.8	131.7	137.4	139.4	135.3	132.7	131.4
France	132	....	....	....	....	....	....	....	....	....	....	132.6	128.5	127.3	124.8	121.5
Germany (1990=100)	134	119.9	119.1	116.4	116.9	113.8	106.4	103.9	103.0	102.3	102.6	103.3	101.0	97.5	93.5	92.5
Ireland	178	93.3	92.9	93.3	97.8	99.4	93.3	93.0	95.9	97.8	107.2	107.4	104.3	101.1	95.0	92.2
Italy	136	121.8	123.5	121.6	121.9	125.1	125.1	123.2	124.4	123.0	123.3	123.9	122.6	119.9	116.6	111.6
Luxembourg (1990=100)	137	82.3	85.1	87.7	90.2	93.7	94.1	92.2	90.9	89.7	90.5	91.2	90.6	89.6	87.6	86.5
Netherlands	138	145.8	144.1	139.9	136.0	134.4	130.1	125.9	121.7	118.1	116.1	115.0	111.7	95.5	103.6	102.5
Spain	184	102.9	103.6	104.9	103.9	105.4	103.9	104.2	103.2	101.2	98.8	94.7	91.5	90.4	89.6	88.6
Denmark (1990=100)	128	....	....	128.6	126.7	123.5	106.7	106.6	106.2	105.1	106.4	103.1	96.1	95.6	97.1	104.0
Greece	174	88.6	94.0	97.5	103.5	104.7	105.6	112.0	117.2	120.9	124.2	125.6	127.0	127.1	125.7	126.1
Norway	142	79.8	80.2	82.9	83.1	83.4	85.1	86.1	87.7	89.2	90.0	92.1	92.9	93.6	94.1	94.7
Sweden	144	138.1	136.8	135.9	138.4	145.9	148.3	142.3	137.1	132.3	133.0	133.2	128.0	123.7	123.2	124.6
Switzerland	146	149.2	147.2	143.4	142.1	141.7	128.8	119.9	119.5	120.0	119.9	121.9	122.0	118.2	114.1	113.4
United Kingdom	112	97.4	97.9	97.9	100.3	100.9	100.6	99.8	97.9	100.8	104.7	101.0	97.3	95.2	95.5	96.4

Sector Coverage

Country		Mining	Mfg.	Util.	Constr.	Serv.	Agri.	Country		Mining	Mfg.	Util.	Constr.	Serv.	Agri.
		Industrial Sector			Other					Industrial Sector			Other		
United States	66..c	x	x	x				Belgium	66..b	x	x				
	65ey		x						65	x	x		x		
	67..c	x	x	x	x	x		Denmark	66..c	x	x				
Canada	66..c	x	x	x					65		x		x		
	65ey		x						67eyc		x				
	67ey		x					Finland	66..c	x	x	x			
Australia	66..c	x	x	x					65ey		x				
	65	x	x	x	x	x	x		67ez	x	x	x			
	67eyc		x					France	66..c	x	x				
Japan	66..c	x	x						65	x	x		x		
	65	x	x	x					67..c	x	x				
	67eyc		x					Germany	66..c	x	x	x	x		
New Zealand	66eyc		x						65..c	x	x	x	x		
	65	x	x	x	x	x	x		67	x	x				
	67ey		x					Greece	66eyb		x				
Austria	66..b	x	x	x					65		x				
	65	x	x	x					67ey	x	x	x			
	67	x	x	x	x	x	x								

Industrial Production

1985	1986	1987	1988	1989	1990	1991	1992	1993	1994	1995	1996	1997	1998	1999		
(66..i)																
82.1	**83.1**	**86.0**	**90.8**	**94.2**	**95.8**	**95.1**	**94.2**	**93.0**	**96.5**	**100.0**	**102.3**	**106.9**	**107.3**	**109.2**	Industrial Countries..........	110
77.0	77.8	81.4	85.1	86.6	86.5	84.7	87.4	90.4	95.4	100.0	104.4	111.0	115.7	119.7	United States	111
83.3	I 83.3	87.3	91.9	91.8	88.8	85.0	I 86.0	89.9	95.7	100.0	101.7	107.3	109.8	114.7	Canada..........	156
80.6	80.4	84.2	88.9	92.9	95.1	I 91.7	92.0	94.7	99.8	100.0	104.3	I 107.3	108.5	111.0	Australia	193
84.6	84.4	87.2	95.6	101.2	105.3	107.2	100.6	96.1	96.7	100.0	102.9	I 107.3	99.7	100.1	Japan	158
95.5	94.1	93.5	89.1	88.9	85.4	81.7	85.1	91.4	96.5	100.0	100.6	102.4	99.8	101.6	New Zealand	196
															Euro Area	
76.6	77.6	77.9	81.5	86.5	93.0	94.4	93.3	91.4	95.0	100.0	100.9	107.9	118.3	124.0	Austria	122
84.6	85.4	87.5	92.7	95.9	99.4	97.4	97.3	92.5	94.1	100.0	100.8	105.1	101.4	110.6	Belgium	124
76.5	77.7	81.7	84.6	87.4	I 87.3	79.9	80.3	84.3	93.8	100.0	103.6	114.1	122.1	....	Finland	172
87.9	88.7	90.4	94.7	98.6	I 100.4	99.2	98.0	94.3	98.0	100.0	100.3	I 104.2	109.6	112.0	France	132
88.1	90.0	90.1	93.3	97.8	103.2	I 103.5	102.0	95.3	99.3	100.0	99.8	102.6	106.2	107.7	Germany	134
41.9	42.8	46.6	53.0	59.4	62.1	63.8	70.1	74.0	83.3	100.0	108.0	125.4	146.1	....	Ireland	178
79.4	82.2	85.4	90.5	93.4	93.5	92.6	92.4	90.2	94.9	100.0	99.1	102.4	104.3	104.4	Italy	136
78.1	80.3	80.7	90.3	97.1	97.5	97.1	96.3	93.7	99.1	100.0	100.7	106.2	114.1	118.1	Luxembourg	137
83.1	83.1	84.0	86.5	89.8	91.5	I 94.0	93.8	92.7	I 97.2	100.0	103.8	106.6	107.7	107.7	Netherlands	138
74.4	79.2	82.8	86.0	91.3	99.9	101.4	99.5	96.4	95.4	100.0	101.4	103.9	107.9	....	Portugal	182
83.4	86.0	90.0	92.7	96.9	96.9	96.2	93.5	89.0	95.6	100.0	99.3	106.1	111.8	114.9	Spain	184
I 79.4	85.3	82.8	84.4	86.5	I 86.5	86.6	89.1	86.6	95.3	100.0	I 101.7	107.4	109.8	112.5	Denmark	128
100.7	100.0	98.0	102.9	105.3	102.3	101.4	100.1	96.6	97.7	100.0	100.3	102.2	106.5	107.1	Greece	174
68.7	71.1	75.7	77.6	85.2	86.5	I 88.5	89.6	92.1	97.2	100.0	102.5	106.0	108.8	....	Norway	142
83.2	83.6	85.7	86.8	90.0	I 87.8	83.3	82.0	82.9	91.5	I 100.0	101.0	107.6	114.1	115.5	Sweden	144
82.0	85.0	86.0	93.0	94.5	97.0	96.9	95.9	93.9	98.0	100.0	100.0	104.6	108.4	....	Switzerland	146
82.8	84.8	88.2	92.5	94.4	94.1	91.0	91.3	93.3	98.3	100.0	101.1	102.1	102.7	103.2	United Kingdom	112

Wages

1985	1986	1987	1988	1989	1990	1991	1992	1993	1994	1995	1996	1997	1998	1999		
(65, 65ey, 65..c)																
57.8	**59.8**	**61.6**	**69.9**	**74.8**	**78.0**	**81.7**	**84.6**	**95.3**	**97.8**	**100.0**	**102.5**	**105.0**	**105.6**	**106.0**	Industrial Countries..........	110
77.1	78.7	80.1	82.4	84.8	87.5	90.4	92.6	95.0	97.5	100.0	103.3	106.4	109.1	112.5	United States	111
71.6	73.9	75.8	79.3	83.6	88.4	93.3	95.6	97.7	98.6	100.0	103.2	104.1	106.3	106.5	Canada	156
58.2	62.7	66.0	70.5	76.2	82.8	86.9	90.4	92.1	95.1	100.0	104.0	108.3	112.7	115.8	Australia	193
76.4	78.6	80.2	83.0	85.6	88.9	91.9	93.9	95.7	97.9	100.0	101.9	103.4	103.1	103.6	Japan	158
....	....	....	....	....	....	....	....	97.5	98.5	100.0	101.9	104.3	106.2	107.8	New Zealand	196
															Euro Area	
63.4	66.3	68.4	70.9	74.1	79.4	83.5	87.5	92.1	95.8	100.0	....	....	....	....	Austria	122
85.9	88.3	I 90.0	90.7	95.8	100.0	105.1	110.1	112.4	114.7						Belgium (1990=100)	124
I 58.3	61.9	I 66.2	71.6	78.1	I 85.8	....	93.0	93.7	95.5	100.0	103.9	....	....	....	Finland	172
71.9	75.1	78.6	81.1	84.9	86.2	90.0	93.4	96.3	99.2	100.0	101.9	104.7	107.6	110.0	France	132
79.3	83.5	87.6	91.0	94.9	100.0	107.2	114.8	121.7	123.6						Germany (1990=100)	134
65.0	69.9	73.4	76.9	80.0	83.1	86.7	90.2	95.1	97.8	100.0	102.5	105.4	110.2	....	Ireland	178
58.1	60.9	64.8	68.8	72.9	78.2	85.9	90.6	93.7	97.0	100.0	103.2	106.9	109.9	112.4	Italy	136
79.9	81.2	82.3	83.4	84.5	87.0	I 90.2	94.1	97.1	I 98.9	100.0	101.7	104.8	108.1	....	Netherlands	138
49.6	55.0	59.1	62.9	67.5	73.4	79.4	85.5	91.3	95.4	100.0	105.3	109.6	....	115.5	Spain	184
75.3	79.4	86.9	92.5	96.2	100.0	104.2	107.2	....	....	....	....	....	....	....	Denmark (1990=100)	128
25.3	28.5	31.2	37.0	44.6	53.2	62.1	70.7	78.1	88.3	100.0	108.6	118.3	123.9	....	Greece	174
29.9	37.5	62.6	79.4	90.0	I 96.9	98.4	98.5	96.3	96.8	100.0	....	....	....	....	Iceland	176
56.4	62.1	72.2	76.0	79.7	84.3	88.7	91.5	93.9	96.6	100.0	104.2	....	....	....	Norway	142
54.3	57.6	62.5	67.5	74.2	81.1	84.9	88.8	91.7	95.5	100.0	107.2	111.4	115.4	118.0	Sweden	144
82.1	85.4	87.5	90.7	94.3	100.0	107.5	113.4	116.2	....	....	....	....	....	....	Switzerland (1990=100)	146
52.4	56.6	61.0	66.3	72.4	79.4	85.6	90.7	93.6	97.0	100.0	103.5	108.0	113.5	119.0	United Kingdom	112

Employment

1985	1986	1987	1988	1989	1990	1991	1992	1993	1994	1995	1996	1997	1998	1999		
(67, 67ey, 67..c, 67eyc)																
96.2	**97.2**	**98.1**	**99.6**	**101.5**	**102.8**	**102.3**	**101.3**	**99.7**	**99.6**	**100.0**	**99.8**	**100.6**	**101.4**	**101.4**	Industrial Countries..........	110
83.1	84.8	87.0	89.8	92.1	93.4	92.4	92.7	94.5	97.4	100.0	102.1	104.7	107.4	109.7	United States	111
100.4	102.5	112.0	113.1	113.7	105.7	92.6	93.5	93.2	96.1	100.0	102.4	106.1	110.3	112.8	Canada	156
101.8	102.1	103.8	107.0	110.5	107.6	101.1	100.1	95.8	99.1	100.0	100.3	101.8	98.5	96.4	Australia	193
96.6	97.2	95.9	96.9	99.1	101.7	104.2	104.9	104.2	101.8	100.0	97.7	96.9	95.6	93.1	Japan	158
89.0	106.5	100.9	92.2	86.7	83.7	80.9	86.4	86.4	96.3	100.0	98.7	94.8	97.1	93.3	New Zealand	196
															Euro Area	
89.9	90.6	90.8	91.6	93.3	95.5	97.7	99.6	99.6	100.1	100.0	99.3	99.6	100.2	101.3	Austria	122
130.7	129.0	124.7	121.2	123.0	121.7	110.0	99.2	92.9	93.3	100.0	100.5	101.4	104.0	106.8	Finland	172
118.2	116.0	113.3	112.1	113.0	113.6	111.5	108.5	103.2	101.0	100.0	97.2	96.5	96.9	96.8	France	132
93.7	95.3	95.2	95.0	97.3	100.0	101.4	99.0	91.9	85.9	....	....	....	....	....	Germany (1990=100)	134
88.4	87.1	86.2	86.4	88.4	90.7	91.7	91.7	90.9	94.2	100.0	105.4	111.2	114.5	....	Ireland	178
109.1	107.3	105.6	106.1	106.1	107.7	108.6	106.8	104.5	102.3	100.0	98.9	98.5	99.5	99.6	Italy	136
87.4	89.2	90.2	93.7	96.2	100.0	95.7	....	....	....	....	....	....	....	....	Luxembourg (1990=100)	137
103.6	105.7	106.7	106.7	108.5	110.9	111.1	110.0	106.7	102.2	100.0	98.9	100.0	....	....	Netherlands	138
87.8	92.3	95.1	97.8	101.8	104.5	104.7	102.7	98.3	97.4	100.0	102.9	106.0	109.7	114.7	Spain	184
108.1	111.2	105.3	102.1	100.0	100.0	96.8	94.7	88.5	....	....	....	....	....	....	Denmark (1990=100)	128
124.6	124.8	123.1	124.4	124.7	122.8	115.2	109.5	103.0	99.9	100.0	99.4	96.2	95.3	....	Greece	174
96.9	100.3	102.3	101.7	98.5	97.7	96.7	96.4	96.5	97.9	100.0	102.8	....	....	....	Norway	142
126.9	128.3	126.2	126.7	127.7	124.6	114.6	104.7	96.1	94.8	100.0	100.9	99.6	100.0	99.4	Sweden	144
114.4	116.0	115.8	115.8	117.0	118.7	116.6	110.7	105.0	101.0	100.0	98.5	95.7	95.9	95.9	Switzerland	146
96.6	96.5	99.1	101.5	103.1	102.5	99.3	97.1	97.8	98.7	100.0	101.3	104.3	106.1	107.4	United Kingdom	112

Sector Coverage

Country		Mining	Mfg.	Util.	Constr.	Serv.	Agri.	Country		Mining	Mfg.	Util.	Constr.	Serv.	Agri.
		Industrial Sector			**Other**					**Industrial Sector**			**Other**		
Iceland	65	x	x		x			Portugal	66..b	x	x	x			
Ireland	66..c	x	x	x				Spain	66..c	x	x	x			
	65ey		x						65	x	x	x	x	x	
	67ey		x						67	x	x	x	x	x	
Italy	66..c	x	x	x				Sweden	66..c	x	x				
	65ey	x	x	x	x				65	x	x				
	67	x	x	x					67	x	x	x			
Luxembourg	66..b	x	x	x				Switzerland	66..b	x	x	x			
	67	x	x	x					65	x	x	x	x		x
Netherlands	66..c	x	x	x					67ey	x		x			
	65		x					United Kingdom	66..c	x	x	x			
	67	x	x	x					65..c	x	x	x	x	x	x
Norway	66..c	x	x	x					67..c	x	x	x	x	x	x
	65		x												
	67	x	x	x											

(For more information please refer to the country notes in the monthly issues of IFS.)

Producer Prices/Wholesale Prices

		1970	1971	1972	1973	1974	1975	1976	1977	1978	1979	1980	1981	1982	1983	1984
													Percent Change over Previous Year:			
World	001	4.9	4.3	5.3	13.8	22.0	10.8	9.3	10.7	7.9	14.1	19.4	14.2	11.8	13.0	14.1
Industrial Countries	110	4.1	3.5	3.9	11.7	18.2	8.9	6.4	7.0	5.7	10.6	13.9	8.7	4.9	2.8	4.2
United States	111	3.6	3.3	4.4	13.1	18.8	9.2	4.6	6.1	7.8	12.5	14.1	9.1	2.0	1.3	2.4
Canada	156	2.5	1.9	4.5	11.1	19.0	11.4	5.1	7.8	9.2	14.5	13.4	10.2	6.7	3.5	4.5
Australia	193	4.3	4.9	4.8	8.6	15.3	15.1	11.3	10.2	8.2	14.8	14.0	8.4	8.9	8.1	5.4
Japan	158	3.6	−.7	.8	15.9	31.4	3.0	5.1	1.9	−2.5	7.3	17.8	1.4	1.8	−2.2	−.3
New Zealand	196	6.0	7.5	6.9	12.7	8.1	13.3	22.4	16.4	11.5	17.7	22.9	16.9	15.1	5.5	7.1
Euro Area																
Austria	122	4.7	5.2	3.9	1.2	15.2	6.4	5.8	3.0	1.0	4.2	8.6	8.0	3.2	.6	3.7
Belgium	124	...	...	...	...	...	...	...	...	...	...	...	14.1	13.5	6.7	7.6
Finland	172	4.4	5.0	8.4	17.5	24.3	13.6	8.2	10.1	5.6	9.7	16.4	12.8	7.2	5.6	5.4
France	132	...	...	...	...	...	...	...	...	...	...	...	11.7	10.7	8.8	9.2
Germany	134	4.9	4.2	2.6	6.6	13.4	4.6	3.7	2.8	1.1	4.8	7.6	7.8	5.9	1.5	2.9
Ireland	178	5.3	5.4	10.4	17.6	13.5	24.5	19.6	17.2	8.9	12.2	10.5	17.3	11.2	6.2	7.7
Italy	136	...	...	...	...	...	...	...	...	...	...	...	13.1	11.0	10.3
Luxembourg	137	...	...	...	...	...	...	...	...	...	...	...	10.7	17.9	4.9	6.2
Netherlands	138	4.7	4.4	4.8	6.2	9.0	6.0	6.9	5.5	1.5	2.6	7.4	8.7	5.7	1.3	4.5
Portugal	182	3.3	2.4	5.5	11.1	28.6	13.2	19.1	29.0	31.4	29.5	6.7	21.4	27.6	16.7	27.5
Spain	184	1.6	5.7	6.9	10.2	18.0	9.1	13.3	20.2	16.4	14.5	17.4	15.7	12.4	14.0	12.2
Denmark	128	7.7	3.3	5.8	14.7	21.7	5.7	8.0	7.4	4.3	9.9	13.7	15.7	10.7	5.0	7.5
Greece	174	3.9	3.5	6.3	23.5	30.9	8.3	14.1	13.7	10.3	21.0	28.4	25.9	16.0	19.8	21.4
Norway	142	...	...	...	...	...	...	...	...	4.0	7.2	13.4	10.5	8.5	6.5	6.9
Sweden	144	6.7	2.3	4.5	11.3	24.8	6.6	8.9	9.5	8.0	11.9	14.1	11.2	12.8	11.1	7.7
Switzerland	146	3.7	4.0	4.1	8.5	14.0	1.2	−1.0	−.1	−1.4	1.9	4.5	5.6	3.7	1.1	2.9
United Kingdom	112	7.1	9.0	5.2	7.5	1.6	22.9	16.5	18.9	9.0	11.8	16.0	10.7	8.5	6.5	6.0
Developing Countries	200	7.8	7.1	10.0	21.2	32.3	16.7	17.9	21.5	14.2	23.2	33.9	29.1	31.2	43.5	42.2
Africa	605	3.7	4.3	6.3	13.8	19.2	12.1	11.9	12.8	9.3	12.9	13.7	14.2	13.7	9.9	10.9
Central African Rep.	626	−.2	5.2	6.2	2.4	19.8	18.8	4.8	7.8	7.6	13.8	16.1	14.6	14.4	8.8	22.7
Congo, Rep. of	634	6.6	.7	12.8	5.3	15.3	14.0	13.5	12.3	9.8	8.9	14.0	13.7	15.3	7.0	14.5
Morocco	686	7.7	4.2	2.1	17.3	23.2	3.7	4.5	14.2	8.7	8.7	8.5	17.6	12.1	7.3	13.7
Sierra Leone	724	...	5.6	11.1	26.2	26.1	16.8	22.5	18.1	17.0	21.1	22.4	22.0	19.7	43.1	44.9
South Africa	199	2.9	5.0	8.3	13.3	17.9	16.8	15.8	13.0	9.9	15.2	16.2	13.7	14.0	10.5	8.4
Tunisia	744	4.0	7.4	1.5	5.4	21.2	9.5	1.2	4.9	3.1	7.3	10.8	12.5	16.9	6.6	8.6
Zambia	754	−2.4	−6.2	5.1	22.0	12.8	−6.7	19.3	22.0	16.4	24.3	13.4	1.4	6.6	24.1	27.9
Zimbabwe	698	...	...	...	...	...	...	...	...	...	...	...	...	...	...	...
Asia	505	4.4	5.3	8.7	17.2	34.6	8.1	5.2	9.1	4.6	18.8	22.4	12.8	4.7	8.9	9.8
China, P.R.: Hong Kong	532	...	...	...	...	...	...	...	...	...	...	...	...	...	...	...
India	534	6.2	5.0	8.8	16.4	28.6	3.9	−2.0	7.6	−.2	11.6	20.1	12.2	2.4	7.9	6.9
Indonesia	536	...	...	13.5	38.2	48.0	6.3	14.7	14.0	9.6	49.6	26.8	11.1	7.4	17.9	11.0
Korea	542	9.2	8.6	13.8	6.9	42.1	26.6	12.1	9.0	11.6	18.8	38.9	20.4	4.7	.2	.7
Malaysia	548	...	...	...	...	...	...	...	...	...	...	...	...	...	...	...
Pakistan	564	2.8	2.8	6.2	17.5	27.3	26.8	9.9	10.2	7.9	6.7	12.3	13.1	9.0	5.4	10.0
Philippines	566	—	15.7	10.1	23.7	47.7	5.4	13.8	7.5	4.8	19.0	18.3	14.6	10.7	16.0	67.3
Singapore	576	...	...	...	...	...	−1.5	6.7	4.5	1.6	14.4	19.6	3.9	−4.2	−3.6	−.6
Sri Lanka	524	...	...	...	...	...	3.4	8.2	21.0	15.8	9.5	33.8	17.0	5.5	25.0	25.6
Thailand	578	−.5	.2	7.8	22.9	28.9	3.7	3.9	7.8	7.5	11.2	20.1	9.5	.9	2.0	−3.1
Europe	170	1.7	2.3	1.9	2.9	3.3	10.6	4.6	2.0	3.7	2.1	6.7	7.9	72.8	11.2	25.8
Armenia	911	...	...	...	...	...	...	...	...	...	...	...	...	...	...	...
Belarus	913	...	...	...	...	...	...	...	...	...	...	...	...	...	...	...
Bulgaria	918	...	...	...	...	...	...	...	...	...	...	...	...	...	...	...
Croatia	960	...	...	...	...	...	...	...	...	...	...	...	...	...	...	...
Cyprus	423	...	...	...	...	...	...	...	...	...	...	...	...	...	...	...
Czech Republic	935	...	...	...	...	...	...	...	...	...	...	...	...	...	...	...
Czechoslovakia	934	...	—	−.1	.1	−.2	−.1	—	4.7	.5	.7	1.7	4.8	7.7	−.3	8.2
Estonia	939	...	...	...	...	...	...	...	...	...	...	...	...	...	...	...
Hungary	944	1.7	2.3	1.9	2.9	3.3	10.6	4.6	2.0	3.7	2.3	15.3	6.3	4.7	5.6	4.2
Kazakhstan	916	...	...	...	...	...	...	...	...	...	...	...	...	...	...	...
Kyrgyz Republic	917	...	...	...	...	...	...	...	...	...	...	...	...	...	...	...
Latvia	941	...	...	...	...	...	...	...	...	...	...	...	...	...	...	...
Lithuania	946	...	...	...	...	...	...	...	...	...	...	...	...	...	...	...
Poland	964	...	...	...	...	...	...	...	...	...	14.9	2.0	4.2	9.2	122.3	15.3	14.5
Romania	968	...	...	...	...	...	...	...	...	...	...	...	...	...	...	...
Russia	922	...	...	...	...	...	...	...	...	...	...	...	...	...	...	...
Slovak Republic	936	...	...	...	...	...	...	...	...	...	...	...	4.3	7.5	.9	8.2
Slovenia	961	...	...	...	...	...	...	...	...	...	...	...	...	...	...	...
Turkey	186	...	...	...	...	...	...	...	...	...	...	...	...	27.0	30.5	50.3
Ukraine	926	...	...	...	...	...	...	...	...	...	...	...	...	...	...	...
Yugoslavia, SFR	188	9.2	15.2	11.0	13.2	29.9	21.6	6.4	9.6	8.1	12.6	28.7	43.4	24.8	32.7	60.0

Calculated from Indices

1985	1986	1987	1988	1989	1990	1991	1992	1993	1994	1995	1996	1997	1998	1999		
11.1	5.8	11.7	18.4	21.7	26.8	13.5	14.1	16.2	24.2	13.4	6.5	4.8	4.3	4.2	World	001
2.0	−2.9	1.0	3.0	4.5	2.8	1.0	.5	.7	1.2	3.3	1.1	.6	−1.3	−.2	Industrial Countries	110
−.5	−2.9	2.6	4.0	5.0	3.6	.2	.6	1.5	1.3	3.6	2.3	—	−2.5	.8	United States	111
2.7	.9	2.8	4.3	2.0	.3	−1.0	.5	3.6	6.1	7.4	.4	.9	−.1	1.6	Canada	156
6.6	5.6	7.3	9.1	5.1	6.0	1.5	1.5	2.0	.8	4.2	.3	1.2	.6	.7	Australia	193
−1.1	−9.1	−3.8	−1.0	2.6	2.1	.2	−1.5	−3.8	−2.0	−.9	.1	1.5	−1.6	−3.4	Japan	158
15.3	5.7	7.9	5.2	7.1	4.7	.9	2.1	2.4	1.3	.8	.5	.4	.7	.8	New Zealand	196
															Euro Area	
2.6	−5.3	−2.0	−.2	1.8	2.9	.8	−.2	−.4	1.3	.3	—	.4	−.5	−.8	Austria	122
2.6	−11.5	−5.0	1.6	6.6	−1.0	−1.0	−1.8	−2.5	1.6	3.2	2.0	3.8	−1.8	.5	Belgium	124
4.5	−5.2	.9	4.1	5.0	3.3	.3	1.1	3.0	1.3	.7	−.9	1.6	−1.4	−.1	Finland	172
4.4	−2.8	.6	5.2	5.5	−1.2	−1.3	−1.6	−2.8	1.1	6.1	−2.7	−.6	−.8	−1.5	France	132
2.4	−2.5	−2.5	1.3	3.2	1.7	2.1	1.4	.2	.6	1.7	−.4	1.1	−.4	−1.0	Germany	134
3.2	−2.2	.6	4.1	5.5	−2.7	1.2	.9	4.7	1.0	2.1	.4	−.4	1.5	.4	Ireland	178
7.7	.2	3.0	3.5	5.9	4.1	3.3	1.9	3.8	3.7	7.9	1.9	1.3	.1	−.3	Italy	136
3.0	−2.5	−6.5	2.6	7.6	−2.0	−2.6	−2.7	−1.3	1.5	3.9	−3.1	1.5	2.4	−3.1	Luxembourg	137
1.6	−2.7	−1.2	.5	3.6	1.0	2.3	1.8	.1	.5	1.5	2.0	1.8	−.2	1.0	Netherlands	138
21.2	9.2	....	....	....	....	....	....	....	....	....	....	....	....	....	Portugal	182
8.0	.9	.8	3.0	4.2	2.1	1.5	1.3	2.5	4.3	6.4	1.7	1.0	−.7	.7	Spain	184
2.9	−6.8	−.2	4.1	5.8	1.0	1.0	−1.1	−.6	.9	2.8	1.1	1.9	−.6	.5	Denmark	128
20.6	16.4	9.8	10.1	13.4	15.9	16.7	11.3	11.9	8.7	7.8	6.1	3.3	3.9	2.1	Greece	174
4.8	−3.4	3.6	4.6	5.4	4.0	2.4	−.4	−1.0	1.3	2.6	2.2	1.4	.6	3.1	Norway	142
5.2	−2.8	2.8	5.3	7.7	4.7	1.7	−1.3	6.2	4.8	7.8	−1.8	1.2	−.6	1.1	Sweden	144
2.0	−1.3	−.7	2.1	3.2	2.3	1.3	.7	.4	−.5	−.1	−1.8	−.7	−1.2	−1.0	Switzerland	146
6.2	1.3	3.5	3.7	4.8	6.2	5.4	3.1	4.0	2.5	4.0	2.6	.9	.5	1.2	United Kingdom	112
36.7	30.2	42.6	65.8	76.2	101.3	46.9	51.0	59.2	75.0	32.5	16.1	12.1	14.5	12.0	Developing Countries	200
14.8	16.3	10.8	9.5	11.8	10.5	11.4	9.6	8.4	7.7	9.8	6.3	4.1	3.5	3.6	Africa	605
6.8	3.7	.4	−15.1	4.0	1.6	−1.2	.3	−1.5	....	....	....	....	—	....	Central African Rep.	626
6.6	3.8	4.6	2.3	2.2	2.0	−3.6	1.7	3.0	....	....	....	....	....	....	Congo, Rep. of	634
9.6	7.8	1.0	4.3	3.8	4.6	6.4	2.8	4.5	2.3	6.5	4.4	−1.6	3.5	.8	Morocco	686
49.2	....	....	....	....	....	....	....	....	....	....	....	....	....	....	Sierra Leone	724
16.8	19.6	13.9	13.1	15.2	12.0	11.3	8.2	6.7	8.2	9.5	7.0	7.1	3.6	5.8	South Africa	199
11.3	9.9	9.2	8.8	5.7	2.8	5.4	3.7	4.7	3.4	3.7	3.7	2.0	3.6	1.4	Tunisia	744
47.2	115.9	84.4	11.6	84.2	115.6	91.7	121.3	140.8	70.6	72.0	....	....	....	....	Zambia	754
....	....	....	....	14.5	18.2	40.7	52.1	20.5	22.3	20.8	17.1	12.9	....	....	Zimbabwe	698
3.8	1.9	8.3	7.6	6.6	7.6	8.9	6.4	4.0	6.8	8.4	5.5	5.3	20.2	.5	Asia	505
....	....	....	....	....	....	3.4	1.8	.7	2.1	2.7	−.1	−.3	−1.8	−1.5	China, P.R.: Hong Kong	532
4.6	5.6	7.0	8.7	6.8	9.0	13.5	11.9	7.5	10.5	9.3	5.9	5.2	6.9	3.5	India	534
5.0	2.2	19.2	4.9	8.6	10.0	5.1	5.2	3.7	5.4	11.4	7.9	9.0	101.8	....	Indonesia	536
.9	−1.5	.5	2.7	1.5	4.2	4.7	2.2	1.5	2.7	4.7	3.2	3.9	12.2	−2.1	Korea	542
−2.1	−6.2	3.7	7.3	3.8	.9	4.0	1.1	1.5	3.9	4.1	2.3	6.6	6.6	....	Malaysia	548
5.2	4.6	5.0	10.0	9.6	7.3	11.7	9.4	7.4	16.4	16.0	11.1	13.0	6.6	6.3	Pakistan	564
18.2	−1.6	9.1	13.4	10.6	10.2	13.5	4.5	−1.1	8.2	3.3	8.9	.5	11.7	5.8	Philippines	566
−2.2	−15.1	7.5	−1.8	2.6	1.7	−4.1	−4.4	−4.4	−.4	—	.1	−1.2	−3.0	2.1	Singapore	576
−15.2	−3.0	13.4	17.8	9.1	22.2	9.2	8.7	7.6	5.0	8.8	20.5	6.9	6.2	−4.3	Sri Lanka	524
....	−.4	5.9	8.2	4.6	3.5	6.8	.2	−.4	4.0	8.2	4.7	3.9	13.8	−6.5	Thailand	578
22.9	16.7	21.1	45.1	84.7	141.8	84.2	57.1	45.3	183.3	117.2	43.2	37.1	19.4	40.3	Europe	170
....	....	....	....	....	....	....	....	....	....	....	....	....	14.6	5.9	Armenia	911
....	....	....	....	....	....	....	....	1,536.3	2,170.8	497.9	35.0	86.5	73.5	355.8	Belarus	913
....	.9	−.3	2.0	.2	11.5	296.3	−60.7	−82.8	1,146.3	55.7	133.9	972.2	16.6	2.9	Bulgaria	918
....	....	100.0	233.3	1,400.0	400.0	166.7	775.0	1,497.1	77.6	.7	2.0	1.2	−1.0	2.4	Croatia	960
....	....	....	....	....	....	....	.1	2.5	3.3	3.6	2.1	2.8	.5	1.2	Cyprus	423
....	....	....	....	....	....	....	....	9.3	5.2	7.6	4.8	4.9	4.8	1.0	Czech Republic	935
1.8	—	.1	—	−.7	4.4	70.0	....	....	....	....	....	....	....	....	Czechoslovakia	934
....	....	....	....	....	....	....	....	....	25.6	14.8	8.4	4.2	−1.2	....	Estonia	939
5.3	2.1	3.5	4.6	15.4	22.0	32.6	12.3	12.0	−27.2	−47.1	21.8	20.3	11.4	4.2	Hungary	944
....	....	....	....	....	....	....	....	....	....	23.9	15.3	.8	19.0	....	Kazakhstan	916
....	....	....	....	....	....	....	....	....	215.3	21.8	23.0	26.3	7.9	53.7	Kyrgyz Republic	917
....	....	....	....	....	....	....	....	117.1	16.8	11.9	13.7	4.1	1.9	−4.0	Latvia	941
....	....	....	....	....	....	....	....	391.9	44.7	28.3	17.3	4.2	−6.7	3.0	Lithuania	946
14.2	16.7	26.5	59.6	218.2	610.1	50.3	27.7	32.2	30.1	25.5	13.2	12.2	7.2	5.5	Poland	964
....	....	....	....	....	....	240.7	203.6	165.0	140.5	35.1	49.9	156.5	33.2	42.2	Romania	968
....	....	....	....	....	....	....	....	943.8	337.0	236.5	50.8	17.2	5.1	58.9	Russia	922
1.8	—	.1	−.2	−2.7	4.8	68.9	5.3	17.2	10.0	9.0	4.1	4.5	3.3	3.8	Slovak Republic	936
....	....	....	....	....	....	166.0	166.0	21.6	17.7	12.8	6.8	6.1	6.0	2.1	Slovenia	961
43.2	29.6	32.0	70.5	64.0	52.3	55.3	62.1	58.0	121.3	86.0	75.9	81.8	71.8	53.1	Turkey	186
....	....	....	....	....	....	....	....	4,619.3	1,143.8	487.9	51.9	7.7	....	....	Ukraine	926
84.4	68.5	94.1	203.0	1,306.3	436.5	113.3	....	....	....	....	....	....	....	....	Yugoslavia, SFR	188

Producer Prices/Wholesale Prices

		1970	1971	1972	1973	1974	1975	1976	1977	1978	1979	1980	1981	1982	1983	1984
														Percent Change over Previous Year:		
Middle East	405	4.5	4.8	4.1	12.0	18.2	10.3	10.6	15.4	13.4	16.1	31.2	22.9	17.5	20.6	22.6
Egypt	469	5.1	.2	1.3	6.8	14.3	7.5	7.8	9.3	14.8	9.7	21.7	8.0	9.3	16.0	10.0
Iran, I.R. of	429	2.9	6.2	5.7	11.3	17.0	8.0	9.0	17.2	10.1	14.1	31.3	23.5	12.7	14.7	7.6
Israel	436	7.2	9.7	10.5	19.1	51.5	40.8	30.8	38.5	53.2	79.0	135.1	122.7	125.7	144.5	396.5
Jordan	439	....	....	....	....	....	....	14.2	6.7	5.4	6.5	14.9	9.0	3.2	4.0	1.7
Kuwait	443	....	....	....	22.0	10.4	7.6	7.6	7.0	-1.2	6.5	10.5	6.9	1.1	1.9	-.6
Saudi Arabia	456	....	....	....	....	....	....	....	....	....	....	....	....	....	....	....
Syrian Arab Rep.	463	9.8	9.0	-4.6	32.6	13.8	7.6	12.0	9.0	12.9	8.7	15.0	19.0	10.9	3.0	8.8
Western Hemisphere	205	13.8	11.4	15.4	33.3	39.0	27.9	34.3	37.7	24.5	33.9	52.5	51.4	57.3	99.4	106.7
Argentina	213	....	....	....	....	....	....	....	....	....	....	....	....	....	....	....
Brazil	223	22.1	20.0	18.6	16.8	29.2	27.2	43.3	42.5	37.6	55.9	106.4	108.2	93.2	167.4	236.3
Chile	228	36.2	18.0	70.0	511.3	1,028.8	481.9	221.1	86.1	43.0	49.4	39.6	9.1	7.2	45.5	24.3
Colombia	233	7.7	11.5	18.3	28.0	36.0	25.4	22.9	26.7	17.6	27.8	24.2	24.1	25.7	21.7	18.3
Costa Rica	238	6.5	6.4	5.5	16.3	39.8	21.6	9.3	7.5	7.8	16.1	23.7	65.3	108.2	26.2	7.7
Ecuador	248	....	....	....	....	....	14.0	16.7	8.2	16.7	10.7	7.3	9.6	16.9	14.9	23.1
El Salvador	253	8.7	-5.4	5.9	21.1	25.3	1.8	34.7	47.3	-19.8	7.6	15.8	10.0	8.5	6.8	5.9
Mexico	273	6.0	3.4	3.1	15.7	22.3	10.7	22.3	41.2	15.8	18.3	24.5	24.5	56.1	107.4	70.3
Panama	283	3.1	5.4	8.5	10.5	30.2	14.0	7.8	7.2	5.4	14.0	15.3	10.0	8.3	-3.8	1.1
Paraguay	288	....	....	....	....	....	....	....	....	....	....	....	....	....	....	....
Peru	293	....	....	....	....	....	....	....	....	....	....	....	68.2	56.6	113.0	120.1
Trinidad and Tobago	369	....	....	....	....	....	....	....	....	....	....	19.4	16.9	13.8	12.5	5.1
Uruguay	298	13.7	20.3	90.2	114.9	78.6	72.4	50.6	50.3	48.6	80.4	41.8	23.4	12.9	73.5	77.4
Venezuela, Rep. Bol.	299	1.6	3.5	3.4	6.7	16.7	13.7	7.2	10.3	7.4	9.3	20.0	13.8	8.6	6.4	17.5
Memorandum Items																
Oil Exporting Countries	999	2.4	5.3	5.0	9.7	25.3	8.6	10.2	14.1	8.6	25.7	25.2	14.8	8.7	13.1	10.4
Non-Oil Developing Countries	201	8.9	8.4	11.6	24.8	27.0	14.9	15.8	18.6	12.5	22.8	35.6	31.9	35.6	49.7	49.4

Indices

Index Numbers:

		1970	1971	1972	1973	1974	1975	1976	1977	1978	1979	1980	1981	1982	1983	1984
World	001	4.0	4.1	4.4	5.0	6.1	6.7	7.3	8.1	8.8	10.0	11.9	13.6	15.2	17.2	19.7
Industrial Countries	110	29.5	30.5	31.7	35.4	41.9	45.6	48.5	51.9	54.9	60.7	69.2	75.2	78.9	81.2	84.5
Developing Countries	200	....	....	....	....	....	....	....	....	....	....	....	....	....	....	....
Africa	605	6.8	7.0	7.5	8.5	10.2	11.4	12.7	14.4	15.7	17.7	20.2	23.0	26.2	28.8	31.9
Asia	505	10.5	11.1	12.0	14.1	19.0	20.5	21.6	23.6	24.6	29.3	35.8	40.4	42.3	46.1	50.6
Europe	170	.1	.1	.1	.1	.1	.1	.1	.1	.1	.1	.1	.1	.1	.2	.3
Middle East	405	2.3	2.4	2.5	2.8	3.3	3.7	4.1	4.7	5.3	6.2	8.1	10.0	11.7	14.2	17.3
Western Hemisphere (1995=10 mil.)	205	1.3	1.4	1.7	2.2	3.1	3.9	5.3	7.3	9.1	12.1	18.5	28.0	44.1	87.9	181.6
Western Hemisphere	205	....	....	....	....	....	....	....	....	....	....	....	....	....	....	....

Calculated from Indices

1985	1986	1987	1988	1989	1990	1991	1992	1993	1994	1995	1996	1997	1998	1999		
19.4	17.3	20.7	21.6	17.5	14.0	16.4	14.6	11.6	14.9	22.3	13.4	5.2	4.1	7.5	**Middle East**	405
13.2	17.3	13.7	26.3	27.3	16.8	17.9	12.1	8.6	4.6	6.3	8.3	4.2	1.4	.9	Egypt	469
5.3	19.0	32.3	22.2	20.4	20.6	25.8	33.0	25.6	37.6	60.6	32.9	10.7	11.9	19.2	Iran, I.R. of	429
266.1	45.1	18.5	17.5	21.1	11.6	16.1	10.2	8.2	7.9	10.7	8.6	6.3	4.2	7.1	Israel	436
1.5	−.3	.9	9.4	33.7	14.4	5.1	4.2	3.4	4.8	−2.4	2.0	1.6	.6	−4.2	Jordan	439
−1.3	.6	3.3	4.6	8.8	3.8	18.6	.4	1.8	−.2	1.4	5.2	−1.3	−1.6	−1.2	Kuwait	443
....	3.8	7.2	13.4	1.2	1.7	3.0	1.3	.6	1.8	7.2	−.3	—	−1.8	.4	Saudi Arabia	456
10.1	40.5	46.7	46.9	13.9	22.0	14.0	2.6	8.5	14.2	6.9	3.2	2.5	−.6	....	Syrian Arab Rep.	463
101.8	84.8	122.1	227.7	271.0	448.0	124.3	168.7	239.2	253.9	38.0	19.7	11.6	8.0	13.6	**Western Hemisphere**	205
....	....	122.9	412.5	3,432.6	1,606.9	110.5	6.0	1.6	.7	7.8	3.7	−1.1	−3.3	....	Argentina	213
229.0	140.2	207.1	697.2	1,268.4	2,703.8	401.4	987.8	2,050.1	2,311.6	57.5	6.2	8.1	3.5	16.6	Brazil	223
43.4	19.8	19.2	5.9	15.1	21.8	21.5	11.7	8.6	7.7	7.6	6.2	1.6	1.9	5.2	Chile	228
24.9	22.0	25.1	28.1	28.2	26.6	27.6	20.1	14.2	17.2	18.1	15.0	15.4	17.3	9.8	Colombia	233
10.4	9.0	10.6	17.9	14.6	14.9	28.1	18.4	5.2	13.1	23.9	16.0	11.6	8.8	10.1	Costa Rica	238
26.1	28.5	31.6	66.8	80.1	45.5	48.0	54.6	39.1	18.2	....	....	....	....	....	Ecuador	248
13.8	32.5	.7	5.5	9.7	18.9	6.9	2.2	7.5	7.9	10.5	4.8	1.0	−6.0	−1.5	El Salvador	253
53.6	88.4	135.6	107.8	16.1	23.3	20.5	13.4	8.9	6.8	39.1	36.3	18.5	13.9	14.7	Mexico	273
−.4	−16.0	1.5	−6.8	2.4	3.9	.5	1.8	−.2	2.0	3.0	2.1	−2.2	−3.9	2.7	Panama	283
....	....	....	....	....	....	....	....	....	....	....	....	1.2	14.9	5.3	Paraguay	288
173.9	60.3	51.5	627.9	2,510.3	6,737.4	306.3	57.2	47.6	17.9	10.5	9.4	7.4	7.3	4.9	Peru	293
4.7	6.5	4.2	5.9	8.9	1.4	.2	.8	5.4	5.4	3.6	2.9	1.9	1.4	....	Trinidad and Tobago	369
76.6	67.2	63.2	57.4	73.2	107.7	87.6	58.3	33.4	34.2	37.7	25.0	16.4	9.3	−.9	Uruguay	298
15.2	17.6	44.8	19.3	97.5	27.2	22.3	23.6	35.0	78.2	57.7	103.2	29.8	22.2	16.2	Venezuela, Rep. Bol.	299

Memorandum Items

1985	1986	1987	1988	1989	1990	1991	1992	1993	1994	1995	1996	1997	1998	1999		
6.5	9.2	23.9	13.0	20.8	13.1	11.9	12.8	11.9	18.4	25.0	20.6	10.1	48.5	....	Oil Exporting Countries	999
43.4	35.4	47.1	80.5	91.5	125.8	54.7	59.7	70.3	87.8	33.9	15.3	12.4	9.2	11.9	Non-Oil Developing Countries	201

Indices

1995=100

1985	1986	1987	1988	1989	1990	1991	1992	1993	1994	1995	1996	1997	1998	1999		
21.8	23.1	25.8	30.6	37.2	47.2	53.6	61.1	71.0	88.2	100.0	106.5	111.5	116.3	121.2	**World**	001
86.2	83.8	84.6	87.2	91.1	93.6	94.5	95.0	95.6	96.8	100.0	101.1	101.7	100.4	100.2	**Industrial Countries**	110
....	....	....	3.4	6.1	12.2	17.9	27.1	43.1	75.4	100.0	116.1	130.1	148.9	166.8	**Developing Countries**	200
36.6	42.6	47.2	51.7	57.8	63.9	71.2	78.0	84.5	91.0	100.0	106.3	110.6	114.5	118.6	Africa	605
52.6	53.6	58.0	62.4	66.6	71.6	78.0	83.1	86.4	92.2	100.0	105.5	111.0	133.5	134.1	Asia	505
.4	.5	.6	.9	1.6	3.9	7.1	11.2	16.3	46.0	100.0	143.2	196.3	234.3	328.8	Europe	170
20.7	24.3	29.3	35.7	41.9	47.8	55.6	63.7	71.2	81.8	100.0	113.4	119.3	124.1	133.4	Middle East	405
366.4	677.0	1,503.9	4,928.2	....	....	....	....	....	....	....	....	....	....	....	Western Hemisphere (1995=10 mil.)	205
....	....	....	—	.2	1.0	2.2	6.0	20.5	72.5	100.0	119.7	133.6	144.3	163.9	Western Hemisphere	205

(See notes in the back of the book.)

Consumer Prices

64 x		1970	1971	1972	1973	1974	1975	1976	1977	1978	1979	1980	1981	1982	1983	1984
													Percent Change over Previous Year;			
World	**001**	**5.8**	**5.6**	**5.8**	**10.1**	**16.3**	**13.9**	**11.9**	**12.3**	**9.3**	**12.6**	**17.2**	**16.5**	**15.2**	**14.8**	**15.3**
Industrial Countries	**110**	**5.6**	**5.4**	**4.9**	**8.0**	**13.5**	**11.5**	**8.7**	**9.0**	**7.5**	**9.6**	**12.3**	**10.4**	**7.7**	**5.3**	**5.0**
United States	111	5.9	4.3	3.3	6.2	11.0	9.1	5.7	6.5	7.6	11.3	I13.5	10.3	6.2	3.2	4.3
Canada	156	3.4	2.8	4.8	7.6	10.9	10.8	7.5	8.0	8.9	9.1	10.2	I12.5	10.8	5.8	4.3
Australia	193	3.9	6.1	5.9	9.5	15.1	15.1	13.5	12.3	7.9	I9.1	10.1	9.7	11.1	10.1	4.0
Japan	158	I7.7	6.4	4.9	11.7	23.1	11.8	9.4	8.2	4.1	3.8	7.8	4.9	2.7	1.9	2.2
New Zealand	196	I6.5	10.3	6.8	8.2	11.3	14.5	16.8	14.6	11.9	13.7	17.1	15.3	16.2	7.4	6.2
Euro Area																
Austria	122	4.4	4.7	6.4	7.5	9.5	8.4	I7.3	5.5	3.6	3.7	6.3	6.8	5.4	3.3	5.7
Belgium	124	3.9	4.3	5.4	7.0	12.7	I12.8	9.2	7.1	4.5	4.5	6.7	7.6	8.7	7.7	I6.3
Finland	172	2.7	6.5	I7.1	11.0	16.7	17.8	14.3	I12.7	7.8	7.5	11.6	I12.0	9.6	8.4	7.1
France	132	5.8	5.4	6.1	7.4	13.6	11.7	9.6	9.5	9.3	10.6	I13.5	13.3	12.0	9.5	7.7
Germany	134	3.4	5.2	5.5	7.0	7.0	5.9	4.3	3.7	2.7	4.1	5.4	6.3	5.3	3.3	2.4
Ireland	178	8.2	9.0	8.6	11.4	17.0	20.9	I18.0	13.6	7.6	13.2	I18.2	20.3	17.1	10.5	8.6
Italy	136	4.8	5.5	5.2	10.7	19.4	16.9	16.6	17.4	12.1	14.6	21.3	17.8	16.4	14.6	10.8
Luxembourg	137	4.6	4.7	5.2	6.1	9.4	10.7	9.8	6.7	3.1	4.5	6.3	8.1	9.4	8.7	I5.6
Netherlands	138	3.7	7.5	7.8	8.0	9.6	10.2	9.1	6.5	4.1	4.2	I6.5	6.7	5.9	2.8	3.3
Portugal	182	4.5	7.5	8.9	10.4	28.0	20.4	18.2	27.1	22.7	23.6	16.6	20.0	22.7	I25.1	29.3
Spain	184	5.7	8.2	8.3	11.4	15.0	17.7	17.6	24.5	19.8	15.7	15.6	14.6	14.4	12.2	11.3
Denmark	128	6.5	5.9	6.6	9.3	15.3	I9.6	9.0	11.1	10.0	9.6	12.3	I11.7	10.1	6.9	6.3
Greece	174	2.9	3.0	4.3	15.5	26.9	13.4	13.3	12.2	12.5	19.0	24.9	I24.5	20.9	20.2	18.4
Iceland	176	13.1	6.7	9.7	21.0	42.7	49.4	I32.8	30.6	44.0	45.4	58.5	50.8	51.0	84.2	29.2
Norway	142	10.6	6.3	7.2	7.4	9.4	11.7	9.2	9.0	8.2	4.8	10.9	13.6	11.4	8.4	6.3
Sweden	144	7.0	7.4	6.0	6.7	9.9	9.8	10.3	11.5	9.9	7.2	I13.7	12.1	8.6	8.9	8.0
Switzerland	146	3.6	6.6	6.7	8.8	9.8	6.7	1.7	1.3	I1.1	3.6	4.0	6.5	I5.7	3.0	2.9
United Kingdom	112	6.4	9.4	7.1	9.2	I15.9	24.2	16.5	15.9	8.2	13.5	18.0	11.9	8.6	4.6	5.0
Developing Countries	**200**	**6.2**	**6.1**	**8.5**	**16.7**	**23.8**	**20.3**	**20.3**	**21.2**	**14.5**	**19.1**	**27.6**	**29.8**	**32.0**	**36.8**	**38.9**
Africa	**605**	**5.8**	**5.9**	**5.8**	**8.8**	**13.7**	**17.9**	**15.4**	**18.7**	**15.2**	**15.1**	**14.5**	**19.3**	**12.9**	**16.7**	**17.3**
Algeria	612	6.6	2.6	3.7	6.2	4.7	8.2	9.4	12.0	17.5	11.3	9.5	14.7	I6.5	6.0	8.1
Angola	614	....	....	....	....	....	....	....	....	....	....	....	....	....	....	....
Benin	638	....	....	....	....	....	....	....	....	....	....	....	....	....	....	....
Botswana	616	....	....	....	....	....	12.0	11.7	13.2	9.0	11.7	13.6	I16.4	11.1	10.5	8.6
Burkina Faso	748	....	....	....	....	....	....	....	....	....	....	....	....	....	....	4.8
Burundi	618	–.2	3.9	3.8	6.0	15.7	15.7	6.9	6.8	23.9	36.5	I2.5	12.2	5.9	8.2	14.3
Cameroon	622	5.9	4.0	8.1	10.4	17.2	13.6	9.9	14.7	12.5	6.6	I9.6	10.7	13.3	16.6	11.4
Central African Rep.	626	....	....	....	....	....	....	....	....	....	....	....	—	13.3	14.6	2.5
Chad	628	....	....	....	....	....	....	....	....	....	....	....	....	....	....	20.3
Congo, Dem. Rep. of	636	8.0	5.8	15.8	15.6	29.5	I28.7	80.4	68.9	48.8	101.1	46.6	35.4	36.7	76.5	52.2
Congo, Rep. of	634	1.5	4.1	9.8	3.5	5.4	17.4	7.2	14.0	10.5	8.1	7.3	I17.0	12.8	7.7	13.2
Côte d'Ivoire	662	8.2	–.4	.3	11.1	17.4	11.4	12.1	27.4	13.2	16.3	14.7	8.8	7.6	5.6	4.3
Equatorial Guinea	642	....	....	....	....	....	....	....	....	....	....	....	....	....	....	....
Ethiopia	644	10.1	.5	–6.1	8.9	8.6	6.6	28.5	16.7	14.3	16.0	4.5	6.1	5.9	–.7	8.4
Gabon	646	3.8	3.9	3.5	6.2	12.1	I28.5	20.2	13.9	10.8	8.0	12.3	8.7	I16.7	10.7	5.9
Gambia, The	648	–2.0	3.1	8.7	6.9	I9.2	25.9	17.0	12.4	8.9	6.1	6.8	5.9	10.9	10.6	22.1
Ghana	652	3.0	9.6	10.1	17.7	18.1	29.8	56.1	116.5	73.1	54.4	50.1	116.5	22.3	122.9	39.7
Guinea-Bissau	654	....	....	....	....	....	....	....	....	....	....	....	....	....	....	....
Kenya	664	2.2	I3.8	5.8	9.3	I17.8	19.1	11.4	14.8	16.9	8.0	I13.9	11.6	20.7	11.4	10.3
Lesotho	666	....	....	....	....	13.4	14.2	11.4	16.7	13.5	16.0	16.3	12.4	12.1	17.5	11.0
Liberia	668	1.6	–.8	3.9	19.6	19.0	14.0	5.6	6.2	7.3	11.6	14.7	7.6	6.0	2.7	1.2
Madagascar	674	2.9	5.4	5.6	6.1	22.1	8.2	5.0	3.1	6.5	14.1	18.2	30.5	31.8	19.3	9.9
Malawi	676	....	....	....	....	....	....	....	....	....	....	....	11.8	9.8	13.5	20.0
Mali	678	....	....	....	....	....	....	....	....	....	....	....	....	....	....	....
Mauritania	682	....	....	....	....	....	....	....	....	....	....	....	....	....	....	....
Mauritius	684	1.5	.3	5.4	13.5	29.1	I14.7	13.0	9.2	8.5	14.5	42.0	I14.5	11.4	5.6	7.4
Morocco	686	1.3	4.2	3.8	I4.1	17.6	7.9	8.5	12.6	9.7	8.3	9.4	12.5	10.5	6.2	12.4
Mozambique	688	....	....	....	....	....	....	....	....	....	....	....	....	....	....	....
Namibia	728	....	....	....	....	....	....	....	....	....	....	....	14.8	15.5	12.0	9.1
Niger	692	1.1	4.2	9.8	11.8	3.4	9.1	23.5	23.3	10.1	7.3	10.3	22.9	11.6	–2.5	8.4
Nigeria	694	13.8	16.0	3.5	5.4	12.7	I33.9	24.3	I13.8	21.7	11.7	10.0	20.8	7.7	23.2	I39.6
Rwanda	714	.5	.5	3.1	9.4	31.1	I30.2	7.2	13.7	13.3	15.7	7.2	6.5	12.6	6.6	5.4
Senegal	722	2.8	3.9	6.2	11.3	16.6	31.7	1.1	11.3	3.4	9.7	8.7	5.9	17.4	11.6	11.8
Seychelles	718	....	14.6	20.9	18.2	24.4	18.6	14.9	I15.0	11.8	12.5	13.6	I10.6	–.9	6.1	4.1
Sierra Leone	724	6.4	–1.3	5.5	5.7	14.4	19.9	17.2	8.3	10.9	I21.3	12.9	23.4	26.9	68.5	66.6
South Africa	199	I4.1	5.8	6.5	9.5	11.8	13.4	11.1	11.2	10.3	13.1	13.9	15.1	14.7	12.4	11.6
Sudan	732	I4.0	1.3	13.6	15.3	26.2	24.0	1.7	17.1	19.2	31.1	25.4	24.6	25.7	30.6	34.1
Swaziland	734	1.8	2.3	2.4	11.5	19.3	12.0	6.5	20.8	8.5	I16.5	18.7	20.1	10.8	I11.6	I12.9
Tanzania	738	3.5	4.8	7.6	10.4	19.6	26.1	6.9	I11.6	6.6	12.9	30.2	25.7	28.9	27.1	36.1
Togo	742	4.5	6.5	7.7	I3.6	12.8	18.0	11.6	22.5	.4	7.5	12.3	19.7	11.1	9.4	–3.5
Tunisia	744	....	....	....	....	....	....	....	....	....	....	....	....	....	....	8.9
Uganda	746	....	....	....	....	....	....	....	....	....	....	....	108.7	49.3	24.1	I42.7
Zambia	754	....	....	....	....	....	....	....	....	....	....	....	....	....	....	....
Zimbabwe	698	2.1	3.0	2.8	3.1	6.6	I10.0	11.0	10.3	5.7	18.2	5.4	13.2	10.6	23.1	20.2
Asia	**505**	**6.7**	**5.0**	**6.3**	**17.6**	**29.7**	**10.4**	**2.8**	**8.6**	**5.9**	**10.1**	**15.3**	**13.3**	**7.4**	**8.2**	**8.5**
Afghanistan, Islamic State of	512	....	....	....	....	....	....	....	....	....	....	....	....	....	....	....
Bangladesh	513	....	....	....	....	....	....	....	....	....	....	.9	4.9	5.8	–3.0	7.7
Bhutan	514	....	....	....	....	....	....	....	....	....	....	....	9.9	9.9	18.0	7.0
Cambodia	522	....	....	....	....	....	....	....	....	....	....	....	....	....	....	....
China, P.R.: Mainland	924	....	....	....	....	....	....	....	....	....	....	....	....	....	....	....
China, P.R.: Hong Kong	532	....	....	....	....	....	....	....	....	....	....	....	....	....	....	....
Fiji	819	4.1	9.1	22.0	11.1	14.5	13.1	11.4	7.0	6.1	7.8	14.5	11.2	7.0	6.7	5.3
India	534	5.1	3.1	6.5	16.9	28.6	5.7	–7.6	8.3	2.5	6.3	11.4	13.1	7.9	11.9	8.3
Indonesia	536	12.3	4.4	6.5	31.0	40.6	19.1	19.9	11.0	8.1	I16.3	18.0	12.2	9.5	11.8	10.5
Korea	542	16.1	13.4	11.7	3.2	24.3	25.3	I15.3	10.2	14.5	18.3	28.7	21.3	7.2	I3.4	2.3
Lao People's Democratic Rep.	544	....	....	....	....	....	....	....	....	....	....	....	....	....	....	....
Malaysia	548	1.8	1.6	3.2	10.6	17.3	4.5	2.6	4.8	4.9	3.7	I6.7	9.7	5.8	3.7	3.9
Maldives	556	....	....	....	....	....	....	....	....	12.7	27.8	23.8	23.7	22.0	....	....
Mongolia	948	....	....	....	....	....	....	....	....	....	....	....	....	....	....	....
Myanmar	518	–4.0	2.1	7.6	25.2	25.2	31.7	22.4	–1.2	–6.0	5.7	.6	I.3	5.3[e]	5.7	I4.8
Nepal	558	15.2	–2.0	8.4	11.4	I19.8	7.6	–3.1	9.9	7.3	3.6	14.7	11.1	11.7	12.4	2.8
Pakistan	564	5.3	I4.7	5.2	23.1	26.7	20.9	7.2	I10.1	6.1	8.3	11.9	11.9	I5.9	6.4	6.1
Papua New Guinea	853	....	....	6.1	8.3	23.2	10.5	7.7	I4.5	5.8	5.8	12.1	8.1	5.5	7.9	7.4
Philippines	566	15.3	21.4	8.2	16.6	34.2	6.8	9.2	9.9	7.3	17.5	18.2	I13.1	9.0	5.3	46.7
Samoa	862	2.7	4.8	I7.5	11.8	25.0	8.8	4.9	14.6	2.1	11.1	I33.0	20.5	18.3	16.5	11.9
Singapore	576	.5	1.8	2.1	19.6	22.4	2.5	–1.8	3.2	4.9	4.1	8.5	8.2	3.9	1.2	2.6
Solomon Islands	813	....	....	6.9	3.2	18.9	I10.1	4.3	8.6	6.3	8.1	13.1	16.4	13.0	6.2	11.0
Sri Lanka	524	5.9	2.7	6.3	9.6	12.3	6.6	1.3	1.2	12.1	10.7	26.1	18.0	10.8	14.0	16.6

Calculated from Indices

1985	1986	1987	1988	1989	1990	1991	1992	1993	1994	1995	1996	1997	1998	1999		
15.7	11.7	14.1	16.6	12.9	27.7	17.1	16.7	18.4	25.2	14.5	8.4	5.9	5.8	5.1	**World**	001
4.4	2.6	3.1	3.4	4.6	5.1	4.2	3.2	2.8	2.3	2.4	2.2	2.0	1.4	1.4	**Industrial Countries**	110
3.6	1.9	3.7	4.0	4.8	5.4	4.2	3.0	3.0	2.6	2.8	2.9	2.3	1.6	2.2	United States	111
4.0	4.2	4.4	4.0	5.0	4.8	5.6	1.5	1.8	.2	I2.2	1.6	1.6	1.0	1.7	Canada	156
6.7	9.1	8.5	7.2	7.6	I7.3	3.2	1.0	1.8	1.9	4.6	2.6	.3	.9	1.5	Australia	193
2.0	.6	.1	.7	2.3	3.1	3.3	1.7	1.3	I.7	-.1	.1	1.7	.6	-.3	Japan	158
I15.4	13.2	15.7	6.4	7.5	5.5	1.7	1.0	1.4	I2.4	3.7	2.3	1.2	1.3	-.1	New Zealand	196
															Euro Area	
3.2	I1.7	1.4	1.9	2.6	3.3	3.3	4.0	3.6	3.0	2.3	I1.8	1.3	.9	.6	Austria	122
4.9	1.3	1.6	I1.2	3.1	3.5	3.2	2.4	2.8	2.4	1.5	I2.1	1.6	1.0	1.1	Belgium	124
I5.9	2.9	4.1	5.1	6.6	6.1	4.1	2.6	2.1	1.1	I1.0	.6	1.2	1.4	1.2	Finland	172
5.8	2.5	3.3	2.7	3.5	I3.4	3.2	2.4	2.1	1.7	1.8	2.0	1.2	I.7	.5	France	132
I2.2	-.1	.2	1.3	I2.8	2.7	I1.7	5.1	4.4	2.8	1.7	1.4	1.9	.9	.6	Germany	134
I5.4	3.8	3.1	2.2	4.1	3.3	3.2	3.1	1.4	2.3	2.5	1.7	I1.4	2.4	1.6	Ireland	178
9.2	5.8	4.7	5.1	6.2	6.5	6.3	5.1	4.5	4.0	I5.2	4.0	2.0	2.0	1.7	Italy	136
4.1	.3	-.1	1.5	3.4	I3.7	3.1	3.2	3.6	2.2	1.9	I1.4	1.4	1.0	1.0	Luxembourg	137
2.2	.1	-.7	.7	1.1	I2.5	3.1	3.2	2.6	2.8	I1.9	2.0	2.2	2.0	2.2	Netherlands	138
19.3	11.7	9.4	9.6	12.6	13.4	I11.4	8.9	6.8	4.9	4.1	3.1	I2.2	2.8	2.3	Portugal	182
8.8	8.8	5.2	4.8	6.8	6.7	5.9	5.9	4.6	4.7	4.7	3.6	2.0	1.8	2.3	Spain	184
4.7	3.7	4.0	4.6	4.8	2.6	2.4	2.1	1.3	2.0	2.1	2.1	2.2	1.8	2.5	Denmark	128
19.3	23.0	16.4	I13.5	13.7	20.4	19.5	15.9	14.4	I10.9	8.9	8.2	5.5	4.8	2.6	Greece	174
31.7	21.9	17.7	25.8	20.8	15.5	6.8	4.0	4.1	1.6	1.7	2.3	1.7	1.7	3.2	Iceland	176
5.7	7.2	8.7	6.7	4.6	4.1	3.4	2.3	2.3	1.4	2.5	1.3	2.6	I2.3	2.3	Norway	142
7.4	4.2	4.2	5.8	6.4	10.5	9.3	2.3	4.6	2.2	2.5	.5	.5	-.1	.5	Sweden	144
3.4	.8	1.4	1.9	3.2	5.4	5.8	I4.1	3.3	.8	1.8	.8	.5	.1	.8	Switzerland	146
6.1	3.4	4.1	4.9	7.8	9.5	5.9	3.7	1.6	2.5	3.4	2.4	3.1	3.4	1.6	United Kingdom	112
41.8	32.3	40.0	50.3	27.3	71.5	39.6	40.7	47.7	57.9	30.0	16.1	10.7	11.2	9.7	**Developing Countries**	200
12.9	13.5	13.8	19.4	19.2	15.1	23.6	31.6	25.4	29.7	28.8	20.1	9.7	6.6	5.6	**Africa**	605
10.5	12.4	7.4	5.9	9.3	I16.6	25.9	31.7	20.5	29.0	29.8	18.7	5.7	5.0	2.5	Algeria	612
....	....	....	....	....	....	83.6	299.1	I1,379.4	948.8	2,671.8	4,145.2	219.2	86.9	286.1	Angola	614
....	....	....	....	....	....	....	....	.4	38.5	14.5	4.9	I3.5	5.8	.3	Benin	638
8.1	10.0	9.8	8.4	11.6	11.4	I11.8	16.2	14.3	10.5	10.5	I10.1	8.6	6.7	7.1	Botswana	616
6.9	-2.6	-2.7	4.1	-.3	-.8	2.5	-2.0	.6	25.2	7.4	6.2	I2.3	5.1	-1.1	Burkina Faso	748
3.8	1.7	7.1	4.5	11.7	7.0	I9.0	1.8	I9.7	14.9	19.3	26.4	31.1	12.5	3.4	Burundi	618
8.5	7.8	13.1	1.7	-1.7	1.1	.1	—	-3.2	I35.1	13.9	4.7	1.0	.1	....	Cameroon	622
10.4	2.1	-6.9	-4.0	.8	-.4	-2.2	-1.4	-2.9	24.6	19.2	3.7	1.6	-1.9	....	Central African Rep.	626
5.2	I-13.1	-6.0	15.5	-3.9		-4.2	-3.1	-7.1	40.4	9.1	12.4	5.6	12.1	-6.8	Chad	628
I23.8	44.4	78.7	I71.1	104.1	81.3	2,154.4	I4,129.2	1,986.9	23,773.1	541.9	658.8	175.5	....	....	Congo, Dem. Rep. of	636
5.6	2.4	2.2	3.8	4.1	-4.8	9.2	2.0	2.0	49.8	21.4	-.2	....	....	....	Congo, Rep. of	634
I1.9	9.7	6.9	6.9	1.0	-.8	1.7	4.2	I2.2	26.1	14.3	I2.5	4.0	4.7	.8	Côte d'Ivoire	662
....	-17.8	-12.9	2.3	5.9	1.1	-3.2	I-7.2	I4.0	36.4	....	....	....	....	....	Equatorial Guinea	642
19.1	-9.8	-2.4	7.1	7.8	5.2	35.7	10.5	3.5	7.6	10.0	-5.1	-3.7	8.2	....	Ethiopia	644
7.4	6.3	-.9	-8.8	6.7	7.7	-11.7	-9.5	.5	36.1	9.6	.7	4.0	....	....	Gabon	646
18.3	56.6	23.5	11.7	8.3	12.2	8.6	9.5	6.5	1.7	7.0	1.1	2.8	1.1	3.8	Gambia, The	648
10.3	24.6	39.8	31.4	25.2	37.3	18.0	10.1	25.0	24.9	59.5	46.6	I27.9	14.6	12.4	Ghana	652
....	....	....	60.3	80.8	33.0	57.6	69.6	48.1	15.2	45.4	50.7	49.1	6.5	-.7	Guinea-Bissau	654
13.0	4.8	7.6	11.2	12.9	15.6	19.8	29.5	45.8	29.0	.8	8.8	12.0	5.8	2.6	Kenya	664
13.3	18.0	11.8	11.5	14.7	11.6	17.7	17.2	13.1	8.2	9.3	9.3	....	....	7.3	Lesotho	666
-1.0	4.0	5.0	9.6	9.1	....	....	....	....	....	....	....	....	....	....	Liberia	668
10.6	14.5	15.0	26.9	9.0	11.8	8.5	14.6	10.0	38.9	49.1	19.8	4.5	6.2	9.9	Madagascar	674
10.5	14.0	25.2	33.9	12.5	11.8	I12.6	23.8	22.8	34.6	83.3	37.6	9.1	29.7	44.9	Malawi	676
....	....	....	....	-.1	.6	1.8	-6.2	-.3	23.2	13.4	6.8	I-.4	4.0	-1.2	Mali	678
....	7.4	8.2	1.3	12.9	I6.6	5.6	10.1	9.4	4.1	6.5	4.7	4.6	8.0	4.1	Mauritania	682
I6.7	1.6	.5	9.2	12.7	13.5	I7.0	4.6	10.5	7.3	6.0	6.6	I6.8	6.8	6.9	Mauritius	684
7.7	8.7	2.7	2.4	3.1	6.9	I8.0	5.7	5.2	5.1	6.1	3.0	.9	2.9	.7	Morocco	686
....	....	91.0	50.1	40.1	I47.0	32.9	45.5	42.2	63.2	I54.4	46.9	6.4	.6	2.0	Mozambique	688
12.0	13.4	12.6	12.9	15.1	12.0	11.9	17.7	8.5	10.8	10.0	8.0	8.8	6.2	8.6	Namibia	728
-.9	-3.2	-6.7	-1.4	-2.8	-.8	I-7.8	-4.5	-1.2	36.0	10.6	5.3	I2.9	4.5	-2.3	Niger	692
7.4	5.7	11.3	54.5	50.5	7.4	13.0	44.6	57.2	57.0	72.8	29.3	8.2	10.3	6.6	Nigeria	694
1.8	-1.1	4.1	3.0	1.0	4.2	19.6	9.6	12.4	....	41.0	7.4	12.0	6.2	-2.4	Rwanda	714
13.0	6.2	-4.1	-1.8	.4	.3	-1.8	-.1	-.6	32.3	7.9	2.8	I1.8	1.2	.8	Senegal	722
.8	.2	2.6	1.8	1.6	3.9	2.0	3.2	1.3	1.8	-.3	-1.1	.6	2.6	....	Seychelles	718
76.6	80.9	178.7	34.3	60.8	110.9	102.7	65.5	I22.2	24.2	26.0	23.1	14.9	35.5	34.1	Sierra Leone	724
16.2	18.7	16.1	12.8	14.7	14.4	15.3	13.9	9.7	9.0	8.6	7.4	8.6	6.9	5.2	South Africa	199
I45.4	24.5	....	I64.7	66.7	65.2	123.6	117.6	101.4	115.4	68.4	132.8	46.7	17.1	16.0	Sudan	732
20.5	13.7	13.4	I21.7	7.5	13.1	8.9	7.6	12.0	13.8	12.3	6.4	7.1	8.1	6.1	Swaziland	734
33.3	32.4	29.9	31.2	I25.8	35.8	28.7	21.8	25.3	33.1	28.4	21.0	16.1	12.8	7.9	Tanzania	738
-1.8	4.1	.1	-.2	-.8	1.0	.4	1.4	I-1.0	39.2	16.4	4.7	I8.3	1.0	-.1	Togo	742
7.3	6.2	8.2	I7.2	7.7	6.5	8.2	5.8	4.0	4.7	6.2	3.7	3.7	3.1	2.7	Tunisia	744
157.7	161.0	200.0	196.1	61.4	33.1	28.1	52.4	6.1	9.7	8.6	7.2	6.9	—	6.4	Uganda	746
....	55.8	47.0	51.0	123.4	107.0	93.2	169.0	188.1	53.6	34.2	46.3	24.8	....	....	Zambia	754
8.5	14.3	12.5	7.4	12.9	I17.4	23.3	42.1	27.6	22.3	22.6	21.4	18.7	31.8	....	Zimbabwe	698
5.2	5.5	6.4	7.4	10.7	6.4	8.1	7.6	9.2	14.6	11.8	7.7	4.7	8.5	2.9	**Asia**	505
112.3	-3.2	19.5	19.9	75.1	41.9	56.7	....	....	....	....	....	....	....	....	Afghanistan, Islamic State of	512
....	....	9.9	7.4	6.0	6.1	6.4	3.6	3.0	5.3	8.5	4.1	5.2	8.3	6.3	Bangladesh	513
1.9	10.0	6.4	10.1	8.8	10.0	12.3	16.0	11.2	7.0	9.5	8.8	6.5	8.5	....	Bhutan	514
....	....	....	....	....	....	....	....	....	....	1.1	10.1	9.2	14.8	4.0	Cambodia	522
....	....	7.2	18.7	18.3	3.1	3.5	6.3	14.6	24.2	16.9	8.3	2.8	-.8	-1.4	China, P.R.: Mainland	924
....	....	....	....	....	....	11.6	9.3	I7.4	8.7	9.1	6.3	5.8	2.8	-4.0	China, P.R.: Hong Kong	532
4.4	I1.8	5.7	11.8	6.2	8.2	6.5	4.9	I5.2	.6	2.2	3.1	3.4	5.7	2.0	Fiji	819
5.6	8.7	8.8	I9.4	6.2	9.0	13.9	11.8	6.4	10.2	10.2	9.0	7.2	13.2	4.7	India	534
4.7	5.8	9.3	8.0	6.4	7.8	9.4	I7.5	9.7	8.5	9.4	I8.0	6.7	57.6	20.5	Indonesia	536
2.5	2.8	3.0	7.1	I5.7	8.6	9.3	I6.2	4.8	6.2	4.5	4.9	4.4	7.5	.8	Korea	542
....	....	....	....	61.3	35.6	13.4	9.9	6.3	6.8	19.6	I13.0	27.5	91.0	128.4	Lao People's Democratic Rep.	544
.3	.7	.3	2.6	2.8	I2.6	4.4	4.8	3.5	I3.7	5.3	3.5	2.7	5.3	2.7	Malaysia	548
....	....	....	....	I7.2	3.6	14.7	I16.8	20.2	3.4	5.4	6.3	7.6	-1.4	3.0	Maldives	556
....	....	....	....	....	....	....	....	268.2	87.6	56.8	I49.3	36.6	9.4	7.6	Mongolia	948
6.8	9.3	24.8	16.0	27.2	17.6	32.3	21.9	31.8	24.1	25.2	16.3	29.7	51.5	18.4	Myanmar	518
8.1	19.0	10.8	I9.0	8.8	8.2	15.6	17.1	7.5	8.3	7.6	9.2	4.0	10.0	8.0	Nepal	558
5.6	3.5	4.7	8.8	7.8	9.1	11.8	I9.5	10.0	12.4	12.3	10.4	11.4	6.2	4.1	Pakistan	564
3.7	5.5	3.3	5.4	4.5	7.0	7.0	4.3	5.0	2.9	17.3	11.6	3.9	13.6	14.9	Papua New Guinea	853
23.2	-.3	3.0	12.2	11.4	13.2	18.5	8.6	6.9	8.4	8.0	9.0	5.9	9.7	6.7	Philippines	566
9.1	5.7	4.6	8.5	6.5	15.2	-1.8	9.0	1.7	12.1	-2.9	5.4	6.9	2.2	....	Samoa	862
.5	-1.4	.5	1.5	2.3	3.5	3.4	2.3	2.3	3.1	1.7	1.4	2.0	I-.3	—	Singapore	576
9.6	13.6	11.0	16.7	14.9	I8.7	15.1	10.8	9.2	13.3	9.6	11.8	8.1	12.4	8.3	Solomon Islands	813
1.5	8.0	7.7	14.0	11.6	21.5	12.2	11.4	11.7	8.4	7.7	15.9	9.6	9.4	4.7	Sri Lanka	524

Consumer Prices

		1970	1971	1972	1973	1974	1975	1976	1977	1978	1979	1980	1981	1982	1983	1984
															Percent Change over Previous Year:	
Asia (cont.)																
Thailand	578	−.1	.5	4.8	15.5	24.3	⌶5.3	4.1	7.6	7.9	9.9	19.7	12.7	5.3	3.7	.9
Tonga	866	....	....	....	....	....	....	7.1	17.5	9.6	5.5	22.4	14.9	10.8	9.8	⌶.1
Vanuatu	846	....	....	....	....	....	....		5.7	6.4	4.2	11.2	26.8	6.7	1.7	5.5
Europe	170	....	7.6	5.2	8.3	10.1	9.5	9.9	13.7	22.4	26.2	44.1	23.9	53.7	−2.5	25.3
Albania	914	....	....	....	....	....	....	....	....	....	....	....	....	....	....	....
Armenia	911	....	....	....	....	....	....	....	....	....	....	....	....	....	....	
Azerbaijan	912	....	....	....	....	....	....	....	....	....	....	....	....	....	....	
Belarus	913	....	....	....	....	....	....	....	....	....	....	....	....	....	....	
Bulgaria	918	....	....	....	....	....	....	....	....	....	....	....	....	....	....	
Croatia	960	....	....	....	....	....	....	....	....	....	....	....	....	....	....	
Cyprus	423	2.4	4.1	4.8	⌶7.8	6.5	⌶14.1	3.9	7.3	7.4	9.5	13.5	⌶10.7	6.4	5.0	6.0
Czech Republic	935	....	....	....	....	....	....	....	....	....	....	....	....	....	....	
Czechoslovakia	934		−.4	−.3	.3	.5	.7	.8	1.3	1.6	3.9	2.9	.8	5.1	.9	.9
Estonia	939	....	....	....	....	....	....	....	....	....	....	....	....	....	....	
Georgia	915	....	....	....	....	....	....	....	....	....	....	....	....	....	....	
Hungary	944	....	....	....	3.4	1.8	3.8	5.2	3.9	4.7	9.0	9.3	4.5	7.0	6.4	8.7
Kazakhstan	916	....	....	....	....	....	....	....	....	....	....	....	....	....	....	
Kyrgyz Republic	917	....	....	....	....	....	....	....	....	....	....	....	....	....	....	
Latvia	941	....	....	....	....	....	....	....	....	....	....	....	....	....	....	
Lithuania	946	....	....	....	....	....	....	....	....	....	....	....	....	....	....	
Macedonia, FYR	962	....	....	....	....	....	....	....	....	....	....	....	....	....	....	
Malta	181	3.7	2.3	3.4	7.7	⌶7.3	8.8	.6	10.0	4.7	7.1	15.7	11.5	5.8	⌶−.9	−.4
Poland	964	....	1.1	−.1	2.5	7.1	2.3	4.4	⌶4.9	8.1	7.0	9.7	19.1	103.6	25.5	15.4
Romania	968	....	....	....	....	....	....	....	....	....	....	....	....	....	....	
Russia	922	....	....	....	....	....	....	....	....	....	....	....	....	....	....	
Slovak Republic	936	....	....	....	....	....	....	....	....	....	....	....	....	....	....	
Slovenia	961	....	....	....	....	....	....	....	....	....	....	....	....	....	....	
Turkey	186	6.9	15.7	11.7	15.4	15.8	19.2	17.4	27.1	45.3	58.7	110.2	36.6	⌶30.8	31.4	48.4
Ukraine	926	....	....	....	....	....	....	....	....	....	....	....	....	....	....	
Yugoslavia, SFR	188	9.5	15.7	15.9	19.5	22.0	23.5	11.2	14.7	14.1	20.7	30.9	39.8	31.5	40.2	54.7
Middle East	405	1.6	3.8	4.8	10.3	15.4	16.0	14.3	17.3	14.8	11.8	20.2	18.5	17.1	17.0	20.2
Bahrain	419	1.6	5.8	5.1	14.3	24.4	16.2	⌶22.5	17.7	15.8	2.2	3.9	11.3	8.9	3.0	⌶.3
Egypt	469	3.8	3.1	2.1	5.1	10.0	9.7	10.3	12.7	11.1	9.9	⌶20.7	10.3	14.8	16.1	17.0
Iran, I.R. of	429	1.7	4.2	6.4	9.8	14.2	12.9	11.3	27.3	11.7	10.5	20.6	24.2	18.7	19.7	12.5
Israel	436	6.1	12.0	12.9	20.0	39.7	⌶39.3	31.4	34.6	50.6	78.3	⌶131.0	116.8	120.4	145.6	⌶373.8
Jordan	439	5.9	4.8	7.7	11.1	19.4	⌶12.0	11.5	14.6	6.9	⌶14.2	11.1	7.7	7.4	5.0	3.8
Kuwait	443	....	....	....	8.3	13.0	8.4	5.2	9.9	⌶8.7	7.1	6.9	7.4	7.8	4.7	1.2
Lebanon	446		1.6	4.9	6.0	11.1	6.1	6.3	6.3	55.2	23.8	10.5	16.0	13.8	7.2	14.6
Libya	672	⌶−5.3	−3.1	−.3	8.0	7.5	9.1	5.5	6.3	29.4	−6.0	....	....	....	....	....
Oman	449	....	....	....	....	....	....	....	....	....	....	....	....	....	....	
Qatar	453	....	....	....	....	....	....	....	....	....	....		6.8	⌶8.5	5.7	2.7	1.1
Saudi Arabia	456	⌶.2	4.5	4.3	16.5	21.4	34.6	31.6	11.4	⌶−1.6	⌶1.9	⌶3.8	2.8	1.0	.2	−1.6
Syrian Arab Rep.	463	4.6	5.6	2.1	20.4	⌶15.5	11.5	11.4	12.0	4.8	4.6	19.3	18.4	14.3	6.1	9.2
Yemen Arab Rep.	473	....	....	....	43.0	26.6	24.0	15.4	26.0	12.4	⌶26.2	5.3	5.0	2.7	5.3	12.8
Yemen, P.D. Rep.	459	5.0	5.3	5.2	19.7	20.3	11.9	3.1	5.5	5.8	7.1	13.7	3.8	9.5	11.0	1.1
Western Hemisphere	205	8.9	11.5	18.8	34.5	32.2	41.4	55.6	44.2	27.4	34.2	44.7	54.0	65.2	95.1	106.2
Antigua and Barbuda	311	....	....	....	....	....	....		13.8	6.1	16.3	19.0	11.5	4.2	2.3	3.9
Argentina	213	....	....	....	....	....	....	....	....	....	....	....	....	....	....	
Aruba	314	....	....	....	....	....	....	....	....	....	....	....	....	....	....	
Bahamas,The	313	6.2	4.6	6.8	5.5	13.1	10.4	4.3	3.2	6.1	9.1	12.1	11.1	⌶6.0	4.0	4.0
Barbados	316	7.3	7.5	11.9	16.9	38.9	20.3	5.0	8.4	9.5	⌶13.2	14.4	14.6	10.3	5.2	4.7
Belize	339	....	....	....	....	....	....	....	....	....	....		11.2ᵉ	6.8ᵉ	5.0	3.4
Bolivia	218	....	....	....	....	....	....	....	....	....	....	....				1,281.3
Brazil	223	....	....	....	....	....	....	....	....	....	....		101.7	100.5	135.0	192.1
Chile	228	32.5	⌶20.0	74.8	361.5	504.7	⌶374.7	211.8	91.9	40.1	33.4	35.1	19.7	⌶9.9	27.3	19.9
Colombia	233	6.8	⌶9.1	13.4	20.8	24.3	22.9	20.2	33.1	17.8	24.7	26.5	27.5	24.5	19.8	16.1
Costa Rica	238	4.7	3.1	4.6	15.2	30.1	⌶17.4	3.5	4.2	6.0	9.2	18.1	37.1	90.1	32.6	12.0
Dominica	321	12.4	3.6	3.7	⌶12.1	34.4	19.9	10.9	86.5	−36.7	....	25.2	13.3	4.4	4.1	2.2
Dominican Republic	243	3.8	3.6	8.6	15.1	13.1	14.5	7.8	12.9	⌶3.5	9.2	⌶16.8	7.5	7.6	5.6	20.2
Ecuador	248	5.1	8.4	7.9	⌶13.0	23.3	15.4	10.7	13.0	11.7	10.3	13.0	⌶16.4	16.3	48.4	31.2
El Salvador	253	2.8	.4	1.5	6.4	16.9	19.1	7.0	11.8	13.3	⌶14.6	17.4	14.8	11.7	13.3	11.5
Grenada	328	....	....	....	....	....	....		18.5	18.1	20.9	21.8	18.8	7.8	6.1	5.7
Guatemala	258	2.3	−.5	.5	13.8	16.5	⌶13.2	⌶10.7	12.3	8.3	11.3	10.8	11.4	.3	4.5	3.4
Guyana	336	....	....	....	....	....	....	....	....	....	....	....	....	....	....	
Haiti	263	1.4	9.6	3.2	22.7	15.0	16.8	7.0	6.5	−2.7	13.1	⌶17.8	10.9	7.4	10.2	6.4
Honduras	268	2.9	2.2	3.6	5.2	12.8	8.4	4.9	8.4	⌶5.7	12.1	18.1	9.4	9.0	8.3	4.7
Jamaica	343	14.7	5.3	5.4	17.7	27.2	17.4	9.8	11.2	34.9	29.1	27.3	12.7	6.5	11.6	27.8
Mexico	273	5.2	5.3	5.0	12.0	23.8	15.2	15.8	29.0	17.5	18.2	26.4	27.9	58.9	101.8	65.5
Netherlands Antilles	353	⌶3.5	2.1	4.1	8.1	19.5	⌶15.6	5.3	5.4	8.2	11.4	14.6	12.2	⌶12.8	2.1	
Nicaragua	278	....	....	....	27.0	13.3	7.5	2.8	11.4	4.6	48.2	⌶35.3	23.9	24.8	31.1	35.4
Panama	283	3.1	1.9	5.4	6.9	16.3	⌶5.9	4.0	4.6	4.2	8.0	13.8	7.3	4.3	2.1	1.6
Paraguay	288	−.7	4.8	9.5	12.5	25.2	6.8	4.6	9.3	10.6	28.3	22.4	14.0	6.8	13.4	20.3
Peru	293	....	....	....	....	....	....	....	....	....	....	....	....	....	....	
St. Kitts and Nevis	361	....	....	....	....	....	....	....	....	....	....		17.7	10.5	5.9	2.3	2.7
St. Lucia	362	13.4	8.4	7.9	13.4	34.2		17.7	9.7	8.9	10.9	9.4	19.5	15.1	4.6	1.5	1.2
St. Vincent & Grenadines	364	....	....	....	....	....		6.8	11.3	10.2	8.4	15.6	17.2	⌶12.7	7.2	5.5	2.7
Suriname	366	2.6	.2	3.2	12.9	16.9	8.4	10.1	9.7	8.8	14.8	⌶14.1	8.8	7.3	4.4	3.7
Trinidad and Tobago	369	2.5	3.5	9.3	14.8	22.0	⌶17.0	10.7	11.7	10.3	14.7	17.5	14.3	⌶11.6	15.2	13.3
Uruguay	298	....	....	....	....	....	....	....	....	....	....	....	....	....	....	
Venezuela, Rep. Bol.	299	2.5	3.2	2.8	4.1	8.3	10.2	7.6	7.8	7.1	12.4	21.5	16.0	9.7	6.3	11.6
Memorandum Items																
Oil Exporting Countries	999	5.3	4.9	4.7	13.1	17.5	14.9	15.0	15.7	10.6	11.1	14.3	14.7	9.2	11.1	11.5
Non-Oil Developing Countries	201	8.6	8.5	11.4	23.4	19.3	16.0	16.6	17.3	11.4	21.4	31.1	33.6	37.9	43.7	46.6

Indices

		1970	1971	1972	1973	1974	1975	1976	1977	1978	1979	1980	1981	1982	1983	1984
															Index Numbers:	
World	001	3.3	3.5	3.7	4.1	4.7	5.4	6.0	6.8	7.4	8.3	9.8	11.4	13.1	15.1	17.4
Industrial Countries	110	22.0	23.2	24.4	26.3	29.9	33.3	36.2	39.5	42.5	46.5	52.2	57.7	62.1	65.4	68.7
Developing Countries	200	.1	.1	.1	.2	.2	.2	.3	.3	.4	.5	.6	.8	1.0	1.4	1.9
Africa	605	2.0	2.1	2.2	2.4	2.7	3.2	3.7	4.4	5.0	5.8	6.7	7.9	9.0	10.5	12.3
Asia	505	10.2	10.7	11.4	13.4	17.4	19.2	19.7	21.4	22.7	25.0	28.8	32.6	35.1	37.9	41.1
Europe (1995=100,000)	170	13.4	14.4	15.2	16.4	18.1	19.8	21.8	24.8	30.3	38.3	55.1	68.3	105.0	102.4	128.3
Europe	170	....	....	....	....	....	....	....	....	....	....	....	....	....	....	
Middle East	405	2.9	3.0	3.2	3.5	4.1	4.7	5.4	6.3	7.2	8.1	9.7	11.5	13.5	15.8	19.0
Western Hemisphere(1995=10 mil.)	205	3.2	3.6	4.2	5.7	7.5	10.6	16.5	23.8	30.3	40.7	58.9	90.6	149.8	292.1	602.3
Western Hemisphere	205	....	....	....	....	....	....	....	....	....	....	....	....	....	....	

Calculated from Indices

1985	1986	1987	1988	1989	1990	1991	1992	1993	1994	1995	1996	1997	1998	1999		
															Asia (cont.)	
2.4	I1.8	2.5	3.8	5.4	I6.0	5.7	4.1	3.4	5.0	5.8	5.8	5.6	8.1	.3	Thailand	578
16.8	21.7	4.7	9.9	4.1	9.7	10.6	7.9	1.0	1.0	I1.4	3.0	2.1	3.3	4.5	Tonga	866
1.1	I4.8	16.0	8.8	7.7	4.8	6.5	1.4	3.6	2.3	2.2	.9	2.8	3.3	....	Vanuatu	846
41.8	21.7	26.3	86.9	84.1	165.3	93.8	92.5	75.8	174.2	117.9	45.6	37.1	30.7	50.1	**Europe**	170
							226.0	85.0	22.6	7.8	12.7	33.2	20.6	.4	Albania	914
									4,962.2	176.0	18.7	I13.9	8.7	.7	Armenia	911
							912.3	I1,129.0	1,664.5	411.7	19.8	3.6	-.7	-8.6	Azerbaijan	912
							966.5	1,190.2	2,221.0	709.3	52.7	63.9	72.9	293.7	Belarus	913
	2.7	2.7	2.4	I6.4	23.8	I338.4	91.3	72.9	96.1	62.1	121.6	1,061.6	18.7	2.6	Bulgaria	918
		133.3	185.7	1,400.0	500.0	122.2	625.0	1,500.0	107.3	4.0	4.3	4.1	6.4	3.7	Croatia	960
5.0	I1.2	2.8	3.4	3.8	4.5	5.0	I6.5	4.9	4.7	2.6	3.0	3.6	2.2	I1.6	Cyprus	423
									10.1	9.1	8.8	8.4	10.7	2.1	Czech Republic	935
2.3	.5	.1	.1	1.4	10.0	I57.7	10.8	....	....						Czechoslovakia	934
								89.8	47.7	28.8	23.1	10.6	8.2	3.3	Estonia	939
								3,378.0	-97.9	162.7	39.4	7.1	3.6	19.1	Georgia	915
I7.0	5.3	8.7	15.8	16.9	29.0	34.2	I22.9	22.5	18.9	28.3	23.5	18.3	14.4	10.3	Hungary	944
									1,876.6	176.2	39.3	17.4	7.1	8.2	Kazakhstan	916
											31.9	23.4	10.5	35.9	Kyrgyz Republic	917
							I243.3	108.8	35.9	25.0	17.6	8.4	4.6	2.4	Latvia	941
								I410.2	72.2	39.7	24.6	8.9	5.1	.8	Lithuania	946
								352.0	126.6	16.4	2.7	1.1	.5	-1.3	Macedonia, FYR	962
-.2	2.0	.4	.9	.8	3.0	I2.5	I1.6	4.1	4.1	4.0	2.5	3.1	2.4	2.1	Malta	181
11.5	16.5	26.4	58.7	244.6	555.4	I76.7	45.3	36.9	33.3	26.8	20.2	15.9	11.7	7.3	Poland	964
						230.6	211.2	255.2	136.8	32.2	38.8	154.8	59.1	45.8	Romania	968
								874.6	307.6	197.5	47.7	14.7	27.7	85.7	Russia	922
						61.2	9.9	23.2	13.4	9.9	I5.8	6.1	6.7	10.6	Slovak Republic	936
							156.6	31.9	19.8	12.6	9.7	9.1	8.6	6.6	Slovenia	961
45.0	34.6	I38.8	73.7	63.3	60.3	66.0	70.1	66.1	I106.3	88.1	80.3	85.7	84.6	64.9	Turkey	186
								4,734.9	891.2	376.7	80.3	15.9	....	....	Ukraine	926
72.3	89.8	120.8	194.1	1,239.9	I583.1	117.4	....	....							Yugoslavia, SFR	188
16.5	18.3	22.9	20.6	15.1	10.5	14.5	13.4	12.0	14.3	22.1	13.1	7.4	7.4	7.3	**Middle East**	405
-2.6	-2.3	-1.7	.3	1.5	.9	.8	-.2	2.5	.8	2.7	-.5	2.4	-.4		Bahrain	419
12.1	23.9	19.7	17.7	21.3	16.8	19.7	13.6	12.1	8.2	I15.7	7.2	I4.6	4.2	3.1	Egypt	469
I4.4	18.4	28.6	28.7	22.3	7.6	I17.1	25.6	21.2	31.5	49.6	28.9	17.2	19.4	21.0	Iran, I.R. of	429
I304.6	I48.1	19.8	16.3	20.2	17.2	19.0	11.9	I10.9	I12.3	10.0	11.3	9.0	5.4	5.2	Israel	436
I3.0	—	-.2	6.6	25.7	16.2	8.2	I4.0	3.3	3.5	2.4	6.5	3.0	4.4	.6	Jordan	439
1.5	1.0	.7	1.5	3.3	9.8	9.1	-.5	.4	2.5	2.7	3.6	.7	.2	....	Kuwait	443
54.5	95.2	487.6	127.8	48.1	62.7	48.4	80.7	15.7	6.8	....					Lebanon	446
															Libya	672
						4.6	1.0	.9	-.4	-1.3	.1	I1.1	-.8	.4	Oman	449
1.9	I1.6	2.7	4.6	3.3	3.0	4.4	3.1	-.9	1.3	3.0	7.4	2.8	....	....	Qatar	453
-3.1	-3.2	-1.5	.9	1.0	2.1	4.9	-.1	1.1	.6	4.9	1.2	—	-.6	-1.4	Saudi Arabia	456
17.3	36.1	59.5	34.6	11.4	I19.4	9.0	11.0	13.2	15.3	8.0	8.2	2.3	-.5	....	Syrian Arab Rep.	463
															Yemen Arab Rep.	473
5.1	....														Yemen, P.D. Rep.	459
124.4	86.5	119.2	106.6	75.2	461.1	139.8	154.4	222.1	219.0	42.2	22.6	13.8	10.4	9.6	**Western Hemisphere**	205
1.0	....														Antigua and Barbuda	311
				3,079.8	2,314.0	171.7	24.9	10.6	4.2	3.4	.2	.5	.9	-1.2	Argentina	213
4.0	1.1	3.6	3.1	4.0	5.8	5.6	3.9	5.2	6.3	3.4	3.2	3.0	1.9	2.3	Aruba	314
4.6	5.4	5.8	4.4	5.4	4.7	7.1	5.7	2.7	1.4	I2.1	1.4	.5	1.3	1.3	Bahamas, The	313
3.9	1.3	3.3	4.9	6.2	3.1	6.3	6.1	1.1	I.1	1.9	2.4	7.7	-1.3	1.6	Barbados	316
4.2	.8	2.0	5.3	—	I3.0	2.2	2.4	1.5	2.6	2.9	6.4	1.0	-.9	-1.2	Belize	339
11,749.6	276.3	14.6	16.0	15.2	17.1	21.4	I12.1	8.5	7.9	10.2	12.4	4.7	7.7	2.2	Bolivia	218
226.0	147.1	228.3	629.1	1,430.7	I2,947.7	432.8	951.6	I1,928.0	2,075.9	66.0	15.8	6.9	3.2	4.9	Brazil	223
29.5	20.6	19.9	14.7	17.0	26.0	21.8	15.4	12.7	11.4	8.2	7.4	6.1	5.1	3.3	Chile	228
24.0	18.9	23.3	I28.1	25.8	29.1	30.4	27.0	22.6	23.8	21.0	I20.2	18.9	20.4	11.2	Colombia	233
15.1	11.8	16.8	20.8	16.5	19.0	28.7	21.8	9.8	I13.5	23.2	17.5	13.2	11.7	10.0	Costa Rica	238
3.7	2.8	4.0	2.9	6.2	3.2	I5.6	5.5	1.6	—	1.3	1.7	2.4	1.0	1.2	Dominica	321
45.3	7.6	13.6	43.9	40.7	50.5	47.1	4.3	5.3	8.3	12.5	5.4	I8.3	4.5	6.5	Dominican Republic	243
28.0	23.0	29.5	58.2	75.6	I48.5	48.8	54.3	45.0	27.4	I22.9	24.4	30.6	36.1	52.2	Ecuador	248
22.3	31.9	24.9	19.8	17.6	24.0	14.4	I11.2	18.5	10.6	10.0	9.8	4.5	2.5	.5	El Salvador	253
2.5	.6	I-.9	4.0	5.6	2.7	2.6	3.8	2.8	3.8	1.9	2.0	1.2	1.4	.2	Grenada	328
18.7	36.9	12.3	10.8	11.4	41.2	33.2	10.0	11.8	10.9	8.4	11.1	9.2	7.0	4.9	Guatemala	258
										12.2	7.1	3.6	4.6	7.5	Guyana	336
10.6	3.3	-11.4	4.1	6.9	21.3	I15.4	I19.4	29.7	39.3	27.6	20.6	20.6	10.6	8.7	Haiti	263
3.4	4.4	2.5	4.5	9.9	23.3	34.0	8.8	10.7	21.7	29.5	23.8	I20.2	13.7	11.7	Honduras	268
25.7	15.1	6.7	I8.3	14.3	22.0	51.1	77.3	22.1	35.1	19.9	26.4	9.7	8.6	6.0	Jamaica	343
57.7	86.2	131.8	114.2	20.0	26.7	22.7	I15.5	9.8	7.0	35.0	34.4	20.6	15.9	16.6	Mexico	273
.5	1.3	3.8	2.6	3.9	I3.7	4.0	1.4	2.0	1.8	2.8	I3.6	3.3	1.1	....	Netherlands Antilles	353
I219.5	681.4	911.9	I10205.0	4,770.2	7,485.5	2,945.1	23.7	20.4	I6.7	10.9	11.6	9.2	13.0	11.2	Nicaragua	278
1.0	-.1	1.0	I.4	.1	.8	1.3	1.8	.5	1.3	1.0	1.3	1.3	.6	1.3	Panama	283
25.2	31.7	21.8	22.6	26.4	I38.2	24.2	15.2	18.2	20.6	13.4	9.8	7.0	11.5	6.8	Paraguay	288
										11.1	11.5	8.6	7.2	3.5	Peru	293
2.6	—	1.0	.2	5.2	4.0	4.3	2.9	1.8	1.4	3.0	2.1	8.9	3.4	3.9	St. Kitts and Nevis	361
I1.4	2.0	7.6	.8	4.1	4.7	5.7	5.1	1.1	2.5	5.7	1.8	.2	2.2	5.4	St. Lucia	362
2.1	1.0	3.3	.2	2.8	7.6	5.5	3.5	4.3	1.0	1.7	4.4	.4	2.1	1.0	St. Vincent & Grenadines	364
10.9	18.7	53.4	7.3	.8	21.7	26.0	43.7	143.5	368.5	235.6	-.7	7.1	19.0	98.9	Suriname	366
7.6	7.7	10.8	7.8	I11.4	11.1	3.8	6.4	10.8	8.8	5.2	3.4	3.6	5.6	3.4	Trinidad and Tobago	369
				80.4	112.5	102.0	68.5	54.1	44.7	42.2	28.3	19.8	10.8	5.7	Uruguay	298
11.4	11.5	28.1	29.5	84.5	40.7	34.2	31.4	38.1	60.8	59.9	99.9	50.0	35.8	I23.6	Venezuela, Rep. Bol.	299
															Memorandum Items	
5.2	8.7	13.7	18.2	18.5	11.2	14.6	17.1	17.8	20.6	25.8	20.3	11.1	29.6	15.2	Oil Exporting Countries	999
52.5	38.6	47.4	60.5	29.0	84.2	44.2	45.0	53.4	64.2	30.6	15.5	10.6	8.8	8.9	Non-Oil Developing Countries	201

Indices

1985	1986	1987	1988	1989	1990	1991	1992	1993	1994	1995	1996	1997	1998	1999		
										1995=100						
20.1	22.5	25.6	29.9	33.7	43.1	50.5	58.9	69.8	87.3	100.0	108.4	114.9	121.6	127.8	World	001
71.7	73.6	75.9	78.4	82.0	86.2	89.9	92.8	95.4	97.6	100.0	102.2	104.3	105.8	107.2	Industrial Countries	110
2.8	3.7	5.1	7.7	9.8	16.8	23.4	33.0	48.7	76.9	100.0	116.1	128.5	142.9	156.6	Developing Countries	200
13.9	15.7	17.9	21.4	25.5	29.3	36.3	47.7	59.8	77.6	100.0	120.1	131.8	140.5	148.4	Africa	605
43.3	45.7	48.6	52.2	57.8	61.4	66.4	71.4	78.0	89.5	100.0	107.7	112.8	122.3	125.9	Asia	505
181.9	221.4	279.6	522.5												Europe (1995=100,000)	170
			.5	1.0	2.6	4.9	9.5	16.7	45.9	100.0	145.6	199.6	260.9	391.6	Europe	170
22.1	26.2	32.1	38.8	44.6	49.3	56.4	64.0	71.7	81.9	100.0	113.1	121.4	130.4	140.0	Middle East	405
1,351.6	2,520.8	5,525.0	11,414.2												Western Hemisphere(1995=10 mil.)	205
			.1	.2	1.1	2.7	6.8	22.0	70.3	100.0	122.6	139.5	154.0	168.8	Western Hemisphere	205

		1970	1971	1972	1973	1974	1975	1976	1977	1978	1979	1980	1981	1982	1983	1984
														Billions of US Dollars		
World	001	300.1	336.4	398.8	552.6	811.3	845.4	953.4	1,080.5	1,251.5	1,618.4	1,931.7	1,924.4	1,777.2	1,736.0	1,840.8
Industrial Countries	110	222.7	248.7	296.7	405.1	541.8	578.0	643.4	729.4	873.1	1,074.2	1,265.1	1,243.9	1,177.2	1,162.7	1,240.5
United States	111	42.659	43.549	49.199	70.823	99.437	I108.856	116.794	I123.182	145.847	186.363	225.566	238.715	216.442	205.639	223.976
Canada	156	16.786	18.374	21.185	26.437	34.508	34.074	40.598	43.545	48.431	58.294	67.734	72.726	71.234	76.749	90.272
Australia	193	4.770	5.213	6.461	9.559	11.016	11.948	13.193	13.367	14.415	18.663	21.944	21.477	21.360	20.113	23.111
Japan	158	19.317	23.995	29.088	37.017	55.469	55.819	67.304	81.083	98.211	102.299	130.441	151.495	138.385	146.965	169.700
New Zealand	196	1.223	1.361	1.792	2.596	2.435	2.162	2.795	3.196	I3.738	4.706	5.421	5.622	5.571	5.414	5.518
Euro Area	163	....	....	....	....	....	....	....	....	....	....	....	....	....	....	....
Austria	122	2.857	3.168	3.883	5.283	7.161	7.519	8.506	9.808	12.175	15.481	17.489	15.841	15.642	15.428	15.739
Belgium	124	....	....	....	....	....	....	....	....	....	....	....	....	....	....	....
Belgium-Luxembourg	126	11.600	12.642	16.152	22.455	28.334	28.804	32.889	37.538	44.947	56.700	64.656	55.694	52.354	51.937	51.891
Finland	172	2.306	2.367	2.913	3.837	5.490	5.502	6.342	7.665	8.570	11.172	14.150	14.004	13.088	12.518	13.471
France	132	18.099	20.811	26.449	36.669	46.259	53.100	56.874	65.130	79.371	100.692	116.030	106.424	96.694	94.943	97.566
Germany	134	34.228	38.845	46.736	67.563	89.368	90.176	102.162	118.072	142.453	171.804	192.860	176.047	176.424	169.417	171.735
Ireland	178	1.120	1.312	1.607	2.131	2.658	3.192	3.315	4.404	5.691	7.143	8.398	7.677	8.067	8.599	9.641
Italy	136	13.205	15.105	18.609	22.226	30.465	34.988	37.265	45.305	56.090	72.233	78.104	77.070	73.791	72.877	74.564
luxembourg	137	.855	.740	1.000	1.490	2.130	1.787	1.830	1.913	2.296	2.926	3.005	2.385	2.237	2.180	2.519
Netherlands	138	13.355	15.773	19.154	27.352	37.423	39.888	46.153	50.110	57.590	73.537	84.948	78.597	75.717	73.692	75.055
Portugal	182	.946	1.049	1.298	1.842	2.277	1.939	1.811	1.970	2.414	3.479	4.640	4.148	4.164	4.599	5.200
Spain	184	2.388	2.964	3.817	5.198	7.091	7.690	8.730	10.223	13.114	18.208	20.720	20.333	20.498	19.734	23.564
Denmark	128	3.356	3.680	4.432	6.248	7.719	8.712	9.115	10.065	11.883	14.696	16.749	16.095	15.397	16.053	15.980
Greece	174	.643	.662	.870	1.456	2.030	2.294	2.561	2.756	3.368	3.885	5.153	4.246	4.298	4.413	4.811
Iceland	176	.147	.150	.189	.290	.331	.306	.401	.512	.641	.782	.918	.894	.685	.740	.739
Norway	142	2.457	2.555	3.283	4.725	6.282	7.232	7.951	8.880	10.882	13.546	18.542	18.217	17.593	17.997	18.886
Sweden	144	6.795	7.463	8.769	12.201	15.939	17.383	18.435	I19.082	21.790	27.602	30.906	28.658	26.808	27.446	29.378
Switzerland	146	5.063	5.738	6.842	9.528	11.934	12.953	14.835	17.614	23.560	I26.538	29.632	27.049	26.019	25.591	25.849
United Kingdom	112	19.430	22.098	23.985	29.637	38.197	43.423	45.356	55.860	67.887	86.397	110.137	102.845	97.017	91.868	93.840
Developing Countries	200	77.33	87.72	102.12	147.55	269.49	267.47	310.04	351.10	378.46	544.19	666.60	680.57	599.98	573.22	600.34
Africa	605	12.682	13.570	15.627	22.396	38.480	36.084	40.042	46.855	48.398	70.694	95.874	80.131	67.185	66.656	66.760
Algeria	612	1.009	.857	1.304	1.887	4.687	4.700	5.259	5.944	6.326	9.551	13.871	14.396	13.170	12.583	12.795
Benin	638	.033	.042	.036	.043	.034	.032	.025	.031	.027	.046	.063	.034	.024	.067	.167
Botswana	616	.026	.042	.058	.085	.121	.142	.170	.186	.233	.451	.504	.398	.475	.644	.751
Burkina Faso	748	.018	.016	.020	.025	.036	.044	.053	.055	.043	.077	.090	.074	.056	.058	.079
Burundi	618	.024	.019	.026	.030	.031	.032	.061	.090	.069	.104	.065	.075	.088	.080	.103
Cameroon	622	.227	.208	.221	.353	.478	.447	.511	.704	.802	1.132	1.384	1.105	1.063	.976	.886
Cape Verde	624	.002	.002	.002	.002	.002	.002	.002	.002	.002	.002	.004	.003	.003	.004	.002
Central African Rep.	626	.031	.032	.039	.037	.048	.047	.061	.082	.072	.080	.116	.079	.107	.074	.085
Chad	628	.030	.028	.036	.038	.037	.048	.063	.107	.099	.088	.071	.083	.058	.105	.131
Comoros	632	.005	.006	.006	.005	.009	.010	.012	.009	.009	.017	.011	.016	.020	.019	.007
Congo, Dem. Rep. of	636	.781	.687	.738	1.013	1.381	.865	.944	.989	.931	1.514	1.627	.544	.399	1.080	1.005
Congo, Rep. of	634	.031	.040	.060	.089	.229	.178	.221	.267	.308	.496	.911	.811	.993	.640	1.183
Côte d'Ivoire	662	.471	.459	.553	.857	1.213	1.181	1.632	2.157	2.322	2.514	3.135	2.533	2.298	2.091	2.707
Djibouti	611	.021	.015	.019	.031	.038	.015	.016	.019	.018	.011	.012	.009	.013	.011	.013
Equatorial Guinea	642	.025	.028	.019	.019	.034	.026	.010	.014	.017	.029	.014	.011	.012	.013	.015
Ethiopia	644	.122	.126	.167	.239	.269	.240	.280	.333	.306	.418	.425	.389	.404	.403	.417
Gabon	646	.144	.179	.228	.331	.768	.943	1.135	1.343	1.107	1.848	2.173	2.201	2.161	2.000	2.011
Gambia, The	648	.017	.013	.019	.025	.043	.044	.035	.047	.039	.058	.031	.027	.044	.048	.049
Ghana	652	.458	.492	.441	.657	.738	.816	.832	1.014	1.093	.995	1.257	1.065	.873	2.624	.528
Guinea-Bissau	654	.004	.002	.003	.004	.004	.007	.006	.013	.012	.013	.011	.014	.012	.009	.017
Kenya	664	.305	.314	.359	.475	.603	.606	.790	1.186	1.023	1.090	1.245	1.139	1.025	.869	1.074
Lesotho	666	.006	.004	.008	.013	.014	.012	.017	.014	.032	.045	.058	.050	.036	.030	.027
Liberia	668	.214	.222	.244	.324	.400	.394	.460	.447	.504	.537	.600	.529	.477	.428	.452
Madagascar	674	.145	.147	.166	.203	.244	.301	.275	.338	.388	.394	.401	.317	.311	.264	.332
Malawi	676	.069	.075	.086	.114	.137	.160	.192	.204	.170	.277	.335	.293	.254	.219	.396
Mali	678	.035	.036	.042	.053	.064	.053	.084	.125	.112	.148	.205	.155	.146	.165	.133
Mauritania	682	.089	.091	.119	.155	.180	.176	.178	.157	.123	.147	.194	.261	.233	.291	.292
Mauritius	684	.069	.066	.106	.137	.312	.298	.265	.309	.325	.381	.435	.332	.366	.366	.372
Morocco	686	.488	.502	.643	.910	1.708	1.543	1.261	1.302	1.508	1.959	2.441	2.386	2.062	2.006	2.171
Mozambique	688	....	....	....	....	....	....	....	....	....	....	....	....	....	....	....
Namibia	728	....	....	....	....	....	....	....	....	....	....	....	....	....	....	....
Niger	692	.032	.039	.054	.062	.053	.091	.134	.161	.282	.448	.566	.455	.332	.299	.259
Nigeria	694	1.240	1.815	2.180	3.462	9.205	7.834	10.566	11.839	9.938	17.334	25.946	18.231	12.196	10.298	11.843
Rwanda	714	.025	.022	.019	.033	.036	.042	.080	.092	.072	.118	.112	.110	.103	.121	.145
Sao Tome & Principe	716	.008	.007	.007	.013	.017	.007	.008	.023	.021	.027	.017	.009			.012
Senegal	722	.153	.126	.216	.195	.391	.461	.485	.624	.449	.535	.477	.500	.548	.618	.634
Seychelles	718	.002	.002	.003	.004	.007	.006	.009	.011	.015	.022	.021	.017	.015	.020	.026
Sierra Leone I	724	.101	.097	.115	.131	.144	.118	.099	.136	.170	.200	.224	.150	.111	.119	.133
South Africa	199	3.344	3.483	4.108	I6.064	8.688	8.789	7.850	9.904	12.772	18.258	I25.540	20.775	17.635	18.532	17.334
Sudan	732	.298	.328	.357	.434	.350	.438	.554	.661	.518	.535	.543	.657	.498	.624	.629
Swaziland	734	.071	.078	.082	.108	.178	.195	.183	.165	.196	.232	.373	.382	.320	.304	.230
Tanzania	738	.252	.268	.324	.368	.403	.372	.440	.507	.476	.497	.511	.568	.449	.372	.298
Togo	742	.055	.050	.050	.061	.189	.126	.105	.159	.234	.218	.338	.212	.178	.163	.192
Tunisia	744	.182	.217	.315	.422	.921	.856	.788	.929	1.126	1.791	2.231	2.500	1.981	1.850	1.797
Uganda	746	.028	.028	.028	.029	.032	.026	.036	.059	.035	.435	.345	.243	.349	.372	.399
Zambia	754	1.001	1.226	.758	1.144	1.407	.810	1.070	.896	.856	1.373	1.305	1.125	1.024	.832	.661
Zimbabwe	698	.370	.404	.515	.688	.863	.932	.891	.877	.885	1.053	1.415	1.266	1.273	1.128	1.147

Billions of US Dollars

1985	1986	1987	1988	1989	1990	1991	1992	1993	1994	1995	1996	1997	1998	1999		
1,875.8	**2,048.5**	**2,419.0**	**2,765.2**	**3,008.5**	**3,423.4**	**3,498.5**	**3,713.9**	**3,752.3**	**4,266.0**	**5,099.8**	**5,267.6**	**5,497.4**	**5,405.8**	**I 5,554.4**	**World**	**001**
1,282.0	**1,485.0**	**1,736.2**	**1,986.5**	**2,127.9**	**2,453.9**	**2,502.2**	**2,650.9**	**2,596.5**	**2,914.1**	**3,469.8**	**3,515.2**	**3,640.9**	**3,665.6**	**I 3,722.5**	**Industrial Countries**	**110**
218.815	227.158	254.122	322.427	363.812	393.592	421.730	448.164	464.773	512.627	584.743	625.073	688.697	682.138	702.098	United States	111
90.950	90.329	98.168	117.105	121.832	127.629	127.163	134.435	145.178	165.376	192.197	201.633	214.422	214.327	238.446	Canada	156
22.604	22.569	26.621	33.233	37.125	39.752	41.854	42.824	42.723	47.528	53.111	60.300	62.910	55.893	56.087	Australia	193
177.164	210.757	231.286	264.856	273.932	287.581	314.786	339.885	362.244	397.005	443.116	410.901	420.957	387.927	419.367	Japan	158
5.720	5.880	7.195	8.850	8.876	9.394	9.619	9.785	10.542	12.185	13.645	14.422	14.076	12.070	12.452	New Zealand	196
....	....	....	....	....	....	....	....	....	....	....	....	....	886.456	881.898	Euro Area	163
17.239	22.522	27.171	31.058	32.492	41.135	41.113	44.411	40.216	45.022	57.642	57.818	58.590	62.742	I 63.407	Austria	122
....	....	....	....	....	....	....	....	125.877	143.658	175.848	175.355	171.881	177.716	I 176.198	Belgium	124
53.742	68.892	83.288	92.135	100.075	118.294	118.279	123.524	119.512	137.257	169.671	165.763	165.544	....	....	Belgium-Luxembourg	126
13.617	16.356	20.037	21.748	23.298	26.571	23.080	23.981	23.446	29.658	39.573	38.435	39.316	42.963	40.665	Finland	172
101.671	124.831	148.382	167.790	179.430	216.591	217.096	235.869	210.444	234.021	284.865	241.068	290.231	306.054	I 300.162	France	132
183.933	243.326	294.369	323.323	341.231	I 410.104	402.843	422.271	382.472	429.722	523.802	524.198	512.427	543.397	541.076	Germany	134
10.357	12.639	15.994	18.742	20.690	23.746	24.215	28.523	29.272	34.149	44.635	48.668	53.512	64.568	70.281	Ireland	178
76.717	97.204	116.711	127.859	140.556	170.304	169.465	178.155	169.153	191.421	233.998	252.039	240.404	245.700	230.193	Italy	136
2.831	3.721	4.375	5.069	5.401	6.305	6.271	6.469	5.892	6.560	7.750	7.210	6.999	7.911	7.888	luxembourg	137
77.872	I 80.255	93.108	103.188	107.854	131.775	133.631	140.335	139.127	155.554	196.276	197.417	194.905	201.374	I 200.286	Netherlands	138
5.685	7.242	9.320	10.989	12.799	16.422	16.329	18.374	15.432	18.006	23.206	24.605	23.973	24.814	I 23.864	Portugal	182
24.247	27.206	34.192	40.341	43.451	55.521	58.621	64.840	60.955	72.927	91.046	101.996	104.359	109.228	I 109.964	Spain	184
17.090	21.286	25.675	27.653	28.107	35.133	36.001	41.053	37.168	41.417	49.754	50.097	47.715	47.477	48.342	Denmark	128
4.539	5.648	6.533	5.429	7.545	8.105	8.673	9.843	8.434	9.384	10.961	9.480	8.626	....	....	Greece	174
.815	1.099	1.375	1.424	1.385	1.592	1.549	1.528	1.399	1.623	1.804	1.639	1.852	2.050	2.005	Iceland	176
19.985	18.092	21.490	22.436	27.107	34.048	34.107	35.178	31.853	34.692	41.992	49.645	48.542	39.645	44.884	Norway	142
30.461	37.263	44.506	49.747	51.547	57.540	55.217	56.118	49.857	61.343	79.801	84.896	82.946	84.780	84.812	Sweden	144
27.433	37.471	45.464	50.704	51.525	63.784	61.517	I 61.377	58.687	66.227	78.040	76.196	72.493	75.431	76.122	Switzerland	146
101.355	106.956	131.193	145.457	153.271	185.268	185.264	190.429	181.362	204.004	242.006	262.096	281.061	271.844	268.211	United Kingdom	112
593.77	**563.47**	**682.78**	**778.70**	**880.55**	**969.57**	**996.35**	**1,063.00**	**1,155.82**	**1,351.93**	**1,629.97**	**1,752.43**	**1,856.56**	**1,740.17**	**1,831.96**	**Developing Countries**	**200**
65.360	**57.061**	**63.097**	**64.346**	**69.588**	**83.954**	**91.076**	**79.147**	**75.102**	**79.662**	**92.780**	**104.786**	**105.815**	**92.027**	**....**	**Africa**	**605**
12.841	7.832	8.225	7.810	9.570	12.930	12.570	11.130	10.230	8.880	10.240	12.620	....	....	....	Algeria	612
.150	.104	.114	.071	.077	.122	.021	.335	.384	.398	.420	.528	.424	.414	.389	Benin	638
.839	1.043	1.896	1.798	1.854	1.785	1.843	1.746	1.757	1.848	2.142	2.536	2.842	1.948	....	Botswana	616
.071	.083	.155	.142	.095	.152	.106	.064	.069	.107	.160	.233	.232	.319	.254	Burkina Faso	748
.112	.154	.090	.133	.078	.075	.091	.073	.062	.121	.106	.040	.087	.065	.054	Burundi	618
.722	.782	.829	.927	1.273	2.002	1.834	1.840	1.429	1.364	1.651	1.769	1.860	....	....	Cameroon	622
.006	.005	.008	.003	.007	.006	.006	.005	.004	.005	.009	....	....	....	....	Cape Verde	624
.092	.066	.130	.066	.134	.120	.047	.107	.110	.151	.171	.147	.154	....	....	Central African Rep.	626
.062	.099	.109	.144	.155	.188	.194	.182	.132	.148	.252	.229	.237	.261	....	Chad	628
.016	.020	.012	.021	.018	.018	.025	.022	.022	.011	.011	....	....	....	....	Comoros	632
.950	1.100	.974	1.120	1.254	.999	.830	.426	.368	.419	.438	.592	....	....	....	Congo, Dem. Rep. of	636
1.087	.777	.973	.937	1.247	.981	1.030	1.179	1.069	.959	1.173	1.555	1.668	....	....	Congo, Rep. of	634
2.969	3.354	3.110	2.770	2.807	3.072	2.686	2.875	2.519	2.742	3.645	4.278	4.179	4.092	4.077	Côte d'Ivoire	662
.014	.020	.028	.023	.025	.025	.017	.016	....	....	....	....	....	....	....	Djibouti	611
.017	.035	.042	.049	.041	.065	.086	.058	.075	.066	.127	.232	.497	.423	....	Equatorial Guinea	642
.333	.455	.355	.429	.440	.298	.189	.169	.199	.372	.423	.417	.587	.561	....	Ethiopia	644
1.951	1.271	1.288	1.196	1.597	2.204	2.243	2.082	2.295	2.350	2.713	3.307	3.110	....	....	Gabon	646
.043	.035	.040	.058	.027	.031	.038	.057	.067	.035	.016	.021	.015	.027	.007	Gambia, The	648
.617	.863	.977	1.009	1.018	....	.617	1.252	.974	1.425	1.724	1.669	1.635	1.795	....	Ghana	652
.012	....	....	.016	.014	.019	.020	.006	.028	.086	.044	.028	.048	.027	.049	Guinea-Bissau	654
.958	1.200	.961	1.067	.951	1.032	1.108	1.339	1.374	1.587	1.879	2.068	2.054	2.008	....	Kenya	664
.022	.025	.047	.064	.066	.062	.067	.109	.132	.143	.160	.187	.196	.194	....	Lesotho	666
.436	.408	.382	.396	.460	....	....	....	....	....	....	....	....	....	....	Liberia	668
.274	.313	.331	.278	.321	.319	.305	.278	.260	.369	.369	.299	.223	.243	....	Madagascar	674
.236	.283	.354	.340	.256	.578	.515	.424	.295	.568	.638	.527	.537	.517	....	Malawi	676
.124	.212	.179	.215	.247	.359	.312	.343	.478	.335	.442	.433	.561	.556	.536	Mali	678
.374	.349	.428	.354	.437	.447	....	....	....	.487	....	....	....	....	....	Mauritania	682
.440	.676	.880	.997	.986	1.194	1.194	1.302	1.299	1.347	1.538	1.802	1.592	1.645	....	Mauritius	684
2.165	2.433	2.807	3.626	3.337	4.265	4.284	3.973	3.055	5.556	6.881	6.881	7.032	7.153	7.367	Morocco	686
....	....	....	....	....	....	....	....	....	.160	.171	.222	.226	.234	.268	Mozambique	688
....	....	....	1.056	1.122	1.086	1.214	1.342	1.290	1.321	....	....	....	....	....	Namibia	728
.259	.317	.312	.289	.244	.283	.307	.333	.287	.225	.287	.325	.272	.298	.276	Niger	692
12.537	5.923	7.344	6.916	7.876	13.596	12.264	11.886	9.908	9.415	I 11.725	16.153	15.213	9.729	....	Nigeria	694
.131	.189	.113	.108	.095	.110	.093	.066	.065	....	.052	.060	.087	.060	.061	Rwanda	714
.006	.010	.007	.010	.005	.004	.006	.005	.005	.006	.005	.005	.005	....	....	Sao Tome & Principe	716
.562	.625	.606	.591	.693	.762	.701	.673	.707	.791	.969	.986	.905	.968	....	Senegal	722
.028	.018	.022	.032	.034	.057	.049	.048	.051	.052	.053	.100	....	....	....	Seychelles	718
.130	.144	.130	.106	.138	.138	.145	.149	.118	.116	.042	.047	.017	.007	.006	Sierra Leone	724
16.330	18.376	21.224	21.814	22.144	23.568	23.279	23.440	24.222	25.308	27.853	29.221	31.027	26.362	26.707	South Africa I	199
.374	.333	.504	.509	.672	.374	.305	.319	.417	.503	I .556	.620	.594	.596	....	Sudan	732
.179	.278	.425	.461	.500	.557	.591	.639	.680	.781	.956	.893	....	....	....	Swaziland	734
.246	.361	.289	.275	.365	.331	.342	.416	.450	.519	.682	.760	.719	.676	.541	Tanzania	738
.190	.204	.244	.242	.245	.268	.253	.275	.136	.328	.378	.441	.424	.411	....	Togo	742
1.738	1.760	2.139	2.395	2.930	3.527	3.699	4.019	3.802	4.657	5.475	5.517	5.559	5.750	5.872	Tunisia	744
.387	.436	.319	.280	.274	.152	.200	.143	.179	.409	.461	.587	.555	.501	.517	Uganda	746
.482	.741	.873	1.178	1.344	1.309	1.083	.756	.826	.927	1.040	1.037	.915	....	....	Zambia	754
1.110	1.301	1.425	1.631	1.548	1.722	1.530	1.442	1.565	1.881	2.114	2.406	....	....	....	Zimbabwe	698

		1970	1971	1972	1973	1974	1975	1976	1977	1978	1979	1980	1981	1982	1983	1984
														Billions of US Dollars		
Asia *	505	16.911	19.213	25.037	37.925	53.546	53.365	66.966	79.434	95.687	125.784	158.998	176.041	172.735	180.891	208.219
Bangladesh	513	....	....	.260	.358	.348	.327	.401	.476	.548	.659	.759	.791	.769	.724	.931
Bhutan	514	....	....	....	....	....	....	....	....	....	....	.017	.020	.017	.016	.018
Cambodia	522	.039	.011	.007	.015	....	....	....	....	....	....	....	....	....	....	....
China, P.R.: Mainland	924	2.307	2.783	3.693	5.876	7.108	7.689	6.943	7.520	9.955	13.614	Ⅰ18.099	22.007	22.321	22.226	26.139
China, P.R.: Hong Kong	532	2.515	2.875	3.436	5.071	5.968	6.026	8.484	9.616	11.453	15.140	19.752	21.827	21.006	21.959	28.323
China, P.R.: Macao	546	.042	.049	.072	.100	.110	.133	.188	.219	.258	.389	.538	.697	.726	.760	.911
Fiji	819	.087	.087	.095	.122	.190	.202	.172	.224	.251	.314	.470	.400	.377	.306	.332
India	534	2.026	2.036	2.448	2.917	3.926	4.355	5.549	6.378	6.671	7.806	8.586	8.295	9.358	9.148	9.451
Indonesia	536	1.108	1.234	1.777	3.211	7.426	7.102	8.547	10.853	11.643	15.591	21.909	25.165	22.328	21.146	21.888
Korea	542	.836	1.067	1.625	3.221	4.462	4.945	7.716	10.048	12.722	15.057	17.512	21.268	21.853	24.446	29.245
Lao People's Democratic Rep.	544	.072	.062	.042	.054	.095	.012	.012	.004	.003	.019	.028	.023	.040	.041	.044
Malaysia	548	1.687	1.644	1.722	3.049	4.236	3.843	5.295	6.079	7.404	11.079	12.945	11.770	12.030	14.104	16.484
Maldives	556	.004	.004	.003	.004	.004	.003	.003	.003	.004	.005	.008	.009	.010	.013	.018
Mongolia	948	....	....	....	....	....	....	....	....	....	....	.403	.469	.562	.610	.674
Myanmar	518	.108	.125	.120	.130	.188	.173	.206	.214	.242	.383	.472	.462	.391	.378	.301
Nepal	558	.042	.048	.058	.063	.066	.100	.098	.081	.091	.109	.080	.141	.088	.093	.127
Pakistan	564	.397	.467	Ⅰ1.026	.919	1.113	1.057	1.172	1.194	1.482	2.066	2.631	2.896	2.667	3.171	2.682
Papua New Guinea	853	.104	.120	.222	.515	.654	.441	.551	.683	.714	.964	1.031	.838	.771	.819	.914
Philippines	566	.914	1.089	1.082	1.507	2.312	2.574	2.300	2.853	3.172	3.957	5.255	5.951	5.240	4.768	5.062
Samoa	862	.005	.006	.005	.007	.013	.007	.007	.015	.011	.017	.017	.011	.013	.018	.019
Singapore	576	1.554	1.761	2.189	3.653	5.810	5.376	6.585	8.241	10.134	14.233	19.375	20.967	20.788	21.833	24.070
Solomon Islands	813	.008	.010	.011	.014	.026	.016	.024	.033	.038	.070	.074	.066	.058	.061	.093
Sri Lanka	524	.342	.344	.338	.410	.527	.569	.572	.761	.845	.981	1.062	1.088	1.031	1.063	1.467
Thailand	578	.710	.831	1.081	1.564	2.444	2.208	2.980	3.490	4.085	5.298	6.505	7.031	6.945	6.368	7.413
Tonga	866	....	....	....	....	....	....	....	....	....	....	....	....	....	....	....
Vanuatu	846	.012	.013	.015	.021	.031	.012	.017	.032	.037	.042	.036	.032	.023	.029	.044
of which:																
Taiwan Province of China	528	1.428	1.998	2.914	4.384	5.518	5.302	8.155	9.349	12.682	16.081	19.786	22.502	22.075	25.086	30.439
Europe	170	....	....	....	....	....	....	....	....	....	....	....	....	....	....	....
Albania	914	....	....	....	....	....	....	....	....	....	....	....	....	....	....	....
Armenia	911	....	....	....	....	....	....	....	....	....	....	....	....	....	....	....
Azerbaijan	912	....	....	....	....	....	....	....	....	....	....	....	....	....	....	....
Belarus	913	....	....	....	....	....	....	....	....	....	....	....	....	....	....	....
Bulgaria	918	2.004	2.182	2.627	3.269	3.836	....	....	....	....	....	....	....	....	....	....
Croatia	960	....	....	....	....	....	....	....	....	....	....	....	....	....	....	....
Cyprus	423	.108	.115	.134	.173	.152	.152	.258	.318	.344	.456	.533	.556	.555	.494	.575
Czech Republic	935	....	....	....	....	....	....	....	....	....	....	....	....	....	....	....
Czechoslovakia	934	....	....	....	....	....	6.154	....	....	....	10.926	12.063	11.611	12.059	12.119	11.775
Estonia	939	....	....	....	....	....	....	....	....	....	....	....	....	....	....	....
Georgia	915	....	....	....	....	....	....	....	....	....	....	....	....	....	....	....
Hungary	944	1.726	1.847	2.403	3.354	3.942	4.519	4.927	5.834	6.408	7.930	8.672	8.707	8.773	8.702	8.563
Kazakhstan	916	....	....	....	....	....	....	....	....	....	....	....	....	....	....	....
Kyrgyz Republic	917	....	....	....	....	....	....	....	....	....	....	....	....	....	....	....
Latvia	941	....	....	....	....	....	....	....	....	....	....	....	....	....	....	....
Lithuania	946	....	....	....	....	....	....	....	....	....	....	....	....	....	....	....
Macedonia, FYR	962	....	....	....	....	....	....	....	....	....	....	....	....	....	....	....
Malta	181	.039	.046	.068	.098	.134	.166	.228	.289	.342	.424	.483	.449	.411	.363	.394
Moldova	921	....	....	....	....	....	....	....	....	....	....	....	....	....	....	....
Poland	964	3.548	3.872	4.927	6.432	8.321	10.289	11.024	10.666	12.238	14.082	14.191	10.675	11.213	11.572	11.750
Romania	968	1.851	2.107	2.601	3.691	4.874	5.341	6.138	7.021	8.086	9.724	11.209	12.610	11.559	11.512	12.646
Russia	922	....	....	....	....	....	....	....	....	....	....	....	....	....	....	....
Slovak Republic	936	....	....	....	....	....	....	....	....	....	....	....	....	....	....	....
Slovenia	961	....	....	....	....	....	....	....	....	....	....	....	....	....	....	....
Turkey	186	.588	.677	.885	1.317	1.532	1.401	1.960	1.753	2.288	2.261	2.910	4.703	5.746	5.728	7.134
Ukraine	926	....	....	....	....	....	....	....	....	....	....	....	....	....	....	....
Yugoslavia, SFR	188	1.679	1.819	2.237	2.853	3.805	4.072	4.878	5.254	5.671	6.491	8.978	10.940	10.284	9.914	10.254
Middle East	405	13.105	18.223	18.024	27.558	82.523	87.101	105.665	115.289	114.590	180.908	204.538	204.700	157.919	126.326	111.385
Bahrain	419	.218	.265	.347	.481	1.272	1.203	1.516	1.845	1.893	2.488	3.594	4.347	3.789	3.199	3.204
Egypt	469	.762	.789	.825	1.121	1.516	1.402	1.522	1.708	1.737	1.840	3.046	3.233	3.120	3.214	3.140
Iran, I.R. of	429	2.403	3.824	1.799	2.669	8.401	7.963	8.935	9.216	8.560	8.310	Ⅰ7.109	Ⅰ3.947	12.968	19.378	12.422
Iraq	433	1.098	1.556	1.086	.836	2.392	15.934	18.250	19.012	21.749	42.402	....	....	....	....	....
Israel	436	.779	.958	1.147	1.449	1.825	1.941	2.415	3.082	3.921	4.546	5.538	5.670	5.255	5.108	5.807
Jordan	439	.034	.032	.048	.073	.155	.153	.207	.249	.298	.403	.574	.733	.752	.580	.752
Kuwait	443	1.693	2.272	2.558	3.815	10.963	9.184	9.846	9.754	10.427	18.404	19.842	16.300	10.961	11.574	12.280
Lebanon	446	.190	.245	.377	.921	1.636	1.233	.546	.760	.830	.850	.955	.920	.800	.760	.378
Libya	672	2.357	2.694	2.938	4.003	8.259	6.834	9.554	11.411	9.895	16.076	21.910	15.571	13.203	12.216	11.148
Oman	449	.143	.154	.167	.239	.823	1.044	1.134	1.139	1.096	1.570	2.387	3.212	2.998	3.074	3.068
Qatar	453	.240	.315	.397	.628	2.015	1.805	2.210	2.072	2.391	3.753	5.680	5.686	4.341	3.357	....
Saudi Arabia	456	2.371	3.850	4.772	8.988	35.555	29.673	38.286	43.466	40.734	63.427	109.116	119.881	79.104	45.827	37.567
Syrian Arab Rep.	463	.203	.195	.287	.351	.782	.930	1.074	1.070	1.060	1.644	2.108	2.103	2.026	1.923	1.853
United Arab Emirates	466	.523	.871	1.157	1.807	6.414	7.262	9.535	9.636	9.126	13.652	20.676	21.238	16.837	14.672	14.192
Yemen Arab Rep.	473	.003	.004	.004	.008	.013	.011	.008	.011	.007	.014	.023	.047	.039	.027	.016
Yemen, P.D. Rep.	459	.012	.096	.008	.007	.016	.017	.007	.181	.192	.466	.777	.607	.795	.674	.645
Yemen, Rep. of	474	....	....	....	....	....	....	....	....	....	....	....	....	....	....	....

Billions of US Dollars

1985	1986	1987	1988	1989	1990	1991	1992	1993	1994	1995	1996	1997	1998	1999		
206.805	225.693	293.815	360.862	404.068	449.603	513.212	581.620	640.660	762.522	924.016	966.194	1,028.201	974.107	1,037.815	Asia *	505
Ɪ.999	.880	1.067	1.291	1.305	1.671	1.689	2.098	2.278	2.661	3.173	3.297	3.778	3.831	3.922	Bangladesh	513
.022	.031	.055	.075	.070	.068	.065	.067	.065	.066	.103	.100	.118	....	....	Bhutan	514
															Cambodia	522
27.350	30.942	39.437	47.516	52.538	62.091	71.910	84.940	90.970	121.047	148.797	151.197	182.877	183.589	195.150	China, P.R.: Mainland	924
30.187	35.439	48.476	63.163	73.140	82.160	98.577	119.487	135.244	151.399	173.750	180.750	188.059	174.002	173.885	China, P.R.: Hong Kong	532
.908	1.034	1.397	1.492	1.640	1.694	1.655	1.749	1.768	1.845	1.977	1.975	2.128	2.122	....	China, P.R.: Macao	546
.307	.336	.380	.372	.442	.497	.450	.443	.450	.572	.623	.750	.620	.510	....	Fiji	819
9.140	9.399	11.298	13.234	15.872	17.969	17.727	19.628	21.572	25.022	30.630	33.105	35.008	33.437	36.316	India	534
18.587	14.805	17.136	19.219	22.160	25.675	29.142	33.967	36.823	40.055	45.417	49.814	53.443	48.847	48.665	Indonesia	536
30.282	34.715	47.281	60.696	62.377	65.016	71.870	76.632	82.236	96.013	125.058	129.715	136.164	132.313	144.745	Korea	542
.054	.055	.064	.058	.063	.079	.097	.133	.241	.301	.311	.323	.359	.370	.311	Lao People's Democratic Rep.	544
15.316	13.689	17.958	21.082	25.048	29.451	34.349	40.772	47.131	58.844	73.914	78.327	78.740	73.304	84.455	Malaysia	548
.023	.025	.031	.040	.045	.052	.054	.040	.035	.046	.050	.059	.073	.074	.064	Maldives	556
.689	.716	.718	.739	.722	.661	.348	.389	.383	.356	.473	.424	.452	.345	.763	Mongolia	948
.303	.288	.219	.166	.210	.325	.419	.531	.586	.798	.851	.746	.866	1.065	1.125	Myanmar	518
.160	.142	.151	.191	.159	.204	.257	.368	.384	.362	.345	.385	.406	.474	....	Nepal	558
2.877	3.505	4.244	4.653	5.035	5.687	6.938	7.435	7.280	7.509	8.247	9.978	9.249	8.913	....	Pakistan	564
.928	1.031	1.241	1.451	1.294	1.177	1.460	1.927	2.585	2.632	2.654	2.529	2.163	1.775	1.877	Papua New Guinea	853
4.998	4.586	5.036	6.331	7.522	7.906	8.411	9.140	10.394	11.996	15.331	18.947	22.512	27.045	32.188	Philippines	566
.016	.010	.012	.015	.013	.009	.006	.006	.006	.004	.009	.010	.015	.015	.020	Samoa	862
22.812	22.495	28.686	39.306	44.661	52.730	58.966	63.472	74.012	96.825	118.268	125.014	124.985	109.895	114.689	Singapore	576
.070	.065	.064	.082	.074	.070	.084	.102	.129	.142	.168	.162	.175	.126	....	Solomon Islands	813
1.333	1.215	1.393	1.476	1.545	1.912	1.987	2.455	2.859	3.208	3.798	4.095	4.633	4.797	4.599	Sri Lanka	524
7.121	8.876	11.727	15.953	20.078	23.068	28.428	32.472	36.969	45.261	56.439	55.721	57.388	54.456	58.392	Thailand	578
									.014	.014	.009	....	....	....	Tonga	866
.031	.017	.018	.020	.022	.019	.018	.024	.023	.025	.028	.030	.035	.034	....	Vanuatu	846
															*of which:	
30.696	39.754	53.820	60.502	66.195	67.079	76.163	81.387	84.641	92.876	111.563	115.730	121.081	110.518	121.496	Taiwan Province of China	528
....	....	....	....	....	....	....	136.726	144.092	184.269	231.307	247.985	260.778	256.650	254.279	Europe	170
							.076	.122	.140	.202	.207	.139	.205	....	Albania	914
								.156	.216	.271	.290	.233	.221	.232	Armenia	911
						1.571	.993	.638	.637	.631	.781	.606	....		Azerbaijan	912
						3.559	1.970	2.510	4.707	5.652	7.301	7.070	5.922		Belarus	913
13.339	14.203	15.864	17.370	16.278	4.822	3.120	3.914	3.729	3.947	5.359	6.602	5.323	4.296	3.925	Bulgaria	918
								3.904	4.260	4.633	4.512	4.171	4.541	4.280	Croatia	960
.476	.502	.621	.709	.793	.951	.952	.987	.867	.969	1.231	1.391	1.250	1.061	.997	Cyprus	423
								Ɪ14.466	Ɪ16.230	Ɪ21.686	21.916	22.746	26.418	26.832	Czech Republic	935
11.900	13.790	15.469	15.322	14.505	11.906	10.939	11.310								Czechoslovakia	934
								.803	Ɪ1.313	1.838	2.077	2.924	3.111	2.939	Estonia	939
											.199	.240	.192	....	Georgia	915
8.538	9.165	9.556	9.949	9.624	9.596	10.199	10.677	8.875	10.689	12.439	12.652	18.628	22.958	24.950	Hungary	944
								3.277	3.231	5.250	5.911	6.497	5.436	5.592	Kazakhstan	916
								.340	.340	.409	.505	.604	.514	.454	Kyrgyz Republic	917
						.778	.998	.991	1.305	1.443	1.672	1.811	1.723		Latvia	941
								2.025	2.029	2.705	3.355	3.860	3.711	3.045	Lithuania	946
								1.055	1.086	1.204					Macedonia, FYR	962
.400	.497	.605	.714	.844	1.130	1.252	1.543	1.355	1.570	1.914	1.731	1.640	1.821	1.989	Malta	181
							.470	.483	.619	.739	.820	.890	.644		Moldova	921
11.489	12.074	12.205	13.960	13.466	13.627	Ɪ14.903	13.324	14.143	17.042	22.895	24.440	25.751	27.191	27.397	Poland	964
12.167	9.763	10.492	11.392	10.487	5.775	4.266	4.363	4.892	6.151	7.910	8.085	8.431	8.300	8.505	Romania	968
							42.039	44.297	Ɪ67.542	81.096	88.599	88.288	74.888	74.663	Russia	922
								5.466	6.709	8.595	8.823	8.254	10.721	10.195	Slovak Republic	936
						3.852	Ɪ6.681	6.083	6.828	8.316	8.312	8.372	9.048	8.604	Slovenia	961
7.958	7.457	10.190	11.662	11.625	12.959	13.594	14.715	15.345	18.106	21.637	23.224	26.261	26.974	26.588	Turkey	186
							8.045	7.817	10.305	13.317	14.441	14.232	12.637	11.582	Ukraine	926
10.700	10.353	11.443	12.663	13.460	14.308	13.953	....								Yugoslavia, SFR	188
102.686	75.400	91.474	88.948	124.471	154.021	112.146	118.595	138.007	142.544	158.258	185.567	183.922	134.378	....	Middle East	405
2.897	2.199	2.430	2.411	2.831	3.761	3.513	3.464	3.726	3.617	4.113	4.702	4.384	3.270	4.088	Bahrain	419
3.714	2.934	4.351	5.706	6.764	4.957	3.705	3.063	2.252	3.450	3.450	3.539	3.921	3.130	3.559	Egypt	469
13.328	7.171	11.916	10.709	13.081	19.305	18.661	19.868	18.080	19.434	18.360	22.391	18.381	....	....	Iran, I.R. of	429
															Iraq	433
6.260	7.154	8.454	8.198	10.738	11.576	11.921	10.019	14.826	16.884	19.046	20.610	22.503	22.993	25.794	Israel	436
.789	.733	.934	1.019	1.107	1.064	1.130	1.219	1.246	1.424	1.769	1.817	1.836	1.802	1.782	Jordan	439
10.597	7.251	8.264	7.758	11.476	7.042	1.088	6.572	10.246	11.260	12.785	14.889	14.224	9.554	....	Kuwait	443
.288	.550	.650	.780	.485	.494	.539	.560	.452	.470	.656	.736	.643	.662	.677	Lebanon	446
12.314	8.215	8.043	6.673	8.034	13.225	11.235	....	....	8.954	8.975	9.903	9.656	6.659	....	Libya	672
3.938	1.835	2.491	2.476	4.068	5.508	4.874	5.553	5.370	5.545	6.068	7.346	7.630	5.508	....	Oman	449
															Qatar	453
27.481	20.185	23.199	24.377	28.382	44.417	47.797	50.286	42.395	42.614	50.040	60.729	62.381	39.775	....	Saudi Arabia	456
1.637	1.325	3.870	1.345	3.006	4.212	3.430	3.093	3.146	3.047	3.563	3.999	3.916	2.890	3.464	Syrian Arab Rep.	463
14.043	12.387	14.165	13.934	17.596	23.544	24.436	24.756	....	....	....	....	....	....	....	United Arab Emirates	466
.013	.008	.048	....	....	....	....	....	....	....	....	....	....	....	....	Yemen Arab Rep.	473
....	.290	....	....	....	....	....	....	....	....	....	....	....	....	....	Yemen, P.D. Rep.	459
						.659	.619	.611	.934	1.945	2.675	2.504	1.497	....	Yemen, Rep. of	474

Exports, f.o.b.

		1970	1971	1972	1973	1974	1975	1976	1977	1978	1979	1980	1981	1982	1983	1984
Western Hemisphere	205	16.433	16.484	18.720	25.722	45.134	41.870	48.253	56.093	60.260	79.950	106.194	115.797	102.921	102.088	112.095
Antigua and Barbuda	311	.011	.016	.018	.026	.029	.020	.009	‡.007	.013	.037	.026	.040	.021	.020	.018
Argentina	213	1.773	1.740	1.941	3.266	3.931	2.961	3.916	5.652	6.400	7.810	8.021	9.143	7.625	7.836	8.107
Bahamas, The	313	.090	.267	.343	.530	1.444	2.508	2.992	3.261	3.058	3.786	5.009	6.189	4.534	3.970	3.393
Barbados	316	.040	.041	.044	.054	.086	.107	.086	.097	.131	.152	.228	.196	.259	‡.323	‡.394
Belize	339	.019	.019	.026	.032	.045	.067	.042	.062	.080	.087	.111	.119	.091	.078	.093
Bolivia	218	.190	.181	.201	.261	.557	.444	.568	.632	.629	.760	.942	.912	.828	.755	.725
Brazil	223	2.739	2.904	3.991	6.199	7.951	8.670	10.128	12.120	12.659	15.244	20.132	23.293	20.175	21.899	27.005
Chile	228	1.249	.997	.855	1.231	2.481	1.552	2.083	2.190	2.478	3.894	4.705	3.837	3.706	3.831	3.651
Colombia	233	.727	.686	.808	1.169	1.509	1.465	1.874	2.403	3.010	3.411	3.924	2.916	3.024	3.001	3.462
Costa Rica	238	.231	.225	.281	.345	.440	.493	.593	.828	.865	.934	1.002	1.008	.870	.873	1.006
Dominica	321	.006	.006	.007	.009	.010	.011	.011	.012	.016	.009	.010	.019	.024	.027	.026
Dominican Republic	243	.249	.243	.348	.442	.637	.894	.716	.780	.676	.869	.962	1.188	.768	.785	.868
Ecuador	248	.190	.199	.326	.532	1.124	.974	1.258	1.436	1.558	2.104	2.481	2.451	2.327	2.348	2.620
El Salvador	253	.229	.228	.273	.352	.463	.531	.743	.972	.848	1.223	.967	.797	.699	.735	.717
Grenada	328	.006	.005	.005	.007	.010	.012	.013	.014	.017	.021	.017	.019	.019	.019	.018
Guatemala	258	.290	.283	.327	.436	.572	.624	.760	1.160	1.089	1.241	1.520	1.226	1.120	1.159	1.129
Guyana	336	.136	.151	.147	.136	.270	.365	.279	.259	.296	.293	.389	.346	.241	.189	.210
Haiti	263	.040	.047	.044	.053	.072	.080	.124	.149	.155	.185	.226	.152	.178	.166	.179
Honduras	268	.179	.189	.205	.259	.289	.295	.400	.513	.608	.734	.829	.761	.660	.672	.725
Jamaica	343	.342	.339	.391	.390	.604	.759	.630	.768	.833	.818	.963	.974	.767	.718	.705
Mexico	273	1.402	1.504	1.694	2.250	2.958	2.904	3.417	4.167	6.005	8.982	‡18.031	23.307	24.055	25.953	29.101
Netherlands Antilles	353	.676	.725	.758	1.369	3.230	2.397	2.524	2.647	2.976	3.966	5.162	5.417	4.891	4.409	3.733
Nicaragua	278	.179	.187	.249	.278	.381	.375	.542	.637	.646	.567	.451	.508	.406	.429	.386
Panama	283	.109	.117	.123	.138	.211	.286	.238	.251	.256	.303	.361	.328	.375	.320	.276
Paraguay	288	.063	.064	.085	.124	.167	.176	.181	.279	.257	.305	.310	.296	.330	.269	.335
Peru	293	1.048	.893	.944	1.112	1.503	‡1.291	1.360	1.726	1.941	3.491	3.898	3.255	3.259	3.015	3.147
St. Kitts and Nevis	361	.004	.004	.006	.008	.012	.022	.018	.015	.017	.017	.024	.024	.019	.018	.020
St. Lucia	362	.009	.006	.008	.010	.016	.017	.021	.025	.029	.036	.058	.046	.045	.055	.049
St. Vincent & Grenadines	364	.004	.003	.003	.005	.007	.008	.009	.010	.016	.015	.015	.024	.032	.041	.054
Suriname	366	.144	.158	.171	.179	.269	.277	.276	.310	.369	‡.444	.514	.474	.429	.367	.356
Trinidad and Tobago	369	.482	.527	.558	.699	2.036	1.771	2.214	2.180	2.040	2.610	4.077	3.761	3.072	2.353	2.173
Uruguay	298	.233	.206	.214	.322	.382	.384	.546	.608	.686	.788	1.059	1.215	1.023	1.045	.934
Venezuela, Rep. Bol.	299	3.169	3.124	3.166	3.298	11.153	8.800	9.299	9.551	9.187	14.317	19.221	20.980	16.590	13.937	15.997

Memorandum Items

		1970	1971	1972	1973	1974	1975	1976	1977	1978	1979	1980	1981	1982	1983	1984
Euro Area	163	....	....	....	....	....	....	....	....	....	....	....	....	....	....	....
Oil Exporting Countries	999	17.354	22.563	23.301	34.844	107.293	108.136	131.421	143.892	141.073	224.387	267.667	264.606	204.697	168.063	157.458
Non-Oil Developing Countries	201	60.220	65.023	79.085	112.922	156.292	153.227	170.971	199.015	229.870	306.972	383.893	401.422	385.152	398.074	437.210

1985	1986	1987	1988	1989	1990	1991	1992	1993	1994	1995	1996	1997	1998	1999		
103.483	88.429	100.463	116.237	129.826	139.828	139.652	147.586	158.269	183.169	223.933	251.233	278.218	275.007	292.812	Western Hemisphere	205
.017	.020	.019	.017	.016	.021	.040	.055	.047	.027	.030	.017	.013	.015	....	Antigua and Barbuda	311
8.396	6.852	6.360	9.135	9.579	12.353	11.978	12.235	13.118	15.659	20.967	23.811	26.370	26.441	23.309	Argentina...................................	213
2.728	2.702	2.722	2.153	2.487	I.238	.225	.192	.162	.167	.176	.180	.181	.300	.380	Bahamas, The........................	313
.357	.278	.161	.177	.188	.215	.207	.190	.187	.182	.239	.281	.283	.252	.229	Barbados.........................	316
.090	.093	.087	.095	.094	.108	.099	.116	.119	.127	.143	.154	.159	.155	.166	Belize	339
.623	.638	.570	.600	.822	.926	.849	.710	.728	1.032	1.101	1.137	1.167	1.104	1.033	Bolivia..............................	218
25.639	22.349	26.224	33.494	34.383	31.414	31.620	35.793	38.555	43.545	46.506	47.747	52.990	51.120	48.011	Brazil..............................	223
3.804	4.191	5.224	7.052	8.078	8.373	8.942	10.007	9.199	11.604	16.024	15.405	16.663	14.830	15.616	Chile	228
3.552	5.102	4.642	5.037	5.717	6.766	7.232	6.917	7.116	8.419	10.056	10.587	11.522	10.852	11.576	Colombia	233
.976	1.121	1.158	1.246	1.415	1.448	1.598	1.841	2.625	2.869	3.453	3.730	4.268	5.511	6.577	Costa Rica	238
.028	.043	.048	.054	.045	.055	.054	.053	.049	.047	.045	.051	.053	.063	.054	Dominica	321
.735	.718	.711	.890	.924	.735	.658	.562	.511	.644	.767	.817	.882	.795	....	Dominican Republic	243
2.905	2.172	1.928	2.192	2.354	2.714	2.852	3.007	2.904	3.820	4.307	4.900	5.264	4.203	4.451	Ecuador	248
.679	.755	.591	.609	.498	.582	.588	.598	.732	.844	.998	1.024	1.359	1.263	1.164	El Salvador	253
.023	.031	.032	.033	.028	.027	.023	.022	.022	.025	.023	.021	....	....	....	Grenada	328
1.057	1.044	.987	1.022	1.108	1.163	1.202	1.295	1.340	1.522	2.156	2.031	2.344	2.582	2.398	Guatemala	258
.166	.222	.267	.230	.227	.257	.246	.292	.414	.456	.455	.517	.644	.484	....	Guyana	336
.168	.184	.214	.179	.144	.160	.167	.073	.080	.082	.110	.090	.120	.175	.196	Haiti	263
.780	.854	.791	.842	.859	.831	.792	.802	.814	.842	1.220	1.316	1.446	1.575	.940	Honduras	268
.566	.589	.706	.880	.998	1.158	1.105	1.047	1.071	1.212	1.427	1.383	1.383	1.312	1.127	Jamaica	343
26.757	21.804	27.600	30.691	35.171	40.711	42.688	46.196	51.886	60.882	79.542	96.000	110.431	117.460	136.703	Mexico	273
1.031	I.924	1.308	1.134	1.454	1.790	1.599	1.559	1.283	1.375	....	....	....	....	....	Netherlands Antilles	353
.302	.247	.273	.233	.311	.331	.272	.223	.267	.352	.526	.671	.704	.573	.544	Nicaragua	278
.336	.349	.358	.307	.318	.340	.358	.502	.553	.583	.625	....	.723	.784	.822	Panama	283
.304	.234	.353	.510	1.006	.959	.737	.657	.725	.817	.919	1.044	1.089	....	....	Paraguay	288
2.979	2.531	2.661	2.701	3.488	3.231	3.329	3.484	3.515	4.555	5.575	5.897	6.841	5.735	6.114	Peru	293
.020	.025	.028	.028	.029	.028	.027	.026	.027	.022	.019	.022	....	....	....	St. Kitts and Nevis..................	361
.057	.087	.080	.116	.109	.127	.110	.123	.120	.106	.124	.082	.066	....	....	St. Lucia	362
.063	.064	.052	.085	.075	.083	.067	.078	.058	.050	.043	.046	.046	.050	.049	St. Vincent & Grenadines	364
.329	.335	.306	.410	.542	.472	.359	.391	1.190	.449	.477	.433	.701	.436	....	Suriname	366
2.139	1.386	1.462	1.412	1.578	1.960	1.985	1.691	1.662	1.867	2.455	2.500	2.542	2.258	....	Trinidad and Tobago	369
.909	1.088	1.189	1.405	1.599	1.693	1.605	1.703	1.645	1.913	2.106	2.397	2.726	2.769	2.232	Uruguay..............................	298
14.438	8.660	10.577	10.244	13.286	17.497	15.155	14.185	14.686	16.089	18.457	23.060	21.624	17.193	19.852	Venezuela, Rep. Bol..................	299

Memorandum Items

1985	1986	1987	1988	1989	1990	1991	1992	1993	1994	1995	1996	1997	1998	1999		
....	....	....	....	....	....	....	....	....	....	....	....	....	886.456	881.898	Euro Area..............................	163
144.307	96.984	113.403	112.326	150.499	196.583	156.380	167.726	183.397	187.131	209.554	249.652	247.533	183.999	....	Oil Exporting Countries	999
444.937	465.964	569.124	667.666	729.323	769.449	842.289	895.405	972.506	1,165.003	1,420.714	1,506.102	1,609.714	1,548.703	1,631.438	Non-Oil Developing Countries	201

(See notes in the back of the book.)

Billions of US Dollars

		1970	1971	1972	1973	1974	1975	1976	1977	1978	1979	1980	1981	1982	1983	1984
World	001	313.9	345.1	406.1	559.6	822.2	869.4	975.8	1,117.0	1,288.7	1,627.8	2,001.2	1,981.9	1,865.9	1,804.0	1,925.7
Industrial Countries	110	232.6	258.0	308.0	423.0	603.3	603.7	696.8	788.9	911.2	1,168.0	1,400.4	1,328.8	1,249.4	1,224.8	1,340.2
United States	111	42.389	48.342	58.862	73.199	110.875	⅋105.880	132.498	⅋160.411	186.045	222.228	256.984	273.352	254.884	269.878	346.364
Canada	156	14.286	16.472	20.038	24.713	34.248	36.106	40.243	42.083	46.278	56.642	62.544	70.010	58.128	64.789	77.789
Australia	193	5.056	5.228	5.028	7.393	11.982	10.697	12.232	13.511	15.567	18.191	22.399	26.215	26.667	21.458	25.919
Japan	158	18.881	19.712	23.863	38.389	61.948	57.860	64.894	71.340	79.922	109.831	141.296	142.866	131.499	126.437	136.176
New Zealand	196	1.245	1.348	1.523	2.176	3.648	3.155	3.254	3.361	⅋3.491	4.553	5.472	5.734	5.782	5.333	6.203
Austria	122	3.549	4.190	5.216	7.119	9.022	9.394	11.523	14.245	16.019	20.252	24.444	21.043	19.502	19.367	19.629
Belgium	124	....	....	....	....	....	....	....	....	....	....	....	....	....	....	....
Belgium-Luxembourg	126	11.412	12.824	15.490	22.075	29.880	30.781	35.519	40.406	48.609	60.914	71.864	62.450	58.227	55.313	55.455
Finland	172	2.638	2.807	3.165	4.341	6.813	7.628	7.392	7.608	7.866	11.398	15.635	14.192	13.401	12.826	12.433
France	132	19.131	21.336	26.999	37.738	52.918	53.947	64.082	70.637	81.788	107.009	134.889	120.953	116.509	106.250	104.372
Germany	134	29.947	34.293	40.378	54.891	69.661	74.930	88.421	101.458	121.754	159.646	188.002	163.941	155.323	152.877	153.022
Ireland	178	1.621	1.837	2.102	2.789	3.814	3.778	4.200	5.396	7.121	9.884	11.153	10.608	9.706	9.170	9.674
Italy	136	14.974	15.969	19.319	27.798	41.089	38.526	43.905	48.092	56.496	77.895	100.741	94.261	87.332	79.808	85.162
Luxembourg	137	.747	.694	.960	1.340	1.739	1.823	1.861	2.037	2.527	3.111	3.612	2.998	2.732	2.664	2.770
Netherlands	138	15.688	17.867	20.667	28.744	38.949	40.897	46.734	52.903	61.314	77.331	88.419	75.940	72.316	68.237	69.254
Portugal	182	1.556	1.803	2.204	3.015	4.496	3.839	4.220	4.744	5.237	6.534	9.309	9.800	9.572	8.240	7.961
Spain	184	4.747	5.009	6.829	9.667	15.428	16.265	17.474	17.836	18.712	25.438	34.078	32.150	31.465	29.193	28.831
Denmark	128	4.407	4.608	5.087	7.802	9.927	10.368	12.427	13.265	14.808	18.401	19.340	17.580	16.492	16.266	16.613
Greece	174	1.958	2.098	2.348	3.477	4.385	5.357	6.059	6.853	7.829	9.614	10.548	8.810	10.026	9.500	9.435
Iceland	176	.157	.210	.231	.359	.518	.484	.467	.605	.675	.815	.999	1.024	.944	.818	.841
Norway	142	3.702	4.075	4.373	6.289	8.420	9.705	11.121	12.883	11.497	13.706	16.926	15.650	15.477	13.497	13.885
Sweden	144	7.007	7.067	8.110	10.907	16.683	17.450	19.628	⅋20.137	20.589	28.735	33.438	28.840	27.585	26.098	26.426
Switzerland	146	6.374	7.191	8.468	11.626	14.445	13.303	14.775	17.940	23.804	⅋29.356	36.341	30.682	28.678	29.192	29.521
United Kingdom	112	21.871	23.858	27.661	38.528	54.190	53.341	55.744	63.191	75.813	99.600	115.545	102.708	99.713	100.234	105.214
Developing Countries	200	81.33	87.06	98.12	136.56	218.85	265.71	279.00	328.09	377.51	459.85	600.88	653.09	616.48	579.27	585.48
Africa	605	12.544	14.341	14.638	19.212	29.183	36.952	37.611	44.938	52.542	54.251	79.725	86.746	74.784	66.024	62.187
Algeria	612	1.257	1.227	1.494	2.236	4.035	5.498	5.081	7.125	8.548	8.403	10.559	11.303	10.754	10.399	10.288
Benin	638	.064	.077	.092	.112	.147	.188	.219	.268	.311	.320	.331	.543	.464	.318	.288
Botswana	616	.057	.083	.110	.166	.184	.216	.209	.286	.371	.538	.693	.828	.722	.750	.713
Burkina Faso	748	.050	.057	.069	.098	.144	.151	.144	.209	.227	.301	.359	.338	.347	.291	.253
Burundi	618	.022	.030	.032	.031	.043	.062	.058	.074	.098	.152	.168	.161	.213	.182	.187
Cameroon	622	.243	.252	.303	.334	.437	.599	.613	.735	1.056	1.275	1.602	1.427	1.211	1.224	1.112
Cape Verde	624	.016	.020	.024	.034	.034	.040	.030	.038	.053	.053	.068	.071	.088	.095	.097
Central African Rep.	626	.034	.033	.034	.052	.046	.069	.055	.063	.057	.070	.081	.095	.123	.068	.087
Chad	628	.062	.063	.062	.082	.087	.133	.116	.189	.217	.085	.074	.108	.109	.157	.181
Comoros	632	.009	.010	.012	.015	.026	.023	.013	.016	.019	.029	.029	.032	.033	.034	.043
Congo, Dem. Rep. of	636	.179	.203	.208	.251	.349	.300	.224	.203	.196	.199	.278	.223	.160	.157	.685
Congo, Rep. of	634	.059	.082	.104	.128	.127	.170	.172	.208	.259	.291	.580	.446	.767	.648	.618
Côte d'Ivoire	662	.390	.402	.454	.710	.969	1.127	1.296	1.756	2.326	2.491	2.991	2.383	2.180	1.839	1.497
Djibouti	611	.049	.053	.066	.072	.082	.140	.120	.107	.164	.188	.213	.224	.226	.221	.222
Equatorial Guinea	642	.024	.028	.027	.027	.015	.020	.004	.010	.009	.019	.026	.027	.031	.019	.018
Ethiopia	644	.172	.188	.189	.214	.283	.313	.352	.352	.455	.567	.722	.739	.786	.876	.928
Gabon	646	.080	.092	.139	.190	.332	.469	.503	.716	.617	.532	.674	.843	.867	.685	.724
Gambia, The	648	.018	.021	.025	.031	.047	.060	.074	.078	.100	.141	.165	.126	.103	.115	.100
Ghana	652	.411	.430	.291	.452	.821	.791	.862	1.038	1.006	.852	1.129	1.106	.705	2.513	.608
Guinea-Bissau	654	.027	.031	.032	.044	.043	.038	.037	.037	.049	.061	.055	.050	.050	.055	....
Kenya	664	.442	.560	.535	.615	1.026	.945	.969	1.289	1.711	1.636	2.125	1.939	1.644	1.334	1.469
Lesotho	666	.032	.039	.056	.088	.120	.164	.212	.234	.281	.328	.427	.461	.458	.483	.435
Liberia	668	.150	.157	.179	.193	.288	.331	.399	.464	.481	.507	.535	.447	.428	.412	.363
Madagascar	674	.170	.214	.205	.203	.281	.366	.285	.347	.443	.641	.600	.545	.417	.387	.366
Malawi	676	.099	.111	.131	.161	.226	.283	.191	.259	.387	.430	.436	.346	.319	.305	.290
Mali	678	.034	.060	.079	.128	.180	.176	.155	.159	.286	.361	.439	.380	.332	.353	.278
Mauritania	682	.056	.057	.069	.128	.120	.161	.179	.206	.181	.259	.286	.265	.276	.227	.208
Mauritius	684	.076	.084	.119	.168	.309	.332	.360	.447	.500	.574	.614	.563	.465	.442	.471
Morocco	686	.684	.701	.779	1.144	1.904	2.568	2.618	3.199	2.970	3.678	4.255	4.400	4.315	3.592	3.911
Mozambique	688	....	....	....	....	....	....	....	....	....	....	....	....	....	....	....
Namibia	728	....	....	....	....	....	....	....	....	....	....	....	....	....	....	....
Niger	692	.059	.054	.066	.086	.097	.101	.126	.197	.305	.461	.594	.510	.466	.324	.288
Nigeria	694	1.059	1.514	1.505	1.862	2.772	6.041	8.213	11.095	12.821	10.218	16.660	20.877	16.061	12.254	9.364
Rwanda	714	.029	.033	.035	.034	.058	.099	.106	.123	.188	.192	.243	.256	.276	.269	.278
Sao Tome & Principe	716	.009	.008	.008	.010	.010	.011	.009	.014	.018	.020	.019	.017	....	....	....
Senegal	722	.195	.220	.280	.361	.498	.583	.636	.764	.755	.931	1.052	1.076	.992	1.025	.981
Seychelles	718	.010	.015	.021	.025	.028	.032	.039	.046	.058	.085	.099	.093	.098	.088	.088
Sierra Leone	724	.116	.113	.119	.155	.222	.185	.153	.181	.279	.316	.427	.328	.298	.160	.157
South Africa ⅋	199	3.843	4.364	3.948	⅋5.163	7.856	8.293	7.285	6.270	7.615	8.989	⅋19.699	22.918	18.499	15.765	16.243
Sudan	732	.288	.331	.320	.436	.642	.887	.980	1.081	1.194	1.109	1.576	1.553	1.282	1.354	1.147
Swaziland	734	.060	.067	.069	.096	.138	.178	.200	.182	.311	.435	.625	.590	.523	.552	.443
Tanzania	738	.318	.382	.404	.496	.753	.778	.638	.744	1.145	1.105	1.258	1.176	1.132	.802	.665
Togo	742	.065	.071	.085	.101	.119	.174	.185	.284	.450	.519	.551	.434	.393	.282	.271
Tunisia	744	.306	.345	.466	.682	1.128	1.424	1.529	1.825	2.138	2.849	3.526	3.791	3.420	3.107	3.221
Uganda	746	.172	.250	.162	.163	.213	.207	.172	.241	.254	.197	.293	.345	.377	.377	.344
Zambia	754	.477	.556	.565	.533	.787	.929	.674	.671	.618	.749	1.088	1.064	1.001	.550	.596
Zimbabwe	698	.378	.456	.478	.606	.865	.932	.703	.710	.685	.929	1.448	1.693	1.644	1.209	1.103

1985	1986	1987	1988	1989	1990	1991	1992	1993	1994	1995	1996	1997	1998	1999		

Billions of US Dollars

1985	1986	1987	1988	1989	1990	1991	1992	1993	1994	1995	1996	1997	1998	1999	Country	Code
1,952.3	2,131.0	2,499.2	2,862.6	3,098.2	3,516.0	3,626.5	3,850.1	3,804.3	4,323.4	5,159.5	5,371.0	5,587.6	5,519.3	Ɪ5,732.9	World	001
1,374.7	1,545.5	1,829.9	2,069.3	2,239.7	2,575.3	2,593.1	2,706.9	2,558.6	2,902.0	3,432.0	3,512.6	3,631.9	3,725.8	Ɪ3,907.5	Industrial Countries	110
352.463	382.295	424.442	459.542	492.922	516.987	508.363	553.923	603.438	689.215	770.852	822.025	899.020	944.353	1,059.435	United States	111
80.640	85.494	92.593	112.711	119.792	123.244	124.782	129.262	139.035	155.072	168.041	174.959	200.873	206.066	220.183	Canada	156
25.889	26.104	29.318	36.095	44.933	41.985	41.648	43.807	45.577	53.425	61.283	65.427	65.892	64.630	69.135	Australia	193
130.488	127.553	151.033	187.378	209.715	235.368	236.999	233.246	241.624	275.235	335.882	349.152	338.754	280.484	311.262	Japan	158
5.992	6.063	7.276	7.342	8.784	9.501	8.381	9.202	9.636	11.913	13.958	14.725	14.518	12.496	14.301	New Zealand	196
20.986	26.843	32.678	36.570	38.923	49.088	50.788	54.112	48.633	55.335	66.386	67.331	64.776	68.183	Ɪ68.755	Austria	122
....	....	....	....	....	....	....	....	114.398	130.067	159.683	163.604	157.260	162.241	Ɪ160.818	Belgium	124
56.190	68.656	83.523	92.439	98.580	120.314	121.059	125.112	112.112	125.639	155.126	152.734	155.435	....	....	Belgium-Luxembourg	126
13.232	15.339	19.634	21.130	24.436	27.001	21.809	21.208	18.032	23.214	28.114	29.264	29.784	32.301	30.726	Finland	172
108.337	129.402	158.477	178.836	192.949	234.447	231.779	239.638	203.202	234.567	281.440	235.098	271.914	290.241	Ɪ289.927	France	132
158.488	190.872	228.441	250.467	269.702	Ɪ346.153	389.908	402.441	346.027	385.351	464.271	458.783	445.616	471.418	472.161	Germany	134
10.015	11.607	13.638	15.569	17.420	20.682	20.750	22.477	21.990	25.909	33.064	35.897	39.238	44.617	46.030	Ireland	178
87.692	99.332	125.661	138.551	153.011	181.968	182.682	188.519	147.336	169.172	206.040	208.092	210.268	218.445	216.621	Italy	136
3.144	4.227	5.239	5.813	6.210	7.596	8.044	8.221	7.687	8.387	9.748	9.667	9.379	7.408	10.929	Luxembourg	137
73.123	Ɪ75.474	91.494	99.444	104.253	126.475	127.213	134.650	124.742	141.317	176.874	180.639	178.130	187.747	Ɪ187.525	Netherlands	138
7.652	9.649	13.967	17.940	19.072	25.264	26.421	30.312	24.273	27.303	33.306	35.177	35.064	38.536	Ɪ38.461	Portugal	182
29.963	35.057	49.113	60.502	70.945	87.554	92.965	99.753	79.665	92.191	113.319	121.782	122.711	133.149	Ɪ144.436	Spain	184
18.245	22.878	25.499	25.941	26.690	32.228	32.402	35.174	30.542	34.878	45.082	44.432	44.039	45.424	43.971	Denmark	128
10.134	11.350	13.168	12.321	16.151	19.777	21.580	23.218	22.010	18.742	22.929	24.136	23.644	23.247	....	Greece	174
.905	1.119	1.590	1.597	1.401	1.680	1.760	1.684	1.341	1.472	1.756	2.032	1.992	2.489	2.503	Iceland	176
15.556	20.301	22.639	23.220	23.676	27.231	25.572	25.905	23.956	27.308	32.968	35.615	35.709	36.193	34.041	Norway	142
28.547	32.693	40.706	45.627	48.975	54.264	49.990	50.017	42.681	51.725	64.743	72.891	65.702	68.237	68.453	Sweden	144
30.696	41.039	50.591	56.363	58.194	69.681	66.485	Ɪ61.737	56.716	64.074	76.985	74.462	71.064	73.877	75.438	Switzerland	146
109.505	126.343	154.387	189.693	199.186	224.412	209.810	221.496	206.101	226.157	265.297	287.426	306.585	314.031	317.968	United Kingdom	112
577.53	585.58	669.32	793.34	858.44	940.66	1,033.39	1,143.19	1,245.67	1,421.32	1,727.48	1,858.36	1,955.70	1,793.51	1,825.42	Developing Countries	200
56.230	54.988	57.750	64.955	67.746	74.478	74.473	79.290	75.139	83.350	101.381	100.844	108.429	106.096	....	Africa	605
9.841	9.228	7.042	7.690	9.470	9.780	7.770	8.550	7.770	9.370	10.250	8.840	....	....	....	Algeria	612
.331	.387	.349	.327	.207	.265	.241	.578	.571	.431	.746	.654	.682	.672	.643	Benin	638
.672	.858	1.106	1.453	1.930	1.947	1.941	1.888	1.766	1.640	1.911	1.723	2.258	2.387	....	Botswana	616
.332	.405	.434	.454	.391	.536	.533	.466	.509	.349	.455	.647	.587	.783	.696	Burkina Faso	748
.186	.202	.212	.204	.187	.231	.255	.221	.196	.225	.234	.127	.121	.158	.118	Burundi	618
1.151	1.704	1.753	1.273	1.261	1.400	1.173	1.163	.885	.717	1.199	1.227	1.359	....	....	Cameroon	622
.086	.143	.100	.106	.112	.136	.147	.180	.154	.209	.252	....	....	....	....	Cape Verde	624
.113	.167	.204	.141	.150	.154	.093	.145	.126	.139	.174	.141	.145	....	....	Central African Rep.	626
.166	.212	.226	.228	.235	.286	.250	.243	.201	.177	.220	.255	.246	.264	....	Chad	628
.036	.037	.052	.053	.043	.052	.058	.069	.059	.053	.063	....	....	....	....	Comoros	632
.792	.875	.756	.763	.850	.888	.711	.420	.372	.382	.397	.424	....	....	....	Congo, Dem. Rep. of	636
.598	.597	.979	1.113	1.030	.621	.594	.451	.582	.631	.670	1.551	....	....	....	Congo, Rep. of	634
1.749	2.055	2.241	2.080	2.111	2.098	2.103	2.352	2.115	1.917	2.931	2.902	2.781	3.196	3.270	Côte d'Ivoire	662
.201	.184	.205	.201	.196	.215	.214	.219	....	....	....	....	....	....	....	Djibouti	611
.020	.052	.058	.061	.055	.062	.117	.093	.038	.024	.031	.168	.080	.032	....	Equatorial Guinea	642
.993	1.102	1.066	1.129	.951	1.081	.472	.839	.787	1.033	1.145	1.401	....	....	1.317	Ethiopia	644
.855	.866	.732	.791	.767	.918	.834	.700	.845	.756	.882	.957	1.104	....	....	Gabon	646
.093	.104	.127	.138	.161	.188	.202	.218	.260	.212	.182	.258	.174	.245	.192	Gambia, The	648
.866	1.046	1.156	.905	1.276	....	1.055	2.169	3.942	2.109	1.907	2.108	2.326	2.563	3.505	Ghana	652
....	....	....	.066	.078	.086	.076	.096	.061	.164	.133	.087	.089	.063	.095	Guinea-Bissau	654
1.436	1.613	1.738	1.988	2.174	2.223	1.935	1.841	1.774	2.091	2.991	2.949	3.279	3.197	....	Kenya	664
.339	.354	.470	.584	.593	.673	.810	.899	.870	.848	.985	.999	1.025	.863	....	Lesotho	666
.284	.259	.308	.272	....	....	....	....	....	....	....	....	....	....	....	Liberia	668
.402	.353	.302	.379	.371	.651	.436	.448	.468	.441	.543	.507	.470	.514	....	Madagascar	674
.339	.244	.366	.533	.540	.641	.833	.852	.504	.449	.345	.414	.781	.382	....	Malawi	676
.299	.444	.374	.504	.340	.602	.460	.608	.634	.589	.792	.843	.760	.762	.751	Mali	678
.234	.221	.235	.240	.222	.220	....	....	....	.403	....	....	....	....	....	Mauritania	682
.529	.684	1.013	1.290	1.325	1.618	1.558	1.625	1.715	1.930	1.976	2.289	2.189	2.073	....	Mauritius	684
3.850	3.803	4.229	4.773	5.492	6.922	6.873	7.348	6.732	8.272	10.023	9.704	9.525	10.290	9.925	Morocco	686
....	....	....	....	....	....	....	....	....	.535	.718	.774	.754	.805	1.161	Mozambique	688
....	....	....	....	....	1.163	1.149	1.283	1.188	1.196	....	....	....	....	....	Namibia	728
.369	.368	.311	.387	.363	.389	.355	.479	.375	.328	.374	.448	.391	.414	.396	Niger	692
8.877	4.034	3.912	4.717	4.187	5.627	8.986	8.275	5.537	7.438	Ɪ7.912	6.932	10.330	10.002	....	Nigeria	694
.298	.349	.352	.370	.333	.288	.306	.288	.332	....	.238	.257	.297	.285	.253	Rwanda	714
.010	.017	.014	.014	.018	.021	.031	.029	.032	.030	.029	.022	.016	....	....	Sao Tome & Principe	716
.826	.961	1.024	1.080	1.221	1.220	1.173	1.034	1.087	1.022	1.412	1.436	1.336	1.437	....	Senegal	722
.099	.105	.114	.159	.165	.187	.173	.191	.238	.207	.233	.274	.340	.403	....	Seychelles	718
.151	.132	.137	.156	.183	.149	.163	.146	.147	.151	.133	.211	.093	.095	.081	Sierra Leone	724
11.440	12.974	15.295	18.670	18.490	18.399	18.828	19.738	19.991	23.363	30.546	30.182	32.998	29.242	26.696	South Africa Ɪ	199
.771	.961	.871	1.060	....	.619	.890	.821	.945	1.227	Ɪ1.219	1.548	1.580	1.915	....	Sudan	732
.316	.353	.437	.511	.585	.664	.715	.866	.870	.927	1.103	1.174	1.192	....	....	Swaziland	734
.845	.937	.929	.823	.990	1.364	1.546	1.510	1.497	1.505	1.675	1.388	1.337	1.453	1.636	Tanzania	738
.288	.312	.424	.487	.472	.581	.444	.395	.179	.222	.594	.664	.645	.631	....	Togo	742
2.757	2.890	3.039	3.689	4.387	5.513	5.189	6.431	6.214	6.581	7.903	7.700	7.914	8.338	8.466	Tunisia	744
.327	.307	.848	.887	.423	.288	.196	.505	....	.875	1.056	1.191	1.316	1.414	1.341	Uganda	746
.722	.597	.736	.839	.906	1.220	.818	.795	.809	.594	.700	.835	.819	....	....	Zambia	754
.896	.985	1.047	1.132	1.614	1.839	2.037	2.201	1.817	2.241	2.661	2.803	....	....	....	Zimbabwe	698

		1970	1971	1972	1973	1974	1975	1976	1977	1978	1979	1980	1981	1982	1983	1984
															Billions of US Dollars	
Asia *	505	21.503	23.481	27.461	40.843	62.729	65.467	70.533	81.591	104.721	136.609	179.382	198.320	193.131	199.103	216.991
Bangladesh	513	....	....	.683	.986	1.078	1.321	.952	1.163	1.513	1.908	2.599	2.699	2.464	2.165	2.825
Bhutan	514	....	....	....	....	....	....	....	....	....	....	.050	.068	.068	.072	.073
Cambodia	522	.054	.057	....	.227	....	....	....	....	....	....	....	....	....	....	....
China, P.R.: Mainland	924	2.279	2.129	2.851	5.208	7.791	7.926	6.660	7.148	11.131	15.621	I 19.941	22.015	19.285	21.390	27.410
China, P.R.: Hong Kong	532	2.905	3.391	3.856	5.655	6.778	6.766	8.838	10.446	13.394	17.127	22.447	24.797	23.575	24.017	28.568
China, P.R.: Macao	546	.065	.075	.104	.158	.134	.161	.161	.198	.249	.351	.544	.720	.719	.727	.795
Fiji	819	.104	.129	.159	.222	.273	.268	.264	.307	.355	.470	.562	.631	.509	.484	.450
India	534	2.124	2.424	2.223	3.211	5.136	6.381	5.665	6.647	7.865	9.827	14.864	15.418	14.786	14.061	15.272
Indonesia	536	1.002	1.103	1.562	2.729	3.842	4.770	5.673	6.230	6.690	7.202	10.834	13.272	16.859	16.352	13.882
Korea	542	1.984	2.394	2.522	4.240	6.852	7.274	8.774	10.811	14.972	20.339	22.292	26.131	24.251	26.192	30.631
Lao People's Democratic Rep.	544	.114	.082	.063	.057	.065	.045	.045	.014	.016	.070	.092	.110	.132	.150	.162
Malaysia	548	1.401	1.447	1.611	2.450	4.114	3.566	3.824	4.542	5.909	7.849	10.779	11.550	12.418	13.262	14.051
Maldives	556	.002	.004	.005	.007	.007	.007	.006	.010	.014	.021	.029	.031	.043	.057	.053
Mongolia	948	....	....	....	....	....	....	....	....	....	....	.548	.704	.791	.928	.975
Myanmar	518	.155	.169	.133	.106	.176	.197	.177	.241	.307	.319	.353	.373	.409	.268	.239
Nepal	558	.075	.085	.085	.104	.134	.172	.163	.168	.221	.254	.342	.369	.395	.464	.417
Pakistan	564	.731	.678	I 1.083	.927	1.737	2.168	2.191	2.458	3.301	4.076	5.376	5.658	6.151	5.520	6.111
Papua New Guinea	853	.302	.355	.332	.356	.518	.592	.502	.642	.770	.903	1.176	1.261	1.170	1.120	1.110
Philippines	566	1.232	1.255	1.374	1.501	2.652	3.729	3.859	4.073	4.581	5.860	7.410	8.549	8.590	7.961	7.088
Samoa	862	.014	.013	.019	.024	.026	.037	.030	I .041	.052	.073	.063	.057	.050	.048	.050
Singapore	576	2.461	2.838	3.395	5.127	8.380	8.133	9.071	10.471	13.061	17.643	24.007	27.572	28.167	28.158	28.667
Solomon Islands	813	.013	.015	.017	.018	.027	.033	.030	.033	.042	.070	.089	.091	.071	.074	.079
Sri Lanka	524	.386	.354	.368	.430	.720	.756	.582	.701	.967	1.451	2.057	1.905	2.015	1.935	1.869
Thailand	578	1.299	1.288	1.484	2.049	3.143	3.280	3.572	4.616	5.356	7.158	9.214	9.955	8.548	10.287	10.398
Tonga	866	....	....	....	....	....	....	....	....	....	....	....	....	....	....	....
Vanuatu	846	.013	.018	.029	.036	.050	.040	.034	.040	.051	.062	.073	.058	.060	.064	.069
*of which:																
Taiwan Province of China	528	1.528	1.849	2.518	3.799	6.983	5.959	7.609	8.522	11.051	14.793	19.764	21.153	18.827	20.308	22.002
Europe	170	....	....	....	....	....	....	....	....	....	....	....	....	....	....	....
Albania	914	....	....	....	....	....	....	....	....	....	....	....	....	....	....	....
Armenia	911	....	....	....	....	....	....	....	....	....	....	....	....	....	....	....
Azerbaijan	912	....	....	....	....	....	....	....	....	....	....	....	....	....	....	....
Belarus	913	....	....	....	....	....	....	....	....	....	....	....	....	....	....	....
Bulgaria	918	1.831	2.120	2.567	3.239	4.326	5.949	6.228	6.329	....	....	....	....	....	....	....
Croatia	960	....	....	....	....	....	....	....	....	....	....	....	....	....	....	....
Cyprus	423	.236	.260	.317	.451	.407	.308	.432	.623	.758	1.010	1.202	1.166	1.215	1.219	1.364
Czech Republic	935	....	....	....	....	....	....	....	....	....	....	....	....	....	....	....
Czechoslovakia	934	....	....	....	....	....	7.050	....	....	....	....	11.940	12.774	11.894	12.271	12.250	11.852
Estonia	939	....	....	....	....	....	....	....	....	....	....	....	....	....	....	....
Georgia	915	....	....	....	....	....	....	....	....	....	....	....	....	....	....	....
Hungary	944	1.877	2.248	2.356	3.018	4.453	5.400	5.533	6.531	7.990	8.682	9.245	9.139	8.819	8.509	8.091
Kazakhstan	916	....	....	....	....	....	....	....	....	....	....	....	....	....	....	....
Kyrgyz Republic	917	....	....	....	....	....	....	....	....	....	....	....	....	....	....	....
Latvia	941	....	....	....	....	....	....	....	....	....	....	....	....	....	....	....
Lithuania	946	....	....	....	....	....	....	....	....	....	....	....	....	....	....	....
Macedonia, FYR	962	....	....	....	....	....	....	....	....	....	....	....	....	....	....	....
Malta	181	.161	.161	.176	.239	.361	.375	.423	.516	.575	.759	.938	.860	.789	.733	.717
Moldova	921	....	....	....	....	....	....	....	....	....	....	....	....	....	....	....
Poland	964	3.608	....	....	....	....	11.155	12.898	13.420	14.744	16.142	16.690	12.792	10.648	10.927	10.985
Romania	968	2.117	2.278	2.827	3.738	5.555	5.769	6.583	7.579	9.638	11.789	13.843	13.454	10.525	10.414	11.161
Russia	922	....	....	....	....	....	....	....	....	....	....	....	....	....	....	....
Slovak Republic	936	....	....	....	....	....	....	....	....	....	....	....	....	....	....	....
Slovenia	961	....	....	....	....	....	....	....	....	....	....	....	....	....	....	....
Turkey	186	.948	1.171	1.563	2.086	3.778	4.739	5.129	5.796	4.599	5.070	7.910	8.933	8.843	9.235	10.757
Ukraine	926	....	....	....	....	....	....	....	....	....	....	....	....	....	....	....
Yugoslavia, SFR	188	2.874	3.252	3.233	4.511	7.542	7.697	7.367	9.634	9.989	12.863	15.076	15.727	13.453	12.154	11.996
Middle East	405	9.086	10.526	12.678	18.733	31.441	45.487	53.723	69.923	80.083	86.914	108.503	126.802	142.035	134.921	123.065
Bahrain	419	.247	.312	.376	.512	1.127	1.189	1.668	2.029	2.045	2.480	3.483	4.124	3.614	3.262	3.480
Egypt	469	.787	.920	.899	.915	2.351	3.934	3.807	4.815	6.727	3.837	4.860	8.782	9.078	10.275	10.766
Iran, I.R. of	429	1.662	1.873	2.409	3.393	5.433	10.343	12.894	14.070	13.549	9.738	I 12.246	14.693	11.955	18.320	15.370
Iraq	433	.508	.702	.705	.894	2.371	4.215	3.897	4.481	4.213	5.888	7.477	7.903	21.534	12.166	11.078
Israel	436	2.079	2.363	2.473	4.240	5.437	5.997	5.669	5.787	7.415	8.576	9.784	10.235	9.655	9.574	9.819
Jordan	439	.184	.215	.274	.330	.488	.732	1.006	1.381	1.504	1.963	2.402	3.165	3.240	3.036	2.784
Kuwait	443	.625	.652	.797	1.049	1.554	2.388	3.327	4.846	4.598	5.201	6.533	6.969	8.285	7.375	6.896
Lebanon	446	.659	.731	.924	1.286	2.355	2.048	.612	1.539	1.922	2.700	3.650	3.499	3.391	3.661	2.948
Libya	672	.554	.703	1.043	1.806	2.762	3.542	3.212	3.773	4.603	5.311	6.777	8.382	7.175	6.029	6.222
Oman	449	.018	.033	.049	.116	.393	.765	.725	.875	.947	1.246	1.732	2.288	2.682	2.492	2.748
Qatar	453	.064	.109	.141	.195	.271	.413	.817	1.225	1.185	1.424	1.423	1.518	1.947	1.456	1.162
Saudi Arabia	456	.693	.808	1.136	1.972	2.860	4.213	8.695	14.656	20.422	24.462	30.171	35.244	40.645	39.205	33.696
Syrian Arab Rep.	463	.360	.439	.540	.613	1.227	1.685	2.383	2.702	2.459	3.329	4.124	5.172	4.028	4.542	4.116
United Arab Emirates	466	.267	.309	.482	.821	1.705	2.685	3.337	5.055	5.371	6.966	8.746	9.646	9.440	8.294	6.936
Yemen Arab Rep.	473	.033	.034	.080	.123	.190	.294	.413	1.040	1.284	1.492	1.853	1.758	1.521	1.618	1.556
Yemen, P.D. Rep.	459	.200	.156	.149	.171	.419	.323	.412	.544	.575	.925	1.527	1.419	1.599	1.483	1.543
Yemen, Rep. of	474	....	....	....	....	....	....	....	....	....	....	....	....	....	....	....

Billions of US Dollars

1985	1986	1987	1988	1989	1990	1991	1992	1993	1994	1995	1996	1997	1998	1999		
222.369	230.707	281.530	364.602	414.656	467.096	537.152	604.879	679.263	795.326	975.426	1,027.358	1,046.500	874.270	936.087	Asia *	505
I2.542	2.546	2.715	3.041	3.650	3.618	3.412	3.732	3.994	4.602	6.502	6.621	6.898	6.974	7.694	Bangladesh	513
.084	.093	.087	.127	.090	.078	.097	.128	.090	.092	.112	.128	.137	....	....	Bhutan	514
															Cambodia	522
42.252	42.904	43.216	55.268	59.140	53.345	63.791	80.585	103.088	115.681	129.113	138.944	142.189	140.305	165.788	China, P.R.: Mainland	924
29.703	35.367	48.465	63.896	72.155	82.490	100.240	123.407	138.650	161.841	192.751	198.550	208.614	184.518	179.520	China, P.R.: Hong Kong	532
.778	.880	1.121	1.290	1.481	1.533	1.841	1.948	2.005	1.978	2.021	1.979	2.062	1.937	....	China, P.R.: Macao	546
.442	.435	.379	.462	.579	.754	.652	.630	.720	.842	.892	.987	.965	.721	....	Fiji	819
15.928	15.421	16.675	19.102	20.549	23.580	20.448	23.579	22.788	26.843	34.707	37.942	41.432	42.980	44.889	India	534
10.259	10.718	12.370	13.249	16.360	21.837	25.869	27.280	28.328	31.983	40.630	42.929	41.694	27.337	24.004	Indonesia	536
31.136	31.585	41.020	51.811	61.465	69.844	81.525	81.775	83.800	102.348	135.119	150.339	144.616	93.282	119.750	Korea	542
.193	.186	.216	.149	.194	.185	.170	.270	.432	.564	.589	.690	.706	.553	.525	Lao People's Democratic Rep.	544
12.253	10.806	12.681	16.506	22.480	29.258	36.648	39.855	45.650	59.600	77.691	78.418	79.030	58.319	64.966	Malaysia	548
.053	.045	.081	.090	.113	.138	.161	.189	.191	.222	.268	.302	.349	.354	.402	Maldives	556
1.096	1.840	1.105	1.114	.963	.924	.361	.418	.379	.258	.415	.451	.468	.503	1.010	Mongolia	948
.283	.304	.268	.244	.191	.270	.646	.651	.814	.886	1.335	1.358	2.037	2.666	2.300	Myanmar	518
.453	.460	.571	.678	.582	.672	.737	.776	.890	1.155	1.333	1.398	1.693	1.246	....	Nepal	558
6.201	5.562	5.926	6.788	7.640	7.514	9.032	9.538	10.265	9.078	11.834	13.093	12.274	9.800	....	Pakistan	564
1.008	1.080	1.165	1.393	1.530	1.193	1.614	1.485	1.299	1.522	1.452	1.741	1.697	1.232	1.188	Papua New Guinea	853
6.090	5.265	5.925	8.024	9.918	12.103	13.180	13.689	16.894	21.058	24.877	32.044	36.041	36.302	31.168	Philippines	566
.051	.047	.062	.076	.075	.081	.094	.105	.105	.081	.095	.100	.097	.097	.115	Samoa	862
26.285	25.511	32.559	43.864	49.656	60.774	66.095	72.171	85.234	102.670	124.507	131.338	132.437	104.719	111.060	Singapore	576
.083	.072	.081	.098	.113	.091	.112	.112	.137	.139	.154	.151	....	....	....	Solomon Islands	813
1.988	1.946	2.053	2.237	2.215	2.688	3.055	3.500	4.005	4.767	5.306	5.442	5.851	5.889	5.893	Sri Lanka	524
9.242	9.178	13.000	20.285	25.770	33.045	37.569	40.686	46.077	54.459	70.786	72.332	62.854	42.971	41.526	Thailand	578
....	....	....	....	....	....	....	....	....	.069	.077	.075	....	....	....	Tonga	866
.070	.057	.070	.070	.071	.096	.083	.082	.079	.089	.095	.098	.094	.088	....	Vanuatu	846
															of which:	
20.124	24.230	34.802	49.763	52.507	54.830	63.078	72.181	77.099	85.507	103.698	101.287	113.924	104.946	110.957	Taiwan Province of China	528
....	....	....	....	....	171.840	158.972	149.576	167.549	192.266	256.300	296.322	317.189	314.092	275.173	Europe	170
....	....	....	....	....	....	.175	.574	.604	.714	.841	.646	.829	....	....	Albania	914
....	....	....	....	....	....	....	.254	.394	.674	.856	.892	.902	....	.800	Armenia	911
....	....	....	....	....	....	.998	.636	.778	.668	.961	.794	1.077	....	....	Azerbaijan	912
....	....	....	....	....	....	3.495	2.539	3.066	5.563	6.939	8.689	8.549	....	6.664	Belarus	913
13.657	15.269	16.169	16.781	15.233	4.710	2.537	4.460	4.720	4.260	5.661	6.861	5.224	4.981	5.409	Bulgaria	918
								4.666	5.229	7.510	7.788	9.104	8.383	7.777	Croatia	960
1.247	1.271	1.484	1.857	2.408	2.796	2.847	3.674	....	....	3.019	3.983	3.698	3.685	3.618	Cyprus	423
								I15.333	I18.376	I26.571	29.107	28.540	30.258	....	Czech Republic	935
12.149	14.666	16.340	15.298	14.988	13.712	10.473	13.207	....	....	....	....	....	....	....	Czechoslovakia	934
....	....	....	....	....	....	....	....	.893	I1.668	2.545	3.224	4.429	4.613	4.093	Estonia	939
....	....	....	....	....	....	....	....	....	....	.687	.944	.887	....	....	Georgia	915
8.224	9.599	9.841	9.345	8.709	8.670	11.417	11.107	12.518	14.386	15.046	15.853	20.668	25.600	27.923	Hungary	944
....	....	....	....	....	....	....	....	3.887	3.561	3.807	4.241	4.301	4.350	3.683	Kazakhstan	916
....	....	....	....	....	....	.418	....	.430	.316	.522	.838	.709	.842	.600	Kyrgyz Republic	917
....	....	....	....	....	....	....	....	.872	1.251	1.818	2.320	2.721	3.191	2.945	Latvia	941
....	....	....	....	....	....	....	....	2.279	2.353	3.649	4.559	5.644	5.794	4.892	Lithuania	946
....	....	....	....	....	....	....	....	1.199	1.484	1.719	....	....	....	....	Macedonia, FYR	962
.759	.887	1.139	1.352	1.480	1.961	2.114	2.349	2.173	2.441	2.944	2.795	2.555	2.686	2.860	Malta	181
....	....	....	....	....	....	....	....	.628	.703	.841	1.079	1.200	1.018	....	Moldova	921
11.855	11.535	11.215	12.712	10.659	8.413	I15.757	15.701	18.834	21.383	29.050	37.137	42.308	46.495	45.903	Poland	964
11.267	11.437	8.978	8.254	9.122	9.843	5.793	6.260	6.522	7.109	10.278	11.435	11.280	11.821	10.392	Romania	968
....	....	....	....	....	....	....	36.984	32.806	I50.518	60.945	68.828	73.660	60.476	40.429	Russia	922
....	....	....	....	....	....	....	....	6.632	6.839	9.225	11.432	10.774	13.604	....	Slovak Republic	936
....	....	....	....	....	....	4.147	I6.142	6.499	7.304	9.492	9.423	9.357	10.110	9.952	Slovenia	961
11.343	11.105	14.158	14.335	15.792	22.302	21.047	22.871	29.428	23.270	35.709	43.627	48.559	45.921	40.692	Turkey	186
....	....	....	....	....	....	....	7.099	9.533	10.748	16.052	18.639	17.114	14.676	11.846	Ukraine	926
12.207	11.751	12.632	13.171	14.829	18.871	14.737	....	....	....	....	....	....	....	....	Yugoslavia, SFR	188
104.155	95.130	104.628	117.073	115.197	122.551	128.080	137.013	135.519	129.461	144.962	157.263	154.689	159.266	....	Middle East	405
3.107	2.405	2.714	2.593	3.134	3.712	4.115	4.263	3.858	3.748	3.716	4.273	4.026	3.566	3.588	Bahrain	419
11.104	11.502	16.225	23.298	18.774	16.783	8.052	8.325	8.214	10.219	11.760	13.038	13.211	16.166	16.022	Egypt	469
11.635	10.521	9.570	9.454	14.794	20.322	27.927	25.860	21.427	13.774	13.882	16.274	14.165	....	....	Iran, I.R. of	429
10.556	10.190	7.415	10.268	....	....	....	....	....	....	....	....	....	....	....	Iraq	433
9.875	10.806	14.348	15.018	14.347	16.794	18.658	15.535	22.624	25.237	29.579	31.620	30.781	29.342	33.160	Israel	436
2.733	2.432	2.708	2.732	2.125	2.600	2.508	3.255	3.539	3.382	3.698	4.293	4.102	3.828	3.728	Jordan	439
6.005	5.717	5.495	6.145	6.301	3.972	4.761	7.257	7.038	6.697	7.790	8.373	8.246	8.619	7.617	Kuwait	443
2.203	2.203	1.880	2.457	2.235	2.525	3.743	4.202	I2.215	2.598	5.480	7.540	7.467	7.070	6.207	Lebanon	446
4.101	4.445	4.334	5.869	4.923	5.336	5.361	....	....	5.548	5.392	5.873	6.123	5.466	....	Libya	672
3.153	2.402	1.822	2.202	2.257	2.681	3.194	3.769	4.114	3.915	4.248	4.578	5.026	5.682	4.674	Oman	449
1.139	1.099	1.134	1.267	1.326	1.695	1.720	2.015	1.891	1.927	3.398	2.868	3.322	....	....	Qatar	453
23.622	19.112	20.110	21.784	21.154	24.069	29.079	33.271	28.198	23.338	28.091	27.765	28.561	30.013	....	Saudi Arabia	456
3.967	2.728	7.112	2.231	2.097	2.400	2.768	3.490	4.140	5.467	4.709	5.380	4.028	3.895	3.832	Syrian Arab Rep.	463
6.549	6.422	7.226	8.522	10.010	11.199	13.746	17.414	19.520	21.024	20.984	22.638	29.952	24.728	....	United Arab Emirates	466
1.313	1.159	.883	1.384	....	....	....	....	....	....	....	....	....	....	....	Yemen Arab Rep.	473
....	.483	....	....	....	....	....	....	....	....	....	....	....	....	....	Yemen, P.D. Rep.	459
....	....	....	....	....	....	2.025	2.587	2.821	2.087	1.582	2.038	2.014	2.167	....	Yemen, Rep. of	474

Imports, c.i.f.

		1970	1971	1972	1973	1974	1975	1976	1977	1978	1979	1980	1981	1982	1983	1984
Western Hemisphere	205	17.396	19.588	21.739	28.589	50.044	53.352	55.835	61.639	69.415	86.295	119.721	128.614	103.898	79.918	81.946
Antigua and Barbuda	311	.036	.044	.047	.048	.070	.067	.035	ⅼ.034	.041	.063	.088	.111	.139	.109	.132
Argentina	213	1.694	1.868	1.905	2.230	3.635	3.947	3.033	4.162	3.834	6.700	10.541	9.430	5.337	4.504	4.585
Aruba	314	....	....	....	....											
Bahamas, The	313	.337	.511	.485	.764	1.908	2.697	3.125	3.568	3.150	3.514	7.546	7.284	6.349	4.616	4.072
Barbados	316	.118	.124	.141	.168	.204	.217	.237	.273	.314	.425	.525	.576	.554	ⅼ.624	ⅼ.662
Belize	339	.033	.036	.043	.044	.064	.088	.073	.090	.106	.132	.150	.162	.128	.112	.130
Bolivia	218	.159	.170	.185	.230	.390	.558	.555	.618	.808	.894	.665	.917	.554	.577	.489
Brazil	223	2.849	3.701	4.783	6.999	14.168	13.592	13.726	13.257	15.054	19.804	24.961	24.079	21.069	16.801	15.210
Chile	228	1.063	1.109	1.086	1.290	2.148	1.525	1.864	2.539	3.408	4.808	5.797	7.181	3.989	3.085	3.574
Colombia	233	.843	.929	.859	1.062	1.597	1.495	1.662	1.880	2.971	3.364	4.739	5.201	5.480	4.963	4.498
Costa Rica	238	.317	.350	.373	.455	.720	.694	.770	1.021	1.166	1.397	1.540	1.209	.889	.988	1.094
Dominica	321	.016	.017	.017	.016	.019	.021	.019	.022	.028	.022	.048	.050	.047	.045	.058
Dominican Republic	243	.304	.358	.388	.489	.808	.889	.878	.975	.987	1.213	1.640	1.668	1.444	1.471	1.446
Ecuador	248	.274	.340	.319	.397	.678	.987	.958	1.189	1.505	1.600	2.253	ⅼ2.246	2.169	1.487	1.616
El Salvador	253	.214	.249	.272	.377	.562	.614	.735	.929	1.028	1.037	.966	.986	.857	.891	.977
Grenada	328	.022	.023	.022	.022	.018	.024	.025	.032	.036	.044	.050	.054	.056	.057	.056
Guatemala	258	.284	.297	.324	.431	.700	.733	.839	1.053	1.286	1.504	1.598	1.688	1.388	1.126	1.279
Guyana	336	.134	.135	.143	.177	.255	.344	.364	.314	.279	.318	.396	.428	.281	.246	.211
Haiti	263	.055	.060	.069	.083	.125	.149	.207	.213	.233	.272	.375	.461	.387	.441	.450
Honduras	268	.221	.194	.193	.262	.382	.400	.456	.575	.693	.826	1.009	.949	.701	.803	.893
Jamaica	343	.525	.552	.638	.677	.936	1.124	.913	.860	.904	.993	1.171	1.473	1.381	1.494	1.146
Mexico	273	2.461	2.407	2.718	3.814	6.057	6.580	6.028	5.489	8.109	12.086	ⅼ22.144	28.462	17.742	12.476	16.691
Netherlands Antilles	353	.798	.882	.870	1.593	3.631	2.827	3.667	3.128	3.491	4.395	5.676	5.862	5.087	4.527	4.032
Nicaragua	278	.199	.210	.218	.327	.562	.517	.532	.762	.596	.360	.887	.999	.776	.826	.848
Panama	283	.357	.396	.440	.502	.822	.892	.848	.861	.942	1.184	1.449	1.540	1.570	1.412	1.423
Paraguay	288	.076	.083	.083	.122	.198	.206	.220	.308	.383	.521	.615	.600	.672	.546	.586
Peru	293	.623	.763	.796	1.019	1.531	ⅼ2.550	2.037	1.911	1.175	1.820	2.499	3.482	3.601	2.548	2.212
St. Kitts and Nevis	361	.012	.015	.016	.018	.019	.024	.022	.022	.024	.032	.045	.048	.044	.051	.052
St. Lucia	362	.027	.035	.036	.038	.044	.046	.048	.059	.083	.101	.124	.129	.118	.144	.119
St. Vincent & Grenadines	364	.015	.018	.018	.019	.025	.025	.024	.030	.036	.047	.057	.058	.065	.070	.077
Suriname	366	.115	.127	.145	.157	.230	.252	.294	.398	.406	ⅼ.411	.504	.568	.511	.453	.346
Trinidad and Tobago	369	.544	.666	.766	.797	1.846	1.469	2.010	1.819	1.967	2.105	3.178	3.125	3.697	2.582	1.919
Uruguay	298	.231	.229	.212	.285	.487	.556	.587	.730	.757	1.206	1.680	1.641	1.110	.788	.777
Venezuela, Rep. Bol.	299	1.869	2.103	2.463	2.812	4.148	6.000	7.663	10.938	11.767	10.670	11.827	13.106	12.944	6.419	7.774
Memorandum Items																
Euro Area	163	....	....	....	....											
Oil Exporting Countries	999	9.579	11.136	13.785	19.885	32.146	50.873	63.534	84.369	94.714	96.731	124.985	145.201	160.281	140.761	125.417
Non-Oil Developing Countries	201	72.097	76.170	84.453	116.759	186.796	213.502	213.237	240.309	279.062	360.103	472.074	502.975	449.655	433.159	456.040

1985	1986	1987	1988	1989	1990	1991	1992	1993	1994	1995	1996	1997	1998	1999		
77.971	80.212	90.689	103.078	112.570	125.146	144.861	173.632	189.610	222.484	251.174	278.435	332.347	361.910	361.919	Western Hemisphere	205
.166	.207	.247	.250	.192	.255	.287	.320	.279	.335	.343	.362	.365	.388	....	Antigua and Barbuda	311
3.814	4.724	5.818	5.322	4.203	4.076	8.275	14.872	16.784	21.527	20.122	23.762	30.450	31.404	25.538	Argentina	213
....	.192	.236	.336	.387	.536	.481	....	....	....	....	....	....	....	....	Aruba	314
3.075	3.284	2.936	2.291	3.235	ɪ 1.074	1.091	1.038	.954	1.056	1.239	1.343	1.622	2.051	1.810	Bahamas, The	313
.611	.591	.518	.582	.677	.704	.699	.524	.577	.614	.771	.834	.996	1.010	1.021	Barbados	316
.128	.122	.143	.181	.216	.211	.256	.274	.281	.260	.257	.255	.286	.325	.366	Belize	339
.691	.674	.766	.591	.611	.687	.970	1.090	1.206	1.209	1.424	1.635	1.851	1.983	1.227	Bolivia	218
14.332	15.557	16.581	16.055	19.875	22.524	22.950	23.068	27.740	35.997	53.783	56.947	65.007	....	....	Brazil	223
3.072	3.436	4.396	5.292	7.233	7.742	8.207	10.183	11.134	11.820	15.900	17.823	19.662	18.779	15.137	Chile	228
4.141	3.862	4.322	5.002	5.004	5.590	4.906	6.516	9.832	11.883	13.853	13.684	15.378	14.635	10.659	Colombia	233
1.098	1.148	1.383	1.410	1.717	1.990	1.877	2.441	3.515	3.789	4.036	4.300	4.924	6.230	6.320	Costa Rica	238
.055	.056	.066	.088	.107	.118	.110	.105	.094	.096	.117	.130	.125	.136	.141	Dominica	321
1.487	1.433	1.830	1.849	2.258	2.062	1.988	2.501	2.436	3.440	3.639	4.118	4.821	5.631	....	Dominican Republic	243
1.767	1.810	2.252	1.714	1.855	1.865	2.399	2.431	2.562	3.622	4.153	3.935	4.955	5.576	3.017	Ecuador	248
.961	.935	.994	1.007	1.161	1.263	1.406	1.699	1.912	2.249	2.853	2.671	2.973	3.112	3.130	El Salvador	253
.069	.084	.089	.092	.099	.105	.121	.107	.144	.119	.130	.152	....	....	....	Grenada	328
1.175	.959	1.447	1.557	1.654	1.649	1.851	2.532	2.599	2.781	3.293	3.146	3.852	4.651	4.382	Guatemala	258
.226	.241	.265	.216	.258	.311	.307	.443	.484	.506	.528	.598	.630	....	....	Guyana	336
.442	.360	.399	.344	.291	.332	.400	.278	.355	.252	.653	.665	.648	.797	1.025	Haiti	263
.888	.875	.827	.940	.969	.935	.955	1.037	1.130	1.056	1.643	1.840	2.149	2.500	2.728	Honduras	268
1.111	.972	1.238	1.454	1.852	1.928	1.823	1.676	2.132	2.224	2.818	2.965	3.132	2.997	2.576	Jamaica	343
19.116	17.573	19.696	29.402	36.400	43.548	52.315	65.049	68.439	83.075	75.858	93.674	114.847	130.948	148.741	Mexico	273
1.388	ɪ 1.112	1.502	1.403	1.610	2.141	2.139	1.868	1.947	1.758	....	....	....	....	....	Netherlands Antilles	353
.964	.857	.827	.805	.615	.638	.751	.855	.744	.875	.962	1.142	1.532	1.492	1.846	Nicaragua	278
1.392	1.229	1.306	.751	.986	1.539	1.695	2.024	2.188	2.404	2.511	2.780	3.002	3.074	3.516	Panama	283
.502	.578	.595	.574	.760	1.352	1.460	1.422	1.689	2.370	3.144	3.204	3.403	....	....	Paraguay	288
1.835	2.909	3.562	3.348	2.749	3.470	4.195	4.861	4.859	6.691	9.224	9.473	10.264	....	....	Peru	293
.051	.063	.079	.093	.102	.110	.110	.095	.118	.128	.133	.149	....	....	....	St. Kitts and Nevis	361
.125	.155	.179	.220	.274	.271	.295	.313	.300	.302	.306	.304	.332	.335	....	St. Lucia	362
.079	.087	.099	.122	.127	.136	.140	.132	.134	.130	.136	.132	.188	.193	.201	St. Vincent & Grenadines	364
.299	.327	.294	.351	.443	.472	.509	.542	.986	.423	.585	.501	.658	.552	....	Suriname	366
1.534	1.350	1.219	1.127	1.221	1.109	1.667	1.104	1.463	1.131	1.714	2.144	2.990	2.999	....	Trinidad and Tobago	369
.708	.870	1.142	1.157	1.203	1.343	1.637	2.045	2.326	2.786	2.867	3.323	3.727	3.811	3.357	Uruguay	298
8.106	8.504	ɪ 9.659	12.726	7.803	7.335	11.147	14.066	12.511	9.187	12.650	9.880	14.606	15.818	14.789	Venezuela, Rep. Bol.	299

Memorandum Items

1985	1986	1987	1988	1989	1990	1991	1992	1993	1994	1995	1996	1997	1998	1999		
....	....	....	....	....	....	....	....	....	....	....	....	....	794.398	821.069	Euro Area	163
103.843	92.391	90.089	103.891	108.483	120.379	139.982	153.526	142.254	134.700	155.881	157.613	164.584	152.802	....	Oil Exporting Countries	999
471.355	491.883	579.009	689.424	750.251	820.489	893.108	989.422	1,103.108	1,286.498	1,571.558	1,701.037	1,791.384	1,640.893	1,678.399	Non-Oil Developing Countries	201

(See notes in the back of the book.)

Export Unit Values/Export Prices

74 *d*

		1970	1971	1972	1973	1974	1975	1976	1977	1978	1979	1980	1981	1982	1983	1984
											Indices of Unit Values (Prices) In Terms of US Dollars:					
World	**001**	**22.2**	**23.3**	**25.5**	**31.3**	**43.3**	**46.9**	**47.3**	**51.8**	**56.9**	**68.2**	**80.8**	**79.9**	**76.4**	**72.9**	**71.3**
Industrial Countries	**110**	**24.3**	**25.6**	**28.0**	**33.9**	**42.4**	**46.9**	**46.6**	**50.5**	**56.9**	**65.8**	**74.4**	**71.5**	**68.9**	**66.5**	**64.6**
United States	**111**	27.4	28.3	29.3	34.1	43.5	48.6	50.3	52.1	55.7	63.3	71.9	78.5	79.4	80.3	81.4
Canada	**156**	32.9	34.3	36.2	41.0	55.8	59.2	62.0	61.6	62.4	73.6	85.7	88.9	87.0	86.9	86.5
Australia	**193**	29.5	30.2	36.4	55.8	66.1	63.1	64.3	65.5	70.0	82.7	96.5	99.0	91.4	87.3	85.3
Japan	**158**	19.4	20.3	23.2	27.4	34.3	34.5	34.4	38.0	45.8	48.0	51.7	54.8	51.0	49.9	49.8
New Zealand	**196**	23.3	25.7	32.6	47.4	47.7	40.6	44.4	49.8	56.5	67.6	74.4	74.9	71.5	67.3	64.8
Euro Area																
Belgium	**124**	....	....	....	....	....	....	....	....	....	....	....	....	....	....	....
Belgium-Luxembourg	**126**	24.6	24.9	28.0	34.1	42.5	46.7	47.0	51.6	58.5	69.0	76.2	65.3	60.6	58.2	55.6
Finland	**172**	16.6	17.7	18.9	23.2	33.3	40.2	39.4	43.7	45.6	54.2	62.9	60.4	57.6	53.4	52.3
France	**132**	22.8	24.3	27.1	33.7	39.4	46.5	45.3	48.7	55.7	64.7	72.3	63.7	59.4	56.1	53.3
Germany	**134**	20.9	22.7	25.7	32.2	38.8	44.2	42.1	46.8	54.7	63.1	69.7	59.6	57.9	55.7	51.7
Ireland	**178**	23.9	26.0	30.5	38.1	42.5	47.7	47.9	53.6	61.7	72.0	80.4	72.2	70.9	67.4	64.1
Italy	**136**	22.5	23.9	26.1	30.9	39.3	43.5	41.6	46.8	52.2	62.5	73.2	67.9	65.8	63.0	59.6
Netherlands	**138**	22.3	23.4	25.9	31.8	42.4	47.3	47.9	53.1	59.1	69.3	79.4	73.3	70.8	66.2	63.4
Portugal (1990=100)	**182**	....	....	....	....	....	....	....	....	....	....	....	....	....	63.2	62.5
Spain	**184**	29.7	29.5	32.9	41.2	51.2	55.3	50.2	52.0	57.8	72.3	80.5	69.2	64.9	58.1	58.3
Denmark	**128**	22.8	23.6	26.5	34.2	40.2	46.8	47.7	51.4	58.1	66.1	70.1	63.3	60.3	57.1	54.2
Greece	**174**	40.3	40.1	41.9	53.7	71.4	74.1	71.3	77.6	81.2	87.0	108.7	103.0	102.6	93.4	84.2
Iceland	**176**	18.1	21.8	22.7	31.9	38.5	35.2	39.8	46.6	50.8	56.4	60.9	60.9	56.6	53.2	50.1
Norway	**142**	28.6	30.1	31.9	40.0	54.6	62.9	61.8	67.5	72.5	88.0	117.5	117.3	111.5	102.0	100.2
Sweden	**144**	27.0	28.6	31.9	38.4	48.3	59.9	60.5	62.1	64.9	77.1	88.8	81.0	73.1	66.8	66.3
Switzerland	**146**	....	....	....	....	....	....	....	....	....	....	....	....	....	....	....
United Kingdom	**112**	22.4	24.1	26.1	28.7	34.8	40.5	39.4	45.3	54.6	66.7	83.5	78.6	72.9	68.5	64.8
Developing Countries	**200**	**17.0**	**18.0**	**19.4**	**25.5**	**49.8**	**50.7**	**53.5**	**60.3**	**61.6**	**82.7**	**110.8**	**117.0**	**110.4**	**101.6**	**101.7**
Africa	**605**	**17.4**	**17.6**	**18.4**	**24.8**	**40.7**	**41.6**	**43.0**	**49.0**	**49.6**	**62.5**	**84.5**	**91.2**	**74.9**	**71.3**	**70.5**
Burkina Faso	**748**	51.8	54.5	56.4	70.2	95.6	108.3	125.0	136.4	141.4	153.6	168.6	144.6	137.7	135.2	121.3
Côte d'Ivoire (1985=100)	**662**	....	33.7	34.8	50.6	60.2	61.1	73.0	112.4	105.9	120.6	134.3	94.3	82.5	81.1	92.8
Ethiopia (1990=100)	**644**	45.6	40.7	46.3	58.6	63.2	56.6	100.4	101.8	101.2	110.0	101.2	....	....	107.3	110.4
Kenya	**664**	33.6	32.2	33.6	39.3	51.0	57.1	67.7	97.3	88.0	97.1	117.6	105.8	96.3	94.8	105.1
Liberia (1985=100)	**668**	38.5	42.8	42.8	47.5	62.5	81.8	84.2	98.1	88.3	103.9	121.1	100.6	109.1	101.9	100.5
Malawi (1985=100)	**676**	55.4	60.3	59.7	65.2	80.6	92.0	97.3	129.7	124.9	116.2	120.9	153.5	142.8	131.0	134.7
Mauritius	**684**	14.7	16.2	19.7	22.6	53.5	66.7	49.3	48.9	51.4	56.7	64.2	59.7	54.3	54.0	51.0
Morocco	**686**	32.0	33.0	36.3	43.8	85.0	98.7	70.9	65.4	75.2	94.8	117.2	106.9	95.8	86.4	86.4
Rwanda	**714**	38.4	31.0	33.7	43.8	47.5	42.5	80.2	134.8	98.7	90.4	75.5	95.5	Ɪ 101.3	123.3	130.4
Senegal (1985=100)	**722**	31.6	35.1	37.6	50.3	88.6	84.2	73.7	86.1	101.2	114.9	113.2	120.7	96.6	92.8	103.1
South Africa	**199**	29.8	28.9	29.0	38.5	49.5	51.5	51.0	55.1	59.4	69.8	86.7	85.1	74.6	81.4	69.7
Tunisia (1990=100)	**744**	14.9	16.3	18.4	26.6	53.7	58.8	48.8	50.5	56.1	79.0	105.1	108.0	98.9	89.2	85.1
Asia	**505**	**25.1**	**25.5**	**27.1**	**35.9**	**53.0**	**50.8**	**52.0**	**58.3**	**61.7**	**74.5**	**87.4**	**87.4**	**83.1**	**79.2**	**82.1**
Bangladesh (1990=100)	**513**	....	....	....	....	....	....	....	....	95.8	112.8	131.4	99.2	88.2	89.9	117.3
Fiji (1985=100)	**819**	36.5	36.3	47.3	59.0	96.0	127.4	101.4	107.7	126.0	126.4	173.7	146.3	131.3	127.3	118.3
India	**534**	36.8	37.9	40.6	44.1	51.3	62.4	62.8	68.2	81.8	82.5	89.5	84.3	87.9	87.6	89.0
Indonesia	**536**	Ɪ 15.6	15.4	18.6	27.0	59.0	62.4	65.6	73.2	74.2	104.3	152.4	152.6	148.9	132.1	130.6
Korea	**542**	30.8	30.4	30.8	38.9	49.3	45.7	51.1	55.9	61.9	74.0	77.3	79.7	77.0	Ɪ 74.1	76.7
Malaysia	**548**	24.2	24.1	22.9	34.4	62.7	58.7	56.3	69.0	71.6	94.0	111.9	107.8	97.9	93.7	103.9
Pakistan	**564**	27.1	25.8	26.7	40.5	52.9	46.7	50.9	60.9	69.5	80.5	85.9	89.1	81.7	79.2	82.4
Papua New Guinea	**853**	....	....	....	38.2	59.2	39.9	47.2	62.8	62.0	83.5	92.1	71.7	64.6	66.5	68.4
Philippines (1990=100)	**566**	53.2	50.6	47.9	69.9	116.1	92.3	80.8	82.0	92.0	113.1	117.8	115.2	95.7	Ɪ 100.5	110.9
Singapore	**576**	....	....	....	....	....	....	....	....	....	82.0	102.7	107.9	103.3	99.7	94.9
Solomon Islands (1990=100)	**813**	60.9	67.0	58.0	83.7	157.3	93.5	136.6	181.2	177.2	256.3	288.0	220.2	201.6	174.2	235.1
Sri Lanka	**524**	26.7	26.8	26.7	29.2	43.6	38.7	37.8	58.0	60.0	65.5	68.9	64.3	58.1	65.9	77.7
Thailand	**578**	26.3	25.4	26.4	41.8	62.6	55.2	53.7	54.8	59.4	70.7	83.3	80.5	71.0	72.1	69.5
Europe	**170**	**121.0**	**124.5**	**135.1**	**163.9**	**197.4**	**213.2**	**221.8**	**253.9**	**273.0**	**303.4**	**336.7**	**343.0**	**338.1**	**330.3**	**297.1**
Cyprus (1985=100)	**423**	58.4	57.8	64.7	81.4	89.5	104.5	99.8	101.0	110.5	124.8	136.1	134.1	116.6	110.3	105.9
Czechoslovakia (1990=100)	**934**	....	....	....	40.5	46.4	50.9	50.7	74.4	79.1	88.0	97.0	112.1	109.8	107.7	91.6
Hungary (1990=100)	**944**	50.1	50.4	55.6	67.2	77.5	84.8	85.6	89.9	96.5	107.1	115.6	113.7	107.6	97.3	90.4
Latvia	**941**	....	....	....	....	....	....	....	....	....	....	....	....	....	....	....
Malta (1985=100)	**181**	46.1	46.3	55.0	62.8	76.3	81.3	82.0	85.6	102.0	118.5	128.3	122.9	118.8	106.3	101.4
Poland	**964**	....	....	....	....	....	91.3	99.0	101.1	109.6	118.1	124.3	115.4	112.3	104.3	96.9
Turkey	**186**	31.6	34.0	37.2	Ɪ 46.3	63.0	59.5	61.8	67.7	71.8	84.5	100.0	88.6	82.9	73.2	74.4
Middle East	**405**	**7.0**	**8.6**	**9.4**	**12.8**	**42.9**	**44.6**	**47.6**	**51.9**	**52.8**	**97.3**	**158.6**	**178.9**	**174.5**	**152.3**	**148.8**
Iran, I.R. of (1985=100)	**429**	5.4	6.7	7.4	9.9	36.3	38.9	41.4	45.6	45.6	68.9	121.9	130.0	109.2	101.2	99.3
Iraq (1985=100)	**433**	5.2	6.5	7.3	9.8	35.6	38.1	40.7	44.7	44.6	65.9	107.2	125.5	118.4	104.4	100.7
Israel	**436**	21.5	22.3	Ɪ 24.3	30.3	35.4	37.0	Ɪ 37.6	44.5	Ɪ 58.8	Ɪ 67.6	Ɪ 76.1	Ɪ 73.5	69.5	Ɪ 67.8	Ɪ 66.6
Jordan	**439**	25.4	23.6	28.4	31.2	64.7	73.9	66.2	66.7	69.2	70.9	85.0	87.9	90.0	79.9	82.2
Kuwait (1985=100)	**443**	5.1	6.6	7.0	9.7	38.4	38.8	41.2	45.3	44.8	67.7	109.2	128.4	118.2	101.8	99.9
Libya (1985=100)	**672**	7.8	9.6	10.2	14.5	43.3	38.8	41.0	46.0	45.5	70.0	119.5	132.8	117.8	102.5	100.0
Oman	**449**	9.9	12.1	13.6	18.6	65.2	68.6	71.0	78.5	79.3	121.8	196.5	223.2	210.5	185.0	174.5
Qatar (1985=100)	**453**	6.0	6.7	7.4	10.1	36.4	38.4	40.3	44.9	44.9	67.2	108.6	127.1	118.7	102.6	100.9
Saudi Arabia	**456**	....	....	....	9.8	34.9	37.5	40.2	43.0	44.1	104.0	173.4	195.6	199.8	173.4	169.1
Syrian Arab Rep.	**463**	48.9	58.6	68.4	85.5	164.5	141.3	173.0	183.1	196.4	256.4	332.9	369.6	323.0	303.0	309.6
United Arab Emirates (1985=100)	**466**	5.8	6.9	7.8	10.9	38.7	39.4	42.2	45.6	46.9	70.1	111.7	128.9	123.1	107.6	104.6
Western Hemisphere	**205**	**35.9**	**35.5**	**39.3**	**49.1**	**74.1**	**72.4**	**80.9**	**101.0**	**92.6**	**100.8**	**119.7**	**110.4**	**101.2**	**105.8**	**105.0**
Argentina	**213**	....	....	....	....	....	....	....	....	....	....	....	....	....	....	....
Bolivia	**218**	21.1	17.1	17.8	49.5	81.8	82.9	88.9	102.0	110.8	144.4	206.0	196.3	186.3	196.7	193.8
Brazil	**223**	33.0	31.9	36.0	49.5	62.4	62.4	72.0	87.8	80.8	88.7	94.0	88.5	83.1	78.6	80.2
Colombia	**233**	Ɪ 37.0	35.1	39.4	49.6	66.5	65.7	96.2	141.4	118.1	116.5	129.9	116.2	115.3	115.6	123.5
Costa Rica (1990=100)	**238**	....	653.9	681.0	766.1	770.5	810.3	916.3	1,171.0	1,092.7	1,144.9	1,292.2	465.5	265.0	238.8	224.3
Dominican Republic	**243**	34.8	20.4	40.2	48.4	66.6	84.3	78.0	101.6	90.2	97.7	100.2	110.4	78.8	77.4	90.9
Ecuador	**248**	28.8	30.1	26.5	31.1	67.2	69.2	73.0	82.1	78.1	122.6	170.8	166.6	159.1	139.2	132.7
Guatemala (1990=100)	**258**	....	....	....	....	....	....	....	....	....	....	....	....	....	....	....
Guyana	**336**	1,374.6	1,468.2	1,658.4	53.0	94.0	117.6	109.9	126.8	114.2	125.1	163.2	5,194.9	4,870.2	4,458.5	136.9
Honduras	**268**	....	....	....	....	....	45.4	56.3	81.4	74.1	70.9	84.4	76.5	74.0	74.6	79.0
Panama (1990=100)	**283**	77.0	73.8	76.8	79.4	88.7	100.2	98.5	91.2	90.2	96.6	104.3	104.5	96.9	104.8	104.5
Paraguay (1985=100)	**288**	97.2	98.8	109.3	137.0	965.6	1,082.8	534.0	854.1	850.1	1,622.6	2,514.1	1,448.6	1,897.4	978.8	1,056.8
Peru	**293**	28.9	27.5	28.0	41.9	111.0	Ɪ 61.7	67.3	74.5	75.3	128.8	174.0	150.7	131.8	130.3	121.2
Suriname (1985=100)	**366**	43.3	44.5	45.2	44.9	61.3	82.6	89.2	99.3	107.4	118.4	143.7	157.3	152.4	138.7	129.4
Trinidad and Tobago (1990=100)	**369**	11.9	13.5	14.1	18.1	46.2	50.5	52.0	57.5	57.5	76.0	121.4	133.9	128.2	127.3	126.5
Memorandum Items																
Oil Exporting Countries	**999**	**7.4**	**9.1**	**10.0**	**13.9**	**46.3**	**48.5**	**51.6**	**56.5**	**56.8**	**101.6**	**167.0**	**186.5**	**180.8**	**157.2**	**153.7**
Non-Oil Developing Countries	**201**	**32.9**	**32.9**	**35.1**	**44.8**	**61.5**	**60.8**	**63.6**	**73.8**	**76.1**	**87.5**	**100.4**	**100.4**	**92.1**	**91.5**	**92.2**

1985	1986	1987	1988	1989	1990	1991	1992	1993	1994	1995	1996	1997	1998	1999		74 d
1995=100																
70.1	**76.2**	**84.3**	**89.2**	**90.7**	**97.7**	**95.7**	**98.0**	**89.6**	**91.3**	**100.0**	**98.1**	**91.9**	**87.2**	**86.5**	**World**	**001**
64.3	**73.4**	**82.0**	**87.2**	**87.4**	**95.5**	**94.6**	**97.1**	**87.6**	**90.6**	**100.0**	**97.9**	**91.1**	**87.8**	**88.8**	**Industrial Countries**	**110**
80.7	81.5	82.9	88.8	91.1	91.9	92.7	92.8	93.2	95.2	100.0	100.6	99.0	95.9	94.7	United States	111
82.7	79.6	84.8	91.9	97.8	98.5	96.8	93.9	92.0	93.0	100.0	101.3	99.3	93.4	95.2	Canada	156
76.3	73.9	80.5	100.4	107.2	106.8	97.4	93.7	87.9	91.9	100.0	101.2	97.7	86.7	82.7	Australia	193
49.2	59.0	64.6	70.2	69.7	69.1	74.0	78.7	86.0	92.6	100.0	92.5	86.5	80.5	85.2	Japan	158
61.4	63.3	75.7	89.2	92.1	90.7	84.0	84.6	87.3	91.9	100.0	101.1	94.7	80.3	80.6	New Zealand	196
															Euro Area	
....	....	....	....	....	....	....	....	82.9	86.6	100.0	97.8	89.1	87.9	83.7	Belgium	124
55.5	68.2	77.3	80.7	81.2	92.8	89.1	93.3	85.8	88.1	100.0	97.1	87.7	....	....	Belgium-Luxembourg	126
52.2	62.5	73.7	81.4	85.2	94.6	89.4	86.0	70.7	78.7	100.0	95.1	85.5	....	....	Finland	172
53.8	65.9	75.4	79.0	78.1	90.0	86.6	89.6	81.1	I 88.5	100.0	97.4	86.5	86.3	....	France	132
52.0	68.2	80.2	82.7	80.8	93.0	90.0	94.9	85.6	86.4	100.0	93.2	81.1	79.5	....	Germany	134
65.1	76.8	84.8	93.1	92.4	97.6	94.3	97.0	90.5	91.6	100.0	99.2	95.1	91.7	....	Ireland	178
59.3	72.4	84.1	88.1	88.9	103.9	103.3	104.8	91.4	92.4	100.0	110.1	99.4	97.8	....	Italy	136
62.5	72.1	79.0	80.9	81.3	93.8	89.9	92.3	84.6	86.7	100.0	95.5	....	....	....	Netherlands	138
62.0	73.0	84.0	90.7	87.9	100.0	98.9	103.6	....	....	....	....	....	....	....	Portugal (1990=100)	182
58.9	68.8	80.1	89.4	92.0	104.8	101.9	104.4	88.1	87.4	100.0	99.5	88.8	87.1	82.7	Spain	184
54.8	69.7	80.9	81.9	80.2	93.2	90.3	93.4	85.1	87.7	100.0	98.2	87.8	85.8	83.1	Denmark	128
78.7	83.5	92.2	106.6	107.1	119.5	113.1	105.6	90.2	94.8	100.0	101.3	85.4	....	....	Greece	174
50.9	63.2	76.7	78.3	72.8	87.3	99.8	99.3	87.4	88.2	100.0	95.8	90.9	....	....	Iceland	176
98.9	86.3	91.5	94.8	100.3	115.5	106.8	102.4	89.7	87.1	100.0	106.1	98.7	81.9	88.4	Norway	142
66.0	79.2	91.4	97.7	99.7	110.6	109.2	110.0	92.3	88.8	100.0	93.6	87.2	82.7	78.7	Sweden	144
....	....	....	I 75.1	71.5	85.0	84.7	86.6	82.4	88.3	100.0	96.6	85.3	84.6	82.7	Switzerland	146
65.9	67.8	78.6	85.9	82.5	92.8	93.2	94.4	90.6	94.2	100.0	99.9	99.2	95.4	93.2	United Kingdom	112
95.6	**86.6**	**92.8**	**95.7**	**102.4**	**105.0**	**98.5**	**99.4**	**96.2**	**93.7**	**100.0**	**98.9**	**94.6**	**85.0**	**83.3**	**Developing Countries**	**200**
63.7	**72.7**	**82.0**	**85.6**	**81.6**	**91.4**	**90.2**	**91.2**	**83.8**	**83.8**	**100.0**	**95.6**	**92.9**	**87.1**	....	**Africa**	**605**
138.6	126.6	151.1	147.8	128.3	165.5	156.1	127.0	114.1	76.3	100.0	95.4	....	....	....	Burkina Faso	748
100.0	108.9	103.2	....	....	....	....	....	....	....	....	....	....	....	....	Côte d'Ivoire (1985=100)	662
110.1	146.0	106.9	111.5	107.9	100.0	105.4	....	....	....	....	....	....	....	....	Ethiopia (1990=100)	644
90.9	98.5	80.5	85.9	79.8	77.6	82.6	79.7	79.4	84.4	100.0	95.6	108.9	107.1	....	Kenya	664
100.0	98.2	93.6	....	....	....	....	....	....	....	....	....	....	....	....	Liberia (1985=100)	668
100.0	103.3	114.1	118.2	128.5	....	....	....	....	....	....	....	....	....	....	Malawi (1985=100)	676
52.0	63.1	73.8	75.2	79.0	84.9	85.8	92.3	88.7	91.2	100.0	107.7	94.8	94.2	....	Mauritius	684
84.9	92.3	95.9	118.5	93.4	99.8	94.1	91.9	84.4	83.6	100.0	103.5	95.5	92.3	....	Morocco	686
117.8	144.4	76.5	....	80.5	73.1	66.2	50.0	56.8	....	100.0	79.8	122.1	78.3	....	Rwanda	714
100.0	90.9	99.6	....	....	....	....	....	....	....	....	....	....	....	....	Senegal (1985=100)	722
58.3	65.6	76.5	78.8	82.0	87.3	863.1	88.0	84.3	87.3	100.0	93.1	91.3	84.1	....	South Africa	199
79.6	75.0	81.9	84.6	87.0	100.0	92.6	94.6	84.2	87.5	....	....	....	....	....	Tunisia (1990=100)	744
76.8	**71.6**	**77.3**	**84.1**	**87.7**	**89.3**	**89.9**	**91.0**	**90.5**	**92.9**	**100.0**	**98.1**	**94.5**	**84.0**	**81.1**	**Asia**	**505**
I 130.6	93.8	92.7	105.5	101.9	100.0	98.9	....	....	....	....	....	....	....	....	Bangladesh (1990=100)	513
100.0	136.7	170.2	141.5	136.5	....	....	....	....	....	....	....	....	....	....	Fiji (1985=100)	819
91.5	90.8	92.5	111.7	114.4	112.2	109.0	109.1	104.1	105.7	100.0	95.5	108.7	....	....	India	534
112.4	74.8	73.4	69.9	74.2	I 90.3	91.0	90.3	88.3	87.6	100.0	105.8	100.5	78.4	....	Indonesia	536
73.8	75.3	82.9	I 94.2	95.9	94.1	94.7	I 93.2	93.6	95.2	100.0	86.6	72.8	63.1	61.5	Korea	542
87.7	55.9	67.5	71.7	70.6	71.9	72.5	76.9	79.7	85.4	100.0	96.1	91.3	....	....	Malaysia	548
72.5	84.2	88.5	86.8	82.2	85.2	80.5	78.4	76.3	82.2	100.0	97.1	97.7	73.2	49.3	Pakistan	564
63.3	64.3	75.1	91.3	77.3	72.6	72.2	72.5	80.0	90.2	100.0	95.7	97.2	77.3	....	Papua New Guinea	853
97.4	86.5	95.1	104.9	102.9	100.0	101.9	....	....	....	....	....	....	....	....	Philippines (1990=100)	566
90.2	78.3	83.7	86.4	I 88.8	96.0	95.3	94.4	93.0	94.4	100.0	99.6	93.2	I 81.1	80.2	Singapore	576
191.4	114.5	107.1	114.0	102.0	100.0	98.6	88.8	....	....	....	....	....	....	....	Solomon Islands (1990=100)	813
64.6	55.8	61.6	66.6	69.3	75.7	74.7	88.5	88.1	90.3	100.0	103.5	105.9	111.9	101.0	Sri Lanka	524
62.1	65.9	72.2	79.5	80.5	82.6	85.6	87.4	88.5	91.5	100.0	108.9	104.9	91.2	87.6	Thailand	578
280.7	**306.7**	**319.3**	**233.4**	**299.2**	**242.8**	**224.8**	**209.1**	**186.5**	**111.3**	**100.0**	**84.0**	**68.5**	**61.8**	....	**Europe**	**170**
100.0	110.1	121.4	....	....	....	....	....	....	....	....	....	....	....	....	Cyprus (1985=100)	423
90.3	103.5	113.4	110.9	111.9	100.0	57.9	....	....	....	....	....	....	....	....	Czechoslovakia (1990=100)	934
89.2	98.7	99.3	98.6	97.2	100.0	110.5	114.3	109.9	113.5	....	....	....	....	....	Hungary (1990=100)	944
....	....	....	....	....	....	....	....	58.4	81.2	100.0	101.8	98.0	96.4	93.6	Latvia	941
100.0	122.3	145.8	168.5	167.4	....	....	....	....	....	....	....	....	....	....	Malta (1985=100)	181
93.5	93.6	90.3	94.6	91.1	85.2	90.8	89.9	85.1	87.9	100.0	97.3	90.2	90.4	85.7	Poland	964
....	....	....	....	1,836.0	1,647.1	1,020.6	627.7	381.8	137.4	100.0	53.8	27.5	15.4	....	Turkey	186
147.2	**86.9**	**97.3**	**83.0**	**93.7**	**113.9**	**99.7**	**101.1**	**91.3**	**91.6**	**100.0**	**113.1**	**107.2**	**77.4**	**101.8**	**Middle East**	**405**
100.0	48.9	64.4	55.1	58.4	....	....	....	....	....	....	....	....	....	....	Iran, I.R. of (1985=100)	429
100.0	54.0	59.8	49.2	....	....	....	....	....	....	....	....	....	....	....	Iraq (1985=100)	433
65.9	68.1	72.5	82.7	88.0	I 95.3	95.7	96.4	96.8	95.4	100.0	99.9	99.1	96.1	97.3	Israel	436
77.7	75.4	72.4	76.2	77.5	79.9	86.7	83.6	82.9	86.1	100.0	105.1	102.0	96.3	92.9	Jordan	439
100.0	73.5	60.8	46.7	....	....	....	....	....	....	....	....	....	....	....	Kuwait (1985=100)	443
100.0	....	....	....	....	....	....	....	....	....	....	....	....	....	....	Libya (1985=100)	672
164.7	82.0	105.3	82.5	....	....	....	109.8	95.2	92.8	100.0	118.5	113.6	72.7	105.8	Oman	449
100.0	....	....	....	....	....	....	....	....	....	....	....	....	....	....	Qatar (1985=100)	453
165.7	118.3	103.9	83.9	96.3	121.9	98.9	103.6	89.9	90.4	100.0	118.1	111.8	72.1	104.6	Saudi Arabia	456
303.0	223.1	206.5	68.9	85.6	111.1	90.0	75.6	74.4	80.0	100.0	105.6	83.3	....	....	Syrian Arab Rep.	463
100.0	49.3	62.7	48.7	....	....	....	....	....	....	....	....	....	....	....	United Arab Emirates (1985=100)	466
91.9	**91.1**	**89.6**	**116.9**	**126.5**	**126.9**	**87.4**	**90.7**	**87.1**	**93.3**	**100.0**	**105.5**	....	....	....	**Western Hemisphere**	**205**
....	....	....	....	....	89.2	88.5	91.7	91.9	94.6	100.0	106.5	102.5	92.9	....	Argentina	213
178.5	143.7	135.3	135.6	157.9	143.0	127.7	108.3	89.1	94.8	100.0	98.6	75.2	67.3	68.1	Bolivia	218
I 75.6	72.1	79.5	85.2	83.8	80.8	81.5	92.4	91.4	96.3	100.0	100.8	....	....	....	Brazil	223
115.4	130.7	100.4	104.9	85.6	89.0	82.7	69.5	69.2	92.2	100.0	93.4	103.0	91.8	85.5	Colombia	233
197.4	200.4	151.0	128.7	116.9	100.0	77.9	71.1	68.7	....	....	....	....	....	....	Costa Rica (1990=100)	238
82.5	82.4	70.6	107.3	116.2	101.3	91.1	89.9	68.8	88.1	100.0	100.7	104.9	82.1	....	Dominican Republic	243
140.6	88.9	99.6	86.5	101.3	116.2	108.8	108.0	88.9	98.9	100.0	115.0	112.3	84.0	101.5	Ecuador	248
....	....	168.6	165.0	154.2	100.0	70.6	67.0	67.6	68.7	....	....	....	....	....	Guatemala (1990=100)	258
121.5	117.0	122.7	127.4	120.8	128.3	161.0	134.7	103.4	101.7	100.0	168.4	97.5	92.0	....	Guyana	336
81.2	97.2	88.2	93.7	94.0	94.4	92.4	72.4	74.2	77.4	100.0	92.9	96.8	94.4	....	Honduras	268
102.6	94.0	103.5	113.5	158.6	100.0	100.9	....	....	....	....	....	....	....	....	Panama (1990=100)	283
100.0	67.2	102.2	137.2	153.0	....	....	....	....	....	....	....	....	....	....	Paraguay (1985=100)	288
107.5	74.6	95.0	93.6	104.2	103.8	84.1	84.9	74.3	84.4	100.0	106.3	102.8	79.9	85.0	Peru	293
100.0	97.9	101.6	137.0	....	....	....	....	....	....	....	....	....	....	....	Suriname (1985=100)	366
118.3	78.4	82.2	73.1	83.6	100.0	....	....	....	....	....	....	....	....	....	Trinidad and Tobago (1990=100)	369
															Memorandum Items	
148.0	**84.1**	**91.2**	**78.0**	**86.8**	**107.0**	**96.8**	**98.5**	**89.5**	**89.4**	**100.0**	**112.6**	**107.0**	**75.0**	....	**Oil Exporting Countries**	**999**
86.0	**86.4**	**92.4**	**98.0**	**104.4**	**104.6**	**98.6**	**99.4**	**97.0**	**94.2**	**100.0**	**97.4**	**93.3**	**86.4**	**82.0**	**Non-Oil Developing Countries**	**201**

(See notes in the back of the book.)

Import Unit Values/Import Prices

Indices of Unit Values (Prices) In Terms of US Dollars:

		1970	1971	1972	1973	1974	1975	1976	1977	1978	1979	1980	1981	1982	1983	1984
World	001	24.6	25.9	27.9	34.2	48.0	52.4	53.1	57.7	62.6	74.0	90.5	90.6	87.0	83.9	82.5
Industrial Countries	110	23.7	25.0	26.9	32.9	46.2	50.5	51.2	55.7	60.3	71.3	87.2	86.7	83.5	79.9	78.5
United States	111	21.1	22.2	23.8	28.3	41.9	45.7	47.1	51.0	55.1	65.7	82.3	86.9	85.5	81.9	83.4
Canada	156	28.7	30.3	31.6	33.6	42.5	47.0	49.7	52.8	55.7	63.7	77.0	85.7	86.8	86.4	87.0
Australia	193	18.6	20.0	21.9	26.1	36.8	42.3	43.3	47.5	52.2	61.7	79.6	81.8	77.1	74.3	74.2
Japan	158	22.0	23.0	24.4	30.1	48.9	52.0	53.3	57.1	59.8	74.7	100.3	103.7	95.8	91.2	88.7
New Zealand	196	23.8	25.6	28.0	33.4	43.5	49.6	50.6	54.3	60.2	66.9	82.6	83.7	80.8	77.9	75.2
Euro Area																
Belgium	124	....	....	....	....	....	....	....	....	....	....	....	....	....	....	....
Belgium-Luxembourg	126	23.5	24.3	26.8	32.3	41.3	46.2	46.9	51.3	58.2	68.3	78.8	70.9	65.9	63.1	60.4
Finland	172	17.9	19.4	20.7	25.2	36.6	40.9	41.6	46.2	50.0	61.4	74.6	72.2	67.7	62.7	60.6
France	132	24.7	25.8	28.5	34.5	47.0	51.6	50.7	55.6	61.0	71.3	85.2	78.6	73.4	68.6	65.6
Germany	134	20.1	21.2	23.5	30.1	39.9	43.2	43.1	48.4	54.4	66.3	78.2	71.6	67.1	63.5	60.4
Ireland	178	21.2	22.8	24.5	27.1	37.8	43.2	41.7	47.5	53.6	65.4	77.9	72.8	69.4	63.4	61.2
Italy	136	20.4	21.7	23.7	30.9	47.4	49.9	49.4	54.0	58.9	71.8	89.7	87.5	82.7	77.2	74.3
Netherlands	138	21.6	23.1	25.1	31.0	43.6	48.5	49.1	54.4	60.6	72.9	84.6	77.6	74.1	70.1	65.7
Portugal (1990=100)	182	34.0	35.0	37.7	47.6	60.2	66.7	67.2	73.6	76.8	83.8	96.0	90.1	82.0	76.8	78.5
Spain	184	27.8	29.5	31.8	40.1	57.6	62.1	58.9	61.5	66.8	78.3	99.8	104.3	98.2	92.1	91.9
Denmark	128	21.1	22.6	24.2	30.8	41.9	46.0	47.3	51.9	56.5	67.5	76.8	71.1	67.0	63.0	60.2
Greece	174	35.5	36.8	40.0	48.3	70.2	77.5	75.8	78.8	84.7	103.1	122.4	108.5	112.2	98.5	95.8
Iceland	176	19.3	20.7	21.8	26.3	35.3	38.4	38.8	44.8	45.5	55.6	62.1	61.0	56.3	55.3	53.7
Norway	142	27.7	29.4	31.8	38.7	50.6	57.1	58.3	64.6	69.0	78.8	90.8	83.6	77.8	72.1	65.7
Sweden	144	28.8	30.7	33.6	41.3	55.5	62.3	62.9	68.1	73.8	89.3	102.7	94.0	86.0	79.4	76.2
Switzerland	146	....	....	....	....	....	....	....	....	....	....	....	....	....	....	....
United Kingdom	112	21.6	23.0	24.5	30.6	42.2	45.6	45.3	50.6	57.2	67.4	80.8	75.5	70.8	67.0	63.8
Developing Countries	200	28.4	29.8	31.4	39.7	55.8	60.4	61.1	66.5	72.4	85.7	104.6	107.5	102.5	101.4	100.3
Africa	605															
Burkina Faso	748	24.8	27.2	32.5	39.3	45.7	59.4	60.5	64.7	68.9	78.8	83.8	78.3	78.7	74.4	67.4
Côte d'Ivoire (1985=100)	662	....	33.5	40.3	47.8	59.6	75.2	77.3	80.1	91.8	110.5	126.5	122.8	120.9	114.2	108.2
Kenya	664	17.3	18.8	21.1	25.5	37.5	46.2	47.1	51.4	58.1	69.6	91.9	96.4	91.8	96.4	91.1
Liberia (1985=100)	668	....	32.8	36.7	42.0	61.6	66.9	64.2	78.9	80.9	93.6	109.0	98.3	103.6	98.6	107.9
Malawi (1985=100)	676	31.6	33.7	36.4	41.5	54.6	64.6	69.9	78.6	84.5	99.4	121.9	126.7	116.5	116.7	115.0
Mauritius	684	19.7	22.0	23.8	30.4	47.3	50.7	51.2	56.4	64.2	75.2	90.2	82.9	84.4	76.8	73.2
Morocco	686	25.6	26.9	31.9	40.0	54.7	59.3	53.7	41.3	50.1	70.4	86.6	84.1	75.1	73.0	71.6
Senegal (1985=100)	722	31.7	37.2	42.1	54.3	71.9	85.5	80.7	85.4	91.8	109.4	143.3	124.9	116.7	110.1	105.3
South Africa	199	19.7	20.4	21.8	26.3	34.8	39.9	41.4	46.8	53.8	68.5	89.1	88.9	86.5	90.6	75.9
Tunisia	744	50.7	52.9	58.8	70.6	91.1	109.1	100.4	102.8	108.3	119.1	134.9	130.4	118.1	107.2	100.2
Asia	505	25.5	26.4	27.9	36.6	54.0	56.3	56.3	59.3	64.1	76.1	92.3	94.4	88.7	85.9	87.9
Bangladesh (1990=100)	513									92.0	92.0	101.9	97.9	91.2	98.3	99.2
India	534	40.6	39.9	40.1	40.6	55.9	93.8	102.1	101.5	99.2	113.7	133.9	138.7	130.0	124.4	102.4
Korea	542	27.6	27.5	28.0	37.2	57.9	59.6	58.3	59.6	63.0	77.0	92.6	97.6	90.4	I86.1	87.2
Malaysia (1985=100)	548	28.9	31.0	35.2	47.1	67.7	72.0	69.0	73.0	79.6	90.3	108.9	117.7	115.6	111.4	107.1
Pakistan	564	21.9	24.0	22.5	27.7	47.5	53.9	51.5	53.3	56.3	63.6	79.4	91.1	86.1	78.1	80.0
Philippines (1990=100)	566	27.3	27.9	29.2	37.7	61.9	64.2	63.5	70.5	71.9	84.6	104.9	116.5	99.6	I100.1	113.1
Singapore	576	....	....	....	....	47.9	48.4	50.6	53.9	60.0	70.8	84.0	86.5	81.7	80.6	79.2
Sri Lanka	524	18.1	19.3	20.3	25.2	42.5	47.0	35.2	40.9	43.1	65.7	78.5	78.2	75.3	69.5	67.4
Thailand	578	15.4	16.2	17.1	20.2	33.0	36.8	38.8	41.7	45.1	51.9	64.3	71.3	69.4	65.5	64.2
Europe	170	128.1	133.1	142.3	179.9	238.3	254.3	260.0	305.5	329.4	376.2	433.1	448.6	443.0	443.8	413.1
Cyprus (1985=100)	423	49.9	53.1	57.9	69.2	89.1	97.2	88.9	94.1	103.3	121.5	140.5	131.4	117.7	107.9	103.3
Czechoslovakia (1990=100)	934	....	....	....	34.0	38.8	44.5	45.8	69.7	75.0	84.9	93.4	111.9	111.5	113.8	105.1
Hungary (1990=100)	944	37.9	38.8	42.9	52.5	67.1	77.3	76.3	83.0	89.6	101.3	108.9	108.0	104.7	97.1	92.2
Malta (1985=100)	181	33.5	35.3	41.0	52.9	68.9	73.8	72.5	79.4	92.4	112.1	125.7	124.0	117.6	112.1	103.2
Poland	964	....	....	....	....	....	102.1	107.1	112.6	121.9	135.1	142.4	131.3	126.7	123.7	114.3
Turkey	186	19.8	21.1	21.7	I26.4	39.0	43.5	44.0	48.5	55.3	65.3	100.0	96.9	95.0	85.4	77.4
Middle East	405	22.7	24.0	25.8	31.6	41.9	45.7	46.6	49.1	58.1	70.6	88.2	94.5	87.6	88.2	87.8
Israel	436	21.9	22.4	I23.9	30.8	41.8	43.7	I42.7	46.5	I57.1	I70.9	I87.1	I84.3	77.1	I73.6	I73.6
Jordan	439	31.7	36.9	40.2	45.8	59.3	82.0	76.9	79.1	82.8	90.2	112.9	123.9	118.0	104.7	109.4
Syrian Arab Rep.	463	29.0	33.6	40.3	49.6	71.4	80.0	96.8	87.5	93.5	116.2	150.9	196.1	184.1	212.7	199.1
Western Hemisphere	205	22.0	23.6	23.6	30.7	46.1	47.9	49.1	52.7	54.6	64.2	86.3	91.8	88.6	81.7	80.7
Argentina	213	....	....	....	....	....	....	....	....	....	....	....	....	....	....	....
Brazil	223	15.5	16.2	15.9	21.6	31.6	34.4	35.3	36.7	39.2	47.0	60.1	66.8	64.6	61.2	58.1
Chile	228	25.2	28.4	26.0	51.4	90.0	59.3	67.3	81.5	74.8	90.1	118.5	123.7	105.1	110.4	113.4
Colombia	233	38.7	39.3	41.9	49.6	63.7	68.0	71.0	75.2	84.2	92.9	101.9	108.1	110.5	108.1	111.5
Costa Rica (1990=100)	238	579.1	I576.7	611.9	676.3	777.0	786.5	747.7	787.4	833.6	956.0	1,084.7	456.4	258.1	225.5	205.0
Guatemala (1990=100)	258	....	....	....	....	....	....	....	....	....	....	....	....	....	....	....
Trinidad and Tobago (1990=100)	369	10.5	11.7	13.1	15.0	32.6	35.4	37.2	38.9	40.6	46.0	69.0	78.0	88.3	88.9	89.0
Memorandum Items																
Oil Exporting Countries	999	....	....	....	....	....	....	....	....	....	....	....	....	....	....	....
Non-Oil Developing Countries	201	28.2	29.5	31.2	39.6	56.1	60.2	61.0	66.5	72.5	85.8	104.7	107.6	102.6	101.6	101.3

1995=100

1985	1986	1987	1988	1989	1990	1991	1992	1993	1994	1995	1996	1997	1998	1999		
80.9	82.2	89.3	88.7	90.8	98.0	96.3	96.8	91.0	91.6	100.0	98.6	93.2	87.0	87.6	World	001
77.3	79.3	87.0	86.7	87.6	96.0	94.4	95.4	88.8	91.0	100.0	98.9	92.6	87.5	87.5	Industrial Countries	110
81.3	78.6	84.3	88.4	91.0	94.0	94.0	94.7	94.1	95.7	100.0	101.0	98.5	92.6	93.4	United States	111
85.1	83.4	86.3	91.4	95.2	98.4	98.9	97.7	96.5	96.9	100.0	100.3	99.4	97.2	97.4	Canada	156
70.1	73.3	81.4	88.8	88.9	91.3	92.0	90.7	90.7	95.2	100.0	99.9	94.6	86.8	87.2	Australia	193
85.2	76.3	82.0	86.8	90.2	95.0	92.5	91.4	92.1	92.3	100.0	100.7	95.1	83.0	83.8	Japan	158
72.5	74.8	80.6	88.9	87.5	87.9	85.9	85.3	85.3	90.4	100.0	101.9	97.1	81.6	82.6	New Zealand	196
															Euro Area	
								81.3	85.6	100.0	98.5	90.5	87.4	85.0	Belgium	124
59.7	68.2	77.0	80.5	80.5	93.3	90.0	92.5	84.0	86.3	100.0	97.0	88.4	....	....	Belgium-Luxembourg	126
60.7	66.4	75.3	81.1	81.8	93.1	90.1	90.0	79.4	84.1	100.0	96.9	88.4	....	....	Finland	172
64.7	70.3	80.0	82.9	83.3	95.9	91.6	93.7	83.3	I88.5	100.0	98.1	87.3	86.4	....	France	132
59.8	68.2	77.4	79.8	80.1	90.9	90.0	92.7	82.8	86.0	100.0	93.4	83.2	80.1	....	Germany	134
61.2	69.2	76.4	83.4	82.6	91.5	91.1	94.4	86.1	89.5	100.0	98.6	94.0	90.3	....	Ireland	178
73.4	77.4	87.7	90.9	92.9	105.6	101.2	101.2	88.6	89.9	100.0	105.6	95.8	89.6	....	Italy	136
64.1	71.7	81.5	83.1	85.1	96.1	93.3	97.1	86.3	88.1	100.0	96.1	....	....	....	Netherlands	138
72.2	75.2	84.8	88.8	87.5	100.0	98.9	100.6	....	....	....	....	....	....	....	Portugal (1990=100)	182
88.0	85.1	93.7	97.2	97.7	109.5	104.5	104.8	88.6	89.2	100.0	98.8	88.5	84.8	81.1	Spain	184
60.1	71.6	80.5	83.1	82.0	93.6	89.6	91.8	83.5	86.1	100.0	97.3	88.1	86.6	82.8	Denmark	128
90.4	100.6	101.6	119.2	116.5	130.6	124.1	119.6	100.7	94.0	100.0	101.4	95.3	....	....	Greece	174
54.0	61.8	70.9	75.7	74.8	87.9	92.0	93.7	87.0	88.9	100.0	99.9	94.3	....	....	Iceland	176
66.4	77.0	86.9	92.6	92.6	102.9	97.7	100.0	88.2	88.9	100.0	97.8	88.3	84.0	79.5	Norway	142
75.7	83.0	96.7	103.5	103.1	114.4	111.3	112.1	97.1	90.9	100.0	95.6	89.2	83.6	82.5	Sweden	144
....	....	....	I80.6	78.2	91.4	88.6	92.4	86.0	88.5	100.0	95.6	85.8	82.4	78.0	Switzerland	146
64.5	70.2	80.3	86.7	82.9	92.2	92.6	93.0	86.9	91.5	100.0	98.9	97.3	92.5	89.1	United Kingdom	112
96.6	94.3	97.0	95.2	103.3	104.0	102.3	99.8	98.4	93.7	100.0	97.8	95.2	85.1	88.0	Developing Countries	200
....	....	....	84.0	82.9	92.8	91.0	91.5	87.7	91.2	100.0	93.4	92.0	84.1	....	Africa	605
70.5	87.7	90.1	90.9	92.0	115.1	103.0	105.5	100.2	84.1	100.0	101.1	....	....	....	Burkina Faso	748
100.0	113.0	129.5	....	....	....	....	....	....	....	....	....	....	....	....	Côte d'Ivoire (1985=100)	662
94.6	90.8	90.8	92.6	96.5	104.1	96.6	95.5	84.0	79.6	100.0	98.3	102.1	102.0	....	Kenya	664
100.0	105.0	111.5	....	....	....	....	....	....	....	....	....	....	....	....	Liberia (1985=100)	668
100.0	118.7	135.7	145.3	154.8	....	....	....	....	....	....	....	....	....	....	Malawi (1985=100)	676
71.9	66.8	72.3	75.6	79.3	86.9	86.4	88.7	86.8	91.4	100.0	103.6	90.4	79.8	....	Mauritius	684
69.6	68.8	73.3	76.4	82.0	92.8	84.8	82.1	82.8	94.6	100.0	103.7	91.7	79.4	....	Morocco	686
100.0	93.9	102.9	....	....	....	....	....	....	....	....	....	....	....	....	Senegal (1985=100)	722
64.3	73.0	85.6	84.0	82.3	89.3	91.9	93.7	88.3	89.8	100.0	89.0	91.0	83.7	....	South Africa	199
100.0	109.3	109.6	....	....	....	....	....	....	....	....	....	....	....	....	Tunisia	744
83.9	78.8	80.4	87.5	90.4	92.8	92.6	91.5	90.9	93.0	100.0	99.5	94.8	84.4	89.2	Asia	505
I97.9	98.8	106.7	97.0	97.0	100.0	114.5	....	....	....	....	....	....	....	....	Bangladesh (1990=100)	513
121.0	117.2	99.1	123.5	129.8	141.5	125.5	118.7	99.1	95.7	100.0	104.3	102.8	....	....	India	534
83.5	78.4	84.2	I93.1	95.0	96.4	96.4	I94.9	91.3	91.8	100.0	98.8	93.7	75.0	74.5	Korea	542
100.0	84.8	87.9	....	....	....	....	....	....	....	....	....	....	....	....	Malaysia (1985=100)	548
73.6	67.1	77.8	83.7	86.2	93.7	91.7	89.2	85.1	91.6	100.0	96.9	98.3	64.2	42.0	Pakistan	564
106.4	87.6	88.0	87.3	92.8	100.0	95.7	....	....	....	....	....	....	....	....	Philippines (1990=100)	566
74.8	66.7	74.7	78.5	I80.9	86.3	87.7	89.8	88.7	92.9	100.0	99.3	92.9	I80.9	81.2	Singapore	576
68.4	61.3	65.8	75.5	79.8	91.3	91.8	90.7	86.7	89.7	100.0	102.4	99.6	....	....	Sri Lanka	524
61.2	58.6	64.9	72.8	76.7	81.0	84.8	85.7	86.0	88.6	100.0	111.1	106.4	97.9	93.0	Thailand	578
390.0	425.1	434.1	238.8	371.1	304.5	284.0	248.4	192.2	110.9	100.0	83.3	65.7	56.2	....	Europe	170
100.0	100.9	103.6	....	....	....	....	....	....	....	....	....	....	....	....	Cyprus (1985=100)	423
102.5	118.3	126.3	120.0	115.1	100.0	82.8	....	....	....	....	....	....	....	....	Czechoslovakia (1990=100)	934
91.8	105.4	105.0	101.8	97.7	100.0	123.4	128.3	120.6	121.8	....	....	....	....	....	Hungary (1990=100)	944
100.0	114.8	131.4	138.8	136.0	....	....	....	....	....	....	....	....	....	....	Malta (1985=100)	181
107.9	106.1	98.7	102.4	84.6	94.0	109.9	99.4	87.8	89.5	100.0	99.8	93.2	91.3	85.5	Poland	964
....	....	....	....	1,842.0	1,577.6	955.9	568.9	333.8	132.6	100.0	52.9	25.9	14.6	....	Turkey	186
83.7	88.4	92.4	85.3	88.4	94.1	90.9	91.0	88.9	91.8	100.0	101.1	96.2	91.0	88.6	Middle East	405
72.0	71.6	78.8	85.4	91.1	I98.1	93.4	93.5	90.3	92.2	100.0	99.3	94.8	89.5	87.1	Israel	436
103.8	88.1	94.6	90.5	85.5	99.6	97.4	92.1	91.8	88.5	100.0	107.8	105.4	104.5	102.3	Jordan	439
167.5	199.1	201.2	86.4	83.9	84.7	97.5	83.1	78.8	89.0	100.0	105.9	90.7	....	....	Syrian Arab Rep.	463
78.9	67.6	69.7	69.2	78.3	81.1	76.4	72.7	77.1	86.0	100.0	99.4	120.7	....	....	Western Hemisphere	205
....	....	....	....	....	101.7	97.8	95.7	93.5	94.9	100.0	98.5	97.1	91.7	....	Argentina	213
I54.7	47.9	49.9	51.6	64.8	73.5	67.7	63.3	66.6	82.7	100.0	92.7	132.5	....	....	Brazil	223
107.5	96.1	93.5	91.1	92.0	92.8	91.1	90.3	90.0	92.1	100.0	106.1	....	....	....	Chile	228
105.3	97.9	97.5	101.3	104.2	99.8	95.5	85.5	84.2	93.5	100.0	101.1	98.5	91.0	84.5	Colombia	233
174.4	140.9	129.2	110.4	107.5	100.0	73.0	69.4	65.9	....	....	....	....	....	....	Costa Rica (1990=100)	238
....	....	178.8	183.1	177.6	100.0	85.8	106.7	94.4	84.8	....	....	....	....	....	Guatemala (1990=100)	258
86.4	79.8	91.4	94.7	98.6	100.0	....	....	....	....	....	....	....	....	....	Trinidad and Tobago (1990=100)	369
															Memorandum Items	
....	....	....	78.6	80.5	81.1	74.1	83.1	84.4	89.7	100.0	101.3	102.7	....	....	Oil Exporting Countries	999
97.0	94.3	97.3	95.3	103.5	104.2	102.5	99.9	98.5	93.7	100.0	97.8	95.1	85.0	87.9	Non-Oil Developing Countries	201

(See notes in the back of the book.)

Terms of Trade

74tx d		1970	1971	1972	1973	1974	1975	1976	1977	1978	1979	1980	1981	1982	1983	1984
															Percent Change over Previous Year:		
World	001	**1.5**	**−.1**	**1.7**	**.1**	**−1.5**	**−.8**	**−.3**	**.6**	**1.4**	**1.3**	**−3.1**	**−1.3**	**−.4**	**−1.0**	**−.5**
Industrial Countries	110	**1.5**	**−.3**	**1.7**	**−.7**	**−11.2**	**1.3**	**−1.9**	**−.5**	**4.2**	**−2.2**	**−7.6**	**−3.4**	**.1**	**.8**	**−1.1**
United States	111	−1.2	−2.0	−3.5	−2.1	−13.8	2.6	.2	−4.2	−.9	−4.6	−9.4	3.5	2.8	5.4	−.4
Canada	156	1.2	−1.0	1.2	6.4	7.6	−4.0	−1.0	−6.4	−4.0	3.1	−3.5	−6.9	−3.3	.3	−1.2
Australia	193	−6.3	−4.8	10.0	28.6	−15.9	−17.0	−.5	−7.2	−2.7	−.1	−9.5	−.1	−2.1	−1.0	−2.1
Japan	158	−1.4	.3	7.5	−3.9	−23.2	−5.3	−2.9	3.4	15.0	−16.1	−19.8	2.5	.8	2.8	2.7
New Zealand	196	−5.8	2.5	15.7	22.0	−22.8	−25.3	7.1	4.5	2.6	7.6	−10.9	−.6	−1.1	−2.5	−.2
Euro Area																
Belgium	124	....	....	....	....	....	....	....	....	....	....	....	....	....	....	....
Belgium-Luxembourg	126	....	....	....	....	....	....	....	....	....	....	....	....	....	....	....
Finland	172	—	−1.5	.4	.8	−1.4	8.2	−3.7	−.3	−3.4	−3.2	−4.4	−.9	1.8	.1	1.3
France	132	−.3	2.0	.6	2.9	−14.2	7.6	−.9	−1.8	4.1	−.6	−6.4	−4.5	−.2	1.2	−.8
Germany	134	2.3	2.6	2.4	−2.1	−9.2	5.2	−4.5	−1.0	4.0	−5.4	−6.4	−6.6	3.7	1.7	−2.3
Ireland	178	.3	1.3	9.2	12.9	−20.0	−1.7	3.9	−1.7	1.9	−4.3	−6.3	−3.8	3.0	3.9	−1.5
Italy	136	.5	−.2	.3	−9.2	−17.3	5.3	−3.3	2.9	2.1	−1.8	−6.2	−4.9	2.5	2.5	−1.6
Netherlands	138	−2.8	−1.9	2.0	−.9	−5.1	.3	—	—	—	−2.6	−1.1	.5	1.2	−1.1	2.3
Portugal	182	....	....	....	....	....	....	....	....	....	....	....	....	....	....	−3.3
Spain	184	−4.1	−6.4	3.7	−.7	−13.6	.4	−4.4	−.8	2.3	6.7	−12.6	−17.7	−.4	−4.6	.7
Denmark	128	—	−3.3	5.0	1.2	−13.4	6.1	−.8	−2.1	3.8	−4.6	−6.8	−2.6	1.0	.8	−.6
Greece	174	−1.6	−3.8	−3.9	6.2	−8.6	−5.9	−1.7	4.7	−2.6	−12.1	5.3	6.9	−3.7	3.8	−7.3
Iceland	176	13.7	12.9	−1.0	16.1	−10.0	−16.0	11.9	8.8	.1	−9.1	−3.4	2.0	−.6	−4.3	−3.0
Norway	142	1.6	−1.0	−1.9	2.9	4.2	2.3	−3.9	−1.3	.5	6.2	15.9	8.4	2.1	−1.2	7.9
Sweden	144	.7	−.8	2.2	−2.3	−6.5	10.7	—	−5.1	−3.6	−1.8	—	−.2	−1.4	−1.1	3.5
Switzerland	146	....	....	....	....	....	....	....	....	....	....	....	....	....	....	....
United Kingdom	112	1.8	1.1	1.7	−11.8	−12.2	7.8	−2.2	3.0	6.5	3.9	4.3	.7	−1.0	−.8	−.6
Developing Countries	200	**1.1**	**1.2**	**1.8**	**4.2**	**39.1**	**−6.2**	**4.4**	**3.6**	**−6.1**	**13.3**	**9.9**	**2.6**	**−1.0**	**−6.9**	**1.2**
Africa	605	....	....	....	....	....	....	....	....	....	....	....	....	....	....	....
Burkina Faso	748	−13.3	−4.0	−13.3	2.9	17.2	−12.8	13.2	2.1	−2.6	−5.1	3.2	−8.2	−5.3	3.9	−.9
Côte d'Ivoire	662			−14.2	22.7	−4.5	−19.6	16.3	48.6	−17.8	−5.4	−2.8	−27.7	−11.1	4.1	20.7
Ethiopia	644	23.2	−15.2	2.0	9.7	−3.1	−15.0	68.1	−5.9	−10.5	.2	−18.1				
Kenya	664	7.2	−11.6	−7.3	−3.4	−16.8	−8.9	16.2	31.5	−19.9	−7.9	−8.2	−14.3	−4.4	−6.3	17.3
Liberia	668			−10.7	−2.9	−10.4	20.6	7.3	−5.2	−12.2	1.6	.1	−7.8	2.8	−1.8	−9.8
Malawi	676	7.7	2.1	−8.5	−4.0	−6.1	−3.6	−2.4	18.6	−10.4	−20.9	−15.1	22.2	1.1	−8.3	4.3
Mauritius	684	7.4	−1.4	12.3	−10.0	52.5	16.3	−26.9	−9.9	−7.6	−5.9	−5.7	1.1	−10.5	9.2	−.9
Morocco	686	−1.5	−2.1	−7.1	−3.6	41.9	7.0	−20.7	20.0	−5.2	−10.4	.5	−6.0	.3	−7.3	2.1
Senegal	722	9.6	−5.2	−5.6	4.0	32.9	−20.2	−7.2	10.4	9.4	−4.8	−24.7	22.2	−14.3	1.8	16.1
Seychelles	718		−1.9	−7.6	23.8	7.4	−29.0	15.0	25.6	11.2	−7.5	−20.2	−.6	−6.7		
South Africa	199	−1.8	−6.2	−6.3	10.1	−2.7	−9.3	−4.7	−4.4	−6.0	−7.7	−4.6	−1.6	−9.8	4.1	2.2
Togo	742	−5.7	−9.9	−10.5	4.5	95.0	−9.7	−35.0	23.2	−9.2	.5	−12.4	−7.3	1.4	−5.9	37.9
Tunisia	744	−3.2	5.1	1.6	20.4	56.5	−8.5	−9.9	1.1	5.4	28.1	17.5	6.3	1.1	−.6	2.0
Asia	505	**4.3**	**−1.8**	**.3**	**1.4**	**−.2**	**−8.0**	**2.4**	**6.5**	**−2.2**	**1.7**	**−3.1**	**−2.4**	**1.3**	**−1.7**	**1.3**
Bangladesh	513	....	....	....	....	....	....	....	....	....	17.7	5.2	−21.4	−4.6	−5.4	29.3
China, P.R.: Hong Kong	532	.2	2.6	2.4	−.4	−6.6	3.2	4.9	−1.6	−.1	−.2	1.0	−2.2	1.3	−1.0	1.3
India	534	1.0	5.0	6.3	7.6	−15.6	−27.5	−7.5	9.3	22.6	−12.0	−7.9	−9.0	11.2	4.1	23.5
Korea	542	.9	−.9	−.4	−5.1	−18.6	−9.7	14.1	7.0	4.8	−2.1	−13.3	−2.1	4.3	.9	2.2
Malaysia	548	18.7	−7.2	−16.4	12.4	26.8	−12.0	.1	15.7	−4.7	15.7	−1.2	−11.0	−7.4	−.6	15.3
Pakistan	564		−13.1	10.3	23.6	−24.1	−22.1	14.0	15.7	8.1	2.4	−14.5	−9.6	−2.9	6.9	1.5
Philippines	566	−2.1	−6.9	−9.6	13.3	1.1	−23.3	−11.5	−8.6	10.0	4.4	−15.9	−12.0	−2.7	4.4	−2.3
Singapore	576	....	....	....	....	....	....	....	....	....	....	5.6	2.1	1.4	−2.2	−3.2
Sri Lanka	524	−6.3	−5.9	−5.6	−11.8	−11.4	−19.8	30.6	31.8	−1.8	−28.3	−12.1	−6.3	−6.2	23.0	21.7
Thailand	578	−12.4	−8.4	−1.5	34.5	−8.6	−20.9	−7.8	−5.0	.2	3.3	−4.8	−12.9	−9.3	7.5	−1.7
Europe	170	....	**−1.0**	**1.5**	**−4.0**	**−9.1**	**1.2**	**1.7**	**−2.6**	**−.3**	**−2.7**	**−3.6**	**−1.6**	**−.2**	**−2.5**	**−3.4**
Cyprus	423	.5	−7.0	2.8	5.1	−14.5	6.9	4.4	−4.3	−.4	−4.0	−5.7	5.4	−2.9	3.1	.3
Czechoslovakia	934					.2	−4.2	−3.2	−3.7	−1.1	−1.8	.3	−3.6	−1.7	−3.9	−7.9
Hungary	944	....	−1.7	−.2	−1.3	−9.6	−5.1	2.3	−3.4	−.6	−1.8	.3	−.8	−2.3	−2.5	−2.1
Malta	181	6.2	−4.6	2.2	−11.4	−6.8	−.6	2.8	−4.7	2.4	−4.3	−3.4	−3.0	1.9	−6.1	3.7
Poland	964	....	....	....	....	....	....	3.4	−2.9	.1	−2.7	−.1	.7	.8	−4.8	.5
Turkey	186	−2.4	.9	6.4	2.5	−8.0	−15.5	2.7	−.5	−7.0	−.2	−22.8	−8.5	−4.7	−1.7	12.0
Yugoslavia, SFR	188	2.1	−.6	.4	−.5	−10.3	3.8	1.5	−1.1	4.1	−2.6	−.9	−1.5	4.4	−1.9	....
Middle East	405	**−3.1**	**15.8**	**1.5**	**11.4**	**153.1**	**−4.8**	**4.7**	**3.4**	**−13.9**	**51.5**	**30.5**	**5.2**	**5.2**	**−13.3**	**−1.8**
Israel	436	−3.3	1.5	2.3	−3.3	−13.9	−.1	4.1	8.4	7.7	−7.5	−8.3	−.2	3.4	2.2	−1.8
Jordan	439	−22.4	−20.2	10.5	−3.7	60.1	−17.4	−4.4	−2.1	−.9	−5.9	−4.3	−5.7	7.5	—	−1.5
Syrian Arab Rep.	463	−5.8	3.4	−2.6	1.6	33.7	−23.4	1.2	17.1	.4	5.1	—	−14.6	−6.9	−18.8	9.2
Western Hemisphere	205	**9.0**	**−7.7**	**10.5**	**−3.9**	**.5**	**−6.0**	**9.1**	**16.3**	**−11.5**	**−7.4**	**−11.7**	**−13.2**	**−5.0**	**13.3**	**.4**
Argentina	213	....	....	....	....	....	....	....	....	....	....	....	....	....	....	....
Brazil	223	10.9	−7.2	14.6	1.4	−13.7	−8.1	12.3	17.4	−13.9	−8.3	−17.3	−15.3	−2.9	−.1	7.4
Chile	228	....	....	....	....	....	....	....	....	....	....	....	−17.1	−24.6	−39.6	−25.8
Colombia	233		−6.5	5.1	6.5	4.4	−7.5	40.3	38.7	−25.4	−10.6	1.7	−15.6	−2.9	2.5	3.5
Costa Rica	238			−1.9	1.8	−12.5	3.9	18.9	21.4	−11.9	−8.6	−.5	−14.4	.6	3.1	3.4
Guatemala	258	....	....	....	....	....	....	....	....	....	....	....	....	....	....	....
Nicaragua	278	−8.7	−3.5	3.6	−1.2	−2.9	−23.1	33.5	17.7	−10.9	−3.9	−10.6	4.3	−2.6	−3.4	6.0
Trinidad and Tobago	369	−2.1	1.9	−6.7	12.2	17.3	.7	−1.9	5.8	−4.3	16.7	6.4	−2.4	−15.4	−1.5	−.7
Memorandum Items																
Oil Exporting Countries	999	....	....	....	....	....	....	....	....	....	....	....	....	....	....	....
Non-Oil Developing Countries	201	1.9	−4.6	1.0	.4	−3.0	−7.7	3.3	6.3	−5.3	−2.8	−6.0	−2.7	−3.7	.3	1.0

Indices

		1970	1971	1972	1973	1974	1975	1976	1977	1978	1979	1980	1981	1982	1983	1984
															Index Numbers:		
World	001	90.0	90.0	91.5	91.6	90.2	89.5	89.2	89.8	91.0	92.2	89.3	88.2	87.8	86.9	86.5
Industrial Countries	110	102.6	102.3	104.0	103.3	91.6	92.9	91.1	90.6	94.4	92.3	85.3	82.4	82.5	83.2	82.3
Developing Countries	200	59.8	60.6	61.7	64.3	89.4	83.9	87.6	90.7	85.1	96.5	106.0	108.8	107.7	100.2	101.4
Africa	605	....	....	....	....	....	....	....	....	....	....	....	....	....	....	....
Asia	505	98.4	96.6	96.8	98.2	98.0	90.2	92.3	98.3	96.2	97.9	94.8	92.5	93.8	92.2	93.4
Europe	170	94.5	93.5	94.9	91.1	82.8	83.8	85.3	83.1	82.9	80.7	77.7	76.5	76.3	74.4	71.9
Middle East	205	163.0	150.5	166.3	159.8	160.7	151.1	164.8	191.6	169.5	157.0	138.6	120.3	114.3	129.5	130.0
Western Hemisphere	405	30.9	35.8	36.3	40.5	102.4	97.4	102.0	105.5	90.9	137.8	179.8	189.2	199.1	172.7	169.6

Terms of Trade

74tx d

Calculated from Indices

1985	1986	1987	1988	1989	1990	1991	1992	1993	1994	1995	1996	1997	1998	1999		
.2	6.9	2.0	6.5	-.7	-.2	-.3	1.8	-2.7	1.2	.4	-.5	-.9	1.6	-1.5	**World**	001
1.1	11.3	1.7	6.8	-.8	-.4	.8	1.6	-3.1	.9	.5	-1.0	-.7	2.0	1.1	**Industrial Countries**	110
1.8	4.5	-5.1	2.1	-.4	-2.2	.9	-.7	1.2	.4	.5	-.4	.9	3.1	-2.1	United States	111
-2.3	-1.7	3.1	2.3	2.1	-2.6	-2.2	-1.8	-.8	.7	4.1	1.0	-1.1	-3.8	1.7	Canada	156
-5.3	-7.4	-1.9	14.5	6.5	-2.9	-9.6	-2.3	-6.3	-.4	3.7	1.3	1.9	-3.2	-5.0	Australia	193
2.9	33.7	1.8	2.7	-4.4	-5.8	10.0	7.6	8.3	7.6	-.4	-8.1	-1.0	6.6	4.8	Japan	158
-1.8	—	11.0	6.8	4.9	-1.9	-5.2	1.4	3.2	-.7	-1.6	-.8	-1.7	1.0	-.9	New Zealand	196
															Euro Area	124
									-.8	-1.2	-.6	-.8	2.1	-2.2	Belgium	126
1.1	7.6	.4	-.2	.7	-1.3	-.6	1.9	1.3	-.1	-2.0	.2	-1.0	....	....	Belgium-Luxembourg	172
-.4	9.5	3.9	2.5	3.8	-2.5	-2.3	-3.8	-6.7	5.0	7.0	-1.9	-1.5	....	....	Finland	132
2.5	12.7	.5	1.1	-1.6	.1	.7	1.2	1.9	2.6	—	-.7	-.1	.7	....	France	134
1.3	15.1	3.7	—	-2.7	1.5	-2.3	2.4	.9	-2.8	-.4	-.2	-2.2	1.8	....	Germany	178
1.6	4.4	—	.6	.2	-4.6	-2.9	-.7	2.3	-2.6	-2.3	.6	.6	.3	....	Ireland	136
.6	15.8	2.5	.9	-1.2	2.9	3.7	1.3	-.3	-.4	-2.7	4.3	-.4	5.2	....	Italy	138
1.0	3.0	-3.5	.4	-1.9	2.2	-1.2	-1.4	3.1	.4	1.6	-.6	....	....	....	Netherlands	182
7.9	13.0	2.1	3.1	-1.6	-.5	—	3.0	....	....	....	....	....	....	....	Portugal	184
5.4	20.9	5.6	7.6	2.5	1.6	1.8	2.3	-.3	-1.4	2.0	.7	-.4	2.4	-.8	Spain	128
1.4	6.6	3.3	-1.9	-.8	1.9	1.3	.9	.2	-.1	-1.9	1.0	-1.3	-.6	1.2	Denmark	174
-1.0	-4.7	9.4	-1.5	2.9	-.5	-.4	-3.1	1.5	12.6	-.9	-.1	-10.2	....	....	Greece	176
1.1	8.5	5.6	-4.2	-6.0	2.0	9.3	-2.3	-5.2	-1.2	.8	-4.2	.6	....	....	Iceland	142
-2.4	-24.8	-6.0	-2.8	5.7	3.7	-2.7	-6.3	-.7	-3.6	2.0	8.6	3.0	-12.8	13.9	Norway	144
.2	9.4	-.9	-.2	2.5	—	1.5	—	-3.1	2.7	2.4	-2.1	-.2	1.3	-3.4	Sweden	146
				-1.9	1.7	2.7	-2.0	2.2	4.3	.2	1.0	-1.6	3.3	3.3	Switzerland	112
.5	-5.5	1.4	1.2	.4	1.2	-.1	.9	2.7	-1.3	-2.8	1.0	.9	1.2	1.4	United Kingdom	
-2.4	-7.2	4.1	5.2	-1.4	1.9	-4.6	3.4	-1.9	2.3	—	1.1	-1.7	.5	-5.2	**Developing Countries**	200
....	....	....	....	-3.3	-.1	.7	.7	-4.2	-3.8	8.9	2.3	-1.3	2.4	....	**Africa**	605
9.2	-26.7	16.3	-3.0	-14.3	3.1	5.4	-20.6	-5.4	-20.3	10.2	-5.7	....	....	....	Burkina Faso	748
16.7	-3.6	-17.3	....	....											Côte d'Ivoire	662
															Ethiopia	644
-16.7	12.9	-18.2	4.6	-10.9	-9.9	14.8	-2.5	13.4	12.2	-5.7	-2.8	9.7	-1.5	....	Kenya	664
7.3	-6.5	-10.3	....	....											Liberia	668
-14.6	-12.9	-3.4	-3.2	2.1	....										Malawi	676
3.8	30.6	8.1	-2.7	....	-1.7	1.6	4.8	-1.8	-2.4	.2	3.9	.9	12.5	....	Mauritius	684
1.1	10.0	-2.5	18.5	-26.6	-5.6	3.2	.8	-8.9	-13.3	13.1	-.1	4.3	11.6	....	Morocco	686
2.1	-3.2	—	....												Senegal	722
															Seychelles	718
-1.3	-.9	-.5	5.0	6.2	-1.9	860.9	-90.0	1.8	1.7	2.9	4.6	-4.0	.1	....	South Africa	199
18.8	....														Togo	742
-6.2	-13.8	9.0	....												Tunisia	744
-2.0	-.6	5.8	—	.9	-.8	.9	2.5	—	.4	—	-1.4	1.1	-.2	-8.6	**Asia**	505
12.9	-28.8	-8.5	25.2	-3.5	-4.8	-13.6	....								Bangladesh	513
3.2	-2.8	-.4	-1.0	1.4	.2	.7	.7	.2	-1.2	-1.5	.9	.7	1.2	-.8	China, P.R.: Hong Kong	532
-13.0	2.4	20.5	-3.1	-2.6	-10.0	9.5	5.8	14.4	5.1	-9.5	-8.4	15.5	....	....	India	534
.5	8.8	2.4	2.8	-.3	-3.3	.6	—	4.4	1.2	-3.6	-12.3	-11.3	8.3	-1.8	Korea	542
-9.7	-24.8	16.5	....	....											Malaysia	548
-4.4	27.5	-9.4	-8.9	-7.9	-4.7	-3.4	.2	2.0	—	11.5	.2	-.8	14.8	2.7	Pakistan	564
-6.7	7.9	9.5	11.0	-7.6	-9.9	6.5	....								Philippines	566
.7	-2.7	-4.5	-1.8	-.4	1.4	-2.3	-3.3	-.2	-3.1	-1.7	.2	—	—	-1.5	Singapore	576
-18.1	-3.6	2.8	-5.8	-1.6	-4.4	-1.9	19.9	4.2	-1.0	-.6	1.0	5.3	....	....	Sri Lanka	524
-6.3	10.8	-1.1	-1.8	-3.9	-2.9	-1.1	1.1	1.0	.3	-3.2	-2.0	.5	-5.4	1.2	Thailand	578
.1	.2	2.0	32.9	-17.5	-1.1	-.7	6.4	15.3	3.4	-.4	.8	3.4	5.5	....	**Europe**	170
-2.4	9.2	7.3	....												Cyprus	423
1.1	-.8	2.6	2.9	5.2	2.8	-30.0	....								Czechoslovakia	934
-.9	-3.6	.9	2.4	2.8	.4	-10.4	-.5	2.3	2.2	....					Hungary	944
1.7	6.5	4.1	9.5	1.4	....										Malta	181
2.3	1.9	3.6	1.0	16.6	-15.9	-8.8	9.5	7.2	1.4	1.8	-2.5	-.7	2.4	1.2	Poland	964
....	....	....	....	....	4.7	2.3	3.3	3.6	-9.4	-3.5	1.7	4.3	-.3	....	Turkey	186
															Yugoslavia, SFR	188
3.7	-44.1	7.2	-7.6	8.9	14.2	-9.3	1.4	-7.7	-2.7	.2	11.8	-.3	-23.6	34.9	**Middle East**	405
1.1	3.9	-3.2	5.3	-.3	.6	5.5	.7	3.9	-3.5	-3.3	.7	3.8	2.8	3.9	Israel	436
-.4	14.3	-10.6	10.2	7.6	-11.5	11.0	2.0	-.6	7.7	2.8	-2.5	-.7	-4.8	-1.4	Jordan	439
16.4	-38.1	-8.3	-22.4	28.0	28.6	-29.6	-1.5	3.8	-4.8	11.2	-.4	-7.8	....	....	Syrian Arab Rep.	463
-10.4	15.7	-4.7	31.4	-4.3	-3.2	-26.8	2.8	-9.4	-4.1	-7.7	6.1	....	....	....	**Western Hemisphere**	205
....	....	....	....	....	....	....	3.3	5.9	2.5	1.5	.3	8.1	-2.4	-3.9	Argentina	213
.1	8.9	5.8	3.7	-21.6	-15.1	9.5	21.3	-6.0	-15.1	-14.2	8.7	....	....	....	Brazil	223
-39.5	-4.4	3.6	18.2	-5.3	....										Chile	228
-1.0	21.8	-22.9	.6	-20.6	8.4	-2.9	-6.1	1.2	20.0	1.4	-7.6	13.2	-3.5	.3	Colombia	233
3.5	25.6	-17.8	-.2	-6.8	-8.0	6.7	-4.0	1.8	....						Costa Rica	238
....	....	....	-4.4	-3.6	15.2	-17.8	-23.6	14.0	13.1	....					Guatemala	258
-12.3	14.1	9.3	-3.4	....											Nicaragua	278
-3.5	-28.3	-8.4	-14.2	9.8	18.0	....									Trinidad and Tobago	369

Memorandum Items

1985	1986	1987	1988	1989	1990	1991	1992	1993	1994	1995	1996	1997	1998	1999		
....	....	....	....	8.6	22.4	-1.1	-9.2	-10.7	-5.9	.3	11.2	-6.3	....	....	Oil Exporting Countries	999
-2.6	3.3	3.7	8.2	-1.9	-.5	-4.2	3.5	-1.1	2.1	-.5	-.4	-1.5	3.6	-8.3	Non-Oil Developing Countries	201

Indices

1995=100

1985	1986	1987	1988	1989	1990	1991	1992	1993	1994	1995	1996	1997	1998	1999		
86.6	92.6	94.5	100.6	99.9	99.7	99.4	101.2	98.5	99.6	100.0	99.5	98.6	100.2	98.7	**World**	001
83.2	92.6	94.2	100.6	99.8	99.4	100.2	101.8	98.6	99.5	100.0	99.0	98.4	100.3	101.4	**Industrial Countries**	110
99.0	91.8	95.6	100.5	99.1	100.9	96.3	99.6	97.8	100.0	100.0	101.1	99.4	99.9	94.7	**Developing Countries**	200
....	....	....	101.9	98.5	98.4	99.1	99.7	95.5	91.9	100.0	102.3	101.0	103.5	....	**Africa**	605
91.5	90.9	96.2	96.1	97.0	96.3	97.1	99.5	99.5	100.0	100.0	98.6	99.7	99.5	90.9	**Asia**	505
72.0	72.1	73.6	97.7	80.6	79.7	79.2	84.2	97.0	100.4	100.0	100.8	104.3	110.0	....	**Europe**	170
116.5	134.8	128.4	168.8	161.6	156.4	114.5	124.7	113.0	108.4	100.0	106.1	....	....	....	**Middle East**	205
175.8	98.3	105.4	97.3	106.0	121.0	109.7	111.2	102.7	99.8	100.0	111.8	111.4	85.1	114.9	**Western Hemisphere**	405

Balance of Payments

Trade Balance

Expressed in Millions of US Dollars

	1983	1984	1985	1986	1987	1988	1989	1990	1991	1992	1993	1994	1995	1996	1997	1998	1999
All Countries	13,417	21,331	14,662	9,910	30,942	36,075	23,638	25,622	34,872	40,757	66,237	97,490	114,167	98,014	117,612	78,056	38,309
Industrial Countries	-26,919	-48,272	-43,141	-11,831	-33,640	-10,276	-29,593	-32,639	3,223	37,888	99,366	94,228	120,882	90,688	95,136	24,831	-110,479
United States	-67,090	-112,480	-122,180	-144,641	-159,239	-126,609	-114,529	-108,248	-72,820	-94,320	-130,716	-164,139	-171,880	-189,369	-194,705	-244,971	-344,822
Canada	14,176	15,611	11,867	7,182	9,170	8,849	6,560	9,513	6,126	7,381	10,136	14,834	25,855	31,091	17,223	12,775	22,756
Australia	26	-742	-968	-1,820	492	-677	-3,350	358	3,528	1,643	-29	-3,277	-4,223	-635	1,849	-5,367	-9,771
Japan	31,460	44,260	55,292	91,188	91,583	92,241	80,122	69,283	96,084	124,764	139,417	144,191	131,787	83,561	101,600	122,389	123,325
New Zealand	337	-452	-61	103	590	2,173	973	815	2,070	1,627	1,719	1,408	895	528	862	937	-421
Euro Area																	
Austria	-3,172	-3,242	-3,137	-4,016	-4,809	-4,765	-5,552	-6,969	-8,560	-7,690	-6,476	-7,914	-6,656	-7,315	-4,274	-3,654	-3,560
Belgium-Luxembourg	-666	-191	492	2,305	1,294	2,703	2,278	1,671	1,999	3,700	5,780	6,901	9,555	8,690	7,703	6,981	7,486
Finland	147	1,480	870	1,704	1,507	1,200	-229	701	2,438	4,009	6,449	7,723	12,437	11,314	11,544	12,490	11,655
France	-8,412	-4,494	-4,814	-1,347	-7,775	-7,656	-10,305	-13,253	-9,714	2,371	7,516	7,249	10,998	14,936	28,069	26,174	20,065
Germany	19,419	21,506	28,421	54,680	68,044	76,348	74,979	68,513	19,441	28,202	41,191	50,915	65,106	69,379	70,811	78,889	70,503
Ireland	-252	237	631	1,145	2,614	3,822	4,003	3,944	4,294	7,045	8,175	9,366	13,557	15,754	18,625	25,653	24,006
Italy	-1,711	-5,132	-5,367	5,048	83	-924	-1,664	-1,474	-2,584	-200	28,889	31,568	38,729	54,118	39,878	35,631	20,385
Luxembourg												-1,601	-1,734	-1,993		-1,999	-2,793
Netherlands	5,553	6,639	6,704	7,408	6,252	10,072	9,825	12,058	11,979	12,309	16,904	18,686	22,102	20,381	18,942	18,020	16,191
Portugal	-2,985	-2,051	-1,430	-1,611	-3,513	-5,377	-4,742	-6,684	-7,688	-9,387	-8,050	-8,321	-8,910	-9,360	-10,041	-12,277	-14,157
Spain	-7,806	-4,643	-4,759	-7,197	-13,742	-18,703	-25,406	-29,158	-30,335	-30,420	-14,999	-14,892	-18,415	-16,283	-13,407	-20,758	-29,208
Denmark	252	-195	-764	-1,050	795	1,883	2,425	4,875	4,748	7,058	7,719	7,441	6,528	7,532	5,369	3,886	6,537
Greece	-4,270	-4,222	-5,013	-4,375	-5,435	-6,027	-7,327	-10,106	-10,022	-11,561	-10,499	-11,273	-14,425	-15,505	-15,375		
Iceland	20	-13		97	-52	-14	134	79	-47	2	181	273	206	19	5	-352	-307
Norway	4,351	5,158	4,728	-2,115	-759	-209	3,770	7,761	8,696	8,254	6,966	7,496	8,571	12,931	11,152	1,566	
Sweden	1,901	3,422	2,385	5,035	4,485	4,880	4,017	3,402	6,357	6,720	7,548	9,558	15,978	18,636	17,999	17,632	
Switzerland	-5,820	-1,613	-2,083	-5,495	-6,017	-5,194	-4,958	-7,174	-4,597	-285	1,571	3,330	3,223	2,250	2,793	988	
United Kingdom	-2,377	-7,114	-3,955	-14,058	-19,209	-38,291	-40,616	-32,549	-18,168	-23,332	-20,028	-16,893	-18,534	-20,232	-19,493	-34,013	-43,069
Developing Countries	40,336	69,603	57,803	21,742	64,582	46,351	53,231	58,261	31,649	2,869	-33,130	3,262	-6,716	7,326	22,476	53,225	148,789
Africa	4,038	8,886	16,165	7,689	11,339	7,143	9,363	16,592	13,814	8,824	7,774	4,373	3,757	16,146	12,435	-2,309	7,894
Algeria	3,199	3,547	4,214	169	2,398	935	1,144	4,179	5,468								
Angola			900	260	1,019	1,120	1,676	2,306	2,102	1,845	1,438	1,563	2,255	3,055			
Benin	-154	-67	-28	-94	-97	-141	-63	-86	-300	-215	-168	-54	-203	-32	-153		
Botswana	25	94	234	244	783	482	635	184	267	187	267	510	555	750	895	77	
Burkina Faso	-196	-129	-222	-292	-245	-237	-257	-262	-221	-222	-243	-129					
Burundi			-36	-36	-61	-42	-58	-116	-103	-105	-99	-92	-63	-60	-9	-59	-42
Cameroon	141	524	490	442	254	620	717	695	850	893	502	402	627				
Cape Verde	-101	-76	-81	-82	-70	-85	-89	-99	-115	-157	-143	-181	-217	-184	-172	-186	
Central African Rep.	-14	-26	-37	-72	-69	-45	-38	-91	-53	-73	-26	15					
Chad	-21	-19	-104	-113	-116	-83	-85	-29	-56	-61	-63	-77					
Comoros	-9	-26	-13	-8	-33	-23	-18	-27	-29	-37	-28	-34	-42				
Congo, Republic of	417	651	515	160	457	320	629	876	613	740	619	346	516	194	941		
Côte d'Ivoire	431	1,137	1,351	1,547	1,086	922	920	1,094	923	995	748	1,289	1,376	1,824	1,819	1,870	
Djibouti											-218	-184	-181	-171			
Equatorial Guinea					-9	-12	-11	-15	-30	-6	10	25	-31	-117			
Ethiopia	-337	-382	-508	-455	-577	-556	-374	-620	-303	-823	-507	-554	-714	-585	-430	-474	
Gabon	1,275	1,285	1,097	95	555	404	874	1,684	1,367	1,373	1,481	1,589	1,744				
Gambia, The	-33	-7	-13	-14	-21	-23	-23	-31	-38	-32	-56	-56	-39	-97	-85		
Ghana	-61	33	-36	14	-107	-112	-203	-308	-321	-470	-664	-342	-257	-367	-638	-806	-1,112
Guinea				84	164	1	64	85	-8	-91	-22	-170	-39	111	118	121	94
Guinea-Bissau	-50	-43	-48	-42	-29	-43	-55	-49	-47	-77	-38	-21	-35	-14			
Kenya	-214	-266	-279	-235	-660	-729	-962	-915	-512	-500	-247	-238	-750	-515	-886	-1,016	
Lesotho	-451	-405	-302	-316	-405	-496	-526	-613	-736	-823	-734	-667	-825	-812	-828	-673	
Liberia	46	121	167	149	63												
Madagascar	-68	-23	-44	-8	11	-34	1	-249	-111	-144	-180	-96	-122	-120	-178	-154	
Malawi	30	150	69	94	100	40	64	126	60	-15	-23	-276					
Mali	-74	-66	-152	-133	-80	-140	-94	-121	-146	-163	-120	-114	-115	-118	10		
Mauritania	-63	-8	38	18	43	89	99	61	37	-55	3	47	184	134	107	40	
Mauritius	-15	-38	-12	76	—	-148	-192	-257	-185	-159	-242	-397	-241	-326	-436	-264	-547
Morocco	-1,227	-1,401	-1,353	-1,053	-1,066	-760	-1,697	-2,108	-1,764	-2,463	-2,065	-2,107	-2,482	-2,193	-1,864	-2,319	
Mozambique	-441	-390	-305	-409	-481	-559	-622	-663	-647	-630	-727	-767	-536	-478	-454	-491	
Namibia								-142	-49	-78	-42	-86	-130	-127	-272	-173	
Niger	4	33	-86	-28	29	-33	-24	-13	-66	-49	-12	-44	-18				
Nigeria	-1,079	3,001	5,667	1,947	3,478	2,520	4,178	8,653	4,441	4,611	3,248	2,948	3,513	9,679	5,706	-240	4,288
Rwanda	-74	-55	-93	-75	-146	-161	-149	-125	-132	-172	-200	-335	-162	-157	-185	-198	
São Tomé & Príncipe	-9	-11	-13	-13	-7	-5	-8	-9									
Senegal	-275	-186	-248	-189	-248	-243	-200	-226	-266	-331	-350	-203	-250	-276	-271		
Seychelles	-70	-69	-80	-85	-88	-118	-120	-109	-114	-132	-165	-136	-161	-185	-188		
Sierra Leone	-18	-11	-5	20	27	-30	-18	8	11	11	-69	-73	-127				
Somalia	-264	-411	-240	-247	-265	-158	-279										
South Africa	4,039	2,174	5,842	7,200	7,163	5,222	5,589	6,783	6,610	6,279	6,232	4,481	2,667	2,695	2,324	2,018	3,751
Sudan	-189	-81	-135	-307	-430	-522	-507	-322	-836	-597	-227	-522	-510	-719	-828	-1,137	-476
Swaziland	-161	-141	-96	-18	43	18	-22	-39	-41	-141	-104	-50	-197	-205	-129	-116	-111
Tanzania	-325	-362	-541	-577	-713	-646	-655	-779	-867	-929	-857	-790	-657	-449	-449	-776	
Togo	-18	28	-22	-56	-40	-69	-58	-89	-53	-128	-111	-37	-129	-127	-108	-133	
Tunisia	-1,084	-1,166	-886	-934	-728	-1,097	-1,207	-1,678	-1,199	-2,037	-2,064	-1,567	-1,989	-1,761	-1,955	-2,152	-2,141
Uganda	25	121	110	46	-142	-257	-311	-313	-204	-271	-278	-251	-367	-348	-467		
Zambia	212	280	226	175	267	502	566	-257	420								
Zimbabwe	84	184	201	311	381	501	375	243	48	-255	122	158					
Africa not specified	569	940	722	325	39	850	492	588	345	311	529	589	615	804	571	555	497

Trade Balance

1983	1984	1985	1986	1987	1988	1989	1990	1991	1992	1993	1994	1995	1996	1997	1998	1999	

Expressed in Millions of US Dollars

1983	1984	1985	1986	1987	1988	1989	1990	1991	1992	1993	1994	1995	1996	1997	1998	1999	
−15,971	−1,477	−9,040	2,875	20,636	12,865	7,005	4,530	2,696	2,870	−10,811	−7,056	−19,856	−27,395	22,172	138,386	134,353	**Asia**
−162	−417	−293	−642	−366	−278	−371	....	....	....	....	....	....	....	....	....	....	Afghanistan, I.S. of
−1,207	−1,408	−1,287	−1,421	−1,369	−1,443	−1,995	−1,587	−1,386	−1,256	−1,113	−1,416	−2,324	−2,275	−1,748	−1,574	−1,962	Bangladesh
....	....	....	....	....	....	....	....	....	....	....	....	....	....	....	....	....	Bhutan
....	....	....	....	....	....	....	....	....	−179	−187	−255	−332	−428	−328	−391	−240	Cambodia
1,990	14	−13,123	−9,140	−1,661	−5,315	−5,620	9,165	8,743	5,183	−10,654	7,290	18,050	19,535	46,222	46,614	36,207	China,P.R.: Mainland
....	....	....	....	....	....	....	....	....	....	....	....	....	....	....	−7,833	−3,159	China,P.R.:Hong Kong
−181	−133	−146	−103	3	−16	−112	−226	−187	−189	−282	−229	−242	−168	−283	−218	....	Fiji
−4,098	−4,025	−5,616	−5,438	−5,777	−6,581	−6,110	−5,151	−2,992	−2,911	−2,093	−4,150	−6,719	−10,052	−10,028	−10,752	−8,029	India
963	5,707	5,822	2,458	4,674	5,678	6,664	5,352	4,801	7,022	8,231	7,901	6,533	5,948	10,075	18,429	20,644	Indonesia
−14	−7	−11	−13	−16	−17	−18	−24	−23	−32	−25	−21	....	....	....	....	....	Kiribati
−1,849	−1,089	−20	4,299	7,529	11,283	4,361	−2,450	−6,803	−1,755	2,319	−2,860	−4,444	−14,965	−3,179	41,627	....	Korea
....	−118	−140	−131	−152	−92	−131	−107	−101	−100	−150	−214	−316	−321	−283	−165	....	Lao People's Dem.Rep
438	2,931	3,573	3,214	5,783	5,427	4,277	2,525	391	3,150	3,037	1,577	−103	3,826	3,876	....	....	Malaysia
−38	−38	−33	−36	−32	−43	−48	−43	−66	−103	−125	−120	−151	−186	−214	−216	−266	Maldives
−806	−713	−799	−951	−864	−873	−963	−497	−101	−29	21	34	25	−36	115	−62	−56	Mongolia
−353	−200	−202	−290	−233	−205	−82	−302	−53	−105	−630	−609	−823	−931	−1,132	−1,386	−991	Myanmar
−367	−273	−283	−294	−350	−471	−407	−449	−482	−376	−462	−790	−961	−1,106	−1,278	−757	−861	Nepal
−2,728	−3,771	−3,245	−2,793	−2,327	−2,705	−2,583	−2,727	−2,272	−2,803	−2,586	−2,239	−2,891	−3,656	−2,399	....	....	Pakistan
−154	−47	51	102	114	91	−23	69	78	625	1,470	1,326	1,408	1,017	677	695	856	Papua New Guinea
−2,482	−679	−482	−202	−1,017	−1,085	−2,598	−4,020	−3,211	−4,695	−6,222	−7,850	−8,944	−11,342	−11,127	−28	4,962	Philippines
−26	−27	−30	−32	−44	−51	−54	−61	−71	−84	−81	−65	−72	−81	−85	−77	....	Samoa
−4,358	−2,643	−1,518	−940	−1,143	28	−313	−1,633	−110	−1,821	−2,724	1,354	977	2,224	1,118	14,811	11,303	Singapore
1	26	−1	−4	−6	−23	−20	−7	−9	14	−8	—	14	11	−28	−18	....	Solomon Islands
−664	−237	−523	−556	−472	−540	−550	−473	−805	−715	−742	−1,085	−985	−800	−640	−567	....	Sri Lanka
−2,861	−1,898	−1,332	388	−424	−2,074	−2,916	−6,751	−5,989	−4,161	−4,297	−3,726	−7,968	−9,488	1,551	16,041	13,477	Thailand
−28	−27	−25	−26	−32	−40	−40	−39	−36	−39	−41	....	....	....	....	....	....	Tonga
−28	−19	−34	−38	−43	−43	−44	−66	−59	−49	−47	−50	−51	−51	−44	−42	....	Vanuatu
5,524	8,285	10,266	15,476	18,937	13,100	15,825	14,875	15,671	12,648	10,385	10,076	10,046	14,339	12,490	9,245	13,986	Asia not specified
7,835	9,537	1,420	3,080	7,118	4,023	−10,755	−34,095	−9,383	−11,435	−27,868	−1,478	−14,940	−27,456	−38,532	−41,239	−11,783	**Europe**
−42	−34	−41	−5	−4	−38	−62	−134	−208	−471	−490	−460	−475	−678	−535	−604	−663	Albania
....	....	....	....	....	....	....	....	....	....	−98	−178	−403	−469	−559	−577	−474	Armenia
....	....	....	....	....	....	....	....	....	....	....	−373	−694	−567	−1,046	−408		Azerbaijan
....	....	....	....	....	....	....	....	....	....	−528	−490	−666	−1,149	−1,335	−1,434	−599	Belarus
−406	−178	−505	−1,183	−1,011	−606	−692	−1,314	−32	−212	−885	−17	121	188	380	−381	−1,064	Bulgaria
....	....	....	....	....	....	....	....	....	−742	−1,172	−3,268	−3,690	−5,224	−4,169	−3,301		Croatia
−598	−652	−647	−646	−799	−1,068	−1,370	−1,553	−1,602	−2,315	−1,507	−1,736	−2,085	−2,183	−2,071	−2,426	−2,309	Cyprus
....	....	....	....	....	....	....	....	....	−517	−1,408	−3,685	−5,877	−4,588	−2,595	−2,069		Czech Republic
348	352	277	−386	−270	385	143	−1,422	−121	−1,834	....	....	....	....	....	....	....	Czechoslovakia
....	....	....	....	....	....	....	....	....	....	−90	−145	−356	−666	−1,019	−1,124	−1,115	−878	Estonia
434	780	448	−465	80	583	1,043	534	358	−11	−4,021	−3,716	−2,433	−2,652	−1,962	−2,354	−2,191	Hungary
....	....	....	....	....	....	....	....	....	....	....	....	114	−335	−276	−801	344	Kazakhstan
....	....	....	....	....	....	....	....	....	....	−107	−86	−122	−252	−15	−221	....	Kyrgyz Republic
....	....	....	....	....	....	....	....	....	−40	3	−301	−580	−798	−848	−1,130	−1,027	Latvia
....	....	....	....	....	....	....	....	....	....	−155	−205	−698	−896	−1,147	−1,518	−1,405	Lithuania
....	....	....	....	....	....	....	....	....	....	....	....	....	−317	−388	−420	−410	Macedonia, FYR
−253	−213	−237	−252	−372	−442	−436	−571	−582	−513	−568	−603	−728	−766	−659	−593	−574	Malta
....	....	....	....	....	....	....	....	....	....	....	−54	−170	−260	−348	−388	−123	Moldova
303	659	347	467	790	1,089	47	3,589	−711	−131	−3,505	−575	−1,646	−7,287	−9,822	−12,836	....	Poland
1,869	2,312	1,772	1,680	2,178	3,750	2,050	−3,344	−1,106	−1,194	−1,128	−411	−1,577	−2,470	−1,980	−2,625	−1,087	Romania
....	....	....	....	....	....	....	....	....	....	....	17,677	20,725	22,934	17,363	17,097	35,301	Russia
....	....	....	....	....	....	....	....	....	....	−912	61	−229	−2,283	−2,084	−2,351	−1,109	Slovak Republic
....	....	....	....	....	....	....	....	....	789	−154	−338	−954	−882	−772	−775	−1,157	Slovenia
−2,990	−2,942	−2,975	−3,081	−3,229	−1,777	−4,219	−9,555	−7,340	−8,190	−14,160	−4,216	−13,212	−10,582	−15,398	−14,332	....	Turkey
....	....	....	....	....	....	....	....	....	....	....	....	....	304	−231	....	....	Turkmenistan
....	....	....	....	....	....	....	....	....	....	....	−2,575	−2,702	−4,296	−4,205	−2,584	−482	Ukraine
−1,231	−789	−588	−702	82	779	58	−2,676	512	....	....	....	....	....	....	....	....	Yugoslavia, SFR
−436	−444	−671	−600	−1,941	−2,180	−2,589	−2,371	4,376	−291	−561	86	170	−1,048	−135	−734	−683	Europe not specified
13,941	13,630	16,018	−8,638	5,217	−1,303	19,727	41,992	13,617	9,244	8,022	22,712	24,397	44,320	42,875	−2,530	28,395	**Middle East**
184	72	101	35	−13	77	11	236	−367	−527	107	120	626	665	605	−28	719	Bahrain
−4,558	−6,216	−5,215	−4,538	−4,980	−6,608	−5,722	−6,379	−5,667	−5,231	−6,378	−5,953	−7,597	−8,390	−8,632	−10,214	−9,928	Egypt
3,480	2,358	2,169	−3,414	−89	101	−367	975	−6,529	−3,406	−1,207	6,817	5,586	7,402	4,258	−626	....	Iran, I.R. of
−3,253	−2,584	−2,382	−1,845	−3,712	−2,907	−1,905	−2,599	−4,961	−4,902	−5,780	−5,555	−7,566	−7,185	−5,174	−3,226	−4,541	Israel
−2,120	−1,721	−1,638	−1,426	−1,467	−1,411	−773	−1,237	−1,173	−1,780	−1,899	−1,579	−1,518	−2,001	−1,813	−1,602	....	Jordan
4,584	5,607	4,655	1,951	3,284	1,709	4,987	3,179	−3,993	−689	3,323	4,669	5,579	6,997	6,534	1,903	5,571	Kuwait
3,370	2,564	4,599	1,468	437	−109	765	3,777	2,664	2,617	113	1,026	2,781	2,519	2,716	471	2,792	Libya
1,895	1,781	1,943	552	2,036	1,235	1,842	2,885	1,759	1,928	1,336	1,849	2,015	2,954	2,982	291	....	Oman
12,646	8,987	7,115	3,119	4,916	4,571	9,154	22,889	21,818	20,039	16,522	21,289	24,390	35,370	34,362	11,287	22,765	Saudi Arabia
−2,106	−1,853	−2,090	−1,326	−869	−639	1,192	2,094	1,084	159	−259	−1,275	−143	−338	454	−172	....	Syrian Arab Republic
−1,756	−1,393	−1,071	−780	−1,141	−862	−677	....	....	....	....	....	....	....	....	....	....	Yemen Arab Rep.
−643	−704	−581	−417	−386	−514	−440	....	....	....	....	....	....	....	....	....	....	Yemen, P.D. Rep.
....	....	....	....	....	....	....	−91	−700	−796	−920	302	−11	−31	−143	−701	....	Yemen, Republic of
2,218	6,730	8,412	−2,017	7,200	4,053	11,660	16,263	9,681	1,830	3,064	1,002	255	6,357	6,726	85	6,308	Middle East not spec

Balance of Payments

Trade Balance

Expressed in Millions of US Dollars

	1983	1984	1985	1986	1987	1988	1989	1990	1991	1992	1993	1994	1995	1996	1997	1998	1999
Western Hemisphere	30,493	39,026	33,240	16,736	20,271	23,622	27,891	29,242	10,904	−6,634	−10,247	−15,289	−74	1,711	−16,474	−39,083	−10,070
Anguilla	....	....	....	....	....	....	....	−28	−28	−33	−33	−37	....	....	....	....	....
Antigua and Barbuda	−63	−115	−147	−181	−196	−176	−217	−202	−209	−208	−221	−254	−249	−263	....	....	....
Argentina	3,716	3,982	4,878	2,446	1,017	4,242	5,709	8,628	4,419	−1,396	−2,364	−4,139	2,357	1,760	−2,123	−3,117	−829
Aruba	....	....	....	−181	−205	−267	−290	−425	−524	−377	−392	−311	−425	−308	−387	−353	−592
Bahamas, The	−534	−546	−563	−606	−673	−672	−911	−797	−817	−768	−738	−815	−931	−1,014	−1,116	−1,374	−1,428
Barbados	−253	−220	−209	−248	−294	−339	−416	−409	−416	−278	−327	−355	−446	−456	−599	−644	....
Belize	....	−23	−24	−16	−24	−42	−64	−59	−98	−104	−119	−75	−66	−58	−90	−105	−129
Bolivia	259	312	161	−51	−128	−48	−6	55	−44	−432	−396	−30	−182	−236	−477	−656	−488
Brazil	6,469	13,086	12,466	8,304	11,158	19,168	16,112	10,747	10,578	15,239	14,329	10,861	−3,157	−5,453	−6,652	−6,603	....
Chile	986	362	884	1,092	1,309	2,210	1,483	1,284	1,485	722	−990	732	1,381	−1,091	−1,558	−2,516	1,664
Colombia	−1,494	246	−23	1,922	1,868	827	1,474	1,971	2,959	1,234	−1,657	−2,240	−2,639	−2,140	−2,715	−2,514	1,734
Costa Rica	−42	5	−62	40	−139	−98	−239	−443	−200	−472	−761	−606	−323	−249	−234	−245	....
Dominica	−15	−25	−24	−5	−10	−20	−48	−48	−41	−38	−44	−48	−57	−48	−51	−37	....
Dominican Republic	−494	−389	−547	−630	−880	−718	−1,039	−1,058	−1,071	−1,612	−1,443	−1,451	−1,391	−1,674	−1,995	−2,617	....
Ecuador	927	1,054	1,294	557	−33	622	662	1,009	643	1,018	592	561	324	1,193	598	−995	1,665
El Salvador	−74	−189	−216	−124	−349	−356	−663	−666	−705	−962	−962	−1,170	−1,462	−1,242	−1,107	−1,267	....
Grenada	−39	−33	−43	−52	−57	−59	−68	−77	−87	−80	−96	−89	−100	−123	....	....	....
Guatemala	36	−50	−17	168	−355	−340	−358	−217	−443	−1,044	−1,021	−997	−875	−643	−940	−1,409	−1,445
Guyana	−32	15	5	....	....	....	....	....	....	−61	−68	−41	−41	....	....	....	....
Haiti	−139	−123	−122	−112	−101	−103	−111	−177	−282	−139	−180	−111	−429	−416	−354	−341	....
Honduras	−49	−139	−86	23	−41	−34	−45	−12	−72	−151	−204	−250	−141	−287	−294	−323	....
Jamaica	−439	−335	−436	−248	−352	−357	−590	−502	−392	−425	−815	−551	−829	−994	−1,132	−1,097	....
Mexico	14,105	13,186	8,399	5,019	8,786	2,611	405	−881	−7,279	−15,934	−13,481	−18,464	7,089	6,531	623	−7,915	−5,360
Montserrat	....	....	....	−16	−19	−21	−31	−41	−33	−28	−22	−27	....	....	....	....	....
Netherlands Antilles	−171	−300	−322	−521	−614	−654	−704	−810	−817	−836	−838	−921	−964	....	....	....	....
Nicaragua	−290	−323	−489	−420	−439	−483	−229	−237	−420	−548	−392	−431	−402	−451	−698	−804	−1,133
Panama	−378	−489	−437	−179	−193	157	−124	−158	−400	−376	−334	−250	−589	−644	−700	−1,371	−1,398
Paraguay	−225	−288	−194	−288	−321	−159	164	361	77	9	79	−243	−194	−503	−207	−114	....
Peru	293	1,007	1,219	−73	−500	−134	1,246	399	−189	−341	−607	−997	−2,168	−1,986	−1,721	−2,465	....
St. Kitts and Nevis	−28	−27	−26	−29	−41	−54	−61	−69	−68	−51	−63	−69	....	....	....	....	....
St. Lucia	−50	−60	−62	−52	−75	−72	−125	−108	−148	−144	−140	−166	−155	−184	....	....	....
St. Vincent & Grens.	−22	−15	−8	−11	−32	−20	−35	−35	−53	−38	−61	−67	−57	−75	....	....	....
Suriname	−62	−31	47	59	115	212	390	163	−2	122	84	99	123	....	....	....	....
Trinidad and Tobago	−131	469	787	169	357	405	506	1,013	564	696	547	741	588	382	−529	−741	....
Uruguay	417	192	178	273	102	292	463	426	61	−122	−387	−706	−563	−687	−704	−772	−868
Venezuela, Rep. Bol.	8,350	8,829	6,977	798	1,694	−1,863	5,694	10,706	4,900	1,322	3,275	7,625	7,013	13,770	10,025	2,748	....
Memorandum Items																	
Oil Exporting Ctys	42,729	51,491	52,984	8,232	31,228	20,288	47,072	80,678	47,836	42,539	45,482	60,688	64,821	102,271	96,175	42,626	88,164
Non-Oil Develop.Ctys	−2,393	18,112	4,818	13,510	33,354	26,063	6,159	−22,417	−16,187	−39,670	−78,612	−57,426	−71,537	−94,945	−73,699	10,599	60,625

Current Account Balance

Excluding Exceptional Financing

Expressed in Millions of US Dollars

1983	1984	1985	1986	1987	1988	1989	1990	1991	1992	1993	1994	1995	1996	1997	1998	1999	
-77,583	-75,889	-84,263	-71,543	-58,349	-68,044	-87,994	-104,553	-111,267	-105,709	-69,125	-43,528	-40,091	-37,946	17,272	-63,902	-152,627	**All Countries**
-30,813	-57,904	-65,839	-37,561	-69,789	-60,146	-78,029	-93,652	-29,318	-35,256	41,147	20,098	55,275	44,012	85,709	-22,018	-207,773	**Industrial Countries**
-44,217	-99,007	-124,470	-149,237	-162,644	-123,055	-98,898	-79,324	4,285	-50,614	-85,293	-121,686	-113,567	-129,294	-143,850	-220,559	-338,916	United States
-2,543	-1,368	-5,734	-11,157	-13,430	-14,818	-21,769	-19,764	-22,345	-21,160	-21,822	-13,024	-4,328	3,378	-10,065	-11,133	-2,273	Canada
-6,330	-8,860	-9,172	-9,807	-7,966	-11,773	-18,205	-16,013	-11,182	-11,190	-9,815	-17,291	-19,640	-15,882	-12,569	-18,035	-22,526	Australia
20,800	35,000	51,129	85,877	84,351	79,249	63,215	44,078	68,203	112,574	131,637	130,255	111,044	65,884	94,354	120,696	106,865	Japan
-960	-3,031	-2,657	-2,826	-2,910	-1,863	-1,525	-1,453	-1,159	-1,071	-746	-2,384	-3,069	-3,935	-4,308	-2,596	-4,334	New Zealand
																	Euro Area
276	-178	-158	204	-263	-242	248	1,166	61	-753	-1,013	-2,992	-5,448	-4,890	-5,221	-4,609	-5,701	Austria
-495	-55	670	3,059	2,797	3,592	3,600	3,627	4,746	6,650	11,237	12,571	14,232	13,762	13,914	12,168	11,961	Belgium-Luxembourg
-1,124	-21	-806	-693	-1,731	-2,694	-5,797	-6,962	-6,807	-5,116	-1,135	1,110	5,231	5,003	6,633	7,371	6,936	Finland
-5,166	-876	-35	2,430	-4,446	-4,619	-4,671	-9,944	-6,518	3,893	8,990	7,415	10,840	20,561	39,474	40,161	37,231	France
4,598	9,571	17,578	40,914	46,444	50,354	57,002	48,303	-17,668	-19,145	-13,871	-20,939	-18,932	-7,969	-2,905	-4,557	-20,901	Germany
-1,219	-1,038	-736	-847	-76	-25	-581	-361	284	607	1,765	1,577	1,721	2,049	1,866	2,142	305	Ireland
699	-3,190	-4,084	2,462	-2,635	-7,181	-12,812	-16,479	-24,463	-29,217	7,802	13,209	25,076	39,999	32,403	19,998	8,239	Italy
....	....	....	....	....	....	....	....	....	....	....	....	2,881	2,780	2,401	2,266	1,562	Luxembourg
5,089	6,380	4,248	4,318	4,187	7,132	10,039	9,221	7,841	7,423	13,594	17,873	24,144	21,637	27,449	25,585	22,597	Netherlands
-1,632	-623	380	1,166	435	-1,066	153	-181	-716	-184	233	-2,196	-132	-4,528	-5,527	-7,250	-9,004	Portugal
-3,013	1,778	2,785	3,914	-263	-3,795	-10,924	-18,009	-19,785	-21,537	-5,804	-6,389	792	407	2,512	-3,135	-12,621	Spain
-1,382	-1,718	-2,767	-4,490	-3,002	-1,340	-1,118	1,372	1,983	4,199	4,832	3,189	1,855	3,090	921	-2,008	2,176	Denmark
-1,878	-2,132	-3,276	-1,676	-1,223	-958	-2,561	-3,537	-1,574	-2,140	-747	-146	-2,864	-4,554	-4,860	....	....	Greece
-56	-133	-115	16	-188	-231	-102	-126	-273	-182	42	109	54	-117	-125	-560	-591	Iceland
1,962	2,886	3,038	-4,551	-4,102	-3,896	212	3,992	5,032	4,471	3,522	3,760	4,854	10,240	8,017	-2,161	....	Norway
-725	736	-1,010	32	-21	-534	-3,101	-6,339	-4,653	-8,827	-4,159	743	4,940	5,892	7,406	4,639	....	Sweden
1,212	6,142	6,039	4,654	6,288	8,846	8,043	6,941	10,374	14,235	17,908	17,372	21,562	21,219	26,960	24,547	....	Switzerland
5,292	1,833	3,314	-1,324	-9,389	-31,230	-38,477	-33,859	-14,972	-18,196	-16,010	-2,038	-5,973	-719	10,828	-1,100	-20,639	United Kingdom
-46,770	-17,985	-18,424	-33,982	11,440	-7,897	-9,965	-10,901	-81,949	-70,453	-110,272	-63,626	-95,367	-81,958	-68,437	-41,885	55,146	**Developing Countries**
-12,477	-5,855	1,373	-5,950	-3,605	-8,262	-5,257	-546	-3,613	-3,070	-6,392	-8,820	-14,100	421	-6,497	-16,651	-6,191	**Africa**
-85	74	1,015	-2,230	141	-2,040	-1,081	1,420	2,367	....	....	....	-295	3,266	....	....	....	Algeria
....	....	195	-303	447	-469	-132	-236	-580	-735	-669	-340	....	....	....	....	....	Angola
-135	-57	-39	-53	-34	-18	37	24	-139	5	16	85	-83	-41	-154	....	....	Benin
-79	-59	82	109	628	194	492	-19	303	198	427	212	300	495	721	170	....	Botswana
-60	-3	-63	-18	-50	-47	99	-77	-91	-23	-71	15	....	....	....	....	....	Burkina Faso
....	....	-41	-36	-95	-70	-11	-69	-33	-60	-28	-17	10	-40	-1	-54	-27	Burundi
-412	-169	-562	-452	-893	-428	-298	-561	-339	-397	-565	-56	90	....	....	....	....	Cameroon
-13	-6	-9	2	-3	—	-13	-4	-7	-12	-24	-46	-62	-35	-30	-58	....	Cape Verde
-29	-33	-49	-87	-73	-35	-33	-89	-62	-83	-13	-25	....	....	....	....	....	Central African Rep.
38	9	-87	-59	-26	26	-56	-46	-66	-86	-117	-38	....	....	....	....	....	Chad
-11	-33	-14	-16	-21	-7	5	-10	-10	-14	10	-7	-19	....	....	....	....	Comoros
-401	210	-161	-601	-223	-445	-85	-251	-462	-317	-553	-793	-650	-1,109	-252	....	....	Congo, Republic of
-931	-77	64	-300	-970	-1,241	-967	-1,214	-1,074	-1,013	-892	-14	-492	-313	-242	-313	....	Côte d'Ivoire
....	....	....	....	....	....	....	....	-87	-34	-46	-23	....	....	....	....	....	Djibouti
....	....	....	-25	-21	-21	-19	-41	-11	3	—	-123	-344	....	....	....	....	Equatorial Guinea
-170	-130	106	-327	-217	-228	-144	-294	103	-120	-50	125	-10	89	-23	134	....	Ethiopia
98	113	-162	-1,057	-449	-616	-192	168	75	-168	-49	317	100	....	....	....	....	Gabon
-32	7	8	3	6	27	14	22	12	38	-5	8	-8	-47	-23	....	....	Gambia, The
-172	-39	-134	-85	-98	-67	-94	-223	-252	-377	-560	-255	-145	-325	-550	-380	-766	Ghana
....	....	....	-124	-38	-222	-180	-203	-289	-263	-57	-248	-216	-177	-91	-184	-152	Guinea
-72	-66	-76	-63	-57	-68	-93	-60	-79	-104	-65	-48	-51	-60	-30	....	....	Guinea-Bissau
-50	-130	-118	-47	-503	-472	-591	-527	-213	-180	71	98	-400	-73	-377	-363	....	Kenya
41	6	-12	-3	24	-25	10	65	83	38	29	108	-323	-303	-269	-280	....	Lesotho
-104	-2	55	-18	-145	....	....	....	....	....	....	....	....	....	....	....	....	Liberia
-247	-193	-184	-143	-141	-150	-84	-265	-230	-198	-258	-277	-276	-291	-266	-301	....	Madagascar
-132	-43	-127	-85	-61	-87	-51	-86	-228	-285	-166	-450	....	....	....	....	....	Malawi
-113	-121	-210	-254	-219	-243	-155	-221	-173	-241	-189	-163	-284	-273	-178	....	....	Mali
-214	-111	-116	-195	-147	-96	-19	-10	-30	-118	-174	-70	22	91	48	77	....	Mauritania
-20	-52	-30	94	65	-56	-104	-119	-17	—	-92	-232	-22	34	-89	3	-52	Mauritius
-886	-984	-891	-209	182	473	-787	-196	-413	-433	-521	-723	-1,296	-58	-169	-236	....	Morocco
-415	-308	-301	-409	-389	-359	-460	-415	-344	-352	-446	-467	-445	-421	-296	-429	....	Mozambique
....	....	....	....	....	....	....	28	105	50	110	85	176	116	90	162	....	Namibia
-64	-7	-69	-156	-177	-230	-257	-236	-176	-159	-97	-126	-152	....	....	....	....	Niger
-4,332	123	2,604	211	-73	-296	1,090	4,988	1,203	2,268	-780	-2,128	-2,578	3,507	552	-4,244	506	Nigeria
-49	-41	-64	-69	-135	-145	-123	-108	-34	-83	-129	-46	57	-8	-62	-143	....	Rwanda
-11	-11	-18	-19	-13	-11	-11	-14	....	....	....	....	....	....	....	....	....	São Tomé & Príncipe
-306	-274	-361	-370	-430	-405	-348	-363	-372	-401	-433	-187	-244	-200	-185	....	....	Senegal
-26	-13	-19	-33	-21	-28	-40	-13	-8	-7	-39	-26	-54	-57	-63	....	....	Seychelles
-18	-23	3	141	-30	-3	-60	-69	15	-5	-58	-89	-127	....	....	....	....	Sierra Leone
-142	-139	-103	-126	-114	-98	-157	....	....	....	....	....	....	....	....	....	....	Somalia
9	-1,589	2,622	3,163	2,934	1,204	1,564	2,065	2,260	1,967	1,502	114	-2,204	-1,881	-2,273	-1,936	-464	South Africa
-219	36	149	-26	-232	-358	-150	-372	-955	-506	-202	-602	-500	-827	-828	-957	-465	Sudan
-107	-77	-38	11	66	95	77	51	47	-41	-6	2	-30	-53	9	-17	17	Swaziland
-305	-360	-375	-322	-407	-357	-335	-559	-737	-714	-1,048	-711	-646	-511	-630	-956	....	Tanzania
-48	16	-33	-66	-61	-87	-51	-100	-147	-141	-82	-56	-122	-154	-117	-140	....	Togo
-570	-765	-581	-605	-54	210	-218	-463	-469	-1,104	-1,323	-537	-774	-478	-595	-735	-503	Tunisia
-72	104	5	-43	-112	-195	-260	-263	-170	-100	-224	-208	-339	-252	-388	....	....	Uganda
-263	-147	-395	-348	-245	-293	-219	-594	-306	....	....	....	....	....	....	....	....	Zambia
-398	-43	-64	17	58	125	17	-140	-457	-604	-116	-425	....	....	....	....	....	Zimbabwe
-289	20	-99	-451	-1,089	-591	-863	-738	-1,034	-865	-529	-529	-432	-261	-546	-579	-737	Africa not specified

Balance of Payments

Current Account Balance

Excluding Exceptional Financing

	1983	1984	1985	1986	1987	1988	1989	1990	1991	1992	1993	1994	1995	1996	1997	1998	1999
									Expressed in Millions of US Dollars								
Asia	**−13,968**	**−4,364**	**−12,523**	**4,973**	**23,484**	**14,722**	**6,251**	**5,077**	**2,738**	**2,135**	**−12,442**	**−2,383**	**−37,031**	**−39,604**	**20,830**	**118,259**	**113,086**
Afghanistan, I.S. of	−139	−451	−243	−537	−167	26	−143	....	....	....	....	....	....	....	....	....	....
Bangladesh	−49	−481	−458	−627	−238	−273	−1,100	−398	65	181	359	200	−824	−991	−327	−35	−292
Bhutan	....	....	....	....	....	....	....	....	....	....	....	....	....	....	....	....	....
Cambodia	....	....	....	....	....	....	....	....	....	−93	−104	−157	−186	−185	−210	−224	−96
China,P.R.: Mainland	4,240	2,030	−11,417	−7,034	300	−3,802	−4,317	11,997	13,272	6,401	−11,609	6,908	1,618	7,243	36,963	31,472	15,667
China,P.R.:Hong Kong																2,901	9,281
Fiji	−55	−18	19	17	27	71	7	−94	−68	−61	−138	−113	−113	14	−34	−55	....
India	−1,953	−2,343	−4,177	−4,598	−5,192	−7,172	−6,826	−7,037	−4,292	−4,485	−1,876	−1,676	−5,563	−5,956	−2,965	−6,903	−2,784
Indonesia	−6,338	−1,856	−1,923	−3,911	−2,098	−1,397	−1,108	−2,988	−4,260	−2,780	−2,106	−2,792	−6,431	−7,663	−4,889	4,096	5,785
Kiribati	1	10	−3	−3	−3	−3	−2	−2	−9	−9	−4	1					
Korea	−1,524	−1,293	−795	4,709	10,058	14,505	5,361	−2,003	−8,317	−3,944	990	−3,867	−8,507	−23,006	−8,167	40,558	....
Lao People's Dem.Rep	....	−164	−164	−142	−165	−103	−137	−111	−115	−111	−139	−284	−346	−347	−306	−150	....
Malaysia	−3,482	−1,657	−600	−101	2,575	1,867	315	−870	−4,183	−2,167	−2,991	−4,520	−8,469	−4,596	−4,792	....	....
Maldives	−24	−16	−6	—	8	9	11	10	−9	−20	−54	−11	−18	−8	−37	−26	−60
Mongolia	−824	−740	−814	−1,061	−991	−1,033	−1,229	−640	−104	−56	31	46	39	−101	55	−129	−112
Myanmar	−350	−218	−205	−294	−180	−176	−68	−431	−267	−114	−228	−130	−258	−280	−412	−495	−222
Nepal	−146	−95	−122	−119	−123	−271	−243	−289	−304	−181	−223	−352	−356	−327	−388	−67	−57
Pakistan	27	−1,200	−1,083	−648	−563	−1,430	−1,340	−1,662	−1,403	−1,877	−2,901	−1,812	−3,349	−4,436	−1,712	....	....
Papua New Guinea	−337	−290	−122	−98	−198	−296	−313	−76	−475	−160	474	402	492	189	−192	−29	95
Philippines	−2,771	−1,294	−36	952	−444	−390	−1,456	−2,695	−1,034	−1,000	−3,016	−2,950	−1,980	−3,953	−4,351	1,546	7,912
Samoa	4	1	2	7	7	8	13	7	−29	−52	−39	6	9	12	9	20	....
Singapore	−610	−385	−4	319	−109	1,937	2,964	3,122	4,880	5,915	4,211	11,400	14,436	13,898	16,912	21,025	21,254
Solomon Islands	−15	—	−28	−12	−17	−38	−33	−28	−36	−1	−8	−3	8	15	−38	8	....
Sri Lanka	−466	1	−418	−417	−326	−394	−414	−298	−595	−451	−382	−757	−770	−683	−395	−288	....
Thailand	−2,873	−2,109	−1,537	247	−366	−1,654	−2,498	−7,281	−7,571	−6,303	−6,364	−8,085	−13,554	−14,691	−3,024	14,048	11,050
Tonga	1	−5	2	2	2	−13	7	6	—	—	−6	....	....	....	....	....	....
Vanuatu	−8	3	−10	−12	−24	−15	−12	−6	−14	−13	−15	−20	−18	−27	−19	5	....
Asia not specified	3,636	5,921	8,161	14,697	16,552	9,334	10,797	10,490	11,855	8,074	5,280	4,225	2,778	8,411	5,288	2,254	4,383
Europe	**9,104**	**11,818**	**3,805**	**5,549**	**11,298**	**8,942**	**−3,034**	**−24,840**	**−526**	**−9,883**	**−22,153**	**8,525**	**−2,558**	**−11,600**	**−23,258**	**−23,495**	**3,793**
Albania	−38	−28	−36	−3	5	−27	−39	−118	−168	−51	15	−157	−12	−107	−272	−65	−155
Armenia	....	....	....	....	....	....	....	....	....	....	−67	−104	−218	−291	−307	−418	−319
Azerbaijan	....	....	....	....	....	....	....	....	....	....	....	....	−401	−931	−916	−1,365	−600
Belarus	....	....	....	....	....	....	....	....	....	....	−435	−444	−458	−516	−788	−931	−257
Bulgaria	36	535	−136	−951	−720	−402	−769	−1,710	−77	−360	−1,099	−32	−26	16	427	−62	−660
Croatia	....	....	....	....	....	....	....	....	....	....	606	826	−1,452	−1,147	−2,344	−1,551	−1,468
Cyprus	−205	−222	−180	−19	−8	−108	−249	−154	−420	−638	110	74	−160	−461	−324	−601	−234
Czech Republic	....	....	....	....	....	....	....	....	....	....	466	−820	−1,374	−4,299	−3,271	−1,392	−1,071
Czechoslovakia	677	708	691	169	371	1,093	936	−1,227	908	−31	....						
Estonia	....	....	....	....	....	....	....	....	....	36	22	−166	−158	−398	−562	−478	−295
Hungary	−181	39	−455	−1,365	−676	−572	−588	379	403	352	−4,262	−4,054	−2,530	−1,689	−982	−2,304	−2,101
Kazakhstan	....	....	....	....	....	....	....	....	....	....	....	....	−213	−751	−799	−1,225	−171
Kyrgyz Republic	....	....	....	....	....	....	....	....	....	....	−88	−84	−235	−425	−139	−371	....
Latvia	....	....	....	....	....	....	....	....	....	191	417	201	−16	−280	−345	−650	−641
Lithuania	....	....	....	....	....	....	....	....	....	....	−86	−94	−614	−723	−981	−1,298	−1,194
Macedonia, FYR	....	....	....	....	....	....	....	....	....	....	....	....	....	−288	−275	−312	−109
Malta	−5	8	−26	7	23	61	−9	−56	−7	30	−84	−132	−352	−352	−201	−200	−128
Moldova	....	....	....	....	....	....	....	....	....	....	....	−82	−98	−201	−286	−347	−33
Poland	−1,581	−1,083	−982	−1,106	−379	−107	−1,409	3,067	−2,146	−3,104	−5,788	954	854	−3,264	−5,744	−6,901	....
Romania	1,160	1,719	1,381	1,395	2,043	3,922	2,514	−3,254	−1,012	−1,506	−1,231	−455	−1,780	−2,579	−2,137	−2,918	−1,303
Russia	....	....	....	....	....	....	....	....	....	....	....	8,848	8,026	12,450	2,548	1,034	24,995
Slovak Republic	....	....	....	....	....	....	....	....	....	....	−580	671	390	−2,090	−1,961	−2,126	−1,155
Slovenia	....	....	....	....	....	....	....	....	....	978	191	600	−23	39	37	−4	−581
Turkey	−1,923	−1,439	−1,013	−1,465	−806	1,596	938	−2,625	250	−974	−6,433	2,631	−2,338	−2,437	−2,679	1,871	....
Turkmenistan	....	....	....	....	....	....	....	....	....	....	....	....	....	....	−580	....	....
Ukraine	....	....	....	....	....	....	....	....	....	....	....	−1,163	−1,152	−1,184	−1,335	−1,296	834
Yugoslavia, SFR	275	478	833	1,100	1,248	2,487	2,427	−2,364	−1,161	....	....	....	....	....	....	....	....
Europe not specified	−523	−516	−769	−693	−1,800	−2,060	−2,452	−2,435	5,593	−287	−637	−52	−111	−1,290	−640	−563	−544
Middle East	**−21,293**	**−18,097**	**−8,344**	**−21,100**	**−9,837**	**−13,015**	**662**	**11,275**	**−62,275**	**−25,791**	**−24,223**	**−10,170**	**−4,492**	**7,708**	**5,703**	**−31,054**	**−832**
Bahrain	103	218	39	−69	−201	192	−193	70	−603	−827	−339	−256	237	261	−31	−778	−420
Egypt	−330	−1,988	−2,166	−1,811	−246	−1,048	−1,309	185	1,903	2,812	2,299	31	−254	−192	−711	−2,566	−1,635
Iran, I.R. of	358	−414	−476	−5,155	−2,090	−1,869	−191	327	−9,448	−6,504	−4,215	4,956	3,358	5,232	2,213	−1,897	....
Israel	−2,099	−1,423	1,157	1,497	−1,227	−638	213	161	−1,315	−979	−2,561	−3,387	−5,196	−5,434	−3,514	−842	−2,601
Jordan	−391	−265	−260	−40	−352	−294	385	−227	−394	−835	−629	−398	−259	−222	29	14	....
Kuwait	5,311	6,428	4,798	5,616	4,561	4,602	9,136	3,886	−26,478	−450	2,498	3,227	5,016	7,107	7,935	2,215	5,062
Libya	−1,643	−1,456	1,906	−166	−1,043	−1,826	−1,026	2,201	−219	1,392	−1,362	29	1,998	1,477	1,875	−391	1,476
Oman	494	303	−10	−1,040	784	−309	305	1,106	−251	−598	−1,190	−805	−801	180	−40	−2,970	....
Saudi Arabia	−16,852	−18,401	−12,932	−11,795	−9,773	−7,340	−9,538	−4,152	−27,546	−17,740	−17,268	−10,487	−5,325	681	305	−13,150	−1,701
Syrian Arab Republic	−844	−794	−958	−504	−298	−151	1,222	1,762	699	55	−203	−791	367	81	483	59	....
Yemen Arab Rep.	−559	−301	−287	−125	−452	−694	−579	....	....	....	....	....	....	....	....	....	....
Yemen, P.D. Rep.	−184	−253	−231	−176	−130	−404	−417	....	....	....	....	....	....	....	....	....	....
Yemen, Republic of	....	....	....	....	....	....	....	739	−663	−1,091	−1,248	366	183	106	52	−228	....
Middle East not spec	−4,657	249	1,077	−7,333	629	−3,234	2,653	5,217	2,039	−1,025	−5	−2,655	−3,816	−1,568	−2,894	−10,521	−3,159

Balance of Payments

Current Account Balance

Excluding Exceptional Financing

1983	1984	1985	1986	1987	1988	1989	1990	1991	1992	1993	1994	1995	1996	1997	1998	1999	
										Expressed in Millions of US Dollars							
−8,136	−1,487	−2,736	−17,454	−9,900	−10,283	−8,586	−1,866	−18,273	−33,842	−45,062	−50,779	−37,186	−38,883	−65,214	−88,944	−54,709	Western Hemisphere
....	....	....	....	....	....	....	−9	−8	−17	−13	−10	....	....	....	....	....	Anguilla
−9	1	−23	−118	−111	−45	−82	−31	−33	−19	—	−18	−1	−40	....	....	....	Antigua and Barbuda
−2,436	−2,495	−952	−2,859	−4,235	−1,572	−1,305	4,552	−647	−5,521	−8,030	−10,992	−4,985	−6,521	−11,954	−14,274	−12,152	Argentina
....	....	....	−19	−23	−44	−47	−158	−209	44	42	81	—	−69	−196	−19	−333	Aruba
−101	−100	−3	23	−55	−67	−84	−37	−180	36	49	−42	−146	−263	−472	−995	−672	Bahamas, The
−44	16	51	7	−19	43	25	−11	−27	140	69	134	89	103	−50	−57	....	Barbados
....	−5	9	12	9	−3	−19	15	−26	−29	−49	−40	−17	−7	−32	−60	−77	Belize
−142	−179	−286	−389	−432	−304	−270	−199	−263	−534	−506	−90	−303	−404	−554	−675	−556	Bolivia
−6,834	33	−280	−5,311	−1,452	4,156	1,002	−3,823	−1,450	6,089	20	−1,153	−18,136	−23,248	−30,491	−33,829	....	Brazil
−1,117	−2,111	−1,413	−1,191	−735	−231	−690	−485	−99	−958	−2,554	−1,585	−1,350	−3,510	−3,728	−4,139	−80	Chile
−3,003	−1,401	−1,809	383	336	−216	−201	542	2,349	901	−2,102	−3,596	−4,624	−4,828	−5,950	−5,272	−979	Colombia
−313	−251	−291	−161	−376	−304	−480	−494	−99	−380	−620	−244	−358	−267	−215	−460	....	Costa Rica
−2	−7	−6	−7	−7	−12	−46	−44	−34	−25	−23	−38	−50	−40	−34	−18	....	Dominica
−418	−163	−108	−183	−364	−19	−327	−280	−157	−708	−533	−283	−183	−213	−163	−336	....	Dominican Republic
−115	−273	76	−582	−1,187	−680	−715	−360	−708	−122	−678	−681	−765	84	−714	−2,169	955	Ecuador
−148	−189	−189	−17	−68	−129	−370	−261	−212	−195	−123	−18	−262	−169	96	−84	....	El Salvador
−15	2	2	−19	−29	−28	−36	−46	−47	−32	−44	−22	−35	−58	....	....	....	Grenada
−224	−377	−246	−18	−443	−414	−367	−233	−184	−706	−702	−625	−572	−452	−634	−1,039	−1,026	Guatemala
−157	−99	−97	....	....	....	....	....	....	−139	−140	−125	−135	....	....	....	....	Guyana
−111	−103	−95	−45	−31	−40	−63	−22	−92	7	−12	−23	−87	−138	−48	−38	....	Haiti
−232	−374	−309	−225	−245	−161	−180	−186	−213	−298	−309	−343	−201	−335	−272	−333	....	Honduras
−339	−315	−273	−18	−126	47	−283	−312	−240	29	−184	93	−74	−112	−312	−255	....	Jamaica
5,866	4,183	800	−1,377	4,247	−2,374	−5,825	−7,451	−14,888	−24,442	−23,400	−29,662	−1,576	−2,328	−7,454	−15,725	−14,016	Mexico
....	....	....	−5	−7	−16	5	−23	−21	−13	−10	−19	....	....	....	....	....	Montserrat
88	175	403	51	−49	75	38	−44	−6	10	1	−98	87	....	....	....	....	Netherlands Antilles
−507	−597	−771	−691	−690	−715	−362	−385	−534	−834	−644	−699	−564	−500	−556	−498	−652	Nicaragua
199	−202	75	−99	545	721	112	209	−241	−267	−96	16	−369	−302	−604	−1,212	−1,333	Panama
−248	−317	−252	−365	−490	−210	256	390	85	−57	59	−274	−279	−495	−238	−106	....	Paraguay
−875	−235	102	−1,393	−2,065	−1,819	−570	−1,384	−1,558	−2,116	−2,327	−2,667	−4,314	−3,643	−3,282	−3,800	....	Peru
−15	−4	−7	−9	−16	−28	−38	−47	−35	−16	−30	−26	....	....	....	....	....	St. Kitts and Nevis
−5	−13	−13	−7	−14	−18	−63	−57	−72	−55	−49	−49	−33	−80	....	....	....	St. Lucia
−3	−1	4	−10	−20	−17	−30	−24	−44	−21	−44	−58	−41	−35	....	....	....	St. Vincent & Grens.
−282	−138	−18	−37	136	114	294	67	−133	25	44	59	73	....	....	....	....	Suriname
−947	−467	−48	−412	−225	−89	−39	459	−5	139	113	218	294	105	−614	−644	....	Trinidad and Tobago
−63	−129	−98	42	−141	22	133	186	42	−9	−244	−438	−213	−233	−287	−476	−605	Uruguay
4,427	4,651	3,327	−2,245	−1,390	−5,809	2,161	8,279	1,736	−3,749	−1,993	2,541	2,014	8,914	3,467	−2,562	....	Venezuela, Rep. Bol.
																	Memorandum Items
−22,140	−9,140	−123	−27,837	−10,152	−18,811	3,003	21,383	−58,334	−23,702	−20,591	−4,200	−2,485	25,568	17,900	−24,258	19,309	Oil Exporting Ctys
−24,630	−8,845	−18,301	−6,145	21,592	10,914	−12,969	−32,284	−23,615	−46,751	−89,681	−59,426	−92,881	−107,527	−86,337	−17,626	35,838	Non-Oil Develop.Ctys

Balance of Payments

Capital and Financial Account

Including Net Errors and Omissions, but Excluding Reserve Assets,
Use of Fund Credit, and Exceptional Financing

	1983	1984	1985	1986	1987	1988	1989	1990	1991	1992	1993	1994	1995	1996	1997	1998	1999
Expressed in Millions of US Dollars																	
All Countries	43,479	67,575	64,230	73,537	178,063	68,084	104,899	136,827	124,500	117,247	142,416	111,234	170,819	204,640	49,285	31,056	291,901
Industrial Countries	35,245	67,639	62,357	60,333	176,927	98,232	104,912	148,528	16,107	28,864	-12,712	15,388	25,760	35,928	-59,543	6,125	270,329
United States	45,413	102,133	128,305	148,927	153,497	126,970	124,185	81,554	-10,041	46,687	86,669	116,336	123,314	122,627	144,862	227,290	330,192
Canada	2,536	-441	2,464	10,738	16,744	22,968	22,462	20,903	20,496	16,375	22,727	12,632	7,039	2,119	7,672	16,129	8,206
Australia	9,361	7,565	6,871	10,510	8,340	17,052	18,805	17,753	10,857	6,464	9,773	16,331	20,036	18,354	15,443	15,994	29,232
Japan	-19,250	-32,880	-51,629	-70,747	-46,301	-61,689	-76,265	-53,168	-76,593	-111,954	-104,164	-104,990	-52,433	-30,746	-87,787	-126,860	-30,609
New Zealand	-154	1,485	620	214	662	-1,057	308	1,632	-353	1,202	672	3,117	3,453	5,708	2,865	2,112	....
Euro Area																	
Austria	-804	245	173	439	595	733	742	-1,181	775	3,341	3,214	3,826	6,839	5,965	2,168	8,112	3,530
Belgium-Luxembourg	760	359	-867	-3,030	-363	-2,731	-3,288	-3,223	-4,162	-6,080	-13,359	-12,351	-13,990	-13,169	-12,858	-14,263	-13,829
Finland	897	1,845	1,389	-1,589	5,764	2,952	4,729	10,893	4,921	2,966	1,426	3,603	-5,603	-8,038	-4,329	-7,075	-7,033
France	8,771	3,810	2,731	-1,249	1,844	-540	3,814	1,324	-5,469	-13,996	-4,968	-10,128	-20,321	-33,534	-20,346	-39,011
Germany	-6,550	-9,919	-15,350	-35,488	-24,949	-65,950	-54,143	-41,050	11,484	56,321	-328	18,903	26,156	6,774	-851	8,572	6,788
Ireland	1,407	995	784	753	962	617	-356	986	179	-2,773	894	-1,752	618	-2,101	-2,974	866	-3,421
Italy	5,177	5,750	-3,502	-115	8,105	15,598	24,170	28,102	17,745	5,224	-10,938	-11,634	-22,272	-28,092	-19,254	-41,470	-17,091
Netherlands	-5,246	-6,392	-3,476	-4,649	-1,493	-5,564	-9,532	-8,954	-7,335	-1,305	-6,952	-17,373	-26,056	-27,331	-30,156	-27,924	-27,691
Portugal	580	529	327	-1,276	1,341	1,933	4,501	3,723	6,430	28	-3,081	765	-168	5,251	6,773	7,758	9,206
Spain	2,748	3,039	-5,061	-1,571	12,969	12,212	15,640	25,197	34,105	3,728	600	6,426	-7,206	23,871	9,244	-11,220	-10,173
Denmark	2,739	1,348	4,299	3,161	6,733	2,776	-2,720	2,013	-4,887	-124	-5,399	-5,041	643	474	5,611	-2,231	7,261
Greece	2,078	1,930	2,880	2,326	2,197	1,895	2,213	3,817	3,778	1,766	4,186	6,455	2,841	8,769	345	....	
Iceland	67	117	179	83	170	232	157	200	282	237	-101	-259	-50	270	81	592	666
Norway	-2,061	181	414	1,340	3,882	3,758	753	-3,578	-7,782	-5,203	4,731	-3,507	-4,279	-3,770	-9,216	-4,224	....
Sweden	-4,756	-6,570	-3,640	145	783	1,472	4,355	13,891	4,590	15,780	6,689	1,639	-6,604	-12,278	-14,118	-1,386	....
Switzerland	-1,411	-4,651	-4,811	-3,564	-3,075	-11,228	-6,674	-5,776	-9,379	-9,875	-17,425	-16,309	-21,509	-18,472	-24,801	-23,649	....
United Kingdom	-7,056	-2,840	-744	4,973	28,518	35,823	31,055	33,901	19,673	11,529	21,448	3,538	5,120	64	-14,729	840	19,604
Developing Countries	8,234	-64	1,872	13,205	1,137	-30,148	-13	-11,701	108,393	88,383	155,128	95,847	145,060	168,712	108,828	24,932	21,573
Africa	7,075	1,788	-4,586	1,262	-4,366	-3,729	-2,632	-1,180	-1,974	-9,065	-2,934	-1,260	157	-6,608	6,256	5,372	2,918
Algeria	-336	-408	6	732	-493	1,081	307	-1,431	-1,319	....	....	....	....	....			
Angola	....	....	-201	44	-779	-456	-798	-973	-920	-403	-651	-688	-944	-505			
Benin	97	34	10	-26	-18	66	-167	-7	-15	40	-103	-22	-50	-120	224		
Botswana	203	183	172	198	-67	188	85	327	71	208	-30	-76	-93	16	-86	-108	....
Burkina Faso	97	39	69	42	60	65	-235	84	98	43	74	-22	....	....			
Burundi	....	....	57	65	93	77	49	66	66	85	44	52	26	5	11	34	26
Cameroon	529	83	621	371	422	265	170	-310	-392	-909	-320	-495	-74	....	....		
Cape Verde	17	2	23	-2	6	-1	28	-3	-9	35	39	68	30	57	30	69	....
Central African Rep.	16	33	24	83	62	21	17	68	22	46	-1	38	....	....			
Chad	-29	8	64	40	26	-60	86	23	46	43	69	43	....	....			
Comoros	13	27	20	19	30	3		6	-16	8	-2	12	9	....			
Congo, Republic of	369	-271	80	202	-265	-22	-318	-113	3	-113	133	639	40	759	-296		
Côte d'Ivoire	230	-400	-233	-92	46	-184	-344	-232	-254	-404	-345	-7	238	-684	-351	-326	....
Djibouti	....	....	....	....	....	....	....	....	....	72	23	47	-1	....			
Equatorial Guinea	....	....	....	....	—	3	11	13	27	-17	-13	-18	112	339	....		
Ethiopia	117	73	56	441	109	205	190	95	-459	-144	82	-126	109	-556	-406	-517	....
Gabon	-187	-100	102	862	314	615	96	-436	-298	-274	-403	-490	-521	....	....		
Gambia, The	10	-23	-14	-25	5	-2	-11	-18	4	-18	16	-2	9	61	30		
Ghana	-9	74	148	25	238	248	250	329	389	254	613	427	395	304	576	488	718
Guinea	....	....	....	11	-59	100	-5	106	131	88	-40	124	144	117	-40	26	72
Guinea-Bissau	54	53	84	30	26	27	22	29	4	53	5	-7	10	17	15	....	
Kenya	148	191	66	184	478	428	713	435	169	-77	341	-36	259	460	497	437	....
Lesotho	-15	2	18	15	-23	18	-18	-48	-41	12	73	13	421	419	410	396	....
Liberia	-24	-151	-259	-276	-155	....	....	....	....	....	....	....	....				
Madagascar	-22	-10	16	26	-22	33	-77	-13	-62	-80	-76	1	-54	197	250	1	....
Malawi	34	46	101	85	106	147	—	115	243	238	190	415	....	....			
Mali	81	122	183	205	205	261	156	156	202	103	91	98	232	302	169	....	
Mauritania	179	97	86	165	16	33	13	-63	46	135	-108	-35	-28	-87	-20	-34	....
Mauritius	-11	9	28	28	154	241	249	351	207	43	99	189	131	14	54	-69	242
Morocco	719	821	859	539	116	-209	808	1,893	1,369	1,223	958	1,206	-599	-615	-820	-483	....
Mozambique	115	-87	-65	437	-660	-13	60	17	-114	-171	-200	-99	58	-3	-183	37	....
Namibia	....	....	....	....	....	....	....	9	-118	-56	-19	-10	-152	-93	-23	-106	
Niger	50	-25	18	36	99	163	246	146	116	64	73	50	134	....			
Nigeria	1,445	-1,093	-3,812	-1,270	-4,465	-4,833	-3,756	-3,947	-2,725	-7,906	-1,131	190	-195	-4,268	-536	1,371	-4,043
Rwanda	30	49	65	99	124	95	56	85	99	79	79	50	-5	29	93	15	....
São Tomé & Príncipe	4	4	7	8	9	6	6	5	....	....	....	....	....				
Senegal	196	176	270	335	334	300	175	226	192	276	292	210	212	173	291	....	
Seychelles	24	12	19	32	25	24	39	17	10	3	29	14	40	43	58	....	
Sierra Leone	-75	-73	-77	-237	-23	-69	11	48	-30	22	65	30	81	....	....		
Somalia	64	112	91	29	16	-83	-33	....	....	....	....	....	....				
South Africa	292	1,008	-3,136	-2,655	-1,587	-2,582	-1,650	-649	-1,113	-1,463	-2,843	569	3,111	609	6,869	2,856	4,419
Sudan	-4	-154	-570	-175	-111	71	-42	128	682	347	244	621	563	864	846	1,030	580
Swaziland	119	69	34	-3	-44	-83	-26	-40	-33	132	—	-14	60	68	16	67	4
Tanzania	217	138	-112	-31	116	-27	8	433	475	510	473	292	288	257	332	447	....
Togo	10	-37	30	22	-70	39	23	56	99	-20	-107	-41	-72	129	130	123	....
Tunisia	605	663	355	390	240	207	319	796	451	1,295	1,390	1,063	871	920	981	562	1,187
Uganda	-9	-37	29	16	58	158	175	221	138	124	99	145	288	243	353	....	
Zambia	241	58	215	214	3	61	112	816	126	....	....	....	....				
Zimbabwe	224	-3	146	39	66	-24	-64	226	502	409	342	339	....	....			
Africa not specified	-63	-448	-237	-115	378	-455	251	-383	-195	-282	-607	-783	-857	-676	-413	-512	-367

Capital and Financial Account

Including Net Errors and Omissions, but Excluding Reserve Assets,
Use of Fund Credit, and Exceptional Financing

Expressed in Millions of US Dollars

1983	1984	1985	1986	1987	1988	1989	1990	1991	1992	1993	1994	1995	1996	1997	1998	1999	
19,212	**12,708**	**21,555**	**20,701**	**18,864**	**1,832**	**8,276**	**17,474**	**37,117**	**28,342**	**55,849**	**69,338**	**83,224**	**105,799**	**-8,176**	**-82,992**	**-7,181**	**Asia**
84	516	269	518	178	-52	123	....	....	....	....	....	....	....	....	....	....	Afghanistan, I.S. of
357	449	374	711	393	405	751	622	369	454	338	492	312	577	191	324	100	Bangladesh
....	....	....	....	....	....	....	....	....	....	....	....	....	....	....	....	....	Bhutan
....	....	....	....	....	....	....	....	....	106	125	193	212	257	244	240	147	Cambodia
-98	-1,892	8,977	4,986	4,483	6,176	3,838	50	1,265	-8,461	13,378	23,545	20,851	24,462	-1,106	-25,224	-7,015	China,P.R.: Mainland
															-9,798	224	China,P.R.:Hong Kong
50	29	-23	13	-74	42	13	159	108	146	125	135	206	65	9	59	....	Fiji
1,201	3,412	3,780	4,189	5,325	7,157	7,063	5,096	4,057	5,557	6,087	12,067	4,831	9,914	8,286	9,974	9,448	India
6,521	2,837	2,433	2,908	2,728	1,284	1,603	5,239	5,788	4,850	2,700	3,576	8,004	12,166	-3,248	-7,789	-3,812	Indonesia
-5	-15	2	1	-3	-1	-4	2	-15	-8	-1	-7	....	....	....	....	....	Kiribati
1,400	1,678	1,006	-4,675	-7,959	-5,178	-1,722	795	7,170	7,667	2,019	8,481	15,546	24,421	-14,812	-14,628	....	Korea
....	31	28	12	13	-1	-27	-15	-10	-11	2	106	196	188	-64	-104	....	Lao People's Dem.Rep
3,469	2,149	1,748	1,563	-1,437	-2,325	920	2,821	5,419	8,785	14,341	1,360	6,703	7,112	933	....	....	Malaysia
20	11	7	-4	-7	5	-8	-10	8	24	54	17	35	36	59	46	69	Maldives
820	754	838	1,075	1,067	1,034	1,358	538	-26	-27	-17	-40	-7	13	-49	76	93	Mongolia
325	209	190	343	218	256	219	440	221	209	151	175	227	255	443	554	178	Myanmar
138	74	28	87	187	265	201	309	468	337	288	414	371	358	557	347	234	Nepal
519	237	664	841	643	1,691	1,146	1,347	1,248	2,268	3,328	3,155	2,145	3,656	2,249	....	....	Pakistan
435	338	120	101	200	243	254	97	66	-166	-727	-572	-531	14	15	-192	30	Papua New Guinea
-725	846	874	182	386	1,064	1,756	2,650	2,789	2,689	3,352	5,277	3,215	8,291	1,257	-267	-4,253	Philippines
4	7	3	—	1	2	-2	4	27	40	29	-10	-7	-5	2	-15	....	Samoa
1,670	1,909	1,341	219	1,203	-278	-226	2,309	-683	185	3,367	-6,664	-5,837	-6,502	-8,972	-18,059	-17,060	Singapore
18	-11	13	-6	10	33	20	14	23	16	6	-1	-9	3	47	9	....	Solomon Islands
463	246	330	325	273	291	465	414	918	652	1,150	1,065	1,009	692	702	513	....	Sri Lanka
2,553	2,638	1,642	467	1,311	4,250	7,527	10,516	12,190	9,333	10,270	12,254	20,713	16,859	-15,226	-17,269	-9,783	Thailand
5	10	—	-8	5	14	-13	1	1	2	4	....	....	....	....	....	....	Tonga
9	-9	10	16	23	11	20	11	11	14	18	14	24	22	17	4	....	Vanuatu
-466	-2,080	-1,915	8,322	11,192	-10,918	-11,802	-14,532	-2,237	-6,635	-3,887	3	-6,794	-7,618	2,574	2,607	14,232	Asia not specified
-12,478	**-14,632**	**-11,187**	**-7,695**	**-13,642**	**-14,491**	**5,830**	**2,000**	**-11,837**	**-4,108**	**12,125**	**-21,959**	**21,888**	**45**	**26,207**	**6,903**	**-9,863**	**Europe**
-3	16	19	2	6	161	364	-120	-56	15	34	164	32	163	312	118	262	Albania
....	....	....	....	....	....	....	....	....	....	80	101	248	245	357	419	323	Armenia
—	—	—	—	—	—	—	—	....	....	....	....	458	846	1,055	1,305	733	Azerbaijan
....	....	....	....	....	....	....	....	....	....	297	127	380	302	853	516	344	Belarus
176	-118	434	66	223	1,059	335	-2,744	-197	629	777	-184	470	-754	718	-33	746	Bulgaria
....	....	....	....	....	....	....	....	....	....	-418	-550	1,492	2,164	2,735	1,711	1,928	Croatia
247	318	151	178	71	178	477	448	355	413	35	173	-203	401	277	518	873	Cyprus
....	....	....	....	....	....	....	....	....	....	2,575	4,294	8,827	3,474	1,512	3,282	2,710	Czech Republic
-640	-542	-802	91	-111	-886	-373	100	-119	-391	....	....	....	....	....	....	....	Czechoslovakia
....	....	....	....	....	....	....	....	....	22	143	184	241	505	778	515	414	Estonia
56	27	991	1,497	395	730	760	-791	1,392	418	6,807	3,579	7,928	445	807	3,255	4,436	Hungary
....	....	....	....	....	....	....	....	....	....	....	....	512	910	1,348	782	424	Kazakhstan
....	....	....	....	....	....	....	....	....	....	58	89	154	405	185	347	....	Kyrgyz Republic
....	....	....	....	....	....	....	....	....	-154	-119	-145	-17	491	447	713	806	Latvia
....	....	....	....	....	....	....	....	....	....	294	207	783	718	1,206	1,725	1,015	Lithuania
....	....	....	....	....	....	....	....	....	....	....	....	193	157	344	228		Macedonia, FYR
109	24	-41	-11	-27	-26	24	-41	-71	14	219	514	45	267	208	391	367	Malta
....	....	....	....	....	....	....	....	....	....	....	95	-77	56	103	6	-89	Moldova
-3,337	-3,187	-1,358	-4,095	-3,227	-10,928	-1,906	-8,569	-4,928	-1,226	2,560	52	8,981	6,901	9,332	12,596	....	Poland
-1,150	-1,591	-1,698	-783	-1,002	-4,207	-1,262	1,760	335	1,368	792	626	1,300	1,997	3,596	2,275	1,537	Romania
....	....	....	....	....	....	....	....	....	....	....	-27,817	-16,324	-29,640	-9,103	-22,357	-26,808	Russia
....	....	....	....	....	....	....	....	....	....	594	535	1,401	2,460	2,060	1,649	1,932	Slovak Republic
....	....	....	....	....	....	....	....	....	-346	-66	50	262	551	1,252	162	500	Slovenia
1,291	-38	229	2,005	1,386	-443	1,772	3,568	-1,449	2,458	6,741	-2,428	6,998	6,981	6,022	-1,430	....	Turkey
....	....	....	....	....	....	....	....	....	....	....	....	....	8	978	....	....	Turkmenistan
....	....	....	....	....	....	....	....	....	....	....	-37	-472	581	632	-2,161	-1,018	Ukraine
-552	-375	-674	-264	-1,010	-534	-496	3,732	-1,636	....	....	....	....	....	....	....	....	Yugoslavia, SFR
752	750	1,004	964	2,100	2,376	2,773	2,645	-3,047	883	792	140	618	974	-21	537	610	Europe not specified
16,388	**10,497**	**12,504**	**11,155**	**12,557**	**5,703**	**7,129**	**-25,007**	**61,831**	**24,987**	**21,339**	**8,341**	**10,148**	**3,256**	**1,608**	**24,922**	**4,139**	**Middle East**
-211	-228	319	-107	-141	-99	5	726	79	736	227	208	-68	-267	134	761	446	Bahrain
417	1,741	1,966	1,780	560	946	775	-10,409	-3,976	548	-2,281	-1,195	-1,573	-1,533	75	1,179	-2,979	Egypt
-1,612	-3,722	1,030	3,941	1,866	859	2,491	-652	7,355	6,484	4,300	-4,049	-491	-2,869	-5,910	328	....	Iran, I.R. of
1,599	876	-758	-504	1,888	-532	463	493	911	-520	2,183	1,234	5,624	6,614	10,709	708	2,822	Israel
444	76	219	82	493	498	80	648	2,419	698	-232	133	87	34	245	-550	....	Jordan
-4,309	-6,311	-4,253	-5,699	-6,408	-6,530	-7,861	-4,784	27,754	2,302	-3,977	-3,174	-5,156	-7,131	-7,928	-1,956	-4,144	Kuwait
-143	-265	456	389	45	434	1,318	-1,043	474	367	-350	266	49	-10	-6	-123	-789	Libya
-143	16	132	427	-676	-158	18	-971	793	898	132	144	369	9	577	2,200	....	Oman
15,343	16,921	12,222	4,176	12,413	5,822	6,030	-1,224	27,595	12,076	18,763	10,341	6,542	5,069	343	12,431	4,516	Saudi Arabia
699	1,010	772	565	377	119	-1,288	-1,726	-627	21	507	1,357	418	798	-29	342	....	Syrian Arab Republic
343	198	237	194	510	408	569	....	....	....	....	....	....	....	....	....	....	Yemen Arab Rep.
187	236	141	118	82	378	401	....	....	....	....	....	....	....	....	....	....	Yemen, P.D. Rep.
....	....	....	....	....	....	....	-996	-30	-157	135	-1,018	-657	-475	-180	-208	....	Yemen, Republic of
3,776	-51	20	5,793	1,549	3,558	4,129	-5,070	-916	1,533	1,931	4,093	5,004	3,018	3,578	9,809	4,388	Middle East not spec

Balance of Payments

Capital and Financial Account

Including Net Errors and Omissions, but Excluding Reserve Assets,
Use of Fund Credit, and Exceptional Financing

	1983	1984	1985	1986	1987	1988	1989	1990	1991	1992	1993	1994	1995	1996	1997	1998	1999
							Expressed in Millions of US Dollars										
Western Hemisphere	−21,964	−10,426	−16,413	−12,219	−12,276	−19,464	−18,615	−4,987	23,255	48,227	68,750	41,386	29,644	66,219	82,932	70,726	31,560
Antigua and Barbuda	3	−1	20	128	109	48	82	30	38	35	−12	26	14	29	....	....	....
Argentina	−2,838	202	106	712	−12	204	−8,332	−5,169	−159	7,404	19,155	10,283	2,770	9,859	15,328	18,392	14,097
Aruba	....	....	....	70	35	44	68	170	232	−21	−8	−84	43	43	177	70	336
Bahamas, The	111	139	21	−54	−5	66	59	48	192	−64	−30	51	143	256	529	1,115	737
Barbados	43	−40	−37	7	22	−10	−71	−31	−17	−115	−49	−96	−47	−17	67	50	....
Belize	....	—	−7	—	2	24	35	—	9	29	34	36	21	27	33	46	69
Bolivia	−486	15	−101	35	−5	11	−34	38	115	402	472	1	395	672	654	777	514
Brazil	−4,417	−5,098	−9,199	−8,116	−10,557	−9,961	−12,222	−5,702	−3,974	4,550	6,870	7,751	31,105	31,644	22,240	17,527	....
Chile	−3,156	110	−1,464	−1,996	−886	−1,025	1,209	2,807	1,356	3,505	2,982	4,736	2,488	6,014	6,912	2,004	−678
Colombia	1,164	1,020	1,963	909	66	409	635	68	−586	374	2,567	3,778	4,619	6,558	6,228	3,882	666
Costa Rica	−71	−226	−144	−204	−315	−39	22	−47	262	395	362	141	574	197	82	−44	....
Dominica	−3	13	6	14	15	11	46	49	38	29	24	35	58	42	35	22	....
Dominican Republic	−82	262	199	253	221	20	64	−195	414	644	−11	−228	329	173	254	346	....
Ecuador	−1,777	−1,310	−954	−1,479	420	−607	−401	706	866	146	1,217	1,020	576	171	977	1,762	−1,281
El Salvador	36	−19	26	−115	−53	−55	259	288	64	61	181	131	410	334	268	387	....
Grenada	15	−4	4	21	33	23	35	49	49	40	45	26	41	58	....	....	....
Guatemala	151	−100	−81	−262	115	76	283	−10	815	692	901	632	420	666	863	1,275	901
Guyana	−73	−39	−42	....	....	....	....	−13	....	77	104	119	92	....	....	....	....
Haiti	83	83	93	49	37	41	49	−13	104	−14	−11	−26	224	87	77	73	....
Honduras	115	276	136	73	63	−48	−187	−124	54	51	−25	273	160	257	454	331	....
Jamaica	−48	469	203	−60	426	31	111	442	219	220	294	265	101	383	142	299	....
Mexico	−6,391	−2,034	−3,529	896	−113	−7,688	5,614	9,669	22,861	26,187	30,632	12,463	−14,735	6,190	21,451	18,918	18,294
Netherlands Antilles	−114	−214	−331	47	20	−42	−82	14	−36	49	43	22	53	....	....	....	....
Nicaragua	−199	145	175	−378	33	295	−144	−310	−598	−478	−375	−830	−538	−299	262	97	199
Panama	−256	84	−204	93	−1,076	−1,726	−944	−345	−87	80	−212	−378	38	569	947	748	1,185
Paraguay	195	304	112	158	417	−18	−264	−273	148	38	−16	575	341	355	42	207	....
Peru	−186	−1,336	−1,696	−1,352	−1,802	−1,237	−2,040	−1,071	161	818	895	3,494	3,001	3,949	3,682	1,649	....
St. Kitts and Nevis	16	6	9	12	17	27	45	47	36	26	33	29	....	....	....	....	....
St. Lucia	5	14	14	18	23	20	69	63	80	62	54	46	38	73	....	....	....
St. Vincent & Grens.	3	6	3	22	15	19	31	29	40	30	43	58	41	36	....	....	....
Suriname	97	47	4	−34	−152	−123	−294	−49	55	−47	−31	−24	24	....	....	....	....
Trinidad and Tobago	74	−226	−253	−310	−31	−141	−138	−637	−272	−243	45	−32	−210	133	807	724	....
Uruguay	−3	44	164	240	189	−46	−74	−54	37	147	437	547	440	386	687	411	575
Venezuela, Rep. Bol.	−3,981	−3,015	−1,628	−1,637	455	1,937	−2,047	−5,803	688	3,087	2,117	−3,485	−3,458	−2,676	−392	−382	....
Memorandum Items																	
Oil Exporting Ctys	16,011	4,926	5,754	10,181	7,413	3,401	2,080	−20,353	61,889	18,219	17,816	−2,415	−228	−8,149	−22,765	9,189	−6,837
Non-Oil Develop.Ctys	−7,777	−4,990	−3,882	3,024	−6,276	−33,548	−2,093	8,652	46,504	70,164	137,312	98,262	145,288	176,861	131,592	15,743	28,410

Balance of Payments

Overall Balance

Excluding Reserves Assets, Use of Fund Credit, and Exceptional Financing

Expressed in Millions of US Dollars

1983	1984	1985	1986	1987	1988	1989	1990	1991	1992	1993	1994	1995	1996	1997	1998	1999	
−34,105	−8,314	−20,034	1,995	119,714	41	16,904	32,274	13,233	11,538	73,291	67,706	127,847	163,914	64,156	−35,112	137,712	**All Countries**
4,432	9,736	−3,482	22,772	107,137	38,085	26,883	54,875	−13,211	−6,393	28,435	35,486	78,154	77,160	23,765	−18,159	60,994	**Industrial Countries**
1,196	3,126	3,835	−310	−9,147	3,915	25,287	2,230	−5,756	−3,927	1,376	−5,350	9,747	−6,667	1,012	6,731	−8,724	United States
−7	−1,809	−3,270	−419	3,313	8,150	693	1,139	−1,848	−4,786	904	−392	2,711	5,498	−2,393	4,996	5,933	Canada
3,030	−1,294	−2,301	703	374	5,279	601	1,740	−324	−4,726	−42	−960	396	2,471	2,873	−2,040	6,705	Australia
1,550	2,120	−500	15,130	38,050	17,560	−13,050	−9,090	−8,389	620	27,473	25,265	58,611	35,139	6,567	−6,164	76,256	Japan
−1,114	−1,546	−2,037	−2,612	−2,248	−2,921	−1,217	179	−1,511	131	−74	733	384	1,772	−1,442	−484	....	New Zealand
																	Euro Area
−528	67	15	643	333	491	990	−15	835	2,588	2,201	834	1,391	1,075	−3,053	3,503	−2,170	Austria
265	305	−197	29	2,434	861	312	404	584	569	−2,122	219	243	593	1,056	−2,095	−1,867	Belgium-Luxembourg
−227	1,824	583	−2,283	4,033	258	−1,068	3,931	−1,886	−2,150	291	4,714	−372	−3,036	2,304	296	−97	Finland
3,605	2,934	2,696	1,181	−2,601	−5,159	−857	10,947	−5,194	−1,576	−5,006	2,448	712	239	5,940	19,815	−1,780	France
−1,952	−348	2,229	5,426	21,495	−15,596	2,860	7,253	−6,185	37,176	−14,199	−2,036	7,224	−1,195	−3,756	4,015	−14,113	Germany
188	−43	48	−94	886	592	−937	626	463	−2,166	2,660	−176	2,339	−52	−1,109	3,007	−3,116	Ireland
5,875	2,560	−7,585	2,348	5,470	8,417	11,358	11,623	−6,718	−23,992	−3,135	1,575	2,804	11,907	13,150	−21,472	−8,852	Italy
−157	−12	771	−330	2,693	1,568	507	268	506	6,118	6,641	500	−1,912	−5,694	−2,707	−2,339	−5,094	Netherlands
−1,053	−95	707	−111	1,777	867	4,654	3,542	5,713	−156	−2,848	−1,430	−300	723	1,246	508	202	Portugal
−265	4,817	−2,275	2,344	12,706	8,416	4,716	7,188	14,307	−17,809	−5,203	36	−6,414	24,279	11,756	−14,355	−22,794	Spain
1,357	−371	1,532	−1,329	3,732	1,436	−3,838	3,385	−2,903	4,075	−567	−1,851	2,498	3,563	6,532	−4,239	9,437	Denmark
200	−202	−396	650	974	937	−348	280	2,204	−374	3,439	6,309	−23	4,215	−4,515	....	....	Greece
11	−15	64	99	−18	1	55	74	9	79	−59	−150	4	153	−44	32	75	Iceland
....	....	....	....	....	....	....	....	....	....	....	....	....	....	....	....	....	Norway
−5,481	−5,834	−4,651	177	762	938	1,254	7,552	−63	6,953	2,530	2,381	−1,664	−6,386	−6,712	3,254	....	Sweden
−199	1,491	1,228	1,091	3,213	−2,382	1,369	1,165	995	4,360	483	1,062	53	2,747	2,159	897	....	Switzerland
−1,764	−1,007	2,570	3,650	19,128	4,593	−7,422	42	4,701	−6,667	5,437	1,500	−853	−654	−3,901	−260	−1,034	United Kingdom
−38,537	−18,050	−16,552	−20,777	12,577	−38,045	−9,978	−22,602	26,444	17,930	44,856	32,220	49,693	86,754	40,391	−16,953	76,719	**Developing Countries**
−5,403	−4,067	−3,213	−4,687	−7,971	−11,991	−7,889	−1,727	−5,587	−12,136	−9,327	−10,080	−13,942	−6,186	−241	−11,279	−3,273	**Africa**
−421	−333	1,020	−1,498	−352	−959	−774	−10	1,047	....	....	....	....	....	....	....	....	Algeria
....	....	−6	−259	−332	−925	−930	−1,209	−1,500	−1,138	−1,320	−1,028	−1,239	2,761	....	....	....	Angola
−37	−23	−29	−79	−52	48	−130	17	−155	46	−88	63	−132	−161	70	....	....	Benin
124	124	254	307	562	382	576	307	374	405	397	135	207	511	635	63	....	Botswana
37	36	6	24	10	18	−135	7	8	20	2	−7	....	....	....	....	....	Burkina Faso
....	....	16	29	−3	7	38	−3	33	26	16	35	37	−35	10	−19	−1	Burundi
117	−86	59	−81	−471	−163	−128	−871	−731	−1,305	−885	−551	15	....	....	....	....	Cameroon
3	−5	14	−1	3	−1	15	−7	−16	23	15	22	−32	22	—	11	....	Cape Verde
−13	—	−25	−4	−12	−13	−17	−21	−40	−37	−14	13	....	....	....	....	....	Central African Rep.
9	17	−24	−19	—	−34	30	−23	−20	−43	−48	6	....	....	....	....	....	Chad
2	−6	6	3	9	−4	5	−5	−26	−6	8	5	−10	....	....	....	....	Comoros
−32	−61	−81	−398	−488	−467	−403	−364	−458	−430	−420	−155	−609	−350	−548	....	....	Congo, Republic of
−701	−477	−169	−392	−924	−1,425	−1,311	−1,447	−1,328	−1,417	−1,237	−20	−254	−997	−593	−639	....	Côte d'Ivoire
....	....	....	....	−26	−17	−10	−6	−14	−16	−12	1	−24	....	....	....	....	Djibouti
....	....	....	....	....	....	....	....	....	−28	−10	−18	−12	−5	....	....	....	Equatorial Guinea
−53	−57	162	114	−107	−22	45	−198	−356	−264	32	—	100	−467	−429	−383	....	Ethiopia
−89	13	−61	−195	−135	−1	−96	−269	−223	−442	−452	−173	−421	....	....	....	....	Gabon
−21	−16	−6	−22	11	25	3	4	16	20	11	6	1	14	7	....	....	Gambia, The
−181	36	14	−61	140	181	157	105	137	−123	53	172	251	−20	27	108	−48	Ghana
....	....	....	−112	−97	−121	−185	−97	−158	−174	−97	−124	−72	−60	−131	−158	−79	Guinea
−18	−12	8	−33	−31	−41	−71	−32	−75	−52	−61	−55	−41	−43	−15	....	....	Guinea-Bissau
98	61	−52	137	−25	−44	122	−93	−44	−257	412	62	−142	387	120	74	....	Kenya
26	9	6	13	1	−6	−8	17	42	50	102	121	98	117	141	116	....	Lesotho
−128	−153	−203	−294	−300	....	....	....	....	....	....	....	....	....	....	....	....	Liberia
−269	−204	−167	−116	−162	−117	−161	−278	−292	−278	−334	−276	−330	−94	−16	−299	....	Madagascar
−98	4	−26	−1	45	60	−52	29	16	−47	24	−35	....	....	....	....	....	Malawi
−32	—	−27	−50	−14	18	1	−65	30	−138	−97	−65	−52	29	−9	....	....	Mali
−35	−14	−31	−29	−132	−63	−6	−72	16	17	−282	−105	−6	4	28	43	....	Mauritania
−31	−44	−3	121	219	185	146	232	191	43	7	−43	109	48	−35	−65	190	Mauritius
−166	−163	−32	331	298	264	21	1,697	956	791	436	483	−1,895	−673	−988	−719	....	Morocco
−301	−396	−366	28	−1,049	−371	−400	−398	−458	−523	−647	−566	−387	−424	−478	−393	....	Mozambique
....	....	....	....	....	....	....	37	−12	−7	91	75	24	23	68	56	....	Namibia
−14	−31	−50	−120	−78	−67	−11	−90	−60	−95	−24	−76	−18	....	....	....	....	Niger
−2,887	−971	−1,209	−1,059	−4,539	−5,129	−2,667	1,041	−1,523	−5,638	−1,911	−1,938	−2,774	−761	15	−2,873	−3,538	Nigeria
−18	8	2	30	−11	−50	−67	−23	65	−4	−50	4	53	20	31	−128	....	Rwanda
−7	−7	−11	−11	−4	−4	−6	−9	....	....	....	....	....	....	....	....	....	São Tomé & Príncipe
−110	−98	−91	−35	−96	−105	−173	−137	−180	−125	−141	23	−33	−27	106	....	....	Senegal
−2	−2	—	−1	4	−4	−1	4	2	−4	−10	−12	−14	−13	−5	....	....	Seychelles
−93	−96	−74	−97	−53	−72	−48	−21	−15	16	8	−59	−46	....	....	....	....	Sierra Leone
−78	−27	−12	−97	−98	−182	−190	....	....	....	....	....	....	....	....	....	....	Somalia
301	−581	−514	508	1,347	−1,379	−86	1,416	1,147	503	−1,341	683	906	−1,272	4,596	920	3,955	South Africa
−223	−118	−421	−201	−343	−287	−193	−244	−273	−159	42	19	63	38	18	73	115	Sudan
12	−8	−5	8	21	12	51	11	14	92	−64	−13	30	15	25	50	22	Swaziland
−88	−221	−487	−353	−292	−384	−327	−126	−262	−204	−575	−419	−359	−254	−297	−509	....	Tanzania
−38	−21	−3	−43	−130	−48	−28	−44	−48	−160	−190	−97	−194	−25	13	−17	....	Togo
35	−102	−226	−215	186	417	101	333	−18	191	67	527	97	442	386	−173	684	Tunisia
−81	67	33	−27	−54	−37	−85	−42	−32	24	−125	−62	−51	−9	−35	....	....	Uganda
−21	−89	−181	−134	−242	−232	−106	222	−179	....	....	....	....	....	....	....	....	Zambia
−174	−46	82	55	124	102	−47	86	45	−195	226	−86	....	....	....	....	....	Zimbabwe
−352	−428	−336	−566	−712	−1,046	−612	−1,121	−1,229	−1,147	−1,136	−1,312	−1,289	−936	−959	−1,091	−1,104	Africa not specified

Balance of Payments

Overall Balance

Excluding Reserves Assets, Use of Fund Credit, and Exceptional Financing

Expressed in Millions of US Dollars

	1983	1984	1985	1986	1987	1988	1989	1990	1991	1992	1993	1994	1995	1996	1997	1998	1999
Asia	5,244	8,344	9,031	25,674	42,348	16,554	14,527	22,551	39,855	30,477	43,407	66,956	46,193	66,195	12,653	35,267	105,905
Afghanistan, I.S. of	-55	65	26	-19	11	-26	-20	....	....	....	....	....	....	....	....	....	....
Bangladesh	308	-32	-84	84	155	132	-348	224	434	635	698	691	-512	-414	-136	288	-192
Bhutan	....	....	....	....	....	....	....	....	....	....	....	....	....	....	....	....	....
Cambodia	....	....	....	....	....	....	....	....	....	13	21	36	26	72	34	16	51
China,P.R.: Mainland	4,142	138	-2,440	-2,048	4,783	2,374	-479	12,047	14,537	-2,060	1,769	30,453	22,469	31,705	35,857	6,248	8,652
China,P.R.:Hong Kong	....	....	....	....	....	....	....	....	....	....	....	....	....	....	....	-6,896	9,505
Fiji	-5	10	-4	29	-46	112	21	65	40	85	-14	23	93	78	-25	5	....
India	-752	1,070	-397	-409	133	-16	237	-1,941	-235	1,072	4,211	10,391	-733	3,958	5,321	3,071	6,664
Indonesia	183	981	510	-1,003	630	-113	495	2,251	1,528	2,070	594	784	1,573	4,503	-8,137	-3,693	1,973
Kiribati	-5	-4	....	-2	-7	-3	-5	-7	-11	-17	-5	-6	....	....	....	....	....
Korea	-124	385	211	34	2,100	9,327	3,639	-1,208	-1,147	3,724	3,009	4,614	7,039	1,416	-22,979	25,930	....
Lao People's Dem.Rep	....	-133	-136	-130	-152	-104	-164	-126	-125	-122	-137	-178	-151	-158	-369	-254	....
Malaysia	-13	492	1,148	1,461	1,139	-458	1,235	1,951	1,236	6,618	11,350	-3,160	-1,767	2,516	-3,859	....	....
Maldives	-4	-5	2	-4	1	14	2	....	-1	5	—	6	17	28	22	20	10
Mongolia	-4	14	25	15	76	1	130	-102	-130	-82	15	6	32	-87	7	-53	-19
Myanmar	-24	-9	-15	49	38	80	151	9	-46	94	-77	45	-32	-25	31	60	-44
Nepal	-8	-21	-93	-33	64	-6	-42	20	163	155	66	63	15	31	169	280	176
Pakistan	546	-963	-419	193	80	261	-194	-314	-155	392	428	1,343	-1,204	-780	538	....	....
Papua New Guinea	97	49	-1	3	2	-53	-59	22	-409	-326	-253	-170	-39	202	-177	-221	125
Philippines	-3,496	-448	838	1,134	-58	674	300	-45	1,755	1,689	336	2,327	1,235	4,338	-3,094	1,279	3,659
Samoa	7	7	5	7	9	10	11	11	-2	-13	-9	-4	2	7	11	6	....
Singapore	1,059	1,524	1,337	538	1,095	1,659	2,738	5,431	4,197	6,100	7,578	4,736	8,599	7,396	7,940	2,966	4,194
Solomon Islands	4	-11	-15	-18	-7	-5	-13	-14	-13	14	-2	-2	-1	18	9	17	....
Sri Lanka	-3	247	-88	-92	-53	-104	52	116	324	202	768	308	239	9	307	224	....
Thailand	-320	529	105	714	945	2,596	5,029	3,235	4,618	3,029	3,907	4,169	7,159	2,167	-18,250	-3,222	1,266
Tonga	5	5	1	-5	6	2	-6	6	1	1	-2	....	....	....	....	....	....
Vanuatu	1	-6	—	5	-1	-5	8	5	-3	1	3	-6	5	-5	-2	8	....
Asia not specified	3,170	3,841	6,246	23,020	27,744	-1,584	-1,005	-4,042	9,618	1,440	1,393	4,228	-4,016	793	7,861	4,861	18,616
Europe	-3,374	-2,814	-7,382	-2,146	-2,343	-5,549	2,796	-22,840	-12,363	-13,991	-10,028	-13,434	19,329	-11,555	2,950	-16,591	-6,070
Albania	-41	-12	-18	-1	12	134	325	-238	-224	-36	49	7	21	56	40	52	107
Armenia	....	....	....	....	....	....	....	....	....	....	13	-3	30	-45	50	1	5
Azerbaijan	—	—	—	—	—	—	—	....	....	....	....	....	58	-85	139	-59	133
Belarus	....	....	....	....	....	....	....	....	....	....	-138	-317	-78	-214	65	-415	87
Bulgaria	212	417	298	-885	-497	657	-434	-4,454	-274	269	-322	-216	445	-739	1,145	-94	87
Croatia	....	....	....	....	....	....	....	....	....	....	188	277	40	1,017	390	161	460
Cyprus	42	96	-30	159	64	71	228	294	-66	-225	145	247	-363	-60	-47	-83	639
Czech Republic	....	....	....	....	....	....	....	....	....	....	3,041	3,474	7,453	-825	-1,758	1,890	1,639
Czechoslovakia	36	166	-112	260	260	207	563	-1,127	789	-422	....	....	....	....	....	....	....
Estonia	....	....	....	....	....	....	....	....	....	58	165	17	84	106	216	37	119
Hungary	-125	66	536	132	-281	158	172	-413	1,795	770	2,545	-475	5,399	-1,244	-175	951	2,335
Kazakhstan	....	....	....	....	....	....	....	....	....	....	....	....	299	159	548	-443	253
Kyrgyz Republic	....	....	....	....	....	....	....	....	....	....	....	-30	5	-81	-20	46	-24
Latvia	....	....	....	....	....	....	....	....	....	37	298	57	-33	211	102	63	165
Lithuania	....	....	....	....	....	....	....	....	....	....	208	113	168	-5	224	427	-179
Macedonia, FYR	....	....	....	....	....	....	....	....	....	....	....	....	....	-95	-119	32	119
Malta	104	32	-67	-5	-5	35	14	-96	-79	45	135	383	-307	-85	7	191	239
Moldova	....	....	....	....	....	....	....	....	....	....	....	13	-175	-145	-182	-342	-122
Poland	-4,918	-4,270	-2,340	-5,201	-3,606	-11,035	-3,315	-5,502	-7,074	-4,330	-3,228	1,006	9,835	3,637	3,588	5,695	....
Romania	10	128	-317	612	1,041	-285	1,252	-1,494	-677	-138	-439	171	-480	-582	1,459	-643	234
Russia	....	....	....	....	....	....	....	....	....	....	....	-18,969	-8,298	-17,190	-6,555	-21,323	-1,813
Slovak Republic	....	....	....	....	....	....	....	....	....	....	14	1,205	1,791	370	99	-478	777
Slovenia	....	....	....	....	....	....	....	....	....	633	125	650	239	590	1,288	158	-81
Turkey	-632	-1,477	-784	540	580	1,153	2,710	943	-1,199	1,484	308	203	4,660	4,544	3,343	441	....
Turkmenistan	....	....	....	....	....	....	....	....	....	....	....	....	....	....	8	398	....
Ukraine	....	....	....	....	....	....	....	....	....	....	....	-1,200	-1,624	-603	-703	-3,457	-184
Yugoslavia, SFR	-277	103	159	836	238	1,953	1,931	1,368	-2,797	....	....	....	....	....	....	....	....
Europe not specified	230	234	235	271	300	316	321	210	2,546	596	154	87	507	-316	-661	-26	66
Middle East	-4,904	-7,599	4,160	-9,944	2,719	-7,312	7,791	-13,733	-444	-804	-2,884	-1,829	5,656	10,965	7,311	-6,132	3,307
Bahrain	-109	-10	357	-176	-343	93	-188	796	-523	-90	-113	-48	169	-6	103	-17	25
Egypt	87	-247	-200	-31	315	-102	-533	-10,224	-2,073	3,360	18	-1,164	-1,827	-1,725	-635	-1,387	-4,614
Iran, I.R. of	-1,254	-4,136	554	-1,214	-224	-1,010	2,300	-325	-2,093	-20	85	907	2,867	2,363	-3,697	-1,569	....
Israel	-500	-547	399	993	661	-1,170	676	654	-403	-1,499	-378	-2,153	427	1,180	7,195	-134	221
Jordan	53	-189	-42	43	141	204	465	421	2,025	-137	-861	-265	-171	-188	275	-536	....
Kuwait	1,002	117	545	-83	-1,847	-1,928	1,275	-897	1,276	1,851	-1,479	53	-140	-24	7	259	918
Libya	-1,786	-1,721	2,362	224	-999	-1,392	292	1,158	255	1,759	-1,712	295	2,047	1,467	1,869	-513	687
Oman	351	319	122	-613	108	-467	324	135	543	300	-1,058	-661	-432	189	537	-770	....
Saudi Arabia	-1,509	-1,480	-709	-7,619	2,640	-1,519	-3,508	-5,376	49	-5,664	1,495	-146	1,217	5,749	648	-719	2,815
Syrian Arab Republic	-145	216	-186	61	79	-32	-66	36	72	76	304	566	785	879	454	401	....
Yemen Arab Rep.	-216	-102	-50	69	58	-286	-10	....	....	....	....	....	....	....	....	....	....
Yemen, P.D. Rep.	3	-17	-90	-58	-48	....	-26	-16	....	....	....	....	....	....	....	....	....
Yemen, Republic of	....	....	....	....	....	....	....	-257	-694	-1,248	-1,113	-653	-475	-368	-129	-436	....
Middle East not spec	-881	198	1,097	-1,540	2,178	324	6,781	146	1,123	508	1,927	1,438	1,189	1,450	684	-712	1,229

Overall Balance

Excluding Reserves Assets, Use of Fund Credit, and Exceptional Financing

Expressed in Millions of US Dollars

1983	1984	1985	1986	1987	1988	1989	1990	1991	1992	1993	1994	1995	1996	1997	1998	1999	
−30,100	−11,912	−19,149	−29,673	−22,176	−29,747	−27,202	−6,853	4,983	14,385	23,688	−9,393	−7,542	27,336	17,719	−18,218	−23,150	Western Hemisphere
....	....	....	....	....	....	....	3	....	1	1	....	....	....	....	....	....	Anguilla
−6	—	−3	10	−2	3	....	−1	5	16	−12	8	14	−11	....	....	....	Antigua and Barbuda
−5,274	−2,293	−846	−2,147	−4,247	−1,368	−9,637	−617	−806	1,883	11,125	−709	−2,215	3,338	3,374	4,118	1,945	Argentina
....	....	....	51	13	—	22	12	23	23	33	−3	43	−26	−18	51	3	Aruba
11	39	19	−31	−60	−1	−25	12	13	−28	19	9	−3	−8	57	119	65	Bahamas, The
—	−24	14	14	4	34	−46	−41	−44	25	20	38	42	86	17	−6	....	Barbados
....	−5	2	12	12	22	16	15	−16	—	−14	−4	4	21	1	−14	−8	Belize
−627	−164	−387	−354	−437	−294	−304	−161	−147	−132	−34	−90	92	268	101	−42	....	Bolivia
−11,251	−5,065	−9,479	−13,427	−12,009	−5,805	−11,220	−9,525	−5,424	10,639	6,890	6,598	12,969	8,396	−8,251	−16,302	....	Brazil
−4,273	−2,001	−2,877	−3,187	−1,621	−1,256	519	2,323	1,257	2,547	428	3,151	1,139	2,504	3,184	−2,135	−758	Chile
−1,839	−381	154	1,292	402	193	434	610	1,763	1,274	464	182	−5	1,730	278	−1,390	−313	Colombia
−384	−477	−435	−365	−692	−343	−458	−541	163	14	−258	−103	216	−69	−132	−505	....	Costa Rica
−4	6	−1	7	8	−1	—	5	4	3	1	−3	8	2	2	4	....	Dominica
−500	98	92	70	−143	1	−263	−474	257	−64	−544	−511	146	−40	91	10	....	Dominican Republic
−1,892	−1,583	−878	−2,061	−767	−1,287	−1,116	346	158	24	539	339	−189	255	263	−407	−326	Ecuador
−111	−208	−163	−132	−122	−184	−111	27	−148	−134	59	113	148	165	364	303	....	El Salvador
—	−2	6	2	4	−5	−1	3	2	8	1	5	6	....	....	....	....	Grenada
−73	−477	−327	−279	−328	−338	−84	−243	631	−14	200	6	−152	214	230	235	−125	Guatemala
−231	−138	−139	....	....	....	....	....	....	−62	−36	−6	−43	....	....	....	....	Guyana
−29	−20	−2	4	6	—	−13	−35	13	−6	−23	−50	137	−50	30	34	....	Haiti
−117	−98	−172	−152	−183	−209	−368	−310	−160	−247	−333	−70	−41	−79	182	−2	....	Honduras
−387	153	−71	−78	300	78	−172	130	−21	248	110	358	27	271	−170	44	....	Jamaica
−525	2,149	−2,729	−481	4,134	−10,062	−211	2,218	7,973	1,745	7,232	−17,199	−16,312	3,863	13,997	3,193	4,278	Mexico
....	....	....	1	1	....	....	3	−4	....	....	2	....	....	....	....	....	Montserrat
−26	−39	72	98	−30	33	−44	−30	−42	59	44	−76	139	....	....	....	....	Netherlands Antilles
−706	−452	−596	−1,068	−657	−420	−506	−695	−1,133	−1,312	−1,019	−1,529	−1,101	−799	−295	−401	−453	Nicaragua
−57	−118	−128	−6	−531	−1,004	−832	−136	−328	−187	−308	−362	−331	267	343	−463	−148	Panama
−53	−14	−140	−206	−73	−228	−8	117	233	−19	43	301	61	−140	−196	100	....	Paraguay
−1,061	−1,571	−1,594	−2,746	−3,867	−3,056	−2,610	−2,455	−1,397	−1,299	−1,432	827	−1,312	306	400	−2,151	....	Peru
1	2	....	3	....	....	6	—	1	10	3	2	....	....	....	....	....	St. Kitts and Nevis
—	—	1	11	9	2	6	6	8	7	4	−2	5	−7	....	....	....	St. Lucia
—	5	6	12	−5	2	1	5	−4	10	−1	—	—	—	....	....	....	St. Vincent & Grens.
−185	−91	−15	−71	−16	−9	—	18	−78	−22	13	34	97	....	....	....	....	Suriname
−873	−693	−301	−722	−256	−229	−177	−178	−277	−104	159	186	84	238	194	80	....	Trinidad and Tobago
−65	−86	66	282	48	−24	60	132	80	138	193	109	228	152	400	−64	−30	Uruguay
446	1,636	1,699	−3,882	−935	−3,872	114	2,476	2,424	−662	124	−944	−1,444	6,238	3,075	−2,944	....	Venezuela, Rep. Bol.

Memorandum Items

1983	1984	1985	1986	1987	1988	1989	1990	1991	1992	1993	1994	1995	1996	1997	1998	1999	
−6,129	−4,214	5,631	−17,656	−2,739	−15,410	5,083	1,030	3,555	−5,482	−2,775	−6,615	−2,713	17,420	−4,864	−15,070	12,471	Oil Exporting Ctys
−32,407	−13,835	−22,183	−3,121	15,316	−22,634	−15,062	−23,631	22,889	23,413	47,631	38,836	52,407	69,334	45,255	−1,883	64,248	Non-Oil Develop.Ctys

Balance of Payments

Exports of Goods and Services

	1983	1984	1985	1986	1987	1988	1989	1990	1991	1992	1993	1994	1995	1996	1997	1998	1999
								As percent of GDP									
All Countries																	
Industrial Countries																	
United States	7.5	7.4	6.9	6.9	7.3	8.4	8.9	9.2	9.7	9.7	9.7	10.0	10.7	10.9	11.3	10.7	10.4
Canada	25.6	28.7	28.5	28.0	27.0	26.9	25.8	26.1	25.3	27.0	30.1	34.0	37.3	38.4	39.5	41.2	43.1
Australia	14.1	14.7	16.3	15.9	16.4	16.2	15.8	16.2	17.1	17.7	18.3	18.1	19.0	19.3	20.5	19.8	18.7
Japan	14.1	15.1	14.7	11.5	10.5	10.2	10.7	10.9	10.4	10.3	9.5	9.5	9.6	10.2	11.4	11.5	10.7
New Zealand	28.8	30.8	31.5	26.4	25.9	26.1	26.6	27.1	29.1	30.9	30.5	30.9	29.9	29.1	28.6	30.3	....
Euro Area																	
Austria	36.2	38.1	40.2	36.4	35.3	37.6	39.7	39.9	39.6	38.4	36.7	37.4	38.2	39.7	42.7	45.1	45.5
Belgium-Luxembourg	68.4	71.7	69.4	64.3	64.4	66.2	68.4	66.6	64.8	62.9	61.3	65.9	64.9	66.1	70.9	71.3	77.3
Finland	30.2	30.6	29.2	27.0	26.0	24.7	23.7	23.1	22.0	26.5	32.5	35.4	37.1	37.5	39.0	39.0	37.7
France	23.9	25.6	25.4	22.4	21.8	22.1	23.6	23.5	23.7	23.7	22.4	22.7	23.4	23.5	26.0	26.8	26.6
Germany	30.3	32.5	34.4	31.6	30.4	31.0	33.0	31.5	26.5	24.7	23.8	24.6	25.5	28.1	29.1	29.4	....
Ireland	51.9	59.0	60.2	52.7	56.3	60.1	63.5	56.8	57.4	60.2	64.9	69.6	75.2	75.9	78.3	111.8	....
Italy	21.8	22.5	22.8	20.1	19.3	18.8	19.8	20.0	18.6	19.2	22.3	23.9	26.9	25.9	26.5	26.2	24.9
Luxembourg	....	....	....	....	....	....	....	....	....	....	....	....	96.7	97.3	104.5	109.7	110.3
Netherlands	58.5	63.4	64.1	53.6	51.9	54.3	58.2	56.6	56.5	54.7	53.4	55.2	56.1	57.3	60.6	59.4	56.7
Portugal	29.5	35.9	37.1	28.6	29.7	29.3	31.3	31.2	27.6	25.2	27.2	28.8	30.8	30.7	31.8	32.4	....
Spain	20.5	22.7	22.7	19.8	19.3	18.9	18.3	17.0	16.9	17.3	19.3	22.3	23.9	25.3	28.4	29.2	27.6
Denmark	36.7	37.5	37.8	32.7	31.8	33.4	35.5	36.7	38.1	37.1	35.7	36.5	36.4	36.8	36.9	36.3	37.6
Greece	20.1	21.2	20.8	19.8	21.7	17.2	16.3	15.7	15.9	15.0	14.5	14.7	13.2	12.3	12.3	....	....
Iceland	39.5	38.8	41.5	39.5	35.5	32.8	35.5	34.4	31.5	30.6	32.9	35.0	35.7	36.3	36.1	34.8	33.8
Norway	42.0	43.5	43.4	34.8	32.8	33.4	38.4	40.8	40.4	38.1	38.3	38.4	38.0	40.6	41.3	37.5	....
Sweden	36.2	36.9	36.0	32.7	32.8	32.9	32.7	30.7	28.9	28.9	33.3	35.7	39.8	38.8	42.5	43.4	....
Switzerland	42.4	47.2	47.8	44.0	41.1	42.5	45.5	42.4	40.4	41.5	40.9	40.3	40.1	41.1	47.0	46.0	....
United Kingdom	26.5	28.4	29.1	25.7	25.5	23.0	23.8	24.2	23.2	23.7	25.4	26.5	28.4	29.2	28.5	26.6	25.7
Developing Countries																	
Africa																	
Algeria	27.5	25.3	23.4	13.7	14.9	15.0	19.5	21.7	27.9	....	....	....	....	....	....	....	....
Angola	....	....	....	....	—	—	—	—	....	....	....	....	....	....	....	....	....
Benin	16.7	26.8	32.1	28.5	29.3	18.7	19.2	19.7	27.7	23.3	25.6	36.1	30.6	29.6	25.2	....	....
Botswana	71.7	73.3	83.6	73.9	111.2	82.5	67.0	57.5	56.1	49.1	51.3	50.4	54.8	55.7	63.3	48.1	....
Burkina Faso	15.1	18.8	10.7	9.7	12.2	11.9	9.6	12.1	11.6	9.6	10.1	14.7	....	....	....	....	....
Burundi	....	....	10.8	11.4	9.5	12.5	9.6	7.8	10.5	8.7	9.1	8.9	10.5	4.5	7.9	6.3	6.3
Cameroon	26.3	27.4	24.5	21.3	16.7	19.1	21.7	20.5	20.5	19.7	16.4	26.2	23.3	....	....	....	....
Cape Verde	26.0	22.5	21.7	18.7	18.9	15.0	....	....	....	....	....	....	....	....	....	....	....
Central African Rep.	24.1	23.4	25.3	19.4	16.4	15.5	17.3	15.2	12.8	11.4	14.2	21.0	....	....	....	....	....
Chad	12.6	16.7	10.9	13.4	14.8	15.9	14.8	16.8	14.0	12.6	13.7	16.1	....	....	....	....	....
Comoros	20.9	9.6	18.6	18.2	15.2	18.5	17.8	14.3	20.3	18.4	19.7	20.5	20.4	....	....	....	....
Congo, Republic of	55.0	61.5	56.4	42.0	42.4	42.3	52.8	53.2	44.3	42.5	43.8	58.0	59.3	68.2	78.7	....	....
Côte d'Ivoire	36.4	43.8	45.3	39.9	34.5	31.7	32.7	32.4	31.6	32.2	30.7	44.4	43.4	46.2	45.7	43.9	....
Djibouti	....	....	....	....	....	....	....	....	....	....	....	....	....	....	....	....	....
Equatorial Guinea	....	....	....	....	33.8	41.9	31.1	29.2	29.4	36.1	43.3	62.1	59.2	66.9	....	....	....
Ethiopia	9.5	11.4	9.9	11.0	9.4	9.3	9.6	7.3	4.7	5.9	8.9	12.9	13.9	13.3	15.8	15.8	....
Gabon	63.5	64.7	59.6	26.1	36.4	37.0	45.7	50.3	47.2	46.6	48.8	61.7	58.8	....	....	....	....
Gambia, The	33.8	46.4	41.2	43.0	60.9	59.9	60.1	57.8	67.5	70.6	83.1	70.9	....	....	....	....	....
Ghana	2.3	8.1	10.6	14.0	18.7	18.4	16.9	15.8	16.7	17.2	20.3	25.5	24.5	24.9	24.0	....	....
Guinea	....	....	....	....	....	....	....	....	....	....	....	....	....	....	....	....	....
Guinea-Bissau	....	....	25.6	—	.2	.5	.8	1.2	2.7	3.2	6.1	6.0	6.4	9.1	21.5	....	....
Kenya	30.1	32.3	25.6	25.8	21.3	22.0	23.1	26.1	27.3	26.2	40.4	37.1	32.6	32.7	27.9	24.6	....
Lesotho	16.8	17.1	16.5	16.5	17.1	19.0	18.7	16.1	15.7	18.2	20.9	21.7	21.3	24.4	27.7	28.2	....
Liberia	40.7	45.7	43.5	44.2	38.1	....	....	....	....	....	....	....	....	....	....	....	....
Madagascar	12.5	13.3	12.2	12.2	16.5	16.5	18.2	15.3	18.1	16.7	15.5	22.0	23.7	20.1	22.2	22.1	....
Malawi	22.5	28.0	24.0	22.7	25.9	24.9	19.7	23.8	23.6	23.1	17.2	32.6	....	....	....	....	....
Mali	16.9	18.8	18.9	16.0	17.2	16.0	17.1	17.2	18.2	16.4	17.8	23.4	22.9	20.6	26.2	....	....
Mauritania	44.0	44.6	57.7	52.5	46.7	49.4	49.1	44.8	42.6	38.5	44.8	42.4	47.6	47.3	43.4	....	....
Mauritius	46.6	48.7	53.4	60.4	64.4	64.6	64.1	65.2	62.9	60.0	59.3	57.3	59.1	64.3	60.8	63.5	63.0
Morocco	20.9	23.5	24.4	21.0	22.3	24.3	21.8	24.0	24.1	25.1	26.1	24.9	27.4	26.3	28.5	28.1	....
Mozambique	11.9	8.1	5.6	4.7	13.0	15.6	15.0	15.9	11.3	15.1	15.1	15.4	17.9	16.5	14.5	13.6	....
Namibia	....	....	....	....	....	....	....	49.9	51.3	50.5	55.7	51.4	52.0	54.6	52.5	....	....
Niger	20.8	22.9	20.7	21.3	24.7	20.8	20.3	21.4	16.8	16.3	14.7	18.1	19.8	....	....	....	....
Nigeria	13.6	14.8	16.6	12.8	28.7	22.6	27.6	44.9	39.7	35.8	25.3	17.5	13.7	13.1	10.8	7.6	....
Rwanda	10.1	11.0	9.4	11.7	7.8	7.2	6.2	5.6	7.3	5.0	5.2	....	5.8	5.9	7.8	5.5	....
São Tomé & Príncipe	....	....	....	....	....	....	....	....	....	....	....	....	....	....	....	....	....
Senegal	38.2	38.5	32.0	27.3	23.3	22.3	26.0	25.5	23.6	22.3	21.2	33.8	33.6	29.4	29.1	....	....
Seychelles	55.9	66.1	69.1	61.1	61.4	64.0	58.6	62.1	57.9	55.8	56.4	51.9	53.4	62.8	61.6	....	....
Sierra Leone	14.3	16.0	18.7	31.1	27.7	14.8	19.1	33.0	33.3	30.1	21.5	23.3	13.6	....	....	....	....
Somalia	....	....	....	....	....	....	....	....	....	....	....	....	....	....	....	....	....
South Africa	25.5	26.7	33.0	32.5	28.7	28.4	27.4	24.2	22.4	21.4	21.5	22.2	23.0	24.5	24.6	25.8	25.4
Sudan	11.1	8.9	13.6	6.8	3.7	5.7	4.5	2.0	1.4	8.8	7.2	10.3	8.2	8.2	6.2	....	....
Swaziland	66.3	61.1	56.7	68.8	81.8	76.9	84.1	76.5	77.9	76.0	78.8	85.1	80.5	77.9	82.7	....	....
Tanzania	8.0	9.0	6.8	9.6	7.7	9.9	12.0	12.6	10.2	12.5	18.0	20.8	24.1	21.1	15.7	13.7	....
Togo	44.0	51.2	49.0	44.2	41.7	39.2	41.5	42.2	42.9	32.8	28.0	40.7	35.6	38.4	36.5	....	....
Tunisia	34.3	32.7	31.8	30.2	34.5	42.1	43.3	42.3	39.2	38.8	39.6	44.2	44.3	41.6	43.2	42.5	41.8
Uganda	9.2	15.9	9.7	9.0	6.4	4.5	5.3	4.8	6.4	5.7	8.7	10.0	10.8	12.4	....	....	....
Zambia	30.8	35.6	38.4	44.0	43.3	34.4	35.7	36.4	37.2	....	....	....	....	....	....	....	....
Zimbabwe	22.0	25.8	24.9	24.0	23.9	23.9	23.7	23.0	24.0	27.2	30.2	34.3	....	....	....	....	....
Asia																	
Afghanistan, I.S. of	11.7	9.5	7.1	5.1	....	....	....	....	....	....	....	....	....	....	....	....	....
Bangladesh	8.0	8.3	8.5	7.2	7.6	8.3	8.0	9.7	9.3	11.1	12.8	13.8	15.3	14.8	17.3	17.8	17.5
Cambodia	....	....	....	....	....	....	....	....	....	....	....	....	....	....	....	....	....
China,P.R.: Mainland	7.5	8.7	9.4	10.1	12.4	11.6	10.9	15.0	16.5	16.8	14.5	22.0	21.0	20.9	22.9	21.5	22.0
China,P.R.:Hong Kong	....	....	....	....	....	....	....	....	....	....	....	....	....	....	....	128.1	131.9
Fiji	43.8	43.0	44.5	41.8	45.0	55.6	62.8	63.2	56.4	51.7	51.2	55.6	54.2	60.4	56.0	57.0	....
India	6.4	6.6	6.1	5.8	5.9	6.1	7.2	7.5	8.5	9.2	9.6	9.8	10.4	10.7	10.7	10.7	....
Indonesia	22.5	24.3	21.9	17.7	23.3	23.6	24.5	25.6	25.3	26.7	25.7	25.5	26.2	25.0	29.3	43.8	39.6
Kiribati	....	....	....	....	....	....	....	....	....	....	....	....	....	....	....	....	....
Korea	33.0	33.6	32.6	36.6	39.5	37.8	32.1	29.0	27.3	27.6	27.5	27.8	30.1	29.5	34.6	49.4	....
Lao People's Dem.Rep	....	7.1	4.9	6.1	10.6	13.2	11.8	11.8	13.1	16.5	25.1	25.4	23.1	23.0	24.3	37.7	....
Malaysia	52.0	54.4	55.0	56.4	62.6	66.2	71.2	74.2	77.5	75.8	78.7	88.9	93.8	90.6	92.7	....	....
Maldives	115.9	118.6	107.7	102.6	121.4	113.7	118.2	122.8	112.0	114.3	98.2	113.3	117.1	122.3	118.8	112.6	112.6
Mongolia	....	....	....	....	....	....	....	....	18.8	35.1	....	60.1	53.1	44.8	64.7	51.9	

Exports of Goods and Services

As percent of GDP

1983	1984	1985	1986	1987	1988	1989	1990	1991	1992	1993	1994	1995	1996	1997	1998	1999	
																	Asia (cont.)
7.1	6.7	5.7	4.9	2.8	1.8	1.5	1.3	1.0	1.6	1.5	1.4	1.2	1.0	.8	.7	.6	Myanmar
11.7	12.1	12.5	12.2	13.0	12.6	11.1	12.0	15.9	18.6	20.7	23.5	24.4	26.1	26.5	23.3	26.0	Nepal
13.1	10.9	11.8	13.0	14.9	14.0	16.0	17.3	18.4	17.5	17.4	17.2	17.1	17.6	16.6	....	....	Pakistan
34.9	41.4	45.0	46.1	51.0	43.7	41.9	42.9	46.2	52.0	56.8	52.8	59.4	56.2	55.3	60.6	....	Papua New Guinea
20.5	22.4	22.3	25.8	24.3	25.0	25.9	25.8	27.5	27.5	29.5	31.6	36.2	40.4	49.1	56.7	51.0	Philippines
26.9	27.6	31.1	26.5	28.3	35.4	40.0	39.8	26.1	27.3	26.5	25.1	33.6	35.3	34.4	....	....	Samoa
171.0	161.1	157.6	152.8	171.0	191.5	185.5	184.0	175.6	168.6	167.4	173.2	177.8	170.5	164.9	156.5	164.0	Singapore
62.7	59.0	50.2	55.5	57.6	60.7	60.4	45.9	52.2	52.9	60.7	60.1	....	....	....	....	....	Solomon Islands
26.3	28.8	26.1	23.6	25.8	26.0	26.5	28.5	28.3	30.1	33.1	33.8	35.4	35.0	36.5	36.0	....	Sri Lanka
20.4	22.3	23.4	25.8	29.0	33.1	35.0	34.2	36.1	37.1	37.6	39.2	42.8	39.3	47.8	53.9	54.8	Thailand
20.8	33.5	38.0	32.4	33.1	23.4	31.5	30.9	22.7	19.7	22.1	....	....	....	....	....	....	Tonga
54.9	73.3	54.9	38.9	50.8	53.3	38.3	48.3	44.4	46.2	44.1	48.1	46.3	....	....	....	....	Vanuatu
																	Europe
....	....	....	....	....	....	....	....	....	....	....	....	....	....	....	....	....	Albania
....	....	....	....	....	....	....	....	....	....	.2	35.3	23.3	23.1	20.2	18.9	....	Armenia
....	....	....	....	....	....	....	....	....	....	....	....	....	....	....	....	....	Azerbaijan
....	....	....	....	....	....	....	....	....	....	....	....	....	....	60.5	....	....	Belarus
....	....	35.2	26.8	27.3	22.7	20.1	33.5	54.2	58.4	45.2	53.5	51.7	63.6	61.7	48.8	46.4	Bulgaria
....	....	....	....	....	....	....	....	....	....	.1	.1	—	—	....	....	....	Croatia
52.0	56.1	50.1	46.7	48.8	49.7	52.9	53.0	48.8	50.8	48.7	48.7	47.8	48.1	48.3	44.9	46.4	Cyprus
....	....	....	....	....	....	....	....	....	....	55.1	53.0	54.2	51.6	56.7	60.9	63.6	Czech Republic
39.7	43.3	35.3	34.9	34.7	34.8	33.9	31.7	40.8	....	....	....	....	....	....	....	....	Czechoslovakia
....	....	....	....	....	....	....	....	....	....	70.1	76.4	72.5	67.0	77.9	80.2	....	Estonia
45.5	47.6	44.6	41.8	41.9	38.6	40.4	36.4	36.5	36.2	28.4	25.9	40.8	45.1	56.0	56.3	....	Hungary
....	....	....	....	....	....	....	....	....	....	....	....	34.7	34.6	36.4	32.1	....	Kazakhstan
....	....	....	....	....	....	....	....	....	....	....	33.6	30.0	32.1	38.2	36.4	....	Kyrgyz Republic
....	....	....	....	....	....	....	....	....	79.9	73.1	46.0	46.9	50.9	50.9	51.3	46.6	Latvia
....	....	....	....	....	....	....	....	....	....	83.3	55.3	53.0	53.4	54.5	47.2	39.8	Lithuania
....	....	....	....	....	....	....	....	....	....	....	....	....	29.5	35.9	40.6	....	Macedonia, FYR
65.1	67.7	69.9	69.4	76.1	78.2	79.9	84.4	85.9	90.9	94.4	96.0	93.3	86.6	84.7	87.4	91.5	Malta
....	....	....	....	....	....	....	....	....	....	....	....	61.3	56.3	54.7	....	....	Moldova
18.0	18.1	18.4	18.9	22.3	23.7	19.5	32.3	23.6	22.2	20.7	25.3	28.1	26.0	27.6	27.2	....	Poland
27.3	35.2	22.9	20.1	19.4	20.4	21.1	16.7	17.1	25.7	21.6	23.9	26.5	27.5	28.5	22.9	29.0	Romania
....	....	....	....	....	....	....	....	....	....	....	27.4	27.7	24.8	24.1	31.4	45.4	Russia
....	....	....	....	....	....	....	....	....	....	61.6	65.2	63.1	58.0	60.7	63.9	....	Slovak Republic
....	....	....	....	....	....	....	....	....	....	59.0	60.0	55.3	55.6	57.4	57.1	....	Slovenia
....	....	....	....	16.3	19.9	17.5	14.0	14.4	14.8	14.0	22.3	21.6	25.1	27.4	27.5	....	Turkey
....	....	....	....	....	....	....	....	....	....	....	....	....	....	....	....	....	Turkmenistan
....	....	....	....	....	....	....	....	....	....	....	45.3	46.2	45.7	41.0	....	....	Ukraine
29.5	31.2	32.3	25.5	23.1	28.7	19.4	....	....	....	....	....	....	....	....	....	....	Yugoslavia, SFR
																	Middle East
91.0	101.8	104.3	97.1	97.1	89.5	94.2	97.4	85.0	84.4	84.1	79.7	82.0	88.0	79.1	64.6	....	Bahrain
18.1	15.1	12.8	9.5	9.2	8.2	8.3	16.0	30.9	27.2	24.4	23.4	21.9	20.9	19.7	15.2	16.5	Egypt
14.2	10.7	8.4	3.6	4.4	3.4	3.5	3.7	2.6	2.0	26.0	27.1	18.5	17.3	12.3	7.6	....	Iran, I.R. of
30.7	35.2	41.3	37.0	36.9	32.9	34.7	32.9	28.4	29.3	31.4	31.8	30.8	30.4	31.1	32.4	36.1	Israel
33.8	36.5	38.2	29.0	34.1	40.1	56.9	62.5	58.9	51.3	50.6	49.1	53.4	55.1	51.2	49.7	....	Jordan
59.1	60.1	53.7	46.2	41.4	42.9	52.4	44.8	18.8	40.5	48.0	51.1	53.6	53.0	53.4	44.9	47.1	Kuwait
41.5	39.6	37.5	26.0	28.0	24.3	29.4	40.1	34.1	31.3	28.6	28.6	30.7	29.1	28.5	....	....	Libya
50.3	47.4	48.0	34.9	44.2	40.0	44.0	47.7	43.5	44.7	43.1	43.0	44.0	48.2	48.3	39.0	....	Oman
46.4	41.8	35.8	31.1	35.0	35.0	37.2	45.3	43.0	43.6	38.5	38.2	41.9	44.9	44.4	33.9	38.5	Saudi Arabia
13.3	12.2	11.8	6.3	6.0	12.2	21.0	21.0	16.2	13.2	13.2	11.5	11.5	10.0	8.7	7.1	....	Syrian Arab Republic
5.1	4.7	3.9	3.6	4.2	....	....	....	....	....	....	....	....	....	....	....	....	Yemen Arab Rep.
....	....	....	....	....	....	....	....	10.9	8.2	7.1	8.1	17.7	32.8	37.5	29.1	....	Yemen, Republic of
....	....	....	....	....	....	....	....	....	....	....	....	....	....	....	....	....	Yemen, P.D. Rep.
																	Western Hemisphere
....	....	....	....	....	....	....	....	....	....	....	....	....	....	....	....	....	Anguilla
64.8	96.4	88.5	83.7	79.2	78.4	77.9	88.2	90.1	96.1	96.2	88.1	81.4	77.6	....	....	....	Antigua and Barbuda
8.9	8.2	11.4	8.0	7.5	8.8	15.4	10.5	7.6	6.7	7.0	7.5	9.7	10.5	10.6	10.4	9.8	Argentina
....	....	....	....	....	....	....	....	....	....	....	....	....	....	....	....	....	Aruba
241.5	210.9	107.0	75.1	68.8	61.5	57.6	58.5	54.8	56.2	57.9	56.0	57.6	....	....	....	....	Bahamas, The
64.5	69.3	66.0	56.8	47.1	50.2	51.9	50.7	48.6	50.8	53.1	57.8	62.1	62.5	57.1	54.7	....	Barbados
....	69.2	70.0	68.9	57.4	61.6	57.9	60.3	57.5	58.4	53.3	50.3	50.7	51.2	53.8	51.9	51.6	Belize
14.3	12.3	11.1	16.8	15.0	14.6	18.4	20.1	17.2	13.7	15.6	19.7	18.4	17.7	17.8	15.9	15.7	Bolivia
12.0	14.5	12.4	9.0	9.5	10.9	9.7	7.6	8.6	10.2	9.9	9.0	7.5	6.8	7.4	7.6	....	Brazil
23.4	22.4	27.3	29.5	30.7	33.7	34.9	33.7	31.9	29.5	26.3	28.4	29.7	27.8	27.6	26.0	28.8	Chile
9.8	13.6	12.9	18.4	18.8	17.2	18.5	21.5	22.1	20.9	19.6	13.4	13.3	13.5	13.3	....	....	Colombia
35.8	34.7	30.9	31.5	31.9	34.9	35.0	34.4	38.8	38.3	38.6	39.9	49.4	52.6	56.4	64.8	....	Costa Rica
45.0	41.6	39.2	52.8	52.5	54.2	46.5	53.8	51.6	52.0	48.2	46.8	44.9	48.2	52.5	53.8	....	Dominica
13.5	11.8	26.2	23.1	26.8	35.4	29.4	25.9	24.5	21.7	49.4	50.1	48.0	46.5	46.8	47.2	....	Dominican Republic
21.0	22.4	20.7	23.4	23.2	26.4	29.2	30.5	29.0	29.4	26.0	27.6	29.2	30.1	30.8	25.4	....	Ecuador
22.0	19.1	15.8	25.0	19.6	17.1	14.1	18.3	16.9	16.4	19.7	20.2	21.5	21.4	24.3	22.9	....	El Salvador
40.5	39.1	41.3	52.2	47.7	46.7	40.0	42.1	40.8	39.6	44.1	48.8	52.3	44.7	....	....	....	Grenada
13.0	13.0	10.4	13.8	16.0	16.2	16.9	20.5	18.0	18.2	17.8	17.3	19.3	17.7	17.9	18.4	19.2	Guatemala
46.4	55.5	56.7	....	....	....	....	....	....	130.4	113.8	107.1	101.2	....	....	....	....	Guyana
17.8	17.6	16.8	13.1	14.8	12.3	9.5	10.7	7.3	5.7	6.6	3.6	8.2	7.0	12.2	13.6	....	Haiti
26.0	25.5	25.0	26.6	22.9	22.2	20.5	33.9	33.1	30.5	34.9	39.2	41.3	47.1	46.4	45.5	....	Honduras
33.9	53.4	56.1	52.9	51.5	47.5	46.8	52.2	58.6	69.6	59.1	76.1	70.4	61.1	54.8	49.2	....	Jamaica
20.2	19.4	17.2	20.5	23.6	20.1	19.0	18.6	16.4	15.3	15.2	16.9	31.2	32.4	30.3	31.2	30.7	Mexico
....	....	....	31.0	....	....	....	31.4	39.3	40.1	....	....	....	....	....	....	....	Montserrat
....	....	....	....	....	....	....	....	....	....	....	....	....	....	....	....	....	Netherlands Antilles
22.3	15.1	11.6	6.4	1.2	22.2	33.6	3.5	19.5	16.8	18.7	25.4	31.3	33.6	41.9	39.1	37.0	Nicaragua
60.7	57.9	61.3	65.0	67.4	73.2	76.2	83.5	92.6	95.3	92.6	96.3	96.3	90.6	95.9	87.7	....	Panama
7.1	10.7	13.6	14.0	17.0	19.3	36.1	47.8	38.9	36.6	48.0	48.2	53.2	45.6	46.9	50.2	....	Paraguay
19.5	19.2	21.7	12.6	8.2	10.6	11.1	12.1	9.9	10.8	10.6	11.3	11.4	12.0	12.8	11.9	....	Peru
52.6	57.8	55.3	61.4	63.9	59.3	55.3	51.7	58.9	61.7	58.3	54.5	....	....	....	....	....	St. Kitts and Nevis
55.9	55.7	54.5	61.6	60.9	71.0	66.1	67.7	63.9	64.9	66.2	65.1	68.7	62.3	....	....	....	St. Lucia
62.4	70.8	73.1	72.5	64.1	75.7	65.1	65.7	53.0	59.3	50.0	46.3	51.6	52.6	....	....	....	St. Vincent & Grens.
78.3	79.2	69.4	64.9	68.2	52.3	67.9	51.2	32.4	23.1	5.5	75.7	119.6	....	....	....	....	Suriname
30.1	31.5	32.6	34.4	33.8	38.7	42.4	45.2	41.1	39.4	40.5	42.5	52.5	49.1	51.2	48.3	....	Trinidad and Tobago
28.1	26.6	26.6	25.7	21.6	23.1	26.1	25.8	21.9	22.2	20.0	18.6	19.4	20.1	21.1	19.9	....	Uruguay
23.4	29.0	25.5	15.6	24.4	18.3	32.7	38.7	30.7	25.7	26.8	30.3	26.8	35.8	28.5	20.0	....	Venezuela, Rep. Bol.

Balance of Payments

Imports of Goods and Services

	1983	1984	1985	1986	1987	1988	1989	1990	1991	1992	1993	1994	1995	1996	1997	1998	1999
							As percent of GDP										
All Countries																	
Industrial Countries																	
United States	9.1	10.2	9.7	10.1	10.6	10.7	10.6	10.6	10.2	10.3	10.7	11.3	12.0	12.2	12.6	12.5	13.3
Canada	22.4	25.3	26.3	27.1	25.9	26.2	25.8	26.0	25.9	27.5	30.2	32.9	34.2	34.4	37.8	39.9	40.2
Australia	15.7	17.1	19.0	18.7	17.5	17.4	18.4	17.3	16.8	18.0	18.8	19.5	20.5	19.5	20.1	21.6	21.3
Japan	12.5	12.6	11.3	7.6	7.6	8.0	9.2	10.0	8.8	8.1	7.2	7.4	8.2	9.7	10.2	9.5	9.1
New Zealand	29.5	34.5	33.4	27.7	25.6	22.5	26.1	27.1	26.1	29.2	28.1	29.0	28.8	28.7	28.3	30.0	....
Euro Area																	
Austria	35.1	37.7	39.9	35.4	34.8	37.1	38.7	38.6	38.6	37.5	36.1	37.7	39.1	40.8	44.3	45.8	46.0
Belgium-Luxembourg	67.6	70.8	67.8	61.1	61.9	63.3	66.7	64.9	63.0	60.3	57.2	61.5	60.8	62.2	66.5	67.4	73.0
Finland	29.8	28.2	28.5	25.6	25.6	25.2	25.7	24.8	23.0	25.5	27.6	29.5	29.2	30.0	30.9	30.1	29.5
France	23.9	24.7	24.4	21.2	21.5	21.8	23.3	23.3	23.1	22.1	20.5	20.9	21.5	21.5	22.7	23.7	23.9
Germany	28.2	29.6	30.3	26.0	25.0	25.7	27.7	28.1	26.6	24.8	22.4	23.2	23.8	24.5	26.7	27.6	28.5
Ireland	54.3	59.2	58.1	50.6	51.0	53.2	57.4	52.1	52.6	52.7	54.5	60.0	64.1	64.8	66.0	96.8	....
Italy	21.3	23.0	23.2	18.6	18.8	18.8	20.0	19.8	18.6	19.2	19.0	20.3	22.8	20.8	22.4	22.8	22.9
Luxembourg	....	....	....	....	....	....	....	....	....	....	....	....	92.5	93.0	99.8	103.9	107.0
Netherlands	54.8	58.5	59.8	50.2	49.6	50.9	54.1	52.1	52.6	50.8	47.8	49.2	49.9	51.1	53.8	53.1	50.8
Portugal	42.8	44.4	40.8	30.9	35.7	38.7	38.4	39.3	36.4	34.4	35.2	36.9	37.8	38.0	40.4	42.4	....
Spain	21.5	20.7	20.6	17.7	19.4	20.3	21.6	20.5	20.4	20.4	20.0	22.3	23.8	24.6	27.2	29.0	28.6
Denmark	35.2	36.5	37.9	33.5	30.6	30.7	32.4	31.1	31.7	30.0	28.6	30.5	32.1	31.7	33.5	34.4	33.5
Greece	28.2	29.5	32.2	26.7	27.8	22.0	23.6	23.6	22.6	21.7	20.8	20.6	21.0	20.6	21.2	....	....
Iceland	36.5	38.0	40.4	35.0	35.8	33.1	32.6	33.0	32.8	30.7	29.8	30.0	32.1	35.7	35.5	39.2	38.1
Norway	34.8	35.2	36.0	38.2	34.9	34.2	34.4	33.7	32.5	31.2	31.7	32.2	32.0	32.0	34.1	37.3	....
Sweden	34.1	33.4	34.2	30.3	31.1	31.4	32.1	30.7	27.4	27.4	29.7	31.6	33.8	32.4	35.7	37.5	....
Switzerland	44.6	45.1	45.8	44.0	40.5	41.6	44.6	42.2	38.7	37.8	36.1	35.3	35.5	36.9	41.6	41.3	....
United Kingdom	25.7	28.7	28.1	26.6	26.7	26.7	27.9	26.8	24.2	24.9	26.5	27.2	28.8	29.8	28.5	27.6	27.5
Developing Countries																	
Africa																	
Algeria	24.5	22.3	19.6	15.7	12.5	14.8	18.7	16.3	17.6	....	....	....	....	....	....	....	....
Angola	....	....	—	—	—	—	—	—	....	....	....	....	....	....	....	....	....
Benin	34.6	36.6	41.8	39.0	38.6	28.2	24.6	24.6	46.0	34.7	35.0	42.3	44.5	33.9	35.0	....	....
Botswana	78.4	72.2	65.0	59.3	65.4	64.1	49.1	57.0	53.6	48.7	47.7	41.3	46.4	42.4	49.4	52.0	....
Burkina Faso	45.6	44.1	32.6	30.7	30.0	29.1	25.4	26.2	25.5	21.3	23.5	26.0	....	....	....	....	....
Burundi	....	....	20.4	21.7	25.1	25.8	21.6	27.7	29.9	29.4	29.5	24.9	21.1	12.2	11.6	15.3	13.3
Cameroon	28.3	24.9	23.9	21.6	19.8	17.7	20.2	20.3	19.4	16.4	15.1	22.7	18.4	....	....	....	....
Cape Verde	82.6	68.3	66.8	52.9	45.6	42.3	....	....	....	....	....	....	....	....	....	....	....
Central African Rep.	36.5	35.5	39.2	35.9	29.3	26.1	26.8	28.5	22.9	24.2	22.7	28.7	....	....	....	....	....
Chad	21.7	24.9	36.9	35.4	35.0	31.5	33.6	30.3	28.6	28.1	31.0	34.9	....	....	....	....	....
Comoros	47.8	69.6	59.9	47.6	50.2	41.8	37.5	36.6	41.0	42.6	37.3	46.9	46.0	....	....	....	....
Congo, Republic of	65.6	46.0	53.5	63.3	41.4	48.9	43.2	45.8	47.0	40.1	50.1	90.9	68.1	86.3	59.8	....	....
Côte d'Ivoire	38.4	33.8	31.1	32.2	31.9	30.3	30.9	31.9	30.3	30.7	29.8	34.2	38.1	37.5	36.4	35.8	....
Djibouti	....	....	....	....	....	....	....	....	....	....	....	....	....	....	....	....	....
Equatorial Guinea	....	....	....	....	67.0	87.3	60.3	61.3	73.9	57.0	55.4	57.7	123.3	176.8	....	....	....
Ethiopia	17.0	19.8	17.7	18.4	17.8	17.8	15.0	15.6	8.1	18.3	18.8	23.8	27.2	22.6	22.9	23.1	....
Gabon	50.7	52.6	54.5	40.6	38.6	42.0	39.5	33.4	32.3	32.4	34.6	38.3	37.3	....	....	....	....
Gambia, The	49.5	49.1	44.5	48.7	68.5	63.6	63.7	66.1	77.7	75.8	101.5	81.8	....	....	....	....	....
Ghana	3.0	9.3	13.3	17.0	24.7	24.3	24.5	24.2	25.1	28.8	36.4	36.8	32.8	34.6	38.3	....	....
Guinea	....	....	....	....	....	....	....	....	....	....	....	....	....	....	....	....	....
Guinea-Bissau	....	....	....	.3	.9	2.4	3.9	4.2	7.5	19.7	17.7	12.4	19.3	27.4	33.5	....	....
Kenya	30.9	34.3	26.6	25.8	26.7	27.4	30.8	31.7	29.0	26.4	36.1	34.4	39.1	37.3	35.3	31.9	....
Lesotho	152.0	154.9	145.4	140.4	118.3	124.9	125.1	121.2	128.6	122.8	114.8	104.5	112.2	112.2	106.7	104.7	....
Liberia	42.8	39.5	32.2	32.3	34.4	....	....	....	....	....	....	....	....	....	....	....	....
Madagascar	19.4	17.5	17.6	16.5	21.1	23.3	22.0	26.2	25.4	24.4	24.2	29.4	31.2	25.1	30.4	30.1	....
Malawi	28.1	25.1	28.3	24.1	27.1	33.8	28.7	29.5	35.5	40.6	29.8	73.8	....	....	....	....	....
Mali	33.0	34.8	48.0	37.7	33.7	35.4	31.4	33.9	35.0	35.4	33.9	44.4	42.9	37.0	36.6	....	....
Mauritania	70.8	66.5	77.6	72.6	61.3	59.1	55.6	49.5	50.2	57.7	61.7	53.1	48.1	53.4	48.8	....	....
Mauritius	47.0	52.0	55.4	53.8	62.3	69.6	71.4	72.5	66.6	63.2	65.4	66.1	61.7	65.2	65.6	65.1	66.2
Morocco	30.0	34.1	33.8	27.3	26.7	24.7	27.3	30.0	29.8	31.8	32.1	30.9	34.1	29.6	31.8	32.0	....
Mozambique	37.2	30.2	18.7	21.3	55.7	70.9	69.3	69.0	38.0	50.6	54.6	56.2	46.1	35.3	28.8	29.1	....
Namibia	....	....	....	....	....	....	....	64.8	65.6	64.8	66.7	61.0	62.9	66.2	65.5	....	....
Niger	26.9	27.0	32.8	27.6	29.8	29.8	29.6	29.3	26.0	24.0	21.8	29.7	28.2	....	....	....	....
Nigeria	17.5	12.8	11.2	10.2	18.3	16.1	16.6	21.3	31.0	25.1	21.4	16.9	14.2	8.7	9.6	10.3	....
Rwanda	20.6	19.6	19.4	21.0	19.3	17.9	15.7	13.9	17.9	17.6	20.7	....	29.1	26.2	25.6	23.8	....
São Tomé & Príncipe	....	....	....	....	....	....	....	....	....	....	....	....	....	....	....	....	....
Senegal	52.8	50.9	45.1	36.4	31.7	29.6	32.8	32.3	31.6	30.6	30.7	41.6	40.7	35.7	35.8	....	....
Seychelles	78.4	79.5	84.9	78.5	72.7	76.3	72.1	67.0	61.6	59.3	65.9	56.6	62.0	74.2	72.9	....	....
Sierra Leone	17.6	18.1	21.5	29.7	23.8	16.4	22.0	33.8	31.1	30.8	30.2	32.0	27.6	....	....	....	....
Somalia	....	....	....	....	....	....	....	....	....	....	....	....	....	....	....	....	....
South Africa	21.5	24.7	23.3	22.4	21.1	23.5	22.3	18.8	17.5	17.3	17.8	19.8	22.1	23.2	23.5	24.4	22.9
Sudan	14.8	10.2	15.3	10.2	7.6	11.5	7.8	3.6	4.9	24.2	12.3	21.9	14.9	18.9	15.7	....	....
Swaziland	107.2	102.2	92.8	79.8	82.1	80.3	86.9	89.3	92.9	101.9	105.9	98.2	100.5	106.2	101.6	....	....
Tanzania	14.1	16.7	16.8	25.0	23.9	25.4	30.4	34.6	30.9	36.4	47.5	40.2	40.7	33.4	25.5	28.1	....
Togo	52.4	52.3	57.9	56.0	51.1	51.1	51.2	53.9	58.1	44.8	40.5	50.0	51.3	53.0	49.9	....	....
Tunisia	42.7	43.1	38.1	37.3	36.0	42.1	48.1	49.0	44.1	46.7	49.1	48.4	48.9	43.5	46.0	45.8	44.0
Uganda	12.3	13.8	9.7	10.5	13.3	12.7	15.6	18.4	20.4	20.6	22.9	21.8	24.1	26.2	....	....	....
Zambia	31.5	33.2	36.7	42.6	38.9	26.9	30.5	50.7	33.0	....	....	....	....	....	....	....	....
Zimbabwe	25.4	26.5	24.3	21.3	21.0	20.3	21.7	22.8	27.8	36.3	31.3	36.8	....	....	....	....	....
Asia																	
Afghanistan, I.S. of	15.6	16.2	11.4	12.9	....	....	....	....	....	....	....	....	....	....	....	....	....
Bangladesh	19.9	20.4	19.1	18.3	16.9	17.8	19.7	18.6	16.5	17.8	19.2	21.0	26.1	23.9	24.6	24.1	24.8
Cambodia	....	....	....	....	....	....	....	....	....	....	....	....	....	....	....	....	....
China,P.R.: Mainland	6.7	8.7	13.6	12.7	12.3	12.6	12.1	12.2	13.6	15.7	16.4	20.6	19.3	18.8	18.2	17.0	19.1
China,P.R.:Hong Kong	....	....	....	....	....	....	....	....	....	....	....	....	....	....	....	127.6	127.4
Fiji	49.2	44.1	44.9	41.6	42.3	51.6	60.5	68.2	59.9	54.2	58.5	58.9	58.0	58.9	57.0	60.4	....
India	8.5	8.8	9.0	8.5	8.7	8.9	10.0	9.7	10.0	10.9	10.9	11.8	13.2	14.3	13.9	13.9	....
Indonesia	25.8	22.0	20.1	18.8	21.7	20.8	21.4	24.0	24.5	25.1	24.2	24.7	26.9	26.1	29.1	35.1	29.9
Kiribati	....	....	....	....	....	....	....	....	....	....	....	....	....	....	....	....	....
Korea	34.8	34.4	32.1	31.4	32.2	30.3	29.9	30.2	30.3	29.1	27.4	28.9	31.7	33.5	36.0	36.1	....
Lao People's Dem.Rep	....	26.5	15.5	16.8	29.6	30.8	30.1	24.5	23.9	25.8	35.6	43.5	42.4	41.5	40.8	46.6	....
Malaysia	57.5	52.6	50.0	50.5	48.7	56.0	65.1	72.2	81.2	74.4	78.8	90.5	97.8	89.6	91.3	....	....
Maldives	145.9	133.6	100.5	91.5	103.6	102.9	110.4	109.1	111.8	113.2	108.2	107.1	115.1	117.2	118.4	108.7	117.2
Mongolia	....	....	....	....	....	....	....	....	25.9	40.9	....	61.9	54.5	53.5	58.1	64.4	....

Balance of Payments

Imports of Goods and Services

As percent of GDP

1983	1984	1985	1986	1987	1988	1989	1990	1991	1992	1993	1994	1995	1996	1997	1998	1999	
																	Asia (cont.)
13.0	9.9	9.0	8.4	4.8	3.4	1.9	2.5	1.2	1.7	2.4	2.0	1.9	1.6	1.4	1.1	.9	Myanmar
24.0	21.0	21.9	21.0	22.0	24.7	21.8	23.7	29.1	27.9	31.5	36.1	38.5	39.6	39.6	31.9	34.6	Nepal
23.7	24.5	23.8	23.2	22.9	22.9	24.2	25.8	25.5	25.6	25.1	23.0	23.7	26.2	22.3	....	....	Pakistan
51.0	55.8	52.9	51.5	57.3	49.8	49.3	46.8	51.4	45.9	37.8	35.3	37.8	43.5	52.0	54.2	....	Papua New Guinea
27.8	23.1	19.5	19.7	23.8	25.0	28.1	31.5	30.5	31.8	38.0	40.6	45.0	49.9	61.4	60.8	48.1	Philippines
56.7	59.3	67.7	61.4	71.1	71.6	78.4	84.7	78.7	85.9	78.9	52.4	60.1	58.8	60.3	....	....	Samoa
172.8	163.8	159.7	152.4	170.8	184.4	177.2	177.1	164.9	158.7	159.5	158.2	162.2	157.2	151.9	136.8	145.1	Singapore
77.7	61.0	71.9	80.9	81.6	99.8	101.1	75.0	81.8	63.5	77.0	77.6	....	....	....	....	....	Solomon Islands
41.3	34.5	38.4	35.3	35.9	36.7	37.5	36.9	39.7	39.6	42.6	45.6	45.9	43.9	43.6	42.4	....	Sri Lanka
27.7	26.7	26.2	23.8	28.5	34.7	37.7	42.0	43.0	41.8	42.1	44.4	50.0	45.9	47.8	39.9	44.3	Thailand
55.4	73.1	82.5	73.6	71.2	67.1	61.1	59.9	48.2	50.0	53.5	....	....	....	....	....	....	Tonga
61.3	70.0	70.3	61.8	74.0	72.8	54.6	67.5	55.4	49.3	48.4	50.4	48.3	....	....	....	....	Vanuatu
																	Europe
....	....	....	....	....	....	....	....	....	....	....	....	....	....	....	....	....	Albania
....	....	....	....	....	....	....	....	....	....	.3	67.0	56.4	55.6	58.1	53.5	....	Armenia
....	....	....	....	....	....	....	....	....	....	....	....	....	....	....	....	....	Azerbaijan
....	....	....	....	....	....	....	....	....	....	....	....	....	....	66.2	....	....	Belarus
....	....	35.6	29.2	28.5	22.8	20.7	38.7	55.8	62.0	53.9	53.5	49.6	60.5	56.3	48.9	52.4	Bulgaria
										—	—	.1	.1				Croatia
64.0	67.1	58.8	48.7	50.2	53.4	59.7	57.0	57.0	60.6	47.7	48.1	50.1	53.4	52.4	51.7	49.5	Cyprus
										53.7	55.3	57.7	58.4	62.1	62.3	65.2	Czech Republic
37.1	40.5	33.2	34.3	33.9	32.5	32.1	34.4	38.3	....	....	....	....	....	....	....	....	Czechoslovakia
										74.4	87.4	80.6	78.5	89.4	90.6	....	Estonia
43.0	43.5	42.9	43.7	41.0	37.2	38.1	33.3	33.9	34.2	38.2	34.5	42.7	45.5	55.3	57.5	....	Hungary
												35.5	37.6	39.0	37.1	....	Kazakhstan
											44.9	48.7	58.8	46.2	57.1	....	Kyrgyz Republic
									73.1	57.8	44.4	49.3	58.9	59.4	64.9	57.6	Latvia
										91.2	61.4	64.8	63.2	65.1	59.1	50.1	Lithuania
													40.2	50.3	57.6	....	Macedonia, FYR
81.9	84.9	87.8	81.9	87.0	89.2	91.6	98.8	97.8	98.9	104.9	106.8	107.3	100.7	93.3	93.2	96.5	Malta
												70.5	75.9	76.6	....	....	Moldova
17.3	17.0	17.5	18.2	20.8	22.0	19.3	25.6	23.7	21.5	24.1	23.0	26.6	28.7	32.2	32.7	....	Poland
23.2	29.0	18.7	16.4	15.2	13.5	16.6	25.9	21.5	33.2	26.3	25.9	31.9	35.6	35.3	30.8	33.4	Romania
											23.4	24.3	20.5	21.3	26.6	28.1	Russia
										66.9	60.0	61.3	69.9	71.0	75.4	....	Slovak Republic
										57.2	57.7	57.1	56.5	58.4	....	....	Slovenia
			17.6	17.7	17.8	17.0	15.8	16.3	18.0	20.2	23.7	27.3	29.8	28.0	....	....	Turkey
																	Turkmenistan
											49.0	49.4	48.2	44.1	....	....	Ukraine
33.6	34.1	34.2	27.3	25.0	29.7	22.2	....	....	....	....	....	....	....	....	....	....	Yugoslavia, SFR
																	Middle East
89.7	93.4	89.9	81.6	87.5	77.3	87.4	94.5	95.6	96.7	80.7	74.0	70.5	76.2	69.5	63.9	....	Bahrain
29.2	29.1	22.9	16.2	14.7	14.2	13.7	22.7	37.2	32.9	32.6	30.3	28.4	27.1	27.7	25.5	24.3	Egypt
14.4	11.2	8.8	6.2	5.2	4.0	4.3	4.1	4.2	2.9	33.7	21.6	14.8	13.5	11.0	8.6	....	Iran, I.R. of
44.5	46.8	49.6	43.7	48.2	40.5	38.8	38.5	37.6	36.4	40.8	40.8	40.1	39.1	37.2	36.4	41.3	Israel
76.6	73.8	72.5	53.5	56.7	62.1	71.4	88.8	81.3	83.1	80.7	72.3	75.3	81.5	74.3	71.0	....	Jordan
50.4	47.3	45.7	51.0	40.3	49.3	43.3	38.8	92.3	59.5	48.1	44.8	47.6	42.0	42.9	52.3	40.7	Kuwait
37.4	37.8	27.1	24.2	32.2	31.1	31.8	31.3	33.9	26.6	32.0	27.6	23.6	24.3	23.2	....	....	Libya
35.9	35.4	36.0	36.4	26.1	31.4	29.8	28.6	35.9	36.6	39.5	35.6	36.5	35.1	36.7	46.0	....	Oman
65.4	61.6	53.3	51.1	50.5	45.6	47.1	42.0	54.9	50.8	42.5	32.6	35.0	35.1	35.7	34.6	32.0	Saudi Arabia
26.1	23.9	23.2	12.0	9.0	15.8	14.0	12.4	12.1	12.2	13.4	13.8	10.9	10.1	7.8	6.9	....	Syrian Arab Republic
43.7	36.1	31.1	24.3	34.7	....	....	....	....	....	....	....	....	....	....	....	....	Yemen Arab Rep.
....	....	....	....	....	....	....	....	....	....	....	....	....	....	....	....	....	Yemen, P.D. Rep.
									22.2	19.0	16.8	8.8	21.2	38.2	46.1	47.2	Yemen, Republic of
																	Western Hemisphere
....	....	....	....	....	....	....	....	....	....	....	....	....	....	....	....	....	Anguilla
77.0	104.2	105.6	119.4	105.8	83.8	90.8	87.0	90.7	93.3	90.7	86.6	90.1	86.7	....	....	....	Antigua and Barbuda
6.1	5.5	6.5	6.5	7.3	6.0	8.7	4.8	6.1	8.4	9.3	10.6	10.1	11.0	12.7	12.9	11.5	Argentina
....	....	....	....	....	....	....	....	....	....	....	....	....	....	....	....	....	Aruba
239.6	207.1	97.5	65.3	63.2	57.2	56.2	54.3	55.2	52.5	52.5	53.7	58.5	....	....	....	....	Bahamas, The
68.3	67.0	59.9	54.6	46.3	45.9	49.0	51.0	49.6	42.5	47.7	49.7	56.6	56.6	59.4	57.0	....	Barbados
....	78.4	77.2	75.6	62.5	68.1	69.1	61.3	67.5	67.3	64.7	57.9	55.5	53.2	60.8	62.0	63.2	Belize
12.3	10.0	10.9	21.3	21.1	18.4	21.8	22.3	20.9	24.0	25.0	22.6	23.4	23.4	26.0	25.8	23.8	Bolivia
9.9	8.8	7.6	6.8	6.6	6.0	6.2	6.1	6.9	7.2	8.0	8.0	9.0	8.5	9.4	9.6	....	Brazil
20.6	23.4	24.3	26.0	26.5	27.4	31.2	30.2	27.6	28.2	29.1	27.2	28.1	29.8	29.6	29.6	26.8	Chile
14.9	13.9	14.6	14.6	15.1	15.8	15.5	17.0	15.4	18.3	22.4	17.4	17.4	17.0	17.3	....	....	Colombia
36.5	34.3	32.7	30.6	36.1	36.9	39.6	41.1	39.6	43.4	45.8	43.2	52.3	55.1	57.8	65.7	....	Costa Rica
62.2	67.0	64.7	59.2	61.3	68.8	78.4	80.5	70.0	65.3	61.0	62.8	64.8	61.5	63.0	58.0	....	Dominica
17.1	13.4	30.9	26.7	33.5	37.3	36.3	31.6	29.1	30.9	57.0	55.7	51.4	51.4	51.6	56.3	....	Dominican Republic
15.1	16.2	14.1	19.8	25.7	21.9	23.6	23.6	26.4	23.8	25.2	26.6	29.5	25.7	31.0	34.1	....	Ecuador
26.6	24.8	20.7	29.1	26.3	23.9	25.0	30.5	30.4	32.3	34.3	35.2	38.2	34.3	34.9	35.6	....	El Salvador
78.7	68.3	67.6	73.5	68.8	65.0	60.4	62.8	61.7	55.1	63.6	59.7	68.5	65.6	....	....	....	Grenada
14.5	15.1	11.2	12.4	22.5	22.1	22.1	23.7	21.6	27.3	26.1	24.6	25.4	22.4	23.6	26.6	27.7	Guatemala
66.8	67.8	67.8	....	....	....	....	....	....	....	155.8	135.4	121.9	113.9	....	....	....	Guyana
30.6	29.0	27.7	21.2	23.2	21.6	17.9	17.3	17.3	12.5	16.6	12.7	34.3	28.7	28.8	29.0	....	Haiti
29.7	32.2	29.9	28.3	25.9	24.7	23.0	37.0	37.1	36.1	42.7	48.4	46.8	55.2	53.2	52.1	....	Honduras
42.2	61.3	67.6	49.2	50.5	51.4	57.4	56.3	60.5	70.7	68.6	76.5	76.8	70.5	65.1	57.8	....	Jamaica
11.0	12.1	13.0	17.1	17.2	18.8	19.1	19.8	19.4	20.4	19.2	22.0	28.7	30.4	30.5	33.4	32.3	Mexico
....	....	....	59.7	....	....	....	89.6	90.9	78.4	....	....	....	....	....	....	....	Montserrat
....	....	....	....	....	....	....	....	....	....	....	....	....	....	....	....	....	Netherlands Antilles
39.0	29.0	31.2	18.7	3.3	69.6	65.7	6.1	47.4	49.9	41.5	51.3	56.5	60.2	77.4	77.8	88.7	Nicaragua
56.6	58.3	59.7	61.7	63.0	58.8	70.4	78.9	93.1	96.3	92.8	95.2	98.2	92.0	99.9	97.0	....	Panama
10.9	16.2	18.5	20.1	25.9	22.1	30.2	41.2	38.1	38.0	49.1	53.4	58.0	52.2	50.3	52.4	....	Paraguay
19.3	15.3	16.0	14.1	10.3	12.0	8.7	12.0	11.3	13.0	13.4	14.2	16.3	16.4	16.7	16.7	....	Peru
96.4	80.5	73.1	77.0	84.5	84.4	83.4	83.1	80.5	69.0	71.1	64.9	....	....	....	....	....	St. Kitts and Nevis
69.9	72.8	68.0	66.4	68.7	75.4	81.8	77.0	76.4	72.0	71.2	71.5	71.1	72.3	....	....	....	St. Lucia
83.3	84.0	79.1	79.9	80.1	82.9	82.6	76.8	72.1	68.3	67.8	70.3	66.1	65.9	....	....	....	St. Vincent & Grens.
104.3	93.0	70.9	68.1	55.6	43.3	49.9	49.5	39.1	23.6	5.1	63.6	104.6	....	....	....	....	Suriname
40.1	32.9	28.2	38.0	32.3	33.8	34.4	28.2	32.9	28.6	31.0	29.8	39.6	38.2	55.3	53.7	....	Trinidad and Tobago
23.8	22.0	21.5	20.4	19.5	18.8	20.0	19.8	19.6	20.9	20.7	20.0	19.8	20.8	22.0	21.5	....	Uruguay
13.4	17.1	15.9	16.4	23.7	24.7	21.7	19.4	25.6	28.4	26.7	22.5	21.8	21.0	21.7	20.9	....	Venezuela, Rep. Bol.

Balance of Payments

Current Account Balance

Excluding Exceptional Financing

	1983	1984	1985	1986	1987	1988	1989	1990	1991	1992	1993	1994	1995	1996	1997	1998	1999
								As percent of GDP									
All Countries																	
Industrial Countries																	
United States	-1.3	-2.5	-3.0	-3.4	-3.4	-2.4	-1.8	-1.4	.1	-.8	-1.3	-1.7	-1.5	-1.7	-1.7	-2.5	-3.7
Canada	-.8	-.4	-1.6	-3.1	-3.2	-3.0	-4.0	-3.4	-3.8	-3.7	-3.9	-2.3	-.7	.6	-1.6	-1.8	-.4
Australia	-3.7	-4.7	-5.5	-5.7	-3.9	-4.6	-6.2	-5.2	-3.6	-3.7	-3.3	-5.1	-5.4	-3.9	-3.1	-5.0	-5.7
Japan	1.8	2.8	3.8	4.3	3.5	2.7	2.2	1.5	2.0	3.0	3.1	2.8	2.2	1.4	2.2	3.2	2.5
New Zealand	-4.1	-13.6	-11.9	-9.9	-8.0	-4.3	-3.6	-3.4	-2.8	-2.7	-1.7	-4.6	-5.1	-6.0	-6.6	-4.9	....
Euro Area																	
Austria	.4	-.3	-.2	.2	-.2	-.2	.2	.7	—	-.4	-.6	-1.5	-2.3	-2.1	-2.5	-2.2	-2.7
Belgium-Luxembourg	-.6	-.1	.8	2.5	1.9	2.2	2.2	1.7	2.2	2.8	4.9	5.1	4.8	4.8	5.3	4.5	4.8
Finland	-2.3	—	-1.5	-1.0	-2.0	-2.6	-5.0	-5.2	-5.5	-4.7	-1.3	1.1	4.0	3.9	5.4	5.7	5.4
France	-1.0	-.2	—	.3	-.5	-.5	-.5	-.8	-.5	.3	.7	.5	.7	1.3	2.8	2.8	2.6
Germany	.7	1.6	2.8	4.6	4.2	4.2	4.8	3.2	-1.0	-.9	-.7	-1.0	-.8	-.3	-.1	-.2	-1.0
Ireland	-6.6	-5.8	-3.9	-3.2	-.2	-.1	-1.6	-.8	.6	1.1	3.5	2.9	2.6	2.8	2.4	2.5	....
Italy	.2	-.8	-1.0	.4	-.3	-.9	-1.5	-1.5	-2.1	-2.4	.8	1.3	2.3	3.3	2.8	1.7	.7
Luxembourg	....	....	....	....	....	....	....	....	....	....	....	....	15.8	15.3	13.8	12.4	8.1
Netherlands	3.8	5.1	3.3	2.4	1.9	3.1	4.4	3.3	2.7	2.3	4.4	5.3	6.1	5.5	7.6	6.8	5.7
Portugal	-7.9	-3.2	1.8	3.4	1.0	-2.2	.3	-.3	-.9	-.2	.3	-2.5	-.1	-4.2	-5.4	-6.8	....
Spain	-1.9	1.1	1.7	1.7	-.1	-1.1	-2.9	-3.7	-3.7	-3.7	-1.2	-1.3	.1	.1	.5	-.6	-2.1
Denmark	-2.4	-3.0	-4.6	-5.3	-2.8	-1.2	-1.0	1.0	1.5	2.9	3.5	2.1	1.0	1.7	.5	-1.2	1.3
Greece	-5.4	-6.3	-9.8	-4.3	-2.6	-1.5	-3.8	-4.3	-1.8	-2.2	-.8	-.1	-2.4	-3.7	-4.0	....	....
Iceland	-2.0	-4.7	-3.9	.4	-3.5	-3.9	-1.9	-2.0	-4.1	-2.3	.7	1.8	.8	-1.6	-1.7	-6.8	-6.7
Norway	3.3	4.8	4.8	-6.0	-4.5	-4.0	.2	3.5	4.3	3.5	3.0	3.1	3.3	6.5	5.2	-1.5	....
Sweden	-.8	.8	-1.0	—	—	—	-.3	-1.6	-2.8	-1.9	-3.6	-2.2	.4	2.1	2.2	3.1	2.0
Switzerland	1.2	6.4	6.3	3.4	3.6	4.7	4.5	3.0	4.5	5.8	7.6	6.6	7.0	7.2	10.5	9.4	....
United Kingdom	1.2	.4	.7	-.2	-1.4	-3.8	-4.6	-3.4	-1.5	-1.7	-1.7	-.2	-.5	-.1	.8	-.1	-1.4
Developing Countries																	
Africa																	
Algeria	-.2	.1	1.7	-3.5	.2	-3.8	-2.1	2.3	5.2	....	....	....	....	....	....	....	....
Angola	....	....	....	....	—	—	—	—	—	....	....	....	....	....	....	....	....
Benin	-12.3	-5.4	-3.7	-4.0	-2.2	-1.1	2.5	1.3	-7.4	.3	.7	5.7	-4.1	-1.9	-7.2	....	....
Botswana	-7.5	-5.5	8.5	8.4	40.8	10.1	17.1	-.6	8.2	5.0	11.4	5.2	6.8	11.6	15.1	3.5	....
Burkina Faso	-6.0	-.4	-4.3	-.9	-2.2	-1.9	4.0	-2.7	-3.1	-.7	-2.5	.8	....	....	....	....	....
Burundi	....	....	-3.5	-2.9	-8.2	-6.4	-1.0	-6.0	-2.9	-5.5	-2.9	-1.6	.9	-3.5	-.1	-4.7	-2.8
Cameroon	-6.0	-2.3	-6.5	-3.8	-7.1	-3.6	-2.8	-4.6	-2.9	-3.3	-4.9	-.8	1.0	....	....	....	....
Cape Verde	-9.4	-4.7	-6.3	.9	-1.0	-.2	....	....	....	....	....	....	....	....	....	....	....
Central African Rep.	-4.4	-5.2	-6.9	-9.1	-6.1	-2.7	-2.7	-6.2	-4.5	-5.9	-1.0	-2.9	....	....	....	....	....
Chad	4.7	1.0	-10.0	-5.6	-2.1	1.8	-4.2	-2.8	-4.1	-5.1	-8.0	-3.2	....	....	....	....	....
Comoros	-10.4	-32.4	-13.3	-10.5	-12.5	-3.1	2.7	-4.3	-4.2	-5.4	3.6	-3.7	-8.4	....	....	....	....
Congo, Republic of	-19.1	9.6	-7.5	-32.5	-9.7	-20.1	-3.6	-9.0	-16.9	-10.8	-20.6	-44.8	-31.0	-45.9	-11.0	....	....
Côte d'Ivoire	-13.6	-1.1	.9	-3.3	-9.6	-12.1	-9.9	-11.2	-10.2	-9.1	-8.6	-.2	-4.9	-2.9	-2.3	-2.7	....
Djibouti	....	....	....	....	....	....	....	....	....	....	....	....	....	....	....	....	....
Equatorial Guinea	....	....	....	....	-19.3	-17.1	-16.9	-13.1	-27.7	-6.6	1.8	-.4	-77.6	-127.6	....	....	....
Ethiopia	-3.0	-2.5	1.7	-5.0	-3.1	-3.1	-1.9	-3.6	1.1	-1.6	-.9	2.4	-.2	1.5	-.4	2.1	....
Gabon	2.8	3.4	-4.6	-23.0	-11.7	-16.2	-4.6	3.1	1.4	-3.0	-.9	7.6	2.0	....	....	....	....
Gambia, The	-13.9	3.2	3.4	2.0	3.0	10.9	5.4	7.4	4.0	11.5	-1.9	2.7	....	....	....	....	....
Ghana	-.8	-.5	-2.1	-1.5	-2.0	-1.3	-1.8	-3.6	-3.8	-5.9	-9.4	-4.7	-2.2	-4.7	-8.0	....	....
Guinea	....	....	....	....	....	....	....	....	....	....	....	....	....	....	....	....	....
Guinea-Bissau	....	....	....	-.2	-.8	-2.2	-3.8	-2.9	-6.3	-18.5	-15.5	-7.3	-10.9	-19.2	-11.4	....	....
Kenya	-1.0	-2.6	-1.9	-.6	-6.3	-5.5	-7.1	-6.2	-2.7	-2.2	1.2	1.4	-4.4	-.8	-3.5	-3.1	....
Lesotho	11.6	2.1	-4.9	-1.0	5.5	-4.9	2.0	10.5	12.0	4.5	3.6	12.9	-34.6	-32.2	-26.3	-31.9	....
Liberia	-9.2	-.2	5.2	-1.7	-12.9	....	....	....	....	....	....	....	....	....	....	....	....
Madagascar	-8.7	-6.6	-6.4	-4.4	-5.5	-6.1	-3.4	-8.6	-8.6	-6.6	-7.7	-9.3	-8.7	-7.3	-7.5	-8.0	....
Malawi	-10.8	-3.5	-11.2	-7.2	-5.1	-6.5	-3.4	-4.6	-10.5	-15.3	-8.2	-38.0	....	....	....	....	....
Mali	-9.2	-9.8	-17.0	-14.8	-11.2	-12.3	-7.7	-9.0	-7.1	-8.9	-7.5	-9.4	-12.3	-10.8	-7.3	....	....
Mauritania	-27.2	-15.4	-16.9	-23.1	-15.7	-10.0	-1.9	-.9	-2.7	-10.7	-18.4	-7.0	2.1	8.4	4.5	....	....
Mauritius	-1.8	-5.0	-2.8	6.4	3.4	-2.6	-4.7	-4.5	-.6	—	-2.9	-6.6	-.6	.8	-2.2	.1	-1.2
Morocco	-6.4	-7.7	-6.9	-1.2	1.0	2.1	-3.4	-.8	-1.5	-1.5	-1.9	-2.4	-3.9	-.2	-.5	-.7	....
Mozambique	-22.3	-16.0	-11.7	-13.6	-28.8	-29.8	-34.6	-28.8	-12.5	-17.5	-21.6	-21.2	-19.4	-14.5	-8.4	-11.0	....
Namibia	....	....	....	....	....	....	....	....	1.1	4.1	1.7	4.0	2.8	5.3	3.6	2.8	....
Niger	-3.5	-.5	-4.8	-8.3	-8.2	-10.3	-12.3	-9.5	-7.4	-6.4	-4.3	-8.9	-9.4	....	....	....	....
Nigeria	-5.5	.1	3.2	.5	-.3	-.9	3.6	15.4	3.6	6.3	-1.8	-3.8	-2.9	2.7	.4	-3.3	....
Rwanda	-3.2	-2.6	-3.7	-3.6	-6.3	-6.3	-5.2	-4.2	-1.8	-4.1	-6.6	....	4.5	-.6	-3.3	-7.1	....
São Tomé & Príncipe	....	....	....	....	....	....	....	....	....	....	....	....	....	....	....	....	....
Senegal	-12.3	-11.7	-14.0	-9.8	-9.4	-8.1	-7.5	-6.4	-6.8	-6.7	-8.0	-5.1	-5.5	-4.3	-4.2	....	....
Seychelles	-17.8	-8.8	-11.4	-15.9	-8.5	-10.0	-13.0	-3.5	-2.2	-1.6	-8.3	-5.4	-10.6	-11.3	-10.9	....	....
Sierra Leone	-1.8	-2.1	.3	28.7	-4.6	-.3	-6.4	-10.9	2.4	-.8	-7.0	-9.6	-13.4	....	....	....	....
Somalia	....	....	....	....	....	....	....	....	....	....	....	....	....	....	....	....	....
South Africa	—	-2.2	4.7	5.0	3.6	1.4	1.7	1.8	1.9	1.5	1.2	.1	-1.5	-1.3	-1.5	-1.4	-.4
Sudan	-3.1	.4	2.5	-.3	-1.9	-3.4	-.8	-1.5	-3.5	-12.1	-3.9	-10.4	-6.0	-10.1	-8.1	....	....
Swaziland	-20.6	-11.7	-10.7	2.4	11.2	13.7	11.1	5.9	5.4	-4.2	-6.4	-2.2	-2.3	-4.4	.7	....	....
Tanzania	-5.0	-6.4	-5.8	-7.1	-7.9	-7.0	-7.6	-13.1	-14.9	-15.5	-24.6	-15.8	-12.3	-7.9	-8.2	-11.4	....
Togo	-6.1	2.3	-4.4	-6.2	-4.9	-6.3	-3.9	-6.4	-10.0	-8.4	-6.6	-5.7	-9.3	-10.6	-8.3	....	....
Tunisia	-6.8	-9.3	-6.9	-6.7	-.6	2.1	-2.2	-3.8	-3.6	-7.1	-9.1	-3.4	-4.3	-2.4	-3.1	-3.7	-2.4
Uganda	-1.8	3.9	.1	-.9	-2.1	-3.3	-4.9	-7.0	-5.6	-3.1	-6.7	-3.9	-5.5	-4.0	....	....	....
Zambia	-7.9	-5.4	-17.5	-20.7	-11.8	-8.1	-5.5	-15.9	-9.0	....	....	....	....	....	....	....	....
Zimbabwe	-6.7	-.8	-1.1	.3	.9	1.6	.2	-1.6	-5.6	-9.0	-1.8	-6.2	....	....	....	....	....
Asia																	
Afghanistan, I.S. of	-2.1	-5.2	-2.6	-5.2	....	....	....	....	....	....	....	....	....	....	....	....	....
Bangladesh	-.4	-3.5	-3.2	-4.1	-1.4	-1.5	-5.4	-1.9	.3	.8	1.5	.8	-2.8	-3.2	-1.0	-.1	-.8
Cambodia	....	....	....	....	....	....	....	....	....	....	....	....	....	....	....	....	....
China,P.R.: Mainland	1.4	.7	-3.8	-2.4	.1	-1.0	-1.0	3.1	3.3	1.4	-1.9	1.3	.2	.9	4.1	3.3	1.6
China,P.R.:Hong Kong	....	....	....	....	....	....	....	....	....	....	....	....	....	....	....	1.8	5.8
Fiji	-4.9	-1.6	1.6	1.3	2.3	6.4	.6	-7.1	-4.9	-3.9	-8.3	-6.1	-5.6	.6	-1.6	-3.5	....
India	-1.0	-1.2	-2.0	-2.0	-2.0	-2.5	-2.4	-2.3	-1.6	-1.6	-.7	-.5	-1.5	-1.5	-.7	-1.6	....
Indonesia	-7.4	-2.1	-2.2	-4.5	-2.7	-1.6	-1.1	-2.6	-3.3	-2.0	-1.3	-1.6	-3.2	-3.4	-2.3	3.3	4.1
Kiribati	....	....	....	....	....	....	....	....	....	....	....	....	....	....	....	....	....
Korea	-1.9	-1.4	-.9	4.4	7.4	8.0	2.4	-.8	-2.8	-1.3	.3	-1.0	-1.7	-4.4	-1.7	12.8	....
Lao People's Dem.Rep	....	-19.7	-10.7	-10.8	-19.2	-18.1	-18.7	-12.8	-11.2	-9.4	-10.5	-18.4	-19.6	-18.7	-17.5	-11.6	....
Malaysia	-11.6	-4.9	-1.9	-.4	8.0	5.3	.8	-2.0	-8.5	-3.7	-4.5	-6.1	-9.5	-4.6	-4.8	....	....
Maldives	-36.6	-22.9	-6.5	-.3	8.7	7.9	8.3	6.8	-5.5	-10.2	-24.8	-4.7	-6.7	-2.5	-10.8	-6.8	-15.2
Mongolia	....	....	....	....	....	....	....	....	-5.2	....	-5.0	....	6.8	4.1	-9.4	5.7	-12.3

Current Account Balance

Excluding Exceptional Financing

As percent of GDP

1983	1984	1985	1986	1987	1988	1989	1990	1991	1992	1993	1994	1995	1996	1997	1998	1999	
																	Asia (cont.)
-5.6	-3.4	-3.1	-3.7	-1.7	-1.5	-.4	-1.8	-.9	-.3	-.4	-.2	-.2	-.2	-.2	-.2	-.1	Myanmar
-6.3	-4.0	-4.8	-4.5	-4.2	-8.2	-7.4	-8.2	-9.4	-5.2	-6.3	-8.7	-8.4	-7.4	-8.0	-1.5	-1.2	Nepal
.1	-4.0	-3.6	-2.1	-1.7	-3.8	-3.6	-4.2	-3.3	-3.9	-6.0	-3.5	-5.6	-7.4	-2.9	....	....	Pakistan
-13.1	-12.2	-5.5	-4.1	-7.5	-8.1	-8.8	-2.3	-12.5	-3.7	9.2	7.4	9.8	3.6	-4.2	-.8	....	Papua New Guinea
-8.3	-4.1	-.1	3.2	-1.3	-1.0	-3.4	-6.1	-2.3	-1.9	-5.5	-4.6	-2.7	-4.8	-5.3	2.4	10.3	Philippines
3.5	.7	2.1	8.0	7.3	6.7	11.7	6.5	-20.1	-33.8	-24.3	3.1	4.9	5.8	3.9	....	....	Samoa
-3.5	-2.1	....	1.8	-.5	7.7	9.9	8.5	11.4	12.0	7.3	16.3	17.3	15.2	17.9	25.4	25.0	Singapore
-11.9	.1	-17.4	-8.2	-11.5	-22.0	-19.8	-13.3	-16.3	-.6	-2.7	-1.1	....	....	....	....	....	Solomon Islands
-9.0	....	-7.0	-6.5	-4.9	-5.7	-5.9	-3.7	-6.6	-4.6	-3.7	-6.5	-5.9	-4.9	-2.6	-1.8	....	Sri Lanka
-7.2	-5.0	-4.0	.6	-.7	-2.7	-3.5	-8.5	-7.7	-5.7	-5.0	-5.7	-8.2	-8.1	-2.0	11.5	8.5	Thailand
.7	-7.4	2.9	3.7	1.9	-11.5	6.4	4.7	—	-.3	-4.1	....	....	....	....	....	....	Tonga
-8.1	3.0	-10.0	-11.6	-24.8	-14.6	-8.7	-4.0	-7.5	-6.9	-7.6	-9.2	-7.7	....	....	....	....	Vanuatu
																	Europe
....	....	....	....	....	....	....	....	....	....	....	....	....	....	....	....	....	Albania
....	....	....	....	....	....	....	....	....	....	-.1	-16.0	-17.0	-18.2	-18.7	-22.0	....	Armenia
....	....	....	....	....	....	....	....	....	....	....	....	....	....	....	....	....	Azerbaijan
....	....	....	....	....	....	....	....	....	....	....	....	....	....	-5.7	....	....	Belarus
		-.4	-2.6	-1.7	-.9	-1.6	-8.3	-1.0	-4.2	-10.1	-.3	-.2	.2	4.2	-.5	-5.3	Bulgaria
....	....	....	....	....	....	....	....	....	....	....	....	....	....	....	....	....	Croatia
-9.5	-9.8	-7.4	-.6	-.2	-2.5	-5.5	-2.8	-7.3	-9.2	1.7	1.0	-1.8	-5.2	-3.8	-6.7	-2.6	Cyprus
										1.4	-2.1	-2.6	-7.4	-6.2	-2.5	-2.0	Czech Republic
1.9	2.2	1.7	.4	.7	2.1	1.9	-2.7	2.7	....	....	....	....	....	....	....	....	Czechoslovakia
										1.3	-7.3	-4.4	-9.1	-12.1	-9.2	....	Estonia
-.9	.2	-2.2	-5.7	-2.6	-2.0	-2.0	1.1	1.2	.9	-11.0	-9.8	-5.7	-3.8	-2.2	-4.9	....	Hungary
											-1.2	-3.7	-3.8	-5.8	....	....	Kazakhstan
										-7.6	-15.7	-24.2	-7.8	-22.6	....	....	Kyrgyz Republic
								14.0	19.2	5.5	-.4	-5.4	-6.1	-10.7	....	-10.2	Latvia
										-3.2	-2.2	-10.2	-9.2	-10.2	-12.1	-11.2	Lithuania
												-6.5	-7.4	-8.9	....	-3.5	Macedonia, FYR
-.5	.8	-2.5	.5	1.4	3.3	-.5	-2.4	-.3	1.1	-3.4	-4.8	-10.9	-10.6	-6.0	-5.7	-3.5	Malta
											-6.8	-12.1	-15.3	....	....	....	Moldova
-2.1	-1.4	-1.4	-1.5	-.6	-.2	-1.7	5.2	-2.8	-3.7	-6.7	1.0	.7	-2.3	-4.0	-4.3	....	Poland
2.6	4.5	2.9	2.7	3.5	6.5	4.7	-8.5	-3.5	-7.7	-4.7	-1.5	-5.0	-7.3	-6.1	-7.0	-3.8	Romania
											-6.8	-12.1	-15.3	....	....	....	Moldova
										-4.8	4.9	2.2	-11.1	-10.1	-10.4	....	Slovak Republic
											1.5	4.2	-.1	.2	.2	—	Slovenia
				-.9	1.8	.9	-1.7	.2	-.6	-3.4	2.0	-1.4	-1.3	-1.4	.9	....	Turkey
....	....	....	....	....	....	....	....	....	....	....	....	....	....	....	....	....	Turkmenistan
											-3.2	-3.1	-2.7	-2.7	....	....	Ukraine
.6	1.1	1.9	1.8	1.8	4.1	2.5										....	Yugoslavia, SFR
																	Middle East
2.7	5.5	1.1	-2.3	-5.9	5.2	-5.0	1.6	-13.1	-17.4	-6.5	-4.6	4.1	4.3	-.5	-12.6	....	Bahrain
-.9	-4.4	-4.0	-2.9	-.3	-1.2	-1.5	.3	5.4	6.7	4.9	.1	-.4	-.3	-.9	-3.1	-1.8	Egypt
.2	-.3	-.3	-2.5	-.7	-.6	—	.1	-1.3	-.6	-5.7	6.8	3.3	3.9	1.4	-1.0	....	Iran, I.R. of
-7.7	-5.5	4.8	5.0	-3.5	-1.5	.5	.3	-.2	-1.5	-3.9	-4.5	-5.9	-5.6	-3.5	-.9	-2.6	Israel
-7.8	-5.1	-5.1	-.6	-5.4	-4.9	9.3	-5.6	-9.3	-16.1	-11.3	-6.5	-4.0	-3.3	.4	.2	....	Jordan
25.4	29.6	22.4	31.4	20.4	22.2	37.6	21.0	-240.4	-2.3	10.4	13.0	18.9	22.9	26.4	8.7	17.1	Kuwait
-5.4	-5.2	6.9	-.7	-4.9	-7.7	-4.1	7.7	-.7	4.3	-4.5	.1	6.8	4.5	5.4	....	....	Libya
5.8	3.2	-.1	-12.6	9.1	-3.7	3.3	9.5	-2.2	-4.8	-9.5	-6.2	-5.8	1.2	-.3	-21.0	....	Oman
-15.6	-18.5	-14.9	-16.1	-13.3	-9.6	-11.5	-4.0	-23.3	-14.4	-14.6	-8.7	-4.2	.5	.2	-10.2	-1.2	Saudi Arabia
-4.5	-4.1	-4.5	-2.0	-.9	....	-.9	6.6	7.4	2.5	.2	-.6	-1.8	.7	.1	.7	.1	Syrian Arab Republic
-11.7	-6.5	-6.8	-3.1	-10.7	....	....	....	....	....	....	....	....	....	....	....	....	Yemen Arab Rep.
....	....	....	....	....	....	....	....	....	....	....	....	....	....	....	....	....	Yemen, P.D. Rep.
									-5.5	-7.1	-6.6	1.5	1.5	1.4	.8	-3.9	Yemen, Republic of
																	Western Hemisphere
....	....	....	....	....	....	....	....	....	....	....	....	....	....	....	....	....	Anguilla
-5.9	.3	-11.4	-48.1	-38.8	-13.3	-21.9	-7.9	-8.1	-4.5	-.1	-3.6	-.1	-7.3	....	....	....	Antigua and Barbuda
-2.3	-2.1	-1.1	-2.7	-3.9	-1.2	-1.7	3.2	-.3	-2.4	-3.4	-4.3	-1.9	-2.4	-4.1	-4.8	-4.3	Argentina
....	....	....	....	....	....	....	....	....	....	....	....	....	....	....	....	....	Aruba
-6.8	-6.3	-.1	1.1	-2.4	-2.6	-2.9	-1.2	-6.2	1.3	1.7	-1.4	-4.8	....	....	....	....	Bahamas, The
-4.1	1.4	4.3	.5	-1.3	2.8	1.5	-.6	-1.6	8.8	4.2	7.7	4.8	5.2	-2.3	-2.4	....	Barbados
....	-2.9	4.9	6.1	3.4	-.8	-5.2	3.8	-6.0	-5.9	-9.1	-7.3	-2.9	-1.1	-5.2	-9.5	-11.2	Belize
-2.4	-2.7	-4.4	-9.8	-9.9	-6.6	-5.7	-4.1	-4.9	-9.5	-8.8	-1.5	-4.5	-5.5	-7.0	-7.9	-6.6	Bolivia
-3.5	—	-.1	-2.0	-.5	1.3	.3	-.8	-.4	1.6	—	-.2	-2.6	-3.0	-3.8	-4.4	....	Brazil
-5.6	-11.0	-8.6	-6.7	-3.6	-1.0	-2.5	-1.6	-.3	-2.3	-5.7	-3.1	-2.1	-5.1	-5.0	-5.7	-.1	Chile
-7.8	-3.7	-5.2	1.1	-.9	-.6	-.5	1.3	5.7	2.0	-4.1	-4.5	-5.0	-5.0	-5.6	....	....	Colombia
-9.9	-6.9	-7.4	-3.6	-8.3	-6.6	-9.2	-8.7	-1.8	-5.6	-8.2	-2.9	-4.0	-2.9	-2.2	-4.3	....	Costa Rica
-2.3	-8.0	-6.5	-6.3	-5.6	-8.6	-29.7	-26.2	-18.6	-13.2	-11.7	-17.8	-22.3	-16.9	-13.7	-6.8	....	Dominica
-4.5	-1.4	-2.1	-3.0	-6.2	-.4	-4.9	-4.0	-2.1	-8.0	-5.5	-2.7	-1.5	-1.6	-1.1	-2.1	....	Dominican Republic
-.9	-2.1	.5	-5.2	-11.3	-6.8	-7.3	-3.4	-6.0	-1.0	-4.7	-4.1	-4.3	.4	-3.6	-11.0	....	Ecuador
-3.6	-4.0	-3.3	-.4	-1.5	-2.4	-5.7	-4.9	-4.0	-3.3	-1.8	-.2	-2.8	-1.6	.9	-.7	....	El Salvador
-16.1	1.8	1.7	-13.3	-17.5	-15.1	-17.0	-20.9	-19.3	-12.9	-17.4	-8.3	-14.7	-19.7	....	....	....	Grenada
-2.5	-4.0	-2.2	-.2	-6.2	-5.3	-4.4	-3.0	-2.0	-6.8	-6.2	-4.8	-3.9	-2.9	-3.6	-5.5	-5.7	Guatemala
-32.5	-22.3	-20.9	....	....	....	....	....	-37.1	-30.1	-22.9	-21.7	....	....	....	....	....	Guyana
-6.8	-5.7	-4.7	-2.0	-1.4	-1.8	-2.5	-.7	-3.0	.4	-.4	-1.3	-3.7	-5.1	-1.5	-1.1	....	Haiti
-7.5	-11.3	-8.5	-5.9	-5.9	-3.5	-3.5	-6.1	-7.0	-8.7	-8.8	-10.0	-5.1	-8.2	-5.8	-6.3	....	Honduras
-9.4	-13.3	-13.0	-.7	-4.1	1.3	-6.9	-7.3	-6.4	.9	-4.6	2.3	-1.5	-2.0	-5.0	-3.7	....	Jamaica
3.9	2.4	.4	-1.1	3.0	-1.3	-2.6	-2.8	-4.7	-6.7	-5.8	-7.0	-.6	-.7	-1.9	-3.8	-2.9	Mexico
....	....	....	-13.0	....	....	....	....	....	....	....	....	....	....	....	....	....	Montserrat
....	....	....	....	....	....	....	-37.6	-42.6	-23.9	....	....	....	....	....	....	....	Netherlands Antilles
-22.7	-19.6	-26.0	-15.5	-2.6	-58.2	-35.7	-3.5	-30.7	-45.2	-32.8	-38.2	-29.8	-25.3	-27.5	-23.4	-28.8	Nicaragua
4.1	-4.0	1.4	-1.8	9.7	14.8	2.3	3.9	-4.1	-4.0	-1.3	.2	-4.7	-3.7	-7.0	-13.3	....	Panama
-3.8	-6.0	-5.5	-6.7	-10.8	-3.5	5.9	7.4	1.4	-.9	.9	.9	-3.1	-5.1	-2.5	-1.2	....	Paraguay
-4.6	-1.2	.6	-5.4	-4.8	-5.4	-1.4	-4.1	-3.7	-5.1	-5.6	-5.3	-7.3	-6.0	-5.0	-6.1	....	Peru
-24.7	-6.2	-8.6	-9.4	-14.9	-21.7	-26.8	-29.5	-21.2	-8.7	-15.2	-11.9	....	....	....	....	....	St. Kitts and Nevis
-2.7	-6.7	-5.6	-2.5	-4.8	-5.3	-16.6	-13.7	-16.0	-11.0	-10.0	-9.4	-6.0	-14.1	....	....	....	St. Lucia
-2.8	-1.0	3.3	-8.0	-14.2	-10.2	-10.2	-11.9	-20.7	-9.0	-18.3	-23.8	-15.6	-12.6	....	....	....	St. Vincent & Grens.
-28.5	-14.2	-1.9	-3.7	12.4	8.8	19.5	3.9	-6.6	.9	.7	12.1	16.8	....	....	....	....	Suriname
-12.1	-6.0	-.6	-8.6	-4.7	-2.0	-.9	9.1	-.1	2.6	2.5	4.4	5.5	1.8	-10.5	-10.6	....	Trinidad and Tobago
-1.2	-2.7	-2.1	.7	-1.9	.3	1.7	2.2	.4	-.1	-1.8	-2.5	-1.2	-1.2	-1.4	-2.3	....	Uruguay
6.5	8.0	5.6	-3.7	-3.0	-9.6	5.0	17.0	3.2	-6.2	-3.3	4.3	2.6	12.6	3.9	-2.7	....	Venezuela, Rep. Bol.

GDP Volume Measures

		1970	1971	1972	1973	1974	1975	1976	1977	1978	1979	1980	1981	1982	1983	1984
													Percent Change over Previous Year:			
World	001	**4.0**	**3.7**	**5.0**	**6.1**	**2.2**	**1.2**	**5.6**	**4.3**	**4.0**	**4.2**	**2.5**	**2.0**	**.6**	**2.9**	**5.2**
Industrial Countries	110	**3.9**	**3.5**	**5.2**	**6.1**	**.7**	**—**	**4.9**	**3.8**	**4.3**	**3.7**	**1.1**	**1.7**	**−.2**	**2.9**	**4.8**
United States	111	.2	3.3	5.4	5.8	−.6	−.4	5.6	4.6	5.5	3.2	−.2	2.5	−2.0	4.3	7.3
Canada	156	2.6	5.8	5.7	7.7	4.4	2.6	6.2	3.6	4.6	3.9	1.5	3.7	−3.2	3.2	6.3
Australia	193	6.2	4.4	2.1	5.6	2.6	1.6	3.8	1.9	2.9	5.2	1.6	4.0	.8	−.2	6.7
Japan	158	9.4	4.2	8.4	7.9	−1.2	2.6	4.8	5.3	5.1	5.2	3.6	3.6	3.2	2.7	4.3
New Zealand	196	3.7	2.5	4.4	7.2	4.0	1.7	.1	−2.7	2.7	2.6	1.1	4.9	−3.3	5.8	5.2
Euro Area	163	....	....	....	....	....	....	....	....	....	....	....	....	....	....	....
Austria	122	7.1	5.3	6.3	5.3	4.3	−1.7	5.8	4.7	−.4	5.5	2.3	−.1	1.9	2.8	.3
Belgium	124															
Finland	172	7.5	2.1	7.6	6.7	3.0	1.1	−.4	.2	2.1	7.0	5.3	1.9	3.2	2.7	3.0
France	132	7.2	4.8	4.4	5.4	3.1	−.3	4.2	3.2	3.3	3.2	1.6	1.2	2.5	.7	1.3
Germany	134	4.9	3.0	4.3	4.8	.3	−1.3	4.9	3.0	3.1	4.3	1.0	.1	−1.0	1.7	2.8
Ireland	178	3.5	3.4	6.5	6.2	4.1	2.4	1.4	8.2	7.2	3.1	3.1	3.3	2.3	−.2	4.3
Italy	136	5.3	1.9	2.9	6.5	4.7	−2.1	6.5	2.9	3.7	5.7	3.5	.5	.5	1.2	2.6
Luxembourg	137	3.9	2.7	6.6	8.3	4.2	−6.6	2.5	1.6	4.1	2.2	1.0	−.6	1.1	3.0	6.2
Netherlands	138	28.8	3.8	2.4	4.8	3.8	.3	4.5	2.9	2.6	−.1	3.2	−1.5	−1.1	1.8	2.9
Portugal	182	9.1	6.6	8.0	11.2	1.1	−4.3	6.9	5.6	2.8	5.6	4.6	1.6	2.1	−.2	−1.9
Spain	184	6.3	4.6	8.1	7.8	5.6	.5	3.3	2.8	1.5	—	1.3	−.2	1.6	2.2	1.5
Denmark	128	2.5	2.6	4.5	3.6	−1.4	−1.7	6.4	1.1	1.8	3.1	−.6	−2.1	2.7	1.7	3.5
Greece	174	7.9	7.1	8.9	7.3	−3.6	6.1	6.4	3.4	6.7	3.7	1.7	.1	.4	.4	2.7
Iceland	176	7.6	13.1	5.8	5.8	6.3	.9	6.1	8.9	7.0	5.5	7.0	4.3	2.0	−2.1	4.1
Norway	142	2.0	4.6	5.2	4.1	5.2	4.2	6.8	3.6	4.7	4.4	5.0	1.0	.2	3.5	5.9
Sweden	144	6.6	.8	2.2	3.9	4.3	2.2	1.2	−2.0	1.3	4.3	2.0	—	1.1	1.8	4.0
Switzerland	146	6.4	4.3	3.5	3.2	1.2	−6.7	−.8	2.4	.6	2.5	4.4	1.6	−1.4	.5	3.0
United Kingdom	112	2.4	2.0	3.6	7.3	−1.7	−.7	2.8	2.4	3.4	2.8	−2.2	−1.3	1.8	3.7	2.4
Developing Countries	200	**3.9**	**4.2**	**4.2**	**5.8**	**6.1**	**4.3**	**7.3**	**5.3**	**3.1**	**5.2**	**5.1**	**2.5**	**2.0**	**2.7**	**5.7**
Africa	605	**8.7**	**6.4**	**5.0**	**4.4**	**7.6**	**−.8**	**4.8**	**4.6**	**−.7**	**6.7**	**4.2**	**−.4**	**1.6**	**−.6**	**1.8**
Benin	638	....	1.9	8.9	2.3	−7.5	4.4	4.3	5.7	2.8	5.0	10.9	5.8	10.8	−4.3	7.9
Botswana	616	14.9	17.2	29.8	24.8	24.2	−1.3	19.0	3.5	19.5	9.9	14.3	9.5	7.5	16.0	11.5
Burkina Faso	748	....	....	....	....	....	....	....	....	....	....	1.7	4.4	2.2	−1.2	1.8
Burundi	618	....	5.1	−8.4	7.2	−.8	1.0	7.9	12.4	−1.1	2.0	7.9	10.9	−.4	3.1	−.1
Cameroon	622	3.6	3.0	4.3	1.5	4.5	5.1	1.9	5.7	10.4	11.2	4.2	17.1	7.6	7.0	7.8
Chad	628	....	1.8	−6.8	−4.9	13.6	17.3	−1.5	−7.4	−.3	−.3	−.3	11.6	11.6	11.6	−5.0
Congo, Dem. Rep. of	636	−.2	6.0	.1	8.1	3.1	−5.0	−5.3	.8	−5.3	.4	2.2	2.4	−.5	1.4	5.5
Congo, Rep. of	634	3.8	5.6	5.1	6.2	15.1	−3.3	−.1	−5.5	−1.6	9.8	15.8	21.2	23.6	5.6	7.2
Côte d'Ivoire	662	....	....	....	....	....	....	....	....	....	....	....	....	....	....	....
Ethiopia	644	3.6	4.5	4.8	2.7	1.4	.1	2.3	.6	−1.1	5.3	5.5	6.1	1.0	7.7	−4.9
Gambia, The	648	....	15.6	7.3	4.5	53.9	−4.1	−1.4	−1.4	8.8	1.6	−54.2	119.4	13.5	2.1	1.6
Ghana	652	6.8	5.6	−2.5	15.3	3.4	−12.9	−3.5	2.3	8.5	−3.2	—	−1.8	−7.2	.7	2.6
Guinea-Bissau	654	....	....	....	....	....	....	....	....	....	....	....	....	....	....	....
Kenya	664	7.4	6.9	72.6	6.8	1.5	3.4	7.0	58.2	−25.8	52.6	4.0	6.0	1.8	4.3	.9
Liberia	668	6.5	5.0	3.8	−2.5	7.4	−15.1	4.0	−.8	4.0	4.4	−4.7	2.2	−2.9	−.7	−.9
Madagascar	674	4.0	2.4	−3.2	−2.0	3.3	3.0	−4.0	3.4	−2.6	9.8	.8	−8.6	−1.8	.8	2.2
Malawi	676	....	....	....	....	7.4	5.5	6.2	4.8	8.3	3.3	−.4	−5.2	2.8	3.5	4.4
Mauritius	684	−.9	4.5	8.0	11.8	8.0	1.3	16.7	6.6	3.8	3.5	−10.1	5.9	5.5	.4	4.8
Morocco	686	5.0	5.8	2.1	3.8	14.3	−1.2	12.8	7.2	2.2	4.8	3.6	−2.8	9.6	−.6	4.3
Mozambique	688	....	....	....	....	....	....	....	....	....	....	....	....	....	....	....
Namibia	728	....	....	....	....	....	....	....	....	....	....	....	....	....	....	....
Niger	692	....	....	....	....	....	....	....	....	....	....	....	....	....	....	....
Nigeria	694	25.0	14.2	3.4	5.4	11.2	−5.2	9.0	6.0	−5.8	6.8	4.2	−13.1	−.2	−5.3	−4.8
Rwanda	714	11.0	1.2	.2	3.4	.7	2.0	1.8	5.2	9.8	9.4	−3.6	2.5	4.1	6.0	−4.2
Senegal	722	8.6	−.1	6.4	−5.6	4.2	7.5	8.9	−2.7	−4.0	7.0	−3.3	−1.2	15.3	2.2	−4.0
Seychelles	718	....	....	....	....	....	....	....	7.9	6.7	15.0	−3.1	−6.6	−1.5	−1.7	8.0
Sierra Leone	724	....	....	−1.1	3.1	4.0	3.0	−3.0	1.4	.3	7.4	3.0	6.2	1.6	−1.4	1.4
South Africa	199	5.2	4.3	1.7	4.6	6.1	1.7	2.2	−.1	3.0	3.8	6.6	5.4	−.4	−1.8	5.1
Swaziland	734	....	....	....	....	....	....	....	....	9.9	14.5	−4.4	6.9	1.2	1.2	6.2
Togo	742	....	6.0	3.8	−4.2	4.3	−.6	−.5	5.6	10.1	5.4	1.9	−3.5	−3.8	.7	1.3
Tunisia	744	7.5	10.0	17.7	−.6	8.1	7.1	7.9	3.4	6.4	6.6	7.4	5.5	−.5	4.7	6.2
Uganda	746	....	....	....	....	....	....	....	....	....	....	....	....	....	....	−4.7
Zambia	754	3.2	−.1	9.2	−.9	6.7	−2.4	4.3	−4.8	.6	−3.0	3.0	6.2	−2.8	−2.0	−.4
Zimbabwe	698	....	....	....	1.7	17.3	−3.6	−1.1	−5.1	−2.2	3.8	10.6	12.5	2.6	1.6	−1.9
Asia	505	**4.8**	**3.6**	**2.6**	**6.6**	**4.4**	**6.2**	**6.1**	**7.0**	**6.8**	**4.0**	**6.5**	**5.9**	**5.3**	**7.3**	**8.3**
Bangladesh	513	....	....	....	....	12.1	3.4	12.3	1.3	6.5	4.6	1.3	6.8	.8	3.6	4.2
China, P.R.: Mainland	924	....	....	....	....	....	....	....	....	....	7.6	7.8	4.5	8.3	10.4	14.6
China, P.R.: Hong Kong	532	9.5	7.4	11.0	12.7	2.1	.4	17.2	12.0	8.8	11.8	10.4	9.4	2.7	6.3	9.8
Fiji	819	12.7	6.9	7.5	11.6	2.5	—	1.8	−3.5	1.8	12.0	−1.7	6.0	−1.1	−4.0	8.4
India	534	5.2	1.8	−.6	3.0	1.2	9.2	1.8	7.2	5.8	−5.3	6.6	6.5	3.8	7.4	3.7
Indonesia	536	7.5	7.0	9.4	11.3	7.6	5.0	6.9	8.8	7.8	6.3	9.9	7.9	2.2	4.2	7.0
Korea	542	8.8	8.6	4.9	12.3	7.4	6.5	11.2	10.0	9.0	7.1	−2.1	6.5	7.2	10.7	8.2
Lao People's Democratic Rep.	544	....	....	....	....	....	....	....	....	....	....	....	15.3	4.7	3.0	6.4
Malaysia	548	....	10.0	9.4	11.7	8.3	.8	11.6	7.8	6.7	9.3	7.4	6.9	6.0	6.2	7.8
Maldives	556	....	....	....	....	....	....	−2.1	26.2	16.1	15.0	10.3	8.6	−3.0	−3.0	16.3	27.0
Mongolia	948	....	....	....	....	....	....	....	....	....	....	....	8.3	8.3	5.8	6.0
Myanmar	518	....	....	....	....	....	....	....	13.0	−1.1	4.7	7.9	6.3	5.4	4.4	4.9
Nepal	558	2.6	−1.2	3.1	−.5	6.3	1.5	4.4	3.0	4.4	2.4	−2.3	8.3	3.8	−3.0	9.7
Pakistan	564	−2.4	.7	.4	6.9	5.5	4.6	4.6	3.8	8.0	4.8	8.7	6.9	6.5	6.8	5.1
Papua New Guinea	853	....	....	....	....	3.8	.9	−1.6	−4.3	8.6	1.8	−2.3	1.1	.8	3.4	−1.0
Philippines	566	3.8	5.4	5.4	8.9	3.6	5.6	8.8	5.6	5.2	5.6	5.1	3.4	3.6	1.9	−7.3
Samoa	862	6.8	13.2	1.7	7.3	−10.6	−4.0	9.5	−1.0	6.3	13.3	−6.1	−9.1	−1.0	1.2	1.3
Singapore	576	13.7	12.5	13.4	11.5	6.3	4.1	7.5	7.8	8.6	9.3	9.7	9.6	6.9	8.2	8.3
Solomon Islands	813	....	....	....	....	....	....	....	....	....	....	....	6.7	−1.1	3.9	8.3
Sri Lanka	524	4.9	.2	3.2	3.7	3.2	2.8	3.0	4.2	8.2	6.3	5.8	5.1	5.1	5.0	5.1
Thailand	578	10.5	5.0	4.1	9.9	4.4	4.8	9.4	9.9	10.4	5.3	4.8	5.9	5.4	5.6	5.8
Tonga	866	....	....	....	....	....	....	.8	4.8	1.9	1.9	15.8	14.0	14.8	5.8	44.1
Vanuatu	846	....	....	....	....	....	....	....	....	....	....	....	....	....	....	6.9

Calculated from Indices

1985	1986	1987	1988	1989	1990	1991	1992	1993	1994	1995	1996	1997	1998	1999		
4.3	3.5	4.0	4.7	3.7	3.3	2.7	3.3	2.9	4.7	4.0	4.4	4.1	2.3	3.9	World	001
3.6	3.1	3.3	4.4	3.6	2.6	1.6	1.8	1.1	3.0	2.4	2.9	3.1	2.5	3.4	Industrial Countries	110
3.8	3.4	3.4	4.2	3.5	1.8	−.5	3.0	2.7	4.0	2.7	3.6	4.2	4.3	4.1	United States	111
4.8	3.3	4.3	4.9	2.4	−.2	−1.8	.8	2.3	4.7	2.8	1.7	4.0	3.6	3.9	Canada	156
5.1	2.2	4.9	4.2	4.6	1.9	−1.1	3.3	3.8	5.2	3.8	4.4	4.1	4.8	4.4	Australia	193
5.0	2.6	4.1	6.2	4.7	4.8	3.8	1.0	.3	.6	1.5	5.1	1.4	−2.9	....	Japan	158
−.2	3.3	.8	1.1	−.1	−.8	−1.1	.8	6.2	5.3	2.9	2.7	3.0	−.7	....	New Zealand	196
....	....	....	....	....	....	....	....	....	....	....	1.3	2.2	2.7	2.4	Euro Area	163
2.2	2.3	1.7	3.2	4.2	4.6	3.4	1.3	.5	2.4	1.7	2.0	1.2	2.9	2.2	Austria	122
....	1.8	2.7	4.6	3.7	2.7	2.0	1.6	−1.5	3.0	2.5	1.0	3.5	2.7	2.6	Belgium	124
3.4	2.4	4.1	4.9	5.5	−.5	−4.8	−3.3	−1.1	4.0	3.8	4.0	6.3	5.0	3.5	Finland	172
1.9	2.5	2.3	4.5	4.3	2.5	1.1	1.3	−.9	1.8	1.9	1.1	1.9	3.2	2.9	France	132
2.3	2.3	1.4	3.6	3.7	5.7	13.2	2.2	−1.1	2.3	1.7	.8	1.5	2.2	1.5	Germany	134
3.1	3.7	4.7	4.3	6.1	7.8	1.9	3.3	2.6	5.8	9.5	7.7	10.7	8.9	....	Ireland	178
2.8	2.8	3.1	3.9	2.9	2.0	1.4	.8	−.9	2.2	2.9	.9	1.5	1.3	2.2	Italy	136
2.9	4.8	2.9	5.7	6.7	3.2	3.1	1.8	....	....	....	....	....	....	....	Luxembourg	137
3.3	3.1	1.4	2.5	4.7	4.0	2.2	2.0	.6	3.2	2.3	3.1	3.6	3.7	7.9	Netherlands	138
2.8	4.1	6.4	7.5	5.4	4.8	2.3	1.9	−1.4	2.4	2.9	3.2	3.5	3.5	....	Portugal	182
2.6	3.2	5.6	5.1	4.8	3.7	2.3	.7	−1.2	2.3	2.7	2.4	3.5	3.8	3.7	Spain	184
3.6	4.0	—	1.2	.2	1.0	1.1	.6	—	5.5	2.8	2.5	3.1	2.5	1.6	Denmark	128
3.1	1.6	−.5	4.5	3.5	−.6	3.5	.4	−.9	1.5	1.9	2.4	3.4	3.7	3.4	Greece	174
3.3	6.4	8.5	−.1	.3	1.2	1.1	−3.3	1.0	3.6	1.0	5.7	3.9	4.7	4.4	Iceland	176
5.2	3.6	2.0	−.1	.9	2.0	3.1	3.3	2.7	5.5	3.8	4.9	4.7	2.0	.9	Norway	142
2.2	2.2	2.8	2.7	2.4	1.4	−1.7	−1.4	−2.2	3.3	3.7	1.1	2.0	3.0	3.8	Sweden	144
3.4	1.6	.7	3.1	4.3	3.7	−.8	−.1	−.5	.5	.5	.3	1.7	2.1	1.7	Switzerland	146
3.8	4.2	4.4	5.2	2.1	.6	−1.5	.1	2.3	4.4	2.8	2.6	3.5	2.2	2.1	United Kingdom	112
5.5	4.1	5.2	5.0	3.6	4.2	4.3	5.7	5.9	6.8	6.1	6.4	5.5	2.2	4.6	Developing Countries	200
4.9	3.1	1.7	5.4	3.4	2.5	2.2	−.4	.7	2.6	2.3	6.2	3.2	3.6	....	Africa	605
7.5	2.1	−1.5	3.4	−2.8	3.2	4.7	4.0	3.5	4.4	4.6	5.5	5.7	4.5	5.0	Benin	638
7.2	7.5	8.9	14.7	22.6	5.5	8.7	6.3	−1	4.2	2.5	6.6	7.0	8.0	4.2	Botswana	616
12.9	9.8	−1.5	6.2	.2	−1.0	9.5	.4	5.1	−4.3	2.7	10.6	5.4	6.2	5.8	Burkina Faso	748
9.5	3.3	5.5	4.9	1.5	3.5	5.3	1.8	−7.0	−3.1	−7.0	−8.6	.4	4.5	....	Burundi	618
8.9	7.2	−2.2	−7.9	−1.8	−6.7	−3.9	−3.0	−3.2	−2.6	3.3	5.0	5.0	....	....	Cameroon	622
26.0	−2.7	−5.6	....	....	....	....	....	....	....	....	....	....	....	....	Chad	628
.5	4.7	2.7	.5	−1.3	−6.6	−8.4	−10.5	−13.5	−3.9	.7	−.9	−5.7	....	....	Congo, Dem. Rep. of	636
−1.2	−6.9	.2	1.8	1.8	2.2	2.4	1.7	−1.0	−5.5	2.2	....	....	....	....	Congo, Rep. of	634
....	....	−.4	1.0	3.0	−1.1	—	−.1	−.4	2.0	7.1	6.9	6.6	6.0	....	Côte d'Ivoire	662
−5.9	6.9	9.6	1.9	1.6	−.4	−6.0	....	....	....	....	....	....	....	....	Ethiopia	644
4.0	2.8	1.5	4.6	5.6	1.7	5.5	.4	6.6	3.6	−4.1	....	....	....	....	Gambia, The	648
5.1	5.2	4.8	5.6	5.1	3.3	5.3	3.9	4.9	3.8	4.5	5.2	5.1	....	....	Ghana	652
....	....	1.5	2.6	4.6	6.1	3.8	1.8	2.5	5.0	3.7	4.8	4.8	....	....	Guinea-Bissau	654
23.4	7.1	5.9	6.2	4.7	4.2	1.4	−.8	.4	2.6	4.4	4.1	3.0	.8	....	Kenya	664
−1.4	2.9	2.7	—	....	....	....	....	....	....	....	....	....	....	....	Liberia	668
1.2	2.0	1.2	3.4	4.1	3.1	−6.3	1.2	2.1	−.1	1.7	2.1	3.7	3.9	4.5	Madagascar	674
4.5	1.1	2.1	3.4	4.0	4.8	7.8	−7.9	10.8	−11.6	9.0	9.5	6.4	6.3	....	Malawi	676
6.9	9.7	10.2	6.8	4.5	7.2	4.3	6.2	5.6	3.9	4.7	5.3	6.3	5.8	3.4	Mauritius	684
6.3	8.3	−2.6	10.4	2.4	2.1	8.9	−4.0	−1.0	10.4	−6.6	12.2	−2.3	6.5	−.1	Morocco	686
1.2	−2.4	14.8	8.6	5.0	−.9	1.9	−8.6	6.8	7.0	3.3	6.8	11.3	12.1	9.0	Mozambique	688
....	3.7	2.3	8.9	2.1	7.9	5.7	7.4	−2.0	6.6	5.1	3.0	....	....	....	Namibia	728
....	....	−1.1	6.5	−.7	−.3	9.5	.8	−1.0	−3.0	2.7	3.3	−.4	8.8	....	Niger	692
9.7	2.5	−.7	9.9	7.2	8.2	4.8	2.9	2.2	−.6	2.6	6.4	3.9	....	....	Nigeria	694
4.4	5.5	−.6	5.0	.5	2.0	−3.8	6.9	−8.4	−49.6	33.9	15.6	13.2	9.5	5.9	Rwanda	714
3.8	4.6	4.0	5.1	−1.4	3.9	−.4	2.2	−2.2	2.9	5.2	5.1	5.0	5.7	....	Senegal	722
10.3	1.2	4.4	5.3	10.3	7.5	2.7	7.2	6.2	−.8	−.6	1.9	22.8	7.4	....	Seychelles	718
−2.7	−2.4	5.4	−7.1	.7	1.0	−2.8	−13.6	−6.2	.2	−2.8	−2.5	−6.6	.1	−11.6	Sierra Leone	724
−1.2	—	2.1	4.2	2.4	−.3	−1.0	−2.1	1.2	3.2	3.1	4.2	2.5	.6	1.2	South Africa	199
3.8	12.3	14.6	6.6	9.1	8.9	2.5	1.3	3.3	3.5	3.0	3.6	3.7	....	....	Swaziland	734
.1	3.8	1.9	6.5	4.6	.5	−.6	−5.3	−18.4	19.4	6.9	9.7	4.2	−1.3	....	Togo	742
3.2	−2.0	4.9	1.6	3.5	7.1	3.9	7.8	2.2	3.2	2.4	7.1	5.4	5.0	6.2	Tunisia	744
.2	6.0	6.4	7.8	6.9	6.2	5.5	4.6	7.1	10.6	9.6	5.9	....	....	....	Uganda	746
1.6	.7	2.7	6.3	−1.0	−.5	—	−1.7	6.8	−3.5	−2.3	6.5	3.5	....	....	Zambia	754
6.4	2.1	1.1	7.6	5.2	7.0	5.5	−9.0	1.3	6.8	−.7	7.6	4.3	....	....	Zimbabwe	698
8.4	6.7	7.8	9.2	5.6	5.6	6.2	9.0	8.5	9.6	8.9	8.0	6.2	2.0	5.7	Asia	505
3.7	4.7	4.2	2.9	2.5	6.6	3.4	4.2	4.5	4.2	4.4	5.4	5.9	5.7	5.2	Bangladesh	513
16.2	8.9	11.6	11.3	4.1	3.8	9.2	14.2	13.5	12.7	10.5	9.6	8.8	7.8	7.1	China, P.R.: Mainland	924
.2	11.1	13.0	8.0	2.6	3.4	5.1	6.3	6.1	5.4	3.9	4.5	5.0	−5.1	3.0	China, P.R.: Hong Kong	532
−5.1	8.1	−6.4	2.2	12.1	4.7	.6	3.1	1.9	....	....	....	....	....	....	Fiji	819
5.5	4.9	4.8	9.9	6.6	5.7	.4	5.4	5.0	7.3	7.7	7.0	4.6	6.8	....	India	534
2.5	5.9	4.9	5.8	7.5	7.2	7.0	6.5	6.5	7.5	8.2	7.8	4.7	−13.2	.2	Indonesia	536
6.5	11.0	11.0	10.5	6.1	9.0	9.2	5.4	5.5	8.3	8.9	6.8	5.0	−6.7	10.7	Korea	542
9.1	4.8	−1.0	−2.1	9.9	6.7	4.0	7.0	4.5	9.5	7.0	6.9	6.9	4.0	....	Lao People's Democratic Rep.	544
−1.1	1.2	5.4	9.0	9.1	9.0	9.5	8.9	9.9	9.2	9.8	10.0	7.3	−7.4	5.6	Malaysia	548
13.8	8.6	8.9	8.7	9.3	16.2	7.6	6.3	6.2	6.6	7.2	7.9	9.1	9.1	8.5	Maldives	556
5.7	9.4	3.5	5.1	4.2	−2.5	−9.2	−9.5	−3.0	2.3	6.3	2.4	4.0	3.5	....	Mongolia	948
2.9	−1.1	−4.0	−11.4	3.7	2.8	−.7	9.7	6.0	7.5	6.9	6.4	5.7	5.8	5.7	Myanmar	518
6.1	4.6	1.7	7.7	4.3	4.6	6.4	4.1	3.4	7.1	.3	5.7	4.8	2.7	3.4	Nepal	558
7.6	5.5	6.5	7.6	5.0	4.5	5.5	7.8	1.9	3.9	5.1	5.0	1.2	3.3	3.9	Pakistan	564
3.6	5.7	2.8	2.9	−1.4	−3.0	9.5	13.8	13.3	....	....	....	....	....	....	Papua New Guinea	853
−7.3	3.4	4.3	6.8	6.2	3.0	−.6	.3	2.1	4.4	4.7	5.8	5.2	−.5	3.2	Philippines	566
6.0	.6	1.0	−.2	1.3	−7.5	−27.9	−2.3	2.4	−3.7	6.8	6.1	1.6	....	....	Samoa	862
−1.6	2.3	7.4	11.6	9.6	9.0	7.1	6.5	12.7	11.4	8.0	7.5	8.4	.4	5.4	Singapore	576
2.6	−2.2	−5.1	....	....	....	....	....	....	....	....	....	....	....	....	Solomon Islands	813
5.0	4.3	1.5	2.7	2.3	6.2	4.6	4.3	6.9	5.6	5.5	3.8	6.3	4.7	....	Sri Lanka	524
4.6	5.5	9.5	13.3	12.2	11.2	8.6	8.1	8.7	8.6	8.8	5.5	−.4	−10.2	3.3	Thailand	578
5.6	8.8	1.7	−3.5	1.1	4.7	5.9	−3.8	−.1	4.8	....	....	....	....	....	Tonga	866
1.1	−2.0	.4	.6	4.5	5.2	10.4	−.7	4.5	2.5	3.2	....	....	....	....	Vanuatu	846

GDP Volume Measures

Percent Change over Previous Year;

	99bp x	1970	1971	1972	1973	1974	1975	1976	1977	1978	1979	1980	1981	1982	1983	1984
Europe	170	....	....	....	....	....	....	....	....	....	....	....	−1.8	.4	4.8	5.7
Armenia	911	....	....	....	....	....	....	....	....	....	....	....	....	....	....	....
Belarus	913	....	....	....	....	....	....	....	....	....	....	....	....	....	....	....
Bulgaria	918	....	....	....	....	....	....	....	....	....	....	....	....	....	....	....
Croatia	960	....	....	....	....	....	....	....	....	....	....	....	....	....	....	....
Kazakhstan	916	....	....	....	....	....	....	....	....	....	....	....	....	....	....	....
Cyprus	423	3.0	13.0	6.8	2.6	−16.9	−19.0	18.0	15.8	7.6	9.9	5.9	3.1	6.3	5.3	8.8
Czech Republic	935	....	....	....	....	....	....	....	....	....	....	....	....	....	....	....
Estonia	939	....	....	....	....	....	....	....	....	....	....	....	....	....	....	....
Hungary	944	....	6.2	6.1	6.9	5.9	6.2	3.6	7.6	4.4	2.7	.2	2.9	2.8	.7	2.6
Kyrgyz Republic	917	....	....	....	....	....	....	....	....	....	....	....	....	....	....	....
Latvia	941	....	....	....	....	....	....	....	....	....	....	....	....	....	....	....
Lithuania	946	....	....	....	....	....	....	....	....	....	....	....	....	....	....	....
Malta	181	12.6	2.5	5.8	9.8	10.0	19.6	17.0	12.2	11.2	10.5	7.0	3.3	2.3	−.6	.9
Poland	964	....	....	....	....	....	....	....	....	....	....	−10.0	−4.8	5.6	5.7	
Romania	968	....	....	....	....	....	....	....	....	....	....		.1	3.9	6.0	6.0
Slovak Republic	936	....	....	....	....	....	....	....	....	....	....	....	....	....	....	....
Slovenia	961	....	....	....	....	....	....	....	....	....	....	....	....	....	....	....
Turkey	186	3.2	5.6	7.4	3.3	5.6	7.2	10.7	3.2	1.5	−.6	−2.4	4.9	3.6	5.0	6.7
Yugoslavia, SFR	188	5.6	8.1	4.3	4.9	8.6	3.6	3.9	8.0	6.9	7.0	2.3	1.4	.5	−1.0	2.0
Middle East	405	**11.4**	**12.4**	**13.4**	**8.9**	**7.4**	**5.2**	**15.8**	**4.1**	**−6.9**	**5.2**	**−1.3**	**−.6**	**−.2**	**5.5**	**2.7**
Bahrain	419	....	....	....	....	....	....	23.7	14.7	8.1	−1.1	6.6	4.4	6.0	8.0	3.8
Egypt	469	....	....	....	....	....	....	....	....	....	....	....	....	....	5.0	9.8
Iran, I.R. of	429	10.6	12.4	16.3	8.6	8.9	2.8	18.3	7.6	−21.1	−9.3	−13.9	−2.5	13.1	13.2	.9
Iraq	433	1.7	4.4	−2.5	18.7	7.2	15.0	12.1	17.3	12.2	11.7	11.7	−18.0	−1.1	−8.3	
Israel	436	33.3	—	—	50.0	—	16.7	3.7	−21.4	13.6	24.0	3.2	4.5	1.3	2.5	2.1
Jordan	439	....	....	....	....	....	....	....	....	....	....	....	....	....	....	....
Kuwait	443	....	18.9	3.9	−6.5	−12.8	−12.1	12.7	−9.2	7.2	13.7	−20.4	−18.9	−11.8	7.9	5.2
Libya	672	3.9	−5.3	9.1	1.9	22.2	4.0	22.6	8.9	2.6	8.3	.6				
Oman	449	3.3	1.0	9.2	−14.0	28.2	28.6	16.0	17.6	17.7	4.6	5.7	17.0	11.5	16.0	16.7
Saudi Arabia	456	15.3	32.0	19.7	15.1	.3	8.6	15.1	5.9	6.7	10.1	7.9	1.7	−10.7	−.1	−2.2
Syrian Arab Rep.	463	−5.9	9.9	25.0	−8.5	24.1	19.5	11.0	−1.3	8.7	3.6	12.0	9.5	2.1	1.4	−4.1
United Arab Emirates	466	....	....	....	14.5	6.2	15.0	17.4	−2.3	24.9	26.4	2.9	−8.3	−2.6	4.5	
Yemen Republic	474	....	....	....	....	....	....	....	....	....	....	....	....	....	....	....
Western Hemisphere	205	**4.8**	**6.5**	**7.1**	**8.0**	**6.6**	**3.6**	**6.1**	**4.7**	**4.8**	**6.6**	**6.3**	**1.0**	**−.8**	**−2.5**	**3.9**
Antigua and Barbuda	311	....	....	....	....	....	....	....	....	4.2	7.3	8.6	4.1	.2	4.7	9.8
Argentina	213	2.6	3.4	1.9	3.2	6.3	−.7	−.2	6.2	−3.3	7.3	1.5	−5.7	−3.1	4.2	2.0
Bahamas, The	313	....	....	....	....	....	....	....	....	....	....	....	....	....	....	....
Barbados	316	9.1	1.6	1.0	2.0	13.4	−2.0	4.5	3.7	4.9	7.9	4.5	−1.9	−4.9	.4	3.7
Belize	339	....	....	....	....	....	....	....	....	....	....	12.9	2.1	−.6	−1.6	1.8
Bolivia	218	7.8	4.9	5.8	6.7	5.1	6.6	6.1	4.2	3.4	1.8	.6	.3	−3.9	−4.0	−.2
Brazil	223	2.6	11.3	12.0	13.9	8.1	5.2	10.2	4.9	5.0	6.8	9.2	−4.2	.8	−2.9	6.4
Chile	228	2.1	9.0	−1.2	−5.6	1.0	−13.3	3.2	8.3	7.8	7.1	7.7	6.7	−13.4	−3.5	6.1
Colombia	233	6.6	6.0	7.7	6.7	5.7	2.3	4.7	4.2	8.5	5.4	4.1	2.3	.9	1.6	3.4
Costa Rica	238	7.5	6.8	8.2	7.7	5.5	2.1	5.5	8.9	6.3	4.9	.8	−2.3	−7.3	2.9	8.0
Dominica	321	....	....	....	....	....	....	....	3.5	11.8	−18.4	12.7	13.6	4.1	2.7	5.4
Dominican Republic	243	9.0	10.9	10.4	12.9	6.0	5.2	6.7	5.0	2.1	4.5	6.1	4.1	1.6	6.9	1.3
Ecuador	248	6.5	6.3	14.4	25.3	6.4	5.6	9.2	6.5	6.6	5.3	4.9	3.9	1.2	−2.8	4.2
El Salvador	253	3.0	4.6	5.7	5.1	6.4	5.6	4.0	6.1	6.4	−1.7	−8.7	−8.3	−5.6	.8	2.3
Grenada	328	....	....	....	....	....	....	9.0	5.7	8.1	2.4	.2	2.1	5.3	25.2	4.7
Guatemala	258	5.7	5.6	7.3	6.8	6.4	1.9	7.4	7.8	5.0	4.7	3.7	.7	−3.5	−2.6	.5
Guyana	336	3.4	2.8	−2.0	1.7	7.0	10.4	2.9	−5.2	−1.3	−11.7	1.6	−.3	−10.4	−9.3	−24.5
Haiti	263	.6	6.5	.9	4.8	5.8	1.1	8.4	.5	4.9	7.6	7.2	−2.7	−3.4	.8	.3
Honduras	268	4.7	5.4	4.0	5.6	−.1	−3.0	10.5	10.4	8.3	6.3	.7	2.5	−1.4	−.9	4.3
Jamaica	343	7.7	4.4	7.8	2.8	−5.4	−1.2	−6.3	−2.4	.7	−1.8	−5.7	2.6	1.2	2.3	−.9
Mexico	273	6.9	4.2	8.5	8.4	6.1	5.6	4.2	3.4	8.3	9.2	8.3	8.5	−.6	−3.5	3.4
Nicaragua	278	1.4	3.3	2.2	6.4	14.2	−.2	5.2	8.4	−7.8	−26.5	4.6	5.4	−.8	4.6	−1.6
Panama	283	7.0	9.6	4.6	5.4	2.4	1.6	1.6	1.1	9.8	20.4	—	9.2	5.3	−4.5	2.7
Paraguay	288	5.2	5.7	6.7	7.5	8.5	7.2	7.3	10.9	11.4	11.4	11.4	8.7	−1.0	−3.0	3.1
Peru	293	5.9	4.2	2.9	5.4	9.3	3.4	2.0	.4	.3	5.8	4.7	5.5	−2.6	−9.9	5.2
St. Kitts and Nevis	361	....	....	....	....	....	....	....	....	7.4	9.2	8.2	1.1	−1.6	−1.0	10.4
St. Lucia	362	....	....	....	....	....	....	....	....	11.3	4.2	−2.1	4.1	2.2	5.4	6.7
St. Vincent & Grenadines	364	....	....	....	....	....	....	10.3	5.8	−5.8	4.7	3.8	6.6	5.8	5.2	5.3
Suriname	366	....	....	....	....	2.6	−10.0	9.0	10.2	5.5	−5.9	−8.6	7.1	−4.2	−3.9	−1.9
Trinidad and Tobago	369	3.5	1.0	5.8	1.7	3.8	1.5	6.4	9.1	10.0	3.6	10.4	4.6	4.0	−9.2	−6.2
Uruguay	298	4.7	.1	−1.6	.4	3.1	5.9	4.0	1.2	5.3	6.2	6.0	1.9	−9.4	−5.9	−1.1
Venezuela, Rep. Bol.	299	8.8	3.0	2.7	6.3	6.1	6.1	8.8	6.7	2.1	1.3	−2.0	−.3	.7	−5.6	−1.4
Memorandum Items																
Oil Exporting Countries	999	11.3	10.9	10.1	7.4	7.4	3.0	12.9	7.2	−4.2	4.5	1.3	−1.0	.4	2.1	1.9
Non-Oil Developing Countries	201	6.9	7.2	7.1	8.4	4.5	3.6	4.6	3.8	4.0	5.3	6.0	3.1	2.3	2.9	6.4

Indices

Index Numbers:

	99bp x	1970	1971	1972	1973	1974	1975	1976	1977	1978	1979	1980	1981	1982	1983	1984
World	001	41.1	42.6	44.8	47.5	48.6	49.2	51.9	54.2	56.3	58.7	60.2	61.4	61.8	63.6	66.8
Industrial Countries	110	48.8	50.5	53.1	56.4	56.7	56.7	59.5	61.8	64.4	66.8	67.5	68.6	68.5	70.5	73.9
Developing Countries	200	31.1	32.4	33.7	35.7	37.9	39.5	42.3	44.6	46.0	48.4	50.8	52.1	53.1	54.6	57.7
Africa	605	49.0	52.1	54.7	57.1	61.5	61.0	63.9	66.9	66.4	70.9	73.9	73.6	74.8	74.3	75.7
Asia	505	20.1	20.8	21.4	22.8	23.8	25.2	26.8	28.6	30.6	31.8	33.9	35.9	37.8	40.6	44.0
Europe	170	....	....	....	....	....	....	....	....	....	....	78.7	77.3	77.6	81.4	86.0
Middle East	405	37.6	42.3	47.9	52.2	56.1	59.0	68.3	71.1	66.3	69.7	68.8	68.4	68.2	72.0	73.9
Western Hemisphere	205	40.2	42.8	45.9	49.5	52.8	54.7	58.0	60.8	63.7	67.9	72.2	72.9	72.3	70.5	73.2

1985	1986	1987	1988	1989	1990	1991	1992	1993	1994	1995	1996	1997	1998	1999		
Calculated from Indices																
3.3	4.7	4.7	2.8	–.6	–2.0	–6.0	.4	4.0	–.5	5.1	4.9	4.9	2.3	....	Europe	170
....	....	....	....	....	....	....	....	....	....	6.9	5.9	3.3	7.2	....	Armenia	911
....	....	....	....	....	....	....	....	–7.6	–12.6	–10.4	2.8	11.4	8.4	3.4	Belarus	913
....	....	....	....	....	–9.1	–8.4	–7.3	–1.5	1.8	2.9	–10.1	–6.9	....	....	Bulgaria	918
....	....	....	....	....	–7.1	–20.6	–11.7	–.9	.6	1.7	4.3	....	....	....	Croatia	960
....	....	....	....	....	....	....	....	....	....	5.0	9.5	1.2	–3.5	....	Kazakhstan	916
4.7	3.6	7.1	8.3	8.1	7.4	.7	9.4	.7	5.9	6.1	1.9	2.5	5.0	4.5	Cyprus	423
....	....	....	....	....	....	....	....	....	2.2	5.9	4.8	–1.0	–2.2	–.2	Czech Republic	935
....	....	....	....	....	....	....	....	–2.0	4.3	3.9	10.6	4.0	....	....	Estonia	939
–.3	2.4	3.8	5.5	.7	–3.5	–11.9	–3.1	–.6	2.9	1.5	....	....	....	....	Hungary	944
....	....	....	....	....	....	....	–13.9	–15.5	–20.1	–5.4	7.1	9.9	2.1	....	Kyrgyz Republic	917
....	....	....	....	....	....	....	–14.9	.6	–.8	3.3	8.6	3.9	.1	....	Latvia	941
....	....	....	....	....	....	....	–16.2	–9.8	3.3	4.7	7.3	5.1	–4.1	....	Lithuania	946
2.6	3.9	4.1	8.4	8.2	6.3	6.3	4.7	4.5	5.7	6.2	4.0	4.9	3.4	4.6	Malta	181
5.1	4.2	2.1	4.0	.3	–11.4	–7.0	2.6	3.8	5.2	7.0	6.0	6.8	4.8	....	Poland	964
–.1	2.3	.8	–.5	–5.8	–5.6	–12.9	–8.8	1.5	3.9	7.1	3.9	–3.9	–7.3	....	Romania	968
....	....	....	....	....	....	....	....	–3.7	4.9	6.9	6.6	6.5	4.4	....	Slovak Republic	936
....	....	....	....	....	....	–8.9	–5.5	2.8	5.3	4.1	3.3	3.8	....	....	Slovenia	961
4.2	7.0	9.5	2.1	.3	9.3	.9	6.0	8.0	–5.5	7.2	7.0	7.5	2.8	....	Turkey	186
.5	3.6	–1.0	–2.0	....	....	....	....	....	....	....	....	....	....	....	Yugoslavia, SFR	188
1.2	–4.4	2.1	—	3.2	8.4	6.1	5.0	3.0	2.9	3.9	4.5	3.8	3.2	....	Middle East	405
–2.8	1.2	10.4	8.6	.4	4.4	11.2	6.7	12.9	–.3	3.9	4.1	3.1	4.8	....	Bahrain	419
5.8	4.7	3.8	5.5	4.9	5.7	1.1	4.5	2.9	4.0	4.6	5.0	5.5	5.6	....	Egypt	469
.2	–15.1	1.2	–8.7	3.3	11.7	11.4	5.7	1.6	.7	4.2	6.7	3.7	1.8	....	Iran, I.R. of	429
—	8.1	19.4	3.1	–8.9	—	....	....	....	....	....	....	....	....	....	Iraq	433
4.0	4.1	6.1	3.1	1.3	5.8	6.2	6.6	3.2	6.8	7.1	4.6	2.9	2.2	2.0	Israel	436
....	7.0	2.9	–1.9	–13.4	1.0	2.3	17.0	5.8	7.6	3.9	1.0	1.3	2.2	....	Jordan	439
–4.3	8.6	8.1	–10.1	25.9	–8.4	–8.4	–8.4	34.0	8.4	1.1	–3.3	....	....	....	Kuwait	443
....	....	....	....	....	....	....	....	....	....	....	....	....	....	....	Libya	672
13.8	2.1	–4.0	5.2	3.0	8.4	6.0	8.5	6.1	3.8	4.8	2.9	6.4	2.7	....	Oman	449
–4.1	5.6	–1.4	7.6	.2	10.7	8.4	2.8	–.6	.5	.5	1.4	2.7	1.6	.4	Saudi Arabia	456
6.1	–4.9	1.9	13.3	–9.0	4.6	7.9	13.5	5.2	7.7	5.8	7.3	2.5	7.8	....	Syrian Arab Rep.	463
–2.5	–21.2	3.6	–.2	15.3	17.5	.8	2.7	....	....	....	....	....	....	....	United Arab Emirates	466
....	....	....	....	....	....	–2.1	4.8	.4	–3.6	7.9	2.9	8.1	5.3	3.8	Yemen Republic	474
3.2	3.5	3.1	1.0	1.7	2.3	3.7	2.9	3.8	5.1	1.2	3.5	5.3	2.2	....	Western Hemisphere	205
8.0	12.7	8.3	5.4	5.8	2.5	2.0	.8	5.4	6.3	–4.2	5.8	....	....	....	Antigua and Barbuda	311
–6.9	7.1	2.6	–1.9	–6.9	–1.8	10.6	9.6	5.7	8.0	–4.0	4.8	8.6	4.2	....	Argentina	213
....	....	....	....	....	–3.3	–3.2	–5.8	–2.1	2.0	1.1	....	....	....	....	Bahamas, The	313
1.1	5.1	2.6	3.5	3.6	–3.3	–4.0	–6.1	1.4	4.0	2.9	4.1	3.0	....	....	Barbados	316
.4	3.0	29.0	9.2	13.0	11.5	2.6	8.2	4.3	3.2	3.5	1.5	3.4	2.4	6.1	Belize	339
–1.7	–2.6	2.5	2.9	3.8	4.6	5.3	1.6	4.3	4.7	4.7	4.4	5.0	5.5	.6	Bolivia	218
7.5	7.0	3.4	–.1	4.0	.4	1.0	–.5	4.9	5.8	4.2	2.7	3.6	–.1	....	Brazil	223
3.5	5.6	6.6	7.3	10.6	3.7	8.0	12.3	7.0	5.7	10.6	7.4	7.4	3.4	–1.1	Chile	228
3.1	5.8	5.4	4.1	3.4	4.3	2.0	4.0	5.4	5.8	5.2	2.1	3.4	....	....	Colombia	233
.7	5.5	4.8	3.4	5.7	3.6	2.3	7.7	6.3	4.5	2.4	–.6	3.7	6.7	8.3	Costa Rica	238
1.3	7.1	7.5	8.6	–.2	5.3	.6	2.0	1.7	1.4	1.7	2.8	1.9	....	....	Dominica	321
–2.1	3.5	10.1	2.2	4.4	–5.5	1.0	8.0	3.0	4.3	4.8	7.3	8.2	7.3	8.3	Dominican Republic	243
4.3	3.1	–6.0	10.5	.3	3.0	5.0	3.6	2.0	4.4	2.3	1.8	3.7	.4	....	Ecuador	248
2.0	.6	2.7	1.6	1.1	3.4	3.6	7.5	7.4	6.0	6.4	1.7	4.2	3.5	2.6	El Salvador	253
8.2	3.9	–14.9	5.3	5.7	5.2	2.9	.6	....	....	....	....	....	....	....	Grenada	328
–.6	.1	3.5	3.9	3.9	3.1	3.6	4.8	3.9	4.0	4.9	2.9	4.4	5.1	3.5	Guatemala	258
35.8	–4.7	.8	–2.6	–3.3	–4.7	6.0	7.8	8.2	....	....	....	....	....	....	Guyana	336
.3	1.0	–.2	–.2	–.4	.2	4.7	–13.2	–2.4	–8.3	4.4	2.7	1.3	3.1	2.4	Haiti	263
4.2	.7	6.0	4.6	4.3	.1	3.3	5.6	6.2	–1.3	4.1	3.6	5.1	2.9	–1.9	Honduras	268
–4.6	1.7	7.8	2.9	6.8	5.5	.7	1.5	1.5	.9	.8	–1.4	–2.1	–.7	....	Jamaica	343
2.2	–3.1	1.7	1.3	4.2	5.1	4.2	3.6	2.0	4.4	–6.2	5.2	6.7	4.8	3.7	Mexico	273
–4.1	–1.0	–.7	–12.4	–1.7	–.1	–.2	.4	–.4	3.3	4.3	4.7	5.1	6.1	5.0	Nicaragua	278
4.9	3.6	–1.8	–13.4	1.6	8.1	9.4	8.2	5.5	2.9	1.8	2.8	4.5	4.1	3.2	Panama	283
4.0	....	4.3	6.4	5.8	3.1	2.5	1.8	4.1	3.1	4.7	1.3	2.6	–.4	.5	Paraguay	288
2.8	10.0	8.0	–8.7	–11.7	–3.7	3.2	–2.0	6.7	12.8	7.3	2.4	6.9	.3	3.8	Peru	293
6.4	11.7	8.7	9.1	7.6	2.3	.4	3.3	–10.0	5.4	3.5	5.9	6.3	....	....	St. Kitts and Nevis	361
7.8	16.7	3.8	14.6	8.1	3.4	–.5	6.5	–.1	2.0	.5	.8	.5	....	....	St. Lucia	362
5.4	7.3	4.6	14.5	2.6	5.1	1.5	5.9	2.4	–2.0	7.6	1.4	3.7	5.2	....	St. Vincent & Grenadines	364
2.0	.8	–6.2	7.8	4.2	—	3.5	5.8	–4.5	–.8	....	....	....	....	....	Suriname	366
–4.1	–3.3	–4.6	–3.9	–.8	1.5	2.7	–1.6	–1.5	3.6	4.0	3.8	3.1	4.4	....	Trinidad and Tobago	369
1.5	8.9	7.9	1.5	1.1	.3	3.6	7.9	2.7	7.3	–1.5	5.4	4.9	4.6	–3.2	Uruguay	298
1.4	6.3	4.5	6.2	–7.8	6.9	9.7	6.1	.3	–2.3	4.0	–.2	6.4	–.1	–7.2	Venezuela, Rep. Bol.	299

Memorandum Items

1985	1986	1987	1988	1989	1990	1991	1992	1993	1994	1995	1996	1997	1998	1999		
1.4	–1.1	2.5	2.0	4.2	8.6	7.6	5.0	3.8	3.5	5.3	5.4	4.4	–6.3	–1.0	Oil Exporting Countries	999
6.2	5.1	5.6	5.6	3.5	3.5	3.8	5.8	6.2	7.3	6.2	6.5	5.7	3.4	5.5	Non-Oil Developing Countries	201

Indices

1995=100

1985	1986	1987	1988	1989	1990	1991	1992	1993	1994	1995	1996	1997	1998	1999		
69.7	72.1	75.0	78.6	81.4	84.1	86.3	89.2	91.8	96.1	100.0	104.4	108.8	111.3	115.7	World	001
76.6	78.9	81.5	85.1	88.2	90.6	92.0	93.7	94.8	97.7	100.0	102.9	106.1	108.7	112.4	Industrial Countries	110
60.9	63.4	66.6	70.0	72.5	75.6	78.8	83.3	88.2	94.2	100.0	106.4	112.3	114.7	120.0	Developing Countries	200
79.3	81.8	83.1	87.6	90.6	92.9	95.0	94.6	95.3	97.8	100.0	106.2	109.6	113.6	....	Africa	605
47.6	50.8	54.8	59.9	63.2	66.8	70.9	77.3	83.8	91.8	100.0	108.0	114.7	116.9	123.6	Asia	505
88.8	93.0	97.4	100.1	99.5	97.5	91.6	92.0	95.6	95.2	100.0	104.9	110.0	112.6	....	Europe	170
74.7	71.4	72.9	72.9	75.2	81.5	86.5	90.8	93.5	96.2	100.0	104.5	108.5	111.9	....	Middle East	405
75.6	78.2	80.7	81.5	82.9	84.8	88.0	90.5	94.0	98.8	100.0	103.5	108.9	111.3	....	Western Hemisphere	205

GDP Deflators

99bi x

	99bi x	1970	1971	1972	1973	1974	1975	1976	1977	1978	1979	1980	1981	1982	1983	1984
													Percent Change over Previous Year;			
World	001	**6.7**	**6.6**	**7.1**	**10.9**	**18.5**	**14.0**	**12.9**	**12.4**	**11.3**	**15.0**	**16.5**	**14.4**	**14.3**	**14.8**	**14.3**
Industrial Countries	110	**6.3**	**6.1**	**5.7**	**8.1**	**12.4**	**11.2**	**8.5**	**8.4**	**8.0**	**8.5**	**9.9**	**9.2**	**7.3**	**5.4**	**4.8**
United States	111	5.3	5.0	4.2	5.6	9.0	9.3	5.7	6.4	7.1	8.3	9.2	9.3	6.2	4.0	3.7
Canada	156	4.6	3.2	5.6	8.9	14.4	9.9	8.7	6.2	6.0	10.0	10.6	10.8	8.7	5.0	3.1
Australia	193	4.8	6.7	8.1	11.9	17.1	16.7	13.5	8.8	7.4	9.8	11.2	9.4	10.6	8.6	6.4
Japan	158	7.7	5.6	5.6	12.9	20.8	7.7	7.2	5.8	4.8	3.0	4.6	3.7	1.7	1.4	2.3
New Zealand	196	9.5	14.9	10.1	8.6	5.5	13.7	20.7	9.2	10.3	13.8	14.9	15.6	16.4	4.9	7.3
Euro Area	163	....	....	....	....	....	....	....	....	....	....	....	....	....	....	....
Austria	122	4.7	6.0	7.5	7.7	9.2	7.9	6.9	5.7	6.0	3.5	5.0	6.6	5.3	3.7	4.6
Belgium	124	4.6	5.4	6.1	7.0	12.2	12.7	7.8	7.3	4.0	4.2	4.3	5.2	6.7	5.4	5.4
Finland	172	3.9	7.6	8.4	14.1	22.5	13.3	13.5	9.9	8.4	8.8	9.7	11.1	8.9	8.6	8.9
France	132	5.6	6.3	7.0	8.5	11.9	13.0	11.1	9.3	10.1	10.1	11.4	11.4	11.7	9.7	7.5
Germany	134	7.7	7.7	5.3	6.4	7.0	5.7	3.6	3.7	4.2	3.8	4.9	4.2	4.4	3.3	2.1
Ireland	178	8.9	10.5	13.4	14.8	5.3	23.9	21.0	13.3	10.5	13.7	14.7	17.4	15.2	11.7	6.4
Italy	136	14.2	6.6	6.2	13.8	20.7	15.9	18.4	19.2	14.0	15.6	20.9	19.1	16.9	14.5	11.6
Luxembourg	137	10.6	−.8	5.8	12.2	17.0	−.8	12.2	1.2	5.1	6.5	7.8	7.2	10.8	6.8	4.4
Netherlands	138	−7.5	8.5	10.4	8.8	9.3	9.8	9.6	6.0	5.3	6.5	3.2	6.4	5.7	1.5	2.1
Portugal	182	2.9	5.1	7.8	8.0	18.9	16.2	16.3	26.4	22.4	19.7	20.6	17.6	20.7	24.6	24.7
Spain	184	6.8	7.8	8.5	11.8	16.0	16.8	16.5	23.4	20.6	16.9	13.4	12.6	13.9	11.8	11.6
Denmark	128	7.9	7.9	9.9	10.8	13.6	13.8	9.0	9.9	9.5	7.9	8.6	11.8	11.1	8.4	6.0
Greece	174	3.9	3.2	5.0	19.4	20.9	12.3	15.4	12.9	13.0	18.6	17.7	19.7	25.1	19.1	20.3
Iceland	176	16.9	12.7	18.3	31.6	37.2	41.9	33.0	32.7	46.2	40.8	51.5	50.8	58.2	76.1	25.5
Norway	142	12.8	6.7	5.0	9.2	10.3	10.0	7.5	8.3	19.5	5.5	13.1	12.9	10.4	7.0	6.3
Sweden	144	6.2	7.3	7.1	7.1	8.3	14.9	11.8	11.0	10.0	7.5	12.1	9.6	8.3	10.0	7.6
Switzerland	146	4.7	8.9	9.5	8.0	7.2	6.5	2.1	.3	3.4	2.0	8.8	5.8	6.8	2.7	3.5
United Kingdom	112	7.4	9.3	8.1	7.2	15.0	27.1	15.2	13.8	11.6	14.5	19.4	11.3	7.4	5.4	4.6
Developing Countries	200	**7.7**	**7.8**	**11.3**	**19.6**	**34.9**	**21.0**	**24.4**	**22.9**	**19.6**	**27.8**	**29.4**	**24.6**	**28.2**	**34.0**	**32.8**
Africa	605	**11.3**	**4.1**	**4.7**	**10.6**	**29.3**	**11.8**	**11.7**	**13.3**	**15.3**	**13.0**	**18.2**	**15.5**	**11.7**	**16.2**	**15.2**
Benin	638	....	3.7	3.5	4.7	30.8	.4	13.5	5.3	5.9	14.1	14.4	15.9	24.9	4.7	2.0
Botswana	616	4.3	9.2	.7	5.5	12.3	19.0	14.2	12.7	−1.6	25.1	19.1	3.6	−4.3	10.4	8.2
Burkina Faso	748	....	....	....	....	....	....	....	....	....	....	6.0	14.2	8.5	7.2	.7
Burundi	618	....	11.5	5.8	5.2	12.6	19.0	9.7	14.1	11.8	21.8	16.5	−6.2	6.1	6.1	17.2
Cameroon	622	17.2	3.9	6.2	10.9	17.7	12.0	11.1	13.7	11.0	5.5	14.6	13.1	12.5	12.6	13.2
Central African Rep.	626	3.8	4.2	4.1	.7	18.8	15.9	7.0	7.5	....	....	....	....	....	....	....
Congo, Dem. Rep. of	636	6.9	5.5	10.1	17.9	18.2	12.2	57.5	37.3	46.3	101.8	252.5	34.3	43.4	78.1	89.6
Côte d'Ivoire	662	....	....	....	....	....	....	....	35.6	2.0	7.0	2.6	3.0	....	....	....
Ethiopia	644	6.2	1.0	−3.9	2.7	9.3	−.6	6.3	13.0	7.7	5.5	.3	11.2	4.5	2.8	−1.8
Gambia, The	648	....	−14.0	24.5	−3.5	−6.2	45.7	3.5	59.4	−6.6	16.0	111.5	−50.0	1.9	12.4	22.9
Ghana	652	5.9	4.9	15.4	7.9	28.7	30.1	28.0	67.3	73.3	38.9	51.8	72.3	28.4	111.4	43.2
Guinea-Bissau	654	....	....	....	....	....	....	....	....	....	....	....	....	....	....	....
Kenya	664	2.8	4.5	−37.9	7.3	17.2	8.9	13.0	−19.1	46.7	−27.2	8.6	9.1	10.8	9.1	8.5
Liberia	668	−2.6	.9	5.0	4.8	13.9	41.6	−.3	12.7	5.4	9.0	9.3	9.1	12.8	1.6	−5.4
Madagascar	674	7.0	5.2	5.1	11.2	21.3	2.9	10.7	7.9	6.8	11.4	15.0	25.2	28.6	21.6	35.8
Malawi	676	....	....	....	....	18.0	8.8	8.8	14.0	1.5	4.5	16.7	16.3	9.3	11.5	13.8
Mauritania	682	....	....	....	....	11.6	33.4	6.1	7.6	2.1	....	....	....	....	....	....
Mauritius	684	2.0	6.0	14.2	15.6	60.8	4.9	3.0	24.5	10.8	17.9	26.6	10.9	8.9	8.4	7.4
Morocco	686	2.9	4.0	3.9	5.8	18.0	9.7	−.1	13.2	8.4	7.3	15.2	9.7	7.2	7.3	8.6
Mozambique	688	....	....	....	....	....	....	....	....	....	....	....	....	....	....	....
Namibia	728	....	....	....	....	....	....	....	....	....	....	....	....	....	....	....
Niger	692	....	....	....	....	....	....	....	....	....	....	....	....	....	....	....
Nigeria	694	51.3	1.3	2.9	5.3	43.9	23.5	14.4	10.7	13.9	11.5	12.4	16.2	2.6	16.1	16.9
Rwanda	714	4.8	−.3	2.0	3.6	17.2	5.2	15.1	10.0	3.2	9.8	15.0	10.7	2.6	2.4	16.9
Senegal	722	2.0	3.0	4.1	7.7	16.8	11.6	3.8	8.2	6.8	9.7	11.5	8.0	9.3	8.9	12.6
Seychelles	718	....	....	....	21.7	15.5	21.1	62.7	25.0	13.1	17.9	20.6	10.5	1.1	4.0	−.1
Sierra Leone	724	....	....	3.2	7.3	16.8	16.4	10.5	19.6	13.9	12.7	9.0	5.3	22.2	18.6	43.5
South Africa	199	4.0	5.8	11.0	18.3	16.2	10.6	10.2	10.9	11.6	15.3	23.6	11.8	13.7	15.7	11.5
Swaziland	734	....	....	....	....	....	....	....	....	....	2.1	3.2	26.6	11.0	7.9	4.8	7.6
Tanzania	738	....	....	....	....	....	....	....	....	....	....	....	....	....	....	....
Togo	742	....	4.6	3.1	7.7	38.6	−1.2	6.7	17.3	1.7	6.8	10.0	12.1	8.7	9.7	3.9
Tunisia	744	3.8	6.0	2.9	8.6	24.4	5.0	2.9	9.7	6.5	10.4	12.8	11.4	16.0	12.7	6.5
Uganda	746	....	6.6	9.1	14.4	23.6	43.3	16.7	80.8	40.1	74.1	40.5	77.2	40.0	−40.7	64.1
Zambia	754	−10.1	−3.1	4.6	19.2	11.2	−14.0	14.8	10.1	12.7	21.9	11.8	7.2	6.1	18.6	18.4
Zimbabwe	698	....	....	....	5.9	1.5	13.0	9.8	7.0	9.7	15.2	10.3	14.4	14.8	13.0	8.9
Asia	505	**5.4**	**5.1**	**9.5**	**18.5**	**25.1**	**9.7**	**6.9**	**7.5**	**9.2**	**16.1**	**11.1**	**9.0**	**6.1**	**6.4**	**7.3**
Bangladesh	513	....	....	....	....	40.6	71.1	−23.9	−3.2	30.4	12.9	13.1	10.3	12.7	5.0	16.4
Bhutan	514	....	....	....	....	....	....	....	....	....	....	6.2	11.1	8.5	9.8
China, P.R.: Mainland	924	....	....	....	....	....	....	....	....	....	....	3.6	3.1	3.5	.2	2.9
China, P.R.: Hong Kong	532	8.6	7.3	8.6	13.9	11.9	4.6	8.7	3.5	7.7	17.3	15.0	10.1	9.8	3.9	9.9
Fiji	819	578.8	3.2	15.7	15.7	33.1	25.4	7.8	1.6	3.5	−84.7	17.6	−.1	8.2	5.3	3.0
India	534	1.6	5.3	10.9	18.1	16.7	−1.5	5.9	5.6	2.5	15.8	11.6	10.3	7.4	8.5	7.5
Indonesia	536	14.3	2.7	13.6	32.9	47.3	12.5	14.5	13.0	10.9	32.5	29.1	18.5	5.1	19.2	8.2
Korea	542	17.6	14.2	17.7	14.8	31.5	26.4	23.1	16.5	23.9	19.6	24.4	17.8	7.1	6.0	5.6
Lao People's Democratic Rep.	544	....	....	....	....	....	....	....	....	....	....	....	....	....	76.5	36.2
Malaysia	548	....	−3.1	.3	17.9	12.7	−3.1	12.7	6.9	9.8	12.1	6.9	1.1	2.5	5.2	5.5
Maldives	556	....	....	....	....	....	....	....	....	....	3.8	19.6	31.8	20.8	18.6	−7.1	−15.2
Mongolia	948	....	....	....	....	....	....	....	....	....	....	....	1.5	2.0	1.0	−3.2
Myanmar	518	8.9	−2.3	.8	10.0	22.1	28.2	7.3	−4.5	8.5	6.1	1.3	4.5	3.6	2.0	2.5
Nepal	558	7.0	3.2	12.5	−3.4	20.8	27.5	.5	−3.6	9.4	10.0	7.6	7.9	9.3	12.3	6.4
Pakistan	564	2.5	5.0	6.6	15.7	23.0	22.4	12.1	10.7	9.0	5.5	10.5	11.1	9.4	5.3	9.7
Papua New Guinea	853	....	....	....	....	27.4	−4.3	8.2	37.9	.3	13.5	7.1	−2.7	3.2	9.2	—
Philippines	566	15.9	12.0	6.1	18.4	32.8	9.2	8.4	8.0	9.5	15.9	6.6	11.7	8.7	14.2	53.3
Samoa	862	3.0	4.6	7.7	12.1	24.8	8.8	5.0	14.5	2.2	11.8	22.0	16.2	20.7	18.1	....
Singapore	576	1.7	4.5	5.4	12.2	15.6	2.4	1.9	1.6	2.4	5.3	11.5	6.7	4.2	3.9	.7
Solomon Islands	813	....	....	....	....	....	....	....	....	....	....	....	10.7	14.0	−14.1	44.8
Sri Lanka	524	−24.9	3.5	4.3	17.4	26.0	7.3	6.0	18.8	7.8	15.7	18.2	20.5	13.6	14.6	17.1
Thailand	578	3.8	−.8	6.5	18.9	20.5	3.6	4.5	6.0	9.6	8.7	13.1	8.4	5.1	3.6	1.4
Vanuatu	846	....	....	....	....	....	....	....	....	....	....	....	....	....	....	−6.4

99bi x

Calculated from Indices

1985	1986	1987	1988	1989	1990	1991	1992	1993	1994	1995	1996	1997	1998	1999		
13.6	**10.6**	**13.5**	**19.5**	**24.0**	**26.3**	**16.2**	**16.3**	**19.5**	**19.5**	**10.0**	**6.6**	**5.1**	**6.0**	. . . .	**World**	**001**
3.7	**3.6**	**3.2**	**3.8**	**4.2**	**4.3**	**4.4**	**3.0**	**2.5**	**1.9**	**2.0**	**1.6**	**1.6**	**1.3**	**1.7**	**Industrial Countries**	**110**
3.2	2.2	3.0	3.4	3.8	3.9	3.6	2.4	2.4	2.1	2.2	1.9	1.9	1.2	1.5	United States	**111**
2.6	2.4	4.6	4.7	4.8	3.1	2.9	2.5	1.5	1.1	2.3	1.6	.8	–.4	2.2	Canada	**156**
5.5	6.0	7.7	8.9	6.8	4.7	2.7	.7	1.4	.7	2.0	1.7	1.2	.6	1.0	Australia	**193**
1.6	2.0	.2	.7	2.1	2.6	2.7	1.7	.6	.2	–.6	–1.4	.4	.7	. . . .	Japan	**158**
15.3	17.0	11.8	6.6	6.6	2.9	1.2	2.4	2.0	1.7	2.7	1.1	.3	1.7	. . . .	New Zealand	**196**
. . . .	. . . .	. . . .	. . . .	. . . .	. . . .	. . . .	. . . .	. . . .	. . . .	. . . .	3.1	–.1	3.1	1.5	Euro Area	**163**
3.1	2.7	2.1	1.6	2.7	3.4	3.7	4.3	2.8	2.8	4.4	1.3	1.6	.6	.5	Austria	**122**
–21.1	3.0	1.4	2.3	4.9	3.0	2.8	3.6	3.7	1.8	1.8	1.2	1.3	1.6	.9	Belgium	**124**
5.3	4.6	4.7	8.5	6.5	5.8	1.6	1.0	1.8	2.0	3.6	–.3	2.7	2.3	. . . .	Finland	**172**
5.8	5.2	3.0	4.4	3.3	2.9	3.0	2.0	2.4	1.8	1.6	1.5	1.3	.7	.3	France	**132**
2.1	3.2	1.9	1.5	2.4	3.4	6.7	5.0	3.7	2.5	2.0	1.0	.8	1.0	1.0	Germany	**134**
5.3	5.8	2.2	3.4	5.4	4.1	1.8	2.8	5.2	1.7	2.7	2.3	3.5	5.6	. . . .	Ireland	**178**
9.0	7.8	6.1	7.1	6.5	8.2	7.6	4.5	3.9	3.5	5.0	5.2	2.6	2.8	1.2	Italy	**136**
15.3	3.6	2.2	5.1	7.5	4.1	5.4	5.2	. . . .	. . . .	. . . .	. . . .	. . . .	. . . .	. . . .	Luxembourg	**137**
2.9	–.2	–.7	1.2	1.2	2.4	2.7	2.4	1.6	1.8	2.7	.3	2.5	2.9	.6	Netherlands	**138**
21.7	37.9	10.1	11.2	12.1	12.4	12.2	10.6	7.0	6.1	5.0	3.1	2.7	4.1	. . . .	Portugal	**182**
7.7	11.1	5.8	5.7	7.0	7.3	7.1	6.9	4.3	4.0	4.8	3.2	2.0	2.2	8.5	Spain	**184**
4.9	4.0	5.1	2.5	5.2	3.7	2.8	2.9	1.4	1.7	1.8	2.5	1.6	2.1	2.6	Denmark	**128**
17.7	17.5	14.3	40.0	14.8	21.3	19.4	15.1	13.7	11.8	11.4	7.4	6.7	4.9	3.0	Greece	**174**
31.3	25.3	19.5	22.8	19.8	16.9	7.8	3.6	2.5	2.0	2.7	1.9	4.8	5.8	4.1	Iceland	**176**
5.2	–.9	6.9	5.0	5.7	3.9	2.4	–.4	2.1	–.2	3.1	4.7	1.6	–.5	7.4	Norway	**142**
6.7	6.9	5.1	6.0	8.0	8.8	8.2	1.0	2.6	2.5	3.7	1.0	1.2	.7	. . . .	Sweden	**144**
2.4	3.1	2.7	2.8	3.1	4.3	6.0	2.7	2.7	1.6	1.1	.4	–.1	.2	.7	Switzerland	**146**
5.6	3.1	5.2	6.1	7.4	7.6	6.7	4.0	2.8	1.5	2.5	3.3	2.9	3.2	2.9	United Kingdom	**112**
33.2	**23.8**	**34.1**	**52.8**	**67.8**	**70.7**	**37.5**	**40.9**	**52.4**	**46.6**	**21.1**	**13.3**	**9.8**	**12.3**	. . . .	**Developing Countries**	**200**
13.6	**10.0**	**21.7**	**16.5**	**21.0**	**15.3**	**23.9**	**34.5**	**27.1**	**17.4**	**27.7**	**14.2**	**8.7**	**6.4**	. . . .	**Africa**	**605**
–4.9	–3.6	3.1	–.3	1.8	1.6	.7	3.4	1.2	33.5	15.4	6.7	4.7	4.2	3.2	Benin	**638**
22.7	23.1	–1.9	18.0	35.3	6.0	6.3	4.2	9.1	16.4	8.9	8.7	15.0	7.8	9.6	Botswana	**616**
50.4	–7.2	1.6	2.6	6.6	1.1	–4.6	.4	–6.1	31.6	10.8	.2	1.6	3.1	–1.3	Burkina Faso	**748**
7.1	–3.5	–3.4	1.5	15.7	5.8	–1.1	8.2	12.7	17.7	22.2	22.7	24.8	12.4	. . . .	Burundi	**618**
11.9	–1.0	–6.5	2.7	–2.6	4.1	1.5	—	7.2	18.9	11.6	5.7	4.0	. . . .	. . . .	Cameroon	**622**
. . . .	. . . .	. . . .	. . . .	. . . .	. . . .	. . . .	. . . .	. . . .	. . . .	. . . .	. . . .	. . . .	. . . .	. . . .	Central African Rep.	**626**
25.8	28.4	73.8	91.6	110.3	109.0	2,202.3	4,078.5	1,662.4	3,820.4	3,820.4	. . . .	. . . .	. . . .	. . . .	Congo, Dem. Rep. of	**636**
. . . .	. . . .	. . . .	. . . .	. . . .	. . . .	. . . .	. . . .	. . . .	. . . .	. . . .	. . . .	. . . .	. . . .	. . . .	Côte d'Ivoire	**662**
26.0	–2.5	–3.2	2.1	3.5	7.4	21.4	.9	14.8	. . . .	. . . .	. . . .	. . . .	. . . .	. . . .	Ethiopia	**644**
11.7	21.4	34.9	5.2	12.5	19.8	5.4	11.6	–19.8	10.6	. . . .	. . . .	. . . .	. . . .	. . . .	Gambia, The	**648**
20.6	41.7	39.2	33.4	28.3	38.8	13.5	11.1	31.7	29.5	42.5	39.1	18.4	. . . .	. . . .	Ghana	**652**
. . . .	. . . .	–28.0	–10.2	23.0	–2.3	–3.4	–16.7	6.5	87.6	–3.8	–5.7	15.8	. . . .	. . . .	Guinea-Bissau	**654**
12.6	8.7	5.4	8.5	8.4	9.4	11.5	20.7	25.5	17.0	11.3	8.9	15.3	10.5	. . . .	Kenya	**664**
2.5	–4.5	3.8	4.8	. . . .	. . . .	. . . .	. . . .	. . . .	. . . .	. . . .	. . . .	. . . .	. . . .	. . . .	Liberia	**668**
10.4	14.2	23.0	21.2	12.0	11.5	13.9	12.5	13.0	41.6	45.1	17.8	7.5	8.5	8.2	Madagascar	**674**
9.0	11.8	16.5	26.4	18.1	15.2	11.7	19.1	19.6	31.7	102.7	42.2	9.9	18.6	. . . .	Malawi	**676**
. . . .	. . . .	. . . .	. . . .	. . . .	. . . .	. . . .	. . . .	. . . .	. . . .	. . . .	. . . .	. . . .	. . . .	. . . .	Mauritania	**682**
8.3	8.0	11.6	10.9	11.0	10.1	8.2	5.5	7.9	7.2	4.7	6.3	5.1	6.9	5.3	Mauritius	**684**
8.4	10.3	3.9	5.3	3.9	8.1	4.0	4.4	3.6	1.6	8.0	1.0	2.0	.7	. . . .	Morocco	**686**
33.7	12.6	180.6	47.8	49.6	36.6	188.6	40.2	48.5	55.4	50.3	48.2	11.5	1.6	2.4	Mozambique	**688**
. . . .	12.9	2.9	17.0	14.6	13.3	6.5	9.4	8.9	14.8	5.4	10.1	. . . .	. . . .	. . . .	Namibia	**728**
. . . .	4.8	.9	–3.0	.2	2.2	–9.3	–2.8	–.8	25.4	.2	–22.4	37.6	2.5	. . . .	Niger	**692**
3.7	–1.5	50.1	21.4	44.4	7.2	20.2	83.6	52.6	28.7	55.8	34.2	10.2	. . . .	. . . .	Nigeria	**694**
4.6	–7.1	1.2	–2.1	7.6	10.1	15.9	5.8	14.4	16.9	51.6	10.6	15.1	2.8	–5.0	Rwanda	**714**
9.3	7.6	2.0	2.1	.9	1.2	.4	.6	–1.4	27.8	5.0	1.3	2.2	2.2	. . . .	Senegal	**722**
2.3	5.8	3.7	3.9	2.1	6.4	–2.0	4.6	3.1	1.2	–.2	.7	–4.6	—	. . . .	Seychelles	**718**
64.4	85.2	170.2	64.3	61.5	70.6	106.0	96.9	52.1	16.2	34.4	26.2	—	26.5	34.1	Sierra Leone	**724**
16.2	16.3	14.2	15.1	17.2	20.8	15.7	14.6	13.1	9.6	10.3	8.3	7.8	7.6	6.9	South Africa	**199**
16.8	13.8	1.1	24.1	6.4	11.7	6.5	12.5	13.0	13.0	18.3	10.1	11.2	. . . .	. . . .	Swaziland	**734**
. . . .	. . . .	. . . .	47.7	20.6	22.4	28.1	25.4	24.5	31.2	26.9	19.3	20.7	24.0	10.2	Tanzania	**738**
7.7	4.0	—	3.6	–3.5	2.6	–2.5	13.0	–2.6	29.5	12.0	3.7	5.7	. . . .	. . . .	Togo	**742**
6.1	4.1	7.0	6.1	7.0	5.3	7.0	5.7	4.7	4.5	5.4	4.4	4.0	3.5	3.4	Tunisia	**744**
166.4	141.0	221.8	162.7	73.7	28.1	31.5	58.6	1.9	16.2	5.4	4.9	. . . .	. . . .	. . . .	Uganda	**746**
41.1	83.9	47.1	42.8	85.7	106.4	92.7	165.5	143.6	56.7	36.9	24.3	25.5	. . . .	. . . .	Zambia	**754**
34.6	10.8	7.3	16.0	17.2	15.5	31.2	27.3	22.2	22.9	10.8	28.3	. . . .	. . . .	. . . .	Zimbabwe	**698**
5.9	**5.2**	**6.7**	**9.9**	**8.5**	**8.5**	**9.6**	**7.1**	**12.8**	**13.2**	**10.4**	**6.9**	**4.1**	**12.5**	**–3.7**	**Asia**	**505**
11.7	9.7	11.2	7.6	7.7	4.9	9.4	4.2	.1	4.3	8.7	5.6	1.8	4.4	7.4	Bangladesh	**513**
10.0	6.5	8.7	7.9	6.9	5.6	6.5	10.7	6.9	9.3	9.7	11.4	14.7	. . . .	. . . .	Bhutan	**514**
5.6	5.9	4.2	12.1	7.6	7.1	6.4	6.4	17.5	20.1	13.4	6.6	.7	–1.1	–4.1	China, P.R.: Mainland	**924**
5.7	3.6	8.9	9.6	12.3	7.5	9.2	9.7	8.5	6.9	2.6	5.9	5.8	.9	–5.6	China, P.R.: Hong Kong	**532**
7.7	4.2	7.1	5.6	–3.9	8.2	7.5	4.8	5.6	–.3	1.7	2.8	5.6	. . . .	. . . .	Fiji	**819**
7.5	6.5	8.6	8.1	8.3	10.9	14.7	8.6	16.0	9.5	8.7	7.7	6.4	8.9	. . . .	India	**534**
6.8	6.2	10.7	9.8	11.9	9.5	10.8	6.1	9.7	7.8	9.9	8.7	12.6	130.1	–11.9	Indonesia	**536**
4.6	5.1	5.6	7.6	5.7	10.7	10.9	7.6	7.1	7.7	7.1	3.9	3.1	5.1	–1.6	Korea	**542**
165.4	41.2	30.7	45.1	71.7	33.1	13.3	9.3	7.7	6.4	19.7	12.7	20.3	86.2	. . . .	Lao People's Democratic Rep.	**544**
–1.4	–8.7	7.5	4.5	4.5	3.8	3.6	2.4	4.0	3.9	3.6	3.7	3.5	8.9	–.4	Malaysia	**548**
5.0	3.3	15.2	7.6	6.3	4.4	12.5	13.2	10.5	10.0	6.9	3.0	3.0	2.0	–4.0	Maldives	**556**
–1.5	–9.2	.8	.9	—	—	99.1	176.4	262.3	66.6	42.5	33.5	24.4	11.5	. . . .	Mongolia	**948**
1.6	6.6	21.2	25.2	57.7	18.5	23.7	21.7	36.2	22.1	19.6	23.0	33.7	35.9	. . . .	Myanmar	**518**
11.4	14.4	12.7	11.8	11.3	10.7	9.4	19.3	10.9	8.5	9.6	7.4	7.6	2.9	9.2	Nepal	**558**
4.5	3.3	4.5	9.6	8.6	6.5	13.1	10.1	8.7	12.9	13.8	8.4	13.3	7.8	6.4	Pakistan	**564**
—	—	—	28.9	–2.5	4.1	7.0	2.9	4.8	. . . .	. . . .	. . . .	. . . .	. . . .	. . . .	Papua New Guinea	**853**
17.6	3.0	7.5	9.6	9.0	13.0	16.5	7.9	6.8	10.0	7.6	7.7	6.0	10.7	8.6	Philippines	**566**
. . . .	. . . .	. . . .	. . . .	. . . .	. . . .	. . . .	. . . .	. . . .	. . . .	. . . .	. . . .	. . . .	. . . .	. . . .	Samoa	**862**
–1.2	–1.4	1.9	5.7	4.7	4.8	3.8	1.5	3.3	2.9	2.6	1.3	.7	–1.8	–1.3	Singapore	**576**
4.2	9.0	22.2	. . . .	. . . .	. . . .	. . . .	. . . .	. . . .	. . . .	. . . .	. . . .	. . . .	. . . .	. . . .	Solomon Islands	**813**
.9	5.8	7.0	11.5	9.6	20.0	11.0	10.0	9.5	9.3	8.4	12.1	—	—	. . . .	Sri Lanka	**524**
2.2	1.7	4.7	5.9	6.1	5.8	5.7	4.5	3.8	3.7	4.5	6.7	3.5	18.4	–5.4	Thailand	**578**
6.9	—	—	—	44.3	3.9	2.9	6.7	5.6	2.4	3.4	. . . .	. . . .	. . . .	. . . .	Vanuatu	**846**

GDP Deflators

99bi x		1970	1971	1972	1973	1974	1975	1976	1977	1978	1979	1980	1981	1982	1983	1984
													Percent Change over Previous Year:			
Europe	170	....	....	....	....	....	....	....	....	....	....	....	13.4	59.2	11.0	10.4
Armenia	911	....	....	....	....	....	....	....	....	....	....	....				
Belarus	913	....	....	....	....	....	....	....	....	....	....	....				
Bulgaria	918	....	....	....	....	....	....	....	....	....	....	....				
Croatia	960	....	....	....	....	....	....	....	....	....	....	....				
Cyprus	423	4.3	2.2	6.3	8.3	11.1	4.2	10.1	9.5	11.2	13.2	14.0	11.8	10.1	5.3	8.1
Czech Republic	935	....	....	....	....	....	....	....	....	....	....	....				
Estonia	939	....	....	....	....	....	....	....	....	....	....	....				
Hungary	944	....	2.1	2.1	2.7	-1.2	1.2	5.8	2.2	3.6	5.5	5.4	5.1	5.7	4.9	6.4
Kazakhstan	916	....	....	....	....	....	....	....	....	....	....	....				
Kyrgyz Republic	917	....	....	....	....	....	....	....	....	....	....	....				
Latvia	941	....	....	....	....	....	....	....	....	....	....	....				
Lithuania	946	....	....	....	....	....	....	....	....	....	....	....				
Malta	181	2.7	.8	-1.4	3.1	3.4	5.4	5.0	4.9	4.1	6.2	12.4	7.8	3.4	-.3	-.2
Poland	964	....	....	....	....	....	....	....	....	....	....	....	21.8	111.5	18.3	17.2
Romania	968	....	....	....	....	....	....	....	....	....	....	....	1.0	12.2	-.3	.2
Slovak Republic	936	....	....	....	....	....	....	....	....	....	....	....				
Slovenia	961	....	....	....	....	....	....	....	....	....	....	....				
Turkey	186	....	....	....	....	....	....	....	....	....	....	....				
Yugoslavia, SFR	188	14.1	17.0	14.7	19.2	19.2	25.6	30.2	13.7	13.4	19.4	30.2	37.8	24.3	37.9	54.6
Middle East	405	-8.6	15.6	8.7	34.4	63.7	9.5	10.7	16.1	7.9	29.7	33.3	19.3	9.8	8.3	16.2
Bahrain	419	....	....	....	....	....	12.6	13.1	9.0	13.5	6.7	7.8	-.8	-2.7	-.8	
Egypt	469	....	....	....	....	....	....	....	....	....	....	....	....	12.0	9.2	
Iran, I.R. of	429	-13.2	11.8	7.3	34.4	60.9	10.6	13.0	17.7	10.3	27.1	29.1	23.8	16.4	12.1	9.7
Iraq	433	6.9	7.1	3.0	-4.9	93.8	3.5	3.3	10.5	6.6	33.1	33.1	-14.8	15.9	13.1	12.4
Israel	436	-11.8	24.5	28.1	-13.8	44.3	19.8	22.0	85.2	45.2	51.1	143.0	127.3	122.0	152.2	384.8
Jordan	439	....	....	....	....	....	....	....	....	....	....	....				
Kuwait	443	....	13.3	1.9	17.2	172.5	4.0	-2.3	16.3	-1.9	41.5	41.9	12.0	—	-9.3	.4
Libya	672	1.1	20.5	1.3	22.5	41.5	-6.4	5.8	7.9	-3.8	27.4	37.9	....	....	....	....
Oman	449	3.4	16.0	3.0	39.9	161.7	-.9	5.3	-9.0	-15.0	30.2	50.1	4.0	-5.9	-3.3	-5.6
Saudi Arabia	456	-5.5	23.1	19.9	112.8	40.2	8.5	8.3	3.8	3.8	40.4	25.0	-.8	-11.3	-10.3	-3.4
Syrian Arab Rep.	463	5.3	7.2	-7.9	16.8	29.5	8.8	8.2	10.7	10.3	16.1	17.5	17.2	2.4	5.0	7.2
United Arab Emirates	466	....	....	....	....	138.3	19.6	12.5	5.5	-2.1	5.7	8.7	7.2	1.2	-6.0	-5.4
Yemen Republic	474	....	....	....	....	....	....	....	....	....	....	....				
Western Hemisphere	205	15.0	14.3	20.2	35.5	37.5	39.2	52.0	44.0	35.4	43.3	58.6	52.5	67.7	96.2	112.9
Antigua and Barbuda	311	....	....	....	....	....	....	....	8.6	14.8	9.9	8.6	10.7	6.1	3.1
Argentina	213	9.7	39.7	58.5	61.5	31.8	194.0	432.1	159.7	158.5	153.8	165.4	106.5	201.9	381.1	608.2
Bahamas, The	313	....	....	....	....	....	....	....	....	....	....	....	-3.5	-.1	6.2	5.3
Barbados	316	6.8	9.2	9.8	14.9	30.3	12.9	7.1	-1.7	5.4	27.0	22.9	12.2	9.9	5.8	5.1
Belize	339	....	....	....	....	27.8	21.6	-2.3	10.9	5.9	-18.1	6.7	-2.0	-7.0	7.8	9.4
Bolivia	218	3.9	4.4	20.4	41.6	58.1	6.5	8.1	10.9	11.6	17.8	35.5	21.7	177.6	262.1	1,406.6
Brazil	223	25.1	19.4	19.9	29.6	34.6	33.9	41.2	45.4	38.2	54.4	91.2	104.7	101.9	136.4	204.4
Chile	228	40.6	18.4	86.9	417.9	694.4	344.3	251.7	106.6	57.2	47.9	29.3	11.0	12.4	30.3	14.6
Colombia	233	12.3	10.8	13.0	20.2	25.4	22.8	25.5	29.2	17.1	24.0	27.6	22.8	24.8	20.4	22.2
Costa Rica	238	7.3	2.4	6.4	14.8	23.2	24.5	16.6	16.9	7.9	9.1	18.8	41.1	84.2	28.9	16.7
Dominica	321	....	....	....	....	....	....	....	31.0	11.1	20.2	18.4	-1.4	4.5	8.0	6.6
Dominican Republic	243	1.4	1.2	8.0	4.5	17.9	16.7	2.9	10.6	1.0	11.1	13.7	5.3	7.9	8.3	24.2
Ecuador	248	9.1	7.6	2.3	6.0	40.0	10.0	12.9	17.5	7.9	16.1	19.5	14.4	17.8	38.7	39.2
El Salvador	253	4.8	.5	.9	10.0	11.2	7.6	22.6	18.4	.9	13.9	13.4	5.7	9.9	12.3	12.3
Grenada	328	....	....	....	....	....	8.3	26.6	10.7	9.4	18.7	14.8	-.5	5.1	4.9	-15.6	3.9
Guatemala	258	5.0	-1.3	-1.3	14.5	15.7	13.1	11.5	16.4	5.5	8.6	10.0	8.5	5.0	6.5	4.2
Guyana	336	3.3	2.4	8.8	5.9	36.9	13.2	-8.0	5.3	13.2	20.5	11.9	6.2	1.1	10.9	54.8
Haiti	263	4.2	3.4	1.3	29.2	-14.6	19.2	19.0	10.9	-1.5	2.9	15.2	5.2	7.8	9.3	11.5
Honduras	268	2.5	1.8	4.3	6.6	11.7	9.6	8.5	12.2	5.1	9.6	15.2	7.2	4.4	7.0	3.4
Jamaica	343	9.4	5.0	4.1	16.3	32.7	21.9	10.6	12.2	25.6	17.1	17.8	8.4	9.2	16.5	35.0
Mexico	273	10.8	5.9	6.2	12.9	22.7	15.8	19.6	30.4	16.8	20.2	34.5	26.5	60.1	89.6	59.0
Nicaragua	278	2.4	3.0	2.5	17.5	23.0	3.1	9.3	8.0	5.0	38.4	37.0	11.7	16.7	11.0	39.0
Panama	283	.5	2.9	5.0	8.5	11.6	10.2	4.5	4.9	8.0	-4.9	35.2	3.6	4.9	7.5	1.6
Paraguay	288	1.6	5.7	8.4	20.4	23.5	5.7	4.8	11.0	9.9	19.9	16.8	16.3	5.0	14.4	26.9
Peru	293	8.8	5.4	8.4	15.7	14.0	18.9	36.3	37.8	58.1	96.6	64.4	66.2	68.6	99.9	109.9
St. Kitts and Nevis	361	....	....	....	....	....	....	....	6.7	6.6	11.3	16.5	7.6	.6	6.3
St. Lucia	362	....	....	....	....	....	....	....	5.2	16.5	19.8	10.0	5.8	2.8	3.4
St. Vincent & Grenadines	364	....	....	....	....	....	....	7.8	9.9	33.8	11.0	8.0	15.1	9.7	6.6	3.3
Suriname	366	....	....	....	....	17.5	26.0	1.5	13.0	8.7	13.1	11.1	4.4	7.4	.5	-.3
Trinidad and Tobago	369	1.9	6.6	11.1	21.2	57.5	24.6	8.0	13.3	3.2	24.7	22.7	5.0	12.1	7.5	6.1
Uruguay	298	13.4	20.0	74.7	105.4	72.1	69.7	48.8	55.8	47.5	75.5	51.0	30.3	16.0	44.8	56.2
Venezuela, Rep. Bol.	299	3.6	6.5	4.3	12.1	44.5	-.8	5.2	8.0	6.3	21.3	24.8	12.5	1.4	5.7	41.6
Memorandum Items																
Oil Exporting Countries	999	4.7	8.9	7.9	28.8	58.5	9.0	10.7	11.4	7.7	24.8	23.6	14.5	4.4	7.9	10.7
Non-Oil Developing Countries	201	10.6	11.7	15.8	31.5	21.3	18.6	21.6	20.0	17.6	28.7	30.8	26.9	34.1	39.7	37.4

Indices

Index Numbers:

		1970	1971	1972	1973	1974	1975	1976	1977	1978	1979	1980	1981	1982	1983	1984
World	001	3.2	3.4	3.6	4.0	4.8	5.4	6.1	6.9	7.7	8.8	10.3	11.8	13.4	15.4	17.6
Industrial Countries	110	23.5	25.0	26.4	28.6	32.1	35.7	38.7	42.0	45.3	49.2	54.0	59.0	63.3	66.8	69.9
Developing Countries	200	.1	.1	.1	.1	.2	.2	.3	.4	.4	.5	.7	.9	1.1	1.5	2.0
Africa	605	2.2	2.3	2.4	2.6	3.4	3.8	4.2	4.8	5.5	6.3	7.4	8.5	9.5	11.1	12.8
Asia	505	9.8	10.3	11.3	13.4	16.8	18.4	19.7	21.1	23.1	26.8	29.8	32.5	34.4	36.6	39.3
Europe	170	....	....	....	....	....	....	....	....	....	....	.4	.5	.8	.8	.9
Middle East	405	2.0	2.3	2.5	3.4	5.5	6.0	6.7	7.7	8.3	10.8	14.4	17.2	18.9	20.5	23.8
Western Hemisphere	205	—	—	—	—	—	—	—	—	—	—	—	—	—	—	—

Calculated from Indices

1985	1986	1987	1988	1989	1990	1991	1992	1993	1994	1995	1996	1997	1998	1999		
9.6	10.6	16.1	35.8	117.7	110.4	72.9	66.3	72.5	59.2	56.6	41.5	60.0	39.4	....	**Europe**	170
....	....	....	....	....	....	....	....	....	....	161.2	19.6	17.7	11.2	....	Armenia	911
....	....	....	....	....	....	....	....	1,063.6	1,967.4	650.6	49.5	73.6	74.9	313.9	Belarus	913
....	....	....	....	....	26.2	226.4	59.6	51.1	72.7	62.8	121.0	950.6	....	....	Bulgaria	918
....	....	....	....	....	....	85.9	629.6	1,506.5	102.6	9.0	5.1	....	....	....	Croatia	960
5.8	4.2	3.9	3.3	4.8	5.5	3.9	6.1	4.8	5.3	3.0	1.7	2.3	1.8	1.0	Cyprus	423
....	....	....	....	....	....	....	....	24.2	12.1	13.5	8.6	7.2	10.2	2.4	Czech Republic	935
....	....	....	....	....	....	....	....	....	39.8	31.9	24.0	10.9	9.4	....	Estonia	939
5.9	2.8	8.5	11.3	18.7	25.7	35.7	21.5	21.3	19.5	25.6	....	....	....	....	Hungary	944
....	....	....	....	....	....	....	....	....	....	120.4	17.9	17.1	6.6	....	Kazakhstan	916
....	....	....	....	....	....	....	830.2	754.9	180.9	42.0	30.0	24.3	9.1	....	Kyrgyz Republic	917
....	....	....	....	....	....	....	....	71.5	38.3	16.0	16.5	6.6	5.5	2.0	Latvia	941
....	....	....	....	....	....	....	....	306.2	61.6	38.0	25.1	13.2	6.7	3.4	Lithuania	946
.6	3.5	3.1	1.9	2.1	3.2	3.4	3.6	2.9	3.5	4.8	.8	2.3	2.3	1.5	Malta	181
15.9	19.0	28.1	68.1	298.2	434.7	55.2	38.5	30.6	37.4	27.9	18.7	14.0	11.8	....	Poland	964
.3	.2	-.1	1.9	-.9	13.6	195.0	199.9	227.3	139.0	35.3	44.6	140.5	58.7	....	Romania	968
....	....	....	....	....	....	....	....	16.2	13.8	9.7	4.5	6.6	5.1	....	Slovak Republic	936
....	....	....	....	....	....	....	....	....	22.6	15.2	11.4	9.6	....	....	Slovenia	961
....	....	....	65.5	74.6	63.2	61.1	67.0	69.0	98.4	87.2	77.8	81.5	74.2	....	Turkey	186
77.8	88.4	125.0	211.8	....	....	....	....	....	....	....	....	....	....	....	Yugoslavia, SFR	188
12.9	8.9	14.3	12.9	15.9	16.1	12.9	14.0	14.1	15.0	16.8	13.9	7.8	3.2	....	**Middle East**	405
-4.8	-17.4	.7	.5	4.0	4.8	-1.9	-3.5	-3.0	7.3	1.1	.2	.9	-7.0	....	Bahrain	419
11.7	12.5	12.4	13.4	18.8	18.4	14.4	19.7	9.9	7.0	11.9	6.1	6.4	3.6	....	Egypt	469
6.3	21.2	21.5	22.4	20.6	18.0	22.7	25.5	38.6	36.1	33.7	23.3	13.9	16.1	....	Iran, I.R. of	429
3.8	-10.1	-.5	6.4	17.6	10.8	....	....	....	....	....	....	....	....	....	Iraq	433
258.1	49.2	20.6	20.3	20.3	17.0	20.0	12.5	11.8	12.9	9.8	11.4	8.8	6.7	6.9	Israel	436
....	.1	-.8	4.5	21.0	11.4	5.1	5.4	3.1	2.3	3.4	2.3	3.7	2.5	....	Jordan	439
4.9	-25.7	10.8	3.0	-1.7	2.0	2.0	2.0	-7.4	-5.9	6.2	21.4	....	....	....	Kuwait	443
....	....	....	....	....	....	....	....	....	....	....	....	....	....	....	Libya	672
-2.3	-14.3	9.9	-7.7	8.5	15.0	-8.5	1.2	-5.5	-.4	1.9	7.6	-2.6	-13.0	....	Oman	449
-6.9	-18.2	3.0	-3.8	8.8	14.0	4.0	1.5	-3.2	.9	5.9	9.1	1.0	-13.7	8.1	Saudi Arabia	456
4.1	26.3	25.4	28.6	23.3	22.8	7.6	5.1	5.9	13.6	6.7	10.1	5.8	-1.6	....	Syrian Arab Rep.	463
—	1.3	6.1	.1	-.1	5.0	—	1.6	....	....	....	....	....	....	....	United Arab Emirates	466
....	....	....	....	....	....	21.3	20.9	23.4	33.2	54.8	39.6	12.4	-11.2	26.4	Yemen Republic	474
123.5	78.8	117.7	222.5	310.9	431.2	125.6	158.3	218.8	230.0	41.1	22.2	12.2	8.1	....	**Western Hemisphere**	205
7.7	8.1	7.6	12.1	4.2	2.3	2.7	2.4	2.2	3.0	3.0	4.0	....	....	....	Antigua and Barbuda	311
620.8	75.7	127.8	385.2	3,038.5	2,064.4	137.3	14.4	-1.4	.8	4.4	.7	-.9	-2.3	....	Argentina	213
2.3	8.3	5.9	-13.7	-13.7	7.1	-2.1	5.0	2.0	4.9	-.5	....	....	....	....	Bahamas, The	313
3.5	4.5	7.4	2.8	6.7	3.8	2.8	-.1	2.3	1.2	4.3	2.9	6.3	....	....	Barbados	316
-1.8	4.1	9.1	4.3	2.0	.1	4.0	3.5	5.0	.8	2.7	1.4	-1.4	-.2	3.1	Belize	339
13,850.2	172.5	14.6	17.5	13.2	16.3	17.7	13.2	6.6	8.0	11.4	11.6	5.7	7.0	2.8	Bolivia	218
249.5	147.5	204.8	648.7	1,121.1	2,775.0	416.7	969.0	1,996.2	2,240.3	77.6	17.4	7.1	4.3	....	Brazil	223
35.4	22.1	24.6	21.5	12.4	21.2	21.2	11.8	10.6	12.6	9.3	1.7	4.0	2.7	3.6	Chile	228
24.9	29.2	23.4	27.7	24.7	28.2	26.5	23.4	24.3	45.4	18.9	16.9	16.8	....	....	Colombia	233
20.6	18.0	10.1	18.8	15.2	18.5	29.1	21.9	10.9	16.9	21.2	18.2	14.4	13.1	9.2	Costa Rica	238
8.3	6.2	4.8	4.8	6.9	3.0	7.8	4.1	2.8	6.0	1.6	3.3	1.4	....	....	Dominica	321
38.4	9.4	14.4	43.5	23.6	50.5	58.2	8.3	4.9	8.3	12.6	5.4	4.8	4.8	6.5	Dominican Republic	243
30.9	20.9	38.0	52.3	70.7	54.0	42.7	52.4	38.6	27.3	23.2	29.6	25.6	35.3	....	Ecuador	248
20.6	37.0	14.0	16.4	16.5	9.5	12.7	8.8	12.8	10.5	10.4	6.8	3.5	3.9	.8	El Salvador	253
16.4	8.1	36.4	4.8	9.3	-1.4	6.1	3.3	....	....	....	....	....	....	....	Grenada	328
18.8	41.5	8.0	11.7	10.9	40.5	33.0	8.8	14.5	11.7	8.7	8.9	8.3	6.8	6.6	Guatemala	258
-14.9	18.6	49.9	26.5	158.2	59.1	134.6	11.3	16.9	....	....	....	....	....	....	Guyana	336
10.4	10.3	-3.3	3.3	12.9	18.9	18.5	20.5	18.7	35.7	21.1	18.0	19.1	11.0	11.3	Haiti	263
5.2	3.9	2.8	6.5	7.1	21.2	26.0	9.1	13.6	28.9	24.9	22.9	22.5	11.0	11.1	Honduras	268
30.8	17.1	11.1	13.7	12.6	23.7	47.1	59.6	34.3	31.4	27.5	21.1	10.9	14.7	....	Jamaica	343
57.0	72.4	141.0	112.8	26.5	28.1	23.3	14.4	9.5	8.3	37.9	29.6	19.0	13.8	17.6	Mexico	273
167.2	281.5	539.5	13,611.6	4,770.1	49,225.8	375.3	23.7	20.4	7.8	10.9	11.7	9.2	10.8	13.4	Nicaragua	278
.8	.3	2.3	-.2	-1.3	.6	.5	5.1	3.6	3.7	.5	.3	1.7	1.4	....	Panama	283
25.2	31.5	30.3	25.1	31.2	36.3	24.8	14.7	19.1	21.0	13.0	10.5	3.0	12.4	....	Paraguay	288
167.4	73.6	84.0	562.6	2,638.5	6,199.5	400.6	61.2	47.6	19.5	12.4	9.6	8.6	5.5	1.3	Peru	293
4.7	8.1	5.7	7.4	5.0	8.7	2.9	7.0	21.2	6.1	.5	.6	2.7	....	....	St. Kitts and Nevis	361
3.1	3.9	5.4	-.5	4.7	5.3	8.3	4.0	—	2.5	6.3	2.3	1.0	....	....	St. Lucia	362
4.2	5.9	6.0	1.0	5.1	6.3	5.7	3.6	-.1	4.0	.8	4.0	1.7	2.4	....	St. Vincent & Grenadines	364
-.9	1.3	17.3	9.9	11.2	12.6	15.4	31.1	132.0	488.3	....	....	....	....	....	Suriname	366
1.3	-1.3	4.9	4.2	7.2	15.5	2.0	4.2	7.5	15.6	4.0	4.7	2.9	.1	....	Trinidad and Tobago	369
74.0	70.9	72.9	75.2	75.6	107.1	100.8	59.4	47.9	39.0	41.0	26.4	19.7	9.7	4.8	Uruguay	298
9.1	3.1	32.1	21.4	84.1	43.6	21.4	28.2	31.6	62.9	51.8	115.5	38.0	20.5	....	Venezuela, Rep. Bol.	299

Memorandum Items

1985	1986	1987	1988	1989	1990	1991	1992	1993	1994	1995	1996	1997	1998	1999		
4.5	3.6	18.3	12.8	23.1	14.9	13.4	17.1	18.8	18.5	21.2	22.6	13.5	57.9	....	Oil Exporting Countries	999
39.4	27.9	37.3	61.6	77.7	81.8	41.7	45.1	58.3	51.3	21.1	12.0	9.2	7.2	....	Non-Oil Developing Countries	201

Indices

1995=100

1985	1986	1987	1988	1989	1990	1991	1992	1993	1994	1995	1996	1997	1998	1999		
20.0	22.2	25.2	30.1	37.3	47.1	54.7	63.6	76.0	90.9	100.0	106.6	112.0	118.7	....	World	001
72.5	75.1	77.5	80.4	83.7	87.4	91.2	93.9	96.2	98.0	100.0	101.6	103.2	104.5	106.3	Industrial Countries	110
2.6	3.2	4.4	6.7	11.2	19.1	26.2	36.9	56.3	82.6	100.0	113.3	124.4	139.7	....	Developing Countries	200
14.5	15.9	19.4	22.6	27.3	31.5	39.0	52.5	66.7	78.3	100.0	114.2	124.2	132.2	....	Africa	605
41.6	43.8	46.7	51.3	55.7	60.4	66.2	70.9	80.0	90.6	100.0	106.9	111.3	125.3	120.6	Asia	505
1.0	1.1	1.3	1.8	3.8	8.1	14.0	23.3	40.1	63.9	100.0	141.5	226.3	315.6	....	Europe	170
26.9	29.2	33.4	37.7	43.7	50.7	57.3	65.3	74.5	85.6	100.0	113.9	122.8	126.6	....	Middle East	405
—	—	—	.1	.2	1.2	2.6	6.7	21.5	70.9	100.0	122.2	137.1	148.3	....	Western Hemisphere	205

Gross Capital Formation as Percentage of GDP

93e r

		1970	1971	1972	1973	1974	1975	1976	1977	1978	1979	1980	1981	1982	1983	1984
																Percentages
World	001	22.3	22.2	22.0	24.3	24.7	22.8	23.4	23.6	24.6	24.9	24.6	24.1	22.7	22.3	22.8
Industrial Countries	110	**24.1**	**23.7**	**23.8**	**25.3**	**25.1**	**21.9**	**22.9**	**23.0**	**23.2**	**24.1**	**23.4**	**22.9**	**21.3**	**20.8**	**21.9**
United States	111	17.4	18.5	19.5	20.3	19.5	17.0	18.7	20.2	21.4	21.6	19.7	20.6	18.2	18.2	20.8
Canada	156	21.6	22.6	22.7	24.1	25.9	25.2	24.8	23.9	23.0	24.8	23.4	24.5	19.1	19.3	20.1
Australia	193	29.1	28.9	26.0	26.0	27.4	23.3	24.1	24.3	24.5	25.8	25.6	27.5	25.7	23.0	25.5
Japan	158	39.0	35.8	35.5	38.1	37.3	32.8	31.8	30.8	30.9	32.5	32.2	31.1	29.9	28.1	28.0
New Zealand	196	24.3	25.1	24.5	27.6	37.0	31.8	30.8	24.6	21.4	22.9	20.5	24.2	25.5	25.8	28.2
Euro Area	163	....	....	....	....	....	....	....	....	....	....	....	....	....	....	....
Austria	122	29.7	29.7	30.6	30.9	31.1	26.0	25.8	26.5	24.9	25.9	27.2	25.3	21.4	20.4	22.0
Belgium	124	24.0	23.2	21.5	22.4	24.6	21.6	21.8	21.6	21.4	21.1	21.5	17.5	17.2	15.4	16.3
Finland	172	30.2	30.8	28.1	30.6	35.4	34.0	27.0	26.1	22.3	25.7	29.2	25.9	25.2	25.1	23.8
France	132	26.9	26.2	26.4	27.2	28.1	23.5	25.4	24.4	23.2	23.7	24.2	21.7	21.9	19.9	19.0
Germany	134	27.6	26.8	25.9	25.2	22.0	19.8	21.6	20.9	21.2	24.8	25.1	23.3	22.0	22.5	22.4
Ireland	178	24.5	24.0	25.1	27.6	29.1	23.3	25.4	27.9	29.0	33.0	27.8	28.4	27.8	23.6	22.6
Italy	136	27.4	24.9	24.0	27.2	30.1	23.9	26.9	24.9	24.1	24.7	27.0	24.7	23.5	22.2	22.9
Luxembourg	137	25.8	29.7	28.5	27.5	21.1	22.9	22.8	20.4	24.9	22.1	25.2	24.5	24.8	24.3	24.7
Netherlands	138	27.9	26.5	24.1	24.5	24.3	20.6	20.6	21.6	21.9	21.5	21.5	18.3	17.9	18.4	19.1
Portugal	182	26.4	27.7	29.3	29.4	28.5	20.3	24.7	29.0	30.9	31.7	34.4	38.6	37.1	29.1	22.2
Spain	184	26.8	24.7	25.8	27.1	30.1	28.5	26.9	24.9	22.9	22.3	23.2	21.9	22.2	21.5	19.7
Denmark	128	26.5	25.5	26.2	27.2	26.3	22.1	25.2	24.2	22.9	23.1	20.1	16.9	18.0	18.1	20.5
Greece	174	28.1	27.9	29.5	35.8	29.3	27.0	26.3	26.4	27.7	30.2	28.6	25.4	21.1	21.9	20.1
Iceland	176	23.1	31.6	26.4	29.7	33.9	33.1	26.6	27.9	23.3	23.9	25.7	25.2	26.9	20.2	21.0
Norway	142	30.5	31.6	27.7	30.1	33.6	35.2	37.1	36.3	29.5	28.5	28.3	27.1	28.2	25.6	26.7
Sweden	144	25.2	22.4	21.7	20.7	23.9	23.3	22.1	20.1	17.2	19.6	21.3	18.2	17.6	17.2	17.8
Switzerland	146	32.3	32.5	31.8	31.3	31.2	23.0	20.7	20.7	21.7	23.9	28.5	26.4	24.1	23.5	25.4
United Kingdom	112	20.4	19.9	19.3	22.8	23.1	19.5	21.2	20.7	20.4	20.5	17.7	16.1	16.8	17.6	18.6
Developing Countries	200	**17.4**	**18.1**	**17.1**	**22.3**	**23.6**	**24.8**	**24.5**	**25.0**	**27.0**	**26.4**	**26.6**	**26.4**	**25.2**	**24.8**	**24.3**
Africa	605	**20.9**	**22.7**	**21.4**	**24.5**	**24.9**	**28.1**	**27.5**	**28.8**	**29.6**	**26.9**	**27.1**	**27.6**	**25.0**	**23.4**	**21.8**
Algeria	612	36.0	36.3	40.2	44.5	39.7	45.2	43.1	46.8	52.1	42.5	39.1	37.0	37.3	37.6	35.1
Benin	638	17.0	16.3	20.5	18.3	20.7	25.5	18.9	18.6	17.8	23.9	23.6	21.7	27.6	17.3	12.8
Botswana	616	39.1	46.5	53.0	52.4	51.7	46.0	38.3	28.1	34.6	34.9	37.7	40.6	43.6	30.1	26.3
Burkina Faso	748	9.9	14.7	17.4	21.2	26.6	25.5	26.4	22.2	20.7	31.6	26.6	23.8	25.5	24.4	24.1
Burundi	618	7.2	5.0	3.2	5.3	4.1	11.1	9.1	11.1	14.1	15.4	13.9	16.1	17.5	17.9	18.1
Cameroon	622	17.0	17.6	19.4	21.0	18.0	20.8	18.5	23.0	24.7	24.0	21.8	27.2	24.8	26.0	25.9
Central African Rep.	626	....	....	....	....	....	....	....	....	....	....	....	....	....	....	....
Congo, Dem. Rep. of	636	26.1	32.9	33.4	30.0	30.6	31.9	25.9	38.5	18.4	19.6	10.7	10.8	8.3	9.3	10.5
Congo, Rep. of	634	....	....	....	....	....	....	....	27.4	31.3	35.8	48.1	60.3	35.6	30.4	
Côte d'Ivoire	662	22.0	21.8	20.6	22.9	22.0	24.3	22.9	26.5	29.8	28.0	26.5	25.9	23.2	18.1	11.6
Ethiopia	644	11.5	11.8	12.7	11.4	9.9	10.5	9.6	8.9	7.5	8.7	10.0	13.6	13.7	12.2	16.8
Ghana	652	14.2	14.1	7.1	9.0	13.0	12.7	8.9	11.1	6.8	6.5	5.6	4.6	3.4	3.7	6.9
Guinea-Bissau	654	....	....	....	....	....	....	....	....	....	....	....	....	....	....	....
Kenya	664	21.9	25.3	23.2	21.2	30.8	20.5	23.0	27.0	34.3	26.1	35.4	33.3	26.4	25.0	25.5
Liberia	668	24.5	23.7	25.6	17.3	24.0	40.5	38.0	40.5	36.3	36.5	33.3	19.4	21.1	20.4	18.4
Madagascar	674	15.6	18.0	13.9	14.3	13.6	12.8	12.8	12.9	14.5	25.3	23.5	18.1	13.4	13.2	10.8
Malawi	676	26.1	19.4	24.7	22.4	27.8	34.1	23.9	24.7	38.4	37.9	31.9	23.3	23.6	27.2	12.9
Mali	678	....	....	....	....	....	....	....	....	....	....	24.5	17.6	19.8	15.2	
Mauritania	682	22.8	23.7	34.0	27.7	44.9	44.4	50.8	43.7	27.0	26.2	32.1	44.1	48.2	45.8	35.3
Mauritius	684	13.8	15.8	16.0	25.9	23.3	33.3	40.5	30.0	30.7	31.2	20.7	25.3	18.2	17.5	22.0
Morocco	686	15.9	15.6	12.6	14.4	20.6	25.2	28.1	34.2	25.7	24.5	24.2	26.1	28.2	24.0	25.3
Mozambique	688	....	....	....	....	....	....	....	....	....	....	19.2	19.5	22.8	20.0	22.0
Namibia	728	....	....	....	....	....	....	....	....	....	....	....	....	....	....	....
Niger	692	9.5	7.4	9.0	14.7	13.9	23.8	26.4	28.9	31.6	31.8	31.5	28.0	21.3	15.6	5.2
Nigeria	694	9.9	12.4	12.7	21.3	16.2	24.0	30.0	29.5	27.4	22.4	22.7	22.8	18.7	13.1	6.7
Rwanda	714	45.8	46.5	47.2	47.2	47.8	13.8	13.9	15.1	16.5	11.9	16.1	13.3	17.7	13.5	15.8
Senegal	722	13.3	13.7	14.5	16.1	19.5	15.2	13.6	14.5	14.3	11.4	11.7	12.8	12.2	12.8	12.8
Seychelles	718	....	....	....	....	....	....	38.9	40.0	43.3	32.9	38.3	32.6	32.3	21.3	21.7
Sierra Leone	724	15.7	15.3	11.7	11.7	15.8	15.7	11.3	13.1	11.3	13.4	16.2	19.1	13.4	14.3	12.7
South Africa	199	28.0	30.4	25.7	26.0	29.6	32.0	28.5	26.9	25.2	26.8	30.8	33.1	25.2	25.8	24.9
Swaziland	734	16.2	22.8	23.3	23.2	26.8	18.6	22.4	27.0	48.0	42.5	40.7	31.0	32.2	35.0	31.6
Tanzania	738	22.5	26.4	21.8	21.1	22.0	21.1	22.9	26.1	25.2	26.1	23.0	24.7	23.3	16.6	16.5
Togo	742	14.4	18.2	20.1	23.6	17.0	28.5	27.0	38.9	49.3	50.7	34.8	30.7	26.3	21.8	15.0
Tunisia	744	19.8	20.2	21.8	21.1	22.7	31.4	29.9	30.1	30.5	29.7	28.8	32.3	31.6	28.4	31.1
Uganda	746	13.8	16.4	10.5	8.5	10.6	7.6	5.7	4.7	3.9	....	....	....	....	8.5	9.9
Zambia	754	29.6	37.3	35.3	29.2	36.4	40.5	23.8	24.7	23.9	14.1	23.3	19.3	16.8	13.8	14.7
Zimbabwe	698	20.4	21.9	20.7	24.8	27.9	27.1	18.9	19.1	11.9	12.7	18.8	23.2	21.1	16.7	18.9
Asia	505	**18.5**	**19.3**	**18.3**	**19.1**	**20.6**	**21.5**	**21.7**	**21.7**	**26.9**	**28.1**	**27.3**	**28.2**	**27.4**	**28.0**	**27.8**
Bangladesh	513	....	....	....	8.9	5.6	5.5	8.7	11.7	11.0	9.6	11.3	10.5	10.4	10.3	11.0
Bhutan	514	....	....	....	....	....	....	....	....	....	....	31.0	38.5	40.5	39.8	36.3
China, P.R.: Mainland	924	....	....	....	....	....	....	....	....	....	36.2	34.9	32.3	32.1	33.0	34.5
China, P.R.: Hong Kong	532	20.5	24.5	23.6	23.0	24.4	23.1	25.5	26.7	28.9	32.9	35.1	35.3	31.3	26.9	24.6
Fiji	819	22.2	24.8	24.0	22.2	18.9	20.6	21.5	23.2	25.3	30.1	31.8	34.3	25.6	21.1	18.9
India	534	17.1	18.5	17.1	18.3	19.8	20.8	20.9	19.8	22.1	22.9	20.9	25.0	22.9	21.1	21.2
Indonesia	536	13.6	15.8	18.8	17.9	16.8	20.3	20.7	20.1	20.5	20.9	20.9	29.8	27.9	28.7	26.2
Korea	542	25.4	25.4	21.4	25.6	32.2	28.7	26.9	28.7	33.2	36.3	31.9	28.4	28.7	29.1	30.4
Malaysia	548	20.3	20.9	21.3	23.6	29.6	25.5	22.8	23.8	26.7	28.9	30.4	35.0	37.3	37.8	33.6
Myanmar	518	11.8	12.2	10.8	10.2	10.3	10.0	10.3	13.0	18.2	22.3	21.5	22.9	22.2	18.0	15.1
Nepal	558	....	....	....	....	....	14.5	15.1	16.0	17.8	15.8	18.3	17.6	17.1	19.6	18.7
Pakistan	564	15.8	15.6	14.2	12.9	13.4	16.4	18.5	19.3	17.9	17.9	18.5	18.8	19.3	18.8	18.3
Papua New Guinea	853	35.4	46.9	38.8	18.6	12.9	22.1	18.1	20.0	19.4	21.7	23.4	25.3	29.8	29.4	27.2
Philippines	566	21.2	20.9	20.6	20.2	25.2	29.5	31.0	28.8	28.9	31.1	29.1	27.5	27.9	29.6	20.3
Singapore	576	38.7	40.2	41.1	39.2	44.6	37.6	40.8	36.2	39.0	43.4	46.3	46.3	47.4	47.9	48.5
Solomon Islands	813	....	....	....	....	....	....	....	....	....	....	....	....	....	....	23.0
Sri Lanka	524	18.9	17.1	17.3	13.7	15.7	15.6	16.2	14.4	20.0	25.8	33.8	27.8	30.8	28.9	25.8
Thailand	578	25.6	24.2	21.7	27.0	26.6	26.7	24.0	26.9	28.2	27.2	29.1	29.7	26.5	30.0	29.5
Vanuatu	846	....	....	....	....	....	....	....	....	....	....	....	....	....	25.7	25.7

Gross Capital Formation as Percentage of GDP

1985	1986	1987	1988	1989	1990	1991	1992	1993	1994	1995	1996	1997	1998	1999		
Percentages																
22.8	**22.5**	**23.0**	**24.1**	**24.7**	**24.1**	**23.3**	**23.0**	**22.9**	**23.2**	**23.4**	**23.1**	**23.3**	**23.1**	**22.3**	**World**	001
21.4	**21.2**	**21.8**	**22.5**	**23.0**	**22.5**	**21.3**	**20.7**	**20.1**	**20.6**	**20.7**	**20.7**	**21.0**	**21.3**	**21.5**	**Industrial Countries**	110
19.7	19.2	19.9	19.0	19.1	18.0	16.6	16.9	17.4	18.5	18.3	18.7	19.4	20.2	20.3	United States	111
20.2	20.6	21.7	22.5	23.0	20.7	19.0	17.9	17.9	18.5	18.5	17.7	17.3	20.0	19.9	Canada	156
26.2	25.0	25.6	26.6	28.2	24.0	20.6	20.9	22.0	23.4	23.1	22.7	22.5	24.4	24.8	Australia	193
28.2	27.7	28.5	30.4	31.3	32.3	32.2	30.8	29.7	28.7	28.6	30.0	28.6	26.3	....	Japan	158
26.1	23.7	21.1	19.3	22.2	18.9	16.1	17.5	20.4	22.0	22.3	22.0	21.1	19.0	....	New Zealand	196
....	....	....	....	....	22.4	22.5	21.4	19.4	20.0	20.2	19.3	19.6	21.2	21.4	Euro Area	163
21.9	21.5	22.2	22.1	22.3	22.9	23.8	22.5	21.5	22.4	23.4	23.3	24.7	26.0	24.3	Austria	122
17.8	17.6	18.4	20.4	21.8	22.3	21.1	20.9	19.8	19.6	20.5	20.0	20.6	21.1	21.2	Belgium	124
25.0	23.2	24.0	28.0	31.1	28.7	22.4	18.8	16.3	17.4	17.7	16.9	19.0	19.0	19.8	Finland	172
18.9	19.6	20.2	22.6	23.4	23.3	22.5	20.9	18.1	19.0	19.2	18.3	17.9	18.8	19.0	France	132
21.8	21.9	21.8	22.8	23.6	24.6	24.3	23.8	22.5	23.2	22.7	21.6	21.6	21.8	22.2	Germany	134
19.8	18.1	16.5	15.5	17.9	21.1	19.3	16.3	15.2	16.2	18.4	19.9	21.9	23.8	....	Ireland	178
22.5	21.1	21.2	22.6	22.4	22.2	21.7	20.8	18.4	18.5	19.3	18.7	19.0	19.8	20.3	Italy	136
16.6	19.7	22.7	24.3	22.4	24.7	27.3	24.0	25.2	21.9	21.3	20.3	21.8	22.9	....	Luxembourg	137
20.0	21.3	20.7	21.4	22.6	22.2	21.4	20.6	18.9	20.0	20.1	19.4	20.4	20.2	22.0	Netherlands	138
20.6	23.2	27.5	30.6	28.9	28.6	26.7	25.9	23.2	23.9	24.4	24.4	25.8	26.5	....	Portugal	182
19.2	20.0	21.5	23.7	25.1	25.4	24.6	22.6	19.9	20.1	21.1	20.6	20.7	24.3	24.2	Spain	184
21.9	23.7	21.5	20.6	21.1	20.3	19.1	18.1	16.4	17.6	19.7	18.9	20.2	21.2	19.5	Denmark	128
21.3	19.8	17.6	22.0	22.2	22.7	23.4	20.9	19.8	18.7	18.9	19.8	20.6	21.3	22.3	Greece	174
18.5	16.8	18.6	18.5	16.4	18.1	19.0	17.4	15.8	15.1	15.1	17.7	18.6	21.9	19.9	Iceland	176
26.4	31.7	30.5	29.2	26.3	23.3	21.4	20.7	21.6	22.3	23.7	23.4	25.2	28.0	24.3	Norway	142
19.2	17.9	18.9	19.9	21.9	21.3	17.9	16.5	13.3	15.9	16.6	15.9	15.5	16.7	16.9	Sweden	144
25.1	25.0	25.3	26.8	28.4	28.3	25.4	22.0	20.7	21.1	21.4	20.3	20.2	21.2	20.5	Switzerland	146
18.4	18.2	19.1	21.5	22.2	20.3	17.1	16.2	15.9	16.5	17.0	16.9	17.2	18.1	17.8	United Kingdom	112
25.1	**24.7**	**25.0**	**26.6**	**27.3**	**26.6**	**26.2**	**26.5**	**27.2**	**27.2**	**27.6**	**26.8**	**26.8**	**25.7**	**23.6**	**Developing Countries**	200
20.7	**20.5**	**19.5**	**19.8**	**20.6**	**20.0**	**19.2**	**17.9**	**18.0**	**19.8**	**20.3**	**19.9**	**20.4**	**....**		**Africa**	605
33.2	33.5	30.0	30.7	32.4	27.2	29.2	25.8	25.1	33.1	35.1	....	....	18.9		Algeria	612
15.8	14.7	14.2	15.6	11.8	14.2	14.6	14.6	14.3	18.5	23.5	17.9	18.4	18.3	18.9	Benin	638
30.4	16.2	26.6	7.9	30.1	30.0	29.8	29.6	28.1	25.9	28.6	25.7	26.8	28.2	35.1	Botswana	616
24.1	22.5	21.5	21.0	22.7	22.5	22.6	22.0	21.9	19.3	22.5	25.4	25.5	25.4	26.8	Burkina Faso	748
14.3	15.7	17.3	14.2	16.4	15.8	16.7	15.2	15.7	8.7	7.8	8.8	6.3	2.7	6.0	Burundi	618
24.5	25.3	25.6	21.3	17.5	18.0	21.4	13.6	16.0	14.1	13.7	15.1	16.1	....	....	Cameroon	622
18.9	15.0	12.6	10.5	11.8	12.7	12.6	12.4	10.6	11.7	14.1	....	....	....	....	Central African Rep.	626
12.5	13.2	14.2	14.4	14.3	9.1	5.6	6.9	1.8	4.1	9.4	....	....	....	....	Congo, Dem. Rep. of	636
30.3	29.5	13.9	18.6	16.2	15.9	20.5	21.6	19.1	46.2	41.9	29.4	22.7	26.0	....	Congo, Rep. of	634
13.0	12.1	12.3	14.4	8.1	8.5	6.3	5.5	8.3	11.8	15.0	13.6	15.6	....	....	Côte d'Ivoire	662
10.7	16.4	15.6	20.4	14.4	12.5	10.4	9.2	14.2	15.2	16.4	19.1	17.0	17.6	....	Ethiopia	644
9.6	9.4	10.4	10.9	13.5	12.3	13.5	13.8	22.2	24.0	20.0	21.5	24.6	....	....	Ghana	652
....	.2	.8	1.7	2.8	2.7	5.0	10.4	12.7	....	....	....	....	....	....	Guinea-Bissau	654
25.5	21.8	24.3	25.0	24.7	24.3	21.3	16.9	17.6	19.3	21.8	20.4	18.4	17.2	16.9	Kenya	664
12.6	11.7	11.4	10.1	8.5	....	....	....	....	....	....	....	....	....	....	Liberia	668
11.5	....	....	....	....	....	....	....	....	....	....	....	....	....	....	Madagascar	674
18.6	12.3	15.4	18.7	21.2	19.1	20.1	18.8	12.3	29.1	16.3	12.1	12.2	13.9	....	Malawi	676
14.5	18.0	21.4	20.3	23.1	20.9	19.2	21.9	17.4	24.9	24.7	21.3	22.0	24.8	....	Mali	678
....	....	....	....	....	....	19.4	25.1	18.6	19.1	20.4	17.8	17.3	....	....	Mauritania	682
23.5	21.9	25.6	31.0	31.1	30.9	28.7	29.3	30.6	32.2	25.8	24.8	29.3	25.6	28.3	Mauritius	684
27.1	22.8	21.1	21.0	23.7	25.0	22.6	23.2	22.5	21.3	20.7	19.6	20.7	22.6	....	Morocco	686
17.1	18.9	45.5	57.4	56.2	59.0	19.4	22.8	23.1	22.6	27.8	20.9	18.0	22.4	....	Mozambique	688
13.5	12.5	14.8	19.1	15.9	27.4	18.1	21.2	16.1	23.1	20.7	22.5	19.7	....	....	Namibia	728
15.3	13.5	10.3	15.9	13.5	16.1	9.0	5.1	5.6	13.4	13.6	14.3	11.7	....	....	Niger	692
7.1	10.6	8.8	6.5	8.2	11.9	10.9	9.5	8.4	6.9	5.8	6.1	9.1	10.0	....	Nigeria	694
17.3	15.9	15.7	15.1	13.6	14.1	12.9	17.0	17.6	10.2	14.8	15.5	15.0	....	....	Rwanda	714
10.5	11.4	12.5	12.7	11.9	13.8	12.5	14.4	13.7	17.0	16.7	18.5	....	....	....	Senegal	722
22.7	24.4	19.8	25.5	27.5	24.6	22.3	21.2	28.7	27.3	30.3	32.4	33.4	37.0	4.4	Seychelles	718
10.9	10.6	10.2	5.9	8.3	9.6	8.5	10.3	4.9	8.2	5.6	4.9	1.3	4.0	4.4	Sierra Leone	724
20.3	19.1	18.5	21.0	21.1	17.2	16.7	14.8	15.3	16.8	18.0	17.1	16.1	16.2	15.2	South Africa	199
26.2	20.0	14.9	23.5	23.9	19.6	20.6	26.1	26.6	32.1	34.1	30.1	33.9	....	....	Swaziland	734
18.6	19.9	22.1	16.5	18.1	26.1	26.3	27.2	25.1	24.6	19.8	16.6	14.9	16.2	15.5	Tanzania	738
25.5	29.1	25.2	24.9	24.0	22.2	21.7	23.8	9.1	14.8	17.2	14.0	13.9	....	....	Togo	742
26.1	23.0	20.5	19.5	23.9	27.1	26.0	29.2	29.2	24.6	24.7	25.1	26.7	27.5	27.8	Tunisia	744
8.1	9.0	11.9	10.9	10.9	14.2	16.4	14.7	16.2	13.8	16.4	15.1	....	....	....	Uganda	746
14.9	23.7	14.4	11.4	10.8	17.3	11.0	11.9	15.0	19.8	30.2	44.9	38.8	....	....	Zambia	754
17.7	18.0	14.9	18.8	15.2	17.5	19.1	20.3	22.8	23.7	19.5	23.2	....	....	....	Zimbabwe	698
29.4	**28.9**	**28.9**	**30.4**	**31.0**	**31.5**	**31.2**	**32.0**	**33.2**	**33.2**	**34.0**	**32.4**	**31.5**	**29.4**	**26.4**	**Asia**	505
10.3	12.3	12.5	14.5	12.9	12.8	11.5	12.1	11.4	13.8	16.6	17.2	15.3	15.0	....	Bangladesh	513
45.3	40.5	30.2	38.6	33.2	33.8	31.1	46.4	44.4	48.2	45.9	44.4	....	....	....	Bhutan	514
38.5	38.0	36.7	37.4	37.0	35.2	35.3	37.3	43.5	41.3	40.8	39.3	38.0	38.1	38.3	China, P.R.: Mainland	924
21.6	23.7	26.4	28.6	26.7	27.4	27.2	28.5	27.6	31.9	34.8	32.1	34.5	29.7	25.4	China, P.R.: Hong Kong	532
19.1	18.2	16.0	14.8	13.4	17.3	14.7	13.3	14.4	13.4	13.8	12.1	12.8	13.3	....	Fiji	819
24.2	23.2	22.5	24.4	24.1	25.2	22.7	24.0	21.3	23.5	26.5	21.9	23.4	21.8	....	India	534
28.1	28.2	31.3	31.5	35.1	36.1	35.5	35.8	29.5	31.1	31.9	30.7	31.8	35.3	11.6	Indonesia	536
30.0	29.1	30.2	31.3	33.9	37.7	39.9	37.3	35.5	36.5	37.2	37.9	34.2	21.2	26.8	Korea	542
27.6	26.0	22.8	25.5	27.7	30.4	36.5	34.6	36.3	39.3	43.6	41.5	42.9	26.7	22.4	Malaysia	548
15.5	12.7	11.6	12.8	9.2	13.4	13.5	13.5	12.4	12.4	14.2	12.3	12.5	12.4	....	Myanmar	518
21.9	19.0	20.2	19.8	21.7	18.4	20.8	21.2	23.1	22.4	24.9	27.3	25.3	20.7	17.3	Nepal	558
18.3	18.8	19.1	18.0	18.9	18.9	19.0	20.1	20.7	19.4	18.4	18.8	17.7	17.1	14.8	Pakistan	564
18.8	18.7	20.0	27.2	23.2	24.4	27.4	23.3	16.8	....	....	....	....	....	....	Papua New Guinea	853
14.3	15.2	17.5	18.7	21.6	24.2	20.2	21.3	24.0	24.1	22.5	24.0	24.9	20.3	18.8	Philippines	566
42.5	37.5	37.9	34.2	35.0	36.6	34.8	36.4	37.9	33.5	34.6	37.1	38.9	34.2	....	Singapore	576
26.2	26.2	23.1	37.1	....	....	....	....	....	....	....	....	....	....	....	Solomon Islands	813
23.8	23.7	23.3	22.8	21.7	22.2	22.9	24.3	25.6	27.0	25.7	24.2	24.4	25.4	....	Sri Lanka	524
28.2	25.9	27.9	32.6	35.1	41.4	42.8	40.0	39.6	40.6	42.3	41.7	33.0	24.0	23.6	Thailand	578
29.7	34.8	33.3	29.5	37.1	43.2	28.3	28.6	27.8	28.8	32.7	....	....	....	....	Vanuatu	846

Gross Capital Formation as Percentage of GDP

		1970	1971	1972	1973	1974	1975	1976	1977	1978	1979	1980	1981	1982	1983	1984
																Percentages
Europe	170	27.5	31.0	31.8	35.5	38.9	36.7	36.5	34.1	37.2	33.1	30.8	25.9	30.0	28.3	28.9
Armenia	911	....	....	....	....	....	....	....	....	....	....	....	....	....	....	....
Belarus	913	....	....	....	....	....	....	....	....	....	....	....	....	....	....	....
Bulgaria	918	....	....	....	....	....	....	....	....	....	....	32.1	34.0	35.5	34.1	32.9	33.2
Cyprus	423	24.4	23.5	23.6	30.2	26.3	22.5	26.6	34.9	37.2	38.7	37.8	33.8	31.7	30.1	33.6
Czech Republic	935	....	....	....	....	....	....	....	....	....	....	....	....	....	....	....
Czechoslovakia	934	26.0	24.5	24.8	26.3	28.4	28.9	29.0	25.2	24.9	24.6	21.2	19.6	19.7	18.8	19.0
Estonia	939	....	....	....	....	....	....	....	....	....	....	....	....	....	....	....
Hungary	944	37.4	38.7	33.4	33.4	40.6	37.8	35.9	37.2	41.3	34.0	30.7	29.7	28.5	26.5	25.7
Kazakhstan	916	....	....	....	....	....	....	....	....	....	....	....	....	....	....	....
Kyrgyz Republic	917	....	....	....	....	....	....	....	....	....	....	....	....	....	....	....
Macedonia, FYR	962	....	....	....	....	....	....	....	....	....	....	....	....	....	....	....
Malta	181	32.7	29.0	25.0	22.1	27.1	23.5	27.5	26.0	23.5	25.5	24.6	27.1	31.5	30.0	28.9
Moldova	921	....	....	....	....	....	....	....	....	....	....	....	....	....	....	....
Poland	964	24.6	28.9	31.7	36.3	38.7	36.7	36.9	33.3	31.8	29.0	26.4	18.5	28.0	25.0	26.3
Romania	968	....	....	....	....	....	....	....	....	....	....	39.8	36.3	33.7	34.0	34.2
Russia	922	....	....	....	....	....	....	....	....	....	....	....	....	....	....	....
Slovak Republic	936	....	....	....	....	....	....	....	....	....	....	....	....	....	....	....
Slovenia	961	....	....	....	....	....	....	....	....	....	....	....	....	....	....	....
Turkey	186	....	....	....	....	....	....	....	....	....	....	....	....	....	....	....
Ukraine	926	....	....	....	....	....	....	....	....	....	....	....	....	....	....	....
Middle East	405	22.5	20.1	22.8	21.0	18.3	26.7	27.1	29.3	27.3	24.7	26.0	24.5	24.6	27.2	27.0
Egypt	469	14.4	13.0	13.7	13.7	17.4	27.2	25.2	29.1	31.0	30.4	28.0	30.4	28.9	31.5	29.7
Iran, I.R. of	429	34.6	28.7	33.6	27.9	18.3	28.8	28.5	27.3	22.2	21.7	29.6	22.8	15.9	23.1	24.3
Iraq	433	15.8	14.6	19.0	22.1	28.1	30.3	22.2	24.5	20.1	28.8	30.5	63.0	57.7	14.9	18.1
Israel	436	28.4	32.0	31.3	25.8	35.7	31.3	27.3	24.4	27.0	27.1	22.4	21.1	23.5	23.3	21.7
Jordan	439	10.4	15.6	16.8	14.8	21.8	23.4	29.3	33.1	29.0	30.6	40.3	49.1	38.3	32.3	28.8
Kuwait	443	12.1	9.4	9.3	9.5	6.8	12.7	16.5	23.3	20.2	13.6	13.9	16.5	22.9	24.8	21.0
Libya	672	17.3	18.5	25.1	29.6	26.5	30.6	24.0	25.0	27.3	25.0	26.3	30.8	30.1	29.1	26.3
Oman	449	13.8	28.5	29.8	26.2	30.6	35.6	35.9	30.6	28.9	26.0	22.7	23.4	27.0	24.2	24.9
Qatar	453	....	....	....	....	....	....	....	....	....	....	17.0	17.7	27.5	21.9	16.6
Saudi Arabia	456	16.1	12.4	13.8	9.3	13.2	20.9	25.4	33.1	27.8	20.7	21.7	19.5	27.2	30.3	33.0
Syrian Arab Rep.	463	11.9	14.5	17.6	18.2	19.6	25.4	31.9	34.1	27.8	26.6	28.0	23.5	24.0	23.9	24.0
United Arab Emirates	466	....	....	27.3	25.4	15.4	30.6	33.3	39.2	38.8	34.5	28.3	26.3	28.6	31.3	28.9
Yemen Arab Rep.	473	16.4	17.6	16.8	20.2	18.5	20.3	21.4	43.4	39.2	44.0	39.5	38.3	29.8	19.4	17.4
Western Hemisphere	205	22.4	22.6	21.8	22.8	25.7	24.1	23.1	23.4	23.9	23.8	25.1	24.5	22.1	18.3	17.6
Antigua and Barbuda	311	....	....	....	....	....	....	20.6	19.3	24.3	34.8	41.9	39.4	20.4	23.6
Argentina	213	22.2	23.1	19.0	17.1	18.4	26.6	27.1	27.2	23.9	22.6	25.3	22.7	21.8	20.9	20.0
Bahamas, The	313	....	....	....	....	....	....	....	....	....	....	....	....	....	....	....
Barbados	316	....	....	....	....	24.0	20.0	27.0	21.8	25.8	23.5	22.1	26.0	21.4	19.9	16.2
Belize	339	....	....	....	29.6	27.8	32.3	37.8	32.5	30.0	33.9	27.6	29.5	23.7	22.9	26.7
Bolivia	218	17.1	17.2	19.8	20.7	16.4	24.4	21.2	20.8	24.7	14.6	13.3	12.5	12.2	10.6
Brazil	223	25.7	27.9	27.7	28.5	33.7	25.7	23.0	22.0	23.0	22.8	23.2	23.2	21.5	17.2	15.3
Chile	228	16.4	14.5	12.2	7.9	21.2	13.1	12.8	14.4	17.8	17.8	21.0	22.7	11.3	9.8	13.6
Colombia	233	20.3	19.9	18.4	18.1	21.5	17.0	17.6	18.8	18.3	18.2	19.1	20.6	20.5	19.9	19.0
Costa Rica	238	20.5	24.3	22.0	24.0	26.7	21.6	23.7	24.3	23.5	25.3	26.6	29.0	24.7	24.2	22.7
Dominican Republic	243	19.1	17.9	19.7	22.1	23.5	24.5	22.3	21.8	23.9	25.4	25.1	23.6	20.0	19.7	19.0
Ecuador	248	18.2	23.2	20.0	19.5	22.5	26.7	23.8	26.5	28.4	25.3	26.1	23.2	25.2	17.6	17.2
El Salvador	253	13.2	15.6	14.2	18.3	22.6	22.1	19.6	23.4	23.8	18.1	13.3	14.2	13.2	12.1	12.0
Grenada	328	....	....	....	....	....	6.5	13.2	15.6	8.4	15.8	27.7	44.3	44.7	40.2	29.7
Guatemala	258	12.8	14.4	12.1	13.7	18.6	16.1	21.4	20.0	21.6	18.7	15.9	17.0	14.1	11.1	11.6
Guyana	336	24.8	19.1	21.7	30.4	32.4	36.8	42.0	29.2	20.8	83.2	81.6	92.8	86.9	27.1	22.9
Haiti	263	8.4	8.8	9.5	8.8	15.2	16.3	16.0	15.8	16.9	16.4	17.9	17.7	16.7	16.4	15.9
Honduras	268	20.9	16.1	15.2	18.4	25.6	19.0	19.2	23.1	27.2	26.5	24.8	21.1	14.1	13.8	17.4
Jamaica	343	31.5	32.1	27.3	31.5	24.3	25.8	18.2	12.2	15.0	19.1	15.9	20.3	20.9	22.3	23.1
Mexico	273	22.7	20.2	20.3	21.4	23.2	23.7	22.3	22.8	23.6	26.0	29.6	27.5	22.7	20.8	19.7
Nicaragua	278	....	....	....	....	....	....	....	....	....	....	....	....	....	....	22.1
Panama	283	27.9	30.5	31.9	33.7	33.8	30.8	31.6	23.6	26.5	27.9	28.1	28.4	26.9	17.9	14.8
Paraguay	288	14.7	14.6	15.1	19.0	21.0	24.1	24.6	24.7	27.2	28.6	28.8	28.8	25.6	21.4	22.9
Peru	293	12.9	15.0	14.2	15.6	18.9	19.8	17.9	15.0	14.2	21.6	28.9	34.3	33.6	24.3	20.2
St. Lucia	362	....	....	....	....	....	46.1	43.0	40.0	48.6	50.0	49.5	47.5	31.9	23.7	23.3
St. Vincent & Grenadines	364	....	....	....	....	....	26.5	21.2	37.5	28.0	34.1	39.3	32.7	28.5	24.7	27.9
Suriname	366	18.3	17.6	21.7	23.0	29.9	38.0	29.5	37.3	32.4	22.8	26.5	31.2	27.7	15.6	11.8
Trinidad and Tobago	369	25.9	34.0	31.3	26.0	21.8	27.3	24.6	26.7	30.2	29.1	30.6	27.6	28.3	26.5	22.1
Uruguay	298	11.6	12.6	11.8	12.6	11.5	13.5	14.8	15.2	16.0	17.3	17.3	15.4	14.4	14.3	12.1
Venezuela, Rep. Bol.	299	29.6	29.7	31.2	29.3	24.0	30.9	34.4	41.5	42.8	31.6	24.7	22.9	25.9	11.8	18.1
Memorandum Items																
Oil Exporting Countries	999	22.6	21.6	24.5	24.2	19.6	27.1	28.4	30.6	29.9	25.4	25.3	25.8	25.5	25.5	24.8
Non-Oil Developing Countries	201	25.4	26.0	25.5	17.1	19.4	19.0	18.4	18.4	26.1	26.6	26.9	26.5	25.1	24.6	24.2

Percentages

1985	1986	1987	1988	1989	1990	1991	1992	1993	1994	1995	1996	1997	1998	1999		
28.9	30.6	29.6	28.9	29.7	26.8	23.7	22.1	24.0	22.2	24.1	24.3	25.0	25.0	....	Europe	170
....	....	....	....	....	47.2	39.7	1.6	9.8	23.5	18.4	20.0	19.1	19.0	....	Armenia	911
....	....	....	....	....	26.9	29.2	32.0	41.0	32.9	25.1	24.5	27.6	27.8	24.0	Belarus	913
31.6	35.9	32.9	34.4	33.1	30.4	22.6	19.9	15.3	9.4	15.7	8.4	11.8	14.7	19.1	Bulgaria	918
30.3	25.9	25.5	27.5	30.9	27.0	25.8	28.7	24.1	25.5	25.3	26.0	24.2	24.7	....	Cyprus	423
....	....	29.3	27.4	26.8	29.3	28.2	26.6	26.8	30.6	34.0	34.9	32.8	29.7	28.5	Czech Republic	935
15.1	16.2	14.9	13.5	12.9	15.7	13.3	....	....	....	....	....	....	....	....	Czechoslovakia	934
....	....	....	....	....	....	24.4	26.7	26.9	27.6	26.7	27.8	31.7	29.3	....	Estonia	939
25.0	26.9	26.7	25.3	26.6	25.4	20.4	16.1	20.0	22.2	24.1	26.9	....	....	....	Hungary	944
....	....	....	....	....	45.1	26.2	31.8	20.9	26.8	22.5	16.9	16.3	18.0	....	Kazakhstan	916
....	....	....	....	....	....	15.4	19.9	11.7	9.0	18.3	26.2	21.7	15.5	....	Kyrgyz Republic	917
....	....	....	....	....	19.0	17.2	15.6	17.9	15.5	20.8	20.1	22.4	23.0	....	Macedonia, FYR	962
28.1	25.5	27.5	28.8	29.6	33.4	31.6	27.5	29.8	30.7	32.0	28.6	25.6	23.2	23.5	Malta	181
....	....	....	....	....	....	29.0	59.8	55.8	28.8	24.9	24.4	24.4	....	....	Moldova	921
27.7	28.9	28.8	32.6	38.5	25.6	19.9	15.2	15.6	17.6	19.7	21.9	24.6	26.2	....	Poland	964
33.0	34.4	31.8	28.4	26.8	30.2	28.0	31.4	28.9	24.8	24.3	26.0	21.8	21.4	19.9	Romania	968
....	....	....	....	....	....	....	34.6	27.0	25.5	25.4	24.6	22.8	15.7	15.5	Russia	922
....	....	....	....	....	....	33.1	28.3	27.4	23.1	28.4	39.4	38.7	39.4	....	Slovak Republic	936
....	....	....	....	....	....	....	....	19.3	20.9	23.4	23.5	24.2	25.2	....	Slovenia	961
....	....	25.8	25.8	24.2	24.6	22.4	23.1	26.5	21.5	25.5	24.6	25.1	24.6	....	Turkey	186
....	....	....	....	....	....	....	34.4	36.3	35.3	26.7	22.7	20.1	....	....	Ukraine	926
23.0	23.5	22.7	22.2	23.0	24.3	25.4	25.3	24.2	22.3	20.7	20.4	20.4	21.8	21.1	Middle East	405
29.3	29.4	26.1	33.2	31.3	29.4	24.0	19.8	19.7	20.3	19.2	19.1	19.4	22.2	24.1	Egypt	469
21.1	22.1	25.5	19.1	23.8	28.6	33.2	35.4	29.0	24.2	19.6	20.9	21.4	21.9	21.2	Iran, I.R. of	429
23.7	19.0	19.7	20.9	19.0	22.5	19.1	14.6	15.5	....	....	....	....	....	....	Iraq	433
19.4	19.1	19.6	18.4	17.3	25.1	25.4	24.9	25.2	24.1	25.4	24.4	21.7	19.5	20.1	Israel	436
20.5	20.5	23.3	23.5	23.7	31.9	25.7	34.2	36.9	34.2	34.1	31.8	26.7	23.5	....	Jordan	439
18.9	22.1	17.6	15.7	12.3	15.9	39.3	19.9	17.2	16.2	15.1	15.3	13.6	16.2	12.6	Kuwait	443
19.3	21.1	17.2	18.7	17.1	18.8	13.3	12.5	13.4	12.4	11.5	15.4	12.3	....	....	Libya	672
25.1	26.1	15.6	15.2	14.1	12.3	15.0	16.4	17.5	15.7	15.0	13.7	17.6	24.0	15.8	Oman	449
17.8	18.5	14.4	16.0	15.3	18.0	19.1	20.6	19.8	24.5	35.1	35.8	39.0	....	....	Qatar	453
20.9	19.9	19.0	20.9	21.6	19.5	21.2	22.2	24.2	20.1	20.7	18.0	19.7	21.3	19.3	Saudi Arabia	456
24.1	22.5	18.2	14.0	16.2	16.5	18.0	23.2	26.0	30.0	27.2	24.2	21.3	21.0	....	Syrian Arab Rep.	463
25.2	30.2	24.0	25.0	23.6	20.5	21.9	24.2	29.3	29.4	28.5	26.4	28.1	30.1	....	United Arab Emirates	466
14.4	13.0	14.6	....	....	....	....	....	....	....	....	....	....	....	....	Yemen Arab Rep.	473
20.0	18.6	20.9	22.2	23.1	19.6	20.0	20.4	20.9	21.5	21.3	21.3	22.7	22.3	....	Western Hemisphere	205
27.8	35.7	45.8	39.8	41.2	32.4	37.6	34.8	31.7	32.4	36.9	39.5	41.1	....	....	Antigua and Barbuda	311
17.6	17.5	19.6	18.6	15.5	14.0	14.6	16.7	19.1	19.9	17.9	....	....	....	....	Argentina	213
....	....	....	....	....	25.1	21.8	22.6	23.2	19.6	21.2	23.2	....	....	....	Bahamas, The	313
15.4	16.0	16.0	17.5	19.1	18.8	17.1	9.5	12.7	13.4	14.1	12.7	15.5	....	....	Barbados	316
24.7	23.6	21.9	25.4	30.3	26.3	30.4	29.1	30.1	24.1	20.9	23.2	25.1	27.5	32.7	Belize	339
16.9	13.6	13.5	14.0	11.6	12.5	15.6	16.7	16.6	14.4	15.2	16.2	19.6	23.1	18.9	Bolivia	218
21.3	19.1	22.2	22.7	28.6	20.2	19.8	18.9	20.8	22.1	22.3	20.9	21.7	21.3	....	Brazil	223
17.2	18.9	22.2	22.8	25.1	25.1	22.6	23.8	26.5	24.1	25.8	26.9	27.2	26.5	21.1	Chile	228
19.0	18.0	20.0	22.0	20.0	18.5	16.0	17.2	21.2	25.5	25.7	22.1	20.8	....	....	Colombia	233
25.9	25.2	27.1	24.5	26.6	27.3	25.1	29.6	30.5	27.6	24.0	26.1	26.5	28.3	26.5	Costa Rica	238
17.8	20.1	24.3	24.7	27.4	25.1	21.7	22.6	26.5	24.0	21.9	21.4	22.3	26.2	27.7	Dominican Republic	243
18.2	20.9	22.7	21.5	20.7	17.5	22.2	21.2	21.1	19.0	18.7	17.3	20.2	24.7	....	Ecuador	248
10.8	13.3	12.4	12.8	15.3	13.9	15.4	18.5	18.6	19.7	20.0	15.2	15.1	17.4	16.2	El Salvador	253
26.5	30.0	33.2	33.7	34.1	38.1	37.9	29.5	31.2	35.8	37.0	35.2	36.6	40.2	....	Grenada	328
11.5	10.3	13.9	13.7	13.5	13.6	14.3	18.3	17.2	15.7	15.1	12.7	13.7	16.0	15.7	Guatemala	258
20.9	26.4	37.2	21.5	34.2	42.3	35.3	53.7	....	....	....	....	....	....	....	Guyana	336
16.6	14.5	14.3	13.5	14.3	7.6	....	....	....	....	....	....	....	....	....	Haiti	263
17.3	13.9	17.4	21.0	19.1	23.0	24.7	26.0	33.6	37.6	31.6	30.4	31.5	30.8	34.9	Honduras	268
24.3	18.5	22.2	25.6	28.6	27.9	26.7	33.0	34.6	33.1	34.4	34.7	35.0	29.0	....	Jamaica	343
20.8	18.1	19.2	22.6	22.9	23.1	23.3	23.3	21.0	21.7	19.8	23.3	26.0	24.4	23.2	Mexico	273
23.1	16.8	15.8	26.8	27.2	19.3	20.3	19.3	18.5	22.4	24.3	26.0	30.5	33.1	42.8	Nicaragua	278
15.2	17.2	18.4	7.5	6.2	16.8	19.2	23.7	24.7	26.8	30.3	30.5	31.1	32.8	....	Panama	283
22.0	25.0	25.1	24.4	23.8	22.9	24.8	22.9	22.9	23.4	23.9	23.4	23.6	23.0	....	Paraguay	288
18.5	20.2	21.1	22.1	18.1	15.6	16.6	16.6	18.6	21.8	24.4	23.3	24.4	24.3	21.7	Peru	293
....	....	....	....	....	....	....	....	....	....	....	....	....	....	....	St. Lucia	362
28.3	30.3	35.2	33.5	31.4	31.0	30.8	26.5	28.4	28.0	33.0	31.2	....	....	....	St. Vincent & Grenadines	364
14.4	22.0	26.0	16.7	21.0	21.8	22.9	23.2	23.6	....	....	....	....	....	....	Suriname	366
18.8	21.6	19.3	13.0	16.6	13.8	16.3	13.8	14.4	20.2	15.9	17.0	26.8	26.4	....	Trinidad and Tobago	369
11.4	11.2	14.3	13.2	11.3	11.0	13.5	13.3	14.6	12.9	12.9	12.6	12.8	15.8	....	Uruguay	298
19.1	20.8	25.2	27.9	12.9	10.2	18.7	23.7	18.8	14.2	18.1	16.6	19.6	19.6	....	Venezuela, Rep. Bol.	299

Memorandum Items

1985	1986	1987	1988	1989	1990	1991	1992	1993	1994	1995	1996	1997	1998	1999		
22.9	23.9	24.7	24.5	25.3	25.8	27.9	28.2	24.7	24.1	24.1	23.4	24.8	26.8	14.7	Oil Exporting Countries	999
25.6	24.8	25.1	27.0	27.7	26.7	26.0	26.2	27.7	27.8	28.3	27.4	27.1	25.6	25.4	Non-Oil Developing Countries	201

Final Consumption Expenditure as Percentage of GDP

		1970	1971	1972	1973	1974	1975	1976	1977	1978	1979	1980	1981	1982	1983	1984
																Percentages
World	001	74.5	73.8	73.6	74.6	75.3	77.4	76.9	76.8	76.0	75.8	76.5	77.0	78.1	78.1	77.4
Industrial Countries	110	77.0	75.9	75.8	74.7	75.8	78.0	77.6	77.4	76.7	76.6	77.7	77.8	79.2	79.6	78.6
United States	111	85.9	81.8	81.1	79.6	80.7	82.1	81.5	81.0	79.8	79.4	80.8	79.9	82.5	83.3	81.8
Canada	156	76.6	76.6	76.6	74.5	73.4	76.3	75.7	76.6	76.5	74.5	74.8	74.4	77.2	77.9	76.6
Australia	193	71.6	71.8	72.0	71.3	73.0	75.8	75.8	76.9	77.7	74.8	75.7	76.1	78.0	79.9	77.0
Japan	158	59.7	61.5	62.2	61.9	63.4	67.2	67.4	67.5	67.4	68.4	68.7	68.1	69.3	70.2	69.2
New Zealand	196	77.4	74.1	73.2	72.4	75.8	75.7	71.6	76.9	77.9	77.6	79.6	77.5	78.3	76.3	76.0
Euro Area	163	....	....	....	....	....	....	....	....	....	....	....	....	....	....	....
Austria	122	69.3	69.6	68.8	68.8	69.2	73.4	74.3	74.4	73.3	73.1	73.3	74.6	75.7	77.0	76.4
Belgium	124	73.7	74.9	75.2	75.6	75.1	78.2	78.0	79.3	79.6	81.0	81.4	84.4	84.7	84.3	83.2
Finland	172	71.1	71.1	71.7	70.0	68.3	72.8	74.4	75.0	74.7	72.9	71.6	72.7	73.9	74.4	73.5
France	132	72.6	72.7	72.6	71.9	72.9	75.3	75.3	75.4	75.5	75.7	77.0	79.1	80.0	80.3	80.4
Germany	134	70.4	71.5	72.1	71.8	73.5	77.2	76.4	76.8	76.3	76.0	77.2	78.3	78.3	77.7	77.3
Ireland	178	83.5	83.3	80.3	79.1	85.5	82.7	82.6	81.2	80.9	83.4	85.7	85.8	79.6	79.2	77.7
Italy	136	73.3	75.3	76.3	75.8	75.0	77.2	75.3	75.5	75.3	76.0	77.2	78.5	79.1	79.0	79.0
Luxembourg	137	61.0	66.5	65.3	60.2	57.6	72.7	71.3	73.4	73.6	73.8	75.4	78.3	76.7	75.4	73.5
Netherlands	138	73.8	73.8	73.2	72.3	73.0	76.0	76.0	77.2	78.0	79.0	79.0	78.2	77.8	77.8	75.7
Portugal	182	80.1	78.9	76.7	77.6	86.8	92.1	88.7	86.6	82.8	81.3	82.5	82.8	83.2	85.6	88.4
Spain	184	74.1	74.5	74.0	73.7	74.7	75.4	77.6	77.1	76.4	77.4	79.1	80.2	79.7	79.4	78.2
Denmark	128	76.4	76.3	73.3	74.6	76.5	78.7	79.3	79.3	79.1	79.9	81.0	82.4	81.6	80.1	78.4
Greece	174	81.8	80.5	77.8	74.9	81.5	82.7	80.8	81.8	81.1	79.7	80.9	85.4	85.7	85.5	84.2
Iceland	176	74.4	74.5	75.0	71.9	75.8	75.0	72.4	72.3	73.0	74.2	73.7	75.7	77.8	77.8	79.2
Norway	142	70.8	71.7	71.6	70.3	69.3	71.5	72.4	74.4	69.8	69.1	65.0	65.5	66.5	66.4	64.3
Sweden	144	74.6	75.3	75.7	75.4	76.5	75.4	77.5	80.8	81.5	81.1	80.8	82.2	83.0	80.7	78.7
Switzerland	146	69.4	69.1	69.1	69.8	70.7	74.2	76.0	76.7	75.9	76.6	74.8	74.5	75.4	76.6	74.9
United Kingdom	112	78.6	79.3	80.3	79.8	82.9	83.3	82.0	79.4	79.0	79.2	80.4	81.7	81.7	81.9	81.6
Developing Countries	200	67.6	68.1	67.6	74.3	73.9	76.1	75.3	75.4	74.9	74.3	74.3	75.8	76.2	75.7	75.6
Africa	605	75.0	76.8	75.9	74.8	71.0	76.6	75.9	76.2	78.4	75.4	75.5	78.3	79.6	79.8	79.8
Algeria	612	70.8	72.9	68.0	69.3	57.0	64.0	61.0	64.4	62.5	56.9	59.2	59.3	60.8	60.3	62.6
Benin	638	90.5	89.1	90.7	91.6	83.4	97.0	99.1	103.6	105.7	100.3	98.4	113.4	93.0	99.3	94.6
Botswana	616	93.3	82.1	72.2	72.6	73.0	78.3	79.1	86.3	87.1	77.8	72.3	75.8	84.0	75.0	70.3
Burkina Faso	748	101.3	101.5	99.4	98.3	91.8	99.2	93.8	101.9	101.9	95.6	102.5	104.8	107.8	106.7	98.6
Burundi	618	92.9	100.7	100.2	97.0	101.7	96.9	93.9	88.2	94.0	95.5	98.0	95.9	97.9	95.2	94.3
Cameroon	622	80.9	85.6	86.7	85.1	76.6	82.1	84.6	79.4	76.0	81.4	82.7	76.9	79.6	75.1	72.4
Central African Rep.	626	96.4	93.5	94.4	92.1	91.5	92.7	88.0	87.8	....	....	....	....	....	....	....
Congo, Dem. Rep. of	636	72.4	76.0	79.0	75.7	76.1	87.2	92.5	91.5	85.9	76.9	89.4	90.9	90.6	89.1	87.7
Congo, Rep. of	634	98.1	97.4	103.4	90.5	83.3	102.6	105.0	101.5	82.4	69.5	58.6	54.2	53.0	54.7	53.6
Côte d'Ivoire	662	75.0	77.5	77.4	77.0	72.6	77.4	71.1	64.2	71.1	75.1	79.6	81.2	79.7	80.7	74.8
Ethiopia	644	88.8	90.1	89.1	86.6	87.0	93.4	91.3	94.2	98.1	96.6	96.3	92.4	94.1	94.5	91.9
Ghana	652	86.5	89.6	87.1	85.7	89.2	86.4	91.5	90.0	94.6	93.4	95.1	96.1	96.3	96.7	93.4
Guinea-Bissau	654	....	....	....	....	....	....	....	....	....	....	....	....	....	....	....
Kenya	664	79.8	81.3	84.0	86.4	85.7	97.6	89.9	82.9	92.6	95.7	96.0	94.4	98.9	95.7	99.2
Liberia	668	56.2	59.0	57.1	61.3	61.2	54.3	58.7	68.4	70.0	67.3	66.8	85.8	78.7	81.5	81.5
Madagascar	674	88.1	88.5	89.4	86.6	90.3	91.5	88.5	88.8	90.9	92.0	93.3	93.0	95.2	93.3	96.0
Malawi	676	86.7	90.7	87.8	87.6	83.6	83.0	82.2	79.9	79.5	79.8	82.1	82.5	82.7	80.4	85.2
Mali	678	....	....	....	....	....	....	79.5	77.4	83.7	86.6	86.2	92.6	99.1	94.4	96.5
Mauritania	682	69.0	68.3	68.5	74.9	74.3	81.1	86.9	92.0	107.5	102.6	100.2	115.2	104.6	98.4	94.1
Mauritius	684	85.9	83.1	80.2	73.3	63.6	67.9	67.4	80.7	81.6	80.5	89.5	85.2	84.6	82.9	81.3
Morocco	686	87.3	86.6	87.5	85.8	78.8	84.4	89.9	84.5	86.6	87.1	87.1	89.1	86.7	86.7	87.8
Mozambique	688	....	....	....	....	....	....	....	....	....	....	100.0	100.0	102.5	105.3	100.0
Namibia	728	....	....	....	....	....	....	....	....	....	....	....	....	....	....	....
Niger	692	97.6	94.4	95.5	93.0	103.8	89.9	83.6	82.3	83.1	79.4	81.3	80.0	85.1	88.8	96.2
Nigeria	694	52.7	55.1	55.0	64.3	62.6	69.4	66.0	68.1	81.4	71.8	73.1	81.1	83.0	85.7	86.3
Rwanda	714	56.4	57.0	57.4	54.2	57.5	94.7	91.0	88.4	92.4	89.8	95.8	98.7	94.8	95.6	91.2
Senegal	722	90.4	92.7	89.0	93.1	85.9	89.4	93.3	93.1	97.9	97.7	105.0	109.1	102.5	101.9	99.3
Seychelles	718	....	....	....	....	....	....	77.1	64.0	57.9	73.0	72.9	84.8	96.7	101.0	91.8
Sierra Leone	724	82.5	85.8	89.7	86.8	86.5	94.3	96.7	94.3	93.6	94.8	99.1	97.6	96.8	96.7	89.1
South Africa	199	73.2	75.3	73.6	69.5	67.2	70.8	71.9	72.0	69.6	67.2	64.6	67.5	70.7	71.8	72.4
Swaziland	734	73.2	67.7	74.6	60.5	48.2	65.1	69.5	76.4	75.8	92.9	92.6	98.6	98.0	101.1	104.6
Tanzania	738	82.9	82.4	83.4	85.8	91.6	91.7	79.3	77.2	90.0	86.7	90.2	83.8	85.9	91.1	91.2
Togo	742	87.9	85.4	87.8	86.5	64.0	89.5	82.9	79.8	80.6	76.7	78.4	85.0	87.8	86.2	85.7
Tunisia	744	85.2	82.9	80.4	83.3	75.6	73.6	77.5	80.5	79.2	75.9	75.7	76.1	78.9	76.9	77.6
Uganda	746	....	....	....	....	....	....	....	....	....	....	....	....	....	105.2	103.6
Zambia	754	56.8	64.8	63.1	55.0	54.1	79.0	71.1	77.9	79.5	76.9	80.7	93.2	92.1	87.4	81.5
Zimbabwe	698	77.4	78.6	76.5	75.9	75.9	75.7	77.2	78.5	84.7	87.5	84.2	84.2	84.4	91.8	80.5
Asia	505	84.2	84.4	83.9	79.4	82.7	82.8	80.3	79.8	73.9	74.2	75.0	74.9	75.1	73.7	73.1
Bangladesh	513	....	....	....	90.1	100.5	100.7	99.8	95.2	85.6	97.4	97.5	98.4	98.3	96.4	95.4
Bhutan	514	....	....	....	....	....	....	....	....	....	....	92.1	93.0	90.7	91.6	92.6
China, P.R.: Mainland	924	....	....	....	....	....	....	....	....	....	64.3	65.4	65.7	66.3	66.2	65.5
China, P.R.: Hong Kong	532	71.8	71.4	68.5	70.7	70.9	71.4	63.9	66.9	70.3	66.2	65.9	66.8	68.8	72.0	67.9
Fiji	819	78.9	84.0	83.6	89.8	86.3	80.0	83.2	78.4	81.7	77.9	74.4	78.9	79.8	85.8	81.5
India	534	84.3	85.5	85.1	78.4	85.7	82.7	80.5	81.1	81.5	81.2	82.6	80.8	80.5	80.5	80.3
Indonesia	536	89.4	86.4	83.6	81.5	75.6	79.1	77.9	76.5	72.6	72.6	70.8	66.7	72.3	71.0	70.3
Korea	542	84.0	84.9	83.1	77.1	79.6	81.8	76.8	73.4	71.5	72.5	76.8	76.4	75.2	71.8	69.6
Malaysia	548	78.0	77.8	79.8	70.7	71.3	76.2	67.7	68.6	67.8	62.2	67.1	71.2	71.4	69.4	64.5
Maldives	556	....	....	....	....	....	....	....	....	....	....	95.4	104.8	98.9	98.8	86.6
Myanmar	518	90.8	90.2	89.4	87.2	90.2	91.1	90.4	88.2	86.2	82.0	82.3	82.1	84.9	85.7	88.4
Nepal	558	....	....	....	....	....	90.0	88.3	86.5	87.1	88.4	88.9	89.1	90.1	91.4	90.1
Pakistan	564	86.9	87.1	87.3	86.5	90.4	92.6	89.2	89.2	91.2	92.9	92.2	90.7	91.7	91.5	92.3
Papua New Guinea	853	96.1	91.7	95.2	83.4	68.8	84.6	89.7	80.0	81.5	78.0	86.4	93.6	91.5	87.8	88.1
Philippines	566	77.9	79.5	80.6	75.3	76.5	76.1	74.1	75.8	76.0	75.8	73.4	73.2	74.7	72.6	76.1
Singapore	576	79.5	79.0	74.3	73.1	71.4	71.4	69.3	68.5	67.9	64.7	61.2	58.3	57.7	55.0	54.7
Solomon Islands	813	101.1	96.8	92.0	....	....	....	....	....	....	....	....	....	....	....	78.5
Sri Lanka	524	84.2	84.9	84.3	87.5	91.8	91.9	86.1	81.9	84.7	86.2	88.8	88.3	88.1	86.2	80.1
Thailand	578	81.3	79.8	80.1	76.8	77.4	80.0	79.6	78.0	75.7	77.1	77.7	78.0	76.7	78.0	76.8
Tonga	866	....	....	....	....	....	101.9	109.9	103.0	108.3	112.7	95.2	112.2	111.1	118.0	....
Vanuatu	846	....	....	....	....	....	....	....	....	....	....	....	....	....	89.8	89.8

1985	1986	1987	1988	1989	1990	1991	1992	1993	1994	1995	1996	1997	1998	1999		96f r
Percentages																
77.4	77.9	77.1	76.2	75.4	75.9	77.0	77.1	77.4	76.8	76.7	76.8	76.4	76.7	....	World	001
78.9	79.0	78.8	78.0	77.6	77.9	78.7	79.1	79.4	78.9	78.7	78.7	78.2	78.4	78.8	Industrial Countries	110
83.0	83.7	83.1	83.1	82.4	83.2	83.7	83.6	83.5	82.8	82.8	82.4	81.6	81.5	82.4	United States	111
77.4	78.6	77.7	76.6	77.3	79.1	82.3	82.0	81.2	78.6	77.3	77.8	78.3	78.6	77.1	Canada	156
77.6	79.1	76.6	74.7	74.2	76.2	79.2	79.9	78.9	77.9	78.4	77.5	77.2	77.2	77.4	Australia	193
68.5	68.3	68.3	67.4	67.3	67.0	66.2	67.0	68.0	69.3	69.9	69.5	69.7	71.3	72.2	Japan	158
77.8	76.6	77.2	77.6	78.0	80.3	80.4	79.6	76.2	75.6	76.3	77.3	78.4	80.3	....	New Zealand	196
....	....	....	....	....	76.0	77.5	78.2	78.8	78.0	77.5	78.0	77.3	76.3	76.8	Euro Area	163
76.5	76.2	76.1	75.9	75.3	74.5	74.0	75.1	76.4	76.4	76.5	77.6	76.6	75.9	76.0	Austria	122
81.1	79.9	79.6	77.0	75.8	75.8	76.9	76.3	76.6	76.4	75.4	76.0	74.9	74.9	74.8	Belgium	124
74.0	75.2	75.4	72.5	70.9	73.0	78.5	80.2	78.8	76.7	74.4	75.4	72.7	72.1	71.9	Finland	172
80.5	79.3	79.7	77.8	77.1	77.1	77.5	78.0	79.8	79.1	78.8	79.5	78.5	78.0	77.9	France	132
76.8	75.2	75.6	74.8	73.7	72.5	75.9	76.4	77.3	76.4	76.6	77.3	76.9	76.5	76.7	Germany	134
78.3	79.6	77.9	77.0	75.1	75.5	76.9	77.2	75.4	75.0	71.0	69.8	67.0	64.8	....	Ireland	178
79.4	78.7	79.2	78.1	78.4	78.3	78.9	79.6	79.1	79.1	77.9	77.8	78.5	78.4	78.7	Italy	136
66.5	64.6	65.9	63.1	59.3	60.1	72.8	70.2	68.3	66.1	65.5	66.8	63.6	61.9	....	Luxembourg	137
75.2	74.9	76.7	74.7	73.5	73.2	73.8	74.9	75.4	74.7	73.3	74.2	73.5	72.9	73.3	Netherlands	138
86.6	82.6	82.3	82.4	82.0	83.0	85.5	86.1	87.3	86.5	85.3	85.4	85.2	86.0	....	Portugal	182
78.8	77.9	78.3	77.5	78.1	78.0	78.6	80.1	80.7	79.7	78.8	78.5	78.1	80.1	76.6	Spain	184
77.8	76.9	76.7	76.5	75.8	74.6	75.0	75.3	76.8	77.1	76.2	76.1	76.3	76.9	76.3	Denmark	128
85.9	86.8	89.0	85.2	87.0	88.5	87.4	88.7	89.7	89.1	88.4	88.2	87.5	86.5	85.2	Greece	174
81.4	79.4	82.5	82.5	81.3	80.5	82.3	82.7	80.9	79.6	81.2	81.7	80.8	82.6	84.4	Iceland	176
66.1	71.7	71.6	71.3	70.0	70.2	70.5	72.4	71.8	71.4	70.3	68.0	67.7	71.1	69.7	Norway	142
78.8	78.6	78.9	78.2	77.5	78.3	80.5	81.8	83.1	79.4	76.5	77.4	77.4	77.0	77.6	Sweden	144
74.5	73.9	73.9	72.8	71.8	71.2	73.2	74.5	74.4	74.4	74.6	75.6	75.4	75.0	74.9	Switzerland	146
80.7	82.6	82.1	82.2	81.8	82.4	83.9	85.0	85.1	84.2	83.4	83.7	82.7	82.8	83.7	United Kingdom	112
74.9	76.0	74.3	73.3	72.1	72.8	74.3	74.0	74.2	73.6	73.6	73.8	73.7	74.0	....	Developing Countries	200
78.6	80.8	79.9	80.7	78.4	79.4	80.9	82.2	80.9	81.9	85.5	83.8	82.2	87.4	....	Africa	605
63.6	70.6	68.1	68.4	66.0	72.7	64.3	69.1	71.9	79.1	77.4	....	....	....	....	Algeria	612
92.1	96.2	95.9	95.4	94.4	93.6	95.3	96.1	96.9	90.0	88.9	90.5	90.5	89.6	88.4	Benin	638
67.1	59.2	66.1	62.0	49.4	64.2	62.1	62.8	67.7	61.6	60.3	57.8	53.1	57.2	66.1	Botswana	616
98.1	98.4	96.1	95.9	93.0	95.1	95.4	97.0	92.5	93.9	92.9	92.5	90.5	89.3	88.0	Burkina Faso	748
93.6	91.3	94.4	95.3	95.8	102.5	101.7	104.1	105.8	107.0	103.2	76.1	77.6	86.2	84.2	Burundi	618
72.2	72.6	81.6	80.9	83.6	81.9	76.7	85.1	78.8	73.9	76.0	75.6	73.1	....	....	Cameroon	622
115.8	114.7	98.1	96.8	94.4	96.1	95.9	97.1	94.9	89.9	90.6	....	....	....	....	Central African Rep.	626
83.6	85.6	88.7	87.9	85.0	83.0	93.1	90.5	96.0	90.8	85.9	....	....	....	....	Congo, Dem. Rep. of	636
58.0	84.4	77.1	81.2	72.9	73.0	78.7	80.3	81.2	71.3	68.9	62.5	66.7	62.0	....	Congo, Rep. of	634
72.7	78.6	83.9	81.9	82.2	76.9	90.7	91.2	90.3	77.2	79.7	75.8	73.4	....	....	Côte d'Ivoire	662
97.2	91.4	92.4	87.5	91.1	92.1	96.6	97.0	94.4	95.0	93.3	93.4	90.1	92.6	....	Ethiopia	644
92.4	92.3	91.8	89.3	94.0	96.4	95.0	97.7	93.4	87.4	88.3	88.1	92.2	....	....	Ghana	652
....	106.5	102.8	112.6	114.0	105.7	107.1	101.1	101.5	104.7	98.9	112.3	103.1	....	....	Guinea-Bissau	654
75.4	78.2	80.8	80.3	82.7	80.9	80.0	83.0	77.6	77.6	84.1	83.7	87.9	90.5	89.9	Kenya	664
80.1	75.5	78.2	74.6	69.1	....	....	....	....	....	....	....	....	....	....	Liberia	668
99.7	94.4	95.8	93.5	90.4	94.5	100.3	97.1	97.8	96.9	95.4	93.9	96.6	95.9	95.1	Madagascar	674
87.1	89.9	87.0	90.8	95.3	90.6	92.1	98.3	103.8	94.7	94.7	100.8	99.1	99.0	....	Malawi	676
108.3	102.2	93.6	95.7	92.8	94.8	96.2	94.8	96.0	97.7	98.3	98.3	89.5	86.0	....	Mali	678
....	....	....	....	....	....	92.3	97.1	98.4	91.6	80.1	88.3	89.5	....	....	Mauritania	682
78.4	71.4	72.4	73.9	76.2	76.4	75.1	73.9	75.5	76.7	76.7	76.0	75.5	75.2	77.2	Mauritius	684
85.2	86.8	87.1	83.4	85.1	80.2	85.3	86.6	86.6	87.7	88.9	88.0	86.4	85.3	....	Morocco	686
95.5	95.9	93.1	94.6	94.6	90.8	113.3	116.6	114.0	110.4	108.7	102.0	99.3	93.9	91.0	Mozambique	688
74.4	77.6	95.8	82.3	84.9	82.4	90.8	87.9	90.4	83.1	87.2	86.5	85.8	....	....	Namibia	728
93.9	93.8	94.8	92.9	95.6	91.2	90.2	93.2	96.1	106.3	93.8	127.4	101.9	....	....	Niger	692
84.9	87.2	78.7	84.2	66.2	60.6	71.6	68.5	61.8	66.8	96.0	88.9	78.9	106.9	....	Nigeria	694
91.7	91.0	94.1	94.6	92.8	94.0	97.3	95.6	97.1	146.7	108.3	104.9	103.1	102.0	94.7	Rwanda	714
102.9	95.8	95.1	93.6	93.6	90.7	90.8	91.5	92.3	84.5	91.3	91.0	87.7	85.7	....	Senegal	722
92.8	92.9	91.5	86.8	87.0	84.9	84.5	84.7	80.5	75.9	76.4	77.6	75.6	78.4	....	Seychelles	718
99.6	85.4	81.0	79.8	85.4	87.9	85.7	79.2	83.2	81.2	84.6	89.3	186.6	91.7	89.5	Sierra Leone	724
71.0	72.5	74.1	74.3	74.2	82.4	83.1	83.9	82.4	82.1	80.9	81.7	82.9	82.6	81.8	South Africa	199
102.0	87.6	78.4	77.5	76.8	79.6	81.8	81.4	73.7	74.0	71.0	81.2	80.5	....	....	Swaziland	734
91.4	95.5	98.6	98.8	98.6	100.6	100.6	102.4	103.1	101.2	99.2	94.6	93.1	95.9	95.1	Tanzania	738
82.8	83.1	84.8	77.5	82.0	82.4	81.7	87.1	100.0	94.5	98.6	95.2	95.1	....	....	Togo	742
78.3	82.1	80.0	80.5	80.3	80.0	79.0	77.7	78.3	78.3	79.2	76.5	75.8	75.7	75.1	Tunisia	744
103.1	98.2	99.6	99.3	102.4	99.5	99.0	99.3	98.1	93.5	93.3	91.8	....	....	....	Uganda	746
84.6	77.1	82.0	81.3	96.2	82.2	85.5	93.6	87.0	84.6	74.7	68.3	73.7	....	....	Zambia	754
81.3	79.4	81.9	78.3	84.3	82.9	84.2	89.3	79.0	78.9	83.8	76.6	....	....	....	Zimbabwe	698
73.1	72.8	70.8	69.6	69.1	68.1	67.8	67.3	67.9	67.0	67.0	67.9	67.6	66.1	71.5	Asia	505
95.5	97.2	96.8	97.4	97.4	97.3	95.9	94.2	93.0	92.6	91.8	92.5	92.5	91.4	91.5	Bangladesh	513
86.4	86.2	81.9	81.3	79.0	70.3	77.1	78.1	66.7	61.7	58.9	65.5	....	....	....	Bhutan	514
65.7	64.6	63.2	63.7	64.1	62.0	61.8	61.7	58.5	57.4	57.5	58.5	58.2	58.1	61.0	China, P.R.: Mainland	924
68.9	67.8	63.7	62.6	61.8	64.2	66.2	66.2	65.4	66.9	69.5	69.3	68.9	69.8	70.1	China, P.R.: Hong Kong	532
82.8	77.0	82.9	90.0	90.0	90.8	94.0	90.0	88.5	87.3	87.0	84.5	84.1	90.2	....	Fiji	819
78.6	79.6	79.0	77.0	75.0	73.2	73.2	72.1	77.9	75.7	74.6	76.2	75.5	75.6	....	India	534
70.2	72.8	67.1	66.1	62.5	63.4	64.1	61.8	67.5	67.8	69.4	69.9	68.5	57.3	80.5	Indonesia	536
69.4	65.9	63.0	61.2	64.1	62.8	62.8	63.7	64.0	64.6	64.4	66.0	66.3	67.3	....	Korea	542
67.3	67.9	63.0	63.4	64.1	65.6	65.9	63.3	60.9	60.4	60.3	57.1	56.2	51.5	52.9	Malaysia	548
101.4	101.3	89.7	79.6	83.6	74.8	....	....	....	....	....	....	....	....	....	Maldives	556
88.5	89.9	92.0	88.9	91.2	88.3	86.0	87.2	88.6	88.3	86.6	88.5	88.2	88.2	....	Myanmar	518
86.6	89.4	88.5	90.1	88.6	92.1	90.4	89.2	86.4	85.3	85.2	86.2	86.0	90.5	89.4	Nepal	558
93.7	89.1	86.1	87.6	87.4	86.5	82.6	83.0	85.4	83.3	84.3	85.6	86.9	84.0	84.9	Pakistan	564
90.4	84.4	84.8	81.5	88.9	83.9	82.5	74.5	67.7	....	....	....	....	....	....	Papua New Guinea	853
81.2	81.0	79.0	78.9	79.7	81.3	83.4	85.1	86.2	85.1	85.5	85.4	86.0	87.6	85.4	Philippines	566
59.4	60.3	60.5	58.6	57.9	56.6	55.3	54.9	54.7	52.7	50.3	50.5	49.9	50.4	....	Singapore	576
92.3	96.4	99.5	105.9	112.7	....	....	....	....	....	....	....	....	....	....	Solomon Islands	813
88.1	88.0	87.2	88.0	87.8	85.7	87.2	85.0	84.0	84.8	84.7	84.7	82.7	81.1	....	Sri Lanka	524
75.7	74.1	71.4	66.8	65.0	66.0	64.2	64.7	64.1	64.3	64.5	64.6	65.6	61.4	65.5	Thailand	578
....	....	....	....	....	....	....	....	....	....	....	....	....	....	....	Tonga	866
94.1	95.3	91.4	93.5	94.3	91.2	84.4	81.9	77.7	76.9	73.9	....	....	....	....	Vanuatu	846

Final Consumption Expenditure as Percentage of GDP

96f r

		1970	1971	1972	1973	1974	1975	1976	1977	1978	1979	1980	1981	1982	1983	1984
																Percentages
Europe	170	**72.6**	**69.8**	**68.5**	**68.1**	**69.4**	**71.1**	**69.5**	**71.1**	**68.3**	**70.1**	**72.3**	**77.3**	**69.6**	**70.1**	**69.4**
Armenia	911	....	....	....	....	....	....	....	....	....	....	....	....	....	....	....
Belarus	913	....	....	....	....	....	....	....	....	....	....	....	....	....	....	....
Bulgaria	918	....	....	....	....	....	....	....	....	....	....	....	....	....	....	....
Cyprus	423	85.2	84.1	83.7	83.3	93.6	98.7	92.0	89.7	87.4	81.0	80.5	80.1	80.9	82.5	77.8
Czech Republic	935	....	....	....	....	....	....	....	....	....	....	....	....	....	....	....
Czechoslovakia	934	70.7	71.8	72.1	73.1	72.5	72.1	73.6	76.5	76.2	75.2	60.3	77.6	76.9	77.7	77.0
Estonia	939	....	....	....	....	....	....	....	....	....	....	....	....	....	....	....
Hungary	944	68.7	68.6	67.0	65.8	68.7	69.7	68.2	67.3	67.9	69.3	71.5	71.4	70.7	71.6	71.1
Kazakhstan	916	....	....	....	....	....	....	....	....	....	....	....	....	....	....	....
Kyrgyz Republic	917	....	....	....	....	....	....	....	....	....	....	....	....	....	....	....
Macedonia, FYR	962	....	....	....	....	....	....	....	....	....	....	....	....	....	....	....
Malta	181	97.3	96.6	98.0	97.6	101.7	90.0	84.2	88.4	83.8	79.7	80.8	81.3	84.6	85.0	86.3
Moldova	921	....	....	....	....	....	....	....	....	....	....	....	....	....	....	....
Poland	964	73.2	69.5	68.2	68.3	68.8	70.9	69.4	71.7	71.5	73.7	76.1	83.6	70.9	73.6	72.6
Romania	968	....	....	....	....	....	....	....	....	....	....	63.0	66.0	64.4	60.3	60.5
Russia	922	....	....	....	....	....	....	....	....	....	....	....	....	....	....	....
Slovak Republic	936	....	....	....	....	....	....	....	....	....	....	....	....	....	....	....
Slovenia	961	....	....	....	....	....	....	....	....	....	....	....	....	....	....	....
Turkey	186	....	....	....	....	....	....	....	....	....	....	....	....	....	....	....
Ukraine	926	....	....	....	....	....	....	....	....	....	....	....	....	....	....	....
Middle East	405	**76.8**	**73.0**	**70.3**	**60.8**	**57.2**	**62.1**	**60.6**	**62.8**	**68.6**	**65.3**	**64.4**	**70.7**	**73.5**	**75.9**	**77.0**
Egypt	469	93.1	91.8	92.0	91.7	94.6	92.0	86.6	80.6	83.0	85.6	87.7	81.6	80.4	80.9	80.9
Iran, I.R. of	429	82.1	81.1	76.2	66.1	58.9	64.0	61.2	64.4	72.4	71.2	74.0	79.0	74.5	74.2	75.1
Iraq	433	68.5	65.2	....	....	....	75.1	74.7	81.0	58.3	40.5	38.0	68.2	82.2	93.0	85.8
Israel	436	96.0	90.7	86.5	98.6	97.8	102.6	103.3	96.6	99.4	97.0	92.8	96.3	95.8	94.3	92.7
Jordan	439	99.9	98.2	97.6	99.2	99.0	98.1	94.0	91.2	92.1	106.3	104.3	107.2	113.8	112.2	110.2
Kuwait	443	52.1	42.9	42.8	40.8	22.1	32.8	38.0	48.1	49.1	36.4	41.1	51.5	73.0	65.4	63.5
Libya	672	50.8	48.4	50.2	52.0	46.1	59.2	51.4	50.0	59.0	49.7	48.1	76.8	67.9	66.9	74.1
Oman	449	32.2	37.9	54.5	61.2	43.4	47.5	47.8	54.4	61.5	53.7	52.6	50.1	57.7	61.4	63.1
Qatar	453	....	....	....	....	....	....	....	....	....	....	35.3	43.0	47.5	59.2	59.8
Saudi Arabia	456	53.3	39.6	32.6	19.8	24.3	32.1	36.8	45.1	56.3	46.6	37.8	48.6	67.0	74.9	79.8
Syrian Arab Rep.	463	90.2	90.5	88.0	85.5	90.1	87.1	82.8	86.5	88.5	90.2	89.2	93.8	87.4	88.8	85.7
United Arab Emirates	466	....	....	27.3	24.6	15.8	24.1	24.1	30.0	34.2	31.0	28.2	38.3	43.4	45.2	44.4
Yemen Arab Rep.	473	107.3	107.3	110.6	107.9	110.3	113.1	128.3	108.2	122.7	124.7	125.5	115.8	117.6	119.2	114.0
Yemen Republic	474	....	....	....	....	....	....	....	....	....	....	....	....	....	....	....
Western Hemisphere	205	**78.4**	**79.4**	**78.8**	**76.0**	**75.1**	**76.7**	**77.6**	**77.2**	**77.6**	**77.5**	**76.8**	**77.4**	**78.2**	**78.4**	**78.7**
Antigua and Barbuda	311	....	....	....	....	....	....	....	84.3	77.2	69.4	84.6	80.4	99.9	94.7	86.7
Argentina	213	77.8	76.9	76.2	80.0	79.6	74.1	68.5	69.7	72.2	77.2	76.2	77.8	75.7	75.8	77.2
Bahamas, The	313	....	....	....	72.6	78.1	73.3	73.8	66.0	63.2	58.9	57.8	56.7	62.1	68.8	69.2
Barbados	316	....	....	95.6	96.4	90.6	85.9	91.3	102.7	98.8	87.1	77.4	81.7	80.0	78.9	79.0
Belize	339	....	....	....	83.0	75.0	73.8	86.8	86.7	82.6	84.5	101.9	108.8	116.1	108.4	95.5
Bolivia	218	83.1	85.6	82.9	80.2	77.1	81.2	81.1	82.0	82.7	82.4	79.9	80.0	77.5	77.7	84.4
Brazil	223	75.7	76.7	75.0	69.8	71.7	73.8	79.0	78.5	78.4	80.6	78.5	77.7	81.0	83.2	82.3
Chile	228	82.9	86.5	91.3	93.9	78.2	88.9	82.9	87.4	85.5	85.0	83.2	87.6	90.6	87.5	87.4
Colombia	233	81.0	84.6	81.4	79.5	79.6	81.2	79.3	77.6	78.9	80.1	80.3	82.9	83.8	82.9	81.6
Costa Rica	238	86.2	86.0	84.3	82.1	88.2	86.8	82.3	81.4	84.4	85.0	83.8	75.9	72.4	76.6	76.9
Dominican Republic	243	88.2	89.2	81.9	80.1	82.9	75.5	81.9	82.4	83.0	81.0	84.6	80.6	84.9	86.4	86.4
Ecuador	248	86.4	86.3	83.6	77.3	72.4	79.7	77.6	76.5	77.2	74.1	74.1	75.8	77.1	78.4	76.3
El Salvador	253	86.5	86.4	84.9	84.7	85.6	84.5	81.7	75.9	85.4	82.1	85.8	92.7	92.5	93.4	94.8
Grenada	328	....	....	....	86.7	89.2	94.1	91.1	94.0	103.4	102.1	100.4	92.1	101.2	94.8	99.1
Guatemala	258	86.4	87.0	87.5	85.6	84.7	85.7	84.6	81.8	84.2	85.8	86.9	89.5	89.8	90.5	90.6
Guyana	336	77.9	77.4	80.3	90.5	73.9	68.7	86.7	89.7	80.6	87.3	95.9	106.8	88.3	93.3	103.5
Haiti	263	104.7	104.3	102.8	96.3	92.1	92.4	93.3	93.8	92.7	93.7	98.8	106.4	97.7	96.5	90.0
Honduras	268	85.7	84.9	84.1	82.7	86.2	90.4	85.8	81.8	77.8	78.3	83.0	85.0	87.3	89.2	88.9
Jamaica	343	72.6	75.0	81.0	78.1	85.9	84.6	90.8	84.9	83.9	82.3	86.2	90.0	90.7	89.8	83.6
Mexico	273	79.2	80.8	80.4	79.7	79.0	79.0	79.1	77.1	77.0	75.3	75.1	75.0	72.3	69.7	72.5
Nicaragua	278	84.1	84.8	81.3	85.8	82.3	88.0	80.3	79.1	83.6	92.1	102.5	96.1	91.5	88.3	90.9
Panama	283	75.9	73.7	73.4	70.6	76.1	76.3	75.3	79.7	77.7	80.2	71.1	69.7	64.6	73.9	81.5
Paraguay	288	86.5	88.0	85.0	80.3	80.7	80.4	78.7	78.3	76.5	76.9	77.5	78.0	82.0	85.6	83.3
Peru	293	82.7	84.3	84.3	85.0	86.0	90.1	87.8	88.6	82.2	66.8	68.2	69.5	69.5	75.5	77.4
St. Kitts and Nevis	361	....	....	....	119.0	105.4	93.4	85.5	78.3	84.2	89.5	92.0	97.3	96.8	105.4	97.8
St. Lucia	362	....	....	....	....	....	97.2	88.8	67.2	73.9	76.7	65.7	69.9	74.3	67.0	68.2
St. Vincent & Grenadines	364	....	....	....	....	....	103.7	100.4	109.3	96.4	110.7	111.7	99.3	101.8	99.5	86.0
Suriname	366	76.7	74.6	72.8	73.8	69.1	68.8	70.7	69.5	69.9	77.5	78.9	82.8	87.7	99.1	93.6
Trinidad and Tobago	369	73.0	71.2	75.3	68.3	53.7	54.9	59.7	60.7	65.4	65.2	57.9	62.7	78.9	82.8	77.4
Uruguay	298	89.9	88.7	87.8	86.2	91.1	90.1	86.0	87.7	86.5	87.2	88.3	88.6	88.7	83.7	82.7
Venezuela, Rep. Bol.	299	65.9	64.1	65.5	61.1	51.3	61.2	64.2	66.2	70.3	66.5	67.1	71.2	77.2	77.4	73.8
Memorandum Items																
Oil Exporting Countries	999	70.7	68.0	65.6	59.9	53.5	60.2	59.4	62.2	66.7	62.3	61.2	66.4	71.0	71.6	72.3
Non-Oil Developing Countries	201	95.3	95.4	94.3	61.4	62.5	63.2	62.5	62.1	76.6	77.0	77.2	77.8	77.4	76.6	76.3

Final Consumption Expenditure as Percentage of GDP

96f r

1985	1986	1987	1988	1989	1990	1991	1992	1993	1994	1995	1996	1997	1998	1999		
Percentages																
68.7	68.6	68.2	69.0	69.4	72.6	76.9	79.6	80.8	81.2	79.8	79.5	80.0	80.6	....	**Europe**	170
....	....	....	....	....	66.9	75.9	112.2	110.6	105.8	117.5	111.7	114.7	111.6	....	Armenia	911
....	....	....	....	....	71.2	67.3	66.5	75.8	80.3	79.7	79.4	77.3	79.8	78.5	Belarus	913
68.6	70.3	69.4	68.2	70.7	74.0	73.1	85.9	92.3	91.2	85.9	88.5	84.1	88.0	90.7	Bulgaria	918
77.9	75.6	76.1	77.4	75.5	77.3	84.0	81.5	75.9	74.5	76.1	79.1	80.7	83.9	81.1	Cyprus	423
....	....	68.7	68.4	69.4	56.1	63.3	72.1	71.6	75.1	70.7	71.4	73.2	71.7	73.1	Czech Republic	935
62.8	63.6	64.6	64.9	65.7	67.4	65.9	....	....	....	....	....	....	....	....	Czechoslovakia	934
....	....	....	....	....	....	67.8	71.0	79.5	84.6	84.3	84.8	81.2	82.2	....	Estonia	939
72.9	74.5	73.8	72.0	70.1	72.0	80.5	84.2	88.2	84.3	78.1	74.6	....	....	....	Hungary	944
....	....	....	....	....	76.8	91.6	82.6	88.3	82.6	81.9	83.9	86.4	86.7	....	Kazakhstan	916
....	....	....	....	....	....	85.9	92.1	96.0	97.3	94.5	104.8	86.2	106.1	....	Kyrgyz Republic	917
....	....	....	....	....	86.3	95.9	95.8	100.8	94.7	89.0	90.2	90.9	91.4	....	Macedonia, FYR	962
87.7	84.6	81.8	81.3	81.3	80.3	79.5	79.5	79.8	79.5	81.7	85.3	82.9	81.9	81.4	Malta	181
....	....	....	....	....	....	72.6	57.5	55.9	75.4	82.9	95.8	95.8	....	....	Moldova	921
70.8	70.2	68.9	65.3	57.3	67.2	82.0	83.3	83.5	80.2	77.9	79.7	79.8	79.0	....	Poland	964
60.2	59.3	61.2	62.1	70.4	79.2	75.9	77.0	76.0	77.3	81.3	83.0	85.3	86.7	84.3	Romania	968
....	....	....	....	....	....	....	48.3	62.2	69.1	71.1	72.0	76.3	78.4	70.6	Russia	922
....	....	....	....	....	....	67.6	75.7	78.2	71.7	69.8	72.6	71.6	71.8	....	Slovak Republic	936
....	....	....	....	....	....	....	....	79.6	76.9	78.3	77.5	76.9	76.3	....	Slovenia	961
....	....	76.4	73.0	77.4	79.6	80.3	79.8	78.9	81.6	81.1	78.8	80.3	81.0	....	Turkey	186
....	....	....	....	....	....	....	....	63.6	64.0	67.8	76.4	79.9	83.7	....	Ukraine	926
78.6	81.3	81.5	84.1	80.4	78.1	86.0	78.5	77.8	76.4	76.6	76.5	77.2	80.4	78.4	**Middle East**	405
79.4	78.9	83.9	84.7	83.1	83.0	83.9	83.0	83.3	84.9	83.1	85.5	85.4	84.2	84.2	Egypt	469
76.5	78.9	74.9	81.2	78.2	76.8	73.9	72.4	69.7	68.7	73.8	73.3	75.8	78.1	77.0	Iran, I.R. of	429
80.9	90.6	83.1	85.3	81.9	76.8	83.5	86.9	86.2	....	....	....	....	....	....	Iraq	433
94.3	93.8	98.3	94.7	91.6	91.2	90.1	88.8	90.9	91.2	89.6	89.7	89.4	89.3	89.7	Israel	436
115.2	105.6	102.2	98.5	95.0	99.0	97.4	98.5	94.0	89.7	87.8	94.6	96.4	97.6	....	Jordan	439
70.2	79.7	67.0	79.7	76.7	97.2	294.3	93.9	79.3	75.3	74.2	71.4	73.0	87.1	77.4	Kuwait	443
66.3	71.0	87.8	88.1	85.4	72.5	83.7	82.2	90.0	86.6	81.4	79.8	82.4	....	....	Libya	672
62.7	75.4	66.2	76.2	71.1	68.0	76.7	74.5	54.6	76.0	76.5	72.2	70.8	83.0	72.2	Oman	449
60.3	75.1	76.4	74.7	71.0	60.7	67.0	63.9	68.8	64.4	63.9	60.3	60.7	....	....	Qatar	453
87.0	90.9	88.3	83.1	77.7	70.4	75.5	72.1	72.5	67.9	66.1	65.5	65.2	73.9	68.7	Saudi Arabia	456
89.4	88.5	95.1	95.3	83.8	83.1	89.7	88.2	87.1	82.4	79.7	84.6	82.1	82.0	....	Syrian Arab Rep.	463
48.2	62.0	59.3	65.8	61.9	54.1	58.2	62.1	62.2	63.1	64.4	61.4	63.1	69.9	....	United Arab Emirates	466
112.9	108.9	109.9	....	....	....	....	....	....	....	....	....	....	....	....	Yemen Arab Rep.	473
....	....	....	....	....	91.0	106.2	100.0	109.1	98.7	99.7	80.0	81.5	85.4	87.1	Yemen Republic	474
76.2	78.8	76.3	75.6	73.7	78.1	79.7	80.7	80.8	80.1	79.3	78.8	79.1	81.1	....	**Western Hemisphere**	205
89.8	86.0	78.0	71.7	68.5	65.6	63.0	62.4	62.8	66.1	71.8	74.9	68.6	....	....	Antigua and Barbuda	311
76.9	80.7	80.1	78.0	78.1	80.2	83.7	84.9	83.3	83.1	82.4	82.5	82.8	82.6	82.6	Argentina	213
64.2	63.5	63.6	58.0	83.7	80.1	89.1	83.1	83.9	84.0	83.4	....	86.2	....	....	Bahamas, The	313
76.7	81.7	83.4	82.0	80.9	83.8	85.6	82.4	81.5	78.6	80.2	81.0	....	86.2	....	Barbados	316
104.2	95.4	80.2	80.7	80.7	74.8	79.7	80.1	81.2	82.4	81.1	79.3	83.5	84.8	82.1	Belize	339
70.9	91.1	94.4	90.4	89.1	88.6	89.9	92.3	92.7	91.2	89.4	88.5	88.6	89.2	90.8	Bolivia	218
75.3	78.2	74.2	72.0	66.5	78.6	79.5	78.6	77.7	77.5	79.5	81.0	80.9	81.4	....	Brazil	223
80.4	78.1	74.9	70.3	70.2	71.6	73.0	74.8	75.9	74.6	72.4	75.3	75.5	77.6	77.0	Chile	228
79.7	75.2	76.0	75.6	75.8	75.7	76.6	80.9	81.1	80.2	80.5	83.4	84.9	....	....	Colombia	233
75.9	73.9	77.0	77.3	77.3	79.6	75.8	76.0	77.1	76.8	76.7	75.7	74.3	72.3	67.7	Costa Rica	238
87.1	83.8	83.1	77.2	79.7	81.3	83.0	86.6	80.7	81.3	81.6	83.5	82.5	83.0	80.7	Dominican Republic	243
75.9	79.0	83.6	80.6	81.1	77.1	76.2	75.0	78.3	78.0	80.3	75.6	78.8	82.0	....	Ecuador	248
96.7	91.1	94.7	93.7	95.1	98.8	97.9	97.8	96.2	95.6	96.1	97.7	95.8	95.6	96.0	El Salvador	253
96.2	76.0	88.8	85.2	87.4	83.7	84.9	89.0	88.0	75.2	79.8	85.5	84.1	71.5	....	Grenada	328
90.1	88.2	92.5	92.1	91.7	90.4	89.7	91.5	90.8	91.6	91.1	92.1	92.0	92.3	91.7	Guatemala	258
90.2	84.5	79.4	83.2	74.4	74.5	67.0	64.0	63.7	63.6	62.3	62.2	65.1	....	....	Guyana	336
94.2	93.6	84.8	82.1	76.6	88.3	82.5	79.2	95.2	112.3	108.2	104.0	103.1	....	....	Haiti	263
87.4	87.9	85.5	81.6	84.2	79.8	78.4	78.1	75.5	72.4	72.8	74.7	74.3	75.3	78.9	Honduras	268
85.5	78.4	77.4	78.9	80.9	76.2	74.6	73.2	83.1	82.2	86.1	86.2	88.3	84.3	....	Jamaica	343
74.1	78.0	74.7	76.0	77.1	78.0	79.6	81.7	82.9	83.1	77.5	74.6	74.0	77.6	78.1	Mexico	273
84.0	91.3	86.2	113.5	105.0	99.1	109.6	113.8	107.8	104.3	102.3	103.2	108.0	109.0	112.2	Nicaragua	278
75.7	73.1	72.8	75.9	85.2	75.0	76.9	72.5	70.8	68.5	66.8	68.3	70.5	74.2	....	Panama	283
82.2	80.5	83.5	78.1	72.5	83.4	83.2	87.6	88.0	95.2	92.5	92.8	92.7	94.0	....	Paraguay	288
75.3	81.1	80.5	80.5	79.3	83.0	85.3	85.6	84.4	78.4	80.6	81.2	79.5	80.5	80.2	Peru	293
92.2	89.4	87.9	70.1	70.8	77.7	77.3	70.7	79.3	86.0	83.5	103.8	....	....	....	St. Kitts and Nevis	361
....	....	....	....	....	....	....	....	....	....	....	....	....	....	....	St. Lucia	362
77.5	76.7	83.5	76.6	88.5	81.2	97.5	84.7	92.1	95.7	84.2	83.4	92.9	92.9	....	St. Vincent & Grenadines	364
88.7	78.2	68.6	78.4	69.9	79.2	84.7	76.9	40.7	....	....	....	....	....	....	Suriname	366
77.1	85.5	79.3	82.1	75.5	69.9	76.2	77.0	80.3	66.4	69.6	72.6	76.3	78.9	....	Trinidad and Tobago	369
83.0	82.9	83.3	82.2	82.4	83.0	83.3	85.8	85.9	81.0	87.2	87.6	87.5	84.7	....	Uruguay	298
74.8	79.6	76.7	78.8	75.5	70.5	76.2	78.8	81.5	77.3	76.6	68.3	72.9	80.4	....	Venezuela, Rep. Bol.	299

Memorandum Items

1985	1986	1987	1988	1989	1990	1991	1992	1993	1994	1995	1996	1997	1998	1999		
73.3	77.5	73.6	74.7	70.1	68.7	73.9	69.2	70.5	70.6	73.8	72.0	71.7	73.1	84.3	Oil Exporting Countries	999
75.3	75.7	74.5	73.1	72.5	73.6	74.4	74.8	74.9	74.1	73.6	74.1	74.0	74.2	....	Non-Oil Developing Countries	201

Commodity Prices

z

		1970	1971	1972	1973	1974	1975	1976	1977	1978	1979	1980	1981	1982	1983	1984
										Wholesale Prices (lines 76) and Unit Values (lines 74)						
Aluminum (US cents/pound)																
All Origins (London) *	156	27.86	28.48	26.77	27.18	34.69	39.39	40.37	51.88	60.10	72.70	80.51	57.28	44.98	65.25	56.77
Bananas (US cents/pound)																
Latin America (US Ports) *	248	7.53	6.37	7.34	7.47	8.34	11.15	11.73	12.38	13.00	14.78	17.01	18.21	17.00	19.47	16.76
Beef (US cents/pound)																
Australia-NZ (US Ports) *	193	59.16	61.05	67.14	91.19	71.77	60.20	71.71	68.33	96.99	130.82	125.19	112.12	108.39	110.67	103.11
United States (New York)	111	46.36	47.68	55.82	71.42	59.67	50.49	58.76	57.10	79.98	102.87	97.32	96.91	110.62	107.26	109.02
Argentina (frozen)	213	33.14	40.16	51.84	71.16	76.26	38.87	41.09	52.61	52.54	83.65	97.41	84.12	64.07	66.59	90.89
Butter (US cents/pound)																
New Zealand (London)	196	33.47	47.16	54.19	44.24	53.06	72.10	76.51	84.22	109.48	130.61	151.39	140.88	129.18	111.41	93.93
New Zealand	196	28.58	38.24	50.62	44.15	44.09	50.46	49.32	57.42	68.08	69.34	73.80	96.88	97.16	91.25	76.27
Coal (US $/metric ton)																
Australia	193	10.96	12.03	13.56	16.19	24.06	38.43	45.33	42.94	45.37	43.84	45.31	52.16	56.69	49.12	45.19
Cocoa Beans (US cents/pound)																
Brazil	223	29.42	23.50	26.24	48.51	73.35	56.59	77.02	183.53	153.53	140.73	107.06	87.50	68.29	83.10	105.32
New York and London *	652	30.57	24.43	29.15	51.29	70.77	56.51	92.79	171.96	154.43	149.36	118.09	94.19	79.01	96.10	108.67
Coconut Oil (US cents/pound)																
Philippines (New York) *	566	17.19	15.99	11.23	23.27	45.26	17.85	18.95	26.23	30.99	44.66	30.51	25.86	21.19	33.10	52.39
Philippines	566	12.80	11.81	8.21	15.94	39.91	17.00	15.71	24.19	27.01	41.95	28.06	23.27	19.75	24.15	44.83
Coffee (US cents/pound)																
Other Milds (New York) *	386	52.01	44.99	50.33	62.31	65.84	65.41	142.75	234.67	162.82	173.53	154.20	128.09	139.72	131.69	144.17
Brazil (New York) *	223	55.80	44.71	52.57	69.19	73.34	82.58	149.48	267.14	165.29	178.47	208.79	186.38	143.68	142.75	149.65
Brazil	223	44.26	33.88	42.73	52.68	56.83	49.57	122.37	203.51	142.11	154.72	143.75	83.34	94.88	101.16	112.72
Uganda (New York) *	799	41.44	42.26	45.18	49.89	58.68	61.05	127.62	223.75	147.48	165.47	147.15	102.91	111.04	124.12	138.18
Copper (US cents/pound)																
United Kingdom (London) *	112	64.04	49.02	48.58	80.58	93.23	56.10	63.64	59.41	61.92	89.49	99.12	79.05	67.21	72.23	62.46
Copra (US $/metric ton)																
Philippines (Europ. Ports) *	566	223.08	189.58	142.33	343.92	668.67	256.00	275.08	402.33	470.58	672.67	453.00	378.92	314.00	496.00	710.08
Cotton (US cents/pound)																
United States (10 markets) *	111	18.98	20.94	25.92	42.42	43.79	34.10	51.43	46.58	43.60	46.98	61.50	54.49	45.42	51.77	51.57
Liverpool Index *	111	28.93	33.88	36.26	62.09	65.13	53.09	77.24	71.33	71.95	77.14	93.73	83.97	72.51	84.10	80.94
Egypt (Liverpool) (1990=100)	469	62.60	61.72	65.09	98.36	153.80	129.41	136.30	149.20	138.60	153.21	153.49	151.99	124.87	139.96	163.82
Egypt (Long Staple)	469	61.06	61.54	64.93	77.79	150.42	138.39	118.46	155.53	119.42	123.40	123.22	121.73	109.69	110.62	142.85
Egypt (Long Medium)	469	49.83	49.22	48.10	62.34	127.61	109.72	84.92	125.75	101.98	109.27	109.17	108.07	80.66	86.85	112.31
Fish Meal (US $/metric ton)																
All Origins (Hamburg) *	293	196.83	168.08	238.67	542.00	372.00	245.33	376.17	453.92	409.92	394.92	504.42	467.50	353.75	452.50	373.17
Iceland	176	185.86	192.75	166.41	415.35	403.38	222.96	277.64	420.08	415.93	375.80	467.76	470.40	313.51	536.62	330.30
Gasoline (US cents/gallon)																
US Gulf Coast *	111	. . . .	. . . .	. . . .	. . . .	. . . .	. . . .	. . . .	. . . .	. . . .	84.40	91.93	100.47	91.95	83.48	76.77
Gold (US $/fine ounce)																
United Kingdom (London) *	112	35.94	40.80	58.16	97.33	159.25	161.03	124.82	147.72	193.24	306.67	607.86	459.75	375.80	422.47	360.36
Groundnuts (US $/metric ton)																
Nigeria (London) *	694	228.18	250.91	253.95	391.31	739.06	432.96	422.99	546.86	630.93	562.74 Ⅰ	1236.58	1,257.42	827.50	965.33	836.58
Groundnut Meal (US $/metric ton)																
All Origins (Europe) *	694	115.34	110.56	137.21	299.29	196.33	157.76	198.02	245.23	230.78	237.72	271.41	269.26	208.33	229.00	187.50
Groundnut Oil (US $/metric ton)																
Any Origin (Europe) *	694	378.25	445.50	425.67	544.00	1,058.25	778.17	690.58	845.75	1,079.17	888.67	858.75	1,042.75	585.17	710.92	1,016.67
Hides (US cents/pound)																
United States (Chicago) *	111	12.90	14.47	29.60	34.30	23.60	23.28	33.57	36.95	47.54	73.13	45.92	41.72	38.56	45.13	58.87
Iron Ore (US cents/pound)																
Brazil (North Sea Ports) *	223	15.22	13.40	12.79	17.13	19.00	22.81	22.72	21.59	19.39	23.44	28.09	28.09	32.50	29.00	26.15
Jute (US $/metric ton)																
Bangladesh (Chitta.-Chalna)	513	269.51	281.40	293.70	284.03	347.67	370.75	295.42	319.00	397.83	384.92	313.50	278.25	283.08	298.25	530.75
Lamb (US cents/pound)																
New Zealand (London) *	196	33.80	36.54	48.66	63.52	65.01	67.79	71.86	78.08	100.65	109.02	131.17	124.98	108.65	87.88	87.70
New Zealand	196	24.33	24.21	27.30	43.51	46.28	39.80	40.90	48.16	55.62	63.94	72.28	78.46	72.04	62.54	57.29
Lead (US cents/pound)																
United Kingdom (London) *	112	13.80	11.50	13.70	19.38	26.80	18.92	20.24	28.02	29.95	54.56	41.07	32.93	24.76	19.29	20.05
United States (New York)	111	16.53	14.63	16.19	17.25	23.46	22.69	24.18	32.34	35.52	55.77	45.81	39.44	28.11	23.73	28.43
Linseed Oil (US $/metric ton)																
Any Origin *	001	216.33	187.08	197.00	544.50	1,094.58	700.75	545.58	461.50	434.17	644.00	697.08	659.92	519.08	484.50	571.50
Maize (US $/bushel)																
United States (Chicago)	111	1.27	1.30	1.21	2.13	2.99	2.68	2.49	2.05	2.15	2.44	2.78	2.93	2.33	2.99	3.02
United States (U.S. Gulf Ports) *	111	1.48	1.48	1.42	2.48	3.36	3.04	2.85	2.42	2.56	2.94	3.19	3.32	2.75	3.45	3.45
Thailand	578	1.66	1.49	1.38	2.64	3.39	3.38	2.92	2.70	2.52	3.49	4.11	3.78	3.25	3.52	3.47
Manganese (US $/long ton)																
India (US Ports)	534	55.33	63.83	64.50	76.17	114.17	140.00	147.33	150.33	144.38	140.00	155.25	167.80	164.12	151.82	143.21
Newsprint (US $/short ton)																
United States (New York)	111	111.21	116.01	120.60	125.94	155.71	189.70	203.95	219.95	233.12	255.11	287.11	316.63	325.67	312.15	333.06
Finland	172	114.89	120.10	125.47	146.55	235.47	315.57	295.04	322.14	332.27	368.04	410.92	405.48	390.37	329.32	317.02
Nickel (US cents/pound)																
United Kingdom(N.Europ.ports)*	156	127.63	133.00	139.67	153.00	173.92	207.33	225.25	236.00	209.17	271.00	295.68	270.03	219.43	211.96	215.56
Palm Kernels (US $/metric ton)																
Malaysia (Rotterdam)	548	367.33	335.50	219.08	489.75	1,045.83	408.58	433.25	620.42	763.92	1,049.25	725.50	588.25	458.17	709.00	1,037.17
Palm Oil (US $/metric ton)																
Malaysia (N.W.Europe) *	548	259.50	262.08	217.42	375.92	691.33	420.25	397.33	530.08	600.33	653.83	583.08	570.67	445.08	501.42	728.83
Malaysia	548	214.82	217.35	187.08	239.32	500.45	474.94	359.85	525.18	533.35	594.21	529.53	490.91	416.81	437.54	650.55
Pepper,Black (US cents/pound)																
Malaysia (New York)	548	57.30	50.06	46.24	57.97	84.86	90.95	89.08	113.62	106.43	96.12	90.43	71.84	70.43	Ⅰ81.40	136.52

*See the Commodity Prices note in the monthly *IFS*.

Country of Origin and,for Wholesale Prices,Pricing Point in Parentheses

1985	1986	1987	1988	1989	1990	1991	1992	1993	1994	1995	1996	1997	1998	1999		
															Aluminum (US cents/pound)	
47.21	52.15	70.99	115.51	88.48	74.37	59.15	56.98	51.71	66.93	81.86	68.34	72.54	61.58	61.69	All Origins (London) *	156
															Bananas (US cents/pound)	
17.15	17.32	17.11	21.73	24.80	24.60	25.46	21.69	20.10	19.91	20.02	21.41	22.25	21.61	19.39	Latin America (US Ports) *	248
															Beef (US cents/pound)	
97.67	94.98	108.18	114.17	116.46	116.27	120.83	111.34	118.74	105.82	86.50	80.97	84.17	78.30	83.14	Australia-NZ (US Ports) *	193
100.68	86.01	91.34	91.52	97.79	105.80	101.49	101.14	104.87	97.34	94.27	95.17	96.49	....	....	United States (New York)	111
86.61	111.04	162.19	154.87	148.59	130.90	194.67	253.91	303.09	229.52	210.56	168.05	180.72	235.34	207.16	Argentina (frozen)	213
															Butter (US cents/pound)	
101.45	115.14	113.49	140.56	148.26	147.93	140.85	150.51	141.00	140.54	164.54	....	147.75	144.64	132.51	New Zealand (London)	196
60.22	56.89	63.64	69.52	90.97	87.34	78.39	91.57	81.65	84.47	99.25	103.17	86.20	87.60	75.03	New Zealand	196
															Coal (US $/metric ton)	
39.92	39.27	34.98	36.29	41.61	42.72	43.66	41.42	39.40	37.35	40.08	43.14	41.42	37.04	....	Australia	193
															Cocoa Beans (US cents/pound)	
94.97	92.04	83.96	72.68	56.85	49.07	47.54	44.99	44.47	55.91	60.46	63.45	72.85	75.09	53.18	Brazil	223
102.27	93.82	90.62	71.84	56.34	57.52	54.10	49.87	50.41	63.31	64.98	66.01	73.43	76.02	51.49	New York and London *	652
															Coconut Oil (US cents/pound)	
26.77	13.45	20.06	25.62	23.44	15.32	19.64	26.22	20.47	27.51	30.37	34.10	29.79	29.95	33.45	Philippines (New York) *	566
24.18	12.10	16.74	23.34	22.39	14.42	16.12	24.74	18.88	25.39	27.96	32.66	28.28	27.15	32.77	Philippines	566
															Coffee (US cents/pound)	
145.56	192.74	112.29	135.10	106.96	89.15	85.03	63.66	69.94	148.53	149.41	120.25	185.02	132.40	101.67	Other Milds (New York) *	386
148.93	231.19	106.37	121.84	98.76	83.80	72.88	56.26	66.58	143.32	145.98	120.29	166.80	121.81	88.92	Brazil (New York) *	223
103.97	190.39	89.98	100.76	74.58	58.80	57.28	43.25	50.08	115.54	123.89	100.21	143.40	106.23	79.56	Brazil	223
121.24	148.32	102.34	95.11	75.69	54.99	49.83	43.63	53.50	119.82	126.83	82.84	80.70	83.93	67.65	Uganda (New York) *	799
															Copper (US cents/pound)	
64.29	62.13	80.79	117.93	129.15	120.72	106.07	103.64	86.86	104.58	133.00	104.03	103.20	75.01	71.33	United Kingdom (London) *	112
															Copra (US $/metric ton)	
386.42	197.58	310.33	395.92	348.02	229.92	295.85	381.85	295.42	416.84	438.50	488.98	433.75	411.03	462.27	Philippines (Europ. Ports) *	566
															Cotton (US cents/pound)	
44.40	39.89	48.01	43.39	48.58	54.34	53.46	41.41	42.26	55.79	71.82	59.77	53.59	51.05	40.18	United States (10 markets) *	111
59.92	47.94	74.77	63.52	75.95	82.56	76.91	57.94	58.02	79.72	98.30	80.54	79.23	65.53	53.13	Liverpool Index *	111
163.97	157.23	162.95	218.45	289.31	300.12	278.66	212.79	201.19	171.54	....	....	....	....	....	Egypt (Liverpool) (1990=100)	469
138.35	142.53	173.66	275.29	617.57	516.94	256.14	164.99	130.01	104.92	110.29	188.31	....	....	....	Egypt (Long Staple)	469
133.21	136.23	132.11	254.53	555.71	436.98	215.20	110.82	99.20	88.41	97.40	110.94	....	....	....	Egypt (Long Medium)	469
															Fish Meal (US $/metric ton)	
280.08	320.58	383.42	544.42	409.08	412.17	477.85	481.52	364.69	376.66	495.00	586.18	606.25	661.55	392.18	All Origins (Hamburg) *	293
304.59	344.64	386.27	476.67	535.48	480.71	499.53	522.16	405.15	452.21	528.38	611.03	673.15	724.26	493.31	Iceland	176
															Gasoline (US cents/gallon)	
76.93	43.62	50.53	47.53	55.76	71.13	63.50	57.46	50.86	47.90	50.92	59.65	58.53	41.30	51.84	US Gulf Coast *	111
															Gold (US $/fine ounce)	
317.18	367.68	446.52	437.15	381.28	383.51	362.18	343.42	359.73	384.22	384.16	387.82	331.10	294.20	278.78	United Kingdom (London)	112
															Groundnuts (US $/metric ton)	
675.75	993.58	758.50	935.75	817.50	1,325.50	1,237.83	799.13	1,092.15	954.80	909.92	962.00	988.42	988.75	834.74	Nigeria (London) *	694
															Groundnut Meal (US $/metric ton)	
146.25	166.00	161.92	209.42	200.42	184.75	150.08	152.58	168.08	168.33	168.58	212.75	221.00	116.17	....	All Origins (Europe) *	694
															Groundnut Oil (US $/metric ton)	
905.25	569.42	499.75	590.50	774.75	963.67	894.83	609.58	737.88	1,022.64	990.92	897.33	1,010.42	908.58	786.67	Any Origin (Europe) *	694
															Hides (US cents/pound)	
51.18	63.96	79.84	87.65	90.02	92.23	79.45	75.86	80.03	86.81	88.14	87.32	88.25	76.69	72.15	United States (Chicago) *	111
															Iron Ore (US $/metric ton)	
26.56	26.26	24.50	23.50	26.50	30.80	33.25	31.60	28.11	25.47	27.00	28.60	28.71	29.69	26.96	Brazil (North Sea Ports) *	223
															Jute (US $/metric ton)	
582.92	271.75	320.58	370.00	373.33	408.33	365.42	279.17	271.25	295.67	365.67	454.25	302.00	259.08	275.67	Bangladesh (Chitta.-Chalna)	513
															Lamb (US cents/pound)	
83.56	92.57	98.45	109.46	105.31	121.14	104.88	115.42	124.12	125.66	113.26	145.44	150.28	116.00	115.84	New Zealand (London) *	196
49.50	49.61	56.93	164.07	69.06	88.53	78.99	82.82	100.78	97.94	100.61	120.28	126.99	108.33	112.87	New Zealand	196
															Lead (US cents/pound)	
17.72	18.40	27.05	29.73	30.51	36.72	25.30	24.65	18.48	24.89	28.55	35.11	28.26	23.90	22.76	United Kingdom (London) *	112
20.67	21.38	37.82	38.50	40.39	47.58	34.82	37.05	33.25	39.14	45.21	52.31	50.41	49.37	46.76	United States (New York)	111
															Linseed Oil (US $/metric ton)	
627.08	419.17	317.50	521.50	756.67	709.25	438.88	396.34	448.50	516.74	657.50	565.83	571.24	707.71	512.54	Any Origin *	001
															Maize (US $/bushel)	
2.46	1.95	1.58	2.32	2.45	2.42	2.32	2.30	2.26	2.40	2.61	3.79	2.64	2.20	1.87	United States (Chicago)	111
2.85	2.23	1.92	2.72	2.83	2.78	2.73	2.65	2.59	2.74	3.14	4.18	2.98	2.58	2.29	United States (U.S. Gulf Ports) *	111
2.59	2.23	2.35	3.17	3.42	3.33	3.17	3.68	3.41	4.13	5.13	....	7.12	3.93	3.65	Thailand	578
															Manganese (US $/long ton)	
141.01	140.83	134.00	149.21	204.75	341.67	391.58	373.75	298.09	212.93	202.79	203.21	203.21	203.21	....	India (US Ports)	534
															Newsprint (US $/short ton)	
342.45	335.36	364.47	386.06	375.21	366.15	370.13	336.26	343.07	356.73	495.63	488.48	410.16	438.75	....	United States (New York)	111
328.07	407.71	465.84	550.46	526.07	575.21	556.29	469.86	377.58	401.99	605.05	650.84	470.85	453.66	....	Finland	172
															Nickel (US cents/pound)	
222.22	176.39	221.00	624.97	603.87	402.07	370.28	318.22	240.78	287.21	373.02	340.38	314.10	209.72	272.27	United Kingdom(N.Europ.ports)*	156
															Palm Kernels (US $/metric ton)	
551.17	288.17	426.08	538.75	472.00	333.58	416.33	581.83	437.84	627.75	677.67	727.97	651.83	686.93	695.03	Malaysia (Rotterdam)	548
															Palm Oil (US $/metric ton)	
500.92	257.00	342.50	437.17	350.42	289.83	339.00	393.69	377.73	529.15	628.58	532.03	545.83	671.30	436.31	Malaysia (N.W.Europe) *	548
493.83	269.89	318.62	416.12	348.83	287.10	329.78	382.41	382.97	482.70	612.41	502.89	504.99	....	....	Malaysia	548
															Pepper,Black (US cents/pound)	
183.10	267.57	263.23	208.74	129.33	81.30	64.34	66.70	104.90	139.41	171.86	167.71	286.88	322.29	....	Malaysia (New York)	548

*See the Commodity Prices note in the monthly *IFS*.

Commodity Prices

Wholesale Prices (lines 76) and Unit Values (lines 74)

		1970	1971	1972	1973	1974	1975	1976	1977	1978	1979	1980	1981	1982	1983	1984
Petroleum, spot (US $/barrel)																
Average Crude Price *	001	2.18	2.66	2.89	3.24	Ɪ11.60	10.96	12.23	13.28	13.39	30.21	36.68	35.27	32.45	Ɪ29.64	28.55
U.K. Brent *	112	2.23	3.21	3.61	4.25	12.93	11.50	13.14	14.31	14.26	32.11	37.89	36.68	33.42	29.78	28.74
West Texas Intermediate *	111	....	....	....	....	....	....	....	....	....	....	....	....	....	30.41	29.39
Alaskan North Slope *	111	2.30	2.30	2.30	2.30	Ɪ9.76	9.85	10.71	11.64	11.67	25.74	32.69	31.38	Ɪ28.98	26.55	Ɪ28.54
Phosphate Rock (US $/metric ton)																
Morocco (Casablanca) *	686	11.00	11.25	11.50	13.75	52.77	68.00	35.83	30.67	29.00	33.00	46.71	49.50	42.38	36.92	38.25
Potash (US $/metric ton)																
Canada (Vancouver) *	156	31.50	32.50	33.50	42.50	60.50	81.33	55.50	51.17	56.38	76.48	115.71	112.46	80.75	75.46	83.71
Plywood (US cents/sheet)																
Philippines (Tokyo)	566	103.06	81.68	96.89	189.78	152.74	121.83	147.71	161.53	189.58	262.49	273.84	245.46	234.35	229.87	227.03
Pulp (US $/metric ton)																
Sweden (North Sea Ports)	144	177.40	188.40	186.00	231.60	333.70	441.40	418.20	391.10	344.00	439.20	536.50	542.90	487.90	427.20	509.30
Rice (US $/metric ton)																
United States (New Orleans)	111	174.71	177.10	200.28	367.32	515.26	388.45	285.67	309.87	370.38	353.68	459.36	524.64	340.21	351.12	352.32
Thailand (Bangkok) *	578	143.00	130.33	149.92	296.58	541.50	363.17	254.08	272.42	368.50	334.33	433.67	482.83	293.38	276.83	252.25
Thailand	578	113.77	88.74	101.00	205.32	466.24	301.85	213.70	222.65	319.06	273.02	340.29	398.55	258.63	252.25	237.66
Myanmar	518	83.33	75.09	75.28	117.32	370.31	257.50	168.04	172.11	201.54	223.85	274.95	311.36	211.00	185.41	186.11
Rubber (US cents/pound)																
All Origins (New York)	111	18.66	15.96	16.04	31.10	35.19	26.45	34.99	36.79	44.18	56.82	65.04	50.45	40.08	49.72	43.89
Malaysia (Singapore) *	548	18.47	15.08	15.05	30.75	34.09	25.44	35.10	36.95	44.71	57.25	64.62	50.93	38.90	48.27	43.44
Thailand	578	17.66	13.49	12.78	25.76	30.92	23.28	31.54	34.10	40.50	52.67	60.13	47.73	34.37	41.88	42.16
Shrimp (US $/pound)																
United States (U.S. Gulf Ports)	111	1.24	1.50	1.88	2.27	2.11	2.67	3.79	3.59	3.64	5.43	4.60	4.41	6.21	6.00	5.24
Silver (US cents/troy ounce)																
United States (New York)	111	177.1	154.6	168.4	255.8	470.8	441.9	435.3	462.3	540.1	1,109.0	2,057.7	1,051.8	794.9	1,144.1	814.1
Sisal (US $/metric ton)																
East African (Europe)	639	152.00	170.00	240.00	526.75	1,055.50	580.33	467.50	511.25	474.83	712.92	764.83	645.25	593.17	570.83	583.75
Sorghum (US $/metric ton)																
United States (US Gulf Ports)	111	51.80	55.70	56.20	93.39	120.94	111.87	105.22	89.24	93.84	108.11	128.86	126.36	108.35	128.73	118.19
Soybeans (US $/metric ton)																
United States (Rotterdam) *	111	116.92	125.58	140.00	290.33	276.92	221.67	231.17	280.17	268.33	297.75	296.25	288.42	244.50	281.67	282.08
Soybean Meal (US $/metric ton)																
United States (Rotterdam) *	111	102.58	101.83	129.17	302.58	184.33	155.00	198.33	229.83	213.33	243.00	258.58	252.67	218.00	237.83	197.17
Soybean Oil (US $/metric ton)																
All Origins (Dutch Ports) *	111	286.33	303.75	240.58	436.00	832.17	563.33	438.33	580.25	607.00	662.17	598.25	506.92	447.33	526.92	725.17
Sugar (US cents/pound)																
EU Import Price *	112	5.09	5.16	6.79	6.66	10.65	15.44	13.39	14.01	15.91	19.29	22.09	18.93	18.12	17.57	16.03
Caribbean (New York) *	001	3.76	4.53	7.48	9.62	29.94	20.56	11.56	8.11	7.82	9.66	28.67	16.89	8.41	8.47	5.20
U.S. Import Price *	111	7.50	7.93	8.53	10.29	29.48	22.47	13.31	11.00	13.97	15.53	30.03	19.73	19.92	22.04	21.74
Brazil	223	5.10	5.50	7.22	8.96	25.38	29.18	11.52	8.24	7.70	8.79	21.79	16.92	9.42	9.46	9.17
Philippines	566	6.62	7.25	7.78	9.24	21.03	27.03	13.25	8.71	8.18	7.61	16.22	20.65	15.09	13.44	12.70
Superphosphate (US $/metric ton)																
United States (US Gulf Ports)	111	42.50	43.00	67.50	100.00	308.00	202.50	91.50	97.92	98.04	143.33	180.33	161.00	138.38	134.67	131.25
Tea (US cents/pound)																
Average Auction (London) *	112	49.55	47.80	47.81	47.97	63.29	62.68	69.70	122.02	99.29	97.87	101.06	91.59	87.62	105.44	156.79
Sri Lanka	524	40.91	42.13	46.42	43.41	52.86	58.78	56.62	96.39	96.52	88.88	91.64	82.83	76.35	101.26	137.66
Timber (US $/cubic meter)																
Hardwood Logs																
Malaysia, Sarawak *	548	43.17	43.26	40.57	68.05	81.53	67.51	92.00	92.57	97.36	170.04	141.51	101.60	101.94	91.24	113.34
Hardwood Sawnwood																
Malaysia *	548	93.23	92.59	109.45	156.09	143.08	166.44	168.13	154.09	205.68	339.08	369.65	314.14	226.31	202.56	251.63
Softwood Logs																
United States *	111	....	....	....	....	....	....	....	....	....	....	....	....	89.43	78.22	73.43
Softwood Sawnwood																
United States *	111	....	....	....	....	....	....	....	....	....	....	....	....	151.63	141.44	137.10
Tin (US cents/pound)																
All Origins (London) *	112	166.63	159.30	169.64	217.83	371.23	311.92	344.08	490.08	584.01	700.68	761.03	642.69	581.95	589.11	554.76
Malaysia	548	160.86	153.59	165.89	201.76	335.35	293.23	334.15	471.98	564.11	665.56	751.14	633.55	593.23	587.60	568.07
Bolivia	218	174.41	158.53	169.63	207.74	361.28	312.55	343.90	475.13	566.91	672.37	760.36	633.80	574.63	586.48	554.40
Thailand	578	158.65	156.53	166.18	197.46	332.00	300.19	329.69	471.06	557.11	656.45	740.28	628.38	615.91	585.81	548.99
Tobacco (US $/metric ton)																
United States (All Markets) *	111	1,055.44	1,100.62	1,073.64	1,128.02	1,482.07	1,841.99	2,186.72	2,253.93	2,268.02	2,344.43	2,275.86	2,321.69	2,563.96	2,656.55	2,786.32
Urea (US $/metric ton)																
Any Origin (Eastern Europe)	170	....	....	....	....	....	....	....	....	....	....	....	....	....	....	....
Wheat (US $/bushel)																
Australia (Sydney)	193	1.48	1.58	1.84	3.97	5.32	4.03	3.50	2.91	3.70	4.28	4.77	4.73	4.35	4.34	3.76
Australia	193	1.42	1.53	1.61	2.03	4.73	4.57	3.92	2.90	3.10	3.94	4.91	5.07	4.41	4.67	3.89
United States (US Gulf Pts) *	111	1.49	1.68	1.90	3.81	4.89	4.06	3.62	2.81	3.48	4.36	4.70	4.76	4.36	4.28	4.15
Argentina	213	1.48	1.62	1.81	2.65	5.26	4.68	3.65	2.63	3.20	3.98	5.01	5.27	4.54	3.91	3.60
Wool (US cents/kilogram)																
Australia-NZ(UK) 48s *	112	120.28	121.70	208.48	364.06	285.13	234.39	320.48	338.57	347.34	422.30	429.78	391.43	342.76	320.24	315.54
Australia-NZ(UK) 64s *	112	196.45	178.38	297.59	698.82	492.00	386.50	398.64	429.53	442.92	524.88	597.25	612.58	572.64	539.86	558.93
New Zealand	196	73.81	72.64	106.86	237.50	214.65	147.59	202.92	256.35	249.63	300.35	316.68	274.56	239.68	221.93	230.74
Zinc (US cents/pound)																
United Kingdom (London) *	112	13.42	14.06	17.14	38.16	56.13	33.83	32.32	26.74	26.92	33.61	34.52	38.37	33.78	34.68	41.82
United States (New York) *	111	22.63	23.02	25.31	30.08	51.12	55.53	53.53	49.28	44.96	53.99	54.40	65.26	57.17	61.19	71.38
Bolivia	218	13.95	15.25	17.64	23.76	34.85	36.93	36.08	33.08	27.48	35.90	35.98	41.04	39.10	36.61	45.86

*See the Commodity Prices note in the monthly *IFS*.

Commodity Prices

Country of Origin and, for Wholesale Prices, Pricing Point in Parentheses

Commodity / Origin	1985	1986	1987	1988	1989	1990	1991	1992	1993	1994	1995	1996	1997	1998	1999	Code
Petroleum, spot (US $/barrel)																
Average Crude Price *	27.37	14.17	18.20	14.77	17.91	22.99	19.37	19.04	16.79	15.95	17.20	20.37	19.27	13.07	18.14	001
U.K. Brent *	27.61	14.43	18.44	14.98	18.25	23.71	19.98	19.41	17.00	15.83	17.06	20.45	19.12	12.72	17.81	112
West Texas Intermediate *	27.99	15.02	19.19	15.97	19.69	24.52	21.51	20.56	18.46	17.18	18.43	22.13	20.59	14.42	19.24	111
Alaskan North Slope *	27.14	13.89	18.08	14.26	17.65	22.03	18.35	18.15	16.40	15.76	17.24	. . . .	. . . .	. . . .	. . . .	111
Phosphate Rock (US $/metric ton)																
Morocco (Casablanca) *	33.92	34.26	31.00	36.00	40.83	40.50	42.50	41.75	33.00	33.00	35.00	39.00	40.83	43.00	44.00	686
Potash (US $/metric ton)																
Canada (Vancouver) *	83.96	68.79	69.04	87.54	98.88	98.13	108.85	112.08	107.42	105.72	117.76	116.93	116.53	116.89	121.64	156
Plywood (US cents/sheet)																
Philippines (Tokyo)	210.91	274.15	398.72	358.84	350.32	354.87	372.38	380.77	661.42	599.50	584.44	529.52	484.96	374.56	440.56	566
Pulp (US $/metric ton)																
Sweden (North Sea Ports)	416.30	490.10	620.20	739.66	829.70	814.50	596.80	562.95	423.91	552.46	853.45	574.12	554.87	508.77	500.14	144
Rice (US $/metric ton)																
United States (New Orleans)	354.87	318.07	300.16	398.85	379.76	361.48	387.94	372.28	361.15	433.10	389.50	463.97	441.53	446.34	449.42	111
Thailand (Bangkok) *	217.42	195.67	214.42	277.25	299.75	270.67	293.67	267.67	237.25	269.46	320.80	338.06	302.47	305.42	248.97	578
Thailand	204.16	170.76	198.64	269.37	288.07	270.20	287.14	291.03	257.18	484.96	314.85	366.67	216.85	321.01	263.90	578
Myanmar	164.87	139.78	119.92	170.19	211.34	205.49	232.27	211.99	173.25	187.15	209.86	219.04	221.07	327.85	. . . .	518
Rubber (US cents/pound)																
All Origins (New York)	36.99	36.47	39.04	43.22	43.13	44.43	42.18	41.34	41.93	43.33	50.17	48.56	47.44	46.61	45.31	111
Malaysia (Singapore) *	34.42	36.58	44.66	53.75	43.99	39.22	37.46	39.08	37.71	51.07	71.68	63.59	46.16	32.73	28.83	548
Thailand	32.84	34.27	40.88	52.00	41.92	35.89	35.20	35.28	35.07	44.08	63.81	59.04	43.30	30.41	23.77	578
Shrimp (US $/pound)																
United States (U.S. Gulf Ports)	4.76	5.85	5.18	5.64	5.09	4.90	5.24	4.97	5.16	5.93	6.13	5.95	6.70	6.45	6.62	111
Silver (US cents/troy ounce)																
United States (New York)	614.2	546.9	700.9	653.5	549.9	482.0	404.0	393.6	429.8	528.4	519.2	518.3	489.2	553.4	525.0	111
Sisal (US $/metric ton)																
East African (Europe)	525.67	514.17	512.08	550.58	653.08	715.00	669.17	505.58	615.42	604.58	710.42	868.25	777.50	821.33	695.75	639
Sorghum (US $/metric ton)																
United States (U.S. Gulf Ports)	103.01	82.41	72.76	98.46	105.94	103.94	105.11	102.76	99.03	103.87	118.97	150.03	109.62	98.04	84.39	111
Soybeans (US $/metric ton)																
United States (Rotterdam) *	224.42	208.42	215.75	303.50	275.00	246.75	239.56	235.52	255.25	252.83	259.25	304.50	295.42	245.42	199.58	111
Soybean Meal (US $/metric ton)																
United States (Rotterdam) *	157.17	184.75	203.25	267.50	247.33	200.08	197.08	204.33	208.08	192.50	196.92	267.58	275.75	170.33	152.00	111
Soybean Oil (US $/metric ton)																
All Origins (Dutch Ports) *	576.00	342.42	334.25	463.42	431.50	447.50	453.90	428.65	479.98	616.20	625.17	551.63	564.75	625.92	428.01	111
Sugar (US cents/pound)																
EU Import Price *	16.12	18.60	21.44	23.82	22.75	26.45	27.77	28.48	28.10	28.20	31.21	31.15	28.38	27.13	26.84	112
Caribbean (New York) *	4.05	6.05	6.76	10.19	12.81	12.51	8.98	9.07	10.02	12.11	13.28	11.96	11.40	8.92	6.27	001
U.S. Import Price *	20.35	20.95	21.83	22.12	22.81	23.25	21.55	21.30	21.61	22.03	23.06	22.36	21.93	22.06	21.14	111
Brazil	6.66	7.03	6.80	8.42	12.14	15.94	11.87	11.12	11.61	13.14	13.75	13.10	12.34	10.37	6.74	223
Philippines	14.94	17.59	16.63	19.01	19.02	19.30	19.09	19.02	14.13	26.01	19.72	19.30	17.66	18.62	26.20	566
Superphosphate (US $/metric ton)																
United States (US Gulf Ports)	121.38	121.17	138.00	158.38	144.00	131.82	133.12	120.74	111.95	132.11	149.63	175.83	171.91	173.67	154.50	111
Tea (US cents/pound)																
Average Auction (London) *	89.98	87.48	77.45	81.18	91.25	92.17	83.57	90.60	84.20	83.15	74.46	80.36	107.59	108.21	105.40	112
Sri Lanka	101.24	72.08	81.60	79.79	84.20	103.91	92.23	84.84	85.58	83.81	90.55	114.51	121.78	129.81	104.74	524
Timber (US $/cubic meter)																
Hardwood Logs																
Malaysia, Sarawak *	82.24	97.29	167.46	167.21	167.34	160.28	179.63	196.69	388.98	316.32	257.68	253.74	238.21	162.86	187.02	548
Hardwood Sawnwood																
Malaysia *	182.58	215.98	371.80	371.23	467.71	517.12	524.76	607.21	758.24	821.44	740.19	740.89	662.33	484.16	601.11	548
Softwood Logs																
United States *	72.30	75.22	88.60	103.41	106.21	123.56	125.67	152.47	217.94	201.23	193.84	204.07	185.31	159.10	164.55	111
Softwood Sawnwood																
United States *	136.07	149.33	160.30	162.65	184.18	206.26	216.17	234.64	277.44	299.55	300.62	309.91	294.13	279.81	300.55	111
Tin (US cents/pound)																
All Origins (London) *	523.40	279.48	303.45	319.86	387.12	276.03	253.83	276.88	234.40	247.66	281.11	279.36	255.85	251.12	244.55	112
Malaysia	524.49	282.68	304.37	322.62	392.91	287.07	266.00	47.64	242.33	238.06	280.51	279.87	242.89	. . . .	. . . .	548
Bolivia	539.32	252.64	308.97	320.22	400.71	286.88	253.36	273.91	249.26	247.62	281.70	278.77	174.28	167.50	168.80	218
Thailand	524.89	283.09	301.24	305.53	381.08	280.53	249.24	261.43	232.36	248.56	276.32	. . . .	. . . .	. . . .	. . . .	578
Tobacco (US $/metric ton)																
United States (All Markets) *	2,611.82	2,659.18	2,745.55	2,467.90	3,167.57	3,392.19	3,500.07	3,439.54	2,695.34	2,641.66	2,643.44	3,056.73	3,531.81	3,336.12	3,101.45	111
Urea (US $/metric ton)																
Any Origin (Eastern Europe)	. . . .	. . . .	. . . .	. . . .	. . . .	130.74	150.95	123.49	94.40	131.39	193.93	187.48	127.93	103.05	77.71	170
Wheat (US $/bushel)																
Australia (Sydney)	3.84	3.26	3.11	4.08	4.81	5.29	3.59	5.41	4.20	4.41	5.38	6.19	5.10	4.22	. . . .	193
Australia	3.50	3.14	2.43	3.71	4.59	4.25	2.91	4.12	3.72	3.50	5.17	5.83	4.59	3.94	3.53	193
United States (US Gulf Pts) *	3.70	3.13	3.07	3.95	4.61	3.69	3.50	4.11	3.82	4.08	4.82	5.64	4.35	3.43	3.05	111
Argentina	3.13	2.66	2.44	3.18	4.05	3.93	2.44	3.27	3.57	3.57	4.47	5.47	4.30	3.35	3.18	213
Wool (US cents/kilogram)																
Australia-NZ(UK) 48s *	301.48	325.99	407.89	467.57	421.67	343.33	262.69	272.34	255.21	318.95	392.55	379.04	328.91	255.74	267.66	112
Australia-NZ(UK) 64s *	495.33	465.48	713.30	1,164.83	926.58	807.83	556.01	498.37	384.74	619.00	651.86	554.28	625.29	429.00	398.76	112
New Zealand	234.94	248.52	333.01	403.17	386.27	341.47	249.33	242.87	234.25	287.90	356.15	348.34	311.95	236.58	232.59	196
Zinc (US cents/pound)																
United Kingdom (London) *	35.53	34.20	36.20	56.26	75.12	68.85	50.86	56.33	43.73	45.28	46.77	46.49	59.64	46.46	48.80	112
United States (New York) *	61.76	57.88	63.00	82.54	110.73	101.92	75.44	81.40	64.77	66.68	71.32	68.89	86.89	68.21	71.59	111
Bolivia	39.41	35.72	37.43	50.55	74.47	67.09	49.63	55.15	43.78	44.56	46.82	45.92	35.17	27.37	28.56	218

*See the Commodity Prices note in the monthly IFS.

Commodity Price Index

d

		1970	1971	1972	1973	1974	1975	1976	1977	1978	1979	1980	1981	1982	1983	1984
														Indices of Wholesale Prices (lines 76) and of Unit Values (lines 74)		
															1995=100	
World (non-fuel comm. with *)	001	32.8	32.2	34.8	56.2	68.2	57.0	62.8	69.5	70.6	85.5	90.7	81.9	73.8	79.1	79.2
Food	001	42.1	43.5	46.9	84.6	104.7	84.0	78.7	76.4	86.6	101.0	109.8	106.3	90.2	97.2	96.6
Beverages	001	39.4	35.7	39.2	49.7	60.2	56.7	104.9	182.2	136.2	141.9	123.9	98.2	98.6	104.7	121.1
Agricultural Raw Materials	001	19.1	18.9	21.6	34.7	35.5	30.3	39.4	40.0	43.1	59.7	65.2	56.9	54.5	55.9	57.0
Metals	001	37.4	34.2	34.7	47.7	64.3	56.0	58.6	61.7	63.6	81.4	89.6	77.5	70.2	79.7	72.8
Fertilizers	001	27.4	28.1	28.7	34.3	131.7	169.7	89.4	76.5	72.4	82.4	116.6	123.5	105.8	96.8	97.7
World Bank LMICs	200	36.0	34.3	36.5	55.8	75.2	61.7	71.7	89.1	83.3	95.3	103.3	88.8	78.4	84.5	86.0
Aluminum (US cents/pound)																
All Origins (London) *	156	34.0	34.8	32.7	33.2	42.4	48.1	49.3	63.4	73.4	88.8	98.4	70.0	54.9	79.7	69.4
Bananas (US cents/pound)																
Latin America (US Ports) *	248	37.6	31.8	36.6	37.3	41.7	55.7	58.6	61.9	65.0	73.8	85.0	90.9	84.9	97.2	83.7
Beef (US cents/pound)																
Australia-NZ (US Ports) *	193	68.4	70.6	77.6	105.4	83.0	69.6	82.9	79.0	112.1	151.2	144.7	129.6	125.3	127.9	119.2
United States (New York)	111	49.2	50.6	59.2	75.8	63.3	53.6	62.3	60.6	84.8	109.1	103.2	102.8	117.3	113.8	115.7
Argentina (frozen)	213	15.7	19.1	24.6	33.8	36.2	18.5	19.5	25.0	25.0	39.7	46.3	40.0	30.4	31.6	43.2
Butter (US cents/pound)																
New Zealand (London)	196	20.3	28.7	32.9	26.9	32.2	43.8	46.5	51.2	66.5	79.4	92.0	85.6	78.5	67.7	57.1
New Zealand	196	28.8	38.5	51.0	44.5	44.4	50.8	49.7	57.9	68.6	69.9	74.4	97.6	97.9	91.9	76.8
Coal (US $/metric ton)																
Australia	193	27.3	30.0	33.8	40.4	60.0	95.9	113.1	107.1	113.2	109.4	113.0	130.1	141.4	122.5	112.7
Cocoa Beans (US cents/pound)																
Brazil	223	48.7	38.9	43.4	80.2	121.3	93.6	127.4	303.5	253.9	232.7	177.1	144.7	112.9	137.4	174.2
New York and London *	652	47.0	37.6	44.9	78.9	108.9	87.0	142.8	264.6	237.7	229.9	181.7	145.0	121.6	147.9	167.2
Coconut Oil (US cents/pound)																
Philippines (New York) *	566	56.6	52.7	37.0	76.6	149.0	58.8	62.4	86.4	102.0	147.0	100.4	85.1	69.8	109.0	172.5
Philippines	566	45.8	42.2	29.4	57.0	142.8	60.6	56.2	86.5	96.6	150.1	100.4	83.2	70.6	86.4	160.4
Coffee (US cents/pound)																
Other Milds (New York) *	386	34.8	30.1	33.7	41.7	44.1	43.8	95.5	157.1	109.0	116.1	103.2	85.7	93.5	88.1	96.5
Brazil (New York) *	223	38.2	30.6	36.0	47.4	50.2	56.6	102.4	183.0	113.2	122.3	143.0	127.7	98.4	97.8	102.5
Brazil	223	35.7	27.3	34.5	42.5	45.9	40.0	98.8	164.3	114.7	124.9	116.0	67.3	76.6	81.7	91.0
Uganda (New York) *	799	32.7	33.3	35.6	39.3	46.3	48.1	100.6	176.4	116.3	130.5	116.0	81.1	87.6	97.9	109.0
Copper (US cents/pound)																
United Kingdom (London) *	112	48.2	36.9	36.5	60.6	70.1	42.2	47.9	44.7	46.6	67.3	74.5	59.4	50.5	54.3	47.0
Copra (US $/metric ton)																
Philippines (Europ. Ports) *	566	50.9	43.2	32.5	78.4	152.5	58.4	62.7	91.8	107.3	153.4	103.3	86.4	71.6	113.1	161.9
Cotton (US cents/pound)																
United States (10 markets) *	111	26.4	29.2	36.1	59.1	61.0	47.5	71.6	64.9	60.7	65.4	85.6	75.9	63.2	72.1	71.8
Liverpool Index *	111	29.4	34.5	36.9	63.2	66.3	54.0	78.6	72.6	73.2	78.5	95.4	85.4	73.8	85.6	82.3
Egypt (Liverpool) (1990=100)	469	20.9	20.6	21.7	32.8	51.2	43.1	45.4	49.7	46.2	51.1	51.1	50.6	41.6	46.6	54.6
Egypt (Long Staple)	469	55.4	55.8	58.9	70.5	136.4	125.5	107.4	141.0	108.3	111.9	111.7	110.4	99.4	100.3	129.5
Egypt (Long Medium)	469	51.2	50.5	49.4	64.0	131.0	112.7	87.2	129.1	104.7	112.2	112.1	111.0	82.8	89.2	115.3
Fish Meal (US $/metric ton)																
All Origins (Hamburg) *	293	39.8	34.0	48.2	109.5	75.2	49.6	76.0	91.7	82.8	79.8	101.9	94.4	71.5	91.4	75.4
Iceland	176	35.2	36.5	31.5	78.6	76.3	42.2	52.5	79.5	78.7	71.1	88.5	89.0	59.3	101.6	62.5
Gasoline (US cents/gallon)																
US Gulf Coast *	111	....	....	....	....	....	....	....	....	....	165.8	180.5	197.3	180.6	163.9	150.8
Gold (US $/fine ounce)																
United Kingdom (London)	112	9.4	10.6	15.1	25.3	41.5	41.9	32.5	38.5	50.3	79.8	158.2	119.7	97.8	110.0	93.8
Groundnuts (US $/metric ton)																
Nigeria (London) *	694	25.1	27.6	27.9	43.0	81.2	47.6	46.5	60.1	69.3	61.8	I135.9	138.2	90.9	106.1	91.9
Groundnut Meal (US $/metric ton)																
All Origins (Europe)	694	68.4	65.6	81.4	177.5	116.5	93.6	117.5	145.5	136.9	141.0	161.0	159.7	123.6	135.8	111.2
Groundnut Oil (US $/metric ton)																
Any Origin (Europe) *	694	38.2	45.0	43.0	54.9	106.8	78.5	69.7	85.4	108.9	89.7	86.7	105.2	59.1	71.7	102.6
Hides (US cents/pound)																
United States (Chicago) *	111	14.6	16.4	33.6	38.9	26.8	26.4	38.1	41.9	53.9	83.0	52.1	47.3	43.8	51.2	66.8
Iron Ore (US $/metric ton)																
Brazil (North Sea Ports) *	223	56.4	49.6	47.4	63.4	70.4	84.5	84.1	79.9	71.8	86.8	104.0	104.0	120.4	107.4	96.9
Jute (US $/metric ton)																
Bangladesh (Chitta.-Chalna)	513	73.7	77.0	80.3	77.7	95.1	101.4	80.8	87.2	108.8	105.3	85.7	76.1	77.4	81.6	145.1
Lamb (US cents/pound)																
New Zealand (London) *	196	29.8	32.3	43.0	56.1	57.4	59.9	63.4	68.9	88.9	96.3	115.8	110.3	95.9	77.6	77.4
New Zealand	196	24.2	24.1	27.1	43.2	46.0	39.6	40.6	47.9	55.3	63.6	71.8	78.0	71.6	62.2	56.9
Lead (US cents/pound)																
United Kingdom (London) *	112	48.3	40.3	48.0	67.9	93.9	66.3	70.9	98.1	104.9	191.1	143.9	115.3	86.7	67.6	70.2
United States (New York)	111	36.6	32.4	35.8	38.2	51.9	50.2	53.5	71.5	78.6	123.3	101.3	87.2	62.2	52.5	62.9
Linseed Oil (US $/metric ton)																
Any Origin *	001	32.9	28.5	30.0	82.8	166.5	106.6	83.0	70.2	66.0	97.9	106.0	100.4	78.9	73.7	86.9
Maize (US $/bushel)																
United States (Chicago)	111	48.7	49.8	46.5	81.7	114.4	102.8	95.4	78.6	82.2	93.4	106.4	112.4	89.4	114.7	115.8
United States (US Gulf Pts) *	111	47.2	47.2	45.1	79.0	107.2	96.8	90.9	77.3	81.6	93.6	101.8	105.8	87.6	110.2	110.0
Thailand	578	32.3	29.0	26.9	51.4	66.1	65.8	56.9	52.6	49.0	67.9	80.1	73.5	63.3	68.6	67.5
Manganese (US $/long ton)																
India (US Ports)	534	27.3	31.5	31.8	37.6	56.3	69.0	72.7	74.1	71.2	69.0	76.6	82.7	80.9	74.9	70.6
Newsprint (US $/short ton)																
United States (New York)	111	22.4	23.4	24.3	25.4	31.4	38.3	41.2	44.4	47.0	51.5	57.9	63.9	65.7	63.0	67.2
Finland	172	19.0	19.8	20.7	24.2	38.9	52.2	48.8	53.2	54.9	60.8	67.9	67.0	64.5	54.4	52.4
Nickel (US cents/pound)																
United Kingdom (N.Europ.ports)*	156	34.2	35.7	37.4	41.0	46.6	55.6	60.4	63.3	56.1	72.7	79.3	72.4	58.8	56.8	57.8
Palm Kernels (US $/metric ton)																
Malaysia (Rotterdam)	548	54.2	49.5	32.3	72.3	154.3	60.3	63.9	91.6	112.7	154.8	107.1	86.8	67.6	104.6	153.0
Palm Oil (US $/metric ton)																
Malaysia (N.W. Europe) *	548	41.3	41.7	34.6	59.8	110.0	66.9	63.2	84.3	95.5	104.0	92.8	90.8	70.8	79.8	115.9
Malaysia	548	35.1	35.5	30.5	39.1	81.7	77.6	58.8	85.8	87.1	97.0	86.5	80.2	68.1	71.4	106.2
Pepper, Black (US cents/pound)																
Malaysia (New York)	548	33.3	29.1	26.9	33.7	49.4	52.9	51.8	66.1	61.9	55.9	52.6	41.8	41.0	I47.4	79.4

*See the Commodity Prices note in
the monthly *IFS*.

Commodity Price Index

Country of Origin and, for Wholesale Prices, Pricing Point in Parentheses
1995=100

1985	1986	1987	1988	1989	1990	1991	1992	1993	1994	1995	1996	1997	1998	1999		
68.8	67.8	74.1	91.9	90.5	84.7	79.9	79.9	81.4	92.3	100.0	98.8	95.7	81.6	75.9	World (non-fuel comm. with *)	001
80.6	70.8	74.2	95.5	97.3	88.0	87.2	89.1	88.0	92.5	100.0	112.2	100.3	87.7	74.0	Food	001
108.4	127.4	89.1	91.5	75.8	66.2	61.9	53.3	56.6	99.1	100.0	82.6	109.5	92.9	73.1	Beverages	001
49.2	51.9	66.5	71.7	74.1	76.2	73.4	75.4	87.6	95.9	100.0	97.3	90.6	75.8	77.5	Agricultural Raw Materials	001
66.9	64.5	79.3	118.6	111.8	99.8	85.6	83.6	71.8	83.7	100.0	88.1	91.3	76.5	75.4	Metals	001
88.2	88.6	89.7	103.5	105.6	100.9	104.2	98.9	83.7	90.4	100.0	113.7	115.0	118.2	113.4	Fertilizers	001
74.9	75.7	76.0	91.0	88.0	81.8	78.1	75.3	74.9	91.5	100.0	94.1	96.2	81.1	72.2	World Bank LMICs	200
															Aluminum (US cents/pound)	
57.7	63.7	86.7	141.1	108.1	90.8	72.3	69.6	63.2	81.8	100.0	83.5	88.6	75.2	75.4	All Origins (London) *	156
															Bananas (US cents/pound)	
85.7	86.5	85.5	108.5	123.9	122.9	127.2	108.4	100.4	99.5	100.0	107.0	111.2	108.0	96.9	Latin America (US Ports) *	248
															Beef (US cents/pound)	
112.9	109.8	125.1	132.0	134.6	134.4	139.7	128.7	137.3	122.3	100.0	93.6	97.3	90.5	96.1	Australia-NZ (US Ports) *	193
106.8	91.2	96.9	97.1	103.7	112.2	107.7	107.3	111.2	103.3	100.0	101.0	102.3	....	....	United States (New York)	111
41.1	52.7	77.0	73.6	70.6	62.2	92.5	120.6	143.9	109.0	100.0	79.8	85.8	111.8	98.4	Argentina (frozen)	213
															Butter (US cents/pound)	
61.7	70.0	69.0	85.4	90.1	89.9	85.6	91.5	85.7	85.4	100.0	....	89.8	87.9	80.5	New Zealand (London)	196
60.7	57.3	64.1	70.0	91.7	88.0	79.0	92.3	82.3	85.1	100.0	104.0	86.9	88.3	75.6	New Zealand	196
															Coal (US $/metric ton)	
99.6	98.0	87.3	90.5	103.8	106.6	108.9	103.3	98.3	93.2	100.0	107.6	103.3	92.4	....	Australia	193
															Cocoa Beans (US cents/pound)	
157.1	152.2	138.9	120.2	94.0	81.2	78.6	74.4	73.5	92.5	100.0	104.9	120.5	124.2	88.0	Brazil	223
157.4	144.4	139.5	110.6	86.7	88.5	83.3	76.7	77.6	97.4	100.0	101.6	113.0	117.0	79.2	New York and London *	652
															Coconut Oil (US cents/pound)	
88.1	44.3	66.0	84.4	77.2	50.4	64.7	86.3	67.4	90.6	100.0	112.3	98.1	98.6	110.1	Philippines (New York) *	566
86.5	43.3	59.9	83.5	80.1	51.6	57.7	88.5	67.5	90.8	100.0	116.8	101.2	97.1	117.2	Philippines	566
															Coffee (US cents/pound)	
97.4	129.0	75.2	90.4	71.6	59.7	56.9	42.6	46.8	99.4	100.0	80.5	123.8	88.6	68.1	Other Milds (New York) *	386
102.0	158.4	72.9	83.5	67.7	57.4	49.9	38.5	45.6	98.2	100.0	82.4	114.3	83.4	60.9	Brazil (New York) *	223
83.9	153.7	72.6	81.3	60.2	47.5	46.2	34.9	40.4	93.3	100.0	80.9	115.7	85.7	64.2	Brazil	223
95.6	117.0	80.7	75.0	59.7	43.4	39.3	34.4	42.2	94.5	100.0	65.3	63.6	66.2	53.3	Uganda (New York) *	799
															Copper (US cents/pound)	
48.3	46.7	60.7	88.7	97.1	90.8	79.8	77.9	65.3	78.6	100.0	78.2	77.6	56.4	53.6	United Kingdom (London) *	112
															Copra (US $/metric ton)	
88.1	45.1	70.8	90.3	79.4	52.4	67.5	87.1	67.4	95.1	100.0	111.5	98.9	93.7	105.4	Philippines (Europ. Ports) *	566
															Cotton (US cents/pound)	
61.8	55.5	66.8	60.4	67.6	75.7	74.4	57.7	58.8	77.7	100.0	83.2	74.6	71.1	55.9	United States (10 markets) *	111
61.0	48.8	76.1	64.6	77.3	84.0	78.2	58.9	59.0	81.1	100.0	81.9	80.6	66.7	54.0	Liverpool Index *	111
54.6	52.4	54.3	72.8	96.4	100.0	92.9	70.9	67.0	57.2	....	....	....	....	....	Egypt (Liverpool) (1990=100)	469
125.4	129.2	157.5	249.6	559.9	468.7	232.2	149.6	117.9	95.1	100.0	170.7	....	....	....	Egypt (Long Staple)	469
136.8	139.9	135.6	261.3	570.6	448.7	220.9	113.8	101.8	90.8	100.0	113.9	....	....	....	Egypt (Long Medium)	469
															Fish Meal (US $/metric ton)	
56.6	64.8	77.5	110.0	82.6	83.3	96.5	97.3	73.7	76.1	100.0	118.4	122.5	133.6	79.2	All Origins (Hamburg) *	293
57.6	65.2	73.1	90.2	101.3	91.0	94.5	98.8	76.7	85.6	100.0	115.6	127.4	137.1	93.4	Iceland	176
															Gasoline (US cents/gallon)	
151.1	85.7	99.2	93.3	109.5	139.7	124.7	112.8	99.9	94.1	100.0	117.1	114.9	81.1	101.8	US Gulf Coast *	111
															Gold (US $/fine ounce)	
82.6	95.7	116.2	113.8	99.3	99.8	94.3	89.4	93.6	100.0	100.0	101.0	86.2	76.6	72.6	United Kingdom (London)	112
															Groundnuts (US $/metric ton)	
74.3	109.2	83.4	102.8	89.8	145.7	136.0	87.8	120.0	104.9	100.0	105.7	108.6	108.7	91.7	Nigeria (London) *	694
															Groundnut Meal (US $/metric ton)	
86.8	98.5	96.0	124.2	118.9	109.6	89.0	90.5	99.7	99.9	100.0	126.2	131.1	68.9	....	All Origins (Europe)	694
															Groundnut Oil (US $/metric ton)	
91.4	57.5	50.4	59.6	78.2	97.3	90.3	61.5	74.5	103.2	100.0	90.6	102.0	91.7	79.4	Any Origin (Europe) *	694
															Hides (US cents/pound)	
58.1	72.6	90.6	99.4	102.1	104.6	90.1	86.1	90.8	98.5	100.0	99.1	100.1	87.0	81.9	United States (Chicago) *	111
															Iron Ore (US $/metric ton)	
98.4	97.3	90.7	87.0	98.1	114.1	123.1	117.0	104.1	94.3	100.0	105.9	106.3	110.0	99.9	Brazil (North Sea Ports) *	223
															Jute (US $/metric ton)	
159.4	74.3	87.7	101.2	102.1	111.7	99.9	76.3	74.2	80.9	100.0	124.2	82.6	70.9	75.4	Bangladesh (Chitta.-Chalna)	513
															Lamb (US cents/pound)	
73.8	81.7	86.9	96.6	93.0	107.0	92.6	101.9	109.6	110.9	100.0	128.4	132.7	102.4	102.3	New Zealand (London) *	196
49.2	49.3	56.6	63.7	68.6	88.0	78.5	82.3	100.2	97.3	100.0	119.5	126.2	107.7	112.2	New Zealand	196
															Lead (US cents/pound)	
62.1	64.5	94.8	104.2	106.9	128.6	88.6	86.4	64.7	87.2	100.0	123.0	99.0	83.7	79.7	United Kingdom (London) *	112
45.7	47.3	83.7	85.2	89.3	105.2	77.0	82.0	73.5	86.6	100.0	115.7	111.5	109.2	103.4	United States (New York)	111
															Linseed Oil (US $/metric ton)	
95.4	63.8	48.3	79.3	115.1	107.9	66.7	60.3	68.2	78.6	100.0	86.1	86.9	107.6	78.0	Any Origin *	001
															Maize (US $/bushel)	
94.4	74.7	60.6	88.9	93.9	92.5	89.0	88.1	86.8	91.8	100.0	145.3	101.0	84.1	71.8	United States (Chicago)	111
91.0	71.1	61.2	86.6	90.2	88.5	87.1	84.4	82.7	87.3	100.0	133.3	94.9	82.3	73.1	United States (US Gulf Pts) *	111
50.4	43.4	45.8	61.6	66.7	64.9	61.7	71.6	66.4	80.5	100.0	....	138.6	76.5	71.1	Thailand	578
															Manganese (US $/long ton)	
69.5	69.4	66.1	73.6	101.0	168.5	193.1	184.3	147.0	105.0	100.0	100.2	100.2	100.2	....	India (US Ports)	534
															Newsprint (US $/short ton)	
69.1	67.7	73.5	77.9	75.7	73.9	74.7	67.8	69.2	72.0	100.0	98.6	82.8	88.5	....	United States (New York)	111
54.2	67.4	77.0	91.0	86.9	95.1	91.9	77.7	62.4	66.4	100.0	107.6	77.8	75.0	....	Finland	172
															Nickel (US cents/pound)	
59.6	47.3	59.2	167.5	161.9	107.8	99.3	85.3	64.5	77.0	100.0	91.3	84.2	56.2	73.0	United Kingdom (N.Europ.ports)*	156
															Palm Kernels (US $/metric ton)	
81.3	42.5	62.9	79.5	69.7	49.2	61.4	85.9	64.6	92.6	100.0	107.4	96.2	101.4	102.6	Malaysia (Rotterdam)	548
															Palm Oil (US $/metric ton)	
79.7	40.9	54.5	69.5	55.7	46.1	53.9	62.6	60.1	84.2	100.0	84.6	86.8	106.8	69.4	Malaysia (N.W. Europe) *	548
80.6	44.1	52.0	67.9	57.0	46.9	53.8	62.4	62.5	78.8	100.0	82.1	82.5	....	....	Malaysia	548
															Pepper, Black (US cents/pound)	
106.5	155.7	153.2	121.5	75.3	47.3	37.4	38.8	61.0	81.1	100.0	97.6	166.9	187.5	....	Malaysia (New York)	548

*See the Commodity Prices note in the monthly *IFS.*

Commodity Price Index

Indices of Wholesale Prices (lines 76) and of Unit Values (lines 74)
1995=100

		1970	1971	1972	1973	1974	1975	1976	1977	1978	1979	1980	1981	1982	1983	1984
Petroleum, spot (US $/barrel)																
Average Crude Price *	001	12.7	15.4	16.8	18.9	I 67.4	63.7	71.1	77.2	77.8	175.6	213.2	205.0	188.6	I 172.3	165.9
U.K. Brent *	112	13.1	18.8	21.2	24.9	75.8	67.4	77.0	83.9	83.6	188.3	222.2	215.0	195.9	174.6	168.5
West Texas Intermediate *	111	....	....	....	....	....	....								165.0	159.4
Alaskan North Slope *	111	13.3	13.3	13.3	13.3	I 56.6	57.1	62.1	67.5	67.7	149.3	189.6	182.0	I 168.1	154.0	I 165.6
Phosphate Rock (US $/metric ton)																
Morocco (Casablanca)	686	31.4	32.1	32.9	39.3	150.8	194.3	102.4	87.6	82.9	94.3	133.5	141.4	121.1	105.5	109.3
Potash (US $/metric ton)																
Canada (Vancouver)	156	26.8	27.6	28.4	36.1	51.4	69.1	47.1	43.5	47.9	64.9	98.3	95.5	68.6	64.1	71.1
Plywood (US cents/sheet)																
Philippines (Tokyo)	566	17.6	14.0	16.6	32.5	26.1	20.8	25.3	27.6	32.4	44.9	46.9	42.0	40.1	39.3	38.8
Pulp (US $/metric ton)																
Sweden (North Sea Ports)	144	20.8	22.1	21.8	27.1	39.1	51.7	49.0	45.8	40.3	51.5	62.9	63.6	57.2	50.1	59.7
Rice (US $/metric ton)																
United States (New Orleans)	111	44.9	45.5	51.4	94.3	132.3	99.7	73.3	79.6	95.1	90.8	117.9	134.7	87.3	90.1	90.5
Thailand (Bangkok) *	578	44.6	40.6	46.7	92.5	168.8	113.2	79.2	84.9	114.9	104.2	135.2	150.5	91.5	86.3	78.6
Thailand	578	36.1	38.2	32.1	65.2	148.1	95.9	67.9	70.7	101.3	86.7	108.1	126.6	82.1	80.1	75.5
Myanmar	518	39.7	35.8	35.9	55.9	176.5	122.7	80.1	82.0	96.0	106.7	131.0	148.4	100.5	88.3	88.7
Rubber (US cents/pound)																
All Origins (New York) *	111	37.2	31.8	32.0	62.0	70.1	52.7	69.7	73.3	88.1	113.3	129.6	100.6	79.9	99.1	87.5
Malaysia (Singapore) *	548	25.8	21.0	21.0	42.9	47.6	35.5	49.0	51.6	62.4	79.9	90.1	71.1	54.3	67.3	60.6
Thailand	578	27.7	21.1	20.0	40.4	48.5	36.5	49.4	53.4	63.5	82.5	94.2	74.8	53.9	65.6	66.1
Shrimp (US $/pound)																
United States (U.S. Gulf Ports)	111	20.2	24.5	30.6	37.1	34.4	43.6	61.8	58.6	59.3	88.5	75.0	71.8	101.2	97.9	85.4
Silver (US cents/troy ounce)																
United States (New York) *	111	34.1	29.8	32.4	49.3	90.7	85.1	83.9	89.0	104.0	213.6	396.3	202.6	153.1	220.4	156.8
Sisal (US $/metric ton)																
East Africa (Europe)	639	21.4	23.9	33.8	74.1	148.6	81.7	65.8	72.0	66.8	100.4	107.7	90.8	83.5	80.4	82.2
Sorghum (US $/metric ton)																
United States (US Gulf Ports)	111	43.5	46.8	47.2	78.5	101.7	94.0	88.4	75.0	78.9	90.9	108.3	106.2	91.1	108.2	99.3
Soybeans (US $/metric ton)																
United States (Rotterdam) *	111	45.1	48.4	54.0	112.0	106.8	85.5	89.2	108.1	103.5	114.9	114.3	111.3	94.3	108.6	108.8
Soybean Meal (US $/metric ton)																
United States (Rotterdam) *	111	52.1	51.7	65.6	153.7	93.6	78.7	100.7	116.7	108.3	123.4	131.3	128.3	110.7	120.8	100.1
Soybean Oil (US $/metric ton)																
All Origins (Dutch Ports) *	111	45.8	48.6	38.5	69.7	133.1	90.1	70.1	92.8	97.1	105.9	95.7	81.1	71.6	84.3	116.0
Sugar (US cents/pound)																
EU Import Price *	112	16.3	16.5	21.8	21.3	34.1	49.5	42.9	44.9	51.0	61.8	70.8	60.6	58.1	56.3	51.4
Caribbean (New York) *	001	28.3	34.1	56.4	72.4	225.5	154.8	87.1	61.1	58.9	72.7	215.9	127.2	63.3	63.8	39.2
U.S. Import Price *	111	32.5	34.4	37.0	44.6	127.9	97.5	57.7	47.7	60.6	67.3	130.3	85.6	86.4	95.6	94.3
Brazil	223	37.1	40.0	52.5	65.2	184.6	212.2	83.8	60.0	56.0	63.9	158.5	123.1	68.5	68.8	66.7
Philippines	566	33.6	36.8	39.4	46.8	106.6	137.0	67.2	44.2	41.5	38.6	82.3	104.7	76.5	68.2	64.4
Superphosphate (US $/metric ton)																
United States (US Gulf Ports)	111	28.4	28.7	45.1	66.8	205.8	135.3	61.2	65.4	65.5	95.8	120.5	107.6	92.5	90.0	87.7
Tea (US cents/pound)																
Average Auction (London) *	112	66.5	64.2	64.2	64.4	85.0	84.2	93.6	163.9	133.4	131.4	135.7	123.0	117.7	141.6	210.6
Sri Lanka	524	45.2	46.5	51.3	47.9	58.4	64.9	62.5	106.4	106.6	98.1	101.2	91.5	84.3	111.8	152.0
Timber (US $/cubic meter)																
Hardwood Logs																
Malaysia, Sarawak *	548	16.8	16.8	15.7	26.4	31.6	26.2	35.7	35.9	37.8	66.0	54.9	39.4	39.6	35.4	44.0
Hardwood Sawnwood																
Malaysia *	548	12.6	12.5	14.8	21.1	19.3	22.5	22.7	20.8	27.8	45.8	49.9	42.4	30.6	27.4	34.0
Softwood Logs																
United States *	111	....	....	....	....	....	....	....	....	....	....	....	46.1	40.4	37.9
Softwood Sawnwood																
United States *	111	....	....	....	....	....	....	....	....	....	....	....	50.4	47.1	45.6
Tin (US cents/pound)																
All Origins (London) *	112	59.3	56.7	60.3	77.5	132.1	111.0	122.4	174.3	207.8	249.3	270.7	228.6	207.0	209.6	197.3
Malaysia	548	57.3	54.8	59.1	71.9	119.5	104.5	119.1	168.3	201.1	237.3	267.8	225.9	211.5	209.5	202.5
Bolivia	218	62.4	56.2	60.2	74.1	127.7	110.6	121.5	169.9	202.2	238.8	269.7	227.4	204.3	208.3	196.4
Thailand	578	57.4	56.6	60.1	71.5	120.2	108.6	119.3	170.5	201.6	237.6	267.9	227.4	222.9	212.0	198.7
Tobacco (US $/metric ton)																
United States (All Markets) *	111	39.9	41.6	40.6	42.7	56.1	69.7	82.7	85.3	85.8	88.7	86.1	87.8	97.0	100.5	105.4
Urea (US $/metric ton)																
Any Origin (Eastern Europe)	170	....	....	....	....	....	....	....	....	....	....	....	....			
Wheat (US $/bushel)																
Australia (Sydney)	193	27.6	29.3	34.2	73.9	99.0	74.9	65.1	54.2	68.7	79.5	88.7	87.9	80.8	80.7	70.0
Australia	193	27.4	29.7	31.1	39.3	91.7	88.6	76.0	56.1	59.9	76.2	95.1	98.2	85.4	90.4	75.3
United States (US Gulf Pts) *	111	31.0	34.9	39.5	79.0	101.6	84.2	75.1	58.3	72.2	90.6	97.6	98.9	90.6	89.0	86.1
Argentina	213	33.1	36.2	40.5	59.3	117.7	104.6	81.6	58.9	71.6	89.0	112.1	117.9	101.5	87.4	80.4
Wool (US cents/kilogram)																
Australia–NZ(UK) 48s *	112	30.6	31.0	53.1	92.7	72.6	59.7	81.6	86.2	88.5	107.6	109.5	99.7	87.3	81.6	80.4
Australia–NZ(UK) 64s *	112	30.1	27.4	45.7	107.2	75.5	59.3	61.2	65.9	67.9	80.5	91.6	94.0	87.8	82.8	85.7
New Zealand	196	20.7	20.4	30.0	66.7	60.3	41.4	57.0	72.0	70.1	84.3	88.9	77.1	67.3	62.3	64.8
Zinc (US cents/pound)																
United Kingdom (London) *	112	28.7	30.1	36.7	81.6	120.0	72.3	69.1	57.2	57.6	71.9	73.8	82.0	72.2	74.1	89.4
United States (New York) *	111	31.7	32.3	35.5	42.2	71.7	77.9	75.1	69.1	63.0	75.7	76.3	91.5	80.2	85.8	100.1
Bolivia	218	29.8	32.6	37.7	50.7	74.4	78.9	77.1	70.7	58.7	76.7	76.9	87.7	83.5	78.2	98.0

*See the Commodity Prices note in the monthly *IFS*.

Country of Origin and,for Wholesale Prices,Pricing Point in Parentheses
1995=100

1985	1986	1987	1988	1989	1990	1991	1992	1993	1994	1995	1996	1997	1998	1999		
															Petroleum, spot (US $/barrel)	
159.1	82.4	105.8	85.8	104.1	133.6	112.6	110.6	97.6	92.7	100.0	118.4	112.0	76.0	105.4	Average Crude Price *	001
161.9	84.6	108.1	87.8	107.0	139.0	117.2	113.8	99.7	92.8	100.0	119.9	112.1	74.6	104.4	U.K. Brent *	112
151.9	81.5	104.1	86.7	106.8	133.0	116.7	111.5	100.1	93.2	100.0	120.1	111.7	78.2	104.4	West Texas Intermediate *	111
157.4	80.6	104.9	82.7	102.4	127.8	106.4	105.3	95.1	91.4	100.0	....	....	....	....	Alaskan North Slope *	111
															Phosphate Rock (US $/metric ton)	
96.9	97.9	88.6	102.9	116.7	115.7	121.4	119.3	94.3	94.3	100.0	111.4	116.7	122.9	125.7	Morocco (Casablanca)	686
															Potash (US $/metric ton)	
71.3	58.4	58.6	74.3	84.0	83.3	92.4	95.2	91.2	89.8	100.0	99.3	99.0	99.3	103.3	Canada (Vancouver)	156
															Plywood (US cents/sheet)	
36.1	46.9	68.2	61.4	59.9	60.7	63.7	65.2	113.2	102.6	100.0	90.6	83.0	64.1	75.4	Philippines (Tokyo)	566
															Pulp (US $/metric ton)	
48.8	57.4	72.7	86.7	97.2	95.4	69.9	66.0	49.7	64.7	100.0	67.3	65.0	59.6	58.6	Sweden (North Sea Ports)	144
															Rice (US $/metric ton)	
91.1	81.7	77.1	102.4	I97.5	92.8	99.6	95.6	92.7	111.2	100.0	119.1	113.4	114.6	115.4	United States (New Orleans)	111
67.8	61.0	66.8	86.4	93.4	84.4	91.5	83.4	74.0	84.0	100.0	105.4	94.3	95.2	77.6	Thailand (Bangkok) *	578
64.8	54.2	63.1	85.6	91.5	85.8	91.2	92.4	81.7	154.0	100.0	116.5	68.9	102.0	83.8	Thailand	578
78.6	66.6	57.1	81.1	100.7	97.9	110.7	101.0	82.6	89.2	100.0	104.4	105.3	156.2	....	Myanmar	518
															Rubber (US cents/pound)	
73.7	72.7	77.8	86.2	I86.0	88.6	84.1	82.4	83.6	86.4	100.0	96.8	94.6	92.9	90.3	All Origins (New York)	111
48.0	51.0	62.3	75.0	61.4	54.7	52.3	54.5	52.6	71.2	100.0	88.7	64.4	45.7	40.2	Malaysia (Singapore) *	548
51.5	53.7	64.1	81.5	65.7	56.2	55.2	55.3	55.0	69.1	100.0	92.5	67.9	47.7	37.3	Thailand	578
															Shrimp (US $/pound)	
77.6	95.5	84.5	92.0	83.1	79.9	85.4	81.0	84.2	96.8	100.0	97.1	109.2	105.1	108.0	United States (U.S. Gulf Ports)	111
															Silver (US cents/troy ounce)	
118.3	105.3	135.0	125.9	105.9	92.8	77.8	75.8	82.8	101.8	100.0	99.8	94.2	106.6	101.1	United States (New York)	111
															Sisal (US $/metric ton)	
74.0	72.4	72.1	77.5	91.9	100.6	94.2	71.2	86.6	85.1	100.0	122.2	109.4	115.6	97.9	East Africa (Europe)	639
															Sorghum (US $/metric ton)	
86.6	69.3	61.2	82.8	89.0	87.4	88.4	86.4	83.2	87.3	100.0	126.1	92.1	82.4	70.9	United States (US Gulf Ports)	111
															Soybeans (US $/metric ton)	
86.6	80.4	83.2	117.1	106.1	95.2	92.4	90.8	98.5	97.5	100.0	117.5	114.0	94.7	77.0	United States (Rotterdam) *	111
															Soybean Meal (US $/metric ton)	
79.8	93.8	103.2	135.8	125.6	101.6	100.1	103.8	105.7	97.8	100.0	135.9	140.0	86.5	77.2	United States (Rotterdam) *	111
															Soybean Oil (US $/metric ton)	
92.1	54.8	53.5	74.1	69.0	71.6	72.6	68.6	76.8	98.6	100.0	88.2	90.3	100.1	68.5	All Origins (Dutch Ports) *	111
															Sugar (US cents/pound)	
51.7	59.6	68.7	76.3	72.9	84.7	89.0	91.2	90.0	90.3	100.0	99.8	90.9	86.9	86.0	EU Import Price *	112
30.5	45.6	50.9	76.8	96.4	94.2	67.6	68.3	75.5	91.2	100.0	90.0	85.9	67.2	47.2	Caribbean (New York) *	001
88.3	90.9	94.7	95.9	98.9	100.9	93.5	92.4	93.7	95.6	100.0	97.0	95.1	95.7	91.7	U.S. Import Price *	111
48.5	51.2	49.5	61.2	88.3	116.0	86.3	80.9	84.4	95.6	100.0	95.3	89.7	75.4	49.0	Brazil	223
75.7	89.2	84.3	96.4	96.4	97.8	96.8	96.4	71.7	131.9	100.0	97.9	89.5	94.4	132.8	Philippines	566
															Superphosphate (US $/metric ton)	
81.1	81.0	92.2	105.8	96.2	88.1	89.0	80.7	74.8	88.3	100.0	117.5	114.9	116.1	103.3	United States (US Gulf Ports)	111
															Tea (US cents/pound)	
120.8	117.5	104.0	109.0	122.6	123.8	112.2	121.7	113.1	111.7	100.0	107.9	144.5	145.3	141.5	Average Auction (London) *	112
111.8	79.6	90.1	88.1	93.0	114.8	101.9	93.7	94.5	92.6	100.0	126.5	134.5	143.4	115.7	Sri Lanka	524
															Timber (US $/cubic meter)	
															Hardwood Logs	
31.9	37.8	65.0	64.9	64.9	62.2	69.7	76.3	151.0	122.8	100.0	98.5	92.4	63.2	72.6	Malaysia, Sarawak *	548
															Hardwood Sawnwood	
24.7	29.2	50.2	50.2	63.2	69.9	70.9	82.0	102.4	111.0	100.0	100.1	89.5	65.4	81.2	Malaysia *	548
															Softwood Logs	
37.3	38.8	45.7	53.3	54.8	63.7	64.8	78.7	112.4	103.8	100.0	105.3	95.6	82.1	84.9	United States *	111
															Softwood Sawnwood	
45.3	49.7	53.3	54.1	61.3	68.6	71.9	78.1	92.3	99.6	100.0	103.1	97.8	93.1	100.0	United States *	111
															Tin (US cents/pound)	
186.2	99.4	107.9	113.8	137.7	98.2	90.3	98.5	83.4	88.1	100.0	99.4	91.0	89.3	87.0	All Origins (London) *	112
187.0	100.8	108.5	115.0	140.1	102.3	94.8	17.0	84.9	84.9	100.0	99.8	86.6	....	....	Malaysia	548
185.8	98.7	109.5	114.3	139.6	100.9	89.7	97.8	83.6	86.8	100.0	98.0	83.9	84.3	82.4	Bolivia	218
190.0	102.5	109.0	110.6	137.9	101.5	90.2	94.6	84.1	90.0	100.0	....	....	....	....	Thailand	578
															Tobacco (US $/metric ton)	
98.8	100.6	103.9	93.4	119.8	128.3	132.4	130.1	102.0	99.9	100.0	115.6	133.6	126.2	117.3	United States (All Markets) *	111
															Urea (US $/metric ton)	
....	....	....	....	....	67.4	77.8	63.7	48.7	67.8	100.0	96.7	66.0	53.1	40.1	Any Origin (Eastern Europe)	170
															Wheat (US $/bushel)	
71.5	60.6	57.9	76.0	89.4	98.3	66.8	100.5	78.2	82.0	100.0	115.1	94.8	78.4	....	Australia (Sydney)	193
67.8	60.8	47.1	71.9	88.8	82.2	56.3	79.7	72.0	67.8	100.0	112.9	88.9	76.3	68.3	Australia	193
76.8	64.9	63.8	82.1	95.6	76.6	72.7	85.4	79.2	84.6	100.0	117.1	90.2	71.3	63.3	United States (US Gulf Pts) *	111
70.1	59.5	54.7	71.2	90.6	87.9	54.6	73.2	79.9	79.8	100.0	122.4	96.1	74.8	71.2	Argentina	213
															Wool (US cents/kilogram)	
76.8	83.0	103.9	119.1	107.4	87.5	66.9	69.4	65.0	81.3	100.0	96.6	83.8	65.1	68.2	Australia-NZ(UK) 48s *	112
76.0	71.4	109.4	178.7	142.1	123.9	85.3	76.5	59.0	95.0	100.0	85.0	95.9	65.8	61.2	Australia-NZ(UK) 64s *	112
66.0	69.8	93.5	113.2	108.5	95.9	70.0	68.2	65.8	80.8	100.0	97.8	87.6	66.4	65.3	New Zealand	196
															Zinc (US cents/pound)	
76.0	73.1	77.4	120.3	160.6	147.2	108.8	120.4	93.5	96.8	100.0	99.4	127.5	99.3	104.3	United Kingdom (London) *	112
86.6	81.2	88.3	115.7	I155.3	142.9	105.8	114.1	90.8	93.5	100.0	96.6	121.8	95.6	100.4	United States (New York) *	111
84.2	76.3	79.9	108.0	159.1	143.3	106.0	117.8	93.5	95.2	100.0	98.1	75.1	58.4	61.0	Bolivia	218

*See the Commodity Prices note in the monthly *IFS*.

COUNTRY
TABLES

Albania

		1970	1971	1972	1973	1974	1975	1976	1977	1978	1979	1980	1981	1982	1983	1984
Exchange Rates															*Leks per SDR:*	
Market Rate	aa	...	...	...	...	...	...	...	...	...	...	...	...	...	...	...
															Leks per US Dollar:	
Market Rate	ae	...	...	...	...	...	...	...	...	...	...	...	...	...	...	...
Market Rate	rf	...	...	...	...	...	...	...	...	...	...	...	...	...	...	...
Fund Position															*Millions of SDRs:*	
Quota	2f. s	—	—	—	—	—	—	—	—	—	—	—	—	—	—	—
SDRs	1b. s	...	...	...	...	...	...	...	...	...	...	...	...	...	...	...
Reserve Position in the Fund	1c. s	...	...	...	...	...	...	...	...	...	...	...	...	...	...	...
Total Fund Cred.&Loans Outstg.	2tl	...	...	...	...	...	...	...	...	...	...	...	...	...	...	...
International Liquidity												*Millions of US Dollars Unless Otherwise Indicated:*				
Total Reserves minus Gold	1l. d	...	...	...	...	...	...	...	...	...	...	...	...	...	...	...
SDRs	1b. d	...	...	...	...	...	...	...	...	...	...	...	...	...	...	...
Reserve Position in the Fund	1c. d	...	...	...	...	...	...	...	...	...	...	...	...	...	...	...
Foreign Exchange	1d. d	...	...	...	...	...	...	...	...	...	...	...	...	...	...	...
Gold (Million Fine Troy Ounces)	1ad	...	...	...	...	...	...	...	...	...	...	...	...	...	...	...
Gold (National Valuation)	1an d	...	...	...	...	...	...	...	...	...	...	...	...	...	...	...
Monetary Authorities															*Billions of Leks:*	
Foreign Assets	11	...	...	...	...	...	...	...	...	...	...	...	...	...	...	...
Claims on Central Government	12a	...	...	...	...	...	...	...	...	...	...	...	...	...	...	...
Claims on Banks	12e	...	...	...	...	...	...	...	...	...	...	...	...	...	...	...
Reserve Money	14	...	...	...	...	...	...	...	...	...	...	...	...	...	...	...
of which: Currency Outside Banks	14a	...	...	...	...	...	...	...	...	...	...	...	...	...	...	...
Foreign Liabilities	16c	...	...	...	...	...	...	...	...	...	...	...	...	...	...	...
Central Government Deposits	16d	...	...	...	...	...	...	...	...	...	...	...	...	...	...	...
Capital Accounts	17a	...	...	...	...	...	...	...	...	...	...	...	...	...	...	...
Other Items (Net)	17r	...	...	...	...	...	...	...	...	...	...	...	...	...	...	...
Banking Institutions															*Billions of Leks:*	
Reserves	20	...	...	...	...	...	...	...	...	...	...	...	...	...	...	...
Foreign Assets	21	...	...	...	...	...	...	...	...	...	...	...	...	...	...	...
Claims on Central Government	22a	...	...	...	...	...	...	...	...	...	...	...	...	...	...	...
Claims on Nonfin.Pub.Enterprises	22c	...	...	...	...	...	...	...	...	...	...	...	...	...	...	...
Claims on Private Sector	22d	...	...	...	...	...	...	...	...	...	...	...	...	...	...	...
Demand Deposits	24	...	...	...	...	...	...	...	...	...	...	...	...	...	...	...
Time and Savings Deposits	25a	...	...	...	...	...	...	...	...	...	...	...	...	...	...	...
Foreign Currency Deposits	25b	...	...	...	...	...	...	...	...	...	...	...	...	...	...	...
Foreign Liabilities	26c	...	...	...	...	...	...	...	...	...	...	...	...	...	...	...
Central Government Deposits	26d	...	...	...	...	...	...	...	...	...	...	...	...	...	...	...
Credit from Monetary Authorities	26g	...	...	...	...	...	...	...	...	...	...	...	...	...	...	...
Capital Accounts	27a	...	...	...	...	...	...	...	...	...	...	...	...	...	...	...
Other Items (Net)	27r	...	...	...	...	...	...	...	...	...	...	...	...	...	...	...
Banking Survey															*Billions of Leks:*	
Foreign Assets (Net)	31n	...	...	...	...	...	...	...	...	...	...	...	...	...	...	...
Domestic Credit	32	...	...	...	...	...	...	...	...	...	...	...	...	...	...	...
Claims on Central Govt. (Net)	32an	...	...	...	...	...	...	...	...	...	...	...	...	...	...	...
Claims on Nonfin.Pub.Enterprises	32c	...	...	...	...	...	...	...	...	...	...	...	...	...	...	...
Claims on Private Sector	32d	...	...	...	...	...	...	...	...	...	...	...	...	...	...	...
Money	34	...	...	...	...	...	...	...	...	...	...	...	...	...	...	...
Quasi-Money	35	...	...	...	...	...	...	...	...	...	...	...	...	...	...	...
Capital Accounts	37a	...	...	...	...	...	...	...	...	...	...	...	...	...	...	...
Other Items (Net)	37r	...	...	...	...	...	...	...	...	...	...	...	...	...	...	...
Money plus Quasi-Money	35l	...	...	...	...	...	...	...	...	...	...	...	...	...	...	...
Interest Rates															*Percent Per Annum*	
Bank Rate *(End of Period)*	60	...	...	...	...	...	...	...	...	...	...	...	...	...	...	...
Treasury Bill Rate	60c	...	...	...	...	...	...	...	...	...	...	...	...	...	...	...
Deposit Rate	60l	...	...	...	...	...	...	...	...	...	...	...	...	...	...	...
Lending Rate	60p	...	...	...	...	...	...	...	...	...	...	...	...	...	...	...
Prices															*Index Numbers (1995=100):*	
Consumer Prices	64	...	...	...	...	...	...	...	...	...	...	...	...	...	...	...
															Number in Thousands:	
Employment	67e	...	...	...	...	...	...	...	...	...	...	...	...	...	...	...
Unemployment	67c	...	...	...	...	...	...	...	...	...	...	...	...	...	...	...
Unemployment Rate (%)	67r	...	...	...	...	...	...	...	...	...	...	...	...	...	...	...

1985	1986	1987	1988	1989	1990	1991	1992	1993	1994	1995	1996	1997	1998	1999		
End of Period															**Exchange Rates**	
....	....	....	....	....	....	....	141.49	135.57	139.55	140.09	148.21	201.23	197.94	185.45	Market Rate.........................	**aa**
End of Period (ae) Period Average (rf)																
....	....	....	....	....	....	....	102.90	98.70	95.59	94.24	103.07	149.14	140.58	135.12	Market Rate.........................	**ae**
							75.03	102.06	94.62	92.70	104.50	148.93	150.63	137.69	Market Rate.........................	**rf**
End of Period															**Fund Position**	
—	—	—	—	—	—	25.00	35.30	35.30	35.30	35.30	35.30	35.30	35.30	48.70	Quota...............................	**2f. s**
....	....	....	....	....	....	—	.04	.01	.20	.10	.52	.46	43.39	56.06	SDRs................................	**1b. s**
....	....	....	....	....	....	—	.01	.01	.01	.01	.01	.01	.01	3.36	Reserve Position in the Fund	**1c. s**
....	....	....	....	....	....	—	9.69	21.60	37.13	43.40	37.70	40.74	45.77	58.69	Total Fund Cred.&Loans Outstg.	**2tl**
End of Period															**International Liquidity**	
....	....	....	....	....	....	....	147.42	204.80	241.05	280.86	308.93	348.50	369.05	Total Reserves minus Gold..............	**1l. d**
....	....	....	....	....	....	—	.06	.01	.30	.14	.75	.62	61.10	76.95	SDRs..............................	**1b. d**
....	....	....	....	....	....	—	.01	.01	.01	.01	.01	.01	.01	4.60	Reserve Position in the Fund	**1c. d**
....	....	....	....	....	....	....	147.40	204.50	240.90	280.10	308.30	287.40	287.50	Foreign Exchange	**1d. d**
....	....	....	....	....	....	....	.05	.05	.06	.12	.12	.12	.12	Gold (Million Fine Troy Ounces).......	**1ad**
....	....	....	....	....	....	....	19.41	20.85	24.30	42.50	33.40	33.70	34.50	Gold (National Valuation)	**1an d**
End of Period															**Monetary Authorities**	
....							....	22.65	46.76	57.02	85.21	91.04	71.08	Foreign Assets	**11**
								69.33	45.69	52.90	86.19	78.20	75.30	Claims on Central Government	**12a**
								3.42	3.31	3.37	7.44	4.56	5.90	Claims on Banks	**12e**
								42.07	53.88	61.39	90.93	89.89	109.31	Reserve Money	**14**
								27.63	41.91	47.81	72.73	68.32	81.34	*of which: Currency Outside Banks*	**14a**
								59.41	33.65	36.81	53.85	55.11	24.15	Foreign Liabilities	**16c**
....								3.75	4.27	3.25	5.62	5.39	5.85	Central Government Deposits	**16d**
....								14.26	10.61	16.83	31.43	38.56	14.82	Capital Accounts	**17a**
....								−24.08	−6.64	−4.99	−3.00	−15.14	−1.85	Other Items (Net)	**17r**
End of Period															**Banking Institutions**	
....							....	11.93	10.30	12.90	16.44	21.57	28.15	Reserves	**20**
								16.94	23.47	35.44	38.96	49.97	57.97	Foreign Assets	**21**
								86.55	108.52	142.51	109.70	127.89	146.89	Claims on Central Government	**22a**
								3.25	3.09	3.41	2.83	1.67	1.67	Claims on Nonfin.Pub.Enterprises...........	**22c**
								7.20	8.35	10.89	13.01	14.86	18.22	Claims on Private Sector	**22d**
								11.14	17.35	42.59	18.94	15.41	21.67	Demand Deposits	**24**
								18.70	28.12	30.24	70.55	115.53	136.66	Time and Savings Deposits	**25a**
								13.30	20.08	33.91	36.33	40.26	53.21	Foreign Currency Deposits	**25b**
								1.82	1.14	1.22	2.02	2.87	4.83	Foreign Liabilities	**26c**
								68.05	75.92	80.41	25.80	1.05	.80	Central Government Deposits	**26d**
								.65	—	1.69	3.64	4.73	1.44	Credit from Monetary Authorities	**26g**
....								6.62	9.76	14.21	25.45	26.46	26.94	Capital Accounts	**27a**
....								5.59	1.36	.89	−1.79	10.80	7.35	Other Items (Net)	**27r**
End of Period															**Banking Survey**	
....							....	−21.63	35.44	54.42	68.30	83.03	100.07	Foreign Assets (Net)	**31n**
								94.52	85.46	126.06	180.31	217.35	235.43	Domestic Credit	**32**
								84.07	74.02	111.76	164.47	199.65	215.54	Claims on Central Govt. (Net)	**32an**
								3.25	3.09	3.41	2.83	1.67	1.67	Claims on Nonfin.Pub.Enterprises........	**32c**
								7.20	8.35	10.89	13.01	14.86	18.22	Claims on Private Sector	**32d**
								38.77	59.25	90.41	91.67	83.73	103.00	Money	**34**
								32.01	48.20	64.15	106.88	155.80	189.87	Quasi-Money.........................	**35**
								20.88	20.37	31.04	56.89	65.02	41.77	Capital Accounts	**37a**
....								−18.76	−6.92	−5.11	−6.83	−4.17	.86	Other Items (Net)	**37r**
....								70.77	107.45	154.55	198.55	239.53	292.87	Money plus Quasi-Money	**35l**
Percent Per Annum															**Interest Rates**	
....	....	....	....	....	....	....	40.0	34.0	25.0	20.5	24.0	32.0	23.4	18.0	Bank Rate *(End of Period)*................	**60**
....	....	....	....	....	....	....	....	....	....	13.8	17.7	32.5	....	....	Treasury Bill Rate	**60c**
....	....	....	....	....	....	....	18.5	ⅈ27.3	19.8	ⅈ15.3	16.8	....	....	12.9	Deposit Rate	**60l**
....	....	....	....	....	....	....	20.6	29.6	23.7	ⅈ19.7	24.0	....	....	21.6	Lending Rate	**60p**
Period Averages															**Prices**	
....	....	....	....	....	....	12.5	40.9	75.7	92.8	100.0	112.7	150.1	181.1	181.8	Consumer Prices.........................	**64**
Period Averages																
776	804	834	856	889	905	851	....	....	....	....	....	....	....	....	Employment........................	**67e**
....	92	89	106	113	151	140	....	....	....	....	....	....	....	....	Unemployment.....................	**67c**
....	6.4	6.1	7.0	7.3	9.5	9.1	....	....	....	....	....	....	....	....	Unemployment Rate (%)................	**67r**

Albania

		1970	1971	1972	1973	1974	1975	1976	1977	1978	1979	1980	1981	1982	1983	1984
International Transactions															*Millions of Leks*	
Exports	70	...	....	...	....	...	...	...	...	...	...	3,573	3,513	3,156	2,992	2,800
Imports, c.i.f.	71	...	....	...	....	...	...	...	...	...	...	3,617	3,391	4,026	3,528	3,257
Balance of Payments															*Millions of US Dollars:*	
Current Account, n.i.e.	78al *d*	...	....	...	....	...	...	...	...	...	...	16.0	45.0	−66.8	−38.3	−28.1
Goods: Exports f.o.b.	78aa *d*	...	....	...	....	...	...	...	...	...	...	367.2	418.0	359.9	341.0	319.1
Goods: Imports f.o.b.	78ab *d*	...	....	...	....	...	...	...	...	...	...	−353.9	−383.2	−437.7	−382.8	−353.2
Trade Balance	78ac *d*	...	....	...	....	...	...	...	...	...	...	13.3	34.8	−77.8	−41.8	−34.1
Services: Credit	78ad *d*	...	....	...	....	...	...	...	...	...	...	10.9	12.0	13.2	13.0	15.4
Services: Debit	78ae *d*	...	....	...	....	...	...	...	...	...	...	−17.5	−19.4	−22.1	−22.1	−19.1
Balance on Goods & Services	78af *d*	...	....	...	....	...	...	...	...	...	...	6.7	27.4	−86.7	−50.9	−37.8
Income: Credit	78ag *d*	...	....	...	....	...	...	...	...	...	...	7.4	12.0	14.7	7.7	4.3
Income: Debit	78ah *d*	...	....	...	....	...	...	...	...	...	...	−3.9	−1.5	−1.3	−1.1	−1.1
Balance on Gds, Serv. & Inc.	78ai *d*	...	....	...	....	...	...	...	...	...	...	10.2	37.9	−73.3	−44.3	−34.6
Current Transfers, n.i.e.: Credit	78aj *d*	...	....	...	....	...	...	...	...	...	...	5.8	7.1	6.5	6.0	6.5
Current Transfers: Debit	78ak *d*	...	....	...	....	...	...	...	...	...	...					
Capital Account, n.i.e.	78bc *d*	...	....	...	....	...	...	...	...	...	...	—	—	—	—	—
Capital Account, n.i.e.: Credit	78ba *d*	...	....	...	....	...	...	...	...	...	...	—	—	—	—	—
Capital Account: Debit	78bb *d*	...	....	...	....	...	...	...	...	...	...	—	—	—	—	—
Financial Account, n.i.e.	78bj *d*	...	....	...	....	...	...	...	...	...	...	−2.0	−39.5	55.2	−29.5	8.5
Direct Investment Abroad	78bd *d*	...	....	...	....	...	...	...	...	...	...	—	—	—	—	—
Dir. Invest. in Rep. Econ., n.i.e.	78be *d*	...	....	...	....	...	...	...	...	...	...	—	—	—	—	—
Portfolio Investment Assets	78bf *d*	...	....	...	....	...	...	...	...	...	...	—	—	—	—	—
Equity Securities	78bk *d*	...	....	...	....	...	...	...	...	...	...	—	—	—	—	—
Debt Securities	78bl *d*	...	....	...	....	...	...	...	...	...	...	—	—	—	—	—
Portfolio Investment Liab., n.i.e.	78bg *d*	...	....	...	....	...	...	...	...	...	...	—	—	—	—	—
Equity Securities	78bm *d*	...	....	...	....	...	...	...	...	...	...	—	—	—	—	—
Debt Securities	78bn *d*	...	....	...	....	...	...	...	...	...	...	—	—	—	—	—
Financial Derivatives Assets	78bw *d*	...	....	...	....	...	...	...	...	...	...	....	....	....	....	....
Financial Derivatives Liabilities	78bx *d*	...	....	...	....	...	...	...	...	...	...	....	....	....	....	....
Other Investment Assets	78bh *d*	...	....	...	....	...	...	...	...	...	...	—	—	—	—	—
Monetary Authorities	78bo *d*	...	....	...	....	...	...	...	...	...	...					
General Government	78bp *d*	...	....	...	....	...	...	...	...	...	...	—	—	—	—	—
Banks	78bq *d*	...	....	...	....	...	...	...	...	...	...	—	—	—	—	—
Other Sectors	78br *d*	...	....	...	....	...	...	...	...	...	...	—	—	—	—	—
Other Investment Liab., n.i.e.	78bi *d*	...	....	...	....	...	...	...	...	...	...	−2.0	−39.5	55.2	−29.5	8.5
Monetary Authorities	78bs *d*	...	....	...	....	...	...	...	...	...	...	7.7	−36.0	58.7	−26.7	11.3
General Government	78bt *d*	...	....	...	....	...	...	...	...	...	...	−9.7	−3.5	−3.5	−2.8	−2.8
Banks	78bu *d*	...	....	...	....	...	...	...	...	...	...	—	—	—	—	—
Other Sectors	78bv *d*	...	....	...	....	...	...	...	...	...	...	—	—	—	—	—
Net Errors and Omissions	78ca *d*	...	....	...	....	...	...	...	...	...	...	−10.6	20.7	−1.9	26.6	7.6
Overall Balance	78cb *d*	...	....	...	....	...	...	...	...	...	...	3.4	26.2	−13.5	−41.2	−12.0
Reserves and Related Items	79da *d*	...	....	...	....	...	...	...	...	...	...	−3.4	−26.2	13.5	41.2	12.0
Reserve Assets	79db *d*	...	....	...	....	...	...	...	...	...	...	−3.4	−26.2	13.5	41.2	12.0
Use of Fund Credit and Loans	79dc *d*	...	....	...	....	...	...	...	...	...	...	—	—	—	—	—
Exceptional Financing	79de *d*	...	....	...	....	...	...	...	...	...	...	—	—	—	—	—
Government Finance															*Millions of Leks:*	
Deficit (-) or Surplus	80	...	....	...	....	...	...	...	...	...	...	....	....	....	....	....
Revenue	81	...	....	...	....	...	...	...	...	...	...	....	....	....	....	....
Grants Received	81z	...	....	...	....	...	...	...	...	...	...	....	....	....	....	....
Expenditure	82	...	....	...	....	...	...	...	...	...	...	....	....	....	....	....
Lending Minus Repayments	83	...	....	...	....	...	...	...	...	...	...	....	....	....	....	....
Financing																
Domestic	84a	...	....	...	....	...	...	...	...	...	...	....	....	....	....	....
Foreign	85a	...	....	...	....	...	...	...	...	...	...	....	....	....	....	....
Debt: Domestic	88a	...	....	...	....	...	...	...	...	...	...	....	....	....	....	....
Foreign	89a	...	....	...	....	...	...	...	...	...	...	....	....	....	....	....
															Millions:	
Population	99z	...	....	...	....	...	...	...	...	...	...	....	....	....	....	....

	Code	1985	1986	1987	1988	1989	1990	1991	1992	1993	1994	1995	1996	1997	1998	1999
International Transactions																
Millions of Leks																
Exports	70	2,665	2,490	2,490	2,549	3,203	2,273	1,252	5,707	12,499	13,092	18,712	21,603	21,044	30,656	37,913
Imports, c.i.f.	71	3,176	2,666	2,650	3,217	3,792	3,797	3,026	13,135	58,536	56,732	66,145	87,995	95,021	124,337	158,959
Balance of Payments																
Minus Sign Indicates Debit																
Current Account, n.i.e.	78al *d*	−36.4	−3.2	5.2	−27.1	−39.3	−118.3	−168.0	−50.7	14.9	−157.3	−11.5	−107.3	−272.2	−65.1	−155.4
Goods: Exports f.o.b.	78aa *d*	303.5	311.3	311.2	344.6	393.7	322.1	73.0	70.0	111.6	141.3	204.9	243.7	158.6	208.0	275.0
Goods: Imports f.o.b.	78ab *d*	−344.1	−316.6	−315.6	−382.3	−455.8	−455.9	−281.0	−540.5	−601.5	−601.0	−679.7	−922.0	−693.6	−811.7	−938.0
Trade Balance	78ac *d*	−40.6	−5.3	−4.4	−37.7	−62.1	−133.8	−208.0	−470.5	−489.9	−459.7	−474.8	−678.3	−535.0	−603.6	−663.0
Services: Credit	78ad *d*	15.0	16.0	22.3	29.6	40.2	31.5	9.2	20.3	77.6	79.1	98.8	129.2	63.8	86.6	269.4
Services: Debit	78ae *d*	−17.9	−19.7	−20.0	−26.2	−27.9	−29.1	−33.4	−89.1	−161.9	−132.5	−156.5	−189.4	−115.2	−129.3	−163.1
Balance on Goods & Services	78af *d*	−43.5	−9.0	−2.1	−34.3	−49.8	−131.4	−232.2	−539.3	−574.2	−513.1	−532.5	−738.5	−586.4	−646.3	−556.7
Income: Credit	78ag *d*	2.3	.8	1.1	.9	.4	—	.8	2.6	64.9	55.1	72.0	83.7	61.4	86.1	85.5
Income: Debit	78ah *d*	−.9	−.7	−.7	−.7	−.5	−1.9	−25.9	−37.7	−31.0	−41.3	−28.4	−11.9	−11.8	−8.7	−10.2
Balance on Gds, Serv. & Inc.	78ai *d*	−42.1	−8.9	−1.7	−34.1	−49.9	−133.3	−257.3	−574.4	−540.3	−499.3	−488.9	−666.7	−536.8	−569.0	−481.4
Current Transfers, n.i.e.: Credit	78aj *d*	5.7	5.7	6.9	7.0	10.6	15.0	89.3	524.0	556.9	347.5	521.2	595.9	299.8	560.8	508.9
Current Transfers: Debit	78ak *d*	—	—	—	—	—	—	—	−.3	−1.7	−5.5	−43.8	−36.5	−35.2	−56.9	−182.9
Capital Account, n.i.e.	78bc *d*	—	—	—	—	—	—	—	—	—	—	389.4	4.8	2.0	31.0	22.6
Capital Account, n.i.e.: Credit	78ba *d*	—	—	—	—	—	—	—	—	—	—	389.4	4.8	2.0	31.0	22.6
Capital Account: Debit	78bb *d*	—	—	—	—	—	—	—	—	—	—	—	—	—	—	—
Financial Account, n.i.e.	78bj *d*	12.8	−1.7	−5.9	139.3	359.4	−117.7	−181.2	−32.2	44.1	40.2	−411.0	61.5	151.4	15.4	33.7
Direct Investment Abroad	78bd *d*											....	—			
Dir. Invest. in Rep. Econ., n.i.e.	78be *d*	—	—	—	—	—	—	—	20.0	58.0	53.0	70.0	90.1	47.5	45.0	41.2
Portfolio Investment Assets	78bf *d*	—	—	—	—	—	—	—	—	—	—	....	....	—	—	—
Equity Securities	78bk *d*	—	—	—	—	—	—	—	—	—	—	....	....	—	—	—
Debt Securities	78bl *d*	—	—	—	—	—	—	—	—	—	—	....	....	—	—	—
Portfolio Investment Liab., n.i.e.	78bg *d*	—	—	—	—	—	—	—	—	—	—	....	....	—	—	—
Equity Securities	78bm *d*	—	—	—	—	—	—	—	—	—	—	....	....	—	—	—
Debt Securities	78bn *d*	—	—	—	—	—	—	—	—	—	—	....	....	—	—	—
Financial Derivatives Assets	78bw *d*	....	....	....	....	....	....	....								
Financial Derivatives Liabilities	78bx *d*	....	....	....	....	....	....	....								
Other Investment Assets	78bh *d*	—	—	—	—	—	—	—	−73.2	−78.6	−97.3	−97.0	−138.6	59.8	−126.9	−130.1
Monetary Authorities	78bo *d*	—	—	—	—	—	—	—	—	—	—	—	—	—	—	—
General Government	78bp *d*	—	—	—	—	—	—	—	—	—	—	—	—	—	—	—
Banks	78bq *d*	—	—	—	—	—	—	—	−50.0	−25.5	−22.9	−68.4	−110.5	81.5	−91.2	−96.8
Other Sectors	78br *d*	—	—	—	—	—	—	—	−23.2	−53.1	−74.4	−28.6	−28.1	−21.7	−35.7	−33.3
Other Investment Liab., n.i.e.	78bi *d*	12.8	−1.7	−5.9	139.3	359.4	−117.7	−181.2	21.0	64.7	84.5	−384.0	110.0	44.1	97.3	122.6
Monetary Authorities	78bs *d*	15.5	.3	−3.9	141.3	361.4	−144.8	−202.6	—	—	—	−9.1	10.4	16.0	10.4	8.9
General Government	78bt *d*	−2.7	−2.0	−2.0	−2.0	−2.0	27.1	21.4	22.4	50.5	74.6	−404.5	61.3	40.3	81.3	97.9
Banks	78bu *d*	—	—	—	—	—	—	—	−1.4	3.4	2.6	−3.3	4.0	−.6	3.5	16.0
Other Sectors	78bv *d*	—	—	—	—	—	—	—	—	10.8	7.3	32.9	34.3	−11.6	2.0	−.2
Net Errors and Omissions	78ca *d*	6.0	3.5	12.3	22.0	4.8	−2.0	125.2	47.4	−10.3	123.9	53.7	96.9	158.4	71.1	206.2
Overall Balance	78cb *d*	−17.6	−1.4	11.6	134.2	324.9	−238.0	−224.0	−35.5	48.7	6.8	20.6	55.9	39.5	52.4	107.1
Reserves and Related Items	79da *d*	17.6	1.4	−11.6	−134.2	−324.9	238.0	224.0	35.5	−48.7	−6.8	−20.6	−55.9	−39.5	−52.4	−107.1
Reserve Assets	79db *d*	17.6	1.4	−11.6	−134.2	−324.9	32.0	28.0	−27.4	−114.9	−55.2	−30.5	−47.6	−43.7	−60.0	−124.7
Use of Fund Credit and Loans	79dc *d*	—	—	—	—	—	—	—	13.9	16.6	22.3	9.9	−8.3	4.2	6.8	17.5
Exceptional Financing	79de *d*	—	—	—	—	—	206.0	196.0	49.0	49.5	26.1	....	....	....	.8	.1

	Code	1985	1986	1987	1988	1989	1990	1991	1992	1993	1994	1995	1996	1997	1998	1999
Government Finance																
Year Ending December 31																
Deficit (−) or Surplus	80	....	....	....	....	....	....	....	....	....	....	−20,157	−34,689	−41,053	−38,972	....
Revenue	81	....	....	....	....	....	....	....	....	....	....	49,068	47,551	53,205	89,145	....
Grants Received	81z	....	....	....	....	....	....	....	....	....	....	598	722	2,304	9,005	....
Expenditure	82	....	....	....	....	....	....	....	....	....	....	69,687	83,553	97,472	137,254	....
Lending Minus Repayments	83	....	....	....	....	....	....	....	....	....	....	136	−591	−910	−132	....
Financing																
Domestic	84a	....	....	....	....	....	....	....	....	....	....	15,919	27,680	36,815	27,464	....
Foreign	85a	....	....	....	....	....	....	....	....	....	....	4,238	7,009	4,238	11,509	....
Debt: Domestic	88a	....	....	....	....	....	....	....	....	....	....	53,876	82,654	120,527	149,439	....
Foreign	89a	....	....	....	....	....	....	....	....	....	....	25,434	42,668	55,432	64,405	....
Midyear Estimates																
Population	99z	2.96	3.02	3.08	3.14	3.20	3.26	3.26	3.36	3.48	3.55	3.61	3.67	3.73	3.79	3.11

(See notes in the back of the book.)

Algeria

		1970	1971	1972	1973	1974	1975	1976	1977	1978	1979	1980	1981	1982	1983	1984
Exchange Rates															*Dinars per SDR:*	
Official Rate	aa	4.937	I 5.042	4.946	5.049	4.894	4.829	5.064	4.901	4.996	4.947	5.065	5.096	5.113	5.147	5.021
															Dinars per US Dollar:	
Official Rate	ae	4.937	I 4.644	4.556	4.185	3.997	4.125	4.359	4.035	3.835	3.756	3.972	4.378	4.636	4.917	5.123
Official Rate	rf	4.937	I 4.913	4.481	3.962	4.181	3.949	4.164	4.147	3.966	3.853	3.837	4.316	4.592	4.789	4.983
															Index Numbers (1995=100):	
Nominal Effective Exchange Rate	ne c	....	....	....	....	....	....	....	....	....	815.55	832.69	907.36	988.99	1,069.23	1,167.29
Real Effective Exchange Rate	re c	....	....	....	....	....	....	....	....	....	....	266.29	295.23	308.88	324.01	353.01
Fund Position															*Millions of SDRs:*	
Quota	2f. s	130	130	130	130	130	130	130	130	285	285	428	428	428	623	623
SDRs	1b. s	14	28	42	42	43	43	43	46	46	76	76	119	140	102	113
Reserve Position in the Fund	1c. s	33	33	33	33	33	33	34	33	32	31	102	117	126	172	165
Total Fund Cred.&Loans Outstg.	2tl	—	—	—	—	—	—	—	—	—	—	—	—	—	—	—
International Liquidity											*Millions of US Dollars Unless Otherwise Indicated:*					
Total Reserves minus Gold	1l. d	148	299	285	912	1,454	1,128	1,765	1,684	1,981	2,659	3,773	3,695	2,422	1,880	1,464
SDRs	1b. d	14	30	45	50	52	50	50	56	60	100	97	138	154	107	111
Reserve Position in the Fund	1c. d	32	35	35	39	40	38	39	40	41	40	130	136	139	180	162
Foreign Exchange	1d. d	101	233	204	823	1,362	1,040	1,676	1,588	1,879	2,518	3,546	3,421	2,129	1,593	1,191
Gold (Million Fine Troy Ounces)	1ad	5.47	5.47	5.47	5.47	5.47	5.47	5.47	5.50	5.53	5.58	5.58	5.58	5.58	5.58	5.58
Gold (National Valuation)	1an d	191	208	208	231	234	224	222	234	252	257	249	227	216	205	192
Monetary Authorities: Other Assets	3..d	3	16	22	16	33	132	64	49	44	5	4	5	4	3	3
Other Liab.	4..d	71	222	114	99	152	55	60	52	60	76	108	54	51	49	47
Deposit Money Banks: Assets	7a. d	58	64	120	172	507	351	497	633	800	656	682	663	649	441	416
Liabilities	7b. d	23	24	168	800	996	1,353	1,433	1,756	2,609	2,972	2,953	2,423	2,001	2,089	2,983
Monetary Authorities															*Billions of Dinars:*	
Foreign Assets	11	1.70	2.39	2.35	4.76	7.03	6.25	8.95	8.03	8.85	11.05	16.06	17.24	12.03	10.24	8.51
Claims on Central Government	12a	3.63	4.39	2.97	.95	.45	.57	2.69	6.43	15.23	14.35	19.74	9.85	16.23	29.24	39.23
Claims on Deposit Money Banks	12e	.17	.91	3.09	4.75	6.29	7.65	8.78	8.52	7.33	11.54	11.78	22.63	27.04	22.20	26.88
Reserve Money	14	4.83	5.96	7.18	9.33	10.61	13.63	18.68	21.96	28.77	35.88	43.26	48.58	50.58	60.99	69.97
of which: Currency Outside DMBs	14a	4.74	5.70	7.05	8.82	10.45	12.74	17.24	20.57	27.37	35.40	42.34	48.06	49.16	60.02	67.46
Foreign Liabilities	16c	.35	1.03	.52	.41	.61	.23	.26	.21	.23	.29	.43	.24	.24	.24	.24
Central Government Deposits	16d	.31	.59	.49	.33	1.84	.56	.18	.12	.08	.09	.31	.10	.32	.54	.44
Other Items (Net)	17r	.02	.11	.22	.40	.71	.05	1.30	.69	2.34	.68	3.59	.79	4.18	-.08	3.97
Deposit Money Banks															*Billions of Dinars:*	
Reserves	20	.15	.16	.14	.51	.14	.89	.85	.98	1.34	.87	.70	.52	1.22	1.09	2.25
Foreign Assets	21	.28	.30	.55	.70	2.03	1.45	2.17	2.55	3.07	2.46	2.71	2.90	3.01	2.17	2.13
Claims on Central Government	22a	1.57	1.07	1.59	3.17	1.97	3.45	3.19	4.11	4.02	5.39	5.22	6.48	7.13	9.17	13.23
Claims on Nonfin.Pub.Enterprises	22c	....	....	....	....	....	....	....	....	....	....	....	....	....	....	....
Claims on Private Sector	22d	6.12	7.73	13.26	15.56	21.52	28.67	36.92	39.77	51.33	59.66	68.20	88.21	112.48	132.63	155.70
Demand Deposits	24	5.78	6.10	8.43	8.68	10.57	15.11	20.56	23.85	28.84	29.49	33.50	40.08	61.99	76.88	95.28
Time Deposits	25	1.45	.97	1.39	1.44	1.52	1.77	2.53	3.40	5.25	7.48	9.11	11.23	12.59	13.17	14.28
Foreign Liabilities	26c	.12	.11	.17	.46	1.28	.98	1.03	1.29	.65	.86	1.83	1.08	.84	.82	1.08
Long-Term Foreign Liabilities	26cl	—	—	.60	2.81	2.70	4.60	5.22	5.79	9.35	10.30	9.90	9.53	8.44	9.45	14.21
Central Government Deposits	26d	.04	.06	.11	.12	.19	.28	.11	.17	.31	.35	.24	.86	1.05	1.04	1.98
Central Govt. Lending Funds	26f	.61	.92	1.54	1.64	2.78	3.13	3.01	2.94	2.55	3.57	3.15	3.66	3.92	6.09	6.62
Credit from Monetary Authorities	26g	.17	.91	3.09	4.75	6.29	7.65	8.78	8.52	7.33	11.54	11.78	22.75	27.16	21.95	27.29
Other Items (Net)	27r	-.04	.18	.20	.04	.33	.94	1.89	1.45	5.47	4.79	7.32	8.91	7.86	15.67	12.57
Post Office: Checking Deposits	24.. i	.66	.92	1.11	1.33	1.96	2.56	2.87	3.46	5.28	6.60	7.83	8.57	12.28	14.07	15.95
Treasury: Checking Deposits	24.. r	.44	.23	.16	.09	1.26	1.56	.40	.67	.72	.73	.77	1.22	1.87	1.80	1.74
Monetary Survey															*Billions of Dinars:*	
Foreign Assets (Net)	31n	1.52	1.54	2.20	4.59	7.17	6.49	9.82	9.08	11.03	12.36	16.51	18.83	13.97	11.35	9.32
Domestic Credit	32	12.42	14.04	18.85	21.00	25.47	36.32	46.12	54.48	76.53	86.61	101.54	113.69	148.97	185.66	223.77
Claims on Central Govt. (Net)	32an	5.97	5.97	5.24	5.10	3.62	7.31	8.86	14.38	24.86	26.62	33.01	25.15	36.15	52.69	67.74
Claims on Nonfin.Pub.Enterprises	32c	....	....	....	....	....	....	....	....	....	....	....	....	....	....	....
Claims on Private Sector	32d	6.45	8.07	13.61	15.90	21.85	29.01	37.25	40.11	51.66	59.99	68.53	88.54	112.82	132.97	156.03
Money	34	11.62	12.95	16.75	18.93	24.25	31.98	41.08	48.55	62.21	72.21	84.43	97.92	125.30	152.76	180.43
Quasi-Money	35	1.45	.97	1.39	1.44	1.52	1.77	2.53	3.40	5.25	7.48	9.11	11.23	12.59	13.17	14.28
Long-Term Foreign Liabilities	36cl	—	—	.60	2.81	2.70	4.60	5.22	5.79	9.35	10.30	9.90	9.53	8.44	9.45	14.21
Central Govt. Lending Funds	36f	.61	.92	1.54	1.64	2.78	3.13	3.01	2.94	2.55	3.57	3.15	3.66	3.92	6.09	6.62
Other Items (Net)	37r	.25	.74	.78	.77	1.39	1.33	4.11	2.89	8.19	5.41	11.47	10.17	12.69	15.54	17.55
Money plus Quasi-Money	35l	13.08	13.93	18.14	20.36	25.77	33.75	43.60	51.95	67.46	79.69	93.54	109.15	137.89	165.93	194.72
Interest Rates															*Percent Per Annum*	
Discount Rate	60	....	....	....	....	2.75	2.75	2.75	2.75	2.75	2.75	2.75	2.75	2.75	2.75	2.75
Money Market Rate	60b	....	....	....	....	....	....	....	....	....	....	....	....	....	....	....
Treasury Bill Rate	60c	....	....	....	....	....	....	....	....	....	....	3.25	3.25	3.25	3.25	3.25
Deposit Rate	60l	....	....	....	....	....	....	....	....	....	....	3.00	3.00	3.00	3.00	3.00
Lending Rate	60p	....	....	....	....	....	....	....	....	....	....	....	....	....	....	....
Other Banking Institutions															*Billions of Dinars:*	
Deposits	45	.38	.66	.86	1.06	1.35	1.69	2.28	3.29	4.61	6.60	10.30	12.08	16.23	19.09	21.92
Liquid Liabilities	55l	13.45	14.59	19.00	21.42	27.12	35.44	45.88	55.24	72.07	86.29	103.84	121.24	154.12	185.02	216.63
Prices, Production, Labor															*Index Numbers (1995=100):*	
Consumer Prices	64	5.3	5.4	5.6	6.0	6.2	6.8	7.4	8.3	9.7	10.8	11.9	13.6	I 14.5	15.3	16.6
Crude Petroleum Production	66aa	132.2	99.7	137.3	140.4	133.5	123.5	140.7	143.7	155.3	145.9	123.4	105.6	90.6	88.3	83.6
															Number in Thousands:	
Employment	67e	....	....	....	....	....	....	....	....	....	....	....	....	....	....	....
Unemployment	67c	....	....	....	....	....	....	....	....	....	....	....	....	....	....	....
Unemployment Rate (%)	67r	....	....	....	....	....	....	....	....	....	....	....	....	....	....	....

1985	1986	1987	1988	1989	1990	1991	1992	1993	1994	1995	1996	1997	1998	1999		
End of Period															**Exchange Rates**	
5.243	5.900	7.003	9.058	10.556	17.343	30.600	31.324	33.134	62.617	77.558	80.793	78.815	84.979	95.135	Official Rate	aa
End of Period (ae) Period Average (rf)																
4.773	4.824	4.936	6.731	8.032	12.191	21.392	22.781	24.123	42.893	52.175	56.186	58.414	60.353	69.314	Official Rate	ae
5.028	4.702	4.850	5.915	7.609	8.958	18.473	21.836	23.345	35.059	47.663	54.749	57.707	58.739	66.574	Official Rate	rf
Period Averages																
1,224.46	1,052.51	907.87	754.30	647.09	512.68	255.36	206.72	214.77	151.51	100.00	88.92	94.55	95.33	87.02	Nominal Effective Exchange Rate	ne c
380.22	351.17	310.72	256.69	219.94	186.15	110.94	113.25	137.69	120.42	100.00	103.94	114.16	119.67	110.17	Real Effective Exchange Rate	re c
End of Period															**Fund Position**	
623	623	623	623	623	623	623	914	914	914	914	914	914	914	1,255	Quota	2f. s
126	137	143	2	3	2	1	1	5	16	1	3	1	1	1	SDRs	1b. s
153	148	108	—	—	—	—	—	—	—	—	—	—	—	85	Reserve Position in the Fund	1c. s
—	—	—	—	471	471	696	578	343	794	994	1,413	1,496	1,428	1,389	Total Fund Cred.&Loans Outstg.	2tl
End of Period															**International Liquidity**	
2,819	1,660	1,640	900	847	725	1,486	1,457	1,475	2,674	2,005	4,235	8,047	6,846	4,526	Total Reserves minus Gold	1l. d
138	167	202	2	4	3	2	1	7	23	1	5	1	2	2	SDRs	1b. d
168	181	153	—	—	—	—	—	—	—	—	—	—	—	117	Reserve Position in the Fund	1c. d
2,513	1,312	1,285	898	843	722	1,484	1,456	1,468	2,651	2,004	4,230	8,046	6,844	4,407	Foreign Exchange	1d. d
5.58	5.58	5.58	5.58	5.58	5.14	5.58	5.58	5.58	5.58	5.58	5.58	5.58	5.58	5.58	Gold (Million Fine Troy Ounces)	1ad
215	239	277	263	257	256	280	269	268	285	290	281	264	275	268	Gold (National Valuation)	1an d
3	3	3	2	2	1	1	13	12	1	4	3	9	....	....	Monetary Authorities: Other Assets	3.. d
51	53	52	38	32	85	152	120	464	466	363	291	414	387	364	Other Liab.	4.. d
382	376	253	569	679	741	1,085	914	683	1,046	638	576	396	456	402	Deposit Money Banks: Assets	7a. d
5,092	7,203	8,305	8,208	7,728	7,941	7,837	7,010	5,201	4,200	2,749	2,088	1,216	1,068	1,015	Liabilities	7b. d
End of Period															**Monetary Authorities**	
14.54	9.19	9.45	7.17	7.89	10.43	35.52	Ɪ36.69	38.66	120.39	111.71	252.88	485.04	423.47	329.89	Foreign Assets	11
42.16	65.86	82.41	104.35	110.40	98.85	100.57	Ɪ162.76	273.80	255.57	243.40	180.87	177.67	174.59	163.48	Claims on Central Government	12a
22.05	23.24	18.17	16.90	30.74	65.70	108.40	Ɪ78.31	29.39	50.45	188.59	255.13	219.06	226.25	310.80	Claims on Deposit Money Banks	12e
78.72	91.06	102.36	111.49	124.97	137.92	160.28	Ɪ196.28	250.41	237.22	255.17	305.91	356.63	403.47	449.46	Reserve Money	14
76.64	89.36	96.87	109.76	119.87	135.26	157.20	Ɪ184.85	211.31	222.99	249.77	290.88	337.62	390.78	440.26	*of which: Currency Outside DMBs*	14a
.25	.25	.26	.26	5.23	9.21	24.54	Ɪ20.84	22.55	69.68	96.06	130.45	142.06	144.70	157.34	Foreign Liabilities	16c
.44	.15	.44	3.89	1.72	5.36	5.97	Ɪ2.31	2.94	9.25	9.80	4.41	21.93	75.32	4.46	Central Government Deposits	16d
-.65	6.82	6.96	12.78	17.11	22.49	53.71	Ɪ58.32	65.96	110.26	182.67	248.11	361.15	200.82	192.89	Other Items (Net)	17r
End of Period															**Deposit Money Banks**	
2.32	1.61	5.66	3.54	4.57	4.04	4.97	5.86	37.89	7.32	5.58	12.79	18.77	15.85	13.37	Reserves	20
1.83	1.81	1.25	3.83	5.45	9.03	23.22	20.82	16.47	44.88	33.30	32.38	23.11	27.50	27.89	Foreign Assets	21
16.82	19.71	20.27	21.12	21.57	44.83	32.14	28.33	300.52	204.63	155.64	141.43	273.15	410.39	459.49	Claims on Central Government	22a
....	....	....	....	....	....	....	....	....	142.04	208.00	461.00	637.71	632.59	760.48	Claims on Nonfin.Pub.Enterprises	22c
174.53	176.84	180.53	191.91	209.30	246.98	325.85	Ɪ76.00	77.12	96.75	103.47	137.85	108.56	128.86	173.89	Claims on Private Sector	22d
104.62	95.94	103.80	115.53	101.89	105.55	133.11	140.84	188.93	196.45	210.78	234.03	254.83	334.52	352.71	Demand Deposits	24
21.63	22.20	33.99	40.76	58.13	72.92	90.28	152.02	198.83	247.68	280.46	325.96	409.95	474.19	578.57	Time Deposits	25
1.23	1.43	1.30	1.46	1.59	3.71	9.89	14.00	12.94	35.14	22.58	20.79	15.71	25.48	30.87	Foreign Liabilities	26c
23.07	33.32	39.70	53.79	60.48	93.09	157.77	145.70	112.52	145.02	120.88	96.51	55.30	39.00	39.46	Long-Term Foreign Liabilities	26cl
2.87	3.85	2.29	1.26	1.29	.87	2.46	5.88	90.19	38.82	44.53	97.53	84.36	55.74	56.66	Central Government Deposits	26d
8.35	9.60	10.31	11.25	12.82	13.56	11.64	14.00	13.19	13.61	13.79	12.30	12.90	13.69	13.22	Central Govt. Lending Funds	26f
23.32	22.43	13.50	10.49	30.74	66.33	108.56	Ɪ78.66	29.39	50.69	190.29	259.13	219.06	226.25	310.80	Credit from Monetary Authorities	26g
10.39	11.21	2.82	-14.14	-26.05	-51.16	-127.53	Ɪ-88.01	-71.95	-165.83	-124.31	-84.09	4.07	15.58	52.82	Other Items (Net)	27r
18.32	18.31	22.25	25.88	26.96	27.16	31.95	39.83	40.98	48.50	53.74	57.96	71.68	81.05	87.34	Post Office: Checking Deposits	24.. i
2.65	1.21	.99	1.04	1.30	2.43	2.21	4.20	5.68	7.89	4.82	6.22	7.43	7.33	9.38	Treasury: Checking Deposits	24.. r
End of Period															**Monetary Survey**	
14.89	9.32	9.15	9.28	6.52	6.54	24.31	Ɪ22.67	19.65	60.45	26.37	134.02	350.38	280.79	169.57	Foreign Assets (Net)	31n
251.25	278.01	303.80	339.24	366.59	414.02	484.29	Ɪ639.24	748.09	774.38	968.93	1,061.39	1,164.93	1,273.45	1,593.76	Domestic Credit	32
76.63	101.09	123.19	147.25	157.21	167.04	158.44	Ɪ226.93	527.84	468.54	403.29	284.55	423.65	542.30	658.66	Claims on Central Govt. (Net)	32an
....	....	....	....	....	....	....	332.07	142.04	208.00	461.00	637.71	632.59	601.86	760.48	Claims on Nonfin.Pub.Enterprises	32c
174.61	176.92	180.61	191.99	209.39	246.98	325.85	Ɪ76.05	77.16	96.79	103.50	137.88	108.63	129.18	174.48	Claims on Private Sector	32d
202.23	204.82	223.91	252.21	250.01	270.40	324.47	Ɪ377.24	450.32	485.65	520.29	589.99	675.96	817.26	889.78	Money	34
21.63	22.20	33.99	40.76	58.13	72.92	90.28	152.02	198.83	247.68	280.46	325.96	409.95	474.19	578.57	Quasi-Money	35
23.07	33.32	39.70	53.79	60.48	93.09	157.77	145.70	112.52	145.02	120.88	96.51	55.30	39.00	39.46	Long-Term Foreign Liabilities	36cl
8.35	9.60	10.31	11.25	12.82	13.56	11.64	14.00	13.19	13.61	13.79	12.30	12.90	13.69	13.22	Central Govt. Lending Funds	36f
10.86	17.40	5.04	-9.49	-8.33	-29.42	-75.55	Ɪ-27.04	-7.12	-57.13	59.89	170.65	361.21	210.10	242.26	Other Items (Net)	37r
223.86	227.02	257.90	292.97	308.15	343.32	414.75	Ɪ529.26	649.15	733.33	800.74	915.95	1,085.91	1,291.46	1,468.36	Money plus Quasi-Money	35l
Percent Per Annum															**Interest Rates**	
2.75	5.00	5.00	5.00	7.00	10.50	11.50	11.50	11.50	21.00	....	13.00	11.00	9.50	8.50	Discount Rate	60
....	....	....	....	....	....	....	....	....	19.80	....	18.50	11.80	10.40	10.40	Money Market Rate	60b
3.25	3.25	3.25	3.25	3.25	3.25	9.50	9.50	9.50	16.50	....	....	....	9.96	10.05	Treasury Bill Rate	60c
3.00	4.00	4.00	4.00	8.00	8.00	8.00	8.00	8.00	12.00	....	17.00	9.50	8.50	8.50	Deposit Rate	60l
....	....	....	....	....	....	....	....	....	16.00	....	21.00	12.50	12.00	11.00	Lending Rate	60p
End of Period															**Other Banking Institutions**	
25.60	30.67	37.99	46.18	58.11	65.07	....	....	....	....	....	....	....	....	....	Deposits	45
249.46	257.68	295.89	339.15	366.26	408.39	....	....	....	....	....	....	....	....	....	Liquid Liabilities	55l
Period Averages															**Prices, Production, Labor**	
18.3	20.6	22.1	23.4	25.6	Ɪ29.9	37.6	49.5	59.7	77.1	100.0	118.7	125.5	131.7	134.9	Consumer Prices	64
82.5	78.5	83.0	83.7	90.8	100.0	104.9	103.1	99.3	96.7	100.0	106.4	110.7	106.6	100.9	Crude Petroleum Production	66aa
Period Averages																
3,884	....	....	....	4,432	4,156	4,538	4,596	....	....	4,928	5,389	5,708	....	....	Employment	67e
....	....	....	....	946	1,156	1,261	1,482	1,519	1,660	2,105	....	2,311	....	....	Unemployment	67c
....	....	....	....	17.0	19.7	21.1	23.8	23.1	24.4	27.9	....	28.7	....	....	Unemployment Rate (%)	67r

Algeria

	1970	1971	1972	1973	1974	1975	1976	1977	1978	1979	1980	1981	1982	1983	1984
International Transactions														*Millions of Dinars*	
Petroleum 70a	3,360	3,016	4,614	6,030	17,838	16,963	19,950	23,064	23,224	33,700	48,532	56,041	....	45,334	45,793
Crude Petroleum 70aa	3,287	2,972	4,565	5,648	16,953	15,885	18,992	22,457	21,518	30,794	40,980	44,302	26,562	32,281	31,780
Refined Petroleum 70ab	73	44	49	382	885	1,078	958	607	1,706	2,906	7,552	11,739	22,896	13,053	14,013
Imports, c.i.f., from DOTS 71y	....	....	....	....	....	....	....	....	....	....	....	48,636	49,311	49,782	52,235
Volume of Exports														*1995=100*	
Petroleum 72a	158	121	162	163	152	150	163	170	181	180	155	145	139	....	....
Crude Petroleum 72aa	292	225	299	289	271	263	290	309	316	315	244	209	138	88	84
Refined Petroleum 72ab	4	2	4	18	17	20	17	10	27	24	53	72	139		
Export Prices														*1995=100:*	
Crude Petroleum .... 76aa *d*	10.6	12.6	15.9	23.9	68.5	68.0	74.6	81.8	80.4	119.5	211.3	225.2	203.8	179.5	173.5
Balance of Payments														*Millions of US Dollars:*	
Current Account, n.i.e. .... 78al *d*	....	....	....	....	....	....	....	−2,325	−3,540	−1,632	249	90	−183	−85	74
Goods: Exports f.o.b. .... 78aa *d*	....	....	....	....	....	....	....	6,009	6,340	9,484	13,652	14,117	13,509	12,742	12,792
Goods: Imports f.o.b. .... 78ab *d*	....	....	....	....	....	....	....	−6,213	−7,316	−7,820	−9,614	−10,105	−9,916	−9,543	−9,245
Trade Balance .... 78ac *d*	....	....	....	....	....	....	....	−204	−976	1,664	4,037	4,012	3,594	3,199	3,547
Services: Credit .... 78ad *d*	....	....	....	....	....	....	....	288	326	468	476	474	528	679	599
Services: Debit .... 78ae *d*	....	....	....	....	....	....	....	−1,520	−1,939	−2,379	−2,697	−2,705	−2,644	−2,410	−2,573
Balance on Goods & Services .... 78af *d*	....	....	....	....	....	....	....	−1,436	−2,589	−247	1,817	1,781	1,477	1,469	1,573
Income: Credit .... 78ag *d*	....	....	....	....	....	....	....	87	69	156	372	481	328	186	179
Income: Debit .... 78ah *d*	....	....	....	....	....	....	....	−1,258	−1,335	−1,863	−2,241	−2,482	−2,318	−1,978	−1,858
Balance on Gds, Serv. & Inc. .... 78ai *d*	....	....	....	....	....	....	....	−2,607	−3,855	−1,953	−52	−219	−512	−323	−106
Current Transfers, n.i.e.: Credit .... 78aj *d*	....	....	....	....	....	....	....	391	451	474	512	513	529	414	350
Current Transfers: Debit .... 78ak *d*	....	....	....	....	....	....	....	−110	−136	−153	−211	−204	−200	−176	−169
Capital Account, n.i.e. .... 78bc *d*	....	....	....	....	....	....	....	—	—	—	—	—	—	—	—
Capital Account, n.i.e.: Credit .... 78ba *d*	....	....	....	....	....	....	....	—	—	—	—	—	—	—	—
Capital Account: Debit .... 78bb *d*	....	....	....	....	....	....	....	—	—	—	—	—	—	—	—
Financial Account, n.i.e. .... 78bj *d*	....	....	....	....	....	....	....	2,038	3,469	2,523	955	16	−799	−529	−211
Direct Investment Abroad .... 78bd *d*	....	....	....	....	....	....	....	−6	—	−16	−34	−15	−11	−15	−15
Dir. Invest. in Rep. Econ., n.i.e. .... 78be *d*	....	....	....	....	....	....	....	178	135	26	349	13	−54	—	1
Portfolio Investment Assets .... 78bf *d*	....	....	....	....	....	....	....	—	—	—	—	—	—	2	—
Equity Securities .... 78bk *d*	....	....	....	....	....	....	....	—	—	—	—	—	—	2	—
Debt Securities .... 78bl *d*	....	....	....	....	....	....	....	—	—	—	—	—	—	—	—
Portfolio Investment Liab., n.i.e. .... 78bg *d*	....	....	....	....	....	....	....	—	—	1	—	—	−3	—	—
Equity Securities .... 78bm *d*	....	....	....	....	....	....	....	—	—	1	—	—	−3	—	—
Debt Securities .... 78bn *d*	....	....	....	....	....	....	....	—	—	—	—	—	—	—	—
Financial Derivatives Assets .... 78bw *d*	....	....	....	....	....	....	....	....	....	....	....	....	....	....	....
Financial Derivatives Liabilities .... 78bx *d*	....	....	....	....	....	....	....	....	....	....	....	....	....	....	....
Other Investment Assets .... 78bh *d*	....	....	....	....	....	....	....	−114	−299	−193	−122	−158	−196	2	49
Monetary Authorities .... 78bo *d*	....	....	....	....	....	....	....	—	—	—	—	—	—	—	—
General Government .... 78bp *d*	....	....	....	....	....	....	....	−212	−118	−126	−34	−132	−250	−224	−67
Banks .... 78bq *d*	....	....	....	....	....	....	....	98	−161	−79	−88	−26	54	226	116
Other Sectors .... 78br *d*	....	....	....	....	....	....	....	—	−20	12	1	—	—	—	—
Other Investment Liab., n.i.e. .... 78bi *d*	....	....	....	....	....	....	....	1,979	3,633	2,705	762	176	−535	−519	−246
Monetary Authorities .... 78bs *d*	....	....	....	....	....	....	....	36	13	28	−23	−93	21	8	−10
General Government .... 78bt *d*	....	....	....	....	....	....	....	68	54	85	−10	−51	−32	−32	−27
Banks .... 78bu *d*	....	....	....	....	....	....	....	247	822	363	74	142	117	20	11
Other Sectors .... 78bv *d*	....	....	....	....	....	....	....	1,628	2,744	2,229	721	178	−640	−514	−220
Net Errors and Omissions .... 78ca *d*	....	....	....	....	....	....	....	−41	143	−407	137	14	−88	193	−197
Overall Balance .... 78cb *d*	....	....	....	....	....	....	....	−328	73	484	1,341	120	−1,070	−421	−333
Reserves and Related Items .... 79da *d*	....	....	....	....	....	....	....	328	−73	−484	−1,341	−120	1,070	421	333
Reserve Assets .... 79db *d*	....	....	....	....	....	....	....	328	−73	−484	−1,341	−120	1,070	421	333
Use of Fund Credit and Loans .... 79dc *d*	....	....	....	....	....	....	....	—	—	—	—	—	—	—	—
Exceptional Financing .... 79de *d*	....	....	....	....	....	....	....	—	—	—	—	—	—	—	—
Government Finance														*Millions of Dinars:*	
Deficit (-) or Surplus 80	−1,989	−1,753	−917	−3,133	2,034	....	....	....	....	....	....	....	....	....	....
Revenue 81	6,704	7,086	9,358	10,925	23,752	....	....	....	....	....	....	....	....	....	....
Expenditure 82	6,014	6,796	7,729	9,913	12,495	....	....	....	....	....	....	....	....	....	....
Lending Minus Repayments 83	2,680	2,043	2,545	4,144	9,223	....	....	....	....	....	....	....	....	....	....
Financing															
Net Borrowing: Domestic 84a	2,420	2,097	1,001	3,181	−1,597	....	....	....	....	....	....	....	....	....	....
Foreign 85a	−431	−348	−49	14	30	....	....	....	....	....	....	....	....	....	....
Use of Cash Balances 87	—	5	−35	−63	−466	....	....	....	....	....	....	....	....	....	....
National Accounts														*Billions of Dinars:*	
Exports of Goods & Services 90c	5.4	4.7	6.9	8.1	21.4	20.7	24.4	26.6	26.7	39.9	55.8	66.2	64.2	65.3	67.7
Government Consumption 91f	4.0	4.3	4.6	5.0	5.9	8.0	9.2	11.6	14.6	17.5	22.4	26.4	30.7	34.7	39.5
Gross Fixed Capital Formation 93e	7.6	8.6	10.3	13.3	17.0	24.0	31.4	38.4	50.8	50.4	54.9	63.0	71.5	80.3	87.5
Increase/Decrease(-) in Stocks 93i	.7	−.1	.8	1.0	5.1	3.9	.6	2.4	3.8	4.1	8.6	7.8	5.9	7.5	5.0
Private Consumption 96f	12.2	12.8	14.1	17.3	25.7	31.5	35.9	44.6	50.9	58.5	70.2	87.2	95.6	106.2	125.8
Imports of Goods & Services 98c	−7.0	−6.9	−9.2	−12.6	−19.6	−26.4	−27.4	−36.3	−42.0	−42.1	−49.3	−59.1	−60.2	−60.3	−61.6
Gross Domestic Product (GDP) 99b	22.9	23.5	27.4	32.1	55.6	61.6	74.1	87.2	104.8	128.2	162.5	191.5	207.6	233.8	263.9
GDP Volume 1974 Prices .... 99b. *p*	....	....	....	48.1	48.5	53.5	58.3	62.7	....	....	....	....	....	....	....
														Millions:	
Population 99z	14.33	14.77	15.27	15.77	16.28	16.78	17.30	17.91	I 17.58	18.19	18.67	19.25	19.86	20.52	21.25

1985	1986	1987	1988	1989	1990	1991	1992	1993	1994	1995	1996	1997	1998	1999		
Millions of Dinars															**International Transactions**	
....	....	....	....	....	....	....	....	....	....	....	....	....	....	....	Petroleum	70a
....	....	....	....	....	....	....	....	....	....	....	....	....	....	....	Crude Petroleum	70aa
....	....	....	....	....	....	....	....	....	....	....	....	....	....	....	Refined Petroleum	70ab
49,491	43,393	34,153	43,765	69,903	86,708	141,932	188,835	204,533	335,522	481,339	498,523	504,982	579,463	651,942	Imports, c.i.f., from DOTS	71y
1995=100															Volume of Exports	
....	....	....	90	90	97	93	94	97	98	100	104	....	....	....	Petroleum	72a
83	78	83	71	84	90	90	84	96	99	100	112	....	....	....	Crude Petroleum	72aa
....	....	....	113	98	105	98	105	98	97	100	95	....	....	....	Refined Petroleum	72ab
Index of Prices in US Dollars															Export Prices	
173.5	....	....	92.1	105.2	138.2	116.3	116.9	98.4	91.8	100.0	121.7	....	....	....	Crude Petroleum	76aa *d*
Minus Sign Indicates Debit															Balance of Payments	
1,015	−2,230	141	−2,040	−1,081	1,420	2,367	....	....	....	....	....	....	....	....	Current Account, n.i.e.	78al *d*
13,034	8,065	9,029	7,620	9,534	12,965	12,330	....	....	....	....	....	....	....	....	Goods: Exports f.o.b.	78aa *d*
−8,820	−7,896	−6,630	−6,685	−8,390	−8,786	−6,862	....	....	....	....	....	....	....	....	Goods: Imports f.o.b.	78ab *d*
4,214	169	2,398	935	1,144	4,179	5,468	....	....	....	....	....	....	....	....	*Trade Balance*	78ac *d*
531	549	565	470	496	497	393	....	....	....	....	....	....	....	....	Services: Credit	78ad *d*
−2,565	−2,019	−1,441	−1,337	−1,214	−1,321	−1,163	....	....	....	....	....	....	....	....	Services: Debit	78ae *d*
2,180	−1,301	1,523	68	425	3,355	4,698	....	....	....	....	....	....	....	....	*Balance on Goods & Services*	78af *d*
191	172	110	71	111	73	70	....	....	....	....	....	....	....	....	Income: Credit	78ag *d*
−1,735	−1,865	−2,009	−2,570	−2,157	−2,341	−2,618	....	....	....	....	....	....	....	....	Income: Debit	78ah *d*
636	−2,994	−376	−2,430	−1,622	1,087	2,151	....	....	....	....	....	....	....	....	*Balance on Gds, Serv. & Inc.*	78ai *d*
529	917	628	477	603	400	269	....	....	....	....	....	....	....	....	Current Transfers, n.i.e.: Credit	78aj *d*
−151	−153	−111	−86	−62	−67	−53	....	....	....	....	....	....	....	....	Current Transfers: Debit	78ak *d*
—	—	—	—	—	—	—	....	....	....	....	....	....	....	....	Capital Account, n.i.e.	78bc *d*
—	—	—	—	—	—	—	....	....	....	....	....	....	....	....	Capital Account, n.i.e.: Credit	78ba *d*
—	—	—	—	—	—	—	....	....	....	....	....	....	....	....	Capital Account: Debit	78bb *d*
−121	590	309	744	755	−1,094	−1,020	....	....	....	....	....	....	....	....	Financial Account, n.i.e.	78bj *d*
−2	5	−15	−5	−8	−5	−50	....	....	....	....	....	....	....	....	Direct Investment Abroad	78bd *d*
—	5	4	13	12	—	12	....	....	....	....	....	....	....	....	Dir. Invest. in Rep. Econ., n.i.e.	78be *d*
—	—	—	2	—	—	—	....	....	....	....	....	....	....	....	Portfolio Investment Assets	78bf *d*
—	—	—	—	—	—	—	....	....	....	....	....	....	....	....	Equity Securities	78bk *d*
—	—	—	2	—	—	—	....	....	....	....	....	....	....	....	Debt Securities	78bl *d*
—	—	—	—	—	—	—	....	....	....	....	....	....	....	....	Portfolio Investment Liab., n.i.e.	78bg *d*
—	—	—	—	—	—	—	....	....	....	....	....	....	....	....	Equity Securities	78bm *d*
—	—	—	—	—	—	—	....	....	....	....	....	....	....	....	Debt Securities	78bn *d*
....	....	....	....	....	....	....	....	....	....	....	....	....	....	....	Financial Derivatives Assets	78bw *d*
....	....	....	....	....	....	....	....	....	....	....	....	....	....	....	Financial Derivatives Liabilities	78bx *d*
−285	−23	73	−131	−97	−229	−145	....	....	....	....	....	....	....	....	Other Investment Assets	78bh *d*
....	....	....	....	....	....	....	....	....	....	....	....	....	....	....	Monetary Authorities	78bo *d*
−85	−74	−122	−45	−14	−4	−37	....	....	....	....	....	....	....	....	General Government	78bp *d*
−199	52	195	−86	−83	−226	−108	....	....	....	....	....	....	....	....	Banks	78bq *d*
															Other Sectors	78br *d*
166	602	248	865	848	−860	−837	....	....	....	....	....	....	....	....	Other Investment Liab., n.i.e.	78bi *d*
11	24	8	7	−6	—	−3	....	....	....	....	....	....	....	....	Monetary Authorities	78bs *d*
20	132	64	240	−51	215	286	....	....	....	....	....	....	....	....	General Government	78bt *d*
8	32	18	8	138	162	90	....	....	....	....	....	....	....	....	Banks	78bu *d*
126	413	158	609	767	−1,237	−1,210	....	....	....	....	....	....	....	....	Other Sectors	78bv *d*
127	142	−802	337	−448	−336	−299	....	....	....	....	....	....	....	....	Net Errors and Omissions	78ca *d*
1,020	−1,498	−352	−959	−774	−10	1,047	....	....	....	....	....	....	....	....	*Overall Balance*	78cb *d*
−1,020	1,498	352	959	774	10	−1,047	....	....	....	....	....	....	....	....	Reserves and Related Items	79da *d*
−1,020	1,498	352	757	121	−138	−1,356	....	....	....	....	....	....	....	....	Reserve Assets	79db *d*
—	—	—	—	584	—	308	....	....	....	....	....	....	....	....	Use of Fund Credit and Loans	79dc *d*
—	—	—	201	69	148	—	....	....	....	....	....	....	....	....	Exceptional Financing	79de *d*
Year Ending December 31															**Government Finance**	
....	....	....	....	....	....	....	....	ℐ−60,354	−28,243	75,258		....	....	....	Deficit (-) or Surplus	80
....	....	....	....	....	....	....	....	ℐ439,199	600,847	825,157		....	....	....	Revenue	81
....	....	....	....	....	....	....	....	ℐ493,626	625,965	749,009		....	....	....	Expenditure	82
....	....	....	....	....	....	....	....		5,927	3,125	890	....	....	....	Lending Minus Repayments	83
															Financing	
....	....	....	....	....	....	....	....		−72,763	−105,101	−162,269	....	....	....	Net Borrowing: Domestic	84a
....	....	....	....	....	....	....	....		141,376	172,158	100,937	....	....	....	Foreign	85a
....	....	....	....	....	....	....	....		−8,259	−38,814	−13,926	....	....	....	Use of Cash Balances	87
Billions of Dinars															**National Accounts**	
68.6	38.7	45.8	ℐ48.9	76.2	135.2	249.3	283.6	261.6	341.9	539.8	791.1	....	....	....	Exports of Goods & Services	90c
45.8	52.9	58.0	ℐ60.0	63.2	82.9	121.4	160.2	198.8	247.1	309.8	....	....	....	....	Government Consumption	91f
92.8	101.3	92.9	ℐ97.3	121.8	135.8	223.9	271.7	300.5	407.5	580.0	690.6	....	....	....	Gross Fixed Capital Formation	93e
4.0	−2.0	1.0	ℐ1.0	5.2	15.2	22.4	−2.0	−9.3	41.7	54.9	....	....	....	....	Increase/Decrease(-) in Stocks	93i
139.7	156.4	154.9	ℐ158.8	195.5	321.2	421.0	561.9	636.4	825.6	1,089.9	....	....	....	....	Private Consumption	96f
−59.5	−50.8	−40.0	ℐ−46.0	−70.1	−134.6	−194.3	−230.3	−255.9	−424.5	−612.7	−614.7	....	....	....	Imports of Goods & Services	98c
291.6	296.6	312.7	ℐ320.0	391.8	555.7	843.7	1,045.1	1,162.1	1,356.5	1,809.2	2,064.5	....	....	....	Gross Domestic Product (GDP)	99b
....	....	....	....	....	....	....	....	....	....	....	....	....	....	....	GDP Volume 1974 Prices	99b. *p*
Midyear Estimates																
21.85	22.52	23.02	23.73	24.33	25.02	25.64	26.27	26.89	27.50	28.06	28.57	29.05	29.80	30.77	**Population**	99z

(See notes in the back of the book.)

Angola

		1970	1971	1972	1973	1974	1975	1976	1977	1978	1979	1980	1981	1982	1983	1984
Exchange Rates											*Readjusted Kwanzas per Thousand SDRs through 1994,*					
Official Rate	aa	29	30	29	31	30	32	35	36	39	39	38	35	33	31	29
											Readjusted Kwanzas per Thousand US Dollars through 1994,					
Official Rate	ae	29	28	27	26	25	27	30	30	30	30	30	30	30	30	30
Official Rate	rf	29	28	27	25	25	26	29	30	30	30	30	30	30	30	30
Fund Position															*Millions of SDRs:*		
Quota	2f. s	—	—	—	—	—	—	—	—	—	—	—	—	—	—	—
SDRs	1b. s	....	....	....	....	....	....	....	....	....	....	....	....	....	....	....
Reserve Position in the Fund	1c. s	....	....	....	....	....	....	....	....	....	....	....	....	....	....	....
Total Fund Cred.&Loans Outstg.	2tl	....	....	....	....	....	....	....	....	....	....	....	....	....	....	....
International Liquidity										*Millions of US Dollars Unless Otherwise Indicated:*						
Total Reserves minus Gold	1l. d	....	....	....	....	....	....	....	....	....	....	....	....	....	....	....
SDRs	1b. d	....	....	....	....	....	....	....	....	....	....	....	....	....	....	....
Reserve Position in the Fund	1c. d	....	....	....	....	....	....	....	....	....	....	....	....	....	....	....
Foreign Exchange	1d. d	....	....	....	....	....	....	....	....	....	....	....	....	....	....	....
Monetary Authorities: Other Assets	3.. d	....	....	....	....	....	....	....	....	....	....	....	....	....	....	....
Other Liab.	4.. d	....	....	....	....	....	....	....	....	....	....	....	....	....	....	....
Banking Institutions: Assets	7a. d	....	....	....	....	....	....	....	....	....	....	....	....	....	....	....
Liabilities	7b. d	....	....	....	....	....	....	....	....	....	....	....	....	....	....	....
Monetary Authorities														*Trillions of Readjusted Kwanzas:*		
Foreign Assets	11	....	....	....	....	....	....	....	....	....	....	....	....	....	....	....
Claims on Central Government	12a	....	....	....	....	....	....	....	....	....	....	....	....	....	....	....
Claims on Nonfin.Pub.Enterprises	12c	....	....	....	....	....	....	....	....	....	....	....	....	....	....	....
Claims on Banking Institutions	12e	....	....	....	....	....	....	....	....	....	....	....	....	....	....	....
Reserve Money	14	....	....	....	....	....	....	....	....	....	....	....	....	....	....	....
of which: Currency Outside Banks	14a	....	....	....	....	....	....	....	....	....	....	....	....	....	....	....
Time & Foreign Currency Deposits	15	....	....	....	....	....	....	....	....	....	....	....	....	....	....	....
Foreign Liabilities	16c	....	....	....	....	....	....	....	....	....	....	....	....	....	....	....
Central Government Deposits	16d	....	....	....	....	....	....	....	....	....	....	....	....	....	....	....
Capital Accounts	17a	....	....	....	....	....	....	....	....	....	....	....	....	....	....	....
Other Items (Net)	17r	....	....	....	....	....	....	....	....	....	....	....	....	....	....	....
Banking Institutions														*Trillions of Readjusted Kwanzas:*		
Reserves	20	....	....	....	....	....	....	....	....	....	....	....	....	....	....	....
Foreign Assets	21	....	....	....	....	....	....	....	....	....	....	....	....	....	....	....
Claims on Central Government	22a	....	....	....	....	....	....	....	....	....	....	....	....	....	....	....
Claims on Private Sector	22d	....	....	....	....	....	....	....	....	....	....	....	....	....	....	....
Demand Deposits	24	....	....	....	....	....	....	....	....	....	....	....	....	....	....	....
Time, Savings,& Fgn.Currency Dep.	25	....	....	....	....	....	....	....	....	....	....	....	....	....	....	....
Foreign Liabilities	26c	....	....	....	....	....	....	....	....	....	....	....	....	....	....	....
Central Government Deposits	26d	....	....	....	....	....	....	....	....	....	....	....	....	....	....	....
Credit from Monetary Authorities	26g	....	....	....	....	....	....	....	....	....	....	....	....	....	....	....
Capital Accounts	27a	....	....	....	....	....	....	....	....	....	....	....	....	....	....	....
Other Items (Net)	27r	....	....	....	....	....	....	....	....	....	....	....	....	....	....	....
Banking Survey														*Trillions of Readjusted Kwanzas:*		
Foreign Assets (Net)	31n	....	....	....	....	....	....	....	....	....	....	....	....	....	....	....
Domestic Credit	32	....	....	....	....	....	....	....	....	....	....	....	....	....	....	....
Claims on Central Govt.(Net)	32an	....	....	....	....	....	....	....	....	....	....	....	....	....	....	....
Claims on Nonfin.Pub.Enterprises	32c	....	....	....	....	....	....	....	....	....	....	....	....	....	....	....
Claims on Private Sector	32d	....	....	....	....	....	....	....	....	....	....	....	....	....	....	....
Money	34	....	....	....	....	....	....	....	....	....	....	....	....	....	....	....
Quasi-Money	35	....	....	....	....	....	....	....	....	....	....	....	....	....	....	....
Capital Accounts	37a	....	....	....	....	....	....	....	....	....	....	....	....	....	....	....
Other Items (Net)	37r	....	....	....	....	....	....	....	....	....	....	....	....	....	....	....
Money plus Quasi-Money	35l	....	....	....	....	....	....	....	....	....	....	....	....	....	....	....
Interest Rates														*Percent Per Annum*		
Discount Rate *(End of Period)*	60	....	....	....	....	....	....	....	....	....	....	....	....	....	....	....
Deposit Rate	60l	....	....	....	....	....	....	....	....	....	....	....	....	....	....	....
Lending Rate	60p	....	....	....	....	....	....	....	....	....	....	....	....	....	....	....
Prices														*Index Numbers (1995=100):*		
Consumer Prices (1995=1 million)	64.a	....	....	....	....	....	....	....	....	....	....	....	....	....	....	....
Consumer Prices	64	....	....	....	....	....	....	....	....	....	....	....	....	....	....	....
International Transactions														*Millions of US Dollars*		
Exports	70.. d	....	....	....	....	....	....	....	....	....	....	....	....	....	....	....
Imports, c.i.f.	71.. d	....	....	....	....	....	....	....	....	....	....	....	....	....	....	....
															Millions:		
Population	99z	5.59	5.70	5.80	5.97	6.11	6.52	6.75	7.00	7.25	7.49	7.72	7.94	8.14	7.57	7.77

1985	1986	1987	1988	1989	1990	1991	1992	1993	1994	1995	1996	1997	1998	1999		
															Exchange Rates	
per SDR Thereafter: End of Period																
33	37	42	40	39	43	257	756	8,928	743,446	‡8,461	290,459	354,011	980,693	7,658,496	Official Rate	aa
per US Dollar Thereafter: End of Period (ae) Period Average (rf)																
30	30	30	30	30	30	180	550	6,500	509,262	‡5,692	201,994	262,376	696,500	5,579,920	Official Rate	ae
30	30	30	30	30	30	55	251	2,660	59,515	‡2,750	128,029	229,040	392,824	2,790,706	Official Rate	rf
End of Period															**Fund Position**	
—	—	—	—	145.00	145.00	145.00	207.30	207.30	207.30	207.30	207.30	207.30	207.30	286.30	Quota	2f. s
....	....	....	—		.08	.09	.09	.10	.10	.11	.11	.12	.12	.13	SDRs	1b. s
....	....	....	—	—	—	—	—	—	—	—	—	—	—	—	Reserve Position in the Fund	1c. s
....	....	....	—	—	—	—	—	—	—	—	—	—	—	—	Total Fund Cred.&Loans Outstg.	2tl
End of Period															**International Liquidity**	
....	....	....	....							212.83	551.62	396.43	203.46	496.10	Total Reserves minus Gold	1l. d
			—		.11	.13	.12	.14	.15	.16	.16	.16	.17	.18	SDRs	1b. d
....	....	....	....												Reserve Position in the Fund	1c. d
....	....	....	....							212.67	551.46	396.27	203.29	495.93	Foreign Exchange	1d. d
....	....	....	....							143.95	6.86	.01	—	—	Monetary Authorities: Other Assets	3.. d
....	....	....	....							1,901.59	348.01	329.78	444.98	195.59	Other Liab.	4.. d
....	....	....	....							264.62	523.49	833.30	682.25	649.04	Banking Institutions: Assets	7a. d
....	....	....	....							69.68	61.07	137.31	199.46	159.68	Liabilities	7b. d
End of Period															**Monetary Authorities**	
....	....	....	....							2.10	112.81	104.02	141.71	2,768.22	Foreign Assets	11
....	....	....	....							4.31	36.23	82.33	330.17	612.82	Claims on Central Government	12a
....	....	....	....							2.91	2.52	3.72	2.53	32.42	Claims on Nonfin.Pub.Enterprises	12c
....	....	....	....							—	—	48.75	61.55	81.72	Claims on Banking Institutions	12e
....	....	....	....							2.57	89.90	172.86	258.63	1,351.72	Reserve Money	14
....	....	....	....							1.24	42.17	101.62	165.69	650.45	*of which: Currency Outside Banks*	14a
....	....	....	....							2.36	58.53	6.77	7.22	7.69	Time & Foreign Currency Deposits	15
....	....	....	....							10.82	70.30	86.53	309.93	1,091.37	Foreign Liabilities	16c
....	....	....	....							.34	21.25	.02	.19	2,591.78	Central Government Deposits	16d
....	....	....	....							-1.18	18.40	15.09	23.25	-649.99	Capital Accounts	17a
....	....	....	....							-5.59	-106.81	-42.43	-63.25	-897.40	Other Items (Net)	17r
End of Period															**Banking Institutions**	
....	....	....	....							1.11	47.73	82.32	92.37	695.51	Reserves	20
....	....	....	....							1.51	105.74	218.64	475.18	3,621.58	Foreign Assets	21
....	....	....	....							.32	1.03	5.85	55.26	69.34	Claims on Central Government	22a
....	....	....	....							.72	26.55	90.56	90.03	433.22	Claims on Private Sector	22d
....	....	....	....							1.23	51.75	93.29	106.58	510.63	Demand Deposits	24
....	....	....	....							.43	77.96	194.50	344.91	2,983.21	Time, Savings,& Fgn.Currency Dep.	25
....	....	....	....							.40	12.33	36.03	138.93	890.97	Foreign Liabilities	26c
....	....	....	....							.02	5.18	6.80	28.94	132.49	Central Government Deposits	26d
....	....	....	....							—	.04	48.00	57.96	49.57	Credit from Monetary Authorities	26g
....	....	....	....							.21	16.08	23.85	100.59	695.15	Capital Accounts	27a
....	....	....	....							1.38	17.69	-5.09	-65.06	-442.37	Other Items (Net)	27r
End of Period															**Banking Survey**	
....	....	....	....							-7.61	135.92	200.10	168.04	4,407.46	Foreign Assets (Net)	31n
....	....	....	....							7.91	39.89	175.66	449.04	-1,576.03	Domestic Credit	32
....	....	....	....							4.28	10.82	81.37	356.31	-2,042.11	Claims on Central Govt.(Net)	32an
....	....	....	....							2.91	2.52	3.72	2.70	32.86	Claims on Nonfin.Pub.Enterprises	32c
....	....	....	....							.72	26.55	90.56	90.03	433.22	Claims on Private Sector	32d
....	....	....	....							2.69	93.92	194.91	272.43	1,161.08	Money	34
....	....	....	....							2.79	136.49	201.26	352.13	2,990.89	Quasi-Money	35
....	....	....	....							-.97	34.49	38.94	123.84	45.16	Capital Accounts	37a
....	....	....	....							-4.21	-89.08	-59.36	-131.32	-1,365.71	Other Items (Net)	37r
....	....	....	....							5.48	230.41	396.17	624.56	4,151.98	Money plus Quasi-Money	35l
Percent Per Annum															**Interest Rates**	
....	....	....	....							160.00	2.00	48.00	58.00	120.00	Discount Rate *(End of Period)*	60
....	....	....	....							125.92	147.13	29.25	36.88	37.50	Deposit Rate	60l
....	....	....	....							206.25	217.88	37.75	45.00	45.00	Lending Rate	60p
Period Averages															**Prices**	
....	....	....	....		31.7	58.3	232.5	3,439.9	36,077.7	....	....	....	....	....	Consumer Prices (1995=1 million)	64.a
....	....	....	....		—	—	—	‡.3	3.6	100.0	4,245.2	13,550.1	25,327.3	97,799.1	Consumer Prices	64
Millions of US Dollars															**International Transactions**	
....	....	....	....				3,754.7	3,762.4	3,018.0	3,641.7	....	....	....	....	Exports	70.. d
....	....	....	....				625.9	214.3	137.8	426.9	....	....	....	....	Imports, c.i.f.	71.. d
Midyear Estimates																
7.98	8.19	8.41	8.70	9.74	10.02	‡9.54	10.61	‡10.24	10.60	10.97	11.34	11.72	12.09	12.48	Population	99z

Antigua and Barbuda

		1970	1971	1972	1973	1974	1975	1976	1977	1978	1979	1980	1981	1982	1983	1984
Exchange Rates											*E. Caribbean Dollars per SDR: End of Period (aa)*					
Official Rate	aa	2.0053	2.0417	2.2194	2.4925	2.5024	2.7770	3.1369	3.2797	3.5175	3.5568	3.4436	3.1427	2.9784	2.8268	2.6466
Official Rate	ae	2.0053	1.8805	2.0442	2.0661	2.0439	2.3721	2.7000	2.7000	2.7000	2.7000	2.7000	2.7000	2.7000	2.7000	2.7000
											Index Numbers (1995=100):					
Official Rate	ahx	134.8	137.3	140.7	137.9	131.6	125.0	103.5	100.0	100.0	100.0	100.0	100.0	100.0	100.0	100.0
Nominal Effective Exchange Rate	ne c	....	....	....	....	....	....	....	....	....	91.4	89.9	93.4	97.6	100.7	105.6
Real Effective Exchange Rate	re c	....	....	....	....	....	....	....	....	....	98.0	100.7	105.4	106.9	107.9	111.7
Fund Position											*Millions of SDRs:*					
Quota	2f. s	—	—	—	—	—	—	—	—	—	....	....	....	3.60	5.00	5.00
SDRs	1b. s	....	....	....	....	....	....	....	....	....	....	....	....	—	—	—
Reserve Position in the Fund	1c. s	....	....	....	....	....	....	....	....	....	....	....	....	—	—	—
Total Fund Cred.&Loans Outstg.	2tl	....	....	....	....	....	....	....	....	....	....	....	....	—	—	—
International Liquidity											*Millions of US Dollars:*					
Total Reserves minus Gold	1l. d	....	....	....	....	....	7.32	9.67	5.10	5.97	11.23	7.82	7.34	8.52	9.93	15.44
SDRs	1b. d	....	....	....	....	....	....	....	....	....	....	....	....	—	—	—
Reserve Position in the Fund	1c. d	....	....	....	....	....	....	....	....	....	....	....	....	—	—	—
Foreign Exchange	1d. d	....	....	....	....	....	7.32	9.67	5.10	5.97	11.23	7.82	7.34	8.52	9.93	15.44
Deposit Money Banks: Assets	7a. d	....	....	....	....	....	14.16	3.68	2.31	4.55	5.58	4.45	8.49	11.02	8.39	19.27
Liabilities	7b. d	....	....	....	....	....	15.91	18.28	10.50	14.87	17.20	14.78	18.16	26.10	30.98	
Monetary Authorities											*Millions of E. Caribbean Dollars:*					
Foreign Assets	11	....	....	....	....	....	17.35	26.10	13.78	16.13	30.33	21.52	20.28	23.67	30.00	37.85
Claims on Central Government	12a	....	....	....	....	....	2.12	5.62	5.77	6.26	6.26	9.40	9.60	11.56	11.56	32.49
Claims on Deposit Money Banks	12e	....	....	....	....	....	—	—	—	—	—	—	—	—	—	4.04
Reserve Money	14	....	....	....	....	....	19.47	31.72	19.55	22.39	36.59	30.51	29.41	34.69	39.79	71.60
of which: Currency Outside DMBs	14a	....	....	....	....	....	10.77	11.92	13.15	15.13	17.09	15.26	16.27	16.32	17.47	23.97
Foreign Liabilities	16c	....	....	....	....	....	—	—	—	—	—	—	—	—	—	—
Central Government Deposits	16d	....	....	....	....	....	—	—	—	—	—	.41	.48	.54	1.78	2.78
Other Items (Net)	17r	....	....	....	....	....	—	—	—	—	—	—	—	—	—	—
Deposit Money Banks											*Millions of E. Caribbean Dollars:*					
Reserves	20	....	....	....	....	....	8.70	19.80	6.40	7.26	19.50	15.24	13.14	18.38	22.31	55.24
Foreign Assets	21	....	....	....	....	....	33.60	9.93	6.24	12.29	15.07	12.02	22.92	29.75	22.67	52.03
Claims on Central Government	22a	....	....	....	....	....	13.29	32.18	20.04	20.02	31.74	34.91	32.99	39.64	38.33	46.59
Claims on Local Government	22b	....	....	....	....	....	—	—	—	—	—	—	—	—	—	—
Claims on Nonfin.Pub.Enterprises	22c	....	....	....	....	....	1.26	2.65	2.33	2.75	6.01	6.24	3.79	8.54	4.56	1.56
Claims on Private Sector	22d	....	....	....	....	....	65.35	74.32	83.74	90.54	85.88	102.72	131.35	137.75	180.13	211.80
Claims on Nonbank Financial Insts	22g	....	....	....	....	....	—	—	—	—	1.44	1.82	1.59	1.65	.36	.11
Demand Deposits	24	....	....	....	....	....	8.20	12.35	17.76	14.24	17.72	23.31	26.89	25.38	33.62	34.44
Time, Savings,& Fgn.Currency Dep.	25	....	....	....	....	....	79.05	82.23	71.61	83.84	95.93	106.79	125.38	149.55	185.71	227.68
Foreign Liabilities	26c	....	....	....	....	....	37.75	49.36	28.36	40.16	46.45	39.90	49.04	70.47	55.73	83.65
Central Government Deposits	26d	....	....	....	....	....	—	—	—	—	—	.63	1.56	1.09	.79	2.73	2.39
Credit from Monetary Authorities	26g	....	....	....	....	....	—	—	—	—	—	—	—	.09	1.42	1.20
Capital Accounts	27a	....	....	....	....	....	3.00	3.00	3.00	3.00	3.26	4.55	5.72	6.92	5.67	15.18
Other Items (Net)	27r	....	....	....	....	....	−5.79	−8.05	−2.00	−8.39	−4.36	−3.17	−2.34	−17.49	−16.51	2.79
Monetary Survey											*Millions of E. Caribbean Dollars:*					
Foreign Assets (Net)	31n	....	....	....	....	....	13.20	−13.33	−8.34	−11.74	−1.05	−6.36	−5.84	−17.05	−3.06	6.23
Domestic Credit	32	....	....	....	....	....	82.02	114.77	111.87	119.57	130.69	153.11	177.75	197.82	230.44	287.37
Claims on Central Govt. (Net)	32an	....	....	....	....	....	15.41	37.80	25.81	26.28	37.37	42.34	41.02	49.88	45.39	73.91
Claims on Local Government	32b	....	....	....	....	....	—	—	—	—	—	—	—	—	—	—
Claims on Nonfin.Pub.Enterprises	32c	....	....	....	....	....	1.26	2.65	2.33	2.75	6.01	6.24	3.79	8.54	4.56	1.56
Claims on Private Sector	32d	....	....	....	....	....	65.35	74.32	83.74	90.54	85.88	102.72	131.35	137.75	180.13	211.80
Claims on Nonbank Financial Inst	32g	....	....	....	....	....	—	—	—	—	1.44	1.82	1.59	1.65	.36	.11
Money	34	....	....	....	....	....	18.97	24.26	30.91	29.37	34.81	38.57	43.16	41.70	51.10	58.40
Quasi-Money	35	....	....	....	....	....	79.05	82.23	71.61	83.84	95.93	106.79	125.38	149.55	185.71	227.68
Capital Accounts	37a	....	....	....	....	....	3.00	3.00	3.00	3.00	3.26	4.55	5.72	6.92	5.67	15.18
Other Items (Net)	37r	....	....	....	....	....	−5.79	−8.05	−2.00	−8.39	−4.36	−3.17	−2.34	−17.41	−15.09	−7.66
Money plus Quasi-Money	35l	....	....	....	....	....	98.02	106.49	102.53	113.21	130.74	145.37	168.54	191.25	236.80	286.08
Interest Rates											*Percent Per Annum*					
Treasury Bill Rate	60c	....	....	....	....	....	....	....	....	....	....	7.0	7.0	7.0	7.0	7.0
Deposit Rate	60l	....	....	....	....	....	....	....	....	....	....	6.0	6.3	7.5	11.0	11.0
Lending Rate	60p	....	....	....	....	....	....	....	....	8.6	8.6	10.0	11.0	13.0	14.0	13.6
Prices											*Index Numbers (1985=100):*					
Consumer Prices	64	....	....	....	....	....	....	48.0	54.6	57.9	67.4	80.2	89.4	93.1	95.3	99.0

	1985	1986	1987	1988	1989	1990	1991	1992	1993	1994	1995	1996	1997	1998	1999	
																Exchange Rates
E. Caribbean Dollars per US Dollar: End of Period (ae)																
	2.9657	3.3026	3.8304	3.6334	3.5482	3.8412	3.8622	3.7125	3.7086	3.9416	4.0135	3.8825	3.6430	3.8017	3.7058	Official Rate.............................. **aa**
	2.7000	2.7000	2.7000	2.7000	2.7000	2.7000	2.7000	2.7000	2.7000	2.7000	2.7000	2.7000	2.7000	2.7000	2.7000	Official Rate.............................. **ae**
Period Averages																
	100.0	100.0	100.0	100.0	100.0	100.0	100.0	100.0	100.0	100.0	100.0	100.0	100.0	100.0	100.0	Official Rate .... **ahx**
	107.9	103.2	99.2	96.3	99.2	95.9	97.1	97.1	103.1	103.2	100.0	101.5	104.7	105.7	106.7	Nominal Effective Exchange Rate .... **ne c**
	110.2	102.9	98.6	98.2	99.2	96.7	98.4[e]	97.0[e]	103.1[e]	103.2	100.0[e]	101.6[e]	105.3[e]	107.5[e]	109.8[e]	Real Effective Exchange Rate .... **re c**
																Fund Position
End of Period																
	5.00	5.00	5.00	5.00	5.00	5.00	5.00	5.00	8.50	8.50	8.50	8.50	8.50	8.50	13.50	Quota .... **2f. s**
	....	....	....	....	—	—	—	—	—	—	—	—	—	—	.01	SDRs .... **1b. s**
	—	—	—	—	—	—	—	—	—	—	—	—	—	—	—	Reserve Position in the Fund .... **1c. s**
	—	—	—	—	—	—	—	—	—	—	—	—	—	—	—	Total Fund Cred.&Loans Outstg. **2tl**
																International Liquidity
End of Period																
	16.58	28.26	25.60	28.03	28.07	27.50	32.54	50.52	37.81	45.81	59.44	47.74	50.70	59.37	69.73	Total Reserves minus Gold..................... **1l. d**
	—	—	—	—	—	—	—	—	.01	.01	.01	.01	.01	.01	.01	SDRs .... **1b. d**
	—	—	—	—	—	—	—	—	—	—	—	—	—	—	—	Reserve Position in the Fund .... **1c. d**
	16.58	28.26	25.60	28.03	28.07	27.50	32.54	50.52	37.80	45.80	59.43	47.73	50.69	59.36	69.72	Foreign Exchange .... **1d. d**
	27.64	19.09	30.99	37.31	29.32	30.28	49.41	53.62	56.99	77.30	77.54	72.02	58.79	71.34	160.10	Deposit Money Banks: Assets .... **7a. d**
	49.21	49.06	51.50	56.23	57.00	55.81	50.14	66.79	52.73	60.72	46.57	76.66	101.70	112.56	209.49	Liabilities........... **7b. d**
																Monetary Authorities
End of Period																
	52.07	78.64	70.50	75.83	76.30	75.07	86.26	134.95	102.00	123.80	160.49	130.16	138.16	161.56	191.56	Foreign Assets **11**
	33.95	37.10	36.38	40.55	38.46	45.78	44.71	36.10	39.48	39.11	31.02	28.01	27.35	25.48	21.74	Claims on Central Government **12a**
	.26	1.92	4.58	7.35	4.15	2.47	1.88	1.60	1.46	1.33	1.18	1.03	.95	.90	.74	Claims on Deposit Money Banks **12e**
	83.15	115.33	109.33	121.49	116.44	120.61	132.75	172.53	142.83	164.12	192.56	159.14	166.37	187.84	213.93	Reserve Money **14**
	26.50	32.46	42.24	51.31	61.47	57.52	57.91	64.31	61.21	65.87	77.22	68.06	66.55	79.78	85.01	*of which: Currency Outside DMBs* **14a**
	—	—	—	—	—	—	—	—	—	—	—	—	—	—	—	Foreign Liabilities............................ **16c**
	3.14	2.33	2.13	2.25	2.48	2.71	.11	.11	.12	.12	.13	.06	.09	.09	.09	Central Government Deposits **16d**
	—	—	—	—	—	—	—	—	—	—	—	—	—	—	—	Other Items (Net) **17r**
																Deposit Money Banks
End of Period																
	61.25	85.53	59.17	65.82	56.66	63.31	77.17	98.34	87.99	96.82	116.90	93.87	99.01	115.73	130.99	Reserves **20**
	74.62	51.54	83.67	100.75	79.18	81.75	133.42	144.76	153.87	208.72	209.36	194.46	158.72	192.61	432.28	Foreign Assets **21**
	48.25	57.57	69.18	85.96	79.98	64.88	80.60	95.19	117.80	124.62	162.83	161.20	192.52	224.83	269.28	Claims on Central Government **22a**
	—	—	—	.12	13.53	19.94	—	.72	.81	.23	.72	.52	.72	1.43	—	Claims on Local Government **22b**
	5.07	8.17	12.04	9.58	9.78	7.27	5.70	9.30	9.69	9.53	33.78	33.25	32.44	53.94	77.60	Claims on Nonfin.Pub.Enterprises **22c**
	258.34	295.34	352.05	412.52	468.64	503.09	547.45	586.67	598.33	613.83	706.86	850.34	1,027.00	1,103.30	1,196.01	Claims on Private Sector **22d**
	1.11	.66	2.29	6.30	13.84	22.35	25.23	6.00	5.92	24.50	7.78	6.73	6.75	9.34	16.43	Claims on Nonbank Financial Insts **22g**
	41.95	54.91	68.39	76.88	79.63	99.22	109.73	118.20	123.26	154.13	202.47	187.25	197.99	250.64	241.08	Demand Deposits **24**
	251.47	290.76	338.82	371.65	425.03	436.34	515.42	539.27	599.16	649.27	773.57	756.28	824.64	929.91	1,058.88	Time, Savings,& Fgn.Currency Dep. **25**
	132.87	132.46	139.04	151.82	153.90	150.68	135.38	180.35	142.36	163.95	125.73	206.99	274.59	303.92	565.62	Foreign Liabilities............................ **26c**
	1.95	4.76	9.43	28.51	27.93	28.18	35.77	49.61	39.82	53.83	65.10	72.77	71.32	69.60	57.57	Central Government Deposits **26d**
	.51	2.20	4.76	8.69	4.83	2.49	1.76	2.12	1.94	1.29	1.17	1.03	4.31	15.63	13.60	Credit from Monetary Authorities **26g**
	17.32	21.84	27.90	27.51	30.75	35.85	96.00	81.18	91.18	110.08	126.40	140.19	161.27	178.04	191.83	Capital Accounts **27a**
	2.57	−8.12	−9.94	15.99	−.46	9.85	−24.51	−29.75	−23.33	−54.32	−56.20	−24.15	−16.96	−46.56	−5.98	Other Items (Net) **27r**
																Monetary Survey
End of Period																
	−6.18	−2.28	15.13	24.76	1.57	6.13	84.30	99.36	113.51	168.57	244.12	117.62	22.29	50.24	58.22	Foreign Assets (Net) **31n**
	341.64	391.76	460.37	524.26	593.82	632.43	667.81	684.25	732.08	757.86	877.76	1,007.22	1,215.36	1,348.62	1,523.39	Domestic Credit **32**
	77.12	87.59	93.99	95.75	88.03	79.78	89.43	81.56	117.35	109.78	128.62	116.38	148.45	180.61	233.35	Claims on Central Govt. (Net) **32an**
	—	—	—	.12	13.53	19.94	—	.72	.81	.23	.72	.52	.72	1.43	—	Claims on Local Government **32b**
	5.07	8.17	12.04	9.58	9.78	7.27	5.70	9.30	9.69	9.53	33.78	33.25	32.44	53.94	77.60	Claims on Nonfin.Pub.Enterprises **32c**
	258.34	295.34	352.05	412.52	468.64	503.09	547.45	586.67	598.33	613.83	706.86	850.34	1,027.00	1,103.30	1,196.01	Claims on Private Sector **32d**
	1.11	.66	2.29	6.30	13.84	22.35	25.23	6.00	5.92	24.50	7.78	6.73	6.75	9.34	16.43	Claims on Nonbank Financial Inst **32g**
	68.45	87.37	110.62	128.19	141.09	156.74	167.64	182.62	184.61	220.18	279.78	255.39	264.61	330.47	326.13	Money **34**
	251.47	290.76	338.82	371.65	425.03	436.34	515.42	539.27	599.16	649.27	773.57	756.28	824.64	929.91	1,058.88	Quasi-Money................................. **35**
	17.32	21.84	27.90	27.51	30.75	35.85	96.00	81.18	91.18	110.08	126.40	140.19	161.27	178.04	191.83	Capital Accounts **37a**
	−1.78	−10.48	−1.84	21.68	−1.48	9.64	−26.95	−19.46	−29.36	−53.10	−57.86	−27.03	−12.87	−39.55	4.78	Other Items (Net) **37r**
	319.92	378.13	449.44	499.84	566.12	593.08	683.06	721.89	783.77	869.45	1,053.35	1,011.67	1,089.25	1,260.38	1,385.00	Money plus Quasi-Money **35l**
																Interest Rates
Percent Per Annum																
	7.0	7.0	7.0	7.0	7.0	7.0	7.0	7.0	7.0	7.0	7.0	7.0	7.0	7.0	7.0	Treasury Bill Rate **60c**
	9.9	7.7	6.5	6.5	6.5	8.4	8.2	7.4	6.7	6.5	5.9	5.5	5.5	5.5	5.5	Deposit Rate.. **60l**
	13.0	14.3	12.4	11.5	12.2	12.4	15.5	13.0	13.0	12.5	11.9	11.4	12.0	12.4	12.1	Lending Rate **60p**
																Prices
Period Averages																
	100.0	....	....	....	....	....	....	....	....	....	....	....	....	....	....	Consumer Prices........................... **64**

Antigua and Barbuda

311		1970	1971	1972	1973	1974	1975	1976	1977	1978	1979	1980	1981	1982	1983	1984
International Transactions															*Millions of E. Caribbean Dollars*	
Exports	70	21.85	32.23	34.64	50.38	58.95	43.00	23.61	⅟17.69	33.85	99.20	70.95	107.50	57.38	53.29	47.49
Imports, c.i.f.	71	72.65	86.77	90.98	94.50	143.75	145.14	91.84	⅟92.89	110.72	169.02	236.25	299.31	375.02	294.06	356.11
Balance of Payments															*Millions of US Dollars:*	
Current Account, n.i.e.	78al d	...	...	...	...	...	...	...	−9.60	−2.20	−19.50	−18.80	−32.70	−41.60	−9.10	.60
Goods: Exports f.o.b.	78aa d	...	...	...	...	...	...	...	6.60	12.60	12.00	59.50	51.40	49.30	36.50	35.20
Goods: Imports f.o.b.	78ab d	...	...	...	...	...	...	...	−37.00	−42.09	−67.72	−114.71	−125.26	−126.71	−99.72	−150.17
Trade Balance	78ac d	...	...	...	...	...	...	...	−30.40	−29.49	−55.72	−55.21	−73.86	−77.41	−63.22	−114.97
Services: Credit	78ad d	...	...	...	...	...	...	...	24.70	29.50	38.20	44.60	52.50	51.70	62.80	132.10
Services: Debit	78ae d	...	...	...	...	...	...	...	−6.50	−7.01	−10.28	−17.09	−19.74	−21.59	−18.28	−30.63
Balance on Goods & Services	78af d	...	...	...	...	...	...	...	−12.20	−7.00	−27.80	−27.70	−41.10	−47.30	−18.70	−13.50
Income: Credit	78ag d	...	...	...	...	...	...	...	.30	.10	.80	2.80	3.20	6.60	5.00	5.10
Income: Debit	78ah d	...	...	...	...	...	...	...	−.50	−.50	−2.60	−4.00	−5.20	−10.30	−6.00	−5.50
Balance on Gds, Serv. & Inc.	78ai d	...	...	...	...	...	...	...	−12.40	−7.40	−29.60	−28.90	−43.10	−51.00	−19.70	−13.90
Current Transfers, n.i.e.: Credit	78aj d	...	...	...	...	...	...	...	2.90	5.40	11.20	12.40	12.60	11.10	12.60	16.60
Current Transfers: Debit	78ak d	...	...	...	...	...	...	...	−.10	−.20	−1.10	−2.30	−2.20	−1.70	−2.00	−2.10
Capital Account, n.i.e.	78bc d	...	...	...	...	...	...	...	—	—	—	—	—	—	—	—
Capital Account, n.i.e.: Credit	78ba d	...	...	...	...	...	...	...	—	—	—	—	—	—	—	—
Capital Account: Debit	78bb d	...	...	...	...	...	...	...	—	—	—	—	—	—	—	—
Financial Account, n.i.e.	78bj d	...	...	...	...	...	...	...	2.81	5.63	18.86	22.29	36.95	35.41	−3.80	−.90
Direct Investment Abroad	78bd d	...	...	...	...	...	...	...	—	—	—	—	—	—	—	—
Dir. Invest. in Rep. Econ., n.i.e.	78be d	...	...	...	...	...	...	...	2.20	−6.90	8.50	19.60	22.40	23.00	5.00	4.40
Portfolio Investment Assets	78bf d	...	...	...	...	...	...	...	—	—	—	—	—	—	—	—
Equity Securities	78bk d	...	...	...	...	...	...	...	—	—	—	—	—	—	—	—
Debt Securities	78bl d	...	...	...	...	...	...	...	—	—	—	—	—	—	—	—
Portfolio Investment Liab., n.i.e.	78bg d	...	...	...	...	...	...	...	—	—	—	—	—	—	—	—
Equity Securities	78bm d	...	...	...	...	...	...	...	—	—	—	—	—	—	—	—
Debt Securities	78bn d	...	...	...	...	...	...	...	—	—	—	—	—	—	—	—
Financial Derivatives Assets	78bw d	...	...	...	...	...	...	...	...	...	...	...	...	...	...	...
Financial Derivatives Liabilities	78bx d	...	...	...	...	...	...	...	...	...	...	...	...	...	...	...
Other Investment Assets	78bh d	...	...	...	...	...	...	...	1.74	−2.24	−.90	1.15	−19.65	7.61	2.70	10.40
Monetary Authorities	78bo d	...	...	...	...	...	...	...	...	...	...	...	...	...	...	...
Financial Derivatives Assets	78bw d	...	...	...	...	...	...	...	...	...	...	...	...	...	...	...
Banks	78bq d	...	...	...	...	...	...	...	1.74	−2.24	−.90	1.15	−3.15	7.61	2.70	10.40
Other Sectors	78br d	...	...	...	...	...	...	...	—	—	—	—	—	—	—	—
Other Investment Liab., n.i.e.	78bi d	...	...	...	...	...	...	...	−1.13	14.77	11.26	1.54	34.20	4.80	−11.50	−15.70
Monetary Authorities	78bs d	...	...	...	...	...	...	...	—	—	—	—	—	—	—	—
Financial Derivatives Liabilities	78bx d	...	...	...	...	...	...	...	—	—	—	—	—	—	—	—
Banks	78bu d	...	...	...	...	...	...	...	−7.78	4.37	2.33	−2.43	3.39	−2.60	−5.40	−10.90
Other Sectors	78bv d	...	...	...	...	...	...	...	1.80	.26	.17	.20	8.51	1.00	2.20	—
Net Errors and Omissions	78ca d	...	...	...	...	...	...	...	2.33	−2.66	5.60	−7.30	−6.13	3.00	6.80	−.10
Overall Balance	78cb d	...	...	...	...	...	...	...	−4.46	.77	4.96	−3.81	−1.88	−3.20	−6.10	−.40
Reserves and Related Items	79da d	...	...	...	...	...	...	...	4.46	−.77	−4.96	3.81	1.88	3.20	6.10	.40
Reserve Assets	79db d	...	...	...	...	...	...	...	4.46	−.77	−5.36	3.21	.38	−1.20	−1.40	−7.10
Use of Fund Credit and Loans	79dc d	...	...	...	...	...	...	...	—	—	—	—	—	—	—	—
Exceptional Financing	79de d	...	...	...	...	...	...	...	—	—	.40	.60	1.50	4.40	7.50	7.50
National Accounts															*Millions of E. Caribbean Dollars*	
Househ.Cons.Expend.,incl.NPISHs	96f								116.1	121.6	126.9	194.0	206.8	301.2	308.6	319.5
Government Consumption Expend.	91f								34.5	34.3	45.9	57.4	63.4	70.8	83.2	86.5
Gross Capital Formation	93e								36.9	39.0	60.5	103.4	140.9	146.9	84.6	110.6
Exports of Goods & Services	90c								85.2	124.5	203.7	200.0	246.1	252.6	253.9	350.2
Imports of Goods & Services	98c								−94.0	−117.3	−187.9	−257.6	−321.2	−399.1	−316.5	−398.2
Gross Domestic Product (GDP)	99b				99.9	111.6	120.6	120.8	⅟178.6	202.1	249.1	297.2	336.1	372.5	413.8	468.5
Net Primary Income from Abroad	98.n								2.2	2.2	4.9	−3.2	−5.1	−10.0	−2.7	−1.1
Gross National Income (GNI)	99a								180.8	204.3	254.0	294.0	331.0	362.5	411.1	467.4
Net Current Transf. from Abroad	98t								3.2	10.0	22.1	24.3	26.5	30.2	27.0	32.1
Gross Nat'l Disposable Inc.(GNDI)	99i								184.0	214.3	276.1	318.3	357.4	392.7	438.1	499.5
Gross Savings	99s								33.5	58.4	103.3	66.9	87.2	20.7	46.3	93.6
GDP Volume 1990 Prices	99b.p								482.3	502.5	539.4	585.7	609.7	610.7	639.3	701.6
GDP Volume (1995=100)	99bv p								41.3	43.0	46.2	50.1	52.2	52.3	54.7	60.1
GDP Deflator (1995=100)	99bi p								⅟32.5	35.3	40.5	44.5	48.3	53.5	56.7	58.5
																Millions:
Population	99z	.07	.07	.07	.07	.07	.07	.07	.07	.07	.07	.08	.08	.08	.07	.08

International Transactions

Millions of E. Caribbean Dollars

1985	1986	1987	1988	1989	1990	1991	1992	1993	1994	1995	1996	1997	1998	1999		
45.04	52.88	52.51	45.91	43.02	55.79	108.14	147.60	127.62	74.03	81.23	45.41	35.00	40.00	....	Exports	70
449.14	560.23	666.94	675.44	519.57	687.69	774.89	864.00	753.20	903.46	925.65	977.00	986.78	1,048.80	....	Imports, c.i.f.	71

Balance of Payments

Minus Sign Indicates Debit

1985	1986	1987	1988	1989	1990	1991	1992	1993	1994	1995	1996	1997	1998	1999		
-23.10	-118.29	-111.29	-45.04	-81.65	-30.99	-33.37	-18.87	-.47	-17.95	-.51	-39.76	....	....	....	Current Account, n.i.e.	78al d
28.30	31.53	26.30	28.19	29.14	33.43	49.50	64.70	62.08	44.45	53.14	54.04	....	....	....	Goods: Exports f.o.b.	78aa d
-174.80	-212.49	-222.01	-204.50	-246.33	-235.44	-258.79	-272.63	-282.58	-298.12	-301.76	-316.61				Goods: Imports f.o.b.	78ab d
-146.50	-180.96	-195.71	-176.31	-217.19	-202.01	-209.29	-207.94	-220.50	-253.67	-248.61	-262.57				*Trade Balance*	78ac d
150.30	174.36	200.68	237.33	261.79	311.87	320.20	342.57	377.20	396.31	348.69	367.51				Services: Credit	78ad d
-38.40	-81.04	-81.13	-79.30	-92.58	-105.12	-113.27	-122.73	-131.57	-134.93	-143.18	-154.50				Services: Debit	78ae d
-34.60	-87.64	-76.16	-18.27	-47.97	4.74	-2.36	11.90	25.14	7.71	-43.10	-49.56				*Balance on Goods & Services*	78af d
2.40	1.44	1.41	1.43	1.20	2.49	2.66	3.70	3.11	4.26	5.21	5.79				Income: Credit	78ag d
-5.10	-37.47	-41.37	-33.06	-46.69	-47.81	-34.98	-33.36	-26.04	-30.81	-31.86	-23.91				Income: Debit	78ah d
-37.30	-123.68	-116.12	-49.90	-93.46	-40.59	-34.67	-17.76	2.20	-18.84	-69.76	-67.69				*Balance on Gds, Serv. & Inc.*	78ai d
16.80	8.94	9.36	9.81	17.28	14.89	9.16	8.54	9.07	10.36	77.94	31.49				Current Transfers, n.i.e.: Credit	78aj d
-2.60	-3.55	-4.53	-4.94	-5.47	-5.29	-7.86	-9.66	-11.75	-9.47	-8.69	-3.56				Current Transfers: Debit	78ak d
—	6.00	5.24	5.49	6.74	5.21	6.43	5.74	6.81	5.91	6.99	3.55				Capital Account, n.i.e.	78bc d
—	6.00	5.24	5.49	6.74	5.23	6.43	5.74	6.81	6.53	6.99	3.55				Capital Account, n.i.e.: Credit	78ba d
—	—	—	—	—	-.02	—	—	—	-.62	—	—				Capital Account: Debit	78bb d
20.20	122.61	92.73	45.83	76.80	60.57	46.44	39.54	.10	13.79	12.07	61.74				Financial Account, n.i.e.	78bj d
											....				Direct Investment Abroad	78bx d
15.60	22.60	38.60	32.95	43.11	60.61	54.71	19.60	14.91	24.81	31.47	18.75				Dir. Invest. in Rep. Econ., n.i.e.	78be d
—	—	—	—	—	—	—	—	—	—	1.19	—				Portfolio Investment Assets	78bf d
—	—	—	—	—	—	—	—	—	—	1.19	—				Equity Securities	78bk d
—	—	—	—	—	—	—	—	—	—	—	—				Debt Securities	78bl d
—	—	—	—	—	—	—	—	—	-1.38	-1.28	-1.59				Portfolio Investment Liab., n.i.e.	78bg d
—	—	—	—	—	—	—	—	—	-1.38	-1.28	-.78				Equity Securities	78bm d
—	—	—	—	—	—	—	—	—	—	—	-.81				Debt Securities	78bn d
											....				Financial Derivatives Assets	78bw d
											....				Financial Derivatives Liabilities	78bx d
17.80	10.64	-7.57	-3.63	8.69	-2.15	-23.97	8.47	-17.85	-13.59	-14.39	35.62				Other Investment Assets	78bh d
											....				Monetary Authorities	78bo d
											....				Financial Derivatives Assets	78bw d
17.80	10.64	-7.57	-3.63	8.69	-2.15	-23.97	8.47	-17.85	-13.59	-14.39	35.62				Banks	78bq d
											....				Other Sectors	78br d
-13.20	89.38	61.71	16.51	25.01	2.11	15.69	11.47	3.04	3.94	-4.91	8.97				Other Investment Liab., n.i.e.	78bi d
—	—	—	—	—	—				—	—					Monetary Authorities	78bs d
											....				Financial Derivatives Liabilities	78bx d
-8.40											....				Banks	78bu d
—	27.74	-2.53	-3.72	-3.02	-7.15	-1.87	5.05	3.03	-1.73	-9.10	10.52				Other Sectors	78bv d
—	-.18	10.83	-3.66	-1.85	-35.39	-14.40	-10.00	-18.65	6.33	-4.96	-36.80				Net Errors and Omissions	78ca d
-2.90	10.14	-2.49	2.62	.04	-.59	5.10	16.40	-12.22	8.08	13.59	-11.26				*Overall Balance*	78cb d
2.90	-10.14	2.49	-2.62	-.04	.59	-5.10	-16.40	12.22	-8.08	-13.59	11.26				Reserves and Related Items	79da d
-3.30	-10.14	2.49	-2.62	-.04	.59	-5.10	-16.40	12.22	-8.08	-13.59	11.26				Reserve Assets	79db d
															Use of Fund Credit and Loans	79dc d
6.20	—	—	—	—	—	—	....	....	....		....				Exceptional Financing	79de d

National Accounts

Millions of E. Caribbean Dollars

1985	1986	1987	1988	1989	1990	1991	1992	1993	1994	1995	1996	1997	1998	1999		
390.7	449.5	475.4	478.8	499.0	503.5	504.0	504.7	544.1	633.8	672.5	791.1	756.2	....	....	Househ.Cons.Expend.,incl.NPISHs	96f
98.7	121.2	128.1	177.0	191.7	189.8	193.9	209.2	230.2	258.2	284.8	307.7	324.7			Government Consumption Expend.	91f
151.6	237.0	354.3	364.3	415.9	343.0	416.7	398.0	390.6	437.4	491.9	578.8	648.3			Gross Capital Formation	93e
409.5	558.5	615.7	720.0	816.7	940.4	998.1	1,099.6	1,186.1	1,190.0	1,084.9	1,145.9	1,174.9			Exports of Goods & Services	90c
-505.4	-702.2	-799.9	-825.7	-915.1	-919.5	-1,004.7	-1,067.5	-1,118.2	-1,169.2	-1,201.3	-1,298.0	-1,328.0			Imports of Goods & Services	98c
545.0	663.9	773.5	914.5	1,008.2	1,057.2	1,108.1	1,144.2	1,232.7	1,350.2	1,332.7	1,466.4	1,576.0			Gross Domestic Product (GDP)	99b
-7.6	-97.3	-107.9	-80.4	-117.8	-117.4	-87.4	-80.1	-61.9	-71.7	-72.0	-62.7	-69.5			Net Primary Income from Abroad	98.n
537.4	566.6	665.6	834.1	890.4	993.9	1,020.7	1,064.1	1,170.7	1,278.6	1,260.8	1,400.7	1,506.5			Gross National Income (GNI)	99a
33.8	25.6	24.8	25.3	24.2	21.3	3.5	-7.2	-7.2	2.4	187.0	85.6	33.2			Net Current Transf. from Abroad	98t
571.2	592.2	690.4	859.4	914.6	961.2	1,024.2	1,061.1	1,163.5	1,281.0	1,447.8	1,486.2	1,539.7			Gross Nat'l Disposable Inc.(GNDI)	99i
81.8	21.6	86.9	203.6	223.9	267.8	326.4	347.1	389.3	389.0	490.5	387.4	458.8			Gross Savings	99s
757.7	854.0	924.6	974.7	1,031.0	1,057.2	1,078.8	1,087.9	1,146.6	1,219.1	1,168.2	1,235.5	....			GDP Volume 1990 Prices	99b.p
64.9	73.1	79.1	83.4	88.3	90.5	92.3	93.1	98.1	104.4	100.0	105.8	....			GDP Volume (1995=100)	99bv p
63.1	68.1	73.3	82.2	85.7	87.7	90.0	92.2	94.2	97.1	100.0	104.0	....			GDP Deflator (1995=100)	99bi p

Midyear Estimates

1985	1986	1987	1988	1989	1990	1991	1992	1993	1994	1995	1996	1997	1998	1999		
.08	.08	.06	.06	.06	.06	.06	.06	.07	.07	.07	.07	.07	.07	.07	Population	99z

Argentina

213

	1970	1971	1972	1973	1974	1975	1976	1977	1978	1979	1980	1981	1982	1983	1984
Exchange Rates															
Pesos per Bill. SDRs through 1977, per Mill. SDRs from 1978 to 1983,															
Official Rate .... aa	.04000	.05429	.05429	.06032	.06122	.71276	3.18922	7.25789	I.01307	.02132	.02541	.08436	.53550	2.43531	I.01752
Pesos per Billion US$ through 1977, per Million US$ from 1978 to 1983,															
Official Rate .... ae	.04000	.05000	.05000	.05000	.05000	.60885	2.74500	5.97500	I.01004	.01619	.01993	.07248	.48545	2.32610	I.01787
Official Rate .... rf	.03792	.04522	.05000	.05000	.05000	.36575	1.39983	4.07633	I.00796	.01317	.01837	.04403	.25923	1.05300	I.00676
Fund Position															*Millions of SDRs:*
Quota .... 2f. s	440.0	440.0	440.0	440.0	440.0	440.0	440.0	440.0	535.0	535.0	802.5	802.5	802.5	1,113.0	1,113.0
SDRs .... 1b. s	59.3	2.8	17.8	66.9	83.8	34.8	78.2	73.9	161.6	247.9	256.6	347.1	—	.3	.6
Reserve Position in the Fund .... 1c. s	130.2	110.0	—	—	11.3	—	—	—	130.5	154.4	262.8	239.2	91.0	—	—
Total Fund Cred.&Loans Outstg. 2tl	—	—	174.0	174.0	64.0	250.1	455.6	344.5	—	—	—	—	—	1,120.6	1,120.6
International Liquidity														*Millions of US Dollars Unless Otherwise Indicated:*	
Total Reserves minus Gold .... 1l. d	533	192	313	1,149	1,144	288	1,445	3,154	4,966	9,388	6,719	3,268	2,506	1,172	1,243
SDRs .... 1b. d	59	3	19	81	103	41	91	90	211	327	327	404	—	—	1
Reserve Position in the Fund .... 1c. d	130	119	—	—	14	—	—	—	170	203	335	278	100	—	—
Foreign Exchange .... 1d. d	343	70	294	1,068	1,028	247	1,354	3,064	4,586	8,858	6,057	2,586	2,406	1,172	1,242
Gold (Million Fine Troy Ounces) 1ad	3.993	2.564	3.993	3.996	3.996	3.996	3.996	4.184	4.278	4.372	4.372	4.372	4.372	4.372	4.372
Gold (National Valuation) 1and	140	97	152	169	169	169	169	177	181	184	185	185	185	1,421	1,421
Monetary Authorities: Other Assets .... 3..d	67	66	121	151	166	389	592	877	1,059	1,069	1,070	1,173	1,247	1,369	1,815
Other Liab. .... 4..d	36	111	176	353	383	457	1,182	871	21	86	194	271	679	1,572	2,155
Deposit Money Banks: Assets .... 7a. d	158	127	183	265	254	329	441	420	478	454	2,155	1,008	751	1,217	1,275
Liabilities .... 7b. d	....	....	....	....	....	....	....	....	....	....	....	7,196	7,172	7,839	7,206
Other Banking Insts.: Assets .... 7e. d	....	....	....	....	....	....	....	....	....	....	....	2	2	2	2
Liabilities .... 7f. d	....	....	....	....	....	....	....	....	....	....	....	8	5	4	3
Monetary Authorities														*Thousandths (.000) of Pesos through 1978; Pesos from 1979 to 1984;*	
Foreign Assets 11	29	17	29	73	74	515	6,052	25,132	62,161	I172	159	335	1,929	9,270	90,586
Claims on Central Government 12a	62	90	140	310	540	1,790	4,760	13,570	30,160	I43	127	485	1,438	16,667	84,202
Claims on Deposit Money Banks 12e	14	19	30	800	1,200	3,600	14,700	4,900	5,700	I8	101	367	4,167	12,308	85,568
Claims on Other Banking Insts 12f	—	—	—	100	200	200	1,200	1,300	600	I2	17	52	617	1,631	9,462
Reserve Money 14	99	141	190	1,300	1,990	5,490	25,140	36,000	71,100	I132	236	513	4,332	19,765	105,849
of which: Currency Outside DMBs 14a	76	100	130	300	400	1,200	4,100	10,700	33,300	I79	164	302	874	4,634	31,340
Foreign Liabilities 16c	1	6	18	28	23	457	4,699	7,706	215	I1	4	20	329	6,386	58,153
Central Government Deposits 16d	—	—	—	10	10	—	120	210	400	I1	—	3	290	903	653
Capital Accounts 17a	2	6	8	9	9	209	686	1,507	2,894	I6	9	66	299	1,509	23,878
Other Items (Net) 17r	3	−26	−17	−64	−19	−51	−3,933	−521	24,012	I85	155	637	2,900	11,313	81,286
Deposit Money Banks														*Thousandths (.000) of Pesos through 1978; Pesos from 1979 to 1984;*	
Reserves 20	24	40	60	1,000	1,590	4,090	19,840	24,000	36,000	I55	75	206	3,190	14,248	71,978
Foreign Assets 21	—	—	—	—	—	—	—	—	—	I—	—	107	365	2,832	23,140
Claims on Central Government 22a	20	20	20	210	200	700	2,500	9,600	33,500	I99	168	644	2,314	7,636	55,179
Claims on State and Local Govts 22b	....	....													
Claims on Official Entities 22bx										I—					4,502
Claims on Private Sector 22d	171	290	460	740	1,170	2,980	12,110	43,350	121,870	I400	835	2,220	6,844	29,079	190,221
Demand Deposits 24	100	100	200	400	700	2,100	8,300	19,400	42,900	I105	196	330	613	2,361	18,191
Time, Savings,& Fgn.Currency Dep. 25	100	100	300	400	600	800	5,900	31,900	95,300	I315	597	1,283	2,970	15,521	122,633
Foreign Liabilities 26c	—	—	—	—	—	—	—	—	—	I—	—	763	3,484	18,243	128,780
Central Government Deposits 26d	—	—	—	—	100	200	500	1,200		I3	5	23	849	3,666	11,078
Credit from Monetary Authorities 26g	57	80	100	900	1,300	3,600	14,500	5,100	5,200	I10	80	266	3,627	7,439	34,349
Capital Accounts 27a	24	62	100	100	100	300	2,200	10,200	27,200	I81	158	482	2,053	9,952	75,135
Other Items (Net) 27r	−67	8	−160	150	260	870	3,350	9,850	19,570	I41	41	79	−884	−3,388	−45,147
Monetary Survey														*Thousandths (.000) of Pesos through 1978; Pesos from 1979 to 1984;*	
Foreign Assets (Net) 31n	28	11	11	45	51	58	1,353	17,426	61,946	I171	155	−341	−1,520	−12,527	−73,207
Domestic Credit 32	253	400	620	1,350	2,100	5,570	20,250	67,110	184,530	I540	1,141	3,376	10,073	50,444	331,835
Claims on Central Govt. (Net) 32an	82	110	160	510	730	2,390	6,940	22,460	62,060	I138	289	1,104	2,612	19,733	127,650
Claims on State and Local Govts 32b	....	....													
Claims on Official Entities 32bx										I—					4,502
Claims on Private Sector 32d	171	290	460	740	1,170	2,980	12,110	43,350	121,870	I400	835	2,220	6,844	29,079	190,221
Claims on Other Banking Insts 32f	—	—	—	100	200	200	1,200	1,300	600	I2	17	52	617	1,631	9,462
Money 34	176	200	330	700	1,100	3,500	13,600	31,900	78,600	I185	362	639	1,623	7,500	51,170
Quasi-Money 35	100	100	300	400	600	800	5,900	31,900	95,300	I315	597	1,283	2,970	15,521	122,633
Capital Accounts 37a	26	68	108	109	109	509	2,886	11,707	30,094	I87	167	549	2,352	11,462	99,013
Other Items (Net) 37r	−21	43	−107	186	341	819	−783	9,029	42,482	I125	171	566	1,608	3,434	−14,188
Money plus Quasi-Money 35l	276	300	630	1,100	1,700	4,300	19,500	63,800	173,900	I500	958	1,921	4,593	23,021	173,803
Other Banking Institutions														*Thousandths (.000) of Pesos through 1978; Pesos from 1979 to 1984;*	
Reserves 40	—	—	—		100	200	1,300	200	500	I1	2	13	138	589	1,952
Foreign Assets 41	—	—	—	—	—	—	—	—	—	I—	—	—	1	4	44
Claims on Central Government 42a	10	—	—	—	—	—	—	240	400	I1	1	10	30	75	311
Claims on Local and State Govts 42b	....	....													
Claims on Official Entities 42bx							100								
Claims on Private Sector 42d	40	10	20	50	80	210	1,770	8,840	23,800	I64	141	288	566	1,707	7,517
Claims on Deposit Money Banks 42e	—	—	—	—	—	—	200	3,200	5,900	I9	8	30	29	104	385
Time, Savings,& Fgn.Currency Dep. 45	20	—	10	20	70	110	1,210	7,910	22,700	I59	120	297	264	1,218	4,513
Foreign Liabilities 46c	—	—	—	—	—	—	—	—	—	I—	—	1	2	8	59
Credit from Monetary Authorities 46g	7	10	10	30	110	200	1,200	1,500	1,800	I2	10	32	490	620	2,139
Capital Accounts 47a	—	—	—	—	—	—	200	800	2,200	I5	11	37	129	510	2,926
Other Items (Net) 47r	23	—	—	—	—	100	660	2,370	3,900	I9	11	−26	−122	123	573
Banking Survey														*Thousandths (.000) of Pesos through 1978; Pesos from 1979 to 1984;*	
Foreign Assets (Net) 51n	28	11	11	45	51	58	1,353	17,426	61,946	I171	155	−341	−1,521	−12,532	−73,222
Domestic Credit 52	303	410	640	1,300	1,980	5,580	20,820	74,990	208,130	I604	1,266	3,621	10,052	50,595	330,201
Claims on Central Govt. (Net) 52an	92	110	160	510	730	2,390	6,940	22,700	62,460	I139	290	1,113	2,642	19,808	127,961
Claims on State and Local Govts 52b	....	....													
Claims on Official Entities 52bx							100			I—					4,502
Claims on Private Sector 52d	211	300	480	790	1,250	3,190	13,880	52,190	145,670	I465	975	2,508	7,409	30,787	197,738
Liquid Liabilities 55l	296	300	640	1,120	1,670	4,210	19,410	71,510	196,100	I558	1,077	2,206	4,720	23,651	176,364
Capital Accounts 57a	26	68	108	109	109	509	3,086	12,507	32,294	I92	178	585	2,481	11,971	101,938
Other Items (Net) 57r	9	53	−97	116	251	919	−323	8,399	41,682	I126	167	489	1,329	2,441	−21,324

1985	1986	1987	1988	1989	1990	1991	1992	1993	1994	1995	1996	1997	1998	1999		
per Thous. SDRs from 1984 to 1988, per SDR thereafter: End of Period															**Exchange Rates**	
.08793	.15375	.53200	1.79920	I.23589	.79456	1.42828	1.36194	1.37150	1.45912	1.48649	1.43724	1.34858	1.40733	1.37182	Official Rate	aa
per Thous.US$ from 1984 to 1988, per US$ after:End Per.(ae) Per.Avg.(rf)																
.08005	.12570	.37500	1.33700	I.17950	.55850	.99850	.99050	.99850	.99950	1.00000	.99950	.99950	.99950	.99950	Official Rate	ae
.06018	.09430	.21443	.87526	I.04233	.48759	.95355	.99064	.99895	.99901	.99975	.99966	.99950	.99950	.99950	Official Rate	rf
End of Period															**Fund Position**	
1,113.0	1,113.0	1,113.0	1,113.0	1,113.0	1,113.0	1,113.0	1,537.1	1,537.1	1,537.1	1,537.1	1,537.1	1,537.1	1,537.1	2,117.1	Quota	2f. s
—	—	—	.3	.2	209.0	134.9	272.8	329.5	385.7	362.7	277.4	123.6	187.7	100.3	SDRs	1b. s
														—	Reserve Position in the Fund	1c. s
2,105.1	2,240.9	2,716.2	2,733.0	2,358.8	2,167.2	1,735.9	1,682.8	2,562.4	2,884.7	4,124.4	4,376.0	4,349.3	3,865.1	3,262.6	Total Fund Cred.&Loans Outstg.	2tl
End of Period															**International Liquidity**	
I3,273	2,718	1,617	3,363	1,463	4,592	6,005	9,990	13,791	14,327	14,288	18,104	22,320	24,752	26,252	Total Reserves minus Gold	1l. d
—	—	—	—	—	297	193	375	453	563	539	399	167	264	138	SDRs	1b. d
														—	Reserve Position in the Fund	1c. d
I3,273	2,718	1,617	3,363	1,463	4,295	5,812	9,615	13,339	13,764	13,749	17,705	22,153	24,488	26,114	Foreign Exchange	1d. d
4.372	4.373	4.373	4.373	4.373	4.233	4.123	4.373	4.373	4.374	4.374	4.374	.361	.360	.338	Gold (Million Fine Troy Ounces)	1ad
1,421	1,421	1,421	1,421	1,421	1,421	1,430	1,446	1,672	1,651	1,679	1,611	120	124	121	Gold (National Valuation)	1an d
2,100	....	....	....	....	1,154	772	—	—	57	22	30	42	30	13	Monetary Authorities: Other Assets	3.. d
4,952	6,506	6,906	7,826	....	7,394	7,629	558	161							Other Liab.	4.. d
1,068	1,063	1,312	1,270	1,557	2,234	2,812	3,642	5,153	5,587	6,302	10,011	17,732	16,895	16,065	Deposit Money Banks: Assets	7a. d
6,732	6,555	7,937	9,338	6,092	7,011	7,869	9,558	9,051	10,995	13,649	15,820	21,048	21,440	22,831	Liabilities	7b. d
4	3	1	1	3	5	10	12	32	26	31	25	24	17	74	Other Banking Insts.: Assets	7e. d
1	1	2		—	2	49	117	26	39	62	84	148	395	434	Liabilities	7f. d
Thousands from 1985 to 1988;Millions Beginning 1989: End of Period															**Monetary Authorities**	
I533	888	2,002	10,635	....	I4,114	9,009	11,236	15,448	I16,035	15,989	19,745	22,806	26,249	27,322	Foreign Assets	11
I715	1,247	4,814	17,641	I475	I5,334	10,879	9,272	11,432	I8,361	8,499	8,223	7,867	7,170	6,350	Claims on Central Government	12a
....	....	....	....	....	I14,510	17,922	23,408	22,527	I22,463	24,129	2,106	1,794	2,070	2,173	Claims on Deposit Money Banks	12e
....	....	....	....	....	I6	6	5	5	I4	3	3	—	—	—	Claims on Other Banking Insts	12f
I515	694	1,352	7,000	I528	I3,617	7,823	11,010	14,989	I16,267	13,769	14,060	15,975	16,392	16,524	Reserve Money	14
I202	399	926	4,319	I182	I2,259	5,222	7,686	10,067	I11,229	11,161	11,736	13,331	13,503	13,736	*of which: Currency Outside DMBs*	14a
I581	1,162	4,035	15,381	....	I5,857	10,102	2,843	3,677	I4,211	6,131	6,293	5,868	5,442	4,478	Foreign Liabilities	16c
I26	10	204	100	I79	I156	1,097	1,378	1,338	I764	1,677	2,242	325	1,343	935	Central Government Deposits	16d
I149	250	1,102	4,477	I446	I5,557	3,786	6,394	7,217	I3,279	3,583	4,053	4,059	4,604	4,415	Capital Accounts	17a
I455	834	4,583	24,604	....	I8,777	15,008	22,296	22,191	I22,342	23,461	3,430	6,242	7,708	9,492	Other Items (Net)	17r
Thousands from 1985 to 1988;Millions Beginning 1989: End of Period															**Deposit Money Banks**	
I309	305	428	2,550	I189	I1,342	2,900	3,481	5,488	I5,203	2,637	2,358	2,673	2,905	3,101	Reserves	20
I86	134	493	1,698	I280	I1,249	2,809	3,606	5,148	I5,587	6,302	10,011	17,732	16,895	16,065	Foreign Assets	21
I247	464	1,552	7,247	I948	I6,197	9,830	9,871	11,657	I6,094	10,299	13,013	14,513	17,433	19,429	Claims on Central Government	22a
									5,008	5,247	5,273	5,950	5,827	7,365	Claims on State and Local Govts	22b
I37	107	310	1,381	I36	I713	795	1,103	1,509	I493	463	565	612	285	340	Claims on Official Entities	22bx
I898	1,650	4,882	22,248	I1,279	I10,702	22,550	34,564	42,600	I51,372	50,780	54,093	63,131	70,525	68,431	Claims on Private Sector	22d
I146	264	491	2,078	I91	I809	2,404	3,678	5,052	I5,133	5,458	7,305	8,151	7,986	6,874	Demand Deposits	24
I568	1,291	3,727	21,528	I379	I4,845	11,471	19,666	30,334	I37,109	35,352	42,710	56,038	64,162	67,081	Time, Savings,& Fgn.Currency Dep.	25
I539	825	2,984	12,485	I1,096	I3,919	7,861	9,462	9,042	I10,995	13,649	15,820	21,048	21,440	22,831	Foreign Liabilities	26c
I167	216	345	1,387	I76	I524	1,976	2,958	5,054	I3,014	2,467	3,054	3,990	4,525	5,060	Central Government Deposits	26d
I240	446	1,363	5,083	I237	I10,082	18,292	22,967	22,336	I2,184	2,650	1,375	409	393	308	Credit from Monetary Authorities	26g
I344	620	1,728	6,073	I533	I5,966	9,608	10,802	12,503	I13,519	13,771	15,065	15,806	16,674	16,437	Capital Accounts	27a
I-429	-1,002	-2,972	-13,511	I319	I-5,942	-12,728	-16,908	-17,919	I1,802	2,381	-18	-830	-1,311	-3,860	Other Items (Net)	27r
Thousands from 1985 to 1988;Millions Beginning 1989: End of Period															**Monetary Survey**	
I-502	-966	-4,524	-15,532	....	I-4,413	-6,145	2,537	7,877	I6,416	2,510	7,643	13,623	16,262	16,078	Foreign Assets (Net)	31n
....	....	....	....	....	I22,272	40,987	50,479	60,811	I67,554	71,148	75,874	87,759	95,372	95,919	Domestic Credit	32
I769	1,485	5,818	23,400	I1,267	I10,851	17,636	14,807	16,697	I10,677	14,654	15,940	18,066	18,735	19,783	Claims on Central Govt. (Net)	32an
									5,008	5,247	5,273	5,950	5,827	7,365	Claims on State and Local Govts	32b
I37	107	310	1,381	I36	I713	795	1,103	1,509	I493	463	565	612	285	340	Claims on Official Entities	32bx
I898	1,650	4,882	22,248	I1,279	I10,702	22,550	34,564	42,600	I51,372	50,780	54,093	63,131	70,525	68,431	Claims on Private Sector	32d
....	....	....	....	....	I6	6	5	5	I4	3	3	—	—	—	Claims on Other Banking Insts	32f
I350	664	1,418	6,402	I273	I3,068	7,626	11,364	15,119	I16,362	16,619	19,042	21,482	21,489	20,610	Money	34
I568	1,291	3,727	21,528	I379	I4,845	11,471	19,666	30,334	I37,109	35,352	42,710	56,038	64,162	67,081	Quasi-Money	35
I494	869	2,829	10,147	I979	I11,523	13,394	17,196	19,720	I16,798	17,354	19,118	19,864	21,279	20,852	Capital Accounts	37a
....	....	....	....	....	I-1,577	2,351	4,790	3,515	I3,701	4,333	2,647	3,997	4,704	3,454	Other Items (Net)	37r
I918	1,955	5,145	27,929	I652	I7,913	19,097	31,030	45,453	I53,471	51,971	61,752	77,520	85,651	87,691	Money plus Quasi-Money	35l
Thousands from 1985 to 1988;Millions Beginning 1989: End of Period															**Other Banking Institutions**	
I2	2	4	21	I1	I7	12	17	20	I20	14	7	6	7	15	Reserves	40
I—	—	—	2	I—	I3	10	12	32	I26	31	25	24	17	74	Foreign Assets	41
I1	1	5	18	I5	I26	37	24	26	I35	37	84	96	114	89	Claims on Central Government	42a
									2	2	—	2	—	—	Claims on Local and State Govts	42b
I—	—	1	11	I—	I2	5	6	—	I—						Claims on Official Entities	42bx
I23	39	87	337	I9	I51	220	441	644	I838	725	846	1,103	1,681	2,147	Claims on Private Sector	42d
I2	3	3	22	I—	I2	5	5	5	I10	13	20	18	22	27	Claims on Deposit Money Banks	42e
I16	38	98	567	I5	I43	121	272	412	I501	284	348	320	333	295	Time, Savings,& Fgn.Currency Dep.	45
I—	—	1	—	I—	I1	49	116	26	I39	62	84	148	395	434	Foreign Liabilities	46c
I10	18	16	35	I1	I6	6	5	5	I4	3	3	—	—	—	Credit from Monetary Authorities	46g
I7	8	19	178	I8	I76	133	167	202	I236	210	190	233	367	468	Capital Accounts	47a
I-5	-18	-33	-368	I1	I-35	-20	-55	82	I151	263	357	547	746	1,155	Other Items (Net)	47r
Thousands from 1985 to 1988;Millions Beginning 1989: End of Period															**Banking Survey**	
I-502	-966	-4,524	-15,530	....	I-4,411	-6,184	2,433	7,883	I6,403	2,480	7,585	13,499	15,884	15,718	Foreign Assets (Net)	51n
I1,728	3,282	11,103	47,395	I2,597	I22,345	41,243	50,945	61,476	I68,424	71,908	76,802	88,959	97,167	98,155	Domestic Credit	52
I769	1,486	5,823	23,418	I1,272	I10,877	17,673	14,831	16,723	I10,711	14,691	16,024	18,163	18,850	19,872	Claims on Central Govt. (Net)	52an
....	....	....	....	....	....	....	....	....	5,009	5,249	5,273	5,951	5,827	7,365	Claims on State and Local Govts	52b
I37	107	311	1,392	I36	I715	800	1,109	1,509	I493	463	565	612	285	340	Claims on Official Entities	52bx
I921	1,688	4,969	22,585	I1,288	I10,753	22,770	35,005	43,244	I52,210	51,505	54,939	64,234	72,206	70,578	Claims on Private Sector	52d
I932	1,991	5,239	28,476	I657	I7,949	19,206	31,285	45,845	I53,952	52,241	62,094	77,835	85,977	87,972	Liquid Liabilities	55l
I501	877	2,848	10,324	I987	I11,599	13,527	17,363	19,922	I17,034	17,564	19,308	20,098	21,646	21,320	Capital Accounts	57a
I-207	-552	-1,509	-6,935	....	I-1,614	2,326	4,730	3,592	I3,841	4,584	2,984	4,526	5,428	4,581	Other Items (Net)	57r

Argentina

213

		1970	1971	1972	1973	1974	1975	1976	1977	1978	1979	1980	1981	1982	1983	1984
Interest Rates														*Percent Per Annum*		
Money Market Rate	60b	…	…	…	…	…	…	…	…	…	…	87	185	202	739	1,182
Money Market Rate (U.S. Dollars)	60ba	…	…	…	…	…	…	…	…	…	…	…	…	…	…	…
Deposit Rate	60l	…	…	…	…	…	…	…	115	132	117	80	157	126	281	397
Lending Rate	60p	…	…	…	…	…	…	…	…	…	…	…	…	…	…	…
Lending Rate (U.S. Dollars)	60pa	…	…	…	…	…	…	…	…	…	…	…	…	…	…	…
Prices, Production, Labor														*Index Numbers (1995=100):*		
Producer Prices	63	…	…	…	…	…	…	…	…	…	…	…	…	…	…	…
Cons.Prices (1995=10 billions)	64.a	—	.1	.1	.2	.2	.6	3.1	8.5	23.6	61.1	122.7	250.9	664.4	2,948.6	21,428.3
Cons.Prices (1995=100,000)	64.b	…	…	…	…	…	…	…	…	…	…	…	…	…	…	.2
Consumer Prices	64	…	…	…	…	…	…	…	…	…	…	…	…	…	…	…
Wages: Monthly Earnings (Mfg)	65ey	…	…	…	…	…	…	…	…	…	…	…	…	…	…	…
Manufacturing Prod., Seas.Adj.	66ey c	…	…	…	…	…	…	…	…	…	…	…	…	…	…	…
Crude Petroleum Production	66aa	54.6	58.9	60.4	58.6	57.6	55.3	55.4	59.9	62.9	65.9	68.5	69.1	68.2	68.2	66.7
															Number in Thousands:	
Labor Force	67d	…	…	…	…	…	…	…	…	…	…	…	…	…	…	…
Employment	67e	…	…	…	…	…	…	…	…	…	…	…	…	…	…	…
Unemployment	67c	…	…	…	…	…	…	…	…	…	…	…	…	…	…	152
Unemployment Rate (%)	67r	…	…	…	…	…	…	…	…	…	…	…	…	…	…	3.8
International Transactions														*Millions of US Dollars*		
Exports	70..d	1,773	1,740	1,941	3,266	3,931	2,961	3,916	5,652	6,400	7,810	8,021	9,143	7,625	7,836	8,107
Meat	70k.d	438.0	412.3	686.3	778.8	437.1	281.5	510.5	622.4	781.0	1,202.5	935.8	907.7	804.9	602.6	404.3
Wheat	70d.d	126	49	110	274	305	301	432	541	174	606	816	764	676	1,474	966
Imports, c.i.f.	71..d	1,694	1,868	1,905	2,230	3,635	3,947	3,033	4,162	3,834	6,700	10,541	9,430	5,337	4,504	4,585
Imports, f.o.b.	71.vd	1,499	1,043	1,686	1,985	3,242	3,512	2,743	3,803	3,492	6,041	9,381	8,430	4,857	4,126	4,201
															1995=100	
Volume of Exports	72	…	…	…	…	…	…	…	…	…	…	…	…	…	…	…
Wheat	72d	33.5	11.7	23.9	43.5	25.2	25.6	45.9	82.0	23.4	62.3	65.4	54.8	55.3	148.2	105.4
Volume of Imports	73	…	…	…	…	…	…	…	…	…	…	…	…	…	…	…
															1995=100:	
Unit Value of Exports	74..d	…	…	…	…	…	…	…	…	…	…	…	…	…	…	…
Frozen Beef	74ka d	15.7	19.1	24.6	33.8	36.2	18.5	19.5	25.0	25.0	39.7	46.3	40.0	30.4	31.6	43.2
Corned Beef	74kd d	38.2	60.0	63.9	80.1	110.0	76.8	72.1	72.9	73.9	115.9	139.8	132.5	97.3	88.8	84.9
Wheat	74d.d	33.1	36.2	40.5	59.3	117.7	104.6	81.6	58.9	71.6	89.0	112.1	117.9	101.5	87.4	80.4
Unit Value of Imports	75..d	…	…	…	…	…	…	…	…	…	…	…	…	…	…	…
Balance of Payments															*Millions of US Dollars:*	
Current Account, n.i.e.	78al d	…	…	…	…	…	…	651	1,126	1,856	−513	−4,774	−4,712	−2,353	−2,436	−2,495
Goods: Exports f.o.b.	78aa d	…	…	…	…	…	…	3,918	5,651	6,401	7,810	8,021	9,143	7,623	7,835	8,100
Goods: Imports f.o.b.	78ab d	…	…	…	…	…	…	−2,765	−3,799	−3,488	−6,028	−9,394	−8,431	−4,859	−4,119	−4,118
Trade Balance	78ac d	…	…	…	…	…	…	1,153	1,852	2,913	1,782	−1,373	712	2,764	3,716	3,982
Services: Credit	78ad d	…	…	…	…	…	…	714	951	1,087	1,369	1,876	1,716	1,574	1,455	1,511
Services: Debit	78ae d	…	…	…	…	…	…	−742	−967	−1,544	−2,814	−3,788	−3,434	−2,018	−2,224	−2,289
Balance on Goods & Services	78af d	…	…	…	…	…	…	1,125	1,836	2,456	337	−3,285	−1,006	2,320	2,947	3,204
Income: Credit	78ag d	…	…	…	…	…	…	59	136	348	737	1,305	946	558	474	298
Income: Debit	78ah d	…	…	…	…	…	…	−551	−877	−1,016	−1,644	−2,817	−4,630	−5,265	−5,873	−5,999
Balance on Gds, Serv. & Inc.	78ai d	…	…	…	…	…	…	633	1,095	1,788	−570	−4,797	−4,690	−2,387	−2,452	−2,497
Current Transfers, n.i.e.: Credit	78aj d	…	…	…	…	…	…	30	43	85	88	85	70	51	35	21
Current Transfers: Debit	78ak d	…	…	…	…	…	…	−12	−12	−17	−31	−62	−92	−17	−19	−19
Capital Account, n.i.e.	78bc d	…	…	…	…	…	…	…	…	…	…	…	…	…	…	…
Capital Account, n.i.e.: Credit	78ba d	…	…	…	…	…	…	—	—	—	—	—	—	—	—	—
Capital Account: Debit	78bb d	…	…	…	…	…	…	—	—	—	—	—	—	—	—	—
Financial Account, n.i.e.	78bj d	…	…	…	…	…	…	−554	605	−70	4,308	2,305	1,355	−1,972	−2,391	257
Direct Investment Abroad	78bd d	…	…	…	…	…	…	—	1	23	59	110	107	30	−2	—
Dir. Invest. in Rep. Econ., n.i.e.	78be d	…	…	…	…	…	…	—	144	250	206	678	837	227	185	268
Portfolio Investment Assets	78bf d	…	…	…	…	…	…	—	—	—	—	—	—	—	—	—
Equity Securities	78bk d	…	…	…	…	…	…	—	—	—	—	—	—	—	—	—
Debt Securities	78bl d	…	…	…	…	…	…	—	—	—	—	—	—	—	—	—
Portfolio Investment Liab., n.i.e.	78bg d	…	…	…	…	…	…	−66	−1	101	222	154	1,125	299	649	372
Equity Securities	78bm d	…	…	…	…	…	…	—	—	—	—	—	—	—	—	—
Debt Securities	78bn d	…	…	…	…	…	…	−66	−1	101	222	154	1,125	299	649	372
Financial Derivatives Assets	78bw d	…	…	…	…	…	…	…	…	…	…	…	…	…	…	…
Financial Derivatives Liabilities	78bx d	…	…	…	…	…	…	…	…	…	…	…	…	…	…	…
Other Investment Assets	78bh d	…	…	…	…	…	…	328	−382	−83	496	−440	−1,605	−552	−374	−241
Monetary Authorities	78bo d	…	…	…	…	…	…	−203	−286	−105	−61	−29	−155	400	−487	−387
General Government	78bp d	…	…	…	…	…	…	6	−10	−1	−10	−11	−14	−17	−12	−20
Banks	78bq d	…	…	…	…	…	…	−17	−87	−27	−285	−368	25	−431	−180	−527
Other Sectors	78br d	…	…	…	…	…	…	542	1	50	852	−32	−1,461	−504	305	693
Other Investment Liab., n.i.e.	78bi d	…	…	…	…	…	…	−816	843	−361	3,325	1,803	891	−1,976	−2,849	−142
Monetary Authorities	78bs d	…	…	…	…	…	…	−99	−275	−901	74	182	84	−200	−703	−123
General Government	78bt d	…	…	…	…	…	…	−48	−10	46	−11	469	977	−15	−841	1,793
Banks	78bu d	…	…	…	…	…	…	41	169	102	197	−60	363	1,050	528	−27
Other Sectors	78bv d	…	…	…	…	…	…	−710	959	392	3,065	1,212	−533	−2,811	−1,833	−1,785
Net Errors and Omissions	78ca d	…	…	…	…	…	…	−218	134	12	243	−308	−205	−401	−447	−55
Overall Balance	78cb d	…	…	…	…	…	…	−121	1,865	1,798	4,038	−2,777	−3,562	−4,726	−5,274	−2,293
Reserves and Related Items	79da d	…	…	…	…	…	…	121	−1,865	−1,798	−4,038	2,777	3,562	4,726	5,274	2,293
Reserve Assets	79db d	…	…	…	…	…	…	−1,156	−1,714	−1,716	−4,225	2,598	3,193	669	1,230	−166
Use of Fund Credit and Loans	79dc d	…	…	…	…	…	…	237	−132	−423	—	—	—	—	1,227	—
Exceptional Financing	79de d	…	…	…	…	…	…	1,040	−20	341	187	179	369	4,057	2,817	2,459

1985	1986	1987	1988	1989	1990	1991	1992	1993	1994	1995	1996	1997	1998	1999		
Percent Per Annum															**Interest Rates**	
1,161	135	253	524	1,387,179	9,695,422	71	15	6	8	9	6	7	7	7	Money Market Rate	60b
....	....	....	....	....	....	....	....	....	....	....	8	6	6	7	6	Money Market Rate (U.S. Dollars)	60ba
630	95	176	372	17,236	1,518	62	17	11	8	12	7	7	8	8	Deposit Rate	60l
....	....	....	....	....	....	....	....	....	10	18	11	9	11	11	Lending Rate	60p
....	....	....	....	....	....	....	....	....	8	14	9	8	9	9	Lending Rate (U.S. Dollars)	60pa
Period Averages															**Prices, Production, Labor**	
....	—	—	.1	2.4	40.7	85.6	90.7	92.2	92.8	100.0	I103.7	102.6	99.2	....	Producer Prices	63
															Cons.Prices (1995=10 billions)	64.a
1.7	3.1	7.3	I32.2	1,024.9	....	....	....	....	....	....	....	....	....	....	Cons.Prices (1995=100,000)	64.b
....	....	....	....	1.0	24.7	67.2	83.9	92.9	96.7	100.0	100.2	100.7	101.6	100.4	Consumer Prices	64
....	....	....	26.1	65.0	84.6	95.2	101.7	100.0	100.7	....	....	....			Wages: Monthly Earnings (Mfg)	65ey
....	....	....	....	....	....	....	....	106.7	100.0	105.1	114.8	116.6	108.1		Manufacturing Prod., Seas.Adj.	66ey c
63.9	60.3	59.4	62.6	63.8	66.9	67.6	77.4	82.5	92.8	100.0	109.2	116.0	117.8	112.3	Crude Petroleum Production	66aa
Period Averages																
					12,091					14,345					Labor Force	67d
						4,373	4,333	4,496	4,609	4,386	4,157				Employment	67e
216	178	230	251	323	441	I696	827	1,062	1,400	1,959	2,047				Unemployment	67c
5.3	4.4	5.3	5.9	7.3	9.2	I6.3	7.2	9.1	11.7	15.9	16.3				Unemployment Rate (%)	67r
Millions of US Dollars															**International Transactions**	
8,396	6,852	6,360	9,135	9,579	12,353	11,978	12,235	13,118	15,659	20,967	23,811	26,370	26,441	23,309	Exports	70..d
385.7	464.7	599.3	607.2	716.3	873.2	....	....	....	....	....	....	....	....	....	Meat	70k.d
1,133	395	351	355	658	871	496	716	735	657	1,005	1,066	1,347	1,308	1,002	Wheat	70d.d
3,814	4,724	5,818	5,322	4,203	4,076	8,275	14,872	16,784	21,527	20,122	23,762	30,450	31,404	25,538	Imports, c.i.f.	71..d
3,515	4,323	5,341	4,890	3,864	3,725	7,525	13,623	14,694	19,661	17,962	22,190	28,553	29,558	24,129	Imports, f.o.b.	71.v d
1995=100																
....	....	....	....	....	66.0	64.6	63.6	68.1	79.9	100.0	106.6	118.7	132.6	....	Volume of Exports	72
139.4	58.5	61.0	39.8	61.3	83.2	79.6	150.4	82.9	75.3	100.0	85.7	126.1	153.0	127.8	Wheat	72d
....	....	....	....	....	19.9	42.1	77.2	89.1	113.1	100.0	119.8	155.3	170.3	....	Volume of Imports	73
Indexes of Unit Values in US Dollars																
....	....	....	....	....	89.2	88.5	91.7	91.9	94.6	100.0	106.5	102.5	92.9	....	Unit Value of Exports	74..d
41.1	52.7	77.0	73.6	70.6	62.2	92.5	120.6	143.9	109.0	100.0	79.8	85.8	111.8	98.4	Frozen Beef	74ka d
80.0	88.2	108.7	80.1	92.7	100.0	116.9	90.9	108.7	116.7	....	....	....	....	....	Corned Beef	74kd d
70.1	59.5	54.7	71.2	90.6	87.9	54.6	73.2	79.9	79.8	100.0	122.4	96.1	74.8	71.2	Wheat	74d.d
....	....	....	....	....	101.7	97.8	95.7	93.5	94.9	100.0	98.5	97.1	91.7	....	Unit Value of Imports	75..d
Minus Sign Indicates Debit															**Balance of Payments**	
-952	-2,859	-4,235	-1,572	-1,305	4,552	-647	-5,521	-8,030	-10,992	-4,985	-6,521	-11,954	-14,274	-12,152	Current Account, n.i.e.	78al d
8,396	6,852	6,360	9,134	9,573	12,354	11,978	12,399	13,269	16,023	21,161	24,043	26,431	26,441	23,316	Goods: Exports f.o.b.	78aa d
-3,518	-4,406	-5,343	-4,892	-3,864	-3,726	-7,559	-13,795	-15,633	-20,162	-18,804	-22,283	-28,554	-29,558	-24,145	Goods: Imports f.o.b.	78ab d
4,878	2,446	1,017	4,242	5,709	8,628	4,419	-1,396	-2,364	-4,139	2,357	1,760	-2,123	-3,117	-829	*Trade Balance*	78ac d
1,651	1,597	1,794	2,015	2,193	2,446	2,408	3,019	3,188	3,428	3,855	4,428	4,509	4,684	4,448	Services: Credit	78ad d
-2,187	-2,500	-2,566	-2,702	-2,793	-3,120	-4,007	-5,482	-6,409	-7,120	-7,181	-7,794	-8,687	-9,015	-8,416	Services: Debit	78ae d
4,342	1,543	245	3,555	5,109	7,954	2,820	-3,859	-5,585	-7,831	-969	-1,606	-6,301	-7,448	-4,797	*Balance on Goods & Services*	78af d
282	392	252	211	276	1,854	1,746	2,354	2,594	3,464	4,413	4,467	5,501	6,183	6,137	Income: Credit	78ag d
-5,576	-4,796	-4,724	-5,338	-6,698	-6,254	-6,006	-4,747	-5,525	-7,031	-8,942	-9,798	-11,590	-13,518	-13,984	Income: Debit	78ah d
-952	-2,861	-4,227	-1,572	-1,313	3,554	-1,440	-6,252	-8,516	-11,398	-5,498	-6,937	-12,390	-14,783	-12,644	*Balance on Gds, Serv. & Inc.*	78ai d
18	21	11	2	18	1,015	821	855	674	628	623	510	542	615	575	Current Transfers, n.i.e.: Credit	78aj d
-18	-19	-19	-2	-10	-17	-28	-124	-188	-222	-110	-94	-106	-106	-83	Current Transfers: Debit	78ak d
—	—	—	—	—	—	....	....	....	....	....	....	....	....	....	Capital Account, n.i.e.	78bc d
—	—	—	—	—	—										Capital Account, n.i.e.: Credit	78ba d
—	—	—	—	—	—										Capital Account: Debit	78bb d
638	410	100	369	-8,083	-5,884	182	7,350	20,328	11,155	4,623	11,175	16,826	17,818	15,146	Financial Account, n.i.e.	78bj d
							-1,166	-704	-1,013	-1,497	-1,600	-3,656	-2,166	-1,195	Direct Investment Abroad	78bd d
919	574	-19	1,147	1,028	1,836	2,439	4,384	2,763	3,490	5,315	6,522	8,755	6,526	23,152	Dir. Invest. in Rep. Econ., n.i.e.	78be d
					-241	-8,261	1,612	-1,555	-1,485	-2,911	-2,483	-1,320	-2,176	-1,977	Portfolio Investment Assets	78bf d
							-295	-1,363	-762	-402	-593	-731	-838	208	Equity Securities	78bk d
					-241	-8,261	1,907	-192	-723	-2,509	-1,890	-589	-1,338	-2,185	Debt Securities	78bl d
-617	-542	-572	-718	-1,098	-1,105	8,227	2,901	35,286	9,874	4,775	12,210	12,407	10,515	-4,641	Portfolio Investment Liab., n.i.e.	78bg d
							1,121	4,979	3,117	1,091	991	1,391	-210	-10,950	Equity Securities	78bm d
-617	-542	-572	-718	-1,098	-1,105	8,227	1,780	30,307	6,757	3,684	11,219	11,016	10,725	6,309	Debt Securities	78bn d
															Financial Derivatives Assets	78bw d
															Financial Derivatives Liabilities	78bx d
26	-286	104	879	-399	661	426	-804	-4,658	-3,169	-8,232	-5,301	-7,131	210	-2,213	Other Investment Assets	78bh d
-207	-198	—		366	-669	273	330								Monetary Authorities	78bo d
-29	-36	-23	—	-48	-81	83	-880	-1,484	442	-686	62		111	-1,530	General Government	78bp d
-231	5	16		—		—	-696	-1,728	-303	-680	-3,010	-5,505	722	853	Banks	78bq d
493	-57	111	879	-717	1,411	70	442	-1,446	-3,308	-6,866	-2,353	-1,537	-623	-1,536	Other Sectors	78br d
310	664	587	-939	-7,614	-7,035	-2,649	423	-10,804	3,458	7,173	1,827	7,771	4,909	2,020	Other Investment Liab., n.i.e.	78bi d
-361	-159	408	426	-1,804	-474	40	-183	-3,999	-18	6	36	-11	-10	-12	Monetary Authorities	78bs d
2,061	860	652	5	-438	-420	-3	-463	-8,712	527	1,883	-261	225	1,794	1,046	General Government	78bt d
898	-28	-49	23	56	100	-31	772	1,158	1,064	3,250	266	3,890	646	1,064	Banks	78bu d
-2,288	-9	-424	-1,393	-5,428	-6,241	-2,655	297	749	1,885	2,034	1,786	3,667	2,479	-78	Other Sectors	78bv d
-532	302	-112	-165	-249	715	-341	54	-1,173	-872	-1,853	-1,316	-1,498	574	-1,049	Net Errors and Omissions	78ca d
-846	-2,147	-4,247	-1,368	-9,637	-617	-806	1,883	11,125	-709	-2,215	3,338	3,374	4,118	1,945	*Overall Balance*	78cb d
846	2,147	4,247	1,368	9,637	617	806	-1,883	-11,125	709	2,215	-3,338	-3,374	-4,118	-1,945	Reserves and Related Items	79da d
-2,016	745	1,302	-1,888	1,826	-3,121	-2,040	-3,264	-4,279	-685	82	-3,875	-3,293	-3,436	-1,186	Reserve Assets	79db d
987	146	615	30	-478	-257	-590	-73	1,211	455	1,924	367	-38	-654	-826	Use of Fund Credit and Loans	79dc d
1,875	1,256	2,330	3,226	8,289	3,996	3,436	1,454	-8,057	938	209	170	-43	-28	68	Exceptional Financing	79de d

		1970	1971	1972	1973	1974	1975	1976	1977	1978	1979	1980	1981	1982	1983	1984
Government Finance											*Thousandths (.000) of Pesos through 1978; Pesos from 1979 to 1984;*					
Deficit (-) or Surplus	80	....	....	....	−100.0	−600.0	−1,700.0	−6,700.0	−8,900.0	−19,800.0	ℐ−43.3	−119.5	−406.1	−923.0	−8,231.6	−29,980.3
Revenue	81	...	...	...	...	...	...	...	...	...	ℐ94.4	170.0	336.1	897.1	4,977.2	35,577.2
Exp. & Lending Minus Repay.	82z	...	...	...	...	...	...	...	...	...	ℐ137.9	289.5	742.2	1,820.1	13,208.8	65,557.5
Expenditure	82	...	...	...	...	...	...	...	...	...	...	...	...	...	...	...
Lending Minus Repayments	83	...	...	...	...	...	...	...	...	...	...	...	...	...	...	...
Total Financing	84	...	...	...	...	...	...	...	...	...	ℐ43.7	119.7	406.4	923.5	8,230.8	29,980.6
Net Borrowing: Domestic	84a										ℐ40.8	117.1	340.9	1,005.8	10,376.7	28,938.5
Foreign	85a										ℐ3.2	2.4	65.4	61.4	−2,145.8	1,042.1
Use of Cash Balances	87	...	...	...						...	ℐ−.3	.2	.1	−143.7	−.1	—
National Accounts											*Thousandths (.000) of Pesos through 1978; Pesos from 1979 to 1984;*					
Exports of Goods & Services	90c	100	100	200	400	500	1,100	9,400	27,300	61,000	ℐ126	194	517	1,986	10,020	60,030
Government Consumption	91f	100	100	200	400	700	1,900	7,400	19,700	60,900	ℐ164	—	—	—	—	—
Gross Fixed Capital Formation	93e	200	300	400	600	900	3,700	20,400	56,900	127,600	ℐ324	970	1,696	4,754	22,870	157,900
Increase/Decrease(-) in Stocks	93i	—	—	—	—	—	100	200	—	−2,700	ℐ−2	—	—	—	—	—
Private Consumption	96f	600	900	1,400	2,400	3,200	8,700	44,600	126,200	317,100	ℐ936	2,925	5,812	16,537	82,990	610,610
Imports of Goods & Services	98c	−100	−100	−200	−300	−400	−1,200	−6,100	−20,800	−40,500	ℐ−122	−249	−551	−1,425	−6,390	−37,620
Gross Domestic Product (GDP)	99b	900	1,300	2,100	3,500	4,900	14,300	75,900	209,300	523,400	ℐ1,425	3,840	7,474	21,852	109,500	790,920
Net Factor Inc/Pmts(-) Abroad	98.n	−11	−20	−29	−40	−30	−200	−1,200	−2,400	−6,200	ℐ−14	−32	−229	−1,266	−6,222	−41,830
Gross National Income (GNI)	99a	800	1,100	2,000	3,200	4,786	14,100	74,700	206,900	517,200	ℐ1,412	2,801	5,247	13,495	62,044	486,270
GDP Vol. 1960 prices(thousandths)	99b.*p*	1	1	1	1	1	1	1	1	1	1	1	...	...	...	...
GDP Vol. 1986 prices(thousands)	99b.*p*	...	...	...	...	...	...	...	...	...	...	10,331	9,738	9,431	9,824	10,020
GDP Vol. 1993 prices(millions)	99b.*p*	...	...	...	...	...	...	...	...	...	...	...	...	...	...	...
GDP Volume (1995=100)	99bv*p*	66.1	69.3	71.9	75.8	80.9	79.8	76.7	81.7	78.9	85.6	85.4	80.5	77.9	81.2	82.8
GDP Deflator (1995=1 trillion)	99bi*p*	5.3	7.4	11.7	18.9	24.8	73.0	388.7	...	...	...	...	...	...	...	...
GDP Deflator (1995=10 billions)	99bi*p*	...	...	...	...	...	...	...	10	26	66	176	363	1,096	5,270	37,324
GDP Deflator (1995=100)	99bi*p*	...	...	...	...	...	...	...	...	...	...	...	...	...	...	...
																Millions:
Population	99z	23.75	24.07	24.39	24.82	25.22	ℐ26.05	26.48	26.91	27.35	27.79	28.24	28.66	29.09	29.51	29.88

Thousands from 1985 to 1988:Millions Beginning 1989: Yr. Ending Dec. 31

	1985	1986	1987	1988	1989	1990	1991	1992	1993	1994	1995	1996	1997	1998	1999		
Government Finance																	
Deficit (-) or Surplus	I-283.7	-239.4	-628.3	-1,487.1	I-21.5	-226.1	-963.0	-73.0	-1,574.0	-1,885.7	I-1426.0	-5,233.6	....	....	....	80
Revenue	I271.2	550.1	1,111.4	3,139.6	I153.4	2,741.2	8,028.5	12,889.0	15,555.0	15,591.8	I38060.9	35,501.0	....	....	....	81
Exp. & Lending Minus Repay.	I554.9	789.5	1,739.7	4,626.6	I174.8	2,967.3	8,991.5	12,962.0	17,129.0	17,477.5	I39486.9	40,734.6	....	....	....	82z
Expenditure	....	....	....	....	....						40,574.5	41,066.1	....	....	....	82
Lending Minus Repayments											-1,087.6	-331.5	....	....	....	83
Total Financing	I283.7	239.3	628.2	1,487.1	I21.5	226.1	963.0	73.0	1,574.0	1,885.7	I1,426.0	5,233.6	....	....	....	84
Net Borrowing: Domestic	I275.7	328.2	181.4	998.9	I-8.6	346.9	869.4	895.0	1,740.0	863.2	....	....	....	....	....	84a
Foreign	I8.4	-89.2	446.9	490.6	I30.1	-86.2	310.8	-118.0	1,283.0	1,256.8	....	....	....	....	....	85a
Use of Cash Balances	I-.3	.4	-.1	-2.4	I—	-34.6	-217.1	-704.0	-1,449.0	-234.3	....	....	....	....	....	87

Thousands from 1985 to 1988; Millions beginning 1989

	1985	1986	1987	1988	1989	1990	1991	1992	1993	1994	1995	1996	1997	1998	1999		
National Accounts																	
Exports of Goods & Services	I623	815	1,837	10,586	I421	7,201	14,046	15,096	I16,458	19,450	25,017	28,470	30,939	31,088	27,827	90c
Government Consumption	I—		—		I—				I31,953	33,948	34,446	34,023	35,325	35,474	36,352	91f
Gross Fixed Capital Formation	I933	1,743	4,563	20,702	I503	9,647	26,478	37,854	I45,069	51,331	46,285	49,211	56,727	59,276	53,909	93e
Increase/Decrease(-) in Stocks	I—								I—							93i
Private Consumption	I4,082	8,057	18,700	86,673	I2,533	55,268	151,448	192,670	I165,067	179,992	178,269	190,522	207,108	210,785	197,195	96f
Imports of Goods & Services	I-333	-631	-1,768	-6,899	I-213	-3,194	-11,074	-18,823	I-22,042	-27,281	-25,985	-30,077	-37,240	-38,491	-32,515	98c
Gross Domestic Product (GDP)	I5,305	9,984	23,332	111,062	I3,244	68,922	180,898	226,847	I236,505	257,440	258,032	272,150	292,859	298,131	282,769	99b
Net Factor Inc/Pmts(-) Abroad	I-346	-417	-982	-3,000	I-145	-1,017	-2,301	-2,065	I-2,931	-3,567	-4,529	-5,331	-6,089	-7,335	-7,847	98.n
Gross National Income (GNI)	I5,000	10,000	22,000	108,000	I3,099	67,906	178,597	224,782	I233,574	253,873	253,503	266,819	286,770	290,796	274,922	99a
GDP Vol. 1960 prices(thousandths)	....	....	....	....	....	....	....	....	....	....	....	....	....	....	....	99b.p
GDP Vol. 1986 prices(thousands)	9,324	9,989	10,248	10,054	9,357	9,185	10,157	11,133	11,770							99b.p
GDP Vol. 1993 prices(millions)	....	....	....	....	....	....	....	....	236,505	250,308	243,186	256,626	277,441	288,195	279,511	99b.p
GDP Volume (1995=100)	77.0	82.5	84.7	83.1	77.3	75.9	83.9	92.0	97.3	102.9	100.0	105.5	114.1	118.5	114.9	99bv p
GDP Deflator (1995=1 trillion)	....	....	....	....	....	....	....	....	....	....	....	....	....	....	....	99bi p
GDP Deflator (1995=10 billions)	269,033	472,616	1,076,565	....	....	....	....	....	....	....	....	....	....	....	....	99bi p
GDP Deflator (1995=100)			—	.1	1.6	35.5	84.2	96.3	I95.0	95.8	100.0	100.7	99.7	97.4	....	99bi p

Midyear Estimates

	1985	1986	1987	1988	1989	1990	1991	1992	1993	1994	1995	1996	1997	1998	1999		
Population	30.32	30.77	31.22	31.64	32.08	32.53	32.97	33.42	33.87	34.32	34.77	35.22	35.67	36.12	36.58	99z

(See notes in the back of the book.)

Armenia

911

	1970	1971	1972	1973	1974	1975	1976	1977	1978	1979	1980	1981	1982	1983	1984
Exchange Rates															*Dram per SDR:*
Official Rate .... aa	....	....	....	....	....	....	....	....	....	....	....	....	....	....	....
															Dram per US Dollar:
Official Rate .... ae	....	....	....	....	....	....	....	....	....	....	....	....	....	....	....
Official Rate .... rf	....	....	....	....	....	....	....	....	....	....	....	....	....	....	....
															Index Numbers (1995=100):
Nominal Effective Exchange Rate .... ne c	....	....	....	....	....	....	....	....	....	....	....	....	....	....	....
Real Effective Exchange Rate .... re c	....	....	....	....	....	....	....	....	....	....	....	....	....	....	....
Fund Position															*Millions of SDRs:*
Quota .... 2f. s	—	—	—	—	—	—	—	—	—	—	—	—	—	—	—
SDRs .... 1b. s	....	....	....	....	....	....	....	....	....	....	....	....	....	....	....
Reserve Position in the Fund .... 1c. s	....	....	....	....	....	....	....	....	....	....	....	....	....	....	....
Total Fund Cred.&Loans Outstg. 2tl	....	....	....	....	....	....	....	....	....	....	....	....	....	....	....
International Liquidity												*Millions of US Dollars Unless Otherwise Indicated:*			
Total Reserves minus Gold .... 1l. d	....	....	....	....	....	....	....	....	....	....	....	....	....	....	....
SDRs .... 1b. d	....	....	....	....	....	....	....	....	....	....	....	....	....	....	....
Reserve Position in the Fund .... 1c. d	....	....	....	....	....	....	....	....	....	....	....	....	....	....	....
Foreign Exchange .... 1d. d	....	....	....	....	....	....	....	....	....	....	....	....	....	....	....
Gold (Million Fine Troy Ounces) 1ad	....	....	....	....	....	....	....	....	....	....	....	....	....	....	....
Gold (National Valuation) .... 1an d	....	....	....	....	....	....	....	....	....	....	....	....	....	....	....
Monetary Authorities: Other Assets .... 3.. d	....	....	....	....	....	....	....	....	....	....	....	....	....	....	....
Other Liab. .... 4.. d	....	....	....	....	....	....	....	....	....	....	....	....	....	....	....
Deposit Money Banks: Assets .... 7a. d	....	....	....	....	....	....	....	....	....	....	....	....	....	....	....
Liabilities .... 7b. d	....	....	....	....	....	....	....	....	....	....	....	....	....	....	....
Monetary Authorities															*Millions of Dram:*
Foreign Assets 11	....	....	....	....	....	....	....	....	....	....	....	....	....	....	....
Claims on General Government 12a	....	....	....	....	....	....	....	....	....	....	....	....	....	....	....
Claims on Deposit Money Banks 12e	....	....	....	....	....	....	....	....	....	....	....	....	....	....	....
Reserve Money 14	....	....	....	....	....	....	....	....	....	....	....	....	....	....	....
of which: Currency Outside DMBs 14a	....	....	....	....	....	....	....	....	....	....	....	....	....	....	....
Time,Savings,& Fgn.Currency Dep. 15	....	....	....	....	....	....	....	....	....	....	....	....	....	....	....
Foreign Liabilities 16c	....	....	....	....	....	....	....	....	....	....	....	....	....	....	....
General Government Deposits 16d	....	....	....	....	....	....	....	....	....	....	....	....	....	....	....
Capital Accounts 17a	....	....	....	....	....	....	....	....	....	....	....	....	....	....	....
Other Items (Net) 17r	....	....	....	....	....	....	....	....	....	....	....	....	....	....	....
Deposit Money Banks															*Millions of Dram:*
Reserves 20	....	....	....	....	....	....	....	....	....	....	....	....	....	....	....
Foreign Assets 21	....	....	....	....	....	....	....	....	....	....	....	....	....	....	....
Claims on General Government 22a	....	....	....	....	....	....	....	....	....	....	....	....	....	....	....
of which: Claims on Local Govts. 22ab	....	....	....	....	....	....	....	....	....	....	....	....	....	....	....
Claims on Other Sectors 22d	....	....	....	....	....	....	....	....	....	....	....	....	....	....	....
Demand Deposits 24	....	....	....	....	....	....	....	....	....	....	....	....	....	....	....
Time,Savings,& Fgn.Currency Dep. 25	....	....	....	....	....	....	....	....	....	....	....	....	....	....	....
Money Market Instruments 26aa	....	....	....	....	....	....	....	....	....	....	....	....	....	....	....
Foreign Liabilities 26c	....	....	....	....	....	....	....	....	....	....	....	....	....	....	....
General Government Deposits 26d	....	....	....	....	....	....	....	....	....	....	....	....	....	....	....
of which: Local Govt. Deposits 26db	....	....	....	....	....	....	....	....	....	....	....	....	....	....	....
Credit from Monetary Authorities 26g	....	....	....	....	....	....	....	....	....	....	....	....	....	....	....
Capital Accounts 27a	....	....	....	....	....	....	....	....	....	....	....	....	....	....	....
Other Items (Net) 27r	....	....	....	....	....	....	....	....	....	....	....	....	....	....	....
Monetary Survey															*Millions of Dram:*
Foreign Assets (Net) 31n	....	....	....	....	....	....	....	....	....	....	....	....	....	....	....
Domestic Credit 32	....	....	....	....	....	....	....	....	....	....	....	....	....	....	....
Claims on General Govt. (Net) 32an	....	....	....	....	....	....	....	....	....	....	....	....	....	....	....
Claims on Other Sectors 32d	....	....	....	....	....	....	....	....	....	....	....	....	....	....	....
Money 34	....	....	....	....	....	....	....	....	....	....	....	....	....	....	....
Quasi-Money 35	....	....	....	....	....	....	....	....	....	....	....	....	....	....	....
Money Market Instruments 36aa	....	....	....	....	....	....	....	....	....	....	....	....	....	....	....
Capital Accounts 37a	....	....	....	....	....	....	....	....	....	....	....	....	....	....	....
Other Items (Net) 37r	....	....	....	....	....	....	....	....	....	....	....	....	....	....	....
Money plus Quasi-Money 35l	....	....	....	....	....	....	....	....	....	....	....	....	....	....	....
Interest Rates															*Percent Per Annum*
Discount Rate (End of Period) 60	....	....	....	....	....	....	....	....	....	....	....	....	....	....	....
Refinancing Rate (End of Period) 60a	....	....	....	....	....	....	....	....	....	....	....	....	....	....	....
Money Market Rate 60b	....	....	....	....	....	....	....	....	....	....	....	....	....	....	....
Treasury Bill Rate 60c	....	....	....	....	....	....	....	....	....	....	....	....	....	....	....
Deposit Rate 60l	....	....	....	....	....	....	....	....	....	....	....	....	....	....	....
Lending Rate 60p	....	....	....	....	....	....	....	....	....	....	....	....	....	....	....
Prices, Production, Labor															*Index Numbers (1995=100):*
Producer Prices (1997=100) 63	....	....	....	....	....	....	....	....	....	....	....	....	....	....	....
Consumer Prices 64	....	....	....	....	....	....	....	....	....	....	....	....	....	....	....
Wages: Avg. Month.Earn.(1997=100) 65	....	....	....	....	....	....	....	....	....	....	....	....	....	....	....
Industrial Production (1997=100) 66	....	....	....	....	....	....	....	....	....	....	....	....	....	....	....
															Number in Thousands:
Employment 67e	....	....	....	....	....	....	....	....	....	....	....	....	....	....	....
Unemployment 67c	....	....	....	....	....	....	....	....	....	....	....	....	....	....	....
Unemployment Rate (%) 67r	....	....	....	....	....	....	....	....	....	....	....	....	....	....	....

	1985	1986	1987	1988	1989	1990	1991	1992	1993	1994	1995	1996	1997	1998	1999		
																Exchange Rates	
End of Period																	
								2.85	103.02	591.98	597.57	625.61	667.85	735.03	718.88	Official Rate	aa
End of Period (ae) Period Average (rf)																	
	....	....	....	....	....	....	....	2.07	75.00	405.51	402.00	435.07	494.98	522.03	523.77	Official Rate	ae
	....	....	....	....	....	....	....	....	9.11	288.65	405.91	414.04	490.85	504.92	535.06	Official Rate	rf
Period Averages																	
	....	....	....	....	....	....	....	....	....	64.99	100.00	217.19	209.90	237.33	324.14	Nominal Effective Exchange Rate	ne c
	....	....	....	....	....	....	....	....	....	57.69	100.00	119.76	104.83	111.47	115.13	Real Effective Exchange Rate	re c
																Fund Position	
End of Period																	
	—	—	—	—	—	—	—	67.50	67.50	67.50	67.50	67.50	67.50	67.50	92.00	Quota	2f. s
								—	—	.19	29.82	28.86	27.63	19.89	29.64	SDRs	1b. s
								.01	.01	.01	.01	.01	—	—	—	Reserve Position in the Fund	1c. s
								—	—	16.88	47.25	81.00	97.88	135.25	146.62	Total Fund Cred.&Loans Outstg.	2tl
																International Liquidity	
End of Period																	
	....	....	....	....	....	....	....	1.29	13.59	32.28	99.58	155.65	228.75	315.29	318.56	Total Reserves minus Gold	1l. d
	....	....	....	....	....	....	....	—	—	.28	44.33	41.50	37.28	28.00	40.68	SDRs	1b. d
	....	....	....	....	....	....	....	.01	.01	.01	.01	.01	.01	.01	—	Reserve Position in the Fund	1c. d
	....	....	....	....	....	....	....	1.28	13.58	31.99	55.24	114.14	191.46	287.28	277.88	Foreign Exchange	1d. d
	....	....	....	....	....	....	....	—	—	.0100	.0300	.0340	.0361	.0432	.0436	Gold (Million Fine Troy Ounces)	1ad
	....	....	....	....	....	....	....	—	—	2.44	10.46	12.82	10.72	12.37	12.69	Gold (National Valuation)	1an d
	....	....	....	....	....	....	....	99.61	2.93	.20	.10	.52	.25	.10	.05	Monetary Authorities: Other Assets	3.. d
	....	....	....	....	....	....	....	5.82	23.96	2.05	1.19	5.09	5.05	2.54	1.59	Other Liab.	4.. d
	....	....	....	....	....	....	....	14.12	22.68	22.03	24.28	18.14	33.28	33.12	70.34	Deposit Money Banks: Assets	7a. d
	....	....	....	....	....	....	....	3.82	3.45	12.98	24.59	50.74	73.39	96.10	111.50	Liabilities	7b. d
																Monetary Authorities	
End of Period																	
	....	....	....	....	....	....	....	209	1,239	14,162	44,278	73,523	118,657	171,103	173,521	Foreign Assets	11
	....	....	....	....	....	....	....	54	1,463	9,536	10,624	27,971	16,491	18,083	18,471	Claims on General Government	12a
	....	....	....	....	....	....	....	81	286	3,629	3,781	3,346	3,345	3,253	1,698	Claims on Deposit Money Banks	12e
	....	....	....	....	....	....	....	108	1,593	15,002	28,806	41,140	51,333	53,863	53,853	Reserve Money	14
	....	....	....	....	....	....	....	60	881	10,056	24,601	34,784	37,596	41,370	42,610	*of which: Currency Outside DMBs*	14a
	....	....	....	....	....	....	....	—	—	781	556	116	187	1,529	1,961	Time,Savings,& Fgn.Currency Dep.	15
	....	....	....	....	....	....	....	12	1,797	10,823	28,715	52,890	67,863	100,741	106,234	Foreign Liabilities	16c
	....	....	....	....	....	....	....	2	76	1,433	423	8,733	8,165	8,813	8,550	General Government Deposits	16d
	....	....	....	....	....	....	....	4	121	596	1,691	7,214	13,733	16,609	12,079	Capital Accounts	17a
	....	....	....	....	....	....	....	218	−599	−1,309	−1,509	−5,254	−2,788	10,882	11,013	Other Items (Net)	17r
																Deposit Money Banks	
End of Period																	
	....	....	....	....	....	....	....	22	529	3,164	3,987	6,083	13,681	12,033	11,082	Reserves	20
	....	....	....	....	....	....	....	29	1,701	8,933	9,759	7,894	16,472	17,287	36,843	Foreign Assets	21
	....	....	....	....	....	....	....	9	199	335	354	5,865	9,198	15,436	12,268	Claims on General Government	22a
	....	....	....	....	....	....	....	—	—	—	—	—	—	2	5	*of which: Claims on Local Govts.*	22ab
	....	....	....	....	....	....	....	125	353	20,718	37,946	37,181	48,486	82,159	90,540	Claims on Other Sectors	22d
	....	....	....	....	....	....	....	55	443	3,188	5,375	4,968	6,372	11,216	9,553	Demand Deposits	24
	....	....	....	....	....	....	....	133	1,584	10,310	9,617	14,424	26,005	42,868	56,881	Time,Savings,& Fgn.Currency Dep.	25
	....	....	....	....	....	....	....	—	—	—	—	—	—	—	24	Money Market Instruments	26aa
	....	....	....	....	....	....	....	8	259	5,262	9,884	22,074	36,328	50,168	58,399	Foreign Liabilities	26c
	....	....	....	....	....	....	....	16	217	1,324	1,748	2,533	2,469	3,662	5,205	General Government Deposits	26d
	....	....	....	....	....	....	....	11	134	790	857	222	577	349	209	*of which: Local Govt. Deposits*	26db
	....	....	....	....	....	....	....	1	4	1,367	4,093	3,539	3,710	3,257	1,701	Credit from Monetary Authorities	26g
	....	....	....	....	....	....	....	−40	165	3,646	7,579	12,315	17,835	28,685	36,366	Capital Accounts	27a
	....	....	....	....	....	....	....	14	112	8,053	13,750	−2,831	−4,882	−12,966	−17,574	Other Items (Net)	27r
																Monetary Survey	
End of Period																	
	....	....	....	....	....	....	....	218	884	7,010	15,438	6,453	30,938	37,481	45,731	Foreign Assets (Net)	31n
	....	....	....	....	....	....	....	182	1,728	27,832	46,753	59,753	63,544	103,205	107,556	Domestic Credit	32
	....	....	....	....	....	....	....	46	1,370	7,113	8,807	22,570	15,055	21,043	16,983	Claims on General Govt. (Net)	32an
	....	....	....	....	....	....	....	125	353	20,718	37,946	37,181	48,486	82,159	90,570	Claims on Other Sectors	32d
	....	....	....	....	....	....	....	115	1,331	13,410	30,078	39,830	44,055	52,678	52,227	Money	34
	....	....	....	....	....	....	....	133	1,584	11,091	10,173	14,540	26,192	44,398	58,842	Quasi-Money	35
	....	....	....	....	....	....	....	—	—	—	—	—	—	—	201	Money Market Instruments	36aa
	....	....	....	....	....	....	....	−35	286	4,242	9,270	19,530	31,568	45,295	48,445	Capital Accounts	37a
	....	....	....	....	....	....	....	188	−590	6,099	12,670	−7,694	−7,333	−1,708	−6,428	Other Items (Net)	37r
	....	....	....	....	....	....	....	248	2,916	24,501	40,251	54,371	70,247	97,075	111,069	Money plus Quasi-Money	35l
																Interest Rates	
Percent Per Annum																	
	....	....	....	....	....	....	....	30.00	210.00	210.00	77.80	26.00	65.10	....	....	Discount Rate *(End of Period)*	60
	....	....	....	....	....	....	....	30.00	210.00	210.00	52.00	60.00	54.00	39.00	‡43.00	Refinancing Rate *(End of Period)*	60a
	....	....	....	....	....	....	....	....	....	....	....	48.56	36.41	27.84	23.65	Money Market Rate	60b
	....	....	....	....	....	....	....	....	....	....	37.81	41.40	55.84	45.84	53.28	Treasury Bill Rate	60c
	....	....	....	....	....	....	....	....	....	....	63.18	32.19	26.08	24.94	27.35	Deposit Rate	60l
	....	....	....	....	....	....	....	....	....	....	111.86	66.36	54.23	48.49	38.85	Lending Rate	60p
																Prices, Production, Labor	
Period Averages																	
	....	....	....	....	....	....	....	....	....	....	....	....	100.0	114.6	121.3	Producer Prices (1997=100)	63
	....	....	....	....	....	....	....	....	1	36	100	119	‡135	147	148	Consumer Prices	64
	....	....	....	....	....	....	....	....	....	....	....	....	100.0	133.0	158.5	Wages: Avg. Month.Earn.(1997=100)	65
	....	....	....	....	....	....	....	....	....	....	....	92.3	100.0	105.3	119.1	Industrial Production (1997=100)	66
Period Averages																	
	....	....	....	....	....	....	....	....	....	....	....	....	1,372.2	1,352.5	....	Employment	67e
	....	....	....	....	....	....	....	....	....	....	....	....	166.1	139.1	....	Unemployment	67c
	....	....	....	....	....	....	....	....	....	....	....	....	10.8	9.3	....	Unemployment Rate (%)	67r

Armenia

911	1970	1971	1972	1973	1974	1975	1976	1977	1978	1979	1980	1981	1982	1983	1984
International Transactions															
Millions of US Dollars															
Exports .... 70..d	....	....	....	....	....	....	....	....	....	....	....	....	....	....	....
Imports, c.i.f. .... 71..d	....	....	....	....	....	....	....	....	....	....	....	....	....	....	....
Imports, f.o.b. 71.vd	....	....	....	....	....	....	....	....	....	....	....	....	....	....	....
Balance of Payments															
Millions of US Dollars:															
Current Account, n.i.e. 78ald	....	....	....	....	....	....	....	....	....	....	....	....	....	....	....
Goods: Exports f.o.b 78aad	....	....	....	....	....	....	....	....	....	....	....	....	....	....	....
Goods: Imports f.o.b 78abd	....	....	....	....	....	....	....	....	....	....	....	....	....	....	....
Trade Balance 78acd	....	....	....	....	....	....	....	....	....	....	....	....	....	....	....
Services: Credit 78add	....	....	....	....	....	....	....	....	....	....	....	....	....	....	....
Services: Debit 78aed	....	....	....	....	....	....	....	....	....	....	....	....	....	....	....
Balance on Goods & Services 78afd	....	....	....	....	....	....	....	....	....	....	....	....	....	....	....
Income: Credit 78agd	....	....	....	....	....	....	....	....	....	....	....	....	....	....	....
Income: Debit 78ahd	....	....	....	....	....	....	....	....	....	....	....	....	....	....	....
Balance on Gds, Serv. & Inc. 78aid	....	....	....	....	....	....	....	....	....	....	....	....	....	....	....
Current Transfers, n.i.e.: Credit 78ajd	....	....	....	....	....	....	....	....	....	....	....	....	....	....	....
Current Transfers: Debit 78akd	....	....	....	....	....	....	....	....	....	....	....	....	....	....	....
Capital Account, n.i.e. 78bcd	....	....	....	....	....	....	....	....	....	....	....	....	....	....	....
Capital Account, n.i.e.: Credit 78bad	....	....	....	....	....	....	....	....	....	....	....	....	....	....	....
Capital Account: Debit 78bbd	....	....	....	....	....	....	....	....	....	....	....	....	....	....	....
Financial Account, n.i.e. 78bjd	....	....	....	....	....	....	....	....	....	....	....	....	....	....	....
Direct Investment Abroad 78bdd	....	....	....	....	....	....	....	....	....	....	....	....	....	....	....
Dir. Invest. in Rep. Econ., n.i.e. 78bed	....	....	....	....	....	....	....	....	....	....	....	....	....	....	....
Portfolio Investment Assets 78bfd	....	....	....	....	....	....	....	....	....	....	....	....	....	....	....
Equity Securities 78bkd	....	....	....	....	....	....	....	....	....	....	....	....	....	....	....
Debt Securities 78bld	....	....	....	....	....	....	....	....	....	....	....	....	....	....	....
Portfolio Investment Liab., n.i.e. 78bgd	....	....	....	....	....	....	....	....	....	....	....	....	....	....	....
Equity Securities 78bmd	....	....	....	....	....	....	....	....	....	....	....	....	....	....	....
Debt Securities 78bnd	....	....	....	....	....	....	....	....	....	....	....	....	....	....	....
Financial Derivatives Assets 78bwd	....	....	....	....	....	....	....	....	....	....	....	....	....	....	....
Financial Derivatives Liabilities 78bxd	....	....	....	....	....	....	....	....	....	....	....	....	....	....	....
Other Investment Assets 78bhd	....	....	....	....	....	....	....	....	....	....	....	....	....	....	....
Monetary Authorities 78bod	....	....	....	....	....	....	....	....	....	....	....	....	....	....	....
General Government 78bpd	....	....	....	....	....	....	....	....	....	....	....	....	....	....	....
Banks 78bqd	....	....	....	....	....	....	....	....	....	....	....	....	....	....	....
Other Sectors 78brd	....	....	....	....	....	....	....	....	....	....	....	....	....	....	....
Other Investment Liab., n.i.e. 78bid	....	....	....	....	....	....	....	....	....	....	....	....	....	....	....
Monetary Authorities 78bsd	....	....	....	....	....	....	....	....	....	....	....	....	....	....	....
General Government 78btd	....	....	....	....	....	....	....	....	....	....	....	....	....	....	....
Banks 78bud	....	....	....	....	....	....	....	....	....	....	....	....	....	....	....
Other Sectors 78bvd	....	....	....	....	....	....	....	....	....	....	....	....	....	....	....
Net Errors and Omissions 78cad	....	....	....	....	....	....	....	....	....	....	....	....	....	....	....
Overall Balance 78cbd	....	....	....	....	....	....	....	....	....	....	....	....	....	....	....
Reserves and Related Items 79dad	....	....	....	....	....	....	....	....	....	....	....	....	....	....	....
Reserve Assets 79dbd	....	....	....	....	....	....	....	....	....	....	....	....	....	....	....
Use of Fund Credit and Loans 79dcd	....	....	....	....	....	....	....	....	....	....	....	....	....	....	....
Exceptional Financing 79ded	....	....	....	....	....	....	....	....	....	....	....	....	....	....	....
International Investment Position															
Millions of US Dollars															
Assets 79aad	....	....	....	....	....	....	....	....	....	....	....	....	....	....	....
Direct Investment Abroad 79abd	....	....	....	....	....	....	....	....	....	....	....	....	....	....	....
Portfolio Investment 79acd	....	....	....	....	....	....	....	....	....	....	....	....	....	....	....
Equity Securities 79add	....	....	....	....	....	....	....	....	....	....	....	....	....	....	....
Debt Securities 79aed	....	....	....	....	....	....	....	....	....	....	....	....	....	....	....
Financial Derivatives 79ald	....	....	....	....	....	....	....	....	....	....	....	....	....	....	....
Other Investment 79afd	....	....	....	....	....	....	....	....	....	....	....	....	....	....	....
Monetary Authorities 79agd	....	....	....	....	....	....	....	....	....	....	....	....	....	....	....
General Government 79ahd	....	....	....	....	....	....	....	....	....	....	....	....	....	....	....
Banks 79aid	....	....	....	....	....	....	....	....	....	....	....	....	....	....	....
Other Sectors 79ajd	....	....	....	....	....	....	....	....	....	....	....	....	....	....	....
Reserve Assets 79akd	....	....	....	....	....	....	....	....	....	....	....	....	....	....	....
Liabilities 79lad	....	....	....	....	....	....	....	....	....	....	....	....	....	....	....
Dir. Invest. in Rep. Economy 79lbd	....	....	....	....	....	....	....	....	....	....	....	....	....	....	....
Portfolio Investment 79lcd	....	....	....	....	....	....	....	....	....	....	....	....	....	....	....
Equity Securities 79ldd	....	....	....	....	....	....	....	....	....	....	....	....	....	....	....
Debt Securities 79led	....	....	....	....	....	....	....	....	....	....	....	....	....	....	....
Financial Derivatives 79lld	....	....	....	....	....	....	....	....	....	....	....	....	....	....	....
Other investment 79lfd	....	....	....	....	....	....	....	....	....	....	....	....	....	....	....
Monetary Authorities 79lgd	....	....	....	....	....	....	....	....	....	....	....	....	....	....	....
General Government 79lhd	....	....	....	....	....	....	....	....	....	....	....	....	....	....	....
Banks 79lid	....	....	....	....	....	....	....	....	....	....	....	....	....	....	....
Other Sectors 79ljd	....	....	....	....	....	....	....	....	....	....	....	....	....	....	....
National Accounts															
Millions of Rubles through 1993;															
Househ.Cons.Expend.,incl.NPISHs 96f	....	....	....	....	....	....	....	....	....	....	....	....	....	....	....
Government Consumption Expend. 91f	....	....	....	....	....	....	....	....	....	....	....	....	....	....	....
Gross Fixed Capital Formation 93e	....	....	....	....	....	....	....	....	....	....	....	....	....	....	....
Changes in Inventories 93i	....	....	....	....	....	....	....	....	....	....	....	....	....	....	....
Exports of Goods and Services 90c	....	....	....	....	....	....	....	....	....	....	....	....	....	....	....
Imports of Goods & Services 98c	....	....	....	....	....	....	....	....	....	....	....	....	....	....	....
Gross Domestic Product (GDP) 99b	....	....	....	....	....	....	....	....	....	....	....	....	....	....	....
Statistical Discrepancy 99bs	....	....	....	....	....	....	....	....	....	....	....	....	....	....	....
GDP Volume (1995=100) 99bvp	....	....	....	....	....	....	....	....	....	....	....	....	....	....	....
GDP Deflator (1995=100) 99bip	....	....	....	....	....	....	....	....	....	....	....	....	....	....	....
Millions:															
Population 99z	....	....	....	....	....	....	....	....	....	....	....	....	....	....	....

	Code	1985	1986	1987	1988	1989	1990	1991	1992	1993	1994	1995	1996	1997	1998	1999
International Transactions *Millions of US Dollars*																
Exports	70..*d*	....	....	....	....	....	....	....	....	156.20	215.50	270.90	290.30	232.55	220.50	232.20
Imports, c.i.f.	71..*d*	....	....	....	....	....	....	....	....	254.20	393.80	673.90	855.80	892.30	902.40	799.70
Imports, f.o.b.	71.v*d*	....	....	....	....	....	....	....	....	233.80	343.80	625.40	757.50	779.40	794.10	703.60
Balance of Payments *Minus Sign Indicates Debit*																
Current Account, n.i.e.	78al*d*	....	....	....	....	....	....	....	....	-66.83	-103.78	-218.37	-290.68	-306.51	-418.08	-318.51
Goods: Exports f.o.b	78aa*d*	....	....	....	....	....	....	....	....	156.19	215.35	270.90	290.44	233.64	228.89	247.31
Goods: Imports f.o.b	78ab*d*	....	....	....	....	....	....	....	....	-254.18	-393.63	-673.87	-759.63	-793.10	-806.38	-721.27
Trade Balance	78ac*d*	....	....	....	....	....	....	....	....	-97.99	-178.28	-402.97	-469.19	-559.46	-577.49	-473.96
Services: Credit	78ad*d*	....	....	....	....	....	....	....	....	17.28	13.67	28.60	77.71	96.60	130.31	135.78
Services: Debit	78ae*d*	....	....	....	....	....	....	....	....	-40.06	-40.70	-52.27	-128.52	-159.38	-208.71	-209.42
Balance on Goods & Services	78af*d*	....	....	....	....	....	....	....	....	-120.77	-205.31	-426.64	-520.00	-622.24	-655.89	-547.60
Income: Credit	78ag*d*	....	....	....	....	....	....	....	....	....	....	54.63	78.04	138.95	103.91	93.57
Income: Debit	78ah*d*	....	....	....	....	....	....	....	....	-1.30	-4.02	-14.61	-33.31	-40.44	-43.51	-38.60
Balance on Gds, Serv. & Inc.	78ai*d*	....	....	....	....	....	....	....	....	-122.07	-209.33	-386.62	-475.27	-523.73	-595.49	-492.63
Current Transfers, n.i.e.: Credit	78aj*d*	....	....	....	....	....	....	....	....	56.29	106.33	169.95	198.99	252.41	203.02	200.57
Current Transfers: Debit	78ak*d*	....	....	....	....	....	....	....	....	-1.05	-.78	-1.70	-14.40	-35.19	-25.61	-26.45
Capital Account, n.i.e.	78bc*d*	....	....	....	....	....	....	....	....	5.10	5.74	8.05	13.40	10.88	9.74	12.55
Capital Account, n.i.e.: Credit	78ba*d*	....	....	....	....	....	....	....	....	5.10	5.74	8.05	13.40	10.88	9.74	16.85
Capital Account: Debit	78bb*d*	....	....	....	....	....	....	....	....	....	....	....	....	....	....	-4.30
Financial Account, n.i.e.	78bj*d*	....	....	....	....	....	....	....	....	57.82	89.94	227.48	216.76	334.82	378.88	279.69
Direct Investment Abroad	78bd*d*	....	....	....	....	....	....	....	....	....	....	....	....	....	-11.55	—
Dir. Invest. in Rep. Econ., n.i.e.	78be*d*	....	....	....	....	....	....	....	....	.80	8.00	25.32	17.57	51.94	220.83	122.04
Portfolio Investment Assets	78bf*d*	....	....	....	....	....	....	....	....	....	....	....	-.01	-.14	.63	.05
Equity Securities	78bk*d*	....	....	....	....	....	....	....	....	....	....	....	-.01	-.03	.53	....
Debt Securities	78bl*d*	....	....	....	....	....	....	....	....	....	....	....	....	-.11	.10	.05
Portfolio Investment Liab., n.i.e.	78bg*d*	....	....	....	....	....	....	....	....	....	....	....	7.23	15.90	-16.57	1.58
Equity Securities	78bm*d*	....	....	....	....	....	....	....	....	....	....	....	1.88	.46	.72	-.32
Debt Securities	78bn*d*	....	....	....	....	....	....	....	....	....	....	....	5.35	15.44	-17.29	1.90
Financial Derivatives Assets	78bw*d*	....	....	....	....	....	....	....	....	....	....	....	....	....	....	....
Financial Derivatives Liabilities	78bx*d*	....	....	....	....	....	....	....	....	....	....	....	....	....	....	....
Other Investment Assets	78bh*d*	....	....	....	....	....	....	....	....	-44.00	35.89	-8.60	35.34	40.76	19.97	2.97
Monetary Authorities	78bo*d*	....	....	....	....	....	....	....	....	-33.40	....	-8.58	-.08	1.36	.07	.06
General Government	78bp*d*	....	....	....	....	....	....	....	....	-10.60	-6.24	....	....	....	-43.27	15.56
Banks	78bq*d*	....	....	....	....	....	....	....	....	....	.27	-.02	7.33	-17.57	6.17	-34.42
Other Sectors	78br*d*	....	....	....	....	....	....	....	....	....	41.86	....	28.09	56.97	57.00	21.77
Other Investment Liab., n.i.e.	78bi*d*	....	....	....	....	....	....	....	....	101.02	46.05	210.76	156.63	226.36	165.57	153.05
Monetary Authorities	78bs*d*	....	....	....	....	....	....	....	....	28.24	-9.18	.53	4.68	-.04	-2.92	-.93
General Government	78bt*d*	....	....	....	....	....	....	....	....	99.05	55.26	151.20	44.21	122.86	35.01	73.68
Banks	78bu*d*	....	....	....	....	....	....	....	....	-26.27	-.03	.03	26.18	29.04	23.99	11.19
Other Sectors	78bv*d*	....	....	....	....	....	....	....	....	....	....	59.00	81.56	74.50	109.49	69.11
Net Errors and Omissions	78ca*d*	....	....	....	....	....	....	....	....	17.17	4.83	12.35	15.06	10.83	30.06	31.06
Overall Balance	78cb*d*	....	....	....	....	....	....	....	....	13.26	-3.27	29.51	-45.46	50.02	.60	4.79
Reserves and Related Items	79da*d*	....	....	....	....	....	....	....	....	-13.26	3.27	-29.51	45.46	-50.02	-.60	-4.79
Reserve Assets	79db*d*	....	....	....	....	....	....	....	....	-13.26	-21.24	-76.22	-60.35	-73.48	-52.13	-20.79
Use of Fund Credit and Loans	79dc*d*	....	....	....	....	....	....	....	....	—	24.50	46.71	49.04	23.46	51.53	16.00
Exceptional Financing	79de*d*	....	....	....	....	....	....	....	....	....	....	....	56.77	....	....	....
International Investment Position *Millions of US Dollars*																
Assets	79aa*d*	....	....	....	....	....	....	....	....	....	....	....	....	381.90	486.26	....
Direct Investment Abroad	79ab*d*	....	....	....	....	....	....	....	....	....	....	....	....	—	—	....
Portfolio Investment	79ac*d*	....	....	....	....	....	....	....	....	....	....	....	....	.61	.05	....
Equity Securities	79ad*d*	....	....	....	....	....	....	....	....	....	....	....	....	.50	.04	....
Debt Securities	79ae*d*	....	....	....	....	....	....	....	....	....	....	....	....	.11	.01	....
Financial Derivatives	79al*d*	....	....	....	....	....	....	....	....	....	....	....	....	—	—	....
Other Investment	79af*d*	....	....	....	....	....	....	....	....	....	....	....	....	141.82	193.09	....
Monetary Authorities	79ag*d*	....	....	....	....	....	....	....	....	....	....	....	....	.18	.10	....
General Government	79ah*d*	....	....	....	....	....	....	....	....	....	....	....	....	18.00	61.27	....
Banks	79ai*d*	....	....	....	....	....	....	....	....	....	....	....	....	37.77	33.85	....
Other Sectors	79aj*d*	....	....	....	....	....	....	....	....	....	....	....	....	85.87	97.87	....
Reserve Assets	79ak*d*	....	....	....	....	....	....	....	....	....	....	....	....	239.47	293.12	....
Liabilities	79la*d*	....	....	....	....	....	....	....	....	....	....	....	....	944.92	1,293.91	....
Dir. Invest. in Rep. Economy	79lb*d*	....	....	....	....	....	....	....	....	....	....	....	....	103.44	316.50	....
Portfolio Investment	79lc*d*	....	....	....	....	....	....	....	....	....	....	....	....	21.18	3.59	....
Equity Securities	79ld*d*	....	....	....	....	....	....	....	....	....	....	....	....	.44	1.09	....
Debt Securities	79le*d*	....	....	....	....	....	....	....	....	....	....	....	....	20.74	2.50	....
Financial Derivatives	79ll*d*	....	....	....	....	....	....	....	....	....	....	....	....	—	—	....
Other investment	79lf*d*	....	....	....	....	....	....	....	....	....	....	....	....	820.30	973.82	....
Monetary Authorities	79lg*d*	....	....	....	....	....	....	....	....	....	....	....	....	132.49	190.45	....
General Government	79lh*d*	....	....	....	....	....	....	....	....	....	....	....	....	496.80	533.87	....
Banks	79li*d*	....	....	....	....	....	....	....	....	....	....	....	....	112.51	133.37	....
Other Sectors	79lj*d*	....	....	....	....	....	....	....	....	....	....	....	....	78.50	116.13	....
National Accounts *Millions of Dram Beginning 1994*																
Househ.Cons.Expend.,incl.NPISHs	96f	....	....	....	....	....	....	....	....	792,436	176,885	555,056	664,002	832,638	962,611	....
Government Consumption Expend.	91f	....	....	....	....	....	....	....	....	150,744	21,086	58,336	74,265	90,220	107,320	....
Gross Fixed Capital Formation	93e	....	....	....	....	....	....	....	....	105,088	37,855	84,365	118,254	130,336	164,881	....
Changes in Inventories	93i	....	....	....	....	....	....	....	....	-21,798	6,012	11,858	14,029	23,015	16,906	....
Exports of Goods and Services	90c	....	....	....	....	....	....	....	....	302,185	73,569	124,965	153,665	163,065	181,510	....
Imports of Goods & Services	98c	....	....	....	....	....	....	....	....	-512,572	-136,746	-324,775	-370,208	-468,722	-499,244	....
Gross Domestic Product (GDP)	99b	....	....	....	....	....	....	....	....	853,063	187,065	522,256	661,209	804,335	958,791	....
Statistical Discrepancy	99bs	....	....	....	....	....	....	....	....	36,980	8,404	12,451	7,202	33,783	24,807	....
GDP Volume (1995=100)	99bv*p*	....	....	....	....	....	....	....	....	....	93.6	100.0	105.9	109.4	117.2	....
GDP Deflator (1995=100)	99bi*p*	....	....	....	....	....	....	....	....	....	38.3	100.0	119.6	140.8	156.6	....
Midyear Estimates																
Population	99z	....	....	....	....	....	....	....	....	3.73	3.75	3.76	3.77	3.79	3.79	3.53

(See notes in the back of the book.)

Aruba

		1970	1971	1972	1973	1974	1975	1976	1977	1978	1979	1980	1981	1982	1983	1984
Exchange Rates																
Official Rate	aa													*Aruban Florins per SDR:*		
		....	....	....	....	....	....	....	....	....	....	....				
Official Rate	ae													*Aruban Florins per US Dollar:*		
Official Rate	rf	....	....	....	....	....	....	....	....	....	....	....				
		....	....	....	....	....	....	....	....	....	....	....	....	....	....	....
International Liquidity														*Millions of US Dollars:*		
Total Reserves minus Gold	1l.d	....	....	....	....	....	....	....	....	....	....	....	....	....	....	....
Foreign Exchange	1d.d	....	....	....	....	....	....	....	....	....	....	....	....	....	....	....
Gold (Million Fine Troy Ounces)	1ad	....	....	....	....	....	....	....	....	....	....	....	....	....	....	....
Gold (National Valuation)	1and	....	....	....	....	....	....	....	....	....	....	....	....	....	....	....
Deposit Money Banks: Assets	7a.d	....	....	....	....	....	....	....	....	....	....	....	....	....	....	....
Liabilities	7b.d	....	....	....	....	....	....	....	....	....	....	....	....	....	....	....
Monetary Authorities														*Millions of Aruban Florins:*		
Foreign Assets	11	....	....	....	....	....	....	....	....	....	....	....	....	....	....	....
Reserve Money	14	....	....	....	....	....	....	....	....	....	....	....	....	....	....	....
of which: Currency Outside DMBs	14a	....	....	....	....	....	....	....	....	....	....	....	....	....	....	....
Central Government Deposits	16d	....	....	....	....	....	....	....	....	....	....	....	....	....	....	....
Capital Accounts	17a	....	....	....	....	....	....	....	....	....	....	....	....	....	....	....
Other Items (Net)	17r	....	....	....	....	....	....	....	....	....	....	....	....	....	....	....
Deposit Money Banks														*Millions of Aruban Florins:*		
Reserves	20	....	....	....	....	....	....	....	....	....	....	....	....	....	....	....
Foreign Assets	21	....	....	....	....	....	....	....	....	....	....	....	....	....	....	....
Claims on Central Government	22a	....	....	....	....	....	....	....	....	....	....	....	....	....	....	....
Claims on Private Sector	22d	....	....	....	....	....	....	....	....	....	....	....	....	....	....	....
Demand Deposits	24	....	....	....	....	....	....	....	....	....	....	....	....	....	....	....
Time and Savings Deposits	25	....	....	....	....	....	....	....	....	....	....	....	....	....	....	....
Bonds	26ab	....	....	....	....	....	....	....	....	....	....	....	....	....	....	....
Foreign Liabilities	26c	....	....	....	....	....	....	....	....	....	....	....	....	....	....	....
Central Government Deposits	26d	....	....	....	....	....	....	....	....	....	....	....	....	....	....	....
Capital Accounts	27a	....	....	....	....	....	....	....	....	....	....	....	....	....	....	....
Other Items (Net)	27r	....	....	....	....	....	....	....	....	....	....	....	....	....	....	....
Monetary Survey														*Millions of Aruban Florins:*		
Foreign Assets (Net)	31n	....	....	....	....	....	....	....	....	....	....	....	....	....	....	....
Domestic Credit	32	....	....	....	....	....	....	....	....	....	....	....	....	....	....	....
Claims on Central Govt. (Net)	32an	....	....	....	....	....	....	....	....	....	....	....	....	....	....	....
Claims on Private Sector	32d	....	....	....	....	....	....	....	....	....	....	....	....	....	....	....
Money	34	....	....	....	....	....	....	....	....	....	....	....	....	....	....	....
Quasi-Money	35	....	....	....	....	....	....	....	....	....	....	....	....	....	....	....
Bonds	36ab	....	....	....	....	....	....	....	....	....	....	....	....	....	....	....
Other Items (Net)	37r	....	....	....	....	....	....	....	....	....	....	....	....	....	....	....
Money plus Quasi-Money	35l	....	....	....	....	....	....	....	....	....	....	....	....	....	....	....
Interest Rates														*Percent Per Annum*		
Discount Rate	60	....	....	....	....	....	....	....	....	....	....	....	....	....	....	....
Deposit Rate	60l	....	....	....	....	....	....	....	....	....	....	....	....	....	....	....
Lending Rate	60p	....	....	....	....	....	....	....	....	....	....	....	....	....	....	....
Prices and Tourism														*Index Numbers (1995=100):*		
Consumer Prices	64	....	....	....	....	....	....	....	....	....	....	....	....	....	....	....
Number of Tourists	66ta	....	....	....	....	....	....	....	....	....	....	....	....	....	....	34
Number of Tourist Nights	66tb	....	....	....	....	....	....	....	....	....	....	26	....	....	....	31
International Transactions														*Millions of Aruban Florins*		
Exports	70..d	....	....	....	....	....	....	....	....	....	....	....	....	....	....	....
Imports, c.i.f.	71..d	....	....	....	....	....	....	....	....	....	....	....	....	....	....	....

1985	1986	1987	1988	1989	1990	1991	1992	1993	1994	1995	1996	1997	1998	1999		
															Exchange Rates	
End of Period																
....	2.1895	2.5394	2.4088	2.3523	2.5466	2.5605	2.4613	2.4587	2.6131	2.6608	2.5739	2.4152	2.5204	2.4568	Official Rate	aa
End of Period (ae) Period Average (rf)																
....	1.7900	1.7900	1.7900	1.7900	1.7900	1.7900	1.7900	1.7900	1.7900	1.7900	1.7900	1.7900	1.7900	1.7900	Official Rate	ae
....	1.7900	1.7900	1.7900	1.7900	1.7900	1.7900	1.7900	1.7900	1.7900	1.7900	1.7900	1.7900	1.7900	1.7900	Official Rate	rf
															International Liquidity	
End of Period																
....	73.63	78.73	90.92	87.07	97.93	119.59	142.11	181.24	177.59	216.67	187.62	172.33	222.19	219.91	Total Reserves minus Gold	1l.d
....	73.63	78.73	90.92	87.07	97.93	119.59	142.11	181.24	177.59	216.67	187.62	172.33	222.19	219.91	Foreign Exchange	1d.d
....	....	....	.100	.100	.100	.100	.100	.100	.100	.100	.100	.100	.100	.100	Gold (Million Fine Troy Ounces)	1ad
....	5.587	5.587	5.587	26.465	26.465	26.465	25.630	25.630	25.630	26.307	27.978	27.978	22.878	22.900	Gold (National Valuation)	1and
....	37.15	64.90	109.14	129.41	160.73	194.37	197.89	213.42	222.37	207.98	233.69	257.38	269.57	280.49	Deposit Money Banks: Assets	7a.d
....	43.52	64.48	121.87	112.54	132.85	153.29	143.36	163.04	150.87	161.08	190.85	217.10	190.79	191.93	Liabilities	7b.d
															Monetary Authorities	
End of Period																
....	142.11	150.94	173.25	203.37	222.78	261.44	300.25	370.30	363.77	434.93	385.91	358.55	438.67	434.74	Foreign Assets	11
....	97.45	116.28	133.47	128.67	152.55	190.64	225.48	249.57	233.57	275.54	236.23	226.35	318.08	338.01	Reserve Money	14
....	32.04	34.56	41.07	48.32	59.22	66.16	76.23	81.66	87.56	93.70	94.87	101.52	104.91	122.44	of which: Currency Outside DMBs	14a
....	30.70	11.57	16.41	13.76	12.54	15.88	23.72	58.57	71.70	99.97	92.55	68.27	65.56	55.64	Central Government Deposits	16d
....	10.00	13.87	19.86	57.84	59.37	59.50	59.80	58.60	56.02	66.40	70.48	76.12	71.71	65.95	Capital Accounts	17a
....	3.96	9.22	3.51	3.10	-1.67	-4.58	-8.74	3.57	2.48	-6.98	-13.35	-12.19	-16.67	-24.87	Other Items (Net)	17r
															Deposit Money Banks	
End of Period																
....	62.88	71.03	85.52	70.08	82.94	112.89	147.13	168.16	147.44	181.48	154.97	119.11	209.55	224.24	Reserves	20
....	66.50	116.16	195.36	231.64	287.71	347.93	354.22	382.02	398.05	372.29	418.30	460.71	482.53	502.08	Foreign Assets	21
....	9.27	29.91	15.66	21.65	23.01	34.34	36.23	43.16	67.94	36.88	59.43	59.50	55.91	61.44	Claims on Central Government	22a
....	286.51	344.33	467.52	539.79	609.05	690.37	742.74	793.09	946.52	1,017.98	1,121.78	1,185.47	1,248.15	1,376.10	Claims on Private Sector	22d
....	66.27	120.59	145.66	192.43	200.69	242.76	252.72	293.14	350.09	343.90	346.37	366.07	433.80	458.88	Demand Deposits	24
....	215.55	274.97	331.13	391.71	478.82	560.40	663.16	673.52	755.64	795.31	853.93	881.59	991.61	1,105.88	Time and Savings Deposits	25
....	....	....	....	....	....	....	....	....	....	....	12.75	—	5.00	5.00	Bonds	26ab
....	77.90	115.41	218.15	201.44	237.80	274.40	256.62	291.84	270.06	288.33	341.61	388.62	341.52	343.55	Foreign Liabilities	26c
....	30.14	14.91	1.97	1.15	4.06	25.96	10.57	20.90	37.90	22.95	16.33	15.89	11.28	7.93	Central Government Deposits	26d
....	40.00	48.71	49.95	55.37	64.53	72.93	62.81	56.56	70.34	85.62	105.49	112.89	105.78	109.64	Capital Accounts	27a
....	-4.68	-13.16	17.29	21.06	16.81	9.08	34.45	50.48	75.91	72.51	78.00	59.73	107.15	133.00	Other Items (Net)	27r
															Monetary Survey	
End of Period																
....	130.39	151.15	149.57	231.13	270.16	334.85	396.84	448.02	478.10	517.80	461.50	428.18	578.01	593.16	Foreign Assets (Net)	31n
....	234.95	347.76	464.81	546.53	615.47	682.86	744.69	756.79	904.86	931.93	1,072.33	1,160.81	1,227.22	1,373.97	Domestic Credit	32
....	-51.57	3.43	-2.72	6.74	6.42	-7.50	1.95	-36.30	-41.66	-86.05	-49.45	-24.66	-20.93	-2.13	Claims on Central Govt. (Net)	32an
....	286.51	344.33	467.52	539.79	609.05	690.37	742.74	793.09	946.52	1,017.98	1,121.78	1,185.47	1,248.15	1,376.10	Claims on Private Sector	32d
....	100.18	157.56	189.82	243.35	264.13	313.97	331.28	377.89	441.45	443.70	447.47	473.18	547.00	589.73	Money	34
....	215.55	285.50	336.28	392.51	481.08	570.04	663.66	674.03	756.17	804.74	855.08	881.76	991.78	1,106.06	Quasi-Money	35
....	....	....	....	....	....	....	....	....	....	....	12.75	—	5.00	5.00	Bonds	36ab
....	49.61	55.85	88.35	141.79	140.42	133.71	146.59	152.88	185.34	201.30	218.52	234.04	261.45	266.35	Other Items (Net)	37r
....	315.73	443.06	526.10	635.87	745.21	884.01	994.94	1,051.93	1,197.62	1,248.44	1,302.55	1,354.94	1,538.78	1,695.79	Money plus Quasi-Money	35l
															Interest Rates	
Percent Per Annum																
....	9.5	9.5	9.5	9.5	9.5	9.5	9.5	9.5	9.5	9.5	9.5	9.5	9.5	6.5	Discount Rate	60
....	6.4	6.7	6.7	6.7	6.7	6.3	5.7	4.2	4.4	4.3	4.2	4.4	....	....	Deposit Rate	60l
....	11.0	10.3	10.3	10.6	10.6	10.6	10.6	10.6	10.6	10.6	10.3	10.0	....	....	Lending Rate	69p
															Prices and Tourism	
Period Averages																
66	67	70	72	75	79	83	86	91	97	100	103	106	108	111	Consumer Prices	64
34	29	37	45	56	70	81	88	91	94	100	104	105	105	110	Number of Tourists	66ta
31	29	36	46	59	76	84	87	90	95	100	105	108	109	115	Number of Tourist Nights	66tb
															International Transactions	
Millions of Aruban Florins																
....	23.7	26.1	30.5	22.9	27.9	25.7	....	....	....	14.7	12.5	24.1	29.1	29.2	Exports	70..d
....	191.9	236.1	336.4	386.6	536.3	481.0	....	....	....	....	....	....	....	....	Imports, c.i.f.	71..d

Aruba

Balance of Payments		1970	1971	1972	1973	1974	1975	1976	1977	1978	1979	1980	1981	1982	1983	1984
														Millions of US Dollars:		
Current Account, n.i.e.	78al d	...	...	...	...	...	...	...	...	...	...	...	...	...	...	...
Goods: Exports f.o.b.	78aa d	...	...	...	...	...	...	...	...	...	...	...	...	...	...	...
Goods: Imports f.o.b.	78ab d	...	...	...	...	...	...	...	...	...	...	...	...	...	...	...
Trade Balance	78ac d	...	...	...	...	...	...	...	...	...	...	...	...	...	...	...
Services: Credit	78ad d	...	...	...	...	...	...	...	...	...	...	...	...	...	...	...
Services: Debit	78ae d	...	...	...	...	...	...	...	...	...	...	...	...	...	...	...
Balance on Goods & Services	78af d	...	...	...	...	...	...	...	...	...	...	...	...	...	...	...
Income: Credit	78ag d	...	...	...	...	...	...	...	...	...	...	...	...	...	...	...
Income: Debit	78ah d	...	...	...	...	...	...	...	...	...	...	...	...	...	...	...
Balance on Gds, Serv. & Inc.	78ai d	...	...	...	...	...	...	...	...	...	...	...	...	...	...	...
Current Transfers, n.i.e.: Credit	78aj d	...	...	...	...	...	...	...	...	...	...	...	...	...	...	...
Current Transfers: Debit	78ak d	...	...	...	...	...	...	...	...	...	...	...	...	...	...	...
Capital Account, n.i.e.	78bc d	...	...	...	...	...	...	...	...	...	...	...	...	...	...	...
Capital Account, n.i.e.: Credit	78ba d	...	...	...	...	...	...	...	...	...	...	...	...	...	...	...
Capital Account: Debit	78bb d	...	...	...	...	...	...	...	...	...	...	...	...	...	...	...
Financial Account, n.i.e.	78bj d	...	...	...	...	...	...	...	...	...	...	...	...	...	...	...
Direct Investment Abroad	78bd d	...	...	...	...	...	...	...	...	...	...	...	...	...	...	...
Dir. Invest. in Rep. Econ., n.i.e.	78be d	...	...	...	...	...	...	...	...	...	...	...	...	...	...	...
Portfolio Investment Assets	78bf d	...	...	...	...	...	...	...	...	...	...	...	...	...	...	...
Equity Securities	78bk d	...	...	...	...	...	...	...	...	...	...	...	...	...	...	...
Debt Securities	78bl d	...	...	...	...	...	...	...	...	...	...	...	...	...	...	...
Portfolio Investment Liab., n.i.e.	78bg d	...	...	...	...	...	...	...	...	...	...	...	...	...	...	...
Equity Securities	78bm d	...	...	...	...	...	...	...	...	...	...	...	...	...	...	...
Debt Securities	78bn d	...	...	...	...	...	...	...	...	...	...	...	...	...	...	...
Financial Derivatives Assets	78bw d	...	...	...	...	...	...	...	...	...	...	...	...	...	...	...
Financial Derivatives Liabilities	78bx d	...	...	...	...	...	...	...	...	...	...	...	...	...	...	...
Other Investment Assets	78bh d	...	...	...	...	...	...	...	...	...	...	...	...	...	...	...
Monetary Authorities	78bo d	...	...	...	...	...	...	...	...	...	...	...	...	...	...	...
General Government	78bp d	...	...	...	...	...	...	...	...	...	...	...	...	...	...	...
Banks	78bq d	...	...	...	...	...	...	...	...	...	...	...	...	...	...	...
Other Sectors	78br d	...	...	...	...	...	...	...	...	...	...	...	...	...	...	...
Other Investment Liab., n.i.e.	78bi d	...	...	...	...	...	...	...	...	...	...	...	...	...	...	...
Monetary Authorities	78bs d	...	...	...	...	...	...	...	...	...	...	...	...	...	...	...
General Government	78bt d	...	...	...	...	...	...	...	...	...	...	...	...	...	...	...
Banks	78bu d	...	...	...	...	...	...	...	...	...	...	...	...	...	...	...
Other Sectors	78bv d	...	...	...	...	...	...	...	...	...	...	...	...	...	...	...
Net Errors and Omissions	78ca d	...	...	...	...	...	...	...	...	...	...	...	...	...	...	...
Overall Balance	78cb d	...	...	...	...	...	...	...	...	...	...	...	...	...	...	...
Reserves and Related Items	79da d	...	...	...	...	...	...	...	...	...	...	...	...	...	...	...
Reserve Assets	79db d	...	...	...	...	...	...	...	...	...	...	...	...	...	...	...
Use of Fund Credit and Loans	79dc d	...	...	...	...	...	...	...	...	...	...	...	...	...	...	...
Exceptional Financing	79de d	...	...	...	...	...	...	...	...	...	...	...	...	...	...	...
																Millions:
Population	99z	...	...	...	...	...	...	...	...	...	...	.06	.07	.06	.06	.06

Minus Sign Indicates Debit

1985	1986	1987	1988	1989	1990	1991	1992	1993	1994	1995	1996	1997	1998	1999	Balance of Payments	
....	-18.7	-22.6	-44.3	-46.7	-158.2	-209.5	43.8	41.7	81.1	-.3	-69.1	-195.8	-18.8	-333.2	Current Account, n.i.e.	78al *d*
....	29.6	45.1	87.4	107.5	155.5	878.8	1,069.2	1,154.4	1,296.8	1,347.2	1,735.7	1,728.7	1,164.8	1,413.5	Goods: Exports f.o.b.	78aa *d*
....	-210.4	-249.8	-354.6	-397.4	-580.8	-1,402.8	-1,446.7	-1,546.5	-1,607.3	-1,772.5	-2,043.4	-2,115.9	-1,518.2	-2,005.2	Goods: Imports f.o.b.	78ab *d*
....	-180.9	-204.7	-267.3	-289.9	-425.4	-524.1	-377.5	-392.1	-310.6	-425.3	-307.7	-387.2	-353.4	-591.7	*Trade Balance*	78ac *d*
....	216.9	260.1	326.2	351.3	411.0	472.7	571.2	604.1	624.2	645.1	769.9	815.8	892.1	989.7	Services: Credit	78ad *d*
....	-50.6	-62.8	-85.3	-100.2	-134.9	-147.8	-159.8	-169.1	-228.7	-245.5	-515.9	-596.1	-553.1	-712.9	Services: Debit	78ae *d*
....	-14.6	-7.4	-26.3	-38.8	-149.3	-199.2	33.9	42.8	85.0	-25.6	-53.6	-167.5	-14.4	-315.0	*Balance on Goods & Services*	78af *d*
....	7.3	8.9	10.9	13.4	14.8	17.9	14.5	13.4	9.6	16.4	19.2	20.7	40.5	37.4	Income: Credit	78ag *d*
....	-13.6	-21.2	-27.9	-24.7	-22.6	-25.7	-21.8	-24.6	-22.3	-24.6	-31.0	-37.9	-40.1	-69.0	Income: Debit	78ah *d*
....	-20.9	-19.7	-43.4	-50.1	-157.0	-207.0	26.5	31.6	72.3	-33.8	-65.5	-184.7	-14.0	-346.6	*Balance on Gds, Serv. & Inc.*	78ai *d*
....	18.4	15.4	14.9	18.0	33.8	38.1	45.9	43.4	47.5	71.5	18.4	18.4	29.3	59.3	Current Transfers, n.i.e.: Credit	78aj *d*
....	-16.1	-18.3	-15.8	-14.6	-34.9	-40.6	-28.7	-33.3	-38.7	-37.9	-22.0	-29.5	-34.1	-45.9	Current Transfers: Debit	78ak *d*
....	—	—	—	—	—	-3.0	-1.5	-1.8	-4.1	-.5	28.0	21.0	5.2	—	Capital Account, n.i.e.	78bc *d*
....	—	—	—	—	—	.8	.9	.9	.3	3.1	28.7	21.6	10.2	.9	Capital Account, n.i.e.: Credit	78ba *d*
....	—	—	—	—	—	-3.8	-2.4	-2.8	-4.4	-3.6	-.7	-.6	-5.0	-.9	Capital Account: Debit	78bb *d*
....	62.8	24.6	56.8	47.8	172.2	228.8	-24.1	-8.4	-75.4	41.6	10.7	158.9	64.2	336.4	Financial Account, n.i.e.	78bj *d*
....	—	—	—	—	—	—	—	—	—	—	—	-.3	1.7	-1.4	8.9	Direct Investment Abroad	78bd *d*
....	—	—	—	—	130.5	184.7	-37.0	-17.9	-73.2	-5.5	84.5	195.9	83.6	392.1	Dir. Invest. in Rep. Econ., n.i.e.	78be *d*
....	—	—	—	—	8.7	13.1	11.3	10.8	16.5	-16.6	-7.8	-1.6	-44.1	-65.6	Portfolio Investment Assets	78bf *d*
....	—	—	—	—	....	....	....	....	....	....	....	....	....	....	Equity Securities	78bk *d*
....	—	—	—	—	8.7	13.1	11.3	10.8	16.5	-16.6	-7.8	-1.6	-44.1	-65.6	Debt Securities	78bl *d*
....	—	—	—	—	-15.1	-25.4	-18.2	-14.6	-25.8	....	1.6	-17.4	-3.4	12.2	Portfolio Investment Liab., n.i.e.	78bg *d*
....	—	—	—	—	....	....	....	....	....	....	....	....	....	....	Equity Securities	78bm *d*
....	—	—	—	—	-15.1	-25.4	-18.2	-14.6	-25.8	....	1.6	-17.4	-3.4	12.2	Debt Securities	78bn *d*
....	....	....	....	....	....	....	....	....	....	....	....	....	....	....	Financial Derivatives Assets	78bw *d*
....	....	....	....	....	....	....	....	....	....	....	....	....	....	....	Financial Derivatives Liabilities	78bx *d*
....	1.1	-27.7	-48.9	-19.4	-10.2	-17.1	13.6	-25.8	5.8	12.5	-11.3	-49.7	29.2	-15.7	Other Investment Assets	78bh *d*
....															Monetary Authorities	78bo *d*
....									-.8						General Government	78bp *d*
....	1.1	-27.7	-48.9	-19.4	-31.3	-33.6	-3.5	-15.7	-3.7	15.6	-17.0	-30.7	-11.5	-12.2	Banks	78bq *d*
....	—	—	—	—	21.2	16.5	17.2	-10.1	10.4	-3.1	5.7	-19.0	40.7	-3.5	Other Sectors	78br *d*
....	61.7	52.3	105.7	67.3	58.3	73.4	6.0	39.2	1.3	51.2	-55.9	30.0	.4	4.5	Other Investment Liab., n.i.e.	78bi *d*
....															Monetary Authorities	78bs *d*
....	27.5	18.2	13.8	12.3	1.2	1.9	10.0	.6	.4	.6	-10.6	-8.9	22.2	7.5	General Government	78bt *d*
....	-1.2	21.0	57.0	-7.4	20.2	19.2	-10.7	18.5	-8.7	10.7	17.0	37.3	-26.4	.5	Banks	78bu *d*
....	35.4	13.1	34.9	62.3	36.9	52.3	6.7	20.1	9.6	39.9	-62.3	1.6	4.6	-3.5	Other Sectors	78bv *d*
....	7.1	10.9	-12.8	20.4	-2.4	6.5	4.4	2.0	-4.7	2.0	4.3	-2.5	.6	-.7	Net Errors and Omissions	78ca *d*
....	51.3	12.9	-.4	21.5	11.7	22.8	22.6	33.4	-3.2	42.7	-26.1	-18.4	51.3	2.5	*Overall Balance*	78cb *d*
....	-51.3	-12.9	.4	-21.5	-11.7	-22.8	-22.6	-33.4	3.2	-42.7	26.1	18.4	-51.3	-2.5	Reserves and Related Items	79da *d*
....	-51.3	-12.9	.4	-21.5	-11.7	-22.8	-22.6	-33.4	3.2	-42.7	26.1	18.4	-51.3	-2.5	Reserve Assets	79db *d*
....	—										....	....	....	....	Use of Fund Credit and Loans	79dc *d*
....	....	....	....	....	....	....	....	....	....	....	....	....	....	....	Exceptional Financing	79de *d*

Midyear Estimates

1985	1986	1987	1988	1989	1990	1991	1992	1993	1994	1995	1996	1997	1998	1999		
.06	.06	.06	.06	.06	.06	.07	.07	.07	.08	.08	.09	.09	.09	.09	**Population**	99z

(See notes in the back of the book.)

Australia

		1970	1971	1972	1973	1974	1975	1976	1977	1978	1979	1980	1981	1982	1983	1984
Exchange Rates														*SDRs per Australian Dollar:*		
Market Rate	ac	1.1150	1.0970	1.1743	1.2335	1.0838	1.0738	.9351	.9396	.8831	.8392	.9257	.9690	.8889	.8616	.8445
														US Dollars per Australian Dollar:		
Market Rate	ag	1.1150	1.1910	1.2750	1.4880	1.3270	1.2571	1.0864	1.1414	1.1505	1.1055	1.1807	1.1279	.9806	.9020	.8278
Market Rate	rh	1.1200	1.1342	1.1923	1.4215	1.4394	1.3102	1.2252	1.1090	1.1447	1.1179	1.1395	1.1493	1.0174	.9024	.8796
														Index Numbers (1995=100):		
Market Rate	ahx	150.2	153.2	160.8	202.8	193.9	176.7	165.2	149.6	154.4	150.8	153.7	155.0	137.2	121.7	118.6
Nominal Effective Exchange Rate	nec	....	....	....	....	....	....	....	....	....	106.0	110.0	121.2	118.4	111.9	117.9
Real Effective Exchange Rate	rec	....	....	....	....	....	....	....	....	....	....	126.0	136.8	137.1	134.4	138.6
Fund Position														*Millions of SDRs:*		
Quota	2f.s	665	665	665	665	665	665	665	665	790	790	1,185	1,185	1,185	1,619	1,619
SDRs	1b.s	90	164	235	235	100	96	36	22	99	32	—	45	78	77	213
Reserve Position in the Fund	1c.s	267	167	167	167	176	167	167	166	161	156	255	252	—	109	187
of which: Outstg.Fund Borrowing	2c															
Total Fund Cred.&Loans Outstg.	2tl	—	—	—	—	—	—	333	333	247	271	62	—	32	—	—
International Liquidity													*Millions of US Dollars Unless Otherwise Indicated:*			
Total Reserves minus Gold	1l.d	1,454	3,034	5,860	5,386	3,953	2,955	2,870	2,058	2,062	1,424	1,690	1,671	6,371	8,962	7,441
SDRs	1b.d	90	178	255	283	122	112	42	27	129	42	—	52	86	81	209
Reserve Position in the Fund	1c.d	267	182	182	201	215	195	194	202	210	206	325	294	—	114	183
Foreign Exchange	1d.d	1,096	2,674	5,423	4,902	3,616	2,647	2,634	1,829	1,723	1,176	1,365	1,325	6,285	8,768	7,049
Gold (Million Fine Troy Ounces)	1ad	6.83	7.43	7.40	7.37	7.38	7.38	7.36	7.65	7.79	7.93	7.93	7.93	7.93	7.93	7.93
Gold (National Valuation)	1and	239	....	280	311	316	299	300	1,228	1,619	3,676	4,722	3,247	3,527	3,080	2,539
Deposit Money Banks: Assets	7a.d	99	157	209	199	202	275	251	183	272	216	367	396	120	179	ℐ913
Liabilities	7b.d	....	143	242	315	390	277	304	310	375	429	655	730	727	647	ℐ1,276
Monetary Authorities													*Millions of Australian Dollars: Average of Weekly*			
Foreign Assets	11	1,542	2,785	4,794	3,953	3,260	2,907	2,772	3,053	3,334	4,148	5,878	4,263	9,745	13,390	12,003
Claims on Central Government	12a	1,138	629	289	584	1,058	2,796	4,741	5,005	5,039	6,562	6,710	7,764	4,102	3,880	5,803
Reserve Money	14	2,695	3,194	3,828	4,830	4,242	5,466	6,123	6,438	6,368	6,932	7,612	8,451	9,199	10,371	11,500
of which: Currency Outside DMBs	14a	1,330	1,477	1,665	1,965	2,355	2,761	3,127	3,550	3,955	4,375	4,975	5,533	6,023	6,882	7,855
Foreign Liabilities	16c	—	—	—	—	—	—	356	354	280	322	67	—	37	—	—
Central Government Deposits	16d	....	....	....	....	....	....									
Other Items (Net)	17r	−15	221	1,254	−293	77	237	1,035	1,266	1,726	3,455	4,910	3,576	4,612	6,899	6,305
Deposit Money Banks													*Millions of Australian Dollars: Average of Weekly*			
Reserves	20	1,341	1,706	2,200	2,771	1,794	2,589	3,059	2,848	2,350	2,518	2,619	2,910	3,264	3,451	3,648
Foreign Assets	21	88	ℐ129	164	134	152	219	231	160	236	195	311	351	122	198	ℐ1,103
Claims on Central Government	22a	4,141	4,339	5,602	5,799	5,724	7,324	7,386	6,718	7,439	7,957	9,201	9,146	10,599	13,137	12,929
Claims on Official Entities	22bx	1,916	2,122	2,380	2,770	3,118	3,731	4,313	4,764	5,255	5,677	6,116	6,557	6,752	7,761	8,114
Claims on Private Sector	22d	8,217	9,286	10,790	14,011	16,683	19,321	23,091	25,860	29,222	33,822	38,015	43,991	48,833	55,334	64,627
Demand Deposits	24	4,111	4,266	5,227	6,076	5,620	6,998	7,550	7,826	8,740	10,266	12,191	12,488	11,960	13,862	14,615
Time and Savings Deposits	25	10,252	11,317	13,525	16,726	19,055	22,798	25,911	27,369	30,116	33,136	37,275	41,819	48,194	54,196	61,300
Foreign Liabilities	26c	....	118	190	212	294	220	280	272	326	388	555	647	741	717	ℐ1,541
Central Government Deposits	26d	396	499	536	756	604	897	1,562	1,626	1,624	1,748	1,033	1,129	1,393	1,261	1,733
Other Items (Net)	27r	945	1,383	1,658	1,714	1,898	2,269	2,775	3,258	3,696	4,632	5,209	6,873	7,282	9,846	ℐ11,231
Monetary Survey													*Millions of Australian Dollars: Average of Weekly*			
Foreign Assets (Net)	31n	1,599	2,796	4,768	3,875	3,118	2,906	2,367	2,587	2,965	3,633	5,567	3,967	9,089	12,871	ℐ11,565
Domestic Credit	32	15,390	16,125	18,724	22,528	26,111	32,433	38,091	41,204	45,575	52,473	59,272	66,685	69,188	79,214	89,890
Claims on Central Govt. (Net)	32an	4,883	4,469	5,355	5,627	6,178	9,222	10,565	10,097	10,853	12,771	14,878	15,781	13,308	15,755	16,999
Claims on Official Entities	32bx	1,916	2,122	2,380	2,770	3,118	3,731	4,313	4,764	5,255	5,677	6,116	6,557	6,752	7,761	8,114
Claims on Private Sector	32d	8,591	9,534	10,990	14,132	16,815	19,480	23,214	26,343	29,466	34,024	38,278	44,347	49,128	55,697	64,778
Money	34	5,446	5,749	6,899	8,050	7,990	9,807	10,681	11,390	12,709	14,661	17,220	18,063	18,032	20,796	22,492
Quasi-Money	35	10,252	11,317	13,525	16,726	19,055	22,798	25,911	27,369	30,116	33,136	37,275	41,819	48,194	54,196	61,300
Other Items (Net)	37r	1,291	1,855	3,068	1,628	2,184	2,734	3,866	5,032	5,715	8,309	10,345	10,770	12,051	17,093	ℐ17,664
Money plus Quasi-Money	35l	15,698	17,066	20,424	24,776	27,045	32,605	36,592	38,759	42,825	47,797	54,495	59,882	66,226	74,992	83,792
Interest Rates														*Percent Per Annum*		
Discount Rate	60	6.03	6.08	4.89	6.13	10.22	8.71	8.67	9.91	9.35	9.53	11.11	13.53	15.76	12.14	12.03
Money Market Rate	60b	5.19	5.46	4.65	4.98	7.52	9.49	7.09	8.49	8.72	8.09	9.49	12.07	13.90	9.50	10.84
Treasury Bill Rate	60c	5.38	5.41	4.32	5.21	9.07	7.51	7.51	8.53	8.65	8.88	10.67	13.25	14.64	11.06	10.99
Deposit Rate	60l	5.00	5.25	5.00	5.50	8.00	9.00	8.63	9.00	8.52	8.25	8.58	10.38	12.33	10.81	9.75
Lending Rate	60p	....	....	....	....	....	11.50	10.50	ℐ10.40	10.35	10.00	10.50	12.74	14.31	13.63	13.58
Govt. Bond Yield: Short-Term	61a	6.26	6.14	4.91	6.30	9.33	8.46	8.69	9.74	8.80	9.62	11.50	13.76	ℐ15.18	12.84	12.25
Long-Term	61	ℐ6.65	6.71	5.83	6.93	9.04	9.74	10.03	10.23	9.39	9.75	11.65	13.96	15.38	13.89	13.53
Prices, Production, Labor														*Index Numbers (1995=100):*		
Share Prices	62	18.9	15.8	19.0	17.7	13.2	12.4	15.3	14.7	16.7	20.5	30.6	31.9	24.4	30.8	35.9
Prices: Manufacturing Output	63	16.7	17.5	18.3	19.9	23.0	26.4	29.4	32.4	35.1	40.3	45.9	49.8	54.2	58.6	61.8
Consumer Prices	64	15.1	16.0	16.9	18.5	21.3	24.5	27.8	31.3	33.7	ℐ36.8	40.5	44.4	49.4	54.4	56.5
Wages, Weekly Earnings	65	11.5	12.8	13.9	15.7	19.2	22.7	25.9	28.7	31.2	33.9	37.9	42.3	ℐ47.3	50.6	55.4
Industrial Production	66..c	57.2	59.4	60.2	66.3	68.4	63.2	66.4	ℐ65.3	66.3	69.8	70.2	72.3	71.9	69.8	74.6
Manufacturing Employment	67eyc	118.4	122.4	119.3	124.0	123.2	113.2	114.8	114.5	109.4	109.5	111.8	112.3	108.8	102.5	102.6
														Number in Thousands:		
Labor Force	67d	....	....	....	....	....	....	....	....	....	....	....	....	....	....	....
Employment	67e	....	....	....	....	....	....	....	....	....	....	....	....	....	....	....
Unemployment	67c	....	....	....	....	....	....	....	....	....	....	....	....	....	....	....
Unemployment Rate (%)	67r	....	....	....	....	....	....	....	....	....	....	....	....	....	....	....

1985	1986	1987	1988	1989	1990	1991	1992	1993	1994	1995	1996	1997	1998	1999		
End of Period															**Exchange Rates**	
.6199	.5435	.5093	.6357	.6032	.5436	.5312	.5008	.4930	.5321	.5012	.5539	.4838	.4360	.4764	Market Rate	**ac**
End of Period (ag)		_Period Average (rh)_														
.6809	.6648	.7225	.8555	.7927	.7733	.7598	.6886	.6771	.7768	.7450	.7965	.6527	.6139	.6538	Market Rate	**ag**
.7008	.6709	.7009	.7842	.7925	.7813	.7791	.7353	.6801	.7317	.7415	.7829	.7441	.6294	.6453	Market Rate	**rh**
Period Averages																
94.5	90.5	94.5	105.8	106.9	105.4	105.1	99.2	91.7	98.7	100.0	105.6	100.3	84.9	87.0	Market Rate	**ahx**
99.2	83.1	80.4	88.9	97.4	98.2	100.1	95.4	94.0	103.3	100.0	109.7	111.1	99.0	100.0	Nominal Effective Exchange Rate	**ne c**
116.7	102.1	101.8	112.7	120.8	117.3	115.8	104.9	98.3	102.3	100.0	110.0	109.4	96.9	98.6	Real Effective Exchange Rate	**re c**
End of Period															**Fund Position**	
1,619	1,619	1,619	1,619	1,619	1,619	1,619	2,333	2,333	2,333	2,333	2,333	2,333	2,333	3,236	Quota	**2f. s**
283	271	260	248	234	218	202	70	60	50	37	25	14	13	53	SDRs	**1b. s**
189	189	189	205	245	245	245	420	400	347	338	335	539	892	1,189	Reserve Position in the Fund	**1c. s**
—	—	—	—	—	—	—	—	—	—	—	—	—	—	75	of which: Outstg.Fund Borrowing	**2c**
—	—	—	—	—	—	—	—	—	—	—	—	—	—	—	Total Fund Cred.&Loans Outstg.	**2tl**
End of Period															**International Liquidity**	
5,768	7,246	8,744	13,598	13,780	16,265	16,535	11,208	11,102	11,285	11,896	14,485	16,845	14,641	21,212	Total Reserves minus Gold	**1l. d**
310	332	369	334	307	311	290	96	82	73	55	37	19	18	72	SDRs	**1b. d**
207	231	268	275	322	349	351	577	550	506	502	482	727	1,256	1,633	Reserve Position in the Fund	**1c. d**
5,250	6,684	8,107	12,989	13,150	15,605	15,894	10,536	10,470	10,706	11,340	13,967	16,099	13,366	19,507	Foreign Exchange	**1d. d**
7.93	7.93	7.93	7.93	7.93	7.93	7.93	7.93	7.90	7.90	7.90	7.90	2.56	2.56	2.56	Gold (Million Fine Troy Ounces)	**1ad**
2,551	3,100	3,855	3,319	3,248	3,064	2,804	2,639	3,086	3,023	3,055	2,918	740	737	743	Gold (National Valuation)	**1and**
1,483	3,631	5,399	6,409	7,184	10,602	8,274	8,218	9,062	10,601	12,049	14,830	15,735	13,065	18,752	Deposit Money Banks: Assets	**7a. d**
2,922	8,967	12,070	13,667	22,074	33,997	37,436	37,770	41,840	39,355	49,238	63,521	64,258	73,409	88,291	Liabilities	**7b. d**
Figures for Last Month of Period															**Monetary Authorities**	
12,412	15,477	17,439	19,561	I21,234	24,205	24,506	20,212	21,415	18,344	20,080	22,581	28,325	27,632	38,596	Foreign Assets	**11**
8,640	9,189	8,031	5,257	I4,200	4,280	5,500	14,303	14,265	13,446	17,700	30,608	18,374	23,703	14,682	Claims on Central Government	**12a**
12,914	14,025	15,683	17,478	I17,559	18,917	19,479	20,648	21,987	23,777	24,969	40,261	32,081	33,780	31,941	Reserve Money	**14**
8,632	9,538	10,841	12,267	I13,018	14,342	15,328	16,326	17,279	18,208	19,092	19,628	21,098	22,784	24,602	of which: Currency Outside DMBs	**14a**
—	—	—	—	I8	37	47	54	38	49	90	63	43	108	84	Foreign Liabilities	**16c**
....	....	....	....	1,576	1,350	1,937	2,719	2,634	999	3,131	4,197	2,782	4,431	9,801	Central Government Deposits	**16d**
8,138	10,641	9,787	7,340	I6,291	8,181	8,543	11,094	11,022	6,965	9,590	8,668	11,792	13,016	11,452	Other Items (Net)	**17r**
Figures for Last Month of Period															**Deposit Money Banks**	
4,280	4,472	4,813	5,111	I4,447	4,281	4,084	4,265	4,674	5,498	5,830	13,378	8,789	9,052	5,052	Reserves	**20**
2,178	5,462	7,473	7,491	I9,456	14,827	12,413	14,968	16,281	17,210	22,562	27,893	35,887	37,706	45,742	Foreign Assets	**21**
14,100	17,930	20,156	21,525	I26,618	21,434	24,902	28,405	30,929	28,457	28,072	25,635	19,991	20,182	23,153	Claims on Central Government	**22a**
7,817	7,016	6,513	7,064	I5,477	6,196	5,395	6,195	4,419	3,233	3,591	3,909	4,659	6,550	11,104	Claims on Official Entities	**22bx**
86,991	105,049	122,489	151,623	I225,978	255,618	262,093	273,139	290,232	320,032	355,318	388,126	427,280	477,178	532,435	Claims on Private Sector	**22d**
14,650	16,391	20,352	23,889	I30,478	32,335	34,851	43,929	53,719	60,496	64,771	75,801	86,965	91,864	101,179	Demand Deposits	**24**
75,505	82,305	94,385	111,923	I150,499	172,064	171,102	177,390	180,265	197,542	215,949	236,124	247,668	271,109	305,051	Time and Savings Deposits	**25**
4,291	13,488	16,706	15,975	I27,847	43,964	49,271	54,850	61,793	50,663	66,091	79,750	98,450	119,579	135,043	Foreign Liabilities	**26c**
1,131	917	595	438	I1,759	1,923	2,694	3,566	3,637	2,988	3,523	3,291	3,578	5,721	5,497	Central Government Deposits	**26d**
19,788	26,828	29,406	40,589	I61,393	52,070	50,968	47,238	47,120	62,741	65,038	63,975	59,947	62,395	70,717	Other Items (Net)	**27r**
Figures for Last Month of Period															**Monetary Survey**	
10,299	7,451	8,206	11,077	I2,835	-4,970	-12,399	-19,724	-24,135	-15,158	-23,540	-29,339	-34,282	-54,348	-50,789	Foreign Assets (Net)	**31n**
116,617	138,326	156,595	185,031	I258,938	284,255	293,259	315,758	333,575	361,180	398,027	440,790	463,945	517,460	566,077	Domestic Credit	**32**
21,609	26,203	27,592	26,344	I27,483	22,441	25,771	36,423	38,924	37,915	39,118	48,755	32,005	33,732	22,537	Claims on Central Govt. (Net)	**32an**
7,817	7,016	6,513	7,064	I5,477	6,196	5,395	6,195	4,419	3,233	3,591	3,909	4,659	6,550	11,104	Claims on Official Entities	**32bx**
87,191	105,108	122,490	151,623	I225,978	255,618	262,093	273,139	290,232	320,032	355,318	388,126	427,280	477,178	532,435	Claims on Private Sector	**32d**
23,298	25,947	31,218	40,470	I43,518	46,698	50,229	60,294	71,026	78,762	83,899	95,641	108,352	114,794	125,943	Money	**34**
75,505	82,305	94,385	111,923	I150,499	172,064	171,102	177,390	180,265	197,542	215,949	236,124	247,668	271,109	305,051	Quasi-Money	**35**
28,112	37,525	39,199	43,715	I67,756	60,524	59,529	58,350	58,149	69,718	74,640	79,686	73,644	77,210	84,294	Other Items (Net)	**37r**
98,803	108,252	125,603	152,393	I194,017	218,762	221,331	237,683	251,291	276,304	299,848	331,765	356,020	385,903	430,994	Money plus Quasi-Money	**35l**
Percent Per Annum															**Interest Rates**	
15.98	16.93	14.95	13.20	17.23	15.24	10.99	6.96	5.83	5.75	5.75	....	....	....	....	Discount Rate	**60**
14.70	15.75	13.06	11.90	16.75	14.81	10.47	6.44	5.11	5.18	I7.50	7.20	5.50	4.99	I4.78	Money Market Rate	**60b**
15.42	15.39	12.80	12.14	16.80	14.15	9.96	6.27	5.00	5.69	I7.64	7.02	5.29	4.84	4.76	Treasury Bill Rate	**60c**
10.46	13.96	13.77	11.92	15.29	13.70	I10.44	6.32	4.76	5.05	7.33	6.86	5.12	4.67	4.59	Deposit Rate	**60l**
15.24	18.09	16.56	15.10	19.58	18.17	14.28	11.06	9.72	9.55	11.12	11.00	9.31	8.04	7.51	Lending Rate	**60p**
14.03	13.97	13.17	12.18	15.14	13.46	9.94	7.25	5.63	I8.19	8.42	7.53	6.00	5.02	5.55	Govt. Bond Yield: Short-Term	**61a**
13.95	13.42	13.19	12.10	13.41	13.18	10.69	9.22	7.28	9.04	9.17	8.17	6.89	5.50	6.08	Long-Term	**61**
Period Averages															**Prices, Production, Labor**	
44.0	59.3	85.1	72.4	77.6	73.4	74.0	77.1	88.8	101.4	100.0	111.6	125.4	131.2	146.2	Share Prices	**62**
65.9	69.5	74.6	81.4	85.5	90.7	92.0	93.4	95.3	96.0	100.0	100.3	101.6	102.2	102.9	Prices: Manufacturing Output	**63**
60.4	65.8	71.4	76.6	82.4	I88.4	91.2	92.1	93.8	95.6	100.0	102.6	102.9	103.7	105.3	Consumer Prices	**64**
58.2	62.7	66.0	70.5	76.2	82.8	86.9	90.4	92.1	95.1	100.0	104.0	108.3	112.7	115.8	Wages, Weekly Earnings	**65**
80.6	80.4	84.2	88.9	92.9	95.1	I91.7	92.0	94.7	99.8	100.0	104.3	I107.3	108.5	111.0	Industrial Production	**66.. c**
101.8	102.1	103.8	107.0	110.5	107.6	101.1	100.1	95.8	99.1	100.0	100.3	100.3	98.5	96.4	Manufacturing Employment	**67ey c**
Period Averages																
....	....	....	....	....	....	8,041	....	8,619	....	9,001	....	9,220	9,343	....	Labor Force	**67d**
6,698	I6,975	7,129	7,398	I7,716	7,837	7,668	7,612	7,645	7,886	8,217	8,328	8,394	8,553	....	Employment	**67e**
603	I613	629	I576	I508	585	815	925	939	856	765	779	787	747	....	Unemployment	**67c**
8.3	I8.1	8.1	7.2	I6.2	6.9	9.6	10.8	10.9	9.7	8.5	8.6	8.6	8.0	....	Unemployment Rate (%)	**67r**

Australia

International Transactions		1970	1971	1972	1973	1974	1975	1976	1977	1978	1979	1980	1981	1982	1983	1984
															Millions of Australian Dollars	
Exports	70	4,259	4,599	5,419	6,719	7,685	9,123	10,774	12,050	12,591	16,711	19,269	18,686	21,032	22,306	26,366
Wheat	70d	363	432	361	201	868	1,062	919	926	765	1,515	1,967	1,471	1,974	1,156	2,454
Coal	70vr	179	210	267	325	489	890	1,185	1,394	1,479	1,608	1,683	2,290	2,533	3,343	3,937
Greasy Wool	70ha	585	467	699	1,212	834	736	1,103	1,068	1,112	1,325	1,300	1,392	1,513	1,525	1,549
Imports, c.i.f.	71	4,515	4,613	4,217	5,177	8,358	8,173	9,999	12,186	13,591	16,279	19,632	22,824	26,210	23,839	29,560
Imports, f.o.b.	71.v	4,056	4,139	3,876	4,840	7,769	7,636	9,134	11,036	12,329	14,801	17,826	20,592	23,194	21,220	25,877
															1995=100	
Volume of Exports	72	18.9	20.8	22.4	22.4	21.0	22.9	24.6	27.4	27.8	33.7	39.3	40.3	41.4	45.0	45.8
Wheat	72d	113.4	126.0	105.9	55.6	103.9	120.0	112.9	140.0	111.7	169.9	180.1	131.6	179.1	88.0	218.6
Coal	72vr	13.4	14.5	17.2	20.9	21.4	22.2	23.5	26.4	27.3	30.0	31.0	37.0	33.3	45.0	56.1
Greasy Wool	72ha	158.9	158.2	168.5	134.4	113.5	125.9	162.5	124.2	129.0	135.9	116.6	116.0	119.6	121.7	115.0
Volume of Imports	73	26.9	26.3	24.1	30.4	38.8	30.7	34.7	35.0	36.3	37.5	39.8	43.7	45.8	40.3	49.4
Export Prices	76	19.6	19.8	22.6	29.1	34.2	‡35.7	39.0	43.8	45.4	54.8	62.8	63.9	66.8	71.8	72.1
Wheat	76d	18.3	19.2	21.3	38.5	51.1	42.4	39.5	36.2	44.5	52.7	57.8	56.7	59.1	66.4	59.1
Coal (Unit Value)	74vr	18.1	19.6	21.0	21.1	30.9	54.3	68.4	71.6	73.3	72.5	73.6	84.0	103.1	100.7	95.0
Greasy Wool (Unit Value)	74ha	16.4	13.2	18.5	40.2	32.8	26.1	30.3	38.3	38.4	43.5	49.7	53.6	56.4	55.9	60.1
Import Prices	76.x	12.3	13.1	13.6	13.6	19.0	23.9	26.3	31.8	33.8	‡40.9	51.8	‡52.7	56.3	61.2	62.7
Balance of Payments															*Millions of US Dollars:*	
Current Account, n.i.e.	78ald	−903	−907	405	358	−2,847	−1,058	−1,941	−3,082	−4,617	−2,738	−4,447	−8,581	−8,512	−6,330	−8,860
Goods: Exports f.o.b.	78aad	4,623	5,065	6,314	9,357	10,907	11,838	13,118	13,351	14,288	18,825	21,892	21,671	21,601	19,766	23,159
Goods: Imports f.o.b.	78abd	−4,109	−4,476	−4,301	−6,488	−10,688	−9,575	−11,031	−12,269	−14,139	−16,248	−20,521	−23,906	−23,775	−19,740	−23,901
Trade Balance	78acd	514	589	2,013	2,868	219	2,262	2,087	1,082	149	2,577	1,371	−2,235	−2,174	26	−742
Services: Credit	78add	930	998	1,109	1,385	1,889	2,021	2,130	2,142	2,749	3,246	3,862	4,284	4,374	4,186	4,543
Services: Debit	78aed	−1,539	−1,682	−1,876	−2,684	−3,728	−3,789	−4,211	−4,310	−5,044	−5,611	−6,568	−7,420	−7,546	−6,990	−8,235
Balance on Goods & Services	78afd	−95	−95	1,247	1,570	−1,620	494	6	−1,086	−2,145	212	−1,334	−5,370	−5,346	−2,778	−4,434
Income: Credit	78agd	179	245	376	664	777	601	531	540	625	752	957	991	1,028	1,275	1,629
Income: Debit	78ahd	−864	−941	−1,051	−1,639	−1,707	−1,846	−2,154	−2,158	−2,543	−3,200	−3,645	−3,827	−3,546	−4,442	−5,740
Balance on Gds, Serv. & Inc.	78aid	−780	−791	572	594	−2,550	−750	−1,617	−2,704	−4,063	−2,236	−4,023	−8,206	−7,864	−5,944	−8,545
Current Transfers, n.i.e.: Credit	78ajd	263	302	357	432	542	728	610	611	682	714	904	1,012	980	970	1,012
Current Transfers: Debit	78akd	−386	−418	−524	−668	−839	−1,036	−933	−990	−1,236	−1,216	−1,328	−1,387	−1,628	−1,356	−1,326
Capital Account, n.i.e.	78bcd	85	58	58	33	8	−49	−9	8	37	72	179	204	203	332	335
Capital Account, n.i.e.: Credit	78bad	166	156	203	242	252	216	228	246	319	387	504	595	615	757	781
Capital Account: Debit	78bbd	−81	−98	−144	−209	−244	−265	−237	−237	−283	−315	−325	−391	−412	−425	−446
Financial Account, n.i.e.	78bjd	1,132	1,947	1,724	−477	841	752	1,860	2,266	3,736	2,127	4,183	7,695	12,656	7,816	6,072
Direct Investment Abroad	78bdd	−112	−104	−129	−259	−245	−160	−266	−266	−236	−343	−461	−733	−697	−521	−1,407
Dir. Invest. in Rep. Econ., n.i.e.	78bed	898	1,149	1,054	147	1,332	455	1,043	1,139	1,678	1,488	1,870	2,347	2,363	2,985	375
Portfolio Investment Assets	78bfd	−10	11	−6	−26	−13	5	−10	−7	−10	−3	−16	−31	−338	−342	−355
Equity Securities	78bkd	−10	11	−6	−26	−13	5	−10	−7	−10	−3	−16	−31	−338	−342	−355
Debt Securities	78bld	—	—	—	—	—	—	—	—	—	—	—	—	—	—	—
Portfolio Investment Liab., n.i.e.	78bhd	333	822	721	−681	−685	358	539	913	1,870	983	1,819	1,103	3,254	1,886	2,008
Equity Securities	78bmd	465	843	717	−516	−549	475	−114	−65	41	360	1,780	520	782	888	−225
Debt Securities	78bnd	−132	−21	5	−165	−136	−117	653	978	1,829	623	39	583	2,473	998	2,233
Financial Derivatives Assets	78bwd	....	....	....	....	....	....	....	....	....	....	....	—	—	—	—
Financial Derivatives Liabilities	78bxd	....	....	....	....	....	....	....	....	....	....	....	—	—	—	—
Other Investment Assets	78bhd	15	11	−135	165	−534	−46	22	−419	−193	−916	−384	437	−427	−293	−1,820
Monetary Authorities	78bod	....	....	....	....	....	....	....	....	....	....	....	....	....	....	....
General Government	78bpd	−16	−25	−30	162	40	−48	−82	−115	—	−109	−52	16	−101	−235	−197
Banks	78bqd	92	29	−42	1	−16	−78	24	67	−77	−58	−113	81	158	146	−66
Other Sectors	78brd	−62	6	−63	1	−558	81	80	−371	−116	−750	−218	340	−485	−205	−1,557
Other Investment Liab., n.i.e.	78bid	9	58	218	177	986	139	531	906	628	919	1,355	4,572	8,501	4,102	7,272
Monetary Authorities	78bsd	7	6	5	18	15	−46	−5	207	−1	−45	−150	207	−171	−1	12
General Government	78btd	16	30	29	16	7	87	−22	−47	204	145	158	−40	353	−67	−173
Banks	78bud	−13	22	185	—	106	−106	75	10	53	68	174	149	292	147	679
Other Sectors	78bvd	—	—	—	143	858	205	484	735	372	752	1,174	4,257	8,028	4,023	6,754
Net Errors and Omissions	78cad	34	273	538	−215	379	−563	−299	−139	756	−208	533	746	385	1,213	1,158
Overall Balance	78cbd	349	1,371	2,725	−301	−1,618	−919	−389	−947	−89	−746	448	64	4,731	3,030	−1,294
Reserves and Related Items	79dad	−349	−1,371	−2,725	301	1,618	919	389	947	89	746	−448	−64	−4,731	−3,030	1,294
Reserve Assets	79dbd	−349	−1,371	−2,725	301	1,618	919	8	947	194	715	−175	8	−4,766	−2,996	1,294
Use of Fund Credit and Loans	79dcd	—	—	—	—	—	—	381	—	−105	31	−272	−71	35	−34	—
Exceptional Financing	79ded	....	....	....	....	....	....	....	....	....	....	....	....	....	....	....
International Investment Position															*Millions of US Dollars*	
Assets	79aad	....	....	....	....	....	....	....	....	....	....	....	....	....	....	....
Direct Investment Abroad	79abd	....	....	....	....	....	....	....	....	....	....	....	....	....	....	....
Portfolio Investment	79acd	....	....	....	....	....	....	....	....	....	....	....	....	....	....	....
Equity Securities	79add	....	....	....	....	....	....	....	....	....	....	....	....	....	....	....
Debt Securities	79aed	....	....	....	....	....	....	....	....	....	....	....	....	....	....	....
Financial Derivatives	79ald	....	....	....	....	....	....	....	....	....	....	....	....	....	....	....
Other Investment	79afd	....	....	....	....	....	....	....	....	....	....	....	....	....	....	....
Monetary Authorities	79agd	....	....	....	....	....	....	....	....	....	....	....	....	....	....	....
General Government	79ahd	....	....	....	....	....	....	....	....	....	....	....	....	....	....	....
Banks	79aid	....	....	....	....	....	....	....	....	....	....	....	....	....	....	....
Other Sectors	79ajd	....	....	....	....	....	....	....	....	....	....	....	....	....	....	....
Reserve Assets	79akd	....	....	....	....	....	....	....	....	....	....	....	....	....	....	....
Liabilities	79lad	....	....	....	....	....	....	....	....	....	....	....	....	....	....	....
Dir. Invest. in Rep. Economy	79lbd	....	....	....	....	....	....	....	....	....	....	....	....	....	....	....
Portfolio Investment	79lcd	....	....	....	....	....	....	....	....	....	....	....	....	....	....	....
Equity Securities	79ldd	....	....	....	....	....	....	....	....	....	....	....	....	....	....	....
Debt Securities	79led	....	....	....	....	....	....	....	....	....	....	....	....	....	....	....
Financial Derivatives	79lld	....	....	....	....	....	....	....	....	....	....	....	....	....	....	....
Other investment	79lfd	....	....	....	....	....	....	....	....	....	....	....	....	....	....	....
Monetary Authorities	79lgd	....	....	....	....	....	....	....	....	....	....	....	....	....	....	....
General Government	79lhd	....	....	....	....	....	....	....	....	....	....	....	....	....	....	....
Banks	79lid	....	....	....	....	....	....	....	....	....	....	....	....	....	....	....
Other Sectors	79ljd	....	....	....	....	....	....	....	....	....	....	....	....	....	....	....

International Transactions

Millions of Australian Dollars

	1985	1986	1987	1988	1989	1990	1991	1992	1993	1994	1995	1996	1997	1998	1999	Code
Exports	32,408	33,716	37,947	42,369	47,005	50,892	53,728	58,363	62,839	64,904	71,657	76,978	84,786	88,977	86,906	70
Wheat	2,570	2,877	2,006	1,409	2,562	2,215	1,582	1,501	2,217	2,283	1,765	3,987	4,407	3,514	3,315	70d
Coal	5,061	5,318	5,043	4,612	5,080	6,157	6,757	7,245	7,712	6,700	7,380	7,758	8,784	9,825	8,390	70vr
Greasy Wool	2,326	2,374	3,457	4,657	4,101	2,281	2,447	2,461	1,951	2,394	2,242	2,108	2,446	1,712	1,499	70ha
Imports, c.i.f.	37,054	39,033	41,816	45,925	56,801	53,785	53,427	59,732	67,027	72,882	82,673	83,543	88,884	102,905	107,118	71
Imports, f.o.b.	33,130	35,716	38,469	42,416	51,726	49,807	49,678	55,513	62,385	68,087	77,467	78,402	83,364	96,723	101,428	71.v

1995=100

	1985	1986	1987	1988	1989	1990	1991	1992	1993	1994	1995	1996	1997	1998	1999	Code
Volume of Exports	52.4	55.9	62.3	62.4	64.7	69.8	80.4	84.4	89.6	96.9	100.0	111.4	126.8	134.4	138.5	72
Wheat	202.2	241.7	227.9	117.1	174.4	160.8	167.4	105.7	160.1	188.0	100.0	211.3	281.1	221.2	239.4	72d
Coal	65.1	66.5	74.0	73.0	70.9	82.5	88.3	94.2	97.5	96.1	100.0	103.1	115.6	121.2	125.6	72vr
Greasy Wool	150.1	146.1	168.1	153.3	148.6	95.0	147.6	142.4	131.4	129.0	100.0	120.7	120.7	93.6	97.9	72ha
Volume of Imports	52.3	51.2	51.9	61.5	74.1	70.8	69.6	75.5	79.6	91.5	100.0	108.5	121.4	135.9	150.3	73
Export Prices	81.0	81.9	85.2	95.3	I 100.5	101.4	92.7	94.5	95.8	93.1	100.0	95.9	97.5	102.3	95.0	76
Wheat	75.9	67.2	61.3	72.1	83.8	93.4	63.6	101.5	85.2	83.1	100.0	109.0	94.7	92.6	....	76d
Coal (Unit Value)	105.4	108.3	92.3	85.6	97.1	101.1	103.7	104.2	107.2	94.4	100.0	101.9	103.0	109.9	90.5	74vr
Greasy Wool (Unit Value)	69.1	72.5	91.7	135.5	123.1	107.1	73.9	77.1	66.2	82.7	100.0	77.9	90.4	81.6	68.4	74ha
Import Prices	74.4	81.3	86.2	84.2	83.4	I 86.7	87.6	91.5	98.9	96.6	100.0	94.6	94.5	102.5	100.2	76.x

Balance of Payments

Minus Sign Indicates Debit

	1985	1986	1987	1988	1989	1990	1991	1992	1993	1994	1995	1996	1997	1998	1999	Code
Current Account, n.i.e.	-9,172	-9,807	-7,966	-11,773	-18,205	-16,013	-11,182	-11,190	-9,815	-17,291	-19,640	-15,882	-12,569	-18,035	-22,526	78ald
Goods: Exports f.o.b.	22,886	22,639	27,377	33,413	37,160	39,642	42,362	42,816	42,637	47,371	53,220	60,397	64,893	55,848	56,044	78aad
Goods: Imports f.o.b.	-23,854	-24,459	-26,885	-34,090	-40,511	-39,284	-38,833	-41,173	-42,666	-50,648	-57,443	-61,032	-63,044	-61,215	-65,815	78abd
Trade Balance	-968	-1,820	492	-677	-3,350	358	3,528	1,643	-29	-3,277	-4,223	-635	1,849	-5,367	-9,771	78acd
Services: Credit	4,219	4,774	6,118	8,433	8,867	10,201	10,998	11,200	11,942	14,185	16,156	18,531	18,533	16,178	17,561	78add
Services: Debit	-7,677	-7,683	-8,771	-10,824	-13,175	-13,772	-13,467	-13,767	-13,412	-15,458	-17,110	-18,606	-18,844	-17,272	-18,265	78aed
Balance on Goods & Services	-4,425	-4,728	-2,161	-3,068	-7,659	-3,213	1,059	-924	-1,500	-4,550	-5,177	-710	1,538	-6,460	-10,476	78afd
Income: Credit	1,431	1,558	2,492	2,988	3,510	3,228	3,285	3,774	4,179	4,462	5,258	6,027	7,162	6,371	6,774	78agd
Income: Debit	-5,934	-6,454	-8,326	-11,395	-14,063	-16,386	-15,453	-13,869	-12,262	-16,820	-19,447	-21,259	-21,039	-17,837	-18,917	78ahd
Balance on Gds, Serv. & Inc.	-8,928	-9,625	-7,995	-11,476	-18,213	-16,371	-11,109	-11,019	-9,583	-16,908	-19,367	-15,942	-12,339	-17,927	-22,619	78aid
Current Transfers, n.i.e.: Credit	930	1,096	1,294	1,576	1,806	2,313	2,145	2,139	2,101	2,206	2,364	2,683	2,742	2,536	2,813	78ajd
Current Transfers: Debit	-1,175	-1,278	-1,265	-1,873	-1,798	-1,955	-2,218	-2,311	-2,333	-2,589	-2,637	-2,623	-2,972	-2,643	-2,720	78akd
Capital Account, n.i.e.	538	627	944	1,838	1,682	1,516	1,633	1,050	260	323	558	967	903	670	860	78bcd
Capital Account, n.i.e.: Credit	877	954	1,287	2,267	2,167	2,114	2,151	1,572	780	908	1,250	1,677	1,606	1,315	1,568	78bad
Capital Account: Debit	-339	-327	-343	-428	-485	-597	-518	-522	-519	-586	-692	-710	-703	-646	-708	78bbd
Financial Account, n.i.e.	7,535	11,441	9,185	15,661	17,301	15,251	8,934	6,621	8,734	14,618	18,821	18,577	15,361	15,516	27,816	78bjd
Direct Investment Abroad	-1,879	-3,327	-5,115	-5,798	-3,238	-1,058	-1,662	-5,033	-2,499	-2,472	-3,796	-5,988	-6,424	-2,329	3,602	78bdd
Dir. Invest. in Rep. Econ., n.i.e.	2,063	5,336	5,264	7,657	7,920	7,465	4,365	5,184	4,032	4,579	12,432	6,200	7,717	6,176	5,431	78bed
Portfolio Investment Assets	-937	-1,848	-950	-2,381	-2,393	367	-4,504	-3,727	-3,882	2,344	-2,461	-3,174	-19	-1,605	-6,327	78bfd
Equity Securities	-937	-1,848	-950	-2,332	-2,240	581	-2,791	-1,639	-2,366	-548	-1,219	-2,171	-530	-1,300	-3,800	78bkd
Debt Securities	—	—	—	-49	-153	-214	-1,713	-2,089	-1,517	2,891	-1,242	-1,003	511	-305	-2,527	78bld
Portfolio Investment Liab., n.i.e.	5,149	5,103	6,820	11,957	10,219	7,103	13,528	4,854	10,964	13,215	13,366	24,782	10,741	4,458	18,630	78bgd
Equity Securities	964	1,014	3,204	1,107	1,401	1,275	2,798	798	6,765	8,120	2,615	3,579	7,121	9,946	10,003	78bmd
Debt Securities	4,185	4,089	3,616	10,850	8,818	5,828	10,731	4,056	4,200	5,095	10,751	21,203	3,620	-5,488	8,627	78bnd
Financial Derivatives Assets	—	—	—	—	—	—	—	—	—	1,004	2,801	974	206	78	-130	78bwd
Financial Derivatives Liabilities	—	—	—	—	—	—	—	—	—	-632	-2,217	-681	1,038	-385	534	78bxd
Other Investment Assets	-1,757	-492	-2,693	-1,302	-1,970	-2,913	-767	1,019	-753	-2,247	-3,668	-5,707	-6,268	-376	-3,906	78bhd
Monetary Authorities	—	—	—	—	—	—	—	—	—	—	—	-246	-414	-180	-327	78bod
General Government	-199	-45	-105	393	108	-26	-189	222	17	137	-57	-93	-490	-407	-841	78bpd
Banks	-258	-611	-357	-1,491	100	-2,920	-159	1,124	57	-2,277	-2,805	-4,656	-4,256	-670	-3,102	78bqd
Other Sectors	-1,300	164	-2,231	-204	-2,178	32	-419	-326	-827	-107	-806	-712	-1,109	880	364	78brd
Other Investment Liab., n.i.e.	4,896	6,669	5,859	5,529	6,763	4,289	-2,026	4,324	872	-1,172	2,364	2,173	8,372	9,498	9,981	78bid
Monetary Authorities	-19	-2	4	28	-28	13	-8	11	13	-4	27	-29	-3	9	61	78bsd
General Government	17	96	-105	198	34	-2	149	-8	25	201	8	103	-340	40	-150	78btd
Banks	1,452	3,719	2,204	2,278	5,318	4,252	-1,804	3,951	1,988	-446	3,872	3,034	7,328	9,210	9,635	78bud
Other Sectors	3,446	2,857	3,756	3,025	1,439	25	-363	370	-1,154	-923	-1,543	-936	1,387	239	435	78bvd
Net Errors and Omissions	-1,201	-1,559	-1,788	-447	-177	986	291	-1,208	779	1,390	656	-1,190	-821	-191	555	78cad
Overall Balance	-2,301	703	374	5,279	601	1,740	-324	-4,726	-42	-960	396	2,471	2,873	-2,040	6,705	78cbd
Reserves and Related Items	2,301	-703	-374	-5,279	-601	-1,740	324	4,726	42	960	-396	-2,471	-2,873	2,040	-6,705	79dad
Reserve Assets	2,301	-703	-374	-5,279	-601	-1,740	324	4,726	42	960	-396	-2,471	-2,873	2,040	-6,705	79dbd
Use of Fund Credit and Loans	—	—	—	—	—	—	—	—	—	—	—	—	—	—	—	79dcd
Exceptional Financing	....	....	....	....	....	....	....	....	....	....	....	....	....	....	....	79ded

International Investment Position

Millions of US Dollars

	1985	1986	1987	1988	1989	1990	1991	1992	1993	1994	1995	1996	1997	1998	1999	Code
Assets	....	35,248	50,055	71,611	78,238	83,525	89,807	86,804	98,984	115,817	129,038	154,200	154,279	160,511	181,478	79aad
Direct Investment Abroad	....	11,613	19,953	28,359	30,363	31,411	32,030	33,998	38,328	42,991	48,237	59,190	56,829	62,152	55,266	79abd
Portfolio Investment	....	5,762	6,500	12,149	15,444	14,911	21,540	24,186	29,834	29,853	35,659	41,921	42,318	45,072	60,379	79acd
Equity Securities	....	5,762	6,500	10,222	13,704	12,282	16,324	17,202	22,168	23,353	27,029	31,424	32,824	34,836	48,131	79add
Debt Securities	....	—	—	1,927	1,740	2,628	5,215	6,984	7,665	6,500	8,630	10,497	9,494	10,236	12,248	79aed
Financial Derivatives	....	—	—	—	—	—	—	—	—	8,924	7,679	6,733	6,485	7,406	8,175	79ald
Other Investment	....	7,526	11,004	14,185	15,403	17,876	16,899	14,772	16,635	19,741	22,515	28,954	31,554	30,504	35,701	79afd
Monetary Authorities	....	—	—	—	—	—	—	—	—	—	—	—	491	766	953	79agd
General Government	....	1,759	2,080	1,063	880	879	1,043	735	705	663	1,208	1,387	1,625	1,910	2,887	79ahd
Banks	....	1,598	2,001	5,994	5,964	8,736	8,266	6,994	7,051	9,202	11,905	16,989	18,862	18,415	22,280	79aid
Other Sectors	....	4,170	6,924	7,129	8,559	8,260	7,590	7,042	8,879	9,875	9,402	10,579	10,576	9,413	9,581	79ajd
Reserve Assets	....	10,347	12,599	16,918	17,028	19,328	19,338	13,848	14,188	14,308	14,949	17,402	17,094	15,377	21,956	79akd
Liabilities	....	108,007	138,241	189,608	206,343	224,314	239,703	231,447	262,488	304,189	333,302	389,407	355,817	369,087	430,232	79lad
Dir. Invest. in Rep. Economy	....	31,256	42,437	62,429	70,250	73,611	77,405	74,288	81,907	92,383	102,113	115,011	98,832	102,420	118,600	79lbd
Portfolio Investment	....	18,816	24,449	89,738	96,270	106,696	120,813	115,151	136,967	159,750	181,333	221,187	202,325	204,693	236,315	79lcd
Equity Securities	....	12,167	15,386	17,755	17,613	19,647	21,956	18,945	35,916	46,544	51,424	61,571	59,589	70,161	90,439	79ldd
Debt Securities	....	6,649	9,063	71,983	78,657	87,049	98,857	96,206	101,051	113,205	129,909	159,616	142,736	134,532	145,876	79led
Financial Derivatives	....	—	—	—	—	—	—	—	—	7,564	7,250	8,275	8,335	8,240	9,710	79lld
Other investment	....	57,936	71,356	37,441	39,823	44,007	41,485	42,007	43,614	44,492	42,605	44,934	46,325	53,735	65,607	79lfd
Monetary Authorities	....	—	—	50	20	33	24	32	43	46	71	45	33	36	100	79lgd
General Government	....	13,166	16,730	296	311	302	566	513	542	827	439	573	138	174	34	79lhd
Banks	....	1,153	1,700	13,467	17,764	21,829	19,756	22,028	24,618	23,779	25,010	28,493	31,270	39,354	50,396	79lid
Other Sectors	....	43,618	52,925	23,627	21,728	21,842	21,138	19,434	18,411	19,840	17,085	15,822	14,884	14,171	15,077	79ljd

Australia

		1970	1971	1972	1973	1974	1975	1976	1977	1978	1979	1980	1981	1982	1983	1984
Government Finance														*Millions of Australian Dollars:*		
Deficit (-) or Surplus	80	ɪ−260	−78	130	−409	−241	−2,479	−3,609	−2,702	−3,290	−3,132	−2,085	−1,078	−590	−4,601	−7,983
Revenue	81	ɪ7,323	8,241	9,131	9,740	12,296	15,749	18,853	22,126	24,315	26,439	30,623	36,305	41,897	45,936	50,450
Expenditure	82	ɪ6,423	7,473	8,284	9,441	11,240	15,679	20,370	23,310	26,269	28,526	31,886	36,419	41,462	49,186	57,315
Lending Minus Repayments	83	ɪ1,160	846	717	708	1,297	2,549	2,092	1,518	1,336	1,045	822	964	1,025	1,351	1,118
Financing (by Residence of Lender)																
Domestic	84a	ɪ391	161	−83	475	371	2,478	3,483	2,345	1,678	1,755	1,837	1,283	222	4,016	7,749
Foreign	85a	ɪ−131	−83	−47	−66	−130	1	126	357	1,612	1,377	248	−205	368	585	234
Debt: Domestic	88a	....	....	....	....	....	....	....	....	20,321	22,865	23,924	25,537	25,707	30,152	38,353
Foreign	89a	....	....	....	....	....	....	....	....	3,635	5,246	5,396	4,652	5,352	6,919	7,084
Financing (by Currency)																
Net Borrowing: Australian Dollars	84b	....	....	....	....	....	....	....	....	....	....	....	....	....	....	....
Foreign Currency	85b	....	....	....	....	....	....	....	....	....	....	....	....	....	....	....
Other Financing	86c	....	....	....	....	....	....	....	....	....	....	....	....	....	....	....
Use of Cash Balances	87	....	....	....	....	....	....	....	....	....	....	....	....	....	....	....
Commonwealth and States																
Debt: Australian Dollars	88b	9,008	9,245	9,964	13,479	14,275	16,587	19,013	21,420	23,287	25,752	27,250	27,820			
Held By: Reserve Bank	88ba	1,190	910	501	611	1,443	1,276	2,739	4,239	4,392	5,197	5,217	4,779	....	....	....
Deposit Money Banks	88bb	3,508	3,749	4,168	5,085	5,164	6,571	6,641	6,395	6,382	7,256	7,548	9,027	....	....	....
Life Insur. Companies	88bc	1,195	1,325	1,483	1,632	1,786	1,862	2,055	2,226	2,447	2,602	2,798	3,012	....	....	....
Others	88be	3,115	3,261	3,812	6,151	5,882	6,878	7,578	8,560	10,066	10,697	11,687	11,002	....	....	....
Intragovernmental Debt	88bg	2,617	2,700	2,628	2,610	2,575	3,052	2,490	2,572	3,114	3,180	....	....	....	....	....
Foreign Currency	89b	1,580	1,545	1,442	1,265	1,032	1,182	1,325	1,870	....	....	....	....	....	....	....
Local and Other Governments																
Total Debt	88.. i	4,903	5,268	6,060	6,609	....	....	....	....	....	....	....	....	....	....	....
National Accounts														*Billions of Australian Dollars*		
Househ.Cons.Expend.,incl.NPISHs	96f. c	20.04	22.19	24.44	28.33	34.38	41.33	48.63	55.02	61.37	68.54	77.97	88.92	101.70	112.53	121.93
Government Consumption Expend	91f. c	5.18	6.00	6.76	8.16	10.55	14.00	16.55	18.22	20.35	22.27	25.88	29.87	34.08	38.30	43.14
Gross Fixed Capital Formation	93e. c	9.63	10.89	11.38	12.99	14.73	17.30	20.31	22.58	25.55	29.03	34.27	41.53	45.48	44.78	50.87
Changes in Inventories	93i. c	.64	.47	−.11	.31	2.17	−.30	.43	.57	.26	2.30	.88	1.44	−.64	−1.36	3.71
Exports of Goods & Services	90c. c	4.96	5.35	6.23	7.55	8.93	10.58	12.48	13.97	14.88	19.76	22.61	22.59	25.58	26.59	31.59
Imports of Goods & Services	98c. c	−5.04	−5.43	−5.18	−6.43	−10.05	−10.21	−12.47	−14.95	−16.75	−19.56	−23.75	−27.27	−30.79	−29.67	−36.69
Gross Domestic Product (GDP)	99b. c	35.24	39.25	43.32	51.20	61.56	72.94	85.93	95.26	105.23	121.46	137.23	156.09	174.17	188.68	214.35
Net Primary Income from Abroad	98.n c	−.61	−.61	−.57	−.69	−.68	−.96	−1.33	−1.46	−1.68	−2.19	−2.36	−2.47	−2.46	−3.52	−4.70
Gross National Income (GNI)	99a. c	34.63	38.64	42.76	50.52	60.88	71.99	84.60	93.80	103.55	119.26	134.87	153.63	171.71	185.16	209.65
Net Current Transf. from Abroad	98t. c	−.1	.2	.5	.3	—	−.1	−.1	−.7	−.9	−1.2	−.2	−.8	−1.5	−.2	1.2
Gross Nat'l Disp. Income(GNDI)	99i. c	34.6	38.8	43.2	50.8	60.9	72.0	84.5	93.1	102.7	118.0	134.6	152.8	170.2	184.9	210.9
Gross Savings	99s. c	9.4	10.6	12.0	14.3	16.0	16.6	19.3	19.9	21.0	27.2	30.8	34.1	34.4	34.1	45.8
GDP Vol. 1997/98 Ref.,Chained	99b. r	230.26	240.28	245.25	259.08	265.93	270.10	280.35	285.61	293.75	308.91	313.96	326.48	329.26	328.44	350.61
GDP Volume (1995=100)	99bv r	45.3	47.3	48.2	51.0	52.3	53.1	55.1	56.2	57.8	60.8	61.8	64.2	64.8	64.6	69.0
GDP Deflator (1995=100)	99bi r	15.8	16.9	18.3	20.4	23.9	27.9	31.7	34.5	37.0	40.7	45.2	49.4	54.7	59.4	63.2
															Millions:	
Population	99z	12.51	12.94	13.18	13.38	13.70	13.89	14.03	14.19	14.36	14.52	14.70	14.92	15.18	15.39	15.56

	1985	1986	1987	1988	1989	1990	1991	1992	1993	1994	1995	1996	1997	1998	1999		
Year Ending June 30																**Government Finance**	
	−6,810	−5,792	−2,781	‡2,324	6,316	7,877	1,951	−9,514	−14,477	−13,674	−11,641	−4,806	2,028	....	....	Deficit (-) or Surplus	80
	59,282	66,660	75,209	‡84,092	91,516	98,410	100,944	96,630	98,460	104,775	114,493	125,861	135,271	....	....	Revenue	81
	65,175	71,633	77,465	‡82,310	85,316	91,754	100,550	108,201	115,441	121,846	127,613	135,843	140,478	....	....	Expenditure	82
	917	819	525	−542	−116	−1,221	−1,557	−2,057	−2,504	−3,397	−1,479	−5,176	−7,235	....	....	Lending Minus Repayments	83
																Financing (by Residence of Lender)	
	5,902	4,521	2,057	−951	−3,166	−8,640	1,242	11,427	11,152	10,062	8,349	−3,098	−4,294	....	....	Domestic	84a
	908	1,271	724	−1,373	−3,150	763	−3,193	−1,913	3,325	3,612	3,292	7,904	2,266	....	....	Foreign	85a
	44,627	49,258	52,710	‡40,430	38,812	29,886	32,106	43,080	58,025	71,221	79,558	78,042	71,869	....	....	Debt: Domestic	88a
	9,857	13,832	15,064	‡22,877	18,576	19,599	17,396	16,794	21,376	22,869	27,943	37,332	42,155	....	....	Foreign	89a
																Financing (by Currency)	
	....	....	....	....	....	....	....	....	....	....	....	....	....	....	....	Net Borrowing: Australian Dollars	84b
	....	....	....	....	....	....	....	....	....	....	....	....	....	....	....	Foreign Currency	85b
	....	....	....	....	....	....	....	....	....	....	....	....	....	....	....	Other Financing	86c
	....	....	....	....	....	....	....	....	....	....	....	....	....	....	....	Use of Cash Balances	87
																Commonwealth and States	
	....	....	....	....	....	....	....	....	....	....	....	....	....	....	....	Debt: Australian Dollars	88b
	....	....	....	....	....	....	....	....	....	....	....	....	....	....	....	Held By: Reserve Bank	88ba
	....	....	....	....	....	....	....	....	....	....	....	....	....	....	....	Deposit Money Banks	88bb
	....	....	....	....	....	....	....	....	....	....	....	....	....	....	....	Life Insur. Companies	88bc
	....	....	....	....	....	....	....	....	....	....	....	....	....	....	....	Others	88be
	....	....	....	....	....	....	....	....	....	....	....	....	....	....	....	Intragovernmental Debt	88bg
	....	....	....	....	....	....	....	....	....	....	....	....	....	....	....	Foreign Currency	89b
																Local and Other Governments	
	....	....	....	....	....	....	....	....	....	....	....	....	....	....	....	Total Debt	88.. *i*
Billions of Australian Dollars																**National Accounts**	
	136.13	149.78	165.99	185.46	206.99	226.40	237.87	249.86	260.43	273.32	292.50	307.53	323.94	342.31	360.46	Househ.Cons.Expend.,incl.NPISHs	96f. *c*
	48.40	53.82	56.97	61.43	66.90	73.70	79.00	82.44	85.17	88.45	92.84	96.89	100.26	104.78	112.24	Government Consumption Expend	91f. *c*
	61.40	65.78	73.85	84.68	98.65	93.84	85.55	88.23	94.19	106.44	111.19	116.54	127.52	137.80	146.23	Gross Fixed Capital Formation	93e. *c*
	.90	−1.42	.75	3.09	5.53	.46	−3.01	−1.46	2.02	2.39	2.49	1.66	−4.05	3.28	5.38	Changes in Inventories	93i. *c*
	38.83	41.01	47.77	53.38	58.20	63.81	68.49	73.60	80.29	84.09	93.56	100.83	112.35	114.56	113.99	Exports of Goods & Services	90c. *c*
	−45.20	−48.05	−50.85	−57.16	−67.95	−67.90	−67.12	−74.92	−82.53	−90.20	−100.57	−101.69	−110.49	−125.09	−130.31	Imports of Goods & Services	98c. *c*
	237.69	257.50	291.09	330.36	368.97	393.66	399.89	416.11	438.11	464.14	491.59	521.70	549.29	579.14	610.67	Gross Domestic Product (GDP)	99b. *c*
	−6.45	−7.31	−8.33	−10.70	−13.35	−16.87	−15.63	−13.71	−11.96	−17.01	−19.36	−19.67	−19.23	−17.85	−18.39	Net Primary Income from Abroad	98.n *c*
	231.24	250.19	282.76	319.66	355.62	376.80	384.26	402.40	426.15	447.13	472.22	502.03	530.06	561.28	592.28	Gross National Income (GNI)	99a. *c*
	−.5	1.4	2.1	−.1	1.1	−.4	−3.2	−3.4	−3.9	−1.3	.6	−3.2	−4.2	2.1	....	Net Current Transf. from Abroad	98t. *c*
	230.7	251.6	284.8	319.6	356.7	376.4	381.0	399.0	422.3	445.9	472.9	201.9	525.9	563.4	....	Gross Nat'l Disp. Income(GNDI)	99i. *c*
	46.2	48.0	61.9	72.7	82.8	76.3	64.2	66.7	76.7	84.1	87.5	−202.5	101.7	116.3	....	Gross Savings	99s. *c*
	368.56	376.69	395.25	411.87	430.71	438.72	434.04	448.44	465.50	489.75	508.41	530.64	552.34	578.97	604.68	GDP Vol. 1997/98 Ref.,Chained	99b. *r*
	72.5	74.1	77.7	81.0	84.7	86.3	85.4	88.2	91.6	96.3	100.0	104.4	108.6	113.9	118.9	GDP Volume (1995=100)	99bv *r*
	66.7	70.7	76.2	83.0	88.6	92.8	95.3	96.0	97.3	98.0	100.0	101.7	102.9	103.5	104.4	GDP Deflator (1995=100)	99bi *r*
Midyear Estimates																	
	15.79	16.02	16.26	16.53	16.81	17.06	17.28	17.49	17.67	17.85	18.07	18.31	18.52	18.73	18.97	**Population**	99z

(See notes in the back of the book.)

Austria

122	1970	1971	1972	1973	1974	1975	1976	1977	1978	1979	1980	1981	1982	1983	1984
Exchange Rates															*Schillings per SDR through 1998,*
Official Rate **aa**	25.880	25.742	I 25.123	23.946	20.973	21.669	19.481	18.385	17.415	16.376	17.612	18.490	18.408	20.249	21.614
															Schillings per US Dollar through 1998,
Official Rate **ae**	25.880	23.710	I 23.140	19.850	17.130	18.510	16.768	15.135	13.368	12.431	13.809	15.885	16.687	19.341	22.050
Official Rate **rf**	26.000	24.986	23.115	19.580	18.693	17.417	17.940	16.527	14.522	13.368	12.938	15.927	17.059	17.963	20.009
															Schillings per ECU:
ECU Rate **ea**	....	....	....	....	....	....	....	....	....	17.9243	18.0843	17.2384	16.1480	16.0027	15.6312
ECU Rate **eb**	....	....	....	....	....	....	....	....	18.5005	18.3216	17.9969	17.8004	16.7387	16.0104	15.7870
															Index Numbers (1995=100):
Official Rate **ahx**	38.9	45.5	43.6	51.8	54.0	57.9	56.2	61.0	69.5	75.4	78.0	63.5	59.1	56.2	50.5
Nominal Effective Exchange Rate **neu**	64.3	64.8	64.5	67.2	70.5	72.3	74.6	78.0	78.5	79.7	82.1	81.4	84.0	85.9	85.9
Real Effective Exchange Rate **reu**	....	....	....	....	....	109.3	110.0	110.3	132.0	128.3	I 124.3	117.7	117.5	117.7	116.0
Fund Position															*Millions of SDRs:*
Quota **2f.s**	175	270	270	270	270	270	270	270	330	330	495	495	495	776	776
SDRs **1b.s**	38	57	86	86	87	87	96	97	105	156	173	186	226	154	224
Reserve Position in the Fund **1c.s**	157	142	132	126	131	177	344	325	254	232	228	224	259	447	447
of which: Outstg.Fund Borrowing **2c**	—	—	—	—	—	24	100	98	79	66	56	43	42	50	47
International Liquidity															*Millions of US Dollars Unless Otherwise Indicated:*
Total Res.Min.Gold (Eurosys.Def) **1l.d**	1,044	1,547	1,927	1,992	2,535	3,583	3,560	3,351	5,047	4,075	5,280	5,285	5,300	4,515	4,244
SDRs **1b.d**	38	62	93	104	107	102	111	117	136	205	221	216	250	161	220
Reserve Position in the Fund **1c.d**	157	155	144	152	160	207	399	394	331	305	291	261	285	468	438
Foreign Exchange **1d.d**	849	1,330	1,690	1,737	2,268	3,273	3,050	2,839	4,579	3,565	4,768	4,808	4,765	3,886	3,586
o/w: Fin.Deriv.Rel.to Reserves **1ddd**	....	....	....	....	....	....	....	....	....	....	....	....	....	....	....
Other Reserve Assets **1e.d**	....	....	....	....	....	....	....	....	....	....	....	....	....	....	....
Gold (Million Fine Troy Ounces) **1ad**	20.39	20.82	20.85	20.88	20.88	20.88	20.88	21.00	21.05	21.11	21.11	21.11	21.12	21.13	21.13
Gold (National Valuation) **1and**	712	756	775	905	1,049	971	1,072	1,195	2,213	3,182	2,863	2,488	2,369	2,044	1,793
Memo: Euro Cl. on Non-EA Res. **1dgd**	....	....	....	....	....	....	....	....	....	....	....	....	....	....	....
Non-Euro Cl. on EA Res. **1dhd**	....	....	....	....	....	....	....	....	....	....	....	....	....	....	....
Mon. Auth.: Other Foreign Assets **3..d**	....	....	....	....	....	....	....	....	....	....	....	....	....	....	....
Foreign Liabilities **4..d**	8	21	26	20	19	24	37	59	202	397	92	31	29	33	52
Banking Insts.: Foreign Assets **7a.d**	1,043	1,479	2,077	3,341	4,518	5,404	7,669	10,290	13,704	19,329	21,711	22,458	25,039	25,743	26,515
Foreign Liab. **7b.d**	962	1,611	2,272	3,358	4,591	5,353	7,974	10,983	14,699	20,272	24,955	25,538	26,118	26,355	28,153
Monetary Authorities															*Billions of Schillings through 1998;*
Fgn. Assets (Cl.on Non-EA Ctys) **11**	45.5	53.9	62.8	57.7	61.2	84.1	77.5	68.6	96.8	90.0	112.4	123.7	128.3	127.1	133.9
Claims on General Government **12a.u**	....	....	....	....	....	....	....	....	....	....	....	....	....	....	....
o/w: Claims on Gen.Govt.in Cty **12a**	6.4	4.6	5.0	5.6	5.7	6.1	6.2	6.2	6.2	5.9	5.9	5.8	6.2	6.7	7.3
Claims on Banking Institutions **12e.u**	....	....	....	....	....	....	....	....	....	....	....	....	....	....	....
o/w: Claims on Bank.Inst.in Cty **12e**	7.6	6.7	8.7	10.4	15.7	7.5	15.9	29.9	28.5	48.6	37.2	42.3	44.2	62.6	66.1
Claims on Other Resident Sectors **12d.u**	....	....	....	....	....	....	....	....	....	....	....	....	....	....	....
o/w: Cl. on Oth.Res.Sect.in Cty **12d**	....	....	....	....	....	....	....	....	....	....	....	....	....	....	....
Claims on ECB **12u**	....	....	....	....	....	....	....	....	....	....	....	....	....	....	....
Currency in Circulation **14a**	37.0	40.5	46.4	50.7	53.7	57.9	60.9	64.4	69.8	74.6	79.7	80.9	83.9	92.3	93.7
Liabilities to Banking Insts **14c.u**	....	....	....	....	....	....	....	....	....	....	....	....	....	....	....
o/w: Liabs to Bank.Inst.in Cty **14c**	12.5	14.9	17.2	14.1	17.6	25.5	26.3	26.6	35.3	32.5	35.0	41.2	42.8	42.7	44.3
Demand Dep. of Other Res.Sect. **14d.u**	....	....	....	....	....	....	....	....	....	....	....	....	....	....	....
o/w: D.Dep.of Oth.Res.Sect.in Cty **14d**	....	....	....	....	....	....	....	....	....	....	....	....	....	....	....
Other Dep. of Other Res.Sect. **15..u**	....	....	....	....	....	....	....	....	....	....	....	....	....	....	....
o/w: O.Dep.of Oth.Res.Sect.in Cty **15**	....	....	....	....	....	....	....	....	....	....	....	....	....	....	....
Money Market Instruments **16m.u**	....	....	....	....	....	....	....	....	....	....	....	....	....	....	....
o/w: MMI Held by Resid.of Cty **16m**	....	....	....	....	....	....	....	....	....	....	....	....	....	....	....
Bonds (Debt Securities) **16n.u**	....	....	....	....	....	....	....	....	....	....	....	....	....	....	....
o/w: Bonds Held by Resid.of Cty **16n**	....	....	....	....	....	....	....	....	....	....	....	....	....	....	....
Foreign Liab. (to Non-EA Ctys) **16c**	.2	.5	.6	.4	.3	.5	.6	.9	2.7	4.9	1.3	.5	.5	.6	1.1
Central Government Deposits **16d.u**	....	....	....	....	....	....	....	....	....	....	....	....	....	....	....
o/w: Cent.Govt.Dep. in Cty **16d**	2.0	3.0	4.5	2.3	2.8	3.2	2.9	3.9	4.0	3.4	2.8	3.8	2.8	3.5	3.4
Liabilities to ECB **16u**	....	....	....	....	....	....	....	....	....	....	....	....	....	....	....
Other Items (Net) **17r**	7.9	6.3	7.8	6.0	8.1	10.5	8.9	8.9	19.7	29.1	36.7	45.4	48.6	57.2	64.8
Banking Institutions															*Billions of Schillings through 1998;*
Claims on Monetary Authorities **20**	15.3	17.9	20.6	18.9	22.8	31.3	32.1	32.2	41.8	40.2	43.4	48.9	50.6	50.6	54.0
Claims on Bk.Inst.in Oth.EA Ctys **20b.u**	....	....	....	....	....	....	....	....	....	....	....	....	....	....	....
Fgn. Assets (Cl.on Non-EA Ctys) **21**	27.1	34.5	48.4	70.1	I 77.4	100.0	128.6	155.7	183.2	240.3	299.8	356.7	417.8	497.9	584.7
Claims on General Government **22a.u**	....	....	....	....	....	....	....	....	....	....	....	....	....	....	....
o/w: Claims on Gen.Govt.in Cty **22a**	32.6	38.3	44.0	56.3	59.9	86.9	116.4	137.2	158.7	183.2	204.5	220.8	255.5	297.4	I 394.2
Claims on Other Resident Sectors **22d.u**	....	....	....	....	....	....	....	....	....	....	....	....	....	....	....
o/w: Cl. on Oth.Res.Sect.in Cty **22d**	178.7	211.1	254.8	282.6	326.7	360.8	440.5	510.1	577.3	679.3	754.2	840.7	896.0	959.8	I 983.1
Demand Deposits **24..u**	....	....	....	....	....	....	....	....	....	....	....	....	....	....	....
o/w: D.Dep.of Oth.Res.Sect.in Cty **24**	30.8	36.4	46.4	49.8	52.7	63.5	70.4	68.6	74.7	58.4	73.5	68.5	77.5	86.3	92.5
Other Deposits **25..u**	....	....	....	....	....	....	....	....	....	....	....	....	....	....	....
o/w: O.Dep.of Oth.Res.Sect.in Cty **25**	150.4	173.3	196.6	227.3	262.3	314.6	377.6	421.6	489.5	552.8	620.0	702.0	782.8	814.3	870.9
Money Market Instruments **26m.u**	....	....	....	....	....	....	....	....	....	....	....	....	....	....	....
o/w: MMI Held by Resid.of Cty **26m**	....	....	....	....	....	....	....	....	....	....	....	....	....	....	....
Bonds (Debt Securities) **26n.u**	....	....	....	....	....	....	....	....	....	....	....	....	....	....	....
o/w: Bonds Held by Resid.of Cty **26n**	15.8	19.9	26.5	29.9	34.8	43.0	55.2	69.7	87.6	127.9	141.6	147.4	161.2	189.0	203.8
Foreign Liab. (to Non-EA Ctys) **26c**	25.0	37.5	52.9	70.4	I 78.7	99.1	133.7	166.2	196.5	252.0	344.6	405.7	435.8	509.7	620.8
Central Government Deposits **26d.u**	....	....	....	....	....	....	....	....	....	....	....	....	....	....	....
o/w: Cent.Govt.Dep. in Cty **26d**	6.6	8.6	11.3	12.9	11.8	17.6	19.3	23.2	25.7	28.0	22.8	26.1	32.3	44.2	49.8
Credit from Monetary Authorities **26g**	7.6	6.7	8.7	10.4	15.7	7.5	15.9	29.9	28.5	48.6	37.2	42.3	44.2	62.6	66.1
Liab. to Bk.Inst.in Oth. EA Ctys **26h.u**	....	....	....	....	....	....	....	....	....	....	....	....	....	....	....
Capital Accounts **27a**	16.5	18.7	20.8	22.7	25.1	28.3	33.3	38.3	44.0	47.1	51.4	54.7	58.9	65.4	72.0
Other Items (Net) **27r**	1.0	.6	4.6	4.6	5.8	5.3	12.1	17.7	14.5	28.1	11.0	20.3	27.2	33.9	39.5
Banking Survey (Nat'l Residency)															*Billions of Schillings through 1998;*
Foreign Assets (Net) **31n**	47.4	50.3	57.6	56.9	I 59.6	84.6	71.8	57.2	80.8	73.3	66.4	74.3	109.8	114.6	96.7
Domestic Credit **32**	209.2	242.4	288.0	329.2	377.6	432.9	540.9	626.4	712.5	837.1	939.1	1,037.3	1,122.6	1,216.1	I 1,331.4
Claims on General Govt. (Net) **32an**	30.5	31.3	33.2	46.6	51.0	72.1	100.4	116.3	135.2	157.8	184.9	196.6	226.6	256.3	I 348.3
Claims on Other Resident Sectors **32d**	178.7	211.1	254.8	282.6	326.7	360.8	440.5	510.1	577.3	679.3	754.2	840.7	896.0	959.8	I 983.1
Currency in Circulation **34a.n**	37.0	40.5	46.4	50.7	53.7	57.9	60.9	64.4	69.8	74.6	79.7	80.9	83.9	92.3	93.7
Demand Deposits **34b.n**	30.8	36.4	46.4	49.8	52.7	63.5	70.4	68.6	74.7	58.4	73.5	68.5	77.5	86.3	92.5
Other Deposits **35..n**	150.4	173.3	196.6	227.3	262.3	314.6	377.6	421.6	489.5	552.8	620.0	702.0	782.8	814.3	870.9
Money Market Instruments **36m**	....	....	....	....	....	....	....	....	....	....	....	....	....	....	....
Bonds (Debt Securities) **36n**	15.8	19.9	26.5	29.9	34.8	43.0	55.2	69.7	87.6	127.9	141.6	147.4	161.2	189.0	203.8
o/w: Bonds Over Two Years **36na**	....	....	....	....	....	....	....	....	....	....	....	....	....	....	....
Other Items (Net) **37r**	22.7	22.7	29.8	28.5	33.8	38.4	48.5	59.3	71.8	96.6	90.7	112.8	126.9	148.6	166.6

1985	1986	1987	1988	1989	1990	1991	1992	1993	1994	1995	1996	1997	1998	1999		
Euros per SDR Thereafter: End of Period															**Exchange Rates**	
18.981	16.770	15.960	16.909	15.527	15.190	15.290	15.612	16.679	16.013	14.996	15.751	17.045	16.540	1.3662	Official Rate	aa
Euros per US Dollar Thereafter: End of Period (ae) Period Average (rf)																
17.280	13.710	11.250	12.565	11.815	10.677	10.689	11.354	12.143	10.969	10.088	10.954	12.633	11.747	.9954	Official Rate	ae
20.690	15.267	12.643	12.348	13.231	11.370	11.676	10.989	11.632	11.422	10.081	10.587	12.204	12.379	.9386	Official Rate	rf
End of Period (ea) Period Average (eb)																
15.3429	14.6752	14.6633	14.7337	14.1426	14.5560	14.3329	13.7486	13.5998	13.4923	13.2581	13.7253	13.9495	13.7058	....	ECU Rate	ea
15.7694	14.9800	14.5934	14.6182	14.5856	14.4738	14.4841	14.2511	13.6360	13.5755	13.1880	13.4234	13.8403	13.8648	....	ECU Rate	eb
Period Averages																
49.1	66.2	79.8	81.7	76.2	88.8	86.6	91.9	86.6	88.4	100.0	95.2	82.6	81.5	....	Official Rate	ahx
86.3	89.7	92.1	91.9	91.5	93.5	93.1	94.7	97.2	97.2	100.0	98.4	96.2	96.4	95.4	Nominal Effective Exchange Rate	neu
114.8	118.4	119.2	114.6	110.6	108.3	104.6	105.2	105.9	103.6	100.0	95.4	90.4	88.6	....	Real Effective Exchange Rate	reu
End of Period															**Fund Position**	
776	776	776	776	776	776	776	1,188	1,188	1,188	1,188	1,188	1,188	1,188	1,872	Quota	2f.s
191	152	206	199	227	196	197	248	161	194	122	136	125	106	106	SDRs	1b.s
405	361	330	289	274	242	276	390	381	364	459	562	714	970	699	Reserve Position in the Fund	1c.s
41	32	19	10	4	—	—	—	—	—	—	—	—	38	—	*of which:* Outstg.Fund Borrowing	2c
End of Period															**International Liquidity**	
4,767	6,162	7,532	7,368	8,598	9,376	10,332	12,383	14,610	16,822	18,730	22,865	19,736	22,432	I 15,120	Total Res.Min.Gold (Eurosys.Def)	1l.d
210	186	292	268	298	278	282	341	220	283	181	195	168	149	145	SDRs	1b.d
445	442	468	389	361	344	395	536	524	531	682	809	963	1,365	959	Reserve Position in the Fund	1c.d
4,112	5,534	6,772	6,711	7,939	8,754	9,655	11,506	13,866	16,008	17,867	21,861	18,605	20,918	14,016	Foreign Exchange	1d.d
....	....	....	....	....	....	....	....	....	....	....	....	....	....	—	*o/w:* Fin.Deriv.Rel.to Reserves	1ddd
....	....	....	....	....	....	....	....	....	....	....	....	....	....	—	Other Reserve Assets	1e.d
21.14	21.14	21.15	21.15	20.66	20.39	20.03	19.93	18.60	18.34	11.99	10.75	7.87	9.64	13.10	Gold (Million Fine Troy Ounces)	1ad
2,283	2,888	3,523	3,153	3,277	3,581	3,510	3,291	2,871	3,135	2,223	1,805	1,168	2,795	3,810	Gold (National Valuation)	1and
....	....	....	....	....	....	....	....	....	....	....	....	....	....	....	Memo: Euro Cl. on Non-EA Res.	1dgd
....	....	....	....	....	....	....	....	....	....	....	....	....	....	2,146	Non-Euro Cl. on EA Res.	1dhd
....	....	....	....	....	....	....	....	....	....	....	....	....	....	....	Mon. Auth.: Other Foreign Assets	3..d
25	37	30	15	20	19	10	15	9	18	19	8	107	....	I 1,584	Foreign Liabilities	4..d
36,754	48,900	58,955	54,604	58,919	65,991	66,189	66,763	68,418	77,885	92,040	89,538	....	....	I 63,219	Banking Insts.: Foreign Assets	7a.d
38,026	50,891	62,440	59,370	65,954	74,306	76,570	77,427	74,089	84,321	99,148	102,739	....	....	I 49,417	Foreign Liab.	7b.d
Billions of Euros Beginning 1999: End of Period															**Monetary Authorities**	
122.4	124.0	123.7	131.9	140.9	137.1	147.5	177.5	211.6	217.4	237.0	268.3	263.4	....	21.95	Fgn. Assets (Cl.on Non-EA Ctys)	11
....	....	....	....	....	....	....	....	....	....	....	....	....	....	1.43	Claims on General Government	12a.u
7.0	6.4	6.0	6.2	6.7	7.6	8.3	8.8	9.2	9.6	9.6	10.6	11.6	....	.22	*o/w:* Claims on Gen.Govt.in Cty	12a
....	....	....	....	....	....	....	....	....	....	....	....	....	....	14.56	Claims on Banking Institutions	12e.u
72.1	76.9	71.8	70.2	75.4	79.3	77.4	70.8	64.0	62.0	47.6	47.2	74.2	....	5.57	*o/w:* Claims on Bank.Inst.in Cty	12e
....	....	....	....	....	....	....	....	....	....	....	....	....	....	2.33	Claims on Other Resident Sectors	12d.u
....	....	....	....	....	....	....	....	....	....	....	....	....	....	.86	*o/w:* Cl. on Oth.Res.Sect.in Cty	12d
....	....	....	....	....	....	....	....	....	....	....	....	....	....	1.63	Claims on ECB	12u
94.5	98.1	102.9	108.4	117.8	124.7	133.4	141.2	149.8	158.3	168.6	176.7	178.8	....	13.92	Currency in Circulation	14a
....	....	....	....	....	....	....	....	....	....	....	....	....	....	16.21	Liabilities to Banking Insts	14c.u
45.4	51.9	43.0	39.2	50.6	43.9	38.5	48.5	55.2	55.9	43.5	50.1	46.3	....	3.28	*o/w:* Liabs to Bank.Inst.in Cty	14c
....	....	....	....	....	....	....	....	....	....	....	....	....	....	.01	Demand Dep. of Other Res.Sect.	14d.u
....	....	....	....	....	....	....	....	....	....	....	....	....	....	.01	*o/w:* D.Dep.of Oth.Res.Sect.in Cty	14d
....	....	....	....	....	....	....	....	....	....	....	....	....	....	—	Other Dep. of Other Res.Sect.	15..u
....	....	....	....	....	....	....	....	....	....	....	....	....	....	—	*o/w:* O.Dep.of Oth.Res.Sect.in Cty	15
....	....	....	....	....	....	....	....	....	....	....	....	....	....	—	Money Market Instruments	16m.u
....	....	....	....	....	....	....	....	....	....	....	....	....	....	....	*o/w:* MMI Held by Resid.of Cty	16m
....	....	....	....	....	....	....	....	....	....	....	....	....	....	—	Bonds (Debt Securities)	16n.u
....	....	....	....	....	....	....	....	....	....	....	....	....	....	....	*o/w:* Bonds Held by Resid.of Cty	16n
.4	.5	.3	.2	.2	.2	.1	.2	.1	.2	.2	.1	1.3	....	1.58	Foreign Liab. (to Non-EA Ctys)	16c
....	....	....	....	....	....	....	....	....	....	....	....	....	....	.01	Central Government Deposits	16d.u
.8	.6	.2	.2	.3	.2	.2	.2	.3	.3	.2	.3	.2	....	.01	*o/w:* Cent.Govt.Dep. in Cty	16d
....	....	....	....	....	....	....	....	....	....	....	....	....	....	—	Liabilities to ECB	16u
60.4	56.2	55.1	60.3	54.1	55.0	61.1	67.0	79.5	74.4	81.6	98.9	122.5	....	10.18	Other Items (Net)	17r
Billions of Euros Beginning 1999: End of Period															**Banking Institutions**	
55.4	62.0	52.7	48.8	65.3	61.8	59.4	69.8	77.4	80.5	74.0	80.1	77.5	....	3.28	Claims on Monetary Authorities	20
....	....	....	....	....	....	....	....	....	....	....	....	....	....	31.08	Claims on Bk.Inst.in Oth.EA Ctys	20b.u
635.1	670.4	663.2	686.1	696.1	704.6	707.5	758.0	830.8	854.3	928.5	980.8	....	....	62.93	Fgn. Assets (Cl.on Non-EA Ctys)	21
....	....	....	....	....	....	....	....	....	....	....	....	....	....	53.53	Claims on General Government	22a.u
330.0	475.5	556.5	566.6	582.4	598.8	632.6	641.7	676.8	805.6	I 833.1	823.9	783.4	....	50.48	*o/w:* Claims on Gen.Govt.in Cty	22a
....	....	....	....	....	....	....	....	....	....	....	....	....	....	207.74	Claims on Other Resident Sectors	22d.u
1,152.0	1,151.3	1,231.6	1,351.5	1,505.8	1,683.2	1,820.6	1,934.4	2,018.6	2,086.2	I 2,228.8	2,376.9	2,595.9	....	196.53	*o/w:* Cl. on Oth.Res.Sect.in Cty	22d
....	....	....	....	....	....	....	....	....	....	....	....	....	....	44.60	Demand Deposits	24..u
97.4	105.7	120.5	133.5	132.4	140.6	152.5	162.0	181.2	201.1	244.0	255.2	273.5	....	42.15	*o/w:* D.Dep.of Oth.Res.Sect.in Cty	24
....	....	....	....	....	....	....	....	....	....	....	....	....	....	130.22	Other Deposits	25..u
928.3	1,012.4	1,083.0	1,139.7	1,234.3	1,363.9	1,465.1	1,567.3	1,643.1	1,721.0	1,770.9	1,812.1	1,840.7	....	123.21	*o/w:* O.Dep.of Oth.Res.Sect.in Cty	25
....	....	....	....	....	....	....	....	....	....	....	....	....	....	—	Money Market Instruments	26m.u
....	....	....	....	....	....	....	....	....	....	....	....	....	....	....	*o/w:* MMI Held by Resid.of Cty	26m
....	....	....	....	....	....	....	....	....	....	....	....	....	....	89.50	Bonds (Debt Securities)	26n.u
236.5	264.4	300.7	332.5	357.6	386.6	401.0	419.7	491.9	538.7	596.8	607.9	630.2	....	....	*o/w:* Bonds Held by Resid.of Cty	26n
657.1	697.7	702.5	746.0	779.2	793.4	818.5	879.1	899.7	924.9	1,000.2	1,125.4	....	....	49.19	Foreign Liab. (to Non-EA Ctys)	26c
....	....	....	....	....	....	....	....	....	....	....	....	....	....	1.61	Central Government Deposits	26d.u
53.6	71.6	73.6	59.1	63.8	58.4	77.9	59.6	55.2	74.0	77.4	77.7	69.7	....	1.61	*o/w:* Cent.Govt.Dep. in Cty	26d
72.1	76.9	71.8	70.2	75.4	79.3	77.4	70.8	64.0	62.0	47.6	47.2	74.2	....	5.56	Credit from Monetary Authorities	26g
....	....	....	....	....	....	....	....	....	....	....	....	....	....	27.53	Liab. to Bk.Inst.in Oth. EA Ctys	26h.u
77.8	90.2	110.6	128.5	147.4	165.7	180.1	194.7	211.4	226.6	238.4	254.7	275.7	....	26.14	Capital Accounts	27a
49.7	40.6	41.2	43.3	59.4	60.6	47.5	50.7	57.0	78.3	89.0	81.6	....	....	–15.80	Other Items (Net)	27r
Billions of Euros Beginning 1999: End of Period															**Banking Survey (Nat'l Residency)**	
100.0	96.2	84.2	71.9	57.5	48.2	36.4	56.3	142.6	146.6	165.1	123.6	....	....	43.05	Foreign Assets (Net)	31n
1,434.6	1,561.0	1,720.3	1,865.0	2,030.8	2,231.1	2,383.4	2,525.1	2,649.0	2,827.2	I 2,993.8	3,133.4	3,321.0	....	246.47	Domestic Credit	32
282.6	409.7	488.7	513.5	525.0	547.9	562.8	590.8	630.5	740.9	I 765.0	756.5	725.1	....	49.08	Claims on General Govt. (Net)	32an
1,152.0	1,151.3	1,231.6	1,351.5	1,505.8	1,683.2	1,820.6	1,934.4	2,018.6	2,086.2	I 2,228.8	2,376.9	2,595.9	....	197.39	Claims on Other Resident Sectors	32d
94.5	98.1	102.9	108.4	117.8	124.7	133.4	141.2	149.8	158.3	168.6	176.7	178.8	....	13.92	Currency in Circulation	34a.n
97.4	105.7	120.5	133.5	132.4	140.6	152.5	162.0	181.2	201.1	244.0	255.2	273.5	....	42.16	Demand Deposits	34b.n
928.3	1,012.4	1,083.0	1,139.7	1,234.3	1,363.9	1,465.1	1,567.3	1,643.1	1,721.0	1,770.9	1,812.1	1,840.7	....	123.21	Other Deposits	35..n
....	....	....	....	....	....	....	....	....	....	....	....	....	....	—	Money Market Instruments	36m
236.5	264.4	300.7	332.5	357.6	386.6	401.0	419.7	491.9	538.7	596.8	607.9	630.2	....	89.50	Bonds (Debt Securities)	36n
....	....	....	....	....	....	....	....	....	....	....	....	....	....	83.41	*o/w:* Bonds Over Two Years	36na
177.9	176.7	197.4	222.7	246.2	263.4	267.8	291.2	325.7	354.7	378.6	405.1	....	....	20.74	Other Items (Net)	37r

Austria

		1970	1971	1972	1973	1974	1975	1976	1977	1978	1979	1980	1981	1982	1983	1984
Banking Survey (EA-Wide Residency)															*Billions of Euros:*	
Foreign Assets (Net)	31n.*u*	....	....	...	....	....	....	....	....	....	....	....	....	....	....	....
Domestic Credit	32..*u*	....	....	...	....	....	....	....	....	....	....	....	....	....	....	....
Claims on General Govt. (Net)	32an*u*	....	....	...	....	....	....	....	....	....	....	....	....	....	....	....
Claims on Other Resident Sect.	32d.*u*	....	....	...	....	....	....	....	....	....	....	....	....	....	....	....
Currency in Circulation	34a.*u*	....	....	...	....	....	....	....	....	....	....	....	....	....	....	....
Demand Deposits	34b.*u*	....	....	...	....	....	....	....	....	....	....	....	....	....	....	....
Other Deposits	35..*u*	....	....	...	....	....	....	....	....	....	....	....	....	....	....	....
o/w: Other Dep. Over Two Yrs	35ab*u*	....	....	...	....	....	....	....	....	....	....	....	....	....	....	....
Money Market Instruments	36m.*u*	....	....	...	....	....	....	....	....	....	....	....	....	....	....	....
Bonds (Debt Securities)	36n.*u*	....	....	...	....	....	....	....	....	....	....	....	....	....	....	....
o/w: Bonds Over Two Years	36na*u*	....	....	...	....	....	....	....	....	....	....	....	....	....	....	....
Other Items (Net)	37r.*u*	....	....	...	....	....	....	....	....	....	....	....	....	....	....	....
Money (National Definitions)															*Billions of Schillings:*	
Central Bank Money	19ma	53.00	60.24	70.32	69.83	78.85	92.26	98.63	104.05	119.11	Ⅰ110.42	117.51	125.90	129.53	138.57	141.42
Extended Monetary Base	19mb														142.48	140.85
Money, M1	39m	70.98	82.88	102.06	108.29	114.05	134.30	146.98	153.66	165.63	Ⅰ142.93	157.14	152.86	165.66	185.02	189.71
Interest Rates															*Percent Per Annum*	
Discount Rate (End of Period)	60	5.00	5.00	5.50	5.50	6.50	6.00	4.00	5.50	4.50	3.75	6.75	6.75	4.75	3.75	4.50
Money Market Rate	60b	5.67	4.39	5.17	6.94	7.26	5.48	4.67	7.49	6.45	5.59	10.38	10.82	8.00	5.36	6.57
Deposit Rate	60l	....	....	....	....	....	....	....	....	5.00	5.00	5.00	5.00	5.00	4.21	4.00
Lending Rate	60p	....	....	....	....	....	....	....	....	....	....	....	....	....	....	....
Government Bond Yield	61	7.82	7.71	7.37	8.25	9.74	9.61	8.75	8.74	8.21	7.96	9.24	10.61	9.92	8.17	8.02
Prices, Production, Labor															*Index Numbers (1995=100):*	
Share Prices	62	27.8	28.2	31.0	36.5	34.5	34.3	34.8	32.5	30.5	31.0	32.0	28.6	25.5	27.6	28.4
Wholesale Prices	63	50.2	52.8	54.9	55.6	64.0	68.1	Ⅰ72.0	74.2	74.9	78.1	84.8	91.6	94.5	95.1	98.7
Consumer Prices	64	32.8	34.4	36.6	39.3	43.1	46.7	Ⅰ50.1	52.9	54.7	56.8	60.4	64.5	68.0	70.2	74.2
Harmonized CPI	64h	....	....	....	....	....	....	....	....	....	....	....	....	....	....	....
Wages: Monthly Earnings	65	18.0	20.5	22.9	25.8	29.9	33.9	36.9	40.1	42.4	44.8	48.4	51.3	54.5	57.0	59.8
Wages (1996=100)	65a															
Industrial Production	66	47.6	Ⅰ50.5	54.5	57.4	60.0	56.3	Ⅰ59.9	62.3	63.8	68.5	70.4	Ⅰ69.6	69.1	69.2	73.3
Employment	67	77.9	80.0	81.9	85.0	86.6	86.6	87.5	89.2	89.9	90.4	90.9	91.2	90.2	89.1	89.5
															Number in Thousands:	
Labor Force	67d	....	....	....	....	....	....	....	....	....	....	....	....	....	....	....
Employment	67e	....	....	....	....	....	....	....	....	....	....	....	....	....	....	....
Unemployment	67c	....	....	....	....	....	....	....	....	....	....	....	....	....	....	....
Unemployment Rate (%)	67r	....	....	....	....	....	....	....	....	....	....	....	....	....	....	130
International Transactions															*Billions of Schillings through 1998;*	
Exports	70	74.27	78.99	89.75	101.98	133.36	130.88	152.11	161.78	176.11	206.25	226.17	251.77	266.86	277.14	314.50
Imports, c.i.f.	71	92.27	104.48	120.58	137.87	168.27	163.38	206.08	234.84	231.89	269.86	315.85	334.51	332.55	348.34	392.09
															1990=100	
Volume of Exports	72	25.9	26.8	29.9	32.5	36.3	33.7	39.1	40.3	44.3	Ⅰ50.1	51.5	54.1	54.7	57.1	62.5
Volume of Imports	73	29.3	31.8	36.4	40.2	41.3	38.5	47.4	52.0	51.2	Ⅰ56.6	59.5	57.0	55.8	59.7	64.9
Export Prices	76	60.9	63.0	64.0	67.6	78.8	81.7	81.7	84.2	84.2	Ⅰ87.7	92.1	97.7	102.1	101.8	105.4
Import Prices	76.x	58.0	60.6	60.9	63.1	75.2	78.0	79.7	82.7	82.6	Ⅰ87.2	96.4	106.5	106.9	105.6	109.6
Balance of Payments															*Millions of US Dollars:*	
Current Account, n.i.e.	78ald	−78	−73	−63	−238	−230	−744	−1,429	−2,801	−1,490	−1,954	−3,865	−3,042	703	276	−178
Goods: Exports f.o.b.	78aad	2,862	3,160	3,890	5,291	7,570	7,620	8,472	9,737	12,203	15,474	17,227	15,769	15,552	15,292	15,475
Goods: Imports f.o.b.	78abd	−3,550	−4,086	−5,018	−6,865	−8,879	−9,587	−11,073	−13,602	−15,504	−19,753	−23,716	−20,713	−18,598	−18,464	−18,717
Trade Balance	78acd	−688	−926	−1,128	−1,574	−1,309	−1,967	−2,602	−3,865	−3,301	−4,279	−6,489	−4,944	−3,046	−3,172	−3,242
Services: Credit	78add	1,335	1,706	2,207	3,017	3,150	3,729	4,359	5,211	6,632	8,166	9,423	8,198	9,557	9,613	9,240
Services: Debit	78aed	−690	−806	−1,026	−1,455	−1,789	−2,223	−2,850	−3,670	−4,330	−5,386	−6,204	−5,752	−5,343	−5,715	−5,768
Balance on Goods & Services	78afd	−42	−26	53	−13	52	−461	−1,094	−2,323	−999	−1,500	−3,271	−2,499	1,169	726	229
Income: Credit	78agd	129	161	169	256	530	598	614	724	974	1,551	2,502	3,168	3,147	2,598	2,876
Income: Debit	78ahd	−175	−212	−253	−390	−637	−735	−829	−1,062	−1,460	−2,035	−3,030	−3,631	−3,559	−2,966	−3,226
Balance on Gds, Serv. & Inc.	78aid	−88	−77	−30	−147	−56	−598	−1,309	−2,661	−1,485	−1,984	−3,799	−2,962	757	359	−120
Current Transfers, n.i.e.: Credit	78ajd	103	120	140	197	254	305	356	416	547	726	778	695	673	619	605
Current Transfers: Debit	78akd	−92	−116	−172	−288	−428	−450	−475	−557	−552	−696	−844	−775	−726	−702	−663
Capital Account, n.i.e.	78bcd	−1	2	−2	4	7	6	6	1	−4	−1	−22	−7	−20	2	−2
Capital Account, n.i.e.: Credit	78bad	4	6	9	13	15	14	16	16	18	21	30	26	20	27	23
Capital Account: Debit	78bbd	−5	−4	−11	−9	−7	−8	−10	−15	−22	−22	−52	−33	−40	−25	−25
Financial Account, n.i.e.	78bjd	94	284	334	−148	667	1,191	766	1,719	1,769	−14	2,891	1,518	−862	−490	188
Direct Investment Abroad	78bdd	−9	−36	−38	−39	−20	−26	−56	−86	−90	−85	−101	−211	−139	−189	−70
Dir. Invest. in Rep. Econ., n.i.e.	78bed	113	143	145	161	177	79	91	97	142	187	239	328	208	216	115
Portfolio Investment Assets	78bfd	−56	−47	−84	−282	−26	−77	−133	−70	−63	−236	−126	−35	−47	−515	−779
Equity Securities	78bkd	−29	−28	−4	−44	−56	−6	−15	−2	−2	10	3	49	28	−58	−139
Debt Securities	78bld	−27	−19	−79	−239	30	−72	−118	−68	−62	−246	−129	−84	−75	−457	−640
Portfolio Investment Liab., n.i.e.	78bgd	−1	8	191	133	309	963	647	1,249	1,267	414	1,701	1,837	1,552	955	1,266
Equity Securities	78bmd	1	4	6	—	−1	5	2	−3	4	−14	10	−1	5	8	3
Debt Securities	78bnd	−2	4	185	133	310	958	645	1,252	1,263	428	1,691	1,839	1,547	947	1,264
Financial Derivatives Assets	78bwd	....	....	....	....	....	....	....	....	....	....	....	....	....	....	....
Financial Derivatives Liabilities	78bxd	....	....	....	....	....	....	....	....	....	....	....	....	....	....	....
Other Investment Assets	78bhd	−393	−290	−550	−1,022	−512	−1,259	−1,604	−1,655	−2,315	−4,654	−5,090	−3,576	−3,938	−4,759	−4,658
Monetary Authorities	78bod	....	....	....	....	....	....	....	....	....	....	....	....	....	....	....
General Government	78bpd	−32	−5	−8	−29	−30	−10	−40	17	−43	−12	−286	208	−143	−106	−66
Banks	78bqd	−352	−281	−547	−981	−474	−1,216	−1,535	−1,681	−1,885	−4,104	−4,399	−3,448	−3,467	−4,093	−3,730
Other Sectors	78brd	−9	−4	4	−12	−8	−32	−29	10	−387	−538	−405	−336	−328	−560	−863
Other Investment Liab., n.i.e.	78bid	441	507	670	901	740	1,511	1,821	2,184	2,828	4,360	6,268	3,176	1,503	3,801	4,314
Monetary Authorities	78bsd	1	11	11	−15	−8	9	8	18	126	177	−262	−55	—	7	24
General Government	78btd	22	−58	−69	−23	128	327	80	182	444	−101	58	358	359	95	148
Banks	78bud	428	489	665	794	518	1,064	1,753	1,601	1,738	3,840	6,128	2,506	1,225	3,212	3,652
Other Sectors	78bvd	−10	66	62	145	102	111	−20	382	520	445	344	366	−81	487	490
Net Errors and Omissions	78cad	167	182	96	210	−56	719	540	731	1,072	940	2,337	1,909	385	−315	60
Overall Balance	78cbd	182	395	365	−172	388	1,172	−116	−350	1,347	−1,029	1,341	379	207	−528	67
Reserves and Related Items	79dad	−182	−395	−365	172	−388	−1,172	116	350	−1,347	1,029	−1,341	−379	−207	528	−67
Reserve Assets	79dbd	−182	−395	−365	172	−388	−1,172	116	350	−1,347	1,029	−1,341	−379	−207	528	−67
Use of Fund Credit and Loans	79dcd	—	—	—	—	—	—	—	—	—	—	—	—	—	—	—
Exceptional Financing	79ded	....	....	....	....	....	....	....	....	....	....	....	....	....	....	....

1985	1986	1987	1988	1989	1990	1991	1992	1993	1994	1995	1996	1997	1998	1999		
End of Period															**Banking Survey (EA-Wide Residency)**	
....	....	....	....	....	....	....	....	....	....	....	....	....	....	34.11	Foreign Assets (Net)	**31n.** *u*
....	....	....	....	....	....	....	....	....	....	....	....	....	....	263.40	Domestic Credit	**32..** *u*
....	....	....	....	....	....	....	....	....	....	....	....	....	....	53.34	Claims on General Govt. (Net)	**32an** *u*
....	....	....	....	....	....	....	....	....	....	....	....	....	....	210.06	Claims on Other Resident Sect.	**32d.** *u*
....	....	....	....	....	....	....	....	....	....	....	....	....	....	13.92	Currency in Circulation	**34a.** *u*
....	....	....	....	....	....	....	....	....	....	....	....	....	....	44.61	Demand Deposits	**34b.** *u*
....	....	....	....	....	....	....	....	....	....	....	....	....	....	130.22	Other Deposits	**35..** *u*
....	....	....	....	....	....	....	....	....	....	....	....	....	....	50.76	o/w: Other Dep. Over Two Yrs	**35ab** *u*
....	....	....	....	....	....	....	....	....	....	....	....	....	....	—	Money Market Instruments	**36m.** *u*
....	....	....	....	....	....	....	....	....	....	....	....	....	....	89.50	Bonds (Debt Securities)	**36n.** *u*
....	....	....	....	....	....	....	....	....	....	....	....	....	....	83.41	o/w: Bonds Over Two Years	**36na** *u*
....	....	....	....	....	....	....	....	....	....	....	....	....	....	19.26	Other Items (Net)	**37r.** *u*
End of Period															**Money (National Definitions)**	
140.71	150.64	146.12	147.82	168.69	168.80	172.09	189.88	205.24	214.47	212.37	227.13	225.38	....	....	*Central Bank Money*	**19ma**
143.04	152.79	161.11	166.89	182.88	195.58	205.76	216.26	224.39	235.17	250.84	260.35	265.81	....	....	*Extended Monetary Base*	**19mb**
192.32	201.58	222.15	240.93	249.20	262.72	284.19	301.81	334.64	355.58	409.19	431.15	452.30	....	....	*Money, M1*	**39m**
Percent Per Annum															**Interest Rates**	
4.00	4.00	3.00	4.00	6.50	6.50	8.00	8.00	5.25	4.50	3.00	2.50	2.50	2.50	....	Discount Rate *(End of Period)*	**60**
6.11	5.19	4.35	4.59	7.46	8.53	9.10	9.35	7.22	5.03	4.36	3.19	3.27	3.36	....	Money Market Rate	**60b**
3.94	3.63	3.03	2.73	2.98	3.41	3.75	3.69	2.98	2.31	2.19	1.71	1.50	I2.65	2.21	Deposit Rate	**60l**
....	....	....	....	....	....	....	....	....	....	....	....	....	6.42	5.64	Lending Rate	**60p**
7.77	7.33	6.91	6.67	7.14	8.74	8.62	8.27	6.64	6.69	6.47	5.30	4.79	4.29	4.09	Government Bond Yield	**61**
Period Averages															**Prices, Production, Labor**	
54.3	67.9	57.8	54.8	94.9	154.0	131.2	103.0	100.9	115.3	100.0	105.2	119.9	135.2	....	Share Prices	**62**
101.2	I95.9	94.0	93.8	95.4	98.2	99.0	98.8	98.4	99.7	100.0	I100.0	100.4	99.8	99.0	Wholesale Prices	**63**
76.6	I77.9	79.0	80.5	82.6	85.3	88.1	91.7	95.0	97.8	100.0	I101.8	103.2	104.1	104.7	Consumer Prices	**64**
....	....	....	....	....	....	....	....	....	....	100.0	101.8	103.0	103.8	104.3	Harmonized CPI	**64h**
63.4	66.3	68.4	70.9	74.1	79.4	83.5	87.5	92.1	95.8	100.0	....	....	....	....	Wages: Monthly Earnings	**65**
....	....	....	....	....	....	....	....	....	....	....	100.0	100.5	104.0	104.6	Wages (1996=100)	**65a**
76.5	I77.4	77.8	81.3	86.3	92.8	I94.2	93.2	91.4	95.0	I100.0	100.9	107.8	118.1	123.7	Industrial Production	**66**
89.9	90.6	90.8	91.6	93.3	95.5	97.7	99.6	99.6	100.1	100.0	99.3	99.6	100.2	101.3	Employment	**67**
Period Averages																
....	....	....	....	....	....	3,607	3,679	3,734	3,881	....	3,870	3,884	3,888	....	Labor Force	**67d**
3,235	3,282	3,300	3,311	3,346	3,420	3,482	3,547	I3,055	3,742	3,759	3,710	3,719	3,723	....	Employment	**67e**
139	152	I164	159	149	166	185	193	222	215	216	231	233	238	222	Unemployment	**67c**
....	5.2	I5.6	5.3	5.0	5.4	5.8	5.9	6.8	6.5	6.6	7.0	7.1	7.2	6.7	Unemployment Rate (%)	**67r**
Billions of Euros Beginning 1999															**International Transactions**	
353.97	342.48	342.43	383.22	429.31	466.07	479.03	487.56	467.66	511.89	580.01	612.19	715.02	774.74	I59.57	Exports	**70**
430.97	407.96	411.85	451.44	514.69	556.23	591.90	593.92	565.56	629.42	668.03	712.76	790.25	842.13	I64.54	Imports, c.i.f.	**71**
1990=100																
68.8	69.3	71.1	I79.6	90.3	100.0	105.7	110.8	108.0	....	....	....	....	....	....	Volume of Exports	**72**
68.0	71.6	75.3	I81.5	90.1	100.0	101.3	106.6	105.8	....	....	....	....	....	....	Volume of Imports	**73**
107.3	104.8	102.2	I102.9	100.3	100.0	96.7	94.8	90.6	....	....	....	....	....	....	Export Prices	**76**
113.8	104.5	99.9	I99.9	102.6	100.0	100.2	98.8	95.5	....	....	....	....	....	....	Import Prices	**76.x**
Minus Sign Indicates Debit															**Balance of Payments**	
−158	204	−263	−242	248	1,166	61	−753	−1,013	−2,992	−5,448	−4,890	−5,221	−4,609	−5,701	Current Account, n.i.e.	**78al** *d*
16,876	21,725	26,626	30,158	31,960	40,414	40,353	44,516	40,271	45,175	57,695	57,937	58,662	62,826	63,695	Goods: Exports f.o.b.	**78aa** *d*
−20,012	−25,741	−31,434	−34,922	−37,512	−47,383	−48,913	−52,205	−46,747	−53,089	−64,352	−65,252	−62,936	−66,480	−67,255	Goods: Imports f.o.b.	**78ab** *d*
−3,137	−4,016	−4,809	−4,765	−5,552	−6,969	−8,560	−7,690	−6,476	−7,914	−6,656	−7,315	−4,274	−3,654	−3,560	*Trade Balance*	**78ac** *d*
9,697	12,561	15,116	17,550	18,377	23,279	25,560	27,326	26,725	28,019	32,211	33,977	29,605	32,347	30,947	Services: Credit	**78ad** *d*
−6,389	−7,627	−9,635	−12,077	−11,527	−14,197	−15,333	−17,956	−19,186	−20,743	−27,703	−29,331	−28,569	−30,161	−28,390	Services: Debit	**78ae** *d*
171	918	672	708	1,298	2,114	1,667	1,680	1,064	−639	−2,149	−2,669	−3,239	−1,468	−1,003	*Balance on Goods & Services*	**78af** *d*
3,194	3,783	4,484	5,324	6,789	9,145	9,544	6,998	7,237	7,074	8,900	9,852	10,393	10,784	10,474	Income: Credit	**78ag** *d*
−3,448	−4,459	−5,346	−6,243	−7,723	−10,087	−11,020	−8,414	−8,310	−8,344	−10,498	−10,291	−10,682	−12,011	−13,186	Income: Debit	**78ah** *d*
−83	242	−190	−210	364	1,172	192	264	−9	−1,909	−3,746	−3,107	−3,527	−2,695	−3,715	*Balance on Gds, Serv. & Inc.*	**78ai** *d*
630	866	1,115	1,258	1,227	1,657	1,699	1,308	1,266	1,370	2,972	3,145	2,912	2,920	2,905	Current Transfers, n.i.e.: Credit	**78aj** *d*
−705	−903	−1,188	−1,289	−1,343	−1,663	−1,830	−2,326	−2,270	−2,453	−4,674	−4,928	−4,605	−4,834	−4,890	Current Transfers: Debit	**78ak** *d*
−17	−3	−7	−5	−12	8	55	−50	−448	−68	−62	78	26	−206	−145	Capital Account, n.i.e.	**78bc** *d*
18	35	36	40	50	63	152	247	246	676	540	591	590	477	531	Capital Account, n.i.e.: Credit	**78ba** *d*
−35	−38	−43	−44	−62	−55	−97	−297	−694	−744	−602	−513	−564	−683	−676	Capital Account: Debit	**78bb** *d*
332	1,670	1,035	415	1,367	−19	−12	2,378	3,970	4,311	7,365	5,325	1,666	8,568	4,913	Financial Account, n.i.e.	**78bj** *d*
−73	−317	−313	−310	−867	−1,701	−1,293	−1,693	−1,189	−1,256	−1,134	−1,848	−1,984	−2,759	−2,712	Direct Investment Abroad	**78bd** *d*
173	187	410	436	587	653	360	1,442	1,129	2,117	1,901	4,485	2,624	6,034	2,979	Dir. Invest. in Rep. Econ., n.i.e.	**78be** *d*
−1,022	−491	−1,185	−1,598	−1,559	−1,608	−2,272	−2,676	−1,912	−4,475	−2,836	−8,296	−10,157	−11,341	−27,664	Portfolio Investment Assets	**78bf** *d*
−71	−199	−274	−572	−524	−430	−60	−178	−618	−842	−545	−1,146	−2,405	−5,209	−5,436	Equity Securities	**78bk** *d*
−951	−292	−911	−1,026	−1,035	−1,178	−2,212	−2,498	−1,294	−3,633	−2,291	−7,150	−7,752	−6,131	−22,228	Debt Securities	**78bl** *d*
1,808	2,822	1,427	3,916	4,193	3,239	2,687	9,164	7,912	4,253	12,292	5,607	10,956	16,570	26,313	Portfolio Investment Liab., n.i.e.	**78bg** *d*
107	104	240	389	864	668	186	158	1,182	1,304	1,262	2,652	2,610	992	2,511	Equity Securities	**78bm** *d*
1,701	2,719	1,188	3,528	3,329	2,571	2,501	9,006	6,729	2,949	11,030	2,955	8,345	15,578	23,803	Debt Securities	**78bn** *d*
....	....	....	....	....	....	....	7	−20	−85	−133	215	−191	−407	−266	Financial Derivatives Assets	**78bw** *d*
....	....	....	....	....	....	....	....	....	....	....	....	223	−100	101	Financial Derivatives Liabilities	**78bx** *d*
−2,261	−1,695	−115	−2,522	−1,606	−1,433	−2,207	−7,301	−5,099	−2,545	−9,923	719	−5,208	−810	−12,401	Other Investment Assets	**78bh** *d*
....	....	....	....	....	....	....	....	....	−17	−131	131	....	−107	−3,561	Monetary Authorities	**78bo** *d*
38	−143	92	−106	−24	−244	−331	259	70	−183	−231	324	−647	−500	331	General Government	**78bp** *d*
−1,817	−1,475	−270	−1,811	−720	−195	−1,144	−5,955	−5,176	−1,307	−10,848	2,292	−3,873	971	−6,045	Banks	**78bq** *d*
−482	−78	63	−604	−862	−994	−732	−1,605	7	−1,039	1,287	−2,027	−687	−1,174	−3,127	Other Sectors	**78br** *d*
1,708	1,164	811	493	618	831	2,714	3,434	3,149	6,303	7,199	4,442	5,403	1,381	18,564	Other Investment Liab., n.i.e.	**78bi** *d*
−58	7	−12	−12	4	−3	4	—	—	—	—	—	—	—	6,412	Monetary Authorities	**78bs** *d*
−98	−353	−327	−721	−402	−211	−36	242	−492	1,558	467	−715	−319	522	101	General Government	**78bt** *d*
1,386	1,592	1,271	749	384	721	2,781	1,887	3,088	4,584	6,077	5,142	5,695	1,644	11,155	Banks	**78bu** *d*
478	−82	−121	478	631	325	−35	1,305	553	160	655	15	27	−786	896	Other Sectors	**78bv** *d*
−143	−1,228	−433	322	−613	−1,170	731	1,013	−308	−417	−464	562	476	−250	−1,238	Net Errors and Omissions	**78ca** *d*
15	643	333	491	990	−15	835	2,588	2,201	834	1,391	1,075	−3,053	3,503	−2,170	Overall Balance	**78cb** *d*
−15	−643	−333	−491	−990	15	−835	−2,588	−2,201	−834	−1,391	−1,075	3,053	−3,503	2,170	Reserves and Related Items	**79da** *d*
−15	−643	−333	−491	−990	15	−835	−2,588	−2,201	−834	−1,391	−1,075	3,053	−3,503	2,170	Reserve Assets	**79db** *d*
—	—	—	—	—	—	—	—	—	—	—	—	—	—	—	Use of Fund Credit and Loans	**79dc** *d*
....	....	....	....	....	....	....	....	....	....	....	....	....	....	....	Exceptional Financing	**79de** *d*

Austria

		1970	1971	1972	1973	1974	1975	1976	1977	1978	1979	1980	1981	1982	1983	1984
International Investment Position																*Millions of US Dollars*
Assets	79aa d	....	....	....	....	....	....	....	....	....	....	36,355	36,298	38,086	37,553	37,646
Direct Investment Abroad	79ab d	....	....	....	....	....	....	....	....	....	....	530	634	676	756	716
Portfolio Investment	79ac d	....	....	....	....	....	....	....	....	....	....	1,892	1,617	1,618	1,600	2,058
Equity Securities	79ad d	....	....	....	....	....	....	....	....	....	....	477	368	321	327	407
Debt Securities	79ae d	....	....	....	....	....	....	....	....	....	....	1,415	1,250	1,297	1,273	1,651
Financial Derivatives	79al d	....	....	....	....	....	....	....	....	....	....	—	—	—	—	—
Other Investment	79af d	....	....	....	....	....	....	....	....	....	....	25,817	26,297	28,145	28,664	28,834
Monetary Authorities	79ag d	....	....	....	....	....	....	....	....	....	....	274	186	323	381	397
General Government	79ah d	....	....	....	....	....	....	....	....	....	....	—	—	—	—	—
Banks	79ai d	....	....	....	....	....	....	....	....	....	....	21,762	22,509	24,290	24,915	25,415
Other Sectors	79aj d	....	....	....	....	....	....	....	....	....	....	3,781	3,601	3,531	3,368	3,023
Reserve Assets	79ak d	....	....	....	....	....	....	....	....	....	....	8,116	7,750	7,648	6,533	6,037
Liabilities	79la d	....	....	....	....	....	....	....	....	....	....	43,664	45,412	42,617	36,225	41,451
Dir. Invest. in Rep. Economy	79lb d	....	....	....	....	....	....	....	....	....	....	3,163	2,898	2,965	2,755	2,512
Portfolio Investment	79lc d	....	....	....	....	....	....	....	....	....	....	7,645	9,256	10,402	10,031	10,231
Equity Securities	79ld d	....	....	....	....	....	....	....	....	....	....	47	39	43	43	40
Debt Securities	79le d	....	....	....	....	....	....	....	....	....	....	7,598	9,216	10,360	9,988	10,191
Financial Derivatives	79ll d	....	....	....	....	....	....	....	....	....	....	—	—	—	—	—
Other investment	79lf d	....	....	....	....	....	....	....	....	....	....	32,857	33,258	29,250	23,439	28,708
Monetary Authorities	79lg d	....	....	....	....	....	....	....	....	....	....	92	31	29	33	52
General Government	79lh d	....	....	....	....	....	....	....	....	....	....	2,214	1,977	2,262	2,045	1,905
Banks	79li d	....	....	....	....	....	....	....	....	....	....	24,955	25,538	21,532	16,666	22,598
Other Sectors	79lj d	....	....	....	....	....	....	....	....	....	....	5,596	5,713	5,426	4,696	4,154
Government Finance																
Federal Government																*Billions of Schillings through 1998;*
Deficit (-) or Surplus	80	I −1.80	.24	−.85	−8.96	−9.76	−26.34	−34.06	−30.21	−34.92	−35.31	−33.57	−32.52	−54.53	−71.84	−58.22
Revenue	81	I 109.24	123.56	141.63	163.39	189.04	204.75	225.96	253.31	288.56	315.84	344.44	379.50	395.04	414.91	454.23
Grants Received	81z	I 1.09	1.21	1.47	.58	.68	1.01	1.11	1.25	1.85	2.32	2.97	3.43	3.04	3.26	3.20
Expenditure	82	I 109.34	122.64	141.00	168.77	192.98	228.37	255.06	280.05	317.46	343.96	371.62	408.40	443.57	477.54	504.95
Lending Minus Repayments	83	I 2.79	1.89	2.95	4.16	6.50	3.73	6.07	4.72	7.87	9.51	9.36	7.05	9.04	12.47	10.70
Financing																
Net Borrowing	84	I 2.93	1.57	3.89	6.67	7.17	37.90	35.77	34.78	35.94	37.17	30.66	30.62	51.19	74.96	59.67
Domestic	84a	I 2.17	2.61	5.49	7.32	2.31	19.80	32.03	21.50	24.13	31.25	22.11	13.99	34.91	63.21	64.32
Foreign	85a	I .76	−1.04	−1.60	−.65	4.86	18.10	3.74	13.28	11.81	5.92	8.55	16.63	16.28	11.75	−4.65
Use of Cash Balances	87	I −1.13	−1.81	−3.04	2.29	2.59	−11.56	−1.71	−4.57	−1.02	−1.86	2.91	1.90	3.34	−3.12	−1.45
Debt: Domestic	88a	33.58	35.00	40.17	47.44	48.13	68.51	98.85	117.95	139.15	167.73	188.62	201.29	233.24	291.21	351.54
Foreign	89a	13.50	12.14	10.31	9.03	13.55	32.07	34.96	47.42	60.02	63.65	72.64	94.56	108.43	125.59	118.96
General Government																*As Percent of*
Deficit (-) or Surplus	80g	....	....	....	....	....	....	....	....	....	....	....	....	....	....	....
Debt	88g	....	....	....	....	....	....	....	....	....	....	....	....	....	....	....
National Accounts																*Billions of Schillings through 1998;*
Househ.Cons.Expend.,incl.NPIS	96f	205.3	230.0	259.8	291.8	330.6	368.3	418.6	466.8	477.5	519.6	559.8	605.5	657.6	717.0	744.8
Government Consumption Expend.	91f	55.2	62.0	70.1	81.9	97.4	113.1	132.5	143.9	158.0	171.7	184.8	201.5	221.1	235.5	248.0
Gross Fixed Capital Formation	93e	97.2	116.9	144.9	155.0	175.7	174.9	168.5	193.0	187.2	207.5	230.9	243.1	237.5	246.1	252.1
Changes in Inventories	93i	14.5	7.7	2.0	12.8	16.9	−4.3	22.8	24.8	29.0	37.8	45.6	30.3	10.8	6.2	34.0
Exports of Goods and Services	90c	116.8	128.7	146.4	165.9	204.2	209.0	236.3	256.9	280.8	327.7	366.2	404.5	425.4	444.4	491.4
Imports of Goods and Services	98c	−113.1	−125.7	−143.7	−163.9	−206.3	−204.8	−247.3	−278.4	−280.4	−331.6	−385.7	−418.5	−406.9	−428.4	−489.6
Gross Domestic Product (GDP)	99b	375.9	419.6	479.6	543.5	618.6	656.1	742.1	820.9	866.8	945.9	1,016.1	1,081.7	1,161.2	1,237.4	1,299.0
Net Current Transf.from Abroad	98.n	−2.0	−1.9	−2.7	−3.4	−3.0	−3.6	−5.0	−6.9	−8.4	−7.8	−8.4	−8.8	−8.4	−8.8	−8.6
Gross National Income (GNI)	99a	373.9	417.7	476.9	540.1	615.6	652.5	753.1	842.4	866.5	949.8	1,035.6	1,095.7	1,142.7	1,221.3	1,297.2
Net National Income	99e	330.1	368.2	420.6	477.7	544.1	575.1	637.2	698.7	736.3	806.5	870.3	918.7	984.4	1,043.2	1,110.0
Net National Income	99e	....	....	....	....	....	....	....	....	....	....	....	....	....	....	....
GDP Volume 1964 Prices	99b.p	301.8	317.8	338.0	355.8	371.0	364.8	385.8	402.6	406.7	427.3	442.9				
GDP Volume 1983 prices	99b.p	....	....	....	....	....	....	....	....	....	....		1,182.3	1,181.1	1,203.6	1,237.4	1,241.5
GDP Volume 1995 Prices	99b.p	....	....	....	....	....	....	....	....	....	....	....	....	....	....	....
GDP Volume (1995=100)	99bv p	50.5	53.1	56.5	59.5	62.0	61.0	64.5	67.5	67.3	70.9	72.6	72.5	73.9	76.0	76.2
GDP Deflator (1995=100)	99bi p	31.4	33.2	35.7	38.5	42.0	45.3	48.4	51.2	54.2	56.1	58.9	62.8	66.2	68.6	71.7
																Millions:
Population	99z	7.43	7.46	7.49	7.53	7.53	I 7.58	7.57	7.57	7.56	7.55	7.55	7.56	7.57	7.55	7.55

	1985	1986	1987	1988	1989	1990	1991	1992	1993	1994	1995	1996	1997	1998	1999		

Millions of US Dollars — **International Investment Position**

1985	1986	1987	1988	1989	1990	1991	1992	1993	1994	1995	1996	1997	1998	1999	Description	Code
57,767	73,093	90,627	85,186	94,658	108,096	111,913	117,479	122,090	137,955	160,211	161,785	166,135	197,275	....	Assets	79aa d
1,343	1,430	1,547	1,616	3,267	4,739	6,502	6,817	8,112	9,390	11,707	11,868	15,159	19,094	....	Direct Investment Abroad	79ab d
3,889	5,405	7,911	8,659	10,961	13,862	14,492	16,866	17,096	22,673	27,389	33,303	44,051	58,738	....	Portfolio Investment	79ac d
602	985	1,502	1,894	2,607	3,362	3,499	3,435	3,722	4,941	5,868	6,454	11,502	17,221	....	Equity Securities	79ad d
3,287	4,420	6,409	6,765	8,354	10,499	10,993	13,431	13,374	17,732	21,521	26,849	32,549	41,517	....	Debt Securities	79ae d
								74	109	169	219	201	741	....	Financial Derivatives	79al d
40,781	51,823	63,396	58,798	63,419	72,595	73,038	74,696	75,113	82,040	95,054	89,730	84,853	92,270	....	Other Investment	79af d
											—	12	238	....	Monetary Authorities	79ag d
550	992	1,120	1,114	1,253	1,564	3,153	2,686	2,528	1,021	1,209	1,607	2,039	2,750	....	General Government	79ah d
34,531	45,018	55,138	50,879	54,515	61,328	61,821	62,780	62,645	70,380	83,267	77,716	73,651	78,114	....	Banks	79ai d
5,700	5,813	7,138	6,805	7,651	9,703	8,064	9,230	9,940	10,639	10,577	10,407	9,150	11,169	....	Other Sectors	79aj d
11,755	14,435	17,773	16,113	17,011	16,900	17,882	19,099	21,695	23,742	25,893	26,666	21,871	26,431	....	Reserve Assets	79ak d
58,513	74,683	93,867	89,733	98,358	114,967	123,342	127,955	133,600	155,538	189,790	189,264	198,918	240,402	....	Liabilities	79la d
3,762	5,222	6,960	7,107	8,261	10,237	11,058	11,221	11,398	13,246	17,536	18,258	19,694	27,428	....	Dir. Invest. in Rep. Economy	79lb d
14,925	20,737	26,613	28,205	33,322	41,538	48,031	55,813	61,896	69,469	89,473	87,676	97,091	121,673	....	Portfolio Investment	79lc d
174	233	293	517	1,244	1,976	2,545	2,633	3,591	5,379	6,989	9,056	15,662	15,621	....	Equity Securities	79ld d
14,751	20,503	26,320	27,688	32,078	39,562	45,486	53,179	58,305	64,090	82,484	78,620	81,430	106,053	....	Debt Securities	79le d
									119	129	110	12	9	....	Financial Derivatives	79ll d
39,826	48,724	60,293	54,421	56,775	63,192	64,253	60,921	60,306	72,705	82,653	83,221	82,121	91,291	....	Other investment	79lf d
									18	20	9	—	—	....	Monetary Authorities	79lg d
2,517	2,458	2,640	1,759	999	721	1,413	1,409	1,359	3,045	4,074	3,478	2,955	3,720	....	General Government	79lh d
31,105	39,643	49,120	44,282	47,059	51,990	52,793	50,167	49,543	57,681	65,385	68,267	68,669	76,752	....	Banks	79li d
6,204	6,623	8,533	8,380	8,718	10,480	10,048	9,345	9,405	11,961	13,174	11,466	10,496	10,820	....	Other Sectors	79lj d

Government Finance

Millions of Euros Beginning 1999: Year Ending December 31 — *Federal Government*

1985	1986	1987	1988	1989	1990	1991	1992	1993	1994	1995	1996	1997	1998	1999	Description	Code
−63.33	−84.22	−81.55	−78.40	−62.84	−80.89	−89.06	−75.48	−107.14	−128.81	−119.88	−99.71	−67.24	....	....	Deficit (-) or Surplus	80
473.11	494.54	513.84	554.26	580.73	626.21	676.73	747.39	777.75	815.10	845.40	903.40	943.11	....	....	Revenue	81
3.59	3.75	3.23	3.78	3.99	3.19	4.36	3.45	3.45	4.03	16.93	12.64	7.71	....	....	Grants Received	81z
530.04	569.22	595.22	629.00	648.44	691.73	749.61	805.16	875.99	917.14	981.20	1,009.89	1,017.87	....	....	Expenditure	82
9.99	13.29	3.40	7.44	−.88	18.56	20.54	21.16	12.49	30.80	1.01	5.86	.19	....	....	Lending Minus Repayments	83

Financing

1985	1986	1987	1988	1989	1990	1991	1992	1993	1994	1995	1996	1997	1998	1999	Description	Code
66.52	101.57	87.33	63.26	70.08	74.60	86.81	68.09	107.42	136.38	126.01	71.86	64.23	....	....	Net Borrowing	84
64.63	95.37	89.86	57.61	66.25	65.68	73.36	46.73	82.11	89.13	84.52	60.00	65.59	....	....	Domestic	84a
1.89	6.20	−2.53	5.65	3.83	8.92	13.45	21.36	25.31	47.25	41.49	11.86	−1.36	....	....	Foreign	85a
−3.19	−17.35	−5.78	15.14	−7.24	6.29	2.25	7.39	−.28	−7.57	−6.13	27.85	3.01	....	....	Use of Cash Balances	87
407.94	494.25	573.81	617.25	677.00	731.80	797.15	828.70	899.56	975.25	1,061.54	1,128.47	1,198.57	....	....	Debt: Domestic	88a
118.72	124.61	124.74	130.80	125.83	135.36	148.46	172.14	212.86	260.94	296.63	296.47	304.93	....	....	Foreign	89a

Gross Domestic Product — *General Government*

1985	1986	1987	1988	1989	1990	1991	1992	1993	1994	1995	1996	1997	1998	1999	Description	Code
....	....	....	....		−2.4	−3.0	−2.0	−4.2	−5.0	−5.1	−3.8	−1.9	−2.5	−2.0	Deficit (-) or Surplus	80g
....	....	....	....		57.9	58.1	58.0	62.7	65.4	69.4	68.3	63.9	63.5	64.9	Debt	88g

National Accounts

Billions of Euros Beginning 1999

1985	1986	1987	1988	1989	1990	1991	1992	1993	1994	1995	1996	1997	1998	1999	Description	Code
783.7	814.0	843.9	886.0	943.3	1,013.0	1,073.0	1,147.7	1,194.1	1,255.1	I 1,332.5	1,406.8	1,433.8	1,465.8	I 109.8	Househ.Cons.Expend.,incl.NPIS	96f
264.3	281.9	292.5	302.5	319.6	338.1	367.8	398.3	429.6	455.0	I 484.1	496.6	499.2	516.5	I 38.4	Government Consumption Expend.	91f
275.5	288.4	306.7	331.3	362.2	397.9	440.3	455.4	455.2	501.6	I 551.4	570.0	582.5	630.9	I 47.4	Gross Fixed Capital Formation	93e
23.7	21.4	24.4	14.9	11.5	17.0	22.0	8.2	2.7	−1.1	3.8	.5	41.4	47.4	—	Changes in Inventories	93i
542.6	516.7	522.9	590.8	669.6	728.3	774.7	791.6	786.5	838.8	I 903.8	969.9	1,074.3	1,172.4	I 89.8	Exports of Goods and Services	90c
−539.9	−504.0	−517.5	−582.6	−653.4	−704.9	−758.0	−772.0	−772.6	−843.0	I −922.7	−996.3	−1,110.7	−1,186.4	I −89.7	Imports of Goods and Services	98c
1,369.1	1,439.0	1,494.1	1,565.8	1,676.7	1,813.5	1,945.8	2,057.3	2,125.3	2,237.9	I 2,375.2	2,453.3	2,522.2	2,611.0	I 194.9	Gross Domestic Product (GDP)	99b
−7.1	−11.9	−12.9	−8.5	−8.9	−7.3	−13.1	−9.7	−9.4	−8.3	−7.7	−7.6	−3.3	−2.4	....	Net Current Transf.from Abroad	98.n
1,366.4	1,426.3	1,488.6	1,557.6	1,660.5	1,790.0	1,929.1	2,037.6	2,111.4	2,242.1	2,338.3	2,428.9	2,528.8	2,617.9	....	Gross National Income (GNI)	99a
1,173.8	1,234.3	1,284.6	1,358.8	1,451.5	1,566.7	1,658.9	1,761.5	1,830.4	....	1,721.9	1,774.8	1,834.8	....	....	Net National Income	99e
....	....	....	....	....	....	....	....	....	....	....	....	....	....	....	Net National Income	99e
....	....	....	....	....	....	....	....	....	....	....	....	....			GDP Volume 1964 Prices	99b.p
1,269.3	1,299.0	1,320.9	1,362.7	1,420.3	1,485.0	1,535.8	1,556.4	1,564.4	1,601.7	I 1,628.7	....	....	....	....	GDP Volume 1983 prices	99b.p
....	....	....	....	....	....	....	....	....	....	2,375.2	2,422.2	2,451.0	2,521.5	I 187.3	GDP Volume 1995 Prices	99b.p
77.9	79.8	81.1	83.7	87.2	91.2	94.3	95.6	96.1	98.3	100.0	102.0	103.2	106.2	I 104.1	GDP Volume (1995=100)	99bv p
74.0	76.0	77.6	78.8	80.9	83.7	86.9	90.6	93.2	95.8	I 100.0	101.3	102.9	103.5	I 104.1	GDP Deflator (1995=100)	99bi p

Midyear Estimates

1985	1986	1987	1988	1989	1990	1991	1992	1993	1994	1995	1996	1997	1998	1999	Description	Code
7.56	7.59	7.60	7.62	7.66	7.73	7.81	7.91	7.99	8.03	8.05	8.06	8.07	8.08	8.18	Population	99z

(See notes in the back of the book.)

Azerbaijan

		1970	1971	1972	1973	1974	1975	1976	1977	1978	1979	1980	1981	1982	1983	1984
Exchange Rates															*Manats per SDR:*	
Official Rate	aa	....	....	....	....	....	....	....	....	....	....	....	....	....	....	....
															Manats per US Dollar:	
Official Rate	ae	....	....	....	....	....	....	....	....	....	....	....	....	....	....	....
Official Rate	rf	....	....	....	....	....	....	....	....	....	....	....	....	....	....	....
Fund Position															*Millions of SDRs:*	
Quota	2f. s	—	—	—	—	—	—	—	—	—	—	—	—	—	—	—
SDRs	1b. s	....	....	....	....	....	....	....	....	....	....	....	....	....	....	....
Reserve Position in the Fund	1c. s	....	....	....	....	....	....	....	....	....	....	....	....	....	....	....
Total Fund Cred.&Loans Outstg.	2tl	....	....	....	....	....	....	....	....	....	....	....	....	....	....	....
International Liquidity										*Millions of US Dollars Unless Otherwise Indicated:*						
Total Reserves minus Gold	1l. d	....	....	....	....	....	....	....	....	....	....	....	....	....	....	....
SDRs	1b. d	....	....	....	....	....	....	....	....	....	....	....	....	....	....	....
Reserve Position in the Fund	1c. d	....	....	....	....	....	....	....	....	....	....	....	....	....	....	....
Foreign Exchange	1d. d	....	....	....	....	....	....	....	....	....	....	....	....	....	....	....
Gold (Million Fine Troy Ounces)	1ad	....	....	....	....	....	....	....	....	....	....	....	....	....	....	....
Gold (National Valuation)	1and	....	....	....	....	....	....	....	....	....	....	....	....	....	....	....
Monetary Authorities: Other Assets	3.. d	....	....	....	....	....	....	....	....	....	....	....	....	....	....	....
Other Liab.	4.. d	....	....	....	....	....	....	....	....	....	....	....	....	....	....	....
Deposit Money Banks: Assets	7a. d	....	....	....	....	....	....	....	....	....	....	....	....	....	....	....
Liabilities	7b. d	....	....	....	....	....	....	....	....	....	....	....	....	....	....	....
Monetary Authorities															*Billions of Manats:*	
Foreign Assets	11	....	....	....	....	....	....	....	....	....	....	....	....	....	....	....
Claims on General Government	12a	....	....	....	....	....	....	....	....	....	....	....	....	....	....	....
Claims on Nonfin.Pub.Enterprises	12c	....	....	....	....	....	....	....	....	....	....	....	....	....	....	....
Claims on Deposit Money Banks	12e	....	....	....	....	....	....	....	....	....	....	....	....	....	....	....
Reserve Money	14	....	....	....	....	....	....	....	....	....	....	....	....	....	....	....
of which: Currency Outside DMBs	14a	....	....	....	....	....	....	....	....	....	....	....	....	....	....	....
Foreign Liabilities	16c	....	....	....	....	....	....	....	....	....	....	....	....	....	....	....
General Government Deposits	16d	....	....	....	....	....	....	....	....	....	....	....	....	....	....	....
Capital Accounts	17a	....	....	....	....	....	....	....	....	....	....	....	....	....	....	....
Other Items (Net)	17r	....	....	....	....	....	....	....	....	....	....	....	....	....	....	....
Deposit Money Banks															*Billions of Manats:*	
Reserves	20	....	....	....	....	....	....	....	....	....	....	....	....	....	....	....
Foreign Assets	21	....	....	....	....	....	....	....	....	....	....	....	....	....	....	....
Claims on General Government	22a	....	....	....	....	....	....	....	....	....	....	....	....	....	....	....
Claims on Nonfin.Pub.Enterprises	22c	....	....	....	....	....	....	....	....	....	....	....	....	....	....	....
Claims on Private Sector	22d	....	....	....	....	....	....	....	....	....	....	....	....	....	....	....
Demand Deposits	24	....	....	....	....	....	....	....	....	....	....	....	....	....	....	....
Time,Savings,& Fgn.Currency Dep.	25	....	....	....	....	....	....	....	....	....	....	....	....	....	....	....
Foreign Liabilities	26c	....	....	....	....	....	....	....	....	....	....	....	....	....	....	....
General Government Deposits	26d	....	....	....	....	....	....	....	....	....	....	....	....	....	....	....
Credit from Monetary Authorities	26g	....	....	....	....	....	....	....	....	....	....	....	....	....	....	....
Liab. to Nonbank Financial Insts	26j	....	....	....	....	....	....	....	....	....	....	....	....	....	....	....
Capital Accounts	27a	....	....	....	....	....	....	....	....	....	....	....	....	....	....	....
Other Items (Net)	27r	....	....	....	....	....	....	....	....	....	....	....	....	....	....	....
Monetary Survey															*Billions of Manats:*	
Foreign Assets (Net)	31n	....	....	....	....	....	....	....	....	....	....	....	....	....	....	....
Domestic Credit	32	....	....	....	....	....	....	....	....	....	....	....	....	....	....	....
Claims on General Govt. (Net)	32an	....	....	....	....	....	....	....	....	....	....	....	....	....	....	....
Claims on Nonfin.Pub.Enterprises	32c	....	....	....	....	....	....	....	....	....	....	....	....	....	....	....
Claims on Private Sector	32d	....	....	....	....	....	....	....	....	....	....	....	....	....	....	....
Claims on Nonbank Fin. Insts	32g	....	....	....	....	....	....	....	....	....	....	....	....	....	....	....
Money	34	....	....	....	....	....	....	....	....	....	....	....	....	....	....	....
Quasi-Money	35	....	....	....	....	....	....	....	....	....	....	....	....	....	....	....
Liab. to Nonbank Financial Insts	36j	....	....	....	....	....	....	....	....	....	....	....	....	....	....	....
Capital Accounts	37a	....	....	....	....	....	....	....	....	....	....	....	....	....	....	....
Other Items (Net)	37r	....	....	....	....	....	....	....	....	....	....	....	....	....	....	....
Money plus Quasi-Money	35l	....	....	....	....	....	....	....	....	....	....	....	....	....	....	....
Interest Rates															*Percent Per Annum*	
Refinancing Rate	60	....	....	....	....	....	....	....	....	....	....	....	....	....	....	....
Lending Rate	60p	....	....	....	....	....	....	....	....	....	....	....	....	....	....	....
Prices and Labor															*Percent Change over*	
Consumer Prices	64.xx	....	....	....	....	....	....	....	....	....	....	....	....	....	....	....
															Number in Thousands:	
Employment	67e	....	....	....	....	....	....	....	....	....	....	....	....	....	....	....
Unemployment	67c	....	....	....	....	....	....	....	....	....	....	....	....	....	....	....
Unemployment Rate (%)	67r	....	....	....	....	....	....	....	....	....	....	....	....	....	....	....

	1985	1986	1987	1988	1989	1990	1991	1992	1993	1994	1995	1996	1997	1998	1999		
End of Period																**Exchange Rates**	
	....	....	....	....	....	....	....	66.83	162.08	6,105.09	6,600.02	5,892.76	5,245.88	5,477.24	6,008.85	Official Rate..	aa
End of Period (ae) Period Average (rf)																	
	....	....	....	....	....	....	....	48.60	118.00	4,182.00	4,440.00	4,098.00	3,888.00	3,890.00	4,378.00	Official Rate..	ae
	....	....	....	....	....	....	....	54.20	99.98	1,570.23	4,413.54	4,301.26	3,985.38	3,869.00	4,120.17	Official Rate	rf
End of Period																**Fund Position**	
	—	—	—	—	—	—	—	78.00	117.00	117.00	117.00	117.00	117.00	117.00	160.90	Quota	2f. s
	....	....	....	....	....	....	....	—	—	—	.84	14.48	4.14	.08	5.15	SDRs	1b. s
	....	....	....	....	....	....	....	—	.01	.01	.01	.01	.01	.01	.01	Reserve Position in the Fund	1c. s
	....	....	....	....	....	....	....	—	—	—	67.86	121.68	197.73	228.14	296.73	Total Fund Cred.&Loans Outstg.	2tl
End of Period																**International Liquidity**	
	....	....	....	....	....	....	....	—	.59	2.03	120.88	211.28	466.09	447.33	672.59	Total Reserves minus Gold....................	1l. d
	....	....	....	....	....	....	....	—	—	—	1.25	20.82	5.59	.11	7.07	SDRs	1b. d
	....	....	....	....	....	....	....	—	.01	.01	.01	.01	.01	.01	.01	Reserve Position in the Fund	1c. d
	....	....	....	....	....	....	....	—	.58	2.02	119.62	190.45	460.49	447.20	665.50	Foreign Exchange	1d. d
	....	....	....	....	....	....	....	—	—	—	—	—	—	—	—	Gold (Million Fine Troy Ounces)...........	1ad
	....	....	....	....	....	....	....	—	—	—	—	2.38	1.38	1.37	—	Gold (National Valuation)	1an d
	....	....	....	....	....	....	....	80.06	54.28	1.93	1.57	1.91	1.53	.46	.40	Monetary Authorities: Other Assets	3..d
	....	....	....	....	....	....	....	124.66	63.09	2.87	1.75	1.33	1.37	2.07	1.96	Other Liab.	4..d
	....	....	....	....	....	....	....	66.15	257.48	135.30	167.69	156.17	154.48	97.27	152.11	Deposit Money Banks: Assets	7a. d
	....	....	....	....	....	....	....	96.79	152.74	41.05	33.95	75.89	53.16	56.08	69.32	Liabilities...........	7b. d
End of Period																**Monetary Authorities**	
	....	....	....	....	....	....	....	3.89	6.47	16.59	543.70	883.38	1,823.46	1,747.21	2,946.37	Foreign Assets	11
	....	....	....	....	....	....	....	2.42	25.73	428.87	333.46	416.73	360.26	345.26	485.26	Claims on General Government	12a
	....	....	....	....	....	....	....	.19	.13	1.02	8.48	8.93	8.76	16.26	12.32	Claims on Nonfin.Pub.Enterprises	12c
	....	....	....	....	....	....	....	2.63	23.93	141.69	1,052.40	893.67	865.45	750.27	755.89	Claims on Deposit Money Banks	12e
	....	....	....	....	....	....	....	2.97	43.84	325.69	911.14	1,071.06	1,514.08	1,145.65	1,328.22	Reserve Money	14
	....	....	....	....	....	....	....	2.72	43.18	276.13	602.40	865.44	1,170.51	926.04	1,135.84	*of which: Currency Outside DMBs*	14a
	....	....	....	....	....	....	....	6.06	7.44	12.02	455.63	722.52	1,042.60	1,257.64	1,791.58	Foreign Liabilities.................................	16c
	....	....	....	....	....	....	....	.29	5.75	235.86	447.68	334.46	367.65	345.83	811.19	General Government Deposits...............	16d
	....	....	....	....	....	....	....	.09	4.08	44.87	405.19	400.30	1,128.62	847.00	1,090.51	Capital Accounts	17a
	....	....	....	....	....	....	....	−.28	−4.85	−30.26	−281.61	−325.63	−995.02	−737.12	−821.67	Other Items (Net)	17r
End of Period																**Deposit Money Banks**	
	....	....	....	....	....	....	....	.98	6.65	43.89	303.17	242.76	301.94	204.07	177.85	Reserves	20
	....	....	....	....	....	....	....	3.21	30.38	565.81	744.55	639.97	600.62	378.37	665.95	Foreign Assets	21
	....	....	....	....	....	....	....	1.69	.33	51.49	12.49	32.03	52.69	30.04	69.44	Claims on General Government	22a
	....	....	....	....	....	....	....	13.95	53.43	623.57	1,403.59	1,719.82	1,635.51	1,658.84	1,722.20	Claims on Nonfin.Pub.Enterprises	22c
	....	....	....	....	....	....	....	2.61	15.08	62.46	126.52	159.32	386.81	530.06	559.69	Claims on Private Sector......................	22d
	....	....	....	....	....	....	....	3.29	22.00	93.70	251.29	250.08	323.80	203.02	215.83	Demand Deposits	24
	....	....	....	....	....	....	....	3.23	20.59	674.36	455.53	418.73	651.71	662.47	826.07	Time,Savings,& Fgn.Currency Dep.	25
	....	....	....	....	....	....	....	4.70	18.02	171.66	150.75	311.00	206.69	218.15	303.46	Foreign Liabilities.................................	26c
	....	....	....	....	....	....	....	4.70	7.19	101.60	98.20	222.31	30.20	82.23	84.95	General Government Deposits...............	26d
	....	....	....	....	....	....	....	3.99	27.06	56.53	893.23	782.36	838.02	615.87	592.89	Credit from Monetary Authorities	26g
	....	....	....	....	....	....	....	.06	.20	.45	2.84	7.44	6.84	5.55	2.17	Liab. to Nonbank Financial Insts	26j
	....	....	....	....	....	....	....	1.16	12.84	121.45	355.30	640.98	831.83	1,020.01	1,152.11	Capital Accounts	27a
	....	....	....	....	....	....	....	1.30	−2.04	127.46	383.18	160.99	88.51	−5.92	17.67	Other Items (Net)	27r
End of Period																**Monetary Survey**	
	....	....	....	....	....	....	....	−3.66	11.39	398.73	681.87	489.83	1,174.80	649.79	1,517.28	Foreign Assets (Net)	31n
	....	....	....	....	....	....	....	15.88	81.77	830.00	1,338.66	1,780.06	2,046.19	2,152.40	1,952.78	Domestic Credit	32
	....	....	....	....	....	....	....	−.88	13.12	142.89	−199.93	−108.00	15.11	−52.76	−341.43	Claims on General Govt. (Net)...........	32an
	....	....	....	....	....	....	....	14.14	53.56	624.59	1,412.07	1,728.75	1,644.27	1,675.10	1,734.52	Claims on Nonfin.Pub.Enterprises	32c
	....	....	....	....	....	....	....	2.61	15.08	62.46	126.52	159.32	386.81	530.06	559.69	Claims on Private Sector....................	32d
	....	....	....	....	....	....	....	.01	.02	.06	—	—	—	—	—	Claims on Nonbank Fin. Insts	32g
	....	....	....	....	....	....	....	6.07	65.52	372.38	858.38	1,119.74	1,524.08	1,134.47	1,357.35	Money	34
	....	....	....	....	....	....	....	3.24	20.59	675.23	455.53	418.76	651.75	662.48	826.08	Quasi-Money	35
	....	....	....	....	....	....	....	.06	.20	.45	2.84	7.44	6.84	5.55	2.17	Liab. to Nonbank Financial Insts	36j
	....	....	....	....	....	....	....	1.24	16.92	166.33	760.50	1,041.28	1,960.45	1,867.02	2,242.62	Capital Accounts	37a
	....	....	....	....	....	....	....	1.62	−10.07	14.34	−56.72	−317.33	−922.14	−867.31	−958.16	Other Items (Net)	37r
	....	....	....	....	....	....	....	9.30	86.11	1,047.62	1,313.92	1,538.50	2,175.83	1,796.95	2,183.42	Money plus Quasi-Money	35l
Percent Per Annum																**Interest Rates**	
	....	....	....	....	....	....	....	12	100	200	80	20	12	14	10	Refinancing Rate	60
	....	....	....	....	....	....	....	....	....	148	163	....	....	....	....	Lending Rate	60p
Previous Period																**Prices and Labor**	
	....	....	....	....	....	....	....	912.30	1,129.04	1,664.53	411.74	19.76	3.60	−.69	−8.59	Consumer Prices.....................................	64.x x
Period Averages																	
	....	....	....	....	....	....	....	2,922.1	2,916.6	2,851.3	2,837.3	2,895.4	2,900.0	....	....	Employment..	67e
	....	....	....	....	....	....	....	....	19.5	23.6	28.3	31.9	38.3	42.3	....	Unemployment..	67c
	....	....	....	....	....	....	....	....	.5	.7	.8	.9	1.0	1.1	....	Unemployment Rate (%)	67r

Azerbaijan

		1970	1971	1972	1973	1974	1975	1976	1977	1978	1979	1980	1981	1982	1983	1984
International Transactions																*Millions of US Dollars*
Exports	70..d	....	....	....	....	....	....	....	....	....	....	....	....	....	....	....
Imports, cif	71..d	....	....	....	....	....	....	....	....	....	....	....	....	....	....	....
Balance of Payments																*Millions of US Dollars:*
Current Account, n.i.e.	78al d	....	....	....	....	....	....	....	....	....	....	....	....	....	....	....
Goods: Exports f.o.b	78aa d	....	....	....	....	....	....	....	....	....	....	....	....	....	....	....
Goods: Imports f.o.b	78ab d	....	....	....	....	....	....	....	....	....	....	....	....	....	....	....
Trade Balance	78ac d	....	....	....	....	....	....	....	....	....	....	....	....	....	....	....
Services: Credit	78ad d	....	....	....	....	....	....	....	....	....	....	....	....	....	....	....
Services: Debit	78ae d	....	....	....	....	....	....	....	....	....	....	....	....	....	....	....
Balance on Goods & Services	78af d	....	....	....	....	....	....	....	....	....	....	....	....	....	....	....
Income: Credit	78ag d	....	....	....	....	....	....	....	....	....	....	....	....	....	....	....
Income: Debit	78ah d	....	....	....	....	....	....	....	....	....	....	....	....	....	....	....
Balance on Gds, Serv., & Inc.	78ai d	....	....	....	....	....	....	....	....	....	....	....	....	....	....	....
Current Transfers, n.i.e.: Credit	78aj d	....	....	....	....	....	....	....	....	....	....	....	....	....	....	....
Current Transfers: Debit	78ak d	....	....	....	....	....	....	....	....	....	....	....	....	....	....	....
Capital Account, n.i.e.	78bc d	....	....	....	....	....	....	....	....	....	....	....	....	....	....	....
Capital Account, n.i.e.: Credit	78ba d	....	....	....	....	....	....	....	....	....	....	....	....	....	....	....
Capital Account: Debit	78bb d	....	....	....	....	....	....	....	....	....	....	....	....	....	....	....
Financial Account, n.i.e.	78bj d	....	....	....	....	....	....	....	....	....	....	....	....	....	....	....
Direct Investment Abroad	78bd d	....	....	....	....	....	....	....	....	....	....	....	....	....	....	....
Dir. Invest. in Rep. Econ., n.i.e.	78be d	....	....	....	....	....	....	....	....	....	....	....	....	....	....	....
Portfolio Investment Assets	78bf d	....	....	....	....	....	....	....	....	....	....	....	....	....	....	....
Equity Securities	78bk d	....	....	....	....	....	....	....	....	....	....	....	....	....	....	....
Debt Securities	78bl d	....	....	....	....	....	....	....	....	....	....	....	....	....	....	....
Portfolio Investment Liab., n.i.e.	78bg d	....	....	....	....	....	....	....	....	....	....	....	....	....	....	....
Equity Securities	78bm d	....	....	....	....	....	....	....	....	....	....	....	....	....	....	....
Debt Securities	78bn d	....	....	....	....	....	....	....	....	....	....	....	....	....	....	....
Financial Derivatives Assets	78bw d	....	....	....	....	....	....	....	....	....	....	....	....	....	....	....
Financial Derivatives Liabilities	78bx d	....	....	....	....	....	....	....	....	....	....	....	....	....	....	....
Other Investment Assets	78bh d	....	....	....	....	....	....	....	....	....	....	....	....	....	....	....
Monetary Authorities	78bo d	....	....	....	....	....	....	....	....	....	....	....	....	....	....	....
General Government	78bp d	....	....	....	....	....	....	....	....	....	....	....	....	....	....	....
Banks	78bq d	....	....	....	....	....	....	....	....	....	....	....	....	....	....	....
Other Sectors	78br d	....	....	....	....	....	....	....	....	....	....	....	....	....	....	....
Other Investment Liab., n.i.e.	78bi d	....	....	....	....	....	....	....	....	....	....	....	....	....	....	....
Monetary Authorities	78bs d	....	....	....	....	....	....	....	....	....	....	....	....	....	....	....
General Government	78bt d	....	....	....	....	....	....	....	....	....	....	....	....	....	....	....
Banks	78bu d	....	....	....	....	....	....	....	....	....	....	....	....	....	....	....
Other Sectors	78bv d	....	....	....	....	....	....	....	....	....	....	....	....	....	....	....
Net Errors and Omissions	78ca d	....	....	....	....	....	....	....	....	....	....	....	....	....	....	....
Overall Balance	78cb d	....	....	....	....	....	....	....	....	....	....	....	....	....	....	....
Reserves and Related Items	79da d	....	....	....	....	....	....	....	....	....	....	....	....	....	....	....
Reserve Assets	79db d	....	....	....	....	....	....	....	....	....	....	....	....	....	....	....
Use of Fund Credit and Loans	79dc d	....	....	....	....	....	....	....	....	....	....	....	....	....	....	....
Exceptional Financing	79de d	....	....	....	....	....	....	....	....	....	....	....	....	....	....	....
Government Finance																*Billions of Manats:*
Deficit(-) / or Surplus	80	....	....	....	....	....	....	....	....	....	....	....	....	....	....	....
Total Revenue and Grants	81y	....	....	....	....	....	....	....	....	....	....	....	....	....	....	....
Revenue	81	....	....	....	....	....	....	....	....	....	....	....	....	....	....	....
Grants	81z	....	....	....	....	....	....	....	....	....	....	....	....	....	....	....
Exp. & Lending Minus Repay.	82z	....	....	....	....	....	....	....	....	....	....	....	....	....	....	....
Expenditure	82	....	....	....	....	....	....	....	....	....	....	....	....	....	....	....
Lending Minus Repayments	83	....	....	....	....	....	....	....	....	....	....	....	....	....	....	....
Total Financing	80h	....	....	....	....	....	....	....	....	....	....	....	....	....	....	....
Domestic	84a	....	....	....	....	....	....	....	....	....	....	....	....	....	....	....
Foreign	85a	....	....	....	....	....	....	....	....	....	....	....	....	....	....	....
Total Debt by Residence	88	....	....	....	....	....	....	....	....	....	....	....	....	....	....	....
Domestic	88a	....	....	....	....	....	....	....	....	....	....	....	....	....	....	....
Foreign	89a	....	....	....	....	....	....	....	....	....	....	....	....	....	....	....
																Millions:
Population	99z	....	....	....	....	....	....	....	....	....	....	....	....	....	....	....

1985	1986	1987	1988	1989	1990	1991	1992	1993	1994	1995	1996	1997	1998	1999		
Millions of US Dollars															**International Transactions**	
....	....	....	....	....	....	....	1,571.2	993.1	637.5	637.2	631.2	781.3	606.2	....	Exports	70..*d*
....	....	....	....	....	....	....	997.9	635.5	777.9	667.6	960.6	794.3	1,077.2	....	Imports, cif	71..*d*
Minus Sign Indicates Debit															Balance of Payments	
....	....	....	....	....	....	....	....	....	....	-400.7	-931.2	-915.8	-1,364.5	-599.7	Current Account, n.i.e.	78al *d*
....	....	....	....	....	....	....	....	....	....	612.3	643.7	808.3	677.8	1,025.2	Goods: Exports f.o.b.	78aa *d*
....	....	....	....	....	....	....	....	....	....	-985.4	-1,337.6	-1,375.2	-1,723.9	-1,433.4	Goods: Imports f.o.b	78ab *d*
....	....	....	....	....	....	....	....	....	....	-373.1	-693.9	-566.9	-1,046.2	-408.2	*Trade Balance*	78ac *d*
....	....	....	....	....	....	....	....	....	....	172.4	149.3	341.8	331.7	256.8	Services: Credit	78ad *d*
....	....	....	....	....	....	....	....	....	....	-304.6	-440.9	-726.0	-700.8	-485.1	Services: Debit	78ae *d*
....	....	....	....	....	....	....	....	....	....	-505.4	-985.6	-951.1	-1,415.2	-636.5	*Balance on Goods & Services*	78af *d*
....	....	....	....	....	....	....	....	....	....	9.9	15.1	22.8	38.3	11.0	Income: Credit	78ag *d*
....	....	....	....	....	....	....	....	....	....	-16.0	-27.2	-32.3	-51.6	-56.0	Income: Debit	78ah *d*
....	....	....	....	....	....	....	....	....	....	-511.4	-997.7	-960.6	-1,428.5	-681.5	*Balance on Gds, Serv., & Inc.*	78ai *d*
....	....	....	....	....	....	....	....	....	....	129.3	107.2	95.7	145.0	134.5	Current Transfers, n.i.e.: Credit	78aj *d*
....	....	....	....	....	....	....	....	....	....	-18.5	-40.7	-50.9	-80.9	-52.8	Current Transfers: Debit	78ak *d*
....	....	....	....	....	....	....	....	....	....	-1.6	—	-10.2	-.7	....	Capital Account, n.i.e.	78bc *d*
....	....	....	....	....	....	....	....	....	....	....	....	....	....	....	Capital Account, n.i.e.: Credit	78ba *d*
....	....	....	....	....	....	....	....	....	....	-1.6	—	-10.2	-.7	....	Capital Account: Debit	78bb *d*
....	....	....	....	....	....	....	....	....	....	400.3	822.5	1,092.1	1,326.0	690.2	Financial Account, n.i.e.	78bj *d*
....	....	....	....	....	....	....	....	....	....						Direct Investment Abroad	78bd *d*
....	....	....	....	....	....	....	....	....	....	330.1	627.3	1,114.8	1,023.0	510.3	Dir. Invest. in Rep. Econ., n.i.e.	78be *d*
....	....	....	....	....	....	....	....	....	....	-1.7	—	1.1	—	....	Portfolio Investment Assets	78bf *d*
....	....	....	....	....	....	....	....	....	....	....	....	....	....	....	Equity Securities	78bk *d*
....	....	....	....	....	....	....	....	....	....	-1.7	—	1.1	—	....	Debt Securities	78bl *d*
....	....	....	....	....	....	....	....	....	....	—	—	—	.4	....	Portfolio Investment Liab., n.i.e.	78bg *d*
....	....	....	....	....	....	....	....	....	....	....	....	....	....	....	Equity Securities	78bm *d*
....	....	....	....	....	....	....	....	....	....	—	—	—	.4	....	Debt Securities	78bn *d*
....	....	....	....	....	....	....	....	....	....	....	....	....	....	....	Financial Derivatives Assets	78bw *d*
....	....	....	....	....	....	....	....	....	....	....	....	....	....	....	Financial Derivatives Liabilities	78bx *d*
....	....	....	....	....	....	....	....	....	....	-22.1	-216.8	-102.6	22.3	-81.0	Other Investment Assets	78bh *d*
....	....	....	....	....	....	....	....	....	....						Monetary Authorities	78bo *d*
....	....	....	....	....	....	....	....	....	....						General Government	78bp *d*
....	....	....	....	....	....	....	....	....	....	-19.6	-136.9	5.3	62.4	-44.2	Banks	78bq *d*
....	....	....	....	....	....	....	....	....	....	-2.5	-79.8	-107.9	-40.1	-36.8	Other Sectors	78br *d*
....	....	....	....	....	....	....	....	....	....	94.1	412.0	78.8	280.4	260.9	Other Investment Liab., n.i.e.	78bi *d*
....	....	....	....	....	....	....	....	....	....						Monetary Authorities	78bs *d*
....	....	....	....	....	....	....	....	....	....	30.0	—	70.8	75.6	161.6	General Government	78bt *d*
....	....	....	....	....	....	....	....	....	....	-.3	26.5	-18.8	-1.7	-.1	Banks	78bu *d*
....	....	....	....	....	....	....	....	....	....	64.3	385.5	26.8	206.5	99.3	Other Sectors	78bv *d*
....	....	....	....	....	....	....	....	....	....	59.7	23.6	-27.0	-20.1	42.4	Net Errors and Omissions	78ca *d*
....	....	....	....	....	....	....	....	....	....	57.8	-85.0	139.2	-59.2	132.9	*Overall Balance*	78cb *d*
....	....	....	....	....	....	....	....	....	....	-57.8	85.0	-139.2	59.2	-132.9	Reserves and Related Items	79da *d*
....	....	....	....	....	....	....	....	....	....	-161.6	7.1	-244.2	18.7	-228.5	Reserve Assets	79db *d*
....	....	....	....	....	....	....	....	....	....	103.8	77.9	105.0	40.5	95.6	Use of Fund Credit and Loans	79dc *d*
....	....	....	....	....	....	....	....	....	....	....	....	....	....	....	Exceptional Financing	79de *d*
Year Ending December 31															**Government Finance**	
....	....	....	....	....	....	....	....	....	-209.21	-545.03	-405.89	-341.84	-623.00	-479.46	Deficit(-) / or Surplus	80
....	....	....	....	....	....	....	....	....	479.70	1,920.25	1,960.77	2,402.03	3,143.02	3,380.17	Total Revenue and Grants	81y
....	....	....	....	....	....	....	....	....	479.70	1,920.25	1,881.02	2,350.03	3,076.02	3,316.97	Revenue	81
....	....	....	....	....	....	....	....	....	—	—	79.76	52.00	67.00	63.20	Grants	81z
....	....	....	....	....	....	....	....	....	688.91	2,465.27	2,366.67	2,743.88	3,766.02	3,859.64	Exp. & Lending Minus Repay.	82z
....	....	....	....	....	....	....	....	....	688.91	2,254.33	2,283.64	3,028.57	3,993.14	4,260.94	Expenditure	82
....	....	....	....	....	....	....	....	....	—	210.94	83.03	-284.70	-227.12	-401.31	Lending Minus Repayments	83
....	....	....	....	....	....	....	....	....	209.21	545.03	405.90	341.84	623.00	479.46	Total Financing	80h
....	....	....	....	....	....	....	....	....	....	....	....	....	....	....	Domestic	84a
....	....	....	....	....	....	....	....	....	....	....	....	....	....	....	Foreign	85a
....	....	....	....	....	....	....	....	....	....	....	....	....	....	....	Total Debt by Residence	88
....	....	....	....	....	....	....	....	....	....	....	....	....	....	....	Domestic	88a
....	....	....	....	....	....	....	....	....	....	....	....	....	....	....	Foreign	89a
Midyear Estimates																
....	....	....	....	....	....	....	7.38	7.49	7.60	7.68	7.76	7.84	7.91	7.98	**Population**	99z

Bahamas, The

313		1970	1971	1972	1973	1974	1975	1976	1977	1978	1979	1980	1981	1982	1983	1984
Exchange Rates																*Bahamian Dollars per SDR:*
Principal Rate.................aa=	**wa**	1.0000	1.0857	1.0857	1.2064	1.2244	1.1707	1.1618	1.2147	1.3028	1.3173	1.2754	1.1640	1.1031	1.0470	.9802
																Bahamian Dollars per US Dollar:
Principal Rate.................ae=	**we**	1.0000	1.0000	1.0000	1.0000	1.0000	1.0000	1.0000	1.0000	1.0000	1.0000	1.0000	1.0000	1.0000	1.0000	1.0000
Secondary Rate	**xe**	....	....	....	....	....	....	....	....	1.1850	1.1750	1.2250	1.2350	1.2350	1.2350	1.1750
Secondary Rate	**xf**	....	....	....	....	....	....	....	....	1.1867	1.1637	1.2135	1.2265	1.2350	1.2350	1.1950
																Index Numbers (1995=100):
Principal Rate	**ahx**	99.7	100.0	100.0	100.0	100.0	100.0	100.0	100.0	100.0	100.0	100.0	100.0	100.0	100.0	100.0
Nominal Effective Exchange Rate	**nec**	....	....	....	....	....	....	....	....	....	75.0	75.7	79.9	83.7	87.5	92.2
Real Effective Exchange Rate	**rec**	....	....	....	....	....	....	....	....	....	....	92.1	96.8	99.4	102.4	105.4
Fund Position																*Millions of SDRs:*
Quota	**2f.s**	—	—	—	20.0	20.0	20.0	20.0	20.0	33.0	33.0	49.5	49.5	49.5	66.4	66.4
SDRs	**1b.s**	....	....	....	—	—	—	—	—	—	3.4	2.7	6.1	5.8	1.1	.7
Reserve Position in the Fund	**1c.s**	....	....	....	—	5.0	5.0	5.0	5.0	4.9	4.7	8.8	6.6	6.7	10.9	10.9
Total Fund Cred.&Loans Outstg.	**2tl**	....	....	....	—	—	—	—	—	—	—	—	—	—	—	—
International Liquidity																*Millions of US Dollars Unless Otherwise Indicated:*
Total Reserves minus Gold	**1l.d**	21.7	29.5	37.1	43.2	49.8	53.3	47.4	I 67.1	58.1	77.5	92.3	100.2	113.5	122.0	161.1
SDRs	**1b.d**	....	....	....	—	—	—	—	—	—	4.5	3.5	7.1	6.3	1.2	.7
Reserve Position in the Fund	**1c.d**	....	....	....	—	6.1	5.9	5.8	6.1	6.3	6.2	11.3	7.7	7.3	11.4	10.7
Foreign Exchange	**1d.d**	21.7	29.5	37.1	43.2	43.7	47.4	41.6	I 61.0	51.8	66.8	77.5	85.4	99.8	109.4	149.8
Deposit Money Banks: Assets	**7a.d**	2,635	4,107	5,840	5,138	11,989	16,480	23,583	26,796	31,863	30,040	33,448	43,289	34,691	31,941	32,078
Liabilities	**7b.d**	2,836	4,270	5,806	5,251	12,127	16,264	23,276	26,622	31,771	29,709	33,246	42,880	34,583	31,775	31,886
Other Banking Insts.: Assets	**7e.d**	....	....	....	13	—	—	4	11	5	348	1,675	1,862	2,079	2,204	2,232
Liabilities	**7f.d**	....	....	....	—	5	2	—	—	—	359	1,681	1,841	2,012	2,106	2,078
Branches of US Banks: Assets	**7k.d**	4,515	8,146	12,472	20,235	26,624	37,505	53,778	61,580	71,407	79,712	88,917	103,698	94,778	99,867	94,148
Liab.	**7m.d**	4,508	8,053	12,479	20,268	26,673	37,333	53,931	61,530	71,898	80,238	89,847	104,531	96,094	101,082	94,979
Monetary Authorities																*Millions of Bahamian Dollars:*
Foreign Assets	**11**	23.7	30.7	36.1	43.5	49.8	53.4	47.5	67.2	58.6	78.2	92.3	100.2	113.5	123.3	161.9
Claims on Central Government	**12a**	9.5	10.7	9.0	.5	9.7	9.9	18.6	12.3	14.9	22.5	42.1	34.2	28.4	35.8	43.8
Claims on Deposit Money Banks	**12e**	1.5	.1	—	.7	1.6	—	—	—	—	2.0	10.0	19.0	19.5	—	—
Claims on Nonbank Financial Insts	**12g**	—	—	—	—	—	—	—	—	—	—	—	—	—	—	—
Reserve Money	**14**	25.9	27.1	37.4	35.6	41.7	44.7	50.3	50.3	57.2	66.1	77.0	76.8	87.4	99.0	117.9
of which: Currency Outside DMBs	**14a**	17.8	15.3	21.3	20.2	19.3	20.1	20.5	23.3	26.5	29.8	33.4	37.4	41.1	45.5	51.0
Central Government Deposits	**16d**	6.7	9.8	4.1	3.2	8.2	9.0	3.5	17.2	1.4	13.4	23.0	28.8	21.7	7.0	33.5
Capital Accounts	**17a**	2.5	3.9	3.1	5.6	10.8	10.6	14.4	15.3	13.3	20.9	38.4	34.8	39.3	49.5	54.6
Other Items (Net)	**17r**	-.4	.7	.5	.3	.4	-1.0	-2.1	-3.3	1.6	2.3	6.0	13.0	13.0	3.6	-.3
Deposit Money Banks																*Millions of Bahamian Dollars:*
Reserves	**20**	8.1	11.8	16.0	15.4	20.7	22.3	21.3	20.4	25.0	30.9	36.4	31.7	38.6	41.8	44.5
Foreign Assets	**21**	2,635.0	4,106.5	5,839.9	5,137.5	11,989.1	16,479.9	23,583.0	26,795.9	31,862.5	30,039.7	33,447.5	43,289.4	34,690.8	31,940.8	32,078.4
Claims on Central Government	**22a**	19.6	156.1	18.9	26.4	59.6	68.8	80.2	94.5	90.6	88.8	69.1	91.2	100.8	126.1	127.2
Claims on Official Entities	**22bx**	—	—	—	—	2.1	.4	10.6	24.6	21.7	20.0	36.9	22.3	47.3	33.2	24.9
Claims on Private Sector	**22d**	349.1	220.8	241.7	369.7	264.8	294.1	264.9	286.6	309.3	348.4	402.8	443.4	483.1	509.7	534.9
Claims on Other Banking Insts	**22f**	—	—	—	76.9	199.2	244.7	242.4	63.5	29.9	46.4	11.6	5.3	4.3	8.2	18.9
Demand Deposits	**24**	62.7	53.5	63.6	55.0	56.2	52.8	55.5	64.1	77.2	101.9	99.6	103.5	115.2	127.9	134.9
Time, Savings,& Fgn.Currency Dep.	**25**	103.1	120.4	119.6	132.2	133.0	155.7	191.3	189.3	212.1	233.8	286.3	323.9	382.1	434.2	469.3
Bonds	**26ab**	—	—	—	3.0	—	—	—	—	—	—	—	—	—	—	—
Foreign Liabilities	**26c**	2,836.1	4,269.7	5,805.8	5,251.0	12,127.1	16,264.2	23,276.4	26,621.9	31,771.2	29,708.7	33,246.2	42,880.1	34,582.6	31,774.5	31,885.5
Central Government Deposits	**26d**	4.6	6.5	.2	2.1	2.4	7.4	6.4	2.7	4.5	12.4	15.9	6.0	5.8	8.2	9.5
Credit from Monetary Authorities	**26g**	—	—	—	3.0	13.0	4.0	—	—	—	2.0	24.0	22.0	12.0	.7	26.0
Liabilities to Other Banking Insts	**26i**	—	—	—	164.0	191.1	543.6	415.1	312.8	27.4	46.8	40.3	27.5	81.3	106.4	40.5
Capital Accounts	**27a**	37.4	41.1	43.4	60.0	14.9	23.4	153.1	106.7	264.6	471.7	327.0	524.7	183.5	203.8	274.2
Other Items (Net)	**27r**	-32.1	4.0	83.9	-44.4	-2.2	59.1	104.6	-12.0	-18.0	-3.1	-35.0	-4.4	2.4	4.1	-11.1
Monetary Survey																*Millions of Bahamian Dollars:*
Foreign Assets (Net)	**31n**	-177.4	-132.5	70.2	-70.0	-88.2	269.1	354.1	241.2	149.9	409.2	293.6	509.5	221.7	289.6	354.8
Domestic Credit	**32**	366.9	371.3	265.3	468.2	524.8	601.5	606.8	461.6	460.5	500.3	523.6	562.0	636.4	697.8	706.7
Claims on Central Govt. (Net)	**32an**	17.8	150.5	23.6	21.6	58.7	62.3	88.9	86.9	99.6	85.5	72.3	90.6	101.7	146.7	128.0
Claims on Official Entities	**32bx**	—	—	—	—	2.1	.4	10.6	24.6	21.7	20.0	36.9	22.3	47.3	33.2	24.9
Claims on Private Sector	**32d**	349.1	220.8	241.7	369.7	264.8	294.1	264.9	286.6	309.3	348.4	402.8	443.4	483.1	509.7	534.9
Claims on Other Banking Insts	**32f**	—	—	—	76.9	199.2	244.7	242.4	63.5	29.9	46.4	11.6	5.7	4.3	8.2	18.9
Claims on Nonbank Financial Inst	**32g**	—	—	—	—	—	—	—	—	—	—	—	—	—	—	—
Money	**34**	80.5	68.8	84.9	75.2	75.5	72.9	82.0	91.3	106.2	133.5	134.9	143.5	158.0	176.5	198.5
Quasi-Money	**35**	103.1	120.4	119.6	132.2	133.0	155.7	191.3	189.3	212.1	233.8	286.3	323.9	382.1	434.2	469.3
Bonds	**36ab**	—	—	—	3.0	—	—	—	—	—	—	—	—	—	—	—
Liabilities to Other Banking Insts	**36i**	—	—	—	164.0	191.1	543.6	415.1	312.8	27.4	46.8	40.3	27.5	81.3	106.4	40.5
Capital Accounts	**37a**	39.9	45.0	46.5	65.6	25.7	34.0	167.5	122.0	277.9	492.6	365.4	559.5	222.8	253.3	328.8
Other Items (Net)	**37r**	-34.0	4.6	84.5	-41.8	11.3	64.4	105.0	-12.6	-13.2	2.8	-9.7	17.1	13.9	17.0	24.4
Money plus Quasi-Money	**35l**	183.6	189.2	204.5	207.4	208.5	228.6	273.3	280.6	318.3	367.3	421.2	467.4	540.1	610.7	667.8
Other Banking Institutions																*Millions of Bahamian Dollars*
Reserves	**40**	....	....	....	—	2.1	2.3	2.5	2.9	3.3	4.2	5.0	5.7	6.8	8.3	9.8
Foreign Assets	**41**	....	....	....	12.6	—	—	4.1	10.5	5.2	348.3	1,675.0	1,861.8	2,078.6	2,204.1	2,231.7
Claims on Central Government	**42a**	....	....	....	2.6	4.0	7.2	6.0	8.6	11.6	9.6	8.2	7.0	6.1	8.4	10.2
Claims on Private Sector	**42d**	....	....	....	51.3	59.9	65.1	65.1	66.6	75.2	93.2	113.2	125.8	142.6	167.1	201.9
Claims on Deposit Money Banks	**42e**	....	....	....	9.3	6.3	4.9	41.6	6.6	4.7	36.2	56.7	49.8	43.3	24.6	25.1
Demand Deposits	**44**	....	....	....	—	—	—	—	—	—	—	—	—	—	—	—
Time, Savings,& Fgn.Currency Dep.	**45**	....	....	....	36.2	41.5	45.7	50.4	57.9	71.0	85.6	99.8	116.7	138.4	168.4	196.6
Foreign Liabilities	**46c**	....	....	....	—	4.7	2.0	—	—	—	358.6	1,681.2	1,841.0	2,011.9	2,105.5	2,078.3
Central Government Deposits	**46d**	....	....	....	—	—	—	—	—	—	—	—	1.1	1.1	1.9	1.1
Credit from Monetary Authorities	**46g**	....	....	....	—	—	—	—	—	—	—	—	.4	—	—	3.0
Credit from Deposit Money Banks	**46h**	....	....	....	1.7	1.0	3.4	.7	1.9	2.2	20.6	6.0	7.7	3.4	3.8	4.5
Capital Accounts	**47a**	....	....	....	22.7	25.3	25.2	31.6	38.0	26.4	27.2	89.9	94.7	123.7	159.1	207.9
Other Items (Net)	**47r**	....	....	....	15.2	-.2	3.2	36.6	-2.6	.4	-.5	-18.8	-11.5	-1.1	-26.2	-12.7
Banking Survey																*Millions of Bahamian Dollars:*
Foreign Assets (Net)	**51n**	....	....	....	-57.4	-92.9	267.1	358.2	251.7	155.1	398.9	287.4	530.3	288.4	388.2	508.2
Domestic Credit	**52**	....	....	....	445.2	389.5	429.1	435.5	473.3	517.4	556.7	633.4	688.0	779.7	863.2	898.8
Claims on Central Govt. (Net)	**52an**	....	....	....	24.2	62.7	69.5	94.9	95.5	111.2	95.1	80.5	96.5	106.7	153.2	137.1
Claims on Official Entities	**52bx**	....	....	....	—	2.1	.4	10.6	24.6	21.7	20.0	36.9	22.3	47.3	33.2	24.9
Claims on Private Sector	**52d**	....	....	....	421.0	324.7	359.2	330.0	353.2	384.5	441.6	516.0	569.2	625.7	676.8	736.8
Claims on Nonbank Financial Inst	**52g**	....	....	....	—	—	—	—	—	—	—	—	—	—	—	—
Liquid Liabilities	**55l**	....	....	....	243.6	247.9	272.0	321.2	335.6	386.0	448.7	516.0	578.4	671.7	770.8	854.6
Bonds	**56ab**	....	....	....	3.0	—	—	—	—	—	—	—	—	—	—	—
Capital Accounts	**57a**	....	....	....	88.3	51.0	59.2	199.1	160.0	304.3	519.8	455.3	654.2	346.5	412.4	536.7
Other Items (Net)	**57r**	....	....	....	52.9	-2.3	365.0	273.4	229.4	-17.8	-12.9	-50.5	-14.3	49.9	68.2	15.7

1985	1986	1987	1988	1989	1990	1991	1992	1993	1994	1995	1996	1997	1998	1999	
End of Period															**Exchange Rates**
1.0984	1.2232	1.4187	1.3457	1.3142	1.4227	1.4304	1.3750	1.3736	1.4599	1.4865	1.4380	1.3493	1.4080	1.3725	Principal Rate aa= wa
End of Period (we and xe) Period Average (xf)															
1.0000	1.0000	1.0000	1.0000	1.0000	1.0000	1.0000	1.0000	1.0000	1.0000	1.0000	1.0000	1.0000	1.0000	1.0000	Principal Rate ae= we
1.1750	1.1750	1.2250	1.2250	1.2250	1.2250	1.2250	1.2250	1.2250	1.2250	1.2250	1.2250	1.2250	1.2250	1.2250	Secondary Rate xe
1.1800	1.1750	1.1989	1.2250	1.2250	1.2250	1.2250	1.2250	1.2250	1.2250	1.2250	1.2250	1.2250	1.2250	1.2250	Secondary Rate xf
Period Averages															
100.0	100.0	100.0	100.0	100.0	100.0	100.0	100.0	100.0	100.0	100.0	100.0	100.0	100.0	100.0	Principal Rate ahx
95.6	91.3	89.3	90.8	96.6	96.9	97.9	98.6	102.2	100.4	100.0	102.2	105.8	107.9	110.6	Nominal Effective Exchange Rate nec
107.6	104.1	101.9	100.6	102.4	99.4	102.7	105.4	107.8	103.5	100.0	100.5	102.7	104.6	107.5	Real Effective Exchange Rate rec
End of Period															**Fund Position**
66.4	66.4	66.4	66.4	66.4	66.4	66.4	94.9	94.9	94.9	94.9	94.9	94.9	94.9	130.3	Quota 2f.s
.4	—	.3	.4	.1	.4	.1	—	—	—	—	—	—	—	—	SDRs 1b.s
10.9	10.9	10.7	9.0	8.6	7.9	7.2	6.8	6.2	6.2	6.2	6.2	6.2	6.2	6.2	Reserve Position in the Fund 1c.s
—	—	—	—	—	—	—	—	—	—	—	—	—	—	—	Total Fund Cred.&Loans Outstg. 2tl
End of Period															**International Liquidity**
182.5	231.5	170.1	172.0	146.8	158.2	181.3	155.3	172.3	176.6	179.2	171.4	227.0	346.5	410.5	Total Reserves minus Gold 1l.d
.4	—	.4	.5	.2	.5	.2	—	—	—	—	—	—	—	—	SDRs 1b.d
12.0	13.4	15.2	12.2	11.4	11.2	10.2	9.4	8.6	9.1	9.3	9.0	8.4	8.8	8.6	Reserve Position in the Fund 1c.d
170.1	218.1	154.5	159.4	135.3	146.4	170.9	145.9	163.7	167.5	169.9	162.4	218.6	337.7	401.9	Foreign Exchange 1d.d
29,385	29,168	39,773	44,475	36,100	33,938	26,707	32,319	35,688	42,817	35,144	41,384	41,310	46,329	58,682	Deposit Money Banks: Assets 7a.d
29,647	29,770	40,868	45,492	37,392	35,820	28,720	33,951	35,958	43,219	35,542	41,796	41,662	47,053	59,127	Liabilities 7b.d
2,639	2,476	2,355	2,414	2,482	2,396	2,355	2,266	1,911	2,232	2,450	2,646	2,836	2,685	2,785	Other Banking Insts.: Assets 7e.d
2,459	2,285	2,156	2,290	2,383	2,230	2,112	1,988	1,541	1,802	1,881	2,084	2,384	2,498	2,626	Liabilities 7f.d
91,390	90,656	104,854	109,722	115,359	103,088	105,310	87,983	87,620	....	....	....	....	....	....	Branches of US Banks: Assets 7k.d
91,657	92,441	106,805	112,386	117,579	105,864	108,549	90,049	89,058	....	....	....	....	....	....	Liab. 7m.d
End of Period															**Monetary Authorities**
182.5	231.5	171.8	172.4	147.2	159.7	172.3	144.0	162.7	170.4	171.3	163.4	219.3	339.0	404.0	Foreign Assets 11
30.3	31.5	53.1	47.0	89.9	111.5	123.1	136.7	114.7	143.6	149.0	152.9	140.8	61.9	73.1	Claims on Central Government 12a
—	—	12.0	21.0	13.0	7.0	—	.5	—	—	—	—	.8	.3	.2	Claims on Deposit Money Banks 12e
1.0	2.1	2.5	2.5	2.5	2.4	2.3	2.1	3.2	3.1	3.6	3.4	4.3	5.0	8.1	Claims on Nonbank Financial Insts 12g
134.8	146.3	151.1	169.8	176.7	187.9	211.9	206.1	205.3	229.9	236.3	230.2	263.5	315.3	380.9	Reserve Money 14
57.8	65.0	74.8	78.8	79.5	80.2	78.7	84.4	83.7	89.4	92.5	97.1	110.2	126.0	149.1	*of which: Currency Outside DMBs* 14a
21.1	55.5	18.1	2.7	6.9	15.8	9.9	6.6	3.2	14.0	7.6	7.6	16.5	4.1	13.9	Central Government Deposits 16d
54.2	50.3	57.6	56.1	60.0	67.7	72.3	72.3	73.5	76.5	78.2	79.7	83.8	86.7	90.3	Capital Accounts 17a
3.7	13.0	12.6	14.3	9.0	9.2	3.6	−1.7	−1.4	−3.3	1.8	2.2	1.4	.1	.3	Other Items (Net) 17r
End of Period															**Deposit Money Banks**
53.7	62.4	58.5	72.4	72.9	86.3	112.5	101.4	105.0	123.0	128.3	118.1	145.6	182.9	226.2	Reserves 20
29,384.6	29,167.5	39,772.5	44,474.6	36,099.6	33,938.1	26,707.0	32,318.7	35,688.2	42,817.2	35,144.4	41,384.0	41,309.8	46,328.8	58,681.7	Foreign Assets 21
122.6	124.3	119.9	164.2	159.8	186.8	220.6	225.1	329.6	295.7	303.2	313.1	356.2	458.4	489.3	Claims on Central Government 22a
9.6	15.6	27.9	39.9	81.9	106.0	113.0	105.5	88.8	72.9	77.1	82.1	79.1	127.6	157.6	Claims on Official Entities 22bx
592.3	677.1	788.5	851.9	927.2	1,122.4	1,163.4	1,215.4	1,400.0	1,591.6	1,777.3	1,952.8	2,488.2	2,767.4	3,071.5	Claims on Private Sector 22d
14.1	12.8	25.3	13.0	6.9	7.3	4.9	5.5	10.6	20.4	18.1	16.4	27.4	29.0	24.7	Claims on Other Banking Insts 22f
146.1	172.4	193.7	214.4	213.9	241.2	266.7	274.4	279.9	308.5	335.6	334.2	398.2	459.9	587.8	Demand Deposits 24
489.5	534.4	628.2	679.0	751.1	885.0	942.4	1,000.4	1,221.4	1,326.4	1,447.2	1,551.3	1,950.2	2,275.0	2,423.4	Time, Savings,& Fgn.Currency Dep. 25
—	—	—	—	—	9.2	8.9	10.0	17.8	6.5	6.5	5.0	3.0	1.3	4.2	Bonds 26ab
29,647.2	29,770.2	40,867.5	45,492.2	37,391.9	35,819.5	28,720.3	33,951.1	35,958.2	43,218.9	35,542.3	41,795.6	41,661.8	47,052.8	59,126.5	Foreign Liabilities 26c
13.0	22.7	21.8	18.4	15.6	19.8	34.6	29.4	29.5	35.7	43.7	59.1	65.0	66.2	67.6	Central Government Deposits 26d
24.0	20.0	33.1	33.0	23.0	19.0	—	.5	—	—	—	—	.8	.3	.2	Credit from Monetary Authorities 26g
18.8	103.2	10.3	7.9	24.2	14.1	26.0	30.2	28.8	27.3	39.6	42.8	43.4	42.1	33.8	Liabilities to Other Banking Insts 26i
−160.2	−568.0	−942.1	−816.1	−1,058.5	−1,553.8	−1,667.3	−1,332.0	78.6	−16.1	12.7	40.7	271.3	−8.7	432.3	Capital Accounts 27a
−1.5	4.8	−19.9	−12.8	−12.9	−7.1	−10.2	7.6	8.0	13.6	20.8	37.8	12.6	5.2	−24.8	Other Items (Net) 27r
End of Period															**Monetary Survey**
−80.1	−371.2	−923.2	−845.2	−1,145.1	−1,721.7	−1,841.0	−1,488.4	−107.3	−231.3	−226.6	−248.2	−132.6	−385.0	−40.8	Foreign Assets (Net) 31n
735.8	785.2	977.3	1,097.4	1,245.7	1,500.8	1,582.8	1,654.3	1,914.2	2,077.6	2,277.0	2,454.0	3,014.4	3,379.0	3,742.8	Domestic Credit 32
118.8	77.6	133.1	190.1	227.2	262.7	299.2	325.8	411.6	389.6	400.9	399.3	415.5	450.0	480.9	Claims on Central Govt. (Net) 32an
9.6	15.6	27.9	39.9	81.9	106.0	113.0	105.5	88.8	72.9	77.1	82.1	79.1	127.6	157.6	Claims on Official Entities 32bx
592.3	677.1	788.5	851.9	927.2	1,122.4	1,163.4	1,215.4	1,400.0	1,591.6	1,777.3	1,952.8	2,488.2	2,767.4	3,071.5	Claims on Private Sector 32d
14.1	12.8	25.3	13.0	6.9	7.3	4.9	5.5	10.6	20.4	18.1	16.4	27.4	29.0	24.7	Claims on Other Banking Insts 32f
1.0	2.1	2.5	2.5	2.5	2.4	2.3	2.1	3.2	3.1	3.6	3.4	4.3	5.0	8.1	Claims on Nonbank Financial Inst 32g
217.2	242.2	270.0	294.5	299.3	342.1	366.1	379.9	381.5	416.4	444.6	446.9	517.1	593.1	747.7	Money 34
489.5	534.4	628.2	679.0	751.1	885.0	942.4	1,000.4	1,221.4	1,326.4	1,447.2	1,551.3	1,950.2	2,275.0	2,423.4	Quasi-Money 35
—	—	—	—	—	9.2	8.9	10.0	17.8	6.5	6.5	5.0	3.0	1.3	4.2	Bonds 36ab
18.8	103.2	10.3	7.9	24.2	14.1	26.0	30.2	28.8	27.3	39.6	42.8	43.4	42.1	33.8	Liabilities to Other Banking Insts 36i
−106.0	−517.7	−884.5	−760.0	−998.5	−1,486.1	−1,595.0	−1,259.7	152.1	60.4	90.9	120.4	355.1	78.0	522.6	Capital Accounts 37a
36.2	51.9	30.1	30.8	24.5	14.8	−6.6	5.1	5.3	9.3	21.6	39.4	13.0	4.5	−29.7	Other Items (Net) 37r
706.7	776.6	898.2	973.5	1,050.4	1,227.1	1,308.5	1,380.3	1,602.9	1,742.8	1,891.8	1,998.2	2,467.3	2,868.1	3,171.1	Money plus Quasi-Money 35l
End of Period															**Other Banking Institutions**
11.8	14.6	17.4	18.7	19.2	16.4	16.5	16.9	12.9	12.8	12.9	13.4	2.9	2.5	4.1	Reserves 40
2,638.8	2,476.1	2,354.7	2,414.3	2,481.5	2,395.7	2,354.5	2,265.7	1,910.6	2,231.7	2,450.1	2,646.3	2,835.6	2,684.9	2,785.4	Foreign Assets 41
12.9	13.5	18.3	21.4	21.8	19.1	20.4	33.6	23.7	22.1	22.3	21.7	3.1	3.2	3.9	Claims on Central Government 42a
248.0	303.6	371.6	388.8	404.5	343.8	351.9	364.4	268.1	266.9	282.8	297.4	62.8	69.4	87.2	Claims on Private Sector 42d
23.0	47.5	21.8	13.5	28.3	13.6	24.3	29.8	25.0	26.8	32.4	42.6	44.7	43.4	59.1	Claims on Deposit Money Banks 42e
—	.1	.1	1.0	3.3	7.1	7.3	9.4	8.3	7.8	10.8	11.5	3.5	4.5	4.6	Demand Deposits 44
245.6	293.9	353.1	363.3	370.2	312.7	317.1	325.8	245.2	242.7	247.6	259.8	38.6	41.2	65.9	Time, Savings,& Fgn.Currency Dep. 45
2,458.8	2,285.1	2,156.2	2,290.4	2,383.4	2,230.2	2,111.5	1,987.8	1,540.9	1,802.0	1,880.8	2,084.4	2,383.9	2,498.2	2,625.9	Foreign Liabilities 46c
1.2	2.3	2.5	3.8	3.5	5.2	1.9	3.1	.3	—	—	—	—	—	—	Central Government Deposits 46d
3.0	3.0	3.0	—	—	—	—	—	—	—	—	—	10.0	15.0	—	Credit from Monetary Authorities 46g
4.6	9.3	21.9	10.5	4.2	4.2	2.1	1.4	3.8	12.6	11.2	11.7	22.5	25.5	16.7	Credit from Deposit Money Banks 46h
251.4	292.7	337.6	269.6	249.4	231.9	272.5	302.2	315.7	323.4	322.5	292.2	253.3	232.7	254.9	Capital Accounts 47a
−30.1	−31.1	−90.6	−81.9	−58.7	−2.7	55.2	80.7	126.1	171.8	327.6	361.8	237.3	−13.7	−28.3	Other Items (Net) 47r
End of Period															**Banking Survey**
99.9	−180.2	−724.7	−721.3	−1,047.0	−1,556.2	−1,598.0	−1,210.5	262.4	198.4	342.7	313.7	319.1	−198.3	118.7	Foreign Assets (Net) 51n
981.4	1,087.2	1,339.4	1,490.8	1,661.6	1,851.2	1,948.3	2,043.7	2,195.1	2,346.2	2,564.0	2,756.7	3,052.9	3,422.6	3,809.2	Domestic Credit 52
130.5	88.8	148.9	207.7	245.5	276.6	317.7	356.3	435.0	411.7	423.2	421.0	418.6	453.2	484.8	Claims on Central Govt. (Net) 52an
9.6	15.6	27.9	39.9	81.9	106.0	113.0	105.5	88.8	72.9	77.1	82.1	79.1	127.6	157.6	Claims on Official Entities 52bx
840.3	980.7	1,160.1	1,240.7	1,331.7	1,466.2	1,515.3	1,579.8	1,668.1	1,858.5	2,060.1	2,250.2	2,551.0	2,836.8	3,158.7	Claims on Private Sector 52d
1.0	2.1	2.5	2.5	2.5	2.4	2.3	2.1	3.2	3.1	3.6	3.4	4.3	5.0	8.1	Claims on Nonbank Financial Inst 52g
940.5	1,056.0	1,234.0	1,319.1	1,404.7	1,530.5	1,616.4	1,698.6	1,843.5	1,980.5	2,137.3	2,256.1	2,506.5	2,911.3	3,237.5	Liquid Liabilities 55l
—	—	—	—	—	9.2	8.9	10.0	17.8	6.5	6.5	5.0	3.0	1.3	4.2	Bonds 56ab
145.4	−225.0	−546.9	−490.4	−749.1	−1,254.2	−1,322.5	−957.5	467.8	383.8	413.4	412.6	608.4	310.7	777.5	Capital Accounts 57a
−4.6	76.0	−72.4	−59.2	−41.0	9.5	47.5	82.1	128.4	173.8	349.5	396.7	254.1	1.0	−91.3	Other Items (Net) 57r

Bahamas, The

		1970	1971	1972	1973	1974	1975	1976	1977	1978	1979	1980	1981	1982	1983	1984
Interest Rates														*Percent Per Annum*		
Bank Rate (End of Period)	60	9.50	9.50	9.50	9.50	9.50	9.50	9.50	9.50	9.50	9.00	11.00	9.00	10.00	9.00	9.50
Treasury Bill Rate	60c	. . .	. . .	7.18	7.02	7.44	6.64	5.32	4.92	3.49	3.07	7.37	8.89	8.76	9.11	6.88
Deposit Rate	60l	. . .	. . .	. . .	. . .	. . .	. . .	. . .	. . .	. . .	. . .	6.96	7.48	7.56	7.47	7.44
Lending Rate	60p	. . .	. . .	. . .	. . .	. . .	. . .	9.50	9.50	9.50	9.13	10.83	11.00	11.00	11.00	11.00
Prices and Labor													*Index Numbers (1995=100):*			
Consumer Prices	64	23.6	24.7	26.4	27.9	31.5	34.8	36.3	37.4	39.7	43.3	48.5	53.9	ʃ57.2	59.5	61.8
														Number in Thousands:		
Labor Force	67d	. . .	. . .	. . .	. . .	. . .	. . .	. . .	. . .	. . .	. . .	. . .	. . .	. . .	. . .	. . .
Employment	67e	. . .	. . .	. . .	. . .	. . .	. . .	. . .	. . .	. . .	. . .	. . .	. . .	. . .	. . .	. . .
Unemployment	67c	. . .	. . .	. . .	. . .	. . .	. . .	. . .	. . .	. . .	. . .	. . .	. . .	. . .	. . .	. . .
Unemployment Rate (%)	67r	. . .	. . .	. . .	. . .	. . .	. . .	. . .	. . .	. . .	. . .	. . .	. . .	. . .	. . .	. . .
International Transactions													*Millions of Bahamian Dollars*			
Exports	70	90	267	343	530	1,444	2,508	2,992	3,261	3,058	3,786	5,009	6,189	4,534	3,970	3,393
Imports, c.i.f.	71	338	511	485	764	1,908	2,697	3,125	3,568	3,150	3,514	7,546	7,284	6,349	4,616	4,098
Balance of Payments														*Millions of US Dollars:*		
Current Account, n.i.e.	78ald							68.1	28.9	2.4	−42.9	−75.3	−139.9	−115.4	−100.6	−100.3
Goods: Exports f.o.b.	78aad							2,694.2	2,637.3	2,192.4	3,577.8	5,006.2	3,670.6	2,555.6	2,669.0	2,437.6
Goods: Imports f.o.b.	78abd							−2,865.5	−2,841.2	−2,455.0	−3,951.5	−5,467.4	−4,171.5	−3,023.4	−3,203.0	−2,983.5
Trade Balance	78acd							−171.3	−203.9	−262.6	−373.7	−461.2	−500.9	−467.8	−534.0	−545.9
Services: Credit	78add							440.0	481.9	583.1	657.1	746.0	787.5	794.1	891.1	931.2
Services: Debit	78aed							−128.0	−155.1	−177.8	−190.9	−226.2	−274.3	−315.9	−329.0	−324.0
Balance on Goods & Services	78afd							140.7	122.9	142.7	92.5	58.6	12.3	10.4	28.1	61.3
Income: Credit	78agd							4.5	4.0	6.9	10.9	13.0	17.0	23.8	15.3	18.8
Income: Debit	78ahd							−80.1	−87.6	−134.7	−144.5	−147.5	−168.9	−155.4	−153.8	−183.9
Balance on Gds, Serv. & Inc.	78aid							65.1	39.3	14.9	−41.1	−75.9	−139.6	−121.2	−110.4	−103.8
Current Transfers, n.i.e.: Credit	78ajd							7.2	7.2	9.0	13.8	19.5	13.3	23.6	19.6	17.5
Current Transfers: Debit	78akd							−4.2	−17.6	−21.5	−15.6	−18.9	−13.6	−17.8	−9.8	−14.0
Capital Account, n.i.e.	78bcd							−14.6	−2.8	−2.2	−2.2	−2.5	−2.5	−2.0	−2.7	−2.7
Capital Account, n.i.e.: Credit	78bad															
Capital Account: Debit	78bbd							−14.6	−2.8	−2.2	−2.2	−2.5	−2.5	−2.0	−2.7	−2.7
Financial Account, n.i.e.	78bjd							−2.4	50.4	−24.8	−24.3	16.8	162.7	83.3	—	−33.6
Direct Investment Abroad	78bdd															
Dir. Invest. in Rep. Econ., n.i.e.	78bed							14.6	31.4	−1.1	9.6	4.1	34.4	2.8	−6.0	−4.9
Portfolio Investment Assets	78bfd							—	—	—	—	—	—	—	—	—
Equity Securities	78bkd							—	—	—	—	—	—	—	—	—
Debt Securities	78bld							—	—	—	—	—	—	—	—	—
Portfolio Investment Liab., n.i.e.	78bgd							−1.5	6.9	−2.3	−3.2	−2.3	−3.0	−3.2	—	—
Equity Securities	78bmd							—	—	—	—	—	—	—	—	—
Debt Securities	78bnd							−1.5	6.9	−2.3	−3.2	−2.3	−3.0	−3.2	—	—
Financial Derivatives Assets	78bwd							. . .	. . .	. . .	. . .	. . .	. . .	. . .	. . .	. . .
Financial Derivatives Liabilities	78bxd							. . .	. . .	. . .	. . .	. . .	. . .	. . .	. . .	. . .
Other Investment Assets	78bhd							−12.0	9.7	.5	−33.1	7.3	17.1	8.5	−19.3	−26.8
Monetary Authorities	78bod							—	—	—	—	—	—	—	—	—
General Government	78bpd							—	—	—	—	—	—	—	—	—
Banks	78bqd							−12.0	9.7	.5	−33.1	7.3	17.1	8.5	−19.3	−26.8
Other Sectors	78brd							—	—	—	—	—	—	—	—	—
Other Investment Liab., n.i.e.	78bid							−3.5	2.4	−21.9	2.4	7.7	114.2	75.2	25.3	−1.9
Monetary Authorities	78bsd							—	—	—	—	—	—	—	—	—
General Government	78btd							−3.5	1.7	−3.4	−4.5	−5.2	34.3	50.8	19.9	1.7
Banks	78bud							—	—	—	—	—	—	—	—	—
Other Sectors	78bvd							—	.7	−18.5	6.9	12.9	79.9	24.4	5.4	−3.6
Net Errors and Omissions	78cad							−57.0	−57.4	15.6	84.2	71.7	−15.0	48.1	113.9	175.7
Overall Balance	78cbd							−5.9	19.1	−9.0	14.8	10.7	5.3	14.0	10.6	39.1
Reserves and Related Items	79dad							5.9	−19.1	9.0	−14.8	−10.7	−5.3	−14.0	−10.6	−39.1
Reserve Assets	79dbd							5.9	−19.1	9.0	−14.8	−10.7	−5.3	−14.0	−10.6	−39.1
Use of Fund Credit and Loans	79dcd							—	—	—	—	—	—	—	—	—
Exceptional Financing	79ded							. . .	. . .	. . .	. . .	. . .	. . .	. . .	. . .	. . .
Government Finance														*Millions of Bahamian Dollars:*		
Deficit (-) or Surplus	80	−17.5	−9.8	1.5	2.9	−32.8	−14.1	−23.3	−27.7	−33.0	−8.2	−7.8	−62.2	−78.2	−68.5	−16.4
Revenue	81	81.3	77.5	97.8	108.8	114.5	118.3	129.3	136.9	164.0	202.1	244.1	282.2	273.5	298.2	333.5
Grants Received	81z	—	—	—	—	—	—	—	—	—	—	—	—	—	—	—
Expenditure	82	97.2	92.1	97.8	107.8	121.5	127.8	151.5	159.7	185.9	205.1	246.9	289.3	302.3	314.3	343.2
Lending Minus Repayments	83	1.6	−4.7	−1.6	−2.0	25.9	4.6	1.2	4.9	11.1	5.2	5.1	55.1	49.5	52.4	6.7
Financing																
Net Borrowing: Domestic	84a	18.2	10.8	−2.9	−17.1	27.1	23.3	25.5	32.0	24.8	34.7	15.6	18.0	17.5	52.0	37.2
Foreign	85a	−1.8	−2.2	−1.8	10.7	2.9	−5.1	−5.0	3.6	−5.8	−7.7	−7.5	31.3	65.9	20.0	1.7
Use of Cash Balances	87	1.0	1.2	3.1	3.4	2.9	−4.1	2.8	−7.9	14.0	−18.7	−.3	12.9	−5.1	−3.5	−22.5
Debt: Domestic	88a	39.1	50.0	46.7	38.5	71.8	95.8	123.4	149.2	173.5	213.5	228.4	235.0	258.1	313.6	328.9
Foreign	89a	22.3	20.1	18.6	33.5	36.4	31.4	26.4	34.8	29.1	21.3	14.7	46.0	93.5	112.9	114.5
National Accounts														*Millions of Bahamian Dollars*		
Househ.Cons.Expend.,incl.NPISHs	96f				345.9	400.2	451.1	482.9	521.0	565.9	617.8	577.7	637.4	713.6	763.1	838.3
Government Consumption Expend.	91f				76.8	85.8	86.9	107.0	109.3	128.4	147.2	173.3	207.3	218.8	250.6	267.6
Gross Fixed Capital Formation	93e				106.7	99.0	75.4	68.1	89.2	94.4	120.3	172.1	266.2	301.1	311.3	300.8
Changes in Inventories	93i												9.0	40.1	14.1	−49.7	3.7
Exports of Goods and Services	90c				465.8	601.4	617.3	676.8	643.4	779.0	947.4	1,156.6	1,200.4	1,189.8	1,238.2	1,293.2
Imports of Goods and Services	98c				−413.0	−564.3	−567.9	−535.9	−407.5	−469.4	−533.8	−788.7	−860.4	−935.7	−1,039.7	−1,106.3
Gross Domestic Product (GDP)	99b				582.2	622.1	733.6	798.9	955.4	1,098.3	1,298.9	1,299.9	1,490.9	1,501.8	1,473.9	1,597.4
Net Primary Income from Abroad	98.n				−61.8	−79.3	−61.6	−64.4	−75.4	−114.4	−125.8	−113.6	−136.4	−115.3	−123.3	−148.5
Gross National Income (GNI)	98a				520.4	542.8	672.0	734.5	880.0	983.9	1,173.1	1,186.3	1,354.5	1,386.5	1,350.6	1,448.9
Net Current Transf.from Abroad	98t				. . .	. . .	. . .	. . .	. . .	. . .	. . .	. . .	. . .	. . .	. . .	. . .
Gross Nat'l Disposable Inc.(GNDI)	99i				. . .	. . .	. . .	. . .	. . .	. . .	. . .	. . .	. . .	. . .	. . .	. . .
Gross Savings	99s				. . .	. . .	. . .	. . .	. . .	. . .	. . .	. . .	. . .	. . .	. . .	. . .
GDP Volume 1995 Prices	99b.p				. . .	. . .	. . .	. . .	. . .	. . .	. . .	. . .	. . .	. . .	. . .	. . .
GDP Volume (1995=100)	99bvp				. . .	. . .	. . .	. . .	. . .	. . .	. . .	. . .	. . .	. . .	. . .	. . .
GDP Deflator (1995=100)	99bip				. . .	. . .	. . .	. . .	. . .	. . .	. . .	. . .	. . .	. . .	. . .	. . .
															Millions:	
Population	99z	.17	.18	.18	.18	.19	.19	.19	.20	.20	.21	.21	.21	.22	.22	.23

1985	1986	1987	1988	1989	1990	1991	1992	1993	1994	1995	1996	1997	1998	1999		
Percent Per Annum															**Interest Rates**	
8.50	7.50	7.50	9.00	9.00	9.00	9.00	7.50	7.00	6.50	6.50	6.50	6.50	6.50	5.75	Bank Rate *(End of Period)*	**60**
5.90	3.47	2.40	4.46	5.21	5.85	6.49	5.32	3.96	1.88	3.01	4.45	4.35	3.84	1.97	Treasury Bill Rate	**60c**
6.40	5.57	5.50	5.97	6.48	6.57	6.92	6.13	5.19	4.30	4.20	5.14	5.23	5.36	4.57	Deposit Rate	**60l**
10.33	9.25	9.00	9.00	9.00	9.00	9.00	8.08	7.46	6.88	6.75	6.75	6.75	6.75	6.38	Lending Rate	**60p**
Period Averages															**Prices and Labor**	
64.7	68.2	72.1	75.3	79.3	83.0	89.0	94.1	96.6	98.0	I100.0	101.4	101.9	103.3	104.6	Consumer Prices	**64**
Period Averages																
....	....	....	....	....	114	....	135	....	137	....	....	....	296	....	Labor Force	**67d**
....	I97	....	111	112	....	114	115	119	120	127	130	135	....	....	Employment	**67e**
....	I14	....	14	15	....	16	20	18	18	16	17	15	....	....	Unemployment	**67c**
....	12.2	....	11.0	11.7	....	12.3	14.8	13.1	13.3	10.9	11.5	9.8	....	....	Unemployment Rate (%)	**67r**
Millions of Bahamian Dollars															**International Transactions**	
2,728	2,702	2,722	2,153	2,487	I238	225	192	162	167	176	180	181	300	380	Exports	**70**
3,078	3,289	3,080	2,291	3,137	I1,112	1,091	1,038	954	1,056	1,243	1,343	1,622	1,872	1,808	Imports, c.i.f.	**71**
Minus Sign Indicates Debit															Balance of Payments	
-2.7	23.0	-54.8	-66.5	-84.2	-36.6	-179.8	35.8	48.7	-42.2	-145.9	-263.3	-472.1	-995.4	-671.9	Current Account, n.i.e.	**78al*d***
862.5	335.3	324.8	310.8	221.0	283.5	229.4	216.6	192.2	198.5	225.4	273.3	295.0	362.9	379.9	Goods: Exports f.o.b.	**78aa*d***
-1,425.8	-940.9	-998.1	-982.9	-1,131.8	-1,080.0	-1,046.3	-984.3	-930.2	-1,013.8	-1,156.7	-1,287.4	-1,410.7	-1,737.1	-1,808.1	Goods: Imports f.o.b.	**78ab*d***
-563.3	-605.6	-673.3	-672.1	-910.8	-796.5	-816.9	-767.7	-738.0	-815.3	-931.3	-1,014.1	-1,115.7	-1,374.2	-1,428.2	*Trade Balance*	**78ac*d***
1,121.9	1,228.7	1,265.6	1,275.2	1,474.3	1,500.1	1,354.0	1,389.6	1,459.0	1,510.6	1,542.3	1,578.2	1,592.9	1,533.0	1,811.2	Services: Credit	**78ad*d***
-383.2	-417.7	-461.9	-491.2	-522.0	-573.0	-549.1	-515.5	-567.7	-627.2	-639.1	-715.8	-836.0	-990.9	-953.8	Services: Debit	**78ae*d***
175.4	205.4	130.4	111.9	41.5	130.6	-12.0	106.4	153.3	68.1	-28.1	-151.7	-358.8	-832.1	-570.8	*Balance on Goods & Services*	**78af*d***
20.4	19.5	18.1	15.3	236.1	232.1	197.9	103.3	112.2	61.2	75.1	84.6	105.7	147.9	229.6	Income: Credit	**78ag*d***
-201.0	-203.1	-201.4	-182.2	-367.7	-404.9	-376.9	-185.9	-240.6	-198.8	-210.8	-233.4	-258.3	-345.4	-367.2	Income: Debit	**78ah*d***
-5.2	21.8	-52.9	-55.0	-90.1	-42.2	-191.0	23.8	24.9	-69.5	-163.8	-300.5	-511.4	-1,029.6	-708.4	*Balance on Gds, Serv. & Inc.*	**78ai*d***
16.8	16.3	16.7	17.4	9.7	12.1	16.0	19.9	33.1	33.1	25.1	45.9	50.0	45.0	49.0	Current Transfers, n.i.e.: Credit	**78aj*d***
-14.3	-15.1	-18.6	-28.9	-3.8	-6.5	-4.8	-7.9	-9.3	-5.8	-7.2	-8.7	-10.7	-10.8	-12.5	Current Transfers: Debit	**78ak*d***
-2.5	-1.5	-1.7	-3.0	-16.6	-7.7	-5.6	-9.8	-9.4	-11.6	-12.5	-24.4	-12.9	-11.7	-14.5	Capital Account, n.i.e.	**78bc*d***
—	—	—	—	—	—	—	—	—	—	—	—	—	—	—	Capital Account, n.i.e.: Credit	**78ba*d***
-2.5	-1.5	-1.7	-3.0	-16.6	-7.7	-5.6	-9.8	-9.4	-11.6	-12.5	-24.4	-12.9	-11.7	-14.5	Capital Account: Debit	**78bb*d***
-11.5	26.2	-14.9	73.2	88.8	66.8	173.0	-4.4	9.3	66.8	104.6	181.1	412.0	817.7	611.4	Financial Account, n.i.e.	**78bj*d***
—	—	—	—	-.4	.1	1.3	-.3	-.1	.1	-.1	.3	-.4	-1.0	-.2	Direct Investment Abroad	**78bd*d***
-30.2	-13.2	10.8	36.7	25.4	-17.3	-1.3	.3	27.1	23.4	106.8	87.8	210.0	146.9	144.6	Dir. Invest. in Rep. Econ., n.i.e.	**78be*d***
—	—	—	—	—	—	—	—	—	—	—	—	—	—	—	Portfolio Investment Assets	**78bf*d***
—	—	—	—	—	—	—	—	—	—	—	—	—	—	—	Equity Securities	**78bk*d***
—	—	—	—	—	—	—	—	—	—	—	—	—	—	—	Debt Securities	**78bl*d***
—	—	—	—	—	—	—	—	—	—	—	—	—	—	—	Portfolio Investment Liab., n.i.e.	**78bg*d***
—	—	—	—	—	—	—	—	—	—	—	—	—	—	—	Equity Securities	**78bm*d***
—	—	—	—	—	—	—	—	—	—	—	—	—	—	—	Debt Securities	**78bn*d***
....	....	....	....	—	—	—	—	—	—	—	—	—	—	—	Financial Derivatives Assets	**78bw*d***
....	....	....	....	—	—	—	—	—	—	—	—	—	—	—	Financial Derivatives Liabilities	**78bx*d***
24.3	27.0	11.9	39.3	8,288.5	2,282.7	7,295.5	-5,520.5	-3,009.4	-7,455.9	7,436.6	-6,428.8	-80.7	-4,872.0	-12,487.1	Other Investment Assets	**78bh*d***
....	....	....	....	—	—	—	—	—	—	—	—	—	—	—	Monetary Authorities	**78bo*d***
—	—	—	—	—	—	—	—	—	—	—	—	—	—	—	General Government	**78bp*d***
24.3	27.0	11.9	39.3	8,288.5	2,282.7	7,295.5	-5,520.5	-3,009.4	-7,455.9	7,436.6	-6,428.8	-80.7	-4,872.0	-12,487.1	Banks	**78bq*d***
—	—	—	—	—	—	—	—	—	—	—	—	—	—	—	Other Sectors	**78br*d***
-5.6	12.4	-37.6	-2.8	-8,224.7	-2,198.7	-7,122.5	5,516.1	2,991.7	7,499.2	-7,438.7	6,521.8	283.1	5,543.8	12,954.1	Other Investment Liab., n.i.e.	**78bi*d***
—	—	—	—	—	—	—	—	—	—	—	—	—	—	—	Monetary Authorities	**78bs*d***
-7.3	10.1	-20.7	-8.1	4.9	12.7	4.1	-4.7	-16.4	-5.8	-26.9	-25.2	19.2	-5.9	11.7	General Government	**78bt*d***
—	—	—	—	-8,249.3	-2,240.1	-7,285.7	5,474.1	3,010.7	7,459.6	-7,417.9	6,451.8	141.9	4,901.8	12,578.9	Banks	**78bu*d***
1.7	2.3	-16.9	5.3	19.7	28.7	159.1	46.7	-2.6	45.4	6.1	95.2	122.0	647.9	363.5	Other Sectors	**78bv*d***
35.4	-78.5	11.5	-4.4	-13.2	-10.8	25.0	-49.6	-30.0	-3.9	50.9	99.0	129.5	308.6	140.2	Net Errors and Omissions	**78ca*d***
18.7	-30.8	-59.9	-.7	-25.2	11.7	12.6	-28.0	18.6	9.1	-2.9	-7.6	56.5	119.2	65.2	*Overall Balance*	**78cb*d***
-18.7	30.8	59.9	.7	25.2	-11.7	-12.6	28.0	-18.6	-9.1	2.9	7.6	-56.5	-119.2	-65.2	Reserves and Related Items	**79da*d***
-18.7	30.8	59.9	.7	25.2	-11.7	-12.6	28.0	-18.6	-9.1	2.9	7.6	-56.5	-119.2	-65.2	Reserve Assets	**79db*d***
—	—	—	—	—	—	—	—	—	—	—	—	—	—	—	Use of Fund Credit and Loans	**79dc*d***
....	....	....	....	....	....	....	....	....	....	....	....	....	....	....	Exceptional Financing	**79de*d***
Year Ending December 31															**Government Finance**	
-28.4	-12.3	-21.4	I-76.0	-123.5	-75.8	-132.5	-88.1	I-85.1	-20.0	-23.2	-64.7	-136.2	-81.2	-50.7	Deficit (-) or Surplus	**80**
376.8	398.8	436.1	I432.6	456.7	497.8	490.4	534.6	I537.1	618.2	660.2	678.8	728.1	760.9	868.8	Revenue	**81**
....	....	....	....	....	....	....	....	....	....	....	....	.5	.5	.3	Grants Received	**81z**
406.0	420.1	462.0	I513.8	580.8	554.2	584.6	597.8	I584.0	604.5	657.3	713.6	829.3	807.2	884.5	Expenditure	**82**
-.9	-9.0	-4.5	I-5.2	-.6	19.4	38.3	24.9	I38.2	33.7	26.1	29.9	35.5	35.4	35.3	Lending Minus Repayments	**83**
															Financing	
48.5	-15.5	26.4	I82.7	134.0	83.9	157.1	85.0	I93.8	47.3	10.1	94.8	87.3	76.0	30.1	Net Borrowing: Domestic	**84a**
-3.6	55.7	-18.5	I-18.1	3.2	7.9	4.1	-4.7	I-14.6	-9.6	14.8	-14.2	63.7	-5.8	17.1	Foreign	**85a**
-16.6	-27.9	13.5	I11.4	-13.7	-16.0	-28.7	7.8	I5.9	-17.7	-1.7	-15.9	-14.3	11.5	3.5	Use of Cash Balances	**87**
365.7	400.2	419.4	I474.0	545.8	643.7	738.1	777.1	I954.1	1,032.9	1,074.9	1,158.6	1,281.4	1,339.9	1,405.8	Debt: Domestic	**88a**
112.5	122.5	108.5	I100.4	126.0	129.4	133.5	125.2	I110.6	100.4	90.9	77.1	90.8	85.0	106.6	Foreign	**89a**
Millions of Bahamian Dollars															**National Accounts**	
897.6	1,015.9	1,137.5	1,126.9	I2,040.7	2,027.1	2,122.8	1,938.2	1,986.0	2,054.1	2,077.4	....	....	....	....	Househ.Cons.Expend.,incl.NPISHs	**96f**
294.4	306.3	333.8	370.1	I423.1	413.8	450.9	434.7	408.4	511.0	483.9	....	....	....	....	Government Consumption Expend.	**91f**
381.3	419.1	512.7	510.7	I726.7	654.2	647.3	650.3	526.4	614.0	698.5	....	....	....	....	Gross Fixed Capital Formation	**93e**
9.6	16.6	6.4	27.5	I13.0	9.6	4.2	13.0	32.8	32.4	13.8	....	....	....	....	Changes in Inventories	**93i**
1,511.9	1,605.1	1,773.0	2,100.8	I1,538.1	1,697.0	1,492.9	1,462.3	1,517.4	1,569.3	1,680.1	....	....	....	....	Exports of Goods and Services	**90c**
-1,239.4	-1,281.2	-1,451.6	-1,557.0	I-1599.1	-1,614.1	-1,609.4	-1,503.8	-1,477.4	-1,633.3	-1,819.6	....	....	....	....	Imports of Goods and Services	**98c**
1,855.4	2,081.7	2,311.7	2,578.9	I2,943.8	3,046.9	2,888.2	2,857.1	2,853.6	3,053.1	3,069.4	....	....	....	....	Gross Domestic Product (GDP)	**99b**
-162.6	-163.8	-162.8	-149.6	I-110.8	-138.3	-132.0	-58.0	-74.5	-89.3	-96.9	....	....	....	....	Net Primary Income from Abroad	**98.n**
1,692.8	1,917.9	2,148.9	2,429.3	I2,833.0	2,908.6	2,756.2	2,799.1	2,779.1	2,963.8	2,972.5	....	....	....	....	Gross National Income (GNI)	**99a**
....	....	....	....	1.0	10.6	20.3	13.4	14.5	15.7	5.4	....	....	....	....	Net Current Transf.from Abroad	**98t**
....	....	....	....	2,834.0	2,919.2	2,776.5	2,812.5	2,793.6	2,979.5	2,977.9	....	....	....	....	Gross Nat'l Disposable Inc.(GNDI)	**99i**
....	....	....	....	370.2	478.3	202.8	439.7	399.1	423.4	416.6	....	....	....	....	Gross Savings	**99s**
....	....	....	....	3,085.6	2,982.7	2,888.2	2,720.9	2,664.8	2,716.8	2,746.1	....	....	....	....	GDP Volume 1995 Prices	**99b.*p***
....	....	....	....	112.4	108.6	105.2	99.1	97.0	98.9	100.0	....	....	....	....	GDP Volume (1995=100)	**99bv*p***
....	....	....	....	I85.4	91.4	89.5	93.9	95.8	100.5	100.0	....	....	....	....	GDP Deflator (1995=100)	**99bi*p***
Midyear Estimates																
.23	.23	.24	.25	.25	.26	.26	.26	.27	.27	.28	.28	.29	.30	.30	**Population**	**99z**

(See notes in the back of the book.)

Bahrain

		1970	1971	1972	1973	1974	1975	1976	1977	1978	1979	1980	1981	1982	1983	1984
Exchange Rates																*SDRs per Dinar:*
Official Rate	ac	2.1000	2.1000	2.1000	2.1000	2.0691	2.1598	2.1754	2.0807	1.9997	2.0135	2.0853	2.2850	2.4110	2.5403	2.7133
																US Dollars per Dinar:
Official Rate	ag	2.1000	2.2800	2.2800	2.5333	2.5333	2.5284	2.5275	2.5275	2.6052	2.6525	2.6596	2.6596	2.6596	2.6596	2.6596
Official Rate	rh	2.1000	2.1064	2.2800	2.5046	2.5333	2.5284	2.5278	2.5275	2.5809	2.6206	2.6525	2.6596	2.6596	2.6596	2.6596
																Index Numbers (1995=100):
Official Rate	ah x	79.0	79.2	85.7	94.2	95.3	95.1	95.0	95.0	97.0	98.5	99.7	100.0	100.0	100.0	100.0
Nominal Effective Exchange Rate	ne c	....	....	....	....	....	....	....	....	....	104.3	104.8	114.2	125.2	131.4	139.2
Real Effective Exchange Rate	re c	....	....	....	....	....	....	....	....	....	....	147.2	162.8	182.4	189.1	193.5
Fund Position																*Millions of SDRs:*
Quota	2f. s	—	—	10.0	10.0	10.0	10.0	10.0	10.0	20.0	20.0	30.0	30.0	30.0	48.9	48.9
SDRs	1b. s	....	....	—	—	—	—	—	—	.1	2.2	1.8	5.2	14.0	12.2	13.1
Reserve Position in the Fund	1c. s	....	....	2.5	2.5	5.5	9.6	4.7	4.8	5.8	5.8	8.5	8.9	12.5	21.4	23.1
International Liquidity												*Millions of US Dollars Unless Otherwise Indicated:*					
Total Reserves minus Gold	1l. d	62.8	86.0	83.5	64.0	131.3	289.5	436.4	503.9	493.4	613.9	953.4	1,544.1	1,534.8	1,426.4	1,302.4
SDRs	1b. d	....	....	—	—	—	—	—	—	.1	2.9	2.2	6.1	15.4	12.8	12.8
Reserve Position in the Fund	1c. d	....	....	2.7	3.0	6.7	11.2	5.5	5.8	7.5	7.6	10.9	10.4	13.8	22.4	22.6
Foreign Exchange	1d. d	62.8	86.0	80.8	61.0	124.6	278.3	430.9	498.1	485.8	603.4	940.3	1,527.7	1,505.6	1,391.2	1,267.0
Monetary Agency	1da d	40.1	50.0	54.8	30.0	43.3	148.8	336.4	443.0	434.5	429.3	544.0	812.4	768.2	762.3	619.4
Government	1db d	22.7	36.0	26.0	31.0	81.3	129.5	94.5	55.1	51.3	174.1	396.3	715.3	737.4	628.9	647.6
Gold (Million Fine Troy Ounces)	1ad	.237	.237	.237	.237	.238	.150	.150	.150	.150	.150	.150	.150	.150	.150	.150
Gold (National Valuation)	1an d	8.3	9.0	8.2	....	10.1	6.3	6.3	6.3	6.5	6.6	6.6	6.6	6.6	6.6	6.6
Monetary Authorities: Other Liab.	4.. d	—	—	—	—	—	16.4	122.1	154.4	97.4	8.5	101.1	48.4	21.8	43.1	3.2
Deposit Money Banks: Assets	7a. d	57.2	87.1	106.6	114.4	250.5	406.0	479.8	566.3	635.1	627.8	851.0	912.6	952.3	1,250.2	1,159.1
Liabilities	7b. d	.9.4	22.8	39.4	58.4	154.2	328.0	389.9	499.8	499.7	625.4	627.7	326.7	333.0	398.7	279.2
OBU: Foreign Assets	7k. d	....	....	....	....	....	1,687	5,568	13,527	20,445	23,074	30,555	41,819	48,890	53,361	53,861
Foreign Liabilities	7m. d	....	....	....	....	....	1,687	5,617	13,561	20,440	23,076	30,349	41,116	48,275	51,864	53,010
Monetary Authorities																*Millions of Dinars:*
Foreign Assets	11	32.52	39.71	33.04	23.56	55.96	116.72	174.68	201.46	195.03	235.96	399.33	601.04	589.37	556.05	536.85
Reserve Money	14	20.06	22.87	25.32	16.15	19.30	49.20	72.80	69.70	76.00	93.60	91.20	105.00	125.80	124.38	116.76
of which: Currency Outside DMBs	14a	18.86	21.23	23.81	14.91	16.88	24.02	34.22	43.78	44.14	49.90	58.32	63.35	70.46	73.53	78.17
Time and Savings Deposits	15	—	—	—	—	—	—	—	6.30	29.90	31.40	37.40	30.20	21.90	14.84	....
Foreign Liabilities	16c	—	—	—	—	—	6.50	48.30	61.10	37.40	3.20	38.00	18.20	8.20	16.20	1.19
Central Government Deposits	16d	9.48	13.80	16.57	13.00	34.86	57.22	44.68	44.86	22.63	80.43	183.34	389.23	334.90	303.04	350.50
Capital Accounts	17a	—	—	—	—	3.60	9.70	15.00	28.00	41.60	49.93	61.99	66.51	86.17	92.46	100.60
Other Items (Net)	17r	2.98	3.04	–8.85	–5.59	–1.80	–5.90	–6.10	–8.50	–12.50	–22.60	–12.60	–8.10	12.40	5.13	–32.20
Deposit Money Banks																*Millions of Dinars:*
Reserves	20	1.20	1.64	1.51	1.24	2.42	25.25	38.46	25.36	33.94	36.89	37.76	40.81	53.93	36.26	39.99
Foreign Assets	21	27.23	38.18	46.76	45.15	98.88	160.59	189.85	224.05	243.79	236.67	319.96	343.12	358.07	470.05	435.82
Claims on Central Government	22a	—	1.90	9.10	2.90	1.13	1.34	3.58	9.17	23.76	26.77	27.16	13.77	26.22	33.68	97.91
Claims on Private Sector	22d	24.73	37.57	53.13	76.36	120.87	160.76	267.90	310.76	325.44	375.84	434.89	487.48	544.64	606.88	640.20
Demand Deposits	24	19.09	27.35	31.40	44.46	44.43	53.75	93.72	108.71	127.20	136.21	133.92	185.42	152.40	133.80	130.10
Time and Savings Deposits	25	18.49	24.56	32.67	40.27	84.52	106.45	175.89	203.01	231.00	225.76	331.83	481.78	198.20	635.79	619.50
Foreign Liabilities	26c	4.50	10.01	17.26	23.05	60.85	129.74	154.24	197.75	191.80	235.79	236.01	122.84	125.21	149.89	104.99
Central Government Deposits	26d	8.23	11.78	13.67	11.30	32.05	50.51	68.67	49.02	66.87	50.77	84.96	59.88	58.91	114.10	240.48
Capital Accounts	27a	1.20	1.96	3.45	6.21	7.61	9.39	14.17	21.50	24.32	34.66	42.57	62.73	122.28	137.59	130.89
Other Items (Net)	27r	1.66	3.64	12.05	.37	–6.16	–1.89	–6.92	–10.66	–14.27	–7.02	–9.52	–27.47	–33.30	–24.29	–12.04
Monetary Survey																*Millions of Dinars:*
Foreign Assets (Net)	31n	55.26	67.88	62.55	45.66	93.99	141.07	161.98	166.65	209.63	233.64	445.28	803.13	814.04	860.01	866.49
Domestic Credit	32	7.02	13.89	31.99	54.96	55.10	54.37	158.12	226.06	259.69	271.41	193.75	52.13	177.04	223.41	147.13
Claims on Central Govt. (Net)	32an	–17.71	–23.68	–21.14	–21.40	–65.77	–106.39	–109.77	–84.71	–65.75	–104.43	–241.14	–435.34	–367.60	–383.46	–493.07
Claims on Private Sector	32d	24.73	37.57	53.13	76.36	120.87	160.76	267.90	310.76	325.44	375.84	434.89	487.48	544.64	606.88	640.20
Money	34	37.95	48.57	55.22	59.37	61.31	77.77	127.94	152.49	171.34	186.11	192.24	248.76	222.85	207.33	208.26
Quasi-Money	35	18.49	24.56	32.67	40.27	84.52	106.45	175.89	209.31	260.90	257.16	369.23	511.98	176.02	607.95	588.47
Other Items (Net)	37r	5.84	8.64	6.65	.99	3.25	11.22	16.27	30.91	37.08	61.78	77.57	94.52	188.97	225.47	185.86
Money plus Quasi-Money	35l	56.44	73.13	87.88	99.64	145.83	184.22	303.83	361.80	432.25	443.27	561.46	760.74	442.95	857.95	827.76
Other Banking Institutions																*Millions of Dinars*
Reserves	40	....	....	....	....	....	....	....	....	....	....	....	....	....	....	....
Other Claims on Monetary Author.	40c	....	....	....	....	....	....	....	....	....	....	....	....	....	....	....
Foreign Assets	41	....	....	....	....	....	....	....	....	....	....	....	....	....	....	....
Claims on Central Government	42a	....	....	....	....	....	....	....	....	....	....	....	....	....	....	....
Claims on Private Sector	42d	....	....	....	....	....	....	....	....	....	....	....	....	....	....	....
Other Claims on Dep.Money Banks	42e	....	....	....	....	....	....	....	....	....	....	....	....	....	....	....
Time and Saving Deposits	45	....	....	....	....	....	....	....	....	....	....	....	....	....	....	....
Liquid Liabilities	45l	....	....	....	....	....	....	....	....	....	....	....	....	....	....	....
Money Market Instruments	46aa	....	....	....	....	....	....	....	....	....	....	....	....	....	....	....
Foreign Liabilities	46c	....	....	....	....	....	....	....	....	....	....	....	....	....	....	....
Central Government Deposits	46d	....	....	....	....	....	....	....	....	....	....	....	....	....	....	....
Credit from Monetary Authorities	46g	....	....	....	....	....	....	....	....	....	....	....	....	....	....	....
Credit from Deposit Money Banks	46h	....	....	....	....	....	....	....	....	....	....	....	....	....	....	....
Capital Accounts	47a	....	....	....	....	....	....	....	....	....	....	....	....	....	....	....
Other Items (Net)	47r	....	....	....	....	....	....	....	....	....	....	....	....	....	....	....
Banking Survey																*millions of dinars*
Foreign Assets (Net)	51n	....	....	....	....	....	....	....	....	....	....	....	....	....	....	....
Domestic Credit	52	....	....	....	....	....	....	....	....	....	....	....	....	....	....	....
Claims on Central Govt. (Net)	52an	....	....	....	....	....	....	....	....	....	....	....	....	....	....	....
Claims on Local Government	52	....	....	....	....	....	....	....	....	....	....	....	....	....	....	....
Claims on Private Sector	52d	....	....	....	....	....	....	....	....	....	....	....	....	....	....	....
Liquid Liabilities	55l	....	....	....	....	....	....	....	....	....	....	....	....	....	....	....
Money Market Instruments	56a	....	....	....	....	....	....	....	....	....	....	....	....	....	....	....
Capital Accounts	57a	....	....	....	....	....	....	....	....	....	....	....	....	....	....	....
Other Items (Net)	57r	....	....	....	....	....	....	....	....	....	....	....	....	....	....	....

1985	1986	1987	1988	1989	1990	1991	1992	1993	1994	1995	1996	1997	1998	1999		
End of Period															**Exchange Rates**	
2.4213	2.1743	1.8747	1.9764	2.0238	1.8695	1.8593	1.9343	1.9363	1.8218	1.7892	1.8495	1.9711	1.8889	1.9377	Official Rate	**ac**
End of Period (ag) Period Average (rh)																
2.6596	2.6596	2.6596	2.6596	2.6596	2.6596	2.6596	2.6596	2.6596	2.6596	2.6596	2.6596	2.6596	2.6596	2.6596	Official Rate	**ag**
2.6596	2.6596	2.6596	2.6596	2.6596	2.6596	2.6596	2.6596	2.6596	2.6596	2.6596	2.6596	2.6596	2.6596	2.6596	Official Rate	**rh**
Period Averages																
100.0	100.0	100.0	100.0	100.0	100.0	100.0	100.0	100.0	100.0	100.0	100.0	100.0	100.0	100.0	Official Rate	**ahx**
143.8	122.3	110.2	104.0	108.3	103.3	103.6	101.8	107.2	105.0	100.0	102.3	108.6	112.6	112.4	Nominal Effective Exchange Rate	**nec**
188.0	153.2	132.4	121.6	123.0	112.6	109.0	103.5	108.8	105.0	100.0	99.6	106.2	107.9	107.6	Real Effective Exchange Rate	**rec**
End of Period															**Fund Position**	
48.9	48.9	48.9	48.9	48.9	48.9	48.9	48.9	82.8	82.8	82.8	82.8	82.8	82.8	135.0	Quota	**2f.s**
13.6	14.1	14.6	15.1	15.9	16.9	17.8	18.7	10.8	11.0	11.3	11.7	11.9	12.1	—	SDRs	**1b.s**
24.6	26.0	27.3	27.7	29.6	28.0	29.6	31.1	40.9	42.2	43.7	45.1	46.7	48.5	62.4	Reserve Position in the Fund	**1c.s**
End of Period															**International Liquidity**	
1,659.7	1,489.4	1,148.5	1,251.7	1,050.0	1,234.9	1,514.6	1,398.5	1,302.2	1,169.7	1,279.9	1,318.4	1,290.3	1,079.2	1,369.0	Total Reserves minus Gold	**1l.d**
15.0	17.3	20.7	20.4	20.9	24.0	25.5	25.7	14.8	16.1	16.8	16.8	16.1	17.1	—	SDRs	**1b.d**
27.0	31.8	38.7	37.3	38.9	39.8	42.4	42.7	56.2	61.6	65.0	64.8	63.0	68.3	85.6	Reserve Position in the Fund	**1c.d**
1,617.7	1,440.3	1,089.1	1,194.0	990.3	1,171.1	1,446.7	1,330.0	1,231.2	1,092.0	1,198.2	1,236.8	1,211.2	993.8	1,283.4	Foreign Exchange	**1d.d**
774.0	740.3	923.5	692.2	693.7	922.2	1,196.3	1,079.6	980.4	841.5	947.3	985.9	960.5	743.0	1,032.9	Monetary Agency	**1dad**
843.7	700.0	165.6	501.8	296.6	248.9	250.4	250.4	250.8	250.5	250.9	250.9	250.7	250.8	250.5	Government	**1dbd**
.150	.150	.150	.150	.150	.150	.150	.150	.150	.150	.150	.150	.150	.150	.150	Gold (Million Fine Troy Ounces)	**1ad**
6.6	6.6	6.6	6.6	6.6	6.6	6.6	6.6	6.6	6.6	6.6	6.6	6.6	6.6	6.6	Gold (National Valuation)	**1and**
27.5	25.4	—	74.7	116.3	16.4	—	—	—	—	—	—	—	—	—	Monetary Authorities: Other Liab.	**4..d**
1,560.6	1,847.4	1,846.7	2,276.3	3,113.0	2,505.1	I 1,975.0	1,855.1	2,272.9	2,761.7	2,592.0	2,557.2	2,863.0	3,164.1	3,410.6	Deposit Money Banks: Assets	**7a.d**
339.5	403.2	390.2	425.9	867.5	762.8	I 599.5	675.5	977.1	1,486.2	1,136.4	1,042.3	1,583.2	1,522.1	2,305.3	Liabilities	**7b.d**
49,148	49,069	57,879	62,942	67,355	56,806	51,187	67,142	57,673	62,363	61,061	64,435	69,382	....	....	OBU: Foreign Assets	**7k.d**
47,939	47,720	56,828	61,613	66,614	56,888	50,585	66,569	57,180	61,875	60,579	64,068	68,644	....	....	Foreign Liabilities	**7m.d**
End of Period															**Monetary Authorities**	
649.79	600.18	470.47	529.62	547.80	473.81	510.84	498.64	481.94	459.09	496.22	494.69	558.44	549.91	530.90	Foreign Assets	**11**
136.00	128.53	142.26	133.50	144.56	158.19	I 249.45	227.08	181.46	173.93	233.97	207.97	234.10	183.20	266.50	Reserve Money	**14**
78.97	79.98	84.06	84.37	84.77	105.25	I 99.05	99.88	103.76	105.53	103.27	102.87	104.60	93.30	113.00	*of which: Currency Outside DMBs*	**14a**
—	—	—	—	—	—	—	5.00	10.00	10.00	20.00	24.50	23.50	35.90	48.40	Time and Savings Deposits	**15**
10.33	9.54	—	28.09	43.73	6.15	—	—	—	—	—	—	—	—	—	Foreign Liabilities	**16c**
386.82	335.65	174.40	249.55	246.57	141.23	118.28	117.74	118.94	120.29	131.35	124.53	122.20	137.53	124.40	Central Government Deposits	**16d**
134.40	151.12	167.77	166.77	170.41	183.85	184.83	198.41	213.30	206.10	240.27	251.02	270.85	291.48	296.50	Capital Accounts	**17a**
-17.75	-24.66	-13.96	-48.29	-57.48	-15.61	I -41.60	-49.60	-41.80	-51.10	-129.30	-113.00	-92.20	-98.20	-204.90	Other Items (Net)	**17r**
End of Period															**Deposit Money Banks**	
56.47	47.39	54.07	48.65	53.46	196.71	I 141.50	116.50	73.30	66.30	124.60	99.00	126.60	89.40	153.70	Reserves	**20**
586.79	694.62	694.34	855.88	1,170.47	941.90	I 742.60	697.50	854.60	1,038.40	974.60	961.50	1,076.50	1,189.70	1,282.40	Foreign Assets	**21**
89.17	126.55	253.00	114.92	127.76	161.21	I 98.00	156.60	132.10	138.50	150.70	166.60	172.10	223.30	323.80	Claims on Central Government	**22a**
598.43	566.09	498.02	491.64	482.37	474.61	I 612.10	676.40	818.50	915.00	947.80	954.70	1,074.30	1,164.20	1,302.50	Claims on Private Sector	**22d**
140.03	131.48	134.80	132.20	126.86	153.30	I 205.80	252.00	261.10	239.20	229.20	232.40	243.10	272.30	313.20	Demand Deposits	**24**
684.31	673.71	749.59	791.03	840.81	672.18	I 841.90	845.60	896.50	992.70	1,095.00	1,132.60	1,238.30	1,477.70	1,482.10	Time and Savings Deposits	**25**
127.65	151.62	146.73	160.13	326.19	286.82	I 225.40	254.00	367.40	558.80	427.30	391.90	595.30	572.30	866.80	Foreign Liabilities	**26c**
242.62	270.82	318.62	334.55	448.13	511.12	I 399.60	284.20	337.00	416.70	358.00	433.30	443.10	409.90	431.00	Central Government Deposits	**26d**
167.79	252.73	201.92	172.34	169.48	132.81	I 111.90	155.70	169.10	194.60	185.50	191.50	199.40	254.90	259.60	Capital Accounts	**27a**
-31.53	-45.70	-52.22	-79.17	-77.40	18.19	I -190.30	-144.60	-152.80	-243.70	-97.40	-200.00	-269.80	-320.40	-290.20	Other Items (Net)	**27r**
End of Period															**Monetary Survey**	
1,098.61	1,133.64	1,018.09	1,197.28	1,348.35	1,122.74	I 1028.04	942.14	969.14	938.69	1,043.52	1,064.29	1,039.64	1,167.31	946.50	Foreign Assets (Net)	**31n**
58.16	86.17	258.00	22.46	-84.57	-16.53	I 192.22	431.06	494.66	516.51	609.15	563.47	681.10	840.07	1,070.90	Domestic Credit	**32**
-540.27	-479.92	-240.02	-469.18	-566.94	-491.15	I -419.88	-245.34	-323.84	-398.49	-338.65	-391.23	-393.20	-324.13	-231.60	Claims on Central Govt. (Net)	**32an**
598.43	566.09	498.02	491.64	482.37	474.61	I 612.10	676.40	818.50	915.00	947.80	954.70	1,074.30	1,164.20	1,302.50	Claims on Private Sector	**32d**
219.00	211.46	218.86	216.57	211.62	258.56	I 304.85	351.88	364.86	344.73	332.47	335.27	347.70	365.60	426.20	Money	**34**
660.17	649.50	721.78	768.72	817.76	672.18	841.90	850.60	906.50	1,002.70	1,115.00	1,157.10	1,261.80	1,513.60	1,530.50	Quasi-Money	**35**
253.46	334.65	307.64	212.13	211.35	175.47	I 73.73	170.61	192.20	108.00	205.17	135.62	111.15	128.28	60.80	Other Items (Net)	**37r**
903.31	885.17	968.45	1,007.60	1,052.43	930.74	1,121.74	1,172.49	1,241.45	1,317.38	1,417.50	1,462.37	1,609.55	1,876.10	1,956.70	Money plus Quasi-Money	**35l**
End of Period															**Other Banking Institutions**	
....	....	....	....	....	....	....	....	....	....	....	....	....	....	....	Reserves	**40**
....	....	....	....	....	....	....	....	....	....	....	....	....	....	....	Other Claims on Monetary Author.	**40c**
....	....	....	....	....	....	51,643.2	67,914.9	58,188.8	62,864.3	62,001.2	65,690.8	70,924.9	86,679.9	87,670.6	Foreign Assets	**41**
....	....	....	....	....	....	.5	.5	.5	.4	.5	.7	.7	41.2	65.7	Claims on Central Government	**42a**
....	....	....	....	....	....	889.0	1,119.0	973.0	981.4	833.8	739.5	929.5	797.4	793.5	Claims on Private Sector	**42d**
....	....	....	....	....	....	....	....	....	....	....	....	....	....	....	Other Claims on Dep.Money Banks	**42e**
....	....	....	....	....	....	....	....	....	....	....	....	....	....	....	Time and Saving Deposits	**45**
....	....	....	....	....	....	631.0	767.0	405.0	474.4	548.3	845.2	1,155.6	1,169.1	1,041.4	Liquid Liabilities	**45l**
....	....	....	....	....	....	....	....	....	....	....	....	....	....	....	Money Market Instruments	**46aa**
....	....	....	....	....	....	50,283.7	66,080.4	56,838.3	62,802.5	60,637.1	63,812.3	68,756.8	84,570.2	85,218.2	Foreign Liabilities	**46c**
....	....	....	....	....	....	810.0	714.0	275.0	464.1	982.2	998.3	648.2	505.4	472.0	Central Government Deposits	**46d**
....	....	....	....	....	....	....	....	....	....	....	....	....	....	....	Credit from Monetary Authorities	**46g**
....	....	....	....	....	....	....	....	....	....	....	....	....	....	....	Credit from Deposit Money Banks	**46h**
....	....	....	....	....	....	....	....	....	....	....	....	....	....	....	Capital Accounts	**47a**
....	....	....	....	....	....	....	....	....	....	....	....	....	....	....	Other Items (Net)	**47r**
End of Period															**Banking Survey**	
....	....	....	....	....	....	....	....	....	....	....	....	....	....	....	Foreign Assets (Net)	**51n**
....	....	....	....	....	....	....	....	....	....	....	....	....	....	....	Domestic Credit	**52**
....	....	....	....	....	....	....	....	....	....	....	....	....	....	....	Claims on Central Govt. (Net)	**52an**
....	....	....	....	....	....	....	....	....	....	....	....	....	....	....	Claims on Local Government	**52**
....	....	....	....	....	....	....	....	....	....	....	....	....	....	....	Claims on Private Sector	**52d**
....	....	....	....	....	....	....	....	....	....	....	....	....	....	....	Liquid Liabilities	**55l**
....	....	....	....	....	....	....	....	....	....	....	....	....	....	....	Money Market Instruments	**56a**
....	....	....	....	....	....	....	....	....	....	....	....	....	....	....	Capital Accounts	**57a**
....	....	....	....	....	....	....	....	....	....	....	....	....	....	....	Other Items (Net)	**57r**

Bahrain

		1970	1971	1972	1973	1974	1975	1976	1977	1978	1979	1980	1981	1982	1983	1984
Interest Rates															*Percent Per Annum*	
Money Market Rate	60b	...	...	...	...	...	...	...	...	...	...	...	...	...	...	...
Treasury Bill Rate	60c	...	...	...	...	...	...	...	...	...	...	...	...	...	...	...
Deposit Rate	60l	...	...	...	...	...	...	6.5	6.5	6.5	6.8	7.9	9.0	8.6	7.0	7.0
Lending Rate	60p	...	...	...	...	...	...	...	...	...	...	...	...	...	...	...
Prices, Production, Labor														*Index Numbers (1995=100):*		
Consumer Prices	64	23.9	25.3	26.6	30.4	37.8	43.9	I 53.8	63.3	73.3	75.0	77.9	86.7	94.4	97.2	I 97.5
Refined Petroleum Production	66ab	101.2	98.1	90.9	93.4	95.5	83.4	85.1	101.5	96.4	97.3	95.8	102.3	77.3	69.6	80.1
															Number in Thousands:	
Labor Force	67d	...	...	...	...	...	...	...	...	...	...	...	...	...	...	...
Employment	67e	...	...	...	...	...	...	...	...	...	...	...	...	...	...	...
Unemployment	67c	...	...	...	...	...	...	...	...	...	...	...	...	...	...	...
International Transactions															*Millions of Dinars*	
Exports	70	103.7	127.5	152.4	191.5	502.0	438.0	522.2	730.1	733.4	949.5	1,359.6	1,634.6	1,424.8	1,172.9	1,204.7
Imports, c.i.f.	71	117.7	148.1	165.1	204.3	445.0	470.4	659.8	802.7	792.2	945.3	1,313.0	1,550.6	1,358.9	1,226.4	1,308.3
Balance of Payments															*Millions of US Dollars:*	
Current Account, n.i.e.	78al d	...	...	...	...	...	−203.0	−360.2	−324.0	−387.7	−222.7	184.4	429.5	425.6	102.7	218.4
Goods: Exports f.o.b.	78aa d	...	...	...	...	...	1,203.0	1,518.0	1,848.9	1,891.8	2,499.1	3,433.2	4,177.1	3,695.0	3,119.4	3,204.0
Goods: Imports f.o.b.	78ab d	...	...	...	...	...	−1,090.0	−1,510.1	−1,837.0	−1,873.3	−2,094.8	−2,987.5	−3,559.3	−3,167.8	−2,935.6	−3,131.6
Trade Balance	78ac d	...	...	...	...	...	113.0	7.8	11.9	18.6	404.3	445.6	617.8	527.2	183.8	72.3
Services: Credit	78ad d	...	...	...	...	...	156.3	201.5	255.8	364.2	313.7	332.9	360.9	567.6	366.8	813.8
Services: Debit	78ae d	...	...	...	...	...	−179.3	−243.2	−296.2	−342.8	−369.7	−473.7	−610.1	−729.8	−499.5	−555.1
Balance on Goods & Services	78af d	...	...	...	...	...	90.0	−33.9	−28.6	40.0	348.3	304.8	368.6	364.9	51.1	331.1
Income: Credit	78ag d	...	...	...	...	...	45.5	66.7	76.3	106.9	112.2	314.1	517.8	489.9	415.7	335.6
Income: Debit	78ah d	...	...	...	...	...	−262.2	−309.4	−369.5	−494.0	−687.6	−522.3	−544.7	−501.3	−404.5	−447.3
Balance on Gds, Serv. & Inc.	78ai d	...	...	...	...	...	−126.7	−276.5	−321.7	−347.1	−227.2	96.6	341.8	353.5	62.2	219.4
Current Transfers, n.i.e.: Credit	78aj d	...	...	...	...	...	—	1.3	100.8	94.7	98.0	183.6	194.4	189.6	142.6	124.5
Current Transfers: Debit	78ak d	...	...	...	...	...	−76.4	−84.9	−103.1	−135.2	−93.5	−95.8	−106.6	−117.6	−102.1	−125.5
Capital Account, n.i.e.	78bc d	...	...	...	...	...	—	—	—	—	—	—	—	—	—	—
Capital Account, n.i.e.: Credit	78ba d	...	...	...	...	...	—	—	—	—	—	—	—	—	—	—
Capital Account: Debit	78bb d	...	...	...	...	...	—	—	—	—	—	—	—	—	—	—
Financial Account, n.i.e.	78bj d	...	...	...	...	...	149.7	353.6	461.3	−3.1	37.2	−238.7	−502.9	−71.0	−166.0	−35.6
Direct Investment Abroad	78bd d	...	...	...	...	...	—	—	—	—	—	—	—	—	—	—
Dir. Invest. in Rep. Econ., n.i.e.	78be d	...	...	...	...	...	—	—	—	23.0	145.2	−418.0	—	28.5	64.1	140.7
Portfolio Investment Assets	78bf d	...	...	...	...	...	—	—	—	−145.3	−83.6	−8.8	−16.8	−16.0	−47.9	—
Equity Securities	78bk d	...	...	...	...	...	—	—	—	−145.3	−83.6	−8.8	−16.8	−16.0	−47.9	—
Debt Securities	78bl d	...	...	...	...	...	—	—	—	—	—	—	—	—	—	—
Portfolio Investment Liab., n.i.e.	78bg d	...	...	...	...	...	96.1	139.0	195.1	112.0	42.2	121.5	69.9	—	—	—
Equity Securities	78bm d	...	...	...	...	...	96.1	139.0	195.1	112.0	42.2	121.5	69.9	—	—	—
Debt Securities	78bn d	...	...	...	...	...	—	—	—	—	—	—	—	—	—	—
Financial Derivatives Assets	78bw d	...	...	...	...	...	...	...	...	...	...	...	...	...	...	...
Financial Derivatives Liabilities	78bx d	...	...	...	...	...	...	...	...	...	...	...	...	...	...	...
Other Investment Assets	78bh d	...	...	...	...	...	−164.1	−98.6	−120.8	−76.7	−6.8	−250.4	−88.6	−127.1	−314.6	−17.6
Monetary Authorities	78bo d	...	...	...	...	...	—	—	—	—	—	—	—	—	—	—
General Government	78bp d	...	...	...	...	...	−8.1	−14.7	−22.0	−4.4	−8.9	−1.3	−2.4	−50.5	−8.0	−6.6
Banks	78bq d	...	...	...	...	...	−156.0	−73.8	−85.4	−52.1	18.6	−221.0	−61.7	−39.9	−297.9	91.0
Other Sectors	78br d	...	...	...	...	...	—	−10.1	−13.4	−20.1	−16.5	−28.1	−24.5	−36.7	−8.8	−101.9
Other Investment Liab., n.i.e.	78bi d	...	...	...	...	...	217.7	313.2	387.0	83.9	−59.7	317.0	−467.6	43.6	132.4	−158.8
Monetary Authorities	78bs d	...	...	...	...	...	16.4	105.7	32.4	−61.2	−89.6	92.3	−52.7	—	—	—
General Government	78bt d	...	...	...	...	...	—	25.3	8.1	77.2	26.5	308.8	−126.9	−121.3	−4.3	17.3
Banks	78bu d	...	...	...	...	...	174.2	61.9	110.2	−15.5	115.3	.5	−301.1	6.4	65.7	−119.4
Other Sectors	78bv d	...	...	...	...	...	27.1	120.3	236.3	83.4	−111.9	−84.6	13.0	158.5	71.0	−56.6
Net Errors and Omissions	78ca d	...	...	...	...	...	222.3	153.2	−70.0	372.8	308.7	396.3	662.7	−358.9	−45.2	−192.8
Overall Balance	78cb d	...	...	...	...	...	168.9	146.6	67.3	−18.0	123.2	342.0	589.3	−4.4	−108.5	−10.1
Reserves and Related Items	79da d	...	...	...	...	...	−168.9	−146.6	−67.3	18.0	−123.2	−342.0	−589.3	4.4	108.5	10.1
Reserve Assets	79db d	...	...	...	...	...	−168.9	−146.6	−67.3	18.0	−123.2	−342.0	−589.3	4.4	108.5	10.1
Use of Fund Credit and Loans	79dc d	...	...	...	...	...	—	—	—	—	—	—	—	—	—	—
Exceptional Financing	79de d	...	...	...	...	...	—	—	—	—	—	—	—	—	—	—
International Investment Position															*Millions of US Dollars*	
Assets	79aa d	...	...	...	...	...	...	...	...	...	...	...	...	...	...	...
Direct Investment Abroad	79ab d	...	...	...	...	...	...	...	...	...	...	...	...	...	...	...
Portfolio Investment	79ac d	...	...	...	...	...	...	...	...	...	...	...	...	...	...	...
Equity Securities	79ad d	...	...	...	...	...	...	...	...	...	...	...	...	...	...	...
Debt Securities	79ae d	...	...	...	...	...	...	...	...	...	...	...	...	...	...	...
Financial Derivatives	79al d	...	...	...	...	...	...	...	...	...	...	...	...	...	...	...
Other Investment	79af d	...	...	...	...	...	...	...	...	...	...	...	...	...	...	...
Monetary Authorities	79ag d	...	...	...	...	...	...	...	...	...	...	...	...	...	...	...
General Government	79ah d	...	...	...	...	...	...	...	...	...	...	...	...	...	...	...
Banks	79ai d	...	...	...	...	...	...	...	...	...	...	...	...	...	...	...
Other Sectors	79aj d	...	...	...	...	...	...	...	...	...	...	...	...	...	...	...
Reserve Assets	79ak d	...	...	...	...	...	...	...	...	...	...	...	...	...	...	...
Liabilities	79la d	...	...	...	...	...	...	...	...	...	...	...	...	...	...	...
Dir. Invest. in Rep. Economy	79lb d	...	...	...	...	...	...	...	...	...	...	...	...	...	...	...
Portfolio Investment	79lc d	...	...	...	...	...	...	...	...	...	...	...	...	...	...	...
Equity Securities	79ld d	...	...	...	...	...	...	...	...	...	...	...	...	...	...	...
Debt Securities	79le d	...	...	...	...	...	...	...	...	...	...	...	...	...	...	...
Financial Derivatives	79ll d	...	...	...	...	...	...	...	...	...	...	...	...	...	...	...
Other Investment	79lf d	...	...	...	...	...	...	...	...	...	...	...	...	...	...	...
Monetary Authorities	79lg d	...	...	...	...	...	...	...	...	...	...	...	...	...	...	...
General Government	79lh d	...	...	...	...	...	...	...	...	...	...	...	...	...	...	...
Banks	79li d	...	...	...	...	...	...	...	...	...	...	...	...	...	...	...
Other Sectors	79lj d	...	...	...	...	...	...	...	...	...	...	...	...	...	...	...

Percent Per Annum

Interest Rates

	1985	1986	1987	1988	1989	1990	1991	1992	1993	1994	1995	1996	1997	1998	1999	
Money Market Rate	....	7.2	7.1	8.0	9.2	8.5	6.3	4.0	3.5	5.2	6.2	5.7	....	5.7	5.6	60b
Treasury Bill Rate			6.4	7.4	9.1	....	5.9	3.8	3.3	4.8	6.1	5.5	5.7	5.5	5.5	60c
Deposit Rate	6.7	5.6	5.0	5.5	7.3	7.5	....	I3.6	3.0	4.0	5.7	5.2	5.3	4.7	4.8	60l
Lending Rate	....	9.0	7.5	7.8	I8.5	8.5	9.5	11.9	11.0	10.8	11.8	12.5	12.3	11.9	11.9	60p

Period Averages

Prices, Production, Labor

	1985	1986	1987	1988	1989	1990	1991	1992	1993	1994	1995	1996	1997	1998	1999	
Consumer Prices	94.9	92.8	91.1	91.4	92.8	93.6	94.3	94.2	96.6	97.4	100.0	99.5	102.0	101.6	....	64
Refined Petroleum Production	74.0	97.8	96.9	96.5	97.0	99.3	102.1	102.6	98.1	98.6	100.0	104.0	100.1	99.0	104.8	66ab

Period Averages

	1985	1986	1987	1988	1989	1990	1991	1992	1993	1994	1995	1996	1997	1998	1999	
Labor Force							226									67d
Employment	112	....	86	86	92	92	93	103	110	116	....	....	124	....	....	67e
Unemployment	6	7	4	4	3	3	3	3	3	4	4	5	....	6	4	67c

International Transactions

Millions of Dinars

	1985	1986	1987	1988	1989	1990	1991	1992	1993	1994	1995	1996	1997	1998	1999	
Exports	1,089.2	827.0	913.5	906.7	1,064.5	1,414.0	1,320.0	1,302.6	1,400.0	1,359.9	1,546.4	1,767.1	1,648.2	1,229.6	1,537.2	70
Imports, c.i.f.	1,168.1	904.3	1,020.3	975.1	1,178.2	1,395.6	1,547.3	1,602.9	1,450.6	1,409.2	1,397.1	1,606.6	1,513.6	1,340.9	1,349.2	71

Balance of Payments

Minus Sign Indicates Debit

	1985	1986	1987	1988	1989	1990	1991	1992	1993	1994	1995	1996	1997	1998	1999	
Current Account, n.i.e.	38.8	-68.9	-201.3	192.0	-193.1	69.7	-602.7	-826.6	-339.4	-255.6	237.2	260.6	-31.1	-777.9	-420.5	78ald
Goods: Exports f.o.b.	2,896.8	2,199.5	2,429.5	2,411.4	2,831.1	3,760.6	3,513.3	3,465.4	3,723.4	3,617.0	4,114.4	4,702.1	4,383.0	3,270.2	4,088.3	78aa d
Goods: Imports f.o.b.	-2,796.0	-2,164.6	-2,442.3	-2,334.0	-2,820.2	-3,524.2	-3,880.6	-3,992.3	-3,616.2	-3,497.3	-3,488.3	-4,037.0	-3,778.2	-3,298.7	-3,369.1	78ab d
Trade Balance	100.8	34.8	-12.8	77.4	10.9	236.4	-367.3	-526.9	107.2	119.7	626.1	665.2	604.8	-28.5	719.1	78ac d
Services: Credit	911.4	764.4	863.6	901.6	809.6	358.5	411.2	542.8	651.9	818.6	683.2	666.2	637.2	724.7	763.6	78ad d
Services: Debit	-488.6	-327.1	-525.0	-529.3	-556.4	-474.5	-534.3	-604.0	-581.9	-621.8	-634.0	-612.8	-634.8	-651.9	-634.6	78ae d
Balance on Goods & Services	523.7	472.1	325.8	449.7	264.1	120.5	-490.4	-588.0	177.1	316.5	675.3	718.6	607.2	44.4	848.1	78af d
Income: Credit	322.6	277.9	282.2	263.0	377.7	5,496.8	3,517.6	2,525.3	2,283.8	3,112.5	4,087.0	3,815.2	4,270.7	4,763.8	4,988.3	78ag d
Income: Debit	-692.8	-675.0	-678.5	-694.1	-738.0	-5,275.3	-3,326.3	-2,493.1	-2,477.7	-3,355.1	-4,146.0	-3,840.2	-4,506.9	-4,926.3	-5,437.5	78ah d
Balance on Gds, Serv. & Inc.	153.5	75.0	-70.5	18.6	-96.3	342.0	-299.2	-555.9	-16.8	73.9	616.2	693.6	371.0	-118.1	398.9	78ai d
Current Transfers, n.i.e.: Credit	120.2	120.7	113.3	368.1	102.1	59.8	65.7	64.9	73.1	101.1	120.7	126.3	232.7	65.2	36.7	78aj d
Current Transfers: Debit	-234.8	-264.6	-244.1	-194.7	-198.9	-332.2	-369.1	-335.6	-395.7	-430.6	-499.7	-559.3	-634.8	-725.0	-856.1	78ak d
Capital Account, n.i.e.	—	—	—	—	—	457.4	101.1	101.1	202.1	319.1	156.9	50.0	125.0	100.0	100.0	78bc d
Capital Account, n.i.e.: Credit	—	—	—	—	—	457.4	101.1	101.1	202.1	319.1	156.9	50.0	125.0	100.0	100.0	78ba d
Capital Account: Debit	—	—	—	—	—					....	....	....	....	....	....	78bb d
Financial Account, n.i.e.	-476.1	-99.7	-55.6	-214.4	-264.6	1,156.6	65.4	397.3	593.9	1,301.1	-1,726.6	-510.4	15.4	22.6	199.5	78bj d
Direct Investment Abroad	—	—	—	—	—	-25.0	-50.0	-52.9	-38.8	-198.7	16.0	-305.1	-47.6	-180.9	-163.3	78bd d
Dir. Invest. in Rep. Econ., n.i.e.	101.3	-31.9	-35.9	222.1	180.9	-182.7	619.4	868.6	-275.0	208.2	430.6	2,048.1	329.3	179.5	447.6	78be d
Portfolio Investment Assets	-28.5	-26.1	-1.9	—	1.1	697.6	-1,063.0	-1,398.1	-1,335.4	-454.0	-113.3	-779.8	-1,150.8	-1,206.6	-2,052.7	78bf d
Equity Securities	-28.5	-26.1	-1.9	—	1.1	....	....	....	....	....	....	....	....	....	....	78bk d
Debt Securities	—	—	—	—	—	697.6	-1,063.0	-1,398.1	-1,335.4	-454.0	-113.3	-779.8	-1,150.8	-1,206.6	-2,052.7	78bl d
Portfolio Investment Liab., n.i.e.	—	—	—	—	—	....	....	....	....	....	....	....	....	357.7	-11.7	78bg d
Equity Securities	—	—	—	—	—	....	....	....	....	....	....	....	....	....	....	78bm d
Debt Securities	—	—	—	—	—	....	....	....	....	....	....	....	....	357.7	-11.7	78bn d
Financial Derivatives Assets																78bw d
Financial Derivatives Liabilities																78bx d
Other Investment Assets	-410.6	-298.9	-7.2	-437.0	-916.8	10,768.6	6,531.4	-14,709.8	10,672.3	-4,527.1	1,124.5	-2,579.8	-4,342.0	-14,677.9	967.0	78bh d
Monetary Authorities																78bo d
General Government	-9.0	-5.3	-3.7	-7.4	-79.8	-13.3	-16.0	-5.3	-5.3	-8.0	-5.3	-8.0	-8.0	-5.1	-7.7	78bp d
Banks	-401.6	-286.7	.8	-429.5	-837.0	10,781.9	6,547.3	-14,704.5	10,677.7	-4,519.1	1,129.8	-2,571.8	-4,334.0	-14,672.9	974.7	78bq d
Other Sectors	—	-6.9	-4.3	....	....	....	....	....	....	....	....	....	....	....	....	78br d
Other Investment Liab., n.i.e.	-138.3	257.2	-10.6	.5	470.2	-10,101.9	-5,972.3	15,689.6	-8,429.3	6,272.6	-3,184.3	1,106.1	5,226.6	15,550.8	1,012.5	78bi d
Monetary Authorities	—	—	12.2	—	17.3	....	....	....	....	....	....	....	....	....	....	78bs d
General Government	-59.3	-16.2	-17.6	-10.1	-7.4	-6.4	-10.9	.8	4.5	4.0	11.2	1.3	52.4	44.1	54.8	78bt d
Banks	60.4	63.8	-13.0	35.9	441.8	-10,025.5	-6,826.6	15,009.3	-8,660.1	6,268.4	-2,901.9	1,056.4	5,175.5	15,231.7	1,006.4	78bu d
Other Sectors	-139.4	209.6	7.7	-25.3	18.6	-69.9	865.2	679.5	226.3	.3	-293.6	48.4	-1.3	275.0	-48.7	78bv d
Net Errors and Omissions	794.7	-7.1	-85.8	114.9	269.3	-887.3	-87.3	238.1	-569.2	-1,412.2	1,501.4	193.3	-6.5	638.7	146.3	78ca d
Overall Balance	357.4	-175.7	-342.7	92.5	-188.5	796.0	-523.5	-90.1	-112.5	-47.5	168.9	-6.4	102.8	-16.6	25.3	78cb d
Reserves and Related Items	-357.4	175.7	342.7	-92.5	188.5	-796.0	523.5	90.1	112.5	47.5	-168.9	6.4	-102.8	16.6	-25.3	79da d
Reserve Assets	-357.4	175.7	342.7	-92.5	188.5	-796.0	523.5	90.1	112.5	47.5	-168.9	6.4	-102.8	16.6	-25.3	79db d
Use of Fund Credit and Loans	—	—	—	—	—	—	—	—	....	....	....	....	....	....	....	79dc d
Exceptional Financing	....	....	....	....	....	—	—	—	....	....	....	....	....	....	....	79de d

International Investment Position

Millions of US Dollars

	1985	1986	1987	1988	1989	1990	1991	1992	1993	1994	1995	1996	1997	1998	1999	
Assets	....	....	....	....	71,586.5	60,934.0	54,976.7	71,035.4	61,614.0	66,735.3	65,872.8	69,518.5	75,156.1	91,199.1	92,459.2	79aa d
Direct Investment Abroad	....	....	....	....	694.4	719.4	769.4	822.3	861.2	1,059.8	1,043.9	1,348.7	1,396.3	1,577.1	1,740.4	79ab d
Portfolio Investment	....	....	....	....	3,109.6	2,413.1	3,476.1	4,870.3	6,201.1	6,647.6	6,760.6	7,538.8	8,696.8	9,899.5	11,947.6	79ac d
Equity Securities																79ad d
Debt Securities	....	....	....	....	3,109.6	2,413.1	3,476.1	4,870.3	6,201.1	6,647.6	6,760.6	7,538.8	8,696.8	9,899.5	11,947.6	79ae d
Financial Derivatives																79al d
Other Investment	....	....	....	....	66,701.7	55,920.0	49,372.5	64,076.9	53,398.6	57,917.7	56,787.9	59,359.7	63,694.0	78,366.6	77,392.2	79af d
Monetary Authorities																79ag d
General Government																79ah d
Banks	....	....	....	....	66,701.7	55,920.0	49,372.5	....	....	....	....	....	....	....	....	79ai d
Other Sectors																79aj d
Reserve Assets	....	....	....	....	1,080.7	1,881.6	1,358.6	1,265.8	1,153.2	1,110.1	1,280.4	1,271.3	1,369.0	1,355.9	1,379.0	79ak d
Liabilities	....	....	....	....	67,376.7	57,317.3	51,100.0	66,979.9	58,049.1	64,529.7	62,081.8	65,187.7	70,744.6	86,515.5	88,016.3	79la d
Dir. Invest. in Rep. Economy	....	....	....	....	734.6	551.6	1,171.0	2,039.6	1,764.6	1,972.9	2,403.5	4,451.6	4,780.8	4,960.4	5,408.0	79lb d
Portfolio Investment	—	—	—	—	—	....	....	....	....	....	....	....	....	357.7	346.0	79lc d
Equity Securities																79ld d
Debt Securities	—	—	—	—	—	....	....	....	....	....	....	....	....	357.7	346.0	79le d
Financial Derivatives																79ll d
Other Investment	....	....	....	....	66,642.1	56,765.7	49,928.9	64,940.0	56,284.5	62,556.8	59,678.4	60,736.3	65,963.7	81,197.5	82,262.4	79lf d
Monetary Authorities																79lg d
General Government																79lh d
Banks	....	....	....	....	66,642.1	56,616.5	49,789.8	....	....	....	....	....	....	....	....	79li d
Other Sectors																79lj d

Bahrain

	1970	1971	1972	1973	1974	1975	1976	1977	1978	1979	1980	1981	1982	1983	1984
Government Finance														*Millions of Dinars:*	
Deficit (-) or Surplus 80	...	...	...	...	39.6	5.5	−36.2	−12.9	−30.6	22.1	68.0	110.8	32.1	−96.2	−23.0
Revenue 81	...	...	...	...	115.3	129.0	186.4	227.4	247.5	277.9	388.9	478.3	497.8	443.5	485.4
Grants Received 81z	...	...	...	...	2.2	—	.3	27.7	26.4	26.4	56.8	58.3	56.4	47.0	37.6
Expenditure 82	...	...	...	...	67.0	112.3	190.9	242.5	285.3	254.5	317.2	380.2	473.7	535.1	538.6
Lending Minus Repayments 83	...	...	...	...	10.9	11.2	32.0	25.5	19.2	27.7	60.5	45.6	48.4	51.6	7.4
Financing															
Total Financing 80h	...	...	...	...	−39.6	−5.5	36.2	12.9	30.6	−22.1	−68.0	−110.8	−32.1	96.2	23.0
Domestic 84a	...	...	...	...	−45.2	−7.9	26.2	10.4	−.7	14.2	3.5	5.6	21.4	52.0	9.5
Foreign 85a	...	...	...	...	5.6	2.4	10.0	2.5	31.3	−36.3	−71.5	−116.4	−53.5	44.2	13.5
Debt: Domestic 88a										20.0	20.0	20.0	20.0	30.0	30.0
Foreign 89a	...	...	...	4.2	9.7	12.1	22.1	24.6	54.5	64.6	77.1	81.3	91.0	87.3	93.8
National Accounts														*Millions of Dinars*	
Exports of Goods & Services 90c	...	...	...	...	...	531.5	674.0	817.0	826.7	1,050.7	1,421.1	1,714.0	1,621.0	1,344.2	1,455.0
Government Consumption 91f						64.6	85.2	111.1	132.3	152.1	150.9	188.6	233.3	254.5	302.2
Gross Fixed Capital Formation 93e						129.1	249.3	349.6	359.5	329.8	356.9	380.5	451.9	536.6	604.1
Increase/Decrease(-) in Stocks 93i						26	18	9	60	92	164	160	57	118	38
Private Consumption 96f						170.8	262.7	336.7	390.6	404.0	370.3	427.7	472.9	481.6	465.6
Imports of Goods & Services 98c						−495.7	−695.4	−853.7	−861.0	−1,010.6	−1,304.8	−1,567.3	−1,465.5	−1,294.4	−1,381.3
Gross Domestic Product (GDP) 99b						425.9	593.5	770.0	907.6	1,018.2	1,158.1	1,303.9	1,370.8	1,440.4	1,483.5
Net Factor Inc/Pmts(-) Abroad 98.n	...	...	...	...	...	...	...	...	...	...	−46.6	−15.0	−38.0	−69.3	−57.5
Gross National Income (GNI) 99a	...	...	...	...	...	...	...	...	...	...	1,111.5	1,288.9	1,332.8	1,370.9	1,426.0
Net National Income 99e	...	...	...	...	...	...	...	...	...	...	991.0	1,153.4	1,183.8	1,203.6	1,211.1
GDP Volume 1977 prices .... 99b. *p*	...	...	...	...	...	543.1	672.0	770.8	833.4	824.1	878.2	916.8	971.8	1,049.7	....
GDP Volume 1989 Prices .... 99b. *p*	...	...	...	...	...	...	...	...	...	...	...	...	...	1,182.3	1,227.3
GDP Volume (1995=100) .... 99bv *p*	...	...	...	...	...	29.0	35.9	41.2	44.6	44.1	46.9	49.0	51.9	56.1	58.2
GDP Deflator (1995=100) .... 99bi *p*	...	...	...	...	...	66.7	75.1	85.0	92.6	105.1	112.2	121.0	120.0	116.7	115.8
															Millions:
Population 99z	.22	.22	.23	.24	.26	.26	.26	.30	.32	.33	.34	.35	.37	.39	.39

Year Ending December 31

Government Finance

	1985	1986	1987	1988	1989	1990	1991	1992	1993	1994	1995	1996	1997	1998	1999		
Deficit (-) or Surplus	13.7	−51.9	−122.2	49.1	−115.8	−103.1	−67.6	−115.2	−1.9	−58.3	−126.6	−55.0	−125.3	−116.5	....		80
Revenue	503.8	422.2	376.4	360.6	403.4	468.8	472.6	464.8	544.8	476.3	526.6	615.5	633.1	516.6	....		81
Grants Received	37.6	37.6	37.6	37.6	37.6	26.3	37.6	37.6	18.8	37.6	37.6	18.8	46.9	37.6	....		81z
Expenditure	508.5	495.1	418.0	445.5	467.5	505.0	502.8	548.8	593.4	623.4	594.1	581.3	620.0	644.6	....		82
Lending Minus Repayments	19.2	16.6	118.2	−96.4	89.3	93.2	75.0	68.8	−27.9	−51.2	96.7	108.0	185.3	26.1	....		83
Financing																	
Total Financing	−13.7	51.9	122.2	−49.1	115.8	103.1	67.6	115.2	1.9	58.3	126.6	55.0	125.3	116.5	....		80h
Domestic	37.5	−3.6	−73.4	80.3	40.3	−35.9	71.7	114.2	−.4	56.6	122.5	54.5	125.1	99.9	....		84a
Foreign	−51.2	55.5	195.6	−129.4	75.5	139.0	−4.1	1.0	2.3	1.7	4.1	.5	.2	16.6	....		85a
Debt: Domestic	30.0	74.1	102.5	193.8	215.4	84.9	233.5	328.5	323.6	318.8	314.0	297.0	319.5	404.5	....		88a
Foreign	71.1	65.2	59.9	60.7	58.1	53.9	50.8	52.0	54.7	55.5	59.6	65.8	85.4	87.6	....		89a

Millions of Dinars

National Accounts

	1985	1986	1987	1988	1989	1990	1991	1992	1993	1994	1995	1996	1997	1998	1999		
Exports of Goods & Services	1,397.4	1,132.9	1,305.6	1,327.2	1,433.0	1,837.8	1,662.4	1,698.7	1,838.7	1,904.7	2,027.4	2,243.9	2,145.5	1,818.9	....		90c
Government Consumption	312.8	312.4	310.1	339.2	356.6	385.1	406.0	426.2	435.5	440.0	458.5	464.3	465.1	482.8	....		91f
Gross Fixed Capital Formation	463.6	370.1	287.3	269.1	287.8	301.0	352.5	394.7	465.4	430.5	381.3	284.1	285.9	326.2	....		93e
Increase/Decrease(-) in Stocks	26	−65	37	12	70	−40	206	198	−55	−17	−47	101	93	84	....		93i
Private Consumption	407.0	370.3	449.6	523.3	578.3	610.8	923.1	957.6	993.5	1,030.6	1,069.2	1,109.2	1,208.3	1,193.8	....		96f
Imports of Goods & Services	−1,233.6	−973.4	−1,114.7	−1,078.8	−1,273.0	−1,504.6	−1,814.1	−1,888.4	−1,723.2	−1,695.1	−1,689.9	−1,908.7	−1,810.3	−1,580.1	....		98c
Gross Domestic Product (GDP)	1,373.1	1,147.7	1,275.4	1,392.1	1,452.7	1,590.4	1,735.7	1,786.3	1,955.4	2,093.3	2,199.4	2,294.3	2,387.3	2,325.2	....		99b
Net Factor Inc/Pmts(-) Abroad	−109.7	−117.9	−121.4	−197.8	−196.8	−258.5	−305.3	−244.0	−239.6	−314.9	−224.6	−259.7	−349.8	−237.4	....		98.n
Gross National Income (GNI)	1,263.4	1,029.8	1,154.0	1,194.3	1,255.9	1,331.9	1,430.4	1,542.3	1,715.8	1,778.4	1,974.8	2,034.6	2,037.5	2,087.8	....		99a
Net National Income	1,057.3	821.2	939.8	967.1	1,020.8	1,083.0	1,168.6	1,279.4	1,408.3	1,451.8	1,642.2	1,705.9	1,705.1	1,737.4	....		99e
GDP Volume 1977 prices	.....	.....	.....	.....	.....	.....	.....	.....	.....	.....	.....	.....	.....	.....	....		99b.p
GDP Volume 1989 Prices	1,193.5	1,207.5	1,333.0	1,447.5	1,452.7	1,517.2	1,687.8	1,800.6	2,032.5	2,027.4	2,107.0	2,193.5	2,261.5	2,369.7	....		99b.p
GDP Volume (1995=100)	56.6	57.3	63.3	68.7	68.9	72.0	80.1	85.5	96.5	96.2	100.0	104.1	107.3	112.5	....		99bv.p
GDP Deflator (1995=100)	110.2	91.1	91.7	92.1	95.8	100.4	98.5	95.0	92.2	98.9	100.0	100.2	101.1	94.0	....		99bi.p

Midyear Estimates

	1985	1986	1987	1988	1989	1990	1991	1992	1993	1994	1995	1996	1997	1998	1999		
Population	.41	.44	.46	.47	.49	.48	.50	.52	.54	.56	.58	.60	.62	.64	.67		99z

(See notes in the back of the book.)

Bangladesh

		1970	1971	1972	1973	1974	1975	1976	1977	1978	1979	1980	1981	1982	1983	1984
Exchange Rates																*Taka per SDR:*
Official Rate.........aa=	wa	....	8.068	8.770	9.849	9.888	17.356	17.373	17.486	19.456	20.607	20.726	23.101	26.556	26.174	25.485
															Taka per US Dollar:	
Official Rate.........ae=	we	....	7.431	8.078	8.164	8.077	14.826	14.953	14.396	14.934	15.643	16.251	19.847	24.074	25.000	26.000
Official Rate.........rf=	wf	....	7.761	7.594	7.742	8.113	12.019	15.347	15.375	15.016	15.552	15.454	17.987	22.118	24.615	25.354
Fund Position																*Millions of SDRs:*
Quota.............................2f. *s*		—	—	125.0	125.0	125.0	125.0	125.0	125.0	152.0	152.0	228.0	228.0	228.0	287.5	287.5
SDRs..............................1b. *s*		....	....	—	—	—	15.4	16.1	3.9	.1	9.2	.4	.1	.8	12.9	.3
Reserve Position in the Fund...1c. *s*		....	....	2.0	1.2	—	—	—	—	—	—	—	—	7.5	22.4	22.4
Total Fund Cred.&Loans Outstg...2tl		....	....	62.5	62.5	133.3	171.6	235.8	207.8	229.4	262.3	332.6	398.9	496.2	540.0	471.6
International Liquidity													*Millions of US Dollars Unless Otherwise Indicated:*			
Total Reserves minus Gold..........1l. *d*		....	....	270.5	143.2	138.2	148.3	288.9	232.7	315.2	386.3	299.6	138.4	182.6	524.1	389.9
SDRs.........................1b. *d*		....	....	—	—	—	18.1	18.7	4.8	.1	12.1	.4	.1	.8	13.5	.3
Reserve Position in the Fund...........1c. *d*		....	....	2.2	1.5	—	—	—	—	—	—	—	—	8.3	23.5	22.0
Foreign Exchange..................1d. *d*		....	....	268.3	141.7	138.2	130.2	270.2	227.9	315.1	374.2	299.2	138.3	173.5	487.1	367.7
Gold (Million Fine Troy Ounces)...1ad		....	....	....	....	....	....	....	.054	.027	.054	.054	.054	.057	.057	.059
Gold (National Valuation)..............1an *d*		....	....	—	—	—	—	—	2.3	1.2	15.7	21.5	16.9	24.5	17.5	15.8
Monetary Authorities: Other Liab...4.. *d*		....	....	....	.1	—	—	21.2	42.2	35.5	80.6	143.1	179.0	197.6	213.6	130.0
Deposit Money Banks: Assets......7a. *d*		....	....	....	....	118.2	121.4	104.2	111.0	127.7	176.1	272.2	228.3	153.0	188.0	221.0
Liabilities...7b. *d*		....	....	....	....	25.2	21.8	26.4	61.2	67.7	77.9	171.0	115.4	94.7	54.0	96.0
Monetary Authorities																*Millions of Taka:*
Foreign Assets........................11		....	....	....	1,174	1,115	2,084	4,318	3,385	4,728	6,332	5,252	3,052	⅃5,710	16,444	13,349
Claims on Central Government.....12a		....	....	3,353	4,240	5,200	5,544	5,696	5,946	5,320	8,782	13,594	10,350	9,833	9,384	
Claims on Nonfin.Pub.Enterprises...12c		....	....	—	160	160	160	160	160	511	460	500	800	750	580	
Claims on Deposit Money Banks......12e		....	....	....	635	1,799	2,220	832	2,625	3,752	5,705	8,554	9,841	15,074	10,596	18,808
Claims on Other Financial Insts......12f		....	....	....	270	223	156	169	172	305	924	1,675	2,138	2,695	3,605	5,644
Reserve Money....................14		....	....	....	4,095	5,157	5,033	5,158	6,679	8,541	9,914	11,767	12,912	⅃14,275	19,140	25,870
of which: Currency Outside DMBs...14a		....	....	....	3,212	4,103	3,618	3,817	4,902	6,329	7,114	8,267	9,143	9,744	13,444	17,250
Liabs. of Central Bank: Securities......16ac																
Foreign Liabilities...................16c		....	....	....	617	1,318	2,979	4,414	4,240	4,994	6,665	9,218	12,769	19,977	20,872	17,721
Central Government Deposits.......16d		....	....	....	—	—	—	—	—	—	—	10	5	⅃13	5	411
Central Govt. Lending Funds......16f		....	....	....	....	....	....	....	....	....	....	....	....	12	907	1,806
Capital Accounts.....................17a		....	....	....	103	133	183	223	263	303	682	1,245	1,862	2,172	2,487	2,867
Other Items (Net)....................17r		....	....	....	617	928	1,626	1,227	856	1,053	1,531	2,484	1,576	⅃−1,819	−2,182	−910
Deposit Money Banks																*Millions of Taka:*
Reserves.............................20		....	....	....	....	1,145	1,276	1,378	1,736	2,051	2,645	3,378	3,798	4,227	5,642	7,867
Other Claims on Monetary Author......20c		....	....	....	....	....	....	....	....	....	....	....	....	....	....	
Foreign Assets.......................21		....	....	....	....	955	1,799	1,558	1,077	1,363	1,919	3,498	4,106	5,702	5,939	6,179
Claims on Central Government.......22a		....	....	....	....	2,401	1,942	2,462	3,185	2,961	4,153	5,423	4,616	5,054	10,362	13,004
Claims on Nonfin.Pub.Enterprises...22c		....	....	....	....	5,194	6,502	6,623	7,622	10,013	12,015	14,774	17,179	22,978	22,567	23,160
Claims on Private Sector..............22d		....	....	....	....	2,603	3,309	4,455	7,450	9,105	12,650	16,205	22,423	26,566	37,799	59,386
Claims on Other Financial Insts......22f		....	....	....	....	690	137	270	318	645	794	1,225	1,243	⅃1,336	1,761	1,823
Demand Deposits....................24		....	....	....	....	4,284	4,662	5,399	6,764	8,306	11,240	11,903	13,570	⅃13,589	18,191	25,016
Time Deposits.......................25		....	....	....	....	5,603	6,458	8,255	9,943	12,667	15,049	20,213	24,443	⅃29,442	42,262	58,315
Foreign Liabilities...................26c		....	....	....	....	155	128	181	564	540	612	1,582	2,291	1,346	2,306	
Central Government Deposits.......26d		....	....	....	....	....	....	....	....	....	....	....	....	1,682	2,634	3,055
Central Govt. Lending Funds......26f		....	....	....	....	480	622	411	432	571	701	1,292	1,741	2,284	3,393	4,383
Credit from Monetary Authorities.....26g		....	....	....	....	1,769	1,962	845	2,446	3,385	5,707	8,995	9,971	15,012	9,985	16,432
Capital Accounts.....................27a		....	....	....	....	431	423	793	920	959	1,039	1,132	1,255	1,523	2,641	3,223
Other Items (Net)....................27r		....	....	....	....	266	712	863	319	−290	−172	−614	93	52	3,619	−1,313
Monetary Survey																*Millions of Taka:*
Foreign Assets (Net)................31n		....	....	....	....	597	776	1,281	−343	557	975	−2,050	−7,902	⅃−10,844	165	−500
Domestic Credit.....................32		....	....	....	....	15,511	17,407	19,683	24,602	29,136	36,365	48,533	61,686	⅃68,083	84,038	109,515
Claims on Central Govt. (Net)......32an		....	....	....	....	6,641	7,142	8,006	8,881	8,907	9,473	14,195	18,205	⅃13,709	17,556	18,922
Claims on Nonfin.Pub.Enterprises...32c		....	....	....	....	5,354	6,662	6,783	7,782	10,173	12,525	15,234	17,679	23,778	23,317	23,740
Claims on Private Sector..............32d		....	....	....	....	2,603	3,309	4,455	7,450	9,105	12,650	16,205	22,423	26,566	37,799	59,386
Claims on Other Financial Insts......32f		....	....	....	....	913	293	439	490	950	1,718	2,899	3,380	⅃4,031	5,366	7,467
Money..............................34		....	....	....	....	8,391	8,283	9,216	11,667	14,636	18,356	20,171	22,716	⅃23,336	31,636	42,269
Quasi-Money.......................35		....	....	....	....	5,603	6,458	8,255	9,943	12,667	15,049	20,213	24,443	⅃29,442	42,262	58,315
Central Govt. Lending Funds......36f		....	....	....	....	480	622	411	432	571	701	1,292	1,741	⅃2,296	4,300	6,189
Capital Accounts.....................37a		....	....	....	....	563	605	1,016	1,183	1,262	1,721	2,376	3,118	3,695	5,128	6,090
Other Items (Net)....................37r		....	....	....	....	1,071	2,215	2,066	1,035	558	1,514	2,431	1,768	−1,530	877	−3,848
Money plus Quasi-Money..........35l		....	....	....	....	13,994	14,741	17,471	21,610	27,302	33,405	40,384	47,159	⅃52,778	73,898	100,584
Interest Rates																*Percent Per Annum*
Discount Rate *(End of Period)*......60		....	5.00	5.00	5.00	8.00	8.00	8.00	8.00	8.00	8.00	10.50	10.50	10.50	10.50	10.50
Deposit Rate.........................60l		....	....	....	....	....	....	6.75	7.00	7.00	7.00	8.25	12.00	12.00	12.00	12.00
Lending Rate........................60p		....	....	....	....	....	....	11.00	11.00	11.00	11.00	11.33	12.00	12.00	12.00	12.00
Prices and Production																*Index Numbers (1995=100):*
Consumer Prices....................64		....	....	....	....	....	....	....	....	....	....	....	....	....	....	....
Industrial Production................66		....	....	....	....	51.4	54.6	52.8	52.7	49.9	⅃48.9	51.3	55.5	52.2	53.0	55.7

	1985	1986	1987	1988	1989	1990	1991	1992	1993	1994	1995	1996	1997	1998	1999		
Exchange Rates																	
End of Period																	
	34.051	37.674	44.262	43.426	42.408	50.917	55.186	53.625	54.736	58.759	60.574	61.041	61.323	68.289	69.998	Official Rate...aa= ...wa	
End of Period (we) Period Average (wf)																	
	31.000	30.800	31.200	32.270	32.270	35.790	38.580	39.000	39.850	40.250	40.750	42.450	45.450	48.500	51.000	Official Rate...ae= ...we	
	I27.995	30.407	30.950	31.733	32.270	34.569	36.596	38.951	39.567	40.212	40.278	41.794	43.892	46.906	49.085	Official Rate...rf= ...wf	
Fund Position																	
End of Period																	
	287.5	287.5	287.5	287.5	287.5	287.5	287.5	392.5	392.5	392.5	392.5	392.5	392.5	392.5	533.3	Quota	2f.s
	11.9	8.4	37.6	40.1	2.3	18.1	49.9	30.1	16.6	24.6	107.3	76.2	21.6	9.1	.7	SDRs	1b.s
	22.4	22.4	22.4	22.4	22.4	—	—	—	.1	.1	.1	.1	.1	.2	.2	Reserve Position in the Fund	1c.s
	473.3	440.5	592.7	623.9	546.8	439.7	523.2	547.7	511.8	473.4	433.1	374.2	287.9	308.4	237.6	Total Fund Cred.&Loans Outstg.	2tl
International Liquidity																	
End of Period																	
	336.5	409.1	843.1	1,046.1	501.5	628.7	1,278.2	1,824.6	2,410.8	3,138.7	2,339.7	1,834.6	1,581.5	1,905.4	1,603.6	Total Reserves minus Gold	1l.d
	13.1	10.3	53.3	54.0	3.0	25.8	71.3	41.4	22.8	36.0	159.5	109.6	29.2	12.9	.9	SDRs	1b.d
	24.6	27.4	31.8	30.1	29.4	—	—	—	.1	.1	.1	.2	.1	.2	.3	Reserve Position in the Fund	1c.d
	298.8	371.4	758.1	961.9	469.0	602.9	1,206.9	1,783.2	2,387.9	3,102.6	2,180.1	1,724.9	1,552.1	1,892.3	1,602.5	Foreign Exchange	1d.d
	.060	.066	.068	.074	.076	.080	.084	.087	.092	.094	.094	.094	.101	.105	.106	Gold (Million Fine Troy Ounces)	1ad
	12.9	16.8	22.8	24.0	21.4	20.8	21.5	22.7	25.9	27.2	26.9	28.0	25.3	22.3	19.6	Gold (National Valuation)	1and
	95.3	74.6	120.7	127.8	83.9	68.4	92.6	38.6	100.2	124.0	171.8	160.9	127.5	257.4	137.6	Monetary Authorities: Other Liab.	4..d
	289.0	273.0	275.8	306.6	391.3	431.7	436.7	356.5	402.5	703.4	730.6	771.6	827.9	794.9	917.0	Deposit Money Banks: Assets	7a.d
	127.0	119.0	160.7	211.3	212.7	237.6	269.0	242.0	241.7	283.7	327.0	399.7	510.7	437.3	463.7	Liabilities	7b.d
Monetary Authorities																	
End of Period																	
	13,360	14,414	29,137	37,415	19,717	27,580	54,175	76,772	101,190	130,167	97,949	80,687	73,398	93,361	82,779	Foreign Assets	11
	10,658	4,454	13,759	9,999	15,384	16,162	12,469	10,426	5,366	5,697	22,783	38,576	36,371	47,968	72,915	Claims on Central Government	12a
	I580	580	1,046	1,079	874	821	825	649	597	594	591	590	590	2,140	2,140	Claims on Nonfin.Pub.Enterprises	12c
	22,681	23,117	23,371	25,389	36,600	37,122	34,292	27,399	24,409	26,275	29,139	34,551	36,220	40,993	41,282	Claims on Deposit Money Banks	12e
	7,261	8,810	7,918	8,228	8,427	8,475	8,440	8,231	11,721	13,153	11,555	11,521	11,493	11,724	12,617	Claims on Other Financial Insts	12f
	29,439	31,536	45,994	51,021	56,878	59,440	58,531	70,950	87,967	114,017	103,458	112,457	122,988	139,489	157,166	Reserve Money	14
	17,672	19,027	22,490	25,282	27,286	29,950	31,330	37,990	44,987	57,248	64,523	68,195	76,074	80,756	93,870	of which: Currency Outside DMBs	14a
	—	—	—	—	—	62	900	900	1,450	4,000	2,755	7,361	—	—	—	Liabs. of Central Bank: Securities	16ac
	21,826	21,116	I29,999	31,215	25,896	24,836	32,450	30,875	32,005	32,807	33,237	29,670	23,454	33,547	23,647	Foreign Liabilities	16c
	10	10	557	980	977	2,180	2,179	3,670	9,717	4,868	3,986	9	13	14	10	Central Government Deposits	16d
	2,418	3,031	3,403	4,865	5,328	9,055	16,100	16,661	13,272	18,977	14,128	11,263	8,452	18,209	22,120	Central Govt. Lending Funds	16f
	3,247	3,627	4,007	4,387	4,650	5,035	5,424	5,966	6,346	6,726	6,665	7,345	8,025	8,705	9,385	Capital Accounts	17a
	-2,399	-7,946	-8,730	-10,358	-12,726	-10,448	-5,381	-5,545	-7,474	-5,509	-2,212	-2,179	-4,860	-3,778	-595	Other Items (Net)	17r
Deposit Money Banks																	
End of Period																	
	9,312	10,387	24,298	27,181	31,140	31,368	29,570	35,787	46,874	56,221	43,333	45,882	48,678	64,661	63,584	Reserves	20
	....	....	—	—	—	62	900	900	1,450	3,994	2,741	7,358	—	—	—	Other Claims on Monetary Author.	20c
	8,945	8,415	I8,606	9,894	12,628	15,450	16,848	13,903	16,039	28,313	29,770	32,753	37,628	38,554	46,766	Foreign Assets	21
	11,927	17,876	I17,486	21,156	19,599	19,271	27,904	47,353	54,135	64,899	64,283	63,790	81,206	99,534	117,884	Claims on Central Government	22a
	26,021	30,385	I27,829	29,840	36,273	37,442	40,592	43,412	45,951	33,731	31,717	39,426	42,900	40,712	40,431	Claims on Nonfin.Pub.Enterprises	22c
	75,530	83,242	99,537	119,538	147,546	167,104	175,944	173,881	191,744	220,332	318,484	359,202	411,731	465,130	509,760	Claims on Private Sector	22d
	1,844	2,031	I5,605	6,012	5,839	5,891	5,865	11,543	11,614	14,644	18,114	20,234	19,231	20,312	25,019	Claims on Other Financial Insts	22f
	28,280	30,968	I28,510	27,883	32,718	35,785	39,474	42,452	48,294	58,717	70,819	73,481	76,559	83,214	91,055	Demand Deposits	24
	68,322	82,794	I106,644	125,955	152,535	168,854	195,821	218,159	236,578	277,489	305,996	347,091	383,813	433,586	504,965	Time Deposits	25
	3,949	3,768	I4,724	6,255	6,219	7,893	9,779	8,873	9,122	11,064	12,993	16,782	23,112	21,115	23,554	Foreign Liabilities	26c
	3,800	5,296	I12,419	15,686	12,565	13,355	18,279	23,726	26,845	32,200	34,509	31,250	39,571	50,076	52,881	Central Government Deposits	26d
	5,615	5,939	5,619	4,208	4,040	4,352	4,458	4,952	5,341	5,423	6,443	5,869	7,164	7,174	6,391	Central Govt. Lending Funds	26f
	20,358	21,551	21,852	25,630	38,210	39,408	35,708	30,019	27,192	28,781	30,843	37,623	39,047	43,789	44,463	Credit from Monetary Authorities	26g
	3,534	3,964	4,962	5,973	6,489	7,023	7,491	13,101	18,515	21,068	21,768	24,551	28,660	30,769	36,644	Capital Accounts	27a
	-277	-1,944	I-1,369	2,031	249	-82	-13,387	-14,503	-4,080	-12,608	25,071	31,998	43,448	59,180	43,491	Other Items (Net)	27r
Monetary Survey																	
End of Period																	
	-3,470	-2,056	I3,019	9,838	231	10,301	28,795	50,927	76,102	114,609	81,489	66,989	64,460	77,253	82,344	Foreign Assets (Net)	31n
	130,011	142,072	160,204	179,186	220,400	239,631	251,581	268,099	284,566	315,982	429,032	502,080	563,938	637,430	735,469	Domestic Credit	32
	18,775	17,024	18,269	14,489	21,441	19,898	19,915	30,383	22,939	33,528	48,571	71,107	77,993	97,412	137,908	Claims on Central Govt. (Net)	32an
	I26,601	30,965	28,875	30,919	37,147	38,263	41,417	44,061	46,548	34,325	32,308	40,016	43,490	42,852	42,571	Claims on Nonfin.Pub.Enterprises	32c
	75,530	83,242	99,537	119,538	147,546	167,104	175,944	173,881	191,744	220,332	318,484	359,202	411,731	465,130	517,354	Claims on Private Sector	32d
	9,105	10,841	13,523	14,240	14,266	14,366	14,305	19,774	23,335	27,797	29,669	31,755	30,724	32,036	37,636	Claims on Other Financial Insts	32f
	45,956	49,996	I51,000	53,165	60,004	65,735	70,804	80,442	93,281	115,965	135,342	141,676	152,633	163,970	184,925	Money	34
	68,322	82,794	I106,644	125,955	152,535	168,854	195,821	218,159	236,578	277,489	305,996	347,091	383,813	433,586	504,965	Quasi-Money	35
	8,033	8,970	9,022	9,073	9,368	13,407	20,558	21,613	18,613	24,400	20,571	17,132	15,616	25,383	28,511	Central Govt. Lending Funds	36f
	6,781	7,591	8,969	10,360	11,139	12,058	12,915	19,067	24,861	27,794	28,433	31,896	36,685	39,474	46,029	Capital Accounts	37a
	-2,548	-9,335	I-12,412	-9,528	-12,415	-10,122	-19,721	-20,255	-12,665	-15,057	20,179	31,274	39,651	52,270	53,383	Other Items (Net)	37r
	114,278	132,790	I157,644	179,120	212,539	234,589	266,625	298,601	329,859	393,454	441,338	488,767	536,446	597,556	689,890	Money plus Quasi-Money	35l
Interest Rates																	
Percent Per Annum																	
	11.25	10.75	10.75	10.75	10.75	9.75	9.25	8.50	6.00	5.50	6.00	7.00	8.00	8.00	7.00	Discount Rate (End of Period)	60
	12.00	12.00	12.00	12.00	12.00	12.04	12.05	10.47	8.18	6.40	6.04	7.28	8.11	8.42	8.74	Deposit Rate	60l
	12.00	16.00	16.00	16.00	16.00	16.00	15.92	15.00	15.00	14.50	14.00	14.00	14.00	14.00	14.13	Lending Rate	60p
Prices and Production																	
Period Averages																	
	....	58.0	63.8	68.5	72.6	77.1	82.0	84.9	87.5	92.1	100.0	104.1	109.5	118.6	126.1	Consumer Prices	64
	56.4	55.3	60.6	I60.8	63.6	63.7	68.5	I75.7	86.6	93.7	100.0	108.8	116.1	120.8	125.1	Industrial Production	66

Bangladesh

		1970	1971	1972	1973	1974	1975	1976	1977	1978	1979	1980	1981	1982	1983	1984
International Transactions																*Millions of Taka*
Exports	70	...	...	1,992	2,764	2,819	3,689	6,150	7,314	8,251	10,242	11,728	14,169	17,049	17,837	23,640
Imports, c.i.f.	71	...	...	5,207	7,624	8,729	16,251	14,584	17,831	22,832	29,762	40,121	48,736	54,240	53,305	71,673
Imports, f.o.b.	71.v	...	...	4,640	6,886	7,783	14,452	12,725	16,157	20,603	26,783	36,108	43,861	45,577	47,975	64,522
																1995=100
Unit Value of Exports	74	...	...	....	....	....	....	....	....	41.6	50.7	58.7	51.6	56.4	64.0	86.0
Unit Value of Imports	75	...	...	....	....	....	....	....	....	40.0	41.4	45.6	51.0	58.4	70.0	72.8
Balance of Payments																*Millions of US Dollars:*
Current Account, n.i.e.	78ald	...	...	....	....	....	....	−278.7	−283.3	−386.4	−418.5	−704.3	−1,019.5	−505.0	−49.5	−481.0
Goods: Exports f.o.b.	78aad	...	...	....	....	....	....	400.5	476.4	549.3	655.6	793.2	790.5	768.4	723.9	931.7
Goods: Imports f.o.b.	78abd	...	...	....	....	....	....	−820.1	−1,019.1	−1,339.6	−1,725.8	−2,352.8	−2,434.8	−2,221.1	−1,930.7	−2,340.0
Trade Balance	78acd	...	...	....	....	....	....	−419.5	−542.6	−790.3	−1,070.2	−1,559.6	−1,644.3	−1,452.6	−1,206.8	−1,408.3
Services: Credit	78add	...	...	....	....	....	....	68.3	64.1	101.0	132.6	211.5	211.1	218.2	215.9	207.5
Services: Debit	78aed	...	...	....	....	....	....	−131.9	−184.9	−253.1	−372.2	−481.2	−463.5	−439.7	−405.1	−478.0
Balance on Goods & Services	78afd	...	...	....	....	....	....	−483.2	−663.4	−942.5	−1,309.8	−1,829.3	−1,896.7	−1,674.2	−1,395.9	−1,678.8
Income: Credit	78agd	...	...	....	....	....	....	16.4	26.5	34.5	64.4	76.3	41.8	28.9	35.9	68.1
Income: Debit	78ahd	...	...	....	....	....	....	−40.2	−58.7	−61.5	−65.9	−69.7	−97.3	−154.2	−117.8	−135.8
Balance on Gds, Serv. & Inc.	78aid	...	...	....	....	....	....	−507.1	−695.5	−969.5	−1,311.3	−1,822.7	−1,952.2	−1,799.4	−1,477.8	−1,746.4
Current Transfers, n.i.e.: Credit	78ajd	...	...	....	....	....	....	229.1	412.8	583.3	893.0	1,118.8	932.9	1,294.6	1,428.6	1,265.6
Current Transfers: Debit	78akd	...	...	....	....	....	....	−.7	−.5	−.3	−.2	−.4	−.2	−.1	−.3	−.2
Capital Account, n.i.e.	78bcd	...	...	....	....	....	....	—	—	—	—	—	—	—	—	—
Capital Account, n.i.e.: Credit	78bad	...	...	....	....	....	....	—	—	—	—	—	—	—	—	—
Capital Account: Debit	78bbd	...	...	....	....	....	....	—	—	—	—	—	—	—	—	—
Financial Account, n.i.e.	78bjd	...	...	....	....	....	....	336.0	264.8	406.5	120.3	569.3	703.2	532.0	383.6	544.5
Direct Investment Abroad	78bdd	...	...	....	....	....	....	—	—	—	—	—	—	—	—	—
Dir. Invest. in Rep. Econ., n.i.e.	78bed	...	...	....	....	....	....	—	—	—	—	—	—	—	.4	−.6
Portfolio Investment Assets	78bfd	...	...	....	....	....	....	—	—	—	—	—	—	—	...	...
Equity Securities	78bkd	...	...	....	....	....	....	—	—	—	—	—	—	—	...	...
Debt Securities	78bld	...	...	....	....	....	....	—	—	—	—	—	—	—	...	...
Portfolio Investment Liab., n.i.e.	78bgd	...	...	....	....	....	....	—	—	—	—	—	—	—	1.3	1.6
Equity Securities	78bmd	...	...	....	....	....	....	—	—	—	—	—	—	—	1.3	1.6
Debt Securities	78bnd	...	...	....	....	....	....	—	—	—	—	—	—	—	—	—
Financial Derivatives Assets	78bwd	...	...	....	....	....	....	—	—	—	—	—	—	—	—	—
Financial Derivatives Liabilities	78bxd	...	...	....	....	....	....	—	—	—	—	—	—	—	—	—
Other Investment Assets	78bhd	...	...	....	....	....	....	−15.4	−73.5	−60.8	−99.0	−76.8	−115.9	−134.3	−91.5	−60.9
Monetary Authorities	78bod	...	...	....	....	....	....	...	...	...	...	...	...	...	...	...
General Government	78bpd	...	...	....	....	....	....	−6.4	−3.5	−10.9	−3.5	52.5	−1.8	−2.3	−2.7	−4.1
Banks	78bqd	...	...	....	....	....	....	−9.0	−70.0	−49.8	−95.5	−129.1	−114.0	−132.0	−88.8	−56.7
Other Sectors	78brd	...	...	....	....	....	....	—	—	—	—	−.2	—	—	—	—
Other Investment Liab., n.i.e.	78bid	...	...	....	....	....	....	351.5	338.3	467.2	219.3	646.1	819.0	666.3	473.4	604.3
Monetary Authorities	78bsd	...	...	....	....	....	....	21.0	5.1	7.4	21.1	114.5	−4.1	43.2	−50.1	−30.2
General Government	78btd	...	...	....	....	....	....	331.3	297.7	412.1	139.9	480.7	537.3	592.4	453.6	543.0
Banks	78bud	...	...	....	....	....	....	−.8	39.2	49.3	29.5	50.8	101.3	142.4	78.8	68.7
Other Sectors	78bvd	...	...	....	....	....	....	—	−3.6	−1.5	28.8	.1	184.6	−111.7	−8.9	22.8
Net Errors and Omissions	78cad	...	...	....	....	....	....	13.8	−14.7	21.6	−4.3	−74.1	93.7	−83.4	−26.4	−95.2
Overall Balance	78cbd	...	...	....	....	....	....	71.2	−33.2	41.6	−302.6	−209.1	−222.6	−56.4	307.7	−31.7
Reserves and Related Items	79dad	...	...	....	....	....	....	−71.2	33.2	−41.6	302.6	209.1	222.6	56.4	−307.7	31.7
Reserve Assets	79dbd	...	...	....	....	....	....	−146.4	63.5	−70.6	−96.0	117.7	140.7	−56.1	−357.6	98.3
Use of Fund Credit and Loans	79dcd	...	...	....	....	....	....	74.5	−32.7	26.5	43.5	89.2	79.1	108.2	46.2	−69.9
Exceptional Financing	79ded	...	...	....	....	....	....	.7	2.3	2.5	355.1	2.2	2.9	4.3	3.7	3.4
Government Finance																*Millions of Taka:*
Deficit (-) or Surplus	80	...	...	...	−864	−330	1,444	−3,728	209	4,274	874	4,976	−7,396	3,135 P	9,003 P	2,873 P
Revenue	81			3,885	5,295	9,087	9,243	12,371	16,361	18,695	22,628	27,604	32,194 P	31,945 P	32,446 P	
Grants Received	81z			138	675	2,776	1,520	3,541	5,311	5,403	5,440	2,474	9,038 P	12,312 P	11,909 P	
Expenditure	82			4,251	5,299	8,153	11,995	13,167	15,085	21,215	20,026	32,445	34,007 P	32,680 P	38,314 P	
Lending Minus Repayments	83			635	1,001	2,266	2,496	2,536	2,313	2,009	3,066	5,029	4,090 P	2,574 P	3,168 P	
Financing																
Total Financing	84			864	330	−1,444	3,728	−209	−4,274	−874	−4,976	7,396	−3,135 P	−9,003 P	−2,873 P	
Net Borrowing: Domestic	84a			913	1,151	855	3,292	−3,586	−6,685	−4,632	....	1,623	....	....	....	
Foreign	85a			—	−211	−368	2,812	875	2,411	3,758	....	5,773	....	....	....	
Use of Cash Balances	87			−49	−610	−1,931	−2,376	2,502	....	....	....	....	....	....	....	
National Accounts																*Billions of Taka:*
Exports of Goods & Services	90c			2.71	2.98	3.14	5.55	6.67	7.18	9.63	10.99	11.48	12.39	18.02	20.14	
Government Consumption	91f			1.82	3.15	4.14	4.64	5.73	6.83	10.62	12.31	15.19	15.47	15.91	18.98	
Gross Fixed Capital Formation	93e			4.03	4.01	6.89	9.34	12.35	16.04	16.01	18.77	17.00	22.32	29.71	38.63	
Increase/Decrease(-) in Stocks	93i			—	—	—	—	—	—	.53	3.52	7.57	5.23	...	...	
Private Consumption	96f			38.82	68.26	122.42	102.62	94.60	118.46	157.75	180.69	214.39	245.28	262.27	314.84	
Imports of Goods & Services	98c			−2.26	−7.32	−10.84	−14.70	−13.99	−18.22	−21.73	−28.31	−32.37	−35.54	−37.47	−42.66	
Gross Domestic Product (GDP)	99b			45.11	71.09	125.74	107.46	105.36	146.37	172.82	197.99	233.26	265.14	288.42	349.92	
Net Factor Inc/Pmts(-) Abroad	98.n			....	....	.29	.31	.43	1.23	1.84	3.47	5.82	5.78	11.63	12.15	
Gross National Income (GNI)	99a			44.42	69.19	124.24	101.70	100.30	140.43	165.75	191.11	225.62	257.10	284.59	343.22	
GDP Volume 1973 prices	99b.p			45.11	50.57	52.28	58.69	59.47	63.34	66.23	67.10	71.64	72.23	74.84	78.00	
GDP Volume 1984/85 Prices	99b.p			....	....	....	....	....	....	....	....	....	....	....	....	
GDP Volume (1995=100)	99bv p			37.1	41.6	43.0	48.2	48.9	52.1	54.4	55.1	58.9	59.4	61.5	64.1	
GDP Deflator (1995=100)	99bi p			10.4	14.6	25.0	19.0	18.4	24.0	27.1	30.7	33.9	38.2	40.1	46.6	
																Millions:
Population	99z	...	...	72.39	74.37	77.03	78.96	80.82	82.72	84.66	86.64	88.68	90.46	92.59	94.65	97.27

	1985	1986	1987	1988	1989	1990	1991	1992	1993	1994	1995	1996	1997	1998	1999		
																	International Transactions	
Millions of Taka																		
	27,997	26,761	33,030	40,967	42,108	57,885	61,866	81,724	90,183	107,013	127,782	137,944	166,087	179,614	192,571	Exports	70
	70,867	77,471	84,087	96,558	117,797	124,880	124,857	145,328	158,123	185,098	261,878	276,838	302,942	327,575	377,496	Imports, c.i.f.	71
	63,780	69,724	75,678	86,902	106,018	113,435	110,430	137,000	142,055	166,246	235,502	248,932	265,565	298,386	342,064	Imports, f.o.b.	71.v
1995=100																		
	105.7	82.5	83.0	96.9	95.1	100.0	104.7	....	....	....	....	....	....	96.9	....	Unit Value of Exports	74
	79.3	86.9	95.5	89.0	90.6	100.0	121.2	....	....	....	....	....	....	....	....	Unit Value of Imports	75
Minus Sign Indicates Debit																	**Balance of Payments**	
	−457.9	−627.0	−237.9	−273.2	−1,099.6	−397.9	64.6	180.8	359.3	199.6	−823.9	−991.4	−327.3	−35.1	−291.5	Current Account, n.i.e.	78al *d*
	999.5	880.0	1,076.9	1,291.0	1,304.8	1,672.4	1,688.7	2,097.9	2,544.7	2,934.4	3,733.3	4,009.3	4,839.9	5,141.4	5,458.3	Goods: Exports f.o.b.	78aa *d*
	−2,286.4	−2,300.7	−2,445.6	−2,734.4	−3,300.1	−3,259.4	−3,074.5	−3,353.8	−3,657.3	−4,350.5	−6,057.4	−6,284.6	−6,587.6	−6,715.7	−7,420.4	Goods: Imports f.o.b.	78ab *d*
	−1,287.0	−1,420.7	−1,368.8	−1,443.4	−1,995.3	−1,587.0	−1,385.8	−1,255.9	−1,112.6	−1,416.1	−2,324.1	−2,275.3	−1,747.7	−1,574.3	−1,962.1	*Trade Balance*	78ac *d*
	237.9	215.0	247.9	277.6	334.4	391.6	431.0	483.4	529.4	589.8	698.2	604.8	687.3	723.9	780.2	Services: Credit	78ad *d*
	−477.9	−503.0	−494.2	−613.1	−726.4	−700.5	−695.3	−788.8	−932.2	−1,025.0	−1,531.2	−1,166.0	−1,287.9	−1,237.1	−1,431.7	Services: Debit	78ae *d*
	−1,527.0	−1,708.7	−1,615.0	−1,778.9	−2,387.3	−1,895.8	−1,650.0	−1,561.4	−1,515.3	−1,851.3	−3,157.1	−2,836.5	−2,348.3	−2,087.4	−2,613.7	*Balance on Goods & Services*	78af *d*
	41.6	31.7	47.4	54.8	88.7	64.2	70.0	100.1	100.1	150.5	270.1	129.4	86.5	91.5	94.4	Income: Credit	78ag *d*
	−153.7	−167.2	−172.5	−180.7	−196.9	−179.8	−166.9	−166.0	−175.8	−188.7	−201.8	−193.1	−196.1	−206.1	−262.7	Income: Debit	78ah *d*
	−1,639.1	−1,844.2	−1,740.1	−1,904.8	−2,495.5	−2,011.4	−1,747.0	−1,627.3	−1,591.0	−1,889.6	−3,088.8	−2,900.2	−2,457.9	−2,202.1	−2,782.0	*Balance on Gds, Serv. & Inc.*	78ai *d*
	1,181.6	1,217.5	1,502.6	1,633.0	1,396.6	1,614.2	1,811.9	1,808.8	1,951.8	2,091.4	2,266.7	1,912.8	2,134.9	2,172.9	2,495.8	Current Transfers, n.i.e.: Credit	78aj *d*
	−.4	−.3	−.4	−1.5	−.7	−.7	−.3	−.7	−1.5	−2.2	−1.8	−4.0	−4.3	−5.9	−5.3	Current Transfers: Debit	78ak *d*
	—	—	—	—	—	—	—	—	—	—	—	371.2	368.1	238.7	362.4	Capital Account, n.i.e.	78bc *d*
	—	—	—	—	—	—	—	—	—	—	—	371.2	368.1	238.7	362.4	Capital Account, n.i.e.: Credit	78ba *d*
	—	—	—	—	—	—	—	—	—	—	—	—	—	—	—	Capital Account: Debit	78bb *d*
	441.8	702.4	516.7	398.6	794.5	697.8	467.6	538.4	268.9	748.8	178.8	92.4	−99.8	−116.0	−526.8	Financial Account, n.i.e.	78bj *d*
	—	—	—	—	—	—	—	—	—	—	—	—	−3.1	−3.0	—	Direct Investment Abroad	78bd *d*
	—	2.4	3.2	1.8	.2	3.2	1.4	3.7	14.0	11.1	1.9	13.5	141.3	190.1	178.6	Dir. Invest. in Rep. Econ., n.i.e.	78be *d*
	—	—	—	—	—	—	—	—	—	—	—	—	—	−.3	4.4	Portfolio Investment Assets	78bf *d*
	—	—	—	—	—	—	—	—	—	—	—	—	—	−.3	4.4	Equity Securities	78bk *d*
	—	—	—	—	—	—	—	—	—	—	—	—	—	—	—	Debt Securities	78bl *d*
	−7.2	—	−.1	—	1.7	.3	2.2	8.7	8.4	105.9	−15.2	−117.0	−14.5	−3.8	−1.0	Portfolio Investment Liab., n.i.e.	78bg *d*
	−7.2	—	−.1	—	1.7	.3	2.2	8.7	8.4	105.9	−15.2	−117.0	−14.5	−4.0	−1.0	Equity Securities	78bm *d*
	—	—	—	—	—	—	—	—	—	—	—	—	—	.1	—	Debt Securities	78bn *d*
	—	—	—	—	—	—	—	—	—	—	—	—	—	—	—	Financial Derivatives Assets	78bw *d*
	—	—	—	—	—	—	—	—	—	—	—	—	—	—	—	Financial Derivatives Liabilities	78bx *d*
	−13.7	−18.0	−21.0	−229.1	−152.0	−207.8	−267.1	−196.0	−178.4	−1.6	−243.9	−426.7	−674.6	−859.7	−1,146.3	Other Investment Assets	78bh *d*
	....	....	....	....	....	....	....	....	....	....	....	....	....	....	....	Monetary Authorities	78bo *d*
	−.1	−1.5	−1.2	−1.6	−.5	−.6	−.4	—	−.7	−.1	—	—	—	—	—	General Government	78bp *d*
	−13.6	−16.5	−19.8	−227.5	−151.4	−206.1	−266.7	−196.0	−177.7	−1.5	−243.9	−41.1	−70.9	−38.1	−130.4	Banks	78bq *d*
	—	—	—	—	—	—	—	—	—	—	—	−385.6	−603.7	−821.6	−1,015.9	Other Sectors	78br *d*
	462.7	717.9	534.6	625.9	944.5	902.0	731.1	722.0	424.8	633.4	436.1	622.6	451.1	560.7	437.4	Other Investment Liab., n.i.e.	78bi *d*
	.5	−40.6	−49.2	−7.0	−35.2	−.1	1.3	−.9	−.2	15.0	58.3	−4.3	−25.5	126.6	−113.7	Monetary Authorities	78bs *d*
	432.1	728.1	583.4	618.9	878.1	827.0	533.1	667.6	379.3	718.5	374.2	511.3	302.1	404.6	453.6	General Government	78bt *d*
	6.5	−.1	9.1	2.8	91.3	40.9	186.8	14.5	—	−116.3	−34.2	83.0	119.1	2.6	28.7	Banks	78bu *d*
	23.6	30.6	−8.8	11.2	10.3	34.2	9.9	40.8	45.8	16.2	37.9	32.7	55.5	26.9	68.9	Other Sectors	78bv *d*
	−67.8	8.7	−123.8	6.6	−43.1	−75.7	−98.4	−84.0	69.4	−257.1	133.3	113.5	−77.3	201.0	264.2	Net Errors and Omissions	78ca *d*
	−83.9	84.1	155.0	132.0	−348.2	224.2	433.8	635.2	697.6	691.3	−511.7	−414.3	−136.3	288.5	−191.6	*Overall Balance*	78cb *d*
	83.9	−84.1	−155.0	−132.0	348.2	−224.2	−433.8	−635.2	−697.6	−691.3	511.7	414.3	136.3	−288.5	191.6	Reserves and Related Items	79da *d*
	79.4	−47.9	−352.3	−176.1	447.8	−78.9	−544.5	−670.1	−647.0	−636.2	572.8	499.9	254.9	−319.1	288.5	Reserve Assets	79db *d*
	1.8	−38.0	196.5	43.6	−99.6	−145.3	110.7	34.9	−50.6	−55.1	−61.0	−85.6	−118.7	30.6	−96.8	Use of Fund Credit and Loans	79dc *d*
	2.8	1.8	.8	.4	—	—	—	—	—	—	—	—	—	....	....	Exceptional Financing	79de *d*
Year Ending June 30																	**Government Finance**	
	−5,924 [P]	....	....	....	....	....	....	....	....	....	....	....	....	....	....	Deficit (-) or Surplus	80
	39,436 [P]	....	....	....	....	....	....	....	....	....	....	....	....	....	....	Revenue	81
	8,688 [P]	....	....	....	....	....	....	....	....	....	....	....	....	....	....	Grants Received	81z
	50,482 [P]	....	....	....	....	....	....	....	....	....	....	....	....	....	....	Expenditure	82
	3,566 [P]	....	....	....	....	....	....	....	....	....	....	....	....	....	....	Lending Minus Repayments	83
																Financing	
	5,924 [P]	....	....	....	....	....	....	....	....	....	....	....	....	....	....	Total Financing	84
	−8,430 [P]	....	....	....	....	....	....	....	....	....	....	....	....	....	....	Net Borrowing: Domestic	84a
	14,354 [P]	....	....	....	....	....	....	....	....	....	....	....	....	....	....	Foreign	85a
																Use of Cash Balances	87
Year Ending June 30																	**National Accounts**	
	23.70	33.86	37.59	45.02	51.19	61.42	73.63	90.70	104.17	121.89	165.71	184.36	216.72	266.81	324.17	Exports of Goods & Services	90c
	20.88	38.08	40.15	48.56	90.46	103.22	114.73	124.94	134.30	147.28	160.80	177.66	198.23	215.11	245.12	Government Consumption	91f
	41.68	46.20	67.50	74.31	85.19	94.43	95.96	109.85	135.38	142.61	193.84	224.37	214.21	232.19	224.67	Gross Fixed Capital Formation	93e
	—	11.07	.08	12.42	—	—	—	—	—	—	—	—	—	—	—	Increase/Decrease(-) in Stocks	93i
	366.34	414.34	482.00	533.30	551.73	614.26	685.20	728.63	747.70	806.32	913.05	1,026.13	1,099.42	1,200.10	1,355.92	Private Consumption	96f
	−54.85	−77.31	−88.11	−101.58	−118.96	−135.75	−135.13	−147.61	−173.49	−187.74	−263.13	−310.91	−325.59	−365.88	−400.63	Imports of Goods & Services	98c
	405.41	465.61	539.20	597.14	659.60	737.57	834.39	906.50	948.06	1,030.36	1,170.26	1,301.60	1,403.05	1,548.33	1,749.26	Gross Domestic Product (GDP)	99b
	8.62	11.93	15.55	20.46	22.53	22.27	26.51	33.85	38.80	48.64	55.67	60.03	71.03	75.18	79.62	Net Factor Inc/Pmts(-) Abroad	98.n
	392.24	452.02	524.67	584.90	682.13	759.84	860.91	940.35	986.86	1,079.00	1,225.93	1,361.63	1,474.07	1,623.52	1,828.87	Gross National Income (GNI)	99a
	80.90	....	....														GDP Volume 1973 prices	99b.*p*
	405.41	424.59	442.35	455.14	466.60	497.53	514.44	536.19	560.23	583.84	609.79	642.44	680.21	718.67	755.73	GDP Volume 1984/85 Prices	99b.*p*
	66.5	69.6	72.5	74.6	76.5	81.6	84.4	87.9	91.9	95.7	100.0	105.4	111.5	117.9	123.9	GDP Volume (1995=100)	99bv *p*
	52.1	57.1	63.5	68.4	73.7	77.2	84.5	88.1	88.2	92.0	100.0	105.6	107.5	112.3	120.6	GDP Deflator (1995=100)	99bi *p*
Midyear Estimates																		
	99.43	101.67	102.56	104.53	106.51	109.47	111.50	113.11	114.90	117.70	119.90	122.10	124.30 ⅰ	124.77	126.95	Population	99z

(See notes in the back of the book.)

Barbados

		1970	1971	1972	1973	1974	1975	1976	1977	1978	1979	1980	1981	1982	1983	1984
Exchange Rates												*Barbados Dollars per SDR: End of Period (aa)*					
Official Rate	aa	2.0053	2.0417	2.2194	2.4925	2.5024	2.3458	2.3281	2.4431	2.6203	2.6495	2.5652	2.3411	2.2187	2.1057	1.9715
Official Rate	ae	2.0053	1.8805	2.0442	2.0661	2.0439	2.0038	2.0038	2.0113	2.0113	2.0113	2.0113	2.0113	2.0113	2.0113	2.0113
Fund Position												*Millions of SDRs:*					
Quota	2f. s	13.00	13.00	13.00	13.00	13.00	13.00	13.00	13.00	17.00	17.00	25.50	25.50	25.50	34.10	34.10
SDRs	1b. s	—	1.39	2.77	2.77	2.77	2.77	2.77	2.72	2.49	3.94	1.56	1.44	.79	.29	.02
Reserve Position in the Fund	1c. s	2.00	2.00	2.00	2.00	2.01	3.26	3.27	3.27	2.98	2.89	5.02	5.01	—	2.15	2.16
Total Fund Cred.&Loans Outstg.	2tl	—	—	—	—	—	—	—	6.50	6.50	6.50	2.27	.77	22.18	35.79	43.59
International Liquidity												*Millions of US Dollars Unless Otherwise Indicated:*					
Total Reserves minus Gold	1l. d	16.58	18.86	27.99	32.37	39.15	39.58	27.98	37.01	59.84	66.12	78.92	100.56	121.60	123.27	132.52
SDRs	1b. d	—	1.51	3.01	3.34	3.39	3.24	3.22	3.30	3.24	5.19	1.99	1.68	.87	.30	.02
Reserve Position in the Fund	1c. d	2.00	2.17	2.17	2.41	2.46	3.82	3.80	3.97	3.88	3.81	6.40	5.83	—	2.25	2.12
Foreign Exchange	1d. d	14.58	15.18	22.81	26.62	33.30	32.52	20.96	29.73	52.71	57.12	70.53	93.05	120.73	120.72	130.38
Monetary Authorities	1da d	8.60	11.01	10.50	16.43	19.06	26.12	12.71	22.03	42.51	45.11	56.33	76.62	101.23	101.07	107.91
Government	1db d	5.98	4.17	I 12.31	10.19	14.24	6.40	8.25	7.70	10.20	12.01	14.20	16.43	19.50	19.65	22.47
Gold (Million Fine Troy Ounces)	1ad	....	....	....	....	....	....	....	....	....	....	.0028	.0061	.0061	.0061	.0061
Gold (National Valuation)	1an d	....	....	....	....	....	....	....	—	.12	.25	1.75	3.36	3.36	3.36	3.36
Monetary Authorities: Other Liab.	4.. d	—	—	—	—	—	—	—	9.94	9.94	7.96	5.97	55.80	60.14	40.85	37.71
Deposit Money Banks: Assets	7a. d	18.70	21.77	19.65	19.39	15.79	16.31	14.48	17.61	15.70	24.26	26.23	25.08	26.28	26.64	46.05
Liabilities	7b. d	27.10	36.43	40.99	51.00	43.36	37.44	41.87	44.66	39.36	42.19	48.36	65.93	65.24	80.84	86.12
Monetary Authorities												*Millions of Barbados Dollars:*					
Foreign Assets	11	33.2	34.7	54.1	69.7	64.4	85.2	58.2	74.7	120.3	135.6	163.9	207.9	251.5	259.9	253.3
Claims on Central Government	12a	3.8	5.8	5.8	11.0	25.8	27.9	38.0	79.5	53.1	89.9	87.4	128.8	126.0	122.8	110.2
Claims on Deposit Money Banks	12e	6.4	4.3	8.8	2.6	2.6	.3	3.0	4.5	—	1.2	1.2	7.5	17.9	22.1	14.9
Claims on Other Banking Insts	12f	—	—	—	—	6.8	12.9	20.1	14.1	24.0	14.4	23.8	50.7	47.8	43.3	70.4
Reserve Money	14	27.0	29.2	33.5	44.4	59.1	80.2	76.5	93.1	109.9	146.5	164.0	180.8	189.6	226.1	233.9
of which: Currency Outside DMBs	14a	21.2	21.4	23.7	26.9	34.1	41.8	47.0	55.7	65.9	80.2	101.6	111.2	110.6	114.1	118.1
Foreign Liabilities	16c	—	—	—	—	—	—	—	35.9	37.0	33.2	17.8	114.0	170.2	157.5	161.8
Central Government Deposits	16d	16.3	12.9	29.6	31.2	29.8	37.6	35.2	26.7	33.1	38.5	47.3	59.8	48.8	45.9	55.0
Capital Accounts	17a	—	2.8	5.5	9.1	12.3	15.2	15.6	17.0	18.6	24.0	28.2	30.8	29.8	28.9	27.9
Other Items (Net)	17r	.1	–.1	.1	–1.3	–1.7	–6.6	–8.1	.1	–1.2	–1.2	19.1	9.4	4.9	–10.4	–29.6
Deposit Money Banks												*Millions of Barbados Dollars:*					
Reserves	20	5.9	7.8	9.8	18.8	14.3	25.8	17.7	33.3	43.6	60.4	58.1	66.1	71.0	78.6	86.9
Foreign Assets	21	37.4	40.1	36.2	40.1	32.3	32.7	29.0	35.4	31.6	48.8	52.8	50.5	52.9	53.6	92.6
Claims on Central Government	22a	8.0	17.4	19.1	9.0	42.5	60.6	82.1	80.0	141.0	138.2	154.8	170.8	201.0	202.9	247.3
Claims on Private Sector	22d	165.8	189.1	214.9	249.9	250.1	271.8	302.9	326.8	362.6	443.9	521.5	618.0	645.0	729.8	741.9
Claims on Other Banking Insts	22f	—	—	—	3.2	5.1	3.5	5.1	7.8	10.7	14.4	12.5	19.0	22.8	29.6	41.7
Demand Deposits	24	34.5	41.1	44.1	47.2	51.5	62.9	65.6	77.0	93.2	140.4	140.5	135.6	137.4	166.7	159.1
Time, Savings,& Fgn.Currency Dep.	25	120.8	146.4	168.5	149.4	190.5	212.3	243.0	256.3	320.2	392.5	449.7	540.6	589.0	618.3	696.2
Foreign Liabilities	26c	54.2	67.1	75.5	105.4	88.6	75.0	83.9	89.8	79.2	84.9	97.3	132.6	131.2	162.6	173.2
Central Government Deposits	26d	12.2	17.9	19.7	35.5	33.3	57.6	50.9	66.2	86.0	91.5	116.8	103.4	110.3	117.8	137.6
Credit from Monetary Authorities	26g	6.4	4.3	8.8	2.6	2.6	.3	3.0	4.5	—	1.2	1.2	5.4	16.2	26.1	24.3
Capital Accounts	27a	—	—	—	1.6	3.7	3.9	2.4	5.3	13.2	16.6	19.9	20.7	18.3	13.1	27.2
Other Items (Net)	27r	–11.0	–22.4	–36.6	–20.6	–26.0	–17.7	–11.9	–15.9	–2.2	–21.2	–25.8	–14.0	–9.8	–10.2	–7.3
Monetary Survey												*Millions of Barbados Dollars:*					
Foreign Assets (Net)	31n	16.4	7.7	14.8	4.4	8.0	42.9	3.3	–15.6	35.7	66.3	101.6	11.7	3.0	–6.7	10.9
Domestic Credit	32	149.1	181.5	190.5	206.4	267.0	281.5	362.0	415.1	472.3	570.8	635.9	824.1	883.5	964.7	1,018.9
Claims on Central Govt. (Net)	32an	–16.7	–7.6	–24.4	–46.6	5.1	–6.7	33.9	66.5	75.1	98.1	78.1	136.4	168.0	161.9	164.9
Claims on Private Sector	32d	165.8	189.1	214.9	249.9	250.1	271.8	302.9	326.8	362.6	443.9	521.5	618.0	645.0	729.8	741.9
Claims on Other Banking Insts	32f	—	—	—	3.2	11.9	16.4	25.2	21.9	34.6	28.8	36.3	69.7	70.6	72.9	112.1
Money	34	55.7	62.5	67.8	74.1	88.6	106.5	113.7	135.7	160.7	222.2	244.8	249.6	251.5	312.9	305.7
Quasi-Money	35	120.8	146.4	168.5	149.4	190.5	212.3	243.0	256.3	320.2	392.5	449.7	540.6	589.0	618.3	696.2
Capital Accounts	37a	—	2.8	5.5	10.7	15.9	19.0	18.0	22.3	31.8	40.6	48.1	51.6	48.1	42.0	55.1
Other Items (Net)	37r	–11.0	–22.5	–36.5	–23.3	–20.0	–13.5	–9.4	–14.7	–4.7	–18.2	–5.1	–5.9	–2.1	–15.2	–27.2
Money plus Quasi-Money	35l	176.5	208.9	236.3	223.5	279.1	318.8	356.7	391.9	480.9	614.7	694.5	790.1	840.5	931.2	1,002.0
Other Banking Institutions												*Millions of Barbados Dollars:*					
Claims on Central Government	42a	12.3	12.6	.5	.5	.5	.5	.9	.4	.6	.5	.5	.8	.5	.1	1.0
Claims on Private Sector	42d	12.4	12.7	2.8	4.9	8.2	13.3	20.2	25.9	34.9	51.4	71.5	105.1	127.6	131.1	141.7
Claims on Deposit Money Banks	42e	2.3	3.5	2.0	4.8	3.3	7.1	4.7	2.3	5.8	7.3	1.9	1.4	6.6	11.0	16.7
Time Deposits	45	17.8	19.7	3.9	8.5	10.5	19.8	23.6	26.0	36.3	39.3	50.3	68.3	88.5	98.7	109.0
Central Government Deposits	46d	—	—	—	—	—	—	—	—	4.2	22.3	19.6	24.6	30.7	27.0	27.5
Credit from Deposit Money Banks	46h	—	—	—	.1	.1	.1	.6	.8	1.7	.9	1.6	5.0	6.6	5.6	8.4
Capital Accounts	47a	6.1	6.5	1.5	1.5	1.5	1.5	1.5	1.8	2.0	2.5	2.5	3.0	3.6	3.6	3.6
Other Items (Net)	47r	3.2	2.6	–.1	.1	—	–.6	.3	—	–3.1	–5.8	–.1	6.3	5.4	7.3	10.9
Banking Survey												*Millions of Barbados Dollars:*					
Foreign Assets (Net)	51n	25.1	17.6	14.8	4.4	8.1	42.9	3.3	–15.6	35.7	66.3	101.6	11.7	3.0	–6.7	10.9
Domestic Credit	52	173.8	206.8	193.8	208.6	263.9	278.9	357.9	419.5	468.9	571.6	652.0	835.7	910.4	996.0	1,022.0
Claims on Central Govt. (Net)	52an	–4.4	5.0	–23.9	–46.1	5.6	–6.2	34.8	66.9	71.4	76.4	59.0	112.6	137.8	135.0	138.4
Claims on Private Sector	52d	178.2	201.8	217.7	254.8	258.3	285.1	323.1	352.7	397.5	495.2	593.0	723.1	772.6	860.9	883.6
Liquid Liabilities	55l	193.9	228.6	240.2	232.0	289.1	337.8	379.9	416.2	512.6	645.9	741.3	856.3	926.5	1,029.9	1,111.0
Capital Accounts	57a	6.1	9.2	7.0	12.2	17.4	20.5	19.5	24.1	33.8	43.1	50.6	54.5	51.7	45.6	58.6
Other Items (Net)	57r	–1.1	–13.4	–38.5	–31.1	–34.6	–36.5	–38.2	–36.3	–41.8	–51.1	–38.3	–63.4	–64.8	–86.1	–136.7
Interest Rates												*Percent Per Annum*					
Bank Rate *(End of Period)*	60	....	....	....	....	....	....	....	6.00	6.00	6.00	7.00	22.00	20.00	16.00	16.00
Treasury Bill Rate	60c	7.01	7.17	5.95	6.57	8.96	5.67	4.43	4.63	4.80	4.88	5.63	9.49	13.25	7.45	6.92
Deposit Rate	60l	....	....	....	....	....	....	....	....	....	....	5.30	7.39	8.83	6.73	6.07
Lending Rate	60p	....	....	....	....	....	....	....	....	....	....	....	11.46	13.38	11.79	11.50

1985	1986	1987	1988	1989	1990	1991	1992	1993	1994	1995	1996	1997	1998	1999		
Barbados Dollars per US Dollar: End of Period (ae)															**Exchange Rates**	
2.2093	2.4464	2.8373	2.6914	2.6283	2.8453	2.8609	2.7500	2.7471	2.9197	2.9730	2.8759	2.6985	2.8161	2.7450	Official Rate	aa
2.0113	2.0000	2.0000	2.0000	2.0000	2.0000	2.0000	2.0000	2.0000	2.0000	2.0000	2.0000	2.0000	2.0000	2.0000	Official Rate	ae
End of Period															**Fund Position**	
34.10	34.10	34.10	34.10	34.10	34.10	34.10	48.90	48.90	48.90	48.90	48.90	48.90	48.90	67.50	Quota	2f. s
.01	—	.63	.46	—	.01	.50	.11	.05	.03	.03	.02	.02	.02	.01	SDRs	1b. s
2.16	2.16	2.17	2.18	2.18	2.18	—	.03	.03	.03	.03	.03	.03	.03	4.68	Reserve Position in the Fund	1c. s
43.59	32.42	15.60	7.75	3.27	.50	—	36.84	36.84	36.84	24.94	6.52	—	—	—	Total Fund Cred.&Loans Outstg.	2tl
End of Period															**International Liquidity**	
139.77	151.71	145.21	135.46	109.46	117.54	87.25	139.96	150.45	195.77	219.10	289.69	264.92	253.23	....	Total Reserves minus Gold	1l. d
.01	—	.89	.62	—	.01	.72	.15	.07	.04	.04	.03	.03	.03	.01	SDRs	1b. d
2.37	2.64	3.08	2.93	2.86	3.10	—	.04	.03	.04	.04	.04	.03	.04	6.42	Reserve Position in the Fund	1c. d
137.39	149.07	141.24	131.91	106.60	114.42	86.53	139.77	150.35	195.69	219.02	289.62	264.85	253.16	....	Foreign Exchange	1d. d
117.24	131.34	125.83	109.10	92.73	104.81	80.06	133.14	143.21	188.28	212.75	280.06	227.62	212.76	....	Monetary Authorities	1da d
20.15	17.73	15.41	22.81	13.87	9.61	6.47	6.63	7.14	7.41	6.27	9.56	37.23	40.40	....	Government	1db d
.0061	.0061	.0061	.0061	.0061	—	—	—	—	—	—	—	—	—	—	Gold (Million Fine Troy Ounces)..........	1ad
3.89	3.89	3.89	3.89	3.11	—	—	—	—	—	—	—	—	—	—	Gold (National Valuation)	1an d
27.92	39.96	33.51	36.18	60.14	76.83	86.11	71.79	55.93	38.20	28.12	16.47	8.72	7.72	6.81	Monetary Authorities: Other Liab.	4.. d
50.12	59.11	120.63	74.85	69.44	77.41	88.48	90.95	95.65	126.53	204.00	341.07	309.48	277.73	338.78	Deposit Money Banks: Assets	7a. d
88.29	107.10	169.40	107.67	107.13	126.18	140.60	143.43	152.56	173.11	274.86	402.14	382.40	400.97	450.04	Liabilities...........	7b. d
End of Period															**Monetary Authorities**	
287.3	327.4	306.2	290.0	250.5	260.0	207.1	315.2	335.8	442.2	502.6	641.5	592.1	571.8	624.9	Foreign Assets	11
134.6	131.3	119.0	110.1	160.4	204.9	266.0	239.4	225.3	219.2	117.6	90.3	64.1	50.0	82.9	Claims on Central Government	12a
1.9	.7	2.4	3.7	29.8	27.8	33.6	31.2	5.0	—	6.0	—	—	23.5	15.0	Claims on Deposit Money Banks	12e
55.7	56.8	58.0	52.4	61.4	69.3	61.3	62.3	25.3	10.1	10.1	9.0	9.0	9.0	9.0	Claims on Other Banking Insts	12f
256.1	260.4	313.6	327.9	317.4	379.0	324.6	367.6	324.6	318.4	368.5	494.4	446.8	486.9	505.5	Reserve Money	14
123.5	137.4	156.6	171.3	182.7	192.9	178.7	176.8	177.0	189.6	200.3	220.1	239.6	268.2	302.7	of which: Currency Outside DMBs	14a
152.5	159.2	111.3	93.2	128.9	155.1	172.2	244.9	213.1	184.0	130.4	51.7	17.4	15.4	13.6	Foreign Liabilities	16c
113.3	141.2	121.1	87.7	121.5	80.5	92.3	112.3	110.1	212.0	197.8	255.5	266.7	244.5	261.7	Central Government Deposits	16d
29.8	31.7	34.8	33.6	28.6	35.3	35.0	34.1	34.1	35.5	35.9	35.1	33.7	34.6	34.1	Capital Accounts	17a
−72.1	−76.3	−95.2	−86.2	−94.3	−88.0	−56.1	−110.7	−90.5	−78.3	−96.3	−95.9	−99.4	−127.1	−83.0	Other Items (Net)	17r
End of Period															**Deposit Money Banks**	
83.0	103.3	122.3	140.4	118.4	181.1	127.2	167.4	129.3	114.1	144.9	243.8	166.5	217.2	195.8	Reserves	20
100.8	118.2	241.3	149.7	138.9	154.8	177.0	181.9	191.3	253.1	408.0	682.1	619.0	555.5	677.6	Foreign Assets	21
263.1	315.7	359.6	394.7	354.3	428.6	441.0	555.1	594.9	603.4	713.5	915.3	981.6	922.9	880.6	Claims on Central Government	22a
769.4	811.0	898.6	965.1	1,102.8	1,104.3	1,144.5	1,121.0	1,128.9	1,268.1	1,470.6	1,536.1	1,839.1	2,138.1	2,445.4	Claims on Private Sector	22d
55.5	44.6	34.4	73.2	79.2	106.9	84.3	66.7	83.7	159.3	39.4	41.2	91.6	108.5	94.1	Claims on Other Banking Insts	22f
198.9	231.0	278.5	329.8	260.3	320.6	293.4	305.1	280.8	309.6	208.4	370.0	350.1	493.3	615.6	Demand Deposits	24
739.9	799.6	899.1	992.2	1,075.3	1,219.3	1,232.0	1,311.0	1,389.0	1,514.5	1,701.6	1,913.3	2,144.3	2,209.2	2,411.4	Time, Savings,& Fgn.Currency Dep.	25
177.6	214.2	338.8	215.3	214.3	252.4	281.2	286.9	305.1	346.2	549.7	804.3	764.8	801.9	900.1	Foreign Liabilities	26c
136.0	112.2	104.6	114.0	125.9	157.2	106.0	125.5	101.3	173.5	215.3	245.8	330.1	287.7	249.8	Central Government Deposits	26d
15.1	13.5	20.3	22.4	40.4	42.9	54.1	38.3	19.7	10.1	24.7	28.7	12.2	22.5	38.5	Credit from Monetary Authorities	26g
26.9	37.9	37.6	36.9	33.6	34.1	32.6	43.5	46.5	92.2	101.0	105.4	117.1	117.6	137.4	Capital Accounts	27a
−22.6	−15.6	−22.7	12.5	43.8	−50.6	−25.3	−18.2	−14.4	−48.2	−24.6	−48.9	−20.8	10.0	−59.4	Other Items (Net)	27r
End of Period															**Monetary Survey**	
58.1	72.2	97.4	131.1	46.3	7.3	−69.3	−34.7	8.9	165.0	230.5	467.7	428.9	309.9	388.8	Foreign Assets (Net)	31n
1,029.0	1,105.9	1,243.9	1,393.8	1,510.7	1,676.3	1,798.8	1,806.7	1,846.5	1,874.6	1,938.0	2,090.7	2,388.7	2,696.3	3,000.6	Domestic Credit	32
148.4	193.5	252.8	303.1	267.3	395.9	508.7	556.7	608.7	437.0	417.9	504.4	449.0	440.8	452.1	Claims on Central Govt. (Net)	32an
769.4	811.0	898.6	965.1	1,102.8	1,104.3	1,144.5	1,121.0	1,128.9	1,268.1	1,470.6	1,536.1	1,839.1	2,138.1	2,445.4	Claims on Private Sector	32d
111.2	101.4	92.5	125.6	140.6	176.1	145.6	129.0	109.0	169.4	49.5	50.2	100.6	117.5	103.1	Claims on Other Banking Insts	32f
353.5	395.4	466.9	524.8	459.0	526.2	495.0	502.3	476.6	516.3	428.5	627.2	620.6	765.7	922.4	Money	34
739.9	799.6	899.1	992.2	1,075.3	1,219.3	1,232.0	1,311.0	1,389.0	1,514.5	1,701.6	1,913.3	2,144.3	2,209.2	2,411.4	Quasi-Money	35
56.7	69.6	72.5	70.6	62.2	69.4	67.6	77.6	80.5	127.7	136.9	140.5	150.8	152.2	171.5	Capital Accounts	37a
−63.0	−86.3	−97.2	−62.6	−39.5	−131.2	−65.2	−118.9	−90.8	−118.9	−98.6	−122.6	−98.1	−120.9	−116.0	Other Items (Net)	37r
1,093.4	1,194.9	1,366.0	1,517.0	1,534.3	1,745.5	1,727.0	1,813.3	1,865.6	2,030.8	2,130.1	2,540.5	2,764.9	2,974.9	3,333.8	Money plus Quasi-Money	35l
End of Period															**Other Banking Institutions**	
1.5	3.7	2.0	1.6	1.4	1.8	1.0	.4	7.1	.5	5.5	4.9	1.3	1.7	1.9	Claims on Central Government	42a
149.3	180.1	231.7	283.3	340.1	360.9	384.4	387.1	403.5	417.5	424.7	443.0	381.8	433.4	378.6	Claims on Private Sector	42d
15.0	9.9	6.0	19.1	1.6	14.4	13.3	15.9	8.6	2.1	6.3	14.8	19.5	14.0	13.9	Claims on Deposit Money Banks	42e
114.9	120.6	201.6	216.2	241.0	269.3	295.4	306.9	339.4	301.8	308.8	326.5	258.8	297.1	241.4	Time Deposits................................	45
33.3	54.0	17.1	45.6	55.4	51.1	50.8	49.8	26.2	34.5	37.7	44.0	31.5	7.5	40.0	Central Government Deposits	46d
1.1	2.5	3.7	10.9	8.6	18.4	17.5	4.6	6.3	46.8	49.2	43.8	70.7	92.6	63.4	Credit from Deposit Money Banks	46h
3.6	4.8	4.8	4.8	4.8	4.8	4.8	4.8	5.0	5.1	5.1	5.1	7.9	10.9	18.9	Capital Accounts	47a
12.9	11.7	12.5	26.5	33.3	33.4	30.2	37.2	42.4	32.0	35.8	43.3	33.7	40.9	30.7	Other Items (Net)	47r
End of Period															**Banking Survey**	
58.1	72.2	97.4	131.1	46.3	7.3	−69.3	−34.7	8.9	165.0	230.5	467.7	428.9	310.0	388.8	Foreign Assets (Net)	51n
1,035.2	1,134.2	1,368.0	1,507.5	1,656.3	1,811.7	1,987.8	2,015.3	2,122.0	2,088.7	2,281.0	2,444.5	2,639.6	3,006.4	3,237.9	Domestic Credit	52
116.6	143.1	237.7	259.1	213.3	346.6	458.9	507.3	589.7	403.0	385.7	465.3	418.7	435.0	414.0	Claims on Central Govt. (Net)	52an
918.7	991.1	1,130.3	1,248.4	1,442.9	1,465.1	1,528.9	1,508.0	1,532.3	1,685.7	1,895.2	1,979.1	2,220.9	2,571.4	2,824.0	Claims on Private Sector	52d
1,208.3	1,315.5	1,567.6	1,733.1	1,775.3	2,014.7	2,022.4	2,120.1	2,205.0	2,332.5	2,438.9	2,867.0	3,023.6	3,271.9	3,575.1	Liquid Liabilities	55l
60.3	74.3	77.2	75.3	67.0	74.2	72.4	82.4	85.5	132.8	142.0	145.6	158.7	163.1	190.4	Capital Accounts	57a
−175.2	−183.4	−179.5	−169.8	−139.8	−269.9	−176.4	−221.9	−159.6	−211.6	−69.5	−100.4	−113.8	−118.7	−138.7	Other Items (Net)	57r
Percent Per Annum															**Interest Rates**	
13.00	8.00	8.00	8.00	13.50	13.50	18.00	12.00	8.00	9.50	12.50	12.50	9.00	9.00	10.00	Bank Rate (End of Period)...................	60
5.53	4.42	4.84	4.75	4.90	7.07	9.34	10.88	5.44	7.26	8.01	6.85	3.61	5.61	5.83	Treasury Bill Rate	60c
5.49	4.28	3.61	4.26	4.78	6.28	6.53	6.68	4.39	4.32	5.11	5.20	4.58	4.20	4.27	Deposit Rate	60l
10.56	9.06	8.75	9.44	9.92	11.42	12.42	13.54	8.92	9.08	10.00	10.00	9.83	9.75	9.40	Lending Rate	60p

Barbados

		1970	1971	1972	1973	1974	1975	1976	1977	1978	1979	1980	1981	1982	1983	1984
Prices, Production, Labor															*Index Numbers (1995=100):*		
Consumer Prices	64	13.1	14.0	15.7	18.4	25.5	30.7	32.2	34.9	38.2	I43.2	49.5	56.7	62.6	65.8	68.9
Industrial Production	66	52.3	57.2	63.8	67.6	64.2	69.2	80.4	82.6	86.3	86.8	89.3	I86.6	82.9	87.0	86.8
															Number in Thousands:		
Labor Force	67d	...	...	...	...	...	...	...	...	...	...	...	...	...	...
Employment	67e	...	...	...	...	...	...	...	...	...	...	...	...	...	...
Unemployment	67c	...	...	...	...	...	...	...	...	...	...	...	...	...	...
Unemployment Rate (%)	67r	...	...	...	...	...	...	...	...	...	...	...	...	...	...
International Transactions															*Millions of Barbados Dollars:*		
Exports	70	79.1	80.3	84.5	103.7	175.0	217.9	172.5	193.0	261.2	303.9	455.4	391.0	517.5	646.0	787.4
Imports, c.i.f.	71	235.0	243.7	270.4	328.6	418.3	437.2	474.1	545.1	628.7	850.8	1,049.1	1,151.1	1,107.5	1,249.0	1,324.7
Balance of Payments															*Millions of US Dollars:*		
Current Account, n.i.e.	78al d	-41.8	-35.1	-43.3	-52.3	-47.8	-41.4	-64.3	-51.6	-31.5	-34.4	-21.8	-118.6	-37.1	-43.6	15.7
Goods: Exports f.o.b.	78aa d	40.4	41.3	44.2	53.4	85.7	108.9	88.0	104.5	131.7	156.0	228.9	193.0	258.2	322.0	393.5
Goods: Imports f.o.b.	78ab d	-106.9	-112.2	-128.0	-152.6	-185.5	-197.1	-219.5	-251.1	-289.7	-381.3	-483.6	-530.2	-510.0	-574.8	-613.5
Trade Balance	78ac d	-66.5	-70.9	-83.9	-99.1	-99.8	-88.3	-131.6	-146.6	-158.0	-225.3	-254.7	-337.2	-251.8	-252.8	-220.0
Services: Credit	78ad d	53.3	61.8	73.2	85.2	91.8	97.1	109.2	143.8	182.1	265.2	345.3	354.2	361.3	359.9	404.3
Services: Debit	78ae d	-34.5	-31.0	-37.1	-44.0	-46.8	-56.1	-59.8	-65.4	-77.9	-98.2	-129.1	-143.3	-155.1	-146.7	-158.1
Balance on Goods & Services	78af d	-47.7	-40.1	-47.8	-57.9	-54.8	-47.3	-82.2	-68.3	-53.8	-58.3	-38.5	-126.3	-45.6	-39.6	26.2
Income: Credit	78ag d	8.0	7.6	7.9	10.7	12.3	15.0	13.5	12.7	17.7	22.9	19.9	22.0	21.0	19.8	27.4
Income: Debit	78ah d	-7.3	-8.1	-9.8	-12.4	-12.3	-16.3	-8.3	-12.0	-12.1	-21.0	-19.6	-28.9	-31.0	-36.0	-44.4
Balance on Gds, Serv. & Inc.	78ai d	-47.0	-40.5	-49.8	-59.6	-54.8	-48.6	-77.0	-67.6	-48.2	-56.4	-38.2	-133.2	-55.6	-55.8	9.2
Current Transfers, n.i.e.: Credit	78aj d	7.7	8.2	9.4	11.2	11.0	11.9	18.4	21.5	22.1	30.9	29.0	34.3	26.5	26.3	26.2
Current Transfers: Debit	78ak d	-2.5	-2.8	-2.9	-3.9	-3.9	-4.7	-5.8	-5.5	-5.4	-8.9	-12.6	-19.6	-8.0	-14.0	-19.6
Capital Account, n.i.e.	78bc d	—	—	—	—	—	—	—	—	—	—	—	...	...	...	...
Capital Account, n.i.e.: Credit	78ba d	—	—	—	—	—	—	—	—	—	—	—	...	...	...	...
Capital Account: Debit	78bb d	—	—	—	—	—	—	—	—	—	—	—	...	...	...	...
Financial Account, n.i.e.	78bj d	11.3	24.6	20.8	34.5	-7.1	21.4	25.2	28.3	16.3	9.3	65.7	162.7	29.4	60.2	-7.4
Direct Investment Abroad	78bd d	-.2	-1.3	.1	-.8	-.1	-.8	-1.0	-.4	.1	-.3	-.6	-1.2	-.5	-1.4	-1.5
Dir. Invest. in Rep. Econ., n.i.e.	78be d	8.7	16.1	17.3	5.6	2.4	22.9	6.9	4.9	9.0	5.4	2.8	8.4	4.7	3.7	.1
Portfolio Investment Assets	78bf d	-.6	-.2	—	-.3	.7	-.1	.1	5.0	—	-3.2	.4	-.5	-2.7	-2.0	-4.0
Equity Securities	78bk d	—	—	—	—	—	—	—	—	—	—	.4	-.1	-2.2	-1.6	-4.6
Debt Securities	78bl d	-.6	-.2	—	-.3	.7	-.1	.1	5.0	—	-3.2	—	-.4	-.5	-.5	.7
Portfolio Investment Liab., n.i.e.	78bg d	—	.8	.5	.4	-.9	.3	.1	.6	2.0	.3	4.9	.6	-3.2	.2	-.2
Equity Securities	78bm d	—	—	—	—	—	—	—	—	—	—	4.8	.8	-3.3	-.4	-.3
Debt Securities	78bn d	—	.8	.5	.4	-.9	.3	.1	.6	2.0	.3	.1	-.2	.1	.5	.5
Financial Derivatives Assets	78bw d	...	...	...	...	...	...	...	...	...	...	...	...	...	...	...
Financial Derivatives Liabilities	78bx d	...	...	...	...	...	...	...	...	...	...	...	...	...	...	...
Other Investment Assets	78bh d	-10.6	-3.4	-4.6	-6.2	1.9	1.6	-6.1	-8.2	-22.8	-41.3	-29.8	-32.3	-55.1	-49.3	-75.8
Monetary Authorities	78bo d															
General Government	78bp d	-.4	-1.6	-1.9	-1.7	-.4	-.5	-.4	-1.2	-.9	—	-1.4	-1.9	-4.6	-1.3	-1.6
Banks	78bq d	-10.7	—	—	—	3.8	-.3	-3.7	-4.0	-5.8	-.5	-2.7	-.9	-.2	-1.6	-21.6
Other Sectors	78br d	.4	-1.8	-2.8	-4.5	-1.5	2.4	-2.0	-3.1	-16.1	-40.8	-25.8	-31.3	-48.3	-46.4	-52.6
Other Investment Liab., n.i.e.	78bi d	14.1	12.7	7.6	35.8	-11.1	-2.4	25.2	26.4	28.0	48.3	88.0	187.6	86.3	109.0	73.6
Monetary Authorities	78bs d	—	2.2	.6	-2.9	.5	—	—	—	.1	.1	-2.0	19.0	-1.5	-1.0	-4.0
General Government	78bt d	—	.4	2.9	21.5	-2.9	—	3.5	5.3	5.7	5.5	25.5	49.1	14.8	30.2	9.0
Banks	78bu d	9.9	6.1	3.0	13.6	-10.4	-6.7	4.4	3.0	-5.4	-3.8	6.2	17.7	-.7	15.7	5.3
Other Sectors	78bv d	4.3	4.0	1.1	3.6	1.8	4.4	17.4	18.2	27.7	46.5	58.3	101.9	73.7	64.1	63.3
Net Errors and Omissions	78ca d	24.6	22.2	25.5	17.4	48.3	28.6	27.1	15.0	36.3	29.9	-31.3	-54.8	4.3	-16.8	-32.1
Overall Balance	78cb d	-5.9	11.7	3.1	-.4	-6.7	8.7	-12.0	-8.3	21.2	4.8	12.6	-10.6	-3.4	-.2	-23.8
Reserves and Related Items	79da d	5.9	-11.7	-3.1	.4	6.7	-8.7	12.0	8.3	-21.2	-4.8	-12.6	10.6	3.4	.2	23.8
Reserve Assets	79db d	5.9	-11.7	-3.1	.4	6.7	-8.7	12.0	-9.2	-21.2	-4.8	-12.0	9.2	-23.8	-22.3	8.5
Use of Fund Credit and Loans	79dc d	—	—	—	—	—	—	—	7.6	—	—	-5.5	-1.7	22.9	14.5	8.1
Exceptional Financing	79de d	—	—	—	—	—	—	—	10.0	—	—	5.0	3.2	4.4	7.9	7.2
Government Finance															*Millions of Barbados Dollars:*		
Total Revenue and Grants	81y	...	...	...	...	140.60	190.64	202.36	227.22	286.22	340.13	420.89	446.65	486.08	545.92	560.58
Revenue	81	...	...	...	...	140.60	190.64	202.36	227.22	286.22	340.13	420.89	446.65	486.08	545.92	560.58
Grants	81z					—	—	—	—	—	—	—	—	—	—	—
Exp. & Lending Minus Repay.	82z	...	...	...	...	188.97	211.89	256.76	312.59	326.08	395.47	471.85	627.64	585.96	633.34	657.49
Expenditure	82					190.69	212.58	257.40	306.73	324.98	393.36	474.19	628.44	585.75	607.60	655.53
Lending Minus Repayments	83					-1.72	-.69	-.64	5.86	1.10	2.11	-2.34	-.80	.21	25.74	1.96
Statistical Discrepancy	80xx	...	...	...	...	...	...	...	...	...	...	...	...	...	...	...
Total Financing	80h	...	...	...	...	...	...	...	...	...	...	...	...	...	...	...
Domestic	84a	...	...	...	...	...	...	...	...	...	...	...	...	...	...	...
Foreign	85a	...	...	...	...	...	...	...	...	...	...	...	...	...	...	...
Total Debt by Residence	88	...	...	...	...	...	...	...	...	340.0	372.1	426.3	493.2	683.4	760.0	861.3	950.9
Domestic	88a									274.8	282.9	314.2	329.3	424.0	473.1	514.0	585.6
Foreign	89a									65.2	89.2	112.1	163.9	259.4	286.9	347.3	365.3
National Accounts															*Millions of Barbados Dollars*		
Exports of Goods & Services	90c	...	...	252	298	386	469	406	493	646	882	1,214	1,138	1,270	1,490	1,656
Government Consumption	91f	...	...	81	111	100	102	151	172	190	210	258	321	329	346	388
Gross Capital Formation	93	...	...	...	...	169	156	236	194	254	317	383	495	425	421	374
Private Consumption	96f	...	...	308	349	539	568	646	742	782	965	1,081	1,235	1,263	1,321	1,432
Imports of Goods & Services	98c	...	...	-329	-398	-472	-515	-566	-607	-760	-1,027	-1,247	-1,315	-1,323	-1,466	-1,547
Gross Domestic Product (GDP)	99b	331	367	407	477	705	780	873	890	984	1,348	1,731	1,905	1,990	2,113	2,303
GDP Volume 1965 prices	99b.p	192.0	195.0	197.0	201.0	228.0	...	...	...	...	...	...	...	...	...	...
GDP Volume 1974 Prices	99b.p	...	...	...	...	640	627	655	679	712	768	802	787	748	751	779
GDP Volume (1995=100)	99bv p	62.7	63.7	64.4	65.7	74.5	73.0	76.3	79.0	82.9	89.4	93.4	91.6	87.1	87.4	90.6
GDP Deflator (1995=100)	99bi p	14.1	15.4	17.0	19.5	25.4	28.7	30.7	30.2	31.8	40.5	49.7	55.8	61.3	64.8	68.2
															Millions:		
Population	99z	.24	.24	.24	.24	.24	.25	.25	.25	.26	.25	.25	.25	.25	.25	.25

1985	1986	1987	1988	1989	1990	1991	1992	1993	1994	1995	1996	1997	1998	1999		
															Prices, Production, Labor	
Period Averages																
71.6	72.6	75.0	78.6	83.5	86.0	91.4	97.0	98.1	‡98.2	100.0	102.4	110.3	108.9	110.6	Consumer Prices	64
91.0	82.1	84.3	97.6	96.1	102.4	96.7	90.6	95.7	98.3	100.0	101.6	106.3	113.3	111.2	Industrial Production	66
Period Averages																
....	....	....	....	....	....	....	125	....	129	137	135	136	....		Labor Force	67d
92	96	98	100	107	105	101	96	100	106	110	114	116	120	....	Employment	67e
21	21	21	21	17	19	21	29	31	28	27	21	20	17	....	Unemployment	67c
18.7	17.7	17.9	17.4	13.7	15.0	17.1	23.0	24.5	21.9	19.7	15.8	14.5	12.3	....	Unemployment Rate (%)	67r
															International Transactions	
Millions of Barbados Dollars																
713.4	556.7	322.5	354.2	375.7	430.2	414.7	380.3	374.0	363.0	477.8	561.2	565.9	503.1	457.1	Exports	70
1,221.6	1,181.1	1,035.9	1,163.9	1,354.3	1,407.9	1,397.7	1,048.5	1,154.1	1,228.6	1,541.2	1,667.3	1,991.0	2,019.6	2,042.5	Imports, c.i.f.	71
															Balance of Payments	
Minus Sign Indicates Debit																
51.3	7.3	−18.9	43.5	25.0	−10.6	−27.1	140.0	68.8	133.6	89.1	102.9	−50.0	−56.5	....	Current Account, n.i.e.	78al *d*
356.9	283.4	167.1	179.6	187.4	219.0	206.5	189.9	187.8	190.0	245.4	286.7	289.0	257.1	....	Goods: Exports f.o.b.	78aa *d*
−565.7	−531.1	−461.5	−518.4	−603.8	−627.6	−622.8	−467.7	−514.3	−544.7	−691.2	−743.0	−887.7	−901.1	....	Goods: Imports f.o.b.	78ab *d*
−208.9	−247.7	−294.5	−338.9	−416.4	−408.6	−416.3	−277.8	−326.6	−354.7	−445.9	−456.3	−598.7	−644.1	....	*Trade Balance*	78ac *d*
438.7	468.6	519.2	598.8	701.4	653.9	617.6	619.1	689.5	813.6	913.2	960.2	959.3	1,023.6	....	Services: Credit	78ad *d*
−155.7	−191.3	−213.2	−193.0	−235.7	−250.2	−218.7	−209.4	−272.6	−319.0	−363.2	−387.1	−409.5	−432.2	....	Services: Debit	78ae *d*
74.2	29.6	11.6	67.0	49.3	−4.9	−17.3	131.9	90.4	140.0	104.2	116.9	−48.9	−52.7	....	*Balance on Goods & Services*	78af *d*
26.3	34.6	32.1	29.1	34.3	30.1	38.0	37.6	40.1	46.1	48.4	54.2	60.5	63.5	....	Income: Credit	78ag *d*
−46.0	−62.2	−65.7	−64.6	−60.2	−75.7	−77.5	−66.5	−81.0	−86.8	−96.1	−106.4	−108.2	−119.5	....	Income: Debit	78ah *d*
54.6	2.0	−22.1	31.5	23.5	−50.6	−56.8	103.0	49.4	99.3	56.5	64.7	−96.6	−108.7	....	*Balance on Gds, Serv. & Inc.*	78ai *d*
24.2	32.7	35.5	43.1	48.1	52.0	45.6	51.7	41.8	54.5	56.2	64.8	71.7	78.4	....	Current Transfers, n.i.e.: Credit	78aj *d*
−27.5	−27.4	−32.4	−31.2	−46.5	−12.0	−15.9	−14.7	−22.5	−20.2	−23.6	−26.6	−25.1	−26.2	....	Current Transfers: Debit	78ak *d*
....	....	....	....	....	....	....	....	....	....	....	.4	−.1	.7	....	Capital Account, n.i.e.	78bc *d*
—	—	—	—	—	—	—	—	—	—	—	.4	—	.7	....	Capital Account, n.i.e.: Credit	78ba *d*
—	—	—	—	—	—	—	—	—	—	—	—	−.1		....	Capital Account: Debit	78bb *d*
−.2	79.2	95.2	37.9	−23.1	42.0	38.1	−80.3	.6	−6.4	−26.4	−22.2	20.0	55.2	....	Financial Account, n.i.e.	78bj *d*
−2.3	−2.8	−2.5	−1.0	−3.0	−1.4	−1.3	−.9	−2.6	−1.1	−3.3	−3.6	−1.2	−1.0	....	Direct Investment Abroad	78bd *d*
4.9	7.8	7.1	11.6	8.4	11.2	7.4	14.5	9.4	13.0	11.8	13.3	14.8	15.8	....	Dir. Invest. in Rep. Econ., n.i.e.	78be *d*
−5.3	−6.7	−1.4	2.0	−5.0	−3.1	−16.9	−4.1	−9.9	−1.8	−3.1	−17.4	−17.3	−23.1	....	Portfolio Investment Assets	78bf *d*
−3.7	−5.9	−1.8	−.6	−5.2	−6.1	−8.3	−4.1	−9.9	−13.3	−7.6	−9.7	−11.3	−14.0	....	Equity Securities	78bk *d*
−1.6	−.8	.5	2.6	.2	3.0	−8.6	—	—	11.5	4.6	−7.8	−6.0	−9.2	....	Debt Securities	78bl *d*
.2	.3	—	40.6	.8	−22.2	14.0	−7.8	1.5	48.7	40.4	−1.6	−25.5	−25.6	....	Portfolio Investment Liab., n.i.e.	78bg *d*
.1	.3	—	.4	.4	—	−.7	.9	—	—	—	−.1	−.1		....	Equity Securities	78bm *d*
.1	—	—	40.2	.4	−22.2	14.7	−7.8	.6	48.7	40.4	−1.6	−25.4	−25.6	....	Debt Securities	78bn *d*
....	....	....	....	....	....	....	....	....	....	....	....	....	....	....	Financial Derivatives Assets	78bw *d*
....	....	....	....	....	....	....	....	....	....	....	....	....	....	....	Financial Derivatives Liabilities	78bx *d*
−15.1	8.6	40.7	−.3	−21.5	−22.4	7.6	−19.3	−8.2	−88.9	−167.0	−210.9	−12.1	−18.5	....	Other Investment Assets	78bh *d*
....	....	....	....	....	....	....	....	....	....	....	....	....	....	....	Monetary Authorities	78bo *d*
−9.7	−.7	−.8	−.6	−.6	−.6	−.5	−3.5	−1.4	−7.8	−9.3	−7.1	−14.1	−12.6	....	General Government	78bp *d*
−6.1	−15.8	−61.6	40.7	−2.4	−19.0	−11.1	−11.1	−14.9	−32.6	−87.5	−154.1	24.5	21.5	....	Banks	78bq *d*
.7	25.0	103.0	−40.5	−18.5	−2.8	19.1	−4.8	8.0	−48.6	−70.3	−49.8	−22.5	−27.4	....	Other Sectors	78br *d*
17.5	72.0	51.3	−15.0	−2.9	79.8	27.3	−62.7	10.4	23.8	94.8	198.0	61.1	107.6	....	Other Investment Liab. n.i.e.	78bi *d*
−3.7	−.7	−7.6	−1.6	—	.7	12.0	9.5	−1.9	−5.2	−8.5	−6.7	−6.7		....	Monetary Authorities	78bs *d*
39.4	54.8	77.4	.4	17.9	25.4	−26.7	−31.3	−25.2	−41.1	−34.4	10.3	7.9	23.9	....	General Government	78bt *d*
2.2	18.3	62.3	−43.4	−16.1	18.4	17.4	13.9	11.2	16.6	101.4	127.3	−19.8	18.6	....	Banks	78bu *d*
−20.5	−.4	−80.9	29.6	−4.8	35.4	24.6	−54.8	26.3	53.5	36.3	67.1	79.6	65.2	....	Other Sectors	78bv *d*
−37.0	−72.2	−72.8	−47.8	−48.2	−72.7	−54.6	−34.4	−49.7	−89.4	−20.6	5.2	47.5	−5.5	....	Net Errors and Omissions	78ca *d*
14.1	14.2	3.5	33.5	−46.3	−41.3	−43.6	25.3	19.6	37.8	42.1	86.4	17.4	−6.1	....	*Overall Balance*	78cb *d*
−14.1	−14.2	−3.5	−33.5	46.3	41.3	43.6	−25.3	−19.6	−37.8	−42.1	−86.4	−17.4	6.1	....	Reserves and Related Items	79da *d*
−22.4	−7.1	15.4	−27.6	48.9	42.3	40.8	−80.3	−21.1	−59.1	−25.0	−61.1	−9.1	5.6	....	Reserve Assets	79db *d*
—	−13.0	−21.6	−10.6	−5.8	−3.7	−.7	51.5	—	—	−18.1	−26.8	−9.0	—	....	Use of Fund Credit and Loans	79dc *d*
8.3	6.0	2.6	4.6	3.2	2.8	3.5	3.4	1.5	21.3	1.0	1.5	.7	.6	....	Exceptional Financing	79de *d*
															Government Finance	
Year Ending December 31																
622.03	657.92	700.14	818.92	1,002.44	931.16	1,016.71	985.05	1,022.79	1,017.43	1,140.52	1,194.44	1,424.53	1,526.78	....	Total Revenue and Grants	81y
622.03	657.92	700.14	818.92	1,002.44	931.16	1,016.71	985.05	1,022.79	1,017.43	1,140.52	1,194.44	1,424.53	1,526.78	....	Revenue	81
....	....	....	....	....	....	....	....	....	....	....	....	....	....	....	Grants	81z
762.41	826.25	890.05	1,024.77	1,077.08	1,175.96	1,085.98	1,017.28	1,109.10	1,098.60	1,113.67	1,324.09	1,463.58	1,566.52	....	Exp. & Lending Minus Repay.	82z
760.10	818.81	882.79	931.71	1,046.64	1,178.49	1,079.70	1,003.95	1,103.97	1,070.34	1,125.78	1,324.26	1,458.02	1,573.67	....	Expenditure	82
2.31	7.44	7.26	93.06	30.44	−2.53	6.28	13.33	5.13	28.26	−12.10	−.17	5.56	−7.15	....	Lending Minus Repayments	83
									−31.79	1.43	−47.47	−10.65	16.51	....	Statistical Discrepancy	80xx
									112.99	−28.28	177.13	49.70	23.23	....	Total Financing	80h
									69.58	−19.30	162.93	83.98	57.78	....	Domestic	84a
									43.41	−8.98	14.20	−34.28	−34.55	....	Foreign	85a
1,095.7	1,266.5	1,461.3	1,611.5	1,695.1	1,857.4	1,901.1	1,991.7	2,322.6	2,492.2	2,479.9	2,721.1	2,737.1	2,796.2	2,872.1	Total Debt by Residence	88
651.7	713.0	754.4	821.8	878.0	1,020.6	1,113.5	1,236.7	1,618.0	1,777.8	1,762.2	1,967.0	2,036.9	2,121.4	2,107.5	Domestic	88a
444.0	553.5	706.9	789.7	817.1	836.8	787.6	755.0	704.6	714.4	717.7	754.1	700.2	674.9	764.6	Foreign	89a
															National Accounts	
Millions of Barbados Dollars																
1,633	1,496	1,340	1,510	1,724	1,689	1,610	1,588	1,727	1,960	2,265	2,450	2,438	....	....	Exports of Goods & Services	90c
456	469	498	537	614	694	642	640	732	707	742	858	934	....	....	Government Consumption	91f
372	424	467	543	656	648	580	301	420	464	527	506	676	....	....	Gross Capital Formation	93
1,392	1,692	1,934	2,004	2,158	2,189	2,262	1,984	1,959	2,024	2,247	2,378	2,834	....	....	Private Consumption	96f
−1,448	−1,435	−1,325	−1,495	−1,725	−1,780	−1,701	−1,330	−1,537	−1,683	−2,053	−2,199	−2,511	....	....	Imports of Goods & Services	98c
2,410	2,646	2,914	3,099	3,427	3,440	3,393	3,183	3,301	3,474	3,728	3,993	4,371	4,680	....	Gross Domestic Product (GDP)	99b
....	....	....	....	....	....	....	....	....	....	....	....	....	....	....	GDP Volume 1965 prices	99b. *p*
787	827	848	878	909	879	844	792	803	835	859	894	921	....	....	GDP Volume 1974 Prices	99b. *p*
91.6	96.3	98.7	102.2	105.8	102.3	98.2	92.2	93.5	97.2	100.0	104.1	107.2	....	....	GDP Volume (1995=100)	99bv *p*
70.6	73.7	79.2	81.4	86.9	90.2	92.7	92.6	94.7	95.9	100.0	102.9	109.3	....	....	GDP Deflator (1995=100)	99bi *p*
Midyear Estimates																
.25	.25	.25	.25	.26	.26	.26	.26	.26	.26	.26	.26	.26	.27	.27	**Population**	99z

(See notes in the back of the book.)

Belarus

		1970	1971	1972	1973	1974	1975	1976	1977	1978	1979	1980	1981	1982	1983	1984
Exchange Rates																*Rubels per SDR:*
Official Rate	aa	....	....	....	....	....	.....	.....	....	....	....	....	....	....	....	....
																Rubels per US Dollar:
Official Rate	ae	....	....	....	....	....	.....	.....	....	....	....	....	....	....	....	....
Official Rate	rf	....	....	....	....	....	.....	.....	....	....	....	....	....	....	....	....
Fund Position																*Millions of SDRs:*
Quota	2f. *s*	—	—	—	—	—	—	—	—	—	—	—	—	—	—	—
SDRs	1b. *s*	—	—	—	—	—	—	—	—	—	—	—	—	—	—	—
Reserve Position in the Fund	1c. *s*	....	....	....	....	....	.....	.....	....	....	....	....	....	....	....	....
Total Fund Cred.&Loans Outstg.	2tl	....	....	....	....	....	.....	.....	....	....	....	....	....	....	....	....
International Liquidity													*Millions of US Dollars Unless Otherwise Indicated:*			
Total Reserves minus Gold	1l. *d*	....	....	....	....	....	.....	.....	....	....	....	....	....	....	....	....
SDRs	1b. *d*	....	....	....	....	....	.....	.....	....	....	....	....	....	....	....	....
Reserve Position in the Fund	1c. *d*	....	....	....	....	....	.....	.....	....	....	....	....	....	....	....	....
Foreign Exchange	1d. *d*	....	....	....	....	....	.....	.....	....	....	....	....	....	....	....	....
Gold (Million Fine Troy Ounces)	1ad	....	....	....	....	....	.....	.....	....	....	....	....	....	....	....	....
Gold (National Valuation)	1an *d*	....	....	....	....	....	.....	.....	....	....	....	....	....	....	....	....
Monetary Authorities: Other Liab.	4.. *d*	....	....	....	....	....	.....	.....	....	....	....	....	....	....	....	....
Dep.Money Banks: Assets Conv.	7ax *d*	....	....	....	....	....	.....	.....	....	....	....	....	....	....	....	....
Assets Nonconv.	7ay *d*	....	....	....	....	....	.....	.....	....	....	....	....	....	....	....	....
Dep.Money Banks: Liab. Conv.	7bx *d*	....	....	....	....	....	.....	.....	....	....	....	....	....	....	....	....
Liab. Nonconv.	7by *d*	....	....	....	....	....	.....	.....	....	....	....	....	....	....	....	....
Monetary Authorities																*Billions of Rubels:*
Foreign Assets	11	....	....	....	....	....	.....	.....	....	....	....	....	....	....	....	....
Claims on Central Government	12a	....	....	....	....	....	.....	.....	....	....	....	....	....	....	....	....
Claims on Local Government	12b	....	....	....	....	....	.....	.....	....	....	....	....	....	....	....	....
Claims on Nonfin.Pub.Enterprises	12c	....	....	....	....	....	.....	.....	....	....	....	....	....	....	....	....
Claims on Private Sector	12d	....	....	....	....	....	.....	.....	....	....	....	....	....	....	....	....
Claims on Banks	12e	....	....	....	....	....	.....	.....	....	....	....	....	....	....	....	....
Reserve Money	14	....	....	....	....	....	.....	.....	....	....	....	....	....	....	....	....
of which: Currency Outside DMBs	14a	....	....	....	....	....	.....	.....	....	....	....	....	....	....	....	....
Time, Savings,& Fgn.Currency Dep.	15	....	....	....	....	....	.....	.....	....	....	....	....	....	....	....	....
Foreign Liabilities	16c	....	....	....	....	....	.....	.....	....	....	....	....	....	....	....	....
Central Government Deposits	16d	....	....	....	....	....	.....	.....	....	....	....	....	....	....	....	....
Capital Accounts	17a	....	....	....	....	....	.....	.....	....	....	....	....	....	....	....	....
Other Items (Net)	17r	....	....	....	....	....	.....	.....	....	....	....	....	....	....	....	....
Deposit Money Banks																*Billions of Rubels:*
Reserves	20	....	....	....	....	....	.....	.....	....	....	....	....	....	....	....	....
Foreign Assets	21	....	....	....	....	....	.....	.....	....	....	....	....	....	....	....	....
Claims on Central Government	22a	....	....	....	....	....	.....	.....	....	....	....	....	....	....	....	....
Claims on Local Government	22b	....	....	....	....	....	.....	.....	....	....	....	....	....	....	....	....
Claims on Nonfin.Pub.Enterprises	22c	....	....	....	....	....	.....	.....	....	....	....	....	....	....	....	....
Claims on Private Sector	22d	....	....	....	....	....	.....	.....	....	....	....	....	....	....	....	....
Claims on Nonbank Financial Insts	22g	....	....	....	....	....	.....	.....	....	....	....	....	....	....	....	....
Demand Deposits	24	....	....	....	....	....	.....	.....	....	....	....	....	....	....	....	....
Time, Savings,& Fgn. Currency Dep.	25	....	....	....	....	....	.....	.....	....	....	....	....	....	....	....	....
Foreign Liabilities	26c	....	....	....	....	....	.....	.....	....	....	....	....	....	....	....	....
Central Government Deposits	26d	....	....	....	....	....	.....	.....	....	....	....	....	....	....	....	....
Credit from Monetary Authorities	26g	....	....	....	....	....	.....	.....	....	....	....	....	....	....	....	....
Capital Accounts	27a	....	....	....	....	....	.....	.....	....	....	....	....	....	....	....	....
Other Items (Net)	27r	....	....	....	....	....	.....	.....	....	....	....	....	....	....	....	....
Monetary Survey																*Billions of Rubels:*
Foreign Assets (Net)	31n	....	....	....	....	....	.....	.....	....	....	....	....	....	....	....	....
Domestic Credit	32	....	....	....	....	....	.....	.....	....	....	....	....	....	....	....	....
Claims on Central Govt. (Net)	32an	....	....	....	....	....	.....	.....	....	....	....	....	....	....	....	....
Claims on Local Government	32b	....	....	....	....	....	.....	.....	....	....	....	....	....	....	....	....
Claims on Nonfin.Pub.Enterprises	32c	....	....	....	....	....	.....	.....	....	....	....	....	....	....	....	....
Claims on Private Sector	32d	....	....	....	....	....	.....	.....	....	....	....	....	....	....	....	....
Claims on Nonbank Financ. Insts	32g	....	....	....	....	....	.....	.....	....	....	....	....	....	....	....	....
Money	34	....	....	....	....	....	.....	.....	....	....	....	....	....	....	....	....
Quasi-Money	35	....	....	....	....	....	.....	.....	....	....	....	....	....	....	....	....
Capital Accounts	37a	....	....	....	....	....	.....	.....	....	....	....	....	....	....	....	....
Other Items (Net)	37r	....	....	....	....	....	.....	.....	....	....	....	....	....	....	....	....
Money plus Quasi-Money	35l	....	....	....	....	....	.....	.....	....	....	....	....	....	....	....	....
Interest Rates																*Percent Per Annum*
Refinancing Rate *(End of Per.)*	60	....	....	....	....	....	.....	.....	....	....	....	....	....	....	....	....
Deposit Rate	60l	....	....	....	....	....	.....	.....	....	....	....	....	....	....	....	....
Lending Rate	60p	....	....	....	....	....	.....	.....	....	....	....	....	....	....	....	....
Prices and Labor																*Percent Change*
Producer Prices	63.x*x*	....	....	....	....	....	.....	.....	....	....	....	....	....	....	....	....
Consumer Prices	64.x*x*	....	....	....	....	....	.....	.....	....	....	....	....	....	....	....	....
Wages	65.x*x*	....	....	....	....	....	.....	.....	....	....	....	....	....	....	....	....
																Number in Thousands:
Unemployment	67c	....	....	....	....	....	.....	.....	....	....	....	....	....	....	....	....
Unemployment Rate (%)	67r	....	....	....	....	....	.....	.....	....	....	....	....	....	....	....	....
International Transactions																*Millions of US Dollars*
Exports	70.. *d*	....	....	....	....	....	.....	.....	....	....	....	....	....	....	....	....
Imports, c.i.f.	71.. *d*	....	....	....	....	....	.....	.....	....	....	....	....	....	....	....	....

1985	1986	1987	1988	1989	1990	1991	1992	1993	1994	1995	1996	1997	1998	1999		
															Exchange Rates	
End of Period																
....	....	....	....	....	....	....	21	960	15,474	17,095	22,288	41,476	309,767	439,203	Official Rate	aa
End of Period (ae) Period Average (rf)																
....	....	....	....	....	....	....	15	699	10,600	11,500	15,500	30,740	220,000	320,000	Official Rate	ae
....	....	....	....	....	....	....	....	....	....	....	....	25,964	....	....	Official Rate	rf
															Fund Position	
End of Period																
—	—	—	—	—	—	—	187.00	280.40	280.40	280.40	280.40	280.40	280.40	386.40	Quota	2f. s
....	....	....	....	....	....	....	—	3.22	.01	3.05	.10	—	.30	.30	SDRs	1b. s
....	....	....	....	....	....	....	.02	.02	.02	.02	.02	.02	.02	.02	Reserve Position in the Fund	1c. s
....	....	....	....	....	....	....	—	70.10	70.10	190.20	190.20	190.20	172.27	129.74	Total Fund Cred.&Loans Outstg.	2tl
															International Liquidity	
End of Period																
....	....	....	....	....	....	....	....	....	100.99	377.02	469.15	393.70	338.83	299.01	Total Reserves minus Gold	1l. d
....	....	....	....	....	....	....	—	4.43	.01	4.54	.14	—	.42	.42	SDRs	1b. d
....	....	....	....	....	....	....	.03	.03	.03	.03	.03	.03	.03	.03	Reserve Position in the Fund	1c. d
....	....	....	....	....	....	....	....	....	100.95	372.45	468.98	393.67	338.39	298.57	Foreign Exchange	1d. d
....	....	....	....	....	....	....	....	....	....	....	....	....	....	....	Gold (Million Fine Troy Ounces)	1ad
....	....	....	....	....	....	....	....	....	....	....	....	....	....	....	Gold (National Valuation)	1and
....	....	....	....	....	....	....	....	....	7.53	11.88	144.97	61.87	78.90	77.31	Monetary Authorities: Other Liab.	4.. d
....	....	....	....	....	....	....	....	....	280.29	261.71	I246.78	276.63	290.03	308.20	Dep.Money Banks: Assets Conv.	7ax d
....	....	....	....	....	....	....	....	....	40.66	27.90	I82.98	93.25	18.54	28.73	Assets Nonconv	7ay d
....	....	....	....	....	....	....	....	....	51.69	88.05	I84.25	89.30	134.49	108.07	Dep.Money Banks: Liab. Conv.	7bx d
....	....	....	....	....	....	....	....	....	36.49	31.68	I58.55	70.10	4.71	7.78	Liab. Nonconv	7by d
															Monetary Authorities	
End of Period																
....	....	....	....	....	....	....	....	....	1,226	4,594	7,411	12,333	76,465	99,873	Foreign Assets	11
....	....	....	....	....	....	....	....	....	1,679	4,876	8,591	14,448	54,930	153,755	Claims on Central Government	12a
....	....	....	....	....	....	....	....	....	—	—	—	—	—	—	Claims on Local Government	12b
....	....	....	....	....	....	....	....	....	12	88	112	101	22	44	Claims on Nonfin.Pub.Enterprises	12c
....	....	....	....	....	....	....	....	....	7	38	32	71	343	2,041	Claims on Private Sector	12d
....	....	....	....	....	....	....	....	....	1,435	2,325	6,719	17,046	51,229	60,226	Claims on Banks	12e
....	....	....	....	....	....	....	....	....	1,757	6,817	12,143	25,214	66,300	184,680	Reserve Money	14
....	....	....	....	....	....	....	....	....	736	3,779	6,199	12,300	27,074	86,852	*of which: Currency Outside DMBs*	14a
....	....	....	....	....	....	....	....	....	15	19	20	23	81	139	Time, Savings,& Fgn.Currency Dep.	15
....	....	....	....	....	....	....	....	....	1,263	3,388	6,486	9,791	70,720	81,722	Foreign Liabilities	16c
....	....	....	....	....	....	....	....	....	379	342	1,107	2,010	6,490	15,072	Central Government Deposits	16d
....	....	....	....	....	....	....	....	....	301	637	1,402	3,694	5,968	24,895	Capital Accounts	17a
....	....	....	....	....	....	....	....	....	643	718	1,708	3,266	33,430	9,430	Other Items (Net)	17r
															Deposit Money Banks	
End of Period																
....	....	....	....	....	....	....	....	....	951	2,842	I5,693	11,889	35,688	92,002	Reserves	20
....	....	....	....	....	....	....	....	....	3,691	3,331	I5,111	11,370	67,886	107,816	Foreign Assets	21
....	....	....	....	....	....	....	....	....	9	640	I2,273	6,084	21,956	53,796	Claims on Central Government	22a
....	....	....	....	....	....	....	....	....	—		I4	22	143	358	Claims on Local Government	22b
....	....	....	....	....	....	....	....	....	2,866	6,571	I9,232	18,565	84,059	170,553	Claims on Nonfin.Pub.Enterprises	22c
....	....	....	....	....	....	....	....	....	3,127	7,360	I12,303	30,292	112,999	279,701	Claims on Private Sector	22d
....	....	....	....	....	....	....	....	....	....	....	302	498	480	1,278	Claims on Nonbank Financial Insts	22g
....	....	....	....	....	....	....	....	....	1,877	6,132	I9,240	21,052	52,487	140,714	Demand Deposits	24
....	....	....	....	....	....	....	....	....	4,238	7,889	I11,609	23,904	136,239	271,888	Time, Savings,& Fgn. Currency Dep.	25
....	....	....	....	....	....	....	....	....	1,014	1,377	I2,213	4,900	30,622	37,073	Foreign Liabilities	26c
....	....	....	....	....	....	....	....	....	238	1,000	I2,848	5,799	20,991	44,722	Central Government Deposits	26d
....	....	....	....	....	....	....	....	....	1,243	2,122	I6,486	15,931	48,371	53,471	Credit from Monetary Authorities	26g
....	....	....	....	....	....	....	....	....	1,107	4,620	I5,277	8,925	25,545	147,109	Capital Accounts	27a
....	....	....	....	....	....	....	....	....	926	-2,396	I-2,753	-1,792	8,955	10,527	Other Items (Net)	27r
															Monetary Survey	
End of Period																
....	....	....	....	....	....	....	....	....	2,640	3,160	I3,823	9,012	43,008	88,894	Foreign Assets (Net)	31n
....	....	....	....	....	....	....	....	....	7,083	18,232	I28,896	62,271	247,452	601,732	Domestic Credit	32
....	....	....	....	....	....	....	....	....	1,071	4,175	I6,909	12,723	49,405	147,757	Claims on Central Govt. (Net)	32an
....	....	....	....	....	....	....	....	....	—	—	I4	22	143	358	Claims on Local Government	32b
....	....	....	....	....	....	....	....	....	2,878	6,659	I9,344	18,665	84,081	170,598	Claims on Nonfin.Pub.Enterprises	32c
....	....	....	....	....	....	....	....	....	3,134	7,398	I12,335	30,363	113,343	281,741	Claims on Private Sector	32d
....	....	....	....	....	....	....	....	....	....	....	302	498	480	1,278	Claims on Nonbank Financ. Insts	32g
....	....	....	....	....	....	....	....	....	2,687	10,027	I15,708	33,852	80,932	233,415	Money	34
....	....	....	....	....	....	....	....	....	4,253	7,908	I11,629	23,927	136,320	272,027	Quasi-Money	35
....	....	....	....	....	....	....	....	....	1,407	5,257	I6,678	12,619	31,513	172,005	Capital Accounts	37a
....	....	....	....	....	....	....	....	....	1,375	-1,800	I-1,297	885	41,694	13,179	Other Items (Net)	37r
....	....	....	....	....	....	....	....	....	6,940	17,934	I27,337	57,779	217,252	505,442	Money plus Quasi-Money	35l
															Interest Rates	
Percent Per Annum																
....	....	....	....	....	....	....	30.0	210.0	480.0	66.0	8.3	8.9	9.6	23.4	Refinancing Rate *(End of Per.)*	60
....	....	....	....	....	....	....	....	65.1	89.6	100.8	32.4	15.6	14.3	23.8	Deposit Rate	60l
....	....	....	....	....	....	....	....	71.6	148.5	175.0	62.3	31.8	27.0	51.0	Lending Rate	60p
															Prices and Labor	
over Previous Period																
....	....	....	....	....	....	....	....	1,536.3	2,170.8	I497.9	35.0	86.5	73.5	355.8	Producer Prices	63.x x
....	....	....	....	....	....	....	966.5	1,190.2	2,221.0	709.3	52.7	63.9	72.9	293.7	Consumer Prices	64.x x
....	....	....	....	....	....	....	....	1,106.8	1,504.4	668.9	60.5	87.3	104.2	322.4	Wages	65.x x
Period Averages																
....	....	....	....	....	....	....	24	66	101	131	183	126	106	....	Unemployment	67c
....	....	....	....	....	....	....	.5	1.4	2.1	2.7	3.9	2.8	2.3	....	Unemployment Rate (%)	67r
Millions of US Dollars																
															International Transactions	
....	....	....	....	....	....	....	3,559	1,970	2,510	4,707	5,652	7,301	7,070	5,922	Exports	70.. d
....	....	....	....	....	....	....	3,495	2,539	3,066	5,563	6,939	8,689	8,549	6,664	Imports, c.i.f.	71.. d

Belarus

		1970	1971	1972	1973	1974	1975	1976	1977	1978	1979	1980	1981	1982	1983	1984
Balance of Payments															*Millions of US Dollars:*	
Current Account, n.i.e.	78al d	...	...	...	...	...	...	...	...	...	...	...	...	...	...	...
Goods: Exports f.o.b.	78aa d	...	...	...	...	...	...	...	...	...	...	...	...	...	...	...
Goods: Imports f.o.b.	78ab d	...	...	...	...	...	...	...	...	...	...	...	...	...	...	...
Trade Balance	78ac d	...	...	...	...	...	...	...	...	...	...	...	...	...	...	...
Services: Credit	78ad d	...	...	...	...	...	...	...	...	...	...	...	...	...	...	...
Services: Debit	78ae d	...	...	...	...	...	...	...	...	...	...	...	...	...	...	...
Balance on Goods & Services	78af d	...	...	...	...	...	...	...	...	...	...	...	...	...	...	...
Income: Credit	78ag d	...	...	...	...	...	...	...	...	...	...	...	...	...	...	...
Income: Debit	78ah d	...	...	...	...	...	...	...	...	...	...	...	...	...	...	...
Balance on Gds, Serv. & Inc.	78ai d	...	...	...	...	...	...	...	...	...	...	...	...	...	...	...
Current Transfers, n.i.e.: Credit	78aj d	...	...	...	...	...	...	...	...	...	...	...	...	...	...	...
Current Transfers: Debit	78ak d	...	...	...	...	...	...	...	...	...	...	...	...	...	...	...
Capital Account, n.i.e.	78bc d	...	...	...	...	...	...	...	...	...	...	...	...	...	...	...
Capital Account, n.i.e.: Credit	78ba d	...	...	...	...	...	...	...	...	...	...	...	...	...	...	...
Capital Account: Debit	78bb d	...	...	...	...	...	...	...	...	...	...	...	...	...	...	...
Financial Account, n.i.e.	78bj d	...	...	...	...	...	...	...	...	...	...	...	...	...	...	...
Direct Investment Abroad	78bd d	...	...	...	...	...	...	...	...	...	...	...	...	...	...	...
Dir. Invest. in Rep. Econ., n.i.e.	78be d	...	...	...	...	...	...	...	...	...	...	...	...	...	...	...
Portfolio Investment Assets	78bf d	...	...	...	...	...	...	...	...	...	...	...	...	...	...	...
Equity Securities	78bk d	...	...	...	...	...	...	...	...	...	...	...	...	...	...	...
Debt Securities	78bl d	...	...	...	...	...	...	...	...	...	...	...	...	...	...	...
Portfolio Investment Liab., n.i.e.	78bg d	...	...	...	...	...	...	...	...	...	...	...	...	...	...	...
Equity Securities	78bm d	...	...	...	...	...	...	...	...	...	...	...	...	...	...	...
Debt Securities	78bn d	...	...	...	...	...	...	...	...	...	...	...	...	...	...	...
Financial Derivatives Assets	78bw d	...	...	...	...	...	...	...	...	...	...	...	...	...	...	...
Financial Derivatives Liabilities	78bx d	...	...	...	...	...	...	...	...	...	...	...	...	...	...	...
Other Investment Assets	78bh d	...	...	...	...	...	...	...	...	...	...	...	...	...	...	...
Monetary Authorities	78bo d	...	...	...	...	...	...	...	...	...	...	...	...	...	...	...
General Government	78bp d	...	...	...	...	...	...	...	...	...	...	...	...	...	...	...
Banks	78bq d	...	...	...	...	...	...	...	...	...	...	...	...	...	...	...
Other Sectors	78br d	...	...	...	...	...	...	...	...	...	...	...	...	...	...	...
Other Investment Liab., n.i.e.	78bi d	...	...	...	...	...	...	...	...	...	...	...	...	...	...	...
Monetary Authorities	78bs d	...	...	...	...	...	...	...	...	...	...	...	...	...	...	...
General Government	78bt d	...	...	...	...	...	...	...	...	...	...	...	...	...	...	...
Banks	78bu d	...	...	...	...	...	...	...	...	...	...	...	...	...	...	...
Other Sectors	78bv d	...	...	...	...	...	...	...	...	...	...	...	...	...	...	...
Net Errors and Omissions	78ca d	...	...	...	...	...	...	...	...	...	...	...	...	...	...	...
Overall Balance	78cb d	...	...	...	...	...	...	...	...	...	...	...	...	...	...	...
Reserves and Related Items	79da d	...	...	...	...	...	...	...	...	...	...	...	...	...	...	...
Reserve Assets	79db d	...	...	...	...	...	...	...	...	...	...	...	...	...	...	...
Use of Fund Credit and Loans	79dc d	...	...	...	...	...	...	...	...	...	...	...	...	...	...	...
Exceptional Financing	79de d	...	...	...	...	...	...	...	...	...	...	...	...	...	...	...
International Investment Position															*Millions of US Dollars*	
Assets	79aa d	...	...	...	...	...	...	...	...	...	...	...	...	...	...	...
Direct Investment Abroad	79ab d	...	...	...	...	...	...	...	...	...	...	...	...	...	...	...
Portfolio Investment	79ac d	...	...	...	...	...	...	...	...	...	...	...	...	...	...	...
Equity Securities	79ad d	...	...	...	...	...	...	...	...	...	...	...	...	...	...	...
Debt Securities	79ae d	...	...	...	...	...	...	...	...	...	...	...	...	...	...	...
Financial Derivatives	79al d	...	...	...	...	...	...	...	...	...	...	...	...	...	...	...
Other Investment	79af d	...	...	...	...	...	...	...	...	...	...	...	...	...	...	...
Monetary Authorities	79ag d	...	...	...	...	...	...	...	...	...	...	...	...	...	...	...
General Government	79ah d	...	...	...	...	...	...	...	...	...	...	...	...	...	...	...
Banks	79ai d	...	...	...	...	...	...	...	...	...	...	...	...	...	...	...
Other Sectors	79aj d	...	...	...	...	...	...	...	...	...	...	...	...	...	...	...
Reserve Assets	79ak d	...	...	...	...	...	...	...	...	...	...	...	...	...	...	...
Liabilities	79la d	...	...	...	...	...	...	...	...	...	...	...	...	...	...	...
Dir. Invest. in Rep. Economy	79lb d	...	...	...	...	...	...	...	...	...	...	...	...	...	...	...
Portfolio Investment	79lc d	...	...	...	...	...	...	...	...	...	...	...	...	...	...	...
Equity Securities	79ld d	...	...	...	...	...	...	...	...	...	...	...	...	...	...	...
Debt Securities	79le d	...	...	...	...	...	...	...	...	...	...	...	...	...	...	...
Financial Derivatives	79ll d	...	...	...	...	...	...	...	...	...	...	...	...	...	...	...
Other Investment	79lf d	...	...	...	...	...	...	...	...	...	...	...	...	...	...	...
Monetary Authorities	79lg d	...	...	...	...	...	...	...	...	...	...	...	...	...	...	...
General Government	79lh d	...	...	...	...	...	...	...	...	...	...	...	...	...	...	...
Banks	79li d	...	...	...	...	...	...	...	...	...	...	...	...	...	...	...
Other Sectors	79lj d	...	...	...	...	...	...	...	...	...	...	...	...	...	...	...

Minus Sign Indicates Debit

1985	1986	1987	1988	1989	1990	1991	1992	1993	1994	1995	1996	1997	1998	1999	Balance of Payments	
....	....	....	....	....	....	....	....	−435.0	−443.8	−458.3	−515.9	−787.6	−931.4	−256.7	Current Account, n.i.e.	78al *d*
....	....	....	....	....	....	....	....	1,970.1	2,510.0	4,803.0	5,790.1	7,382.6	7,134.5	5,949.3	Goods: Exports f.o.b.	78aa *d*
....	....	....	....	....	....	....	....	−2,498.0	−2,999.8	−5,468.7	−6,938.6	−8,718.0	−8,568.6	−6,547.8	Goods: Imports f.o.b.	78ab *d*
....	....	....	....	....	....	....	....	−527.9	−489.8	−665.7	−1,148.5	−1,335.4	−1,434.1	−598.5	*Trade Balance*	78ac *d*
....	....	....	....	....	....	....	....	184.9	251.4	466.1	908.0	918.8	875.9	733.8	Services: Credit	78ad *d*
....	....	....	....	....	....	....	....	−136.8	−199.3	−283.7	−335.9	−364.8	−436.1	−435.8	Services: Debit	78ae *d*
....	....	....	....	....	....	....	....	−479.8	−437.7	−483.3	−576.4	−781.4	−994.3	−300.5	*Balance on Goods & Services*	78af *d*
....	....	....	....	....	....	....	....	.1	.5	1.9	74.1	31.2	26.5	29.0	Income: Credit	78ag *d*
....	....	....	....	....	....	....	....	−7.5	−29.3	−52.9	−104.9	−115.8	−104.0	−93.6	Income: Debit	78ah *d*
....	....	....	....	....	....	....	....	−487.2	−466.5	−534.3	−607.2	−866.0	−1,071.8	−365.1	*Balance on Gds, Serv. & Inc.*	78ai *d*
....	....	....	....	....	....	....	....	64.6	50.9	107.2	135.5	106.1	165.7	136.2	Current Transfers, n.i.e.: Credit	78aj *d*
....	....	....	....	....	....	....	....	−12.4	−28.2	−31.2	−44.2	−27.7	−25.3	−27.8	Current Transfers: Debit	78ak *d*
....	....	....	....	....	....	....	....	—	23.8	7.3	101.1	133.2	170.1	60.4	Capital Account, n.i.e.	78bc *d*
....	....	....	....	....	....	....	....	—	23.8	7.3	257.2	248.0	261.3	131.1	Capital Account, n.i.e.: Credit	78ba *d*
....	....	....	....	....	....	....	....	....	....	....	−156.1	−114.8	−91.2	−70.7	Capital Account: Debit	78bb *d*
....	....	....	....	....	....	....	....	294.1	144.6	204.0	346.8	586.4	249.3	249.3	Financial Account, n.i.e.	78bj *d*
....	....	....	....	....	....	....	....	....	....	....		−2.1	−2.3	−.8	Direct Investment Abroad	78bd *d*
....	....	....	....	....	....	....	....	17.6	10.5	14.7	72.6	200.0	143.8	225.0	Dir. Invest. in Rep. Econ., n.i.e.	78be *d*
....	....	....	....	....	....	....	....	....	....	....	−17.7	−61.6	28.0	−13.9	Portfolio Investment Assets	78bf *d*
....	....	....	....	....	....	....	....	....	....	....		−.6	.3	−7.3	Equity Securities	78bk *d*
....	....	....	....	....	....	....	....	....	....	....	−17.7	−61.0	27.7	−6.6	Debt Securities	78bl *d*
....	....	....	....	....	....	....	....	....	....	....	3.2	41.8	−13.4	−18.3	Portfolio Investment Liab., n.i.e.	78bg *d*
....	....	....	....	....	....	....	....	....	....	....		....	2.7		Equity Securities	78bm *d*
....	....	....	....	....	....	....	....	....	....	....	3.2	41.8	−16.1	−18.3	Debt Securities	78bn *d*
....	....	....	....	....	....	....	....	....	....	....		....	....	....	Financial Derivatives Assets	78bw *d*
....	....	....	....	....	....	....	....	....	....	....		....	....	....	Financial Derivatives Liabilities	78bx *d*
....	....	....	....	....	....	....	....	−118.1	−232.5	−155.4	−131.5	49.8	240.4	−33.0	Other Investment Assets	78bh *d*
....	....	....	....	....	....	....	....	....	....	....		1.5	—	1.1	Monetary Authorities	78bo *d*
....	....	....	....	....	....	....	....	—	—	14.0		−8.9			General Government	78bp *d*
....	....	....	....	....	....	....	....	−60.6	−94.2	58.6	−40.2	−3.8	61.3	−12.8	Banks	78bq *d*
....	....	....	....	....	....	....	....	−57.5	−138.3	−228.0	−91.3	61.0	179.1	−21.3	Other Sectors	78br *d*
....	....	....	....	....	....	....	....	394.6	366.6	344.7	420.2	358.5	−147.2	90.3	Other Investment Liab., n.i.e.	78bi *d*
....	....	....	....	....	....	....	....	—	−.3	3.7	133.1	−86.8	16.9	.7	Monetary Authorities	78bs *d*
....	....	....	....	....	....	....	....	243.9	239.4	81.7	33.4	62.4	22.0	−41.5	General Government	78bt *d*
....	....	....	....	....	....	....	....	−4.8	34.9	24.1	23.1	11.5	−20.2	−23.1	Banks	78bu *d*
....	....	....	....	....	....	....	....	155.5	92.6	235.2	230.6	371.4	−165.9	154.2	Other Sectors	78bv *d*
....	....	....	....	....	....	....	....	3.4	−41.6	168.6	−146.2	133.1	97.0	34.3	Net Errors and Omissions	78ca *d*
....	....	....	....	....	....	....	....	−137.5	−317.0	−78.4	−214.2	65.1	−415.0	87.3	*Overall Balance*	78cb *d*
....	....	....	....	....	....	....	....	137.5	317.0	78.4	214.2	−65.1	415.0	−87.3	Reserves and Related Items	79da *d*
....	....	....	....	....	....	....	....	12.5	−58.6	−283.7	−78.6	75.3	53.7	34.6	Reserve Assets	79db *d*
....	....	....	....	....	....	....	....	98.2	—	177.8	—	—	−24.4	−58.1	Use of Fund Credit and Loans	79dc *d*
....	....	....	....	....	....	....	....	26.8	375.6	184.3	292.8	−140.4	385.7	−63.8	Exceptional Financing	79de *d*

Millions of US Dollars

1985	1986	1987	1988	1989	1990	1991	1992	1993	1994	1995	1996	1997	1998	1999	International Investment Position	
....	....	....	....	....	....	....	....	....	....	....	1,331.9	1,270.2	987.9	1,000.6	Assets	79aa *d*
....	....	....	....	....	....	....	....	....	....	....	—	2.1	4.4	5.2	Direct Investment Abroad	79ab *d*
....	....	....	....	....	....	....	....	....	....	....	18.0	79.6	51.6	65.5	Portfolio Investment	79ac *d*
....	....	....	....	....	....	....	....	....	....	....	.3	.9	.6	7.9	Equity Securities	79ad *d*
....	....	....	....	....	....	....	....	....	....	....	17.7	78.7	51.0	57.6	Debt Securities	79ae *d*
....	....	....	....	....	....	....	....	....	....	....	—	—	—	—	Financial Derivatives	79al *d*
....	....	....	....	....	....	....	....	....	....	....	844.8	794.9	592.9	625.3	Other Investment	79af *d*
....	....	....	....	....	....	....	....	....	....	....	9.0	7.5	8.4	7.3	Monetary Authorities	79ag *d*
....	....	....	....	....	....	....	....	....	....	....	—	—	—	—	General Government	79ah *d*
....	....	....	....	....	....	....	....	....	....	....	291.7	304.3	285.4	298.2	Banks	79ai *d*
....	....	....	....	....	....	....	....	....	....	....	544.1	483.1	299.1	319.8	Other Sectors	79aj *d*
....	....	....	....	....	....	....	....	....	....	....	469.1	393.6	339.0	304.6	Reserve Assets	79ak *d*
....	....	....	....	....	....	....	....	....	....	....	2,032.8	2,473.2	2,843.9	2,973.9	Liabilities	79la *d*
....	....	....	....	....	....	....	....	....	....	....	122.4	322.4	471.6	696.6	Dir. Invest. in Rep. Economy	79lb *d*
....	....	....	....	....	....	....	....	....	....	....	34.6	76.4	63.0	44.7	Portfolio Investment	79lc *d*
....	....	....	....	....	....	....	....	....	....	....	5.5	5.5	8.2	8.2	Equity Securities	79ld *d*
....	....	....	....	....	....	....	....	....	....	....	29.1	70.9	54.8	36.5	Debt Securities	79le *d*
....	....	....	....	....	....	....	....	....	....	....	—	—	—	—	Financial Derivatives	79ll *d*
....	....	....	....	....	....	....	....	....	....	....	1,875.8	2,074.4	2,309.3	2,232.6	Other Investment	79lf *d*
....	....	....	....	....	....	....	....	....	....	....	409.9	303.4	298.6	230.0	Monetary Authorities	79lg *d*
....	....	....	....	....	....	....	....	....	....	....	639.5	683.0	738.8	685.7	General Government	79lh *d*
....	....	....	....	....	....	....	....	....	....	....	142.8	159.4	139.1	115.7	Banks	79li *d*
....	....	....	....	....	....	....	....	....	....	....	683.6	928.6	1,132.8	1,201.2	Other Sectors	79lj *d*

Belarus

		1970	1971	1972	1973	1974	1975	1976	1977	1978	1979	1980	1981	1982	1983	1984
Government Finance																*Billions of Rubels:*
Deficit (-) or Surplus	80	...	...	...	...	...	...	...	...	...	...	...	...	...	...	...
Total Revenue and Grants	81y	...	...	...	...	...	...	...	...	...	...	...	...	...	...	...
Revenue	81	...	...	...	...	...	...	...	...	...	...	...	...	...	...	...
Grants	81z	...	...	...	...	...	...	...	...	...	...	...	...	...	...	...
Exp. & Lending Minus Repay.	82z	...	...	...	...	...	...	...	...	...	...	...	...	...	...	...
Expenditure	82	...	...	...	...	...	...	...	...	...	...	...	...	...	...	...
Lending Minus Repayments	83	...	...	...	...	...	...	...	...	...	...	...	...	...	...	...
Total Financing	80h	...	...	...	...	...	...	...	...	...	...	...	...	...	...	...
Domestic	84a	...	...	...	...	...	...	...	...	...	...	...	...	...	...	...
Foreign	85a	...	...	...	...	...	...	...	...	...	...	...	...	...	...	...
Total Debt by Residence	88	...	...	...	...	...	...	...	...	...	...	...	...	...	...	...
Domestic	88a	...	...	...	...	...	...	...	...	...	...	...	...	...	...	...
Foreign	89a	...	...	...	...	...	...	...	...	...	...	...	...	...	...	...
National Accounts																*Billions of Rubels*
Househ.Cons.Expend.,incl.NPISHs	96f	...	...	...	...	...	...	...	...	...	...	...	...	...	...	...
Government Consumption Expend.	91f	...	...	...	...	...	...	...	...	...	...	...	...	...	...	...
Gross Fixed Capital Formation	93e	...	...	...	...	...	...	...	...	...	...	...	...	...	...	...
Changes in Inventories	93i	...	...	...	...	...	...	...	...	...	...	...	...	...	...	...
Exports of Goods and Services	90c	...	...	...	...	...	...	...	...	...	...	...	...	...	...	...
Imports of Goods and Services	98c	...	...	...	...	...	...	...	...	...	...	...	...	...	...	...
Gross Domestic Product (GDP)	99b	...	...	...	...	...	...	...	...	...	...	...	...	...	...	...
GDP Volume 1995 Ref., Chained	99b.p	...	...	...	...	...	...	...	...	...	...	...	...	...	...	...
GDP Volume (1995=100)	99bv p	...	...	...	...	...	...	...	...	...	...	...	...	...	...	...
GDP Deflator (1995=100)	99bi p	...	...	...	...	...	...	...	...	...	...	...	...	...	...	...
																Millions:
Population	99z	...	...	...	...	...	...	...	...	...	...	...	...	...	...	...

1985	1986	1987	1988	1989	1990	1991	1992	1993	1994	1995	1996	1997	1998	1999	Government Finance	
Year Ending December 31																
....	....	....	....	....	....	....	−5	−35	−325	−3,221	−3,464	−5,724	−5,991	....	Deficit (-) or Surplus	80
....	....	....	....	....	....	....	30	381	6,014	37,105	58,993	117,871	206,594	....	Total Revenue and Grants	81y
....	....	....	....	....	....	....	29	381	6,014	37,105	58,993	117,871	206,594	....	Revenue	81
....	....	....	....	....	....	....	1	—	—	—	—	—	—	....	Grants	81z
....	....	....	....	....	....	....	35	416	6,339	40,325	62,458	123,595	212,585	....	Exp. & Lending Minus Repay.	82z
....	....	....	....	....	....	....	35	416	6,339	40,325	62,515	121,793	213,225	....	Expenditure	82
....	....	....	....	....	....	....	—	—	—	—	−57	1,801	−640	....	Lending Minus Repayments	83
....	....	....	....	....	....	....	5	35	325	3,221	3,464	5,724	5,991	....	Total Financing	80h
....	....	....	....	....	....	....	2	−3	−127	2,789	3,687	4,115	7,970	....	Domestic	84a
....	....	....	....	....	....	....	3	38	452	431	−223	1,609	−1,979	....	Foreign	85a
....	....	....	....	....	....	....	24	51	13,515	20,493	22,100	44,649	141,700	....	Total Debt by Residence	88
....	....	....	....	....	....	....	11	51	509	3,035	7,423	14,633	33,555	....	Domestic	88a
....	....	....	....	....	....	....	12	—	13,006	17,458	14,677	30,015	108,145	....	Foreign	89a
Billions of Rubels															**National Accounts**	
....	....	....	....	....	....	....	47	572	10,717	72,356	109,603	202,875	399,844	1,685,796	Househ.Cons.Expend.,incl.NPISHs..........	96f
....	....	....	....	....	....	....	14	175	3,581	23,157	36,627	72,441	139,142	581,868	Government Consumption Expend.	91f
....	....	....	....	....	....	....	23	334	5,918	29,984	40,438	92,555	182,103	740,550	Gross Fixed Capital Formation	93e
....	....	....	....	....	....	....	6	70	−58	63	4,681	5,891	5,458	−47,667	Changes in Inventories...........................	93i
....	....	....	....	....	—	—	55	651	12,644	59,890	88,876	217,574	415,224	1,786,834	Exports of Goods and Services	90c
....	....	....	....	....	....	....	−53	−817	−14,988	−65,637	−96,050	−239,975	−449,248	1,869,663	Imports of Goods and Services..............	98c
....	....	....	....	....	....	....	92	986	17,815	119,813	184,174	356,080	675,159	2,890,320	Gross Domestic Product (GDP)	99b
....	....	....	....	....	....	165,582	152,998	133,720	119,813	123,195	137,239	148,747	153,864		GDP Volume 1995 Ref., Chained	99b.*p*
....	....	....	....	....	....		138.2	127.7	111.6	100.0	102.8	114.5	124.1	128.4	GDP Volume (1995=100)	99bv*p*
....	....	....	....	....	....		.1	.6	13.3	100.0	149.5	259.5	453.9	1,878.5	GDP Deflator (1995=100)..................	99bi*p*
Midyear Estimates																
....	....	....	....	....	....		10.31	10.36	10.31	10.28	10.25	10.22	10.19	10.16	**Population**..	99z

(See notes in the back of the book.)

Belgium

124

	1970	1971	1972	1973	1974	1975	1976	1977	1978	1979	1980	1981	1982	1983	1984
Exchange Rates															*Francs per SDR through 1998,*
Market Rate....aa=.... wa	49.675	48.591	47.839	49.846	44.227	46.273	41.806	40.013	37.520	36.948	40.205	44.766	51.758	58.252	61.832
															Francs per US Dollar through 1998,
Market Rate....ae=.... we	49.675	44.755	44.063	41.320	36.123	39.528	35.983	32.940	28.800	28.048	31.523	38.460	46.920	55.640	63.080
Market Rate....rf=.... wf	49.650	48.781	44.015	38.977	38.952	36.779	38.605	35.843	31.492	29.319	29.242	37.129	45.691	51.132	57.784
Secondary Rate.... xe	49.70	44.75	44.38	41.24	36.10	40.32	35.70	32.99	29.39	28.99	31.65	42.55	48.10	56.55	63.30
Secondary Rate.... xf	50.17	48.56	43.96	39.01	39.76	37.80	40.24	35.89	31.95	30.14	29.66	39.31	49.05	52.02	58.65
															Francs per ECU:
ECU Rate.... ea	....	....	....	....	....	....	....	....	....	40.318	41.335	41.747	45.321	46.097	44.717
ECU Rate.... eb	....	....	....	....	....	....	42.921	40.884	40.059	40.166	40.601	41.301	44.680	45.430	45.438
															Index Numbers (1995=100):
Market Rate.... ahx	59.3	68.4	66.9	75.8	75.7	80.3	76.4	82.2	93.6	100.5	100.8	79.7	64.8	57.8	51.1
Nominal Effective Exchange Rate.... neu	80.4	80.1	82.6	84.0	85.5	86.8	89.8	94.9	97.6	98.4	97.8	93.4	85.2	83.2	82.0
Real Effective Exchange Rate.... reu	....	....	....	....	....	148.5	149.6	153.1	139.7	130.0	I 123.8	112.4	94.0	92.0	91.2
Fund Position															*Millions of SDRs:*
Quota.... 2f.s	650	650	650	650	650	650	650	650	890	890	1,335	1,335	1,335	2,080	2,080
SDRs.... 1b.s	205	405	523	626	584	615	397	407	414	476	497	628	672	399	454
Reserve Position in the Fund.... 1c.s	392	599	516	492	511	591	814	779	606	524	489	390	328	496	521
of which: Outstg.Fund Borrowing.... 2c	—	—	—	—	—	50	200	230	207	151	117	75	28	10	7
International Liquidity															*Millions of US Dollars Unless Otherwise Indicated:*
Total Res.Min.Gold (Eurosys.Def).... 1l.d	1,377	1,797	2,232	3,319	3,538	4,069	3,491	3,956	3,966	5,443	7,823	4,952	3,927	4,714	4,564
SDRs.... 1b.d	205	440	568	756	715	720	462	495	540	627	633	731	741	418	445
Reserve Position in the Fund.... 1c.d	392	651	560	594	626	692	946	947	789	690	624	454	362	520	511
Foreign Exchange.... 1d.d	780	706	1,104	1,969	2,197	2,656	2,083	2,515	2,637	4,126	6,565	3,767	2,824	3,776	3,608
o/w: Fin.Deriv.Rel.to Reserves.... 1ddd	....	....	....	....	....	....	....	....	....	....	....	....	....	....	....
Other Reserve Assets.... 1e.d	....	....	....	....	....	....	....	....	....	....	....	....	....	....	....
Gold (Million Fine Troy Ounces).... 1ad	42.01	44.12	43.08	42.17	42.17	42.17	42.17	42.45	42.59	34.21	34.18	34.18	34.18	34.18	34.18
Gold (National Valuation).... 1and	1,470	1,723	1,682	1,780	1,780	1,780	1,780	1,793	1,797	1,445	I 1,443	1,443	1,443	1,443	1,443
Memo: Euro Cl. on Non-EA Res.... 1dgd	....	....	....	....	....	....	....	....	....	....	....	....	....	....	....
Non-Euro Cl. on EA Res.... 1dhd	....	....	....	....	....	....	....	....	....	....	....	....	....	....	....
Mon. Auth.: Other Foreign Assets.... 3..d	40	130	375	409	332	300	386	621	908	789	247	838	701	560	194
Foreign Liabilities.... 4..d	20	78	38	79	91	91	92	823	1,132	1,191	222	315	524	985	98
Banking Insts.: Foreign Assets.... 7a.d	4,922	6,611	8,207	12,049	16,577	17,777	21,505	28,543	39,438	49,162	60,680	69,943	65,748	66,202	71,607
Foreign Liab.... 7b.d	5,734	7,386	9,222	13,708	19,254	20,148	23,914	31,852	44,514	58,635	72,953	83,102	78,374	80,196	86,376
Monetary Authorities															*Billions of Francs through 1998;*
Fgn. Assets (Cl.on Non-EA Ctys).... 11	144.4	166.9	194.9	222.5	227.3	253.2	226.9	247.9	243.1	253.9	I 324.1	250.4	233.5	298.4	325.5
Claims on General Government.... 12a.u	....	....	....	....	....	....	....	....	....	....	....	....	....	....	....
o/w: Claims on Gen.Govt.in Cty.... 12a	49.5	40.8	37.1	42.9	46.1	45.5	61.9	78.7	78.7	79.4	I 168.2	242.5	276.0	284.8	298.1
Claims on Banking Institutions.... 12e.u	....	....	....	....	....	....	....	....	....	....	....	....	....	....	....
o/w: Claims on Bank.Inst.in Cty.... 12e	....	....	....	....	....	....	....	....	....	....	57.5	86.1	85.0	97.2	13.0
Claims on Other Resident Sectors.... 12d.u	....	....	....	....	....	....	....	....	....	....	....	....	....	....	....
o/w: Cl. on Oth.Res.Sect.in Cty.... 12d	....	....	....	....	....	....	....	....	....	....	....	....	....	....	....
Claims on ECB.... 12u	....	....	....	....	....	....	....	....	....	....	....	....	....	....	....
Currency in Circulation.... 14a	188.2	201.8	222.6	238.5	256.1	288.4	307.2	335.4	359.9	371.8	I 390.7	397.9	397.6	411.4	413.8
Liabilities to Banking Insts.... 14c.u	....	....	....	....	....	....	....	....	....	....	....	....	....	....	....
o/w: Liabs to Bank.Inst.in Cty.... 14c	1.2	1.0	8.8	21.9	15.6	.7	.7	.5	.6	.3	I 1.2	1.0	1.3	1.1	1.2
Demand Dep. of Other Res.Sect.... 14d.u	....	....	....	....	....	....	....	....	....	....	....	....	....	....	....
o/w: D.Dep.of Oth.Res.Sect.in Cty.... 14d	....	....	....	....	....	....	....	....	....	....	....	....	....	....	....
Other Dep. of Other Res.Sect.... 15..u	....	....	....	....	....	....	....	....	....	....	....	....	....	....	....
o/w: O.Dep.of Oth.Res.Sect.in Cty.... 15	....	....	....	....	....	....	....	....	....	....	....	....	....	....	....
Money Market Instruments.... 16m.u	....	....	....	....	....	....	....	....	....	....	....	....	....	....	....
o/w: MMI Held by Resid.of Cty.... 16m	....	....	....	....	....	....	....	....	....	....	....	....	....	....	....
Bonds (Debt Securities).... 16n.u	....	....	....	....	....	....	....	....	....	....	....	....	....	....	....
o/w: Bonds Held by Resid.of Cty.... 16n	....	....	....	....	....	....	....	....	....	....	—	—	—	—	—
Foreign Liab. (to Non-EA Ctys).... 16c	1.0	3.5	1.7	3.2	3.3	3.6	3.3	27.1	32.6	33.4	I 7.1	12.3	24.7	55.1	6.5
Central Government Deposits.... 16d.u	....	....	....	....	....	....	....	....	....	....	....	....	....	....	....
o/w: Cent.Govt.Dep. in Cty.... 16d	....	....	....	....	....	....	....	....	....	....	—	—	—	—	—
Liabilities to ECB.... 16u	....	....	....	....	....	....	....	....	....	....	....	....	....	....	....
Capital Accounts.... 17a	....	....	....	....	....	....	....	....	....	....	8.4	9.6	11.1	12.3	13.8
Other Items (Net).... 17r	3.1	.8	−1.7	1.3	−1.9	5.1	−23.6	−36.9	−72.1	−72.9	I 147.9	162.7	162.0	202.9	202.1
Banking Institutions															*Billions of Francs through 1998;*
Claims on Monetary Authorities.... 20	13.3	14.8	20.7	30.1	26.7	14.3	14.5	14.8	15.4	19.3	19.5	17.1	17.0	16.9	21.7
Claims on Bk.Inst.in Oth.EA Ctys.... 20b.u	....	....	....	....	....	....	....	....	....	....	....	....	....	....	....
Fgn. Assets (Cl.on Non-EA Ctys).... 21	246.1	296.3	367.8	486.0	598.8	702.7	773.8	940.2	1,135.8	1,378.9	1,912.8	2,690.0	3,084.9	3,683.5	4,517.0
Claims on General Government.... 22a.u	....	....	....	....	....	....	....	....	....	....	....	....	....	....	....
o/w: Claims on Gen.Govt.in Cty.... 22a	212.6	234.0	276.0	323.0	355.1	395.6	445.1	467.5	526.3	609.9	737.1	864.0	1,051.5	1,325.8	1,457.3
Claims on Other Resident Sectors.... 22d.u	....	....	....	....	....	....	....	....	....	....	....	....	....	....	....
o/w: Cl. on Oth.Res.Sect.in Cty.... 22d	238.8	271.5	329.4	386.6	435.5	524.1	599.0	706.6	782.5	921.6	1,014.8	1,060.0	1,090.3	1,144.6	1,244.5
Demand Deposits.... 24..u	....	....	....	....	....	....	....	....	....	....	....	....	....	....	....
o/w: D.Dep.of Oth.Res.Sect.in Cty.... 24	201.7	231.8	273.0	289.6	307.5	362.9	389.8	419.5	439.7	452.0	450.2	458.7	491.0	551.1	556.3
Other Deposits.... 25..u	....	....	....	....	....	....	....	....	....	....	....	....	....	....	....
o/w: O.Dep.of Oth.Res.Sect.in Cty.... 25	204.4	240.1	283.9	355.3	399.1	457.5	550.5	596.9	654.0	722.9	771.4	853.8	941.6	1,016.9	1,102.2
Money Market Instruments.... 26m.u	....	....	....	....	....	....	....	....	....	....	....	....	....	....	....
o/w: MMI Held by Resid.of Cty.... 26m	25.5	30.4	35.8	41.8	48.7	58.2	74.3	104.4	125.6	153.0	201.0	245.0	300.2	356.8	393.5
Bonds (Debt Securities).... 26n.u	....	....	....	....	....	....	....	....	....	....	....	....	....	....	....
o/w: Bonds Held by Resid.of Cty.... 26n	....	....	....	....	....	....	....	....	....	....	....	....	....	....	....
Foreign Liab. (to Non-EA Ctys).... 26c	286.7	331.0	413.3	552.9	695.5	796.4	860.5	1,049.2	1,282.0	1,644.6	2,299.7	3,196.1	3,677.3	4,462.1	5,448.6
Central Government Deposits.... 26d.u	....	....	....	....	....	....	....	....	....	....	....	....	....	....	....
o/w: Cent.Govt.Dep. in Cty.... 26d	....	....	....	....	....	....	....	....	....	....	....	....	....	....	....
Credit from Monetary Authorities.... 26g	....	....	....	....	....	....	....	....	....	....	....	....	....	....	....
Liab. to Bk.Inst.in Oth. EA Ctys.... 26h.u	....	....	....	....	....	....	....	....	....	....	....	....	....	....	....
Capital Accounts.... 27a	....	....	....	....	....	....	....	....	....	....	....	....	....	....	....
Other Items (Net).... 27r	−7.3	−16.6	−12.3	−14.4	−34.8	−39.2	−42.7	−40.9	−41.3	−42.8	−38.1	−122.5	−166.4	−216.1	−260.1

1985	1986	1987	1988	1989	1990	1991	1992	1993	1994	1995	1996	1997	1998	1999		
Euros per SDR Thereafter: End of Period															**Exchange Rates**	
55.316	49.429	47.032	50.255	46.994	44.078	44.730	45.623	49.599	46.478	43.725	46.022	49.814	48.682	1.3662	Market Rate aa=	wa
Euros per US Dollar Thereafter: End of Period (we) Period Average (wf)																
50.360	40.410	33.153	37.345	35.760	30.983	31.270	33.180	36.110	31.838	29.415	32.005	36.920	34.575	.9954	Market Rate ae=	we
59.378	44.672	37.334	36.768	39.404	33.418	34.148	32.150	34.597	33.456	29.480	30.962	35.774	36.299	.9386	Market Rate rf=	wf
50.68	40.82	33.22	37.28	35.59	....	....	....	....	....	....	....	....	....	....	Secondary Rate	xe
59.74	45.08	37.57	37.01	39.51	....	....	....	....	....	....	....	....	....	....	Secondary Rate	xf
End of Period (ea) Period Average (eb)																
44.645	43.233	43.154	43.576	42.592	42.184	41.931	40.178	40.287	39.161	38.698	40.102	40.771	40.340	....	ECU Rate	ea
44.913	43.803	43.039	43.427	43.378	42.423	42.222	41.604	40.466	39.662	38.537	39.290	40.529	40.623	....	ECU Rate	eb
Period Averages																
50.0	66.2	79.0	80.3	74.8	88.4	86.6	91.8	85.2	88.2	100.0	95.1	82.4	81.2	....	Market Rate	ahx
82.7	86.5	89.4	88.3	87.6	91.5	91.4	93.2	94.4	96.1	100.0	97.9	93.9	93.9	92.8	Nominal Effective Exchange Rate	neu
90.2	92.2	93.8	91.1	91.2	94.0	95.4	95.0	96.8	96.5	100.0	97.3	93.1	92.1	....	Real Effective Exchange Rate	reu
End of Period															**Fund Position**	
2,080	2,080	2,080	2,080	2,080	2,080	2,080	3,102	3,102	3,102	3,102	3,102	3,102	3,102	4,605	Quota	2f.s
328	280	494	418	423	398	411	124	125	123	331	346	363	433	197	SDRs	1b.s
472	462	392	345	342	326	367	586	560	556	676	747	876	1,348	1,668	Reserve Position in the Fund	1c.s
4	1	—	—	—	—	—	—	—	—	—	—	—	140	—	*of which:* Outstg.Fund Borrowing	2c
End of Period															**International Liquidity**	
4,849	5,538	9,620	9,333	10,766	12,151	12,180	13,801	11,415	13,876	16,177	16,953	16,190	18,272	I 10,937	Total Res.Min.Gold (Eurosys.Def)	1l.d
361	342	700	563	556	566	588	171	171	180	492	498	489	610	271	SDRs	1b.d
519	565	557	464	449	464	524	806	769	812	1,005	1,075	1,182	1,899	2,290	Reserve Position in the Fund	1c.d
3,969	4,630	8,363	8,306	9,760	11,121	11,068	12,825	10,474	12,884	14,680	15,380	14,519	15,763	8,377	Foreign Exchange	1d.d
....	....	....	....	....	....	....	....	....	....	....	....	....	....	....	*o/w:* Fin.Deriv.Rel.to Reserves	1ddd
....	....	....	....	....	....	....	....	....	....	....	....	....	....	—	Other Reserve Assets	1e.d
34.18	34.18	33.63	33.67	30.23	30.23	30.23	25.04	25.04	25.04	20.54	15.32	15.32	9.52	8.30	Gold (Million Fine Troy Ounces)	1ad
1,443	1,443	1,421	1,421	1,277	9,017	10,774	8,321	9,955	8,482	7,306	6,171	5,140	2,565	2,413	Gold (National Valuation)	1and
....	....	....	....	....	....	....	....	....	....	....	....	....	....	257	Memo: Euro Cl. on Non-EA Res.	1dgd
....	....	....	....	....	....	....	....	....	....	....	....	....	....	139	Non-Euro Cl. on EA Res.	1dhd
335	109	82	86	512	609	254	165	140	115	113	100	91	97	I —	Mon. Auth.: Other Foreign Assets	3..d
133	144	151	273	131	274	339	241	341	477	629	144	81	382	I 7,341	Foreign Liabilities	4..d
92,631	117,926	149,126	150,374	164,516	192,031	192,024	I 197,574	211,230	238,602	273,058	267,758	262,470	....	I 113,285	Banking Insts.: Foreign Assets	7a.d
112,925	144,838	184,795	186,432	205,526	239,787	229,933	I 231,022	228,782	263,337	302,856	293,657	280,033	....	I 183,066	Foreign Liab.	7b.d
Millions of Euros Beginning 1999: End of Period															**Monetary Authorities**	
291.2	270.9	365.2	396.1	435.5	743.6	730.2	716.9	764.7	729.1	692.6	741.4	793.7	712.1	13,303	Fgn. Assets (Cl.on Non-EA Ctys)	11
....	....	....	....	....	....	....	....	....	....	....	....	....	....	3,683	Claims on General Government	12a.u
281.3	310.4	231.5	214.1	176.9	151.5	67.0	71.6	90.3	79.3	86.3	91.0	94.1	47.0	1,123	*o/w:* Claims on Gen.Govt.in Cty	12a
....	....	....	....	....	....	....	....	....	....	....	....	....	....	24,362	Claims on Banking Institutions	12e.u
25.7	2.0	.4	.7	39.5	33.5	104.9	82.5	155.4	128.3	151.3	151.4	150.5	185.0	20,457	*o/w:* Claims on Bank.Inst.in Cty	12e
....	....	....	....	....	....	....	....	....	....	....	....	....	....	92	Claims on Other Resident Sectors	12d.u
....	....	....	....	....	....	....	....	....	....	....	....	....	....	3	*o/w:* Cl. on Oth.Res.Sect.in Cty	12d
....	....	....	....	....	....	....	....	....	....	....	....	....	....	1,433	Claims on ECB	12u
409.2	430.2	440.3	445.9	458.8	446.3	450.1	448.0	459.3	431.4	465.9	486.2	501.1	505.8	13,545	Currency in Circulation	14a
....	....	....	....	....	....	....	....	....	....	....	....	....	....	17,488	Liabilities to Banking Insts	14c.u
1.0	.5	1.3	.8	1.0	.5	3.8	3.8	5.5	2.3	7.6	4.7	1.2	279.0	3,509	*o/w:* Liabs to Bank.Inst.in Cty	14c
....	....	....	....	....	....	....	....	....	....	....	....	....	....	19	Demand Dep. of Other Res.Sect.	14d.u
....	....	....	....	....	....	....	....	....	....	....	....	....	....	19	*o/w:* D.Dep.of Oth.Res.Sect.in Cty	14d
....	....	....	....	....	....	....	....	....	....	....	....	....	....	—	Other Dep. of Other Res.Sect.	15..u
....	....	....	....	....	....	....	....	....	....	....	....	....	....	—	*o/w:* O.Dep.of Oth.Res.Sect.in Cty	15
....	....	....	....	....	....	....	....	....	....	....	....	....	....	—	Money Market Instruments	16m.u
....	....	....	....	....	....	....	....	....	....	....	....	....	....	....	*o/w:* MMI Held by Resid.of Cty	16m
....	....	....	....	....	....	....	....	....	....	....	....	....	....	—	Bonds (Debt Securities)	16n.u
—	—	—	—	—	—	—	—	—	—	—	230.0	230.0	—	....	*o/w:* Bonds Held by Resid.of Cty	16n
7.0	6.1	5.3	10.5	5.1	8.5	10.7	8.4	12.3	15.2	18.5	4.6	3.0	13.2	7,307	Foreign Liab. (to Non-EA Ctys)	16c
....	....	....	....	....	....	....	....	....	....	....	....	....	....	64	Central Government Deposits	16d.u
—	—	—	—	—	—	—	—	1.3	1.0	.5	.7	.1	.4	64	*o/w:* Cent.Govt.Dep. in Cty	16d
....	....	....	....	....	....	....	....	....	....	....	....	....	....	12	Liabilities to ECB	16u
15.7	18.7	22.3	25.7	30.1	33.3	36.8	40.0	43.6	46.5	48.6	50.6	53.1	53.6	5,369	Capital Accounts	17a
167.9	133.5	131.8	128.0	156.7	439.9	400.6	370.8	488.5	440.2	389.1	206.9	249.8	92.3	–931	Other Items (Net)	17r
Millions of Euros Beginning 1999: End of Period															**Banking Institutions**	
20.0	22.9	21.6	20.9	23.2	23.2	17.3	I 35.4	34.3	35.1	37.9	245.8	228.6	....	3,509	Claims on Monetary Authorities	20
....	....	....	....	....	....	....	....	....	....	....	....	....	....	95,580	Claims on Bk.Inst.in Oth.EA Ctys	20b.u
4,664.9	4,765.4	4,943.9	5,615.7	5,883.1	5,949.6	6,004.6	I 6,555.5	7,627.5	7,596.5	8,032.0	8,569.6	9,690.4	....	112,766	Fgn. Assets (Cl.on Non-EA Ctys)	21
....	....	....	....	....	....	....	....	....	....	....	....	....	....	176,820	Claims on General Government	22a.u
1,668.7	1,823.1	1,915.1	1,983.5	2,089.4	2,231.6	2,191.4	I 5,267.1	5,528.2	6,101.4	6,215.7	6,296.0	6,236.2	....	134,603	*o/w:* Claims on Gen.Govt.in Cty	22a
....	....	....	....	....	....	....	....	....	....	....	....	....	....	218,674	Claims on Other Resident Sectors	22d.u
1,272.9	1,388.4	1,546.4	1,834.1	2,293.6	2,420.0	2,637.2	I 5,695.7	5,794.3	5,979.9	6,099.0	6,402.6	6,749.2	....	191,886	*o/w:* Cl. on Oth.Res.Sect.in Cty	22d
....	....	....	....	....	....	....	....	....	....	....	....	....	....	53,236	Demand Deposits	24..u
588.3	646.8	682.9	738.0	789.9	813.4	820.1	I 966.4	1,060.6	1,111.3	1,152.7	1,200.0	1,237.0	....	50,136	*o/w:* D.Dep.of Oth.Res.Sect.in Cty	24
....	....	....	....	....	....	....	....	....	....	....	....	....	....	188,240	Other Deposits	25..u
1,179.8	1,328.8	1,495.0	1,573.0	1,787.4	1,900.2	2,047.8	I 4,148.9	4,560.7	4,706.0	4,936.3	5,490.4	5,915.4	....	157,609	*o/w:* O.Dep.of Oth.Res.Sect.in Cty	25
....	....	....	....	....	....	....	....	....	....	....	....	....	....	1,029	Money Market Instruments	26m.u
444.5	451.1	461.4	468.7	530.0	676.1	809.3	I 3,422.9	3,583.8	3,703.8	3,691.3	3,593.6	3,291.5	....	....	*o/w:* MMI Held by Resid.of Cty	26m
....	....	....	....	....	....	....	....	....	....	....	....	....	....	80,701	Bonds (Debt Securities)	26n.u
....	....	....	....	....	....	....	....	....	....	....	....	....	....	....	*o/w:* Bonds Held by Resid.of Cty	26n
5,686.9	5,852.9	6,126.4	6,962.3	7,349.6	7,429.2	7,190.0	I 7,665.3	8,261.3	8,384.0	8,908.5	9,398.5	10,338.8	....	182,228	Foreign Liab. (to Non-EA Ctys)	26c
....	....	....	....	....	....	....	....	....	....	....	....	....	....	1,282	Central Government Deposits	26d.u
....	....	....	....	....	....	....	238.1	270.3	217.0	78.8	60.6	245.6	....	923	*o/w:* Cent.Govt.Dep. in Cty	26d
....	....	....	....	....	....	....	66.1	139.0	123.8	106.7	121.7	75.5	....	20,457	Credit from Monetary Authorities	26g
....	....	....	....	....	....	....	....	....	....	....	....	....	....	57,421	Liab. to Bk.Inst.in Oth. EA Ctys	26h.u
....	....	....	....	....	....	....	728.8	787.6	856.8	894.7	1,621.1	2,077.7	....	29,498	Capital Accounts	27a
–273.0	–279.5	–338.8	–288.0	–168.0	–194.5	–18.7	I 317.0	321.3	609.7	615.3	27.9	–277.3	....	–6,743	Other Items (Net)	27r

Belgium

	1970	1971	1972	1973	1974	1975	1976	1977	1978	1979	1980	1981	1982	1983	1984
Banking Survey (Nat'l Residency)															*Billions of Francs through 1998;*
Foreign Assets (Net) ... 31n	102.8	128.7	147.7	152.4	127.3	155.9	136.9	111.8	64.3	−45.2	ɪ−69.9	−268.0	−383.6	−535.3	−612.6
Domestic Credit ... 32	500.9	546.3	642.5	752.5	836.7	965.2	1,106.0	1,252.8	1,387.5	1,610.9	ɪ1,920.1	2,166.5	2,417.8	2,755.2	2,999.9
Claims on General Govt. (Net) ... 32an	262.1	274.8	313.1	365.9	401.2	441.1	507.0	546.2	605.0	689.3	ɪ905.3	1,106.5	1,327.5	1,610.6	1,755.4
Claims on Other Resident Sectors ... 32d	238.8	271.5	329.4	386.6	435.5	524.1	599.0	706.6	782.5	921.6	1,014.8	1,060.0	1,090.3	1,144.6	1,244.5
Currency in Circulation ... 34a.n	188.2	201.8	222.6	238.5	256.1	288.4	307.2	335.7	359.9	371.8	ɪ390.7	397.9	397.6	411.4	413.8
Demand Deposits ... 34b.n	202.9	232.8	281.8	311.5	323.1	364.5	390.5	420.0	440.2	452.3	451.4	459.7	492.3	552.2	557.5
Other Deposits ... 35.n	204.4	240.1	283.9	355.3	399.1	457.5	550.5	596.9	654.0	722.9	771.4	853.8	941.6	1,016.9	1,102.2
Money Market Instruments ... 36m	25.5	30.4	35.8	41.8	48.7	58.2	74.3	104.4	125.6	153.0	201.0	245.0	300.2	356.8	393.5
Bonds (Debt Securities) ... 36n	....	....	....	....	....	....	....	....	....	....	....	....	....	....	....
o/w: Bonds Over Two Years ... 36na	....	....	....	....	....	....	....	....	....	....	....	....	....	....	....
Capital Accounts ... 37a	....	....	....	....	....	....	....	....	....	....	8.4	9.6	11.1	12.3	13.8
Other Items (Net) ... 37r	−17.5	−30.6	−34.7	−43.2	−63.4	−48.4	−80.8	−92.6	−128.8	−135.0	ɪ32.8	−63.0	−106.4	−127.3	−92.7
Banking Survey (EA-Wide Residency)															*Millions of Euros:*
Foreign Assets (Net) ... 31n.u	....	....	....	....	....	....	....	....	....	....	....	....	....	....	....
Domestic Credit ... 32..u	....	....	....	....	....	....	....	....	....	....	....	....	....	....	....
Claims on General Govt. (Net) ... 32anu	....	....	....	....	....	....	....	....	....	....	....	....	....	....	....
Claims on Other Resident Sect. ... 32d.u	....	....	....	....	....	....	....	....	....	....	....	....	....	....	....
Currency in Circulation ... 34a.u	....	....	....	....	....	....	....	....	....	....	....	....	....	....	....
Demand Deposits ... 34b..u	....	....	....	....	....	....	....	....	....	....	....	....	....	....	....
Other Deposits ... 35..u	....	....	....	....	....	....	....	....	....	....	....	....	....	....	....
o/w: Other Dep. Over Two Yrs ... 35abu	....	....	....	....	....	....	....	....	....	....	....	....	....	....	....
Money Market Instruments ... 36m.u	....	....	....	....	....	....	....	....	....	....	....	....	....	....	....
Bonds (Debt Securities) ... 36n.u	....	....	....	....	....	....	....	....	....	....	....	....	....	....	....
o/w: Bonds Over Two Years ... 36nau	....	....	....	....	....	....	....	....	....	....	....	....	....	....	....
Capital Accounts ... 37a	....	....	....	....	....	....	....	....	....	....	....	....	....	....	....
Other Items (Net) ... 37r.u	....	....	....	....	....	....	....	....	....	....	....	....	....	....	....
Interest Rates															*Percent Per Annum*
Discount Rate *(End of Period)* ... 60	6.50	5.50	5.00	7.75	8.75	6.00	9.00	9.00	6.00	10.50	12.00	15.00	11.50	10.00	11.00
Money Market Rate ... 60b	6.26	3.72	2.51	4.80	9.24	4.68	8.31	5.49	5.23	7.97	11.22	11.47	11.44	8.18	9.47
Treasury Bill Rate ... 60c	7.05	6.83	6.68	7.17	9.87	6.49	9.53	6.64	6.89	10.51	13.90	14.88	13.96	10.38	11.60
Deposit Rate ... 60l	5.92	4.65	2.90	4.27	6.75	5.41	5.62	5.46	4.50	5.50	7.69	7.50	7.46	6.67	7.44
Lending Rate ... 60p	....	....	....	....	....	....	....	....	....	....	....	18.00	15.50	13.75	14.00
Government Bond Yield ... 61	7.81	7.35	7.04	7.44	8.68	8.54	9.05	8.80	8.45	9.51	12.04	13.71	13.56	11.86	11.98
Prices, Production, Labor															*Index Numbers (1995=100):*
Industrial Share Prices ... 62	29	32	36	43	35	33	31	28	29	31	31	25	29	37	47
Producer Prices															
Home and Import Goods ... 63	....	....	....	....	....	....	....	....	....	....	73.2	83.5	94.8	101.1	108.8
Industrial Production Prices ... 63b	....	....	....	....	....	....	....	....	....	....	72.6	81.5	90.6	96.3	102.2
Consumer Prices ... 64	27.9	29.1	30.7	32.9	37.0	ɪ41.8	45.6	48.8	51.0	53.3	56.8	61.2	66.5	71.6	ɪ76.1
Harmonized CPI ... 64h															
Wages: Hourly Earnings ... 65	19.6	22.0	25.1	29.2	35.3	42.4	47.1	51.4	55.0	ɪ59.3	64.8	71.3	75.7	79.0	82.9
Industrial Production ... 66..b	65.6	67.3	71.5	75.9	78.7	71.2	77.4	77.4	79.0	82.6	81.6	79.4	79.6	81.1	83.2
															Number in Thousands:
Labor Force ... 67d	....	....	....	....	....	....	....	....	....	....	....	....	....	....	....
Employment ... 67e	....	....	....	....	....	....	....	....	....	....	....	....	....	....	....
Unemployment ... 67c	....	....	....	....	....	....	....	....	....	....	....	....	....	....	596
Unemployment Rate (%) ... 67r	....	....	....	....	....	....	....	....	....	....	....	....	....	....	....
International Transactions															
(For Belgium Only)															*Billions of Francs*
Exports ... 70	....	....	....	....	....	....	....	....	....	....	....	....	....	....	....
Imports, c.i.f. ... 71	....	....	....	....	....	....	....	....	....	....	....	....	....	....	....
															1995=100
Volume of Exports ... 72	....	....	....	....	....	....	....	....	....	....	....	....	....	....	....
Volume of Imports ... 73	....	....	....	....	....	....	....	....	....	....	....	....	....	....	....
Unit Value of Exports ... 74	....	....	....	....	....	....	....	....	....	....	....	....	....	....	....
Unit Value of Imports ... 75	....	....	....	....	....	....	....	....	....	....	....	....	....	....	....
Import Price (1990=100) ... 76.x	41	40	41	49	61	57	60	60	58	66	ɪ71	83	95	102	111
(BLEU: Country Code 126)															*Billions of Francs*
Exports ... 70	580.0	620.2	711.0	870.1	1,099.8	1,056.9	1,266.5	1,344.7	1,410.3	1,661.2	1,890.4	2,062.3	2,393.2	2,651.3	2,992.1
Imports, c.i.f. ... 71	570.6	629.1	681.8	856.1	1,160.7	1,130.9	1,369.0	1,448.0	1,526.0	1,784.4	2,100.8	2,309.8	2,653.4	2,820.9	3,195.8
															1995=100
Volume of Exports ... 72	29	31	35	39	40	37	42	ɪ43	45	48	ɪ49	49	50	52	54
Volume of Imports ... 73	31	34	37	43	45	42	48	ɪ49	51	55	ɪ56	54	54	53	56
Unit Value of Exports ... 74	42	41	42	45	56	58	62	ɪ63	63	69	ɪ76	82	94	101	109
Unit Value of Imports ... 75	40	40	40	43	55	58	61	ɪ62	62	68	ɪ78	89	102	109	118

	1985	1986	1987	1988	1989	1990	1991	1992	1993	1994	1995	1996	1997	1998	1999	
Millions of Euros Beginning 1999: End of Period																**Banking Survey (Nat'l Residency)**
	−737.8	−822.7	−822.6	−961.0	−1,036.1	−744.5	−465.9	I−401.3	118.6	−73.6	−202.4	−92.1	142.3	....	11,352	Foreign Assets (Net) **31n**
	3,222.9	3,521.9	3,693.0	4,031.7	4,559.9	4,803.1	4,895.6	I10796.3	11,141.2	11,942.6	12,321.7	12,728.3	12,833.8	....	326,628	Domestic Credit **32**
	1,950.0	2,133.5	2,146.6	2,197.6	2,266.3	2,383.1	2,258.4	I5,100.6	5,346.9	5,962.7	6,222.7	6,325.7	6,084.6	....	134,739	Claims on General Govt. (Net).......... **32an**
	1,272.9	1,388.4	1,546.4	1,834.1	2,293.6	2,420.0	2,637.2	I5,695.7	5,794.3	5,979.9	6,099.0	6,402.6	6,749.2	....	191,889	Claims on Other Resident Sectors **32d**
	409.2	430.2	440.3	445.9	458.8	446.3	450.1	448.0	459.3	431.4	465.9	486.2	501.1	505.8	13,545	Currency in Circulation **34a.***n*
	589.3	647.3	684.2	738.8	790.9	813.9	823.9	I966.4	1,060.6	1,111.3	1,152.7	1,200.0	1,237.0	....	50,155	Demand Deposits **34b.***n*
	1,179.8	1,328.8	1,495.0	1,573.0	1,787.4	1,900.2	2,047.8	I4,148.9	4,560.7	4,706.0	4,936.3	5,490.4	5,915.4	....	157,609	Other Deposits **35.***n*
	444.5	451.1	461.4	468.7	530.0	676.1	809.3	I3,422.9	3,583.8	3,703.8	3,691.3	3,593.6	3,291.5	....	1,029	Money Market Instruments **36m**
	—	—	—	—	—	—	—	—	—	—	—	230.0	230.0	—	80,701	Bonds (Debt Securities)........................... **36n**
														....	67,530	*o/w:* Bonds Over Two Years.............. **36na**
	15.7	18.7	22.3	25.7	30.1	33.3	36.8	I768.8	831.2	903.3	943.3	1,671.7	2,130.8	....	34,867	Capital Accounts **37a**
	−150.8	−170.9	−229.0	−181.6	−74.0	188.7	259.7	I639.8	764.6	1,012.6	929.5	−36.0	−329.9	....	73.7	Other Items (Net) **37r**
End of Period																**Banking Survey (EA-Wide Residency)**
	....	....	....	....	....	....	....	....	....	....	....	....	....	....	−63,466	Foreign Assets (Net) **31n.***u*
	....	....	....	....	....	....	....	....	....	....	....	....	....	....	397,923	Domestic Credit .... **32..***u*
	....	....	....	....	....	....	....	....	....	....	....	....	....	....	179,157	Claims on General Govt. (Net) **32an***u*
	....	....	....	....	....	....	....	....	....	....	....	....	....	....	218,766	Claims on Other Resident Sect. **32d.***u*
	....	....	....	....	....	....	....	....	....	....	....	....	....	....	13,545	Currency in Circulation **34a.***u*
	....	....	....	....	....	....	....	....	....	....	....	....	....	....	53,255	Demand Deposits **34b.***u*
	....	....	....	....	....	....	....	....	....	....	....	....	....	....	188,240	Other Deposits .... **35..***u*
	....	....	....	....	....	....	....	....	....	....	....	....	....	....	19,713	*o/w:* Other Dep. Over Two Yrs........ **35ab***u*
	....	....	....	....	....	....	....	....	....	....	....	....	....	....	1,029	Money Market Instruments **36m.***u*
	....	....	....	....	....	....	....	....	....	....	....	....	....	....	80,701	Bonds (Debt Securities)....................... **36n.***u*
	....	....	....	....	....	....	....	....	....	....	....	....	....	....	67,530	*o/w:* Bonds Over Two Years.............. **36na***u*
	....	....	....	....	....	....	....	....	....	....	....	....	....	....	34,867	Capital Accounts **37a**
	....	....	....	....	....	....	....	....	....	....	....	....	....	....	−37,180	Other Items (Net) **37r.***u*
Percent Per Annum																**Interest Rates**
	9.75	8.00	7.00	7.75	10.25	10.50	8.50	7.75	5.25	4.50	3.00	2.50	2.75	2.75	....	Discount Rate *(End of Period)*.................... **60**
	8.27	6.64	5.67	5.04	7.00	8.29	I9.38	9.38	8.21	5.72	4.80	3.24	3.46	3.58	....	Money Market Rate **60b**
	9.44	8.09	7.00	6.61	8.45	9.62	9.24	9.36	8.52	5.57	4.67	3.19	3.38	3.51	2.72	Treasury Bill Rate **60c**
	6.69	5.33	5.00	4.54	5.13	6.13	6.25	6.25	I7.11	4.86	4.04	2.66	2.88	3.01	2.42	Deposit Rate **60l**
	12.54	10.44	9.33	8.92	11.08	13.00	12.88	13.00	11.81	9.42	8.42	7.17	7.06	7.25	6.71	Lending Rate **60p**
	10.61	7.93	7.83	7.85	8.64	10.09	9.26	8.64	7.19	7.82	7.45	6.45	5.74	4.72	4.81	Government Bond Yield **61**
Period Averages																**Prices, Production, Labor**
	52	75	89	88	101	94	91	89	93	106	100	....	....	....	....	Industrial Share Prices **62**
																Producer Prices
	111.6	98.8	93.9	95.5	101.7	100.7	I99.7	97.9	95.4	96.9	100.0	102.0	105.9	103.9	104.4	Home and Import Goods **63**
	105.0	95.5	91.3	92.4	97.7	98.3	I97.2	97.4	96.5	97.8	100.0	100.6	102.3	101.0	100.6	Industrial Production Prices **63b**
	79.8	80.9	82.1	I83.1	85.7	88.6	91.5	93.7	96.3	98.6	100.0	I102.1	103.7	104.7	105.9	Consumer Prices....................................... **64**
	....	....	....	....	....	....	....	....	....	....	100.0	101.8	103.3	104.2	105.4	Harmonized CPI **64h**
	85.9	88.3	I90.0	90.7	95.8	100.0	105.1	110.1	112.4	114.7	....	....	....	....	....	Wages: Hourly Earnings.......................... **65**
	84.6	85.4	87.5	92.7	95.9	99.4	97.4	97.3	92.5	94.1	100.0	100.8	105.1	101.4	110.6	Industrial Production .... **66..***b*
Period Averages																
	....	....	....	....	4,144	4,179	4,210	4,237	....	4,160	4,185	4,196	4,214	4,241	....	Labor Force **67d**
	3,514	3,525	3,480	3,496	3,595	3,637	3,731	3,773	3,746	3,755	3,794	3,792	3,839	....	....	Employment **67e**
	I558	517	501	459	419	403	430	473	550	589	597	587	568	541	508	Unemployment... **67c**
	13.6	12.6	12.2	11.1	10.1	9.6	10.2	11.2	12.9	13.9	14.1	13.8	13.3	12.6	11.7	Unemployment Rate (%) **67r**
																International Transactions
Billions of Euros																(For Belgium Only)
	....	....	....	....	....	....	....	....	4,349.1	4,792.7	5,177.8	5,430.2	6,142.9	6,442.0	I165.43	Exports... **70**
	....	....	....	....	....	....	....	....	3,953.6	4,339.7	4,702.0	5,065.8	5,619.2	5,880.0	I150.99	Imports, c.i.f. **71**
1995=100																
	....	....	....	....	....	....	....	....	86	94	100	102	110	115	119	Volume of Exports **72**
	....	....	....	....	....	....	....	....	88	95	100	104	109	117	117	Volume of Imports **73**
	....	....	....	....	....	....	....	....	97	98	100	103	108	108	107	Unit Value of Exports **74**
	....	....	....	....	....	....	....	....	95	97	100	103	110	108	109	Unit Value of Imports **75**
	114	99	93	95	102	100	99	96	....	....	....	....	....	....	....	Import Price (1990=100) **76.x**
Billions of Francs																(BLEU: Country Code 126)
	3,167.7	3,070.3	3,100.1	3,382.3	3,943.1	3,944.5	4,023.4	3,969.8	4,129.0	4,579.0	4,996.1	5,133.1	5,916.2	....	....	Exports... **70**
	3,317.8	3,065.2	3,110.1	3,393.6	3,883.9	4,011.6	4,116.3	4,023.3	3,875.0	4,192.0	4,568.4	4,729.1	5,554.4	....	....	Imports, c.i.f. **71**
1995=100																
	56	59	62	66	72	74	77	77	I84	93	100	103	110	....	....	Volume of Exports **72**
	57	61	66	70	75	79	82	82	I83	95	100	106	111	....	....	Volume of Imports **73**
	112	103	98	101	109	105	103	102	I101	100	100	102	106	....	....	Unit Value of Exports **74**
	120	103	98	100	108	106	104	101	I99	98	100	102	107	....	....	Unit Value of Imports **75**

Belgium

124		1970	1971	1972	1973	1974	1975	1976	1977	1978	1979	1980	1981	1982	1983	1984
Balance of Payments																*Millions of US Dollars:*
(BLEU: Country Code 126)																
Current Account, n.i.e.	78al*d*	....	....	....	....	....	181	435	-554	-823	-3,080	-4,931	-4,168	-2,594	-495	-55
Goods: Exports f.o.b.	78aa*d*	....	....	....	....	....	23,797	26,886	32,699	40,055	51,410	57,573	50,719	48,243	47,598	48,001
Goods: Imports f.o.b.	78ab*d*	....	....	....	....	....	-24,191	-27,574	-34,537	-41,267	-54,426	-61,432	-54,193	-50,543	-48,264	-48,192
Trade Balance	78ac*d*	....	....	....	....	....	-394	-687	-1,838	-1,212	-3,016	-3,859	-3,474	-2,300	-666	-191
Services: Credit	78ad*d*	....	....	....	....	....	5,555	6,018	8,277	9,006	11,016	12,925	12,341	10,971	10,770	10,423
Services: Debit	78ae*d*	....	....	....	....	....	-4,957	-5,136	-7,071	-8,659	-10,703	-12,827	-11,804	-9,908	-9,392	-9,464
Balance on Goods & Services	78af*d*	....	....	....	....	....	204	195	-632	-865	-2,703	-3,761	-2,937	-1,237	712	768
Income: Credit	78ag*d*	....	....	....	....	....	4,479	4,430	5,263	7,380	11,527	18,427	24,197	22,883	18,333	18,943
Income: Debit	78ah*d*	....	....	....	....	....	-3,889	-3,670	-4,563	-6,585	-11,007	-18,366	-24,189	-23,063	-18,441	-18,934
Balance on Gds, Serv. & Inc.	78ai*d*	....	....	....	....	....	795	955	68	-71	-2,184	-3,700	-2,928	-1,417	604	776
Current Transfers, n.i.e.: Credit	78aj*d*	....	....	....	....	....	755	918	1,232	1,588	1,928	1,743	1,403	1,249	1,259	1,300
Current Transfers: Debit	78ak*d*	....	....	....	....	....	-1,368	-1,438	-1,854	-2,341	-2,825	-2,973	-2,643	-2,426	-2,358	-2,131
Capital Account, n.i.e.	78bc*d*	....	....	....	....	....	—	—	—	—	—	—	—	—	—	—
Capital Account, n.i.e.: Credit	78ba*d*	....	....	....	....	....	—	—	—	—	—	—	—	—	—	—
Capital Account: Debit	78bb*d*	....	....	....	....	....	—	—	—	—	—	—	—	—	—	—
Financial Account, n.i.e.	78bj*d*	....	....	....	....	....	-55	-1,183	848	330	2,313	4,083	3,115	2,300	1,187	208
Direct Investment Abroad	78bd*d*	....	....	....	....	....	-238	-352	-465	-560	-1,341	-196	-104	69	-355	-293
Dir. Invest. in Rep. Econ., n.i.e.	78be*d*	....	....	....	....	....	955	872	1,275	1,436	1,130	1,545	1,386	1,472	1,290	389
Portfolio Investment Assets	78bf*d*	....	....	....	....	....	-1,039	-763	-1,373	-864	-216	-789	-1,583	-2,237	-3,788	-4,141
Equity Securities	78bk*d*	....	....	....	....	....	-183	97	82	64	146	165	37	173	-11	62
Debt Securities	78bl*d*	....	....	....	....	....	-856	-860	-1,455	-927	-361	-954	-1,620	-2,410	-3,776	-4,203
Portfolio Investment Liab., n.i.e.	78bg*d*	....	....	....	....	....	-35	213	230	-94	829	1,485	812	246	113	161
Equity Securities	78bm*d*	....	....	....	....	....	-16	-34	11	-13	74	-1	-27	12	12	-86
Debt Securities	78bn*d*	....	....	....	....	....	-18	247	219	-82	755	1,486	839	234	101	247
Financial Derivatives Assets	78bw*d*	....	....	....	....	....	....	....	....	....	....	....	....	....	....	....
Financial Derivatives Liabilities	78bx*d*	....	....	....	....	....	....	....	....	....	....	....	....	....	....	....
Other Investment Assets	78bh*d*	....	....	....	....	....	-8,376	-9,946	-14,827	-18,165	-32,136	-45,092	-17,604	-27,519	-4,785	-31,332
Monetary Authorities	78bo*d*	....	....	....	....	....	....	....	....	....	....	....	....	....	....	....
General Government	78bp*d*	....	....	....	....	....	-87	-54	-47	-131	-152	-101	-116	-122	-139	-114
Banks	78bq*d*	....	....	....	....	....	-8,563	-8,521	-14,164	-16,593	-28,113	-42,259	-14,597	-26,373	-3,929	-30,199
Other Sectors	78br*d*	....	....	....	....	....	275	-1,370	-615	-1,441	-3,871	-2,731	-2,891	-1,024	-717	-1,019
Other Investment Liab., n.i.e.	78bi*d*	....	....	....	....	....	8,678	8,792	16,008	18,577	34,046	47,130	20,208	30,269	8,712	35,424
Monetary Authorities	78bs*d*	....	....	....	....	....	29	-20	728	791	318	-703	1,768	1,442	925	-583
General Government	78bt*d*	....	....	....	....	....	—	-6	27	17	68	905	1,324	1,845	453	1,187
Banks	78bu*d*	....	....	....	....	....	8,444	8,488	15,112	17,348	30,877	45,519	15,400	26,732	6,730	33,521
Other Sectors	78bv*d*	....	....	....	....	....	205	330	141	421	2,782	1,409	1,717	250	603	1,299
Net Errors and Omissions	78ca*d*	....	....	....	....	....	419	113	129	219	-138	981	-1,341	-294	-428	152
Overall Balance	78cb*d*	....	....	....	....	....	546	-635	422	-275	-906	133	-2,394	-588	265	305
Reserves and Related Items	79da*d*	....	....	....	....	....	-546	635	-422	275	906	-133	2,394	588	-265	-305
Reserve Assets	79db*d*	....	....	....	....	....	-546	635	-422	275	906	-133	2,394	588	-265	-305
Use of Fund Credit and Loans	79dc*d*	....	....	....	....	....	—	—	—	—	—	—	—	—	—	—
Exceptional Financing	79de*d*	....	....	....	....	....	....	....	....	....	....	....	....	....	....	....
International Investment Position																*Millions of US Dollars*
(For Belgium Only)																
Assets	79aa*d*	597	1,091	1,128	1,350	1,341	1,413	1,408	1,441	1,329	1,317	1,258	119,152	118,878	118,766	122,580
Direct Investment Abroad	79ab*d*	....	....	....	....	....	....	....	....	....	....	....	6,292	5,499	6,111	6,072
Portfolio Investment	79ac*d*	....	....	....	....	....	....	....	....	....	....	....	13,651	12,660	16,499	19,103
Equity Securities	79ad*d*	....	....	....	....	....	....	....	....	....	....	....	4,290	2,920	4,170	4,090
Debt Securities	79ae*d*	....	....	....	....	....	....	....	....	....	....	....	9,360	9,740	12,329	15,013
Financial Derivatives	79al*d*	....	....	....	....	....	....	....	....	....	....	....	—	—	—	—
Other Investment	79af*d*	....	....	....	....	....	....	....	....	....	....	—	79,511	80,413	77,516	81,341
Monetary Authorities	79ag*d*	....	....	....	....	....	....	....	....	....	....	....	130	85	90	32
General Government	79ah*d*	....	....	....	....	....	....	....	....	....	....	—	676	597	557	539
Banks	79ai*d*	....	....	....	....	....	....	....	....	....	....	....	62,246	61,743	60,694	66,027
Other Sectors	79aj*d*	....	....	....	....	....	....	....	....	....	....	—	16,459	17,988	16,175	14,743
Reserve Assets	79ak*d*	597	1,091	1,128	1,350	1,341	1,413	1,408	1,441	1,329	1,317	1,258	19,698	20,306	18,641	16,064
Liabilities	79la*d*	—	—	—	—	—	—	—	—	—	—	—	106,344	108,781	111,862	119,673
Dir. Invest. in Rep. Economy	79lb*d*	....	....	....	....	....	....	....	....	....	....	....	10,088	11,125	12,311	12,032
Portfolio Investment	79lc*d*	....	....	....	....	....	....	....	....	....	....	....	9,984	12,830	13,659	14,822
Equity Securities	79ld*d*	....	....	....	....	....	....	....	....	....	....	....	312	405	449	380
Debt Securities	79le*d*	....	....	....	....	....	....	....	....	....	....	....	9,672	12,425	13,210	14,442
Financial Derivatives	79ll*d*	....	....	....	....	....	....	....	....	....	....	....	—	—	—	—
Other Investment	79lf*d*	—	—	—	—	—	—	—	—	—	—	—	86,271	84,825	85,891	92,819
Monetary Authorities	79lg*d*	—	—	—	—	—	—	—	—	—	—	—	598	426	359	317
General Government	79lh*d*	....	....	....	....	....	....	....	....	....	....	....	26	64	72	—
Banks	79li*d*	....	....	....	....	....	....	....	....	....	....	....	75,689	74,233	76,042	83,291
Other Sectors	79lj*d*	....	....	....	....	....	....	....	....	....	....	....	9,958	10,102	9,418	9,211
Government Finance																
Central Government																*Billions of Francs through 1998;*
Deficit (-) or Surplus	80	I -21.2	-39.6	-67.9	-61.8	-46.6	-109.0	-147.5	-168.3	-209.2	-247.7	-282.0	-446.9	-431.6	-515.9	-596.1
Revenue	81	I 448.1	493.7	553.6	646.9	779.0	924.8	1,056.1	1,180.1	1,296.8	1,393.4	1,508.6	1,595.5	1,781.9	1,857.3	2,040.0
Grants Received	81z	I 1.3	2.0	2.4	3.2	2.6	3.1	3.9	3.4	3.9	4.7	2.4	3.0	2.9	2.8	3.1
Expenditure	82	I 468.3	530.6	619.9	706.8	820.2	1,025.9	1,194.0	1,340.2	1,482.3	1,625.6	1,758.3	2,016.1	2,185.0	2,346.9	2,493.6
Lending Minus Repayments	83	I 2.3	4.7	4.0	5.1	8.0	11.0	13.5	11.6	27.6	20.2	34.7	29.3	31.4	29.1	145.6
Financing																
Net Borrowing: National Currency	84a	I 33.1	69.1	82.3	68.4	40.6	109.1	150.7	167.4	172.7	207.1	211.5	234.6	220.4	394.0	405.8
Foreign Currency	85a	I -11.3	-28.5	-15.0	-3.5	-1.4	.2	-.4	-.3	13.4	43.0	83.5	214.1	189.4	127.0	181.1
Use of Cash Balances	87	I -.6	-1.0	.6	-3.1	7.4	-.3	-2.8	1.2	23.1	-2.4	-13.0	-1.8	21.8	-5.1	9.2
Debt: National Currency	88a	I 554.2	615.7	693.7	749.1	807.9	917.0	1,050.4	1,218.2	1,387.5	1,556.3	1,761.0	2,000.3	2,299.2	2,706.0	3,077.3
Foreign Currency	89a	I 55.0	26.8	11.8	8.3	6.9	7.1	6.7	6.4	19.9	62.9	154.9	374.4	591.0	724.8	882.0
General Government																*As Percent of*
Deficit (-) or Surplus	80g	....	....	....	....	....	....	....	....	....	....	....	....	....	....	....
Debt	88g	....	....	....	....	....	....	....	....	....	....	....	....	....	....	....

	1985	1986	1987	1988	1989	1990	1991	1992	1993	1994	1995	1996	1997	1998	1999	

Minus Sign Indicates Debit

Balance of Payments (BLEU: Country Code 126)

	1985	1986	1987	1988	1989	1990	1991	1992	1993	1994	1995	1996	1997	1998	1999	
Current Account, n.i.e.	670	3,059	2,797	3,592	3,600	3,627	4,746	6,650	11,237	12,571	14,232	13,762	13,914	12,168	11,961	78ald
Goods: Exports f.o.b.	49,178	62,914	77,948	87,436	92,123	110,188	107,990	116,841	106,302	122,795	155,219	154,695	149,497	153,558	152,713	78aad
Goods: Imports f.o.b.	-48,686	-60,608	-76,653	-84,733	-89,845	-108,517	-105,991	-113,141	-100,522	-115,895	-145,664	-146,004	-141,794	-146,577	-145,227	78abd
Trade Balance	492	2,305	1,294	2,703	2,278	1,671	1,999	3,700	5,780	6,901	9,555	8,690	7,703	6,981	7,486	78acd
Services: Credit	10,796	14,618	18,908	21,045	21,840	28,417	30,583	33,658	33,366	40,440	35,466	34,702	35,503	38,081	40,372	78add
Services: Debit	-9,941	-13,163	-16,464	-18,898	-21,314	-26,581	-28,789	-30,999	-29,995	-36,500	-33,134	-32,069	-31,664	-34,411	-36,946	78aed
Balance on Goods & Services	1,346	3,760	3,739	4,851	2,805	3,507	3,793	6,359	9,151	10,841	11,887	11,322	11,542	10,651	10,912	78afd
Income: Credit	20,830	23,665	27,496	33,127	48,276	65,544	75,452	88,295	83,011	89,403	74,798	62,884	58,237	65,251	65,229	78agd
Income: Debit	-20,851	-23,420	-27,011	-32,631	-45,592	-63,228	-72,274	-85,309	-78,138	-84,166	-67,990	-55,838	-51,882	-59,315	-59,596	78ahd
Balance on Gds, Serv. & Inc.	1,325	4,005	4,224	5,347	5,489	5,824	6,971	9,345	14,024	16,078	18,695	18,368	17,896	16,588	16,544	78aid
Current Transfers, n.i.e.: Credit	1,524	1,968	2,500	2,602	2,329	3,825	4,160	4,368	4,198	4,501	7,822	7,474	7,142	7,006	6,638	78ajd
Current Transfers: Debit	-2,180	-2,913	-3,927	-4,357	-4,217	-6,022	-6,385	-7,063	-6,986	-8,009	-12,285	-12,081	-11,124	-11,426	-11,221	78akd
Capital Account, n.i.e.	—	—	—	—	—	—	—	—	—	....	378	179	403	-113	-63	78bcd
Capital Account, n.i.e.: Credit	—	—	—	—	—	—	—	—	—	....	734	673	783	323	459	78bad
Capital Account: Debit	—	—	—	—	—	—	—	—	—	....	-356	-494	-379	-436	-522	78bbd
Financial Account, n.i.e.	-605	-3,248	-349	-2,793	-2,664	-1,651	-3,155	-7,806	-13,563	-10,182	-12,912	-12,257	-12,091	-16,043	-13,310	78bjd
Direct Investment Abroad	-296	-1,723	-2,782	-3,784	-6,486	-6,314	-6,271	-11,407	-4,904	-1,371	-11,603	-8,026	-7,252	-28,845	-24,967	78bdd
Dir. Invest. in Rep. Econ., n.i.e.	1,051	730	2,355	5,212	7,020	8,047	9,363	11,286	10,750	8,514	10,689	14,064	11,998	22,690	15,956	78bed
Portfolio Investment Assets	-6,269	-7,039	-4,435	-12,302	-14,324	-9,443	-29,570	-62,887	-58,431	-40,963	-29,472	-48,409	-62,657	-100,234	-155,533	78bfd
Equity Securities	-96	-644	31	-332	-3,839	1,530	-659	-115	-9,465	-10,649	-3,525	-3,582	-21,006	-29,087	-44,738	78bkd
Debt Securities	-6,172	-6,395	-4,466	-11,970	-10,485	-10,973	-28,911	-62,773	-48,966	-30,314	-25,946	-44,827	-41,651	-71,147	-110,795	78bld
Portfolio Investment Liab., n.i.e.	267	447	2,006	7,729	11,050	7,946	27,490	59,016	50,472	17,445	4,649	36,666	54,047	59,253	147,265	78bgd
Equity Securities	185	608	1,433	6,362	10,082	7,014	20,816	56,272	46,838	22,489	6,505	34,243	47,207	58,418	92,716	78bmd
Debt Securities	82	-161	573	1,368	968	932	6,674	2,743	3,634	-5,043	-1,856	2,423	6,840	835	54,548	78bnd
Financial Derivatives Assets	....	....	....	....	—	—	—	—	—	....	1,213	-970	-330	489	1,151	78bwd
Financial Derivatives Liabilities	....	....	....	....	—	—	—	—	—	....	630	483	444	302	1,141	78bxd
Other Investment Assets	-51,671	-61,223	-122,240	6,361	-55,626	-64,422	-22,023	-49,920	-51,772	11,269	-23,445	-14,977	-48,692	7,467	-73,625	78bhd
Monetary Authorities	....	....	....	....	—	—	—	—	—	....	....	....	....	-147	-11,077	78bod
General Government	-98	-143	-163	-99	-242	-184	-440	-536	-802	-294	-72	-372	-306	371	-2,237	78bpd
Banks	-50,970	-59,184	-119,861	8,613	-55,225	-67,666	-25,042	-49,101	-45,916	9,829	-16,926	9,164	-28,220	3,886	-14,855	78bqd
Other Sectors	-604	-1,896	-2,216	-2,153	-159	3,429	3,459	-277	-5,054	1,734	-6,447	-23,769	-20,166	3,357	-45,456	78brd
Other Investment Liab., n.i.e.	56,313	65,561	124,747	-6,010	55,701	62,536	17,857	46,107	40,321	-5,076	34,426	8,913	40,352	22,836	75,303	78bid
Monetary Authorities	-602	1,161	998	2,741	—	—	—	—	—	....	223	-458	-50	193	29,651	78bsd
General Government	892	346	-566	-135	2,167	948	2,417	-2,887	10,758	-5,233	322	-40	-161	203	1,923	78btd
Banks	55,827	62,395	120,145	-10,449	52,731	56,431	7,262	32,419	19,043	64	42,121	6,469	31,211	18,087	9,697	78bud
Other Sectors	196	1,659	4,171	1,833	804	5,156	8,178	16,575	10,520	93	-8,240	2,941	9,352	4,352	34,032	78bvd
Net Errors and Omissions	-263	218	-14	61	-624	-1,572	-1,007	1,726	204	-2,169	-1,456	-1,091	-1,171	1,893	-456	78cad
Overall Balance	-197	29	2,434	861	312	404	584	569	-2,122	219	243	593	1,056	-2,095	-1,867	78cbd
Reserves and Related Items	197	-29	-2,434	-861	-312	-404	-584	-569	2,122	-219	-243	-593	-1,056	2,095	1,867	79dad
Reserve Assets	197	-29	-2,434	-861	-312	-404	-584	-569	2,122	-219	-243	-593	-1,056	2,095	1,867	79dbd
Use of Fund Credit and Loans	—	—	—	—	—	—	—	—	—	—	—	—	—	—	—	79dcd
Exceptional Financing	....	....	....	....												79ded

Millions of US Dollars

International Investment Position (For Belgium Only)

	1985	1986	1987	1988	1989	1990	1991	1992	1993	1994	1995	1996	1997	1998	1999	
Assets	159,100	212,984	277,043	282,724	332,353	401,644	426,728	439,946	469,094	533,478	578,243	580,701	573,800P	629,965P	....	79aad
Direct Investment Abroad	9,551	15,194	19,606	24,903	34,676	40,636	48,385	55,636	62,642	69,541	83,325	87,861	92,308P	124,485P	....	79abd
Portfolio Investment	29,408	44,593	58,155	70,130	86,885	106,350	116,565	124,141	145,694	161,256	186,945	189,033	192,091P	200,668P	....	79acd
Equity Securities	6,652	11,383	13,212	19,708	27,629	33,858	38,727	42,616	59,319	59,804	60,105	58,710	56,717P	68,750P	....	79add
Debt Securities	22,756	33,210	44,944	50,422	59,256	72,493	77,838	81,525	86,375	101,453	126,840	130,323	135,374P	131,918P	....	79aed
Financial Derivatives											646	1,375	1,869P	2,054P	....	79ald
Other Investment	103,296	133,531	172,174	163,610	186,997	229,775	237,544	237,342	238,244	279,199	283,835	279,394	266,143P	282,260P	....	79afd
Monetary Authorities	79	198	211	161	196	258	927	784	775	597	1,632	1,031	135P	405P	....	79agd
General Government	735	965	1,418	1,259	1,314	1,775	2,271	2,140	2,049	1,947	2,074	1,906	1,652P	1,764P	....	79ahd
Banks	83,836	108,018	138,994	132,253	148,294	181,490	183,019	177,366	178,926	203,816	218,664	206,811	197,671P	196,214P	....	79aid
Other Sectors	18,646	24,350	31,551	29,937	37,192	46,252	51,327	57,052	56,494	72,839	61,465	69,645	66,685P	83,877P	....	79ajd
Reserve Assets	16,845	19,665	27,107	24,082	23,796	24,883	24,233	22,827	22,514	23,482	23,492	23,038	21,389P	20,499P	....	79akd
Liabilities	157,903	211,086	270,900	278,538	328,384	391,963	408,826	416,667	437,690	495,611	546,864	539,010	528,738P	588,383P	....	79lad
Dir. Invest. in Rep. Economy	18,447	27,394	30,646	39,309	52,824	58,388	70,163	75,678	94,295	105,881	120,211	132,542	140,818P	189,880P	....	79lbd
Portfolio Investment	19,619	28,483	39,605	44,183	53,160	64,036	78,286	80,530	93,603	103,808	100,323	92,361	85,861P	79,394P	....	79lcd
Equity Securities	814	2,054	2,805	3,749	4,754	5,616	5,980	5,937	8,253	9,737	10,539	12,061	13,787P	20,391P	....	79ldd
Debt Securities	18,805	26,429	36,800	40,434	48,406	58,420	72,306	74,593	85,350	94,071	89,784	80,300	72,075P	59,003P	....	79led
Financial Derivatives											578	937	1,273P	1,764P	....	79lld
Other Investment	119,837	155,209	200,649	195,046	222,399	269,539	260,377	260,458	249,792	285,921	325,752	313,170	300,785P	317,345P	....	79lfd
Monetary Authorities	377	445	513	616	503	678	768	663	665	848	1,122	531	460P	839P	....	79lgd
General Government	20	49	181	80	419	355	416	573	305	942	850	687	379P	406P	....	79lhd
Banks	108,519	142,217	185,114	179,328	203,160	240,813	229,645	227,818	219,247	251,590	302,193	289,455	276,165P	285,818P	....	79lid
Other Sectors	10,921	12,497	14,841	15,022	18,317	27,693	29,549	31,404	29,576	32,540	21,588	22,496	23,781P	30,282P	....	79ljd

Government Finance

Central Government

Millions of Euros Beginning 1999: Year Ending December 31

	1985	1986	1987	1988	1989	1990	1991	1992	1993	1994	1995	1996	1997	1998	1999	
Deficit (-) or Surplus	-537.6	-497.3	-404.0	-364.0	-397.0	-364.6	-416.2	-486.1	-450.2	-324.9	-259.1	I-210.2	-176.0	....	....	80
Revenue	2,201.6	2,271.4	2,369.9	2,459.7	2,603.4	2,818.9	2,949.4	3,094.5	3,263.4	3,476.4	3,567.5	I3,685.2	3,822.5	....	....	81
Grants Received	2.5	2.6	2.7	2.2	2.8	2.0	2.4	5.8	4.6	5.7	11.1	I5.0	20.3	....	....	81z
Expenditure	2,624.5	2,727.4	2,735.4	2,798.4	2,973.0	3,154.7	3,353.9	3,575.3	3,699.5	3,821.3	3,885.6	I3,909.5	4,045.6	....	....	82
Lending Minus Repayments	117.2	43.9	41.2	27.5	30.2	30.8	14.1	11.1	18.7	-14.3	-47.9	I-9.1	-26.8	....	....	83

Financing

	1985	1986	1987	1988	1989	1990	1991	1992	1993	1994	1995	1996	1997	1998	1999	
Net Borrowing: National Currency	504.4	423.2	372.2	341.1	328.2	384.2	548.6	619.5	112.3	360.1	380.1	I612.9	115.6	....	....	84a
Foreign Currency	26.8	74.1	31.8	22.9	68.8	-19.6	-8.0	-107.6	454.9	-152.4	-262.0	I-334.1	-1.0	....	....	85a
Use of Cash Balances	6.4	—	—	—	—	—	-124.4	-25.8	-117.0	117.2	141.0	I-68.6	61.4	....	....	87
Debt: National Currency	3,694.2	4,632.5	5,237.4	5,693.5	6,064.2	6,581.4	7,248.0	7,899.7	8,075.9	8,623.7	9,063.4	I9,576.7	9,702.8	....	....	88a
Foreign Currency	919.8	1,020.4	1,045.9	1,087.4	1,131.0	1,111.8	1,107.0	1,010.5	1,519.9	1,349.5	1,085.3	I734.0	784.4	....	....	89a

General Government

Gross Domestic Product

	1985	1986	1987	1988	1989	1990	1991	1992	1993	1994	1995	1996	1997	1998	1999	
Deficit (-) or Surplus	....	....	....	....	....	-5.5	-6.3	-6.9	-7.1	-4.9	-4.0	-3.7	-2.0	-1.0	-.9	80g
Debt	....	....	....	....	....	125.7	127.5	129.0	135.2	133.2	132.2	128.3	123.0	117.4	114.4	88g

Belgium

National Accounts		1970	1971	1972	1973	1974	1975	1976	1977	1978	1979	1980	1981	1982	1983	1984
														Billions of Francs through 1998;		
Househ.Cons.Expend.,incl.NPISHs	96f	769	848	948	1,084	1,256	1,421	1,613	1,769	1,890	2,057	2,241	2,415	2,644	2,802	2,990
Government Consumption Expend.	91f	175	202	232	264	314	388	441	489	544	588	616	669	707	729	765
Gross Fixed Capital Formation	93e	288	306	328	374	467	512	565	606	646	668	724	642	672	669	709
Changes in Inventories	93i	20	18	10	25	46	−13	10	8	8	20	29	−4	8	−22	26
Exports Of goods and services	90c	562	609	683	846	1,116	1,065	1,266	1,474	1,540	1,798	2,170	2,439	2,794	3,079	3,505
Imports of Goods and Services	98c	−533	−581	−633	−811	−1,109	−1,061	−1,261	−1,499	−1,570	−1,866	−2,258	−2,497	−2,834	−3,004	−3,429
Gross Domestic Product (GDP)	99b	1,281	1,402	1,569	1,782	2,091	2,313	2,633	2,847	3,058	3,265	3,508	3,655	3,957	4,189	4,513
Net Primary Income from Abroad	98.n	11	10	12	9	12	13	17	12	10	−4	−26	−30	−58	−63	−60
Gross National Income (GNI)	99a	1,292	1,412	1,581	1,792	2,103	2,326	2,650	2,859	3,068	3,261	3,502	3,647	3,925	4,152	4,478
GDP Volume 1990 prices	99b.*p*	....	....	....	....	....	....	....	....	....	....	....	....	....	....	....
GDP Volume 1995 prices	99b.*p*	....	....	....	....	....	....	....	....	....	....	....	....	....	....	....
GDP Volume (1995=100)	99bv *p*	....	....	....	....	....	....	....	....	....	....	....	....	....	....	....
GDP Deflator (1995=100)	99bi *p*	38.9	41.0	43.5	46.6	52.3	58.9	63.5	68.1	70.8	73.8	77.0	81.0	86.4	91.0	95.9
																Millions:
Population	99z	9.66	9.67	9.71	9.74	9.77	9.79	9.81	9.82	9.83	9.84	9.85	9.85	9.86	9.86	9.86

1985	1986	1987	1988	1989	1990	1991	1992	1993	1994	1995	1996	1997	1998	1999	National Accounts	
Billions of Euros Beginning 1999																
₤2,851	2,934	3,049	3,192	3,446	3,658	3,865	4,024	4,094	4,281	4,385	4,504	4,671	4,890		₤125 Househ.Cons.Expend.,incl.NPISHs..........	**96f**
₤1,129	1,174	1,212	1,219	1,278	1,339	1,448	1,528	1,599	1,671	1,745	1,807	1,851	1,917		₤49 Government Consumption Expend.	**91f**
₤874	911	978	1,156	1,363	1,523	1,487	1,546	1,523	1,558	1,653	1,686	1,817	1,894		₤49 Gross Fixed Capital Formation	**93e**
₤1	−4	9	14	−4	−51	−30	−28	−54	−33	17	−29	−20	24		₤— Changes in Inventories.............................	**93i**
₤3,556	3,414	3,464	3,942	4,573	4,700	4,813	4,934	4,849	5,319	5,703	5,917	6,608	6,868		₤177 Exports Of goods and services	**90c**
₤−3,506	−3,289	−3,359	−3,791	−4,425	−4,577	−4,674	−4,731	−4,583	−5,003	−5,373	−5,584	−6,214	−6,502		₤168 Imports of Goods and Services	**98c**
₤4,905	5,140	5,354	5,730	6,231	6,593	6,910	7,273	7,431	7,792	8,129	8,304	8,713	9,088		₤233 Gross Domestic Product (GDP)	**99b**
₤−37	−25	−25	−43	−97	−49	−27	−8	97	132	84	107	82	87		₤2 Net Primary Income from Abroad........	**98.n**
₤4,867	5,115	5,328	5,688	6,135	6,544	6,883	7,265	7,526	7,926	8,212	8,411	8,794	9,175		₤236 Gross National Income (GNI)	**99a**
3,645	3,722	3,801	3,957	7,333	7,534	7,685	7,809	7,694	7,924	8,132	8,203	8,466	8,712	....	GDP Volume 1990 prices	**99b.** *p*
6,487	6,602	6,780	7,092	7,351	7,550	7,699	7,820	7,702	7,931	8,129	8,209	8,499	8,727	₤221.9	GDP Volume 1995 prices	**99b.** *p*
79.8	81.2	83.4	87.2	90.4	92.9	94.7	96.2	94.7	97.6	100.0	101.0	104.6	107.4	₤110.1	GDP Volume (1995=100)	**99bv** *p*
₤75.6	77.9	79.0	80.8	84.8	87.3	89.8	93.0	96.5	98.2	100.0	101.2	102.5	104.1	₤105.1	GDP Deflator (1995=100)	**99bi** *p*
Midyear Estimates																
9.86	9.86	9.87	9.90	9.94	9.97	9.98	10.05	10.08	10.09	10.14	10.16	10.19	10.21	10.15	**Population**..	**99z**

(See notes in the back of the book.)

Belize

339		1970	1971	1972	1973	1974	1975	1976	1977	1978	1979	1980	1981	1982	1983	1984
Exchange Rates																*Belize Dollars per SDR: End of Period (aa)*
Official Rate	aa	1.6711	1.7014	I 1.8495	2.0770	2.0853	2.3141	2.7299	2.4294	2.6056	2.6347	2.5508	2.3279	2.2062	2.0939	1.9604
Official Rate	ae	1.6711	1.5671	I 1.7035	1.7218	1.7032	1.9768	2.3496	2.0000	2.0000	2.0000	2.0000	2.0000	2.0000	2.0000	2.0000
																Index Numbers (1995=100):
Official Rate	ahx	119.8	122.2	125.1	122.6	117.0	111.1	90.3	100.0	100.0	100.0	100.0	100.0	100.0	100.0	100.0
Nominal Effective Exchange Rate	nec	....	....	....	....	....	....	....	....	....	52.9	52.9	57.2	61.4	65.6	70.6
Real Effective Exchange Rate	rec	....	....	....	....	....	....	....	....	....	....	102.7	111.4[e]	118.6[e]	125.2	130.3
Fund Position																*Millions of SDRs:*
Quota	2f.s	—	—	—	—	—	—	—	—	—	—	—	—	7.20	9.50	9.50
SDRs	1b.s	....	....	....	....	....	....	....	....	....	....	....	....	—	.02	.01
Reserve Position in the Fund	1c.s	....	....	....	....	....	....	....	....	....	....	....	....	1.32	1.90	1.90
Total Fund Cred.&Loans Outstg.	2tl	....	....	....	....	....	....	....	....	....	....	....	....	—	3.60	4.80
International Liquidity																*Millions of US Dollars Unless Otherwise Indicated:*
Total Reserves minus Gold	1l.d	....	....	....	....	....	....	5.49	8.02	13.98	10.46	12.68	10.33	9.84	9.31	6.07
SDRs	1b.d	....	....	....	....	....	....	....	....	....	....	....	....	—	.02	.01
Reserve Position in the Fund	1c.d	....	....	....	....	....	....	....	....	....	....	....	....	1.46	1.99	1.86
Foreign Exchange	1d.d	....	....	....	....	....	....	5.49	8.02	13.98	10.46	12.68	10.33	8.38	7.30	4.20
Monetary Authorities: Other Liab.	4..d	....	....	....	....	....	....	—	.26	1.08	.45	.45	.19	.19	.45	1.77
Deposit Money Banks: Assets	7a.d	....	....	....	....	....	....	1.31	4.79	7.68	12.71	13.51	14.05	7.79	9.36	9.77
Liabilities	7b.d	....	....	....	....	....	....	4.59	6.31	6.41	14.81	17.29	19.04	23.68	23.04	26.11
Other Banking Insts.: Assets	7e.d	....	....	....	....	....	....	....	....	—	.01	.01	.01	.01	.01	1.59
Liabilities	7f.d	....	....	....	....	....	....	....	....	6.04	6.61	8.51	10.77	12.00	12.98	16.06
Monetary Authorities																*Millions of Belize Dollars:*
Foreign Assets	11	....	....	....	....	....	....	12.90	16.04	27.96	20.93	25.35	20.67	19.67	18.63	12.34
Claims on Central Government	12a	....	....	....	....	....	....	1.90	4.67	4.73	10.77	11.91	28.08	33.70	39.52	56.70
Claims on Deposit Money Banks	12e	....	....	....	....	....	....	—	—	—	—	.81	—	—	—	—
Reserve Money	14	....	....	....	....	....	....	13.64	18.58	25.45	22.92	26.11	31.58	37.15	34.99	47.14
of which: Currency Outside DMBs	14a	....	....	....	....	....	....	11.27	12.55	16.72	16.68	17.51	19.01	20.61	21.53	22.77
Foreign Liabilities	16c	....	....	....	....	....	....	—	.52	2.16	.91	.90	.39	.38	8.45	12.94
Central Government Deposits	16d	....	....	....	....	....	....	—	—	.49	—	1.52	5.34	—	—	—
Capital Accounts	17a	....	....	....	....	....	....	.64	2.00	4.74	7.99	9.55	10.46	10.46	11.14	11.73
Other Items (Net)	17r	....	....	....	....	....	....	.52	–.39	–.15	–.11	–.02	.99	5.38	3.57	–2.78
Deposit Money Banks																*Millions of Belize Dollars:*
Reserves	20	....	....	....	....	....	....	2.37	5.79	8.38	6.22	8.49	12.54	16.52	13.70	19.81
Foreign Assets	21	....	....	....	....	....	....	3.09	9.59	15.36	25.41	27.02	28.11	15.58	18.71	19.55
Claims on Central Government	22a	....	....	....	....	....	....	1.57	3.50	7.01	2.59	9.82	6.68	16.17	32.07	30.10
Claims on Official Entities	22bx	....	....	....	....	....	....	4.04	4.38	6.25	8.13	7.00	8.66	9.58	7.00	13.05
Claims on Private Sector	22d	....	....	....	....	....	....	57.66	52.68	55.32	70.73	77.32	90.79	107.66	117.16	116.14
Demand Deposits	24	....	....	....	....	....	....	10.03	12.14	19.26	20.19	24.03	20.52	18.76	20.84	22.67
Time, Savings,& Fgn.Currency Dep.	25	....	....	....	....	....	....	50.28	48.74	56.92	59.04	66.55	78.25	85.67	105.75	104.62
Foreign Liabilities	26c	....	....	....	....	....	....	10.79	12.62	12.82	29.62	34.59	38.08	47.35	46.09	52.22
Central Government Deposits	26d	....	....	....	....	....	....	.76	.75	1.09	1.41	.57	2.38	6.18	8.37	10.96
Credit from Monetary Authorities	26g	....	....	....	....	....	....	—	—	—	—	.40	—	—	—	6.80
Capital Accounts	27a	....	....	....	....	....	....	.70	5.40	5.21	7.25	7.63	8.23	8.35	10.30	10.61
Other Items (Net)	27r	....	....	....	....	....	....	–3.82	–3.71	–2.97	–4.43	–4.12	–.69	–.82	–2.71	–9.23
Monetary Survey																*Millions of Belize Dollars:*
Foreign Assets (Net)	31n	....	....	....	....	....	....	5.19	12.49	28.34	15.82	16.88	10.31	–12.48	–17.19	–33.28
Domestic Credit	32	....	....	....	....	....	....	64.42	64.48	71.73	90.81	103.95	126.63	161.15	187.53	205.23
Claims on Central Govt. (Net)	32an	....	....	....	....	....	....	2.71	7.42	10.16	11.95	19.64	27.04	43.69	63.22	75.84
Claims on Official Entities	32bx	....	....	....	....	....	....	4.04	4.38	6.25	8.13	7.00	8.66	9.58	7.00	13.05
Claims on Private Sector	32d	....	....	....	....	....	....	57.66	52.68	55.32	70.73	77.32	90.79	107.66	117.16	116.14
Money	34	....	....	....	....	....	....	21.30	24.69	36.01	36.89	41.65	39.56	39.40	42.41	50.01
Quasi-Money	35	....	....	....	....	....	....	50.28	48.74	56.92	59.04	66.55	78.25	85.67	105.75	104.62
Capital Accounts	37a	....	....	....	....	....	....	1.34	7.40	9.94	15.23	17.18	18.69	18.81	21.44	22.34
Other Items (Net)	37r	....	....	....	....	....	....	–3.31	–3.85	–2.80	–4.55	–4.54	.44	4.78	.73	–5.02
Money plus Quasi-Money	35l	....	....	....	....	....	....	71.58	73.43	92.93	95.94	108.20	117.81	125.07	148.16	154.63
Other Banking Institutions																*Millions of Belize Dollars:*
Reserves	40	....	....	....	....	....	....	....	....	1.01	.83	.91	.53	.89	2.31	.95
Foreign Assets	41	....	....	....	....	....	....	....	....	.01	.03	.02	.02	.02	.02	3.19
Claims on Central Government	42a	....	....	....	....	....	....	....	....	1.66	1.41	1.09	.64	.24	.77	.64
Claims on Official Entities	42bx	....	....	....	....	....	....	....	....	1.67	1.67	1.60	1.38	1.39	1.49	1.29
Claims on Private Sector	42d	....	....	....	....	....	....	....	....	12.00	12.74	17.12	22.04	24.20	27.35	30.01
Foreign Liabilities	46c	....	....	....	....	....	....	....	....	12.07	13.23	17.02	21.55	23.99	25.96	32.13
Central Government Deposits	46d	....	....	....	....	....	....	....	....	—	—	—	—	—	—	—
Credit from Monetary Authorities	46g	....	....	....	....	....	....	....	....	—	—	.41	—	—	.75	—
Capital Accounts	47a	....	....	....	....	....	....	....	....	2.41	3.61	4.47	3.90	4.72	4.98	4.70
Other Items (Net)	47r	....	....	....	....	....	....	....	....	1.86	–.16	–1.15	–.82	–1.98	.25	–.75
Banking Survey																*Millions of Belize Dollars:*
Foreign Assets (Net)	51n	....	....	....	....	....	....	....	....	16.28	2.62	–.11	–11.22	–36.45	–43.13	–62.22
Domestic Credit	52	....	....	....	....	....	....	....	....	87.06	106.62	123.76	150.70	186.97	217.14	237.17
Claims on Central Govt. (Net)	52an	....	....	....	....	....	....	....	....	11.82	13.36	20.73	27.68	43.94	63.99	76.48
Claims on Official Entities	52bx	....	....	....	....	....	....	....	....	7.92	9.79	8.60	10.05	10.97	8.49	14.34
Claims on Private Sector	52d	....	....	....	....	....	....	....	....	67.32	83.47	94.43	112.84	131.86	144.51	146.15
Liquid Liabilities	55l	....	....	....	....	....	....	....	....	91.92	95.11	107.29	117.28	124.18	145.85	153.68
Capital Accounts	57a	....	....	....	....	....	....	....	....	12.36	18.84	21.65	22.58	23.54	26.42	27.04
Other Items (Net)	57r	....	....	....	....	....	....	....	....	–.94	–4.70	–5.29	–.38	2.80	1.73	–5.76
Interest Rates																*Percent Per Annum*
Discount Rate *(End of Period)*	60	....	....	....	....	....	....	....	7.00	7.50	10.00	14.00	14.50	13.50	11.50	12.00
Treasury Bill Rate	60c	....	....	....	....	....	....	....	5.91	6.40	6.40	10.29	11.68	12.00	10.51	9.55
Deposit Rate	60l	....	....	....	....	....	....	7.10	6.70	6.80	6.80	11.18	14.68	14.87	11.30	9.08
Lending Rate	60p	....	....	....	....	....	....	11.50	11.30	11.30	11.60	16.50	19.28	....	....	....

	1985	1986	1987	1988	1989	1990	1991	1992	1993	1994	1995	1996	1997	1998	1999		
Belize Dollars per US Dollar: End of Period (ae)																**Exchange Rates**	
	2.1968	2.4464	2.8373	2.6914	2.6283	2.8453	2.8609	2.7500	2.7471	2.9197	2.9730	2.8759	2.6985	2.8161	2.7450	Official Rate	**aa**
	2.0000	2.0000	2.0000	2.0000	2.0000	2.0000	2.0000	2.0000	2.0000	2.0000	2.0000	2.0000	2.0000	2.0000	2.0000	Official Rate	**ae**
Period Averages																	
	100.0	100.0	100.0	100.0	100.0	100.0	100.0	100.0	100.0	100.0	100.0	100.0	100.0	100.0	100.0	Official Rate	**ah x**
	77.1	73.7	71.3	72.7	79.3	82.7	85.7	87.6	95.1	99.6	100.0	103.1	107.8	110.9	111.9	Nominal Effective Exchange Rate	**ne c**
	138.3	123.7	114.7	113.5	111.7	104.8	103.3	100.7	106.6	102.3	100.0	105.3	108.6	108.2	105.6	Real Effective Exchange Rate	**re c**
End of Period																**Fund Position**	
	9.50	9.50	9.50	9.50	9.50	9.50	9.50	13.50	13.50	13.50	13.50	13.50	13.50	13.50	18.80	Quota	**2f. s**
	—	—	.06	.02	—	.01	.08	.15	.29	.37	.47	.61	.71	.82	1.01	SDRs	**1b. s**
	1.90	1.90	1.91	1.91	1.91	1.91	1.91	2.91	2.91	2.91	2.91	2.91	2.91	2.91	4.24	Reserve Position in the Fund	**1c. s**
	9.54	9.54	8.03	5.79	2.52	.30	—	—	—	—	—	—	—	—	—	Total Fund Cred.&Loans Outstg.	**2tl**
End of Period																**International Liquidity**	
	14.81	26.90	36.41	51.66	59.88	69.78	53.02	52.94	38.75	34.52	37.61	58.40	59.42	44.09	71.31	Total Reserves minus Gold	**1l. d**
	—	—	.09	.03	—	.01	.11	.21	.39	.54	.70	.88	.96	1.16	1.39	SDRs	**1b. d**
	2.09	2.32	2.71	2.57	2.51	2.72	2.73	4.00	4.00	4.25	4.33	4.19	3.93	4.10	5.82	Reserve Position in the Fund	**1c. d**
	12.73	24.57	33.62	49.06	57.37	67.05	50.17	48.74	34.35	29.72	32.58	53.34	54.53	38.82	64.10	Foreign Exchange	**1d. d**
	.68	.58	.86	.56	1.65	4.14	7.51	8.79	6.81	6.21	5.31	1.77	3.64	1.61	1.04	Monetary Authorities: Other Liab.	**4.. d**
	10.17	8.48	8.04	6.95	12.38	19.39	16.31	12.31	23.64	24.27	26.21	38.45	35.84	37.94	45.64	Deposit Money Banks: Assets	**7a. d**
	21.74	13.17	11.14	10.51	8.53	4.58	12.54	23.60	49.15	51.68	39.59	41.40	43.71	50.69	43.06	Liabilities	**7b. d**
	1.35	.59	.36	.12	.25	—	—	.01	—	—	—	—	—	—	—	Other Banking Insts.: Assets	**7e. d**
	11.81	17.93	19.37	19.42	17.67	16.79	16.05	15.53	14.11	14.20	14.33	13.64	17.88	17.97	21.11	Liabilities	**7f. d**
End of Period																**Monetary Authorities**	
	29.63	53.55	73.15	103.51	120.22	139.84	105.88	105.86	77.27	68.94	75.24	116.85	118.89	88.23	142.90	Foreign Assets	**11**
	65.57	61.47	50.45	33.64	27.00	5.19	21.95	31.40	61.47	67.54	81.72	110.78	89.86	94.89	67.38	Claims on Central Government	**12a**
	—	—	—	—	—	—	—	10.00	8.50	7.84	7.06	6.39	4.18	2.25	1.00	Claims on Deposit Money Banks	**12e**
	54.09	63.94	71.45	68.31	85.16	83.72	86.79	105.38	104.63	102.50	116.21	119.64	125.81	135.57	165.22	Reserve Money	**14**
	22.64	25.90	29.56	34.11	40.44	43.46	47.91	50.98	54.19	56.74	61.42	63.61	66.45	70.38	84.15	*of which: Currency Outside DMBs*	**14a**
	22.31	24.50	24.50	16.70	9.93	9.13	15.01	17.58	13.62	12.41	10.62	3.54	7.29	3.22	2.08	Foreign Liabilities	**16c**
	3.77	6.41	7.63	39.41	33.28	35.28	10.08	13.30	15.06	17.88	19.42	65.93	47.31	21.48	25.87	Central Government Deposits	**16d**
	15.24	15.36	14.84	15.49	15.99	16.91	17.36	19.85	17.18	17.78	18.50	19.30	20.19	20.82	21.30	Capital Accounts	**17a**
	−.22	4.81	5.18	−2.76	2.86	−.01	−1.41	−8.85	−3.25	−6.24	−.73	25.62	12.35	4.29	−3.19	Other Items (Net)	**17r**
End of Period																**Deposit Money Banks**	
	21.07	22.74	25.43	29.43	42.32	37.91	37.30	53.40	49.95	45.13	53.77	54.71	58.68	64.85	59.02	Reserves	**20**
	20.34	16.95	16.08	13.90	24.76	38.78	32.62	24.62	47.28	48.53	52.42	56.90	71.68	75.89	91.27	Foreign Assets	**21**
	33.58	47.98	48.32	39.87	37.24	51.20	45.44	60.75	48.93	52.99	63.88	39.77	61.92	58.39	80.11	Claims on Central Government	**22a**
	3.16	2.74	9.04	7.96	5.45	7.25	4.88	1.16	.31	.27	2.73	2.81	5.18	9.36	4.99	Claims on Official Entities	**22bx**
	120.47	119.77	146.60	197.95	231.08	268.35	331.10	372.01	385.99	405.27	436.44	478.03	540.03	610.72	641.14	Claims on Private Sector	**22d**
	24.44	29.60	36.80	42.92	56.58	59.45	68.97	74.45	81.65	86.81	93.32	99.12	99.03	115.85	141.86	Demand Deposits	**24**
	109.13	128.06	157.35	170.33	187.40	224.80	245.90	285.11	288.57	316.35	388.84	421.56	486.98	504.93	552.39	Time, Savings,& Fgn.Currency Dep.	**25**
	43.48	26.34	22.28	21.03	17.07	9.17	25.07	47.21	98.30	103.36	79.18	82.79	87.42	101.39	86.12	Foreign Liabilities	**26c**
	12.20	15.43	16.44	31.64	58.30	75.19	86.80	74.24	49.30	43.86	23.59	27.78	26.89	40.68	21.56	Central Government Deposits	**26d**
	.61	1.35	5.84	4.76	3.60	2.86	2.20	7.98	5.32	1.66	1.48	1.28	1.09	.88	.63	Credit from Monetary Authorities	**26g**
	11.29	12.13	13.36	17.08	19.00	21.25	25.06	28.41	31.00	31.04	39.40	43.54	49.77	51.73	69.71	Capital Accounts	**27a**
	−2.51	−2.73	−6.59	1.34	−1.10	10.78	−2.66	−5.47	−21.67	−30.89	−16.57	−23.85	−13.70	3.76	4.26	Other Items (Net)	**27r**
End of Period																**Monetary Survey**	
	−15.82	19.67	42.45	79.68	117.98	160.33	98.42	65.70	12.64	1.70	37.85	107.43	95.86	59.51	145.97	Foreign Assets (Net)	**31n**
	207.05	210.41	230.69	208.37	209.19	221.53	306.49	377.78	432.35	464.44	541.76	537.72	622.80	711.44	747.57	Domestic Credit	**32**
	83.18	87.61	74.70	2.46	−27.34	−54.08	−29.49	4.60	46.03	58.80	102.59	56.83	77.58	91.13	100.07	Claims on Central Govt. (Net)	**32an**
	3.16	2.74	9.04	7.96	5.45	7.25	4.88	1.16	.31	.27	2.73	2.81	5.18	9.36	4.99	Claims on Official Entities	**32bx**
	120.47	119.77	146.60	197.95	231.08	268.35	331.10	372.01	385.99	405.27	436.44	478.03	540.03	610.72	641.14	Claims on Private Sector	**32d**
	58.61	71.03	84.30	81.78	99.87	105.99	118.30	126.33	136.35	144.18	155.47	164.02	166.17	186.65	248.24	Money	**34**
	109.13	128.06	157.35	170.33	187.40	224.80	245.90	285.11	288.57	316.35	388.84	421.56	486.98	504.93	552.39	Quasi-Money	**35**
	26.53	27.49	28.20	32.57	34.99	38.16	42.42	48.26	48.18	48.82	57.90	62.84	69.95	72.55	91.00	Capital Accounts	**37a**
	−3.04	3.49	3.28	3.36	4.91	12.90	−1.70	−16.23	−28.11	−43.20	−22.59	−3.28	−4.45	6.83	1.92	Other Items (Net)	**37r**
	167.73	199.10	241.65	252.11	287.27	330.80	364.20	411.45	424.92	460.53	544.31	585.58	653.15	691.58	800.62	Money plus Quasi-Money	**35l**
End of Period																**Other Banking Institutions**	
	.11	1.34	1.09	2.49	.83	3.44	4.91	2.38	1.28	1.41	2.47	.93	3.17	1.58	11.35	Reserves	**40**
	2.70	1.17	.71	.23	.50	—	—	.02	—	—	—	—	—	—	—	Foreign Assets	**41**
	—	1.09	1.11	—	—	—	—	—	—	—	—	—	—	—	—	Claims on Central Government	**42a**
	—	1.03	.94	.55	.50	.52	.17	.17	.17	—	—	—	—	—	—	Claims on Official Entities	**42bx**
	32.26	36.84	34.65	34.64	35.55	33.71	32.87	36.59	40.66	45.70	47.03	53.75	60.78	65.96	61.92	Claims on Private Sector	**42d**
	23.62	35.86	38.74	38.84	35.34	33.57	32.10	31.05	28.22	28.41	28.66	27.29	35.77	35.93	42.22	Foreign Liabilities	**46c**
	—	—	—	—	.40	.26	.26	.80	1.23	1.40	1.07	1.20	2.71		27.06	Central Government Deposits	**46d**
	—	—	—	—	—	—	—	3.08	3.35	4.07	6.30	6.02	5.77	5.36	Credit from Monetary Authorities	**46g**
	5.39	5.41	5.72	5.61	4.14	−3.85	−6.36	−1.52	−.26	1.21	3.48	8.69	10.68	11.88	13.80	Capital Accounts	**47a**
	6.05	.21	−5.96	−6.54	−2.10	7.55	11.95	9.36	10.29	12.90	11.89	11.34	10.29	11.25	−15.17	Other Items (Net)	**47r**
End of Period																**Banking Survey**	
	−36.74	−15.02	4.42	41.07	83.14	126.76	66.32	34.66	−15.58	−26.70	9.20	80.14	60.09	23.58	103.75	Foreign Assets (Net)	**51n**
	239.30	249.37	267.38	243.56	245.24	255.36	339.26	414.29	472.39	508.91	587.39	590.40	682.38	774.70	782.43	Domestic Credit	**52**
	83.18	88.70	75.81	2.46	−27.34	−54.47	−29.75	4.35	45.24	57.57	101.20	55.76	76.38	88.42	73.01	Claims on Central Govt. (Net)	**52an**
	3.16	2.74	9.04	7.96	5.95	7.77	5.05	1.33	.48	.27	2.73	2.81	5.18	9.36	4.99	Claims on Official Entities	**52bx**
	152.73	156.61	181.25	232.59	266.63	302.06	363.97	408.60	426.66	450.97	483.47	531.79	600.81	676.69	703.06	Claims on Private Sector	**52d**
	167.63	197.76	240.56	249.62	286.44	327.36	359.28	409.07	423.64	459.12	541.85	584.65	649.98	690.00	789.27	Liquid Liabilities	**55l**
	31.92	32.89	33.92	38.18	39.13	34.31	36.06	46.75	47.92	50.04	61.38	71.53	80.63	84.43	104.80	Capital Accounts	**57a**
	3.01	3.70	−2.68	−3.18	2.81	20.45	10.25	−6.87	−14.74	−26.95	−6.63	14.36	11.86	23.86	−7.89	Other Items (Net)	**57r**
Percent Per Annum																**Interest Rates**	
	20.00	12.00	12.00	10.00	12.00	12.00	12.00	12.00	12.00	12.00	12.00	12.00	12.00	12.00	12.00	Discount Rate *(End of Period)*	**60**
	12.76	10.81	8.80	8.32	7.36	7.37	6.71	5.38	4.59	4.27	4.10	3.78	3.51	3.83	5.91	Treasury Bill Rate	**60c**
	11.63	11.83	9.58	8.42	7.86	8.14	8.42	8.15	8.13	8.55	9.37	9.08	9.19	8.76	8.12	Deposit Rate	**60l**
	....	14.69	14.14	13.56	13.77	14.04	14.24	14.32	14.37	14.78	15.69	16.30	16.29	16.50	16.27	Lending Rate	**60p**

Belize

339

		1970	1971	1972	1973	1974	1975	1976	1977	1978	1979	1980	1981	1982	1983	1984
Prices and Labor														*Index Numbers (1995=100):*		
Consumer Prices	64	...	...	...	...	...	...	...	...	...	...	59.5	66.2[e]	70.7[e]	74.2	76.7
															Number in Thousands:	
Labor Force	67d	...	...	...	...	...	...	...	...	...	...	...	...	...	...	...
Employment	67e	...	...	...	...	...	...	...	...	...	...	...	...	...	...	...
Unemployment	67c	...	...	...	...	...	...	...	...	...	...	...	...	...	...	...
Unemployment Rate (%)	67r	...	...	...	...	...	...	...	...	...	...	...	...	...	...	...
International Transactions														*Millions of Belize Dollars*		
Exports	70	31.33	31.69	40.89	52.69	76.86	120.40	94.04	124.16	159.57	173.46	221.30	238.01	182.03	155.46	186.40
Imports, c.i.f.	71	55.61	58.59	69.26	72.32	109.18	159.23	161.51	180.15	212.99	263.68	299.51	323.93	256.00	223.58	260.27
Balance of Payments														*Millions of US Dollars:*		
Current Account, n.i.e.	78al d	...	...	...	...	...	...	...	...	...	...	...	...	...	...	−5.3
Goods: Exports f.o.b.	78aa d															93.2
Goods: Imports f.o.b.	78ab d															−116.3
Trade Balance	78ac d															−23.1
Services: Credit	78ad d															35.4
Services: Debit	78ae d															−29.4
Balance on Goods & Services	78af d															−17.1
Income: Credit	78ag d															1.3
Income: Debit	78ah d															−14.8
Balance on Gds, Serv. & Inc.	78ai d															−30.6
Current Transfers, n.i.e.: Credit	78aj d															27.9
Current Transfers: Debit	78ak d															−2.6
Capital Account, n.i.e.	78bc d	...	...	...	...	...	...	...	...	...	...	...	...	...	...	3.6
Capital Account, n.i.e.: Credit	78ba d															—
Capital Account: Debit	78bb d															—
Financial Account, n.i.e.	78bj d															−3.6
Direct Investment Abroad	78bd d															—
Dir. Invest. in Rep. Econ., n.i.e.	78be d															−3.7
Portfolio Investment Assets	78bf d															—
Equity Securities	78bk d															—
Debt Securities	78bl d															—
Portfolio Investment Liab., n.i.e.	78bg d															.7
Equity Securities	78bm d															—
Debt Securities	78bn d															.7
Financial Derivatives Assets	78bw d															...
Financial Derivatives Liabilities	78bx d															...
Other Investment Assets	78bh d															—
Monetary Authorities	78bo d															—
General Government	78bp d															—
Banks	78bq d															—
Other Sectors	78br d															—
Other Investment Liab., n.i.e.	78bi d															−.6
Monetary Authorities	78bs d															—
General Government	78bt d															4.3
Banks	78bu d															−1.8
Other Sectors	78bv d															−3.0
Net Errors and Omissions	78ca d															3.6
Overall Balance	78cb d															−5.3
Reserves and Related Items	79da d															5.3
Reserve Assets	79db d															2.9
Use of Fund Credit and Loans	79dc d															1.2
Exceptional Financing	79de d															1.2
Government Finance														*Thousands of Belize Dollars:*		
Deficit (-) or Surplus	80	...	...	...	...	...	...	...	−12,112	−2,613	‡−5,018	‡−5,916	...	...	...	−5,214
Revenue	81								41,913	54,914	‡63,326	‡80,565	83,621	79,514	78,908	92,795
Grants Received	81z								8,167	7,577	‡8,359	‡4,688	5,461	18,426	16,954	5,600
Expenditure	82								61,296	62,568	‡73,914	‡89,072	102,989	107,655	105,856	105,026
Lending Minus Repayments	83								896	2,536	‡2,789	‡2,097	...	...	...	−1,417
Financing																
Domestic	84a								8,237	2,513	‡6,223	‡4,857	...	...	...	
Foreign	85a								3,875	100	‡−1,205	‡1,059	...	...	...	
Debt: Domestic	88a	...	...	...	...	...	...	...	...	...	...	...	...	...	...	
Foreign	89a	...	...	...	...	...	...	...	...	...	...	...	...	...	...	
National Accounts														*Millions of Belize Dollars*		
Exports of Goods & Services	90c	...	...	...	63.1	111.4	150.1	113.9	155.7	205.9	173.8	215.7	206.0	172.0	185.5	263.4
Government Consumption	91f	...	...	...	16.5	22.0	22.8	27.1	29.5	33.9	53.0	66.8	70.6	74.7	79.0	83.5
Gross Fixed Capital Formation	93e	...	...	...	27.0	38.6	53.0	58.0	62.9	69.1	81.0	88.2	95.6	80.8	71.5	85.7
Increase/Decrease(-) in Stocks	93i	...	...	...	5.7	4.2	8.0	11.2	5.8	3.3	14.7	5.7	4.9	−6.4	4.9	13.6
Private Consumption	96f	...	...	...	75.0	93.6	116.6	131.9	154.0	165.7	185.5	280.2	299.4	290.4	282.8	271.4
Imports of Goods & Services	98c	...	...	...	−77.1	−115.6	−161.7	−159.0	−196.3	−236.5	−225.6	−267.1	−290.7	−253.0	−245.7	−295.9
Gross Domestic Product (GDP)	99b	...	...	...	110.3	154.2	188.8	183.2	211.6	241.7	282.4	340.3	340.2	314.5	333.6	371.5
Net Factor Inc/Pmts(-) Abroad	98.n	...	...	...	...	...	...	...	...	...	−2.2	−3.8	−3.8	−9.8	−11.0	−18.6
Gross National Income (GNI)	99a	...	...	...	110.9	145.1	176.4	180.9	...	...	280.2	385.6	382.0	348.7	367.0	403.2
GDP Volume 1984 Prices	99b.p										323.8	365.7	373.2	370.9	365.1	371.5
GDP Volume (1995=100)	99bv p	...	...	...	...	...	...	...	...	...	38.4	43.4	44.2	44.0	43.3	44.0
GDP Deflator (1995=100)	99bi p	...	...	...	...	...	...	...	...	...	62.7	66.9	65.5	61.0	65.7	71.9
															Millions:	
Population	99z	.12	.12	.13	.13	.13	.13	.14	.14	.14	.14	.14	.15	.15	.16	.16

268   INTERNATIONAL FINANCIAL STATISTICS YEARBOOK   2000

	1985	1986	1987	1988	1989	1990	1991	1992	1993	1994	1995	1996	1997	1998	1999		
																Prices and Labor	
Period Averages																	
	79.9	80.5	82.2	86.5	86.5	189.2	91.2	93.4	94.7	97.2	100.0	106.4	107.5	106.6	105.3	Consumer Prices	**64**
Period Averages																	
	....	....	.....	.....	.....	.....	55	....	....	70	....	....	....	....	....	Labor Force	**67d**
	....	....	.....	.....	.....	.....	....	....	62	62	66	....	....	....	....	Employment	**67e**
	....	....	.....	.....	.....	.....	....	....	7	8	....	....	....	....	....	Unemployment	**67c**
	....	....	.....	.....	.....	.....	....	....	9.8	11.1	....	....	....	....	....	Unemployment Rate (%)	**67r**
																International Transactions	
Millions of Belize Dollars																	
	179.39	185.21	205.66	232.51	249.07	265.92	243.44	281.01	272.97	301.98	323.25	335.27	352.16	381.48	338.33	Exports	**70**
	256.26	243.93	285.89	361.95	431.39	422.59	512.49	548.06	561.92	519.86	514.43	510.97	572.43	649.88	748.85	Imports, c.i.f.	**71**
Minus Sign Indicates Debit																Balance of Payments	
	9.1	12.0	9.4	−2.6	−19.1	15.4	−25.8	−28.6	−48.5	−40.1	−17.2	−6.6	−31.9	−59.8	−77.4	Current Account, n.i.e.	**78ald**
	90.2	92.6	102.9	119.4	124.4	129.2	126.1	140.6	132.0	156.5	164.6	171.3	193.4	186.2	201.5	Goods: Exports f.o.b.	**78aad**
	−113.8	−108.3	−127.0	−161.3	−188.5	−188.4	−223.6	−244.5	−250.5	−231.9	−230.6	−229.5	−282.9	−290.9	−330.3	Goods: Imports f.o.b.	**78abd**
	−23.7	−15.7	−24.1	−41.9	−64.1	−59.2	−97.5	−103.9	−118.5	−75.4	−66.1	−58.2	−89.5	−104.7	−128.8	*Trade Balance*	**78acd**
	38.1	42.8	56.0	74.5	85.9	115.4	122.7	142.6	150.5	121.1	132.8	137.9	137.8	140.5	154.1	Services: Credit	**78add**
	−27.6	−40.2	−46.0	−53.4	−62.5	−60.0	−68.2	−81.6	−92.5	−88.0	−94.9	−91.3	−91.7	−99.0	−105.1	Services: Debit	**78aed**
	−13.1	−13.1	−14.1	−20.8	−40.8	−3.9	−43.0	−42.9	−60.5	−42.2	−28.1	−11.7	−43.3	−63.3	−79.8	*Balance on Goods & Services*	**78afd**
	2.9	9.2	5.9	8.0	9.7	10.6	8.3	6.7	2.9	2.8	2.8	6.3	7.5	7.2	7.3	Income: Credit	**78agd**
	−13.2	−11.6	−13.4	−15.7	−19.1	−20.8	−19.1	−22.8	−23.4	−28.2	−25.1	−32.4	−30.8	−39.3	−41.5	Income: Debit	**78ahd**
	−23.4	−15.5	−21.6	−28.5	−50.2	−14.1	−53.8	−59.0	−78.0	−67.5	−50.4	−37.8	−66.7	−95.4	−114.0	*Balance on Gds, Serv. & Inc.*	**78aid**
	34.5	31.3	35.1	29.4	34.5	33.6	32.3	35.4	33.8	34.4	38.3	34.2	38.2	38.4	40.0	Current Transfers, n.i.e.: Credit	**78ajd**
	−2.1	−3.9	−4.1	−3.6	−3.4	−4.2	−4.3	−5.0	−4.3	−6.9	−5.2	−3.1	−3.4	−2.8	−3.5	Current Transfers: Debit	**78akd**
	—	—	—	—	—	—	—	—	—	—	—	−2.2	−3.4	−1.9	−2.0	Capital Account, n.i.e.	**78bcd**
	—	—	—	—	—	—	—	—	—	—	—	—	—	—	.5	Capital Account, n.i.e.: Credit	**78bad**
	—	—	—	—	—	—	—	—	—	—	—	−2.2	−3.4	−1.9	−2.4	Capital Account: Debit	**78bbd**
	9.4	.7	2.7	27.3	25.5	25.1	22.2	22.4	32.8	3.6	−1.0	11.0	27.6	23.5	66.8	Financial Account, n.i.e.	**78bjd**
	—	—	—	—	—	—	—	—	—	—	—	−5.7	−3.9	−4.5	48.9	Direct Investment Abroad	**78bdd**
	3.7	4.6	6.9	14.0	18.7	17.2	13.6	15.6	9.2	15.4	21.1	16.6	12.0	17.7	3.5	Dir. Invest. in Rep. Econ., n.i.e.	**78bed**
	—	—	—	—	—	—	—	—	—	—	—	—	—	....	−.7	Portfolio Investment Assets	**78bfd**
	—	—	—	—	—	—	—	—	—	—	—	—	—	—	—	Equity Securities	**78bkd**
	—	—	—	—	—	—	—	—	—	—	—	—	—	—	−.7	Debt Securities	**78bld**
	.7	—	—	—	—	—	.2	7.0	6.1	3.5	10.1	10.2	12.5	33.6		Portfolio Investment Liab., n.i.e.	**78bgd**
	—	—	—	—	—	—	—	—	—	—	—	—	—	—	—	Equity Securities	**78bmd**
	.7	—	—	—	—	—	.2	7.0	6.1	3.5	10.1	10.2	12.5	33.6		Debt Securities	**78bnd**
	....	....	.....	.....	.....	.....	....	....	....	....	....	—	—	—	—	Financial Derivatives Assets	**78bwd**
	....	....	.....	.....	.....	.....	....	....	....	....	....	—	—	—	—	Financial Derivatives Liabilities	**78bxd**
	—	—	—	1.8	—	—	3.0	3.7	−11.6	−17.1	−14.1	−12.2	2.8	—	−8.9	Other Investment Assets	**78bhd**
	—	—	—	—	—	—	—	—	—	—	—	—	—	—	—	Monetary Authorities	**78bod**
	—	—	—	.2	—	—	—	—	—	—	—	—	—	—	—	General Government	**78bpd**
	—	—	—	1.6	—	—	3.0	3.7	−11.6	−3.3	−1.7	−12.2	2.8	—	−6.3	Banks	**78bqd**
	—	—	—	—	—	—	—	—	—	−13.8	−12.4	—	—	—	−2.7	Other Sectors	**78brd**
	5.0	−3.9	−4.2	11.6	6.9	7.9	5.6	3.0	28.2	−.8	−11.5	2.2	6.5	−2.2	−9.5	Other Investment Liab., n.i.e.	**78bid**
	—	—	—	—	—	—	—	—	—	—	—	—	—	—	—	Monetary Authorities	**78bsd**
	12.4	3.7	.6	9.5	11.3	7.9	10.2	6.1	16.3	8.9	−2.6	19.7	11.5	8.8	—	General Government	**78btd**
	−.9	−5.0	−.2	—	−9.0	−2.0	2.9	9.1	18.7	−9.3	−12.1	−6.3	4.8	7.2	−8.9	Banks	**78bud**
	−6.5	−2.6	−4.6	2.1	4.6	2.1	−7.5	−12.2	−6.8	−.3	3.2	−11.2	−9.8	−18.2	−.6	Other Sectors	**78bvd**
	−16.1	−.9	−.2	−2.9	9.1	−25.0	−12.8	6.3	1.5	32.8	22.4	18.4	9.1	24.5	4.3	Net Errors and Omissions	**78cad**
	2.3	11.8	11.9	21.8	15.5	15.4	−16.4	.1	−14.2	−3.6	4.1	20.6	1.4	−13.7	−8.3	*Overall Balance*	**78cbd**
	−2.3	−11.8	−11.9	−21.8	−15.5	−15.4	16.4	−.1	14.2	3.6	−4.1	−20.6	−1.4	13.7	8.3	Reserves and Related Items	**79dad**
	−7.2	−11.8	−9.9	−18.7	−11.3	−12.5	16.8	−.1	14.2	3.6	−4.1	−20.6	−1.4	13.7	−27.5	Reserve Assets	**79dbd**
	4.9	—	−2.0	−3.0	−4.2	−3.0	−.4	—	—	—	—	—	—	—	—	Use of Fund Credit and Loans	**79dcd**
															35.8	Exceptional Financing	**79ded**
																Government Finance	
Year Beginning April 1																	
	−14,208	....	....	44,922	−5,733	5,633	−27,701	−44,411	−82,365	−70,802	−39,698	−15,671	−32,588[f]	....	....	Deficit (-) or Surplus	**80**
	96,896	....	....	161,443	190,169	210,747	216,191	245,281	247,864	258,978	261,658	288,256	283,357[f]	....	....	Revenue	**81**
	1,400	....	....	1,868	5,600	13,000	12,836	9,848	6,953	13,264	1,079	4,076	41,191[f]	....	....	Grants Received	**81z**
	111,895	....	....	152,670	202,550	228,824	278,901	332,438	342,935	348,953	306,090	317,781	362,261[f]	....	....	Expenditure	**82**
	609	....	....	−34,281	−1,048	−10,710	−22,173	−32,898	−5,753	−5,909	−3,655	−9,778	−5,125[f]	....	....	Lending Minus Repayments	**83**
																Financing	
	....	....	....	−54,966	−1,651	−25,951	8,318	5,348	42,583	45,433	41,604	−33,262	....	....	....	Domestic	**84a**
	....	....	....	10,044	7,384	20,318	19,383	39,063	39,782	25,369	−1,906	48,933	....	....	....	Foreign	**85a**
	....	....	....	77,270	75,272	73,808	77,626	113,070	136,104	145,985	167,747	168,330	....	....	....	Debt: Domestic	**88a**
	....	....	....	123,962	140,002	145,516	177,141	228,555	259,453	285,800	282,610	329,798	....	....	....	Foreign	**89a**
Millions of Belize Dollars																**National Accounts**	
	202.8	253.0	334.4	390.5	419.2	489.2	495.3	568.3	565.9	579.2	601.6	618.2	662.6	666.2	707.2	Exports of Goods & Services	**90c**
	88.3	93.4	98.9	104.4	110.4	116.8	122.1	146.4	171.4	186.8	186.9	196.5	209.5	219.1	235.2	Government Consumption	**91f**
	72.7	79.5	118.8	161.6	198.8	211.9	253.2	276.0	317.0	254.3	257.8	273.7	289.8	307.3	408.4	Gross Fixed Capital Formation	**93e**
	17.7	13.3	2.5	−1.8	21.2	1.2	9.8	6.2	1.9	11.7	−12.9	5.8	19.1	38.5	42.2	Increase/Decrease(-) in Stocks	**93i**
	293.2	281.5	344.8	403.9	475.6	489.7	567.7	630.3	690.2	723.1	764.3	761.0	818.4	847.5	895.4	Private Consumption	**96f**
	−256.4	−264.9	−346.2	−428.8	−498.9	−496.8	−583.0	−651.6	−685.5	−639.4	−637.4	−642.2	−749.2	−781.6	−870.7	Imports of Goods & Services	**98c**
	366.2	392.8	553.0	629.8	726.3	810.8	865.2	969.3	1,061.0	1,104.0	1,173.2	1,207.2	1,231.1	1,258.5	1,376.6	Gross Domestic Product (GDP)	**99b**
	−19.8	−8.8	−14.2	−17.8	−24.9	−13.5	−20.6	−33.5	−37.4	−43.8	−46.0	−52.0	−47.6	−64.4	−68.0	Net Factor Inc/Pmts(-) Abroad	**98.n**
	398.6	447.0	538.8	612.0	712.9	784.1	833.4	935.8	1,023.1	1,060.2	1,127.2	1,155.2	1,183.5	1,794.1	1,308.6	Gross National Income (GNI)	**99a**
	373.0	384.3	495.9	541.5	612.0	682.2	699.8	757.4	789.6	815.0	843.4	856.1	885.2	906.8	961.8	GDP Volume 1984 Prices	**99b.p**
	44.2	45.6	58.8	64.2	72.6	80.9	83.0	89.8	93.6	96.6	100.0	101.5	105.0	107.5	114.0	GDP Volume (1995=100)	**99bvp**
	70.6	73.5	80.2	83.6	85.3	85.4	88.9	92.0	96.6	97.4	100.0	101.4	100.0	99.8	102.9	GDP Deflator (1995=100)	**99bip**
Midyear Estimates																	
	.17	.17	.17	.18	.18	.19	.19	.20	.21	.21	.22	.22	.23	.24	.24	Population	**99z**

(See notes in the back of the book.)

Benin

		1970	1971	1972	1973	1974	1975	1976	1977	1978	1979	1980	1981	1982	1983	1984
Exchange Rates															*Francs per SDR:*	
Official Rate	aa	276.02	283.61	278.00	284.00	272.08	262.55	288.70	285.76	272.28	264.78	287.99	334.52	370.92	436.97	470.11
															Francs per US Dollar:	
Official Rate	ae	276.02	261.22	256.05	235.42	222.22	224.27	248.49	235.25	209.00	201.00	225.80	287.40	336.25	417.37	479.60
Official Rate	rf	276.40	275.59	252.03	222.89	240.70	214.31	238.95	245.68	225.66	212.72	211.28	271.73	328.61	381.07	436.96
Fund Position															*Millions of SDRs:*	
Quota	2f. s	13.0	13.0	13.0	13.0	13.0	13.0	13.0	13.0	16.0	16.0	24.0	24.0	24.0	31.3	31.3
SDRs	1b. s	1.7	3.1	4.5	4.5	4.5	4.5	4.5	4.4	4.4	6.1	1.7	2.9	2.0	1.1	.2
Reserve Position in the Fund	1c. s	2.1	2.1	2.1	2.1	2.1	2.1	2.1	2.1	2.0	1.9	2.0	2.0	2.0	2.0	2.0
Total Fund Cred.&Loans Outstg.	2tl	—	—	—	—	—	—	—	—	5.4	5.4	12.7	12.7	12.7	12.5	11.4
International Liquidity													*Millions of US Dollars Unless Otherwise Indicated:*			
Total Reserves minus Gold	1l. d	15.5	24.6	28.4	33.1	34.6	15.0	19.2	20.4	15.5	14.2	8.1	57.6	4.9	3.7	2.5
SDRs	1b. d	1.7	3.3	4.8	5.4	5.4	5.2	5.2	5.4	5.8	8.0	2.2	3.4	2.2	1.2	.1
Reserve Position in the Fund	1c. d	2.1	2.3	2.3	2.6	2.6	2.5	2.5	2.6	2.6	2.6	2.6	2.4	2.2	2.1	2.0
Foreign Exchange	1d. d	11.7	19.0	21.3	25.2	26.6	7.3	11.6	12.4	7.1	3.6	3.4	51.9	.5	.4	.3
Gold (Million Fine Troy Ounces)	1ad	. . . .	. . . .	. . . .	. . . .	. . . .	. . . .	—	.006	.008	.011	.011	.011	.011	.011	.011
Gold (National Valuation)	1an d	. . . .	. . . .	. . . .	. . . .	. . . .	. . . .	—	.2	.4	.5	.5	4.7	4.7	4.3	3.7
Monetary Authorities: Other Liab.	4.. d	.1	—	.3	.2	.1	.9	1.0	1.8	10.6	22.8	8.7	4.1	12.2	47.9	41.6
Deposit Money Banks: Assets	7a. d	5.2	7.8	3.6	5.1	13.6	60.4	7.2	8.2	6.6	5.5	3.6	6.1	2.9	16.8	14.5
Liabilities	7b. d	7.7	11.0	10.8	21.5	19.8	52.0	65.6	70.6	75.6	80.6	85.6	90.6	95.6	100.6	37.2
Monetary Authorities															*Billions of Francs:*	
Foreign Assets	11	4.3	6.3	7.3	7.6	7.7	3.4	4.8	4.8	3.2	2.9	1.8	16.6	1.7	1.5	1.2
Claims on Central Government	12a	.5	—	.9	1.3	1.3	.8	.4	—	2.3	5.6	6.5	8.0	10.0	13.8	15.2
Claims on Deposit Money Banks	12e	1.5	1.0	1.4	1.1	2.3	7.9	7.7	9.3	11.3	15.0	22.8	19.9	34.9	39.3	40.0
Reserve Money	14	4.8	5.4	6.4	6.5	6.7	8.7	10.3	10.5	10.0	14.4	17.9	29.0	29.8	23.8	29.3
of which: Currency Outside DMBs	14a	4.5	5.0	5.8	6.0	6.1	8.4	9.4	9.9	8.0	13.3	16.3	28.1	28.8	22.5	28.1
Foreign Liabilities	16c	—	—	.1	—	—	.2	.2	.4	5.2	7.5	9.1	9.0	12.3	28.9	28.5
Central Government Deposits	16d	1.1	1.0	1.9	2.2	3.3	1.9	1.0	2.0	1.9	1.4	5.5	7.6	5.8	3.7	.9
Other Items (Net)	17r	.5	.9	1.2	1.2	1.3	1.2	1.3	1.3	−.3	.2	−1.5	−1.1	−1.4	−1.7	−2.3
Deposit Money Banks															*Billions of Francs:*	
Reserves	20	.2	.4	.6	.3	.6	.4	.5	.6	3.6	1.4	1.4	1.7	1.8	1.3	1.2
Foreign Assets	21	1.4	2.0	.9	1.2	3.0	13.6	. . . .	. . . .	. . . .	1.1	.8	1.7	1.0	7.0	7.0
Claims on Central Government	22a	.2	.2	.4	—	.1	—	.1	.1	.3	1.8	.6	2.7	3.0	3.4	3.7
Claims on Private Sector	22d	7.4	8.5	10.4	12.7	16.5	32.4	32.1	37.6	45.1	63.5	85.0	87.0	125.9	132.9	116.9
Claims on Other Financial Insts	22f	. . . .	. . . .	. . . .	. . . .	. . . .	. . . .	. . . .	. . . .	. . . .	. . . .	. . . .	. . . .	. . . .	. . . .	. . . .
Demand Deposits	24	4.5	5.9	6.1	5.4	8.7	17.3	14.7	17.6	20.6	18.1	26.0	30.0	52.0	56.6	59.6
Time Deposits	25	.4	.7	1.2	2.5	2.7	5.0	5.0	5.6	8.0	17.0	16.0	15.0	15.0	15.0	21.1
Foreign Liabilities	26c	1.7	2.1	2.0	4.3	3.6	11.2	15.6	15.7	14.2	14.1	16.7	22.2	27.0	42.0	17.8
Long-Term Foreign Liabilities	26cl	.4	.7	.7	.7	.8	.7	.7	.9	1.6	2.1	2.6	3.8	5.2	—	—
Central Government Deposits	26d	.4	.6	.7	1.3	1.4	3.0	3.3	6.0	8.0	24.1	19.2	24.0	20.0	17.0	6.4
Credit from Monetary Authorities	26g	1.5	1.0	1.4	1.1	2.3	7.9	7.7	9.3	11.3	15.0	22.8	19.9	34.9	39.3	40.0
Other Items (Net)	27r	.3	.1	.1	−.9	.6	1.4	−12.6	−15.0	−13.4	−13.5	−15.4	−21.0	−22.4	−25.3	−16.1
Treasury Claims: Private Sector	22d. i															
Post Office: Checking Deposits	24.. i	.6	.6	.8	.9	1.0	1.2	1.6	1.8	2.5	2.4	2.4	2.3	2.6	2.9	3.0
Monetary Survey															*Billions of Francs:*	
Foreign Assets (Net)	31n	4.0	6.2	6.1	4.5	7.0	5.5	6.3	6.3	.9	−17.7	−23.2	−12.9	−36.7	−62.4	−38.1
Domestic Credit	32	7.3	7.7	9.9	11.6	14.0	29.5	29.8	31.5	40.2	46.9	69.8	68.4	115.7	132.3	131.5
Claims on Central Govt. (Net)	32an	−.1	−.8	−.5	−1.2	−2.4	−3.0	−2.3	−6.1	−4.9	−16.6	−15.2	−18.6	−10.2	−.6	14.6
Claims on Private Sector	32d	7.4	8.5	10.4	12.7	16.5	32.4	32.1	37.6	45.1	63.5	85.0	87.0	125.9	132.9	116.9
Claims on Other Financial Insts	32f	. . . .	. . . .	. . . .	. . . .	. . . .	. . . .	. . . .	. . . .	. . . .	. . . .	. . . .	. . . .	. . . .	. . . .	. . . .
Money	34	9.6	11.5	12.7	12.3	15.7	26.9	25.6	29.3	31.0	33.7	44.7	60.4	83.4	82.0	90.6
Quasi-Money	35	.4	.7	1.2	2.5	2.7	5.0	5.0	5.6	8.0	17.0	16.0	15.0	15.0	15.0	21.1
Long-Term Foreign Liabilities	36cl	.4	.7	.7	.7	.8	.7	.7	.9	1.6	2.1	2.6	3.8	5.2	—	—
Other Items (Net)	37r	.8	.9	1.4	.6	1.8	2.4	4.8	1.9	.5	−13.6	−16.7	−23.7	−24.6	−27.0	−18.4
Money plus Quasi-Money	35l	10.0	12.3	13.9	14.8	18.4	31.9	30.6	34.9	39.0	40.7	60.7	75.4	98.4	97.0	111.7
Other Banking Institutions															*Billions of Francs:*	
Savings Deposits	45	.5	.5	.6	.6	.7	.8	.9	.9	1.0	1.0	1.1	1.5	1.6	1.7	1.7
Liquid Liabilities	55l	10.5	12.8	14.5	15.4	19.1	32.7	31.5	35.8	40.0	41.7	61.8	76.9	100.0	98.7	113.4
Interest Rates															*Percent Per Annum:*	
Discount Rate (End of Period)	60	3.50	3.50	3.50	5.50	5.50	8.00	8.00	8.00	8.00	8.00	10.50	10.50	12.50	10.50	10.50
Money Market Rate	60b	. . . .	. . . .	. . . .	. . . .	. . . .	. . . .	7.28	7.38	7.40	7.72	10.13	13.68	14.66	12.23	11.84
Deposit Rate	60l	3.00	3.00	3.00	5.75	5.75	5.88	6.00	6.00	6.00	6.00	6.19	6.25	7.75	7.50	7.25
Lending Rate	60p	. . . .	. . . .	. . . .	. . . .	. . . .	. . . .	. . . .	12.00	12.00	12.00	14.50	14.50	16.00	14.50	14.50
Prices and Labor															*Index Numbers (1995=100):*	
Consumer Prices	64	. . . .	. . . .	. . . .	. . . .	. . . .	. . . .	. . . .	. . . .	. . . .	. . . .	. . . .	. . . .	. . . .	. . . .	. . . .
															Number in Thousands:	
Labor Force	67d	. . . .	. . . .	. . . .	. . . .	. . . .	. . . .	. . . .	. . . .	. . . .	. . . .	. . . .	. . . .	. . . .	. . . .	. . . .
Employment	67e	. . . .	. . . .	. . . .	. . . .	. . . .	. . . .	. . . .	. . . .	. . . .	. . . .	. . . .	. . . .	. . . .	. . . .	. . . .

	1985	1986	1987	1988	1989	1990	1991	1992	1993	1994	1995	1996	1997	1998	1999		
																Exchange Rates	
End of Period																	
	415.26	394.78	378.78	407.68	380.32	364.84	370.48	378.57	404.89	I 780.44	728.38	753.06	807.94	791.61	I 896.19	Official Rate	**aa**
End of Period (ae) Period Average (rf)																	
	378.05	322.75	267.00	302.95	289.40	256.45	259.00	275.32	294.77	I 534.60	490.00	523.70	598.81	562.21	I 652.95	Official Rate	**ae**
	449.26	346.31	300.54	297.85	319.01	272.26	282.11	264.69	283.16	I 555.20	499.15	511.55	583.67	589.95	I 615.70	Official Rate	**rf**
																Fund Position	
End of Period																	
	31.3	31.3	31.3	31.3	31.3	31.3	31.3	45.3	45.3	45.3	45.3	45.3	45.3	45.3	61.9	Quota	**2f. s**
	—	—	.1	.1	—	.1	.2	—	.1	—	.1	.2	—	—	.2	SDRs	**1b. s**
	2.0	2.0	2.0	2.0	2.0	2.0	2.0	2.1	2.1	2.1	2.1	2.2	2.2	2.2	2.2	Reserve Position in the Fund	**1c. s**
	10.3	7.8	5.3	3.0	7.8	6.3	15.7	15.7	31.3	48.8	56.6	68.9	70.3	66.4	67.1	Total Fund Cred.&Loans Outstg.	**2tl**
																International Liquidity	
End of Period																	
	4.1	3.9	3.6	4.2	3.4	64.9	191.6	245.2	244.0	258.2	197.9	261.8	253.1	261.5	400.0	Total Reserves minus Gold	**1l. d**
	—	—	.1	.1	—	.1	.2	—	.1	—	.1	.3	.1	.1	.2	SDRs	**1b. d**
	2.2	2.5	2.9	2.7	2.7	2.9	2.9	2.8	2.9	3.1	3.2	3.1	2.9	3.1	3.0	Reserve Position in the Fund	**1c. d**
	1.9	1.4	.6	1.4	.7	61.9	188.5	242.4	241.0	255.1	194.7	258.4	250.1	258.4	396.8	Foreign Exchange	**1d. d**
	.011	.011	.011	.011	.011	.011	.011	.011	.011	.011	.011	.011	.011	.011	.011	Gold (Million Fine Troy Ounces)	**1ad**
	3.6	4.5	5.2	4.6	4.3	4.2	3.9	3.8	4.1	4.1	4.3	4.2	3.4	3.3	3.3	Gold (National Valuation)	**1an d**
	63.7	74.9	128.7	143.9	26.4	5.7	8.1	4.7	13.6	3.8	6.1	10.9	12.8	2.6	2.0	Monetary Authorities: Other Liab.	**4.. d**
	13.3	23.2	20.6	18.5	8.9	25.9	52.9	72.7	96.2	143.9	239.3	278.8	265.0	288.9	253.9	Deposit Money Banks: Assets	**7a. d**
	48.5	56.4	111.7	67.4	72.3	81.1	71.2	56.2	50.7	30.4	50.2	102.0	53.1	89.5	107.3	Liabilities	**7b. d**
																Monetary Authorities	
End of Period																	
	1.6	1.3	1.0	1.3	1.0	16.6	49.6	67.5	71.9	138.1	97.0	137.1	151.5	147.0	261.2	Foreign Assets	**11**
	13.7	16.1	15.5	16.9	21.0	30.6	29.5	28.7	23.2	28.3	41.9	42.6	55.1	52.0	52.7	Claims on Central Government	**12a**
	42.4	44.5	48.9	63.4	51.8	50.8	50.3	50.3	50.3	—	—	2.0	1.0	—	—	Claims on Deposit Money Banks	**12e**
	24.0	28.4	23.4	28.2	50.6	80.8	100.6	123.3	107.4	108.9	80.5	87.9	105.4	100.7	177.0	Reserve Money	**14**
	20.3	26.2	19.6	23.7	36.4	41.1	46.5	51.7	25.5	77.3	50.6	68.9	80.8	70.4	160.3	*of which: Currency Outside DMBs*	**14a**
	31.2	30.5	38.4	45.9	11.2	3.8	7.9	7.2	16.7	40.1	44.2	57.6	64.5	54.1	61.4	Foreign Liabilities	**16c**
	4.6	3.7	2.1	4.4	9.0	9.5	16.7	11.6	17.4	18.7	15.1	37.0	31.1	36.7	71.1	Central Government Deposits	**16d**
	-2.0	-.6	1.4	3.0	3.0	3.9	4.3	4.4	3.9	-1.4	-.9	-.8	6.6	7.5	4.4	Other Items (Net)	**17r**
																Deposit Money Banks	
End of Period																	
	3.4	2.1	3.6	1.5	7.7	36.1	52.6	71.0	93.2	30.9	32.4	17.1	31.9	31.5	16.5	Reserves	**20**
	5.0	7.5	5.5	5.6	2.6	6.6	13.7	20.0	28.4	76.9	117.3	146.0	158.7	162.4	165.8	Foreign Assets	**21**
	3.8	3.7	7.0	12.5	13.6	14.6	7.2	6.4	7.1	44.4	40.6	44.2	32.9	30.7	25.9	Claims on Central Government	**22a**
	145.4	132.6	124.8	137.8	103.4	102.1	86.2	69.4	67.7	75.0	80.4	102.4	71.7	100.1	161.7	Claims on Private Sector	**22d**
	—	—	—	—	—	—	—	—	—	1.0	1.0	—	—	—	—	Claims on Other Financial Insts	**22f**
	63.6	49.9	38.9	42.3	39.9	58.5	67.4	72.9	84.6	106.3	107.8	114.8	107.5	108.4	104.2	Demand Deposits	**24**
	24.5	30.2	35.0	25.9	19.8	29.5	31.7	47.9	59.3	66.1	86.0	90.5	99.6	98.3	110.2	Time Deposits	**25**
	18.3	14.2	24.7	16.5	16.1	15.9	14.8	14.9	14.0	14.9	24.1	52.8	31.0	49.6	67.6	Foreign Liabilities	**26c**
	—	4.0	5.1	3.9	4.8	4.9	3.7	.6	.9	1.3	.5	.6	.8	.7	2.4	Long-Term Foreign Liabilities	**26cl**
	10.3	10.9	11.4	22.2	31.6	26.9	29.5	19.7	25.6	35.0	34.0	35.1	39.8	56.1	74.4	Central Government Deposits	**26d**
	40.7	45.0	48.9	64.2	51.8	57.0	50.8	50.3	50.3	—	—	4.0	1.0	—	—	Credit from Monetary Authorities	**26g**
	.1	-8.3	-23.1	-17.6	-36.7	-33.3	-38.0	-39.4	-38.4	4.5	19.3	12.0	15.5	11.6	10.9	Other Items (Net)	**27r**
	—	—	—	—	—	—	—	—	—	—	—	—	—	—	—	Treasury Claims: Private Sector	**22d. i**
	2.9	2.7	3.0	3.4	3.5	1.6	1.5	1.9	.6	2.0	2.8	5.3	4.4	4.7	5.1	Post Office: Checking Deposits	**24.. i**
																Monetary Survey	
End of Period																	
	-43.0	-35.9	-56.6	-55.6	-23.8	3.6	40.7	65.4	69.5	159.9	146.0	172.7	214.7	205.7	298.0	Foreign Assets (Net)	**31n**
	150.9	140.5	136.7	144.0	100.9	112.4	78.2	75.2	55.7	97.0	117.7	122.4	93.2	94.7	99.9	Domestic Credit	**32**
	5.5	7.9	11.9	6.2	-2.5	10.4	-8.1	5.8	-12.1	21.0	36.3	20.0	21.5	-5.4	-61.7	Claims on Central Govt. (Net)	**32an**
	145.4	132.6	124.8	137.8	103.4	102.1	86.2	69.4	67.7	75.0	80.4	102.4	71.7	100.1	161.7	Claims on Private Sector	**32d**
	—	—	—	—	—	—	—	—	—	1.0	1.0	—	—	—	—	Claims on Other Financial Insts	**32f**
	87.1	78.9	61.8	72.0	84.4	104.6	116.7	128.2	111.3	186.2	161.7	189.5	193.4	184.2	270.6	Money	**34**
	24.5	30.2	35.0	25.9	19.8	29.5	31.7	47.9	59.3	66.1	86.0	90.5	99.6	98.3	110.2	Quasi-Money	**35**
	—	4.0	5.1	3.9	4.8	4.9	3.7	.6	.9	1.3	.5	.6	.8	.7	2.4	Long-Term Foreign Liabilities	**36cl**
	-3.6	-8.5	-21.8	-13.3	-31.8	-22.9	-33.2	-36.1	-46.3	3.3	15.4	14.5	14.2	17.2	14.6	Other Items (Net)	**37r**
	111.6	109.1	96.8	97.9	104.2	134.0	148.3	176.1	170.6	252.3	247.7	280.0	293.0	282.5	380.8	Money plus Quasi-Money	**35l**
																Other Banking Institutions	
End of Period																	
	2.1	2.4	3.3	3.1	3.1	. . . .	. . . .	. . . .	. . . .	. . . .	. . . .	. . . .	. . . .	—	—	Savings Deposits	**45**
	113.7	111.5	100.1	101.0	107.3	. . . .	. . . .	. . . .	. . . .	. . . .	. . . .	280.0	293.0	282.5	380.8	Liquid Liabilities	**55l**
																Interest Rates	
Percent Per Annum																	
	10.50	8.50	8.50	9.50	11.00	11.00	11.00	12.50	10.50	10.00	7.50	6.50	6.00	6.25	5.75	Discount Rate *(End of Period)*	**60**
	10.66	8.58	8.37	8.72	10.07	10.98	10.94	11.44	. . . .	. . . .	. . . .	. . . .	. . . .	4.81	4.95	Money Market Rate	**60b**
	7.25	6.08	5.25	5.25	6.42	7.00	7.00	7.75	. . . .	. . . .	. . . .	. . . .	. . . .	3.50	3.50	Deposit Rate	**60l**
	14.50	13.50	13.50	13.58	15.08	16.00	16.00	16.75	. . . .	. . . .	. . . .	. . . .	. . . .	. . . .	. . . .	Lending Rate	**60p**
																Prices and Labor	
Period Averages																	
	. . . .	. . . .	. . . .	. . . .	. . . .	. . . .	. . . .	62.8	63.1	87.4	100.0	104.9	I 108.6	114.8	115.2	Consumer Prices	**64**
Period Averages																	
	. . . .	. . . .	. . . .	. . . .	. . . .	. . . .	. . . .	. . . .	. . . .	. . . .	. . . .	3,211	. . . .	. . . .	. . . .	Labor Force	**67d**
	81	77	78	78	47	51	52	56	. . . .	. . . .	. . . .	. . . .	. . . .	. . . .	. . . .	Employment	**67e**

Benin

		1970	1971	1972	1973	1974	1975	1976	1977	1978	1979	1980	1981	1982	1983	1984
International Transactions																*Billions of Francs*
Exports	70	9.06	11.65	9.19	9.79	8.31	6.79	5.96	7.64	6.14	9.77	13.27	9.14	7.84	25.35	72.82
Imports, c.i.f.	71	17.66	21.20	23.09	24.86	35.30	40.28	52.30	65.79	70.20	68.10	69.97	147.50	152.55	121.02	125.88
Balance of Payments																*Millions of US Dollars:*
Current Account, n.i.e.	78al *d*	....	....	....	....	−29.3	−53.4	−72.8	−60.7	−96.4	−51.9	−35.7	−93.4	−377.2	−134.8	−57.1
Goods: Exports f.o.b.	78aa *d*	....	....	....	....	93.0	116.1	85.9	129.1	125.6	132.9	164.0	388.0	135.4	132.3	223.8
Goods: Imports f.o.b.	78ab *d*	....	....	....	....	−148.3	−205.6	−208.6	−255.5	−284.8	−289.0	−312.2	−526.8	−514.5	−286.3	−290.9
Trade Balance	78ac *d*	....	....	....	....	−55.3	−89.5	−122.7	−126.4	−159.2	−156.1	−148.3	−138.8	−379.1	−154.0	−67.1
Services: Credit	78ad *d*	....	....	....	....	22.0	28.1	30.8	32.5	38.7	43.4	62.3	66.8	48.0	50.2	58.3
Services: Debit	78ae *d*	....	....	....	....	−40.6	−57.9	−61.0	−71.3	−85.5	−94.9	−108.6	−142.7	−133.7	−92.4	−93.8
Balance on Goods & Services	78af *d*	....	....	....	....	−73.9	−119.3	−152.9	−165.2	−206.0	−207.6	−194.6	−214.6	−464.8	−196.3	−102.6
Income: Credit	78ag *d*	....	....	....	....	4.1	3.5	3.2	3.4	3.9	6.0	15.1	10.6	10.7	4.9	7.4
Income: Debit	78ah *d*	....	....	....	....	−1.8	−4.8	−3.2	−3.6	−3.7	−4.8	−6.9	−10.0	−29.6	−51.8	−55.4
Balance on Gds, Serv. & Inc.	78ai *d*	....	....	....	....	−71.6	−120.6	−152.8	−165.4	−205.8	−206.3	−186.5	−214.1	−483.7	−243.2	−150.7
Current Transfers, n.i.e.: Credit	78aj *d*	....	....	....	....	46.9	72.3	83.2	108.6	114.4	160.7	157.5	127.2	111.1	113.2	100.2
Current Transfers: Debit	78ak *d*	....	....	....	....	−4.6	−5.1	−3.2	−3.9	−5.0	−6.2	−6.8	−6.5	−4.5	−4.8	−6.6
Capital Account, n.i.e.	78bc *d*	....	....	....	....	—	—	—	—	—	—	—	—	—	—	—
Capital Account, n.i.e.: Credit	78ba *d*	....	....	....	....	—	—	—	—	—	—	—	—	—	—	—
Capital Account: Debit	78bb *d*	....	....	....	....	—	—	—	—	—	—	—	—	—	—	—
Financial Account, n.i.e.	78bj *d*	....	....	....	....	19.1	10.6	45.1	36.7	63.6	36.1	37.9	127.5	318.2	87.4	−1.9
Direct Investment Abroad	78bd *d*	....	....	....	....	—	—	—	—	—	−.2	—	—	−.5	−.5	−.5
Dir. Invest. in Rep. Econ., n.i.e.	78be *d*	....	....	....	....	−2.3	1.9	2.5	3.1	.8	3.6	4.3	2.1			
Portfolio Investment Assets	78bf *d*	....	....	....	....	—	—	—	—	—	—	—	—	—	—	—
Equity Securities	78bk *d*	....	....	....	....	—	—	—	—	—	—	—	—	—	—	—
Debt Securities	78bl *d*	....	....	....	....	—	—	—	—	—	—	—	—	—	—	—
Portfolio Investment Liab., n.i.e.	78bg *d*	....	....	....	....	—	—	—	—	—	—	—	—	—	—	—
Equity Securities	78bm *d*	....	....	....	....	—	—	—	—	—	—	—	—	—	—	—
Debt Securities	78bn *d*	....	....	....	....	—	—	—	—	—	—	—	—	—	—	—
Financial Derivatives Assets	78bw *d*	....	....	....	....	....	....	....	....	....	....	....	....	....	....	....
Financial Derivatives Liabilities	78bx *d*	....	....	....	....	....	....	....	....	....	....	....	....	....	....	....
Other Investment Assets	78bh *d*	....	....	....	....	−15.0	−71.6	−26.0	−38.0	−30.5	−41.8	16.8	−98.4	106.5	−29.6	−9.1
Monetary Authorities	78bo *d*	....	....	....	....	....	....	....	....	....	....	....	....	....	....	....
General Government	78bp *d*	....	....	....	....	−.5	−1.0	−.4	−1.0	−.2	−1.0	−1.5	−.3	−1.2	−1.3	−.6
Banks	78bq *d*	....	....	....	....	−10.5	−71.0	−28.8	−28.5	−26.8	−37.8	96.8	20.0	3.8	4.0	−10.2
Other Sectors	78br *d*	....	....	....	....	−4.0	.5	3.2	−8.5	−3.5	−3.1	−78.5	−118.1	103.9	−32.2	1.8
Other Investment Liab., n.i.e.	78bi *d*	....	....	....	....	36.4	80.3	68.6	71.5	93.3	74.6	16.8	223.9	212.2	117.5	7.7
Monetary Authorities	78bs *d*	....	....	....	....	.1	.8	−.1	.7	14.8	10.8	−12.5	−2.5	8.2	40.9	−.1
General Government	78bt *d*	....	....	....	....	6.2	9.7	16.2	13.6	23.0	25.4	10.5	35.4	145.8	54.0	1.0
Banks	78bu *d*	....	....	....	....	−2.7	40.3	19.8	14.8	14.7	43.0	3.9	−19.8	−13.6	−13.9	1.5
Other Sectors	78bv *d*	....	....	....	....	32.8	29.5	32.7	42.4	40.8	−4.5	14.9	210.8	71.8	36.5	5.2
Net Errors and Omissions	78ca *d*	....	....	....	....	10.7	23.0	24.9	20.1	13.6	12.1	−24.7	−3.0	10.9	10.0	35.6
Overall Balance	78cb *d*	....	....	....	....	.5	−19.9	−2.8	−3.9	−19.2	−3.6	−22.6	31.2	−48.1	−37.4	−23.3
Reserves and Related Items	79da *d*	....	....	....	....	−.5	19.9	2.8	3.9	19.2	3.6	22.6	−31.2	48.1	37.4	23.3
Reserve Assets	79db *d*	....	....	....	....	−.5	19.9	−5.2	−.1	6.5	3.6	7.5	−51.6	45.9	1.4	1.3
Use of Fund Credit and Loans	79dc *d*	....	....	....	....	—	—	—	—	6.7	—	9.6	.1	—	−.2	−1.1
Exceptional Financing	79de *d*	....	....	....	....	—	—	8.0	4.0	6.1	—	5.4	20.3	2.2	36.2	23.1
Government Finance																*Millions of Francs:*
Deficit (-) or Surplus	80	....	....	....	....	....	....	....	1,434	5,052	−1,010	....	....	....	....	....
Revenue	81	....	....	....	....	....	....	24,781	27,518	31,611	34,200	....	....	....	....	....
Grants Received	81z	....	....	....	....	....	....	....	14,477	9,096	11,705	....	....	....	....	....
Expenditure	82	....	....	....	....	....	....	....	37,006	34,304	42,065	....	....	....	....	....
Lending Minus Repayments	83	....	....	....	....	....	....	....	3,555	1,351	4,850	....	....	....	....	....
Financing																
Net Borrowing: Domestic	84a	....	....	....	....	....	....	....	−430	2,071	147	....	....	....	....	....
Foreign	85a	....	....	....	....	....	....	....	887	1,802	2,457	....	....	....	....	....
Use of Cash Balances	87	....	....	....	....	....	....	....	−1,891	−8,925	−1,594	....	....	....	....	....
National Accounts																*Billions of Francs*
Exports of Goods & Services	90c	19.3	23.6	21.6	25.4	27.8	30.6	31.6	43.3	50.0	50.3	59.5	65.1	107.6	83.5	130.7
Government Consumption	91f	9.0	9.3	10.5	11.2	11.8	13.4	12.8	14.7	14.4	17.4	21.7	65.2	43.7	60.2	62.6
Gross Fixed Capital Formation	93e	10.2	10.3	14.9	14.1	20.2	22.8	22.0	22.9	23.2	38.8	48.2	52.3	112.7	69.4	57.3
Increase/Decrease(-) in Stocks	93i	1.6	1.7	2.2	2.2	2.1	6.0	3.3	4.8	5.5	7.5	9.7	13.1	2.3	2.9	1.5
Private Consumption	96f	54.1	56.4	64.8	70.4	77.9	96.0	119.5	139.1	156.3	176.7	220.0	276.1	343.8	354.1	372.0
Imports of Goods & Services	98c	−24.5	−27.5	−30.9	−33.2	−35.4	−55.7	−54.8	−73.7	−80.9	−97.2	−113.5	−130.7	−193.6	−152.8	−164.7
Gross Domestic Product (GDP)	99b	69.7	73.7	83.1	89.0	107.6	112.8	133.5	148.5	161.6	193.5	245.6	301.0	416.6	417.4	459.3
Net Factor Inc/Pmts(-) Abroad	98.n	.7	−.7	....	....	−.3	−.1	.2	.1	.2	.2	.2	−.2	....	....	−11.7
Gross National Income (GNI)	99a	....	....	....	....	....	....	....	134.5	151.3	168.8	193.7	245.8	300.8	....	447.6
Net National Income	99e	57.1	....	....	....	103.5	107.7	126.0	142.4	157.9	181.3	226.0	277.8			
GDP Volume 1985 Prices	99b.*p*	....	....	....	....	....	....	....	....	....	....	....	....	423.2	404.8	436.9
GDP Volume (1995=100)	99bv *p*	41.4	42.2	46.0	47.0	43.5	45.4	47.3	50.0	51.4	53.9	59.8	63.3	70.1	67.1	72.4
GDP Deflator (1995=100)	99bi *p*	16.8	17.4	18.0	18.9	24.7	24.8	28.1	29.6	31.4	35.8	40.9	47.4	59.2	62.1	63.3
																Millions:
Population	99z	2.72	2.79	2.87	2.95	3.03	3.11	3.20	3.29	3.38	⅔3.38	3.46	3.58	3.69	3.81	3.93

Billions of Francs

1985	1986	1987	1988	1989	1990	1991	1992	1993	1994	1995	1996	1997	1998	1999	International Transactions	
67.35	36.01	34.27	21.00	24.58	33.25	5.98	88.80	108.60	220.90	209.50	269.90	247.50	244.50	239.00	Exports	70
148.78	133.85	104.98	97.26	66.13	72.19	68.05	153.02	161.78	239.35	372.20	334.70	397.90	396.70	398.30	Imports, c.i.f.	71

Minus Sign Indicates Debit

Balance of Payments

1985	1986	1987	1988	1989	1990	1991	1992	1993	1994	1995	1996	1997	1998	1999		
−39.0	−52.8	−34.3	−18.2	37.3	23.9	−139.4	5.4	15.7	84.6	−82.6	−41.0	−154.0	....	....	Current Account, n.i.e.	78al d
297.8	308.7	366.3	190.2	187.9	237.5	373.5	345.1	393.5	397.9	419.9	527.7	424.0	....	....	Goods: Exports f.o.b.	78aa d
−326.3	−402.2	−463.2	−331.4	−250.6	−323.4	−673.4	−560.5	−561.4	−451.5	−622.5	−559.7	−576.9	....	....	Goods: Imports f.o.b.	78ab d
−28.5	−93.6	−96.8	−141.2	−62.7	−85.9	−299.8	−215.5	−167.9	−53.6	−202.5	−32.0	−152.9	....	....	*Trade Balance*	78ac d
37.6	71.6	90.8	114.4	100.5	126.4	146.0	156.0	146.6	142.2	194.3	126.1	116.0	....	....	Services: Credit	78ad d
−111.3	−119.3	−139.4	−126.6	−119.1	−130.6	−189.6	−186.2	−175.1	−181.4	−272.2	−188.8	−172.3	....	....	Services: Debit	78ae d
−102.2	−141.2	−145.4	−153.4	−81.2	−90.1	−343.4	−245.6	−196.4	−92.8	−280.4	−94.7	−209.2	....	....	*Balance on Goods & Services*	78af d
6.7	2.9	3.3	4.7	5.6	12.2	24.1	34.1	37.8	18.8	23.5	36.5	25.4	....	....	Income: Credit	78ag d
−34.7	−28.9	−32.0	−37.0	−36.1	−37.7	−39.5	−27.1	−32.8	−21.7	−31.1	−57.5	−45.4	....	....	Income: Debit	78ah d
−130.2	−167.2	−174.0	−185.6	−111.8	−115.6	−358.8	−238.6	−191.4	−95.7	−288.0	−115.6	−229.2	....	....	*Balance on Gds, Serv. & Inc.*	78ai d
95.7	120.1	146.4	191.7	171.1	169.4	249.1	272.1	235.2	206.3	235.9	108.9	93.7	....	....	Current Transfers: Credit	78aj d
−4.5	−5.8	−6.7	−24.2	−22.0	−29.9	−29.7	−28.1	−28.1	−25.9	−30.5	−34.2	−18.5	....	....	Current Transfers: Debit	78ak d
—	—	—	—	4.7	7.3	1.8	1.1	1.1	1.1	1.2	6.4	84.5	....	....	Capital Account, n.i.e.	78bc d
—	—	—	—	4.7	7.3	1.8	1.1	1.1	1.1	1.2	6.4	84.5	....	....	Capital Account, n.i.e.: Credit	78ba d
—	—	—	—	—	—	—	—	—	—	—	—	—	....	....	Capital Account: Debit	78bb d
−6.7	−26.9	34.6	65.2	−185.4	−25.2	−19.2	30.1	−96.4	−6.9	−50.0	−132.8	132.4	....	....	Financial Account, n.i.e.	78bj d
											−21.9	−13.1	....	....	Direct Investment Abroad	78bd d
—	—	—	—	62.1	62.4	120.8	77.6	1.4	13.6	13.3	35.5	27.0	....	....	Dir. Invest. in Rep. Econ., n.i.e.	78be d
—	—	—	.3	−.7	−4.6	3.7	−5.6	−9.1	−26.4	−64.2	−7.7	−7.8	....	....	Portfolio Investment Assets	78bf d
											1.4	—	....	....	Equity Securities	78bk d
—	—	—	.3	−.7	−4.6	3.7	−5.6	−9.1	−26.4	−64.2	−9.1	−7.7	....	....	Debt Securities	78bl d
—	—	—	—	—	.1	—	—	—	—	.3	−3.9	−9.4	....	....	Portfolio Investment Liab., n.i.e.	78bg d
—	—	—	—	—	.1	—	—	—	—	.3	2.5	2.0	....	....	Equity Securities	78bm d
—	—	—	—	—	—	—	—	—	—	—	−6.5	−11.4	....	....	Debt Securities	78bn d
....	....	....	....	....	....	....	—	—	—	—	....	....	....	....	Financial Derivatives Assets	78bw d
....	....	....	....	....	....	....	....	....	....	....	....	....	....	....	Financial Derivatives Liabilities	78bx d
5.6	−5.2	41.6	21.5	−2.9	−6.2	−1.9	−83.6	−73.9	−52.2	−62.1	−4.0	−12.4	....	....	Other Investment Assets	78bh d
....	....	—	—	—	—	—	....	—	—	—	—	—	....	....	Monetary Authorities	78bo d
—	—	—	−.2	−.4	−.7	−.2	−.4	−2.2	11.9	−6.9	—	−.1	....	....	General Government	78bp d
5.6	−5.2	41.6	5.3	11.8	−3.8	−26.8	−23.5	−48.9	−50.8	−44.2	11.8	−41.1	....	....	Banks	78bq d
—	—	—	16.4	−14.3	−1.7	25.0	−59.7	−22.9	−13.3	−10.9	−15.8	28.8	....	....	Other Sectors	78br d
−12.2	−21.7	−7.0	43.4	−243.8	−76.7	−141.9	41.7	−14.8	58.1	62.6	−130.8	148.1	....	....	Other Investment Liab., n.i.e.	78bi d
....	....	....	31.0	−112.6	−22.3	2.0	−2.2	8.6	.6	−2.7	5.2	4.7	....	....	Monetary Authorities	78bs d
−12.9	−22.8	−8.3	91.9	−181.4	−49.2	−246.0	46.9	−6.0	9.3	48.0	−157.9	17.8	....	....	General Government	78bt d
—	—	—	3.5	−1.6	1.5	−11.2	−5.0	−1.0	6.4	16.0	4.5	−12.8	....	....	Banks	78bu d
.7	1.2	1.3	−83.1	51.8	−6.7	113.2	2.0	−16.5	41.8	1.3	17.4	138.4	....	....	Other Sectors	78bv d
16.2	.4	−52.6	.4	13.6	11.1	2.1	9.1	−8.1	−16.3	−1.0	6.3	6.7	....	....	Net Errors and Omissions	78ca d
−29.5	−79.2	−52.3	47.5	−129.7	17.2	−154.7	45.8	−87.8	62.5	−132.4	−161.1	69.7	....	....	*Overall Balance*	78cb d
29.5	79.2	52.3	−47.5	129.7	−17.2	154.7	−45.8	87.8	−62.5	132.4	161.1	−69.7	....	....	Reserves and Related Items	79da d
−1.1	.7	.9	−.9	.8	−57.7	−117.0	−67.3	−15.4	−117.7	81.9	−78.3	−24.5	....	....	Reserve Assets	79db d
−1.1	−2.9	−3.2	−3.1	5.9	−1.9	12.5	—	21.9	24.9	12.2	18.0	1.9	....	....	Use of Fund Credit and Loans	79dc d
31.6	81.4	54.6	−43.5	123.0	42.5	259.3	21.5	81.3	30.2	38.2	221.4	−47.1	....	....	Exceptional Financing	79de d

Year Ending December 31

Government Finance

1985	1986	1987	1988	1989	1990	1991	1992	1993	1994	1995	1996	1997	1998	1999		
....	....	....	....	....	....	....	....	....	....	....	....	....		....	Deficit (-) or Surplus	80
....	....	....	....	....	....	....	....	....	....	....	....	....		....	Revenue	81
....	....	....	....	....	....	....	....	....	....	....	....	....		....	Grants Received	81z
....	....	....	....	....	....	....	....	....	....	....	....	....		....	Expenditure	82
....	....	....	....	....	....	....	....	....	....	....	....	....		....	Lending Minus Repayments	83
															Financing	
....	....	....	....	....	....	....	....	....	....	....	....	....		....	Net Borrowing: Domestic	84a
....	....	....	....	....	....	....	....	....	....	....	....	....		....	Foreign	85a
....	....	....	....	....	....	....	....	....	....	....	....	....		....	Use of Cash Balances	87

Billions of Francs

National Accounts

1985	1986	1987	1988	1989	1990	1991	1992	1993	1994	1995	1996	1997	1998	1999		
156.5	129.5	128.7	93.4	87.6	102.4	117.7	138.1	144.7	248.9	269.9	300.2	337.2	367.8	403.8	Exports of Goods & Services	90c
58.8	63.8	65.7	63.7	62.3	66.2	64.0	65.9	69.4	90.1	100.1	108.3	113.8	119.6	125.6	Government Consumption	91f
63.0	68.2	66.7	72.8	59.7	67.4	72.6	79.8	89.4	144.1	190.0	196.7	223.1	242.0	271.5	Gross Fixed Capital Formation	93e
11.2	−.2	−.1	2.6	−3.1	4.0	4.6	3.6	−3.9	10.0	45.8	5.6	6.2	6.8	7.3	Increase/Decrease(-) in Stocks	93i
374.1	381.1	384.5	398.7	390.1	404.1	440.9	481.1	508.9	657.8	791.2	913.9	1,017.2	1,099.4	1,177.1	Private Consumption	96f
−194.0	−179.9	−179.0	−146.8	−117.4	−141.6	−170.0	−199.0	−212.0	−319.9	−394.0	−395.1	−447.7	−474.8	−511.8	Imports of Goods & Services	98c
469.9	462.5	469.7	484.4	479.2	502.3	529.7	569.5	596.4	831.1	1,002.9	1,129.5	1,249.8	1,360.6	1,473.6	Gross Domestic Product (GDP)	99b
−10.7	−10.4	−8.6	−7.4	−12.2	−9.4	−4.9	−6.9	−1.8	−14.5	−22.1	....	....	....	....	Net Factor Inc/Pmts(-) Abroad	98.n
459.1	452.1	461.0	477.0	467.0	492.9	524.9	562.6	594.6	816.6	980.8	....	....	....	....	Gross National Income (GNI)	99a
....	....	....	....	....	....	....	....	....	....	....	....	....	....	....	Net National Income	99e
469.8	479.9	472.7	488.9	474.9	490.1	513.4	533.9	552.7	576.9	603.5	636.9	673.3	703.7	738.6	GDP Volume 1985 Prices	99b.p
77.8	79.5	78.3	81.0	78.7	81.2	85.1	88.5	91.6	95.6	100.0	105.5	111.6	116.6	122.4	GDP Volume (1995=100)	99bv p
60.2	58.0	59.8	59.6	60.7	61.7	62.1	64.2	64.9	86.7	100.0	106.7	111.7	116.3	120.1	GDP Deflator (1995=100)	99bi p

Midyear Estimates

1985	1986	1987	1988	1989	1990	1991	1992	1993	1994	1995	1996	1997	1998	1999		
4.06	4.19	4.32	4.46	4.61	4.74	4.89	4.92	5.08	5.24	5.41	5.59	5.83	6.04	6.06	**Population**	99z

(See notes in the back of the book.)

Bhutan

514

		1970	1971	1972	1973	1974	1975	1976	1977	1978	1979	1980	1981	1982	1983	1984
Exchange Rates															*Ngultrum per SDR:*	
Official Rate	aa	7.576	7.903	8.773	9.896	9.978	10.462	10.318	9.971	10.668	10.416	10.114	10.591	10.627	10.986	12.205
															Ngultrum per US Dollar:	
Official Rate	ae	7.576	7.279	8.080	8.203	8.150	8.937	8.881	8.209	8.188	7.907	7.930	9.099	9.634	10.493	12.451
Official Rate	rf	7.500	7.492	7.594	7.742	8.102	8.376	8.960	8.739	8.193	8.126	7.863	8.659	9.455	10.099	11.363
Fund Position															*Millions of SDRs:*	
Quota	2f. s	—	—	—	—	—	—	—	—	—	—	—	1.700	1.700	1.700	2.500
SDRs	1b. s	...	...	...	...	...	...	...	...	...	...	...	—	—	.020	.050
Reserve Position in the Fund	1c. s	...	...	...	...	...	...	...	...	...	...	...	—			
Total Fund Cred.&Loans Outstg.	2tl	...	...	...	...	...	...	...	...	...	...	...		.370	.370	.570
International Liquidity												*Millions of US Dollars Unless Otherwise Indicated:*				
Total Reserves minus Gold	1l. d	...	...	...	...	...	...	...	...	...	...	...	31.11	35.51	40.22	44.81
SDRs	1b. d	...	...	...	...	...	...	...	...	...	...	...		—	.02	.05
Reserve Position in the Fund	1c. d	...	...	...	...	...	...	...	...	...	...	...		.41	.39	.56
Foreign Exchange	1d. d	...	...	...	...	...	...	...	...	...	...	...	31.11	35.10	39.81	44.21
of which: Convertible Currency	1dx d	...	...	...	...	...	...	...	...	...	...	...			4.22	7.12
Deposit Money Banks: Assets	7a. d	...	...	...	...	...	...	...	...	...	...	...			30.58	34.78
Liabilities	7b. d	...	...	...	...	...	...	...	...	...	...	...			2.53	3.68
Monetary Authorities															*Millions of Ngultrum*	
Foreign Assets	11	...	...	...	...	...	...	...	...	...	...	...			51	103
Claims on Central Government	12a	...	...	...	...	...	...	...	...	...	...	...				
Claims on Deposit Money Banks	12e	...	...	...	...	...	...	...	...	...	...	...				
Claims on Other Financial Insts	12f	...	...	...	...	...	...	...	...	...	...	...			—	14
Reserve Money	14	...	...	...	...	...	...	...	...	...	...	...			39	85
of which: Currency Outside DMBs	14a	...	...	...	...	...	...	...	...	...	...	...			22	46
Bonds	16ab	...	...	...	...	...	...	...	...	...	...	...				
Foreign Liabilities	16c	...	...	...	...	...	...	...	...	...	...	...				
Central Government Deposits	16d	...	...	...	...	...	...	...	...	...	...	...				
Other Items (Net)	17r	...	...	...	...	...	...	...	...	...	...	...			13	24
of which: Valuation Adjustment	17rv	...	...	...	...	...	...	...	...	...	...	...			−1	8
Deposit Money Banks															*Millions of Ngultrum*	
Reserves	20	...	...	...	...	...	...	...	...	...	...	...			9	13
Foreign Assets	21	...	...	...	...	...	...	...	...	...	...	...			321	433
Claims on Central Government	22a	...	...	...	...	...	...	...	...	...	...	...			23	59
Claims on Nonfin.Pub.Enterprises	22c	...	...	...	...	...	...	...	...	...	...	...			57	41
Claims on Private Sector	22d	...	...	...	...	...	...	...	...	...	...	...			43	58
Demand Deposits	24	...	...	...	...	...	...	...	...	...	...	...			155	164
Time & Foreign Currency Deposits	25	...	...	...	...	...	...	...	...	...	...	...			147	157
Foreign Liabilities	26c	...	...	...	...	...	...	...	...	...	...	...			27	46
Central Government Deposits	26d	...	...	...	...	...	...	...	...	...	...	...			—	89
Capital Accounts	27a	...	...	...	...	...	...	...	...	...	...	...			121	111
Other Items (Net)	27r	...	...	...	...	...	...	...	...	...	...	...			4	38
Monetary Survey															*Millions of Ngultrum:*	
Foreign Assets (Net)	31n	...	...	...	...	...	...	...	...	...	...	...			346	490
Domestic Credit	32	...	...	...	...	...	...	...	...	...	...	...			110	59
Claims on Central Govt. (Net)	32an	...	...	...	...	...	...	...	...	...	...	...			10	−54
Claims on Nonfin.Pub.Enterprises	32c	...	...	...	...	...	...	...	...	...	...	...			57	41
Claims on Private Sector	32d	...	...	...	...	...	...	...	...	...	...	...			43	58
Claims on Other Financial Insts	32f	...	...	...	...	...	...	...	...	...	...	...			—	14
Money	34	...	...	...	...	...	...	...	...	...	...	...			177	210
Quasi-Money	35	...	...	...	...	...	...	...	...	...	...	...			147	157
Other Items (Net)	37r	...	...	...	...	...	...	...	...	...	...	...			132	182
Money plus Quasi-Money	35l	...	...	...	...	...	...	...	...	...	...	...			325	367
Interest Rates															*Percent Per Annum*	
Deposit Rate	60l	...	...	...	...	...	...	...	...	...	...	...			5.5	5.5
Lending Rate	60p	...	...	...	...	...	...	...	...	...	...	...			15.0	15.0

1985	1986	1987	1988	1989	1990	1991	1992	1993	1994	1995	1996	1997	1998	1999		
Exchange Rates																
End of Period																
13.363	16.051	18.268	20.117	22.387	25.712	36.953	36.025	43.102	45.810	52.295	51.666	52.999	59.813	59.690	Official Rate	aa
End of Period (ae) Period Average (rf)																
12.166	13.122	12.877	14.949	17.035	18.073	25.834	26.200	31.380	31.380	35.180	35.930	39.280	42.480	43.490	Official Rate	ae
12.369	12.611	12.962	13.917	16.226	17.505	22.742	25.918	30.493	31.374	32.427	35.433	36.313	41.259	43.055	Official Rate	rf
Fund Position																
End of Period																
2.500	2.500	2.500	2.500	2.500	2.500	2.500	4.500	4.500	4.500	4.500	4.500	4.500	4.500	6.300	Quota	2f. s
.080	.110	.140	.160	.200	.250	.300	.340	.376	.405	.438	.471	.504	.541	.134	SDRs	1b. s
.570	.570	.570	.570	.570	.570	.570	.570	.570	.570	.570	.570	.570	.570	1.020	Reserve Position in the Fund	1c. s
—	—	—	—	—	—	—	—	—	—	—	—	—	—	—	Total Fund Cred.&Loans Outstg.	2tl
International Liquidity																
End of Period																
50.30	61.00	74.94	94.12	98.51	86.01	98.92	77.87	....	115.20	124.29	183.99	181.18	249.63	274.41	Total Reserves minus Gold	1l. d
.09	.13	.20	.22	.26	.36	.43	.47	.52	.59	.65	.68	.68	.76	.18	SDRs	1b. d
.63	.70	.81	.75	.75	.81	.82	.78	.78	.83	.85	.82	.77	.80	1.40	Reserve Position in the Fund	1c. d
49.59	60.17	83.54	91.69	85.31	84.85	97.68	76.62	....	113.78	I122.79	182.49	179.73	248.07	272.82	Foreign Exchange	1d. d
17.42	21.59	35.26	44.57	46.39	61.29	85.44	75.29	....	110.39	I121.00	144.86	147.73	182.38	195.56	*of which:* Convertible Currency	1dx d
34.60	33.06	49.46	49.09	40.67	25.50	13.50	8.11	13.84	8.88	7.17	43.01	38.86	72.22	93.24	Deposit Money Banks: Assets	7a. d
4.38	2.84	3.32	3.08	5.13	6.53	5.30	13.63	18.09	—	—	—	—	—	—	Liabilities	7b. d
Monetary Authorities																
End of Period																
228	304	483	697	841	1,145	2,268	2,027	I2,945	3,533	4,337	5,284	6,065	8,022	8,841	Foreign Assets	11
....	....	....	....	....	....	....	....	74	—	50	—	51	—	—	Claims on Central Government	12a
....	....	....	....	....	....	....	....	108	7	3	308	3	1,193	1,188	Claims on Deposit Money Banks	12e
16	17	24	24	30	39	48	44	I—	55	5	5	5	—	—	Claims on Other Financial Insts	12f
204	259	433	384	691	1,260	1,593	1,257	I1,931	1,287	2,149	2,328	2,545	3,954	4,971	Reserve Money	14
70	91	104	149	188	194	246	345	I335	348	433	423	721	769	969	*of which:* Currency Outside DMBs	14a
....	....	....	....	....	....	....	....		600	550	1,000	681	560	487	Bonds	16ab
....	....	....	....	....	....	....	....	—	617	161	250	250	250	—	Foreign Liabilities	16c
22	19	9	180	78	65	116	20	I25	30	29	334	28	1,207	1,234	Central Government Deposits	16d
18	42	65	156	102	–141	607	794	I1,170	1,062	1,506	1,685	2,619	3,244	3,335	Other Items (Net)	17r
....	....	....	....	....	....	....	....			1,451	1,653	2,013	1,905	1,610	*of which:* Valuation Adjustment	17rv
Deposit Money Banks																
End of Period																
119	143	310	244	502	1,009	1,253	828	I1,001	1,416	2,382	2,085	3,009	2,901	3,675	Reserves	20
421	434	637	734	693	461	349	213	I434	279	252	1,545	1,526	3,068	4,055	Foreign Assets	21
120	104	12	3	3	3	3	3	I2	5	2	100	201	50	50	Claims on Central Government	22a
27	20	14	32	28	53	65	770	I796	561	535	484	449	411	372	Claims on Nonfin.Pub.Enterprises	22c
55	67	82	116	192	216	306	426	I489	724	751	748	1,472	1,472	1,490	Claims on Private Sector	22d
191	186	213	263	358	345	504	496	I487	697	890	1,652	1,447	1,860	2,755	Demand Deposits	24
202	222	236	312	430	539	648	746	I1,120	1,351	1,926	1,465	3,458	3,782	4,741	Time & Foreign Currency Deposits	25
53	37	43	46	87	118	137	357	I568	—	—	—	—	—	—	Foreign Liabilities	26c
78	118	307	221	202	299	315	200	I311	140	344	459	209	322	914	Central Government Deposits	26d
133	150	176	177	229	240	236	534	I330	324	371	371	539	561	633	Capital Accounts	27a
85	55	80	110	110	200	136	–95	I–90	473	390	1,016	1,007	1,365	599	Other Items (Net)	27r
Monetary Survey																
End of Period																
595	700	1,077	1,384	1,446	1,488	2,480	1,883	I2,811	3,195	4,429	6,579	7,341	10,840	12,896	Foreign Assets (Net)	31n
118	71	–185	–227	–27	–54	–10	1,022	I1,024	1,175	969	545	1,941	404	–236	Domestic Credit	32
20	–33	–305	–399	–277	–361	–428	–218	I–261	–165	–321	–692	15	–1,480	–2,098	Claims on Central Govt. (Net)	32an
27	20	14	32	28	53	65	770	I796	561	535	484	449	411	372	Claims on Nonfin.Pub.Enterprises	32c
55	67	82	116	192	216	306	426	I489	724	751	748	1,472	1,472	1,490	Claims on Private Sector	32d
16	17	24	24	30	39	48	44	I—	55	5	5	5	—	—	Claims on Other Financial Insts	32f
262	277	317	412	546	540	750	841	I822	1,044	1,322	2,074	2,168	2,629	3,724	Money	34
202	222	236	312	430	539	648	746	I1,120	1,351	1,926	1,465	3,458	3,782	4,741	Quasi-Money	35
249	272	339	434	442	355	1,072	1,317	I1,897	1,975	2,149	3,585	3,658	4,823	4,193	Other Items (Net)	37r
464	499	553	724	977	1,079	1,398	1,587	I1,942	2,395	3,249	3,540	5,626	6,410	8,465	Money plus Quasi-Money	35l
Interest Rates																
Percent Per Annum																
6.1	6.5	6.5	6.5	6.5	6.5	6.5	8.0	8.0	8.0	8.0	....	....	....	....	Deposit Rate	60l
15.0	15.0	15.0	15.0	15.0	15.0	15.0	17.0	17.0	16.6	16.0	....	....	....	....	Lending Rate	60p

Bhutan

	1970	1971	1972	1973	1974	1975	1976	1977	1978	1979	1980	1981	1982	1983	1984
Prices, Production, and Tourism													*Index Numbers (1995=100):*		
Consumer Prices 64	...	...	...	...	...	...	...	...	...	...	24.6	27.1	29.7	35.1	37.6
Electricity Production 66ae	...	...	...	...	...	...	...	...	...	...	...	...	...	...	1.5
Tourist Arrivals 66ta	...	...	...	...	...	...	...	...	...	...	29.5	25.8	33.7	40.0	39.9
International Transactions													*Millions of Ngultrum:*		
Exports 70	...	...	...	...	...	...	...	...	...	...	131.5	171.7	159.4	160.7	206.4
Imports, c.i.f. 71	...	...	...	...	...	...	...	...	...	...	394.6	585.9	646.5	730.0	825.2
Government Finance													*Millions of Ngultrum:*		
Deficit (-) or Surplus.................. 80	...	...	...	...	...	...	...	...	...	...	...	...	10.3	−23.4	31.8
Revenue 81	...	...	...	...	...	...	...	...	...	...	...	...	137.8	197.3	278.1
Grants Received 81z	...	...	...	...	...	...	...	...	...	...	...	...	360.3	478.4	512.1
Expenditure 82	...	...	...	...	...	...	...	...	...	...	...	...	487.8	697.5	753.4
Lending Minus Repayments 83	...	...	...	...	...	...	...	...	...	...	...	...	—	1.6	5.0
Financing															
Total Financing 84	...	...	...	...	...	...	...	...	...	...	...	...	−10.3	23.4	−31.8
Domestic 84a	...	...	...	...	...	...	...	...	...	...	...	...	−18.9	14.4	−49.8
Foreign 85a	...	...	...	...	...	...	...	...	...	...	...	...	8.6	9.0	18.0
Debt: Domestic 88a	...	...	...	...	...	...	...	...	...	...	...	...	12.6	37.2	14.1
Foreign 89a	...	...	...	...	...	...	...	...	...	...	...	...	12.2	22.4	45.8
National Accounts													*Millions of Ngultrum:*		
Exports of Goods & Services 90c	...	...	...	...	...	...	...	...	...	...	145	207	213	228	290
Government Consumption 91f	...	...	...	...	...	...	...	...	...	...	276	287	327	443	513
Gross Fixed Capital Formation 93e	...	...	...	...	...	...	...	...	...	...	330	426	556	691	755
Increase/Decrease(-) in Stocks 93i	...	...	...	...	...	...	...	...	...	...	15	75	60	21	10
Private Consumption 96f	...	...	...	...	...	...	...	...	...	...	749	922	1,054	1,195	1,436
Imports of Goods & Services 98c	...	...	...	...	...	...	...	...	...	...	−402	−616	−688	−789	−899
Gross Domestic Product (GDP) 99b	...	...	...	...	...	...	...	...	...	...	1,113	1,301	1,522	1,789	2,106
Net Factor Inc/Pmts(-) Abroad 98.n	...	...	...	...	...	...	...	...	...	...	−200	−270	−322	−457	−388
Gross National Income (GNI) 99a	...	...	...	...	...	...	...	...	...	...	913	1,032	1,200	1,332	1,718
GDP at Factor Cost 99ba	...	...	...	...	...	...	...	...	...	...	1,095	1,280	1,498	1,754	2,060
GDP Vol. at Fac.Cost,1980 Prices ...... 99ba p	...	...	...	...	...	...	...	...	...	...	1,095	1,205	1,269	1,370	1,466
GDP Volume (1995=100) .... 99bv p	...	...	...	...	...	...	...	...	...	...	37.5	41.3	43.5	46.9	50.2
GDP Deflator (1995=100) .... 99bi p	...	...	...	...	...	...	...	...	...	...	30.4	32.3	35.8	38.9	42.7
													Millions:		
Population................................ 99z	...	...	...	...	...	...	...	...	...	...	1.24	1.27	1.29	1.32	1.35

	1985	1986	1987	1988	1989	1990	1991	1992	1993	1994	1995	1996	1997	1998	1999		
Period Averages																**Prices, Production, and Tourism**	
	38.3	42.1	44.7	49.3	53.6	58.9	66.2	76.8	85.4	91.3	100.0	108.8	115.9	....	....	Consumer Prices	**64**
	1.3	23.7	95.9	80.9	99.7	100.0	100.2	....	....	....	....	....	....	....	....	Electricity Production	**66ae**
	39.8	50.5	53.0	46.1	31.1	32.3	43.1	59.9	62.9	83.3	100.0	107.7	113.6	....	....	Tourist Arrivals	**66ta**
Year Ending June 30																**International Transactions**	
	272.0	387.4	715.0	1,042.0	1,132.3	1,192.4	1,478.9	1,738.2	1,990.4	2,082.7	3,349.1	3,553.8	4,274.1	....	....	Exports	**70**
	1,041.6	1,168.0	1,124.2	1,772.7	1,464.7	1,368.0	2,197.2	3,317.1	2,745.3	2,876.4	3,641.9	4,525.2	4,978.0	....	....	Imports, c.i.f.	**71**
Year Ending June 30																**Government Finance**	
	−207.2	−98.3	....	I 31.9	I−470.6	−390.0	−47.0	−247.3	312.2	−45.1	7.8	238.6	−300.9	−60.1 [f]	....	Deficit (-) or Surplus	**80**
	268.3	345.0	....	I 841.7	I 829.0	945.7	996.6	1,207.5	1,650.9	1,666.3	1,877.4	2,127.7	2,424.2	2,882.4 [f]	....	Revenue	**81**
	701.7	777.4	....	I 929.9	I 791.0	523.0	752.7	785.9	1,230.1	1,456.2	1,773.2	2,363.6	2,232.1	3,162.5 [f]	....	Grants Received	**81z**
	1,098.1	1,064.3	....	I 1,621.3	I 1,538.2	1,774.8	1,752.2	2,138.9	2,397.3	2,891.0	3,655.6	4,152.6	4,630.6	6,060.4 [f]	....	Expenditure	**82**
	79.1	156.4	....	I 118.4	I 552.4	83.9	44.1	101.8	171.5	276.6	−12.8	100.1	326.6	44.6 [f]	....	Lending Minus Repayments	**83**
																Financing	
	207.2	98.3	....	I−31.9	I 470.6	390.0	47.0	247.4	−312.2	45.1	−7.8	−238.6	300.9	60.1 [f]	....	Total Financing	**84**
	115.9	−73.6	....	I−242.2	I−20.7	332.7	−6.2	157.0	−334.7	21.0	−1.1	−211.8	176.6	−1.8 [f]	....	Domestic	**84a**
	91.3	171.9	....	I 210.3	I 491.3	57.3	53.2	90.4	22.5	24.1	−6.7	−26.8	124.3	61.9 [f]	....	Foreign	**85a**
	126.3	77.8	....	I 8.9	I 4.3	231.3	104.8	226.3	19.3	....	....	....	....	....	....	Debt: Domestic	**88a**
	135.5	316.2	....	I 560.8	I 2,357.6	2,455.7	2,594.1	2,730.2	2,801.8	....	....	....	....	....	....	Foreign	**89a**
Calendar Year																**National Accounts**	
	368	551	768	1,101	1,239	1,408	1,829	2,079	2,264	2,508	3,712	3,973	....	....	....	Exports of Goods & Services	**90c**
	561	576	634	641	879	783	1,015	1,215	1,383	2,106	2,727	3,445	....	....	....	Government Consumption	**91f**
	1,003	1,103	1,250	1,508	1,574	1,716	1,782	2,597	3,299	3,871	4,417	5,046	....	....	....	Gross Fixed Capital Formation	**93e**
	82	32	−161	10	−121	−34	−71	351	−102	229	156	157	....	....	....	Increase/Decrease(-) in Stocks	**93i**
	1,507	1,838	2,321	2,558	2,582	2,718	3,229	3,745	3,411	3,136	3,147	4,224	....	....	....	Private Consumption	**96f**
	−1,128	−1,298	−1,203	−1,885	−1,771	−1,609	−2,281	−3,634	−3,163	−3,349	−4,190	−5,133	....	....	....	Imports of Goods & Services	**98c**
	2,392	2,801	3,608	3,934	4,381	4,982	5,503	6,354	7,192	8,501	9,968	11,714	14,477	....	....	Gross Domestic Product (GDP)	**99b**
	−428	−467	−350	−344	−172	−326	−491	−734	−734	−634	−1,208	−1,396	−1,605	....	....	Net Factor Inc/Pmts(-) Abroad	**98.n**
	1,964	2,334	3,259	3,589	4,210	4,656	5,012	5,619	6,358	7,867	8,760	10,317	12,287	....	....	Gross National Income (GNI)	**99a**
	2,350	2,759	3,531	3,851	4,308	4,848	5,342	6,178	7,008	8,151	9,611	11,355	13,971	....	....	GDP at Factor Cost	**99ba**
	1,520	1,675	1,973	1,994	2,087	2,225	2,303	2,407	2,553	2,716	2,918	3,095	3,321	....	....	GDP Vol. at Fac.Cost,1980 Prices	**99ba** *p*
	52.1	57.4	67.6	68.3	71.5	76.3	78.9	82.5	87.5	93.1	100.0	106.1	113.8	....	....	GDP Volume (1995=100)	**99bv** *p*
	46.9	50.0	54.3	58.6	62.7	66.2	70.4	77.9	83.3	91.1	100.0	111.4	127.7	....	....	GDP Deflator (1995=100)	**99bi** *p*
Midyear Estimates																	
	1.38	1.41	1.45	1.48	1.52	1.54	1.57	1.58	1.60	1.61	1.64	1.81	1.86	2.00	2.06	**Population**	**99z**

(See notes in the back of the book.)

Bolivia

218

		1970	1971	1972	1973	1974	1975	1976	1977	1978	1979	1980	1981	1982	1983	1984
Exchange Rates																
										Bolivianos per Million SDRs through 1983; per Thousand SDRs in 1984:						
Market Rate	aa	11.880	12.898	21.714	24.127	24.487	23.413	23.237	24.294	26.056	32.288	31.260	28.529	218.305	528.605	‡8.609
										Bolivianos per Million US$ through 1983; per Thousand US$ in 1984:						
Market Rate	ae	11.880	11.880	20.000	20.000	20.000	20.000	20.000	20.000	20.000	24.510	24.510	24.510	197.900	504.900	‡8.783
Market Rate	rf	11.880	11.880	13.295	20.010	20.010	20.010	20.010	20.010	20.010	20.403	24.520	24.520	64.072	231.630	‡3.136
											Index Numbers (1995=100):					
Market Rate	ah x	....	....	....	....	....	....	....	....	....	....	....	....	....	....	363,927.4
Nominal Effective Exchange Rate	ne c	....	....	....	....	....	....	....	....	....	38,511.3	37,392.4	46,987.1	33,557.7	10,897.5	2,402.0
Real Effective Exchange Rate	re c	....	....	....	....	....	....	....	....	....	....	171.4	217.6	234.9	219.1	289.1
Fund Position															*Millions of SDRs:*		
Quota	2f. s	37.0	37.0	37.0	37.0	37.0	37.0	37.0	37.0	45.0	45.0	67.5	67.5	67.5	90.7	90.7
SDRs	1b. s	2.7	2.4	3.0	2.2	2.6	7.0	6.9	5.7	14.1	—	—	.1		.1	
Reserve Position in the Fund	1c. s							6.4	7.4	9.0						
Total Fund Cred.&Loans Outstg.	2tl	6.1	6.6	7.9	18.1	14.3	13.9			30.3	30.3	99.0	97.3	114.3	121.4	98.0
International Liquidity											*Millions of US Dollars Unless Otherwise Indicated:*						
Total Reserves minus Gold	1l. d	32.8	39.6	44.3	54.9	176.2	139.5	151.1	211.1	169.8	178.2	106.1	99.8	155.9	160.1	251.6
SDRs	1b. d	2.7	2.6	3.3	2.6	3.2	8.2	8.0	6.9	18.4	—	—	.1		.1	
Reserve Position in the Fund	1c. d	—						7.5	9.0	11.7						
Foreign Exchange	1d. d	30.1	37.0	41.0	52.3	173.0	131.3	135.6	195.2	139.7	178.2	106.1	99.7	155.9	160.0	251.6
Gold (Million Fine Troy Ounces)	1ad	.362	.384	.407	.407	.408	.410	.414	.602	.645	.683	.759	.829	.890	.914	.913
Gold (National Valuation)	1an d	12.8	13.6	15.4	15.5	17.2	17.3	17.6	25.4	27.2	28.8	31.2	34.2	36.1	37.0	37.9
Monetary Authorities: Other Liab.	4.. d	14.7	18.8	13.6	28.7	30.4	33.0	29.0	33.1	28.6	218.5	190.7	443.4	557.7	693.2	618.6
Deposit Money Banks: Assets	7a. d	2.9	4.1	6.4	5.1	7.2	14.9	21.0	22.9	23.9	32.8	43.2	36.8	18.0	34.0	25.0
Liabilities	7b. d	3.1	7.2	8.1	15.0	36.0	41.0	41.0	90.0	173.0	203.0	161.0	191.0	182.0	314.0	282.0
Other Banking Insts.: Assets	7e. d	.5	.3	.3	.9	−.9	.6	.3	.4	1.6	−1.3	−.5	−1.3	−1.5	−.9	4.9
Liabilities	7f. d	14.1	16.8	12.3	16.8	24.1	37.7	51.9	56.9	65.0	62.5	67.5	60.1	48.7	47.6	
Monetary Authorities											*Bolivianos through 1982; Thousands from 1983 to 1984;*						
Foreign Assets	11	541	573	1,196	1,384	3,868	3,142	3,853	4,726	4,004	5,534	3,482	3,989	41,972	‡120	2,814
Claims on Central Government	12a	1,711	2,039	2,805	3,330	3,666	5,681	8,941	12,173	13,842	21,593	32,163	43,298	241,541	‡726	13,115
Claims on State and Local Govts	12b	—	—	—	—	—	—	—	—	—	—	—	—	—	‡—	—
Claims on Nonfin.Pub.Enterprises	12c	—	—	—	—	—	—	—	—	—	—	—	—	—	‡—	—
Claims on Private Sector	12d	—	—	—	—	—	—	—	—	—	—	—	—	—	‡—	—
Claims on Deposit Money Banks	12e	132	102	262	601	621	935	765	791	1,212	1,775	2,618	3,230	13,334	‡27	542
Claims on Other Banking Insts	12f	84	179	218	459	648	661	973	1,454	1,461	1,151	1,363	1,540	7,704	‡27	428
Claims on Nonbank Financial Insts	12g															
Reserve Money	14	1,414	1,679	1,974	2,768	3,668	4,348	6,315	7,884	8,836	9,832	13,741	16,195	63,726	‡195	3,345
of which: Currency Outside DMBs	14a	1,153	1,281	1,598	2,073	2,746	3,054	3,968	4,864	5,810	7,211	9,461	10,852	39,093	‡125	2,888
Time, Savings,& Fgn.Currency Dep.	15	—	—	—	—	—	—	—	—	—	—	—	—	—	‡—	—
of which: Fgn. Currency Deposits	15b															
Foreign Liabilities	16c	109	173	222	613	546	569	330	439	587	5,476	5,851	9,970	105,586	‡144	1,974
Long-Term Foreign Liabilities	16cl	137	135	222	396	413	417	250	224	776	860	1,918	3,673	29,729	‡270	4,303
Central Government Deposits	16d	474	564	1,004	1,452	3,258	4,410	6,875	9,861	9,972	13,711	19,005	26,586	154,752	‡450	10,189
Central Govt. Lending Funds	16f	—	—	—	—	—	—	—	—	—	—	—	—	—	‡—	—
Capital Accounts	17a	—	—	—	—	—	—	—	—	—	—	—	—	—	‡—	—
Other Items (Net)	17r	334	344	1,060	545	918	676	762	737	348	174	−888	−4,368	−49,243	‡−159	−2,911
Deposit Money Banks											*Bolivianos through 1982; Thousands from 1983 to 1984;*						
Reserves	20	261	346	357	677	929	1,269	2,314	2,918	2,947	2,800	4,010	5,332	25,717	‡73	674
Foreign Assets	21	35	48	129	101	145	298	419	459	479	803	1,058	902	3,553	‡17	226
Claims on Central Government	22a	—	—	—	—	—	—	—	—	—	—	—	—	—	‡—	—
Claims on State and Local Govts	22b	—	—	—	—	—	—	—	—	—	—	—	—	—	‡—	—
Claims on Nonfin.Pub.Enterprises	22c	—	—	—	—	—	—	—	—	—	—	—	—	—	‡—	—
Claims on Private Sector	22d	692	798	1,143	1,830	3,005	3,713	5,136	7,365	9,746	12,241	14,350	18,546	69,281	‡141	1,526
Claims on Other Banking Insts	22f	—	—	—	—	—	—	—	—	—	—	—	—	—	‡—	—
Claims on Nonbank Financial Insts	22g	—	—	—	—	—	—	—	—	—	—	—	—	—	‡—	—
Demand Deposits	24	365	429	576	849	1,461	1,607	2,430	2,882	2,856	2,924	4,820	6,299	17,699	‡50	432
Time, Savings,& Fgn.Currency Dep.	25	379	491	631	804	1,189	1,952	3,401	4,957	5,643	6,317	8,419	11,820	39,206	‡88	684
of which: Fgn. Currency Deposits	25b	37	35	50	143	244	454	830	1,455	1,972	2,731	2,712	3,195	849	‡1	9
Foreign Liabilities	26c	37	86	162	252	552	794	807	1,610	2,666	2,561	1,970	2,197	17,889	‡112	1,859
Long-Term Foreign Liabilities	26cl	—	—	—	56	169	32	5	184	802	2,422	1,974	2,484	17,676	‡45	678
Central Government Deposits	26d	—	—	—	—	—	—	—	—	—	—	—	—	—	‡—	—
Credit from Monetary Authorities	26g	118	100	166	491	531	654	719	792	966	1,592	2,405	3,229	9,818	‡14	297
Liabilities to Other Banking Insts	26i	—	—	—	—	—	—	—	—	—	—	—	—	—	‡—	—
Liab. to Nonbank Financial Insts	26j	—	—	—	—	—	—	—	—	—	—	—	—	—	‡—	—
Capital Accounts	27a	136	163	238	290	377	573	793	1,243	1,347	1,458	1,936	1,993	11,347	‡26	698
Other Items (Net)	27r	−47	−77	−145	−133	−200	−332	−286	−927	−1,108	−1,429	−2,105	−3,243	−15,083	‡−104	−2,220
Monetary Survey											*Bolivianos through 1982; Thousands from 1983 to 1984;*						
Foreign Assets (Net)	31n	430	363	940	620	2,914	2,078	3,135	3,136	1,229	−1,699	−3,280	−7,276	−77,950	‡−119	−792
Domestic Credit	32	2,071	2,510	3,219	4,223	4,118	5,702	8,232	11,188	15,135	21,274	28,871	36,796	163,773	‡445	4,881
Claims on Central Govt. (Net)	32an	1,295	1,533	1,858	1,935	465	1,328	2,123	2,369	3,927	7,882	13,159	16,711	86,789	‡276	2,927
Claims on State and Local Govts	32b	—	—	—	—	—	—	—	—	—	—	—	—	—	‡—	—
Claims on Nonfin.Pub.Enterprises	32c	—	—	—	—	—	—	—	—	—	—	—	—	—	‡—	—
Claims on Private Sector	32d	692	798	1,143	1,830	3,005	3,713	5,136	7,365	9,746	12,241	14,350	18,546	69,281	‡141	1,526
Claims on Other Banking Insts	32f	84	179	218	459	648	661	973	1,454	1,461	1,151	1,363	1,540	7,704	‡27	428
Claims on Nonbank Financial Inst	32g	—	—	—	—	—	—	—	—	—	—	—	—	—	‡—	—
Money	34	1,532	1,766	2,210	2,969	4,257	4,759	6,497	7,855	8,831	10,304	14,694	17,587	57,827	‡178	3,370
Quasi-Money	35	381	493	634	807	1,192	1,956	3,405	4,960	5,650	6,328	8,430	11,831	39,375	‡88	684
Long-Term Foreign Liabilities	36cl	137	135	222	453	582	449	255	408	1,578	3,282	3,893	6,157	47,404	‡315	4,981
Central Govt. Lending Funds	36f	—	—	—	—	—	—	—	—	—	—	—	—	—	‡—	—
Liabilities to Other Banking Insts	36i	—	—	—	—	—	—	—	—	—	—	—	—	—	‡—	—
Liab. to Nonbank Financial Insts	36j	—	—	—	—	—	—	—	—	—	—	—	—	—	‡—	—
Capital Accounts	37a	136	163	238	290	377	573	793	1,243	1,347	1,458	1,936	1,993	11,347	‡26	698
Other Items (Net)	37r	314	316	855	326	624	43	417	−141	−1,041	−1,797	−3,361	−8,048	−70,130	‡−281	−5,644
Money plus Quasi-Money	35l	1,913	2,259	2,844	3,776	5,449	6,715	9,903	12,815	14,481	16,631	23,124	29,418	97,201	‡265	4,053

Exchange Rates

and per SDR thereafter: End of Period

and per US$ thereafter: End of Period (ae) Period Average (rf)

Period Averages

1985	1986	1987	1988	1989	1990	1991	1992	1993	1994	1995	1996	1997	1998	1999		
I1.859	2.352	3.135	3.324	3.916	4.837	5.357	5.631	6.147	6.854	7.336	7.456	7.239	7.948	8.221	Market Rate	aa
I1.692	1.923	2.210	2.470	2.980	3.400	3.745	4.095	4.475	4.695	4.935	5.185	5.365	5.645	5.990	Market Rate	ae
I.440	1.922	2.055	2.350	2.692	3.173	3.581	3.901	4.265	4.621	4.800	5.075	5.254	5.510	5.812	Market Rate	rf
9,881.3	249.9	233.9	204.4	179.0	151.5	134.1	123.2	112.6	103.9	100.0	94.6	91.4	87.1	82.6	Market Rate	ahx
109.8	3.3	3.8	5.4	10.6	21.4	28.7	39.3	61.3	97.9	100.0	98.2	100.9	100.5	103.4	Nominal Effective Exchange Rate	nec
496.1	145.6	139.5	134.4	127.5	106.6	110.5	108.9	108.2	102.7	100.0	105.0	109.4	114.9	118.4	Real Effective Exchange Rate	rec

Fund Position

End of Period

1985	1986	1987	1988	1989	1990	1991	1992	1993	1994	1995	1996	1997	1998	1999		
90.7	90.7	90.7	90.7	90.7	90.7	90.7	126.2	126.2	126.2	126.2	126.2	126.2	126.2	171.5	Quota	2f. s
—	2.0	—	—	—	.7	.1	.1	10.2	17.0	26.9	26.8	26.8	26.8	27.3	SDRs	1b. s
—	—	—	—	—	—	—	8.9	8.9	8.9	8.9	8.9	8.9	8.9	8.9	Reserve Position in the Fund	1c. s
74.9	157.3	130.9	155.3	191.6	180.7	171.1	181.1	160.5	180.5	180.1	192.0	183.9	187.6	180.0	Total Fund Cred.&Loans Outstg.	2tl

International Liquidity

End of Period

1985	1986	1987	1988	1989	1990	1991	1992	1993	1994	1995	1996	1997	1998	1999		
200.0	163.7	97.3	105.8	204.9	166.8	106.4	181.8	223.4	451.0	660.0	955.0	1,086.6	884.6	916.5	Total Reserves minus Gold	1l. d
—	2.5	—	—	—	1.0	.1	—	14.0	24.8	40.0	38.5	36.2	37.7	37.4	SDRs	1b. d
—	—	—	—	—	—	—	12.2	12.2	13.0	13.2	12.8	12.0	12.5	12.2	Reserve Position in the Fund	1c. d
200.0	161.2	97.3	105.8	204.9	165.8	106.3	169.5	197.2	413.2	606.8	903.7	1,038.5	834.4	866.9	Foreign Exchange	1d. d
.894	.894	.894	.894	.894	.894	.894	.894	.894	.893	.893	.939	.939	.939	.943	Gold (Million Fine Troy Ounces)	1ad
37.8	37.8	37.8	37.8	37.8	37.8	37.8	37.8	39.6	37.7	37.7	39.6	39.6	234.9	235.7	Gold (National Valuation)	1an d
260.0	362.3	371.5	407.5	520.4	435.4	414.0	486.9	432.1	503.9	545.9	659.8	597.1	578.8	542.0	Monetary Authorities: Other Liab.	4.. d
15.0	41.6	50.1	52.1	66.0	61.3	62.4	79.3	72.2	84.5	103.6	124.4	137.9	409.8	471.8	Deposit Money Banks: Assets	7a. d
156.6	157.0	89.5	67.0	50.1	60.0	101.0	189.0	318.1	476.8	544.0	540.9	721.4	879.7	744.6	Liabilities	7b. d
5.7	—	6.2	3.9	.8	1.8	.2	—	—	—	—	3.8	6.6	46.9	9.7	Other Banking Insts.: Assets	7e. d
54.0	30.5	31.6	6.2	7.1	5.6	4.1	4.1	4.1	—	—	2.5	2.4	8.1	13.3	Liabilities	7f. d

Monetary Authorities

Millions of Bolivianos Beginning 1985: End of Period

1985	1986	1987	1988	1989	1990	1991	1992	1993	1994	1995	1996	1997	1998	1999		
I463	963	I1,138	1,288	1,475	1,714	1,969	2,343	2,917	3,702	4,538	I7,032	7,735	8,217	8,906	Foreign Assets	11
I2,444	2,673	I2,375	2,797	3,208	4,189	5,108	5,906	4,700	5,009	4,328	I3,889	3,475	3,598	4,123	Claims on Central Government	12a
I—	—	I76	89	111	125	129	150	20	18	—	I—	—	—	—	Claims on State and Local Govts	12b
I—	—	I570	621	846	1,086	1,240	1,461	814	891	113	I119	—	—	—	Claims on Nonfin.Pub.Enterprises	12c
I—	—	—	—	—	—	—	—	—	—	—	I2	2	2	2	Claims on Private Sector	12d
I80	227	I361	631	942	1,039	1,538	1,789	1,392	2,405	3,032	I3,394	3,427	3,444	3,506	Claims on Deposit Money Banks	12e
I50	133	I179	223	327	404	—	—	—	—	—	I107	66	72	42	Claims on Other Banking Insts	12f
I—	—	I1	18	27	54	73	84	91	108	119	I—	—	—	206	Claims on Nonbank Financial Insts	12g
I201	380	I533	873	1,110	1,413	1,827	1,925	2,557	2,668	3,291	I4,194	5,036	3,989	4,441	Reserve Money	14
I174	294	I398	529	502	642	754	886	1,034	1,406	1,694	I1,802	2,061	2,193	2,173	of which: Currency Outside DMBs	14a
I—	—	I417	351	226	438	526	570	568	1,682	897	I547	452	451	994	Time, Savings,& Fgn.Currency Dep.	15
I—	—	I280	227	145	304	257	284	244	1,235	522	I573	442	446	990	of which: Fgn. Currency Deposits	15b
I304	367	I539	600	1,011	882	705	786	606	800	753	I1,432	1,331	1,491	1,480	Foreign Liabilities	16c
I391	700	I692	893	1,166	1,253	1,398	1,641	1,674	1,898	2,217	I2,175	1,987	1,830	1,782	Long-Term Foreign Liabilities	16cl
I2,649	3,211	I2,998	3,340	3,621	4,415	5,390	6,220	2,524	2,589	3,565	I4,460	3,591	3,489	3,642	Central Government Deposits	16d
I—	—	I81	263	637	1,033	1,369	1,741	2,238	2,684	1,240	I1,081	919	989	999	Central Govt. Lending Funds	16f
I—	—	I435	412	392	599	341	205	1,075	1,673	2,516	I1,057	1,442	3,287	3,857	Capital Accounts	17a
I-509	-662	I-997	-1,066	-1,226	-1,422	-1,499	-1,355	-1,307	-1,861	-2,347	I-405	-53	-193	-410	Other Items (Net)	17r

Deposit Money Banks

Millions of Bolivianos Beginning 1985: End of Period

1985	1986	1987	1988	1989	1990	1991	1992	1993	1994	1995	1996	1997	1998	1999		
I111	183	I111	251	563	664	974	1,030	1,539	1,133	1,450	I2,788	3,588	1,426	1,459	Reserves	20
I25	80	I111	129	197	209	234	325	323	397	511	I645	740	2,313	2,826	Foreign Assets	21
I—	—	I—	—	7	4	8	114	29	103	572	I1,522	1,590	1,322	924	Claims on Central Government	22a
I—	—	I—	—	—	—	—	—	—	—	—	I—	—	—	—	Claims on State and Local Govts	22b
I—	—	I—	—	—	—	—	—	—	—	—	I—	5	1	2	Claims on Nonfin.Pub.Enterprises	22c
I291	732	I1,086	1,543	2,311	3,320	5,093	7,599	10,740	13,452	15,152	I17,568	21,017	26,103	27,331	Claims on Private Sector	22d
I—	—	I—	—	—	—	—	—	—	—	—	I—	—	11	10	Claims on Other Banking Insts	22f
I—	—	I—	—	—	—	—	—	—	—	—	I153	131	309	291	Claims on Nonbank Financial Insts	22g
I24	69	I110	159	206	350	693	1,037	1,466	1,826	2,219	I867	1,036	1,124	1,031	Demand Deposits	24
I89	448	I643	978	1,537	2,349	3,723	5,167	7,175	7,809	8,887	I13,542	15,916	18,237	19,203	Time, Savings,& Fgn.Currency Dep.	25
I36	282	I510	841	1,418	2,203	3,564	5,039	7,036	7,568	8,700	I13,201	15,546	17,799	18,737	of which: Fgn. Currency Deposits	25b
I117	150	I144	129	39	84	164	402	1,028	1,570	1,955	I2,088	2,717	3,364	2,868	Foreign Liabilities	26c
I148	152	I54	36	111	120	215	372	396	669	730	I717	1,153	1,602	1,592	Long-Term Foreign Liabilities	26cl
I—	—	I10	13	14	18	20	38	49	74	179	I935	1,319	260	97	Central Government Deposits	26d
I53	144	I235	472	829	929	1,014	1,297	1,334	2,260	2,984	I3,830	3,721	3,499	3,920	Credit from Monetary Authorities	26g
I—	—	I—	—	—	—	—	—	—	—	—	I—	—	95	93	Liabilities to Other Banking Insts	26i
I—	—	I—	—	—	—	—	—	—	—	—	I—	310	520	894	Liab. to Nonbank Financial Insts	26j
I165	206	I421	500	668	766	976	1,283	1,577	1,899	2,043	I2,352	2,821	3,822	4,626	Capital Accounts	27a
I-170	-174	I-309	-364	-325	-417	-495	-527	-393	-1,023	-1,312	I-1,655	-1,921	-1,037	-1,482	Other Items (Net)	27r

Monetary Survey

Millions of Bolivianos Beginning 1985: End of Period

1985	1986	1987	1988	1989	1990	1991	1992	1993	1994	1995	1996	1997	1998	1999		
I67	526	I565	688	622	957	1,335	1,480	1,607	1,730	2,341	I4,157	4,427	5,675	7,384	Foreign Assets (Net)	31n
I136	327	I1,279	1,937	3,202	4,749	6,242	9,056	13,821	16,917	16,541	I17,964	21,377	27,669	29,192	Domestic Credit	32
I-205	-538	I-632	-556	-420	-240	-294	-238	2,156	2,449	1,156	I16	155	1,171	1,308	Claims on Central Govt. (Net)	32an
I—	—	I76	89	111	125	129	150	20	18	—	I—	—	—	—	Claims on State and Local Govts	32b
I—	—	I570	621	846	1,086	1,240	1,461	814	891	113	I119	5	1	2	Claims on Nonfin.Pub.Enterprises	32c
I291	732	I1,086	1,543	2,311	3,320	5,093	7,599	10,740	13,452	15,152	I17,570	21,019	26,105	27,333	Claims on Private Sector	32d
I50	133	I179	223	327	404	—	—	—	—	—	I107	66	83	52	Claims on Other Banking Insts	32f
I—	—	I1	18	27	54	73	84	91	108	119	I153	131	309	497	Claims on Nonbank Financial Inst	32g
I198	369	I516	698	715	997	1,447	1,923	2,499	3,232	3,913	I3,055	3,636	3,895	3,670	Money	34
I89	448	I1,060	1,329	1,762	2,787	4,249	5,737	7,743	9,490	9,784	I14,089	16,368	18,688	20,197	Quasi-Money	35
I539	852	I746	929	1,277	1,373	1,613	2,013	2,069	2,567	2,947	I2,892	3,140	3,432	3,374	Long-Term Foreign Liabilities	36cl
I—	—	I140	356	760	1,172	1,502	1,901	2,238	2,684	1,240	I1,081	919	989	999	Central Govt. Lending Funds	36f
I—	—	I—	—	—	—	—	—	—	—	—	I—	—	95	93	Liabilities to Other Banking Insts	36i
I—	—	I—	—	—	—	—	—	—	—	—	I—	310	520	894	Liab. to Nonbank Financial Insts	36j
I165	206	I857	912	1,060	1,365	1,317	1,488	2,652	3,573	4,559	I3,409	4,263	7,109	8,483	Capital Accounts	37a
I-788	-1,022	I-1,474	-1,599	-1,748	-1,988	-2,552	-2,525	-1,773	-2,899	-3,560	I-2,406	-2,832	-1,383	-1,135	Other Items (Net)	37r
I287	817	I1,576	2,027	2,477	3,784	5,696	7,660	10,242	12,722	13,697	I17,145	20,004	22,583	23,867	Money plus Quasi-Money	35l

Bolivia

		1970	1971	1972	1973	1974	1975	1976	1977	1978	1979	1980	1981	1982	1983	1984
Other Banking Institutions											*Bolivianos through 1982; Thousands from 1983 to 1984;*					
Reserves	40	22	48	33	39	59	94	102	124	172	178	283	283	1,100	‡ 5	70
Foreign Assets	41	5	4	5	17	−17	11	5	8	32	−31	−13	−32	−300	‡—	43
Claims on Central Government	42a	—	—	—	—	—	—	—	—	—	—	—	—	—	‡—	—
Claims on State and Local Govts	42b	—	—	—	—	—	—	—	—	—	—	—	—	—	‡—	—
Claims on Nonfin.Pub.Enterprises	42c	—	—	—	—	—	—	—	—	—	—	—	—	—	‡—	—
Claims on Private Sector	42d	369	388	551	949	1,421	1,905	2,335	2,887	3,275	3,889	4,664	5,529	27,800	‡ 74	1,240
Claims on Deposit Money Banks	42e	—	—	—	—	—	—	—	—	—	—	—	—	—	‡—	—
Claims on Nonbank Financial Insts	42g	—	—	—	—	—	—	—	—	—	—	—	—	—	‡—	—
Demand Deposits	44	—	—	—	—	—	—	—	—	—	—	—	—	—	‡—	—
Time, Savings,& Fgn.Currency Dep.	45	30	36	28	157	47	187	217	270	330	236	376	629	2,100	‡ 6	102
of which: Fgn. Currency Deposits	45b	—	—	—	—	—	—	—	—	—	—	—	—	—	‡—	—
Foreign Liabilities	46c	—	—	—	—	—	—	—	—	—	—	—	—	—	‡—	—
Long-Term Foreign Liabilities	46cl	167	200	245	336	483	754	1,038	1,137	1,301	1,532	1,655	1,670	11,900	‡ 25	418
Central Government Deposits	46d	27	22	22	64	83	116	115	45	72	80	129	119	800	‡ 3	80
Credit from Monetary Authorities	46g	61	156	207	340	614	823	916	1,289	1,477	1,127	1,541	1,876	4,000	‡ 19	409
Credit from Deposit Money Banks	46h	—	—	—	—	—	—	—	—	—	—	—	—	—	‡—	—
Liabs. to Nonbank Financial Insts	46j	—	—	—	—	—	—	—	—	—	—	—	—	—	‡—	—
Capital Accounts	47a	120	114	105	118	89	292	455	700	952	1,811	1,973	1,792	2,900	‡ 8	684
Other Items (Net)	47r	−9	−89	−18	−9	147	−162	−300	−423	−653	−750	−741	−306	6,900	‡ 17	−340
Banking Survey											*Bolivianos through 1982; Thousands from 1983 to 1984;*					
Foreign Assets (Net)	51n	435	366	946	637	2,897	2,089	3,140	3,144	1,261	−1,730	−3,294	−7,308	−78,250	‡ −119	−749
Domestic Credit	52	2,329	2,697	3,530	4,650	4,808	6,830	9,478	12,576	16,876	23,933	32,043	40,667	183,070	‡ 488	5,612
Claims on Central Govt. (Net)	52an	1,268	1,511	1,836	1,871	382	1,212	2,008	2,324	3,855	7,803	13,030	16,592	85,989	‡ 272	2,847
Claims on State and Local Govts	52b	—	—	—	—	—	—	—	—	—	—	—	—	—	‡—	—
Claims on Nonfin.Pub.Enterprises	52c	—	—	—	—	—	—	—	—	—	—	—	—	—	‡—	—
Claims on Private Sector	52d	1,061	1,186	1,694	2,779	4,426	5,618	7,471	10,252	13,021	16,131	19,014	24,075	97,081	‡ 215	2,766
Claims on Nonbank Financial Inst	52g	—	—	—	—	—	—	—	—	—	—	—	—	—	‡—	—
Liquid Liabilities	55l	1,921	2,247	2,840	3,894	5,437	6,807	10,018	12,961	14,639	16,689	23,217	29,764	98,201	‡ 266	4,086
Long-Term Foreign Liabilities	56cl	305	335	467	789	1,064	1,203	1,293	1,545	2,878	4,814	5,548	7,827	59,304	‡ 340	5,399
Central Govt. Lending Funds	56f	—	—	—	—	—	—	—	—	—	—	—	—	—	‡—	—
Liab. to Nonbank Financial Insts	56j	—	—	—	—	—	—	—	—	—	—	—	—	—	‡—	—
Capital Accounts	57a	256	277	343	407	467	866	1,248	1,942	2,299	3,270	3,909	3,785	14,247	‡ 34	1,382
Other Items (Net)	57r	281	204	827	197	738	44	59	−728	−1,679	−2,571	−3,924	−8,017	−66,932	‡ −272	−6,003
Money (National Definitions)											*Bolivianos through 1982; Thousands from 1983 to 1984;*					
Reserve Money	19ma	....	....	....	....	....	....	....	7,883	8,836	9,841	13,741	16,195	63,726	‡ 195	3,345
M1	59ma	....	....	....	....	....	....	....	7,730	8,633	10,085	14,238	17,153	56,555	‡ 175	3,296
M'1	59mb	....	....	....	....	....	....	....	7,730	8,633	10,085	14,238	17,153	56,555	‡ 175	3,296
M2	59mc	....	....	....	....	....	....	....	10,117	11,172	12,676	18,556	23,895	75,246	‡ 227	3,603
M'2	59md	....	....	....	....	....	....	....	10,117	11,172	12,676	18,556	23,895	75,246	‡ 227	3,603
M3	59me	....	....	....	....	....	....	....	11,394	12,447	13,694	20,249	26,346	97,101	‡ 265	3,975
M'3	59mf	....	....	....	....	....	....	....	12,933	14,537	16,684	23,092	29,574	98,534	‡ 266	3,986
M4	59mg	....	....	....	....	....	....	....	....	....	....	....	....	....	....	....
M'4	59mh	....	....	....	....	....	....	....	....	....	....	....	....	....	....	....
Interest Rates														*Percent Per Annum*		
Discount Rate *(End of Period)*	60	12.00	13.00	11.00	11.00	13.00	13.00	13.00	13.00	13.00	18.00	19.90	26.00	37.00	61.00	149.00
Discount Rate (Fgn.Cur.)*(End per)*	60.. f	....	....	....	....	....	....	....	....	....	....	....	....	....	....	....
Money Market Rate	60b	....	....	....	....	....	....	....	....	....	....	....	....	....	....	....
Money Market Rate (Fgn.Cur)	60b. f	....	....	....	....	....	....	....	....	....	....	....	....	....	....	....
Treasury Bill Rate	60c	....	....	....	....	....	....	....	....	....	....	....	....	....	....	....
Treasury Bill Rate (Fgn.Currency)	60c. f	....	....	....	....	....	....	....	....	....	....	....	....	....	....	....
Savings Rate	60k	....	....	....	....	....	....	....	....	....	....	....	....	....	43.00	110.00
Savings Rate (Fgn.Currency)	60k. f	....	....	....	....	....	....	....	....	....	....	....	....	....	....	....
Deposit Rate	60l	....	....	....	....	....	....	....	....	....	16.00	18.00	28.42	30.33	39.83	108.33
Deposit Rate (Fgn.Currency)	60l. f	....	....	....	....	....	....	....	....	....	....	....	....	....	....	....
Lending Rate	60p	....	....	....	....	....	....	....	....	....	27.00	28.00	42.50	45.00	56.83	120.67
Lending Rate (Fgn.Currency)	60p. f	....	....	....	....	....	....	....	....	....	....	....	....	....	....	....
Prices, Production, Labor														*Index Numbers (1995=100):*		
Consumer Prices (1995=100,000)	64.a	.08	.09	.09	.12	.20	.21	.22	.24	.26	.32	.46	.61	1.37	5.16	71.24
Consumer Prices	64															.1
Crude Petroleum Production	66aa	85.2	127.6	154.3	166.8	160.4	141.9	143.6	122.5	114.5	98.4	84.1	78.2	86.3	78.1	73.7
															Number in Thousands:	
Labor Force	67d	....	....	....	....	....	....	....	....	....	....	....	....	....	....	....
Employment	67e	....	....	....	....	....	....	....	....	....	....	....	....	....	....	....
Unemployment	67c	....	....	....	....	....	....	....	....	....	....	....	....	....	....	....
Unemployment Rate (%)	67r	....	....	....	....	....	....	....	....	....	....	....	....	....	....	....
International Transactions														*Millions of US Dollars*		
Exports	70..d	190.2	181.1	201.2	260.5	556.5	444.1	568.2	631.7	628.8	759.8	942.2	912.4	827.7	755.2	724.5
Tin	70q.d	108.1	105.9	113.5	131.0	230.1	171.4	216.3	328.8	374.2	395.6	378.2	343.1	278.4	207.9	247.8
Zinc	70t.d	14.3	15.3	15.4	26.0	37.7	40.3	39.1	44.7	31.5	42.7	36.7	40.4	38.4	33.4	37.3
Imports, c.i.f.	71..d	159.2	169.6	185.4	230.2	390.0	557.9	554.6	617.9	807.8	894.3	665.4	917.1	554.1	576.7	488.5
Imports, f.o.b.	71.vd	135.2	144.2	142.8	194.0	364.0	531.5	562.3	644.0	689.8	673.6	574.4	827.7	496.0	496.0	412.3
															1995=100	
Volume of Exports	72	142.7	156.0	161.3	95.9	95.5	89.6	99.1	105.1	97.3	97.8	91.1	99.3	90.1	80.1	80.4
Tin	72q	195.5	212.6	213.0	199.5	203.4	175.0	200.9	218.4	208.9	186.9	158.2	170.3	153.8	112.7	142.4
Zinc	72t	31.7	31.0	27.1	33.8	33.4	33.8	33.6	41.8	35.5	36.8	31.5	30.5	30.4	28.2	25.1
															1995=100:	
Unit Value of Exports	74..d	21.1	17.1	17.8	49.5	81.8	82.9	88.9	102.0	110.8	144.4	206.0	196.3	186.3	196.7	193.8
Tin	74q.d	62.4	56.2	60.2	74.1	127.7	110.6	121.5	169.9	202.2	238.8	269.7	227.4	204.3	208.3	196.4
Zinc	74t.d	29.8	32.6	37.7	50.7	74.4	78.9	77.1	70.7	58.7	76.7	76.9	87.7	83.5	78.2	98.0

1985	1986	1987	1988	1989	1990	1991	1992	1993	1994	1995	1996	1997	1998	1999		

Other Banking Institutions

Millions of Bolivianos Beginning 1985: End of Period

1985	1986	1987	1988	1989	1990	1991	1992	1993	1994	1995	1996	1997	1998	1999		
I2	6	I4	15	8	7	3	—	—	1	—	I160	192	80	361	Reserves	40
I13	14	I14	10	3	6	1	—	—	—	—	I20	35	265	58	Foreign Assets	41
I—	I—	I—	—	—	1	1	2	3	3	3	I106	91	118	14	Claims on Central Government	42a
I—	I—	—	—	—	—	—	—	—	—	—	I—	—	—	—	Claims on State and Local Govts	42b
—	—	—	—	—	—	—	—	—	—	—	I—	—	—	—	Claims on Nonfin.Pub.Enterprises	42c
I160	244	I290	309	318	390	390	393	389	349	386	I2,226	3,249	3,885	3,703	Claims on Private Sector	42d
I—	I—	—	—	—	—	—	—	—	—	—	I—	—	140	86	Claims on Deposit Money Banks	42e
I—	—	—	—	—	—	—	—	—	—	—	I4	4	26	57	Claims on Nonbank Financial Insts	42g
I—	—	I1	—	—	—	—	—	—	—	—	I—	1	1	1	Demand Deposits	44
I18	12	I24	20	2	1	2	1	1	1	—	I2,305	3,185	3,693	3,480	Time, Savings,& Fgn.Currency Dep.	45
I—	—	I23	20	2	1	2	1	1	1	—	I2,251	3,114	3,619	3,429	*of which: Fgn. Currency Deposits*	45b
I—	—	I10	12	—	5	—	—	—	—	—	I2	6	12	6	Foreign Liabilities	46c
I91	97	I58	66	19	19	21	17	18	19	—	I11	7	34	74	Long-Term Foreign Liabilities	46cl
I10	3	I6	7	6	2	1	1	1	1	—	I6	14	16	8	Central Government Deposits	46d
I56	120	I26	33	61	92	112	307	292	272	548	I4	6	8	11	Credit from Monetary Authorities	46g
I—	—	I—	—	—	—	—	—	—	—	—	I86	100	72	55	Credit from Deposit Money Banks	46h
I—	—	—	—	—	—	—	—	—	—	—	I245	303	294	301	Liabs. to Nonbank Financial Insts	46j
I100	135	I328	366	325	434	257	73	34	21	-289	I447	579	775	819	Capital Accounts	47a
I-100	-103	I-144	-169	-82	-149	2	-5	46	40	130	I-592	-630	-391	-476	Other Items (Net)	47r

Banking Survey

Millions of Bolivianos Beginning 1985: End of Period

1985	1986	1987	1988	1989	1990	1991	1992	1993	1994	1995	1996	1997	1998	1999		
I80	540	I568	685	625	958	1,336	1,480	1,607	1,730	2,341	I4,175	4,456	5,928	7,436	Foreign Assets (Net)	51n
I235	435	I1,384	2,017	3,188	4,734	6,631	9,450	14,211	17,269	16,930	I20,187	24,641	31,599	32,907	Domestic Credit	52
I-215	-541	I-638	-563	-426	-241	-295	-237	2,158	2,452	1,160	I116	232	1,273	1,314	Claims on Central Govt. (Net)	52an
I—	—	I76	89	111	125	129	150	20	18	—	I—	—	—	—	Claims on State and Local Govts	52b
I—	—	I570	621	846	1,086	1,240	1,461	814	891	113	I119	5	1	2	Claims on Nonfin.Pub.Enterprises	52c
I451	976	I1,376	1,852	2,629	3,710	5,483	7,992	11,128	13,801	15,538	I19,796	24,268	29,991	31,037	Claims on Private Sector	52d
I—	—	I1	18	27	54	73	84	91	108	119	I157	135	335	554	Claims on Nonbank Financial Inst	52g
I303	823	I1,596	2,032	2,471	3,778	5,694	7,661	10,243	12,723	13,697	I19,291	22,998	26,198	26,987	Liquid Liabilities	55l
I630	949	I803	996	1,295	1,392	1,634	2,029	2,087	2,587	2,947	I2,903	3,147	3,465	3,448	Long-Term Foreign Liabilities	56cl
I—	—	I149	356	771	1,187	1,512	2,023	2,238	2,684	1,240	I1,081	919	989	999	Central Govt. Lending Funds	56f
I—	—	I—	—	—	—	—	—	—	—	—	I245	613	813	1,195	Liab. to Nonbank Financial Insts	56j
I265	341	I1,184	1,278	1,384	1,799	1,574	1,561	2,686	3,593	4,270	I3,856	4,842	7,885	9,303	Capital Accounts	57a
I-882	-1,138	I-1,780	-1,959	-2,108	-2,464	-2,448	-2,344	-1,435	-2,588	-2,882	I-3,015	-3,422	-1,822	-1,589	Other Items (Net)	57r

Money (National Definitions)

Millions of Bolivianos Beginning 1985: End of Period

1985	1986	1987	1988	1989	1990	1991	1992	1993	1994	1995	1996	1997	1998	1999		
I201	384	519	693	816	1,073	1,411	1,776	2,352	2,760	3,105	3,963	4,731	3,560	3,685	*Reserve Money*	19ma
I199	363	506	663	647	830	1,039	1,236	1,417	1,890	2,333	2,580	3,006	3,276	3,152	*M1*	59ma
I199	363	508	685	706	988	1,447	1,924	2,499	3,232	3,913	4,768	5,682	6,342	5,892	*M'1*	59mb
I233	452	616	784	744	947	1,134	1,312	1,499	1,997	2,425	2,791	3,300	3,589	3,479	*M2*	59mc
I233	452	619	826	904	1,358	1,956	2,646	3,544	4,534	5,460	8,028	10,163	11,533	11,211	*M'2*	59md
I256	532	639	800	765	976	1,198	1,364	1,555	2,132	2,520	2,983	3,470	3,766	3,644	*M3*	59me
I290	822	1,175	1,683	2,245	3,339	5,171	7,092	9,675	11,767	12,880	18,430	21,983	25,118	25,776	*M'3*	59mf
....	....	....	800	765	976	1,198	1,364	1,555	2,136	2,523	3,106	3,476	3,766	3,645	*M4*	59mg
			1,683	2,245	3,339	5,171	7,092	9,675	12,036	13,330	18,948	22,353	25,552	26,846	*M'4*	59mh

Interest Rates

Percent Per Annum

1985	1986	1987	1988	1989	1990	1991	1992	1993	1994	1995	1996	1997	1998	1999		
....	....	....	....	....	....	....	....	....	....	....	16.50	13.25	14.10	12.50	Discount Rate *(End of Period)*	60
....	....	....	....	....	....	....	....	....	....	....	9.89	8.58	9.30	9.04	Discount Rate *(Fgn.Cur.)(End per)*	60..f
....	....	....	....	....	....	....	....	....	....	22.42	20.27	13.97	12.57	13.49	Money Market Rate	60b
....	....	....	....	....	....	....	....	....	....	14.16	9.54	7.85	9.26	8.29	Money Market Rate (Fgn.Cur)	60b.f
....	....	....	....	....	....	....	....	....	17.89	24.51	19.93	13.65	12.33	14.07	Treasury Bill Rate	60c
....	....	....	....	....	....	....	....	....	8.22	13.20	9.89	7.15	7.48	7.84	Treasury Bill Rate (Fgn.Currency)	60c.f
99.60	29.57	24.69	22.76	19.04	18.67	18.65	20.28	20.92	17.46	16.52	16.43	14.30	12.08	10.79	Savings Rate	60k
....	....	....	7.23	7.42	8.48	8.35	8.14	7.97	7.16	7.03	7.20	6.60	5.93	5.50	Savings Rate (Fgn.Currency)	60k.f
68.75	I33.39	30.35	27.74	23.67	23.83	23.78	23.22	22.18	18.43	18.87	19.16	14.73	12.82	12.26	Deposit Rate	60l
11.20	14.97	16.33	16.74	15.69	14.70	12.93	11.40	11.19	9.89	10.36	10.13	8.32	7.96	8.78	Deposit Rate (Fgn.Currency)	60l.f
172.15	I65.78	49.41	39.79	37.27	41.81	41.15	45.51	53.88	55.57	51.02	55.97	50.05	39.41	35.37	Lending Rate	60p
17.80	23.01	26.75	25.67	24.34	23.03	21.51	19.13	18.46	16.46	16.86	17.64	16.48	15.66	16.03	Lending Rate (Fgn.Currency)	60p.f

Prices, Production, Labor

Period Averages

1985	1986	1987	1988	1989	1990	1991	1992	1993	1994	1995	1996	1997	1998	1999		
....														....	Consumer Prices (1995=100,000)	64.a
8.4	31.8	36.4	42.2	48.6	57.0	69.2	I77.5	84.1	90.8	100.0	112.4	117.7	126.8	129.5	Consumer Prices	64
70.0	62.0	66.6	67.8	70.3	73.8	78.2	74.9	78.4	90.7	100.0	103.2	107.5	133.0	114.5	Crude Petroleum Production	66aa

Period Averages

1985	1986	1987	1988	1989	1990	1991	1992	1993	1994	1995	1996	1997	1998	1999		
....	....	....	....	....	....	....	2,365	....	....	....	1,369	3,645	....	....	Labor Force	67d
1,686	1,661	1,670	1,769	1,662	1,843	I988	1,016	1,091	1,195	1,257	1,355	....	....	....	Employment	67e
58	46	78	....	I95	72	62	59	70	39	47	59	....	....	....	Unemployment	67c
....	....	....	10.0	7.3	5.9	5.5	6.0	3.1	3.6	4.2	....	....	....	....	Unemployment Rate (%)	67r

International Transactions

Millions of US Dollars

1985	1986	1987	1988	1989	1990	1991	1992	1993	1994	1995	1996	1997	1998	1999		
623.4	637.8	569.5	600.2	821.8	926.1	848.6	710.1	727.5	1,032.4	1,100.7	1,137.1	1,166.5	1,103.9	1,033.4	Exports	70..d
186.7	103.3	68.9	76.9	126.5	106.5	99.7	107.3	83.3	91.1	88.6	85.5	75.1	59.9	64.8	Tin	70q.d
29.5	28.0	32.7	60.2	132.2	146.0	139.7	173.0	119.5	105.3	151.3	153.4	119.3	92.3	89.8	Zinc	70t.d
690.9	674.0	766.3	590.5	610.9	687.2	969.5	1,090.3	1,205.9	1,209.0	1,423.8	1,635.0	1,850.9	1,983.0	1,227.3	Imports, c.i.f.	71..d
565.1	564.0	646.3	495.1	563.1	633.5	893.7	1,005.0	1,111.6	1,121.7	1,263.2	1,450.5	1,698.1	1,824.4	1,076.3	Imports, f.o.b.	71.v d

1995=100

1985	1986	1987	1988	1989	1990	1991	1992	1993	1994	1995	1996	1997	1998	1999		
68.8	75.0	66.6	72.3	90.7	99.2	106.8	107.7	95.1	93.2	100.0	102.4	107.2	102.1	93.3	Volume of Exports	72
113.4	118.2	71.0	75.9	102.3	119.1	125.4	123.9	112.4	118.5	100.0	98.5	101.0	80.2	88.8	Tin	72q
23.1	24.3	27.0	36.8	54.9	67.3	87.1	97.1	84.4	73.1	100.0	103.3	104.9	104.4	97.3	Zinc	72t

Indices of Unit Values in US Dollars

1985	1986	1987	1988	1989	1990	1991	1992	1993	1994	1995	1996	1997	1998	1999		
178.5	143.7	135.3	135.6	157.9	143.0	127.7	108.3	89.1	94.8	100.0	98.6	75.2	67.3	68.1	Unit Value of Exports	74..d
185.8	98.7	109.5	114.3	139.6	100.9	89.7	83.6	83.6	86.8	100.0	98.0	83.9	84.3	82.4	Tin	74q.d
84.2	76.3	79.9	108.0	159.1	143.3	106.0	117.8	93.5	95.2	100.0	98.1	75.1	58.4	61.0	Zinc	74t.d

Bolivia

218		1970	1971	1972	1973	1974	1975	1976	1977	1978	1979	1980	1981	1982	1983	1984
Balance of Payments																*Millions of US Dollars:*
Current Account, n.i.e.	78al *d*	....	....	....	....	....	....	–53.5	–117.9	–331.5	–397.0	–6.4	–468.5	–174.4	–141.6	–178.5
Goods: Exports f.o.b.	78aa *d*	....	....	....	....	....	....	563.0	634.3	627.3	759.8	942.2	912.4	827.7	755.1	724.5
Goods: Imports f.o.b.	78ab *d*	....	....	....	....	....	....	–512.3	–579.0	–723.9	–738.4	–574.4	–827.7	–496.0	–496.0	–412.3
Trade Balance	78ac *d*	....	....	....	....	....	....	50.7	55.3	–96.6	21.4	367.8	84.7	331.7	259.1	312.2
Services: Credit	78ad *d*	....	....	....	....	....	....	60.4	60.8	76.2	105.2	87.9	93.0	82.3	103.0	93.5
Services: Debit	78ae *d*	....	....	....	....	....	....	–147.1	–181.9	–224.2	–392.5	–258.5	–319.8	–221.7	–244.6	–253.5
Balance on Goods & Services	78af *d*	....	....	....	....	....	....	–36.0	–65.8	–244.6	–265.9	197.2	–142.1	192.3	117.5	152.2
Income: Credit	78ag *d*	....	....	....	....	....	....	12.8	5.6	2.5	8.4	15.6	16.2	8.4	40.9	30.0
Income: Debit	78ah *d*	....	....	....	....	....	....	–44.3	–72.7	–116.4	–190.7	–278.7	–378.4	–419.1	–402.7	–444.9
Balance on Gds, Serv. & Inc.	78ai *d*	....	....	....	....	....	....	–67.5	–132.9	–358.5	–448.2	–65.9	–504.3	–218.4	–244.3	–262.7
Current Transfers, n.i.e.: Credit	78aj *d*	....	....	....	....	....	....	16.0	18.0	30.0	53.0	62.0	38.0	46.2	106.8	87.0
Current Transfers: Debit	78ak *d*	....	....	....	....	....	....	–2.0	–3.0	–3.0	–1.8	–2.5	–2.2	–2.2	–4.1	–2.8
Capital Account, n.i.e.	78bc *d*	....	....	....	....	....	....	—	—	—	—	—	2.8	.7	2.7	3.6
Capital Account, n.i.e.: Credit	78ba *d*	....	....	....	....	....	....	—	—	—	—	—	3.0	1.0	3.0	3.8
Capital Account: Debit	78bb *d*	....	....	....	....	....	....	—	—	—	—	—	–.2	–.3	–.3	–.2
Financial Account, n.i.e.	78bj *d*	....	....	....	....	....	....	168.1	227.3	350.4	301.9	27.2	438.5	–49.4	–554.0	29.0
Direct Investment Abroad	78bd *d*	....	....	....	....	....	....	—	—	—	—	–.5	–.1	–.1	–.1	—
Dir. Invest. in Rep. Econ., n.i.e.	78be *d*	....	....	....	....	....	....	–8.1	–1.2	11.5	67.0	91.0	148.9	61.2	13.0	13.0
Portfolio Investment Assets	78bf *d*	....	....	....	....	....	....	—	—	—	2.5	–2.6	—	—	—	—
Equity Securities	78bk *d*	....	....	....	....	....	....	—	—	—	2.5	–2.6	—	—	—	—
Debt Securities	78bl *d*	....	....	....	....	....	....	—	—	—	—	—	—	—	—	—
Portfolio Investment Liab., n.i.e.	78bg *d*	....	....	....	....	....	....	—	—	—	–1.1	–.9	–.9	–15.0	–1.8	–.9
Equity Securities	78bm *d*	....	....	....	....	....	....	—	—	—	—	—	—	—	—	—
Debt Securities	78bn *d*	....	....	....	....	....	....	—	—	—	–1.1	–.9	–.9	–15.0	–1.8	–.9
Financial Derivatives Assets	78bw *d*	....	....	....	....	....	....	....	....	....	....	....	....	....	....	....
Financial Derivatives Liabilities	78bx *d*	....	....	....	....	....	....	....	....	....	....	....	....	....	....	....
Other Investment Assets	78bh *d*	....	....	....	....	....	....	–20.1	–135.1	–63.7	–8.8	–15.3	–4.0	–156.4	–101.5	178.6
Monetary Authorities	78bo *d*	....	....	....	....	....	....	....	....	....	....	....	....	....	....	....
General Government	78bp *d*	....	....	....	....	....	....	–2.1	–10.0	–9.1	–3.1	–1.6	–10.6	–28.4	–4.1	–6.6
Banks	78bq *d*	....	....	....	....	....	....	–6.0	–2.1	–4.6	–5.7	–13.7	6.6	19.3	.9	–3.3
Other Sectors	78br *d*	....	....	....	....	....	....	–12.0	–123.0	–50.0	—	—	—	–147.3	–98.3	188.5
Other Investment Liab., n.i.e.	78bi *d*	....	....	....	....	....	....	196.3	363.6	402.6	242.3	–44.5	294.6	60.9	–463.6	–161.7
Monetary Authorities	78bs *d*	....	....	....	....	....	....	–11.0	3.5	–15.3	67.6	–2.5	214.0	153.3	–239.1	–16.2
General Government	78bt *d*	....	....	....	....	....	....	148.5	180.5	103.4	81.7	66.9	78.5	–43.0	–118.1	–119.9
Banks	78bu *d*	....	....	....	....	....	....	1.0	40.1	55.2	59.7	–59.7	7.8	–25.1	–32.1	5.0
Other Sectors	78bv *d*	....	....	....	....	....	....	57.8	139.5	259.3	33.3	–49.2	–5.7	–24.3	–74.3	–30.6
Net Errors and Omissions	78ca *d*	....	....	....	....	....	....	–63.4	–79.0	–84.9	–36.1	–456.0	–260.3	4.1	65.5	–18.1
Overall Balance	78cb *d*	....	....	....	....	....	....	51.2	30.4	–66.0	–131.2	–435.2	–287.5	–219.0	–627.4	–164.0
Reserves and Related Items	79da *d*	....	....	....	....	....	....	–51.2	–30.4	66.0	131.2	435.2	287.5	219.0	627.4	164.0
Reserve Assets	79db *d*	....	....	....	....	....	....	–35.1	–67.4	64.8	–18.5	96.1	—	–46.5	–49.3	–95.0
Use of Fund Credit and Loans	79dc *d*	....	....	....	....	....	....	–16.1	—	38.2	—	89.5	–2.0	18.6	8.3	–24.0
Exceptional Financing	79de *d*	....	....	....	....	....	....	—	37.0	–37.0	149.7	249.7	289.6	246.9	668.4	282.9
International Investment Position																*Millions of US Dollars*
Assets	79aa *d*	....	....	....	....	....	....	....	....	....	....	....	....	....	....	....
Direct Investment Abroad	79ab *d*	....	....	....	....	....	....	....	....	....	....	....	....	....	....	....
Portfolio Investment	79ac *d*	....	....	....	....	....	....	....	....	....	....	....	....	....	....	....
Equity Securities	79ad *d*	....	....	....	....	....	....	....	....	....	....	....	....	....	....	....
Debt Securities	79ae *d*	....	....	....	....	....	....	....	....	....	....	....	....	....	....	....
Financial Derivatives	79al *d*	....	....	....	....	....	....	....	....	....	....	....	....	....	....	....
Other Investment	79af *d*	....	....	....	....	....	....	....	....	....	....	....	....	....	....	....
Monetary Authorities	79ag *d*	....	....	....	....	....	....	....	....	....	....	....	....	....	....	....
General Government	79ah *d*	....	....	....	....	....	....	....	....	....	....	....	....	....	....	....
Banks	79ai *d*	....	....	....	....	....	....	....	....	....	....	....	....	....	....	....
Other Sectors	79aj *d*	....	....	....	....	....	....	....	....	....	....	....	....	....	....	....
Reserve Assets	79ak *d*	....	....	....	....	....	....	....	....	....	....	138.1	146.9	195.3	245.4	341.3
Liabilities	79la *d*	....	....	....	....	....	....	....	....	....	....	....	....	....	....	....
Dir. Invest. in Rep. Economy	79lb *d*	....	....	....	....	....	....	....	....	....	....	....	....	....	....	....
Portfolio Investment	79lc *d*	....	....	....	....	....	....	....	....	....	....	....	....	....	....	....
Equity Securities	79ld *d*	....	....	....	....	....	....	....	....	....	....	....	....	....	....	....
Debt Securities	79le *d*	....	....	....	....	....	....	....	....	....	....	....	....	....	....	....
Financial Derivatives	79ll *d*	....	....	....	....	....	....	....	....	....	....	....	....	....	....	....
Other Investment	79lf *d*	....	....	....	....	....	....	....	....	....	....	....	....	....	....	....
Monetary Authorities	79lg *d*	....	....	....	....	....	....	....	....	....	....	....	....	....	....	....
General Government	79lh *d*	....	....	....	....	....	....	....	....	....	....	....	....	....	....	....
Banks	79li *d*	....	....	....	....	....	....	....	....	....	....	....	....	....	....	....
Other Sectors	79lj *d*	....	....	....	....	....	....	....	....	....	....	....	....	....	....	....
Government Finance																*Bolivianos through 1982; Thousands from 1983 to 1984;*
Deficit (-) or Surplus	80	–238	–522	–595	–873	–455	–707	–1,399	–3,313	–3,002	–6,651	–9,729	–10,217	–110,959	I –309	–7,661
Revenue	81	1,131	1,151	1,389	2,479	5,070	5,689	6,841	7,641	8,540	8,384	11,793	14,069	19,316	I 47	560
Grants Received	81z	29	35	34	18	....	....	....	....	....	....	....	....	....	....	....
Expenditure	82	1,399	1,708	2,019	3,370	5,525	6,395	8,240	10,954	11,542	15,035	21,522	24,286	130,275	I 356	8,221
Financing																
Domestic	84a	19	352	434	357	....	....	....	....	....	....	....	....	....	....	....
Foreign	85a	219	171	161	516	....	....	....	....	....	....	....	....	....	....	....
National Accounts																*Bolivianos through 1982; Thousands from 1983 to 1984;*
Exports of Goods & Services	90c	2,494	2,336	2,963	5,878	12,448	10,474	12,698	14,512	17,000	21,800	31,500	40,000	140,000	I 430	2,910
Government Consumption	91f	1,324	1,520	1,920	2,814	4,461	5,699	6,700	8,559	9,500	13,600	15,900	20,000	40,000	I 110	4,700
Gross Fixed Capital Formation	93e	1,792	1,951	2,623	4,519	6,550	9,055	10,685	12,414	16,400	17,400	17,500	20,000	50,000	I 160	2,260
Increase/Decrease(-) in Stocks	93i	319	375	797	878	558	2,971	1,264	1,149	2,200	1,400	500	—	—	I 10	–50
Private Consumption	96f	9	10	12	18	29	34	39	45	53	61	82	100	270	I 1	13
Imports of Goods & Services	98c	–2,514	–2,713	–3,430	–6,114	–9,620	–13,242	–13,956	–16,354	–22,600	–24,700	–24,800	–30,000	–100,000	I –300	–1,860
Gross Domestic Product (GDP)	99b	12,370	13,543	17,249	26,056	43,325	49,201	56,447	65,220	75,200	90,200	122,900	150,000	400,000	I 1,390	20,900
Net Factor Inc/Pmts(-) Abroad	98.n	–284	–179	–309	–488	–822	–792	–896	–1,684	–2,334	–3,572	....	....	....	....	....
Gross National Income (GNI)	99a	11,330	12,489	15,791	23,957	40,207	45,516	52,138	59,172	69,194	82,543	113,832	....	....	....	....
GDP Volume 1970 Prices (bolivianos)	99b.*p*	12,370	12,976	13,729	14,646	15,400	16,417	17,418	18,151	18,760	19,104	19,212	....	....	....	....
GDP Volume 1990 Prices (millions)	99b.*p*	....	....	....	....	....	....	....	....	....	....	15,261	15,303	14,701	14,106	14,078
GDP Volume (1995=100)	99bv *p*	52.1	54.6	57.8	61.6	64.8	69.1	73.3	76.4	78.9	80.4	80.8	81.1	77.9	74.7	74.6
GDP Deflator (1995=10 billions)	99bi *p*	7,372	7,694	9,262	13,116	20,740	22,094	23,891	26,490	29,552	34,808	47,160	57,401	159,346	577,054	8,694,004
GDP Deflator (1995=100)	99bi *p*	....	....	....	....	....	....	....	....	....	....	....	....	....	....	.1
																Millions:
Population	99z	4.58	4.62	4.64	4.67	4.75	I 4.89	5.03	5.16	5.30	5.45	5.60	5.76	5.92	6.08	I 5.78

1985	1986	1987	1988	1989	1990	1991	1992	1993	1994	1995	1996	1997	1998	1999		
Minus Sign Indicates Debit															Balance of Payments	
-285.8	-388.9	-432.3	-304.4	-270.1	-198.9	-262.6	-533.9	-505.5	-90.2	-302.5	-404.3	-553.5	-675.2	-556.0	Current Account, n.i.e.	78al*d*
623.4	545.5	518.7	542.5	723.5	830.8	760.3	608.4	715.5	985.1	1,041.4	1,132.0	1,166.6	1,104.0	1,051.1	Goods: Exports f.o.b.	78aa*d*
-462.8	-596.5	-646.3	-590.9	-729.5	-775.6	-804.2	-1,040.8	-1,111.7	-1,015.3	-1,223.7	-1,368.0	-1,643.6	-1,759.5	-1,539.1	Goods: Imports f.o.b.	78ab*d*
160.6	-51.0	-127.6	-48.4	-6.0	55.2	-43.9	-432.4	-396.2	-30.2	-182.3	-236.0	-477.0	-655.5	-488.0	*Trade Balance*	78ac*d*
96.5	121.1	131.5	128.3	143.3	145.9	157.0	164.6	181.4	196.0	192.4	180.9	247.2	253.5	259.3	Services: Credit	78ad*d*
-246.1	-245.8	-270.2	-254.8	-298.2	-310.6	-311.2	-311.0	-321.7	-337.5	-350.2	-363.4	-418.7	-441.1	-449.5	Services: Debit	78ae*d*
11.0	-175.7	-266.3	-174.9	-160.9	-109.5	-198.1	-578.8	-536.5	-171.7	-340.1	-418.5	-648.5	-843.1	-678.3	*Balance on Goods & Services*	78af*d*
17.5	17.6	16.2	18.2	23.9	18.8	24.6	17.7	9.2	18.7	28.3	28.6	98.2	127.4	157.1	Income: Credit	78ag*d*
-390.4	-326.1	-293.9	-283.0	-283.0	-267.4	-271.6	-215.4	-215.1	-201.2	-234.9	-236.8	-294.7	-289.4	-358.5	Income: Debit	78ah*d*
-361.9	-484.2	-544.0	-439.7	-420.0	-358.1	-445.1	-776.5	-742.4	-354.2	-546.7	-626.7	-845.0	-1,005.1	-879.6	*Balance on Gds, Serv. & Inc.*	78ai*d*
80.3	97.0	113.9	140.0	152.5	161.2	185.8	246.3	241.0	269.2	248.0	226.2	300.3	341.6	352.2	Current Transfers, n.i.e.: Credit	78aj*d*
-4.2	-1.7	-2.2	-4.7	-2.6	-2.0	-3.3	-3.7	-4.1	-5.2	-3.8	-3.8	-8.8	-11.7	-28.6	Current Transfers: Debit	78ak*d*
3.4	4.7	5.5	1.3	5.9	.8	.5	.6	1.0	1.2	2.0	2.8	25.3	9.9	—	Capital Account, n.i.e.	78bc*d*
4.2	5.0	5.5	1.3	5.9	.8	.5	.6	1.0	1.2	2.0	2.8	25.3	9.9	—	Capital Account, n.i.e.: Credit	78ba*d*
-.8	-.3	—	—	—	—	—	—	—	—	—	—	—	—	....	Capital Account: Debit	78bb*d*
-285.7	-95.7	-155.5	-37.1	-7.7	48.1	61.7	367.4	347.1	315.3	505.2	701.0	889.8	999.1	732.2	Financial Account, n.i.e.	78bj*d*
—	—	-1.7	-1.9	-1.0	-1.1	-2.0	-2.0	-2.0	-2.2	-2.0	-2.1	-2.5	-2.6	-2.5	Direct Investment Abroad	78bd*d*
19.0	20.0	67.8	-10.1	-24.4	27.2	52.0	93.1	123.8	130.2	392.7	474.1	730.6	872.4	953.5	Dir. Invest. in Rep. Econ., n.i.e.	78be*d*
—	—	—	—	—	—	—	—	—	—	—	.3	-53.2	-74.5	-44.4	Portfolio Investment Assets	78bf*d*
—	—	—	—	—	—	—	—	—	—	—	—	—	—	....	Equity Securities	78bk*d*
—	—	—	—	—	—	—	—	—	—	—	.3	-53.2	-74.5	-44.4	Debt Securities	78bl*d*
-.9	—	—	—	—	—	—	—	—	—	—	—	—	—	-16.9	Portfolio Investment Liab., n.i.e.	78bg*d*
—	—	—	—	—	—	—	—	—	—	—	—	—	—	....	Equity Securities	78bm*d*
-.9	—	—	—	—	—	—	—	—	—	—	—	—	—	-16.9	Debt Securities	78bn*d*
....	....	....	....	....	....	....	....	....	....	....	....	—	—	....	Financial Derivatives Assets	78bw*d*
....	....	....	....	....	....	....	....	....	....	....	....	—	—	....	Financial Derivatives Liabilities	78bx*d*
15.2	112.2	-98.7	-85.5	-161.8	-32.1	-16.3	-13.0	17.1	-104.0	-38.4	12.2	-19.9	-106.2	-125.1	Other Investment Assets	78bh*d*
....	....	....	....	....	....	....	....	....	....	....	....	—	—	....	Monetary Authorities	78bo*d*
-5.5	-12.6	-8.8	-2.4	-23.0	-7.4	-9.3	-6.4	-6.1	—	—	-.2	—	—	....	General Government	78bp*d*
-2.5	—	6.4	-2.2	-10.9	3.0	-3.4	-14.3	-6.4	-104.0	-38.4	12.4	-19.9	66.7	-25.2	Banks	78bq*d*
23.2	124.8	-96.3	-80.9	-127.9	-27.7	-3.6	7.7	29.6	—	—	—	—	-172.9	-99.9	Other Sectors	78br*d*
-319.0	-227.9	-122.9	60.4	179.5	54.1	28.0	289.3	208.2	291.3	152.9	216.5	234.8	310.0	-32.4	Other Investment Liab., n.i.e.	78bi*d*
-108.8	-31.5	7.5	81.4	216.3	28.8	8.6	75.2	42.5	40.8	78.0	11.7	1.5	-46.4	-11.8	Monetary Authorities	78bs*d*
-141.6	-170.7	-132.1	2.2	-3.3	-60.2	-77.6	-42.6	-23.7	-16.9	-41.0	206.9	199.7	138.6	121.0	General Government	78bt*d*
-32.8	-25.7	-11.4	-44.7	-42.7	30.2	32.9	86.5	124.4	206.3	78.8	2.8	169.7	142.7	-134.6	Banks	78bu*d*
-35.8	—	13.1	21.5	9.2	55.3	64.1	170.2	65.0	61.1	37.1	-4.9	-136.1	75.1	-7.0	Other Sectors	78bv*d*
181.0	126.3	144.9	46.6	-32.1	-11.4	53.2	34.3	123.6	-315.8	-112.3	-31.6	-260.6	-232.1	-218.0	Net Errors and Omissions	78ca*d*
-387.1	-353.6	-437.4	-293.6	-304.0	-161.4	-147.2	-131.6	-33.7	-89.5	92.4	268.0	101.0	101.7	-41.8	*Overall Balance*	78cb*d*
387.1	353.6	437.4	293.6	304.0	161.4	147.2	131.6	33.7	89.5	-92.4	-268.0	-101.0	-101.7	41.8	Reserves and Related Items	79da*d*
58.0	-214.5	82.0	12.8	57.3	-5.0	-8.4	-41.2	-81.7	-26.4	-147.4	-310.1	-89.6	-133.2	-32.0	Reserve Assets	79db*d*
-23.5	99.8	-33.6	30.5	47.5	-13.2	-13.9	14.7	-28.7	28.7	-1.1	17.1	-11.4	5.7	-10.9	Use of Fund Credit and Loans	79dc*d*
352.6	468.3	389.0	250.2	199.2	179.5	169.5	158.1	144.2	87.3	56.1	25.1	—	25.9	84.7	Exceptional Financing	79de*d*
Millions of US Dollars															International Investment Position	
....	....	....	....	....	....	....	....	....	....	....	....	1,996.1	2,442.0	....	Assets	79aa*d*
....	....	....	....	....	....	....	....	....	....	....	....	21.9	24.5	....	Direct Investment Abroad	79ab*d*
....	....	....	....	....	....	....	....	....	....	....	....	60.0	117.5	....	Portfolio Investment	79ac*d*
....	....	....	....	....	....	....	....	....	....	....	....	60.0	117.5	....	Equity Securities	79ad*d*
....	....	....	....	....	....	....	....	....	....	....	....	—	—	....	Debt Securities	79ae*d*
....	....	....	....	....	....	....	....	....	....	....	....	—	—	....	Financial Derivatives	79al*d*
....	....	....	....	....	....	....	....	....	....	....	....	599.9	972.5	....	Other Investment	79af*d*
....	....	....	....	....	....	....	....	....	....	....	....	121.2	121.2	....	Monetary Authorities	79ag*d*
....	....	....	....	....	....	....	....	....	....	....	....	—	—	....	General Government	79ah*d*
....	....	....	....	....	....	....	....	....	....	....	....	128.7	401.3	....	Banks	79ai*d*
....	....	....	....	....	....	....	....	....	....	....	....	350.0	450.0	....	Other Sectors	79aj*d*
293.8	507.8	426.0	413.4	....	....	....	....	....	....	....	....	1,314.3	1,327.5	....	Reserve Assets	79ak*d*
....	....	....	....	....	....	....	....	....	....	....	....	7,739.4	9,061.7	....	Liabilities	79la*d*
....	....	....	....	....	....	....	....	....	....	....	....	2,414.7	3,286.6	....	Dir. Invest. in Rep. Economy	79lb*d*
....	....	....	....	....	....	....	....	....	....	....	....	15.1	37.0	....	Portfolio Investment	79lc*d*
....	....	....	....	....	....	....	....	....	....	....	....	—	—	....	Equity Securities	79ld*d*
....	....	....	....	....	....	....	....	....	....	....	....	15.1	37.0	....	Debt Securities	79le*d*
....	....	....	....	....	....	....	....	....	....	....	....	—	—	....	Financial Derivatives	79ll*d*
....	....	....	....	....	....	....	....	....	....	....	....	5,309.6	5,738.1	....	Other Investment	79lf*d*
....	....	....	....	....	....	....	....	....	....	....	....	733.4	767.0	....	Monetary Authorities	79lg*d*
....	....	....	....	....	....	....	....	....	....	....	....	3,118.4	3,399.8	....	General Government	79lh*d*
....	....	....	....	....	....	....	....	....	....	....	....	845.4	949.2	....	Banks	79li*d*
....	....	....	....	....	....	....	....	....	....	....	....	612.4	622.1	....	Other Sectors	79lj*d*
Millions of Bolivianos Beginning 1985: Year Ending December 31															**Government Finance**	
I -1,182	-126	-32	-45	....	....	....	....	I -1,161	-902	-697	-869	-1,783	-1,275	-1,969	Deficit (-) or Surplus	80
I 202	841	1,027	1,247	....	....	....	....	I 5,273	6,532	7,687	9,014	9,884	11,699	12,131	Revenue	81
....	....	....	....	....	....	....	....	....	....	....	....	....	....	....	Grants Received	81z
I 1,384	967	1,058	1,293	....	....	....	....	I 6,434	7,434	8,384	9,883	11,667	12,973	14,100	Expenditure	82
															Financing	
....	....	....	....	....	....	....	....	I 259	165	-327	-355	602	4	860	Domestic	84a
....	....	....	....	....	....	....	....	I 903	737	1,024	1,224	1,181	1,271	1,109	Foreign	85a
Millions of Bolivianos Beginning 1985															**National Accounts**	
I 830	1,623	1,754	2,028	2,856	3,517	4,109	4,413	4,667	5,987	7,270	8,476	8,791	9,417 p	8,446 p	Exports of Goods & Services	90c
I 238	719	994	1,230	1,516	1,815	2,310	2,833	3,270	3,750	4,375	5,003	5,790	6,624 p	7,088 p	Government Consumption	91f
I 336	1,018	1,080	1,372	1,522	1,939	2,771	3,592	4,076	4,104	5,007	6,072	7,899	10,721 p	9,451 p	Gross Fixed Capital Formation	93e
I 148	13	127	138	-51	-4	209	86	-25	-133	-93	23	276	143 p	-278 p	Increase/Decrease(-) in Stocks	93i
I 2	6	7	9	10	12	15	17	19	21	24	28	31	35 p	37 p	Private Consumption	96f
I -479	-1,956	-2,144	-2,500	-2,939	-3,695	-5,159	-6,398	-6,943	-7,516	-8,764	-10,238	-12,226	-15,217 p	-13,153 p	Imports of Goods & Services	98c
I 2,867	7,610	8,934	10,806	12,694	15,443	19,132	22,014	24,459	27,636	32,235	37,537	41,644	47,001 p	48,605 p	Gross Domestic Product (GDP)	99b
....	....	....	....	....	....	....	....	....	....	....	....	....	....	....	Net Factor Inc/Pmts(-) Abroad	98.n
....	....	....	....	....	....	....	....	....	....	....	....	....	....	....	Gross National Income (GNI)	99a
....	....	....	....	....	....	....	....	....	....	....	....	....	....	....	GDP Volume 1970 Prices (bolivianos)	99b.*p*
13,842	13,486	13,818	14,220	14,759	15,443	16,257	16,524	17,230	18,034	18,877	19,701	20,677	21,817	21,949	GDP Volume 1990 Prices (millions)	99b.*p*
73.3	71.4	73.2	75.3	78.2	81.8	86.1	87.5	91.3	95.5	100.0	104.4	109.5	115.6	116.3	GDP Volume (1995=100)	99bv*p*
....	....	....	....	....	....	....	....	....	....	....	....	....	....	....	GDP Deflator (1995=10 billions)	99bi*p*
12.1	33.0	37.9	44.5	50.4	58.6	68.9	78.0	83.1	89.7	100.0	111.6	117.9	126.2 p	129.7 p	GDP Deflator (1995=100)	99bi*p*
Midyear Estimates																
5.90	6.02	6.16	6.29	6.43	6.57	6.73	6.90	7.07	7.24	7.41	7.59	7.77	7.95	8.14	**Population**	99z

(See notes in the back of the book.)

Botswana

		1970	1971	1972	1973	1974	1975	1976	1977	1978	1979	1980	1981	1982	1983	1984
Exchange Rates															*Pula per SDR:*	
Official Rate	aa	.7172	.8308	.8499	.8097	.8444	1.0180	1.0103	1.0060	1.0789	1.0390	.9461	1.0244	1.1704	1.2098	1.5292
															Pula per US Dollar:	
Official Rate	ae	.7172	.7653	.7828	.6712	.6896	.8696	.8696	.8282	.8282	.7887	.7418	.8801	1.0610	1.1555	1.5601
Official Rate	rf	.7143	.7152	.7687	.6940	.6795	.7395	.8696	.8420	.8282	.8150	.7772	.8367	1.0297	1.0969	1.2984
Fund Position															*Millions of SDRs:*	
Quota	2f. s	5.00	5.00	5.00	5.00	5.00	5.00	5.00	5.00	9.00	9.00	13.50	13.50	13.50	22.10	22.10
SDRs	1b. s	.50	1.04	1.57	1.57	1.57	1.57	1.57	1.57	1.57	2.50	2.45	5.25	6.19	7.26	8.53
Reserve Position in the Fund	1c. s	.61	.61	.61	.62	.62	.62	.61	1.24	1.22	2.18	5.12	9.13	9.15	11.31	12.34
Total Fund Cred.&Loans Outstg.	2tl	—	—	—	—	—	—	—	—	—	—	—	—	—	—	—
International Liquidity														*Millions of US Dollars Unless Otherwise Indicated:*		
Total Reserves minus Gold	1l. d	....	....	....	....	....	....	74.86	100.11	150.57	267.28	343.69	253.43	292.97	395.67	474.29
SDRs	1b. d	.50	1.13	1.70	1.89	1.92	1.84	1.82	1.91	2.05	3.29	3.12	6.11	6.83	7.60	8.36
Reserve Position in the Fund	1c. d	.61	.66	.66	.75	.76	.73	.71	1.51	1.59	2.87	6.53	10.63	10.09	11.84	12.10
Foreign Exchange	1d. d	....	....	....	....	....	....	72.32	96.70	146.94	261.12	334.04	236.69	276.05	376.23	453.83
Deposit Money Banks: Assets	7a. d	....	....	26.31	37.64	50.13	69.11	.68	3.37	3.23	4.97	3.29	1.64	4.65	6.34	20.01
Liabilities	7b. d	....	....	7.58	5.17	19.82	33.99	1.13	3.08	3.31	2.84	3.97	7.67	3.06	10.78	11.01
Monetary Authorities															*Millions of Pula:*	
Foreign Assets	11	....	....	....	....	....	....	65	83	125	211	255	223	311	457	711
Reserve Money	14	....	....	....	....	....	....	33	36	36	57	62	53	47	49	57
of which: Currency Outside DMBs	14a	....	....	....	....	....	....	10	12	16	18	24	30	29	30	35
Time Deposits	15	....	....	....	....	....	....	—	1	8	50	91	30	15	65	12
Liabs. of Central Bank: Securities	16ac	....	....	....	....	....	....	—	—	—	—	—	—	50	58	71
Central Government Deposits	16d	....	....	....	....	....	....	29	39	63	84	91	76	105	185	368
Capital Accounts	17a	....	....	....	....	....	....	5	8	17	15	18	38	61	65	65
Other Items (Net)	17r	....	....	....	....	....	....	-2	-1	1	4	-8	26	33	36	138
Deposit Money Banks															*Millions of Pula:*	
Reserves	20	....	....	1	2	2	3	22	24	20	38	36	22	18	22	17
Other Claims on Monetary Author.	20c	....	....	—	—	—	—	—	—	—	—	—	—	50	58	71
Foreign Assets	21	....	....	21	27	35	60	1	3	3	4	2	1	5	7	31
Claims on Central Government	22a	....	....	2	1	1	3	12	13	9	7	5	9	—	—	—
Claims on Local Government	22b	....	....	—	—	—	—	—	—	—	1	1	—	—	—	—
Claims on Nonfin.Pub.Enterprises	22c	....	....	1	—	1	2	1	4	4	—	2	5	8	15	18
Claims on Private Sector	22d	....	....	12	21	36	51	66	68	69	84	93	136	135	155	204
Claims on Other Financial Insts	22f	....	....	—	—	—	—	—	1	1	2	3	4	6	8	16
Demand Deposits	24	....	....	13	17	20	21	33	46	45	64	66	85	98	107	115
Time and Savings Deposits	25	....	....	12	17	21	26	43	50	52	67	55	81	103	114	206
Foreign Liabilities	26c	....	....	6	4	14	30	1	3	3	2	3	7	3	12	17
Central Government Deposits	26d	....	....	7	12	21	42	22	13	4	1	13	1	—	—	—
Capital Accounts	27a	....	....	—	—	—	—	4	6	7	9	9	14	21	25	30
Other Items (Net)	27r	....	....	-2	1	-2	-1	—	-5	-5	-7	-5	-10	-4	6	-10
Monetary Survey															*Millions of Pula:*	
Foreign Assets (Net)	31n	....	....	....	....	....	....	65	83	125	212	254	218	313	452	725
Domestic Credit	32	....	....	....	....	....	....	27	32	17	8	6	77	43	-8	-130
Claims on Central Govt. (Net)	32an	....	....	....	....	....	....	-40	-40	-57	-79	-92	-67	-106	-185	-368
Claims on Local Government	32b	....	....	....	....	....	....	—	—	—	1	1	—	—	—	—
Claims on Nonfin.Pub.Enterprises	32c	....	....	....	....	....	....	1	4	4	—	2	5	8	15	18
Claims on Private Sector	32d	....	....	....	....	....	....	66	68	69	84	93	136	135	155	204
Claims on Other Financial Insts	32f	....	....	....	....	....	....	—	1	1	2	3	4	6	8	16
Money	34	....	....	....	....	....	....	44	58	61	82	91	115	127	137	151
Quasi-Money	35	....	....	....	....	....	....	43	50	60	117	146	112	118	179	218
Liabs. of Central Bank: Securities	36ac															
Capital Accounts	37a	....	....	....	....	....	....	8	14	25	24	27	52	82	90	94
Other Items (Net)	37r	....	....	....	....	....	....	-2	-7	-4	-2	-4	16	28	39	132
Money plus Quasi-Money	35l	....	....	....	....	....	....	86	109	121	199	237	226	246	316	369
Interest Rates															*Percent Per Annum*	
Bank Rate (End of Period)	60	....	....	....	....	....	....	8.25	7.75	6.75	5.75	5.75	8.50	12.00	10.50	9.00
Deposit Rate	60l	....	....	....	....	....	....	....	....	....	....	5.00	8.67	10.75	11.88	10.00
Lending Rate	60p	....	....	....	....	....	....	....	....	....	....	8.48	9.63	24.21	13.38	12.00
Prices, Production, Labor															*Index Numbers (1995=100):*	
Consumer Prices	64	....	....	....	....	10.3	11.5	12.9	14.6	15.9	17.8	20.2	‡23.5	26.1	28.9	31.4
Mining Production	66zx	....	2.0	7.8	8.0	11.5	14.1	20.1	20.9	24.9	29.5	32.4	‡34.0	48.3	67.2	79.1
															Number in Thousands:	
Labor Force	67d	....	....	....	....	....	....	....	....	....	....	....	....	....	....	....
Employment	67e	....	....	....	....	....	....	....	....	....	....	....	....	....	....	....
International Transactions															*Millions of Pula:*	
Exports	70	18.3	30.3	44.8	59.2	82.0	105.0	153.2	156.7	192.7	367.3	391.3	347.8	494.3	707.5	857.1
Imports, c.i.f.	71	40.9	59.1	84.2	115.0	125.4	159.3	181.4	239.6	307.1	438.3	537.6	695.1	742.7	818.3	895.2

1985	1986	1987	1988	1989	1990	1991	1992	1993	1994	1995	1996	1997	1998	1999		
Exchange Rates																
End of Period																
2.3076	2.2477	2.2212	2.6049	2.4605	2.6622	2.9646	3.1031	3.5229	3.9670	4.1944	5.2404	5.1400	6.2774	6.3572	Official Rate	aa
End of Period (ae) Period Average (rf)																
2.1008	1.8376	1.5657	1.9357	1.8723	1.8713	2.0725	2.2568	2.5648	2.7174	2.8217	3.6443	3.8095	4.4583	4.6318	Official Rate	ae
1.9026	1.8791	1.6789	1.8286	2.0149	1.8605	2.0216	2.1097	2.4231	2.6846	2.7722	3.3242	3.6508	4.2259	4.6244	Official Rate	rf
Fund Position																
End of Period																
22.10	22.10	22.10	22.10	22.10	22.10	22.10	36.60	36.60	36.60	36.60	36.60	36.60	36.60	63.00	Quota	2f. s
9.70	14.01	15.38	16.79	18.91	21.70	24.10	22.46	24.03	25.39	27.06	28.71	30.36	32.41	28.05	SDRs	1b. s
12.93	15.58	15.73	13.64	19.22	16.17	13.45	14.79	16.60	16.34	19.28	19.91	18.13	27.61	22.59	Reserve Position in the Fund	1c. s
—	—	—	—	—	—	—	—	—	—	—	—	—	—	—	Total Fund Cred.&Loans Outstg.	2tl
International Liquidity																
End of Period																
783.21	1,197.67	2,057.08	2,258.09	2,841.11	3,385.34	3,772.37	3,844.64	4,153.14	4,462.40	4,764.36	5,097.57	5,740.42	6,025.17	6,298.72	Total Reserves minus Gold	1l. d
10.65	17.14	21.82	22.59	24.85	30.87	34.47	30.88	33.00	37.07	40.22	41.28	40.96	45.63	38.50	SDRs	1b. d
14.20	19.06	22.32	18.36	25.26	23.00	19.24	20.34	22.79	23.86	28.66	28.63	24.46	38.87	31.00	Reserve Position in the Fund	1c. d
758.35	1,161.48	2,012.95	2,217.14	2,791.00	3,331.46	3,718.66	3,793.42	4,097.34	4,401.47	4,695.48	5,027.66	5,675.00	5,940.67	6,229.21	Foreign Exchange	1d. d
17.49	22.77	31.27	33.78	24.06	80.39	74.31	64.91	61.17	63.42	69.60	124.51	211.33	317.73	290.52	Deposit Money Banks: Assets	7a. d
10.33	19.30	25.91	23.86	19.72	34.14	23.80	19.40	54.32	24.22	35.05	41.61	31.61	38.49	34.79	Liabilities	7b. d
Monetary Authorities																
End of Period																
1,645	2,201	3,152	4,371	5,225	6,257	7,708	8,561	10,506	10,567	12,115	18,356	21,637	26,502	28,867	Foreign Assets	11
60	86	104	138	191	256	512	424	395	392	405	453	572	707	808	Reserve Money	14
43	59	69	96	118	144	158	163	180	195	223	247	276	353	404	of which: Currency Outside DMBs	14a
183	188	480	482	832	359	491	605	38	46	48	47	63	26	172	Time Deposits	15
102	80	175	261	311	192	207	344	1,201	1,451	1,964	2,816	3,308	3,246	4,230	Liabs. of Central Bank: Securities	16ac
642	1,270	1,817	2,348	3,059	4,001	4,287	5,100	5,630	6,734	6,507	7,267	15,407	19,122	20,256	Central Government Deposits	16d
465	385	374	829	847	866	1,464	1,365	2,167	2,935	2,942	6,107	1,888	3,229	3,415	Capital Accounts	17a
194	193	203	313	-16	585	747	725	1,075	-990	250	1,666	399	172	-14	Other Items (Net)	17r
Deposit Money Banks																
End of Period																
16	23	23	52	66	99	220	124	194	160	166	177	271	331	353	Reserves	20
102	80	175	261	311	192	207	344	361	493	832	1,192	1,572	1,322	1,718	Other Claims on Monetary Author.	20c
37	42	49	65	45	150	154	146	157	172	196	454	805	1,417	1,346	Foreign Assets	21
—	—	—	—	—	—	—	—	—	2	—	—	—	—	—	Claims on Central Government	22a
—	—	—	1	—	1	2	2	3	2	3	2	2	14	15	Claims on Local Government	22b
25	34	22	26	55	57	60	76	94	148	95	70	61	267	528	Claims on Nonfin.Pub.Enterprises	22c
182	217	261	321	435	662	945	1,285	1,434	1,600	1,560	1,626	1,775	2,461	3,518	Claims on Private Sector	22d
17	21	1	21	39	37	33	35	32	95	122	100	61	231	130	Claims on Other Financial Insts	22f
145	185	244	311	389	442	456	444	516	579	607	704	762	1,160	1,371	Demand Deposits	24
186	175	221	340	458	601	1,084	1,267	1,386	1,573	1,809	2,192	3,003	4,183	5,282	Time and Savings Deposits	25
22	35	41	46	37	64	49	44	139	66	99	152	120	172	161	Foreign Liabilities	26c
—	—	—	2	3	5	14	9	31	16	19	40	36	29	66	Central Government Deposits	26d
40	41	56	63	99	119	160	221	244	308	337	402	464	568	732	Capital Accounts	27a
-15	-19	-29	-13	-34	-33	-140	27	-43	131	103	131	162	-70	-5	Other Items (Net)	27r
Monetary Survey																
End of Period																
1,660	2,207	3,161	4,390	5,234	6,344	7,813	8,664	10,524	10,673	12,213	18,658	22,321	27,747	30,051	Foreign Assets (Net)	31n
-419	-997	-1,532	-1,981	-2,533	-3,250	-3,260	-3,711	-4,099	-4,904	-4,747	-5,509	-13,543	-16,179	-16,131	Domestic Credit	32
-643	-1,270	-1,817	-2,350	-3,062	-4,006	-4,301	-5,108	-5,662	-6,748	-6,526	-7,307	-15,442	-19,151	-20,322	Claims on Central Govt. (Net)	32an
—	—	—	1	—	1	2	2	3	2	3	2	2	14	15	Claims on Local Government	32b
25	34	22	26	55	57	60	76	94	148	95	70	61	267	528	Claims on Nonfin.Pub.Enterprises	32c
182	217	261	321	435	662	945	1,285	1,434	1,600	1,560	1,626	1,775	2,461	3,518	Claims on Private Sector	32d
17	21	1	21	39	37	33	35	32	95	122	100	61	231	130	Claims on Other Financial Insts	32f
188	243	312	406	506	586	614	607	696	774	829	951	1,038	1,513	1,775	Money	34
369	363	701	822	1,291	960	1,575	1,871	1,424	1,619	1,856	2,239	3,066	4,209	5,454	Quasi-Money	35
—	—	—	—	—	—	—	—	840	958	1,132	1,623	1,736	1,924	2,513	Liabs. of Central Bank: Securities	36ac
505	426	430	892	946	984	1,624	1,585	2,412	3,243	3,279	6,509	2,352	3,797	4,147	Capital Accounts	37a
179	178	186	289	-42	564	740	889	1,053	-823	369	1,827	587	126	32	Other Items (Net)	37r
557	606	1,013	1,228	1,797	1,546	2,188	2,478	2,121	2,392	2,686	3,190	4,104	5,722	7,228	Money plus Quasi-Money	35l
Interest Rates																
Percent Per Annum																
9.00	9.00	8.50	6.50	6.50	8.50	12.00	14.25	14.25	13.50	13.00	13.00	12.50	12.50	13.25	Bank Rate (End of Period)	60
9.00	8.67	7.50	5.00	5.58	6.11	11.40	12.50	13.49	10.39	9.98	10.43	9.25	8.72	9.46	Deposit Rate	60l
11.50	11.00	10.00	7.83	7.67	7.88	11.83	14.00	14.92	13.88	14.29	14.50	14.08	13.53	14.63	Lending Rate	60p
Prices, Production, Labor																
Period Averages																
33.9	37.3	40.9	44.4	49.5	55.1	‡61.6	71.6	81.9	90.5	100.0	‡110.1	119.6	127.6	136.6	Consumer Prices	64
77.5	79.8	80.3	93.2	91.6	103.4	99.0	96.4	89.3	94.0	100.0	....	....	....	....	Mining Production	66zx
Period Averages																
....	....	....	....	....	....	432	....	....	....	437	....	....	....	....	Labor Force	67d
117	130	150	170	190	209	226	226	227	231	232	230	233	....	....	Employment	67e
International Transactions																
Millions of Pula																
1,384.3	1,619.3	2,664.7	2,678.3	3,742.6	3,319.1	3,738.0	3,675.0	4,270.9	4,965.0	5,941.5	8,141.8	10,390.7	10,286.7	....	Exports	70
1,095.2	1,331.4	1,572.5	2,172.2	3,019.6	3,619.3	3,927.7	3,970.1	4,285.0	4,407.3	5,305.1	5,742.9	8,250.0	10,069.0	....	Imports, c.i.f.	71

Botswana

616

	Code	1970	1971	1972	1973	1974	1975	1976	1977	1978	1979	1980	1981	1982	1983	1984
Balance of Payments																*Millions of US Dollars*
Current Account, n.i.e.	**78al d**	....	....	....	....	....	-35.6	-20.4	-27.0	-115.6	-60.6	-151.1	-303.7	-144.6	-78.9	-58.8
Goods: Exports f.o.b.	**78aa d**	....	....	....	....	....	142.0	169.7	191.6	223.4	442.2	544.5	401.3	460.6	640.3	677.7
Goods: Imports f.o.b.	**78ab d**	....	....	....	....	....	-181.2	-180.2	-226.4	-295.0	-442.1	-602.5	-687.1	-579.8	-615.3	-583.4
Trade Balance	**78ac d**	....	....	....	....	....	-39.2	-10.5	-34.8	-71.6	.1	-58.0	-285.8	-119.2	25.1	94.3
Services: Credit	**78ad d**	....	....	....	....	....	30.8	46.8	51.4	50.5	61.1	100.9	97.0	102.5	113.0	107.2
Services: Debit	**78ae d**	....	....	....	....	....	-76.0	-78.4	-89.9	-101.9	-155.1	-215.9	-211.8	-181.6	-209.4	-190.2
Balance on Goods & Services	**78af d**	....	....	....	....	....	-84.4	-42.1	-73.3	-123.0	-93.9	-173.1	-400.5	-198.3	-71.4	11.2
Income: Credit	**78ag d**	....	....	....	....	....	47.1	59.3	68.3	58.9	72.3	102.2	106.0	82.4	82.7	92.7
Income: Debit	**78ah d**	....	....	....	....	....	6.9	-51.9	-54.4	-68.5	-69.4	-135.1	-49.7	-45.1	-129.9	-190.6
Balance on Gds, Serv. & Inc.	**78ai d**	....	....	....	....	....	-30.4	-34.6	-59.4	-132.6	-91.0	-206.0	-344.2	-161.0	-118.6	-86.7
Current Transfers, n.i.e.: Credit	**78aj d**	....	....	....	....	....	30.6	57.7	95.0	80.7	109.1	144.4	141.6	115.0	145.7	124.8
Current Transfers: Debit	**78ak d**	....	....	....	....	....	-35.7	-43.5	-62.6	-63.6	-78.6	-89.4	-101.1	-98.6	-106.0	-96.9
Capital Account, n.i.e.	**78bc d**	....	....	....	....	....	—	5.6	6.1	4.1	6.6	8.2	8.7	6.7	7.3	7.3
Capital Account, n.i.e.: Credit	**78ba d**	....	....	....	....	....	—	5.6	6.1	6.4	7.4	9.1	9.6	7.8	8.4	7.9
Capital Account: Debit	**78bb d**	....	....	....	....	....	—	—	—	-2.3	-.7	-.9	-.8	-1.1	-1.1	-.5
Financial Account, n.i.e.	**78bj d**	....	....	....	....	....	43.5	73.6	15.9	90.4	87.5	144.0	110.9	90.8	94.7	112.5
Direct Investment Abroad	**78bd d**	....	....	....	....	....	—	-.1	-.2	—	—	-2.3	.1	—	1.3	.2
Dir. Invest. in Rep. Econ., n.i.e.	**78be d**	....	....	....	....	....	-38.3	11.3	12.2	40.8	127.9	111.6	88.4	21.1	23.8	62.2
Portfolio Investment Assets	**78bf d**	....	....	....	....	....	—	—	—	—	—	—	—	—	—	—
Equity Securities	**78bk d**	....	....	....	....	....	—	—	—	—	—	—	—	—	—	—
Debt Securities	**78bl d**	....	....	....	....	....	—	—	—	—	—	—	—	—	—	—
Portfolio Investment Liab., n.i.e.	**78bg d**	....	....	....	....	....	—	—	—	4.2	—	—	—	—	—	—
Equity Securities	**78bm d**	....	....	....	....	....	—	—	—	4.2	—	—	—	—	—	—
Debt Securities	**78bn d**	....	....	....	....	....	—	—	—	—	—	—	—	—	—	—
Financial Derivatives Assets	**78bw d**	....	....	....	....	....	....	....	....	....	....	....	....	....	....	....
Financial Derivatives Liabilities	**78bx d**	....	....	....	....	....	....	....	....	....	....	....	....	....	....	....
Other Investment Assets	**78bh d**	....	....	....	....	....	-50.4	72.6	10.2	5.6	-28.0	-12.7	-25.3	-17.5	6.6	-16.7
Monetary Authorities	**78bo d**	....	....	....	....	....	....	....	....	....	....	....	....	....	....	....
General Government	**78bp d**	....	....	....	....	....	-5.1	-7.2	-.7	-9.2	-20.0	-2.4	-15.2	-13.0	2.5	1.5
Banks	**78bq d**	....	....	....	....	....	-34.5	68.1	-2.3	.1	-1.6	1.9	-3.1	-8.8	5.3	-18.4
Other Sectors	**78br d**	....	....	....	....	....	-10.8	11.7	13.2	14.6	-6.4	-12.2	-7.1	4.4	-1.2	.2
Other Investment Liab., n.i.e.	**78bi d**	....	....	....	....	....	132.3	-10.1	-6.3	39.8	-12.4	47.5	47.7	87.2	63.1	66.9
Monetary Authorities	**78bs d**	....	....	....	....	....	—	—	.4	-.2	-.2	2.8	.4	-2.0	1.5	-1.8
General Government	**78bt d**	....	....	....	....	....	22.3	5.4	-25.2	15.3	-5.3	13.4	15.7	55.4	14.1	17.6
Banks	**78bu d**	....	....	....	....	....	21.5	-32.9	1.9	.2	.6	-1.8	7.3	-5.7	-3.5	3.7
Other Sectors	**78bv d**	....	....	....	....	....	88.4	17.4	16.6	24.5	-7.5	33.1	24.4	39.6	50.9	47.3
Net Errors and Omissions	**78ca d**	....	....	....	....	....	-8.0	13.0	23.1	60.1	82.5	89.3	110.3	102.0	100.6	63.2
Overall Balance	**78cb d**	....	....	....	....	....	—	71.9	18.1	39.1	116.0	90.4	-73.8	54.9	123.6	124.3
Reserves and Related Items	**79da d**	....	....	....	....	....	—	-71.9	-18.1	-39.1	-116.0	-90.4	73.8	-54.9	-123.6	-124.3
Reserve Assets	**79db d**	....	....	....	....	....	—	-71.9	-18.1	-39.1	-116.0	-90.4	73.8	-54.9	-123.6	-124.3
Use of Fund Credit and Loans	**79dc d**	....	....	....	....	....	—	—	—	—	—	—	—	—	—	—
Exceptional Financing	**79de d**	....	....	....	....	....	....	....	....	....	....	....	....	....	....	....
International Investment Position																*Millions of US Dollars*
Assets	**79aa d**	....	....	....	....	....	....	....	....	....	....	....	....	....	....	....
Direct Investment Abroad	**79ab d**	....	....	....	....	....	....	....	....	....	....	....	....	....	....	....
Portfolio Investment	**79ac d**	....	....	....	....	....	....	....	....	....	....	....	....	....	....	....
Equity Securities	**79ad d**	....	....	....	....	....	....	....	....	....	....	....	....	....	....	....
Debt Securities	**79ae d**	....	....	....	....	....	....	....	....	....	....	....	....	....	....	....
Financial Derivatives	**79al d**	....	....	....	....	....	....	....	....	....	....	....	....	....	....	....
Other Investment	**79af d**	....	....	....	....	....	....	....	....	....	....	....	....	....	....	....
Monetary Authorities	**79ag d**	....	....	....	....	....	....	....	....	....	....	....	....	....	....	....
General Government	**79ah d**	....	....	....	....	....	....	....	....	....	....	....	....	....	....	....
Banks	**79ai d**	....	....	....	....	....	....	....	....	....	....	....	....	....	....	....
Other Sectors	**79aj d**	....	....	....	....	....	....	....	....	....	....	....	....	....	....	....
Reserve Assets	**79ak d**	....	....	....	....	....	....	....	....	....	....	....	....	....	....	....
Liabilities	**79la d**	....	....	....	....	....	....	....	....	....	....	....	....	....	....	....
Dir. Invest. in Rep. Economy	**79lb d**	....	....	....	....	....	....	....	....	....	....	....	....	....	....	....
Portfolio Investment	**79lc d**	....	....	....	....	....	....	....	....	....	....	....	....	....	....	....
Equity Securities	**79ld d**	....	....	....	....	....	....	....	....	....	....	....	....	....	....	....
Debt Securities	**79le d**	....	....	....	....	....	....	....	....	....	....	....	....	....	....	....
Financial Derivatives	**79ll d**	....	....	....	....	....	....	....	....	....	....	....	....	....	....	....
Other Investment	**79lf d**	....	....	....	....	....	....	....	....	....	....	....	....	....	....	....
Monetary Authorities	**79lg d**	....	....	....	....	....	....	....	....	....	....	....	....	....	....	....
General Government	**79lh d**	....	....	....	....	....	....	....	....	....	....	....	....	....	....	....
Banks	**79li d**	....	....	....	....	....	....	....	....	....	....	....	....	....	....	....
Other Sectors	**79lj d**	....	....	....	....	....	....	....	....	....	....	....	....	....	....	....

Balance of Payments

Minus Sign Indicates Debit

1985	1986	1987	1988	1989	1990	1991	1992	1993	1994	1995	1996	1997	1998	1999		Code
81.9	108.7	628.5	193.9	491.9	−19.3	302.9	197.7	426.9	211.6	299.7	495.0	721.5	170.1	....	Current Account, n.i.e.	78al d
727.6	852.5	1,586.6	1,468.9	1,819.7	1,795.4	1,871.1	1,743.9	1,722.2	1,874.3	2,160.2	2,217.5	2,819.8	2,060.6	....	Goods: Exports f.o.b.	78aa d
−493.8	−608.4	−803.9	−986.9	−1,185.1	−1,610.9	−1,604.0	−1,556.6	−1,455.4	−1,364.3	−1,605.4	−1,467.7	−1,924.4	−1,983.1	....	Goods: Imports f.o.b.	78ab d
233.8	244.0	782.7	482.0	634.6	184.4	267.2	187.3	266.8	510.0	554.8	749.8	895.4	77.5	....	*Trade Balance*	78ac d
76.3	100.0	125.1	110.3	110.5	209.5	209.9	189.2	191.3	186.1	260.4	163.0	210.2	255.3	....	Services: Credit	78ad d
−130.5	−155.0	−203.4	−238.8	−228.0	−375.9	−382.5	−360.1	−325.6	−322.0	−444.2	−343.6	−440.7	−522.4	....	Services: Debit	78ae d
179.7	189.1	704.4	353.6	517.1	18.0	94.5	16.4	132.5	374.2	370.9	569.2	664.9	−189.6	....	*Balance on Goods & Services*	78af d
84.9	116.5	171.8	220.1	244.8	416.2	483.1	542.1	554.5	230.8	483.2	501.7	622.1	622.7	....	Income: Credit	78ag d
−216.3	−245.7	−415.3	−546.8	−483.6	−522.1	−420.2	−429.7	−260.9	−455.1	−515.6	−754.8	−766.9	−503.1	....	Income: Debit	78ah d
48.2	60.0	460.9	26.9	278.3	−87.9	157.4	128.8	426.1	149.9	338.5	316.1	520.1	−70.0	....	*Balance on Gds, Serv. & Inc.*	78ai d
102.7	133.5	280.8	301.8	266.8	330.7	421.6	344.5	275.9	356.8	330.7	355.4	456.8	460.9	....	Current Transfers, n.i.e.: Credit	78aj d
−68.9	−84.8	−113.2	−134.7	−53.2	−262.1	−276.0	−275.6	−275.1	−295.1	−369.5	−176.6	−255.5	−220.8	....	Current Transfers: Debit	78ak d
5.2	2.5	5.8	—	6.3	64.7	37.5	53.2	84.9	19.2	14.4	6.2	16.9	31.8	....	Capital Account, n.i.e.	78bc d
5.6	3.2	7.0	—	7.0	65.6	38.5	53.8	86.1	19.6	15.4	18.0	29.4	44.2	....	Capital Account, n.i.e.: Credit	78ba d
−.4	−.7	−1.1	—	−.7	−.9	−1.0	−.5	−1.3	−.4	−.9	−11.9	−12.5	−12.4	....	Capital Account: Debit	78bb d
123.1	105.6	−89.8	−25.3	113.0	82.6	123.3	275.8	−40.3	41.1	−33.9	42.4	5.6	−202.4	....	Financial Account, n.i.e.	78bj d
−1.5	....	....	....	....	−7.4	−8.5	−9.9	−9.5	−9.5	−40.9	1.1	−4.1	−3.5	....	Direct Investment Abroad	78bd d
53.6	70.4	113.6	39.9	42.2	95.9	−8.2	−1.6	−286.9	−14.2	70.4	71.2	100.1	95.3	....	Dir. Invest. in Rep. Econ., n.i.e.	78be d
....	....	....	....	....	....	....	....	....	....	−36.2	−35.5	−28.5	−42.8	....	Portfolio Investment Assets	78bf d
....	....	....	....	....	....	....	....	....	....	−30.8	−26.7	−33.1	−16.9	....	Equity Securities	78bk d
....	....	....	....	....	....	....	....	....	....	−5.4	−8.9	4.7	−25.9	....	Debt Securities	78bl d
—	—	—	—	1.3	−1.2	.1	.2	−.1	—	5.5	28.9	10.8	−14.1	....	Portfolio Investment Liab., n.i.e.	78bg d
—	—	—	—	....	....	....	....	....	....	5.5	28.7	10.8	−14.1	....	Equity Securities	78bm d
—	—	—	—	1.3	−1.2	.1	.2	−.1	—	—	.2	—	—	....	Debt Securities	78bn d
....	....	....	....	....	....	....	....	....	....	−.2	....	−15.4	5.2	....	Financial Derivatives Assets	78bw d
....	....	....	....	....	....	....	....	....	....	.3	2.1	....	....	....	Financial Derivatives Liabilities	78bx d
−16.7	−28.7	−251.6	−68.3	−34.6	−136.9	−53.0	148.9	63.4	15.8	−88.7	−95.6	−166.5	−310.8	....	Other Investment Assets	78bh d
															Monetary Authorities	78bo d
−10.1	−35.8	11.4	−41.4	−45.0	−91.8	11.7	139.9	56.1	19.7	−46.1	−28.7	−78.0	−101.1	....	General Government	78bp d
−2.9	−2.7	−4.2	−8.9	10.4	−33.5	−23.4	−7.0	14.3	.4	−8.7	−35.1	−76.9	−139.7	....	Banks	78bq d
−3.7	9.7	−258.8	−18.0	—	−11.7	−41.3	16.1	−6.9	−4.3	−34.0	−31.8	−11.6	−70.0	....	Other Sectors	78br d
87.7	63.9	48.3	3.1	105.4	129.7	194.2	138.2	192.5	49.0	55.9	70.3	109.3	68.2	....	Other Investment Liab., n.i.e.	78bi d
															Monetary Authorities	78bs d
9.4	40.3	38.5	—	28.2	12.3	77.9	54.4	67.0	6.5	−12.3	−19.6	51.3	22.2	....	General Government	78bt d
30.5	−21.3	3.0	3.1	−4.6	9.5	−3.6	−5.6	23.1	−2.8	−2.5	17.8	−3.4	−3.5	....	Banks	78bu d
47.7	44.9	6.7	—	81.8	108.0	119.9	89.4	102.4	45.3	70.7	72.1	61.4	49.5	....	Other Sectors	78bv d
44.0	90.2	16.9	213.7	−34.7	179.2	−89.7	−121.4	−74.5	−136.7	−73.6	−32.9	−108.9	63.0	....	Net Errors and Omissions	78ca d
254.3	306.9	561.5	382.3	576.5	307.2	374.1	405.3	397.0	135.2	206.6	510.7	635.1	62.6	....	*Overall Balance*	78cb d
−254.3	−306.9	−561.5	−382.3	−576.5	−307.2	−374.1	−405.3	−397.0	−135.2	−206.6	−510.7	−635.1	−62.6	....	Reserves and Related Items	79da d
−254.3	−306.9	−561.5	−382.3	−576.5	−307.2	−374.1	−405.3	−397.0	−135.2	−206.6	−510.7	−635.1	−62.6	....	Reserve Assets	79db d
—	—	—	—	—	—	—	—	—	....	....	—	....	—	....	Use of Fund Credit and Loans	79dc d
....	....	....	....	....	....	....	....	....	....	....	—	....	—	....	Exceptional Financing	79de d

International Investment Position

Millions of US Dollars

1985	1986	1987	1988	1989	1990	1991	1992	1993	1994	1995	1996	1997	1998	1999		Code
....	....	....	....	....	....	....	....	....	5,084.0	5,643.9	6,001.0	6,566.0	6,884.5	....	Assets	79aa d
....	....	....	....	....	....	....	....	....	484.5	650.1	576.7	404.5	257.5	....	Direct Investment Abroad	79ab d
....	....	....	....	....	....	....	....	....	26.9	61.5	139.1	187.6	244.0	....	Portfolio Investment	79ac d
....	....	....	....	....	....	....	....	....	16.1	45.8	105.8	143.4	169.1	....	Equity Securities	79ad d
....	....	....	....	....	....	....	....	....	10.9	15.8	33.3	44.3	74.9	....	Debt Securities	79ae d
....	....	....	....	....	....	....	....	....	—	.2	—	17.1	9.6	....	Financial Derivatives	79al d
....	....	....	....	....	....	....	....	....	171.3	239.1	253.1	280.3	433.0	....	Other Investment	79af d
....	....	....	....	....	....	....	....	....	—	—	—	—	—	....	Monetary Authorities	79ag d
....	....	....	....	....	....	....	....	....							General Government	79ah d
....	....	....	....	....	....	....	....	....	63.3	69.5	99.9	186.2	291.5	....	Banks	79ai d
....	....	....	....	....	....	....	....	....	107.9	169.6	153.3	94.2	141.5	....	Other Sectors	79aj d
....	....	....	....	....	....	....	....	....	4,401.3	4,693.0	5,032.1	5,676.5	5,940.3	....	Reserve Assets	79ak d
....	....	....	....	....	....	....	....	....	2,005.3	1,995.1	1,941.9	2,151.9	2,248.7	....	Liabilities	79la d
....	....	....	....	....	....	....	....	....	998.5	1,126.4	1,058.1	1,172.9	1,294.8	....	Dir. Invest. in Rep. Economy	79lb d
....	....	....	....	....	....	....	....	....	10.9	15.9	50.4	60.5	34.2	....	Portfolio Investment	79lc d
....	....	....	....	....	....	....	....	....	10.9	15.9	50.4	60.0	33.4	....	Equity Securities	79ld d
....	....	....	....	....	....	....	....	....	—	—	—	.5	.8	....	Debt Securities	79le d
....	....	....	....	....	....	....	....	....	—	.2	1.9	—	—	....	Financial Derivatives	79ll d
....	....	....	....	....	....	....	....	....	996.0	852.6	831.5	918.5	919.7	....	Other Investment	79lf d
....	....	....	....	....	....	....	....	....							Monetary Authorities	79lg d
....	....	....	....	....	....	....	....	....	496.9	495.8	387.9	483.1	482.6	....	General Government	79lh d
....	....	....	....	....	....	....	....	....	38.9	35.1	27.4	23.7	16.8	....	Banks	79li d
....	....	....	....	....	....	....	....	....	460.1	321.7	416.2	411.7	420.3	....	Other Sectors	79lj d

Botswana

		1970	1971	1972	1973	1974	1975	1976	1977	1978	1979	1980	1981	1982	1983	1984
Government Finance															*Millions of Pula*	
Deficit (-) or Surplus	80	....	−11.22	−21.00	−14.05	−5.67	1.24	−20.75	−4.58	−6.91	21.38	−1.27	−18.34	−20.09	103.22	188.32
Revenue	81	....	16.44	27.12	39.36	60.60	77.92	68.39	97.39	132.24	206.09	263.88	275.27	340.39	507.97	750.82
Grants Received	81z	....	2.74	1.73	6.27	5.29	11.36	16.48	18.09	28.58	37.08	37.81	39.79	47.21	48.20	40.33
Exp. & Lending Minus Repay.	82z	....	30.40	49.85	59.68	71.56	88.04	105.62	120.06	167.73	221.79	302.96	333.40	407.69	452.95	602.83
Expenditure	82	....	23.14	29.74	42.38	62.11	77.61	98.24	112.71	156.34	200.43	261.91	300.13	372.61	401.16	526.23
Lending Minus Repayments	83	....	7.26	20.11	17.30	9.45	10.43	7.38	7.35	11.39	21.36	41.05	33.27	35.08	51.79	76.60
Financing																
Net Borrowing: Domestic	84a	....	.42	2.43	.26	1.04	2.51	5.41	2.92	−3.48	.53	−3.31	−11.65	1.47	−2.16	1.82
Foreign	85a	....	11.80	24.57	21.69	18.03	13.65	10.74	6.15	14.54	12.02	10.86	11.85	58.86	20.13	33.67
Other Financing	86	....	....	....	....	....	....	....	....	....	....	....	....	....	....	....
Use of Cash Balances	87	....	−1.00	−6.00	−7.90	−13.40	−17.40	4.60	−4.49	−4.15	−33.93	−6.28	18.14	−40.24	−121.19	−223.81
Debt: Domestic	88a	....	....	....	....	....	....	....	15.35	14.49	14.28	14.67	1.35	.57	.58	.50
Foreign	89a	....	....	....	....	....	....	....	101.66	109.50	87.61	98.73	132.45	199.23	232.37	380.62
National Accounts															*Millions of Pula:*	
Exports of Goods & Services	90c	....	....	39.8	....	76.4	93.8	135.2	190.8	196.3	312.8	410.5	464.5	428.7	711.7	884.9
Government Consumption	91f	....	....	16.0	....	31.7	41.5	58.2	80.2	95.9	110.7	148.7	203.2	242.6	301.9	362.8
Gross Fixed Capital Formation	93e	....	....	53.1	....	79.6	57.3	79.1	77.8	110.1	162.9	248.8	306.6	304.6	320.3	337.6
Increase/Decrease(-) in Stocks	93i	....	....	1.3	....	17.8	44.4	35.9	20.9	32.4	34.7	42.1	49.2	87.9	26.8	28.7
Private Consumption	96f	....	....	58.1	....	105.7	131.8	179.6	222.6	262.9	330.4	408.9	460.3	513.2	563.2	615.1
Imports of Goods & Services	98c	....	....	−65.7	....	−121.8	−147.6	−187.5	−241.6	−285.5	−384.6	−487.4	−608.3	−677.1	−770.8	−838.2
Gross Domestic Product (GDP)	99b	61.3	78.5	102.6	135.0	188.3	221.2	300.5	350.7	412.1	566.9	771.6	875.5	899.9	1,153.1	1,390.9
Net Factor Inc/Pmts(-) Abroad	98.n	....	....	—	....	9.3	15.1	18.5	−24.4	−31.9	−44.7	....	....	64.9	125.1	104.9
Gross National Income (GNI)	99a	....	....	....	....	....	....	....	....	....	....	725.1	764.4	835.0	1,028.0	1,286.0
GDP Volume 1968 prices	99b.p	57.9	67.9	88.1	109.9	121.2	119.6	....	....	....	....	....	....	....	....	....
GDP Volume 1985/86 Prices	99b.p	....	....	....	....	....	746.0	887.7	919.2	1,098.2	1,207.3	1,379.9	1,511.1	1,623.8	1,884.1	2,101.2
GDP Volume 1993/94 Prices	99b.p	....	....	....	....	....	....	....	....	....	....	....	....	....	....	....
GDP Volume (1995=100)	99bv p	6.6	7.8	10.1	12.6	15.7	15.5	18.4	19.1	22.8	25.1	28.6	31.4	33.7	39.1	43.6
GDP Deflator (1995=100)	99bi p	7.5	8.2	8.3	8.7	9.8	11.7	13.3	15.0	14.8	18.5	22.0	22.8	21.8	24.1	26.0
																Millions:
Population	99z	.58	.59	.63	.65	.66	.69	.69	.71	.73	.79	.89	.94	.97	1.01	1.05

	1985	1986	1987	1988	1989	1990	1991	1992	1993	1994	1995	1996	1997	1998	1999		
Year Beginning April 1																**Government Finance**	
	413.83	539.77	502.42	789.71	571.48	793.37	760.50	897.40	913.00	212.50	356.40	1,368.60	....	....	....	Deficit (-) or Surplus	**80**
	1,079.45	1,444.37	1,705.64	2,427.73	2,694.16	3,596.48	3,969.00	4,503.60	5,103.00	4,352.90	5,377.70	7,251.90	....	....	....	Revenue	**81**
	41.23	67.62	97.29	117.71	41.48	117.77	70.00	90.10	226.50	72.20	37.90	85.20	....	....	....	Grants Received	**81z**
	706.85	972.22	1,300.51	1,755.73	2,164.16	2,920.88	3,278.50	3,696.30	4,416.50	4,212.60	5,059.20	5,968.50	....	....	....	Exp. & Lending Minus Repay.	**82z**
	642.83	909.17	1,169.39	1,469.79	1,847.90	2,368.33	2,691.30	3,209.30	3,924.50	4,017.80	4,760.70	5,764.00	....	....	....	Expenditure	**82**
	64.02	63.05	131.12	285.94	316.26	552.55	587.20	487.00	492.00	194.80	298.50	204.50	....	....	....	Lending Minus Repayments	**83**
																Financing	
	.49	−1.37	22.01	3.39	19.91	−53.41	140.40	−136.70	120.00	31.50	32.80	11.90	....	....	....	Net Borrowing: Domestic	**84a**
	13.22	73.09	75.40	92.35	56.52	2.49	36.00	79.50	43.60	−19.00	−51.00	89.60	....	....	....	Foreign	**85a**
	....	....	....	....	....	....	....	....	....	....	....	....	....	....	....	Other Financing	**86**
	−427.54	−611.49	−599.83	−885.45	−647.91	−742.45	−936.90	−840.20	−1,076.60	−225.00	−338.20	−1,470.10	....	....	....	Use of Cash Balances	**87**
	.50	.50	.34	—	—	—	—	—	—	—	—	—	....	....	....	Debt: Domestic	**88a**
	410.96	474.12	557.51	713.95	751.88	801.92	965.80	1,096.30	1,254.50	1,377.00	1,438.90	1,797.90	....	....	....	Foreign	**89a**
Year Ending June 30																**National Accounts**	
	1,074.5	1,737.5	1,838.8	3,119.0	3,701.6	3,658.3	4,107.1	4,346.6	4,082.8	5,421.8	5,974.9	7,509.6	10,110.8	11,484.7	9,863.9	Exports of Goods & Services	**90c**
	443.1	531.8	722.6	1,052.3	1,182.9	1,435.7	1,902.2	2,016.4	2,595.2	3,179.5	3,603.5	4,175.2	4,925.3	5,872.8	6,705.7	Government Consumption	**91f**
	484.0	457.9	669.9	1,081.8	1,692.9	2,080.9	2,365.3	2,473.4	2,388.3	2,749.5	3,073.9	3,546.5	4,176.5	5,047.1	6,433.8	Gross Fixed Capital Formation	**93e**
	71.6	−64.6	18.6	−804.3	56.1	....	....	−13.3	156.7	90.8	428.4	101.6	512.3	699.5	1,730.8	Increase/Decrease(-) in Stocks	**93i**
	784.8	901.8	987.4	1,116.0	1,682.8	2,732.2	2,750.6	3,197.8	3,528.0	3,578.0	3,789.2	4,036.9	4,368.0	5,774.2	8,673.2	Private Consumption	**96f**
	−1,029.4	−1,143.8	−1,427.5	−1,769.2	−2,479.5	−3,369.8	−3,649.9	−3,648.3	−3,625.0	−3,987.8	−4,617.9	−5,168.0	−6,590.0	−8,449.9	10,148.5	Imports of Goods & Services	**98c**
	1,828.6	2,420.6	2,585.3	3,498.7	5,803.5	6,490.7	7,496.5	8,298.6	9,045.4	10,972.5	12,252.0	14,201.8	17,485.7	20,363.1	23,258.9	Gross Domestic Product (GDP)	**99b**
	195.2	322.8	251.7	465.1	....	....	....	....	....	....	....	....	....	....	....	Net Factor Inc/Pmts(-) Abroad	**98.n**
	1,633.4	2,097.8	2,558.2	3,316.1	....	....	....	....	....	....	....	....	....	....	....	Gross National Income (GNI)	**99a**
	....	....	....	....	....	....	....	....	....	....	....	....	....	....	....	GDP Volume 1968 prices	**99b.**p
	2,251.9	2,420.6	2,636.1	....	....	....	....	....	....	....	....	....	....	....	....	GDP Volume 1985/86 Prices	**99b.**p
	....	....	6,153.3	7,056.0	8,651.8	9,127.4	9,918.7	10,541.3	10,532.7	10,972.2	11,249.2	11,995.2	12,838.3	13,868.5	14,450.9	GDP Volume 1993/94 Prices	**99b.**p
	46.7	50.2	54.7	62.7	76.9	81.1	88.2	93.7	93.6	97.5	100.0	106.6	114.1	123.3	128.5	GDP Volume (1995=100)	**99bv** p
	31.9	39.3	38.6	45.5	61.6	65.3	69.4	72.3	78.9	91.8	100.0	108.7	125.1	134.8	147.8	GDP Deflator (1995=100)	**99bi** p
Midyear Estimates																	
	1.09	1.13	1.17	1.21	1.24	1.30	1.33	1.36	1.39	1.42	1.46	1.50	1.53	1.57	1.61	**Population**	**99z**

Brazil

		1970	1971	1972	1973	1974	1975	1976	1977	1978	1979	1980	1981	1982	1983	1984
Exchange Rates										*Reais per Trillion SDRs through 1983, per Bill. 1984-88, per Mill.*						
Principal Rate	aa	1.80	2.23	2.46	2.73	3.32	3.86	5.22	7.09	9.91	20.37	30.38	54.09	101.35	374.62	‡1.13
										Reais per Trillion US$ through 1983, per Bill.US$ 1984-88, per Mill.US$						
Principal Rate	ae	1.80	2.05	2.27	2.27	2.71	3.30	4.49	5.84	7.61	15.47	23.82	46.47	91.88	357.82	‡1.16
Principal Rate	rf	1.67	1.92	2.16	2.23	2.47	2.95	3.88	5.14	6.57	9.79	19.16	33.85	65.25	209.73	‡.67
Fund Position														*Millions of SDRs*		
Quota	2f. s	440	440	440	440	440	440	440	440	665	665	998	998	998	1,461	1,461
SDRs	1b. s	62	110	157	157	163	163	171	173	184	291	301	388	—	—	1
Reserve Position in the Fund	1c. s	117	116	116	116	116	116	162	160	139	183	270	227	260	—	—
Total Fund Cred.&Loans Outstg.	2tl	—	—	—	—	—	—	—	—	—	—	—	—	499	2,526	4,270
International Liquidity											*Millions of US Dollars Unless Otherwise Indicated:*					
Total Reserves minus Gold	1l. d	1,142	1,696	4,133	6,360	5,216	3,980	6,488	7,192	11,826	8,966	5,769	6,604	3,928	4,355	11,508
SDRs	1b. d	62	120	170	190	199	191	199	210	239	383	384	452	—	—	1
Reserve Position in the Fund	1c. d	117	126	126	140	142	136	188	195	181	241	344	264	287	—	—
Foreign Exchange	1d. d	962	1,450	3,836	6,030	4,874	3,653	6,101	6,787	11,406	8,342	5,042	5,888	3,641	4,355	11,507
Other Liquid Foreign Assets	1e. d	....	....	....	....	....	....	....	....	....	....	....	....	....	....	....
Gold (Million Fine Troy Ounces)	1ad	1.29	1.32	1.33	1.33	1.33	1.33	1.33	1.52	1.61	1.70	1.88	2.20	.15	.54	1.47
Gold (National Valuation)	1and	45	50	50	56	56	56	56	64	68	75	1,143	905	65	207	488
Monetary Authorities: Other Assets	3.. d	299	316	476	665	896	1,195	1,473	1,599	1,513	1,613	4,333	3,050	2,804	3,818	4,463
Other Liab.	4.. d	440	405	618	574	940	1,162	1,765	1,956	3,286	4,504	6,810	6,846	8,557	14,928	18,888
Deposit Money Banks: Assets	7a. d	192	335	436	895	1,161	929	1,175	1,214	2,043	1,817	1,489	2,088	2,099	1,924	2,274
Liabilities	7b. d	1,633	893	1,452	2,258	2,973	2,778	4,797	5,849	8,365	8,109	11,292	15,764	18,150	16,997	17,325
Other Banking Insts.: Assets	7e. d	....	....	....	....	....	....	....	....	....	....	....	24	99	401	136
Liabilities	7f. d	204	357	1,290	1,613	1,757	2,111	2,276	2,704	4,183	4,823	5,337	6,336	6,794	7,032	6,564
Monetary Authorities										*Millionths of Reais through 1974; Thousandths 1975-85; Reais 1986-89;*						
Foreign Assets	11	2,659	‡4,000	10,182	15,636	16,000	‡16	34	48	‡102	165	267	488	621	2,984	18,960
Claims on Central Government	12a	930	‡-2,545	-727	-2,545	-9,455	‡-17	-20	-18	‡35	43	157	330	618	1,235	3,144
Claims on State and Local Govts	12b	323	‡—	—	—	—	‡—	—	1	‡6	8	9	19	30	67	92
Claims on Private Sector	12d	4,428	‡9,455	12,727	18,182	32,000	‡54	86	125	‡154	253	435	720	1,253	2,504	5,876
Claims on Deposit Money Banks	12e	560	‡1,455	2,182	3,273	6,545	‡12	17	24	‡26	35	57	129	244	486	1,769
Claims on Other Banking Insts	12f	—	‡364	1,091	1,455	5,091	‡9	16	28	‡25	27	37	66	89	132	191
Claims on Nonbank Financial Insts	12g	....	....	....	....	....	....	....	....	....	....	....	....	....	....	....
Reserve Money	14	6,649	‡8,000	9,091	13,455	18,545	‡26	40	60	‡86	160	252	429	801	1,649	5,409
of which: Currency Outside DMBs	14a	2,443	‡3,273	4,364	5,818	8,000	‡11	17	24	‡34	61	105	190	367	684	2,272
Liabs. of Central Bank: Securities	16ac	....	....	....	....	....	....	....	....	....	....	....	....	....	....	....
Restricted Deposits	16b	218	‡—	—	—	—	‡3	15	16	‡23	30	12	5	3	1	35
Foreign Liabilities	16c	4	‡727	1,091	1,091	1,091	‡1	4	6	‡3	4	41	84	629	2,535	8,086
Long-Term Foreign Liabilities	16cl	1,801	‡364	364	364	1,455	‡3	4	5	‡22	65	120	233	204	3,720	18,495
Central Government Deposits	16d	....	....	....	....	....	....	....	....	88	79	171	478	636	808	7,861
Capital Accounts	17a	2,545	‡3,636	6,182	8,727	15,636	‡24	36	55	‡64	88	76	-17	-424	-3,272	-12,809
Other Items (Net)	17r	-2,317	‡—	8,727	12,364	13,455	‡18	35	67	‡62	107	289	541	1,006	1,965	2,957
Deposit Money Banks										*Millionths of Reais through 1974; Thousandths 1975-85; Reais 1986-89;*						
Reserves	20	1,513	‡2,182	2,545	3,636	4,000	‡4	9	19	‡29	51	84	132	276	552	1,906
Other Claims on Monetary Author.	20c	....	....	....	....	....	....	....	....	....	....	....	....	....	....	....
Blocked Financial Assets	20d	....	....	....	....	....	....	....	....	....	....	....	....	....	....	....
Foreign Assets	21	344	‡727	1,091	2,182	3,273	‡3	5	7	‡15	28	35	97	192	685	2,620
Claims on Central Government	22a	1,152	‡1,818	2,909	4,364	5,818	‡9	15	19	‡26	37	90	269	524	1,091	4,616
Claims on State and Local Govts	22b	679	‡1,091	1,455	1,818	1,818	‡3	6	10	‡19	38	73	219	498	1,521	4,874
Claims on Nonfin.Pub.Enterprises	22c	....	....	....	....	....	....	....	....	23	49	98	251	583	2,037	6,415
Claims on Private Sector	22d	9,036	‡13,091	19,273	27,636	41,455	‡63	95	143	‡205	337	572	1,170	2,377	5,731	19,269
Claims on Other Banking Insts	22f	—	‡—	—	364	364	‡—	—	1	‡1	4	11	26	98	241	537
Demand Deposits	24	7,808	‡10,182	14,182	21,091	28,364	‡41	55	77	‡103	176	304	561	900	1,866	5,418
Time and Savings Deposits	25	1,858	‡1,091	2,182	2,545	2,909	‡4	7	16	‡34	56	67	152	412	1,448	7,287
Money Market Instruments	26aa	....	....	....	....	....	....	....	....	....	....	....	....	....	....	....
Restricted Deposits	26b	....	....	....	....	....	....	....	....	....	....	....	....	....	....	....
Foreign Liabilities	26c	2,104	‡727	1,091	2,545	3,636	‡3	10	15	‡30	51	120	309	586	1,966	7,914
Long-Term Foreign Liabilities	26cl	727	‡1,091	2,182	2,545	4,364	‡6	11	19	‡33	73	153	449	1,075	4,085	11,751
Central Government Deposits	26d	—	‡364	364	364	364	‡1	1	1	‡47	57	104	247	489	745	2,692
Credit from Monetary Authorities	26g	609	‡1,455	2,182	3,273	6,182	‡12	17	25	‡21	33	60	132	246	555	1,809
Liabilities to Other Banking Insts	26i	....	....	....	....	....	....	....	....	....	....	....	....	....	....	....
Liab. to Nonbank Financial Insts	26j	....	....	....	....	....	....	....	....	....	....	....	....	....	....	....
Capital Accounts	27a	2,043	‡2,909	4,000	5,455	7,273	‡10	16	26	‡47	64	111	289	656	2,007	6,881
Other Items (Net)	27r	-2,426	‡1,091	1,091	2,182	3,636	‡6	14	19	‡3	34	45	26	184	-813	-3,516
Monetary Survey										*Millionths of Reais through 1974; Thousandths 1975-85; Reais 1986-89;*						
Foreign Assets (Net)	31n	894	‡3,273	9,091	14,182	14,545	‡15	25	34	‡85	138	141	192	-401	-832	5,579
Domestic Credit	32	16,549	‡22,909	36,364	50,909	76,727	‡121	197	309	‡368	683	1,234	2,408	5,024	14,036	39,106
Claims on Central Govt. (Net)	32an	2,083	‡-1,091	1,818	1,455	-4,000	‡-9	-7	—	‡-74	-55	-28	-126	17	773	-2,792
Claims on State and Local Govts	32b	1,002	‡1,091	1,455	1,818	1,818	‡3	6	11	‡25	46	83	239	528	1,588	4,966
Claims on Nonfin.Pub.Enterprises	32c	—	‡—	—	—	—	‡—	—	1	‡32	70	125	313	662	3,067	11,059
Claims on Private Sector	32d	13,465	‡22,545	32,000	45,818	73,455	‡117	181	269	‡359	590	1,006	1,890	3,629	8,235	25,145
Claims on Other Banking Insts	32f	—	‡364	1,091	1,818	5,455	‡9	16	29	‡26	32	48	92	187	372	728
Claims on Nonbank Financial Inst	32g	....	....	....	....	....	....	....	....	....	....	....	....	....	....	....
Money	34	11,523	‡15,636	21,455	31,273	42,909	‡61	84	116	‡158	276	468	855	1,441	2,922	8,887
Quasi-Money	35	2,191	‡3,273	2,182	2,545	2,909	‡4	7	16	‡34	56	67	152	412	1,448	7,287
Money Market Instruments	36aa	....	....	....	....	....	....	....	....	....	....	....	....	....	....	....
Liabs. of Central Bank: Securities	36ac	....	....	....	....	....	....	....	....	....	....	....	....	....	....	....
Restricted Deposits	36b	218	‡—	—	—	—	‡3	15	16	‡23	30	12	5	3	1	35
Long-Term Foreign Liabilities	36cl	2,529	‡1,455	2,545	2,909	5,818	‡8	15	24	‡56	139	273	682	1,279	7,806	30,246
Liabilities to Other Banking Insts	36i	....	....	....	....	....	....	....	....	....	....	....	....	....	....	....
Liab. to Nonbank Financial Insts	36j	....	....	....	....	....	....	....	....	....	....	....	....	....	....	....
Capital Accounts	37a	4,589	‡6,545	10,182	14,182	22,909	‡33	52	81	‡111	152	188	271	233	-1,265	-5,928
Other Items (Net)	37r	-3,606	‡-727	9,091	14,182	16,727	‡25	49	91	‡73	168	367	635	1,256	2,292	4,159
Money plus Quasi-Money	35l	13,714	‡18,909	23,636	33,818	45,818	‡65	91	132	‡192	332	535	1,007	1,853	4,370	16,174

1985	1986	1987	1988	1989	1990	1991	1992	1993	1994	1995	1996	1997	1998	1999		
1989-92, per Thous.SDRs thereafter: End of Period															**Exchange Rates**	
4.19	6.63	37.27	374.50	I5.43	91.60	555.94	6,193.75	I162.88	1,235.03	1,446.35	1,494.62	1,506.30	1,701.89	2,455.42	Principal Rate	**aa**
1989-92, per Thous.US$ thereafter: End of Per.(ae) Per. Average (rf)																
3.81	5.42	26.27	278.29	I4.13	64.39	388.65	4,504.55	I118.58	846.00	973.00	1,039.40	1,116.40	1,208.70	1,789.00	Principal Rate	**ae**
2.25	4.96	14.26	95.27	I1.03	24.84	147.86	1,641.09	I32.16	639.30	917.67	1,005.10	1,077.99	1,160.52	1,814.73	Principal Rate	**rf**
End of Period															**Fund Position**	
1,461	1,461	1,461	1,461	1,461	1,461	1,461	2,171	2,171	2,171	2,171	2,171	2,171	2,171	3,036	Quota	**2f.s**
1	—	—	—	—	8	9	1	2	—	1	1	—	1	7	SDRs	**1b.s**
—	—	—	—	—	—	—	—	—	—	—	—	—	—	—	Reserve Position in the Fund	**1c.s**
4,205	3,680	2,803	2,477	1,843	1,280	865	581	221	128	95	47	23	3,427	6,431	Total Fund Cred.&Loans Outstg.	**2tl**
End of Period															**International Liquidity**	
10,605	I5,803	6,299	6,972	7,535	7,441	8,033	22,521	30,604	37,070	49,708	58,323	50,827	42,580	34,796	Total Reserves minus Gold	**1l.d**
1	—	—	—	—	11	13	1	2	—	1	1	1	2	10	SDRs	**1b.d**
—	—	—	—	—	—	—	—	—	—	—	—	—	—	—	Reserve Position in the Fund	**1c.d**
10,604	I5,803	6,299	6,971	7,535	7,430	8,020	22,520	30,602	37,069	49,707	58,322	50,826	42,578	34,786	Foreign Exchange	**1d.d**
....	....	....	1,024	950	798	643	486	501	319	365	467	503	585	618	Other Liquid Foreign Assets	**1e.d**
3.10	2.43	2.43	2.73	2.98	4.57	2.02	2.23	2.93	3.71	4.58	3.69	3.03	4.60	3.17	Gold (Million Fine Troy Ounces)	**1ad**
1,004	958	1,159	1,144	1,194	1,735	731	747	1,107	1,418	1,767	1,381	903	1,358	929	Gold (National Valuation)	**1and**
4,965	2,445	3,315	2,446	2,751	2,425	2,095	2,331	2,056	1,851	4,077	5,050	4,935	5,456	5,334	Monetary Authorities: Other Assets	**3..d**
19,198	29,939	46,405	46,024	46,728	28,502	56,762	47,253	48,399	6,888	5,614	3,239	2,948	8,284	5,288	Other Liab.	**4..d**
1,983	3,379	3,544	5,551	8,186	8,628	9,573	11,763	15,196	20,855	18,682	20,345	19,550	17,621	16,618	Deposit Money Banks: Assets	**7a.d**
14,053	14,128	13,138	14,167	15,252	15,696	16,776	21,472	31,054	36,771	42,494	51,432	54,756	50,580	41,066	Liabilities	**7b.d**
8	7	9	127	77	100	27	141	702	1,504	393	177	143	74	65	Other Banking Insts.: Assets	**7e.d**
6,539	6,287	6,307	4,183	2,849	2,352	2,013	2,242	2,527	2,224	2,247	3,211	4,398	9,406	6,282	Liabilities	**7f.d**
Thousands 1990-92; Millions Beginning 1993: End of Period															**Monetary Authorities**	
62,094	I47	269	I3,257	49,425	I675	4,028	111,731	I3,968	35,326	55,218	69,829	61,745	55,053	69,273	Foreign Assets	**11**
12,698	I224	901	I18,140	300,863	I5,747	29,354	363,345	I7,941	26,509	31,221	27,713	41,233	136,916	121,463	Claims on Central Government	**12a**
257	I—	—	I—	—	I194	862	172	I9	—	—	—	—	—	—	Claims on State and Local Govts	**12b**
23,337	I—	—	I8	49	I—	—	2	I—	3	5	5	5	—	—	Claims on Private Sector	**12d**
4,977	I114	445	I66	3,733	I153	662	17,299	I120	20,557	34,576	67,642	68,012	40,368	31,151	Claims on Deposit Money Banks	**12e**
756	I2	9	I2	474	I6	6	163	I1	5	5	3	902	—	—	Claims on Other Banking Insts	**12f**
....	I—	1	I20	8	I—	1	5	I—	—	—	6	7	1,926	2,036	Claims on Nonbank Financial Insts	**12g**
18,981	I75	413	I1,686	42,411	I821	4,897	61,120	I1,543	36,130	40,430	49,638	66,636	59,213	63,849	Reserve Money	**14**
8,671	I31	92	I760	14,677	I356	1,314	14,564	I340	8,700	12,517	15,316	18,141	21,185	25,978	*of which: Currency Outside DMBs*	**14a**
....	I74	594	I—	—	I11	987	94,933	I867	39,289	52,457	83,106	65,724	104,709	62,468	Liabs. of Central Bank: Securities	**16ac**
134	I33	152	I1,148	16,137	I1,498	4,449	5,014	I75	306	190	125	12	10	13	Restricted Deposits	**16b**
21,143	I30	270	I1,096	14,227	I203	7,303	28,125	I807	895	478	143	167	7,723	15,942	Foreign Liabilities	**16c**
69,276	I156	1,047	I12,571	187,771	I1,656	15,237	188,322	I4,968	5,075	5,116	3,292	3,157	8,111	9,297	Long-Term Foreign Liabilities	**16cl**
31,981	I36	134	I780	35,195	I874	3,036	42,889	I1,023	12,094	22,239	25,143	41,135	50,403	75,779	Central Government Deposits	**16d**
–38,888	I35	48	I4,468	42,509	I128	727	70,673	I1,838	998	1,408	4,190	4,198	3,809	–4,496	Capital Accounts	**17a**
1,491	I–52	–1,034	I–257	16,303	I1,585	–1,722	1,642	I918	–12,387	–1,293	–438	–9,125	285	1,070	Other Items (Net)	**17r**
Thousands 1990-92; Millions Beginning 1993: End of Period															**Deposit Money Banks**	
5,900	I41	351	I1,597	21,710	I387	2,325	30,779	I901	22,956	22,126	22,035	42,494	32,716	38,024	Reserves	**20**
....	....	....	97	299	I9	119	46,131	I320	5,192	6,578	18,932	11,603	37,545	28,845	Other Claims on Monetary Author.	**20c**
....	....	....	—	—	I1,251	3,612	1	I—	—	—	—	—	—	—	Blocked Financial Assets	**20d**
7,528	I18	93	I1,537	33,645	I529	3,720	52,983	I1,802	17,602	18,159	21,130	21,810	21,284	29,716	Foreign Assets	**21**
17,369	I28	88	I1,596	122,967	I336	1,055	27,547	I1,027	7,850	16,118	29,224	92,061	74,110	114,723	Claims on Central Government	**22a**
17,612	I36	220	I2,960	44,977	I669	3,770	57,656	I1,522	27,480	20,284	55,986	39,229	20,007	10,437	Claims on State and Local Govts	**22b**
21,781	I105	673	I2,931	53,009	I636	3,040	42,715	I1,158	10,243	6,093	18,669	5,620	12,553	15,193	Claims on Nonfin.Pub.Enterprises	**22c**
67,785	I286	949	I20,041	305,429	I3,595	19,971	348,163	I11,589	158,826	199,138	204,681	225,197	259,983	272,575	Claims on Private Sector	**22d**
3,646	I5	59	I10	2,903	I18	135	3,046	I79	873	770	1,078	3,353	3,284	2,903	Claims on Other Banking Insts	**22f**
25,740	I125	265	I1,748	22,619	I550	2,581	24,073	I497	13,979	14,034	14,320	27,912	29,059	36,242	Demand Deposits	**24**
29,729	I100	311	I10,816	172,322	I2,000	16,548	312,748	I9,980	119,979	159,901	173,714	203,992	225,619	238,503	Time and Savings Deposits	**25**
....	....	....	5	4,909	I53	328	9,140	I283	3,320	4,744	7,029	10,283	8,936	9,627	Money Market Instruments	**26aa**
....	....	....	—	—	I1,645	4,396	18	I—	98	1,806	227	—	—	—	Restricted Deposits	**26b**
22,805	I40	210	I809	19,268	I275	1,736	70,000	I2,568	21,212	28,209	37,441	38,539	31,974	48,834	Foreign Liabilities	**26c**
30,547	I36	134	I3,114	43,416	I688	4,783	26,719	I1,115	9,823	13,095	15,976	22,547	29,122	24,601	Long-Term Foreign Liabilities	**26cl**
6,707	I15	35	I6,024	111,428	I654	3,194	44,638	I1,411	18,288	14,670	16,074	17,939	9,964	6,620	Central Government Deposits	**26d**
1,950	I115	784	I133	5,335	I181	646	16,508	I146	20,455	23,407	39,025	30,272	11,623	521	Credit from Monetary Authorities	**26g**
....	....	....	1,083	16,385	I164	1,228	31,305	I1,081	11,914	9,396	22,017	21,973	26,774	28,473	Liabilities to Other Banking Insts	**26i**
....	....	....	12	696	I2	13	442	I1	92	111	60	234	159	268	Liab. to Nonbank Financial Insts	**26j**
24,946	I77	370	I5,855	121,551	I1,471	10,726	143,861	I4,069	44,094	57,704	74,127	95,976	115,114	131,644	Capital Accounts	**27a**
–802	I10	325	I1,170	67,008	I–250	–8,435	–70,431	I–2,752	–12,232	–37,811	–28,275	–28,300	–26,862	–12,917	Other Items (Net)	**27r**
Thousands 1990-92; Millions Beginning 1993: End of Period															**Monetary Survey**	
25,675	I–5	–118	I2,889	49,575	I726	–1,291	66,589	I2,395	30,821	44,690	53,375	44,849	36,640	34,212	Foreign Assets (Net)	**31n**
157,157	I609	2,654	I38,905	684,056	I9,674	51,964	755,285	I20,892	201,407	236,725	296,148	348,533	448,412	456,931	Domestic Credit	**32**
–8,621	I175	742	I12,932	277,207	I4,555	24,180	303,364	I6,535	3,977	10,430	15,720	74,220	150,659	153,787	Claims on Central Govt. (Net)	**32an**
17,869	I36	220	I2,960	44,977	I863	4,632	57,828	I1,531	27,480	20,284	55,986	39,229	20,007	10,437	Claims on State and Local Govts	**32b**
52,386	I105	674	I2,931	53,009	I636	3,040	42,715	I1,158	10,243	6,093	18,669	5,620	12,553	15,193	Claims on Nonfin.Pub.Enterprises	**32c**
91,122	I286	949	I20,049	305,478	I3,595	19,971	348,165	I11,589	158,829	199,143	204,686	225,202	259,983	272,575	Claims on Private Sector	**32d**
4,402	I7	68	I12	3,377	I24	140	3,209	I79	878	775	1,081	4,255	3,284	2,903	Claims on Other Banking Insts	**32f**
....	I—	1	I20	8	I—	1	5	I—	—	—	6	7	1,926	2,036	Claims on Nonbank Financial Inst	**32g**
38,600	I166	524	I2,623	37,697	I917	4,856	52,539	I1,113	25,540	32,094	41,683	50,999	54,819	62,278	Money	**34**
29,729	I100	311	I10,816	172,322	I2,000	16,548	312,748	I9,980	119,979	159,901	173,714	203,992	225,619	238,503	Quasi-Money	**35**
....	....	....	5	4,909	I53	328	9,140	I283	3,320	4,744	7,029	10,283	8,936	9,627	Money Market Instruments	**36aa**
....	I74	594	I–97	–299	I2	868	48,802	I547	34,097	45,879	64,174	54,121	67,164	33,623	Liabs. of Central Bank: Securities	**36ac**
134	I33	152	I1,148	16,137	I3,143	8,845	5,032	I75	404	1,996	352	12	10	13	Restricted Deposits	**36b**
99,823	I193	1,181	I15,685	231,187	I2,344	20,020	215,041	I6,083	14,898	18,211	19,268	25,704	37,233	33,898	Long-Term Foreign Liabilities	**36cl**
....	....	....	1,083	16,385	I164	1,228	31,305	I1,081	11,914	9,396	22,017	21,973	26,774	28,473	Liabilities to Other Banking Insts	**36i**
....	....	....	12	696	I2	13	442	I1	92	111	60	234	159	268	Liab. to Nonbank Financial Insts	**36j**
–13,942	I112	418	I10,323	164,000	I1,599	11,453	214,533	I5,908	45,092	59,112	78,317	100,174	118,923	127,148	Capital Accounts	**37a**
28,488	I–73	–643	I195	90,536	I178	–13,488	–67,706	I–1,783	–23,108	–50,029	–57,090	–74,110	–54,585	–42,688	Other Items (Net)	**37r**
68,329	I266	834	I13,440	210,019	I2,918	21,404	365,286	I11,092	145,519	191,995	215,397	254,991	280,438	300,781	Money plus Quasi-Money	**35l**

	1970	1971	1972	1973	1974	1975	1976	1977	1978	1979	1980	1981	1982	1983	1984
Other Banking Institutions									*Millionths of Reais through 1974; Thousandths 1975-85; Reais 1986-89;*						
Reserves 40	364	I364	727	727	1,091	I1	2	2	I2	4	4	12	25	49	156
Other Claims on Monetary Author. 40c	....	....	....	....	....										
Blocked Financial Assets 40d	....	....	....	....	....										
Foreign Assets 41	—	I—	—	—	—	I—			I—	—	—	1	9	143	157
Claims on Central Government 42a	727	I1,091	2,545	3,636	5,818	I11	18	28	I43	81	129	374	909	2,641	7,771
Claims on State and Local Govts 42b	364	I—	364	364	364	I—	1	2	I7	16	32	60	180	574	1,999
Claims on Nonfin.Pub.Enterprises 42c									33	59	102	291	686	1,735	4,532
Claims on Private Sector 42d	8,364	I12,727	20,727	32,000	51,636	I84	143	224	I304	516	907	2,013	4,452	11,843	38,604
Claims on Deposit Money Banks 42e	364	I727	1,091	1,818	4,000	I7	13	22	I23	50	106	252	530	1,351	4,153
Demand Deposits 44	727	I727	727	1,091	1,455	I2	4	5	I5	9	18	34	60	128	361
Time and Savings Deposits 45	1,818	I3,636	6,545	11,636	18,909	I34	59	97	I153	272	499	1,214	2,807	8,482	29,133
Money Market Instruments 46aa	727	I1,091	1,818	2,182	2,909	I3	4	4	I4	5	6	10	11	29	49
Restricted Deposits 46b			....	....	....										
Foreign Liabilities 46c	....	....	....	....	....										
Long-Term Foreign Liabilities 46cl	364	I727	2,909	3,636	4,727	I7	10	16	I32	75	126	294	621	2,504	7,562
Central Government Deposits 46d	....	....	....	....	....				130	230	419	957	2,159	6,056	20,002
Credit from Monetary Authorities 46g	—	I364	727	1,455	3,273	I6	10	17	I25	32	34	62	104	173	404
Credit from Deposit Money Banks 46h															
Capital Accounts 47a	2,909	I4,727	6,545	9,818	15,636	I24	37	51	I71	109	186	422	1,061	2,974	10,040
Other Items (Net) 47r	3,636	I3,636	6,182	8,727	16,000	I27	52	88	I-8	-5	-6	9	-33	-2,010	-10,179
Banking Survey									*Millionths of Reais through 1974; Thousandths 1975-85; Reais 1986-89;*						
Foreign Assets (Net) 51n	894	I3,273	9,091	14,182	14,545	I15	25	34	I85	138	141	193	-392	-689	5,736
Domestic Credit 52	26,004	I36,364	58,909	85,091	129,091	I207	343	535	I600	1,094	1,938	4,096	8,904	24,400	71,282
Claims on Central Govt. (Net) 52an	2,810	I—	4,364	5,091	1,818	I2	11	28	I-161	-203	-317	-709	-1,234	-2,643	-15,023
Claims on State and Local Govts 52b	1,365	I1,091	1,818	2,182	2,182	I4	7	13	I32	61	115	299	708	2,163	6,965
Claims on Nonfin.Pub.Enterprises 52c	....	....	....	....	....	I—	—	1	I66	129	227	604	1,348	4,802	15,591
Claims on Private Sector 52d	21,828	I35,273	52,727	77,818	125,091	I201	324	493	I663	1,106	1,913	3,903	8,081	20,078	63,749
Claims on Nonbank Financial Inst 52g	....	....	....	....	....										
Liquid Liabilities 55l	15,896	I22,909	30,182	45,818	65,091	I100	152	232	I348	609	1,047	2,243	4,695	12,931	45,511
Money Market Instruments 56aa	727	I1,091	1,818	2,182	2,909	I3	4	4	I4	5	6	10	11	29	49
Liabs. of Central Bank: Securities 56ac															
Restricted Deposits 56b	218	I—	—	—	—	I3	15	16	I23	30	12	5	3	1	35
Long-Term Foreign Liabilities 56cl	2,892	I2,182	5,455	6,545	10,545	I15	25	40	I88	213	399	976	1,900	10,309	37,808
Liab. to Nonbank Financial Insts 56j															
Capital Accounts 57a	7,498	I11,273	16,727	24,000	38,545	I57	89	132	I182	262	374	693	1,293	1,709	4,112
Other Items (Net) 57r	-333	I2,182	13,818	20,727	26,545	I43	83	145	I41	113	241	362	610	-1,268	-10,496
Nonbank Financial Institutions									*Reais through 1989; Thousands of Reais from 1990 through 1992;*						
Reserves .... 40..n	....	....	....	....	....										
Other Claims on Monetary Auth. 40c.n	....	....	....	....	....										
Blocked Financial Assets 40d.n	....	....	....	....	....										
Foreign Assets .... 41..n	....	....	....	....	....										
Claims on Central Government 42a.n	....	....	....	....	....										
Claims on State and Local Govt. 42b.n	....	....	....	....	....										
Claims on Nonfin.Pub.Enterprises 42c.n	....	....	....	....	....										
Claims on Private Sector 42d.n	....	....	....	....	....										
Claims on Deposit Money Banks 42e.n	....	....	....	....	....										
Claims on Other Banking Insts 42f.n	....	....	....	....	....										
Money Market Instruments 46aan	....	....	....	....	....										
Restricted Deposits 46b.n	....	....	....	....	....										
Foreign Liabilities 46c.n	....	....	....	....	....										
Long-Term Foreign Liabilities 46cln	....	....	....	....	....										
Central Government Deposits 46d.n	....	....	....	....	....										
Liabilities to Other Banking Insts 46i.n	....	....	....	....	....										
Capital Accounts 47a.n	....	....	....	....	....										
Other Items (Net) 47r.n	....	....	....	....	....										
Money (National Definitions)									*Millionths of Reais through 1974; Thousandths 1975-85; Reais 1986-89;*						
Reserve Money 19ma	4,495	5,964	7,006	10,261	13,421	I18	29	47	70	133	211	353	707	1,271	4,627
M1 .... 59ma	12,727	16,727	23,273	34,182	45,455	I65	91	125	176	305	540	1,014	1,689	3,337	10,072
M2 .... 59mb	17,091	22,182	32,727	47,636	64,727	I100	152	210	307	479	821	1,953	3,834	7,772	32,468
M3 .... 59mc	17,818	23,636	35,273	52,727	75,273	I120	191	275	412	669	1,179	2,857	5,914	14,374	55,199
M4 .... 59md	22,182	32,364	49,091	74,909	102,909	I160	243	353	542	875	1,487	3,533	7,605	19,068	73,092
BA .... 19ma a	....	....	....	....	....										
B2 .... 19ma b	....	....	....	....	....										
M2A .... 59mb a	....	....	....	....	....										
M3A .... 59mc a	....	....	....	....	....										
M4A .... 59md a	....	....	....	....	....										
Interest Rates															*Percent Per Annum*
Discount Rate (End of Period) 60															
Money Market Rate 60b	20.00	20.00	20.00	18.00	18.00	18.00	25.33	28.33	31.50	33.58	I47.33	89.74	120.66	203.23	257.32
Treasury Bill Rate 60c	....	....	....	....	....										....
Treasury Bill Rate (Fgn.Currency) ..... 60c. f	....	....	....	....	....										....
Savings Rate 60k	....	....	....	....	....										....
Deposit Rate 60l	....	....	....	....	....						115.00	108.00	156.10	154.56	267.63
Prices, Production, Labor														*Index Numbers (1995=100):*	
Share Prices 62															
W'sale Prices (1995=1 trillion) 63.a	.3	.4	.5	.6	.7	.9	1.3	1.9	2.6	4.1	8.4	17.4	33.6	89.9	302.4
W'sale Prices(1995=1 million) 63.b	....	....	....	....	....										
Wholesale Prices 63	....	....	....	....	....										
Consumer Prices (1995=10 billion) 64.a	....	....	....	....	....							.1	.2	.4	.9	2.7
Consumer Prices (1995=1 million) 64.b	....	....	....	....	....										
Consumer Prices 64	....	....	....	....	....										
Industrial Production .... 66..c	....	....	....	....	....										
															Number in Thousands:
Labor Force 67d	....	....	....	....	....										
Employment 67e	....	....	....	....	....										
Unemployment 67c	....	....	....	....	....										2,234
Unemployment Rate (%) 67r	....	....	....	....	....										4.3

1985	1986	1987	1988	1989	1990	1991	1992	1993	1994	1995	1996	1997	1998	1999		
Thousands 1990-92; Millions Beginning 1993: End of Period															**Other Banking Institutions**	
3,488	....	....	I 443	3,260	I 15	113	2,064	I 53	1,526	611	768	1,174	881	224	Reserves	40
....	....	....	1	—	I —	—	829	I 15	113	459	1,195	3,015	734	211	Other Claims on Monetary Author.	40c
....	....	....	—	—	I 74	265	—	I —	—	—	—	—	—	—	Blocked Financial Assets	40d
31	I —	—	I 35	315	I 6	11	634	I 83	1,269	382	184	159	89	117	Foreign Assets	41
20,817	....	....	I 229	1,671	I 3	17	2,965	I 95	525	1,633	1,644	3,800	9,204	2,044	Claims on Central Government	42a
7,328	I 13	86	I 701	7,763	I 113	434	5,852	I 156	918	931	1,160	2,400	2,524	3,112	Claims on State and Local Govts	42b
26,232	I 40	188	I 1,845	22,984	I 311	1,703	15,257	I 355	2,705	3,372	3,547	2,811	3,199	1,869	Claims on Nonfin.Pub.Enterprises	42c
119,282	....	....	I 6,629	72,398	I 898	5,766	82,942	I 1,981	25,796	27,332	31,802	41,440	51,742	58,542	Claims on Private Sector	42d
17,997	....	....	I 663	8,845	I 397	2,144	31,115	I 1,025	11,506	15,624	19,438	22,749	26,983	37,447	Claims on Deposit Money Banks	42e
1,487	I 7	17	I —	—	I —	—	—	I —	—	—	—	—	—	—	Demand Deposits	44
98,264	....	....	I 2,953	20,834	I 146	856	25,462	I 684	7,865	5,298	6,339	7,281	7,505	4,528	Time and Savings Deposits	45
46	....	....	I 131	603	I 7	26	427	I 9	179	143	563	497	357	442	Money Market Instruments	46aa
....	....	....	—	—	I 98	242	4	I —	—	—	—	—	—	—	Restricted Deposits	46b
....	....	....	10	120	I 2	3	1,068	I 39	239	43	699	550	398	816	Foreign Liabilities	46c
24,823	I 34	165	I 1,148	11,589	I 142	780	9,032	I 261	1,638	2,141	2,636	4,356	10,964	10,417	Long-Term Foreign Liabilities	46cl
70,455	I 81	429	I 4,237	62,980	I 599	3,170	40,373	I 1,086	10,432	12,308	14,607	16,443	20,649	23,841	Central Government Deposits	46d
1,257	I 2	16	I 281	3,993	I 45	188	2,537	I 57	778	1,035	1,065	2,020	354	385	Credit from Monetary Authorities	46g
....	....	....	1,107	18,033	I 177	672	7,865	I 145	958	1,162	1,152	3,804	1,279	1,197	Credit from Deposit Money Banks	46h
32,843	....	....	I 2,624	39,943	I 467	3,824	54,101	I 1,382	16,756	21,323	18,350	19,931	19,697	20,936	Capital Accounts	47a
-33,999	....	....	I -1,945	-40,859	I 135	693	788	I 100	5,513	6,891	14,327	22,666	34,153	41,004	Other Items (Net)	47r
Thousands 1990-92; Millions Beginning 1993: End of Period															**Banking Survey**	
25,706	I -5	-118	I 2,914	49,770	I 730	-1,283	66,155	I 2,440	31,851	45,029	52,860	44,458	36,331	33,513	Foreign Assets (Net)	51n
255,960	....	....	I 44,060	722,515	I 10,376	56,574	818,719	I 22,314	220,041	256,910	318,613	378,286	491,148	495,754	Domestic Credit	52
-58,259	....	....	I 8,925	215,898	I 3,960	21,027	265,956	I 5,545	-5,930	-245	2,757	61,577	139,214	131,990	Claims on Central Govt. (Net)	52an
25,196	I 49	306	I 3,661	52,740	I 976	5,066	63,679	I 1,687	28,398	21,215	57,146	41,629	22,531	13,549	Claims on State and Local Govts	52b
78,618	I 145	862	I 4,776	75,992	I 947	4,743	57,972	I 1,513	12,948	9,465	22,216	8,431	15,752	17,062	Claims on Nonfin.Pub.Enterprises	52c
210,404	....	....	I 26,678	377,876	I 4,493	25,737	431,107	I 13,570	184,625	226,475	236,488	266,642	311,725	331,117	Claims on Private Sector	52d
....	I —	1	I 20	8	I —	1	5	I —	—	—	6	7	1,926	2,036	Claims on Nonbank Financial Inst	52g
164,591	....	....	I 15,950	227,593	I 3,049	22,147	388,684	I 11,724	151,858	196,682	220,968	261,098	287,062	305,085	Liquid Liabilities	55l
46	....	....	I 136	5,512	I 59	355	9,567	I 292	3,499	4,887	7,592	10,780	9,293	10,069	Money Market Instruments	56aa
....	I 74	594	I -97	-299	I 2	868	47,972	I 532	33,984	45,420	62,979	51,106	66,430	33,412	Liabs. of Central Bank: Securities	56ac
134	I 33	152	I 1,148	16,137	I 3,241	9,087	5,035	I 75	404	1,996	352	12	10	13	Restricted Deposits	56b
124,646	I 227	1,346	I 16,833	242,777	I 2,486	20,800	224,073	I 6,344	16,536	20,352	21,904	30,060	48,197	44,315	Long-Term Foreign Liabilities	56cl
....	....	....	12	696	I 2	13	442	I 1	92	111	60	234	159	268	Liab. to Nonbank Financial Insts	56j
18,901	....	....	I 12,947	204,003	I 2,066	15,277	268,634	I 7,289	61,848	80,435	96,667	120,105	138,620	148,084	Capital Accounts	57a
-26,653	....	....	I 45	75,865	I 202	-13,256	-59,534	I -1,503	-16,329	-47,944	-39,048	-50,651	-22,292	-11,979	Other Items (Net)	57r
Millions of Reais Beginning 1993: End of Period															**Nonbank Financial Institutions**	
....	....	....	33	456	I 7	38	353	I —	3	6	31	14	3	4	Reserves	40..*n*
....	....	....	56	5	I 1	4	2,804	I 8	405	154	350	364	667	333	Other Claims on Monetary Auth.	40c.*n*
....	....	....	—	—	I 26	91	1	I —	—	—	—	—	—	—	Blocked Financial Assets	40d.*n*
....	....	....	—	25	I —	1	277	I 11	76	87	93	45	44	104	Foreign Assets	41..*n*
....	....	....	163	20,154	I 48	57	1,528	I 65	17	42	1,090	1,228	1,103	2,153	Claims on Central Government	42a.*n*
....	....	....	449	11,326	I 55	56	547	I 26	360	330	408	103	552	142	Claims on State and Local Govt.	42b.*n*
....	....	....	109	2,605	I 34	171	1,775	I 4	36	8	14	14	13	7	Claims on Nonfin.Pub.Enterprises	42c.*n*
....	....	....	2,196	2,430	I 12	309	1,515	I 91	2,074	2,458	3,599	3,601	18,825	16,075	Claims on Private Sector	42d.*n*
....	....	....	223	5,147	I 51	135	6,165	I 178	1,405	1,709	3,062	2,810	4,064	3,402	Claims on Deposit Money Banks	42e.*n*
....	....	....	9	67	I —	1	13	I 1	14	5	12	35	20	9	Claims on Other Banking Insts	42f.*n*
....	....	....	47	486	I 7	208	3,919	I 131	1,181	3,901	5,482	8,307	9,243	7,000	Money Market Instruments	46aa*n*
....	....	....	—	—	I 6	15	8	I —	—	—	—	—	—	—	Restricted Deposits	46b.*n*
....	....	....	—	—	I —	—	—	I —	—	—	22	176	182	630	Foreign Liabilities	46c.*n*
....	....	....	130	2,397	I 34	315	4,757	I 170	1,529	2,293	2,972	3,552	4,041	4,401	Long-Term Foreign Liabilities	46cl*n*
....	....	....	—	—	I —	—	5	I —	—	—	1	1	3	4	Central Government Deposits	46d.*n*
....	....	....	149	2,079	I 14	125	2,873	I 118	1,517	1,619	3,670	4,093	5,176	4,324	Liabilities to Other Banking Insts	46i.*n*
....	....	....	552	12,104	I 131	1,025	15,086	I 444	5,767	8,783	10,848	11,187	13,141	16,032	Capital Accounts	47a.*n*
....	....	....	2,360	25,149	I 41	-822	-11,669	I -479	-5,604	-11,797	-14,336	-19,102	-6,495	-10,162	Other Items (Net)	47r.*n*
Thousands 1990-92; Millions Beginning 1993: End of Period															**Money (National Definitions)**	
16,534	I 65	183	1,323	24,522	I 590	2,306	25,167	I 517	17,685	21,682	19,796	31,828	39,184	48,430	*Reserve Money*	19ma
40,719	I 165	377	2,525	37,476	I 913	3,932	38,027	I 848	22,733	28,493	29,807	47,363	50,707	62,226	*M1*	59ma
146,887	I 318	1,356	13,837	304,868	I 1,952	13,647	237,364	I 6,809	72,538	107,157	166,687	202,433	252,023	347,833	*M2*	59mb
226,027	I 438	2,159	23,296	422,116	I 2,814	19,609	329,403	I 9,893	117,483	170,792	238,712	299,495	359,445	458,565	*M3*	59mc
292,254	I 561	2,535	26,952	480,230	I 3,779	26,124	492,451	I 14,820	175,136	250,616	322,140	392,389	453,348	550,204	*M4*	59md
....	....	....	....	....	....	....	....	....	80,734	122,291	184,050	280,070	352,345	447,132	*BA*	19ma *a*
....	....	....	....	....	....	....	....	....	101,902	156,428	231,898	318,599	374,282	458,567	*B2*	19ma *b*
....	....	....	....	....	....	....	....	....	60,443	72,380	60,084	63,353	63,170	271,272	*M2A*	59mb *a*
....	....	....	....	....	....	....	....	....	119,882	143,410	142,159	173,436	185,294	385,863	*M3A*	59mc *a*
....	....	....	....	....	....	....	....	....	174,523	259,381	342,305	422,306	480,202	575,147	*M4A*	59md *a*
Percent Per Annum															**Interest Rates**	
....	....	....	....	....	....	....	....	....	....	....	25.34	45.09	39.41	21.37	Discount Rate *(End of Period)*	60
281.65	105.22	424.38	1,192.87	6,404.97	15,778.57	847.54	1,574.28	3,284.44	4,820.64	53.37	27.45	25.00	29.50	26.26	Money Market Rate	60b
....	....	....	....	....	....	....	....	....	....	49.93	25.73	24.79	28.57	26.23	Treasury Bill Rate	60c
....	....	....	....	....	....	....	....	....	....	17.78	15.13	11.60	15.04	....	Treasury Bill Rate (Fgn.Currency)	60c. *f*
254.69	113.75	511.32	1,100.72	3,477.82	21,938.25	689.88	1,254.90	2,743.33	4,206.04	40.26	16.39	16.62	14.48	12.31	Savings Rate	60k
295.42	109.48	401.03	859.43	I 5844.98	9,394.29	913.47	1,560.18	3,293.50	5,175.24	52.25	26.45	24.35	28.00	26.02	Deposit Rate	60l
Period Averages															**Prices, Production, Labor**	
—	—	—	—	—	—	.01	.08	2.77	85.11	100.00	151.59	263.62	233.93	291.21	Share Prices	62
995.1	2,390.1	7,339.1	58,505.3	....	....	....	....	....	....	....	....	....	....	....	W'sale Prices (1995=1 trillion)	63.a
....	....	....	....	.8	22.4	112.5	1,224.3	26,323.2	....	....	....	....	....	....	W'sale Prices(1995=1 million)	63.b
....	....	....	....	....	....	....	.1	2.6	63.5	I 100.0	106.2	114.9	119.0	138.7	Wholesale Prices	63
8.8	21.8	71.6	522.2	7,994.2	....	....	....	....	....	....	....	....	....	....	Consumer Prices (1995=10 billion)	64.a
....	....	....	....	.8	24.4	129.8	1,365.1	27,684.5	....	....	....	....	....	....	Consumer Prices (1995=1 million)	64.b
....	....	....	....	....	....	....	.1	I 2.8	60.2	100.0	115.8	123.8	127.7	133.9	Consumer Prices	64
....	....	....	....	98.9	90.2	87.7	84.6	91.0	98.0	100.0	I 100.9	105.1	102.9	102.1	Industrial Production	66..*c*
Period Averages																
....	....	....	....	....	....	....	66,139	67,159	....	70,539	70,182	75,213	....	....	Labor Force	67d
53,761	55,436	57,410	58,729	60,622	62,100	....	I 65,395	66,570	....	69,629	67,920	69,332	....	....	Employment	67e
1,875	1,380	2,133	2,319	1,891	2,368	....	I 4,574	4,396	....	4,510	5,076	5,882	....	....	Unemployment	67c
3.4	2.4	3.6	3.8	3.0	3.7	....	I 6.5	I 5.3	5.1	4.6	....	....	....	....	Unemployment Rate (%)	67r

Brazil

		1970	1971	1972	1973	1974	1975	1976	1977	1978	1979	1980	1981	1982	1983	1984
International Transactions																*Millions of US Dollars*
Exports	70..d	2,739	2,904	3,991	6,199	7,951	8,670	10,128	12,120	12,659	15,244	20,132	23,293	20,175	21,899	27,005
Coffee	70e..d	939	773	989	1,244	864	855	2,173	2,299	1,947	1,918	2,486	1,517	1,858	2,096	2,564
Imports, c.i.f.	71..d	2,849	3,701	4,783	6,999	14,168	13,592	13,726	13,257	15,054	19,804	24,961	24,079	21,069	16,801	15,210
Imports, f.o.b.	71.v d	2,507	3,247	4,232	6,192	12,642	12,210	12,383	12,023	13,683	18,084	22,955	22,091	19,395	15,429	13,916
																1995=100
Volume of Exports	72	I20	22	23	32	39	46	45	41	44	49	54	62	60	59	71
Coffee	72e	133	143	146	149	96	108	112	71	86	78	109	114	123	130	143
Volume of Imports	73	27	I33	38	50	55	53	61	62	70	75	72	64	60	55	54
																1995=100:
Unit Value of Exports	74..d	33	32	36	50	62	62	72	88	81	89	94	88	83	79	80
Coffee (Unit Value)	74e.d	36	27	34	43	46	40	99	164	115	125	116	67	77	82	91
Coffee (Wholesale Price)	76eb d	38	31	36	47	50	57	102	183	113	122	143	128	98	98	103
Unit Value of Imports	75..d	16	16	16	22	32	34	35	37	39	47	60	67	65	61	58
Balance of Payments																*Millions of US Dollars:*
Current Account, n.i.e.	78al d	....	....	....	....	....	−6,968	−6,520	−5,049	−6,996	−10,516	−12,831	−11,764	−16,317	−6,834	33
Goods: Exports f.o.b.	78aa d	....	....	....	....	....	8,492	9,961	11,923	12,473	15,244	20,132	23,276	20,173	21,898	27,002
Goods: Imports f.o.b.	78ab d	....	....	....	....	....	−12,042	−12,347	−12,023	−13,631	−17,961	−22,955	−22,091	−19,395	−15,429	−13,916
Trade Balance	78ac d	....	....	....	....	....	−3,550	−2,386	−100	−1,158	−2,717	−2,823	1,185	778	6,469	13,086
Services: Credit	78ad d	....	....	....	....	....	1,060	1,018	1,207	1,350	1,475	1,737	2,265	1,809	1,724	1,947
Services: Debit	78ae d	....	....	....	....	....	−2,504	−2,603	−2,793	−3,074	−3,799	−4,871	−5,138	−5,397	−4,131	−3,696
Balance on Goods & Services	78af d	....	....	....	....	....	−4,994	−3,971	−1,686	−2,882	−5,041	−5,957	−1,688	−2,810	4,062	11,337
Income: Credit	78ag d	....	....	....	....	....	387	304	380	666	1,279	1,406	1,382	1,487	719	1,256
Income: Debit	78ah d	....	....	....	....	....	−2,404	−2,891	−3,806	−4,892	−6,733	−8,424	−11,644	−14,981	−11,726	−12,722
Balance on Gds, Serv. & Inc.	78ai d	....	....	....	....	....	−7,011	−6,558	−5,112	−7,108	−10,495	−12,975	−11,950	−16,304	−6,945	−129
Current Transfers, n.i.e.: Credit	78aj d	....	....	....	....	....	71	49	85	157	180	308	336	184	145	182
Current Transfers: Debit	78ak d	....	....	....	....	....	−28	−11	−22	−45	−201	−164	−150	−197	−34	−20
Capital Account, n.i.e.	78bc d	....	....	....	....	....	−40	−34	−63	−40	38	25	13	5	−3	9
Capital Account, n.i.e.: Credit	78ba d	....	....	....	....	....	62	62	42	96	50	29	34	11	4	10
Capital Account: Debit	78bb d	....	....	....	....	....	−102	−96	−105	−136	−12	−4	−21	−6	−7	−1
Financial Account, n.i.e.	78bj d	....	....	....	....	....	6,381	8,735	6,261	11,363	6,344	9,677	12,791	9,146	−3,828	−5,506
Direct Investment Abroad	78bd d	....	....	....	....	....	−112	−183	−146	−124	−196	−367	−207	−376	−187	−42
Dir. Invest. in Rep. Econ., n.i.e.	78be d	....	....	....	....	....	1,302	1,555	1,833	2,006	2,419	1,911	2,520	2,910	1,609	1,594
Portfolio Investment Assets	78bf d	....	....	....	....	....	—	—	—	—	3	—	−3	−3	−8	−4
Equity Securities	78bk d	....	....	....	....	....	—	—	—	—	−2	−2	−4	−4	−8	−4
Debt Securities	78bl d	....	....	....	....	....	—	—	—	—	5	2	1	1	—	—
Portfolio Investment Liab., n.i.e.	78bg d	....	....	....	....	....	—	—	—	—	657	354	1	2	−278	−268
Equity Securities	78bm d	....	....	....	....	....	—	—	—	—	−2	−11	14	16	−3	−3
Debt Securities	78bn d	....	....	....	....	....	—	—	—	—	659	365	−13	−14	−275	−265
Financial Derivatives Assets	78bw d	....	....	....	....	....										
Financial Derivatives Liabilities	78bx d	....	....	....	....	....										
Other Investment Assets	78bh d	....	....	....	....	....	165	−516	−260	−653	16	−405	−1,397	−553	348	−3,325
Monetary Authorities	78bo d	....	....	....	....	....	8	−9	−7	41	5	12	4	4	1	—
General Government	78bp d	....	....	....	....	....	−19	−38	−126	159	381	−638	−226	−290	178	−111
Banks	78bq d	....	....	....	....	....	248	−213	−38	−481	171	−256	−598	17	176	−353
Other Sectors	78br d	....	....	....	....	....	−72	−256	−89	−372	−541	477	−577	−284	−7	−2,861
Other Investment Liab., n.i.e.	78bi d	....	....	....	....	....	5,026	7,879	4,834	10,134	3,445	8,184	11,877	7,166	−5,312	−3,461
Monetary Authorities	78bs d	....	....	....	....	....	−37	400	−234	49	−144	69	−47	1,538	−3,950	−7,555
General Government	78bt d	....	....	....	....	....	1,694	1,612	2,454	4,215	3,402	511	324	2,031	2,297	6,573
Banks	78bu d	....	....	....	....	....	82	2,205	727	3,232	−108	2,969	5,691	1,528	−2,404	−50
Other Sectors	78bv d	....	....	....	....	....	3,287	3,662	1,887	2,638	295	4,635	5,909	2,069	−1,255	−2,429
Net Errors and Omissions	78ca d	....	....	....	....	....	−438	491	−628	301	1,234	−340	−418	−375	−586	399
Overall Balance	78cb d	....	....	....	....	....	−1,065	2,672	521	4,628	−2,900	−3,469	622	−7,541	−11,251	−5,065
Reserves and Related Items	79da d	....	....	....	....	....	1,065	−2,672	−521	−4,628	2,900	3,469	−622	7,541	11,251	5,065
Reserve Assets	79db d	....	....	....	....	....	1,065	−2,672	−521	−4,628	2,900	3,469	−622	4,655	−269	−7,169
Use of Fund Credit and Loans	79dc d	....	....	....	....	....	—	—	—	—	—	—	—	546	2,160	1,801
Exceptional Financing	79de d	....	....	....	....	....	—	—	—	—	—	—	—	2,340	9,360	10,434
Government Finance												*Millionths of Reais through 1974; Thousandths 1975-85; Reais 1986-89;*				
Deficit (-) or Surplus	80	I−444	−811	−524	585	3,171	I−2	−1	−8	−23	−13	−111	−218	−463	−1,762	−6,829
Revenue	81	I12,625	17,211	23,807	34,189	50,149	I71	116	203	301	493	1,009	2,183	4,604	11,267	33,010
Grants Received	81z	I18	127	178	211	258	I—	1	2	1	4	7	26	46	116	371
Expenditure	82	I12,429	16,713	22,004	29,098	42,447	I67	106	169	260	398	912	1,814	3,840	9,069	28,990
Lending Minus Repayments	83	I658	1,436	2,505	4,716	4,789	I7	12	44	65	111	215	613	1,272	4,076	11,219
Financing																
Domestic	84a	....	....	....	....	....	....						221	529	1,545	5,996
Foreign	85a	....	....	....	....	....	....						−3	−69	218	833
Debt: Domestic	88a	....	....	....	....	....	....					365	909	1,558	3,480	10,139
Foreign	89a	....	....	....	....	....	....					153	248	248	455	1,287
National Accounts												*Millionths of Reais through 1974; Thousandths 1975-85; Reais 1986-89;*				
Exports of Goods & Services	90c	5,091	6,182	9,091	14,545	20,727	I27	42	66	88	157	408	840	1,399	4,870	19,020
Government Consumption	91f	8,000	10,545	13,455	18,545	25,455	I39	62	85	127	215	414	831	1,839	4,119	11,632
Gross Fixed Capital Formation	93e	17,092	23,638	31,638	45,457	72,004	I89	133	193	293	507	1,031	2,046	3,940	7,731	22,182
Increase/Decrease(-) in Stocks	93i	1,091	2,545	3,273	7,636	19,273	I9	4	6	10	−13	20	13	−63	−617	−1,600
Private Consumption	96f	45,455	61,455	81,091	111,273	168,728	I243	407	626	904	1,532	3,139	6,064	12,785	30,378	98,771
Imports of Goods & Services	98c	−5,455	−7,636	−11,273	−16,727	−36,000	I−42	−56	−72	−104	−202	−509	−874	−1,521	−3,841	−11,125
Gross Domestic Product (GDP)	99b	70,655	93,927	126,036	186,109	270,945	I382	594	907	1,315	2,168	4,527	8,876	18,065	41,455	134,218
Net Factor Inc/Pmts(-) Abroad	98.n	726	1,089	1,089	1,815	2,178	I5	9	15	30	59	−147	−368	−940	−2,483	−7,964
Gross National Income (GNI)	99a	70,503	94,125	124,289	174,077	255,120	I362	581	889	1,337	2,235	4,353	8,501	17,112	38,948	126,182
Net National Income	99e	66,909	89,091	117,818	165,091	241,818	I343	552	845	1,272	2,125	4,409	8,489	15,745	....	....
GDP Vol.1990 Prices (thousands)	99b.p	4,078	4,540	5,083	5,792	6,263	6,589	7,264	7,622	8,001	8,542	9,330	8,935	9,008	8,744	9,300
GDP Volume (1995=100)	99bv p	30.4	33.8	37.8	43.1	46.6	49.1	54.1	56.7	59.6	63.6	69.5	66.5	67.1	65.1	69.2
GDP Deflator (1995=1 trillion)	99bi p	.4	.4	.5	.7	.9	1.2	1.7	2.5	3.4	5.3	10.1	20.7	41.7	98.5	300.0
GDP Deflator (1995=10 billions)	99bi p	....	....	....	....	....	....	....	....	....	....	....	....	....	....	
GDP Deflator (1995=100)	99bi p	....	....	....	....	....	....	....	....	....	....	....	....	....	....	3
																Millions:
Population	99z	92.52	95.17	97.85	99.92	102.40	104.94	107.54	110.21	112.94	115.74	121.29	124.07	126.90	129.77	132.66

1985	1986	1987	1988	1989	1990	1991	1992	1993	1994	1995	1996	1997	1998	1999		
Millions of US Dollars															**International Transactions**	
25,639	22,349	26,224	33,494	34,383	31,414	31,620	35,793	38,555	43,545	46,506	47,747	52,990	51,120	48,011	Exports	70..d
2,369	2,006	1,959	2,009	1,560	1,106	1,382	970	1,065	2,219	1,970	1,719	2,745	2,330	2,230	Coffee	70e.d
14,332	15,557	16,581	16,055	19,875	22,524	22,950	23,068	27,740	35,997	53,783	56,947	65,007	....	....	Imports, c.i.f.	71..d
13,153	14,044	15,052	14,605	18,263	20,661	21,041	20,554	25,256	33,079	49,972	53,346	59,755	57,731	49,214	Imports, f.o.b.	71.vd
1995=100																
73	67	71	85	88	84	83	83	91	97	100	99	104	115	114	Volume of Exports	72
143	66	137	125	132	118	152	141	134	121	100	108	120	138	176	Coffee	72e
49	60	62	58	57	57	63	68	77	81	100	108	91	92	85	Volume of Imports	73
Indices of Unit Values in US Dollars																
I 76	72	80	85	84	81	81	92	91	96	100	101	....	....	....	Unit Value of Exports	74..d
84	154	73	81	60	47	46	35	40	93	100	81	116	86	64	Coffee (Unit Value)	74e.d
102	158	73	83	68	57	50	39	46	98	100	82	114	83	61	Coffee (Wholesale Price)	76ebd
I 55	48	50	52	65	74	68	63	67	83	100	93	132	....	....	Unit Value of Imports	75..d
Minus Sign Indicates Debit															Balance of Payments	
-280	-5,311	-1,452	4,156	1,002	-3,823	-1,450	6,089	20	-1,153	-18,136	-23,248	-30,491	-33,829	....	Current Account, n.i.e.	78ald
25,634	22,348	26,210	33,773	34,375	31,408	31,619	35,793	39,630	44,102	46,506	47,851	53,189	51,136	....	Goods: Exports f.o.b.	78aad
-13,168	-14,044	-15,052	-14,605	-18,263	-20,661	-21,041	-20,554	-25,301	-33,241	-49,663	-53,304	-59,841	-57,739	....	Goods: Imports f.o.b.	78abd
12,466	8,304	11,158	19,168	16,112	10,747	10,578	15,239	14,329	10,861	-3,157	-5,453	-6,652	-6,603	....	*Trade Balance*	78acd
2,086	1,816	1,952	2,279	3,132	3,762	3,319	4,088	3,965	4,908	6,135	4,655	5,989	7,631	....	Services: Credit	78add
-3,790	-4,389	-4,316	-5,302	-5,917	-7,523	-7,210	-7,430	-9,555	-10,254	-13,630	-12,714	-15,298	-16,676	....	Services: Debit	78aed
10,762	5,731	8,794	16,145	13,327	6,986	6,687	11,897	8,739	5,515	-10,652	-13,512	-15,961	-15,648	....	*Balance on Goods & Services*	78afd
1,589	967	568	771	1,310	1,157	904	1,118	1,308	2,202	3,457	5,350	5,344	4,914	....	Income: Credit	78agd
-12,779	-12,089	-10,882	-12,851	-13,856	-12,765	-10,555	-9,115	-11,630	-11,293	-14,562	-17,527	-21,688	-24,531	....	Income: Debit	78ahd
-428	-5,391	-1,520	4,065	781	-4,622	-2,964	3,900	-1,583	-3,576	-21,757	-25,689	-32,305	-35,265	....	*Balance on Gds, Serv. & Inc.*	78aid
171	134	158	127	238	840	1,556	2,260	1,704	2,577	3,861	2,699	2,130	1,795	....	Current Transfers, n.i.e.: Credit	78ajd
-23	-54	-90	-36	-17	-41	-42	-71	-101	-154	-240	-258	-316	-359	....	Current Transfers: Debit	78akd
7	7	5	3	23	35	42	54	81	173	352	494	482	375	....	Capital Account, n.i.e.	78bcd
8	14	10	4	27	36	43	54	86	175	363	507	519	488	....	Capital Account, n.i.e.: Credit	78bad
-1	-7	-5	-1	-4	-1	-1	—	-5	-2	-11	-13	-37	-113	....	Capital Account: Debit	78bbd
-8,676	-8,189	-9,757	-9,137	-11,426	-5,441	-4,868	5,889	7,604	8,020	29,306	33,142	24,918	20,063	....	Financial Account, n.i.e.	78bjd
-81	-143	-138	-175	-523	-665	-1,014	-137	-491	-1,037	-1,384	467	-1,042	-2,721	....	Direct Investment Abroad	78bdd
1,441	345	1,169	2,804	1,131	989	1,103	2,061	1,292	3,072	4,859	11,200	19,650	31,913	....	Dir. Invest. in Rep. Econ., n.i.e.	78bed
-3	1	—	—	-30	-67	—	—	-606	-3,052	-936	-257	-335	-594	....	Portfolio Investment Assets	78bfd
-4	1	—	—	—	—	—	—	-607	—	-168	-49	-306	-553	....	Equity Securities	78bkd
1	—	—	—	-30	-67	—	—	1	-3,052	-768	-208	-29	-41	....	Debt Securities	78bld
-234	-451	-428	-498	-391	579	3,808	7,366	12,928	47,784	10,171	21,089	10,393	19,013	....	Portfolio Investment Liab., n.i.e.	78bgd
-11	9	61	189	-57	103	578	1,704	6,570	7,280	2,775	5,785	5,099	-1,768	....	Equity Securities	78bmd
-223	-460	-489	-687	-334	476	3,230	5,662	6,358	40,504	7,396	15,304	5,294	20,781	....	Debt Securities	78bnd
....	....	....	....	....	....	....	....	—	—	....	....	....	....	....	Financial Derivatives Assets	78bwd
....	....	....	....	....	....	....	....	—	—	....	....	....	....	....	Financial Derivatives Liabilities	78bxd
190	1,385	-401	-1,994	-894	-2,864	-3,140	-99	-2,696	-4,368	-1,783	-3,327	2,251	-5,992	....	Other Investment Assets	78bhd
—	71	—	-17	-5	22	8	—	-34	—	....	-44	-67	-84	....	Monetary Authorities	78bod
-100	-46	-121	-98	-62	-108	-17	-44	29	—	....	....	2,146	60	....	General Government	78bpd
275	687	-47	-328	-591	-2,758	-3,357	-37	-2,980	-4,077	-228	-4,610	5,133	3,383	....	Banks	78bqd
15	673	-233	-1,551	-236	-20	226	-18	289	-291	-1,555	1,327	-4,961	-9,351	....	Other Sectors	78brd
-9,989	-9,326	-9,959	-9,274	-10,719	-3,413	-5,625	-3,302	-2,823	-34,379	18,379	3,970	-5,999	-21,556	....	Other Investment Liab., n.i.e.	78bid
-6,344	-720	-1,278	3,303	1,366	-637	-1,012	-277	-140	-545	-1,652	-3,773	-1,698	-1,704	....	Monetary Authorities	78bsd
3,397	-307	259	-3,729	-6,132	-2,715	-2,876	-1,968	-2,622	-35,609	....	-286	....	....	....	General Government	78btd
-3,511	-3,641	-1,730	-1,786	-2,115	-229	386	1,167	-2,269	-1,439	7,071	6,450	-897	-8,570	....	Banks	78bud
-3,531	-4,658	-7,210	-7,062	-3,838	168	-2,123	-2,224	2,208	3,214	12,960	1,579	-3,404	-11,282	....	Other Sectors	78bvd
-530	66	-805	-827	-819	-296	852	-1,393	-815	-442	1,447	-1,992	-3,160	-2,911	....	Net Errors and Omissions	78cad
-9,479	-13,427	-12,009	-5,805	-11,220	-9,525	-5,424	10,639	6,890	6,598	12,969	8,396	-8,251	-16,302	....	*Overall Balance*	78cbd
9,479	13,427	12,009	5,805	11,220	9,525	5,424	-10,639	-6,890	-6,598	-12,969	-8,396	8,251	16,302	....	Reserves and Related Items	79dad
573	3,856	-1,014	-1,250	-893	-474	369	-14,670	-8,709	-7,215	-12,920	-8,326	8,284	6,990	....	Reserve Assets	79dbd
-62	-625	-1,151	-462	-808	-771	-566	-399	-504	-133	-49	-70	-33	4,773	....	Use of Fund Credit and Loans	79dcd
8,968	10,195	14,174	7,516	12,921	10,771	5,621	4,430	2,323	750	—	....	—	4,539	....	Exceptional Financing	79ded
Thousands 1990-92; Millions Beg. 1993: Year Ending December 31															**Government Finance**	
-56,093	I -178	-507	-4,777	-74,282	I -672	-257	-24,389	I -1,315	-21,270	....	....	....	....	....	Deficit (-) or Surplus	80
132,883	I 297	1,441	6,318	102,300	I 3,628	15,553	173,586	I 4,272	108,280	....	....	....	....	....	Revenue	81
836	I 4	13	38	997	I 8	40	115	I 2	125	....	....	....	....	....	Grants Received	81z
127,735	I 371	1,044	9,852	160,561	I 4,027	14,683	187,242	I 5,250	117,906	....	....	....	....	....	Expenditure	82
62,079	I 108	917	1,280	17,018	I 281	1,167	10,848	I 338	11,769	....	....	....	....	....	Lending Minus Repayments	83
															Financing	
57,222	I 177	....	....	....	....	....	....	....	....	....	....	....	....	....	Domestic	84a
-1,127	I 1	....	....	....	....	....	....	....	....	....	....	....	....	....	Foreign	85a
74,070	I 227	....	....	....	....	....	....	....	....	....	....	....	....	....	Debt: Domestic	88a
169	I 1	....	....	....	....	....	....	....	....	....	....	....	....	....	Foreign	89a
Thousands 1990-92; Millions Beginning 1993															**National Accounts**	
61,455	I 117	397	3,427	38,004	I 947	5,231	69,661	I 1,481	33,220	49,917	54,430	65,491	66,862	....	Exports of Goods & Services	90c
49,455	I 142	510	3,951	65,948	I 2,228	10,791	109,367	I 2,490	62,388	126,652	144,001	154,239	159,921	....	Government Consumption	91f
96,364	I 255	936	7,151	114,496	I 2,386	10,917	118,086	I 2,718	72,453	132,753	150,050	172,212	179,203	....	Gross Fixed Capital Formation	93e
11,273	I —	—	—	—	I -57	1,001	3,277	I 220	4,880	11,274	12,903	15,343	12,271	....	Increase/Decrease(-) in Stocks	93i
330,572	I 902	2,612	18,727	200,000	I 6,849	37,117	394,313	I 8,470	208,256	386,910	486,813	545,113	572,391	....	Private Consumption	96f
-35,636	I -85	-260	-1,792	-23,243	I -804	-4,771	-53,745	I -1,282	-31,993	-61,314	-69,311	-88,287	-90,833	....	Imports of Goods & Services	98c
504,364	I 1,336	4,209	31,491	400,000	I 11,549	60,286	640,959	I 14,097	349,205	646,192	778,887	864,111	899,814	....	Gross Domestic Product (GDP)	99b
-26,909	I -59	-159	-1,200	-13,954	I -300	-1,000	-12,000	I -343	-5,913	-10,154	-12,228	-17,110	-22,362	....	Net Factor Inc/Pmts(-) Abroad	98.n
477,455	I 1,276	4,050	30,230	448,503	I 10,700	59,300	629,000	I 13,754	343,292	636,038	766,659	847,001	877,452	....	Gross National Income (GNI)	99a
....	....	....	....	....	....	....	....	....	....	....	....	....	....	....	Net National Income	99e
10,000	10,700	11,062	11,055	11,500	11,549	11,668	11,605	12,176	12,888	13,432	13,789	14,286	14,269	....	GDP Vol.1990 Prices (thousands)	99b.p
74.4	79.7	82.4	82.3	85.6	86.0	86.9	86.4	90.6	95.9	100.0	102.7	106.4	106.2	....	GDP Volume (1995=100)	99bvp
....	....	....	....	....	....	....	....	....	....	....	....	....	....	....	GDP Deflator (1995=1 trillion)	99bip
10	26	79	592	7,230	207,864	1,073,987	....	....	....	....	....	....	....	....	GDP Deflator (1995=10 billions)	99bip
....	....	....	....	....	....	.01	.11	2.41	56.32	100.00	117.41	125.73	131.08	....	GDP Deflator (1995=100)	99bip
Midyear Estimates																
I 133.56	134.65	137.27	139.82	142.31	144.72	147.07	149.36	151.57	153.73	155.82	157.87	159.64	161.79	163.95	**Population**	99z

(See notes in the back of the book.)

Bulgaria

918

		1970	1971	1972	1973	1974	1975	1976	1977	1978	1979	1980	1981	1982	1983	1984
Exchange Rates															*Leva per SDR:*	
Official Rate	aa	.0012	.0012	.0012	.0012	.0012	....	....	....	....	....	....	....	....	....	
															Leva per US Dollar:	
Official Rate	ae	.0012	.0011	.0011	.0010	.0010	....	....	....	....	....	....	....	....	....	
Official Rate	rf	.0012	.0012	.0011	.0010	.0010	....	....	....	....	....	....	....	....	....	
														Index Numbers (1995=100):		
Nominal Effective Exchange Rate	ne c	....	....	....	....	....	....	....	....	....	....	....	....	....	....	
Real Effective Exchange Rate	re c	....	....	....	....	....	....	....	....	....	....	....	....	....	....	
Fund Position															*Millions of SDRs:*	
Quota	2f. s	—	—	—	—	—	—	—	—	—	—	—	—	—	—	—
SDRs	1b. s	....	....	....	....	....	....	....	....	....	....	....	....	....	....	
Reserve Position in the Fund	1c. s	....	....	....	....	....	....	....	....	....	....	....	....	....	....	
Total Fund Cred.&Loans Outstg.	2tl	....	....	....	....	....	....	....	....	....	....	....	....	....	....	
International Liquidity									*Millions of US Dollars Unless Otherwise Indicated:*							
Total Reserves minus Gold	1l. d	....	....	....	....	....	....	....	....	....	....	....	....	....	....	
SDRs	1b. d	....	....	....	....	....	....	....	....	....	....	....	....	....	....	
Reserve Position in the Fund	1c. d	....	....	....	....	....	....	....	....	....	....	....	....	....	....	
Foreign Exchange	1d. d	....	....	....	....	....	....	....	....	....	....	....	....	....	....	
Gold (Million Fine Troy Ounces)	1ad	....	....	....	....	....	....	....	....	....	....	....	....	....	....	
Gold (National Valuation)	1an d	....	....	....	....	....	....	....	....	....	....	....	....	....	....	
Monetary Authorities: Other Liab.	4..d	....	....	....	....	....	....	....	....	....	....	....	....	....	....	
Deposit Money Banks: Assets	7a. d	....	....	....	....	....	....	....	....	....	....	....	....	....	....	
Liabilities	7b. d	....	....	....	....	....	....	....	....	....	....	....	....	....	....	
Monetary Authorities															*Millions of Leva:*	
Foreign Assets	11	....	....	....	....	....	....	....	....	....	....	....	....	....	....	
Claims on Central Government	12a	....	....	....	....	....	....	....	....	....	....	....	....	....	....	
Claims on Nonfin.Pub.Enterprises	12c	....	....	....	....	....	....	....	....	....	....	....	....	....	....	
Claims on Deposit Money Banks	12e	....	....	....	....	....	....	....	....	....	....	....	....	....	....	
Reserve Money	14	....	....	....	....	....	....	....	....	....	....	....	....	....	....	
of which: Currency Outside Banks	14a	....	....	....	....	....	....	....	....	....	....	....	....	....	....	
Time, Savings,& Fgn.Currency Dep.	15	....	....	....	....	....	....	....	....	....	....	....	....	....	....	
Restricted Deposits	16b	....	....	....	....	....	....	....	....	....	....	....	....	....	....	
Foreign Liabilities	16c	....	....	....	....	....	....	....	....	....	....	....	....	....	....	
Central Government Deposits	16da	....	....	....	....	....	....	....	....	....	....	....	....	....	....	
Capital Accounts	17a	....	....	....	....	....	....	....	....	....	....	....	....	....	....	
Other Items (Net)	17r	....	....	....	....	....	....	....	....	....	....	....	....	....	....	
Deposit Money Banks															*Millions of Leva:*	
Reserves	20	....	....	....	....	....	....	....	....	....	....	....	....	....	....	
Foreign Assets	21	....	....	....	....	....	....	....	....	....	....	....	....	....	....	
Claims on Central Government	22a	....	....	....	....	....	....	....	....	....	....	....	....	....	....	
Claims on Local Government	22b	....	....	....	....	....	....	....	....	....	....	....	....	....	....	
Claims on Nonfin.Pub.Enterprises	22c	....	....	....	....	....	....	....	....	....	....	....	....	....	....	
Claims on Private Sector	22d	....	....	....	....	....	....	....	....	....	....	....	....	....	....	
Claims on Other Financial Insts	22f	....	....	....	....	....	....	....	....	....	....	....	....	....	....	
Demand Deposits	24	....	....	....	....	....	....	....	....	....	....	....	....	....	....	
Time, Savings,& Fgn.Currency Dep.	25	....	....	....	....	....	....	....	....	....	....	....	....	....	....	
Money Market Instruments	26aa	....	....	....	....	....	....	....	....	....	....	....	....	....	....	
Restricted Deposits	26b	....	....	....	....	....	....	....	....	....	....	....	....	....	....	
Foreign Liabilities	26c	....	....	....	....	....	....	....	....	....	....	....	....	....	....	
Central Government Deposits	26da	....	....	....	....	....	....	....	....	....	....	....	....	....	....	
Local Government Deposits	26db	....	....	....	....	....	....	....	....	....	....	....	....	....	....	
Credit from Central Bank	26g	....	....	....	....	....	....	....	....	....	....	....	....	....	....	
Capital Accounts	27a	....	....	....	....	....	....	....	....	....	....	....	....	....	....	
Other Items (Net)	27r	....	....	....	....	....	....	....	....	....	....	....	....	....	....	
Monetary Survey															*Millions of Leva:*	
Foreign Assets (Net)	31n	....	....	....	....	....	....	....	....	....	....	....	....	....	....	
Domestic Credit	32	....	....	....	....	....	....	....	....	....	....	....	....	....	....	
Claims on General Govt. (Net)	32an	....	....	....	....	....	....	....	....	....	....	....	....	....	....	
Claims on Nonfin.Pub.Enterprises	32c	....	....	....	....	....	....	....	....	....	....	....	....	....	....	
Claims on Private Sector	32d	....	....	....	....	....	....	....	....	....	....	....	....	....	....	
Claims on Other Financial Insts	32f	....	....	....	....	....	....	....	....	....	....	....	....	....	....	
Money	34	....	....	....	....	....	....	....	....	....	....	....	....	....	....	
Quasi-Money	35	....	....	....	....	....	....	....	....	....	....	....	....	....	....	
Money Market Instruments	36aa	....	....	....	....	....	....	....	....	....	....	....	....	....	....	
Restricted Deposits	36b	....	....	....	....	....	....	....	....	....	....	....	....	....	....	
Other Items (Net)	37r	....	....	....	....	....	....	....	....	....	....	....	....	....	....	
Money plus Quasi-Money	35l	....	....	....	....	....	....	....	....	....	....	....	....	....	....	
Interest Rates															*Percent Per Annum*	
Discount Rate (End of Period)	60	....	....	....	....	....	....	....	....	....	....	....	....	....	....	
Money Market Rate	60b	....	....	....	....	....	....	....	....	....	....	....	....	....	....	
Treasury Bill Yield	60c	....	....	....	....	....	....	....	....	....	....	....	....	....	....	
Deposit Rate	60l	....	....	....	....	....	....	....	....	....	....	....	....	....	....	
Lending Rate	60p	....	....	....	....	....	....	....	....	....	....	....	....	....	....	
Government Bond Yield	61	....	....	....	....	....	....	....	....	....	....	....	....	....	....	

	1985	1986	1987	1988	1989	1990	1991	1992	1993	1994	1995	1996	1997	1998	1999		
Exchange Rates																	
End of Period																	
	.0011	.0011	.0012	.0011	.0011	.0040	.0312	.0337	.0449	.0964	.1051	.7008	2.3969	2.3586	2.6721	Official Rate	aa
End of Period (ae)	*Period Average (rf)*																
	.0010	.0009	.0009	.0008	.0008	.0028	.0218	.0245	.0327	.0660	.0707	.4874	1.7765	1.6751	1.9469	Official Rate	ae
	.0010	.0009	.0009	.0008	.0008	.0022	.0178	.0233	.0276	.0541	.0672	.1779	1.6819	1.7604	1.8364	Official Rate	rf
Period Averages																	
	....	....	....	....	....	....	....	115.64	164.54	118.51	100.00	56.87	5.55	5.39	5.82	Nominal Effective Exchange Rate	ne c
								63.62	97.79	89.06	100.00	86.05	102.61	116.26	117.98	Real Effective Exchange Rate	re c
Fund Position																	
End of Period																	
	—	—	—	—	—	310.00	310.00	464.90	464.90	464.90	464.90	464.90	464.90	464.90	640.20	Quota	2f. s
	....	....	....	....	....	—	5.86	.32	.83	10.39	20.08	8.31	8.37	21.38	59.53	SDRs	1b. s
	....	....	....	....	....	—	.01	38.73	32.63	32.63	32.63	32.63	32.63	32.63	32.69	Reserve Position in the Fund	1c. s
	....	....	....	....	....	—	289.23	428.90	459.90	644.41	482.12	407.25	698.02	792.27	910.74	Total Fund Cred.&Loans Outstg.	2tl
International Liquidity																	
End of Period																	
	....	....	....	....	....		311	902	655	1,002	1,236	484	2,249	2,831	3,083	Total Reserves minus Gold	1l. d
	....	....	....	....	....	—	8.38	.44	1.14	15.16	29.84	11.95	11.29	30.10	81.70	SDRs	1b. d
	....	....	....	....	....	—	.01	53.25	44.82	47.63	48.50	46.92	44.03	45.95	44.87	Reserve Position in the Fund	1c. d
	....	....	....	....	....		302	849	609	939	1,158	425	2,193	2,755	2,957	Foreign Exchange	1d. d
	....	....	....	....	....		1.017	1.017	1.017	1.031	1.031	1.031	1.031	1.031	1.031	Gold (Million Fine Troy Ounces)	1ad
	....	....	....	....	....		305	305	305	309	309	309	I 290	296	265	Gold (National Valuation)	1an d
	....	....	....	....	....		200.50	350.40	355.42	635.08	657.61	689.55	—	—	—	Monetary Authorities: Other Liab.	4.. d
	....	....	....	....	....		....	....	....	....		1,426	1,248	1,603	1,688	1,565	Deposit Money Banks: Assets	7a. d
	....	....	....	....	....		....	....	....	....		2,375	1,661	663	582	459	Liabilities	7b. d
Monetary Authorities																	
End of Period																	
	....	....	....	....	....		14.8	31.9	33.9	124.6	154.0	710.6	I 4,884.5	5,441.9	6,432.7	Foreign Assets	11
	....	....	....	....	....		9.8	23.5	34.8	54.2	100.7	410.9	1,632.1	1,665.9	2,203.2	Claims on Central Government	12a
	....	....	....	....	....		—	—	—	—	.3	.5	.6	1.4	2.1	Claims on Nonfin.Pub.Enterprises	12c
	....	....	....	....	....		25.5	20.7	32.1	54.8	44.0	262.5	334.6	256.5	228.6	Claims on Deposit Money Banks	12e
	....	....	....	....	....		29.6	44.7	54.9	88.7	154.3	351.6	2,174.2	2,387.4	2,721.7	Reserve Money	14
	....	....	....	....	....		11.9	18.3	25.2	38.5	61.6	126.5	1,314.1	1,742.0	1,957.4	of which: Currency Outside Banks	14a
	....	....	....	....	....		.3	.8	.3	—	—	3.6	.7	10.3	.3	Time, Savings,& Fgn.Currency Dep.	15
	....	....	....	....	....		—	—	—	—	—	.1	16.2	17.8	—	Restricted Deposits	16b
	....	....	....	....	....		13.4	23.0	32.3	104.0	97.2	621.4	I 1,673.1	1,868.6	2,433.6	Foreign Liabilities	16c
	....	....	....	....	....		5.5	10.5	11.8	42.2	51.0	192.4	1,703.7	1,947.8	2,693.4	Central Government Deposits	16da
	....	....	....	....	....		13.7	17.2	30.5	91.3	102.2	307.3	961.7	916.3	1,019.5	Capital Accounts	17a
	....	....	....	....	....		-12.5	-20.1	-28.9	-92.7	-105.8	-91.9	I 322.2	217.5	-2.0	Other Items (Net)	17r
Deposit Money Banks																	
End of Period																	
	....	....	....	....	....		20.4	26.7	24.6	43.5	I 92.8	223.2	818.4	651.2	753.5	Reserves	20
	....	....	....	....	....		32.2	37.1	43.5	109.5	I 100.8	608.1	2,848.1	2,828.2	3,047.7	Foreign Assets	21
	....	....	....	....	....		55.6	82.8	179.6	283.6	I 271.1	863.3	2,510.6	1,656.9	1,300.8	Claims on Central Government	22a
	....	....	....	....	....		—	1.4	2.4	2.8	I .4	.4	—	17.1	31.8	Claims on Local Government	22b
	....	....	....	....	....		102.6	138.7	187.5	239.1	I 161.0	462.4	1,253.4	944.2	711.0	Claims on Nonfin.Pub.Enterprises	22c
	....	....	....	....	....		9.8	11.6	11.1	19.8	I 185.4	622.1	2,151.8	2,733.7	3,321.2	Claims on Private Sector	22d
	....	....	....	....	....		....	....	....	....	4.7	24.2	89.0	38.0	47.1	Claims on Other Financial Insts	22f
	....	....	....	....	....		15.0	19.6	23.2	36.6	I 46.0	110.0	I 944.7	1,013.6	1,039.3	Demand Deposits	24
	....	....	....	....	....		72.5	111.1	181.3	334.0	I 463.4	1,004.3	I 3,271.2	3,414.7	3,917.1	Time, Savings,& Fgn.Currency Dep.	25
	....	....	....	....	....		....	....	....	....		.3	I 4.3	7.6	56.4	Money Market Instruments	26aa
	....	....	....	....	....		3.6	3.4	4.2	8.9	I 12.3	65.3	I 459.3	391.2	380.6	Restricted Deposits	26b
	....	....	....	....	....		240.2	288.0	385.2	236.2	I 167.9	809.3	1,177.0	974.1	893.0	Foreign Liabilities	26c
	....	....	....	....	....		11.3	5.1	5.8	13.6	I 33.1	173.6	730.1	807.7	623.7	Central Government Deposits	26da
	....	....	....	....	....		—	—	—	—	I 4.8	7.1	67.4	74.5	62.5	Local Government Deposits	26db
	....	....	....	....	....		6.8	6.4	9.6	28.7	I 34.5	128.1	341.7	277.3	273.8	Credit from Central Bank	26g
	....	....	....	....	....		15.0	22.0	36.1	79.0	I 87.1	771.6	306.9	159.8	417.4	Capital Accounts	27a
	....	....	....	....	....		-144.0	-157.3	-196.6	-38.8	I -32.9	-266.2	2,368.8	1,748.7	1,549.1	Other Items (Net)	27r
Monetary Survey																	
End of Period																	
	....	....	....	....	....		-206.7	-242.0	-340.1	-106.1	I -10.2	-112.0	I 4,882.5	5,427.4	6,153.7	Foreign Assets (Net)	31n
	....	....	....	....	....		160.8	242.4	397.9	543.7	I 634.7	2,010.5	5,136.5	4,227.0	4,237.4	Domestic Credit	32
	....	....	....	....	....		48.5	92.0	199.3	284.9	I 283.4	901.3	1,641.6	509.8	156.0	Claims on General Govt. (Net)	32an
	....	....	....	....	....		102.6	138.7	187.5	239.1	I 161.2	462.9	1,254.1	945.6	713.1	Claims on Nonfin.Pub.Enterprises	32c
	....	....	....	....	....		9.8	11.6	11.1	19.8	I 185.4	622.1	2,151.8	2,733.7	3,321.2	Claims on Private Sector	32d
	....	....	....	....	....		—	—	—	—	I 4.7	24.2	89.0	38.0	47.1	Claims on Other Financial Insts	32f
	....	....	....	....	....		24.8	38.0	50.3	76.0	I 107.9	236.6	I 2,266.9	2,755.6	2,996.6	Money	34
	....	....	....	....	....		72.7	112.0	181.6	334.0	I 463.4	1,007.9	I 3,271.9	3,425.0	3,917.4	Quasi-Money	35
	....	....	....	....	....		—	—	—	—		.1	I 4.3	7.6	56.4	Money Market Instruments	36aa
	....	....	....	....	....		3.6	3.4	4.2	8.9	I 12.3	65.4	I 475.5	409.0	380.7	Restricted Deposits	36b
	....	....	....	....	....		-147.0	-153.0	-178.2	18.7	I 40.8	588.2	I 4,000.4	3,057.2	3,040.0	Other Items (Net)	37r
	....	....	....	....	....		97.5	150.0	231.9	410.0	I 571.3	1,244.6	I 5,538.8	6,180.6	6,914.0	Money plus Quasi-Money	35l
Interest Rates																	
Percent Per Annum																	
	....	....	....	....	....		54.00	41.00	52.00	78.50	37.31	192.00	....	....	....	Discount Rate (End of Period)	60
	....	....	....	....	....		48.67	52.39	48.07	66.43	53.09	119.88	66.43	2.48	2.93	Money Market Rate	60b
	....	....	....	....	....		....	48.11	45.45	57.72	48.27	114.31	78.35	6.02	5.43	Treasury Bill Yield	60c
	....	....	....	....	....		39.49	45.01	42.56	51.14	35.94	74.68	46.83	3.00	3.21	Deposit Rate	60l
	....	....	....	....	....		48.37	56.67	58.30	72.58	58.98	123.48	83.96	13.30	12.79	Lending Rate	60p
	....	....	....	....	....		....	....	....	56.86	49.76	....	....	10.10	10.05	Government Bond Yield	61

Bulgaria

918

		1970	1971	1972	1973	1974	1975	1976	1977	1978	1979	1980	1981	1982	1983	1984
Prices and Labor																*Index Numbers (1995=100):*
Producer Prices	63	...	...	...	...	...	...	...	...	...	...	...	...	...	...	...
Consumer Prices	64	...	...	...	...	...	...	...	...	...	...	...	...	...	...	...
Employment	67e															*Number in Thousands:*
Employment	67e	...	...	...	...	...	...	...	...	...	...	...	...	...	...	4,098
Unemployment	67c	...	...	...	...	...	...	...	...	...	...	...	...	...	...	...
Unemployment Rate (%)	67r	...	...	...	...	...	...	...	...	...	...	...	...	...	...	...
International Transactions																*Millions of Leva*
Exports	70	2.3	2.6	2.8	3.2	3.7	4.5	5.2	6.0	6.7	7.7	8.9	9.8	10.9	11.8	13.0
Imports, c.i.f.	71	2.1	2.5	2.8	3.2	4.2	5.2	5.4	6.1	6.8	7.4	8.3	10.0	11.0	12.0	12.8
Balance of Payments																*Millions of US Dollars:*
Current Account, n.i.e.	78ald	...	...	...	...	...	...	...	...	...	...	954.0	122.0	177.0	36.0	535.0
Goods: Exports f.o.b	78aa d	...	...	...	...	...	...	...	...	...	...	8,091.0	8,052.0	7,894.0	8,829.0	9,671.0
Goods: Imports f.o.b	78ab d	...	...	...	...	...	...	...	...	...	...	−7,445.0	−8,360.0	−8,184.0	−9,235.0	−9,849.0
Trade Balance	78ac d											646.0	−308.0	−290.0	−406.0	−178.0
Services: Credit	78ad d											1,211.0	1,284.0	1,207.0	1,059.0	1,273.0
Services: Debit	78ae d											−549.0	−683.0	−630.0	−598.0	−581.0
Balance on Goods & Services	78af d											1,308.0	293.0	287.0	55.0	514.0
Income: Credit	78ag d											141.0	182.0	160.0	161.0	173.0
Income: Debit	78ah d											−553.0	−443.0	−372.0	−289.0	−233.0
Balance on Gds, Serv. & Inc.	78ai d											896.0	32.0	75.0	−73.0	454.0
Current Transfers, n.i.e.: Credit	78aj d											80.0	106.0	123.0	134.0	109.0
Current Transfers: Debit	78ak d											−22.0	−16.0	−21.0	−25.0	−28.0
Capital Account, n.i.e.	78bc d	...	...	...	...	...	...	...	...	...	...	—	—	—	—	—
Capital Account, n.i.e.: Credit	78ba d											—	—	—	—	—
Capital Account: Debit	78bb d											—	—	—	—	—
Financial Account, n.i.e.	78bj d	...	...	...	...	...	...	...	...	...	...	−870.0	−395.0	−57.0	−347.0	−238.0
Direct Investment Abroad	78bd d	...	...	...	...	...	...	...	...	...	...	—	—	—	—	—
Dir. Invest. in Rep. Econ., n.i.e.	78be d	...	...	...	...	...	...	...	...	...	...	—	—	—	—	—
Portfolio Investment Assets	78bf d	...	...	...	...	...	...	...	...	...	...	—	—	—	—	—
Equity Securities	78bk d	...	...	...	...	...	...	...	...	...	...	—	—	—	—	—
Debt Securities	78bl d	...	...	...	...	...	...	...	...	...	...	—	—	—	—	—
Portfolio Investment Liab., n.i.e.	78bg d	...	...	...	...	...	...	...	...	...	...	—	—	—	—	—
Equity Securities	78bm d	...	...	...	...	...	...	...	...	...	...	—	—	—	—	—
Debt Securities	78bn d	...	...	...	...	...	...	...	...	...	...	—	—	—	—	—
Financial Derivatives Assets	78bw d	...	...	...	...	...	...	...	...	...	...	...	...	...	...	...
Financial Derivatives Liabilities	78bx d	...	...	...	...	...	...	...	...	...	...	...	...	...	...	...
Other Investment Assets	78bh d	...	...	...	...	...	...	...	...	...	...	−130.0	−74.0	−57.0	−44.0	−332.0
Monetary Authorities	78bo d	...	...	...	...	...	...	...	...	...	...	—	—	—	—	—
General Government	78bp d	...	...	...	...	...	...	...	...	...	...	—	—	—	—	—
Banks	78bq d	...	...	...	...	...	...	...	...	...	...	−130.0	−74.0	−57.0	−44.0	−332.0
Other Sectors	78br d	...	...	...	...	...	...	...	...	...	...	—	—	—	—	—
Other Investment Liab., n.i.e.	78bi d	...	...	...	...	...	...	...	...	...	...	−740.0	−321.0	—	−303.0	94.0
Monetary Authorities	78bs d	...	...	...	...	...	...	...	...	...	...	—	—	—	—	—
General Government	78bt d	...	...	...	...	...	...	...	...	...	...	—	—	—	—	—
Banks	78bu d	...	...	...	...	...	...	...	...	...	...	−740.0	−321.0	—	−303.0	94.0
Other Sectors	78bv d	...	...	...	...	...	...	...	...	...	...	—	—	—	—	—
Net Errors and Omissions	78ca d	...	...	...	...	...	...	...	...	...	...	151.0	−88.0	6.0	523.0	120.0
Overall Balance	78cb d											235.0	−361.0	126.0	212.0	417.0
Reserves and Related Items	79da d	...	...	...	...	...	...	...	...	...	...	−235.0	361.0	−126.0	−212.0	−417.0
Reserve Assets	79db d											−235.0	361.0	−126.0	−212.0	−417.0
Use of Fund Credit and Loans	79dc d											—	—	—	—	—
Exceptional Financing	79de d											—	—	—	—	—
International Investment Position																*Millions of US Dollars*
Assets	79aa d	...	...	...	...	...	...	...	...	...	...	...	...	...	...	...
Direct Investment Abroad	79ab d	...	...	...	...	...	...	...	...	...	...	...	...	...	...	...
Portfolio Investment	79ac d	...	...	...	...	...	...	...	...	...	...	...	...	...	...	...
Equity Securities	79ad d	...	...	...	...	...	...	...	...	...	...	...	...	...	...	...
Debt Securities	79ae d	...	...	...	...	...	...	...	...	...	...	...	...	...	...	...
Financial Derivatives	79al d	...	...	...	...	...	...	...	...	...	...	...	...	...	...	...
Other Investment	79af d	...	...	...	...	...	...	...	...	...	...	...	...	...	...	...
Monetary Authorities	79ag d	...	...	...	...	...	...	...	...	...	...	...	...	...	...	...
General Government	79ah d	...	...	...	...	...	...	...	...	...	...	...	...	...	...	...
Banks	79ai d	...	...	...	...	...	...	...	...	...	...	...	...	...	...	...
Other Sectors	79aj d	...	...	...	...	...	...	...	...	...	...	...	...	...	...	...
Reserve Assets	79ak d	...	...	...	...	...	...	...	...	...	...	...	...	...	...	...
Liabilities	79la d	...	...	...	...	...	...	...	...	...	...	...	...	...	...	...
Dir. Invest. in Rep. Economy	79lb d	...	...	...	...	...	...	...	...	...	...	...	...	...	...	...
Portfolio Investment	79lc d	...	...	...	...	...	...	...	...	...	...	...	...	...	...	...
Equity Securities	79ld d	...	...	...	...	...	...	...	...	...	...	...	...	...	...	...
Debt Securities	79le d	...	...	...	...	...	...	...	...	...	...	...	...	...	...	...
Financial Derivatives	79ll d	...	...	...	...	...	...	...	...	...	...	...	...	...	...	...
Other Investment	79lf d	...	...	...	...	...	...	...	...	...	...	...	...	...	...	...
Monetary Authorities	79lg d	...	...	...	...	...	...	...	...	...	...	...	...	...	...	...
General Government	79lh d	...	...	...	...	...	...	...	...	...	...	...	...	...	...	...
Banks	79li d	...	...	...	...	...	...	...	...	...	...	...	...	...	...	...
Other Sectors	79lj d	...	...	...	...	...	...	...	...	...	...	...	...	...	...	...

Prices and Labor

Period Averages

1985	1986	1987	1988	1989	1990	1991	1992	1993	1994	1995	1996	1997	1998	1999		
16.8	17.0	16.9	17.3	17.3	19.3	I76.4	I30.0	5.2	64.2	I100.0	233.9	2,508.2	2,925.7	3,009.2	Producer Prices	63
1.5	1.6	1.6	1.6	I1.8	2.2	I9.5	18.2	31.5	61.7	100.0	221.6	2,573.9	3,056.4	3,135.0	Consumer Prices	64

Period Averages

1985	1986	1987	1988	1989	1990	1991	1992	1993	1994	1995	1996	1997	1998	1999		
4,095	4,077	4,109	4,078	4,085	3,846	3,205	2,663	2,267	2,032	1,910	1,852	....	....	....	Employment	67e
....	....	....	....	....	65	419	577	601	488	424	479	524	465	....	Unemployment	67c
....	....	....	....	....	1.7	11.1	15.3	16.4	12.4	11.1	12.5	13.7	....	....	Unemployment Rate (%)	67r

International Transactions

Millions of Leva

1985	1986	1987	1988	1989	1990	1991	1992	1993	1994	1995	1996	1997	1998	1999		
13.7	13.4	13.8	14.4	13.7	10.6	57.4	91.5	102.9	216.2	359.7	859.8	8,281.4	7,570.1	7,230.7	Exports	70
14.1	14.4	14.1	13.9	12.8	10.3	45.1	104.3	131.5	227.0	380.0	892.1	8,268.5	8,765.2	9,971.4	Imports, c.i.f.	71

Balance of Payments

Minus Sign Indicates Debit

1985	1986	1987	1988	1989	1990	1991	1992	1993	1994	1995	1996	1997	1998	1999		
-136.0	-951.0	-720.0	-402.0	-769.0	-1,710.0	-76.9	-359.9	-1,098.8	-31.8	-25.8	15.7	426.9	-61.8	-659.6	Current Account, n.i.e.	78al d
10,313.0	8,862.0	10,297.0	9,283.0	8,268.0	6,113.0	3,737.0	3,956.4	3,726.5	3,935.1	5,345.0	4,890.2	4,939.6	4,193.5	3,967.2	Goods: Exports f.o.b	78aa d
-10,818.0	-10,045.0	-11,308.0	-9,889.0	-8,960.0	-7,427.0	-3,769.0	-4,168.7	-4,611.9	-3,951.9	-5,224.0	-4,702.6	-4,559.3	-4,574.2	-5,031.3	Goods: Imports f.o.b	78ab d
-505.0	-1,183.0	-1,011.0	-606.0	-692.0	-1,314.0	-32.0	-212.3	-885.4	-16.8	121.0	187.6	380.3	-380.7	-1,064.1	*Trade Balance*	78ac d
1,047.0	958.0	1,158.0	1,186.0	1,223.0	837.0	399.9	1,070.3	1,171.3	1,256.9	1,431.4	1,366.0	1,337.4	1,787.9	1,784.3	Services: Credit	78ad d
-654.0	-631.0	-661.0	-656.0	-785.0	-600.0	-485.8	-1,165.2	-1,229.3	-1,246.1	-1,277.9	-1,245.9	-1,171.0	-1,415.1	-1,466.8	Services: Debit	78ae d
-112.0	-856.0	-514.0	-76.0	-254.0	-1,077.0	-117.9	-307.2	-943.4	-6.0	274.5	307.7	546.7	-7.9	-746.6	*Balance on Goods & Services*	78af d
160.0	138.0	115.0	82.0	127.0	120.0	55.6	125.1	92.6	84.6	149.7	181.0	210.8	306.6	266.8	Income: Credit	78ag d
-257.0	-300.0	-429.0	-511.0	-719.0	-878.0	-83.7	-220.7	-284.9	-277.1	-581.9	-577.2	-567.4	-590.3	-479.6	Income: Debit	78ah d
-209.0	-1,018.0	-828.0	-505.0	-846.0	-1,835.0	-146.0	-402.8	-1,135.7	-198.5	-157.7	-88.5	190.1	-291.6	-959.4	*Balance on Gds, Serv. & Inc.*	78ai d
98.0	89.0	161.0	183.0	143.0	232.0	123.4	114.1	285.9	357.1	256.8	231.8	275.5	261.4	328.7	Current Transfers, n.i.e.: Credit	78aj d
-25.0	-22.0	-53.0	-80.0	-66.0	-107.0	-54.3	-71.2	-249.0	-190.4	-124.9	-127.6	-38.7	-31.6	-28.9	Current Transfers: Debit	78ak d
—	—	—	—	—	—	....	—	—	763.3	—	65.9	—	—	-4.8	Capital Account, n.i.e.	78bc d
—	—	—	—	—	—	....	—	—	763.3	—	65.9	—	—	—	Capital Account, n.i.e.: Credit	78ba d
—	—	—	—	—	—	....	—	—	—	—	....	—	—	-4.8	Capital Account: Debit	78bb d
-165.0	412.0	480.0	1,545.0	-40.0	-2,814.0	-428.6	613.9	759.0	-1,018.7	326.6	-715.0	462.0	266.7	659.4	Financial Account, n.i.e.	78bj d
—	—	—	—	—	—	....	—	—	—	8.0	28.5	1.7	-.1	-4.9	Direct Investment Abroad	78bd d
—	—	—	—	—	4.0	55.9	41.5	40.0	105.4	90.4	109.0	504.8	537.2	770.4	Dir. Invest. in Rep. Econ., n.i.e.	78be d
—	—	—	—	—	—	....	—	—	-222.0	9.7	-7.1	-13.7	-129.5	-207.8	Portfolio Investment Assets	78bf d
—	—	—	—	—	—	....	—	—	—	9.7	-7.1	-8.5	-10.7	—	Equity Securities	78bk d
—	—	—	—	—	—	....	—	—	-222.0	—	—	-5.2	-118.8	-207.8	Debt Securities	78bl d
—	—	—	—	—	—	....	—	—	-9.8	-75.4	-122.2	146.5	-112.0	8.0	Portfolio Investment Liab., n.i.e.	78bg d
—	—	—	—	—	—	....	—	—	—	—	2.0	52.0	19.2	1.9	Equity Securities	78bm d
—	—	—	—	—	—	....	—	—	-9.8	-75.4	-124.2	94.5	-131.2	6.1	Debt Securities	78bn d
....	....	....	....	—	—	....	....	....	—	—	—	—	—	....	Financial Derivatives Assets	78bw d
															Financial Derivatives Liabilities	78bx d
-349.0	-478.0	-442.0	-548.0	-488.0	384.0	-191.9	244.3	338.4	-209.2	404.2	-568.1	-53.9	222.2	13.5	Other Investment Assets	78bh d
....	....	....	—												Monetary Authorities	78bo d
—	—	—	-401.0	-204.0	277.0	92.4	307.7	285.5	90.1	292.6	293.7	106.5	-19.8	-17.5	General Government	78bp d
-349.0	-478.0	-442.0	-147.0	-284.0	107.0	-284.3	-63.4	52.9	-299.3	111.6	113.7	-440.6	103.0	22.6	Banks	78bq d
											-975.5	280.2	139.0	8.4	Other Sectors	78br d
184.0	890.0	922.0	2,093.0	448.0	-3,202.0	-292.6	328.1	380.6	-683.1	-110.3	-155.1	-123.4	-251.1	80.2	Other Investment Liab., n.i.e.	78bi d
—	—	—	—	—	—	—	89.9	3.0							Monetary Authorities	78bs d
								-59.6	-951.0	-1.9	44.0	-82.1	-213.7	-114.2	General Government	78bt d
184.0	890.0	922.0	2,093.0	448.0	-3,202.0	-292.6	-279.8	10.2	-39.2	-94.8	-179.7	-52.3	-65.1	10.3	Banks	78bu d
						—	518.0	427.0	307.1	-13.6	-19.4	11.0	27.7	184.1	Other Sectors	78bv d
599.0	-346.0	-257.0	-486.0	375.0	70.0	231.5	14.7	18.1	71.6	143.8	-105.3	256.4	-299.2	91.6	Net Errors and Omissions	78ca d
298.0	-885.0	-497.0	657.0	-434.0	-4,454.0	-274.0	268.7	-321.7	215.6	444.6	-738.7	1,145.3	-94.3	86.6	*Overall Balance*	78cb d
-298.0	885.0	497.0	-657.0	434.0	4,454.0	274.0	-268.7	321.7	-215.6	-444.6	738.7	-1,145.3	94.3	-86.7	Reserves and Related Items	79da d
-298.0	885.0	497.0	-657.0	434.0	878.0	-318.4	-637.0	247.0	-341.6	-233.7	750.9	-1,641.3	-461.5	-517.8	Reserve Assets	79db d
—	—	—	—	—	—	399.9	196.1	42.7	262.4	-245.9	-108.7	396.9	129.4	161.9	Use of Fund Credit and Loans	79dc d
—	—	—	—	—	3,576.0	192.5	172.2	32.0	294.8	35.0	96.5	99.1	426.4	269.3	Exceptional Financing	79de d

International Investment Position

Millions of US Dollars

1985	1986	1987	1988	1989	1990	1991	1992	1993	1994	1995	1996	1997	1998	1999		
....	....	....	....	....	....	....	....	....	....	....	....	....	8,562.8	....	Assets	79aa d
....	....	....	....	....	....	....	....	....	....	....	....	....	3.5	....	Direct Investment Abroad	79ab d
....	....	....	....	....	....	....	....	....	....	....	....	....	602.1	....	Portfolio Investment	79ac d
....	....	....	....	....	....	....	....	....	....	....	....	....	20.6	....	Equity Securities	79ad d
....	....	....	....	....	....	....	....	....	....	....	....	....	581.5	....	Debt Securities	79ae d
....	....	....	....	....	....	....	....	....	....	....	....	....		....	Financial Derivatives	79al d
....	....	....	....	....	....	....	....	....	....	....	....	....	4,900.8	....	Other Investment	79af d
....	....	....	....	....	....	....	....	....	....	....	....	....	.5	....	Monetary Authorities	79ag d
....	....	....	....	....	....	....	....	....	....	....	....	....	2,242.4	....	General Government	79ah d
....	....	....	....	....	....	....	....	....	....	....	....	....	1,524.6	....	Banks	79ai d
....	....	....	....	....	....	....	....	....	....	....	....	....	1,133.3	....	Other Sectors	79aj d
....	....	....	....	....	....	....	....	....	....	....	....	....	3,056.4	....	Reserve Assets	79ak d
....	....	....	....	....	....	....	....	....	....	....	....	....	11,776.1	....	Liabilities	79la d
....	....	....	....	....	....	....	....	....	....	....	....	....	1,348.3	....	Dir. Invest. in Rep. Economy	79lb d
....	....	....	....	....	....	....	....	....	....	....	....	....	5,148.9	....	Portfolio Investment	79lc d
....	....	....	....	....	....	....	....	....	....	....	....	....	89.3	....	Equity Securities	79ld d
....	....	....	....	....	....	....	....	....	....	....	....	....	5,059.6	....	Debt Securities	79le d
....	....	....	....	....	....	....	....	....	....	....	....	....		....	Financial Derivatives	79ll d
....	....	....	....	....	....	....	....	....	....	....	....	....	5,278.9	....	Other Investment	79lf d
....	....	....	....	....	....	....	....	....	....	....	....	....	1,115.5	....	Monetary Authorities	79lg d
....	....	....	....	....	....	....	....	....	....	....	....	....	3,440.5	....	General Government	79lh d
....	....	....	....	....	....	....	....	....	....	....	....	....	454.5	....	Banks	79li d
....	....	....	....	....	....	....	....	....	....	....	....	....	268.4	....	Other Sectors	79lj d

Bulgaria

	1970	1971	1972	1973	1974	1975	1976	1977	1978	1979	1980	1981	1982	1983	1984
Government Finance														*Millions of Leva:*	
Deficit (-) or Surplus 80	....	....	....	....	....	....	....	....	....	....	....	....	....	....	....
Total Revenue and Grants 81y	....	....	....	....	....	....	....	....	....	....	....	....	....	....	....
Revenue 81	....	....	....	....	....	....	....	....	....	....	....	....	....	....	....
Grants 81z	....	....	....	....	....	....	....	....	....	....	....	....	....	....	....
Exp. & Lending Minus Repay. 82z	....	....	....	....	....	....	....	....	....	....	....	....	....	....	....
Expenditure 82	....	....	....	....	....	....	....	....	....	....	....	....	....	....	....
Lending Minus Repayments 83	....	....	....	....	....	....	....	....	....	....	....	....	....	....	....
Total Financing 80h	....	....	....	....	....	....	....	....	....	....	....	....	....	....	....
Total Net Borrowing 84	....	....	....	....	....	....	....	....	....	....	....	....	....	....	....
Net Domestic 84a	....	....	....	....	....	....	....	....	....	....	....	....	....	....	....
Net Foreign 85a	....	....	....	....	....	....	....	....	....	....	....	....	....	....	....
Use of Cash Balances 87	....	....	....	....	....	....	....	....	....	....	....	....	....	....	....
Total Debt by Residence 88	....	....	....	....	....	....	....	....	....	....	....	....	....	....	....
Domestic 88a	....	....	....	....	....	....	....	....	....	....	....	....	....	....	....
Foreign 89a	....	....	....	....	....	....	....	....	....	....	....	....	....	....	....
National Accounts														*Millions of Leva*	
Househ.Cons.Expend.,incl.NPISHs 96f	....	....	....	....	....	....	....	....	....	....	....	....	....	....	....
Government Consumption Expend. 91f	....	....	....	....	....	....	....	....	....	....	....	....	....	....	....
Gross Fixed Capital Formation 93e										6	7	8	8	8	8
Changes in Inventories 93i										1	1	2	2	2	2
Exports of Goods and Services 90c	....	....	....	....	....	....	....	....	....	....	....	....	....	....	....
Imports of Goods and Services............. 98c	....	....	....	....	....	....	....	....	....	....	....	....	....	....	....
Gross Domestic Product (GDP) 99b	11	10	11	12	13	14	15	15	....	22	26	28	29	30	32
GDP Volume (1995=100) .... 99bv p	....	....	....	....	....	....	....	....	....	....	....	....	....	....	....
GDP Deflator (1995=100) .... 99bi p	....	....	....	....	....	....	....	....	....	....	....	....	....	....	....
														Millions:	
Population 99z	8.49	8.54	8.58	8.62	8.68	8.72	8.76	8.80	8.81	8.95	8.86	8.89	8.92	8.94	8.96

Year Ending December 31

1985	1986	1987	1988	1989	1990	1991	1992	1993	1994	1995	1996	1997	1998	1999	Government Finance	
....	....	....	-1.6	-.4	-3.7	-6.1	-9.9	-36.1	I-24.5	-46.2	-332.8	353.3	599.2	....	Deficit (-) or Surplus	80
....	....	....	20.2	21.5	22.8	49.9	71.8	100.0	I209.3	315.5	703.3	5,662.1	7,530.6	....	Total Revenue and Grants	81y
....	....	....	19.9	21.0	22.3	49.5	71.6	99.9	I209.3	314.6	699.1	5,558.0	7,380.3	....	Revenue	81
....	....	....	.3	.5	.5	.4	.2	.1	I—	.9	4.2	104.1	150.3	....	Grants	81z
....	....	....	21.8	21.9	26.5	56.0	81.7	136.1	I233.8	361.7	1,036.1	5,308.8	6,931.4	....	Exp. & Lending Minus Repay.	82z
....	....	....	20.2	20.7	25.0	54.5	81.6	133.9	I235.9	360.6	1,040.9	5,733.2	7,227.6	....	Expenditure	82
....	....	....	1.6	1.2	1.5	1.5	.1	2.2	I-2.1	1.1	-4.8	-424.4	-296.2	....	Lending Minus Repayments	83
....	....	....	1.6	.4	3.7	6.1	9.9	36.1	I24.5	46.2	332.8	-353.3	-599.3	....	Total Financing	80h
....	....	....	1.7	1.4	3.7	11.3	16.5	35.5	I53.0	58.7	295.5	1,261.0	-213.3	....	Total Net Borrowing	84
....	....	....	2.2	1.9	4.1	7.5	13.6	38.3	I44.6	65.5	331.3	1,204.3	-65.8	....	Net Domestic	84a
....	....	....	-.5	-.5	-.4	3.8	2.9	-2.8	I8.4	-6.8	-35.8	56.7	-147.5	....	Net Foreign	85a
....	....	....	-.1	-1.0	—	-5.2	-6.6	.6	I-28.5	-12.5	37.3	-1,614.3	-386.0	....	Use of Cash Balances	87
....	....	....	....	....	....	....	....	....	....	....	....	....	....	....	Total Debt by Residence	88
....	....	....	7.3	9.3	15.7	23.1	39.8	112.0	I275.1	345.4	1,052.8	....	....	....	Domestic	88a
....	....	....	....	....	....	....	....	....	....	....	....	....	....	....	Foreign	89a

Millions of Leva

1985	1986	1987	1988	1989	1990	1991	1992	1993	1994	1995	1996	1997	1998	1999	National Accounts	
....	....	....	....	....	....	73	132	220	389	622	1,340	12,274	15,734	17,037	Househ.Cons.Expend.,incl.NPISHs	96f
....	....	....	....	....	....	26	41	56	90	134	207	2,116	3,255	3,612	Government Consumption Expend.	91f
9	9	10	10	10	10	I25	33	39	72	134	238	1,932	2,496	3,632	Gross Fixed Capital Formation	93e
2	3	2	3	3	4	I6	7	7	-23	4	-92	93	686	707	Changes in Inventories	93i
....	....	....	....	....	....	59	95	114	237	393	1,100	10,478	9,755	10,054	Exports of Goods and Services	90c
....	....	....	....	....	....	-53	-106	-137	-240	-407	-1,046	-9,529	-9,983	-11,819	Imports of Goods and Services	98c
33	34	37	38	40	45	I136	201	299	526	880	1,749	17,103	21,577	22,776	Gross Domestic Product (GDP)	99b
....	....	....	....	125.6	I114.1	I104.5	I96.9	I95.5	I97.2	I100.0	I89.9	83.7	....	....	GDP Volume (1995=100)	99bv p
....	....	....	....	3.6	4.5	I14.7	23.5	35.6	61.4	100.0	221.0	2,321.3	....	....	GDP Deflator (1995=100)	99bi p

Midyear Estimates

1985	1986	1987	1988	1989	1990	1991	1992	1993	1994	1995	1996	1997	1998	1999		
8.96	8.96	8.97	8.98	8.99	8.99	8.98	I8.54	8.47	8.44	8.41	8.36	8.31	8.25	8.21	Population	99z

(See notes in the back of the book.)

Burkina Faso

748

		1970	1971	1972	1973	1974	1975	1976	1977	1978	1979	1980	1981	1982	1983	1984
Exchange Rates															*Francs per SDR:*	
Official Rate	aa	276.02	283.61	278.00	284.00	272.08	262.55	288.70	285.76	272.28	264.78	287.99	334.52	370.92	436.97	470.11
															Francs per US Dollar:	
Official Rate	ae	276.02	261.22	256.05	235.42	222.22	224.27	248.49	235.25	209.00	201.00	225.80	287.40	336.25	417.37	479.60
Official Rate	rf	276.40	275.59	252.03	222.89	240.70	214.31	238.95	245.68	225.66	212.72	211.28	271.73	328.61	381.07	436.96
Fund Position															*Millions of SDRs:*	
Quota	2f. s	13.0	13.0	13.0	13.0	13.0	13.0	13.0	13.0	16.0	16.0	24.0	24.0	24.0	24.0	31.6
SDRs	1b. s	1.7	3.1	4.4	4.4	4.4	4.4	4.4	4.4	4.4	6.1	5.8	7.5	7.5	7.5	5.6
Reserve Position in the Fund	1c. s	1.4	2.5	3.1	3.3	3.3	3.3	3.3	4.6	4.6	4.6	5.6	5.6	5.6	5.6	7.5
Total Fund Cred.&Loans Outstg.	2tl	—	—	—	—	—	—	—	—	—	5.4	9.3	12.7	12.7	12.5	11.4
International Liquidity												*Millions of US Dollars Unless Otherwise Indicated:*				
Total Reserves minus Gold	1l. d	36.4	42.9	47.5	62.6	83.6	76.5	71.4	56.2	36.3	61.6	68.2	70.8	61.8	85.0	106.3
SDRs	1b. d	1.7	3.3	4.8	5.3	5.4	5.2	5.1	5.4	5.8	8.0	7.4	8.7	8.3	7.9	5.5
Reserve Position in the Fund	1c. d	1.4	2.7	3.4	3.9	4.0	3.8	3.8	5.6	6.0	6.0	7.2	6.6	6.2	5.9	7.4
Foreign Exchange	1d. d	33.3	36.9	39.3	53.4	74.2	67.5	62.5	45.2	24.6	47.5	53.6	55.6	47.3	71.2	93.4
Gold (Million Fine Troy Ounces)	1ad	....	....	....	....	....	....	—	.006	.008	.011	.011	.011	.011	.011	.011
Gold (National Valuation)	1and	....	....	....	....	....	....	—	.2	.4	.5	.5	4.7	4.8	4.3	3.7
Monetary Authorities: Other Liab.	4. d	.1	.2	.3	—	2.3	5.1	11.1	2.4	5.2	6.4	7.2	5.1	8.6	6.0	12.6
Deposit Money Banks: Assets	7a. d	1.2	4.9	.5	6.4	2.7	3.1	1.2	3.8	4.2	1.4	7.0	3.5	2.8	4.7	5.8
Liabilities	7b. d	6.0	9.6	8.3	12.5	23.3	22.2	28.6	53.9	58.3	61.9	56.5	55.2	53.0	51.6	32.4
Monetary Authorities															*Billions of Francs:*	
Foreign Assets	11	10.1	11.0	12.1	14.4	18.6	17.2	17.7	13.2	7.6	12.4	15.4	20.4	20.8	35.5	51.0
Claims on Central Government	12a	—	—	—	—	—	—	—	2.0	3.5	4.4	5.1	6.1	10.1	12.4	13.8
Claims on Deposit Money Banks	12e	.1	.2	.3	.4	1.5	2.5	6.1	7.5	13.3	11.5	11.8	8.9	10.5	11.2	9.6
Claims on Other Financial Insts	12f	—	—	—	—	—	—	.2	.4	.4	.3	.4	.5	.6	.8	.8
Reserve Money	14	5.9	5.8	6.2	7.6	9.0	11.7	13.3	15.7	15.2	19.9	21.6	26.3	28.6	42.0	57.3
of which: Currency Outside DMBs	14a	5.7	5.7	5.8	7.1	8.5	10.7	12.8	14.7	13.5	17.4	19.9	24.8	27.0	31.7	31.2
Foreign Liabilities	16c	—	.1	.1	—	.5	1.1	2.8	.6	4.1	6.3	8.8	9.2	11.1	11.4	14.6
Central Government Deposits	16d	3.9	4.4	4.8	5.9	9.4	5.7	6.6	5.6	5.4	3.3	3.5	1.3	2.7	7.2	4.8
Other Items (Net)	17r	.5	1.0	1.3	1.4	1.3	1.0	1.4	1.3	.2	-.9	-1.2	-.9	-.4	-.8	-1.5
Deposit Money Banks															*Billions of Francs:*	
Reserves	20	.1	.1	.4	.4	.4	1.1	.6	.9	1.5	2.1	1.6	1.4	2.0	10.2	25.8
Foreign Assets	21	.3	1.2	.1	1.5	.6	.7	.3	.9	.9	.3	1.6	1.0	.9	1.9	2.8
Claims on Central Government	22a	—	—	—	.1	.3	5.3	4.8	1.9	5.9	8.6	14.1	13.4	12.5	12.7	
Claims on Private Sector	22d	5.5	6.0	7.1	9.0	15.2	21.4	31.9	45.3	54.8	⅄56.7	58.7	65.0	73.4	76.1	74.4
Claims on Other Financial Insts	22f	....	....	....	....	....	....	....	....	....	.5	.5	.6	1.2	1.5	1.7
Demand Deposits	24	3.0	3.4	3.6	5.8	7.3	10.7	13.6	14.7	18.8	⅄15.8	20.3	22.5	26.0	27.3	33.4
Time Deposits	25	.2	.5	.7	1.0	1.2	1.8	4.0	4.8	8.1	⅄11.5	11.5	14.9	17.0	19.7	26.3
Foreign Liabilities	26c	.8	1.4	.6	.6	1.3	.8	2.6	7.7	7.0	7.2	8.4	11.5	13.5	17.1	12.8
Long-Term Foreign Liabilities	26cl	.9	1.0	1.6	2.3	3.8	4.2	4.5	5.0	5.2	5.2	4.4	4.4	4.3	4.4	2.7
Central Government Deposits	26d	.3	.3	.6	.7	.5	5.3	5.6	6.6	8.3	⅄10.7	13.4	17.1	19.2	24.0	28.0
Credit from Monetary Authorities	26g	.1	.2	.3	.4	1.5	2.5	6.1	7.5	13.3	11.5	11.8	8.9	10.5	11.2	9.6
Other Items (Net)	27r	.7	.6	.4	.1	.8	3.1	1.0	2.8	2.4	4.3	1.1	2.7	.3	-1.4	4.5
Treasury Claims: Private Sector	22d. i	.1	.1	.2	.2	.2	.3	.5	.8	1.1	1.0	1.6	1.8	2.5	1.9	1.8
Post Office: Checking Deposits	24.. i	.4	.4	.5	.5	.6	1.1	1.1	1.4	2.1	1.6	1.4	1.4	1.4	1.3	1.8
Monetary Survey															*Billions of Francs:*	
Foreign Assets (Net)	31n	9.6	10.8	11.6	15.3	17.3	15.9	12.6	5.9	-2.6	-.9	-.2	.7	-2.9	8.9	26.3
Domestic Credit	32	1.8	1.7	2.2	2.9	6.1	16.7	25.6	38.8	53.1	⅄56.2	57.7	69.3	78.2	73.4	72.4
Claims on Central Govt. (Net)	32an	-3.8	-4.5	-5.1	-6.3	-9.3	-4.9	-7.0	-7.7	-3.3	⅄-2.3	-3.4	1.5	.6	-6.9	-6.2
Claims on Private Sector	32d	5.6	6.1	7.3	9.2	15.4	21.7	32.4	46.1	56.0	⅄57.7	60.2	66.7	75.9	78.0	76.2
Claims on Other Financial Insts	32f	—	—	—	—	—	—	.2	.4	.4	⅄.9	.9	1.1	1.8	2.3	2.5
Money	34	9.1	9.5	9.9	13.5	16.4	22.5	27.6	30.8	34.4	⅄34.8	41.7	48.8	54.4	60.3	66.5
Quasi-Money	35	.2	.5	.7	1.0	1.2	1.8	4.0	4.8	8.1	⅄11.5	11.5	14.9	17.0	19.7	26.3
Long-Term Foreign Liabilities	36cl	.9	1.0	1.6	2.3	3.8	4.2	4.5	5.0	5.2	5.2	4.4	4.4	4.3	4.4	2.7
Other Items (Net)	37r	1.2	1.5	1.7	1.4	2.1	4.2	2.2	4.1	2.8	3.9	—	1.9	-.4	-2.2	3.3
Money plus Quasi-Money	35l	9.4	9.9	10.6	14.5	17.5	24.3	31.6	35.6	42.5	⅄46.2	53.2	63.7	71.4	80.1	92.8
Other Banking Institutions															*Billions of Francs:*	
Savings Deposits	45	1.00	1.05	1.12	1.37	1.65	2.04	2.50	2.82	2.94	3.37	3.81	4.27	4.36	4.25	4.08
Liquid Liabilities	55l	10.4	11.0	11.7	15.9	19.2	26.4	34.1	38.4	45.5	⅄49.6	57.0	68.0	75.7	84.3	96.9
Interest Rates															*Percent Per Annum*	
Discount Rate (End of Period)	60	3.50	3.50	3.50	5.50	5.50	8.00	8.00	8.00	8.00	8.00	10.50	10.50	12.50	10.50	10.50
Money Market Rate	60b	....	....	....	....	....	....	7.28	7.27	7.42	7.72	10.55	13.68	14.66	12.23	11.84
Deposit Rate	60l	3.00	3.00	3.00	5.75	5.75	5.88	6.00	6.00	6.00	6.00	6.19	6.25	7.75	7.50	7.25
Lending Rate	60p	....	....	....	....	....	....	....	12.00	12.00	12.00	14.50	14.50	16.00	14.50	14.50
Prices and Labor															*Index Numbers (1995=100):*	
Consumer Prices	64	....	....	....	....	....	....	....	....	....	....	....	....	....	67.4	70.6
															Number in Thousands:	
Employment	67e	....	....	....	....	....	....	....	....	....	....	....	....	....	....	....
Unemployment	67c	....	....	....	....	....	....	....	....	....	....	....	....	....	....	....

302 INTERNATIONAL FINANCIAL STATISTICS YEARBOOK 2000

	1985	1986	1987	1988	1989	1990	1991	1992	1993	1994	1995	1996	1997	1998	1999		
																Exchange Rates	
End of Period																	
	415.26	394.78	378.78	407.68	380.32	364.84	370.48	378.57	404.89	‡780.44	728.38	753.06	807.94	791.61	‡896.19	Official Rate	**aa**
End of Period (ae)	*Period Average (rf)*																
	378.05	322.75	267.00	302.95	289.40	256.45	259.00	275.32	294.77	‡534.60	490.00	523.70	598.81	562.21	‡652.95	Official Rate	**ae**
	449.26	346.31	300.54	297.85	319.01	272.26	282.11	264.69	283.16	‡555.20	499.15	511.55	583.67	589.95	‡615.70	Official Rate	**rf**
End of Period																**Fund Position**	
	31.6	31.6	31.6	31.6	31.6	31.6	31.6	44.2	44.2	44.2	44.2	44.2	44.2	44.2	60.2	Quota	**2f. s**
	5.6	5.6	5.7	5.6	5.6	5.7	5.6	5.6	5.6	5.6	5.5	1.8	1.6	.5	.5	SDRs	**1b. s**
	7.5	7.5	7.5	7.5	7.5	7.2	7.2	7.2	7.2	7.2	7.2	7.2	7.2	7.2	7.2	Reserve Position in the Fund	**1c. s**
	9.3	6.7	4.2	1.9	.4	.1	6.3	6.3	15.2	32.8	50.5	56.5	68.5	79.6	87.9	Total Fund Cred.&Loans Outstg.	**2tl**
End of Period																**International Liquidity**	
	139.5	233.5	322.6	320.9	265.5	300.5	346.1	341.3	382.3	237.2	347.4	338.6	344.8	373.3	295.0	Total Reserves minus Gold	**1l. d**
	6.2	6.9	8.0	7.6	7.4	8.0	8.0	7.7	7.7	8.1	8.2	2.6	2.2	.8	.7	SDRs	**1b. d**
	8.3	9.2	10.7	10.1	9.9	10.2	10.3	9.9	9.9	10.5	10.7	10.4	9.7	10.2	9.9	Reserve Position in the Fund	**1c. d**
	125.1	217.4	303.9	303.1	248.2	282.2	327.7	323.7	364.7	218.6	328.4	325.6	332.9	362.4	284.3	Foreign Exchange	**1d. d**
	.011	.011	.011	.011	.011	.011	.011	.011	.011	.011	.011	.011	.011	.011	.011	Gold (Million Fine Troy Ounces)	**1ad**
	3.6	4.5	5.2	4.6	4.3	4.2	3.9	3.8	4.1	4.1	4.3	4.2	3.4	3.3	3.3	Gold (National Valuation)	**1and**
	21.4	46.3	59.6	53.7	42.6	41.8	40.4	32.5	29.8	14.9	4.1	5.8	29.0	43.9	29.3	Monetary Authorities: Other Liab.	**4.. d**
	9.0	10.3	34.8	30.9	43.5	54.9	38.7	48.6	53.1	155.5	253.5	212.8	167.5	167.5	232.9	Deposit Money Banks: Assets	**7a. d**
	45.4	41.4	50.6	45.7	57.8	75.7	66.6	43.1	42.5	39.7	58.7	44.0	54.5	67.0	129.1	Liabilities	**7b. d**
End of Period																**Monetary Authorities**	
	52.7	75.4	86.1	97.2	76.8	77.1	89.6	94.0	112.7	126.8	170.2	177.3	206.5	209.9	192.6	Foreign Assets	**11**
	11.9	12.2	16.6	17.2	18.2	19.3	21.6	22.6	26.3	44.8	55.7	59.3	80.1	92.9	103.7	Claims on Central Government	**12a**
	7.0	7.5	8.1	4.5	4.3	3.9	9.0	9.0	9.0	—	2.5	4.0	14.6	24.7	3.9	Claims on Deposit Money Banks	**12e**
	.8	1.1	1.2	1.3	1.6	1.6	1.3	1.0	.9	.4	.3	.4	.7	1.1	1.1	Claims on Other Financial Insts	**12f**
	51.8	73.3	86.6	94.9	81.0	82.1	99.2	105.2	121.4	120.4	149.3	156.3	193.1	186.2	160.0	Reserve Money	**14**
	31.0	43.4	43.7	49.3	53.3	58.7	60.9	65.8	78.5	94.9	123.5	139.6	170.1	165.0	142.5	of which: Currency Outside DMBs	**14a**
	14.5	20.4	19.1	17.8	12.7	10.8	12.8	11.3	14.9	33.6	38.8	45.6	72.7	87.7	97.9	Foreign Liabilities	**16c**
	5.2	2.6	4.0	4.0	4.1	5.3	5.5	6.0	8.4	19.5	37.4	37.3	29.5	48.4	45.0	Central Government Deposits	**16d**
	1.0	–.1	2.2	3.5	3.2	3.8	4.0	3.9	4.1	–1.4	3.2	1.7	6.6	6.2	–1.6	Other Items (Net)	**17r**
End of Period																**Deposit Money Banks**	
	20.2	29.3	41.9	42.4	26.2	22.3	36.4	37.7	41.0	20.9	17.7	9.1	15.7	14.4	19.8	Reserves	**20**
	3.4	3.3	9.3	9.3	12.6	14.1	10.0	13.4	15.7	83.1	124.2	111.5	100.3	94.2	152.1	Foreign Assets	**21**
	6.7	6.8	5.6	6.9	14.7	19.7	15.2	14.0	13.5	35.3	27.3	26.1	28.1	32.7	26.1	Claims on Central Government	**22a**
	91.1	96.2	102.1	114.5	136.0	141.4	108.4	94.9	87.6	72.3	79.0	89.9	163.2	180.9	186.5	Claims on Private Sector	**22d**
	1.7	2.0	1.5	1.5	1.6	—	1.6	1.2	.3	.3	—	—	—	—		Claims on Other Financial Insts	**22f**
	36.4	39.7	44.1	47.2	48.5	42.1	45.8	41.4	42.0	69.8	81.5	80.2	90.7	89.5	107.7	Demand Deposits	**24**
	23.8	28.8	36.3	47.8	48.9	49.9	51.0	56.8	57.4	62.6	71.0	70.7	83.7	94.3	108.5	Time Deposits	**25**
	14.5	9.8	9.5	9.2	10.3	14.5	11.2	6.4	6.9	12.2	19.7	23.1	30.5	33.0	77.2	Foreign Liabilities	**26c**
	2.7	3.5	4.0	4.7	6.5	4.9	6.1	5.4	5.6	9.0	9.1	—	2.1	4.7	7.1	Long-Term Foreign Liabilities	**26cl**
	31.1	39.5	53.2	57.9	68.6	75.8	51.4	50.9	47.8	59.0	61.3	54.6	57.5	58.0	60.5	Central Government Deposits	**26d**
	7.0	7.5	8.1	4.5	4.3	3.9	9.0	9.0	9.0	—	2.5	—	14.6	25.2	4.4	Credit from Monetary Authorities	**26g**
	7.6	8.8	5.1	3.3	4.1	6.5	–2.9	–8.8	–10.5	–.7	3.1	7.9	28.3	17.6	19.2	Other Items (Net)	**27r**
	1.9	1.9	1.0	1.6	1.3	1.3	1.8	2.2	.9	1.7	1.6	1.6	1.8	1.4	1.1	Treasury Claims: Private Sector	**22d. i**
	2.0	2.1	2.8	1.8	2.3	2.3	1.9	1.7	1.6	2.4	2.7	2.7	2.1	2.3	2.3	Post Office: Checking Deposits	**24.. i**
End of Period																**Monetary Survey**	
	27.1	48.5	66.8	79.6	66.5	65.9	75.7	89.6	106.5	164.2	236.0	220.1	203.5	183.4	169.6	Foreign Assets (Net)	**31n**
	77.8	78.4	72.5	81.3	101.7	103.2	93.1	78.4	74.1	77.0	66.3	86.5	187.3	203.5	214.2	Domestic Credit	**32**
	–17.7	–22.8	–33.3	–37.7	–38.8	–41.2	–20.0	–20.9	–15.7	2.4	–14.6	–5.4	21.5	20.1	25.4	Claims on Central Govt. (Net)	**32an**
	93.1	98.1	103.1	116.1	137.3	142.8	110.2	97.1	88.5	73.9	80.6	91.5	165.0	182.3	187.6	Claims on Private Sector	**32d**
	2.5	3.1	2.7	2.8	3.2	1.6	2.8	2.2	1.2	.6	.3	.4	.7	1.1	1.1	Claims on Other Financial Insts	**32f**
	69.5	85.4	91.2	100.9	105.4	103.6	109.3	109.9	122.6	170.3	213.7	228.7	268.9	261.9	256.9	Money	**34**
	23.8	28.8	36.3	47.8	48.9	49.9	51.0	56.8	57.4	62.6	71.0	70.7	83.7	94.3	108.5	Quasi-Money	**35**
	2.7	3.5	4.0	4.7	6.5	4.9	6.1	5.4	5.6	9.0	9.1	—	2.1	4.7	7.1	Long-Term Foreign Liabilities	**36cl**
	9.0	9.2	7.7	7.5	7.5	10.7	2.3	–4.2	–5.0	–.8	8.5	7.2	36.2	26.0	11.4	Other Items (Net)	**37r**
	93.3	114.2	127.5	148.7	154.3	153.5	160.4	166.7	180.0	232.9	284.7	299.4	352.5	356.2	365.3	Money plus Quasi-Money	**35l**
End of Period																**Other Banking Institutions**	
	5.47	6.58	6.69	6.68	6.80	6.56	6.63	10.17	. . . .	. . . .	—	—	—	—	—	Savings Deposits	**45**
	98.8	120.8	134.2	155.4	161.1	160.1	167.0	176.9	. . . .	. . . .	. . . .	299.4	352.5	356.2	365.3	Liquid Liabilities	**55l**
Percent Per Annum																**Interest Rates**	
	10.50	8.50	8.50	9.50	11.00	11.00	11.00	12.50	10.50	10.00	7.50	6.50	6.00	6.25	5.75	Discount Rate (End of Period)	**60**
	10.67	8.58	8.37	8.72	10.07	10.98	10.94	11.44	. . . .	. . . .	. . . .	. . . .	. . . .	4.81	4.95	Money Market Rate	**60b**
	7.25	6.08	5.25	5.25	6.42	7.00	7.00	7.75	. . . .	. . . .	. . . .	. . . .	. . . .	3.50	3.50	Deposit Rate	**60l**
	14.50	13.50	13.50	13.58	15.13	16.00	16.00	16.75	. . . .	. . . .	. . . .	. . . .	. . . .			Lending Rate	**60p**
Period Averages																**Prices and Labor**	
	75.5	73.5	71.6	74.5	74.3	73.6	75.5	74.0	74.4	93.1	100.0	106.2	‡108.6	114.2	112.9	Consumer Prices	**64**
Period Averages																	
	. . . .	128	134	138	146	152	158	163	. . . .	. . . .	. . . .	. . . .	. . . .	. . . .	. . . .	Employment	**67e**
	33	32	35	‡35	38	42	35	30	30	27	. . . .	. . . .	. . . .	. . . .	. . . .	Unemployment	**67c**

Burkina Faso

748

International Transactions		1970	1971	1972	1973	1974	1975	1976	1977	1978	1979	1980	1981	1982	1983	1984
															Billions of Francs	
Exports	70	5.06	4.41	5.14	5.60	8.70	9.37	12.69	13.61	9.60	16.24	19.07	19.92	18.11	21.71	34.87
Imports, c.i.f.	71	13.70	15.61	17.27	21.69	34.66	32.39	34.42	51.36	51.08	63.92	75.61	91.44	114.01	109.57	111.26
															1995=100	
Unit Value of Exports	74	28.7	30.1	28.5	31.4	46.1	‡46.5	59.8	67.1	63.9	65.5	71.4	78.7	90.6	103.2	106.2
Unit Value of Imports	75	13.8	15.0	16.4	17.6	22.0	‡25.5	29.0	31.8	31.1	33.6	35.5	42.6	51.8	56.8	59.0
Balance of Payments															*Millions of US Dollars:*	
Current Account, n.i.e.	78ald	....	....	....	....	−5.3	−54.3	−33.5	−84.3	−59.5	−63.8	−48.7	−42.1	−92.1	−60.1	−3.5
Goods: Exports f.o.b.	78aad					66.0	73.5	83.1	94.8	107.8	132.7	160.6	159.4	126.4	112.9	140.9
Goods: Imports f.o.b.	78abd					−147.8	−187.8	−167.4	−220.7	−255.4	−312.1	−368.3	−348.4	−359.9	−308.9	−270.1
Trade Balance	78acd					−81.8	−114.3	−84.4	−125.9	−147.6	−179.4	−207.7	−191.1	−233.4	−196.0	−129.2
Services: Credit	78add					9.4	14.3	17.0	17.5	23.7	41.6	49.1	40.9	48.3	37.7	27.1
Services: Debit	78aed					−51.5	−74.2	−77.2	−95.1	−135.2	−178.6	−209.0	−185.4	−174.0	−146.9	−124.3
Balance on Goods & Services	78afd					−123.9	−174.2	−144.5	−203.5	−259.1	−316.5	−367.6	−333.6	−359.2	−305.2	−226.4
Income: Credit	78agd					9.0	7.4	6.4	6.2	4.9	7.1	15.6	8.9	9.0	5.9	7.0
Income: Debit	78ahd					−11.3	−19.3	−15.8	−26.2	−15.5	−16.0	−19.1	−18.4	−19.2	−16.0	−14.4
Balance on Gds, Serv. & Inc.	78aid					−126.1	−186.1	−153.9	−223.4	−269.7	−325.5	−371.1	−343.1	−369.4	−315.2	−233.8
Current Transfers, n.i.e.: Credit	78ajd					134.9	157.3	147.9	171.9	255.6	315.3	387.2	354.3	319.9	301.2	270.9
Current Transfers: Debit	78akd					−14.0	−25.4	−27.5	−32.8	−45.4	−53.6	−64.8	−53.2	−42.6	−46.1	−40.5
Capital Account, n.i.e.	78bcd					—	—	—	—	—	—	—	—	—	—	—
Capital Account, n.i.e.: Credit	78bad					—	—	—	—	—	—	—	—	—	—	—
Capital Account: Debit	78bbd					—	—	—	—	—	—	—	—	—	—	—
Financial Account, n.i.e.	78bjd					19.9	32.6	32.7	55.3	27.7	67.5	63.3	64.4	76.5	87.2	33.1
Direct Investment Abroad	78bdd					−.4	−.7	−.3	−.4	−.8	−.4	—	—	−.2	—	—
Dir. Invest. in Rep. Econ., n.i.e.	78bed					2.7	.3	2.1	5.0	1.2	1.5	—	2.4	1.9	2.0	1.7
Portfolio Investment Assets	78bfd					−.6	−.8	−.9	−1.4	.4	—	−1.1	−.2	.9	.4	—
Equity Securities	78bkd					—	—	—	—	—	−1.0	—	—	—	—	—
Debt Securities	78bld					−.6	−.8	−.9	−1.4	1.3	—	−1.1	−.2	.9	.4	—
Portfolio Investment Liab., n.i.e.	78bgd					.2	.2	1.2	.1	.4	—	.5	—	—	—	—
Equity Securities	78bmd					.2	.2	1.2	.1	.4	—	.5	—	—	—	—
Debt Securities	78bnd					—	—	—	—	—	—	—	—	—	—	—
Financial Derivatives Assets	78bwd					....	....	....	....	....	....	....	....	....	....	....
Financial Derivatives Liabilities	78bxd					....	....	....	....	....	....	....	....	....	....	....
Other Investment Assets	78bhd					−4.6	7.1	−7.5	−2.1	−2.0	−3.6	−13.1	−4.4	−7.0	−10.7	−7.5
Monetary Authorities	78bod															
General Government	78bpd							−.2	−.1	−.1	−.1	−3.2	−6.1	−6.9	−2.8	−1.8
Banks	78bqd					3.2	−.7	−.1	−3.1	−.3	2.1	−11.6	2.3	−2.4	−2.1	−2.5
Other Sectors	78brd					−7.8	7.8	−7.2	.9	−1.5	−5.6	1.7	−.6	2.2	−5.8	−3.2
Other Investment Liab., n.i.e.	78bid					22.5	26.5	38.1	54.1	28.5	69.9	77.0	66.6	80.9	95.5	38.9
Monetary Authorities	78bsd															
General Government	78btd					11.0	23.2	22.4	6.1	19.3	53.0	51.0	35.7	56.2	59.0	40.8
Banks	78bud					13.0	−2.0	8.3	21.6	−1.4	1.4	7.8	21.1	11.3	11.6	−18.0
Other Sectors	78bvd					−1.5	5.3	7.4	26.3	10.5	15.5	18.2	9.8	13.4	24.9	16.1
Net Errors and Omissions	78cad					1.7	15.5	1.3	9.2	.6	4.6	−7.9	−8.1	15.4	9.5	6.2
Overall Balance	78cbd					16.3	−6.3	.5	−19.8	−31.2	8.3	6.6	14.2	−.2	36.6	35.9
Reserves and Related Items	79dad					−16.3	6.3	−.5	19.8	31.2	−8.3	−6.6	−14.2	.2	−36.6	−35.9
Reserve Assets	79dbd					−16.3	6.3	−1.5	18.4	24.6	−20.6	−10.9	−14.3	.2	−36.3	−34.8
Use of Fund Credit and Loans	79dcd					—	—	—	—	—	6.7	5.1	4.3	.1	—	−1.1
Exceptional Financing	79ded					—	—	1.0	1.3	—	7.2	—	—	—	−.2	—
Government Finance															*Millions of Francs:*	
Deficit (-) or Surplus	80	....	....	....	354	2,212	−1,664	−1,272	‡4,313	1,495	−5,622	879	−4,674	−6,185	562	−3,350
Total Revenue and Grants	81y				12,862	15,973	15,785	21,430	‡28,765	32,235	35,071	43,139	48,720	54,560	54,540	63,088
Revenue	81				12,111	14,998	15,235	20,630	‡27,965	32,235	34,071	42,461	45,809	54,170	53,529	62,278
Grants	81z				751	975	550	800	‡800	—	1,000	678	2,911	390	1,011	810
Exp. & Lending Minus Repay.	82z				12,508	13,761	18,326	23,037	‡27,101	31,047	41,173	42,260	53,394	60,745	53,978	66,438
Expenditure	82				11,804	13,181	16,246	20,963	‡26,954	30,734	40,319	44,047	50,063	63,037	52,614	64,691
Lending Minus Repayments	83				704	580	2,080	2,074	‡147	313	854	−1,787	3,331	−2,292	1,364	1,747
Adjustment to Cash Basis	80x				....	....	....	....	....							
Total Financing	80h				....	....	....	....	....	....	....	−879	4,674	6,185	−562	3,350
National Accounts															*Billions of Francs*	
Exports of Goods & Services	90c	8.6	9.1	11.6	11.8	18.7	18.4	23.9	27.4	29.0	36.2	43.6	53.6	56.2	55.9	88.1
Government Consumption	91f	7.9	8.5	9.5	10.9	13.4	23.2	21.2	26.5	30.0	49.2	47.4	60.9	72.5	78.8	76.9
Gross Fixed Capital Formation	93e	7.5	12.2	15.5	20.0	28.8	29.5	33.2	35.9	39.2	74.8	66.0	69.9	84.0	90.3	90.8
Increase/Decrease(-) in Stocks	93i	2.3	2.7	3.5	3.3	6.0	5.6	6.2	5.1	6.8	5.0	6.4	7.2	7.8	2.6	3.3
Private Consumption	96f	92.1	94.6	99.2	96.9	106.9	113.4	118.9	161.9	196.7	192.1	231.3	278.7	315.1	327.6	308.3
Imports of Goods & Services	98c	−19.6	−25.5	−29.9	−33.2	−42.8	−52.4	−54.0	−71.9	−79.2	−104.8	−122.7	−146.1	−176.0	−174.2	−176.8
Gross Domestic Product (GDP)	99b	98.7	101.6	109.4	109.7	131.0	137.7	149.4	184.9	222.5	252.5	272.0	324.2	359.6	381.0	390.6
Net Factor Inc/Pmts(-) Abroad	98.n	−10.1	−13.0	−2.2	−.2	−.2	.3	.5	−.8	−1.5	−1.3	1.1	−.5	−1.0	−.7	−.8
Gross National Income (GNI)	99a	88.6	88.6	107.2	109.5	130.8	138.0	149.4	184.1	221.1	252.2	273.1	323.7	358.6	380.3	389.8
GDP Volume 1979 prices	99b.p	....	....	....	....	....	....	....	....	....	252.5	256.7	268.0	274.0	270.7	275.5
GDP Volume 1985 Prices	99b.p	....	....	....	....	....	....	....	....	....	....	....	....	....	....	....
GDP Volume (1995=100)	99bvp										62.8	63.8	66.6	68.1	67.3	68.5
GDP Deflator (1995=100)	99bip	....								....	34.3	36.4	41.5	45.0	48.3	48.6
															Millions:	
Population	99z	5.38	5.49	5.61	‡5.45	5.54	5.64	5.74	5.84	5.94	6.04	6.91	7.09	7.28	7.48	7.68

	1985	1986	1987	1988	1989	1990	1991	1992	1993	1994	1995	1996	1997	1998	1999		
Billions of Francs																**International Transactions**	
	31.16	28.67	46.59	41.95	30.27	41.28	29.89	16.83	19.66	59.22	80.10	119.04	133.62	190.44	156.60	Exports	70
	146.24	139.64	130.53	134.94	125.35	145.83	150.26	123.36	144.02	193.70	227.16	330.96	342.35	460.33	428.26	Imports, c.i.f.	71
1995=100																	
	124.8	87.8	I91.0	88.2	82.0	90.3	88.2	67.3	64.7	84.8	100.0	97.8	....	....	....	Unit Value of Exports	74
	63.4	60.9	I54.2	54.2	58.8	62.8	58.2	55.9	56.8	93.5	100.0	103.7	....	....	....	Unit Value of Imports	75
Minus Sign Indicates Debit																Balance of Payments	
	-63.0	-18.0	-49.8	-46.5	99.3	-76.9	-90.6	-23.0	-71.1	14.9	....	....	....	....	....	Current Account, n.i.e.	78al*d*
	130.5	148.8	229.8	240.0	184.6	280.5	269.1	237.2	226.1	215.6	....	....	....	....	....	Goods: Exports f.o.b.	78aa*d*
	-352.4	-441.3	-475.1	-477.4	-441.7	-542.5	-490.5	-458.9	-469.1	-344.3	....	....	....	....	....	Goods: Imports f.o.b.	78ab*d*
	-221.9	-292.4	-245.3	-237.3	-257.2	-261.9	-221.4	-221.7	-243.0	-128.7	....	....	....	....	....	*Trade Balance*	78ac*d*
	27.1	39.7	45.8	54.7	51.4	68.7	68.4	64.5	64.6	56.3	....	....	....	....	....	Services: Credit	78ad*d*
	-129.3	-157.1	-200.2	-243.0	-185.6	-215.7	-253.2	-207.7	-209.0	-138.3	....	....	....	....	....	Services: Debit	78ae*d*
	-324.1	-409.8	-399.6	-425.6	-391.3	-409.0	-406.2	-364.9	-387.4	-210.7	....	....	....	....	....	*Balance on Goods & Services*	78af*d*
	9.8	12.2	12.7	18.1	17.8	17.6	16.5	21.7	21.5	8.7	....	....	....	....	....	Income: Credit	78ag*d*
	-14.7	-17.7	-21.5	-26.9	-24.2	-17.7	-16.2	-19.1	-28.6	-38.1	....	....	....	....	....	Income: Debit	78ah*d*
	-329.0	-415.3	-408.4	-434.4	-397.7	-409.2	-406.0	-362.3	-394.5	-240.1	....	....	....	....	....	*Balance on Gds, Serv. & Inc.*	78ai*d*
	310.2	453.1	423.8	452.0	571.6	430.2	413.1	419.2	389.6	308.0	....	....	....	....	....	Current Transfers, n.i.e.: Credit	78aj*d*
	-44.2	-55.8	-65.1	-64.1	-74.6	-97.9	-97.7	-79.9	-66.3	-53.0	....	....	....	....	....	Current Transfers: Debit	78ak*d*
	—	—	—	—	—	—	—	—	—	—	....	....	....	....	....	Capital Account, n.i.e.	78bc*d*
	—	—	—	—	—	—	—	—	—	—	....	....	....	....	....	Capital Account, n.i.e.: Credit	78ba*d*
	—	—	—	—	—	—	—	—	—	....	....	....	....	....	....	Capital Account: Debit	78bb*d*
	51.5	39.6	55.6	63.5	-228.6	82.4	104.8	34.7	69.1	-13.9	....	....	....	....	....	Financial Account, n.i.e.	78bj*d*
	—	—	—	—	—	—	—	—	—	....	....	....	....	....	....	Direct Investment Abroad	78bd*d*
	-1.4	3.1	1.3	3.7	5.7	—	—	—	—	—	....	....	....	....	....	Dir. Invest. in Rep. Econ., n.i.e.	78be*d*
	—	—	—	—	—	—	—	—	—	....	....	....	....	....	....	Portfolio Investment Assets	78bf*d*
	—	—	—	—	—	—	—	—	—	....	....	....	....	....	....	Equity Securities	78bk*d*
	—	—	—	—	—	—	—	—	—	....	....	....	....	....	....	Debt Securities	78bl*d*
	—	—	—	—	—	—	—	—	—	....	....	....	....	....	....	Portfolio Investment Liab., n.i.e.	78bg*d*
	—	—	—	—	—	—	—	—	—	....	....	....	....	....	....	Equity Securities	78bm*d*
	—	—	—	—	—	—	—	—	—	....	....	....	....	....	....	Debt Securities	78bn*d*
	....	....	....	....	....	....	....	....	....	....	....	....	....	....	....	Financial Derivatives Assets	78bw*d*
	....	....	....	....	....	....	....	....	....	....	....	....	....	....	....	Financial Derivatives Liabilities	78bx*d*
	-3.2	-26.0	-35.7	-2.3	-26.7	-6.6	.5	-45.2	24.2	-139.2	....	....	....	....	....	Other Investment Assets	78bh*d*
	....	....	....	....	....	....	....	....	....	....	....	....	....	....	....	Monetary Authorities	78bo*d*
	-1.4	-2.8	—	—	—	—	—	—	—	—	....	....	....	....	....	General Government	78bp*d*
	-1.3	.2	-22.4	-.8	-12.8	-3.0	15.9	-21.7	24.2	-135.2	....	....	....	....	....	Banks	78bq*d*
	-.5	-23.4	-13.3	-1.5	-13.8	-3.7	-15.4	-23.4	—	-4.0	....	....	....	....	....	Other Sectors	78br*d*
	56.1	62.5	89.9	62.1	-207.6	89.1	104.3	79.9	44.9	125.3	....	....	....	....	....	Other Investment Liab., n.i.e.	78bi*d*
	—	—	—	—	—	—	—	-6.6	—	—	....	....	....	....	....	Monetary Authorities	78bs*d*
	35.8	46.5	69.3	48.4	-226.5	64.3	78.4	100.0	84.4	29.3	....	....	....	....	....	General Government	78bt*d*
	4.5	-11.8	-2.6	1.5	13.0	9.2	-7.0	-12.1	-47.1	41.9	....	....	....	....	....	Banks	78bu*d*
	15.9	27.8	23.2	12.1	6.0	15.6	32.9	-1.3	7.7	54.0	....	....	....	....	....	Other Sectors	78bv*d*
	17.2	2.9	4.0	1.1	-5.9	1.6	-6.6	8.3	4.6	-8.3	....	....	....	....	....	Net Errors and Omissions	78ca*d*
	5.7	24.5	9.7	18.1	-135.2	7.1	7.7	20.0	2.5	-7.3	....	....	....	....	....	*Overall Balance*	78cb*d*
	-5.7	-24.5	-9.7	-18.1	135.2	-7.1	-7.7	-20.0	-2.5	7.3	....	....	....	....	....	Reserves and Related Items	79da*d*
	-5.5	-48.6	-28.8	-29.7	50.0	-6.6	-43.6	-15.9	-53.5	-17.4	....	....	....	....	....	Reserve Assets	79db*d*
	-2.2	-3.0	-3.3	-3.1	-1.9	-.5	8.7	—	12.5	25.5	....	....	....	....	....	Use of Fund Credit and Loans	79dc*d*
	2.0	27.1	22.3	14.8	87.1	—	27.3	-4.2	38.5	-.7	....	....	....	....	....	Exceptional Financing	79de*d*
Year Ending December 31																**Government Finance**	
	I6,339	-35,330	-29,840	-36,870	24,960	-29,213	-37,680	-34,620	-37,540	-46,806	-37,971	-23,579	-50,500	-50,300	-70,300	Deficit (-) or Surplus	80
	I71,588	95,840	122,130	112,070	162,980	114,340	145,490	128,000	139,800	189,669	225,178	223,280	279,200	303,100	379,200	Total Revenue and Grants	81y
	I70,798	68,460	79,210	79,290	79,850	91,470	108,490	93,000	100,800	114,325	137,183	160,812	181,400	199,400	238,500	Revenue	81
	I790	27,380	42,920	32,780	83,130	22,870	37,000	35,000	39,000	75,344	87,995	62,468	97,800	103,700	140,700	Grants	81z
	I65,249	133,720	158,290	154,170	140,610	131,490	164,090	164,400	181,940	225,115	244,859	229,859	323,200	347,900	439,600	Exp. & Lending Minus Repay.	82z
	I62,883	131,390	155,680	153,660	138,910	132,760	163,220	164,400	183,940	227,449	247,053	231,552	325,700	348,500	439,300	Expenditure	82
	I2,366	2,330	2,610	510	1,700	-1,270	870	—	-2,000	-2,334	-2,194	-1,693	-2,500	-600	300	Lending Minus Repayments	83
	....	2,550	6,320	5,230	2,590	-12,063	-19,080	1,780	4,600	-11,360	-18,290	-17,000	-6,500	-5,500	-9,900	Adjustment to Cash Basis	80x
	....	35,330	29,840	36,870	-24,960	29,213	37,680	34,620	37,540	46,806	37,971	23,579	50,500	50,300	70,300	Total Financing	80h
Billions of Francs																**National Accounts**	
	69.2	63.0	81.0	86.0	73.0	88.0	92.0	92.0	92.2	135.6	152.6	150.3	188.0	213.1	229.3	Exports of Goods & Services	90c
	86.3	95.0	98.0	105.0	110.0	121.0	122.0	128.0	121.0	160.2	165.1	170.4	174.2	180.1	194.7	Government Consumption	91f
	133.5	145.0	150.6	152.1	173.0	170.6	185.5	190.1	170.8	216.5	279.1	337.1	385.0	413.4	439.9	Gross Fixed Capital Formation	93e
	26.6	7.0	-5.0	3.0	6.0	7.0	—	-8.0	8.4	-18.3	-15.7	-7.1	-30.4	-26.3	-13.1	Increase/Decrease(-) in Stocks	93i
	563.9	570.0	552.0	602.0	622.0	628.0	663.0	676.0	635.2	806.0	923.5	1,030.2	1,083.9	1,179.7	1,205.0	Private Consumption	96f
	-216.4	-204.0	-200.0	-211.0	-197.0	-227.0	-240.0	-249.0	-209.8	-270.7	-332.6	-382.6	-410.5	-437.7	-465.8	Imports of Goods & Services	98c
	663.1	676.0	676.6	737.1	787.0	787.6	822.5	829.1	817.8	1,029.3	1,172.0	1,298.3	1,390.2	1,522.3	1,590.0	Gross Domestic Product (GDP)	99b
	-15.2	.6	-.8	1.9	1.5	-.1	-.8	1.1	1.0	-3.3	-.7	.1	2.4	3.8	-7.8	Net Factor Inc/Pmts(-) Abroad	98.n
	749.3	676.6	675.8	739.0	788.5	787.5	821.7	830.2	818.8	1,026.0	1,171.3	2,824.5	1,392.6	1,526.1	1,582.2	Gross National Income (GNI)	99a
	311.1	....	....	....	....	....	....	....	....	....	....	....	....	....	....	GDP Volume 1979 prices	99b.*p*
	663.1	728.4	717.4	762.0	763.5	755.5	827.4	830.4	872.4	834.5	857.2	948.0	998.8	1,060.7	1,122.2	GDP Volume 1985 Prices	99b.*p*
	77.4	85.0	83.7	88.9	89.1	88.1	96.5	96.9	101.8	97.4	100.0	110.6	116.5	123.7	130.9	GDP Volume (1995=100)	99bv*p*
	73.1	67.9	69.0	70.7	75.4	76.2	72.7	73.0	68.6	90.2	100.0	100.2	101.8	105.0	103.6	GDP Deflator (1995=100)	99bi*p*
Midyear Estimates																	
	7.89	8.10	8.31	8.54	8.77	9.00	9.19	9.43	9.68	9.89	10.20	10.78	11.09	I10.68	11.62	**Population**	99z

(See notes in the back of the book.)

Burundi

		1970	1971	1972	1973	1974	1975	1976	1977	1978	1979	1980	1981	1982	1983	1984
Exchange Rates															*Francs per SDR:*	
Official Rate	aa	87.50	95.00	95.00	95.00	96.42	92.19	104.56	109.32	117.25	118.56	114.79	104.76	99.28	122.70	122.70
															Francs per US Dollar:	
Official Rate	ae	87.50	87.50	87.50	78.75	78.75	78.75	90.00	90.00	90.00	90.00	90.00	90.00	90.00	117.41	124.95
Official Rate	rf	87.50	87.50	87.50	80.03	78.75	78.75	86.25	90.00	90.00	90.00	90.00	90.00	90.00	92.95	119.71
															Index Numbers (1995=100):	
Official Rate	ahx	284.6	137.8	284.6	311.6	316.2	316.2	289.9	276.7	276.7	276.7	276.7	276.7	276.7	269.5	208.2
Nominal Effective Exchange Rate	nec	....	....	....	....	....	....	....	....	....	108.4	108.6	129.0	147.1	157.2	135.5
Real Effective Exchange Rate	rec	....	....	....	....	....	....	....	....	....	144.3	133.0	160.3	176.6	190.5	176.6
Fund Position															*Millions of SDRs:*	
Quota	2f.s	19.00	19.00	19.00	19.00	19.00	19.00	19.00	19.00	23.00	23.00	34.50	34.50	34.50	42.70	42.70
SDRs	1b.s	2.18	1.81	3.65	3.60	3.56	3.24	3.03	2.82	2.76	5.32	4.14	5.53	4.16	.99	.11
Reserve Position in the Fund	1c.s	—	—	.28	.39	—	—	—	—	4.75	4.47	7.34	7.34	7.37	9.42	9.42
Total Fund Cred.&Loans Outstg.	2tl	7.67	5.34	—	—	—	1.20	1.21	3.25	7.87	23.13	28.00	28.07	27.97	22.69	16.36
International Liquidity														*Millions of US Dollars Unless Otherwise Indicated:*		
Total Reserves minus Gold	1l.d	15.36	17.69	18.49	21.48	14.19	30.71	49.03	94.41	81.30	89.99	94.50	61.30	29.49	26.94	19.73
SDRs	1b.d	2.18	1.97	3.96	4.34	4.36	3.79	3.52	3.43	3.60	7.01	5.28	6.44	4.59	1.04	.11
Reserve Position in the Fund	1c.d	—	—	.30	.47	—	—	—	—	6.19	5.89	9.36	8.54	8.13	9.86	9.23
Foreign Exchange	1d.d	13.18	15.72	14.22	16.67	9.83	26.92	45.51	90.98	71.52	77.09	79.86	46.32	16.77	16.04	10.39
Gold (Million Fine Troy Ounces)	1ad	.001	.001	.001	.001	.001	.001	.001	.009	.009	.013	.017	.017	.017	.017	.017
Gold (National Valuation)	1and	.03	.03e			.16	.13	.13	1.50	2.05	8.87	10.15	6.85	7.87	6.60	5.33
Monetary Authorities: Other Liab.	4..d	10.39	8.44	3.76	2.74	1.91	4.41	5.98	7.04	5.26	22.65	21.33	18.13	19.85	10.56	7.11
Deposit Money Banks: Assets	7a.d	2.13	2.38	2.12	1.96	3.00	1.75	2.99	3.57	5.57	8.07	3.47	3.74	1.63	5.64	6.41
Liabilities	7b.d	.70	.66	2.03	1.31	2.27	2.71	4.35	3.85	4.49	3.57	6.22	4.24	5.57	9.25	4.46
Other Banking Insts.: Assets	7e.d	....	....	....	....	....	....	....	....	....	....	—	.24	.65	2.73	.81
Liabilities	7f.d	—	—	—	—	—	.65	2.38	4.23	4.65	6.70	5.87	6.15	5.58	6.28	6.77
Monetary Authorities															*Millions of Francs:*	
Foreign Assets	11	1,347	1,550	1,621	1,695	1,130	2,429	4,424	8,632	7,502	8,897	9,419	6,134	3,363	3,934	3,134
Claims on Central Government	12a	855	705	833	1,031	1,192	860	1,509	1,880	2,909	5,170	5,808	7,959	9,299	12,355	14,588
Claims on Nonfin.Pub.Enterprises	12c	—	—	—	—	—	5	5	5	5	14	1,381	598	482	412	362
Claims on Private Sector	12d	127	126	127	135	127	26	32	65	93	116	110	110	111	124	134
Claims on Deposit Money Banks	12e	4	113	83	46	959	—	16	—	—	1,166	506	3,075	2,095	640	498
Claims on Other Financial Insts	12f	10	10	10	10	10	70	26	108	306	155	144	161	510	693	335
Reserve Money	14	1,332	1,547	1,631	1,753	2,103	2,052	3,452	4,788	5,617	5,346	5,916	8,145	6,999	8,916	9,607
of which: Currency Outside DMBs	14a	1,192	1,333	1,370	1,548	1,873	1,710	2,411	3,225	4,542	4,876	5,001	7,073	6,437	7,293	7,519
Nonfin.Pub.Ent. Deps.	14e	111	164	112	91	207	117	612	478	514	407	521	646	372	532	1,222
Bonds	16ab	134	127	147	166	243	233	349	259	364	889	971	992	568	768	1,032
Restricted Deposits	16b	101	93	186	212	238	183	345	546	683	530	549	750	382	804	766
Stabilization Fund	16bb	15	48	55	20	128	2	413	1,727	470	1,065	547	21	94	338	510
Foreign Liabilities	16c	909	738	329	216	151	347	539	846	1,342	3,607	4,043	3,577	3,625	3,441	2,895
Central Government Deposits	16d	161	227	251	410	399	332	1,076	2,197	1,718	1,773	2,113	1,592	1,658	1,548	1,550
Capital Accounts	17a	724	773	1,036	996	934	1,241	992	1,741	2,529	3,989	4,241	3,663	4,052	3,598	3,838
Other Items (Net)	17r	–942	–1,050	–960	–855	–876	–1,003	–1,153	–1,413	–1,239	–1,639	–1,015	–707	–1,504	–1,237	–1,147
Deposit Money Banks																
Commercial Banks															*Millions of Francs:*	
Reserves	20	29	48	150	109	22	237	448	1,379	457	108	79	65	71	1,095	595
Foreign Assets	21	186	208	186	154	237	138	269	321	501	727	312	337	147	662	801
Claims on Central Government	22a	163	263	233	311	162	713	680	462	103	203	4	5	13	49	317
Claims on Nonfin.Pub.Enterprises	22c	....	....	....	....	....	....	....	....	....	....	....	....	....	....	2,525
Claims on Private Sector	22d	698	932	945	1,149	2,459	932	1,454	1,507	3,309	5,106	5,592	8,415	7,422	6,949	4,559
Claims on Other Financial Insts	22f	19	19	19	15	15	15	15	15	15	15	32	32	382	1,070	889
Demand Deposits	24	759	891	1,035	1,274	1,485	1,507	2,201	2,779	3,274	3,834	3,840	3,871	3,927	5,183	5,325
Savings Deposits	25	138	124	131	295	199	274	256	529	725	639	499	1,254	1,453	2,818	2,227
Foreign Liabilities	26c	61	57	177	103	179	214	391	346	404	289	492	334	453	1,048	531
Central Government Deposits	26d	34	41	30	38	48	8	10	8	3	4	8	4	4		
Credit from Monetary Authorities	26g	4	13	83	—	966	3	—	—	—	1,197	906	2,884	1,561	48	415
Capital Accounts	27a	159	164	168	233	252	265	307	313	301	402	512	583	733	845	919
Other Items (Net)	27r	14	254	80	26	–28	68	109	62	120	197	518	76	115	–86	–76
Other Monetary Institutions															*Millions of Francs:*	
Reserves	20..h	....	....	....	....	....	23	49	63	198	889	1,828	373	146	147	294
Claims on Central Government	22a.h	30	6	8	10	10	14	14	43	45	997	1,615	1,900	188	148	156
Claims on Nonfin.Pub.Enterprises	22c.h	....	....	....	....	....	....	....	....	....	111	305	675	1,178	1,438	1,493
Claims on Private Sector	22d.h	26	34	29	37	37	43	68	112	296	391	711	739	855	1,107	1,110
Claims on Other Financial Insts	22f.h	....	....	....	....	....	....	....	....	....	101	200	270	20	20	40
Demand Deposits	24..h	7	6	8	9	10	13	12	21	29	38	69	103	65	139	148
Time and Savings Deposits	25..h	—	—	—	—	—	—	—	—	—	—	1	1	1	1	1
Foreign Liabilities	26c.h	....	....	....	....	....	....	....	....	....	33	69	48	48	38	27
Central Government Deposits	26d.h	10	9	11	21	26	50	86	96	154	472	676	958	890	933	1,360
Cred.from Monetary Authorities	26g.h	....	....	....	....	....	....	....	....	....	....	....	—	472	535	
Other Items (Net)	27r.h	....	....	....	....	....	....	....	....	....	20	1–130	–93	122	9	7
Monetary Survey															*Millions of Francs:*	
Foreign Assets (Net)	31n	563	963	1,300	1,530	1,037	2,007	3,763	7,760	6,257	5,696	5,128	2,512	–616	69	482
Domestic Credit	32	1,684	1,793	1,895	2,213	3,429	2,293	2,664	2,166	6,159	10,960	13,106	18,308	19,907	23,915	23,848
Claims on Central Govt. (Net)	32an	823	701	785	896	908	1,232	1,103	137	1,291	3,595	3,691	6,368	7,738	11,005	13,511
Claims on Nonfin.Pub.Enterprises	32c	—	—	—	—	—	55	21	291	1,101	1,358	1,687	1,273	1,660	1,850	4,379
Claims on Private Sector	32d	824	1,057	1,072	1,283	2,486	958	1,487	1,572	3,401	5,613	6,414	9,264	8,388	8,180	4,693
Claims on Other Financial Insts	32f	29	29	29	25	25	85	41	123	321	270	376	462	911	1,783	1,265
Money	34	2,069	2,394	2,526	2,922	3,575	3,347	5,235	6,503	8,358	9,156	9,431	11,693	10,801	13,145	14,214
Quasi-Money	35	138	124	131	295	199	274	256	529	725	639	500	1,255	1,453	2,819	2,227
Other Items (Net)	37r	203	311	710	757	898	981	1,327	2,940	3,333	5,416	7,037	5,548	4,082	4,499	5,793
Money plus Quasi-Money	35l	2,199	2,512	2,648	3,208	3,764	3,608	5,480	7,010	9,054	9,757	9,862	12,845	12,190	15,826	16,293

1985	1986	1987	1988	1989	1990	1991	1992	1993	1994	1995	1996	1997	1998	1999		
															Exchange Rates	
End of Period																
122.70	151.50	161.00	201.00	232.14	232.14	273.07	322.90	362.99	360.78	413.37	462.63	551.56	710.64	860.83	Official Rate	aa
End of Period (ae) Period Average (rf)																
111.97	124.17	114.47	149.94	175.43	165.35	191.10	236.55	264.38	246.94	277.92	322.35	408.38	505.16	628.58	Official Rate	ae
120.69	114.17	123.56	140.40	158.67	171.26	181.51	208.30	242.78	252.66	249.76	302.75	352.35	447.77	563.56	Official Rate	rf
Period Averages																
206.6	218.8	201.7	179.0	157.2	145.6	138.1	119.9	102.7	98.7	100.0	82.6	70.9	56.0	44.4	Official Rate	ahx
141.3	123.8	102.7	90.2	86.2	80.8	86.6	82.5	90.4	102.6	100.0	86.3	81.4	66.9	55.7	Nominal Effective Exchange Rate	nec
180.2	154.9	132.6	116.6	118.1	103.5	106.4	90.3	90.1	94.6	100.0	105.1	124.9	111.8	89.9	Real Effective Exchange Rate	rec
															Fund Position	
End of Period																
42.70	42.70	42.70	42.70	42.70	42.70	42.70	57.20	57.20	57.20	57.20	57.20	57.20	57.20	77.00	Quota	2f.s
.11	.53	.04	.08	.01	.04	2.62	1.08	.51	.14	.05	.08	.05	.07	.07	SDRs	1b.s
9.16	9.16	9.16	9.16	9.16	7.55	7.24	5.86	5.86	5.86	5.86	5.86	5.86	5.86	5.86	Reserve Position in the Fund	1c.s
13.24	18.08	14.48	24.12	29.96	34.16	47.39	44.40	40.13	34.16	28.18	22.20	15.37	9.82		Total Fund Cred.&Loans Outstg.	2tl
															International Liquidity	
End of Period																
29.47	69.07	60.73	69.38	99.62	105.04	141.38	174.17	162.98	204.70	209.45	139.60	113.04	65.52	47.98	Total Reserves minus Gold	11.d
.12	.65	.06	.11	.01	.06	3.75	1.49	.70	.21	.07	.11	.06	.09	.10	SDRs	1b.d
10.06	11.20	12.99	12.33	12.04	10.74	10.36	8.06	8.05	8.56	8.71	8.43	7.91	8.25	8.04	Reserve Position in the Fund	1c.d
19.29	57.22	47.68	56.95	87.57	94.24	127.28	164.63	154.23	195.94	200.67	131.06	105.07	57.18	39.84	Foreign Exchange	1d.d
.017	.017	.017	.017	.017	.017	.017	.017	.017	.017	.017	.017	.017	.017	.017	Gold (Million Fine Troy Ounces)	1ad
5.62	6.93	8.53	7.14	7.03	6.55	6.44	5.79	6.66	6.59	6.66	6.36	4.99	4.95	5.00	Gold (National Valuation)	1an.d
4.07	23.72	17.50	29.59	41.18	46.92	52.69	54.84	48.45	42.95	32.02	20.54	12.53	9.13	6.15	Monetary Authorities: Other Liab.	4..d
5.24	9.70	6.11	5.32	4.46	5.32	6.64	6.51	9.66	19.33	17.13	24.53	11.99	5.25	13.41	Deposit Money Banks: Assets	7a.d
6.67	9.42	6.32	4.93	3.65	5.50	8.77	8.08	7.70	12.95	10.97	7.68	7.46	7.51	7.71	Liabilities	7b.d
1.72	1.49	1.31	.79	.84	—	—	—	—	—	—	—	—	—	—	Other Banking Insts.: Assets	7e.d
7.50	6.92	10.69	11.65	13.23	11.54	12.68	12.24	14.00	18.21	18.41	16.20	13.72	12.25	10.35	Liabilities	7f.d
															Monetary Authorities	
End of Period																
3,962	9,508	7,881	10,621	18,792	18,270	28,244	43,387	46,912	54,230	61,439	48,407	49,620	37,711	33,642	Foreign Assets	11
17,119	16,414	17,161	15,837	15,237	15,040	13,450	11,885	9,170	8,698	10,504	12,443	20,702	27,498	41,685	Claims on Central Government	12a
324	303	306	312	315	316	25	25	25	25	25	25	25	25	25	Claims on Nonfin.Pub.Enterprises	12c
148	126	140	213	244	265	276	325	421	420	1,486	1,563	1,181	1,220	703	Claims on Private Sector	12d
51	215	61	2,683	2,153	4,872	2,827	550	3,355	2,538	2,210	9,239	3,838	15,460	13,983	Claims on Deposit Money Banks	12e
112	105	105	117	446	272	915	1,616	1,487	634	1,307	761	162	781	117	Claims on Other Financial Insts	12f
11,962	12,160	12,176	11,763	12,478	13,068	15,121	16,797	17,617	22,292	22,114	26,346	26,854	27,566	37,387	Reserve Money	14
7,270	8,059	8,780	9,643	9,930	10,824	11,499	12,933	14,440	19,073	19,495	23,974	23,693	24,180	32,087	*of which:* Currency Outside DMBs	14a
1,966	2,210	1,416	1,315	1,525	1,302	990	990	1,118	649	577	371	749	860	710	Nonfin.Pub.Ent. Deps.	14e
765	660	886	2,961	1,422	1,481	2,091	2,743	2,174	2,701	2,329	2,531	2,400	1,915	3,924	Bonds	16ab
910	1,109	580	954	1,294	979	1,429	1,123	1,019	842	1,164	540	2,230	3,014	1,752	Restricted Deposits	16b
300	1,190	527	1,143	590	1	68	452	4	4	74	16	20	—	4	Stabilization Fund	16bb
2,080	4,355	2,962	4,995	7,375	7,775	10,070	12,972	12,809	10,607	8,899	6,621	5,117	4,613	3,868	Foreign Liabilities	16c
2,477	3,539	4,334	3,338	6,533	8,967	6,307	6,966	8,299	7,710	10,764	7,290	6,062	7,629	7,108	Central Government Deposits	16d
3,644	4,492	4,981	5,717	8,020	6,918	9,730	11,654	12,490	12,744	15,926	17,531	20,418	20,262	22,482	Capital Accounts	17a
-420	-834	-793	-1,089	-524	-154	922	5,081	6,958	9,645	15,703	11,562	12,426	17,694	13,631	Other Items (Net)	17r
															Deposit Money Banks	
															Commercial Banks	
End of Period																
2,075	463	1,678	353	812	737	2,525	2,469	1,761	2,171	1,290	1,716	2,852	2,839	4,754	Reserves	20
587	1,204	699	798	782	879	1,269	1,539	2,553	4,773	4,760	7,907	4,898	2,650	8,427	Foreign Assets	21
778	776	1,179	1,597	1,157	1,017	901	460	2,441	5,311	6,799	8,824	10,524	10,879	9,888	Claims on Central Government	22a
3,576	3,782	3,926	5,398	6,128	7,123	6,338	5,793	1,591	2,749	1,322	1,673	2,213	3,515	4,538	Claims on Nonfin.Pub.Enterprises	22c
4,812	5,986	5,930	8,839	12,137	16,437	22,500	23,862	31,557	34,022	29,162	35,886	39,516	52,948	69,385	Claims on Private Sector	22d
607	231	346	887	827	1,124	346	127	114	142	284	1,748	104	106	105	Claims on Other Financial Insts	22f
8,185	8,729	8,637	8,768	9,025	10,399	12,462	13,525	14,721	19,095	18,730	18,038	22,235	22,180	34,296	Demand Deposits	24
2,432	881	1,382	3,664	7,334	8,067	11,147	10,695	10,135	14,951	10,681	16,373	17,038	15,955	26,144	Savings Deposits	25
717	1,140	689	672	593	863	1,636	1,872	1,969	3,155	3,048	2,447	3,019	3,796	4,848	Foreign Liabilities	26c
—	—	—	—	—	—	—	—	25	526	76	192	14	—	150	Central Government Deposits	26d
—	250	59	2,821	2,147	4,269	2,845	1,134	4,044	2,602	806	8,020	1,128	14,518	13,199	Credit from Monetary Authorities	26g
1,068	1,148	1,180	2,131	2,423	3,211	3,924	5,111	7,085	8,281	8,221	11,446	12,625	14,510	17,470	Capital Accounts	27a
-191	294	1,810	-184	322	509	1,866	1,888	1,536	1,008	1,939	1,414	4,064	1,798	989	Other Items (Net)	27r
															Other Monetary Institutions	
End of Period																
654	679	304	309	219	303	1 1	4	169	72	....	7	342	....	....	Reserves	20..h
280	262	345	476	332	261	2,097	1,473	1,089	1,376	....	1,264	1,556	1,602	2,203	Claims on Central Government	22a.h
1,458	1,436	1,589	2,021	2,184	2,092	1,876	1,379	1,286	1,071	....	1,896	1,312	....	....	Claims on Nonfin.Pub.Enterprises	22c.h
1,111	1,737	1,936	1,672	1,699	2,533	1 388	530	1,404	1,675	....	2,690	2,133	....	....	Claims on Private Sector	22d.h
680	70	—	356	116	6	6	6	6	6	....	6	6	....	....	Claims on Other Financial Insts	22f.h
247	253	329	348	314	242	396	506	1,021	1,329	....	1,259	1,527	1,595	2,200	Demand Deposits	24..h
1	1	3	2	2	2	2	2	347	598	....	1,484	2,052	2	2	Time and Savings Deposits	25..h
29	29	34	67	47	47	41	41	66	43	....	29	29	....	....	Foreign Liabilities	26c.h
1,862	1,962	1,643	2,085	2,442	1,843	1 2,172	2,186	1,779	1,811	....	639	500	....	....	Central Government Deposits	26d.h
—	—	11	—	—	476	189	469	749	303	....	1,195	1,172	....	....	Cred.from Monetary Authorities	26g.h
32	8	12	126	16	1,272	706	-157	-7	115	....	1,256	69	4	1	Other Items (Net)	27r.h
															Monetary Survey	
End of Period																
1,723	5,188	4,895	5,685	11,558	10,464	17,767	30,042	34,621	45,198	54,252	47,217	46,352	31,952	33,353	Foreign Assets (Net)	31n
27,417	25,951	26,691	32,713	32,591	34,986	40,638	38,304	39,985	46,531	39,933	60,834	72,872	90,764	121,389	Domestic Credit	32
15,701	13,912	14,351	14,571	10,192	7,351	7,969	4,642	2,096	5,788	6,347	14,587	26,220	32,169	46,517	Claims on Central Govt. (Net)	32an
5,357	5,521	5,820	7,730	8,627	9,531	8,239	7,197	2,902	3,844	1,347	3,593	3,550	3,540	4,563	Claims on Nonfin.Pub.Enterprises	32c
4,960	6,112	6,070	9,052	12,382	16,702	23,164	24,717	33,381	36,117	30,648	40,138	42,830	54,168	70,087	Claims on Private Sector	32d
1,399	406	450	1,360	1,390	1,403	1,267	1,749	1,607	782	1,591	2,516	273	887	222	Claims on Other Financial Insts	32f
17,667	19,251	19,162	20,074	20,793	22,767	25,347	27,955	31,300	40,146	38,802	43,642	48,203	48,816	69,293	Money	34
2,432	881	1,386	3,666	7,336	8,069	11,149	10,697	10,482	15,549	10,681	17,857	19,089	15,957	26,146	Quasi-Money	35
6,668	9,352	9,947	12,769	14,381	13,498	21,046	29,349	32,824	36,034	44,703	46,552	51,932	57,943	59,304	Other Items (Net)	37r
19,853	19,879	20,218	23,392	27,816	30,593	36,100	38,145	40,761	54,366	49,482	60,240	65,766	63,177	93,239	Money plus Quasi-Money	35l

Burundi

	1970	1971	1972	1973	1974	1975	1976	1977	1978	1979	1980	1981	1982	1983	1984
Other Banking Institutions														*Millions of Francs:*	
Cash..40.. *f*	....	....	....	....	....	....	....	....	....	....	....	....	....	....	....
Foreign Assets.............................41.. *f*	....	....	....	....	....	....	....	....	....	....	....	22	59	321	101
Claims on Central Government ....42a. *f*	....	....	....	....	....	....	....	....	....	....	—	....	....	....	....
Claims on Private Sector ....42d. *f*	....	....	....	....	....	....	....	....	....	....	....	....	....	....	....
Bonds...46ab *f*	....	....	....	....	....	....	....	....	....	....	....	....	....	....	....
Long-Term Foreign Liabilities ....46cl *f*	....	....	....	....	....	....	....	....	....	....	....	....	....	....	....
Central Govt. Lending Funds ....46f. *f*	....	....	....	....	....	87	87	87	124	110	62	82	182	221	240
Credit from Monetary Authorities ....46g. *f*	—	2	—	—	—	—	6	86	286	166	105	120	430	617	224
Credit from Depos. Money Banks ....46h. *f*	—	—	—	—	—	—	14	—	—	—	—	—	350	1,039	789
Capital Accounts.............................47a. *f*	....	....	....	....	....	....	....	....	....	....	....	....	....	....	....
Other Items (Net)............................47r. *f*	....	....	....	....	....	....	....	....	....	....	....	....	....	....	....
Banking Survey														*Millions of Francs:*	
Foreign Assets (Net) 51n	....	....	....	....	....	....	....	....	....	....	5,127	2,533	−559	388	579
Domestic Credit 52	1,782	1,923	1,997	2,329	3,568	2,551	3,130	2,758	6,847	11,899	14,414	20,069	21,924	26,858	₹27,887
Claims on Central Govt. (Net) 52an	831	706	794	905	918	1,246	1,116	180	1,336	3,718	4,630	7,309	8,959	12,288	14,197
Claims on Nonfin.Pub.Enterprises........52c	—	—	—	—	—	55	21	291	1,101	1,358	1,687	1,273	1,660	1,850	4,379
Claims on Private Sector 52d	951	1,217	1,203	1,424	2,650	1,251	1,993	2,287	4,410	6,822	8,097	11,486	11,316	12,719	₹9,311
Liquid Liabilities 55l	2,137	2,441	2,439	2,988	3,451	3,349	4,713	6,550	8,902	9,477	12,844	15,849	15,238	19,414	20,162
Other Items (Net)....................................57r	....	....	....	....	....	....	....	....	....	....	8,414	7,329	5,446	5,584	8,305
Interest Rates														*Percent Per Annum*	
Discount Rate *(End of Period)* 60	....	....	....	....	5.50	5.50	5.50	5.50	5.50	7.00	7.00	7.00	7.00	7.00	7.00
Deposit Rate 60l	....	....	....	....	2.50	2.50	2.50	2.50	2.50	2.50	2.50	4.50	5.00	4.50	4.50
Lending Rate 60p	....	....	....	....	....	....	....	....	12.00	12.00	12.00	12.00	12.00	12.00	12.00
Prices and Labor														*Index Numbers (1995=100):*	
Consumer Prices 64	9.6	9.9	10.3	10.9	12.6	14.6	15.6	16.7	20.7	28.2	₹28.9	32.5	34.4	37.2	42.5
														Number in Thousands:	
Employment 67e	....	....	....	....	....	....	....	....	....	....	....	....	....	....	....
Unemployment 67c	....	....	....	....	....	....	....	....	....	....	....	....	....	....	....
International Transactions														*Millions of Francs:*	
Exports 70	2,132	1,622	2,276	2,371	2,439	2,515	5,415	8,073	6,244	9,360	5,885	6,742	7,899	7,494	12,318
Imports, c.i.f. 71	1,955	2,613	2,765	2,495	3,394	4,847	5,022	6,677	8,846	13,721	15,119	14,511	19,159	16,863	22,383
Balance of Payments														*Millions of US Dollars:*	
Current Account, n.i.e. ....78al *d*	....	....	....	....	....	....	....	....	....	....	....	....	....	....	....
Goods: Exports f.o.b. ....78aa *d*	....	....	....	....	....	....	....	....	....	....	....	....	....	....	....
Goods: Imports f.o.b. ....78ab *d*	....	....	....	....	....	....	....	....	....	....	....	....	....	....	....
Trade Balance..............................78ac *d*	....	....	....	....	....	....	....	....	....	....	....	....	....	....	....
Services: Credit ....78ad *d*	....	....	....	....	....	....	....	....	....	....	....	....	....	....	....
Services: Debit................................78ae *d*	....	....	....	....	....	....	....	....	....	....	....	....	....	....	....
Balance on Goods & Services ....78af *d*	....	....	....	....	....	....	....	....	....	....	....	....	....	....	....
Income: Credit ....78ag *d*	....	....	....	....	....	....	....	....	....	....	....	....	....	....	....
Income: Debit..................................78ah *d*	....	....	....	....	....	....	....	....	....	....	....	....	....	....	....
Balance on Gds, Serv. & Inc. ....78ai *d*	....	....	....	....	....	....	....	....	....	....	....	....	....	....	....
Current Transfers, n.i.e.: Credit ....78aj *d*	....	....	....	....	....	....	....	....	....	....	....	....	....	....	....
Current Transfers: Debit ....78ak *d*	....	....	....	....	....	....	....	....	....	....	....	....	....	....	....
Capital Account, n.i.e. ....78bc *d*	....	....	....	....	....	....	....	....	....	....	....	....	....	....	....
Capital Account, n.i.e.: Credit..........78ba *d*	....	....	....	....	....	....	....	....	....	....	....	....	....	....	....
Capital Account: Debit ....78bb *d*	....	....	....	....	....	....	....	....	....	....	....	....	....	....	....
Financial Account, n.i.e. ....78bj *d*	....	....	....	....	....	....	....	....	....	....	....	....	....	....	....
Direct Investment Abroad ....78bd *d*	....	....	....	....	....	....	....	....	....	....	....	....	....	....	....
Dir. Invest. in Rep. Econ., n.i.e. ....78be *d*	....	....	....	....	....	....	....	....	....	....	....	....	....	....	....
Portfolio Investment Assets ....78bf *d*	....	....	....	....	....	....	....	....	....	....	....	....	....	....	....
Equity Securities.............................78bk *d*	....	....	....	....	....	....	....	....	....	....	....	....	....	....	....
Debt Securities................................78bl *d*	....	....	....	....	....	....	....	....	....	....	....	....	....	....	....
Portfolio Investment Liab., n.i.e. ......78bg *d*	....	....	....	....	....	....	....	....	....	....	....	....	....	....	....
Equity Securities.............................78bm *d*	....	....	....	....	....	....	....	....	....	....	....	....	....	....	....
Debt Securities................................78bn *d*	....	....	....	....	....	....	....	....	....	....	....	....	....	....	....
Financial Derivatives Assets ....78bw *d*	....	....	....	....	....	....	....	....	....	....	....	....	....	....	....
Financial Derivatives Liabilities ....78bx *d*	....	....	....	....	....	....	....	....	....	....	....	....	....	....	....
Other Investment Assets ....78bh *d*	....	....	....	....	....	....	....	....	....	....	....	....	....	....	....
Monetary Authorities.....................78bo *d*	....	....	....	....	....	....	....	....	....	....	....	....	....	....	....
General Government......................78bp *d*	....	....	....	....	....	....	....	....	....	....	....	....	....	....	....
Banks ....78bq *d*	....	....	....	....	....	....	....	....	....	....	....	....	....	....	....
Other Sectors ....78br *d*	....	....	....	....	....	....	....	....	....	....	....	....	....	....	....
Other Investment Liab., n.i.e. ....78bi *d*	....	....	....	....	....	....	....	....	....	....	....	....	....	....	....
Monetary Authorities.....................78bs *d*	....	....	....	....	....	....	....	....	....	....	....	....	....	....	....
General Government......................78bt *d*	....	....	....	....	....	....	....	....	....	....	....	....	....	....	....
Banks ....78bu *d*	....	....	....	....	....	....	....	....	....	....	....	....	....	....	....
Other Sectors ....78bv *d*	....	....	....	....	....	....	....	....	....	....	....	....	....	....	....
Net Errors and Omissions...................78ca *d*	....	....	....	....	....	....	....	....	....	....	....	....	....	....	....
Overall Balance ....78cb *d*	....	....	....	....	....	....	....	....	....	....	....	....	....	....	....
Reserves and Related Items ....79da *d*	....	....	....	....	....	....	....	....	....	....	....	....	....	....	....
Reserve Assets ....79db *d*	....	....	....	....	....	....	....	....	....	....	....	....	....	....	....
Use of Fund Credit and Loans ....79dc *d*	....	....	....	....	....	....	....	....	....	....	....	....	....	....	....
Exceptional Financing ....79de *d*	....	....	....	....	....	....	....	....	....	....	....	....	....	....	....

Other Banking Institutions

End of Period

	1985	1986	1987	1988	1989	1990	1991	1992	1993	1994	1995	1996	1997	1998	1999	
Cash	....	....	....	....	....	....	....	....	....	....	....	....	478	102	....	**40..** f
Foreign Assets	193	185	151	119	147	—	—	—	—	—	—	—	—	—	....	**41.** f
Claims on Central Government	....	....	....	....	....	....	....	....	....	....	....	....	405	1,057	....	**42a.** f
Claims on Private Sector	....	....	....	....	....	....	....	....	....	....	....	....	15,376	16,637	....	**42d.** f
Bonds	....	....	....	....	....	....	....	....	....	....	....	....	2,829	2,561	....	**46ab** f
Long-Term Foreign Liabilities	....	....	....	....	....	....	....	....	....	....	....	....	6,057	6,641	....	**46cl** f
Central Govt. Lending Funds	266	2,213	3,942	974	891	897	1,040	1,213	....	1,151	1,185	1,045	914	1,371	1,340	**46f.** f
Credit from Monetary Authorities	10	—	—	98	293	110	777	1,347	....	228	1,043	599	—	623	118	**46g.** f
Credit from Depos. Money Banks	817	—	200	739	766	587	—	—	....	—	—	4	375	1	—	**46h.** f
Capital Accounts	....	....	....	....	....	....	....	....	....	....	....	....	7,125	7,834	....	**47a.** f
Other Items (Net)	....	....	....	....	....	....	....	....	....	....	....	....	-667	-1,235	....	**47r.** f

Banking Survey

End of Period

	1985	1986	1987	1988	1989	1990	1991	1992	1993	1994	1995	1996	1997	1998	1999	
Foreign Assets (Net)	1,916	5,373	5,045	5,804	11,706	10,464	17,767	30,042	34,621	45,198	54,252	47,217	46,352	31,952	33,353	**51n**
Domestic Credit	31,193	31,440	35,683	41,904	42,189	44,916	50,306	48,373	....	58,377	....	72,709	85,811	104,239	....	**52**
Claims on Central Govt. (Net)	15,926	14,183	16,166	16,622	11,644	8,756	8,727	4,850	2,168	5,840	....	14,674	26,625	33,226	....	**52an**
Claims on Nonfin.Pub.Enterprises	5,357	5,521	5,820	7,730	8,627	9,531	8,239	7,197	2,902	3,844	1,347	3,593	3,550	3,540	4,563	**52c**
Claims on Private Sector	9,909	11,736	13,697	17,551	21,918	26,630	33,340	36,326	....	48,693	43,967	54,442	55,637	67,473	84,152	**52d**
Liquid Liabilities	23,933	23,330	22,452	28,217	31,789	35,341	37,246	38,948	....	55,563	....	61,308	66,815	64,671	....	**55l**
Other Items (Net)	9,175	13,483	18,277	19,491	22,106	20,039	30,828	39,467	....	48,012	54,331	58,618	65,349	71,520	....	**57r**

Interest Rates

Percent Per Annum

	1985	1986	1987	1988	1989	1990	1991	1992	1993	1994	1995	1996	1997	1998	1999	
Discount Rate *(End of Period)*	7.00	5.00	7.00	7.00	7.00	8.00	10.70	9.80	9.80	9.40	9.90	....	....	12.40	12.09	**60**
Deposit Rate	4.50	5.96	5.33	4.00	....	....	....	....	....	....	....	....	....	....	....	**60l**
Lending Rate	12.00	12.00	12.00	12.00	12.00	12.34	12.78	13.66	13.77	14.20	15.26	....	....	....	15.24	**60p**

Prices and Labor

Period Averages

	1985	1986	1987	1988	1989	1990	1991	1992	1993	1994	1995	1996	1997	1998	1999	
Consumer Prices	44.1	44.9	48.0	50.2	56.0	60.0	I65.4	66.6	I73.0	83.8	100.0	126.4	165.8	186.5	192.8	**64**

Period Averages

	1985	1986	1987	1988	1989	1990	1991	1992	1993	1994	1995	1996	1997	1998	1999	
Employment	45	47	50	54	49	47	45	....	....	....	....	....	....	....	....	**67e**
Unemployment	2	7	8	9	11	15	14	7	....	....	....	....	....	....	....	**67c**

International Transactions

Millions of Francs

	1985	1986	1987	1988	1989	1990	1991	1992	1993	1994	1995	1996	1997	1998	1999	
Exports	13,522	17,675	11,117	18,591	12,305	12,774	16,698	15,355	15,019	30,034	25,982	11,372	30,767	28,635	30,971	**70**
Imports, c.i.f.	22,435	23,080	26,141	28,632	29,667	39,371	46,154	46,106	47,435	56,511	58,186	37,332	43,250	70,274	66,308	**71**

Balance of Payments

Minus Sign Indicates Debit

	1985	1986	1987	1988	1989	1990	1991	1992	1993	1994	1995	1996	1997	1998	1999	
Current Account, n.i.e.	-41.3	-36.2	-95.2	-70.1	-11.5	-69.4	-33.3	-59.6	-28.1	-16.9	10.4	-40.0	-1.0	-53.6	-27.0	**78al** d
Goods: Exports f.o.b.	113.6	129.1	98.3	124.4	93.2	72.8	93.0	77.0	73.9	80.7	112.9	40.4	87.5	64.0	55.0	**78aa** d
Goods: Imports f.o.b.	-149.7	-165.3	-159.2	-166.1	-151.4	-189.0	-195.9	-181.8	-172.8	-172.6	-175.6	-100.0	-96.1	-123.5	-97.3	**78ab** d
Trade Balance	-36.1	-36.2	-60.8	-41.7	-58.2	-116.3	-103.0	-104.8	-99.0	-91.9	-62.7	-59.6	-8.6	-59.5	-42.3	**78ac** d
Services: Credit	13.2	11.7	11.9	11.9	15.3	16.7	25.7	17.5	14.6	14.9	16.4	10.5	8.7	7.6	6.3	**78ad** d
Services: Debit	-89.3	-102.9	-132.1	-114.9	-92.6	-129.2	-141.3	-137.3	-114.8	-93.9	-83.3	-38.4	-45.4	-49.5	-32.6	**78ae** d
Balance on Goods & Services	-112.2	-127.3	-181.0	-144.7	-135.5	-228.8	-218.6	-224.7	-199.2	-170.9	-129.6	-87.4	-45.3	-101.3	-68.7	**78af** d
Income: Credit	1.6	2.1	2.9	2.9	8.9	8.2	9.7	14.0	11.2	8.1	10.4	6.4	4.3	3.6	1.9	**78ag** d
Income: Debit	-19.9	-22.7	-31.3	-25.8	-26.5	-23.0	-20.7	-27.6	-22.2	-19.5	-22.9	-20.4	-16.8	-11.9	-11.3	**78ah** d
Balance on Gds, Serv. & Inc.	-130.5	-147.9	-209.4	-167.6	-153.1	-243.6	-229.7	-238.2	-210.2	-182.3	-142.1	-101.4	-57.8	-109.6	-78.1	**78ai** d
Current Transfers, n.i.e.: Credit	93.6	115.8	118.3	103.4	142.7	175.5	198.1	180.6	183.8	167.0	154.7	62.5	61.3	59.3	52.9	**78aj** d
Current Transfers: Debit	-4.3	-4.0	-4.1	-5.9	-1.1	-1.3	-1.7	-1.9	-1.8	-1.6	-2.1	-1.1	-4.5	-3.3	-1.8	**78ak** d
Capital Account, n.i.e.	-.8	-1.4	-1.2	-.5	-.6	-.5	-.7	-.8	-1.2	-.2	-.8	-.3	-.1	—	—	**78bc** d
Capital Account, n.i.e.: Credit	—	—	—	—	—	—	—	—	—	—	—	—	—	—	—	**78ba** d
Capital Account: Debit	-.8	-1.4	-1.2	-.5	-.6	-.5	-.7	-.8	-1.2	-.2	-.8	-.3	-.1	—	—	**78bb** d
Financial Account, n.i.e.	66.1	85.0	131.1	84.3	64.4	78.0	70.4	98.7	52.5	31.1	21.1	14.1	13.7	63.9	38.7	**78bj** d
Direct Investment Abroad	—	—	—	—	-.1	—	—	—	-.1	-.1	-.6	—	—	—	—	**78bd** d
Dir. Invest. in Rep. Econ., n.i.e.	.5	1.5	1.4	1.2	.6	1.3	.9	.6	.5	—	2.0	—	—	—	.2	**78be** d
Portfolio Investment Assets	—	—	—	—	—	—	—	—	—	—	—	—	—	—	—	**78bf** d
Equity Securities	—	—	—	—	—	—	—	—	—	—	—	—	—	—	—	**78bk** d
Debt Securities	—	—	—	—	—	—	—	—	—	—	—	—	—	—	—	**78bl** d
Portfolio Investment Liab., n.i.e.	—	—	—	—	—	—	—	—	—	—	—	—	—	—	—	**78bg** d
Equity Securities	—	—	—	—	—	—	—	—	—	—	—	—	—	—	—	**78bm** d
Debt Securities	—	—	—	—	—	—	—	—	—	—	—	—	—	—	—	**78bn** d
Financial Derivatives Assets	....	....	....	....	....	....	....	....	....	....	....	....	....	....	....	**78bw** d
Financial Derivatives Liabilities																**78bx** d
Other Investment Assets	.3	8.0	1.4	-11.5	-7.6	4.1	-3.5	-1.0	-1.5	-1.6	8.2	6.6	15.3	45.8	35.4	**78bh** d
Monetary Authorities	....	....	....	....	....	....	....	....	....	....	....	....	....	....	....	**78bo** d
General Government	-1.6	-7.0	-10.0	-5.8	-1.9	-1.0	-1.1	-.6	-.3	-.8	-.4	-.3	-.4	-.3	-.3	**78bp** d
Banks	1.8	-5.4	4.1	-.7	.1	-.6	-2.1	-1.3	-4.2	-8.8	.1	-10.4	8.5	5.0	-10.3	**78bq** d
Other Sectors	.2	20.4	7.2	-5.0	-5.7	5.7	-.4	1.0	3.0	7.9	8.6	17.3	7.1	41.1	46.0	**78br** d
Other Investment Liab., n.i.e.	65.2	75.4	128.3	94.6	71.5	72.7	73.1	99.1	53.6	32.9	11.5	7.6	-1.6	18.1	3.1	**78bi** d
Monetary Authorities	—	—	—	—	—	—	—	—	—	—	—	—	—	—	—	**78bs** d
General Government	56.5	67.2	124.5	83.9	65.4	62.1	57.0	90.8	47.2	25.2	4.9	7.3	-8.0	15.3	.2	**78bt** d
Banks	—	3.6	-3.0	1.3	-.6	1.6	1.4	1.1	.4	4.7	-.4	-2.0	1.6	1.7	1.9	**78bu** d
Other Sectors	8.7	4.6	6.8	9.4	6.6	9.0	14.6	7.1	6.0	3.0	7.0	2.2	4.8	1.1	1.1	**78bv** d
Net Errors and Omissions	-8.1	-18.9	-37.3	-6.6	-14.3	-11.3	-3.9	-12.7	-7.2	21.1	5.9	-9.2	-2.4	-29.7	-13.0	**78ca** d
Overall Balance	15.9	28.5	-2.6	7.1	38.0	-3.2	32.6	25.5	16.0	35.2	36.7	-35.3	10.2	-19.5	-1.2	**78cb** d
Reserves and Related Items	-15.9	-28.5	2.6	-7.1	-38.0	3.2	-32.6	-25.5	-16.0	-35.2	-36.7	35.3	-10.2	19.5	1.2	**79da** d
Reserve Assets	-12.7	-34.5	7.3	-20.5	-46.1	4.0	-38.4	-44.0	-11.9	-29.0	-27.6	44.0	-2.0	28.7	8.8	**79db** d
Use of Fund Credit and Loans	-3.2	6.0	-4.6	13.3	8.1	-.8	5.8	18.5	-4.1	-6.1	-9.0	-8.7	-8.3	-9.3	-7.6	**79dc** d
Exceptional Financing	....	....	....	....	....	....	....	....	....	....	....	....	....	....	....	**79de** d

Burundi

		1970	1971	1972	1973	1974	1975	1976	1977	1978	1979	1980	1981	1982	1983	1984
Government Finance																*Millions of Francs:*
Deficit (-) or Surplus	80	103.5	307.5	183.2	113.2	219.5	−136.6	162.4	390.7	−19.8	67.1	−1,708.0	−1,873.0	−1,362.1	−917.8	231.4
Total Revenue and Grants	81y	2,159.2	2,368.1	2,588.4	2,805.8	3,221.3	3,168.7	5,030.1	7,138.3	9,239.5	11,052.3	11,441.0	12,321.1	14,046.8	12,855.9	16,350.6
Revenue	81	....	....	....	....	....	....	....	....	....	....	....	....	....	....	....
Grants	81z	....	....	....	....	....	....	....	....	....	....	....	....	....	....	....
Exp. & Lending Minus Repay.	82z	2,055.7	2,060.6	2,405.2	2,692.6	3,001.8	3,305.3	4,867.7	6,747.6	9,259.3	10,985.2	13,149.0	14,194.1	15,408.9	13,773.7	16,119.2
Expenditure	82	2,046.6	2,045.9	2,377.0	2,663.4	2,937.9	3,267.8	4,839.9	6,714.3	9,264.1	10,986.9	13,149.8	14,194.2	15,409.0	13,773.7	16,119.2
Lending Minus Repayments	83	9.1	14.7	28.2	29.2	63.9	37.5	27.8	33.3	−4.8	−1.7	−.8	−.1	−.1	—	—
Statistical Discrepancy	80xx															
Total Financing	80h	−103.5	−307.5	−183.2	−113.2	−219.5	136.6	−162.4	−390.7	19.8	−67.1	1,708.0	1,873.0	1,362.1	917.8	−231.4
Domestic	84a	−120.1	−289.2	−136.7	−59.7	−171.5	98.5	50.8	−152.7	218.4	162.1	1,700.7	2,231.1	1,680.7	1,487.9	579.4
Foreign	85a	16.6	−18.3	−46.5	−53.5	−48.0	38.1	−213.2	−238.0	−198.6	−229.2	7.3	−358.1	−318.6	−570.1	−810.8
Total Debt by Residence	88	1,793	1,796	1,783	2,037	2,103	3,451	4,599	6,321	9,341	14,797	19,216	23,663	28,795	47,992	59,732
Domestic	88a	1,154	1,145	1,194	1,475	1,474	1,726	2,573	2,872	3,989	6,361	8,186	10,638	12,519	15,624	18,633
Foreign	89a	639	651	589	562	629	1,726	2,026	3,449	5,353	8,437	11,030	13,025	16,276	32,368	41,099
National Accounts																*Millions of Francs*
Exports of Goods & Services	90c	2,735	1,866	2,534	2,683	2,652	2,899	5,309	8,671	6,661	9,985	7,328	6,999	8,697	9,683	11,782
Government Consumption	91f	2,615	2,342	2,791	2,821	2,652	4,642	3,368	5,495	9,574	11,436	13,746	15,583	18,183	20,414	21,132
Gross Fixed Capital Formation	93e	1,265	1,121	1,137	1,392	1,768	4,181	3,515	5,517	7,709	10,505	10,955	11,948	17,170	19,541	20,364
Increase/Decrease(-) in Stocks	93i	113	—	−450	−98	−666	−556	—	—	—	—	921	2,429	−741	−1,083	1,410
Private Consumption	96f	15,052	20,084	18,839	20,805	24,238	27,029	32,938	38,227	41,932	53,586	70,133	69,823	73,894	77,516	92,484
Imports of Goods & Services	98c	−2,766	−3,135	−3,256	−3,247	−4,224	−5,523	−6,454	−8,332	−11,055	−17,426	−17,476	−17,696	−23,109	−23,179	−26,721
Gross Domestic Product (GDP)	99b	19,014	22,278	21,595	24,355	27,190	32,672	38,676	49,578	54,821	68,086	85,607	89,086	94,094	102,892	120,451
Net Factor Inc/Pmts(-) Abroad	98.n	....	....	−997	−669	−708	−681	−971	−1,231	−1,301	−914	822	455	68	−382	−980
Gross National Income (GNI)	99a	....	24,818	20,598	23,686	26,482	32,472	37,705	48,347	53,520	67,172	86,429	89,541	94,162	102,510	119,471
GDP Volume 1971 prices	99b.p	21,199	22,278	20,406	21,871	21,689	21,908	23,633	26,558	26,266	26,784	....	....	....	....	....
GDP Volume 1980 Prices	99b.p	....	....	....	....	....	....	....	....	....	79,321	85,607	94,949	94,540	97,479	97,382
GDP Volume (1995=100)	99bvp	54.6	57.4	52.5	56.3	55.8	56.4	60.9	68.4	67.6	69.0	74.4	82.6	82.2	84.8	84.7
GDP Deflator (1995=100)	99bip	11.4	12.7	13.4	14.1	15.9	18.9	20.7	23.6	26.4	32.2	37.5	35.2	37.3	39.6	46.4
																Millions:
Population	99z	3.62	3.69	3.74	3.80	3.86	‡ 3.74	3.82	3.90	3.98	4.03	4.12	4.23	4.34	4.46	4.58

Government Finance

Year Ending December 31

Item	Code	1985	1986	1987	1988	1989	1990	1991	1992	1993	1994	1995	1996	1997	1998	1999
Deficit (-) or Surplus	80	-148.5	3,475.0	-1,433.2	1,116.1	4,649.1	1,273.7	4,219.3	1,796.8	3,442.6	6,743.1	2,630.0	-7,890.5	ℐ-16777.4	-15,069.5	-34,350.8
Total Revenue and Grants	81y	19,254.1	23,133.4	20,060.8	25,084.9	38,583.8	37,079.4	42,820.3	45,618.7	49,933.2	48,525.1	49,001.6	39,330.5	ℐ52717.4	74,005.8	78,593.9
Revenue	81	....	....	....	....	....	....	....	....	....	....	....	....	42,446.9	63,531.5	67,239.3
Grants	81z													10,270.5	10,474.3	11,354.6
Exp. & Lending Minus Repay.	82z	19,402.6	19,658.4	21,494.0	23,968.8	33,934.7	35,805.7	38,601.0	43,821.9	46,490.6	41,782.0	46,371.6	47,221.0	ℐ69494.8	89,075.3	112,944.7
Expenditure	82	19,402.6	19,658.4	21,494.0	23,968.8	33,934.7	35,805.7	38,601.0	43,821.9	46,490.6	41,782.0	46,371.6	47,221.0	ℐ70716.6	90,413.7	113,927.1
Lending Minus Repayments	83	—	—	—	—	—	—	—	—	—	—	—	—	ℐ-1221.8	-1,338.4	-982.4
Statistical Discrepancy	80xx	....	....	....	....	....	....	....	....	....	....	....	....	-3,605.9	-10,054.2	-21,205.9
Total Financing	80h	148.5	-3,475.0	1,433.2	-1,116.1	-4,649.1	-1,273.7	-4,219.3	-1,796.8	-3,442.6	-6,743.1	-2,630.0	7,890.5	ℐ20383.3	24,027.7	36,741.1
Domestic	84a	1,551.3	-3,151.3	217.9	-1,007.9	-4,950.1	-1,420.7	-4,483.0	-4,088.5	-2,787.7	-2,803.1	1,452.1	11,412.2	ℐ11351.0	9,223.1	24,568.1
Foreign	85a	-1,402.8	-323.7	1,215.3	-108.2	301.0	147.0	263.7	2,291.7	-654.9	-3,940.0	-4,082.1	-3,521.7	ℐ9,032.3	14,804.6	12,173.0
Total Debt by Residence	88	69,066	87,584	107,766	142,412	170,205	161,951	188,322	235,307	272,757	278,759	323,954	380,464	ℐ464,228	605,411	740,305
Domestic	88a	21,986	22,169	24,455	25,937	22,935	22,662	18,080	15,591	13,784	13,630	17,785	27,384	ℐ39,989	49,659	64,528
Foreign	89a	47,080	65,415	83,311	116,475	147,270	139,289	170,242	219,716	258,973	265,129	306,169	353,080	ℐ424,239	555,752	675,777

National Accounts

Millions of Francs

Item	Code	1985	1986	1987	1988	1989	1990	1991	1992	1993	1994	1995	1996	1997	1998	1999
Exports of Goods & Services	90c	13,937	15,625	13,015	17,298	15,697	15,641	20,013	15,346	21,641	24,029	32,197	15,289	33,760	32,019	31,185
Government Consumption	91f	22,793	24,252	28,570	31,491	36,547	38,344	40,227	44,429	30,280	32,459	33,578	34,474	37,068	47,400	51,000
Gross Fixed Capital Formation	93e	20,113	18,860	21,114	25,701	26,115	32,234	34,282	36,425	36,193	23,446	24,064	32,711	21,976	24,000	34,314
Increase/Decrease(-) in Stocks	93i	73	3,247	3,762	-4,029	3,247	-1,177	19	-2,158	1,002	53	-199	-2,351	5,205	-10,529	-991
Private Consumption	96f	109,478	104,340	107,015	114,298	135,449	163,216	168,216	190,669	220,231	256,549	283,108	227,328	297,563	389,268	413,900
Imports of Goods & Services	98c	-25,047	-25,482	-29,886	-31,852	-37,507	-51,602	-57,716	-58,854	-69,709	-66,592	-68,173	-41,454	-49,473	-77,775	-71,177
Gross Domestic Product (GDP)	99b	141,347	140,842	143,590	152,907	179,548	196,656	204,951	225,857	236,676	270,051	306,897	344,182	431,037	506,305	552,037
Net Factor Inc/Pmts(-) Abroad	98.n	-1,436	-1,697	-2,092	-2,457	-2,008	-2,550	-2,041	-2,845	-2,674	-2,876	-3,152	-4,223	-4,416	-3,699	-4,902
Gross National Income (GNI)	99a	139,911	139,145	141,498	150,450	177,540	194,106	202,910	223,012	234,002	267,175	303,745	339,959	426,621	502,606	547,135
GDP Volume 1971 prices	99b.p	....	....	....	....	....	....	....	....	....	....	....	....	....	....	....
GDP Volume 1980 Prices	99b.p	106,671	110,138	116,199	121,884	123,692	128,021	134,849	137,284	127,635	123,698	115,013	105,113	105,512	110,249	....
GDP Volume (1995=100)	99bv p	92.7	95.8	101.0	106.0	107.5	111.3	117.2	119.4	111.0	107.6	100.0	91.4	91.7	95.9	....
GDP Deflator (1995=100)	99bi p	49.7	47.9	46.3	47.0	54.4	57.6	57.0	61.7	69.5	81.8	100.0	122.7	153.1	172.1	....

Midyear Estimates

Item	Code	1985	1986	1987	1988	1989	1990	1991	1992	1993	1994	1995	1996	1997	1998	1999
Population	99z	4.72	4.86	5.00	5.15	5.30	5.46	5.62	5.78	ℐ5.77	5.87	5.98	6.09	6.19	6.30	6.48

(See notes in the back of the book.)

Cambodia

		1970	1971	1972	1973	1974	1975	1976	1977	1978	1979	1980	1981	1982	1983	1984
Exchange Rates															*Riels per SDR:*	
Official Rate	aa	55.5	141.1	203.0	331.7	....	....	....	....	....	....	....	....	....	....	
															Riels per US Dollar:	
Official Rate	ae	55.5	130.0	187.0	275.0	....	....	....	....	....	....	....	....	....	....	
Official Rate	rf	55.5	75.8	162.3	244.9	....	....	....	....	....	....	....	....	....	....	
Fund Position															*Millions of SDRs:*	
Quota	2f. s	25.00	25.00	25.00	25.00	25.00	25.00	25.00	25.00	25.00	25.00	25.00	25.00	25.00	25.00	25.00
SDRs	1b. s	1.59	1.73	4.24	.48	1.08	.64	.33	.01	—	1.90	3.78	4.54	3.12	1.58	
Reserve Position in the Fund	1c. s	6.25	—	.01	.01	.01	.01	.01	.01	.01	.01	.01	.01	.01	.01	.01
Total Fund Cred.&Loans Outstg.	2tl	—	—	6.25	12.50	12.50	12.50	12.50	12.50	12.50	12.50	12.50	12.50	12.50	12.50	12.50
International Liquidity											*Millions of US Dollars Unless Otherwise Indicated:*					
Total Reserves minus Gold	1l. d	....	....													
SDRs	1b. d	1.59	1.88	4.60	.58	1.32	.75	.38	.01	—	2.50	4.82	5.28	3.44	1.65	—
Reserve Position in the Fund	1c. d	6.25	—	.01	.01	.01	.01	.01	.01	.01	.01	.01	.01	.01	.01	.01
Foreign Exchange	1d. d	....	....	....	....	....	....	....	....	....	....	....	....	....	....	
Deposit Money Banks: Assets	7a. d	....	....	....	....	....	....	....	....	....	....	....	....	....	....	
Liabilities	7b. d	....	....	....	....	....	....	....	....	....	....	....	....	....	....	
Monetary Authorities															*Billions of Riels:*	
Foreign Assets	11	....	....	....	....	....	....	....	....	....	....	....	....	....	....	
Claims on Central Government	12a	....	....	....	....	....	....	....	....	....	....	....	....	....	....	
Claims on Private Sector	12d	....	....	....	....	....	....	....	....	....	....	....	....	....	....	
Claims on Deposit Money Banks	12e	....	....	....	....	....	....	....	....	....	....	....	....	....	....	
Reserve Money.............................	14	....	....	....	....	....	....	....	....	....	....	....	....	....	....	
of which: Currency Outside DMBs	14a	....	....	....	....	....	....	....	....	....	....	....	....	....	....	
Restricted Deposits	16b	....	....	....	....	....	....	....	....	....	....	....	....	....	....	
Foreign Liabilities	16c	....	....	....	....	....	....	....	....	....	....	....	....	....	....	
Central Government Deposits	16d	....	....	....	....	....	....	....	....	....	....	....	....	....	....	
Capital Accounts	17a	....	....	....	....	....	....	....	....	....	....	....	....	....	....	
Other Items (Net).........................	17r	....	....	....	....	....	....	....	....	....	....	....	....	....	....	
Deposit Money Banks															*Billions of Riels:*	
Reserves....................................	20	....	....	....	....	....	....	....	....	....	....	....	....	....	....	
Foreign Assets	21	....	....	....	....	....	....	....	....	....	....	....	....	....	....	
Claims on Central Government	22a	....	....	....	....	....	....	....	....	....	....	....	....	....	....	
Claims on Nonfin.Pub.Enterprises	22c	....	....	....	....	....	....	....	....	....	....	....	....	....	....	
Claims on Private Sector	22d	....	....	....	....	....	....	....	....	....	....	....	....	....	....	
Demand Deposits	24	....	....	....	....	....	....	....	....	....	....	....	....	....	....	
Time and Savings Deposits	25a	....	....	....	....	....	....	....	....	....	....	....	....	....	....	
Foreign Currency Deposits	25b	....	....	....	....	....	....	....	....	....	....	....	....	....	....	
Restricted Deposits	26b	....	....	....	....	....	....	....	....	....	....	....	....	....	....	
Foreign Liabilities	26c	....	....	....	....	....	....	....	....	....	....	....	....	....	....	
Central Government Deposits	26d	....	....	....	....	....	....	....	....	....	....	....	....	....	....	
Credit from Monetary Authorities	26g	....	....	....	....	....	....	....	....	....	....	....	....	....	....	
Capital Accounts	27a	....	....	....	....	....	....	....	....	....	....	....	....	....	....	
Other Items (Net).........................	27r	....	....	....	....	....	....	....	....	....	....	....	....	....	....	
Monetary Survey															*Billions of Riels:*	
Foreign Assets (Net)	31n	....	....	....	....	....	....	....	....	....	....	....	....	....	....	
Domestic Credit	32	....	....	....	....	....	....	....	....	....	....	....	....	....	....	
Claims on Central Govt. (Net)	32an	....	....	....	....	....	....	....	....	....	....	....	....	....	....	
Claims on Nonfin.Pub.Enterprises........	32c	....	....	....	....	....	....	....	....	....	....	....	....	....	....	
Claims on Private Sector	32d	....	....	....	....	....	....	....	....	....	....	....	....	....	....	
Money.....................................	34	....	....	....	....	....	....	....	....	....	....	....	....	....	....	
Quasi-Money...............................	35	....	....	....	....	....	....	....	....	....	....	....	....	....	....	
Capital Accounts..........................	37a	....	....	....	....	....	....	....	....	....	....	....	....	....	....	
Other Items (Net).........................	37r	....	....	....	....	....	....	....	....	....	....	....	....	....	....	
Money plus Quasi-Money.......................	35l	....	....	....	....	....	....	....	....	....	....	....	....	....	....	
Interest Rates															*Percent Per Annum*	
Deposit Rate	60l	....	....	....	....	....	....	....	....	....	....	....	....	....	....	
Lending Rate	60p	....	....	....	....	....	....	....	....	....	....	....	....	....	....	
Prices															*Index Numbers (1995=100):*	
Consumer Prices	64	....	....	....	....	....	....	....	....	....	....	....	....	....	....	

1985	1986	1987	1988	1989	1990	1991	1992	1993	1994	1995	1996	1997	1998	1999		
End of Period															**Exchange Rates**	
....	....	....	....	283.9	853.6	743.8	2,750.0	3,166.1	3,759.1	3,754.9	3,901.2	4,657.6	5,308.3	5,174.4	Official Rate	aa
End of Period (ae) Period Average (rf)																
....	....	....	....	216.0	600.0	520.0	2,000.0	2,305.0	2,575.0	2,526.0	2,713.0	3,452.0	3,770.0	3,770.0	Official Rate	ae
....	....	....	....	....	....	....	1,266.6	2,689.0	2,545.3	2,450.8	2,624.1	2,946.3	3,744.4	3,807.8	Official Rate	rf
End of Period															**Fund Position**	
25.00	25.00	25.00	25.00	25.00	25.00	25.00	25.00	25.00	65.00	65.00	65.00	65.00	65.00	87.50	Quota	2f. s
—	—	—	—	—	—	—	—		11.42	10.89	10.21	9.51	8.77	6.95	3.78	SDRs	1b. s
.01	.01	.01	.01	.01	.01	.01	.93	—	—	—	—	—	—	—	Reserve Position in the Fund	1c. s
12.50	12.50	12.50	12.50	12.50	12.50	12.50	6.25	6.25	20.25	48.25	48.25	48.25	47.21	53.12	Total Fund Cred.&Loans Outstg.	2tl
End of Period															**International Liquidity**	
....	....	....	....	....	....	....	....	24.18	118.50	191.98	265.78	298.53	324.28	393.19	Total Reserves minus Gold	1l. d
								15.68	15.90	15.18	13.68	11.83	9.78	5.19	SDRs	1b. d
.01	.01	.01	.01	.01	.01	.01	1.28	—	—	—	—	—	—	—	Reserve Position in the Fund	1c. d
....	....	....	....	....	....	....	....	8.50	102.60	176.80	252.10	286.70	314.50	388.00	Foreign Exchange	1d. d
....	....	....	....	....	....	....	....	103.96	126.75	163.27	186.96	163.28	140.07	155.06	Deposit Money Banks: Assets	7a. d
....	....	....	....	....	....	....	....	68.43	63.93	65.78	59.55	58.03	59.51	56.88	Liabilities	7b. d
End of Period															**Monetary Authorities**	
....	....	....	....	....	....	....	....	56.44	305.09	484.88	720.91	1,033.02	1,675.22	1,923.51	Foreign Assets	11
								206.26	215.02	217.11	213.58	211.28	288.55	283.04	Claims on Central Government	12a
								3.93	2.70	—	—	—	—	—	Claims on Private Sector	12d
								32.49	34.20	10.09	9.48	6.19	8.10	4.94	Claims on Deposit Money Banks	12e
....	....	....	....	....	....	....	....	228.09	285.91	314.53	449.83	545.33	802.61	929.87	Reserve Money	14
								189.72	176.30	250.92	299.84	356.06	509.06	489.86	*of which: Currency Outside DMBs*	14a
								16.23	26.17	24.55	70.93	42.94	68.67	75.52	Restricted Deposits	16b
								19.79	76.12	181.17	188.23	224.73	250.59	274.88	Foreign Liabilities	16c
								5.59	70.12	62.36	81.86	153.49	106.11	176.26	Central Government Deposits	16d
								57.61	127.43	115.88	200.72	391.56	839.61	870.12	Capital Accounts	17a
								−28.17	−28.75	13.59	−47.62	−107.54	−95.72	−115.24	Other Items (Net)	17r
End of Period															**Deposit Money Banks**	
....	....	....	....	....	....	....	....	13.49	88.75	88.15	178.43	199.61	346.00	503.74	Reserves	20
								239.62	326.39	412.41	507.22	563.63	528.07	584.58	Foreign Assets	21
								.07	.01	.31	.31	.31	.31	.31	Claims on Central Government	22a
								6.21	6.00	5.11	5.22	5.93	5.86	10.14	Claims on Nonfin.Pub.Enterprises	22c
								157.67	234.39	293.40	434.55	636.79	654.60	763.23	Claims on Private Sector	22d
								11.77	20.94	27.29	29.09	28.70	34.21	42.09	Demand Deposits	24
								8.51	17.80	5.07	7.85	13.21	19.77	31.71	Time and Savings Deposits	25a
								121.13	232.57	365.55	574.84	664.90	667.03	878.84	Foreign Currency Deposits	25b
								10.30	3.22	4.04	11.45	4.23	3.97	4.04	Restricted Deposits	26b
								157.74	164.61	166.15	161.56	200.32	224.37	214.45	Foreign Liabilities	26c
								25.43	1.75	7.14	4.38	4.26	4.20	4.15	Central Government Deposits	26d
								3.03	2.96	4.81	3.51	7.02	5.87	7.52	Credit from Monetary Authorities	26g
								121.81	356.49	356.11	454.98	602.77	689.78	767.43	Capital Accounts	27a
								−42.65	−144.79	−136.78	−121.93	−119.15	−114.37	−88.23	Other Items (Net)	27r
End of Period															**Monetary Survey**	
....	....	....	....	....	....	....	....	118.54	390.75	549.97	878.35	1,171.59	1,728.33	2,018.76	Foreign Assets (Net)	31n
								343.14	386.25	446.43	567.41	696.55	839.01	876.31	Domestic Credit	32
								175.32	143.16	147.92	127.64	53.84	178.55	102.95	Claims on Central Govt. (Net)	32an
								6.21	6.00	5.11	5.22	5.93	5.86	10.14	Claims on Nonfin.Pub.Enterprises	32c
								161.61	237.09	293.40	434.55	636.79	654.60	763.23	Claims on Private Sector	32d
								203.82	201.68	278.49	328.93	384.76	543.27	531.95	Money	34
								129.65	250.37	370.62	582.69	678.11	686.80	910.55	Quasi-Money	35
								179.42	483.92	472.00	655.71	994.33	1,529.39	1,637.64	Capital Accounts	37a
								−51.21	−158.96	−124.70	−121.57	−189.05	−192.12	−185.06	Other Items (Net)	37r
....	....	....	....	....	....	....	....	333.47	452.05	649.11	911.62	1,062.87	1,230.07	1,442.50	Money plus Quasi-Money	35l
Percent Per Annum															**Interest Rates**	
....	....	....	....	....	....	....	....	....	....	8.7	8.8	8.0	7.8	7.3	Deposit Rate	60l
										18.7	18.8	18.4	18.3	17.6	Lending Rate	60p
Period Averages															**Prices**	
....	....	....	....	....	....	....	....	....	99.0	100.0	110.1	113.6	130.3	135.6	Consumer Prices	64

Cambodia

International Transactions		1970	1971	1972	1973	1974	1975	1976	1977	1978	1979	1980	1981	1982	1983	1984
Balance of Payments																*Millions of US Dollars:*
Current Account, n.i.e.	78al d	....	....	....	....	....	....	....	....	....	....	....	....	....	....	....
Goods: Exports f.o.b.	78aa d	....	....	....	....	....	....	....	....	....	....	....	....	....	....	....
Goods: Imports f.o.b.	78ab d	....	....	....	....	....	....	....	....	....	....	....	....	....	....	....
Trade Balance	78ac d	....	....	....	....	....	....	....	....	....	....	....	....	....	....	....
Services: Credit	78ad d	....	....	....	....	....	....	....	....	....	....	....	....	....	....	....
Services: Debit	78ae d	....	....	....	....	....	....	....	....	....	....	....	....	....	....	....
Balance on Goods & Services	78af d	....	....	....	....	....	....	....	....	....	....	....	....	....	....	....
Income: Credit	78ag d	....	....	....	....	....	....	....	....	....	....	....	....	....	....	....
Income: Debit	78ah d	....	....	....	....	....	....	....	....	....	....	....	....	....	....	....
Balance on Gds, Serv. & Inc.	78ai d	....	....	....	....	....	....	....	....	....	....	....	....	....	....	....
Current Transfers, n.i.e.: Credit	78aj d	....	....	....	....	....	....	....	....	....	....	....	....	....	....	....
Current Transfers: Debit	78ak d	....	....	....	....	....	....	....	....	....	....	....	....	....	....	....
Capital Account, n.i.e.	78bc d	....	....	....	....	....	....	....	....	....	....	....	....	....	....	....
Capital Account, n.i.e.: Credit	78ba d	....	....	....	....	....	....	....	....	....	....	....	....	....	....	....
Capital Account: Debit	78bb d	....	....	....	....	....	....	....	....	....	....	....	....	....	....	....
Financial Account, n.i.e.	78bj d	....	....	....	....	....	....	....	....	....	....	....	....	....	....	....
Direct Investment Abroad	78bd d	....	....	....	....	....	....	....	....	....	....	....	....	....	....	....
Dir. Invest. in Rep. Econ., n.i.e.	78be d	....	....	....	....	....	....	....	....	....	....	....	....	....	....	....
Portfolio Investment Assets	78bf d	....	....	....	....	....	....	....	....	....	....	....	....	....	....	....
Equity Securities	78bk d	....	....	....	....	....	....	....	....	....	....	....	....	....	....	....
Debt Securities	78bl d	....	....	....	....	....	....	....	....	....	....	....	....	....	....	....
Portfolio Investment Liab., n.i.e.	78bg d	....	....	....	....	....	....	....	....	....	....	....	....	....	....	....
Equity Securities	78bm d	....	....	....	....	....	....	....	....	....	....	....	....	....	....	....
Debt Securities	78bn d	....	....	....	....	....	....	....	....	....	....	....	....	....	....	....
Financial Derivatives Assets	78bw d	....	....	....	....	....	....	....	....	....	....	....	....	....	....	....
Financial Derivatives Liabilities	78bx d	....	....	....	....	....	....	....	....	....	....	....	....	....	....	....
Other Investment Assets	78bh d	....	....	....	....	....	....	....	....	....	....	....	....	....	....	....
Monetary Authorities	78bo d	....	....	....	....	....	....	....	....	....	....	....	....	....	....	....
General Government	78bp d	....	....	....	....	....	....	....	....	....	....	....	....	....	....	....
Banks	78bq d	....	....	....	....	....	....	....	....	....	....	....	....	....	....	....
Other Sectors	78br d	....	....	....	....	....	....	....	....	....	....	....	....	....	....	....
Other Investment Liab., n.i.e.	78bi d	....	....	....	....	....	....	....	....	....	....	....	....	....	....	....
Monetary Authorities	78bs d	....	....	....	....	....	....	....	....	....	....	....	....	....	....	....
General Government	78bt d	....	....	....	....	....	....	....	....	....	....	....	....	....	....	....
Banks	78bu d	....	....	....	....	....	....	....	....	....	....	....	....	....	....	....
Other Sectors	78bv d	....	....	....	....	....	....	....	....	....	....	....	....	....	....	....
Net Errors and Omissions	78ca d	....	....	....	....	....	....	....	....	....	....	....	....	....	....	....
Overall Balance	78cb d	....	....	....	....	....	....	....	....	....	....	....	....	....	....	....
Reserves and Related Items	79da d	....	....	....	....	....	....	....	....	....	....	....	....	....	....	....
Reserve Assets	79db d	....	....	....	....	....	....	....	....	....	....	....	....	....	....	....
Use of Fund Credit and Loans	79dc d	....	....	....	....	....	....	....	....	....	....	....	....	....	....	....
Exceptional Financing	79de d	....	....	....	....	....	....	....	....	....	....	....	....	....	....	....
International Investment Position																*Millions of US Dollars*
Assets	79aa d	....	....	....	....	....	....	....	....	....	....	....	....	....	....	....
Direct Investment Abroad	79ab d	....	....	....	....	....	....	....	....	....	....	....	....	....	....	....
Portfolio Investment	79ac d	....	....	....	....	....	....	....	....	....	....	....	....	....	....	....
Equity Securities	79ad d	....	....	....	....	....	....	....	....	....	....	....	....	....	....	....
Debt Securities	79ae d	....	....	....	....	....	....	....	....	....	....	....	....	....	....	....
Financial Derivatives	79al d	....	....	....	....	....	....	....	....	....	....	....	....	....	....	....
Other Investment	79af d	....	....	....	....	....	....	....	....	....	....	....	....	....	....	....
Monetary Authorities	79ag d	....	....	....	....	....	....	....	....	....	....	....	....	....	....	....
General Government	79ah d	....	....	....	....	....	....	....	....	....	....	....	....	....	....	....
Banks	79ai d	....	....	....	....	....	....	....	....	....	....	....	....	....	....	....
Other Sectors	79aj d	....	....	....	....	....	....	....	....	....	....	....	....	....	....	....
Reserve Assets	79ak d	....	....	....	....	....	....	....	....	....	....	....	....	....	....	....
Liabilities	79la d	....	....	....	....	....	....	....	....	....	....	....	....	....	....	....
Dir. Invest. in Rep. Economy	79lb d	....	....	....	....	....	....	....	....	....	....	....	....	....	....	....
Portfolio Investment	79lc d	....	....	....	....	....	....	....	....	....	....	....	....	....	....	....
Equity Securities	79ld d	....	....	....	....	....	....	....	....	....	....	....	....	....	....	....
Debt Securities	79le d	....	....	....	....	....	....	....	....	....	....	....	....	....	....	....
Financial Derivatives	79ll d	....	....	....	....	....	....	....	....	....	....	....	....	....	....	....
Other Investment	79lf d	....	....	....	....	....	....	....	....	....	....	....	....	....	....	....
Monetary Authorities	79lg d	....	....	....	....	....	....	....	....	....	....	....	....	....	....	....
General Government	79lh d	....	....	....	....	....	....	....	....	....	....	....	....	....	....	....
Banks	79li d	....	....	....	....	....	....	....	....	....	....	....	....	....	....	....
Other sectors	79lj d	....	....	....	....	....	....	....	....	....	....	....	....	....	....	....
																Millions:
Population	99z	7.06	7.26	7.46	7.71	7.92	I 7.10	6.97	6.78	6.59	6.44	6.40	6.46	6.61	6.89	7.29

Cambodia

International Transactions

Minus Sign Indicates Debit

1985	1986	1987	1988	1989	1990	1991	1992	1993	1994	1995	1996	1997	1998	1999		
															Balance of Payments	
....	....	....	....	....	....	....	-93.0	-103.9	-156.6	-185.7	-184.9	-209.9	-223.9	-96.2	Current Account, n.i.e.	78ald
....	....	....	....	....	....	....	264.5	283.7	489.9	855.2	643.6	736.0	705.4	971.3	Goods: Exports f.o.b.	78aad
....	....	....	....	....	....	....	-443.4	-471.1	-744.4	-1,186.8	-1,071.8	-1,064.0	-1,096.8	-1,211.6	Goods: Imports f.o.b.	78abd
....	....	....	....	....	....	....	-178.9	-187.4	-254.5	-331.6	-428.2	-328.0	-391.4	-240.3	*Trade Balance*	78acd
....	....	....	....	....	....	....	49.7	63.9	54.5	114.0	162.8	160.4	109.8	129.5	Services: Credit	78add
....	....	....	....	....	....	....	-63.6	-120.5	-139.6	-187.9	-214.8	-188.0	-189.4	-195.0	Services: Debit	78aed
....	....	....	....	....	....	....	-192.8	-244.0	-339.6	-405.5	-480.2	-355.6	-471.0	-305.8	*Balance on Goods & Services*	78afd
....	....	....	....	....	....	....	....	.5	2.1	9.7	12.6	16.0	17.9	20.5	Income: Credit	78agd
....	....	....	....	....	....	....	-20.6	-16.6	-49.1	-66.9	-98.3	-58.5	-68.2	-45.4	Income: Debit	78ahd
....	....	....	....	....	....	....	-213.4	-260.1	-386.6	-462.7	-565.9	-398.1	-521.3	-330.7	*Balance on Gds, Serv. & Inc.*	78aid
....	....	....	....	....	....	....	120.4	156.4	230.0	277.9	383.4	188.5	298.0	235.9	Current Transfers, n.i.e.: Credit	78ajd
....	....	....	....	....	....	....	....	-.2	—	-.9	-2.4	-.3	-.6	-1.4	Current Transfers: Debit	78akd
....	....	....	....	....	....	....	126.3	123.4	73.2	78.0	75.8	65.2	61.6	44.0	Capital Account, n.i.e.	78bcd
....	....	....	....	....	....	....	126.3	123.4	73.2	78.0	75.8	65.2	61.6	44.0	Capital Account, n.i.e.: Credit	78bad
....	....	....	....	....	....	....	....	....							Capital Account: Debit	78bbd
....	....	....	....	....	....	....	13.9	.2	54.0	122.4	259.1	219.8	122.8	104.0	Financial Account, n.i.e.	78bjd
....	....	....	....	....	....	....									Direct Investment Abroad	78bdd
....	....	....	....	....	....	....	33.0	54.1	68.9	150.8	293.6	203.7	120.7	125.5	Dir. Invest. in Rep. Econ., n.i.e.	78bed
....	....	....	....	....	....	....	....	....	....	....			....	....	Portfolio Investment Assets	78bfd
....	....	....	....	....	....	....									Equity Securities	78bkd
....	....	....	....	....	....	....									Debt Securities	78bld
....	....	....	....	....	....	....									Portfolio Investment Liab., n.i.e.	78bgd
....	....	....	....	....	....	....									Equity Securities	78bmd
....	....	....	....	....	....	....									Debt Securities	78bnd
....	....	....	....	....	....	....									Financial Derivatives Assets	78bwd
....	....	....	....	....	....	....									Financial Derivatives Liabilities	78bxd
....	....	....	....	....	....	....	-24.1	-51.1	-46.8	-103.4	-118.0	-23.6	-41.6	-61.1	Other Investment Assets	78bhd
....	....	....	....	....	....	....	....	....							Monetary Authorities	78bod
....	....	....	....	....	....	....		-.4							General Government	78bpd
....	....	....	....	....	....	....	....	-25.6	—	-39.8	-23.6	23.6	23.2	-15.1	Banks	78bqd
....	....	....	....	....	....	....	-24.1	-25.1	-46.8	-63.6	-94.4	-47.2	-64.8	-46.0	Other Sectors	78brd
....	....	....	....	....	....	....	5.0	-2.8	31.9	75.0	83.5	39.7	43.7	39.6	Other Investment Liab., n.i.e.	78bid
....	....	....	....	....	....	....	—								Monetary Authorities	78bsd
....	....	....	....	....	....	....	-2.1	3.2	51.4	73.1	89.7	41.2	42.4	42.3	General Government	78btd
....	....	....	....	....	....	....	7.1	-6.0	-19.5	1.9	-6.2	-1.5	1.3	-2.7	Banks	78bud
....	....	....	....	....	....	....									Other Sectors	78bvd
....	....	....	....	....	....	....	-34.0	1.0	65.6	11.5	-78.0	-41.2	55.3	-1.3	Net Errors and Omissions	78cad
....	....	....	....	....	....	....	13.2	20.8	36.2	26.2	72.0	33.9	15.8	50.5	*Overall Balance*	78cbd
....	....	....	....	....	....	....	-13.2	-20.8	-36.2	-26.2	-72.0	-33.9	-15.8	-50.5	Reserves and Related Items	79dad
....	....	....	....	....	....	....	-4.5	-23.0	-71.2	-73.2	-68.9	-34.3	-25.2	-68.2	Reserve Assets	79dbd
....	....	....	....	....	....	....	-8.7	—	19.8	42.3	—		-1.4	8.3	Use of Fund Credit and Loans	79dcd
....	....	....	....	....	....	....	....	2.2	15.2	4.7	-3.1	.4	10.8	9.4	Exceptional Financing	79ded

Millions of US Dollars

1985	1986	1987	1988	1989	1990	1991	1992	1993	1994	1995	1996	1997	1998	1999		
															International Investment Position	
....	....	....	....	....	....	....	....	....	....	374.4	711.0	798.4	834.8	993.2	Assets	79aad
....	....	....	....	....	....	....	....	....	....	—	—	—	—	—	Direct Investment Abroad	79abd
....	....	....	....	....	....	....	....	....	....	—	—	—	—	—	Portfolio Investment	79acd
....	....	....	....	....	....	....	....	....	....	—	—	—	—	—	Equity Securities	79add
....	....	....	....	....	....	....	....	....	....	—	—	—	—	—	Debt Securities	79aed
....	....	....	....	....	....	....	....	....	....	—	—	—	—	—	Financial Derivatives	79ald
....	....	....	....	....	....	....	....	....	....	182.3	206.9	223.2	206.1	225.0	Other Investment	79afd
....	....	....	....	....	....	....	....	....	....					—	Monetary Authorities	79agd
....	....	....	....	....	....	....	....	....	....						General Government	79ahd
....	....	....	....	....	....	....	....	....	....	163.3	186.9	163.2	140.1	155.0	Banks	79aid
....	....	....	....	....	....	....	....	....	....	19.0	20.0	60.0	66.0	70.0	Other Sectors	79ajd
....	....	....	....	....	....	....	....	....	....	192.1	504.1	575.2	628.7	768.2	Reserve Assets	79akd
....	....	....	....	....	....	....	....	....	....	1,108.0	1,351.2	1,210.5	1,252.9	1,455.4	Liabilities	79lad
....	....	....	....	....	....	....	....	....	....	498.1	677.6	580.4	680.9	724.5	Dir. Invest. in Rep. Economy	79lbd
....	....	....	....	....	....	....	....	....	....	—	—	—	—	—	Portfolio Investment	79lcd
....	....	....	....	....	....	....	....	....	....	—	—	—	—	—	Equity Securities	79ldd
....	....	....	....	....	....	....	....	....	....	—	—	—	—	—	Debt Securities	79led
....	....	....	....	....	....	....	....	....	....	—	—	—	—	—	Financial Derivatives	79lld
....	....	....	....	....	....	....	....	....	....	609.9	673.6	630.1	572.0	730.9	Other Investment	79lfd
....	....	....	....	....	....	....	....	....	....	71.7	69.4	65.1	66.5	72.9	Monetary Authorities	79lgd
....	....	....	....	....	....	....	....	....	....	472.5	544.7	506.9	446.0	601.1	General Government	79lhd
....	....	....	....	....	....	....	....	....	....	65.7	59.6	58.1	59.5	56.9	Banks	79lid
....	....	....	....	....	....	....	....	....	....	—	—	—	—	—	Other sectors	79ljd

Midyear Estimates

1985	1986	1987	1988	1989	1990	1991	1992	1993	1994	1995	1996	1997	1998	1999		
7.56	7.82	8.07	8.32	8.33	8.57	8.78	9.00	9.23	9.46	9.69	9.94	10.18	11.44	I 10.95	**Population**	99z

(See notes in the back of the book.)

Cameroon

		1970	1971	1972	1973	1974	1975	1976	1977	1978	1979	1980	1981	1982	1983	1984
Exchange Rates															*Francs per SDR:*	
Official Rate	aa	276.02	283.61	278.00	284.00	272.08	262.55	288.70	285.76	272.28	264.78	287.99	334.52	370.92	436.97	470.11
															Francs per US Dollar:	
Official Rate	ae	276.02	261.22	256.05	235.42	222.22	224.27	248.49	235.25	209.00	201.00	225.80	287.40	336.25	417.37	479.60
Official Rate	rf	276.40	275.59	252.03	222.89	240.70	214.31	238.95	245.68	225.66	212.72	211.28	271.73	328.61	381.07	436.96
														Index Numbers (1995=100):		
Official Rate	ahx	180.5	98.6	197.9	224.6	207.2	233.0	209.0	203.0	221.4	234.6	236.4	184.6	152.6	131.5	114.5
Nominal Effective Exchange Rate	nec	....	....	....	....	....	....	....	....	....	90.9	93.0	87.2	83.4	81.1	80.5
Real Effective Exchange Rate	rec	....	....	....	....	....	....	....	....	....	....	131.7	120.9	118.2	122.9	125.1
Fund Position															*Millions of SDRs:*	
Quota	2f.s	35.00	35.00	35.00	35.00	35.00	35.00	35.00	35.00	45.00	45.00	67.50	67.50	67.50	92.70	92.70
SDRs	1b.s	3.06	6.80	10.51	10.51	10.47	10.11	8.79	6.75	3.23	.01	—	.23	1.64	.62	6.23
Reserve Position in the Fund	1c.s	6.90	6.90	6.90	6.90	—	—	—	—	3.47	—	12.04	12.04	12.04	13.90	.20
Total Fund Cred.&Loans Outstg.	2tl	—	—	—	—	4.62	12.13	33.89	33.89	47.27	49.92	46.04	37.68	34.74	33.60	30.70
International Liquidity												*Millions of US Dollars Unless Otherwise Indicated:*				
Total Reserves minus Gold	1l.d	80.81	73.60	43.64	51.15	78.53	28.83	43.80	42.39	52.28	125.70	188.86	85.19	67.23	159.09	53.85
SDRs	1b.d	3.06	7.38	11.41	12.68	12.82	11.84	10.21	8.20	4.21	.01	—	.27	1.81	.65	6.11
Reserve Position in the Fund	1c.d	6.90	7.49	7.49	8.32	—	—	—	—	4.52	8.42	15.36	14.01	15.33	7.54	.20
Foreign Exchange	1d.d	70.85	58.73	24.74	30.15	65.71	16.99	33.59	34.19	43.56	117.27	173.50	70.90	50.08	150.90	47.55
Gold (Million Fine Troy Ounces)	1ad	....	....	....	....	....	....	.015	.015	.030	.030	.030	.030	.030	.030	.030
Gold (National Valuation)	1and	....	....	....	....	....	....	....	2.46	2.95	15.59	17.65	11.99	13.45	11.33	9.27
Monetary Authorities: Other Liab.	4..d	.14	.06	.06	.05	8.59	2.80	4.38	2.89	3.78	2.85	2.12	.98	1.20	.92	2.89
Deposit Money Banks: Assets	7a.d	9.81	11.29	8.51	16.39	6.73	5.85	14.68	28.57	34.00	32.24	34.31	151.65	71.16	129.92	279.74
Liabilities	7b.d	29.14	24.75	30.95	23.54	26.92	32.41	20.29	51.35	109.22	126.81	326.04	195.46	333.63	228.43	167.14
Monetary Authorities															*Billions of Francs:*	
Foreign Assets	11	22.44	18.83	11.16	11.78	17.45	6.47	10.88	10.55	11.55	28.42	46.65	27.93	27.12	71.17	30.27
Claims on Central Government	12a	—	—	—	2.00	7.65	15.77	25.35	26.01	34.44	36.34	38.60	42.38	44.83	60.79	77.22
Claims on Deposit Money Banks	12e	13.64	14.59	17.17	20.28	18.77	25.07	24.97	44.32	61.20	61.11	68.99	107.19	132.02	162.67	162.33
Claims on Other Banking Insts	12f	....	....	....	....	....	....	....	....	....	....	....	....	....	....	....
Reserve Money	14	22.73	23.78	24.38	28.66	34.98	36.39	43.09	56.13	65.33	77.58	89.78	119.76	126.50	162.95	159.97
of which: Currency Outside DMBs	14a	20.63	22.18	22.78	26.65	32.20	33.71	38.85	50.72	60.05	70.27	80.84	105.26	111.02	131.24	141.08
Foreign Liabilities	16c	.04	.02	.02	.01	3.17	3.81	10.87	10.36	17.61	20.44	23.55	24.33	25.98	29.75	30.25
Central Government Deposits	16d	12.49	7.34	.90	2.21	4.24	3.91	3.45	9.87	19.26	18.11	29.85	19.24	36.17	85.25	61.27
Capital Accounts	17a	—	—	—	.06	.06	.06	.06	.05	.05	.05	3.78	3.23	4.41	4.67	4.35
Other Items (Net)	17r	.82	2.29	3.04	3.22	1.42	3.14	3.74	4.46	4.92	9.71	7.29	10.94	10.92	12.11	13.97
Deposit Money Banks															*Billions of Francs:*	
Reserves	20	2.11	1.61	1.60	2.02	2.79	2.67	4.24	5.41	5.29	7.30	8.94	14.51	15.48	31.71	18.89
Foreign Assets	21	2.72	2.89	2.18	3.86	1.50	1.31	3.65	I 6.72	7.11	6.48	7.75	43.58	23.93	54.23	134.16
Claims on Central Government	22a	3.58	4.18	5.25	5.73	7.31	8.59	10.96	15.85	21.06	21.47	29.23	35.35	49.81	61.87	69.38
Claims on Nonfin.Pub.Enterprises	22c	....	....	....	....	....	....	....	....	....	....	....	....	....	....	....
Claims on Private Sector	22d	45.20	48.16	57.67	64.90	89.30	114.79	144.09	I 204.59	266.82	323.75	416.61	559.68	678.74	808.76	806.13
Claims on Other Banking Insts	22f	....	....	....	....	....	....	....	....	....	....	....	....	....	....	....
Claims on Nonbank Financial Insts	22g	....	....	....	....	....	....	....	....	....	....	....	....	....	....	....
Demand Deposits	24	18.85	21.97	24.57	28.93	41.46	43.49	57.34	I 77.70	88.48	116.01	130.15	157.12	190.89	249.43	276.35
Time and Savings Deposits	25	7.07	8.39	10.35	15.06	21.60	30.05	37.96	56.87	65.37	75.84	107.18	146.69	184.92	235.35	325.47
Bonds	26ab															
Foreign Liabilities	26c	6.53	4.99	6.49	3.98	4.12	6.04	3.76	11.04	20.77	11.14	45.17	15.50	47.42	50.74	19.22
Long-Term Foreign Liabilities	26cl	1.56	1.34	1.43	1.56	1.86	1.23	1.29	1.04	2.06	14.35	28.45	40.67	64.77	44.60	60.94
Central Government Deposits	26d	4.39	4.01	4.82	5.59	6.84	9.38	29.26	34.19	43.99	66.90	76.16	173.82	158.06	127.47	138.50
Credit from Monetary Authorities	26g	13.64	14.59	17.17	20.28	23.99	27.56	28.75	47.82	65.77	64.38	71.14	110.72	132.02	162.67	162.33
Capital Accounts	27a	3.94	5.34	5.97	7.20	8.31	11.36	12.67	13.53	17.46	24.33	26.84	42.16	49.24	62.36	46.64
Other Items (Net)	27r	−2.37	−3.80	−4.10	−6.09	−7.30	−1.74	−8.09	I −9.63	−3.62	−13.94	−22.47	−33.56	−59.36	23.94	−.88
Monetary Survey															*Billions of Francs:*	
Foreign Assets (Net)	31n	18.59	16.71	6.84	11.64	11.66	−2.08	−.09	I −4.13	−19.73	3.32	−14.32	31.68	−22.35	44.90	114.96
Domestic Credit	32	31.91	40.99	57.21	64.83	93.17	125.86	147.69	I 202.38	259.07	296.55	378.52	444.35	579.15	718.80	752.96
Claims on Central Govt. (Net)	32an	−13.30	−7.17	−.47	−.07	3.87	11.07	3.60	−2.21	−7.75	−27.20	−38.09	−115.33	−99.59	−89.96	−53.17
Claims on Nonfin.Pub.Enterprises	32c	....	....	....	....	....	....	....	....	....	....	....	....	....	....	....
Claims on Private Sector	32d	45.20	48.16	57.67	64.90	89.30	114.79	144.09	I 204.59	266.82	323.75	416.61	559.68	678.74	808.76	806.13
Claims on Other Banking Insts	32f	....	....	....	....	....	....	....	....	....	....	....	....	....	....	....
Claims on Nonbank Financial Inst	32g	....	....	....	....	....	....	....	....	....	....	....	....	....	....	....
Money	34	39.48	44.14	47.35	55.57	73.66	77.20	96.19	I 128.42	148.53	186.28	210.99	262.37	301.91	380.67	417.43
Quasi-Money	35	7.07	8.39	10.35	15.06	21.60	30.05	37.96	56.87	65.37	75.84	107.18	146.69	184.92	235.35	325.47
Bonds	36ab															
Other Items (Net)	37r	3.95	5.17	6.35	5.95	9.56	16.53	13.44	I 12.95	25.45	37.75	46.03	66.97	69.97	147.68	125.02
Money plus Quasi-Money	35l	48.51	54.75	60.13	73.61	99.28	111.77	139.81	I 193.11	222.91	273.17	331.59	426.31	507.36	642.00	774.23
Interest Rates															*Percent Per Annum*	
Discount Rate (End of Period)	60	4.50	4.50	4.50	4.50	5.50	5.50	6.50	6.50	6.50	8.50	8.50	8.50	8.50	8.50	8.50
Deposit Rate	60l	....	....	....	....	....	....	....	....	....	6.50	7.50	7.50	7.50	7.50	7.50
Lending Rate	60p	....	....	....	....	....	....	....	....	....	10.25	13.00	13.00	13.00	14.50	14.50
Prices															*Index Numbers (1995=100):*	
Consumer Prices	64	11.3	11.7	12.7	14.0	16.4	18.6	20.4	23.5	26.4	28.1	I 30.8	34.1	38.6	45.0	50.2
															Number in Thousands:	
Employment	67e	....	....	....	....	....	....	....	....	....	....	....	....	....	....	....

1985	1986	1987	1988	1989	1990	1991	1992	1993	1994	1995	1996	1997	1998	1999		
End of Period															**Exchange Rates**	
415.26	394.78	378.78	407.68	380.32	364.84	370.48	378.57	404.89	I 780.44	728.38	753.06	807.94	791.61	I 896.19	Official Rate..............	aa
End of Period (ae)	*Period Average (rf)*															
378.05	322.75	267.00	302.95	289.40	256.45	259.00	275.32	294.77	I 534.60	490.00	523.70	598.81	562.21	I 652.95	Official Rate...............	ae
449.26	346.31	300.54	297.85	319.01	272.26	282.11	264.69	283.16	I 555.20	499.15	511.55	583.67	589.95	I 615.70	Official Rate...............	rf
Period Averages																
111.9	144.3	166.1	167.8	156.5	183.7	177.4	188.9	176.3	90.0	100.0	97.5	85.6	84.7	81.1	Official Rate................	ahx
83.7	90.5	94.9	98.7	103.6	122.9	129.8	148.0	164.6	91.9	100.0	100.7	96.8	99.0	100.9	Nominal Effective Exchange Rate	ne c
130.7	144.7	161.9	157.8	145.5	149.6	143.1	144.2	134.5	86.6	100.0	101.5	96.9	102.1	109.7	Real Effective Exchange Rate	re c
End of Period															**Fund Position**	
92.70	92.70	92.70	92.70	92.70	92.70	92.70	135.10	135.10	135.10	135.10	135.10	135.10	135.10	185.70	Quota........................	2f. s
4.21	2.82	.18	.02	.22	.45	3.89	.20	.06	.03	.03	.11	—	.01	1.90	SDRs.........................	1b. s
.20	.20	.20	.22	.22	.22	.23	.29	.34	.34	.36	.37	.41	.45	.50	Reserve Position in the Fund	1c. s
24.95	18.13	11.32	74.64	86.18	85.11	84.28	45.66	11.86	29.91	34.41	50.11	68.91	110.94	142.65	Total Fund Cred.&Loans Outstg.	2tl
End of Period															**International Liquidity**	
132.46	59.02	63.76	175.85	79.86	25.54	43.04	20.37	2.45	2.26	3.79	2.77	.86	1.29	4.43	Total Reserves minus Gold.....................	1l. d
4.62	3.45	.26	.03	.29	.64	5.56	.28	.09	.05	.04	.16	—	.02	2.61	SDRs........................	1b. d
.22	.24	.28	.30	.29	.31	.33	.40	.47	.49	.53	.53	.55	.63	.69	Reserve Position in the Fund	1c. d
127.62	55.32	63.22	175.52	79.28	24.59	37.15	19.70	1.90	1.72	3.22	2.08	.31	.64	1.13	Foreign Exchange	1d. d
.030	.030	.030	.030	.030	.030	.030	.030	.030	.030	.030	.030	.030	....	....	Gold (Million Fine Troy Ounces)...........	1ad
9.70	11.74	14.45	12.17	12.01	11.48	10.58	9.95	11.91	I 11.33	11.56	11.04	8.72	8.61	....	Gold (National Valuation)	1an d
.97	1.46	1.63	I 440.82	368.76	471.54	506.92	637.31	762.34	650.63	713.03	537.11	300.24	238.09	188.63	Monetary Authorities: Other Liab.	4.. d
431.08	127.71	279.70	396.82	481.78	142.84	173.78	98.99	88.27	135.55	131.07	90.23	105.23	122.82	163.34	Deposit Money Banks: Assets	7a. d
268.42	394.45	567.80	759.14	791.18	338.28	301.01	90.26	125.49	50.01	81.98	71.50	62.51	85.92	84.52	Liabilities...........	7b. d
End of Period															**Monetary Authorities**	
53.78	22.83	20.91	I 56.99	26.59	9.51	13.89	8.35	4.17	7.37	7.53	7.25	5.70	5.57	8.57	Foreign Assets	11
74.24	113.86	95.29	I 117.18	133.24	131.32	I 320.40	331.57	319.09	340.51	338.23	340.59	338.61	358.64	403.25	Claims on Central Government	12a
129.98	192.56	341.55	I 327.91	294.33	273.36	I 77.58	51.63	52.06	27.07	21.41	4.93	4.07	13.51	2.17	Claims on Deposit Money Banks	12e
....	....	....	....	....	....	....	....	....	....	....	....	....	....	—	Claims on Other Banking Insts	12f
183.44	216.13	200.71	I 206.40	219.98	200.59	199.14	168.61	129.79	180.77	142.77	183.17	256.74	282.83	305.91	Reserve Money	14
155.94	171.52	175.28	I 166.12	162.85	155.98	170.25	149.02	116.13	136.33	102.29	95.32	180.28	205.76	237.40	*of which: Currency Outside DMBs*	14a
21.09	14.79	9.01	I 163.97	139.49	151.98	162.52	192.75	229.52	371.17	374.45	319.02	235.47	221.67	251.01	Foreign Liabilities...........................	16c
37.64	86.94	223.70	I 123.32	82.72	52.00	43.38	23.62	14.85	44.83	63.03	59.71	49.52	63.96	57.54	Central Government Deposits	16d
3.61	3.97	4.17	I 14.30	13.21	12.19	12.58	12.16	13.59	22.17	20.38	20.99	22.19	21.44	25.23	Capital Accounts	17a
12.22	7.42	20.16	I -5.92	-1.24	-2.57	-5.77	-5.59	-12.43	-243.99	-233.45	-230.12	-215.54	-212.19	-226.67	Other Items (Net)	17r
End of Period															**Deposit Money Banks**	
27.50	44.57	25.41	I 30.91	48.78	41.25	27.69	17.22	12.39	42.57	37.49	82.48	70.57	68.60	62.66	Reserves	20
162.97	41.22	74.68	I 120.22	139.43	36.63	45.01	27.25	26.02	72.46	64.22	47.25	63.01	69.05	106.65	Foreign Assets	21
82.40	115.69	140.92	I 125.18	119.49	86.05	108.85	I 126.05	154.08	185.76	187.67	159.72	171.59	173.66	173.85	Claims on Central Government	22a
....	....	....	132.76	191.13	182.57	171.91	77.03	52.68	39.45	42.06	36.26	39.76	53.95	54.35	Claims on Nonfin.Pub.Enterprises	22c
878.29	986.21	1,014.56	I 897.65	887.42	894.45	892.95	400.06	368.81	369.54	371.39	385.89	348.14	428.82	481.46	Claims on Private Sector	22d
....	....	....	.01	.31	....	.01	....	.01	.03	.19	.05	.06	.19	.08	Claims on Other Banking Insts	22f
....	....	....	2.49	2.60	2.10	2.96	3.06	3.05	4.43	8.83	9.16	11.95	14.57	5.41	Claims on Nonbank Financial Insts	22g
278.38	280.31	215.90	I 246.49	281.20	259.29	258.45	159.94	150.06	223.09	213.97	213.45	237.72	271.06	294.49	Demand Deposits	24
437.84	383.07	290.71	I 303.19	316.98	337.98	340.37	290.32	278.67	329.79	329.30	268.89	267.45	259.81	306.43	Time and Savings Deposits	25
....	....	....	16.88	16.50	15.00	15.93	6.22	5.01	3.85	3.85	.90	5.30	.90	.90	Bonds	26ab
50.14	83.61	98.90	I 132.47	151.48	54.22	I 47.17	22.92	32.58	17.44	36.08	34.84	34.74	43.80	47.21	Foreign Liabilities	26c
51.33	43.70	52.71	I 97.51	77.49	32.53	I 30.80	1.93	4.41	9.30	4.09	2.60	2.69	4.50	7.98	Long-Term Foreign Liabilities	26cl
143.65	120.76	221.57	I 177.08	189.77	199.60	189.05	I 82.24	77.65	97.04	94.00	109.15	55.43	85.19	101.56	Central Government Deposits	26d
129.98	192.56	341.55	I 327.91	294.33	273.37	I 77.58	51.63	52.06	27.07	21.41	4.93	4.07	13.51	2.17	Credit from Monetary Authorities	26g
64.22	82.43	101.34	I 95.05	119.51	131.29	I 370.23	77.27	75.87	84.39	62.25	102.79	112.58	129.23	150.84	Capital Accounts	27a
-4.38	1.25	-67.11	I -87.37	-58.11	-60.24	-80.20	I -41.80	-59.27	-77.72	-53.09	-16.75	-14.91	.84	-18.68	Other Items (Net)	27r
End of Period															**Monetary Survey**	
145.51	-34.35	-12.31	I -206.28	-194.18	-184.89	I -181.58	-181.99	-236.32	-318.07	-342.86	-301.96	-204.18	-195.36	-190.98	Foreign Assets (Net)	31n
853.64	1,008.05	805.50	I 974.85	1,061.70	1,044.88	1,264.64	I 831.91	805.22	797.85	791.34	762.82	806.10	881.16	959.54	Domestic Credit	32
-24.64	21.84	-209.06	I -58.05	-19.76	-34.24	196.81	I 351.76	380.67	384.40	368.88	331.46	405.25	383.15	418.00	Claims on Central Govt. (Net)	32an
....	....	....	132.76	191.13	182.57	171.91	77.03	52.68	39.45	42.06	36.26	39.76	53.95	54.35	Claims on Nonfin.Pub.Enterprises	32c
878.29	986.21	1,014.56	I 897.65	887.42	894.45	892.95	400.06	368.81	369.54	371.39	385.89	348.14	428.82	481.46	Claims on Private Sector	32d
....	....	....	.01	.31	....	.01	....	.01	.03	.19	.05	.06	.19	.08	Claims on Other Banking Insts	32f
....	....	....	2.49	2.60	2.10	2.96	3.06	3.05	4.43	8.83	9.16	12.89	15.06	5.64	Claims on Nonbank Financial Inst	32g
434.32	451.87	391.21	I 421.98	452.40	418.63	429.90	311.33	267.46	361.29	319.24	314.14	423.90	485.29	537.73	Money..	34
437.84	383.07	290.71	I 303.19	316.98	337.98	340.37	290.32	278.67	329.79	329.30	268.89	267.45	259.81	306.43	Quasi-Money	35
....	....	....	16.88	16.50	15.00	15.93	6.22	5.01	3.85	3.85	.90	5.30	.90	.90	Bonds	36ab
127.00	138.77	111.27	I 26.52	81.64	88.38	I 296.85	I 42.04	17.77	-215.15	-203.91	-123.08	-94.74	-60.19	-69.05	Other Items (Net)..........................	37r
908.94	870.15	710.67	I 725.18	769.38	756.61	770.28	601.65	546.13	691.08	648.55	583.03	691.35	745.09	844.17	Money plus Quasi-Money	35l
Percent Per Annum															**Interest Rates**	
9.00	8.00	8.00	9.50	10.00	11.00	10.75	12.00	11.50	I 7.75	8.60	7.75	7.50	7.00	7.30	Discount Rate *(End of Period)*..................	60
7.50	7.35	7.15	7.21	7.50	I 7.50	7.50	7.50	7.75	8.08	5.50	5.38	5.04	5.00	5.00	Deposit Rate	60l
14.50	13.50	13.00	13.46	15.00	I 18.50	18.15	17.77	17.46	17.50	16.00	22.00	22.00	22.00	22.00	Lending Rate	60p
Period Averages															**Prices**	
54.4	58.7	66.4	67.5	66.4	67.1	67.1	67.1	65.0	I 87.8	100.0	104.7	105.8	105.9	....	Consumer Prices................................	64
Period Averages																
3,989	4,920	....	....	....	....	....	....	....	....	....	....	....	....	....	Employment.................................	67e

Cameroon

		1970	1971	1972	1973	1974	1975	1976	1977	1978	1979	1980	1981	1982	1983	1984
International Transactions															*Billions of Francs:*	
Exports	70	62.78	57.28	55.70	78.32	114.90	96.13	122.03	172.88	181.70	240.62	290.62	299.72	348.23	372.22	381.33
Imports, c.i.f.	71	67.24	69.37	76.47	74.23	104.84	128.10	146.98	180.68	237.25	271.14	337.61	386.09	394.58	466.98	484.43
Balance of Payments															*Millions of US Dollars:*	
Current Account, n.i.e.	78ald	....	....	....	....	....	....	....	−93.1	−187.1	−126.5	−446.0	−482.1	−386.0	−411.9	−168.9
Goods: Exports f.o.b.	78aad	....	....	....	....	....	....	....	809.1	1,095.8	1,354.1	1,657.5	1,410.6	1,357.9	1,366.7	1,588.9
Goods: Imports f.o.b.	78abd	....	....	....	....	....	....	....	−719.2	−951.5	−1,270.8	−1,620.3	−1,368.8	−1,217.6	−1,225.2	−1,064.7
Trade Balance	78acd	....	....	....	....	....	....	....	89.9	144.3	83.3	37.2	41.8	140.3	141.5	524.2
Services: Credit	78add	....	....	....	....	....	....	....	161.8	206.5	351.5	401.0	389.5	427.3	440.8	414.7
Services: Debit	78aed	....	....	....	....	....	....	....	−335.1	−464.1	−464.7	−716.8	−723.3	−752.1	−717.3	−755.8
Balance on Goods & Services	78afd	....	....	....	....	....	....	....	−83.4	−113.3	−29.9	−278.6	−292.0	−184.4	−135.0	183.1
Income: Credit	78agd	....	....	....	....	....	....	....	8.1	16.3	12.4	38.3	29.8	14.9	28.2	35.7
Income: Debit	78ahd	....	....	....	....	....	....	....	−49.3	−90.4	−108.3	−214.5	−213.2	−209.1	−307.4	−363.1
Balance on Gds, Serv. & Inc.	78aid	....	....	....	....	....	....	....	−124.6	−187.5	−125.8	−454.8	−475.4	−378.6	−414.3	−144.4
Current Transfers, n.i.e.: Credit	78ajd	....	....	....	....	....	....	....	64.2	53.1	71.0	140.2	132.7	118.3	145.9	107.0
Current Transfers: Debit	78akd	....	....	....	....	....	....	....	−32.7	−52.7	−71.7	−131.4	−139.4	−125.6	−143.5	−131.6
Capital Account, n.i.e.	78bcd	....	....	....	....	....	....	....	—	—	—	—	—	—	—	—
Capital Account, n.i.e.: Credit	78bad	....	....	....	....	....	....	....	—	—	—	—	—	—	—	—
Capital Account: Debit	78bbd	....	....	....	....	....	....	....	—	—	—	—	—	—	—	—
Financial Account, n.i.e.	78bjd	....	....	....	....	....	....	....	90.9	173.9	183.6	530.0	418.1	371.6	523.5	204.6
Direct Investment Abroad	78bdd	....	....	....	....	....	....	....	−4.4	−6.9	2.2	8.2	.4	−4.3	−5.2	−10.1
Dir. Invest. in Rep. Econ., n.i.e.	78bed	....	....	....	....	....	....	....	8.7	40.5	62.1	129.8	135.4	111.4	213.8	17.7
Portfolio Investment Assets	78bfd	....	....	....	....	....	....	....	—	—	—	—	—	—	—	—
Equity Securities	78bkd	....	....	....	....	....	....	....	—	—	—	—	—	—	—	—
Debt Securities	78bld	....	....	....	....	....	....	....	—	—	—	—	—	—	—	—
Portfolio Investment Liab., n.i.e.	78bgd	....	....	....	....	....	....	....	—	—	—	—	—	—	—	—
Equity Securities	78bmd	....	....	....	....	....	....	....	—	—	—	—	—	—	—	—
Debt Securities	78bnd	....	....	....	....	....	....	....	—	—	—	—	—	—	—	—
Financial Derivatives Assets	78bwd	....	....	....	....	....	....	....	....	....	....	....	....	....	....	....
Financial Derivatives Liabilities	78bxd	....	....	....	....	....	....	....	....	....	....	....	....	....	....	....
Other Investment Assets	78bhd	....	....	....	....	....	....	....	−42.7	8.3	−90.5	−213.6	−185.8	−64.9	−271.6	−418.0
Monetary Authorities	78bod	....	....	....	....	....	....	....								
General Government	78bpd	....	....	....	....	....	....	....	.3	.4	−.3	−.9	.2	.2	.1	−.7
Banks	78bqd	....	....	....	....	....	....	....	−13.5	16.6	−10.2	27.7	−131.9	59.8	−79.5	−183.2
Other Sectors	78brd	....	....	....	....	....	....	....	−29.5	−8.7	−80.0	−240.4	−54.2	−125.0	−192.2	−234.2
Other Investment Liab., n.i.e.	78bid	....	....	....	....	....	....	....	129.3	131.9	209.8	605.5	468.2	329.4	586.5	615.0
Monetary Authorities	78bsd	....	....	....	....	....	....	....	−1.5	.4	−1.5	−.8	.4	.4	−.1	.5
General Government	78btd	....	....	....	....	....	....	....	77.9	55.0	120.3	180.0	186.7	74.3	81.5	122.8
Banks	78bud	....	....	....	....	....	....	....	20.1	21.4	−44.0	161.0	−109.2	97.1	10.9	−65.2
Other Sectors	78bvd	....	....	....	....	....	....	....	32.8	55.0	135.1	265.2	390.2	157.5	494.2	556.9
Net Errors and Omissions	78cad	....	....	....	....	....	....	....	−2.1	.6	.9	−6.4	4.3	3.9	5.2	−121.6
Overall Balance	78cbd	....	....	....	....	....	....	....	−4.3	−12.6	58.0	77.5	−59.7	−10.4	116.7	−85.9
Reserves and Related Items	79dad	....	....	....	....	....	....	....	4.3	12.6	−58.0	−77.5	59.7	10.4	−116.7	85.9
Reserve Assets	79dbd	....	....	....	....	....	....	....	3.6	−4.7	−62.2	−72.9	69.4	13.5	−115.6	88.9
Use of Fund Credit and Loans	79dcd	....	....	....	....	....	....	....	—	16.6	3.5	−5.3	−10.2	−3.2	−1.2	−3.0
Exceptional Financing	79ded	....	....	....	....	....	....	....	.7	.7	.8	.6	.5	.1	.1	....
Government Finance															*Billions of Francs:*	
Deficit (−) or Surplus	80	....	....	....	....	....	−12.98	−15.85	−3.02	4.07	31.72	7.24	−58.50	−55.22	33.87	....
Revenue	81	....	....	....	....	....	86.82	104.32	128.16	178.78	222.43	230.64	314.54	390.44	612.27	790.52
Grants Received	81z	....	....	....	....	....	4.14	5.29	4.59	—	—	.10	—	—	59.56	4.89
Expenditure	82	....	....	....	....	....	103.12	125.27	133.53	168.45	188.98	221.92	371.63	445.56	546.71	....
Lending Minus Repayments	83	....	....	....	....	....	.82	.19	2.24	6.26	1.73	1.58	1.41	.10	91.25	....
Financing																
Domestic	84a	....	....	....	....	....	5.20	6.61	−16.50	−4.33	−26.47	−17.17	....	....	−56.47	....
Foreign	85a	....	....	....	....	....	7.78	9.24	19.52	.26	−5.25	9.93	....	....	22.60	....
Adj. to Total Financing	84x															
Debt: Domestic	88a	....	....	....	....	....	....	....	....	....	....	....	....	....	....	112.56
Foreign	89a	....	....	....	....	....	....	130.70	209.23	....	....	....	291.89	359.54	431.53	
National Accounts															*Billions of Francs:*	
Exports of Goods & Services	90c	85.1	82.0	73.7	89.7	137.9	145.6	150.4	202.6	249.9	259.4	378.6	388.5	434.8	547.5	646.5
Government Consumption	91f	39.1	41.5	46.0	49.0	57.3	68.4	74.8	81.9	102.8	116.3	136.8	159.1	192.0	248.7	306.4
Gross Fixed Capital Formation	93e	44.7	50.5	60.3	74.0	74.7	99.2	118.7	163.5	204.7	251.7	282.4	441.4	507.2	654.5	809.5
Increase/Decrease(−) in Stocks	93i	6.3	6.2	8.6	10.3	14.0	21.3	3.0	18.3	34.1	20.9	13.5	47.0	31.5	25.6	19.4
Private Consumption	96f	203.7	233.6	262.6	291.9	320.0	408.1	481.4	545.3	632.9	807.8	985.3	1,222.5	1,538.5	1,716.5	2,008.0
Imports of Goods & Services	98c	−78.5	−92.5	−95.2	−114.4	−111.3	−162.5	−171.1	−221.7	−256.3	−310.1	−386.5	−462.1	−531.2	−574.7	−594.7
Gross Domestic Product (GDP)	99b	300.3	321.3	355.9	400.5	492.6	580.2	657.2	789.9	968.1	1,135.4	1,356.2	1,796.4	2,172.8	2,618.1	3,195.0
Net Factor Inc/Pmts(−) Abroad	98.n	11.0	.3	−52.2	−63.9	−108.8	−109.2	−119.6	−162.0	....	....	....	....	....	....	....
Gross National Income (GNI)	99a	311.4	321.6	303.7	336.6	383.8	471.0	537.6	627.9	....	....	....	....	....	....	....
Net National Income	99e	272.7	307.6	338.8	373.6	415.1	515.3	583.1	709.5	872.0	1,047.8	1,283.2	1,619.8	1,965.6	2,400.3	2,967.7
GDP Volume 1966 prices	99b.p	258.3														
GDP Volume 1970 prices	99b.p	300.4	309.4	322.8	327.5	342.1	359.7	366.6	387.4	427.7	475.6	495.6	....	....	....	....
GDP Volume 1980 prices	99b.p	....	....	....	....	....	....	....	....	....	....	1,356.2	1,650.7	1,775.5	1,900.5	2,049.3
GDP Volume 1985 Prices	99b.p	....	....	....	....	....	....	....	....	....	....	....	....	....	....	....
GDP Volume (1995=100)	99bvp	47.6	49.0	51.1	51.9	54.2	57.0	58.1	61.4	67.8	75.3	78.5	91.9	98.9	105.8	114.1
GDP Deflator (1995=100)	99bip	14.5	15.0	15.9	17.7	20.8	23.3	25.9	29.5	32.7	34.5	39.6	44.8	50.3	56.7	64.1
															Millions:	
Population	99z	6.78	6.92	7.06	7.21	7.37	7.53	7.70	7.91	8.18	8.40	8.50	8.97	9.28	9.57	9.87

International Transactions

Billions of Francs

Item	Code	1985	1986	1987	1988	1989	1990	1991	1992	1993	1994	1995	1996	1997	1998	1999
Exports	70	321.75	271.64	248.77	275.12	405.99	545.11	517.39	487.13	404.70	757.12	824.28	904.87	1,084.51	....	....
Imports, c.i.f.	71	508.76	590.44	526.19	378.73	402.24	381.15	330.96	307.79	250.50	398.33	598.71	627.42	793.93	....	....

Balance of Payments

Minus Sign Indicates Debit

Item	Code	1985	1986	1987	1988	1989	1990	1991	1992	1993	1994	1995	1996	1997	1998	1999
Current Account, n.i.e.	78al d	-561.5	-451.8	-892.7	-428.3	-298.0	-560.7	-338.8	-396.6	-565.4	-56.1	89.9	....	....		
Goods: Exports f.o.b.	78aa d	1,626.3	2,076.9	1,688.6	1,841.2	1,853.8	2,125.4	1,957.4	1,934.1	1,507.7	1,454.2	1,735.9				
Goods: Imports f.o.b.	78ab d	-1,135.9	-1,634.5	-1,434.8	-1,220.8	-1,136.8	-1,430.0	-1,107.2	-1,041.4	-1,005.3	-1,052.3	-1,109.0				
Trade Balance	78ac d	490.4	442.5	253.9	620.5	717.0	695.3	850.2	892.7	502.4	401.9	626.9				
Services: Credit	78ad d	498.7	467.2	411.4	458.9	475.7	382.2	406.0	407.5	390.9	330.8	304.4				
Services: Debit	78ae d	-936.2	-944.0	-1,052.5	-901.4	-1,032.4	-1,045.1	-1,122.3	-907.3	-741.1	-493.2	-498.6				
Balance on Goods & Services	78af d	53.0	-34.4	-387.2	178.0	160.3	32.4	133.9	392.8	152.2	239.6	432.6				
Income: Credit	78ag d	38.1	36.9	12.4	16.9	16.8	8.3	18.3	41.8	17.0	19.9	12.4				
Income: Debit	78ah d	-634.0	-354.4	-419.0	-510.9	-430.8	-566.1	-442.7	-823.9	-669.5	-336.4	-424.6				
Balance on Gds, Serv. & Inc.	78ai d	-542.9	-351.9	-793.7	-316.0	-253.7	-525.4	-290.4	-389.3	-500.3	-76.9	20.4				
Current Transfers, n.i.e.: Credit	78aj d	147.6	71.8	61.2	63.8	88.0	82.3	57.0	141.0	65.2	83.8	100.7				
Current Transfers: Debit	78ak d	-166.2	-171.8	-160.2	-176.0	-132.3	-117.5	-105.4	-148.3	-130.2	-63.0	-31.2				
Capital Account, n.i.e.	78bc d	—	7.3	—	6.4	5.0	2.8	7.9	17.0	6.3	14.1	20.4				
Capital Account, n.i.e.: Credit	78ba d	—	7.7	—	6.4	5.0	2.9	8.0	17.1	6.4	14.1	21.1				
Capital Account: Debit	78bb d	—	-.4	—	—	-.1	-.1	-.1	-.1	-.1	—	-.7				
Financial Account, n.i.e.	78bj d	511.8	392.9	826.0	39.4	325.6	-227.3	-361.1	-342.9	-310.0	-626.4	43.3				
Direct Investment Abroad	78bd d	-10.6	-15.7	-11.5	-28.6	-26.1	-15.1	-21.5	-23.5	-22.1	-.4	-.6				
Dir. Invest. in Rep. Econ., n.i.e.	78be d	316.2	-90.7	115.9	92.4	-85.7	-112.8	-14.5	29.2	5.1	-9.0	7.3				
Portfolio Investment Assets	78bf d	—	11.0	—	-10.9	-1.0	55.6	-2.2	-46.5	-106.3	-74.6	-26.2				
Equity Securities	78bk d	—	82.9	—	3.1	.2	104.1	18.6	53.4	8.0	6.4	—				
Debt Securities	78bl d	—	-71.8	—	-14.0	-1.2	-48.4	-20.8	-99.9	-114.4	-81.1	-26.2				
Portfolio Investment Liab., n.i.e.	78bg d	—	—	—	—	—	—	—	—	—	—	—				
Equity Securities	78bm d	—	—	—	—	—	—	—	—	—	—	—				
Debt Securities	78bn d	—	—	—	—	—	—	—	—	—	—	—				
Financial Derivatives Assets	78bw d	....	....	....	....	....	....	....	....	....	....	....				
Financial Derivatives Liabilities	78bx d	....	....	....	....	....	....	....	....	....	....	....				
Other Investment Assets	78bh d	-141.3	490.5	299.7	-93.9	-8.9	481.5	-112.3	16.8	105.5	138.4	-146.8				
Monetary Authorities	78bo d	.1			-.1		.3			.1						
General Government	78bp d	-64.1	351.6	-111.3	-145.2	-67.4	377.6	-29.7	26.0	42.8	-27.9	6.6				
Banks	78bq d	-77.4	138.9	411.0	51.4	58.5	103.6	-82.6	-9.2	62.6	166.3	-153.4				
Other Sectors	78br d	347.5	-2.2	421.9	80.5	447.3	-636.5	-210.6	-309.4	-292.2	-680.7	209.6				
Other Investment Liab., n.i.e.	78bi d	.5	.4	-1.1	.7	6.2	-.4	1.1	3.5	-5.4	-181.3	666.9				
Monetary Authorities	78bs d	94.0	174.3	401.7	226.1	352.0	-84.6	64.1	-175.8	-22.5	-272.3	-457.0				
General Government	78bt d	64.3	55.4	47.1	-62.4	301.3	-397.0	-31.2	-41.3	-104.1	-76.2	17.0				
Banks	78bu d	188.7	-232.3	-25.8	-83.9	-212.3	-154.6	-244.6	-95.8	-160.1	-150.9	-17.3				
Other Sectors	78bv d															
Net Errors and Omissions	78ca d	108.9	-29.0	-403.9	219.1	-160.7	-85.4	-39.1	-582.6	-16.2	117.0	-138.1				
Overall Balance	78cb d	59.3	-80.7	-470.7	-163.4	-128.0	-870.6	-731.1	-1,305.2	-885.3	-551.3	15.4				
Reserves and Related Items	79da d	-59.3	80.7	470.7	163.4	128.0	870.6	731.1	1,305.2	885.3	551.3	-15.4				
Reserve Assets	79db d	-53.5	88.6	7.3	-94.6	96.8	64.6	-31.6	20.9	14.9	.4	14.5				
Use of Fund Credit and Loans	79dc d	-5.8	-8.0	-8.7	81.6	14.5	-1.4	-1.2	-54.6	-47.4	25.3	6.7				
Exceptional Financing	79de d	—	—	472.1	176.4	16.7	807.4	763.9	1,338.9	917.8	525.6	-36.6				

Government Finance

Year Ending June 30

Item	Code	1985	1986	1987	1988	1989	1990	1991	1992	1993	1994	1995	1996	1997	1998	1999
Deficit (-) or Surplus	80	....	....	....	....	-110.24	I-198.44	-174.88	I-81.16	-54.74	-99.05	I8.25	....	....		
Revenue	81	....	919.06	742.78	633.08	601.65	I517.51	547.90	I498.47	448.41	385.90	I536.54	....	....		
Grants Received	81z	.12	4.80	—	.12	—	I—	—	I—	—	—	I—	....	....		
Expenditure	82	813.81	....	....	....	707.47	I709.71	719.76	I578.43	501.15	483.49	I525.27	....	....		
Lending Minus Repayments	83	41.36	....	....	....	4.42	I6.24	3.02	I1.20	2.00	1.46	I3.02	....	....		
Financing																
Domestic	84a	....	....	....	....	14.53	I39.68	37.27	I14.27	12.45	-13.09	I-13.17	....	....		
Foreign	85a	....	....	....	....	95.71	I176.01	141.09	I106.73	61.16	120.84	I14.42	....	....		
Adj. to Total Financing	84x	....	....	....	....	—	I-17.25	-3.48	I-39.84	-18.87	-8.70	I-9.50	....	....		
Debt: Domestic	88a	125.88	172.74	228.30	153.87	....	I141.50	356.43	I377.90	374.16	1,179.18	I1419.89	....	....		
Foreign	89a	....	....	....	....		I1054.40	1,275.81	I1496.02	1,852.61	4,084.80	I4343.87	....	....		

National Accounts

Year Ending June 30

Item	Code	1985	1986	1987	1988	1989	1990	1991	1992	1993	1994	1995	1996	1997	1998	1999
Exports of Goods & Services	90c	799.9	997.0	710.7	630.2	726.4	682.3	699.8	649.5	531.3	768.5	1,068.3	1,116.3	1,335.8	....	....
Government Consumption	91f	345.3	360.5	429.0	412.0	434.0	427.6	412.3	387.1	343.0	257.5	299.9	305.0	332.1	....	....
Gross Fixed Capital Formation	93e	939.0	1,018.2	962.3	757.6	638.2	581.2	693.2	457.1	492.5	533.0	597.5	729.3	850.5	....	....
Increase/Decrease(-) in Stocks	93i	16.3	29.4	6.4	4.1	-37.6	16.0	.9	-27.3	29.8	—	—				
Private Consumption	96f	2,466.3	2,642.0	2,658.4	2,482.6	2,428.9	2,298.2	2,079.5	2,292.4	2,233.6	2,538.9	3,018.9	3,354.8	3,537.2	....	....
Imports of Goods & Services	98c	-727.9	-941.0	-844.8	-642.0	-677.0	-671.1	-566.4	-584.4	-504.7	-681.8	-834.5	-950.4	-1,038.2	....	....
Gross Domestic Product (GDP)	99b	3,896.0	4,135.0	3,783.2	3,578.7	3,423.5	3,326.7	3,246.8	3,150.0	3,270.8	3,786.0	4,365.5	4,844.0	5,290.5	5,604.0	....
Net Factor Inc/Pmts(-) Abroad	98.n	....	-245.8	-141.9	-118.0	-154.1	-162.7	-146.8	-174.6	-198.9	-190.0	-168.5	-284.0	-299.0	....	....
Gross National Income (GNI)	99a	....	3,860.4	3,780.0	3,526.5	3,358.9	3,171.5	3,172.4	2,999.7	2,926.6	3,226.0	3,981.7	4,271.0	4,718.4	....	....
Net National Income	99e	....	....	....	....	....	....	....	....	....	....	....	....	....	....	....
GDP Volume 1966 prices	99b.p	....	....	....	....	....	....	....	....	....	....	....	....	....	....	....
GDP Volume 1970 prices	99b.p	....	....	....	....	....	....	....	....	....	....	....	....	....	....	....
GDP Volume 1980 prices	99b.p	2,232.4	2,393.7	....	....	....	....	....	....	....	....	....	....	....		
GDP Volume 1985 Prices	99b.p	....	4,099.6	4,011.4	3,695.9	3,630.5	3,388.4	3,256.6	3,158.7	3,058.3	2,977.6	3,075.9	3,229.7	3,391.1	....	....
GDP Volume (1995=100)	99bv p	124.3	133.3	130.4	120.2	118.0	110.2	105.9	102.7	99.4	96.8	100.0	105.0	110.2	....	....
GDP Deflator (1995=100)	99bi p	71.8	71.1	66.5	68.2	66.4	69.2	70.2	70.3	75.4	89.6	100.0	105.7	109.9	....	....

Midyear Estimates

Item	Code	1985	1986	1987	1988	1989	1990	1991	1992	1993	1994	1995	1996	1997	1998	1999
Population	99z	10.17	10.46	10.82	10.88	11.54	I11.47	11.80	12.13	12.47	12.82	13.28	13.55	13.92	14.31	14.69

(See notes in the back of the book.)

		1970	1971	1972	1973	1974	1975	1976	1977	1978	1979	1980	1981	1982	1983	1984
Exchange Rates														*Canadian Dollars per SDR:*		
Market Rate	aa	1.0112	1.0881	1.0809	1.2013	1.2136	1.1899	1.1725	1.3294	1.5451	1.5388	1.5237	1.3803	1.3562	1.3028	1.2952
														Canadian Dollars per US Dollar:		
Market Rate	ae	1.0112	1.0022	.9956	.9958	.9912	1.0164	1.0092	1.0944	1.1860	1.1681	1.1947	1.1859	1.2294	1.2444	1.3214
Market Rate	rf	1.0449	1.0098	.9899	1.0001	.9780	1.0172	.9860	1.0635	1.1407	1.1714	1.1692	1.1989	1.2337	1.2324	1.2951
														Index Numbers (1995=100):		
Market Rate	ahx	131.5	135.9	138.6	137.2	140.3	134.9	139.2	129.1	120.3	117.1	117.4	114.5	111.3	111.3	106.0
Nominal Effective Exchange Rate	neu	144.5	148.7	149.3	145.2	149.5	143.3	149.7	138.0	121.3	121.3	121.5	121.1	120.4	121.8	117.6
Real Effective Exchange Rate	reu	....	....	....	....	....	95.2	104.2	96.9	105.6	101.9	I 102.1	104.8	107.8	112.7	108.8
Fund Position														*Millions of SDRs:*		
Quota	2f. s	1,100	1,100	1,100	1,100	1,100	1,100	1,100	1,100	1,357	1,357	2,036	2,036	2,036	2,941	2,941
SDRs	1b. s	182	372	465	467	469	474	480	416	401	445	355	150	64	20	74
Reserve Position in the Fund	1c. s	670	333	316	280	433	554	813	701	427	297	454	346	331	672	692
of which: Outstg.Fund Borrowing	2c	120	—	—	—	141	247	247	205	129	26	13	13	13	124	164
International Liquidity													*Millions of US Dollars Unless Otherwise Indicated:*			
Total Reserves minus Gold	1l. d	3,888	4,839	5,216	4,841	4,885	4,426	4,964	3,672	3,557	2,864	3,093	3,537	3,011	3,466	2,491
SDRs	1b. d	182	404	505	564	574	555	558	505	522	586	453	174	71	21	72
Reserve Position in the Fund	1c. d	670	361	343	338	530	648	944	852	557	391	579	402	365	703	678
Foreign Exchange	1d. d	3,037	4,074	4,368	3,940	3,781	3,223	3,462	2,315	2,478	1,888	2,061	2,961	2,575	2,742	1,741
of which: US Dollars	1dxd	3,022	4,061	4,355	3,927	3,768	3,207	3,446	2,299	2,463	1,864	2,038	2,865	2,455	2,373	1,692
Gold (Million Fine Troy Ounces)	1ad	22.59	22.69	21.95	21.95	21.95	21.95	21.62	22.01	22.13	22.18	20.98	20.46	20.26	20.17	20.14
Gold (National Valuation)	1and	791	792	834	927	941	899	879	936	1,009	1,023	937	834	782	739	691
Deposit Money Banks: Assets	7a. d	7,600	6,993	8,203	12,343	13,942	13,852	17,237	18,150	21,657	25,406	35,194	38,160	38,150	40,965	41,212
Liabilities	7b. d	5,501	6,282	8,134	12,632	13,333	14,095	16,475	18,874	24,645	32,042	42,959	61,040	57,738	61,289	61,619
Monetary Authorities														*Billions of Canadian Dollars:*		
Foreign Assets	11	4.73	5.71	6.02	5.74	5.77	5.41	5.90	5.04	5.42	4.54	4.81	5.18	4.66	5.23	4.20
Claims on Central Government	12a	4.14	5.04	5.91	6.88	7.54	8.80	9.47	11.29	13.34	15.17	17.06	18.54	18.61	19.00	19.17
Reserve Money	14	5.28	6.08	7.03	8.16	9.31	10.75	11.76	13.18	14.74	16.01	17.62	18.02	18.82	19.08	19.44
of which: Currency Outside DMBs	14a	3.51	3.95	4.55	5.30	5.99	6.92	7.36	8.13	8.98	9.70	10.45	10.88	11.87	12.92	13.93
Central Government Deposits	16d	4.13	5.05	5.26	4.88	4.70	4.22	4.47	3.68	4.29	3.56	3.82	4.94	4.29	4.50	3.28
Other Items (Net)	17r	-.53	-.38	-.35	-.41	-.70	-.76	-.86	-.53	-.27	.14	.43	.77	.16	.64	.66
Deposit Money Banks														*Billions of Canadian Dollars:*		
Reserves	20	1.70	2.07	2.45	2.94	3.44	4.02	4.48	5.13	5.83	6.63	7.28	7.36	7.15	6.08	5.85
Foreign Assets	21	7.69	7.01	8.17	11.90	13.41	13.61	16.93	19.39	25.24	29.19	41.60	44.19	45.29	49.23	52.17
Claims on Central Government	22a	6.60	7.33	7.13	7.24	8.06	7.73	8.58	9.51	9.75	9.93	9.75	9.85	11.55	16.10	14.72
Claims on Local Government	22b	1.69	1.79	1.86	2.19	2.45	3.04	3.05	2.65	2.64	2.73	2.88	4.32	4.08	3.56	2.96
Claims on Private Sector	22d	21.17	25.86	31.45	38.90	47.92	56.05	67.34	80.03	100.24	120.00	136.54	I 189.24	193.70	185.80	199.78
Demand Deposits	24	11.82	13.59	15.18	16.23	15.90	19.12	18.94	20.92	22.02	21.91	24.32	I 26.00	28.16	31.11	38.86
Savings & Fgn Currency Deposits	25	18.63	19.53	22.93	29.99	39.53	44.82	58.02	67.09	81.36	100.80	110.18	I 140.62	146.34	140.45	143.14
Foreign Liabilities	26c	5.56	6.30	8.10	11.49	11.62	12.27	14.65	18.27	26.73	34.69	48.48	68.85	67.37	73.11	78.04
Central Government Deposits	26d	1.26	2.24	2.41	2.36	4.68	3.66	3.10	4.73	6.47	2.42	4.09	7.14	6.91	6.06	2.80
Other Items (Net)	27r	1.58	2.40	2.44	3.09	3.54	4.59	5.68	5.69	7.13	8.66	10.97	I 12.35	12.99	10.05	12.65
Monetary Survey														*Billions of Canadian Dollars:*		
Foreign Assets (Net)	31n	6.83	6.40	6.05	6.12	7.48	6.71	8.08	6.05	3.87	-1.05	-2.13	-19.63	-17.55	-18.75	-21.85
Domestic Credit	32	28.69	33.24	39.27	48.70	57.55	68.76	81.73	95.74	115.74	142.19	158.48	I 209.88	216.75	213.89	230.55
Claims on Central Govt. (Net)	32an	5.36	5.08	5.37	6.89	6.22	8.64	10.48	12.38	12.34	19.12	18.89	16.32	18.97	24.53	27.82
Claims on Local Government	32b	1.69	1.79	1.86	2.19	2.45	3.04	3.05	2.65	2.64	2.73	2.88	4.32	4.08	3.56	2.96
Claims on Private Sector	32d	21.64	26.37	32.04	39.62	48.88	57.08	68.20	80.72	100.76	120.34	136.71	I 189.24	193.70	185.80	199.78
Money	34	15.34	17.56	19.73	21.55	21.91	26.05	26.31	29.06	31.03	31.62	34.80	I 36.92	40.08	44.22	52.87
Quasi-Money	35	18.63	19.53	22.93	29.99	39.53	44.82	58.02	67.09	81.36	100.80	110.18	I 140.62	146.34	140.45	143.14
Other Items (Net)	37r	1.54	2.56	2.65	3.28	3.59	4.60	5.48	5.64	7.21	8.72	11.37	I 12.71	12.80	10.48	12.70
Money plus Quasi-Money	35l	33.97	37.09	42.67	51.54	61.44	70.87	84.34	96.15	112.39	132.42	144.98	I 177.54	186.41	184.66	196.00
Other Banking Institutions														*Billions of Canadian Dollars:*		
Cash	40	1.10	1.41	2.12	I 1.54	1.91	2.66	2.85	3.36	3.83	4.01	4.04	5.28	6.31	4.86	9.47
Claims on Central Government	42a	....	....	....	.56	.49	.49	.55	.75	.98	1.20	1.93	1.61	2.19	3.39	3.28
Claims on State and Local Govts	42b	1.03	1.33	1.31	I 1.17	1.11	1.10	1.10	1.20	1.19	1.16	1.54	1.43	1.61	1.66	2.26
Claims on Private Sector	42d	11.66	13.31	15.95	I 25.45	30.30	35.08	41.25	48.81	57.81	67.70	74.81	78.70	78.94	87.24	98.42
Demand Deposits	44	.55	.61	.71	I .74	.66	.79	.81	.94	1.04	1.02	1.56	1.86	2.47	3.66	5.29
Time and Savings Deposits	45	16.27	18.95	21.87	I 18.51	22.16	26.60	32.39	39.05	46.94	55.41	63.45	69.46	74.75	81.48	88.31
Money Market Instruments	46aa	....	....	....	2.92	3.55	3.54	3.86	4.18	4.93	5.65	6.27	I 4.31	3.89	5.84	7.50
Bonds	46ab	....	....	....	3.00	3.21	3.70	4.78	5.25	5.60	5.98	5.80	I 4.61	3.68	3.15	3.34
Capital Accounts	47a	2.58	2.73	3.08	I 4.76	5.16	5.95	6.74	7.71	8.69	9.17	9.66	I 6.01	5.67	6.09	5.99
Other Items (Net)	47r	-5.61	-6.24	-6.27	I -1.21	-.93	-1.25	-2.83	-3.01	-3.38	-3.17	-4.42	I .76	-1.39	-3.07	2.99
Banking Survey														*Billions of Canadian Dollars:*		
Foreign Assets (Net)	51n	6.83	6.40	6.05	6.12	7.48	6.71	8.08	6.05	3.87	-1.05	-2.13	-19.63	-17.55	-18.75	-21.85
Domestic Credit	52	41.38	47.89	56.53	I 75.87	89.45	105.42	124.62	146.50	175.73	212.23	236.76	I 291.61	299.49	306.18	334.51
Claims on Central Govt. (Net)	52an	5.36	5.08	5.37	7.45	6.71	9.14	11.03	13.13	13.32	20.31	20.82	17.93	21.16	27.92	31.09
Claims on State and Local Govts	52b	2.72	3.13	3.17	I 3.36	3.56	4.13	4.14	3.84	3.84	3.88	4.41	5.75	5.70	5.22	5.22
Claims on Private Sector	52d	33.30	39.68	47.99	I 65.06	79.18	92.15	109.45	129.53	158.57	188.04	211.53	I 267.93	272.64	273.04	298.20
Liquid Liabilities	55l	49.69	55.24	63.12	I 69.26	82.35	95.60	114.68	132.79	156.54	184.84	205.96	I 243.58	257.31	264.95	280.14
Money Market Instruments	56aa	....	....	....	2.92	3.55	3.54	3.86	4.18	4.93	5.65	6.27	I 4.31	3.89	5.84	7.50
Bonds	56ab	....	....	....	3.00	3.21	3.70	4.78	5.25	5.60	5.98	5.80	I 4.61	3.68	3.15	3.34
Other Items (Net)	57r	-1.49	-.96	-.54	I 6.82	7.82	9.29	9.39	10.34	12.52	14.72	16.61	I 19.48	17.07	13.49	21.68

	1985	1986	1987	1988	1989	1990	1991	1992	1993	1994	1995	1996	1997	1998	1999		Code
End of Period																**Exchange Rates**	
	1.5350	1.6886	1.8440	1.6050	1.5215	1.6507	1.6530	1.7478	1.8186	2.0479	2.0294	1.9694	1.9282	2.1550	1.9809	Market Rate	aa
End of Period (ae) Period Average (rf)																	
	1.3975	1.3805	1.2998	1.1927	1.1578	1.1603	1.1556	1.2711	1.3240	1.4028	1.3652	1.3696	1.4291	1.5305	1.4433	Market Rate	ae
	1.3655	1.3895	1.3260	1.2307	1.1840	1.1668	1.1457	1.2087	1.2901	1.3656	1.3724	1.3635	1.3846	1.4835	1.4857	Market Rate	rf
Period Averages																	
	100.5	98.7	103.5	111.5	115.9	117.6	119.8	113.6	106.4	100.5	100.0	100.6	99.1	92.6	92.4	Market Rate	ahx
	112.1	105.0	107.2	114.2	120.2	120.5	122.5	115.3	108.7	102.0	100.0	101.7	101.9	95.8	95.2	Nominal Effective Exchange Rate	neu
	104.4	97.7	101.4	108.5	117.6	122.3	125.1	119.3	108.9	100.5	100.0	99.7	101.0	96.0	....	Real Effective Exchange Rate	reu
End of Period																**Fund Position**	
	2,941	2,941	2,941	2,941	2,941	2,941	2,941	4,320	4,320	4,320	4,320	4,320	4,320	4,320	6,369	Quota	2f. s
	198	202	281	1,017	1,048	1,072	1,106	756	773	786	792	812	834	780	384	SDRs	1b. s
	647	561	466	375	402	364	414	735	690	629	836	853	1,167	1,633	2,308	Reserve Position in the Fund	1c. s
	161	155	120	30	—	—	—	—	—	—	—	—	—	—	204	of which: Outstg.Fund Borrowing	2c
End of Period																**International Liquidity**	
	2,503	3,251	7,277	15,391	16,055	17,845	16,252	11,431	12,481	12,286	15,049	20,422	17,823	23,308	28,126	Total Reserves minus Gold	1l. d
	218	247	399	1,369	1,377	1,526	1,582	1,039	1,062	1,148	1,177	1,168	1,126	1,098	527	SDRs	1b. d
	711	686	661	505	528	517	592	1,011	948	919	1,243	1,226	1,575	2,299	3,168	Reserve Position in the Fund	1c. d
	1,574	2,318	6,218	13,517	14,150	15,802	14,079	9,382	10,471	10,219	12,629	18,028	15,122	19,911	24,432	Foreign Exchange	1d. d
	1,524	2,274	6,163	12,608	11,489	11,476	9,440	7,864	9,950	9,693	12,117	17,521	14,630	15,907	18,838	of which: US Dollars	1dx d
	20.11	19.72	18.52	17.14	16.10	14.76	12.96	9.94	6.05	3.89	3.41	3.09	3.09	2.49	1.81	Gold (Million Fine Troy Ounces)	1ad
	773	845	920	807	741	735	649	478	292	198	178	155	146	122	524	Gold (National Valuation)	1and
	44,169	50,745	50,734	46,804	48,819	52,070	46,033	46,851	41,114	54,614	64,061	76,144	84,432	86,456	79,191	Deposit Money Banks: Assets	7a. d
	64,637	68,905	71,734	69,480	70,807	77,946	76,711	73,613	67,151	80,507	77,143	87,951	108,978	111,723	95,543	Liabilities	7b. d
End of Period																**Monetary Authorities**	
	4.58	5.65	10.65	19.32	19.45	21.56	19.53	15.14	16.91	17.51	20.79	28.18	25.68	35.86	40.72	Foreign Assets	11
	17.55	21.06	23.39	24.10	25.04	25.37	26.38	27.83	29.63	30.41	30.09	31.03	31.81	32.41	41.68	Claims on Central Government	12a
	20.56	22.15	24.11	25.32	26.32	26.92	28.64	29.31	30.93	31.65	32.08	33.46	34.58	36.86	45.83	Reserve Money	14
	15.06	16.02	17.39	18.79	20.10	20.89	22.07	23.60	25.57	27.30	27.99	28.78	30.15	32.32	38.72	of which: Currency Outside DMBs	14a
	3.96	4.50	9.43	17.57	17.47	19.41	17.14	12.58	14.41	15.01	17.69	25.01	22.09	30.83	35.85	Central Government Deposits	16d
	-2.39	.06	.50	.53	.70	.61	.14	1.08	1.20	1.26	1.11	.75	.82	.57	.72	Other Items (Net)	17r
End of Period																**Deposit Money Banks**	
	5.68	6.24	6.77	6.71	6.29	6.58	7.15	5.88	5.92	5.04	4.67	5.24	4.79	4.89	8.56	Reserves	20
	59.91	68.41	63.92	52.88	53.09	57.13	50.81	57.44	51.74	73.94	83.18	97.07	109.86	122.51	105.26	Foreign Assets	21
	14.84	17.40	15.18	20.94	20.58	24.47	38.35	50.68	69.59	78.33	84.20	81.50	72.55	71.89	70.75	Claims on Central Government	22a
	3.21	2.59	3.84	3.99	4.53	4.91	7.78	8.90	9.67	13.15	13.01	12.91	14.80	15.24	15.95	Claims on Local Government	22b
	216.85	223.58	244.52	272.27	306.67	334.55	348.75	372.22	415.63	450.77	474.89	531.94	607.32	617.22	643.28	Claims on Private Sector	22d
	54.98	64.31	67.91	71.54	75.47	75.92	79.02	84.73	91.87	97.84	109.89	126.60	139.61	147.08	160.95	Demand Deposits	24
	137.07	142.03	156.35	177.06	207.78	230.30	241.87	266.81	301.19	326.97	342.32	348.69	377.66	380.37	388.15	Savings & Fgn Currency Deposits	25
	86.57	90.46	87.33	76.73	74.38	82.41	81.13	87.68	82.23	105.94	97.52	113.51	146.31	160.94	127.04	Foreign Liabilities	26c
	4.35	2.05	1.82	1.84	2.08	3.23	2.08	1.41	2.44	2.78	6.19	4.22	6.63	5.89	11.59	Central Government Deposits	26d
	17.52	19.39	20.82	29.62	31.45	35.77	48.74	54.50	74.83	87.70	104.04	135.63	139.12	137.48	156.00	Other Items (Net)	27r
End of Period																**Monetary Survey**	
	-22.20	-16.48	-13.11	-4.75	-2.14	-4.01	-11.22	-15.49	-13.94	-14.99	5.98	11.55	-10.91	-2.67	18.67	Foreign Assets (Net)	31n
	244.14	258.08	275.68	301.89	337.28	366.66	402.05	445.64	507.67	554.86	578.31	628.15	697.75	700.04	724.22	Domestic Credit	32
	24.08	31.91	27.32	25.63	26.07	27.21	45.52	64.52	82.36	90.94	90.41	83.30	75.64	67.58	64.99	Claims on Central Govt. (Net)	32an
	3.21	2.59	3.84	3.99	4.53	4.91	7.78	8.90	9.67	13.15	13.01	12.91	14.80	15.24	15.95	Claims on Local Government	32b
	216.85	223.58	244.52	272.27	306.67	334.55	348.75	372.22	415.63	450.77	474.89	531.94	607.32	617.22	643.28	Claims on Private Sector	32d
	70.30	80.65	85.66	90.67	95.90	97.06	101.35	108.54	117.58	125.32	138.07	155.56	169.92	179.62	199.95	Money	34
	137.07	142.03	156.35	177.06	207.78	230.30	241.87	266.81	301.19	326.97	342.32	348.69	377.66	380.37	388.15	Quasi-Money	35
	14.58	18.93	20.56	29.40	31.45	35.29	47.61	54.80	74.96	87.58	103.90	135.45	139.27	137.39	154.79	Other Items (Net)	37r
	207.37	222.68	242.01	267.74	303.68	327.36	343.22	375.35	418.77	452.29	480.40	504.25	547.57	559.99	588.09	Money plus Quasi-Money	35l
End of Period																**Other Banking Institutions**	
	9.44	11.07	11.87	12.71	13.50	14.54	16.13	16.91	15.11	15.07	17.14	16.63	15.67	18.19	20.95	Cash	40
	3.50	5.23	3.87	4.84	6.87	8.49	9.25	8.96	7.55	6.74	7.41	7.58	5.18	5.47	6.49	Claims on Central Government	42a
	1.98	1.98	1.85	2.47	2.02	2.28	2.48	3.04	2.13	1.63	1.48	1.33	1.26	.94	.84	Claims on State and Local Govts	42b
	110.83	123.81	142.37	162.44	184.40	196.15	197.83	196.71	166.38	161.64	161.55	168.30	165.10	172.58	178.69	Claims on Private Sector	42d
	7.77	8.43	8.92	9.87	11.51	11.43	11.62	11.45	9.47	8.96	8.37	8.69	7.87	8.07	8.11	Demand Deposits	44
	95.27	108.63	121.48	140.20	158.62	173.21	177.00	178.95	148.27	141.95	143.53	145.42	131.64	136.34	141.39	Time and Savings Deposits	45
	8.06	9.26	9.62	9.17	11.00	10.14	9.18	7.73	7.00	9.51	10.17	13.63	18.34	20.86	20.43	Money Market Instruments	46aa
	4.13	5.35	6.89	8.38	8.27	9.25	9.73	8.94	8.83	9.45	11.12	11.41	16.83	23.41	23.82	Bonds	46ab
	6.07	6.34	7.71	8.94	10.12	11.03	11.45	11.22	10.27	9.40	9.54	9.84	9.60	9.91	10.18	Capital Accounts	47a
	4.45	4.08	5.34	5.90	7.28	6.39	6.72	7.32	7.33	5.79	4.85	4.85	2.93	-1.41	3.04	Other Items (Net)	47r
End of Period																**Banking Survey**	
	-22.20	-16.48	-13.11	-4.75	-2.14	-4.01	-11.22	-15.49	-13.94	-14.99	5.98	11.55	-10.91	-2.67	18.67	Foreign Assets (Net)	51n
	360.44	389.10	423.76	471.64	530.57	573.58	611.62	654.34	683.73	724.87	748.75	805.36	869.29	879.02	910.23	Domestic Credit	52
	27.58	37.14	31.18	30.47	32.94	35.70	54.77	73.47	89.91	97.68	97.82	90.88	80.82	73.05	71.48	Claims on Central Govt. (Net)	52an
	5.19	4.56	5.69	6.46	6.56	7.19	10.27	11.95	11.80	14.79	14.49	14.23	16.06	16.18	16.79	Claims on State and Local Govts	52b
	327.67	347.40	386.89	434.71	491.07	530.69	546.58	568.92	582.01	612.41	636.44	700.24	772.41	789.80	821.97	Claims on Private Sector	52d
	300.97	328.67	360.53	405.10	460.30	497.46	515.70	548.84	561.40	588.14	615.16	641.72	671.41	686.20	716.64	Liquid Liabilities	55l
	8.06	9.26	9.62	9.17	11.00	10.14	9.18	7.73	7.00	9.51	10.17	13.63	18.34	20.86	20.43	Money Market Instruments	56aa
	4.13	5.35	6.89	8.38	8.27	9.25	9.73	8.94	8.83	9.45	11.12	11.41	16.83	23.41	23.82	Bonds	56ab
	25.09	29.34	33.61	44.24	48.86	52.70	65.78	73.35	92.55	102.78	118.29	150.14	151.81	145.88	168.02	Other Items (Net)	57r

Canada

156

	1970	1971	1972	1973	1974	1975	1976	1977	1978	1979	1980	1981	1982	1983	1984
Nonbank Financial Institutions													*Millions of Canadian Dollars:*		
Cash ......40.. s	.13	.13	.21	.19	.17	.27	.32	.44	.44	.57	.69	1.14	1.38	.95	1.15
Claims on Central Government ......42a. s	.50	.49	.55	.48	.51	.55	.75	.99	1.65	2.60	3.09	3.48	4.46	5.38	7.74
Claims on Local Government ......42b. s	1.78	1.86	2.01	2.11	2.14	2.25	2.61	2.90	3.19	3.29	3.50	4.17	4.63	5.20	6.53
Claims on Private Sector ......42d. s	11.29	12.07	13.90	15.36	16.70	18.69	20.46	22.83	25.30	27.99	31.95	34.94	37.14	40.71	42.39
Incr.in Total Assets(Within Per.) ......49z. s	.63	2.07	1.39	1.64	1.61	2.44	2.66	3.21	3.96	4.50	5.49	4.97	5.21	6.08	6.68
Interest Rates													*Percent Per Annum*		
Bank Rate (End of Period) 60	6.00	4.75	4.75	7.25	8.75	9.00	8.50	7.50	10.75	14.00	17.26	14.66	10.26	10.04	10.16
Money Market Rate 60b	....	....	....	....	....	9.23	8.45	5.88	6.61	13.21	18.96	12.82	10.38	9.07	10.05
Corporate Paper Rate 60bc	7.34	4.51	5.10	7.45	10.51	7.94	9.17	7.48	8.83	12.07	13.15	18.33	14.15	9.45	11.19
Treasury Bill Rate 60c	5.99	3.56	3.56	5.47	7.82	7.40	8.87	7.33	8.68	11.69	12.79	17.72	13.66	9.31	11.06
Deposit Rate 60l	....	4.75	5.36	6.87	9.97	7.78	9.31	7.53	8.83	12.05	12.87	18.16	13.74	7.91	10.06
Lending Rate 60p	8.17	6.48	6.00	7.65	10.75	9.42	10.04	8.50	9.69	12.90	14.25	19.29	15.81	11.17	12.06
Govt. Bond Yield: Med.-Term 61a	7.11	5.56	6.26	6.98	8.12	7.72	8.35	7.90	9.00	10.42	12.37	15.68	14.00	10.61	11.91
Long-Term 61	7.91	6.95	7.23	7.56	8.90	9.04	9.18	8.70	9.27	10.21	12.48	15.22	14.26	11.79	12.75
Prices, Production, Labor													*Index Numbers (1995=100):*		
Industrial Share Prices 62	20.5	21.8	25.7	27.4	22.9	22.6	23.3	22.8	26.1	35.6	47.9	48.7	37.0	53.4	52.8
Prices: Industry Selling 63	23.4	23.8	24.9	27.7	32.9	36.6	38.5	41.5	45.4	52.0	58.9	64.9	69.3	71.7	74.9
Consumer Prices 64	23.2	23.9	25.0	26.9	29.8	33.1	35.6	38.4	41.8	45.6	50.3	I 56.6	62.7	66.3	69.2
Wages: Hourly Earnings (Mfg) 65ey	17.9	19.5	21.0	22.9	26.0	30.0	34.2	37.9	40.6	44.2	48.6	54.5	60.9	I 65.1	69.0
Industrial Production ......66.. c	51.6	I 54.4	58.5	64.3	66.5	62.5	65.9	67.4	70.2	I 74.3	71.8	73.3	66.1	70.4	78.9
Gold Production 66kr	50.6	47.5	43.6	41.0	35.7	34.1	35.5	36.4	36.4	34.5	33.1	31.8	43.7	49.6	56.3
Manufacturing Employment 67ey	109.0	108.0	109.9	115.3	118.8	112.2	113.7	112.2	113.3	116.7	114.5	115.3	104.5	I 101.5	98.4
													Number in Thousands:		
Labor Force 67d	....	....	....	....	....	....	....	....	....	....	....	....	....	....	....
Employment 67e	....	....	....	....	....	....	....	....	....	....	....	....	....	....	....
Unemployment 67c	....	....	....	....	....	....	....	....	....	....	....	....	....	....	....
Unemployment Rate (%) 67r	....	....	....	....	....	....	....	....	....	....	....	....	....	....	....
International Transactions													*Millions of Canadian Dollars*		
Exports 70	17,527	18,552	20,955	26,438	33,743	34,662	40,015	46,337	55,311	68,269	79,208	87,164	87,911	94,603	116,965
Imports, f.o.b. 71.v	14,454	16,135	19,231	24,027	32,674	35,761	38,619	43,634	51,613	64,756	71,353	81,867	69,892	77,855	98,339
													1995=100		
Volume of Exports 72	24.6	25.9	28.4	31.4	30.2	28.0	31.4	34.2	37.6	38.3	37.8	I 38.8	38.6	41.4	49.1
Volume of Imports 73	22.0	24.1	28.2	32.8	36.1	34.1	36.8	37.0	38.2	42.4	40.0	I 41.1	34.4	38.2	45.7
Unit Value of Exports 74	25.0	25.2	26.1	29.9	39.7	43.9	44.5	47.7	51.9	62.8	73.0	I 77.6	78.2	78.0	81.6
Unit Value of Imports 75	21.9	22.3	22.8	24.5	30.3	I 34.8	35.7	40.9	46.3	54.4	65.6	74.9	78.0	77.6	82.1
Balance of Payments													*Millions of US Dollars:*		
Current Account, n.i.e. ......78al d	494	–1,039	–2,405	–2,056	–4,570	–8,196	–7,639	–7,003	–8,188	–8,385	–6,088	–12,505	1,816	–2,543	–1,368
Goods: Exports f.o.b. ......78aa d	16,731	18,175	21,177	26,500	34,277	33,780	39,696	42,883	47,942	57,300	67,532	71,931	70,259	75,376	89,283
Goods: Imports f.o.b. ......78ab d	–13,682	–15,628	–19,041	–23,357	–32,518	–34,371	–38,144	–39,990	–43,876	–53,379	–59,593	–66,466	–55,162	–61,200	–73,672
Trade Balance ......78ac d	3,049	2,548	2,135	3,144	1,759	–591	1,553	2,893	4,066	3,921	7,939	5,464	15,097	14,176	15,611
Services: Credit ......78ad d	2,477	2,642	2,789	3,233	4,163	4,313	5,017	5,002	5,469	6,495	7,445	8,385	8,036	8,750	9,235
Services: Debit ......78ae d	–3,301	–3,590	–3,924	–4,578	–5,734	–6,797	–8,086	–8,405	–8,868	–9,232	–10,666	–11,964	–11,628	–12,545	–13,147
Balance on Goods & Services ......78af d	2,224	1,600	1,000	1,798	189	–3,076	–1,516	–510	667	1,184	4,717	1,886	11,505	10,381	11,699
Income: Credit ......78ag d	1,922	1,689	1,271	2,723	3,926	3,492	3,266	3,981	4,312	7,679	7,868	9,157	11,283	8,137	10,868
Income: Debit ......78ah d	–3,540	–4,259	–4,559	–6,477	–8,583	–8,357	–9,205	–10,253	–12,862	–17,055	–18,631	–23,522	–20,846	–20,724	–23,278
Balance on Gds, Serv. & Inc. ......78ai d	606	–970	–2,288	–1,956	–4,468	–7,941	–7,455	–6,782	–7,883	–8,191	–6,046	–12,480	1,942	–2,205	–711
Current Transfers, n.i.e.: Credit ......78aj d	366	436	465	539	681	709	787	813	844	1,037	1,310	1,389	1,463	1,362	1,296
Current Transfers: Debit ......78ak d	–479	–505	–583	–639	–783	–965	–971	–1,033	–1,149	–1,230	–1,352	–1,414	–1,589	–1,700	–1,954
Capital Account, n.i.e. ......78bc d	182	245	284	345	550	486	530	429	111	465	424	527	1,262	1,085	1,058
Capital Account: Credit ......78ba d	374	428	448	520	717	653	737	649	541	682	552	658	1,407	1,241	1,208
Capital Account: Debit ......78bb d	–191	–183	–164	–176	–167	–167	–207	–220	–429	–218	–129	–131	–145	–155	–149
Financial Account, n.i.e. ......78bj d	1,035	2,856	3,830	1,995	4,934	7,873	10,699	6,621	5,084	9,169	5,008	16,663	–2,786	4,187	4,092
Direct Investment Abroad ......78bd d	–929	–458	–80	–1,166	–1,357	–1,249	–1,003	–1,631	–2,277	–3,829	–4,093	–5,546	–2,371	–2,629	–3,663
Dir. Invest. in Rep. Econ., n.i.e. ......78be d	1,826	2,273	2,112	3,185	3,723	3,386	2,451	3,372	3,740	5,308	5,813	664	90	1,999	4,754
Portfolio Investment Assets ......78bf d	59	194	246	71	49	–20	79	207	25	–496	–154	–24	–439	–1,035	–1,600
Equity Securities ......78bk d	79	218	275	118	69	40	21	228	67	–522	–97	2	–250	–669	–559
Debt Securities ......78bl d	–20	–25	–29	–48	–20	–60	58	–21	–42	27	–57	–26	–189	–366	–1,040
Portfolio Investment Liab., n.i.e. ......78bg d	694	183	1,211	742	1,971	4,797	9,823	5,383	2,544	3,370	5,388	10,126	8,511	5,784	7,369
Equity Securities ......78bm d	–76	–124	–24	13	–142	85	–57	–97	–235	451	1,283	–528	–250	740	117
Debt Securities ......78bn d	770	307	1,235	729	2,112	4,712	9,880	5,481	2,779	2,919	4,106	10,655	8,761	5,044	7,252
Financial Derivatives Assets ......78bw d	....	....	....	....	....	....	....	....	....	....	....	....	....	....	....
Financial Derivatives Liabilities ......78bx d	....	....	....	....	....	....	....	....	....	....	....	....	....	....	....
Other Investment Assets ......78bh d	–1,869	–840	–2,162	–5,359	–1,944	–1,031	–4,899	–4,052	–6,641	–6,859	–13,962	–12,770	–5,498	–3,943	–5,481
Monetary Authorities ......78bo d	....	....	....	....	....	....	....	....	....	....	....	....	....	....	....
General Government ......78bp d	–74	–129	–214	–227	–318	–333	–422	–472	–209	–442	–410	–491	–364	–502	–480
Banks ......78bq d	–1,391	396	–1,273	–3,880	–1,501	116	–3,262	–880	–3,479	–4,010	–10,293	–4,432	–108	–3,525	–1,610
Other Sectors ......78br d	–404	–1,107	–675	–1,252	–124	–814	–1,215	–2,700	–2,953	–2,406	–3,260	–7,847	–5,025	84	–3,391
Other Investment Liab., n.i.e. ......78bi d	1,253	1,504	2,502	4,523	2,492	1,990	4,248	3,341	7,693	11,674	12,016	24,213	–3,079	4,011	2,713
Monetary Authorities ......78bs d	....	....	....	....	....	....	....	....	....	....	....	....	....	....	....
General Government ......78bt d	–91	25	8	63	98	–49	118	569	1,686	–405	509	–85	–492	–117	–1
Banks ......78bu d	1,142	875	1,981	3,544	687	947	2,463	2,268	4,727	9,022	10,920	18,739	–2,893	3,590	2,242
Other Sectors ......78bv d	202	604	513	916	1,708	1,091	1,667	504	1,280	3,057	587	5,559	306	538	471
Net Errors and Omissions ......78ca d	–182	–1,290	–1,459	–751	–889	–560	–3,021	–1,403	–2,118	–1,133	121	–3,712	–1,880	–2,737	–5,591
Overall Balance ......78cb d	1,528	772	249	–468	25	–398	569	–1,356	–5,111	116	–536	973	–1,588	–7	–1,809
Reserves and Related Items ......79da d	–1,528	–772	–249	468	–25	398	–569	1,356	5,111	–116	536	–973	1,588	7	1,809
Reserve Assets ......79db d	–1,528	–772	–249	468	–25	398	–569	1,356	183	900	–84	–387	496	–490	854
Use of Fund Credit and Loans ......79dc d	—	—	—	—	—	—	—	—	—	—	—	—	—	—	—
Exceptional Financing ......79de d	....	....	....	....	....	....	....	....	4,928	–1,015	620	–586	1,092	497	956

	Code	1985	1986	1987	1988	1989	1990	1991	1992	1993	1994	1995	1996	1997	1998	1999
Nonbank Financial Institutions		*End of Period*														
Cash	40.. *s*	1.36	1.45	....	....	....	....	....	....	....	....	....	....	....	....	....
Claims on Central Government	42a. *s*	10.33	10.18	....	....	....	....	....	....	....	....	....	....	....	....	....
Claims on Local Government	42b. *s*	7.43	7.99	....	....	....	....	....	....	....	....	....	....	....	....	....
Claims on Private Sector	42d. *s*	47.34	53.45	....	....	....	....	....	....	....	....	....	....	....	....	....
Incr.in Total Assets(Within Per.)	49z. *s*	9.06	7.66	....	....	....	....	....	....	....	....	....	....	....	....	....
Interest Rates		*Percent Per Annum*														
Bank Rate *(End of Period)*	60	9.49	8.49	8.66	11.17	12.47	11.78	7.67	7.36	4.11	7.43	5.79	3.25	4.50	5.25	5.00
Money Market Rate	60b	9.84	8.16	8.50	10.35	12.06	11.62	7.40	6.79	3.79	5.54	5.71	3.01	4.34	5.11	4.76
Corporate Paper Rate	60bc	9.56	9.16	8.38	9.67	12.21	13.03	8.91	6.74	4.97	5.66	7.22	4.35	3.61	5.05	4.94
Treasury Bill Rate	60c	9.43	8.97	8.15	9.48	12.05	12.81	8.73	6.59	4.84	5.54	6.89	4.21	3.26	4.73	4.72
Deposit Rate	60l	8.40	8.25	7.67	9.54	12.09	12.81	8.62	6.67	4.92	5.59	7.15	4.33	3.59	5.03	4.91
Lending Rate	60p	10.58	10.52	9.52	10.83	13.33	14.06	9.94	7.48	5.94	6.88	8.65	6.06	4.96	6.60	6.44
Govt. Bond Yield: Med.-Term	61a	10.39	9.21	9.42	9.77	10.20	11.19	9.16	7.43	6.46	7.79	7.64	6.21	5.33	5.16	5.50
Long-Term	61	11.04	9.52	9.95	10.22	9.92	10.85	9.76	8.77	7.85	8.63	8.28	7.50	6.42	5.47	5.69
Prices, Production, Labor		*Period Averages*														
Industrial Share Prices	62	61.2	67.9	80.5	74.5	85.7	77.2	78.2	76.7	88.1	96.6	100.0	118.8	145.7	152.4	159.2
Prices: Industry Selling	63	77.0	77.6	79.8	83.2	84.9	85.2	84.3	84.7	87.8	93.1	100.0	100.4	101.3	101.2	102.9
Consumer Prices	64	71.9	74.9	78.2	81.3	85.4	89.5	94.5	95.9	97.7	97.9	I 100.0	101.6	103.2	104.2	106.0
Wages: Hourly Earnings (Mfg)	65ey	71.6	73.9	75.8	79.3	83.6	88.4	93.3	95.6	97.7	98.6	100.0	103.2	104.1	106.3	106.5
Industrial Production	66.. c	83.3	I 83.3	87.3	91.9	91.8	88.8	85.0	I 86.0	89.9	95.7	100.0	101.7	107.3	109.8	114.7
Gold Production	66kr	59.1	69.5	78.2	91.0	106.3	111.0	115.6	105.7	100.9	97.8	100.0	....	....	....	....
Manufacturing Employment	67ey	100.4	102.5	112.0	113.1	113.7	105.7	92.6	93.5	93.2	96.1	100.0	102.4	106.1	110.3	112.8
		Period Averages														
Labor Force	67d	....	....	....	....	....	....	....	....	13,946	14,832	14,928	15,145	15,354	15,632	....
Employment	67e	11,742	12,095	12,422	12,819	13,086	13,165	12,916	12,842	13,015	13,292	I 13,506	13,676	13,941	14,326	....
Unemployment	67c	1,381	1,283	1,208	1,082	1,065	1,164	1,492	1,640	1,649	1,541	I 1,422	1,469	1,414	1,305	1,216
Unemployment Rate (%)	67r	10.5	9.6	8.9	7.8	7.5	8.1	10.4	11.3	11.2	10.4	I 9.6	9.7	9.2	8.3	....
International Transactions		*Millions of Canadian Dollars*														
Exports	70	124,249	125,497	130,089	144,038	144,248	148,912	145,658	162,596	187,346	225,908	263,697	274,884	296,928	317,903	354,108
Imports, f.o.b.	71.v	107,477	115,887	119,725	135,416	138,406	140,329	139,427	152,435	175,049	206,626	224,977	232,672	271,422	298,076	319,008
		1995=100														
Volume of Exports	72	52.3	I 54.7	56.6	61.9	62.7	65.7	66.4	I 72.2	81.1	90.8	100.0	106.1	114.8	124.2	137.3
Volume of Imports	73	50.4	I 54.5	57.9	66.1	69.7	69.8	71.4	I 76.4	83.5	92.8	100.0	105.3	125.0	130.5	145.0
Unit Value of Exports	74	82.3	I 80.6	82.0	82.4	84.4	83.8	80.8	I 82.7	86.5	92.6	100.0	100.6	100.2	100.9	103.0
Unit Value of Imports	75	84.7	I 84.4	83.3	81.9	82.2	83.7	82.5	I 86.0	90.7	96.4	100.0	99.6	100.3	105.0	105.5
Balance of Payments		*Minus Sign Indicates Debit*														
Current Account, n.i.e.	78al *d*	-5,734	-11,157	-13,430	-14,818	-21,769	-19,764	-22,345	-21,160	-21,822	-13,024	-4,328	3,378	-10,065	-11,133	-2,273
Goods: Exports f.o.b.	78aa *d*	89,913	90,097	99,187	116,693	124,130	130,328	128,914	135,153	147,418	166,990	193,373	205,443	217,739	217,406	242,820
Goods: Imports f.o.b.	78ab *d*	-78,045	-82,915	-90,017	-107,843	-117,569	-120,815	-122,788	-127,772	-137,281	-152,155	-167,517	-174,352	-200,516	-204,631	-220,064
Trade Balance	78ac *d*	11,867	7,182	9,170	8,849	6,560	9,513	6,126	7,381	10,136	14,834	25,855	31,091	17,223	12,775	22,756
Services: Credit	78ad *d*	9,827	11,806	13,083	15,680	17,550	19,210	20,368	20,785	21,868	23,958	26,128	29,243	31,407	32,907	34,854
Services: Debit	78ae *d*	-13,912	-15,858	-17,646	-21,024	-24,425	-28,303	-30,326	-30,868	-32,446	-32,530	-33,473	-35,906	-38,182	-37,660	-38,921
Balance on Goods & Services	78af *d*	7,782	3,130	4,607	3,505	-315	419	-3,832	-2,702	-442	6,262	18,510	24,428	10,448	8,022	18,690
Income: Credit	78ag *d*	9,837	8,036	8,831	13,232	13,432	15,072	12,936	11,413	10,697	15,443	18,888	19,204	22,501	20,772	21,283
Income: Debit	78ah *d*	-22,653	-22,046	-25,982	-30,706	-33,915	-34,460	-30,334	-28,925	-31,499	-34,382	-41,609	-40,755	-43,564	-40,435	-42,923
Balance on Gds, Serv. & Inc.	78ai *d*	-5,033	-10,880	-12,544	-13,968	-20,798	-18,968	-21,230	-20,214	-21,243	-12,676	-4,211	2,877	-10,615	-11,641	-2,950
Current Transfers, n.i.e.: Credit	78aj *d*	1,234	1,868	1,668	2,219	2,227	2,530	2,537	2,564	2,593	2,625	2,878	3,594	3,653	3,342	3,654
Current Transfers: Debit	78ak *d*	-1,935	-2,145	-2,554	-3,068	-3,198	-3,326	-3,652	-3,510	-3,172	-2,973	-2,995	-3,092	-3,104	-2,834	-2,978
Capital Account, n.i.e.	78bc *d*	1,066	1,313	2,803	3,924	4,629	5,331	5,596	7,105	8,292	7,498	4,950	5,833	5,429	3,335	3,428
Capital Account, n.i.e.: Credit	78ba *d*	1,288	1,551	3,076	4,324	5,096	6,203	6,069	7,470	8,908	7,876	5,416	6,262	5,862	3,794	3,887
Capital Account: Debit	78bb *d*	-223	-238	-272	-400	-467	-872	-473	-365	-617	-378	-466	-429	-433	-459	-459
Financial Account, n.i.e.	78bj *d*	5,650	10,801	16,280	18,716	19,395	17,283	15,068	6,244	19,505	5,159	-1,277	-9,277	3,835	9,397	-1,868
Direct Investment Abroad	78bd *d*	-3,864	-3,504	-7,121	-6,221	-5,270	-5,229	-5,837	-3,547	-5,711	-9,303	-11,490	-13,107	-22,521	-31,041	-17,842
Dir. Invest. in Rep. Econ., n.i.e.	78be *d*	1,357	2,849	8,115	6,071	6,027	7,581	2,874	4,777	4,749	8,224	9,319	9,635	11,758	21,677	25,129
Portfolio Investment Assets	78bf *d*	-1,400	-2,106	-2,222	-3,659	-4,625	-2,239	-10,179	-9,800	-13,784	-6,587	-5,328	-14,183	-8,568	-15,106	-15,443
Equity Securities	78bk *d*	-855	-1,974	-1,561	-3,588	-3,269	-2,177	-8,736	-8,586	-9,886	-6,898	-4,570	-12,661	-3,777	-10,428	-13,851
Debt Securities	78bl *d*	-545	-132	-661	-70	-1,356	-62	-1,442	-1,214	-3,898	311	-759	-1,522	-4,792	-4,678	-1,591
Portfolio Investment Liab., n.i.e.	78bg *d*	7,681	17,853	12,405	18,671	19,674	15,964	27,527	20,506	41,352	17,155	18,402	13,718	11,487	16,973	3,686
Equity Securities	78bm *d*	1,133	1,342	4,974	-1,935	3,287	-1,502	-856	830	9,334	4,718	-3,077	5,900	5,461	9,173	9,534
Debt Securities	78bn *d*	6,548	16,512	7,431	20,606	16,386	17,466	28,383	19,676	32,018	12,437	21,479	7,818	6,026	7,800	-5,848
Financial Derivatives Assets	78bw *d*	....	....	....	....	....	....	....	....	....	....	....	....	....	....	....
Financial Derivatives Liabilities	78bx *d*	....	....	....	....	....	....	....	....	....	....	....	....	....	....	....
Other Investment Assets	78bh *d*	-230	-8,196	-162	3,668	-6,152	-8,442	934	-3,536	-415	-20,378	-8,328	-21,064	-16,282	10,253	8,396
Monetary Authorities	78bo *d*	....	....	....	....	....	....	....	....	....	....	....	....	....	....	....
General Government	78bp *d*	-479	-477	-324	-293	-361	193	-359	-403	-230	-436	-336	-119	-530	-597	-331
Banks	78bq *d*	-909	-6,247	1,121	5,599	-2,972	-3,936	5,852	-59	5,848	-12,575	-8,314	-13,847	-5,419	969	13,378
Other Sectors	78br *d*	1,158	-1,473	-960	-1,638	-2,820	-4,699	-4,559	-3,074	-6,033	-7,366	322	-7,098	-10,333	9,881	-4,651
Other Investment Liab., n.i.e.	78bi *d*	2,107	3,906	5,266	185	9,742	9,648	-251	-2,156	-6,686	16,049	-3,852	15,724	27,962	6,641	-5,796
Monetary Authorities	78bs *d*	—	—	—	—	—	—	—	—	—	—	—	—	—	—	—
General Government	78bt *d*	1,570	-1,248	556	-860	-770	-389	-109	-278	-179	586	-484	-508	-321	-269	-313
Banks	78bu *d*	1,628	4,865	1,716	-3,373	1,951	6,603	-2,075	-3,202	-6,649	15,233	-4,579	12,707	24,630	2,701	-13,004
Other Sectors	78bv *d*	-1,091	289	2,994	4,418	8,561	3,434	1,933	1,324	142	230	1,211	3,525	3,652	4,208	7,522
Net Errors and Omissions	78ca *d*	-4,252	-1,376	-2,340	328	-1,562	-1,710	-168	3,025	-5,070	-26	3,366	5,563	-1,592	3,397	6,647
Overall Balance	78cb *d*	-3,270	-419	3,313	8,150	693	1,139	-1,848	-4,786	904	-392	2,711	5,498	-2,393	4,996	5,933
Reserves and Related Items	79da *d*	3,270	419	-3,313	-8,150	-693	-1,139	1,848	4,786	-904	392	-2,711	-5,498	2,393	-4,996	-5,933
Reserve Assets	79db *d*	63	-636	-3,877	-8,150	-693	-1,139	1,848	4,786	-904	392	-2,711	-5,498	2,393	-4,996	-5,933
Use of Fund Credit and Loans	79dc *d*	—	—	—	—	—	—	—	—	—	—	—	—	—	—	—
Exceptional Financing	79de *d*	3,207	1,055	564	....	....	....	....	....	....	....	....	....	....	....	....

Canada

		1970	1971	1972	1973	1974	1975	1976	1977	1978	1979	1980	1981	1982	1983	1984
International Investment Position															*Millions of US Dollars*	
Assets	79aa d	27,531	30,132	33,409	40,050	44,068	45,920	52,790	56,111	63,786	72,964	92,330	110,267	114,079	117,462	124,866
Direct Investment Abroad	79ab d	6,448	6,874	7,107	8,290	9,790	10,912	11,997	13,005	14,589	18,487	23,783	30,071	30,474	35,830	39,941
Portfolio Investment	79ac d	2,788	3,003	3,370	3,656	3,879	4,181	4,576	4,854	5,403	7,035	7,943	8,407	8,660	10,231	11,981
Equity Securities	79ad d	2,319	2,485	2,822	3,053	3,254	3,512	3,934	4,176	4,667	6,321	7,163	7,587	7,574	8,627	9,164
Debt Securities	79ae d	469	519	547	604	626	669	642	678	736	714	780	820	1,085	1,604	2,817
Financial Derivatives	79al d	—	—	—	—	—	—	—	—	—	—	—	—	—	—	—
Other Investment	79af d	13,617	14,624	16,886	22,335	24,576	25,503	30,376	33,646	39,225	43,559	56,577	67,419	71,154	67,197	69,761
Monetary Authorities	79ag d	—	—	—	—	—	—	—	—	—	—	—	—	—	—	—
General Government	79ah d	2,120	2,444	2,829	3,126	3,966	4,474	4,597	4,944	5,413	6,485	7,117	7,913	9,804	9,653	10,492
Banks	79ai d	7,691	7,226	8,545	12,356	13,987	13,885	17,479	18,451	21,889	25,957	35,866	38,766	38,536	42,106	42,958
Other Sectors	79aj d	3,806	4,955	5,511	6,853	6,622	7,144	8,300	10,251	11,924	11,118	13,595	20,740	22,813	15,438	16,312
Reserve Assets	79ak d	4,679	5,631	6,047	5,769	5,823	5,324	5,842	4,606	4,569	3,883	4,027	4,370	3,792	4,205	3,183
Liabilities	79la d	57,252	62,265	68,471	77,874	86,630	95,538	113,537	118,844	138,070	161,272	184,635	224,727	225,190	233,435	241,715
Dir. Invest. in Rep. Economy	79lb d	27,071	28,925	30,698	34,120	37,890	38,103	41,244	41,239	42,234	48,613	54,163	59,303	59,227	64,022	65,070
Portfolio Investment	79lc d	16,502	17,196	18,931	20,255	22,541	28,854	38,616	41,413	50,524	56,504	62,211	71,968	79,132	83,279	88,501
Equity Securities	79ld d	4,480	4,500	4,707	5,191	5,470	6,119	6,331	6,666	6,709	8,820	11,247	11,671	10,704	9,904	9,869
Debt Securities	79le d	12,022	12,696	14,224	15,064	17,071	22,735	32,285	34,747	43,815	47,683	50,964	60,297	68,428	73,374	78,632
Financial Derivatives	79ll d	—	—	—	—	—	—	—	—	—	—	—	—	—	—	—
Other investment	79lf d	13,680	16,144	18,842	23,499	26,198	28,581	33,678	36,192	45,312	56,156	68,261	93,456	86,831	86,135	88,144
Monetary Authorities	79lg d	—	—	—	—	—	—	—	—	—	—	—	—	—	—	—
General Government	79lh d	70	107	169	249	297	282	338	943	1,543	2,957	2,910	3,057	2,441	2,506	3,012
Banks	79li d	6,270	7,154	9,136	12,689	13,429	14,316	16,830	19,073	25,465	33,255	44,286	63,554	59,645	63,199	64,883
Other Sectors	79lj d	7,340	8,883	9,537	10,561	12,472	13,983	16,510	16,176	18,304	19,943	21,066	26,845	24,745	20,431	20,249
Government Finance															*Billions of Canadian Dollars:*	
Deficit (-) or Surplus	80	−.99	−1.91	−1.74	−1.70	ɪ−1.97	−5.70	−6.30	−9.41	−11.95	−10.56	−10.73	−8.43	−20.81	−25.16	−28.87
Revenue	81	17.23	19.11	22.04	25.85	ɪ31.62	34.89	37.72	38.24	41.64	48.22	57.49	72.28	73.24	77.33	85.30
Grants Received	81z	....	....	....	....	ɪ	—	—	—	—	—	—	—	—	—	—
Expenditure	82	15.99	18.42	21.32	24.68	ɪ30.08	36.00	39.69	45.06	50.51	55.54	65.52	76.15	89.36	98.81	111.38
Lending Minus Repayments	83	2.23	2.60	2.45	2.88	ɪ3.51	4.59	4.33	2.59	3.08	3.23	2.70	4.56	4.68	3.67	2.79
Financing																
Total Net Borrowing	84	1.41	2.16	2.25	1.37	ɪ3.67	4.79	5.40	9.80	15.64	5.42	12.25	9.35	21.84	25.67	28.48
Net Domestic	84a	....	....	....	....	ɪ3.73	4.82	5.40	9.80	9.59	6.50	10.50	8.02	20.59	24.50	20.38
Net Foreign	85a	....	....	....	....	ɪ−.06	−.04	—	.01	6.05	−1.08	1.75	1.33	1.26	1.17	8.10
Use of Cash Balances	87	−.42	−.25	−.51	.33	ɪ−1.70	.91	.89	−.39	−3.68	5.14	−1.51	−.92	−1.03	−.51	.40
Total Debt	88z	....	....	....	....	ɪ34.73	39.45	44.10	53.54	69.08	74.34	86.14	95.28	117.19	145.97	177.17
Domestic	88a	....	....	....	....	ɪ34.53	39.28	43.94	51.30	60.79	67.12	77.17	84.99	105.63	133.26	156.36
Foreign	89a	....	....	....	....	ɪ.20	.16	.16	2.25	8.29	7.22	8.97	10.30	11.55	12.72	20.81
Other Finan.Institutions	88ac	2,251	2,118	2,220	1,971	....	....	....	....	....	....	....	....	....	....	....
Other Dom. Investors	88ae	10,865	12,720	13,613	13,102	....	....	....	....	....	....	....	....	....	....	....
Foreigners	88c	726	681	844	741	....	....	....	....	....	....	....	....	....	....	....
Intragovernmental Debt	88s	1,005	569	611	607	....	....	....	....	....	....	....	....	....	....	....
National Accounts															*Billions of Canadian Dollars*	
Househ.Cons.Expend.,incl.NPISHs	96f. c	51.85	56.27	63.02	72.07	84.23	97.57	111.50	123.56	137.43	153.39	172.42	196.19	210.51	231.45	251.65
Government Consumption Expend	91f. c	16.45	18.23	20.14	22.85	27.48	33.27	38.27	43.41	47.39	52.29	59.25	68.79	78.66	84.57	89.09
Gross Fixed Capital Formation	93e. c	19.01	21.57	23.88	28.86	35.78	41.85	46.71	50.23	54.58	63.44	72.29	86.12	81.33	81.23	84.70
Changes in Inventories	93i. c	.24	.37	.78	1.86	3.59	1.37	2.33	1.86	1.05	4.99	−.34	1.19	−9.75	−2.85	4.76
Exports of Goods and Services	90c. c	20.08	21.17	23.74	29.77	37.81	38.95	44.25	51.18	61.15	75.07	87.58	96.88	96.65	103.44	126.04
Imports of Goods & Services	98c. c	−17.83	−19.53	−22.78	−28.02	−37.37	−41.36	−45.28	−51.25	−60.05	−73.28	−81.93	−93.00	−82.60	−89.83	−110.63
Gross Domestic Product (GDP)	99b. c	89.12	97.29	108.63	127.37	152.11	171.54	197.92	217.88	241.60	276.10	309.89	355.99	374.44	405.72	444.74
Net Primary Income from Abroad	98.n c	−1.35	−1.51	−1.46	−1.73	−2.24	−2.54	−3.54	−4.57	−5.95	−7.16	−7.83	−11.34	−12.67	−11.60	−13.49
Gross National Income (GNI)	99a. c	87.77	95.78	107.17	125.64	149.87	169.00	194.39	213.31	235.65	268.94	302.06	344.66	361.77	394.11	431.25
Net National Income	99e. c	77.82	85.02	95.43	112.01	133.43	150.24	172.93	189.51	209.04	238.20	266.54	303.98	317.42	347.05	380.37
GDP Volume 1986 Prices	99b. r	271.37	287.00	303.45	326.85	341.24	350.11	371.69	385.12	402.74	418.33	424.54	440.13	425.97	439.45	467.17
GDP Volume 1992 Prices	99b. r	....	....	....	....	....	....	....	....	....	....	....	....	....	....	....
GDP Volume (1995=100)	99bv r	44.1	46.6	49.3	53.1	55.4	56.9	60.4	62.5	65.4	67.9	68.9	71.5	69.2	71.4	75.9
GDP Deflator (1995=100)	99bi r	25.1	25.9	27.3	29.7	34.0	37.4	40.6	43.2	45.8	50.4	55.7	61.7	67.1	70.4	72.6
																Millions:
Population	99z	21.32	21.59	21.83	22.07	22.40	22.73	23.03	23.28	23.49	23.70	24.04	24.34	24.58	24.79	24.98

	1985	1986	1987	1988	1989	1990	1991	1992	1993	1994	1995	1996	1997	1998	1999		

Millions of US Dollars — **International Investment Position**

1985	1986	1987	1988	1989	1990	1991	1992	1993	1994	1995	1996	1997	1998	1999		
129,772	146,175	163,760	184,684	205,558	227,461	243,944	234,853	246,426	281,124	320,266	365,919	405,823	431,243	459,835	Assets	79aa d
43,143	46,935	57,037	66,876	77,605	84,808	94,382	87,870	92,468	104,302	118,105	131,875	146,720	160,936	178,347	Direct Investment Abroad	79ab d
13,735	16,143	20,600	25,917	31,132	34,641	43,773	45,380	53,200	57,385	61,696	73,279	82,746	94,095	113,409	Portfolio Investment	79ac d
10,052	11,911	14,744	19,490	22,510	25,870	34,021	35,204	39,982	44,327	47,909	57,754	63,277	71,335	88,184	Equity Securities	79ad d
3,682	4,231	5,856	6,427	8,622	8,771	9,753	10,175	13,218	13,057	13,787	15,525	19,469	22,761	25,225	Debt Securities	79ae d
—	—	—	—	—	—	—	—	—	—	—	—	—	—	—	Financial Derivatives	79al d
69,617	79,001	77,929	75,694	80,018	89,438	88,889	89,696	88,007	106,962	125,250	140,174	158,373	152,744	139,346	Other Investment	79af d
—	—	—	—	—	—	—	—	—	—	—	—	—	—	—	Monetary Authorities	79ag d
10,479	10,296	10,799	11,457	12,121	13,124	14,459	15,341	14,966	15,419	15,656	15,868	16,759	18,716	20,792	General Government	79ah d
44,406	51,123	50,861	44,628	46,961	50,345	43,931	43,015	37,279	49,976	60,268	73,657	75,960	74,501	60,124	Banks	79ai d
14,733	17,582	16,269	19,609	20,936	25,968	30,499	31,339	35,762	41,567	49,326	50,649	65,655	59,527	58,431	Other Sectors	79aj d
3,277	4,096	8,194	16,197	16,803	18,575	16,900	11,908	12,751	12,476	15,216	20,591	17,984	23,467	28,732	Reserve Assets	79ak d
257,023	288,742	327,309	365,706	406,007	445,099	475,328	469,385	490,942	520,374	563,437	598,271	625,578	644,430	667,929	Liabilities	79la d
64,657	69,579	81,502	95,728	105,945	112,844	117,025	108,503	106,868	110,204	123,181	131,731	138,468	143,234	166,266	Dir. Invest. in Rep. Economy	79lb d
98,995	121,362	139,002	162,355	182,392	202,704	228,222	234,585	266,961	281,767	311,054	323,821	322,872	336,737	343,321	Portfolio Investment	79lc d
10,829	11,769	14,001	15,184	17,791	17,806	15,269	14,083	17,685	22,001	27,170	34,515	35,973	41,467	50,057	Equity Securities	79ld d
88,166	109,593	125,001	147,171	164,600	184,898	212,953	220,502	249,276	259,766	283,885	289,306	286,899	295,270	293,265	Debt Securities	79le d
—	—	—	—	—	—	—	—	—	—	—	—	—	—	—	Financial Derivatives	79ll d
93,371	97,801	106,805	107,623	117,671	129,551	130,081	126,297	117,113	128,403	129,201	142,720	164,238	164,459	158,342	Other investment	79lf d
—	—	—	—	—	—	—	—	—	—	—	—	—	—	—	Monetary Authorities	79lg d
4,354	4,837	6,475	5,555	4,416	4,177	4,254	3,819	3,889	4,568	4,059	3,329	2,790	2,648	2,544	General Government	79lh d
67,905	72,531	75,966	72,594	74,889	82,598	80,132	75,630	68,757	83,691	79,735	92,486	115,625	118,010	103,565	Banks	79li d
21,112	20,433	24,364	29,473	38,366	42,776	45,696	46,849	44,468	40,145	45,407	46,905	45,822	43,802	52,232	Other Sectors	79lj d

Year Beginning April 1 — **Government Finance**

1985	1986	1987	1988	1989	1990	1991	1992	1993	1994	1995	1996	1997	1998	1999		
−28.68	−20.11	−14.00	‡−24.67	−25.89	−32.78	−38.64	−42.37	−42.36	−36.02	−27.78	....	....	....	....	Deficit (-) or Surplus	80
91.10	99.21	111.55	‡121.50	133.75	140.21	145.07	146.51	144.72	153.63	160.33	....	....	....	....	Revenue	81
—	.02	.11	‡.37	.44	.46	.49	.46	.54	.53	.52	....	....	....	....	Grants Received	81z
117.20	119.33	127.08	‡147.34	160.94	172.00	183.82	187.93	187.23	191.38	194.53	....	....	....	....	Expenditure	82
2.58	.01	−1.41	‡−.80	−.86	1.45	.38	1.40	.39	−1.20	−5.91	....	....	....	....	Lending Minus Repayments	83
															Financing	
28.15	25.88	22.14	‡29.26	26.38	39.50	39.26	39.29	44.04	34.77	39.02	....	....	....	....	Total Net Borrowing	84
22.89	15.62	14.29	‡26.38	23.71	38.28	38.18	41.25	49.30	41.02	38.91	....	....	....	....	Net Domestic	84a
5.26	10.26	7.85	‡2.88	2.66	1.23	1.08	−1.97	−5.26	−6.25	.11	....	....	....	....	Net Foreign	85a
.53	−5.78	−8.13	‡−4.59	−.49	−6.72	−.62	3.09	−1.68	1.25	−11.24	....	....	....	....	Use of Cash Balances	87
205.61	231.28	253.36	‡379.99	406.61	444.56	476.10	514.36	557.60	595.88	634.94	....	....	....	....	Total Debt	88z
179.53	194.94	209.76	‡369.21	398.42	437.39	469.93	506.39	544.61	577.02	616.23	....	....	....	....	Domestic	88a
26.08	36.34	43.60	‡10.79	8.19	7.17	6.17	7.97	13.00	18.86	18.71	....	....	....	....	Foreign	89a
....	....	....	....	....	....	....	....	....	....	....	....	....	....	....	Other Finan.Institutions	88ac
....	....	....	....	....	....	....	....	....	....	....	....	....	....	....	Other Dom. Investors	88ae
....	....	....	....	....	....	....	....	....	....	....	....	....	....	....	Foreigners	88c
....	....	....	....	....	....	....	....	....	....	....	....	....	....	....	Intragovernmental Debt	88s

Billions of Canadian Dollars — **National Accounts**

1985	1986	1987	1988	1989	1990	1991	1992	1993	1994	1995	1996	1997	1998	1999		
274.50	297.48	322.77	349.94	378.94	394.32	411.96	422.52	436.54	452.44	463.25	479.43	511.16	532.93	558.57	Househ.Cons.Expend.,incl.NPISHs	96f. c
95.52	100.13	105.79	114.47	124.11	135.15	144.89	150.39	152.16	150.59	160.94	169.49	173.26	175.86	180.00	Government Consumption Expend	91f. c
94.20	101.56	116.72	132.79	146.08	141.38	132.01	128.92	128.88	138.12	134.83	142.66	165.16	174.08	186.55	Gross Fixed Capital Formation	93e. c
2.28	2.56	3.07	3.80	3.62	−2.84	−3.24	−3.70	1.10	3.97	7.67	1.44	9.27	5.74	3.88	Changes in Inventories	93i. c
134.92	138.12	145.42	159.31	163.90	168.92	164.85	181.19	209.37	250.88	296.35	320.70	345.06	373.18	414.29	Exports of Goods and Services	90c. c
−123.39	−133.37	−140.50	−156.38	−166.09	−171.13	−172.81	−187.25	−212.53	−246.46	−275.07	−288.40	−329.88	−360.36	−385.94	Imports of Goods & Services	98c. c
477.99	505.67	551.60	605.91	650.75	669.51	676.48	698.54	724.96	767.51	807.09	833.92	873.95	901.31	957.91	Gross Domestic Product (GDP)	99b. c
−14.33	−16.40	−16.45	−18.71	−21.50	−23.86	−21.87	−24.24	−23.99	−27.10	−27.82	−27.15	−28.30	−29.55	−29.62	Net Primary Income from Abroad	98.n c
463.66	489.26	535.15	587.19	629.25	645.61	654.61	665.88	688.86	720.16	760.22	797.52	843.40	872.25	928.29	Gross National Income (GNI)	99a. c
407.73	428.67	471.04	519.07	556.90	567.02	572.28	580.58	600.96	627.24	661.45	691.73	733.42	756.70	808.19	Net National Income	99e. c
489.44	505.67	527.23	552.96	566.49	565.16	555.05	559.31	....	....	....	....	....	....	....	GDP Volume 1986 Prices	99b. r
....	....	....	....	....	....	....	698.54	714.58	748.35	769.08	782.13	813.03	842.00	875.25	GDP Volume 1992 Prices	99b. r
79.5	82.1	85.6	89.8	92.0	91.8	90.1	‡90.8	92.9	97.3	100.0	101.7	105.7	109.5	113.8	GDP Volume (1995=100)	99bv r
74.5	76.3	79.8	83.6	87.6	90.4	93.0	95.3	96.7	97.7	100.0	101.6	102.4	102.0	104.3	GDP Deflator (1995=100)	99bi r

Midyear Estimates

1985	1986	1987	1988	1989	1990	1991	1992	1993	1994	1995	1996	1997	1998	1999		
25.16	25.35	25.62	26.89	27.29	27.70	28.03	28.38	28.70	29.04	29.35	29.67	29.99	30.25	30.49	**Population**	99z

(See notes in the back of the book.)

Cape Verde

		1970	1971	1972	1973	1974	1975	1976	1977	1978	1979	1980	1981	1982	1983	1984
Exchange Rates														*Escudos per SDR:*		
Official Rate	aa	28.750	29.922	29.314	31.178	30.114	32.160	36.655	41.179	46.822	50.467	54.192	59.199	69.540	83.730	91.174
														Escudos per US Dollar:		
Official Rate	ae	28.750	27.560	27.000	25.845	24.596	27.472	31.549	33.900	35.940	38.310	42.490	50.860	63.040	79.975	93.015
Official Rate	rf	28.750	28.360	27.053	24.515	25.408	25.543	30.229	34.046	35.501	37.433	40.175	48.695	58.293	71.686	84.878
Fund Position														*Millions of SDRs:*		
Quota	2f. s	—	—	—	—	—	—	—	—	2.00	2.00	3.00	3.00	3.00	4.50	4.50
SDRs	1b. s	...	...	...	...	...	...	...	...	—	—	.01	—	.15	.11	.10
Reserve Position in the Fund	1c. s	...	...	...	...	...	...	...	...	—	—	.32	.58	.58	.95	.95
Total Fund Cred.&Loans Outstg.	2tl	...	...	...	...	...	...	...	...	—	—	—	—	—	—	—
International Liquidity												*Millions of US Dollars Unless Otherwise Indicated:*				
Total Reserves minus Gold	1l. d	...	...	...	...	...	...	32.70	42.02	39.37	42.32	42.40	37.83	42.74	45.90	40.99
SDRs	1b. d	...	...	...	...	...	...	...	...	—	.01	.21	.17	.12	.10
Reserve Position in the Fund	1c. d	...	...	...	...	...	...	...	...	—	.42	.74	.68	.64	.99	.93
Foreign Exchange	1d. d	...	...	...	...	...	...	32.70	42.02	39.37	41.89	41.66	36.94	41.93	44.79	39.96
Monetary Authorities: Other Liab.	4.. d	...	...	...	...	...	...	.47	.11	2.27	1.75	.42	2.14	3.36	7.32	2.87
Deposit Money Banks: Assets	7a. d	...	...	...	...	...	...	...	...	...	...	...	...	...	...	...
Liabilities	7b. d	...	...	...	...	...	...	...	...	...	...	...	...	...	...	...
Monetary Authorities														*Millions of Escudos:*		
Foreign Assets	11	...	...	...	...	...	...	1,031.5	1,424.6	1,414.9	1,621.4	1,801.6	1,924.0	2,694.3	3,671.1	3,812.7
Claims on Central Government	12a	...	...	...	...	...	...	87.9	91.8	91.8	121.8	157.0	548.1	547.7	669.0	727.1
Claims on Local Government	12b	...	...	...	...	...	...	—	—	.9	.6	3.5	19.6	31.8	32.9	34.9
Claims on Nonfin.Pub.Enterprises	12c	...	...	...	...	...	...	—	—	125.3	142.8	587.1	770.6	1,046.1	1,030.0	1,346.1
Claims on Private Sector	12d	...	...	...	...	...	...	316.4	308.3	435.0	591.1	506.3	720.3	802.6	1,222.8	1,437.6
Claims on Deposit Money Banks	12e	...	...	...	...	...	...	...	...	...	...	...	...	...	...	...
Claims on Other Banking Insts	12f	...	...	...	...	...	...	1.5	1.5	1.5	1.5	1.5	1.5	1.5	1.5	1.5
Claims on Nonbank Financial Insts	12g	...	...	...	...	...	...	...	...	...	...	...	...	...	...	...
Reserve Money	14	...	...	...	...	...	...	1,000.4	1,411.3	1,614.8	1,822.6	2,302.0	2,552.7	3,227.8	3,956.2	4,201.6
of which: Currency Outside DMBs	14a	...	...	...	...	...	...	464.8	537.2	638.3	736.4	872.2	1,040.5	1,251.9	1,332.9	1,433.6
Time & Foreign Currency Deposits	15	...	...	...	...	...	...	17.1	23.8	52.3	135.2	254.1	486.1	616.1	628.3	914.7
Foreign Liabilities	16c	...	...	...	...	...	...	14.9	3.8	81.5	67.1	17.9	109.0	211.7	585.4	267.2
Central Government Deposits	16d	...	...	...	...	...	...	252.8	214.6	88.2	50.8	130.9	119.4	235.3	188.2	364.9
Capital Accounts	17a	...	...	...	...	...	...	186.6	357.1	515.0	723.0	880.9	982.3	1,358.7	1,844.4	1,936.9
Other Items (Net)	17r	...	...	...	...	...	...	−34.5	−184.4	−282.4	−319.5	−528.8	−265.4	−525.6	−575.2	−325.4
Deposit Money Banks														*Millions of Escudos:*		
Reserves	20	...	...	...	...	...	...	...	...	...	...	...	...	...	...	...
Foreign Assets	21	...	...	...	...	...	...	...	...	...	...	...	...	...	...	...
Claims on Central Government	22a	...	...	...	...	...	...	...	...	...	...	...	...	...	...	...
Claims on Local Government	22b	...	...	...	...	...	...	...	...	...	...	...	...	...	...	...
Claims on Nonfin.Pub.Enterprises	22c	...	...	...	...	...	...	...	...	...	...	...	...	...	...	...
Claims on Private Sector	22d	...	...	...	...	...	...	...	...	...	...	...	...	...	...	...
Demand Deposits	24	...	...	...	...	...	...	...	...	...	...	...	...	...	...	...
Time, Savings,& Fgn.Currency Dep.	25	...	...	...	...	...	...	...	...	...	...	...	...	...	...	...
Restricted Deposits	26b	...	...	...	...	...	...	...	...	...	...	...	...	...	...	...
Foreign Liabilities	26c	...	...	...	...	...	...	...	...	...	...	...	...	...	...	...
Central Government Deposits	26d	...	...	...	...	...	...	...	...	...	...	...	...	...	...	...
Counterpart Funds	26e	...	...	...	...	...	...	...	...	...	...	...	...	...	...	...
Credit from Monetary Authorities	26g	...	...	...	...	...	...	...	...	...	...	...	...	...	...	...
Liab. to Nonbank Financial Insts	26j	...	...	...	...	...	...	...	...	...	...	...	...	...	...	...
Capital Accounts	27a	...	...	...	...	...	...	...	...	...	...	...	...	...	...	...
Other Items (Net)	27r	...	...	...	...	...	...	...	...	...	...	...	...	...	...	...
Monetary Survey														*Millions of Escudos:*		
Foreign Assets (Net)	31n	...	...	...	...	...	...	1,016.6	1,420.8	1,333.4	1,554.3	1,783.7	1,815.0	2,482.6	3,085.7	3,545.5
Domestic Credit	32	...	...	...	...	...	...	153.0	187.0	566.3	807.0	1,124.5	1,940.7	2,194.4	2,768.0	3,182.3
Claims on Central Govt. (Net)	32an	...	...	...	...	...	...	−164.9	−122.8	3.6	71.0	26.1	428.7	312.4	480.8	362.2
Claims on Local Government	32b	...	...	...	...	...	...	—	—	.9	.6	3.5	19.6	31.8	32.9	34.9
Claims on Nonfin.Pub.Enterprises	32c	...	...	...	...	...	...	—	—	125.3	142.8	587.1	770.6	1,046.1	1,030.0	1,346.1
Claims on Private Sector	32d	...	...	...	...	...	...	316.4	308.3	435.0	591.1	506.3	720.3	802.6	1,222.8	1,437.6
Claims on Other Banking Insts	32f	...	...	...	...	...	...	1.5	1.5	1.5	1.5	1.5	1.5	1.5	1.5	1.5
Claims on Nonbank Financial Inst	32g	...	...	...	...	...	...	...	...	...	...	...	...	...	...	...
Money	34	...	...	...	...	...	...	1,000.4	1,411.3	1,614.8	1,822.6	2,302.0	2,552.7	3,227.8	3,956.2	4,201.6
Quasi-Money	35	...	...	...	...	...	...	17.1	23.8	52.3	135.2	254.1	486.1	616.1	628.3	914.7
Restricted Deposits	36b	...	...	...	...	...	...	4.1	6.2	6.9	7.9	7.1	8.0	10.0	13.5	296.7
Counterpart Funds	36e	...	...	...	...	...	...	...	...	...	...	...	...	...	...	...
Liab. to Nonbank Financial Insts	36j	...	...	...	...	...	...	...	...	...	...	...	...	...	...	...
Capital Accounts	37a	...	...	...	...	...	...	186.6	357.1	515.0	723.0	880.9	982.3	1,358.7	1,844.4	1,936.9
Other Items (Net)	37r	...	...	...	...	...	...	−38.6	−190.6	−289.3	−327.4	−535.9	−273.4	−535.6	−588.7	−622.1
Money plus Quasi-Money	35l	...	...	...	...	...	...	1,017.5	1,435.1	1,667.1	1,957.8	2,556.1	3,038.8	3,843.9	4,584.5	5,116.3
Other Banking Institutions														*Millions of Escudos:*		
Cash	40	...	...	...	...	...	...	31.5	38.8	46.2	50.7	21.4	16.6	21.8	75.0	6.7
Foreign Assets	41	...	...	...	...	...	...	.1	.1	.1	.1	.3	.3	.3	.3	.3
Claims on Private Sector	42d	...	...	...	...	...	...	84.1	86.6	96.6	121.2	178.2	217.3	230.2	265.6	232.2
Time, Savings,& Fgn.Currency Dep.	45	...	...	...	...	...	...	57.0	64.6	81.8	99.0	116.7	150.5	167.3	235.4	230.2
Credit from Monetary Authorities	46g	...	...	...	...	...	...	1.5	1.5	1.5	1.5	1.5	1.5	1.5	1.5	—
Capital Accounts	47a	...	...	...	...	...	...	...	...	...	...	...	...	...	...	...
Other Items (Net)	47r	...	...	...	...	...	...	57.2	59.4	59.6	71.5	81.5	82.1	83.5	104.0	9.0
Banking Survey														*Millions of Escudos:*		
Foreign Assets (Net)	51n	...	...	...	...	...	...	1,016.7	1,420.9	1,333.5	1,554.4	1,783.8	1,815.0	2,482.9	3,086.0	3,545.8
Domestic Credit	52	...	...	...	...	...	...	250.4	286.0	674.0	936.9	1,309.9	2,163.8	2,429.0	3,036.6	3,416.1
Claims on Central Govt. (Net)	52an	...	...	...	...	...	...	−164.7	−122.6	3.8	71.2	26.3	428.9	312.6	481.0	362.4
Claims on Local Government	52b	...	...	...	...	...	...	7.4	7.1	7.5	5.7	8.0	23.5	35.1	35.6	37.0
Claims on Nonfin.Pub.Enterprises	52c	...	...	...	...	...	...	7.2	6.6	131.1	147.7	591.0	773.8	1,048.5	1,031.6	1,346.9
Claims on Private Sector	52d	...	...	...	...	...	...	400.5	394.9	531.6	712.3	684.5	937.6	1,032.8	1,488.4	1,669.8
Liquid Liabilities	55l	...	...	...	...	...	...	1,043.0	1,460.9	1,702.7	2,006.1	2,651.4	3,172.7	3,989.4	4,744.9	5,339.8
Restricted Deposits	56b	...	...	...	...	...	...	4.1	6.2	6.9	7.9	7.1	8.0	10.0	13.5	296.7
Capital Accounts	57a	...	...	...	...	...	...	186.6	357.1	515.0	723.0	880.9	982.3	1,358.7	1,844.4	1,936.9
Other Items (Net)	57r	...	...	...	...	...	...	33.4	−117.3	−217.1	−245.7	−445.7	−184.0	−446.2	−480.2	−611.5

		1985	1986	1987	1988	1989	1990	1991	1992	1993	1994	1995	1996	1997	1998	1999
Exchange Rates		*End of Period*														
Official Rate	aa	93.778	93.654	93.312	99.131	95.993	94.016	95.081	100.497	118.115	118.452	115.136	122.464	129.845	132.714	147.648
		End of Period (ae) Period Average (rf)														
Official Rate	ae	85.375	76.565	65.775	73.665	73.045	66.085	66.470	73.089	85.992	81.140	77.455	85.165	96.235	94.255	107.575
Official Rate	rf	91.632	80.145	72.466	72.068	77.978	70.031	71.408	68.018	80.427	81.891	76.853	82.591	93.177	98.158	102.700
Fund Position		*End of Period*														
Quota	2f.*s*	4.50	4.50	4.50	4.50	4.50	4.50	4.50	7.00	7.00	7.00	7.00	7.00	7.00	7.00	9.60
SDRs	1b.*s*	.10	.10	.07	.03	.04	.03	.04	.05	.02	.05	.02	.04	.02	.04	.01
Reserve Position in the Fund	1c.*s*	.95	—	—	—	—	—	—	—	—	—	—	—	—	—	—
Total Fund Cred.&Loans Outstg.	2tl	—	—	—	—	—	—	—	—	—	—	—	—	—	—	—
International Liquidity		*End of Period*														
Total Reserves minus Gold	1l.*d*	55.36	56.36	80.73	81.33	74.74	76.97	65.10	75.76	57.69	42.08	57.34	51.76	41.76	37.15	60.39
SDRs	1b.*d*	.11	.12	.10	.04	.05	.04	.06	.07	.03	.07	.03	.06	.03	.06	.02
Reserve Position in the Fund	1c.*d*	1.04	—	—	—	—	—	—	—	—	—	—	—	—	—	—
Foreign Exchange	1d.*d*	54.20	56.24	80.63	81.29	74.69	76.93	65.04	75.69	57.66	42.01	57.31	51.69	41.73	37.09	60.37
Monetary Authorities: Other Liab.	4..*d*	8.02	.93	1.73	1.65	1.23	1.13	2.49	2.90	.80	.60	6.47	3.51	2.60	.94	1.11
Deposit Money Banks: Assets	7a.*d*	....	....	....	....	....	....	....	....	14.47	31.60	10.62	32.35	23.89	33.41	30.71
Liabilities	7b.*d*	....	....	....	....	....	....	....	....	2.47	3.38	6.32	5.73	9.95	11.16	15.52
Monetary Authorities		*End of Period*														
Foreign Assets	11	4,726.2	4,315.2	5,310.0	5,991.4	5,459.2	5,086.5	4,327.2	5,536.9	4,999.9	3,483.1	I 5,154.8	4,838.5	4,521.9	3,584.9	6,595.6
Claims on Central Government	12a	938.0	1,248.8	1,441.8	1,653.9	1,902.8	2,217.0	3,101.0	4,118.6	5,068.2	4,446.4	I 4,964.4	4,315.8	6,001.6	5,615.2	5,865.2
Claims on Local Government	12b	32.2	34.5	28.3	48.3	60.0	79.7	70.3	68.8	27.6	—	I —	—	—	—	—
Claims on Nonfin.Pub.Enterprises	12c	1,483.4	1,517.3	1,422.1	2,724.6	2,986.1	3,151.2	3,602.4	3,694.1	2,136.9	119.7	I 118.8	113.9	.1	—	86.8
Claims on Private Sector	12d	2,110.2	2,565.1	3,179.0	2,223.3	2,877.3	3,444.5	3,948.0	4,731.8	2,005.7	1,091.2	I 1,099.4	2,049.4	1,151.9	1,142.7	1,100.8
Claims on Deposit Money Banks	12e	....	....	....	....	....	....	....	....	612.8	592.1	I 632.7	630.3	519.8	361.6	331.4
Claims on Other Banking Insts	12f	—	—	32.7	137.2	214.2	258.4	308.0	301.4	—	—	I —	—	—	—	—
Claims on Nonbank Financial Insts	12g	....	....	....	....	....	....	....	....	....	....	—	—	—	5.5	5.5
Reserve Money	14	4,843.2	5,620.6	5,710.4	6,037.9	6,410.5	6,926.4	7,538.1	9,906.6	14,205.4	8,685.9	I 10655.6	9,982.8	10,035.2	10,971.4	11,701.4
of which: Currency Outside DMBs	14a	1,628.1	1,826.4	1,955.9	2,219.2	2,490.3	2,842.4	2,971.9	3,191.3	3,549.4	3,929.7	I 4,635.1	4,513.0	4,853.6	5,059.8	6,026.1
Time & Foreign Currency Deposits	15	1,297.1	1,966.0	2,527.1	3,591.6	4,659.4	5,754.3	7,195.0	6,730.7	—	173.9	I 101.4	—	—	—	—
Foreign Liabilities	16c	685.0	71.1	114.0	121.8	89.5	74.6	165.3	211.8	69.2	48.7	I 500.9	298.8	249.8	88.8	119.7
Central Government Deposits	16d	689.6	640.0	722.6	929.6	928.9	968.9	649.0	803.9	—	—	I 245.9	230.8	944.7	516.6	838.1
Capital Accounts	17a	2,300.0	2,277.7	2,434.1	2,213.3	2,459.5	2,970.3	2,725.2	3,002.9	2,190.4	2,069.3	I 2,338.7	2,739.2	3,114.5	3,051.5	2,374.7
Other Items (Net)	17r	–524.9	–894.5	–94.3	–115.5	–1,048.2	–2,457.2	–2,915.7	–2,204.3	–1,613.9	–1,245.3	I –1872.4	–1,303.7	–2,149.0	–3,918.4	–1,048.6
Deposit Money Banks		*End of Period*														
Reserves	20	....	....	....	....	....	....	....	....	10,604.3	4,803.9	I 5,987.1	5,472.5	5,701.4	5,820.3	5,653.0
Foreign Assets	21	....	....	....	....	....	....	....	....	1,244.4	2,563.7	I 822.3	2,754.7	2,299.1	3,149.0	3,303.5
Claims on Central Government	22a	....	....	....	....	....	....	....	....	—	6,046.7	I 7,557.0	8,944.3	10,357.8	10,347.4	10,238.3
Claims on Local Government	22b	....	....	....	....	....	....	....	....	48.7	76.2	I 97.1	109.1	.2	10.7	238.0
Claims on Nonfin.Pub.Enterprises	22c	....	....	....	....	....	....	....	....	433.9	432.7	I 545.0	378.5	24.2	21.4	425.3
Claims on Private Sector	22d	....	....	....	....	....	....	....	....	5,495.8	6,473.9	I 9,292.1	10,159.8	13,540.5	15,308.7	17,292.7
Demand Deposits	24	....	....	....	....	....	....	....	....	7,049.3	7,542.3	I 7,232.4	8,609.7	11,106.4	10,573.4	12,216.4
Time, Savings,& Fgn.Currency Dep.	25	....	....	....	....	....	....	....	....	9,039.4	10,394.4	I 12974.5	14,251.9	14,386.0	15,557.7	17,494.4
Restricted Deposits	26b	....	....	....	....	....	....	....	....	300.9	203.8	I 257.6	491.7	398.1	710.0	242.6
Foreign Liabilities	26c	....	....	....	....	....	....	....	....	212.8	274.3	I 489.7	488.3	957.1	1,051.5	1,669.6
Central Government Deposits	26d	....	....	....	....	....	....	....	....	847.8	1,035.7	I 2,401.0	2,539.4	2,038.2	2,100.4	1,169.0
Counterpart Funds	26e	....	....	....	....	....	....	....	....	....	....	—	—	2.0	3.4	—
Credit from Monetary Authorities	26g	....	....	....	....	....	....	....	....	612.8	592.1	I 573.5	551.4	519.8	361.6	331.4
Liab. to Nonbank Financial Insts	26j	....	....	....	....	....	....	....	....	3.4	20.3	I 181.1	298.7	125.6	36.2	306.0
Capital Accounts	27a	....	....	....	....	....	....	....	....	1,292.9	1,638.8	I 2,833.5	3,433.6	4,426.3	5,365.6	5,579.6
Other Items (Net)	27r	....	....	....	....	....	....	....	....	–1,532.2	–1,304.6	I –2642.8	–2,845.9	–2,036.3	–1,102.3	–1,858.2
Monetary Survey		*End of Period*														
Foreign Assets (Net)	31n	4,041.2	4,244.1	5,196.0	5,869.6	5,369.7	5,011.9	4,161.9	5,325.1	5,962.3	5,723.8	I 4,986.5	6,806.0	5,614.0	5,593.6	8,109.8
Domestic Credit	32	3,874.2	4,725.7	5,381.3	5,857.7	7,111.5	8,181.9	10,380.7	12,110.8	14,369.0	17,651.1	I 21026.9	23,300.6	28,093.4	29,834.6	33,245.5
Claims on Central Govt. (Net)	32an	248.4	608.8	719.2	724.3	973.9	1,248.1	2,452.0	3,314.7	4,220.4	9,457.4	I 9,874.5	10,489.9	13,376.5	13,345.6	14,096.4
Claims on Local Government	32b	32.2	34.5	28.3	48.3	60.0	79.7	70.3	68.8	76.3	76.2	I 97.1	109.1	.2	10.7	238.0
Claims on Nonfin.Pub.Enterprises	32c	1,483.4	1,517.3	1,422.1	2,724.6	2,986.1	3,151.2	3,602.4	3,694.1	2,570.8	552.4	I 663.8	492.4	24.3	21.4	512.1
Claims on Private Sector	32d	2,110.2	2,565.1	3,179.0	2,223.3	2,877.3	3,444.5	3,948.0	4,731.8	7,501.5	7,565.1	I 10391.5	12,209.2	14,692.4	16,451.4	18,393.5
Claims on Other Banking Insts	32f	—	—	32.7	137.2	214.2	258.4	308.0	301.4	—	—	I —	—	—	—	—
Claims on Nonbank Financial Inst	32g	....	....	....	....	....	....	....	....	....	....	—	—	—	5.5	5.5
Money	34	4,843.2	5,620.6	5,710.4	6,037.9	6,410.5	6,926.4	7,538.1	9,906.6	10,598.7	11,472.0	I 11867.5	13,122.7	15,960.0	15,633.2	18,332.6
Quasi-Money	35	1,297.1	1,966.0	2,527.1	3,591.6	4,659.4	5,754.3	7,195.0	6,730.7	9,039.4	10,568.3	I 13075.9	14,251.9	14,386.0	15,557.7	17,494.4
Restricted Deposits	36b	379.2	272.0	228.1	321.8	185.2	289.2	141.6	142.5	300.9	203.8	I 257.6	491.7	398.1	710.0	242.6
Counterpart Funds	36e	....	....	....	....	....	....	....	....	....	....	—	—	2.0	3.4	—
Liab. to Nonbank Financial Insts	36j	....	....	....	....	....	....	....	....	3.4	20.3	I 181.1	298.7	125.6	36.2	306.0
Capital Accounts	37a	2,300.0	2,277.7	2,434.1	2,213.3	2,459.5	2,970.3	2,725.2	3,002.9	3,483.3	3,708.1	I 5,172.2	6,172.8	7,540.8	8,417.1	7,954.3
Other Items (Net)	37r	–904.1	–1,166.5	–322.4	–437.3	–1,233.4	–2,746.4	–3,057.3	–2,346.8	–3,094.4	–2,597.6	I –4541.0	–4,231.2	–4,705.1	–4,929.4	–2,974.6
Money plus Quasi-Money	35l	6,140.3	7,586.6	8,237.5	9,629.5	11,069.9	12,680.7	14,733.1	16,637.3	19,638.1	22,040.3	I 24943.4	27,374.6	30,346.0	31,190.9	35,827.0
Other Banking Institutions		*End of Period*														
Cash	40	9.5	54.3	33.4	42.6	43.8	47.6	57.0	74.6	....	....	....	....	....	....	....
Foreign Assets	41	.3	.2	.2	.2	.2	.2	.2	.2	....	....	....	....	....	....	....
Claims on Private Sector	42d	274.2	254.2	378.5	548.5	717.5	1,013.3	1,016.1	1,126.4	....	....	....	....	....	....	....
Time, Savings,& Fgn.Currency Dep.	45	257.1	256.5	308.5	368.4	432.0	506.7	569.7	623.8	....	....	....	....	....	....	....
Credit from Monetary Authorities	46g	—	—	33.8	137.5	214.2	245.4	327.6	301.4	....	....	....	....	....	....	....
Capital Accounts	47a	—	—	—	—	—	—	—	—	....	....	....	....	....	....	....
Other Items (Net)	47r	26.9	52.2	69.8	85.4	115.3	309.0	176.0	276.0	....	....	....	....	....	....	....
Banking Survey		*End of Period*														
Foreign Assets (Net)	51n	4,041.5	4,244.3	5,196.2	5,869.8	5,369.9	5,012.1	4,162.1	5,325.3	....	....	....	....	....	....	....
Domestic Credit	52	4,150.9	4,979.9	5,727.1	6,269.1	7,614.8	8,936.8	11,088.8	12,935.8	....	....	....	....	....	....	....
Claims on Central Govt. (Net)	52an	248.6	608.8	719.2	724.3	973.9	1,248.1	2,452.0	3,314.7	....	....	....	....	....	....	....
Claims on Local Government	52b	33.7	34.5	28.3	48.4	60.0	79.7	70.3	68.8	....	....	....	....	....	....	....
Claims on Nonfin.Pub.Enterprises	52c	1,484.2	1,517.3	1,422.1	2,724.6	2,986.1	3,151.2	3,602.4	3,694.1	....	....	....	....	....	....	....
Claims on Private Sector	52d	2,384.4	2,819.3	3,557.5	2,771.8	3,594.8	4,457.8	4,964.1	5,858.2	....	....	....	....	....	....	....
Liquid Liabilities	55l	6,387.9	7,788.8	8,512.6	9,955.3	11,458.1	13,139.8	15,245.8	17,186.5	....	....	....	....	....	....	....
Restricted Deposits	56b	379.2	272.0	228.1	321.8	185.2	289.2	141.6	142.5	....	....	....	....	....	....	....
Capital Accounts	57a	2,300.0	2,277.7	2,434.1	2,213.3	2,459.5	2,970.3	2,725.2	3,002.9	....	....	....	....	....	....	....
Other Items (Net)	57r	–874.7	–1,114.3	–251.5	–351.5	–1,118.1	–2,450.4	–2,861.7	–2,070.8	....	....	....	....	....	....	....

Cape Verde

	1970	1971	1972	1973	1974	1975	1976	1977	1978	1979	1980	1981	1982	1983	1984
Interest Rates														*Percent Per Annum*	
Deposit Rate 601	....	....	....	....	....	....	....	....	....	....	....	....	....	....	....
Lending Rate 60p	....	....	....	....	6.5	6.5	6.5	6.5	6.5	6.5	6.5	6.5	6.5	6.5	6.5
Prices													*Index Numbers (1995=100):*		
Consumer Prices 64														46	51
International Transactions													*Millions of Escudos*		
Exports 70	48	46	48	48	53	61	48	75	75	92	170	147	191	246	212
Imports, c.i.f. 71	469	574	657	833	869	1,011	912	1,285	1,908	1,987	2,742	3,452	5,102	6,237	7,036
Balance of Payments													*Millions of US Dollars:*		
Current Account, n.i.e. .... 78al d	....	....	....	....	....	....	....	5.84	−8.57	−1.02	4.32	−21.61	−14.84	−13.35	−6.42
Goods: Exports f.o.b. .... 78aa d	....	....	....	....	....	....	....	1.24	3.07	4.12	9.12	6.26	3.97	3.30	6.93
Goods: Imports f.o.b. .... 78ab d	....	....	....	....	....	....	....	−45.08	−58.75	−71.25	−79.97	−85.90	−96.71	−104.59	−82.47
Trade Balance..................... 78ac d								−43.84	−55.67	−67.12	−70.85	−79.64	−92.74	−101.29	−75.54
Services: Credit .... 78ad d	....	....	....	....	....	....	....	.96	4.68	8.19	10.08	17.39	27.45	33.48	23.73
Services: Debit .... 78ae d	....	....	....	....	....	....	....	−3.66	−4.62	−5.48	−7.47	−17.17	−12.62	−12.20	−10.45
Balance on Goods & Services ..... 78af d								−46.54	−55.61	−64.41	−68.24	−79.42	−77.90	−80.01	−62.26
Income: Credit .... 78ag d	....	....	....	....	....	....	....	1.13	.90	2.12	3.48	2.88	1.66	1.32	1.62
Income: Debit .... 78ah d	....	....	....	....	....	....	....	−.14	−.26	−.83	−.09	−2.36	−6.13	−8.19	−6.12
Balance on Gds, Serv. & Inc. ...... 78ai d								−45.55	−54.98	−63.12	−64.85	−78.90	−82.37	−86.88	−66.75
Current Transfers, n.i.e.: Credit .... 78aj d	....	....	....	....	....	....	....	52.95	48.69	65.59	73.48	61.39	71.29	77.58	63.99
Current Transfers: Debit .... 78ak d	....	....	....	....	....	....	....	−1.57	−2.29	−3.49	−4.30	−4.11	−3.76	−4.05	−3.65
Capital Account, n.i.e. .... 78bc d	....	....	....	....	....	....	....	—	—	—	—	—	—	—	—
Capital Account, n.i.e.: Credit.......... 78ba d	....	....	....	....	....	....	....	—	—	—	—	—	—	—	—
Capital Account: Debit .... 78bb d	....	....	....	....	....	....	....	—	—	—	—	—	—	—	—
Financial Account, n.i.e. .... 78bj d	....	....	....	....	....	....	....	2.02	3.75	.42	1.14	20.56	21.66	20.24	6.41
Direct Investment Abroad .... 78bd d	....	....	....	....	....	....	....	—	—	—	—	—	—	—	—
Dir. Invest. in Rep. Econ., n.i.e. .... 78be d	....	....	....	....	....	....	....	—	—	—	—	—	—	—	—
Portfolio Investment Assets .... 78bf d	....	....	....	....	....	....	....	—	—	—	—	—	—	—	—
Equity Securities..................... 78bk d	....	....	....	....	....	....	....	—	—	—	—	—	—	—	—
Debt Securities .... 78bl d	....	....	....	....	....	....	....	—	—	—	—	—	—	—	—
Portfolio Investment Liab., n.i.e. .... 78bg d	....	....	....	....	....	....	....	—	—	—	—	—	—	—	—
Equity Securities..................... 78bm d	....	....	....	....	....	....	....	—	—	—	—	—	—	—	—
Debt Securities .... 78bn d	....	....	....	....	....	....	....	—	—	—	—	—	—	—	—
Financial Derivatives Assets .... 78bw d	....	....	....	....	....	....	....	—	—	—	—	—	—	—	—
Financial Derivatives Liabilities .... 78bx d	....	....	....	....	....	....	....	—	—	—	—	—	—	—	—
Other Investment Assets .... 78bh d	....	....	....	....	....	....	....	—	—	—	—	—	—	—	—
Monetary Authorities................. 78bo d	....	....	....	....	....	....	....	—	—	—	—	—	—	—	—
General Government .... 78bp d	....	....	....	....	....	....	....	—	—	—	—	—	—	—	—
Banks .... 78bq d	....	....	....	....	....	....	....	—	—	—	—	—	—	—	—
Other Sectors .... 78br d	....	....	....	....	....	....	....	—	—	—	—	—	—	—	—
Other Investment Liab., n.i.e. .... 78bi d	....	....	....	....	....	....	....	2.02	3.75	.42	1.14	20.56	21.66	20.24	6.41
Monetary Authorities .... 78bs d	....	....	....	....	....	....	....	−.33	2.19	−.38	−1.22	1.87	1.76	5.21	−3.75
General Government .... 78bt d	....	....	....	....	....	....	....	2.28	1.56	.80	2.33	18.67	18.50	14.74	10.23
Banks .... 78bu d	....	....	....	....	....	....	....								
Other Sectors .... 78bv d	....	....	....	....	....	....	....	.07	—	.01	.03	.02	1.40	.29	−.07
Net Errors and Omissions................ 78ca d	....	....	....	....	....	....	....	1.47	2.17	3.27	−5.63	−3.69	−1.86	−3.69	−4.84
Overall Balance .... 78cb d								9.33	−2.66	2.67	−.18	−4.74	4.96	3.20	−4.84
Reserves and Related Items .... 79da d	....	....	....	....	....	....	....	−9.33	2.66	−2.67	.18	4.74	−4.96	−3.20	4.84
Reserve Assets .... 79db d	....	....	....	....	....	....	....	−9.33	2.66	−2.67	.18	4.74	−4.96	−3.20	4.84
Use of Fund Credit and Loans .... 79dc d	....	....	....	....	....	....	....	—	—	—	—	—	—	—	—
Exceptional Financing .... 79de d	....	....	....	....	....	....	....	—	—	—	—	—	—	—	—
National Accounts													*Millions of Escudos*		
Exports of Goods & Services 90c	....	....	....	321	....	....	185	325	437	610	1,089	1,588	1,880	2,451	2,562
Government Consumption 91f	....	....	....	124	....	....	368	498	628	649	807	980	1,495	1,954	2,438
Gross Fixed Capital Formation 93e	....	....	....	279	....	....	553	847	1,537	1,655	2,214	3,271	4,222	4,840	4,966
Net Increase/Decrease(-) in Stocks....... 93i	....	....	....	56	....	....	−34	121	11	24	214	−175	149	21	−37
Private Consumption 96f	....	....	....	1,312	....	....	2,574	2,955	3,605	4,282	5,386	6,141	7,113	8,498	10,193
Imports of Goods & Services 98c	....	....	....	−1,016	....	....	−1,199	−1,684	−2,187	−2,711	−3,793	−4,753	−6,420	−7,622	−8,575
Gross Domestic Product (GDP) 99b	....	....	....	1,075	....	....	2,424	3,172	4,038	4,569	5,919	7,053	8,438	10,140	11,548
GDP Volume 1980 Prices................... 99b.p	....	....	....	....	....	....	....	....	....	....	5,919	6,296	6,520	7,121	7,381
GDP Volume (1995=100) .... 99bv p	....	....	....	....	....	....	....	....	....	....	48.2	51.3	53.1	58.0	60.1
GDP Deflator (1985=100)................. 99bi p	....	....	....	....	....	....	....	....	....	....	60.2	67.4	77.9	85.7	94.1
															Millions:
Population.................................. 99z	.27	.27	.29	.29	.29	.29	.30	.29	.29	.30	.30	.29	.30	.32	.33

Cape Verde

624

	1985	1986	1987	1988	1989	1990	1991	1992	1993	1994	1995	1996	1997	1998	1999		
Percent Per Annum																**Interest Rates**	
	4.0	4.0	4.0	4.0	4.0	4.0	4.0	4.0	4.0	4.0	I5.0	5.0	5.0	5.3	4.8	Deposit Rate	**601**
	10.0	10.0	10.0	10.0	10.0	10.0	10.0	10.0	10.0	10.7	12.0	12.0	12.1	12.5	12.0	Lending Rate	**60p**
Period Averages																**Prices**	
	54	60	62	65	67	75	82	I84	89	92	100	106	115	120	....	Consumer Prices	**64**
Millions of Escudos																**International Transactions**	
	524	355	567	237	527	398	438	327	312	407	686	...	...	...	....	Exports	**70**
	7,663	8,601	7,281	7,652	8,706	9,495	10,469	12,234	12,387	17,110	19,394	...	...	...	....	Imports, c.i.f.	**71**
Minus Sign Indicates Debit																Balance of Payments	
	-8.94	1.73	-2.57	-.49	-12.83	-3.83	-6.96	-12.15	-23.93	-45.73	-61.62	-35.04	-29.72	-58.00	....	Current Account, n.i.e.	**78al d**
	6.12	4.00	24.04	17.47	23.18	21.90	14.25	11.39	9.05	14.16	16.58	23.88	43.24	32.69	....	Goods: Exports f.o.b.	**78aa d**
	-86.74	-85.93	-93.59	-102.80	-111.71	-121.07	-128.82	-168.50	-151.95	-195.26	-233.63	-207.52	-215.10	-218.33	....	Goods: Imports f.o.b.	**78ab d**
	-80.61	-81.93	-69.54	-85.33	-88.53	-99.17	-114.56	-157.12	-142.90	-181.10	-217.05	-183.64	-171.87	-185.64	....	*Trade Balance*	**78ac d**
	24.81	32.25	22.79	25.63	26.70	34.94	33.89	39.31	40.09	47.01	66.90	77.52	91.31	86.45	....	Services: Credit	**78ad d**
	-8.60	-16.78	-19.57	-18.38	-26.62	-27.88	-20.54	-25.34	-29.39	-34.52	-60.50	-70.03	-71.90	-90.57	....	Services: Debit	**78ae d**
	-64.40	-66.45	-66.32	-78.07	-88.45	-92.11	-101.22	-143.14	-132.20	-168.61	-210.65	-176.15	-152.46	-189.76	....	*Balance on Goods & Services*	**78af d**
	1.90	2.64	4.17	5.28	7.60	6.41	5.85	5.68	4.81	4.22	4.00	2.98	4.87	2.51	....	Income: Credit	**78ag d**
	-5.98	-5.33	-4.39	-4.53	-3.61	-4.12	-4.65	-4.40	-3.85	-4.56	-6.57	-7.38	-8.46	-8.07	....	Income: Debit	**78ah d**
	-68.47	-69.14	-66.54	-77.32	-84.46	-89.82	-100.02	-141.86	-131.24	-168.95	-213.22	-180.55	-156.05	-195.32	....	*Balance on Gds, Serv. & Inc.*	**78ai d**
	63.37	72.29	64.72	78.08	72.65	87.11	95.14	133.81	110.41	125.55	155.96	148.38	129.91	142.46	....	Current Transfers, n.i.e.: Credit	**78aj d**
	-3.84	-1.41	-.75	-1.25	-1.03	-1.12	-2.08	-4.09	-3.11	-2.33	-4.36	-2.87	-3.58	-5.15	....	Current Transfers: Debit	**78ak d**
	—	—	1.66	2.08	1.92	1.62	7.78	9.17	19.02	20.07	20.88	12.83	6.30	19.01	....	Capital Account, n.i.e.	**78bc d**
	—	—	1.66	2.08	1.92	1.62	7.78	9.17	19.02	20.07	20.88	12.83	6.30	19.01	....	Capital Account, n.i.e.: Credit	**78ba d**
	—	—	—	—	—	—	—	—							....	Capital Account: Debit	**78bb d**
	18.24	9.23	9.69	.89	12.93	-19.38	16.84	16.82	17.52	39.60	44.51	46.00	44.06	36.97	....	Financial Account, n.i.e.	**78bj d**
	—	—	—	-.18	-.77	-.32	-.54	-1.20	-.66	-.42	-.57	-.26	-.05	...	....	Direct Investment Abroad	**78bd d**
	—	-.01	2.79	.60	.17	.25	1.74	.45	3.64	2.13	26.18	28.53	11.58	9.03	....	Dir. Invest. in Rep. Econ., n.i.e.	**78be d**
	—	—	—	—	—	—	—	—	...	...	...	...	...	...	....	Portfolio Investment Assets	**78bf d**
	—	—	—	—	—	—	—	—	...	...	...	...	...	...	....	Equity Securities	**78bk d**
	—	—	—	—	—	—	—	—	...	...	...	...	...	...	....	Debt Securities	**78bl d**
	—	—	—	—	—	—	—	—	...	...	...	...	...	...	....	Portfolio Investment Liab., n.i.e.	**78bg d**
	—	—	—	—	—	—	—	—	...	...	...	...	...	...	....	Equity Securities	**78bm d**
	—	—	—	—	—	—	—	—	...	...	...	...	...	...	....	Debt Securities	**78bn d**
	...	...	...	...	...	...	...	...	...	...	...	...	...	...	....	Financial Derivatives Assets	**78bw d**
	...	...	...	...	...	...	...	...	...	...	...	...	...	...	....	Financial Derivatives Liabilities	**78bx d**
	—	—	-.56	-.56	.42	-28.99	6.99	.57	-6.75	1.61	-1.67	-2.25	-1.79	-22.44	....	Other Investment Assets	**78bh d**
	...	...	-.56	-.56	.42	-28.99	6.99	.57	-6.75	1.61	2.32	-2.34	-1.84	4.02	....	Monetary Authorities	**78bo d**
	—	—	—	—	—	—	—	—	...	...	-3.99	.09	.05	-28.39	....	General Government	**78bp d**
														3.02	....	Banks	**78bq d**
														-1.09	....	Other Sectors	**78br d**
	18.24	9.24	7.47	1.04	13.11	9.67	8.65	17.01	21.29	36.28	20.57	19.99	34.33	50.39	....	Other Investment Liab., n.i.e.	**78bi d**
	4.56	-7.66	—	-.27	-.43	-.21	1.27	.68	.88	-1.21	-.93	-.12	-.12	-.01	....	Monetary Authorities	**78bs d**
	14.92	12.09	12.17	4.92	13.82	7.54	8.79	18.16	19.69	22.74	17.57	22.88	19.79	28.49	....	General Government	**78bt d**
	—	—	—	—	—	—	—	—	2.65	1.11	2.38	.02	4.94	8.00	....	Banks	**78bu d**
	-1.24	4.81	-4.70	-3.62	-.27	2.34	-1.41	-1.84	-1.93	13.64	1.55	-2.80	9.72	13.91	....	Other Sectors	**78bv d**
	4.94	-11.57	-5.78	-3.52	13.40	14.62	-33.94	8.71	2.38	8.31	-35.64	-1.34	-20.40	12.78	....	Net Errors and Omissions	**78ca d**
	14.24	-.61	3.00	-1.04	15.42	-6.97	-16.28	22.55	14.99	22.24	-31.87	22.46	.24	10.76	....	*Overall Balance*	**78cb d**
	-14.24	.61	-3.00	1.04	-15.42	6.97	16.28	-22.55	-14.99	-22.24	31.87	-22.46	-.24	-10.76	....	Reserves and Related Items	**79da d**
	-14.24	-.89	.04	1.52	-14.02	12.29	19.31	-18.46	-11.50	-20.78	30.93	-19.76	9.84	-8.50	....	Reserve Assets	**79db d**
	—	—	—	—	—	—	—	—	—	—	—	—	—	—	....	Use of Fund Credit and Loans	**79dc d**
	—	1.50	-3.04	-.48	-1.40	-5.32	-3.04	-4.09	-3.49	-1.46	.95	-2.70	-10.08	-2.26	....	Exceptional Financing	**79de d**
Millions of Escudos																**National Accounts**	
	2,887	2,733	2,984	3,190	....	....	....	....	....	....	....			....		Exports of Goods & Services	**90c**
	2,748	3,380	3,673	3,968	....	....	....	....	....	....	....			....		Government Consumption	**91f**
	5,957	6,440	7,053	7,721	....	....	....	....	....	....	....			....		Gross Fixed Capital Formation	**93e**
	-246	439	328	-434	....	....	....	....	....	....	....			....		Net Increase/Decrease(-) in Stocks	**93i**
	11,471	13,407	15,134	17,848	....	....	....	....	....	....	....			....		Private Consumption	**96f**
	-9,736	-10,841	-11,189	-11,653	....	....	....	....	....	....	....			....		Imports of Goods & Services	**98c**
	13,081	15,558	17,984	20,640	....	....	....	....	....	....	....			....		Gross Domestic Product (GDP)	**99b**
	7,870	8,096	8,444	8,951	9,461	9,526	9,660	9,954	10,682	11,422	12,278			....		GDP Volume 1980 Prices	**99b.p**
	64.1	65.9	68.8	72.9	77.1	77.6	78.7	81.1	87.0	93.0	100.0			....		GDP Volume (1995=100)	**99bv p**
	100.0	115.6	128.1	138.7	....	....	....	....	....	....	....			....		GDP Deflator (1985=100)	**99bi p**
Midyear Estimates																	
	.33	.34	.35	.33	.33	.34	.35	.36	.37	.38	.39	.40	.41	.42	.42	Population	**99z**

(See notes in the back of the book.)

Central African Rep.

		1970	1971	1972	1973	1974	1975	1976	1977	1978	1979	1980	1981	1982	1983	1984
Exchange Rates														*Francs per SDR:*		
Official Rate	aa	276.02	283.61	278.00	284.00	272.08	262.55	288.70	285.76	272.28	264.78	287.99	334.52	370.92	436.97	470.11
														Francs per US Dollar:		
Official Rate	ae	276.02	261.22	256.05	235.42	222.22	224.27	248.49	235.25	209.00	201.00	225.80	287.40	328.61	417.37	479.60
Official Rate	rf	276.40	275.59	252.03	222.89	240.70	214.31	238.95	245.68	225.66	212.72	211.28	271.73	328.61	381.07	436.96
														Index Numbers (1995=100):		
Official Rate	ahx	180.5	98.6	197.9	224.6	207.2	233.0	209.0	203.0	221.4	234.6	236.4	184.6	152.6	131.5	114.5
Nominal Effective Exchange Rate	nec	....	....	....	....	....	....	....	....	....	69.3	71.7	68.6	67.1	66.8	68.9
Real Effective Exchange Rate	rec	....	....	....	....	....	....	....	....	....	....	....	187.3	180.7	177.8	182.4	171.9
Fund Position														*Millions of SDRs:*		
Quota	2f.s	13.00	13.00	13.00	13.00	13.00	13.00	13.00	13.00	16.00	16.00	24.00	24.00	24.00	30.40	30.40
SDRs	1b.s	.01	—	1.21	1.02	.81	2.25	1.62	1.56	1.30	1.36	—	.07	.17	.71	2.59
Reserve Position in the Fund	1c.s	1.33	.14	.29	.44	—	—	—	—	1.66	1.85	—	—	1.21	1.61	.11
Total Fund Cred.&Loans Outstg.	2tl	—	—	—	—	2.66	4.85	9.59	9.59	15.67	13.57	18.43	32.41	34.19	38.15	35.77
International Liquidity												*Millions of US Dollars Unless Otherwise Indicated:*				
Total Reserves minus Gold	1l.d	1.39	.21	1.72	1.78	1.74	3.83	18.83	25.35	24.13	44.11	54.98	69.27	46.37	46.79	52.68
SDRs	1b.d	.01	—	1.31	1.23	.99	2.63	1.88	1.89	1.69	1.79	—	.08	.19	.74	2.54
Reserve Position in the Fund	1c.d	1.33	.15	.31	.53	—	—	—	—	2.16	2.44	—	—	1.33	1.69	.11
Foreign Exchange	1d.d	.05	.06	.09	.02	.75	1.19	16.95	23.46	20.28	39.88	54.98	69.19	44.85	44.36	50.03
Gold (Million Fine Troy Ounces)	1ad	....	....	....	....	....	....	—	.006	.009	.011	.011	.011	.011	.011	.011
Gold (National Valuation)	1and	....	....	....	....	....	—	—	.92	1.94	5.79	6.56	4.45	5.00	4.21	3.44
Monetary Authorities: Other Liab.	4..d	.16	.31	.32	.27	2.40	2.37	1.08	1.85	1.21	2.23	1.59	.70	1.74	2.60	1.47
Deposit Money Banks: Assets	7a.d	6.55	6.69	6.96	12.91	.83	.77	8.56	4.10	8.36	12.23	14.61	11.70	5.65	9.11	9.68
Liabilities	7b.d	9.36	10.33	9.46	16.71	23.29	24.14	20.20	24.17	26.57	25.16	23.83	17.87	4.16	1.31	2.46
Monetary Authorities														*Billions of Francs:*		
Foreign Assets	11	.39	.05	.44	.41	.39	.86	4.68	6.18	5.45	10.04	13.90	21.19	17.27	21.30	26.91
Claims on Central Government	12a	2.15	1.73	2.27	2.63	3.09	3.88	5.38	5.84	9.13	8.49	12.31	19.44	20.48	27.27	26.73
Claims on Deposit Money Banks	12e	5.32	4.78	5.29	6.66	7.23	6.80	3.37	3.42	7.67	8.47	11.69	11.12	16.40	15.74	12.13
Claims on Other Banking Insts	12f	....	....	....	....	....	....	....	....	....	....	....	....	....	....	....
Reserve Money	14	5.24	5.14	5.78	5.99	7.58	7.87	9.28	11.49	13.73	18.16	24.81	32.43	31.77	35.41	37.91
of which: Currency Outside DMBs	14a	5.19	5.05	5.71	5.85	7.44	7.52	8.99	11.19	13.45	17.98	24.38	31.99	31.39	34.93	37.33
Foreign Liabilities	16c	.04	.08	.08	.06	1.26	1.80	3.04	3.18	5.99	5.47	9.31	15.29	17.98	23.21	22.88
Central Government Deposits	16d	1.94	.75	.19	2.54	.20	1.39	.35	.19	.88	.59	.54	.85	.68	.89	.77
Capital Accounts	17a	—	—	—	.01	.01	.01	.02	.01	.01	.01	1.53	1.30	1.69	1.78	1.65
Other Items (Net)	17r	.62	.59	1.94	1.10	1.67	.46	.74	.57	1.63	2.76	1.72	1.87	2.04	3.02	2.55
Deposit Money Banks														*Billions of Francs:*		
Reserves	20	.05	.10	.07	.14	.14	.36	.29	.30	.28	.18	.43	.43	.38	.48	.58
Foreign Assets	21	1.82	1.71	1.78	2.97	.18	.17	2.13	1.97	1.75	2.46	3.30	3.36	1.90	3.80	4.64
Claims on Central Government	22a	.59	1.40	1.22	2.63	4.31	5.29	5.06	5.25	5.36	5.22	5.17	5.31	1.44	.51	1.01
Claims on Nonfin.Pub.Enterprises	22c	....	....	....	....	....	....	....	....	....	....	....	....	....	....	....
Claims on Private Sector	22d	10.27	8.13	8.98	9.83	14.62	13.33	12.04	14.73	18.24	15.62	23.47	24.43	30.35	30.84	30.62
Claims on Other Banking Insts	22f	....	....	....	....	....	....	....	....	....	....	....	....	....	....	....
Claims on Nonbank Financial Insts	22g	....	....	....	....	....	....	....	....	....	....	....	....	....	....	....
Demand Deposits	24	2.48	2.72	3.42	3.38	4.88	4.62	7.94	7.04	7.16	8.19	10.25	10.37	9.34	10.47	11.01
Time and Savings Deposits	25	.81	.79	.81	1.13	1.09	1.35	2.22	2.29	1.99	.97	2.01	3.01	2.73	3.15	3.87
Foreign Liabilities	26c	1.72	1.90	1.68	3.24	4.67	4.96	4.57	4.78	4.65	5.06	5.38	5.14	1.40	.55	1.18
Long-Term Foreign Liabilities	26cl	.88	.74	.74	.60	.50	.45	.45	.91	.91	....	....	....	....	....	....
Central Government Deposits	26d	.20	.16	.19	.25	.22	.20	.26	.28	.31	.04	.41	1.53	1.45	3.14	4.94
Credit from Monetary Authorities	26g	5.32	4.78	5.29	6.66	7.23	6.80	3.37	3.42	7.67	8.47	11.69	11.12	16.40	15.74	12.13
Capital Accounts	27a	1.24	.58	.52	.73	.92	1.09	1.27	3.27	3.60	3.70	3.67	4.78	5.76	6.33	8.60
Other Items (Net)	27r	.08	-.33	-.58	-.42	-.26	-.33	-.55	-.74	-.66	-2.95	-1.03	-2.41	-3.02	-3.75	-4.87
Post Office: Checking Deposits	24..i	.16	.15	.16	.16	.27	.39	.45	.33	.30	.23	.30	.38	.33	.37	.32
Postal Debt	26c.i	.41	1.21	1.03	2.39	3.88	4.74	4.47	4.87	5.03	4.95	4.84	4.81	.95	—	—
Monetary Survey														*Billions of Francs:*		
Foreign Assets (Net)	31n	.44	-.22	.46	.08	-5.36	-5.73	-.80	-.81	-3.44	1.97	2.51	4.12	-.21	1.35	7.50
Domestic Credit	32	10.87	10.35	12.09	12.31	21.60	20.91	21.87	25.34	31.53	28.71	40.00	46.79	50.14	54.59	52.64
Claims on Central Govt. (Net)	32an	.60	2.22	3.11	2.48	6.98	7.58	9.83	10.61	13.29	13.09	16.53	22.36	19.80	23.75	22.03
Claims on Nonfin.Pub.Enterprises	32c	....	....	....	....	....	....	....	....	....	....	....	....	....	....	....
Claims on Private Sector	32d	10.27	8.13	8.98	9.83	14.62	13.33	12.04	14.73	18.24	15.62	23.47	24.43	30.35	30.84	30.62
Claims on Other Banking Insts	32f	....	....	....	....	....	....	....	....	....	....	....	....	....	....	....
Claims on Nonbank Financial Inst	32g	....	....	....	....	....	....	....	....	....	....	....	....	....	....	....
Money	34	7.67	7.77	9.13	9.23	12.32	12.13	16.93	18.23	20.61	26.17	34.63	42.36	40.73	45.40	48.33
Quasi-Money	35	.81	.79	.81	1.13	1.09	1.35	2.22	2.29	1.99	.97	2.01	3.01	2.73	3.15	3.87
Other Items (Net)	37r	2.83	1.57	2.61	2.03	2.83	1.69	1.93	4.02	5.50	3.53	5.88	5.55	6.47	7.39	7.94
Money plus Quasi-Money	35l	8.49	8.56	9.94	10.36	13.41	13.49	19.15	20.51	22.60	27.15	36.63	45.37	43.46	48.55	52.20
Interest Rates														*Percent Per Annum*		
Discount Rate (End of Period)	60	4.50	4.50	4.50	4.50	5.50	5.50	6.50	6.50	6.50	8.50	8.50	8.50	8.50	8.50	8.50
Deposit Rate	60l	....	....	....	....	....	....	....	....	5.50	4.00	5.50	7.50	7.50	7.50	7.50
Lending Rate	60p	....	....	....	....	....	....	....	....	9.50	8.50	10.50	12.00	12.00	12.50	12.50
Prices and Labor														*Index Numbers (1995=100):*		
Wholesale Prices (1990=100)	63	21.9	23.1	24.5	25.1	30.0	35.7	37.4	40.3	43.4	49.4	57.3	65.7	75.1	81.7	100.3
Consumer Prices	64	....	....	....	....	....	....	....	....	....	....	53.3	53.3	60.4	69.2	71.0
														Number in Thousands:		
Employment	67e	....	....	....	....	....	....	....	....	....	....	....	....	....	....	....
Unemployment	67c	....	....	....	....	....	....	....	....	....	....	....	....	....	....	....
International Transactions														*Millions of Francs:*		
Exports	70	8,434	8,939	9,930	8,328	11,622	10,120	14,623	20,033	16,182	16,937	24,384	21,323	35,461	28,405	37,022
Imports, c.i.f.	71	9,492	9,053	8,547	11,496	11,090	14,615	13,155	15,540	12,775	14,816	17,009	25,646	41,306	25,951	38,193

1985	1986	1987	1988	1989	1990	1991	1992	1993	1994	1995	1996	1997	1998	1999		
															Exchange Rates	
End of Period																
415.26	394.78	378.78	407.68	380.32	364.84	370.48	378.57	404.89	I780.44	728.38	753.06	807.94	791.61	I896.19	Official Rate	aa
End of Period (ae) Period Average (rf)																
378.05	322.75	267.00	302.95	289.40	256.45	259.00	275.32	294.77	I534.60	490.00	523.70	598.81	562.21	I652.95	Official Rate	ae
449.26	346.31	300.54	297.85	319.01	272.26	282.11	264.69	283.16	I555.20	499.15	511.55	583.67	589.95	I615.70	Official Rate	rf
Period Averages																
111.9	144.3	166.1	167.8	156.5	183.7	177.4	188.9	176.3	90.0	100.0	97.5	85.6	84.7	81.1	Official Rate	ah x
74.1	80.6	85.2	88.8	93.9	107.5	115.5	133.2	147.3	92.4	100.0	105.0	104.4	105.5	105.2	Nominal Effective Exchange Rate	ne c
183.3	192.3	177.6	164.1	156.9	157.8	146.7	144.2	135.2	84.7	100.0	102.2	99.1	96.5	92.1	Real Effective Exchange Rate	re c
															Fund Position	
End of Period																
30.40	30.40	30.40	30.40	30.40	30.40	30.40	41.20	41.20	41.20	41.20	41.20	41.20	41.20	55.70	Quota	2f. s
1.54	.43	4.93	9.15	—	3.42	.49	.04	.03	.01	.02	.01	—	.01	.04	SDRs	1b. s
.11	.11	.11	.11	.11	.09	.09	.09	.09	.09	.09	.10	.10	.10	.10	Reserve Position in the Fund	1c. s
35.49	34.13	36.58	37.33	26.88	25.73	23.28	22.09	20.96	28.34	23.48	19.22	13.80	12.47	17.09	Total Fund Cred.&Loans Outstg.	2tl
															International Liquidity	
End of Period																
49.62	65.35	96.73	108.47	113.06	118.63	102.98	100.12	111.98	210.01	233.64	232.24	178.56	145.70	136.28	Total Reserves minus Gold	1l. d
1.69	.53	6.99	12.31	—	4.87	.70	.06	.04	.01	.02	.01	—	.01	.05	SDRs	1b. d
.12	.13	.16	.15	.14	.13	.13	.12	.13	.14	.14	.14	.13	.13	.13	Reserve Position in the Fund	1c. d
47.81	64.69	89.58	96.01	112.92	113.63	102.15	99.94	111.81	209.86	233.48	232.09	178.43	145.56	136.10	Foreign Exchange	1d. d
.011	.011	.011	.011	.011	.011	.011	.011	.011	.011	.011	.011	.011	....	....	Gold (Million Fine Troy Ounces)	1ad
3.60	4.36	5.37	4.52	3.52	3.98	3.94	3.70	4.42	I4.21	4.29	4.10	3.24	3.20	....	Gold (National Valuation)	1an d
1.12	.52	1.14	I25.44	19.72	17.35	16.77	21.20	12.45	12.57	12.79	12.43	11.87	12.90	17.24	Monetary Authorities: Other Liab.	4.. d
21.94	28.04	29.74	13.02	10.57	12.65	9.43	9.12	6.85	11.45	6.39	4.41	4.99	5.91	10.48	Deposit Money Banks: Assets	7a. d
3.26	12.24	12.67	16.24	14.24	16.18	13.22	14.34	12.04	12.10	7.93	7.35	6.36	7.43	8.81	Liabilities	7b. d
															Monetary Authorities	
End of Period																
20.12	22.50	27.27	I34.25	34.01	31.52	27.69	28.59	34.29	114.56	116.59	123.77	108.86	83.71	91.10	Foreign Assets	11
24.22	24.35	22.65	I22.68	17.94	17.41	I27.66	28.23	28.34	41.99	36.97	37.69	32.76	32.28	37.86	Claims on Central Government	12a
18.13	18.85	13.11	I9.15	7.60	11.67	I2.51	2.18	3.66	—	1.60	1.24	.50	5.00	4.79	Claims on Deposit Money Banks	12e
....	....	....	...	...	...	...	...	...	...	...	...	...	...	—	Claims on Other Banking Insts	12f
38.27	43.03	42.89	I39.00	42.82	43.13	43.14	43.80	52.46	96.65	101.04	108.82	95.35	76.11	81.96	Reserve Money	14
38.03	40.95	42.28	I38.71	42.24	41.84	42.26	43.36	52.16	88.53	98.97	104.00	92.96	75.25	81.12	of which: Currency Outside DMBs	14a
19.16	16.44	15.89	I22.93	15.93	13.84	12.97	14.20	12.16	28.84	23.37	20.98	18.25	17.13	26.57	Foreign Liabilities	16c
.90	1.19	1.72	I5.14	1.09	2.05	.59	.63	1.69	1.89	1.58	2.82	1.36	.91	3.45	Central Government Deposits	16d
1.36	1.41	1.44	I1.46	1.34	1.11	1.23	.99	1.27	1.02	.83	.90	.65	.64	.97	Capital Accounts	17a
2.79	3.63	1.09	I-2.45	-1.62	.47	-.07	-.62	-1.28	28.15	28.35	29.18	26.51	26.20	20.81	Other Items (Net)	17r
															Deposit Money Banks	
End of Period																
.24	2.07	.61	I.29	.58	1.29	.88	.44	.30	8.11	2.07	4.82	2.38	.86	.84	Reserves	20
8.29	9.05	7.94	I4.01	3.06	3.24	2.44	2.51	2.02	6.12	3.13	2.31	2.99	3.32	6.84	Foreign Assets	21
.40	3.15	1.72	I1.96	2.20	2.28	3.76	I4.22	5.21	5.07	4.35	3.33	4.47	3.50	3.96	Claims on Central Government	22a
....	....	....	4.45	6.32	11.03	9.35	4.25	4.54	5.84	7.65	7.14	6.37	7.97	14.71	Claims on Nonfin.Pub.Enterprises	22c
35.03	31.97	29.46	I27.96	30.21	29.15	26.60	16.85	15.93	18.70	23.16	23.25	24.17	27.95	27.77	Claims on Private Sector	22d
....	....	....	—	—	—	—	—	—	—	—	—	—	—	—	Claims on Other Banking Insts	22f
....	....	....	...	...	...	...	...	...	...	...	...	...	...	.92	Claims on Nonbank Financial Insts	22g
14.39	11.58	12.09	I11.03	14.42	12.71	10.77	7.68	7.26	14.86	12.27	12.64	14.22	12.33	17.53	Demand Deposits	24
5.01	6.17	6.48	I7.32	7.75	7.47	6.49	6.20	5.16	11.89	8.98	9.42	9.14	9.97	9.69	Time and Savings Deposits	25
1.23	3.95	3.38	I2.77	2.43	2.66	I1.83	3.53	3.18	5.80	3.45	3.43	3.45	3.52	5.66	Foreign Liabilities	26c
—	—	—	I2.15	1.69	1.49	I1.60	.42	.37	.66	.44	.42	.36	.66	.10	Long-Term Foreign Liabilities	26cl
2.16	1.64	1.59	I3.01	3.75	5.59	5.30	I2.41	1.98	3.55	7.22	7.77	7.04	4.73	6.25	Central Government Deposits	26d
18.15	18.85	13.11	I9.15	7.60	11.67	I2.51	2.18	3.66	—	1.60	1.24	.50	5.00	4.79	Credit from Monetary Authorities	26g
8.87	10.70	10.75	I7.19	7.49	7.74	I19.97	8.01	8.10	8.70	9.35	7.78	7.44	8.20	13.35	Capital Accounts	27a
-5.84	-6.65	-7.66	I-3.95	-2.75	-2.34	-5.43	I-2.15	-1.71	-1.62	-2.94	-1.85	-1.77	-.79	-2.31	Other Items (Net)	27r
.32	.31	.31	.31	....	....	....	....	....	....	....	....	....	....	....	Post Office: Checking Deposits	24.. i
—	2.35	1.17													Postal Debt	26c. i
															Monetary Survey	
End of Period																
8.02	11.16	15.94	I13.97	19.52	18.94	I13.74	12.95	20.60	85.38	92.47	101.25	89.79	65.73	65.62	Foreign Assets (Net)	31n
56.60	56.64	50.52	I48.90	51.83	52.23	I61.47	I50.52	50.35	66.15	63.33	60.82	59.38	66.06	75.53	Domestic Credit	32
21.57	24.67	21.06	I16.49	15.30	12.05	I25.53	I29.41	29.88	41.61	32.52	30.44	28.84	30.14	32.13	Claims on Central Govt. (Net)	32an
....	....	....	4.45	6.32	11.03	9.35	4.25	4.54	5.84	7.65	7.14	6.37	7.97	14.71	Claims on Nonfin.Pub.Enterprises	32c
35.03	31.97	29.46	I27.96	30.21	29.15	26.60	16.85	15.93	18.70	23.16	23.25	24.17	27.95	27.77	Claims on Private Sector	32d
....	....	....	—	—	—	—	—	—	—	—	—	—	—	—	Claims on Other Banking Insts	32f
....	....	....	...	...	...	...	...	...	...	...	...	...	...	.92	Claims on Nonbank Financial Inst	32g
52.42	52.54	54.37	I49.74	56.66	54.56	53.03	51.05	59.42	103.40	111.24	116.64	107.19	87.58	98.64	Money	34
5.01	6.17	6.48	I7.32	7.75	7.47	6.49	6.20	5.16	11.89	8.98	9.42	9.14	9.97	9.69	Quasi-Money	35
7.19	9.09	5.61	I5.81	6.94	9.14	I15.70	I6.23	6.38	36.25	35.58	36.00	32.84	34.25	32.81	Other Items (Net)	37r
57.43	58.71	60.85	I57.06	64.41	62.03	59.52	57.24	64.58	115.29	120.22	126.07	116.33	97.54	108.34	Money plus Quasi-Money	35l
															Interest Rates	
Percent Per Annum																
9.00	8.00	8.00	9.50	10.00	11.00	10.75	12.00	11.50	I7.75	8.60	7.75	7.50	7.00	7.60	Discount Rate (End of Period)	60
7.50	7.35	7.19	7.44	7.50	I7.50	7.50	7.50	7.75	8.08	5.50	5.46	5.00	5.00	5.00	Deposit Rate	60l
12.50	12.00	11.42	12.25	13.00	I18.50	18.15	17.77	17.46	17.50	16.00	22.00	22.00	22.00	22.00	Lending Rate	60p
															Prices and Labor	
Period Averages																
107.1	111.1	111.5	94.7	98.4	100.0	98.8	99.1	97.7	....	....	....	150.6	150.5	....	Wholesale Prices (1990=100)	63
78.4	80.1	74.6	71.6	72.2	71.9	70.4	69.4	67.4	83.9	100.0	103.7	105.4	103.4	....	Consumer Prices	64
Period Averages																
19	18	18	17	14	15	12	14	....	....	....	....	....	....	....	Employment	67e
8	10	9	9	8	8	8	6	6	10	8	....	....	....	....	Unemployment	67c
															International Transactions	
Millions of Francs																
41,217	22,975	39,180	19,769	42,866	32,770	13,209	28,328	31,079	83,900	85,300	75,100	89,700	....	....	Exports	70
50,686	57,841	61,370	42,002	47,994	42,050	26,186	38,469	35,559	77,300	86,900	72,300	84,400	....	....	Imports, c.i.f.	71

Central African Rep.

		1970	1971	1972	1973	1974	1975	1976	1977	1978	1979	1980	1981	1982	1983	1984
Balance of Payments															*Millions of US Dollars:*	
Current Account, n.i.e.	78ald	...	...	...	...	...	...	...	−19.0	−23.1	−16.1	−43.1	−4.3	−42.6	−29.3	−33.4
Goods: Exports f.o.b.	78aad	...	...	...	...	...	...	...	104.5	110.3	122.2	147.2	117.7	124.4	123.4	114.4
Goods: Imports f.o.b.	78abd	...	...	...	...	...	...	...	−103.9	−117.7	−132.9	−185.1	−144.6	−149.7	−137.5	−140.1
Trade Balance	78acd	...	...	...	...	...	...	...	.6	−7.4	−10.7	−37.9	−26.9	−25.3	−14.1	−25.6
Services: Credit	78add	...	...	...	...	...	...	...	23.4	32.7	35.0	53.8	51.7	41.6	35.7	34.8
Services: Debit	78aed	...	...	...	...	...	...	...	−70.2	−87.9	−113.3	−142.3	−92.1	−106.4	−103.7	−86.4
Balance on Goods & Services	78afd	...	...	...	...	...	...	...	−46.3	−62.6	−89.0	−126.4	−67.2	−90.1	−82.1	−77.2
Income: Credit	78agd	...	...	...	...	...	...	...	2.8	3.7	2.6	4.4	8.0	5.0	3.1	2.7
Income: Debit	78ahd	...	...	...	...	...	...	...	−3.4	−2.5	−8.0	−1.8	−4.7	−12.2	−13.8	−12.4
Balance on Gds, Serv. & Inc.	78aid	...	...	...	...	...	...	...	−46.9	−61.5	−94.4	−123.8	−63.9	−97.4	−92.8	−86.9
Current Transfers, n.i.e.: Credit	78ajd	...	...	...	...	...	...	...	43.0	56.7	89.9	107.6	81.6	76.8	86.2	75.7
Current Transfers: Debit	78akd	...	...	...	...	...	...	...	−15.1	−18.3	−11.5	−26.8	−22.0	−22.1	−22.7	−22.3
Capital Account, n.i.e.	78bcd	...	...	...	...	...	...	...	—	—	—	—	—	—	—	—
Capital Account, n.i.e.: Credit	78bad	...	...	...	...	...	...	...	—	—	—	—	—	—	—	—
Capital Account: Debit	78bbd	...	...	...	...	...	...	...	—	—	—	—	—	—	—	—
Financial Account, n.i.e.	78bjd	...	...	...	...	...	...	...	15.7	3.9	43.9	61.5	13.5	−1.7	8.3	26.3
Direct Investment Abroad	78bdd	...	...	...	...	...	...	...	−.1	1.3	−.3	—	—	−.3	−.4	−.3
Dir. Invest. in Rep. Econ., n.i.e.	78bed	...	...	...	...	...	...	...	−2.8	6.1	22.8	5.3	5.8	9.2	4.5	5.1
Portfolio Investment Assets	78bfd	...	...	...	...	...	...	...	—	—	—	—	—	—	—	—
Equity Securities	78bkd	...	...	...	...	...	...	...	—	—	—	—	—	—	—	—
Debt Securities	78bld	...	...	...	...	...	...	...	—	—	—	—	—	—	—	—
Portfolio Investment Liab., n.i.e.	78bgd	...	...	...	...	...	...	...	—	—	—	—	—	—	—	—
Equity Securities	78bmd	...	...	...	...	...	...	...	—	—	—	—	—	—	—	—
Debt Securities	78bnd	...	...	...	...	...	...	...	—	—	—	—	—	—	—	—
Financial Derivatives Assets	78bwd	...	...	...	...	...	...	...	...	...	...	...	...	...	...	...
Financial Derivatives Liabilities	78bxd	...	...	...	...	...	...	...	...	...	...	...	...	...	...	...
Other Investment Assets	78bhd	...	...	...	...	...	...	...	.5	−12.7	−6.0	−4.0	−28.0	.4	−17.7	−8.7
Monetary Authorities	78bod	...	...	...	...	...	...	...	...	...	...	...	...	...	...	...
General Government	78bpd	...	...	...	...	...	...	...	−.1	−1.0	—	—	−2.9	−2.1	−.9	—
Banks	78bqd	...	...	...	...	...	...	...	3.2	−4.4	−2.4	−4.0	−.2	4.5	−5.0	−1.9
Other Sectors	78brd	...	...	...	...	...	...	...	−2.5	−7.3	−3.6	—	−24.9	−1.9	−11.7	−6.7
Other Investment Liab., n.i.e.	78bid	...	...	...	...	...	...	...	18.1	9.2	27.5	60.1	35.8	−10.9	21.9	30.1
Monetary Authorities	78bsd	...	...	...	...	...	...	...	1.1	1.5	1.3	7.1	5.1	−7.8	.7	−1.0
General Government	78btd	...	...	...	...	...	...	...	6.3	.3	3.5	40.1	6.5	−15.1	14.8	23.0
Banks	78bud	...	...	...	...	...	...	...	4.2	−.6	−.2	1.5	−.9	1.9	−1.2	1.7
Other Sectors	78bvd	...	...	...	...	...	...	...	6.4	7.9	22.9	11.4	25.0	10.1	7.7	6.4
Net Errors and Omissions	78cad	...	...	...	...	...	...	...	9.3	8.2	−10.0	−12.1	−11.4	2.1	7.6	6.7
Overall Balance	78cbd	...	...	...	...	...	...	...	6.0	−11.0	17.8	6.3	−2.2	−42.2	−13.4	−.4
Reserves and Related Items	79dad	...	...	...	...	...	...	...	−6.0	11.0	−17.8	−6.3	2.2	42.2	13.4	.4
Reserve Assets	79dbd	...	...	...	...	...	...	...	−6.1	3.1	−16.9	−14.5	−25.5	21.4	−3.2	−5.0
Use of Fund Credit and Loans	79dcd	...	...	...	...	...	...	...	—	7.5	−2.7	6.3	17.0	2.0	4.3	−2.5
Exceptional Financing	79ded	...	...	...	...	...	...	...	.1	.4	1.9	1.9	10.6	18.9	12.3	7.9
Government Finance															*Millions of Francs:*	
Deficit (-) or Surplus	80	...	...	...	...	...	...	...	...	...	...	...	−6,671	...	...	...
Revenue	81	...	...	...	...	...	...	...	...	...	...	...	30,365	...	...	...
Grants Received	81z	...	...	...	...	...	...	...	...	...	...	...	4,686	...	...	...
Expenditure	82	...	...	...	...	...	...	...	...	...	...	...	41,538	...	...	...
Lending Minus Repayments	83	...	...	...	...	...	...	...	...	...	...	...	618	...	...	...
Overall Cash Adjustment	80x	...	...	...	...	...	...	...	...	...	...	...	434	...	...	...
Financing																
Net Borrowing: Domestic	84a	...	...	...	...	...	...	...	...	...	...	...	4,489	...	...	...
Foreign	85a	...	...	...	...	...	...	...	...	...	...	...	3,925	...	...	...
Use of Cash Balances	87	...	...	...	...	...	...	...	...	...	...	...	−1,743	...	...	...
National Accounts															*Billions of Francs:*	
Exports of Goods & Services	90c	14	14	12	14	16	13	18	22	...	...	...	...	...	...	...
Government Consumption	91f	11	11	11	12	14	16	18	21	...	...	...	...	...	...	...
Gross Fixed Capital Formation	93e	9	10	11	13	17	20	22	24	...	...	...	...	...	...	...
Increase/Decrease(-) in Stocks	93i	...	...	...	...	...	...	...	...	...	...	...	...	...	...	...
Private Consumption	96f	37	39	42	41	52	62	65	73	...	...	...	...	...	...	...
Imports of Goods & Services	98c	−22	−21	−20	−23	−26	−30	−29	−33	...	...	...	...	...	...	...
Gross Domestic Product (GDP)	99b	50	53	56	57	72	84	94	107	121	135	168	218	248	252	279
																Millions:
Population	99z	1.82	1.87	1.91	1.96	2.01	2.05	2.10	2.17	2.22	2.28	2.31	2.38	2.44	2.50	2.56

	1985	1986	1987	1988	1989	1990	1991	1992	1993	1994	1995	1996	1997	1998	1999	
																Balance of Payments
Minus Sign Indicates Debit																
	–48.6	–86.5	–73.4	–34.6	–33.4	–89.1	–61.8	–83.1	–13.0	–24.7	....	....	....	....	....	Current Account, n.i.e. .... 78al *d*
	131.0	129.5	128.9	133.7	148.1	150.5	125.6	115.9	132.5	145.9	....	....	....	....	....	Goods: Exports f.o.b. .... 78aa *d*
	–167.7	–201.0	–197.7	–179.1	–186.0	–241.6	–178.7	–189.0	–158.1	–130.6	....	....	....	....	....	Goods: Imports f.o.b. .... 78ab *d*
	–36.7	–71.5	–68.8	–45.4	–37.9	–91.1	–53.0	–73.2	–25.7	15.3						*Trade Balance* .... 78ac *d*
	46.8	56.0	67.8	62.3	65.6	69.1	50.5	45.1	49.3	33.1						Services: Credit .... 78ad *d*
	–108.0	–141.6	–154.4	–151.0	–144.4	–168.5	–136.7	–152.7	–131.9	–113.8						Services: Debit .... 78ae *d*
	–98.0	–157.2	–155.4	–134.1	–116.8	–190.5	–139.2	–180.7	–108.3	–65.4						*Balance on Goods & Services* .... 78af *d*
	6.7	2.8	2.8	—	.7	.8	5.5	6.4	4.5	—						Income: Credit .... 78ag *d*
	–14.0	–15.2	–21.9	–21.2	–21.4	–22.4	–19.0	–22.2	–23.2	–22.7						Income: Debit .... 78ah *d*
	–105.3	–169.5	–174.5	–155.3	–137.5	–212.1	–152.7	–196.5	–127.1	–88.1						*Balance on Gds, Serv. & Inc.* .... 78ai *d*
	78.9	111.5	136.3	156.7	138.3	164.2	129.7	151.0	152.4	92.6						Current Transfers, n.i.e.: Credit .... 78aj *d*
	–22.2	–28.5	–35.2	–36.0	–34.2	–41.2	–38.8	–37.6	–38.3	–29.2	....	....	....	....	....	Current Transfers: Debit .... 78ak *d*
	—	—	—	—	—	—	—	—	....	....	....	....	....	....	....	Capital Account, n.i.e. .... 78bc *d*
	—	—	—	—	—	—	—	—								Capital Account, n.i.e.: Credit .... 78ba *d*
	—	—	—	—	—	—	—	—								Capital Account: Debit .... 78bb *d*
	31.5	76.0	63.4	9.6	15.4	66.7	24.0	20.3	–7.1	52.8	....	....	....	....	....	Financial Account, n.i.e. .... 78bj *d*
	–.6	–1.3	–2.6	–4.8	–3.8	–3.8	–3.5	–5.9	–5.3	–7.2						Direct Investment Abroad .... 78bd *d*
	3.0	8.2	11.9	–3.8	1.3	.7	–4.9	–10.7	–10.0	3.6						Dir. Invest. in Rep. Econ., n.i.e. .... 78be *d*
	—	—	—	—	—	—	—	—	....	....						Portfolio Investment Assets .... 78bf *d*
	—	—	—	—	—	—	—	—								Equity Securities .... 78bk *d*
	—	—	—	—	—	—	—	—								Debt Securities .... 78bl *d*
	—	—	—	—	—	—	—	—	....	....						Portfolio Investment Liab., n.i.e. .... 78bg *d*
	—	—	—	—	—	—	—	—								Equity Securities .... 78bm *d*
	—	—	—	—	—	—	—	—								Debt Securities .... 78bn *d*
	....	....	....	....	....	....	....	....								Financial Derivatives Assets .... 78bw *d*
	....	....	....	....	....	....	....	....								Financial Derivatives Liabilities .... 78bx *d*
	–22.3	–16.8	–12.7	–9.0	–13.3	–16.3	–11.2	–33.2	–18.2	8.1	....	....	....	....	....	Other Investment Assets .... 78bh *d*
	....	....	....	....	....	....	....	....								Monetary Authorities .... 78bo *d*
	–2.7	—	–.2	–.1	–.1	–.2	—	—	....	....						General Government .... 78bp *d*
	–8.1	–2.2	3.7	11.8	1.1	–.7	2.8	—	2.5	—						Banks .... 78bq *d*
	–11.5	–14.6	–16.2	–20.7	–14.3	–15.4	–14.0	–33.2	–20.7	8.1						Other Sectors .... 78br *d*
	51.4	85.9	66.8	27.2	31.3	86.0	43.6	70.0	26.4	48.3						Other Investment Liab., n.i.e. .... 78bi *d*
	–.1	–.3	–.1	–1.0	–5.3	–2.9	–.5	1.6	–8.4	—						Monetary Authorities .... 78bs *d*
	46.4	79.8	68.8	26.9	30.5	83.9	52.3	57.7	23.2	43.9						General Government .... 78bt *d*
	.6	2.5	–1.9	—	.6	.1	–2.5	1.2	3.2	5.9						Banks .... 78bu *d*
	4.5	3.9	—	1.3	5.5	4.9	–5.7	9.4	8.4	–1.6						Other Sectors .... 78bv *d*
	–7.8	7.0	–1.6	11.7	1.4	1.4	–1.9	26.2	6.3	–15.0	....	....	....	....	....	Net Errors and Omissions .... 78ca *d*
	–24.9	–3.6	–11.6	–13.3	–16.6	–21.1	–39.6	–36.6	–13.7	13.1						*Overall Balance* .... 78cb *d*
	24.9	3.6	11.6	13.3	16.6	21.1	39.6	36.6	13.7	–13.1	....	....	....	....	....	Reserves and Related Items .... 79da *d*
	18.6	–4.9	–14.2	–32.4	.8	9.4	13.8	–2.8	–20.1	–56.0						Reserve Assets .... 79db *d*
	–.5	–1.3	3.1	1.1	–13.4	–1.6	–3.3	–1.7	–1.6	10.3						Use of Fund Credit and Loans......... 79dc *d*
	6.7	9.7	22.7	44.6	29.3	13.3	29.2	41.0	35.4	32.6						Exceptional Financing .... 79de *d*
																Government Finance
Year Ending December 31																
	....	....	....	....	....	....	....	....	....	....	....	....	....	....	....	Deficit (-) or Surplus 80
	....	....	....	....	....	....	....	....	....	....	....	....	....	....	....	Revenue 81
	....	....	....	....	....	....	....	....	....	....	....	....	....	....	....	Grants Received 81z
	....	....	....	....	....	....	....	....	....	....	....	....	....	....	....	Expenditure....................................... 82
	....	....	....	....	....	....	....	....	....	....	....	....	....	....	....	Lending Minus Repayments 83
	....	....	....	....	....	....	....	....	....	....	....	....	....	....	....	Overall Cash Adjustment 80x
																Financing
	....	....	....	....	....	....	....	....	....	....	....	....	....	....	....	Net Borrowing: Domestic 84a
	....	....	....	....	....	....	....	....	....	....	....	....	....	....	....	Foreign 85a
	....	....	....	....	....	....	....	....	....	....	....	....	....	....	....	Use of Cash Balances 87
																National Accounts
Billions of Francs																
	86	71	64	67	80	67	67	68	63	62	111	....	....	....	....	Exports of Goods & Services 90c
	59	61	63	61	62	60	65	64	55	78	83	....	....	....	....	Government Consumption................... 91f
	48	50	46	37	41	46	47	45	36	56	73	....	....	....	....	Gross Fixed Capital Formation 93e
	12	—	–1	3	5	4	2	1	3	–1	6	....	....	....	....	Increase/Decrease(-) in Stocks 93i
	307	319	291	304	309	317	308	299	289	347	422	....	....	....	....	Private Consumption 96f
	–123	–111	–103	–94	–104	–102	–102	–99	–83	–118	–146	....	....	....	....	Imports of Goods & Services 98c
	316	331	361	377	394	392	389	374	362	473	557	527	566	621	....	Gross Domestic Product (GDP) 99b
Midyear Estimates																
	2.61	2.74	2.72	2.88	2.99	2.94	3.01	3.08	3.15	3.22	3.29	3.35	I 3.25	3.49	3.55	Population... 99z

(See notes in the back of the book.)

Chad

		1970	1971	1972	1973	1974	1975	1976	1977	1978	1979	1980	1981	1982	1983	1984
Exchange Rates														*Francs per SDR:*		
Official Rate	aa	276.02	283.61	278.00	284.00	272.08	262.55	288.70	285.76	272.28	264.78	287.99	334.52	370.92	436.97	470.11
														Francs per US Dollar:		
Official Rate	ae	276.02	261.22	256.05	235.42	222.22	224.27	248.49	235.25	209.00	201.00	225.80	287.40	336.25	417.37	479.60
Official Rate	rf	276.40	275.59	252.03	222.89	240.70	214.31	238.95	245.68	225.66	212.72	211.28	271.73	328.61	381.07	436.96
Fund Position															*Millions of SDRs:*	
Quota	2f. s	13.00	13.00	13.00	13.00	13.00	13.00	13.00	13.00	16.00	16.00	24.00	24.00	24.00	30.60	30.60
SDRs	1b. s	.04	—	1.12	.38	2.41	2.27	1.91	1.70	1.46	1.55	—	.02	.26	1.47	.37
Reserve Position in the Fund	1c. s	—	—	—	—	—	—	—	—	1.24	1.84	3.84	3.84	5.06	3.46	.26
Total Fund Cred.&Loans Outstg.	2tl	2.47	2.32	2.18	1.02	3.11	2.97	9.47	9.47	13.54	12.99	10.81	12.49	12.49	12.26	8.52
International Liquidity											*Millions of US Dollars Unless Otherwise Indicated:*					
Total Reserves minus Gold	1l. d	2.31	11.22	10.07	1.47	15.27	3.06	23.27	18.78	11.79	11.27	5.05	7.31	12.41	28.00	44.16
SDRs	1b. d	.04	—	1.22	.46	2.95	2.66	2.22	2.07	1.90	2.04	—	.02	.29	1.54	.36
Reserve Position in the Fund	1c. d	—	—	—	—	—	—	—	—	1.62	2.42	4.90	4.47	5.58	3.62	.25
Foreign Exchange	1d. d	2.27	11.22	8.86	1.01	12.32	.40	21.06	16.72	8.27	6.80	.16	2.82	6.54	22.84	43.54
Gold (Million Fine Troy Ounces)	1ad	....	....	....	....	....	....	—	.006	.009	.011	.011	.011	.011	.011	.011
Gold (National Valuation)	1and	....	....	....	....	....	—	—	.92	1.94	5.79	6.56	4.45	5.00	4.21	3.44
Monetary Authorities: Other Liab.	4.. d	−.13	—	−.14	−.16	−.95	−.95	−.72	−.82	−1.03	7.14	6.30	5.64	5.27	1.61	2.07
Deposit Money Banks: Assets	7a. d	2.82	2.86	3.24	6.74	2.69	5.73	8.84	6.32	14.83	16.05	14.29	10.85	9.25	7.27	17.42
Liabilities	7b. d	5.22	4.45	6.19	6.94	9.43	10.52	7.95	10.11	11.00	7.65	6.81	6.48	3.54	3.46	3.50
Monetary Authorities															*Billions of Francs:*	
Foreign Assets	11	.64	2.86	2.57	.23	3.50	.78	5.87	4.71	3.49	3.46	2.66	4.19	6.04	13.86	23.07
Claims on Central Government	12a	2.40	1.98	2.24	2.99	3.22	3.30	4.79	5.84	6.79	9.57	9.37	10.43	9.74	9.51	10.14
Claims on Deposit Money Banks	12e	3.45	3.16	3.46	4.07	5.10	11.16	7.27	8.55	14.80	23.95	23.23	17.97	17.81	17.81	22.36
Claims on Other Banking Insts	12f															
Reserve Money	14	5.61	6.32	7.06	6.97	9.21	11.81	14.04	15.38	17.64	23.97	20.87	22.83	24.64	30.18	46.36
of which: Currency Outside DMBs	14a	5.31	6.20	6.90	6.49	8.53	10.88	13.00	14.37	16.49	22.54	17.45	22.14	23.61	29.20	44.93
Foreign Liabilities	16c	.65	.64	.57	.25	.63	.57	2.55	2.51	4.94	6.30	6.09	7.60	8.41	8.28	6.92
Central Government Deposits	16d	.59	.74	.33	.31	.17	.61	.67	.55	1.08	.84	.66	.39	.42	1.08	2.97
Capital Accounts	17a	—	—	—	.02	.02	.02	.03	.03	.03	.02	1.40	1.19	1.62	1.72	1.60
Other Items (Net)	17r	.39	.85	.99	1.05	1.48	3.16	1.85	2.02	4.24	7.40	7.98	1.81	.52	1.98	1.78
Deposit Money Banks															*Billions of Francs:*	
Reserves	20	.29	.12	.16	.48	.68	.92	1.04	1.01	1.15	1.43	3.42	.69	1.03	.99	1.43
Foreign Assets	21	⅃.78	.73	.83	1.55	.60	1.28	2.20	1.49	3.10	3.23	3.23	3.12	3.11	3.03	8.35
Claims on Central Government	22a	.18	.16	.16	.15	.16	.14	.14	.14	.12	.17	.17	.17	.18	.18	.18
Claims on Nonfin.Pub.Enterprises	22c	....	....	....	....	....	....	....	....	....	....	....	....	....	....	....
Claims on Private Sector	22d	⅃9.97	8.94	9.09	10.89	14.59	22.25	19.28	23.45	31.09	38.17	37.48	31.26	29.99	32.46	45.93
Claims on Other Banking Insts	22f	....	....	....	....	....	....	....	....	....	....	....	....	....	....	....
Claims on Nonbank Financial Insts	22g	....	....	....	....	....	....	....	....	....	....	....	....	....	....	....
Demand Deposits	24	⅃3.17	2.94	2.57	3.16	5.42	4.44	6.33	7.92	10.87	8.83	8.83	9.34	9.35	11.36	20.00
Time and Savings Deposits	25	.59	.51	.49	.86	.98	1.18	1.34	1.19	⅃1.85	1.66	1.66	1.48	1.49	1.64	2.63
Foreign Liabilities	26c	⅃.48	.20	.65	.77	1.23	1.49	1.64	2.15	1.89	1.16	1.16	1.49	.81	.81	1.30
Long-Term Foreign Liabilities	26cl	⅃.97	.94	.94	.82	.87	.87	.34	.23	.41	.38	.38	.38	.38	.38	.38
Central Government Deposits	26d	.25	.23	.09	.10	.11	.69	1.17	1.06	.73	.69	.69	.89	.90	2.35	
Credit from Monetary Authorities	26g	4.19	3.73	4.16	5.29	5.10	12.37	8.58	10.19	16.79	23.95	23.23	18.01	17.81	17.81	22.36
Capital Accounts	27a	⅃1.61	1.81	1.90	2.83	4.16	5.00	4.78	5.09	5.04	5.04	5.04	5.16	5.16	5.16	5.52
Other Items (Net)	27r	⅃−.04	−.40	−.57	−.77	−1.85	−1.49	−1.48	−1.74	−2.12	1.29	3.30	⅃−1.49	−1.58	−1.40	1.35
Post Office: Checking Deposits	24.. i	.12	.13	.16	.15	.19	.19	.17	.22	.20	.20	.20	.20	.20	.20	.20
Postal Debt	26c. i	.30	.39	1.08	1.78	2.09	2.76	3.73	3.28	2.82	2.81	2.81	2.81	2.81	2.81	2.80
Monetary Survey															*Billions of Francs:*	
Foreign Assets (Net)	31n	⅃−.01	2.35	1.11	−1.02	.15	−2.75	.15	−1.75	−3.05	−3.59	−4.17	−4.59	−2.88	4.99	20.40
Domestic Credit	32	⅃12.12	10.64	12.31	15.56	19.95	27.34	26.25	31.34	39.22	49.40	48.68	43.58	41.62	43.18	53.93
Claims on Central Govt. (Net)	32an	1.16	1.23	2.89	4.27	5.11	4.93	6.90	7.75	8.01	11.22	11.20	12.32	11.62	10.73	8.00
Claims on Nonfin.Pub.Enterprises	32c	....	....	....	....	....	....	....	....	....	....	....	....	....	....	....
Claims on Private Sector	32d	⅃10.97	9.41	9.42	11.29	14.84	22.41	19.35	23.60	31.20	38.17	37.48	31.26	29.99	32.46	45.93
Claims on Other Banking Insts	32f	....	....	....	....	....	....	....	....	....	....	....	....	....	....	....
Claims on Nonbank Financial Inst	32g	....	....	....	....	....	....	....	....	....	....	....	....	....	....	....
Money	34	8.54	9.17	9.46	9.45	14.20	15.59	19.77	22.51	⅃27.57	31.57	26.48	31.68	33.16	40.75	65.13
Quasi-Money	35	⅃.49	.51	.48	.86	.98	1.18	1.34	1.20	1.85	1.66	1.66	1.48	1.49	1.64	2.63
Other Items (Net)	37r	⅃2.70	2.83	3.02	4.35	3.79	7.93	6.28	7.01	9.18	13.75	17.72	5.51	4.10	5.74	6.48
Money plus Quasi-Money	35l	⅃9.10	9.78	10.12	10.66	15.11	16.69	20.83	23.71	29.42	33.24	28.14	33.16	34.65	42.39	67.76
Interest Rates															*Percent Per Annum*	
Discount Rate (End of Period)	60	4.50	4.50	4.50	4.50	5.50	5.50	6.50	6.50	6.50	8.50	8.50	8.50	8.50	9.00	9.00
Deposit Rate	60l	....	....	....	....	....	....	....	....	4.75	4.50	5.50	5.50	5.50	5.50	5.50
Lending Rate	60p	....	....	....	....	....	....	....	....	10.50	8.50	11.00	11.00	11.00	11.50	11.50
Prices and Labor															*Index Numbers (1995=100):*	
Consumer Prices	64	....	....	....	....	....	....	....	....	....	....	....	....	....	60.8	73.1
															Number in Thousands:	
Labor Force	67d	....	....	....	....	....	....	....	....	....	....	....	....	....	....	....
Employment	67e	....	....	....	....	....	....	....	....	....	....	....	....	....	....	....

1985	1986	1987	1988	1989	1990	1991	1992	1993	1994	1995	1996	1997	1998	1999		
															Exchange Rates	
End of Period																
415.26	394.78	378.78	407.68	380.32	364.84	370.48	378.57	404.89	I780.44	728.38	753.06	807.94	791.61	I896.19	Official Rate	aa
End of Period (ae) Period Average (rf)																
378.05	322.75	267.00	302.95	289.40	256.45	259.00	275.32	294.77	I534.60	490.00	523.70	598.81	562.21	I652.95	Official Rate	ae
449.26	346.31	300.54	297.85	319.01	272.26	282.11	264.69	283.16	I555.20	499.15	511.55	583.67	589.95	I615.70	Official Rate	rf
															Fund Position	
End of Period																
30.60	30.60	30.60	30.60	30.60	30.60	30.60	41.30	41.30	41.30	41.30	41.30	41.30	41.30	56.00	Quota	2f. s
3.52	1.69	6.35	5.72	1.34	.10	.11	.02	.01	—	.02	.16	.01	.01	.02	SDRs	1b. s
.26	.26	.26	.26	.26	.26	.27	.27	.28	.28	.28	.28	.28	.28	.28	Reserve Position in the Fund	1c. s
10.90	8.93	13.97	12.24	17.92	21.42	21.42	21.42	20.20	29.30	32.97	45.20	45.31	45.34	50.17	Total Fund Cred.&Loans Outstg.	2tl
															International Liquidity	
End of Period																
33.46	15.91	52.11	63.08	111.73	127.78	119.79	80.48	38.94	76.01	142.52	164.48	135.82	120.09	95.02	Total Reserves minus Gold	1l. d
3.87	2.07	9.01	7.70	1.76	.14	.16	.03	.01	—	.03	.24	.01	.01	.03	SDRs	1b. d
.29	.32	.37	.35	.34	.37	.39	.37	.38	.41	.42	.40	.38	.40	.39	Reserve Position in the Fund	1c. d
29.31	13.52	42.73	55.04	109.63	127.27	119.25	80.08	38.54	75.60	142.07	163.84	135.44	119.68	94.60	Foreign Exchange	1d. d
.011	.011	.011	.011	.011	.011	.011	.011	.011	.011	.011	.011	.011	....	....	Gold (Million Fine Troy Ounces)	1ad
3.60	4.36	5.37	4.52	3.52	3.98	3.94	3.70	4.42	....	....	....	....	I3.20	....	Gold (National Valuation)	1and
4.05	3.60	4.76	18.95	19.62	21.27	22.49	18.94	.01	.75	.44	1.10	16.61	12.47	18.56	Monetary Authorities: Other Liab.	4..d
26.99	16.86	18.58	15.63	18.66	57.22	31.08	31.02	8.55	11.09	9.91	10.55	32.35	24.20	39.72	Deposit Money Banks: Assets	7a. d
3.20	4.17	13.61	13.12	22.32	22.99	25.12	28.40	26.43	22.36	17.37	8.83	14.78	8.59	14.56	Liabilities	7b. d
															Monetary Authorities	
End of Period																
14.36	6.98	15.56	I20.49	33.63	33.87	32.04	23.18	12.75	42.93	75.53	88.29	83.26	69.31	64.15	Foreign Assets	11
8.48	9.71	11.34	I10.93	11.60	13.43	I13.32	29.91	33.79	48.48	49.71	61.94	65.56	64.83	72.61	Claims on Central Government	12a
36.68	42.93	38.64	I28.12	20.46	15.12	19.52	13.18	9.69	.50	1.00	7.66	5.20	10.70	4.05	Claims on Deposit Money Banks	12e
....	....	....	4.62	4.56	4.44	4.32	—	—	—	—	—	1.50	3.85	3.30	Claims on Other Banking Insts	12f
47.79	47.35	52.20	I46.52	53.23	49.06	50.47	47.94	38.25	47.24	74.73	98.29	94.13	84.51	79.22	Reserve Money	14
47.35	46.67	46.70	40.27	43.06	46.81	49.45	46.95	35.84	39.69	61.98	89.36	78.81	73.62	68.25	of which: Currency Outside DMBs	14a
7.31	5.45	6.88	I10.73	12.49	13.27	13.76	13.32	8.18	23.27	24.23	34.62	46.55	42.91	57.08	Foreign Liabilities	16c
3.65	2.21	4.15	I5.10	1.67	2.42	.28	.44	.56	3.61	10.78	6.99	3.40	9.87	3.27	Central Government Deposits	16d
1.34	1.41	1.51	I5.31	4.95	4.58	4.77	4.58	5.06	8.38	8.44	8.81	9.03	8.94	9.93	Capital Accounts	17a
1.44	5.15	1.12	I-3.49	-.12	1.35	.02	-.02	4.12	9.41	8.06	9.18	2.40	2.46	-5.40	Other Items (Net)	17r
															Deposit Money Banks	
End of Period																
.44	.67	5.49	I6.19	9.57	2.18	.93	.86	1.98	6.17	10.08	7.39	12.77	10.13	10.35	Reserves	20
10.20	5.44	4.96	I4.78	5.40	14.68	I8.05	8.54	2.52	5.93	4.86	5.52	19.37	13.61	25.94	Foreign Assets	21
.18	.18	.63	I.87	.98	1.14	4.45	5.71	6.37	7.98	8.19	2.22	2.49	1.88	1.60	Claims on Central Government	22a
....	....	....	34.08	24.05	16.06	23.38	12.95	6.71	7.13	7.25	17.24	20.77	19.95	15.05	Claims on Nonfin.Pub.Enterprises	22c
64.95	75.00	74.17	I34.65	33.54	34.44	31.54	31.22	20.86	23.75	27.79	29.95	29.16	34.03	33.89	Claims on Private Sector	22d
....	....	....													Claims on Other Banking Insts	22f
....	....	....	—	.01	—	—	.03	—	—	—	—	—	.36	.27	Claims on Nonbank Financial Insts	22g
20.79	22.34	23.68	I21.25	23.35	19.45	19.32	15.79	9.19	18.73	20.68	22.98	27.11	25.38	27.80	Demand Deposits	24
3.55	3.58	4.79	I3.91	4.31	3.73	I4.12	3.62	2.20	2.86	7.87	5.36	5.87	5.77	6.11	Time and Savings Deposits	25
.83	.97	1.75	I2.29	2.04	1.49	I2.31	3.14	7.58	11.22	8.42	4.62	8.79	4.83	7.52	Foreign Liabilities	26c
.38	.38	1.89	I4.40	4.42	4.40	I4.20	4.67	.21	.73	.09	—	.06		1.99	Long-Term Foreign Liabilities	26cl
6.52	6.46	7.35	I11.11	10.78	14.77	I13.06	8.14	6.53	4.91	10.84	13.27	24.60	21.36	23.71	Central Government Deposits	26d
36.68	42.93	38.64	I28.12	20.46	15.12	I16.45	9.83	5.88	.50	1.00	7.66	5.20	10.70	4.05	Credit from Monetary Authorities	26g
7.58	8.74	8.59	I7.04	7.63	9.08	I9.45	27.43	10.64	11.95	11.57	13.45	15.52	15.83	17.83	Capital Accounts	27a
-.56	-1.80	-1.43	I2.23	.10	-1.98	-.54	-13.35	-3.79	.06	-2.30	-5.01	-2.60	-3.90	-1.91	Other Items (Net)	27r
.20	.13	.22	.21	....	....	....	....	....	....	....	....	....	....	....	Post Office: Checking Deposits	24.. i
2.80	2.80	2.80	....	....	....	....	....	....	....	....	....	....	....	....	Postal Debt	26c. i
															Monetary Survey	
End of Period																
13.62	3.21	9.09	I10.58	22.46	31.85	19.83	10.58	-.70	13.64	47.64	54.57	47.23	35.18	23.50	Foreign Assets (Net)	31n
66.45	81.46	77.67	I72.06	65.72	54.27	63.66	71.24	60.64	78.82	71.33	91.09	91.48	93.68	99.74	Domestic Credit	32
1.50	6.46	3.49	I-1.30	3.56	-.67	4.43	27.03	33.07	47.94	36.28	43.90	40.06	35.48	47.23	Claims on Central Govt. (Net)	32an
....	....	....	34.08	24.05	16.06	23.38	12.95	6.71	7.13	7.25	17.24	20.77	19.95	15.05	Claims on Nonfin.Pub.Enterprises	32c
64.95	75.00	74.17	I34.65	33.54	34.44	31.54	31.22	20.86	23.75	27.79	29.95	29.16	34.03	33.89	Claims on Private Sector	32d
....	....	....	4.62	4.56	4.44	4.32	—	—	—	—	—	1.50	3.85	3.30	Claims on Other Banking Insts	32f
....	....	....	—	.01	—	—	.03	—	—	—	—	—	.36	.27	Claims on Nonbank Financial Inst	32g
68.34	69.14	70.60	61.57	66.46	66.34	68.86	62.86	45.47	59.79	85.33	113.88	108.47	99.75	96.67	Money	34
3.55	3.58	4.79	I3.91	4.31	2.75	4.12	3.62	2.20	2.86	7.87	5.36	5.87	5.77	6.11	Quasi-Money	35
8.46	12.09	8.29	11.34	13.01	15.46	I10.62	15.30	12.22	29.80	25.76	26.43	24.36	23.33	20.45	Other Items (Net)	37r
71.90	72.71	75.38	I65.48	70.77	69.08	72.98	66.48	47.67	62.66	93.20	119.23	114.35	105.52	102.78	Money plus Quasi-Money	35l
															Interest Rates	
Percent Per Annum																
9.00	8.00	8.00	9.50	10.00	11.00	10.75	12.00	11.50	I7.75	8.60	7.75	7.50	7.00	7.60	Discount Rate (End of Period)	60
5.50	5.50	5.33	4.31	4.25	I7.50	7.50	7.50	7.75	8.08	5.50	5.46	5.00	5.00	5.00	Deposit Rate	60l
11.50	11.00	10.50	10.79	11.50	I18.50	18.15	17.77	17.46	17.50	16.00	22.00	22.00	22.00	22.00	Lending Rate	60p
															Prices and Labor	
Period Averages																
76.9	I66.9	62.9	72.6	69.7	69.6	72.5	70.3	65.3	91.7	100.0	112.4	118.7	133.1	124.1	Consumer Prices	64
Period Averages																
....	....	....	....	....	....	....	2,316	....	....	....	....	....	....	....	Labor Force	67d
....	9	9	11	11	10	13	....	....	....	....	....	....	....	....	Employment	67e

Chad

		1970	1971	1972	1973	1974	1975	1976	1977	1978	1979	1980	1981	1982	1983	1984
International Transactions															*Millions of Francs*	
Exports	70	8,206	7,787	9,028	8,483	9,056	10,103	14,861	26,177	22,329	18,776	14,999	22,665	18,968	39,824	57,384
Imports, c.i.f.	71	17,216	17,219	15,675	18,213	20,859	28,325	27,593	46,465	49,034	18,132	15,533	29,349	35,701	59,707	79,272
Volume of Exports																*1995=100*
Cotton	72f	52	46	54	48	50	72	79	....	....	....	....	....	33	50	67
Balance of Payments															*Millions of US Dollars:*	
Current Account, n.i.e.	78al d	...	...	...	...	...	...	...	−28.5	−46.4	−8.3	8.6	20.4	18.5	38.0	9.0
Goods: Exports f.o.b.	78aa d	...	...	...	...	...	...	...	106.5	99.0	88.3	71.0	83.4	57.7	78.2	109.7
Goods: Imports f.o.b.	78ab d	...	...	...	...	...	...	...	−142.2	−163.4	−64.1	−55.3	−81.2	−81.7	−99.1	−128.3
Trade Balance	78ac d	...	...	...	...	...	...	...	−35.7	−64.4	24.2	15.7	2.2	−24.0	−20.9	−18.7
Services: Credit	78ad d	...	...	...	...	...	...	...	24.2	20.6	4.6	.4	4.1	2.4	24.2	36.8
Services: Debit	78ae d	...	...	...	...	...	...	...	−103.4	−104.1	−54.4	−24.2	−25.3	−22.1	−77.6	−90.1
Balance on Goods & Services	78af d	...	...	...	...	...	...	...	−114.9	−148.0	−25.6	−8.1	−19.0	−43.7	−74.3	−71.9
Income: Credit	78ag d	...	...	...	...	...	...	...	1.6	—	—	—	—	1.9	4.4	1.3
Income: Debit	78ah d	...	...	...	...	...	...	...	−3.9	−3.7	−8.6	−3.7	−1.1	−1.0	−3.3	−6.3
Balance on Gds, Serv. & Inc.	78ai d	...	...	...	...	...	...	...	−117.2	−151.6	−34.2	−11.8	−20.1	−42.7	−73.3	−76.8
Current Transfers, n.i.e.: Credit	78aj d	...	...	...	...	...	...	...	106.2	118.8	35.9	24.5	41.1	61.9	118.0	94.0
Current Transfers: Debit	78ak d	...	...	...	...	...	...	...	−17.6	−13.6	−10.0	−4.1	−.6	−.7	−6.9	−8.1
Capital Account, n.i.e.	78bc d	...	...	...	...	...	...	...	—	—	—	—	—	—	—	—
Capital Account, n.i.e.: Credit	78ba d	...	...	...	...	...	...	...	—	—	—	—	—	—	—	—
Capital Account: Debit	78bb d	...	...	...	...	...	...	...	—	—	—	—	—	—	—	—
Financial Account, n.i.e.	78bj d	...	...	...	...	...	...	...	30.9	26.1	−19.0	−11.4	−3.8	−6.3	−21.6	−6.0
Direct Investment Abroad	78bd d	...	...	...	...	...	...	...	—	1.0	−1.3	−.4	−.1	−.1	−.1	—
Dir. Invest. in Rep. Econ., n.i.e.	78be d	...	...	...	...	...	...	...	21.2	34.1	—	—	—	—	—	9.2
Portfolio Investment Assets	78bf d	...	...	...	...	...	...	...	—	—	—	—	—	—	—	—
Equity Securities	78bk d	...	...	...	...	...	...	...	—	—	—	—	—	—	—	—
Debt Securities	78bl d	...	...	...	...	...	...	...	—	—	—	—	—	—	—	—
Portfolio Investment Liab., n.i.e.	78bg d	...	...	...	...	...	...	...	—	—	—	—	—	—	—	—
Equity Securities	78bm d	...	...	...	...	...	...	...	—	—	—	—	—	—	—	—
Debt Securities	78bn d	...	...	...	...	...	...	...	—	—	—	—	—	—	—	—
Financial Derivatives Assets	78bw d	...	...	...	...	...	...	...	...	...	...	...	...	...	...	...
Financial Derivatives Liabilities	78bx d	...	...	...	...	...	...	...	...	...	...	...	...	...	...	...
Other Investment Assets	78bh d	...	...	...	...	...	...	...	−3.4	−2.1	−.3	—	—	—	—	−12.0
Monetary Authorities	78bo d	...	...	...	...	...	...	...	—	—	—	—	—	—	—	—
General Government	78bp d	...	...	...	...	...	...	...	—	−2.1	—	—	—	—	—	−.1
Banks	78bq d	...	...	...	...	...	...	...	−1.9	—	−.3	—	—	—	—	−11.9
Other Sectors	78br d	...	...	...	...	...	...	...	−1.5	—	—	—	—	—	—	—
Other Investment Liab., n.i.e.	78bi d	...	...	...	...	...	...	...	13.1	−7.0	−17.5	−11.0	−3.7	−6.2	−21.5	−3.1
Monetary Authorities	78bs d	...	...	...	...	...	...	...	−.6	.1	−.1	−.2	−.2	.3	−.1	−.1
General Government	78bt d	...	...	...	...	...	...	...	9.3	.3	−2.7	−3.7	−1.8	−1.0	−18.0	−6.7
Banks	78bu d	...	...	...	...	...	...	...	1.4	−1.2	—	—	—	1.2	−.2	—
Other Sectors	78bv d	...	...	...	...	...	...	...	3.0	−6.2	−14.9	−7.2	−1.6	−6.2	−3.6	3.7
Net Errors and Omissions	78ca d	...	...	...	...	...	...	...	−7.0	−5.4	−2.4	−21.0	−1.9	−7.8	−7.5	13.7
Overall Balance	78cb d	...	...	...	...	...	...	...	−4.7	−25.7	−29.8	−23.8	14.7	4.4	8.9	16.7
Reserves and Related Items	79da d	...	...	...	...	...	...	...	4.7	25.7	29.8	23.8	−14.7	−4.4	−8.9	−16.7
Reserve Assets	79db d	...	...	...	...	...	...	...	4.7	7.6	3.0	8.0	−.9	−2.4	−17.7	−21.6
Use of Fund Credit and Loans	79dc d	...	...	...	...	...	...	...	—	5.0	−.7	−2.9	2.5	—	−.2	−3.7
Exceptional Financing	79de d	...	...	...	...	...	...	...	—	13.0	27.5	18.7	−16.4	−2.0	9.0	8.6
Government Finance															*Millions of Francs:*	
Deficit (-) or Surplus	80	...	...	−2,783	−3,910	−2,543	−2,130	−2,848	...	...	...	...	...	...	...	...
Total Revenue and Grants	81y	...	...	12,852	13,450	16,707	18,191	20,292	...	...	...	...	...	...	...	...
Revenue	81	...	...	11,295	11,478	13,836	14,290	15,122	...	...	...	...	...	...	...	...
Grants	81z	...	...	1,557	1,972	2,871	3,901	5,170	...	...	...	...	...	...	...	...
Exp. & Lending Minus Repay.	82z	...	...	15,635	17,360	19,250	20,321	23,140	...	...	...	...	...	...	...	...
Expenditure	82	...	...	15,637	17,373	19,245	20,341	23,169	...	...	...	...	...	...	...	...
Lending Minus Repayments	83	...	...	−2	−13	5	−20	−29	...	...	...	...	...	...	...	...
Statistical Discrepancy	80xx	...	...	—	—	—	—	—	...	...	...	...	...	...	...	...
Total Financing	80h	...	...	2,783	3,910	2,543	2,130	2,848	...	...	...	...	...	...	...	...
Domestic	84a	...	...	2,128	2,793	1,733	584	1,399	...	...	...	...	...	...	...	...
Foreign	85a	...	...	655	1,117	810	1,546	1,449	...	...	...	...	...	...	...	...
Total Debt by Residence	88	...	...	...	...	...	...	...	...	...	...	...	...	...	...	...
Domestic	88a	...	...	...	...	...	...	...	...	...	...	...	...	...	...	...
Foreign	89a	...	...	...	...	...	...	...	...	...	...	...	...	...	...	...
National Accounts															*Billions of Francs:*	
Gross Domestic Product (GDP)	99b	90,500	98,400	93,600	102,300	119,900	149,400	162,200	161,300	208,600	....	....	....	187,600	311,000	384,000
GDP Volume 1983 Prices	99b.p	146.6	149.3	139.2	132.3	150.4	176.4	173.8	160.9	....	....	159.4	....	221.5	210.4
GDP Volume (1985=100)	99bv p	55.3	56.3	52.5	49.9	56.7	66.6	65.6	60.7	....	....	60.1	....	83.6	79.4
GDP Deflator (1985=100)	99bi p	41.9	44.8	45.7	52.5	54.2	57.6	63.4	68.2	....	....	....	....	95.4	124.0
																Millions:
Population	99z	3.64	3.72	3.79	3.86	3.95	4.03	4.12	4.21	4.31	4.38	4.48	4.58	4.68	4.80	4.91

	1985	1986	1987	1988	1989	1990	1991	1992	1993	1994	1995	1996	1997	1998	1999	
International Transactions																
Millions of Francs																
Exports	27,781	34,145	32,892	42,900	49,570	51,202	54,600	48,250	37,330	82,160	125,600	117,230	138,100	154,250	....	70
Imports, c.i.f.	74,708	73,437	67,894	68,000	75,100	77,742	70,500	64,320	56,910	98,310	109,720	130,660	143,800	155,880	....	71
1995=100																
Volume of Exports — Cotton	28	48	43	56	64	100	....	....	....	....	....	....	....	....	....	72f
Balance of Payments																
Minus Sign Indicates Debit																
Current Account, n.i.e.	-87.2	-59.4	-25.5	25.5	-55.9	-45.6	-65.6	-85.7	-116.6	-37.7	....					78al d
Goods: Exports f.o.b.	61.8	98.6	109.4	145.9	155.4	230.3	193.5	182.3	151.8	135.3						78aa d
Goods: Imports f.o.b.	-166.3	-212.1	-225.9	-228.4	-240.3	-259.5	-249.9	-243.0	-215.2	-212.1						78ab d
Trade Balance	-104.5	-113.5	-116.5	-82.5	-84.9	-29.2	-56.3	-60.7	-63.5	-76.8						78ac d
Services: Credit	32.6	44.5	70.4	78.7	42.3	40.9	30.9	26.7	47.1	54.8						78ad d
Services: Debit	-153.9	-165.7	-198.0	-217.9	-210.0	-228.2	-208.0	-224.1	-235.1	-199.4						78ae d
Balance on Goods & Services	-225.7	-234.7	-244.0	-221.7	-252.6	-216.5	-233.4	-258.1	-251.4	-221.4						78af d
Income: Credit	5.0	3.5	2.9	2.1	1.3	3.0	8.9	17.5	4.3	5.0						78ag d
Income: Debit	-7.3	-12.4	-13.1	-15.5	-10.8	-23.8	-11.2	-14.9	-15.7	-12.4						78ah d
Balance on Gds, Serv. & Inc.	-228.0	-243.5	-254.2	-235.0	-262.0	-237.2	-235.7	-255.5	-262.9	-228.7						78ai d
Current Transfers, n.i.e.: Credit	153.5	204.7	257.0	301.4	241.4	239.3	215.5	222.3	192.4	209.4						78aj d
Current Transfers: Debit	-12.8	-20.6	-28.3	-40.8	-35.2	-47.7	-45.3	-52.5	-46.2	-18.4						78ak d
Capital Account, n.i.e.	—	—	—	—	—	—	—	—	—	—						78bc d
Capital Account, n.i.e.: Credit	—	—	—	—	—	—	—	—	—	—						78ba d
Capital Account: Debit	—	—	—	—	—	—	—	—	—	—						78bb d
Financial Account, n.i.e.	69.2	30.8	9.1	24.2	74.4	56.1	59.0	33.7	68.8	76.3						78bj d
Direct Investment Abroad	-.3	-.4	-8.0	-13.8	-12.5	—	-10.5	-13.8	-10.9	-.6						78bd d
Dir. Invest. in Rep. Econ., n.i.e.	53.7	28.2	8.2	1.3	18.7	—	4.2	2.0	15.2	27.1						78be d
Portfolio Investment Assets	—	—	—	—	—	—	—	—	—	—						78bf d
Equity Securities	—	—	—	—	—	—	—	—	—	—						78bk d
Debt Securities	—	—	—	—	—	—	—	—	—	—						78bl d
Portfolio Investment Liab., n.i.e.	—	—	—	—	—	—	—	—	—	—						78bg d
Equity Securities	—	—	—	—	—	—	—	—	—	—						78bm d
Debt Securities	—	—	—	—	—	—	—	—	—	—						78bn d
Financial Derivatives Assets	....	....	....	....	....	....	....	....	....	....						78bw d
Financial Derivatives Liabilities	....	....	....	....	....	....	....	....	....	....						78bx d
Other Investment Assets	-4.1	13.1	12.1	10.3	3.5	—	24.2	3.9	42.1	.6						78bh d
Monetary Authorities	....	....														78bo d
General Government	—	-.6														78bp d
Banks	-4.1	13.7	1.6	.8	-3.1	—	23.5	-1.8	31.0	-4.8						78bq d
Other Sectors	—	—	10.5	9.5	6.6	—	.7	5.7	11.0	5.4						78br d
Other Investment Liab., n.i.e.	19.9	-10.1	-3.1	26.4	64.7	56.1	41.1	41.6	22.5	49.2						78bi d
Monetary Authorities	-.4	-1.5	.5	-.2	-.1	—	-.9	-6.3	-5.2	-.1						78bs d
General Government	17.8	17.6	38.2	46.1	79.0	103.4	81.3	71.3	102.1	49.8						78bt d
Banks	-.2	.4	2.6	1.1	—	-36.7	2.2	5.0	—	—						78bu d
Other Sectors	2.7	-26.6	-44.4	-20.6	-14.2	-10.6	-41.5	-28.3	-74.4	-.6						78bv d
Net Errors and Omissions	-5.5	9.7	16.5	-83.7	11.1	-33.3	-13.0	9.2	-.1	-33.0						78ca d
Overall Balance	-23.6	-18.9	.1	-34.0	29.6	-22.9	-19.6	-42.8	-47.9	5.5						78cb d
Reserves and Related Items	23.6	18.9	-.1	34.0	-29.6	22.9	19.6	42.8	47.9	-5.5						79da d
Reserve Assets	18.6	17.5	-25.0	14.8	-41.3	3.6	8.2	32.9	39.4	-30.7						79db d
Use of Fund Credit and Loans	2.5	-2.2	6.6	-2.3	6.9	4.6	—	—	-1.7	12.7						79dc d
Exceptional Financing	2.4	3.6	18.3	21.5	4.8	14.7	11.4	9.9	10.2	12.4						79de d
Government Finance																
Year Ending December 31																
Deficit (-) or Surplus	....	‡-9,029	-8,365	-11,893	-25,458	-22,451	‡-42,416	-53,105	-24,723	-56,900	-43,003	-105,521	-79,501	-65,161	-100,307 f	80
Total Revenue and Grants	....	‡61,530	73,380	73,490	85,789	80,801	‡57,101	55,832	50,531	87,587	96,573	101,538	118,888	115,415	154,203	81y
Revenue	....	‡17,577	19,471	24,775	28,022	31,567	‡32,243	31,420	29,148	31,959	44,834	58,458	72,359	77,347	104,854	81
Grants	....	‡43,953	53,909	48,715	57,767	49,234	‡24,858	24,412	21,383	55,628	51,739	43,080	46,529	38,068	49,349	81z
Exp. & Lending Minus Repay.	....	‡70,559	81,745	85,383	111,247	103,252	‡99,517	108,937	75,254	144,487	139,576	207,059	198,389	180,576	254,510	82z
Expenditure	....	‡70,559	81,745	85,341	110,945	103,252	‡80,657	99,147	78,024	122,997	125,846	150,750	163,389	153,028	211,666	82
Lending Minus Repayments	....	‡—	—	42	302	—	‡18,860	9,790	-2,770	21,490	13,730	56,309	35,000	27,548	42,844	83
Statistical Discrepancy	....	‡—	—	—	—	—	‡-3,008	1,029	-6,197	23,957	33,842	14,775	32,529	13,208	20,226	80xx
Total Financing	....	‡9,029	8,365	11,893	25,458	22,451	‡39,408	54,134	18,526	80,857	76,845	120,296	112,030	78,369	120,533	80h
Domestic	....	‡1,845	660	-1,506	-4,629	-1,185	‡-281	19,927	9,916	-460	-5,817	14,546	28,432	5,041	17,000	84a
Foreign	....	‡7,184	7,705	13,399	30,087	23,636	‡39,689	34,207	8,610	81,317	82,662	105,750	83,598	73,328	103,533	85a
Total Debt by Residence	....	....	....	....	....	153,893	‡7,156	7,129	10,171	14,528	11,108	15,574	15,416	525,250	607,173 f	88
Domestic	....	....	....	....	....	29,975	‡3,316	3,119	4,236	6,503	5,481	7,020	7,108	7,310	9,073 f	88a
Foreign	....	....	....	96,923	114,997	123,918	‡3,840	4,010	5,935	8,025	5,627	8,554	8,308	517,940	598,100 f	89a
National Accounts																
Billions of Francs																
Gross Domestic Product (GDP)	390,000	370,000	364,000	422,000	427,400	438,800	451,000	440,800	412,000	655,000	717,800	830,000	889,000	993,000	967,000	99b
GDP Volume 1983 Prices	265.1	258.0	243.7	....	....	....	....	....	....	....	....	....	....	....	....	99b.p
GDP Volume (1985=100)	100.0	97.3	91.9	....	....	....	....	....	....	....	....	....	....	....	....	99bv p
GDP Deflator (1985=100)	100.0	97.5	101.5	....	....	....	....	....	....	....	....	....	....	....	....	99bi p
Midyear Estimates																
Population	5.02	5.12	5.22	5.32	5.56	5.69	5.82	5.96	6.10	6.21	6.71	6.90	7.09	7.27	7.46	99z

(See notes in the back of the book.)

Chile

228

		1970	1971	1972	1973	1974	1975	1976	1977	1978	1979	1980	1981	1982	1983	1984
Exchange Rates																*Pesos per Thousand SDRs through 1973*
Market Rate	aa	10.00	32.57	54.29	904.76	I2.45	9.95	20.24	33.96	44.23	51.38	49.74	45.39	64.50	76.23	87.26
																Pesos per Thousand US Dollars through 1973
Market Rate	ae	10.00	30.00	50.00	750.00	I2.00	8.50	17.42	27.96	33.95	39.00	39.00	39.00	58.47	72.81	89.02
Market Rate	rf	11.28	12.21	20.84	71.64	I.59	4.91	13.05	21.54	31.66	37.25	39.00	39.00	50.91	78.79	98.48
																Index Numbers (1995=100):
Market Rate	ahx	....	....	....	963,665.1	77,520.0	9,915.9	3,135.7	1,875.5	1,255.7	1,066.6	1,016.1	1,016.1	826.1	504.5	409.1
Nominal Effective Exchange Rate	nec	....	....	....	....	....	....	....	....	....	64.2	66.3	78.3	75.7	57.7	58.5
Real Effective Exchange Rate	rec	....	....	....	....	....	....	....	....	....	....	162.6	192.6	173.7	142.3	141.1
Fund Position																*Millions of SDRs:*
Quota	2f.s	158.0	158.0	158.0	158.0	158.0	158.0	158.0	158.0	217.0	217.0	325.5	325.5	325.5	440.5	440.5
SDRs	1b.s	21.8	38.3	2.0	.3	13.8	20.9	48.3	54.7	20.7	22.0	3.0	16.4	17.7	5.2	11.7
Reserve Position in the Fund	1c.s	—	—	—	—	—	—	—	—	38.3	37.1	64.3	64.3	70.5	—	—
Total Fund Cred.&Loans Outstg.	2tl	1.5	39.5	79.0	79.0	160.0	330.8	402.2	300.6	266.5	135.9	96.3	41.8	5.7	579.0	795.0
International Liquidity																*Millions of US Dollars Unless Otherwise Indicated:*
Total Reserves minus Gold	1l.d	341.8	170.1	96.8	121.6	41.1	55.9	405.1	426.5	1,090.1	1,938.3	3,123.2	3,213.3	1,815.0	2,036.3	2,303.2
SDRs	1b.d	21.8	41.6	2.2	.4	16.9	24.5	56.1	66.4	27.0	28.9	3.8	19.1	19.5	5.4	11.5
Reserve Position in the Fund	1c.d	—	—	—	—	—	—	—	—	49.9	48.9	82.0	74.8	77.8	—	—
Foreign Exchange	1d.d	320.0	128.5	94.6	121.2	24.2	31.4	349.0	360.1	1,013.2	1,860.5	3,037.5	3,119.4	1,717.7	2,030.9	2,291.7
Gold (Million Fine Troy Ounces)	1ad	1.334	1.346	1.355	1.376	1.438	1.297	1.336	1.364	1.390	1.524	1.704	1.702	1.712	....	....
Gold (National Valuation)	1and	46.7	47.1	51.5	58.1	60.7	54.8	56.4	57.6	58.7	439.5	963.4	660.4	655.9	566.7[e]	540.1
Monetary Authorities: Other Liab.	4..d	61.2	85.5	274.2	490.8	490.8	603.3	157.2	687.4	595.3	1,260.2	1,184.3	836.0	766.9	2,218.8	3,717.9
Deposit Money Banks: Assets	7a.d	82.0	63.3	40.0	66.7	98.4	96.1	124.2	104.7	143.8	298.8	548.2	881.4	959.2	814.0	722.0
Liabilities	7b.d	82.0	126.6	240.0	336.1	368.4	323.6	296.5	410.9	831.0	1,579.4	3,535.3	6,238.2	7,282.2	6,311.0	6,733.0
Monetary Authorities																*Thousands of Pesos through 1971; Millions from 1972 to 1976;*
Foreign Assets	11	4,833.7	3,436.8	I3.9	87.9	445.2	1,635.7	I10476.0	I18.9	48.6	109.7	165.6	147.1	185.5	231.3	364.1
Claims on Central Government	12a	9,575.0	29,917.0	I88.1	759.8	3,737.1	18,708.2	I39597.0	I87.8	92.1	116.8	108.6	58.0	53.5	163.2	425.8
Claims on Nonfin.Pub.Enterprises	12c	....	....	....	....	....	....	1,616.0	I1.9	2.1	.7	1.3	.5	.9	.6	.8
Claims on Private Sector	12d	745.0	416.0	I.5	6.8	41.5	120.1	I7,874.0	I2.1	34.0	52.5	54.6	59.7	176.4	228.6	278.6
Claims on Deposit Money Banks	12e	686.0	1,871.0	I6.9	8.5	216.2	875.7	I3,176.0	I6.1	18.0	20.8	25.4	39.2	152.3	601.8	876.1
Claims on Other Banking Insts	12f	....	....	....	....	....	....	253.0	I.6	.9	1.0	3.0	2.5	12.9	26.3	47.9
Reserve Money	14	7,740.0	21,442.0	I60.0	310.9	1,003.5	3,568.2	I15110.0	I29.2	50.2	72.4	117.8	106.1	226.5	520.1	918.7
of which: Currency Outside DMBs	14a	4,380.0	8,973.0	I28.2	95.7	349.3	1,358.2	I4,480.0	I9.3	16.4	24.9	35.6	44.5	43.0	51.9	64.2
Time, Savings,& Fgn.Currency Dep.	15	....	....	....	....	....	....	5,435.0	I6.3	8.0	8.1	11.0	11.3	72.1	158.4	165.5
Foreign Liabilities	16c	767.2	2,028.7	I8.7	211.2	1,283.8	8,424.0	I—	I—	—	—	—	—	15.2	79.3	161.1
Long-Term Foreign Liabilities	16cl	....	....	....	....	....	....	10,879.0	I25.3	26.7	43.5	36.9	20.6	46.8	181.9	412.9
Central Government Deposits	16d	330.0	808.0	I3.2	49.4	177.8	505.2	I5,701.0	I12.9	25.5	50.6	43.5	33.0	22.9	22.6	29.2
Capital Accounts	17a	1,775.0	3,432.0	I6.4	70.9	475.1	2,384.4	I8,985.0	I22.3	51.7	121.5	143.5	139.4	198.9	230.3	173.7
Other Items (Net)	17r	5,227.5	7,930.1	I21.1	220.6	1,499.8	6,457.9	I16882.0	I21.4	33.6	5.4	5.8	–3.3	–.7	59.4	132.1
Deposit Money Banks																*Thousands of Pesos through 1971; Millions from 1972 to 1976;*
Reserves	20	3,598.0	12,209.0	I33.5	241.1	764.5	3,281.0	I9,742.0	I20.5	31.1	41.8	55.5	40.0	24.4	39.4	43.0
Foreign Assets	21	826.0	713.0	I1.3	24.4	183.7	817.3	I2,159.0	I3.4	5.7	12.4	21.6	35.5	70.6	71.3	96.7
Claims on Central Government	22a	1,822.0	3,439.0	I10.9	85.2	343.0	1,359.4	I1,090.0	I2.2	3.4	8.5	1.5	1.9	56.5	75.2	109.7
Claims on Local Government	22b	....	....	....	....	....	....	1.0	I—	—	—	.1	—	—	.2	.1
Claims on Nonfin.Pub.Enterprises	22c	....	....	....	....	....	....	3,179.0	I3.2	3.4	3.3	5.7	7.8	13.9	15.7	24.9
Claims on Private Sector	22d	7,446.0	11,474.0	I22.3	69.9	541.0	2,952.7	I12844.0	I55.5	107.1	211.4	412.1	590.8	845.5	925.8	1,256.5
Claims on Other Banking Insts	22f	....	....	....	....	....	....	—	I—	.1	.7	9.0	21.1	1.3	.9	1.4
Demand Deposits	24	5,647.0	12,300.0	I25.9	132.9	487.4	1,620.5	I6,141.0	I8.9	22.0	40.4	63.8	65.5	70.5	78.8	97.1
Time, Savings,& Fgn.Currency Dep.	25	4,976.0	9,027.0	I20.0	93.0	441.0	2,218.0	I9,838.0	I27.3	56.2	97.5	167.4	237.5	298.7	298.8	393.5
Bonds	26ab	....	....	....	....	....	....	—	I—	1.3	8.3	28.3	48.5	82.1	110.5	155.0
Foreign Liabilities	26c	685.0	1,562.0	I6.0	121.0	689.0	2,751.2	I5,165.0	I15.1	17.0	27.3	52.2	76.0	147.4	124.4	85.2
Long-Term Foreign Liabilities	26cl	....	....	....	....	....	....	—	I—	11.3	39.7	96.7	193.9	388.2	428.0	775.3
Central Government Deposits	26d	2,332.0	4,892.0	I17.7	142.7	476.6	2,069.8	I4,655.0	I15.1	17.5	27.3	72.5	59.5	49.0	52.8	59.5
Credit from Monetary Authorities	26g	993.0	2,184.0	I8.9	25.0	237.8	701.2	I2,113.0	I8.9	15.8	21.6	26.3	34.6	48.1	463.5	663.1
Liabilities to Other Financ. Insts	26i	....	....	....	....	....	....	—	I—	—	.7	1.9	4.9	10.8	3.5	16.0
Capital Accounts	27a	2,012.0	2,372.0	I4.0	45.0	617.0	3,642.9	I10688.0	I20.1	25.7	41.9	66.8	78.3	99.2	93.7	93.4
Other Items (Net)	27r	–2,953.0	–4,502.0	I–14.5	–139.0	–1,116.6	–4,593.2	I–9585.0	I–10.6	–16.0	–26.7	–70.4	–101.7	–181.8	–525.4	–805.6
Monetary Survey																*Thousands of Pesos through 1971; Millions from 1972 to 1976;*
Foreign Assets (Net)	31n	4,207.5	559.2	I–9.5	–219.9	–1,343.9	–8,722.2	I–3409.0	I–18.1	–.7	11.7	1.4	–107.9	–341.5	–510.9	–973.8
Domestic Credit	32	16,926.0	39,546.0	I100.9	729.6	4,008.2	20,565.4	I56098.0	I125.3	200.0	316.9	479.8	649.8	1,089.2	1,361.2	2,057.1
Claims on Central Govt. (Net)	32an	8,735.0	27,656.0	I78.1	652.9	3,425.7	17,492.6	I30331.0	I62.0	52.5	47.3	–5.9	–32.7	38.2	163.1	446.8
Claims on Local Government	32b	....	....	....	....	....	....	1.0	I—	—	—	.1	—	—	.2	.1
Claims on Nonfin.Pub.Enterprises	32c	....	....	....	....	....	....	4,795.0	I5.1	5.5	4.0	7.0	8.3	14.8	16.3	25.7
Claims on Private Sector	32d	8,191.0	11,890.0	I22.8	76.7	582.5	3,072.8	I20718.0	I57.6	141.1	263.9	466.7	650.5	1,021.9	1,154.4	1,535.2
Claims on Other Banking Insts	32f	....	....	....	....	....	....	253.0	I.6	1.0	1.7	12.0	23.6	14.3	27.3	49.3
Money	34	10,027.0	21,273.0	I54.1	228.6	836.7	2,978.7	I11502.0	I19.8	39.4	66.8	101.0	110.6	113.7	131.5	161.4
Quasi-Money	35	4,976.0	9,027.0	I20.0	93.0	441.0	2,218.0	I15273.0	I33.6	64.2	105.6	178.4	248.8	370.9	457.2	559.0
Bonds	36ab	....	....	....	....	....	....	—	I—	1.3	8.3	28.3	48.5	82.1	110.5	155.0
Liabilities to Other Financ. Insts	36i	....	....	....	....	....	....	—	I—	—	.7	1.9	4.9	10.8	3.5	16.0
Capital Accounts	37a	3,787.0	5,804.0	I10.4	115.9	1,092.1	6,027.3	I19673.0	I42.4	77.3	163.5	210.3	217.6	298.1	323.9	267.1
Other Items (Net)	37r	2,343.5	4,001.2	I6.9	72.2	294.5	619.2	I6,241.0	I11.4	17.0	–16.2	–38.7	–88.5	–127.9	–176.3	–75.2
Money plus Quasi-Money	35l	15,003.0	30,300.0	I74.1	321.6	1,277.7	5,196.7	I26775.0	I53.4	103.6	172.4	279.5	359.4	484.6	588.6	720.4
Other Banking Institutions																*Billions of Pesos:*
Reserves	40	....	....	....	....	....	....	....	....	....	.9	4.9	1.7	1.4	4.7	8.0
Foreign Assets	41	....	....	....	....	....	....	....	....	....	—	—	—	—	.1	.1
Claims on Central Government	42a	....	....	....	....	....	....	....	....	....	4.5	—	—	.1	.6	.5
Claims on Local Government	42b	....	....	....	....	....	....	....	....	....	—	—	—	—	—	—
Claims on Nonfin.Pub.Enterprises	42c	....	....	....	....	....	....	....	....	....	.1	.1	.1	.4	.4	.1
Claims on Private Sector	42d	....	....	....	....	....	....	....	....	....	16.0	37.1	26.2	20.0	18.5	25.5
Claims on Deposit Money Banks	42e	....	....	....	....	....	....	....	....	....	.9	2.3	1.6	2.8	1.9	2.7
Time, Savings,& Fgn.Currency Dep.	45	....	....	....	....	....	....	....	....	....	16.8	28.3	19.6	15.0	15.9	23.0
Bonds	46ab	....	....	....	....	....	....	....	....	....	—	.1	2.1	1.9	2.3	3.6
Foreign Liabilities	46c	....	....	....	....	....	....	....	....	....	—	—	—	—	—	—
Long-Term Foreign Liabilities	46cl	....	....	....	....	....	....	....	....	....	.8	.9	1.2	.8	.9	.8
Central Government Deposits	46d	....	....	....	....	....	....	....	....	....	—	.1	—	.1	.5	.2
Credit from Monetary Authorities	46g	....	....	....	....	....	....	....	....	....	.1	1.5	—	4.1	4.8	4.9
Credit from Deposit Money Banks	46h	....	....	....	....	....	....	....	....	....	1.7	8.8	3.3	1.3	.2	1.0
Capital Accounts	47a	....	....	....	....	....	....	....	....	....	3.1	4.7	3.5	3.2	3.0	3.7
Other Items (Net)	47r	....	....	....	....	....	....	....	....	....	—	—	–.2	–1.6	–1.4	–.4

	Code	1985	1986	1987	1988	1989	1990	1991	1992	1993	1994	1995	1996	1997	1998	1999
Exchange Rates																
and per SDR thereafter: End of Period																
Market Rate	aa	201.74	250.75	337.80	333.05	389.75	479.24	536.23	525.70	592.06	589.91	605.19	611.09	593.41	667.08	727.53
and per US Dollar thereafter: End of Period (ae) Period Average (rf)																
Market Rate	ae	183.66	205.00	238.11	247.49	296.58	336.86	374.87	382.33	431.04	404.09	407.13	424.97	439.81	473.77	530.07
Market Rate	rf	160.86	192.93	219.41	245.01	266.95	304.90	349.22	362.58	404.17	420.18	396.77	412.27	419.30	460.29	508.78
Period Averages																
Market Rate	ahx	249.9	205.6	181.0	161.8	149.0	130.2	113.6	109.4	98.1	94.3	100.0	96.1	94.5	86.1	78.0
Nominal Effective Exchange Rate	nec	45.1	37.0	33.8	37.2	51.0	62.6	63.6	70.4	79.9	94.7	100.0	99.8	105.5	100.5	93.7
Real Effective Exchange Rate	rec	112.4	95.8	88.5	83.9	85.4	82.3	84.5	89.5	91.6	94.3	100.0	103.4	113.1	111.1	105.4
Fund Position																
End of Period																
Quota	2f.s	440.5	440.5	440.5	440.5	440.5	440.5	440.5	621.7	621.7	621.7	621.7	621.7	621.7	621.7	856.1
SDRs	1b.s	.3	.2	28.8	32.9	18.5	.7	.5	.5	.9	.5	2.1	1.3	1.0	5.9	13.5
Reserve Position in the Fund	1c.s	—	—	—	—	—	—	—	—	—	—	—	35.0	232.0	429.6	299.4
Total Fund Cred.&Loans Outstg.	2tl	990.6	1,088.3	1,032.4	982.6	966.5	812.9	669.4	525.0	346.5	199.5	—	—	—	—	—
International Liquidity																
End of Period																
Total Reserves minus Gold	1l.d	2,449.9	2,351.3	2,504.2	3,160.5	3,628.6	6,068.5	7,041.3	9,167.7	9,640.3	13,087.6	14,139.8	14,833.2	17,305.8	15,662.6	14,406.8
SDRs	1b.d	.3	.2	40.8	44.3	24.4	1.0	.8	.6	1.3	.7	3.1	1.9	1.3	8.3	18.5
Reserve Position in the Fund	1c.d	—	—	—	—	—	—	—	—	—	—	—	50.4	313.1	604.9	411.0
Foreign Exchange	1d.d	2,449.6	2,351.1	2,463.4	3,116.2	3,604.2	6,067.5	7,040.5	9,167.0	9,639.0	13,086.9	14,136.7	14,780.9	16,991.4	15,049.4	13,977.3
Gold (Million Fine Troy Ounces)	1ad	....	1.795	1.811	1.824	1.752	1.858	1.863	1.867	1.865	1.864	1.861	1.859	1.858	1.222	1.220
Gold (National Valuation)	1and	518.6	668.1	757.4	679.4	592.0	641.5	596.9	574.0	612.0	652.0	642.8	637.4	533.0	321.9	316.9
Monetary Authorities: Other Liab.	4..d	4,420.8	4,423.5	4,912.1	3,921.8	2,605.2	2,380.4	2,103.0	1,995.2	1,917.0	2,388.1	1,491.6	3.4	3.1	2.9	2.4
Deposit Money Banks: Assets	7a.d	413.0	480.0	342.0	395.0	378.0	507.0	526.6	520.0	524.0	547.0	490.0	605.0	1,257.2	2,111.6	4,961.5
Liabilities	7b.d	6,572.0	6,221.0	5,071.0	4,197.0	3,331.0	2,972.0	2,354.2	3,505.0	3,793.0	4,258.0	3,962.0	3,634.0	2,116.7	2,203.7	1,419.0
Monetary Authorities																
Billions of Pesos Beginning 1977: End of Period																
Foreign Assets	11	534.7	630.0	783.3	971.9	1,209.2	2,313.6	2,923.2	4,115.5	4,749.6	5,999.0	6,439.5	7,230.9	8,440.9	7,590.6	7,972.6
Claims on Central Government	12a	1,129.9	1,519.4	1,879.5	2,177.3	2,197.4	2,795.4	3,143.0	3,432.4	3,814.8	3,597.8	3,805.1	3,817.6	3,852.4	3,637.4	3,817.3
Claims on Nonfin.Pub.Enterprises	12c	.8	.9	—	.6	—	—	—	—	—	—	—	—	—	—	—
Claims on Private Sector	12d	357.5	412.8	465.7	511.7	86.6	106.9	127.1	146.7	167.5	188.0	200.8	224.8	301.6	311.3	321.8
Claims on Deposit Money Banks	12e	1,695.6	1,886.9	2,039.0	1,826.0	1,879.9	2,168.9	2,378.0	2,393.0	2,484.2	2,397.3	2,453.8	2,256.8	1,146.2	1,161.7	1,099.3
Claims on Other Banking Insts	12f	53.8	43.1	45.7	42.3	53.6	56.7	58.1	56.1	51.1	43.4	.8	.3	.9	.2	—
Reserve Money	14	1,918.4	2,328.9	2,515.6	2,568.6	2,521.9	3,892.9	4,813.8	5,859.8	6,658.9	8,039.8	9,157.9	10,613.0	12,308.1	11,863.9	12,974.3
of which: Currency Outside DMBs	14a	79.5	108.5	135.7	181.6	221.8	285.5	368.4	480.5	582.1	667.3	784.2	859.5	985.3	977.3	1,185.6
Time, Savings,& Fgn.Currency Dep.	15	285.9	328.9	404.7	441.1	545.1	570.4	365.7	303.7	285.7	258.9	110.9	62.7	71.2	62.5	58.4
Foreign Liabilities	16c	254.2	267.5	392.5	330.1	358.7	407.1	362.3	305.3	222.0	155.4	1.1	1.8	3.1	3.4	101.1
Long-Term Foreign Liabilities	16cl	735.3	891.8	1,096.8	979.3	735.6	770.9	804.3	843.8	888.6	1,002.2	648.8	1.6	1.4	1.3	1.3
Central Government Deposits	16d	87.7	118.4	188.4	219.7	245.1	473.2	806.3	1,200.6	1,371.0	1,573.3	1,753.7	2,011.3	2,390.9	2,085.4	1,495.2
Capital Accounts	17a	224.6	263.7	327.6	378.6	478.8	624.9	402.3	802.5	520.7	–113.3	374.1	268.3	–492.0	–892.2	–767.2
Other Items (Net)	17r	266.2	294.0	287.6	612.4	541.6	702.1	1,074.8	827.8	1,320.4	1,309.1	853.5	571.9	–540.8	–423.1	–651.9
Deposit Money Banks																
Billions of Pesos Beginning 1977: End of Period																
Reserves	20	96.0	102.2	127.5	160.3	153.1	178.1	337.0	528.6	575.8	711.9	721.7	746.7	564.1	897.9	896.7
Foreign Assets	21	63.8	96.6	81.0	98.7	107.0	179.4	197.3	207.9	225.7	221.0	199.4	256.5	552.4	999.7	2,617.4
Claims on Central Government	22a	191.9	187.5	163.6	23.4	22.2	23.0	26.3	27.8	51.3	56.6	84.0	137.0	306.4	188.7	179.8
Claims on Local Government	22b	.1	.2	.2	.4	.3	.4	—	.4	.4	.4	.5	.5	.4	.3	.3
Claims on Nonfin.Pub.Enterprises	22c	52.3	74.2	98.1	50.9	81.2	301.6	247.1	174.7	165.8	124.5	95.4	88.7	136.4	672.2	219.2
Claims on Private Sector	22d	1,448.4	1,696.3	2,122.2	2,606.7	3,531.5	4,152.1	5,155.6	6,892.8	8,933.2	10,452.6	13,429.8	16,081.7	18,837.3	20,577.1	22,483.0
Claims on Other Banking Insts	22f	1.8	1.5	2.0	1.9	2.5	.9	2.5	.4	9.9	5.5	26.9	21.7	47.7	23.7	17.7
Demand Deposits	24	120.8	178.5	211.7	327.2	374.6	449.7	695.7	863.1	1,046.3	1,224.6	1,528.3	1,826.6	2,242.6	1,821.9	2,533.0
Time, Savings,& Fgn.Currency Dep.	25	574.8	713.4	1,042.6	1,331.6	1,851.5	2,391.6	3,305.7	4,192.1	5,290.7	5,871.6	7,672.8	9,322.2	10,741.0	12,525.0	13,883.0
Bonds	26ab	199.3	241.9	284.2	336.1	440.9	610.8	843.3	1,086.3	1,449.9	2,090.4	2,902.4	3,717.6	4,586.4	4,844.9	5,263.9
Foreign Liabilities	26c	92.0	164.1	218.9	309.7	452.6	608.6	564.8	1,173.1	1,316.6	1,359.4	1,155.6	1,020.0	332.2	422.1	140.9
Long-Term Foreign Liabilities	26cl	926.4	1,089.1	978.2	734.5	489.3	443.2	317.3	316.4	318.4	361.3	457.5	524.4	598.7	621.9	607.9
Central Government Deposits	26d	86.0	105.0	134.4	192.5	156.4	255.9	301.6	357.7	425.4	488.8	707.6	684.2	894.1	749.1	979.4
Credit from Monetary Authorities	26g	1,150.9	1,183.2	1,167.3	912.1	901.0	841.4	836.7	692.0	538.2	439.9	361.1	326.3	236.4	177.0	120.0
Liabilities to Other Financ. Insts	26i	40.6	86.1	158.9	218.8	230.1	322.0	345.3	270.6	287.2	437.4	425.3	323.1	953.0	1,415.4	2,491.7
Capital Accounts	27a	699.9	859.0	998.4	823.7	1,080.7	1,385.4	1,161.1	1,278.7	1,619.7	2,291.5	3,101.1	3,701.1	5,023.1	4,645.1	6,001.7
Other Items (Net)	27r	–2,036.2	–2,461.7	–2,600.0	–2,243.8	–2,079.4	–2,473.1	–2,405.4	–2,397.6	–2,330.4	–2,992.3	–3,754.0	–4,112.9	–5,163.0	–3,862.7	–5,607.5
Monetary Survey																
Billions of Pesos Beginning 1977: End of Period																
Foreign Assets (Net)	31n	–1,409.4	–1,685.9	–1,822.1	–1,283.0	–720.0	263.2	1,071.9	1,684.7	2,229.8	3,341.8	4,376.0	5,939.7	8,057.8	7,541.6	9,738.8
Domestic Credit	32	3,062.9	3,712.5	4,454.2	5,003.0	5,573.7	6,707.9	7,652.0	9,172.8	11,397.4	12,406.6	15,182.0	17,676.8	20,198.1	22,576.5	24,564.6
Claims on Central Govt. (Net)	32an	1,148.1	1,483.5	1,720.2	1,788.5	1,818.1	2,089.3	2,061.4	1,901.8	2,069.6	1,592.2	1,427.8	1,259.1	873.8	991.6	1,522.5
Claims on Local Government	32b	.1	.2	.2	.4	.3	.4	—	.4	.4	.4	.5	.5	.4	.3	.3
Claims on Nonfin.Pub.Enterprises	32c	53.1	75.1	98.1	51.5	81.2	301.7	247.1	174.7	165.8	124.5	95.4	88.7	136.4	672.2	219.2
Claims on Private Sector	32d	1,805.9	2,109.1	2,587.9	3,118.4	3,618.1	4,258.9	5,282.8	7,039.5	9,100.7	10,640.5	13,630.6	16,306.5	19,139.0	20,888.5	22,804.9
Claims on Other Banking Insts	32f	55.6	44.6	47.7	44.2	56.0	57.6	60.6	56.4	60.9	48.9	27.6	22.0	48.6	23.9	17.7
Money	34	200.5	287.2	347.5	509.1	596.5	735.4	1,064.5	1,344.0	1,628.9	1,892.3	2,312.9	2,686.7	3,228.1	2,799.4	3,718.9
Quasi-Money	35	860.7	1,042.2	1,447.3	1,772.7	2,396.6	2,962.1	3,671.3	4,495.9	5,576.3	6,130.5	7,783.7	9,384.8	10,812.2	12,587.5	13,941.4
Bonds	36ab	199.3	241.9	284.2	336.1	440.9	610.8	843.3	1,086.3	1,449.9	2,090.4	2,902.4	3,717.6	4,586.4	4,844.9	5,263.9
Liabilities to Other Financ. Insts	36i	40.6	86.1	158.9	218.8	230.1	322.0	345.3	270.6	287.2	437.4	425.3	323.1	953.0	1,415.4	2,491.7
Capital Accounts	37a	924.4	1,122.7	1,326.0	1,202.2	1,559.5	2,010.3	1,563.4	2,081.2	2,140.4	2,178.1	3,475.2	3,969.4	4,531.2	3,752.9	5,234.5
Other Items (Net)	37r	–572.0	–753.5	–931.8	–318.8	–370.0	330.6	1,236.1	1,579.6	2,544.4	3,019.6	2,658.5	3,534.7	4,144.9	4,717.9	3,653.0
Money plus Quasi-Money	35l	1,061.2	1,329.4	1,794.8	2,281.8	2,993.1	3,697.5	4,735.8	5,839.8	7,205.3	8,022.8	10,096.6	12,071.6	14,040.4	15,386.9	17,660.2
Other Banking Institutions																
End of Period																
Reserves	40	8.0	4.4	4.4	5.0	5.2	8.4	19.3	22.2	12.9	13.0	9.4	11.6	14.7	35.9	33.8
Foreign Assets	41	—	—	—	—	—	—	—	—	—	—	—	—	—	—	—
Claims on Central Government	42a	1.5	2.3	2.3	.7	.4	.4	—	—	—	—	—	—	—	—	—
Claims on Local Government	42b	—	—	—	—	—	—	—	—	—	—	—	—	—	—	—
Claims on Nonfin.Pub.Enterprises	42c	.1	.5	.7	.2	.3	2.3	.1	—	4.7	.1	—	—	—	—	—
Claims on Private Sector	42d	32.5	34.7	44.9	58.9	84.6	100.6	141.4	249.1	390.9	500.6	441.7	593.4	747.8	742.5	355.3
Claims on Deposit Money Banks	42e	4.1	1.9	3.8	4.6	6.1	6.4	14.6	16.6	29.7	28.7	26.9	24.8	24.6	39.4	12.2
Time, Savings,& Fgn.Currency Dep.	45	27.0	27.6	37.8	46.9	62.0	75.4	119.9	211.9	313.3	378.8	348.4	466.4	593.0	629.9	298.6
Bonds	46ab	4.8	5.4	5.3	5.2	5.8	6.7	7.9	10.4	15.0	24.3	1.6	10.5	21.4	24.2	—
Foreign Liabilities	46c	.2	—	—	—	—	—	—	—	—	—	—	—	—	—	—
Long-Term Foreign Liabilities	46cl	.5	.2	—	—	—	—	—	—	—	—	—	—	—	—	—
Central Government Deposits	46d	.3	.7	.9	1.9	.5	.3	.3	.8	.6	1.4	1.0	2.0	1.2	1.3	1.2
Credit from Monetary Authorities	46g	6.5	4.6	4.8	3.1	3.3	2.4	2.6	2.8	3.9	3.4	.6	.3	.9	.2	—
Credit from Deposit Money Banks	46h	3.1	3.2	2.8	3.1	9.3	4.1	6.4	17.0	35.2	39.3	56.4	73.1	80.1	80.2	40.4
Capital Accounts	47a	4.7	3.3	4.5	5.5	7.5	13.3	16.4	24.1	32.9	43.0	31.9	42.5	56.3	61.2	35.6
Other Items (Net)	47r	–.8	–1.2	—	3.8	8.1	15.9	21.8	21.0	37.2	52.1	38.1	35.0	34.3	20.8	25.5

Chile

		1970	1971	1972	1973	1974	1975	1976	1977	1978	1979	1980	1981	1982	1983	1984
Banking Survey																*Billions of Pesos:*
Foreign Assets (Net)	51n	...	...	...	...	...	...	...	...	...	11.0	.5	−109.0	−342.3	−511.7	−974.5
Domestic Credit	52	...	...	...	...	...	...	...	...	...	335.8	504.9	652.4	1,095.4	1,353.0	2,033.6
Claims on Central Govt. (Net)	52an										51.9	−6.0	−32.7	38.3	163.2	447.1
Claims on Local Government	52b										—	.1	—	.2	.1
Claims on Nonfin.Pub.Enterprises	52c										4.0	7.1	8.3	15.2	16.7	25.8
Claims on Private Sector	52d										279.9	503.8	676.7	1,042.0	1,172.9	1,560.6
Liquid Liabilities	55l										188.3	302.9	377.3	498.1	599.8	735.4
Bonds	56ab										8.3	28.3	50.6	84.1	112.9	158.6
Capital Accounts	57a										166.6	215.0	221.1	301.3	326.9	270.8
Other Items (Net)	57r	...	...	...	...	...	...	...	...	...	−16.3	−40.8	−105.7	−130.3	−198.3	−105.7
Nonbank Financial Institutions																*Billions of Pesos*
Claims on Monetary Authorities	40x.p	...	...	...	...	...	...	...	...	...	...	...	...	...	...	26.8
Foreign Assets	41..p	...	...	...	...	...	...	...	...	...	...	...	...	...	...	—
Claims on Central Government	42a.p	...	...	...	...	...	...	...	...	...	...	...	...	...	...	41.6
Claims on Private Sector	42d.p	...	...	...	...	...	...	...	...	...	...	...	...	...	...	2.9
Claims on Deposit Money Banks	42e.p	...	...	...	...	...	...	...	...	...	...	...	...	...	...	90.5
Reserve Funds and Capital	47a.p															161.6
Other Items (Net)	47r.p															—
Interest Rates																*Percent Per Annum*
Deposit Rate	60l	...	...	...	...	...	...	...	94.92	63.53	45.19	37.72	40.90	48.68	28.01	27.63
Lending Rate	60p	...	...	...	...	...	...	...	163.15	86.13	62.11	47.14	52.02	63.86	42.82	38.33
Prices, Production, Labor																*Index Numbers (1995=100):*
Industrial Share Prices	62	...	...	...	...	...	—	—	.1	Ɪ.3	.5	Ɪ1.5	1.2	1.0	.8	1.1
Prices: Home & Import Goods	63	—	—	—	—	Ɪ—	1	2	3	4	7	9	10	11	15	19
Home Goods	63a	—	—	—	—	Ɪ—	1	2	3	4	6	9	9	10	14	18
Consumer Prices	64	—	Ɪ—	—	—	—	Ɪ1	2	3	5	6	8	10	Ɪ11	14	17
Wages, Hourly (April 93=100)	65a															
Manufacturing Production	66ey	54	62	64	61	59	42	44	49	52	56	60	60	51	53	59
Mining Production	66zx	34	34	33	34	41	38	43	44	43	45	47	49	56	55	58
Copper Production	66c	29	29	29	30	37	34	41	43	42	43	43	44	51	51	53
																Number in Thousands:
Labor Force	67d	...	...	...	...	...	...	...	...	...	...	...	...	...	...	...
Employment	67e	...	...	...	...	...	...	...	...	...	...	...	...	...	...	...
Unemployment	67c	...	...	...	...	...	...	...	...	...	...	...	...	...	...	...
Unemployment Rate (%)	67r	...	...	...	...	...	...	...	...	...	...	...	...	...	...	...
International Transactions																*Millions of US Dollars*
Exports	70..d	1,249	997	855	1,231	2,481	1,552	2,083	2,190	2,478	3,894	4,705	3,837	3,706	3,831	3,651
Imports, c.i.f.	71..d	1,063	1,109	1,086	1,290	2,148	1,525	1,864	2,539	3,408	4,808	5,797	7,181	3,989	3,085	3,574
Imports, f.o.b.	71.vd	941	980	941	1,098	1,911	1,338	Ɪ1,643	2,259	3,002	4,218	5,469	6,513	3,643	2,845	3,288
																1995=100
Import Prices	76.x	—	—	—	—	Ɪ.1	.7	2.2	4.4	6.0	8.5	11.6	12.2	13.5	21.9	28.1
Balance of Payments																*Millions of US Dollars:*
Current Account, n.i.e.	78ald	...	...	...	...	...	−490	148	−551	−1,088	−1,189	−1,971	−4,733	−2,304	−1,117	−2,111
Goods: Exports f.o.b.	78aad						1,590	2,116	2,186	2,460	3,835	4,705	3,836	3,706	3,831	3,650
Goods: Imports f.o.b.	78abd						−1,520	−1,473	−2,151	−2,886	−4,190	−5,469	−6,513	−3,643	−2,845	−3,288
Trade Balance	78acd						70	643	35	−426	−355	−764	−2,677	63	986	362
Services: Credit	78add						248	297	417	481	785	1,263	1,172	936	797	664
Services: Debit	78aed						−535	−515	−734	−751	−1,048	−1,583	−1,780	−1,410	−1,236	−1,207
Balance on Goods & Services	78afd						−217	425	−282	−696	−618	−1,084	−3,285	−411	547	−181
Income: Credit	78agd						4	12	18	43	126	308	606	512	203	322
Income: Debit	78ahd						−289	−337	−383	−532	−802	−1,308	−2,162	−2,514	−1,964	−2,359
Balance on Gds, Serv. & Inc.	78aid						−502	100	−647	−1,185	−1,294	−2,084	−4,841	−2,413	−1,214	−2,218
Current Transfers, n.i.e.: Credit	78ajd						16	52	101	127	143	194	193	186	161	165
Current Transfers: Debit	78akd						−4	−4	−5	−30	−38	−81	−85	−77	−64	−58
Capital Account, n.i.e.	78bcd						—	—	—	—	—	—	—	—	—	—
Capital Account, n.i.e.: Credit	78bad						—	—	—	—	—	—	—	—	—	—
Capital Account: Debit	78bbd						—	—	—	—	—	—	—	—	—	—
Financial Account, n.i.e.	78bjd						−67	247	601	1,960	2,161	3,241	4,768	834	−3,224	−80
Direct Investment Abroad	78bdd						—	—	−5	−4	−11	—	—	—	—	−11
Dir. Invest. in Rep. Econ., n.i.e.	78bed						50	−1	21	181	244	213	383	401	135	78
Portfolio Investment Assets	78bfd						—	—	—	—	—	−43	−21	−17	−3	—
Equity Securities	78bkd						—	—	—	—	—	−43	−21	−17	−3	—
Debt Securities	78bld						—	—	—	—	—	—	—	—	—	—
Portfolio Investment Liab., n.i.e.	78bgd						−6	−6	−7	—	50	—	—	—	—	—
Equity Securities	78bmd						—	—	—	—	50	—	—	—	—	—
Debt Securities	78bnd						−6	−6	−7	—	—	—	—	—	—	—
Financial Derivatives Assets	78bwd															
Financial Derivatives Liabilities	78bxd															
Other Investment Assets	78bhd						185	67	50	108	5	128	−484	−720	242	153
Monetary Authorities	78bod															
General Government	78bpd						—	−5	−19	—	—	—	−11	−2	—	−5
Banks	78bqd						11	−28	19	−39	−138	−235	−378	−51	122	99
Other Sectors	78brd						174	100	50	147	143	363	−95	−667	120	59
Other Investment Liab., n.i.e.	78bid						−296	187	542	1,675	1,873	2,943	4,890	1,170	−3,598	−300
Monetary Authorities	78bsd						−83	145	−4	304	319	−36	−320	−58	12	47
General Government	78btd						−28	−62	−97	−124	−315	−56	−39	10	−57	147
Banks	78bud						−57	−27	115	388	701	2,141	3,126	446	−2,261	−393
Other Sectors	78bvd						−128	131	528	1,107	1,168	894	2,123	772	−1,292	−101
Net Errors and Omissions	78cad						−109	69	114	−128	−12	51	102	−69	68	190
Overall Balance	78cbd						−666	464	164	744	961	1,321	137	−1,539	−4,273	−2,001
Reserves and Related Items	79dad						666	−464	−164	−744	−961	−1,321	−137	1,539	4,273	2,001
Reserve Assets	79dbd						80	−413	−51	−700	−887	−1,269	−73	1,379	−94	−312
Use of Fund Credit and Loans	79dcd						207	82	−118	−44	−170	−52	−64	−40	623	220
Exceptional Financing	79ded						380	−133	5	—	96	—	—	200	3,744	2,094

		1985	1986	1987	1988	1989	1990	1991	1992	1993	1994	1995	1996	1997	1998	1999
Banking Survey		*End of Period*														
Foreign Assets (Net)	51n	-1,410.1	-1,686.2	-1,822.2	-1,283.0	-720.0	263.2	1,071.9	1,684.7	2,229.8	3,341.8	4,376.0	5,939.7	8,057.8	7,541.6	9,738.8
Domestic Credit	52	3,041.1	3,704.7	4,453.5	5,016.7	5,602.5	6,753.3	7,732.6	9,364.7	11,731.5	12,856.9	15,595.1	18,246.2	20,896.2	23,293.8	24,901.0
Claims on Central Govt. (Net)	52an	1,149.3	1,485.1	1,721.6	1,787.3	1,818.1	2,089.4	2,061.1	1,901.0	2,069.1	1,590.8	1,426.8	1,257.1	872.6	990.3	1,521.3
Claims on Local Government	52b	.1	.2	.2	.4	.3	.4	—	.4	.4	.4	.5	.5	.4	.3	.3
Claims on Nonfin.Pub.Enterprises	52c	53.2	75.6	98.9	51.7	81.5	304.0	247.2	174.7	170.5	124.6	95.4	88.7	136.4	672.2	219.2
Claims on Private Sector	52d	1,838.4	2,143.8	2,632.9	3,177.3	3,702.7	4,359.5	5,424.2	7,288.6	9,491.6	11,141.1	14,072.3	16,899.9	19,886.8	21,631.0	23,160.2
Liquid Liabilities	55l	1,080.2	1,352.6	1,828.2	2,323.6	3,049.9	3,764.5	4,836.4	6,029.5	7,505.7	8,388.6	10,435.6	12,526.3	14,618.7	15,980.9	17,925.1
Bonds	56ab	204.1	247.3	289.5	341.3	446.7	617.4	851.2	1,096.7	1,464.9	2,114.8	2,904.1	3,728.1	4,607.8	4,869.2	5,263.9
Capital Accounts	57a	929.1	1,126.0	1,330.5	1,207.7	1,567.0	2,023.6	1,579.8	2,105.3	2,173.3	2,221.2	3,507.1	4,012.0	4,587.4	3,814.1	5,270.1
Other Items (Net)	57r	-582.3	-707.4	-816.9	-138.9	-181.1	611.0	1,537.1	1,817.9	2,817.4	3,474.1	3,124.3	3,919.4	5,140.1	6,171.3	6,180.7
Nonbank Financial Institutions		*End of Period*														
Claims on Monetary Authorities	40x.p	57.4	112.9	192.1	267.4	508.7	956.3	1,412.4	1,904.5	2,656.8	3,462.9	3,883.0	4,538.6	4,937.3	5,521.9	5,670.3
Foreign Assets	41..p	—	—	—	—	—	—	—	—	38.7	80.5	21.0	63.1	154.8	828.4	2,423.9
Claims on Central Government	42a.p	62.7	89.7	75.3	48.4	46.4	35.9	34.7	35.5	32.8	108.3	195.7	384.5	428.7	505.2	655.9
Claims on Private Sector	42d.p	3.1	19.9	57.0	129.2	256.2	505.0	1,320.1	1,601.7	2,693.5	3,536.8	3,848.1	3,832.4	3,924.8	3,114.6	3,339.1
Claims on Deposit Money Banks	42e.p	158.4	211.4	319.6	446.4	523.4	751.5	1,006.9	1,195.8	1,415.5	1,807.2	2,391.5	2,872.4	4,083.6	4,715.4	6,163.9
Reserve Funds and Capital	47a.p	281.8	433.4	644.7	885.9	1,329.3	2,244.5	3,769.2	4,736.5	6,831.4	8,983.6	10,231.0	11,555.6	13,405.8	14,552.5	18,093.0
Other Items (Net)	47r.p	—	—	—	—	—	—	—	—	—	—	—	—	—	—	—
Interest Rates		*Percent Per Annum*														
Deposit Rate	60l	31.97	18.99	25.22	15.11	27.72	40.27	22.32	18.26	18.24	15.08	13.73	13.46	12.02	14.91	8.55
Lending Rate	60p	40.81	26.27	32.80	21.17	35.92	48.83	28.55	23.92	24.30	20.34	18.16	17.37	15.67	20.17	12.62
Prices, Production, Labor		*Period Averages*														
Industrial Share Prices	62	1.4	3.0	5.4	8.1	13.0	20.0	36.2	49.9	56.4	78.5	100.0	89.2	80.9	60.5	65.7
Prices: Home & Import Goods	63	28	33	39	I42	48	59	71	80	86	93	100	106	108	110	116
Home Goods	63a	25	31	37	I39	46	56	69	78	85	92	100	107	109	111	115
Consumer Prices	64	21	26	31	35	42	52	64	74	83	92	100	107	114	120	124
Wages, Hourly (April 93=100)	65a	....	....	....	....	....	....	....	....	84	89	100	115	125	135	142
Manufacturing Production	66ey	59	63	66	71	77	77	I81	91	93	95	100	104	109	109	108
Mining Production	66zx	60	60	60	62	I68	69	77	82	85	90	100	123	134	143	166
Copper Production	66c	55	57	57	59	I66	65	74	79	84	89	100	125	137	148	177
		Period Averages														
Labor Force	67d	....	....	....	....	....	....	....	4,990	5,219	5,300	5,274	5,601	5,684	5,852	....
Employment	67e	3,721	3,896	4,011	4,266	4,425	4,460	4,540	4,773	4,986	I5,036	5,095	5,182	5,281	5,375	5,255
Unemployment	67c	517	374	344	286	250	269	254	217	234	I427	402	350	344	384	572
Unemployment Rate (%)	67r	12.1	8.8	7.9	6.3	5.3	5.6	5.3	4.4	4.5	I7.9	7.3	6.4	6.1	6.4	....
International Transactions		*Millions of US Dollars*														
Exports	70..d	3,804	4,191	5,224	7,052	8,078	8,373	8,942	10,007	9,199	11,604	16,024	15,405	16,663	14,830	15,616
Imports, c.i.f.	71..d	3,072	3,436	4,396	5,292	7,233	7,742	8,207	10,183	11,134	11,820	15,900	17,823	19,662	18,779	15,137
Imports, f.o.b.	71.vd	2,920	3,099	3,994	4,833	6,595	7,089	7,456	9,285	10,189	10,872	14,643	16,496	18,220	17,346	13,951
		1995=100														
Import Prices	76.x	43.6	46.7	51.7	I56.3	61.9	71.3	80.2	82.5	91.7	97.5	100.0	110.2	....	....	....
Balance of Payments		*Minus Sign Indicates Debit*														
Current Account, n.i.e.	78ald	-1,413	-1,191	-735	-231	-690	-485	-99	-958	-2,554	-1,585	-1,350	-3,510	-3,728	-4,139	-80
Goods: Exports f.o.b.	78aad	3,804	4,191	5,303	7,054	8,078	8,373	8,942	10,007	9,199	11,604	16,025	15,405	16,663	14,831	15,616
Goods: Imports f.o.b.	78abd	-2,920	-3,099	-3,994	-4,844	-6,595	-7,089	-7,456	-9,285	-10,189	-10,872	-14,644	-16,496	-18,221	-17,347	-13,952
Trade Balance	78acd	884	1,092	1,309	2,210	1,483	1,284	1,485	722	-990	732	1,381	-1,091	-1,558	-2,516	1,664
Services: Credit	78add	692	1,042	1,045	1,089	1,535	1,849	2,127	2,358	2,512	2,840	3,333	3,661	4,109	4,122	3,790
Services: Debit	78aed	-1,080	-1,506	-1,499	-1,780	-1,994	-2,077	-2,094	-2,535	-2,740	-2,989	-3,657	-3,921	-4,063	-4,236	-4,106
Balance on Goods & Services	78afd	496	628	855	1,519	1,024	1,055	1,518	545	-1,218	583	1,057	-1,351	-1,512	-2,630	1,348
Income: Credit	78agd	201	228	176	185	243	484	576	558	502	556	869	795	1,086	1,135	1,103
Income: Debit	78ahd	-2,256	-2,132	-1,904	-2,116	-2,182	-2,222	-2,504	-2,438	-2,158	-3,056	-3,582	-3,461	-3,823	-3,107	-2,983
Balance on Gds, Serv. & Inc.	78aid	-1,560	-1,276	-873	-412	-916	-682	-410	-1,336	-2,874	-1,916	-1,657	-4,017	-4,249	-4,602	-532
Current Transfers, n.i.e.: Credit	78ajd	203	106	172	218	385	354	501	536	536	449	482	664	877	815	793
Current Transfers: Debit	78akd	-56	-22	-34	-37	-158	-157	-189	-158	-216	-118	-175	-157	-356	-352	-341
Capital Account, n.i.e.	78bcd	—	—	—	—	—	—	—	—	—	—	—	—	—	—	....
Capital Account, n.i.e.: Credit	78bad	—	—	—	—	—	—	—	—	—	—	—	—	—	—	....
Capital Account: Debit	78bbd	—	—	—	—	—	—	—	—	—	—	—	—	—	—	....
Financial Account, n.i.e.	78bjd	-1,394	-2,219	-743	-903	1,241	2,857	964	3,132	2,995	5,294	2,357	6,665	7,355	3,181	-829
Direct Investment Abroad	78bdd	-2	-3	-6	-16	-7	-8	-125	-398	-434	-911	-752	-1,188	-1,865	-2,798	-4,855
Dir. Invest. in Rep. Econ., n.i.e.	78bed	144	316	891	968	1,284	661	822	935	1,034	2,583	2,957	4,634	5,219	4,638	9,221
Portfolio Investment Assets	78bfd	—	—	—	—	—	—	—	—	-90	-351	-14	-131	-238	-1,420	-2,366
Equity Securities	78bkd	—	—	—	—	—	—	—	—	-90	-351	-14	-131	-238	-1,420	-2,366
Debt Securities	78bld	—	—	—	—	—	—	—	—	—	—	—	—	—	—	....
Portfolio Investment Liab., n.i.e.	78bgd	—	-78	-8	-8	83	361	189	458	820	1,259	48	1,231	2,603	591	2,496
Equity Securities	78bmd	—	—	—	—	90	367	24	338	816	1,259	-249	661	1,709	529	442
Debt Securities	78bnd	—	-78	-8	-8	-7	-6	165	120	4	—	297	570	894	62	2,054
Financial Derivatives Assets	78bwd	—	—	—	—	—	—	—	—	—	—	—	—	—	—	....
Financial Derivatives Liabilities	78bxd	—	—	—	—	—	—	—	—	—	—	—	—	—	—	....
Other Investment Assets	78bhd	435	576	256	370	165	355	1,168	-323	726	-152	-309	-327	-843	-2,546	-6,390
Monetary Authorities	78bod	—	—	—	—	—	-66	12	-15	-4	-57	10	18	-121	16	-3
General Government	78bpd	-4	-9	-10	-17	-37	37	—	47	—	—	—	—	—	—	....
Banks	78bqd	170	-59	13	-56	27	-145	-62	-21	7	-26	57	-117	-654	-855	-3,052
Other Sectors	78brd	269	644	254	443	175	530	1,218	-334	723	-70	-376	-228	-68	-1,707	-3,335
Other Investment Liab., n.i.e.	78bid	-1,972	-3,031	-1,876	-2,218	-284	1,488	-1,089	2,460	939	2,865	427	2,445	2,479	4,716	1,065
Monetary Authorities	78bsd	-260	-597	-52	-948	-696	-400	-66	10	-240	-99	-402	-178	-25	-74	-65
General Government	78btd	179	53	77	108	127	206	80	157	-119	-99	-1,323	-545	-387	-171	-101
Banks	78bud	-1,230	-1,478	-1,652	-1,188	-566	-320	-570	1,589	61	407	-322	-444	-1,498	-65	-840
Other Sectors	78bvd	-660	-1,008	-249	-190	852	2,002	-533	704	1,237	2,656	2,474	3,612	4,390	5,026	2,071
Net Errors and Omissions	78cad	-70	223	-142	-122	-33	-50	392	373	-13	-558	132	-651	-443	-1,177	151
Overall Balance	78cbd	-2,877	-3,187	-1,621	-1,256	519	2,323	1,257	2,547	428	3,151	1,139	2,504	3,184	-2,135	-758
Reserves and Related Items	79dad	2,877	3,187	1,621	1,256	-519	-2,323	-1,257	-2,547	-428	-3,151	-1,139	-2,504	-3,184	2,135	758
Reserve Assets	79dbd	-103	137	-66	-756	-548	-2,121	-1,049	-2,344	-170	-2,918	-740	-1,107	-3,184	2,135	758
Use of Fund Credit and Loans	79dcd	205	115	-70	-70	-21	-209	-197	-203	-249	-210	-298	—	—	—	—
Exceptional Financing	79ded	2,774	2,935	1,756	2,082	50	8	-11	—	-9	-22	-101	-1,397	—	—	....

Chile

		1970	1971	1972	1973	1974	1975	1976	1977	1978	1979	1980	1981	1982	1983	1984
International Investment Position																*Millions of US Dollars*
Assets	79aa d	....	....	....	....	....	....	....	....	....	....	....	....	....	....	....
Direct Investment Abroad	79ab d	....	....	....	....	....	....	....	....	....	....	....	....	....	....	....
Portfolio Investment	79ac d	....	....	....	....	....	....	....	....	....	....	....	....	....	....	....
Equity Securities	79ad d	....	....	....	....	....	....	....	....	....	....	....	....	....	....	....
Debt Securities	79ae d	....	....	....	....	....	....	....	....	....	....	....	....	....	....	....
Financial Derivatives	79al d	....	....	....	....	....	....	....	....	....	....	....	....	....	....	....
Other Investment	79af d	....	....	....	....	....	....	....	....	....	....	....	....	1,722	1,450	1,481
Monetary Authorities	79ag d	....	....	....	....	....	....	....	....	....	....	....	....	—	—	—
General Government	79ah d	....	....	....	....	....	....	....	....	....	....	....	....			
Banks	79ai d	....	....	....	....	....	....	....	....	....	....	....	....	960	834	743
Other Sectors	79aj d	....	....	....	....	....	....	....	....	....	....	....	....			
Reserve Assets	79ak d	....	....	....	....	....	....	....	....	....	....	4,436	4,134	2,712	2,770	3,051
Liabilities	79la d	....	....	....	....	....	....	....	....	....	....	....	....	....	....	....
Dir. Invest. in Rep. Economy	79lb d	....	....	....	....	....	....	....	....	....	....	....	....	....	....	....
Portfolio Investment	79lc d	....	....	....	....	....	....	....	....	....	....	....	....	....	....	....
Equity Securities	79ld d	....	....	....	....	....	....	....	....	....	....	....	....	....	....	....
Debt Securities	79le d	....	....	....	....	....	....	....	....	....	....	....	....	....	....	....
Financial Derivatives	79ll d	....	....	....	....	....	....	....	....	....	....	....	....	....	....	....
Other Investment	79lf d	....	....	....	....	....	....	....	....	....	....	....	....	18,408	18,920	20,700
Monetary Authorities	79lg d	....	....	....	....	....	....	....	....	....	....	....	554	568	1,293	1,474
General Government	79lh d	....	....	....	....	....	....	....	....	....	....	....				
Banks	79li d	....	....	....	....	....	....	....	....	....	....	....				
Other Sectors	79lj d	....	....	....	....	....	....	....	....	....	....	....		7,452	6,859	6,969
Government Finance														*Thousands of Pesos through 1971; Millions from 1972 to 1976;*		
Deficit (-) or Surplus	80	-2,800.0	-10,000.0	‡-30.0	-84.0	-495.0	45.0	1,756.0	‡-3.2	-.5	37.2	58.2	33.0	-12.2	-40.9	‡-56.2
Total Revenue and Grants	81y	....	....	‡71.0	326.0	2,607.0	12,459.0	41,047.0	‡91.5	157.4	263.5	367.1	419.3	374.4	432.2	‡547.4
Revenue	81	16,000.0	23,100.0	‡71.0	326.0	2,548.0	11,450.0	39,192.0	‡87.9	150.7	251.8	352.4	401.1	365.7	432.2	‡547.4
Grants	81z	....	....	‡—	—	59.0	1,009.0	1,855.0	‡3.6	6.7	11.7	14.7	18.2	8.7	—	‡—
Exp. & Lending Minus Repay.	82z	....	....	‡101.0	410.0	3,102.0	12,414.0	39,291.0	‡94.7	157.9	226.3	308.9	386.3	386.6	473.0	‡603.6
Expenditure	82	18,800.0	33,100.0	‡98.0	399.0	3,042.0	12,164.0	38,757.0	‡92.1	155.0	221.6	301.2	374.9	422.8	497.2	‡617.1
Lending Minus Repayments	83	....	....	‡3.0	11.0	60.0	250.0	534.0	‡2.6	2.9	4.7	7.7	11.4	-36.2	-24.2	‡-13.6
Financing																
Net Borrowing	84	3,100.0	10,000.0	‡32.0	146.0	684.0	970.0	1,547.0	‡13.4	4.3	-10.7	-50.8	-45.0	-7.1	40.9	‡56.2
Net Borrowing: Domestic	84a	....	....	‡32.0	149.0	592.0	1,916.0	4,176.0	‡16.8	6.6	-3.3	-42.7	-38.3	-3.4	41.2	‡42.0
Foreign	85a	....	....	‡—	-3.0	92.0	-946.0	-2,629.0	‡-3.4	-2.3	-7.5	-8.1	-6.7	-3.7	-.3	‡14.2
Use of Cash Balances	87	-300.0	—	‡-2.0	-62.0	-189.0	-1,016.0	-3,303.0	‡-10.2	-3.8	-26.5	-7.4	12.0	19.3	....	....
Total Debt by Residence	88	....	....	....	....	....	....	....	....	....	....	....	....	1,460.0	....	....
Domestic	88a	....	....	....	....	....	....	....	....	....	....	....	....	122.0	....	....
Foreign	89a	....	....	....	....	....	....	....	....	....	....	....	....	1,338.0	....	....
Intragovernmental Debt	88s	....	....	....	....	....	....	....	....	....	....	....	....	26.8	....	....
National Accounts														*Thousands of Pesos through 1971; Millions from 1972 to 1996;*		
Househ.Cons.Expend.,incl.NPISHs	96f	69,001	90,493	‡176	927	5,742	25,941	88,669	‡210	347	546	760	948	933	1,142	1,382
Government Consumption Expend.	91f	12,588	19,381	‡38	151	1,448	5,560	17,990	‡42	70	110	134	167	190	221	274
Gross Fixed Capital Formation	93e	14,771	18,500	‡31	147	1,559	6,271	17,068	‡38	72	115	179	237	181	187	234
Changes in Inventories	93i	1,405	-96	‡-2	-56	386	-1,626	-621	‡3	15	22	47	52	-42	-34	24
Exports of Goods and Services	90c	14,591	13,900	‡23	138	1,880	9,040	32,320	‡59	100	180	245	209	240	374	24
Imports of Goods & Services	98c	-143,580	-152,000	‡-392	-166	-1,815	-9,726	-26,752	‡-65	-117	-202	-290	-341	-263	-332	-480
Gross Domestic Product (GDP)	99b	98,417	126,979	‡234	1,147	9,199	35,447	128,676	‡288	488	772	1,075	1,273	1,239	1,558	1,893
Net Primary Income from Abroad	98.n	-2,324	-1,461	‡-1	-12	-144	-1,388	-4,204	‡-8	-13	-25	-36	-57	-96	-134	-193
Gross National Income (GNI)	99a	96,093	125,518	‡233	1,134	9,055	34,058	124,472	‡280	474	747	1,039	1,216	1,107	1,398	1,705
Net National Income	99e	88,930	115,168	‡214	1,016	8,055	29,106	108,303	‡249	423	676	940	1,100	1,016	1,217	1,479
GDP Volume 1977 prices	99b.p	283.1	308.4	304.7	287.8	290.6	....	....	....	....	....	....	....	....	....	....
GDP Volume 1986 Prices	99b.p	....	....	....	....	2,745.6	2,381.1	2,457.7	2,660.8	2,867.1	3,071.5	3,308.9	3,529.8	3,056.1	2,949.4	3,129.1
GDP Volume (1995=100)	99bv p	39.3	42.9	42.3	40.0	40.4	35.0	36.1	39.1	42.2	45.2	48.7	51.9	44.9	43.4	46.0
GDP Deflator (1995=10 millions)	99bi p	96.7	114.5	214.1	1,108.6	8,806.1	39,126.6	....	....	....	....	....	....	....	....	....
GDP Deflator (1995=100)	99bi p	....	....	....	....	....	.4	1.4	2.8	4.5	6.6	8.5	9.5	10.7	13.9	15.9
Population	99z	9.37	9.53	9.70	9.86	10.03	10.20	10.37	10.55	‡10.82	10.98	11.14	11.33	11.52	11.72	11.92 *Millions:*

Millions of US Dollars

International Investment Position

1985	1986	1987	1988	1989	1990	1991	1992	1993	1994	1995	1996	1997	1998	1999		
....	....	....			....	....	....	....	....	....	16,257	19,259	18,014	19,234	Assets	79aa d
....	....	....			....	....	....	....	....	....	—	—	—	—	Direct Investment Abroad	79ab d
....	....	....			....	....	....	....	....	....	—	—	—	—	Portfolio Investment	79ac d
....	....	....			....	....	....	....	....	....	—	—	—	—	Equity Securities	79ad d
....	....	....			....	....	....	....	....	....	—	—	—	—	Debt Securities	79ae d
....	....	....			....	....	....	....	....	....	—	—	—	—	Financial Derivatives	79al d
1,006	....	....			....	....	....	....	....	....	597	1,256	1,930	4,492	Other Investment	79af d
—	....	....			....	....	....	....	....	....	—	—	—	—	Monetary Authorities	79ag d
....	....	....			....	....	....	....	....	....					General Government	79ah d
286	....	....			....	....	....	....	....	....	597	1,256	1,930	4,492	Banks	79ai d
....	....	....			....	....	....	....	....	....					Other Sectors	79aj d
3,163	....	....	4,227	4,702	6,957	8,052	10,236	10,585	14,040	15,065	15,660	18,003	16,084	14,742	Reserve Assets	79ak d
....	....	....			....	....	....	....	....	....	27,863	32,312	34,914	37,870	Liabilities	79la d
....	....	....			....	....	....	....	....	....					Dir. Invest. in Rep. Economy	79lb d
....	....	....			....	....	....	....	....	....	6,496	9,039	7,669	10,430	Portfolio Investment	79lc d
....	....	....			....	....	....	....	....	....	5,302	6,991	5,586	6,293	Equity Securities	79ld d
....	....	....			39	200	320	324	324	624	1,194	2,048	2,083	4,137	Debt Securities	79le d
....	....	....			....	....	....	....	....	....					Financial Derivatives	79ll d
21,606	....	....			....	....	....	....	....	....	21,367	23,273	27,245	27,440	Other Investment	79lf d
1,624	....	....			....	....	....	....	....	....	189	165	92	26	Monetary Authorities	79lg d
....	....	....			....	....	....	....	....	....	2,653	2,269	2,169	2,583	General Government	79lh d
6,607	....	....			....	....	....	....	....	....	3,599	2,091	2,041	1,403	Banks	79li d
....	....	....			....	....	....	....	....	....	14,926	18,748	22,943	23,428	Other Sectors	79lj d

Billions of Pesos Beginning 1977: Year Ending December 31

Government Finance

1985	1986	1987	1988	1989	1990	1991	1992	1993	1994	1995	1996	1997	1998	1999		
−60.7	−31.4	I 86.3	61.0	108.4	74.3	186.1	346.4	356.5	361.9	667.6	657.8	623.2	131.3	....	Deficit (-) or Surplus	80
752.1	921.0	I 1,155.7	1,334.3	1,610.3	1,917.3	2,702.8	3,495.1	4,177.5	4,829.3	5,754.0	6,633.9	7,366.6	7,733.1	....	Total Revenue and Grants	81y
752.1	921.0	I 1,155.7	1,334.3	1,610.3	1,917.3	2,702.8	3,495.1	4,177.5	4,829.3	5,754.0	6,633.9	7,366.6	7,733.1	....	Revenue	81
		I												....	Grants	81z
812.8	952.4	I 1,069.4	1,273.3	1,501.9	1,843.1	2,516.8	3,148.7	3,821.0	4,467.4	5,086.4	5,976.1	6,743.4	7,601.8	....	Exp. & Lending Minus Repay.	82z
806.1	969.3	I 1,129.9	1,370.9	1,571.1	1,884.5	2,542.0	3,152.0	3,842.7	4,482.0	5,137.1	5,982.8	6,695.4	7,576.3	....	Expenditure	82
6.7	−16.9	I −60.5	−97.7	−69.2	−41.4	−25.3	−3.3	−21.7	−14.6	−50.6	−6.7	48.1	25.4	....	Lending Minus Repayments	83
															Financing	
60.7	31.4	....	....	....	....	....	....	....	....	....	....	....	....	....	Net Borrowing	84
−5.5	−72.4	....	....	....	....	....	....	....	....	....	....	....	....	....	Net Borrowing: Domestic	84a
66.2	103.8	....	....	....	....	....	....	....	....	....	....	....	....	....	Foreign	85a
....	....	....			....	....	....	....	....	....	....	....	....	....	Use of Cash Balances	87
....	....	....	3,288.2	3,580.8	4,365.0	4,978.2	5,162.6	5,686.4	5,477.7	5,056.4	4,719.1	4,594.8	4,657.6	....	Total Debt by Residence	88
....	....	....	2,127.0	2,209.9	2,530.5	2,844.4	2,981.6	3,431.6	3,305.6	3,432.1	3,392.0	3,483.8	3,491.6	....	Domestic	88a
....	....	....	1,161.2	1,370.9	1,834.5	2,133.8	2,181.0	2,254.8	2,172.1	1,624.3	1,327.1	1,111.0	1,165.9	....	Foreign	89a
....	....	....	....	....	....	....	....	....	....	....	....	....	....	....	Intragovernmental Debt	88s

Billions of Pesos Beginning 1977

National Accounts

1985	1986	1987	1988	1989	1990	1991	1992	1993	1994	1995	1996	1997	1998	1999		
1,776	2,239	2,906	3,545	4,422	5,720	7,661	9,894	11,847	13,829	16,187	18,362	20,515	22,309	22,383	Househ.Cons.Expend.,incl.NPISHs	96f
356	430	494	613	742	902	1,170	1,469	1,804	2,129	2,543	2,918	3,320	3,708	4,060	Government Consumption Expend.	91f
447	586	882	1,202	1,734	2,140	2,412	3,405	4,480	4,980	6,177	7,040	8,044	8,461	7,302	Gross Fixed Capital Formation	93e
9	60	128	146	116	182	317	210	285	175	497	559	551	413	−47	Changes in Inventories	93i
746	995	1,374	2,046	2,639	3,201	4,012	4,655	4,943	6,270	7,905	8,126	8,878	9,004	9,989	Exports of Goods and Services	90c
−682	−890	−1,244	−1,634	−2,298	−2,899	−3,471	−4,447	−5,383	−5,988	−7,434	−8,735	−9,740	−10,383	−9,361	Imports of Goods & Services	98c
2,652	3,419	4,541	5,918	7,354	9,246	12,101	15,185	17,975	21,395	25,876	28,268	31,567	33,513	34,327	Gross Domestic Product (GDP)	99b
−335	−374	−384	−485	−532	−536	−684	−696	−690	−1,072	−1,106	−1,154	−1,142	−899	−946	Net Primary Income from Abroad	98.n
2,317	3,045	4,156	5,433	6,822	8,709	11,416	14,489	17,285	20,323	24,769	27,115	30,426	32,615	33,381	Gross National Income (GNI)	99a
2,339	3,064	4,184	5,477	6,880	8,769	11,525	14,634	17,415	20,462	24,893	27,322	30,643	32,828	33,614	Net National Income	99e
....	....	....	....	....	....	....	....	....	....	....	....	....	....	....	GDP Volume 1977 prices	99b.p
3,238.0	3,419.2	3,644.7	3,911.2	4,324.2	4,484.1	4,841.4	5,435.9	5,815.6	6,147.6	6,801.0	7,305.1	7,845.1	8,109.4	8,020.7	GDP Volume 1986 Prices	99b.p
47.6	50.3	53.6	57.5	63.6	65.9	71.2	79.9	85.5	90.4	100.0	107.4	115.4	119.2	117.9	GDP Volume (1995=100)	99bv p
....	....	....	....	....	....	....	....	....	....	....	....	....	....	....	GDP Deflator (1995=10 millions)	99bi p
21.5	26.3	32.7	39.8	44.7	54.2	65.7	73.4	81.2	91.5	100.0	101.7	105.8	108.6	112.5	GDP Deflator (1995=100)	99bi p

Midyear Estimates

1985	1986	1987	1988	1989	1990	1991	1992	1993	1994	1995	1996	1997	1998	1999		
12.12	12.33	12.54	12.75	12.96	13.10	13.32	13.54	13.77	13.99	14.20	14.42	14.62	14.82	15.02	Population	99z

(See notes in the back of the book.)

924	1970	1971	1972	1973	1974	1975	1976	1977	1978	1979	1980	1981	1982	1983	1984
Exchange Rates															*Yuan per SDR:*
Market Rate ....aa= ....wa	2.4618	2.6728	2.4321	2.4371	2.2524	2.3019	2.1846	2.1014	2.0546	1.9710	1.9518	2.0317	2.1209	2.0739	2.7404
															Yuan per US Dollar:
Market Rate ....ae= ....we	2.4618	2.4618	2.2401	2.0202	1.8397	1.9663	1.8803	1.7300	1.5771	1.4962	1.5303	1.7455	1.9227	1.9809	2.7957
Market Rate ....rf= ....wf	2.4618	2.4618	2.2451	1.9894	1.9612	1.8598	1.9414	1.8578	1.6836	1.5550	1.4984	1.7045	1.8925	1.9757	2.3200
														Index Numbers (1995=100):	
Nominal Effective Exchange Rate ne c	....	....	....	....	....	....	....	....	....	361.52	387.82	378.79	389.18	408.68	388.51
Real Effective Exchange Rate re c	....	....	....	....	....	....	....	....	....	....	367.01	327.43	312.56	307.27	273.91
Fund Position															*Millions of SDRs:*
Quota 2f. s	—	—	—	—	—	—	—	—	—	—	1,800	1,800	1,800	2,391	2,391
SDRs 1b. s	—	—	—	—	—	—	—	—	—	—	72	236	194	320	414
Reserve Position in the Fund 1c. s	—	—	—	—	—	—	—	—	—	—	150	—	—	168	261
Total Fund Cred.&Loans Outstg. 2tl	—	—	—	—	—	—	—	—	—	—		760	760	310	310
International Liquidity											*Millions of US Dollars Unless Otherwise Indicated:*				
Total Reserves Minus Gold 1l. d	....	....	....	....	....	....	....	2,345	1,557	2,154	2,545	5,058	11,349	14,987	I17,366
SDRs 1b. d	—	—	—	—	—	—	—	—	—	—	92	275	214	335	406
Reserve Position in the Fund 1c. d	—	—	—	—	—	—	—	—	—	—	191	—	—	176	255
Foreign Exchange 1d. d	....	....	....	....	....	....	....	2,345	1,557	2,154	2,262	4,783	11,135	14,476	I16,705
Gold (Million Fine Troy Ounces) 1ad	....	....	....	....	....	....	....	12.8	12.8	12.8	12.8	12.7	12.7	12.7	12.7
Gold (National Valuation) 1an d	....	....	....	....	....	....	....	544	584	590	571	516	491	464	435
Monetary Authorities: Other Assets 3.. d	....	....	....	....	....	....	....	322	701	828	908	798	742	829	897
Banking Institutions: Liabilities 7b. d	....	....	....	....	....	....	....	1,916	2,542	4,373	5,667	3,874	2,907	3,337	3,646
Monetary Authorities															*Billions of Yuan:*
Foreign Assets 11	....	....	....	....	....	....	....	....	....	....	....	....	....	....	....
Claims on Central Government 12a	....	....	....	....	....	....	....	....	....	....	....	....	....	....	....
Claims on Other Sectors 12d	....	....	....	....	....	....	....	....	....	....	....	....	....	....	....
Claims on Deposit Money Banks 12e	....	....	....	....	....	....	....	....	....	....	....	....	....	....	....
Claims on Other Banking Insts 12f	....	....	....	....	....	....	....	....	....	....	....	....	....	....	....
Reserve Money 14	....	....	....	....	....	....	....	....	....	....	....	....	....	....	....
Currency Outside Banking Insts. 14a	....	....	....	....	....	....	....	....	....	....	....	....	....	....	....
Reserves of Deposit Money Banks 14c	....	....	....	....	....	....	....	....	....	....	....	....	....	....	....
Deposits of Other Sectors 14d	....	....	....	....	....	....	....	....	....	....	....	....	....	....	....
Deposits of Other Banking Insts. 14f	....	....	....	....	....	....	....	....	....	....	....	....	....	....	....
Bonds 16ab															
Foreign Liabilities 16c	—	—	—	—	—	—	—	—	—	—	—	1.54	1.61	.64	.85
Central Government Deposits 16d	....	....	....	....	....	....	....	....	....	....	....	....	....	....	....
Capital Accounts 17a	....	....	....	....	....	....	....	....	....	....	....	....	....	....	....
Other Items (Net) 17r	....	....	....	....	....	....	....	....	....	....	....	....	....	....	....
Banking Institutions															*Billions of Yuan:*
Reserves 20	....	....	....	....	....	....	....	....	....	....	....	....	....	....	....
Foreign Assets 21	....	....	....	....	....	....	....	....	....	....	....	....	....	....	....
Claims on Central Government 22a	....	....	....	....	....	....	....	....	....	....	....	....	....	....	....
Claims on Other Sectors 22d	....	....	....	....	....	....	....	....	....	....	....	....	....	....	....
Demand Deposits 24	....	....	....	....	....	....	....	....	....	....	....	....	....	....	....
Savings Deposits 25aa	....	....	....	....	....	....	....	....	....	....	....	....	....	....	....
Time Deposits 25ab	....	....	....	....	....	....	....	....	....	....	....	....	....	....	....
Other Deposits 25e	....	....	....	....	....	....	....	....	....	....	....	....	....	....	....
Bonds 26ab	....	....	....	....	....	....	....	....	....	....	....	....	....	....	....
Foreign Liabilities 26c	....	....	....	....	....	....	....	3.31	4.01	6.54	8.67	6.76	5.59	6.61	10.19
Credit from Monetary Authorities 26g	....	....	....	....	....	....	....	....	....	....	....	....	....	....	....
Capital Accounts 27a	....	....	....	....	....	....	....	....	....	....	....	....	....	....	....
Other Items (Net) 27r	....	....	....	....	....	....	....	....	....	....	....	....	....	....	....
Banking Survey															*Billions of Yuan:*
Foreign Assets (Net) 31n	....	....	....	....	....	....	....	2.41	.54	-1.64	-2.78	2.67	16.14	23.95	27.03
Domestic Credit 32	....	....	....	....	....	....	....	126.24	139.31	198.11	242.25	273.99	304.67	343.70	451.45
Claims on Central Govt. (Net) 32an	....	....	....	....	....	....	....	-40.09	-45.69	-5.85	.82	-2.48	-.56	.59	9.49
Claims on Other Sectors 32d	....	....	....	....	....	....	....	166.33	185.00	203.96	241.43	276.47	305.23	343.11	441.96
Money 34	....	....	....	....	....	....	....	58.01	58.04	92.15	114.88	134.52	148.84	174.89	244.94
Quasi-Money 35	....	....	....	....	....	....	....	27.83	30.93	40.63	52.23	63.25	77.73	96.39	114.91
Bonds 36ab	....	....	....	....	....	....	....	....	....	....	....	....	....	....	....
Capital Accounts 37a	....	....	....	....	....	....	....	....	....	....	....	....	....	....	....
Other Items (Net) 37r	....	....	....	....	....	....	....	42.81	50.88	50.56	55.19	55.97	65.76	66.39	85.29
Money plus Quasi-Money 35l	....	....	....	....	....	....	....	85.84	88.97	132.78	167.11	197.77	226.57	271.28	359.85
Interest Rates															*Percent per Annum*
Bank Rate 60	....	....	....	....	....	....	....	....	....	....	....	....	....	....	....
Deposit Rate 60l	....	....	....	....	....	....	....	....	....	....	5.40	5.40	5.76	5.76	5.76
Lending Rate 60p	....	....	....	....	....	....	....	....	....	....	5.04	5.04	7.20	7.20	7.20
Prices, Production, Labor															*Percent Change over Corresponding*
Consumer Prices 64..x	....	....	....	....	....	....	....	....	....	....	....	....	....	....	....
Industrial Production 66..x	....	....	....	....	....	....	....	....	....	....	....	....	....	....	....
															Number in Thousands:
Employment 67e	....	....	....	....	....	....	....	....	....	....	....	....	....	....	....
Unemployment 67c	....	....	....	....	....	....	....	....	....	....	....	....	....	....	....
Unemployment Rate (%) 67r	....	....	....	....	....	....	....	....	....	....	....	....	....	....	....

1985	1986	1987	1988	1989	1990	1991	1992	1993	1994	1995	1996	1997	1998	1999		
End of Period															**Exchange Rates**	
3.5166	4.5528	5.2804	5.0088	6.2056	7.4293	7.7732	7.9087	7.9666	12.3302	12.3637	11.9325	11.1715	11.6567	11.3637	Market Rate ....aa=	wa
End of Period (we) Period Average (wf)																
3.2015	3.7221	3.7221	3.7221	4.7221	5.2221	5.4342	5.7518	5.8000	8.4462	8.3174	8.2982	8.2798	8.2787	8.2795	Market Rate ....ae=	we
2.9367	3.4528	3.7221	3.7221	3.7651	4.7832	5.3234	5.5146	5.7620	8.6187	8.3514	8.3142	8.2898	8.2790	8.2783	Market Rate ....rf=	wf
Period Averages																
332.49	242.54	207.46	159.23	179.02	173.83	157.40	139.29	111.83	101.23	100.00	104.23	111.08	116.15	113.65	Nominal Effective Exchange Rate	ne c
232.48	169.30	146.70	122.11	140.84	125.26	110.42	98.39	85.86	91.51	100.00	107.39	112.16	112.35	106.93	Real Effective Exchange Rate	re c
End of Period															**Fund Position**	
2,391	2,391	2,391	2,391	2,391	2,391	2,391	3,385	3,385	3,385	3,385	3,385	3,385	3,385	4,687	Quota	2f. s
440	465	451	436	411	395	404	305	352	369	392	427	447	480	540	SDRs	1b. s
303	303	303	303	303	303	303	551	513	517	818	971	1,682	2,523	1,685	Reserve Position in the Fund	1c. s
310	876	814	752	691	330	—	—	—	—	—	—	—	—	—	Total Fund Cred.&Loans Outstg.	2tl
End of Period															**International Liquidity**	
12,728	11,453	16,305	18,541	17,960	29,586	43,674	I 20,620	22,387	52,914	75,377	107,039	142,762	149,188	157,728	Total Reserves Minus Gold	1l. d
483	569	640	586	540	562	577	419	484	539	582	614	602	676	741	SDRs	1b. d
332	370	429	407	398	430	433	758	704	755	1,216	1,396	2,270	3,553	2,312	Reserve Position in the Fund	1c. d
11,913	10,514	15,236	17,548	17,022	28,594	42,664	I 19,443	21,199	51,620	73,579	105,029	139,890	144,959	154,675	Foreign Exchange	1d. d
12.7	12.7	12.7	12.7	12.7	12.7	12.7	12.7	12.7	12.7	12.7	12.7	12.7	12.7	12.7	Gold (Million Fine Troy Ounces)	1ad
486	541	629	594	587	623	634	610	612	646	660	637	601	624	608	Gold (National Valuation)	1an d
943	1,108	1,450	1,399	1,127	2,006	1,575	1,786	1,498	....	....	....	....	....	....	Monetary Authorities: Other Assets	3.. d
6,634	8,389	10,155	11,660	10,582	12,868	19,918	19,398	21,925	31,298	50,666	....	....	....	....	Banking Institutions: Liabilities	7b. d
End of Period															**Monetary Authorities**	
6.10	6.67	14.59	15.67	14.29	24.11	21.97	21.21	I 154.95	445.13	666.95	956.22	1,345.21	1,376.17	1,485.75	Foreign Assets	11
27.51	37.01	51.50	57.65	68.46	80.11	106.78	124.11	158.27	168.77	158.28	158.28	158.28	158.28	158.28	Claims on Central Government	12a
7.84	12.82	22.68	30.56	34.53	40.67	44.91	53.39	I 68.23	72.83	68.01	65.87	17.10	10.38	10.15	Claims on Other Sectors	12d
224.86	268.16	275.64	336.44	420.95	509.07	591.81	678.02	I 960.95	1,045.10	1,151.03	1,451.84	1,435.79	1,305.75	1,537.39	Claims on Deposit Money Banks	12e
—	1.23	1.74	2.36	3.65	5.70	7.37	20.11	25.17	26.99	18.16	11.77	207.23	296.28	383.31	Claims on Other Banking Insts	12f
228.41	281.86	318.17	398.36	491.12	638.73	793.14	922.80	I 1314.70	1,721.78	2,075.98	2,688.85	3,145.45	3,233.94	3,478.81	Reserve Money	14
98.78	121.84	145.45	213.26	234.21	264.12	317.40	432.94	I 577.65	728.44	788.19	879.89	1,017.46	1,120.07	1,345.21	*Currency Outside Banking Insts.*	14a
96.37	120.08	127.41	145.38	208.15	312.66	399.98	420.51	I 557.85	745.44	932.03	1,383.52	1,599.29	1,489.35	1,581.49	*Reserves of Deposit Money Banks*	14c
33.26	39.94	45.31	39.72	48.76	61.95	75.76	69.35	I 129.17	186.56	251.33	309.88	435.84	553.06	498.99	*Deposits of Other Sectors*	14d
....	....	....	....	....	....	....	....	50.03	61.34	104.43	115.56	92.86	71.46	53.12	*Deposits of Other Banking Insts.*	14f
								—		19.71	—	11.89	11.89	11.89	Bonds	16ab
1.09	3.99	4.30	3.77	4.29	2.45	....	....	—	—	—	—	22.29	20.14	39.90	Foreign Liabilities	16c
36.84	31.15	30.70	27.11	43.80	38.04	48.58	23.06	I 47.34	83.33	97.34	122.54	I 66.42	72.20	61.73	Central Government Deposits	16d
23.36	23.23	26.38	26.40	30.62	36.29	52.70	68.27	32.92	29.49	40.04	39.51	39.27	39.44	39.37	Capital Accounts	17a
-23.39	-14.34	-13.40	-12.95	-27.95	-55.84	-121.58	-117.30	I -27.39	-75.78	-170.64	-206.92	-121.70	-230.76	-56.82	Other Items (Net)	17r
End of Period															**Banking Institutions**	
96.07	111.56	113.99	128.86	178.15	263.81	359.32	367.80	I 594.32	768.59	1,006.41	1,387.00	1,645.68	1,511.15	1,610.78	Reserves	20
29.67	31.40	45.83	52.76	54.17	91.39	113.86	147.05	I 294.87	440.47	390.50	428.68	531.95	600.90	646.58	Foreign Assets	21
								7.45	47.82	105.73	182.30	151.98	498.79	607.94	Claims on Central Government	22a
594.44	775.50	927.39	1,092.54	1,290.60	1,586.18	1,899.56	2,295.48	I 3294.48	4,104.28	5,098.70	6,357.18	7,689.33	8,947.18	9,982.84	Claims on Other Sectors	22d
169.69	224.12	266.64	295.76	300.45	374.88	505.62	669.14	I 969.29	1,238.99	1,520.16	1,876.49	2,381.03	2,648.57	3,235.62	Demand Deposits	24
39.69	50.58	70.75	94.80	94.62	115.15	145.07	214.06	I 1458.29	2,051.60	2,804.55	3,637.34	4,363.52	5,020.57	5,580.51	Savings Deposits	25aa
21.61	27.96	41.01	59.72	61.37	76.43	101.70	154.83	218.88	194.31	332.42	504.19	673.85	830.19	947.68	Time Deposits	25ab
....	....	....	....	....	....	....	....	214.80	292.13	377.70	401.74	315.07	383.55	496.20	Other Deposits	25e
								24.79	21.30	18.91	29.98	354.18	520.38	635.46	Bonds	26ab
21.24	31.22	37.80	43.40	49.97	67.20	108.24	111.57	I 227.53	379.15	418.95	464.61	488.80	452.72	389.61	Foreign Liabilities	26c
224.86	268.39	274.99	336.10	420.15	508.29	590.56	670.99	I 971.56	1,034.44	1,119.78	1,423.29	1,403.85	1,206.98	828.92	Credit from Monetary Authorities	26g
65.34	74.13	81.46	91.42	99.32	111.49	131.30	131.30	I 283.72	343.25	351.58	411.37	428.59	658.27	626.34	Capital Accounts	27a
53.41	72.52	92.06	103.17	107.73	130.81	107.98	14.31	I -83.62	-194.06	-344.23	-392.77	-389.95	-163.21	107.83	Other Items (Net)	27r
End of Period															**Banking Survey**	
I 13.44	2.86	18.32	21.26	14.21	45.86	27.59	56.68	I 222.29	506.45	638.50	920.29	1,366.07	1,504.20	1,702.82	Foreign Assets (Net)	31n
I 592.95	794.18	970.87	1,153.64	1,349.79	1,668.92	2,002.67	2,449.92	I 3481.09	4,310.37	5,333.38	6,641.09	7,950.27	9,542.44	10,697.47	Domestic Credit	32
I -9.33	5.86	20.80	30.54	24.66	42.07	58.20	101.05	I 118.38	133.26	166.67	218.04	243.84	584.88	704.49	Claims on Central Govt. (Net)	32an
I 602.28	788.32	950.07	1,123.10	1,325.13	1,626.85	1,944.47	2,348.87	I 3362.71	4,177.11	5,166.71	6,423.05	7,706.44	8,957.56	9,992.99	Claims on Other Sectors	32d
I 301.73	385.90	457.40	548.74	583.42	700.95	898.78	1,171.43	I 1676.11	2,153.99	2,559.68	3,066.26	3,834.33	4,321.70	5,079.82	Money	34
I 185.76	248.96	338.34	411.47	555.89	767.24	961.11	1,261.30	I 1891.97	2,538.04	3,514.67	4,543.27	5,352.45	6,234.31	7,024.39	Quasi-Money	35
								24.79	21.30	38.62	29.98	366.07	532.27	647.35	Bonds	36ab
88.70	97.36	107.84	117.82	129.94	147.78	184.00	199.57	I 316.64	372.74	391.62	450.88	467.86	697.71	665.70	Capital Accounts	37a
I 30.16	64.84	85.62	96.88	94.74	98.82	-13.63	-125.70	I -112.01	-269.30	-534.23	-527.93	-704.36	-739.35	-1,016.94	Other Items (Net)	37r
I 487.49	634.86	795.74	960.21	1,139.31	1,468.19	1,859.89	2,432.73	I 3568.08	4,692.03	6,074.35	7,609.53	9,186.78	10,556.01	12,104.21	Money plus Quasi-Money	35l
Percent per Annum															**Interest Rates**	
....	....	....	....	7.92	7.20	7.20	10.08	10.08	10.44	9.00	8.55	4.59	3.24		Bank Rate	60
7.20	7.20	7.20	8.64	11.34	8.64	7.56	7.56	10.98	10.98	10.98	7.47	5.67	3.78	2.25	Deposit Rate	60l
7.92	7.92	7.92	9.00	I 11.34	9.36	8.64	8.64	10.98	10.98	12.06	10.08	8.64	6.39	5.85	Lending Rate	60p
Period of Previous Year															**Prices, Production, Labor**	
....	....	7.2	18.7	18.3	3.1	3.5	6.3	14.6	24.2	16.9	8.3	2.8	-.8	-1.4	Consumer Prices	64..x
....	....	....	....	....	....	—	21.2	....	21.4	16.1	15.1	13.2	9.6	9.8	Industrial Production	66..x
Period Averages																
498,730	512,820	527,830	543,340	553,290	639,090	647,990	655,540	663,730	671,990	679,470	688,500	696,000	699,570	....	Employment	67e
2,385	2,644	2,766	2,960	3,779	3,832	3,522	3,603	4,201	4,764	5,196	5,528	5,768	5,710	....	Unemployment	67c
1.8	2.0	2.0	2.0	2.6	2.5	2.3	2.3	2.6	2.8	2.9	3.0	3.0	3.1	....	Unemployment Rate (%)	67r

China,P.R.: Mainland

		1970	1971	1972	1973	1974	1975	1976	1977	1978	1979	1980	1981	1982	1983	1984
International Transactions														*Millions of US Dollars*		
Exports	70..d	2,307	2,783	3,693	5,876	7,108	7,689	6,943	7,520	9,955	13,614	Ɪ18,099	22,007	22,321	22,226	26,139
Imports, c.i.f.	71..d	2,279	2,129	2,851	5,208	7,791	7,926	6,660	7,148	11,131	15,621	Ɪ19,941	22,015	19,285	21,390	27,410
Balance of Payments														*Millions of US Dollars:*		
Current Account, n.i.e.	78al d	....	....	....	....	....	....	....	....	....	....	....	....	5,674	4,240	2,030
Goods: Exports f.o.b.	78aa d	....	....	....	....	....	....	....	....	....	....	....	....	21,125	20,707	23,905
Goods: Imports f.o.b.	78ab d	....	....	....	....	....	....	....	....	....	....	....	....	−16,876	−18,717	−23,891
Trade Balance	78ac d	....	....	....	....	....	....	....	....	....	....	....	....	4,249	1,990	14
Services: Credit	78ad d	....	....	....	....	....	....	....	....	....	....	....	....	2,512	2,479	2,811
Services: Debit	78ae d	....	....	....	....	....	....	....	....	....	....	....	....	−2,024	−1,994	−2,857
Balance on Goods & Services	78af d	....	....	....	....	....	....	....	....	....	....	....	....	4,737	2,475	−32
Income: Credit	78ag d	....	....	....	....	....	....	....	....	....	....	....	....	1,092	1,549	2,008
Income: Debit	78ah d	....	....	....	....	....	....	....	....	....	....	....	....	−641	−295	−388
Balance on Gds, Serv. & Inc.	78ai d	....	....	....	....	....	....	....	....	....	....	....	....	5,188	3,729	1,588
Current Transfers, n.i.e.: Credit	78aj d	....	....	....	....	....	....	....	....	....	....	....	....	672	620	596
Current Transfers: Debit	78ak d	....	....	....	....	....	....	....	....	....	....	....	....	−186	−109	−154
Capital Account, n.i.e.	78bc d	....	....	....	....	....	....	....	....	....	....	....	....	—	—	—
Capital Account, n.i.e.: Credit	78ba d	....	....	....	....	....	....	....	....	....	....	....	....	—	—	—
Capital Account: Debit	78bb d	....	....	....	....	....	....	....	....	....	....	....	....	—	—	—
Financial Account, n.i.e.	78bj d	....	....	....	....	....	....	....	....	....	....	....	....	338	−226	−1,003
Direct Investment Abroad	78bd d	....	....	....	....	....	....	....	....	....	....	....	....	−44	−93	−134
Dir. Invest. in Rep. Econ., n.i.e.	78be d	....	....	....	....	....	....	....	....	....	....	....	....	430	636	1,258
Portfolio Investment Assets	78bf d	....	....	....	....	....	....	....	....	....	....	....	....	−20	−641	−1,721
Equity Securities	78bk d	....	....	....	....	....	....	....	....	....	....	....	....	—	—	—
Debt Securities	78bl d	....	....	....	....	....	....	....	....	....	....	....	....	−20	−641	−1,721
Portfolio Investment Liab., n.i.e.	78bg d	....	....	....	....	....	....	....	....	....	....	....	....	41	20	83
Equity Securities	78bm d	....	....	....	....	....	....	....	....	....	....	....	....	—	—	—
Debt Securities	78bn d	....	....	....	....	....	....	....	....	....	....	....	....	41	20	83
Financial Derivatives Assets	78bw d	....	....	....	....	....	....	....	....	....	....	....	....	....	....	....
Financial Derivatives Liabilities	78bx d	....	....	....	....	....	....	....	....	....	....	....	....	....	....	....
Other Investment Assets	78bh d	....	....	....	....	....	....	....	....	....	....	....	....	−790	−638	−625
Monetary Authorities	78bo d	....	....	....	....	....	....	....	....	....	....	....	....			
General Government	78bp d	....	....	....	....	....	....	....	....	....	....	....	....	−472	−388	−303
Banks	78bq d	....	....	....	....	....	....	....	....	....	....	....	....			
Other Sectors	78br d	....	....	....	....	....	....	....	....	....	....	....	....	−318	−250	−322
Other Investment Liab., n.i.e.	78bi d	....	....	....	....	....	....	....	....	....	....	....	....	721	490	136
Monetary Authorities	78bs d	....	....	....	....	....	....	....	....	....	....	....	....	−13	27	4
General Government	78bt d	....	....	....	....	....	....	....	....	....	....	....	....	514	304	937
Banks	78bu d	....	....	....	....	....	....	....	....	....	....	....	....	−503	8	38
Other Sectors	78bv d	....	....	....	....	....	....	....	....	....	....	....	....	723	151	−843
Net Errors and Omissions	78ca d	....	....	....	....	....	....	....	....	....	....	....	....	293	128	−889
Overall Balance	78cb d	....	....	....	....	....	....	....	....	....	....	....	....	6,305	4,142	138
Reserves and Related Items	79da d	....	....	....	....	....	....	....	....	....	....	....	....	−6,305	−4,142	−138
Reserve Assets	79db d	....	....	....	....	....	....	....	....	....	....	....	....	−6,305	−3,658	−138
Use of Fund Credit and Loans	79dc d	....	....	....	....	....	....	....	....	....	....	....	....	—	—	—
Exceptional Financing	79de d	....	....	....	....	....	....	....	....	....	....	....	....	—	−483	—
Government Finance														*Billions of Yuan:*		
Deficit (-) or Surplus	80								3.10	1.01	−17.06	−12.75	−2.55	−2.93	−4.35	−4.45
Revenue	81								87.45	112.11	110.33	108.52	108.95	112.40	124.90	150.19
Expenditure	82								84.35	111.10	127.39	121.27	111.50	115.33	129.25	154.64
National Accounts														*Billions of Yuan:*		
Exports (Net)	90n	....	....	....	....	....	....	....	....	−1.1	−2.0	−1.5	1.1	9.1	5.1	.1
Government Consumption	91f	....	....	....	....	....	....	....	....	48.0	61.4	65.9	70.5	77.0	83.8	102.0
Gross Fixed Capital Formation	93e	....	....	....	....	....	....	....	....	107.4	115.1	131.8	125.3	149.3	170.9	212.6
Increase/Decrease(-) in Stocks	93i	....	....	....	....	....	....	....	....	30.4	32.3	27.2	32.8	26.7	29.6	34.3
Private Consumption	96f	....	....	....	....	....	....	....	....	175.9	200.5	231.7	260.4	286.8	318.3	367.5
Gross Domestic Product (GDP)	99b	....	....	....	....	....	....	....	....	....	407.4	455.1	490.1	548.9	607.6	716.4
Net Factor Inc/Pmts(-) Abroad	98.n	....	....	....	....	....	....	....	....	....	....	—	−.7	1.3	1.9	3.2
Gross National Income (GNI)	99a	....	....	....	....	....	....	....	....	362.4	398.8	455.1	489.4	550.2	609.5	719.6
GDP Volume 1995 Prices	99b.p	....	....	....	....	....	....	....	....	1,178.5	1,268.0	1,367.0	1,428.3	1,546.1	1,707.6	1,956.2
GDP Volume (1995=100)	99bv p	....	....	....	....	....	....	....	....	20.1	21.7	23.4	24.4	26.4	29.2	33.4
GDP Deflator (1995=100)	99bi p	....	....	....	....	....	....	....	....	....	32.1	33.3	34.3	35.5	35.6	36.6
														Millions:		
Population	99z	829.9	852.3	871.8	892.1	908.6	924.2	937.2	949.7	962.6	975.4	996.1	1,008.4	1,020.6	1,039.6	1,054.9

1985	1986	1987	1988	1989	1990	1991	1992	1993	1994	1995	1996	1997	1998	1999	International Transactions	
Millions of US Dollars																
27,350	30,942	39,437	47,516	52,538	62,091	71,910	84,940	90,970	121,047	148,797	151,197	182,877	183,589	195,150	Exports	70..*d*
42,252	42,904	43,216	55,268	59,140	53,345	63,791	80,585	103,088	115,681	129,113	138,944	142,189	140,305	165,788	Imports, c.i.f.	71..*d*
Minus Sign Indicates Debit															Balance of Payments	
−11,417	−7,034	300	−3,802	−4,317	11,997	13,272	6,401	−11,609	6,908	1,618	7,243	36,963	31,472	15,667	Current Account, n.i.e.	78al *d*
25,108	25,756	34,734	41,054	43,220	51,519	58,919	69,568	75,659	102,561	128,110	151,077	182,670	183,529	194,716	Goods: Exports f.o.b.	78aa *d*
−38,231	−34,896	−36,395	−46,369	−48,840	−42,354	−50,176	−64,385	−86,313	−95,271	−110,060	−131,542	−136,448	−136,915	−158,509	Goods: Imports f.o.b.	78ab *d*
−13,123	−9,140	−1,661	−5,315	−5,620	9,165	8,743	5,183	−10,654	7,290	18,050	19,535	46,222	46,614	36,207	*Trade Balance*	78ac *d*
3,055	3,827	4,437	4,858	4,603	5,855	6,979	9,249	11,193	16,620	19,130	20,601	24,569	23,895	23,778	Services: Credit	78ad *d*
−2,524	−2,276	−2,485	−3,603	−3,910	−4,352	−4,121	−9,434	−12,036	−16,299	−25,223	−22,585	−27,967	−26,672	−31,288	Services: Debit	78ae *d*
−12,592	−7,589	291	−4,060	−4,927	10,668	11,601	4,998	−11,497	7,611	11,958	17,551	42,824	43,837	28,697	*Balance on Goods & Services*	78af *d*
1,478	1,100	976	1,469	1,894	3,017	3,719	5,595	4,390	5,737	5,191	7,318	5,710	5,584	10,571	Income: Credit	78ag *d*
−546	−924	−1,191	−1,630	−1,665	−1,962	−2,879	−5,347	−5,674	−6,775	−16,965	−19,755	−16,715	−22,228	−28,545	Income: Debit	78ah *d*
−11,660	−7,413	76	−4,221	−4,698	11,723	12,441	5,246	−12,781	6,573	184	5,114	31,819	27,193	10,723	*Balance on Gds, Serv. & Inc.*	78ai *d*
439	516	389	568	477	376	890	1,206	1,290	1,269	1,827	2,368	5,477	4,661	5,368	Current Transfers, n.i.e.: Credit	78aj *d*
−196	−137	−165	−149	−96	−102	−59	−51	−118	−934	−392	−239	−333	−382	−424	Current Transfers: Debit	78ak *d*
—	—	—	—	—	—	—	—	—	—	—	—	−21	−47	−26	Capital Account, n.i.e.	78bc *d*
—	—	—	—	—	—	—	—	—	—	—	—	—	—	—	Capital Account, n.i.e.: Credit	78ba *d*
—	—	—	—	—	—	—	—	—	—	—	—	−21	−47	−26	Capital Account: Debit	78bb *d*
8,971	5,944	6,001	7,133	3,723	3,255	8,032	−250	23,474	32,645	38,674	39,966	21,037	−6,275	7,667	Financial Account, n.i.e.	78bj *d*
−629	−450	−645	−850	−780	−830	−913	−4,000	−4,400	−2,000	−2,000	−2,114	−2,563	−2,634	−1,775	Direct Investment Abroad	78bd *d*
1,659	1,875	2,314	3,194	3,393	3,487	4,366	11,156	27,515	33,787	35,849	40,180	44,237	43,751	38,753	Dir. Invest. in Rep. Econ., n.i.e.	78be *d*
2,263	−40	−140	−340	−320	−241	−330	−450	−597	−380	79	−628	−899	−3,830	−10,535	Portfolio Investment Assets	78bf *d*
															Equity Securities	78bk *d*
2,263	−40	−140	−340	−320	−241	−330	−450	−597	−380	79	−628	−899	−3,830	−10,535	*Debt Securities*	78bl *d*
764	1,608	1,191	1,216	140	—	565	393	3,646	3,923	710	2,372	7,842	98	−699	Portfolio Investment Liab., n.i.e.	78bg *d*
—	—	—	—	—	—	—	—	—	—	—	—	5,657	765	612	*Equity Securities*	78bm *d*
764	1,608	1,191	1,216	140	—	565	393	3,646	3,923	710	2,372	2,185	−667	−1,311	*Debt Securities*	78bn *d*
....	....	....	....	....	....	....	....	....	....	....	....	....	....	....	Financial Derivatives Assets	78bw *d*
....	....	....	....	....	....	....	....	....	....	....	....	....	....	....	Financial Derivatives Liabilities	78bx *d*
−1,101	−328	82	−781	−229	−231	−156	−3,267	−2,114	−1,189	−1,081	−1,126	−39,608	−35,041	−24,394	Other Investment Assets	78bh *d*
												−7,977	−2,417	−5,715	Monetary Authorities	78bo *d*
−104	145	151	−729	−121	−116	−48	−3,351	−1,741	−1,136	−367	−1,102	....	....	....	General Government	78bp *d*
												−12,572	2,841	6,075	Banks	78bq *d*
−997	−473	−69	−52	−108	−115	−108	84	−373	−53	−714	−24	−19,059	−35,465	−24,754	Other Sectors	78br *d*
6,015	3,279	3,199	4,694	1,519	1,070	4,500	−4,082	−576	−1,496	5,116	1,282	12,028	−8,619	6,317	Other Investment Liab., n.i.e.	78bi *d*
68	509	−112	198	50	−115	—	140	175	1,004	1,154	1,256	−2,037	−5,441	−1,472	Monetary Authorities	78bs *d*
1,219	3,945	1,158	3,895	4,699	3,129	2,284	−18	1,564	5,178	6,021	4,995	....	....	3,232	General Government	78bt *d*
4,688	−1,685	1,884	1,108	−2,661	−2,315	1,655	−786	−415	−5,222	−4,045	−5,959	6,968	−3,150	−5,021	Banks	78bu *d*
40	510	269	−507	−569	371	561	−3,418	−1,900	−2,456	1,986	990	7,097	−28	9,578	Other Sectors	78bv *d*
6	−958	−1,518	−957	115	−3,205	−6,767	−8,211	−10,096	−9,100	−17,823	−15,504	−22,122	−18,902	−14,656	Net Errors and Omissions	78ca *d*
−2,440	−2,048	4,783	2,374	−479	12,047	14,537	−2,060	1,769	30,453	22,469	31,705	35,857	6,248	8,652	*Overall Balance*	78cb *d*
2,440	2,048	−4,783	−2,374	479	−12,047	−14,537	2,060	−1,769	−30,453	−22,469	−31,705	−35,857	−6,248	−8,652	Reserves and Related Items	79da *d*
2,440	1,369	−4,704	−2,291	558	−11,555	−14,083	2,060	−1,769	−30,453	−22,469	−31,705	−35,857	−6,248	−8,652	Reserve Assets	79db *d*
—	679	−79	−82	−79	−492	−454	—	—	—	—	—	—	—	....	Use of Fund Credit and Loans	79dc *d*
....	....	....	....	....	....	....	....	....	....	....	....	....	....	....	Exceptional Financing	79de *d*
Year Ending December 31															Government Finance	
2.16	−8.29	−6.28	−13.40	−15.89	−14.65	−23.71	−25.88	−29.33	−57.45	−58.15	−52.96	−58.25	−92.20	−176.00	Deficit (-) or Surplus	80
186.64	212.20	219.94	235.72	266.49	293.71	314.95	348.34	434.90	521.81	624.22	740.80	865.11	987.60	1,137.70	Revenue	81
184.48	220.49	226.22	249.12	282.38	308.36	338.66	374.22	464.23	579.26	682.37	793.76	923.36	1,079.80	1,313.70	Expenditure	82
Billions of Yuan															National Accounts	
−36.7	−25.5	1.1	−15.1	−18.6	51.0	61.8	27.6	−68.0	63.4	99.9	145.9	285.7	305.2	241.8	Exports (Net)	90n
118.4	136.7	149.0	172.7	203.3	225.2	283.0	349.2	450.0	598.6	669.1	785.2	872.5	948.5	1,062.3	Government Consumption	91f
264.1	309.8	374.2	462.4	433.9	473.2	594.0	831.7	1,298.0	1,685.6	2,030.1	2,333.6	2,515.4	2,818.1	2,964.6	Gross Fixed Capital Formation	93e
74.5	74.8	58.0	87.1	175.6	171.2	157.7	131.9	201.8	240.4	357.7	353.1	330.3	221.5	177.0	Increase/Decrease(-) in Stocks	93i
458.9	517.5	596.1	763.3	852.4	911.3	1,031.6	1,246.0	1,568.2	2,081.0	2,694.5	3,215.2	3,485.5	3,692.1	3,943.2	Private Consumption	96f
879.2	1,013.3	1,178.4	1,470.4	1,646.6	1,832.0	2,128.0	2,586.4	3,450.1	4,669.1	5,851.1	6,833.0	7,489.5	7,985.3	8,205.4	Gross Domestic Product (GDP)	99b
2.5	−.1	−.8	−.6	.9	5.1	4.5	1.4	−7.4	−8.9	−98.3	....	....	....	....	Net Factor Inc/Pmts(-) Abroad	98.n
881.7	1,013.2	1,177.6	1,469.8	1,647.5	1,837.0	2,132.5	2,587.7	3,442.7	4,660.1	5,752.7	....	....	....	....	Gross National Income (GNI)	99a
2,273.2	2,474.8	2,761.1	3,072.2	3,197.2	3,319.7	3,624.9	4,141.1	4,699.7	5,294.8	5,851.1	6,412.0	6,976.5	7,520.9	8,055.9	GDP Volume 1995 Prices	99b.*p*
38.9	42.3	47.2	52.5	54.6	56.7	62.0	70.8	80.3	90.5	100.0	109.6	119.2	128.5	137.7	GDP Volume (1995=100)	99bv *p*
38.7	40.9	42.7	47.9	51.5	55.2	58.7	62.5	73.4	88.2	100.0	106.6	107.4	106.2	101.9	GDP Deflator (1995=100)	99bi *p*
Midyear																
1,070.2	1,086.7	1,104.2	1,121.9	1,139.2	1,155.3	1,170.1	1,183.6	1,196.4	1,208.8	1,220.5	1,232.5	1,244.2	1,255.7	1,266.8	Population	99z

(See notes in the back of the book.)

China,P.R.:Hong Kong

532		1970	1971	1972	1973	1974	1975	1976	1977	1978	1979	1980	1981	1982	1983	1984
Exchange Rates													*Hong Kong Dollars per SDR:*			
Market Rate	aa	6.0766	6.1870	I 6.1820	6.1403	6.0116	5.8919	5.4292	5.6059	6.2573	6.5181	6.5429	6.6055	7.1647	8.1453	7.6682
														Hong Kong Dollars per US Dollar:			
Market Rate	ae	6.0766	5.6985	I 5.6940	5.0900	4.9100	5.0330	4.6730	4.6150	4.8030	4.9480	5.1300	5.6750	6.4950	7.7800	7.8230
Market Rate	rf	6.0606	5.9774	5.6414	5.1465	5.0316	4.9352	4.9048	4.6620	4.6837	5.0027	4.9761	5.5893	6.0699	7.2652	7.8180
														Index Numbers (1995=100)			
Nominal Effective Exchange Rate	ne c	....	....	....	....		....		....	....	136.26	137.95	132.26	132.69	114.31	111.81
Fund Position														*Millions of SDRs:*			
Reserve Position in the Fund	1c. s	—	—	—	—	—	—	—	—	—	—	—	—	—	—	—
of which: Outstg.Fund Borrowing	2c	—	—	—	—	—	—	—	—	—	—	—	—	—	—	—
International Liquidity												*Billions of US Dollars Unless Otherwise Indicated:*					
Total Reserves minus Gold	1l. d	....	....	....	....	....	....	....	....	....	....	....	....	....	....	....
Reserve Position in the Fund	1c. d	—	—	—	—	—	—	—	—	—	—	—	—	—	—	—
Foreign Exchange	1d. d	....	....	....	....	....	....	....	....	....	....	....	....	....	....	....
Gold (Million Fine Troy Ounces)	1ad	....	....	....	....	....	....	....	....	....	....	....	....	....	....	....
Gold (National Valuation)	1and	....	....	....	....	....	....	....	....	....	....	....	....	....	....	....
Banking Institutions: Assets	7a. d	1.24	1.76	I 2.40	2.83	5.15	6.64	9.12	11.82	14.06	24.99	34.52	46.19	58.23	67.56	78.75
Liabilities	7b. d	.36	.53	.96	2.55	4.94	6.61	9.20	13.07	16.38	21.12	32.59	45.24	54.12	59.63	65.94
Monetary Authorities														*Billions of Hong Kong Dollars:*			
Foreign Assets	11	....	....	....	....	....	....	....	....	....	....	....	....	....	....	....
Reserve Money	14	....	....	....	....	....	....	....	....	....	....	....	....	....	....	....
of which: Currency Outside Banks	14a	....	....	....	....	....	....	....	....	....	....	....	....	....	....	....
Foreign Liabilities	16c	....	....	....	....	....	....	....	....	....	....	....	....	....	....	....
Government Deposits	16d	....	....	....	....	....	....	....	....	....	....	....	....	....	....	....
Capital Accounts	17a	....	....	....	....	....	....	....	....	....	....	....	....	....	....	....
Other Items (Net)	17r	....	....	....	....	....	....	....	....	....	....	....	....	....	....	....
Banking Institutions														*Billions of Hong Kong Dollars:*			
Reserves	20	....	....	....	....	....	....	....	....	....	....	....	....	....	....	....
Foreign Assets	21	....	....	....	....	....	....	....	....	....	....	....	....	....	....	....
Claims on Government	22a	....	....	....	....	....	....	....	....	....	....	....	....	....	....	....
Claims on Other Sectors	22d	....	....	....	....	....	....	....	....	....	....	....	....	....	....	....
Demand Deposits	24	....	....	....	....	....	....	....	....	....	....	....	....	....	....	....
Time, Savings,& Fgn.Currency Dep.	25	....	....	....	....	....	....	....	....	....	....	....	....	....	....	....
Money Market Instruments	26aa	....	....	....	....	....	....	....	....	....	....	....	....	....	....	....
Foreign Liabilities	26c	....	....	....	....	....	....	....	....	....	....	....	....	....	....	....
Government Deposits	26d	....	....	....	....	....	....	....	....	....	....	....	....	....	....	....
Capital Accounts	27a	....	....	....	....	....	....	....	....	....	....	....	....	....	....	....
Other Items (Net)	27r	....	....	....	....	....	....	....	....	....	....	....	....	....	....	....
Banking Survey														*Billions of Hong Kong Dollars:*			
Foreign Assets (Net)	31n	....	....	....	....	....	....	....	....	....	....	....	....	....	....	....
Domestic Credit	32	....	....	....	....	....	....	....	....	....	....	....	....	....	....	....
Claims on Government (net)	32an	....	....	....	....	....	....	....	....	....	....	....	....	....	....	....
Claims on Other Sectors	32d	....	....	....	....	....	....	....	....	....	....	....	....	....	....	....
Money	34	....	....	....	....	....	....	....	....	....	....	....	....	....	....	....
Quasi-Money	35	....	....	....	....	....	....	....	....	....	....	....	....	....	....	....
Money Market Instruments	36aa	....	....	....	....	....	....	....	....	....	....	....	....	....	....	....
Capital Accounts	37a	....	....	....	....	....	....	....	....	....	....	....	....	....	....	....
Other Items (Net)	37r	....	....	....	....	....	....	....	....	....	....	....	....	....	....	....
Money plus Quasi-Money	35l	....	....	....	....	....	....	....	....	....	....	....	....	....	....	....
Interest Rates														*Percent Per Annum*			
Discount Rate (End of Period)	60	....	....	....	....	....	....	....	....	....	....	....	....	....	....	....
Money Market Rate	60b	....	....	....	....	....	....	....	....	....	....	....	....	....	....	....
Treasury Bill Rate	60c	....	....	....	....	....	....	....	....	....	....	....	....	....	....	....
Deposit Rate	60l	....	....	....	....	....	....	....	....	....	....	....	....	....	....	....
Lending Rate	60p	....	....	....	....	....	....	....	....	....	....	....	....	....	....	....
Prices, Production, Labor														*Index Numbers (1995=100):*			
Share Prices	62	....	....	....	....	....	....	....	....	....	....	....	....	....	....	....
Producer Prices	63	....	....	....	....	....	....	....	....	....	....	....	....	....	....	....
Consumer Prices	64	....	....	....	....	....	....	....	....	....	....	....	....	....	....	....
Wages: Avg.Earnings(Mfg)	65	....	....	....	....	....	....	....	....	....	....	....	....	....	....	....
Wage Rates (Manufacturing)	65a	....	....	....	....	....	....	....	....	....	....	....	....	....	....	....
Manufacturing Production	66ey	....											....	54.3	61.8	71.7
														Number in Thousands:			
Labor Force	67d	....	....	....	....	....	....	....	....	....	....	....	....	....	....	....
Employment	67e	....	....	....	....	....	....	....	....	....	....	....	....	....	....	....
Unemployment	67c	....	....	....	....	....	....	....	....	....	....	....	....	....	....	....
Unemployment Rate (%)	67r	....	....	....	....	....	....	....	....	....	....	....	....	....	....	....

Exchange Rates

End of Period

1985	1986	1987	1988	1989	1990	1991	1992	1993	1994	1995	1996	1997	1998	1999		
8.5798	9.5348	11.0088	10.5072	10.2596	11.0982	11.1302	10.6466	10.6121	11.2963	11.4935	11.1241	10.4513	10.9066	10.6658	Market Rate	aa

End of Period (ae) Period Average (rf)

1985	1986	1987	1988	1989	1990	1991	1992	1993	1994	1995	1996	1997	1998	1999		
7.8110	7.7950	7.7600	7.8080	7.8070	7.8010	7.7810	7.7430	7.7260	7.7380	7.7320	7.7360	7.7460	7.7460	7.7710	Market Rate	ae
7.7908	7.8033	7.7983	7.8060	7.7999	7.7898	7.7712	7.7406	7.7356	7.7284	7.7358	7.7343	7.7421	7.7453	7.7575	Market Rate	rf

Period Averages

1985	1986	1987	1988	1989	1990	1991	1992	1993	1994	1995	1996	1997	1998	1999		
117.60	103.45	94.99	92.80	95.32	95.21	97.03	97.89	104.72	104.88	100.00	103.48	109.06	115.28	112.08	Nominal Effective Exchange Rate	ne c

Fund Position

End of Period

1985	1986	1987	1988	1989	1990	1991	1992	1993	1994	1995	1996	1997	1998	1999		
—	—	—	—	—	—	—	—	—	—	—	—	—	31.34	—	Reserve Position in the Fund	1c. s
—	—	—	—	—	—	—	—	—	—	—	—	—	31.34	—	of which: Outstg.Fund Borrowing	2c

International Liquidity

End of Period

1985	1986	1987	1988	1989	1990	1991	1992	1993	1994	1995	1996	1997	1998	1999		
....	....	....	....	....	24.57	28.81	35.17	42.99	49.25	55.40	63.81	92.80	89.65	96.24	Total Reserves minus Gold	1l.d
—	....	—	—	—	—	—	—	—	—	—	—	—	.04	—	Reserve Position in the Fund	1c.d
....	....	....	....	....	24.57	28.81	35.17	42.99	49.25	55.40	63.81	I92.80	I89.60	96.24	Foreign Exchange	1d.d
					.228	.228	.228	.068	.068	.067	.067	.067	.067	.067	Gold (Million Fine Troy Ounces)	1ad
					.089	.081	.076	.026	.026	.026	.025	.019	.019	.019	Gold (National Valuation)	1and
101.17	155.23	266.05	309.74	355.64	464.09	503.20	507.32	518.78	614.80	655.58	608.62	600.63	501.17	475.68	Banking Institutions: Assets	7a.d
83.33	125.78	229.43	269.58	310.13	402.69	461.89	463.87	477.58	582.33	620.40	579.85	597.32	447.35	371.87	Liabilities	7b.d

Monetary Authorities

End of Period

1985	1986	1987	1988	1989	1990	1991	1992	1993	1994	1995	1996	1997	1998	1999		
....	....	....	....	....	123.50	161.40	199.10	290.52	297.27	376.59	463.89	549.97	672.68	691.27	Foreign Assets	11
					43.27	49.21	62.17	72.79	79.88	82.96	87.12	92.71	94.77	I234.39	Reserve Money	14
					37.22	42.14	51.70	62.89	67.31	70.87	76.05	80.34	80.92	99.27	of which: Currency Outside Banks	14a
					.01	.02	.02	.03	1.54	.03	.32	.04	.27	.04	Foreign Liabilities	16c
					63.23	69.80	96.15	115.68	131.24	125.92	145.90	237.63	424.56	392.21	Government Deposits	16d
					82.64	98.65	106.64	127.54	125.77	160.13	172.86	190.21	242.22	290.86	Capital Accounts	17a
					−65.64	−56.27	−65.88	−25.52	−41.17	7.56	57.69	29.38	−89.15	−226.22	Other Items (Net)	17r

Banking Institutions

End of Period

1985	1986	1987	1988	1989	1990	1991	1992	1993	1994	1995	1996	1997	1998	1999		
....	....	....	....	....	6.05	7.07	10.47	9.91	12.57	12.09	11.07	12.37	13.85	32.67	Reserves	20
....	....	....	....	....	3,620.34	3,915.38	3,928.17	4,008.11	4,757.31	5,068.93	4,708.31	4,652.49	3,882.07	3,696.49	Foreign Assets	21
....	....	....	....	....	17.78	17.89	29.72	56.77	106.77	57.25	104.74	143.61	140.34	166.64	Claims on Government	22a
....	....	....	....	....	962.04	948.88	1,045.40	1,256.02	1,506.39	1,671.93	1,935.32	2,324.36	2,181.93	1,965.58	Claims on Other Sectors	22d
....	....	....	....	....	....	57.56	72.85	87.71	83.38	80.32	98.33	87.44	79.07	85.35	Demand Deposits	24
....	....	....	....	....	....	1,115.20	1,193.40	1,357.87	1,534.82	1,713.81	1,923.57	2,113.05	2,374.65	2,560.47	Time, Savings,& Fgn.Currency Dep.	25
....	....	....	....	....	....	45.86	38.51	46.83	71.26	82.62	107.13	118.16	116.51	110.77	Money Market Instruments	26aa
....	....	....	....	....	....	3,594.00	3,591.78	3,689.75	4,506.08	4,796.95	4,485.74	4,626.87	3,465.16	2,889.79	Foreign Liabilities	26c
....	....	....	....	....	6.13	13.69	11.30	26.60	18.87	14.43	19.09	5.16	6.15	3.78	Government Deposits	26d
....	....	....	....	....	....	63.55	90.86	104.85	113.03	132.61	153.91	170.34	153.67	154.22	Capital Accounts	27a
....	....	....	....	−171.19	−23.35	−.64	15.04	17.20	55.58	−10.56	−28.33	11.78	22.98	57.00	Other Items (Net)	27r

Banking Survey

End of Period

1985	1986	1987	1988	1989	1990	1991	1992	1993	1994	1995	1996	1997	1998	1999		
....	....	....	....	....	....	482.77	535.47	608.86	546.96	648.53	686.14	575.54	1,089.32	1,497.93	Foreign Assets (Net)	31n
....	....	....	....	....	910.46	883.27	967.68	1,170.50	1,463.04	1,588.84	1,875.07	2,225.17	1,891.55	1,736.24	Domestic Credit	32
....	....	....	....	....	−51.57	−65.60	−77.73	−85.51	−43.34	−83.10	−60.25	−99.18	−290.38	−229.34	Claims on Government (net)	32an
....	....	....	....	....	962.04	948.88	1,045.40	1,256.02	1,506.39	1,671.93	1,935.32	2,324.36	2,181.93	1,965.58	Claims on Other Sectors	32d
....	....	....	....	....	....	99.70	124.55	150.60	150.70	151.19	174.38	167.78	159.99	184.62	Money	34
....	....	....	....	....	....	1,115.20	1,193.40	1,357.87	1,534.82	1,713.81	1,923.57	2,113.05	2,374.65	2,560.47	Quasi-Money	35
....	....	....	....	....	....	45.86	38.51	46.83	71.26	82.62	107.13	118.16	116.51	110.77	Money Market Instruments	36aa
....	....	....	....	....	....	162.20	197.50	232.39	238.81	292.75	326.77	360.55	395.89	445.08	Capital Accounts	37a
....	....	....	....	....	−88.99	−56.91	−50.83	−8.32	14.40	−3.00	29.36	41.16	−66.17	−66.76	Other Items (Net)	37r
						1,214.89	1,317.95	1,508.46	1,685.52	1,865.00	2,097.95	2,280.84	2,534.64	2,745.08	Money plus Quasi-Money	35l

Interest Rates

Percent Per Annum

1985	1986	1987	1988	1989	1990	1991	1992	1993	1994	1995	1996	1997	1998	1999		
....	....	....	....	....			4.00	4.00	5.75	6.25	6.00	7.00	6.25	7.00	Discount Rate (End of Period)	60
....	....	....	....	....	11.50	4.63	3.81	4.00	5.44	6.00	5.13	4.50	5.50	5.75	Money Market Rate	60b
....	....	....	....	....			3.83	3.17	5.66	5.55	4.45	7.50	5.04	4.94	Treasury Bill Rate	60c
....	....	....	....	....	6.67	5.46	3.07	2.25	3.54	5.63	4.64	5.98	6.62	4.50	Deposit Rate	60l
....	....	....	....	....	10.00	8.50	6.50	6.50	8.50	8.75	8.50	9.50	9.00	8.50	Lending Rate	60p

Prices, Production, Labor

Period Averages

1985	1986	1987	1988	1989	1990	1991	1992	1993	1994	1995	1996	1997	1998	1999		
....	....	....	....	....	33.7	42.2	60.9	82.9	105.9	100.0	127.5	148.6	104.8	140.8	Share Prices	62
....	....	....	....	....	89.9	93.0	94.7	95.3	97.3	100.0	99.9	99.6	97.8	96.3	Producer Prices	63
....	....	....	....	....	64.3	71.8	78.5	I84.3	91.7	100.0	106.3	112.5	115.7	111.1	Consumer Prices	64
....	....	....	....	....					90.3	100.0	107.7	116.5	123.8	123.1	Wages: Avg.Earnings(Mfg)	65
....	....	....	....	....	65.4	72.2	I79.6	87.6	94.7	100.0	107.5	113.2	114.1	113.5	Wage Rates (Manufacturing)	65a
68.6	79.5	92.1	97.7	98.1	97.3	97.9	99.9	99.3	99.1	100.0	96.3	95.5	87.3	81.7	Manufacturing Production	66ey

Period Averages

1985	1986	1987	1988	1989	1990	1991	1992	1993	1994	1995	1996	1997	1998	1999		
								2,873	2,972	3,001	3,094	3,216	3,359	....	Labor Force	67d
2,543	2,624	2,681	2,725	2,723	I2,712	2,753	2,738	2,816	2,915	2,971	I3,008	3,145	3,201	....	Employment	67e
....	76	47	38	30	I37	50	55	57	57	98	I86	71	158	217	Unemployment	67c
....	2.8	1.7	1.4	1.1	I1.3	1.8	2.0	2.0	1.9	3.2	I2.8	2.2	4.7	....	Unemployment Rate (%)	67r

China,P.R.:Hong Kong

		1970	1971	1972	1973	1974	1975	1976	1977	1978	1979	1980	1981	1982	1983	1984
International Transactions															*Billions of US Dollars*	
Exports	70..d	2.51	2.87	3.44	5.07	5.97	6.03	8.48	9.62	11.45	15.14	19.75	21.83	21.01	21.96	28.32
Imports, c.i.f.	71..d	2.91	3.39	3.86	5.66	6.78	6.77	8.84	10.45	13.39	17.13	22.45	24.80	23.58	24.02	28.57
																1995=100
Volume of Exports	72	4.9	5.2	5.7	6.4	6.1	6.1	7.9	8.2	9.3	11.3	13.3	15.3	14.8	17.0	20.7
Volume of Imports	73	5.2	5.8	5.9	6.6	5.9	6.3	7.8	8.3	10.2	11.7	14.1	15.7	15.3	16.8	19.2
Unit Value of Exports	74	22.8	24.0	25.2	29.9	35.7	35.1	38.1	39.2	42.2	49.2	53.9	58.6	62.7	69.1	78.1
Unit Value of Imports	75	23.6	24.2	24.8	29.5	37.8	36.0	37.2	39.0	41.9	49.0	53.2	59.1	62.4	69.6	77.6
Balance of Payments															*Millions of US Dollars:*	
Current Account, n.i.e.	78al d	....	....	....	....	....	....	....	....	....	....	....	....	....	....	....
Goods: Exports f.o.b.	78aa d	....	....	....	....	....	....	....	....	....	....	....	....	....	....	....
Goods: Imports f.o.b.	78ab d	....	....	....	....	....	....	....	....	....	....	....	....	....	....	....
Trade Balance	78ac d	....	....	....	....	....	....	....	....	....	....	....	....	....	....	....
Services: Credit	78ad d	....	....	....	....	....	....	....	....	....	....	....	....	....	....	....
Services: Debit	78ae d	....	....	....	....	....	....	....	....	....	....	....	....	....	....	....
Balance on Goods & Services	78af d	....	....	....	....	....	....	....	....	....	....	....	....	....	....	....
Income: Credit	78ag d	....	....	....	....	....	....	....	....	....	....	....	....	....	....	....
Income: Debit	78ah d	....	....	....	....	....	....	....	....	....	....	....	....	....	....	....
Balance on Gds, Serv. & Inc.	78ai d	....	....	....	....	....	....	....	....	....	....	....	....	....	....	....
Current Transfers, n.i.e.: Credit	78aj d	....	....	....	....	....	....	....	....	....	....	....	....	....	....	....
Current Transfers: Debit	78ak d	....	....	....	....	....	....	....	....	....	....	....	....	....	....	....
Capital Account, n.i.e.	78bc d	....	....	....	....	....	....	....	....	....	....	....	....	....	....	....
Capital Account, n.i.e.: Credit	78ba d	....	....	....	....	....	....	....	....	....	....	....	....	....	....	....
Capital Account: Debit	78bb d	....	....	....	....	....	....	....	....	....	....	....	....	....	....	....
Financial Account, n.i.e.	78bj d	....	....	....	....	....	....	....	....	....	....	....	....	....	....	....
Direct Investment Abroad	78bd d	....	....	....	....	....	....	....	....	....	....	....	....	....	....	....
Dir. Invest. in Rep. Econ., n.i.e.	78be d	....	....	....	....	....	....	....	....	....	....	....	....	....	....	....
Portfolio Investment Assets	78bf d	....	....	....	....	....	....	....	....	....	....	....	....	....	....	....
Equity Securities	78bk d	....	....	....	....	....	....	....	....	....	....	....	....	....	....	....
Debt Securities	78bl d	....	....	....	....	....	....	....	....	....	....	....	....	....	....	....
Portfolio Investment Liab., n.i.e.	78bg d	....	....	....	....	....	....	....	....	....	....	....	....	....	....	....
Equity Securities	78bm d	....	....	....	....	....	....	....	....	....	....	....	....	....	....	....
Debt Securities	78bn d	....	....	....	....	....	....	....	....	....	....	....	....	....	....	....
Financial Derivatives (Assets)	78bw d	....	....	....	....	....	....	....	....	....	....	....	....	....	....	....
Financial Derivatives(liabilities)	78bx d	....	....	....	....	....	....	....	....	....	....	....	....	....	....	....
Other Investment Assets	78bh d	....	....	....	....	....	....	....	....	....	....	....	....	....	....	....
Monetary Authorities	78bo d	....	....	....	....	....	....	....	....	....	....	....	....	....	....	....
General Government	78bp d	....	....	....	....	....	....	....	....	....	....	....	....	....	....	....
Banks	78bq d	....	....	....	....	....	....	....	....	....	....	....	....	....	....	....
Other Sectors	78br d	....	....	....	....	....	....	....	....	....	....	....	....	....	....	....
Other Investment Liab., n.i.e.	78bi d	....	....	....	....	....	....	....	....	....	....	....	....	....	....	....
Monetary Authorities	78bs d	....	....	....	....	....	....	....	....	....	....	....	....	....	....	....
General Government	78bt d	....	....	....	....	....	....	....	....	....	....	....	....	....	....	....
Banks	78bu d	....	....	....	....	....	....	....	....	....	....	....	....	....	....	....
Other Sectors	78bv d	....	....	....	....	....	....	....	....	....	....	....	....	....	....	....
Net Errors and Omissions	78ca d	....	....	....	....	....	....	....	....	....	....	....	....	....	....	....
Overall Balance	78cb d	....	....	....	....	....	....	....	....	....	....	....	....	....	....	....
Reserves and Related Items	79da d	....	....	....	....	....	....	....	....	....	....	....	....	....	....	....
Reserve Assets	79db d	....	....	....	....	....	....	....	....	....	....	....	....	....	....	....
Use of Fund Credit and Loans	79dc d	....	....	....	....	....	....	....	....	....	....	....	....	....	....	....
Exceptional Financing	79de d	....	....	....	....	....	....	....	....	....	....	....	....	....	....	....
National Accounts															*Billions of Hong Kong Dollars*	
Exports of Goods & Services	90c	22	24	27	45	52	54	72	78	94	126	157	193	207	253	278
Government Consumption	91f	2	2	2	3	3	3	4	5	5	7	9	12	15	16	18
Gross Fixed Capital Formation	93e	5	6	7	9	11	11	13	18	23	34	46	56	59	53	57
Increase/Decrease(-) in Stocks	93i	—	—	—	—	1	1	3	2	2	3	4	4	1	4	6
Private Consumption	96f	15	17	20	26	30	32	36	44	54	67	85	102	118	137	156
Imports of Goods & Services	98c	−20	−23	−25	−33	−39	−39	−50	−57	−73	−100	−129	−161	−168	−205	−259
Gross Domestic Product (GDP)	99b	23	27	32	41	47	49	63	73	85	112	142	171	192	213	256
Net Factor Inc/Pmts(-) Abroad	98.n	....	....	....	....	....	....	....	....	....	....	....	....	....	....	....
Gross National Income (GNI)	99a	....	....	....	....	....	....	....	....	....	....	....	....	....	....	....
GDP Volume 1973 Prices	99b.p	26	27	29	34	35	35	42	46	51	58	64	71	73	....	....
GDP Volume 1980 Prices	99b.p	....	....	....	....	....	....	....	....	....	....	....	....	154	163	179
GDP Volume 1990 Prices	99b.p	....	....	....	....	....	....	....	....	....	....	....	....	....	....	....
GDP Volume (1995=100)	99bv p	16.8	18.1	20.1	22.6	23.1	23.2	27.2	30.4	33.1	37.0	40.9	44.7	45.9	48.8	53.5
GDP Deflator (1995=100)	99bi p	12.7	13.6	14.8	16.8	18.9	19.7	21.4	22.2	23.9	28.0	32.2	35.5	39.0	40.5	44.5
																Millions:
Population	99z	3.96	4.05	4.12	4.21	4.32	4.40	4.44	I4.51	4.67	4.93	5.06	5.18	5.26	5.35	5.40

	1985	1986	1987	1988	1989	1990	1991	1992	1993	1994	1995	1996	1997	1998	1999	International Transactions	
Billions of US Dollars																	
	30.19	35.44	48.48	63.16	73.14	82.16	98.58	119.49	135.24	151.40	173.75	180.75	188.06	174.00	173.89	Exports	70..d
	29.70	35.37	48.46	63.90	72.15	82.49	100.24	123.41	138.65	161.84	192.75	198.55	208.61	184.52	179.52	Imports, c.i.f.	71..d
1995=100																	
	21.9	25.3	33.3	I42.1	46.3	50.7	59.5	71.2	80.9	89.3	100.0	104.8	111.2	106.4	110.3	Volume of Exports	72
	20.4	23.2	30.6	I38.7	42.2	47.0	55.9	68.4	77.1	87.9	100.0	104.3	111.9	103.9	104.1	Volume of Imports	73
	78.5	80.2	83.2	I85.8	90.1	92.5	94.9	95.7	95.4	96.8	100.0	99.6	98.1	94.4	91.8	Unit Value of Exports	74
	75.6	79.4	82.6	I86.1	89.2	91.4	93.1	93.3	92.8	95.3	100.0	98.8	96.5	91.8	89.9	Unit Value of Imports	75

Minus Sign Indicates Debit

Balance of Payments

	1998	1999		
	2,901	9,281	Current Account, n.i.e.	78al d
	175,833	174,719	Goods: Exports f.o.b.	78aa d
	-183,666	-177,878	Goods: Imports f.o.b.	78ab d
	-7,833	-3,159	*Trade Balance*	78ac d
	33,653	34,850	Services: Credit	78ad d
	-25,036	-24,456	Services: Debit	78ae d
	784	7,235	*Balance on Goods & Services*	78af d
	46,831	47,296	Income: Credit	78ag d
	-43,117	-43,780	Income: Debit	78ah d
	4,498	10,751	*Balance on Gds, Serv. & Inc.*	78ai d
	669	708	Current Transfers, n.i.e.: Credit	78aj d
	-2,265	-2,178	Current Transfers: Debit	78ak d
	-2,382	-1,774	Capital Account, n.i.e.	78bc d
	377	101	Capital Account, n.i.e.: Credit	78ba d
	-2,759	-1,875	Capital Account: Debit	78bb d
	-8,476	1,498	Financial Account, n.i.e.	78bj d
	-16,973	-19,905	Direct Investment Abroad	78bd d
	14,776	23,068	Dir. Invest. in Rep. Econ., n.i.e.	78be d
	25,492	-25,467	Portfolio Investment Assets	78bf d
	8,507	-29,159	Equity Securities	78bk d
	16,985	3,692	Debt Securities	78bl d
	-3,407	57,734	Portfolio Investment Liab., n.i.e.	78bg d
	-2,106	58,829	Equity Securities	78bm d
	-1,301	-1,095	Debt Securities	78bn d
	10,799	24,037	Financial Derivatives (Assets)	78bw d
	-7,523	-11,729	Financial Derivatives (Liabilities)	78bx d
	119,830	42,236	Other Investment Assets	78bh d
	....	....	Monetary Authorities	78bo d
	....	....	General Government	78bp d
	101,774	33,338	Banks	78bq d
	18,057	8,898	Other Sectors	78br d
	-151,470	-88,477	Other Investment Liab., n.i.e.	78bi d
	....	....	Monetary Authorities	78bs d
	....	....	General Government	78bt d
	-148,616	-83,980	Banks	78bu d
	-2,854	-4,497	Other Sectors	78bv d
	1,061	500	Net Errors and Omissions	78ca d
	-6,896	9,505	*Overall Balance*	78cb d
	6,896	-9,505	Reserves and Related Items	79da d
	6,896	-9,505	Reserve Assets	79db d
	....	....	Use of Fund Credit and Loans	79dc d
	....	....	Exceptional Financing	79de d

National Accounts

	1985	1986	1987	1988	1989	1990	1991	1992	1993	1994	1995	1996	1997	1998	1999		
Billions of Hong Kong Dollars																	
	296	348	470	604	698	782	927	1,114	1,262	1,411	1,610	1,694	1,754	1,615	1,626	Exports of Goods & Services	90c
	20	23	26	30	36	43	51	64	73	84	94	104	114	118	121	Government Consumption	91f
	57	68	92	116	136	154	178	214	245	301	330	372	445	387	316	Gross Fixed Capital Formation	93e
	1	6	10	14	3	6	4	8	2	21	46	10	12	-11	-4	Increase/Decrease(-) in Stocks	93i
	167	189	219	255	288	330	391	452	514	593	654	722	798	767	742	Private Consumption	96f
	-271	-322	-432	-564	-637	-733	-883	-1,073	-1,199	-1,398	-1,657	-1,711	-1,800	-1,609	-1,570	Imports of Goods & Services	98c
	272	313	384	455	524	583	669	779	897	1,011	1,077	1,192	1,324	1,267	1,232	Gross Domestic Product (GDP)	99b
									13	12	21	—	10	29	27	Net Factor Inc/Pmts(-) Abroad	98.n
									911	1,023	1,098	1,192	1,334	1,296	1,260	Gross National Income (GNI)	99a
	....	....	....	....	....	....	....	....	....	....	....	....	....	....	....	GDP Volume 1973 Prices	99b.p
	180	199	....													GDP Volume 1980 Prices	99b.p
	....	450	509	549	563	583	612	650	690	728	756	790	829	786	810	GDP Volume 1990 Prices	99b.p
	53.6	59.6	67.3	72.7	74.5	77.1	81.0	86.0	91.3	96.3	100.0	104.5	109.7	104.0	107.2	GDP Volume (1995=100)	99bv p
	47.0	48.7	53.0	58.1	65.2	70.2	76.6	84.1	91.2	97.5	100.0	105.9	112.1	113.0	106.7	GDP Deflator (1995=100)	99bi p
Midyear Estimates																	
	5.46	5.52	5.58	5.63	5.69	5.70	5.75	5.80	5.90	6.04	6.16	6.31	6.50	6.69	6.84	**Population**	99z

(See notes in the back of the book.)

Colombia

		1970	1971	1972	1973	1974	1975	1976	1977	1978	1979	1980	1981	1982	1983	1984
Exchange Rates															*Pesos per SDR:*	
Principal Rate	aa	19.09	22.70	24.74	29.91	35.05	38.58	42.20	46.11	53.41	57.96	64.94	68.76	77.54	92.94	111.64
															Pesos per US Dollar:	
Principal Rate	ae	19.09	20.91	22.79	24.79	28.63	32.96	36.32	37.96	41.00	44.00	50.92	59.07	70.29	88.77	113.89
Principal Rate	rf	18.44	19.93	21.87	23.64	26.06	30.93	34.69	36.77	39.09	42.55	47.28	54.49	64.08	78.85	100.82
															Index Numbers (1995=100):	
Principal Rate	ahx	4,953.6	4,584.5	4,178.9	3,865.3	3,508.4	2,957.4	2,633.9	2,484.0	2,337.1	2,146.9	1,933.8	1,678.8	1,428.5	1,164.4	909.2
Nominal Effective Exchange Rate	ne c	....	....	....	....	....	....	....	....	....	336.5	320.2	314.1	305.0	289.0	264.6
Real Effective Exchange Rate	re c	....	....	....	....	....	....	....	....	....	....	146.7	158.4	168.5	168.6	155.8
Fund Position															*Millions of SDRs:*	
Quota	2f. s	157	157	157	157	157	157	157	157	193	193	290	290	290	394	394
SDRs	1b. s	—	8	18	23	25	20	24	26	38	72	85	119	162	189	—
Reserve Position in the Fund	1c. s	—	—	—	39	39	39	45	77	70	74	115	152	175	262	—
Total Fund Cred.&Loans Outstg.	2tl	55	53	—												
International Liquidity												*Millions of US Dollars Unless Otherwise Indicated:*					
Total Reserves minus Gold	1l.d	189	188	309	516	431	475	1,101	1,747	2,366	3,844	4,831	4,741	3,861	1,901	1,364
SDRs	1b.d	—	9	19	28	30	24	28	31	49	95	109	139	179	198	—
Reserve Position in the Fund	1c.d	—	—	—	47	48	46	53	93	91	97	146	177	193	274	—
Foreign Exchange	1d.d	189	179	290	441	353	405	1,020	1,623	2,226	3,652	4,576	4,425	3,489	1,429	1,364
Gold (Million Fine Troy Ounces)	1ad	.486	.400	.429	.429	.429	1.126	1.413	1.731	1.961	2.317	2.787	3.366	3.817	4.223	1.367
Gold (National Valuation)	1and	17	14	16	16	18	48	60	73	137	215	525	764	933	1,025e	426
Monetary Authorities: Other Assets	3..d	12	24	24	—	—	28	8	18	—	7	77	57	7	23	6
Other Liab.	4..d	64	73	112	132	137	135	142	175	229	259	302	321	334	348	345
Deposit Money Banks: Assets	7a.d	6	4	5	21	35	57	62	64	89	145	170	179	177	385	528
Liabilities	7b.d	239	331	325	310	578	533	637	476	486	869	1,093	1,147	1,222	1,151	1,202
Other Banking Insts.: Liabilities	7f.d	....	....	....	....	102	152	139	175	229	292	435	466	539	530	608
Monetary Authorities														*Millions of Pesos through 1973;*		
Foreign Assets	11	4,040.0	4,560.0	7,780.0	12,675.1	I11.6	16.4	40.7	69.4	98.6	175.9	259.3	308.0	314.8	242.6	145.4
Claims on Central Government	12a	5,611.0	6,832.0	6,990.0	6,200.0	I8.0	10.9	9.0	8.8	I9.5	9.7	13.1	13.7	46.7	106.8	252.3
Claims on Nonfin.Pub.Enterprises	12c				334.0	I.3	.3	.2	.2	.2	.1	.1	.1	-1.0	2.2	—
Claims on Private Sector	12d	3,987.0	2,745.0	3,464.0	3,545.0	I1.8	2.2	3.0	3.6	4.5	6.3	5.3	8.0	10.2	14.1	13.2
Claims on Deposit Money Banks	12e	3,249.0	3,618.0	3,394.0	5,790.0	I7.6	8.1	7.4	13.9	I32.1	36.0	38.0	48.6	67.8	104.3	121.1
Claims on Other Banking Insts	12f	3,689.0	4,772.0	5,875.0	8,055.0	I11.3	19.2	20.6	35.3	I27.8	25.2	27.3	30.0	34.3	53.3	84.4
Claims on Nonbank Financial Insts	12g															
Reserve Money	14	13,700.0	15,363.0	18,919.0	24,808.0	I30.1	37.7	53.4	74.9	I115.0	148.7	192.4	239.1	281.2	333.4	411.9
of which: Currency Outside DMBs	14a	7,809.0	8,534.0	10,729.0	12,424.0	I15.9	20.8	28.8	40.5	I53.7	67.3	84.1	101.6	130.3	167.7	211.7
Time, Savings,& Fgn.Currency Dep.	15	....	....	....	....	....										
Money Market Instruments	16aa				504.0	I1.0	1.6	5.1	16.3	I27.3	39.9	62.0	65.8	106.7	69.6	69.1
Restricted Deposits	16b	2,401.0	2,144.0	2,496.0	3,661.0	I3.8	2.0	.9	5.1	I5.9	10.1	12.8	12.0	10.0	25.6	35.9
Foreign Liabilities	16c	1,226.0	1,121.0	297.0	812.0	I1.0	.2	.2	.2	I.4	.3	.2	.1	.1	7.4	8.3
Long-Term Foreign Liabilities	16cl	1,046.0	1,621.0	2,264.0	2,464.0	I3.0	4.3	5.0	6.4	I9.0	11.1	15.2	18.8	23.4	23.5	31.0
Central Government Deposits	16d	1,632.0	1,304.0	1,536.0	1,594.0	I1.9	1.8	2.8	4.1	I5.8	28.7	30.4	32.5	19.3	42.1	39.3
Capital Accounts	17a				2,530.0	I2.4	2.5	2.7	2.9	I3.6	5.1	7.4	10.0	11.8	15.5	48.5
Other Items (Net)	17r	571.0	974.0	1,991.0	226.1	I-2.7	7.0	10.8	21.2	I5.5	9.2	22.8	29.9	20.3	6.1	-27.5
Deposit Money Banks														*Millions of Pesos through 1973;*		
Reserves	20	5,209.0	5,410.0	6,758.0	10,690.0	I12.6	17.0	24.8	34.3	I60.5	79.3	106.0	134.5	149.7	169.5	202.2
Foreign Assets	21	113.0	85.0	109.0	510.0	I1.0	1.9	2.2	2.4	I3.6	6.0	8.4	10.3	12.2	28.3	50.9
Claims on Central Government	22a	1,990.0	2,352.0	2,968.0	4,822.0	I6.9	6.9	9.3	14.6	I15.1	15.6	15.5	22.6	30.2	40.6	62.0
Claims on Local Government	22b	....	....	....	....	....										
Claims on Nonfin.Pub.Enterprises	22c									1.6	1.0	1.1	2.8	3.4	10.9	13.5
Claims on Private Sector	22d	17,582.0	21,515.0	25,095.0	29,976.0	I45.1	55.6	73.5	88.6	I108.0	138.1	220.7	298.1	374.2	479.2	584.8
Claims on Other Banking Insts	22f	1,840.0	2,240.0	3,081.0	4,465.0	I7.0	10.5	12.1	14.7	I9.1	12.0	15.0	18.6	22.3	26.3	28.7
Demand Deposits	24	14,005.0	15,647.0	20,055.0	28,151.0	I31.7	40.9	54.8	69.4	I76.5	93.6	121.4	147.2	180.8	220.9	267.3
Time, Savings,& Fgn.Currency Dep.	25	2,972.0	3,545.0	5,127.0	7,408.0	I13.1	17.0	24.0	34.3	I44.0	51.7	103.2	171.4	196.8	250.6	309.1
Money Market Instruments	26aa															
Bonds	26ab															
Restricted Deposits	26b															
Foreign Liabilities	26c	4,285.0	6,576.0	7,068.0	7,363.0	I16.2	17.3	22.9	17.8	I19.3	37.7	55.2	67.4	85.7	102.0	136.8
Long-Term Foreign Liabilities	26cl	287.0	338.0	331.0	334.0	I.3	.3	.2	.2	I.3	.3	.2	.2	.1	.1	—
Central Government Deposits	26d										.7	.9	1.3	1.5	2.5	2.8	3.2
Credit from Monetary Authorities	26g	3,018.0	2,751.0	2,394.0	4,320.0	I6.2	6.4	5.2	16.0	I31.5	35.5	36.7	47.0	68.4	101.2	119.1
Liabilities to Other Banking Insts	26i															
Capital Accounts	27a	3,752.0	4,456.0	5,183.0	6,102.0	I5.6	6.8	9.1	11.6	I22.9	28.8	40.3	52.4	66.3	71.9	75.9
Other Items (Net)	27r	-1,585.0	-1,711.0	-2,147.0	-3,215.0	I-.4	3.1	5.8	5.5	I2.8	3.6	8.3	-.1	-8.7	5.3	30.7
Monetary Survey														*Millions of Pesos through 1973;*		
Foreign Assets (Net)	31n	-1,358.0	-3,052.0	524.0	5,010.1	I-4.5	.8	19.8	53.7	I82.4	143.9	212.3	250.7	241.2	161.5	51.3
Domestic Credit	32	33,060.0	39,145.0	45,937.0	55,469.0	I78.7	104.5	124.4	161.6	I169.3	178.4	266.5	364.6	498.5	686.5	996.5
Claims on Central Govt. (Net)	32an	4,696.0	6,333.0	6,413.0	5,800.0	I8.8	10.8	14.9	19.2	I18.1	-4.3	-3.1	2.3	55.1	102.5	271.8
Claims on Local Government	32b	....	....	....	....	....										
Claims on Nonfin.Pub.Enterprises	32c				334.0	I.3	.3	.2	.2	1.8	1.1	1.2	2.9	2.4	13.1	13.5
Claims on Private Sector	32d	21,569.0	24,260.0	28,559.0	33,521.0	I47.4	58.9	76.5	92.3	I112.4	144.4	226.0	306.1	384.4	493.3	598.0
Claims on Other Banking Insts	32f	5,529.0	7,012.0	8,956.0	12,520.0	I18.4	29.7	32.7	50.1	I36.9	37.2	42.3	48.6	56.6	79.7	113.1
Claims on Nonbank Financial Inst	32g															
Money	34	22,397.0	25,063.0	31,854.0	41,647.0	I49.1	58.9	79.4	103.5	I132.9	165.9	212.4	256.4	321.4	396.7	492.4
Quasi-Money	35	3,381.0	4,127.0	5,856.0	9,250.0	I14.6	19.6	25.8	37.2	I47.1	55.1	108.1	178.4	204.2	262.5	324.4
Money Market Instruments	36aa				504.0	I1.1	1.6	5.1	16.3	27.3	39.9	62.0	70.0	106.7	69.6	69.1
Bonds	36ab															
Restricted Deposits	36b	2,402.0	2,144.0	2,496.0	3,661.0	I3.8	2.0	.9	5.1	I5.9	10.1	12.8	12.0	10.0	25.6	35.9
Long-Term Foreign Liabilities	36cl	1,333.0	1,959.0	2,595.0	2,798.0	I3.3	4.5	5.2	6.7	I9.3	11.4	15.4	19.0	23.5	23.6	31.0
Liabilities to Other Banking Insts	36i	....	....	....												
Capital Accounts	37a				8,632.0	I8.0	9.4	11.8	14.6	I26.5	34.0	47.7	62.4	78.1	87.5	124.5
Other Items (Net)	37r	2,189.0	2,800.0	3,660.0	-6,012.9	I-5.7	9.4	16.1	32.0	I2.7	5.9	20.4	17.1	-4.3	-17.6	-29.6
Money plus Quasi-Money	35l	25,778.0	29,190.0	37,710.0	50,897.0	I63.7	78.5	105.1	140.7	I180.0	221.0	320.5	434.7	525.6	659.2	816.8

1985	1986	1987	1988	1989	1990	1991	1992	1993	1994	1995	1996	1997	1998	1999		
End of Period															**Exchange Rates**	
189.15	267.88	374.10	451.97	570.24	809.11	1,011.11	1,116.18	1,260.01	1,213.53	1,468.13	1,445.62	1,745.36	2,122.63	2,571.77	Principal Rate	aa
End of Period (ae) Period Average (rf)																
172.20	219.00	263.70	335.86	433.92	568.73	706.86	811.77	917.33	831.27	987.65	1,005.33	1,293.58	1,507.52	1,873.77	Principal Rate	ae
I 142.31	194.26	242.61	299.17	382.57	502.26	633.05	759.28	863.06	844.84	912.83	1,036.69	1,140.96	1,426.04	1,756.23	Principal Rate	rf
Period Averages																
649.0	470.5	376.0	305.6	239.0	182.2	144.2	119.5	105.5	107.8	100.0	87.8	80.3	64.0	52.2	Principal Rate	ahx
215.4	151.3	125.4	116.4	115.9	105.6	95.2	94.9	98.1	110.0	100.0	93.3	91.4	75.5	63.0	Nominal Effective Exchange Rate	nec
135.9	101.2	90.0	87.3	83.7	73.5	75.6	82.4	87.3	98.4	100.0	107.0	119.0	113.5	102.7	Real Effective Exchange Rate	rec
End of Period															**Fund Position**	
394	394	394	394	394	394	394	561	561	561	561	561	561	561	774	Quota	2f.s
—	114	114	114	114	114	114	42	115	116	119	123	128	139	95	SDRs	1b.s
—	—	—	—	—	—	—	69	80	87	135	165	263	408	286	Reserve Position in the Fund	1c.s
—	—	—	—	—	—	—	—	—	—	—	—	—	—	—	Total Fund Cred.&Loans Outstg.	2tl
End of Period															**International Liquidity**	
1,595	2,696	3,086	3,248	3,616	4,628	6,533	7,746	7,930	8,103	8,452	9,938	9,907	8,754	8,103	Total Reserves minus Gold	1l.d
—	140	162	154	150	163	163	58	158	170	177	177	172	196	131	SDRs	1b.d
—	—	—	—	—	—	—	95	110	127	201	237	355	575	392	Reserve Position in the Fund	1c.d
1,595	2,556	2,924	3,094	3,466	4,465	6,370	7,593	7,663	7,806	8,074	9,524	9,379	7,983	7,580	Foreign Exchange	1d.d
1.842	2.009	.682	1.102	.614	.626	.863	.484	.302	.293	.267	.252	.358	.358	.328	Gold (Million Fine Troy Ounces)	1ad
597	698	290	468	249	248	323	172	119	112	119	94	104	103	95	Gold (National Valuation)	1and
10	1	—	—	246	356	388	402	398	445	440	250	439	442	438	Monetary Authorities: Other Assets	3..d
607	776	694	580	829	860	870	800	602	383	473	355	249	238	211	Other Liab.	4..d
272	312	321	492	....	269	420	425	544	506	443	484	1,031	944	552	Deposit Money Banks: Assets	7a.d
1,096	961	944	1,176	....	984	782	1,019	1,655	1,854	2,136	2,654	3,316	2,868	1,712	Liabilities	7b.d
....	....	....	....	....	1,201	1,338	1,785	2,271	3,182	3,476	4,241	3,834	3,352	2,837	Other Banking Insts.: Liabilities	7f.d
Billions of Pesos Beginning 1974: End of Period															**Monetary Authorities**	
360.5	987.9	1,182.9	1,212.8	I 1,786.3	2,738.3	4,377.1	6,047.5	6,709.4	7,073.1	8,760.5	10,402.8	13,295.7	13,841.5	15,954.0	Foreign Assets	11
310.9	410.6	466.5	526.2	I 513.0	543.7	759.7	777.3	679.6	711.1	565.0	725.0	574.3	951.6	2,397.2	Claims on Central Government	12a
.3	47.9	97.7	130.2	I 221.3	263.6	9.2	9.7	9.3	—	—	—	—	—	—	Claims on Nonfin.Pub.Enterprises	12c
43.2	21.3	41.9	65.6	I 10.3	4.8	3.7	4.5	6.2	52.2	81.6	105.8	128.3	538.7	577.4	Claims on Private Sector	12d
140.3	132.3	135.3	158.1	I 396.8	445.0	148.8	117.1	75.6	66.3	239.9	62.6	416.3	885.4	2,510.0	Claims on Deposit Money Banks	12e
94.9	126.1	130.3	171.3	I 297.8	246.9	285.4	290.1	322.6	339.0	436.9	264.9	286.0	392.6	435.5	Claims on Other Banking Insts	12f
....	....	....	....	....	—	—	—	—	—	—	133.1	408.8	579.5	681.6	Claims on Nonbank Financial Insts	12g
483.6	581.5	848.9	1,017.6	I 1,695.6	2,086.2	2,663.6	3,665.9	4,605.8	5,902.5	6,301.1	7,415.6	8,640.7	7,165.0	10,014.0	Reserve Money	14
186.7	....	418.8	530.7	....	I 837.0	1,054.9	1,438.6	1,804.4	2,373.3	2,994.3	3,536.0	4,453.0	4,997.3	6,507.4	*of which: Currency Outside DMBs*	14a
....	....	....	....	279.5	303.5	21.5	28.5	31.7	49.6	9.9	14.0	.8	120.4	101.3	Time, Savings,& Fgn.Currency Dep.	15
178.7	474.9	504.3	547.1	I 173.5	319.8	1,283.5	1,627.2	1,231.7	392.2	214.7	723.0	.5	15.8	—	Money Market Instruments	16aa
54.1	62.0	84.5	125.3	I 128.5	157.7	.4	.4	.4	.4	.4	.4	.3	.3	.3	Restricted Deposits	16b
43.2	11.7	11.7	14.5	I 54.6	51.7	50.4	7.7	22.1	83.8	131.2	43.8	3.9	1.4	2.6	Foreign Liabilities	16c
61.4	158.2	171.4	180.2	I 293.6	421.9	499.9	582.4	461.4	234.0	335.1	312.3	316.7	358.1	393.2	Long-Term Foreign Liabilities	16cl
78.7	270.5	247.4	79.3	I 282.5	375.6	530.3	589.4	414.3	475.6	128.4	247.3	349.0	251.4	235.4	Central Government Deposits	16d
61.8	74.9	144.7	223.0	I 255.4	383.5	408.2	498.2	1,104.3	1,388.1	3,110.2	3,231.1	6,120.0	9,644.1	12,087.7	Capital Accounts	17a
–11.6	92.3	41.5	77.1	I 62.3	142.4	126.1	246.5	–69.0	–284.5	–147.1	–293.3	–322.6	–367.4	–278.8	Other Items (Net)	17r
Billions of Pesos Beginning 1974: End of Period															**Deposit Money Banks**	
268.8	....	483.9	560.8	....	I 1,000.6	1,323.1	1,791.6	2,461.1	2,937.1	2,736.3	2,890.2	3,544.7	2,157.1	3,242.9	Reserves	20
44.7	....	83.7	166.7	....	I 148.0	265.6	313.6	437.3	419.9	437.0	485.9	1,326.9	1,427.0	1,033.9	Foreign Assets	21
52.5	....	79.5	101.0	....	I 138.2	98.3	158.1	337.8	430.9	463.7	617.1	1,441.0	2,454.1	2,167.1	Claims on Central Government	22a
....	....	....	....	....	146.5	240.7	233.0	347.3	1,009.7	1,407.0	1,715.4	3,214.1	3,498.4	3,577.6	Claims on Local Government	22b
16.8	....	38.3	40.3	....	I 69.8	59.2	50.0	8.1	68.7	100.0	89.1	136.4	301.4	295.5	Claims on Nonfin.Pub.Enterprises	22c
747.8	....	1,229.3	1,680.3	....	I 3,142.1	3,481.2	4,902.7	7,701.0	11,266.6	15,162.0	18,547.0	26,167.9	33,048.8	31,334.5	Claims on Private Sector	22d
34.5	....	61.4	68.5	....	I 157.0	351.6	581.2	560.7	1,081.2	1,581.3	2,714.1	2,970.9	3,125.2	6,597.7	Claims on Other Banking Insts	22f
341.2	....	577.4	723.0	....	I 1,140.8	1,502.7	2,164.1	2,883.8	3,626.1	4,271.9	5,272.8	6,251.6	5,673.3	6,533.1	Demand Deposits	24
417.8	....	739.6	817.7	....	I 1,476.8	1,898.3	2,777.6	4,217.7	6,447.3	8,005.4	10,036.5	16,709.5	23,452.4	25,587.6	Time, Savings,& Fgn.Currency Dep.	25
....	....	....	....	....	193.8	246.0	191.5	221.5	294.7	247.4	185.1	122.9	103.7	56.9	Money Market Instruments	26aa
2.1	....	26.1	28.8	....	I —	—	40.5	69.7	670.5	823.2	1,715.6	2,772.2	2,826.9	1,684.7	Bonds	26ab
....	....	....	....	....	147.1	34.6	8.2	5.8	18.5	21.8	25.6	32.6	37.9	29.8	Restricted Deposits	26b
188.7	....	249.0	394.9	....	I 463.4	444.9	745.3	1,283.3	1,448.5	2,003.0	2,557.8	3,889.9	4,048.0	3,009.3	Foreign Liabilities	26c
—	....	—	—	....	I 79.0	49.6	6.5	46.6	88.7	104.6	106.4	377.8	285.4	195.7	Long-Term Foreign Liabilities	26cl
3.8	....	6.8	8.7	....	I 230.4	374.4	589.8	816.7	1,015.3	1,319.0	1,666.7	2,333.0	2,457.4	2,243.1	Central Government Deposits	26d
148.2	....	173.3	273.2	....	I 416.4	207.5	138.5	119.6	122.9	119.4	104.0	73.3	934.0	2,471.6	Credit from Monetary Authorities	26g
....	....	....	....	....	377.5	740.0	1,026.1	1,484.5	1,878.4	2,474.4	2,708.5	3,011.4	4,250.2	3,586.7	Liabilities to Other Banking Insts	26i
21.9	....	75.4	155.3	....	I 508.9	696.1	1,076.4	1,719.5	2,676.0	3,558.6	4,808.3	6,159.0	5,179.0	6,120.2	Capital Accounts	27a
41.4	....	128.6	216.1	....	I –231.9	–374.4	–734.3	–1,015.4	–1,072.8	–1,061.4	–2,128.5	–2,931.3	–3,236.2	–3,269.5	Other Items (Net)	27r
Billions of Pesos Beginning 1974: End of Period															**Monetary Survey**	
173.3	....	1,006.0	970.1	....	I 2,371.2	4,147.3	5,608.1	5,841.3	5,960.7	7,063.2	8,287.1	10,728.8	11,219.1	13,975.9	Foreign Assets (Net)	31n
1,218.3	....	1,890.7	2,695.4	....	I 4,106.4	4,384.3	5,827.4	8,741.6	13,468.5	18,350.1	22,997.5	32,645.6	42,181.4	45,585.7	Domestic Credit	32
280.8	....	291.8	539.2	....	I 75.8	–46.7	–243.8	–213.6	–348.9	–418.7	–571.9	–666.7	696.9	2,085.8	Claims on Central Govt. (Net)	32an
....	....	....	....	....	146.5	240.7	233.0	347.3	1,009.7	1,407.0	1,715.4	3,214.1	3,498.4	3,577.6	Claims on Local Government	32b
17.1	....	136.0	170.5	....	I 333.4	68.4	59.7	17.4	68.7	100.0	89.1	136.4	301.4	295.5	Claims on Nonfin.Pub.Enterprises	32c
791.0	....	1,271.1	1,745.9	....	I 3,146.9	3,484.9	4,907.2	7,707.2	11,318.8	15,243.6	18,652.8	26,296.2	33,587.5	31,912.0	Claims on Private Sector	32d
129.4	....	191.7	239.8	....	I 403.9	637.0	871.3	883.3	1,420.2	2,018.2	2,979.0	3,256.9	3,517.8	7,033.2	Claims on Other Banking Insts	32f
....	....	....	....	....	—	—	—	—	—	—	133.1	408.8	579.5	681.6	Claims on Nonbank Financial Inst	32g
545.3	....	1,019.6	1,282.0	....	I 2,125.0	2,802.1	4,067.0	5,211.3	6,722.4	8,078.5	9,966.0	11,697.9	10,785.7	13,404.5	Money	34
436.8	....	795.7	916.4	....	I 1,780.3	1,919.8	2,806.1	4,249.4	6,496.9	8,015.3	10,050.5	16,710.3	23,572.8	25,688.9	Quasi-Money	35
180.8	....	530.4	575.9	....	I 513.6	1,529.5	1,818.7	1,453.2	686.9	462.1	908.1	123.4	119.5	56.9	Money Market Instruments	36aa
2.1	....	26.1	28.8	....	I —	—	40.5	69.7	670.5	823.2	1,715.6	2,772.2	2,826.9	1,684.7	Bonds	36ab
54.1	....	84.5	125.3	....	I 304.8	35.0	8.6	6.2	18.9	22.2	26.0	32.9	38.2	30.2	Restricted Deposits	36b
61.4	....	171.4	180.2	....	I 500.9	549.5	588.9	508.0	322.7	439.7	418.7	694.5	643.5	588.9	Long-Term Foreign Liabilities	36cl
....	....	....	....	....	377.5	740.0	1,026.1	1,484.5	1,878.4	2,474.4	2,708.5	3,011.4	4,250.2	3,586.7	Liabilities to Other Banking Insts	36i
83.8	....	220.1	378.3	....	I 892.4	1,104.3	1,574.6	2,823.8	4,064.1	6,668.8	8,039.4	12,279.0	14,823.1	18,207.9	Capital Accounts	37a
27.3	....	48.7	178.7	....	I –16.8	–148.5	–495.0	–1,223.2	–1,431.6	–1,570.8	–2,548.2	–3,947.3	–3,659.5	–3,686.9	Other Items (Net)	37r
982.1	....	1,815.3	2,198.4	....	I 3,905.3	4,721.9	6,873.1	9,460.7	13,219.3	16,093.8	20,016.5	28,408.2	34,358.5	39,093.3	Money plus Quasi-Money	35l

Colombia

		1970	1971	1972	1973	1974	1975	1976	1977	1978	1979	1980	1981	1982	1983	1984
Other Banking Institutions														*Millions of Pesos through 1973;*		
Reserves	40	...	...	...	...	‡13.1	4.5	6.0	8.8	11.6	13.9	19.3	28.1	33.3	29.1	43.0
Foreign Assets	41	...	...	...	...	‡.3	.4	.5	.7	.6	.4	1.0	.8	2.4	3.3	4.3
Claims on Central Government	42a	...	...	...	...	‡.5	1.2	2.9	2.1	3.6	4.1	7.0	9.0	11.3	28.1	34.2
Claims on Local Government	42b	...	...	...	...	...	...	...	...	...	...					
Claims on Nonfin.Pub.Enterprises	42c	...	...	...	...	‡.3	.4	.5	.5	.5	.5	1.1	1.4	1.9	2.5	3.3
Claims on Private Sector	42d	...	...	...	...	‡48.1	61.8	75.7	103.6	140.5	178.9	255.0	344.8	469.0	628.5	841.3
Claims on Deposit Money Banks	42e	...	...	...	...	‡2.8	3.5	5.2	6.8	8.9	12.4	15.4	21.1	25.2	30.3	37.5
Demand Deposits	44	733.0	798.0	1,030.0	1,450.0	‡1.8	2.4	3.1	4.2	4.7	6.8	8.7	10.6	14.6	20.2	24.4
Time, Savings,& Fgn.Currency Dep.	45	...	...	...	...	‡13.3	21.0	32.9	45.7	66.9	87.7	137.2	198.2	267.0	360.0	445.5
Money Market Instruments	46aa	...	...	...	...	...	...	...	...	...	...					
Bonds	46ab	...	...	...	...	‡11.5	12.0	12.8	8.4	16.6	25.0	32.6	44.9	49.9	58.5	74.0
Restricted Deposits	46b	...	...	...	...	...	...	...	...	...	...					
Foreign Liabilities	46c	...	...	...	...	‡1.6	1.8	1.7	2.6	4.3	5.9	11.1	14.3	19.3	22.7	18.2
Long-Term Foreign Liabilities	46cl	...	...	...	...	‡1.3	3.2	3.3	4.0	5.0	7.0	11.0	13.3	18.6	24.3	51.0
Central Government Deposits	46d	...	...	...	...	‡.3	.4	.4	.3	.5	.5	.1	—	—	—	—
Credit from Monetary Authorities	46g	...	...	...	...	‡11.8	13.6	13.6	21.1	28.5	25.2	23.9	31.5	40.8	63.3	102.4
Credit from Deposit Money Banks	46h	...	...	...	...	‡5.7	6.5	7.8	9.6	12.6	10.1	11.3	13.4	23.9	29.1	33.4
Capital Accounts	47a	...	...	...	...	‡6.2	6.7	11.0	14.4	19.9	26.1	36.6	47.4	72.4	88.8	112.0
Other Items (Net)	47r	...	...	...	...	‡11.9	4.2	4.2	12.2	6.6	16.1	26.0	31.7	36.7	55.0	102.7
Banking Survey														*Millions of Pesos through 1973;*		
Foreign Assets (Net)	51n	...	...	...	...	‡−5.6	−.2	19.0	52.3	78.7	138.5	202.1	237.2	224.3	142.0	37.3
Domestic Credit	52	...	...	...	...	‡104.6	134.1	164.7	217.7	276.4	324.3	487.1	666.3	924.1	1,285.4	1,762.3
Claims on Central Govt. (Net)	52an	...	...	...	...	‡9.0	11.6	10.9	21.1	21.2	−.7	3.7	11.3	66.3	130.6	306.1
Claims on Local Government	52b	...	...	...	...	...	...	...	...	...	...					
Claims on Nonfin.Pub.Enterprises	52c	17,582.0	21,516.0	25,095.0	334.0	‡.6	.7	.7	.7	2.3	1.7	2.3	4.2	4.3	15.6	16.8
Claims on Private Sector	52d	...	...	...	...	‡95.5	120.7	152.2	195.9	252.9	323.3	481.1	650.9	853.4	1,121.9	1,439.4
Claims on Nonbank Financial Inst.	52g	...	...	...	...	...	...	...	...	...	...					
Liquid Liabilities	55l	...	...	...	...	‡52.8	68.8	103.1	181.8	240.0	301.5	447.2	615.3	773.9	1,010.3	1,243.7
Money Market Instruments	56aa	...	...	...	...	‡12.5	13.6	17.9	24.7	43.9	64.9	94.6	114.9	156.6	128.1	143.0
Bonds	56ab	...	...	...	...	...	...	...	...	16.6	25.0	32.6	44.9	49.9	58.5	74.0
Restricted Deposits	56b	2,400.0	2,140.0	2,500.0	3,661.0	‡3.8	2.0	.1	5.1	5.9	10.1	12.8	12.0	10.0	25.6	35.9
Long-Term Foreign Liabilities	56cl	...	...	...	...	‡4.6	7.7	8.5	10.7	14.3	18.3	26.5	32.3	42.1	47.9	82.0
Capital Accounts	57a	...	...	...	...	‡14.2	16.0	15.4	29.0	46.3	60.1	84.3	109.8	150.5	176.3	236.5
Other Items (Net)	57r	...	...	...	...	‡11.0	25.7	38.7	18.7	−12.1	−17.2	−8.7	−25.7	−34.5	−19.2	−15.6
Money (National Definitions)														*Millions of Pesos through 1973;*		
Reserve Money	19ma	13,112.0	14,098.0	17,636.0	23,504.0	‡28.4	37.0	51.8	72.4	101.3	132.0	179.4	219.6	258.5	289.1	335.3
M1	39ma	21,627.0	23,993.0	29,842.0	38,572.0	‡46.1	58.9	79.4	103.5	134.9	167.6	216.5	259.2	321.5	405.1	499.7
M2	59ma	25,052.0	28,141.0	35,864.0	51,205.0	‡66.7	90.1	125.3	164.7	235.5	293.6	446.0	631.9	771.6	1,011.8	1,252.3
M3	59mb	...	...	...	...	...	...	...	...	...	...	459.5	661.8	802.3	1,039.0	1,292.9
M3 +Bonds	59mc	...	...	...	...	...	...	...	...	...	...	459.5	674.5	818.2	1,059.0	1,311.0
Interest Rates														*Percent Per Annum*		
Discount Rate (End of Period)	60	14.0	14.0	14.0	14.0	16.0	16.0	20.0	20.0	22.0	30.0	30.0	30.0	27.0	27.0	27.0
Money Market Rate	60b	...	...	...	...	...	...	...	...	...	...					
Deposit Rate	60l	...	...	...	...	...	...	...	...	...	...					
Lending Rate	60p	...	...	...	...	...	...	...	...	...	...					
Prices, Production, Labor														*Index Numbers (1995=100):*		
Share Prices	62	1.0	.9	.7	.8	.8	.7	.8	1.2	1.8	2.3	2.0	2.3	3.4	2.6	2.1
Producer Prices	63	‡.6	.6	.7	.9	1.3	1.6	2.0	2.5	2.9	3.7	4.6	5.8	7.2	8.8	10.4
Consumer Prices	64	.6	‡.6	.7	.9	1.1	1.3	1.6	2.1	2.5	3.1	3.9	5.0	6.2	7.5	8.7
Manufacturing Production	66ey	...	...	...	...	...	...	...	...	...	...	64.2	63.0	60.4	60.1	66.1
Vol.of Gold Produced(1990=100)	66kr	21.3	20.0	19.8	22.7	27.9	32.5	32.0	27.1	25.7	28.8	52.4	54.4	48.4	45.4	77.0
Crude Petroleum Production	66aa	37.6	36.9	33.6	31.5	28.8	26.9	25.1	23.6	22.4	21.3	21.6	22.9	24.3	25.5	28.6
														Number in Thousands:		
Labor Force	67d	...	...	...	...	...	...	...	...	...	...					
Employment	67e	...	...	...	...	...	...	...	...	...	...					
Unemployment	67c	...	...	...	...	...	...	...	...	...	...					
Unemployment Rate (%)	67r	...	...	...	...	...	...	...	...	...	...					
International Transactions														*Millions of US Dollars*		
Exports	70..d	726.7	686.0	807.5	1,168.6	1,508.6	1,465.0	1,873.8	2,403.4	3,009.8	3,410.6	3,924.3	2,916.3	3,023.6	3,000.6	3,461.6
Coffee	70e.d	466.9	399.7	430.4	597.9	624.8	674.5	977.4	1,525.7	1,993.9	2,024.3	2,375.2	1,458.8	1,577.4	1,536.6	1,798.8
Imports, c.i.f.	71..d	843.0	929.4	858.9	1,061.5	1,597.2	1,494.8	1,661.9	1,880.0	2,971.0	3,364.1	4,738.6	5,200.8	5,479.8	4,963.4	4,497.5
Imports, f.o.b.	71.vd	746.0	813.8	756.7	918.3	1,431.2	1,345.5	1,544.4	1,825.7	2,555.2	2,912.8	4,200.5	4,685.4	4,936.8	4,471.6	4,052.1
Volume of Exports															*1995=100*	
Coffee	72e	67	67	67	69	71	84	64	54	92	114	114	93	91	94	104
Export Prices in Pesos	76	1	1	1	1	2	2	4	6	5	5	7	7	8	10	14
Import Prices in Pesos	76.x	1	1	1	1	2	2	3	3	4	4	5	6	8	9	12
Export Prices															*1995=100:*	
Coffee	76e.d	34.9	30.2	34.3	44.8	48.0	50.3	96.5	148.8	114.1	113.0	110.2	78.9	86.1	81.1	88.9

1985	1986	1987	1988	1989	1990	1991	1992	1993	1994	1995	1996	1997	1998	1999	Other Banking Institutions	
....	....	....	....	....	I237.2	240.7	513.4	548.5	702.0	988.1	1,282.4	1,103.8	334.8	641.8	Reserves	40
....	....	....	....	....	I8.7	68.3	53.7	120.0	140.2	132.0	258.5	256.7	244.9	394.2	Foreign Assets	41
....	....	....	....	....	I114.4	105.0	172.7	202.0	273.7	131.1	155.7	265.2	1,306.3	3,607.2	Claims on Central Government	42a
....	....	....	....	....	1.6	11.2	13.1	30.8	783.2	1,294.4	1,472.6	1,256.2	870.9	649.1	Claims on Local Government	42b
4.9	....	....	....	....	I452.6	945.1	1,191.3	1,329.9	676.7	765.9	974.7	1,329.3	2,244.4	1,759.3	Claims on Nonfin.Pub.Enterprises	42c
....	....	....	....	....	I3,079.5	3,803.4	5,122.1	7,623.3	10,207.6	13,978.3	17,955.1	19,457.4	18,014.6	18,975.6	Claims on Private Sector	42d
....	....	89.4	124.0	....	I80.7	799.4	1,234.2	1,560.4	2,271.5	2,993.6	3,275.9	3,466.2	4,692.0	4,633.3	Claims on Deposit Money Banks	42e
33.1	41.5	53.2	64.8	....	I4.7	4.3	6.8	—	—	—	—	—	—	—	Demand Deposits	44
....	....	....	....	....	I2,357.8	3,266.9	4,360.4	6,064.6	9,501.0	12,870.1	15,339.3	15,222.5	13,657.5	15,000.6	Time, Savings,& Fgn.Currency Dep.	45
....	....	....	....	....	9.9	20.3	16.3	15.2	89.4	35.0	15.1	13.1	16.9	1.5	Money Market Instruments	46aa
....	....	135.0	78.0	....	I272.6	652.1	625.3	869.0	578.8	1,052.1	3,379.5	3,577.5	2,976.2	2,534.3	Bonds	46ab
....	....	....	....	....	17.5	3.8	28.4	7.6	7.1	6.4	5.9	.7	.7	3.1	Restricted Deposits	46b
....	....	....	....	....	I175.2	125.9	387.6	741.6	1,380.0	1,456.9	1,709.9	1,951.6	1,942.3	1,710.0	Foreign Liabilities	46c
....	....	—	....	....	I486.5	720.1	929.4	1,083.3	1,258.9	1,973.4	2,548.4	2,983.2	3,122.8	3,600.9	Long-Term Foreign Liabilities	46cl
....	....	....	....	....	I96.1	215.0	215.5	261.5	322.8	390.7	357.4	266.1	420.8	598.8	Central Government Deposits	46d
....	....	....	....	....	I140.6	203.7	215.5	250.2	280.5	232.4	209.5	96.6	362.7	533.7	Credit from Monetary Authorities	46g
....	....	....	....	....	I39.6	340.4	437.4	628.0	1,112.2	1,632.2	1,617.5	2,176.8	2,505.6	5,695.9	Credit from Deposit Money Banks	46h
....	....	....	....	....	I489.6	1,073.6	1,544.8	1,985.7	2,874.4	4,034.8	5,214.9	6,004.5	7,076.0	7,952.5	Capital Accounts	47a
....	....	....	....	....	I-115.4	-653.0	-466.9	-491.8	-2,350.2	-3,400.7	-5,022.6	-5,157.8	-4,373.4	-6,970.7	Other Items (Net)	47r

Billions of Pesos Beginning 1974: End of Period

1985	1986	1987	1988	1989	1990	1991	1992	1993	1994	1995	1996	1997	1998	1999	Banking Survey	
....	....	....	....	....	I2,204.7	4,089.8	5,274.2	5,219.7	4,720.9	5,738.3	6,835.8	9,033.8	9,521.6	12,660.1	Foreign Assets (Net)	51n
....	....	....	....	....	I7,254.6	8,397.0	11,239.8	16,782.8	23,666.7	32,110.9	40,219.2	51,430.7	60,679.1	62,944.9	Domestic Credit	52
....	....	....	....	....	I94.1	-156.7	-286.6	-273.1	-398.0	-678.3	-773.6	-667.6	1,582.4	5,094.2	Claims on Central Govt. (Net)	52an
....	....	....	....	....	148.1	251.9	246.1	378.1	1,792.9	2,701.4	3,188.0	4,470.3	4,369.3	4,226.8	Claims on Local Government	52b
22.0	....	....	....	....	I786.0	1,013.5	1,251.0	1,347.3	745.4	865.9	1,063.8	1,465.7	2,545.8	2,054.8	Claims on Nonfin.Pub.Enterprises	52c
....	....	....	....	....	I6,226.4	7,288.3	10,029.3	15,330.5	21,526.4	29,221.9	36,608.0	45,753.6	51,602.1	50,887.6	Claims on Private Sector	52d
....	....	....	....	....	....	....	....	....	....	....	133.1	408.8	579.5	681.6	Claims on Nonbank Financial Inst	52g
....	....	....	....	....	I6,030.6	7,752.4	10,726.9	14,976.8	22,018.3	27,975.8	34,073.4	42,527.0	47,681.3	53,452.1	Liquid Liabilities	55l
....	....	....	....	....	I523.5	1,549.8	1,835.0	1,468.4	776.3	497.1	923.2	136.5	136.4	58.4	Money Market Instruments	56aa
....	....	161.1	106.7	....	I272.6	652.1	665.8	938.7	1,249.3	1,875.3	5,095.1	6,349.7	5,803.1	4,219.0	Bonds	56ab
54.1	62.0	84.5	125.3	....	I322.3	38.8	37.0	13.8	26.0	28.6	31.9	33.6	38.9	33.2	Restricted Deposits	56b
....	....	....	....	....	I987.4	1,269.6	1,518.3	1,591.3	1,581.6	2,413.1	2,967.2	3,677.6	3,766.3	4,189.8	Long-Term Foreign Liabilities	56cl
....	....	....	....	....	I1,382.0	2,177.9	3,119.4	4,809.5	6,938.5	10,703.6	13,254.3	18,283.5	21,899.1	26,160.4	Capital Accounts	57a
....	....	....	....	....	I-59.0	-953.8	-1,388.4	-1,796.0	-4,202.4	-5,644.3	-9,290.1	-10,543.4	-9,124.3	-12,507.8	Other Items (Net)	57r

Billions of Pesos Beginning 1974: End of Period

1985	1986	1987	1988	1989	1990	1991	1992	1993	1994	1995	1996	1997	1998	1999	Money (National Definitions)	
429.3	549.8	715.8	914.9	1,171.7	1,493.5	2,290.0	3,312.5	4,419.0	5,634.4	6,267.1	6,627.6	8,287.1	6,923.1	9,739.6	*Reserve Money*	19ma
640.4	784.5	1,044.6	1,314.5	1,694.7	2,122.5	2,795.4	3,941.8	5,124.6	6,419.0	7,717.8	8,992.8	10,948.0	10,526.5	12,856.8	*M1*	39ma
1,680.9	2,172.0	2,795.3	3,455.9	4,582.6	6,034.2	8,061.7	11,119.6	15,817.3	22,569.1	28,961.3	34,815.5	43,794.6	48,558.1	53,726.5	*M2*	59ma
1,732.1	2,235.7	2,909.9	3,625.6	4,866.3	6,383.9	8,489.5	11,767.6	16,791.8	23,884.0	30,478.9	36,751.8	46,961.0	52,081.8	56,992.4	*M3*	59mb
1,750.0	2,249.8	2,923.3	3,641.4	4,892.5	6,411.1	8,579.1	11,956.3	17,222.7	24,623.9	31,900.8	41,299.2	52,334.7	56,456.7	60,001.7	*M3 +Bonds*	59mc

Percent Per Annum

1985	1986	1987	1988	1989	1990	1991	1992	1993	1994	1995	1996	1997	1998	1999	Interest Rates	
27.0	I33.8	34.8	34.3	36.9	I46.5	45.0	34.4	33.5	44.9	40.4	35.1	31.3	42.3	23.1	Discount Rate *(End of Period)*	60
....	....	....	....	....	....	....	....	....	....	22.4	28.4	23.8	35.0	18.8	Money Market Rate	60b
....	31.4	30.8	33.5	33.7	36.4	37.2	26.7	25.8	29.4	32.3	31.2	24.1	32.6	21.3	Deposit Rate	60l
....	40.8	41.1	42.7	43.0	45.2	47.1	37.3	35.8	40.5	42.7	42.0	34.2	42.2	30.4	Lending Rate	60p

Period Averages

1985	1986	1987	1988	1989	1990	1991	1992	1993	1994	1995	1996	1997	1998	1999	Prices, Production, Labor	
1.9	2.9	5.5	7.5	8.2	10.1	I19.2	58.7	65.9	120.1	100.0	104.7	155.9	135.6	121.0	Share Prices	62
13.0	I15.9	19.8	25.4	32.6	41.3	I52.7	63.3	72.3	84.7	100.0	I115.0	132.8	155.8	171.1	Producer Prices	63
10.8	12.8	15.8	I20.2	25.5	32.9	42.9	54.4	66.8	82.7	100.0	I120.2	142.9	172.0	191.3	Consumer Prices	64
67.9	72.6	77.8	80.7	82.0	I86.3	86.0	92.0	94.7	97.9	100.0	97.3	99.7	98.2	....	Manufacturing Production	66ey
120.4	134.8	89.9	98.3	100.0	100.0	117.6	108.8	92.8	71.1	....	....	....	....	....	Vol.of Gold Produced(1990=100)	66kr
30.2	52.0	66.0	64.4	69.3	75.3	72.9	75.3	77.6	77.7	100.0	107.6	109.1	129.6	141.4	Crude Petroleum Production	66aa

Period Averages

1985	1986	1987	1988	1989	1990	1991	1992	1993	1994	1995	1996	1997	1998	1999		
....	....	....	....	....	....	5,286	....	5,261	....	6,153	6,452	6,653	....		Labor Force	67d
3,100	3,248	3,443	3,572	3,668	4,325	I4,843	5,053	5,333	5,408	5,494	5,451	5,702	5,655	....	Employment	67e
500	483	429	403	357	492	I528	509	450	444	525	740	786	998	....	Unemployment	67c
....	....	....	....	8.9	10.2	I9.8	9.2	7.8	7.6	8.7	11.9	12.1	15.0	....	Unemployment Rate (%)	67r

Millions of US Dollars

1985	1986	1987	1988	1989	1990	1991	1992	1993	1994	1995	1996	1997	1998	1999	International Transactions	
3,551.6	5,101.6	4,642.2	5,037.0	5,716.5	6,765.8	7,232.1	6,916.5	7,115.9	8,418.5	10,056.2	10,587.0	11,522.4	10,852.1	11,576.4	Exports	70..d
1,784.0	3,046.0	1,688.5	1,646.1	1,583.5	1,414.7	1,336.4	1,258.9	1,139.7	1,990.1	1,831.8	1,576.5	2,259.0	1,891.0	1,324.0	Coffee	70e.d
4,140.9	3,861.5	4,321.9	5,001.8	5,004.1	5,589.5	4,906.1	6,516.4	9,831.5	11,882.9	13,852.9	13,683.6	15,377.7	14,634.5	10,658.6	Imports, c.i.f.	71..d
3,731.5	3,564.0	3,907.2	4,531.6	4,573.3	5,144.8	4,512.9	5,980.2	9,085.7	11,039.3	12,921.2	12,793.7	14,408.9	13,726.2	9,990.1	Imports, f.o.b.	71.vd

1995=100 — Volume of Exports

1985	1986	1987	1988	1989	1990	1991	1992	1993	1994	1995	1996	1997	1998	1999		
102	116	115	100	111	143	129	169	139	120	100	108	112	115	102	Coffee	72e
18	I28	27	34	36	49	57	58	65	85	100	I106	129	143	164	Export Prices in Pesos	76
16	I21	26	33	44	55	66	71	80	87	100	I115	123	142	163	Import Prices in Pesos	76.x

Indices of Prices in US Dollars — Export Prices

1985	1986	1987	1988	1989	1990	1991	1992	1993	1994	1995	1996	1997	1998	1999		
89.7	119.8	69.2	83.2	65.9	54.9	52.3	39.2	44.4	81.3	100.0	81.0	123.9	90.1	....	Coffee	76e.d

Colombia

		1970	1971	1972	1973	1974	1975	1976	1977	1978	1979	1980	1981	1982	1983	1984
Balance of Payments																*Millions of US Dollars:*
Current Account, n.i.e.	78al d	-293	-454	-191	-55	-352	-172	163	375	258	438	-206	-1,961	-3,054	-3,003	-1,401
Goods: Exports f.o.b.	78aa d	788	754	979	1,263	1,495	1,683	2,202	2,660	3,155	3,441	3,986	3,158	3,114	2,970	4,273
Goods: Imports f.o.b.	78ab d	-802	-903	-850	-983	-1,511	-1,415	-1,654	-1,970	-2,552	-2,978	-4,283	-4,730	-5,358	-4,464	-4,027
Trade Balance	78ac d	-14	-148	129	280	-17	268	548	690	603	463	-297	-1,572	-2,244	-1,494	246
Services: Credit	78ad d	192	218	226	281	366	431	568	730	780	1,105	1,342	1,148	1,335	844	927
Services: Debit	78ae d	-334	-382	-383	-440	-566	-597	-647	-773	-857	-941	-1,170	-1,295	-1,346	-1,302	-1,298
Balance on Goods & Services	78af d	-156	-313	-28	121	-217	102	468	647	526	627	-126	-1,719	-2,255	-1,952	-125
Income: Credit	78ag d	39	25	24	44	88	66	80	112	164	305	532	708	525	289	128
Income: Debit	78ah d	-212	-200	-222	-255	-273	-388	-437	-430	-505	-596	-777	-1,192	-1,494	-1,504	-1,703
Balance on Gds, Serv. & Inc.	78ai d	-329	-488	-226	-89	-403	-220	112	329	185	336	-371	-2,203	-3,223	-3,167	-1,700
Current Transfers, n.i.e.: Credit	78aj d	50	46	46	45	61	80	83	84	109	114	178	257	187	186	316
Current Transfers: Debit	78ak d	-14	-12	-11	-11	-10	-32	-32	-38	-36	-12	-13	-15	-17	-22	-17
Capital Account, n.i.e.	78bc d	—	—	—	—	—	—	—	—	—	—	—	—	—	—	—
Capital Account, n.i.e.: Credit	78ba d	—	—	—	—	—	—	—	—	—	—	—	—	—	—	—
Capital Account: Debit	78bb d	—	—	—	—	—	—	—	—	—	—	—	—	—	—	—
Financial Account, n.i.e.	78bj d	329	346	251	151	278	112	203	-24	102	977	945	2,039	2,232	1,434	944
Direct Investment Abroad	78bd d	-4	-3	-1	-1	-6	-4	-11	-22	-41	-24	-106	-37	-29	-104	-23
Dir. Invest. in Rep. Econ., n.i.e.	78be d	43	43	18	24	41	37	25	65	107	127	157	265	366	618	584
Portfolio Investment Assets	78bf d	—	—	—	—	—	—	—	—	—	—	—	—	—	—	—
Equity Securities	78bk d	—	—	—	—	—	—	—	—	—	—	—	—	—	—	—
Debt Securities	78bl d	—	—	—	—	—	—	—	—	—	—	—	—	—	—	—
Portfolio Investment Liab., n.i.e.	78bg d	-2	-6	-1	42	-4	-2	-2	-3	-2	-11	-3	-2	-7	-2	-3
Equity Securities	78bm d	—	—	—	—	—	—	—	—	—	—	—	—	—	—	—
Debt Securities	78bn d	-2	-6	-1	42	-4	-2	-2	-3	-2	-11	-3	-2	-7	-2	-3
Financial Derivatives Assets	78bw d	....	....	....	....	....	....	....	....	....	....	....	....	....	....	....
Financial Derivatives Liabilities	78bx d	....	....	....	....	....	....	....	....	....	....	....	....	....	....	....
Other Investment Assets	78bh d	-32	-19	-52	-57	-238	-7	—	-9	-244	80	-303	-33	-42	-360	-562
Monetary Authorities	78bo d	—	-10	-1	10	10	-19	-3	7	-34	-19	-58	-11	63	-11	23
General Government	78bp d	—	-7	-25	-23	-7	-1	-4	-8	-33	-18	-40	31	-4	—	—
Banks	78bq d	-1	-1	-12	-18	-30	-24	-2	-1	19	-34	-11	11	23	-194	-133
Other Sectors	78br d	-31	-1	-14	-26	-210	37	9	-7	-196	151	-194	-64	-124	-155	-452
Other Investment Liab., n.i.e.	78bi d	324	331	286	144	485	88	192	-55	282	805	1,199	1,846	1,944	1,282	948
Monetary Authorities	78bs d	-12	16	52	30	24	9	39	24	95	50	52	69	-3	97	-14
General Government	78bt d	126	100	158	176	85	160	-8	-6	20	371	460	590	310	105	368
Banks	78bu d	58	94	-2	-62	291	-12	77	-190	17	448	211	72	96	258	-55
Other Sectors	78bv d	152	120	78	—	84	-68	83	117	150	-64	477	1,115	1,541	822	649
Net Errors and Omissions	78ca d	-18	90	106	70	-14	118	255	298	236	98	168	-99	-52	-270	76
Overall Balance	78cb d	18	-18	165	166	-88	59	621	649	596	1,513	908	-21	-874	-1,839	-381
Reserves and Related Items	79da d	-18	18	-165	-166	88	-59	-621	-649	-596	-1,513	-908	21	874	1,839	381
Reserve Assets	79db d	33	20	-107	-166	88	-59	-621	-649	-596	-1,513	-908	21	874	1,839	381
Use of Fund Credit and Loans	79dc d	-51	-2	-58	—	—	—	—	—	—	—	—	—	—	—	—
Exceptional Financing	79de d	....	....	....	....	....	....	....	....	....	....	....	....	....	....	....
International Investment Position																*Millions of US Dollars*
Assets	79aa d	....	....	....	....	....	....	....	....	....	....	5,948	6,138	5,373	3,925	2,854
Direct Investment Abroad	79ab d	....	....	....	....	....	....	....	....	....	....	136	140	170	274	295
Portfolio Investment	79ac d	....	....	....	....	....	....	....	....	....	....	—	—	—	—	—
Equity Securities	79ad d	....	....	....	....	....	....	....	....	....	....	—	—	—	—	—
Debt Securities	79ae d	....	....	....	....	....	....	....	....	....	....	—	—	—	—	—
Financial Derivatives	79al d	....	....	....	....	....	....	....	....	....	....	—	—	—	—	—
Other Investment	79af d	....	....	....	....	....	....	....	....	....	....	449	418	345	546	653
Monetary Authorities	79ag d	....	....	....	....	....	....	....	....	....	....	—	—	—	—	—
General Government	79ah d	....	....	....	....	....	....	....	....	....	....	359	339	280	291	269
Banks	79ai d	....	....	....	....	....	....	....	....	....	....	90	79	56	250	383
Other Sectors	79aj d	....	....	....	....	....	....	....	....	....	....	—	—	9	5	1
Reserve Assets	79ak d	....	....	....	....	....	....	....	....	....	....	5,363	5,581	4,858	3,105	1,906
Liabilities	79la d	....	....	....	....	....	....	....	....	....	....	8,117	9,865	12,218	13,567	14,786
Dir. Invest. in Rep. Economy	79lb d	....	....	....	....	....	....	....	....	....	....	1,464	1,607	1,720	1,837	2,163
Portfolio Investment	79lc d	....	....	....	....	....	....	....	....	....	....	31	29	23	20	17
Equity Securities	79ld d	....	....	....	....	....	....	....	....	....	....	—	—	—	—	—
Debt Securities	79le d	....	....	....	....	....	....	....	....	....	....	31	29	23	20	17
Financial Derivatives	79ll d	....	....	....	....	....	....	....	....	....	....	—	—	—	—	—
Other investment	79lf d	....	....	....	....	....	....	....	....	....	....	6,622	8,229	10,475	11,710	12,606
Monetary Authorities	79lg d	....	....	....	....	....	....	....	....	....	....	501	570	565	662	650
General Government	79lh d	....	....	....	....	....	....	....	....	....	....	....	2,713	2,998	3,074	3,412
Banks	79li d	....	....	....	....	....	....	....	....	....	....	1,159	1,231	1,327	1,585	1,530
Other Sectors	79lj d	....	....	....	....	....	....	....	....	....	....	2,824	3,715	5,585	6,389	7,014

Minus Sign Indicates Debit

Balance of Payments

1985	1986	1987	1988	1989	1990	1991	1992	1993	1994	1995	1996	1997	1998	1999		
-1,809	383	336	-216	-201	542	2,349	901	-2,102	-3,596	-4,624	-4,828	-5,950	-5,272	-979	Current Account, n.i.e.	78al d
3,650	5,331	5,661	5,343	6,031	7,079	7,507	7,263	7,429	9,058	10,528	10,952	12,059	11,493	12,045	Goods: Exports f.o.b.	78aa d
-3,673	-3,409	-3,793	-4,516	-4,557	-5,108	-4,548	-6,029	-9,086	-11,298	-13,167	-13,092	-14,774	-14,007	-10,311	Goods: Imports f.o.b.	78ab d
-23	1,922	1,868	827	1,474	1,971	2,959	1,234	-1,657	-2,240	-2,639	-2,140	-2,715	-2,514	1,734	*Trade Balance*	78ac d
855	1,108	1,166	1,408	1,291	1,600	1,593	1,983	2,520	1,647	1,763	2,187	2,134	2,062	1,904	Services: Credit	78ad d
-1,427	-1,684	-1,709	-1,670	-1,565	-1,750	-1,812	-2,028	-2,321	-2,631	-2,889	-3,378	-3,631	-3,535	-3,283	Services: Debit	78ae d
-595	1,346	1,325	565	1,200	1,821	2,740	1,189	-1,458	-3,224	-3,765	-3,331	-4,212	-3,987	355	*Balance on Goods & Services*	78af d
111	175	202	257	287	347	390	449	561	702	667	707	891	912	796	Income: Credit	78ag d
-1,786	-1,923	-2,192	-2,002	-2,586	-2,652	-2,480	-2,471	-2,344	-2,164	-2,283	-2,795	-3,240	-2,644	-2,919	Income: Debit	78ah d
-2,270	-402	-665	-1,180	-1,099	-484	651	-833	-3,240	-4,686	-5,381	-5,419	-6,561	-5,719	-1,768	*Balance on Gds, Serv. & Inc.*	78ai d
479	801	1,022	994	928	1,043	1,743	1,871	1,350	1,284	988	811	830	611	970	Current Transfers, n.i.e.: Credit	78aj d
-18	-16	-21	-30	-30	-17	-45	-137	-212	-194	-231	-220	-219	-164	-181	Current Transfers: Debit	78ak d
—	—	—	—	—	—	—	—	—	....	....	....	....	....	....	Capital Account, n.i.e.	78bc d
—	—	—	—	—	—	—	—	—	....	....	....	....	....	....	Capital Account, n.i.e.: Credit	78ba d
									....	....	....	....	....	....	Capital Account: Debit	78bb d
2,236	1,160	-1	939	478	-2	-777	183	2,701	3,421	4,687	6,707	7,095	4,542	378	Financial Account, n.i.e.	78bj d
-7	-32	-26	-44	-29	-16	-24	-50	-240	-149	-256	-328	-810	-529	6	Direct Investment Abroad	78bd d
1,023	674	319	203	576	500	457	729	959	1,445	969	3,112	5,639	2,961	1,008	Dir. Invest. in Rep. Econ., n.i.e.	78be d
—	—	—	—	—	—	....	....	....	-1,380	393	-586	-616	660	-1,378	Portfolio Investment Assets	78bf d
—	—	—	—	—	—	—	—	—	-1,149	864					Equity Securities	78bk d
—	—	—	—	—	—	....	....	....	-231	-471	-586	-616	660	-1,378	Debt Securities	78bl d
-1	30	48	—	179	-4	86	126	498	1,467	1,041	2,195	1,673	978	663	Portfolio Investment Liab., n.i.e.	78bg d
—	—	—	—	—	—	....	....	....	478	165	292	278	47	-27	Equity Securities	78bm d
-1	30	48	—	179	-4	86	126	498	989	876	1,903	1,395	931	690	Debt Securities	78bn d
....	....	....	....	....	....	....	....	....	—	—	....	....	....	....	Financial Derivatives Assets	78bw d
....	....	....	....	....	....	....	....	....	—	—	....	290	-39	100	Financial Derivatives Liabilities	78bx d
-111	-217	-295	-315	-95	-102	-522	-637	160	162	322	-754	-1,094	-293	-74	Other Investment Assets	78bh d
4	42	-3	-1	24	....	....	....	-40	....	....	—	1	7	5	Monetary Authorities	78bo d
-6	—	—	—	—	-82	-100	-346	267	—	—	—	-23	-15		General Government	78bp d
256	-65	-45	-117	41	17	-272	-110	-74	-69	59	-80	-256	-175	165	Banks	78bq d
-365	-194	-247	-197	-160	-37	-150	-182	7	231	263	-674	-816	-110	-244	Other Sectors	78br d
1,332	705	-47	1,095	-153	-380	-774	15	1,325	1,876	2,218	3,068	2,013	804	53	Other Investment Liab., n.i.e.	78bi d
30	108	23	-4	89	-27	—	-131	-99	-190	53	15	-12	-17	-14	Monetary Authorities	78bs d
283	377	-225	371	69	95	-14	-78	-329	-383	-80	-264	-53	347	909	General Government	78bt d
-253	-1,247	-190	318	39	10	-362	785	710	730	592	-3	483	-860	-1,177	Banks	78bu d
1,272	1,467	345	410	-350	-458	-397	-561	1,043	1,719	1,653	3,320	1,595	1,334	335	Other Sectors	78bv d
-273	-251	67	-530	157	70	191	191	-135	357	-68	-149	-867	-660	288	Net Errors and Omissions	78ca d
154	1,292	402	193	434	610	1,763	1,274	464	182	-5	1,730	278	-1,390	-313	*Overall Balance*	78cb d
-154	-1,292	-402	-193	-434	-610	-1,763	-1,274	-464	-182	5	-1,730	-278	1,390	313	Reserves and Related Items	79da d
-154	-1,292	-402	-193	-434	-610	-1,763	-1,274	-464	-182	5	-1,730	-278	1,390	313	Reserve Assets	79db d
—	—	—	—	—	—	—	—	—	—	—	—	—	—	—	Use of Fund Credit and Loans	79dc d
....	....	....	....	....	....	....	....	....	....	....	....	....	....	....	Exceptional Financing	79de d

Millions of US Dollars

International Investment Position

1985	1986	1987	1988	1989	1990	1991	1992	1993	1994	1995	1996	1997	1998	1999		
2,899	4,638	4,735	5,157	5,295	5,832	8,041	9,212	12,701	15,149	16,445	16,840	19,362	18,320	19,080	Assets	79aa d
301	316	335	371	392	402	422	472	592	744	1,028	1,096	1,893	2,381	2,315	Direct Investment Abroad	79ab d
—	—	—	—	—	—	—	—	—	447	1,171	2,452	3,114	2,455	3,833	Portfolio Investment	79ac d
—	—	—	—	—	—	—	—	—	447	1,171	—	—	—	—	Equity Securities	79ad d
—	—	—	—	—	—	—	—	—	—	—	2,452	3,114	2,455	3,833	Debt Securities	79ae d
—	—	—	—	—	—	—	—	—	—	—	—	....	....	....	Financial Derivatives	79al d
407	739	817	852	811	699	1,012	927	4,163	5,845	5,786	3,353	4,448	4,752	4,831	Other Investment	79af d
—	—	—	—	—	—	—	—	40	40	40	5	5	12	7	Monetary Authorities	79ag d
271	229	235	24	—	—	100	—	561	1,545	1,052	—	23	38	38	General Government	79ah d
127	176	187	215	191	128	528	554	1,109	1,150	1,051	323	580	753	588	Banks	79ai d
9	334	395	613	620	571	384	373	2,452	3,110	3,643	3,025	3,840	3,949	4,198	Other Sectors	79aj d
2,191	3,583	3,583	3,934	4,092	4,731	6,607	7,813	7,946	8,114	8,462	9,939	9,908	8,733	8,102	Reserve Assets	79ak d
16,837	18,939	20,374	20,839	21,464	23,145	22,890	23,047	24,937	30,129	35,297	43,266	55,396	53,867	50,825	Liabilities	79la d
2,654	3,311	3,624	3,827	4,404	4,904	5,362	6,152	5,779	6,916	8,563	11,773	19,770	16,854	13,346	Dir. Invest. in Rep. Economy	79lb d
16	46	105	104	276	275	360	419	741	2,026	2,591	5,531	7,520	7,812	8,183	Portfolio Investment	79lc d
—	—	—	—	—	—	—	—	215	693	858	942	1,553	880	586	Equity Securities	79ld d
16	46	105	104	276	275	360	419	525	1,333	1,733	4,589	5,967	6,932	7,597	Debt Securities	79le d
—	—	—	—	—	—	—	—	—	—	—	—	290	251	351	Financial Derivatives	79ll d
14,167	15,582	16,645	16,908	16,784	17,966	17,168	16,476	18,417	21,187	24,144	25,962	27,816	28,950	28,945	Other investment	79lf d
668	790	853	597	687	761	763	650	452	231	301	174	147	134	117	Monetary Authorities	79lg d
3,726	4,199	4,189	4,548	4,855	5,468	5,405	5,589	5,202	5,102	5,144	4,722	4,515	4,999	5,934	General Government	79lh d
1,277	1,256	1,041	1,130	1,166	1,176	855	1,628	3,741	4,518	5,169	5,558	6,167	5,373	4,092	Banks	79li d
8,496	9,337	10,562	10,633	10,076	10,561	10,145	8,609	9,023	11,336	13,530	15,508	16,987	18,444	18,802	Other Sectors	79lj d

Colombia

		1970	1971	1972	1973	1974	1975	1976	1977	1978	1979	1980	1981	1982	1983	1984
Government Finance															*Millions of Pesos through 1973;*	
Deficit (-) or Surplus	80	-1,139.0	-1,236.0	-3,676.0	-2,377.0	Ɪ-2.8	-1.1	4.5	5.8	6.0	6.0	-10.8	-10.0	-33.7	-53.8	-130.5
Total Revenue and Grants	81y	11,953.0	14,417.0	16,084.0	20,074.0	Ɪ26.2	38.4	48.8	63.4	84.1	114.6	152.5	205.0	257.5	290.9	299.2
Revenue	81	....	....	....	....	....	....	....	....	....	....	....	....	....	....	....
Grants	81z	....	....	....	....	....	....	....	....	....	....	....	....	....	....	....
Exp. & Lending Minus Repay.	82z	13,092.0	15,653.0	19,760.0	22,451.0	Ɪ29.0	39.6	44.3	57.6	78.1	108.6	163.2	215.0	291.1	344.7	429.7
Expenditure	82	....	....	....	....	....	....	....	....	....	....	....	....	....	....	....
Lending Minus Repayments	83	....	....	....	....	....	....	....	....	....	....	....	....	....	....	....
Total Financing	80h	1,138.0	1,234.0	3,678.0	2,380.0	Ɪ2.8	1.1	-4.5	-5.8	-6.0	-6.0	10.8	10.0	33.7	53.8	130.5
Domestic	84a	-320.0	6.0	395.0	-619.0	Ɪ2.5	1.7	-3.3	-4.2	-3.8	-11.2	-5.7	-9.5	18.8	60.0	128.9
Foreign	85a	1,458.0	1,228.0	3,283.0	2,999.0	Ɪ.3	-.5	-1.2	-1.6	-2.2	5.2	16.5	19.5	14.9	-6.1	1.6
Total Debt by Currency	88z	22,058.0	26,490.0	33,205.0	39,615.0	Ɪ42.3	52.7	60.4	65.4	68.0	99.7	134.0	157.7	200.5	....	....
National	88b	9,776.0	10,012.0	12,086.0	13,435.0	Ɪ14.6	17.8	20.2	19.5	18.6	23.1	27.7	28.0	37.7	104.2	287.7
Foreign	89b	12,282.0	16,478.0	21,119.0	26,180.0	Ɪ27.8	34.9	40.2	45.9	49.5	76.6	106.4	129.7	162.9		
National Accounts															*Millions of Pesos through 1973;*	
Househ.Cons.Expend.,incl.NPISHs	96f	Ɪ95,330	114,840	136,230	170,230	Ɪ229	293	378	500	640	841	1,109	1,438	1,820	2,197	2,722
Government Consumption Expend.	91f	Ɪ12,280	17,100	18,140	23,010	Ɪ28	36	44	55	78	111	159	207	273	335	426
Gross Fixed Capital Formation	93e	Ɪ24,000	28,000	31,000	38,000	Ɪ53	62	85	104	140	183	265	350	436	525	654
Changes in Inventories	93i	Ɪ2,940	2,960	3,890	6,010	Ɪ16	7	9	30	26	32	36	59	76	83	77
Exports of Goods and Services	90c	Ɪ17,620	18,650	25,130	36,290	Ɪ47	64	91	121	151	181	256	235	273	319	458
Imports of Goods & Services	98c	Ɪ-19,320	-24,970	-24,270	-30,790	Ɪ-50	-57	-74	-95	-126	-160	-246	-306	-379	-404	-481
Gross Domestic Product (GDP)	99b	Ɪ132,770	155,890	189,610	243,160	Ɪ322	405	532	716	909	1,189	1,579	1,983	2,497	3,054	3,857
Net Primary Income from Abroad	98.n	-2,830	-2,820	-3,600	-4,480	Ɪ-4	-7	-9	-8	-8	-7	-6	-11	-51	-54	-99
Gross National Income (GNI)	99a	Ɪ129,940	153,070	186,010	238,680	Ɪ319	399	523	708	902	1,182	1,573	1,972	2,447	3,000	3,758
GDP Volume 1975 Prices	99b.p	308	326	351	374	396	405	424	442	479	505	526	538	543	551	570
GDP Volume 1994 Prices	99b.p	....	....	....	....	....	....	....	....	....	....	....	....	....	....	....
GDP Volume (1995=100)	99bv p	33.6	35.6	38.3	40.9	43.3	44.3	46.4	48.3	52.4	55.2	57.4	58.8	59.3	60.2	62.3
GDP Deflator (1995=100)	99bi p	.5	.5	.6	.7	.9	1.1	1.4	1.8	2.1	2.6	3.3	4.0	5.0	6.0	7.3
																Millions:
Population	99z	20.53	21.09	21.67	22.34	22.98	23.64	24.33	Ɪ24.23	24.91	25.38	25.89	26.43	26.97	27.50	28.06

	1985	1986	1987	1988	1989	1990	1991	1992	1993	1994	1995	1996	1997	1998	1999		
Billions of Pesos Beginning 1974: Year Ending December 31																**Government Finance**	
	−131.8	−90.0	−39.4	−159.8	−499.1	−163.7	25.2	−1,117.3	−329.2	−1,027.2	−1,939.8	−3,780.2	−4,504.1	−6,940.6	−8,888.9	Deficit (-) or Surplus	**80**
	446.5	655.5	912.2	1,207.2	1,271.0	2,070.9	3,221.6	4,113.0	5,715.3	7,656.1	9,521.2	12,007.3	15,282.6	16,880.2	20,144.0	Total Revenue and Grants	**81y**
	....	....	....	....	....	....	....	....	....	7,656.1	9,521.2	12,007.3	15,282.6	16,880.2	20,144.0	Revenue	**81**
	....	....	....	....	....	....	....	....	....	—	—	—	—	—	—	Grants	**81z**
	578.3	745.5	951.6	1,367.0	1,770.1	2,234.6	3,196.4	5,230.2	6,044.6	8,683.3	11,461.0	15,787.5	19,786.7	23,820.8	29,032.9	Exp. & Lending Minus Repay.	**82z**
	....	....	....	....	....	....	....	....	....	8,553.8	11,289.5	15,610.9	19,583.6	23,492.0	28,153.8	Expenditure	**82**
	....	....	....	....	....	....	....	....	....	129.5	171.5	176.6	203.1	328.8	879.1	Lending Minus Repayments	**83**
	131.8	90.0	39.4	159.8	499.1	163.7	−25.3	1,117.3	329.1	1,027.2	1,939.8	3,780.2	4,504.5	6,940.4	8,889.6	Total Financing	**80h**
	84.5	−11.9	113.0	61.8	402.1	5.9	−25.2	1,093.2	809.8	907.7	1,717.5	2,516.5	3,140.9	4,521.9	4,570.4	Domestic	**84a**
	47.3	101.9	−73.6	98.0	97.1	157.8	−.1	24.1	−480.6	119.5	222.3	1,263.7	1,363.6	2,418.5	4,319.2	Foreign	**85a**
	....	....	700.3	....	....	....	....	....	....	....	....	....	....	....	....	Total Debt by Currency	**88z**
	455.0	595.1	700.3	....	....	....	....	....	....	....	....	....	....	....	....	National	**88b**
	....	....	....	....	....	....	....	....	....	....	....	....	....	....	....	Foreign	**89b**
Billions of Pesos Beginning 1974																**National Accounts**	
	3,425	4,436	5,835	7,684	9,876	13,239	17,317	23,133	30,513	44,419	55,350	65,835	79,037	....	....	Househ.Cons.Expend.,incl.NPISHs	**96f**
	531	666	868	1,183	1,597	2,077	2,685	3,965	5,108	9,774	12,622	18,123	24,246	....	....	Government Consumption Expend.	**91f**
	870	1,204	1,537	2,288	2,733	3,365	3,810	5,212	8,251	15,727	18,911	21,749	24,592	....	....	Gross Fixed Capital Formation	**93e**
	75	18	227	292	288	387	354	552	1,049	1,497	2,806	462	708	....	....	Changes in Inventories	**93i**
	686	1,279	1,496	1,911	2,723	4,160	5,572	5,936	7,212	10,129	12,272	15,308	18,063	....	....	Exports of Goods and Services	**90c**
	−622	−814	−1,140	−1,626	−2,090	−2,998	−3,631	−5,282	−8,235	−14,127	−17,701	−20,993	−25,261	....	....	Imports of Goods & Services	**98c**
	4,966	6,788	8,824	11,731	15,127	20,228	26,107	33,515	43,898	67,533	84,439	100,711	121,708	....	....	Gross Domestic Product (GDP)	**99b**
	−142	−150	−187	−196	−423	−560	−154	−104	245	−1,200	−1,442	−2,128	−2,706	....	....	Net Primary Income from Abroad	**98.n**
	4,824	6,638	8,638	11,536	14,704	19,669	25,952	33,411	44,143	66,333	82,997	98,583	119,002	....	....	Gross National Income (GNI)	**99a**
	588	622	655	682	705	735	750	780	822	870	....	....	....	....	....	GDP Volume 1975 Prices	**99b.p**
	....	....	....	....	....	....	....	....	....	67,533	71,046	72,507	74,994	....	....	GDP Volume 1994 Prices	**99b.p**
	64.2	67.9	71.6	74.5	77.0	80.3	81.9	85.3	89.8	95.1	100.0	102.1	105.6	....	....	GDP Volume (1995=100)	**99bvp**
	9.2	11.8	14.6	18.7	23.3	29.8	37.7	46.6	57.9	84.1	100.0	116.9	136.5	....	....	GDP Deflator (1995=100)	**99bip**
Midyear Estimates																	
	28.62	30.02	30.58	31.14	34.31	34.97	35.69	36.41	37.13	37.85	38.54	39.30	40.06	40.83	41.59	**Population**	**99z**

(See notes in the back of the book.)

Comoros

632

		1970	1971	1972	1973	1974	1975	1976	1977	1978	1979	1980	1981	1982	1983	1984
Exchange Rates														*Francs per SDR:*		
Official Rate	aa	276.02	283.61	277.99	284.00	272.08	262.55	288.70	285.76	272.28	264.78	287.98	334.52	370.92	436.97	470.10
														Francs per US Dollar:		
Official Rate	ae	276.02	261.22	256.05	235.42	222.22	224.27	248.49	235.25	209.00	201.00	225.80	287.40	336.25	417.37	479.60
Official Rate	rf	276.40	275.59	252.03	222.89	240.70	214.31	238.95	245.68	225.65	212.72	211.28	271.73	328.60	381.06	436.95
Fund Position														*Millions of SDRs:*		
Quota	2f. s	—	—	—	—	—	—	1.90	1.90	2.30	2.30	3.50	3.50	3.50	3.50	4.50
SDRs	1b. s	....	....	....	....	....	....	—	—	—	.24	—	.01	—	—	.23
Reserve Position in the Fund	1c. s	....	....	....	....	....	....	—	—	—	—	.30	—	—	—	—
Total Fund Cred.&Loans Outstg.	2tl	....	....	....	....	....	....	—	—	—	—	—	—	—	—	—
International Liquidity													*Millions of US Dollars Unless Otherwise Indicated:*			
Total Reserves minus Gold	1l. d	....	....	....	....	....	....	....	....	....	....	6.37	8.39	10.83	10.79	3.51
SDRs	1b. d	....	....	....	....	....	....	....	....	....	.32	—	.01	—	—	.23
Reserve Position in the Fund	1c. d	....	....	....	....	....	....	—	—	—	—	.38	—	—	—	—
Foreign Exchange	1d. d	....	....	....	....	....	....	....	....	....	....	5.99	8.38	10.83	10.79	3.28
Gold (Million Fine Troy Ounces)	1ad	....	....	....	....	....	....	....	....	....	....	....	....	....	.001	.001
Gold (National Valuation)	1an d	....	....	....	....	....	....	....	....	....	....	....	....	—	.22	.19
Deposit Money Banks: Assets	7a. d	....	....	....	....	....	....	....	....	....	....	....	....	2.36	1.61	.15
Liabilities	7b. d	....	....	....	....	....	....	....	....	....	....	....	....	.12	.33	.10
Monetary Authorities														*Millions of Francs:*		
Foreign Assets	11	....	....	....	....	....	....	....	....	....	....	....	....	3,642	4,597	1,775
Claims on Central Government	12a	....	....	....	....	....	....	....	....	....	....	....	....	670	786	978
Claims on Private Sector	12d	....	....	....	....	....	....	....	....	....	....	....	....	....	....	....
Claims on Other Banking Insts	12f	....	....	....	....	....	....	....	....	....	....	....	....	....	....	....
Reserve Money	14	....	....	....	....	....	....	....	....	....	....	....	....	3,583	3,976	3,475
of which: Currency Outside DMBs	14a	....	....	....	....	....	....	....	....	....	....	....	....	2,434	3,427	3,142
Foreign Liabilities	16c	....	....	....	....	....	....	....	....	....	....	....	....	171	335	177
Central Government Deposits	16d	....	....	....	....	....	....	....	....	....	....	....	....	92	337	80
Counterpart Funds	16e	....	....	....	....	....	....	....	....	....	....	....	....	....	....	....
Central Govt. Lending Funds	16f	....	....	....	....	....	....	....	....	....	....	....	....	....	....	....
Capital Accounts	17a	....	....	....	....	....	....	....	....	....	....	....	....	1,289	1,469	1,674
Other Items (Net)	17r	....	....	....	....	....	....	....	....	....	....	....	....	−823	−734	−2,653
Deposit Money Banks														*Millions of Francs:*		
Reserves	20	....	....	....	....	....	....	....	....	....	....	....	....	481	266	419
Foreign Assets	21	....	....	....	....	....	....	....	....	....	....	....	....	795	671	73
Claims on Central Government	22a	....	....	....	....	....	....	....	....	....	....	....	....	457	457	457
Claims on Private Sector	22d	....	....	....	....	....	....	....	....	....	....	....	....	3,485	4,436	6,313
Demand Deposits	24	....	....	....	....	....	....	....	....	....	....	....	....	1,688	2,783	2,016
Foreign Currency Deposits	25a	....	....	....	....	....	....	....	....	....	....	....	....	1,168	1,229	959
Restricted Deposits	26b	....	....	....	....	....	....	....	....	....	....	....	....	....	....	....
Foreign Liabilities	26c	....	....	....	....	....	....	....	....	....	....	....	....	42	139	50
Central Government Deposits	26d	....	....	....	....	....	....	....	....	....	....	....	....	129	70	206
Credit From Monetary Authorities	26g	....	....	....	....	....	....	....	....	....	....	....	....	—	—	2,516
Capital Accounts	27a	....	....	....	....	....	....	....	....	....	....	....	....	350	514	581
Other Items (Net)	27r	....	....	....	....	....	....	....	....	....	....	....	....	1,841	1,094	934
Monetary Survey														*Millions of Francs:*		
Foreign Assets (Net)	31n	....	....	....	....	....	....	....	....	....	....	....	....	4,224	4,794	1,621
Domestic Credit	32	....	....	....	....	....	....	....	....	....	....	....	....	4,993	6,120	8,399
Claims on Central Govt. (Net)	32an	....	....	....	....	....	....	....	....	....	....	....	....	1,447	1,621	2,046
Claims on Private Sector	32d	....	....	....	....	....	....	....	....	....	....	....	....	3,546	4,499	6,353
Claims on Other Banking Insts	32f	....	....	....	....	....	....	....	....	....	....	....	....	....	....	....
Money	34	....	....	....	....	....	....	....	....	....	....	....	....	5,231	7,404	6,268
Quasi-Money	35	....	....	....	....	....	....	....	....	....	....	....	....	1,168	1,229	959
Restricted Deposits	36b	....	....	....	....	....	....	....	....	....	....	....	....	....	....	....
Counterpart Funds	36e	....	....	....	....	....	....	....	....	....	....	....	....	....	....	....
Central Govt. Lending Funds	36f	....	....	....	....	....	....	....	....	....	....	....	....	....	....	....
Other Items (Net)	37r	....	....	....	....	....	....	....	....	....	....	....	....	2,818	2,280	2,793
Money plus Quasi-Money	35l	....	....	....	....	....	....	....	....	....	....	....	....	6,399	8,633	7,227
Other Banking Institutions														*Millions of Francs:*		
Reserves	40	....	....	....	....	....	....	....	....	....	....	....	....	245	137	60
Foreign Assets	41	....	....	....	....	....	....	....	....	....	....	....	....	....	....	....
Claims on Central Government	42a	....	....	....	....	....	....	....	....	....	....	....	....	2	5	16
Claims on Private Sector	42d	....	....	....	....	....	....	....	....	....	....	....	....	576	925	1,226
Time Deposits	45	....	....	....	....	....	....	....	....	....	....	....	....	97	182	277
Central Government Deposits	46d	....	....	....	....	....	....	....	....	....	....	....	....	—	—	38
Long-Term Foreign Liabilities	46cl	....	....	....	....	....	....	....	....	....	....	....	....	—	—	—
Central Govt. Lending Funds	46f	....	....	....	....	....	....	....	....	....	....	....	....	413	514	643
Capital Accounts	47a	....	....	....	....	....	....	....	....	....	....	....	....	348	392	433
Other Items (Net)	47r	....	....	....	....	....	....	....	....	....	....	....	....	−35	−21	−89
Banking Survey														*Millions of Francs:*		
Foreign Assets (Net)	51n	....	....	....	....	....	....	....	....	....	....	....	....	4,224	4,794	1,621
Domestic Credit	52	....	....	....	....	....	....	....	....	....	....	....	....	5,571	7,050	9,603
Claims on Central Govt. (Net)	52an	....	....	....	....	....	....	....	....	....	....	....	....	1,449	1,626	2,024
Claims on Private Sector	52d	....	....	....	....	....	....	....	....	....	....	....	....	4,122	5,424	7,579
Liquid Liabilities	55l	....	....	....	....	....	....	....	....	....	....	....	....	6,495	8,814	7,503
Money	54	....	....	....	....	....	....	....	....	....	....	....	....	5,230	7,403	6,267
Quasi-Money	55	....	....	....	....	....	....	....	....	....	....	....	....	1,265	1,411	1,236
Restricted Deposits	56b	....	....	....	....	....	....	....	....	....	....	....	....	....	....	....
Counterpart Funds	56e	....	....	....	....	....	....	....	....	....	....	....	....	....	....	....
Central Govt. Lending Funds	56f	....	....	....	....	....	....	....	....	....	....	....	....	763	864	993
Other Items (Net)	57r	....	....	....	....	....	....	....	....	....	....	....	....	2,537	2,165	2,728

1985	1986	1987	1988	1989	1990	1991	1992	1993	1994	1995	1996	1997	1998	1999		
															Exchange Rates	
End of Period (aa)																
415.25	394.78	378.78	407.68	380.31	364.84	370.48	378.57	404.89	I585.32	546.28	564.79	605.95	593.70	I672.14	Official Rate	**aa**
End of Period (ae)		*Period Average (rf)*														
378.05	322.75	267.00	302.95	256.45	259.00	275.32	294.77	I400.95	367.50	392.77	449.10	421.65	I489.72		Official Rate	**ae**
449.26	346.30	300.53	297.85	319.01	272.26	282.10	264.69	283.16	I416.40	374.36	383.66	437.75	442.46	I461.77	Official Rate	**rf**
End of Period															**Fund Position**	
4.50	4.50	4.50	4.50	4.50	4.50	4.50	6.50	6.50	6.50	6.50	6.50	6.50	6.50	8.90	Quota	**2f. s**
.21	.18	.14	.11	.06	.08	.02	.02	.07	.03	.07	.04	.10	—	.12	SDRs	**1b. s**
—	—	—	—	—	—	—	.50	.50	.52	.54	.54	.54	.54	.54	Reserve Position in the Fund	**1c. s**
—	—	—	—	—	—	.90	.90	.90	2.25	2.25	2.25	2.07	1.89	1.58	Total Fund Cred.&Loans Outstg.	**2tl**
End of Period															**International Liquidity**	
11.75	17.55	30.67	23.54	30.77	29.69	29.18	27.09	38.63	44.03	44.48	50.55	40.48	39.14	37.15	Total Reserves minus Gold	**1l. d**
.23	.22	.20	.15	.08	.11	.03	.03	.09	.05	.11	.05	.13	.01	.16	SDRs	**1b. d**
—	—	—	—	—	—	—	.69	.69	.76	.80	.78	.73	.76	.74	Reserve Position in the Fund	**1c. d**
11.52	17.33	30.48	23.39	30.69	29.58	29.15	26.38	37.85	43.22	43.58	49.72	39.62	38.37	36.24	Foreign Exchange	**1d. d**
.001	.001	.001	.001	.001	.001	.001	.001	.001	.001	.001	.001	.001	....	....	Gold (Million Fine Troy Ounces)	**1ad**
.20	.24	.30	.24	.24	.22	.21	.19	.22	.22	.22	.21	.18	.17	....	Gold (National Valuation)	**1an d**
3.76	2.11	.40	5.50	3.90	3.89	5.84	4.35	2.73	.29	2.42	2.16	4.29	I2.04	8.10	Deposit Money Banks: Assets	**7a. d**
1.21	3.81	6.26	6.30	5.46	6.28	6.93	4.76	2.66	.01	.25	.02	—	I1.99	2.45	Liabilities	**7b. d**
End of Period															**Monetary Authorities**	
4,515	5,740	8,275	7,205	8,977	7,654	7,595	7,512	11,475	17,729	16,422	19,950	18,305	I16,581	18,295	Foreign Assets	**11**
1,202	1,251	1,312	1,624	1,830	1,819	2,475	2,510	2,648	3,483	3,589	3,569	3,646	I3,806	3,814	Claims on Central Government	**12a**
....	....	....	....	....	....	....	....	....	....	....	....	....	57	49	Claims on Private Sector	**12d**
....	....	....	....	....	....	....	....	....	....	....	....	....	50	75	Claims on Other Banking Insts	**12f**
3,881	5,205	7,358	5,772	7,801	6,508	5,954	6,085	8,539	9,756	8,760	11,936	10,454	I9,326	11,104	Reserve Money	**14**
3,448	3,118	3,151	3,688	3,618	4,274	4,046	4,082	4,402	5,100	5,672	5,639	5,433	I5,418	6,310	of which: Currency Outside DMBs	**14a**
172	193	88	115	182	196	575	505	524	1,428	1,421	1,393	1,385	I1,183	1,171	Foreign Liabilities	**16c**
189	161	959	1,638	230	752	756	657	2,287	1,743	1,279	1,723	1,515	I542	518	Central Government Deposits	**16d**
....	....	....	....	....	....	....	....	....	....	....	....	....	56	49	Counterpart Funds	**16e**
													504	314	Central Govt. Lending Funds	**16f**
1,540	1,724	1,706	1,809	2,585	2,728	2,802	2,976	2,972	8,492	8,673	8,670	8,770	I9,243	9,279	Capital Accounts	**17a**
−65	−292	−523	−505	8	−711	−18	−200	−198	−206	−121	−203	−173	I−361	−200	Other Items (Net)	**17r**
End of Period															**Deposit Money Banks**	
66	1,804	3,774	1,722	3,728	1,637	1,261	1,599	2,972	3,082	1,631	4,719	4,024	I5,195	3,796	Reserves	**20**
1,420	681	106	1,667	1,130	997	1,512	1,198	804	115	889	848	1,927	I859	3,966	Foreign Assets	**21**
458	385	328	273	178	51	....	....	....	....	....	415	94	I358	554	Claims on Central Government	**22a**
3,428	3,982	4,734	6,826	6,277	9,023	9,627	9,998	8,829	8,579	9,452	6,712	8,458	I6,948	8,600	Claims on Private Sector	**22d**
2,636	2,904	3,024	3,831	4,065	4,244	3,465	3,866	3,710	3,954	4,170	4,487	4,518	I4,250	4,386	Demand Deposits	**24**
1,015	1,432	3,035	3,559	4,608	4,574	5,829	5,720	5,781	5,910	5,442	6,167	7,771	I5,737	6,974	Foreign Currency Deposits	**25a**
....	....	....	....	....	....	....	....	....	....	....	....	....	260	618	Restricted Deposits	**26b**
457	1,231	1,671	1,908	1,580	1,611	1,795	1,311	783	3	93	8	—	I840	1,200	Foreign Liabilities	**26c**
—	348	277	83	127	—	—	—	377	—	167	132	209	I362	240	Central Government Deposits	**26d**
17	—	—	—		84	—	—	87	122	—	—	—	I—		Credit From Monetary Authorities	**26g**
617	566	592	632	835	951	1,174	1,405	1,586	1,850	2,194	2,022	2,235	I2,667	3,368	Capital Accounts	**27a**
630	373	343	475	98	244	137	493	281	−63	−94	−123	−230	I−776	70	Other Items (Net)	**27r**
End of Period															**Monetary Survey**	
5,306	4,997	6,622	6,849	8,345	6,844	6,737	6,894	10,972	16,413	15,797	19,397	18,847	I15,417	19,890	Foreign Assets (Net)	**31n**
5,820	5,984	6,516	8,163	10,067	11,918	13,277	14,403	11,465	12,497	12,449	10,213	10,474	I10,315	12,342	Domestic Credit	**32**
2,392	1,982	1,763	1,304	3,727	2,829	3,523	4,316	2,566	3,822	2,924	3,422	2,016	I3,260	3,610	Claims on Central Govt. (Net)	**32an**
3,428	4,002	4,753	6,859	6,340	9,089	9,754	10,087	8,899	8,675	9,525	6,791	8,458	I7,005	8,649	Claims on Private Sector	**32d**
....	....	....	....	....	....	....	....	....	....	....	....	....	50	83	Claims on Other Banking Insts	**32f**
7,313	7,256	7,931	9,110	10,302	10,916	10,122	11,069	11,575	12,714	12,040	13,021	10,603	I10,015	11,662	Money	**34**
1,015	1,432	3,035	3,559	4,608	4,574	5,829	5,720	5,781	5,910	5,442	6,167	7,771	I5,758	7,036	Quasi-Money	**35**
....	....	....	....	....	....	....	....	....	....	....	....	....	260	618	Restricted Deposits	**36b**
....	....	....	....	....	....	....	....	....	....	....	....	....	56	49	Counterpart Funds	**36e**
													504	314	Central Govt. Lending Funds	**36f**
2,798	2,295	2,173	2,343	3,501	3,272	4,062	4,509	5,082	10,287	10,765	10,421	10,947	I9,140	12,557	Other Items (Net)	**37r**
8,328	8,688	10,966	12,669	14,910	15,490	15,951	16,789	17,356	18,624	17,482	19,188	18,374	I15,773	18,698	Money plus Quasi-Money	**35l**
End of Period															**Other Banking Institutions**	
143	134	148	129	337	267	443	511	697	1,340	1,250	856	88	I475	1,060	Reserves	**40**
1	1	1	2	1	2	—	2	2	4	2	5	—	I89	96	Foreign Assets	**41**
12	70	163	116	162	166	246	....	526	11	....	....	....	I—	....	Claims on Central Government	**42a**
1,498	1,749	2,052	2,114	1,995	1,922	2,000	1,991	1,916	1,985	2,200	3,029	4,022	I4,038	3,329	Claims on Private Sector	**42d**
318	375	397	345	308	376	456	472	473	387	267	694	760	I709	768	Time Deposits	**45**
32	66	75	3	4	4	4	....	....	....	....	....	....	I263	153	Central Government Deposits	**46d**
—	—	221	448	713	635	1,042	1,284	1,551	1,838	1,964	1,588	1,633	I845	688	Long-Term Foreign Liabilities	**46cl**
896	1,089	1,156	1,008	866	595	445	235	233	230	296	317	306	I883	896	Central Govt. Lending Funds	**46f**
511	520	562	607	687	807	825	854	887	918	1,018	1,399	1,494	I2,090	1,971	Capital Accounts	**47a**
−106	−96	−47	−50	−83	−60	−83	−341	−2	−34	−93	−108	−84	I−189	7	Other Items (Net)	**47r**
End of Period															**Banking Survey**	
5,307	4,998	6,402	6,403	7,633	6,211	5,695	5,612	9,423	14,579	13,835	17,814	17,214	I14,661	19,298	Foreign Assets (Net)	**51n**
7,298	7,737	8,656	10,390	12,220	14,002	15,519	16,394	13,907	14,493	14,649	13,242	14,496	I14,040	15,435	Domestic Credit	**52**
2,372	1,986	1,851	1,417	3,885	2,991	3,765	4,316	3,092	3,833	2,924	3,422	2,016	I2,997	3,457	Claims on Central Govt. (Net)	**52an**
4,926	5,751	6,805	8,973	8,335	11,011	11,754	12,078	10,815	10,660	11,725	9,820	12,480	I11,043	11,978	Claims on Private Sector	**52d**
8,504	8,933	11,213	12,889	14,887	15,617	15,981	16,781	17,172	17,704	16,525	19,002	19,114	I16,166	18,522	Liquid Liabilities	**55l**
7,171	7,126	7,781	8,985	9,971	10,667	9,696	10,589	10,918	11,407	10,816	12,141	10,583	I9,699	10,718	Money	**54**
1,333	1,807	3,432	3,904	4,916	4,950	6,285	6,192	6,254	6,297	5,709	6,861	8,531	I6,467	7,804	Quasi-Money	**55**
....	....	....	....	....	....	....	....	....	....	....	....	....	260	618	Restricted Deposits	**56b**
....	....	....	....	....	....	....	....	....	....	....	....	....	56	49	Counterpart Funds	**56e**
1,246	1,439	1,506	1,358	1,216	945	795	585	583	230	296	317	306	I1,387	1,210	Central Govt. Lending Funds	**56f**
2,852	2,365	2,340	2,546	3,749	3,651	4,437	4,641	5,577	11,138	11,664	11,736	12,289	I10,829	14,336	Other Items (Net)	**57r**

Comoros

		1970	1971	1972	1973	1974	1975	1976	1977	1978	1979	1980	1981	1982	1983	1984
Interest Rates															*Percent Per Annum*	
Discount Rate *(End of Period)*	60	....	....	....	....	....	....	....	....	....	....	....	....		10.00	10.00
Deposit Rate	60l	....	....	....	....	....	....	....	....	....	....	....	....		7.50	7.50
Lending Rate	60p	....	....	....	....	....	....	....	....	....	....	....	....		15.00	15.00
International Transactions															*Millions of Francs*	
Exports	70	1,278	1,572	1,511	1,106	2,138	2,036	2,824	2,203	2,099	3,701	2,364	4,462	6,435	7,419	3,079
Imports, c.i.f.	71	2,373	2,835	2,932	3,369	6,203	4,974	3,119	4,053	4,329	6,135	6,147	8,791	10,725	13,099	18,778
Balance of Payments															*Millions of US Dollars:*	
Current Account, n.i.e.	78ald	....	....	....	....	....	....	....	....	....	....	−8.91	−8.16	−10.96	−11.05	−32.72
Goods: Exports f.o.b.	78aad	....	....	....	....	....	....	....	....	....	....	11.19	16.42	19.58	19.47	7.05
Goods: Imports f.o.b.	78abd	....	....	....	....	....	....	....	....	....	....	−22.37	−24.89	−25.10	−28.80	−32.65
Trade Balance	78acd	....	....	....	....	....	....	....	....	....	....	−11.18	−8.47	−5.52	−9.33	−25.60
Services: Credit	78add	....	....	....	....	....	....	....	....	....	....	2.24	1.10	2.56	2.64	2.65
Services: Debit	78aed	....	....	....	....	....	....	....	....	....	....	−11.92	−25.31	−25.41	−21.85	−37.66
Balance on Goods & Services	78afd	....	....	....	....	....	....	....	....	....	....	−20.86	−32.67	−28.38	−28.54	−60.61
Income: Credit	78agd	....	....	....	....	....	....	....	....	....	....	.63	.81	1.27	1.27	1.04
Income: Debit	78ahd	....	....	....	....	....	....	....	....	....	....	−.04	−.56	−.71	−1.73	−1.61
Balance on Gds, Serv. & Inc.	78aid	....	....	....	....	....	....	....	....	....	....	−20.27	−32.43	−27.82	−29.00	−61.18
Current Transfers, n.i.e.: Credit	78ajd	....	....	....	....	....	....	....	....	....	....	12.88	28.09	21.85	22.09	33.89
Current Transfers: Debit	78akd	....	....	....	....	....	....	....	....	....	....	−1.52	−3.82	−4.98	−4.14	−5.43
Capital Account, n.i.e.	78bcd	....	....	....	....	....	....	....	....	....	....	—	—	—	—	—
Capital Account, n.i.e.: Credit	78bad	....	....	....	....	....	....	....	....	....	....	—	—	—	—	—
Capital Account: Debit	78bbd	....	....	....	....	....	....	....	....	....	....	—	—	—	—	—
Financial Account, n.i.e.	78bjd	....	....	....	....	....	....	....	....	....	....	20.59	14.86	18.42	15.21	27.36
Direct Investment Abroad	78bdd	....	....	....	....	....	....	....	....	....	....					
Dir. Invest. in Rep. Econ., n.i.e.	78bed	....	....	....	....	....	....	....	....	....	....					
Portfolio Investment Assets	78bfd	....	....	....	....	....	....	....	....	....	....	−.41	−.31	.40	—	—
Equity Securities	78bkd	....	....	....	....	....	....	....	....	....	....	−.41	−.31	.40	—	—
Debt Securities	78bld	....	....	....	....	....	....	....	....	....	....	—	—	—	—	—
Portfolio Investment Liab., n.i.e.	78bgd	....	....	....	....	....	....	....	....	....	....					
Equity Securities	78bmd	....	....	....	....	....	....	....	....	....	....					
Debt Securities	78bnd	....	....	....	....	....	....	....	....	....	....					
Financial Derivatives Assets	78bwd	....	....	....	....	....	....	....	....	....	....	....	....	....	....	....
Financial Derivatives Liabilities	78bxd	....	....	....	....	....	....	....	....	....	....	....	....	....	....	....
Other Investment Assets	78bhd	....	....	....	....	....	....	....	....	....	....	—	—	—	−.53	—
Monetary Authorities	78bod	....	....	....	....	....	....	....	....	....	....					
General Government	78bpd	....	....	....	....	....	....	....	....	....	....					
Banks	78bqd	....	....	....	....	....	....	....	....	....	....	—	—	—	−.53	—
Other Sectors	78brd	....	....	....	....	....	....	....	....	....	....	—	—	—	—	—
Other Investment Liab., n.i.e.	78bid	....	....	....	....	....	....	....	....	....	....	21.00	15.17	18.01	15.74	27.36
Monetary Authorities	78bsd	....	....	....	....	....	....	....	....	....	....	—	—	—	—	—
General Government	78btd	....	....	....	....	....	....	....	....	....	....	22.14	13.90	14.32	15.50	26.77
Banks	78bud	....	....	....	....	....	....	....	....	....	....	−1.14	1.27	1.42	.24	1.46
Other Sectors	78bvd	....	....	....	....	....	....	....	....	....	....	—	—	2.27	—	−.88
Net Errors and Omissions	78cad	....	....	....	....	....	....	....	....	....	....	−15.19	−3.19	−3.75	−2.08	−.49
Overall Balance	78cbd	....	....	....	....	....	....	....	....	....	....	−3.51	3.51	3.71	2.08	−5.85
Reserves and Related Items	79dad	....	....	....	....	....	....	....	....	....	....	3.51	−3.51	−3.71	−2.08	5.85
Reserve Assets	79dbd	....	....	....	....	....	....	....	....	....	....	3.51	−3.51	−3.71	−2.08	5.85
Use of Fund Credit and Loans	79dcd	....	....	....	....	....	....	....	....	....	....	—	—	—	—	—
Exceptional Financing	79ded	....	....	....	....	....	....	....	....	....	....	—	—	—	—	—
Government Finance															*Millions of Francs:*	
Deficit (-) or Surplus	80	....	....	....	....	....	....	....	....	....	....	....	....	−4,084	−6,353	−8,587
Revenue	81	....	....	....	....	....	....	....	....	....	....	....	....	5,036	6,844	6,977
Grants Received	81z	....	....	....	....	....	....	....	....	....	....	....	....	4,750	6,868	9,279
Cash Adj.& Unall.Rev. & Grants	81x	....	....	....	....	....	....	....	....	....	....	....	....	−235	−211	−145
Expenditure	82	....	....	....	....	....	....	....	....	....	....	....	....	13,706	19,825	24,636
Lending Minus Repayments	83	....	....	....	....	....	....	....	....	....	....	....	....	−70	28	61
Financing																
Domestic	84a	....	....	....	....	....	....	....	....	....	....	....	....	154	238	−391
Foreign	85a	....	....	....	....	....	....	....	....	....	....	....	....	3,930	6,115	8,977
Debt: Domestic	88a	....	....	....	....	....	....	....	....	....	....	....	....	....	....	797
Foreign	89a	....	....	....	....	....	....	....	....	....	....	....	....	....	....	81,626
National Accounts															*Billions of Francs:*	
Gross Domestic Product (GDP)	99b	8.0	8.9	10.0	11.0	16.8	15.0	14.4	....	....	....	....	....	....	40.4	44.2
															Millions:	
Population	99z	.27	.28	.28	.29	.31	.32	.34	.35	.36	.38	.38	.41	.42	.42	.44

	1985	1986	1987	1988	1989	1990	1991	1992	1993	1994	1995	1996	1997	1998	1999		
Interest Rates																	
Percent Per Annum																	
Discount Rate (End of Period)	10.00	10.00	8.50	8.50	....	....	....	....	....	....	....	....	....	....	....	Discount Rate (End of Period)	60
Deposit Rate	7.50	7.50	6.50	6.50	....	....	....	....	....	....	....	....	....	....	....	Deposit Rate	60l
Lending Rate	15.00	15.00	13.00	13.00	....	....	....	....	....	....	....	....	....	....	....	Lending Rate	60p
International Transactions																	
Millions of Francs																	
Exports	7,048	7,053	3,485	6,399	5,809	4,883	7,028	5,847	6,189	4,688	4,236	....	....	....	....	Exports	70
Imports, c.i.f.	16,495	12,849	15,560	15,647	13,576	14,041	16,399	18,139	16,817	21,929	23,411	....	....	....	....	Imports, c.i.f.	71
Balance of Payments																	
Minus Sign Indicates Debit																	
Current Account, n.i.e.	-14.26	-15.69	-21.37	-6.52	5.41	-10.48	-10.25	-14.19	9.57	-7.22	-18.96	....	....	....	....	Current Account, n.i.e.	78al d
Goods: Exports f.o.b.	15.69	20.37	11.60	21.48	18.05	17.93	24.36	21.43	21.58	10.79	11.32					Goods: Exports f.o.b.	78aa d
Goods: Imports f.o.b.	-28.22	-28.54	-44.15	-44.29	-35.65	-45.23	-53.60	-58.27	-49.54	-44.94	-53.50					Goods: Imports f.o.b.	78ab d
Trade Balance	-12.53	-8.17	-32.55	-22.81	-17.60	-27.29	-29.24	-36.84	-27.96	-34.16	-42.18					*Trade Balance*	78ac d
Services: Credit	4.22	6.76	14.44	16.85	17.55	16.86	24.70	26.59	31.06	28.84	34.51					Services: Credit	78ad d
Services: Debit	-35.89	-42.27	-41.80	-42.29	-39.61	-43.92	-45.72	-52.97	-49.87	-45.59	-49.85					Services: Debit	78ae d
Balance on Goods & Services	-44.21	-43.68	-59.91	-48.26	-39.66	-54.36	-50.26	-63.22	-46.77	-50.91	-57.53					*Balance on Goods & Services*	78af d
Income: Credit	.57	1.50	1.80	1.76	4.30	3.35	2.81	3.49	3.30	2.62	3.40					Income: Credit	78ag d
Income: Debit	-1.97	-3.13	-2.92	-3.94	-2.94	-4.21	-3.74	.46	-1.27	-2.69	-2.39					Income: Debit	78ah d
Balance on Gds, Serv. & Inc.	-45.60	-45.32	-61.03	-50.44	-38.31	-55.21	-51.19	-59.27	-44.74	-50.98	-56.52					*Balance on Gds, Serv. & Inc.*	78ai d
Current Transfers, n.i.e.: Credit	36.61	36.97	45.86	48.40	49.17	49.41	47.44	56.11	59.83	49.95	41.06					Current Transfers, n.i.e.: Credit	78aj d
Current Transfers: Debit	-5.27	-7.34	-6.19	-4.48	-5.45	-4.67	-6.50	-11.04	-5.52	-6.19	-3.50					Current Transfers: Debit	78ak d
Capital Account, n.i.e.	—	—	—	—	—	—	—	—	—	—	—					Capital Account, n.i.e.	78bc d
Capital Account, n.i.e.: Credit	—	—	—	—	—	—	—	—	—	—	—					Capital Account, n.i.e.: Credit	78ba d
Capital Account: Debit	—	—	—	—	—	—	—	—	—	—	—					Capital Account: Debit	78bb d
Financial Account, n.i.e.	18.60	21.18	29.51	4.19	7.54	13.72	-.43	13.48	4.05	18.54	10.87					Financial Account, n.i.e.	78bj d
Direct Investment Abroad	—	—	—	—	—	-1.10	—	—	—	—	—					Direct Investment Abroad	78bd d
Dir. Invest. in Rep. Econ., n.i.e.	—	—	7.55	3.77	3.27	.39	2.51	-1.45	.19	.18	.89					Dir. Invest. in Rep. Econ., n.i.e.	78be d
Portfolio Investment Assets	.02	—	—	—	—	—	—	—	—	—	—					Portfolio Investment Assets	78bf d
Equity Securities	.02	—	—	—	—	—	—	—	—	—	—					Equity Securities	78bk d
Debt Securities	—	—	—	—	—	—	—	—	—	—	—					Debt Securities	78bl d
Portfolio Investment Liab., n.i.e.	-.24	—	—	—	—	—	—	—	—	—	—					Portfolio Investment Liab., n.i.e.	78bg d
Equity Securities	—	—	—	—	—	—	—	—	—	—	—					Equity Securities	78bm d
Debt Securities	-.24	—	—	—	—	—	—	—	—	—	—					Debt Securities	78bn d
Financial Derivatives Assets	....	....	....	....	....	....	....	....	....	....	....					Financial Derivatives Assets	78bw d
Financial Derivatives Liabilities	....	....	....	....	....	....	....	....	....	....	....					Financial Derivatives Liabilities	78bx d
Other Investment Assets	-3.00	-1.49	8.83	-13.71	-6.73	.60	-2.23	.24	-1.45	1.66	-1.83					Other Investment Assets	78bh d
Monetary Authorities	....	....	....	....	....	....	....	....	....	....	....					Monetary Authorities	78bo d
General Government	—	—	4.58	—	—	—	—	—	—	—	—					General Government	78bp d
Banks	-3.00	2.13	1.91	-5.24	.66	.60	-2.23	.24	-1.45	1.66	-1.83					Banks	78bq d
Other Sectors	—	-3.63	2.34	-8.46	-7.39	—	—	—	—	—	—					Other Sectors	78br d
Other Investment Liab., n.i.e.	21.82	22.68	13.14	14.13	11.01	13.82	-.71	14.69	5.30	16.70	11.81					Other Investment Liab., n.i.e.	78bi d
Monetary Authorities	—	—	6.82	8.46	7.20	8.07	9.23	-.29	2.99	7.93	2.02					Monetary Authorities	78bs d
General Government	20.27	19.79	5.26	1.31	2.79	.66	-13.02	12.03	2.06	10.63	8.72					General Government	78bt d
Banks	1.55	-.17	.32	.80	—	—	—	—	—	—	—					Banks	78bu d
Other Sectors	—	3.06	.74	3.57	1.01	5.09	3.08	2.96	.25	-1.86	1.06					Other Sectors	78bv d
Net Errors and Omissions	1.77	-2.02	.65	-1.39	-7.60	-8.08	-15.18	-5.32	-5.84	-6.33	-1.77					Net Errors and Omissions	78ca d
Overall Balance	6.12	3.48	8.79	-3.72	5.35	-4.84	-25.85	-6.03	7.78	4.99	-9.86					*Overall Balance*	78cb d
Reserves and Related Items	-6.12	-3.48	-8.79	3.72	-5.35	4.84	25.85	6.03	-7.78	-4.99	9.86					Reserves and Related Items	79da d
Reserve Assets	-6.12	-3.48	-8.79	3.72	-5.35	4.84	1.78	-.39	-14.00	-14.97	3.37					Reserve Assets	79db d
Use of Fund Credit and Loans	—	—	—	—	—	—	1.19	—	—	1.89	—					Use of Fund Credit and Loans	79dc d
Exceptional Financing	—	—	—	—	—	—	22.89	6.42	6.22	8.09	6.49					Exceptional Financing	79de d
Government Finance																	
Year Ending December 31																	
Deficit (-) or Surplus	-8,126	-4,816	....	....	....	....	....	....	....	....	....	....	....	....	....	Deficit (-) or Surplus	80
Revenue	6,482	8,979	6,820^P	....	....	....	....	....	....	....	....	....	....	....	....	Revenue	81
Grants Received	9,532	9,496	....	....	....	....	....	....	....	....	....	....	....	....	....	Grants Received	81z
Cash Adj.& Unall.Rev. & Grants	3	35	....	....	....	....	....	....	....	....	....	....	....	....	....	Cash Adj.& Unall.Rev. & Grants	81x
Expenditure	24,142	23,326	21,037^P	....	....	....	....	....	....	....	....	....	....	....	....	Expenditure	82
Lending Minus Repayments	1	—	67^P	....	....	....	....	....	....	....	....	....	....	....	....	Lending Minus Repayments	83
Financing																	
Domestic	563	2,357	....	....	....	....	....	....	....	....	....	....	....	....	....	Domestic	84a
Foreign	7,563	2,460	....	....	....	....	....	....	....	....	....	....	....	....	....	Foreign	85a
Debt: Domestic	....	....	....	....	....	....	....	....	....	....	....	....	....	....	....	Debt: Domestic	88a
Foreign	....	....	....	....	....	....	....	....	....	....	....	....	....	....	....	Foreign	89a
National Accounts																	
Billions of Francs																	
Gross Domestic Product (GDP)	48.1	51.5	51.5	61.7	64.0	66.4	68.3	69.1	75.5	80.4	84.1	....	....	....	....	Gross Domestic Product (GDP)	99b
Midyear Estimates																	
Population	.45	.48	.49	.51	.51	.52	.54	.56	.57	.59	.61	.62	.65	.66	.66	Population	99z

(See notes in the back of the book.)

Congo, Dem. Rep. of

		1970	1971	1972	1973	1974	1975	1976	1977	1978	1979	1980	1981	1982	1983	1984
Exchange Rates									*N.Zaïres per Bill.SDRs through 1980, per Mill. SDRs 1981-90, per Thous.*							
Market Rate	aa	166.7	181.0	181.0	201.1	204.1	195.1	333.4	336.4	437.1	889.1	1,268.9	‡2.1	2.1	10.5	13.2
										N.Zaïres per Bill. US$ through 1980, per Mill. US$ 1981-90, per Thous.							
Market Rate	ae	166.7	166.7	166.7	166.7	166.7	166.7	287.0	277.0	335.5	674.9	994.9	‡1.8	1.9	10.0	13.5
Market Rate	rf	166.6	166.6	166.6	166.6	166.6	166.6	264.0	285.6	278.6	576.1	933.1	‡1.5	1.9	4.3	12.0
													Index Numbers (1995=100):			
Market Rate	ahx	125,497.3	8,124.9	125,497.3	9,912.8	9,912.8	9,912.8	6,581.5	73,241.1	75,558.8	36,884.2	22,747.5	15,434.9	10,916.9	7,896.2	1,746.0
Nominal Effective Exchange Rate	nec	....	....	....	....	....	....	....	....	....	14,208.3	8,949.5	7,093.4	5,951.5	4,934.4	1,295.5
Real Effective Exchange Rate	rec	....	....	....	....	....	....	....	....	....	....	453.7	420.3	442.7	515.9	179.1
Fund Position														*Millions of SDRs:*		
Quota	2f.s	113.00	113.00	113.00	113.00	113.00	113.00	113.00	113.00	152.00	152.00	228.00	228.00	228.00	291.00	291.00
SDRs	1b.s	15.62	15.71	7.36	6.88	6.39	19.96	27.10	.03	4.39	.12	—	.56	.02	20.97	—
Reserve Position in the Fund	1c.s	28.27	28.27	28.27	28.27	28.27	—	—	—	—	—	—	23.46	—	—	—
Total Fund Cred.&Loans Outstg.	2tl	—	—	28.23	28.23	28.23	73.25	180.64	220.33	247.11	271.57	292.75	407.45	492.93	593.87	688.45
International Liquidity										*Millions of US Dollars Unless Otherwise Indicated:*							
Total Reserves minus Gold	1l.d	136.00	90.87	123.18	172.79	118.80	47.91	50.28	133.87	125.75	206.69	204.11	151.55	38.87	101.56	137.37
SDRs	1b.d	15.62	17.06	7.99	8.30	7.82	23.37	31.49	.04	5.72	.16	—	.65	.02	21.95	—
Reserve Position in the Fund	1c.d	28.27	30.69	30.69	34.10	34.61	—	—	—	—	—	—	27.31	—	—	—
Foreign Exchange	1d.d	92.11	43.12	84.50	130.39	76.36	24.54	18.79	133.83	120.03	206.53	204.11	123.59	38.85	79.61	137.37
Gold (Million Fine Troy Ounces)	1ad	1.425	1.439	1.454	1.464	.500	.260	.260	.260	.308	.252	.298	.358	.410	.440	.466
Gold (National Valuation)	1and	49.88	50.37	50.89	51.24	17.50	9.10	10.98	10.98	58.52	91.44	153.07	136.12	156.94	154.55	141.13
Monetary Authorities: Other Liab.	4..d	.10	.19	.74	.39	20.82	28.62	18.63	56.86	48.19	47.73	133.13	61.33	168.56	6,572.27	301.01
Deposit Money Banks: Assets	7a.d	37.16	35.51	37.56	50.53	72.62	105.20	113.39	149.33	162.29	131.99	171.65	171.65	146.62	110.66	74.65
Liabilities	7b.d	2.14	5.70	11.57	14.87	17.04	149.65	48.73	57.34	41.92	47.79	43.97	39.59	50.28	24.69	12.63
Monetary Authorities										*Thousandths (.000) of New Zaïres through 1979; New Zaïres 1980-87;*							
Foreign Assets	11	30,880	23,545	29,150	37,145	22,716	9,612	30,088	40,136	61,888	201,692	‡355	526	542	28,659	2,570
Claims on Central Government	12a	56,278	39,374	48,431	57,322	100,734	139,243	249,291	368,144	620,305	827,651	‡944	1,554	3,096	23,450	4,547
Claims on Nonfin.Pub.Enterprises	12c	—	—	—	—	—	—	—	—	—	—	‡—	—	—	—	45
Claims on Private Sector	12d	—	—	—	—	—	—	9,693	10,680	10,789	1,438	‡1	2	37	—	34
Claims on Deposit Money Banks	12e	—	—	—	1,600	6,100	4,500	700	6,967	3,633	5,933	‡43	17	11	191	383
Claims on Other Banking Insts	12f	66	100	148	148	148	173	173	174	358	358	‡—	—	1	1	7
Reserve Money	14	47,583	41,408	52,188	61,248	74,819	105,140	191,862	247,423	386,327	316,048	‡677	1,078	2,065	33,041	5,220
of which: Currency Outside DMBs	14a	24,960	27,766	32,552	40,061	53,029	68,457	95,577	155,203	266,599	136,193	‡418	697	1,094	2,047	2,934
Time & Foreign Currency Deposits	15	1,396	6,536	3,305	16,014	16,891	1,003	3,010	4,456	13,954	32,011	‡20	46	97	17	36
Restricted Deposits	16b	614	1,495	1,457	2,037	11,865	7,071	13,923	77,878	149,118	195,836	‡146	139	272	60,119	751
Foreign Liabilities	16c	17	32	5,231	5,741	9,231	19,062	65,573	89,875	124,190	273,653	‡504	976	1,364	72,228	13,158
Central Government Deposits	16d	29,456	3,736	3,891	4,077	6,820	8,110	9,205	11,973	89,841	121,779	‡107	247	408	17,829	140
Counterpart Funds	16e	1,917	2,247	1,635	1,318	748	582	2,044	4,617	8,655	12,691	‡1	3	6	621	36
Capital Accounts	17a	5,835	7,727	9,942	9,632	9,659	9,826	49,897	43,358	82,114	100,599	‡183	222	196	89,990	1,428
Other Items (Net)	17r	407	−161	81	−3,851	−335	2,735	−45,569	−53,483	−157,226	−15,544	‡−294	−611	−292	−221,545	−11,897
Deposit Money Banks										*Thousandths (.000) of New Zaïres through 1979; New Zaïres 1980-87;*							
Reserves	20	18,648	10,802	15,825	15,692	18,868	26,567	90,321	77,147	116,734	137,408	‡237	337	800	1,037	2,015
Foreign Assets	21	6,193	5,918	6,261	8,422	12,103	17,533	32,538	41,359	54,456	89,063	‡171	267	212	1,099	1,006
Claims on Central Government	22a	5,834	8,336	8,114	7,637	12,853	15,613	29,778	30,050	39,320	42,217	‡54	58	58	59	84
Claims on Nonfin.Pub.Enterprises	22c	414	577	582	2,580	4,275	11,499	8,547	9,489	4,910	4,027	‡2	10	5	5	21
Claims on Private Sector	22d	13,717	17,992	28,600	43,041	73,438	94,344	109,035	158,357	199,540	276,831	‡367	422	597	939	1,469
Claims on Other Banking Insts	22f	—	—	—	—	—	17	20	30	30	30	‡—	—	—	—	—
Demand Deposits	24	32,852	31,399	40,649	50,146	71,813	73,576	113,691	166,342	257,547	364,600	‡453	637	1,227	2,079	2,739
Time & Foreign Currency Deposits	25	5,733	6,100	9,886	12,990	20,080	29,163	29,950	55,953	70,969	96,764	‡138	167	254	297	414
Restricted Deposits	26b	2,703	1,723	1,505	2,137	6,305	6,725	20,648	26,640	21,320	18,338	‡32	124	28	83	61
Foreign Liabilities	26c	357	950	1,928	2,478	2,840	24,941	13,983	15,880	14,067	32,254	‡44	72	96	248	170
Central Government Deposits	26d	284	523	837	857	944	1,262	2,907	2,883	9,781	15,933	‡22	27	42	268	133
Counterpart Funds	26e	940	34	1	5	3	—	—	56	59	3	‡—	—	—	—	—
Credit from Monetary Authorities	26g	—	—	—	1,600	6,100	4,500	700	6,967	3,633	5,933	‡43	17	11	191	383
Capital Accounts	27a	3,547	4,331	6,782	7,432	8,633	10,090	15,156	17,355	20,538	34,888	‡56	86	128	259	469
Other Items (Net)	27r	−1,612	−1,435	−2,208	−272	4,820	15,317	73,205	24,354	17,076	−19,136	‡42	−34	−116	−286	228
Post Office: Checking Deposits	24..i	617	710	959	1,248	1,658	2,151	2,168	2,116	2,006	2,248	‡3	3	3	3	4
Monetary Survey										*Thousandths (.000) of New Zaïres through 1979; New Zaïres 1980-87;*							
Foreign Assets (Net)	31n	36,700	28,481	28,251	37,349	22,748	−16,858	−16,931	−24,261	−21,913	−15,153	‡−21	−255	−707	−42,717	−9,752
Domestic Credit	32	47,185	62,829	82,105	107,043	185,342	253,668	396,594	564,182	777,636	1,017,089	‡1,241	1,776	3,346	6,359	5,939
Claims on Central Govt. (Net)	32an	32,988	44,160	52,776	61,274	107,481	147,635	269,126	385,453	562,009	734,405	‡871	1,341	2,707	5,414	4,362
Claims on Nonfin.Pub.Enterprises	32c	414	577	582	2,580	4,275	11,499	8,547	9,489	4,910	4,027	‡2	10	5	5	67
Claims on Private Sector	32d	13,717	17,992	28,600	43,041	73,438	94,344	118,728	169,037	210,329	278,269	‡368	424	634	939	1,503
Claims on Other Banking Insts	32f	66	100	148	148	148	189	193	204	388	388	‡—	—	1	1	7
Money	34	62,272	62,146	77,659	96,217	129,474	152,964	219,867	342,183	536,191	523,345	‡903	1,400	2,469	33,903	5,811
Quasi-Money	35	7,129	12,636	13,191	29,004	36,971	30,166	32,959	60,410	84,923	128,774	‡158	213	351	314	450
of which: Fgn. Currency Deposits	35x	....	....	....	....	....	....	....	....	....	....			77	87	118
Restricted Deposits	36b	3,318	3,217	2,962	4,174	18,170	13,795	34,571	104,519	170,438	214,173	‡178	262	300	60,202	813
Counterpart Funds	36e	2,856	2,281	1,636	1,323	751	582	2,044	4,674	8,715	12,694	‡1	3	6	621	36
Capital Accounts	37a	9,382	12,058	16,725	17,064	18,292	19,916	65,053	60,714	102,652	135,488	‡239	308	325	90,249	1,897
Revaluation Accounts	37ar	....	....	....	....	....	....	....	....	....	....				—	−7,208
Other Items (Net)	37r	−1,072	−1,027	−1,816	−3,391	4,432	19,386	25,169	−32,577	−147,196	−12,538	‡−260	−665	−813	−221,648	−4,325
Money plus Quasi-Money	35l	69,401	74,782	90,850	125,221	166,445	183,130	252,827	402,593	621,114	652,120	‡1,061	1,613	2,821	34,217	6,261

1985	1986	1987	1988	1989	1990	1991	1992	1993	1994	1995	1996	1997	1998	1999		
SDRs 191-92, per SDR thereafter: End of Period															**Exchange Rates**	
20.4	29.0	62.2	122.9	199.1	948.4	I30.4	912.1	I48.1	4,744.5	22,046.1	....	143,020.5	....	....	Market Rate	aa
US$ 1991-92, per US$ thereafter: End of Period (ae) Period Average (rf)																
18.6	23.7	43.8	91.3	151.5	666.7	I21.2	663.3	I35.0	3,250.0	14,831.0	....	106,000.0	....	...	Market Rate	ae
16.6	19.9	37.5	62.3	127.1	239.5	I5.2	215.1	I2.5	1,194.1	7,024.4	....	....	....	...	Market Rate	rf
Period Averages																
1,265.7	1,056.7	573.3	348.0	167.6	100.0	11.5	.3	—	—	100.0	....	....	....	...	Market Rate	ahx
1,077.6	795.0	401.0	262.7	159.2	100.0	11.8	.3	—	—	100.0	....	....	....	...	Nominal Effective Exchange Rate	nec
162.0	161.8	138.9	145.1	143.6	119.3	115.7	112.9	149.7	113.8	100.0	99.5	122.1	126.8	340.7	Real Effective Exchange Rate	rec
End of Period															**Fund Position**	
291.00	291.00	291.00	291.00	291.00	291.00	291.00	291.00	291.00	291.00	291.00	291.00	291.00	291.00	291.00	Quota	2f. s
.19	—	.08	—	3.74	—	—	—	—	—	—	—	—	—	—	SDRs	1b. s
—	—	—	—	—	—	—	—	—	—	—	—	—	—	—	Reserve Position in the Fund	1c. s
735.11	699.67	681.26	584.07	478.19	366.28	330.31	330.31	330.31	327.27	326.37	301.26	301.26	300.71	300.03	Total Fund Cred.&Loans Outstg.	2tl
End of Period															**International Liquidity**	
189.71	268.62	180.77	186.94	195.08	219.07	182.85	156.73	46.20	120.69	146.60	82.50	....	....	—	Total Reserves minus Gold	1l. d
.21	—	.11	—	4.91	—	—	—	—	—	—	—	—	—	—	SDRs	1b. d
—	—	—	—	—	—	—	—	—	—	—	—	—	—	—	Reserve Position in the Fund	1c. d
189.50	268.62	180.66	186.94	190.17	219.07	182.85	156.73	46.20	120.69	146.60	82.50	....		...	Foreign Exchange	1d. d
.445	.467	.488	.450	.216	.108	.029	.028	.022	.028	.028	....	.054		...	Gold (Million Fine Troy Ounces)	1ad
145.52	182.55	237.41	184.57	86.62	42.23	10.25	9.32	8.59	10.71	10.83	....	15.80		...	Gold (National Valuation)	1and
801.06	487.75	248.25	264.07	198.67	217.99	305.63	290.50	272.40	280.95	331.50	....	....		...	Monetary Authorities: Other Liab.	4.. d
77.49	104.39	125.48	94.58	174.81	131.61	86.13	68.00	62.37	81.18	69.18	....	....		...	Deposit Money Banks: Assets	7a. d
17.97	43.50	48.33	47.34	67.55	53.13	39.62	27.72	27.31	31.29	16.75	....	....		...	Liabilities	7b. d
Thousands 1988-91; Millions 1992-93; Billions Beg. 1994: End of Period															**Monetary Authorities**	
2,844	10,641	16,901	I26	53	171	4,664	I122	6,682	I515	2,528	....			...	Foreign Assets	11
4,756	8,255	10,805	I44	115	541	7,928	I243	4,183	I168	167	....			...	Claims on Central Government	12a
57	81	102	I1	1	8	431	I1	2	I1	32	....			...	Claims on Nonfin.Pub.Enterprises	12c
44	402	486	I1	2	3	20	I3	80	I3	70	....			...	Claims on Private Sector	12d
727	1,243	5,075	I5	13	16	6	I—	127	I16	823	....			...	Claims on Deposit Money Banks	12e
55	111	134	I—	—	1	3	I—	7	I1	93	....			...	Claims on Other Banking Insts	12f
6,666	10,703	21,497	I47	84	239	5,817	I258	6,999	I235	1,767	....			...	Reserve Money	14
4,098	6,329	12,085	I28	51	142	3,615	I121	4,693	I277	1,684	....			...	*of which: Currency Outside DMBs*	14a
98	72	133	I—	1	11	512	I3	688	I71	152	....			...	Time & Foreign Currency Deposits	15
299	1,032	1,439	I4	7	41	1,117	I20	1,262	I100	487	....			...	Restricted Deposits	16b
29,914	31,843	53,245	I96	125	493	16,515	I494	25,414	I2,466	12,112	....			...	Foreign Liabilities	16c
168	397	406	I4	10	24	148	I3	34	I30	66	....			...	Central Government Deposits	16d
51	38	35	I—	—	—	—	I—	—	I—	—	....			...	Counterpart Funds	16e
2,930	5,115	8,081	I27	40	117	2,982	I107	4,537	I412	2,484	....			...	Capital Accounts	17a
-30,034	-26,821	-49,137	I-100	-83	-185	-14,037	I-517	-27,853	I-2,611	-13,353	....			...	Other Items (Net)	17r
Thousands 1988-91; Millions 1992-93; Billions Beg. 1994: End of Period															**Deposit Money Banks**	
2,241	4,026	9,077	I15	29	64	1,759	I131	2,122	I26	64	....			...	Reserves	20
1,441	2,474	5,500	I9	26	88	1,828	I45	2,183	I264	1,026	....			...	Foreign Assets	21
95	213	839	I1	2	4	14	I—	23	I18	8	....			...	Claims on Central Government	22a
4	26	—	I—	—	2	21	I—	8	I8	17	....			...	Claims on Nonfin.Pub.Enterprises	22c
1,824	3,190	7,644	I13	21	38	322	I14	246	I70	351	....			...	Claims on Private Sector	22d
—	—	—	I—	—	—	—	I—	—	I—	—	....			...	Claims on Other Banking Insts	22f
3,173	5,416	10,319	I19	33	70	1,961	I126	1,618	I92	187	....			...	Demand Deposits	24
519	851	2,284	I8	9	36	652	I23	1,077	I141	630	....			...	Time & Foreign Currency Deposits	25
429	604	1,209	I1	6	18	158	I2	194	I6	21	....			...	Restricted Deposits	26b
334	1,031	2,118	I4	10	35	841	I18	956	I102	248	....			...	Foreign Liabilities	26c
167	145	435	I1	2	5	60	I5	100	I—	—	....			...	Central Government Deposits	26d
—	—	144	I—	—	—	—	I—	—	I—	—	....			...	Counterpart Funds	26e
727	1,243	5,075	I5	13	16	6	I—	127	I16	823	....			...	Credit from Monetary Authorities	26g
728	1,576	1,809	I4	11	32	213	I10	114	I20	412	....			...	Capital Accounts	27a
-472	-938	-332	I-4	-6	-17	52	I5	396	I9	-856	....			...	Other Items (Net)	27r
5	8	40	I—	—	—	—	I—	—	I—	—	....			...	Post Office: Checking Deposits	24.. i
Thousands 1988-91; Millions 1992-93; Billions Beg. 1994: End of Period															**Monetary Survey**	
-25,963	-19,759	-32,962	I-65	-56	-270	-10,864	I-345	-17,505	I-1,789	-8,806	....			...	Foreign Assets (Net)	31n
6,506	11,745	19,208	I55	129	567	8,531	I253	4,415	I238	673	....			...	Domestic Credit	32
4,522	7,935	10,843	I41	104	516	7,734	I235	4,072	I156	109	....			...	Claims on Central Govt. (Net)	32an
61	107	102	I1	1	9	452	I1	10	I8	49	....			...	Claims on Nonfin.Pub.Enterprises	32c
1,868	3,592	8,130	I13	23	41	342	I16	326	I73	421	....			...	Claims on Private Sector	32d
55	111	134	I—	—	1	3	I—	7	I1	93	....			...	Claims on Other Banking Insts	32f
7,495	11,966	22,829	I50	88	242	6,019	I254	6,495	I373	1,889	....			...	Money	34
617	924	2,417	I8	10	47	1,164	I26	1,765	I211	783	....			...	Quasi-Money	35
268	305	736	I2	5	34	1,088	I23	1,627	I209	774	....			...	*of which: Fgn. Currency Deposits*	35x
729	1,636	2,647	I5	13	59	1,275	I23	1,456	I107	508	....			...	Restricted Deposits	36b
51	38	179	I—	—	—	—	I—	—	I—	—	....			...	Counterpart Funds	36e
3,659	6,691	9,890	I31	51	149	3,195	I117	4,651	I432	2,897	....			...	Capital Accounts	37a
-10,019	169	-5,523	I-29	121	301	-7,861	I-287	-11,572	I-1,435	-6,858	....			...	Revaluation Accounts	37ar
-20,379	-27,793	-43,997	I-74	-211	-500	-6,125	I-225	-15,885	I-1,239	-7,352	....			...	Other Items (Net)	37r
8,112	12,890	25,246	I58	98	289	7,182	I280	8,260	I584	2,672	....			...	Money plus Quasi-Money	35l

Congo, Dem. Rep. of

636

	1970	1971	1972	1973	1974	1975	1976	1977	1978	1979	1980	1981	1982	1983	1984
Other Banking Institutions										*Thousandths (.000) of New Zaïres through 1979;*					
Claims on Private Sector 42d	....	....	—	—	—	—	—	—	—	—	I—	....	....	....	....
Sight Deposits 44	....	....	—	—	—	—	—	—	—	—	I—	....	....	....	....
Time and Savings Deposits......... 45	....	....	—	—	—	—	—	—	—	—	I—	....	....	....	....
Central Govt. Lending Funds 46f	—	—	—	—	—	—	—	—	—	—	I—	....	....	....	....
Other Items (Net) 47r	....	....	—	—	—	—	—	—	—	—	I—	....	....	....	....
Interest Rates														*Percent Per Annum*	
Discount Rate *(End of Period)* 60	....	....	....	....	....	....	....	12.0	12.0	12.0	12.0	15.0	20.0	20.0	
Prices													*Index Numbers (1995=100):*		
Consumer Prices 64	—	—	—	—	—	I—	—	—	—	—	—	—	—	—	—
Mining Production(1980=100)........... 66zx	91.7	95.1	100.3ᵉ	109.7	113.1	109.9	98.1	103.5	94.6	88.7	100.0	106.6	102.1	106.0	110.5
International Transactions													*Millions of US Dollars*		
Exports .... 70..d	781	687	738	1,013	1,381	865	944	989	931	1,514	1,627	544	399	1,080	1,005
Imports, c.i.f. .... 71..d	179	203	208	251	349	300	224	203	196	199	278	223	160	157	685
Government Finance									*Thousandths (.000) of New Zaïres through 1979; New Zaïres 1980-87;*						
Deficit (-) or Surplus............. 80	-6,767	I-25,533	-27,333	-47,000	-108,100	-72,033	-209,000	-149,867	-198,467	-182,867	I-111	-719	-1,161	....	....
Revenue 81	107,333	I98,733	102,100	128,433	178,033	145,033	163,533	229,367	246,333	660,100	I1,266	1,581	2,060	3,821	8,950
Grants Received 81z	9,967	I10,867	12,667	18,100	18,000	18,467	27,400	47,167	57,033	158,567	I284	387	335	....	....
Expenditure 82	123,267	I132,300	141,567	192,733	285,400	235,933	402,033	426,100	502,067	1,000,267	I1,660	2,688	3,549	....	....
Lending Minus Repayments 83	800	I2,833	533	800	18,733	-400	-2,100	300	-233	1,267	I1	—	7	....	....
Financing															
Domestic 84a	4,200	I10,600	9,267	10,633	68,600	37,433	173,700	97,467	175,200	161,633	I69	479	1,069	....	....
Foreign 85a	2,567	I14,933	18,067	36,367	39,500	34,600	35,300	52,400	23,267	21,233	I42	241	92	....	....
Debt: Domestic 88a	....	I47,067	57,233	65,367	114,067	154,100	277,467	381,600	568,900	812,967	I1,041	1,660	2,731	....	....
Foreign 89a	....	I53,400	47,700	88,900	127,233	159,567	304,100	358,167	477,767	951,333	I2,532	4,378	2,693	....	58,580
National Accounts									*Thousandths (.000) of New Zaïres through 1979; New Zaïres 1980-87;*						
Exports of Goods & Services 90c	138,333	124,567	125,833	187,233	272,400	173,167	308,867	372,267	405,433	914,033	I2,333	3,000	3,667	8,667	23,667
Government Consumption 91f	88,500	94,967	88,333	104,100	142,600	150,633	185,100	257,400	297,800	619,000	I919	2,000	2,467	3,567	6,200
Gross Fixed Capital Formation 93e	67,500	99,767	123,767	124,000	183,667	182,500	218,600	457,200	316,733	508,633	I1,145	1,558	2,433	4,767	10,033
Increase/Decrease(-) in Stocks 93i	14,000	15,433	5,133	23,333	—	21,767	28,600	50,633	18,933	217,700	I281	431	-267	-367	-100
Private Consumption 96f	137,733	170,733	216,600	268,300	313,500	406,767	696,400	949,533	1,270,733	2,228,767	I11,000	14,667	21,233	38,567	76,800
Imports of Goods & Services 98c	-133,533	-155,767	-173,900	-215,167	-312,467	-295,133	-484,167	-768,300	-482,800	-786,467	I-2,126	-3,000	-3,333	-8,000	-22,000
Gross Domestic Product (GDP) 99b	312,533	349,700	385,767	491,800	599,700	639,333	953,333	1,318,667	1,826,667	3,701,667	I13,333	18,333	26,167	47,267	94,600
Net Factor Inc/Pmts(-) Abroad .. 98.n	-18,633	-18,500	-19,167	-25,067	-35,033	-31,367	-38,933	-50,200	-59,833	-128,067	I-247	-667	-633	-1,367	-5,533
Gross National Income (GNI) 99a	262,300	283,867	314,000	421,967	505,533	528,433	777,900	1,050,633	1,420,000	2,827,467	I13,000	18,000	25,733	46,267	89,567
Net National Income 99e	275,767	291,733	279,333	378,333	463,367	487,200	719,467	848,133	1,186,767	2,323,033	I12,667	17,333	24,933	44,833	86,733
GDP Vol.1987 Prices(Thousands)....... 99b.p	234	248	248	268	277	263	249	251	237	238	244	249	248	252	266
GDP Volume (1995=100) .... 99bv p	128.0	135.7	135.9	146.9	151.5	144.0	136.3	137.4	130.0	130.6	133.5	136.6	136.0	137.9	145.5
GDP Deflator (1995=1 trillion) .... 99bi p	6.1	6.4	7.1	8.4	9.9	11.1	17.5	24.0	35.1	70.8	249.5	335.2	480.6	856.0	1,623.3
GDP Deflator (1995=10 billions)........ 99bi p	....	....	....	....	....	....	....	....	....	....	....	....	....	....	....
GDP Deflator (1995=100) .... 99bi p	....	....	....	....	....	....	....	....	....	....	....	....	....	....	....
														Millions:	
Population........................... 99z	21.64	22.22	22.86	23.51	24.17	I22.58	23.29	24.02	24.78	I25.56	26.38	27.23	28.12	29.04	29.92

	1985	1986	1987	1988	1989	1990	1991	1992	1993	1994	1995	1996	1997	1998	1999		

New Zaïres in 1980: End of Period

	1985	1986	1987	1988	1989	1990	1991	1992	1993	1994	1995	1996	1997	1998	1999	Series	Code
																Other Banking Institutions	
	....	....	....	....	....	....	....	....	....	....	....	....	....	....	....	Claims on Private Sector	42d
	....	....	....	....	....	....	....	....	....	....	....	....	....	....	....	Sight Deposits	44
	....	....	....	....	....	....	....	....	....	....	....	....	....	....	....	Time and Savings Deposits	45
	....	....	....	....	....	....	....	....	....	....	....	....	....	....	....	Central Govt. Lending Funds	46f
	....	....	....	....	....	....	....	....	....	....	....	....	....	....	....	Other Items (Net)	47r

Percent Per Annum

	1985	1986	1987	1988	1989	1990	1991	1992	1993	1994	1995	1996	1997	1998	1999	Series	Code
																Interest Rates	
	26.0	26.0	29.0	37.0	50.0	45.0	55.0	55.0	95.0	145.0	125.0	238.0	....	....	....	Discount Rate *(End of Period)*	60

Period Averages

	1985	1986	1987	1988	1989	1990	1991	1992	1993	1994	1995	1996	1997	1998	1999	Series	Code
																Prices	
	I—	—	—	I—	—	—	—	I—	.1	15.6	100.0	758.8	2,090.7	....	....	Consumer Prices	64
	....	....	....	....	....	....	....	....	....	....	....	....	....	....	....	Mining Production(1980=100)	66zx

Millions of US Dollars

	1985	1986	1987	1988	1989	1990	1991	1992	1993	1994	1995	1996	1997	1998	1999	Series	Code
																International Transactions	
	950	1,100	974	1,120	1,254	999	830	426	368	419	438	592	....	....	....	Exports	70..d
	792	875	756	763	850	888	711	420	372	382	397	424	....	....	....	Imports, c.i.f.	71..d

Thousands 1988-91; Millions 1992-93; Billions Beg. 1994: Yr.End. Dec. 31

	1985	1986	1987	1988	1989	1990	1991	1992	1993	1994	1995	1996	1997	1998	1999	Series	Code
																Government Finance	
	....	....	....	I-44	—	-146	-6,782	I-265	-3,694	I-123	8	-934	-6,291	....	....	Deficit (-) or Surplus	80
	14,240	16,683	29,347	I54	131	226	2,351	I59	1,216	I208	2,120	15,688	40,364	....	....	Revenue	81
	....	....	....	I13	25	48	529	I6	30	I17	1,177	17,091	32,298	....	....	Grants Received	81z
	....	....	....	I111	156	420	9,662	I306	4,831	I331	3,289	33,713	78,953	....	....	Expenditure	82
				I—	—	—	—	I24	109	I17	—	—	—	....	....	Lending Minus Repayments	83
																Financing	
	....	....	....	I44	-3	146	6,782	I254	3,596	I106	-8	934	6,291	....	....	Domestic	84a
				I—	4	—	—	I11	99	I17	—	—	—	....	....	Foreign	85a
	4,950	8,313	11,100	I45	30	176	7,734	I235	4,072	I156	175	3,654	30,363	....	....	Debt: Domestic	88a
				I642	1,090	6,314	49,057	I2,038	23,925	I11,645	92,166	701,896	1,187,133	....	....	Foreign	89a

Thousands 1988-91; Millions 1992-93; Billions in 1995

	1985	1986	1987	1988	1989	1990	1991	1992	1993	1994	1995	1996	1997	1998	1999	Series	Code
																National Accounts	
	32,333	39,667	74,667	I141	292	621	10,323	I381	3,050	....	11,291	....	....	....	....	Exports of Goods & Services	90c
	9,200	12,867	28,500	I70	116	258	6,282	I384	4,154	....	1,968	....	....	....	....	Government Consumption	91f
	13,333	20,633	39,833	I81	153	288	2,878	I125	606	....	3,827	....	....	....	....	Gross Fixed Capital Formation	93e
	1,600	600	800	I-1	11	-85	-245	I-4	-131	....	-54	....	....	....	....	Increase/Decrease(-) in Stocks	93i
	90,767	124,767	226,100	I415	860	1,600	37,688	I1,214	21,698	....	32,419	....	....	....	....	Private Consumption	96f
	-27,667	-37,667	-82,667	I-154	-285	-630	-11,000	I-309	-2,453	....	-9,406	....	....	....	....	Imports of Goods & Services	98c
	119,600	160,867	287,000	I552	1,147	2,239	47,208	I1,765	26,924	....	40,045	....	....	....	....	Gross Domestic Product (GDP)	99b
	9,300	-8,800	-13,400	I-20	-47	-63	-647	I1	-37	....	....	....	....	....	....	Net Factor Inc/Pmts(-) Abroad	98.n
	111,100	153,267	276,267	I536	1,109	2,183	46,699	I1,766	26,886	....	....	....	....	....	....	Gross National Income (GNI)	99a
	107,500	148,433	267,667	I519	1,075	2,117	45,298	I1,713	26,832	....	33,205	....	....	....	....	Net National Income	99e
	267	280	287	288	285	266	244	218	189	181	183	181	171	....	....	GDP Vol.1987 Prices(Thousands)	99b.p
	146.2	153.1	157.2	157.9	155.9	145.7	133.4	119.4	103.3	99.3	100.0	99.1	93.4	....	....	GDP Volume (1995=100)	99bv p
	2,042.8	2,623.9	4,559.2	8,734.7	....	....	....				....	....	....	....	....	GDP Deflator (1995=1 trillion)	99bi p
				87	184	384	8,835	369,187	6,506,440		....	....	....	....	....	GDP Deflator (1995=10 billions)	99bi p
	....	....	....	....	....	....	....		.1	....	100.0	....	....	....	....	GDP Deflator (1995=100)	99bi p

Midyear Estimates

	1985	1986	1987	1988	1989	1990	1991	1992	1993	1994	1995	1996	1997	1998	1999	Series	Code
	30.98	31.50	32.46	33.46	34.49	35.56	36.67	I40.53	42.25	43.90	45.42	46.77	47.99	49.14	50.34	**Population**	99z

(See notes in the back of the book.)

Congo, Republic of

		1970	1971	1972	1973	1974	1975	1976	1977	1978	1979	1980	1981	1982	1983	1984
Exchange Rates															*Francs per SDR:*	
Official Rate	aa	276.02	283.61	278.00	284.00	272.08	262.55	288.70	285.76	272.28	264.78	287.99	334.52	370.92	436.97	470.11
															Francs per US Dollar:	
Official Rate	ae	276.02	261.22	256.05	235.42	222.22	224.27	248.49	235.25	209.00	201.00	225.80	287.40	336.25	417.37	479.60
Official Rate	rf	276.40	275.59	252.03	222.89	240.70	214.31	238.95	245.68	225.66	212.72	211.28	271.73	328.61	381.07	436.96
Fund Position															*Millions of SDRs:*	
Quota	2f. s	13.00	13.00	13.00	13.00	13.00	13.00	13.00	13.00	17.00	17.00	25.50	25.50	25.50	37.30	37.30
SDRs	1b. s	.03	1.32	2.58	2.46	2.33	2.15	2.06	1.48	1.31	1.20	—	.90	.96	.21	2.13
Reserve Position in the Fund	1c. s	1.56	1.65	1.75	1.84	1.93	2.03	2.03	—	—	—	2.06	3.30	2.98	.48	
Total Fund Cred.&Loans Outstg.	2tl	—	—	—	—	—	—	—	9.34	16.68	21.58	17.44	12.70	12.63	12.27	11.12
International Liquidity												*Millions of US Dollars Unless Otherwise Indicated:*				
Total Reserves minus Gold	1l. d	8.88	10.82	10.34	7.86	24.10	13.81	12.17	13.53	9.43	42.23	85.90	123.37	37.01	7.36	4.11
SDRs	1b. d	.03	1.43	2.80	2.97	2.85	2.52	2.39	1.80	1.71	1.58	—	1.05	1.06	.22	2.09
Reserve Position in the Fund	1c. d	1.56	1.79	1.90	2.22	2.37	2.38	2.36	—	—	—	2.40	3.64	3.12	.47	
Foreign Exchange	1d. d	7.29	7.59	5.63	2.67	18.88	8.92	7.41	11.73	7.72	40.65	85.90	119.92	32.32	4.02	1.56
Gold (Million Fine Troy Ounces)	1ad	....	....	....	....	....	....	—	.006	.009	.011	.011	.011	.011	.011	.011
Gold (National Valuation)	1an d	....	....	....	....	....	—	.92	1.94	5.79	6.56	4.45	5.00	4.21	3.44	
Monetary Authorities: Other Liab.	4..d	.03	.09	.09	.04	.08	.06	3.62	3.96	2.76	2.14	1.65	1.53	.72	.47	1.40
Deposit Money Banks: Assets	7a. d	2.65	4.82	2.59	3.35	4.99	3.21	5.80	6.84	14.11	15.93	13.89	26.31	19.88	13.84	20.93
Liabilities	7b. d	7.63	7.37	11.78	9.10	12.06	21.07	24.97	57.31	63.37	64.79	56.79	93.93	81.13	95.05	106.82
Monetary Authorities															*Billions of Francs:*	
Foreign Assets	11	2.47	2.77	2.64	1.81	5.36	3.10	3.02	3.40	2.38	9.66	20.89	37.02	14.12	4.84	3.62
Claims on Central Government	12a	2.03	1.59	2.65	3.98	4.20	7.86	9.06	11.47	15.18	16.41	17.65	16.30	36.39	40.96	51.45
Claims on Deposit Money Banks	12e	2.78	3.81	4.74	5.41	4.55	5.91	7.58	8.77	11.24	10.27	4.08	8.82	21.94	30.68	38.27
Claims on Other Banking Insts	12f	....	....	....	....	....	....	....	....	....	....	....	....	....	....	....
Reserve Money	14	6.48	7.13	8.36	9.43	12.35	15.31	16.43	17.30	17.55	21.26	27.73	33.03	46.00	47.90	47.39
of which: Currency Outside DMBs	14a	6.02	6.71	7.99	9.15	11.86	14.34	15.29	16.13	16.53	19.17	23.06	31.21	44.21	44.33	45.03
Foreign Liabilities	16c	.01	.02	.02	.01	.02	.01	.90	4.00	6.59	8.61	9.04	8.94	9.61	10.92	11.13
Central Government Deposits	16d	.25	.09	.36	.34	.44	.29	.72	.41	1.31	1.62	2.03	16.61	12.48	12.17	29.11
Capital Accounts	17a	—	—	—	.02	.02	.02	.04	.04	.04	.04	1.42	1.21	1.61	1.70	1.57
Other Items (Net)	17r	.54	.91	1.29	1.40	1.28	1.23	1.56	1.89	3.32	4.82	2.40	2.35	2.76	3.79	4.14
Deposit Money Banks															*Billions of Francs:*	
Reserves	20	.46	.43	.37	.29	.48	.97	1.14	1.17	1.02	2.09	4.67	1.83	1.78	3.58	2.36
Foreign Assets	21	.74	1.23	.66	.77	1.11	.72	1.44	Ⅰ1.61	2.95	3.20	3.14	7.56	6.69	5.78	10.04
Claims on Central Government	22a	1.84	1.90	2.73	2.60	3.92	5.45	6.36	9.14	10.54	9.02	10.15	12.73	17.54	28.15	40.24
Claims on Nonfin.Pub.Enterprises	22c	....	....	....	....	....	....	....	....	....	....	....	....	....	....	....
Claims on Private Sector	22d	12.38	14.25	16.06	18.50	21.26	28.23	35.83	Ⅰ38.93	39.42	45.59	56.00	94.20	131.15	151.95	180.56
Claims on Other Banking Insts	22f	....	....	....	....	....	....	....	....	....	....	....	....	....	....	....
Claims on Nonbank Financial Insts	22g	....	....	....	....	....	....	....	....	....	....	....	....	....	....	....
Demand Deposits	24	7.06	7.40	6.93	8.03	12.13	12.83	16.06	Ⅰ14.76	16.65	20.65	31.50	44.47	54.41	47.58	57.66
Time and Savings Deposits	25	.92	1.12	1.27	1.41	1.86	2.14	2.61	3.87	3.92	5.30	7.06	17.01	18.35	23.33	20.92
Foreign Liabilities	26c	1.89	1.67	2.89	1.23	1.20	2.01	2.25	8.50	7.75	7.52	6.98	13.79	9.46	25.29	19.36
Long-Term Foreign Liabilities	26cl	.23	.21	.12	.87	1.48	2.71	3.95	4.98	5.49	5.50	5.84	13.21	17.82	14.39	31.88
Central Government Deposits	26d	.73	1.49	1.34	1.38	1.54	1.67	1.32	2.28	1.50	.97	1.37	4.86	17.38	33.02	41.95
Credit from Monetary Authorities	26g	2.35	3.25	4.21	4.54	4.27	5.55	6.66	8.77	11.24	10.27	5.08	9.11	21.94	30.68	38.27
Capital Accounts	27a	2.20	2.52	2.86	3.19	3.70	4.33	6.61	6.46	7.04	9.03	12.81	13.17	20.99	23.74	28.70
Other Items (Net)	27r	.03	.14	.20	1.52	.61	4.13	5.32	Ⅰ1.22	.33	.65	3.32	.72	–3.19	–8.63	–5.53
Post Office: Checking Deposits	24.. i	.32	.26	.31	.28	.43	.55	.60	.53	.53	.53	.53	.53	2.59	3.65	5.07
Postal Debt	26c. i	.89	.89	1.61	1.45	2.36	3.03	3.99	6.06	6.78	6.05	6.19	5.56	1.18	3.20	2.57
Monetary Survey															*Billions of Francs:*	
Foreign Assets (Net)	31n	1.31	2.30	.39	1.35	5.25	1.79	1.31	Ⅰ–7.49	–9.01	–3.27	8.00	21.85	1.74	–25.59	–16.83
Domestic Credit	32	15.27	16.15	19.74	23.37	27.41	39.59	49.20	Ⅰ56.85	62.33	68.43	80.40	101.76	155.23	175.87	201.19
Claims on Central Govt. (Net)	32an	2.89	1.90	3.68	4.87	6.14	11.35	13.37	17.92	22.91	22.85	24.40	7.56	24.07	23.92	20.63
Claims on Nonfin.Pub.Enterprises	32c	....	....	....	....	....	....	....	....	....	....	....	....	....	....	....
Claims on Private Sector	32d	12.38	14.25	16.06	18.50	21.26	28.23	35.83	Ⅰ38.93	39.42	45.59	56.00	94.20	131.15	151.95	180.56
Claims on Other Banking Insts	32f	....	....	....	....	....	....	....	....	....	....	....	....	....	....	....
Claims on Nonbank Financial Inst	32g	....	....	....	....	....	....	....	....	....	....	....	....	....	....	....
Money	34	13.08	14.11	14.92	17.18	24.00	27.17	31.34	Ⅰ30.89	33.18	39.82	54.56	75.67	98.62	91.91	102.69
Quasi-Money	35	.92	1.12	1.27	1.41	1.86	2.14	2.61	3.87	3.92	5.30	7.06	17.01	18.35	23.33	20.92
Other Items (Net)	37r	2.58	3.23	3.94	6.14	6.80	12.07	16.56	Ⅰ14.60	16.21	20.04	26.78	30.93	39.99	35.05	60.75
Money plus Quasi-Money	35l	14.00	15.23	16.19	18.58	25.85	29.31	33.95	Ⅰ34.76	37.10	45.12	61.62	92.68	116.97	115.24	123.61
Interest Rates															*Percent Per Annum:*	
Discount Rate *(End of Period)*	60	4.50	4.50	4.50	4.50	5.50	5.50	6.50	6.50	6.50	8.50	8.50	8.50	8.50	8.50	8.50
Deposit Rate	60l	....	....	....	....	....	....	....	....	5.75	5.50	6.50	6.50	6.50	7.50	7.50
Lending Rate	60p	....	....	....	....	....	....	....	....	13.00	9.00	11.00	11.00	11.00	12.00	12.00
Prices and Production															*Index Numbers (1995=100):*	
Wholesale Prices (1990=100)	63	18.5	18.6	21.0	22.1	25.5	29.0	32.9	Ⅰ37.0	40.6	44.3	50.5	57.4	66.2	70.8	81.1
Consumer Prices	64	11.6	12.0	13.2	13.7	14.4	16.9	18.1	20.7	22.8	24.7	26.5	Ⅰ31.0	34.9	37.6	42.6
Crude Petroleum Production	66aa	.2	.2	3.6	22.6	24.7	19.3	22.7	19.9	26.4	29.5	35.4	44.3	49.1	57.9	65.0

1985	1986	1987	1988	1989	1990	1991	1992	1993	1994	1995	1996	1997	1998	1999		
															Exchange Rates	
End of Period																
415.26	394.78	378.78	407.68	380.32	364.84	370.48	378.57	404.89	I780.44	728.38	753.06	807.94	791.61	I896.19	Official Rate	aa
End of Period (ae) Period Average (rf)																
378.05	322.75	267.00	302.95	289.40	256.45	259.00	275.32	294.77	I534.60	490.00	523.70	598.81	562.21	I652.95	Official Rate	ae
449.26	346.31	300.54	297.85	319.01	272.26	282.11	264.69	283.16	I555.20	499.15	511.55	583.67	589.95	I615.70	Official Rate	rf
															Fund Position	
End of Period																
37.30	37.30	37.30	37.30	37.30	37.30	37.30	57.90	57.90	57.90	57.90	57.90	57.90	57.90	84.60	Quota	2f. s
1.51	3.80	1.91	.84	1.21	1.17	.04	.04	.01	.03	.02	.01	.01	—	.08	SDRs	1b. s
.48	.48	.48	.48	.48	.47	.47	.47	.47	.47	.50	.54	.54	.54	.54	Reserve Position in the Fund	1c. s
8.99	16.03	13.56	11.40	8.75	7.61	4.00	4.00	3.50	14.00	12.50	26.40	24.83	24.26	21.14	Total Fund Cred.&Loans Outstg.	2tl
															International Liquidity	
End of Period																
3.96	6.82	3.40	4.70	6.10	5.91	4.76	4.01	1.34	50.36	59.30	90.99	59.92	.84	39.35	Total Reserves minus Gold	1l. d
1.66	4.65	2.71	1.13	1.59	1.66	.06	.06	.02	.05	.03	.02	.01	.01	.11	SDRs	1b. d
.53	.59	.68	.65	.63	.67	.67	.65	.64	.68	.75	.77	.72	.75	.74	Reserve Position in the Fund	1c. d
1.78	1.58	.01	2.93	3.88	3.58	4.03	3.31	.68	49.63	58.52	90.20	59.19	.08	38.51	Foreign Exchange	1d. d
.011	.011	.011	.011	.011	.011	.011	.011	.011	.011	.011	.011	.011	....	....	Gold (Million Fine Troy Ounces)	1ad
3.60	4.36	5.37	4.52	3.52	3.98	3.94	3.70	4.42	I4.21	4.29	4.10	3.24	3.21	2.10	Gold (National Valuation)	1an d
.85	.69	1.50	I130.34	144.14	34.87	66.41	43.48	38.71	17.20	18.62	16.48	13.53	35.97	25.10	Monetary Authorities: Other Liab.	4.. d
32.19	30.89	38.61	47.75	39.22	48.90	50.71	68.00	82.84	41.43	33.16	33.17	27.79	29.01	34.07	Deposit Money Banks: Assets	7a. d
138.92	169.43	85.21	71.80	60.61	59.31	63.58	96.22	58.86	50.04	28.91	25.81	14.13	41.82	39.17	Liabilities	7b. d
															Monetary Authorities	
End of Period																
2.87	3.60	2.35	I5.81	5.87	6.74	2.25	2.12	1.67	29.21	31.17	49.81	37.81	2.27	27.80	Foreign Assets	11
45.12	60.81	59.95	I53.37	53.37	55.19	I51.63	73.25	72.61	77.25	80.75	92.48	110.27	123.14	120.76	Claims on Central Government	12a
40.65	46.11	41.55	I28.66	31.44	28.14	I14.85	6.84	1.51	1.54	4.26	3.70	5.01	7.16	6.20	Claims on Deposit Money Banks	12e
....	....	....	12.39	11.94	13.03	12.26	—	—	—	—	—	—	—	—	Claims on Other Banking Insts	12f
52.94	53.91	59.53	I53.72	52.70	71.02	57.29	66.33	63.50	85.97	93.09	101.08	112.80	89.44	120.07	Reserve Money	14
50.19	51.09	56.87	I51.20	49.91	66.20	53.28	59.32	53.71	69.49	81.58	87.35	93.26	73.26	102.34	of which: Currency Outside DMBs	14a
7.79	9.13	7.08	I44.13	45.04	11.72	18.68	13.49	12.83	20.12	18.23	28.51	28.17	39.43	35.33	Foreign Liabilities	16c
22.33	36.83	28.86	I2.48	4.51	17.40	4.22	4.01	4.95	22.34	15.87	24.01	19.59	11.33	12.77	Central Government Deposits	16d
1.35	1.47	1.51	I5.42	5.08	4.74	4.90	5.44	6.10	9.35	8.51	8.68	9.00	8.50	9.82	Capital Accounts	17a
4.23	9.18	6.87	I-5.53	-4.72	-1.77	-4.09	-7.06	-11.58	-29.78	-19.53	-16.30	-16.47	-16.13	-23.24	Other Items (Net)	17r
															Deposit Money Banks	
End of Period																
2.75	2.78	2.63	I2.35	2.46	4.09	3.84	4.42	9.68	12.05	7.41	8.99	15.08	13.85	12.72	Reserves	20
12.17	9.97	10.31	I14.03	11.35	12.54	13.13	18.72	24.42	22.15	16.25	17.37	16.64	16.31	22.25	Foreign Assets	21
38.42	44.01	30.95	I45.16	41.45	39.81	36.96	I36.78	17.84	30.76	28.91	29.45	25.74	28.74	20.12	Claims on Central Government	22a
....	....	....	38.92	32.17	27.23	27.62	26.78	11.28	10.17	13.75	13.96	13.35	16.16	13.98	Claims on Nonfin.Pub.Enterprises	22c
201.24	202.88	186.91	I107.02	112.32	119.58	122.97	122.33	66.02	75.62	85.68	98.09	106.53	112.01	158.00	Claims on Private Sector	22d
....	....	....	.53	.95	1.09	1.26	.41	.06	.01	.02	.01	.30	.13	.78	Claims on Other Banking Insts	22f
....	....	....	.78	.29	.69	.62	.26	.40	.60	.84	1.05	1.16	1.33	.63	Claims on Nonbank Financial Insts	22g
63.73	48.12	47.08	I46.17	46.35	54.10	58.73	57.40	41.94	60.57	49.16	61.08	68.85	68.39	76.68	Demand Deposits	24
35.62	32.99	36.13	I39.07	45.13	46.84	48.61	49.86	28.48	24.78	24.34	31.00	35.14	31.94	26.84	Time and Savings Deposits	25
14.89	13.39	12.70	I13.41	14.60	12.87	I12.81	24.81	17.18	26.75	14.04	13.51	8.45	23.51	25.57	Foreign Liabilities	26c
37.63	41.30	10.06	I3.03	2.94	2.34	I3.66	1.68	.17		.13	.01	.01			Long-Term Foreign Liabilities	26cl
42.15	53.15	49.93	I52.16	16.95	17.15	19.48	I18.08	2.61	6.10	11.03	12.65	10.95	17.44	25.53	Central Government Deposits	26d
40.65	41.55	41.55	I28.66	31.44	28.14	I14.85	6.84	1.51	1.54	4.26	3.70	5.01	7.16	6.20	Credit from Monetary Authorities	26g
33.95	39.53	40.75	I36.59	54.45	57.07	I56.84	57.41	36.24	41.05	54.40	59.64	62.30	45.04	62.95	Capital Accounts	27a
-14.04	-14.93	-7.38	I-10.30	-10.86	-13.50	-8.58	I-6.38	1.57	-9.42	-4.51	-12.65	-11.91	-4.96	4.70	Other Items (Net)	27r
5.43	5.46	5.26	2.56	....	....	....	....	....	....	....	....	....	....	....	Post Office: Checking Deposits	24.. i
.35	.83	1.17	....	....	....	....	....	....	....	....	....	....	....	....	Postal Debt	26c. i
															Monetary Survey	
End of Period																
-7.63	-8.94	-7.11	I-40.73	-45.36	-7.65	I-19.77	-19.13	-4.09	4.49	15.02	25.15	17.82	-44.36	-10.86	Foreign Assets (Net)	31n
220.31	217.72	199.02	I203.52	231.04	222.06	I229.61	I237.72	160.65	165.98	183.04	198.39	226.80	252.73	275.96	Domestic Credit	32
19.06	14.84	12.11	I43.88	73.37	60.45	I64.89	I87.94	82.89	79.58	82.75	85.27	105.46	123.10	102.58	Claims on Central Govt. (Net)	32an
....	....	....	38.92	32.17	27.23	27.62	26.78	11.28	10.17	13.75	13.96	13.35	16.16	13.98	Claims on Nonfin.Pub.Enterprises	32c
201.24	202.88	186.91	I107.02	112.32	119.58	122.97	122.33	66.02	75.62	85.68	98.09	106.53	112.01	158.00	Claims on Private Sector	32d
....	....	....	12.92	12.89	14.12	13.52	.41	.06	.01	.02	.01	.30	.13	.78	Claims on Other Banking Insts	32f
....	....	....	.78	.29	.69	.62	.26	.40	.60	.84	1.05	1.16	1.33	.63	Claims on Nonbank Financial Inst	32g
113.92	99.24	103.98	I97.54	96.59	121.03	112.17	119.32	95.76	134.49	134.85	153.18	166.56	143.98	184.03	Money	34
35.62	32.99	36.13	I39.07	45.13	46.84	48.61	49.86	28.48	24.78	24.34	31.00	35.14	31.94	26.84	Quasi-Money	35
63.13	76.56	51.81	I26.18	43.96	46.54	I49.06	I49.41	32.32	11.20	38.87	39.37	42.92	32.45	54.23	Other Items (Net)	37r
149.54	132.22	140.10	I136.61	141.72	167.87	160.79	169.17	124.24	159.27	159.19	184.17	201.70	175.92	210.87	Money plus Quasi-Money	35l
															Interest Rates	
Percent Per Annum																
9.00	8.00	8.00	9.50	10.00	11.00	10.75	12.00	11.50	I7.75	8.60	7.75	7.50	7.00	7.60	Discount Rate (*End of Period*)	60
8.25	8.10	7.79	7.81	8.00	I7.50	7.50	7.50	7.75	8.08	5.50	5.46	5.00	5.00	5.00	Deposit Rate	60l
12.00	11.50	11.13	11.79	12.50	I18.50	18.15	17.77	17.46	17.50	16.00	22.00	22.00	22.00	22.00	Lending Rate	60p
															Prices and Production	
Period Averages																
86.4	89.7	93.8	96.0	98.1	100.0	96.4	98.0	101.0	....	....	....	....	....	....	Wholesale Prices (1990=100)	63
45.0	46.1	47.1	48.9	50.9	48.4	52.9	53.9	55.0	82.4	100.0	99.8	....	....	....	Consumer Prices	64
64.1	64.2	68.2	75.9	85.9	86.6	86.9	93.2	102.9	97.4	100.0	112.0	125.0	132.3	346.1	Crude Petroleum Production	66aa

Congo, Republic of

		1970	1971	1972	1973	1974	1975	1976	1977	1978	1979	1980	1981	1982	1983	1984
International Transactions																*Billions of Francs*
Exports	70	8.56	10.96	15.00	19.62	54.86	38.25	52.95	65.51	69.56	105.43	192.40	220.43	326.15	243.82	516.76
Imports, c.i.f.	71	16.39	22.57	26.27	28.56	30.54	36.33	41.16	50.82	58.26	61.95	122.54	121.31	251.90	246.97	269.95
Imports, f.o.b.	71.v	14.59	19.89	23.03	22.62	25.21	30.04	34.68	43.19	47.69	53.39	100.29	98.92	205.75	200.96	219.60
Balance of Payments																*Millions of US Dollars:*
Current Account, n.i.e.	78al d	....	....	....	....	....	....	....	....	−180.6	−99.4	−166.7	−460.7	−331.5	−400.9	210.2
Goods: Exports f.o.b.	78aa d	....	....	....	....	....	....	....	....	308.2	495.7	910.6	1,072.7	1,108.5	1,066.2	1,268.4
Goods: Imports f.o.b.	78ab d	....	....	....	....	....	....	....	....	−282.1	−363.0	−545.2	−803.6	−663.8	−649.5	−617.6
Trade Balance	78ac d	....	....	....	....	....	....	....	....	26.1	132.7	365.4	269.1	444.7	416.7	650.8
Services: Credit	78ad d	....	....	....	....	....	....	....	....	68.8	69.7	110.6	84.0	77.6	87.8	80.3
Services: Debit	78ae d	....	....	....	....	....	....	....	....	−259.2	−219.8	−480.1	−713.3	−697.3	−727.4	−391.3
Balance on Goods & Services	78af d	....	....	....	....	....	....	....	....	−164.3	−17.4	−4.0	−360.2	−175.1	−222.9	339.8
Income: Credit	78ag d	....	....	....	....	....	....	....	....	3.4	3.3	8.0	16.6	19.6	5.4	6.5
Income: Debit	78ah d	....	....	....	....	....	....	....	....	−58.0	−96.3	−169.6	−128.8	−158.0	−179.3	−133.5
Balance on Gds, Serv. & Inc.	78ai d	....	....	....	....	....	....	....	....	−218.9	−110.4	−165.6	−472.3	−313.4	−396.8	212.9
Current Transfers, n.i.e.: Credit	78aj d	....	....	....	....	....	....	....	....	67.1	50.5	85.3	71.6	37.2	51.3	55.1
Current Transfers: Debit	78ak d	....	....	....	....	....	....	....	....	−28.7	−39.4	−86.4	−59.9	−55.3	−55.4	−57.8
Capital Account, n.i.e.	78bc d	....	....	....	....	....	....	....	....							
Capital Account, n.i.e.: Credit	78ba d	....	....	....	....	....	....	....	....	—	—	—	—	—	—	—
Capital Account: Debit	78bb d	....	....	....	....	....	....	....	....	—	—	—	—	—	—	—
Financial Account, n.i.e.	78bj d	....	....	....	....	....	....	....	....	168.4	91.8	174.9	327.8	202.1	297.9	−291.5
Direct Investment Abroad	78bd d	....	....	....	....	....	....	....	....							
Dir. Invest. in Rep. Econ., n.i.e.	78be d	....	....	....	....	....	....	....	....	4.1	16.5	40.0	30.8	35.3	56.1	34.9
Portfolio Investment Assets	78bf d	....	....	....	....	....	....	....	....	—	—	—	—	—	—	
Equity Securities	78bk d	....	....	....	....	....	....	....	....	—	—	—	—	—	—	
Debt Securities	78bl d	....	....	....	....	....	....	....	....	—	—	—	—	—	—	
Portfolio Investment Liab., n.i.e.	78bg d	....	....	....	....	....	....	....	....	—	—	—	—	—	—	
Equity Securities	78bm d	....	....	....	....	....	....	....	....	—	—	—	—	—	—	
Debt Securities	78bn d	....	....	....	....	....	....	....	....	—	—	—	—	—	—	
Financial Derivatives Assets	78bw d	....	....	....	....	....	....	....	....	....	....	....	....	....	....	....
Financial Derivatives Liabilities	78bx d	....	....	....	....	....	....	....	....	....	....	....	....	....	....	....
Other Investment Assets	78bh d	....	....	....	....	....	....	....	....	−17.7	−14.0	−93.8	−183.8	−44.4	33.9	−255.5
Monetary Authorities	78bo d	....	....	....	....	....	....	....	....		—	—	—	—		
General Government	78bp d	....	....	....	....	....	....	....	....		−1.5	.1	.3	.3	1.4	
Banks	78bq d	....	....	....	....	....	....	....	....	—	.1	−.3	−16.3	2.3	1.0	−9.8
Other Sectors	78br d	....	....	....	....	....	....	....	....	−7.2	−.9	−.3	−16.3	2.3	1.0	−9.8
Other Investment Liab., n.i.e.	78bi d	....	....	....	....	....	....	....	....	−10.5	−11.6	−93.6	−167.5	−47.0	31.5	−245.8
Monetary Authorities	78bs d	....	....	....	....	....	....	....	....	182.0	89.3	228.7	480.8	211.1	208.0	−70.9
General Government	78bt d	....	....	....	....	....	....	....	....	1.5	−.8	−.3	.2	−.6	−.1	.6
Banks	78bu d	....	....	....	....	....	....	....	....	98.9	35.4	119.6	−4.4	183.3	77.7	31.1
Other Sectors	78bv d	....	....	....	....	....	....	....	....	−3.8	−1.1	2.2	21.4	.2	36.3	−2.6
										85.5	55.8	107.2	463.6	28.2	94.0	−100.1
Net Errors and Omissions	78ca d	....	....	....	....	....	....	....	....	−1.4	29.9	38.5	174.6	45.0	70.9	20.5
Overall Balance	78cb d	....	....	....	....	....	....	....	....	−13.6	22.3	46.7	41.8	−84.5	−32.1	−60.8
Reserves and Related Items	79da d	....	....	....	....	....	....	....	....	13.6	−22.3	−46.7	−41.8	84.5	32.1	60.8
Reserve Assets	79db d	....	....	....	....	....	....	....	....	4.6	−28.5	−49.3	−57.1	82.2	32.4	7.8
Use of Fund Credit and Loans	79dc d	....	....	....	....	....	....	....	....	9.0	6.4	−5.3	−5.7	−.1	−.4	−1.2
Exceptional Financing	79de d	....	....	....	....	....	....	....	....	—	−.1	7.8	21.0	2.4	—	54.2
Government Finance																*Billions of Francs:*
Deficit (-) or Surplus	80	−1.1	−2.4	....	....	....	....	....	....	....	....	ⱡ −18.8	.4	−93.4	−26.7	....
Revenue	81	16.7	17.6	18.8	20.1	44.1	47.8	48.3	....	....	....	ⱡ 157.4	214.3	261.7	280.5	....
Grants Received	81z	—	—	—	—	—	—	—	....	....	....	ⱡ 2.6	.8	1.2	3.5	....
Expenditure	82	17.8	20.0	....	....	....	....	....	....	....	....	ⱡ 177.9	214.3	355.6	310.5	....
Lending Minus Repayments	83	—	—	....	....	....	....	....	....	....	....	ⱡ .9	.4	.7	.2	....
Financing																
Domestic	84a	....	....	....	....	....	....	....	....	....	....	ⱡ 4.9	−.3	24.2	−15.0	....
Foreign	85a	....	....	....	....	....	....	....	....	....	....	ⱡ 13.9	−.1	69.2	41.6	....
National Accounts																*Billions of Francs*
Exports of Goods & Services	90c	26.4	28.9	29.3	38.2	75.0	59.4	71.2	....	78.6	....	203.0	314.3	383.5	454.2	590.7
Government Consumption	91f	18.1	22.9	27.6	28.2	37.8	54.3	61.2	61.2	45.5	....	63.4	72.8	95.8	120.0	141.7
Gross Fixed Capital Formation	93e	18.9	19.9	21.2	23.9	31.7	41.2	36.1	32.8	46.4	....	118.7	239.7	404.7	280.2	277.3
Increase/Decrease(-) in Stocks	93i									7.9	....	10.2	21.1	24.0	4.3	14.0
Private Consumption	96f	55.0	57.3	66.5	64.7	76.3	109.5	120.9	123.2	117.9	....	147.9	220.6	281.6	317.0	372.2
Imports of Goods & Services	98c	−43.9	−46.7	−53.6	−52.4	−83.3	−104.8	−116.0	....	−97.9	....	−182.8	−326.9	−478.1	−376.3	−437.3
Gross Domestic Product (GDP)	99b	74.5	82.3	91.0	102.6	137.0	159.6	173.4	181.7	198.3	254.5	360.4	541.7	711.5	799.4	958.5
Net Factor Inc/Pmts(-) Abroad	98.n	−2.2	−4.9	−4.6	−10.5	....	....	....	....	....	....	−32.7	−33.2	−59.6	−62.9	−67.6
Gross National Income (GNI)	99a											327.7	508.5	650.4	736.4	890.9
GDP Volume 1975 Prices	99b.p	121.5	128.3	134.9	143.3	165.0	159.6	159.4	150.6	148.2	162.7	188.4				
GDP Volume 1978 Prices	99b.p	....	....	....	....	....	....	....	....	....	....	248.6	301.4	372.4	393.3	421.7
GDP Volume (1995=100)	99bv p	39.1	41.3	43.4	46.1	53.1	51.4	51.3	48.5	47.7	52.4	60.6	73.5	90.8	95.9	102.8
GDP Deflator (1995=100)	99bi p	18.2	19.0	20.0	21.3	24.6	29.7	32.3	35.8	39.7	46.4	56.8	70.4	74.8	79.6	89.0
Population	99z	1.20	1.23	1.26	1.29	1.32	1.35	1.39	1.44	1.45	1.49	1.53	1.72	1.77	1.81	1.87

Millions:

	1985	1986	1987	1988	1989	1990	1991	1992	1993	1994	1995	1996	1997	1998	1999		Code
International Transactions																	
Billions of Francs																	
Exports	488.52	268.99	292.40	279.20	397.70	267.10	290.50	312.00	302.63	532.40	585.30	795.30	973.70	....	....	Exports	70
Imports, c.i.f.	268.70	206.65	294.37	331.45	328.49	169.02	167.68	119.48	164.79	350.41	334.18	793.31	....	....	....	Imports, c.i.f.	71
Imports, f.o.b.	218.63	168.14	239.52	269.69	267.26	137.54	136.44	97.22	134.08	340.20	324.50	695.30	524.90	....	....	Imports, f.o.b.	71.v
Balance of Payments																	
Minus Sign Indicates Debit																	
Current Account, n.i.e.	-161.3	-600.7	-222.7	-445.5	-85.0	-251.2	-461.5	-316.6	-552.7	-793.4	-649.7	-1,109.0	-251.9	....	....	Current Account, n.i.e.	78al d
Goods: Exports f.o.b.	1,144.7	672.6	876.7	843.2	1,160.5	1,388.7	1,107.7	1,178.7	1,119.1	958.9	1,167.0	1,554.5	1,744.1	....	....	Goods: Exports f.o.b.	78aa d
Goods: Imports f.o.b.	-630.1	-512.4	-419.9	-522.7	-532.0	-512.7	-494.5	-438.2	-500.1	-612.7	-650.7	-1,361.0	-802.9	....	....	Goods: Imports f.o.b.	78ab d
Trade Balance	514.7	160.2	456.8	320.5	628.5	876.0	613.2	740.5	619.1	346.2	516.3	193.5	941.3			*Trade Balance*	78ac d
Services: Credit	74.7	103.1	97.2	92.3	95.3	99.2	99.3	66.1	56.2	67.0	76.3	91.1	55.7			Services: Credit	78ad d
Services: Debit	-525.6	-656.8	-532.1	-560.1	-494.0	-769.1	-786.6	-737.5	-845.5	-995.8	-778.5	-721.1	-565.2			Services: Debit	78ae d
Balance on Goods & Services	63.8	-393.5	21.9	-147.4	229.8	206.0	-74.1	69.1	-170.2	-582.7	-185.9	-436.5	431.8			*Balance on Goods & Services*	78af d
Income: Credit	9.1	8.1	30.5	7.5	2.2	14.7	18.8	12.5	11.3	2.0	3.0	11.7	5.1			Income: Credit	78ag d
Income: Debit	-237.2	-234.2	-286.2	-313.3	-363.3	-474.9	-401.6	-379.7	-384.9	-291.1	-459.4	-670.1	-668.9			Income: Debit	78ah d
Balance on Gds, Serv. & Inc.	-164.2	-619.6	-233.8	-453.2	-131.3	-254.2	-456.9	-298.1	-543.9	-871.8	-642.3	-1,094.9	-232.0			*Balance on Gds, Serv. & Inc.*	78ai z
Current Transfers, n.i.e.: Credit	51.0	69.1	88.8	79.8	119.7	86.3	74.1	54.8	50.5	111.3	30.9	29.9	24.7			Current Transfers, n.i.e.: Credit	78aj d
Current Transfers: Debit	-48.0	-50.3	-77.7	-72.0	-73.4	-83.4	-78.7	-73.3	-59.3	-33.0	-38.3	-44.0	-44.5			Current Transfers: Debit	78ak d
Capital Account, n.i.e.	—	—	—	—	—	—	—	—	—	—	—	—	—	....		Capital Account, n.i.e.	78bc d
Capital Account, n.i.e.: Credit	—	—	—	—	—	—	—	—	—	—	—	—	—			Capital Account, n.i.e.: Credit	78ba d
Capital Account: Debit	—	—	—	—	—	—	—	—	—	—	—	—	—			Capital Account: Debit	78bb d
Financial Account, n.i.e.	38.6	154.3	-293.1	-62.3	-326.7	-72.0	9.6	-153.8	-111.2	605.4	-80.3	657.2	-173.7	....		Financial Account, n.i.e.	78bj d
Direct Investment Abroad	—	—	—	—	—	—	—	—	—	—	—	—	—			Direct Investment Abroad	78bd d
Dir. Invest. in Rep. Econ., n.i.e.	12.7	22.4	43.4	9.1	—	—	—	—	—	—	—	—	—	....		Dir. Invest. in Rep. Econ., n.i.e.	78be d
Portfolio Investment Assets	—	—	—	—	—	—	—	—	—	—	—	—	—			Portfolio Investment Assets	78bf d
Equity Securities	—	—	—	—	—	—	—	—	—	—	—	—	—			Equity Securities	78bk d
Debt Securities	—	—	—	—	—	—	—	—	—	—	—	—	—			Debt Securities	78bl d
Portfolio Investment Liab., n.i.e.	—	—	—	—	—	—	—	—	—	—	—	—	—			Portfolio Investment Liab., n.i.e.	78bg d
Equity Securities	—	—	—	—	—	—	—	—	—	—	—	—	—			Equity Securities	78bm d
Debt Securities	—	—	—	—	—	—	—	—	—	—	—	—	—			Debt Securities	78bn d
Financial Derivatives Assets	....	....	....	....	....	....	....	....	....	....	....	....	....			Financial Derivatives Assets	78bw d
Financial Derivatives Liabilities	....	....	....	....	....	....	....	....	....	....	....	....	....			Financial Derivatives Liabilities	78bx d
Other Investment Assets	8.6	157.8	-150.8	-59.0	-7.8	-67.9	35.1	-24.9	-22.6	35.5	-10.4	.4	-3.6			Other Investment Assets	78bh d
Monetary Authorities	....	....	....	....	....	....	....	....	....	....	....	....	....			Monetary Authorities	78bo d
General Government	—	—	—	—	—	—	—	—	—	—	—	—	—			General Government	78bp d
Banks	-4.7	6.3	-1.1	-13.9	—	-56.2	2.5	-18.5	-14.8	33.9	-13.4	-3.5	-7.4			Banks	78bq d
Other Sectors	13.4	151.5	-149.6	-45.0	-7.8	-11.8	32.6	-6.4	-7.8	1.6	3.0	3.9	3.8			Other Sectors	78br d
Other Investment Liab., n.i.e.	17.3	-26.0	-185.8	-12.4	-318.9	-4.0	-25.5	-128.8	-88.6	569.9	-69.9	656.8	-170.1			Other Investment Liab., n.i.e.	78bi d
Monetary Authorities	-.3	-.1	.3	-.4	-1.4	—	—	—	—	—	—	—	—			Monetary Authorities	78bs d
General Government	-8.0	-177.3	-106.1	-66.5	-233.8	-110.9	-227.6	-257.3	-288.9	88.4	-432.5	-317.3	-386.7			General Government	78bt d
Banks	-12.6	-11.4	-3.4	—	—	—	—	—	—	—	—	—	—			Banks	78bu d
Other Sectors	38.2	162.8	-76.5	54.4	-83.7	106.9	201.1	128.5	200.2	481.4	362.6	974.1	216.6			Other Sectors	78bv d
Net Errors and Omissions	41.7	48.1	27.6	40.6	8.5	-40.6	-6.3	40.4	244.0	33.1	120.7	102.1	-122.1			Net Errors and Omissions	78ca d
Overall Balance	-81.0	-398.2	-488.2	-467.2	-403.2	-363.9	-458.2	-429.9	-420.0	-154.9	-609.3	-349.7	-547.7			*Overall Balance*	78cb d
Reserves and Related Items	81.0	398.2	488.2	467.2	403.2	363.9	458.2	429.9	420.0	154.9	609.3	349.7	547.7			Reserves and Related Items	79da d
Reserve Assets	1.8	-2.0	4.7	-1.7	—	-112.9	32.1	-26.8	-1.7	-55.5	-6.4	-16.8	21.6			Reserve Assets	79db d
Use of Fund Credit and Loans	-2.2	8.7	-3.1	-2.9	-3.4	-1.5	-4.9	—	-.7	15.0	-2.3	20.1	-2.1			Use of Fund Credit and Loans	79dc d
Exceptional Financing	81.4	391.6	486.6	471.8	406.6	478.2	431.0	456.8	422.4	195.4	618.1	346.4	528.2			Exceptional Financing	79de d
Government Finance																	
Year Ending December 31																	
Deficit (-) or Surplus	....	....	....	....	....	....	....	-109.7	-95.9	-130.0	-86.5	-24.6	-116.2	....		Deficit (-) or Surplus	80
Revenue	....	....	....	....	....	....	....	174.4	183.1	220.1	249.4	357.7	398.2	....		Revenue	81
Grants Received	....	....	....	....	....	....	....	.1	10.4	10.7	4.3	1.4		....		Grants Received	81z
Expenditure	....	....	....	....	....	....	....	276.3	279.1	360.5	346.6	386.6	515.8	....		Expenditure	82
Lending Minus Repayments	....	....	....	....	....	....	....	7.8	—	—	—	—	—			Lending Minus Repayments	83
Financing																	
Domestic	....	....	....	....	....	....	....	....	....	....	....	....	....			Domestic	84a
Foreign	....	....	....	....	....	....	....	....	....	....	....	....	....			Foreign	85a
National Accounts																	
Billions of Francs																	
Exports of Goods & Services	551.9	255.2	288.3	267.7	368.1	382.4	314.9	323.1	323.5	557.6	588.2	829.4	976.0	835.3	....	Exports of Goods & Services	90c
Government Consumption	159.7	159.8	142.1	138.7	144.6	153.5	186.3	192.4	182.3	200.8	189.0	189.1	337.4	199.1	....	Government Consumption	91f
Gross Fixed Capital Formation	276.9	182.9	104.0	129.2	126.7	131.2	151.1	159.8	140.7	439.6	426.2	337.0	299.0	322.9	....	Gross Fixed Capital Formation	93e
Increase/Decrease(-) in Stocks	17.1	5.7	-7.8	-6.5	-3.8	-10.1	6.7	7.9	4.2	13.8	12.4	25.6	4.1	—	....	Increase/Decrease(-) in Stocks	93i
Private Consumption	403.6	380.5	390.7	396.3	408.5	403.2	418.7	430.1	434.7	499.9	532.4	582.0	552.9	572.3	....	Private Consumption	96f
Imports of Goods & Services	-438.3	-343.7	-266.7	-266.4	-270.6	-298.2	-309.0	-336.9	-325.3	-725.4	-692.0	-669.3	-834.3	-685.9	....	Imports of Goods & Services	98c
Gross Domestic Product (GDP)	970.8	640.1	690.6	659.0	758.2	762.1	768.7	775.5	760.2	982.3	1,047.0	1,234.7	1,334.6	1,243.7	....	Gross Domestic Product (GDP)	99b
Net Factor Inc/Pmts(-) Abroad	-102.4	-41.9	-76.7	-90.2	-112.8	-125.3	-108.0	-97.4	-105.8	-160.5	-198.9	-232.9	-264.0	....		Net Factor Inc/Pmts(-) Abroad	98.n
Gross National Income (GNI)	868.4	598.5	613.8	568.7	645.4	636.8	660.7	684.9	662.6	780.9	881.3	962.7	932.0			Gross National Income (GNI)	99a
GDP Volume 1975 Prices	....	....	....	....	....	....	....	....	....	....	....	....	....			GDP Volume 1975 Prices	99b.p
GDP Volume 1978 Prices	416.8	388.1	388.8	395.7	402.7	411.7	421.4	428.7	424.5	401.3	410.1	....	....			GDP Volume 1978 Prices	99b.p
GDP Volume (1995=100)	101.6	94.6	94.8	96.5	98.2	100.4	102.8	104.5	103.5	97.9	100.0	....	....			GDP Volume (1995=100)	99bv p
GDP Deflator (1995=100)	91.2	64.6	69.6	65.2	73.7	72.5	71.5	70.9	70.1	95.9	100.0	....	....			GDP Deflator (1995=100)	99bi p
Midyear Estimates																	
Population	1.92	1.98	2.04	2.10	2.16	2.22	2.23	2.35	2.42	2.49	2.56	2.63	2.71	2.79	2.86	Population	99z

(See notes in the back of the book.)

		1970	1971	1972	1973	1974	1975	1976	1977	1978	1979	1980	1981	1982	1983	1984
Exchange Rates														*Colones per SDR:*		
Market Rate	aa	6.63	7.20	7.20	8.02	10.49	10.03	9.96	10.41	11.16	11.29	10.93	42.01	44.40	45.44	46.81
														Colones per US Dollar:		
Market Rate	ae	6.64	6.64	6.64	6.65	8.57	8.57	8.57	8.57	8.57	8.57	8.57	36.09	40.25	43.40	47.75
Market Rate	rf	6.63	6.63	6.64	6.65	7.93	8.57	8.57	8.57	8.57	8.57	8.57	21.76	37.41[e]	41.09	44.53
														Index Numbers (1995=100):		
Market Rate	ahx	2,702.5	2,702.5	2,702.5	2,697.8	2,282.5	2,092.3	2,092.3	2,092.3	2,092.3	2,092.3	2,092.3	909.9	480.8[e]	437.9	403.1
Nominal Effective Exchange Rate	ne c	....	....	....	....	....	....	....	....	....	....	527.0	542.1	252.8	147.8	150.0	152.9
Real Effective Exchange Rate	re c	....	....	....	....	....	....	....	....	....	....	159.6	86.9	89.3	108.2	110.9
Fund Position														*Millions of SDRs:*		
Quota	2f. s	32.00	32.00	32.00	32.00	32.00	32.00	32.00	32.00	41.00	41.00	61.50	61.50	61.50	84.10	84.10
SDRs	1b. s	.20	.06	3.99	3.88	1.96	3.81	1.24	5.53	3.00	4.46	—	—	.07	2.85	.11
Reserve Position in the Fund	1c. s	6.03	.29	.28	.28	—	—	—	—	7.78	7.54	—	—	—	—	—
Total Fund Cred.&Loans Outstg.	2tl	—	—	—	—	18.84	29.96	32.30	29.31	24.32	43.81	44.64	88.16	84.18	183.28	158.98
International Liquidity													*Millions of US Dollars Unless Otherwise Indicated:*			
Total Reserves minus Gold	1l. d	14.16	27.19	40.62	48.49	42.13	48.82	95.41	190.49	193.89	118.63	145.57	131.42	226.12	311.27	405.00
SDRs	1b. d	.20	.07	4.33	4.68	2.40	4.46	1.44	6.72	3.91	5.88	—	—	.08	2.98	.11
Reserve Position in the Fund	1c. d	6.03	.31	.30	.34	—	—	—	—	10.14	9.93	—	—	—	—	—
Foreign Exchange	1d. d	7.93	26.81	35.98	43.47	39.73	44.36	93.97	183.77	179.85	102.82	145.57	131.42	226.04	308.29	404.89
Gold (Million Fine Troy Ounces)	1ad	.060	.060	.060	.060	.060	.060	.060	.073	.080	.087	.087	.029	.052	.088	.023
Gold (National Valuation)	1and	2.10	2.10	2.28	2.54	2.53	2.53	2.53	11.69	15.46	36.00	53.86	7.19	22.60	—	—
Monetary Authorities: Other Liab.	4..d	7.55	11.20	25.98	19.61	50.04	68.26	100.47	149.16	238.47	385.30	832.81	921.97	792.03	1,773.48	1,830.95
Deposit Money Banks: Assets	7a. d	10.88	11.88	18.20	27.55	22.89	11.74	28.67	40.28	55.15	47.06	30.05	65.47	69.44	60.30	38.91
Liabilities	7b. d	21.01	20.47	24.15	36.80	31.20	45.12	65.99	94.92	87.63	120.04	126.72	131.10	139.95	68.41	88.65
Other Banking Insts.: Liabilities	7f. d	17.37	17.10	16.95	11.98	8.73	7.93	7.41	9.85	8.59	7.27	5.93	71.21	71.73	68.80	59.48
Monetary Authorities															*Billions of Colones:*	
Foreign Assets	11	.12	.23	.32	.40	.38	.44	.84	1.73	1.79	1.32	3.38	5.29	9.78	18.43	20.58
Claims on Central Government	12a	.33	.34	.42	.38	.54	.76	1.13	1.64	2.31	3.16	4.09	9.65	6.07	9.33	9.79
Claims on Nonfin.Pub.Enterprises	12c	—	—	—	—	—	—	—	—	1.38	2.15	3.10	3.86	7.15	20.09	23.36
Claims on Deposit Money Banks	12e	.23	.25	.29	.28	.81	.85	.79	1.06	1.27	3.94	6.19	1.78	1.73	6.35	5.45
Claims on Other Banking Insts	12f	.06	.08	.08	.11	.12	.14	.17	.21	.31	.41	.47	.61	.77	1.13	1.41
Reserve Money	14	.60	.77	.93	1.08	1.24	1.65	2.21	3.24	3.22	4.98	5.91	13.10	14.28	19.01	23.02
of which: Currency Outside DMBs	14a	.38	.43	.52	.64	.73	.85	1.12	1.41	1.70	1.95	2.26	3.50	5.44	6.94	8.59
Time, Savings,& Fgn.Currency Dep.	15	—	—	—	.06	.01	.21	.34	.65	1.73	1.91	6.72	3.23	3.35	2.79	
Liabs. of Central Bank: Securities	16ac	.01	—	—	—	—	—	—	.30	.42	.37	.30	1.54	5.26	5.08	4.90
Restricted Deposits	16b	—	—	—	—	—	—	—	—	—	—	.03	.27			
Foreign Liabilities	16c	.01	.01	.07	.03	.40	.30	.36	.39	.79	1.02	3.76	17.90	12.34	15.17	12.33
Long-Term Foreign Liabilities	16cl	.04	.07	.10	.10	.23	.58	.82	1.19	1.53	2.77	3.87	19.07	23.28	70.12	82.54
Central Government Deposits	16d	.14	.10	.12	.13	.24	.20	.36	.27	.30	.23	.68	1.04	2.36	3.68	3.45
Counterpart Funds	16e	—	—	—	—	—	—	—	—	—	—	—	—	—	—	—
Capital Accounts	17a	.05	.08	.10	.11	.15	.15	.15	.13	.15	.20	.25	1.29	1.40	1.80	1.98
Other Items (Net)	17r	−.10	−.11	−.20	−.29	−.45	−.69	−1.17	−1.22	—	−.33	.52	−39.73	−36.66	−62.90	−70.41
of which: Valuation Adjustment	17rv	....	....	....	....	....	....	....	....	−.84	−.78	−.84	−34.10	−47.65	−58.98	−84.06
Deposit Money Banks															*Billions of Colones:*	
Reserves	20	.21	.32	.40	.44	.48	.77	1.07	1.57	1.43	2.97	3.30	8.18	8.63	11.47	14.62
Other Claims on Monetary Author.	20c	—	—	—	—	—	—	—	—	—	—	—	—	—	—	—
Foreign Assets	21	.07	.08	.12	.18	.20	.10	.25	.35	.47	.40	.26	2.36	2.80	2.62	1.86
Claims on Central Government	22a	.03	.06	.12	.17	.32	.48	.58	.86	1.15	3.21	5.31	1.42	3.07	3.98	4.23
Claims on Nonfin.Pub.Enterprises	22c	—	—	—	—	—	—	—	—	.18	.18	.28	.28	.43	.75	1.06
Claims on Private Sector	22d	1.20	1.57	1.79	2.03	3.05	4.18	5.12	6.02	7.47	8.94	10.21	11.19	16.07	24.82	29.24
Claims on Other Banking Insts	22f	.05	.10	.10	.09	.18	.18	.13	.13	.18	.32	.25	.38	.40	.65	.93
Demand Deposits	24	.62	.88	.97	1.23	1.40	1.89	2.27	3.07	3.86	4.23	4.86	7.19	12.89	18.40	21.40
Time, Savings,& Fgn.Currency Dep.	25	.27	.49	.67	.77	1.24	2.13	2.98	3.82	4.79	6.91	8.06	14.72	19.31	27.17	32.84
Bonds	26ab	—	—	—	—	—	—	—	—	—	—	—	—	.01	.01	.06
Restricted Deposits	26b	—	—	—	—	—	—	—	—	—	—	—	—	—	—	—
Foreign Liabilities	26c	.01	.03	.04	.05	.05	.04	.03	.07	.09	.18	.41	1.93	2.10	1.00	1.59
Long-Term Foreign Liabilities	26cl	.13	.11	.12	.19	.22	.35	.54	.74	.66	.85	.67	2.80	3.53	1.97	2.65
Central Government Deposits	26d	.12	.14	.17	.20	.34	.30	.58	.48	.55	.61	.71	1.40	.42	.63	.63
Credit from Monetary Authorities	26g	.22	.24	.28	.27	.80	.85	.80	1.06	1.27	3.89	6.15	1.75	1.68	6.18	5.18
Capital Accounts	27a	.24	.24	.25	.26	.28	.30	.30	.32	.33	.36	.37	4.20	.58	1.10	1.90
Other Items (Net)	27r	−.05	—	.02	−.06	−.09	−.13	−.35	−.62	−.66	−1.01	−1.64	−10.18	−9.12	−12.18	−14.30
Monetary Survey															*Billions of Colones:*	
Foreign Assets (Net)	31n	.17	.28	.33	.49	.13	.20	.69	1.61	1.38	.52	−.54	−12.18	−1.87	4.88	8.52
Domestic Credit	32	1.42	1.91	2.22	2.44	3.65	5.29	6.24	8.18	12.20	17.60	22.36	25.00	31.18	56.42	65.94
Claims on Central Govt. (Net)	32an	.11	.17	.26	.22	.29	.75	.77	1.75	2.62	5.53	8.00	8.63	6.36	8.99	9.95
Claims on Nonfin.Pub.Enterprises	32c	—	—	—	—	—	—	—	—	1.56	2.33	3.38	4.14	7.58	20.84	24.41
Claims on Private Sector	32d	1.20	1.57	1.79	2.03	3.05	4.22	5.17	6.08	7.54	9.01	10.27	11.24	16.07	24.82	29.24
Claims on Other Banking Insts	32f	.12	.17	.18	.19	.31	.32	.30	.34	.49	.72	.72	.99	1.17	1.77	2.34
Money	34	1.01	1.32	1.50	1.87	2.15	2.77	3.41	4.50	5.62	6.23	7.27	10.83	18.45	25.62	30.13
Quasi-Money	35	.27	.49	.67	.77	1.30	2.13	3.18	4.16	5.44	8.64	9.96	21.44	22.55	30.52	35.63
Bonds	36ab	—	—	—	—	—	—	—	—	—	—	—	—	—	—	—
Liabs. of Central Bank: Securities	36ac	.01	—	—	—	—	—	—	.30	.42	.37	.30	1.54	5.26	5.08	4.90
Restricted Deposits	36b	—	—	—	—	—	—	—	—	—	—	.03	.27	—	—	—
Long-Term Foreign Liabilities	36cl	.17	.18	.22	.28	.44	.93	1.36	1.93	2.18	3.62	4.54	21.87	26.81	72.09	85.19
Counterpart Funds	36e	—	—	—	—	—	—	—	—	—	—	—	—	—	—	—
Capital Accounts	37a	.29	.32	.36	.37	.43	.45	.44	.46	.48	.56	.62	5.49	1.98	2.90	3.87
Other Items (Net)	37r	−.16	−.12	−.19	−.37	−.55	−.79	−1.46	−1.57	−.57	−1.31	−.90	−48.63	−45.74	−74.93	−85.31
Money plus Quasi-Money	35l	1.28	1.81	2.17	2.64	3.45	4.90	6.59	8.66	11.07	14.87	17.24	32.27	40.99	56.14	65.76

1985	1986	1987	1988	1989	1990	1991	1992	1993	1994	1995	1996	1997	1998	1999	Item	Code
															Exchange Rates	
End of Period																
58.99	72.02	98.24	106.98	110.85	147.32	193.72	188.97	208.01	240.98	289.72	316.51	329.61	382.17	409.27	Market Rate	aa
End of Period (ae) Period Average (rf)																
53.70	58.88	69.25	79.50	84.35	103.55	135.43	137.43	151.44	165.07	194.90	220.11	244.29	271.42	298.19	Market Rate	ae
50.45	55.99	62.78	75.80	81.50	91.58	122.43	134.51	142.17	157.07	179.73	207.69	232.60	257.23	285.68	Market Rate	rf
Period Averages																
354.8	320.5	286.2	236.7	220.0	196.5	147.3	133.4	126.2	114.2	100.0	86.5	77.2	69.8	62.8	Market Rate	ah x
154.0	143.7	132.8	120.4	128.3	130.3	105.4	102.9	111.1	113.3	100.0	89.8	84.1	78.5	72.0	Nominal Effective Exchange Rate	ne c
114.1	105.2	100.7	94.8	99.8	97.7	90.5	95.8	98.9	98.1	100.0	100.7	103.2	104.9	103.5	Real Effective Exchange Rate	re c
															Fund Position	
End of Period																
84.10	84.10	84.10	84.10	84.10	84.10	84.10	119.00	119.00	119.00	119.00	119.00	119.00	119.00	164.10	Quota	2f. s
.02	.01	.01	.01	.04	1.14	.21	.17	.12	.12	.04	.01	.02	.05	.59	SDRs	1b. s
—	—	—	—	—	—	—	8.73	8.73	8.73	8.73	8.73	8.73	8.73	20.00	Reserve Position in the Fund	1c. s
171.64	140.95	93.27	53.03	26.94	7.94	58.03	59.28	59.28	45.46	16.32	.50	—	—	—	Total Fund Cred.&Loans Outstg.	2tl
															International Liquidity	
End of Period																
506.37	523.37	488.86	667.98	742.57	520.63	919.80	1,018.65	1,024.03	893.20	1,046.64	1,000.23	1,261.82	1,063.39	1,460.40	Total Reserves minus Gold	1l. d
.02	.01	.01	.01	.05	1.62	.30	.23	.16	.06	.01	.03	.07	.81		SDRs	1b. d
							12.00	11.98	12.74	12.97	12.55	11.77	12.29	27.45	Reserve Position in the Fund	1c. d
506.35	523.36	488.85	667.97	742.52	519.01	919.50	1,006.41	1,011.89	880.28	1,033.61	987.67	1,250.02	1,051.04	1,432.14	Foreign Exchange	1d. d
.058	.069	.021	.008	.011	.032	.040	.035	.034	.034	.002	.002	.002	.002	.002	Gold (Million Fine Troy Ounces)	1ad
19.05	26.10	24.91	9.26	3.37	4.32	12.00	95.97	13.46	....	....		.03	.02	.02	Gold (National Valuation)	1an d
1,996.51	2,152.13	2,116.11	2,084.06	1,959.77	1,593.10	1,563.21	1,533.13	1,452.73	1,294.60	1,217.58	1,115.12	1,047.67	1,078.46	1,013.79	Monetary Authorities: Other Liab.	4..d
48.51	74.07	86.89	85.96	100.57	96.51	136.31	200.90	151.99	199.11	203.90	248.10	251.59	324.56	271.57	Deposit Money Banks: Assets	7a. d
79.44	61.32	55.45	50.67	54.80	58.64	51.06	49.73	90.29	102.24	166.96	200.85	293.53	333.73	387.14	Liabilities	7b. d
54.69	32.70	4.62	1.85	5.12	4.70	4.27	4.21	3.81	3.58	....	....	....	....	....	Other Banking Insts.: Liabilities	7f. d
															Monetary Authorities	
End of Period																
28.27	32.43	35.48	53.44	62.42	58.12	130.93	148.63	162.32	155.90	196.71	203.73	I364.00	370.61	556.35	Foreign Assets	11
10.81	17.27	18.07	21.86	25.33	31.80	37.94	42.76	51.97	71.53	100.17	283.39	I359.68	416.84	312.07	Claims on Central Government	12a
24.29	30.87	30.62	34.77	32.80	37.45	40.52	34.28	28.76	23.54	23.40	25.41	I8.74	9.34	9.87	Claims on Nonfin.Pub.Enterprises	12c
8.79	13.45	18.40	19.58	20.39	24.29	28.00	28.78	30.91	62.74	38.32	43.39	I22.01	20.77	22.93	Claims on Deposit Money Banks	12e
1.68	1.43	1.30	3.28	2.97	2.87	4.15	3.52	3.49	3.30	3.07	3.25	I.95	.88	.81	Claims on Other Banking Insts	12f
32.92	42.59	48.81	70.61	82.24	99.50	161.47	190.26	208.40	269.98	313.66	382.25	I446.77	496.95	533.51	Reserve Money	14
9.94	13.24	14.78	24.73	21.92	27.51	34.67	47.86	54.67	74.86	84.75	91.74	I106.84	124.17	154.88	of which: Currency Outside DMBs	14a
.87	.68	.43	.71	5.89	10.29	7.62	9.20	8.86	4.79	4.74	8.16	I4.19	4.28	3.69	Time, Savings,& Fgn.Currency Dep.	15
5.59	6.23	11.44	23.38	30.83	28.60	33.98	39.61	45.48	78.94	128.50	46.78	I196.45	184.24	379.39	Liabs. of Central Bank: Securities	16ac
												I.29	.29	.29	Restricted Deposits	16b
13.63	14.04	14.19	11.50	8.71	16.82	20.94	17.70	14.34	11.64	4.94	.34	I8.53	9.19	14.55	Foreign Liabilities	16c
103.71	122.82	141.51	159.86	159.58	149.31	202.00	204.20	218.00	213.01	237.09	245.26	I247.40	283.53	287.75	Long-Term Foreign Liabilities	16cl
5.86	7.80	2.57	9.28	12.54	16.51	16.87	11.69	14.09	9.33	28.53	111.86	I63.15	60.80	80.43	Central Government Deposits	16d
												I8.63	10.80	2.53	Counterpart Funds	16e
3.33	4.64	5.18	5.95	8.64	9.92	15.79	24.47	25.06	26.80	28.98	126.88	I126.50	105.85	-220.97	Capital Accounts	17a
-92.08	-103.34	-120.27	-148.35	-164.52	-176.42	-217.13	-239.17	-256.79	-297.48	-384.78	-362.37	I-346.53	-337.48	-179.14	Other Items (Net)	17r
-110.46	-125.16	-161.56	-188.26	-213.40	-257.57	-248.81	-274.58	-293.34	-335.01	-415.03	-401.27	I-353.05	-346.54	-196.58	of which: Valuation Adjustment	17rv
															Deposit Money Banks	
End of Period																
23.69	28.73	34.94	52.50	61.01	78.95	129.24	142.10	155.73	196.21	232.32	289.87	I248.78	282.46	282.65	Reserves	20
—	—	—	—	.61	.63	.72	2.59	1.51	7.74	36.07	30.31	I109.45	36.73	169.92	Other Claims on Monetary Author.	20c
2.61	4.36	6.02	6.83	8.48	9.99	18.46	27.61	23.02	32.87	39.74	54.61	I61.46	88.09	80.98	Foreign Assets	21
5.24	5.31	5.68	10.28	12.95	21.33	14.14	7.77	6.56	34.58	28.38	89.72	I130.06	133.07	129.49	Claims on Central Government	22a
.99	.78	.83	1.25	2.35	3.26	3.10	2.60	2.65	2.76	2.36	2.48	I7.30	7.04	9.64	Claims on Nonfin.Pub.Enterprises	22c
34.14	40.19	51.34	59.27	66.16	78.94	93.12	138.70	190.34	222.92	223.00	329.90	I434.26	670.63	804.84	Claims on Private Sector	22d
.93	.91	1.06	1.09	1.77	1.75	1.61	2.75	2.93	2.58	.07	.05	I9.62	26.42	30.69	Claims on Other Banking Insts	22f
22.37	29.02	27.62	40.19	41.90	38.78	45.04	61.10	62.44	86.60	67.03	84.89	I243.70	279.60	330.68	Demand Deposits	24
42.70	48.99	64.10	84.25	104.97	146.18	210.71	252.34	301.35	355.06	389.71	620.66	I578.07	763.81	919.74	Time, Savings,& Fgn.Currency Dep.	25
.05	.04	.04	.03	.03	.03	.03	—	—	.02	—	—	I6.98	16.32	17.19	Bonds	26ab
												I.26	.08	.03	Restricted Deposits	26b
.52	.78	1.44	1.46	1.11	2.33	2.57	3.10	8.58	7.28	13.43	22.15	I64.28	75.66	99.94	Foreign Liabilities	26c
3.74	2.83	2.40	2.57	3.51	3.74	4.35	3.74	5.10	9.60	19.11	22.06	I7.43	14.92	15.50	Long-Term Foreign Liabilities	26cl
1.24	1.07	1.59	1.58	1.70	3.88	3.70	4.99	5.61	41.40	15.03	3.41	I—			Central Government Deposits	26d
9.21	9.96	14.53	17.42	18.00	20.63	19.21	18.68	17.40	45.83	14.47	10.99	I9.19	7.95	7.48	Credit from Monetary Authorities	26g
3.81	4.55	6.49	11.35	14.42	20.38	31.41	35.52	43.04	31.83	63.72	95.47	I185.63	229.10	269.86	Capital Accounts	27a
-16.06	-16.95	-18.36	-27.62	-32.33	-41.09	-56.63	-55.36	-60.78	-77.96	-20.55	-62.68	I-94.62	-142.99	-152.22	Other Items (Net)	27r
															Monetary Survey	
End of Period																
16.72	21.98	25.87	47.33	61.08	48.96	125.88	155.44	162.42	169.84	218.07	235.84	I352.65	373.86	522.84	Foreign Assets (Net)	31n
70.98	87.89	104.72	120.94	130.08	157.01	174.00	215.69	266.99	310.50	336.88	618.93	I887.45	1,203.42	1,216.98	Domestic Credit	32
8.94	13.71	19.58	21.28	24.04	32.74	31.51	33.84	38.83	55.39	84.99	257.84	I426.59	489.12	361.13	Claims on Central Govt. (Net)	32an
25.28	31.65	31.45	36.02	35.15	40.71	43.63	36.87	31.41	26.30	25.76	27.89	I16.04	16.38	19.52	Claims on Nonfin.Pub.Enterprises	32c
34.14	40.19	51.34	59.27	66.16	78.94	93.12	138.70	190.34	222.92	223.00	329.90	I434.26	670.63	804.84	Claims on Private Sector	32d
2.62	2.35	2.36	4.37	4.73	4.42	5.75	6.27	6.41	5.89	3.13	3.30	I10.57	27.30	31.50	Claims on Other Banking Insts	32f
32.44	42.49	42.61	65.27	63.98	66.48	79.79	109.52	117.19	161.57	151.90	177.52	I354.65	415.43	516.56	Money	34
43.56	49.67	64.54	84.96	110.86	156.46	218.33	261.54	310.21	359.85	394.44	628.82	I582.26	768.09	923.43	Quasi-Money	35
.05	.04	.04	.03	.03	.03	.03	—	—	.02	—	—	I6.98	16.32	17.19	Bonds	36ab
5.59	6.23	11.44	23.38	30.22	27.97	33.27	37.03	43.98	71.20	92.43	16.48	I87.00	147.51	209.48	Liabs. of Central Bank: Securities	36ac
												I.55	.37	.32	Restricted Deposits	36b
107.45	125.65	143.91	162.43	163.09	153.05	206.34	207.94	223.09	222.61	256.20	267.32	I254.83	298.45	303.25	Long-Term Foreign Liabilities	36cl
												I8.63	10.80	2.53	Counterpart Funds	36e
7.14	9.19	11.67	17.30	23.06	30.31	47.20	59.99	68.10	58.64	92.70	222.35	I312.13	334.95	48.89	Capital Accounts	37a
-108.54	-123.41	-143.62	-185.10	-200.08	-228.33	-285.07	-304.89	-333.16	-393.54	-432.71	-457.71	I-366.93	-414.64	-281.83	Other Items (Net)	37r
76.00	92.16	107.15	150.23	174.83	222.95	298.12	371.06	427.40	521.41	546.34	806.33	I936.91	1,183.52	1,439.99	Money plus Quasi-Money	35l

Costa Rica

		1970	1971	1972	1973	1974	1975	1976	1977	1978	1979	1980	1981	1982	1983	1984
Other Banking Institutions																*Billions of Colones:*
Cash	40	—	—	—	.01				.02	—	—	—	.07	.27	.23	.58
Claims on Central Government	42a	—	.01	.01	.01	.01	.01	.01	—	—	—	.01		.07	.04	.02
Claims on Official Entities	42bx	—	—	—	—	—	—	—	—	—	—	—	.02	.02	.02	.02
Claims on Private Sector	42d	.46	.54	.58	.57	.65	.73	.80	.92	1.14	1.25	1.28	2.06	2.20	2.83	3.22
Demand Deposits	44												.03	.03	.04	.04
Time, Savings,& Fgn.Currency Dep.	45	—	—	—	—	—	—	—	—	.02	.08	.13	.22	.39	.78	1.21
Bonds	46ab	.13	.13	.14	.14	.08	.12	.18	.21	.28	.18	.23	.35	.28	.29	.33
Long-Term Foreign Liabilities	46cl	.12	.11	.11	.08	.07	.07	.06	.08	.07	.06	.05	2.57	2.89	2.99	2.84
Central Government Deposits	46d	—	—	—	—	—	—	—	—	—	—	—	.01	.01	.01	.01
Credit from Monetary Authorities	46g	.06	.09	.10	.11	.13	.14	.18	.21	.27	.31	.31	.61	.77	1.13	1.42
Credit from Deposit Money Banks	46h	.05	.10	.10	.08	.18	.17	.17	.13	.17	.31	.25	.12	.18	.44	.70
Capital Accounts	47a	.10	.11	.12	.11	.11	.12	.13	.13	.14	.14	.14	.25	.28	.33	.34
Other Items (Net)	47r	—	.01	.03	.07	.08	.11	.14	.19	.19	.17	.19	-2.00	-2.26	-2.88	-3.06
Banking Survey																*Billions of Colones:*
Foreign Assets (net)	51n	.17	.28	.33	.49	.13	.20	.69	1.61	1.38	.52	-.54	-12.18	-1.87	4.88	8.52
Domestic Credit	52	1.77	2.29	2.63	2.83	3.99	5.70	6.75	8.76	12.86	18.14	22.95	26.09	32.29	57.54	66.86
Claims on Central Govt. (Net)	52an	.11	.18	.27	.23	.29	.75	.78	1.76	2.62	5.54	8.02	8.63	6.42	9.03	9.97
Claims on Official Entities	52bx									1.56	2.33	3.38	4.16	7.61	20.86	24.43
Claims on Private Sector	52d	1.66	2.11	2.37	2.60	3.70	4.95	5.97	7.01	8.68	10.26	11.55	13.30	18.27	27.65	32.45
Liquid Liabilities	55l	1.28	1.81	2.17	2.64	3.45	4.90	6.59	8.64	11.08	14.95	17.37	32.45	41.14	56.73	66.44
Bonds	56ab	.14	.14	.14	.14	.08	.12	.18	.50	.70	.55	.53	1.90	5.55	5.38	5.28
Long-Term Foreign Liabilities	56cl	.29	.29	.33	.36	.52	1.00	1.42	2.02	2.26	3.69	4.59	24.44	29.69	75.08	88.03
Capital Accounts	57a	.39	.43	.47	.47	.54	.57	.57	.59	.62	.70	.77	5.74	2.25	3.24	4.22
Other Items (Net)	57r	-.15	-.10	-.14	-.30	-.47	-.69	-1.32	-1.38	-.42	-1.24	-.84	-50.62	-48.22	-78.02	-88.59
Interest Rates																*Percent Per Annum*
Discount Rate *(End of Period)*	60	5.00	5.00	5.00	5.00	7.00	7.00	8.00	8.00	15.40	14.80	23.50	23.50	30.00	30.00	28.00
Deposit Rate	60l	....	....	....	....	....	....	....	....	....	....	....	....	18.29	19.50	14.50
Lending Rate	60p	....	....	....	....	....	....	....	....	....	....	....	....	25.00	23.25	18.00
Prices and Labor																*Index Numbers (1995=100):*
Producer Prices	63	1.1	1.2	1.3	1.5	2.1	2.5	2.8	3.0	‡3.2	3.7	4.6	7.7	15.9	20.1	21.7
Consumer Prices	64	1.5	1.6	1.6	1.9	2.5	‡2.9	3.0	3.1	3.3	3.6	4.3	5.8	11.1	14.7	16.5
																Number in Thousands:
Labor Force	67d	....	....	....	....	....	....	....	....	....	....	....	....	....	....	....
Employment	67e	....	....	....	....	....	....	....	....	....	....	....	....	....	....	....
Unemployment	67c	....	....	....	....	....	....	....	....	....	....	....	....	....	....	....
Unemployment Rate (%)	67r	....	....	....	....	....	....	....	....	....	....	....	....	....	....	....
International Transactions																*Millions of US Dollars:*
Exports	70..d	231.2	225.4	280.9	344.5	440.3	493.3	592.9	828.2	864.9	934.4	1,001.7	1,008.1	870.4	872.6	1,006.4
Imports, c.i.f.	71..d	316.7	349.7	372.8	455.3	719.7	694.0	770.4	1,021.4	1,165.7	1,396.8	1,540.4	1,208.5	889.0	987.8	1,093.7
Balance of Payments																*Millions of US Dollars:*
Current Account, n.i.e.	78al d	....	....	....	....	....	....	....	-225.6	-363.2	-558.2	-663.9	-409.1	-271.7	-312.6	-251.1
Goods: Exports f.o.b.	78aa d								827.8	863.9	942.1	1,000.9	1,002.6	869.0	852.5	997.5
Goods: Imports f.o.b.	78ab d								-925.1	-1,049.4	-1,257.2	-1,375.2	-1,090.6	-804.9	-894.3	-992.9
Trade Balance	78ac d								-97.3	-185.5	-315.1	-374.3	-88.0	64.1	-41.8	4.6
Services: Credit	78ad d								129.9	141.9	154.8	194.2	170.8	242.2	275.2	272.5
Services: Debit	78ae d								-199.0	-228.7	-266.8	-286.2	-217.0	-240.3	-253.4	-261.3
Balance on Goods & Services	78af d								-166.4	-272.3	-427.1	-466.3	-134.2	66.0	-20.0	15.8
Income: Credit	78ag d								11.4	19.2	14.4	23.5	25.9	32.2	44.9	43.7
Income: Debit	78ah d								-86.4	-126.7	-157.7	-235.6	-327.9	-400.8	-373.8	-351.5
Balance on Gds, Serv. & Inc.	78ai d								-241.4	-379.8	-570.4	-678.4	-436.2	-302.6	-348.9	-292.0
Current Transfers, n.i.e.: Credit	78aj d								26.4	28.0	30.1	33.5	36.9	38.9	45.6	51.3
Current Transfers: Debit	78ak d								-10.6	-11.4	-17.9	-19.0	-9.8	-8.0	-9.3	-10.4
Capital Account, n.i.e.	78bc d								—	—	—	—	—	—	—	—
Capital Account, n.i.e.: Credit	78ba d								—	—	—	—	—	—	—	—
Capital Account: Debit	78bb d								—	—	—	—	—	—	—	—
Financial Account, n.i.e.	78bj d								355.8	423.0	317.0	373.9	-32.2	-226.3	-149.3	-330.4
Direct Investment Abroad	78bd d								—	-1.6	-1.1	-4.5	-3.4	-2.4	-5.4	-3.9
Dir. Invest. in Rep. Econ., n.i.e.	78be d								62.5	48.6	43.5	52.6	69.6	28.9	60.7	55.9
Portfolio Investment Assets	78bf d								—	—	—	—	-.5	-.3	—	—
Equity Securities	78bk d								—	—	—	—	—	—	—	—
Debt Securities	78bl d								—	—	—	—	-.5	-.3	—	—
Portfolio Investment Liab., n.i.e.	78bg d								3.5	20.9	—	122.0	-1.9	-1.6	-2.6	-.2
Equity Securities	78bm d								—	—	—	—	—	—	—	—
Debt Securities	78bn d								3.5	20.9	—	122.0	-1.9	-1.6	-2.6	-.2
Financial Derivatives Assets	78bw d															
Financial Derivatives Liabilities	78bx d								....	....	....	....	....	....	....	....
Other Investment Assets	78bh d								-22.6	-49.2	-113.7	-163.2	-131.2	-145.7	-25.8	-161.8
Monetary Authorities	78bo d								—	—	—	—	—	—	—	—
General Government	78bp d								-.1	-6.9	-3.2	-5.4	-3.6	-13.1	-1.2	-14.2
Banks	78bq d								—	—	—	—	—	—	—	—
Other Sectors	78br d								-22.5	-42.3	-110.5	-157.8	-127.6	-132.6	-24.6	-147.6
Other Investment Liab., n.i.e.	78bi d								312.4	404.3	388.3	367.0	35.2	-105.2	-176.2	-220.4
Monetary Authorities	78bs d								46.0	89.9	98.3	146.8	56.4	-35.4	-103.3	-173.9
General Government	78bt d								31.3	70.6	85.7	60.3	33.5	-9.6	14.7	18.2
Banks	78bu d								42.4	-9.2	40.8	41.5	-50.9	-15.7	-49.3	-16.6
Other Sectors	78bv d								192.7	253.0	163.5	118.4	-3.8	-44.5	-38.3	-48.1
Net Errors and Omissions	78ca d								-27.4	-50.5	79.2	-69.5	69.6	163.7	78.4	104.4
Overall Balance	78cb d								102.8	9.3	-162.0	-359.5	-334.3	-383.6	-477.2
Reserves and Related Items	79da d								-102.8	-9.3	162.0	359.5	371.7	334.3	383.6	477.2
Reserve Assets	79db d								-107.3	-20.8	93.2	-92.9	-1.5	-120.9	-152.7	79.7
Use of Fund Credit and Loans	79dc d								-3.5	-6.6	25.3	.8	50.1	-4.4	105.6	-24.5
Exceptional Financing	79de d								8.0	18.1	43.5	451.7	323.0	459.6	430.6	422.0

Other Banking Institutions — *End of Period*

1985	1986	1987	1988	1989	1990	1991	1992	1993	1994	1995	1996	1997	1998	1999		
.43	.24	—	.05	.95	.71	.85	.02	.06	.04	...	...	...	...	...	Cash	40
.03	.29	.08	.03	.16	.08	.41	.61	.77	.45	...	...	...	...	...	Claims on Central Government	42a
.11	.02									...	...	...	...	...	Claims on Official Entities	42bx
3.51	3.93	2.61	2.83	3.41	3.86	3.85	4.77	4.99	7.28	...	...	...	...	...	Claims on Private Sector	42d
.07	.24	.21	—	.01	—	—	—	—	—	...	...	...	...	...	Demand Deposits	44
.56	.29	.41	.46	.90	.95	1.17	.55	.43	.47	...	...	...	...	...	Time, Savings,& Fgn.Currency Dep.	45
.51	1.12	.48	.71	.72	.61	.92	1.40	2.01	2.09	...	...	...	...	...	Bonds	46ab
2.94	1.93	.32	.15	.43	.49	.58	.58	.58	.59	...	...	...	...	...	Long-Term Foreign Liabilities	46cl
.01	.01	—	—	—	—	—	—	—	—	...	...	...	...	...	Central Government Deposits	46d
1.88	2.94	.48	.44	.80	.84	1.02	.65	.65	2.45	...	...	...	...	...	Credit from Monetary Authorities	46g
.93	.83	.80	1.01	1.82	1.82	1.68	2.15	2.31	2.15	...	...	...	...	...	Credit from Deposit Money Banks	46h
.36	.42	.23	.24	.23	.19	.20	.16	.14	.18	...	...	...	...	...	Capital Accounts	47a
-3.17	-3.29	-.25	-.09	-.39	-.24	-.46	-.09	-.30	-.14	...	...	...	...	...	Other Items (Net)	47r

Banking Survey — *End of Period*

1985	1986	1987	1988	1989	1990	1991	1992	1993	1994	1995	1996	1997	1998	1999		
16.72	21.98	25.87	47.33	61.08	48.96	125.88	155.44	162.42	169.84	...	...	...	...	...	Foreign Assets (net)	51n
72.00	89.78	105.04	119.43	128.92	156.33	172.50	214.79	266.33	312.34	...	...	...	...	...	Domestic Credit	52
8.96	13.99	19.66	21.31	24.20	32.82	31.91	34.45	39.60	55.84	...	...	...	...	...	Claims on Central Govt. (Net)	52an
25.39	31.67	31.45	36.02	35.15	40.71	43.63	36.87	31.41	26.30	...	...	...	...	...	Claims on Official Entities	52bx
37.65	44.12	53.94	62.10	69.57	82.80	96.96	143.47	195.32	230.21	...	...	...	...	...	Claims on Private Sector	52d
76.20	92.45	107.77	150.63	174.79	223.18	298.44	371.58	427.77	521.84	...	...	...	...	...	Liquid Liabilities	55l
6.15	7.39	11.96	24.12	30.97	28.60	34.22	38.43	45.99	73.31	...	...	...	...	...	Bonds	56ab
110.39	127.58	144.23	162.58	163.52	153.54	206.92	208.52	223.67	223.20	...	...	...	...	...	Long-Term Foreign Liabilities	56cl
7.50	9.61	11.90	17.53	23.30	30.50	47.39	60.15	68.25	58.81	...	...	...	...	...	Capital Accounts	57a
-111.51	-125.28	-144.94	-188.11	-202.58	-230.54	-288.58	-308.45	-336.92	-394.97	...	...	...	...	...	Other Items (Net)	57r

Interest Rates — *Percent Per Annum*

1985	1986	1987	1988	1989	1990	1991	1992	1993	1994	1995	1996	1997	1998	1999		
28.00	27.50	31.38	31.50	31.61	37.80	42.50	29.00	35.00	37.75	38.50	35.00	31.00	37.00	34.00	Discount Rate (End of Period)	60
16.50	16.67	14.06	15.18	15.62	21.16	27.32	15.80	16.90	17.72	23.88	17.29	13.03	12.76	14.31	Deposit Rate	60l
20.92	21.80	23.82	28.69	29.17	32.56	38.88	28.46	30.02	33.03	36.70	26.27	22.48	22.47	25.74	Lending Rate	60p

Prices and Labor — *Period Averages*

1985	1986	1987	1988	1989	1990	1991	1992	1993	1994	1995	1996	1997	1998	1999		
23.9	26.1	28.8	34.0	38.9	44.7	57.3	67.9	71.4	80.7	100.0	116.0	129.5	140.9	155.2	Producer Prices	63
19.0	21.2	24.8	30.0	34.9	41.5	53.5	65.1	71.5	81.2	100.0	117.5	133.1	148.6	163.5	Consumer Prices	64

Period Averages

1985	1986	1987	1988	1989	1990	1991	1992	1993	1994	1995	1996	1997	1998	1999		
							1,063	1,119	1,160	...	1,199	1,277	1,377	...	Labor Force	67d
827	854	923	951	987	1,017	1,007	1,043	1,096	1,138	1,174	1,145	1,227	1,300	...	Employment	67e
61	57	55	55	39	50	59	44	47	49	64	76	74	77	...	Unemployment	67c
6.8	6.2	5.6	5.5	3.8	4.6	5.5	4.1	4.1	4.2	5.2	6.2	5.7	5.6	...	Unemployment Rate (%)	67r

International Transactions — *Millions of US Dollars*

1985	1986	1987	1988	1989	1990	1991	1992	1993	1994	1995	1996	1997	1998	1999		
976.0	1,120.5	1,158.3	1,245.7	1,414.6	1,448.2	1,597.7	1,840.8	2,624.6	2,869.4	3,453.0	3,730.2	4,267.6	5,511.3	6,577.2	Exports	70..d
1,098.2	1,147.5	1,382.5	1,409.8	1,717.4	1,989.7	1,876.6	2,440.7	3,514.9	3,789.0	4,036.1	4,299.5	4,924.0	6,230.4	6,320.1	Imports, c.i.f.	71..d

Balance of Payments — *Minus Sign Indicates Debit*

1985	1986	1987	1988	1989	1990	1991	1992	1993	1994	1995	1996	1997	1998	1999		
-291.1	-160.6	-376.4	-303.5	-479.9	-494.0	-99.2	-380.4	-620.2	-244.0	-358.1	-266.5	-214.7	-460.3	...	Current Account, n.i.e.	78al d
939.1	1,084.8	1,106.7	1,180.7	1,333.4	1,354.2	1,498.1	1,739.1	1,866.8	2,122.0	3,481.8	3,774.1	4,349.5	5,546.8		Goods: Exports f.o.b.	78aa d
-1,001.0	-1,045.2	-1,245.2	-1,278.6	-1,572.0	-1,796.7	-1,697.6	-2,210.9	-2,627.6	-2,727.8	-3,804.4	-4,023.3	-4,583.9	-5,791.3		Goods: Imports f.o.b.	78ab d
-61.9	39.6	-138.5	-97.9	-238.6	-442.5	-199.5	-471.8	-760.8	-605.8	-322.6	-249.2	-234.4	-244.5		*Trade Balance*	78ac d
274.7	303.0	337.1	430.3	497.9	609.0	691.4	841.3	1,039.3	1,195.0	969.1	1,053.6	1,129.1	1,329.7		Services: Credit	78ad d
-281.7	-303.6	-391.1	-423.7	-496.0	-549.7	-534.8	-710.6	-816.4	-860.1	-913.0	-1,033.5	-1,031.2	-1,182.9		Services: Debit	78ae d
-68.9	39.0	-192.5	-91.3	-236.7	-383.2	-42.9	-341.1	-537.9	-270.9	-266.5	-229.1	-136.5	-97.7		*Balance on Goods & Services*	78af d
56.4	52.4	48.5	47.8	119.9	130.3	111.4	112.8	111.2	154.6	146.4	142.4	180.4	179.9		Income: Credit	78ag d
-332.2	-323.3	-338.4	-390.4	-489.5	-363.0	-285.3	-315.4	-336.6	-283.0	-371.9	-326.8	-373.0	-647.5		Income: Debit	78ah d
-344.7	-231.9	-482.4	-433.9	-606.3	-615.9	-216.8	-543.7	-763.3	-399.3	-492.0	-413.5	-329.1	-565.3		*Balance on Gds, Serv. & Inc.*	78ai d
64.2	82.1	117.2	141.9	130.5	126.0	121.1	168.9	149.3	164.5	165.2	190.1	182.2	197.2		Current Transfers, n.i.e.: Credit	78aj d
-10.6	-10.8	-11.2	-11.5	-4.1	-4.1	-3.5	-5.6	-6.2	-9.2	-31.3	-43.1	-67.8	-92.2		Current Transfers: Debit	78ak d
—	—	—	—	—	—	—	—	—	—	—	28.2	...	...		Capital Account, n.i.e.	78bc d
—	—	—	—	—	—	—	—	—	—	—	28.2	...	...		Capital Account, n.i.e.: Credit	78ba d
											...	...			Capital Account: Debit	78bb d
-286.9	-301.6	-446.7	-263.9	-186.7	-90.8	162.1	192.8	62.8	-108.4	517.3	47.6	199.6	192.4		Financial Account, n.i.e.	78bj d
-4.7	-3.6	-4.5	-.9	-6.0	-2.1	-5.6	-4.4	-2.3	-4.7	-5.5	-5.7	-7.0	-7.5		Direct Investment Abroad	78bd d
69.9	61.0	80.3	122.3	101.2	162.5	178.4	226.0	246.7	297.6	336.9	427.0	482.5	559.0		Dir. Invest. in Rep. Econ., n.i.e.	78be d
.7	—	—	—	—	—	—	—	—	-.4	...	...	...	...		Portfolio Investment Assets	78bf d
.7	—	—	—	—	—	—	—	—	-.4	...	...	...	...		Equity Securities	78bk d
															Debt Securities	78bl d
-14.2	-2.5	—	-6.0	-13.2	-28.2	-13.0	-16.9	-5.1	-1.2	-24.4	-21.5	-139.3	-90.0		Portfolio Investment Liab., n.i.e.	78bg d
	-2.5														Equity Securities	78bm d
-14.2		—	-6.0	-13.2	-28.2	-13.0	-16.9	-5.1	-1.2	-24.4	-21.5	-139.3	-90.0		Debt Securities	78bn d
															Financial Derivatives Assets	78bw d
															Financial Derivatives Liabilities	78bx d
-95.8	-42.4	-72.4	-77.3	-5.9	-124.7	75.6	84.8	54.5	-76.2	16.8	-159.3	-100.0	-28.8		Other Investment Assets	78bh d
										.1	-6.3	-3.7	...		Monetary Authorities	78bo d
—	-12.9	-.9	-.1	-4.9	-4.7	1.2	-8.5	34.9	-4.4						General Government	78bp d
										-9.8	-17.8	98.5	-29.8		Banks	78bq d
-95.8	-29.5	-71.5	-77.2	-1.0	-120.0	74.4	93.3	19.6	-71.8	26.5	-135.2	-194.8	1.0		Other Sectors	78br d
-242.8	-314.1	-450.1	-302.0	-262.8	-98.3	-73.3	-96.7	-231.0	-323.9	193.9	-192.9	-36.6	-240.3		Other Investment Liab., n.i.e.	78bi d
-178.0	-213.9	-404.3	-284.8	-293.3	-141.3	-25.5	-76.6	-256.8	-216.1	-94.4	-104.0	-121.8	-109.5		Monetary Authorities	78bs d
-39.5	1.3	-27.4	-36.1	-17.8	-28.1	-68.3	-47.8	-25.7	-106.2	12.9	-85.2	-87.8	-112.5		General Government	78bt d
-16.3	-11.6	.1	-13.5	4.4	-1.0	-8.7	7.1	27.7	-18.8	23.0	48.7	-4.0	5.0		Banks	78bu d
-9.0	-89.9	-18.5	32.4	43.9	72.1	29.2	20.6	23.8	17.2	252.4	-52.4	177.0	-23.3		Other Sectors	78bv d
142.9	97.5	131.2	224.6	208.9	43.4	99.9	201.9	299.0	249.1	57.1	121.4	-117.2	-236.7		Net Errors and Omissions	78ca d
-435.1	-364.7	-691.9	-342.8	-457.7	-541.4	162.8	14.3	-258.4	-103.3	216.2	-69.3	-132.3	-504.6		*Overall Balance*	78cb d
435.1	364.7	691.9	342.8	457.7	541.4	-162.8	-14.3	258.4	103.3	-216.2	69.3	132.3	504.6		Reserves and Related Items	79da d
-72.1	-58.0	25.0	-188.0	-112.3	197.2	-416.1	-176.8	59.6	65.5	-179.2	77.3	-215.7	149.1		Reserve Assets	79db d
12.2	-36.4	-62.3	-54.1	-33.4	-25.6	67.7	1.7	—	-20.3	-44.4	-23.1	-.7	—		Use of Fund Credit and Loans	79dc d
495.0	459.2	729.2	585.0	603.3	369.8	185.6	160.8	198.8	58.1	7.4	15.1	348.7	355.5		Exceptional Financing	79de d

Costa Rica

		1970	1971	1972	1973	1974	1975	1976	1977	1978	1979	1980	1981	1982	1983	1984
Government Finance																*Millions of Colones:*
Deficit (-) or Surplus	**80**	−5	−244	−267	−339	−176	−386	−974	−746	−1,316	−2,310	−3,356	−1,381	−936	−2,464	−187
Total Revenue and Grants	**81y**	883	910	1,041	1,387	1,936	2,279	2,692	3,487	4,111	4,344	5,258	7,453	12,948	21,057	27,281
Revenue	**81**	883	910	1,041	1,387	1,936	2,279	2,692	3,487	4,111	4,344	5,258	7,453	12,948	21,057	27,281
Grants	**81z**	—	—	—	—	—	—	—	—	—	—	—	—	—	—	....
Exp. & Lending Minus Repay.	**82z**	....	....	....	....	....	....	....	....	....	....	....	....	....	....	....
Expenditure	**82**	888	1,154	1,309	1,726	2,112	2,665	3,666	4,233	5,426	6,654	8,614	8,834	13,885	23,521	27,469
Lending Minus Repayments	**83**	—	—	—	—	—	—	—	—	—	—	—	—	—	—	....
Total Financing	**80h**	5	244	267	....	....	386	974	746	1,316	2,310	3,356	1,381	936	2,464	187
Domestic	**84a**	9	174	136	....	....	234	744	443	1,102	1,918	2,931	1,125	454	480	−1,853
Foreign	**85a**	−4	70	132	....	....	152	230	304	214	392	425	256	482	1,983	2,040
Total Debt by Residence	**88**	1,876	2,181	2,628	3,351	4,030	4,402	6,127	7,354	12,652	13,728	15,689	18,510	31,179	38,605	41,312
Domestic Debt	**88a**	1,528	1,698	2,054	2,626	2,961	3,135	4,633	5,471	9,821	10,200	10,931	13,134	17,687	23,409	23,830
Foreign Debt	**89a**	349	484	574	725	1,069	1,267	1,493	1,882	2,831	3,528	4,758	5,376	13,492	15,196	17,482
National Accounts																*Millions of Colones*
Exports of Goods & Services	**90c**	1,816	1,912	2,483	3,130	4,380	5,052	5,977	8,128	8,509	9,311	10,963	24,708	43,959	46,601	56,046
Government Consumption	**91f**	820	990	1,182	1,417	1,889	2,558	3,306	4,208	5,069	6,243	7,544	8,987	14,192	19,527	25,503
Gross Fixed Capital Formation	**93e**	1,270	1,579	1,800	2,252	3,175	3,695	4,846	5,889	6,952	9,050	9,895	13,737	19,808	23,269	32,679
Increase/Decrease(-) in Stocks	**93i**	70	158	10	187	359	−58	46	502	132	−295	1,109	2,837	4,262	8,001	4,324
Private Consumption	**96f**	4,805	5,146	5,748	6,924	9,772	12,036	13,718	17,171	20,412	23,139	27,140	34,344	56,397	79,481	99,837
Imports of Goods & Services	**98c**	−2,256	−2,648	−3,007	−3,747	−6,360	−6,478	−7,218	−9,567	−10,879	−12,863	−15,245	−27,510	−41,113	−47,565	−55,378
Gross Domestic Product (GDP)	**99b**	6,525	7,137	8,216	10,162	13,216	16,805	20,676	26,331	30,194	34,584	41,405	57,103	97,505	129,314	163,011
Net Factor Inc/Pmts(-) Abroad	**98.n**	−88	−98	−253	−285	−312	−543	−627	−655	−903	−1,279	−1,987	−6,434	−16,087	−13,673	−13,804
Gross National Income (GNI)	**99a**	6,436	7,033	7,958	9,875	12,910	16,283	20,077	25,705	29,315	33,307	39,417	50,669	81,418	115,641	149,207
Net National Income	**99e**	6,020	6,583	7,454	9,308	12,212	15,391	18,953	24,352	27,730	31,461	37,237	47,958	77,531	111,431	144,346
GDP Volume 1966 Prices	**99b.p**	5,574	5,951	6,438	6,934	7,319	7,473	7,885	8,587	9,125	9,576	9,648	9,430	8,743	8,993	9,715
GDP Volume (1995=100)	**99bvp**	36.3	38.8	42.0	45.2	47.7	48.7	51.4	56.0	59.5	62.4	62.9	61.5	57.0	58.6	63.3
GDP Deflator (1995=100)	**99bip**	1.1	1.1	1.2	1.4	1.7	2.1	2.5	2.9	3.1	3.4	4.1	5.7	10.6	13.6	15.9
																Millions:
Population	**99z**	1.73	1.80	1.84	1.87	1.92	1.96	2.01	2.07	2.12	2.17	2.25	2.27	2.42	2.50	2.57

	1985	1986	1987	1988	1989	1990	1991	1992	1993	1994	1995	1996	1997	1998	1999		Code
Government Finance																	
Year Ending December 31																	
Deficit (-) or Surplus	1,775	−4,171	‡−4,912	−5,429	−14,086	−17,458	−23,308	−16,047	−24,131	−85,361	−84,575	−95,471	−81,769	−89,435	−98,989		80
Total Revenue and Grants	29,725	39,922	‡44,025	53,436	63,765	74,975	100,875	142,671	166,065	191,247	253,699	302,497	363,540	444,486	547,436		81y
Revenue	29,725	39,922	‡44,025	53,436	63,765	74,975	100,875	142,671	166,065	191,247	253,699	302,497	363,540	444,486	547,436		81
Grants																	81z
Exp. & Lending Minus Repay.	....	....	‡48,937	58,865	77,851	92,433	124,183	158,718	190,196	276,608	338,274	397,968	445,309	533,921	646,424		82z
Expenditure	27,950	44,093	‡48,937	58,865	77,851	92,433	124,183	158,718	190,196	276,608	338,274	397,968	445,309	533,921	646,424		82
Lending Minus Repayments																	83
Total Financing	−1,774	4,171	‡4,912	5,429	14,086	17,459	23,308	16,047	24,131	85,361	84,575	95,471	81,769	89,435	98,991		80h
Domestic	−2,320	4,140	‡4,841	6,833	11,518	15,949	17,007	13,919	33,742	88,500	101,353	120,982	106,561	39,828	34,516		84a
Foreign	546	31	‡71	−1,404	2,568	1,510	6,301	2,128	−9,611	−3,139	−16,778	−25,511	−24,792	49,607	64,476		85a
Total Debt by Residence	45,452	64,656	‡60,654	64,079	82,239	97,405	269,047	338,524	398,135	506,771	671,357	922,811	1,080,891	1,283,354	1,427,974		88
Domestic Debt	26,434	44,072	‡40,375	44,029	61,393	77,883	125,013	176,706	228,678	320,272	463,933	697,676	706,375	977,150	1,064,311		88a
Foreign Debt	19,018	20,584	‡20,279	20,050	20,846	19,522	144,034	161,818	169,457	186,499	207,424	225,135	374,516	306,204	363,663		89a
Millions of Colones																	
National Accounts																	
Exports of Goods & Services	60,807	77,280	90,005	118,998	148,435	178,763	264,832	343,845	407,357	512,604	686,269	847,105	1,042,560	1,353,953	1,639,994		90c
Government Consumption	31,175	37,951	42,652	54,630	72,283	94,948	111,876	144,448	178,453	223,549	284,971	326,419	377,765	446,971	500,919		91f
Gross Fixed Capital Formation	38,240	46,023	56,313	66,211	87,224	117,071	136,098	188,318	248,535	258,940	309,783	335,996	434,586	590,456	679,561		93e
Increase/Decrease(-) in Stocks	13,000	16,139	20,857	19,358	26,009	25,786	37,413	80,098	78,090	101,202	79,577	161,428	163,489	180,701	175,660		93i
Private Consumption	118,974	144,381	176,475	215,794	256,923	321,143	411,105	544,609	648,464	779,307	958,024	1,115,129	1,301,652	1,526,594	1,683,564		96f
Imports of Goods & Services	−64,277	−75,195	−101,768	−125,247	−164,963	−214,864	−271,166	−394,878	−491,499	−569,805	−698,191	−881,511	1,059,572	1,368,941	1,451,269		98c
Gross Domestic Product (GDP)	197,920	246,579	284,533	349,743	425,911	522,848	690,158	906,440	1,069,400	1,305,796	1,620,433	1,904,566	2,260,479	2,729,735	3,228,429		99b
Net Factor Inc/Pmts(-) Abroad	−14,115	−15,099	−18,616	−25,661	−30,739	−21,480	−22,180	−28,083	−32,684	−21,402	−40,668	−39,340	−50,248	−119,869	−345,896		98.n
Gross National Income (GNI)	183,805	231,481	265,917	324,082	395,171	501,368	667,979	878,357	1,036,716	1,284,394	1,579,765	1,865,226	2,210,231	2,609,866	2,882,533		99a
Net National Income	178,317	225,351	258,803	315,163	384,550	488,151	649,618	856,133	1,010,976	1,254,018	1,539,888	1,816,473	2,153,719	2,541,622	2,801,822		99e
GDP Volume 1966 Prices	9,784	10,326	10,818	11,190	11,824	12,244	12,521	13,490	14,345	14,986	15,343	15,257	15,825	16,891	18,294		99b.p
GDP Volume (1995=100)	63.8	67.3	70.5	72.9	77.1	79.8	81.6	87.9	93.5	97.7	100.0	99.4	103.1	110.1	119.2		99bv p
GDP Deflator (1995=100)	19.2	22.6	24.9	29.6	34.1	40.4	52.2	63.6	70.6	82.5	100.0	118.2	135.2	153.0	167.1		99bi p
Midyear Estimates																	
Population	2.64	2.72	2.78	2.85	2.92	2.99	3.06	3.13	3.20	3.27	3.33	3.40	3.46	3.53	3.59		99z

(See notes in the back of the book.)

Côte d'Ivoire

		1970	1971	1972	1973	1974	1975	1976	1977	1978	1979	1980	1981	1982	1983	1984
Exchange Rates																*Francs per SDR:*
Official Rate	aa	276.02	283.61	278.00	284.00	272.08	262.55	288.70	285.76	272.28	264.78	287.99	334.52	370.92	436.97	470.11
															Francs per US Dollar:	
Official Rate	ae	276.02	261.22	256.05	235.42	222.22	224.27	248.49	235.25	209.00	201.00	225.80	287.40	336.25	417.37	479.60
Official Rate	rf	276.40	275.59	252.03	222.89	240.70	214.31	238.95	245.68	225.66	212.72	211.28	271.73	328.61	381.07	436.96
															Index Numbers (1995=100):	
Official Rate	ahx	180.5	98.6	197.9	224.6	207.2	233.0	209.0	203.0	221.4	234.6	236.4	184.6	152.6	131.5	114.5
Nominal Effective Exchange Rate	nec	....	....	....	....	....	....	....	....	....	....	52.9	54.7	50.5	48.2	52.3
Real Effective Exchange Rate	rec	....	....	....	....	....	....	....	....	....	....	149.3	128.2	116.8	112.7	108.4
Fund Position																*Millions of SDRs:*
Quota	2f.s	52.0	52.0	52.0	52.0	52.0	52.0	52.0	52.0	76.0	76.0	114.0	114.0	114.0	165.5	165.5
SDRs	1b.s	3.2	9.8	15.3	15.3	15.2	14.5	11.8	8.6	7.4	17.9	2.7	10.6	.1	15.5	.2
Reserve Position in the Fund	1c.s	10.8	10.8	10.8	10.8	—	—	—	—	10.4	12.2	9.5	—	—	—	—
Total Fund Cred.&Loans Outstg.	2tl	—	—	—	—	11.2	11.2	23.4	13.4	21.6	21.6	50.6	370.0	485.4	640.3	649.7
International Liquidity													*Millions of US Dollars Unless Otherwise Indicated:*			
Total Reserves minus Gold	1l.d	118.8	89.4	87.2	88.4	65.7	102.8	76.4	184.8	448.0	147.0	19.7	17.8	2.2	19.7	5.4
SDRs	1b.d	3.2	10.6	16.6	18.5	18.6	16.9	13.7	10.4	9.6	23.6	3.5	12.3	.1	16.2	.2
Reserve Position in the Fund	1c.d	10.7	11.7	11.7	13.0	—	—	—	—	13.5	16.1	12.1	—	—	—	—
Foreign Exchange	1d.d	104.9	67.2	58.9	56.9	47.1	85.8	62.7	174.4	424.9	107.3	4.1	5.6	2.1	3.5	5.2
Gold (Million Fine Troy Ounces)	1ad	....	....	....	....	....	....	—	.022	.034	.045	.045	.045	.045	.045	.045
Gold (National Valuation)	1and	....	....	....	....	....	....	—	1.0	1.5	2.1	2.0	18.7	19.0	17.2	14.8
Monetary Authorities: Other Liab.	4..d	3.2	.5	1.0	7.3	4.1	11.5	2.8	10.7	31.7	31.5	483.0	590.8	453.7	571.8	380.8
Deposit Money Banks: Assets	7a.d	91.1	101.2	31.6	47.9	165.5	36.9	111.0	147.0	118.6	94.9	95.0	100.9	122.8	99.6	146.5
Liabilities	7b.d	50.6	54.5	63.5	85.3	116.1	149.9	215.3	212.3	371.7	495.1	612.0	483.3	433.2	422.8	247.6
Monetary Authorities																*Billions of Francs:*
Foreign Assets	11	29.1	22.9	22.3	20.3	14.6	23.0	19.0	43.5	93.6	29.6	4.4	5.1	.7	8.2	2.6
Claims on Central Government	12a	—	1.5	4.8	.1	—	—	9.3	—	6.0	36.0	91.9	166.0	245.3	316.4	333.5
Claims on Deposit Money Banks	12e	22.9	29.2	35.0	51.5	91.1	90.4	103.0	165.2	173.6	197.7	266.2	366.8	405.7	466.9	433.3
Claims on Other Financial Insts	12f	—	—	—	—	—	—	2.9	4.4	5.7	6.4	5.7	5.5	6.4	7.8	8.6
Reserve Money	14	45.0	50.2	56.7	62.5	87.5	99.3	120.6	167.4	221.0	230.1	232.6	255.2	239.6	257.6	309.2
of which: Currency Outside DMBs	14a	39.8	47.0	51.5	57.0	77.5	89.6	106.7	137.3	164.5	193.7	210.9	229.8	219.1	232.0	278.7
Foreign Liabilities	16c	.9	.1	.3	1.7	3.9	5.5	7.4	6.3	18.5	18.0	137.5	307.5	346.5	532.4	500.8
Central Government Deposits	16d	5.2	.8	1.1	3.8	13.4	6.7	2.4	33.2	40.7	21.0	3.5	2.9	87.0	37.7	19.7
Other Items (Net)	17r	.9	2.5	4.0	4.0	.8	2.1	3.8	6.2	-1.4	.6	-5.4	-22.1	-14.9	-28.4	-51.7
Deposit Money Banks																*Billions of Francs:*
Reserves	20	4.7	3.1	5.0	5.1	9.1	8.2	12.0	30.0	55.5	32.6	31.5	25.0	20.9	26.6	39.2
Foreign Assets	21	25.3	25.9	8.1	11.0	36.8	8.3	27.6	34.6	24.8	19.1	21.4	29.0	41.3	41.6	70.3
Claims on Central Government	22a	.1	.2	.2	.2	.3	.3	5.1	2.8	6.4	I 24.8	12.6	13.9	17.0	17.4	19.4
Claims on Private Sector	22d	89.3	107.5	128.8	167.4	238.5	286.4	377.3	581.7	673.3	I 773.7	861.2	947.7	1,010.3	1,091.1	1,076.8
Claims on Other Financial Insts	22f	....	....	....	....	....	....	....	....	....	I 11.2	17.5	16.6	13.9	15.9	18.9
Demand Deposits	24	42.0	43.2	50.0	59.5	82.8	87.9	151.7	243.4	248.3	I 240.0	227.7	234.5	238.2	253.1	290.6
Time Deposits	25	23.2	25.5	19.7	30.0	60.4	64.7	89.7	141.4	166.1	I 132.4	143.1	175.3	200.0	203.9	251.5
Foreign Liabilities	26c	8.4	8.1	10.0	12.6	18.0	23.5	41.7	35.7	61.0	73.5	111.7	110.5	108.7	137.5	70.8
Long-Term Foreign Liabilities	26cl	5.7	5.9	6.2	7.1	7.8	10.1	11.8	14.3	16.7	26.0	26.6	28.4	36.9	39.0	48.0
Central Government Deposits	26d	9.5	15.3	11.5	15.1	25.2	16.8	23.6	28.6	64.4	I 141.5	140.6	106.4	89.3	78.0	90.8
Credit from Monetary Authorities	26g	22.9	29.2	35.0	51.5	91.1	90.4	103.4	165.2	173.5	196.6	270.0	365.2	407.0	457.0	449.3
Other Items (Net)	27r	7.8	9.6	9.7	8.0	-.6	9.6	.2	20.6	30.1	51.3	24.7	12.0	23.2	24.2	23.6
Treasury Claims: Private Sector	22d.i	3.4	3.9	4.2	7.9	5.2	6.2	11.7	19.4	17.3	12.2	15.1	9.3	12.0	10.2	11.8
Post Office: Checking Deposits	24..i	1.7	1.9	1.6	1.4	2.5	2.3	1.6	2.4	2.6	—	—	—	2.9	2.8	5.0
Monetary Survey																*Billions of Francs:*
Foreign Assets (Net)	31n	45.2	40.5	20.1	17.1	29.5	2.3	-2.6	36.1	38.9	-42.9	-223.3	-383.9	-413.2	-620.0	-498.7
Domestic Credit	32	76.4	95.1	122.7	150.2	205.6	267.2	370.4	529.5	588.8	I 689.6	844.9	1,040.5	1,119.6	1,335.7	1,351.6
Claims on Central Govt. (Net)	32an	-16.2	-16.2	-10.2	-25.2	-38.1	-25.3	-21.6	-76.0	-107.5	I -114.0	-54.7	61.5	77.0	210.7	235.6
Claims on Private Sector	32d	92.7	111.4	132.9	175.4	243.7	292.5	389.0	601.2	690.7	I 785.9	876.3	957.0	1,022.3	1,101.3	1,088.6
Claims on Other Financial Insts	32f	....	....	....	....	....	....	2.9	4.4	5.7	I 17.7	23.2	22.0	20.3	23.7	27.4
Money	34	83.5	92.1	103.2	117.9	162.8	179.8	260.1	383.1	415.6	I 433.8	438.7	464.4	460.3	488.0	574.6
Quasi-Money	35	23.2	25.5	19.7	30.0	60.4	64.7	89.7	141.4	166.1	I 132.4	143.1	175.3	200.0	203.9	251.5
Long-Term Foreign Liabilities	36cl	5.7	5.9	6.2	7.1	7.8	10.1	11.8	14.3	16.7	26.0	26.6	28.4	36.9	39.0	48.0
Other Items (Net)	37r	9.2	12.2	13.7	12.3	4.1	14.9	6.2	26.8	29.5	54.5	13.2	-11.5	9.1	-15.2	-21.1
Money plus Quasi-Money	35l	106.8	117.6	122.8	147.9	223.2	244.6	349.8	524.5	581.6	I 566.2	581.8	639.7	660.3	692.0	826.1
Other Banking Institutions																*Billions of Francs:*
Savings Deposits	45	1.0	1.1	1.2	1.3	1.5	1.5	1.8	2.1	2.1	....	....	....	....	....	....
Liquid Liabilities	55l	107.7	118.7	124.0	149.2	224.7	246.1	351.5	526.6	583.7	....	....	....	....	....	....
Interest Rates																*Percent Per Annum:*
Discount Rate *(End of Period)*	60	3.50	3.50	3.50	5.50	5.50	8.00	8.00	8.00	8.00	8.00	10.50	10.50	12.50	10.50	10.50
Money Market Rate	60b	....	....	....	....	....	....	7.28	7.38	7.40	7.72	10.13	13.68	14.66	12.23	11.84
Deposit Rate	60l	3.00	3.00	3.00	5.75	5.75	5.88	6.00	6.00	6.00	6.00	6.19	6.25	7.75	7.50	7.25
Lending Rate	60p	....	....	....	....	....	....	12.00	12.00	12.00	14.50	14.50	16.00	14.50	14.50	
Prices and Production																*Index Numbers (1995=100):*
Consumer Prices	64	12.4	12.3	12.4	13.7	16.1	18.0	20.2	25.7	29.1	33.8	38.8	42.2	45.4	48.0	50.0
Industrial Production	66	24.4	28.8	32.6	37.6	39.8	48.6	60.7	70.6	81.3	I 88.2	101.6	102.6	98.7	84.0	I 91.0
International Transactions																*Billions of Francs*
Exports	70	130.19	126.56	139.54	190.86	291.77	254.57	392.50	529.21	524.38	534.85	663.92	689.30	747.45	796.77	1,184.34
Imports, c.i.f.	71	107.70	110.84	114.32	157.52	232.29	241.39	311.61	429.57	522.50	528.85	636.96	653.32	718.59	704.25	658.57
																1985=100

	1985	1986	1987	1988	1989	1990	1991	1992	1993	1994	1995	1996	1997	1998	1999		
Exchange Rates																	
End of Period																Official Rate	aa
	415.26	394.78	378.78	407.68	380.32	364.84	370.48	378.57	404.89	†780.44	728.38	753.06	807.94	791.61	†896.19		
End of Period (ae) Period Average (rf)																Official Rate	ae
	378.05	322.75	267.00	302.95	289.40	256.45	259.00	275.32	294.77	†534.60	490.00	523.70	598.81	562.21	†652.95		
	449.26	346.31	300.54	297.85	319.01	272.26	282.11	264.69	283.16	†555.20	499.15	511.55	583.67	589.95	†615.70	Official Rate	rf
Period Averages																	
	111.9	144.3	166.1	167.8	156.5	183.7	177.4	188.9	176.3	90.0	100.0	97.5	85.6	84.7	81.1	Official Rate	ahx
	57.2	67.8	77.5	84.8	94.9	119.6	127.0	144.9	162.5	93.9	100.0	100.6	96.9	101.2	100.1	Nominal Effective Exchange Rate	ne c
	108.3	130.2	144.6	147.9	139.6	141.3	136.3	142.4	140.4	86.5	100.0	100.5	98.9	105.5	103.5	Real Effective Exchange Rate	re c
Fund Position																	
End of Period																	
	165.5	165.5	165.5	165.5	165.5	165.5	165.5	238.2	238.2	238.2	238.2	238.2	238.2	238.2	325.2	Quota	2f.s
	.1	7.0	.2	.5	3.9	.8	1.4	.2	.8	.1	1.2	.8	—	.1	2.5	SDRs	1b.s
	—	—	—	—	—	—	—	—	.1	.1	.1	.1	.2	.2	.2	Reserve Position in the Fund	1c.s
	605.5	538.7	425.8	377.9	281.3	303.1	259.7	194.5	159.1	224.8	287.1	349.6	333.5	457.3	451.4	Total Fund Cred.&Loans Outstg.	2tl
International Liquidity																	
End of Period																	
	4.7	19.6	8.9	10.4	15.0	4.0	13.4	6.9	2.3	204.3	529.0	605.8	618.4	855.5	630.4	Total Reserves minus Gold	1l.d
	.1	8.5	.2	.7	5.1	1.2	2.0	.3	1.1	.2	1.8	1.2	—	.2	3.4	SDRs	1b.d
	—	—	—	—	—	—	—	—	.1	.1	.1	.2	.2	.3	.3	Reserve Position in the Fund	1c.d
	4.7	11.0	8.7	9.7	9.8	2.8	11.4	6.7	1.1	204.0	527.0	604.4	618.1	855.0	626.6	Foreign Exchange	1d.d
	.045	.045	.045	.045	.045	.045	.045	.045	.045	.045	.045	.045	.045	.045	.045	Gold (Million Fine Troy Ounces)	1ad
	14.4	18.0	21.0	18.5	17.4	16.9	15.8	15.4	16.6	16.6	17.1	16.7	13.6	13.1	13.1	Gold (National Valuation)	1and
	190.7	274.1	597.8	845.5	1,019.8	1,330.7	1,316.0	1,519.8	1,382.4	1.7	9.6	7.8	10.6	14.4	7.6	Monetary Authorities: Other Liab.	4..d
	174.8	167.4	191.8	154.6	141.3	189.6	163.6	206.9	176.5	202.1	352.6	268.5	266.8	311.3	351.9	Deposit Money Banks: Assets	7a.d
	388.3	520.7	775.3	713.5	687.1	614.6	558.6	449.6	486.4	299.8	400.6	312.0	295.4	363.0	389.7	Liabilities	7b.d
Monetary Authorities																	
End of Period																	
	1.8	6.3	2.4	3.2	4.3	1.0	3.5	1.9	.7	109.2	259.2	317.2	370.3	481.0	411.6	Foreign Assets	11
	327.4	327.6	289.6	279.1	245.6	250.3	245.0	239.1	273.2	433.2	382.6	439.8	449.3	572.3	596.4	Claims on Central Government	12a
	392.2	412.9	498.8	497.5	452.0	523.9	521.5	533.6	506.6	130.0	140.8	125.8	104.7	114.6	99.8	Claims on Deposit Money Banks	12e
	9.9	11.1	11.7	11.9	10.7	10.1	9.4	9.3	10.6	5.1	12.3	14.4	13.4	14.7	14.2	Claims on Other Financial Insts	12f
	389.1	406.4	413.2	356.4	278.8	296.4	305.1	271.1	295.8	462.4	516.0	550.8	615.7	733.1	676.7	Reserve Money	14
	307.1	318.7	305.0	298.5	254.1	270.7	258.3	252.1	272.5	392.6	451.4	473.2	571.8	652.1	615.5	of which: Currency Outside DMBs	14a
	334.4	332.3	328.4	413.8	403.5	451.9	437.1	492.1	471.9	176.3	213.8	267.3	275.8	370.2	409.5	Foreign Liabilities	16c
	25.0	27.0	33.0	1.9	3.1	16.7	18.5	8.2	13.1	45.8	43.0	49.5	27.8	51.1	56.7	Central Government Deposits	16d
	-17.2	11.3	27.9	19.6	27.3	20.3	18.7	12.5	10.3	-6.9	22.0	29.5	18.4	28.2	-20.8	Other Items (Net)	17r
Deposit Money Banks																	
End of Period																	
	78.1	90.3	107.7	61.7	26.9	24.8	38.9	22.1	20.6	66.6	58.1	74.7	45.4	67.2	60.7	Reserves	20
	66.1	54.0	51.2	46.8	40.9	48.6	42.4	57.0	52.0	108.0	172.8	140.6	159.8	175.0	229.8	Foreign Assets	21
	52.7	74.5	98.4	107.0	81.3	76.6	83.1	226.8	224.7	314.9	371.1	413.4	415.9	412.6	382.8	Claims on Central Government	22a
	1,053.8	1,061.8	1,142.8	1,143.8	1,091.8	1,062.7	1,053.7	928.9	878.5	828.2	997.1	1,016.0	1,147.4	1,186.7	1,084.5	Claims on Private Sector	22d
	21.4	30.7	37.6	29.9	27.3	20.5	11.7	11.2	6.2	5.8	1.7	—	—	—	—	Claims on Other Financial Insts	22f
	311.2	317.1	292.3	278.3	255.6	254.4	250.1	234.5	219.2	403.3	490.7	489.0	502.8	562.0	576.7	Demand Deposits	24
	319.3	327.5	331.4	366.0	356.5	319.0	336.3	346.9	331.0	412.1	485.3	519.6	527.7	485.1	477.7	Time Deposits	25
	78.7	89.8	109.3	124.5	128.6	93.0	82.3	78.1	95.8	112.5	160.1	128.2	153.8	172.3	207.1	Foreign Liabilities	26c
	68.1	78.2	97.7	91.7	70.3	64.6	62.4	45.7	47.6	47.8	36.2	35.2	23.1	31.7	47.4	Long-Term Foreign Liabilities	26cl
	121.5	118.6	164.2	114.4	80.7	97.7	82.5	74.9	92.5	171.1	183.1	243.3	278.9	325.7	234.4	Central Government Deposits	26d
	393.5	414.5	480.7	458.4	444.9	514.7	516.4	524.7	497.3	134.4	152.2	124.3	104.7	116.0	91.0	Credit from Monetary Authorities	26g
	-20.2	-34.5	-37.9	-44.1	-68.3	-110.1	-100.3	-58.9	-101.3	42.3	93.0	105.0	177.6	148.7	123.5	Other Items (Net)	27r
	13.6	12.2	7.4	6.4	14.7	10.0	12.3	17.5	17.8	26.7	19.0	22.7	22.0	—	16.0	Treasury Claims: Private Sector	22d.i
	1.8	1.4	1.6	1.1	1.5	1.2	1.4	2.5	1.7	2.1	1.5	2.4	3.6	2.0	3.0	Post Office: Checking Deposits	24..i
Monetary Survey																	
End of Period																	
	-345.2	-342.7	-384.2	-488.3	-486.8	-495.3	-473.6	-511.3	-515.0	-71.5	58.1	62.3	100.5	113.5	24.8	Foreign Assets (Net)	31n
	1,320.5	1,361.4	1,384.5	1,456.5	1,374.3	1,307.1	1,303.3	1,334.6	1,289.3	1,372.4	1,540.1	1,593.1	1,722.9	1,811.5	1,789.8	Domestic Credit	32
	221.8	245.7	185.0	264.5	229.9	203.8	216.3	367.7	376.1	506.5	510.1	540.0	540.1	610.1	675.1	Claims on Central Govt. (Net)	32an
	1,067.4	1,074.0	1,150.2	1,150.3	1,106.5	1,072.7	1,065.9	946.4	896.3	854.9	1,016.0	1,038.7	1,169.4	1,186.7	1,100.5	Claims on Private Sector	32d
	31.2	41.7	49.3	41.8	38.0	30.6	21.0	20.5	16.9	10.9	13.9	14.4	13.4	14.7	14.2	Claims on Other Financial Insts	32f
	620.2	637.4	598.9	578.0	511.2	526.4	510.1	489.4	494.0	798.8	944.5	966.4	1,080.0	1,219.3	1,198.0	Money	34
	319.3	327.5	331.4	366.0	356.5	319.0	336.3	346.9	331.0	412.1	485.3	519.6	527.7	485.1	477.7	Quasi-Money	35
	68.1	78.2	97.7	91.7	70.3	64.6	62.4	45.7	47.6	47.8	36.2	35.2	23.1	31.7	47.4	Long-Term Foreign Liabilities	36cl
	-32.3	-24.3	-27.7	-67.4	-50.5	-98.2	-79.1	-58.7	-98.3	42.1	132.0	134.2	192.6	188.9	91.6	Other Items (Net)	37r
	939.4	964.9	930.3	944.0	867.7	845.4	846.4	836.4	825.0	1,210.9	1,429.9	1,486.0	1,607.7	1,704.4	1,675.7	Money plus Quasi-Money	35l
Other Banking Institutions																	
End of Period																	
	....	....	....	....	....	....	....	....	....	....	—	—	—	—	—	Savings Deposits	45
	....	....	....	....	....	....	....	....	....	....	....	1,486.0	1,607.7	1,704.4	1,675.7	Liquid Liabilities	55l
Interest Rates																	
Percent Per Annum																	
	10.50	8.50	8.50	9.50	11.00	11.00	11.00	12.50	10.50	10.00	7.50	6.50	6.00	6.25	5.75	Discount Rate (End of Period)	60
	10.66	8.58	8.37	8.72	10.07	10.98	10.94	11.44	....	....	....	....	....	4.81	4.95	Money Market Rate	60b
	7.25	6.08	5.25	5.25	6.42	7.00	7.00	7.75	....	....	....	....	....	3.50	3.50	Deposit Rate	60l
	14.50	13.50	13.50	13.58	15.08	16.00	16.00	16.75	....	....	....	....	....	....	....	Lending Rate	60p
Prices and Production																	
Period Averages																	
	†51.0	55.9	59.8	63.9	64.6	64.1	65.2	67.9	†69.4	87.5	100.0	†102.5	106.6	111.6	112.5	Consumer Prices	64
	93.8	101.4	101.4	98.6	96.9	91.0	88.6	90.0	89.1	91.9	100.0	113.3	126.8	141.0	....	Industrial Production	66
International Transactions																	
Billions of Francs																	
	1,318.06	1,160.44	929.14	826.47	895.60	836.43	757.76	751.70	713.20	1,522.50	1,819.30	2,188.30	2,439.00	2,414.00	2,510.00	Exports	70
	772.98	709.04	673.90	619.92	673.45	571.10	593.37	613.17	599.00	1,064.60	1,463.00	1,484.50	1,623.10	1,885.60	2,013.60	Imports, c.i.f.	71

1985=100

Côte d'Ivoire

662

	Code	1970	1971	1972	1973	1974	1975	1976	1977	1978	1979	1980	1981	1982	1983	1984
Balance of Payments																*Millions of US Dollars:*
Current Account, n.i.e.	78al *d*	....	....	....	....	....	-378.9	-249.3	-177.3	-839.2	-1,383.3	-1,826.5	-1,411.4	-1,017.3	-931.1	-76.8
Goods: Exports f.o.b.	78aa *d*	....	....	....	....	....	1,238.8	1,735.1	2,412.1	2,615.9	2,722.8	3,012.6	2,435.1	2,347.2	2,066.3	2,624.7
Goods: Imports f.o.b.	78ab *d*	....	....	....	....	....	-1,012.1	-1,161.3	-1,597.2	-2,042.9	-2,233.4	-2,613.6	-2,067.9	-1,789.7	-1,635.1	-1,487.3
Trade Balance	78ac *d*	....	....	....	....	....	226.8	573.8	814.9	573.0	489.4	399.0	367.3	557.5	431.2	1,137.4
Services: Credit	78ad *d*	....	....	....	....	....	225.8	235.2	324.8	410.4	510.5	564.2	434.3	450.7	425.1	370.5
Services: Debit	78ae *d*	....	....	....	....	....	-550.1	-642.1	-823.9	-1,097.0	-1,363.8	-1,531.1	-1,225.5	-1,163.4	-990.1	-824.3
Balance on Goods & Services	78af *d*	....	....	....	....	....	-97.5	166.8	315.8	-113.6	-363.9	-568.0	-423.9	-155.2	-133.8	683.6
Income: Credit	78ag *d*	....	....	....	....	....	38.7	28.0	42.3	60.3	59.2	62.9	46.0	46.0	46.7	37.5
Income: Debit	78ah *d*	....	....	....	....	....	-178.2	-185.0	-235.3	-367.4	-506.8	-615.8	-554.2	-545.3	-548.5	-530.9
Balance on Gds, Serv. & Inc.	78ai *d*	....	....	....	....	....	-237.0	9.9	122.8	-420.7	-811.4	-1,120.8	-932.2	-654.6	-635.6	190.2
Current Transfers, n.i.e.: Credit	78aj *d*	....	....	....	....	....	130.2	128.7	160.3	186.0	199.1	242.3	205.2	189.4	174.2	149.9
Current Transfers: Debit	78ak *d*	....	....	....	....	....	-272.0	-387.9	-460.4	-604.5	-771.0	-948.0	-684.5	-552.0	-469.7	-417.0
Capital Account, n.i.e.	78bc *d*	....	....	....	....	....	—	—	—	—	—	—	—	—	—	—
Capital Account, n.i.e.: Credit	78ba *d*	....	....	....	....	....	—	—	—	—	—	—	—	—	—	—
Capital Account: Debit	78bb *d*	....	....	....	....	....	—	—	—	—	—	—	—	—	—	—
Financial Account, n.i.e.	78bj *d*	....	....	....	....	....	288.8	254.4	351.7	1,023.7	1,132.0	1,215.5	906.0	749.5	384.4	-280.8
Direct Investment Abroad	78bd *d*	....	....	....	....	....	—	—	—	—	—	—	—	—	—	—
Dir. Invest. in Rep. Econ., n.i.e.	78be *d*	....	....	....	....	....	69.1	44.8	14.7	83.3	74.7	94.7	32.8	47.5	37.5	21.7
Portfolio Investment Assets	78bf *d*	....	....	....	....	....	-.9	-5.0	-9.4	-6.6	1.4	2.8	.7	—	1.3	-.9
Equity Securities	78bk *d*	....	....	....	....	....	-.9	-.8	-9.4	-6.6	-.9	.5	.7	.3	1.6	-.7
Debt Securities	78bl *d*	....	....	....	....	....	—	-4.2	—	—	2.4	2.4	—	-.3	-.3	-.2
Portfolio Investment Liab., n.i.e.	78bg *d*	....	....	....	....	....	-.5	.8	-2.4	.4	—	—	—	-1.2	-1.0	-.7
Equity Securities	78bm *d*	....	....	....	....	....	1.9	1.7	—	1.8	—	—	—	—	—	—
Debt Securities	78bn *d*	....	....	....	....	....	-2.3	-.8	-2.4	-1.3	—	—	—	-1.2	-1.0	-.7
Financial Derivatives Assets	78bw *d*	....	....	....	....	....	....	....	....	....	....	....	....	....	....	....
Financial Derivatives Liabilities	78bx *d*	....	....	....	....	....	....	....	....	....	....	....	....	....	....	....
Other Investment Assets	78bh *d*	....	....	....	....	....	-14.9	-190.4	-371.2	-24.4	205.0	-30.3	-27.6	-10.7	-64.0	-94.5
Monetary Authorities	78bo *d*	....	....	....	....	....	....	....	....	....	....	....	....	....	....	....
General Government	78bp *d*	....	....	....	....	....	-50.4	-27.2	-143.7	56.3	111.4	-34.6	29.8	3.7	17.8	-2.5
Banks	78bq *d*	....	....	....	....	....	30.8	-95.8	-66.8	-96.6	175.8	-33.6	-45.6	-12.5	-12.1	-95.0
Other Sectors	78br *d*	....	....	....	....	....	4.7	-67.4	-160.8	16.0	-82.3	37.9	-11.8	-1.8	-69.8	3.0
Other Investment Liab., n.i.e.	78bi *d*	....	....	....	....	....	236.1	404.3	720.0	970.9	850.9	1,148.2	900.2	713.9	410.7	-206.4
Monetary Authorities	78bs *d*	....	....	....	....	....	7.9	-7.5	8.1	15.1	-.9	-23.7	-.7	4.0	-1.6	1.8
General Government	78bt *d*	....	....	....	....	....	104.5	127.6	352.9	528.7	461.6	751.6	656.5	604.4	139.9	-228.4
Banks	78bu *d*	....	....	....	....	....	56.9	98.3	14.7	170.6	181.0	227.7	18.4	68.2	157.7	-43.7
Other Sectors	78bv *d*	....	....	....	....	....	66.7	185.8	344.4	256.6	209.2	192.6	226.0	37.4	114.7	63.9
Net Errors and Omissions	78ca *d*	....	....	....	....	....	5.6	-3.7	-48.2	-32.2	-78.8	-76.9	-98.8	-35.2	-154.1	-119.1
Overall Balance	78cb *d*	....	....	....	....	....	-84.5	1.4	126.3	152.4	-330.1	-687.9	-604.2	-302.9	-700.8	-476.7
Reserves and Related Items	79da *d*	....	....	....	....	....	84.5	-1.4	-126.3	-152.4	330.1	687.9	604.2	302.9	700.8	476.7
Reserve Assets	79db *d*	....	....	....	....	....	84.5	-37.1	-115.2	-164.1	329.9	135.5	6.2	20.3	-19.1	10.0
Use of Fund Credit and Loans	79dc *d*	....	....	....	....	....	—	14.6	-11.6	9.9	—	37.0	372.0	125.6	165.3	9.9
Exceptional Financing	79de *d*	....	....	....	....	....	—	21.1	.5	1.9	.2	515.4	226.1	157.0	554.6	456.7
International Investment Position																*Millions of US Dollars*
Assets	79aa *d*	....	....	....	....	....	....	....	....	....	....	....	....	....	....	....
Direct Investment Abroad	79ab *d*	....	....	....	....	....	....	....	....	....	....	....	....	....	....	....
Portfolio Investment	79ac *d*	....	....	....	....	....	....	....	....	....	....	....	....	....	....	....
Equity Securities	79ad *d*	....	....	....	....	....	....	....	....	....	....	....	....	....	....	....
Debt Securities	79ae *d*	....	....	....	....	....	....	....	....	....	....	....	....	....	....	....
Financial Derivatives	79al *d*	....	....	....	....	....	—	—	—	—	—	—	—	—	—	—
Other Investment	79af *d*	....	....	....	....	....	....	....	....	....	....	....	....	....	....	....
Monetary Authorities	79ag *d*	....	....	....	....	....	....	....	....	....	....	....	....	....	....	....
General Government	79ah *d*	....	....	....	....	....	....	....	....	....	....	....	....	....	....	....
Banks	79ai *d*	....	....	....	....	....	....	....	....	....	....	....	....	....	....	....
Other Sectors	79aj *d*	....	....	....	....	....	....	....	....	....	....	....	....	....	....	....
Reserve Assets	79ak *d*	....	....	....	....	....	....	....	....	....	....	....	....	....	....	....
Liabilities	79la *d*	....	....	....	....	....	....	....	....	....	....	....	....	....	....	....
Dir. Invest. in Rep. Economy	79lb *d*	....	....	....	....	....	....	....	....	....	....	....	....	....	....	....
Portfolio Investment	79lc *d*	....	....	....	....	....	....	....	....	....	....	....	....	....	....	....
Equity Securities	79ld *d*	....	....	....	....	....	....	....	....	....	....	....	....	....	....	....
Debt Securities	79le *d*	....	....	....	....	....	....	....	....	....	....	....	....	....	....	....
Financial Derivatives	79ll *d*	....	....	....	....	....	—	—	—	—	—	—	—	—	—	—
Other Investment	79lf *d*	....	....	....	....	....	....	....	....	....	....	....	....	....	....	....
Monetary Authorities	79lg *d*	....	....	....	....	....	....	....	....	....	....	....	....	....	....	....
General Government	79lh *d*	....	....	....	....	....	....	....	....	....	....	....	....	....	....	....
Banks	79li *d*	....	....	....	....	....	....	....	....	....	....	....	....	....	....	....
Other Sectors	79lj *d*	....	....	....	....	....	....	....	....	....	....	....	....	....	....	....

Balance of Payments

Minus Sign Indicates Debit

1985	1986	1987	1988	1989	1990	1991	1992	1993	1994	1995	1996	1997	1998	1999		
63.7	−300.3	−970.0	−1,241.2	−967.3	−1,214.3	−1,074.1	−1,012.7	−891.7	−13.8	−492.4	−313.4	−241.7	−312.6	....	Current Account, n.i.e.	78al *d*
2,761.0	3,187.4	2,949.7	2,691.3	2,696.8	2,912.6	2,705.0	2,946.8	2,518.7	2,895.9	3,805.9	4,446.1	4,298.7	4,575.1	....	Goods: Exports f.o.b.	78aa *d*
−1,409.9	−1,639.9	−1,863.3	−1,769.4	−1,777.1	−1,818.8	−1,781.6	−1,952.1	−1,770.4	−1,606.8	−2,430.3	−2,622.4	−2,479.5	−2,705.1	....	Goods: Imports f.o.b.	78ab *d*
1,351.1	1,547.5	1,086.4	921.9	919.7	1,093.8	923.4	994.7	748.3	1,289.1	1,375.5	1,823.7	1,819.2	1,870.0	....	*Trade Balance*	78ac *d*
399.1	471.5	535.4	555.7	485.9	590.2	614.3	649.2	675.9	507.7	530.9	565.9	532.3	549.9	....	Services: Credit	78ad *d*
−763.5	−1,313.6	−1,352.6	−1,342.3	−1,230.4	−1,626.0	−1,393.8	−1,477.2	−1,331.7	−1,011.1	−1,375.7	−1,443.4	−1,367.7	−1,474.4	....	Services: Debit	78ae *d*
986.7	705.4	269.2	135.3	175.2	58.0	143.9	166.8	92.5	785.7	530.7	946.1	983.8	945.5	....	*Balance on Goods & Services*	78af *d*
39.4	67.3	77.9	71.8	55.8	58.0	60.3	18.9	97.8	133.8	189.5	171.0	167.4	169.8	....	Income: Credit	78ag *d*
−705.4	−714.1	−957.3	−992.8	−995.9	−1,149.2	−1,171.9	−1,099.8	−887.8	−817.5	−976.1	−939.5	−895.4	−879.6	....	Income: Debit	78ah *d*
320.7	58.6	−610.2	−785.6	−764.9	−1,033.2	−967.7	−914.1	−697.5	102.0	−255.8	177.7	255.8	235.8	....	*Balance on Gds, Serv. & Inc.*	78ai *d*
130.5	184.2	276.1	208.8	316.0	370.2	413.7	404.6	270.9	246.8	277.7	55.5	50.0	50.9	....	Current Transfers, n.i.e.: Credit	78aj *d*
−387.5	−543.2	−635.9	−664.4	−518.5	−551.3	−520.0	−503.2	−465.1	−362.6	−514.3	−546.6	−547.6	−599.2	....	Current Transfers: Debit	78ak *d*
—	—	—	—	—	—	—	—	—	527.6	291.3	49.8	39.7	36.3	....	Capital Account, n.i.e.	78bc *d*
—	—	—	—	—	—	—	—	—	527.6	291.3	49.8	39.7	36.3	....	Capital Account, n.i.e.: Credit	78ba *d*
—	—	—	—	—	—	—	—	—	—	—	—	—	—	....	Capital Account: Debit	78bb *d*
−317.2	−36.4	33.3	−159.1	−305.3	−122.7	−151.4	−450.7	−356.0	−523.1	−88.6	−697.3	−455.6	−533.9	....	Financial Account, n.i.e.	78bj *d*
											−.4			....	Direct Investment Abroad	78bd *d*
29.2	70.7	87.5	51.7	18.5	48.1	16.3	−230.8	87.9	78.0	211.5	269.2	341.3	435.3	....	Dir. Invest. in Rep. Econ., n.i.e.	78be *d*
−1.1	−.3	−5.3	−13.4	1.9	4.4	6.4	—	7.4	−27.4	−8.4	−15.8	−15.4	−14.2	....	Portfolio Investment Assets	78bf *d*
−1.1	−.3	−4.3	−13.4	1.9	4.4	6.4	—	7.4	7.7	1.2	−1.4			....	Equity Securities	78bk *d*
		−1.0							−35.1	−9.6	−14.5	−15.4	−14.2	....	Debt Securities	78bl *d*
−.2	—	−2.7	−.7	−.6	—	—	—	—	−.7	10.0	26.6	30.7	38.5	....	Portfolio Investment Liab., n.i.e.	78bg *d*
—	—	—	—	—	—	—	—	—	1.1	1.2	11.7			....	Equity Securities	78bm *d*
−.2	—	−2.7	−.7	−.6	—	—	—	—	−1.8	8.8	14.9	30.7	38.5	....	Debt Securities	78bn *d*
											−3.3			....	Financial Derivatives Assets	78bw *d*
....	....	....	....	....	....	....	....	—	—	—		....	....	....	Financial Derivatives Liabilities	78bx *d*
−30.3	96.2	−3.0	50.4	21.6	−91.8	−25.2	169.6	51.9	−39.6	−323.2	−254.1	−278.4	−324.3	....	Other Investment Assets	78bh *d*
								—	—	—				....	Monetary Authorities	78bo *d*
−4.7	4.0	−11.3	8.4	−25.1	−1.8	−3.2	—	—	−11.9	−14.2	−22.3			....	General Government	78bp *d*
−26.7	82.6	23.3	49.4	36.0	−66.1	2.8	63.8	72.7	−95.3	−33.1	37.5	−278.4	−324.3	....	Banks	78bq *d*
1.1	9.5	−15.0	−7.4	10.7	−23.9	−24.8	105.8	−20.8	67.5	−275.9	−269.4			....	Other Sectors	78br *d*
−314.7	−203.0	−43.3	−247.1	−346.7	−83.4	−148.9	−389.5	−503.2	−533.3	21.4	−719.4	−533.7	−669.2	....	Other Investment Liab., n.i.e.	78bi *d*
6.9	−12.7	9.0	−21.5	−.9	55.1	−10.3	−33.2	−44.1	−726.6	1.8	−1.2		—	....	Monetary Authorities	78bs *d*
−239.1	−262.5	−139.4	−353.5	−482.4	−75.7	−141.1	−207.4	−444.6	249.8	−105.8	−601.1	−471.8	−596.8	....	General Government	78bt *d*
−42.5	145.2	159.4	65.5	−29.8	−124.5	−18.8	−134.9	7.8	75.1	77.1	−42.4			....	Banks	78bu *d*
−40.1	−73.1	−72.2	62.4	166.5	61.7	21.3	−14.0	−22.2	−131.7	48.3	−74.7	−61.9	−72.4	....	Other Sectors	78bv *d*
84.2	−55.3	12.6	−24.4	−38.8	−109.6	−102.2	46.6	11.1	−11.1	35.6	−36.2	64.8	340.0	....	Net Errors and Omissions	78ca *d*
−169.2	−392.0	−924.2	−1,424.8	−1,311.5	−1,446.6	−1,327.6	−1,416.9	−1,236.6	−20.3	−254.2	−997.0	−592.8	−638.9	....	*Overall Balance*	78cb *d*
169.2	392.0	924.2	1,424.8	1,311.5	1,446.6	1,327.6	1,416.9	1,236.6	20.3	254.2	997.0	592.8	638.9	....	Reserves and Related Items	79da *d*
4.8	−10.7	−17.2	−.3	11.3	16.3	−.5	−84.4	4.4	−194.5	−302.5	−113.4	−94.4	−291.4	....	Reserve Assets	79db *d*
−45.4	−78.4	−145.8	−63.0	−123.9	33.4	−58.5	−91.9	−49.0	94.3	94.9	90.3	−22.3	168.8	....	Use of Fund Credit and Loans	79dc *d*
209.8	481.1	1,087.1	1,488.0	1,424.1	1,396.9	1,386.7	1,593.2	1,281.2	120.5	461.8	1,020.0	709.5	761.4	....	Exceptional Financing	79de *d*

International Investment Position

Millions of US Dollars

1985	1986	1987	1988	1989	1990	1991	1992	1993	1994	1995	1996	1997	1998	1999		
....	....	....	....	....	....	....	....	....	541.8	909.5	875.3	889.9	....	....	Assets	79aa *d*
....	....	....	....	....	....	....	....	....	—	—	—	—	....	....	Direct Investment Abroad	79ab *d*
....	....	....	....	....	....	....	....	....	—	—	—	—	....	....	Portfolio Investment	79ac *d*
....	....	....	....	....	....	....	....	....	—	—	—	—	....	....	Equity Securities	79ad *d*
....	....	....	....	....	....	....	....	....	—	—	—	—	....	....	Debt Securities	79ae *d*
—	—	—	—	—	—	—	—	—	—	—	—	—	—	—	Financial Derivatives	79al *d*
....	....	....	....	....	....	....	....	....	337.4	378.6	268.3	266.9	....	....	Other Investment	79af *d*
....	....	....	....	....	....	....	....	....	—	—	—	—	....	....	Monetary Authorities	79ag *d*
....	....	....	....	....	....	....	....	....	230.5	249.8	81.0	100.7	—	....	General Government	79ah *d*
....	....	....	....	....	....	....	....	....						....	Banks	79ai *d*
....	....	....	....	....	....	....	....	....	204.4	531.0	607.0	623.0	....	....	Other Sectors	79aj *d*
....	....	....	....	....	....	....	....	....	15,272.6	17,009.2	16,101.1	14,046.3	....	....	Reserve Assets	79ak *d*
....	....	....	....	....	....	....	....	....	—	—	—	—	....	....	Liabilities	79la *d*
....	....	....	....	....	....	....	....	....	—	—	—	—	....	....	Dir. Invest. in Rep. Economy	79lb *d*
....	....	....	....	....	....	....	....	....	—	—	—	—	....	....	Portfolio Investment	79lc *d*
....	....	....	....	....	....	....	....	....	—	—	—	—	....	....	Equity Securities	79ld *d*
—	—	—	—	—	—	—	—	—	—	—	—	—	—	—	Debt Securities	79le *d*
															Financial Derivatives	79lf *d*
....	....	....	....	....	....	....	....	....	15,272.6	17,009.2	16,101.1	14,046.3	....	....	Other Investment	79lg *d*
....	....	....	....	....	....	....	....	....	329.8	436.8	510.7	461.3	....	....	Monetary Authorities	79lh *d*
....	....	....	....	....	....	....	....	....	....	....	....	....	....	....	General Government	79li *d*
....	....	....	....	....	....	....	....	....	743.5	522.9	266.2	295.4	....	....	Banks	79lj *d*
....	....	....	....	....	....	....	....	....	....	....	....	....	....	....	Other Sectors	79lj *d*

Côte d'Ivoire

		1970	1971	1972	1973	1974	1975	1976	1977	1978	1979	1980	1981	1982	1983	1984
Government Finance																*Billions of Francs:*
Deficit (-) or Surplus	80	....	....	....	....	....	....	....	....	....	....	....	....	....	....	....
Total Revenue and Grants	81y	....	....	....	....	....	....	....	....	....	....	....	....	....	....	....
Revenue	81	....	....	....	....	....	....	....	....	....	....	....	....	....	....	....
Grants	81z	....	....	....	....	....	....	....	....	....	....	....	....	....	....	....
Exp. & Lending Minus Repay.	82z	....	....	....	....	....	....	....	....	....	....	....	....	....	....	....
Expenditure	82	....	....	....	....	....	....	....	....	....	....	....	....	....	....	....
Lending Minus Repayments	83	....	....	....	....	....	....	....	....	....	....	....	....	....	....	....
Total Financing	80h	....	....	....	....	....	....	....	....	....	....	....	....	....	....	....
Domestic	84a	....	....	....	....	....	....	....	....	....	....	....	....	....	....	....
Foreign	85a	....	....	....	....	....	....	....	....	....	....	....	....	....	....	....
Total Debt by Residence	88	....	....	....	....	....	....	....	....	....	....	....	....	....	....	....
Domestic	88a	....	....	....	....	....	....	....	....	....	....	....	....	....	....	....
Foreign	89a	....	....	....	....	....	....	....	....	....	....	....	....	....	....	....
National Accounts																*Billions of Francs*
Exports of Goods & Services	90c	150.6	153.1	170.2	215.8	337.6	315.2	465.0	656.1	651.0	673.1	752.5	806.0	905.7	963.1	1,354.6
Government Consumption	91f	64.9	73.9	77.2	95.6	118.7	141.8	180.3	209.7	290.4	353.8	362.4	403.6	432.5	439.3	453.3
Gross Fixed Capital Formation	93e	83.9	92.4	94.3	122.0	143.6	199.4	247.2	397.7	529.0	526.7	523.6	558.4	538.7	461.8	387.5
Increase/Decrease(-) in Stocks	93i	7.4	3.6	3.1	7.8	19.1	3.4	8.9	23.1	1.8	16.9	46.9	36.0	37.8	8.9	−39.3
Private Consumption	96f	246.1	267.1	287.8	340.1	418.1	504.1	616.4	811.9	978.1	1,106.7	1,349.8	1,456.3	1,549.7	1,663.5	1,783.7
Imports of Goods & Services	98c	−129.6	−141.6	−149.6	−203.4	−286.6	−326.0	−403.8	−559.2	−667.3	−732.5	−885.3	−968.9	−977.9	−930.7	−950.4
Gross Domestic Product (GDP)	99b	414.9	439.9	471.8	566.2	739.0	834.5	1,120.4	1,590.4	1,783.0	1,944.7	2,149.9	2,291.4	2,486.5	2,605.9	2,989.4
Net Factor Inc/Pmts(-) Abroad	98.n	−11.5	−15.2	−12.7	−12.6	−20.5	−27.2	−41.1	−50.5	−69.4	....	....	....	....	....	....
Gross National Income (GNI)	99a	403.4	424.6	459.1	553.6	718.5	807.3	1,072.9	1,488.8	1,713.6	....	....	....	....	....	....
Net National Income	99e	388.4	405.6	437.1	528.6	688.5	767.3	1,017.9	1,406.8	1,591.2	1,702.0	....	....	....	....	....
GDP Volume (1980=100)	99bv*p*	....	....	....	....	....	....	79.2	82.9	91.1	92.8	100.0	103.5	....	....	....
GDP Deflator (1980=100)	99bi*p*	....	....	....	....	....	....	65.8	89.2	91.0	97.4	100.0	103.0	....	....	....
																Millions:
Population	99z	5.55	5.58	5.86	6.15	6.43	6.77	7.05	7.34	7.61	7.92	8.33	8.52	8.85	9.30	9.56

1985	1986	1987	1988	1989	1990	1991	1992	1993	1994	1995	1996	1997	1998	1999		
Year Ending December 31															**Government Finance**	
....	....	....	....	....	....	....	....	....	−280.1	−147.3	−57.7	23.3	−83.0	−11.0	Deficit (-) or Surplus	**80**
....	....	....	....	....	....	....	....	....	878.7	1,142.2	1,274.5	1,374.3	1,443.7	1,482.1	Total Revenue and Grants	**81y**
....	....	....	....	....	....	....	....	....	849.0	1,107.2	1,234.0	1,330.2	1,392.2	1,442.1	Revenue	**81**
....	....	....	....	....	....	....	....	....	29.7	35.0	40.5	44.1	51.5	40.0	Grants	**81z**
....	....	....	....	....	....	....	....	....	1,158.8	1,289.5	1,332.2	1,351.0	1,526.7	1,493.1	Exp. & Lending Minus Repay.	**82z**
....	....	....	....	....	....	....	....	....	1,166.0	1,322.6	1,385.2	1,494.5	1,557.3	1,533.1	Expenditure	**82**
....	....	....	....	....	....	....	....	....	−7.2	−33.1	−53.0	−143.5	−30.6	−40.0	Lending Minus Repayments	**83**
....	....	....	....	....	....	....	....	....	....	....	....	....	....	....	Total Financing	**80h**
....	....	....	....	....	....	....	....	....	....	....	....	....	....	....	Domestic	**84a**
....	....	....	....	....	....	....	....	....	433.2	208.9	165.2	6.2	47.7	115.2	Foreign	**85a**
....	....	....	....	....	....	....	....	....	9,148.6	9,392.7	9,606.0	10,056.3	7,620.7	....	Total Debt by Residence	**88**
....	....	....	....	....	....	....	....	....	1,320.4	1,230.7	1,137.8	1,070.6	1,039.5	....	Domestic	**88a**
....	....	....	....	....	....	....	....	....	7,828.2	8,162.0	8,468.2	8,985.7	6,581.2	....	Foreign	**89a**
Billions of Francs															**National Accounts**	
1,466.3	1,252.7	1,013.5	788.7	885.1	812.7	888.0	857.3	851.3	1,730.5	2,051.0	2,396.2	2,553.1	....	....	Exports of Goods & Services	**90c**
441.6	485.9	501.8	530.0	576.0	499.0	484.0	473.2	487.0	599.4	606.0	611.5	633.4	....	....	Government Consumption	**91f**
369.1	374.8	356.8	336.6	248.8	218.2	220.7	210.0	231.7	454.9	641.0	688.2	887.7	....	....	Gross Fixed Capital Formation	**93e**
37.0	7.7	16.6	104.7	3.2	31.3	−33.0	−46.6	13.7	46.9	105.0	67.7	76.4	....	....	Increase/Decrease(-) in Stocks	**93i**
1,836.4	2,007.8	2,041.0	1,971.1	1,979.3	1,761.8	2,199.5	2,220.5	2,174.3	2,684.3	3,367.0	3,592.6	3,898.8	....	....	Private Consumption	**96f**
−1,015.6	−957.2	−898.0	−663.9	−705.1	−627.9	−799.1	−810.5	−811.5	−1,379.8	−1,782.0	−1,877.3	−2,046.2	....	....	Imports of Goods & Services	**98c**
3,134.8	3,174.0	3,031.8	3,054.5	3,109.5	2,939.7	2,958.9	2,953.0	2,946.2	4,256.0	4,987.7	5,548.2	6,176.2	6,893.3	....	Gross Domestic Product (GDP)	**99b**
....	−237.0	−285.8	−300.2	−359.4	−374.3	−411.3	....	....	....	....	....	....	....	....	Net Factor Inc/Pmts(-) Abroad	**98.n**
....	2,934.7	2,745.9	2,754.3	2,753.4	2,565.0	2,548.7	....	....	....	....	....	....	....	....	Gross National Income (GNI)	**99a**
....	....	....	....	....	....	....	....	....	....	....	....	....	....	....	Net National Income	**99e**
....	....	....	....	....	....	....	....	....	....	....	....	....	....	....	GDP Volume (1980=100)	**99bv** *p*
....	....	....	....	....	....	....	....	....	....	....	....	....	....	....	GDP Deflator (1980=100)	**99bi** *p*
Midyear Estimates																
9.93	10.32	10.72	10.82	11.26	11.72	12.19	12.67	13.18	13.70	14.23	14.78	‖14.06	14.29	14.53	Population	**99z**

(See notes in the back of the book.)

Croatia

960

		1970	1971	1972	1973	1974	1975	1976	1977	1978	1979	1980	1981	1982	1983	1984
Exchange Rates																*Kuna per SDR:*
Official Rate	aa	....	....	....	....	....	....	....	....	....	....	....	....	....	....	....
																Kuna per US Dollar:
Official Rate	ae	....	....	....	....	....	....	....	....	....	....	....	....	....	....	....
Official Rate	rf	....	....	....	....	....	....	....	....	....	....	....	....	....	....	....
															Index Numbers (1995=100):	
Nominal Effective Exchange Rate	ne c	....	....	....	....	....	....	....	....	....	....	....	....	....	....	....
Real Effective Exchange Rate	re c	....	....	....	....	....	....	....	....	....	....	....	....	....	....	....
Fund Position																*Millions of SDRs:*
Quota	2f. s	—	—	—	—	—	—	—	—	—	—	—	—	—	—	—
SDRs	1b. s	....	....	....	....	....	....	....	....	....	....	....	....	....	....	....
Reserve Position in the Fund	1c. s	....	....	....	....	....	....	....	....	....	....	....	....	....	....	....
Total Fund Cred.&Loans Outstg.	2tl	....	....	....	....	....	....	....	....	....	....	....	....	....	....	....
International Liquidity														*Millions of US Dollars Unless Otherwise Indicated:*		
Total Reserves minus Gold	1l. d	....	....	....	....	....	....	....	....	....	....	....	....	....	....	....
SDRs	1b. d	....	....	....	....	....	....	....	....	....	....	....	....	....	....	....
Reserve Position in the Fund	1c. d	....	....	....	....	....	....	....	....	....	....	....	....	....	....	....
Foreign Exchange	1d. d	....	....	....	....	....	....	....	....	....	....	....	....	....	....	....
Gold (Million Fine Troy Ounces)	1ad	....	....	....	....	....	....	....	....	....	....	....	....	....	....	....
Gold (National Valuation)	1an d	....	....	....	....	....	....	....	....	....	....	....	....	....	....	....
Monetary Authorities: Other Liab.	4.. d	....	....	....	....	....	....	....	....	....	....	....	....	....	....	....
Deposit Money Banks: Assets	7a. d	....	....	....	....	....	....	....	....	....	....	....	....	....	....	....
Liabilities	7b. d	....	....	....	....	....	....	....	....	....	....	....	....	....	....	....
Monetary Authorities																*Millions of Kuna:*
Foreign Assets	11	....	....	....	....	....	....	....	....	....	....	....	....	....	....	....
Claims on Central Government	12a	....	....	....	....	....	....	....	....	....	....	....	....	....	....	....
Claims on Private Sector	12d	....	....	....	....	....	....	....	....	....	....	....	....	....	....	....
Claims on Deposit Money Banks	12e	....	....	....	....	....	....	....	....	....	....	....	....	....	....	....
Reserve Money	14	....	....	....	....	....	....	....	....	....	....	....	....	....	....	....
of which: Currency Outside DMBs	14a	....	....	....	....	....	....	....	....	....	....	....	....	....	....	....
Restricted Deposits	16b	....	....	....	....	....	....	....	....	....	....	....	....	....	....	....
Foreign Liabilities	16c	....	....	....	....	....	....	....	....	....	....	....	....	....	....	....
Central Government Deposits	16d	....	....	....	....	....	....	....	....	....	....	....	....	....	....	....
Capital Accounts	17a	....	....	....	....	....	....	....	....	....	....	....	....	....	....	....
Other Items (Net)	17r	....	....	....	....	....	....	....	....	....	....	....	....	....	....	....
Deposit Money Banks																*Millions of Kuna:*
Reserves	20	....	....	....	....	....	....	....	....	....	....	....	....	....	....	....
Foreign Assets	21	....	....	....	....	....	....	....	....	....	....	....	....	....	....	....
Claims on Central Government	22a	....	....	....	....	....	....	....	....	....	....	....	....	....	....	....
Claims on Local Government	22b	....	....	....	....	....	....	....	....	....	....	....	....	....	....	....
Claims on Nonfin.Pub.Enterprises	22c	....	....	....	....	....	....	....	....	....	....	....	....	....	....	....
Claims on Private Sector	22d	....	....	....	....	....	....	....	....	....	....	....	....	....	....	....
Claims on Other Banking Insts	22f	....	....	....	....	....	....	....	....	....	....	....	....	....	....	....
Claims on Nonbank Financial Insts	22g	....	....	....	....	....	....	....	....	....	....	....	....	....	....	....
Demand Deposits	24	....	....	....	....	....	....	....	....	....	....	....	....	....	....	....
Time, Savings,& Fgn.Currency Dep.	25	....	....	....	....	....	....	....	....	....	....	....	....	....	....	....
Money Market Instruments	26aa	....	....	....	....	....	....	....	....	....	....	....	....	....	....	....
Bonds	26ab	....	....	....	....	....	....	....	....	....	....	....	....	....	....	....
Restricted Deposits	26b	....	....	....	....	....	....	....	....	....	....	....	....	....	....	....
Foreign Liabilities	26c	....	....	....	....	....	....	....	....	....	....	....	....	....	....	....
Central Government Deposits	26d	....	....	....	....	....	....	....	....	....	....	....	....	....	....	....
Credit from Monetary Authorities	26g	....	....	....	....	....	....	....	....	....	....	....	....	....	....	....
Capital Accounts	27a	....	....	....	....	....	....	....	....	....	....	....	....	....	....	....
Other Items (Net)	27r	....	....	....	....	....	....	....	....	....	....	....	....	....	....	....
Monetary Survey																*Millions of Kuna:*
Foreign Assets (Net)	31n	....	....	....	....	....	....	....	....	....	....	....	....	....	....	....
Domestic Credit	32	....	....	....	....	....	....	....	....	....	....	....	....	....	....	....
Claims on Central Govt. (Net)	32an	....	....	....	....	....	....	....	....	....	....	....	....	....	....	....
Claims on Local Government	32b	....	....	....	....	....	....	....	....	....	....	....	....	....	....	....
Claims on Nonfin.Pub.Enterprises	32c	....	....	....	....	....	....	....	....	....	....	....	....	....	....	....
Claims on Private Sector	32d	....	....	....	....	....	....	....	....	....	....	....	....	....	....	....
Claims on Other Banking Insts	32f	....	....	....	....	....	....	....	....	....	....	....	....	....	....	....
Claims on Nonbank Financial Inst	32g	....	....	....	....	....	....	....	....	....	....	....	....	....	....	....
Money	34	....	....	....	....	....	....	....	....	....	....	....	....	....	....	....
Quasi-Money	35	....	....	....	....	....	....	....	....	....	....	....	....	....	....	....
Money Market Instruments	36aa	....	....	....	....	....	....	....	....	....	....	....	....	....	....	....
Bonds	36ab	....	....	....	....	....	....	....	....	....	....	....	....	....	....	....
Restricted Deposits	36b	....	....	....	....	....	....	....	....	....	....	....	....	....	....	....
Capital Accounts	37a	....	....	....	....	....	....	....	....	....	....	....	....	....	....	....
Other Items (Net)	37r	....	....	....	....	....	....	....	....	....	....	....	....	....	....	....
Money plus Quasi-Money	35l	....	....	....	....	....	....	....	....	....	....	....	....	....	....	....
Interest Rates																*Percent Per Annum*
Discount Rate *(End of Period)*	60	....	....	....	....	....	....	....	....	....	....	....	....	....	....	....
Money Market Rate	60b	....	....	....	....	....	....	....	....	....	....	....	....	....	....	....
Deposit Rate	60l	....	....	....	....	....	....	....	....	....	....	....	....	....	....	....
Lending Rate	60p	....	....	....	....	....	....	....	....	....	....	....	....	....	....	....
Prices, Production, Labor																*Index Numbers (1995=100):*
Wholesale Prices	63	....	....	....	....	....	....	....	....	....	....	....	....	....	....	....
Consumer Prices	64	....	....	....	....	....	....	....	....	....	....	....	....	....	....	....
Wages	65	....	....	....	....	....	....	....	....	....	....	....	....	....	....	....
Industrial Production	66	....	....	....	....	....	....	....	....	....	....	....	....	....	....	....
Total Employment	67	....	....	....	....	....	....	....	....	....	....	97.3	....	....	102.8	104.4
																Number in Thousands:
Employment	67e	....	....	....	....	....	....	....	....	....	....	....	....	....	....	....
Unemployment	67c	....	....	....	....	....	....	....	....	....	....	....	....	....	....	....
Unemployment Rate (%)	67r	....	....	....	....	....	....	....	....	....	....	....	....	....	....	....

Croatia

960

1985	1986	1987	1988	1989	1990	1991	1992	1993	1994	1995	1996	1997	1998	1999		
End of Period															**Exchange Rates**	
....	....	....	....	....	....	....	1.098	9.013	8.217	7.902	7.966	8.504	8.797	10.496	Official Rate	aa
End of Period (ae) Period Average (rf)																
....	....	....	....	....	....	....	.798	6.562	5.629	5.316	5.540	6.303	6.248	7.648	Official Rate	ae
....	....	....	....	....	....	....	....	3.577	5.996	5.230	5.434	6.101	6.362	7.112	Official Rate	rf
Period Averages																
....	....	....	....	....	....	....	2,506.77	244.19	97.87	100.00	104.34	105.06	104.41	98.43	Nominal Effective Exchange Rate	ne c
....	....	....	....	....	....	....	67.57	86.00	102.15	100.00	103.19	103.57	105.26	100.92	Real Effective Exchange Rate	re c
End of Period															**Fund Position**	
—	—	—	—	—	—	—	—	261.6	261.6	261.6	261.6	261.6	261.6	365.1	Quota	2f. s
....	....	....	....	....	....	....	—	.8	3.1	94.4	87.3	109.0	164.2	138.1	SDRs	1b. s
....	....	....	....	....	....	....	—	—	—	—	—	.1	.1	.1	Reserve Position in the Fund	1c. s
....	....	....	....	....	....	....	—	14.8	87.1	148.6	145.4	172.7	166.1	143.2	Total Fund Cred.&Loans Outstg.	2tl
End of Period															**International Liquidity**	
....	....	....	....	....	....	....	166.8	616.2	1,405.0	1,895.7	2,314.0	2,539.1	2,815.7	3,025.0	Total Reserves minus Gold	1l. d
....	....	....	....	....	....	....	—	1.1	4.5	140.3	125.6	147.1	231.2	189.5	SDRs	1b. d
....	....	....	....	....	....	....	—	—	—	—	—	.1	.2	.2	Reserve Position in the Fund	1c. d
....	....	....	....	....	....	....	166.8	615.1	1,400.5	1,755.4	2,188.4	2,391.9	2,584.4	2,835.3	Foreign Exchange	1d. d
....	....	....	....	....	....	....	—	—	—	—	—	—	—	—	Gold (Million Fine Troy Ounces)	1ad
....	....	....	....	....	....	....	—	—	—	—	—	—	—	—	Gold (National Valuation)	1an d
....	....	....	....	....	....	....	—	.1	.1	.2	.3	.5	.7	22.2	Monetary Authorities: Other Liab.	4.. d
....	....	....	....	....	....	....	....	946.7	1,258.3	1,748.8	2,265.4	2,567.9	2,042.9	1,621.4	Deposit Money Banks: Assets	7a. d
....	....	....	....	....	....	....	....	1,838.9	2,333.5	2,849.8	2,250.6	2,190.5	2,589.3	2,245.1	Liabilities	7b. d
End of Period															**Monetary Authorities**	
....	....	....	....	....	....	—	133.2	4,026.5	7,908.3	10,077.7	12,818.8	16,005.6	17,592.6	23,135.7	Foreign Assets	11
....	....	....	....	....	....	15.5	52.7	535.1	250.6	390.1	218.8	—	3.8	24.1	Claims on Central Government	12a
....	....	....	....	....	....	—	.1	.3	.7	.9	1.1	24.4	1.0	276.1	Claims on Private Sector	12d
....	....	....	....	....	....	25.7	107.7	191.6	223.8	220.2	213.9	33.5	1,043.7	1,139.4	Claims on Deposit Money Banks	12e
....	....	....	....	....	....	34.1	205.5	2,248.9	4,714.2	6,744.1	8,770.3	10,346.2	9,954.3	10,309.9	Reserve Money	14
....	....	....	....	....	....	18.3	130.8	1,367.0	2,658.2	3,365.1	4,366.2	5,319.6	5,730.1	5,958.9	*of which: Currency Outside DMBs*	14a
....	....	....	....	....	....	—	.1	1.4	40.3	212.2	243.2	101.1	119.1	380.6	Restricted Deposits	16b
....	....	....	....	....	....	—	—	133.9	716.2	1,175.2	1,160.4	1,471.4	1,465.4	1,672.9	Foreign Liabilities	16c
....	....	....	....	....	....	—	—	—	793.8	395.5	557.6	1,032.7	434.8	397.2	Central Government Deposits	16d
....	....	....	....	....	....	1.9	114.4	2,366.0	2,066.0	2,019.4	1,900.1	2,361.8	2,902.1	4,535.5	Capital Accounts	17a
....	....	....	....	....	....	5.2	–26.4	3.2	52.9	142.5	621.0	750.4	3,765.3	7,279.1	Other Items (Net)	17r
End of Period															**Deposit Money Banks**	
....	....	....	....	....	....	....	....	862.1	2,039.7	3,508.3	4,573.9	5,056.7	5,908.1	8,987.9	Reserves	20
....	....	....	....	....	....	....	....	6,212.1	7,082.5	9,296.6	12,549.6	16,185.8	12,763.1	12,400.0	Foreign Assets	21
....	....	....	....	....	....	....	....	19,971.9	17,837.0	17,188.1	16,693.4	15,238.8	14,864.2	16,264.4	Claims on Central Government	22a
....	....	....	....	....	....	....	....	11.4	112.9	147.1	145.4	308.8	654.0	905.6	Claims on Local Government	22b
....	....	....	....	....	....	....	....	1,802.4	2,141.4	1,896.2	1,943.8	2,182.5	2,291.8	1,794.2	Claims on Nonfin.Pub.Enterprises	22c
....	....	....	....	....	....	....	....	18,447.9	25,344.4	30,674.5	31,600.7	46,100.9	56,650.9	52,699.9	Claims on Private Sector	22d
....	....	....	....	....	....	....	....	10.2	—	—	—	—	.4	45.4	Claims on Other Banking Insts	22f
....	....	....	....	....	....	....	....	15.7	62.1	100.8	140.2	246.8	193.9	154.0	Claims on Nonbank Financial Insts	22g
....	....	....	....	....	....	....	....	1,758.7	3,969.7	4,870.0	7,007.5	8,423.8	7,808.9	7,891.5	Demand Deposits	24
....	....	....	....	....	....	....	....	6,878.3	10,828.8	16,257.4	25,204.1	36,876.9	43,654.7	42,363.6	Time, Savings,& Fgn.Currency Dep.	25
....	....	....	....	....	....	....	....	3.3	1.5	.2	.9	7.0	4.5	1.4	Money Market Instruments	26aa
....	....	....	....	....	....	....	....	45.0	207.0	130.5	127.2	126.6	149.7	474.6	Bonds	26ab
....	....	....	....	....	....	....	....	14,261.5	12,087.7	10,662.4	8,223.6	5,852.3	4,196.0	3,434.2	Restricted Deposits	26b
....	....	....	....	....	....	....	....	12,066.4	13,134.8	15,150.0	12,467.4	13,807.1	16,176.8	17,169.9	Foreign Liabilities	26c
....	....	....	....	....	....	....	....	1,437.8	1,675.0	2,025.6	1,720.9	6,874.7	7,298.3	5,828.6	Central Government Deposits	26d
....	....	....	....	....	....	....	....	275.2	224.6	182.6	267.7	33.7	1,049.2	1,125.3	Credit from Monetary Authorities	26g
....	....	....	....	....	....	....	....	11,203.3	13,883.6	15,392.4	15,441.8	17,023.6	19,786.8	21,975.4	Capital Accounts	27a
....	....	....	....	....	....	....	....	–595.9	–1,392.6	–1,859.2	–2,813.9	–3,705.5	–6,798.4	–7,013.1	Other Items (Net)	27r
End of Period															**Monetary Survey**	
....	....	....	....	....	....	....	....	–1,961.7	1,139.8	3,049.2	11,740.6	16,912.9	12,713.5	16,692.9	Foreign Assets (Net)	31n
....	....	....	....	....	....	....	....	39,357.0	43,280.3	47,976.5	48,464.9	56,194.8	66,937.0	65,937.9	Domestic Credit	32
....	....	....	....	....	....	....	....	19,069.1	15,618.7	15,157.1	14,633.7	7,331.4	7,134.9	10,062.7	Claims on Central Govt. (Net)	32an
....	....	....	....	....	....	....	....	11.4	112.9	147.1	145.4	308.8	654.0	905.6	Claims on Local Government	32b
....	....	....	....	....	....	....	....	1,802.4	2,141.4	1,896.2	1,943.8	2,182.5	2,291.8	1,794.2	Claims on Nonfin.Pub.Enterprises	32c
....	....	....	....	....	....	....	....	18,448.2	25,345.1	30,675.3	31,601.8	46,125.3	56,651.9	52,976.0	Claims on Private Sector	32d
....	....	....	....	....	....	....	....	10.2	—	—	—	—	10.5	45.4	Claims on Other Banking Insts	32f
....	....	....	....	....	....	....	....	15.7	62.1	100.8	140.2	246.8	193.9	154.0	Claims on Nonbank Financial Inst	32g
....	....	....	....	....	....	....	....	3,133.9	6,648.8	8,283.6	11,419.6	13,814.3	13,621.1	13,858.9	Money	34
....	....	....	....	....	....	....	....	6,878.3	10,828.8	16,257.4	25,204.1	36,876.9	43,654.7	42,363.6	Quasi-Money	35
....	....	....	....	....	....	....	....	3.3	1.5	.2	.9	7.0	4.5	1.4	Money Market Instruments	36aa
....	....	....	....	....	....	....	....	45.0	207.0	130.5	127.2	126.6	149.7	474.6	Bonds	36ab
....	....	....	....	....	....	....	....	14,262.9	12,128.0	10,874.6	8,466.8	5,953.4	4,315.1	3,814.8	Restricted Deposits	36b
....	....	....	....	....	....	....	....	13,569.3	15,949.6	17,411.8	17,341.9	19,385.4	22,688.9	26,510.9	Capital Accounts	37a
....	....	....	....	....	....	....	....	–497.5	–1,343.4	–1,932.0	–2,354.7	–3,055.9	–4,783.5	–4,393.5	Other Items (Net)	37r
....	....	....	....	....	....	....	....	10,012.2	17,477.6	24,541.0	36,623.7	50,691.2	57,275.8	56,222.5	Money plus Quasi-Money	35l
Percent Per Annum															**Interest Rates**	
....	....	....	....	....	....	....	1,889.39	34.49	8.50	8.50	6.50	5.90	5.90	7.90	Discount Rate *(End of Period)*	60
....	....	....	....	....	....	....	951.20	1,370.50	26.93	21.13	19.26	10.18	14.48	13.72	Money Market Rate	60b
....	....	....	....	....	....	....	658.51	379.31	6.52	5.53	5.59	4.30	4.62	4.31	Deposit Rate	60l
....	....	....	....	....	....	....	1,157.79	1,443.61	22.91	20.24	22.52	15.47	15.75	14.94	Lending Rate	60p
Period Averages															**Prices, Production, Labor**	
....	....	—	—	—	.1	.4	3.5	55.9	99.3	100.0	102.0	103.2	102.2	104.6	Wholesale Prices	63
....	....	—	—	—	.2	.4	2.9	46.4	96.2	100.0	104.3	108.7	115.6	119.9	Consumer Prices	64
....	....	—	–.1	–.4	–.3	.4	1.8	29.4	68.6	100.0	111.7	130.6	147.4	167.9	Wages	65
191.0	199.8	204.6	201.8	200.6	177.9	127.2	108.6	102.3	99.8	100.0	103.0	110.1	113.9	112.3	Industrial Production	66
109.5	112.6	114.8	114.6	114.2	110.9	101.9	104.5	102.1	101.4	100.0	93.9	92.5	97.7	94.4	Total Employment	67
Period Averages																
....	....	....	....	....	....	....	1,159	1,108	1,061	1,027	1,012	996	962	....	Employment	67e
....	....	....	....	....	....	....	267	251	243	241	261	278	288	322	Unemployment	67c
....	....	....	....	....	....	....	17.2	16.8	....	....	....	....	....	....	Unemployment Rate (%)	67r

Croatia

960

	1970	1971	1972	1973	1974	1975	1976	1977	1978	1979	1980	1981	1982	1983	1984

International Transactions

Millions of US Dollars

Exports .... 70..*d*	....	....	....	....	....	....	....	....	....	....	....	....	....	....	....
Imports, c.i.f. .... 71..*d*	....	....	....	....	....	....	....	....	....	....	....	....	....	....	....

Balance of Payments

Millions of US Dollars:

Current Account, n.i.e. .... 78al *d*	....	....	....	....	....	....	....	....	....	....	....	....	....	....	....
Goods: Exports f.o.b. .... 78aa *d*	....	....	....	....	....	....	....	....	....	....	....	....	....	....	....
Goods: Imports f.o.b. .... 78ab *d*	....	....	....	....	....	....	....	....	....	....	....	....	....	....	....
Trade Balance .... 78ac *d*	....	....	....	....	....	....	....	....	....	....	....	....	....	....	....
Services: Credit .... 78ad *d*	....	....	....	....	....	....	....	....	....	....	....	....	....	....	....
Services: Debit .... 78ae *d*	....	....	....	....	....	....	....	....	....	....	....	....	....	....	....
Balance on Goods & Services .... 78af *d*	....	....	....	....	....	....	....	....	....	....	....	....	....	....	....
Income: Credit .... 78ag *d*	....	....	....	....	....	....	....	....	....	....	....	....	....	....	....
Income: Debit .... 78ah *d*	....	....	....	....	....	....	....	....	....	....	....	....	....	....	....
Balance on Gds, Serv. & Inc. .... 78ai *d*	....	....	....	....	....	....	....	....	....	....	....	....	....	....	....
Current Transfers, n.i.e.: Credit .... 78aj *d*	....	....	....	....	....	....	....	....	....	....	....	....	....	....	....
Current Transfers: Debit .... 78ak *d*	....	....	....	....	....	....	....	....	....	....	....	....	....	....	....
Capital Account, n.i.e. .... 78bc *d*	....	....	....	....	....	....	....	....	....	....	....	....	....	....	....
Capital Account, n.i.e.: Credit .... 78ba *d*	....	....	....	....	....	....	....	....	....	....	....	....	....	....	....
Capital Account: Debit .... 78bb *d*	....	....	....	....	....	....	....	....	....	....	....	....	....	....	....
Financial Account, n.i.e. .... 78bj *d*	....	....	....	....	....	....	....	....	....	....	....	....	....	....	....
Direct Investment Abroad .... 78bd *d*	....	....	....	....	....	....	....	....	....	....	....	....	....	....	....
Dir. Invest. in Rep. Econ., n.i.e. ... 78be *d*	....	....	....	....	....	....	....	....	....	....	....	....	....	....	....
Portfolio Investment Assets .... 78bf *d*	....	....	....	....	....	....	....	....	....	....	....	....	....	....	....
Equity Securities....................... 78bk *d*	....	....	....	....	....	....	....	....	....	....	....	....	....	....	....
Debt Securities .... 78bl *d*	....	....	....	....	....	....	....	....	....	....	....	....	....	....	....
Portfolio Investment Liab., n.i.e. ...... 78bg *d*	....	....	....	....	....	....	....	....	....	....	....	....	....	....	....
Equity Securities....................... 78bm *d*	....	....	....	....	....	....	....	....	....	....	....	....	....	....	....
Debt Securities .... 78bn *d*	....	....	....	....	....	....	....	....	....	....	....	....	....	....	....
Financial Derivatives Assets .... 78bw *d*	....	....	....	....	....	....	....	....	....	....	....	....	....	....	....
Financial Derivatives Liabilities ...... 78bx *d*	....	....	....	....	....	....	....	....	....	....	....	....	....	....	....
Other Investment Assets .... 78bh *d*	....	....	....	....	....	....	....	....	....	....	....	....	....	....	....
Monetary Authorities.................. 78bo *d*	....	....	....	....	....	....	....	....	....	....	....	....	....	....	....
General Government .... 78bp *d*	....	....	....	....	....	....	....	....	....	....	....	....	....	....	....
Banks .... 78bq *d*	....	....	....	....	....	....	....	....	....	....	....	....	....	....	....
Other Sectors .... 78br *d*	....	....	....	....	....	....	....	....	....	....	....	....	....	....	....
Other Investment Liab., n.i.e. .... 78bi *d*	....	....	....	....	....	....	....	....	....	....	....	....	....	....	....
Monetary Authorities.................... 78bs *d*	....	....	....	....	....	....	....	....	....	....	....	....	....	....	....
General Government .... 78bt *d*	....	....	....	....	....	....	....	....	....	....	....	....	....	....	....
Banks .... 78bu *d*	....	....	....	....	....	....	....	....	....	....	....	....	....	....	....
Other Sectors .... 78bv *d*	....	....	....	....	....	....	....	....	....	....	....	....	....	....	....
Net Errors and Omissions.................. 78ca *d*	....	....	....	....	....	....	....	....	....	....	....	....	....	....	....
Overall Balance .... 78cb *d*	....	....	....	....	....	....	....	....	....	....	....	....	....	....	....
Reserves and Related Items .... 79da *d*	....	....	....	....	....	....	....	....	....	....	....	....	....	....	....
Reserve Assets .... 79db *d*	....	....	....	....	....	....	....	....	....	....	....	....	....	....	....
Use of Fund Credit and Loans .... 79dc *d*	....	....	....	....	....	....	....	....	....	....	....	....	....	....	....
Exceptional Financing .... 79de *d*	....	....	....	....	....	....	....	....	....	....	....	....	....	....	....

Government Finance

Millions of Kuna:

Deficit (-) or Surplus............................. 80	....	....	....	....	....	....	....	....	....	....	....	....	....	....	....
Total Revenue and Grants................... 81y	....	....	....	....	....	....	....	....	....	....	....	....	....	....	....
Revenue 81	....	....	....	....	....	....	....	....	....	....	....	....	....	....	....
Grants 81z	....	....	....	....	....	....	....	....	....	....	....	....	....	....	....
Exp. & Lending Minus Repay. 82z	....	....	....	....	....	....	....	....	....	....	....	....	....	....	....
Expenditure 82	....	....	....	....	....	....	....	....	....	....	....	....	....	....	....
Lending Minus Repayments................. 83	....	....	....	....	....	....	....	....	....	....	....	....	....	....	....
Total Financing 80h	....	....	....	....	....	....	....	....	....	....	....	....	....	....	....
Domestic 84a	....	....	....	....	....	....	....	....	....	....	....	....	....	....	....
Foreign 85a	....	....	....	....	....	....	....	....	....	....	....	....	....	....	....
Total Debt by Residence 88	....	....	....	....	....	....	....	....	....	....	....	....	....	....	....
Domestic 88a	....	....	....	....	....	....	....	....	....	....	....	....	....	....	....
Foreign 89a	....	....	....	....	....	....	....	....	....	....	....	....	....	....	....

National Accounts

Billions of Kuna:

GDP Volume 1990 Prices..................... 99b.*p*	....	....	....	....	....	....	....	....	....	....	....	....	....	....	....
GDP Volume (1995=100) .... 99bv *p*	....	....	....	....	....	....	....	....	....	....	....	....	....	....	....

Millions:

Population... 99z	....	....	....	....	....	....	....	....	....	....	....	....	....	....	....

	1985	1986	1987	1988	1989	1990	1991	1992	1993	1994	1995	1996	1997	1998	1999	
Millions of US Dollars																**International Transactions**
	....	....	....	....	....	....	....	....	3,903.8	4,260.4	4,632.7	4,511.8	4,170.7	4,541.1	4,279.7	Exports... 70..*d*
									4,666.4	5,229.3	7,509.9	7,787.9	9,104.0	8,383.1	7,777.4	Imports, c.i.f. .... 71..*d*
Minus Sign Indicates Debit																**Balance of Payments**
	....	....	....	....	....	....	....	....	606.2	826.3	−1,451.6	−1,147.2	−2,344.1	−1,550.7	−1,468.2	Current Account, n.i.e. .... 78al *d*
	....	....	....	....	....	....	....	....	3,903.8	4,260.4	4,632.7	4,545.9	4,210.4	4,604.5	4,371.2	Goods: Exports f.o.b. .... 78aa *d*
	....	....	....	....	....	....	....	....	−4,645.3	−5,432.3	−7,900.7	−8,235.7	−9,434.7	−8,773.5	−7,671.8	Goods: Imports f.o.b. .... 78ab *d*
	....	....	....	....	....	....	....	....	−741.5	−1,171.9	−3,268.0	−3,689.8	−5,224.3	−4,169.0	−3,300.6	*Trade Balance* .... 78ac *d*
	....	....	....	....	....	....	....	....	2,285.8	2,857.1	2,451.3	3,296.8	4,010.9	3,964.0	3,707.9	Services: Credit .... 78ad *d*
	....	....	....	....	....	....	....	....	−1,147.6	−1,224.0	−1,410.2	−1,717.0	−1,980.1	−1,889.5	−2,029.2	Services: Debit .... 78ae *d*
	....	....	....	....	....	....	....	....	396.7	461.2	−2,226.9	−2,110.0	−3,193.5	−2,094.5	−1,621.9	*Balance on Goods & Services* ..... 78af *d*
	....	....	....	....	....	....	....	....	128.0	149.0	218.8	269.9	363.6	394.9	265.4	Income: Credit .... 78ag *d*
	....	....	....	....	....	....	....	....	−247.5	−313.1	−247.6	−339.5	−385.8	−558.9	−611.7	Income: Debit .... 78ah *d*
	....	....	....	....	....	....	....	....	277.2	297.1	−2,255.7	−2,179.6	−3,215.7	−2,258.5	−1,968.2	*Balance on Gds, Serv. & Inc.* ..... 78ai *d*
	....	....	....	....	....	....	....	....	509.0	672.0	973.0	1,183.2	966.1	921.1	833.2	Current Transfers, n.i.e.: Credit .... 78aj *d*
	....	....	....	....	....	....	....	....	−180.0	−142.8	−168.9	−150.8	−94.5	−213.3	−333.2	Current Transfers: Debit .... 78ak *d*
	....	....	....	....	....	....	....	....	—	—	—	16.2	21.3	19.1	25.0	Capital Account, n.i.e. .... 78bc *d*
	....	....	....	....	....	....	....	....	—	—	—	18.0	23.5	24.1	28.2	Capital Account, n.i.e.: Credit .... 78ba *d*
	....	....	....	....	....	....	....	....	—	—	—	−1.8	−2.2	−5.0	−3.2	Capital Account: Debit .... 78bb *d*
	....	....	....	....	....	....	....	....	−163.4	37.5	1,132.1	3,075.1	3,021.3	1,600.8	1,846.1	Financial Account, n.i.e. .... 78bj *d*
	....	....	....	....	....	....	....	....	−18.5	−6.7	−5.6	−24.4	−186.1	−93.2	−43.0	Direct Investment Abroad .... 78bd *d*
	....	....	....	....	....	....	....	....	96.3	113.1	101.2	533.3	509.8	893.9	1,347.4	Dir. Invest. in Rep. Econ., n.i.e. ...... 78be *d*
	....	....	....	....	....	....	....	....	−.4	1.0	.2	6.2	11.2	−.1	−.3	Portfolio Investment Assets .... 78bf *d*
	....	....	....	....	....	....	....	....	−.4	1.0	.2	6.2	.2	−.1	−.3	Equity Securities........................... 78bk *d*
	....	....	....	....	....	....	....	....	—	—	—	—	11.0	—	—	Debt Securities .... 78bl *d*
	....	....	....	....	....	....	....	....	.4	7.6	4.5	622.0	565.3	15.0	576.2	Portfolio Investment Liab., n.i.e. ...... 78bg *d*
	....	....	....	....	....	....	....	....	.4	7.6	4.5	−6.8	15.4	1.3	−16.9	Equity Securities........................... 78bm *d*
	....	....	....	....	....	....	....	....	—	—	—	628.8	549.9	13.7	593.1	Debt Securities .... 78bn *d*
	....	....	....	....	....	....	....	....	....	....	....	....	....	....	....	Financial Derivatives Assets .... 78bw *d*
	....	....	....	....	....	....	....	....	—	—	—	....	....	....	....	Financial Derivatives Liabilities....... 78bx *d*
	....	....	....	....	....	....	....	....	−148.8	11.4	429.6	850.8	190.3	368.3	−523.4	Other Investment Assets .... 78bh *d*
	....	....	....	....	....	....	....	....					—	—	—	Monetary Authorities .... 78bo *d*
	....	....	....	....	....	....	....	....								General Government .... 78bp *d*
	....	....	....	....	....	....	....	....	−210.6	−189.5	−467.1	−622.6	−341.1	383.8	340.5	Banks .... 78bq *d*
	....	....	....	....	....	....	....	....	61.8	200.9	896.7	1,473.4	531.4	−15.5	−863.9	Other Sectors............................... 78br *d*
	....	....	....	....	....	....	....	....	−92.4	−88.9	602.2	1,087.2	1,930.8	416.9	489.2	Other Investment Liab., n.i.e. .... 78bi *d*
	....	....	....	....	....	....	....	....								Monetary Authorities .... 78bs *d*
	....	....	....	....	....	....	....	....	−119.3	−131.5	−47.2	268.8	95.7	−61.3	183.3	General Government .... 78bt *d*
	....	....	....	....	....	....	....	....	−20.6	52.5	492.5	226.2	672.2	137.3	−31.3	Banks .... 78bu *d*
	....	....	....	....	....	....	....	....	47.5	−9.9	156.9	592.1	1,162.9	340.9	337.2	Other Sectors............................... 78bv *d*
	....	....	....	....	....	....	....	....	−254.5	−587.3	359.9	−926.8	−308.1	91.3	57.2	Net Errors and Omissions .... 78ca *d*
	....	....	....	....	....	....	....	....	188.3	276.5	40.4	1,017.3	390.4	160.5	460.1	*Overall Balance*.............................. 78cb *d*
	....	....	....	....	....	....	....	....	−188.3	−276.5	−40.4	−1,017.3	−390.4	−160.5	−460.1	Reserves and Related Items .... 79da *d*
	....	....	....	....	....	....	....	....	−466.4	−742.8	−443.2	−533.4	−428.0	−151.7	−428.6	Reserve Assets .... 79db *d*
	....	....	....	....	....	....	....	....	19.8	107.0	97.1	−4.5	37.5	−8.9	−31.5	Use of Fund Credit and Loans .... 79dc *d*
	....	....	....	....	....	....	....	....	258.3	359.3	305.7	−479.4	—	—	—	Exceptional Financing .... 79de *d*
Year Ending December 31																**Government Finance**
	....	....	....	....	....	....	....	....	....	543.9	−715.4	−133.8	−1,160.2	1,256.7	−2,522.0	Deficit (-) or Surplus............................... 80
	....	....	....	....	....	....	....	....	....	22,817.3	27,485.1	30,813.1	33,702.4	42,376.2	40,277.9	Total Revenue and Grants 81y
	....	....	....	....	....	....	....	....	....	22,817.3	27,385.1	30,813.1	33,702.4	42,376.2	40,277.9	Revenue 81
	....	....	....	....	....	....	....	....	....	—	100.0	—	—	—	—	Grants 81z
	....	....	....	....	....	....	....	....	....	22,273.4	28,200.5	30,946.9	34,862.5	41,119.6	42,799.9	Exp. & Lending Minus Repay. 82z
	....	....	....	....	....	....	....	....	....	22,282.8	28,475.6	30,971.2	34,395.2	41,390.4	47,379.6	Expenditure 82
	....	....	....	....	....	....	....	....	....	−9.3	−275.1	−24.3	467.4	−270.8	−4,579.7	Lending Minus Repayments 83
	....	....	....	....	....	....	....	....	....	−543.9	715.3	134.0	1,160.2	−1,256.7	2,521.9	Total Financing 80h
	....	....	....	....	....	....	....	....	....	−591.2	29.3	−669.9	−1,825.7	−1,247.6	−2,093.1	Domestic 84a
	....	....	....	....	....	....	....	....	....	47.3	686.0	804.0	2,985.9	−9.1	4,615.0	Foreign 85a
	....	....	....	....	....	....	....	....	....	....	....	27,739.7	29,814.0	32,760.0	....	Total Debt by Residence............................ 88
	....	....	....	....	....	....	18,502.1	17,218.4	20,768.6	17,284.7	16,405.4	16,533.7	14,501.6	13,697.5	13,944.0	Domestic 88a
	....	....	....	....	....	....	....	....	....	....	11,334.3	13,280.3	18,258.4	....	....	Foreign 89a
Billions of Kuna:																**National Accounts**
	....	....	....	....	....	....	....	....	192	193	196	205	....	....	....	GDP Volume 1990 Prices 99b.*p*
	....	....	....	....	....	....	....	....	97.7	98.3	100.0	104.3	....	....	....	GDP Volume (1995=100) .... 99bv *p*
Midyear Estimates																
	....	....	....	....	....	....	4.51	4.47	4.64	4.65	4.67	̌4.49	4.57	4.50	4.48	Population... 99z

(See notes in the back of the book.)

Cyprus

		1970	1971	1972	1973	1974	1975	1976	1977	1978	1979	1980	1981	1982	1983	1984
Exchange Rates															*SDRs per Pound:*	
Official Rate	ac	2.4000	2.3524	2.4026	2.2983	2.2841	2.1719	2.0911	2.1532	2.1853	2.1965	2.1495	1.9859	1.8570	1.7169	1.5838
															US Dollars per Pound:	
Official Rate	ag	2.4000	2.5540	2.6085	2.7725	2.7965	2.5425	2.4295	2.6155	2.8470	2.8935	2.7415	2.3115	2.0485	1.7975	1.5525
Official Rate	rh	2.4000	2.4355	2.6071	2.8612	2.7426	2.7162	2.4371	2.4510	2.6796	2.8220	2.8338	2.3829	2.1071	1.9015	1.7039
														Index Numbers (1995=100):		
Official Rate	ahx	108.5	110.5	117.9	129.4	124.0	122.8	110.2	110.8	121.2	127.6	128.2	107.8	95.3	86.0	77.1
Nominal Effective Exchange Rate	nec	....	....	....	....	....	....	....	....	....	74.2	76.0	75.3	76.5	77.7	79.6
Real Effective Exchange Rate	rec	....	....	....	....	....	....	....	....	....	....	119.5	115.1	112.4	110.0	109.0
Fund Position															*Millions of SDRs:*	
Quota	2f.s	26.0	26.0	26.0	26.0	26.0	26.0	26.0	26.0	34.0	34.0	51.0	51.0	51.0	69.7	69.7
SDRs	1b.s	3.9	7.7	10.4	10.5	10.4	10.0	7.9	5.1	1.7	9.9	6.5	3.4	.2	.2	.1
Reserve Position in the Fund	1c.s	6.5	6.5	6.5	6.5	—	—	—	—	6.5	6.1	—	—	—	4.7	4.7
Total Fund Cred.&Loans Outstg.	2tl	—	—	—	—	6.4	8.1	43.1	43.1	32.9	38.0	30.6	21.6	12.3	5.5	3.2
International Liquidity												*Millions of US Dollars Unless Otherwise Indicated:*				
Total Reserves minus Gold	1l.d	194.0	268.7	303.3	288.7	250.1	197.7	274.5	313.5	345.7	353.1	368.3	426.4	523.2	519.1	540.5
SDRs	1b.d	3.9	8.3	11.3	12.6	12.8	11.8	9.2	6.2	2.2	13.0	8.3	4.0	.2	.2	.1
Reserve Position in the Fund	1c.d	6.5	7.1	7.1	7.9	—	—	—	—	8.5	8.0	—	—	—	4.9	4.6
Foreign Exchange	1d.d	183.6	253.3	284.9	268.2	237.3	185.9	265.3	307.3	335.0	332.0	360.0	422.4	523.0	514.0	535.9
Gold (Million Fine Troy Ounces)	1ad	.428	.428	.428	.428	.428	.428	.428	.440	.443	.459	.459	.459	.459	.459	.459
Gold (National Valuation)	1and	15.0	....	....	18.1	17.5	15.9	15.2	16.8	19.1	20.8	19.7	16.7	14.8	13.0	11.2
Monetary Authorities: Other Liab.	4..d	1.4	4.6	4.9	2.5	4.4	7.7	8.4	7.6	10.2	6.7	1.2	1.3	1.0	1.0	.8
Deposit Money Banks: Assets	7a.d	15.9	16.5	13.7	16.0	19.4	11.7	20.8	21.1	33.4	43.9	45.8	55.5	60.7	66.8	84.6
Liabilities	7b.d	32.0	42.9	47.5	58.2	50.5	37.1	48.3	64.9	83.5	118.1	147.7	174.2	212.3	249.1	286.2
Other Banking Insts.: Liabilities	7f.d	8.9	9.8	12.2	13.5	15.5	11.9	11.2	14.4	19.8	28.0	31.7	36.1	35.5	29.8	24.5
Monetary Authorities															*Millions of Pounds:*	
Foreign Assets	11	88.2	110.9	118.0	110.8	102.0	85.9	122.2	127.7	128.6	129.9	142.0	191.9	262.9	298.4	356.1
Claims on Central Government	12a	–.6	–2.0	–.3	—	12.9	12.8	28.3	25.1	31.5	59.9	87.5	92.9	75.3	84.2	89.1
Claims on Deposit Money Banks	12e	—	—	.8	.1	—	.9	2.3	5.1	5.5	9.8	14.2	14.9	20.7	24.5	31.4
Reserve Money	14	41.4	54.2	64.7	67.8	78.0	79.2	97.6	110.1	127.8	153.1	195.4	240.0	297.5	344.5	404.9
of which: Currency Outside DMBs	14a	18.4	21.8	26.3	29.7	35.8	33.7	39.3	43.2	51.2	64.0	76.0	89.5	101.6	115.9	122.2
Foreign Liabilities	16c	.6	1.8	1.9	.9	4.4	6.7	24.1	22.9	18.7	19.6	14.7	11.5	7.1	3.7	2.5
Central Government Deposits	16d	37.0	43.1	43.4	32.9	22.9	6.9	23.6	17.7	10.5	12.6	14.5	20.5	20.6	18.3	21.3
Other Items (Net)	17r	8.7	9.9	8.6	9.3	9.6	6.8	7.6	7.2	8.6	14.3	19.1	27.7	33.6	40.5	47.8
Deposit Money Banks															*Millions of Pounds:*	
Reserves	20	23.1	32.1	38.0	37.4	42.3	35.0	47.5	54.9	58.7	66.6	94.0	118.9	154.8	181.0	228.0
Foreign Assets	21	6.6	6.3	5.3	5.5	7.0	4.6	8.6	8.1	11.7	15.2	16.7	24.0	29.6	37.2	54.5
Claims on Central Government	22a	9.0	15.9	18.8	13.9	13.6	15.3	34.1	21.0	20.7	18.1	31.6	47.0	54.7	69.4	90.5
Claims on Private Sector	22d	88.2	98.3	119.2	147.3	172.1	178.4	195.6	247.7	292.2	354.6	402.4	460.0	539.7	605.6	683.9
Demand Deposits	24	24.2	25.0	31.2	31.1	31.3	28.4	40.7	42.8	49.6	65.5	77.2	98.4	116.6	132.5	137.1
Time and Savings Deposits	25	76.1	95.8	114.8	132.4	157.6	164.4	191.5	226.0	257.5	296.9	341.2	406.6	483.8	534.6	631.0
Foreign Liabilities	26c	13.3	16.5	18.2	20.1	18.1	14.6	19.9	24.8	29.3	40.8	53.9	75.4	103.6	138.6	184.3
Central Government Deposits	26d	3.4	3.5	3.8	4.6	4.4	5.0	6.8	7.6	10.7	15.7	28.3	18.9	15.0	20.6	21.3
Credit from Monetary Authorities	26g	—	—	.8	.1	—	.9	2.3	5.1	5.5	9.8	14.2	14.9	20.7	24.5	31.4
Other Items (Net)	27r	9.9	12.0	12.5	15.9	23.7	20.1	24.6	25.4	30.8	25.7	29.7	35.7	39.1	42.4	51.7
Monetary Survey															*Millions of Pounds:*	
Foreign Assets (Net)	31n	81.0	99.0	103.1	95.4	86.5	69.2	86.8	88.1	92.3	84.7	90.1	129.1	181.8	193.2	223.7
Domestic Credit	32	56.4	65.7	90.7	123.9	171.8	195.3	228.2	269.1	323.9	406.3	481.0	562.9	637.0	724.2	825.6
Claims on Central Govt. (Net)	32an	–31.9	–32.6	–28.6	–23.6	–.8	16.2	32.1	20.7	31.0	49.6	76.2	100.6	94.3	114.7	137.0
Claims on Local Government	32b	....	....	....	....	....	....	....	....	....	....	....	....	....	....	....
Claims on Nonfin.Pub.Enterprises	32c	....	....	....	....	....	....	....	....	....	....	....	....	....	....	....
Claims on Private Sector	32d	88.4	98.3	119.3	147.5	172.6	179.1	196.1	248.4	292.9	356.7	404.7	462.4	542.7	609.5	688.7
Money	34	42.6	46.7	57.4	60.9	67.0	62.1	80.0	85.9	100.8	129.5	153.3	188.3	218.5	248.5	259.4
Quasi-Money	35	77.8	98.3	117.7	136.1	161.4	167.6	195.1	230.1	262.5	304.0	347.9	413.2	491.0	542.7	640.1
Other Items (Net)	37r	17.0	19.7	18.6	22.3	29.9	34.8	39.9	41.2	52.9	57.4	69.9	90.6	109.3	126.3	149.8
Money plus Quasi-Money	35l	120.4	145.0	175.2	197.0	228.5	229.7	275.1	316.0	363.3	433.5	501.2	601.4	709.5	791.1	899.4
Other Banking Institutions															*Millions of Pounds:*	
Reserves	40	6.4	6.0	6.5	8.5	5.5	4.6	7.2	7.2	8.6	12.0	14.5	15.9	19.3	21.1	23.1
Foreign Assets	41	—	—	—	—	—	—	—	—	—	—	—	—	—	—	—
Claims on Private Sector	42d	14.2	16.2	21.2	26.7	29.9	30.9	33.5	43.2	50.9	56.4	65.1	69.1	73.8	74.8	83.5
Liquid Liabilities	45l	13.0	13.4	17.2	23.3	22.0	22.6	26.2	33.7	39.8	42.2	46.6	49.4	55.7	61.2	70.4
Foreign Liabilities	46c	3.7	3.8	4.7	4.7	5.5	4.7	4.6	5.5	7.0	9.7	11.6	15.6	17.3	16.6	15.8
Capital Accounts	47a	2.6	2.8	3.1	3.4	4.0	4.8	5.5	6.7	7.9	9.8	11.4	14.7	15.1	10.9	13.6
Other Items (Net)	47r	1.3	2.2	2.8	3.8	3.9	3.6	4.4	4.5	4.9	6.8	10.0	5.3	4.9	7.1	6.8
Banking Survey															*Millions of Pounds:*	
Foreign Assets (Net)	51n	77.3	95.3	98.5	90.7	81.0	64.5	82.2	82.6	85.4	75.0	78.6	113.4	164.4	176.7	207.9
Domestic Credit	52	70.4	81.9	111.8	150.3	201.1	225.4	261.4	312.3	375.0	461.5	544.7	630.7	711.1	797.9	909.2
Claims on Central Govt. (Net)	52an	–32.0	–32.6	–28.5	–23.7	–.9	16.1	32.3	21.4	31.9	50.5	77.2	101.7	97.7	117.5	141.8
Claims on Local Government	52b	....	....	....	....	....	....	....	....	....	....	....	....	....	....	....
Claims on Nonfin.Pub.Enterprises	52c	....	....	....	....	....	....	....	....	....	....	....	....	....	....	....
Claims on Private Sector	52d	102.4	114.5	140.4	174.0	202.0	209.3	229.1	291.0	343.1	411.0	467.5	529.0	613.4	680.4	767.4
Monetary Liabilities	54	37.1	42.2	53.6	56.0	64.7	63.4	78.8	90.1	103.4	130.3	148.9	182.7	210.5	239.0	249.1
Quasi-Monetary Liabilities	55	90.0	110.2	132.3	155.8	180.2	187.4	218.9	256.6	296.0	340.5	391.1	458.8	542.7	600.3	706.7
Other Items (Net)	57r	20.7	24.7	24.5	29.2	37.1	39.1	46.0	48.2	60.9	65.7	83.2	102.7	122.4	135.2	161.3
Liquid Liabilities	55l	127.0	152.5	185.8	211.9	245.0	247.6	294.1	342.5	394.5	463.7	533.3	634.9	745.9	831.2	946.7
Interest Rates															*Percent Per Annum*	
Discount Rate (End of Period)	60	6.00	6.00	6.00	6.00	6.00	6.00	6.00	6.00	6.00	6.00	6.00	6.00	6.00	6.00	6.00
Deposit Rate	60l	....	5.00	5.00	5.00	5.00	5.06	5.75	5.75	5.75	5.75	5.75	5.75	5.75	5.75	5.75
Lending Rate	60p	6.00	6.00	6.00	6.00	....	9.00	9.00	9.00	9.00	9.00	9.00	9.00	9.00	9.00	9.00

1985	1986	1987	1988	1989	1990	1991	1992	1993	1994	1995	1996	1997	1998	1999		
End of Period															**Exchange Rates**	
1.6756	1.5979	1.6061	1.5936	1.5892	1.6174	1.5923	1.5056	1.4006	1.4384	1.4735	1.4800	1.4097	1.4255	1.2680	Official Rate	ac
End of Period (ag) Period Average (rh)																
1.8405	1.9545	2.2785	2.1445	2.0885	2.3010	2.2777	2.0702	1.9238	2.0998	2.1903	2.1282	1.9021	2.0071	1.7404	Official Rate	ag
1.6407	1.9353	2.0802	2.1447	2.0228	2.1874	2.1585	2.2212	2.0120	2.0347	2.2113	2.1446	1.9476	1.9342	1.8440	Official Rate	rh
Period Averages																
74.2	87.5	94.1	97.0	91.5	98.9	97.6	100.4	91.0	92.0	100.0	97.0	88.1	87.5	83.4	Official Rate	ahx
83.0	83.2	80.8	82.1	85.1	87.9	89.9	92.1	93.0	96.3	100.0	102.0	102.8	108.3	106.0	Nominal Effective Exchange Rate	ne c
109.2	105.0	99.6	97.7	95.5	93.5	93.7	96.1	96.6	99.0	100.0	100.3	100.1	103.3	99.7	Real Effective Exchange Rate	re c
End of Period															**Fund Position**	
69.7	69.7	69.7	69.7	69.7	69.7	69.7	100.0	100.0	100.0	100.0	100.0	100.0	100.0	139.6	Quota	2f. s
.1	.1	.3	.1	.1	.1	.1	.1	.1	.1	—	—	—	.2	.4	SDRs	1b. s
4.7	4.7	4.7	11.7	18.1	15.1	17.9	25.5	25.5	25.5	25.5	25.5	25.5	25.5	35.4	Reserve Position in the Fund	1c. s
—	—	—	—	—	—	—	—	—	—	—	—	—	—	—	Total Fund Cred.&Loans Outstg.	2tl
End of Period															**International Liquidity**	
595.3	752.7	873.5	927.9	1,124.0	1,506.9	1,390.2	1,027.9	1,096.7	1,464.5	1,116.9	1,541.9	1,391.6	1,379.7	1,832.9	Total Reserves minus Gold	1l. d
.1	.1	.4	.1	.1	.1	.1	.1	.1	.1	.2	—	.3	.3	.5	SDRs	1b. d
5.1	5.7	6.6	15.7	23.7	21.5	25.5	35.0	35.0	37.2	37.8	36.6	34.3	35.8	48.5	Reserve Position in the Fund	1c. d
590.0	747.0	866.5	912.1	1,100.2	1,485.3	1,364.5	992.8	1,061.6	1,427.2	1,079.0	1,505.3	1,356.9	1,343.6	1,783.8	Foreign Exchange	1d. d
.459	.459	.459	.459	.459	.459	.459	.459	.460	.459	.460	.440	.462	.462	.464	Gold (Million Fine Troy Ounces)	1ad
13.3	14.1	16.4	15.5	15.1	16.6	16.4	15.0	14.2	15.6	16.7	170.2	133.9	132.9	142.6	Gold (National Valuation)	1an d
2.7	2.8	11.0	23.7	29.4	69.1	76.8	77.2	53.9	55.7	89.6	56.4	73.2	57.1	49.7	Monetary Authorities: Other Liab.	4..d
124.3	178.4	232.0	318.7	553.2	701.9	1,093.0	1,396.6	1,554.3	1,915.4	3,083.3	3,255.1	3,612.4	3,519.3	3,902.3	Deposit Money Banks: Assets	7a. d
364.5	462.7	600.2	714.8	924.8	1,400.0	1,728.8	2,010.5	2,187.8	2,697.5	3,738.3	4,302.8	4,694.4	4,790.3	5,461.7	Liabilities	7b. d
335.6	389.6	578.6	735.1	1,271.1	1,837.0	1,639.4	1,647.7	1,722.9	2,052.7	2,257.4	3,189.6	13,090.6	8,607.2	8,060.5	Other Banking Insts.: Liabilities	7f. d
End of Period															**Monetary Authorities**	
331.5	393.3	408.0	440.9	546.0	662.3	618.0	504.3	578.1	705.6	518.2	805.2	802.7	754.4	1,135.8	Foreign Assets	11
122.1	86.7	119.1	166.5	92.5	186.1	240.8	415.2	407.3	398.5	607.2	570.5	558.4	596.7	534.9	Claims on Central Government	12a
42.6	58.7	69.0	83.7	10.4	24.1	24.6	34.2	13.4	12.4	22.4	6.5	.1	104.6	—	Claims on Deposit Money Banks	12e
419.2	453.0	501.8	I 569.2	506.9	696.7	714.0	763.6	775.6	872.4	834.6	761.5	755.5	878.0	1,010.7	Reserve Money	14
127.9	130.7	142.6	157.6	169.1	183.5	195.5	215.1	229.4	246.6	257.1	265.8	276.3	290.1	313.8	of which: Currency Outside DMBs	14a
1.5	1.4	4.8	11.0	14.1	30.1	33.7	37.3	28.0	26.6	40.9	26.5	38.5	28.4	28.5	Foreign Liabilities	16c
21.0	17.4	18.2	23.9	94.6	111.0	115.8	131.7	154.8	175.2	227.3	342.9	339.5	325.7	314.0	Central Government Deposits	16d
54.5	67.0	71.2	I 87.0	33.3	34.8	19.9	21.1	40.4	42.4	45.1	251.3	227.7	223.6	317.4	Other Items (Net)	17r
End of Period															**Deposit Money Banks**	
230.4	253.7	278.0	327.3	334.8	485.6	504.4	542.0	538.0	612.4	555.1	479.7	452.9	455.4	671.8	Reserves	20
67.6	91.3	101.8	148.6	264.9	305.0	479.9	674.6	807.9	912.2	1,407.7	1,529.5	1,899.1	1,753.4	2,242.2	Foreign Assets	21
98.0	121.5	181.2	222.8	234.6	285.6	310.2	342.5	519.9	566.5	463.7	722.1	834.5	854.0	965.6	Claims on Central Government	22a
788.6	874.7	981.0	I 1,147.1	1,345.6	1,611.6	1,839.3	2,158.9	2,436.7	2,754.3	3,225.3	3,667.0	4,109.7	4,635.2	5,184.3	Claims on Private Sector	22d
157.2	151.4	171.1	201.2	214.4	245.3	265.7	289.3	317.2	326.1	353.9	386.5	427.2	439.2	719.6	Demand Deposits	24
696.4	801.0	911.0	1,084.2	1,289.0	1,529.1	1,793.7	2,064.1	2,440.9	2,785.4	3,131.2	3,487.3	3,890.0	4,243.3	4,691.4	Time and Savings Deposits	25
198.1	236.7	263.4	333.3	442.8	608.4	759.0	971.2	1,137.3	1,284.6	1,706.8	2,021.8	2,468.0	2,386.7	3,138.2	Foreign Liabilities	26c
33.6	31.4	35.0	35.3	36.1	34.3	36.4	36.4	38.1	38.4	42.7	40.7	44.8	50.3	51.6	Central Government Deposits	26d
42.6	58.7	69.0	83.7	10.4	24.1	24.6	34.2	13.4	12.4	22.4	6.5	.1	5.6	—	Credit from Monetary Authorities	26g
56.7	61.9	92.4	108.7	187.2	246.6	254.3	322.8	355.5	398.5	394.8	455.5	466.2	573.1	463.1	Other Items (Net)	27r
End of Period															**Monetary Survey**	
199.5	246.4	241.6	245.2	353.9	328.9	305.2	170.4	220.8	306.6	178.3	286.4	195.4	92.7	211.2	Foreign Assets (Net)	31n
958.4	1,039.2	1,234.0	I 1,496.8	1,558.9	1,969.3	2,279.6	2,797.6	3,225.9	3,579.3	4,108.1	4,670.8	5,229.1	5,847.5	6,469.5	Domestic Credit	32
165.5	159.4	247.0	330.1	196.4	326.5	398.8	589.6	734.2	751.5	800.9	908.9	1,008.6	1,074.8	1,134.9	Claims on Central Govt. (Net)	32an
....	....	....	6.3	9.8	19.3	28.7	34.5	37.5	42.9	46.8	55.6	65.4	79.3	86.5	Claims on Local Government	32b
....	....	....	7.0	6.0	7.3	10.3	12.0	14.9	28.1	34.8	38.9	45.0	57.9	63.3	Claims on Nonfin.Pub.Enterprises	32c
792.9	879.8	987.0	I 1,153.4	1,346.7	1,616.3	1,841.8	2,161.5	2,439.2	2,756.8	3,225.7	3,667.4	4,110.0	4,635.6	5,184.9	Claims on Private Sector	32d
285.3	282.5	314.0	358.9	385.0	429.1	462.4	506.3	549.1	576.2	612.2	653.5	704.5	730.3	1,033.9	Money	34
707.0	813.0	924.4	I 1,102.7	1,300.8	1,539.7	1,800.2	2,070.2	2,448.0	2,794.3	3,142.2	3,495.6	3,900.4	4,255.6	4,706.9	Quasi-Money	35
165.6	190.2	237.1	I 280.3	227.0	329.4	322.1	391.5	449.5	515.4	532.0	808.1	819.6	954.4	939.9	Other Items (Net)	37r
992.3	1,095.5	1,238.4	I 1,461.7	1,685.8	1,968.8	2,262.6	2,576.5	2,997.1	3,370.5	3,754.4	4,149.1	4,604.9	4,985.9	5,740.8	Money plus Quasi-Money	35l
End of Period															**Other Banking Institutions**	
27.1	29.3	27.0	27.6	18.6	24.1	9.7	10.1	18.3	27.0	25.1	20.6	32.3	39.6	35.2	Reserves	40
—	.1	.1	I 340.1	606.0	795.7	718.6	795.1	894.9	977.1	1,030.2	1,498.4	6,901.6	4,290.9	4,647.4	Foreign Assets	41
93.0	106.2	115.2	I 635.4	768.3	909.0	1,059.4	1,235.1	1,405.8	1,599.8	1,826.0	2,056.5	2,244.4	2,431.6	2,747.0	Claims on Private Sector	42d
81.9	88.5	99.6	I 712.3	835.1	977.8	1,111.1	1,276.6	1,475.7	1,685.0	1,897.6	2,095.8	2,327.6	2,582.7	2,554.2	Liquid Liabilities	45l
25.3	22.9	20.8	I 342.8	608.6	798.3	719.8	795.9	895.6	977.6	1,030.6	1,498.7	6,882.2	4,288.4	4,631.4	Foreign Liabilities	46c
16.0	18.2	20.2	23.5	26.6	30.5	33.3	34.9	38.3	41.9	39.9	42.9	43.8	48.6	80.0	Capital Accounts	47a
−3.1	6.0	1.7	I −75.5	−77.5	−77.9	−76.5	−67.0	−90.6	−100.6	−86.8	−62.0	−75.2	−157.6	164.0	Other Items (Net)	47r
End of Period															**Banking Survey**	
174.2	223.6	220.9	I 242.5	351.3	326.2	304.0	169.6	220.1	306.1	177.8	286.0	214.8	95.2	227.3	Foreign Assets (Net)	51n
1,060.6	1,147.5	1,347.3	I 2,132.1	2,342.0	2,886.5	3,343.2	4,035.8	4,635.8	5,182.2	5,940.0	6,737.5	7,482.1	8,292.5	9,229.6	Domestic Credit	52
179.1	166.6	251.2	335.6	212.4	339.4	405.5	595.3	740.9	757.2	807.2	919.5	1,017.5	1,088.5	1,148.6	Claims on Central Govt. (Net)	52an
....	....	....	6.3	9.8	19.3	28.7	34.5	37.5	42.9	46.8	55.6	65.4	79.3	86.5	Claims on Local Government	52b
....	....	....	7.0	6.0	7.3	10.3	12.0	14.9	28.1	34.8	38.9	45.0	57.9	63.3	Claims on Nonfin.Pub.Enterprises	52c
881.6	980.9	1,096.1	I 1,783.1	2,113.8	2,520.6	2,898.7	3,394.0	3,842.5	4,354.1	5,051.3	5,723.5	6,354.1	7,066.8	7,931.2	Claims on Private Sector	52d
273.0	267.0	302.3	346.5	381.0	427.8	460.2	503.8	539.8	560.1	601.7	644.7	685.1	708.3	1,020.6	Monetary Liabilities	54
784.7	899.8	1,022.1	I 1,794.3	2,121.6	2,504.3	2,903.7	3,339.3	3,915.3	4,468.6	5,026.2	5,580.0	6,214.4	6,822.0	7,242.8	Quasi-Monetary Liabilities	55
177.1	204.4	243.8	I 233.8	190.7	280.6	283.3	362.3	400.8	459.6	489.9	798.7	797.4	857.5	1,193.5	Other Items (Net)	57r
1,047.1	1,154.8	1,311.0	I 2,146.3	2,502.3	2,922.5	3,364.0	3,843.0	4,454.6	5,028.4	5,626.9	6,224.4	6,900.2	7,529.1	8,259.8	Liquid Liabilities	55l
Percent Per Annum															**Interest Rates**	
6.00	6.00	6.00	6.00	6.50	6.50	6.50	6.50	6.50	6.50	6.50	I 7.50	7.00	7.00	7.00	Discount Rate (End of Period)	60
5.75	5.75	5.75	5.75	5.75	5.75	5.75	5.75	5.75	5.75	5.75	5.75	....	....	....	Deposit Rate	60l
9.00	9.00	9.00	9.00	9.00	9.00	9.00	9.00	9.00	8.83	8.50	8.50	....	....	....	Lending Rate	60p

Cyprus

423		1970	1971	1972	1973	1974	1975	1976	1977	1978	1979	1980	1981	1982	1983	1984
Prices, Production, Labor																*Index Numbers (1995=100):*
Wholesale Prices	63	....	....	....	....	....	....	....	....	....	....	....	....	....	....	....
Wholesale Prices: Home Goods	63a	24.2	24.5	I25.4	28.3	35.5	39.5	I41.3	44.1	44.9	51.4	65.9	75.2	79.8	81.1	84.5
Consumer Prices	64	23.2	24.1	25.3	I27.3	29.0	I33.1	34.4	36.9	39.7	43.5	49.3	I54.6	58.1	61.1	64.7
Industrial Production	66	40.2	44.3	50.4	53.3	40.8	34.8	I42.1	48.7	I53.8	58.2	62.5	66.2	67.9	70.0	73.8
Mining Production	66zx	186.8	203.9	190.6	196.3	133.4	I108.6	108.6	119.5	I145.6	138.8	139.9	121.0	112.5	105.2	89.9
																Number in Thousands:
Labor Force	67d	....	....	....	....	....	....	....	....	....	....	....	....	....	....	....
Employment	67e	....	....	....	....	....	....	....	....	....	....	....	....	....	....	....
Unemployment	67c	....	....	....	....	....	....	....	....	....	....	....	....	....	....	....
Unemployment Rate (%)	67r	....	....	....	....	....	....	....	....	....	....	....	....	....	....	....
International Transactions																*Millions of Pounds*
Exports	70	45.19	47.28	51.31	60.47	55.29	56.01	106.33	129.75	128.37	161.87	188.04	234.77	263.81	260.53	336.83
Imports, c.i.f.	71	98.23	106.87	121.48	157.44	148.03	113.71	177.76	254.01	282.69	357.60	424.29	489.54	577.55	641.96	796.52
																1985=100
Volume of Exports	72	48	53	52	I55	43	38	63	80	76	88	94	105	104	97	113
Volume of Imports	73	40	42	47	I55	39	27	41	56	62	70	73	75	88	96	104
Unit Value of Exports	74	40	39	41	I46	53	63	67	67	67	72	78	92	90	95	102
Unit Value of Imports	75	34	36	36	I40	53	59	60	63	63	70	81	90	91	93	99
Balance of Payments																*Millions of US Dollars:*
Current Account, n.i.e.	78al*d*	....	....	....	....	....	....	-26.6	-104.6	-185.0	-239.8	-258.3	-171.8	-178.2	-205.1	-221.6
Goods: Exports f.o.b.	78aa*d*	....	....	....	....	....	....	254.1	312.4	339.2	451.1	527.7	551.5	554.1	495.4	573.1
Goods: Imports f.o.b.	78ab*d*	....	....	....	....	....	....	-397.8	-558.9	-683.8	-906.2	-1,079.2	-1,042.6	-1,090.3	-1,093.5	-1,224.9
Trade Balance	78ac*d*	....	....	....	....	....	....	-143.7	-246.5	-344.6	-455.1	-551.5	-491.2	-536.2	-598.1	-651.8
Services: Credit	78ad*d*	....	....	....	....	....	....	175.9	206.6	258.6	371.3	481.8	526.5	577.2	627.4	701.6
Services: Debit	78ae*d*	....	....	....	....	....	....	-111.6	-143.6	-169.5	-226.8	-267.7	-273.6	-294.5	-287.7	-300.5
Balance on Goods & Services	78af*d*	....	....	....	....	....	....	-79.4	-183.5	-255.4	-310.6	-337.3	-238.2	-253.5	-258.4	-250.7
Income: Credit	78ag*d*	....	....	....	....	....	....	29.5	46.6	60.8	74.2	97.7	102.3	115.3	102.9	110.0
Income: Debit	78ah*d*	....	....	....	....	....	....	-24.1	-25.7	-35.1	-50.2	-63.4	-74.5	-89.4	-103.3	-105.5
Balance on Gds, Serv. & Inc.	78ai*d*	....	....	....	....	....	....	-74.1	-162.7	-229.7	-286.6	-303.1	-210.5	-227.6	-258.8	-246.3
Current Transfers, n.i.e.: Credit	78aj*d*	....	....	....	....	....	....	49.2	59.8	46.6	49.1	46.2	39.9	50.5	54.9	25.8
Current Transfers: Debit	78ak*d*	....	....	....	....	....	....	-1.7	-1.7	-1.9	-2.3	-1.4	-1.2	-1.1	-1.1	-1.2
Capital Account, n.i.e.	78bc*d*	....	....	....	....	....	....	13.2	14.7	22.8	24.8	28.6	24.0	22.1	20.5	18.9
Capital Account, n.i.e.: Credit	78ba*d*	....	....	....	....	....	....	14.6	16.2	24.1	26.5	31.2	26.1	24.2	22.4	20.7
Capital Account: Debit	78bb*d*	....	....	....	....	....	....	-1.5	-1.5	-1.3	-1.7	-2.5	-2.1	-2.1	-1.9	-1.9
Financial Account, n.i.e.	78bj*d*	....	....	....	....	....	....	51.9	99.7	160.1	171.8	250.7	238.5	275.8	215.5	269.6
Direct Investment Abroad	78bd*d*	....	....	....	....	....	....	—	—	—	—	—	—	—	—	—
Dir. Invest. in Rep. Econ., n.i.e.	78be*d*	....	....	....	....	....	....	32.4	41.4	57.0	70.5	85.0	78.3	71.5	68.4	52.7
Portfolio Investment Assets	78bf*d*	....	....	....	....	....	....	—	—	—	—	—	—	—	—	—
Equity Securities	78bk*d*	....	....	....	....	....	....	—	—	—	—	—	—	—	—	—
Debt Securities	78bl*d*	....	....	....	....	....	....	—	—	—	—	—	—	—	—	—
Portfolio Investment Liab., n.i.e.	78bg*d*	....	....	....	....	....	....	—	—	—	—	—	—	—	—	—
Equity Securities	78bm*d*	....	....	....	....	....	....	—	—	—	—	—	—	—	—	—
Debt Securities	78bn*d*	....	....	....	....	....	....	—	—	—	—	—	—	—	—	—
Financial Derivatives Assets	78bw*d*	....	....	....	....	....	....	....	....	....	....	....	....	....	....	....
Financial Derivatives Liabilities	78bx*d*	....	....	....	....	....	....	....	....	....	....	....	....	....	....	....
Other Investment Assets	78bh*d*	....	....	....	....	....	....	-12.2	5.4	-7.5	-9.6	-9.1	-16.6	-16.8	-21.1	-32.8
Monetary Authorities	78bo*d*	....	....	....	....	....	....	-2.2	3.9	2.9	—	—	—	—	-.4	—
General Government	78bp*d*	....	....	....	....	....	....	-.5	.2	-.5	-.3	-.3	1.2	-.2	-.4	—
Banks	78bq*d*	....	....	....	....	....	....	-9.5	1.2	-9.9	-9.3	-4.2	-16.8	-11.4	-14.6	-29.4
Other Sectors	78br*d*	....	....	....	....	....	....	—	—	—	—	-4.5	-.9	-5.3	-5.7	-3.4
Other Investment Liab., n.i.e.	78bi*d*	....	....	....	....	....	....	31.7	52.9	110.6	110.9	174.8	176.8	221.1	168.2	249.7
Monetary Authorities	78bs*d*	....	....	....	....	....	....	1.2	-6.4	1.9	-3.4	-5.4	.2	-.2	.2	—
General Government	78bt*d*	....	....	....	....	....	....	23.4	38.7	34.5	33.9	88.9	56.9	108.5	48.6	87.0
Banks	78bu*d*	....	....	....	....	....	....	13.2	13.0	12.3	32.4	37.1	51.0	59.5	66.3	77.7
Other Sectors	78bv*d*	....	....	....	....	....	....	-6.1	7.6	61.8	48.0	54.1	68.6	53.2	53.2	85.0
Net Errors and Omissions	78ca*d*	....	....	....	....	....	....	6.3	5.8	20.3	31.1	16.1	-2.7	20.5	10.8	29.1
Overall Balance	78cb*d*	....	....	....	....	....	....	44.8	15.6	18.2	-12.0	37.1	88.0	140.2	41.7	95.9
Reserves and Related Items	79da*d*	....	....	....	....	....	....	-44.8	-15.6	-18.2	12.0	-37.1	-88.0	-140.2	-41.7	-95.9
Reserve Assets	79db*d*	....	....	....	....	....	....	-85.3	-23.2	-5.9	5.4	-27.8	-77.3	-129.9	-34.3	-93.5
Use of Fund Credit and Loans	79dc*d*	....	....	....	....	....	....	40.5	—	-12.8	6.6	-9.3	-10.6	-10.3	-7.4	-2.3
Exceptional Financing	79de*d*	....	....	....	....	....	....	—	7.6	.5	—	—	—	—	—	....
Government Finance																*Millions of Pounds:*
Deficit (-) or Surplus	80	1.42	.32	-4.81	-12.14	-20.90	-20.38	-24.90	-12.71	-28.84	-41.64	-70.01	-46.75	-48.48	-110.13	-71.03
Revenue	81	41.37	46.91	52.28	60.42	54.82	59.48	64.29	83.20	100.00	123.52	161.22	191.25	232.83	275.62	333.39
Grants Received	81z	—	.12	.10	—	6.33	7.41	14.48	23.61	13.50	13.25	12.55	12.09	19.52	13.79	10.96
Expenditure	82	38.35	45.36	54.14	70.26	79.20	84.58	100.39	116.52	136.63	174.11	221.52	255.58	297.03	389.13	406.54
Lending Minus Repayments	83	1.60	1.35	3.05	2.30	2.85	2.69	3.28	3.00	5.71	4.30	22.26	-5.49	3.80	10.41	8.84
Financing																
Net Borrowing: Domestic	84a	3.98	4.63	6.58	-4.49	2.98	5.42	14.43	-6.29	17.82	28.93	40.62	26.72	8.54	38.63	44.11
Foreign	85a	.74	-.99	.15	1.66	.84	1.98	10.92	16.20	18.42	11.68	29.61	25.45	51.96	63.93	36.49
Use of Cash Balances	87	-6.14	-3.96	-1.92	14.97	17.08	12.98	-.45	2.80	-7.40	1.03	-.22	-5.42	-12.02	7.57	-9.57
Debt: Domestic	88a	13.93	18.56	25.15	27.58	32.73	35.36	49.99	43.98	57.29	87.74	131.95	156.17	164.48	202.90	246.88
Foreign	89a	5.17	4.23	4.27	6.66	8.82	10.69	23.22	39.79	59.26	70.14	95.44	133.95	199.05	308.89	372.43
National Accounts																*Millions of Pounds*
Exports of Goods & Services	90c	85.9	99.0	115.3	131.6	115.8	91.2	166.1	202.3	214.4	281.4	344.1	440.2	521.9	573.0	731.0
Government Consumption	91f	21.6	25.5	29.6	35.8	43.1	44.9	54.5	59.2	66.3	80.5	103.4	127.5	151.5	171.9	188.7
Gross Fixed Capital Formation	93e	53.3	58.5	67.2	94.3	80.0	50.5	70.3	124.6	170.4	219.5	260.0	275.9	304.7	316.0	412.5
Increase/Decrease(-) in Stocks	93i	1.9	3.0	2.8	5.4	.1	7.4	18.4	23.0	18.1	24.4	27.5	20.3	20.4	26.3	36.8
Private Consumption	96f	171.5	194.3	218.9	238.9	242.1	208.7	252.7	320.4	376.6	429.7	508.4	573.8	678.0	765.8	851.5
Imports of Goods & Services	98c	-107.6	-118.8	-136.7	-176.1	-176.5	-145.7	-209.1	-286.7	-318.7	-401.6	-479.5	-554.7	-658.4	-727.2	-897.4
Gross Domestic Product (GDP)	99b	226.6	261.5	296.9	329.9	304.6	257.0	333.9	423.1	506.5	629.8	760.4	876.0	1,024.9	1,136.7	1,337.4
Net Factor Inc/Pmts(-) Abroad	98.n	7.4	8.1	8.9	11.1	11.9	14.2	13.9	18.8	20.2	22.1	26.6	27.0	30.5	21.8	24.2
Gross National Income (GNI)	99a	234.0	269.6	306.0	341.0	316.5	271.2	347.8	441.9	526.7	651.9	787.0	903.0	1,055.4	1,158.5	1,361.6
Net National Income	99e	223.5	257.5	292.0	307.0	284.8	244.1	319.6	408.2	484.2	597.6	716.6	814.2	951.3	1,039.5	1,221.1
GDP Volume 1967 prices	99b.*p*	201.3	227.4	242.8	249.0	....	....	....	....	....	....	....	....	....	....	....
GDP Volume 1973 prices	99b.*p*	....	....	....	329.9	274.1	222.0	261.9	....	....	....	....	....	....	....	....
GDP Volume 1980 prices	99b.*p*	....	....	....	....	....	....	524.3	607.0	653.4	717.9	760.4	783.6	832.8	877.0	954.5
GDP Volume 1985 prices	99b.*p*	....	....	....	....	....	....	....	....	....	....	....	....	....	....	....
GDP Volume 1990 Prices	99b.*p*	....	....	....	....	....	....	....	....	....	....	....	....	....	....	....
GDP Volume (1995=100)	99bv*p*	30.7	34.7	37.0	38.0	31.6	25.6	30.2	34.9	37.6	41.3	43.7	45.1	47.9	50.5	54.9
GDP Deflator (1995=100)	99bi*p*	18.5	18.9	20.1	21.8	24.2	25.2	27.7	30.4	33.8	38.2	43.6	48.7	53.6	56.5	61.0
																Millions:
Population	99z	.61	.61	.61	.62	.63	.62	.61	.61	.62	.62	.63	.63	.64	.65	.66

1985	1986	1987	1988	1989	1990	1991	1992	1993	1994	1995	1996	1997	1998	1999		
Period Averages															**Prices, Production, Labor**	
....	....	....	....	....	....	91.1	91.1	93.4	96.5	100.0	102.1	105.0	105.5	106.8	Wholesale Prices	63
87.2	78.5	76.3	78.3	78.9	82.7	....	....	....	....	I 100.0	102.8	106.2	108.6	110.2	Wholesale Prices: Home Goods	63a
68.0	I 68.8	70.7	73.2	75.9	79.3	83.3	I 88.8	93.1	97.5	100.0	103.0	106.7	109.1	I 110.8	Consumer Prices	64
72.9	I 75.2	82.5	88.7	92.0	I 97.3	97.9	101.6	95.1	98.5	100.0	97.0	96.8	99.5	....	Industrial Production	66
105.3	95.7	101.6	99.4	81.9	I 82.1	80.5	82.1	100.4	108.6	100.0	102.4	102.6	121.0	....	Mining Production	66zx
Period Averages																
....	....	....	....	....	....	280	287	....	....	303	....	....	....	....	Labor Force	67d
....	....	....	....	....	....	256	267	267	271	282	285	285	287	....	Employment	67e
8	9	9	7	6	5	8	5	8	8	8	9	10	10	....	Unemployment	67c
3.3	3.7	3.4	2.8	2.3	1.8	3.0	1.8	2.6	2.7	2.6	3.1	3.4	3.3	....	Unemployment Rate (%)	67r
Millions of Pounds															**International Transactions**	
290.61	260.16	297.99	330.86	393.05	435.60	441.79	443.72	431.40	475.98	555.61	649.03	640.01	551.13	542.71	Exports	70
762.31	659.07	711.42	866.77	1,192.90	1,278.54	1,321.13	1,653.36	1,316.08	1,482.22	1,670.41	1,857.51	1,899.34	1,904.71	1,970.67	Imports, c.i.f.	71
1985=100																
100	95	115	....	....	....	....	....	....	....	....	....	....	....	....	Volume of Exports	72
100	108	117	....	....	....	....	....	....	....	....	....	....	....	....	Volume of Imports	73
100	93	95	....	....	....	....	....	....	....	....	....	....	....	....	Unit Value of Exports	74
100	85	81	....	....	....	....	....	....	....	....	....	....	....	....	Unit Value of Imports	75
Minus Sign Indicates Debit															Balance of Payments	
-180.2	-18.9	-7.7	-107.6	-248.7	-154.3	-420.3	-638.2	109.8	74.4	-160.5	-461.3	-324.0	-600.6	-233.7	Current Account, n.i.e.	78al*d*
474.9	502.8	619.6	709.1	795.4	951.6	951.7	985.9	867.7	967.5	1,228.7	1,392.4	1,245.8	1,064.6	1,000.3	Goods: Exports f.o.b.	78aa*d*
-1,121.9	-1,148.3	-1,418.6	-1,777.4	-2,165.5	-2,504.4	-2,553.5	-3,301.1	-2,374.5	-2,703.0	-3,314.2	-3,575.7	-3,317.2	-3,490.4	-3,309.5	Goods: Imports f.o.b.	78ab*d*
-647.0	-645.6	-799.0	-1,068.3	-1,370.1	-1,552.8	-1,601.8	-2,315.2	-1,506.8	-1,735.5	-2,085.5	-2,183.3	-2,071.4	-2,425.7	-2,309.2	*Trade Balance*	78ac*d*
738.4	938.5	1,187.9	1,411.6	1,618.6	2,003.6	1,857.1	2,521.4	2,335.1	2,646.7	2,991.2	2,872.5	2,827.6	2,954.7	3,184.7	Services: Credit	78ad*d*
-301.7	-354.5	-441.1	-501.7	-559.0	-673.9	-729.1	-884.0	-765.0	-862.1	-1,105.6	-1,160.8	-1,109.4	-1,140.7	-1,157.2	Services: Debit	78ae*d*
-210.3	-61.6	-52.2	-158.4	-310.5	-223.1	-473.7	-677.8	63.3	49.2	-199.8	-471.6	-353.2	-611.8	-281.8	*Balance on Goods & Services*	78af*d*
115.6	68.5	77.5	87.9	119.1	158.9	175.3	156.8	131.9	121.5	282.7	274.5	297.5	327.9	330.4	Income: Credit	78ag*d*
-107.3	-128.3	-140.7	-160.7	-172.3	-216.8	-230.8	-234.9	-198.4	-211.1	-312.5	-314.8	-309.2	-348.4	-369.3	Income: Debit	78ah*d*
-201.9	-121.4	-115.4	-231.2	-363.7	-281.0	-529.3	-755.9	-3.2	-40.4	-229.7	-511.9	-364.9	-632.3	-320.7	*Balance on Gds, Serv. & Inc.*	78ai*d*
22.7	105.4	110.4	126.9	118.5	131.0	114.3	123.2	118.4	125.0	134.8	127.8	118.7	132.7	194.7	Current Transfers, n.i.e.: Credit	78aj*d*
-1.0	-2.9	-2.7	-3.2	-3.4	-4.4	-5.4	-5.6	-5.4	-10.2	-65.6	-77.2	-77.8	-101.0	-107.7	Current Transfers: Debit	78ak*d*
19.1	....	....	....	....	....	....	....	....	....	....	....	....	....	....	Capital Account, n.i.e.	78bc*d*
20.6	....	....	....	....	....	....	....	....	....	....	....	....	....	....	Capital Account, n.i.e.: Credit	78ba*d*
-1.5	....	....	....	....	....	....	....	....	....	....	....	....	....	....	Capital Account: Debit	78bb*d*
112.5	205.0	146.5	166.3	451.5	436.0	278.2	323.4	-3.8	185.7	-150.7	401.9	358.6	595.2	929.7	Financial Account, n.i.e.	78bj*d*
-.2	—	-2.3	-.6	-.8	-4.6	-14.6	-14.7	-12.3	-6.1	-27.6	-48.3	-44.2	-84.6	-158.2	Direct Investment Abroad	78bd*d*
58.0	46.3	52.0	62.1	69.7	126.6	81.8	107.4	83.4	75.2	82.4	50.0	68.1	56.0	65.4	Dir. Invest. in Rep. Econ., n.i.e.	78be*d*
—	-.2	....	....	....	....	....	-5.1	-18.9	-244.6	-44.4	-117.5	-125.9	-106.2	-474.8	Portfolio Investment Assets	78bf*d*
—	....	....	....	....	....	....	....	....	....	....	....	....	....	....	Equity Securities	78bk*d*
—	-.2	....	....	....	....	....	-5.1	-18.9	-244.6	-44.4	-117.5	-125.9	-106.2	-474.8	Debt Securities	78bl*d*
—	....	....	....	92.6	-38.0	125.7	57.6	-33.4	84.5	-27.4	69.7	268.3	303.0	476.5	Portfolio Investment Liab., n.i.e.	78bg*d*
—	....	....	....	....	....	....	....	....	....	2.0	2.8	3.1	-12.0	139.2	Equity Securities	78bm*d*
—	....	....	....	92.6	-38.0	125.7	57.6	-33.4	84.5	-29.4	66.9	265.2	315.0	337.2	Debt Securities	78bn*d*
....	....	....	....	....	....	....	....	....	....	....	....	....	....	....	Financial Derivatives Assets	78bw*d*
....	....	....	....	....	....	....	....	....	....	....	....	....	....	....	Financial Derivatives Liabilities	78bx*d*
-68.2	-7.3	-.2	-118.5	-231.7	-114.6	-379.0	-321.2	-231.2	56.3	-1,075.5	-158.0	-700.5	580.5	-385.1	Other Investment Assets	78bh*d*
.3	....	....	....	....	....	....	....	....	....	....	....	....	....	....	Monetary Authorities	78bo*d*
-8.2	36.5	49.1	-30.4	-18.6	-29.7	-16.8	57.4	10.1	1.0	-11.9	-7.7	-22.8	32.4	.6	General Government	78bp*d*
-21.4	-43.8	-19.3	-82.5	-234.7	-83.0	-362.2	-395.5	-246.1	55.3	-1,063.6	-150.3	-677.8	548.1	-385.7	Banks	78bq*d*
-39.0	....	-29.9	-5.6	21.6	-2.0	....	16.9	4.8	....	....	....	....	....	....	Other Sectors	78br*d*
122.9	166.2	97.1	223.3	521.6	466.5	464.2	499.4	208.5	220.4	941.8	606.0	892.8	-153.5	1,406.0	Other Investment Liab., n.i.e.	78bi*d*
-.5	—	7.1	13.3	6.1	34.9	6.9	9.8	-23.1	.4	29.2	-36.2	20.6	-24.3	-5.7	Monetary Authorities	78bs*d*
36.7	124.7	27.4	28.7	110.6	-12.4	60.5	-169.1	-155.0	-228.6	-147.2	-95.4	-112.9	-6.6	-38.9	General Government	78bt*d*
20.9	76.0	55.3	150.0	221.2	361.5	359.8	463.4	331.3	301.5	964.4	693.3	872.0	-136.1	1,384.1	Banks	78bu*d*
65.8	-34.5	7.3	31.3	183.8	82.5	37.0	195.3	55.3	147.1	95.5	44.4	113.1	13.5	66.5	Other Sectors	78bv*d*
19.0	-26.6	-75.2	12.0	25.3	12.2	76.5	89.9	38.8	-13.2	-51.8	-.4	-81.6	-77.1	-57.0	Net Errors and Omissions	78ca*d*
-29.6	159.5	63.7	70.7	228.0	293.8	-65.6	-224.9	144.8	246.9	-363.1	-59.8	-47.0	-82.5	639.0	*Overall Balance*	78cb*d*
29.6	-159.5	-63.7	-70.7	-228.0	-293.8	65.6	224.9	-144.8	-246.9	363.1	59.8	47.0	82.5	-639.0	Reserves and Related Items	79da*d*
32.8	-159.5	-63.7	-70.7	-228.0	-293.8	65.6	224.9	-144.8	-246.9	363.1	59.8	47.0	82.5	-639.0	Reserve Assets	79db*d*
-3.2	—	—	—	—	—	—	—	—	—	—	—	—	—	—	Use of Fund Credit and Loans	79dc*d*
....	....	....	....	....	....	....	....	....	....	....	....	....	....	....	Exceptional Financing	79de*d*
Year Ending December 31															**Government Finance**	
-78.50	-49.13	-103.74	-93.42	-65.97	-136.08	-182.39	-147.56	-77.82	-51.85	-39.90	-142.08	-231.22	-257.56	....	Deficit (-) or Surplus	80
380.39	418.10	454.73	529.10	627.24	706.42	720.83	873.99	987.93	1,140.55	1,266.90	1,321.30	1,373.39	1,473.17	....	Revenue	81
9.71	8.99	6.98	6.96	5.37	4.04	3.78	1.14	3.75	3.97	3.90	2.35	1.64	.74	....	Grants Received	81z
450.54	468.37	549.47	619.47	691.23	836.34	888.91	1,007.37	1,053.83	1,192.36	1,306.10	1,462.72	1,603.53	1,731.70	....	Expenditure	82
18.06	7.85	15.98	10.01	7.35	10.20	18.09	15.32	15.67	4.01	4.60	3.01	2.72	-.23	....	Lending Minus Repayments	83
															Financing	
69.35	1.35	102.27	112.49	-2.08	168.55	125.75	249.03	219.76	106.87	117.40	203.91	143.13	109.31	....	Net Borrowing: Domestic	84a
28.21	65.34	13.34	21.11	107.41	-22.37	82.85	-54.63	-91.04	-65.02	-77.50	-61.83	88.08	148.28	....	Foreign	85a
-19.06	-17.56	-11.87	-40.18	-39.36	-10.10	-26.21	-46.84	-50.90	10.00	—	—	—	—	....	Use of Cash Balances	87
316.26	318.34	411.02	533.73	531.71	700.02	826.36	1,075.44	1,295.36	1,402.51	1,583.40	1,837.56	1,987.35	2,130.72	....	Debt: Domestic	88a
386.92	490.15	506.83	511.02	616.92	595.60	682.79	665.27	627.81	556.65	479.27	402.95	515.33	664.77	....	Foreign	89a
Millions of Pounds															**National Accounts**	
722.4	721.0	841.8	959.6	1,161.4	1,316.8	1,260.8	1,544.4	1,555.2	1,741.1	1,865.6	1,946.9	2,053.4	2,041.1	2,166.6	Exports of Goods & Services	90c
208.5	229.9	295.7	332.5	360.7	443.1	493.3	590.7	552.5	608.1	655.2	745.0	805.6	895.7	945.0	Government Consumption	91f
403.0	384.0	417.9	490.8	621.4	628.5	650.2	795.9	741.2	751.5	769.7	843.8	801.0	836.0	....	Gross Fixed Capital Formation	93e
46.7	31.0	36.6	57.2	75.8	62.3	41.0	94.6	47.6	180.0	240.0	230.0	250.0	310.2	....	Increase/Decrease(-) in Stocks	93i
945.8	979.2	1,059.8	1,210.2	1,343.3	1,532.2	1,754.1	1,938.6	1,934.3	2,111.0	2,382.8	2,526.1	2,694.2	2,994.5	3,027.1	Private Consumption	96f
-872.0	-779.2	-894.9	-1,067.9	-1,351.3	-1,456.3	-1,526.9	-1,881.6	-1,569.4	-1,755.5	-1,999.7	-2,208.8	-2,274.8	-2,398.3	-2,411.1	Imports of Goods & Services	98c
1,482.2	1,599.7	1,781.1	1,992.4	2,256.2	2,555.7	2,674.7	3,102.9	3,274.6	3,650.7	3,990.1	4,134.6	4,337.1	4,637.7	4,897.2	Gross Domestic Product (GDP)	99b
25.8	21.1	24.1	23.3	35.0	41.6	44.8	39.6	47.2	41.3	43.7	24.6	33.9	31.7	19.6	Net Factor Inc/Pmts(-) Abroad	98.n
1,508.0	1,620.8	1,805.2	2,015.7	2,291.2	2,597.3	2,719.5	3,142.5	3,322.0	3,692.0	4,033.8	4,159.2	4,371.0	4,669.4	4,916.8	Gross National Income (GNI)	99a
1,349.7	1,450.0	1,615.7	1,803.8	2,050.7	2,324.6	2,434.0	2,812.5	2,973.2	3,304.3	3,610.3	3,722.5	3,912.0	4,179.1	4,400.5	Net National Income	99e
....	....	....	....	....	....	....	....	....	....	....	....	....	....	....	GDP Volume 1967 prices	99b.*p*
....	....	....	....	....	....	....	....	....	....	....	....	....	....	....	GDP Volume 1973 prices	99b.*p*
999.8	....	....	....	....	....	....	....	....	....	....	....	....	....	....	GDP Volume 1980 prices	99b.*p*
1,482.2	1,535.3	1,644.9	1,781.7	1,925.8	2,068.4	....	....	....	....	....	....	....	....	....	GDP Volume 1985 prices	99b.*p*
....	....	....	....	....	2,555.7	2,574.6	2,815.7	2,834.7	3,001.1	3,184.2	3,244.8	3,325.9	3,492.2	3,649.6	GDP Volume 1990 Prices	99b.*p*
57.5	59.6	63.8	69.1	74.7	80.3	80.9	88.4	89.0	94.2	100.0	101.9	104.5	109.7	114.6	GDP Volume (1995=100)	99bv*p*
64.6	67.3	69.9	72.2	75.7	79.8	82.9	87.9	92.2	97.1	100.0	101.7	104.1	106.0	107.1	GDP Deflator (1995=100)	99bi*p*
Midyear Estimates																
.67	.65	.66	.66	.67	.68	.69	.71	.72	.73	.73	.74	.74	.75	.78	**Population**	99z

(See notes in the back of the book.)

		1970	1971	1972	1973	1974	1975	1976	1977	1978	1979	1980	1981	1982	1983	1984
Exchange Rates																*Koruny per SDR:*
Official Rate	aa	....	....	....	....	....	....	....	....	....	....	....	....	....	....	....
																Koruny per US Dollar:
Official Rate	ae	....	....	....	....	....	....	....	....	....	....	....	....	....	....	....
Official Rate	rf	....	....	....	....	....	....	....	....	....	....	....	....	....	....	....
																Index Numbers (1995=100):
Nominal Effective Exchange Rate	ne c	....	....	....	....	....	....	....	....	....	....	....	....	....	....	....
Real Effective Exchange Rate	re c	....	....	....	....	....	....	....	....	....	....	....	....	....	....	....
Fund Position																*Millions of SDRs:*
Quota	2f. s	—	—	—	—	—	—	—	—	—	—	—	—	—	—	—
SDRs	1b. s	......	......	......	......	......	......	......	......	......	......	......	......	......	......	......
Reserve Position in the Fund	1c. s	......	......	......	......	......	......	......	......	......	......	......	......	......	......	......
Total Fund Cred.&Loans Outstg.	2tl	......	......	......	......	......	......	......	......	......	......	......	......	......	......	......
International Liquidity														*Millions of US Dollars Unless Otherwise Indicated:*		
Total Reserves minus Gold	1l. d	....	....	....	....	....	....	....	....	....	....	....	....	....	....	....
SDRs	1b. d	....	....	....	....	....	....	....	....	....	....	....	....	....	....	....
Reserve Position in the Fund	1c. d	....	....	....	....	....	....	....	....	....	....	....	....	....	....	....
Foreign Exchange	1d. d	....	....	....	....	....	....	....	....	....	....	....	....	....	....	....
Gold (Million Fine Troy Ounces)	1ad	....	....	....	....	....	....	....	....	....	....	....	....	....	....	....
Gold (National Valuation)	1and	....	....	....	....	....	....	....	....	....	....	....	....	....	....	....
Monetary Authorities: Other Assets	3.. d	....	....	....	....	....	....	....	....	....	....	....	....	....	....	....
Other Liab.	4.. d	....	....	....	....	....	....	....	....	....	....	....	....	....	....	....
Deposit Money Banks: Assets	7a. d	....	....	....	....	....	....	....	....	....	....	....	....	....	....	....
Liabilities	7b. d	....	....	....	....	....	....	....	....	....	....	....	....	....	....	....
Monetary Authorities																*Billions of Koruny:*
Foreign Assets	11	....	....	....	....	....	....	....	....	....	....	....	....	....	....	....
Claims on Central Government	12a	....	....	....	....	....	....	....	....	....	....	....	....	....	....	....
Claims on Nonfin.Pub.Enterprises	12c	....	....	....	....	....	....	....	....	....	....	....	....	....	....	....
Claims on Deposit Money Banks	12e	....	....	....	....	....	....	....	....	....	....	....	....	....	....	....
Claims on Nonbank Financial Insts	12g	....	....	....	....	....	....	....	....	....	....	....	....	....	....	....
Reserve Money	14	....	....	....	....	....	....	....	....	....	....	....	....	....	....	....
of which: Currency Outside DMBs	14a	....	....	....	....	....	....	....	....	....	....	....	....	....	....	....
Time Deposits	15	....	....	....	....	....	....	....	....	....	....	....	....	....	....	....
Foreign Liabilities	16c	....	....	....	....	....	....	....	....	....	....	....	....	....	....	....
Long-Term Foreign Liabilities	16cl	....	....	....	....	....	....	....	....	....	....	....	....	....	....	....
Central Government Deposits	16d	....	....	....	....	....	....	....	....	....	....	....	....	....	....	....
Capital Accounts	17a	....	....	....	....	....	....	....	....	....	....	....	....	....	....	....
Other Items (Net)	17r	....	....	....	....	....	....	....	....	....	....	....	....	....	....	....
Deposit Money Banks																*Billions of Koruny:*
Reserves	20	....	....	....	....	....	....	....	....	....	....	....	....	....	....	....
Foreign Assets	21	....	....	....	....	....	....	....	....	....	....	....	....	....	....	....
Claims on General Government	22a	....	....	....	....	....	....	....	....	....	....	....	....	....	....	....
of which: Clms.on Natl.Prop.Fd.	22ae	....	....	....	....	....	....	....	....	....	....	....	....	....	....	....
Claims on Nonfin.Pub.Enterprises	22c	....	....	....	....	....	....	....	....	....	....	....	....	....	....	....
Claims on Private Sector	22d	....	....	....	....	....	....	....	....	....	....	....	....	....	....	....
Claims on Nonbank Financial Insts	22g	....	....	....	....	....	....	....	....	....	....	....	....	....	....	....
Demand Deposits	24	....	....	....	....	....	....	....	....	....	....	....	....	....	....	....
Time & Foreign Currency Deposits	25	....	....	....	....	....	....	....	....	....	....	....	....	....	....	....
of which: Fgn. Currency Deposits	25b	....	....	....	....	....	....	....	....	....	....	....	....	....	....	....
Bonds	26ab	....	....	....	....	....	....	....	....	....	....	....	....	....	....	....
Foreign Liabilities	26c	....	....	....	....	....	....	....	....	....	....	....	....	....	....	....
Long-Term Foreign Liabilities	26cl	....	....	....	....	....	....	....	....	....	....	....	....	....	....	....
General Government Deposits	26d	....	....	....	....	....	....	....	....	....	....	....	....	....	....	....
of which: Natl.Prop.Fd.Deposits	26de	....	....	....	....	....	....	....	....	....	....	....	....	....	....	....
Credit from Monetary Authorities	26g	....	....	....	....	....	....	....	....	....	....	....	....	....	....	....
Capital Accounts	27a	....	....	....	....	....	....	....	....	....	....	....	....	....	....	....
Other Items (Net)	27r	....	....	....	....	....	....	....	....	....	....	....	....	....	....	....
Monetary Survey																*Billions of Koruny:*
Foreign Assets (Net)	31n	....	....	....	....	....	....	....	....	....	....	....	....	....	....	....
Domestic Credit	32	....	....	....	....	....	....	....	....	....	....	....	....	....	....	....
Claims on General Govt. (Net)	32an	....	....	....	....	....	....	....	....	....	....	....	....	....	....	....
Claims on Nonfin.Pub.Enterprises	32c	....	....	....	....	....	....	....	....	....	....	....	....	....	....	....
Claims on Private Sector	32d	....	....	....	....	....	....	....	....	....	....	....	....	....	....	....
Claims on Nonbank Fin. Insts	32g	....	....	....	....	....	....	....	....	....	....	....	....	....	....	....
Money	34	....	....	....	....	....	....	....	....	....	....	....	....	....	....	....
Quasi-Money	35	....	....	....	....	....	....	....	....	....	....	....	....	....	....	....
Bonds	36ab	....	....	....	....	....	....	....	....	....	....	....	....	....	....	....
Long-Term Foreign Liabilities	36cl	....	....	....	....	....	....	....	....	....	....	....	....	....	....	....
Capital Accounts	37a	....	....	....	....	....	....	....	....	....	....	....	....	....	....	....
Other Items (Net)	37r	....	....	....	....	....	....	....	....	....	....	....	....	....	....	....
Money plus Quasi-Money	35l	....	....	....	....	....	....	....	....	....	....	....	....	....	....	....
Interest Rates																*Percent Per Annum*
Discount Rate (End of Period)	60	....	....	....	....	....	....	....	....	....	....	....	....	....	....	....
Refinancing Rate	60a	....	....	....	....	....	....	....	....	....	....	....	....	....	....	....
Deposit Rate	60l	....	....	....	....	....	....	....	....	....	....	....	....	....	....	....
Lending Rate	60p	....	....	....	....	....	....	....	....	....	....	....	....	....	....	....
Prices, Production, Labor																*Index Numbers (1995=100):*
Producer Prices	63	....	....	....	....	....	....	....	....	....	....	....	....	....	....	....
Consumer Prices	64	....	....	....	....	....	....	....	....	....	....	....	....	....	....	....
Wages	65	....	....	....	....	....	....	....	....	....	....	....	....	....	....	....
Industrial Production	66	....	....	....	....	....	....	....	....	....	....	....	....	....	....	....
Industrial Employment	67	....	....	....	....	....	....	....	....	....	....	....	....	....	....	....
																Number in Thousands:
Labor Force	67d	....	....	....	....	....	....	....	....	....	....	....	....	....	....	....
Employment	67e	....	....	....	....	....	....	....	....	....	....	....	....	....	....	....
Unemployment	67c	....	....	....	....	....	....	....	....	....	....	....	....	....	....	....
Unemployment Rate (%)	67r	....	....	....	....	....	....	....	....	....	....	....	....	....	....	....
International Transactions																*Millions of Koruny*
Exports	70	....	....	....	....	....	....	....	....	....	....	....	....	....	....	....
Imports, f.o.b.	71.v	....	....	....	....	....	....	....	....	....	....	....	....	....	....	....

	1985	1986	1987	1988	1989	1990	1991	1992	1993	1994	1995	1996	1997	1998	1999		
End of Period																**Exchange Rates**	
	....	....	....	....	....	....	....	....	41.145	40.947	39.544	39.302	46.733	42.037	49.382	Official Rate	aa
End of Period (ae) Period Average (rf)																	
	....	....	....	....	....	....	....	....	29.955	28.049	26.602	27.332	34.636	29.855	35.979	Official Rate	ae
	....	....	....	....	....	....	....	....	29.153	28.785	26.541	27.145	31.698	32.281	34.569	Official Rate	rf
Period Averages																	
	....	....	....	....	....	131.27	91.32	92.50	97.67	100.00	100.00	101.90	98.38	99.04	99.23	Nominal Effective Exchange Rate	ne c
	....	....	....	....	....	81.92	75.67	79.17	92.06	96.71	100.00	106.66	107.46	116.29	114.76	Real Effective Exchange Rate	re c
End of Period																**Fund Position**	
	—	—	—	—	—	—	—	—	589.6	589.6	589.6	589.6	589.6	589.6	819.3	Quota	2f. s
	....	....	....	....	....	....	....	....	6.0	—	.1	—	—	—	—	SDRs	1b. s
	....	....	....	....	....	....	....	....	—	—	—	—	—	—	—	Reserve Position in the Fund	1c. s
	....	....	....	....	....	....	....	....	780.7	—	—	—	—	—	—	Total Fund Cred.&Loans Outstg.	2tl
End of Period																**International Liquidity**	
	....	....	....	....	....	....	....	....	3,789	6,145	13,843	12,352	9,734	12,542	12,806	Total Reserves minus Gold	1l. d
	....	....	....	....	....	....	....	....	8	—	—	—	—	—	—	SDRs	1b. d
	....	....	....	....	....	....	....	....	—	—	—	—	—	—	—	Reserve Position in the Fund	1c. d
	....	....	....	....	....	....	....	....	3,781	6,145	13,843	12,352	9,734	12,542	12,806	Foreign Exchange	1d. d
	....	....	....	....	....	....	....	....	1.950	2.098	1.990	1.985	1.041	.288	.446	Gold (Million Fine Troy Ounces)	1ad
	....	....	....	....	....	....	....	....	129	140	141	137	57	18	23	Gold (National Valuation)	1an d
	....	....	....	....	....	....	....	....	2,264	1,043	1,084	1,161	843	946	1,285	Monetary Authorities: Other Assets	3.. d
	....	....	....	....	....	....	....	....	2,905	1,791	1,802	658	696	381	849	Other Liab.	4.. d
	....	....	....	....	....	....	....	....	2,802	3,203	3,783	5,767	8,585	11,793	22,530	Deposit Money Banks: Assets	7a. d
	....	....	....	....	....	....	....	....	1,459	2,464	6,428	9,048	9,124	10,799	15,278	Liabilities	7b. d
End of Period																**Monetary Authorities**	
	....	....	....	....	....	....	....	....	185.20	205.53	400.83	373.08	368.28	403.23	507.82	Foreign Assets	11
	....	....	....	....	....	....	....	....	44.98	39.73	12.63	.32	—	—	—	Claims on Central Government	12a
	....	....	....	....	....	....	....	....	1.99	1.27	.70	.71	I .55	.28	.16	Claims on Nonfin.Pub.Enterprises	12c
	....	....	....	....	....	....	....	....	78.40	77.71	74.84	84.88	100.49	74.91	50.47	Claims on Deposit Money Banks	12e
	....	....	....	....	....	....	....	....	.16	.04	—	—	2.48	15.81	15.81	Claims on Nonbank Financial Insts	12g
	....	....	....	....	....	....	....	....	166.12	223.23	342.77	344.40	I 344.60	422.24	459.78	Reserve Money	14
	....	....	....	....	....	....	....	....	59.04	83.58	104.27	118.90	118.74	127.16	125.76	*of which: Currency Outside DMBs*	14a
	....	....	....	....	....	....	....	....	.14	9.22	52.68	40.27	I .68	.79	.85	Time Deposits	15
	....	....	....	....	....	....	....	....	37.40	1.10	.75	5.73	1.49	.43	18.02	Foreign Liabilities	16c
	....	....	....	....	....	....	....	....	81.75	49.15	47.17	12.25	22.62	10.95	12.53	Long-Term Foreign Liabilities	16cl
	....	....	....	....	....	....	....	....	33.41	51.86	41.15	43.09	I 68.46	63.07	62.44	Central Government Deposits	16d
	....	....	....	....	....	....	....	....	9.90	18.00	27.34	29.56	60.56	39.07	82.84	Capital Accounts	17a
	....	....	....	....	....	....	....	....	-17.20	-27.44	-22.86	-16.30	-26.62	-42.33	-62.19	Other Items (Net)	17r
End of Period																**Deposit Money Banks**	
	....	....	....	....	....	....	....	....	71.45	80.78	160.93	158.50	214.94	288.85	669.40	Reserves	20
	....	....	....	....	....	....	....	....	83.95	89.84	100.64	157.64	297.34	352.08	810.60	Foreign Assets	21
	....	....	....	....	....	....	....	....	64.94	49.17	75.07	82.22	73.77	79.36	215.93	Claims on General Government	22a
	....	....	....	....	....	....	....	....	10.80	12.20	27.80	18.00	17.00	15.00	15.00	*of which: Clms.on Natl.Prop.Fd.*	22ae
	....	....	....	....	....	....	....	....	222.92	221.00	234.82	274.46	I 155.57	120.02	99.68	Claims on Nonfin.Pub.Enterprises	22c
	....	....	....	....	....	....	....	....	508.67	683.19	801.73	879.38	I 1094.54	1,055.83	1,229.35	Claims on Private Sector	22d
	....	....	....	....	....	....	....	....	....	....	....	....	.28	.40	1.74	Claims on Nonbank Financial Insts	22g
	....	....	....	....	....	....	....	....	201.96	307.64	310.89	317.46	297.24	275.68	288.88	Demand Deposits	24
	....	....	....	....	....	....	....	....	428.21	426.43	601.90	663.78	755.75	809.54	938.01	Time & Foreign Currency Deposits	25
	....	....	....	....	....	....	....	....	56.73	59.06	57.66	69.33	133.60	137.80	285.73	*of which: Fgn. Currency Deposits*	25b
	....	....	....	....	....	....	....	....	3.78	21.21	46.68	60.88	81.58	113.38	415.42	Bonds	26ab
	....	....	....	....	....	....	....	....	37.51	61.17	156.31	214.67	234.91	244.43	408.35	Foreign Liabilities	26c
	....	....	....	....	....	....	....	....	6.20	7.95	14.68	32.62	81.10	77.97	141.33	Long-Term Foreign Liabilities	26cl
	....	....	....	....	....	....	....	....	78.73	90.33	92.38	88.19	51.87	55.31	56.04	General Government Deposits	26d
	....	....	....	....	....	....	....	....	43.48	29.94	40.91	33.95	1.76	8.77	11.06	*of which: Natl.Prop.Fd.Deposits*	26de
	....	....	....	....	....	....	....	....	63.11	32.25	18.15	58.17	108.64	58.46	108.45	Credit from Monetary Authorities	26g
	....	....	....	....	....	....	....	....	160.75	185.37	195.88	204.28	I 348.20	395.15	890.78	Capital Accounts	27a
	....	....	....	....	....	....	....	....	-28.25	-8.29	-63.62	-87.77	-122.85	-133.39	-220.55	Other Items (Net)	27r
End of Period																**Monetary Survey**	
	....	....	....	....	....	....	....	....	194.24	233.10	344.40	310.32	429.22	510.44	892.05	Foreign Assets (Net)	31n
	....	....	....	....	....	....	....	....	731.37	852.20	991.45	1,105.86	I 1225.97	1,185.74	1,489.33	Domestic Credit	32
	....	....	....	....	....	....	....	....	-2.22	-53.28	-45.83	-48.74	I -46.57	-39.02	97.45	Claims on General Govt. (Net)	32an
	....	....	....	....	....	....	....	....	224.91	222.27	235.52	275.17	I 156.12	120.30	99.84	Claims on Nonfin.Pub.Enterprises	32c
	....	....	....	....	....	....	....	....	508.68	683.21	801.77	879.43	I 1113.66	1,088.24	1,274.48	Claims on Private Sector	32d
	....	....	....	....	....	....	....	....	....	....	....	....	2.76	16.22	17.55	Claims on Nonbank Fin. Insts	32g
	....	....	....	....	....	....	....	....	268.98	403.97	431.08	451.55	I 418.39	404.00	415.67	Money	34
	....	....	....	....	....	....	....	....	428.35	435.65	654.58	704.05	I 756.44	810.33	938.85	Quasi-Money	35
	....	....	....	....	....	....	....	....	3.78	21.21	46.68	60.88	81.58	113.38	415.42	Bonds	36ab
	....	....	....	....	....	....	....	....	87.95	57.10	61.85	44.87	103.72	88.92	153.86	Long-Term Foreign Liabilities	36cl
	....	....	....	....	....	....	....	....	170.10	202.22	221.26	231.06	I 408.76	434.22	973.62	Capital Accounts	37a
	....	....	....	....	....	....	....	....	-33.85	-35.89	-80.72	-74.59	-113.69	-154.69	-516.04	Other Items (Net)	37r
	....	....	....	....	....	....	....	....	697.33	839.62	1,085.66	1,155.59	I 1174.83	1,214.33	1,354.52	Money plus Quasi-Money	35l
Percent Per Annum																**Interest Rates**	
	....	....	....	....	....	....	....	....	8.00	8.50	9.50	10.50	13.00	7.50	5.00	Discount Rate *(End of Period)*	60
	....	....	....	....	....	....	....	....	11.50	11.00	12.50	14.00	23.00	12.50	7.50	Refinancing Rate	60a
	....	....	....	....	....	....	....	....	7.03	7.07	6.96	6.79	7.71	8.08	4.48	Deposit Rate	60l
	....	....	....	....	....	....	....	....	14.07	13.12	12.80	12.54	13.20	12.81	8.68	Lending Rate	60p
Period Averages																**Prices, Production, Labor**	
	41.5	....	....	....	....	....	....	....	88.3	92.9	100.0	104.8	109.9	115.3	116.4	Producer Prices	63
	....	....	....	....	....	....	....	....	83.3	91.7	100.0	108.8	118.0	130.6	133.4	Consumer Prices	64
	....	....	....	....	....	....	....	....	71.2	84.4	100.0	118.4	130.8	143.1	155.1	Wages	65
	....	....	....	....	....	....	....	....	90.1	92.0	100.0	101.9	106.5	109.7	106.7	Industrial Production	66
	....	....	....	....	....	....	....	....	117.2	111.6	100.0	95.3	107.7	107.3	101.2	Industrial Employment	67
Period Averages																	
	....	....	....	....	....	....	....	....	....	....	....	5,199	5,215	5,233	....	Labor Force	67d
	....	....	....	....	....	....	....	....	5,011	5,945	5,103	I 4,971	4,937	4,866	....	Employment	67e
	....	....	....	....	....	....	....	....	200	202	181	206	248	317	447	Unemployment	67c
	....	....	....	....	....	....	....	....	3.8	3.9	3.5	4.0	4.8	6.5	....	Unemployment Rate (%)	67r
Millions of Koruny																**International Transactions**	
	....	....	....	....	....	....	....	....	421,601	466,403	574,722	594,630	722,501	850,240	929,196	Exports	70
	....	....	....	....	....	....	....	....	426,084	501,549	670,445	752,343	861,770	926,559	997,320	Imports, f.o.b.	71.v

Czech Republic

	1970	1971	1972	1973	1974	1975	1976	1977	1978	1979	1980	1981	1982	1983	1984
Balance of Payments													*Millions of US Dollars:*		
Current Account, n.i.e. 78ald	...	...	...	...	...	...	...	...	...	...	...	...	...	...	...
Goods: Exports f.o.b. .... 78aa d	...	...	...	...	...	...	...	...	...	...	...	...	...	...	...
Goods: Imports f.o.b. .... 78ab d	...	...	...	...	...	...	...	...	...	...	...	...	...	...	...
Trade Balance .... 78ac d	...	...	...	...	...	...	...	...	...	...	...	...	...	...	...
Services: Credit................................. 78ad d	...	...	...	...	...	...	...	...	...	...	...	...	...	...	...
Services: Debit.................................. 78ae d	...	...	...	...	...	...	...	...	...	...	...	...	...	...	...
Balance on Goods & Services .... 78af d	...	...	...	...	...	...	...	...	...	...	...	...	...	...	...
Income: Credit................................... 78ag d	...	...	...	...	...	...	...	...	...	...	...	...	...	...	...
Income: Debit.................................... 78ah d	...	...	...	...	...	...	...	...	...	...	...	...	...	...	...
Balance on Gds, Serv. & Inc. .... 78ai d	...	...	...	...	...	...	...	...	...	...	...	...	...	...	...
Current Transfers, n.i.e.: Credit .... 78aj d	...	...	...	...	...	...	...	...	...	...	...	...	...	...	...
Current Transfers: Debit .... 78ak d	...	...	...	...	...	...	...	...	...	...	...	...	...	...	...
Capital Account, n.i.e. .... 78bc d	...	...	...	...	...	...	...	...	...	...	...	...	...	...	...
Capital Account, n.i.e.: Credit .... 78ba d	...	...	...	...	...	...	...	...	...	...	...	...	...	...	...
Capital Account: Debit .... 78bb d	...	...	...	...	...	...	...	...	...	...	...	...	...	...	...
Financial Account, n.i.e.................... 78bj d	...	...	...	...	...	...	...	...	...	...	...	...	...	...	...
Direct Investment Abroad .... 78bd d	...	...	...	...	...	...	...	...	...	...	...	...	...	...	...
Dir. Invest. in Rep. Econ., n.i.e. .... 78be d	...	...	...	...	...	...	...	...	...	...	...	...	...	...	...
Portfolio Investment Assets .... 78bf d	...	...	...	...	...	...	...	...	...	...	...	...	...	...	...
Equity Securities............................ 78bk d	...	...	...	...	...	...	...	...	...	...	...	...	...	...	...
Debt Securities .... 78bl d	...	...	...	...	...	...	...	...	...	...	...	...	...	...	...
Portfolio Investment Liab., n.i.e. ...... 78bg d	...	...	...	...	...	...	...	...	...	...	...	...	...	...	...
Equity Securities........................... 78bm d	...	...	...	...	...	...	...	...	...	...	...	...	...	...	...
Debt Securities .... 78bn d	...	...	...	...	...	...	...	...	...	...	...	...	...	...	...
Financial Derivatives Assets .... 78bw d	...	...	...	...	...	...	...	...	...	...	...	...	...	...	...
Financial Derivatives Liabilities .... 78bx d	...	...	...	...	...	...	...	...	...	...	...	...	...	...	...
Other Investment Assets .... 78bh d	...	...	...	...	...	...	...	...	...	...	...	...	...	...	...
Monetary Authorities...................... 78bo d	...	...	...	...	...	...	...	...	...	...	...	...	...	...	...
General Government .... 78bp d	...	...	...	...	...	...	...	...	...	...	...	...	...	...	...
Banks .... 78bq d	...	...	...	...	...	...	...	...	...	...	...	...	...	...	...
Other Sectors .... 78br d	...	...	...	...	...	...	...	...	...	...	...	...	...	...	...
Other Investment Liab., n.i.e. .... 78bi d	...	...	...	...	...	...	...	...	...	...	...	...	...	...	...
Monetary Authorities .... 78bs d	...	...	...	...	...	...	...	...	...	...	...	...	...	...	...
General Government .... 78bt d	...	...	...	...	...	...	...	...	...	...	...	...	...	...	...
Banks .... 78bu d	...	...	...	...	...	...	...	...	...	...	...	...	...	...	...
Other Sectors .... 78bv d	...	...	...	...	...	...	...	...	...	...	...	...	...	...	...
Net Errors and Omissions.................. 78ca d	...	...	...	...	...	...	...	...	...	...	...	...	...	...	...
Overall Balance .... 78cb d	...	...	...	...	...	...	...	...	...	...	...	...	...	...	...
Reserves and Related Items .... 79da d	...	...	...	...	...	...	...	...	...	...	...	...	...	...	...
Reserve Assets .... 79db d	...	...	...	...	...	...	...	...	...	...	...	...	...	...	...
Use of Fund Credit and Loans .... 79dc d	...	...	...	...	...	...	...	...	...	...	...	...	...	...	...
Exceptional Financing .... 79de d	...	...	...	...	...	...	...	...	...	...	...	...	...	...	...
International Investment Position													*Millions of US Dollars*		
Assets .... 79aa d	...	...	...	...	...	...	...	...	...	...	...	...	...	...	...
Direct Investment Abroad .... 79ab d	...	...	...	...	...	...	...	...	...	...	...	...	...	...	...
Portfolio Investment .... 79ac d	...	...	...	...	...	...	...	...	...	...	...	...	...	...	...
Equity Securities............................ 79ad d	...	...	...	...	...	...	...	...	...	...	...	...	...	...	...
Debt Securities .... 79ae d	...	...	...	...	...	...	...	...	...	...	...	...	...	...	...
Financial Derivatives........................ 79al d	...	...	...	...	...	...	...	...	...	...	...	...	...	...	...
Other Investment .... 79af d	...	...	...	...	...	...	...	...	...	...	...	...	...	...	...
Monetary Authorities .... 79ag d	...	...	...	...	...	...	...	...	...	...	...	...	...	...	...
General Government...................... 79ah d	...	...	...	...	...	...	...	...	...	...	...	...	...	...	...
Banks .... 79ai d	...	...	...	...	...	...	...	...	...	...	...	...	...	...	...
Other Sectors .... 79aj d	...	...	...	...	...	...	...	...	...	...	...	...	...	...	...
Reserve Assets .... 79ak d	...	...	...	...	...	...	...	...	...	...	...	...	...	...	...
Liabilities .... 79la d	...	...	...	...	...	...	...	...	...	...	...	...	...	...	...
Dir. Invest. in Rep. Economy........... 79lb d	...	...	...	...	...	...	...	...	...	...	...	...	...	...	...
Portfolio Investment .... 79lc d	...	...	...	...	...	...	...	...	...	...	...	...	...	...	...
Equity Securities .... 79ld d	...	...	...	...	...	...	...	...	...	...	...	...	...	...	...
Debt Securities .... 79le d	...	...	...	...	...	...	...	...	...	...	...	...	...	...	...
Financial Derivatives .... 79ll d	...	...	...	...	...	...	...	...	...	...	...	...	...	...	...
Other investment.............................. 79lf d	...	...	...	...	...	...	...	...	...	...	...	...	...	...	...
Monetary Authorities .... 79lg d	...	...	...	...	...	...	...	...	...	...	...	...	...	...	...
General Government...................... 79lh d	...	...	...	...	...	...	...	...	...	...	...	...	...	...	...
Banks .... 79li d	...	...	...	...	...	...	...	...	...	...	...	...	...	...	...
Other Sectors................................. 79lj d	...	...	...	...	...	...	...	...	...	...	...	...	...	...	...

Minus Sign Indicates Debit

1985	1986	1987	1988	1989	1990	1991	1992	1993	1994	1995	1996	1997	1998	1999	Balance of Payments	
....	....	....	....	....	....	....	....	466	−820	−1,374	−4,299	−3,271	−1,392	−1,071	Current Account, n.i.e.	78al d
....	....	....	....	....	....	....	....	14,231	15,964	21,477	21,693	22,737	26,395	26,840	Goods: Exports f.o.b.	78aa d
....	....	....	....	....	....	....	....	−14,748	−17,372	−25,162	−27,571	−27,325	−28,989	−28,909	Goods: Imports f.o.b.	78ab d
....	....	....	....	....	....	....	....	−517	−1,408	−3,685	−5,877	−4,588	−2,595	−2,069	*Trade Balance*	78ac d
....	....	....	....	....	....	....	....	4,721	5,167	6,725	8,181	7,132	7,513	6,928	Services: Credit	78ad d
....	....	....	....	....	....	....	....	−3,709	−4,685	−4,882	−6,264	−5,389	−5,724	−5,702	Services: Debit	78ae d
....	....	....	....	....	....	....	....	496	−926	−1,842	−3,961	−2,845	−806	−843	*Balance on Goods & Services*	78af d
....	....	....	....	....	....	....	....	548	791	1,197	1,170	1,405	1,427	1,652	Income: Credit	78ag d
....	....	....	....	....	....	....	....	−664	−812	−1,301	−1,892	−2,197	−2,421	−2,390	Income: Debit	78ah d
....	....	....	....	....	....	....	....	379	−947	−1,945	−4,683	−3,636	−1,800	−1,581	*Balance on Gds, Serv. & Inc.*	78ai d
....	....	....	....	....	....	....	....	242	298	664	617	866	781	1,061	Current Transfers, n.i.e.: Credit	78aj d
....	....	....	....	....	....	....	....	−154	−171	−92	−233	−501	−373	−552	Current Transfers: Debit	78ak d
....	....	....	....	....	....	....	....	−563	—	7	1	11	2	−2	Capital Account, n.i.e.	78bc d
....	....	....	....	....	....	....	....	208	—	12	1	17	14	18	Capital Account, n.i.e.: Credit	78ba d
....	....	....	....	....	....	....	....	−771	—	−5	—	−5	−12	−20	Capital Account: Debit	78bb d
....	....	....	....	....	....	....	....	3,043	4,504	8,225	4,202	1,122	2,913	2,490	Financial Account, n.i.e.	78bj d
....	....	....	....	....	....	....	....	−90	−116	−37	−155	−28	−75	−196	Direct Investment Abroad	78bd d
....	....	....	....	....	....	....	....	654	878	2,568	1,435	1,286	2,737	5,091	Dir. Invest. in Rep. Econ., n.i.e.	78be d
....	....	....	....	....	....	....	....	−232	−47	−325	−50	−159	−44	−1,882	Portfolio Investment Assets	78bf d
....	....	....	....	....	....	....	....	−232	−47	−325	−50	3	119	−524	Equity Securities	78bk d
....	....	....	....	....	....	....	....	....	....	....	....	−162	−163	−1,358	Debt Securities	78bl d
....	....	....	....	....	....	....	....	1,840	893	1,695	771	1,152	1,146	500	Portfolio Investment Liab., n.i.e.	78bg d
....	....	....	....	....	....	....	....	1,125	497	1,236	601	378	1,096	120	Equity Securities	78bm d
....	....	....	....	....	....	....	....	715	396	460	170	774	49	380	Debt Securities	78bn d
....	....	....	....	....	....	....	....	....	....	....	....	....	....	....	Financial Derivatives Assets	78bw d
....	....	....	....	....	....	....	....	....	....	....	....	....	....	....	Financial Derivatives Liabilities	78bx d
....	....	....	....	....	....	....	....	−2,867	−2,437	−2,492	−2,370	−4,427	−1,600	−2,703	Other Investment Assets	78bh d
....	....	....	....	....	....	....	....								Monetary Authorities	78bo d
....	....	....	....	....	....	....	....	−3,054	−2,362	−2,138	48	16	20	28	General Government	78bp d
....	....	....	....	....	....	....	....	36	−163	−224	−2,317	−4,161	−1,652	−2,642	Banks	78bq d
....	....	....	....	....	....	....	....	151	88	−130	−101	−281	31	−89	Other Sectors	78br d
....	....	....	....	....	....	....	....	3,738	5,333	6,816	4,571	3,298	749	1,679	Other Investment Liab., n.i.e.	78bi d
....	....	....	....	....	....	....	....	106	−47	40	−2	−11	−7	−57	Monetary Authorities	78bs d
....	....	....	....	....	....	....	....	3,037	2,821	1,657	−295	−360	−364	−185	General Government	78bt d
....	....	....	....	....	....	....	....	4	888	3,310	2,858	1,638	388	875	Banks	78bu d
....	....	....	....	....	....	....	....	591	1,671	1,809	2,011	2,030	732	1,046	Other Sectors	78bv d
....	....	....	....	....	....	....	....	95	−210	596	−729	379	367	222	Net Errors and Omissions	78ca d
....	....	....	....	....	....	....	....	3,041	3,474	7,453	−825	−1,758	1,890	1,639	*Overall Balance*	78cb d
....	....	....	....	....	....	....	....	−3,041	−3,474	−7,453	825	1,758	−1,890	−1,639	Reserves and Related Items	79da d
....	....	....	....	....	....	....	....	−3,039	−2,357	−7,453	825	1,758	−1,890	−1,639	Reserve Assets	79db d
....	....	....	....	....	....	....	....	−3	−1,117	—	—	—	—	—	Use of Fund Credit and Loans	79dc d
....	....	....	....	....	....	....	....	....	....	....	....	....	....	....	Exceptional Financing	79de d

Millions of US Dollars

1985	1986	1987	1988	1989	1990	1991	1992	1993	1994	1995	1996	1997	1998	1999	International Investment Position	
....	....	....	....	....	....	....	....	17,906	20,424	29,347	30,587	29,743	36,380	37,651	Assets	79aa d
....	....	....	....	....	....	....	....	181	300	345	498	548	804	908	Direct Investment Abroad	79ab d
....	....	....	....	....	....	....	....	276	433	755	1,372	1,032	1,202	2,900	Portfolio Investment	79ac d
....	....	....	....	....	....	....	....	264	334	693	748	417	449	1,843	Equity Securities	79ad d
....	....	....	....	....	....	....	....	12	99	62	624	615	752	1,057	Debt Securities	79ae d
....	....	....	....	....	....	....	....	—	—	—	—	—	—	—	Financial Derivatives	79al d
....	....	....	....	....	....	....	....	13,578	13,448	14,224	16,281	18,389	21,757	21,018	Other Investment	79af d
....	....	....	....	....	....	....	....	820	876	984	956	754	875	—	Monetary Authorities	79ag d
....	....	....	....	....	....	....	....	6,425	6,231	5,938	5,889	5,888	5,856	5,804	General Government	79ah d
....	....	....	....	....	....	....	....	2,837	2,944	3,469	5,622	8,308	11,263	11,841	Banks	79ai d
....	....	....	....	....	....	....	....	3,495	3,396	3,833	3,814	3,440	3,763	3,373	Other Sectors	79aj d
....	....	....	....	....	....	....	....	3,872	6,243	14,023	12,435	9,774	12,617	12,825	Reserve Assets	79ak d
....	....	....	....	....	....	....	....	14,123	18,088	27,182	33,151	32,863	40,361	39,976	Liabilities	79la d
....	....	....	....	....	....	....	....	3,423	4,547	7,350	8,572	9,234	14,375	16,246	Dir. Invest. in Rep. Economy	79lb d
....	....	....	....	....	....	....	....	1,956	2,910	4,696	5,298	4,880	5,564	4,602	Portfolio Investment	79lc d
....	....	....	....	....	....	....	....	1,101	1,331	2,642	3,398	3,028	3,793	2,724	Equity Securities	79ld d
....	....	....	....	....	....	....	....	855	1,579	2,055	1,900	1,853	1,771	1,878	Debt Securities	79le d
....	....	....	....	....	....	....	....	—	—	—	—	—	—	—	Financial Derivatives	79ll d
....	....	....	....	....	....	....	....	8,744	10,631	15,136	19,280	18,749	20,422	19,127	Other investment	79lf d
....	....	....	....	....	....	....	....	1,272	62	98	85	64	64	9	Monetary Authorities	79lg d
....	....	....	....	....	....	....	....	2,747	2,907	2,041	1,622	1,105	800	578	General Government	79lh d
....	....	....	....	....	....	....	....	1,283	2,402	6,007	8,964	9,009	10,640	9,682	Banks	79li d
....	....	....	....	....	....	....	....	3,442	5,260	6,989	8,610	8,570	8,917	8,858	Other Sectors	79lj d

Czech Republic

935

Government Finance

Billions of Koruny:

	1970	1971	1972	1973	1974	1975	1976	1977	1978	1979	1980	1981	1982	1983	1984
Deficit (-) or Surplus 80	....	....	....	....	....	....	....	....	....	....	....	....	....	....	....
Total Revenue and Grants 81y	....	....	....	....	....	....	....	....	....	....	....	....	....	....	....
Revenue 81	....	....	....	....	....	....	....	....	....	....	....	....	....	....	....
Grants 81z	....	....	....	....	....	....	....	....	....	....	....	....	....	....	....
Exp. & Lending Minus Repay. ... 82z	....	....	....	....	....	....	....	....	....	....	....	....	....	....	....
Expenditure 82	....	....	....	....	....	....	....	....	....	....	....	....	....	....	....
Lending Minus Repayments 83	....	....	....	....	....	....	....	....	....	....	....	....	....	....	....
Total Financing 80h	....	....	....	....	....	....	....	....	....	....	....	....	....	....	....
Domestic 84a	....	....	....	....	....	....	....	....	....	....	....	....	....	....	....
Foreign 85a	....	....	....	....	....	....	....	....	....	....	....	....	....	....	....
Total Debt by Residence 88	....	....	....	....	....	....	....	....	....	....	....	....	....	....	....
Domestic 88a	....	....	....	....	....	....	....	....	....	....	....	....	....	....	....
Foreign 89a	....	....	....	....	....	....	....	....	....	....	....	....	....	....	....

National Accounts

Billions of Koruny

	1970	1971	1972	1973	1974	1975	1976	1977	1978	1979	1980	1981	1982	1983	1984
Househ.Cons.Expend.,incl.NPISHs ... 96f	....	....	....	....	....	....	....	....	....	....	....	....	....	....	....
Government Consumption Expend. ... 91f	....	....	....	....	....	....	....	....	....	....	....	....	....	....	....
Gross Fixed Capital Formation 93e	....	....	....	....	....	....	....	....	....	....	....	....	....	....	....
Changes in Inventories 93i	....	....	....	....	....	....	....	....	....	....	....	....	....	....	....
Exports of Goods and Services 90c	....	....	....	....	....	....	....	....	....	....	....	....	....	....	....
Imports of Goods and Services 98c	....	....	....	....	....	....	....	....	....	....	....	....	....	....	....
Gross Domestic Product (GDP) 99b	....	....	....	....	....	....	....	....	....	....	....	....	....	....	....
Net Primary Income from Abroad ... 98.n	....	....	....	....	....	....	....	....	....	....	....	....	....	....	....
Gross National Income (GNI) 99a	....	....	....	....	....	....	....	....	....	....	....	....	....	....	....
GDP Volume 1995 Prices .... 99b. *p*	....	....	....	....	....	....	....	....	....	....	....	....	....	....	....
GDP Volume (1995=100) .... 99bv *p*	....	....	....	....	....	....	....	....	....	....	....	....	....	....	....
GDP Deflator (1995=100) .... 99bi *p*	....	....	....	....	....	....	....	....	....	....	....	....	....	....	....

Millions:

	1970	1971	1972	1973	1974	1975	1976	1977	1978	1979	1980	1981	1982	1983	1984
Population 99z	....	....	....	....	....	....	....	....	....	....	....	....	....	....	....

1985	1986	1987	1988	1989	1990	1991	1992	1993	1994	1995	1996	1997	1998	1999	Government Finance	
Year Ending December 31																
....	....	....	....	....	....	....	....	1.1	10.4	7.2	−1.8	−15.9	−29.2	−29.7	Deficit (-) or Surplus	80
....	....	....	....	....	....	....	....	349.0	381.3	440.4	476.4	500.8	530.6	563.3	Total Revenue and Grants	81y
....	....	....	....	....	....	....	....	349.0	381.3	440.4	476.4	500.8	530.6	563.3	Revenue	81
....	....	....	....	....	....	....	....	—	—	—	—	—	—	—	Grants	81z
....	....	....	....	....	....	....	....	347.9	370.9	433.2	478.2	516.7	559.8	593.0	Exp. & Lending Minus Repay.	82z
....	....	....	....	....	....	....	....	351.9	373.1	433.9	480.6	521.2	561.6	593.8	Expenditure	82
....	....	....	....	....	....	....	....	−4.0	−2.2	−.7	−2.4	−4.5	−1.8	−.8	Lending Minus Repayments	83
....	....	....	....	....	....	....	....	−1.1	−10.4	−7.2	1.7	15.9	29.3	29.6	Total Financing	80h
....	....	....	....	....	....	....	....	−1.1	−10.4	−7.2	1.7	15.9	29.3	29.6	Domestic	84a
....	....	....	....	....	....	....	....	—	—	—	—	—	—	—	Foreign	85a
....	....	....	....	....	....	....	....	158.9	161.7	154.4	155.2	167.2	194.5	228.3	Total Debt by Residence......................	88
....	....	....	....	....	....	....	....	86.5	90.2	101.3	110.9	128.9	169.9	207.1	Domestic	88a
....	....	....	....	....	....	....	....	72.4	71.5	53.1	44.3	38.3	24.6	21.2	Foreign	89a
Billions of Koruny															National Accounts	
....	....							496.3	607.0	‡701.7	810.7	889.6	949.3	980.0	Househ.Cons.Expend.,incl.NPISHs..........	96f
....	....							221.6	255.5	‡275.1	312.5	331.8	340.9	362.5	Government Consumption Expend.	91f
....	....							280.8	339.8	‡442.4	500.6	514.4	508.1	484.5	Gross Fixed Capital Formation	93e
....	....							−11.7	12.2	‡27.6	48.9	33.0	25.6	38.1	Changes in Inventories............................	93i
....	....							523.6	597.1	‡740.8	831.3	949.7	1,092.1	1,168.4	Exports of Goods and Services	90c
....	....							−508.3	−628.8	‡−806.5	−931.7	−1,049.7	−1,117.7	−1,197.2	Imports of Goods and Services	98c
....	....							1,002.3	1,148.6	1,381.1	1,572.3	1,668.8	1,798.3	1,836.3	Gross Domestic Product (GDP)	99b
....	....							−4.3	−2.0	−7.1	−17.3	−20.2	−31.8	−25.6	Net Primary Income from Abroad........	98.n
....	....							1,017.4	1,180.8	1,373.9	1,555.0	1,648.6	1,771.8	1,815.9	Gross National Income (GNI)	99a
....	....							1,275.3	1,303.6	1,381.1	1,447.7	1,432.8	1,401.3	1,397.9	GDP Volume 1995 Prices	99b.p
....	....							92.3	94.4	100.0	104.8	103.7	101.5	101.2	GDP Volume (1995=100)	99bv p
....	....							78.6	88.1	100.0	108.6	116.5	128.3	131.4	GDP Deflator (1995=100)	99bi p
Midyear Estimates																
....	....	....	....	....	....	....	....	10.33	10.34	10.33	10.32	10.30	10.29	10.28	Population..	99z

(See notes in the back of the book.)

Denmark

		1970	1971	1972	1973	1974	1975	1976	1977	1978	1979	1980	1981	1982	1983	1984
Exchange Rates															*Kroner per SDR:*	
Market Rate	aa	7.489	7.667	7.434	‖7.588	6.918	7.232	6.724	7.018	6.631	7.067	7.672	8.526	9.248	10.339	11.037
															Kroner per US Dollar:	
Market Rate	ae	7.489	7.062	6.847	‖6.290	5.650	6.178	5.788	5.778	5.090	5.365	6.015	7.325	8.384	9.875	11.260
Market Rate	rf	7.500	7.426	6.949	6.050	6.095	5.746	6.045	6.003	5.515	5.636	5.636	7.123	8.332	9.145	10.357
										Kroner per ECU through 1998; Kroner per Euro Beginning 1999:						
Euro Rate	ea	....	....	....	....	....	....	....	....	....	7.7010	7.8494	7.9408	8.1149	8.1827	7.9881
Euro Rate	eb	....	....	....	....	....	....	6.7627	6.8529	7.0188	7.2105	7.8283	7.9241	8.1544	8.1300	8.1457
															Index Numbers (1995=100):	
Market Rate	ahx	74.6	141.9	80.5	92.8	92.0	97.6	92.6	93.2	101.6	106.4	99.4	78.9	67.4	61.4	54.2
Nominal Effective Exchange Rate	neu	96.9	95.8	95.4	98.9	98.9	101.0	102.8	101.7	101.5	100.1	92.2	87.3	84.0	84.7	82.6
Real Effective Exchange Rate	reu	....	....	....	....	....	95.5	96.7	95.0	96.7	96.2	‖87.2	82.4	80.2	82.5	81.8
Fund Position															*Millions of SDRs:*	
Quota	2f. s	260.0	260.0	260.0	260.0	260.0	260.0	260.0	260.0	310.0	310.0	465.0	465.0	465.0	711.0	711.0
SDRs	1b. s	17.4	44.8	72.2	119.3	91.5	81.9	81.9	97.1	97.9	137.6	137.6	172.6	176.4	118.7	158.1
Reserve Position in the Fund	1c. s	26.4	52.3	65.0	119.1	72.9	61.1	67.0	72.8	68.7	76.8	110.9	105.3	99.8	205.0	214.4
of which: Outstg.Fund Borrowing	2c	—	—	—	—	—	—	—	—	—	—	—	—	—	—	—
International Liquidity												*Millions of US Dollars Unless Otherwise Indicated:*				
Total Reserves minus Gold	1l. d	419	653	786	1,247	858	803	841	1,589	3,129	3,236	3,387	2,548	2,266	3,621	3,009
SDRs	1b. d	17	49	78	144	112	96	95	118	128	181	175	201	195	124	155
Reserve Position in the Fund	1c. d	26	57	71	144	89	72	78	88	89	101	141	123	110	215	210
Foreign Exchange	1d. d	375	548	637	960	656	635	669	1,383	2,912	2,953	3,070	2,224	1,961	3,282	2,644
Gold (Million Fine Troy Ounces)	1ad	2	2	2	2	2	2	2	2	2	2	2	2	2	2	2
Gold (National Valuation)	1and	65	68e	69e	77	85	78	87	100	117	92	‖542	784	568	573	545
Monetary Authorities: Other Liab.	4..d	23	42	43	43	41	29	142	66	67	75	80	48	83	60	51
Deposit Money Banks: Assets	7a. d	364	398	449	723	1,289	1,068	1,764	2,734	3,832	4,812	4,833	5,265	5,865	6,654	7,975
Liabilities	7b. d	364	459	409	766	920	992	1,468	2,238	3,763	4,465	4,877	5,271	5,844	7,104	8,289
Monetary Authorities															*Billions of Kroner:*	
Foreign Assets	11	3.63	5.08	5.87	8.32	5.33	5.44	5.37	9.76	16.53	16.82	22.18	21.31	21.71	37.85	38.29
Claims on Central Government	12a	2.26	.50	.54	.58	1.07	4.03	8.49	11.33	12.09	24.00	35.87	55.53	74.55	87.25	89.96
Claims on Private Sector	12d	7.33	7.99	8.74	9.31	10.87	11.93	18.25	14.49	12.61	12.08	13.15	13.79	14.44	14.61	14.98
Claims on Deposit Money Banks	12e	2.35	2.11	3.08	3.95	5.12	1.01	1.61	4.14	4.50	4.51	1.75	1.27	6.18	5.42	9.71
Claims on Other Banking Insts	12f	....	....	....	....	....	....	....	....	....	....	....	....	....		
Reserve Money	14	7.56	7.85	8.25	8.44	8.88	12.33	12.85	11.22	12.08	13.71	14.31	15.58	15.97	17.11	18.84
of which: Currency Outside DMBs	14a	4.87	4.92	5.56	5.99	6.04	7.63	8.44	9.91	10.75	11.57	12.36	13.57	14.18	15.42	16.37
Foreign Liabilities	16c	.17	.29	.30	.27	.23	.19	.82	.38	.34	.40	.48	.35	.70	.59	.57
Central Government Deposits	16d	6.46	5.42	6.87	10.74	10.03	7.20	16.46	24.41	29.91	37.98	47.17	59.41	81.47	105.39	102.92
Other Items (Net)	17r	1.38	2.13	2.80	2.70	3.24	2.69	3.60	3.70	3.41	5.31	10.99	16.57	18.74	22.03	30.60
Deposit Money Banks															*Billions of Kroner:*	
Reserves	20	2.15	2.18	2.03	1.73	2.15	3.61	3.17	.82	.80	1.52	1.14	1.74	1.59	1.27	2.09
Foreign Assets	21	2.65	2.78	3.14	4.54	7.20	7.38	10.66	15.85	20.16	26.27	31.33	41.53	53.17	72.90	104.60
Claims on Central Government	22a	1.64	1.77	1.72	3.47	4.25	4.82	8.55	9.50	10.65	15.74	20.17	27.91	37.83	61.96	77.07
Claims on Private Sector	22d	34.82	37.91	43.87	50.11	53.62	64.49	71.75	79.14	84.07	87.14	94.04	99.41	111.53	132.85	162.01
Claims on Other Banking Insts	22f	....	....	....	....	....	....	....	....	....	....	....	....	....		
Demand Deposits	24	17.26	19.10	21.92	24.13	26.09	31.46	32.66	34.58	40.64	44.23	47.78	55.15	56.74	72.88	80.10
Time and Savings Deposits	25	15.10	16.92	19.70	23.27	26.45	36.08	43.36	47.46	45.30	49.57	58.60	63.28	77.48	103.78	126.95
Foreign Liabilities	26c	2.76	3.21	2.86	4.81	5.14	6.50	8.67	12.99	19.06	23.81	30.36	40.08	50.79	74.16	103.47
Credit from Monetary Authorities	26g	2.35	2.55	3.55	4.52	5.32	1.41	1.53	3.87	4.21	4.39	1.91	1.72	5.12	4.50	7.34
Capital Accounts	27a	4.57	4.94	5.47	6.58	7.09	7.66	10.67	11.47	12.91	14.48	16.39	19.18	21.62	25.57	35.44
Other Items (Net)	27r	−.78	−2.08	−2.73	−3.46	−2.87	−2.80	−2.77	−5.06	−6.45	−5.82	−8.41	−8.81	−7.64	−11.90	−9.36
Other Monetary Institutions															*Billions of Kroner:*	
Reserves	20..h	.39	.39	.31	.41	.53	1.04	1.25	.54	.56	.71	.78	.74	.66	.59	.80
Claims on Central Govt. (Net)	22anh	1.31	.90	1.20	1.12	.13	−.06	.28	1.60	.28	7.44	10.86	13.53	16.56	24.89	37.24
Claims on Private Sector	22d.h	18.09	19.83	22.92	26.68	29.01	34.64	38.41	41.97	45.66	47.97	50.26	52.14	56.52	64.94	72.27
Demand Deposits	24..h	7.04	7.54	9.27	10.39	10.83	14.25	14.89	16.15	18.88	21.34	21.97	23.65	25.88	31.03	39.44
Time and Savings Deposits	25..h	11.82	12.68	13.79	15.42	16.88	19.04	21.60	24.66	26.08	28.93	31.88	34.90	37.68	47.22	54.76
Other Items (Net)	27r.h	.95	.89	1.37	2.40	1.98	2.33	3.44	3.31	5.31	5.85	8.03	7.86	10.19	12.17	16.11
Monetary Survey															*Billions of Kroner:*	
Foreign Assets (Net)	31n	3.34	4.37	5.80	7.73	7.11	6.14	6.57	13.14	17.45	19.48	23.20	23.14	23.83	35.34	38.26
Domestic Credit	32	58.99	63.47	72.12	80.52	88.91	112.65	129.27	133.62	139.23	156.40	177.16	202.91	229.96	281.11	350.62
Claims on Central Govt. (Net)	32an	−1.25	−2.25	−3.40	−5.58	−4.59	1.59	.86	−1.98	−3.11	9.21	19.72	37.57	47.47	68.71	101.34
Claims on Local Government	32b	....	....	....	....	....	....	....	....	....	....	....	....	....		
Claims on Private Sector	32d	60.24	65.72	75.52	86.09	93.49	111.06	128.41	135.60	142.34	147.19	157.44	165.34	182.49	212.40	249.27
Claims on Other Banking Insts	32f	....	....	....	....	....	....	....	....	....	....	....	....	....	—	—
Money	34	27.47	29.61	33.64	37.59	39.36	49.86	52.34	56.08	65.06	71.88	77.51	88.03	91.67	113.30	128.08
Quasi-Money	35	26.92	29.60	33.48	38.68	43.34	55.12	64.96	72.11	71.38	78.50	90.48	98.18	115.16	151.00	181.71
Other Items (Net)	37r	7.96	8.63	10.79	11.98	13.34	13.81	18.53	18.58	20.24	25.49	32.31	39.84	46.96	52.15	77.25
Money plus Quasi-Money	35l	54.39	59.21	67.12	76.27	82.70	104.99	117.30	128.19	136.44	150.38	167.99	186.21	206.83	264.31	309.79
Money (National Definitions)															*Billions of Kroner:*	
Broad Money	39m	....	....	....	....	....	....	....	....	....	....	....	156.58	172.27	217.41	259.45
Interest Rates															*Percent Per Annum*	
Discount Rate (End of Period)	60	9.00	7.50	7.00	9.00	10.00	7.50	10.00	9.00	8.00	11.00	11.00	11.00	10.00	7.00	7.00
Money Market Rate	60b	....	....	6.26	8.10	13.34	6.47	10.28	14.48	15.42	12.63	16.93	14.84	‖16.92	12.81	11.77
Deposit Rate	60l	....	....	....	....	....	....	....	....	....	....	10.8	10.8	13.0	12.9	9.0
Lending Rate	60p	....	....	....	....	....	....	....	....	13.9	15.3	17.2	17.7	18.6	14.5	13.4
Government Bond Yield	61	10.57	10.67	10.37	11.08	14.55	13.10	13.21	13.38e	14.54	15.82	17.66	18.92	20.39	14.46	‖13.96
Mortgage Bond Yield	61a	10.92	10.96	10.57	11.83	15.12	12.96	15.03	15.74	16.51	16.91	19.03	‖19.64	‖21.35	15.34	14.63

Item	1985	1986	1987	1988	1989	1990	1991	1992	1993	1994	1995	1996	1997	1998	1999	Code
Exchange Rates																
End of Period																
Market Rate	9.852	8.981	8.649	9.250	8.683	8.217	8.459	8.601	9.302	8.880	8.244	8.548	9.210	8.992	10.155	aa
End of Period (ae) Period Average (rf)																
Market Rate	8.969	7.343	6.097	6.874	6.608	5.776	5.914	6.256	6.773	6.083	5.546	5.945	6.826	6.387	7.399	ae
Market Rate	10.596	8.091	6.840	7.310	6.189	6.396	6.036	6.484	6.361	5.602	5.799	6.604	6.701	6.976		rf
End of Period (ea) Period Average (eb)																
Euro Rate	7.9567	7.8619	7.9446	8.0298	7.8816	7.8826	7.9295	7.5748	7.5508	7.4823	7.2940	7.4466	7.5312	7.4488	1.0046	ea
Euro Rate	8.0183	7.9360	7.8829	7.9517	8.0487	7.8561	7.9082	7.8119	7.5916	7.5415	7.3271	7.3598	7.4830	7.4999	1.0668	eb
Period Averages																
Market Rate	53.2	69.4	81.9	83.3	76.7	90.6	87.8	92.9	86.4	88.2	100.0	96.5	84.8	83.6	80.3	ahx
Nominal Effective Exchange Rate	83.8	87.4	89.9	88.4	86.5	91.4	90.2	92.3	96.2	96.3	100.0	98.6	95.9	96.5	95.4	neu
Real Effective Exchange Rate	85.3	88.7	96.8	96.0	94.5	99.0	94.5	95.2	98.8	97.5	100.0	97.7	95.6	95.9	....	reu
Fund Position																
End of Period																
Quota	711.0	711.0	711.0	711.0	711.0	711.0	711.0	1,069.9	1,069.9	1,069.9	1,069.9	1,069.9	1,069.9	1,069.9	1,642.8	2f.s
SDRs	178.7	207.2	214.5	167.0	213.1	151.6	169.0	66.7	62.4	124.6	106.8	116.7	248.7	246.0	249.9	1b.s
Reserve Position in the Fund	207.5	127.2	123.2	234.7	254.9	219.8	248.6	345.7	309.1	294.6	400.0	421.8	467.9	827.5	582.1	1c.s
of which: Outstg.Fund Borrowing	—	—	—	—	—	—	—	—	—	—	—	—	—	34.2		2c
International Liquidity																
End of Period																
Total Reserves minus Gold	5,429	4,964	10,066	10,765	6,397	10,591	7,404	11,044	10,301	9,056	11,016	14,140	19,124	15,264	22,287	1l.d
SDRs	196	253	304	225	280	216	242	92	86	182	159	168	336	346	343	1b.d
Reserve Position in the Fund	228	156	175	316	335	313	356	475	425	430	595	607	631	1,165	799	1c.d
Foreign Exchange	5,004	4,555	9,587	10,224	5,782	10,063	6,807	10,477	9,791	8,444	10,262	13,366	18,157	13,753	21,145	1d.d
Gold (Million Fine Troy Ounces)	2	2	2	2	2	2	2	2	2	2	2	2	2	2	2	1ad
Gold (National Valuation)	631	650	767	713	711	780	638	580	478	703	714	590	545	677	531	1and
Monetary Authorities: Other Liab.	72	803	131	230	220	235	658	4,609	117	253	397	275	124	196	297	4..d
Deposit Money Banks: Assets	14,158	16,033	24,155	28,781	34,661	45,546	I49,066	45,629	57,272	50,945	56,593	62,392	65,675	76,754	68,432	7a.d
Liabilities	14,852	16,405	23,421	27,899	35,228	44,803	I47,379	36,845	27,128	30,141	33,246	40,172	50,347	61,484	63,340	7b.d
Monetary Authorities																
End of Period																
Foreign Assets	56.89	42.03	I67.07	74.07	49.77	67.64	46.44	72.32	70.88	63.18	69.34	86.25	129.49	101.85	169.06	11
Claims on Central Government	.64	.64	I6.40	5.93	8.06	10.35	16.48	6.79	10.04	20.05	14.83	15.47	15.19	15.50	14.80	12a
Claims on Private Sector	14.84	26.15	I.49	.77	1.27	1.43	.91	1.40	.24	2.86	1.64	6.14	3.44	1.67	2.50	12d
Claims on Deposit Money Banks	22.63	42.42	I17.70	1.33	18.41	4.07	1.09	24.86	79.21	57.28	45.33	40.72	31.57	36.96	70.19	12e
Claims on Other Banking Insts	—	—	29.72	31.28	34.59	36.44	28.15	28.90	30.95	24.99	19.97	21.26	20.24	22.95	24.56	12f
Reserve Money	47.24	31.32	I36.60	38.17	36.62	44.79	43.55	38.18	62.70	63.15	71.69	95.55	125.31	97.00	192.86	14
of which: Currency Outside DMBs	17.57	18.82	I19.82	21.39	22.38	22.58	24.24	24.97	25.72	28.93	30.59	30.94	33.25	34.49	36.86	14a
Foreign Liabilities	.60	5.90	I.80	1.57	1.45	1.36	3.89	28.78	.79	1.54	2.20	1.63	.88	1.25	2.43	16c
Central Government Deposits	18.33	49.92	I56.85	45.32	37.08	39.50	11.43	31.27	89.57	56.91	35.44	31.65	30.73	34.03	36.49	16d
Other Items (Net)	28.83	24.11	I27.12	28.30	36.94	34.27	34.20	36.04	38.26	46.77	41.78	41.00	43.00	46.66	49.33	17r
Deposit Money Banks																
End of Period																
Reserves	25.80	11.23	I4.70	8.37	9.12	8.70	I19.38	16.31	35.33	32.69	39.57	51.62	70.63	54.20	96.26	20
Foreign Assets	144.27	137.42	I147.26	197.84	229.03	263.07	I290.15	285.43	387.88	309.90	313.87	370.89	448.30	490.19	506.32	21
Claims on Central Government	86.60	83.64	I92.90	104.77	96.39	82.18	I103.85	103.49	70.18	124.60	99.53	85.34	69.80	71.14	65.37	22a
Claims on Private Sector	190.41	251.92	I370.84	371.77	415.79	429.18	I371.95	361.76	317.67	297.74	312.89	331.06	357.73	405.37	420.62	22d
Claims on Other Banking Insts	....	....	....	....	....	....	49.92	46.51	136.53	108.44	125.15	157.66	181.52	218.24	189.06	22f
Demand Deposits	99.81	106.45	I155.78	195.30	192.53	205.86	I233.09	229.77	255.44	248.31	259.86	287.09	304.47	321.44	336.34	24
Time and Savings Deposits	146.39	160.95	I238.86	225.83	230.79	242.24	I247.58	246.11	318.06	262.20	282.89	296.17	320.02	325.42	298.27	25
Foreign Liabilities	146.35	135.43	I142.79	191.78	232.77	258.78	I280.18	230.49	183.73	183.35	184.38	238.80	343.67	392.67	468.64	26c
Credit from Monetary Authorities	20.37	31.74	I17.73	3.32	19.79	4.72	I7.07	26.50	80.56	58.66	45.94	35.73	21.46	34.03	34.01	26g
Capital Accounts	40.86	53.00	I75.38	83.67	92.58	91.81	I78.01	86.11	72.13	79.54	75.37	77.42	82.25	87.64	91.43	27a
Other Items (Net)	-6.69	-3.35	I-14.83	-17.14	-18.13	-20.30	I-10.67	-5.48	37.67	41.31	42.58	61.35	56.11	77.93	48.94	27r
Other Monetary Institutions																
End of Period																
Reserves	3.93	2.45	.99	....	....	....	....	....	....	....	....	....	....	....	....	20..h
Claims on Central Govt. (Net)	41.22	39.94	35.94	....	....	....	....	....	....	....	....	....	....	....	....	22an h
Claims on Private Sector	83.76	111.29	....	....	....	....	....	....	....	....	....	....	....	....	....	22d.h
Demand Deposits	46.96	49.27	....	....	....	....	....	....	....	....	....	....	....	....	....	24..h
Time and Savings Deposits	63.78	72.28	....	....	....	....	....	....	....	....	....	....	....	....	....	25..h
Other Items (Net)	18.18	32.09	....	....	....	....	....	....	....	....	....	....	....	....	....	27r.h
Monetary Survey																
End of Period																
Foreign Assets (Net)	53.21	40.13	I70.74	78.56	44.58	70.57	I52.52	98.49	274.24	188.19	196.62	216.70	233.24	198.12	204.31	31n
Domestic Credit	399.15	463.67	I443.50	469.19	519.00	520.07	I565.73	523.25	482.44	528.22	545.50	592.83	629.40	714.58	695.15	32
Claims on Central Govt. (Net)	110.14	74.31	I42.44	65.38	67.36	53.03	I108.90	79.00	-9.36	87.74	78.91	69.16	54.26	52.62	43.68	32an
Claims on Local Government	....	....	....	....	....	....	5.90	5.67	6.40	6.44	6.93	7.56	12.22	13.73	14.74	32b
Claims on Private Sector	289.01	389.37	I371.34	372.54	417.06	430.61	I372.86	363.16	317.91	300.61	314.53	337.19	361.17	407.04	423.12	32d
Claims on Other Banking Insts	—	—	29.72	31.28	34.59	36.44	I78.07	75.41	167.48	133.43	145.13	178.91	201.75	241.19	213.62	32f
Money	156.49	167.97	I188.45	225.11	226.11	244.48	I258.27	256.00	283.00	279.05	291.98	325.52	344.05	360.74	381.77	34
Quasi-Money	210.18	233.23	I238.86	225.83	230.79	242.24	I247.58	246.11	318.06	262.20	282.89	296.17	320.02	325.42	298.27	35
Other Items (Net)	85.69	102.55	I86.93	96.81	106.68	103.92	I112.41	119.62	155.62	175.16	167.25	187.84	198.57	226.54	219.42	37r
Money plus Quasi-Money	366.67	401.19	I427.31	450.95	456.90	486.72	I505.85	502.11	601.06	541.25	574.87	621.69	664.08	686.16	680.04	35l
Money (National Definitions)																
End of Period																
Broad Money	306.49	333.74	343.57	358.25	368.16	391.73	379.42	373.90	416.42	394.03	410.01	439.74	462.66	476.23	495.94	39m
Interest Rates																
Percent Per Annum																
Discount Rate (End of Period)	7.00	7.00	7.00	7.00	7.00	8.50	9.50	9.50	6.25	5.00	4.25	3.25	3.50	3.50	3.00	60
Money Market Rate	10.33	9.22	10.20	8.52	9.66	10.97	9.78	11.35	I11.49	6.30	6.19	3.98	3.71	4.27	3.37	60b
Deposit Rate	8.2	6.6	7.1	7.8	8.3	I7.9	7.2	7.5	6.5	I3.5	3.9	2.8	2.7	3.1	2.4	60l
Lending Rate	14.7	13.0	13.6	12.6	13.4	I14.1	11.4	11.8	10.5	I10.0	10.3	8.7	7.7	7.9	7.1	60p
Government Bond Yield	11.31	9.91	11.06	9.78	9.75	10.74	9.59	9.47	7.08	7.41	7.58	6.04	5.08	4.59	4.30	61
Mortgage Bond Yield	12.19	10.50	12.54	11.28	10.16	10.97	10.09	10.14	8.17	8.34	8.97	7.84	7.14	6.04	6.08	61a

Denmark

Prices, Production, Labor		1970	1971	1972	1973	1974	1975	1976	1977	1978	1979	1980	1981	1982	1983	1984
														Index Numbers (1995=100):		
Share Prices: Industrial	62a	‖7	7	10	15	11	12	16	16	15	15	14	23	29	51	55
Shipping	62b	‖4	4	5	9	8	8	10	11	12	11	12	19	20	23	27
Prices: Home & Import Goods	63	25.1	26.0	27.5	31.5	38.3	‖40.5	43.8	47.0	49.0	53.9	63.2	73.1	80.9	85.0	‖91.3
Home Goods	63a	25.4	26.3	28.1	32.3	37.5	‖40.5	43.8	47.0	49.8	53.1	60.8	68.8	76.2	80.5	‖86.5
Consumer Prices	64	20.0	21.2	22.6	24.7	28.4	‖31.2	34.0	37.8	41.5	45.5	51.1	‖57.1	62.9	67.3	71.5
Harmonized CPI	64h															
Wages: Hourly Earn. (1990=100)	65	15.1	17.4	19.5	22.4	26.9	32.0	35.6	39.2	43.2	48.1	53.6	58.3	64.4	68.7	72.0
Industrial Production	66..c	‖52.5	53.6	57.4	59.5	‖57.4	54.3	59.8	60.5	62.2	64.6	64.8	64.9	66.3	68.6	76.0
Agricultural Production	66bx	72.2	73.2	72.5	73.6	74.5	‖74.2	74.4	76.2	79.3	83.4	‖85.2	85.3	85.9	89.8	88.7
Manufacturing Empl. (1990=100)	67ey c	....	....	128.6	126.7	123.5	106.7	106.6	106.2	105.1	106.4	103.1	96.1	95.6	97.1	104.0
														Number in Thousands:		
Labor Force	67d	....	....	....	....	....	....	....	....	....	....	....	....	....	....	....
Employment	67e	....	....	....	....	....	....	....	....	....	....	....	....	....	....	....
Unemployment	67c	....	....	....	....	....	....	....	....	....	....	....	....	....	....	....
Unemployment Rate (%)	67r	....	....	....	....	....	....	....	....	....	....	....	....	....	....	....

International Transactions

		1970	1971	1972	1973	1974	1975	1976	1977	1978	1979	1980	1981	1982	1983	1984
														Millions of Kroner		
Exports	70	25,171	27,303	30,789	37,549	46,920	50,030	55,035	60,436	65,314	77,321	94,359	114,263	128,194	146,761	165,335
Imports, c.i.f.	71	33,054	34,196	35,337	46,969	60,479	59,707	75,009	79,638	81,404	96,837	108,894	124,710	138,879	148,916	171,827
														1995=100		
Volume of Exports	72	29	‖31	33	35	‖37	36	37	39	41	46	49	51	52	54	58
Volume of Imports	73	46	‖44	45	55	‖52	48	57	56	58	62	57	54	55	54	62
Unit Value of Exports	74	30	‖31	33	37	‖44	48	52	55	57	62	71	80	90	93	100
Unit Value of Imports	75	28	‖30	30	33	‖46	47	51	56	56	63	77	90	100	103	111
Import Prices	76.x	25	25	27	30	39	‖41	43	47	48	55	68	81	89	93	‖100

Balance of Payments

		1975	1976	1977	1978	1981	1982	1983	1984
								Millions of US Dollars:	
Current Account, n.i.e.	78al d	−490	−1,914	−1,722	−1,502	−1,875	−2,259	−1,382	−1,718
Goods: Exports f.o.b.	78aa d	8,652	9,053	10,011	11,807	16,136	15,685	16,226	16,090
Goods: Imports f.o.b.	78ab d	−9,956	−11,931	−12,725	−14,163	−17,063	−16,479	−15,974	−16,285
Trade Balance	78ac d	−1,304	−2,878	−2,715	−2,356	−927	−794	252	−195
Services: Credit	78ad d	3,223	3,586	4,113	4,785	5,853	5,410	5,131	5,049
Services: Debit	78ae d	−2,159	−2,480	−2,958	−3,596	−4,663	−4,538	−4,501	−4,301
Balance on Goods & Services	78af d	−240	−1,771	−1,559	−1,167	262	78	882	553
Income: Credit	78ag d	249	255	363	543	1,187	1,146	909	1,227
Income: Debit	78ah d	−574	−616	−911	−1,429	−3,164	−3,298	−2,984	−3,567
Balance on Gds, Serv. & Inc.	78ai d	−566	−2,132	−2,107	−2,053	−1,715	−2,074	−1,194	−1,787
Current Transfers, n.i.e.: Credit	78aj d	448	641	944	1,196	753	654	729	935
Current Transfers: Debit	78ak d	−373	−424	−559	−645	−914	−839	−917	−866
Capital Account, n.i.e.	78bc d								
Capital Account, n.i.e.: Credit	78ba d	—	—	—	—	—	—	—	—
Capital Account: Debit	78bb d	—	—	—	—	—	—	—	—
Financial Account, n.i.e.	78bj d	552	1,819	2,501	2,899	1,414	2,491	2,853	1,743
Direct Investment Abroad	78bd d	−79	−64	−161	−33	−139	−82	−150	−289
Dir. Invest. in Rep. Econ., n.i.e.	78be d	267	−190	76	89	99	134	60	−15
Portfolio Investment Assets	78bf d	—	—	−18	−63	−18	−95	−61	−142
Equity Securities	78bk d	—	—	−5	—				
Debt Securities	78bl d	—	—	−13	−63	−18	−95	−61	−142
Portfolio Investment Liab., n.i.e.	78bg d	—	—	283	541	81	−46	363	823
Equity Securities	78bm d	—	—	−29	−11				
Debt Securities	78bn d	—	—	311	552	81	−46	363	823
Financial Derivatives Assets	78bw d								
Financial Derivatives Liabilities	78bx d								
Other Investment Assets	78bh d	−172	−563	−1,420	−1,016	−1,213	−1,102	−1,727	−2,270
Monetary Authorities	78bo d	−67	38	−74	−139				
General Government	78bp d								
Banks	78bq d	116	−497	−938	−614	−1,213	−1,102	−1,727	−2,270
Other Sectors	78br d	−221	−104	−408	−263	—			
Other Investment Liab., n.i.e.	78bi d	535	2,636	3,741	3,380	2,603	3,682	4,367	3,637
Monetary Authorities	78bs d	−6	70	−74	2	−22	40	−18	−4
General Government	78bt d	128	1,597	1,405	1,335	1,015	2,792	1,818	−629
Banks	78bu d	206	369	761	1,147	1,300	1,155	2,294	2,250
Other Sectors	78bv d	208	600	1,650	897	311	−304	273	2,019
Net Errors and Omissions	78ca d	−104	114	−62	99	−273	−489	−114	−396
Overall Balance	78cb d	−42	19	717	1,496	−735	−257	1,357	−371
Reserves and Related Items	79da d	42	−19	−717	−1,496	735	257	−1,357	371
Reserve Assets	79db d	42	−19	−717	−1,496	735	257	−1,357	371
Use of Fund Credit and Loans	79dc d	—	—	—	—	—	—	—	—
Exceptional Financing	79de d	—	—	—	—	—	—	—	—

International Investment Position

Millions of US Dollars

Assets	79aa d	....
Direct Investment Abroad	79ab d	....
Portfolio Investment	79ac d	....
Equity Securities	79ad d	....
Debt Securities	79ae d	....
Financial Derivatives	79al d	....
Other Investment	79af d	....
Monetary Authorities	79ag d	....
General Government	79ah d	....
Banks	79ai d	....
Other Sectors	79aj d	....
Reserve Assets	79ak d	....
Liabilities	79la d	....
Dir. Invest. in Rep. Economy	79lb d	....
Portfolio Investment	79lc d	....
Equity Securities	79ld d	....
Debt Securities	79le d	....
Financial Derivatives	79ll d	....
Other investment	79lf d	....
Monetary Authorities	79lg d	....
General Government	79lh d	....
Banks	79li d	....
Other Sectors	79lj d	....

	1985	1986	1987	1988	1989	1990	1991	1992	1993	1994	1995	1996	1997	1998	1999		
Prices, Production, Labor																	
Period Averages																	
	57	57	48	54	75	83	90	82	84	100	100	122	162	175	155	Share Prices: Industrial	**62a**
	28	25	25	33	80	94	94	86	98	107	100	120	215	223	252	Shipping	**62b**
	94.0	87.6	87.4	91.0	96.2	97.1	98.1	96.9	I 96.4	97.3	100.0	101.1	103.0	102.4	102.9	Prices: Home & Import Goods	**63**
	89.1	86.2	87.2	90.6	95.5	96.8	98.0	97.4	I 96.9	....	100.0	101.6	103.5	102.9	103.9	Home Goods	**63a**
	74.8	77.6	80.7	84.4	88.4	90.7	92.9	94.9	96.0	98.0	100.0	102.1	104.4	106.3	108.9	Consumer Prices	**64**
	....	....	....	....	....	....	....	....	....	....	100.0	102.1	104.1	105.4	107.6	Harmonized CPI	**64h**
	75.3	79.4	86.9	92.5	96.2	100.0	104.2	107.2	....	....	....	....	....	....	....	Wages: Hourly Earn. (1990=100)	**65**
	I 79.4	85.3	82.8	84.4	86.5	I 86.5	86.6	89.1	86.6	95.3	100.0	I 101.7	107.4	109.8	112.5	Industrial Production	**66..c**
	I 89.2	91.9	89.2	88.9	88.3	90.0	91.9	96.4	I 101.7	101.1	100.0	100.2	101.0	104.6	104.8	Agricultural Production	**66bx**
	108.1	111.2	I 105.3	I 102.1	100.9	100.0	96.8	94.7	88.5	....	....	....	....	....	....	Manufacturing Empl. (1990=100)	**67ey c**
Period Averages																	
	....	....	....	....	....	....	2,912	....	2,893	2,777	....	2,822	2,856	2,848	....	Labor Force	**67d**
	2,553	2,663	2,679	2,695	2,645	2,670	2,647	2,652	2,584	I 2,555	2,607	2,627	2,682	2,692	....	Employment	**67e**
	252	220	222	244	265	272	296	318	349	343	288	246	217	180	155	Unemployment	**67c**
	9.1	7.9	7.9	8.7	9.5	9.7	10.6	11.3	12.4	12.2	10.3	8.7	7.8	6.5	5.6	Unemployment Rate (%)	**67r**
International Transactions																	
Millions of Kroner																	
	179,578	171,720	175,187	185,819	205,300	216,444	229,764	247,254	241,034	262,365	278,515	290,543	315,001	317,422	337,309	Exports	**70**
	191,562	184,737	173,837	174,429	195,117	198,782	206,799	212,088	197,957	220,769	252,344	257,654	290,648	303,705	306,747	Imports, c.i.f.	**71**
1995=100																	
	I 61	61	63	66	71	73	81	85	82	89	100	103	109	111	117	Volume of Exports	**72**
	I 67	66	70	69	71	72	77	81	75	85	100	101	111	115	117	Volume of Imports	**73**
	I 104	101	99	98	105	103	103	101	99	100	100	102	104	103	103	Unit Value of Exports	**74**
	I 114	103	98	100	107	103	102	99	97	98	100	101	104	104	103	Unit Value of Imports	**75**
	103	90	88	91	97	98	98	96	I 95	98	100	100	102	102	101	Import Prices	**76.x**
Balance of Payments																	
Minus Sign Indicates Debit																	
	−2,767	−4,490	−3,002	−1,340	−1,118	1,372	1,983	4,199	4,832	3,189	1,855	3,090	921	−2,008	2,176	Current Account, n.i.e.	**78al *d***
	17,123	21,307	25,695	27,537	28,728	36,072	36,783	40,504	36,948	41,741	50,348	50,735	48,103	47,908	49,548	Goods: Exports f.o.b.	**78aa *d***
	−17,887	−22,357	−24,900	−25,654	−26,304	−31,197	−32,035	−33,446	−29,229	−34,300	−43,821	−43,203	−42,734	−44,021	−43,011	Goods: Imports f.o.b.	**78ab *d***
	−764	−1,050	795	1,883	2,425	4,875	4,748	7,058	7,719	7,441	6,528	7,532	5,369	3,886	6,537	*Trade Balance*	**78ac *d***
	5,487	6,372	7,848	9,623	9,570	12,830	14,264	14,083	12,564	13,661	15,307	16,502	14,044	15,212	15,823	Services: Credit	**78ad *d***
	−4,794	−6,066	−7,302	−8,427	−8,638	−10,218	−10,420	−10,736	−10,467	−12,067	−14,040	−14,771	−13,727	−15,779	−15,201	Services: Debit	**78ae *d***
	−71	−743	1,342	3,078	3,356	7,487	8,592	10,405	9,816	9,035	7,795	9,263	5,685	3,319	7,158	*Balance on Goods & Services*	**78af *d***
	1,409	1,995	2,627	3,677	4,718	6,011	8,855	15,956	23,091	22,743	28,433	37,626	18,774	10,401	8,602	Income: Credit	**78ag *d***
	−3,970	−5,464	−6,750	−7,876	−9,049	−11,719	−14,599	−21,282	−27,480	−27,385	−32,982	−42,235	−22,203	−14,247	−11,463	Income: Debit	**78ah *d***
	−2,632	−4,212	−2,781	−1,121	−975	1,779	2,848	5,079	5,427	4,394	3,246	4,655	2,256	−527	4,298	*Balance on Gds, Serv. & Inc.*	**78ai *d***
	825	1,341	1,546	1,799	1,608	2,007	2,083	2,136	2,442	2,261	2,580	2,398	3,633	3,443	3,433	Current Transfers, n.i.e.: Credit	**78aj *d***
	−960	−1,619	−1,766	−2,018	−1,750	−2,415	−2,948	−3,016	−3,037	−3,466	−3,970	−3,963	−4,968	−4,924	−5,554	Current Transfers: Debit	**78ak *d***
	—	—	—	—	—	—	—	—	—	....	....	....	128	50	129	Capital Account, n.i.e.	**78bc *d***
	—	—	—	—	—	—	—	—	—	....	....	....	128	81	167	Capital Account, n.i.e.: Credit	**78ba *d***
	—	—	—	—	—	—	—	—	—	....	....	....	—	−31	−38	Capital Account: Debit	**78bb *d***
	4,603	3,446	6,648	3,395	−2,373	4,420	−2,703	423	−6,545	−5,647	−432	1,882	8,496	−1,488	7,341	Financial Account, n.i.e.	**78bj *d***
	−306	−654	−619	−720	−2,066	−1,482	−1,852	−2,236	−1,373	−4,162	−2,969	−2,510	−4,355	−4,215	−9,784	Direct Investment Abroad	**78bd *d***
	111	163	85	503	1,090	1,132	1,553	1,017	1,713	5,006	4,139	773	2,792	6,675	8,479	Dir. Invest. in Rep. Econ., n.i.e.	**78be *d***
	−346	−2,223	797	−585	−1,527	−1,168	−4,378	1,420	2	−1,175	−1,171	−2,349	−6,239	−7,563	−9,578	Portfolio Investment Assets	**78bf *d***
	—	—	—	—	—	—	—	—	—	....	....	....	....	....	....	Equity Securities	**78bk *d***
	−346	−2,223	797	−585	−1,527	−1,168	−4,378	1,420	2	−1,175	−1,171	−2,349	....	....	....	Debt Securities	**78bl *d***
	1,579	144	2,886	1,815	−1,222	4,068	6,232	8,707	12,659	−10,596	7,487	7,865	11,186	−2,598	5,929	Portfolio Investment Liab., n.i.e.	**78bg *d***
	—	—	—	—	—	—	—	—	—	....	....	....	....	....	....	Equity Securities	**78bm *d***
	1,579	144	2,886	1,815	−1,222	4,068	6,232	8,707	12,659	−10,596	7,487	7,865	....	....	....	Debt Securities	**78bn *d***
	....	....	....	....	....	....	....	....	....	....	....	....	....	....	....	Financial Derivatives Assets	**78bw *d***
	....	....	....	....	....	....	....	....	....	....	....	....	....	....	....	Financial Derivatives Liabilities	**78bx *d***
	−3,816	1,359	−4,174	−7,443	−4,242	−5,442	−3,012	432	−14,812	12,136	−1,330	−9,339	−8,033	−1,797	1,072	Other Investment Assets	**78bh *d***
	....	....	....	....	....	....	....	....	....	....	....	....	....	....	....	Monetary Authorities	**78bo *d***
	—	—	—	—	—	—	—	—	—	....	....	....	....	....	....	General Government	**78bp *d***
	−3,816	1,359	−4,174	−7,443	−4,242	−5,442	−3,012	432	−14,812	12,136	−1,330	−9,339	....	....	....	Banks	**78bq *d***
	—	—	—	—	—	—	—	—	—	....	....	....	....	....	....	Other Sectors	**78br *d***
	7,380	4,658	7,672	9,825	5,594	7,312	−1,246	−8,918	−4,734	−6,856	−6,589	7,442	13,146	8,010	11,223	Other Investment Liab., n.i.e.	**78bi *d***
	10	650	−712	120	−16	11	399	4,301	−4,419	122	133	−108	—	—	—	Monetary Authorities	**78bs *d***
	671	4,473	2,465	−1,480	−679	443	−5,078	1,309	8,648	−4,058	−3,380	−1,563	....	....	....	General Government	**78bt *d***
	4,071	−1,708	3,381	8,249	5,449	3,867	1,648	−9,476	−6,497	414	15	9,343	....	....	....	Banks	**78bu *d***
	2,629	1,242	2,538	2,936	840	2,991	1,785	−5,052	−2,467	−3,333	−3,357	−231	....	....	....	Other Sectors	**78bv *d***
	−304	−285	85	−619	−347	−2,407	−2,183	−547	1,146	606	1,075	−1,408	−3,013	−793	−208	Net Errors and Omissions	**78ca *d***
	1,532	−1,329	3,732	1,436	−3,838	3,385	−2,903	4,075	−567	−1,851	2,498	3,563	6,532	−4,239	9,437	*Overall Balance*	**78cb *d***
	−1,532	1,329	−3,732	−1,436	3,838	−3,385	2,903	−4,075	567	1,851	−2,498	−3,563	−6,532	4,239	−9,437	Reserves and Related Items	**79da *d***
	−1,532	1,329	−3,732	−1,436	3,838	−3,385	2,903	−4,075	567	1,851	−2,498	−3,563	−6,532	4,239	−9,437	Reserve Assets	**79db *d***
	—	—	—	—	—	—	—	—	—	—	—	—	—	—	—	Use of Fund Credit and Loans	**79dc *d***
	....	....	....	....	....	....	....	....	....	....	....	....	....	....	....	Exceptional Financing	**79de *d***
International Investment Position																	
Millions of US Dollars																	
	....	....	....	....	....	....	102,567	104,156	111,991	109,111	123,004	145,614	156,402	187,059	208,743	Assets	**79aa *d***
	....	....	....	....	....	....	15,558	16,306	15,799	19,892	24,702	27,589	28,128	34,135	37,303	Direct Investment Abroad	**79ab *d***
	....	....	....	....	....	....	19,954	16,625	17,866	17,261	22,899	29,944	37,064	51,828	67,984	Portfolio Investment	**79ac *d***
	....	....	....	....	....	....	6,426	6,394	7,973	8,877	10,819	16,149	22,414	32,569	48,386	Equity Securities	**79ad *d***
	....	....	....	....	....	....	13,528	10,231	9,893	8,384	12,081	13,794	14,650	19,259	19,598	Debt Securities	**79ae *d***
	....	....	....	....	....	....	—	—	—	—	—	—	—	—	—	Financial Derivatives	**79al *d***
	....	....	....	....	....	....	58,679	59,628	67,183	62,798	63,469	73,513	71,931	85,023	80,824	Other Investment	**79af *d***
	....	....	....	....	....	....	—	—	—	—	—	—	—	—	—	Monetary Authorities	**79ag *d***
	....	....	....	....	....	....	2,706	2,718	2,362	2,795	2,524	2,187	2,051	2,662	2,298	General Government	**79ah *d***
	....	....	....	....	....	....	42,276	39,965	51,384	46,359	49,766	55,177	56,255	65,607	62,983	Banks	**79ai *d***
	....	....	....	....	....	....	13,697	16,945	13,437	13,645	11,179	16,149	13,624	16,754	15,543	Other Sectors	**79aj *d***
	....	....	....	....	....	....	8,376	11,597	11,142	9,160	11,933	14,569	19,279	16,073	22,632	Reserve Assets	**79ak *d***
	....	....	....	....	....	....	158,451	154,104	155,186	151,734	170,934	187,737	197,480	233,774	232,200	Liabilities	**79la *d***
	....	....	....	....	....	....	14,712	14,387	14,618	18,083	23,801	22,205	22,268	30,533	33,384	Dir. Invest. in Rep. Economy	**79lb *d***
	....	....	....	....	....	....	59,018	65,063	84,016	72,826	88,713	101,607	106,505	118,218	105,693	Portfolio Investment	**79lc *d***
	....	....	....	....	....	....	2,875	2,398	3,248	6,740	8,294	12,448	20,363	20,512	20,409	Equity Securities	**79ld *d***
	....	....	....	....	....	....	56,143	62,665	80,768	66,086	80,418	89,158	86,141	97,706	85,284	Debt Securities	**79le *d***
	....	....	....	....	....	....	—	—	—	—	—	—	—	—	—	Financial Derivatives	**79ll *d***
	....	....	....	....	....	....	84,721	74,654	56,552	60,825	58,420	63,925	68,708	85,023	93,123	Other investment	**79lf *d***
	....	....	....	....	....	....	676	4,476	148	329	361	336	146	157	270	Monetary Authorities	**79lg *d***
	....	....	....	....	....	....	3,044	2,877	2,067	3,123	1,983	1,178	732	939	405	General Government	**79lh *d***
	....	....	....	....	....	....	39,570	30,853	22,444	27,289	29,210	35,159	42,631	54,490	62,037	Banks	**79li *d***
	....	....	....	....	....	....	41,431	36,448	31,894	30,084	26,866	27,252	25,198	29,437	30,410	Other Sectors	**79lj *d***

Denmark

	1970	1971	1972	1973	1974	1975	1976	1977	1978	1979	1980	1981	1982	1983	1984
Government Finance														*Millions of Kroner:*	
Deficit (-) or Surplus.............. 80	Ɪ 2,950	3,569	4,089	6,140	1,335	–4,350	Ɪ –519	–2,730	–1,066	–2,584	–10,002	–24,690	–37,522	–35,154	–22,241
Revenue 81	Ɪ 41,605	47,319	53,380	58,268	66,918	69,810	Ɪ 80,981	90,422	105,617	120,393	136,398	145,706	163,129	188,365	218,810
Grants Received 81z	Ɪ 336	400	376	524	557	1,593	Ɪ 3,189	1,491	1,804	2,307	2,499	2,633	3,349	4,220	4,883
Expenditure 82	Ɪ 38,295	43,557	48,968	51,826	65,085	74,767	Ɪ 83,604	93,654	107,137	124,520	147,376	171,020	202,363	225,514	243,895
Lending Minus Repayments 83	Ɪ 696	593	699	826	1,055	986	Ɪ 1,085	989	1,350	764	1,523	2,009	1,637	2,225	2,039
Net Borrowing: Kroner 84b	....	....	....	....	....	....	....	....	....	....	....	....	....	....	....
Foreign Currency 85b	....	....	....	....	....	....	....	....	....	....	....	....	....	....	....
Finance from Foreign Aid 86a	....	....	....	....	....	....	....	....	....	....	....	....	....	....	....
Use of Cash Balances 87	....	....	....	....	....	....	....	....	....	....	....	....	....	....	....
Debt: Kroner 88b	....	....	....	....	....	....	....	....	....	....	....	....	....	....	....
Debt: Foreign 89a	Ɪ 3,699	5,292	6,106	6,517	7,243	10,429	Ɪ 16,456	24,410	29,139	35,744	45,346	57,521	79,142	102,514	98,534
Foreign Currency 89b	....	....	....	....	....	....	....	....	....	....	....	....	....	....	....
National Accounts														*Billions of Kroner*	
Househ.Cons.Expend.,incl.NPISHs 96f	67.8	73.1	79.6	93.6	104.6	119.3	141.4	157.6	173.3	193.5	207.2	228.3	255.4	277.1	302.7
Government Consumption Expend. 91f	25.5	30.0	34.2	39.3	48.2	56.5	64.1	70.7	80.8	91.8	105.3	119.8	138.3	148.6	155.0
Gross Fixed Capital Formation 93e	31.2	33.7	40.2	46.1	50.0	49.8	62.7	67.5	74.1	80.0	78.1	71.4	85.0	95.7	111.4
Changes in Inventories 93i	1.1	.8	.4	2.4	2.5	–.4	2.6	2.2	–.5	2.4	–.4	–.1	1.8	.5	7.9
Exports of Goods and Services 90c	33.3	36.5	41.0	49.6	61.8	65.4	72.9	81.0	87.1	102.8	124.3	151.9	172.2	190.1	211.9
Imports of Goods and Services 98c	–36.8	–38.8	–40.2	–52.8	–67.4	–67.3	–84.5	–91.1	–93.7	–113.2	–128.6	–149.0	–170.5	–180.2	–205.4
Gross Domestic Product (GDP) 99b	122.1	135.3	155.3	178.2	199.7	223.4	259.2	288.0	321.1	357.3	385.8	422.4	482.2	531.7	583.5
Net Primary Income from Abroad ... 98.n	–.1	–.3	–.2	1.0	.3	.3	.9	2.0	2.7	–.3	–3.7	–7.5	–12.1	–12.3	–16.5
Gross National Income (GNI) 99a	122.1	135.0	155.1	179.2	200.0	223.7	260.1	290.0	323.8	357.0	382.2	414.9	470.1	519.4	567.0
GDP Volume 1995 Prices 99b.p	647.9	664.7	694.8	719.5	709.6	697.4	742.3	750.5	764.3	788.3	783.8	767.7	788.8	802.5	830.7
GDP Volume (1995=100) .... 99bv p	64.2	65.8	68.8	71.3	70.3	69.1	73.5	74.3	75.7	78.1	77.6	76.0	78.1	79.5	82.3
GDP Deflator (1995=100) .... 99bi p	18.9	20.3	22.4	24.8	28.1	32.0	34.9	38.4	42.0	45.3	49.2	55.0	61.1	66.3	70.3
															Millions:
Population 99z	4.93	4.96	4.99	5.02	5.05	5.06	5.07	5.09	5.10	5.12	5.12	5.12	5.12	5.11	5.11

	1985	1986	1987	1988	1989	1990	1991	1992	1993	1994	1995	1996	1997	1998	1999		
Government Finance																		
Year Ending December 31																Deficit (-) or Surplus	**80**
	−3,726	30,082	27,410	16,077	8,164	−5,550	−9,669	−13,386	−19,715	−21,778 P	−19,293 P	....	....	....	....	Deficit (-) or Surplus	**80**
	246,846	281,324	291,516	303,078	312,992	314,135	327,485	341,939	361,185	384,684 P	400,199 P	....	....	....	....	Revenue	**81**
	4,664	4,328	4,133	4,380	3,824	4,276	4,518	4,449	5,646	5,683 P	3,933 P	....	....	....	....	Grants Received	**81z**
	253,940	255,127	266,843	289,116	307,738	321,978	337,991	359,660	383,834	412,145 P	419,725 P	....	....	....	....	Expenditure	**82**
	1,296	443	1,396	2,265	914	1,983	3,681	114	2,712	— P	3,700 P	....	....	....	....	Lending Minus Repayments	**83**
	....	....	....	....	....	....	....	....	....	....	....	....	....	....	....	Net Borrowing: Kroner	**84b**
	....	....	....	....	....	....	....	....	....	....	....	....	....	....	....	Foreign Currency	**85b**
	....	....	....	....	....	....	....	....	....	....	....	....	....	....	....	Finance from Foreign Aid	**86a**
	....	....	....	....	....	....	....	....	....	....	....	....	....	....	....	Use of Cash Balances	**87**
	92,930	119,913	127,637	124,333	116,031	119,101	92,339	104,633	....	....	....	....	....	....	....	Debt: Kroner	**88b**
																Debt: Foreign	**89a**
	....	....	....	....	....	....	....	....	....	....	....	....	....	....	....	Foreign Currency	**89b**
National Accounts																		
Billions of Kroner																		
	329.2	358.4	367.1	375.8	393.3	404.9	423.0	439.3	450.2	493.8	509.6	533.2	564.0	594.3	613.7	Househ.Cons.Expend.,incl.NPISHs	**96f**
	164.2	168.9	186.0	196.6	204.6	210.9	220.5	229.2	240.9	250.3	260.3	274.6	284.5	300.1	312.5	Government Consumption Expend.	**91f**
	132.5	155.7	159.7	154.9	163.2	166.0	165.6	161.0	155.7	168.4	189.3	198.4	218.0	236.3	237.9	Gross Fixed Capital Formation	**93e**
	6.5	6.4	−4.6	−.6	3.2	1.6	−1.9	−.2	−7.9	1.6	9.3	2.5	6.5	10.9	−1.6	Changes in Inventories	**93i**
	230.6	218.9	225.2	248.4	276.7	295.7	319.1	324.2	318.6	342.6	357.5	379.4	405.7	410.7	444.0	Exports of Goods and Services	**90c**
	−229.0	−222.8	−212.5	−227.0	−252.2	−253.8	−268.7	−265.6	−257.3	−291.0	−316.1	−327.2	−366.8	−388.5	−393.1	Imports of Goods and Services	**98c**
	634.0	685.6	720.9	748.3	788.6	825.3	857.7	887.9	900.2	965.7	1,009.8	1,060.9	1,112.0	1,163.8	1,213.3	Gross Domestic Product (GDP)	**99b**
	−18.7	−18.5	−16.8	−18.2	−21.7	−24.8	−26.4	−22.3	−16.0	−16.0	−12.7	−14.0	−17.5	−18.4	−13.7	Net Primary Income from Abroad	**98.n**
	615.3	667.1	704.2	730.1	766.9	800.6	831.3	865.5	884.2	949.7	997.1	1,046.9	1,094.5	1,145.4	1,199.6	Gross National Income (GNI)	**99a**
	860.2	894.7	894.9	905.8	907.2	915.9	926.1	931.8	931.8	982.7	1,009.8	1,035.2	1,067.7	1,094.8	1,112.0	GDP Volume 1995 Prices	**99b**, *p*
	85.2	88.6	88.6	89.7	89.8	90.7	91.7	92.3	92.3	97.3	100.0	102.5	105.7	108.4	110.1	GDP Volume (1995=100)	**99bv** *p*
	73.7	76.6	80.6	82.6	86.9	90.1	92.6	95.3	96.6	98.3	100.0	102.5	104.1	106.3	109.1	GDP Deflator (1995=100)	**99bi** *p*
Midyear Estimates																		
	5.11	5.12	5.13	5.13	5.13	5.14	5.15	5.17	5.19	5.20	5.23	5.26	5.28	5.30	5.32	**Population**	**99z**

(See notes in the back of the book.)

Djibouti

611

		1970	1971	1972	1973	1974	1975	1976	1977	1978	1979	1980	1981	1982	1983	1984
Exchange Rates																*Francs per SDR:*
Official Rate	aa	214.39	214.39	214.39	214.39	217.59	208.05	206.48	215.88	231.53	234.12	226.67	206.86	196.05	186.07	174.20
																Francs per US Dollar:
Official Rate	ae	214.39	197.47	197.47	177.72	177.72	177.72	177.72	177.72	177.72	177.72	177.72	177.72	177.72	177.72	177.72
Official Rate	rf	214.39	213.78	197.47	179.94	177.72	177.72	177.72	177.72	177.72	177.72	177.72	177.72	177.72	177.72	177.72
Fund Position																*Millions of SDRs:*
Quota	2f. s	—	—	—	—	—	—	—	—	3.80	3.80	5.70	5.70	5.70	5.70	8.00
SDRs	1b. s	....	....	....	....	....	....	....	....	—	.08	.13	.50	.46	.43	.40
Reserve Position in the Fund	1c. s	....	....	....	....	....	....	....	....	—	.76	1.23	1.23	1.24	1.24	1.24
Total Fund Cred.&Loans Outstg.	2tl	....	....	....	....	....	....	....	....	—						
International Liquidity																*Millions of US Dollars Unless Otherwise Indicated:*
Total Reserves minus Gold	1l. d	....	....	....	....	....	....	....	....	....	....	....	....	....	....	44.93
SDRs	1b. d	....	....	....	....	....	....	....	....	—	.11	.17	.58	.51	.45	.39
Reserve Position in the Fund	1c. d	....	....	....	....	....	....	....	....	....	1.00	1.57	1.43	1.37	1.30	1.22
Foreign Exchange	1d. d	....	....	....	....	....	....	....	....	....						43.33
Deposit Money Banks: Assets	7a. d	....	....	....	....	....	....	....	....	....	....	....	....	....	....	170.13
Liabilities	7b. d															95.37
Other Banking Insts.: Liabilities	7f. d	....	....	....	....	....	....	....	....	....	....	....	....	....	....	
Monetary Authorities																*Millions of Francs:*
Foreign Assets	11	....	....	....	....	....	....	....	....	....	....	....	....	....	....	7,986
Claims on Deposit Money Banks	12e	....	....	....	....	....	....	....	....	....	....	....	....	....	....	—
Reserve Money	14	....	....	....	....	....	....	....	....	....	....	....	....	....	....	7,471
of which: Currency Outside DMBs	14a	....	....	....	....	....	....	....	....	....	....	....	....	....	....	6,671
Central Government Deposits	16d	....	....	....	....	....	....	....	....	....	....	....	....	....	....	225
Capital Accounts	17a	....	....	....	....	....	....	....	....	....	....	....	....	....	....	357
Other Items (Net)	17r	....	....	....	....	....	....	....	....	....	....	....	....	....	....	−70
Deposit Money Banks																*Millions of Francs:*
Reserves	20	....	....	....	....	....	....	....	....	....	....	....	....	....	....	800
Foreign Assets	21	....	....	....	....	....	....	....	....	....	....	....	....	....	....	30,236
Claims on Nonfin.Pub.Enterprises	22c	....	....	....	....	....	....	....	....	....	....	....	....	....	....	561
Claims on Private Sector	22d	....	....	....	....	....	....	....	....	....	....	....	....	....	....	29,114
Demand Deposits	24	....	....	....	....	....	....	....	....	....	....	....	....	....	....	12,690
Time Deposits	25	....	....	....	....	....	....	....	....	....	....	....	....	....	....	18,264
Foreign Liabilities	26c	....	....	....	....	....	....	....	....	....	....	....	....	....	....	16,949
Central Government Deposits	26d	....	....	....	....	....	....	....	....	....	....	....	....	....	....	—
Credit From Monetary Authorities	26g	....	....	....	....	....	....	....	....	....	....	....	....	....	....	3,458
Capital Accounts	27a	....	....	....	....	....	....	....	....	....	....	....	....	....	....	8,220
Other Items (Net)	27r	....	....	....	....	....	....	....	....	....	....	....	....	....	....	1,129
Monetary Survey																*Millions of Francs:*
Foreign Assets (Net)	31n	....	....	....	....	....	....	....	....	....	....	....	....	....	....	21,273
Domestic Credit	32	....	....	....	....	....	....	....	....	....	....	....	....	....	....	26,565
Claims on Central Govt. (Net)	32an	....	....	....	....	....	....	....	....	....	....	....	....	....	....	−3,952
Claims on Nonfin.Pub.Enterprises	32c	....	....	....	....	....	....	....	....	....	....	....	....	....	....	561
Claims on Private Sector	32d	....	....	....	....	....	....	....	....	....	....	....	....	....	....	29,956
Money	34	....	....	....	....	....	....	....	....	....	....	....	....	....	....	19,934
Quasi-Money	35	....	....	....	....	....	....	....	....	....	....	....	....	....	....	18,264
Other Items (Net)	37r	....	....	....	....	....	....	....	....	....	....	....	....	....	....	9,636
Money plus Quasi-Money	35l	....	....	....	....	....	....	....	....	....	....	....	....	....	....	38,198
Other Banking Institutions																*Millions of Francs:*
Reserves	40	....	....	....	....	....	....	....	....	....	....	....	....	....	....	195
Claims on Private Sector	42d	....	....	....	....	....	....	....	....	....	....	....	....	....	....	795
Long-Term Foreign Liabilities	46cl	....	....	....	....	....	....	....	....	....	....	....	....	....	....	—
Central Govt. Lending Funds	46f	....	....	....	....	....	....	....	....	....	....	....	....	....	....	270
Capital Accounts	47a	....	....	....	....	....	....	....	....	....	....	....	....	....	....	477
Other Items (Net)	47r	....	....	....	....	....	....	....	....	....	....	....	....	....	....	243
International Transactions																*Millions of Francs*
Exports	70	4,523	3,219	3,829	5,493	6,733	2,639	2,835	3,364	3,154	2,023	2,221	1,554	2,232	1,919	2,362
Imports, c.i.f.	71	10,593	11,335	12,935	12,935	14,496	24,933	21,284	18,949	29,117	33,454	37,920	39,865	40,197	39,307	39,425

1985	1986	1987	1988	1989	1990	1991	1992	1993	1994	1995	1996	1997	1998	1999		
															Exchange Rates	
End of Period (aa)																
195.21	217.39	252.13	239.16	233.55	252.84	254.22	244.37	244.11	259.45	264.18	255.56	239.79	250.24	243.92	Official Rate..............................	aa
End of Period (ae)		*Period Average (rf)*														
177.72	177.72	177.72	177.72	177.72	177.72	177.72	177.72	177.72	177.72	177.72	177.72	177.72	177.72	177.72	Official Rate..............................	ae
177.72	177.72	177.72	177.72	177.72	177.72	177.72	177.72	177.72	177.72	177.72	177.72	177.72	177.72	177.72	Official Rate..............................	rf
															Fund Position	
End of Period																
8.00	8.00	8.00	8.00	8.00	8.00	8.00	11.50	11.50	11.50	11.50	11.50	11.50	11.50	15.90	Quota	2f. s
.37	.35	.33	.30	.27	.23	.19	.15	.15	.11	.06	.10	.55	.27	.06	SDRs	1b. s
1.24	1.24	1.24	1.24	1.24	1.24	1.24	2.11	—	—	—				1.10	Reserve Position in the Fund	1c. s
—	—	—	—	—	—	—	—	—	—	—	2.88	3.98	6.30	9.28	Total Fund Cred.&Loans Outstg.	2tl
															International Liquidity	
End of Period																
50.94	53.62	63.53	64.36	59.15	93.64	100.00	83.40	75.10	73.76	72.16	76.97	66.57	66.45	70.61	Total Reserves minus Gold....................	1l. d
.41	.43	.47	.40	.35	.33	.27	.21	.21	.16	.09	.15	.75	.38	.09	SDRs	1b. d
1.36	1.52	1.76	1.67	1.63	1.76	1.77	2.90	—	—	—				1.51	Reserve Position in the Fund	1c. d
49.17	51.67	61.30	62.29	57.17	91.55	97.95	80.29	74.89	73.60	72.07	76.82	65.82	66.07	69.01	Foreign Exchange	1d. d
195.86	186.92	198.14	198.39	238.27	209.40	225.35	200.09	219.26	211.53	209.96	173.31	167.22	169.95	....	Deposit Money Banks: Assets	7a. d
102.73	79.08	79.01	62.80	95.85	68.92	72.10	84.45	84.81	88.65	91.10	89.01	83.33	88.47	....	Liabilities..........	7b. d
		.62	1.28	2.56	3.36	1.18	2.97	3.62	4.01	3.43	3.21	3.26	....	....	Other Banking Insts.: Liabilities	7f. d
															Monetary Authorities	
End of Period																
9,053	9,529	11,290	11,438	10,513	16,642	17,772	14,822	13,347	13,990	12,688	13,683	12,064	11,518	....	Foreign Assets	11
—	—	3,023	2,616	3,117	35	37	39	40	40	42	44	44	44	....	Claims on Deposit Money Banks	12e
7,237	7,994	9,366	9,301	8,960	9,875	9,899	12,187	11,250	11,869	10,370	9,989	9,783	9,575	....	Reserve Money	14
6,686	7,180	8,013	8,439	8,197	9,035	9,263	11,331	10,401	10,693	9,367	9,686	9,450	9,099	....	*of which: Currency Outside DMBs*	14a
1,357	992	4,366	3,690	3,545	2,637	2,490	114	716	797	1,074	284	106	676	....	Central Government Deposits	16d
470	593	792	861	935	1,037	1,244	1,436	1,425	1,390	1,712	1,729	1,872	2,361	....	Capital Accounts	17a
–12	–52	–211	201	189	3,125	4,179	1,124	–4	–23	–426	1,725	347	–1,051	....	Other Items (Net)	17r
															Deposit Money Banks	
End of Period																
551	790	1,432	929	748	894	647	868	925	1,148	1,065	638	778	575	....	Reserves	20
34,809	33,219	35,214	35,258	42,346	37,214	40,049	35,561	38,967	37,594	37,314	30,801	29,719	30,204	....	Foreign Assets	21
563	494	459	609	221	572	489	444	483	419	464	599	778	2,115	....	Claims on Nonfin.Pub.Enterprises..........	22c
32,965	35,701	35,684	36,529	38,062	36,165	35,105	34,712	32,057	33,382	37,783	38,826	38,469	42,098	....	Claims on Private Sector....................	22d
13,418	15,601	16,905	18,142	16,444	17,944	20,761	21,595	22,209	21,814	21,157	18,738	17,506	20,146	....	Demand Deposits	24
24,694	27,050	26,346	28,391	31,619	31,462	29,554	22,986	22,094	23,030	26,841	23,185	23,943	24,845	....	Time Deposits	25
18,257	14,055	14,041	11,161	17,034	12,249	12,814	15,008	15,073	15,755	16,191	15,819	14,810	15,723	....	Foreign Liabilities	26c
2,625	1,651	587	1,448	1,814	1,842	1,095	929	925	2,089	727	568	605	877	....	Central Government Deposits	26d
—	—	3,024	1,970	3,127	47	69	39	40	40	40	52	406	40	....	Credit From Monetary Authorities	26g
7,649	8,435	8,300	8,643	8,355	7,833	7,961	7,466	8,082	9,854	10,051	10,053	9,609	9,814	....	Capital Accounts	27a
2,245	3,411	3,584	3,569	2,984	3,468	4,035	3,562	4,010	–40	1,619	2,452	2,866	3,547	....	Other Items (Net)	27r
															Monetary Survey	
End of Period																
25,605	28,693	32,463	35,535	35,825	41,607	45,007	35,358	37,222	35,815	33,794	27,904	25,959	24,336	....	Foreign Assets (Net)	31n
29,975	34,061	31,603	32,485	33,467	32,641	33,634	36,168	35,446	39,075	45,598	48,918	47,278	45,560	....	Domestic Credit	32
–4,490	–2,883	–5,251	–5,198	–5,259	–4,463	–2,307	739	2,158	5,180	7,233	9,384	7,928	1,347	....	Claims on Central Govt. (Net)	32an
563	494	459	609	221	572	489	444	483	419	464	599	778	2,115	....	Claims on Nonfin.Pub.Enterprises	32c
33,902	36,450	36,395	37,074	38,505	36,532	35,452	34,985	32,805	33,476	37,901	38,935	38,572	42,098	....	Claims on Private Sector	32d
20,533	23,290	25,331	27,066	25,184	27,362	31,649	34,981	36,404	37,608	36,998	35,925	32,478	29,245	....	Money	34
24,694	27,050	26,346	28,391	31,619	31,462	29,554	22,986	22,094	23,030	26,841	23,185	23,943	24,845	....	Quasi-Money	35
10,352	12,411	12,387	12,561	12,488	15,421	17,440	13,559	14,171	14,254	15,553	17,715	16,817	15,805	....	Other Items (Net)	37r
45,227	50,340	51,677	55,457	56,803	58,824	61,203	57,967	58,498	60,638	63,839	59,110	56,421	54,090	....	Money plus Quasi-Money	35l
															Other Banking Institutions	
End of Period																
295	184	310	721	561	656	510	251	261	167	80	30	....	....	....	Reserves	40
468	636	791	975	1,044	1,790	2,860	4,202	4,472	4,277	4,126	3,537	....	....	....	Claims on Private Sector	42d
—	111	228	455	597	210	527	644	712	610	570	580	....	....	....	Long-Term Foreign Liabilities	46cl
270	240	390	740	690	1,607	1,463	1,999	1,788	1,542	1,533	1,180	....	....	....	Central Govt. Lending Funds	46f
483	486	485	436	364	342	1,133	1,529	1,557	1,557	1,817	1,696	....	....	....	Capital Accounts	47a
10	–16	–2	63	–46	287	247	281	676	735	286	111	....	....	....	Other Items (Net)	47r
															International Transactions	
Millions of Francs																
2,488	3,628	4,976	4,116	4,423	4,420	3,083	2,800	....	....	....	....	....	....	....	Exports.....................................	70
35,670	32,731	36,487	35,771	34,920	38,174	38,103	38,860	....	....	....	....	....	....	....	Imports, c.i.f.	71

Djibouti

		1970	1971	1972	1973	1974	1975	1976	1977	1978	1979	1980	1981	1982	1983	1984
Balance of Payments														*Millions of US Dollars:*		
Current Account, n.i.e.	78al d	...	...	...	...	...	...	...	...	...	...	...	...	...	...	...
Goods: Exports f.o.b.	78aa d	...	...	...	...	...	...	...	...	...	...	...	...	...	...	...
Goods: Imports f.o.b.	78ab d	...	...	...	...	...	...	...	...	...	...	...	...	...	...	...
Trade Balance	78ac d	...	...	...	...	...	...	...	...	...	...	...	...	...	...	...
Services: Credit	78ad d	...	...	...	...	...	...	...	...	...	...	...	...	...	...	...
Services: Debit	78ae d	...	...	...	...	...	...	...	...	...	...	...	...	...	...	...
Balance on Goods & Services	78af d	...	...	...	...	...	...	...	...	...	...	...	...	...	...	...
Income: Credit	78ag d	...	...	...	...	...	...	...	...	...	...	...	...	...	...	...
Income: Debit	78ah d	...	...	...	...	...	...	...	...	...	...	...	...	...	...	...
Balance on Gds, Serv. & Inc.	78ai d	...	...	...	...	...	...	...	...	...	...	...	...	...	...	...
Current Transfers, n.i.e.: Credit	78aj d	...	...	...	...	...	...	...	...	...	...	...	...	...	...	...
Current Transfers: Debit	78ak d	...	...	...	...	...	...	...	...	...	...	...	...	...	...	...
Capital Account, n.i.e.	78bc d	...	...	...	...	...	...	...	...	...	...	...	...	...	...	...
Capital Account, n.i.e.: Credit	78ba d	...	...	...	...	...	...	...	...	...	...	...	...	...	...	...
Capital Account: Debit	78bb d	...	...	...	...	...	...	...	...	...	...	...	...	...	...	...
Financial Account, n.i.e.	78bj d	...	...	...	...	...	...	...	...	...	...	...	...	...	...	...
Direct Investment Abroad	78bd d	...	...	...	...	...	...	...	...	...	...	...	...	...	...	...
Dir. Invest. in Rep. Econ., n.i.e.	78be d	...	...	...	...	...	...	...	...	...	...	...	...	...	...	...
Portfolio Investment Assets	78bf d	...	...	...	...	...	...	...	...	...	...	...	...	...	...	...
Equity Securities	78bk d	...	...	...	...	...	...	...	...	...	...	...	...	...	...	...
Debt Securities	78bl d	...	...	...	...	...	...	...	...	...	...	...	...	...	...	...
Portfolio Investment Liab., n.i.e.	78bg d	...	...	...	...	...	...	...	...	...	...	...	...	...	...	...
Equity Securities	78bm d	...	...	...	...	...	...	...	...	...	...	...	...	...	...	...
Debt Securities	78bn d	...	...	...	...	...	...	...	...	...	...	...	...	...	...	...
Financial Derivatives Assets	78bw d	...	...	...	...	...	...	...	...	...	...	...	...	...	...	...
Financial Derivatives Liabilities	78bx d	...	...	...	...	...	...	...	...	...	...	...	...	...	...	...
Other Investment Assets	78bh d	...	...	...	...	...	...	...	...	...	...	...	...	...	...	...
Monetary Authorities	78bo d	...	...	...	...	...	...	...	...	...	...	...	...	...	...	...
General Government	78bp d	...	...	...	...	...	...	...	...	...	...	...	...	...	...	...
Banks	78bq d	...	...	...	...	...	...	...	...	...	...	...	...	...	...	...
Other Sectors	78br d	...	...	...	...	...	...	...	...	...	...	...	...	...	...	...
Other Investment Liab., n.i.e.	78bi d	...	...	...	...	...	...	...	...	...	...	...	...	...	...	...
Monetary Authorities	78bs d	...	...	...	...	...	...	...	...	...	...	...	...	...	...	...
General Government	78bt d	...	...	...	...	...	...	...	...	...	...	...	...	...	...	...
Banks	78bu d	...	...	...	...	...	...	...	...	...	...	...	...	...	...	...
Other Sectors	78bv d	...	...	...	...	...	...	...	...	...	...	...	...	...	...	...
Net Errors and Omissions	78ca d	...	...	...	...	...	...	...	...	...	...	...	...	...	...	...
Overall Balance	78cb d	...	...	...	...	...	...	...	...	...	...	...	...	...	...	...
Reserves and Related Items	79da d	...	...	...	...	...	...	...	...	...	...	...	...	...	...	...
Reserve Assets	79db d	...	...	...	...	...	...	...	...	...	...	...	...	...	...	...
Use of Fund Credit and Loans	79dc d	...	...	...	...	...	...	...	...	...	...	...	...	...	...	...
Exceptional Financing	79de d	...	...	...	...	...	...	...	...	...	...	...	...	...	...	...
Government Finance															*Millions of Francs:*	
Deficit (-) or Surplus	80	...	...	...	...	...	...	...	...	...	ƚ1,872	ƚ4,062	ƚ5,268	2,798	4,587	2,729
Revenue	81	...	...	...	...	...	...	...	...	...	ƚ13,918	ƚ17,922	ƚ23,058	24,904	26,706	23,644
Grants Received	81z	...	...	...	...	...	...	...	...	...	ƚ8,433	ƚ13,460	ƚ96	2,896	1,916	1,473
Expenditure	82	...	...	...	...	...	...	...	...	...	ƚ20,397	ƚ26,916	ƚ16,396	24,190	24,035	22,182
Lending Minus Repayments	83	...	...	...	...	...	...	...	...	...	ƚ82	ƚ404	ƚ1,490	812	—	206
Financing																
Domestic	84a	...	...	...	...	...	...	...	...	...	ƚ163	ƚ−241	...	...	...	...
Foreign	85a	...	...	...	...	...	...	...	...	...	ƚ−2,035	ƚ−3,821	...	...	...	...
National Accounts															*Billions of Francs:*	
Gross Domestic Product (GDP)	99b	10	17	19	22	27	30	36	35	38	46	60	67	70	72	...
																Millions:
Population	99z	ƚ.16	...	...	...	...	.21	.23	.25	.27	.29	.36	.37	.37	.38	.41

1985	1986	1987	1988	1989	1990	1991	1992	1993	1994	1995	1996	1997	1998	1999		
Minus Sign Indicates Debit															**Balance of Payments**	
....	....	....	....	....	....	....	-87.5	-34.3	-46.1	-23.0	....	....	....	....	Current Account, n.i.e.	78al *d*
....	....	....	....	....	....	....	53.2	71.2	56.4	33.5	....	....	....	....	Goods: Exports f.o.b.	78aa *d*
....	....	....	....	....	....	....	-271.0	-255.1	-237.1	-205.0	....	....	....	....	Goods: Imports f.o.b.	78ab *d*
....	....	....	....	....	....	....	-217.8	-183.9	-180.7	-171.5	....	....	....	....	*Trade Balance*	78ac *d*
....	....	....	....	....	....	....	145.1	156.9	152.3	151.4	....	....	....	....	Services: Credit	78ad *d*
....	....	....	....	....	....	....	-109.3	-110.8	-89.7	-87.2	....	....	....	....	Services: Debit	78ae *d*
....	....	....	....	....	....	....	-182.0	-137.8	-118.1	-107.3	....	....	....	....	*Balance on Goods & Services*	78af *d*
....	....	....	....	....	....	....	29.4	30.3	23.7	25.9	....	....	....	....	Income: Credit	78ag *d*
....	....	....	....	....	....	....	-9.4	-7.2	-7.0	-8.7	....	....	....	....	Income: Debit	78ah *d*
....	....	....	....	....	....	....	-162.0	-114.8	-101.4	-90.0	....	....	....	....	*Balance on Gds, Serv. & Inc.*	78ai *d*
....	....	....	....	....	....	....	90.7	96.6	73.7	85.4	....	....	....	....	Current Transfers, n.i.e.: Credit	78aj *d*
....	....	....	....	....	....	....	-16.3	-16.1	-18.3	-18.4	....	....	....	....	Current Transfers: Debit	78ak *d*
....	....	....	....	....	....	....	—	—	—	—	....	....	....	....	Capital Account, n.i.e.	78bc *d*
....	....	....	....	....	....	....	—	—	—	—	....	....	....	....	Capital Account, n.i.e.: Credit	78ba *d*
....	....	....	....	....	....	....	—	—	—	—	....	....	....	....	Capital Account: Debit	78bb *d*
....	....	....	....	....	....	....	74.0	16.6	39.0	-2.1	....	....	....	....	Financial Account, n.i.e.	78bj *d*
....	....	....	....	....	....	....					....	....	....	....	Direct Investment Abroad	78bd *d*
....	....	....	....	....	....	....	2.3	1.4	1.4	3.2	....	....	....	....	Dir. Invest. in Rep. Econ., n.i.e.	78be *d*
....	....	....	....	....	....	....	—	—	—	—	....	....	....	....	Portfolio Investment Assets	78bf *d*
....	....	....	....	....	....	....	—	—	—	—	....	....	....	....	Equity Securities	78bk *d*
....	....	....	....	....	....	....	—	—	—	—	....	....	....	....	Debt Securities	78bl *d*
....	....	....	....	....	....	....	—	—	—	—	....	....	....	....	Portfolio Investment Liab., n.i.e.	78bg *d*
....	....	....	....	....	....	....	—	—	—	—	....	....	....	....	Equity Securities	78bm *d*
....	....	....	....	....	....	....	—	—	—	—	....	....	....	....	Debt Securities	78bn *d*
....	....	....	....	....	....	....	....	....	....	....	....	....	....	....	Financial Derivatives Assets	78bw *d*
....	....	....	....	....	....	....	....	....	....	....	....	....	....	....	Financial Derivatives Liabilities	78bx *d*
....	....	....	....	....	....	....	—	—	—	—	....	....	....	....	Other Investment Assets	78bh *d*
....	....	....	....	....	....	....					....	....	....	....	Monetary Authorities	78bo *d*
....	....	....	....	....	....	....					....	....	....	....	General Government	78bp *d*
....	....	....	....	....	....	....	—	—	—	—	....	....	....	....	Banks	78bq *d*
....	....	....	....	....	....	....	—	—	—	—	....	....	....	....	Other Sectors	78br *d*
....	....	....	....	....	....	....	71.7	15.2	37.6	-5.4	....	....	....	....	Other Investment Liab., n.i.e.	78bi *d*
....	....	....	....	....	....	....					....	....	....	....	Monetary Authorities	78bs *d*
....	....	....	....	....	....	....	8.1	15.9	12.0	-9.4	....	....	....	....	General Government	78bt *d*
....	....	....	....	....	....	....	37.6	-18.8	11.6	4.0	....	....	....	....	Banks	78bu *d*
....	....	....	....	....	....	....	26.0	18.1	14.1	.1	....	....	....	....	Other Sectors	78bv *d*
....	....	....	....	....	....	....	-2.0	6.0	7.9	.7	....	....	....	....	Net Errors and Omissions	78ca *d*
....	....	....	....	....	....	....	-15.5	-11.7	.8	-24.5	....	....	....	....	*Overall Balance*	78cb *d*
....	....	....	....	....	....	....	15.5	11.7	-.8	24.5	....	....	....	....	Reserves and Related Items	79da *d*
....	....	....	....	....	....	....	15.5	11.3	-3.4	7.3	....	....	....	....	Reserve Assets	79db *d*
....	....	....	....	....	....	....	—	—	—	—	....	....	....	....	Use of Fund Credit and Loans..........	79dc *d*
....	....	....	....	....	....	....	—	.4	2.6	17.2	....	....	....	....	Exceptional Financing	79de *d*
Year Ending December 31															**Government Finance**	
922	I-1,470	....	I-733	....	....	....	....				....	....	....	....	Deficit (-) or Surplus......................	80
22,485	I21,024	....	I20,101	....	....	....	....				....	....	....	....	Revenue....................................	81
1,445	I2,404	....	I1,400	....	....	....	....				....	....	....	....	Grants Received..........................	81z
22,918	I24,383	....	I22,234	....	....	....	....				....	....	....	....	Expenditure................................	82
90	I515	....	I—	....	....	....	....				....	....	....	....	Lending Minus Repayments	83
															Financing	
....	I1,693	....	....	....	....	....	....				....	....	....	....	Domestic	84a
....	I-223	....	....	....	....	....	....				....	....	....	....	Foreign	85a
Billions of Francs															**National Accounts**	
....	....	66	70	73	75	....	....	....	....	....	....	....	....	....	Gross Domestic Product (GDP)	99b
Midyear Estimates																
.43	.46	.44	.47	.49	.52	.54	.56	.57	.59	.60	.61	.62	.62	.63	**Population**...................................	99z

(See notes in the back of the book.)

Dominica

321

		1970	1971	1972	1973	1974	1975	1976	1977	1978	1979	1980	1981	1982	1983	1984
Exchange Rates											*E.Caribbean Dollars per SDR: End of Period (aa)*					
Official Rate	aa	2.0053	2.0417	2.2194	2.4925	2.5024	2.7770	3.1369	3.2797	3.5175	3.5568	3.4436	3.1427	2.9784	2.8268	2.6466
Official Rate	ae	2.0053	1.8805	2.0442	2.0661	2.0439	2.3721	2.7000	2.7000	2.7000	2.7000	2.7000	2.7000	2.7000	2.7000	2.7000
												Index Numbers (1995=100):					
Nominal Effective Exchange Rate	ne c	....	....	....	....	....	....	....	....	....	62.21	60.28	64.10	68.39	73.89	84.39
Real Effective Exchange Rate	re c	....	....	....	....	....	....	....	....	....	87.99	94.79	102.43	105.83	112.62	121.92
Fund Position												*Millions of SDRs:*					
Quota	2f. s	—	—	—	—	—	—	—	—	1.90	1.90	2.90	2.90	2.90	4.00	4.00
SDRs	1b. s	....	....	....	....	....	....	....	....	—	—	—	.70	.26	.40	—
Reserve Position in the Fund	1c. s	....	....	....	....	....	....	....	....	—	—	—	—	—	—	.01
Total Fund Cred.&Loans Outstg.	2tl	....	....	....	....	....	....	....	....	—	1.90	1.65	6.47	9.32	11.00	10.66
International Liquidity											*Millions of US Dollars Unless Otherwise Indicated:*						
Total Reserves minus Gold	1l. d	....	....	....	....	....	.35	1.17	2.23	1.93	9.84	5.08	3.06	4.33	1.48	5.25
SDRs	1b. d	....	....	....	....	....	....	....	....	—	—	—	.81	.29	.42	—
Reserve Position in the Fund	1c. d	....	....	....	....	....	....	....	....	—	—	—	—	—	—	.01
Foreign Exchange	1d. d	....	....	....	....	....	.35	1.17	2.23	1.93	9.84	5.08	2.24	4.04	1.06	5.24
Deposit Money Banks: Assets	7a. d	....	....	....	....	....	1.77	.86	1.43	1.50	6.40	4.41	6.28	6.79	7.77	5.53
Liabilities	7b. d	....	....	....	....	....	3.96	3.88	5.00	5.44	6.69	7.64	10.18	8.86	7.61	8.21
Monetary Authorities												*Millions of E. Caribbean Dollars:*					
Foreign Assets	11	....	....	....	....	....	.82	3.17	6.02	5.20	26.56	13.71	8.25	11.69	3.99	19.85
Claims on Central Government	12a	....	....	....	....	....	3.30	3.30	3.70	3.70	11.08	11.49	24.45	33.36	37.68	42.86
Claims on Deposit Money Banks	12e	....	....	....	....	....										
Reserve Money	14	....	....	....	....	....	4.12	6.47	9.72	8.90	30.88	19.52	12.37	17.29	10.58	34.49
of which: Currency Outside DMBs	14a	....	....	....	....	....	2.77	3.65	4.81	5.15	7.33	7.48	7.73	6.58	6.39	12.22
Foreign Liabilities	16c	....	....	....	....	....	—	—	—	—	6.76	5.68	20.33	27.76	31.09	28.21
Central Government Deposits	16d	....	....	....	....	....	—	—	—	—	—	—	—	—	—	—
Other Items (Net)	17r	....	....	....	....	....	—	—	—	—	—	—	—	—	—	—
Deposit Money Banks												*Millions of E. Caribbean Dollars:*					
Reserves	20	....	....	....	....	....	1.35	2.81	4.91	3.75	23.54	12.04	4.64	10.71	4.19	23.00
Foreign Assets	21	....	....	....	....	....	4.19	2.31	3.87	4.04	17.28	11.92	16.96	18.32	20.97	14.93
Claims on Central Government	22a	....	....	....	....	....	9.04	10.95	16.94	12.76	13.50	18.49	18.25	18.72	19.04	13.13
Claims on Local Government	22b	....	....	....	....	....										
Claims on Nonfin.Pub.Enterprises	22c	....	....	....	....	....	1.00	1.00	1.00	1.00	3.76	2.20	8.87	4.82	3.31	9.02
Claims on Private Sector	22d	....	....	....	....	....	25.53	28.82	25.86	34.27	36.76	49.78	60.50	67.49	79.07	81.32
Claims on Nonbank Financial Insts	22g	....	....	....	....	....	—	—	—	—	.01	.17	.13	.13	6.16	5.49
Demand Deposits	24	....	....	....	....	....	5.77	5.70	6.72	12.34	22.75	19.63	18.71	18.83	19.01	20.18
Time, Savings,& Fgn.Currency Dep.	25	....	....	....	....	....	28.11	31.89	33.63	36.45	47.52	52.36	54.84	70.86	80.31	90.19
Foreign Liabilities	26c	....	....	....	....	....	9.39	10.48	13.51	14.69	18.07	20.63	27.49	23.93	20.55	22.16
Central Government Deposits	26d	....	....	....	....	....	—	—	—	—	—	.22	3.76	2.98	5.50	4.19
Credit from Monetary Authorities	26g	....	....	....	....	....	—	—	—	—	—	—	—	—	—	—
Capital Accounts	27a	....	....	....	....	....	1.00	1.80	1.80	1.80	1.84	1.82	2.80	2.95	4.28	4.78
Other Items (Net)	27r	....	....	....	....	....	–3.16	–3.99	–3.07	–9.47	4.66	–.06	1.75	.66	3.09	5.39
Monetary Survey												*Millions of E. Caribbean Dollars:*					
Foreign Assets (Net)	31n	....	....	....	....	....	–4.38	–5.01	–3.62	–5.45	19.00	–.69	–22.61	–21.68	–26.68	–15.59
Domestic Credit	32	....	....	....	....	....	38.87	44.07	47.50	51.72	65.10	81.92	108.45	121.55	139.76	147.62
Claims on Central Govt. (Net)	32an	....	....	....	....	....	12.34	14.25	20.64	16.46	24.57	29.77	38.95	49.10	51.22	51.79
Claims on Local Government	32b	....	....	....	....	....	—	—	—	—	—	—	—	—	—	—
Claims on Nonfin.Pub.Enterprises	32c	....	....	....	....	....	1.00	1.00	1.00	1.00	3.76	2.20	8.87	4.82	3.31	9.02
Claims on Private Sector	32d	....	....	....	....	....	25.53	28.82	25.86	34.27	36.76	49.78	60.50	67.49	79.07	81.32
Claims on Nonbank Financial Inst	32g	....	....	....	....	....	—	—	—	—	.01	.17	.13	.13	6.16	5.49
Money	34	....	....	....	....	....	8.54	9.36	11.53	17.49	30.09	27.11	26.44	25.41	25.40	32.40
Quasi-Money	35	....	....	....	....	....	28.11	31.89	33.63	36.45	47.52	52.36	54.84	70.86	80.31	90.19
Capital Accounts	37a	....	....	....	....	....	1.00	1.80	1.80	1.80	2.55	3.20	4.66	4.70	5.95	6.34
Other Items (Net)	37r	....	....	....	....	....	–3.16	–3.99	–3.07	–9.47	3.95	–1.44	–.10	–1.10	1.43	3.10
Money plus Quasi-Money	35l	....	....	....	....	....	36.65	41.25	45.15	53.94	77.60	79.47	81.29	96.26	105.71	122.59
Interest Rates												*Percent Per Annum*					
Treasury Bill Rate	60c	....	....	....	....	....	....	....	....	....	....	6.5	6.5	6.5	6.5	6.5
Deposit Rate	60l	....	....	....	....	....	....	....	....	4.0	4.0	4.0	5.0	5.0	5.0	5.0
Lending Rate	60p	....	....	....	....	....	....	....	....	8.5	8.5	8.5	9.0	9.5	9.5	10.4
Prices												*Index Numbers (1995=100):*					
Consumer Prices	64	13.9	14.4	15.0	I 16.8	22.6	27.0	30.0	55.9	35.4	....	55.4	62.8	65.5	68.2	69.7
International Transactions												*Millions of E. Caribbean Dollars*					
Exports	70	11.81	12.28	13.50	16.74	20.95	24.65	29.05	32.30	42.89	25.39	26.30	51.76	66.01	74.00	69.23
Imports, c.i.f.	71	31.51	33.02	32.88	32.29	38.92	45.04	49.83	59.08	76.77	59.97	128.73	134.10	128.19	121.71	156.10

1985	1986	1987	1988	1989	1990	1991	1992	1993	1994	1995	1996	1997	1998	1999		
E.Caribbean Dollars per US Dollar: End of Period (ae)															**Exchange Rates**	
2.9657	3.3026	3.8304	3.6334	3.5482	3.8412	3.7125	3.7086	3.9416	4.0135	3.8825	3.6430	3.8017		3.7058	Official Rate	**aa**
2.7000	2.7000	2.7000	2.7000	2.7000	2.7000	2.7000	2.7000	2.7000	2.7000	2.7000	2.7000	2.7000	2.7000	2.7000	Official Rate	**ae**
Period Averages																
89.68	84.60	80.52	77.72	81.30	83.40	86.93	90.20	98.38	103.11	100.00	102.92	108.88	115.49	114.43	Nominal Effective Exchange Rate	**ne** c
125.31	116.27	111.83	105.16	109.51	104.28	106.09	107.02	110.07	106.17	100.00	101.40	106.98	112.15	111.16	Real Effective Exchange Rate	**re** c
End of Period															**Fund Position**	
4.00	4.00	4.00	4.00	4.00	4.00	4.00	6.00	6.00	6.00	6.00	6.00	6.00	6.00	8.20	Quota	**2f.** s
—	.81	.70	.55	.32	.21	.01	.07	—	—	—	—	—	—	.01	SDRs	**1b.** s
.01	.01	.01	.01	.01	.01	.01	.01	.01	.01	.01	.01	.01	.01	.01	Reserve Position in the Fund	**1c.** s
9.17	8.63	8.23	6.57	4.99	4.00	3.32	2.78	2.26	1.71	1.15	.59	.19	.03	—	Total Fund Cred.&Loans Outstg.	**2tl**
End of Period															**International Liquidity**	
3.27	9.59	18.43	14.06	11.68	14.46	17.77	20.41	19.92	15.41	22.12	22.89	23.89	27.67	31.57	Total Reserves minus Gold	**1l.** d
—	.99	.99	.74	.42	.30	.01	.10	—	—	—	—	—	—	.01	SDRs	**1b.** d
.01	.01	.01	.01	.01	.01	.01	.01	.01	.01	.01	.01	.01	.01	.01	Reserve Position in the Fund	**1c.** d
3.26	8.59	17.42	13.31	11.25	14.15	17.74	20.30	19.90	15.40	22.11	22.88	23.88	27.65	31.55	Foreign Exchange	**1d.** d
6.87	14.88	28.64	40.19	32.54	23.16	22.88	28.13	24.13	26.62	28.14	38.81	43.08	51.84	60.28	Deposit Money Banks: Assets	**7a.** d
8.76	13.95	15.42	16.77	18.63	20.40	23.08	27.73	30.94	39.49	34.45	35.35	43.00	45.73	45.38	Liabilities	**7b.** d
End of Period															**Monetary Authorities**	
10.63	25.91	47.77	37.96	31.54	39.04	47.93	55.10	53.71	41.71	60.54	62.64	64.63	74.70	85.39	Foreign Assets	**11**
46.05	47.29	50.41	39.54	35.68	38.33	37.08	27.85	24.04	26.16	19.74	14.78	13.19	11.30	10.77	Claims on Central Government	**12a**
—	.72	.38	1.30	.72	4.05	.02	.02	.02	.37	2.04	.01	.01	.03	.01	Claims on Deposit Money Banks	**12e**
29.48	45.42	67.04	54.94	50.23	66.06	72.21	72.64	69.73	63.18	74.91	74.44	76.42	85.19	95.60	Reserve Money	**14**
9.64	6.64	20.77	22.83	20.69	24.96	30.76	31.13	27.86	24.49	29.16	28.53	28.21	29.13	34.09	*of which: Currency Outside DMBs*	**14a**
27.20	28.50	31.52	23.87	17.71	15.36	12.82	10.32	8.38	6.72	4.60	2.28	.68	.10	—	Foreign Liabilities	**16c**
—	—	—	—	—	—	—	—	—	—	.79	.72	.75	.74	.57	Central Government Deposits	**16d**
—	—	—	—	—	—	—	—	—	—	—	—	—	—	—	Other Items (Net)	**17r**
End of Period															**Deposit Money Banks**	
25.33	39.31	46.46	29.19	29.98	38.33	41.65	41.68	42.78	33.46	45.86	46.52	44.93	56.16	68.92	Reserves	**20**
18.55	40.18	77.34	108.51	87.86	62.53	61.78	75.95	65.16	71.88	75.98	104.78	116.31	139.96	162.76	Foreign Assets	**21**
15.60	24.94	10.36	9.14	11.45	28.00	37.28	42.17	53.46	66.56	77.86	79.34	87.40	87.73	95.35	Claims on Central Government	**22a**
—	—	—	—	—	—	—	.01	.05	.23	.17	.17	.17	.09	.06	Claims on Local Government	**22b**
7.36	2.38	1.03	6.01	8.27	18.47	24.65	21.40	26.40	29.07	29.13	19.27	21.77	23.05	23.04	Claims on Nonfin.Pub.Enterprises	**22c**
89.03	86.16	93.59	128.73	171.49	211.13	234.43	263.99	289.57	312.48	344.63	358.48	386.35	409.97	419.77	Claims on Private Sector	**22d**
5.35	2.92	5.33	1.50	4.12	1.54	1.57	1.62	1.29	.42	.46	1.57	1.48	1.52	1.22	Claims on Nonbank Financial Insts	**22g**
21.58	30.39	37.89	34.37	35.39	44.96	42.81	54.96	47.87	49.88	62.25	67.43	67.63	74.09	95.00	Demand Deposits	**24**
96.98	110.24	132.18	127.06	150.05	183.65	218.76	241.38	244.57	260.18	319.08	342.74	358.88	379.83	398.90	Time, Savings,& Fgn.Currency Dep.	**25**
23.65	37.67	41.63	45.27	50.31	55.09	62.32	74.88	83.54	106.61	93.02	95.45	116.10	123.48	122.54	Foreign Liabilities	**26c**
2.17	3.35	8.07	52.55	43.81	29.63	24.72	29.81	43.14	55.43	56.21	48.45	61.70	70.32	65.29	Central Government Deposits	**26d**
.47	.91	.42	1.90	2.68	1.54	—	9.68	2.00	—	—	—	2.80	.85		Credit from Monetary Authorities	**26g**
6.09	7.35	10.00	15.07	16.88	26.08	41.18	40.18	44.26	49.91	55.09	62.59	68.69	83.51	97.16	Capital Accounts	**27a**
10.29	5.99	4.33	8.32	14.85	17.92	10.02	5.61	5.66	-9.90	-11.55	-6.53	-14.63	-15.55	-8.62	Other Items (Net)	**27r**
End of Period															**Monetary Survey**	
-21.67	-.08	51.95	77.33	51.38	31.12	34.56	45.85	26.95	.25	38.90	69.69	64.16	91.07	125.62	Foreign Assets (Net)	**31n**
161.22	160.34	152.65	132.36	187.21	267.84	310.29	327.23	351.67	379.50	415.00	424.45	447.86	462.60	484.34	Domestic Credit	**32**
59.48	68.88	52.70	-3.87	3.32	36.70	49.64	40.21	34.36	37.30	40.60	44.95	38.14	27.97	40.25	Claims on Central Govt. (Net)	**32an**
—	—	—	—	—	—	—	.01	.05	.23	.17	.17	.17	.09	.06	Claims on Local Government	**32b**
7.36	2.38	1.03	6.01	8.27	18.47	24.65	21.40	26.40	29.07	29.13	19.27	21.77	23.05	23.04	Claims on Nonfin.Pub.Enterprises	**32c**
89.03	86.16	93.59	128.73	171.49	211.13	234.43	263.99	289.57	312.48	344.63	358.48	386.35	409.97	419.77	Claims on Private Sector	**32d**
5.35	2.92	5.33	1.50	4.12	1.54	1.57	1.62	1.29	.42	.46	1.57	1.48	1.52	1.22	Claims on Nonbank Financial Inst	**32g**
31.22	37.03	58.67	57.19	56.08	69.92	73.51	86.21	75.80	74.45	92.36	97.04	96.71	104.21	130.18	Money	**34**
96.98	110.24	132.18	127.06	150.05	183.65	218.76	241.38	244.57	260.18	319.08	342.74	358.88	379.83	398.90	Quasi-Money	**35**
7.84	9.30	12.26	17.22	18.97	28.35	43.46	42.37	46.44	52.24	57.46	64.88	70.84	85.75	99.35	Capital Accounts	**37a**
3.52	3.69	1.49	8.22	13.49	17.04	9.12	3.12	11.80	-7.11	-15.00	-10.52	-14.40	-16.11	-18.47	Other Items (Net)	**37r**
128.20	147.27	190.85	184.26	206.13	253.57	292.27	327.59	320.37	334.63	411.44	439.78	455.59	484.03	529.08	Money plus Quasi-Money	**35l**
Percent Per Annum															**Interest Rates**	
6.5	6.5	6.5	6.5	6.5	6.5	6.5	6.5	6.4	6.4	6.4	6.4	6.4	6.4	6.4	Treasury Bill Rate	**60c**
5.0	4.9	5.0	5.0	4.5	4.2	4.4	4.1	4.0	4.0	4.0	4.0	4.0	4.0	4.9	Deposit Rate	**60l**
10.0	10.3	10.5	10.5	10.5	10.5	10.3	10.0	10.0	9.6	10.3	10.5	10.5	10.5	10.5	Lending Rate	**60p**
Period Averages															**Prices**	
72.4	74.4	77.4	79.6	84.6	87.3	I 92.1	97.2	98.7	98.7	100.0	101.7	104.2	105.2	106.4	Consumer Prices	**64**
Millions of E. Caribbean Dollars															**International Transactions**	
76.77	117.24	129.59	146.41	121.77	148.59	146.62	144.35	131.67	127.30	121.81	138.46	143.01	170.34	146.53	Exports	**70**
149.38	150.69	179.22	236.34	289.09	318.39	295.98	284.69	252.99	260.10	316.66	350.85	336.31	367.18	380.11	Imports, c.i.f.	**71**

Dominica

Balance of Payments		1970	1971	1972	1973	1974	1975	1976	1977	1978	1979	1980	1981	1982	1983	1984
														Millions of US Dollars:		
Current Account, n.i.e.	78al d	...	...	...	...	...	...	-1.10	-1.50	-1.30	6.30	-14.30	-12.81	-8.24	-1.83	-7.23
Goods: Exports f.o.b.	78aa d	...	...	...	...	...	...	11.10	12.00	15.90	9.80	10.10	19.70	25.10	27.80	25.60
Goods: Imports f.o.b.	78ab d	...	...	...	...	...	...	-17.27	-19.91	-25.91	-35.82	-48.36	-45.18	-43.18	-42.81	-50.72
Trade Balance	78ac d	...	...	...	...	...	...	-6.17	-7.91	-10.01	-26.02	-38.26	-25.48	-18.08	-15.01	-25.12
Services: Credit	78ad d	...	...	...	...	...	...	2.50	3.00	3.10	9.50	5.60	3.70	6.60	8.20	11.80
Services: Debit	78ae d	...	...	...	...	...	...	-1.83	-2.29	-3.39	-4.48	-6.34	-6.92	-6.92	-6.89	-9.48
Balance on Goods & Services	78af d	...	...	...	...	...	...	-5.50	-7.20	-10.30	-21.00	-39.00	-28.70	-18.40	-13.70	-22.80
Income: Credit	78ag d	...	...	...	...	...	...	.40	.30	.20	.30	.60	1.00	1.00	1.26	—
Income: Debit	78ah d	...	...	...	...	...	...	-.20	-.30	-.40	-.40	-.30	-.50	-.80	-1.70	-1.90
Balance on Gds, Serv. & Inc.	78ai d	...	...	...	...	...	...	-5.30	-7.20	-10.50	-21.10	-38.70	-28.20	-18.20	-14.14	-24.70
Current Transfers, n.i.e.: Credit	78aj d	...	...	...	...	...	...	4.20	7.20	11.40	29.30	26.70	18.09	12.86	16.71	21.97
Current Transfers: Debit	78ak d	...	...	...	...	...	...	—	-1.50	-2.20	-1.90	-2.30	-2.70	-2.90	-4.40	-4.50
Capital Account, n.i.e.	78bc d	...	...	...	...	...	...	—	—	—	—	—	—	—	—	—
Capital Account, n.i.e.: Credit	78ba d	...	...	...	...	...	...	—	—	—	—	—	—	—	—	—
Capital Account: Debit	78bb d	...	...	...	...	...	...	—	—	—	—	—	—	—	—	—
Financial Account, n.i.e.	78bj d	...	...	...	...	...	...	.90	2.74	1.27	-1.89	3.59	3.35	7.03	1.37	11.43
Direct Investment Abroad	78bd d	...	...	...	...	...	...	—	—	—	—	—	—	—	—	—
Dir. Invest. in Rep. Econ., n.i.e.	78be d	...	...	...	...	...	...	—	—	—	—	—	—	.20	.20	2.30
Portfolio Investment Assets	78bf d	...	...	...	...	...	...	—	—	—	—	—	—	—	—	—
Equity Securities	78bk d	...	...	...	...	...	...	—	—	—	—	—	—	—	—	—
Debt Securities	78bl d	...	...	...	...	...	...	—	—	—	—	—	—	—	—	—
Portfolio Investment Liab., n.i.e.	78bg d	...	...	...	...	...	...	—	—	—	—	-.20	—	.09	.09	—
Equity Securities	78bm d	...	...	...	...	...	...	—	—	—	—	—	—	—	—	—
Debt Securities	78bn d	...	...	...	...	...	...	—	—	—	—	-.20	—	.09	.09	—
Financial Derivatives Assets	78bw d	...	...	...	...	...	...	...	...	...	...	...	...	...	...	...
Financial Derivatives Liabilities	78bx d	...	...	...	...	...	...	...	...	...	...	...	...	...	...	...
Other Investment Assets	78bh d	...	...	...	...	...	...	-.80	-.58	-.06	-3.84	1.17	-1.87	-.50	-3.38	2.24
Monetary Authorities	78bo d	...	...	...	...	...	...	—	—	—	—	—	—	—	—	—
General Government	78bp d	...	...	...	...	...	...	—	—	—	—	—	—	—	—	—
Banks	78bq d	...	...	...	...	...	...	-.80	-.58	-.06	-3.84	1.17	-1.87	-.50	-.98	2.24
Other Sectors	78br d	...	...	...	...	...	...	—	—	—	—	—	—	—	-2.40	—
Other Investment Liab., n.i.e.	78bi d	...	...	...	...	...	...	1.70	3.32	1.34	1.95	2.61	5.22	7.24	4.46	6.90
Monetary Authorities	78bs d	...	...	...	...	...	...	—	—	—	—	—	—	—	—	—
General Government	78bt d	...	...	...	...	...	...	—	.70	.10	.10	.96	.18	4.49	2.61	4.00
Banks	78bu d	...	...	...	...	...	...	—	1.12	.44	1.25	.95	2.54	-1.32	-1.25	.60
Other Sectors	78bv d	...	...	...	...	...	...	1.70	1.50	.80	.60	.70	2.50	4.07	3.10	2.30
Net Errors and Omissions	78ca d	...	...	...	...	...	...	.60	-.29	.12	1.14	6.77	.94	-.76	-3.99	1.43
Overall Balance	78cb d	...	...	...	...	...	...	.40	.96	.10	5.56	-3.94	-8.52	-1.98	-4.46	5.64
Reserves and Related Items	79da d	...	...	...	...	...	...	-.40	-.96	-.10	-5.56	3.94	8.52	1.98	4.46	-5.64
Reserve Assets	79db d	...	...	...	...	...	...	-.40	-.96	-.10	-8.05	4.26	2.72	-1.60	2.56	-5.39
Use of Fund Credit and Loans	79dc d	...	...	...	...	...	...	—	—	—	2.49	-.32	5.80	3.14	1.81	-.37
Exceptional Financing	79de d	...	...	...	...	...	...	—	—	—	—	—	.01	.44	.08	.12
Government Finance													*Millions of E. Caribbean Dollars:*			
Deficit (-) or Surplus	80	...	...	...	...	...	...	-4.49	.20	-2.72	-8.11	...	...	...	...	...
Revenue	81	...	...	...	...	...	...	15.83	23.46	31.46	32.46	...	...	...	...	...
Grants Received	81z	...	...	...	...	...	...	5.85	7.54	11.84	19.67	...	...	...	...	...
Expenditure	82	...	...	...	...	...	...	23.21	27.74	44.20	53.40	...	...	...	...	...
Lending Minus Repayments	83	...	...	...	...	...	...	2.96	3.06	1.82	6.84	...	...	...	...	...
National Accounts													*Millions of E. Caribbean Dollars*			
Gross Domestic Product (GDP)	99b	...	...	...	...	56.5	62.9	72.5	98.2	122.0	119.6	159.6	178.8	194.5	215.8	242.6
GDP Volume 1990 Prices	99b. p	...	...	...	...	...	...	...	256.7	286.9	234.0	263.7	299.7	312.1	320.5	337.9
GDP Deflator (1995=100)	99bi p	...	...	...	...	...	...	23.5	30.8	34.2	41.1	48.7	48.0	50.1	54.2	57.7
															Millions:	
Population	99z	.07	.07	.07	.07	.07	.07	.07	.08	.08	.07	.07	.07	.08	.08	.08

1985	1986	1987	1988	1989	1990	1991	1992	1993	1994	1995	1996	1997	1998	1999		
Minus Sign Indicates Debit															**Balance of Payments**	
-6.43	-7.11	-7.06	-12.30	-45.54	-43.53	-33.61	-25.41	-23.41	-38.42	-49.76	-39.92	-33.55	-17.52	....	Current Account, n.i.e.	78al *d*
28.40	44.58	49.29	57.04	46.30	56.07	55.62	55.10	48.15	47.84	46.12	52.74	53.76	62.25	....	Goods: Exports f.o.b.	78aa *d*
-52.00	-49.16	-58.86	-77.24	-94.42	-103.95	-96.47	-92.79	-91.96	-95.76	-103.21	-100.50	-104.31	-98.81	....	Goods: Imports f.o.b.	78ab *d*
-23.60	-4.58	-9.57	-20.21	-48.12	-47.88	-40.86	-37.70	-43.81	-47.92	-57.09	-47.75	-50.55	-36.56	....	*Trade Balance*	78ac *d*
10.20	14.63	17.00	20.89	24.95	33.38	37.41	44.59	48.42	52.96	53.93	61.29	74.53	75.94	....	Services: Credit	78ad *d*
-11.80	-17.20	-18.64	-21.64	-25.84	-30.00	-29.84	-32.43	-30.32	-39.48	-41.11	-44.83	-51.17	-50.23	....	Services: Debit	78ae *d*
-25.20	-7.16	-11.21	-20.96	-49.01	-44.50	-33.29	-25.54	-25.71	-34.43	-44.26	-31.30	-27.19	-10.84	....	*Balance on Goods & Services*	78af *d*
—	1.98	2.69	4.33	3.60	4.03	2.60	2.50	2.97	3.07	3.24	2.85	3.61	4.48	....	Income: Credit	78ag *d*
-1.90	-4.39	-5.03	-5.89	-7.59	-8.92	-10.27	-9.86	-9.37	-14.13	-16.61	-21.64	-20.46	-21.94	....	Income: Debit	78ah *d*
-27.10	-9.57	-13.55	-22.52	-53.00	-49.39	-40.95	-32.90	-32.11	-45.49	-57.63	-50.09	-44.04	-28.30	....	*Balance on Gds, Serv. & Inc.*	78ai *d*
25.27	5.54	9.54	13.16	10.24	10.39	11.20	10.88	12.42	14.86	16.26	17.83	17.57	17.51	....	Current Transfers, n.i.e.: Credit	78aj *d*
-4.60	-3.09	-3.05	-2.93	-2.78	-4.53	-3.87	-3.38	-3.73	-7.79	-8.39	-7.66	-7.09	-6.72	....	Current Transfers: Debit	78ak *d*
—	12.48	7.07	11.37	13.58	13.50	13.19	9.80	9.73	8.57	24.54	25.30	22.53	13.92	....	Capital Account, n.i.e.	78bc *d*
—	16.52	8.70	12.85	15.58	14.96	14.74	11.28	11.21	9.37	24.65	25.42	22.64	14.05	....	Capital Account, n.i.e.: Credit	78ba *d*
—	-4.04	-1.63	-1.48	-2.00	-1.45	-1.56	-1.48	-1.48	-.80	-.11	-.12	-.12	-.13	....	Capital Account: Debit	78bb *d*
6.51	3.34	8.20	5.11	32.03	29.32	24.59	22.79	19.97	29.80	45.02	9.73	15.25	2.24	....	Financial Account, n.i.e.	78bj *d*
												-.85	-2.45	....	Direct Investment Abroad	78bd *d*
3.00	5.19	13.52	11.93	17.20	12.89	15.22	20.58	13.20	22.63	54.09	17.79	21.71	11.17	....	Dir. Invest. in Rep. Econ., n.i.e.	78be *d*
—	—	—	—	—	—	—	—	—	.01	—	.48	.08	.78	....	Portfolio Investment Assets	78bf *d*
—	—	—	—	—	—	—	—	—	.01	—			—	....	Equity Securities......................	78bk *d*
—	—	—	—	—	—	—	—	—	—	—	.48	.07	.77	....	Debt Securities	78bl *d*
—	—	—	—	-.37	—	—	—	-.10	—	-7.96	-.02	-.26	—	....	Portfolio Investment Liab., n.i.e.	78bg *d*
—	—	—	—	-.37	—	—	—	-.10	—	-7.96	—	—	—	....	Equity Securities......................	78bm *d*
—	—	—	—	—	—	—	—	—	—	—	-.02	-.26	—	....	Debt Securities	78bn *d*
....	....	....	....	....	....	....	....	....	....	....	....	....	....	....	Financial Derivatives Assets	78bw *d*
....	....	....	....	....	....	....	....	....	....	....	....	....	....	....	Financial Derivatives Liabilities........	78bx *d*
-1.31	-2.81	-11.41	-8.48	8.18	10.78	3.06	-.60	7.20	6.05	-6.55	-9.76	3.38	-6.03	....	Other Investment Assets	78bh *d*
—	—	—	—	—	—	—	—	—	—	—	—	—	—	....	Monetary Authorities	78bo *d*
—	—	—	—	—	—	—	—	—	—	—	—	—	—	....	General Government	78bp *d*
-1.31	-2.81	-11.41	-8.48	8.18	10.78	3.06	-.60	7.20	6.05	-6.55	-9.76	3.38	-6.03	....	Banks	78bq *d*
—	—	—	—	—	—	—	—	—	—	....	....	....	....	....	Other Sectors............................	78br *d*
4.82	.97	6.09	1.67	6.66	6.02	6.31	2.81	-.33	1.11	5.44	1.24	-8.81	-1.23	....	Other Investment Liab., n.i.e.	78bi *d*
—	—	—	—	—	—	—	—	—	—	—	—	—	—	....	Monetary Authorities	78bs *d*
3.20	1.30	6.06	1.83	6.95	7.14	8.01	4.04	.16	1.64	5.82	4.98	-10.32	1.68	....	General Government	78bt *d*
-.18	—	—	—	—	—	—	—	—	—	....	....	....	....	....	Banks	78bu *d*
1.80	-.32	.03	-.16	-.30	-1.11	-1.70	-1.23	-.49	-.54	-.37	-3.74	1.51	-2.91	....	Other Sectors............................	78bv *d*
-.69	-2.15	.18	-5.22	.11	5.75	.07	-3.82	-5.66	-3.18	-11.78	7.13	-2.39	5.35	....	Net Errors and Omissions	78ca *d*
-.61	6.57	8.39	-1.03	.18	5.05	4.22	3.36	.62	-3.23	8.02	2.24	1.84	3.99	....	*Overall Balance*	78cb *d*
.61	-6.57	-8.39	1.03	-.18	-5.05	-4.22	-3.36	-.62	3.23	-8.02	-2.24	-1.84	-3.99	....	Reserves and Related Items	79da *d*
2.00	-6.04	-7.92	3.23	1.83	-3.70	-3.29	-2.60	.11	4.03	-7.16	-1.43	-1.29	-3.77	....	Reserve Assets	79db *d*
-1.52	-.61	-.53	-2.27	-2.03	-1.35	-.94	-.76	-.73	-.80	-.86	-.81	-.55	-.22	....	Use of Fund Credit and Loans........	79dc *d*
.13	.09	.05	.07	.03	—	—	—	—	—	—	—	....	....	....	Exceptional Financing	79de *d*
Year Ending June 30															**Government Finance**	
....	....	....	....	....	....	....	....	....	....	....	....	....	....	....	Deficit (-) or Surplus	80
....	....	....	....	....	....	....	....	....	....	....	....	....	....	....	Revenue	81
....	....	....	....	....	....	....	....	....	....	....	....	....	....	....	Grants Received..........................	81z
....	....	....	....	....	....	....	....	....	....	....	....	....	....	....	Expenditure	82
....	....	....	....	....	....	....	....	....	....	....	....	....	....	....	Lending Minus Repayments	83
Millions of E. Caribbean Dollars															**National Accounts**	
266.2	302.6	341.1	388.2	414.1	449.1	487.2	517.8	541.1	581.7	601.2	638.4	660.0	693.6	....	Gross Domestic Product (GDP)	99b
342.2	366.4	394.0	427.7	426.7	449.1	451.8	461.1	468.8	475.5	483.5	496.9	506.6	....	....	GDP Volume 1990 Prices	99b. *p*
62.6	66.4	69.6	73.0	78.1	80.4	86.7	90.3	92.8	98.4	100.0	103.3	104.8	....	....	GDP Deflator (1995=100)	99bi *p*
Midyear Estimates																
.08	.08	.08	.07	.07	.07	.07	.07	.07	.07	.08	.07	.08	.08	1.07	Population................................	99z

Dominican Republic

243		1970	1971	1972	1973	1974	1975	1976	1977	1978	1979	1980	1981	1982	1983	1984
Exchange Rates																*Pesos per SDR:*
Market Rate ..... aa=	wa	1.000	1.086	1.086	1.206	1.224	1.171	1.162	1.215	1.303	1.317	1.275	1.164	1.103	1.047	.980
																Pesos per US Dollar:
Market Rate ..... ae=	we	1.000	1.000	1.000	1.000	1.000	1.000	1.000	1.000	1.000	1.000	1.000	1.000	1.000	1.000	1.000
Market Rate ..... rf=	wf	1.000	1.000	1.000	1.000	1.000	1.000	1.000	1.000	1.000	1.000	1.000	1.000	1.000	1.000	1.000
Secondary Rate	xe	....	....	....	....	....	....	....	1.250	1.280	1.236	1.232	1.315	1.536	1.800	3.105
Secondary Rate	xf	1.137	1.131	1.112	1.124	1.130	1.170	1.190	1.213	1.245	1.217	1.255	1.278	1.457	....	2.737
																Index Numbers (1995=100):
Market Rate	ahx	1,359.6	800.0	1,359.6	311.1	1,359.6	1,359.6	1,359.6	1,359.6	1,359.6	1,359.6	1,359.6	1,359.6	1,359.6	1,359.6	1,359.6
Nominal Effective Exchange Rate	nec	....	....	....	....	....	....	....	....	....	393.3	403.1	436.9	458.6	458.6	301.6
Real Effective Exchange Rate	rec	....	....	....	....	....	....	....	....	....	....	149.3	151.7	138.5	136.7	97.1
Fund Position																*Millions of SDRs:*
Quota	2f.s	43.0	43.0	43.0	43.0	43.0	43.0	43.0	43.0	55.0	55.0	82.5	82.5	82.5	112.1	112.1
SDRs	1b.s	—	—	6.9	6.8	7.2	6.5	6.0	5.2	4.7	7.2	—	1.6	.5	.2	.4
Reserve Position in the Fund	1c.s	—	—	—	10.8	—	—	—	—	—	—	—	—	—	7.4	—
Total Fund Cred.&Loans Outstg.	2tl	6.6	10.8	3.8	—	—	—	21.5	36.5	36.5	94.3	38.0	19.8	64.1	235.2	225.7
International Liquidity																*Millions of US Dollars Unless Otherwise Indicated:*
Total Reserves minus Gold	1l.d	29.1	52.8	55.3	84.3	87.1	112.6	123.5	180.1	154.0	238.6	201.8	225.2	129.0	171.3	253.5
SDRs	1b.d	—	—	7.5	8.2	8.8	7.6	7.0	6.3	6.1	9.5	—	1.9	.6	.2	.4
Reserve Position in the Fund	1c.d	—	—	—	13.0	—	—	—	—	—	—	—	—	—	7.7	—
Foreign Exchange	1d.d	29.1	52.8	47.8	63.2	78.3	105.0	116.5	173.8	147.9	229.1	201.8	223.3	128.4	163.3	253.1
Gold (Million Fine Troy Ounces)	1ad	.086	.086	.086	.086	.086	.086	.086	.104	.104	.113	.131	.142	.091	.077	.018
Gold (National Valuation)	1and	3.0	3.3	3.3	3.6	3.6	3.6	3.6	4.4	20.2	48.4	72.8	58.7	43.7	31.3	7.9
Monetary Authorities: Other Liab.	4..d	22.5	20.3	14.9	10.3	32.5	72.0	106.6	139.0	152.0	252.8	519.2	748.0	990.5	1,138.9	1,243.8
Deposit Money Banks: Assets	7a.d	7.4	11.4	9.2	8.1	9.8	17.0	36.1	40.4	25.3	56.9	127.4	272.5	292.0	42.8	58.7
Liabilities	7b.d	11.3	25.4	22.3	37.1	69.1	36.5	47.9	76.1	78.9	73.9	154.8	341.3	314.1	93.7	85.1
Other Banking Insts.: Liabilities	7f.d	....	42.0	35.0	34.2	36.2	39.6	48.2	51.1	51.5	46.1	38.9	30.6	26.9	23.3	21.0
Monetary Authorities																*Millions of Pesos:*
Foreign Assets	11	43	68	74	107	113	141	154	211	203	312	308	320	212	244	311
Claims on Central Government	12a	139	157	173	189	249	256	260	270	295	335	364	492	660	867	938
Claims on Nonfin.Pub.Enterprises	12c	1	2	2	2	2	2	2	2	2	2	53	56	137	238	258
Claims on Private Sector	12d	—	—	—	5	2	2	6	6	6	6	76	76	76	76	76
Claims on Deposit Money Banks	12e	61	57	64	77	110	142	153	184	301	346	383	543	683	747	723
Claims on Other Banking Insts	12f	42	49	49	55	75	90	117	117	130	196	266	306	327	360	271
Reserve Money	14	181	211	229	288	422	389	390	500	542	587	566	713	731	850	1,097
of which: Currency Outside DMBs	14a	81	84	99	116	141	158	172	203	224	274	275	324	358	415	593
Liabs.of Centl.Bank: Securities	16ac	—	—	—	—	—	—	—	—	—	—	6	1	—	—	8
Foreign Liabilities	16c	29	32	19	10	32	72	132	183	200	377	568	771	1,061	1,385	1,465
Long-Term Foreign Liabilities	16cl	25	30	30	56	42	54	64	34	87	103	126	111	89	59	31
Central Government Deposits	16d	13	7	11	18	2	61	62	39	4	6	10	6	8	30	2
Counterpart Funds	16e	—	—	—	—	—	—	—	—	—	—	—	—	—	—	—
Capital Accounts	17a	33	42	49	55	58	62	63	69	73	80	81	66	72	112	131
Other Items (Net)	17r	6	10	23	8	–5	–6	–19	–37	31	42	93	125	132	95	–158
of which: Revaluation of Reserves	17rv	—	–2	—	—	—	—	—	—	—	—	—	—	—	—	—
Deposit Money Banks																*Millions of Pesos:*
Reserves	20	109	136	144	187	317	260	255	349	365	375	346	462	444	592	692
Foreign Assets	21	7	11	9	8	10	17	36	40	25	57	127	272	292	43	59
Claims on Central Government	22a	31	39	57	58	63	102	95	86	78	102	133	133	154	159	195
Claims on Local Government	22b	2	2	3	3	2	2	3	6	12	13	15	17	16	17	16
Claims on Nonfin.Pub.Enterprises	22c	19	21	26	41	67	65	56	91	131	135	142	300	392	474	486
Claims on Private Sector	22d	180	217	282	386	578	685	789	851	885	990	1,166	1,158	1,262	1,363	1,504
Claims on Other Banking Insts	22f	36	39	36	41	42	49	55	63	70	63	84	77	76	93	101
Demand Deposits	24	104	124	143	179	266	275	263	314	321	419	459	456	502	562	768
Time, Savings,& Fgn.Currency Dep.	25	101	130	181	245	360	454	458	540	527	510	544	610	650	812	897
Bonds	26ab	—	—	—	—	—	—	—	—	—	—	—	—	—	—	—
Foreign Liabilities	26c	11	25	22	37	69	37	48	76	79	74	155	341	314	94	85
Central Government Deposits	26d	28	27	35	40	54	56	79	84	108	57	54	39	51	96	86
Credit from Monetary Authorities	26g	65	57	64	79	123	138	161	166	223	271	327	447	532	518	569
Capital Accounts	27a	23	26	32	44	64	108	124	136	148	163	183	212	219	252	281
Other Items (Net)	27r	51	77	80	98	143	114	156	170	162	242	291	313	368	408	366
Monetary Survey																*Millions of Pesos:*
Foreign Assets (Net)	31n	10	22	42	68	21	49	10	–8	–50	–82	–287	–520	–871	–1,192	–1,180
Domestic Credit	32	409	493	582	720	1,024	1,136	1,241	1,368	1,497	1,780	2,234	2,569	3,040	3,520	3,756
Claims on Central Govt. (Net)	32an	129	162	184	188	256	241	213	232	261	374	433	580	755	900	1,045
Claims on Local Government	32b	2	2	3	3	2	2	3	6	12	13	15	17	16	17	16
Claims on Nonfin.Pub.Enterprises	32c	20	22	28	43	69	66	58	93	133	137	195	356	529	712	744
Claims on Private Sector	32d	180	217	282	391	580	687	794	857	891	996	1,241	1,234	1,337	1,438	1,579
Claims on Other Banking Insts	32f	78	89	85	96	117	139	172	179	201	259	350	383	403	453	372
Money	34	188	211	248	299	414	444	438	519	545	695	738	781	866	985	1,411
Quasi-Money	35	101	130	181	245	360	454	458	540	527	510	544	610	650	812	897
Bonds	36ab	—	—	—	—	—	—	—	—	—	—	—	—	—	—	—
Liabs.of Centl.Bank: Securities	36ac	—	—	—	—	—	—	—	—	—	—	6	1	—	—	8
Long-Term Foreign Liabilities	36cl	25	30	30	56	42	54	64	34	87	103	126	111	89	59	31
Capital Accounts	37a	56	68	81	99	122	170	187	206	221	243	263	278	291	364	412
Other Items (Net)	37r	49	75	83	90	108	63	105	61	67	146	270	268	272	109	–184
Money plus Quasi-Money	35l	289	341	429	544	774	898	896	1,059	1,072	1,205	1,282	1,392	1,516	1,797	2,308
Other Banking Institutions																*Millions of Pesos:*
Reserves	40	....	—	—	—	2	1	2	3	4	4	7	8	11	12	20
Claims on Central Government	42a	....	43	43	42	46	69	75	85	94	39	51	94	74	82	145
Claims on Nonfin.Pub.Enterprises	42c	....	1	5	5	2	2	2	2	6	5	6	8	4	4	4
Claims on Private Sector	42d	....	133	137	153	206	259	332	437	538	702	879	1,006	1,412	1,597	1,780
Claims on Deposit Money Banks	42e	....	17	37	61	51	54	61	37	35	63	88	131	214	261	300
Time, Savings,& Fgn.Currency Dep.	45	....	23	32	55	75	101	124	156	196	242	327	395	470	547	619
Bonds	46ab	....	6	5	5	5	14	23	41	65	112	159	214	513	642	768
Long-Term Foreign Liabilities	46cl	....	42	35	34	36	40	48	51	52	46	39	31	27	23	21
Credit from Monetary Authorities	46g	....	40	48	63	48	70	86	105	127	145	206	241	254	279	308
Credit from Deposit Money Banks	46h	....	6	5	8	9	10	10	11	9	16	7	9	15	18	26
Capital Accounts	47a	....	101	116	119	123	129	139	150	180	207	234	300	319	361	431
Other Items (Net)	47r	....	–24	–20	–22	11	22	43	51	48	44	58	58	117	87	76

Dominican Republic

243

1985	1986	1987	1988	1989	1990	1991	1992	1993	1994	1995	1996	1997	1998	1999	
End of Period															**Exchange Rates**
3.229	3.763	7.037	8.532	8.332	16.147	18.109	17.291	17.536	19.071	20.015	20.220	19.383	22.230	22.014	Market Rate....................aa= .... wa
End of Period (we) Period Average (wf)															
2.940	3.077	4.960	6.340	6.340	11.350	12.660	12.575	12.767	13.064	13.465	14.062	14.366	15.788	16.039	Market Rate....................ae= .... we
3.113	2.904	3.845	6.113	6.340	8.525	12.692	12.774	12.676	13.160	13.597	13.775	14.265	15.267	16.033	Market Rate....................rf= .... wf
....	....	....	....	....	....	....	....	....	....	....	....	....	....	....	Secondary Rate.. xe
....	....	....	....	....	....	....	....	....	....	....	....	....	....	....	Secondary Rate.. xf
Period Averages															
437.1	467.3	362.1	226.1	211.2	170.0	106.5	106.4	107.3	103.3	100.0	98.7	95.3	88.9	84.8	Market Rate .... ah*x*
268.4	247.7	196.9	133.3	139.5	116.3	84.0	88.7	97.3	104.5	100.0	100.3	99.6	96.2	91.2	Nominal Effective Exchange Rate .... ne*c*
108.5	103.0	88.0	73.8	89.0	87.9	88.8	89.3	93.2	97.2	100.0	102.3	107.3	106.6	105.6	Real Effective Exchange Rate .... re*c*
End of Period															**Fund Position**
112.1	112.1	112.1	112.1	112.1	112.1	112.1	158.8	158.8	158.8	158.8	158.8	158.8	158.8	218.9	Quota 2f.*s*
28.8	—	—	—	—	—	—	.1	10.3	2.5	.3	.3	.2	.2	.2	SDRs 1b.*s*
—	—	—	—	—	—	—	—	—	—	—	—	—	—	—	Reserve Position in the Fund 1c.*s*
270.4	248.8	199.9	161.8	93.2	50.4	62.4	89.4	135.5	129.9	107.5	66.5	21.1	39.7	39.7	Total Fund Cred.&Loans Outstg. 2tl
End of Period															**International Liquidity**
340.1	376.3	182.2	254.0	164.0	61.6	441.9	499.8	651.2	252.1	365.6	350.3	391.0	501.9	689.4	Total Reserves minus Gold..................... 1l.*d*
31.6	—	—	—	—	—	.1	.1	14.1	3.7	.5	.4	.3	.3	.3	SDRs 1b.*d*
—	—	—	—	—	—	—	—	—	—	—	—	—	—	—	Reserve Position in the Fund 1c.*d*
308.5	376.3	182.2	254.0	164.0	61.6	441.8	499.7	637.1	248.4	365.0	349.8	390.7	501.6	689.1	Foreign Exchange 1d.*d*
.018	.018	.018	.018	.018	.018	.018	.018	.018	.018	.018	.018	.018	.018	.018	Gold (Million Fine Troy Ounces)........... 1ad
5.9	7.1	8.8	7.6	7.5	6.8	6.5	6.1	6.9	6.8	6.8	6.7	5.5	5.3	....	Gold (National Valuation) 1an*d*
1,395.8	229.0	257.7	139.7	202.6	180.5	150.8	26.0	22.3	90.8	102.4	89.5	88.6	50.8	42.1	Monetary Authorities: Other Liab. .... 4..*d*
41.9	55.9	215.8	248.3	233.6	219.6	230.4	232.5	191.8	189.4	183.8	174.5	236.7	307.0	322.5	Deposit Money Banks: Assets 7a.*d*
13.3	26.2	210.6	212.9	212.2	220.5	226.1	218.2	184.0	183.3	55.0	97.6	188.6	401.4	458.9	Liabilities........... 7b.*d*
24.0	22.4	60.9	107.8	12.9	28.1	41.8	49.3	62.7	91.2	8.4	10.9	6.3	17.2	22.7	Other Banking Insts.: Liabilities 7f.*d*
End of Period															**Monetary Authorities**
1,190	1,327	1,185	1,981	1,411	2,086	6,326	7,128	9,008	4,804	6,577	6,962	7,696	10,071	13,599	Foreign Assets 11
953	941	1,046	1,087	1,104	1,146	1,972	1,953	938	558	605	1,236	1,537	1,632	2,416	Claims on Central Government 12a
209	151	285	291	323	334	979	585	738	2,959	1,609	1,632	1,665	1,987	2,520	Claims on Nonfin.Pub.Enterprises........... 12c
76	76	76	76	96	103	537	550	550	45	45	45	45	5	5	Claims on Private Sector........................ 12d
724	815	840	896	1,092	1,103	1,349	1,383	1,343	2,075	2,092	3,108	2,161	2,917	2,992	Claims on Deposit Money Banks 12e
305	324	349	536	532	353	441	1,087	923	292	307	320	388	384	375	Claims on Other Banking Insts 12f
1,085	2,112	1,983	4,001	5,170	6,801	10,277	11,602	14,889	14,956	17,412	19,306	22,963	28,110	32,328	Reserve Money 14
677	937	1,313	1,876	2,683	3,733	4,586	5,913	6,905	7,679	8,892	9,635	11,534	12,568	16,889	*of which: Currency Outside DMBs* 14a
55	101	156	211	126	138	646	518	196	743	1,991	4,099	4,357	3,499	5,135	Liabs.of Centl.Bank: Securities 16ac
4,977	1,641	2,685	2,266	2,061	2,863	3,039	1,873	2,661	3,663	3,529	2,602	1,682	1,684	1,549	Foreign Liabilities 16c
97	3,632	5,711	8,078	8,492	16,095	17,585	15,734	15,793	10,780	11,652	12,454	12,205	13,110	13,207	Long-Term Foreign Liabilities 16cl
68	51	463	111	262	198	1,496	2,308	2,179	151	344	400	351	424	479	Central Government Deposits 16d
—	—	—	—	—	—	—	—	—	—	—	—	—	—	—	Counterpart Funds 16e
175	-84	-90	-575	-1,068	-1,630	-892	501	-922	-491	-1,482	-2,915	-4,143	-5,523	-6,957	Capital Accounts 17a
-2,999	-3,817	-7,126	-9,225	-10,486	-19,340	-20,545	-19,849	-21,295	-19,069	-22,210	-22,644	-23,924	-24,307	-23,834	Other Items (Net) 17r
-385	-3,389	-5,423	-7,780	-8,318	-14,570	-17,568	-17,627	-17,883	-16,415	-16,961	-17,326	-17,376	-17,872	-18,169	*of which:* Revaluation of Reserves 17rv
End of Period															**Deposit Money Banks**
770	1,797	1,258	2,909	3,315	4,268	7,302	7,438	8,992	9,214	10,654	10,761	12,964	16,947	17,331	Reserves 20
123	172	1,070	1,574	1,481	2,493	2,917	2,924	2,449	2,474	2,475	2,453	3,400	4,846	5,172	Foreign Assets 21
190	448	214	423	410	552	470	465	371	540	505	536	1,934	1,998	4,144	Claims on Central Government 22a
17	16	17	17	10	7	6	3	5	6	29	4	6	4	14	Claims on Local Government 22b
608	589	789	990	1,130	1,129	1,446	1,424	1,431	1,470	2,366	4,485	4,426	3,938	4,715	Claims on Nonfin.Pub.Enterprises........... 22c
1,852	2,766	3,442	4,455	6,858	8,924	11,126	15,806	19,442	22,166	27,688	34,500	44,404	52,744	66,877	Claims on Private Sector........................ 22d
111	290	366	180	256	606	555	965	805	799	554	778	764	957	760	Claims on Other Banking Insts 22f
985	1,662	1,895	3,081	3,527	5,160	6,610	7,221	8,104	8,470	10,064	13,540	16,081	16,782	18,884	Demand Deposits 24
1,037	2,256	2,287	3,301	4,580	6,262	9,610	13,322	17,092	19,854	23,458	27,022	34,725	43,380	54,211	Time, Savings,& Fgn.Currency Dep.......... 25
—	—	—	—	—	—	—	—	133	122	80	138	76	17	398	Bonds 26ab
39	81	1,045	1,350	1,345	2,503	2,863	2,743	2,349	2,394	740	1,372	2,710	6,337	7,361	Foreign Liabilities..................................... 26c
182	423	324	498	556	733	1,535	2,774	2,568	1,746	2,533	2,594	3,076	2,500	3,578	Central Government Deposits 26d
582	683	706	864	1,026	1,437	1,214	1,103	902	1,334	1,310	1,220	1,532	2,222	2,449	Credit from Monetary Authorities 26g
371	504	640	1,188	1,575	2,122	2,951	3,028	3,388	4,050	4,581	5,203	6,524	8,220	10,224	Capital Accounts 27a
475	469	260	266	851	-239	-962	-1,165	-1,042	-1,301	1,506	2,428	3,175	1,975	1,907	Other Items (Net) 27r
End of Period															**Monetary Survey**
-3,703	-223	-1,474	-61	-514	-787	3,341	5,435	6,447	1,221	4,784	5,441	6,704	6,896	9,862	Foreign Assets (Net) 31n
4,072	5,127	5,797	7,444	9,900	12,221	14,503	17,757	20,457	26,938	30,832	40,542	51,742	60,726	77,768	Domestic Credit 32
894	916	473	901	696	767	-588	-2,665	-3,438	-798	-1,766	-1,221	43	706	2,503	Claims on Central Govt. (Net) 32an
17	16	17	17	10	7	6	3	5	6	29	4	6	4	14	Claims on Local Government 32b
817	739	1,074	1,281	1,453	1,463	2,425	2,010	2,170	4,429	3,975	6,117	6,092	5,925	7,235	Claims on Nonfin.Pub.Enterprises 32c
1,927	2,841	3,518	4,530	6,954	9,026	11,664	16,356	19,992	22,211	27,733	34,545	44,449	52,749	66,881	Claims on Private Sector 32d
416	614	715	715	788	958	996	2,053	1,728	1,091	861	1,098	1,152	1,342	1,135	Claims on Other Banking Insts 32f
1,683	2,611	3,216	4,967	6,266	9,196	11,297	13,231	15,065	16,198	18,996	23,225	27,703	29,416	35,840	Money 34
1,037	2,256	2,287	3,301	4,580	6,262	9,610	13,322	17,092	19,854	23,458	27,022	34,725	43,380	54,211	Quasi-Money.. 35
—	—	—	—	—	—	—	—	133	122	80	138	76	17	398	Bonds 36ab
55	101	156	211	126	138	646	518	196	743	1,991	4,099	4,357	3,499	5,135	Liabs.of Centl.Bank: Securities 36ac
97	3,632	5,711	8,078	8,492	16,095	17,585	15,734	15,793	10,780	11,652	12,454	12,205	13,110	13,207	Long-Term Foreign Liabilities 36cl
546	419	550	612	507	492	2,059	3,528	2,466	3,558	3,098	2,288	2,381	2,696	3,267	Capital Accounts 37a
-3,048	-4,114	-7,597	-9,786	-10,585	-20,748	-23,353	-23,141	-23,842	-23,097	-23,659	-23,243	-23,001	-24,496	-24,428	Other Items (Net) 37r
2,720	4,866	5,503	8,268	10,846	15,458	20,908	26,553	32,157	36,052	42,454	50,247	62,428	72,795	90,051	Money plus Quasi-Money 35l
End of Period															**Other Banking Institutions**
33	47	80	130	210	309	327	415	316	329	332	353	429	483	796	Reserves 40
161	164	173	80	13	200	311	277	474	522	774	569	452	837	971	Claims on Central Government 42a
5	5	5	5	5	5	8	11	10	12	19	18	18	19	19	Claims on Nonfin.Pub.Enterprises........... 42c
2,255	2,811	3,708	4,725	6,422	7,535	8,828	10,088	10,365	12,263	12,513	13,797	16,324	19,797	24,062	Claims on Private Sector........................ 42d
309	653	687	942	1,059	1,092	1,748	2,589	3,388	2,358	3,097	3,674	4,303	5,368	6,418	Claims on Deposit Money Banks 42e
837	869	1,167	1,386	1,683	1,957	2,706	3,444	3,647	3,679	3,981	4,499	5,464	6,731	6,778	Time, Savings,& Fgn.Currency Dep.......... 45
944	1,682	2,087	2,499	3,292	3,939	5,018	6,310	6,589	7,290	8,474	9,418	11,295	13,120	17,634	Bonds 46ab
71	69	302	684	82	319	529	620	800	1,192	113	153	90	271	364	Long-Term Foreign Liabilities 46cl
364	414	410	627	872	926	1,067	1,216	1,641	1,623	1,464	1,434	1,360	1,298	1,112	Credit from Monetary Authorities 46g
20	28	78	68	177	311	298	354	429	424	460	478	457	539	458	Credit from Deposit Money Banks 46h
529	652	812	1,115	1,429	1,823	2,122	2,554	2,543	2,667	2,818	2,855	3,390	4,430	5,831	Capital Accounts 47a
-3	-33	-204	-497	174	-135	-517	-1,119	-1,096	-1,390	-576	-428	-530	114	89	Other Items (Net) 47r

Dominican Republic

		1970	1971	1972	1973	1974	1975	1976	1977	1978	1979	1980	1981	1982	1983	1984
Banking Survey															*Millions of Pesos:*	
Foreign Assets (Net)	51n	....	22	42	68	21	49	10	−8	−50	−82	−287	−520	−871	−1,192	−1,180
Domestic Credit	52	....	581	681	824	1,162	1,327	1,479	1,713	1,935	2,266	2,820	3,294	4,126	4,750	5,313
Claims on Central Govt. (Net)	52an	....	205	227	230	303	310	288	317	356	413	484	674	829	981	1,190
Claims on Local Government	52b	....	2	3	3	2	2	3	6	12	13	15	17	16	17	16
Claims on Nonfin.Pub.Enterprises	52c	....	24	32	47	71	69	61	95	138	142	201	363	533	716	748
Claims on Private Sector	52d	....	350	419	544	786	946	1,127	1,294	1,429	1,698	2,120	2,239	2,749	3,036	3,359
Liquid Liabilities	55l	....	364	461	599	848	998	1,018	1,212	1,265	1,442	1,602	1,778	1,975	2,332	2,907
Bonds	56ab	....	6	5	5	5	14	23	41	65	112	159	214	513	642	768
Liabs.of Centl.Bank: Securities	56ac		—	—	—	—	—	—	—	—	—	6	1	—	—	8
Long-Term Foreign Liabilities	56cl	....	72	65	90	78	94	112	85	139	149	165	142	116	82	52
Capital Accounts	57a	....	169	197	218	245	299	325	355	401	450	498	578	610	724	843
Other Items (Net)	57r	....	−9	−5	−20	7	−29	10	11	15	30	104	62	41	−222	−444
Interest Rates															*Percent Per Annum*	
Money Market Rate	60b	....	....	....	....	....	....	....	....	....	....	....	....	....	....	....
Savings Rate	60k	....	....	....	....	....	....	....	....	....	....	....	....	....	....	....
Deposit Rate	60l	....	....	....	....	....	....	....	....	....	....	....	....	....	....	....
Lending Rate	60p	....	....	....	....	....	....	....	....	....	....	....	....	....	....	....
Prices and Labor															*Index Numbers (1995=100):*	
Consumer Prices	64	2.4	2.5	2.7	3.1	3.5	4.0	4.3	4.9	15.0	5.5	16.4	6.9	7.4	7.8	9.4
															Number in Thousands:	
Labor Force	67d	....	....	....	....	....	....	....	....	....	....	....	....	....	....	....
Employment	67e	....	....	....	....	....	....	....	....	....	....	....	....	....	....	....
Unemployment	67c	....	....	....	....	....	....	....	....	....	....	....	....	....	....	....
Unemployment Rate (%)	67r	....	....	....	....	....	....	....	....	....	....	....	....	....	....	....
International Transactions															*Millions of US Dollars*	
Exports	70..d	249.1	243.0	347.6	442.1	636.8	893.8	716.4	780.4	675.5	868.6	961.9	1,188.0	767.7	785.2	868.1
Imports, f.o.b.	71.vd	266.8	311.1	337.7	421.9	673.0	772.7	763.6	847.8	859.7	1,054.6	1,425.7	1,450.2	1,255.8	1,279.0	1,257.1
															1995=100	
Volume of Exports	72	94	111	148	165	166	147	159	168	135	161	119	130	118	142	143
															1995=100:	
Unit Value of Exports	74..d	35	20	40	48	67	84	78	102	90	98	100	110	79	77	91
Balance of Payments															*Millions of US Dollars:*	
Current Account, n.i.e.	78ald	−101.9	−129.4	−47.0	−96.6	−241.0	−72.8	−129.2	−128.6	−311.9	−331.3	−719.9	−389.4	−442.6	−417.9	−163.4
Goods: Exports f.o.b.	78aad	214.0	240.7	347.6	442.1	636.8	893.8	716.4	780.5	675.5	868.6	961.9	1,188.0	767.7	785.2	868.1
Goods: Imports f.o.b.	78abd	−278.0	−309.7	−337.7	−421.9	−673.0	−772.7	−763.6	−849.3	−862.4	−1,137.5	−1,519.7	−1,451.7	−1,257.3	−1,279.0	−1,257.1
Trade Balance	78acd	−64.0	−69.0	9.9	20.2	−36.2	121.1	−47.2	−68.8	−186.9	−268.9	−557.8	−263.7	−489.6	−493.8	−389.0
Services: Credit	78add	43.0	49.5	63.5	71.5	93.4	116.2	127.8	146.7	152.5	266.3	309.4	324.6	374.1	456.6	501.5
Services: Debit	78aed	−86.2	−98.5	−104.1	−142.0	−243.4	−236.3	−226.4	−247.7	−291.6	−346.8	−399.0	−366.7	−277.3	−298.6	−299.5
Balance on Goods & Services	78afd	−107.2	−118.0	−30.7	−50.3	−186.2	1.0	−145.8	−169.8	−326.0	−349.4	−647.4	−305.8	−392.8	−335.8	−187.0
Income: Credit	78agd	1.5	1.5	1.5	2.8	5.0	5.2	8.9	12.3	20.8	31.9	41.8	11.8	4.4	6.9	5.8
Income: Debit	78ahd	−27.4	−30.3	−48.4	−79.7	−94.8	−118.0	−118.1	−110.7	−156.5	−219.6	−318.8	−288.4	−259.2	−304.0	−247.2
Balance on Gds, Serv. & Inc.	78aid	−133.1	−146.8	−77.6	−127.2	−276.0	−111.8	−255.0	−268.2	−461.7	−537.1	−924.4	−582.4	−647.6	−632.9	−428.4
Current Transfers, n.i.e.: Credit	78ajd	35.4	21.0	34.3	34.0	37.9	41.3	127.5	141.5	150.2	207.5	204.8	193.0	205.0	215.0	265.0
Current Transfers: Debit	78akd	−4.2	−3.6	−3.7	−3.4	−2.9	−2.3	−1.7	−1.9	−.4	−1.7	−.3				
Capital Account, n.i.e.	78bcd	—	—	—	—	—	—	—	—	—	—	—	—	—	—	—
Capital Account, n.i.e.: Credit	78bad	—	—	—	—	—	—	—	—	—	—	—	—	—	—	—
Capital Account: Debit	78bbd	—	—	—	—	—	—	—	—	—	—	—	—	—	—	—
Financial Account, n.i.e.	78bjd	109.2	102.1	93.6	69.9	239.6	179.2	166.9	194.0	121.6	308.4	626.1	413.0	147.2	−92.7	231.9
Direct Investment Abroad	78bdd	—	—	—	—	—	—	—	—	—	—	—	—	—	—	—
Dir. Invest. in Rep. Econ., n.i.e.	78bed	71.6	65.0	43.5	34.5	53.6	63.9	60.0	71.5	63.6	17.1	92.7	79.7	−1.4	48.2	68.5
Portfolio Investment Assets	78bfd	—	—	—	—	—	—	—	—	—	—	—	—	—	—	—
Equity Securities	78bkd	—	—	—	—	—	—	—	—	—	—	—	—	—	—	—
Debt Securities	78bld	—	—	—	—	—	—	—	—	—	—	—	—	—	—	—
Portfolio Investment Liab. n.i.e.	78bgd	—	—	—	—	—	—	—	—	—	—	—	—	—	—	—
Equity Securities	78bmd	—	—	—	—	—	—	—	—	—	—	—	—	—	—	—
Debt Securities	78bnd	—	—	—	—	—	—	—	—	—	—	—	—	—	—	—
Financial Derivatives Assets	78bwd	....	....	....	....	....	....	....	....	....	....	....	....	....	....	....
Financial Derivatives Liabilities	78bxd	....	....	....	....	....	....	....	....	....	....	....	....	....	....	....
Other Investment Assets	78bhd	−2.1	−4.7	−1.0	−1.4	−1.7	−7.2	−5.8	8.1	15.2	−17.3	10.7	6.4	−19.1	−4.9	−19.6
Monetary Authorities	78bod	....														
General Government	78bpd	—	−.7	−3.2	−2.5	—	—	3.7	−1.4	.2	−6.7	—	—	—	—	—
Banks	78bqd	−2.1	−4.0	2.2	1.1	−1.7	−7.2	−9.5	9.5	15.0	−10.6	10.7	6.4	−19.1	−4.9	−19.6
Other Sectors	78brd															
Other Investment Liab., n.i.e.	78bid	39.7	41.8	51.1	36.8	187.7	122.5	112.7	114.4	42.8	308.6	522.7	326.9	167.7	−136.0	183.0
Monetary Authorities	78bsd	.1	.1	3.4	3.5	4.3	39.7	−7.5	3.6	−39.3	−134.5	33.4	−26.7	−46.8	−153.2	−149.1
General Government	78btd	30.6	14.9	31.8	23.5	61.7	49.0	59.1	82.2	129.7	314.1	241.7	241.7	331.8	202.8	273.0
Banks	78bud	−5.8	14.0	−3.0	14.7	32.1	−32.6	1.5	−.8	3.6	−19.2	−.2	34.9	−27.6	33.6	−4.4
Other Sectors	78bvd	14.8	12.8	18.9	−4.9	89.6	66.4	59.6	29.4	−51.2	148.2	247.8	77.0	−89.7	−219.2	63.5
Net Errors and Omissions	78cad	−16.8	40.3	−32.8	50.4	1.5	−68.8	−70.9	−16.8	69.2	−73.5	48.0	−54.5	−31.1	10.6	29.7
Overall Balance	78cbd	−9.5	13.0	13.8	23.7	.1	37.6	−33.2	48.6	−121.1	−96.4	−45.8	−30.9	−326.5	−500.0	98.2
Reserves and Related Items	79dad	9.5	−13.0	−13.8	−23.7	−.1	−37.6	33.2	−48.6	121.1	96.4	45.8	30.9	326.5	500.0	−98.2
Reserve Assets	79dbd	13.1	−19.5	2.4	−28.4	−4.1	−27.5	−10.4	−66.9	39.0	−72.3	39.5	−16.8	96.9	−46.3	−87.3
Use of Fund Credit and Loans	79dcd	−8.0	4.2	−7.6	−4.5	—	—	24.8	17.4	—	75.4	−72.1	−22.0	49.9	185.3	−9.8
Exceptional Financing	79ded	4.5	2.3	−8.6	9.2	4.0	−10.1	18.8	.9	82.1	93.2	78.4	69.7	179.7	361.1	−1.1

End of Period — Banking Survey

1985	1986	1987	1988	1989	1990	1991	1992	1993	1994	1995	1996	1997	1998	1999		Code
-3,703	-223	-1,474	-61	-514	-787	3,341	5,435	6,447	1,221	4,784	5,441	6,704	6,896	9,862	Foreign Assets (Net)	51n
6,076	7,492	8,967	11,538	15,552	19,003	22,654	26,080	29,577	38,644	43,277	53,828	67,384	80,036	101,685	Domestic Credit	52
1,055	1,080	646	980	709	967	-277	-2,388	-2,964	-276	-992	-652	496	1,543	3,474	Claims on Central Govt. (Net)	52an
17	16	17	17	10	7	6	3	5	6	29	4	6	4	14	Claims on Local Government	52b
821	744	1,079	1,285	1,458	1,468	2,433	2,020	2,180	4,440	3,994	6,134	6,110	5,944	7,254	Claims on Nonfin.Pub.Enterprises	52c
4,183	5,652	7,225	9,255	13,376	16,561	20,491	26,444	30,356	34,474	40,246	48,342	60,772	72,545	90,944	Claims on Private Sector	52d
3,524	5,688	6,590	9,524	12,319	17,105	23,287	29,582	35,488	39,401	46,103	54,392	67,464	79,043	96,033	Liquid Liabilities	55l
944	1,682	2,087	2,499	3,292	3,939	5,018	6,310	6,722	7,412	8,554	9,556	11,371	13,137	18,032	Bonds	56ab
55	101	156	211	126	138	646	518	196	743	1,991	4,099	4,357	3,499	5,135	Liabs.of Centl.Bank: Securities	56ac
168	3,700	6,013	8,762	8,574	16,414	18,113	16,354	16,593	11,972	11,765	12,607	12,295	13,381	13,571	Long-Term Foreign Liabilities	56cl
1,075	1,071	1,362	1,727	1,936	2,315	4,181	6,082	5,009	6,225	5,916	5,144	5,771	7,127	9,098	Capital Accounts	57a
-3,392	-4,973	-8,714	-11,246	-11,209	-21,695	-25,249	-27,331	-27,984	-25,889	-26,268	-26,529	-27,170	-29,255	-30,321	Other Items (Net)	57r

Percent Per Annum — Interest Rates

1985	1986	1987	1988	1989	1990	1991	1992	1993	1994	1995	1996	1997	1998	1999		Code
....	....	....	....	....	....	6.20	5.58	5.00	4.87	....	14.70	13.01	16.68	15.30	Money Market Rate	60b
....	....	....	....	....	....	....	....	....	4.66	5.00	4.74	4.51	4.54	....	Savings Rate	60k
....	....	....	....	....	....	20.02	16.70	14.04	13.70	14.94	13.91	13.40	17.65	16.07	Deposit Rate	60l
....	....	....	....	....	....	35.26	28.34	29.89	28.68	30.68	23.73	21.01	25.64	25.05	Lending Rate	60p

Period Averages (1995=100) — Prices and Labor

1985	1986	1987	1988	1989	1990	1991	1992	1993	1994	1995	1996	1997	1998	1999		Code
13.7	14.7	16.7	24.0	33.8	50.9	74.8	78.0	82.1	88.9	100.0	105.4	114.1	119.3	127.0	Consumer Prices	64

Period Averages

1985	1986	1987	1988	1989	1990	1991	1992	1993	1994	1995	1996	1997	1998	1999		Code
....	....	....	....	....	....	....	....	....	....	3,008	2,920	3,594	....	....	Labor Force	67d
....	....	....	....	....	....	2,252	2,406	2,417	2,401	2,401	2,523	2,652	....	....	Employment	67e
....	....	....	....	....	....	548	612	599	457	452	494	504	....	....	Unemployment	67c
....	....	....	....	....	....	19.7	20.3	19.9	16.0	15.9	16.7	15.9	....	....	Unemployment Rate (%)	67r

Millions of US Dollars — International Transactions

1985	1986	1987	1988	1989	1990	1991	1992	1993	1994	1995	1996	1997	1998	1999		Code
735.2	717.6	711.3	889.7	924.4	734.5	658.3	562.4	511.0	644.0	766.7	816.7	881.7	795.0	....	Exports	70..d
1,293.0	1,245.8	1,591.5	1,608.0	1,963.8	1,792.8	1,728.8	2,174.6	2,118.4	2,991.7	3,164.2	3,580.7	4,192.0	4,896.6	....	Imports, f.o.b.	71.vd

1995=100

1985	1986	1987	1988	1989	1990	1991	1992	1993	1994	1995	1996	1997	1998	1999		Code
127	101	125	126	131	107	102	95	99	96	100	106	109	103	....	Volume of Exports	72

Indices of Unit Values in US Dollars

1985	1986	1987	1988	1989	1990	1991	1992	1993	1994	1995	1996	1997	1998	1999		Code
82	82	71	107	116	101	91	90	69	88	100	101	105	82	....	Unit Value of Exports	74..d

Minus Sign Indicates Debit — Balance of Payments

1985	1986	1987	1988	1989	1990	1991	1992	1993	1994	1995	1996	1997	1998	1999		Code
-107.6	-183.4	-364.1	-18.9	-327.3	-279.6	-157.3	-707.9	-532.9	-283.0	-182.8	-212.7	-163.0	-335.7	....	Current Account, n.i.e.	78ald
738.5	722.1	711.3	889.7	924.4	734.5	658.3	562.5	3,211.0	3,452.5	3,779.5	4,052.8	4,613.7	4,980.5	....	Goods: Exports f.o.b.	78aad
-1,285.9	-1,351.7	-1,591.5	-1,608.0	-1,963.8	-1,792.8	-1,728.8	-2,174.3	-4,654.2	-4,903.2	-5,170.4	-5,727.0	-6,608.7	-7,597.3	....	Goods: Imports f.o.b.	78abd
-547.4	-629.6	-880.2	-718.3	-1,039.4	-1,058.3	-1,070.5	-1,611.8	-1,443.2	-1,450.7	-1,390.9	-1,674.2	-1,995.0	-2,616.8	....	Trade Balance	78acd
584.3	692.9	852.0	1,013.4	1,041.1	1,097.2	1,198.7	1,348.6	1,537.1	1,787.6	1,951.3	2,140.0	2,446.6	2,501.5	....	Services: Credit	78add
-274.5	-283.1	-360.4	-397.0	-464.7	-440.4	-479.3	-555.1	-823.8	-921.1	-966.4	-1,121.4	-1,171.3	-1,319.5	....	Services: Debit	78aed
-237.6	-219.8	-388.6	-101.9	-463.0	-401.5	-351.1	-818.3	-729.9	-583.9	-406.0	-655.6	-719.7	-1,434.8	....	Balance on Goods & Services	78afd
21.6	17.0	11.6	8.5	107.1	86.3	87.2	54.7	103.6	101.4	128.1	130.3	140.4	168.2	....	Income: Credit	78agd
-247.9	-266.7	-317.7	-279.1	-355.8	-335.0	-279.9	-376.1	-800.6	-783.3	-897.1	-855.1	-935.8	-1,055.6	....	Income: Debit	78ahd
-463.9	-469.5	-694.7	-372.5	-711.7	-650.2	-543.8	-1,139.7	-1,426.9	-1,265.8	-1,175.0	-1,380.4	-1,515.1	-2,322.2	....	Balance on Gds, Serv. & Inc.	78aid
356.3	286.1	330.6	353.6	384.4	370.6	386.5	431.8	908.4	996.8	1,007.7	1,187.6	1,373.1	2,016.9	....	Current Transfers, n.i.e.: Credit	78ajd
								-14.4	-14.0	-15.5	-19.9	-21.0	-30.4	....	Current Transfers: Debit	78akd
—	—	—	—	—	—	—	—	—	—	—	—	—	—	....	Capital Account, n.i.e.	78bcd
—	—	—	—	—	—	—	—	—	—	—	—	—	—	....	Capital Account, n.i.e.: Credit	78bad
—	—	—	—	—	—	—	—	—	—	—	....	....	....	....	Capital Account: Debit	78bbd
43.6	171.1	-27.5	-15.6	137.9	-73.8	-134.1	74.8	-226.6	368.0	253.6	64.1	447.6	696.0	....	Financial Account, n.i.e.	78bjd
—	—	—	—	—	—	—	—	—	—	—	....	....	....	....	Direct Investment Abroad	78bdd
36.2	50.0	89.0	106.1	110.0	132.8	145.0	179.7	189.3	206.8	414.3	96.5	420.6	699.8	....	Dir. Invest. in Rep. Econ., n.i.e.	78bed
—	—	—	—	—	—	—	—	....	-38.9	-2.9	-7.3	-5.6	-17.5	....	Portfolio Investment Assets	78bfd
—	—	—	—	—	—	—	—	....	....	....	-4.0	-2.1	-13.7	....	Equity Securities	78bkd
—	—	—	—	—	—	—	—	....	-38.9	-2.9	-3.3	-3.5	-3.8	....	Debt Securities	78bld
—	—	—	—	—	—	—	—	....	....	....	....	-1.9	-3.8	....	Portfolio Investment Liab., n.i.e.	78bgd
—	—	—	—	—	—	—	—	....	....	....	....	....	....	....	Equity Securities	78bmd
—	—	—	—	—	—	—	—	....	....	....	....	-1.9	-3.8	....	Debt Securities	78bnd
....	....	....	....	....	....	....	....	....	....	....	....	....	....	....	Financial Derivatives Assets	78bwd
....	....	....	....	....	....	....	....	....	....	....	....	....	....	....	Financial Derivatives Liabilities	78bxd
-64.2	34.2	-34.7	-83.0	-98.0	89.3	-196.6	128.8	-49.2	176.8	-263.1	42.3	-220.1	-66.4	....	Other Investment Assets	78bhd
....	....	....	....	....	....	....	....	....	-15.2	-.6	-.9	-.9	-1.0	....	Monetary Authorities	78bod
....	....	....	....	....	....	....	....	....	....	....	....	....	....	....	General Government	78bpd
-64.2	34.2	-34.7	-83.0	82.0	-.7	-6.6	-1.2	-26.7	18.0	-39.0	17.0	-40.7	-53.2	....	Banks	78bqd
—	—	—	—	-180.0	90.0	-190.0	130.0	-22.5	174.0	-223.5	26.2	-178.5	-12.2	....	Other Sectors	78brd
71.6	86.9	-81.8	-38.7	125.9	-295.9	-82.5	-233.7	-366.7	23.3	105.3	-67.4	254.6	83.9	....	Other Investment Liab., n.i.e.	78bid
-73.3	-177.8	-244.3	-210.6	68.9	-255.5	-72.1	-131.6	-465.2	31.1	27.1	-22.8	-17.3	-88.7	....	Monetary Authorities	78bsd
202.7	220.0	153.5	124.8	-4.2	-64.4	-20.0	-66.2	-75.9	-59.5	-18.8	-35.3	-64.2	-68.4	....	General Government	78btd
-45.8	44.7	9.0	47.1	-3.8	40.8	-4.7	-12.7	-9.5	45.4	32.1	89.7	172.3	223.2	....	Banks	78bud
-12.0	—	—	—	65.0	-16.8	14.3	-23.2	183.9	6.3	64.9	-99.0	163.8	17.8	....	Other Sectors	78bvd
155.7	82.3	248.9	35.6	-73.6	-120.7	548.3	569.0	215.1	-596.0	75.3	108.5	-193.3	-350.5	....	Net Errors and Omissions	78cad
91.7	70.0	-142.7	1.1	-263.0	-474.1	256.9	-64.0	-544.4	-511.0	146.1	-40.1	91.3	9.8	....	*Overall Balance*	78cbd
-91.7	-70.0	142.7	-1.1	263.0	474.1	-256.9	64.0	544.4	511.0	-146.1	40.1	-91.3	-9.8	....	Reserves and Related Items	79dad
-91.9	-18.0	209.7	-58.9	90.0	49.0	-357.4	-63.5	-153.5	384.7	-131.2	15.2	-39.5	-98.2	....	Reserve Assets	79dbd
49.2	-26.1	-62.9	-51.2	-88.0	-56.9	15.9	37.3	63.9	-8.1	-34.0	-59.4	-62.4	26.8	....	Use of Fund Credit and Loans	79dcd
-49.0	-25.9	-4.1	109.0	261.0	482.0	84.6	90.2	634.0	134.4	19.1	84.4	10.6	61.6	....	Exceptional Financing	79ded

Dominican Republic

	1970	1971	1972	1973	1974	1975	1976	1977	1978	1979	1980	1981	1982	1983	1984
Government Finance														*Millions of Pesos:*	
Deficit (-) or Surplus................ 80	-10.1	-19.7	-7.3	-15.5	-26.0	12.5	29.5	3.4	-67.4	-268.8	-162.7	-141.8	-232.1	-214.2	-71.1
Total Revenue and Grants.......... 81y	244.4	276.4	316.8	361.0	474.2	652.4	584.7	629.3	596.2	690.8	890.8	926.0	755.6	925.4	1,173.5
Revenue 81	244.4	276.4	316.8	361.0	474.2	652.4	584.7	629.3	596.2	690.1	889.4	919.4	752.8	924.0	1,167.8
Grants 81z	—	—	—	—	—	—	—	—	—	.7	1.4	6.6	2.8	1.4	5.7
Exp. & Lending Minus Repay. ... 82z	....	....	....	....	....	....	....	....	....	959.6	1,053.5	1,067.8	987.7	1,139.6	1,244.6
Expenditure 82	254.5	296.1	324.1	376.5	500.2	639.9	555.2	625.9	663.6	897.9	1,053.5	1,067.9	988.8	1,136.1	1,236.9
Lending Minus Repayments 83	....	....	....	....	....	....	....	....	....	61.7	—	-.1	-1.1	3.5	7.7
Total Financing 80h	10.1	19.7	7.3	15.3	26.0	-12.6	-29.5	-3.5	67.4	268.8	162.7	141.7	232.2	214.2	71.1
Domestic 84a	-.1	11.3	6.5	5.4	30.9	-6.7	-20.1	6.4	78.7	89.0	70.0	88.0	183.8	175.8	-26.2
Foreign 85a	10.2	8.4	.8	9.9	-4.9	-5.9	-9.4	-9.9	-11.3	179.8	92.7	53.7	48.4	38.4	97.3
National Accounts														*Millions of Pesos*	
Exports of Goods & Services 90c	256	292	411	513	730	1,009	840	918	828	1,135	1,271	1,513	1,142	1,962	3,780
Government Consumption 91f	172	169	178	194	292	222	152	189	271	420	504	693	779	786	871
Gross Fixed Capital Formation 93e	246	294	427	498	644	803	780	939	1,032	1,335	1,584	1,655	1,491	1,754	2,169
Increase/Decrease(-) in Stocks 93i	38	4	-35	20	45	79	101	60	98	60	82	61	99	62	34
Private Consumption 96f	1,138	1,318	1,449	1,685	2,139	2,496	3,083	3,589	3,659	4,034	5,109	5,163	5,986	7,180	9,145
Imports of Goods & Services 98c	-365	-410	-442	-565	-917	-1,010	-1,005	-1,109	-1,154	-1,484	-1,919	-1,818	-1,533	-2,524	-4,405
Gross Domestic Product (GDP) 99b	1,486	1,667	1,987	2,345	2,931	3,599	3,952	4,587	4,734	5,499	6,631	7,267	7,964	9,220	11,594
Net Factor Inc/Pmts(-) Abroad 98.n	-26	-29	-47	-77	-90	-113	-124	-123	-136	-188	-210	-277	-254	-475	-683
Gross National Income (GNI) 99a	1,460	1,638	1,941	2,268	2,841	3,486	3,828	4,464	4,599	5,311	6,421	6,990	7,710	8,745	10,911
Net National Income 99e	1,371	1,538	1,821	2,127	2,666	3,270	3,591	4,191	4,323	4,984	6,025	6,558	7,236	8,197	10,241
GDP Volume 1970 Prices.................. 99b.p	1,486	1,647	1,818	2,053	2,176	2,289	2,443	2,565	2,620	2,738	2,904	3,022	3,069	3,280	3,322
GDP Volume (1995=100) .... 99bv p	32.4	35.9	39.6	44.8	47.4	49.9	53.3	55.9	57.1	59.7	63.3	65.9	66.9	71.5	72.4
GDP Deflator (1995=100)................ 99bi p	2.8	2.9	3.1	3.2	3.8	4.4	4.6	5.1	5.1	5.7	6.5	6.8	7.3	7.9	9.9
														Millions:	
Population................................... 99z	4.06	4.20	4.34	4.48	4.61	4.75	4.89	5.03	5.17	5.30	5.44	5.54	5.98	6.12	6.27

	1985	1986	1987	1988	1989	1990	1991	1992	1993	1994	1995	1996	1997	1998	1999	Government Finance	
Year Ending December 31																	
	−205.1	125.8	−69.5	−73.5	143.7	367.3	1,013.7	3,763.3	288.1	−690.6	1,720.3	540.6	2,038.0	2,109.8	−1,286.6	Deficit (-) or Surplus	80
	1,638.8	2,352.7	2,941.8	4,557.4	5,846.7	6,917.8	10,180.2	17,842.0	20,188.0	21,499.9	24,890.8	27,133.6	34,729.1	38,867.3	43,947.3	Total Revenue and Grants	81y
	1,636.4	2,148.2	2,877.0	4,424.1	5,785.7	6,867.8	10,113.3	17,572.0	19,776.1	21,482.3	24,890.8	26,921.3	34,729.1	38,564.8	43,483.6	Revenue	81
	2.4	204.5	64.8	133.3	61.0	50.0	66.9	270.0	411.9	17.6	—	212.3	—	302.5	463.7	Grants	81z
	1,843.9	2,226.9	3,011.3	4,630.9	5,703.0	6,550.5	9,166.5	14,078.7	19,899.9	22,190.5	23,170.5	26,593.0	32,691.1	36,757.5	45,233.9	Exp. & Lending Minus Repay.	82z
	1,829.3	2,222.7	3,009.3	4,626.7	5,701.4	6,548.2	9,165.2	14,078.7	19,899.9	22,190.5	23,170.5	26,593.0	32,691.1	36,757.5	45,164.7	Expenditure	82
	14.6	4.2	2.0	4.2	1.6	2.3	1.3	—	—	—	—	—	—	—	69.2	Lending Minus Repayments	83
	205.2	−125.8	69.6	73.5	−143.7	−367.3	−1,013.7	−3,763.3	−288.1	690.6	−1,720.3	−540.6	−2,038.4	−2,110.0	1,217.1	Total Financing	80h
	−21.7	−264.8	−62.4	240.7	−97.8	−294.5	−269.6	−2,225.7	1,708.5	2,522.1	1.8	1,289.3	379.2	−8.4	1,862.4	Domestic	84a
	226.9	139.0	132.0	−167.2	−45.9	−72.8	−744.1	−1,537.6	−1,996.6	−1,831.5	−1,722.1	−1,829.9	−2,417.6	−2,101.6	−645.4	Foreign	85a
Millions of Pesos																**National Accounts**	
	4,088	4,041	5,847	11,000	12,795	16,880	23,588	24,185	59,648	67,795	77,058	84,485	100,513	113,752	130,085	Exports of Goods & Services	90c
	1,112	1,297	1,205	1,783	1,251	1,765	2,433	3,480	5,398	6,692	8,331	10,413	16,403	19,949	22,797	Government Consumption	91f
	2,747	3,492	5,319	8,034	11,505	15,041	20,821	25,307	32,169	32,785	35,265	38,984	47,674	63,099	76,808	Gross Fixed Capital Formation	93e
	52	85	118	89	100	120	127	150	158	175	209	236	277	312	359	Increase/Decrease(-) in Stocks	93i
	12,562	13,606	17,410	23,593	32,552	47,290	77,517	94,108	92,958	105,107	124,052	142,927	160,937	180,841	202,394	Private Consumption	96f
	−4,859	−4,741	−7,495	−11,649	−15,810	−20,791	−28,153	−34,531	−68,524	−74,989	−82,632	−93,513	−110,739	−135,542	−153,504	Imports of Goods & Services	98c
	15,702	17,780	22,404	32,850	42,393	60,305	96,333	112,698	121,808	137,566	162,283	183,532	215,065	241,910	278,939	Gross Domestic Product (GDP)	99b
	−706	−722	−1,160	−1,837	−888	−760	−1,862	−3,893	−8,761	−8,851	−10,405	−9,966	−11,342	−13,565	−15,266	Net Factor Inc/Pmts(-) Abroad	98.n
	14,996	17,058	21,244	31,199	41,517	59,589	94,471	108,803	113,047	128,715	151,878	173,566	203,722	228,345	263,674	Gross National Income (GNI)	99a
	14,062	16,000	19,912	29,242	38,995	55,971	88,691	102,041	105,738	120,461	142,141	162,554	190,818	213,830	246,937	Net National Income	99e
	3,251	3,366	3,706	3,786	3,953	3,737	3,773	4,076	4,199	4,378	4,587	4,920	5,324	5,714	6,188	GDP Volume 1970 Prices	99b.p
	70.9	73.4	80.8	82.5	86.2	81.5	82.3	88.9	91.5	95.4	100.0	107.3	116.1	124.6	134.9	GDP Volume (1995=100)	99bv p
	13.7	14.9	17.1	24.5	30.3	45.6	72.2	78.2	82.0	88.8	100.0	105.4	114.2	119.7	127.4	GDP Deflator (1995=100)	99bi p
Midyear Estimates																	
	6.42	6.56	6.71	6.87	7.02	7.11	7.32	7.47	7.62	7.77	7.71	7.83	7.97	8.10	8.33	Population	99z

(See notes in the back of the book.)

Ecuador

		1970	1971	1972	1973	1974	1975	1976	1977	1978	1979	1980	1981	1982	1983	1984
Exchange Rates																*Sucres per SDR:*
Principal Rate	aa	25.0	27.1	27.1	30.2	30.6	29.3	29.0	30.4	32.6	32.9	31.9	29.1	36.6	56.6	65.8
																Sucres per US Dollar:
Principal Rate	ae	25.0	25.0	25.0	25.0	25.0	25.0	25.0	25.0	25.0	25.0	25.0	25.0	33.2	54.1	67.2
Principal Rate	rf	20.9	25.0	25.0	25.0	25.0	25.0	25.0	25.0	25.0	25.0	25.0	25.0	30.0	44.1	62.5
																Index Numbers (1995=100):
Principal Rate	ahx	12,342.7	3,045.3	10,223.6	275.6	10,223.6	10,223.6	10,223.6	10,223.6	10,223.6	10,223.6	10,223.6	10,223.6	8,673.7	5,943.5	4,107.0
Nominal Effective Exchange Rate	ne c	...	...	...	...	...	...	...	...	...	1,445.2	1,527.8	1,706.4	1,625.9	1,194.0	844.9
Real Effective Exchange Rate	re c	...	...	...	...	...	...	...	...	...	...	173.0	193.9	189.5	181.0	150.3
Fund Position																*Millions of SDRs:*
Quota	2f. s	33.0	33.0	33.0	33.0	33.0	33.0	33.0	33.0	70.0	70.0	105.0	105.0	105.0	150.7	150.7
SDRs	1b. s	.1	3.4	6.7	5.6	6.5	6.3	6.3	8.2	10.6	19.2	19.0	28.9	—	.1	.5
Reserve Position in the Fund	1c. s	—	—	—	5.6	9.2	13.2	—	—	8.0	9.4	21.8	24.8	—	11.4	—
Total Fund Cred.&Loans Outstg.	2tl	13.8	5.5	8.3	—	—	—	—	—	—	—	—	—	—	203.5	242.9
International Liquidity															*Millions of US Dollars Unless Otherwise Indicated:*
Total Reserves minus Gold	1l. d	55.2	37.1	121.1	210.4	318.6	253.4	477.4	623.1	635.8	722.0	1,013.0	632.4	304.2	644.5	611.2
SDRs	1b. d	.1	3.6	7.3	6.7	7.9	7.4	7.3	10.0	13.8	25.2	24.2	33.6	—	.1	.5
Reserve Position in the Fund	1c. d	—	—	—	6.8	11.3	15.5	—	—	10.4	12.4	27.8	28.8	—	12.0	—
Foreign Exchange	1d. d	55.1	33.5	113.8	196.9	299.4	230.5	470.1	613.1	611.5	684.4	961.0	570.0	304.2	632.4	610.7
Gold (Million Fine Troy Ounces)	1ad	.546	.533	.355	.386	.386	.386	.386	.400	.407	.414	.414	.414	.414	.414	.414
Gold (National Valuation)	1and	19.0	18.6	12.4	16.3	16.3	16.3	16.3	16.9	17.2	17.5	17.5	17.5	124.3	124.3	124.3
Monetary Authorities: Other Liab.	4.. d	19.2	37.2	9.4	13.9	62.9	62.9	80.6	99.7	84.2	153.2	227.5	115.0	245.6	1,286.1	2,043.8
Deposit Money Banks: Assets	7a. d	.9	3.5	4.6	9.7	14.3	25.7	43.9	74.2	79.8	96.9	115.4	135.6	127.6	171.7	73.5
Liabilities	7b. d	—	1.9	4.4	6.4	10.7	14.2	21.8	31.8	33.2	43.0	40.3	58.1	40.7	42.7	64.3
Other Banking Insts.: Assets	7e. d	...	...	...	...	...	...	...	...	...	...	...	...	...	...	...
Liabilities	7f. d	4.7	5.8	7.4	8.6	10.0	15.7	18.8	37.7	21.6	24.0	32.5	38.5	47.2	44.6	43.0
Monetary Authorities																*Millions of Sucres through 1978;*
Foreign Assets	11	2,082.0	1,577.5	3,557.8	5,871.3	8,743.8	7,154.8	11,836.8	16,096.0	16,874.4	‡19.5	27.0	17.0	15.1	43.3	50.2
Claims on Central Government	12a	3,269.0	3,430.7	4,236.7	4,434.6	6,280.2	6,003.9	5,958.0	5,206.0	4,163.0	‡4.1	3.7	3.5	3.8	71.9	84.7
Claims on Nonfin.Pub.Enterprises	12c										‡—		.2			
Claims on Private Sector	12d	1,094.2	1,154.0	1,055.9	1,057.0	1,406.2	2,178.5	3,329.0	4,050.0	5,867.0	‡8.6	11.4	17.3	16.3	19.0	24.0
Claims on Deposit Money Banks	12e	128.2	51.6	65.4	108.4	402.2	765.5	1,323.0	2,578.0	5,020.0	‡6.7	9.0	14.2	21.7	47.7	79.5
Claims on Other Banking Insts	12f	473.2	514.1	502.1	748.3	1,852.3	3,504.5	4,318.0	3,913.0	4,008.0	‡5.3	7.6	11.4	13.9	28.5	53.0
Reserve Money	14	4,504.6	4,986.2	6,457.3	9,112.8	12,896.5	12,828.1	15,556.0	18,891.0	22,098.0	‡28.4	32.1	34.6	37.6	45.2	63.0
of which: Currency Outside DMBs	14a	2,329.2	2,414.1	2,889.8	3,617.8	4,776.3	5,385.7	7,569.6	9,126.4	10,274.2	‡12.3	15.3	17.4	20.5	25.4	35.3
Time, Savings,& Fgn.Currency Dep.	15	15.7	28.1	39.4	24.6	222.1	591.8	4,994.0	4,479.0	4,381.0	‡7.8	12.5	12.7	21.4	28.3	44.8
Bonds	16ab			3.0	360.0	183.4	327.5	474.0	1,679.0	1,613.0	‡1.5	1.8	1.1	2.0	1.5	1.1
Restricted Deposits	16b	1,180.5	693.0	1,148.9	13.5	7.5	859.0	2,643.0	2,846.0	2,459.0	‡2.9	3.8	5.1	9.6	17.0	26.2
Foreign Liabilities	16c	823.3	1,079.6	457.8	347.6	1,572.8	1,571.5	2,016.0	2,492.0	2,104.0	‡3.8	5.7	2.9	8.1	34.5	38.8
Long-Term Foreign Liabilities	16cl										‡—				46.6	114.5
Central Government Deposits	16d	948.6	679.5	1,548.1	2,642.9	4,496.5	5,769.1	5,184.0	5,448.0	7,862.0	‡6.2	7.5	11.4	6.5	83.1	124.2
Central Govt. Lending Funds	16f	—	20.0	25.0	59.0	285.0	285.0	299.0	306.0	361.0	‡.4	.3	.5	.7	1.9	1.5
Capital Accounts	17a	205.3	298.8	399.6	508.1	1,035.5	1,009.2	1,201.0	1,020.0	1,458.0	‡1.8	3.7	4.5	2.8	−20.5	−75.8
Other Items (Net)	17r	−631.4	−1,057.3	−661.2	−848.9	−2,014.6	−3,634.0	−5,602.2	−5,318.0	−6,403.6	‡−8.7	−8.5	−9.1	−17.8	−27.1	−46.8
Deposit Money Banks																*Millions of Sucres through 1978;*
Reserves	20	1,681.5	2,101.9	2,463.4	3,366.6	4,682.2	5,437.0	7,247.7	8,599.9	9,747.9	‡10.4	13.0	12.7	13.9	17.4	31.6
Foreign Assets	21	22.6	87.1	114.2	242.3	357.6	642.9	1,097.4	1,854.0	1,996.2	‡2.4	2.9	3.4	4.2	9.3	4.9
Claims on Central Government	22a	32.7	42.9	40.1	66.4	125.0	128.5	153.5	130.4	55.4	‡.1	—	—	—	—	—
Claims on Nonfin.Pub.Enterprises	22c															
Claims on Private Sector	22d	4,795.4	5,365.5	6,207.1	7,551.0	9,754.2	12,127.1	15,926.3	21,721.0	26,631.7	‡33.5	42.4	53.8	76.7	130.4	175.0
Claims on Other Banking Insts	22f	59.8	130.1	168.2	261.3	305.6	353.6	404.3	497.1	544.1	‡.6	.7	.8	1.1	1.4	2.0
Demand Deposits	24	2,955.1	3,502.7	4,126.5	5,426.8	7,991.4	9,336.5	12,836.9	15,811.6	18,118.6	‡21.2	28.0	31.0	37.3	49.4	72.4
Time, Savings,& Fgn.Currency Dep.	25	1,730.2	2,147.3	2,555.5	3,107.0	3,944.7	4,148.7	5,028.0	5,534.0	6,002.3	‡6.9	8.3	9.1	12.1	16.5	28.2
Bonds	26ab	1,452.1	1,612.9	1,836.3	2,122.9	2,536.8	3,340.5	4,057.5	4,637.8	5,370.2	‡6.3	8.8	11.4	13.8	17.2	25.8
Foreign Liabilities	26c	—	47.7	110.8	161.1	267.7	354.3	544.6	794.5	830.2	‡1.1	1.0	1.5	1.3	2.3	4.3
Long-Term Foreign Liabilities	26cl	...	...	...	...	...	...	...	...	...						
Central Government Deposits	26d										‡—					
Credit from Monetary Authorities	26g	122.5	42.2	60.1	110.8	214.5	545.0	920.2	4,056.6	5,366.7	‡6.8	9.0	13.6	20.7	58.8	76.8
Liabilities to Other Banking Insts	26i	—	—	—	—	—	—	—	—	—	‡—	—	.1	.3	.4	.7
Capital Accounts	27a	764.4	900.9	991.1	1,172.7	1,412.2	1,879.2	2,348.6	3,085.2	4,207.9	‡5.5	7.0	9.1	10.7	13.7	18.8
Other Items (Net)	27r	−432.3	−526.2	−687.3	−613.7	−1,142.7	−915.1	−906.6	−1,117.3	−920.6	‡−.7	−3.1	−5.0	−.3	.2	−13.3
Monetary Survey																*Millions of Sucres through 1978;*
Foreign Assets (Net)	31n	1,281.3	537.3	3,103.4	5,604.9	7,260.9	5,871.9	10,373.6	14,663.5	15,936.4	‡17.0	23.2	16.0	9.8	15.8	12.1
Domestic Credit	32	9,037.0	10,324.3	11,243.8	12,373.0	17,282.7	21,120.1	24,936.9	30,111.1	33,441.1	‡46.0	58.4	75.7	105.3	168.3	214.5
Claims on Central Govt. (Net)	32an	2,353.1	2,794.1	2,728.7	1,858.1	1,908.7	363.3	927.5	−111.6	−3,643.6	‡−2.1	−3.7	−7.8	−2.7	−11.1	−39.6
Claims on State and Local Govts	32b	261.3	366.5	581.8	897.3	2,055.7	2,593.1	31.8	41.6	33.9	‡—	—	—	—	—	—
Claims on Nonfin.Pub.Enterprises	32c										‡—		.2			
Claims on Private Sector	32d	5,889.6	6,519.5	7,263.0	8,608.0	11,160.4	14,305.6	19,255.3	25,771.0	32,498.7	‡42.1	53.8	71.1	93.0	149.5	199.0
Claims on Other Banking Insts	32f	533.0	644.2	670.3	1,009.6	2,157.9	3,858.1	4,722.3	4,410.1	4,552.1	‡5.9	8.3	12.2	15.0	29.9	55.0
Money	34	5,988.6	6,718.6	8,371.5	11,223.1	16,665.5	17,782.2	21,911.5	28,562.0	31,342.8	‡39.7	49.2	55.2	62.9	83.0	115.8
Quasi-Money	35	1,745.9	2,175.4	2,594.9	3,131.6	4,166.8	4,740.5	10,022.0	10,013.0	10,383.3	‡14.7	20.8	21.7	33.5	44.8	73.0
Bonds	36ab	1,452.1	1,612.9	1,839.3	2,482.9	2,720.2	3,668.0	4,531.5	6,316.8	6,983.2	‡7.8	10.5	12.5	15.8	18.7	26.8
Restricted Deposits	36b	1,180.5	693.0	1,148.9	13.5	7.5	859.0	2,643.0	2,846.0	2,459.0	‡2.9	3.8	5.1	9.6	17.0	26.2
Long-Term Foreign Liabilities	36cl										‡—				46.6	114.5
Central Govt. Lending Funds	36f	—	20.0	25.0	59.0	285.0	285.0	299.0	306.0	361.0	‡.4	.3	.5	.7	1.9	1.5
Liabilities to Other Banking Insts	36i										‡—		.1	.3	.4	.7
Capital Accounts	37a	969.7	1,199.7	1,390.7	1,680.8	2,447.7	2,888.4	3,549.6	4,105.2	5,665.9	‡7.3	10.7	13.6	13.5	−6.8	−57.0
Other Items (Net)	37r	−1,018.5	−1,558.0	−1,023.1	−613.0	−1,749.1	−3,231.1	−7,646.1	−7,374.4	−7,817.7	‡−9.9	−13.8	−17.0	−21.0	−21.6	−74.9
Money plus Quasi-Money	35l	7,734.5	8,894.0	10,966.4	14,354.7	20,832.3	22,522.7	31,933.5	38,575.0	41,726.1	‡54.5	70.1	76.9	96.4	127.8	188.8

Ecuador

248

	1985	1986	1987	1988	1989	1990	1991	1992	1993	1994	1995	1996	1997	1998	1999		
Exchange Rates																	
End of Period																	
Principal Rate	105.2	179.2	314.2	582.0	852.1	1,249.4	1,817.5	2,535.8	2,807.3	3,312.4	4,345.8	5,227.0	5,974.5	9,609.8	27,783.7	aa
End of Period (ae) Period Average (rf)																	
Principal Rate	95.8	146.5	221.5	432.5	648.4	878.2	1,270.6	1,844.3	2,043.8	2,269.0	2,923.5	3,635.0	4,428.0	6,825.0	20,243.0	ae
Principal Rate	69.6	122.8	170.5	301.6	526.3	767.8	1,046.2	1,534.0	1,919.1	2,196.7	2,564.5	3,189.5	3,998.3	5,446.6	11,786.8	rf
Period Averages																	
Principal Rate	3,710.1	2,129.7	1,528.3	899.5	492.2	335.7	245.5	170.9	132.7	116.5	100.0	81.5	63.9	47.9	23.4	ahx
Nominal Effective Exchange Rate	783.2	570.9	381.4	222.7	191.1	163.4	138.2	109.1	107.6	115.4	100.0	83.2	70.3	53.9	27.5	nec
Real Effective Exchange Rate	156.1	125.6	96.4	72.8	83.8	76.1	80.6	81.0	94.8	101.6	100.0	99.3	106.6	107.7	80.4	rec
Fund Position																	
End of Period																	
Quota	150.7	150.7	150.7	150.7	150.7	150.7	150.7	219.2	219.2	219.2	219.2	219.2	219.2	219.2	302.3	2f.s
SDRs	26.2	45.7	.7	1.0	.7	10.3	28.9	.1	3.2	3.0	2.1	1.9	.4	.2	1.7	1b.s
Reserve Position in the Fund	—	—	—	—	—	—	—	17.1	17.1	17.1	17.2	17.2	17.2	17.2	17.2	1c.s
Total Fund Cred.&Loans Outstg.	327.3	397.7	345.2	300.7	247.2	186.0	127.5	72.6	51.8	135.7	116.7	100.9	98.9	49.5	—	2tl
International Liquidity																	
End of Period																	
Total Reserves minus Gold	718.2	644.1	491.1	397.6	540.4	838.5	924.3	868.2	1,379.9	1,844.2	1,627.6	1,858.5	2,092.8	1,619.7	1,642.4	1l.d
SDRs	28.8	55.9	.9	1.3	.9	14.7	41.4	.1	4.3	4.3	3.1	2.7	.5	.3	2.3	1b.d
Reserve Position in the Fund	—	—	—	—	—	—	—	23.6	23.5	25.0	25.5	24.7	23.1	24.2	23.5	1c.d
Foreign Exchange	689.4	588.2	490.2	396.3	539.5	823.8	882.9	844.5	1,352.1	1,814.9	1,599.0	1,831.1	2,069.1	1,595.3	1,616.5	1d.d
Gold (Million Fine Troy Ounces)	.414	.414	.414	.414	.414	.443	.443	.443	.414	.414	.414	.414	.414	.414	.414	1ad
Gold (National Valuation)	124.3	124.3	165.7	165.7	165.7	165.7	165.7	165.7	165.6	165.6	166.6	166.6	166.7	166.7	166.4	1and
Monetary Authorities: Other Liab.	3,532.8	2,501.3	1,635.0	3,343.1	2,214.8	3,513.6	4,484.7	4,119.3	4,109.6	4,003.3	196.2	178.7	147.1	430.3	608.5	4..d
Deposit Money Banks: Assets	63.6	65.6	67.2	63.1	66.2	90.5	98.8	138.0	153.5	303.4	373.5	544.2	867.3	901.4	652.2	7a.d
Liabilities	51.6	53.1	88.2	55.3	54.5	261.3	263.2	307.4	207.7	572.7	792.5	849.5	1,317.1	1,484.4	837.6	7b.d
Other Banking Insts.: Assets	....	....	....	....	....	8.5	16.2	24.1	26.9	50.8	24.8	17.0	71.6	30.7	24.5	7e.d
Liabilities	46.0	113.4	178.3	200.8	195.4	109.8	109.9	117.6	183.4	272.0	281.8	380.3	479.3	545.8	383.9	7f.d
Monetary Authorities																	
Billions of Sucres Beginning 1979: End of Period																	
Foreign Assets	83.7	75.6	59.3	237.1	293.6	I 382.9	412.2	389.3	3,043.3	4,508.4	5,106.3	7,241.4	9,984.5	I 11581.4	25,217.7	11
Claims on Central Government	140.5	142.4	184.3	644.9	631.8	I 620.7	940.4	1,237.7	8,021.0	9,124.3	569.1	603.9	571.0	I 1,975.7	27,050.8	12a
Claims on Nonfin.Pub.Enterprises	—	—	—	—	—	I .3	.3	.3	.2	.2	—	—	—	I —	—	12c
Claims on Private Sector	24.6	19.3	16.1	24.1	47.6	I 49.9	30.5	26.3	29.9	48.1	17.9	29.9	31.8	I 120.0	151.9	12d
Claims on Deposit Money Banks	81.8	89.1	88.4	71.7	64.5	I 128.4	138.3	172.1	149.3	31.0	387.6	970.6	198.3	I 6,128.4	8,796.0	12e
Claims on Other Banking Insts	63.8	77.0	79.2	78.7	101.3	I 33.6	40.0	19.5	9.9	4.6	155.7	1.3	.2	I 73.7	103.8	12f
Reserve Money	81.7	109.8	153.3	257.8	376.7	I 672.3	924.3	1,514.9	2,467.2	2,808.6	3,275.3	4,356.8	5,690.1	I 6,872.6	16,393.0	14
of which: Currency Outside DMBs	42.7	54.6	74.8	124.0	176.3	I 272.7	383.9	597.3	853.8	1,122.4	1,375.8	1,882.4	2,384.6	I 2,911.7	9,287.7	14a
Time, Savings,& Fgn.Currency Dep.	33.6	36.1	57.9	98.8	105.2	I 116.5	132.4	84.1	259.6	404.3	385.2	445.3	501.6	I —	—	15
Bonds	5.6	5.3	32.7	50.9	62.0	I 62.3	89.0	127.2	180.8	81.7	57.8	34.3	1.9	I 2,085.4	6,249.9	16ab
Restricted Deposits	11.5	10.7	27.2	46.0	10.7	I 2.2	.8	.7	.7	.6	.6	.6	.6	I —	—	16b
Foreign Liabilities	67.0	107.2	141.0	331.3	299.7	I 155.9	119.0	84.1	500.6	589.3	557.6	599.4	691.9	I 587.8	3,262.0	16c
Long-Term Foreign Liabilities	305.7	330.5	329.6	1,289.6	1,347.0	I 1,317.6	1,701.2	1,561.4	7,982.1	9,061.5	522.7	574.9	553.2	I 2,824.5	9,055.6	16cl
Central Government Deposits	99.6	92.4	85.5	182.1	265.1	I 492.9	515.0	761.7	1,281.5	1,851.7	1,853.8	2,542.2	2,659.0	I 2,548.9	7,168.9	16d
Central Govt. Lending Funds	1.5	2.3	3.7	11.2	22.5	I 27.0	36.7	68.3	84.4	94.5	92.1	62.3	66.9	I —	—	16f
Capital Accounts	−182.6	−225.4	−273.2	−1,051.1	−1,143.7	I −1500.9	−1,796.6	39.4	618.7	783.2	970.0	1,937.6	1,987.6	I 7,983.3	24,950.5	17a
Other Items (Net)	−29.0	−65.4	−130.4	−160.1	−206.5	I −130.0	−160.1	−2,396.6	−2,122.0	−1,958.8	−1,478.4	−1,706.2	−1,367.0	I −3023.2	−5,759.7	17r
Deposit Money Banks																	
Billions of Sucres Beginning 1979: End of Period																	
Reserves	36.4	47.8	56.3	104.2	152.1	I 253.0	406.7	684.3	875.1	900.2	1,243.0	1,861.5	2,378.2	I 4,310.1	8,228.4	20
Foreign Assets	6.1	9.6	14.9	27.3	42.9	I 79.9	126.6	254.3	313.2	690.9	1,092.3	1,977.6	3,837.8	I 6,151.9	13,202.3	21
Claims on Central Government	2.0	3.7	.6	1.3	.3	I 11.4	10.5	19.6	59.5	117.9	370.3	765.6	1,693.5	I 5,848.2	7,543.9	22a
Claims on Nonfin.Pub.Enterprises	....	....	....	....	....	29.0	26.1	16.0	43.6	—	—	—	—	I —	—	22c
Claims on Private Sector	219.5	258.9	336.8	393.9	539.6	I 951.3	1,634.0	2,636.2	4,736.4	8,470.0	12,607.0	16,472.2	24,534.7	I 38653.3	80,270.3	22d
Claims on Other Banking Insts	3.2	4.6	6.9	11.0	15.5	I 25.0	50.1	68.7	48.4	16.0	552.3	1,242.5	105.0	I 589.7	1,191.2	22f
Demand Deposits	91.7	104.8	136.0	201.4	279.6	I 465.1	693.9	1,026.1	1,644.3	2,217.8	2,239.2	2,977.2	3,911.2	I 4,975.4	7,134.1	24
Time, Savings,& Fgn.Currency Dep.	49.5	70.2	115.8	178.3	264.4	I 812.9	1,363.4	2,239.1	3,516.4	5,902.1	9,610.2	14,535.8	19,530.1	I 26303.6	51,368.6	25
Bonds	67.0	89.8	117.6	139.0	209.9	I 53.5	64.2	92.0	104.5	92.0	439.4	1,496.3	2,250.8	I 2,251.6	3,093.8	26ab
Foreign Liabilities	4.9	7.8	19.5	23.9	35.4	I 30.1	45.2	104.4	183.2	971.8	1,935.5	2,523.6	4,949.9	I 9,286.1	15,016.3	26c
Long-Term Foreign Liabilities	....	....	....	....	....	200.8	291.8	462.4	240.6	332.3	382.0	563.4	878.3	I 845.2	1,938.9	26cl
Central Government Deposits	—	—	—	—	—	—	—	—	—	—	7.6	15.0	28.6	I 500.8	952.9	26d
Credit from Monetary Authorities	71.8	75.8	73.4	58.1	45.6	I 117.5	136.6	168.7	179.8	57.8	395.8	483.0	24.0	I 5,081.4	6,174.7	26g
Liabilities to Other Banking Insts	1.3	1.9	3.9	5.4	6.1	I 15.5	22.5	35.1	110.5	292.0	611.2	84.8	80.0	I 235.6	1,780.7	26i
Capital Accounts	25.6	36.3	49.6	83.8	124.9	I 230.6	447.4	757.5	1,342.9	2,182.0	3,726.0	5,261.7	7,793.5	I 11737.8	22,344.0	27a
Other Items (Net)	−44.7	−62.1	−100.3	−152.2	−215.4	I −576.5	−810.9	−1,206.1	−1,245.9	−1,852.9	−3,482.1	−5,621.3	−6,897.2	I −5664.3	632.0	27r
Monetary Survey																	
Billions of Sucres Beginning 1979: End of Period																	
Foreign Assets (Net)	17.9	−29.7	−86.3	−90.8	1.4	I 276.9	374.5	455.1	2,672.7	3,638.1	3,705.5	6,096.0	8,180.5	I 7,859.4	20,141.6	31n
Domestic Credit	354.0	413.4	538.2	971.7	1,071.0	I 1,228.2	2,217.0	3,262.6	11,667.5	15,929.2	12,410.9	16,558.2	24,248.5	I 44211.0	108,190.2	32
Claims on Central Govt. (Net)	42.9	53.7	99.4	464.0	367.0	I 139.1	436.0	495.6	6,799.0	7,390.5	−922.0	−1,187.7	−423.2	I 4,773.8	26,472.5	32an
Claims on State and Local Govts	—	—	—	—	—	I —	—	—	—	—	—	—	—	I .4	.4	32b
Claims on Nonfin.Pub.Enterprises	—	—	—	—	—	I 29.3	26.4	16.3	43.8	.2	—	—	—	I —	—	32c
Claims on Private Sector	244.1	278.2	352.8	418.0	587.2	I 1,001.2	1,664.5	2,662.5	4,766.3	8,518.0	12,624.9	16,502.1	24,566.5	I 38773.4	80,422.2	32d
Claims on Other Banking Insts	66.9	81.6	86.1	89.7	116.8	I 58.6	90.1	88.2	58.4	20.6	708.0	1,243.8	105.2	I 663.4	1,295.1	32f
Money	145.4	174.6	235.1	359.0	516.2	I 856.5	1,256.1	1,864.1	3,051.0	4,041.5	4,151.2	5,349.5	6,955.9	I 9,081.9	19,129.2	34
Quasi-Money	83.0	106.2	173.8	277.1	369.6	I 929.4	1,495.8	2,323.1	3,776.0	6,306.3	9,995.4	14,981.0	20,031.6	I 26303.6	51,368.6	35
Bonds	72.6	95.1	150.3	189.9	271.9	I 115.8	153.1	219.2	285.3	173.6	497.3	1,530.5	2,252.7	I 4,337.0	9,343.7	36ab
Restricted Deposits	11.5	10.7	27.2	46.0	10.7	I 2.2	.8	.7	.7	.6	.6	.6	.6	I —	—	36b
Long-Term Foreign Liabilities	305.7	330.5	329.6	1,289.6	1,347.0	I 1,518.4	1,993.0	2,023.8	8,222.8	9,393.8	904.7	1,138.3	1,431.5	I 3,669.7	10,994.5	36cl
Central Govt. Lending Funds	1.5	2.3	3.7	11.2	22.5	I 27.0	36.7	68.3	84.4	94.5	92.1	62.3	66.9	I —	—	36f
Liabilities to Other Banking Insts	1.3	1.9	3.9	5.4	6.1	I 15.5	22.5	35.1	110.5	292.0	611.2	84.8	80.0	I 235.6	1,780.7	36i
Capital Accounts	−157.0	−189.0	−223.6	−967.3	−1,018.8	I −1270.3	−1,349.3	796.8	1,961.6	2,965.1	4,696.0	7,199.3	9,781.2	I 19721.0	47,294.5	37a
Other Items (Net)	−92.1	−148.6	−247.9	−329.9	−452.8	I −689.4	−1,017.3	−3,613.5	−3,152.0	−3,700.2	−4,832.0	−7,692.2	−8,171.3	I −11278.4	−11,579.3	37r
Money plus Quasi-Money	228.4	280.8	408.8	636.1	885.8	I 1,785.9	2,751.9	4,187.2	6,827.0	10,347.8	14,146.6	20,330.5	26,987.6	I 35385.5	70,497.8	35l

Ecuador

	1970	1971	1972	1973	1974	1975	1976	1977	1978	1979	1980	1981	1982	1983	1984
Other Banking Institutions												*Millions of Sucres through 1978;*			
Reserves ... 40	153.7	179.4	238.8	271.1	451.5	339.9	634.5	745.4	994.3	‡1.0	1.4	2.1	1.0	1.9	1.6
Foreign Assets ... 41	....	....	....	—	—	—	....	....	....	....	—	—	—	—	—
Claims on Central Government ... 42a	—	—	—	—	—	—	....	....	....	‡—	—	—	—	—	—
Claims on Private Sector ... 42d	1,659.3	1,860.1	2,088.7	2,889.1	5,425.6	7,920.2	9,741.8	10,458.5	11,221.3	‡11.7	13.2	15.4	14.8	22.2	31.9
Claims on Deposit Money Banks ... 42e	3.6	6.5	8.0	293.4	434.5	638.7	748.7	1,111.1	1,249.2	‡1.3	1.3	1.5	1.8	1.9	2.4
Demand Deposits ... 44	191.6	266.4	422.6	627.2	1,338.5	1,631.9	2,366.5	2,791.8	2,543.0	‡2.6	3.5	4.6	4.5	6.1	7.6
Time, Savings,& Fgn.Currency Dep. ... 45	187.6	257.0	309.3	493.9	814.1	842.5	1,064.1	1,287.0	1,297.0	‡1.5	1.7	2.0	2.0	2.7	4.7
Bonds ... 46ab	17.4	10.8	6.4	3.7	1.6	.8	....	....	....	‡—	—	.5	1.1	2.3	4.1
Foreign Liabilities ... 46c	....	....	....	....	....	....	....	....	....	‡—	—	—	—	—	—
Long-Term Foreign Liabilities ... 46cl	116.5	144.8	185.4	214.3	251.1	392.6	469.3	942.5	539.9	‡.6	.8	1.0	1.6	2.4	2.9
Credit from Monetary Authorities ... 46g	452.5	519.4	530.3	854.6	1,981.8	3,418.9	4,453.9	3,304.1	3,042.2	‡3.8	4.6	5.4	5.6	7.7	9.5
Credit from Deposit Money Banks ... 46h	88.4	126.2	167.8	212.9	312.9	379.8	455.3	580.9	566.4	‡1.3	.6	.8	.8	.9	1.2
Capital Accounts ... 47a	707.0	761.5	735.3	891.9	1,761.1	2,205.0	2,925.2	3,341.5	5,436.1	‡5.1	5.0	5.4	4.9	5.4	9.2
Other Items (Net) ... 47r	55.6	−40.1	−21.6	155.1	−149.5	27.3	−609.3	67.2	40.2	‡.1	−.4	−.7	−2.8	−1.4	−3.3
Banking Survey												*Millions of Sucres through 1978;*			
Foreign Assets (Net) ... 51n	1,281.3	537.3	3,103.4	5,604.9	7,260.9	5,871.9	10,373.6	14,663.5	15,936.4	‡17.0	23.2	16.0	9.8	15.8	12.1
Domestic Credit ... 52	10,163.3	11,540.2	12,662.2	14,252.5	20,550.4	25,182.2	29,956.4	36,159.5	40,110.3	‡51.8	63.3	78.9	105.2	160.6	191.4
Claims on Central Govt. (Net) ... 52an	2,353.1	2,794.1	2,728.7	1,858.1	1,908.7	363.3	927.5	−111.6	−3,643.6	‡−2.1	−3.7	−7.8	−2.7	−11.1	−39.6
Claims on State and Local Govts ... 52b	261.3	366.5	581.8	897.3	2,055.7	2,593.1	31.8	41.6	33.9	‡—	—	—	—	—	—
Claims on Nonfin.Pub.Enterprises ... 52c										‡—	—	.2	—	—	—
Claims on Private Sector ... 52d	7,548.9	8,379.6	9,351.7	11,497.1	16,586.0	22,225.8	28,997.1	36,229.5	43,720.0	‡53.8	67.0	86.5	107.8	171.7	230.9
Liquid Liabilities ... 55l	7,960.0	9,238.0	11,459.5	15,204.7	22,533.4	24,657.2	34,729.6	41,908.4	44,571.8	‡57.5	73.9	81.5	101.8	134.6	199.5
Bonds ... 56ab	1,469.5	1,623.7	1,845.7	2,486.6	2,721.8	3,668.8	4,531.5	6,316.8	6,983.2	‡7.8	10.6	13.0	16.9	21.0	30.9
Restricted Deposits ... 56b	1,180.5	693.0	1,148.9	13.5	7.5	859.0	2,643.0	2,846.0	2,459.0	‡2.9	3.8	5.1	9.6	17.0	26.2
Long-Term Foreign Liabilities ... 56cl	116.5	144.8	185.4	214.3	251.1	392.6	469.3	942.5	539.9	‡.6	.8	1.0	1.6	49.0	117.4
Central Govt. Lending Funds ... 56f	—	20.0	25.0	59.0	285.0	285.0	299.0	306.0	361.0	‡.4	.3	.5	.7	1.9	1.5
Capital Accounts ... 57a	1,676.7	1,961.2	2,126.0	2,572.7	4,208.8	5,093.4	6,474.8	7,446.7	11,102.0	‡12.4	15.7	19.0	18.4	−1.3	−47.8
Other Items (Net) ... 57r	−958.6	−1,603.2	−1,024.9	−693.4	−2,196.3	−3,901.9	−8,817.2	−8,943.4	−9,970.2	‡−12.9	−18.5	−25.2	−33.9	−45.7	−124.2
Interest Rates												*Percent Per Annum*			
Discount Rate *(End of Period)* ... 60	8.00	8.00	8.00	8.00	8.00	8.00	8.00	8.00	8.00	8.00	8.00	15.00	15.00	19.00	23.00
Deposit Rate ... 60l	....	....	....	....	....	....	....	....	....	....	....	....	....	16.00	18.17
Lending Rate ... 60p	....	....	....	....	....	....	....	....	....	....	9.00	9.00	9.25	12.33	16.17
Prices, Production, Labor												*Index Numbers (1995=100):*			
Wholesale Prices (1990=100) ... 63	....	....	....	....	3.0	3.4	3.9	4.3	5.0	5.5	5.9	6.5	7.6	8.7	10.7
Consumer Prices ... 64	.3	.3	.3	1.3	.4	.5	.5	.6	.7	.8	.9	‡1.0	1.2	1.7	2.3
Crude Petroleum Production ... 66aa	1.1	1.0	20.4	54.4	46.1	41.9	48.8	47.7	52.5	55.7	53.3	54.9	55.0	61.8	67.0
												Number in Thousands:			
Labor Force ... 67d	....	....	....	....	....	....	....	....	....	....	....	....	....	....	....
Employment ... 67e	....	....	....	....	....	....	....	....	....	....	....	....	....	....	....
Unemployment ... 67c	....	....	....	....	....	....	....	....	....	....	....	....	....	....	....
Unemployment Rate (%) ... 67r	....	....	....	....	....	....	....	....	....	....	....	....	....	....	....
International Transactions												*Millions of US Dollars*			
Exports ... 70..d	189.9	199.1	326.3	532.0	1,123.5	973.9	1,257.5	1,436.3	1,557.5	2,104.2	2,480.8	2,451.4	2,327.4	2,347.7	2,620.4
Imports, c.i.f. ... 71..d	273.9	340.1	318.6	397.3	678.2	987.0	958.3	1,188.5	1,505.1	1,599.7	2,253.3	‡2,246.1	2,168.9	1,487.4	1,616.3
Imports, f.o.b. ... 71.vd	238.3	297.4	274.9	344.6	589.8	863.8	850.2	1,041.5	1,324.8	1,416.8	1,989.8	‡1,895.2	1,897.7	1,304.6	1,395.5
												1995=100			
Volume of Exports ... 72	....	....	....	....	....	....	....	....	....	....	....	....	....	....	....
Volume of Imports ... 73	....	....	....	....	....	....	....	....	....	....	....	....	....	....	....
												1995=100:			
Unit Value of Exports ... 74..d	28.8	30.1	26.5	31.1	67.2	69.2	73.0	82.1	78.1	122.6	170.8	166.6	159.1	139.2	132.7
Balance of Payments												*Millions of US Dollars:*			
Current Account, n.i.e. ... 78ald							−10	−343	−703	−630	−642	−998	−1,182	−115	−273
Goods: Exports f.o.b. ... 78aad							1,307	1,401	1,529	2,151	2,520	2,527	2,327	2,348	2,621
Goods: Imports f.o.b. ... 78abd							−1,048	−1,361	−1,704	−2,097	−2,242	−2,353	−2,187	−1,421	−1,567
Trade Balance ... 78acd							259	40	−175	54	278	174	140	927	1,054
Services: Credit ... 78add							111	202	174	260	367	399	381	315	291
Services: Debit ... 78aed							−268	−426	−475	−569	−704	−834	−723	−491	−535
Balance on Goods & Services ... 78afd							103	−183	−475	−256	−59	−262	−202	751	810
Income: Credit ... 78agd							13	24	35	62	88	69	26	23	59
Income: Debit ... 78ahd							−153	−220	−304	−467	−701	−831	−1,026	−913	−1,162
Balance on Gds, Serv. & Inc. ... 78aid							−37	−380	−744	−660	−672	−1,023	−1,202	−139	−293
Current Transfers, n.i.e.: Credit ... 78ajd							30	42	43	32	36	35	30	38	25
Current Transfers: Debit ... 78akd							−2	−6	−2	−2	−6	−10	−10	−14	−5
Capital Account, n.i.e. ... 78bcd							3	—	—	—	—	—	—	—	—
Capital Account, n.i.e.: Credit ... 78bad							3	—	—	—	—	—	—	—	—
Capital Account: Debit ... 78bbd							—	—	—	—	—	—	—	—	—
Financial Account, n.i.e. ... 78bjd							223	503	663	666	980	717	766	−2,571	−1,407
Direct Investment Abroad ... 78bdd							—	—	—	—	—	—	—	—	—
Dir. Invest. in Rep. Econ., n.i.e. ... 78bed							−20	35	49	63	70	60	40	50	50
Portfolio Investment Assets ... 78bfd							—	—	—	—	—	—	—	—	—
Equity Securities ... 78bkd							—	—	—	—	—	—	—	—	—
Debt Securities ... 78bld							—	—	—	—	—	—	—	—	—
Portfolio Investment Liab., n.i.e. ... 78bgd							6	52	—	—	—	—	—	—	—
Equity Securities ... 78bmd							—	—	—	—	—	—	—	—	—
Debt Securities ... 78bnd							6	52	—	—	—	—	—	—	—
Financial Derivatives Assets ... 78bwd							—	—	—	—	—	—	—	—	—
Financial Derivatives Liabilities ... 78bxd							—	—	—	—	—	—	—	—	—
Other Investment Assets ... 78bhd							−102	−41	−104	−34	−231	−449	503	−168	−26
Monetary Authorities ... 78bod							—	—	—	—	—	—	—	—	—
General Government ... 78bpd							−25	−37	−13	−48	−66	90	−15	−15	−27
Banks ... 78bqd							−15	−31	1	−3	−34	−21	25	−84	11
Other Sectors ... 78brd							−62	26	−92	17	−132	−518	493	−69	−10
Other Investment Liab., n.i.e. ... 78bid							339	458	718	636	1,141	1,106	223	−2,453	−1,431
Monetary Authorities ... 78bsd							44	25	−11	70	75	−107	183	96	−107
General Government ... 78btd							234	352	379	331	570	916	247	−1,699	−164
Banks ... 78bud							—	5	65	−6	22	17	25	84	−4
Other Sectors ... 78bvd							61	77	286	241	475	280	−232	−934	−1,156
Net Errors and Omissions ... 78cad							−13	−48	46	8	−68	−89	−802	794	97
Overall Balance ... 78cbd							203	112	6	44	270	−370	−1,218	−1,892	−1,583
Reserves and Related Items ... 79dad							−203	−112	−6	−44	−270	370	1,218	1,892	1,583
Reserve Assets ... 79dbd							−203	−112	−6	−44	−270	370	339	−327	60
Use of Fund Credit and Loans ... 79dcd							—	—	—	—	—	—	—	214	40
Exceptional Financing ... 79ded							—	—	—	—	—	—	879	2,005	1,483

1985	1986	1987	1988	1989	1990	1991	1992	1993	1994	1995	1996	1997	1998	1999		
Billions of Sucres Beginning 1979: End of Period															**Other Banking Institutions**	
2.5	4.8	12.3	5.9	9.6	I 7.6	18.7	31.5	68.6	120.9	122.0	139.8	151.9	I 162.0	544.6	Reserves	40
....	....	....	....	....	7.5	20.8	44.4	54.8	115.6	72.5	61.8	316.9	I 209.7	495.6	Foreign Assets	41
—	—	—	—	—	I .4	—	1.4	8.8	27.9	7.8	38.8	23.5	I 169.8	5,621.4	Claims on Central Government	42a
46.4	78.1	104.9	165.5	242.7	I 238.5	312.3	614.6	1,131.7	2,076.4	3,143.6	3,853.0	5,312.5	I 9,333.7	17,942.6	Claims on Private Sector	42d
3.4	4.1	5.3	5.9	7.9	I 5.1	7.8	12.0	12.5	27.0	30.7	23.0	31.5	I 86.4	94.2	Claims on Deposit Money Banks	42e
10.3	13.8	17.8	17.6	23.9	I —	—	—	—	—	—	—	—	I —	—	Demand Deposits	44
6.9	9.2	12.8	17.4	21.9	I 136.4	188.9	266.6	448.2	881.7	1,287.8	1,272.9	1,662.6	I 2,189.5	4,409.3	Time, Savings,& Fgn.Currency Dep.	45
5.5	11.8	12.2	11.8	14.7	I 27.4	45.9	61.7	18.0	48.0	32.6	350.9	794.7	I 1,592.5	3,040.9	Bonds	46ab
....	....	....	....	....	27.9	58.9	28.4	53.7	129.7	101.8	37.6	260.8	I 938.1	727.9	Foreign Liabilities	46c
4.4	16.6	39.5	86.9	126.7	I 69.1	81.8	188.4	320.7	489.7	722.3	1,344.3	1,860.1	I 2,787.3	7,043.5	Long-Term Foreign Liabilities	46cl
14.6	23.1	26.3	31.7	60.2	I 16.7	5.9	6.8	3.2	1.3	80.1	.1	6.1	I 20.2	8.4	Credit from Monetary Authorities	46g
1.9	1.8	1.6	1.6	3.9	I 2.6	7.3	15.2	46.3	86.1	172.7	54.2	128.6	I 303.7	269.2	Credit from Deposit Money Banks	46h
16.2	15.9	17.2	17.4	21.3	I 97.5	128.1	378.9	661.7	1,101.3	1,576.4	2,010.3	2,383.5	I 3,510.5	11,879.7	Capital Accounts	47a
-7.4	-5.2	-4.9	-7.1	-12.4	I -118.4	-157.1	-242.0	-275.3	-370.0	-597.3	-953.9	-1,260.1	I -1380.1	-2,680.5	Other Items (Net)	47r
Billions of Sucres Beginning 1979: End of Period															**Banking Survey**	
17.9	-29.7	-86.3	-90.8	1.4	I 256.5	336.4	471.2	2,673.9	3,624.0	3,676.2	6,120.1	8,236.7	I 7,131.1	19,909.3	Foreign Assets (Net)	51n
333.4	410.0	557.0	1,047.5	1,196.9	I 1,408.4	2,439.2	3,790.4	12,749.7	18,013.0	14,854.3	19,206.2	29,479.3	I 53051.0	130,459.2	Domestic Credit	52
42.9	53.7	99.4	464.0	367.0	I 139.5	436.0	497.0	6,807.8	7,418.4	-914.2	-1,148.9	-399.6	I 4,943.6	32,093.9	Claims on Central Govt. (Net)	52an
—	—	—	—	—	I —	—	—	—	—	—	—	—	I .4	.4	Claims on State and Local Govts	52b
—	—	—	—	—	I 29.3	26.4	16.3	43.8	.2	—	—	—	I —	—	Claims on Nonfin.Pub.Enterprises	52c
290.5	356.3	457.7	583.5	829.9	I 1,239.7	1,976.9	3,277.1	5,898.0	10,594.4	15,768.5	20,355.1	29,879.0	I 48107.0	98,364.8	Claims on Private Sector	52d
243.1	299.0	427.1	665.1	922.0	I 1,914.7	2,922.1	4,422.3	7,206.7	11,108.6	15,312.4	21,463.6	28,498.2	I 37413.0	74,362.4	Liquid Liabilities	55l
78.1	106.9	162.4	201.7	286.6	I 143.2	199.1	281.0	303.2	221.6	529.9	1,881.5	3,047.4	I 5,929.5	12,384.6	Bonds	56ab
11.5	10.7	27.2	46.0	10.7	I 2.2	.8	.7	.7	.6	.6	.6	.6	I —	—	Restricted Deposits	56b
310.1	347.1	369.1	1,376.5	1,473.8	I 1,587.5	2,074.8	2,212.2	8,543.4	9,883.5	1,627.0	2,482.5	3,291.6	I 6,457.0	18,038.1	Long-Term Foreign Liabilities	56cl
1.5	2.3	3.7	11.2	22.5	I 27.0	36.7	68.3	84.4	94.5	92.1	62.3	66.9	I —	—	Central Govt. Lending Funds	56f
-140.8	-173.1	-206.4	-949.9	-997.5	I -1172.8	-1,221.2	1,175.7	2,623.3	4,066.5	6,272.5	9,209.6	12,164.7	I 23231.6	59,174.2	Capital Accounts	57a
-152.2	-212.7	-312.3	-393.9	-519.8	I -836.8	-1,236.6	-3,898.7	-3,338.2	-3,738.4	-5,304.0	-9,773.8	-9,353.4	I -12848.9	-13,590.8	Other Items (Net)	57r
Percent Per Annum															**Interest Rates**	
23.00	23.00	23.00	23.00	32.00	35.00	49.00	49.00	33.57	44.88	59.41	46.38	37.46	61.84	64.40	Discount Rate *(End of Period)*	60
21.00	21.39	25.34	34.00	40.24	43.55	41.54	46.81	31.97	33.65	43.31	41.50	28.09	39.39	48.93	Deposit Rate	60l
18.00	18.00	18.42	23.00	30.08	37.50	46.67	60.17	47.83	43.99	55.67	54.50	43.02	49.55	64.02	Lending Rate	60p
Period Averages															**Prices, Production, Labor**	
13.5	17.4	I 22.9	38.2	68.7	100.0	148.0	228.9	318.3	376.4	....	....	....	....	....	Wholesale Prices (1990=100)	63
2.9	3.6	4.6	7.4	12.9	I 19.2	28.5	44.0	63.9	81.4	I 100.0	124.4	162.5	221.1	336.7	Consumer Prices	64
73.0	75.9	58.7	80.5	74.4	75.6	77.7	83.4	89.3	98.7	100.0	100.2	101.1	97.7	97.2	Crude Petroleum Production	66aa
Period Averages																
....	....	....	....	....	3,220	....	....	....	....	....	3,169	3,326	3,560	....	Labor Force	67d
....	....	1,148	2,068	2,192	I 2,331	2,562	2,693	2,651	2,698	2,892	2,889	3,062	3,151	....	Employment	67e
....	....	90	155	187	I 150	158	263	241	207	213	335	312	409	....	Unemployment	67c
....	....	7.2	7.0	7.9	I 6.1	5.8	8.9	8.3	7.1	6.9	10.4	9.2	11.5	....	Unemployment Rate (%)	67r
Millions of US Dollars															**International Transactions**	
2,904.7	2,171.5	1,927.8	2,192.4	2,353.8	2,714.3	2,851.5	3,007.4	2,903.7	3,819.9	4,307.2	4,899.9	5,264.4	4,202.9	4,451.0	Exports	70..d
1,766.6	1,810.2	2,251.5	1,713.5	1,854.8	1,865.1	2,399.0	2,431.0	2,562.2	3,622.0	4,152.6	3,934.5	4,954.9	5,575.7	3,017.3	Imports, c.i.f.	71..d
1,543.9	1,575.0	1,981.7	1,517.4	1,634.1	1,644.5	2,115.5	1,975.5	2,223.0	3,252.5	3,774.8	3,570.9	4,520.1	5,012.7	2,736.9	Imports, f.o.b.	71.vd
1995=100																
....	....	....	....	....	65.0	69.6	75.3	80.5	89.4	100.0	102.4	102.1	96.7	92.9	Volume of Exports	72
....	....	....	....	....	72.7	70.8	73.4	49.3	74.6	100.0	96.3	132.6	166.1	95.6	Volume of Imports	73
Indices of Unit Values in US Dollars																
140.6	88.9	99.6	86.5	101.3	116.2	108.8	108.0	88.9	98.9	100.0	115.0	112.3	84.0	101.5	Unit Value of Exports	74..d
Minus Sign Indicates Debit															Balance of Payments	
76	-582	-1,187	-680	-715	-360	-708	-122	-678	-681	-765	84	-714	-2,169	955	Current Account, n.i.e.	78ald
2,905	2,200	2,021	2,205	2,354	2,724	2,851	3,101	3,066	3,843	4,381	4,873	5,264	4,203	4,451	Goods: Exports f.o.b.	78aad
-1,611	-1,643	-2,054	-1,583	-1,692	-1,715	-2,208	-2,083	-2,474	-3,282	-4,057	-3,680	-4,666	-5,198	-2,786	Goods: Imports f.o.b.	78abd
1,294	557	-33	622	662	1,009	643	1,018	592	561	324	1,193	598	-995	1,665	*Trade Balance*	78acd
397	441	421	440	516	538	556	617	652	742	850	854	826	808	812	Services: Credit	78add
-636	-583	-648	-606	-626	-804	-900	-933	-1,126	-1,127	-1,234	-1,210	-1,459	-1,531	-1,304	Services: Debit	78aed
1,055	415	-260	456	552	743	299	702	118	176	-60	837	-35	-1,718	1,173	*Balance on Goods & Services*	78afd
29	32	28	17	20	25	31	35	28	55	86	77	102	82	49	Income: Credit	78agd
-1,088	-1,074	-1,087	-1,250	-1,384	-1,235	-1,148	-979	-954	-1,057	-1,022	-1,120	-1,172	-1,309	-1,368	Income: Debit	78ahd
-4	-627	-1,319	-777	-812	-467	-818	-242	-808	-826	-996	-206	-1,105	-2,945	-146	*Balance on Gds, Serv. & Inc.*	78aid
85	51	135	104	106	119	123	134	145	164	250	359	438	840	1,151	Current Transfers, n.i.e.: Credit	78ajd
-5	-6	-3	-7	-9	-12	-13	-14	-15	-19	-19	-69	-47	-64	-50	Current Transfers: Debit	78akd
—	—	—	—	—	—	—	—	....	....	....	....	....	....	....	Capital Account, n.i.e.	78bcd
—	—	—	—	—	—	—	....	....	....	....	....	....	....	....	Capital Account, n.i.e.: Credit	78bad
—	—	—	—	—	—	—	....	....	....	....	....	....	....	....	Capital Account: Debit	78bbd
-1,122	-1,033	-209	-632	-515	580	732	361	1,309	998	1,883	1,514	1,454	2,114	743	Financial Account, n.i.e.	78bjd
—	—	—	—	—	—	—	—	....	....	....	....	....	....	....	Direct Investment Abroad	78bdd
62	81	123	155	160	126	160	178	469	531	470	491	625	814	690	Dir. Invest. in Rep. Econ., n.i.e.	78bed
—	—	—	—	—	—	—	—	....	....	....	....	....	....	....	Portfolio Investment Assets	78bfd
—	—	—	—	—	—	—	—	....	....	....	....	....	....	....	Equity Securities	78bkd
—	—	—	—	—	—	—	—	....	....	....	....	....	....	....	Debt Securities	78bld
—	—	—	—	—	—	—	—	....	....	....	....	....	....	....	Portfolio Investment Liab., n.i.e.	78bgd
—	—	—	—	—	—	—	—	....	....	....	....	....	....	....	Equity Securities	78bmd
—	—	—	—	—	—	—	—	....	....	....	....	....	....	....	Debt Securities	78bnd
....	....	....	....	....	....	....	....	....	....	....	....	....	....	....	Financial Derivatives Assets	78bwd
....	....	....	....	....	....	....	....	....	....	....	....	....	....	....	Financial Derivatives Liabilities	78bxd
54	-23	4	14	-68	—	—	—	....	....	....	....	....	....	....	Other Investment Assets	78bhd
....	....	....	....	....	....	....	....	....	....	....	....	....	....	....	Monetary Authorities	78bod
-5	-2	-4	1	-15	—	—	—	....	....	....	....	....	....	....	General Government	78bpd
-28	-15	26	3	-32	—	—	—	....	....	....	....	....	....	....	Banks	78bqd
87	-6	-18	10	-21	—	—	—	....	....	....	....	....	....	....	Other Sectors	78brd
-1,238	-1,091	-336	-801	-607	454	572	183	840	467	1,413	1,023	829	1,300	53	Other Investment Liab., n.i.e.	78bid
-63	188	21	70	-221	-53	-6	-4	69	-118	-42	-15	-17	-14	97	Monetary Authorities	78bsd
-649	-1,192	-357	-856	-426	-508	-585	-678	-684	-524	809	367	176	513	270	General Government	78btd
-35	8	—	-15	-3	—	—	—	....	....	....	....	....	....	....	Banks	78bud
-491	-95	—	—	43	1,015	1,163	865	1,455	1,109	646	671	670	801	-314	Other Sectors	78bvd
168	-446	629	25	114	126	134	-215	-92	22	-1,307	-1,343	-477	-352	-2,024	Net Errors and Omissions	78cad
-878	-2,061	-767	-1,287	-1,116	346	158	24	539	339	-189	255	263	-407	-326	*Overall Balance*	78cbd
878	2,061	767	1,287	1,116	-346	-158	-24	-539	-339	189	-255	-263	407	326	Reserves and Related Items	79dad
-97	124	185	26	-118	-261	-79	54	-510	-461	218	-232	-260	474	394	Reserve Assets	79dbd
89	83	-69	-58	-69	-85	-79	-77	-29	122	-29	-23	-3	-67	-68	Use of Fund Credit and Loans	79dcd
886	1,854	650	1,319	1,303	—	—	—	....	....	....	....	....	....	....	Exceptional Financing	79ded

Ecuador

		1970	1971	1972	1973	1974	1975	1976	1977	1978	1979	1980	1981	1982	1983	1984
Government Finance													*Millions of Sucres through 1978;*			
Deficit (-) or Surplus	80	−1,545.0	−1,733.0	−893.0	I 124.0	−3.0	−666.0	−2,160.0	−5,388.0	−2,296.0	I −1.5	−4.1	−16.8	−18.5	−14.0	−6.8
Revenue	81	3,716.0	4,423.0	5,514.0	I 7,973.0	11,390.0	12,391.0	14,653.0	16,452.0	19,057.0	I 23.1	37.5	39.3	46.0	60.2	99.9
Expenditure	82	5,261.0	6,156.0	6,407.0	I 7,849.0	11,393.0	13,057.0	16,813.0	21,840.0	21,353.0	I 24.6	41.7	56.1	64.5	74.2	106.7
Financing																
Domestic	84a	1,574.0	1,642.0	163.0	I −73.0	130.0	902.0	1,774.0	4,307.0	3,264.0	I 2.6	2.6	9.2	8.5	16.3	10.8
Foreign	85a	11.0	−56.0	954.0	I −51.0	−127.0	−236.0	386.0	1,081.0	−968.0	I −1.1	1.6	7.7	10.0	−2.3	−4.1
Use of Cash Balances	87	−40.0	147.0	−224.0	....	....	....	....	....	....	....	....	....	....	....	....
Debt: Sucres	88b	5,590.0	6,516.0	6,548.0	....	....	....	....	....	....	....	....	....	....	....	....
Debt: Foreign Currency	89b	....	....	....	....	....	....	....	....	....	....	....	....	....	....	....
National Accounts													*Millions of Sucres through 1978;*			
Exports of Goods & Services	90c	4,909	5,986	8,808	15,506	33,589	28,242	34,171	41,315	40,831	I 61	74	76	88	133	210
Government Consumption	91f	3,864	4,117	4,744	6,394	11,646	15,624	18,629	24,656	26,450	I 30	43	50	58	70	100
Gross Fixed Capital Formation	93e	5,842	8,704	8,441	10,885	16,859	24,907	29,470	39,285	50,085	I 55	69	78	94	93	125
Increase/Decrease(-) in Stocks	93i	529	574	936	1,230	3,991	3,890	2,109	4,852	4,347	I 4	7	3	11	5	15
Private Consumption	96f	26,375	30,436	34,429	41,711	55,506	70,298	84,517	102,578	121,244	I 143	175	215	262	369	521
Imports of Goods & Services	98c	−6,500	−9,769	−10,499	−13,497	−28,828	−35,221	−35,983	−46,310	−51,612	I −59	−75	−72	−97	−111	−157
Gross Domestic Product (GDP)	99b	35,019	40,048	46,859	62,229	92,763	107,740	132,913	166,376	191,345	I 234	293	349	416	560	813
Net Factor Inc/Pmts(-) Abroad	98.n	−670	−920	−1,680	−3,540	−5,670	−2,470	−4,060	−4,480	−5,520	I −10	−15	−18	−31	−42	−73
Gross National Income (GNI)	99a	34,347	39,126	45,181	58,687	87,098	105,272	128,852	161,898	185,822	I 224	279	330	385	518	740
Net National Income	99e	32,865	35,726	40,943	53,303	80,484	96,423	117,776	147,764	169,110	I 202	230	294	340	456	643
GDP Volume 1975 Prices (Billions)	99b.p	62.9	66.9	76.5	95.9	102.0	107.7	117.7	125.4	133.6	140.7	147.6	153.4	155.3	150.9	157.2
GDP Volume (1995=100)	99bv p	29.2	31.1	35.6	44.6	47.4	50.1	54.7	58.3	62.1	65.4	68.6	71.3	72.2	70.1	73.1
GDP Deflator (1995=100)	99bi p	.3	.3	.3	.3	.4	.5	.5	.6	.7	.8	.9	1.1	1.3	1.7	2.4
																Millions:
Population	99z	5.96	6.17	6.38	6.60	6.82	7.03	7.24	7.45	7.67	7.89	8.12	8.36	8.61	8.64	8.87

Billions of Sucres Beginning 1979: Year Ending December 31

1985	1986	1987	1988	1989	1990	1991	1992	1993	1994	1995	1996	1997	1998	1999		
															Government Finance	
22.0	I-31.1	-41.8	-1.4	97.2	147.6	186.0	461.0	550.7	115.2	-420.2	-282.8	-1,165.2	374.3	-1,167.1	Deficit (-) or Surplus	80
189.5	I186.9	236.8	415.5	835.4	1,355.2	1,820.1	3,008.6	4,314.6	5,647.6	8,030.4	10,633.9	13,515.3	17,866.6	31,884.4	Revenue	81
167.5	I218.0	278.6	416.8	738.2	1,207.6	1,634.1	2,547.6	3,763.9	5,532.5	8,450.6	10,916.7	14,680.5	17,492.3	33,051.5	Expenditure	82
															Financing	
-18.2	I8.6	29.1	36.7	-5.7	4.8	91.9	29.9	-59.3	521.8	937.2	479.1	3,296.2	-374.7	380.2	Domestic	84a
-3.8	I22.5	12.7	-35.4	-91.5	-152.4	-277.9	-490.9	-491.4	-637.0	-517.0	-196.3	-2,131.0	.4	787.0	Foreign	85a
....	....	....	....	....	....	....	....	....	....	....	....	....	....	....	Use of Cash Balances	87
....	....	....	....	....	....	....	....	....	....	....	....	....	....	....	Debt: Sucres	88b
....	....	....	....	....	....	....	....	....	....	....	....	....	....	....	Debt: Foreign Currency	89b

Billions of Sucres Beginning 1979

1985	1986	1987	1988	1989	1990	1991	1992	1993	1994	1995	1996	1997	1998	1999		
															National Accounts	
297	315	432	859	1,520	2,686	3,858	6,119	7,184	9,743	13,658	18,514	23,711	27,170	....	Exports of Goods & Services	90c
127	167	230	347	485	706	936	1,407	2,117	3,427	5,789	7,146	9,147	12,524	....	Government Consumption	91f
178	260	407	643	1,071	1,513	2,417	3,784	5,457	6,852	8,537	10,798	15,053	22,550	....	Gross Fixed Capital Formation	93e
23	28	—	6	-1	-77	309	333	330	82	59	-300	902	3,938	....	Increase/Decrease(-) in Stocks	93i
716	926	1,269	2,087	3,706	5,622	8,432	13,148	19,375	25,025	31,134	38,791	53,153	75,610	....	Private Consumption	96f
-232	-313	-544	-922	-1,611	-2,246	-3,655	-5,378	-7,011	-8,651	-13,171	-14,223	-22,926	-34,371	....	Imports of Goods & Services	98c
1,110	1,383	1,795	3,020	5,171	8,204	12,296	19,414	27,451	36,478	46,005	60,727	79,040	107,421	....	Gross Domestic Product (GDP)	99b
-82	-112	-122	-207	-384	-629	-737	-931	-1,098	-2,810	-3,238	-4,158	-6,107	....	....	Net Factor Inc/Pmts(-) Abroad	98.n
1,028	1,272	1,672	2,813	4,786	7,575	11,560	18,483	26,353	33,669	42,768	56,569	73,356	....	....	Gross National Income (GNI)	99a
893	1,072	1,357	2,271	3,851	6,159	9,534	15,476	21,986	28,309	35,965	45,334	....	....	....	Net National Income	99e
164.1	169.1	159.0	175.7	176.2	181.5	190.6	197.4	201.4	210.2	215.1	219.0	227.0	228.0	....	GDP Volume 1975 Prices (Billions)	99b.p
76.3	78.6	73.9	81.7	81.9	84.4	88.6	91.8	93.6	97.7	100.0	101.8	105.5	106.0	....	GDP Volume (1995=100)	99bv p
3.2	3.8	5.3	8.0	13.7	21.1	30.2	46.0	63.7	81.1	100.0	129.6	162.8	220.3	....	GDP Deflator (1995=100)	99bi p

Midyear Estimates

1985	1986	1987	1988	1989	1990	1991	1992	1993	1994	1995	1996	1997	1998	1999		
9.10	9.33	9.56	9.79	10.03	10.26	10.50	10.74	10.98	11.22	11.46	11.70	11.94	12.17	12.41	**Population**	99z

(See notes in the back of the book.)

Egypt

	1970	1971	1972	1973	1974	1975	1976	1977	1978	1979	1980	1981	1982	1983	1984
Exchange Rates														*Pounds per SDR:*	
Market Rate ......aa= wa	.4348	.4720	.4720	.5245	.4791	.4581	.4546	.4753	.5098	.9221	.8928	.8148	.7722	.7329	.6861
														Pounds per US Dollar:	
Market Rate ......ae= we	.4348	.4348	.4348	.4348	.3913	.3913	.3913	.3913	.3913	.7000	.7000	.7000	.7000	.7000	.7000
Secondary Rate ...... xe	...	...	...	...	...	...	.7000	.7000	.7000	...	...	.8317	.8317	.8317	.8317
Secondary Rate ...... xf	...	...	...	...	...	...	...	.7000	...	...	.7390	...	.8317	.8317	.8317
Tertiary Rate ...... yf	...	...	...	...	...	...	...	...	...	...	...	...	...	1.1453	1.2543
Fund Position														*Millions of SDRs:*	
Quota 2f.s	188	188	188	188	188	188	188	188	228	228	342	342	342	463	463
SDRs 1b.s	—	7	5	31	31	14	20	24	8						
Reserve Position in the Fund 1c.s												24		30	
Total Fund Cred.&Loans Outstg. 2tl	49	70	24	62	93	68	178	275	374	381	322	269	236	228	210
International Liquidity										*Millions of US Dollars Unless Otherwise Indicated:*					
Total Reserves minus Gold 1l.d	74	57	52	260	252	194	240	431	492	529	1,046	716	698	771	736
SDRs 1b.d	—	8	6	38	38	17	24	29	11						
Reserve Position in the Fund 1c.d												28		32	
Foreign Exchange 1d.d	74	49	46	222	214	177	216	402	481	529	1,046	688	698	739	736
Gold (Million Fine Troy Ounces) 1ad	2.434	2.432	2.432	2.432	2.432	2.432	2.432	2.432	2.473	2.472	2.432	2.432	2.432	2.432	2.432
Gold (National Valuation) 1and	85	85	85	85	103	103	103	103	104	104	103	775	578	757	679
Monetary Authorities: Other Assets ...... 3..d	101	90	75	124	265	631	300	347	510	409	529	849	1,106	1,349	1,625
Other Liab. ...... 4..d	532	677	673	791	978	2,554	2,798	4,041	8,915	5,173	I 5,082	4,768	5,126	4,487	4,403
Deposit Money Banks: Assets 7a.d	108.3	97.5	138.7	374.0	1,042.4	1,265.3	1,965.5	3,406.5	4,420.6	2,745.1	I 4,633.7	4,711.9	7,444.6	9,063.1	8,377.7
Liabilities 7b.d	186.3	200.6	211.4	302.2	957.8	1,789.9	1,961.6	1,598.0	1,942.5	1,228.4	I 2,598.9	3,702.4	5,099.7	6,283.1	6,252.7
Other Banking Insts.: Assets 7e.d	2.3	2.3	2.3	2.3	2.6	2.6	...	2.6	2.6	5.7	I 5.6	11.1	14.3	10.3	8.3
Liabilities 7f.d	...							20.7	43.4	41.4	I 63.1	99.4	149.0	377.1	388.9
Monetary Authorities														*Millions of Pounds:*	
Foreign Assets 11	102	100	92	185	201	265	251	344	590	763	I 1,187	1,639	1,667	2,030	1,888
Claims on Central Government 12a	517	592	668	823	982	1,511	1,594	1,878	4,178	6,211	I 6,184	8,093	10,393	12,627	14,377
Claims on Nonfin.Pub.Enterprises 12c	12	—	—	—	—	—	—	—	—	—	I 625	676	329	351	334
Claims on Deposit Money Banks 12e	417	390	383	395	580	775	1,105	1,544	1,633	1,153	I 1,757	333	357	643	898
Claims on Other Banking Insts 12f	6	6	6	6	5	5	5	104	170	121	I 213	314	518	551	665
Reserve Money 14	751	703	802	1,000	1,270	1,446	1,730	2,083	2,655	3,402	I 5,611	7,056	9,281	11,875	13,544
of which: Currency Outside DMBs 14a	525	559	631	777	948	1,156	1,388	1,750	2,184	2,657	I 3,398	4,291	5,503	6,475	7,098
Foreign Liabilities 16c	253	327	304	376	427	1,031	1,176	1,712	3,679	3,972	I 3,845	3,557	3,770	3,308	3,226
Central Government Deposits 16d	15	18	18	20	34	38	40	47	101	693	I 362	406	300	847	1,062
Other Items (Net) 17r	35	40	26	13	37	43	9	30	136	181	I 148	36	−88	172	330
Deposit Money Banks														*Millions of Pounds:*	
Reserves 20	236	142	185	260	382	370	451	495	505	803	I 1,325	2,392	3,557	5,039	6,124
Foreign Assets 21	47	42	60	163	408	495	769	1,333	1,730	1,922	I 3,244	3,298	5,211	6,344	5,864
Claims on Central Government 22a	583	663	704	741	923	1,369	1,646	1,816	2,393	2,546	I 2,775	1,335	1,785	1,206	1,973
Claims on Nonfin.Pub.Enterprises 22c	...										2,685	3,809	3,950	5,576	7,145
Claims on Private Sector 22d	381	417	425	410	587	881	1,147	1,537	1,790	2,396	I 2,174	4,242	5,549	6,876	8,284
Claims on Other Banking Insts 22f	123	126	122	115	196	207	174	102	67	136	I 119	304	272	309	391
Demand Deposits 24	258	287	357	425	553	706	849	1,194	1,369	1,697	I 2,504	2,886	3,498	3,798	4,554
Time, Savings,& Fgn.Currency Dep. 25	270	238	266	331	498	567	822	1,160	1,659	2,490	I 3,589	5,920	8,240	10,884	13,486
Bonds 26ab															
Restricted Deposits 26b											897	1,279	1,478	1,677	1,753
Foreign Liabilities 26c	81	87	92	131	375	700	768	625	760	860	I 1,819	2,592	3,570	4,398	4,377
Central Government Deposits 26d	105	126	130	128	184	211	247	366	596	821	I 349	494	488	545	555
Credit from Monetary Authorities 26g	416	385	383	395	578	771	1,105	1,530	1,589	1,078	I 1,780	372	552	858	1,108
Other Items (Net) 27r	240	268	268	278	308	367	397	409	512	857	I 1,384	1,837	2,500	3,189	3,949
Monetary Survey														*Millions of Pounds:*	
Foreign Assets (Net) 31n	−185	−272	−244	−160	−193	−971	−923	−660	−2,119	−2,148	I −1,234	−1,211	−461	668	150
Domestic Credit 32	1,502	1,660	1,777	1,947	2,475	3,725	4,279	5,024	7,901	9,897	I 14,065	17,871	22,008	26,104	31,553
Claims on Central Govt. (Net) 32an	980	1,111	1,224	1,416	1,686	2,632	2,953	3,282	5,874	7,243	I 8,248	8,527	11,390	12,441	14,733
Claims on Nonfin.Pub.Enterprises 32c	...										3,310	4,485	4,279	5,927	7,479
Claims on Private Sector 32d	394	418	426	411	587	881	1,147	1,537	1,790	2,396	I 2,174	4,242	5,549	6,876	8,284
Claims on Other Banking Insts 32f	129	132	127	120	201	212	179	206	237	257	I 333	617	790	865	1,056
Money 34	783	846	989	1,205	1,503	1,863	2,239	2,943	3,553	4,354	I 6,775	7,646	9,552	10,933	12,443
of which: Foreign Currency Deps. 34a											874	1,030	1,361	1,612	1,913
Quasi-Money 35	270	238	266	331	498	567	822	1,160	1,659	2,490	I 3,589	5,920	8,240	10,885	13,486
of which: Fgn. Currency Deposits 35a											1,493	2,524	3,640	4,301	4,616
Bonds 36ab											—				
Restricted Deposits 36b											897	1,279	1,478	1,677	1,753
Other Items (Net) 37r	265	304	278	251	281	325	295	262	570	904	I 1,571	1,815	2,277	3,277	4,020
Money plus Quasi-Money 35l	1,053	1,085	1,255	1,536	2,000	2,430	3,061	4,103	5,212	6,844	I 10,364	13,566	17,792	21,817	25,929
Other Banking Institutions															
Specialized Banks														*Millions of Pounds:*	
Cash 40	...								1	1	I 49	49	33	36	25
Foreign Assets 41	...	1	1	1	1	1	1	1	1	4	I 4	8	10	7	6
Claims on Nonfin.Pub.Enterprises 42c											130	215	390	492	651
Claims on Private Sector 42d	122	154	140	153	154	137	138	185	210	243	I 327	511	674	1,182	1,490
Demand Deposits 44	17	20	23	25	28	29	36	40	54	93	I 89	96	155	142	172
Time and Savings Deposits 45											47	85	138	258	296
Restricted Deposits 46b											8	12	16	23	26
Foreign Liabilities 46c								8	17	29	I 44	70	104	264	272
Central Government Deposits 46d	3	9	12	13	23	23	28	48	58	70	I 67	97	111	194	168
Credit from Monetary Authorities 46g	6	6	6	6	6	6	7	106	175	125	I 213	309	519	556	665
Credit from Deposit Money Banks 46h	123	126	121	115	194	203	175	102	61	118	I 119	303	267	375	501
Other Items (Net) 47r	−27	−6	−21	−6	−96	−123	−105	−117	−152	−187	I −78	−189	−203	−94	72
Post Office: Savings Deposits ...... 45..i	77	81	90	101	119	136	152	163	187	203	216	261	300	353	403
Banking Survey														*Millions of Pounds:*	
Foreign Assets (Net) 51n											−1,274	−1,273	−555	411	−117
Domestic Credit 52											14,342	18,147	22,475	27,083	32,883
Claims on Central Govt. (Net) 52an											8,401	8,694	11,583	12,606	14,978
Claims on Nonfin.Pub.Enterprises 52c											3,440	4,700	4,669	6,419	8,131
Claims on Private Sector 52d											2,501	4,753	6,223	8,058	9,774
Liquid Liabilities 55l											10,668	13,959	18,351	22,534	26,776
Bonds 56ab															
Restricted Deposits 56b											905	1,291	1,494	1,700	1,779
Other Items (Net) 57r											1,496	1,624	2,075	3,260	4,211

1985	1986	1987	1988	1989	1990	1991	1992	1993	1994	1995	1996	1997	1998	1999		
															Exchange Rates	
End of Period																
.7689	.8562	.9931	.9420	1.4456	2.8453	4.7665	4.5906	4.6314	4.9504	5.0392	4.8718	4.5713	4.7704	4.6734	Market Rate aa=	wa
End of Period																
.7000	.7000	.7000	.7000	1.1000	2.0000	3.3322	3.3386	3.3718	3.3910	3.3900	3.3880	3.3880	3.3880	3.4050	Market Rate ae=	we
1.3300	1.3600	1.8700	2.3529	2.5580	2.8736	....	....	....	....	....	....	....	....	....	Secondary Rate	xe
1.3010	1.3503	1.5183	2.2233	2.5171	2.7072	....	....	....	....	....	....	....	....	....	Secondary Rate	xf
1.5488	1.8838	2.1838	2.3731	2.6949	2.7978	....	....	....	....	....	....	....	....	....	Tertiary Rate	yf
End of Period															**Fund Position**	
463	463	463	463	463	463	463	678	678	678	678	678	678	678	944	Quota	2f.s
—	—	—	—	—	—	1	43	50	59	70	86	84	114	30	SDRs	1b.s
—	—	—	—	—	—	—	54	54	54	54	54	54	54	120	Reserve Position in the Fund	1c.s
167	118	185	141	122	88	89	147	147	132	70	11	—	—	—	Total Fund Cred.&Loans Outstg.	2tl
End of Period															**International Liquidity**	
792	829	1,378	1,263	1,520	2,684	5,325	10,810	12,904	13,481	16,181	17,398	18,665	18,124	14,484	Total Reserves minus Gold	1l.d
—	—	—	—	—	1	1	59	69	86	103	123	113	160	41	SDRs	1b.d
—	—	—	—	—	—	—	74	74	78	80	77	73	76	165	Reserve Position in the Fund	1c.d
792	829	1,378	1,263	1,520	2,683	5,324	10,677	12,761	13,316	15,998	17,198	18,479	17,888	14,278	Foreign Exchange	1d.d
2.432	2.432	2.432	2.432	2.432	2.432	2.432	2.432	2.432	2.432	2.432	2.432	2.432	2.432	2.432	Gold (Million Fine Troy Ounces)	1ad
578	622	814	794	679	641	656	616	616	694	704	695	609	541	475	Gold (National Valuation)	1and
1,290	1,439	255	618	604	1,078	1,287	1,280	1,274	1,293	1,131	1,003	938	874	....	Monetary Authorities: Other Assets	3..d
4,133	4,732	9,136	12,620	16,108	15,622	11,852	12,457	11,842	12,551	13,298	12,324	11,384	11,873	11,296	Other Liab.	4..d
8,774.9	13,208.3	20,829.4	24,290.9	8,481.6	10,365.5	12,606.9	11,326.8	10,786.5	11,432.3	11,070.3	10,736.2	9,153.2	7,815.1	7,441.1	Deposit Money Banks: Assets	7a.d
6,239.3	9,392.9	11,673.7	12,171.9	3,485.4	3,714.3	3,423.6	2,343.2	1,782.0	1,465.3	1,500.2	1,844.2	3,555.7	4,995.3	4,318.3	Liabilities	7b.d
6.9	45.6	24.7	32.6	40.0	35.1	33.6	42.9	51.2	29.5	29.8	22.0	16.9	14.8	7.3	Other Banking Insts.: Assets	7e.d
501.3	594.9	790.7	1,100.7	770.5	530.7	423.3	436.1	486.5	457.1	275.5	255.4	267.4	219.9	215.1	Liabilities	7f.d
End of Period															**Monetary Authorities**	
1,888	2,128	2,646	2,704	3,639	11,029	26,086	45,911	55,894	60,529	61,901	65,189	68,799	66,782	52,923	Foreign Assets	11
15,966	17,841	21,058	24,588	34,263	52,238	56,562	56,993	52,849	50,978	51,615	47,015	44,368	61,209	75,447	Claims on Central Government	12a
425	492	545	559	694	722	725	823	820	799	799	900	849	817	1,029	Claims on Nonfin.Pub.Enterprises	12c
1,075	1,173	1,992	2,191	3,309	4,608	6,157	8,279	11,655	12,224	12,892	12,700	12,438	8,359	6,462	Claims on Deposit Money Banks	12e
837	1,078	1,155	1,256	1,425	1,624	1,823	1,974	2,134	2,040	2,095	2,147	2,261	2,275	3,336	Claims on Other Banking Insts	12f
15,814	17,655	18,714	19,476	21,082	27,137	32,356	35,712	42,554	47,888	52,357	54,562	60,610	72,336	73,522	Reserve Money	14
8,285	8,803	9,537	10,406	10,934	12,410	13,524	15,241	17,818	20,612	22,750	24,954	28,215	31,502	35,310	*of which: Currency Outside DMBs*	14a
3,021	3,413	6,579	8,967	17,895	31,494	39,917	42,264	40,609	43,215	45,430	41,807	38,570	40,224	38,464	Foreign Liabilities	16c
933	1,209	1,626	1,289	2,308	9,211	18,634	35,109	38,481	33,617	29,661	28,476	26,738	22,296	23,298	Central Government Deposits	16d
422	435	477	1,566	2,045	2,379	445	894	1,707	1,851	1,855	3,105	2,797	4,586	3,913	Other Items (Net)	17r
End of Period															**Deposit Money Banks**	
7,164	9,262	10,545	11,054	12,068	14,726	19,330	19,540	23,097	25,402	28,094	28,146	30,241	33,262	34,636	Reserves	20
6,142	9,246	14,581	17,004	21,696	29,786	41,980	37,722	36,370	38,767	37,528	36,374	31,011	26,477	25,337	Foreign Assets	21
2,684	3,911	5,233	7,302	7,360	6,747	17,699	40,681	41,262	42,398	41,882	47,567	54,479	47,244	40,363	Claims on Central Government	22a
8,529	9,683	11,148	13,091	16,615	23,026	28,214	23,928	29,283	29,998	33,180	37,481	38,643	38,801	42,109	Claims on Nonfin.Pub.Enterprises	22c
10,145	12,888	14,881	17,330	20,428	24,454	24,816	30,978	36,885	48,831	66,777	83,810	105,545	133,799	159,958	Claims on Private Sector	22d
686	1,123	1,284	1,629	1,695	2,095	2,056	1,250	1,432	1,284	1,630	2,424	2,988	4,251	2,958	Claims on Other Banking Insts	22f
5,606	6,135	7,460	8,308	9,742	10,849	12,703	13,985	14,940	15,919	17,282	18,026	18,920	19,335	20,506	Demand Deposits	24
15,978	21,127	26,635	33,969	41,619	56,302	70,126	86,761	98,598	109,810	121,175	135,764	150,966	162,512	174,713	Time, Savings,& Fgn.Currency Dep.	25
—	—	—	—	—	—	—	—	—	—	—	800	1,675	1,675	2,238	Bonds	26ab
1,942	3,108	5,079	5,070	6,023	7,423	8,152	7,076	8,239	9,182	10,858	12,513	14,081	15,771	18,113	Restricted Deposits	26b
4,368	6,575	8,172	8,520	8,916	10,673	11,400	7,804	6,009	4,969	5,086	6,248	12,047	16,924	14,704	Foreign Liabilities	26c
663	1,059	1,201	1,415	1,373	2,070	5,778	10,206	6,907	7,805	11,016	13,638	14,670	18,906	23,889	Central Government Deposits	26d
1,242	1,550	2,401	2,726	4,142	5,930	7,859	9,613	15,598	17,571	20,842	20,648	20,938	11,244	7,256	Credit from Monetary Authorities	26g
5,551	6,558	6,723	7,402	8,048	7,588	18,076	18,654	18,040	21,423	22,832	28,165	29,609	37,468	43,943	Other Items (Net)	27r
End of Period															**Monetary Survey**	
641	1,386	2,476	2,220	−1,476	−1,353	16,748	33,566	45,646	51,111	48,914	53,508	49,194	36,111	25,092	Foreign Assets (Net)	31n
37,674	44,747	52,476	63,052	78,798	99,625	107,483	111,311	119,278	134,906	157,300	179,230	207,724	247,195	278,013	Domestic Credit	32
17,053	19,484	23,464	29,186	37,941	47,705	49,848	52,358	48,724	51,953	52,820	52,467	57,439	67,252	68,623	Claims on Central Govt. (Net)	32an
8,953	10,175	11,692	13,651	17,309	23,748	28,940	24,751	30,103	30,797	33,979	38,381	39,492	39,618	43,138	Claims on Nonfin.Pub.Enterprises	32c
10,145	12,888	14,881	17,330	20,428	24,454	24,816	30,978	36,885	48,831	66,777	83,810	105,545	133,799	159,958	Claims on Private Sector	32d
1,523	2,200	2,439	2,885	3,120	3,720	3,879	3,224	3,566	3,324	3,724	4,571	5,248	6,526	6,294	Claims on Other Banking Insts	32f
14,696	15,973	18,241	20,579	22,471	26,205	28,337	30,832	34,571	38,275	41,540	44,521	48,708	58,577	59,066	Money	34
2,454	2,848	3,878	4,484	5,588	8,249	11,104	10,253	10,918	9,892	10,980	10,260	9,332	10,225	11,148	*of which: Foreign Currency Deps.*	34a
15,980	21,129	26,637	33,970	41,623	56,303	70,127	86,762	98,602	109,834	121,227	135,882	151,129	162,795	174,844	Quasi-Money	35
5,230	8,645	12,214	17,124	21,749	29,802	36,093	27,608	25,964	30,851	33,335	32,015	31,792	33,271	37,435	*of which: Fgn. Currency Deposits*	35a
—	—	—	—	—	—	—	—	—	—	—	800	1,675	1,675	2,238	Bonds	36ab
1,942	3,108	5,079	5,070	6,023	7,423	8,152	7,076	8,239	9,182	10,858	12,513	14,081	15,771	18,113	Restricted Deposits	36b
5,697	5,922	4,994	5,654	7,206	8,342	17,616	20,207	23,512	28,727	32,590	39,021	41,325	44,489	48,845	Other Items (Net)	37r
30,676	37,102	44,878	54,549	64,094	82,508	98,464	117,594	133,174	148,109	162,766	180,404	199,837	221,372	233,909	Money plus Quasi-Money	35l
															Other Banking Institutions	
End of Period															Specialized Banks	
28	44	59	69	82	94	180	134	184	169	262	288	300	467	382	Cash	40
5	32	17	23	44	70	112	143	173	100	101	74	57	50	25	Foreign Assets	41
808	1,004	1,147	1,289	1,435	1,584	1,758	1,881	1,961	2,067	2,130	2,170	2,112	2,073	2,397	Claims on Nonfin.Pub.Enterprises	42c
1,794	2,472	2,983	3,596	4,047	4,950	5,442	5,458	6,361	7,425	8,785	11,355	13,814	17,607	20,657	Claims on Private Sector	42d
221	234	307	351	481	475	458	575	722	912	1,195	1,434	2,010	2,366	652	Demand Deposits	44
383	455	666	775	849	875	1,291	1,330	1,705	2,322	2,751	3,464	4,297	5,703	8,835	Time and Savings Deposits	45
2	10	27	25	27	21	19	19	32	20	32	36	42	59	53	Restricted Deposits	46b
351	416	554	771	848	1,061	1,411	1,456	1,640	1,550	934	865	906	745	732	Foreign Liabilities	46c
89	87	153	418	465	573	194	427	592	713	893	1,614	1,980	1,712	1,860	Central Government Deposits	46d
844	1,076	1,145	1,256	1,426	1,630	1,830	2,008	2,067	2,043	2,112	2,155	2,279	2,299	3,375	Credit from Monetary Authorities	46g
623	1,088	1,150	1,489	1,524	1,888	1,945	1,236	1,410	1,021	1,500	2,292	2,790	3,932	2,442	Credit from Deposit Money Banks	46h
123	186	205	−109	−12	175	345	565	509	1,180	1,861	2,027	1,980	3,381	5,513	Other Items (Net)	47r
459	531	589	643	694	773	894	1,046	1,335	1,866	2,591	3,524	4,877	6,680	8,783	Post Office: Savings Deposits	45..i
End of Period															**Banking Survey**	
295	1,001	1,940	1,473	−2,280	−2,344	15,450	32,253	44,178	49,661	48,081	52,717	48,346	35,416	24,384	Foreign Assets (Net)	51n
39,134	46,481	54,630	65,297	81,406	102,675	111,585	116,128	124,880	142,295	166,797	190,938	222,041	266,064	301,818	Domestic Credit	52
17,434	19,943	23,927	29,431	38,187	47,940	50,629	53,060	49,570	53,175	55,127	55,223	61,079	72,968	75,668	Claims on Central Govt. (Net)	52an
9,761	11,179	12,839	14,940	18,744	25,331	30,698	26,632	32,064	32,864	36,108	40,551	41,603	41,691	45,535	Claims on Nonfin.Pub.Enterprises	52c
11,940	15,360	17,864	20,926	24,475	29,404	30,258	36,436	43,246	56,256	75,562	95,164	119,359	151,406	180,615	Claims on Private Sector	52d
31,710	38,277	46,380	56,249	66,036	84,537	100,927	120,411	136,752	153,040	169,041	188,538	210,721	235,654	251,797	Liquid Liabilities	55l
—	—	—	—	—	—	—	—	—	—	—	800	1,675	1,675	2,238	Bonds	56ab
1,944	3,118	5,106	5,095	6,050	7,443	8,171	7,095	8,271	9,202	10,890	12,550	14,123	15,830	18,166	Restricted Deposits	56b
5,775	6,087	5,083	5,425	7,041	8,352	17,937	20,876	24,035	29,714	34,948	41,768	43,868	48,322	54,003	Other Items (Net)	57r

Egypt

		1970	1971	1972	1973	1974	1975	1976	1977	1978	1979	1980	1981	1982	1983	1984
Interest Rates															*Percent Per Annum*	
Discount Rate *(End of Period)*	60	5.00	5.00	5.00	5.00	5.00	5.00	6.00	7.00	8.00	9.00	11.00	12.00	13.00	13.00	13.00
Treasury Bill Rate	60c	….	….	….	….	….	….									….
Deposit Rate	60l	….	….	….	….	….	….	3.0	4.7	5.9	7.0	8.3	10.0	11.0	11.0	11.0
Lending Rate	60p	….	….	….	….	….	….	8.0	8.8	10.2	12.0	13.3	15.0	15.0	15.0	15.0
Prices and Labor														*Index Numbers (1995=100):*		
Industrial Share Price (1992=100)	62															
Wholesale Prices	63	ɪ6.1	6.1	6.2	6.6	7.6	8.1	8.8	9.6	11.0	12.1	14.7	15.9	17.3	20.1	22.1
Consumer Prices	64	4.5	4.6	4.7	5.0	5.5	6.0	6.6	7.5	8.3	9.1	ɪ11.0	12.1	13.9	16.2	18.9
															Number in Thousands:	
Labor Force	67d	….	….	….	….	….	….	….	….	….	….	….	….	….	….	….
Employment	67e	….	….	….	….	….	….	….	….	….	….	….	….	….	….	….
Unemployment	67c	….	….	….	….	….	….	….	….	….	….	….	….	….	….	….
Unemployment Rate (%)	67r	….	….	….	….	….	….	….	….	….	….	….	….	….	….	….
International Transactions															*Millions of Pounds:*	
Exports	70	331.2	343.2	358.8	444.2	593.3	548.6	595.5	668.5	679.8	1,287.8	2,132.2	2,263.0	2,184.1	2,250.1	2,197.9
Suez Canal Dues	70.s	—	—	—	—	—	33.2	121.7	167.4	201.1	412.1	464.3	621.8	657.8	678.8	665.4
Imports, c.i.f.	71	342.0	399.9	390.8	361.1	920.1	1,539.3	1,489.8	1,884.3	2,632.2	2,686.0	3,401.9	6,147.4	6,354.5	7,192.7	7,536.1
Balance of Payments															*Millions of US Dollars:*	
Current Account, n.i.e.	78ald	….	….	….	….	….	−1,200	−1,220	−1,542	−438	−2,136	−1,851	−330	−1,988		
Goods: Exports f.o.b.	78aad	….	….	….	….	….	1,974	1,939	2,424	3,854	3,999	4,018	3,693	3,864		
Goods: Imports f.o.b.	78abd	….	….	….	….	….	−4,038	−4,743	−6,002	−6,814	−7,918	−7,733	−8,251	−10,080		
Trade Balance	78acd	….	….	….	….	….	−2,064	−2,804	−3,578	−2,960	−3,919	−3,715	−4,558	−6,216		
Services: Credit	78add	….	….	….	….	….	1,601	1,633	1,788	2,393	2,537	2,800	3,133	2,990		
Services: Debit	78aed	….	….	….	….	….	−1,448	−1,548	−1,773	−2,343	−2,487	−2,727	−2,767	−3,096		
Balance on Goods & Services	78afd	….	….	….	….	….	−1,912	−2,719	−3,563	−2,911	−3,869	−3,642	−4,192	−6,323		
Income: Credit	78agd	….	….	….	….	….	39	86	172	270	401	402	437	522		
Income: Debit	78ahd	….	….	….	….	….	−315	−412	−420	−589	−897	−1,092	−1,080	−1,092		
Balance on Gds, Serv. & Inc.	78aid	….	….	….	….	….	−2,188	−3,044	−3,811	−3,230	−4,366	−4,332	−4,835	−6,892		
Current Transfers, n.i.e.: Credit	78ajd	….	….	….	….	….	988	1,824	2,269	2,791	2,230	2,481	4,505	4,904		
Current Transfers: Debit	78akd	….	….	….	….	….										
Capital Account, n.i.e.	78bcd	….	….	….	….	….	—	—	—	—	—	—	—	—		
Capital Account, n.i.e.: Credit	78bad	….	….	….	….	….	—	—	—	—	—	—	—	—		
Capital Account: Debit	78bbd	….	….	….	….	….	—	—	—	—	—	—	—	—		
Financial Account, n.i.e.	78bjd	….	….	….	….	….	−773	143	1,488	956	2,046	1,458	285	1,718		
Direct Investment Abroad	78bdd	….	….	….	….	….	−7	−20	−5	−7	−6	−8	−19	−16		
Dir. Invest. in Rep. Econ., n.i.e.	78bed	….	….	….	….	….	105	318	1,216	548	753	294	490	729		
Portfolio Investment Assets	78bfd	….	….	….	….	….	6	4	3	5	7	—	6	1		
Equity Securities	78bkd	….	….	….	….	….	—	—	—	—	—	—	—	—		
Debt Securities	78bld	….	….	….	….	….	6	4	3	5	7	—	6	1		
Portfolio Investment Liab., n.i.e.	78bgd	….	….	….	….	….	—	—	—	—	—	—	—	—		
Equity Securities	78bmd	….	….	….	….	….	—	—	—	—	—	—	—	—		
Debt Securities	78bnd	….	….	….	….	….	—	—	—	—	—	—	—	—		
Financial Derivatives Assets	78bwd	….	….	….	….	….										
Financial Derivatives Liabilities	78bxd	….	….	….	….	….										
Other Investment Assets	78bhd	….	….	….	….	….	−136	−194	−407	−249	379	250	−389	488		
Monetary Authorities	78bod	….	….	….	….	….	−6	−16	−9	−16	−6	−11	−11	−10		
General Government	78bpd	….	….	….	….	….	−56	−25	−18	−10	−14	−3	−2	−2		
Banks	78bqd	….	….	….	….	….	−74	−153	−380	−223	399	265	−376	500		
Other Sectors	78brd	….	….	….	….	….										
Other Investment Liab., n.i.e.	78bid	….	….	….	….	….	−741	34	680	658	914	922	196	516		
Monetary Authorities	78bsd	….	….	….	….	….	−239	−264	−253	−326	−499	−351	−373	−288		
General Government	78btd	….	….	….	….	….	569	843	734	729	1,853	1,559	1,143	838		
Banks	78bud	….	….	….	….	….	−930	−341	279	340	−343	−166	−1	−40		
Other Sectors	78bvd	….	….	….	….	….	−141	−204	−80	−85	−97	−121	−573	6		
Net Errors and Omissions	78cad	….	….	….	….	….	66	13	39	92	143	148	131	24		
Overall Balance	78cbd	….	….	….	….	….	−1,906	−1,064	−16	610	53	−245	87	−247		
Reserves and Related Items	79dad	….	….	….	….	….	1,906	1,064	16	−610	−53	245	−87	247		
Reserve Assets	79dbd	….	….	….	….	….	−130	22	−52	−559	−105	−178	−152	55		
Use of Fund Credit and Loans	79dcd	….	….	….	….	….	114	125	10	−77	−63	−36	−9	−18		
Exceptional Financing	79ded	….	….	….	….	….	1,922	917	58	26	115	460	74	210		
Government Finance															*Millions of Pounds:*	
Deficit (-) or Surplus	80						−938	−1,557	−1,114	−1,246	−1,964	….	ɪ−1,096	−3,554	−2,364	−3,258
Revenue	81						2,039	2,306	3,388	3,758	4,666	….	ɪ8,072	9,711	10,977	12,345
Grants Received	81z						250	223	60	62	20	….	ɪ9	6	100	1
Expenditure	82						2,912	3,774	3,911	4,151	5,590	….	ɪ7,892	11,595	11,195	13,361
Lending Minus Repayments	83						315	312	651	915	1,060	….	ɪ1,285	1,676	2,246	2,243
Financing																
Domestic	84a						461	917	588	945	1,567	….	ɪ731	3,019	2,034	3,001
Foreign	85a						477	640	526	301	397	….	ɪ365	535	330	257
National Accounts															*Millions of Pounds:*	
Exports of Goods & Services	90c	ɪ439	447	457	531	890	894	1,034	1,470	1,945	3,251	ɪ4,322	5,307	5,913	6,159	6,387
Government Consumption	91f	ɪ756	821	905	1,020	1,101	1,213	1,571	1,697	1,841	2,059	ɪ2,549	2,841	3,584	4,160	4,957
Gross Fixed Capital Formation	93e	ɪ353	356	405	462	640	1,228	1,385	1,825	2,618	3,346	ɪ4,062	5,108	6,150	8,164	8,921
Increase/Decrease(-) in Stocks	93i	ɪ74	60	62	40	90	100	195	561	416	450	ɪ266	100	351	150	500
Private Consumption	96f	ɪ2,011	2,119	2,237	2,339	2,871	3,281	3,863	4,917	6,279	8,623	ɪ11,023	ɪ11,155	14,485	17,208	20,684
Imports of Goods & Services	98c	ɪ−574	−600	−649	−729	−1,395	−1,831	−1,772	−2,260	−3,316	−5,254	ɪ−6,410	−7,361	−8,504	−8,981	−10,357
Gross Domestic Product (GDP)	99b	ɪ2,971	3,203	3,417	3,663	4,197	4,886	6,276	8,210	9,783	12,475	ɪ15,410	17,150	22,465	26,424	31,693
Net Factor Inc/Pmts(-) Abroad	98.n	ɪ−44	−117	−14	−29	−112	−148	133	433	983	785	ɪ1,685	742	446	1,217	2,005
Gross National Income (GNI)	99a	ɪ3,059	3,086	3,403	3,634	4,085	4,738	6,409	8,643	10,766	13,260	ɪ17,231	17,892	21,327	26,051	30,605
GDP Volume 1981/82 Prices	99b.p													22,460	23,590	25,900
GDP Volume 1986/87 Prices	99b.p													….	….	….
GDP Volume 1991/92 Prices	99b.p													….	….	….
GDP Volume 1996/97 Prices	99b.p													….	….	….
GDP Volume (1995=100)	99bvp													54.5	57.2	62.8
GDP Deflator (1995=100)	99bip													20.1	22.5	24.6
															Millions:	
Population	99z	33.33	34.08	34.84	35.62	36.42	37.23	37.87	38.79	39.82	40.98	42.13	41.67	42.84	44.02	45.23

1985	1986	1987	1988	1989	1990	1991	1992	1993	1994	1995	1996	1997	1998	1999		
Percent Per Annum															**Interest Rates**	
13.00	13.00	13.00	13.00	14.00	14.00	20.00	18.40	16.50	14.00	13.50	13.00	12.25	12.00	12.00	Discount Rate *(End of Period)*	60
....	....	....	....	....	....	....	....	....	....	....	....	8.8	8.8	9.0	Treasury Bill Rate	60c
11.0	11.0	11.0	11.0	11.7	12.0	12.0	12.0	12.0	11.8	10.9	10.5	9.8	9.4	9.2	Deposit Rate	60l
15.0	15.0	16.3	17.0	18.3	19.0	....	20.3	18.3	16.5	16.5	15.6	13.8	13.0	13.0	Lending Rate	60p
Period Averages															**Prices and Labor**	
....	....	....	....	....	....	....	....	....	....	....	....	449.11	474.64	586.65	Industrial Share Price (1992=100)	62
25.0	29.4	33.4	42.1	53.6	62.6	73.9	82.8	I 89.9	94.1	100.0	108.3	112.8	114.4	115.4	Wholesale Prices	63
21.2	26.3	31.4	37.0	44.9	52.4	62.7	71.3	79.9	86.4	I 100.0	107.2	I 112.1	116.8	120.4	Consumer Prices	64
Period Averages																
....	....	....	....	15,698	15,964	15,599	15,862	16,494	17,174	17,365	....	....	....	....	Labor Force	67d
....	....	....	....	I 14,926	14,361	13,827	14,399	I 14,703	15,241	15,344	....	....	....	....	Employment	67e
....	....	....	....	1,108	1,347	1,463	1,416	1,801	1,877	1,917	....	....	....	....	Unemployment	67c
....	....	....	....	6.9	8.6	9.6	9.0	10.9	11.0	11.3	....	....	....	....	Unemployment Rate (%)	67r
Millions of Pounds															**International Transactions**	
2,600.0	2,054.0	3,046.0	3,994.4	5,734.7	6,953.8	11,764.6	10,173.4	7,558.8	11,767.9	11,703.8	12,004.1	13,285.9	10,605.9	12,086.1	Exports	70
654.2	769.0	844.5	904.6	1,506.8	3,177.6	5,707.9	6,187.9	6,628.4	6,998.1	6,692.9	6,381.4	6,072.5	6,108.9	6,015.3	Suez Canal Dues	70.s
7,772.8	8,051.4	11,357.8	16,308.6	16,623.7	24,823.2	25,216.2	27,656.1	27,553.8	34,598.9	39,892.0	44,218.0	44,769.0	54,771.0	54,399.0	Imports, c.i.f.	71
Minus Sign Indicates Debit															Balance of Payments	
-2,166	-1,811	-246	-1,048	-1,309	185	1,903	2,812	2,299	31	-254	-192	-711	-2,566	-1,635	Current Account, n.i.e.	78al*d*
3,836	2,632	3,115	2,770	3,119	3,924	4,164	3,670	3,545	4,044	4,670	4,779	5,525	4,403	5,237	Goods: Exports f.o.b.	78aa*d*
-9,050	-7,170	-8,095	-9,378	-8,841	-10,303	-9,831	-8,901	-9,923	-9,997	-12,267	-13,169	-14,157	-14,617	-15,165	Goods: Imports f.o.b.	78ab*d*
-5,215	-4,538	-4,980	-6,608	-5,722	-6,379	-5,667	-5,231	-6,378	-5,953	-7,597	-8,390	-8,632	-10,214	-9,928	*Trade Balance*	78ac*d*
3,024	3,358	3,627	4,408	4,203	5,971	6,783	7,716	7,895	8,070	8,590	9,271	9,380	8,141	9,494	Services: Credit	78ad*d*
-3,190	-3,012	-2,742	-3,082	-3,283	-3,788	-3,364	-4,867	-5,367	-5,645	-4,873	-5,084	-6,770	-6,492	-6,452	Services: Debit	78ae*d*
-5,381	-4,192	-4,095	-5,283	-4,802	-4,196	-2,248	-2,382	-3,850	-3,528	-3,880	-4,203	-6,021	-8,565	-6,886	*Balance on Goods & Services*	78af*d*
418	406	503	575	709	857	860	915	1,110	1,330	1,578	1,901	2,122	2,030	1,788	Income: Credit	78ag*d*
-1,211	-1,126	-983	-776	-1,389	-1,879	-2,143	-2,797	-1,967	-2,114	-1,983	-1,556	-1,185	-1,075	-1,045	Income: Debit	78ah*d*
-6,174	-4,912	-4,575	-5,484	-5,482	-5,218	-3,531	-4,264	-4,707	-4,312	-4,285	-3,858	-5,085	-7,610	-6,143	*Balance on Gds, Serv. & Inc.*	78ai*d*
4,007	3,101	4,329	4,436	4,183	5,417	5,434	7,076	7,006	4,622	4,284	3,888	4,738	5,166	4,564	Current Transfers, n.i.e.: Credit	78aj*d*
—	—	—	—	-10	-14	—	—	—	-279	-253	-222	-363	-122	-55	Current Transfers: Debit	78ak*d*
—	—	—	—	—	—	—	—	—	—	—	—	....	....	....	Capital Account, n.i.e.	78bc*d*
—	—	—	—	—	—	—	—	—	—	—	—	....	....	....	Capital Account, n.i.e.: Credit	78ba*d*
—	—	—	—	—	—	—	—	—	—	—	—	....	....	....	Capital Account: Debit	78bb*d*
1,381	1,936	-332	1,308	361	-11,039	-4,706	-168	-762	-1,450	-1,845	-1,459	1,958	1,901	-1,421	Financial Account, n.i.e.	78bj*d*
-3	-6	-19	-12	-23	-12	-62	-4	—	-43	-93	-5	-129	-45	-38	Direct Investment Abroad	78bd*d*
1,178	1,217	948	1,190	1,250	734	253	459	493	1,256	598	636	891	1,076	1,065	Dir. Invest. in Rep. Econ., n.i.e.	78be*d*
20	—	2	—	—	15	21	6	—	—	....	—	....	-63	-22	Portfolio Investment Assets	78bf*d*
—	—	—	—	—	—	—	—	—	—	....	—	....	-63	-22	Equity Securities	78bk*d*
20	—	2	—	—	15	21	6	—	—	....	—	....	....	....	Debt Securities	78bl*d*
—	—	—	—	—	—	—	—	4	3	20	545	816	-537	617	Portfolio Investment Liab., n.i.e.	78bg*d*
—	—	—	—	—	—	—	—	—	—	....	—	515	-160	658	Equity Securities	78bm*d*
—	—	—	—	—	—	—	—	4	3	20	545	301	-377	-41	Debt Securities	78bn*d*
....	....	....	....	....	....	....	....	....	—	....	—	....	....	....	Financial Derivatives Assets	78bw*d*
....	....	....	....	....	....	....	....	....	—	....	—	....	....	....	Financial Derivatives Liabilities	78bx*d*
-369	479	-909	546	-1,299	-1,921	-2,298	1,183	319	-905	-396	-565	-170	39	-1,805	Other Investment Assets	78bh*d*
-15	-4	-10	-7	-25	-16	-46	-13	-21	-25	65	65	37	24	-14	Monetary Authorities	78bo*d*
-2	—	-1	-17	-26	-2	-18	-104	-4	—	....	—	....	....	....	General Government	78bp*d*
-352	483	-898	571	-1,249	-1,904	-2,234	1,300	523	-634	371	338	1,599	1,357	372	Banks	78bq*d*
—	—	—	—	—	—	—	—	-179	-246	-832	-968	-1,806	-1,342	-2,163	Other Sectors	78br*d*
555	245	-354	-416	432	-9,855	-2,620	-1,812	-1,578	-1,761	-1,974	-2,070	551	1,431	-1,240	Other Investment Liab., n.i.e.	78bi*d*
-585	-438	-832	-250	-372	-29	-113	-42	629	-5	-21	-4	-19	-204	-3	Monetary Authorities	78bs*d*
890	1,105	754	387	688	-10,032	-2,204	-1,175	-1,761	-1,536	-1,783	-2,578	-1,506	-946	-989	General Government	78bt*d*
16	-316	-537	-749	-138	237	-333	-383	-202	-256	-148	324	1,715	1,393	-692	Banks	78bu*d*
233	-106	261	196	254	-31	30	-212	-244	36	-22	188	361	1,188	444	Other Sectors	78bv*d*
585	-156	892	-362	414	630	730	716	-1,519	255	272	-74	-1,882	-722	-1,558	Net Errors and Omissions	78ca*d*
-200	-31	315	-102	-533	-10,224	-2,073	3,360	18	-1,164	-1,827	-1,725	-635	-1,387	-4,614	*Overall Balance*	78cb*d*
200	31	-315	102	533	10,224	2,073	-3,360	-18	1,164	1,827	1,725	635	1,387	4,614	Reserves and Related Items	79da*d*
-107	-282	-669	153	435	-2,508	-2,775	-6,330	-2,809	-1,193	-409	-1,010	-1,185	535	4,027	Reserve Assets	79db*d*
-43	-57	89	-59	-24	-48	—	81	—	-22	-95	-85	-15	—	—	Use of Fund Credit and Loans	79dc*d*
350	370	266	7	122	12,781	4,849	2,889	2,791	2,379	2,331	2,820	1,836	852	587	Exceptional Financing	79de*d*
Year Ending June 30															**Government Finance**	
-3,439	-4,655	-2,613	-4,716	-4,126	-5,494	-1,067	-4,831	2,681	589	1,828	I -4,411	-5,178	....	....	Deficit (-) or Surplus	80
13,681	15,508	16,764	19,916	22,601	23,435	35,430	49,678	59,443	67,828	73,654	I 69,233	72,782	....	....	Revenue	81
219	374	1,087	548	1,023	1,428	2,820	3,337	3,269	2,811	2,056	I 1,954	1,392	....	....	Grants Received	81z
14,945	17,552	18,091	22,548	23,913	26,738	35,499	54,649	56,143	65,382	68,689	I 74,400	78,503	....	....	Expenditure	82
2,394	2,985	2,373	2,632	3,837	3,619	3,818	3,197	3,888	4,668	5,193	I 1,198	849	....	....	Lending Minus Repayments	83
															Financing	
2,947	4,432	2,298	5,033	4,551	6,164	2,296	6,708	-1,319	1,454	-60	I 5,844	6,785	....	....	Domestic	84a
492	223	315	-317	-425	-670	-1,229	-1,877	-1,362	-2,043	-1,768	I -1,433	-1,607	....	....	Foreign	85a
Year Ending June 30															**National Accounts**	
6,597	6,034	6,476	10,700	13,800	19,400	31,000	40,400	43,500	40,100	45,100	48,450	51,700	47,200	48,440	Exports of Goods & Services	90c
5,668	6,462	7,350	8,600	9,700	10,850	12,450	14,500	16,000	18,000	21,500	23,600	26,050	28,250	30,420	Government Consumption	91f
10,389	12,753	14,100	20,150	23,100	26,500	27,850	28,700	31,000	35,600	38,600	42,100	49,400	59,600	64,430	Gross Fixed Capital Formation	93e
600	240	-650	300	900	1,800	-1,200	-1,200	—	—	700	1,550	200	2,730	8,460	Increase/Decrease(-) in Stocks	93i
24,076	28,338	35,900	43,550	54,100	68,950	80,900	101,000	115,000	130,500	148,900	171,700	192,700	207,740	224,250	Private Consumption	96f
-10,636	-9,837	-11,740	-21,700	-24,800	-31,400	-39,800	-44,300	-48,200	-49,200	-49,800	-59,100	-63,800	-65,300	-73,700	Imports of Goods & Services	98c
37,451	44,131	51,526	61,600	76,800	96,100	111,200	139,100	157,300	175,000	205,000	228,300	256,250	280,220	302,300	Gross Domestic Product (GDP)	99b
1,681	1,176	2,768	6,730	7,524	....	....	....	....	....	....	....	....	....	....	Net Factor Inc/Pmts(-) Abroad	98.n
35,892	39,397	46,818	....	....	....	....	....	....	....	....	....	....	....	....	Gross National Income (GNI)	99a
27,400	28,700	29,800	....	....	....	....	....	....	....	....	....	....	....	....	GDP Volume 1981/82 Prices	99b.*p*
....	....	51,530	54,340	57,010	60,250	60,920	63,650	....	....	....	....	....	....	....	GDP Volume 1986/87 Prices	99b.*p*
....	....	....	....	....	....	....	139,100	143,140	148,820	155,730	163,500	172,480	....	....	GDP Volume 1991/92 Prices	99b.*p*
....	....	....	....	....	....	....	....	....	....	....	....	256,250	270,590	....	GDP Volume 1996/97 Prices	99b.*p*
66.5	69.6	72.3	76.3	80.0	84.5	85.5	89.3	91.9	95.6	100.0	105.0	110.8	117.0	....	GDP Volume (1995=100)	99bv*p*
27.5	30.9	34.8	39.4	46.8	55.4	63.5	76.0	83.5	89.3	100.0	106.1	112.9	116.9	....	GDP Deflator (1995=100)	99bi*p*
Midyear Estimates																
46.47	47.81	49.05	50.27	50.86	51.91	52.99	54.08	55.20	56.34	57.51	59.31	I 64.73	65.98	67.23	**Population**	99z

(See notes in the back of the book.)

El Salvador

		1970	1971	1972	1973	1974	1975	1976	1977	1978	1979	1980	1981	1982	1983	1984
Exchange Rates														*Colones per SDR: End of Period (aa)*		
Market Rate	aa	2.500	2.714	2.714	3.016	3.061	2.927	2.905	3.037	3.257	3.293	3.189	2.910	2.758	2.617	2.451
Market Rate	ae	2.500	2.500	2.500	2.500	2.500	2.500	2.500	2.500	2.500	2.500	2.500	2.500	2.500	2.500	2.500
Fund Position															*Millions of SDRs:*	
Quota	2f. s	35.0	35.0	35.0	35.0	35.0	35.0	35.0	35.0	43.0	43.0	64.5	64.5	64.5	89.0	89.0
SDRs	1b. s	—	2.2	3.7	3.8	3.6	3.9	4.0	7.8	7.6	13.2	—	.1	1.7	.1	
Reserve Position in the Fund	1c. s								5.1	8.8	8.5	—	—	—		
Total Fund Cred.&Loans Outstg.	2tl	6.5	10.2	8.8	—	17.9	17.9	12.8	—	—	—	25.0	57.3	117.1	132.6	127.2
International Liquidity													*Millions of US Dollars Unless Otherwise Indicated:*			
Total Reserves minus Gold	1l. d	45.4	46.2	63.9	41.3	77.6	107.0	185.4	211.2	268.1	142.6	77.7	71.9	108.5	160.2	165.8
SDRs	1b. d	—	2.4	4.1	4.6	4.4	4.6	4.7	9.5	9.9	17.4	—	.1	1.8	.1	
Reserve Position in the Fund	1c. d	—	—	—	—	—	—	—	6.2	11.4	11.2	—	—	—		
Foreign Exchange	1d. d	45.4	43.8	59.8	36.7	73.2	102.4	180.7	195.6	246.8	114.0	77.7	71.8	106.7	160.1	165.8
Gold (Million Fine Troy Ounces)	1ad	.494	.492	.486	.486	.486	.486	.486	.501	.501	.508	.516	.516	.516	.469	.469
Gold (National Valuation)	1an d	17.3	17.2	18.5	20.5	20.5	20.5	20.5	21.1	21.1	21.5	21.8	21.8	21.8	19.8	19.8
Monetary Authorities: Other Liab.	4.. d	25.2	26.9	28.0	19.1	80.9	83.9	96.4	79.3	165.5	177.4	428.0	559.9	568.6	574.8	572.4
Deposit Money Banks: Assets	7a. d	9.2	7.5	8.0	14.4	21.0	14.6	15.7	10.6	24.3	14.6	43.0	67.5	39.0	87.0	104.7
Liabilities	7b. d	13.5	8.7	7.6	22.2	33.3	9.9	21.5	37.7	55.8	43.9	9.1	22.4	22.5	37.0	47.0
Other Banking Insts.: Assets	7e. d	....	....	....	....	....	....	....	....	....	....	....	....	....	....	....
Liabilities	7f. d	....	....	....	....	....	....	....	....	....	....	....	....	....	....	....
Monetary Authorities														*Millions of Colones:*		
Foreign Assets	11	157	158	206	154	245	319	515	581	723	404	249	234	286	406	416
Claims on Central Government	12a	116	136	152	131	253	281	295	391	401	688	1,158	1,781	1,675	1,601	2,014
Claims on Local Government	12b	....	....	....	....	....	....	....	....	....	....	....	....	—	2	2
Claims on Nonfin.Pub.Enterprises	12c	....	....	....	....	....	....	....	....	....	....	....	....	264	268	277
Claims on Private Sector	12d	44	65	77	90	128	194	231	275	306	360	878	887	⎸50	54	118
Claims on Deposit Money Banks	12e	130	145	149	222	287	243	285	336	316	533	606	586	638	788	677
Claims on Other Banking Insts	12f	....	....	....	....	....	....	....	....	....	....	....	....	860	669	803
Reserve Money	14	149	166	209	239	277	353	476	504	386	357	457	537	1,447	1,505	1,678
of which: Currency Outside DMBs	14a	136	145	175	201	241	253	380	432	500	743	719	703	732	724	836
Time, Savings,& Fgn.Currency Dep.	15	....	....	....	....	....	....	....	....	....	....	....	....	2	2	—
Bonds	16ab	—	—	—	—	—	—	—	—	—	—	—	—	—	—	—
Foreign Liabilities	16c	19	30	28	6	67	60	45	2	55	15	499	823	928	635	585
Long-Term Foreign Liabilities	16cl	60	65	66	42	190	202	233	196	358	429	651	743	816	1,149	1,158
Central Government Deposits	16d	35	40	31	47	72	85	131	235	213	195	260	305	158	216	590
Counterpart Funds	16e	....	....	....	....	....	....	....	....	....	....	....	....	52	—	—
Central Govt. Lending Funds	16f	....	....	....	....	....	....	....	....	....	....	....	....	97	103	52
Capital Accounts	17a	62	80	99	77	94	103	118	138	181	248	310	343	347	358	380
Other Items (Net)	17r	121	124	151	186	214	234	323	508	553	743	715	736	⎸−75	−178	−136
Deposit Money Banks														*Millions of Colones:*		
Reserves	20	163	177	218	256	295	378	484	529	419	393	508	567	⎸624	693	784
Foreign Assets	21	23	19	20	36	52	36	39	27	61	37	108	169	⎸97	218	262
Claims on Central Government	22a	7	7	7	9	22	18	31	52	54	91	34	154	⎸101	150	208
Claims on Local Government	22b	....	....	....	....	....	....	....	....	....	....	....	....			
Claims on Private Sector	22d	588	640	720	909	1,072	1,128	1,350	1,647	1,914	2,128	2,124	2,244	⎸2,574	2,848	3,081
Claims on Other Banking Insts	22f	....	....	....	....	....	....	....	....	....	....	....	....	6	2	3
Demand Deposits	24	157	167	208	263	314	392	512	550	579	567	693	693	⎸755	746	879
Time, Savings,& Fgn.Currency Dep.	25	300	343	418	492	560	705	854	1,015	1,154	1,125	1,135	1,397	⎸1,470	1,834	2,144
Bonds	26ab	126	124	120	121	135	117	123	139	149	162	178	191	⎸246	263	241
Foreign Liabilities	26c	30	18	16	52	81	22	52	94	139	110	15	48	⎸49	88	114
Long-Term Foreign Liabilities	26cl	4	4	3	3	3	2	2	—	—	—	8	7	⎸7	5	4
Central Government Deposits	26d	9	12	13	13	17	21	24	44	50	48	66	60	⎸54	60	121
Credit from Monetary Authorities	26g	125	140	143	218	287	243	285	336	316	533	606	586	⎸638	788	677
Liabilities to Other Banking Insts	26i	....	....	....	....	....	....	....	....	....	....	....	....	152	114	183
Liab. to Nonbank Financial Insts	26j	....	....	....	....	....	....	....	....	....	....	....	....	32	68	136
Capital Accounts	27a	59	62	70	83	79	90	107	131	149	164	181	181	⎸211	211	215
Other Items (Net)	27r	−29	−26	−26	−35	−33	−32	−55	−54	−90	−60	−108	−30	⎸−211	−266	−374
Monetary Survey														*Millions of Colones:*		
Foreign Assets (Net)	31n	131	129	182	132	150	273	457	511	589	316	−157	−469	⎸−594	−99	−21
Domestic Credit	32	710	796	912	1,079	1,386	1,516	1,753	2,086	2,413	3,025	3,868	4,700	⎸5,344	5,341	5,818
Claims on Central Govt. (Net)	32an	78	91	115	80	186	193	171	164	192	537	866	1,570	⎸1,565	1,476	1,512
Claims on Local Government	32b	4	5	3	4	8	7	14	30	37	78	25	47	⎸—	2	2
Claims on Nonfin.Pub.Enterprises	32c	....	....	....	....	....	....	....	....	....	....	....	....	290	289	299
Claims on Private Sector	32d	631	705	797	998	1,200	1,322	1,582	1,922	2,220	2,488	3,002	3,130	⎸2,624	2,902	3,199
Claims on Other Banking Insts	32f	....	....	....	....	....	....	....	....	....	....	....	....	865	672	806
Money	34	295	315	390	466	557	648	917	988	1,087	1,321	1,429	1,437	⎸1,578	1,557	1,773
Quasi-Money	35	300	343	418	492	560	705	854	1,015	1,154	1,125	1,135	1,397	⎸1,471	1,835	2,144
Bonds	36ab	127	124	120	121	135	117	123	221	230	243	190	250	⎸246	263	241
Long-Term Foreign Liabilities	36cl	64	69	69	45	193	204	235	196	358	429	659	750	⎸823	1,154	1,161
Counterpart Funds	36e	....	....	....	....	....	....	....	....	....	....	....	....	52	—	—
Central Govt. Lending Funds	36f	....	....	....	....	....	....	....	....	....	....	....	....	97	103	52
Liabilities to Other Banking Insts	36i	....	....	....	....	....	....	....	....	....	....	....	....	152	114	183
Liab. to Nonbank Financial Insts	36j	....	....	....	....	....	....	....	....	....	....	....	....	32	68	136
Capital Accounts	37a	121	141	169	160	173	193	225	270	330	412	491	524	⎸558	569	594
Other Items (Net)	37r	−66	−66	−72	−73	−81	−78	−144	−93	−158	−189	−193	−127	⎸−259	−424	−488
Money plus Quasi-Money	35l	595	658	807	958	1,116	1,353	1,770	2,004	2,241	2,446	2,563	2,834	⎸3,049	3,393	3,917

	1985	1986	1987	1988	1989	1990	1991	1992	1993	1994	1995	1996	1997	1998	1999		
Colones per US Dollar: End of Period (ae)																**Exchange Rates**	
	2.746	6.116	7.093	6.729	6.571	11.424	11.558	12.609	11.909	12.774	13.014	12.589	11.813	12.327	12.016	Market Rate	**aa**
	2.500	5.000	5.000	5.000	5.000	8.030	8.080	9.170	8.670	8.750	8.755	8.755	8.755	8.755	8.755	Market Rate	**ae**
End of Period																**Fund Position**	
	89.0	89.0	89.0	89.0	89.0	89.0	89.0	125.6	125.6	125.6	125.6	125.6	125.6	125.6	171.3	Quota	**2f. s**
	—	—	—	—	—	—	—	—	—	.1	25.0	25.0	25.0	25.0	25.0	SDRs	**1b. s**
	—	—	—	—	—	—	—	—	—	—	—	—	—	—	—	Reserve Position in the Fund	**1c. s**
	100.6	50.9	15.8	8.0	4.1	.1	—	—	—	—	—	—	—	—	—	Total Fund Cred.&Loans Outstg.	**2tl**
End of Period																**International Liquidity**	
	179.6	169.7	186.1	161.6	265.9	414.8	287.2	422.1	536.2	649.4	758.3	936.9	1,307.9	1,613.1	2,003.8	Total Reserves minus Gold	**1l. d**
	—	—	—	—	—	—	—	—	—	.1	37.1	35.9	33.7	35.2	34.3	SDRs	**1b. d**
	—	—	—	—	—	—	—	—	—	—	—	—	—	—	—	Reserve Position in the Fund	**1c. d**
	179.6	169.7	186.1	161.6	265.9	414.8	287.2	422.1	536.2	649.3	721.2	901.0	1,274.2	1,577.9	1,969.5	Foreign Exchange	**1d. d**
	.469	.469	.469	.469	.469	.469	.469	.469	.469	.469	.469	.469	.469	.469	.469	Gold (Million Fine Troy Ounces)	**1ad**
	19.8	19.8	19.8	19.8	19.8	19.8	19.8	19.8	19.8	19.8	19.8	19.8	19.8	19.8	19.8	Gold (National Valuation)	**1an d**
	561.3	501.5	395.1	374.0	484.8	546.7	342.1	368.1	293.1	158.6	175.6	217.9	244.4	169.5	166.5	Monetary Authorities: Other Liab.	**4.. d**
	148.4	94.5	81.8	72.3	93.1	86.9	65.8	81.1	94.0	59.3	67.4	103.2	111.7	118.8	124.3	Deposit Money Banks: Assets	**7a. d**
	42.2	23.7	17.0	29.1	51.8	17.1	18.0	31.4	48.5	140.8	348.0	397.2	532.2	512.0	543.5	Liabilities	**7b. d**
	....	....	....	....	....	....	....	....	....	.3	2.5	3.0	1.7	2.5	1.0	Other Banking Insts.: Assets	**7e. d**
	....	....	....	....	....	....	....	....	....	1.5	13.7	7.4	2.7	2.5	6.1	Liabilities	**7f. d**
End of Period																**Monetary Authorities**	
	446	1,322	1,398	1,275	1,966	4,391	3,734	5,094	6,385	7,473	8,211	9,721	12,720	15,556	17,258	Foreign Assets	**11**
	2,157	2,105	2,214	2,494	3,474	5,170	6,330	6,867	6,825	6,314	6,200	5,813	5,688	5,383	5,579	Claims on Central Government	**12a**
	1	1	2	2	5	5	11	12	12	12	11	10	9	8	7	Claims on Local Government	**12b**
	305	345	414	382	334	—	—	13	—	—	—	—	—	—	—	Claims on Nonfin.Pub.Enterprises	**12c**
	98	64	55	7	—	—	10	—	—	—	—	—	—	—	—	Claims on Private Sector	**12d**
	886	817	1,098	1,261	2,094	2,249	1,094	1,243	1,317	—	—	—	172	711	1,160	Claims on Deposit Money Banks	**12e**
	916	945	1,003	1,307	1,303	556	629	638	657	2,292	2,979	3,510	3,514	3,456	3,381	Claims on Other Banking Insts	**12f**
	2,058	2,076	2,595	3,011	3,332	4,318	5,289	6,086	8,730	10,762	12,101	13,313	15,084	16,339	18,004	Reserve Money	**14**
	1,080	1,157	1,298	1,326	1,727	1,856	2,023	2,433	2,655	2,999	3,161	3,130	3,250	3,531	4,716	of which: Currency Outside DMBs	**14a**
	3	13	23	15	278	546	773	693	853	841	887	327	74	56	26	Time, Savings,& Fgn.Currency Dep.	**15**
	8	—	90	8	91	596	1,815	2,935	3,347	2,836	1,844	2,581	3,741	4,192	5,219	Bonds	**16ab**
	531	735	327	357	683	1,430	356	551	300	63	79	26	25	—	25	Foreign Liabilities	**16c**
	1,149	2,083	1,760	1,567	1,768	2,962	2,407	2,825	2,242	1,325	1,458	1,882	2,115	1,484	1,433	Long-Term Foreign Liabilities	**16cl**
	610	1,093	907	1,213	1,137	1,521	1,772	1,446	1,496	2,009	1,767	1,214	1,220	4,100	4,623	Central Government Deposits	**16d**
	150	250	1,098	1,214	1,727	900	528	716	99	54	18	13	15	11	11	Counterpart Funds	**16e**
	52	105	105	105	362	105	517	22	20	1	1	1	1	—	—	Central Govt. Lending Funds	**16f**
	398	493	528	533	551	1,474	1,573	1,982	2,158	2,235	1,989	1,978	2,022	2,183	2,331	Capital Accounts	**17a**
	−150	−1,248	−1,249	−1,292	−752	−1,478	−3,223	−3,389	−4,047	−4,033	−2,744	−2,281	−2,192	−3,251	−4,287	Other Items (Net)	**17r**
End of Period																**Deposit Money Banks**	
	902	833	1,193	1,577	1,525	2,874	3,175	4,252	6,341	8,383	8,470	9,279	11,426	12,056	15,936	Reserves	**20**
	371	473	409	362	465	698	532	744	815	519	591	903	978	1,040	1,088	Foreign Assets	**21**
	291	418	485	446	645	557	774	765	1,009	1,347	1,368	1,346	1,261	791	1,123	Claims on Central Government	**22a**
	—	—	—	—	—	—	—	—	—	—	—	—	17	25	70	Claims on Local Government	**22b**
	3,977	4,917	5,345	6,063	6,604	7,345	8,598	12,267	14,405	19,638	24,636	29,341	37,566	42,891	47,352	Claims on Private Sector	**22d**
	3	2	2	3	2	4	4	5	2	27	19	40	26	—	692	Claims on Other Banking Insts	**22f**
	1,095	1,451	1,278	1,459	1,474	2,045	2,139	3,059	3,506	3,539	3,934	4,996	4,921	5,268	5,416	Demand Deposits	**24**
	2,805	3,586	3,977	4,584	4,887	6,618	8,297	11,206	14,934	20,312	22,185	26,560	33,919	38,131	41,736	Time, Savings,& Fgn.Currency Dep.	**25**
	246	226	215	223	244	171	158	150	112	100	397	1,040	1,642	1,677	2,113	Bonds	**26ab**
	103	107	80	143	258	136	144	288	420	1,157	2,787	2,816	3,502	2,613	2,458	Foreign Liabilities	**26c**
	3	11	6	2	1	1	2	—	—	75	260	662	1,157	1,869	2,301	Long-Term Foreign Liabilities	**26cl**
	190	262	338	392	383	462	521	541	562	873	1,432	1,609	2,046	2,827	2,645	Central Government Deposits	**26d**
	886	817	1,098	1,261	2,094	2,249	1,094	1,238	1,317	—	—	—	172	711	1,297	Credit from Monetary Authorities	**26g**
	201	426	402	372	358	412	330	284	274	2,251	2,579	2,641	2,949	3,398	3,778	Liabilities to Other Banking Insts	**26i**
	115	199	299	361	330	435	432	574	616	675	695	777	1,208	1,131	707	Liab. to Nonbank Financial Insts	**26j**
	237	273	311	386	416	409	743	809	860	2,102	2,620	3,352	4,310	5,125	5,579	Capital Accounts	**27a**
	−336	−717	−568	−732	−1,203	−1,461	−776	−117	−29	−1,170	−1,805	−3,543	−4,553	−5,947	−1,769	Other Items (Net)	**27r**
End of Period																**Monetary Survey**	
	184	952	1,400	1,137	1,491	3,523	3,765	4,999	6,480	6,772	5,936	7,782	10,171	13,983	15,863	Foreign Assets (Net)	**31n**
	6,966	7,457	8,290	9,110	10,859	11,667	14,065	18,579	20,852	26,749	32,014	37,237	44,816	45,628	50,978	Domestic Credit	**32**
	1,648	1,168	1,454	1,335	2,599	3,744	4,812	5,645	5,777	4,779	4,369	4,335	3,683	−753	−566	Claims on Central Govt. (Net)	**32an**
	1	1	2	2	5	5	11	12	12	12	11	10	26	33	77	Claims on Local Government	**32b**
	323	360	429	393	347	12	1	13	—	—	—	—	—	—	41	Claims on Nonfin.Pub.Enterprises	**32c**
	4,075	4,981	5,400	6,070	6,604	7,345	8,608	12,267	14,405	19,638	24,636	29,341	37,566	42,891	47,352	Claims on Private Sector	**32d**
	919	947	1,005	1,310	1,305	560	633	643	659	2,320	2,997	3,551	3,541	3,456	4,074	Claims on Other Banking Insts	**32f**
	2,251	2,694	2,680	2,892	3,281	4,017	4,745	6,142	7,198	7,569	8,766	9,898	9,693	10,064	10,880	Money	**34**
	2,808	3,599	3,999	4,598	5,165	7,165	9,070	11,900	15,787	21,153	23,072	26,887	33,993	38,187	41,761	Quasi-Money	**35**
	254	226	305	230	335	766	1,973	3,085	3,459	2,936	2,241	3,622	5,383	5,869	7,332	Bonds	**36ab**
	1,152	2,095	1,766	1,569	1,769	2,963	2,409	2,825	2,242	1,400	1,718	2,543	3,272	3,353	3,734	Long-Term Foreign Liabilities	**36cl**
	150	250	1,098	1,214	1,727	900	528	716	99	54	18	13	15	11	11	Counterpart Funds	**36e**
	52	105	105	105	362	105	517	22	20	1	1	1	1	—	—	Central Govt. Lending Funds	**36f**
	201	426	402	372	358	412	330	284	274	2,251	2,579	2,641	2,949	3,398	3,778	Liabilities to Other Banking Insts	**36i**
	115	199	299	361	330	435	432	574	616	675	695	777	1,208	1,131	707	Liab. to Nonbank Financial Insts	**36j**
	635	766	839	918	966	1,883	2,316	2,792	3,018	4,337	4,609	5,330	6,331	7,308	7,910	Capital Accounts	**37a**
	−468	−1,949	−1,802	−2,012	−1,943	−3,455	−4,490	−4,760	−5,378	−6,854	−5,750	−6,692	−7,859	−9,711	−9,274	Other Items (Net)	**37r**
	5,059	6,293	6,680	7,491	8,447	11,181	13,815	18,042	22,984	28,722	31,839	36,784	43,686	48,251	52,641	Money plus Quasi-Money	**35l**

		1970	1971	1972	1973	1974	1975	1976	1977	1978	1979	1980	1981	1982	1983	1984
Other Banking Institutions														*Millions of Colones:*		
Reserves	40	...	...	...	...	...	...	...	...	...	...	...	...	...	...	...
Foreign Assets	41	...	...	...	...	...	...	...	...	...	...	...	...	...	...	...
Claims on Central Government	42a	...	...	...	...	...	...	...	...	...	...	...	...	...	...	...
Claims on Private Sector	42d	...	...	...	...	...	...	...	...	...	...	...	...	...	...	...
Claims on Deposit Money Banks	42e	...	...	...	...	...	...	...	...	...	...	...	...	...	...	...
Time, Savings,& Fgn.Currency Dep.	45	...	...	...	...	...	...	...	...	...	...	...	...	...	...	...
Money Market Instruments	46aa	...	...	...	...	...	...	...	...	...	...	...	...	...	...	...
Foreign Liabilities	46c	...	...	...	...	...	...	...	...	...	...	...	...	...	...	...
Long-Term Foreign Liabilities	46cl	...	...	...	...	...	...	...	...	...	...	...	...	...	...	...
Central Government Deposits	46d	...	...	...	...	...	...	...	...	...	...	...	...	...	...	...
Credit from Monetary Authorities	46g	...	...	...	...	...	...	...	...	...	...	...	...	...	...	...
Credit from Deposit Money Banks	46h	...	...	...	...	...	...	...	...	...	...	...	...	...	...	...
Capital Accounts	47a	...	...	...	...	...	...	...	...	...	...	...	...	...	...	...
Other Items (Net)	47r	...	...	...	...	...	...	...	...	...	...	...	...	...	...	...
Banking Survey														*Millions of Colones:*		
Foreign Assets (Net)	51n	...	...	...	...	...	...	...	...	...	...	...	...	...	...	...
Domestic Credit	52	...	...	...	...	...	...	...	...	...	...	...	...	...	...	...
Claims on Central Govt. (Net)	52an	...	...	...	...	...	...	...	...	...	...	...	...	...	...	...
Claims on Local Government	52b	...	...	...	...	...	...	...	...	...	...	...	...	...	...	...
Claims on Nonfin.Pub.Enterprises	52c	...	...	...	...	...	...	...	...	...	...	...	...	...	...	...
Claims on Private Sector	52d	...	...	...	...	...	...	...	...	...	...	...	...	...	...	...
Liquid Liabilities	55l	...	...	...	...	...	...	...	...	...	...	...	...	...	...	...
Money Market Instruments	56aa	...	...	...	...	...	...	...	...	...	...	...	...	...	...	...
Bonds	56ab	...	...	...	...	...	...	...	...	...	...	...	...	...	...	...
Long-Term Foreign Liabilities	56cl	...	...	...	...	...	...	...	...	...	...	...	...	...	...	...
Counterpart Funds	56e	...	...	...	...	...	...	...	...	...	...	...	...	...	...	...
Central Govt. Lending Funds	56f	...	...	...	...	...	...	...	...	...	...	...	...	...	...	...
Liab. to Nonbank Financial Insts	56j	...	...	...	...	...	...	...	...	...	...	...	...	...	...	...
Capital Accounts	57a	...	...	...	...	...	...	...	...	...	...	...	...	...	...	...
Other Items (Net)	57r	...	...	...	...	...	...	...	...	...	...	...	...	...	...	...
Interest Rates														*Percent Per Annum*		
Money Market Rate	60b	...	...	...	...	...	...	...	...	...	...	...	...	...	...	...
Deposit Rate	60l	...	...	...	...	...	...	...	...	...	...	...	...	...	12.50	12.50
Deposit Rate (Fgn. Currency)	60l. f	...	...	...	...	...	...	...	...	...	...	...	...	...	...	...
Lending Rate	60p	...	...	...	...	...	...	...	...	...	...	...	...	...	15.00	14.00
Lending Rate (Fgn. Currency)	60p. f	...	...	...	...	...	...	...	...	...	...	...	...	...	...	...
Prices and Labor														*Index Numbers (1995=100):*		
Wholesale Prices	63	8.3	7.8	8.3	10.0	12.6	12.8	17.2	25.4	‡20.3	21.9	25.3	27.9	30.2	32.3	34.2
Consumer Prices	64	3.5	3.5	3.5	3.8	4.4	5.2	5.6	6.3	7.1	‡8.1	9.6	11.0	12.3	13.9	15.5
															Number in Thousands:	
Labor Force	67d	...	...	...	...	...	...	...	...	...	...	...	...	...	...	...
Employment	67e	...	...	...	...	...	...	...	...	...	...	...	...	...	...	...
Unemployment	67c	...	...	...	...	...	...	...	...	...	...	...	...	...	...	...
Unemployment Rate (%)	67r	...	...	...	...	...	...	...	...	...	...	...	...	...	...	...
International Transactions														*Millions of US Dollars*		
Exports	70..d	229.4	228.2	273.3	352.0	462.6	531.4	743.3	972.4	848.4	1,223.2	966.8	796.6	699.4	735.3	717.3
Imports, c.i.f.	71..d	214.4	249.4	272.4	377.2	562.5	614.0	734.7	929.1	1,028.0	1,037.0	966.1	985.6	856.8	891.5	977.4
Balance of Payments														*Millions of US Dollars:*		
Current Account, n.i.e.	78al d							23.6	37.4	−278.7	32.2	33.9	−250.5	−120.0	−147.8	−188.7
Goods: Exports f.o.b.	78aa d							744.6	973.5	801.6	1,132.3	1,075.3	798.0	699.6	758.0	725.9
Goods: Imports f.o.b.	78ab d							−681.0	−861.0	−951.1	−954.7	−897.0	−898.4	−799.8	−832.2	−914.5
Trade Balance	78ac d							63.7	112.5	−149.4	177.6	178.4	−100.3	−100.2	−74.3	−188.6
Services: Credit	78ad d							116.1	113.0	121.0	133.0	138.8	124.7	117.4	135.8	165.4
Services: Debit	78ae d							−171.4	−208.6	−256.8	−300.6	−273.5	−263.4	−253.0	−246.3	−242.0
Balance on Goods & Services	78af d							8.4	16.8	−285.3	10.0	43.7	−239.0	−235.9	−184.7	−265.1
Income: Credit	78ag d							38.9	39.9	37.0	90.4	56.6	47.5	50.9	37.0	62.9
Income: Debit	78ah d							−52.8	−65.5	−88.8	−130.3	−118.6	−119.3	−142.4	−151.6	−159.1
Balance on Gds, Serv. & Inc.	78ai d							−5.6	−8.7	−337.2	−30.0	−18.3	−310.9	−327.4	−299.3	−361.3
Current Transfers, n.i.e.: Credit	78aj d							38.1	50.0	61.8	65.6	52.9	75.2	210.5	154.1	176.1
Current Transfers: Debit	78ak d							−8.9	−3.9	−3.4	−3.3	−.6	−14.8	−3.1	−2.6	−3.5
Capital Account, n.i.e.	78bc d							—	−6.5	−7.1	−10.8	−3.3	—	—	—	—
Capital Account, n.i.e.: Credit	78ba d							—	—	—	—	—	—	—	—	—
Capital Account: Debit	78bb d							—	−6.5	−7.1	−10.8	−3.3	—	—	—	—
Financial Account, n.i.e.	78bj d							85.6	43.9	340.4	−49.0	30.6	187.6	138.6	87.0	32.7
Direct Investment Abroad	78bd d							—	—	—	—	—	—	—	—	—
Dir. Invest. in Rep. Econ., n.i.e.	78be d							13.0	18.6	23.4	−10.0	5.9	−5.7	−1.0	28.1	12.4
Portfolio Investment Assets	78bf d							—	−.8	−1.1	—	—	—	—	—	—
Equity Securities	78bk d							—	—	—	—	—	—	—	—	—
Debt Securities	78bl d							—	−.8	−1.1	—	—	—	—	—	—
Portfolio Investment Liab., n.i.e.	78bg d							17.8	1.5	5.1	−5.7	−1.0	—	−1.0	.1	—
Equity Securities	78bm d							3.3	−1.4	2.1	−2.2	—	—	—	—	—
Debt Securities	78bn d							14.5	2.9	3.0	−3.5	−1.0	—	−1.0	.1	—
Financial Derivatives Assets	78bw d							...	...	...	...	...	...	...	...	...
Financial Derivatives Liabilities	78bx d							...	...	...	...	...	...	...	...	...
Other Investment Assets	78bh d							−30.2	−143.4	−33.0	7.3	−24.3	−22.4	−1.2	−45.2	−20.7
Monetary Authorities	78bo d							—	—	—	—	—	—	—	—	—
General Government	78bp d							−1.1	−2.0	−1.6	−1.0	−4.2	−4.6	−21.1	−1.6	−2.2
Banks	78bq d							−1.2	5.1	−13.7	9.7	−28.4	−24.5	28.6	−48.1	−17.7
Other Sectors	78br d							−27.9	−146.5	−17.7	−1.4	8.2	6.7	−8.7	4.5	−.8
Other Investment Liab., n.i.e.	78bi d							85.0	167.9	346.0	−40.7	50.0	215.7	141.8	104.0	41.0
Monetary Authorities	78bs d							−8.4	5.0	58.6	13.4	73.9	63.7	7.3	−12.4	−74.6
General Government	78bt d							25.2	20.6	52.0	55.9	110.5	154.9	119.6	161.0	88.8
Banks	78bu d							12.9	15.2	17.6	−11.9	−35.6	13.3	.2	14.6	10.0
Other Sectors	78bv d							55.2	127.0	217.8	−98.1	−98.8	−16.2	14.7	−59.3	16.8
Net Errors and Omissions	78ca d							−24.9	−33.8	−29.1	−106.2	−318.2	−58.6	−61.4	−50.5	−51.9
Overall Balance	78cb d							84.3	40.9	25.4	−133.8	−257.0	−121.6	−42.9	−111.3	−207.9
Reserves and Related Items	79da d							−84.3	−40.9	−25.4	133.8	257.0	121.6	42.9	111.3	207.9
Reserve Assets	79db d							−78.4	−26.0	−55.4	133.8	68.1	11.3	−36.5	−40.2	−1.4
Use of Fund Credit and Loans	79dc d							−5.9	−14.9	—	—	33.4	36.8	65.1	16.5	−5.3
Exceptional Financing	79de d							—	—	30.0	—	155.5	73.5	14.3	135.0	214.6

Other Banking Institutions

End of Period

1985	1986	1987	1988	1989	1990	1991	1992	1993	1994	1995	1996	1997	1998	1999	Item	Code
…	…	…	…	…	…	…	…	…	732	1,203	1,235	488	197	17	Reserves	40
…	…	…	…	…	…	…	…	…	2	22	27	15	22	9	Foreign Assets	41
…	…	…	…	…	…	…	…	…	—	—	146	—	—	—	Claims on Central Government	42a
…	…	…	…	…	…	…	…	…	3,409	4,944	4,179	2,012	1,229	590	Claims on Private Sector	42d
…	…	…	…	…	…	…	…	…	181	147	283	73	3	4	Claims on Deposit Money Banks	42e
…	…	…	…	…	…	…	…	…	3,701	5,015	4,985	1,886	917	226	Time, Savings,& Fgn.Currency Dep.	45
…	…	…	…	…	…	…	…	…	80	173	75	—	—	—	Money Market Instruments	46aa
…	…	…	…	…	…	…	…	…	13	120	57	24	22	54	Foreign Liabilities	46c
…	…	…	…	…	…	…	…	…	—	—	8	—	—	—	Long-Term Foreign Liabilities	46cl
…	…	…	…	…	…	…	…	…	149	124	55	1	—	—	Central Government Deposits	46d
…	…	…	…	…	…	…	…	…	17	—	—	63	—	—	Credit from Monetary Authorities	46g
…	…	…	…	…	…	…	…	…	60	91	10	26	25	2	Credit from Deposit Money Banks	46h
…	…	…	…	…	…	…	…	…	281	407	548	-27	-130	-248	Capital Accounts	47a
…	…	…	…	…	…	…	…	…	23	385	132	614	617	586	Other Items (Net)	47r

Banking Survey

End of Period

1985	1986	1987	1988	1989	1990	1991	1992	1993	1994	1995	1996	1997	1998	1999	Item	Code
…	…	…	…	…	…	…	…	…	6,761	5,837	7,752	10,162	13,983	15,818	Foreign Assets (Net)	51n
…	…	…	…	…	…	…	…	…	27,688	33,837	37,956	43,286	43,400	47,494	Domestic Credit	52
…	…	…	…	…	…	…	…	…	4,630	4,245	4,426	3,682	-753	-566	Claims on Central Govt. (Net)	52an
…	…	…	…	…	…	…	…	…	12	11	10	26	33	77	Claims on Local Government	52b
…	…	…	…	…	…	…	…	…	—	—	—	—	—	41	Claims on Nonfin.Pub.Enterprises	52c
…	…	…	…	…	…	…	…	…	23,047	29,580	33,520	39,578	44,120	47,942	Claims on Private Sector	52d
…	…	…	…	…	…	…	…	…	31,691	35,652	40,534	45,084	48,971	52,850	Liquid Liabilities	55l
…	…	…	…	…	…	…	…	…	80	173	75	—	—	—	Money Market Instruments	56aa
…	…	…	…	…	…	…	…	…	2,936	2,241	3,622	5,383	5,869	7,332	Bonds	56ab
…	…	…	…	…	…	…	…	…	1,400	1,718	2,551	3,272	3,353	3,734	Long-Term Foreign Liabilities	56cl
…	…	…	…	…	…	…	…	…	54	18	13	15	11	11	Counterpart Funds	56e
…	…	…	…	…	…	…	…	…	1	1	1	1	—	—	Central Govt. Lending Funds	56f
…	…	…	…	…	…	…	…	…	675	695	777	1,208	1,131	707	Liab. to Nonbank Financial Insts	56j
…	…	…	…	…	…	…	…	…	4,618	5,016	5,878	6,304	7,178	7,663	Capital Accounts	57a
…	…	…	…	…	…	…	…	…	-7,004	-5,839	-7,742	-7,820	-9,130	-8,985	Other Items (Net)	57r

Interest Rates

Percent Per Annum

1985	1986	1987	1988	1989	1990	1991	1992	1993	1994	1995	1996	1997	1998	1999	Item	Code
											…	10.43	9.43	10.68	Money Market Rate	60b
12.50	15.00	15.00	15.00	16.25	18.00	16.11	11.51	15.27	13.57	14.37	13.98	11.77	10.32	10.75	Deposit Rate	60l
											8.38	7.68	6.86	6.61	Deposit Rate (Fgn. Currency)	60l. f
14.00	17.00	17.00	17.00	18.50	21.17	19.67	16.43	19.42	19.03	19.00	18.57	16.05	14.98	15.46	Lending Rate	60p
											12.53	10.82	9.93	10.38	Lending Rate (Fgn. Currency)	60p. f

Prices and Labor

Period Averages

1985	1986	1987	1988	1989	1990	1991	1992	1993	1994	1995	1996	1997	1998	1999	Item	Code
38.9	51.5	51.9	54.8	60.1	71.4	76.4	78.1	83.9	90.5	100.0	104.8	105.9	99.5	98.1	Wholesale Prices	63
18.9	25.0	31.2	37.4	44.0	54.5	62.4	I69.4	82.2	90.9	100.0	109.8	114.7	117.6	118.2	Consumer Prices	64

Period Averages

1985	1986	1987	1988	1989	1990	1991	1992	1993	1994	1995	1996	1997	1998	1999	Item	Code
…	…	…	…	…	…	939	1,683	…	2,010	2,051	2,140	2,188	…	…	Labor Force	67d
1,373	299	…	I717	790	885	890	I1,782	…	1,951	1,973	2,056	2,076	…	…	Employment	67e
280	I28	…	I74	72	98	72	81	I109	162	163	171	180	…	…	Unemployment	67c
16.9	I7.9	…	I9.4	8.4	10.0	7.5	7.9	I9.9	7.7	7.7	7.7	8.0	…	…	Unemployment Rate (%)	67r

International Transactions

Millions of US Dollars

1985	1986	1987	1988	1989	1990	1991	1992	1993	1994	1995	1996	1997	1998	1999	Item	Code
679.0	754.9	590.9	608.8	497.5	581.5	588.0	597.5	731.7	843.9	998.0	1,024.4	1,359.1	1,262.8	1,164.1	Exports	70..d
961.4	934.9	994.1	1,007.0	1,161.3	1,262.5	1,405.9	1,698.5	1,912.2	2,248.7	2,853.3	2,670.9	2,973.4	3,112.4	3,129.8	Imports, c.i.f.	71..d

Balance of Payments

Minus Sign Indicates Debit

1985	1986	1987	1988	1989	1990	1991	1992	1993	1994	1995	1996	1997	1998	1999	Item	Code
-188.7	-17.1	-68.2	-129.2	-369.7	-260.8	-212.4	-195.1	-122.8	-18.0	-261.6	-169.0	96.0	-84.4	…	Current Account, n.i.e.	78al d
679.0	777.9	589.6	610.6	557.5	643.9	586.8	598.1	1,031.8	1,252.3	1,651.1	1,787.4	2,414.2	2,450.5	…	Goods: Exports f.o.b.	78aa d
-895.0	-902.3	-938.7	-966.5	-1,220.2	-1,309.5	-1,291.4	-1,560.5	-1,994.0	-2,422.3	-3,113.5	-3,029.7	-3,520.9	-3,717.5	…	Goods: Imports f.o.b.	78ab d
-216.0	-124.4	-349.1	-355.9	-662.7	-665.6	-704.6	-962.3	-962.3	-1,170.0	-1,462.3	-1,242.3	-1,106.8	-1,267.0	…	*Trade Balance*	78ac d
223.9	241.1	318.1	328.0	351.0	329.2	310.9	377.1	335.5	387.2	388.6	414.4	291.7	290.1	…	Services: Credit	78ad d
-290.8	-281.0	-280.1	-341.4	-392.1	-314.7	-322.9	-364.7	-386.7	-428.9	-509.8	-504.6	-364.3	-548.8	…	Services: Debit	78ae d
-282.8	-164.4	-311.1	-369.3	-703.9	-651.1	-716.6	-949.9	-1,013.4	-1,211.7	-1,583.5	-1,332.5	-1,179.4	-1,525.7	…	*Balance on Goods & Services*	78af d
48.5	36.9	42.9	24.2	26.1	29.5	30.3	31.7	30.8	35.5	54.0	44.1	75.0	111.4	…	Income: Credit	78ag d
-137.9	-138.9	-134.9	-129.6	-127.4	-161.1	-151.1	-128.9	-142.4	-130.1	-120.7	-134.4	-162.3	-177.5	…	Income: Debit	78ah d
-372.3	-266.4	-403.1	-474.7	-805.2	-782.7	-837.4	-1,047.1	-1,125.0	-1,306.4	-1,650.2	-1,422.8	-1,266.6	-1,591.8	…	*Balance on Gds, Serv. & Inc.*	78ai d
186.7	251.8	336.8	347.6	437.6	524.6	627.5	852.8	1,004.7	1,290.9	1,393.2	1,258.6	1,362.7	1,514.7	…	Current Transfers, n.i.e.: Credit	78aj d
-3.1	-2.5	-1.9	-2.1	-2.1	-2.7	-2.5	-.7	-2.5	-2.5	-4.6	-4.8	—	-7.3	…	Current Transfers: Debit	78ak d
—	—	—	—	—	—	—	—	—	—	—	—	—	1.3	…	Capital Account, n.i.e.	78bc d
—	—	—	—	—	—	—	—	—	—	—	—	—	1.3	…	Capital Account, n.i.e.: Credit	78ba d
—	—	—	—	—	—	—	—	—	—	—	—	—	—	…	Capital Account: Debit	78bb d
2.9	26.7	-60.3	52.3	118.2	-11.4	-61.1	-4.3	73.9	115.8	438.3	358.1	379.6	635.6	…	Financial Account, n.i.e.	78bj d
											-2.4			…	Direct Investment Abroad	78bd d
12.4	24.1	18.3	17.0	14.4	1.9	25.2	15.3	16.4	—	38.0	-4.8	—	872.3	…	Dir. Invest. in Rep. Econ., n.i.e.	78be d
												.5		…	Portfolio Investment Assets	78bf d
												.5		…	Equity Securities	78bk d
														…	Debt Securities	78bl d
	-3.1										68.5	150.0	110.9	-221.4	Portfolio Investment Liab., n.i.e.	78bg d
														…	Equity Securities	78bm d
	-3.1										68.5	150.0	110.9	-221.4	Debt Securities	78bn d
														…	Financial Derivatives Assets	78bw d
														…	Financial Derivatives Liabilities	78bx d
-51.6	54.4	9.7	10.6	-1.1	-20.9	15.0	—	18.5	-8.7	24.2	4.7	2.1	-82.5	…	Other Investment Assets	78bh d
								14.4	—	35.0	—	—	—	…	Monetary Authorities	78bo d
-10.4	-1.5	-1.2	-.4	-.3	-.6	-.2							-22.0	…	General Government	78bp d
-43.8	55.6	12.6	9.5	.8	-17.2	21.3	—	4.1	-8.7	-10.2	—	2.1	-8.0	…	Banks	78bq d
2.5	.3	-1.8	1.5	-1.7	-3.1	-6.0				-.6	4.7	—	-52.4	…	Other Sectors	78br d
42.2	-48.8	-88.3	24.7	104.9	7.5	-101.3	-19.6	39.0	124.5	307.5	210.2	266.7	67.2	…	Other Investment Liab., n.i.e.	78bi d
-45.7	-81.0	-121.1	-42.1	-17.7	-51.1	-139.4	-92.8	-91.1	-147.2	38.2	51.2	28.0	-72.2	…	Monetary Authorities	78bs d
104.2	62.5	52.0	67.1	103.2	84.5	14.3	42.2	115.4	177.0	46.4	162.8	108.0	160.8	…	General Government	78bt d
-4.6	-18.0	-7.2	11.4	12.0	-25.3	.7	—	14.7	94.7	219.9	-3.2	130.6	-21.9	…	Banks	78bu d
-11.8	-12.4	-11.9	-11.7	7.4	-.7	23.0	31.0	—	—	3.1	-.6	—	.5	…	Other Sectors	78bv d
23.0	-141.8	6.9	-107.1	140.9	299.4	125.6	65.6	107.6	15.4	-28.4	-24.2	-111.4	-249.4	…	Net Errors and Omissions	78ca d
-162.8	-132.2	-121.6	-184.1	-110.6	27.1	-147.9	-133.8	58.6	113.3	148.3	164.8	364.3	303.0	…	*Overall Balance*	78cb d
162.8	132.2	121.6	184.1	110.6	-27.1	147.9	133.8	-58.6	-113.3	-148.3	-164.8	-364.3	-303.0	…	Reserves and Related Items	79da d
—	14.1	-36.8	30.1	-110.0	-164.6	70.0	-91.6	-111.9	-113.3	-148.3	-164.8	-364.3	-303.0	…	Reserve Assets	79db d
-27.2	-57.9	-45.0	-10.5	-5.0	-5.2	-.2	—	—	—	—	—	—	—	…	Use of Fund Credit and Loans	79dc d
190.0	176.1	203.5	164.5	225.7	142.7	78.1	225.5	53.3	—	—	—	—	—	…	Exceptional Financing	79de d

El Salvador

		1970	1971	1972	1973	1974	1975	1976	1977	1978	1979	1980	1981	1982	1983	1984
International Investment Position														*Millions of US Dollars*		
Assets	79aa d	....	....	....	....	....	....	....	....	....	....	....	....	....	....	....
Direct Investment Abroad	79ab d	....	....	....	....	....	....	....	....	....	....	....	....	....	....	....
Portfolio Investment	79ac d	....	....	....	....	....	....	....	....	....	....	....	....	....	....	....
Equity Securities	79ad d	....	....	....	....	....	....	....	....	....	....	....	....	....	....	....
Debt Securities	79ae d	....	....	....	....	....	....	....	....	....	....	....	....	....	....	....
Financial Derivatives	79al d	....	....	....	....	....	....	....	....	....	....	....	....	....	....	....
Other Investment	79af d	....	....	....	....	....	....	....	....	....	....	....	....	....	....	....
Monetary Authorities	79ag d	....	....	....	....	....	....	....	....	....	....	....	....	....	....	....
General Government	79ah d	....	....	....	....	....	....	....	....	....	....	....	....	....	....	....
Banks	79ai d	....	....	....	....	....	....	....	....	....	....	....	....	....	....	....
Other Sectors	79aj d	....	....	....	....	....	....	....	....	....	....	....	....	....	....	....
Reserve Assets	79ak d	....	....	....	....	....	....	....	....	....	....	....	....	....	....	....
Liabilities	79la d	....	....	....	....	....	....	....	....	....	....	....	....	....	....	....
Dir. Invest. in Rep. Economy	79lb d	....	....	....	....	....	....	....	....	....	....	....	....	....	....	....
Portfolio Investment	79lc d	....	....	....	....	....	....	....	....	....	....	....	....	....	....	....
Equity Securities	79ld d	....	....	....	....	....	....	....	....	....	....	....	....	....	....	....
Debt Securities	79le d	....	....	....	....	....	....	....	....	....	....	....	....	....	....	....
Financial Derivatives	79ll d	....	....	....	....	....	....	....	....	....	....	....	....	....	....	....
Other Investment	79lf d	....	....	....	....	....	....	....	....	....	....	....	....	....	....	....
Monetary Authorities	79lg d	....	....	....	....	....	....	....	....	....	....	....	....	....	....	....
General Government	79lh d	....	....	....	....	....	....	....	....	....	....	....	....	....	....	....
Banks	79li d	....	....	....	....	....	....	....	....	....	....	....	....	....	....	....
Other Sectors	79lj d	....	....	....	....	....	....	....	....	....	....	....	....	....	....	....
Government Finance															*Millions of Colones:*	
Deficit (-) or Surplus	80	.9	−30.2	−24.2	11.7	−54.3	−24.7	−21.4	179.7	−122.3	−121.9	−396.7	−549.2	−607.3	−324.4	−382.4
Total Revenue and Grants	81y	284.1	297.7	326.5	403.1	488.1	580.8	805.2	1,256.6	1,048.4	1,171.1	1,028.9	1,068.2	1,091.3	1,258.2	1,573.9
Revenue	81	....	....	....	....	....	....	....	....	....	....	....	....	....	....	....
Grants	81z	....	....	....	....	....	....	....	....	....	....	....	....	....	....	....
Exp. & Lending Minus Repay.	82z	283.2	327.9	350.7	391.4	542.4	605.5	826.6	1,076.9	1,170.7	1,293.0	1,425.6	1,617.4	1,698.6	1,582.6	1,956.3
Expenditure	82	283.2	327.9	350.7	391.4	542.4	605.5	826.6	1,076.9	1,184.2	1,280.1	1,422.4	1,581.5	1,694.6	1,571.4	1,820.7
Lending Minus Repayments	83	—	—	—	—	—	—	—	—	−13.5	12.9	3.2	35.9	4.0	11.2	135.6
Total Financing	80h	−.9	30.0	24.1	−11.6	54.1	24.8	21.6	−179.5	122.4	122.0	396.8	549.2	607.3	324.4	382.4
Domestic	84a	−8.1	22.3	8.7	−46.8	−8.1	9.9	−1.4	−179.1	86.8	93.7	375.1	488.0	483.8	285.9	350.8
Foreign	85a	7.2	7.7	15.4	35.2	62.2	14.9	23.0	−.4	35.6	28.3	21.7	61.2	123.5	38.5	31.6
Use of Cash Balances	87	−2.1	1.5	1.7	−7.0	−12.8	6.7	−26.8	−88.8	32.6	21.0	−54.2	−13.3	47.2	−10.3	9.3
Total Debt by Residence	88	321.0	345.6	405.7	459.4	604.9	817.2	1,002.5	999.9	1,307.7	1,577.4	2,150.5	3,406.3	4,264.6	4,732.0	5,504.5
Domestic	88a	97.6	117.2	129.5	138.5	160.3	194.2	289.2	299.0	459.9	581.0	962.8	1,774.2	2,225.1	2,245.4	2,790.0
Foreign	89a	223.4	228.4	276.2	320.9	444.6	623.0	713.3	700.9	847.8	996.4	1,187.7	1,632.1	2,039.5	2,486.6	2,714.5
National Accounts															*Millions of Colones*	
Exports of Goods & Services	90c	639	666	839	998	1,279	1,480	2,028	2,735	2,328	3,182	3,046	2,307	2,042	2,486	2,536
Government Consumption	91f	276	275	308	349	429	501	686	805	996	1,133	1,247	1,369	1,415	1,607	1,869
Gross Fixed Capital Formation	93e	308	359	474	521	719	1,031	1,145	1,521	1,652	1,512	1,210	1,173	1,130	1,180	1,336
Increase/Decrease(-) in Stocks	93i	33	62	−66	88	174	−40	−26	158	183	45	−27	58	56	44	59
Private Consumption	96f	1,948	2,061	2,138	2,474	2,946	3,283	3,973	4,634	5,574	5,933	6,405	6,644	6,877	7,871	9,184
Imports of Goods & Services	98c	−631	−720	−811	−1,099	−1,610	−1,711	−2,101	−2,686	−3,041	−3,197	−2,964	−2,904	−2,553	−3,036	−3,327
Gross Domestic Product (GDP)	99b	2,571	2,704	2,882	3,332	3,944	4,478	5,706	7,167	7,692	8,607	8,917	8,647	8,966	10,152	11,657
Net Factor Inc/Pmts(-) Abroad	98.n	−21	−25	−27	−38	−53	−69	−17	−72	−130	−60	−128	−149	−229	−370	−343
Gross National Income (GNI)	99a	2,550	2,679	2,855	3,294	3,891	4,409	5,689	7,095	7,562	8,547	8,789	8,498	8,737	9,782	11,314
Net National Income	99e	2,425	2,545	2,718	3,146	3,714	4,210	5,458	6,826	7,244	8,191	8,420	8,140	8,367	9,362	10,832
GDP Volume 1962 Prices	99b.p	2,394	2,504	2,646	2,780	2,958	3,123	3,247	3,444	3,665	3,602	3,289	3,017	2,848	2,870	2,936
GDP Volume 1990 Prices	99b.p	....	....	....	....	....	....	....	....	....	....	....	....	....	....	....
GDP Volume (1995=100)	99bv p	54.0	56.5	59.7	62.7	66.7	70.4	73.2	77.7	82.7	81.2	74.2	68.1	64.2	64.8	66.2
GDP Deflator (1995=100)	99bi p	5.7	5.8	5.8	6.4	7.1	7.6	9.4	11.1	11.2	12.7	14.5	15.3	16.8	18.9	21.2
															Millions:	
Population	99z	3.44	3.55	13.67	3.77	3.89	4.01	4.12	4.26	4.35	4.44	4.51	4.59	4.66	4.72	4.78

	1985	1986	1987	1988	1989	1990	1991	1992	1993	1994	1995	1996	1997	1998	1999		

Millions of US Dollars

International Investment Position

	1985	1986	1987	1988	1989	1990	1991	1992	1993	1994	1995	1996	1997	1998	1999		
Assets	....	....	....	....	....	....	....	....	758.7	872.8	1,029.7	1,240.4	1,575.7	1,959.5	....	79aa d
Direct Investment Abroad	....	....	....	....	....	....	....	....	—	—	—	—	—	—	....	79ab d
Portfolio Investment	....	....	....	....	....	....	....	....	—	—	—	—	—	—	....	79ac d
Equity Securities	....	....	....	....	....	....	....	....	....	....	....	—	—	—	....	79ad d
Debt Securities	....	....	....	....	....	....	....	....	....	....	....	—	—	—	....	79ae d
Financial Derivatives	....	....	....	....	....	....	....	....							....	79al d
Other Investment	....	....	....	....	....	....	....	....	51.4	59.9	70.1	115.7	113.8	194.1	....	79af d
Monetary Authorities	....	....	....	....	....	....	....	....				—	—	20.2	....	79ag d
General Government	....	....	....	....	....	....	....	....				—	—	22.0	....	79ah d
Banks	....	....	....	....	....	....	....	....				115.7	113.8	121.8	....	79ai d
Other Sectors	....	....	....	....	....	....	....	....				—	—	30.0	....	79aj d
Reserve Assets	....	....	....	....	....	....	....	....	707.3	812.9	959.6	1,124.7	1,461.9	1,765.4	....	79ak d
Liabilities	....	....	....	....	....	....	....	....	2,042.7	2,198.3	2,530.1	2,921.9	3,310.0	4,090.7	....	79la d
Dir. Invest. in Rep. Economy	....	....	....	....	....	....	....	....						872.8	....	79lb d
Portfolio Investment	....	....	....	....	....	....	....	....	—	—	—	141.4	350.7	129.2	....	79lc d
Equity Securities	....	....	....	....	....	....	....	....				—	—	—	....	79ld d
Debt Securities	....	....	....	....	....	....	....	....	....	....	....	141.4	350.7	129.2	....	79le d
Financial Derivatives	....	....	....	....	....	....	....	....							....	79ll d
Other Investment	....	....	....	....	....	....	....	....	2,042.7	2,198.3	2,530.1	2,780.5	2,959.3	3,088.7	....	79lf d
Monetary Authorities	....	....	....	....	....	....	....	....				240.8	237.5	165.4	....	79lg d
General Government	....	....	....	....	....	....	....	....				2,133.8	2,184.8	2,350.0	....	79lh d
Banks	....	....	....	....	....	....	....	....				405.9	537.1	572.9	....	79li d
Other Sectors	....	....	....	....	....	....	....	....				—	—	.5	....	79lj d

Year Ending December 31

Government Finance

	1985	1986	1987	1988	1989	1990	1991	1992	1993	1994	1995	1996	1997	1998	1999		
Deficit (-) or Surplus	-192.6	42.1	85.8	-175.1	-730.5	-27.1	-1,184.9	-1,839.3	-1,284.4	I -521.8	-455.2	-1,841.3	-1,102.1	-1,920.9	-2,456.0	80
Total Revenue and Grants	1,901.9	2,821.9	2,981.0	2,927.6	2,631.2	3,852.7	4,072.1	5,715.6	7,215.7	I 9,529.7	11,436.9	12,248.9	12,204.7	13,202.2	12,570.2	81y
Revenue														13,104.2	12,471.4	81
Grants	....	....	....											98.0	98.8	81z
Exp. & Lending Minus Repay.	2,094.5	2,779.8	2,895.2	3,102.7	3,361.7	3,879.8	5,257.0	7,554.9	8,500.1	I 10051.5	11,892.1	14,090.2	13,306.8	15,123.1	15,026.2	82z
Expenditure	2,149.6	2,723.1	3,022.8	3,095.8	3,306.7	3,854.7	4,927.9	7,253.7	8,314.0	I 9,970.9	11,755.7	14,070.3	13,533.6	15,227.1	15,094.3	82
Lending Minus Repayments	-55.1	56.7	-127.6	6.9	55.0	25.1	329.1	301.2	186.1	I 80.6	136.4	19.9	-226.8	-104.0	-68.1	83
Total Financing	192.6	-42.1	-85.8	175.1	730.5	27.1	....	....	....	I 521.9	455.2	1,841.3	1,102.1	1,920.1	2,456.0	80h
Domestic	191.3	42.0	-189.7	-127.3	471.6	117.1	....	....	....	I -844.2	-542.3	-86.2	-553.4	2,159.8	1,296.7	84a
Foreign	1.3	-84.1	103.9	302.4	258.9	-90.0	....	....	1,305.0	I 1,366.1	997.5	1,927.5	1,655.5	-239.7	1,159.3	85a
Use of Cash Balances	49.3	8.7	-172.3	-381.3	-218.5	-74.0	....	....	....	-527.8	-313.6					87
Total Debt by Residence	5,956.7	9,390.6	11,786.2	11,364.7	13,880.2	19,119.2	23,697.4	25,142.3	25,292.0	I 21305.8	22,066.6	23,968.0	24,759.7	24,663.7	27,714.1	88
Domestic	3,021.3	3,120.1	5,226.2	4,494.7	6,293.7	7,472.5	9,050.3	9,494.8	9,995.6	I 8,463.0	8,226.3	7,883.7	7,460.9	7,119.9	8,015.2	88a
Foreign	2,935.4	6,270.5	6,560.0	6,870.0	7,586.5	11,646.7	14,647.1	15,647.5	15,296.4	I 12842.8	13,840.3	16,084.3	17,298.8	17,543.8	19,698.9	89a

Millions of Colones

National Accounts

	1985	1986	1987	1988	1989	1990	1991	1992	1993	1994	1995	1996	1997	1998	1999		
Exports of Goods & Services	3,199	4,875	4,395	4,327	4,261	6,771	7,332	8,019	11,683	14,126	17,987	19,023	23,470	23,661	27,035	90c
Government Consumption	2,220	2,803	3,181	3,484	3,930	3,618	4,236	4,670	5,196	5,942	7,184	8,438	8,842	10,178	10,902	91f
Gross Fixed Capital Formation	1,723	2,594	3,158	3,456	4,293	5,004	6,456	8,561	10,737	13,067	15,557	14,266	15,663	17,365	17,619	93e
Increase/Decrease(-) in Stocks	-169	26	-297	45	646	54	107	673	478	865	1,106	-559	-936	860	-53	93i
Private Consumption	11,640	15,206	18,744	22,153	26,729	32,435	37,463	44,082	52,854	61,658	72,683	79,719	84,481	89,998	93,141	96f
Imports of Goods & Services	-4,283	-5,740	-6,040	-6,099	-7,636	-11,394	-13,000	-16,166	-20,588	-24,909	-31,388	-30,627	-34,091	-37,285	-40,243	98c
Gross Domestic Product (GDP)	14,331	19,763	23,141	27,366	32,224	36,488	42,594	49,839	60,359	70,748	83,130	90,261	97,428	104,777	108,401	99b
Net Factor Inc/Pmts(-) Abroad	-354	-471	-525	-509	-568	-971	-1,145	-901	-979	-804	-839	-1,062	-827	-791	-2,159	98.n
Gross National Income (GNI)	13,977	19,292	22,616	26,857	31,656	35,517	41,449	48,938	59,380	69,944	82,291	89,199	96,601	103,986	106,242	99a
Net National Income	13,385	18,477	21,661	25,728	30,327	35,517	41,449	48,938	59,380	69,944	82,291	89,199	96,601	103,986	106,242	99e
GDP Volume 1962 Prices	2,994	3,013	3,094	3,144	3,177	3,285	....	....	....	....	....	....	....	....	....	99b.p
GDP Volume 1990 Prices	....	....	....	....	....	36,487	37,791	40,643	43,638	46,278	49,238	50,078	52,204	54,022	55,429	99b.p
GDP Volume (1995=100)	67.5	68.0	69.8	70.9	71.7	74.1	76.8	82.5	88.6	94.0	100.0	101.7	106.0	109.7	112.6	99bv p
GDP Deflator (1995=100)	25.5	35.0	39.9	46.4	54.1	59.2	66.8	72.6	81.9	90.5	100.0	106.8	110.5	114.9	115.8	99bi p

Midyear Estimates

	1985	1986	1987	1988	1989	1990	1991	1992	1993	1994	1995	1996	1997	1998	1999		
Population	4.86	4.95	5.05	5.09	5.19	5.03	5.35	5.48	5.39	5.53	5.67	5.79	5.91	6.03	6.15	99z

(See notes in the back of the book.)

Equatorial Guinea

642

		1970	1971	1972	1973	1974	1975	1976	1977	1978	1979	1980	1981	1982	1983	1984
Exchange Rates														*Bipkwele per SDR through 1984;*		
Official Rate	aa	276.02	283.61	278.00	284.00	272.08	262.55	288.70	285.76	272.28	264.78	287.99	334.52	370.92	436.97	470.11
														Bipkwele per US Dollar through 1984;		
Official Rate	ae	276.02	261.22	256.05	235.42	222.22	224.27	248.49	235.25	209.00	201.00	225.80	287.40	336.25	417.37	479.60
Official Rate	rf	276.40	275.59	252.03	222.89	240.70	214.31	238.95	245.68	225.66	212.72	211.28	271.73	328.61	381.07	436.96
														Index Numbers (1995=100):		
Nominal Effective Exchange Rate	ne c	....	....	....	....	....	....	....	....	....	....	1,072.36	787.98	506.02	498.21	480.93	500.28
Real Effective Exchange Rate	re c	....	....	....	....	....	....	....	....	....	....	....	....	....			
Fund Position														*Millions of SDRs:*		
Quota	2f. s	8.00	8.00	8.00	8.00	8.00	8.00	8.00	8.00	10.00	10.00	15.00	15.00	15.00	18.40	18.40
SDRs	1b. s	1.01	1.86	1.87	1.86	1.85	1.81	1.77	1.74	1.70	.65	.02	.12	.02	—	—
Reserve Position in the Fund	1c. s	1.00	1.00	.01	.01	.01	.01	1.76	—	—	.18		.24	.50	—	—
Total Fund Cred.&Loans Outstg.	2tl	—	—	—	—	—	—	—	—	—	—	12.62	19.24	19.24	19.24	13.19
International Liquidity													*Millions of US Dollars Unless Otherwise Indicated:*			
Total Reserves minus Gold	1l. d	....	....	....	....	....	....	....	....	....	....	....	....	2.77	1.30	1.38
SDRs	1b. d	1.01	2.02	2.03	2.24	2.27	2.12	2.06	2.11	2.21	.86	.03	.14	.02	—	—
Reserve Position in the Fund	1c. d	1.00	1.09	.01	.01	.01	.01	2.04	—	—	.24	—	.28	.55	—	—
Foreign Exchange	1d. d	....	....	....	....	....	....	....	....	....	....	....	....	2.20	1.30	1.38
Monetary Authorities: Other Liab.	4..d	....	....	....	....	....	....	....	....	....	....	....	....	−12.51	−11.85	−4.53
Deposit Money Banks: Assets	7a. d	....	....	....	....	....	....	....	....	....	....	....	....	....	....	....
Liabilities	7b. d	....	....	....	....	....	....	....	....	....	....	....	....	....	....	....
Monetary Authorities														*Billions of Francs:*		
Foreign Assets	11	....	....	....	....	....	....	....	....	....	....	....	....	....	....	....
Claims on Central Government	12a	....	....	....	....	....	....	....	....	....	....	....	....	....	....	....
Claims on Deposit Money Banks	12e	....	....	....	....	....	....	....	....	....	....	....	....	....	....	....
Claims on Other Banking Insts	12f	....	....	....	....	....	....	....	....	....	....	....	....	....	....	....
Reserve Money	14	....	....	....	....	....	....	....	....	....	....	....	....	....	....	....
of which: Currency Outside DMBs	14a	....	....	....	....	....	....	....	....	....	....	....	....	....	....	....
Foreign Liabilities	16c	....	....	....	....	....	....	....	....	....	....	....	....	....	....	....
Central Government Deposits	16d	....	....	....	....	....	....	....	....	....	....	....	....	....	....	....
Capital Accounts	17a	....	....	....	....	....	....	....	....	....	....	....	....	....	....	....
Other Items (Net)	17r	....	....	....	....	....	....	....	....	....	....	....	....	....	....	....
Deposit Money Banks														*Billions of Francs:*		
Reserves	20	....	....	....	....	....	....	....	....	....	....	....	....	....	....	....
Foreign Assets	21	....	....	....	....	....	....	....	....	....	....	....	....	....	....	....
Claims on Central Government	22a	....	....	....	....	....	....	....	....	....	....	....	....	....	....	....
Claims on Nonfin.Pub.Enterprises	22c	....	....	....	....	....	....	....	....	....	....	....	....	....	....	....
Claims on Private Sector	22d	....	....	....	....	....	....	....	....	....	....	....	....	....	....	....
Claims on Other Banking Insts	22f	....	....	....	....	....	....	....	....	....	....	....	....	....	....	....
Claims on Nonbank Financial Insts	22g	....	....	....	....	....	....	....	....	....	....	....	....	....	....	....
Demand Deposits	24	....	....	....	....	....	....	....	....	....	....	....	....	....	....	....
Time and Savings Deposits	25	....	....	....	....	....	....	....	....	....	....	....	....	....	....	....
Foreign Liabilities	26c	....	....	....	....	....	....	....	....	....	....	....	....	....	....	....
Long-Term Foreign Liabilities	26cl	....	....	....	....	....	....	....	....	....	....	....	....	....	....	....
Central Government Deposits	26d	....	....	....	....	....	....	....	....	....	....	....	....	....	....	....
Credit from Monetary Authorities	26g	....	....	....	....	....	....	....	....	....	....	....	....	....	....	....
Capital Accounts	27a	....	....	....	....	....	....	....	....	....	....	....	....	....	....	....
Other Items (Net)	27r	....	....	....	....	....	....	....	....	....	....	....	....	....	....	....
Monetary Survey														*Billions of Francs:*		
Foreign Assets (Net)	31n	....	....	....	....	....	....	....	....	....	....	....	....	....	....	....
Domestic Credit	32	....	....	....	....	....	....	....	....	....	....	....	....	....	....	....
Claims on Central Govt. (Net)	32an	....	....	....	....	....	....	....	....	....	....	....	....	....	....	....
Claims on Nonfin.Pub.Enterprises	32c	....	....	....	....	....	....	....	....	....	....	....	....	....	....	....
Claims on Private Sector	32d	....	....	....	....	....	....	....	....	....	....	....	....	....	....	....
Claims on Other Banking Insts	32f	....	....	....	....	....	....	....	....	....	....	....	....	....	....	....
Claims on Nonbank Financial Inst	32g	....	....	....	....	....	....	....	....	....	....	....	....	....	....	....
Money	34	....	....	....	....	....	....	....	....	....	....	....	....	....	....	....
Quasi-Money	35	....	....	....	....	....	....	....	....	....	....	....	....	....	....	....
Other Items (Net)	37r	....	....	....	....	....	....	....	....	....	....	....	....	....	....	....
Money plus Quasi-Money	35l	....	....	....	....	....	....	....	....	....	....	....	....	....	....	....
Interest Rates														*Percent Per Annum*		
Discount Rate (End of Period)	60	....	....	....	....	....	....	....	....	....	....	....	....	....	....	....
Deposit Rate	60l	....	....	....	....	....	....	....	....	....	....	....	....	....	....	....
Lending Rate	60p	....	....	....	....	....	....	....	....	....	....	....	....	....	....	....
Prices														*Index Numbers (1990=100):*		
Consumer Prices	64	....	....	....	....	....	....	....	....	....	....	....	....	....	....	....

1985	1986	1987	1988	1989	1990	1991	1992	1993	1994	1995	1996	1997	1998	1999	
															Exchange Rates
Francs per SDR Beginning 1985: End of Period															
415.26	394.78	378.78	407.68	380.32	364.84	370.48	378.57	404.89	‡780.44	728.38	753.06	807.94	791.61	‡896.19	Official Rate ... aa
Francs per US Dollar Beginning 1985: End of Period(ae)Period Average(rf)															
378.05	322.75	267.00	302.95	289.40	256.45	259.00	275.32	294.77	‡534.60	490.00	523.70	598.81	562.21	‡652.95	Official Rate ... ae
449.26	346.31	300.54	297.85	319.01	272.26	282.11	264.69	283.16	‡555.20	499.15	511.55	583.67	589.95	‡615.70	Official Rate ... rf
Period Averages															
97.43	108.00	115.57	117.42	120.69	134.73	136.07	144.72	153.62	95.56	100.00	99.53	96.39	98.07	96.67	Nominal Effective Exchange Rate ... ne c
176.27	148.61	128.42	122.58	119.85	119.66	110.28	105.70	111.48	79.65	100.00[e]	126.96[e]	159.00[e]	208.43[e]	263.49[e]	Real Effective Exchange Rate ... re c
															Fund Position
End of Period															
18.40	18.40	18.40	18.40	18.40	18.40	18.40	24.30	24.30	24.30	24.30	24.30	24.30	24.30	32.60	Quota ... 2f. s
3.09	.61	.15	.03	.09	.05	5.57	5.52	.28	.01	.01	.01	—	.01	—	SDRs ... 1b. s
—	—	—	—	—	—	—	—	—	—	—	—	—	—	—	Reserve Position in the Fund ... 1c. s
11.70	9.01	8.11	10.61	6.72	4.10	9.20	9.20	11.96	13.43	12.70	11.93	9.75	7.64	5.80	Total Fund Cred.&Loans Outstg. ... 2tl
															International Liquidity
End of Period															
3.47	2.68	.57	5.50	5.97	.71	9.47	13.41	.48	.39	.04	.52	4.93	.80	3.35	Total Reserves minus Gold ... 1l. d
3.39	.75	.21	.04	.12	.07	7.96	7.59	.38	.02	.01	.01	—	.01	—	SDRs ... 1b. d
—	—	—	—	—	—	—	—	—	—	—	—	—	—	—	Reserve Position in the Fund ... 1c. d
.07	1.93	.36	5.46	5.85	.64	1.51	5.82	.10	.37	.03	.51	4.93	.79	3.35	Foreign Exchange ... 1d. d
5.07	.34	11.01	22.19	16.50	25.45	33.31	41.54	12.78	11.57	5.42	2.49	2.33	15.55	15.42	Monetary Authorities: Other Liab. ... 4..d
5.40	2.04	7.49	4.15	3.37	5.10	5.68	6.08	4.07	5.78	5.08	4.92	2.38	18.07	39.45	Deposit Money Banks: Assets ... 7a. d
—	—	.30	1.17	1.72	3.49	2.34	2.96	2.17	2.67	3.56	1.96	6.18	5.22	19.31	Liabilities ... 7b. d
															Monetary Authorities
End of Period															
1.31	.86	.15	‡1.67	1.73	.18	‡2.45	3.69	.14	.21	.02	.27	2.95	.45	2.19	Foreign Assets ... 11
6.46	5.11	4.62	‡6.06	4.25	3.09	9.27	9.71	12.18	17.84	17.42	17.33	15.86	14.03	20.90	Claims on Central Government ... 12a
3.21	4.26	3.82	‡3.24	3.24	4.65	‡—	—	—	—	—	—	—	—	—	Claims on Deposit Money Banks ... 12e
....	....	....	....	....	....	....	—	—	—	—	—	—	—	—	Claims on Other Banking Insts ... 12f
5.68	8.93	6.88	‡3.28	5.59	1.74	1.92	3.09	2.46	4.38	8.72	9.99	10.97	8.79	17.17	Reserve Money ... 14
5.24	7.48	6.69	‡1.96	4.79	.90	1.09	1.62	1.21	3.77	6.78	8.50	6.59	5.79	12.06	of which: Currency Outside DMBs ... 14a
6.78	3.67	6.01	‡11.05	7.33	8.02	12.04	14.92	8.09	15.38	10.70	9.05	7.94	13.58	14.17	Foreign Liabilities ... 16c
1.02	.27	.72	‡1.74	.26	.07	.25	.35	.17	.06	.07	.08	.48	1.08	1.19	Central Government Deposits ... 16d
....	....	....	2.36	2.22	2.12	2.40	2.42	2.55	4.82	4.53	4.63	4.95	4.83	5.56	Capital Accounts ... 17a
-2.49	-2.62	-5.02	‡-7.46	-6.18	-4.05	‡-4.89	-7.38	-.95	-6.58	-6.58	-6.15	-5.54	-13.80	-14.99	Other Items (Net) ... 17r
															Deposit Money Banks
End of Period															
.44	1.45	.20	‡1.31	.80	.84	.84	1.47	1.25	.62	1.95	1.49	4.38	3.00	5.11	Reserves ... 20
2.04	.66	2.00	‡1.26	.98	1.31	‡1.47	1.67	1.20	3.09	2.49	2.57	1.43	10.16	25.76	Foreign Assets ... 21
—	—	—	‡.57	.62	.78	‡1.08	2.76	.05	.23	.25	.51	1.63	.94	.46	Claims on Central Government ... 22a
—	—	—	.24	.47	.64	.04	.29	.44	.72	.72	.96	.80	.72	.03	Claims on Nonfin.Pub.Enterprises ... 22c
6.53	8.36	7.52	‡7.37	7.79	7.87	‡12.45	7.92	1.99	2.25	3.40	6.20	12.02	14.13	21.29	Claims on Private Sector ... 22d
....	....	....	—	—	—	—	—	—	—	—	—	—	—	—	Claims on Other Banking Insts ... 22f
—	—	—	—	—	—	—	—	—	—	—	—	—	—	—	Claims on Nonbank Financial Insts ... 22g
2.81	2.44	2.32	‡3.26	2.46	2.23	‡1.55	1.95	1.34	2.24	2.73	5.78	7.07	9.19	16.39	Demand Deposits ... 24
.93	.62	.43	‡.38	.63	.67	‡.70	.80	.69	1.76	2.05	2.23	4.38	5.86	6.72	Time and Savings Deposits ... 25
—	—	—	‡.17	.25	.65	‡.36	.56	.41	1.24	1.60	.92	3.67	2.94	12.61	Foreign Liabilities ... 26c
—	—	.08	‡.18	.25	.25	‡.25	.25	.23	.19	.14	.11	.03	—	—	Long-Term Foreign Liabilities ... 26cl
.50	.18	.09	.76	.75	1.07	‡1.10	1.05	.53	.46	.88	1.86	3.10	6.12	10.76	Central Government Deposits ... 26d
3.21	4.26	3.82	‡3.24	3.24	4.64	‡—	—	—	—	—	—	—	—	—	Credit from Monetary Authorities ... 26g
.67	.71	1.16	‡2.36	2.54	2.70	‡10.49	9.63	1.67	1.36	2.30	1.26	3.02	5.26	6.67	Capital Accounts ... 27a
.90	2.25	1.82	‡.43	.53	-.77	‡1.43	-.13	.07	-.33	-.91	-.43	-1.03	-.42	-.50	Other Items (Net) ... 27r
															Monetary Survey
End of Period															
-3.43	-2.14	-3.86	‡-8.48	-5.13	-7.43	‡-8.72	-10.37	-7.39	-13.51	-9.94	-7.23	-7.26	-5.91	1.18	Foreign Assets (Net) ... 31n
11.47	13.02	11.33	‡11.74	12.12	11.24	‡21.49	19.29	13.96	20.52	20.83	23.05	26.72	22.66	30.73	Domestic Credit ... 32
4.94	4.66	3.81	‡4.12	3.86	2.73	‡9.00	11.07	11.53	17.55	16.72	15.90	13.90	7.78	9.41	Claims on Central Govt. (Net) ... 32an
....	....	....	.24	.47	.64	.04	.29	.44	.72	.72	.96	.80	.72	.03	Claims on Nonfin.Pub.Enterprises ... 32c
6.53	8.36	7.52	‡7.37	7.79	7.87	‡12.45	7.92	1.99	2.25	3.40	6.20	12.02	14.13	21.29	Claims on Private Sector ... 32d
....	....	....	—	—	—	—	—	—	—	—	—	—	—	—	Claims on Other Banking Insts ... 32f
—	—	—	—	—	—	—	—	—	—	—	—	—	—	.03	Claims on Nonbank Financial Inst ... 32g
8.05	9.92	9.00	‡5.22	7.25	3.12	2.64	3.57	2.55	6.01	9.51	14.28	13.66	14.99	28.45	Money ... 34
.93	.62	.43	‡1.38	.63	.67	.70	.80	.69	1.76	2.05	2.23	4.38	5.86	6.72	Quasi-Money ... 35
-.93	.34	-2.05	‡-.06	.74	1.37	9.43	4.54	3.34	-.73	-.66	-.68	1.41	-4.13	-3.26	Other Items (Net) ... 37r
8.97	10.54	9.43	‡5.60	7.88	3.79	3.34	4.37	3.24	7.76	11.56	16.51	18.04	20.85	35.16	Money plus Quasi-Money ... 35l
															Interest Rates
Percent Per Annum															
9.00	8.00	8.00	9.50	10.00	11.00	10.75	12.00	11.50	‡7.75	8.60	7.75	7.50	7.00	7.60	Discount Rate (End of Period) ... 60
7.50	8.25	7.88	6.33	6.50	‡7.50	7.50	7.50	7.75	8.08	5.50	5.46	5.00	5.00	5.00	Deposit Rate ... 60l
15.00	14.50	14.13	14.79	15.50	‡18.50	18.15	17.77	17.46	17.50	16.00	22.00	22.00	22.00	22.00	Lending Rate ... 60p
															Prices
Period Averages															
127.42	104.76	91.28	93.40	98.91	100.00	96.84	‡89.90	‡93.49	127.54	....	....	....	....	....	Consumer Prices ... 64

Equatorial Guinea

		1970	1971	1972	1973	1974	1975	1976	1977	1978	1979	1980	1981	1982	1983	1984
International Transactions																*Millions of Francs*
Exports	70	...	...	...	...	...	...	...	...	...	...	...	3,067	3,797	5,074	6,526
Imports, c.i.f.	71	...	...	...	...	...	...	...	...	...	...	...	7,390	10,029	7,250	7,656
Balance of Payments																*Millions of US Dollars:*
Current Account, n.i.e.	78al d	...	...	...	...	...	...	...	...	...	...	...	...	...	...	...
Goods: Exports f.o.b.	78aa d	...	...	...	...	...	...	...	...	...	...	...	...	...	...	...
Goods: Imports f.o.b.	78ab d	...	...	...	...	...	...	...	...	...	...	...	...	...	...	...
Trade Balance	78ac d	...	...	...	...	...	...	...	...	...	...	...	...	...	...	...
Services: Credit	78ad d	...	...	...	...	...	...	...	...	...	...	...	...	...	...	...
Services: Debit	78ae d	...	...	...	...	...	...	...	...	...	...	...	...	...	...	...
Balance on Goods & Services	78af d	...	...	...	...	...	...	...	...	...	...	...	...	...	...	...
Income: Credit	78ag d	...	...	...	...	...	...	...	...	...	...	...	...	...	...	...
Income: Debit	78ah d	...	...	...	...	...	...	...	...	...	...	...	...	...	...	...
Balance on Gds, Serv. & Inc.	78ai d	...	...	...	...	...	...	...	...	...	...	...	...	...	...	...
Current Transfers, n.i.e.: Credit	78aj d	...	...	...	...	...	...	...	...	...	...	...	...	...	...	...
Current Transfers: Debit	78ak d	...	...	...	...	...	...	...	...	...	...	...	...	...	...	...
Capital Account, n.i.e.	78bc d	...	...	...	...	...	...	...	...	...	...	...	...	...	...	...
Capital Account, n.i.e.: Credit	78ba d	...	...	...	...	...	...	...	...	...	...	...	...	...	...	...
Capital Account: Debit	78bb d	...	...	...	...	...	...	...	...	...	...	...	...	...	...	...
Financial Account, n.i.e.	78bj d	...	...	...	...	...	...	...	...	...	...	...	...	...	...	...
Direct Investment Abroad	78bd d	...	...	...	...	...	...	...	...	...	...	...	...	...	...	...
Dir. Invest. in Rep. Econ., n.i.e.	78be d	...	...	...	...	...	...	...	...	...	...	...	...	...	...	...
Portfolio Investment Assets	78bf d	...	...	...	...	...	...	...	...	...	...	...	...	...	...	...
Equity Securities	78bk d	...	...	...	...	...	...	...	...	...	...	...	...	...	...	...
Debt Securities	78bl d	...	...	...	...	...	...	...	...	...	...	...	...	...	...	...
Portfolio Investment Liab., n.i.e.	78bg d	...	...	...	...	...	...	...	...	...	...	...	...	...	...	...
Equity Securities	78bm d	...	...	...	...	...	...	...	...	...	...	...	...	...	...	...
Debt Securities	78bn d	...	...	...	...	...	...	...	...	...	...	...	...	...	...	...
Financial Derivatives Assets	78bw d	...	...	...	...	...	...	...	...	...	...	...	...	...	...	...
Financial Derivatives Liabilities	78bx d	...	...	...	...	...	...	...	...	...	...	...	...	...	...	...
Other Investment Assets	78bh d	...	...	...	...	...	...	...	...	...	...	...	...	...	...	...
Monetary Authorities	78bo d	...	...	...	...	...	...	...	...	...	...	...	...	...	...	...
General Government	78bp d	...	...	...	...	...	...	...	...	...	...	...	...	...	...	...
Banks	78bq d	...	...	...	...	...	...	...	...	...	...	...	...	...	...	...
Other Sectors	78br d	...	...	...	...	...	...	...	...	...	...	...	...	...	...	...
Other Investment Liab., n.i.e.	78bi d	...	...	...	...	...	...	...	...	...	...	...	...	...	...	...
Monetary Authorities	78bs d	...	...	...	...	...	...	...	...	...	...	...	...	...	...	...
General Government	78bt d	...	...	...	...	...	...	...	...	...	...	...	...	...	...	...
Banks	78bu d	...	...	...	...	...	...	...	...	...	...	...	...	...	...	...
Other Sectors	78bv d	...	...	...	...	...	...	...	...	...	...	...	...	...	...	...
Net Errors and Omissions	78ca d	...	...	...	...	...	...	...	...	...	...	...	...	...	...	...
Overall Balance	78cb d	...	...	...	...	...	...	...	...	...	...	...	...	...	...	...
Reserves and Related Items	79da d	...	...	...	...	...	...	...	...	...	...	...	...	...	...	...
Reserve Assets	79db d	...	...	...	...	...	...	...	...	...	...	...	...	...	...	...
Use of Fund Credit and Loans	79dc d	...	...	...	...	...	...	...	...	...	...	...	...	...	...	...
Exceptional Financing	79de d	...	...	...	...	...	...	...	...	...	...	...	...	...	...	...
National Accounts																*Millions of Francs*
Exports of Goods & Services	90c	...	...	...	...	...	...	...	...	...	...	...	...	...	1,477	1,886
Government Consumption	91f	...	...	...	...	...	...	...	...	...	...	...	...	...	7,080	8,505
Gross Fixed Capital Formation	93e	...	...	...	...	...	...	...	...	...	...	...	...	...	3,018	3,224
Increase/Decrease(-) in Stocks	93i	...	...	...	...	...	...	...	...	...	...	...	...	...	−158	418
Private Consumption	96f	...	...	...	...	...	...	...	...	...	...	...	...	...	16,083	17,511
Imports of Goods & Services	98c	...	...	...	...	...	...	...	...	...	...	...	...	...	−1,851	−2,012
Gross Domestic Product (GDP)	99b	...	...	...	...	...	...	...	...	...	...	...	...	...	25,649	29,532
GDP Volume 1995 Prices	99b. p	...	...	...	...	...	...	...	...	...	...	...	...	...	...	...
GDP Volume (1995=100)	99bv p	...	...	...	...	...	...	...	...	...	...	...	...	...	...	...
																Millions:
Population	99z	.29	.29	.30	.31	.32	.32	.33	.33	.34	.35	.35	.23	.25	.27	.29

Millions of Francs (International Transactions) — *Minus Sign Indicates Debit* (Balance of Payments) — *Millions of Francs* (National Accounts) — *Midyear Estimates* (Population)

1985	1986	1987	1988	1989	1990	1991	1992	1993	1994	1995	1996	1997	1998	1999	Item	Code
															International Transactions	
7,441	12,100	12,600	14,719	12,925	17,665	24,148	15,309	21,103	36,849	63,631	118,554	290,362	249,609	....	Exports	70
8,947	17,900	17,300	18,230	17,473	16,776	33,017	24,638	10,722	13,335	15,438	85,812	46,461	18,598	....	Imports, c.i.f.	71
															Balance of Payments	
....	....	-25.44	-20.57	-21.00	-18.99	-40.72	-10.57	2.84	-.38	-123.40	-344.04	....	....	....	Current Account, n.i.e.	78al d
....	....	38.48	44.65	32.71	37.82	37.35	49.54	61.06	62.00	89.93	175.31	....	....	....	Goods: Exports f.o.b.	78aa d
....	....	-47.87	-56.51	-43.61	-53.17	-67.24	-56.00	-51.03	-36.95	-120.57	-292.04	....	....	....	Goods: Imports f.o.b.	78ab d
....	....	-9.38	-11.86	-10.91	-15.36	-29.89	-6.47	10.03	25.05	-30.64	-116.73	....	....	....	*Trade Balance*	78ac d
....	....	6.11	5.87	5.84	4.51	5.84	8.15	8.99	3.36	4.18	4.88	....	....	....	Services: Credit	78ad d
....	....	-40.68	-48.69	-31.22	-35.76	-41.45	-35.17	-38.53	-23.82	-75.54	-184.58	....	....	....	Services: Debit	78ae d
....	....	-43.96	-54.68	-36.29	-46.61	-65.50	-33.49	-19.51	4.59	-102.00	-296.43	....	....	....	*Balance on Goods & Services*	78af d
....	....	....	....	....	....	....	1.32	—	—	.10	.16	....	....	....	Income: Credit	78ag d
....	....	-6.51	-7.93	-8.55	-10.25	-9.20	-4.92	-9.30	-8.75	-25.03	-45.18	....	....	....	Income: Debit	78ah d
....	....	-50.46	-62.61	-44.84	-56.86	-74.70	-37.09	-28.80	-4.16	-126.93	-341.44	....	....	....	*Balance on Gds, Serv. & Inc.*	78ai d
....	....	28.66	46.90	36.84	54.92	42.40	33.63	37.76	5.67	6.83	4.03	....	....	....	Current Transfers, n.i.e.: Credit	78aj d
....	....	-3.64	-4.87	-12.99	-17.05	-8.42	-7.11	-6.11	-1.89	-3.30	-6.62	....	....	....	Current Transfers: Debit	78ak d
....	....	—	—	—	—	—	—	—	—	—	—	....	....	....	Capital Account, n.i.e.	78bc d
....	....	—	—	—	—	—	—	—	—	—	—	....	....	....	Capital Account, n.i.e.: Credit	78ba d
....	....	—	—	—	—	—	—	—	—	—	—	....	....	....	Capital Account: Debit	78bb d
....	....	-.95	4.90	10.02	11.68	28.51	-16.08	13.95	-15.04	101.56	313.75	....	....	....	Financial Account, n.i.e.	78bj d
....	....	—	—	—	—	—	—	—	—	—	—	....	....	....	Direct Investment Abroad	78bd d
....	....	—	—	.89	11.07	41.32	6.02	22.30	17.00	126.92	376.18	....	....	....	Dir. Invest. in Rep. Econ., n.i.e.	78be d
....	....	—	—	—	—	—	—	—	—	—	—	....	....	....	Portfolio Investment Assets	78bf d
....	....	—	—	—	—	—	—	—	—	—	—	....	....	....	Equity Securities	78bk d
....	....	—	—	—	—	—	—	—	—	—	—	....	....	....	Debt Securities	78bl d
....	....	—	—	—	—	—	—	—	—	—	—	....	....	....	Portfolio Investment Liab., n.i.e.	78bg d
....	....	—	—	—	—	—	—	—	—	—	—	....	....	....	Equity Securities	78bm d
....	....	—	—	—	—	—	—	—	—	—	—	....	....	....	Debt Securities	78bn d
....	....	....	....	....	....	....	....	....	....	....	....	....	....	....	Financial Derivatives Assets	78bw d
....	....	....	....	....	....	....	....	....	....	....	....	....	....	....	Financial Derivatives Liabilities	78bx d
....	....	-4.91	-1.12	—	—	—	—	—	—	—	—	....	....	....	Other Investment Assets	78bh d
....	....	....	....	....	....	....	....	....	....	....	....	....	....	....	Monetary Authorities	78bo d
....	....	-1.27	-1.12	—	—	—	—	—	—	—	—	....	....	....	General Government	78bp d
....	....	-3.64	—	—	—	—	—	—	—	—	—	....	....	....	Banks	78bq d
....	....	....	....	....	....	....	....	....	....	....	....	....	....	....	Other Sectors	78br d
....	....	3.95	6.02	9.13	.61	-12.81	-22.09	-8.35	-32.04	-25.36	-62.43	....	....	....	Other Investment Liab., n.i.e.	78bi d
....	....	....	....	....	....	....	....	....	....	....	....	....	....	....	Monetary Authorities	78bs d
....	....	5.98	10.38	11.51	2.94	-9.87	1.17	-3.12	-7.32	-13.95	-3.84	....	....	....	General Government	78bt d
....	....	—	2.92	1.60	.38	-1.73	.01	1.05	-1.98	1.84	-1.57	....	....	....	Banks	78bu d
....	....	-2.03	-7.28	-3.97	-2.71	-1.21	-23.28	-6.28	-22.73	-13.25	-57.02	....	....	....	Other Sectors	78bv d
....	....	.82	-1.70	.77	1.61	-1.64	-1.13	-27.17	-2.93	10.33	24.82	....	....	....	Net Errors and Omissions	78ca d
....	....	-25.58	-17.37	-10.20	-5.70	-13.85	-27.78	-10.38	-18.35	-11.52	-5.46	....	....	....	*Overall Balance*	78cb d
....	....	25.58	17.37	10.20	5.70	13.85	27.78	10.38	18.35	11.52	5.46	....	....	....	Reserves and Related Items	79da d
....	....	3.64	-7.11	.74	-3.27	-11.27	4.36	-1.02	-.93	-8.98	-3.59	....	....	....	Reserve Assets	79db d
....	....	-1.14	3.44	-5.01	-3.53	7.18	—	3.79	2.08	-1.11	-1.11	....	....	....	Use of Fund Credit and Loans	79dc d
....	....	23.08	21.05	14.47	12.50	17.94	23.42	7.61	17.20	21.61	10.17	....	....	....	Exceptional Financing	79de d
															National Accounts	
10,388	12,092	18,568	19,187	17,083	26,483	13,174	15,269	19,837	36,308	45,088	105,083	292,158	....	....	Exports of Goods & Services	90c
5,909	7,240	5,210	7,804	9,397	6,765	6,696	5,294	7,996	6,938	10,791	18,274	27,811	....	....	Government Consumption	91f
4,551	7,590	10,190	11,133	8,285	15,328	8,525	15,885	17,620	55,126	64,528	176,141	197,359	....	....	Gross Fixed Capital Formation	93e
-1,721	-624	654	-685	-7	-1,365	-1,091	-987	531	-20	-9	-11	-13	....	....	Increase/Decrease(-) in Stocks	93i
30,566	28,754	26,630	29,096	22,956	23,593	35,225	31,042	25,150	2,430	18,646	49,826	157,939	....	....	Private Consumption	96f
-11,626	-17,847	-21,930	-23,786	-15,458	-26,455	-13,174	-24,133	-25,361	-42,332	-59,662	-211,429	-358,965	....	....	Imports of Goods & Services	98c
38,067	37,205	39,700	35,900	39,600	39,500	41,500	42,336	45,774	58,450	79,382	137,884	316,290	....	....	Gross Domestic Product (GDP)	99b
38,756	37,286	40,074	42,189	41,025	....	....	42,311	46,323	53,358	61,956	89,995	182,536	....	....	GDP Volume 1995 Prices	99b.p
62.6	60.2	64.7	68.1	66.2	....	....	68.3	74.8	86.1	100.0	145.3	294.6	....	....	GDP Volume (1995=100)	99bv p
.31	.32	.33	.33	.34	.35	.36	.37	.38	.39	.40	.41	.42	.43	.44	Population	99z

(See notes in the back of the book.)

Estonia

		1970	1971	1972	1973	1974	1975	1976	1977	1978	1979	1980	1981	1982	1983	1984

Exchange Rates
Krooni per SDR:
Official Rate .... aa
Krooni per US Dollar:
Official Rate .... ae
Official Rate .... rf

Fund Position
Millions of SDRs:
Quota .... 2f. *s*
SDRs .... 1b. *s*
Reserve Position in the Fund .... 1c. *s*
Total Fund Cred.&Loans Outstg. 2tl

International Liquidity
Millions of US Dollars Unless Otherwise Indicated:
Total Reserves minus Gold .... 1l. *d*
SDRs .... 1b. *d*
Reserve Position in the Fund .... 1c. *d*
Foreign Exchange .... 1d. *d*
Gold (Million Fine Troy Ounces) 1ad
Gold (National Valuation) .... 1an *d*
Monetary Authorities: Other Liab. .... 4.. *d*
Banks: Assets .... 7a. *d*
        Liabilities .... 7b. *d*

Monetary Authorities
Millions of Krooni:
Foreign Assets 11
Claims on General Government 12a
Claims on Nonfin.Pub.Enterprises 12c
Claims on Private Sector 12d
Claims on Banks 12e

Reserve Money 14
    of which: Currency Outside Banks 14a
Foreign Liabilities 16c
General Government Deposits 16d
Capital Accounts 17a
Other Items (Net) 17r

Banking Institutions
Millions of Krooni:
Reserves 20
Foreign Assets 21
Claims on General Government 22a
Claims on Nonfin.Pub.Enterprises 22c
Claims on Private Sector 22d
Claims on Nonbank Financial Insts 22g

Demand Deposits 24
Time, Savings,& Fgn.Currency Dep. 25
Money Market Instruments 26aa
Bonds 26ab
Foreign Liabilities 26c
General Government Deposits 26d
Counterpart Funds 26e
Government Lending Funds 26f
Credit from Monetary Authorities 26g
Capital Accounts 27a
Other Items (Net) 27r

Banking Survey
Millions of Krooni:
Foreign Assets (Net) 31n
Domestic Credit 32
    Claims on General Govt. (Net) 32an
    Claims on Nonfin.Pub.Enterprises 32c
    Claims on Private Sector 32d
    Claims on Nonbank Financial Inst 32g

Money 34
Quasi-Money 35
Money Market Instruments 36aa
Bonds 36ab
Counterpart Funds 36e
Government Lending Funds 36f
Capital Accounts 37a
Other Items (Net) 37r

Money plus Quasi-Money 35l

Interest Rates
Percent Per Annum
Money Market Rate 60b
Deposit Rate 60l
Lending Rate 60p

Prices and Labor
Index Numbers (1995=100):
Producer Prices 63
Consumer Prices 64
Monthly Earnings 65

Number in Thousands:
Unemployment 67c
Unemployment Rate (%) 67r

International Transactions
Millions of Krooni
Exports 70
Imports, c.i.f. 71
Imports, f.o.b. 71.v

1985	1986	1987	1988	1989	1990	1991	1992	1993	1994	1995	1996	1997	1998	1999	
End of Period															**Exchange Rates**
....	....	....	....	....	....	....	17.754	19.062	18.088	17.038	17.888	19.343	18.882	21.359	Official Rate.............. aa
End of Period (ae) Period Average (rf)															
....	....	....	....	....	....	....	12.912	13.878	12.390	11.462	12.440	14.336	13.410	15.562	Official Rate............. ae
....	....	....	....	....	....	....	....	13.223	12.991	11.465	12.034	13.882	14.075	14.678	Official Rate .... rf
End of Period															**Fund Position**
....	....	....	....	....	....	....	46.50	46.50	46.50	46.50	46.50	46.50	46.50	65.20	Quota................... 2f. s
....	....	....	....	....	....	....	7.72	41.56	1.09	.20	.12	.01	.05	.99	SDRs.................. 1b. s
....	....	....	....	....	....	....	—	.01	.01	.01	.01	.01	.01	.01	Reserve Position in the Fund ... 1c. s
....	....	....	....	....	....	....	7.75	41.85	41.85	61.81	54.15	40.01	21.31	18.41	Total Fund Cred.&Loans Outstg. ... 2tl
End of Period															**International Liquidity**
....	....	....	....	....	....	....	170.18	386.12	443.35	579.91	636.82	757.72	810.60	853.06	Total Reserves minus Gold.......... 1l. d
....	....	....	....	....	....	....	10.62	57.08	1.58	.29	.17	.01	.07	1.36	SDRs................ 1b. d
....	....	....	....	....	....	....	—	—	.01	.01	.01	.01	.01	.01	Reserve Position in the Fund ... 1c. d
....	....	....	....	....	....	....	159.56	329.04	441.76	579.61	636.64	757.70	810.53	851.69	Foreign Exchange .... 1d. d
....	....	....	....	....	....	....	.0820	.0080	.0080	.0080	.0080	.0080	.0080	.0080	Gold (Million Fine Troy Ounces)...... 1ad
....	....	....	....	....	....	....	25.36	3.22	3.61	3.19	3.03	2.39	2.37	2.38	Gold (National Valuation) .... 1an d
....	....	....	....	....	....	....	42.44	ⅼ11.15	15.17	7.55	3.56	1.67	.77	.44	Monetary Authorities: Other Liab. ... 4., d
....	....	....	....	....	....	....	122.81	103.10	243.80	322.58	322.30	563.45	483.29	552.49	Banks: Assets .... 7a. d
....	....	....	....	....	....	....	7.95	14.34	55.98	140.83	305.07	913.11	884.58	879.19	Liabilities .... 7b. d
End of Period															**Monetary Authorities**
....	....	....	....	....	....	1,782.8	3,596.7	ⅼ5,353.3	5,595.1	6,686.6	7,956.1	10,901.9	10,884.0	13,430.7	Foreign Assets.................. 11
....	....	....	....	....	....	—	—	ⅼ45.2	—	3.0	3.3	3.6	2.9	4.0	Claims on General Government ... 12a
....	....	....	....	....	....	651.9	—	ⅼ63.5	14.8	.8	—	.2	—	17.5	Claims on Nonfin.Pub.Enterprises... 12c
....	....	....	....	....	....	14.6	—	ⅼ4.6	8.2	14.5	18.6	26.3	39.5	49.2	Claims on Private Sector........... 12d
....	....	....	....	....	....	275.4	583.7	ⅼ576.7	480.9	194.0	141.0	78.0	280.5	266.4	Claims on Banks............. 12e
....	....	....	....	....	....	732.7	1,862.8	ⅼ3,846.6	4,285.1	5,100.6	6,192.9	8,526.7	9,070.3	11,526.0	Reserve Money............. 14
....	....	....	....	....	....	212.4	1,040.7	ⅼ2,440.6	3,131.3	3,837.5	4,270.5	4,588.5	4,538.6	5,741.3	of which: Currency Outside Banks......... 14a
....	....	....	....	....	....	444.8	685.6	ⅼ952.5	945.0	1,139.6	1,013.0	797.8	412.8	400.0	Foreign Liabilities............. 16c
....	....	....	....	....	....	30.4	.3	ⅼ5.1	.2	.1	.3	355.3	6.5	27.0	General Government Deposits ... 16d
....	....	....	....	....	....	1,094.9	1,672.7	ⅼ2,101.9	1,822.3	1,891.4	2,028.0	2,212.7	2,289.3	2,259.8	Capital Accounts 17a
....	....	....	....	....	....	421.9	–41.0	ⅼ–862.7	–953.5	–1,232.7	–1,115.3	–882.6	–571.9	–445.0	Other Items (Net) 17r
End of Period															**Banking Institutions**
....	....	....	....	....	....	598.3	835.0	1,437.7	1,208.4	1,293.1	1,922.5	3,885.3	4,509.5	5,790.9	Reserves 20
....	....	....	....	....	....	852.9	1,585.7	1,430.8	3,020.7	3,697.4	4,009.4	8,077.7	6,480.9	8,597.9	Foreign Assets 21
....	....	....	....	....	....	1.8	14.5	294.6	405.3	649.3	1,006.8	1,086.9	945.9	1,170.3	Claims on General Government ... 22a
....	....	....	....	....	....	202.4	644.4	416.7	346.0	334.5	424.8	320.0	225.8	372.5	Claims on Nonfin.Pub.Enterprises... 22c
....	....	....	....	....	....	330.1	986.1	2,409.8	4,176.0	6,041.3	9,465.4	16,619.8	18,500.7	19,771.7	Claims on Private Sector........... 22d
....	....	....	....	....	....	—	—	8.7	12.2	628.9	2,026.3	4,980.2	6,325.7	6,524.1	Claims on Nonbank Financial Insts ... 22g
....	....	....	....	....	....	451.4	1,813.8	2,847.4	3,248.6	4,399.6	6,513.9	8,582.5	8,207.7	11,174.7	Demand Deposits 24
....	....	....	....	....	....	696.0	1,123.1	852.0	1,558.6	2,140.6	3,369.8	6,286.0	8,047.5	9,008.3	Time, Savings,& Fgn.Currency Dep. ... 25
....	....	....	....	....	....	—	—	.6	220.2	11.5	—	—	—	—	Money Market Instruments 26aa
....	....	....	....	....	....	—	—	—	40.0	82.5	535.5	368.9	200.7	447.7	Bonds 26ab
....	....	....	....	....	....	19.4	102.6	199.0	693.5	1,614.2	3,795.1	13,090.4	11,862.2	13,682.0	Foreign Liabilities............. 26c
....	....	....	....	....	....	60.5	154.9	916.9	1,711.1	2,370.8	2,438.7	3,428.8	2,411.7	1,787.2	General Government Deposits ... 26d
....	....	....	....	....	....	—	51.5	114.3	112.0	102.0	72.5	68.1	—	—	Counterpart Funds 26e
....	....	....	....	....	....	—	9.8	151.8	487.1	819.5	915.2	671.7	555.2	540.7	Government Lending Funds 26f
....	....	....	....	....	....	122.6	271.0	337.9	401.7	88.6	47.9	23.2	14.5	11.4	Credit from Monetary Authorities ... 26g
....	....	....	....	....	....	228.8	493.9	776.8	994.4	1,834.9	2,773.5	5,796.0	8,796.9	9,289.1	Capital Accounts 27a
....	....	....	....	....	....	406.9	45.1	–198.5	–298.6	–819.7	–1,606.9	–3,345.8	–3,107.9	–3,713.7	Other Items (Net) 27r
End of Period															**Banking Survey**
....	....	....	....	....	....	2,171.5	4,394.2	ⅼ5,632.6	6,977.3	7,630.3	7,157.5	5,091.4	5,089.9	7,946.6	Foreign Assets (Net) 31n
....	....	....	....	....	....	1,110.0	1,489.8	ⅼ2,321.2	3,251.2	5,301.4	10,506.1	19,252.8	23,622.3	26,095.2	Domestic Credit 32
....	....	....	....	....	....	–89.0	–140.7	ⅼ–582.1	–1,306.0	–1,718.6	–1,428.9	–2,693.6	–1,469.4	–639.8	Claims on General Govt. (Net)... 32an
....	....	....	....	....	....	854.4	644.4	ⅼ480.1	360.8	335.3	424.8	320.1	225.8	390.0	Claims on Nonfin.Pub.Enterprises... 32c
....	....	....	....	....	....	344.7	986.1	ⅼ2,414.5	4,184.3	6,055.8	9,484.0	16,646.1	18,540.2	19,820.9	Claims on Private Sector......... 32d
....	....	....	....	....	....	—	—	8.7	12.2	628.9	2,026.3	4,980.2	6,325.7	6,524.1	Claims on Nonbank Financial Inst ... 32g
....	....	....	....	....	....	729.2	2,854.6	ⅼ5,288.2	6,379.9	8,237.1	10,786.0	13,223.3	12,750.0	16,918.6	Money 34
....	....	....	....	....	....	1,596.1	1,123.1	ⅼ852.0	1,601.7	2,140.6	3,369.8	6,286.0	8,047.5	9,008.3	Quasi-Money 35
....	....	....	....	....	....	—	—	.6	220.2	11.5	—	—	—	—	Money Market Instruments 36aa
....	....	....	....	....	....	—	—	—	40.0	82.5	535.5	368.9	200.7	447.7	Bonds 36ab
....	....	....	....	....	....	—	51.5	114.3	112.0	102.0	72.5	68.1	—	—	Counterpart Funds 36e
....	....	....	....	....	....	—	9.8	151.8	487.1	819.5	915.2	671.7	555.2	540.7	Government Lending Funds......... 36f
....	....	....	....	....	....	1,323.8	2,166.6	ⅼ2,878.8	2,816.7	3,726.3	4,801.5	8,008.8	11,086.2	11,548.9	Capital Accounts 37a
....	....	....	....	....	....	–367.5	–321.7	ⅼ–1332.0	–1,429.0	–2,187.8	–2,817.0	–4,282.6	–3,927.5	–4,422.5	Other Items (Net) 37r
....	....	....	....	....	....	2,325.3	3,977.7	ⅼ6,140.1	7,981.6	10,377.8	14,155.9	19,509.4	20,797.5	25,927.0	Money plus Quasi-Money 35l
Percent Per Annum															**Interest Rates**
....	....	....	....	....	....	....	....	5.67	4.94	3.53	6.45	11.66	4.92		Money Market Rate 60b
....	....	....	....	....	....	....	....	11.51	8.74	6.05	6.19	8.07	4.19		Deposit Rate 60l
....	....	....	....	....	....	30.50	27.30	23.08	15.95	13.67	19.82	16.67	8.70		Lending Rate 60p
Period Averages															**Prices and Labor**
....	....	....	....	....	....	....	....	79.6	100.0	114.8	ⅼ124.4	129.7	128.1		Producer Prices 63
....	....	....	....	....	....	27.7	52.6	77.7	100.0	123.1	136.1	147.2	152.1		Consumer Prices 64
....	....	....	....	....	....	100.0	194.2	73.0	100.0	....	....	....	....		Monthly Earnings............. 65
Period Averages															
....	....	....	....	....	....	29	50	57	71	72	ⅼ69	68	....		Unemployment.............. 67c
....	....	....	....	....	....	3.7	6.5	7.6	9.7	10.0	ⅼ9.7	9.6	....		Unemployment Rate (%) 67r
Millions of Krooni															**International Transactions**
....	....	....	....	....	....	5,549	10,642	ⅼ16,941	21,040	25,024	40,662	43,952	43,178		Exports 70
....	....	....	....	....	....	5,128	11,848	ⅼ21,525	29,101	38,887	61,610	64,897	60,248		Imports, c.i.f. 71
....	....	....	....	....	....	4,736	10,944	ⅼ19,883	26,881	35,920	....	....	....		Imports, f.o.b. 71.v

Estonia

		1970	1971	1972	1973	1974	1975	1976	1977	1978	1979	1980	1981	1982	1983	1984

Balance of Payments — *Millions of US Dollars:*

	Code	1970	1971	1972	1973	1974	1975	1976	1977	1978	1979	1980	1981	1982	1983	1984
Current Account, n.i.e.	78al d	...	...	...	...	...	...	...	...	...	...	...	...	...	...	...
Goods: Exports f.o.b.	78aa d	...	...	...	...	...	...	...	...	...	...	...	...	...	...	...
Goods: Imports f.o.b.	78ab d	...	...	...	...	...	...	...	...	...	...	...	...	...	...	...
Trade Balance	78ac d	...	...	...	...	...	...	...	...	...	...	...	...	...	...	...
Services: Credit	78ad d	...	...	...	...	...	...	...	...	...	...	...	...	...	...	...
Services: Debit	78ae d	...	...	...	...	...	...	...	...	...	...	...	...	...	...	...
Balance on Goods & Services	78af d	...	...	...	...	...	...	...	...	...	...	...	...	...	...	...
Income: Credit	78ag d	...	...	...	...	...	...	...	...	...	...	...	...	...	...	...
Income: Debit	78ah d	...	...	...	...	...	...	...	...	...	...	...	...	...	...	...
Balance on Gds, Serv. & Inc.	78ai d	...	...	...	...	...	...	...	...	...	...	...	...	...	...	...
Current Transfers, n.i.e.: Credit	78aj d	...	...	...	...	...	...	...	...	...	...	...	...	...	...	...
Current Transfers: Debit	78ak d	...	...	...	...	...	...	...	...	...	...	...	...	...	...	...
Capital Account, n.i.e.	78bc d	...	...	...	...	...	...	...	...	...	...	...	...	...	...	...
Capital Account, n.i.e.: Credit	78ba d	...	...	...	...	...	...	...	...	...	...	...	...	...	...	...
Capital Account: Debit	78bb d	...	...	...	...	...	...	...	...	...	...	...	...	...	...	...
Financial Account, n.i.e.	78bj d	...	...	...	...	...	...	...	...	...	...	...	...	...	...	...
Direct Investment Abroad	78bd d	...	...	...	...	...	...	...	...	...	...	...	...	...	...	...
Dir. Invest. in Rep. Econ., n.i.e.	78be d	...	...	...	...	...	...	...	...	...	...	...	...	...	...	...
Portfolio Investment Assets	78bf d	...	...	...	...	...	...	...	...	...	...	...	...	...	...	...
Equity Securities	78bk d	...	...	...	...	...	...	...	...	...	...	...	...	...	...	...
Debt Securities	78bl d	...	...	...	...	...	...	...	...	...	...	...	...	...	...	...
Portfolio Investment Liab., n.i.e.	78bg d	...	...	...	...	...	...	...	...	...	...	...	...	...	...	...
Equity Securities	78bm d	...	...	...	...	...	...	...	...	...	...	...	...	...	...	...
Debt Securities	78bn d	...	...	...	...	...	...	...	...	...	...	...	...	...	...	...
Financial Derivatives Assets	78bw d	...	...	...	...	...	...	...	...	...	...	...	...	...	...	...
Financial Derivatives Liabilities	78bx d	...	...	...	...	...	...	...	...	...	...	...	...	...	...	...
Other Investment Assets	78bh d	...	...	...	...	...	...	...	...	...	...	...	...	...	...	...
Monetary Authorities	78bo d	...	...	...	...	...	...	...	...	...	...	...	...	...	...	...
General Government	78bp d	...	...	...	...	...	...	...	...	...	...	...	...	...	...	...
Banks	78bq d	...	...	...	...	...	...	...	...	...	...	...	...	...	...	...
Other Sectors	78br d	...	...	...	...	...	...	...	...	...	...	...	...	...	...	...
Other Investment Liab., n.i.e.	78bi d	...	...	...	...	...	...	...	...	...	...	...	...	...	...	...
Monetary Authorities	78bs d	...	...	...	...	...	...	...	...	...	...	...	...	...	...	...
General Government	78bt d	...	...	...	...	...	...	...	...	...	...	...	...	...	...	...
Banks	78bu d	...	...	...	...	...	...	...	...	...	...	...	...	...	...	...
Other Sectors	78bv d	...	...	...	...	...	...	...	...	...	...	...	...	...	...	...
Net Errors and Omissions	78ca d	...	...	...	...	...	...	...	...	...	...	...	...	...	...	...
Overall Balance	78cb d	...	...	...	...	...	...	...	...	...	...	...	...	...	...	...
Reserves and Related Items	79da d	...	...	...	...	...	...	...	...	...	...	...	...	...	...	...
Reserve Assets	79db d	...	...	...	...	...	...	...	...	...	...	...	...	...	...	...
Use of Fund Credit and Loans	79dc d	...	...	...	...	...	...	...	...	...	...	...	...	...	...	...
Exceptional Financing	79de d	...	...	...	...	...	...	...	...	...	...	...	...	...	...	...

International Investment Position — *Millions of US Dollars*

	Code	1970	1971	1972	1973	1974	1975	1976	1977	1978	1979	1980	1981	1982	1983	1984
Assets	79aa d	...	...	...	...	...	...	...	...	...	...	...	...	...	...	...
Direct Investment Abroad	79ab d	...	...	...	...	...	...	...	...	...	...	...	...	...	...	...
Portfolio Investment	79ac d	...	...	...	...	...	...	...	...	...	...	...	...	...	...	...
Equity Securities	79ad d	...	...	...	...	...	...	...	...	...	...	...	...	...	...	...
Debt Securities	79ae d	...	...	...	...	...	...	...	...	...	...	...	...	...	...	...
Financial Derivatives	79al d	...	...	...	...	...	...	...	...	...	...	...	...	...	...	...
Other Investment	79af d	...	...	...	...	...	...	...	...	...	...	...	...	...	...	...
Monetary Authorities	79ag d	...	...	...	...	...	...	...	...	...	...	...	...	...	...	...
General Government	79ah d	...	...	...	...	...	...	...	...	...	...	...	...	...	...	...
Banks	79ai d	...	...	...	...	...	...	...	...	...	...	...	...	...	...	...
Other Sectors	79aj d	...	...	...	...	...	...	...	...	...	...	...	...	...	...	...
Reserve Assets	79ak d	...	...	...	...	...	...	...	...	...	...	...	...	...	...	...
Liabilities	79la d	...	...	...	...	...	...	...	...	...	...	...	...	...	...	...
Dir. Invest. in Rep. Economy	79lb d	...	...	...	...	...	...	...	...	...	...	...	...	...	...	...
Portfolio Investment	79lc d	...	...	...	...	...	...	...	...	...	...	...	...	...	...	...
Equity Securities	79ld d	...	...	...	...	...	...	...	...	...	...	...	...	...	...	...
Debt Securities	79le d	...	...	...	...	...	...	...	...	...	...	...	...	...	...	...
Financial Derivatives	79ll d	...	...	...	...	...	...	...	...	...	...	...	...	...	...	...
Other Investment	79lf d	...	...	...	...	...	...	...	...	...	...	...	...	...	...	...
Monetary Authorities	79lg d	...	...	...	...	...	...	...	...	...	...	...	...	...	...	...
General Government	79lh d	...	...	...	...	...	...	...	...	...	...	...	...	...	...	...
Banks	79li d	...	...	...	...	...	...	...	...	...	...	...	...	...	...	...
Other Sectors	79lj d	...	...	...	...	...	...	...	...	...	...	...	...	...	...	...

Government Finance — *Millions of Krooni:*

	Code	1970	1971	1972	1973	1974	1975	1976	1977	1978	1979	1980	1981	1982	1983	1984
Deficit (-) or Surplus	80	...	...	...	...	...	...	...	...	...	...	...	...	...	...	...
Revenue	81	...	...	...	...	...	...	...	...	...	...	...	...	...	...	...
Grants Received	81z	...	...	...	...	...	...	...	...	...	...	...	...	...	...	...
Expenditure	82	...	...	...	...	...	...	...	...	...	...	...	...	...	...	...
Lending Minus Repayments	83	...	...	...	...	...	...	...	...	...	...	...	...	...	...	...
Financing																
Domestic	84a	...	...	...	...	...	...	...	...	...	...	...	...	...	...	...
Foreign	85a	...	...	...	...	...	...	...	...	...	...	...	...	...	...	...

National Accounts — *Millions of Krooni*

	Code	1970	1971	1972	1973	1974	1975	1976	1977	1978	1979	1980	1981	1982	1983	1984
Househ.Cons.Expend.,incl.NPISHs	96f	...	...	...	...	...	...	...	...	...	...	...	...	...	...	...
Government Consumption Expend.	91f	...	...	...	...	...	...	...	...	...	...	...	...	...	...	...
Gross Fixed Capital Formation	93e	...	...	...	...	...	...	...	...	...	...	...	...	...	...	...
Changes in Inventories	93i	...	...	...	...	...	...	...	...	...	...	...	...	...	...	...
Exports of Goods and Services	90c	...	...	...	...	...	...	...	...	...	...	...	...	...	...	...
Imports of Goods & Services	98c	...	...	...	...	...	...	...	...	...	...	...	...	...	...	...
Gross Domestic Product (GDP)	99b	...	...	...	...	...	...	...	...	...	...	...	...	...	...	...
GDP Volume 1995 Prices	99b. p	...	...	...	...	...	...	...	...	...	...	...	...	...	...	...
GDP Volume (1995=100)	99bv p	...	...	...	...	...	...	...	...	...	...	...	...	...	...	...
GDP Deflator (1995=100)	99bi p	...	...	...	...	...	...	...	...	...	...	...	...	...	...	...

Millions:

	Code	1970	1971	1972	1973	1974	1975	1976	1977	1978	1979	1980	1981	1982	1983	1984
Population	99z	...	...	...	...	...	...	...	...	...	...	...	...	...	...	...

1985	1986	1987	1988	1989	1990	1991	1992	1993	1994	1995	1996	1997	1998	1999		
Minus Sign Indicates Debit															**Balance of Payments**	
....	....	....	....	....	....	....	36.2	21.6	-166.3	-157.8	-398.3	-561.9	-477.9	-294.7	Current Account, n.i.e.	78al d
....	....	....	....	....	....	....	460.7	811.7	1,225.0	1,696.3	1,812.3	2,291.3	2,690.1	2,453.0	Goods: Exports f.o.b.	78aa d
....	....	....	....	....	....	....	-551.1	-956.6	-1,581.4	-2,362.3	-2,831.5	-3,415.6	-3,804.9	-3,330.6	Goods: Imports f.o.b.	78ab d
....	....	....	....	....	....	....	-90.4	-144.9	-356.5	-666.0	-1,019.2	-1,124.3	-1,114.8	-877.5	*Trade Balance*	78ac d
....	....	....	....	....	....	....	203.1	334.6	515.3	876.8	1,108.3	1,318.0	1,479.6	1,489.7	Services: Credit	78ad d
....	....	....	....	....	....	....	-160.4	-259.4	-410.2	-497.7	-589.8	-726.6	-910.1	-917.6	Services: Debit	78ae d
....	....	....	....	....	....	....	-47.7	-69.7	-251.3	-286.9	-500.7	-532.9	-545.3	-305.4	*Balance on Goods & Services*	78af d
....	....	....	....	....	....	....	.5	26.9	37.3	63.6	112.2	115.1	133.5	133.8	Income: Credit	78ag d
....	....	....	....	....	....	....	-13.6	-40.8	-66.9	-60.8	-110.3	-260.8	-214.5	-235.5	Income: Debit	78ah d
....	....	....	....	....	....	....	-60.8	-83.6	-280.9	-284.1	-498.8	-678.6	-626.3	-407.1	*Balance on Gds, Serv. & Inc.*	78ai d
....	....	....	....	....	....	....	97.4	108.4	120.3	134.5	116.8	135.3	172.9	153.7	Current Transfers, n.i.e.: Credit	78aj d
....	....	....	....	....	....	....	-.3	-3.2	-5.7	-8.2	-16.3	-18.6	-24.5	-41.3	Current Transfers: Debit	78ak d
....	....	....	....	....	....	....	27.4	—	-.6	-.8	-.7	-.2	1.8	1.2	Capital Account, n.i.e.	78bc d
....	....	....	....	....	....	....	27.4	—	.5	1.4	.2	.7	2.1	1.4	Capital Account, n.i.e.: Credit	78ba d
....	....	....	....	....	....	....	—	—	-1.1	-2.2	-.8	-.9	-.3	-.2	Capital Account: Debit	78bb d
....	....	....	....	....	....	....	-1.3	188.9	167.2	233.4	540.9	802.8	508.1	418.2	Financial Account, n.i.e.	78bj d
....	....	....	....	....	....	....	-1.9	-6.2	-2.4	-2.5	-40.1	-136.6	-6.3	-82.9	Direct Investment Abroad	78bd d
....	....	....	....	....	....	....	82.3	162.2	214.4	201.5	150.2	266.2	580.5	305.2	Dir. Invest. in Rep. Econ., n.i.e.	78be d
....	....	....	....	....	....	....	—	-.4	-22.5	-33.2	-52.7	-165.0	-10.9	-132.3	Portfolio Investment Assets	78bf d
....	....	....	....	....	....	....	—	-.4	-14.5	5.1	-15.0	-87.8	35.1	12.9	Equity Securities	78bk d
....	....	....	....	....	....	....	—	—	-8.0	-38.2	-37.6	-77.2	-46.0	-145.2	Debt Securities	78bl d
....	....	....	....	....	....	....	—	.2	8.4	11.1	198.1	427.5	1.1	153.3	Portfolio Investment Liab., n.i.e.	78bg d
....	....	....	....	....	....	....	—	.1	8.4	9.9	172.3	127.8	25.7	235.4	Equity Securities	78bm d
....	....	....	....	....	....	....	—	.1	—	1.2	25.8	299.7	-24.6	-82.1	Debt Securities	78bn d
....	....	....	....	....	....	....	....	....	....	....	....	....	....	....	Financial Derivatives Assets	78bw d
....	....	....	....	....	....	....	....	....	....	....	....	....	....	....	Financial Derivatives Liabilities	78bx d
....	....	....	....	....	....	....	-122.4	-144.7	-146.7	-98.9	-7.3	-334.2	-168.5	-110.3	Other Investment Assets	78bh d
....	....	....	....	....	....	....	-72.8	5.7	.1	.1	.1			-18.3	Monetary Authorities	78bo d
....	....	....	....	....	....	....	—	-17.1	.4	-.4	-3.3	-24.7	-61.9	-60.8	General Government	78bp d
....	....	....	....	....	....	....	-48.5	-44.7	-102.8	-41.1	20.8	-195.9	61.3	-53.8	Banks	78bq d
....	....	....	....	....	....	....	-1.1	-88.6	-44.4	-57.5	-24.9	-113.5	-167.9	22.5	Other Sectors	78br d
....	....	....	....	....	....	....	40.7	177.8	115.9	155.4	292.6	744.8	112.1	285.2	Other Investment Liab., n.i.e.	78bi d
....	....	....	....	....	....	....	8.1	14.9	6.2	-13.5	-6.7	-2.5	-1.1	7.3	Monetary Authorities	78bs d
....	....	....	....	....	....	....	11.1	77.3	19.8	61.0	31.3	-3.3	4.4	9.8	General Government	78bt d
....	....	....	....	....	....	....	7.2	7.2	37.5	82.2	173.7	492.4	-17.3	188.3	Banks	78bu d
....	....	....	....	....	....	....	14.3	78.4	52.3	25.7	94.4	258.2	126.0	79.8	Other Sectors	78bv d
....	....	....	....	....	....	....	-4.4	-45.9	17.2	8.7	-35.6	-24.9	5.3	-5.4	Net Errors and Omissions	78ca d
....	....	....	....	....	....	....	57.9	164.6	17.5	83.5	106.3	215.9	37.3	119.3	*Overall Balance*	78cb d
....	....	....	....	....	....	....	-57.9	-164.6	-17.5	-83.5	-106.3	-215.9	-37.3	-119.3	Reserves and Related Items	79da d
....	....	....	....	....	....	....	-69.2	-212.4	-17.5	-112.9	-95.3	-196.4	-11.7	-115.3	Reserve Assets	79db d
....	....	....	....	....	....	....	11.3	47.7	—	29.4	-11.1	-19.4	-25.6	-4.0	Use of Fund Credit and Loans	79dc d
....	....	....	....	....	....	....	....	....	....	....	....	....	....	....	Exceptional Financing	79de d
Millions of US Dollars															**International Investment Position**	
....	....	....	....	....	....	....	....	....	....	....	1,344.1	2,045.5	2,300.4	2,414.7	Assets	79aa d
....	....	....	....	....	....	....	....	....	....	....	107.7	215.3	198.4	281.2	Direct Investment Abroad	79ab d
....	....	....	....	....	....	....	....	....	....	....	121.0	249.3	211.2	305.2	Portfolio Investment	79ac d
....	....	....	....	....	....	....	....	....	....	....	26.1	98.5	31.5	12.4	Equity Securities	79ad d
....	....	....	....	....	....	....	....	....	....	....	94.9	150.9	179.7	292.9	Debt Securities	79ae d
....	....	....	....	....	....	....	....	....	....	....					Financial Derivatives	79al d
....	....	....	....	....	....	....	....	....	....	....	475.9	820.4	1,077.4	972.4	Other Investment	79af d
....	....	....	....	....	....	....	....	....	....	....					Monetary Authorities	79ag d
....	....	....	....	....	....	....	....	....	....	....	4.6	26.7	97.7	129.6	General Government	79ah d
....	....	....	....	....	....	....	....	....	....	....	246.9	392.8	360.9	374.4	Banks	79ai d
....	....	....	....	....	....	....	....	....	....	....	224.3	400.8	618.7	468.4	Other Sectors	79aj d
....	....	....	....	....	....	....	....	....	....	....	639.6	760.5	813.5	855.8	Reserve Assets	79ak d
....	....	....	....	....	....	....	....	....	....	....	2,007.8	3,789.0	4,481.9	5,224.9	Liabilities	79la d
....	....	....	....	....	....	....	....	....	....	....	824.6	1,147.9	1,821.7	2,467.3	Dir. Invest. in Rep. Economy	79lb d
....	....	....	....	....	....	....	....	....	....	....	117.4	954.2	702.9	771.8	Portfolio Investment	79lc d
....	....	....	....	....	....	....	....	....	....	....	76.3	572.9	301.2	500.7	Equity Securities	79ld d
....	....	....	....	....	....	....	....	....	....	....	41.1	381.3	401.7	271.2	Debt Securities	79le d
....	....	....	....	....	....	....	....	....	....	....					Financial Derivatives	79ll d
....	....	....	....	....	....	....	....	....	....	....	1,065.9	1,686.9	1,957.3	1,985.7	Other Investment	79lf d
....	....	....	....	....	....	....	....	....	....	....	151.4	55.7	30.8	25.8	Monetary Authorities	79lg d
....	....	....	....	....	....	....	....	....	....	....	208.2	192.6	203.5	203.9	General Government	79lh d
....	....	....	....	....	....	....	....	....	....	....	299.1	747.1	692.7	778.2	Banks	79li d
....	....	....	....	....	....	....	....	....	....	....	407.1	691.5	1,030.3	977.8	Other Sectors	79lj d
Year Ending December 31															**Government Finance**	
....	....	....	....	....	....	7.2	163.3	-458.5	416.8	-233.6	-433.7	1,632.4	-42.3	....	Deficit (-) or Surplus	80
....	....	....	....	....	....	448.1	2,994.8	6,320.3	10,566.8	14,649.3	17,544.8	22,360.5	24,006.5	....	Revenue	81
....	....	....	....	....	....	14.9	219.9	243.7	—	132.0	—	25.0	124.0	....	Grants Received	81z
....	....	....	....	....	....	404.7	3,024.0	6,088.5	9,590.3	14,523.5	17,713.7	20,551.8	24,103.3	....	Expenditure	82
....	....	....	....	....	....	51.1	27.4	934.0	559.7	491.4	264.8	201.3	69.5	....	Lending Minus Repayments	83
															Financing	
....	....	....	....	....	....	-7.2	-172.1	....	....	-150.2	49.3	-974.0	524.0	....	Domestic	84a
....	....	....	....	....	....	—	8.8	....	....	383.8	384.4	-658.4	-481.7	....	Foreign	85a
Millions of Krooni															**National Accounts**	
....	....	....	....	....	....	1,002	7,261	12,711	18,248	23,959	31,845	37,990	43,656	....	Househ.Cons.Expend.,incl.NPISHs	96f
....	....	....	....	....	....	241	2,084	4,474	6,790	10,350	12,632	14,219	16,534	....	Government Consumption Expend.	91f
....	....	....	....	....	....	357	2,755	5,280	8,004	10,576	14,015	17,962	21,311	....	Gross Fixed Capital Formation	93e
....	....	....	....	....	....	91	763	541	181	305	564	2,423	170	....	Changes in Inventories	93i
....	....	....	....	....	....	584	7,893	15,197	22,486	29,451	35,186	50,238	58,394	....	Exports of Goods and Services	90c
....	....	....	....	....	....	-495	-7,121	-16,125	-25,739	-32,736	-41,229	-57,661	-65,464	....	Imports of Goods & Services	98c
....	....	....	....	....	....	1,832	13,158	21,610	29,600	40,705	52,446	64,324	73,213	....	Gross Domestic Product (GDP)	99b
....	....	....	....	....	....	....	....	39,827	39,031	40,705	42,297	46,789	48,682	....	GDP Volume 1995 Prices	99b.p
....	....	....	....	....	....	....	....	97.8	95.9	100.0	103.9	114.9	119.6	....	GDP Volume (1995=100)	99bv p
....	....	....	....	....	....	....	....	54.3	75.8	100.0	124.0	137.5	150.4	....	GDP Deflator (1995=100)	99bi p
Midyear Estimates																
....	....	....	....	....	....	....	1.54	1.52	1.50	1.48	1.47	1.46	1.45	1.41	**Population**	99z

(See notes in the back of the book.)

Ethiopia

644

		1970	1971	1972	1973	1974	1975	1976	1977	1978	1979	1980	1981	1982	1983	1984
Exchange Rates															*Birr per SDR*	
Official Rate	aa	2.5000	2.4971	2.4971	2.4971	2.5344	2.4233	2.4050	2.5144	2.6968	2.7269	2.6401	2.4094	2.2834	2.1672	2.0290
															Birr per US Dollar	
Official Rate	ae	2.5000	2.3000	2.3000	2.0700	2.0700	2.0700	2.0700	2.0700	2.0700	2.0700	2.0700	2.0700	2.0700	2.0700	2.0700
Official Rate	rf	2.5000	2.4935	2.3000	2.0988	2.0700	2.0700	2.0700	2.0700	2.0700	2.0700	2.0700	2.0700	2.0700	2.0700	2.0700
Fund Position															*Millions of SDRs:*	
Quota	2f. s	27.0	27.0	27.0	27.0	27.0	27.0	27.0	27.0	36.0	36.0	54.0	54.0	54.0	70.6	70.6
SDRs	1b. s	—	—	—	—	—	—	—	—	—	.4	—	10.4	3.2	2.3	3.0
Reserve Position in the Fund	1c. s	6.8	6.8	6.8	6.8	6.8	6.8	6.8	7.3	—	—	4.1	—	—	4.2	—
Total Fund Cred.&Loans Outstg.	2tl	—	—	—	—	—	—	—	—	11.2	55.8	62.3	124.4	145.6	127.6	100.2
International Liquidity														*Millions of US Dollars Unless Otherwise Indicated:*		
Total Reserves minus Gold	1l. d	63.3	59.3	83.2	166.0	263.6	276.7	294.7	213.3	152.9	172.7	80.1	266.7	181.8	125.9	44.3
SDRs	1b. d	—	—	—	—	—	—	—	—	—	.5	—	12.1	3.5	2.4	2.9
Reserve Position in the Fund	1c. d	6.8	7.4	7.4	8.2	8.4	8.0	7.9	8.9	—	—	5.2	—	—	4.4	—
Foreign Exchange	1d. d	56.5	51.9	75.8	157.8	255.2	268.7	286.8	204.4	152.9	172.2	74.9	254.6	178.3	119.1	41.4
Gold (Million Fine Troy Ounces)	1ad	.226	.237	.249	.257	.275	.275	.275	.286	.286	.286	.309	.260	.209	.209	.209
Gold (National Valuation)	1and	7.9	9.0	9.5	10.8	11.0	11.0	10.8	11.3	11.3	11.8	24.5	23.3	21.3	21.3	21.3
Monetary Authorities: Other Liab.	4..d	2.0	3.2	1.0	2.3	3.5	4.5	5.1	4.3	6.5	3.4	5.2	9.6	7.4	10.4	6.0
Deposit Money Banks: Assets	7a. d	12.1	13.6	21.1	52.5	48.1	40.3	38.8	57.9	45.4	70.0	50.8	63.8	90.1	71.9	64.9
Liabilities	7b. d	25.6	27.7	24.5	23.6	21.4	23.0	22.4	25.0	22.2	23.8	40.7	60.0	71.6	66.7	62.1
Other Banking Insts.: Assets	7e. d	.1	.1	.2	.2	.5	.7	.3	.4	3.6	1.2	1.7	.2	.6	.6	.5
Liabilities	7f. d	12.7	13.2	12.4	20.5	24.0	31.4	33.5	37.1	46.4	49.1	73.6	36.4	32.5	29.2	29.1
Monetary Authorities															*Millions of Birr*	
Foreign Assets	11	178	157	213	366	563	591	622	494	391	400	203	575	413	295	130
Claims on Central Government	12a	147	158	171	148	126	307	512	605	787	950	1,093	1,033	1,284	1,574	1,892
Claims on Other Financial Insts	12f	—	—	—	—	—	83	105	167	282	441	692	855	982	845	1,014
Reserve Money	14	375	354	393	472	603	835	1,004	1,001	1,097	1,209	1,355	1,554	1,690	1,690	2,027
of which: Currency Outside DMBs	14a	323	304	340	404	533	689	575	769	895	1,012	1,029	1,039	1,150	1,251	1,272
Foreign Liabilities	16c	5	7	2	5	7	9	11	9	44	159	175	319	348	298	216
Central Government Deposits	16d	44	50	49	65	93	87	123	134	148	144	95	107	118	170	208
Capital Accounts	17a	38	37	49	47	65	77	97	122	151	174	178	187	192	200	210
Other Items (Net)	17r	−137	−132	−109	−74	−79	−28	5	—	21	105	185	295	331	355	375
Deposit Money Banks															*Millions of Birr*	
Reserves	20	56	52	56	70	72	155	435	229	201	194	325	514	540	†440	757
Foreign Assets	21	30	31	49	109	100	83	80	120	94	145	105	132	187	†149	134
Claims on Central Government	22a	19	13	14	43	52	65	86	158	198	229	217	292	363	†914	951
Claims on Private Sector	22d	387	419	444	473	545	464	467	568	732	†880	875	1,005	1,064	†988	870
Claims on Other Financial Insts	22f	28	30	26	18	24	30	30	14	16	†51	72	90	89	†84	84
Demand Deposits	24	130	133	151	215	221	253	378	409	484	559	539	681	742	†892	1,037
Time, Savings,& Fgn.Currency Dep.	25	187	215	265	363	381	302	450	473	483	536	628	718	797	†1,056	1,140
Foreign Liabilities	26c	34	27	23	17	15	21	21	29	25	31	68	110	136	†128	121
Long-Term Foreign Liabilities	26cl	30	37	34	32	29	27	25	23	21	18	16	14	12	10	8
Central Government Deposits	26d	13	13	13	14	21	25	31	24	28	39	68	89	98	†117	89
Capital Accounts	27a	56	57	60	61	64	65	74	83	81	89	85	232	223	†318	339
Other Items (Net)	27r	70	63	43	11	63	105	119	48	119	227	188	190	233	†54	62
Monetary Survey															*Millions of Birr*	
Foreign Assets (Net)	31n	169	155	237	453	640	645	671	575	416	355	65	278	115	†18	−73
Domestic Credit	32	524	557	594	604	635	837	1,047	1,355	1,840	†2,368	2,785	3,079	3,565	†4,118	4,514
Claims on Central Govt. (Net)	32an	109	109	124	113	65	259	445	606	809	996	1,146	1,129	1,431	†2,201	2,546
Claims on Private Sector	32d	387	419	444	473	545	464	467	568	732	†880	875	1,005	1,064	†988	870
Claims on Other Financial Insts	32f	28	30	26	19	24	113	135	181	299	†492	764	945	1,071	†930	1,098
Money	34	453	437	491	619	754	942	953	1,179	1,378	1,572	1,568	1,720	1,892	†2,142	2,309
Quasi-Money	35	187	215	265	363	381	302	450	473	483	536	628	718	797	†1,056	1,140
Long-Term Foreign Liabilities	36cl	30	37	34	32	29	27	25	23	21	18	16	14	12	10	8
Capital Accounts	37a	94	94	109	108	129	142	171	205	232	262	264	419	415	†519	550
Other Items (Net)	37r	−70	−71	−68	−65	−18	69	119	51	141	334	374	485	564	†409	435
Money plus Quasi-Money	35l	640	651	756	982	1,135	1,244	1,403	1,652	1,861	2,108	2,196	2,438	2,689	†3,198	3,449
Other Banking Institutions															*Millions of Birr*	
Cash	40	2	6	8	15	9	9	31	43	41	30	49	53	34	75	64
Foreign Assets	41	—	—	1	1	1	2	1	1	8	2	4	—	1	1	1
Claims on Nonfin.Pub.Enterprises	42c															
Claims on Private Sector	42d	132	126	154	201	245	369	391	459	621	838	1,161	1,149	1,262	1,138	1,347
Demand Deposits	44															
Time and Savings Deposits	45	11	14	28	34	42	58	77	86	124	144	228	179	229	251	267
Foreign Liabilities	46c	32	30	29	42	50	65	69	77	96	102	152	75	67	61	60
Central Govt. Lending Funds	46f	19	21	18	31	32	29	24	24	24	23	22	15	15	14	14
Credit from Monetary Authorities	46g	—	—	—	—	—	83	105	167	282	441	692	855	982	845	1,014
Credit from Deposit Money Banks	46h	27	29	23	22	29	34	29	31	35	40	53	70	24	23	
Capital Accounts	47a	48	40	69	88	105	115	115	118	118	115	115	104	91	73	81
Other Items (Net)	47r	−2	−2	−3	−3	−2	−3	3	1	−8	4	−49	−95	−112	−52	−45
Liquid Liabilities	55l	649	659	776	1,001	1,167	1,293	1,449	1,695	1,944	2,222	2,375	2,565	2,884	3,374	3,652
Interest Rates															*Percent Per Annum*	
Discount Rate	60	....	....	....	....	....	....	....	....	....	....	....	....	....	....	....
Treasury Bill Rate	60c	....	....	....	....	....	....	....	....	2.03	2.02	2.80	2.80	3.00	3.00	3.00
Deposit Rate	60l	....	....	....	....	....	....	....	....	....	....	....	....	....	....	....
Lending Rate	60p	....	....	....	....	....	....	....	....	....	....	....	....	....	....	....
Government Bond Yield	61	....	....	....	....	....	....	....	....	....	....	....	....	....	....	....
Prices and Labor															*Index Numbers (1995=100):*	
Consumer Prices	64	14.3	14.4	13.5	14.7	16.0	17.0	21.9	25.5	29.1	33.8	35.3	37.5	39.7	39.4	42.8
															Number in Thousands:	
Labor Force	67d	....	....	....	....	....	....	....	....	....	....	....	....	....	....	....
Employment	67e	....	....	....	....	....	....	....	....	....	....	....	....	....	....	....
Unemployment	67c	....	....	....	....	....	....	....	....	....	....	....	....	....	....	....
Unemployment Rate (%)	67r	....	....	....	....	....	....	....	....	....	....	....	....	....	....	54.7

	1985	1986	1987	1988	1989	1990	1991	1992	1993	1994	1995	1996	1997	1998	1999		
Exchange Rates																	
End of Period																	
	2.2737	2.5320	2.9366	2.7856	2.7203	2.9449	2.9610	6.8750	6.8678	8.6861	9.3946	9.2403	9.2613	10.5644	11.1640	Official Rate	aa
End of Period (ae) Period Average (rf)																	
	2.0700	2.0700	2.0700	2.0700	2.0700	2.0700	2.0700	5.0000	5.0000	5.9500	6.3200	6.4260	6.8640	7.5030	8.1340	Official Rate	ae
	2.0700	2.0700	2.0700	2.0700	2.0700	2.0700	2.0700	2.8025	5.0000	5.4650	6.1583	6.3517	6.7093	7.1159	7.9423	Official Rate	rf
Fund Position																	
End of Period																	
	70.6	70.6	70.6	70.6	70.6	70.6	70.6	98.3	98.3	98.3	98.3	98.3	98.3	98.3	133.7	Quota	2f. s
	.2	—	1.2	—	—	.2	.1	.1	.2	.3	.2	—	.1	.1	—	SDRs	1b. s
	—	—	—	—	—	—	—	6.9	7.0	7.0	7.0	7.1	7.1	7.1	7.1	Reserve Position in the Fund	1c. s
	64.8	68.8	53.4	40.8	23.0	4.5	—	14.1	35.3	49.4	49.4	64.2	64.2	76.1	69.0	Total Fund Cred.&Loans Outstg.	2tl
International Liquidity																	
End of Period																	
	148.0	250.5	122.7	64.2	46.1	20.2	54.5	232.4	455.8	544.2	771.5	732.2	501.1	511.1	458.5	Total Reserves minus Gold	1l. d
	.2	—	1.7	—	.1	.3	.2	.1	.3	.4	.3	—	.1	.1	.1	SDRs	1b. d
	—	—	—	—	—	—	—	9.5	9.6	10.2	10.5	10.1	9.5	10.0	9.7	Reserve Position in the Fund	1c. d
	147.8	250.5	121.0	64.2	46.0	19.9	54.3	222.8	445.9	533.6	760.8	722.0	491.4	501.0	448.7	Foreign Exchange	1d. d
	.209	.209	.209	.209	.192	.091	.147	.113	.113	.113	.113	.002	.002	.030	.030	Gold (Million Fine Troy Ounces)	1ad
	21.3	21.3	21.3	21.3	17.3	9.4	15.1	11.4	11.4	11.4	11.4	.4	.4	.3		Gold (National Valuation)	1an d
	12.9	12.5	18.1	37.8	48.8	60.8	18.9	174.0	161.5	146.5	134.8	169.2	90.1	107.2	95.1	Monetary Authorities: Other Liab.	4.. d
	57.4	72.6	52.3	71.6	64.1	43.6	151.4	192.2	236.2	533.3	454.2	428.6	672.1	647.8	536.1	Deposit Money Banks: Assets	7a. d
	59.2	57.0	56.2	62.3	60.9	67.9	77.5	65.9	91.4	134.8	216.0	229.1	249.6	252.6	282.3	Liabilities	7b. d
	1.4	.9	4.0	.9	1.3	3.1	2.5	2.2	1.0	3.5	2.5	8.6	9.3	9.2	6.8	Other Banking Insts.: Assets	7e. d
	33.4	43.0	50.4	63.2	73.2	112.7	132.6	55.5	58.9	52.8	45.0	39.0	36.9	27.2	28.1	Liabilities	7f. d
Monetary Authorities																	
End of Period																	
	350	558	337	177	131	67	144	1,219	2,726	3,464	4,946	4,707	3,441	3,878	3,652	Foreign Assets	11
	1,722	2,061	2,047	2,492	2,838	3,553	4,668	5,724	6,584	8,444	8,131	7,656	8,529	9,201	10,301	Claims on Central Government	12a
	1,194	1,333	1,588	1,786	1,945	2,064	2,081	2,102	2,118	464	465	465	465	465	465	Claims on Other Financial Insts	12f
	2,117	2,638	2,596	3,085	3,515	4,028	5,137	6,120	6,421	7,084	7,977	6,653	7,236	6,346	5,673	Reserve Money	14
	1,418	1,640	1,744	1,962	2,341	3,081	4,007	4,709	4,776	5,380	5,718	5,401	4,964	3,978	4,507	of which: Currency Outside DMBs	14a
	174	200	194	192	163	139	39	967	1,050	1,301	1,316	1,544	1,076	1,297	1,215	Foreign Liabilities	16c
	339	374	313	387	363	453	661	590	2,038	1,787	1,809	1,750	2,195	2,070	2,522	Central Government Deposits	16d
	218	266	358	318	330	334	342	518	466	733	880	1,159	1,198	1,272	1,423	Capital Accounts	17a
	419	473	510	473	543	729	715	850	1,453	1,465	1,561	1,722	730	2,559	3,585	Other Items (Net)	17r
Deposit Money Banks																	
End of Period																	
	703	998	852	1,126	1,169	941	1,130	1,413	1,635	1,666	2,197	1,228	2,173	2,312	1,315	Reserves	20
	119	150	108	148	133	90	313	961	1,181	3,173	2,871	2,754	4,613	4,861	4,361	Foreign Assets	21
	1,451	1,449	1,476	1,498	1,869	2,639	2,630	2,617	2,617	2,617	2,773	2,613	2,361	2,629	5,234	Claims on Central Government	22a
	861	943	1,224	1,272	1,253	1,194	1,184	1,450	2,865	3,618	5,336	8,243	9,595	10,253	12,014	Claims on Private Sector	22d
	91	91	89	119	118	116	115	144	141	160	274	629	574	607	849	Claims on Other Financial Insts	22f
	1,285	1,633	1,597	1,759	1,981	2,192	2,192	2,433	2,674	3,646	3,562	3,872	5,123	5,326	6,018	Demand Deposits	24
	1,292	1,195	1,413	1,570	1,726	1,894	2,188	2,607	3,252	4,379	5,325	6,699	8,224	8,488	8,477	Time, Savings,& Fgn.Currency Dep.	25
	117	115	115	129	126	140	160	329	457	802	1,365	1,472	1,713	1,895	2,296	Foreign Liabilities	26c
	5	3	1	—	—	—	—	—	—	—	—	—	—	—	—	Long-Term Foreign Liabilities	26cl
	81	123	130	150	149	153	178	243	412	619	810	737	974	1,153	1,176	Central Government Deposits	26d
	354	399	432	438	466	493	538	548	825	979	1,238	2,028	2,566	3,078	3,219	Capital Accounts	27a
	91	162	61	118	92	107	116	424	818	809	1,150	659	715	723	2,587	Other Items (Net)	27r
Monetary Survey																	
End of Period																	
	178	394	136	4	−26	−122	258	884	2,400	4,534	5,136	4,445	5,264	5,547	4,501	Foreign Assets (Net)	31n
	4,900	5,379	5,981	6,629	7,510	8,960	9,840	11,203	11,875	12,897	14,361	17,119	18,355	19,934	25,165	Domestic Credit	32
	2,753	3,012	3,080	3,453	4,195	5,586	6,460	7,508	6,751	8,654	8,286	7,782	7,721	8,608	11,837	Claims on Central Govt. (Net)	32an
	861	943	1,224	1,272	1,253	1,194	1,184	1,450	2,865	3,618	5,336	8,243	9,595	10,253	12,014	Claims on Private Sector	32d
	1,286	1,423	1,677	1,905	2,063	2,180	2,196	2,246	2,259	624	740	1,094	1,039	1,073	1,314	Claims on Other Financial Insts	32f
	2,702	3,273	3,341	3,722	4,322	5,273	6,199	7,142	7,450	9,027	9,280	9,273	10,087	9,304	10,524	Money	34
	1,292	1,195	1,413	1,570	1,726	1,894	2,188	2,607	3,252	4,379	5,325	6,699	8,224	8,488	8,477	Quasi-Money	35
	5	3	1	—	—	—	—	—	—	—	—	—	—	—	—	Long-Term Foreign Liabilities	36cl
	571	665	790	755	796	827	880	1,066	1,291	1,712	2,118	3,187	3,764	4,351	4,641	Capital Accounts	37a
	507	636	571	587	640	843	831	1,272	2,282	2,313	2,773	2,405	1,544	3,338	6,024	Other Items (Net)	37r
	3,994	4,468	4,754	5,291	6,048	7,167	8,387	9,749	10,702	13,405	14,605	15,972	18,311	17,792	19,001	Money plus Quasi-Money	35l
Other Banking Institutions																	
End of Period																	
	38	217	211	208	351	331	308	297	369	234	10	8	23	8	12	Cash	40
	3	2	8	2	3	7	5	11	5	21	16	55	64	69	55	Foreign Assets	41
	—	—	—	—	—	—	—	—	—	—	—	492	575	397	300	258	Claims on Nonfin.Pub.Enterprises	42c
	1,553	1,705	2,013	2,335	2,479	3,067	3,113	2,701	954	1,206	701	1,173	1,774	2,476	2,917	Claims on Private Sector	42d
	—	—	—	—	—	—	—	—	—	—	10	22	31	16	26	Demand Deposits	44
	279	425	456	557	657	677	641	497	530	538	49	2	234	681	735	Time and Savings Deposits	45
	69	89	104	131	152	233	274	278	295	314	285	250	254	204	228	Foreign Liabilities	46c
	14	14	23	34	28	28	27	29	100	54	14	14	14	14	14	Central Govt. Lending Funds	46f
	1,194	1,333	1,588	1,786	1,945	2,064	2,081	2,102	2,118	464	465	465	465	465	465	Credit from Monetary Authorities	46g
	22	24	18	27	2	1	1	97	−1,563	116	415	685	958	894	1,416	Credit from Deposit Money Banks	46h
	95	125	142	128	154	87	61	−41	−106	101	177	391	361	381	397	Capital Accounts	47a
	−79	−86	−98	−119	−106	314	339	47	−44	−128	−194	−18	−61	197	−39	Other Items (Net)	47r
	4,235	4,676	4,999	5,640	6,354	7,514	8,721	9,949	10,863	13,710	14,644	15,966	18,523	18,465	19,724	Liquid Liabilities	55l
Interest Rates																	
Percent Per Annum																	
	6.00	6.00	3.00	3.00	3.00	3.00	3.00	5.25	12.00	12.00	12.00	....	....	....	....	Discount Rate	60
	3.00	3.00	3.00	3.00	3.00	3.00	3.00	5.25	12.00	12.00	12.00	7.22	3.97	3.48	3.65	Treasury Bill Rate	60c
	6.00	6.35	6.70	6.70	6.70	2.43	5.00	3.63	11.50	11.50	11.46	9.42	7.00	6.00	6.32	Deposit Rate	60l
	8.50	7.25	6.00	6.00	6.00	6.00	6.00	8.00	14.00	14.33	15.08	13.92	10.50	10.50	10.50	Lending Rate	60p
	....	6.00	5.00	5.00	5.00	5.00	5.00	7.00	13.00	13.00	13.00	13.00	....	....	....	Government Bond Yield	61
Prices and Labor																	
Period Averages																	
	50.9	45.9	44.8	48.0	51.7	54.4	73.8	81.6	84.5	90.9	100.0	94.9	91.4	98.9	....	Consumer Prices	64
Period Averages																	
	....	....	....	....	....	....	....	....	....	....	....	....	26,408	....	....	Labor Force	67d
	....	....	539	....	....	....	....	....	683	....	....	....	....	....	....	Employment	67e
	56	53	58	55	51	44	44	71	63	65	23	28	35	....	....	Unemployment	67c
	56.4	52.6	58.2	55.3	51.3	44.2	44.3	70.9	62.9	....	....	....	....	....	....	Unemployment Rate (%)	67r

Ethiopia

		1970	1971	1972	1973	1974	1975	1976	1977	1978	1979	1980	1981	1982	1983	1984
International Transactions																*Millions of Birr*
Exports	70	305.9	314.4	384.1	502.4	556.2	497.8	580.6	689.0	633.6	864.3	878.8	805.1	835.5	833.3	862.7
Imports, c.i.f.	71	429.1	469.6	435.6	448.2	586.0	647.9	729.5	727.8	942.7	1,174.6	1,494.7	1,528.9	1,627.8	1,813.3	1,921.4
Balance of Payments																*Millions of US Dollars:*
Current Account, n.i.e.	78al *d*	....	....	....	....	....	....	....	−82.6	−111.7	−91.4	−226.1	−249.5	−194.9	−169.9	−130.1
Goods: Exports f.o.b.	78aa *d*	....	....	....	....	....	....	....	333.3	306.2	430.3	419.3	374.1	402.8	402.6	416.8
Goods: Imports f.o.b.	78ab *d*	....	....	....	....	....	....	....	−417.0	−436.5	−522.9	−649.6	−629.8	−675.2	−740.0	−798.4
Trade Balance	78ac *d*	....	....	....	....	....	....	....	−83.7	−130.3	−92.5	−230.3	−255.7	−272.4	−337.3	−381.5
Services: Credit	78ad *d*	....	....	....	....	....	....	....	83.9	79.5	86.3	125.4	132.4	135.1	138.9	186.5
Services: Debit	78ae *d*	....	....	....	....	....	....	....	−139.5	−151.1	−175.3	−208.3	−206.6	−212.4	−224.8	−252.6
Balance on Goods & Services	78af *d*	....	....	....	....	....	....	....	−139.2	−201.9	−181.4	−313.1	−329.9	−349.7	−423.2	−447.7
Income: Credit	78ag *d*	....	....	....	....	....	....	....	19.3	18.1	20.5	28.1	24.8	41.4	30.7	23.8
Income: Debit	78ah *d*	....	....	....	....	....	....	....	−19.1	−12.6	−12.5	−13.5	−13.3	−27.4	−28.0	−37.5
Balance on Gds, Serv. & Inc.	78ai *d*	....	....	....	....	....	....	....	−139.1	−196.4	−173.5	−298.6	−318.4	−335.7	−420.6	−461.4
Current Transfers, n.i.e.: Credit	78aj *d*	....	....	....	....	....	....	....	59.3	86.8	85.4	74.3	70.3	143.4	254.3	332.5
Current Transfers: Debit	78ak *d*	....	....	....	....	....	....	....	−2.8	−2.1	−3.2	−1.8	−1.4	−2.7	−3.6	−1.2
Capital Account, n.i.e.	78bc *d*	....	....	....	....	....	....	....	−1.4	−.9	−.7	−.6	−.4	−.3	−.5	−.3
Capital Account, n.i.e.: Credit	78ba *d*	....	....	....	....	....	....	....	—	—	—	—	—	—	—	—
Capital Account: Debit	78bb *d*	....	....	....	....	....	....	....	−1.4	−.9	−.7	−.6	−.4	−.3	−.5	−.3
Financial Account, n.i.e.	78bj *d*	....	....	....	....	....	....	....	17.7	−4.9	53.4	158.2	365.9	109.0	171.6	224.2
Direct Investment Abroad	78bd *d*	....	....	....	....	....	....	....	—	—	—	—	—	—	—	—
Dir. Invest. in Rep. Econ., n.i.e.	78be *d*	....	....	....	....	....	....	....	5.8	—	—	—	—	—	—	—
Portfolio Investment Assets	78bf *d*	....	....	....	....	....	....	....	—	—	—	—	—	—	—	—
Equity Securities	78bk *d*	....	....	....	....	....	....	....	—	—	—	—	—	—	—	—
Debt Securities	78bl *d*	....	....	....	....	....	....	....	—	—	—	—	—	—	—	—
Portfolio Investment Liab., n.i.e.	78bg *d*	....	....	....	....	....	....	....	—	—	—	—	—	—	—	—
Equity Securities	78bm *d*	....	....	....	....	....	....	....	—	—	—	—	—	—	—	—
Debt Securities	78bn *d*	....	....	....	....	....	....	....	—	—	—	—	—	—	—	—
Financial Derivatives Assets	78bw *d*	....	....	....	....	....	....	....	....	....	....	....	....	....	....	....
Financial Derivatives Liabilities	78bx *d*	....	....	....	....	....	....	....	....	....	....	....	....	....	....	....
Other Investment Assets	78bh *d*	....	....	....	....	....	....	....	−26.7	−35.2	−23.6	63.9	21.1	17.6	−23.9	24.3
Monetary Authorities	78bo *d*	....	....	....	....	....	....	....	....	....	....	....	....	....	....	....
General Government	78bp *d*	....	....	....	....	....	....	....	−20.1	−17.0	15.0	11.2	—	—	—	—
Banks	78bq *d*	....	....	....	....	....	....	....	—	—	—	—	—	—	—	—
Other Sectors	78br *d*	....	....	....	....	....	....	....	−6.6	−18.2	−38.6	52.8	21.1	17.6	−23.9	24.3
Other Investment Liab., n.i.e.	78bi *d*	....	....	....	....	....	....	....	38.5	30.3	77.0	94.3	344.8	91.4	195.5	200.0
Monetary Authorities	78bs *d*	....	....	....	....	....	....	....	−.7	2.2	−4.1	18.5	76.5	11.4	2.7	−3.3
General Government	78bt *d*	....	....	....	....	....	....	....	39.3	36.7	73.1	46.1	215.7	72.9	221.1	98.2
Banks	78bu *d*	....	....	....	....	....	....	....	2.7	−2.8	1.5	−.5	19.3	11.7	−14.0	−1.9
Other Sectors	78bv *d*	....	....	....	....	....	....	....	−2.8	−5.7	6.4	30.2	33.3	−4.5	−14.3	107.0
Net Errors and Omissions	78ca *d*	....	....	....	....	....	....	....	3.3	29.2	19.5	−33.4	−7.5	10.8	−54.1	−150.6
Overall Balance	78cb *d*	....	....	....	....	....	....	....	−63.0	−88.4	−19.2	−101.9	108.4	−75.4	−52.9	−56.8
Reserves and Related Items	79da *d*	....	....	....	....	....	....	....	63.0	88.4	19.2	101.9	−108.4	75.4	52.9	56.8
Reserve Assets	79db *d*	....	....	....	....	....	....	....	63.0	74.4	−39.0	93.4	−180.9	51.7	72.1	83.7
Use of Fund Credit and Loans	79dc *d*	....	....	....	....	....	....	....	—	14.0	58.2	8.5	72.6	23.7	−19.2	−28.0
Exceptional Financing	79de *d*	....	....	....	....	....	....	....	—	—	—	—	.1	−.1	—	1.2
Government Finance																*Millions of Birr:*
Deficit (-) or Surplus	80	−46.8	−51.0	Ɪ−64.2	−49.2	−43.8	−226.2	−325.1	−232.5	−421.9	−254.5	−380.5	−334.2	Ɪ−491.5	−1,350.8	−621.5
Total Revenue and Grants	81y	514.8	559.4	Ɪ587.0	652.7	717.6	806.5	855.1	1,096.3	1,256.1	1,436.8	1,604.0	1,794.7	Ɪ1,878.4	2,188.4	2,303.9
Revenue	81	426.8	466.0	Ɪ494.1	561.0	619.7	710.4	777.9	1,013.7	1,184.3	1,410.1	1,597.1	1,791.7	Ɪ1,865.3	2,158.4	2,283.2
Grants	81z	88.0	93.4	Ɪ92.9	91.7	97.9	96.1	77.2	82.6	71.8	26.7	6.9	3.0	Ɪ13.1	30.0	20.7
Exp. & Lending Minus Repay.	82z	561.6	610.4	Ɪ651.2	701.9	761.4	1,032.7	1,180.2	1,328.8	1,678.0	1,691.3	1,984.5	2,128.9	Ɪ2,369.9	3,539.2	2,925.4
Expenditure	82	550.4	603.8	Ɪ647.9	678.6	733.0	985.4	1,144.5	1,320.0	1,664.1	1,690.5	1,994.9	2,136.3	Ɪ2,377.4	3,159.2	2,874.6
Lending Minus Repayments	83	11.2	6.6	Ɪ3.3	23.3	28.4	47.3	35.7	8.8	13.9	.8	−10.4	−7.4	Ɪ−7.5	380.0	50.8
Total Financing	80h	46.8	51.1	Ɪ64.2	49.2	43.8	226.2	325.1	232.5	421.9	254.5	380.5	334.2	Ɪ491.5	1,350.8	621.5
Domestic	84a	19.5	11.3	Ɪ20.1	9.4	−3.1	127.9	220.9	145.7	348.2	83.7	230.0	203.7	Ɪ16.6	929.8	413.0
Foreign	85a	27.3	39.8	Ɪ44.1	39.8	46.9	98.3	104.2	86.8	73.7	170.8	150.5	130.5	Ɪ474.9	421.0	208.5
Financing																
Net Borrowing: Domestic	84a	27.3	511.4	Ɪ561.3	593.0	647.1	891.5	1,199.5	1,431.7	1,853.6	2,108.1	2,488.6	2,822.8	Ɪ3,314.3	4,666.6	5,288.1
Domestic	88a	....	205.7	Ɪ225.9	225.1	237.1	383.2	587.0	732.4	1,080.6	1,164.3	1,394.3	1,598.0	Ɪ1,614.6	2,544.4	2,957.4
Foreign	89a	....	305.7	Ɪ335.4	367.9	410.0	508.3	612.5	699.3	773.0	943.8	1,094.3	1,224.8	Ɪ1,699.7	2,122.2	2,330.7
National Accounts																*Millions of Birr:*
Exports of Goods & Services	90c	489	469	491	654	828	682	760	822	866	943	1,210	1,072	Ɪ1,007	1,065	1,165
Government Consumption	91f	443	461	508	538	586	730	866	967	1,240	1,314	1,346	1,429	Ɪ1,630	1,973	1,905
Gross Capital Formation	93	512	554	603	569	549	579	578	606	545	699	854	1,367	Ɪ1,457	1,436	1,851
Private Consumption	96f	3,519	3,782	3,720	3,797	4,244	4,428	4,618	5,461	5,885	6,483	6,881	7,886	Ɪ8,375	9,158	8,192
Imports of Goods & Services	98c	−504	−556	−578	−552	−655	−896	−818	−1,030	−1,271	−1,368	−1,749	−1,676	Ɪ−1,833	−1,856	−2,125
Gross Domestic Product (GDP)	99b	4,461	4,710	4,744	5,006	5,552	5,523	6,004	6,826	7,265	8,071	8,541	10,079	Ɪ10,636	11,775	10,988
Net Factor Inc/Pmts(-) Abroad	98.n	−20	−19	−29	−47	−36	−35	−3	−6	−9	−8	−14	−14	Ɪ−17	−27	−37
Gross National Income (GNI)	99a	4,441	4,691	4,715	4,958	5,515	5,489	6,001	6,820	7,256	8,063	8,527	10,065	Ɪ10,619	11,994	11,299
GDP at Factor Cost	99ba	....	....	....	....	....	....	5,530	6,146	6,487	7,087	7,625	9,324	Ɪ9,812	11,118	10,008
GDP Vol. Fact.Cost,'60/61 Prices	99ba *p*	....	....	....	....	....	....	4,031	4,055	4,009	4,222	4,454	4,586	24,807	....	....
GDP Vol. Fact.Cost,'80/81 Prices	99ba *p*	....	....	....	....	....	....	....	....	....	....	....	....	9,979	10,254	9,608
GDP Volume (1995=100)	99bv *p*	....	....	....	....	....	....	68.4	68.8	68.0	71.6	75.5	77.8	78.9	81.1	76.0
GDP Deflator (1990=100)	99bi *p*	42.7	43.2	41.5	42.6	46.6	46.3	49.2	55.6	59.9	63.2	63.3	70.4	Ɪ73.6	75.6	74.2
																Millions:
Population	99z	24.63	25.25	25.89	26.19	26.78	27.47	28.19	Ɪ35.92	36.76	37.63	38.75	39.59	40.41	41.18	42.69

International Transactions

Millions of Birr

1985	1986	1987	1988	1989	1990	1991	1992	1993	1994	1995	1996	1997	1998	1999	Item	Code
689.4	941.6	735.2	888.6	911.5	615.8	390.5	448.4	994.2	2,062.4	2,602.9	2,650.6	3,941.3	3,966.0	....	Exports	70
2,056.4	2,280.4	2,205.9	2,336.2	1,967.9	2,238.5	976.8	2,604.3	3,936.7	5,658.0	7,052.5	8,899.2	....	....	10,514.7	Imports, c.i.f.	71

Balance of Payments

Minus Sign Indicates Debit

1985	1986	1987	1988	1989	1990	1991	1992	1993	1994	1995	1996	1997	1998	1999	Item	Code
106.3	−327.1	−216.9	−227.5	−144.4	−293.8	103.1	−120.0	−50.0	125.4	−9.7	89.4	−23.0	134.0	....	Current Account, n.i.e.	78ald
332.9	477.1	355.2	400.0	443.8	292.0	167.6	169.9	198.8	372.0	423.0	417.5	588.3	568.3	....	Goods: Exports f.o.b.	78aad
−840.5	−932.6	−932.7	−956.0	−817.9	−912.1	−470.8	−992.7	−706.0	−925.7	−1,136.7	−1,002.2	−1,018.7	−1,042.2	....	Goods: Imports f.o.b.	78abd
−507.7	−455.4	−577.4	−556.0	−374.1	−620.1	−303.2	−822.9	−507.1	−553.7	−713.7	−584.7	−430.5	−473.9	....	*Trade Balance*	78acd
288.8	243.9	296.9	271.7	289.2	304.6	268.3	267.6	277.2	294.6	344.5	377.2	390.7	431.3	....	Services: Credit	78add
−270.8	−271.7	−307.7	−330.1	−323.4	−358.8	−284.3	−368.3	−299.0	−310.4	−357.9	−349.8	−396.2	−418.5	....	Services: Debit	78aed
−489.6	−483.2	−588.3	−614.4	−408.3	−674.3	−319.3	−923.5	−528.9	−569.5	−727.1	−557.2	−436.0	−461.1	....	*Balance on Goods & Services*	78afd
24.7	34.0	21.9	17.1	12.7	9.2	14.4	22.3	25.9	42.9	68.3	51.3	37.2	47.8	....	Income: Credit	78agd
−39.9	−61.1	−58.7	−72.8	−85.0	−77.7	−96.7	−104.1	−78.4	−74.6	−87.2	−76.1	−67.0	−59.6	....	Income: Debit	78ahd
−504.7	−510.3	−625.1	−670.0	−480.6	−742.9	−401.5	−1,005.3	−581.4	−601.1	−745.9	−582.0	−465.8	−472.9	....	*Balance on Gds, Serv. & Inc.*	78aid
612.5	184.2	412.9	443.2	337.5	451.3	505.9	887.4	532.6	728.5	737.3	679.0	450.4	627.9	....	Current Transfers, n.i.e.: Credit	78ajd
−1.4	−1.0	−4.6	−.7	−1.3	−2.2	−1.3	−2.0	−1.2	−2.0	−1.1	−7.5	−7.6	−21.0	....	Current Transfers: Debit	78akd
−.4	−.1	−.6	−.3	−.1	—	—	—	—	—	3.7	—	—	—	....	Capital Account, n.i.e.	78bcd
—	—	—	—	—	—	—	—	—	—	3.7	—	—	—	....	Capital Account, n.i.e.: Credit	78bad
−.4	−.1	−.6	−.3	−.1	—	—	—	—	—	—	—	—	—	....	Capital Account: Debit	78bbd
225.0	239.6	292.8	299.6	222.0	230.0	−204.1	−62.9	97.7	−199.0	158.3	−499.6	241.2	−23.5	....	Financial Account, n.i.e.	78bjd
—	—	—	—	—	—	—	—	—	—	—	—	—	—	....	Direct Investment Abroad	78bdd
—	—	—	—	—	—	—	—	—	—	—	—	—	—	....	Dir. Invest. in Rep. Econ., n.i.e.	78bed
—	—	—	—	—	—	—	—	—	—	—	—	—	—	....	Portfolio Investment Assets	78bfd
—	—	—	—	—	—	—	—	—	—	—	—	—	—	....	Equity Securities	78bkd
—	—	—	—	—	—	—	—	—	—	—	—	—	—	....	Debt Securities	78bld
—	—	—	—	—	—	—	—	—	—	—	—	—	—	....	Portfolio Investment Liab., n.i.e.	78bgd
—	—	—	—	—	—	—	—	—	—	—	—	—	—	....	Equity Securities	78bmd
—	—	—	—	—	—	—	—	—	—	—	—	—	—	....	Debt Securities	78bnd
														....	Financial Derivatives Assets	78bwd
														....	Financial Derivatives Liabilities	78bxd
12.3	—	—	—	50.0	87.0	−166.7	−87.1	−31.7	−318.5	57.7	−306.8	318.5	45.1	....	Other Investment Assets	78bhd
														....	Monetary Authorities	78bod
—	—	—	—	19.2	28.0	−108.9	−26.7	−40.2	−358.5	44.7	−283.0	350.7	11.7	....	General Government	78bpd
12.3	—	—	—	30.8	59.0	−57.8	−60.4	8.4	40.0	13.1	−23.7	−32.2	33.5	....	Banks	78bqd
														....	Other Sectors	78brd
212.7	239.6	292.8	299.6	171.9	143.0	−37.4	24.2	129.4	119.5	100.5	−192.8	−77.3	−68.6	....	Other Investment Liab., n.i.e.	78bid
6.7	—	—	—	8.6	12.0	−41.8	37.3	−50.9	25.4	.4	−7.9	−.1	−.4	....	Monetary Authorities	78bsd
179.4	194.8	239.3	290.7	266.2	121.7	−41.7	1.0	209.1	82.4	37.7	−131.5	−91.0	−79.9	....	General Government	78btd
−4.5	−1.0	—	6.8	−3.5	−2.6	8.3	1.1	26.5	55.3	91.2	205.6	15.0	14.8	....	Banks	78bud
31.1	45.7	53.5	2.1	−99.4	11.9	37.9	−15.2	−55.2	−43.6	−28.8	−259.0	−1.3	−3.1	....	Other Sectors	78bvd
−168.8	201.6	−182.8	−94.0	−32.0	−134.6	−254.9	−81.2	−15.2	69.5	−49.0	−56.6	−646.7	−493.5	....	Net Errors and Omissions	78cad
162.2	113.9	−107.4	−22.3	45.5	−198.3	−355.9	−264.0	32.4	−.4	99.6	−466.7	−428.6	−383.1	....	*Overall Balance*	78cbd
−162.2	−113.9	107.4	22.3	−45.5	198.3	355.9	264.0	−32.4	.4	−99.6	466.7	428.6	383.1	....	Reserves and Related Items	79dad
−126.0	−117.4	126.9	39.1	−22.7	34.7	−37.2	−95.9	−296.2	−124.7	−204.8	20.0	192.1	178.9	....	Reserve Assets	79dbd
−36.2	3.5	−19.9	−16.8	−22.8	−25.2	−6.5	19.9	29.7	20.8	.4	21.2	—	16.9	....	Use of Fund Credit and Loans	79dcd
—	—	.4	—	—	188.8	399.6	340.0	234.0	104.3	105.2	425.5	236.4	187.2	....	Exceptional Financing	79ded

Government Finance

Year Ending July 7

1985	1986	1987	1988	1989	1990	1991	1992	1993	1994	1995	1996	1997	1998	1999	Item	Code
−861.8	−805.0	−689.1	−784.2	−1,028.0	−1,739.1	−1,684.5	I−1454.3	−1,465.3	−2,814.8	−1,379.3	−749.2	−635.8	−1,786.5	−2,524.3	Deficit (−) or Surplus	80
2,345.4	2,781.6	2,927.6	3,478.7	4,072.9	3,170.7	2,784.2	I2,751.0	3,733.5	5,060.7	6,874.1	7,824.0	9,381.4	9,673.5	8,265.5	Total Revenue and Grants	81y
2,266.0	2,730.4	2,847.8	3,432.3	3,882.0	3,103.9	2,680.0	I2,208.0	3,206.6	3,842.6	5,839.2	6,817.3	7,877.4	8,400.2	7,847.0	Revenue	81
79.4	51.2	79.8	46.4	190.9	66.8	104.2	543.0	526.9	1,218.1	1,034.9	1,006.7	1,504.0	1,273.3	418.5	Grants	81z
3,207.2	3,586.6	3,616.7	4,262.9	5,100.9	4,909.8	4,468.7	I4,205.3	5,198.8	7,875.5	8,253.4	8,573.2	10,017.2	11,460.0	10,789.8	Exp. & Lending Minus Repay.	82z
3,150.3	3,540.5	3,604.1	4,161.5	4,785.7	4,832.3	4,421.1	....	....	....	....	....	....	....	....	Expenditure	82
56.9	46.1	12.6	101.4	315.2	77.5	47.6	....	....	....	....	....	....	....	....	Lending Minus Repayments	83
861.8	805.0	689.1	784.2	1,028.0	1,739.1	1,684.5	1,454.3	1,465.3	2,814.8	1,379.3	749.2	635.8	1,786.5	2,524.3	Total Financing	80h
533.1	334.8	362.3	382.2	426.4	1,243.2	1,263.7	1,155.1	750.8	709.6	60.0	−652.6	−92.1	1,007.0	1,175.8	Domestic	84a
328.7	470.2	326.8	402.0	601.6	495.9	420.8	299.2	714.5	2,105.2	1,319.3	1,401.8	727.9	779.5	1,348.7	Foreign	85a

Financing

1985	1986	1987	1988	1989	1990	1991	1992	1993	1994	1995	1996	1997	1998	1999	Item	Code
6,156.9	6,916.6	7,671.5	8,503.6	9,517.1	12,186.2	14,182.0	13,051.0	714.5	2,105.2	1,319.3	1,401.8	727.9	779.5	1,348.7	Net Borrowing: Domestic	84a
3,490.5	3,825.4	4,187.7	4,564.3	4,990.6	6,272.5	7,536.2	8,691.4	9,474.5	....	....	....	....	....	....	Domestic	88a
2,666.4	3,091.2	3,483.8	3,939.3	4,526.5	5,913.7	6,645.8	4,359.6	....	....	....	....	....	....	....	Foreign	89a

National Accounts

Year Ending July 7

1985	1986	1987	1988	1989	1990	1991	1992	1993	1994	1995	1996	1997	1998	1999	Item	Code
1,057	1,272	1,187	1,205	1,423	1,295	1,062	I937	2,223	3,223	4,852	4,962	6,731	7,251	....	Exports of Goods & Services	90c
1,997	2,143	2,262	2,707	3,061	3,232	3,166	I2,108	2,819	3,155	3,675	4,158	4,526	6,251	....	Government Consumption	91f
1,394	2,226	2,245	3,061	2,269	2,101	1,996	I1,911	3,792	4,294	5,569	7,246	7,049	7,927	....	Gross Capital Formation	93
10,661	10,261	11,036	10,396	11,281	12,258	15,369	I18,059	22,359	23,748	27,942	31,291	32,831	35,472	....	Private Consumption	96f
−2,083	−2,326	−2,338	−2,398	−2,292	−2,060	−2,398	I−2,223	−4,521	−6,091	−8,154	−9,719	−9,672	−11,866	....	Imports of Goods & Services	98c
13,027	13,575	14,391	14,971	15,742	16,826	19,195	I20,792	26,671	28,329	33,885	37,938	41,465	45,035	....	Gross Domestic Product (GDP)	99b
−64	−61	−89	−126	−158	−130	−142	I−179	−414	−460	−378	−275	−224	−178	....	Net Factor Inc/Pmts(−) Abroad	98.n
13,503	14,176	14,773	14,845	15,585	16,696	19,053	I20,613	26,257	27,869	33,508	37,662	41,241	44,857	....	Gross National Income (GNI)	99a
12,102	12,565	13,313	13,787	14,550	15,699	17,979	I19,897	25,209	26,283	31,434	35,093	38,189	41,358	....	GDP at Factor Cost	99ba
....	....	....	....	....	....	....	....	....	....	....	....	....	....	....	GDP Vol. Fact.Cost,'60/61 Prices	99ba p
8,677	9,536	10,875	10,948	10,986	11,433	10,938	10,535	11,724	11,910	12,645	13,987	14,708	14,631	....	GDP Vol. Fact.Cost,'80/81 Prices	99ba p
68.6	75.4	86.0	86.6	86.9	90.4	86.5	83.3	92.7	94.2	100.0	110.6	116.3	115.7	....	GDP Volume (1995=100)	99bv p
93.5	91.1	88.2	90.0	93.2	100.0	121.4	122.5	140.6	....	....	....	....	....	....	GDP Deflator (1990=100)	99bi p

Midyear Estimates

1985	1986	1987	1988	1989	1990	1991	1992	1993	1994	1995	1996	1997	1998	1999	Item	Code
44.25	45.74	44.15	45.45	46.93	48.36	49.95	51.57	53.24	54.94	I54.65	56.37	58.12	59.88	61.67	Population	99z

(See notes in the back of the book.)

		1970	1971	1972	1973	1974	1975	1976	1977	1978	1979	1980	1981	1982	1983	1984
Exchange Rates																*Euros per SDR:*
Market Rate	aa	....	....	....	....	....	....	....	....	....	....	....	....	....	....	....
Market Rate	ae	....	....	....	....	....	....	....	....	....	....	....	....	....	....	*Euros per US Dollar:*
Market Rate	rf	....	....	....	....	....	....	....	....	....	....	....	....	....	....	....
														Index Numbers (1995=100):		
Nominal Effective Exchange Rate	ne u	90.75	91.21	94.60	102.07	101.94	106.93	104.43	105.60	104.93	108.32	106.10	91.38	87.79	84.41	79.90
Real Effective Exchange Rate	re u									105.94	107.55	102.80	87.86	85.69	84.81	81.84
International Liquidity												*Millions of US Dollars Unless Otherwise Indicated:*				
Tot.Res.minus Gold (Eurosyst.Def)	1l. d	....	....	....	....	....	....	....	....	....	....	....	....	....	....	....
SDRs	1b. d	976	2,419	3,524	3,902	3,954	3,798	3,816	3,332	3,744	5,365	5,358	5,934	6,106	3,944	4,157
Reserve Position in the Fund	1c. d	2,445	3,783	3,664	3,681	3,751	4,406	5,938	6,138	7,489	5,992	6,266	6,009	6,470	8,651	8,633
Foreign Exchange	1d. d	....	....	....	....	....	....	....	....	....	....	....	....	....	....	....
of which: Fin.Deriv.rel.to Res.	1dd d	....	....	....	....	....	....	....	....	....	....	....	....	....	....	....
Other Reserve Assets	1e. d	....	....	....	....	....	....	....	....	....	....	....	....	....	....	....
Gold (Million Fine Troy Ounces)	1ad d	....	....	....	....	....	....	....	....	....	....	....	....	....	....	....
Gold (EMU Valuation)	1an d	....	....	....	....	....	....	....	....	....	....	....	....	....	....	....
Memo: Euro Cl. on Non-EA Res.	1dg d	....	....	....	....	....	....	....	....	....	....	....	....	....	....	....
Non-Euro Cl. on EA Res.	1dh d	....	....	....	....	....	....	....	....	....	....	....	....	....	....	....
Mon. Auth.: Other Foreign Assets	3.. d	....	....	....	....	....	....	....	....	....	....	....	....	....	....	....
Foreign Liabilities	4.. d	....	....	....	....	....	....	....	....	....	....	....	....	....	....	....
Banking Insts: Foreign Assets	7a. d	....	....	....	....	....	....	....	....	....	....	....	....	....	....	....
Foreign Liabs.	7b. d	....	....	....	....	....	....	....	....	....	....	....	....	....	....	....
Monetary Authorities (Eurosyst.)																*Billions of Euros:*
Foreign Assets (on Non-EA Ctys)	11	....	....	....	....	....	....	....	....	....	....	....	....	....	....	....
Claims on General Government	12a. u	....	....	....	....	....	....	....	....	....	....	....	....	....	....	....
Claims on EA Banking Sector	12e. u	....	....	....	....	....	....	....	....	....	....	....	....	....	....	....
Claims on Other Resident Sectors	12d. u	....	....	....	....	....	....	....	....	....	....	....	....	....	....	....
Currency in Circulation	14a	....	....	....	....	....	....	....	....	....	....	....	....	....	....	....
Liabilities to EA Banking Sector	14c. u	....	....	....	....	....	....	....	....	....	....	....	....	....	....	....
Deposits of Other Resident Sect.	15.. u	....	....	....	....	....	....	....	....	....	....	....	....	....	....	....
Money Market Instruments	16m. u	....	....	....	....	....	....	....	....	....	....	....	....	....	....	....
Bonds (Debt Securities)	16n. u	....	....	....	....	....	....	....	....	....	....	....	....	....	....	....
Foreign Liabs. (to Non-EA Ctys)	16c	....	....	....	....	....	....	....	....	....	....	....	....	....	....	....
Central Government Deposits	16d. u	....	....	....	....	....	....	....	....	....	....	....	....	....	....	....
Capital Accounts	17a	....	....	....	....	....	....	....	....	....	....	....	....	....	....	....
Other Items (Net)	17r	....	....	....	....	....	....	....	....	....	....	....	....	....	....	....
Banking Institutions (Oth.MFIs)																*Billions of Euros:*
Claims on EA Banking Sector	20.. u	....	....	....	....	....	....	....	....	....	....	....	....	....	....	....
Foreign Assets (on Non-EA Ctys)	21	....	....	....	....	....	....	....	....	....	....	....	....	....	....	....
Claims on General Government	22a. u	....	....	....	....	....	....	....	....	....	....	....	....	....	....	....
Claims on Oth. Resident Sectors	22d. u	....	....	....	....	....	....	....	....	....	....	....	....	....	....	....
Demand (Overnight) Deposits	24.. u	....	....	....	....	....	....	....	....	....	....	206.8	219.7	238.0	262.0	287.0
Deposits with Agreed Maturity	25a. u	....	....	....	....	....	....	....	....	....	....	....	....	....	....	....
Deposits Redeemable at Notice	25b. u	....	....	....	....	....	....	....	....	....	....	....	....	....	....	....
Repurchase Agreements	25f. u	....	....	....	....	....	....	....	....	....	....	....	....	....	....	....
Money Market Instruments	26m. u	....	....	....	....	....	....	....	....	....	....	....	....	....	....	....
Bonds (Debt Securities)	26n. u	....	....	....	....	....	....	....	....	....	....	....	....	....	....	....
Foreign Liabs. (to Non-EA Ctys)	26c	....	....	....	....	....	....	....	....	....	....	....	....	....	....	....
Central Government Deposits	26d. u	....	....	....	....	....	....	....	....	....	....	....	....	....	....	....
Credit fr. EA Banking Sector	26g. u	....	....	....	....	....	....	....	....	....	....	....	....	....	....	....
Capital Accounts	27a	....	....	....	....	....	....	....	....	....	....	....	....	....	....	....
Other Items (Net)	27r	....	....	....	....	....	....	....	....	....	....	....	....	....	....	....
Banking Survey																*Billions of Euros:*
Foreign Assets (Net)	31n. u	....	....	....	....	....	....	....	....	....	....	....	....	....	....	....
Domestic Credit	32.. u	....	....	....	....	....	....	....	....	....	....	....	....	....	....	....
Claims on General Govt. (Net)	32an u	....	....	....	....	....	....	....	....	....	....	....	....	....	....	....
Claims on Oth. Resident Sectors	32d. u	....	....	....	....	....	....	....	....	....	....	....	....	....	....	....
Currency in Circulation	34a. u	....	....	....	....	....	....	....	....	....	....	111.9	118.5	127.2	138.9	145.7
Demand (Overnight) Deposits	34b. u	....	....	....	....	....	....	....	....	....	....	208.8	222.0	241.3	265.7	290.7
Deposits with Agreed Maturity	35a. u	....	....	....	....	....	....	....	....	....	....	....	....	....	....	....
of which: Over 2-Yr. Maturity	35ab u	....	....	....	....	....	....	....	....	....	....	....	....	....	....	....
Deposits Redeemable at Notice	35b. u	....	....	....	....	....	....	....	....	....	....	....	....	....	....	....
of which: Over 3-Mos Notice	35bb u	....	....	....	....	....	....	....	....	....	....	....	....	....	....	....
Repurchase Agreements	35f. u	....	....	....	....	....	....	....	....	....	....	....	....	....	....	....
Money Market Instruments	36m. u	....	....	....	....	....	....	....	....	....	....	....	....	....	....	....
Bonds	36n. u	....	....	....	....	....	....	....	....	....	....	....	....	....	....	....
of which: Over 2-Yr. Maturity	36na u	....	....	....	....	....	....	....	....	....	....	....	....	....	....	....
Capital Accounts	37a	....	....	....	....	....	....	....	....	....	....	....	....	....	....	....
Other Items (Net)	37r. u	....	....	....	....	....	....	....	....	....	....	....	....	....	....	....
Money (Eurosystem Definition)																*Billions of Euros:*
M1	39ma u	....	....	....	....	....	....	....	....	....	....	492.7	519.1	570.6	628.7	682.5
M2	39mb u	....	....	....	....	....	....	....	....	....	....	1,198.1	1,308.3	1,449.9	1,579.3	1,710.9
M3	39mc u	....	....	....	....	....	....	....	....	....	....	1,230.5	1,356.9	1,511.7	1,647.6	1,788.8
Nonmonetary Liabs. of MFIs	39md u	....	....	....	....	....	....	....	....	....	....	....	....	....	....	....
Interest Rates																*Percent Per Annum*
Eurosyst.Marg.Lending Fac.Rate	60	....	....	....	....	....	....	....	....	....	....	....	....	....	....	....
Eurosyst. Refinancing Rate	60r	....	....	....	....	....	....	....	....	....	....	....	....	....	....	....
Eurosyst. Deposit Facility Rate	60x	....	....	....	....	....	....	....	....	....	....	....	....	....	....	....
Interbank Rate (Overnight)	60a	....	....	....	....	....	....	....	....	....	....	....	....	....	....	....
Interbank Rate (3-Mos Maturity)	60b	....	....	....	....	....	....	....	....	....	....	....	....	....	....	....
Deposit Rate	60l	....	....	....	....	....	....	....	....	....	....	....	....	....	....	....
Lending Rate	60p	....	....	....	....	....	....	....	....	....	....	....	....	....	....	....
Government Bond Yield	61	....	....	....	....	....	....	....	....	....	....	....	....	....	....	....

1985	1986	1987	1988	1989	1990	1991	1992	1993	1994	1995	1996	1997	1998	1999		
End of Period															**Exchange Rates**	
....	....	....	....	....	....	....	....	....	....	....	....	....	....	1.36623	Market Rate..	aa
End of Period (ae) Period Average (rf)																
....	....	....	....	....	....	....	....	....	....	....	....	....	....	.99542	Market Rate..	ae
....	....	....	....	....	....	....	....	....	....	....	....	....	....	.93863	Market Rate..	rf
Period Averages																
78.69	88.58	94.59	91.58	91.24	100.46	97.82	101.14	97.47	95.74	100.00	100.13	91.28	91.24	87.12	Nominal Effective Exchange Rate .... ne*u*	
81.39	90.17	94.98	91.79	91.32	99.74	96.78	99.88	97.66	95.55	100.00	100.04	89.00	85.48	....	Real Effective Exchange Rate .... re*u*	
End of Period															**International Liquidity**	
														257,077	Tot.Res.minus Gold (Eurosyst.Def) 1l.*d*	
4,565	6,019	7,418	6,896	6,906	6,986	6,853	2,778	3,039	3,519	5,572	5,440	5,359	6,015	4,546	SDRs 1b.*d*	
9,016	9,631	10,442	9,358	9,179	9,434	11,018	13,709	12,691	12,941	16,100	16,572	18,637	27,364	24,245	Reserve Position in the Fund 1c.*d*	
....	....	....	....	....	....	....	....	....	....	....	....	....	....	226,250	Foreign Exchange 1d.*d*	
....	....	....	....	....	....	....	....	....	....	....	....	....	....	....	of which: Fin.Deriv.rel.to Res. 1dd*d*	
....	....	....	....	....	....	....	....	....	....	....	....	....	....	2,036	Other Reserve Assets 1e.*d*	
....	....	....	....	....	....	....	....	....	....	....	....	....	....	402.76	Gold (Million Fine Troy Ounces)............ 1a*d*	
....	....	....	....	....	....	....	....	....	....	....	....	....	....	117,085	Gold (EMU Valuation) 1an*d*	
....	....	....	....	....	....	....	....	....	....	....	....	....	....	....	Memo: Euro Cl. on Non-EA Res. 1dg*d*	
....	....	....	....	....	....	....	....	....	....	....	....	....	....	14,481	Non-Euro Cl. on EA Res. 1dh*d*	
....	....	....	....	....	....	....	....	....	....	....	....	....	....	....	Mon. Auth.: Other Foreign Assets .... 3..*d*	
....	....	....	....	....	....	....	....	....	....	....	....	....	....	49,993	Foreign Liabilities............... 4..*d*	
....	....	....	....	....	....	....	....	....	....	....	....	....	....	1,710,821	Banking Insts: Foreign Assets 7a.*d*	
....	....	....	....	....	....	....	....	....	....	....	....	....	....	1,782,896	Foreign Liabs.................. 7b.*d*	
End of Period															**Monetary Authorities (Eurosyst.)**	
												324.1	322.3	400.6	Foreign Assets (on Non-EA Ctys) 11	
												132.9	106.6	105.8	Claims on General Government 12a.*u*	
												216.2	205.7	424.0	Claims on EA Banking Sector 12e.*u*	
												4.5	4.3	11.5	Claims on Other Resident Sectors 12d.*u*	
												354.9	359.1	393.0	Currency in Circulation 14a	
												91.9	94.2	277.1	Liabilities to EA Banking Sector 14c.*u*	
												3.4	3.5	8.8	Deposits of Other Resident Sect. .... 15..*u*	
												13.4	8.5	3.3	Money Market Instruments 16m.*u*	
												14.8	5.3	4.6	Bonds (Debt Securities)...................... 16n.*u*	
												33.4	18.6	49.8	Foreign Liabs. (to Non-EA Ctys) 16c	
												51.7	54.4	53.4	Central Government Deposits 16d.*u*	
												106.0	97.1	175.1	Capital Accounts 17a	
												8.1	−1.6	−23.2	Other Items (Net) 17r	
End of Period															**Banking Institutions (Oth.MFIs)**	
												3,541.1	3,902.8	4,246.6	Claims on EA Banking Sector .... 20..*u*	
												1,594.8	1,579.9	1,703.0	Foreign Assets (on Non-EA Ctys) 21	
												1,872.0	1,923.5	1,949.2	Claims on General Government 22a.*u*	
												5,127.0	5,585.2	6,127.8	Claims on Oth. Resident Sectors 22d.*u*	
307.4	333.6	353.4	384.6	423.5	544.9	545.2	568.9	600.1	621.7	949.9	1,072.7	1,229.6	1,382.7	1,532.3	Demand (Overnight) Deposits .... 24..*u*	
												1,901.2	1,924.1	2,037.4	Deposits with Agreed Maturity 25a.*u*	
												1,326.3	1,388.8	1,327.1	Deposits Redeemable at Notice 25b.*u*	
												205.4	176.7	144.2	Repurchase Agreements........................ 25f.*u*	
												390.8	402.1	551.8	Money Market Instruments 26m.*u*	
												1,924.8	2,116.0	2,364.2	Bonds (Debt Securities)...................... 26n.*u*	
												1,373.5	1,500.4	1,774.7	Foreign Liabs. (to Non-EA Ctys) 26c	
												102.1	95.3	88.6	Central Government Deposits 26d.*u*	
												3,009.3	3,311.7	3,579.8	Credit fr. EA Banking Sector 26g.*u*	
												687.5	742.4	836.4	Capital Accounts 27a	
												−15.5	−48.6	−210.0	Other Items (Net) 27r	
End of Period															**Banking Survey**	
												511.9	383.3	279.1	Foreign Assets (Net) 31n.*u*	
												6,982.6	7,470.0	8,052.3	Domestic Credit .... 32..*u*	
												1,851.1	1,880.4	1,913.1	Claims on General Govt. (Net)......... 32an*u*	
												5,131.5	5,589.6	6,139.2	Claims on Oth. Resident Sectors 32d.*u*	
153.2	163.8	178.2	196.8	211.8	224.5	242.0	264.7	277.1	292.2	303.8	313.3	320.6	323.4	349.6	Currency in Circulation 34a.*u*	
310.5	337.2	357.7	389.7	428.8	552.0	552.5	570.8	602.9	624.6	952.6	1,075.7	1,233.0	1,386.2	1,541.1	Demand (Overnight) Deposits 34b.*u*	
												1,901.2	1,924.1	2,037.4	Deposits with Agreed Maturity 35a.*u*	
												1,004.9	1,030.2	1,160.3	of which: Over 2-Yr. Maturity 35ab*u*	
												1,326.3	1,388.8	1,327.1	Deposits Redeemable at Notice 35b.*u*	
												219.8	214.8	112.8	of which: Over 3-Mos Notice............ 35bb*u*	
												205.4	176.7	144.2	Repurchase Agreements....................... 35f.*u*	
												304.4	303.5	425.2	Money Market Instruments 36m.*u*	
												1,303.4	1,398.9	1,540.3	Bonds 36n.*u*	
												1,232.2	1,329.2	1,452.3	of which: Over 2-Yr. Maturity 36na*u*	
												698.8	714.3	869.8	Capital Accounts 37a	
												201.5	237.4	96.6	Other Items (Net) 37r.*u*	
End of Period															**Money (Eurosystem Definition)**	
732.8	796.0	853.4	925.6	1,015.2	1,128.5	1,171.5	1,215.3	1,287.9	1,343.2	1,423.2	1,528.5	1,623.4	1,776.9	1,959.0	*M1* 39ma*u*	
1,833.6	1,955.3	2,080.9	2,233.0	2,419.2	2,658.7	2,808.4	2,939.9	3,150.4	3,243.9	3,397.5	3,562.5	3,680.0	3,905.8	4,119.5	*M2* 39mb*u*	
1,928.0	2,059.0	2,221.6	2,410.0	2,660.0	2,980.0	3,204.7	3,433.2	3,651.9	3,735.9	3,937.5	4,090.4	4,260.9	4,455.6	4,776.9	*M3* 39mc*u*	
....	....	....	....	....	....	....	....	....	....	....	....	3,155.6	3,288.5	3,595.2	Nonmonetary Liabs. of MFIs 39md*u*	
Percent Per Annum															**Interest Rates**	
												....	....	4.00	Eurosyst.Marg.Lending Fac.Rate 60	
												....	....	2.71	Eurosyst. Refinancing Rate 60r	
														1.71	Eurosyst. Deposit Facility Rate.............. 60x	
									6.18	6.09	4.58	4.02	3.73	2.74	Interbank Rate (Overnight) 60a	
									6.33	6.58	4.92	4.25	3.83	2.97	Interbank Rate (3-Mos Maturity)........... 60b	
											4.08	3.41	3.20	2.44	Deposit Rate 60l	
										....	8.85	7.58	6.74	5.66	Lending Rate 60p	
									8.18	8.73	7.23	5.96	4.70	4.66	Government Bond Yield 61	

	1970	1971	1972	1973	1974	1975	1976	1977	1978	1979	1980	1981	1982	1983	1984

Prices, Production, Labor — *Index Numbers (1995=100):*

Producer Prices 63	...	...	...	...	...	...	...	...	...	...	...	...	...	...	...
Harmonized CPI (hcpi) 64h	...	...	...	...	...	...	...	...	...	...	...	...	...	...	...
Wages/Labor Costs (1996=100) .... 65.. c	...	...	...	...	...	...	...	...	...	...	...	...	...	...	...
Industrial Production .... 66.. c	...	...	...	...	...	...	...	...	...	...	...	...	...	...	...
Employment 67	...	...	...	...	...	...	...	...	...	...	...	...	...	...	...

International Transactions — *Billions of Ecus through 1998;*

Exports 70	...	...	...	...	...	...	...	...	...	...	...	...	...	...	...
Imports, c.i.f. 71	...	...	...	...	...	...	...	...	...	...	...	...	...	...	...

1995=100

Volume of Exports 72	...	...	...	...	...	...	...	...	...	...	...	...	...	...	...
Volume of Imports 73	...	...	...	...	...	...	...	...	...	...	...	...	...	...	...
Unit Value of Exports 74	...	...	...	...	...	...	...	...	...	...	...	...	...	...	...
Unit Value of Imports 75	...	...	...	...	...	...	...	...	...	...	...	...	...	...	...

Balance of Payments — *Billions of US Dollars*

Current Account, n.i.e. .... 78al d	...	...	...	...	...	...	...	...	...	...	...	...	...	...	...
Goods: Exports f.o.b. .... 78aa d	...	...	...	...	...	...	...	...	...	...	...	...	...	...	...
Goods: Imports f.o.b. .... 78ab d	...	...	...	...	...	...	...	...	...	...	...	...	...	...	...
Trade Balance .... 78ac d	...	...	...	...	...	...	...	...	...	...	...	...	...	...	...
Services: Credit .... 78ad d	...	...	...	...	...	...	...	...	...	...	...	...	...	...	...
Services: Debit .... 78ae d	...	...	...	...	...	...	...	...	...	...	...	...	...	...	...
Balance on Goods & Services .... 78af d	...	...	...	...	...	...	...	...	...	...	...	...	...	...	...
Income: Credit .... 78ag d	...	...	...	...	...	...	...	...	...	...	...	...	...	...	...
Income: Debit .... 78ah d	...	...	...	...	...	...	...	...	...	...	...	...	...	...	...
Balance on Gds, Serv. & Inc. .... 78ai d	...	...	...	...	...	...	...	...	...	...	...	...	...	...	...
Current Transfers, n.i.e.: Credit .... 78aj d	...	...	...	...	...	...	...	...	...	...	...	...	...	...	...
Current Transfers: Debit .... 78ak d	...	...	...	...	...	...	...	...	...	...	...	...	...	...	...
Capital Account, n.i.e. .... 78bc d	...	...	...	...	...	...	...	...	...	...	...	...	...	...	...
Capital Account, n.i.e.: Credit .... 78ba d	...	...	...	...	...	...	...	...	...	...	...	...	...	...	...
Capital Account: Debit .... 78bb d	...	...	...	...	...	...	...	...	...	...	...	...	...	...	...
Financial Account, n.i.e. .... 78bj d	...	...	...	...	...	...	...	...	...	...	...	...	...	...	...
Direct Investment Abroad .... 78bd d	...	...	...	...	...	...	...	...	...	...	...	...	...	...	...
Dir. Invest. in Rep. Econ., n.i.e. .... 78be d	...	...	...	...	...	...	...	...	...	...	...	...	...	...	...
Portfolio Investment Assets .... 78bf d	...	...	...	...	...	...	...	...	...	...	...	...	...	...	...
Equity Securities.......................... 78bk d	...	...	...	...	...	...	...	...	...	...	...	...	...	...	...
Debt Securities .... 78bl d	...	...	...	...	...	...	...	...	...	...	...	...	...	...	...
Portfolio Investment Liab., n.i.e. ...... 78bg d	...	...	...	...	...	...	...	...	...	...	...	...	...	...	...
Equity Securities.......................... 78bm d	...	...	...	...	...	...	...	...	...	...	...	...	...	...	...
Debt Securities .... 78bn d	...	...	...	...	...	...	...	...	...	...	...	...	...	...	...
Financial Derivatives Assets .... 78bw d	...	...	...	...	...	...	...	...	...	...	...	...	...	...	...
Financial Derivatives Liabilities ...... 78bx d	...	...	...	...	...	...	...	...	...	...	...	...	...	...	...
Other Investment Assets .... 78bh d	...	...	...	...	...	...	...	...	...	...	...	...	...	...	...
Monetary Authorities.................... 78bo d	...	...	...	...	...	...	...	...	...	...	...	...	...	...	...
General Government .... 78bp d	...	...	...	...	...	...	...	...	...	...	...	...	...	...	...
Banks .... 78bq d	...	...	...	...	...	...	...	...	...	...	...	...	...	...	...
Other Sectors .... 78br d	...	...	...	...	...	...	...	...	...	...	...	...	...	...	...
Other Investment Liab., n.i.e. .... 78bi d	...	...	...	...	...	...	...	...	...	...	...	...	...	...	...
Monetary Authorities.................... 78bs d	...	...	...	...	...	...	...	...	...	...	...	...	...	...	...
General Government .... 78bt d	...	...	...	...	...	...	...	...	...	...	...	...	...	...	...
Banks .... 78bu d	...	...	...	...	...	...	...	...	...	...	...	...	...	...	...
Other Sectors .... 78bv d	...	...	...	...	...	...	...	...	...	...	...	...	...	...	...
Net Errors and Omissions................... 78ca d	...	...	...	...	...	...	...	...	...	...	...	...	...	...	...
Overall Balance .... 78cb d	...	...	...	...	...	...	...	...	...	...	...	...	...	...	...
Reserves and Related Items .... 79da d	...	...	...	...	...	...	...	...	...	...	...	...	...	...	...
Reserve Assets .... 79db d	...	...	...	...	...	...	...	...	...	...	...	...	...	...	...
Use of Fund Credit and Loans .... 79dc d	...	...	...	...	...	...	...	...	...	...	...	...	...	...	...
Exceptional Financing .... 79de d	...	...	...	...	...	...	...	...	...	...	...	...	...	...	...

Government Finance — *As Percent of*

Deficit (-) or Surplus........................... 80g	...	...	...	...	...	...	...	...	...	...	...	...	...	...	...
Debt 88g	...	...	...	...	...	...	...	...	...	...	...	...	...	...	...

National Accounts — *Billions of Ecus through 1998;*

Househ.Cons.Expend.,incl.NPISHs....... 96f. c	...	...	...	...	...	...	...	...	...	...	...	...	...	...	...
Government Consumption Exp. .... 91f. c	...	...	...	...	...	...	...	...	...	...	...	...	...	...	...
Gross Fixed Capital Formation .... 93e. c	...	...	...	...	...	...	...	...	...	...	...	...	...	...	...
Changes in Inventories.................... 93i. c	...	...	...	...	...	...	...	...	...	...	...	...	...	...	...
Exports of Goods and Services .... 90c. c	...	...	...	...	...	...	...	...	...	...	...	...	...	...	...
Imports of Goods and Services .... 98c. c	...	...	...	...	...	...	...	...	...	...	...	...	...	...	...
Gross Domestic Product (GDP) .... 99b. c	...	...	...	...	...	...	...	...	...	...	...	...	...	...	...
Net Primary Income from Abroad....... 98.n c	...	...	...	...	...	...	...	...	...	...	...	...	...	...	...
GDP Volume 1995 Prices .... 99b. r	...	...	...	...	...	...	...	...	...	...	...	...	...	...	...
GDP Deflator (1995=100) .... 99bi r	...	...	...	...	...	...	...	...	...	...	...	...	...	...	...

	1985	1986	1987	1988	1989	1990	1991	1992	1993	1994	1995	1996	1997	1998	1999		
Period Averages																**Prices, Production, Labor**	
	...	...	...	...	...	...	...	...	...	...	...	...	...	100.6	100.6	Producer Prices	63
	...	...	...	...	...	...	...	...	...	...	...	...	...	104.9	106.1	Harmonized CPI (hcpi)	64h
	...	...	...	...	...	...	...	...	...	...	...	...	...	104.7	....	Wages/Labor Costs (1996=100)	65..c
	...	...	...	...	...	...	...	...	...	...	...	...	...	109.1	110.4	Industrial Production	66..c
	...	...	...	...	...	...	...	...	...	...	...	...	...	101.9	....	Employment	67
Billions of Euros beginning 1999																**International Transactions**	
	...	...	...	...	...	...	...	...	...	...	...	...	...	791.5	829.2	Exports	70
	...	...	...	...	...	...	...	...	...	...	...	...	...	709.3	771.7	Imports, c.i.f.	71
1995=100																	
	...	...	...	...	...	...	...	...	...	...	...	...	...	124.5	127.2	Volume of Exports	72
	...	...	...	...	...	...	...	...	...	...	...	...	...	129.2	135.5	Volume of Imports	73
	...	...	...	...	...	...	...	...	...	...	...	...	...	106.6	108.9	Unit Value of Exports	74
	...	...	...	...	...	...	...	...	...	...	...	...	...	102.8	106.1	Unit Value of Imports	75
Minus Sign Indicates Debit																**Balance of Payments**	
	...	...	...	...	...	...	...	...	...	...	...	...	...	67.55	40.79	Current Account, n.i.e.	78al d
	...	...	...	...	...	...	...	...	...	...	...	...	...	865.28	847.07	Goods: Exports f.o.b.	78aa d
	...	...	...	...	...	...	...	...	...	...	...	...	...	-731.97	-741.23	Goods: Imports f.o.b.	78ab d
	...	...	...	...	...	...	...	...	...	...	...	...	...	133.30	105.85	*Trade Balance*	78ac d
	...	...	...	...	...	...	...	...	...	...	...	...	...	259.94	251.00	Services: Credit	78ad d
	...	...	...	...	...	...	...	...	...	...	...	...	...	-260.98	-259.03	Services: Debit	78ae d
	...	...	...	...	...	...	...	...	...	...	...	...	...	132.26	97.82	*Balance on Goods & Services*	78af d
	...	...	...	...	...	...	...	...	...	...	...	...	...	222.34	214.65	Income: Credit	78ag d
	...	...	...	...	...	...	...	...	...	...	...	...	...	-235.59	-226.45	Income: Debit	78ah d
	...	...	...	...	...	...	...	...	...	...	...	...	...	119.01	86.02	*Balance on Gds, Serv. & Inc.*	78ai d
	...	...	...	...	...	...	...	...	...	...	...	...	...	68.07	71.74	Current Transfers, n.i.e.: Credit	78aj d
	...	...	...	...	...	...	...	...	...	...	...	...	...	-119.53	-116.98	Current Transfers: Debit	78ak d
	...	...	...	...	...	...	...	...	...	...	...	...	...	14.21	14.11	Capital Account, n.i.e.	78bc d
	...	...	...	...	...	...	...	...	...	...	...	...	...	19.96	20.85	Capital Account, n.i.e.: Credit	78ba d
	...	...	...	...	...	...	...	...	...	...	...	...	...	-5.75	-6.74	Capital Account: Debit	78bb d
	...	...	...	...	...	...	...	...	...	...	...	...	...	-88.76	-84.96	Financial Account, n.i.e.	78bj d
	...	...	...	...	...	...	...	...	...	...	...	...	...	-206.39	-225.78	Direct Investment Abroad	78bd d
	...	...	...	...	...	...	...	...	...	...	...	...	...	89.04	79.15	Dir. Invest. in Rep. Econ., n.i.e.	78be d
	...	...	...	...	...	...	...	...	...	...	...	...	...	-336.60	-335.40	Portfolio Investment Assets	78bf d
	...	...	...	...	...	...	...	...	...	...	...	...	...	-109.86	-162.55	Equity Securities	78bk d
	...	...	...	...	...	...	...	...	...	...	...	...	...	-226.74	-172.85	Debt Securities	78bl d
	...	...	...	...	...	...	...	...	...	...	...	...	...	240.61	301.81	Portfolio Investment Liab., n.i.e.	78bg d
	...	...	...	...	...	...	...	...	...	...	...	...	...	111.11	101.85	Equity Securities	78bm d
	...	...	...	...	...	...	...	...	...	...	...	...	...	129.52	199.97	Debt Securities	78bn d
	...	...	...	...	...	...	...	...	...	...	...	...	...	—	—	Financial Derivatives Assets	78bw d
	...	...	...	...	...	...	...	...	...	...	...	...	...	-9.44	-2.06	Financial Derivatives Liabilities	78bx d
	...	...	...	...	...	...	...	...	...	...	...	...	...	-70.74	-63.40	Other Investment Assets	78bh d
	...	...	...	...	...	...	...	...	...	...	...	...	...	-.84	10.09	Monetary Authorities	78bo d
	...	...	...	...	...	...	...	...	...	...	...	...	...	-1.21	-.99	General Government	78bp d
	...	...	...	...	...	...	...	...	...	...	...	...	...	-21.94	-26.77	Banks	78bq d
	...	...	...	...	...	...	...	...	...	...	...	...	...	-46.73	-45.72	Other Sectors	78br d
	...	...	...	...	...	...	...	...	...	...	...	...	...	204.75	160.70	Other Investment Liab., n.i.e.	78bi d
	...	...	...	...	...	...	...	...	...	...	...	...	...	4.01	—	Monetary Authorities	78bs d
	...	...	...	...	...	...	...	...	...	...	...	...	...	-8.62	-14.30	General Government	78bt d
	...	...	...	...	...	...	...	...	...	...	...	...	...	195.90	148.06	Banks	78bu d
	...	...	...	...	...	...	...	...	...	...	...	...	...	13.46	26.94	Other Sectors	78bv d
	...	...	...	...	...	...	...	...	...	...	...	...	...	-2.85	15.22	Net Errors and Omissions	78ca d
	...	...	...	...	...	...	...	...	...	...	...	...	...	-9.87	-14.86	*Overall Balance*	78cb d
	...	...	...	...	...	...	...	...	...	...	...	...	...	9.87	14.86	Reserves and Related Items	79da d
	...	...	...	...	...	...	...	...	...	...	...	...	...	9.87	14.86	Reserve Assets	79db d
	...	...	...	...	...	...	...	...	...	...	...	...	...	—	—	Use of Fund Credit and Loans	79dc d
	...	...	...	...	...	...	...	...	...	...	...	...	...	—	—	Exceptional Financing	79de d
Gross Domestic Product																**Government Finance**	
	...	...	...	...	...	-4.1	-4.4	-4.6	-5.6	-5.1	-4.8	-4.2	-2.6	-2.0	-1.2	Deficit (-) or Surplus	80g
	...	...	...	...	...	58.4	58.3	61.8	68.3	70.7	73.4	74.4	74.0	73.4	72.2	Debt	88g
Billions of Euros beginning 1999																**National Accounts**	
	...	...	...	...	...	...	...	...	...	...	...	...	...	3,309.5	3,469.1	Househ.Cons.Expend.,incl.NPISHs	96f. c
	...	...	...	...	...	...	...	...	...	...	...	...	...	1,168.0	1,223.1	Government Consumption Exp.	91f. c
	...	...	...	...	...	...	...	...	...	...	...	...	...	1,186.8	1,266.2	Gross Fixed Capital Formation	93e. c
	...	...	...	...	...	...	...	...	...	...	...	...	...	59.9	42.3	Changes in Inventories	93i. c
	...	...	...	...	...	...	...	...	...	...	...	...	...	1,925.5	2,020.2	Exports of Goods and Services	90c. c
	...	...	...	...	...	...	...	...	...	...	...	...	...	-1,778.2	-1,913.3	Imports of Goods and Services	98c. c
	...	...	...	...	...	...	...	...	...	...	...	...	...	5,871.3	6,107.7	Gross Domestic Product (GDP)	99b. c
	...	...	...	...	...	...	...	...	...	...	...	...	...	-35.6	....	Net Primary Income from Abroad	98.n c
	...	...	...	...	...	...	...	...	...	...	...	...	...	5,647.3	5,787.7	GDP Volume 1995 Prices	99b. r
	...	...	...	...	...	...	...	...	...	...	...	...	...	106.2	I 107.8	GDP Deflator (1995=100)	99bi r

(See notes in the back of the book.)

Fiji

		1970	1971	1972	1973	1974	1975	1976	1977	1978	1979	1980	1981	1982	1983	1984
Exchange Rates														*Fiji Dollars per SDR:*		
Official Rate	aa	.8731	.8890	.9155	.9762	.9795	1.0104	1.0939	1.0575	1.0679	1.1077	1.0089	1.0205	1.0450	1.0954	1.1204
														Fiji Dollars per US Dollar:		
Official Rate	ae	.8731	.8188	.8432	.8092	.8000	.8631	.9415	.8705	.8197	.8409	.7911	.8767	.9473	1.0462	1.1430
Official Rate	rf	.8708	.8588	.8252	.7942	.8056	.8219	.8977	.9174	.8468	.8357	.8180	.8546	.9324	1.0170	1.0826
														Index Numbers (1995=100):		
Official Rate	ahx	161.2	164.4	170.5	177.2	174.6	171.3	156.8	153.3	166.1	168.3	172.0	164.8	150.9	138.4	130.1
Nominal Effective Exchange Rate	ne c	....	....	....	....	....	....	....	....	....	....	115.5	119.8	123.6	127.6	131.3
Real Effective Exchange Rate	re c	....	....	....	....	....	....	....	....	....	....	....	137.9	141.6	142.2	141.5	143.5
Fund Position														*Millions of SDRs:*		
Quota	2f. s	....	13.00	13.00	13.00	13.00	13.00	13.00	13.00	18.00	18.00	27.00	27.00	27.00	36.50	36.50
SDRs	1b. s	....		1.38	1.38	1.37	1.33	1.33	1.27	1.30	3.10	2.71	4.52	3.72	.28	6.31
Reserve Position in the Fund	1c. s	....	2.30	2.30	2.30		3.25	3.25	3.25	3.15	3.06	5.34	5.36	5.40	7.79	7.81
Total Fund Cred.&Loans Outstg.	2tl	....	—	—	—	.34	—	—	6.50	6.50	6.50	—	—	13.50	13.50	13.50
International Liquidity											*Millions of US Dollars Unless Otherwise Indicated:*						
Total Reserves minus Gold	1l. d	27.35	39.62	69.42	73.95	109.15	148.59	116.32	147.13	134.70	136.48	167.51	135.08	126.92	115.82	117.42
SDRs	1b. d	—		1.50	1.66	1.68	1.56	1.55	1.54	1.69	4.08	3.46	5.26	4.10	.29	6.19
Reserve Position in the Fund	1c. d	—	2.50	2.50	2.77	—	3.80	3.78	3.95	4.10	4.03	6.81	6.24	5.96	8.16	7.66
Foreign Exchange	1d. d	27.35	37.12	65.42	69.51	107.47	143.23	111.00	141.64	128.90	128.37	157.24	123.58	116.86	107.37	103.58
Gold (Million Fine Troy Ounces)	1ad	....	....	....	....	....	....	—	.006	.008	.011	.011	.011	.011	.011	.011
Gold (National Valuation)	1and	—	—	—	—	—	—	—	.24	.38	.51	.50	.45	.43	.41	.38
Deposit Money Banks: Assets	7a. d	20.06	23.64	18.31	8.61	9.55	6.37	4.96	4.83	5.16	3.66	8.38	10.02	4.95	7.87	8.42
Liabilities	7b. d	1.17	2.81	7.27	14.47	20.77	18.65	22.25	22.79	13.24	13.62	16.27	19.98	23.53	18.67	14.82
Monetary Authorities														*Millions of Fiji Dollars:*		
Foreign Assets	11	27.0	35.0	54.5	67.8	91.6	129.1	110.3	128.7	110.3	116.9	132.5	116.0	123.4	122.5	130.0
Claims on Central Government	12a	3.5	3.5	3.6	2.6	2.8	3.0	2.8	1.6	5.1	10.4	6.1	4.6	11.1	8.2	16.7
Claims on Official Entities	12bx	—	—	—	.4	.1	—	.3	1.3	2.9	9.4	2.9	1.0	2.8	11.4	6.5
Reserve Money	14	17.3	20.4	24.9	37.6	48.5	63.4	54.5	56.4	64.1	72.0	66.2	76.4	81.6	86.9	100.5
of which: Currency Outside DMBs	14a	11.2	13.1	14.9	17.2	21.5	27.3	30.7	34.0	38.8	45.2	44.1	48.7	52.8	58.7	61.0
Bonds	16aa	—	—	—	—	—	—	—	—	—	—	—	—	—	—	—
Central Government Deposits	16d	8.4	12.3	12.7	19.7	13.7	24.2	20.6	21.3	15.1	16.1	29.3	16.9	13.1	13.3	10.6
Capital Accounts	17a	.6	2.3	2.0	9.1	10.8	10.8	20.4	18.2	19.4	24.7	16.2	23.4	28.4	34.0	36.3
Other Items (Net)	17r	4.2	3.5	18.5	14.4	21.5	33.7	18.0	35.8	19.8	23.9	29.8	4.7	14.2	7.9	5.9
Deposit Money Banks														*Millions of Fiji Dollars:*		
Reserves	20	2.3	3.0	12.6	16.7	18.6	25.3	18.1	20.8	19.1	20.4	22.2	23.3	28.2	28.3	39.5
Reserve Bank Bonds	20r	—	—	—	—	—	—	—	—	—	—	—	—	—	—	—
Foreign Assets	21	17.5	19.0	13.9	7.0	7.6	5.5	4.7	4.2	4.2	3.1	6.6	8.8	4.7	8.2	9.6
Claims on Central Government	22a	6.7	7.4	8.8	10.0	16.2	22.2	27.0	31.4	39.6	42.8	53.0	40.3	51.6	52.9	44.8
Claims on Official Entities	22bx	2.3	2.9	6.8	7.1	7.5	10.0	13.7	13.3	17.7	16.7	18.3	25.0	46.4	61.8	52.0
Claims on Private Sector	22d	23.8	30.8	40.4	57.7	75.5	78.2	102.3	119.5	127.2	167.9	188.7	233.2	245.9	275.3	324.8
Demand Deposits	24	22.4	25.3	31.5	35.4	39.4	47.3	47.9	48.4	53.5	61.8	56.6	65.4	70.1	76.0	74.9
Time Deposits	25	28.1	35.2	43.1	50.6	65.9	80.8	96.6	119.1	140.0	174.9	205.4	234.1	257.5	297.5	344.1
Foreign Liabilities	26c	1.0	2.3	5.5	11.7	16.6	16.1	21.0	19.8	10.8	11.5	12.9	17.5	22.3	19.5	16.9
Central Government Deposits	26d	5.3	4.2	3.7	4.0	5.3	2.7	5.0	5.1	5.3	7.1	8.1	7.7	11.1	14.9	21.7
Other Items (Net)	27r	-4.3	-3.9	-1.3	-3.3	-1.8	-5.7	-4.7	-3.3	-1.9	-4.3	5.7	6.0	15.8	18.7	13.1
Monetary Survey														*Millions of Fiji Dollars:*		
Foreign Assets (Net)	31n	43.5	51.8	62.9	63.1	82.2	118.4	94.1	106.2	96.8	101.3	126.3	107.3	91.7	96.4	107.6
Domestic Credit	32	22.5	28.1	43.2	54.1	83.1	86.6	120.5	140.7	172.0	224.1	231.5	279.4	333.7	381.5	412.6
Claims on Central Govt. (Net)	32an	-3.6	-5.6	-4.0	-11.1	—	-1.6	4.2	6.7	24.2	30.0	21.6	20.2	38.6	32.9	29.3
Claims on Official Entities	32bx	2.3	2.9	6.8	7.5	7.6	10.0	14.0	14.6	20.5	26.2	21.2	25.9	49.3	73.3	58.5
Claims on Private Sector	32d	23.8	30.8	40.4	57.7	75.5	78.2	102.3	119.5	127.2	167.9	188.7	233.2	245.9	275.3	324.8
Money	34	37.3	42.7	52.3	56.5	69.1	84.0	85.4	84.1	98.4	112.3	100.7	118.4	123.6	134.8	136.0
Quasi-Money	35	28.1	35.2	43.1	51.6	81.4	107.2	108.5	146.0	149.0	186.0	234.4	234.2	257.6	297.5	344.1
Reserve Bank Bonds	36aa	—	—	—	—	—	—	—	—	—	—	—	—	—	—	—
Capital Accounts	37a	.6	2.3	2.0	9.1	10.8	10.8	20.4	18.2	19.4	24.7	16.2	23.4	28.4	34.0	36.3
Other Items (Net)	37r	-.2	-.4	8.7	-.1	4.1	2.9	.3	-1.3	1.9	2.4	6.5	10.6	15.8	11.7	3.8
Money plus Quasi-Money	35l	65.5	78.0	95.4	108.1	150.5	191.3	193.9	230.1	247.4	298.3	335.1	352.6	381.2	432.2	480.1
Nonbank Financial Institutions														*Millions of Fiji Dollars:*		
Claims on Central Government	42a. l	8.1	8.6	9.3	9.6	10.9	9.3	9.6	13.7	18.4	23.1	26.8	30.8	34.3	39.2	44.1
Claims on Local Government	42b. l	2.7	3.8	4.4	5.1	5.1	5.2	5.2	5.5	5.6	6.4	6.3	8.9	8.6	10.6	11.1
Claims on Nonfin.Pub.Enterprises	42c. l	—	—	—	.1	.1	.2	.4	.8	1.7	2.4	4.6	5.2	5.5	6.7	7.8
Claims on Private Sector	42d. l	2.9	3.1	3.3	4.7	5.7	6.7	7.6	8.0	9.4	10.7	12.1	14.2	19.4	21.8	24.2
Incr.in Total Assets(Within Per.)	49z. l	1.4	1.9	1.9	2.8	2.9	2.3	4.2	8.3	6.1	7.3	7.7	9.5	11.4	12.1	13.5
Interest Rates														*Percent Per Annum*		
Bank Rate (End of Period)	60	....	....	....	....	6.38	6.25	5.50	5.50	5.58	6.50	7.50	8.83	9.50	10.17	11.00
Money Market Rate	60b	....	....	....	....									5.07	6.20	8.74
Treasury Bill Rate	60c	....	....	....	....	4.34	4.34	4.34	4.50	5.32	5.36	5.72	5.96	6.17	7.09
Deposit Rate	60l	....	....	....	....	3.96	4.00	4.00	4.04	4.04	4.50	4.50	6.00	6.00	6.00	6.00
Lending Rate	60p	....	8.00	10.00	10.00	10.00	10.00	10.00	10.00	10.50	10.50	12.00	13.50	13.50	13.50	13.50
Prices, Production, Labor														*Index Numbers (1995=100):*		
Consumer Prices	64	14.4	15.7	19.1	21.2	24.3	27.5	30.6	32.8	34.8	37.5	42.9	47.7	51.1	54.5	57.4
Wage Rates	65	17.0	18.7	21.2	27.4	33.7	41.1	46.0	48.9	54.3	58.4	63.9	69.9	75.4	80.4	81.5
Industrial Production	66	....	....	....	....	....	....	....	....	....	92.0	84.9	93.5	98.1	82.7	98.3
Tourist Arrivals	66.t	....	....	....	....	....	....	....	....	....			61.5	59.6	63.8	60.2	73.9
Industrial Employment	67	....	....	....	....	....	....	....	....	78.7	80.7	82.7	83.7	80.5	82.3	80.8
														Number in Thousands:		
Labor Force	67d	....	....	....	....	....	....	....	....	....	....	....	....	....	....	....
Employment	67e	....	....	....	....	....	....	....	....	....	....	....	....	....	....	....
Unemployment	67c	....	....	....	....	....	....	....	....	....	....	....	....	....	....	....
Unemployment Rate (%)	67r	....	....	....	....	....	....	....	....	....	....	....	....	....	....	....

	1985	1986	1987	1988	1989	1990	1991	1992	1993	1994	1995	1996	1997	1998	1999		
End of Period																**Exchange Rates**	
	1.2307	1.4010	2.0436	1.8906	1.9632	2.0760	2.1067	2.1511	2.1164	2.0570	2.1248	1.9900	2.0902	2.7965	2.6981	Official Rate	aa
End of Period (ae) Period Average (rf)																	
	1.1204	1.1453	1.4405	1.4049	1.4939	1.4592	1.4728	1.5645	1.5408	1.4090	1.4294	1.3839	1.5492	1.9861	1.9658	Official Rate	ae
	1.1536	1.1329	1.2439	1.4303	1.4833	1.4809	1.4756	1.5030	1.5418	1.4641	1.4063	1.4033	1.4437	1.9868	1.9696	Official Rate	rf
Period Averages																	
	122.0	124.2	114.9	98.4	94.9	95.0	95.3	93.6	91.2	96.1	100.0	100.2	97.5	70.8	71.4	Official Rate	ahx
	137.9	130.1	113.0	93.7	97.8	98.8	99.3	97.8	99.1	100.8	100.0	101.3	104.7	83.5	82.7	Nominal Effective Exchange Rate	nec
	145.5	130.8	111.2	95.2	95.0	95.3	98.2	98.7	102.6	101.9	100.0	101.9	106.9	88.7	88.9	Real Effective Exchange Rate	rec
End of Period																**Fund Position**	
	36.50	36.50	36.50	36.50	36.50	36.50	36.50	51.10	51.10	51.10	51.10	51.10	51.10	51.10	70.30	Quota	2f. s
	5.14	5.82	9.90	15.08	15.90	16.48	9.26	5.97	6.26	7.39	7.67	7.99	8.29	8.62	4.10	SDRs	1b. s
	7.83	7.85	7.87	7.87	7.89	7.12	6.76	10.43	9.95	9.99	10.00	10.05	10.08	10.12	14.94	Reserve Position in the Fund	1c. s
	13.19	6.44	4.75	2.97	.59	—	—	—	—	—	—	—	—	—	—	Total Fund Cred.&Loans Outstg.	2tl
End of Period																**International Liquidity**	
	130.84	171.05	132.17	233.36	211.59	260.79	271.43	316.87	269.46	273.14	349.03	427.24	360.29	385.42	428.69	Total Reserves minus Gold	1l. d
	5.65	7.12	14.04	20.29	20.90	23.45	13.25	8.21	8.59	10.79	11.41	11.49	11.18	12.14	5.63	SDRs	1b. d
	8.60	9.60	11.16	10.59	10.37	10.13	9.67	14.34	13.67	14.58	14.87	14.45	13.60	14.25	20.50	Reserve Position in the Fund	1c. d
	116.59	154.33	106.96	202.48	180.33	227.22	248.51	294.32	247.19	247.77	322.76	401.30	335.51	359.04	402.55	Foreign Exchange	1d. d
	.011	.011	.001	.001	.001	.001	.001	.001	.001	.001	.001	.001	.001	.001	.001	Gold (Million Fine Troy Ounces)	1ad
	.43	.47	.41	.41	.30	.32	.29	.28	.33	.32	.32	.31	.24	.24	.24	Gold (National Valuation)	1and
	44.42	111.97	26.29	38.35	51.99	77.88	49.90	44.47	58.69	62.91	50.13	78.07	89.31	136.34	200.07	Deposit Money Banks: Assets	7a. d
	55.56	120.11	25.05	41.56	54.40	83.02	66.05	67.17	64.30	65.66	73.89	124.33	123.48	108.04	159.49	Liabilities	7b. d
End of Period																**Monetary Authorities**	
	146.5	195.9	190.2	326.8	316.1	380.5	399.7	498.0	414.8	384.9	498.9	591.2	558.1	765.5	842.7	Foreign Assets	11
	4.3	1.8	26.9	1.5	9.0	.1	.1	—	6.7	—	—	—	—	—	50.7	Claims on Central Government	12a
	6.2	.3	5.3	—	.1	.1	.1	.1	2.2	.1	.1	—	—	—	—	Claims on Official Entities	12bx
	103.0	116.7	111.6	199.3	152.1	169.3	189.1	226.4	219.9	223.6	243.4	247.9	260.4	276.8	434.2	Reserve Money	14
	61.8	63.1	64.9	67.7	78.0	86.0	91.0	103.1	112.4	115.6	117.8	125.4	134.0	159.8	189.9	of which: Currency Outside DMBs	14a
	—	—	—	—	56.9	96.2	95.4	163.9	108.9	126.6	220.5	253.3	210.7	252.9	255.8	Bonds	16aa
	7.4	13.9	.9	49.0	42.9	36.2	31.7	21.8	14.3	14.8	6.8	47.2	40.0	22.3	42.6	Central Government Deposits	16d
	47.7	69.9	110.8	76.1	80.6	83.5	73.0	82.8	62.7	45.8	49.3	42.3	50.5	197.1	169.0	Capital Accounts	17a
	-1.1	-2.5	-.8	4.0	-7.5	-4.5	10.7	3.3	17.9	-25.8	-21.0	.4	-3.4	16.4	-8.3	Other Items (Net)	17r
End of Period																**Deposit Money Banks**	
	41.4	53.4	46.7	131.5	73.1	83.2	97.8	123.3	107.5	107.9	125.5	120.2	126.4	111.5	237.3	Reserves	20
	—	—	—	—	20.3	60.7	39.9	60.2	44.6	44.0	104.1	106.0	60.4	44.4	54.5	Reserve Bank Bonds	20r
	49.8	128.2	37.9	53.9	77.7	113.6	73.5	69.6	90.4	88.6	71.7	108.0	138.4	270.8	393.3	Foreign Assets	21
	50.2	77.2	62.5	83.6	71.6	60.8	82.2	91.6	88.9	80.7	65.4	78.8	87.0	107.0	117.8	Claims on Central Government	22a
	53.4	56.1	60.9	70.4	67.9	75.2	97.5	118.4	141.9	144.4	137.7	145.8	164.5	154.4	137.1	Claims on Official Entities	22bx
	350.4	367.6	393.6	411.5	540.8	676.4	802.9	880.4	994.4	1,080.9	1,112.2	1,165.0	1,013.9	963.8	997.0	Claims on Private Sector	22d
	76.0	108.8	103.4	205.2	184.5	179.2	183.1	211.0	251.4	229.0	268.3	328.7	311.3	328.6	497.6	Demand Deposits	24
	351.6	402.9	429.9	448.4	525.6	722.9	855.4	977.4	1,013.7	1,069.7	1,089.6	1,032.1	913.2	859.9	851.6	Time Deposits	25
	62.2	137.6	36.1	58.4	81.3	121.1	97.3	105.1	99.1	92.5	105.6	172.1	191.3	214.6	313.5	Foreign Liabilities	26c
	17.3	17.7	7.5	26.4	18.2	13.6	15.1	6.8	21.5	40.5	40.1	21.0	37.8	78.6	122.5	Central Government Deposits	26d
	38.0	15.5	24.8	12.5	41.8	33.0	42.8	43.2	81.9	114.7	112.8	170.1	136.9	170.2	151.8	Other Items (Net)	27r
End of Period																**Monetary Survey**	
	117.7	177.6	182.3	316.7	311.3	373.0	376.0	462.5	406.2	381.0	464.9	527.2	505.2	821.7	922.5	Foreign Assets (Net)	31n
	439.9	471.3	540.9	491.6	628.2	762.7	935.9	1,061.9	1,198.2	1,250.7	1,268.3	1,321.3	1,187.6	1,124.3	1,137.5	Domestic Credit	32
	29.8	47.3	81.0	9.7	19.4	11.1	35.5	63.0	59.8	25.3	18.4	10.5	9.1	6.1	3.3	Claims on Central Govt. (Net)	32an
	59.6	56.4	66.2	70.4	68.0	75.2	97.6	118.5	144.1	144.5	137.8	145.8	164.5	154.4	137.1	Claims on Official Entities	32bx
	350.4	367.6	393.6	411.5	540.8	676.4	802.9	880.4	994.4	1,080.9	1,112.2	1,165.0	1,013.9	963.8	997.0	Claims on Private Sector	32d
	137.8	172.1	168.3	272.9	263.6	265.3	274.4	314.1	363.8	344.6	386.2	456.3	445.3	493.9	694.5	Money	34
	351.6	402.9	429.9	448.4	525.6	722.9	855.4	977.4	1,013.7	1,069.7	1,089.6	1,032.1	913.2	859.9	851.6	Quasi-Money	35
	—	—	—	—	36.6	35.5	55.6	103.7	64.4	82.5	116.4	147.3	150.3	208.4	201.3	Reserve Bank Bonds	36aa
	47.7	69.9	110.8	76.1	80.6	83.5	73.0	82.8	62.7	45.8	49.3	42.3	50.5	197.1	169.0	Capital Accounts	37a
	20.6	4.0	14.2	10.9	33.1	28.5	53.5	46.4	99.8	88.9	91.8	170.5	133.4	186.6	143.5	Other Items (Net)	37r
	489.4	575.0	598.2	721.3	789.2	988.2	1,129.8	1,291.5	1,377.5	1,414.4	1,475.7	1,488.4	1,358.5	1,353.8	1,546.1	Money plus Quasi-Money	35l
End of Period																**Nonbank Financial Institutions**	
	46.6	54.7	58.1	63.9	67.2	61.7	54.4	55.6	55.3	58.1	58.2	77.4	127.7	127.0	134.8	Claims on Central Government	42a. l
	12.7	14.1	13.5	12.7	10.7	12.9	14.1	14.1	14.9	20.6	26.8	26.9	—	—	—	Claims on Local Government	42b. l
	9.3	11.6	11.4	13.1	13.0	13.7	11.9	14.2	15.2	26.7	36.2	54.4	—	—	—	Claims on Nonfin.Pub.Enterprises	42c. l
	28.1	32.5	37.2	32.8	36.1	29.1	33.0	37.6	42.6	59.0	68.3	73.8	93.5	100.5	119.8	Claims on Private Sector	42d. l
	15.2	16.4	10.5	5.0	11.4	12.2	14.0	19.9	22.1	23.2	27.6	15.1	-14.4	14.8	28.7	Incr.in Total Assets(Within Per.)	49z. l
Percent Per Annum																**Interest Rates**	
	11.00	8.00	11.00	11.00	8.00	8.00	8.00	6.00	6.00	6.00	6.00	6.00	1.88	2.50	2.50	Bank Rate (End of Period)	60
	6.61	6.55	9.02	1.49	2.34	2.92	4.28	3.06	2.91	4.10	3.95	2.43	1.91	1.27	1.27	Money Market Rate	60b
	7.03	6.36	9.76	1.78	2.75	4.40	5.61	3.65	2.91	2.69	3.15	2.98	2.60	2.00	2.00	Treasury Bill Rate	60c
	6.00	6.00	6.00	4.88	4.00	4.06	4.04	4.10	3.69	3.15	3.18	3.38	3.08	2.17	1.24	Deposit Rate	60l
	13.50	13.50	13.50	20.46	11.64	11.86	12.25	12.35	11.74	11.28	11.06	11.33	11.03	9.66	8.77	Lending Rate	60p
Period Averages																**Prices, Production, Labor**	
	59.9	⅃61.0	64.5	72.1	76.5	82.8	88.2	92.5	⅃97.3	97.9	100.0	103.1	106.5	112.6	114.8	Consumer Prices	64
	82.6	82.6	87.0	89.2	87.0	92.2	82.7	88.4	95.8	98.7	100.0	112.3	104.1	....	....	Wage Rates	65
	87.4	74.8	67.7	71.2	78.1	83.7	86.0	87.6	92.7	97.2	100.0	91.9	90.9	....	....	Industrial Production	66
	71.6	80.9	59.6	65.4	78.7	87.6	81.4	87.5	90.3	100.1	100.0	106.6	112.8	116.6	128.7	Tourist Arrivals	66.t
	83.3	82.1	80.3	79.7	92.4	92.5	94.3	96.1	97.5	98.0	100.0	113.2	118.0	116.4	....	Industrial Employment	67
Period Averages																	
	....	....	....	....	250	253	265	269	....	....	....	....	....	....		Labor Force	67d
	81	80	78	78	88	89	92	92	94	95	97	....	....	....		Employment	67e
	19	18	23	23	15	16	15	14	16	16	15	....	....	....		Unemployment	67c
	8.1	7.5	9.3	9.4	6.1	6.4	5.9	5.4	5.9	5.7	5.4	....	....	....		Unemployment Rate (%)	67r

Fiji

819

		1970	1971	1972	1973	1974	1975	1976	1977	1978	1979	1980	1981	1982	1983	1984
International Transactions															*Millions of Fiji Dollars*	
Exports	70	75.36	74.59	79.38	96.48	152.11	168.64	155.61	204.15	211.10	262.50	381.45	344.21	353.92	312.04	362.40
Imports, c.i.f.	71	90.52	110.80	131.55	176.34	219.33	220.97	238.04	281.01	300.00	392.87	458.75	539.91	475.58	493.17	486.99
Imports, f.o.b.	71.v	81.55	97.54	115.87	155.50	189.56	190.77	205.40	242.48	256.56	345.63	403.72	475.13	418.51	433.99	428.54
															1985=100	
Unit Value of Exports	74	27.5	27.0	I 33.9	40.6	67.1	90.8	78.9	I 85.7	92.5	91.6	123.1	108.4	106.2	112.3	111.1
Balance of Payments															*Millions of US Dollars:*	
Current Account, n.i.e.	78al d	....	....	....	....	....	....	....	....	....	−58.8	−17.5	−161.3	−84.3	−55.4	−18.4
Goods: Exports f.o.b.	78aa d	....	....	....	....	....	....	....	....	....	270.2	373.6	314.7	286.9	240.9	258.1
Goods: Imports f.o.b.	78ab d	....	....	....	....	....	....	....	....	....	−412.6	−492.1	−545.1	−441.0	−421.7	−390.7
Trade Balance	78ac d	....	....	....	....	....	....	....	....	....	−142.5	−118.6	−230.3	−154.0	−180.8	−132.6
Services: Credit	78ad d	....	....	....	....	....	....	....	....	....	191.3	200.5	219.7	236.2	251.2	249.0
Services: Debit	78ae d	....	....	....	....	....	....	....	....	....	−106.7	−124.3	−167.7	−154.7	−130.5	−128.5
Balance on Goods & Services	78af d	....	....	....	....	....	....	....	....	....	−57.9	−42.3	−178.4	−72.5	−60.1	−12.0
Income: Credit	78ag d	....	....	....	....	....	....	....	....	....	14.0	23.0	30.9	22.5	20.6	20.9
Income: Debit	78ah d	....	....	....	....	....	....	....	....	....	−27.5	−40.2	−41.7	−58.7	−48.7	−49.0
Balance on Gds, Serv. & Inc.	78ai d	....	....	....	....	....	....	....	....	....	−71.3	−59.5	−189.2	−108.7	−88.1	−40.1
Current Transfers, n.i.e.: Credit	78aj d	....	....	....	....	....	....	....	....	....	19.3	48.5	44.1	42.4	47.1	36.5
Current Transfers: Debit	78ak d	....	....	....	....	....	....	....	....	....	−6.7	−6.5	−16.2	−17.9	−14.4	−14.7
Capital Account, n.i.e.	78bc d	....	....	....	....	....	....	....	....	....	−7.9	−9.4	−10.9	−6.9	−8.0	−6.9
Capital Account, n.i.e.: Credit	78ba d	....	....	....	....	....	....	....	....	....	.9	.6	1.4	1.2	.7	1.3
Capital Account: Debit	78bb d	....	....	....	....	....	....	....	....	....	−8.8	−9.9	−12.3	−8.2	−8.7	−8.2
Financial Account, n.i.e.	78bj d	....	....	....	....	....	....	....	....	....	57.0	71.7	139.5	85.3	67.9	35.0
Direct Investment Abroad	78bd d	....	....	....	....	....	....	....	....	....	—	−2.2	1.5	−.8	−.1	−.6
Dir. Invest. in Rep. Econ., n.i.e.	78be d	....	....	....	....	....	....	....	....	....	10.2	36.3	36.2	36.8	31.9	23.3
Portfolio Investment Assets	78bf d	....	....	....	....	....	....	....	....	....	—	—	—	—	—	—
Equity Securities	78bk d	....	....	....	....	....	....	....	....	....	—	—	—	—	—	—
Debt Securities	78bl d	....	....	....	....	....	....	....	....	....	—	—	—	—	—	—
Portfolio Investment Liab., n.i.e.	78bg d	....	....	....	....	....	....	....	....	....	—	—	—	—	—	—
Equity Securities	78bm d	....	....	....	....	....	....	....	....	....	—	—	—	—	—	—
Debt Securities	78bn d	....	....	....	....	....	....	....	....	....	—	—	—	—	—	—
Financial Derivatives Assets	78bw d													....	....	....
Financial Derivatives Liabilities	78bx d													....	....	....
Other Investment Assets	78bh d	....	....	....	....	....	....	....	....	....	1.4	−18.9	12.7	5.6	2.8	5.0
Monetary Authorities	78bo d	....	....	....	....	....	....	....	....	....	....	....	....	....	....	....
General Government	78bp d	....	....	....	....	....	....	....	....	....	—	−1.1	—	—	—	—
Banks	78bq d	....	....	....	....	....	....	....	....	....	1.4	−4.3	−2.5	4.4	−3.5	−1.2
Other Sectors	78br d	....	....	....	....	....	....	....	....	....	—	−13.4	15.2	1.2	6.2	6.3
Other Investment Liab., n.i.e.	78bi d	....	....	....	....	....	....	....	....	....	45.5	56.5	89.0	43.7	33.3	7.2
Monetary Authorities	78bs d	....	....	....	....	....	....	....	....	....	....	....	....	....	....	....
General Government	78bt d	....	....	....	....	....	....	....	....	....	22.9	57.6	78.9	43.4	34.0	6.4
Banks	78bu d	....	....	....	....	....	....	....	....	....	−.4	1.6	.7	2.5	−.1	1.0
Other Sectors	78bv d	....	....	....	....	....	....	....	....	....	23.0	−2.7	9.4	−2.3	−.6	−.2
Net Errors and Omissions	78ca d	....	....	....	....	....	....	....	....	....	15.0	−5.1	10.8	−15.8	−9.9	.8
Overall Balance	78cb d	....	....	....	....	....	....	....	....	....	5.4	39.8	−21.9	−21.7	−5.4	10.5
Reserves and Related Items	79da d	....	....	....	....	....	....	....	....	....	−5.4	−39.8	21.9	21.7	5.4	−10.5
Reserve Assets	79db d	....	....	....	....	....	....	....	....	....	−5.4	−31.2	21.9	6.4	5.4	−10.5
Use of Fund Credit and Loans	79dc d	....	....	....	....	....	....	....	....	....	—	−8.6	—	15.3	—	—
Exceptional Financing	79de d	....	....	....	....	....	....	....	....	....	....	....	....	....	....	....
Government Finance															*Millions of Fiji Dollars:*	
Deficit (-) or Surplus	80	−5.3	−3.2	−4.0	−11.2	−16.0	−7.7	−23.6	−35.2	−30.6	−24.8	−29.5	−45.3	−70.3	−43.3	−38.7
Total Revenue and Grants	81y	43.4	50.2	55.1	68.2	80.0	109.3	124.1	134.1	157.0	194.0	224.4	262.9	264.8	293.7	329.2
Revenue	81	40.2	48.2	53.2	64.9	76.7	107.4	122.7	131.6	152.8	188.7	220.4	255.2	254.7	283.7	319.1
Grants	81z	3.1	2.0	1.9	3.3	3.3	1.9	1.4	2.5	4.3	5.3	3.9	7.7	10.1	10.0	10.1
Exp. & Lending Minus Repay.	82z	48.6	53.4	59.1	79.4	96.1	117.0	147.7	169.3	187.6	218.8	253.9	308.1	335.1	336.9	367.9
Expenditure	82	49.5	56.6	58.2	79.0	94.3	115.1	147.0	168.1	185.9	219.6	255.3	292.2	323.9	329.5	366.1
Lending Minus Repayments	83	−.9	−3.2	.9	.4	1.8	1.9	.7	1.2	1.7	−.8	−1.5	15.9	11.3	7.4	1.8
Total Financing	80h	5.3	3.2	4.0	11.2	16.0	7.7	23.6	35.2	30.6	24.8	29.5	45.3	70.3	43.3	38.7
Domestic	84a	5.7	3.2	4.2	5.7	9.8	2.1	13.8	16.0	32.8	16.6	4.8	13.4	52.4	38.1	34.4
Foreign	85a	−.5	.1	−.1	5.5	6.2	5.5	9.9	19.2	−2.2	8.2	24.8	31.9	18.0	5.2	4.3
Total Debt by Residence	88	39.1	49.4	46.7	73.6	83.5	99.1	121.7	154.0	168.0	193.7	247.2	292.2	358.1	399.2	446.4
Domestic	88a	30.4	39.2	36.5	47.2	51.5	63.0	75.7	91.5	109.6	125.5	157.1	168.8	216.0	250.8	289.4
Foreign	89a	8.7	10.2	10.2	26.4	32.0	36.1	45.9	62.5	58.4	68.3	90.2	123.4	142.1	148.4	157.0
National Accounts															*Millions of Fiji Dollars:*	
Exports of Goods & Services	90c	92.8	105.5	119.9	153.2	221.1	241.8	235.1	289.9	299.5	385.8	477.5	454.4	481.3	498.1	546.2
Government Consumption	91f	26.8	30.7	37.9	42.4	54.0	67.5	85.3	102.3	115.1	143.9	156.7	173.1	203.8	231.6	244.8
Gross Fixed Capital Formation	93e	34.8	45.9	53.1	65.7	74.2	103.4	119.5	128.9	149.8	197.3	249.8	280.5	262.6	239.2	218.0
Increase/Decrease(-) in Stocks	93i	7.7	6.7	9.5	9.9	10.9	12.6	14.5	24.1	27.8	59.6	63.4	81.7	21.9	2.3	23.3
Private Consumption	96f	124.6	147.3	180.5	261.3	334.4	382.5	433.7	415.1	458.2	519.6	574.7	660.0	684.7	748.2	794.1
Imports of Goods & Services	98c	−99.0	−122.0	−144.2	−198.8	−244.6	−245.4	−264.6	−308.1	−330.5	−432.1	−510.4	−606.6	−552.6	−560.1	−559.8
Gross Domestic Product (GDP)	99b	191.8	211.9	261.2	338.3	450.0	562.4	623.5	660.0	702.1	852.1	983.7	1,056.1	1,113.4	1,142.2	1,275.3
Net Factor Inc/Pmts(-) Abroad	98.n	−8.2	−10.1	−9.1	−4.6	−1.8	−6.0	−1.0	−8.6	−4.5	−12.5	−14.6	−9.2	−33.8	−28.2	−30.3
Gross National Income (GNI)	99a	183.6	201.8	252.2	333.7	448.2	556.4	622.5	651.4	697.6	839.6	969.2	1,046.9	1,079.6	1,114.0	1,245.0
Net National Income	99e	174.6	191.9	239.4	318.7	431.2	539.7	593.9	616.3	654.2	787.1	903.7	969.4	991.7	1,034.4	1,156.7
GDP at Factor Cost	99ba	168.9	184.7	230.5	300.6	410.5	515.4	570.6	605.7	642.9	779.4	901.0	953.6	1,020.5	1,031.8	1,151.7
GDP Vol.at Fact.Cost,'68 Prices	99ba p	148.7	157.6	170.0	191.6	196.6	196.8	202.1	211.1	....	....	....	....	....	....	....
GDP Vol.at Fact.Cost,'77 Prices	99ba p	....	....	....	....	....	....	....	605.7	616.6	690.9	679.3	719.9	712.2	683.9	741.3
GDP Vol.at Fact.Cost,'89 Prices	99ba p	....	....	....	....	....	....	....	....	....	....	....	....	....	....	....
GDP Volume (1995=100)	99bv p	44.0	46.6	50.3	56.7	58.1	58.2	59.8	62.4	63.6	71.2	70.0	74.2	73.4	70.5	76.4
GDP Deflator (1995=100)	99bi p	113.6	117.2	135.6	156.9	208.8	261.9	282.3	286.9	297.1	45.6	53.6	53.5	57.9	60.9	62.8
																Millions:
Population	99z	.55	.53	.54	.55	.56	.57	.58	.60	.61	.62	.63	.65	.66	.67	.69

1985	1986	1987	1988	1989	1990	1991	1992	1993	1994	1995	1996	1997	1998	1999		
Millions of Fiji Dollars															**International Transactions**	
352.23	383.02	483.12	531.19	658.62	731.87	664.60	666.98	692.40	833.60	875.90	1,052.10	896.50	1,016.20	....	Exports	70
508.00	493.60	465.11	658.82	860.44	1,112.90	961.77	947.11	1,109.81	1,229.10	1,253.90	1,384.50	1,392.50	1,433.80	....	Imports, c.i.f.	71
447.18	434.51	409.43	579.95	638.26	950.20	810.60	809.80	1,006.50	1,053.70	1,070.80	1,178.70	1,182.20	1,221.00	....	Imports, f.o.b.	71.v
1985=100																
100.0	134.3	183.5	175.4	175.5	....	....	....	....	....	....	....	....	....	....	Unit Value of Exports	74
Minus Sign Indicates Debit															Balance of Payments	
18.7	16.8	27.3	70.5	7.5	–94.0	–68.2	–61.3	–138.1	–112.8	–112.7	13.5	–34.1	–54.6	....	Current Account, n.i.e.	78al*d*
235.3	275.8	328.5	372.9	377.1	415.6	362.6	349.8	370.9	490.2	519.6	672.2	535.6	393.4	....	Goods: Exports f.o.b.	78aa*d*
–381.7	–379.2	–325.0	–389.2	–489.0	–641.6	–549.4	–538.8	–652.8	–719.7	–761.4	–839.9	–818.9	–611.6	....	Goods: Imports f.o.b.	78ab*d*
–146.4	–103.4	3.5	–16.3	–111.8	–226.1	–186.8	–189.0	–281.9	–229.5	–241.8	–167.7	–283.2	–218.1	....	*Trade Balance*	78ac*d*
272.9	263.1	201.8	244.7	365.1	417.0	427.6	453.2	481.1	534.7	564.1	612.6	667.9	506.4	....	Services: Credit	78ad*d*
–130.9	–157.7	–173.1	–183.2	–226.4	–257.4	–289.2	–303.7	–321.1	–366.0	–398.6	–412.9	–405.6	–340.8	....	Services: Debit	78ae*d*
–4.4	2.1	32.2	45.2	26.8	–66.5	–48.3	–39.5	–121.8	–60.8	–76.3	31.9	–20.9	–52.5	....	*Balance on Goods & Services*	78af*d*
35.0	41.2	40.0	46.2	51.2	49.1	51.8	52.3	52.1	49.2	55.4	63.6	61.7	53.7	....	Income: Credit	78ag*d*
–45.8	–49.4	–49.7	–61.6	–75.7	–75.2	–72.4	–79.8	–80.4	–105.7	–94.6	–91.6	–99.2	–86.5	....	Income: Debit	78ah*d*
–15.2	–6.1	22.4	29.9	2.4	–92.6	–68.9	–66.9	–150.1	–117.3	–115.5	4.0	–58.4	–85.3	....	*Balance on Gds, Serv. & Inc.*	78ai*d*
51.4	37.4	28.2	53.6	27.0	24.3	32.4	34.9	40.2	38.1	36.0	44.1	54.6	45.3	....	Current Transfers, n.i.e.: Credit	78aj*d*
–17.5	–14.6	–23.3	–12.9	–21.8	–25.7	–31.8	–29.3	–28.2	–33.5	–33.1	–34.6	–30.3	–14.7	....	Current Transfers: Debit	78ak*d*
–10.4	–13.4	–13.6	–12.1	48.4	47.6	71.1	72.5	57.1	43.4	87.0	70.8	48.5	65.2	....	Capital Account, n.i.e.	78bc*d*
.6	.7	.1	.1	70.0	69.6	97.9	96.7	83.7	76.0	120.1	114.5	88.9	105.0	....	Capital Account, n.i.e.: Credit	78ba*d*
–11.0	–14.1	–13.7	–12.2	–21.6	–22.0	–26.8	–24.2	–26.7	–32.6	–33.1	–43.8	–40.5	–39.8	....	Capital Account: Debit	78bb*d*
–2.0	–1.1	–72.8	46.6	–26.2	82.2	13.1	84.0	45.1	61.0	88.3	3.6	–15.1	25.6	....	Financial Account, n.i.e.	78bj*d*
–13.0	.7	–29.2	–1.5	–28.6	–13.1	6.8	–25.8	–28.9	.3	2.8	–9.8	–30.0	–31.3	....	Direct Investment Abroad	78bd*d*
21.7	8.0	16.2	31.6	8.8	91.9	5.2	103.6	91.2	67.5	69.5	2.4	15.6	75.5	....	Dir. Invest. in Rep. Econ., n.i.e.	78be*d*
—	—	—	—	—	—	—	—	—	—	—	—	—	—	....	Portfolio Investment Assets	78bf*d*
—	—	—	—	—	—	—	—	—	—	—	—	—	—	....	Equity Securities	78bk*d*
—	—	—	—	—	—	—	—	—	—	—	—	—	—	....	Debt Securities	78bl*d*
—	—	—	—	—	—	—	—	—	—	—	—	—	—	....	Portfolio Investment Liab., n.i.e.	78bg*d*
—	—	—	—	—	—	—	—	—	—	—	—	—	—	....	Equity Securities	78bm*d*
—	—	—	—	—	—	—	—	—	—	—	—	—	—	....	Debt Securities	78bn*d*
....	....	....	....	—	—	—	—	—	—	—	—	—	—	....	Financial Derivatives Assets	78bw*d*
....	....	....	....	—	—	—	—	—	—	—	—	—	—	....	Financial Derivatives Liabilities	78bx*d*
–47.9	–61.5	45.3	–6.8	–22.3	–18.0	27.2	2.6	–13.5	1.2	12.0	–25.9	–21.1	–69.7	....	Other Investment Assets	78bh*d*
....	....	....	....	—	—	—	—	—	—	—	—	—	—	....	Monetary Authorities	78bo*d*
—	—	—	—	—	—	—	—	—	—	—	—	—	—	....	General Government	78bp*d*
–34.8	–62.4	72.6	–11.2	–22.3	–18.0	27.2	2.6	–13.5	1.2	12.0	–25.9	–21.1	–69.7	....	Banks	78bq*d*
–13.1	.9	–27.3	4.4	—	—	—	—	—	—	—	—	—	—	....	Other Sectors	78br*d*
37.2	51.7	–105.1	23.3	15.9	21.3	–26.0	3.7	–3.8	–8.1	3.9	36.8	20.4	51.0	....	Other Investment Liab., n.i.e.	78bi*d*
—	—	—	—	—	—	—	—	—	—	—	—	—	—	....	Monetary Authorities	78bs*d*
—	.2	–11.2	9.7	—	—	—	—	—	—	—	—	—	—	....	General Government	78bt*d*
36.3	61.1	–80.2	14.3	15.9	21.3	–26.0	3.7	–3.8	–8.1	3.9	36.8	20.4	51.0	....	Banks	78bu*d*
.9	–9.5	–13.7	–.7	—	—	—	—	—	—	—	—	—	—	....	Other Sectors	78bv*d*
–10.6	27.2	12.8	7.1	–9.1	29.2	23.9	–10.6	22.4	30.9	30.4	–9.7	–24.3	–31.5	....	Net Errors and Omissions	78ca*d*
–4.2	29.5	–46.2	112.2	20.6	65.0	39.9	84.6	–13.6	22.5	93.0	78.1	–25.1	4.7	....	*Overall Balance*	78cb*d*
4.2	–29.5	46.2	–112.2	–20.6	–65.0	–39.9	–84.6	13.6	–22.5	–93.0	–78.1	25.1	–4.7	....	Reserves and Related Items	79da*d*
4.8	–21.5	48.4	–109.8	15.5	–34.1	–8.9	–59.3	45.2	10.7	–76.6	–71.1	29.7	–27.0	....	Reserve Assets	79db*d*
–.6	–7.9	–2.1	–2.4	–3.1	–.8	—	—	—	—	—	—	—	—	....	Use of Fund Credit and Loans	79dc*d*
....	....	....	....	–33.0	–30.1	–31.0	–25.3	–31.7	–33.2	–16.4	–7.0	–4.6	22.3	....	Exceptional Financing	79de*d*
Year Ending December 31															**Government Finance**	
–35.4	–70.6	–73.9	–11.9	–54.8	I –54.7	–103.4	–112.1	–158.7	–114.6	–92.7	–211.4	–281.9	–104.3	....	Deficit (-) or Surplus	80
339.7	340.1	336.2	389.8	459.8	I 551.2	576.4	602.5	654.0	697.9	718.9	743.6	803.4	1,141.2	....	Total Revenue and Grants	81y
329.2	330.6	324.8	367.6	447.9	I 542.5	569.1	595.3	649.9	693.4	712.6	736.3	798.5	1,138.6	....	Revenue	81
10.5	9.5	11.4	22.2	11.9	I 8.7	7.3	7.2	4.1	4.5	6.3	7.3	4.9	2.6	....	Grants	81z
375.1	410.6	410.1	401.7	514.7	I 605.9	679.8	714.6	812.7	812.5	811.6	955.0	1,085.3	1,245.5	....	Exp. & Lending Minus Repay.	82z
371.7	383.3	398.2	397.2	477.9	I 596.9	667.3	708.3	799.1	794.4	803.6	945.2	1,081.8	1,231.5	....	Expenditure	82
3.4	27.3	11.9	4.5	36.7	I 9.0	12.5	6.3	13.6	18.1	8.0	9.8	3.5	14.0	....	Lending Minus Repayments	83
35.4	70.6	73.9	11.9	54.8	I 54.7	103.4	112.1	158.7	114.6	92.7	211.4	281.9	104.3	....	Total Financing	80h
33.4	73.7	88.8	29.4	83.7	I 34.3	80.7	100.7	146.9	83.6	71.5	193.9	273.2	93.5	....	Domestic	84a
2.1	–3.2	–14.9	–17.5	–28.9	I 20.4	22.7	11.4	11.8	31.0	21.2	17.5	8.7	10.8	....	Foreign	85a
475.9	546.2	....	....	....	I 775.5	805.0	843.5	923.7	981.8	1,001.8	1,133.5	1,356.3	1,454.9	....	Total Debt by Residence	88
319.0	389.3	498.3	....	....	I 547.1	593.9	638.1	733.3	792.2	807.3	942.8	1,156.1	1,060.6	....	Domestic	88a
157.0	156.9	....	....	....	I 228.4	211.1	205.4	190.4	189.6	194.5	190.7	200.2	394.3	....	Foreign	89a
Millions of Fiji Dollars															**National Accounts**	
583.6	609.0	663.9	894.8	1,099.4	1,231.5	1,164.5	1,205.2	1,311.6	1,498.5	1,522.2	1,772.6	1,727.5	2,094.0	....	Exports of Goods & Services	90c
252.4	252.6	255.1	263.4	303.9	329.3	360.2	418.3	466.4	454.2	458.7	463.4	466.6	565.0	....	Government Consumption	91f
239.1	215.4	229.9	223.1	211.2	303.5	278.3	280.8	331.8	322.5	357.9	320.4	349.8	377.6	....	Gross Fixed Capital Formation	93e
12.2	51.1	4.5	12.6	24.5	35.0	26.0	30.0	38.0	40.0	30.0	40.0	46.0	40.0	....	Increase/Decrease(-) in Stocks	93i
838.1	873.3	959.6	1,166.0	1,273.7	1,442.7	1,581.8	1,683.2	1,802.3	1,901.5	1,986.7	2,058.1	2,141.4	2,261.0	....	Private Consumption	96f
–588.6	–577.0	–616.3	–814.6	–1,058.9	–1,329.7	–1,235.5	–1,264.2	–1,499.0	–1,587.7	–1,629.7	–1,752.5	–1,798.0	–2,163.4	....	Imports of Goods & Services	98c
1,316.5	1,461.7	1,465.2	1,587.6	1,752.8	1,951.9	2,066.3	2,334.8	2,564.9	2,697.2	2,811.5	2,983.5	3,102.4	3,134.2	....	Gross Domestic Product (GDP)	99b
–36.3	–34.3	–47.9	–35.2	–36.3	–41.8	–40.4	–28.3	–32.0	....	....	....	....	....	....	Net Factor Inc/Pmts(-) Abroad	98.n
1,280.2	1,427.4	1,417.3	1,552.6	1,716.5	1,910.1	2,025.9	2,167.2	2,337.2	3,001.0	....	....	....	....	....	Gross National Income (GNI)	99a
1,185.2	1,324.5	1,306.2	1,433.7	1,576.6	1,756.3	1,858.4	1,983.9	....	....	....	....	....	....	....	Net National Income	99e
1,177.7	1,326.1	1,329.2	1,433.3	1,555.3	1,744.3	1,827.0	2,033.8	2,201.6	2,307.3	2,407.1	2,556.6	2,658.4	2,678.6	....	GDP at Factor Cost	99ba
....	....	....	....	....	....	....	....	....	....	....	....	....	....	....	GDP Vol.at Fact.Cost,'68 Prices	99ba*p*
703.7	760.5	711.5	726.8	820.5	....	....	....	....	....	....	....	....	....	....	GDP Vol.at Fact.Cost,'77 Prices	99ba*p*
....	....	....	....	1,555.3	1,611.5	1,568.1	1,640.4	1,707.5	1,794.4	1,838.9	1,897.1	1,864.8	1,840.6	....	GDP Vol.at Fact.Cost,'89 Prices	99ba*p*
72.5	78.4	73.3	74.9	84.6	87.6	85.3	89.2	92.9	97.6	100.0	103.2	101.4	100.1	....	GDP Volume (1995=100)	99bv*p*
67.6	70.4	75.5	79.7	76.6	82.9	89.1	93.4	98.6	98.3	100.0	102.8	108.6	....	....	GDP Deflator (1995=100)	99bi*p*
Midyear Estimates																
.70	.71	.72	.72	I .75	.73	.74	.75	.77	.78	.80	.78	.79	.80	.81	**Population**	99z

(See notes in the back of the book.)

Finland

		1970	1971	1972	1973	1974	1975	1976	1977	1978	1979	1980	1981	1982	1983	1984
Exchange Rates															*Markkaa per SDR through 1998;*	
Official Rate	aa	4.1800	4.5057	4.5383	‡4.6384	4.3477	4.5070	4.3766	4.8807	5.1148	4.8886	4.8976	5.0714	5.8366	6.0828	6.4008
															Markkaa per US Dollar through 1998;	
Official Rate	ae	4.1800	4.1500	4.1800	‡3.8450	3.5510	3.8500	3.7670	4.0180	3.9260	3.7110	3.8400	4.3570	5.2910	5.8100	6.5300
Official Rate	rf	4.2000	4.1844	4.1463	3.8212	3.7738	3.6787	3.8644	4.0294	4.1173	3.8953	3.7301	4.3153	4.8204	5.5701	6.0100
															Markkaa per ECU:	
ECU Rate	ea	....	....	....	....	....	....	....	....		5.3509	5.0289	4.7282	5.1201	4.8072	4.6291
ECU Rate	eb	....	....	....	....	....	....	....	....	5.2453	5.3388	5.1886	4.8229	4.7298	4.9645	....
															Index Numbers (1995=100):	
Official Rate	ahx	104.3	147.6	105.2	114.3	115.7	118.8	112.9	108.4	106.0	112.0	117.0	101.3	91.0	78.4	72.7
Nominal Effective Exchange Rate	neu	127.4	125.0	117.5	115.8	118.8	117.7	120.3	114.1	102.7	102.5	106.2	109.1	110.9	106.0	103.2
Real Effective Exchange Rate	reu	....	....	....	....	....	100.1	106.3	100.6	125.3	123.2	‡126.2	131.7	134.0	128.5	131.3
Fund Position															*Millions of SDRs:*	
Quota	2f.s	190.0	190.0	190.0	190.0	190.0	190.0	190.0	190.0	262.0	262.0	393.0	393.0	393.0	574.9	574.9
SDRs	1b.s	23.3	47.0	67.5	67.8	68.1	66.2	56.1	41.8	61.8	88.1	81.3	124.2	104.3	37.0	145.7
Reserve Position in the Fund	1c.s	66.8	63.8	63.8	63.8	63.8	—	—	—	46.1	44.7	77.4	77.4	77.5	123.0	133.7
of which: Outstg.Fund Borrowing	2c	—	—	—	—	—	—	—	—	—	—	—	—	—	—	—
Total Fund Cred.&Loans Outstg.	2tl	—	—	—	—	—	71.3	186.4	186.4	152.1	66.4	66.4	52.1	14.4	—	—
International Liquidity												*Millions of US Dollars Unless Otherwise Indicated:*					
Total Res.Min.Gold (Eurosys.Def)	1l.d	424.6	623.1	667.6	574.3	595.9	433.2	462.1	531.1	1,222.9	1,540.0	1,870.2	1,483.7	1,517.5	1,237.7	2,754.3
SDRs	1b.d	23.3	51.0	73.2	81.8	83.4	77.5	65.2	50.8	80.4	116.1	103.7	144.6	115.0	38.7	142.8
Reserve Position in the Fund	1c.d	66.7	69.2	69.2	76.9	78.1	—	—	—	60.0	58.9	98.8	90.1	85.5	128.7	131.1
Foreign Exchange	1d.d	334.5	502.9	525.2	415.6	434.4	355.7	396.9	480.3	1,082.4	1,365.1	1,667.7	1,249.0	1,317.0	1,070.3	2,480.4
o/w: Fin.Deriv.Rel.to Reserves	1ddd	....	....	....	....	....	....	....	....	....	....	....	....	....	....	....
Other Reserve Assets	1e.d	....	....	....	....	....	....	....	....	....	....	....	....	....	....	....
Gold (Million Fine Troy Ounces)	1ad	.825	1.396	1.397	.823	.823	.823	.823	.905	.945	.986	.986	1.269	1.270	1.270	1.270
Gold (National Valuation)	1and	28.8	48.8	50.0e	31.0	34.1	31.4	32.1	33.1	43.0	289.1	279.4	317.2	261.2	238.0	211.8
Memo: Euro Cl. on Non-EA Res.	1dgd	....	....	....	....	....	....	....	....	....	....	....	....	....	....	....
Non-Euro Cl. on EA Res.	1dhd	....	....	....	....	....	....	....	....	....	....	....	....	....	....	....
Mon. Auth.: Other Foreign Assets	3..d	6.5	7.0	25.5	92.7	4.6	129.0	125.5	143.1	132.4	45.5	58.7	476.0	306.0	101.3	62.5
Foreign Liabilities	4..d	25.2	77.9	29.6	37.6	128.7	44.6	26.9	349.1	15.4	228.0	255.9	21.9	504.9	356.4	123.9
Banking Insts.: Foreign Assets	7a.d	218	300	418	531	686	593	718	1,136	1,401	2,026	2,762	3,231	4,154	4,777	6,258
Foreign Liab.	7b.d	283	320	354	490	815	1,209	1,332	1,693	1,778	2,788	4,566	4,909	6,293	7,205	9,441
Monetary Authorities												*Millions of Markkaa through 1998;*					
Fgn. Assets (Cl.on Non-EA Ctys)	11	1,932	2,798	3,047	2,710	2,258	2,290	2,339	2,848	5,501	6,970	8,480	9,920	13,263	11,387	20,126
Claims on General Government	12a.u	....	....	....	....	....	....	....	....							
o/w: Claims on Gen.Govt.in Cty	12a	140	167	196	223	300	335	442	391	633	884	1,226	1,236	1,041	2,178	1,951
Claims on Banking Institutions	12e.u	....	....	....	....	....	....	....	....							
o/w: Claims on Bank.Inst.in Cty	12e	1,110	1,137	946	2,792	3,558	4,260	3,845	4,979	2,220	4,229	6,035	3,769	4,542	8,464	6,727
Claims on Other Resident Sectors	12d.u	....	....	....	....	....	....	....	....							
o/w: Cl. on Oth.Res.Sect.in Cty	12d	291	291	328	393	763	1,181	1,586	1,559	1,418	1,698	2,424	3,390	4,386	4,793	5,068
Claims on ECB	12u	....	....	....	....	....	....	....	....	....	....	....	....	....	....	....
Currency in Circulation	14a	1,471	1,629	1,895	2,098	2,462	2,855	2,885	3,167	3,822	4,375	4,954	5,595	6,062	6,574	7,442
Liabilities to Banking Insts	14c.u	....	....	....	....	....	....	....	....							
o/w: Liabs to Bank.Inst.in Cty	14c	5	11	2	2	8	4	4	5	2	1,768	3,318	2,492	3,138	5,041	8,843
Demand Dep. of Other Res.Sect.	14d.u	....	....	....	....	....	....	....	....							
o/w: D.Dep.of Oth.Res.Sect.in Cty	14d	3	2	1	8	1	3	—	—	7	1	1	1	1	2	62
Other Dep. of Other Res.Sect.	15..u	....	....	....	....	....	....	....	....							
o/w: O.Dep.of Oth.Res.Sect.in Cty	15	311	385	688	25	34	118	80	167	89	137	850	1,455	1,426	1,325	2,146
Money Market Instruments	16m.u	....	....	....	....	....	....	....	....	....	....	....	....	....	....	....
o/w: MMI Held by Resid.of Cty	16m	....	....	....	....	....	....	....	....	....	....	....	....	....	....	....
Bonds (Debt Securities)	16n.u	....	....	....	....	....	....	....	....	....	....	....	....	....	....	....
o/w: Bonds Held by Resid.of Cty	16n	....	....	....	....	....	....	....	....	....	....	....	....	....	....	....
Foreign Liab. (to Non-EA Ctys)	16c	106	327	122	147	457	493	917	2,312	838	1,171	1,308	359	2,755	2,071	809
Central Government Deposits	16d.u	....	....	....	....	....	....	....	....							
o/w: Cent.Govt.Dep. in Cty	16d	323	291	189	1,985	1,598	408	62	368	1,153	2,069	2,491	2,178	1,701	3,001	4,277
Liabilities to ECB	16u	....	....	....	....	....	....	....	....	....	....	....	....	....	....	....
Capital Accounts	17a	689	806	932	972	1,021	1,896	1,992	2,136	2,259	2,469	2,408	4,476	4,865	5,237	6,955
Other Items (Net)	17r	567	942	690	883	1,298	2,291	2,272	1,622	1,602	1,789	2,836	1,757	3,284	3,572	3,338
Banking Institutions												*Millions of Markkaa through 1998;*					
Claims on Monetary Authorities	20	216	165	366	335	319	351	345	342	342	486	3,971	3,263	4,028	5,985	10,415
Claims on Bk.Inst.in Oth.EA Ctys	20b.u	....	....	....	....	....	....	....	....							
Fgn. Assets (Cl.on Non-EA Ctys)	21	916	1,261	1,714	2,072	2,436	2,282	2,706	4,565	5,502	7,519	10,605	14,077	21,979	27,754	40,865
Claims on General Government	22a.u	....	....	....	....	....	....	....	....							
o/w: Claims on Gen.Govt.in Cty	22a	781	634	568	494	242	461	127	148	392	347	1,110	976	1,958	3,485	3,662
Claims on Other Resident Sectors	22d.u	....	....	....	....	....	....	....	....							
o/w: Cl. on Oth.Res.Sect.in Cty	22d	19,176	22,077	25,299	31,382	39,167	47,208	52,392	59,229	65,222	76,418	90,309	103,913	123,875	146,111	170,515
Demand Deposits	24..u	....	....	....	....	....	....	....	....							
o/w: D.Dep.of Oth.Res.Sect.in Cty	24	2,156	2,547	3,413	4,325	5,116	7,261	7,057	7,029	8,006	10,178	10,673	12,361	14,746	15,798	19,007
Other Deposits	25..u	....	....	....	....	....	....	....	....							
o/w: O.Dep.of Oth.Res.Sect.in Cty	25	15,728	17,846	20,712	23,555	27,601	32,854	37,010	42,068	48,388	56,524	65,600	75,758	85,719	98,611	113,168
Money Market Instruments	26m.u	....	....	....	....	....	....	....	....	....	....	....	....	....	....	....
o/w: MMI Held by Resid.of Cty	26m	....	....	....	....	....	....	....	....	....	....	....	....	....	....	....
Bonds (Debt Securities)	26n.u	....	....	....	....	....	....	....	....	....	....	....	....	....	....	....
o/w: Bonds Held by Resid.of Cty	26n	....	....	....	....	....	....	....	....	....	....	....	....	....	....	....
Foreign Liab. (to Non-EA Ctys)	26c	1,190	1,344	1,451	1,909	2,893	4,654	5,017	6,802	6,980	10,345	17,533	21,389	33,295	41,861	61,652
Central Government Deposits	26d.u	....	....	....	....	....	....	....	....							
o/w: Cent.Govt.Dep. in Cty	26d	970	1,207	1,543	2,170	2,633	1,766	2,663	2,618	4,315	3,371	3,420	4,769	6,193	5,959	6,820
Credit from Monetary Authorities	26g	1,111	1,138	941	2,757	3,508	3,911	4,912	4,894	2,256	3,356	6,044	3,722	4,493	8,432	6,670
Liab. to Bk.Inst.in Oth. EA Ctys	26h.u	....	....	....	....	....	....	....	....							
Capital Accounts	27a	988	1,146	1,303	1,786	1,638	1,880	1,934	1,969	2,095	2,428	2,872	3,012	3,936	4,873	6,669
Other Items (Net)	27r	−1,055	−1,089	−1,417	−2,219	−1,225	−2,026	−3,024	−1,097	−584	−1,432	−148	1,216	3,457	7,801	11,471

1985	1986	1987	1988	1989	1990	1991	1992	1993	1994	1995	1996	1997	1998	1999		
Euros per SDR Thereafter: End of Period															**Exchange Rates**	
5.9501	5.8640	5.5980	5.6102	5.3342	5.1699	5.9120	7.2119	7.9454	6.9244	6.4790	6.6777	7.3139	7.1753	1.3662	Official Rate	**aa**
Euros per US Dollar Thereafter: End of Period (ae) Period Average (rf)																
5.4170	4.7940	3.9460	4.1690	4.0590	3.6340	4.1330	5.2450	5.7845	4.7432	4.3586	4.6439	5.4207	5.0960	.9954	Official Rate	**ae**
6.1979	5.0695	4.3956	4.1828	4.2912	3.8235	4.0440	4.4794	5.7123	5.2235	4.3667	4.5936	5.1914	5.3441	.9386	Official Rate	**rf**
End of Period (ea) Period Average (eb)																
4.8098	5.1315	5.1432	4.8886	4.8586	4.9542	5.5419	6.3512	6.4785	5.8343	5.7282	5.8188	5.9856	5.9458	....	ECU Rate	**ea**
4.7240	4.9742	5.0739	4.9520	4.7307	4.8673	5.0166	5.8090	6.6963	6.2084	5.7122	5.8245	5.8874	5.9855	....	ECU Rate	**eb**
Period Averages																
70.8	86.1	99.4	104.0	101.8	114.3	108.2	97.8	76.4	83.9	100.0	95.0	84.1	81.7	....	Official Rate	**ahx**
108.8	106.9	107.9	109.2	113.6	114.6	110.3	96.1	84.1	90.8	100.0	96.6	94.2	93.4	91.8	Nominal Effective Exchange Rate	**neu**
130.6	126.2	124.5	127.9	132.3	134.0	123.2	100.4	85.2	89.7	100.0	93.8	89.3	89.2	....	Real Effective Exchange Rate	**reu**
End of Period															**Fund Position**	
574.9	574.9	574.9	574.9	574.9	574.9	574.9	861.8	861.8	861.8	861.8	861.8	861.8	861.8	1,263.8	Quota	**2f.s**
156.4	167.3	160.5	199.8	182.0	152.5	157.7	78.4	83.8	222.7	241.6	201.6	241.7	247.5	211.3	SDRs	**1b.s**
130.3	135.0	141.6	167.6	178.9	151.0	192.3	241.0	220.4	196.1	259.5	292.8	414.2	595.0	464.3	Reserve Position in the Fund	**1c.s**
—	—	—	—	—	—	—	—	—	—	—	—	—	31.3	—	*of which:* Outstg.Fund Borrowing	**2c**
—	—	—	—	—	—	—	—	—	—	—	—	—	—	—	Total Fund Cred.&Loans Outstg.	**2tl**
End of Period															**International Liquidity**	
3,749.9	1,787.1	6,417.5	6,369.2	5,111.2	9,644.1	7,608.7	5,213.4	5,410.8	10,662.0	10,038.3	6,916.3	8,416.6	9,694.5	I 8,207.3	Total Res.Min.Gold (Eurosys.Def)	**1l.d**
171.8	204.6	227.7	268.9	239.2	216.9	225.6	107.8	115.1	325.1	359.2	289.9	326.1	348.5	290.1	SDRs	**1b.d**
143.1	165.2	200.8	225.6	235.0	214.8	275.1	331.3	302.7	286.3	385.8	421.1	558.8	837.8	637.3	Reserve Position in the Fund	**1c.d**
3,435.0	1,417.4	5,989.0	5,874.7	4,636.9	9,212.4	7,108.0	4,774.3	4,993.0	10,050.6	9,293.4	6,205.3	7,531.7	8,508.2	6,747.0	Foreign Exchange	**1d.d**
....	....	....	....	....	....	....	....	....	....	....	....	....	....	—	*o/w:* Fin.Deriv.Rel.to Reserves	**1ddd**
....	....	....	....	....	....	....	....	....	....	....	....	....	....	533	Other Reserve Assets	**1e.d**
1.912	1.912	1.955	1.955	2.002	2.002	2.002	2.002	2.002	2.003	1.600	1.600	1.600	2.002	1.577	Gold (Million Fine Troy Ounces)	**1ad**
384.2	434.1	539.3	510.4	537.1	599.9	527.5	415.6	376.9	459.6	399.7	375.1	321.4	427.8	459.0	Gold (National Valuation)	**1and**
....	....	....	....	....	....	....	....	....	....	....	....	....	....	2,686	Memo: Euro Cl. on Non-EA Res.	**1dgd**
....	....	....	....	....	....	....	....	....	....	....	....	....	....	682	Non-Euro Cl. on EA Res.	**1dhd**
47.2	716.6	325.4	257.4	22.7	20.6	8.2	....	....	....	....	....	....	....	I —	Mon. Auth.: Other Foreign Assets	**3..d**
106.3	6.4	34.1	59.3	171.8	270.6	11.2	452.7	33.4	27.5	278.6	201.2	107.8	143.9	I 437.0	Foreign Liabilities	**4..d**
7,671	14,310	18,825	20,542	22,242	27,000	24,272	21,499	21,608	22,295	24,169	26,986	21,364	21,845	I 15,715	Banking Insts.: Foreign Assets	**7a.d**
12,812	20,531	32,917	37,756	42,581	59,906	53,452	40,169	31,854	30,679	29,269	25,884	17,916	19,991	I 9,370	Foreign Liab.	**7b.d**
Millions of Euros Beginning 1999: End of Period															**Monetary Authorities**	
22,651	14,084	30,668	31,759	24,216	37,678	34,095	29,928	33,478	52,752	48,916	36,461	51,505	51,999	10,926	Fgn. Assets (Cl.on Non-EA Ctys)	**11**
....	....	....	....	....	....	....	....	....	....	....	....	....	....	91	Claims on General Government	**12a.u**
1,023	1,002	977	1,039	1,137	1,314	1,376	2,447	1,788	1,806	1,882	1,907	2,015	2,074	—	*o/w:* Claims on Gen.Govt.in Cty	**12a**
....	....	....	....	....	....	....	....	....	....	....	....	....	....	3,866	Claims on Banking Institutions	**12e.u**
7,596	13,314	3,639	12,095	36,542	13,075	15,648	11,547	7,575	1,718	8,415	13,301	2,837	19	1,513	*o/w:* Claims on Bank.Inst.in Cty	**12e**
....	....	....	....	....	....	....	....	....	....	....	....	....	....	535	Claims on Other Resident Sectors	**12d.u**
5,143	5,479	5,188	5,204	4,681	3,793	3,054	2,921	4,404	3,951	3,302	2,462	1,877	1,541	234	*o/w:* Cl. on Oth.Res.Sect.in Cty	**12d**
....	....	....	....	....	....	....	....	....	....	....	....	....	....	699	Claims on ECB	**12u**
8,072	8,667	9,990	11,550	13,129	14,555	14,528	14,508	14,994	14,315	15,611	16,891	17,817	17,689	3,350	Currency in Circulation	**14a**
....	....	....	....	....	....	....	....	....	....	....	....	....	....	8,238	Liabilities to Banking Insts	**14c.u**
10,222	9,270	16,668	20,170	26,037	17,819	21,447	23,295	23,037	43,148	42,766	22,359	18,412	17,888	4,884	*o/w:* Liabs to Bank.Inst.in Cty	**14c**
....	....	....	....	....	....	....	....	....	....	....	....	....	....	—	Demand Dep. of Other Res.Sect.	**14d.u**
67	56	36	31	38	36	—	—	—	—	—	—	—	—	—	*o/w:* D.Dep.of Oth.Res.Sect.in Cty	**14d**
....	....	....	....	....	....	....	....	....	....	....	....	....	....	1	Other Dep. of Other Res.Sect.	**15..u**
3,863	4,690	4,831	6,497	10,228	9,925	7,057	3,362	2,087	1,549	994	574	32	6	1	*o/w:* O.Dep.of Oth.Res.Sect.in Cty	**15**
....	....	....	....	....	....	....	....	....	....	....	....	....	....	—	Money Market Instruments	**16m.u**
....	....	....	....	....	....	....	....	....	....	....	....	....	....	....	*o/w:* MMI Held by Resid.of Cty	**16m**
....	....	....	....	....	....	....	....	....	....	....	....	....	....	—	Bonds (Debt Securities)	**16n.u**
....	....	....	....	....	....	....	....	....	....	....	....	....	....	....	*o/w:* Bonds Held by Resid.of Cty	**16n**
576	31	135	247	697	983	46	2,375	193	130	1,214	934	584	733	435	Foreign Liab. (to Non-EA Ctys)	**16c**
....	....	....	....	....	....	....	....	....	....	....	....	....	....	—	Central Government Deposits	**16d.u**
4,301	2,001	901	1,903	5,324	1,321	4	90	784	93	75	—	—	—	—	*o/w:* Cent.Govt.Dep. in Cty	**16d**
....	....	....	....	....	....	....	....	....	....	....	....	....	....	—	Liabilities to ECB	**16u**
7,013	6,723	6,728	6,288	6,594	6,904	6,607	6,790	6,895	6,749	6,691	6,716	6,810	6,785	4,552	Capital Accounts	**17a**
2,300	2,442	1,183	3,412	4,529	4,317	4,483	–3,577	–745	–5,756	–4,836	6,658	14,579	12,533	–459	Other Items (Net)	**17r**
Millions of Euros Beginning 1999: End of Period															**Banking Institutions**	
12,159	11,592	18,642	23,990	29,863	22,400	27,162	29,983	27,638	46,653	45,976	25,604	21,711	20,774	4,884	Claims on Monetary Authorities	**20**
....	....	....	....	....	....	....	....	....	....	....	....	....	....	5,775	Claims on Bk.Inst.in Oth.EA Ctys	**20b.u**
41,553	68,603	74,283	85,641	90,280	98,117	100,316	112,765	124,993	105,751	105,344	125,320	115,806	111,320	15,643	Fgn. Assets (Cl.on Non-EA Ctys)	**21**
....	....	....	....	....	....	....	....	....	....	....	....	....	....	8,690	Claims on General Government	**22a.u**
2,050	2,624	2,662	2,487	2,205	1,993	I 3,426	7,568	11,117	15,630	37,442	30,796	37,738	41,067	7,792	*o/w:* Claims on Gen.Govt.in Cty	**22a**
....	....	....	....	....	....	....	....	....	....	....	....	....	....	65,481	Claims on Other Resident Sectors	**22d.u**
203,221	231,015	271,469	348,149	402,750	449,853	467,798	437,016	398,932	360,408	350,038	347,768	337,266	358,798	64,975	*o/w:* Cl. on Oth.Res.Sect.in Cty	**22d**
....	....	....	....	....	....	....	....	....	....	....	....	....	....	38,335	Demand Deposits	**24..u**
21,483	21,425	23,047	27,472	32,634	34,837	I 121,832	125,425	131,365	143,547	163,521	191,188	201,557	211,632	38,277	*o/w:* D.Dep.of Oth.Res.Sect.in Cty	**24**
....	....	....	....	....	....	....	....	....	....	....	....	....	....	22,246	Other Deposits	**25..u**
134,052	146,223	165,112	204,011	218,087	228,976	I 158,200	154,861	153,618	145,670	142,710	104,963	102,154	103,542	22,209	*o/w:* O.Dep.of Oth.Res.Sect.in Cty	**25**
....	....	....	....	....	....	....	....	....	....	....	....	....	....	19,086	Money Market Instruments	**26m.u**
....	....	....	....	....	....	....	....	....	....	....	....	....	....	....	*o/w:* MMI Held by Resid.of Cty	**26m**
....	....	....	....	....	....	....	....	....	....	....	....	....	....	6,227	Bonds (Debt Securities)	**26n.u**
....	....	....	....	....	....	....	....	....	....	....	....	....	....	....	*o/w:* Bonds Held by Resid.of Cty	**26n**
69,401	98,424	129,890	157,404	172,837	217,697	220,917	210,685	184,260	145,519	127,572	120,204	97,118	101,876	9,327	Foreign Liab. (to Non-EA Ctys)	**26c**
....	....	....	....	....	....	....	....	....	....	....	....	....	....	2,553	Central Government Deposits	**26d.u**
7,467	15,510	17,715	17,068	16,884	21,058	11,314	9,843	10,174	11,250	19,057	19,881	27,569	17,951	2,552	*o/w:* Cent.Govt.Dep. in Cty	**26d**
7,572	13,140	2,843	10,844	36,011	12,419	I 15,648	13,132	7,576	1,718	8,415	13,301	2,837	19	1,514	Credit from Monetary Authorities	**26g**
....	....	....	....	....	....	....	....	....	....	....	....	....	....	3,153	Liab. to Bk.Inst.in Oth. EA Ctys	**26h.u**
7,488	9,175	10,618	14,842	20,404	38,623	49,103	38,497	38,496	31,789	31,579	29,799	34,003	34,113	6,763	Capital Accounts	**27a**
11,519	9,936	17,832	28,626	28,242	18,754	I 21,689	34,890	37,190	48,948	45,947	50,152	47,285	62,826	–8,733	Other Items (Net)	**27r**

Finland

	1970	1971	1972	1973	1974	1975	1976	1977	1978	1979	1980	1981	1982	1983	1984
Banking Survey (Nat'l Residency)													*Millions of Markkaa through 1998;*		
Foreign Assets (Net) **31n**	1,552	2,388	3,188	2,727	1,345	−575	−889	−1,702	3,184	2,973	244	2,248	−809	−4,790	−1,471
Domestic Credit **32**	19,096	21,672	24,659	28,337	36,241	47,011	51,821	58,341	62,197	73,906	89,158	102,567	123,365	147,606	170,100
Claims on General Govt. (Net) **32an**	−372	−696	−969	−3,438	−3,689	−1,378	−2,156	−2,447	−4,443	−4,209	−3,575	−4,736	−4,896	−3,297	−5,483
Claims on Other Resident Sectors **32d**	19,468	22,368	25,628	31,775	39,930	48,389	53,978	60,788	66,640	78,115	92,733	107,303	128,261	150,903	175,583
Currency in Circulation **34a.**n	1,471	1,629	1,895	2,098	2,462	2,855	2,885	3,167	3,822	4,375	4,954	5,595	6,062	6,574	7,442
Demand Deposits **34b.**n	2,159	2,549	3,413	4,333	5,117	7,264	7,057	7,029	8,013	10,179	10,674	12,362	14,747	15,799	19,069
Other Deposits .... **35..**n	16,039	18,231	21,400	23,579	27,635	32,972	37,089	42,235	48,477	56,661	66,451	77,213	87,146	99,936	115,313
Money Market Instruments **36m**	....	....	....	....	....	....	....	....	....	....	....	....	....	....	....
Bonds (Debt Securities) **36n**	....	....	....	....	....	....	....	....	....	....	....	....	....	....	....
o/w: Bonds Over Two Years **36na**	....	....	....	....	....	....	....	....	....	....	....	....	....	....	....
Capital Accounts **37a**	1,677	1,952	2,235	2,758	2,659	3,776	3,926	4,105	4,354	4,897	5,279	7,489	8,801	10,111	13,624
Other Items (Net) **37r**	−698	−300	−1,097	−1,704	−287	−430	−25	102	715	767	2,044	2,156	5,801	10,397	13,181
Money plus Quasi-Money **35l**	19,484	22,256	26,359	29,694	34,902	42,744	46,690	52,107	59,973	70,748	81,429	94,400	107,063	121,363	140,259
Banking Survey (EA-Wide Residency)													*Millions of Euros:*		
Foreign Assets (Net) **31n.**u	....	....	....	....	....	....	....	....	....	....	....	....	....	....	....
Domestic Credit **32.**u	....	....	....	....	....	....	....	....	....	....	....	....	....	....	....
Claims on General Govt. (Net) **32an**u	....	....	....	....	....	....	....	....	....	....	....	....	....	....	....
Claims on Other Resident Sect. **32d.**u	....	....	....	....	....	....	....	....	....	....	....	....	....	....	....
Currency in Circulation **34a.**u	....	....	....	....	....	....	....	....	....	....	....	....	....	....	....
Demand Deposits **34b.**u	....	....	....	....	....	....	....	....	....	....	....	....	....	....	....
Other Deposits .... **35..**u	....	....	....	....	....	....	....	....	....	....	....	....	....	....	....
o/w: Other Dep. Over Two Yrs **35ab**u	....	....	....	....	....	....	....	....	....	....	....	....	....	....	....
Money Market Instruments **36m.**u	....	....	....	....	....	....	....	....	....	....	....	....	....	....	....
Bonds (Debt Securities) **36n.**u	....	....	....	....	....	....	....	....	....	....	....	....	....	....	....
o/w: Bonds Over Two Years **36na**u	....	....	....	....	....	....	....	....	....	....	....	....	....	....	....
Capital Accounts **37a**	....	....	....	....	....	....	....	....	....	....	....	....	....	....	....
Other Items (Net) **37r.**u	....	....	....	....	....	....	....	....	....	....	....	....	....	....	....
Liquid Liabilities **55l**	20,058	22,898	27,079	30,499	35,823	43,838	47,955	53,458	61,318	71,849	82,503	95,428	108,096	122,453	141,388
Interest Rates													*Percent Per Annum*		
Discount Rate *(End of Period)* **60**	7.00	8.50	7.75	9.25	9.25	9.25	9.25	8.25	7.25	8.50	9.25	9.25	8.50	9.50	9.50
Money Market Rate **60b**	....	....	....	....	....	....	....	....	....	11.75	9.26	12.35	11.46	11.66	14.67	16.50
Deposit Rate **60l**	....	....	....	....	....	....	....	....	....	....	....	9.00	8.56	8.75	9.25
Lending Rate **60p**	....	....	....	....	....	....	....	8.85	8.22	8.03	9.77	9.84	9.32	9.56	10.49
Government Bond Yield **61**	....	....	....	....	....	....	....	....	....	....	....	....	....	....	....
Prices, Production, Labor													*Index Numbers (1995=100):*		
Industrial Share Prices........................ **62**	4.1	4.6	6.1	9.5	9.2	8.3	7.4	6.1	5.9	7.2	7.7	7.9	10.6	16.1	22.6
Prices: Domestic Supply........................... **63**	20.4	21.4	23.2	27.3	33.9	Ⅰ38.5	41.7	45.9	48.5	53.2	Ⅰ61.9	69.8	74.8	79.0	83.2
Producer, Manufacturing........... **63ey**	19.7	20.7	21.9	26.5	33.3	Ⅰ38.2	40.8	44.6	46.7	51.2	Ⅰ59.4	64.5	71.2	74.8	79.0
Consumer Prices **64**	16.1	17.2	Ⅰ18.4	20.4	23.8	28.1	32.1	Ⅰ36.2	39.0	41.9	46.8	Ⅰ52.4	57.4	62.2	66.6
Harmonized CPI **64h**	....	....	....	....	....	....	....	....	....	....	....	....	....	....	....
Wages: Hourly Earnings **65ey**	9.7	11.1	12.7	14.8	17.7	Ⅰ21.2	24.7	27.1	29.1	32.2	36.2	40.9	45.3	49.7	54.2
Industrial Production .... **66..**c	42.0	42.6	47.8	51.2	53.6	51.6	52.1	52.4	55.1	60.9	Ⅰ65.9	67.7	68.2	70.4	73.7
Industrial Employment........................ **67ey** c	....	....	....	....	....	....	131.8	130.4	126.8	131.7	137.4	139.4	135.3	132.7	131.4
													Number in Thousands:		
Labor Force................................. **67d**	....	....	....	....	....	....	....	....	....	....	....	....	....	....	....
Employment **67e**	....	....	....	....	....	....	....	....	....	....	....	....	....	....	....
Unemployment **67c**	....	....	....	....	....	....	....	....	....	....	....	....	....	....	....
Unemployment Rate (%)................... **67r**	....	....	....	....	....	....	....	....	....	....	....	....	....	....	....
International Transactions													*Millions of Markkaa through 1998*		
Exports **70**	9,687	9,898	12,082	14,609	20,687	20,246	24,506	30,931	35,206	43,430	52,804	60,308	63,026	69,751	80,923
Newsprint **70ul**	631	647	751	816	1,114	993	1,089	1,201	1,679	2,200	2,419	2,972	2,761	2,967	3,519
Imports, c.i.f............................... **71**	11,078	11,739	13,126	16,548	25,676	28,011	28,555	30,707	32,338	44,221	58,247	61,269	64,751	71,519	74,685
													1995=100		
Volume of Exports............................ **72**	Ⅰ34	33	38	41	41	34	40	Ⅰ44	47	51	56	58	56	58	65
Newsprint **72ul**	108	107	120	121	104	71	79	77	102	127	131	141	122	134	153
Volume of Imports............................ **73**	Ⅰ51	50	52	59	64	64	61	Ⅰ56	53	63	71	67	67	69	70
Unit Value of Exports **74**	Ⅰ16	17	18	20	29	34	35	Ⅰ40	43	48	54	60	64	68	72
Newsprint **74ul**	18	19	20	21	34	44	43	49	52	54	58	66	71	69	72
Unit Value of Imports **75**	Ⅰ17	19	20	22	32	34	37	Ⅰ43	47	55	64	71	75	80	83
Import Prices **76.x**	23	24	26	31	39	Ⅰ42	44	49	55	63	73	82	Ⅰ85	90	95

1985	1986	1987	1988	1989	1990	1991	1992	1993	1994	1995	1996	1997	1998	1999	
Millions of Euros Beginning 1999: End of Period															**Banking Survey (Nat'l Residency)**
−5,773	−15,768	−25,074	−40,251	−59,038	−82,886	−86,552	−70,367	−25,982	12,854	25,474	40,643	69,609	60,710	20,914	Foreign Assets (Net) **31n**
199,670	222,610	261,680	337,909	388,565	434,574	I464,336	440,018	405,283	370,451	373,532	363,052	351,327	385,529	70,449	Domestic Credit **32**
−8,694	−13,884	−14,977	−15,445	−18,867	−19,072	I−6,516	81	1,947	6,092	20,192	12,821	12,184	25,190	5,240	Claims on General Govt. (Net).......... **32an**
208,364	236,494	276,657	353,353	407,431	453,646	470,852	439,937	403,335	364,359	353,340	350,231	339,143	360,339	65,209	Claims on Other Resident Sectors **32d**
8,072	8,667	9,990	11,550	13,129	14,555	14,528	14,508	14,994	14,315	15,611	16,891	17,817	17,689	3,350	Currency in Circulation **34a.**n
21,550	21,481	23,083	27,503	32,672	34,873	121,832	125,425	131,365	143,547	163,521	191,188	201,557	211,632	38,277	Demand Deposits **34b.**n
137,915	150,913	169,942	210,508	228,315	238,901	165,257	158,223	155,705	147,218	143,704	105,537	102,186	103,548	22,210	Other Deposits .... **35..**n
....	....	....	....	....	....	....	....	....	....	....	....	....	....	19,086	Money Market Instruments **36m**
														6,227	Bonds (Debt Securities)........ **36n**
														4,985	*o/w:* Bonds Over Two Years........ **36na**
14,501	15,898	17,345	21,130	26,997	45,527	55,709	45,287	45,391	38,538	38,270	36,514	40,813	40,897	11,315	Capital Accounts **37a**
11,859	9,882	16,245	26,967	28,413	17,833	20,457	26,209	31,846	39,688	37,901	53,564	58,563	72,473	−9,104	Other Items (Net) **37r**
165,608	178,751	200,284	246,429	269,758	283,330	I295,902	293,052	297,464	301,576	319,626	310,371	318,260	329,983	....	Money plus Quasi-Money **35l**
End of Period															**Banking Survey (EA-Wide Residency)**
....	....	....	....	....	....	....	....	....	....	....	....	....	....	16,807	Foreign Assets (Net) **31n.**u
....	....	....	....	....	....	....	....	....	....	....	....	....	....	72,244	Domestic Credit .... **32..**u
....	....	....	....	....	....	....	....	....	....	....	....	....	....	6,228	Claims on General Govt. (Net) **32an**u
....	....	....	....	....	....	....	....	....	....	....	....	....	....	66,016	Claims on Other Resident Sect. **32d.**u
....	....	....	....	....	....	....	....	....	....	....	....	....	....	3,350	Currency in Circulation **34a.**u
....	....	....	....	....	....	....	....	....	....	....	....	....	....	38,335	Demand Deposits **34b.**u
....	....	....	....	....	....	....	....	....	....	....	....	....	....	22,247	Other Deposits .... **35..**u
....	....	....	....	....	....	....	....	....	....	....	....	....	....	2,088	*o/w:* Other Dep. Over Two Yrs........ **35ab**u
....	....	....	....	....	....	....	....	....	....	....	....	....	....	19,086	Money Market Instruments **36m.**u
....	....	....	....	....	....	....	....	....	....	....	....	....	....	6,227	Bonds (Debt Securities) **36n.**u
....	....	....	....	....	....	....	....	....	....	....	....	....	....	4,985	*o/w:* Bonds Over Two Years............ **36na**u
....	....	....	....	....	....	....	....	....	....	....	....	....	....	11,315	Capital Accounts **37a**
....	....	....	....	....	....	....	....	....	....	....	....	....	....	−11,511	Other Items (Net) **37r.**u
166,752	179,907	201,436	247,681	271,105	284,690	I297,849	295,786	300,560	303,261	320,845	311,794	319,857	331,750	....	Liquid Liabilities **551**
Percent Per Annum															**Interest Rates**
9.00	7.00	7.00	8.00	8.50	8.50	8.50	9.50	5.50	5.25	4.88	4.00	4.00	3.50	....	Discount Rate *(End of Period)*........ **60**
13.46	11.90	10.03	9.97	12.56	14.00	13.08	13.25	7.77	5.35	5.75	3.63	3.23	3.57	2.97	Money Market Rate **60b**
8.75	7.33	7.00	7.75	5.75	7.50	7.50	7.50	4.75	3.27	3.19	2.35	2.00	1.22		Deposit Rate **60l**
10.41	9.08	8.91	9.72	10.31	11.62	11.80	12.14	9.92	7.91	7.75	6.16	5.29	5.35	4.71	Lending Rate **60p**
....	....	....	....	....	....	....	....	8.8	9.0	8.8	....	....	....	4.7	Government Bond Yield **61**
Period Averages															**Prices, Production, Labor**
19.4	29.7	I46.9	62.3	66.6	50.2	36.7	34.6	58.4	90.2	100.0	88.3	117.2	165.8	285.5	Industrial Share Prices **62**
86.9	82.4	83.2	86.5	I90.9	93.9	94.2	95.2	I98.0	99.3	100.0	99.1	100.6	99.2	99.1	Prices: Domestic Supply **63**
82.3	78.8	79.4	83.0	I87.9	89.8	89.6	91.9	95.2	96.7	100.0	100.1	....	....	....	Producer, Manufacturing **63ey**
I70.5	72.6	75.5	79.4	84.6	89.8	93.5	95.9	98.0	99.0	I100.0	100.6	101.8	103.2	104.4	Consumer Prices **64**
										100.0	101.1	102.3	103.7	105.0	Harmonized CPI **64h**
I58.3	61.9	I66.2	71.6	78.1	I85.8	....	93.0	93.7	95.5	100.0	103.9	....	....	....	Wages: Hourly Earnings **65ey**
76.5	77.7	81.7	84.6	87.4	I87.3	79.9	80.3	84.3	93.8	100.0	103.6	114.1	122.1	....	Industrial Production .... **66..** c
130.7	129.0	124.7	121.2	123.0	121.7	110.0	99.2	92.9	93.3	100.0	100.5	101.4	104.0	106.8	Industrial Employment .... **67ey** c
Period Averages															
....	....	....	....	....	....	....	....	2,507	....	2,521	2,531	2,560	2,532	....	Labor Force **67d**
2,466	2,458	2,452	2,458	2,531	2,525	2,402	2,233	I2,099	2,080	2,128	2,158	I2,194	2,247	2,296	Employment **67e**
129	138	130	116	89	88	193	328	444	456	430	408	I315	285	261	Unemployment **67c**
5.0	5.4	5.0	4.5	3.4	3.4	7.5	13.0	17.9	18.4	17.2	16.3	I12.6	11.4	10.2	Unemployment Rate (%) **67r**
Millions of Euros Beginning 1999															**International Transactions**
83,976	82,699	87,706	90,901	99,854	101,380	93,088	107,471	133,962	153,690	172,380	176,592	204,202	229,233	I38,212	Exports **70**
3,685	3,350	3,250	3,053	2,687	2,917	2,875	2,656	2,955	2,915	3,187	3,342	3,169	3,205	I593	Newsprint **70ul**
81,350	77,631	85,799	88,555	104,782	103,066	87,821	94,984	103,162	119,897	122,428	134,422	154,681	172,315	I28,858	Imports, c.i.f. **71**
1995=100															
64	65	66	68	67	70	64	69	82	93	100	106	118	....	....	Volume of Exports **72**
150	134	132	110	99	110	106	105	114	115	100	93	107	110	112	Newsprint **72ul**
74	78	84	92	102	98	82	79	77	93	100	108	117	....	....	Volume of Imports **73**
74	73	74	78	84	83	83	88	92	94	100	100	102	....	....	Unit Value of Exports **74**
77	78	78	87	85	83	85	80	82	79	100	113	93	92	....	Newsprint **74ul**
86	77	76	78	80	82	83	92	104	101	100	102	105	....	....	Unit Value of Imports **75**
97	82	81	80	I84	84	85	91	100	100	100	102	....	....	....	Import Prices **76.x**

Finland

		1970	1971	1972	1973	1974	1975	1976	1977	1978	1979	1980	1981	1982	1983	1984
Balance of Payments															*Millions of US Dollars:*	
Current Account, n.i.e.	78ald	....	....	....	....	....	−2,140	−1,114	−99	680	−163	−1,403	−478	−923	−1,124	−21
Goods: Exports f.o.b.	78aa d	....	....	....	....	....	5,508	6,295	7,609	8,504	11,100	14,070	13,662	12,842	12,172	13,087
Goods: Imports f.o.b.	78ab d	....	....	....	....	....	−7,241	−6,978	−7,182	−7,427	−10,755	−14,752	−13,307	−12,641	−12,025	−11,607
Trade Balance	78ac d	....	....	....	....	....	−1,733	−684	427	1,077	345	−683	354	201	147	1,480
Services: Credit	78ad d	....	....	....	....	....	1,100	1,253	1,455	1,861	2,249	2,733	2,915	2,723	2,532	2,438
Services: Debit	78ae d	....	....	....	....	....	−1,103	−1,208	−1,376	−1,614	−2,009	−2,555	−2,603	−2,523	−2,515	−2,672
Balance on Goods & Services	78af d	....	....	....	....	....	−1,736	−639	506	1,324	584	−505	666	401	164	1,245
Income: Credit	78ag d	....	....	....	....	....	134	132	147	225	368	530	683	571	520	872
Income: Debit	78ah d	....	....	....	....	....	−504	−566	−709	−823	−1,011	−1,313	−1,716	−1,766	−1,670	−1,967
Balance on Gds, Serv. & Inc.	78ai d	....	....	....	....	....	−2,107	−1,073	−55	726	−59	−1,288	−367	−794	−986	150
Current Transfers, n.i.e.: Credit	78aj d	....	....	....	....	....	28	28	29	37	50	68	90	86	78	84
Current Transfers: Debit	78ak d	....	....	....	....	....	−61	−69	−73	−83	−154	−182	−201	−216	−216	−255
Capital Account, n.i.e.	78bc d	....	....	....	....	....	−2	−3	−6	−6	−6	−7	−5	−6	−5	−4
Capital Account, n.i.e.: Credit	78ba d	....	....	....	....	....	—	—	—	—	—	—	—	—	—	—
Capital Account: Debit	78bb d	....	....	....	....	....	−2	−3	−6	−6	−6	−7	−5	−6	−5	−4
Financial Account, n.i.e.	78bj d	....	....	....	....	....	2,166	725	498	−54	638	1,515	120	1,130	814	2,344
Direct Investment Abroad	78bd d	....	....	....	....	....	−26	−31	−72	−63	−125	−137	−129	−78	−139	−492
Dir. Invest. in Rep. Econ., n.i.e.	78be d	....	....	....	....	....	68	58	48	34	28	28	100	1	84	136
Portfolio Investment Assets	78bf d	....	....	....	....	....	—	—	—	—	−13	−120	13	−3	−31	−66
Equity Securities	78bk d	....	....	....	....	....	—	—	—	—	—	−1	−1	−1	—	−13
Debt Securities	78bl d	....	....	....	....	....	—	—	—	—	−13	−119	14	−2	−31	−53
Portfolio Investment Liab., n.i.e.	78bg d	....	....	....	....	....	233	174	224	694	162	154	317	517	364	1,339
Equity Securities	78bm d	....	....	....	....	....	—	—	—	—	—	—	—	—	—	—
Debt Securities	78bn d	....	....	....	....	....	233	174	224	694	162	154	317	517	364	1,339
Financial Derivatives Assets	78bw d	....	....	....	....	....	....	....	....	....	....	....	....	....	....	....
Financial Derivatives Liabilities	78bx d	....	....	....	....	....	....	....	....	....	....	....	....	....	....	....
Other Investment Assets	78bh d	....	....	....	....	....	−98	−428	−507	−691	−765	−1,480	−1,812	−2,237	−1,332	−1,652
Monetary Authorities	78bo d	....	....	....	....	....										
General Government	78bp d	....	....	....	....	....	−268	15	86	−19	87	−32	−456	−310	108	356
Banks	78bq d	....	....	....	....	....	2	−106	−341	−188	−444	−725	−859	−1,786	−1,064	−2,200
Other Sectors	78br d	....	....	....	....	....	168	−336	−252	−483	−407	−723	−497	−142	−376	193
Other Investment Liab., n.i.e.	78bi d	....	....	....	....	....	1,989	951	804	−28	1,351	3,071	1,631	2,931	1,867	3,079
Monetary Authorities	78bs d	....	....	....	....	....	−76	−19	322	−334	207	38	−220	485	−139	−218
General Government	78bt d	....	....	....	....	....	101	119	129	152	282	127	214	300	146	146
Banks	78bu d	....	....	....	....	....	466	92	335	18	860	1,890	744	2,038	1,328	2,707
Other Sectors	78bv d	....	....	....	....	....	1,497	759	19	136	2	1,015	893	108	532	444
Net Errors and Omissions	78ca d	....	....	....	....	....	−240	281	−348	89	−84	175	143	−5	89	−495
Overall Balance	78cb d	....	....	....	....	....	−217	−112	45	709	385	280	−220	196	−227	1,824
Reserves and Related Items	79da d	....	....	....	....	....	217	112	−45	−709	−385	−280	220	−196	227	−1,824
Reserve Assets	79db d	....	....	....	....	....	129	−20	−45	−665	−274	−280	237	−155	243	−1,824
Use of Fund Credit and Loans	79dc d	....	....	....	....	....	89	132	—	−44	−110	—	−17	−42	−16	—
Exceptional Financing	79de d	....	....	....	....	....	....	....	....	....	....	....	....	....	....	....
International Investment Position															*Millions of US Dollars*	
Assets	79aa d	....	....	....	....	....	3,746	4,321	4,811	6,425	8,179	10,064	10,473	11,310	11,658	14,365
Direct Investment Abroad	79ab d	....	....	....	....	....	318	356	397	471	626	737	550	671	754	1,306
Portfolio Investment	79ac d	....	....	....	....	....	34	—	—	—	13	132	104	90	111	159
Equity Securities	79ad d	....	....	....	....	....	—	—	—	—	—	2	3	3	3	15
Debt Securities	79ae d	....	....	....	....	....	34	—	—	—	13	130	101	86	108	144
Financial Derivatives	79al d	....	....	....	....	....										
Other Investment	79af d	....	....	....	....	....	2,929	3,469	3,848	4,685	5,707	7,046	8,018	8,771	9,319	9,879
Monetary Authorities	79ag d	....	....	....	....	....	337	345	374	412	330	460	845	1,076	960	497
General Government	79ah d	....	....	....	....	....	247	279	165	210	227	241	266	266	286	300
Banks	79ai d	....	....	....	....	....	516	593	1,004	1,222	1,765	2,356	2,852	3,815	4,424	5,916
Other Sectors	79aj d	....	....	....	....	....	1,830	2,252	2,305	2,842	3,385	3,989	4,055	3,615	3,648	3,167
Reserve Assets	79ak d	....	....	....	....	....	466	495	565	1,268	1,832	2,150	1,801	1,779	1,476	3,020
Liabilities	79la d	....	....	....	....	....	8,837	10,421	11,645	13,048	14,809	17,536	18,831	20,068	21,249	23,755
Dir. Invest. in Rep. Economy	79lb d	....	....	....	....	....	292	397	427	480	533	540	1,202	1,044	1,013	1,040
Portfolio Investment	79lc d	....	....	....	....	....	873	1,118	1,512	2,438	2,582	2,640	2,825	3,220	3,556	4,539
Equity Securities	79ld d	....	....	....	....	....	—	—	—	—	—	—	—	—	—	—
Debt Securities	79le d	....	....	....	....	....	873	1,118	1,512	2,438	2,582	2,640	2,825	3,220	3,556	4,539
Financial Derivatives	79ll d	....	....	....	....	....										
Other investment	79lf d	....	....	....	....	....	7,672	8,906	9,706	10,130	11,695	14,356	14,805	15,803	16,680	18,177
Monetary Authorities	79lg d	....	....	....	....	....	339	467	807	495	601	742	451	869	832	558
General Government	79lh d	....	....	....	....	....	232	350	505	719	1,021	1,085	1,252	1,459	1,487	1,460
Banks	79li d	....	....	....	....	....	1,205	1,325	1,630	1,685	2,659	4,410	4,807	6,146	7,025	8,849
Other Sectors	79lj d	....	....	....	....	....	5,896	6,765	6,765	7,231	7,413	8,119	8,295	7,328	7,336	7,310
Government Finance																
Central Government													*Millions of Markkaa through 1998;*			
Deficit (-) or Surplus	80	418	332	‡715	2,044	755	−2,315	−32	−1,938	−2,645	−4,105	−4,154	−1,968	−5,070	−7,965	−3,111
Revenue	81	10,231	11,340	‡15,359	19,212	23,355	28,604	35,865	38,897	40,280	44,938	52,050	61,518	68,775	77,049	87,235
Grants Received	81z			‡286	306	346	496	696	734	781	882	910	1,022	1,297	1,498	1,798
Expenditure	82	9,113	9,940	‡14,073	16,275	21,465	28,920	33,305	37,679	41,275	47,702	53,858	61,878	72,671	84,892	90,321
Lending Minus Repayments	83	700	1,068	‡857	1,199	1,481	2,495	3,288	3,890	2,431	2,223	3,256	2,630	2,471	1,620	1,823
Financing (By Residence of Lender)																
Domestic	84a	....	....	‡−679	−1,882	−567	1,927	−556	1,210	−358	1,822	2,632	−349	2,297	5,541	414
Foreign	85a	....	....	‡−36	−162	−188	388	588	728	3,003	2,283	1,522	2,317	2,773	2,424	2,697
Debt: Domestic	88a	....	‡2,530	2,325	1,797	1,566	2,021	2,379	3,039	4,867	6,254	7,642	8,778	11,443	15,958	19,119
Foreign	89a	....	‡1,524	1,517	1,395	1,152	1,609	2,248	3,679	7,360	8,964	10,341	13,331	18,808	21,723	24,945
Financing (By Currency)																
Net Borrowing	84	−486	−310	....	....	....	....	....	....	....	....	....	....	....	....	....
Markkaa	84b	−434	−190													
Foreign Currency	85b	−52	−120													
Use of Cash Balances	87	68	−22													
Debt: Markkaa	88b	2,202	....													
Foreign Currency	89b	1,548	....													
General Government															*As Percent of*	
Deficit (-) or Surplus	80g	....	....	....	....	....	....	....	....	....	....	....	....	....	....	....
Debt	88g	....	....	....	....	....	....	....	....	....	....	....	....	....	....	....

Minus Sign Indicates Debit

1985	1986	1987	1988	1989	1990	1991	1992	1993	1994	1995	1996	1997	1998	1999	Balance of Payments	
−806	−693	−1,731	−2,694	−5,797	−6,962	−6,807	−5,116	−1,135	1,110	5,231	5,003	6,633	7,371	6,936	Current Account, n.i.e.	78ald
13,351	16,291	19,526	22,202	23,249	26,531	23,098	24,101	23,587	29,881	40,558	40,725	41,148	43,393	41,983	Goods: Exports f.o.b.	78aa d
−12,481	−14,587	−18,019	−21,001	−23,479	−25,829	−20,660	−20,093	−17,138	−22,158	−28,121	−29,411	−29,604	−30,903	−30,328	Goods: Imports f.o.b.	78ab d
870	1,704	1,507	1,200	−229	701	2,438	4,009	6,449	7,723	12,437	11,314	11,544	12,490	11,655	*Trade Balance*	78ac d
2,429	2,606	3,338	3,833	4,057	4,649	4,101	4,656	4,412	5,490	7,415	7,129	6,640	6,759	6,646	Services: Credit	78ad d
−2,920	−3,333	−4,521	−5,507	−6,198	−7,627	−7,684	−7,577	−6,637	−7,335	−9,584	−8,817	−8,235	−7,802	−7,682	Services: Debit	78ae d
379	977	324	−474	−2,371	−2,276	−1,145	1,088	4,225	5,878	10,268	9,627	9,949	11,448	10,619	*Balance on Goods & Services*	78af d
999	1,023	1,496	2,368	2,513	3,505	2,598	1,536	1,154	1,789	2,879	2,868	4,136	4,237	4,973	Income: Credit	78ag d
−2,014	−2,309	−3,074	−4,090	−5,192	−7,239	−7,279	−6,946	−6,086	−6,103	−7,318	−6,503	−6,600	−7,320	−7,644	Income: Debit	78ah d
−635	−310	−1,253	−2,196	−5,050	−6,010	−5,827	−4,322	−707	1,564	5,828	5,992	7,485	8,365	7,948	*Balance on Gds, Serv. & Inc.*	78ai d
91	83	111	367	222	288	345	427	475	410	1,536	1,253	1,210	1,523	1,600	Current Transfers, n.i.e.: Credit	78aj d
−262	−466	−589	−865	−969	−1,240	−1,326	−1,221	−903	−863	−2,133	−2,242	−2,062	−2,517	−2,612	Current Transfers: Debit	78ak d
−5	—	—	—	—	—	−71	—	—	—	66	56	247	91	4	Capital Account, n.i.e.	78bc d
—	—	—	—	—	—	—	—	—	—	114	130	247	91	43	Capital Account, n.i.e.: Credit	78ba d
−5	—	—	—	—	—	−71	—	—	—	−48	−74	—	—	−38	Capital Account: Debit	78bb d
1,433	−2,079	7,135	2,101	3,471	12,405	4,196	3,071	374	4,093	−4,284	−7,718	−2,976	−2,186	−4,206	Financial Account, n.i.e.	78bj d
−348	−760	−1,141	−2,624	−2,968	−2,782	120	757	−1,401	−4,354	−1,494	−3,583	−5,260	−18,698	−4,759	Direct Investment Abroad	78bd d
113	348	265	532	490	812	−233	396	864	1,496	1,044	1,118	2,129	12,029	3,344	Dir. Invest. in Rep. Econ., n.i.e.	78be d
−191	−516	−612	−481	−61	−469	−334	−622	−604	775	204	−4,186	−4,600	−3,906	−12,944	Portfolio Investment Assets	78bf d
14	−1	−9	−14	−62	1	87	−10	−151	−78	−209	−736	−1,694	−2,099	−4,583	Equity Securities	78bk d
−205	−514	−603	−467	1	−470	−421	−612	−452	853	414	−3,450	−2,906	−1,807	−8,361	Debt Securities	78bl d
1,534	1,992	2,227	3,538	3,752	5,696	8,610	8,243	6,836	6,180	−1,779	1,153	3,843	3,866	13,231	Portfolio Investment Liab., n.i.e.	78bg d
....	203	133	111	304	96	20	89	2,216	2,541	2,027	1,915	4,023	7,931	10,279	Equity Securities	78bm d
1,534	1,790	2,093	3,427	3,448	5,600	8,590	8,154	4,620	3,640	−3,807	−761	−181	−4,065	2,952	Debt Securities	78bn d
....	....	....	....	....	....	—	—	—	51	38	38	−72	89	....	Financial Derivatives Assets	78bw d
....	....	....	....	—	—	—	—	—	5	600	325	114	−725	−420	Financial Derivatives Liabilities	78bx d
−177	−2,434	1,261	−1,723	−1,717	720	−2,965	−3,285	−1,832	−668	−2,863	−4,683	−2,201	−132	−4,473	Other Investment Assets	78bh d
....	−629	52	85	428	151	−1	−416	−29	99	146	27	94	145	−1,940	Monetary Authorities	78bo d
−28	−81	−75	−97	−97	−82	−83	−275	−344	−445	−366	−719	−609	−589	−636	General Government	78bp d
−31	−1,666	1,326	−1,155	−1,208	935	−1,900	−896	−987	−511	−1,926	−3,815	−1,725	41	−1,284	Banks	78bq d
−118	−59	−42	−555	−840	−284	−981	−1,698	−472	189	−717	−175	39	270	−612	Other Sectors	78br d
502	−708	5,136	2,858	3,974	8,428	−1,003	−2,418	−3,488	607	−35	2,099	3,072	5,292	1,815	Other Investment Liab., n.i.e.	78bi d
−26	−116	−16	−11	59	96	−251	1,244	−298	−107	92	−96	−173	−180	761	Monetary Authorities	78bs d
−1	−35	−62	−436	−344	−104	257	255	983	965	−331	764	1,478	394	−420	General Government	78bt d
1,069	1,215	4,635	3,336	1,936	4,764	−414	−5,034	−4,970	−1,088	869	−626	1,876	3,607	80	Banks	78bu d
−540	−1,772	579	−31	2,323	3,672	−595	1,117	796	837	−666	2,056	−110	1,471	1,394	Other Sectors	78bv d
−38	489	−1,371	851	1,258	−1,512	796	−105	1,053	−489	−1,384	−375	−1,600	−4,980	−2,832	Net Errors and Omissions	78ca d
583	−2,283	4,033	258	−1,068	3,931	−1,886	−2,150	291	4,714	−372	−3,036	2,304	296	−97	*Overall Balance*	78cb d
−583	2,283	−4,033	−258	1,068	−3,931	1,886	2,150	−291	−4,714	372	3,036	−2,304	−296	97	Reserves and Related Items	79da d
−583	2,283	−4,033	−258	1,068	−3,931	1,886	2,150	−291	−4,714	372	3,036	−2,304	−296	97	Reserve Assets	79db d
—	—	—	—	—	—	—	—	—	—	—	—	—	—	—	Use of Fund Credit and Loans	79dc d
—	—	—	—	—	—	—	—	—	—	—	—	—	—	—	Exceptional Financing	79de d

Millions of US Dollars

1985	1986	1987	1988	1989	1990	1991	1992	1993	1994	1995	1996	1997	1998	1999	International Investment Position	
17,769	20,880	30,344	32,180	35,473	45,048	44,118	39,957	40,838	51,570	57,970	65,385	71,601	86,831	106,923	Assets	79aa d
1,829	2,342	4,433	5,708	7,938	11,227	10,845	8,565	9,178	12,534	14,993	17,666	20,297	29,407	31,803	Direct Investment Abroad	79ab d
438	1,040	1,949	2,330	2,280	2,582	2,803	3,257	4,067	3,417	3,572	7,713	11,659	16,777	30,678	Portfolio Investment	79ac d
3	5	17	30	96	210	103	89	308	418	738	1,564	3,245	5,250	12,752	Equity Securities	79ad d
435	1,036	1,932	2,300	2,185	2,372	2,700	3,168	3,758	2,999	2,835	6,149	8,414	11,527	17,926	Debt Securities	79ae d
—	—	—	—	—	—	—	—	77	103	41	−5	259	151	3,469	Financial Derivatives	79al d
11,368	15,277	17,005	17,262	19,606	20,994	22,333	22,510	21,729	24,395	28,153	32,173	29,895	30,709	32,410	Other Investment	79af d
536	1,256	1,430	1,276	848	729	659	928	874	969	911	830	617	1,078	2,841	Monetary Authorities	79ag d
415	553	755	811	936	1,411	1,415	1,521	1,841	2,481	2,966	3,636	4,007	4,636	5,134	General Government	79ah d
5,926	8,455	8,830	8,896	10,487	10,997	12,164	11,301	10,933	12,021	14,203	17,872	18,430	18,004	17,291	Banks	79ai d
4,491	5,013	5,990	6,279	7,335	7,857	8,095	8,759	8,081	8,924	10,073	9,835	6,842	6,992	7,145	Other Sectors	79aj d
4,134	2,221	6,957	6,880	5,648	10,245	8,137	5,626	5,788	11,122	11,210	7,839	9,490	9,787	8,562	Reserve Assets	79ak d
27,947	32,880	47,511	51,754	61,646	84,362	86,073	83,423	85,949	107,281	111,245	118,245	119,705	186,123	319,974	Liabilities	79la d
1,339	1,680	2,620	3,040	3,965	5,132	4,220	3,689	4,217	6,714	8,465	8,797	9,530	16,455	16,540	Dir. Invest. in Rep. Economy	79lb d
6,851	10,014	14,358	17,193	21,277	34,243	40,475	44,974	53,875	69,508	69,408	75,311	76,436	131,124	263,470	Portfolio Investment	79lc d
—	702	1,159	1,279	2,007	1,390	1,004	979	5,251	12,767	14,625	23,457	28,870	79,722	217,069	Equity Securities	79ld d
6,851	9,312	13,198	15,914	19,270	32,853	39,471	43,995	48,624	56,741	54,782	51,855	47,566	51,403	46,401	Debt Securities	79le d
—	—	—	—	—	—	—	—	—	−1,055	354	723	1,153	229	2,965	Financial Derivatives	79ll d
19,757	21,186	30,533	31,521	36,404	44,987	41,378	34,760	28,913	32,151	33,018	33,414	32,586	38,315	36,999	Other investment	79lf d
595	546	649	610	690	876	558	1,301	908	996	1,176	1,018	713	734	1,329	Monetary Authorities	79lg d
1,746	2,028	2,429	1,791	1,403	1,412	1,551	1,689	2,767	4,016	3,886	4,299	5,340	6,133	5,347	General Government	79lh d
9,798	12,236	19,413	21,525	24,323	27,789	25,905	19,348	12,708	12,620	13,824	12,527	13,003	16,135	15,107	Banks	79li d
7,619	6,376	8,042	7,595	9,988	14,909	13,363	12,423	12,530	14,519	14,133	15,570	13,530	15,313	15,216	Other Sectors	79lj d

Millions of Euros Beginning 1999: Year Ending December 31

1985	1986	1987	1988	1989	1990	1991	1992	1993	1994	1995	1996	1997	1998	1999	Government Finance	
															Central Government	
−2,702	394	−6,690	1,754	8,807	945	−34,096	−70,346	−64,554	−58,781	−53,599	−36,571	−15,523	....	....	Deficit (-) or Surplus	80
98,617	111,091	114,733	134,761	151,922	160,241	154,141	156,114	160,235	168,307	178,584	192,955	199,126	....	....	Revenue	81
1,865	2,305	2,355	2,512	3,633	3,867	4,173	5,881	5,585	5,520	9,370	6,318	6,744	....	....	Grants Received	81z
100,887	110,383	121,278	132,038	143,593	158,673	184,225	203,201	218,612	223,119	232,883	231,425	219,527	....	....	Expenditure	82
2,297	2,619	2,500	3,481	3,155	4,490	8,185	29,140	11,762	9,489	8,670	4,419	1,867	....	....	Lending Minus Repayments	83
															Financing (By Residence of Lender)	
1,096	−322	4,176	−59	−5,920	−4,377	11,301	19,449	15,431	26,024	53,823	36,203	34,419	....	....	Domestic	84a
1,606	−72	2,514	−1,695	−2,887	3,432	22,795	50,897	49,123	32,757	−224	368	−18,896	....	....	Foreign	85a
21,100	24,871	29,831	31,805	32,331	27,444	30,216	51,956	87,588	123,434	174,874	196,836	210,088	....	....	Debt: Domestic	88a
25,676	26,981	28,680	26,279	23,063	29,210	57,699	119,974	175,490	190,851	187,328	199,882	209,258	....	....	Foreign	89a
															Financing (By Currency)	
....	....	....	....	....											Net Borrowing	84
....	....	....	....	....											Markkaa	84b
....	....	....	....	....											Foreign Currency	85b
....	....	....	....	....											Use of Cash Balances	87
....	....	....	....	....											Debt: Markkaa	88b
....	....	....	....	....											Foreign Currency	89b

Gross Domestic Product

1985	1986	1987	1988	1989	1990	1991	1992	1993	1994	1995	1996	1997	1998	1999		
															General Government	
....	....	....	....	....	5.4	−1.5	−5.9	−8.0	−6.4	−4.6	−3.2	−1.5	1.3	2.3	Deficit (-) or Surplus	80g
....	....	....	....	....	14.5	23.0	41.5	58.0	59.6	58.1	57.1	54.1	49.0	47.1	Debt	88g

Finland

National Accounts		1970	1971	1972	1973	1974	1975	1976	1977	1978	1979	1980	1981	1982	1983	1984
														Billions of Markkaa through 1998;		
Househ.Cons.Expend.,incl.NPISHs	96f	25.90	28.11	33.04	39.27	47.81	57.50	65.71	72.65	80.38	91.31	103.55	117.28	134.23	149.62	165.15
Government Consumption Expend.	91f	6.61	7.62	8.97	10.70	13.70	17.59	21.02	23.74	25.94	29.41	34.39	40.18	45.84	52.45	58.84
Gross Fixed Capital Formation	93e	12.01	13.82	16.37	20.56	26.86	32.72	32.97	35.26	34.48	38.79	48.70	54.78	61.65	69.55	73.01
Changes in Inventories	93i	1.79	1.64	.08	1.29	4.99	2.36	−1.43	−1.74	−2.75	3.73	7.44	1.32	−.17	−1.39	−.46
Exports of Goods & Services	90c	11.75	12.22	14.95	18.15	24.79	24.76	29.54	36.97	43.04	52.55	63.49	72.36	75.80	82.74	94.19
Imports of Goods & Services	98c	−12.31	−13.15	−14.80	−18.60	−28.10	−30.92	−31.82	−34.73	−37.39	−49.95	−65.02	−69.25	−73.76	−81.36	−86.14
Gross Domestic Product (GDP)	99b	45.75	50.26	58.61	71.37	90.05	103.17	116.64	128.55	142.29	165.55	192.56	216.66	243.59	271.61	304.60
Net Primary Income from Abroad	98.n	−.42	−.49	−.65	−.82	−1.04	−1.53	−1.86	−2.48	−2.69	−2.77	−3.24	−4.83	−6.14	−6.88	−7.19
Gross National Income (GNI)	99a	45.32	49.77	57.97	70.56	89.01	101.65	114.79	126.07	139.60	162.78	188.13	211.83	237.44	264.73	297.41
Net Current Transf. from Abroad	98t	....	....	....	....	....	....									
Net National Income	99e	39.80	43.32	50.44	61.22	76.75	87.17	98.03	106.66	117.77	138.27	159.79	179.61	201.66	224.24	252.92
Gross Nat'l Disposable Inc.(GNDI)	99i	....	....	....	....	....	98.59	118.17	129.67	142.91	166.49	191.97	216.36	242.40	269.90	303.19
Gross Savings	99s	....	....	....	....	....	28.97	30.57	32.27	35.83	44.77	52.81	57.84	61.44	67.19	78.82
GDP Volume 1980 prices	99b.p	134.81	137.63	148.12	158.07	162.86	164.73	....	....	....	....	....	....	....	....	....
GDP Volume 1990 Prices	99b.p	....	....	....	....	....	330.36	328.96	329.76	336.67	360.09	379.29	386.36	398.91	409.69	422.05
GDP Volume 1995 Prices	99b.p	....	....	....	....	....	....	....	....	....	....	....	....	....	....	....
GDP Volume (1995=100)	99bv p	53.8	54.9	59.1	63.1	65.0	65.7	65.5	65.6	67.0	71.6	75.5	76.9	79.4	81.5	84.0
GDP Deflator (1995=100)	99bi p	15.1	16.2	17.6	20.0	24.5	27.8	31.6	34.7	37.6	40.9	44.9	49.9	54.4	59.0	64.2
																Millions:
Population	99z	4.61	4.62	4.64	4.67	4.69	4.71	4.73	4.74	4.75	4.76	4.78	4.80	4.83	4.86	4.88

	1985	1986	1987	1988	1989	1990	1991	1992	1993	1994	1995	1996	1997	1998	1999	National Accounts	
Billions of Euros Beginning in 1999																	
	180.89	194.01	211.53	228.67	251.18	263.64	268.71	267.29	269.25	279.14	291.75	306.72	321.67	345.64	⅃61.07	Househ.Cons.Expend.,incl.NPISHs	96f
	66.97	72.85	80.05	90.60	99.70	112.63	123.37	123.34	119.13	121.47	128.18	134.85	140.46	149.20	⅃25.70	Government Consumption Expend.	91f
	79.42	82.91	92.54	115.39	143.25	148.18	120.30	95.52	79.33	79.52	90.51	98.06	112.29	127.45	⅃23.33	Gross Fixed Capital Formation	93e
	4.31	−.51	.46	7.84	10.60	−.27	−8.62	−4.13	.78	11.23	9.41	1.04	8.49	3.26	⅃.57	Changes in Inventories	93i
	98.03	95.63	100.05	108.67	117.35	119.00	109.89	128.77	159.92	183.33	209.32	220.92	249.68	267.85	⅃45.56	Exports of Goods & Services	90c
	−94.64	−89.90	−97.78	−110.84	−127.24	−127.75	−114.28	−123.87	−135.80	−152.39	−164.60	−175.72	−197.05	−206.66	⅃−35.57	Imports of Goods & Services	98c
	334.99	354.99	386.86	440.33	494.84	515.43	499.36	486.92	492.61	522.31	564.57	585.87	635.53	686.74	⅃120.76	Gross Domestic Product (GDP)	99b
	−6.99	−7.38	−7.67	−9.15	−13.71	−15.87	−20.27	−25.54	−28.93	−23.09	−23.51	−20.38	−16.16	−18.15	....	Net Primary Income from Abroad	98.n
	324.64	347.61	379.19	433.16	483.34	506.83	479.21	463.01	464.98	498.69	537.88	566.86	616.18	671.33	⅃118.09	Gross National Income (GNI)	99a
	....	....	....	−.96	−2.96	−3.64	−3.90	−3.51	−2.45	−2.42	1.38	−.61	−3.12	−1.91	....	Net Current Transf. from Abroad	98t
	276.12	295.41	322.09													Net National Income	99e
	330.64	352.86	383.49	435.25	481.25	505.21	476.61	459.23	462.08	497.14	543.19	565.19	619.23	665.92	⅃117.13	Gross Nat'l Disposable Inc.(GNDI)	99i
	82.37	86.00	92.91	115.89	129.68	128.40	84.12	67.96	73.21	96.29	122.15	121.06	153.02	171.07	⅃30.38	Gross Savings	99s
	....	....	....	....	....	....	....	....	....	....	....	....	....	....	....	GDP Volume 1980 prices	99b.*p*
	436.26	446.61	464.92	487.72	....	....	....	....	....	....	....	....	....	....	....	GDP Volume 1990 Prices	99b.*p*
	....	....	....	547.88	577.96	575.31	547.42	529.24	523.16	543.85	564.57	587.20	624.15	655.59	114.16	GDP Volume 1995 Prices	99b.*p*
	86.8	88.9	92.5	97.0	102.4	101.9	97.0	93.7	92.7	96.3	100.0	104.0	110.6	116.1	120.2	GDP Volume (1995=100)	99bv*p*
	67.7	70.8	74.1	80.4	85.6	90.6	92.0	93.0	94.7	96.5	100.0	99.7	102.4	104.8	105.8	GDP Deflator (1995=100)	99bi*p*
Midyear Estimates																	
	4.90	4.92	4.93	4.95	4.96	4.99	5.01	5.04	5.07	5.09	5.11	5.12	5.14	5.15	5.17	**Population**	99z

(See notes in the back of the book.)

France

		1970	1971	1972	1973	1974	1975	1976	1977	1978	1979	1980	1981	1982	1983	1984
Exchange Rates																*Francs per SDR through 1998,*
Market Rate	aa	5.5542	5.5542	5.5542	5.6801	5.4416	5.2510	5.7740	5.7152	5.4457	5.2957	5.7598	6.6904	7.4184	8.7394	9.4022
																Francs per US Dollar through 1998,
Market Rate	ae	5.5542	5.1157	5.1157	4.7085	4.4445	4.4855	4.9698	4.7050	4.1800	4.0200	4.5160	5.7480	6.7250	8.3475	9.5920
Market Rate	rf	5.5542	5.5406	5.0445	4.4528	4.8096	4.2878	4.8029	4.9052	4.5131	4.2544	4.2256	5.4346	6.5721	7.6213	8.7391
																Francs per ECU:
ECU Rate	ea	....	....	....	....	....	....				5.7931	5.9392	6.2018	6.5221	6.9036	6.8307
ECU Rate	eb	....	....	....	....	....	....	5.3446	5.6060	5.7396	5.8288	5.8694	6.0405	6.4255	6.7689	6.8714
																Index Numbers (1995=100):
Market Rate	ahx	90.2	90.5	98.9	112.4	103.8	116.4	104.0	101.7	110.7	117.3	118.2	92.3	76.3	65.8	57.2
Nominal Effective Exchange Rate...........	neu	111.9	109.6	111.8	115.6	108.1	118.4	115.3	111.0	109.6	109.2	109.7	103.0	95.4	89.9	87.0
Real Effective Exchange Rate	reu	....	....	....	....	....	109.9	107.9	103.8	109.3	109.9	ꙇ112.8	109.9	110.9	107.8	106.3
Fund Position																*Millions of SDRs:*
Quota	2f. s	1,500	1,500	1,500	1,500	1,500	1,500	1,500	1,500	1,919	1,919	2,879	2,879	2,879	4,483	4,483
SDRs	1b. s	171	348	581	73	202	244	227	233	286	644	733	1,080	887	422	584
Reserve Position in the Fund	1c. s	—	436	460	377	429	623	843	736	461	479	837	884	868	1,292	1,291
of which: Outstg.Fund Borrowing.........	2c	—	—	—	—	—	—	—	—	38	16					
International Liquidity															*Millions of US Dollars Unless Otherwise Indicated:*	
Total Res.Min.Gold (Eurosys.Def)	1l. d	1,428	4,428	6,189	4,268	4,526	8,457	5,620	5,872	9,278	17,579	27,340	22,262	16,531	19,851	20,940
SDRs	1b. d	171	378	630	88	248	286	263	284	373	849	935	1,257	979	442	572
Reserve Position in the Fund	1c. d	—	473	499	455	525	729	979	895	600	630	1,067	1,029	958	1,352	1,265
Foreign Exchange	1d. d	1,257	3,577	5,059	3,725	3,753	7,442	4,377	4,694	8,305	16,100	25,338	19,976	14,594	18,057	19,102
o/w: Fin.Deriv.Rel.to Reserves	1dd d	....	....	....	....	....	....	....	....	....	....	....	....	....	....	....
Other Reserve Assets	1e. d	....	....	....	....	....	....	....	....	....	....	....	....	....	....	....
Gold (Million Fine Troy Ounces)	1ad	100.91	100.66	100.69	100.91	100.93	100.93	101.02	101.67	101.99	81.92	81.85	81.85	81.85	81.85	81.85
Gold (National Valuation)	1and	3,532	3,825	3,826	4,261	4,261	14,133	12,840	16,717	22,340	34,195	49,991	33,877	36,848	30,786	26,832
Memo: Euro Cl. on Non-EA Res.	1dg d	....	....	....	....	....	....	....	....	....	....	....	....	....	....	....
Non-Euro Cl. on EA Res.	1dh d	....	....	....	....	....	....	....	....	....	....	....	....	....	....	....
Mon. Auth.: Other Foreign Assets	3.. d	....	....	....	....	....	....	....	....	....	....	....	....	....	....	....
Foreign Liabilities	4.. d	437	240	221	356	605	934	942	ꙇ453	849	8,570	13,926	11,188	10,155	12,882	10,897
Banking Insts.: Foreign Assets	7a. d	10,144	14,467	19,806	32,215	33,120	41,173	41,292	ꙇ72,689	ꙇ108,876	137,587	160,208	158,090	162,959	156,322	158,643
Foreign Liab.	7b. d	10,833	16,553	23,090	33,516	35,691	41,924	51,500	66,835	ꙇ95,239	119,652	146,678	153,793	164,669	167,068	174,374
Monetary Authorities													*Billions of Francs through 1998;*			
Fgn. Assets (Cl.on Non-EA Ctys)	11	29	47	54	44	44	ꙇ101	94	110	136	ꙇ254	420	377	397	460	488
Claims on General Government	12a.u	....	....	....	....	....	....	....	....	....	....	....	....	....	....	....
o/w: Claims on Gen.Govt.in Cty	12a	12	13	13	11	11	22	22	18	23	24	24	11	25	39	66
Claims on Banking Institutions	12e.u	....	....	....	....	....	....	....	....	....	....	....	....	....	....	....
o/w: Claims on Bank.Inst.in Cty	12e	51	41	66	86	98	51	54	59	89	87	90	116	221	175	154
Claims on Other Resident Sectors	12d.u	....	....	....	....	....	....	....	....	....	....	....	....	....	....	....
o/w: Cl. on Oth.Res.Sect.in Cty	12d	....	....	....	....	....	....	....	1	1	1	1	1	2	1	1
Claims on ECB	12u	....	....	....	....	....	....	....	....	....	....	....	....	....	....	....
Currency in Circulation	14a	78	80	87	93	101	111	119	126	136	145	149	167	184	200	209
Liabilities to Banking Insts	14c.u	....	....	....	....	....	....	....	....	....	....	....	....	....	....	....
o/w: Liabs to Bank.Inst.in Cty	14c	7	14	37	40	49	7	7	12	18	21	42	32	52	49	65
Demand Dep. of Other Res.Sect.	14d.u	....	....	....	....	....	....	....	....	....	....	....	....	....	....	....
o/w: D.Dep.of Oth.Res.Sect.in Cty	14d	1	1	1	2	2	2	2	2	2	3	2	2	3	3	4
Other Dep. of Other Res.Sect.	15..u	....	....	....	....	....	....	....	....	....	....	....	....	....	....	....
o/w: O.Dep.of Oth.Res.Sect.in Cty	15	....	....	....	....	....	....	....	....	....	....	....	....	....	....	....
Money Market Instruments	16m.u	....	....	....	....	....	....	....	....	....	....	....	....	....	....	....
o/w: MMI Held by Resid.of Cty	16m	....	....	....	....	....	....	....	....	....	....	....	....	....	....	....
Bonds (Debt Securities)	16n.u	....	....	....	....	....	....	....	....	....	....	....	....	....	....	....
o/w: Bonds Held by Resid.of Cty	16n	....	....	....	....	....	....	....	....	....	....	....	....	....	....	....
Foreign Liab. (to Non-EA Ctys)	16c	6	1	1	2	3	4	5	2	4	34	63	64	68	108	105
Central Government Deposits	16d.u	....	....	....	....	....	....	....	....	....	....	....	....	....	....	....
o/w: Cent.Govt.Dep. in Cty	16d	....	....	....	....	....	....	....	3	27	23	28	24	58	38	58
Liabilities to ECB	16u	....	....	....	....	....	....	....	....	....	....	....	....	....	....	....
Capital Accounts	17a	....	....	....	....	....	....	....	65	79	ꙇ160	273	235	302	319	318
Other Items (Net)	17r	—	4	6	6	−2	ꙇ50	37	−22	−18	ꙇ−18	−22	−19	−22	−40	−50

	1985	1986	1987	1988	1989	1990	1991	1992	1993	1994	1995	1996	1997	1998	1999		

Exchange Rates

Euros per SDR Thereafter: End of Period

| 8.3052 | 7.8957 | 7.5756 | 8.1536 | 7.6064 | 7.2968 | 7.4096 | 7.5714 | 8.0978 | 7.8044 | 7.2838 | 7.5306 | 8.0794 | 7.9161 | 1.3662 | Market Rate.. | aa |

Euros per US Dollar Thereafter: End of Period (ae) Period Average (rf)

| 7.5610 | 6.4550 | 5.3400 | 6.0590 | 5.7880 | 5.1290 | 5.1800 | 5.5065 | 5.8955 | 5.3460 | 4.9000 | 5.2370 | 5.9881 | 5.6221 | .9954 | Market Rate.. | ae |
| 8.9852 | 6.9261 | 6.0107 | 5.9569 | 6.3801 | 5.4453 | 5.6421 | 5.2938 | 5.6632 | 5.5520 | 4.9915 | 5.1155 | 5.8367 | 5.8995 | .9386 | Market Rate.. | rf |

End of Period (ea) Period Average (eb)

| 6.7047 | 6.8750 | 6.9834 | 7.0982 | 6.9204 | 6.9501 | 6.9534 | 6.6678 | 6.5742 | 6.5758 | 6.4458 | 6.5619 | 6.6135 | 6.5596 | .... | ECU Rate.. | ea |
| 6.7951 | 6.7981 | 6.9289 | 7.0361 | 7.0237 | 6.9141 | 6.9733 | 6.8496 | 6.6334 | 6.5796 | 6.5250 | 6.4928 | 6.6122 | 6.6015 | .... | ECU Rate.. | eb |

Period Averages

56.0	72.1	83.1	83.9	78.3	91.8	88.7	94.4	88.2	90.0	100.0	97.5	85.6	84.7	....	Market Rate..	ah x
88.2	90.6	90.6	88.7	87.8	91.6	90.1	92.9	96.2	97.1	100.0	99.9	96.7	97.2	95.8	Nominal Effective Exchange Rate..........	ne u
109.4	111.0	108.2	104.6	101.6	103.0	98.9	99.3	100.2	99.0	100.0	96.9	92.3	90.9	....	Real Effective Exchange Rate.................	re u

End of Period

Fund Position

4,483	4,483	4,483	4,483	4,483	4,483	4,483	7,415	7,415	7,415	7,415	7,415	7,415	7,415	10,739	Quota...	2f. s
819	1,054	1,059	1,033	1,011	902	927	118	241	248	643	682	720	786	253	SDRs...	1b. s
1,247	1,419	1,349	1,200	1,076	1,004	1,165	1,805	1,682	1,627	1,854	1,875	2,119	3,162	3,950	Reserve Position in the Fund	1c. s
—	—	—	—	—	—	—	—	—	—	—	—	—	—	382	of which: Outstg.Fund Borrowing ..	2c

End of Period

International Liquidity

26,589	31,454	33,049	25,364	24,611	36,778	31,284	27,028	22,649	26,257	26,853	26,796	30,927	44,312	⊥39,701	Total Res.Min.Gold (Eurosys.Def)........	1l. d
900	1,290	1,502	1,390	1,329	1,283	1,326	163	331	362	955	981	971	1,107	347	SDRs...	1b. d
1,370	1,736	1,914	1,615	1,414	1,428	1,666	2,482	2,310	2,375	2,756	2,695	2,859	4,452	5,421	Reserve Position in the Fund	1c. d
24,319	28,428	29,634	22,359	21,868	34,067	28,292	24,384	20,008	23,520	23,142	23,120	27,097	38,753	33,933	Foreign Exchange	1d. d
....	....	....	....	....	....	....	....	....	....	....	....	....	....	—	o/w: Fin.Deriv.Rel.to Reserves........	1dd d
....	....	....	....	....	....	....	....	....	....	....	....	....	....	—	Other Reserve Assets	1e. d
81.85	81.85	81.85	81.85	81.85	81.85	81.85	81.85	81.85	81.85	81.85	81.85	81.85	81.89	102.37	97.24	Gold (Million Fine Troy Ounces)...........	1ad
27,580	33,932	41,496	33,686	33,982	31,321	31,704	26,313	30,729	30,730	31,658	30,368	25,002	29,871	28,284	Gold (National Valuation)	1an d
....	....	....	....	....	....	....	....	....	....	....	....	....	....	—	Memo: Euro Cl. on Non-EA Res.	1dg d
....	....	....	....	....	....	....	....	....	....	....	....	....	....	3,330	Non-Euro Cl. on EA Res.	1dh d
															Mon. Auth.: Other Foreign Assets ..	3.. d
10,891	11,552	19,554	13,601	13,022	12,338	12,795	29,541	20,553	11,650	11,649	⊥796	618	1,014	⊥7,678	Foreign Liabilities..............	4.. d
184,380	217,992	290,077	299,721	358,829	455,781	457,104	512,485	581,393	599,906	705,082	684,056	736,795	....	⊥417,477	Banking Insts.: Foreign Assets	7a. d
197,183	228,288	296,772	315,902	384,692	519,809	523,456	526,214	523,077	592,630	662,469	671,759	694,578	....	⊥329,796	Foreign Liab.	7b. d

Millions of Euros Beginning 1999: End of Period

Monetary Authorities

446	495	474	430	405	407	396	345	351	372	346	309	335	420	68,150	Fgn. Assets (Cl.on Non-EA Ctys)............	11
....	....	....	....	....	....	....	....	....	....	....	....	....	....	4,051	Claims on General Government	12a. u
59	62	63	63	57	81	74	95	75	72	59	58	52	51	4,051	o/w: Claims on Gen.Govt.in Cty	12a
....	....	....	....	....	....	....	....	....	....	....	....	....	....	52,255	Claims on Banking Institutions.......	12e. u
159	130	212	238	271	162	166	294	372	200	147	143	125	167	48,448	o/w: Claims on Bank.Inst.in Cty	12e
....	....	....	....	....	....	....	....	....	....	....	....	....	....	380	Claims on Other Resident Sectors	12d. u
1	1	3	2	3	4	4	4	4	4	6	18	19	20	380	o/w: Cl. on Oth.Res.Sect.in Cty	12d
....	....	....	....	....	....	....	....	....	....	....	....	....	....	10,675	Claims on ECB...................................	12u
217	224	235	247	259	270	270	271	267	270	275	278	283	287	49,282	Currency in Circulation	14a
....	....	....	....	....	....	....	....	....	....	....	....	....	....	49,076	Liabilities to Banking Insts	14c. u
104	104	128	115	103	78	68	22	14	10	30	33	36	129	24,359	o/w: Liabs to Bank.Inst.in Cty	14c
....	....	....	....	....	....	....	....	....	....	....	....	....	....	1,573	Demand Dep. of Other Res.Sect.	14d. u
3	3	5	4	4	4	4	3	3	3	4	4	4	4	1,573	o/w: D.Dep.of Oth.Res.Sect.in Cty ...	14d
....	....	....	....	....	....	....	....	....	....	....	....	....	....	—	Other Dep. of Other Res.Sect.	15.. u
....	....	....	....	....	....	....	....	....	....	....	....	....	....	—	o/w: O.Dep.of Oth.Res.Sect.in Cty	15
....	....	....	....	....	....	....	....	....	....	....	....	....	....	—	Money Market Instruments	16m. u
....	....	....	....	....	....	....	....	....	....	....	....	....	....	....	o/w: MMI Held by Resid.of Cty	16m
....	....	....	....	....	....	....	....	....	....	....	....	....	....	—	Bonds (Debt Securities).........................	16n. u
....	....	....	....	....	....	....	....	....	....	....	....	....	....	—	o/w: Bonds Held by Resid.of Cty	16n
82	75	104	82	75	63	66	163	121	62	57	4	4	6	7,643	Foreign Liab. (to Non-EA Ctys)	16c
....	....	....	....	....	....	....	....	....	....	....	....	....	....	1,057	Central Government Deposits	16d. u
47	57	120	76	107	104	86	148	198	123	58	20	43	89	1,057	o/w: Cent.Govt.Dep. in Cty.................	16d
....	....	....	....	....	....	....	....	....	....	....	....	....	....	—	Liabilities to ECB................................	16u
260	269	276	255	244	201	205	182	225	201	177	191	201	168	35,675	Capital Accounts	17a
−49	−44	−116	−45	−56	−67	−59	−51	−26	−23	−44	−3	−39	−25	−8,796	Other Items (Net)	17r

France

Banking Institutions

Billions of Francs through 1998;

	1970	1971	1972	1973	1974	1975	1976	1977	1978	1979	1980	1981	1982	1983	1984
Claims on Monetary Authorities 20	9	16	38	40	50	10	11	I16	I22	25	47	38	58	57	74
Claims on Bk.Inst.in Oth.EA Ctys 20b.u	....	....	....	....	....	....	....	....	....	....	....	....	....	....	....
Fgn. Assets (Cl.on Non-EA Ctys) 21	56	74	101	148	147	185	205	I342	I455	553	724	909	1,096	1,305	1,522
Claims on General Government 22a.u	....	....	....	....	....	....	....	....	....	....	....	....	....	....	....
o/w: Claims on Gen.Govt.in Cty 22a	18	17	13	4	4	33	34	34	I268	297	308	374	478	529	584
Claims on Other Resident Sectors 22d.u	....	....	....	....	....	....	....	....	....	....	....	....	....	....	....
o/w: Cl. on Oth.Res.Sect.in Cty 22d	271	321	396	468	551	629	767	I926	I1,623	1,848	2,107	2,383	2,739	3,065	3,398
Demand Deposits .... 24..u	....	....	....	....	....	....	....	....	....	....	....	....	....	....	....
o/w: D.Dep.of Oth.Res.Sect.in Cty 24	123	145	174	192	219	262	279	I313	I532	610	655	737	805	914	1,016
Other Deposits .... 25..u	....	....	....	....	....	....	....	....	....	....	....	....	....	....	....
o/w: O.Dep.of Oth.Res.Sect.in Cty 25	111	147	185	226	275	331	392	I465	I1,015	1,171	1,300	1,423	1,593	1,753	1,888
Money Market Instruments 26m.u	....	....	....	....	....	....	....	....	....	....	....	....	....	....	....
o/w: MMI Held by Resid.of Cty 26m	....	....	....	....	....	....	....	....	....	1	1	1	1	1	1
Bonds (Debt Securities) 26n.u	....	....	....	....	....	....	....	....	....	....	....	....	....	....	....
o/w: Bonds Held by Resid.of Cty 26n	....	....	....	....	....	....	....	77	I177	200	250	303	363	445	530
Foreign Liab. (to Non-EA Ctys) 26c	60	85	118	154	159	188	256	314	I398	481	662	884	1,107	1,395	1,673
Central Government Deposits 26d.u	....	....	....	....	....	....	....	....	....	....	....	....	....	....	....
o/w: Cent.Govt.Dep. in Cty 26d	....	....	....	....	....	....	....	....	58	61	71	69	76	81	84
Credit from Monetary Authorities 26g	51	41	66	86	98	51	54	59	89	87	90	116	221	175	154
Liab. to Bk.Inst.in Oth. EA Ctys 26h.u	....	....	....	....	....	....	....	....	....	....	....	....	....	....	....
Capital Accounts 27a	....	....	....	....	....	....	....	72	I112	146	170	193	223	261	300
Other Items (Net) 27r	8	9	6	—	—	26	35	15	I-4	-13	16	35	62	38	65

Banking Survey (Nat'l Residency)

Billions of Francs through 1998;

	1970	1971	1972	1973	1974	1975	1976	1977	1978	1979	1980	1981	1982	1983	1984
Foreign Assets (Net) 31n	20	35	36	37	30	I94	39	I144	I192	295	422	342	323	269	239
Domestic Credit 32	301	351	422	483	566	685	824	976	I1,831	2,086	2,342	2,677	3,110	3,516	3,907
Claims on General Govt. (Net) 32an	30	30	26	16	16	55	56	49	I207	237	233	292	369	450	508
Claims on Other Resident Sectors 32d	271	321	396	468	551	629	767	I927	I1,624	1,849	2,109	2,385	2,741	3,067	3,399
Currency in Circulation 34a.n	78	80	87	93	101	111	119	I126	I136	145	149	167	184	200	209
Demand Deposits 34b.n	124	147	175	194	221	263	281	I315	I534	612	657	739	808	917	1,020
Other Deposits .... 35..n	111	147	185	226	275	331	392	I465	I1,015	1,171	1,300	1,423	1,593	1,753	1,888
Money Market Instruments 36m	....	....	....	....	....	....	....	....	1	1	1	1	1	1	1
Bonds (Debt Securities) 36n	....	....	....	....	....	....	....	77	177	200	250	303	363	445	530
o/w: Bonds Over Two Years 36na	....	....	....	....	....	....	....	....	....	....	....	....	....	....	....
Capital Accounts 37a	....	....	....	....	....	....	....	137	192	I306	443	428	525	580	617
Other Items (Net) 37r	7	11	12	7	-3	I72	68	I206	I-35	-57	-40	-47	-46	-117	-126

Banking Survey (Nat'l Residency)

Millions of Euros Beginning 1999: End of Period

	1985	1986	1987	1988	1989	1990	1991	1992	1993	1994	1995	1996	1997	1998	1999	
Foreign Assets (Net)	267	353	334	250	180	15	−14	106	573	349	497	369	584	....	276,417	31n
Domestic Credit	4,241	4,685	5,077	5,643	6,229	6,909	7,188	7,484	7,342	7,560	7,903	8,118	8,390	....	1,363,863	32
Claims on General Govt. (Net)	594	628	529	567	529	547	523	550	626	968	1,152	1,447	1,586	....	305,565	32an
Claims on Other Resident Sectors	3,647	4,057	4,548	5,076	5,700	6,362	6,665	6,934	6,716	6,593	6,751	6,671	6,804	....	1,058,298	32d
Currency in Circulation	217	224	235	247	259	270	270	271	267	270	275	278	283	287	49,282	34a.n
Demand Deposits	1,105	1,193	1,248	1,294	1,378	1,434	1,355	1,352	1,368	1,418	1,561	1,557	1,674	....	243,949	34b.n
Other Deposits	2,006	2,165	2,228	2,350	2,451	2,519	2,565	2,619	2,776	3,012	3,374	3,582	3,855	....	632,781	35..n
Money Market Instruments	9	39	163	274	426	781	851	1,128	1,174	1,062	973	859	827	....	314,039	36m
Bonds (Debt Securities)	629	793	900	1,053	1,166	1,230	1,315	1,458	1,500	1,475	1,575	1,407	1,324	....	360,322	36n
o/w: Bonds Over Two Years														....	336,089	36na
Capital Accounts	604	708	860	918	1,018	1,082	1,195	1,287	1,465	1,494	1,462	1,479	1,521	....	269,379	37a
Other Items (Net)	−63	−83	−223	−245	−289	−391	−376	−525	−633	−824	−819	−675	−509	....	−229,473	37r

Banking Institutions

Millions of Euros Beginning 1999: End of Period

	1985	1986	1987	1988	1989	1990	1991	1992	1993	1994	1995	1996	1997	1998	1999	
Claims on Monetary Authorities	112	113	138	125	114	91	80	34	27	26	47	51	48	....	24,371	20
Claims on Bk.Inst.in Oth.EA Ctys														....	192,393	20b.u
Fgn. Assets (Cl.on Non-EA Ctys)	1,394	1,407	1,549	1,816	2,077	2,338	2,368	2,822	3,428	3,207	3,455	3,582	4,412	....	415,565	21
Claims on General Government														....	386,731	22a.u
o/w: Claims on Gen.Govt in Cty	670	724	704	695	696	681	630	699	798	1,074	1,275	1,566	1,729	....	312,415	22a
Claims on Other Resident Sectors														....	1,100,899	22d.u
o/w: Cl. on Oth.Res.Sect.in Cty	3,646	4,056	4,545	5,074	5,698	6,358	6,661	6,930	6,712	6,589	6,745	6,653	6,785	....	1,057,918	22d
Demand Deposits														....	246,895	24..u
o/w: D.Dep.of Oth.Res.Sect.in Cty	1,102	1,189	1,243	1,291	1,375	1,430	1,351	1,349	1,364	1,415	1,557	1,554	1,670	....	242,376	24
Other Deposits														....	649,980	25..u
o/w: O.Dep.of Oth.Res.Sect.in Cty	2,006	2,165	2,228	2,350	2,451	2,519	2,565	2,619	2,776	3,012	3,374	3,582	3,855	....	632,781	25
Money Market Instruments														....	314,039	26m.u
o/w: MMI Held by Resid.of Cty	9	39	163	274	426	781	851	1,128	1,174	1,062	973	859	827	....		26m
Bonds (Debt Securities)														....	360,322	26n.u
o/w: Bonds Held by Resid.of Cty	629	793	900	1,053	1,166	1,230	1,315	1,458	1,500	1,475	1,575	1,407	1,324	....		26n
Foreign Liab. (to Non-EA Ctys)	1,491	1,474	1,585	1,914	2,227	2,666	2,712	2,898	3,084	3,168	3,246	3,518	4,159	....	328,286	26c
Central Government Deposits														....	10,109	26d.u
o/w: Cent.Govt.Dep. in Cty	88	102	117	116	118	111	95	96	50	55	124	156	152	....	9,844	26d
Credit from Monetary Authorities	159	130	212	238	271	162	166	294	372	200	147	143	125	167	48,448	26g
Liab. to Bk.Inst.in Oth. EA Ctys														....	150,237	26h.u
Capital Accounts	344	439	584	664	774	881	989	1,105	1,240	1,293	1,284	1,288	1,320	....	233,704	27a
Other Items (Net)	−6	−30	−97	−189	−222	−311	−306	−462	−595	−785	−759	−654	−459	....	−222,061	27r

France

	1970	1971	1972	1973	1974	1975	1976	1977	1978	1979	1980	1981	1982	1983	1984
Banking Survey (EA-Wide Residency)															*Millions of Euros:*
Foreign Assets (Net) .... **31n.** *u*	....	....	....	....	....	....	....	....	....	....	....	....	....	....	....
Domestic Credit .... **32..** *u*	....	....	....	....	....	....	....	....	....	....	....	....	....	....	....
Claims on General Govt. (Net) .... **32an** *u*	....	....	....	....	....	....	....	....	....	....	....	....	....	....	....
Claims on Other Resident Sect. .... **32d.** *u*	....	....	....	....	....	....	....	....	....	....	....	....	....	....	....
Currency in Circulation .... **34a.** *u*	....	....	....	....	....	....	....	....	....	....	....	....	....	....	....
Demand Deposits .... **34b.** *u*	....	....	....	....	....	....	....	....	....	....	....	....	....	....	....
Other Deposits .... **35..** *u*	....	....	....	....	....	....	....	....	....	....	....	....	....	....	....
o/w: Other Dep. Over Two Yrs ...... **35ab** *u*	....	....	....	....	....	....	....	....	....	....	....	....	....	....	....
Money Market Instruments .... **36m.** *u*	....	....	....	....	....	....	....	....	....	....	....	....	....	....	....
Bonds (Debt Securities) .... **36n.** *u*	....	....	....	....	....	....	....	....	....	....	....	....	....	....	....
o/w: Bonds Over Two Years .... **36na** *u*	....	....	....	....	....	....	....	....	....	....	....	....	....	....	....
Capital Accounts **37a**	....	....	....	....	....	....	....	....	....	....	....	....	....	....	....
Other Items (Net) .... **37r.** *u*	....	....	....	....	....	....	....	....	....	....	....	....	....	....	....
Money (National Definitions)															*Billions of Francs:*
M1 .... **39ma**	....	....	....	....	....	....	....	602	665	750	800	899	983	1,104	1,215
M1, Seasonally Adjusted .... **39ma** *c*	....	....	....	....	....	....	....	579	603	680	740	824	921	1,007	1,105
M2 .... **39mb**	....	....	....	....	....	....	....	1,069	1,212	1,370	1,481	1,683	1,885	2,136	2,333
M2, Seasonally Adjusted .... **39mb** *c*	....	....	....	....	....	....	....	1,040	1,105	1,264	1,378	1,540	1,752	1,957	2,162
M3 .... **39mc**	....	....	....	....	....	....	....	1,404	1,583	1,805	1,979	2,196	2,450	2,735	3,005
M3, Seasonally Adjusted .... **39mc** *c*	....	....	....	....	....	....	....	1,376	1,466	1,664	1,850	2,072	2,313	2,551	2,812
M4 .... **39md**	....	....	....	....	....	....	....	1,404	1,583	1,805	1,979	2,196	2,450	2,735	3,005
M4, Seasonally Adjusted .... **39md** *c*	....	....	....	....	....	....	....	1,378	1,466	1,664	1,850	2,072	2,313	2,551	2,812
Interest Rates															*Percent Per Annum*
Repurchase of Agreements **60a**	....	....	....	....	11.23	7.72	7.56	8.92	6.32	8.98	11.90	....	14.53	12.35	11.68
Money Market Rate **60b**	8.68	5.84	4.95	8.91	12.91	7.92	8.56	9.07	7.98	9.04	11.85	15.30	14.87	12.53	11.74
Treasury Bill Rate **60c**	8.93	6.29	5.51	9.13	13.02	7.84	8.69	9.22	8.16	9.48	12.20	15.26	14.73	12.63	11.88
Deposit Rate **60l**	4.13	4.25	4.25	4.25	6.25	7.50	6.50	6.50	6.50	6.50	7.25	7.75	8.50	8.08	7.08
Lending Rate **60p**	7.98	6.92	6.38	8.57	11.98	10.00	9.08	9.50	9.12	9.81	12.54	14.28	13.63	12.25	12.15
Government Bond Yield **61**	8.06	7.73	7.36	8.27	10.48	9.57	9.32	9.87	9.50	9.81	13.03	15.79	15.69	13.63	12.54
Prices, Production, Labor															*Index Numbers (1995=100):*
Share Prices **62**	15.9	15.3	‡17.1	18.9	14.1	15.6	15.0	12.1	15.8	20.0	23.2	‡20.4	19.8	‡26.7	‡36.1
Producer Prices															
Indust. Goods,Tax Incl.(1985=100) **63**	28.5	29.1	30.4	34.9	45.1	42.5	45.6	48.2	50.3	57.0	62.0	68.8	76.4	84.9	96.1
Intermediate Indust. Goods **63a**	....	....	....	....	....	....	....	....	....	....	60.0	67.1	74.3	80.8	88.3
Imported Raw Materials **63b**	28.1	27.2	27.8	35.0	46.7	38.4	43.4	46.9	‡47.6	56.2	65.7	77.4	82.7	93.9	109.7
Consumer Prices **64**	19.4	20.4	21.7	23.3	26.4	29.5	32.4	35.4	38.7	42.8	‡48.6	55.1	61.7	67.6	72.7
Harmonized CPI **64h**															
Labor Costs **65**	9.7	10.9	12.2	‡13.8	16.5	19.8	23.1	26.4	30.1	34.7	40.3	46.1	55.4	62.5	67.8
Industrial Production .... **66.. c**	66.4	70.3	74.3	79.6	81.6	76.3	82.3	83.6	85.6	88.9	‡89.6	88.7	88.1	87.5	87.7
Industrial Employment .... **67.. c**											132.6	128.5	127.3	124.8	121.5
															Number in Thousands:
Labor Force **67d**	....	....	....	....	....	....	....	....	....	....	....	....	....	....	....
Employment **67e**	....	....	....	....	....	....	....	....	....	....	....	....	....	....	....
Unemployment **67c**	....	....	....	....	....	....	....	....	....	....	....	....	....	....	....
Unemployment Rate (%) **67r**	....	....	....	....	....	....	....	....	....	....	....	....	....	....	....
International Transactions															*Billions of Francs through 1998;*
Exports **70**	101	115	133	162	222	227	273	319	358	428	491	577	633	723	851
Imports, c.i.f. **71**	106	118	136	167	254	231	308	346	369	455	570	655	764	807	910
Imports, f.o.b. **71.v**	100	111	127	156	239	221	294	331	355	438	551	636	705	758	871
															1995=100
Volume of Exports **72**	27.3	29.6	33.9	‡37.3	40.9	‡39.2	42.8	45.6	48.3	53.2	54.3	55.9	54.2	56.1	59.1
Volume of Imports **73**	28.2	30.3	34.6	‡39.3	41.0	‡38.1	46.0	46.4	48.8	54.5	57.9	56.0	57.9	56.8	58.2
Unit Value of Exports........................ **74**	25.5	27.0	27.3	‡30.0	37.8	‡39.9	43.6	47.9	50.2	55.1	61.2	‡69.1	78.0	85.6	93.1
Unit Value of Imports **75**	27.4	28.3	28.6	‡30.7	45.1	‡44.3	48.9	54.6	55.2	60.8	72.0	‡85.4	96.6	104.5	114.7

Banking Survey (EA-Wide Residency)

End of Period

Item	1999	Code
Foreign Assets (Net)	147,786	31n.*u*
Domestic Credit	1,480,895	32..*u*
Claims on General Govt. (Net)	379,616	32an *u*
Claims on Other Resident Sect.	1,101,279	32d.*u*
Currency in Circulation	49,282	34a.*u*
Demand Deposits	248,468	34b.*u*
Other Deposits	649,980	35..*u*
o/w: Other Dep. Over Two Yrs	299,588	35ab *u*
Money Market Instruments	314,039	36m.*u*
Bonds (Debt Securities)	360,322	36n.*u*
o/w: Bonds Over Two Years	336,089	36na *u*
Capital Accounts	269,379	37a
Other Items (Net)	−262,790	37r.*u*

Money (National Definitions)

End of Period

1985	1986	1987	1988	1989	1990	1991	1992	1993	1994	1995	1996	1997	1998	1999	Item	Code
1,294	1,386	1,446	1,506	1,622	1,685	1,606	1,603	1,626	1,671	1,800	1,815	1,933	1,993	....	M1	39ma
1,198	1,298	1,360	1,396	1,475	1,535	1,532	1,521	1,513	1,559	1,581	1,666	1,735	1,884	....	M1, Seasonally Adjusted	39ma c
2,471	2,585	2,696	2,796	2,918	2,944	2,845	2,807	2,854	3,003	3,246	3,363	3,624	3,781	....	M2	39mb
2,322	2,469	2,556	2,651	2,755	2,786	2,766	2,719	2,696	2,806	2,935	3,143	3,356	3,641	....	M2, Seasonally Adjusted	39mb c
3,218	3,425	3,808	4,117	4,523	4,930	5,029	5,287	5,134	5,225	5,463	5,281	5,385	5,532	....	M3	39mc
3,058	3,282	3,569	3,919	4,257	4,635	4,920	5,138	5,217	5,083	5,283	5,318	5,263	5,492	....	M3, Seasonally Adjusted	39mc c
3,221	3,448	3,848	4,157	4,586	4,979	5,078	5,343	5,184	5,296	5,541	5,364	5,511	5,622	....	M4	39md
3,058	3,305	3,610	3,965	4,315	4,688	4,975	5,190	5,273	5,142	5,360	5,409	5,369	5,590	....	M4, Seasonally Adjusted	39md c

Interest Rates

Percent Per Annum

1985	1986	1987	1988	1989	1990	1991	1992	1993	1994	1995	1996	1997	1998	1999	Item	Code
9.85	7.52	7.75	7.16	8.64	9.55	9.07	9.56	7.60	5.44	4.96	3.60	3.15	3.28	....	Repurchase of Agreements	60a
9.93	7.74	7.98	7.52	9.07	9.85	9.49	10.35	8.75	5.69	6.35	3.73	3.24	3.39	....	Money Market Rate	60b
10.08	7.79	8.22	7.88	9.34	I10.18	9.69	10.49	8.41	5.79	6.58	3.84	3.35	3.45	2.72	Treasury Bill Rate	60c
6.25	5.00	4.50	4.50	4.50	4.50	4.50	4.50	4.50	4.50	4.50	3.67	3.50	3.21	2.69	Deposit Rate	60l
11.09	9.89	9.60	9.43	10.00	10.57	10.22	10.00	8.90	7.89	8.12	6.77	6.34	6.55	6.36	Lending Rate	60p
10.94	8.44	9.43	9.06	8.79	9.94	9.05	8.60	6.91	7.35	7.59	6.39	5.63	4.72	4.69	Government Bond Yield	61

Prices, Production, Labor

Period Averages

1985	1986	1987	1988	1989	1990	1991	1992	1993	1994	1995	1996	1997	1998	1999	Item	Code
I42.2	64.6	74.9	I68.4	95.4	97.5	94.3	99.8	109.8	109.7	100.0	113.0	148.3	200.1	248.1	Share Prices	62
															Producer Prices	
100.0	....	....	....	....	....	....	....	....	....	....	....	....	....	....	Indust. Goods,Tax Incl.(1985=100)	63
92.2	89.6	90.2	94.8	100.0	98.8	97.5	95.9	I93.2	94.2	100.0	97.3	96.7	95.9	94.5	Intermediate Indust. Goods	63a
102.1	77.8	I80.7	103.1	127.9	101.7	91.4	82.2	I74.7	88.3	100.0	87.1	96.8	81.4	83.1	Imported Raw Materials	63b
77.0	78.9	81.5	83.7	86.7	I89.6	92.5	94.7	96.6	98.3	100.0	102.0	103.2	I103.9	104.5	Consumer Prices	64
....	....	....	....	....	....	....	....	....	....	100.0	102.1	103.4	104.1	104.7	Harmonized CPI	64h
71.9	75.1	78.6	81.1	84.9	86.2	90.0	93.4	96.3	99.2	100.0	I101.9	104.7	107.6	110.0	Labor Costs	65
87.9	88.7	90.4	94.7	98.6	I100.4	99.2	98.0	94.3	98.0	100.0	100.3	I104.2	109.6	112.0	Industrial Production	66..c
118.2	116.0	113.3	112.1	113.0	113.6	111.5	108.5	103.2	101.0	100.0	97.2	96.5	96.9	96.8	Industrial Employment	67..c

Period Averages

1985	1986	1987	1988	1989	1990	1991	1992	1993	1994	1995	1996	1997	1998	1999	Item	Code
								25,756	....	26,803	26,404	26,404	....	....	Labor Force	67d
21,450	21,551	21,631	21,830	22,154	21,454	21,595	21,609	I20,432	20,120	20,010	20,088	20,087	....	....	Employment	67e
....	2,517	2,622	2,563	2,532	2,505	2,709	2,911	3,172	3,329	I2,893	3,063	3,102	2,977	2,772	Unemployment	67c
10.2	10.4	10.5	10.0	9.4	8.9	9.4	I10.1	11.1	12.4	11.6	12.1	12.3	11.8	....	Unemployment Rate (%)	67r

International Transactions

Billions of Euros Beginning 1999

1985	1986	1987	1988	1989	1990	1991	1992	1993	1994	1995	1996	1997	1998	1999	Item	Code
907	864	889	998	1,143	1,177	1,221	1,249	1,190	1,295	1,420	1,234	1,693	1,802	I281.95	Exports	70
968	896	950	1,063	1,230	1,274	1,303	1,268	1,149	1,298	1,404	1,203	1,585	1,709	I272.31	Imports, c.i.f.	71
931	863	921	1,030	1,187	1,227	1,251	1,218	1,101	1,244	1,358	1,394	1,522	1,638	I264.16	Imports, f.o.b.	71.v

1995=100

1985	1986	1987	1988	1989	1990	1991	1992	1993	1994	1995	1996	1997	1998	1999	Item	Code
60.7	I61.0	63.2	68.7	74.1	77.8	I81.4	I84.4	85.9	93.0	100.0	103.9	I114.5	122.1	....	Volume of Exports	72
60.6	I62.6	67.0	71.4	77.6	81.5	I83.4	I84.6	87.0	95.1	100.0	102.4	I110.3	118.9	....	Volume of Imports	73
96.3	91.5	90.7	94.2	99.8	98.0	97.6	95.0	92.0	I98.3	100.0	99.9	101.2	102.0	....	Unit Value of Exports	74
116.0	97.6	96.3	98.8	106.4	104.4	103.3	99.3	94.4	I98.3	100.0	100.6	102.0	102.1	....	Unit Value of Imports	75

France

		1970	1971	1972	1973	1974	1975	1976	1977	1978	1979	1980	1981	1982	1983	1984
Balance of Payments														*Billions of US Dollars:*		
Current Account, n.i.e.	78al d	...	...	...	...	...	2.74	-3.36	-.41	7.06	5.14	-4.21	-4.81	-12.08	-5.17	-.88
Goods: Exports f.o.b.	78aa d	...	...	...	...	...	50.42	54.05	61.99	75.19	95.51	109.69	102.58	93.38	91.32	93.37
Goods: Imports f.o.b.	78ab d	...	...	...	...	...	-49.39	-59.05	-65.34	-75.22	-99.14	-123.77	-112.72	-108.83	-99.73	-97.87
Trade Balance	78ac d	...	...	...	...	...	1.03	-4.99	-3.35	-.03	-3.63	-14.08	-10.14	-15.45	-8.41	-4.49
Services: Credit	78ad d	...	...	...	...	...	18.18	19.23	22.86	30.13	36.26	43.51	41.24	35.84	34.25	34.33
Services: Debit	78ae d	...	...	...	...	...	-13.99	-15.39	-17.72	-21.02	-25.70	-32.15	-33.29	-28.04	-25.66	-25.43
Balance on Goods & Services	78af d	...	...	...	...	...	5.22	-1.15	1.79	9.08	6.94	-2.72	-2.19	-7.64	.17	4.41
Income: Credit	78ag d	...	...	...	...	...	5.14	5.33	6.36	9.29	14.35	20.92	26.16	25.44	20.22	20.42
Income: Debit	78ah d	...	...	...	...	...	-5.00	-5.10	-5.72	-8.03	-12.12	-18.24	-24.55	-25.25	-21.74	-22.81
Balance on Gds, Serv. & Inc.	78ai d	...	...	...	...	...	5.37	-.91	2.42	10.34	9.17	-.04	-.58	-7.46	-1.35	2.02
Current Transfers, n.i.e.: Credit	78aj d	...	...	...	...	...	2.58	2.66	3.22	4.08	5.54	6.16	5.33	4.93	5.05	5.01
Current Transfers: Debit	78ak d	...	...	...	...	...	-5.21	-5.10	-6.04	-7.35	-9.56	-10.33	-9.56	-9.55	-8.87	-7.91
Capital Account, n.i.e.	78bc d	...	...	...	...	...	—	—	—	—	—	—	—	—	—	—
Capital Account, n.i.e.: Credit	78ba d	...	...	...	...	...	—	—	—	—	—	—	—	—	—	—
Capital Account: Debit	78bb d	...	...	...	...	...	—	—	—	—	—	—	—	—	—	—
Financial Account, n.i.e.	78bj d	...	...	...	...	...	-.58	-.48	-.39	-3.71	-3.89	8.49	3.51	9.27	8.41	3.16
Direct Investment Abroad	78bd d	...	...	...	...	...	-1.34	-1.64	-1.00	-1.90	-1.99	-3.10	-4.55	-2.85	-1.71	-2.12
Dir. Invest. in Rep. Econ., n.i.e.	78be d	...	...	...	...	...	1.56	.98	1.90	2.47	2.59	3.28	2.47	1.59	1.73	2.40
Portfolio Investment Assets	78bf d	...	...	...	...	...	-.58	-.68	-.45	-1.02	-1.88	-2.07	-2.17	.19	-1.63	-.47
Equity Securities	78bk d	...	...	...	...	...	...	...	...	...	...	...	...	...	-.31	.15
Debt Securities	78bl d	...	...	...	...	...	-.58	-.68	-.45	-1.02	-1.88	-2.07	-2.17	.19	-1.32	-.62
Portfolio Investment Liab., n.i.e.	78bg d	...	...	...	...	...	1.69	1.99	1.41	.93	.28	2.37	1.84	7.00	7.40	7.46
Equity Securities	78bm d	...	...	...	...	...	...	...	...	...	...	...	...	...	.38	.20
Debt Securities	78bn d	...	...	...	...	...	1.69	1.99	1.41	.93	.28	2.37	1.84	7.00	7.02	7.25
Financial Derivatives Assets	78bw d	...	...	...	...	...	...	...	...	...	...	...	...	...	...	...
Financial Derivatives Liabilities	78bx d	...	...	...	...	...	...	...	...	...	...	...	...	...	...	...
Other Investment Assets	78bh d	...	...	...	...	...	-9.71	-14.65	-17.99	-20.97	-28.16	-31.46	-17.25	-11.51	-5.98	-13.54
Monetary Authorities	78bo d	...	...	...	...	...	—	—	—	—	—	—	—	—	—	—
General Government	78bp d	...	...	...	...	...	-.33	-.38	-.36	—	-.68	-1.88	-1.37	-1.48	-1.79	-1.66
Banks	78bq d	...	...	...	...	...	-10.02	-11.17	-16.58	-21.23	-22.71	-25.62	-8.79	-9.83	-1.69	-9.28
Other Sectors	78br d	...	...	...	...	...	.63	-3.09	-1.05	.26	-4.78	-3.96	-7.09	-.20	-2.50	-2.61
Other Investment Liab., n.i.e.	78bi d	...	...	...	...	...	7.80	13.52	15.74	16.78	25.27	39.46	23.17	14.85	8.61	9.43
Monetary Authorities	78bs d	...	...	...	...	...	.16	.26	-.46	.49	-.04	.67	1.64	1.59	-1.89	-.17
General Government	78bt d	...	...	...	...	...	.01	.03	.01	.02	-.06	-.03	.04	1.99	5.10	-.08
Banks	78bu d	...	...	...	...	...	7.35	9.80	12.78	14.26	19.73	29.26	14.44	7.23	2.78	6.92
Other Sectors	78bv d	...	...	...	...	...	.28	3.42	3.41	2.01	5.64	9.56	7.04	4.05	2.62	2.77
Net Errors and Omissions	78ca d	...	...	...	...	...	1.83	1.00	.92	-.06	.56	2.27	-2.28	-.96	.36	.65
Overall Balance	78cb d	...	...	...	...	...	3.99	-2.83	.13	3.30	1.81	6.56	-3.59	-3.77	3.61	2.93
Reserves and Related Items	79da d	...	...	...	...	...	-3.99	2.83	-.13	-3.30	-1.81	-6.56	3.59	3.77	-3.61	-2.93
Reserve Assets	79db d	...	...	...	...	...	-3.99	2.83	-.13	-3.30	-1.81	-6.56	3.59	3.77	-3.61	-2.93
Use of Fund Credit and Loans	79dc d	...	...	...	...	...	—	—	—	—	—	—	—	—	—	—
Exceptional Financing	79de d	...	...	...	...	...	...	...	...	...	...	...	...	...	...	...
International Investment Position														*Billions of US Dollars*		
Assets	79aa d	...	...	...	...	...	...	...	...	...	...	...	...	...	...	...
Direct Investment Abroad	79ab d	...	...	...	...	...	...	...	...	...	...	...	...	...	...	...
Portfolio Investment	79ac d	...	...	...	...	...	...	...	...	...	...	...	...	...	...	...
Equity Securities	79ad d	...	...	...	...	...	...	...	...	...	...	...	...	...	...	...
Debt Securities	79ae d	...	...	...	...	...	...	...	...	...	...	...	...	...	...	...
Financial Derivatives	79al d	...	...	...	...	...	...	...	...	...	...	...	...	...	...	...
Other Investment	79af d	...	...	...	...	...	...	...	...	...	...	...	...	158.59	152.41	154.38
Monetary Authorities	79ag d	...	...	...	...	...	...	...	...	...	...	...	...	—	—	—
General Government	79ah d	...	...	...	...	...	...	...	...	...	...	...	...	...	...	...
Banks	79ai d	...	...	...	...	...	...	...	...	...	...	...	...	147.00	141.37	143.44
Other Sectors	79aj d	...	...	...	...	...	...	...	...	...	...	...	...	...	...	...
Reserve Assets	79ak d	...	...	...	...	...	...	...	...	...	...	79.76	56.23	53.37	51.63	47.83
Liabilities	79la d	...	...	...	...	...	...	...	...	...	...	...	...	...	...	...
Dir. Invest. in Rep. Economy	79lb d	...	...	...	...	...	...	...	...	...	...	...	...	...	...	...
Portfolio Investment	79lc d	...	...	...	...	...	...	...	...	...	...	...	...	...	...	...
Equity Securities	79ld d	...	...	...	...	...	...	...	...	...	...	...	...	...	...	...
Debt Securities	79le d	...	...	...	...	...	...	...	...	...	...	...	...	...	...	...
Financial Derivatives	79ll d	...	...	...	...	...	...	...	...	...	...	...	...	...	...	...
Other investment	79lf d	...	...	...	...	...	...	...	...	...	...	...	...	174.88	178.53	167.77
Monetary Authorities	79lg d	...	...	...	...	...	...	...	...	...	...	...	...	3.76	2.39	1.94
General Government	79lh d	...	...	...	...	...	...	...	...	...	...	...	...	2.39	7.54	7.38
Banks	79li d	...	...	...	...	...	...	...	...	...	...	131.82	138.35	141.54	139.41	140.25
Other Sectors	79lj d	...	...	...	...	...	...	...	...	...	...	...	...	27.19	29.18	18.20

1985	1986	1987	1988	1989	1990	1991	1992	1993	1994	1995	1996	1997	1998	1999	Balance of Payments	
Minus Sign Indicates Debit																
-.03	2.43	-4.45	-4.62	-4.67	-9.94	-6.52	3.89	8.99	7.42	10.84	20.56	39.47	40.16	37.23	Current Account, n.i.e.	78al d
97.10	120.53	143.00	161.59	172.19	208.93	209.17	227.44	199.04	230.81	278.63	281.85	284.20	301.70	298.15	Goods: Exports f.o.b.	78aa d
-101.92	-121.88	-150.78	-169.24	-182.49	-222.19	-218.89	-225.07	-191.53	-223.56	-267.63	-266.91	-256.13	-275.53	-278.08	Goods: Imports f.o.b.	78ab d
-4.81	-1.35	-7.78	-7.66	-10.31	-13.25	-9.71	2.37	7.52	7.25	11.00	14.94	28.07	26.17	20.07	*Trade Balance*	78ac d
35.56	43.08	50.49	54.52	59.94	76.46	80.10	91.77	86.38	75.52	84.09	83.53	81.14	85.42	83.34	Services: Credit	78ad d
-25.89	-33.03	-40.11	-43.84	-46.34	-61.05	-63.69	-72.65	-69.54	-57.67	-66.12	-67.28	-63.65	-66.72	-64.26	Services: Debit	78ae d
4.85	8.70	2.61	3.03	3.29	2.15	6.70	21.49	24.36	25.10	28.97	31.19	45.56	44.88	39.15	*Balance on Goods & Services*	78af d
21.79	24.24	27.56	34.02	41.29	55.74	69.77	87.60	98.99	41.56	45.18	47.55	52.76	62.39	67.85	Income: Credit	78ag d
-24.05	-25.92	-29.20	-34.97	-41.57	-59.63	-75.50	-96.21	-108.16	-48.32	-54.15	-50.25	-50.06	-58.01	-56.80	Income: Debit	78ah d
2.59	7.02	.97	2.08	3.01	-1.75	.96	12.87	15.19	18.34	20.01	28.48	48.25	49.26	50.19	*Balance on Gds, Serv. & Inc.*	78ai d
5.89	9.49	10.87	13.01	11.52	14.79	18.76	20.73	16.74	18.22	22.01	22.76	20.99	20.97	18.80	Current Transfers, n.i.e.: Credit	78aj d
-8.52	-14.08	-16.28	-19.71	-19.21	-22.99	-26.24	-29.71	-22.94	-29.15	-31.17	-30.68	-29.77	-30.07	-31.76	Current Transfers: Debit	78ak d
—	—	—	-.19	-.21	-4.13	-.03	.66	.03	-4.18	.51	1.23	1.48	1.47	1.47	Capital Account, n.i.e.	78bc d
—	—	—	.22	.23	.22	.25	.93	.30	.99	1.16	1.88	2.41	2.10	2.02	Capital Account, n.i.e.: Credit	78ba d
—	—	—	-.40	-.45	-4.35	-.28	-.27	-.28	-5.16	-.66	-.65	-.93	-.63	-.54	Capital Account: Debit	78bb d
2.44	-2.06	.99	-1.31	10.36	24.76	-3.07	-8.04	-16.67	-4.78	-7.33	-22.34	-39.91	-40.80	-41.80	Financial Account, n.i.e.	78bj d
-2.24	-5.40	-9.21	-14.50	-19.50	-34.82	-23.93	-31.27	-20.60	-24.44	-15.82	-30.36	-35.48	-40.80	-106.83	Direct Investment Abroad	78bd d
2.60	3.26	5.14	8.49	10.30	13.18	15.15	21.84	20.75	15.80	23.73	21.97	23.04	28.00	38.82	Dir. Invest. in Rep. Econ., n.i.e.	78be d
-2.47	-5.96	-3.27	-4.15	-6.65	-8.41	-15.33	-19.51	-31.16	-21.96	-7.42	-46.63	-60.79	-103.82	-129.84	Portfolio Investment Assets	78bf d
.68	-1.17	-1.98	-1.16	-1.46	.50	-2.98	-1.55	-2.52	....	1.78	-1.08	-9.67	-24.32	-19.05	Equity Securities	78bk d
-3.15	-4.79	-1.29	-2.99	-5.20	-8.91	-12.35	-17.96	-28.64	....	-9.20	-45.55	-51.12	-79.50	-110.79	Debt Securities	78bl d
8.95	7.83	8.71	11.95	32.04	43.22	29.54	52.50	34.52	-27.90	13.08	-15.35	35.32	56.18	115.44	Portfolio Investment Liab., n.i.e.	78bg d
2.00	4.19	3.41	1.75	7.00	5.90	7.66	5.41	13.58	....	6.82	12.20	11.96	15.77	45.14	Equity Securities	78bm d
6.95	3.64	5.30	10.20	25.05	37.32	21.87	47.09	20.94	....	6.26	-27.56	23.36	40.40	70.30	Debt Securities	78bn d
....	....	....	....	....	....	-.39	1.04	-.34	....	—	-6.47	-9.75	-15.49	....	Financial Derivatives Assets	78bw d
....	....	....	....	....	....	....	....	....	....	1.00	7.81	10.14	12.37	-2.20	Financial Derivatives Liabilities	78bx d
-6.86	-9.87	-47.04	-28.18	-62.79	-61.54	.15	-61.09	-13.38	23.06	-40.16	26.31	-51.86	25.94	-31.23	Other Investment Assets	78bh d
—	—	—	—	—	—	—	—	—	-.24	.50	.13	-.43	-.05	-11.30	Monetary Authorities	78bo d
-1.77	-2.93	-5.67	-5.16	-4.47	-1.57	-5.13	-4.96	-3.91	3.08	-.65	1.11	1.18	.86	.94	General Government	78bp d
-6.11	-8.55	-36.85	-23.52	-52.30	-52.83	8.74	-65.09	-46.69	22.72	-43.19	28.59	-46.70	41.73	-11.98	Banks	78bq d
1.02	1.61	-4.52	.50	-6.02	-7.14	-3.46	8.96	37.22	-2.50	3.18	-3.52	-5.91	-16.60	-1.83	Other Sectors	78br d
2.47	8.09	46.66	25.08	56.96	73.14	-8.26	28.44	-6.46	30.67	18.26	20.38	49.48	7.00	74.05	Other Investment Liab., n.i.e.	78bi d
.31	.07	7.09	-4.10	3.54	-.33	.64	22.02	-1.07	-14.41	.45	-.47	-.24	.61	27.94	Monetary Authorities	78bs d
-2.04	-3.87	-.37	-.23	-.02	-.56	-.13	.11	.23	3.16	1.10	-.01	4.67	.15	1.13	General Government	78bt d
3.52	12.20	33.99	27.36	57.50	80.26	-5.07	10.39	-5.69	32.11	13.12	15.83	39.05	2.26	42.77	Banks	78bu d
.67	-.30	5.95	2.06	-4.07	-6.24	-3.69	-4.08	.07	9.81	3.59	5.04	6.00	3.98	2.21	Other Sectors	78bv d
.29	.81	.85	.95	-6.34	.26	4.42	1.90	2.65	3.99	-3.31	.79	4.89	8.82	1.31	Net Errors and Omissions	78ca d
2.70	1.18	-2.60	-5.16	-.86	10.95	-5.19	-1.58	-5.01	2.45	.71	.24	5.94	19.82	-1.78	*Overall Balance*	78cb d
-2.70	-1.18	2.60	5.16	.86	-10.95	5.19	1.58	5.01	-2.45	-.71	-.24	-5.94	-19.82	1.45	Reserves and Related Items	79da d
-2.70	-1.18	2.60	5.16	.86	-10.95	5.19	1.58	5.01	-2.45	-.71	-.24	-5.94	-19.82	1.45	Reserve Assets	79db d
—	—	—	—	—	—	—	—	—	—	—	—	—	—	—	Use of Fund Credit and Loans	79dc d
—	—	—	—	—	—	—	—	—	—	—	—	—	—	—	Exceptional Financing	79de d
Billions of US Dollars															International Investment Position	
....	....	....	....	587.46	736.31	754.91	812.07	905.94	1,077.09	1,207.51	1,227.58	1,319.57	1,556.94	....	Assets	79aa d
....	....	51.69	51.46	75.41	110.12	129.90	140.58	141.43	184.87	208.08	215.35	218.62	275.43	....	Direct Investment Abroad	79ab d
....	....	....	....	73.65	81.05	91.51	96.10	130.18	186.23	205.10	260.68	337.92	489.50	....	Portfolio Investment	79ac d
....	....	....	....	45.23	40.20	44.42	42.51	51.84	53.76	58.31	73.50	99.51	148.08	....	Equity Securities	79ad d
....	....	....	....	28.42	40.85	47.08	53.59	78.35	132.47	146.80	187.19	238.41	341.42	....	Debt Securities	79ae d
....	....	....	....	....	....	....	....	....	24.80	31.37	34.73	38.54	50.03	....	Financial Derivatives	79al d
178.15	206.31	278.86	289.40	379.60	476.45	470.24	521.77	581.82	623.25	704.33	659.48	668.88	667.79	....	Other Investment	79af d
—	—	—	—	—	—	—	—	—	1.25	.92	.76	1.17	2.12	....	Monetary Authorities	79ag d
....	....	....	....	35.18	40.48	44.79	46.47	54.21	38.53	43.69	42.10	38.11	40.38	....	General Government	79ah d
162.52	184.82	247.79	257.87	313.85	388.96	382.75	431.52	464.58	461.95	521.49	475.86	498.47	479.59	....	Banks	79ai d
....	....	....	....	30.56	47.01	42.70	43.78	63.02	121.51	138.22	140.75	131.13	145.71	....	Other Sectors	79aj d
54.75	65.36	75.33	59.76	58.80	68.70	63.26	53.62	52.51	57.94	58.63	57.33	55.62	74.18	....	Reserve Assets	79ak d
....	....	....	....	561.52	757.99	813.85	848.02	955.81	1,085.11	1,223.90	1,235.99	1,285.13	1,531.19	....	Liabilities	79la d
....	....	....	—	60.52	84.93	97.45	100.21	103.20	158.17	185.37	192.69	190.73	232.56	....	Dir. Invest. in Rep. Economy	79lb d
....	....	....	....	153.44	215.27	260.85	287.42	366.13	366.65	417.94	424.10	475.69	632.02	....	Portfolio Investment	79lc d
....	....	....	....	50.29	54.83	71.18	71.39	103.60	102.28	120.82	155.28	197.98	288.15	....	Equity Securities	79ld d
....	....	24.47	27.48	103.14	160.44	189.67	216.04	262.52	264.37	297.12	268.82	277.72	343.88	....	Debt Securities	79le d
....	....	....	....	....	....	....	....	....	20.26	32.98	38.29	41.01	52.88	....	Financial Derivatives	79ll d
182.00	204.03	272.67	280.13	347.55	457.80	455.54	460.39	486.49	540.03	587.61	580.92	577.70	613.72	....	Other investment	79lf d
2.91	3.43	6.80	6.73	8.32	8.43	8.21	26.26	18.37	1.76	2.06	2.31	2.35	2.70	....	Monetary Authorities	79lg d
5.29	1.56	5.72	.96	.93	.49	.37	.38	.31	9.41	11.27	10.64	13.98	15.19	....	General Government	79lh d
153.57	178.40	237.69	252.74	318.62	427.18	424.39	413.30	389.41	435.02	466.37	468.95	472.85	497.25	....	Banks	79li d
20.22	20.64	22.45	19.71	19.68	21.70	22.57	20.45	78.40	93.85	107.92	99.03	88.51	98.58	....	Other Sectors	79lj d

France

		1970	1971	1972	1973	1974	1975	1976	1977	1978	1979	1980	1981	1982	1983	1984
Government Finance																
Central Government														*Billions of Francs through 1998;*		
Deficit (-) or Surplus	80	3.7	−3.5	I 6.8	4.7	5.8	−37.8	−17.1	−22.3	−29.6	−37.0	−2.0	−73.2	−121.9	−140.7	−116.3
Revenue	81	169.9	180.2	I 331.3	372.0	455.9	512.6	625.5	695.6	787.1	935.4	1,112.9	1,275.5	1,482.4	1,652.5	1,817.7
Grants Received	81z	....	....	I 3.3	3.5	3.8	5.4	6.1	6.3	7.0	7.7	12.2	13.5	16.6	21.3	19.8
Exp. & Lending Minus Repay.	82z	166.2	183.7	I 329.1	366.0	453.3	555.5	642.4	719.8	835.4	970.0	1,121.9	1,353.1	1,638.8	1,805.3	1,971.6
Expenditure	82	....	....	I 320.2	356.7	440.4	536.9	620.7	701.2	818.6	945.4	1,110.0	1,328.2	1,570.5	1,774.1	1,943.4
Lending Minus Repayments	83	....	....	I 8.9	9.3	12.9	18.6	21.7	18.6	16.8	24.6	11.9	24.9	68.3	31.2	28.2
Overall Adj. to Cash Basis	80x	....	....	I 1.3	−4.8	−.6	−.3	−6.3	−4.4	11.7	−10.1	−5.2	−9.1	17.9	−9.2	17.8
Financing																
Net Borrowing	84	−4.3	−2.5	I 1.8	.1	−4.0	46.3	20.8	35.7	56.0	40.0	31.6	83.8	185.3	119.8	160.4
Domestic	84a	....	....	I 1.7	−1.2	−4.9	46.2	19.4	34.0	56.2	38.5	31.5	82.5	185.5	117.7	161.9
Foreign	85a	....	....	I .1	1.3	.9	.1	1.4	1.7	−.2	1.5	.1	1.3	−.2	2.1	−1.5
Finance from Foreign Aid	86a	—	—	....	....	....	....	....	....	....	....	....	....	....	....	....
Use of Cash Balances	87	.6	5.9	I −8.3	−5.6	−.7	−8.6	−3.3	−13.1	−26.4	−3.0	−29.6	−10.6	−63.4	20.9	−44.1
Adj. to Total Financing	84x	....	....	I −.3	.8	−1.1	.1	−.4	−.3							
Debt: Francs	88b	89.2	87.4	78.1	77.7	87.4	123.3	133.9	149.7	188.1	362.5	404.4	485.3	599.4	751.0	883.7
Foreign Currency	89b	9.7	8.8	8.3	8.3	8.2	5.9	4.8	5.7	9.6	10.3	13.9	15.1	17.3	29.4	31.7
General Government															*As Percent of*	
Deficit (-) or Surplus	80g	....	....	....	....	....	....	....	....	....	....	....	....	....	....	....
Debt	88g	....	....	....	....	....	....	....	....	....	....	....	....	....	....	....
National Accounts														*Billions of Francs through 1998;*		
Househ.Cons.Expend.,incl.NPISHs	96f. c	457.2	508.4	567.3	641.6	745.6	857.8	988.4	1,111.4	1,257.5	1,434.8	1,645.0	1,897.8	2,190.4	2,424.1	2,639.2
Government Consumption Expend	91f. c	119.0	134.6	149.8	171.1	204.2	247.9	292.9	335.2	390.1	443.8	517.5	604.3	711.8	793.5	866.4
Gross Fixed Capital Formation	93e. c	192.9	218.3	244.4	285.2	336.1	354.3	407.2	439.4	488.5	555.1	645.8	694.6	774.3	809.7	840.4
Changes in Inventories	93i. c	20.2	13.3	16.1	22.1	30.1	−10.0	24.5	29.4	17.5	32.5	34.3	−7.5	18.9	−14.0	−12.4
Exports of Goods & Services	90c. c	125.4	145.2	165.1	198.6	269.6	279.8	333.0	392.8	445.4	527.0	604.4	714.2	790.4	900.6	1,053.3
Imports of Goods & Services	98c. c	−121.2	−135.6	−154.9	−188.7	−282.7	−262.3	−345.4	−390.5	−416.4	−512.1	−638.7	−744.8	−859.6	−907.4	−1,025.0
Gross Domestic Product (GDP)	99b. c	793.5	884.2	987.9	1,129.8	1,303.0	1,467.9	1,700.6	1,917.8	2,182.6	2,481.1	2,808.3	3,164.8	3,626.0	4,006.5	4,361.9
Net Primary Income from Abroad	98.n c	3.3	2.9	2.2	2.4	4.1	2.4	2.9	3.9	4.7	8.6	12.6	10.3	2.0	−11.7	−23.5
Gross National Income (GNI)	99a. c	796.8	887.1	990.1	1,132.2	1,307.1	1,470.3	1,703.5	1,921.7	2,187.3	2,489.7	2,820.9	3,175.1	3,628.0	3,994.8	4,338.4
GDP Volume 1980 prices	99b. r	2,028.9	2,126.0	2,220.2	2,340.9	2,413.7	2,407.0	2,509.1	2,589.9	2,676.6	2,763.4	2,808.3	2,841.3	2,913.7	2,933.9	2,972.5
GDP Vol. 1995 Ref., Chained	99b. r	....	....	....	....	....	....	....	....	....	....	....	....	....	....	....
GDP Volume (1995=100)	99bv r	54.4	57.0	59.5	62.7	64.7	64.5	67.2	69.4	71.7	74.0	75.2	76.1	78.1	78.6	79.6
GDP Deflator (1995=100)	99bi r	18.8	20.0	21.4	23.2	26.0	29.4	32.6	35.7	39.3	43.2	48.2	53.6	59.9	65.8	70.7
																Millions:
Population	99z	50.77	51.25	51.70	52.13	52.49	52.79	52.91	53.15	53.38	53.61	53.88	54.18	54.48	54.73	54.95

	1985	1986	1987	1988	1989	1990	1991	1992	1993	1994	1995	1996	1997	1998	1999		
																Government Finance	
																Central Government	
Millions of Euros Beginning 1999: Year Ending December 31	-127.7	-170.2	-64.5	-134.2	-118.6	-136.5	-85.6	-274.0	-402.0	-412.0	-502.6	-413.3	-284.4	....	....	Deficit (-) or Surplus	80
	1,962.4	2,076.6	2,206.9	2,342.8	2,495.6	2,638.7	2,766.2	2,845.5	2,871.3	2,983.5	3,116.5	3,271.2	3,438.7	....	....	Revenue	81
	18.9	26.4	26.3	35.5	33.2	34.6	51.7	47.2	50.2	48.8	53.0	46.6	51.8	....	....	Grants Received	81z
	2,122.8	2,268.7	2,313.8	2,480.3	2,612.8	2,761.6	2,983.3	3,159.0	3,319.0	3,429.8	3,662.0	3,740.9	3,797.3	....	....	Exp. & Lending Minus Repay.	82z
	2,099.4	2,228.7	2,325.8	2,462.9	2,595.3	2,770.0	2,950.5	3,154.7	3,336.9	3,458.2	3,564.7	3,687.2	3,789.2	....	....	Expenditure	82
	23.4	40.0	-12.0	17.4	17.5	-8.4	32.8	4.3	-17.9	-28.4	97.3	53.7	8.1	....	....	Lending Minus Repayments	83
	13.8	-4.5	16.1	-32.2	-34.6	-48.2	79.8	-7.7	-4.5	-14.5	-10.1	9.8	22.4	....	....	Overall Adj. to Cash Basis	80x
																Financing	
	164.3	135.5	128.5	84.1	151.9	152.7	84.7	328.8	460.3	326.7	451.5	364.9	....	....	....	Net Borrowing	84
	163.5	135.3	121.1	60.3	105.8	81.9	66.1	293.9	420.5	375.9	396.1	350.0	....	....	....	Domestic	84a
	.8	.2	7.4	23.8	46.1	70.8	18.6	34.9	39.8	-49.2	55.4	14.9	....	....	....	Foreign	85a
	....	....	....	....	....	....	....	....	....	....	....	....	....	....	....	Finance from Foreign Aid	86a
	-36.6	34.8	-64.0	50.1	-33.3	-16.2	.9	-54.8	-58.3	85.3	51.1	48.4	....	....	....	Use of Cash Balances	87
	—	—	—	—	—	—	—	—	—	—	—	—	....	....	....	Adj. to Total Financing	84x
	1,030.8	1,162.9	1,248.5	1,438.3	1,582.0	1,744.1	1,827.1	2,056.6	2,417.1	2,859.2	3,214.2	3,506.8	3,738.2	3,977.9	....	Debt: Francs	88b
	40.0	31.9	33.4	36.7	40.4	38.4	37.8	55.4	57.9	62.6	58.6	57.1	56.4	49.8	....	Foreign Currency	89b
																General Government	
Gross Domestic Product	....	....	....	....	....	-1.6	-2.1	-3.9	-5.8	-5.8	-4.9	-4.2	-3.0	-2.7	-1.8	Deficit (-) or Surplus	80g
	....	....	....	....	....	35.5	35.8	39.8	45.3	48.5	52.8	57.1	59.0	59.3	58.6	Debt	88g
																National Accounts	
Billions of Euros Beginning 1999	2,858.4	3,049.5	3,235.6	I 3,203.3	3,437.7	3,633.9	3,790.0	3,911.9	3,999.4	4,111.6	I 4,260.1	4,394.9	4,459.1	4,645.1	I 729.3	Househ.Cons.Expend.,incl.NPISHs	96f. c
	923.0	972.8	1,018.6	I 1,325.5	1,398.1	1,473.9	1,551.6	1,644.9	1,768.9	1,809.7	I 1,851.5	1,922.9	1,986.2	2,009.6	I 318.2	Government Consumption Expend	91f. c
	905.3	977.5	1,054.8	I 1,277.3	1,414.9	1,494.9	1,512.5	1,490.7	1,398.8	1,428.7	I 1,458.2	1,469.2	1,473.0	1,564.9	I 255.4	Gross Fixed Capital Formation	93e. c
	-17.9	17.2	20.7	40.5	53.7	49.8	35.5	-2.9	-90.4	-6.2	I 31.0	-12.2	-7.4	42.3	I -.1	Changes in Inventories	93i. c
	1,123.9	1,074.1	1,101.4	I 1,188.2	1,364.4	1,411.2	1,479.1	1,529.3	1,494.7	1,610.2	I 1,747.7	1,831.4	2,093.3	2,228.8	I 350.3	Exports of Goods & Services	90c. c
	-1,092.6	-1,021.8	-1,094.3	-1,236.8	-1,422.2	-1,473.5	-1,510.4	-1,488.6	-1,386.4	-1,509.5	I -1637.2	-1,700.2	-1,849.2	-2,006.3	I -318.3	Imports of Goods & Services	98c. c
	4,700.1	5,069.3	5,336.6	I 5,824.8	6,275.5	6,621.3	6,891.0	7,120.4	7,227.1	7,488.4	I 7,752.4	7,951.4	8,207.1	8,536.3	I 1,344.0	Gross Domestic Product (GDP)	99b. c
	-25.6	-16.6	-12.5	-31.8	-36.3	-32.1	-38.3	-57.6	-56.2	-52.9	-40.9	-4.6	19.0	33.7	I 7.1	Net Primary Income from Abroad	98.n c
	4,674.5	5,052.7	5,324.2	5,703.3	6,123.4	6,452.2	6,710.6	6,918.4	7,022.9	7,329.9	7,711.5	7,946.8	8,226.1	8,570.0	I 1,351.5	Gross National Income (GNI)	99a. c
	3,028.4	3,104.6	3,174.5	3,317.3	....	....	....	....	....	....	....	....	....	....	....	GDP Volume 1980 prices	99b. r
	....	....	....	6,892.7	7,191.4	7,373.9	7,451.8	7,549.5	7,480.9	7,615.0	7,756.0	7,840.1	7,988.5	8,247.7	I 1,294.3	GDP Vol. 1995 Ref., Chained	99b. r
	81.1	83.2	85.0	88.9	92.7	95.1	96.1	97.3	96.5	98.2	100.0	101.1	103.0	106.3	I 109.5	GDP Volume (1995=100)	99bv r
	74.7	78.6	80.9	I 84.5	87.3	89.8	92.5	94.4	96.7	98.4	I 100.0	101.5	102.8	103.5	I 103.9	GDP Deflator (1995=100)	99bi r
Midyear Estimates	55.17	55.55	55.82	55.12	56.42	56.73	57.05	57.37	57.65	57.90	58.14	58.37	58.61	58.85	59.10	Population	99z

(See notes in the back of the book.)

Gabon

		1970	1971	1972	1973	1974	1975	1976	1977	1978	1979	1980	1981	1982	1983	1984
Exchange Rates																*Francs per SDR:*
Official Rate	aa	276.02	283.61	278.00	284.00	272.08	262.55	288.70	285.76	272.28	264.78	287.99	334.52	370.92	436.97	470.11
																Francs per US Dollar:
Official Rate	ae	276.02	261.22	256.05	235.42	222.22	224.27	248.49	235.25	209.00	201.00	225.80	287.40	336.25	417.37	479.60
Official Rate	rf	276.40	275.59	252.03	222.89	240.70	214.31	238.95	245.68	225.66	212.72	211.28	271.73	328.61	381.07	436.96
															Index Numbers (1995=100):	
Official Rate	ahx	180.5	98.6	197.9	224.6	207.2	233.0	209.0	203.0	221.4	234.6	236.4	184.6	152.6	131.5	114.5
Nominal Effective Exchange Rate	nec	....	....	....	....	....	....	....	....	....	104.2	107.8	100.8	97.6	96.1	96.4
Real Effective Exchange Rate	rec	....	....	....	....	....	....	....	....	....	....	204.6	182.1	183.8	180.9	173.5
Fund Position																*Millions of SDRs:*
Quota	2f.s	15.00	15.00	15.00	15.00	15.00	15.00	15.00	15.00	30.00	30.00	45.00	45.00	45.00	73.10	73.10
SDRs	1b.s	1.60	3.17	4.73	4.70	4.66	4.63	4.62	4.61	4.55	7.21	5.64	6.97	.74	.42	5.82
Reserve Position in the Fund	1c.s	2.37	2.40	2.43	2.46	2.49	2.53	2.53	2.53				.03	.04	7.03	.03
Total Fund Cred.&Loans Outstg.	2tl									7.61	15.22	11.36	11.34	9.35	1.85	
International Liquidity														*Millions of US Dollars Unless Otherwise Indicated:*		
Total Reserves minus Gold	1l.d	14.74	25.39	23.23	47.86	103.29	146.07	116.16	9.91	22.57	20.13	107.50	198.85	311.88	186.90	199.45
SDRs	1b.d	1.60	3.44	5.14	5.67	5.71	5.42	5.37	5.60	5.93	9.50	7.19	8.11	.82	.44	5.70
Reserve Position in the Fund	1c.d	2.37	2.61	2.64	2.97	3.05	2.97	2.94	3.08		—		.03	.04	7.36	.03
Foreign Exchange	1d.d	10.77	19.34	15.45	39.22	94.53	137.68	107.84	1.23	16.65	10.64	100.31	190.71	311.02	179.10	193.72
Gold (Million Fine Troy Ounces)	1ad	....	....	....	....	....	....		.006	.010	.013	.013	.013	.013	.013	.013
Gold (National Valuation)	1and	....	....	....	....	....	....			1.06	2.24	6.68	7.57	5.14	5.77	4.86	3.97
Monetary Authorities: Other Liab.	4..d	.04	.06	.08	.05	.02	.03	.04	.04	.11	.35	.16	.20	.18	.35	.52	3.17
Deposit Money Banks: Assets	7a.d	.60	3.17	6.97	6.48	10.31	11.31	30.26	25.39	18.61	32.81	17.74	30.43	34.60	23.24	15.56
Liabilities	7b.d	17.88	13.09	16.44	21.85	43.42	39.62	54.01	131.16	125.31	108.73	80.92	105.51	83.10	36.35	16.73
Monetary Authorities																*Billions of Francs:*
Foreign Assets	11	4.09	6.49	5.94	11.02	22.95	32.76	28.86	2.58	5.19	5.40	25.99	58.63	106.81	80.05	97.56
Claims on Central Government	12a	1.61	—	—		1.00	4.10	9.27	27.03	28.57	33.98	23.90	3.79	5.16	.81	
Claims on Deposit Money Banks	12e	1.16	2.48	4.39	5.37	7.02	6.84	4.81	17.15	11.88	12.07	8.83	7.14	6.21	7.27	8.03
Claims on Other Banking Insts	12f	....	....	....	....	....	....	....	....	....	....	....	....	....	....	....
Reserve Money	14	5.73	6.95	7.93	10.26	18.95	24.44	40.27	40.94	35.72	37.91	45.06	48.26	52.59	57.53	68.00
of which: Currency Outside DMBs	14a	5.26	6.18	7.38	9.56	15.63	22.22	33.65	34.27	31.34	30.34	35.85	37.82	45.45	50.24	54.29
Foreign Liabilities	16c	.01	.02	.02	.01	.01	.01	.01	.03	2.15	4.06	3.32	3.84	3.59	1.02	1.52
Central Government Deposits	16d	.63	1.04	1.01	4.50	10.45	17.34	.21	3.21	3.15	2.15	1.79	9.12	55.89	25.19	33.33
Capital Accounts	17a	—	—	—	.02	.02	.03	.03	.04	.04	.05	1.64	1.39	1.98	2.10	1.93
Other Items (Net)	17r	.49	.97	1.37	1.59	1.55	1.89	2.43	2.55	4.57	7.28	6.92	6.94	4.12	2.29	.82
Deposit Money Banks																*Billions of Francs:*
Reserves	20	.48	.77	.55	.70	3.32	2.22	6.62	6.66	4.39	7.58	9.21	10.44	7.15	7.29	13.72
Foreign Assets	21	.17	.81	1.78	1.49	2.29	2.54	7.52	‡5.97	3.89	6.60	4.01	8.75	11.63	9.70	7.46
Claims on Central Government	22a	1.94	2.06	3.38	4.95	13.22	11.61	34.80	39.63	27.45	27.07	30.56	30.36	49.38	55.49	83.50
Claims on Nonfin.Pub.Enterprises	22c	....	....	....	....	....	....	....	....	....	....	....	....	....	....	....
Claims on Private Sector	22d	15.90	19.49	24.78	33.13	48.77	66.63	99.75	‡124.71	129.98	123.35	142.59	170.99	184.98	229.11	251.83
Claims on Other Banking Insts	22f	....	....	....	....	....	....	....	....	....	....	....	....	....	....	....
Claims on Nonbank Financial Insts	22g	....	....	....	....	....	....	....	....	....	....	....	....	....	....	....
Demand Deposits	24	7.55	8.70	11.41	13.70	22.82	37.26	71.33	‡65.26	59.37	55.56	59.03	77.76	81.58	94.20	115.11
Time and Savings Deposits	25	.95	.83	1.30	3.27	5.89	11.98	28.43	33.82	22.94	36.94	58.11	61.67	74.08	92.73	105.05
Bonds	26ab	....	....	....	....	....	....	....	....	....	....	....	....	....	....	....
Foreign Liabilities	26c	2.73	1.06	1.80	2.40	6.80	5.43	9.42	26.77	22.45	17.68	10.91	25.06	19.75	7.86	1.56
Long-Term Foreign Liabilities	26cl	2.24	2.29	2.40	2.63	2.85	3.46	4.00	4.09	3.74	4.17	7.37	5.27	8.20	7.31	6.47
Central Government Deposits	26d	1.57	2.84	4.34	6.38	13.93	9.40	17.71	19.31	37.19	22.60	17.62	22.22	26.23	48.52	65.31
Credit from Monetary Authorities	26g	1.16	2.48	4.39	5.37	6.16	6.18	4.33	16.16	11.32	11.63	8.48	6.65	6.21	7.27	8.03
Capital Accounts	27a	2.47	2.87	3.36	4.27	5.20	7.01	10.19	14.40	19.36	23.72	25.68	36.40	36.83	46.75	49.41
Other Items (Net)	27r	-.18	2.06	1.50	2.26	3.95	2.28	3.28	‡-2.82	-10.66	-7.70	-.83	-14.47	.26	-3.05	5.57
Monetary Survey																*Billions of Francs:*
Foreign Assets (Net)	31n	1.52	6.23	5.90	10.10	18.44	29.86	26.95	‡-18.24	-15.52	-9.75	15.77	38.47	95.10	80.87	101.94
Domestic Credit	32	17.25	17.67	22.81	27.20	38.60	55.60	125.90	‡168.86	145.66	159.66	177.64	173.81	157.39	211.69	236.69
Claims on Central Govt. (Net)	32an	1.35	-1.82	-1.96	-5.93	-10.17	-11.03	26.15	44.15	15.68	36.30	35.05	2.82	-27.58	-17.41	-15.14
Claims on Nonfin.Pub.Enterprises	32c	....	....	....	....	....	....	....	....	....	....	....	....	....	....	....
Claims on Private Sector	32d	15.90	19.49	24.78	33.13	48.77	66.63	99.75	‡124.71	129.98	123.35	142.59	170.99	184.98	229.11	251.83
Claims on Other Banking Insts	32f	....	....	....	....	....	....	....	....	....	....	....	....	....	....	....
Claims on Nonbank Financial Inst	32g	....	....	....	....	....	....	....	....	....	....	....	....	....	....	....
Money	34	12.81	14.88	18.79	23.26	38.44	59.48	104.97	‡99.53	90.70	85.90	94.88	115.58	127.02	144.43	169.40
Quasi-Money	35	.95	.83	1.30	3.27	5.89	11.98	28.43	33.82	22.94	36.94	58.11	61.67	74.08	92.73	105.05
Bonds	36ab	....	....	....	....	....	....	....	....	....	....	....	....	....	....	....
Other Items (Net)	37r	5.01	8.19	8.63	10.77	12.71	14.01	19.45	‡17.27	16.51	27.08	40.42	35.03	51.39	55.40	64.19
Money plus Quasi-Money	35l	13.76	15.71	20.09	26.53	44.33	71.46	133.40	‡133.35	113.64	122.83	152.99	177.25	201.11	237.16	274.44
Interest Rates																*Percent Per Annum:*
Discount Rate *(End of Period)*	60	4.50	4.50	4.50	4.50	5.50	5.50	6.50	6.50	6.50	8.50	8.50	8.50	8.50	8.50	8.50
Deposit Rate	60l	....	....	....	....	....	....	....	....	7.50	6.50	7.50	7.50	7.50	7.50	7.50
Lending Rate	60p	....	....	....	....	....	....	....	....	10.50	8.50	12.50	12.50	12.46	13.00	13.00
Prices and Production																*Index Numbers (1995=100):*
Consumer Prices	64	15.7	16.3	16.9	17.9	20.1	‡25.8	31.0	35.3	39.0	42.2	47.4	51.5	‡60.1	66.5	70.4
Crude Petroleum	66aa	....	....	....	....	....	....	....	....	65.9	59.9	51.4	44.0	45.2	45.9	44.8

1985	1986	1987	1988	1989	1990	1991	1992	1993	1994	1995	1996	1997	1998	1999		
															Exchange Rates	
End of Period																
415.26	394.78	378.78	407.68	380.32	364.84	370.48	378.57	404.89	I780.44	728.38	753.06	807.94	791.61	I896.19	Official Rate	aa
End of Period (ae) Period Average (rf)																
378.05	322.75	267.00	302.95	289.40	256.45	259.00	275.32	294.77	I534.60	490.00	523.70	598.81	562.21	I652.95	Official Rate	ae
449.26	346.31	300.54	297.85	319.01	272.26	282.11	264.69	283.16	I555.20	499.15	511.55	583.67	589.95	I615.70	Official Rate	rf
Period Averages																
111.9	144.3	166.1	167.8	156.5	183.7	177.4	188.9	176.3	90.0	100.0	97.5	85.6	84.7	81.1	Official Rate	ahx
102.0	111.1	118.9	126.6	138.3	162.1	163.2	173.5	179.0	96.0	100.0	100.5	97.1	99.5	97.0	Nominal Effective Exchange Rate	nec
178.9	194.8	191.4	165.5	167.2	181.4	153.4	138.5	134.3	90.6	100.0	98.9	97.4	100.8	96.2	Real Effective Exchange Rate	rec
															Fund Position	
End of Period																
73.10	73.10	73.10	73.10	73.10	73.10	73.10	110.30	110.30	110.30	110.30	110.30	110.30	110.30	154.30	Quota	2f.s
2.08	10.05	8.19	6.54	.17	.19	4.44	.08	.03	.17	—	.02	—	.01	—	SDRs	1b.s
.03	.03	.03	.03	.04	.04	.05	.05	.05	.05	.05	.07	.07	.07	.11	Reserve Position in the Fund	1c.s
—	27.41	42.50	98.68	102.69	98.49	84.34	58.55	32.89	61.42	64.95	83.26	97.20	80.52	62.60	Total Fund Cred.&Loans Outstg.	2tl
															International Liquidity	
End of Period																
192.55	126.35	12.00	67.44	34.43	273.76	327.48	71.21	.75	175.19	148.09	248.72	282.60	15.41	17.95	Total Reserves minus Gold	1l.d
2.28	12.29	11.62	8.80	.22	.27	6.35	.10	.03	.25	—	.03	—	.01	.01	SDRs	1b.d
.03	.04	.04	.04	.05	.06	.07	.07	.07	.08	.08	.09	.09	.09	.15	Reserve Position in the Fund	1c.d
190.23	114.02	.34	58.59	34.15	273.44	321.05	71.04	.64	174.86	148.01	248.59	282.51	15.30	17.79	Foreign Exchange	1d.d
.013	.013	.013	.013	.013	.013	.013	.013	.013	.013	.013	.013	.013	....	....	Gold (Million Fine Troy Ounces)	1ad
4.16	5.03	6.19	5.21	4.07	4.59	4.55	4.28	5.11	I4.85	4.95	4.73	3.74	3.69	....	Gold (National Valuation)	1and
1.35	.65	64.52	I125.25	73.66	76.97	74.50	45.95	35.48	33.67	34.56	33.52	53.73	34.62	46.34	Monetary Authorities: Other Liab.	4..d
26.49	43.01	39.44	40.77	82.79	89.44	88.02	61.55	53.13	82.23	75.69	159.03	64.55	71.56	74.88	Deposit Money Banks: Assets	7a.d
94.46	122.00	57.85	33.13	142.16	143.75	154.76	117.45	89.15	41.28	79.93	94.16	50.58	56.73	77.78	Liabilities	7b.d
															Monetary Authorities	
End of Period																
74.38	42.40	4.87	I22.02	11.45	71.48	85.99	20.78	1.70	96.30	74.99	132.74	171.45	10.74	14.15	Foreign Assets	11
—	28.51	81.99	I90.14	101.00	40.26	I42.53	58.00	62.47	95.83	101.92	123.60	87.49	211.13	200.78	Claims on Central Government	12a
26.98	22.83	28.82	I19.77	17.39	16.70	I11.77	23.54	19.82	.16	3.74	.75	—	8.11	11.63	Claims on Deposit Money Banks	12e
....	....	....	4.48	7.67	7.91	9.00	3.11	—	—	—	—	—	—	—	Claims on Other Banking Insts	12f
62.68	55.56	58.65	I54.63	63.28	69.02	88.44	63.58	58.38	133.91	128.24	165.20	167.93	153.60	141.52	Reserve Money	14
57.39	49.12	51.46	I48.13	57.50	61.88	62.88	56.79	50.47	76.93	100.69	110.88	121.03	124.72	105.26	*of which:* Currency Outside DMBs	14a
.51	11.03	33.33	I78.17	60.37	55.67	50.54	34.82	23.78	65.94	64.24	80.26	110.71	83.21	86.36	Foreign Liabilities	16c
35.25	8.34	12.44	I11.34	31.05	23.87	22.41	7.97	3.11	18.51	10.67	32.35	16.13	12.14	26.10	Central Government Deposits	16d
1.92	1.96	2.05	I7.67	7.09	6.90	7.16	6.97	7.59	12.49	11.53	11.89	12.31	11.87	13.75	Capital Accounts	17a
1.00	16.84	9.21	I-15.39	-24.28	-19.12	I-19.26	-7.90	-8.87	-38.56	-34.03	-32.61	-48.15	-30.85	-41.17	Other Items (Net)	17r
															Deposit Money Banks	
End of Period																
5.29	6.44	7.19	I5.81	5.53	7.07	25.49	5.94	7.86	56.87	27.06	48.32	44.10	27.47	34.75	Reserves	20
10.02	13.88	10.53	I12.38	23.96	22.94	22.80	16.95	15.66	43.96	37.09	83.28	38.65	40.23	48.89	Foreign Assets	21
109.78	81.37	90.40	I102.34	102.20	101.17	95.20	I105.35	99.25	172.94	161.16	152.37	143.46	135.76	137.99	Claims on Central Government	22a
....	....	....	22.49	22.84	19.06	19.90	8.78	9.88	10.17	9.49	13.60	26.91	23.20	22.32	Claims on Nonfin.Pub.Enterprises	22c
303.20	336.33	293.33	I192.09	208.58	210.54	224.39	162.01	157.91	157.20	196.08	191.93	269.89	285.12	286.06	Claims on Private Sector	22d
....	....	....	.17	—	.01				.88	.88	.91	1.39	.60	.74	Claims on Other Banking Insts	22f
....	....	....	2.18	2.64	4.06	4.04	4.65	4.22	7.07	10.22	7.99	7.66	7.55	10.53	Claims on Nonbank Financial Insts	22g
120.78	105.00	83.80	I114.24	113.40	118.98	132.48	84.71	86.92	117.96	117.90	159.11	174.41	156.99	168.61	Demand Deposits	24
129.41	122.51	105.46	I99.98	107.72	107.01	112.54	99.11	99.87	130.98	139.87	144.78	169.98	176.47	177.21	Time and Savings Deposits	25
....	....	....	.23	.16	.11	1.01	.90	1.20	.30	.23	.15	.08	3.09	5.55	Bonds	26ab
29.99	33.77	-6.74	I9.43	4.76	12.45	I21.78	19.86	19.37	13.73	36.34	46.79	28.24	22.66	38.99	Foreign Liabilities	26c
5.72	5.60	22.19	I34.97	36.44	24.42	I18.31	12.48	6.91	8.34	2.83	2.52	2.05	9.24	11.80	Long-Term Foreign Liabilities	26cl
62.75	57.60	51.27	I39.59	35.32	34.31	39.42	I22.88	16.72	32.21	15.35	20.93	20.62	21.82	29.67	Central Government Deposits	26d
26.98	24.83	28.82	I19.77	17.39	16.70	I11.77	23.54	19.82	.16	3.74	.75	—	8.11	11.63	Credit from Monetary Authorities	26g
58.20	62.56	77.28	I19.22	56.45	54.15	I58.91	54.68	54.55	133.44	128.50	123.58	115.89	122.47	120.48	Capital Accounts	27a
-5.54	28.15	39.37	I.02	-5.90	-3.27	-4.40	I-14.49	-10.58	11.97	-2.78	-.21	20.78	-.92	-15.89	Other Items (Net)	27r
															Monetary Survey	
End of Period																
53.90	11.48	-11.18	I-88.18	-66.16	1.88	I18.16	-29.43	-32.70	52.25	8.68	86.45	69.10	-64.14	-74.10	Foreign Assets (Net)	31n
314.98	380.27	402.00	I362.96	378.57	324.83	I333.22	I311.04	313.90	393.36	453.74	437.12	500.04	629.38	602.65	Domestic Credit	32
11.78	43.94	108.68	I141.55	136.83	83.25	I75.90	I132.50	141.89	218.05	237.06	222.68	194.19	312.92	283.00	Claims on Central Govt. (Net)	32an
....	....	....	22.49	22.84	19.06	19.90	8.78	9.88	10.17	9.49	13.60	26.91	23.20	22.32	Claims on Nonfin.Pub.Enterprises	32c
303.20	336.33	293.33	I192.09	208.58	210.54	224.39	162.01	157.91	157.20	196.08	191.93	269.89	285.12	286.06	Claims on Private Sector	32d
....	....	....	4.65	7.67	7.92	9.00	3.11	—	.88	.88	.91	1.39	.60	.74	Claims on Other Banking Insts	32f
....	....	....	2.18	2.64	4.06	4.04	4.65	4.22	7.07	10.22	7.99	7.66	7.55	10.53	Claims on Nonbank Financial Inst	32g
178.16	154.11	135.26	I163.06	171.16	180.93	195.43	142.35	137.44	195.01	219.09	276.00	298.25	283.12	268.61	Money	34
129.41	122.51	105.46	I99.98	107.72	107.01	112.54	99.11	99.87	130.98	139.87	144.78	169.98	176.47	177.21	Quasi-Money	35
....	....	....	.23	.16	.11	1.01	.90	1.20	.30	.23	.15	.08	3.09	5.55	Bonds	36ab
61.30	115.12	150.10	I11.52	33.37	38.65	I42.41	I39.26	42.69	119.33	103.23	102.64	100.84	102.57	77.17	Other Items (Net)	37r
307.58	276.62	240.72	I263.04	278.87	287.94	307.97	241.46	237.31	325.98	358.96	420.78	468.22	459.59	445.82	Money plus Quasi-Money	35l
															Interest Rates	
Percent Per Annum																
9.00	8.00	8.00	9.50	10.00	11.00	10.75	12.00	11.50	I7.75	8.60	7.75	7.50	7.00	7.60	Discount Rate (*End of Period*)	60
7.67	8.00	7.94	8.17	8.75	I7.50	7.50	7.50	7.75	8.08	5.50	5.46	5.00	5.00	5.00	Deposit Rate	60l
12.67	11.50	11.13	11.79	12.50	I18.50	18.15	17.77	17.46	17.50	16.00	22.00	22.00	22.00	22.00	Lending Rate	60p
															Prices and Production	
Period Averages																
75.5	80.3	79.5	72.6	77.4	83.4	73.7	66.6	67.0	91.2	100.0	100.7	104.7	....		Consumer Prices	64
44.9	47.6	45.8	51.4	64.6	81.4	82.5	87.5	86.4	96.7	100.0	105.5	107.6	103.5	99.6	Crude Petroleum	66aa

Gabon

		1970	1971	1972	1973	1974	1975	1976	1977	1978	1979	1980	1981	1982	1983	1984
International Transactions															*Billions of Francs*	
Exports	70	39.87	49.43	57.50	73.10	184.36	201.92	271.48	329.96	249.85	393.19	459.06	598.00	710.00	762.20	878.90
Imports, c.i.f.	71	22.23	25.31	35.00	42.29	79.89	100.56	120.24	176.00	139.17	113.11	142.31	229.00	285.00	261.10	316.20
Imports, c.i.f., from DOTS	71y	....	....	....	....	....	....	....	....	....	....	....	228.10	262.39	261.24	345.81
Balance of Payments															*Millions of US Dollars:*	
Current Account, n.i.e.	78al d	....	....	....	....	....	....	....	....	73.9	247.6	383.9	403.3	309.4	97.9	112.7
Goods: Exports f.o.b.	78aa d	....	....	....	....	....	....	....	....	1,308.6	1,815.0	2,084.4	2,200.2	2,160.4	2,000.1	2,017.8
Goods: Imports f.o.b.	78ab d	....	....	....	....	....	....	....	....	−557.9	−554.8	−686.1	−841.2	−722.6	−725.5	−733.2
Trade Balance	78ac d									750.7	1,260.2	1,398.3	1,359.0	1,437.8	1,274.6	1,284.6
Services: Credit	78ad d									169.9	208.8	324.6	307.6	170.3	200.8	137.8
Services: Debit	78ae d									−577.6	−741.9	−789.4	−868.2	−926.1	−1,031.4	−1,018.5
Balance on Goods & Services	78af d									343.0	727.1	933.5	798.4	681.9	444.0	403.9
Income: Credit	78ag d									4.4	7.3	24.9	25.2	20.0	43.2	47.7
Income: Debit	78ah d									−231.1	−368.8	−450.5	−355.2	−333.3	−299.8	−271.8
Balance on Gds, Serv. & Inc.	78ai d									116.2	365.6	507.9	468.4	368.6	187.4	179.8
Current Transfers, n.i.e.: Credit	78aj d									57.9	69.8	72.7	61.6	36.8	43.0	50.3
Current Transfers: Debit	78ak d									−100.2	−187.7	−196.8	−126.7	−96.0	−132.4	−117.4
Capital Account, n.i.e.	78bc d									—	—	—	—	—	—	—
Capital Account, n.i.e.: Credit	78ba d									—	—	—	—	—	—	—
Capital Account: Debit	78bb d									—	—	—	—	—	—	—
Financial Account, n.i.e.	78bj d									−20.2	−234.2	−265.9	−277.6	−111.3	−91.5	−15.8
Direct Investment Abroad	78bd d									—	−6.7	−8.0	−7.1	−4.8	−5.7	−3.4
Dir. Invest. in Rep. Econ., n.i.e.	78be d									56.5	55.0	31.5	54.6	131.7	111.8	8.1
Portfolio Investment Assets	78bf d	....	....	....	....	....	....	....	....	—	—	—	—	—	—	—
Equity Securities	78bk d									—	—	—	—	—	—	—
Debt Securities	78bl d									—	—	—	—	—	—	—
Portfolio Investment Liab., n.i.e.	78bg d									—	—	—	—	—	—	—
Equity Securities	78bm d									—	—	—	—	—	—	—
Debt Securities	78bn d									—	—	—	—	—	—	—
Financial Derivatives Assets	78bw d									....	....	....	....	....	....	....
Financial Derivatives Liabilities	78bx d															
Other Investment Assets	78bh d									−17.8	−177.3	−205.6	−239.1	−263.7	−175.7	−237.9
Monetary Authorities	78bo d									—	—	—	—	−.5	—	—
General Government	78bp d									−2.8	1.2	−1.6	−.6	—	—	—
Banks	78bq d									14.8	−16.5	17.5	−14.4	−8.8	5.1	5.1
Other Sectors	78br d									−29.8	−162.0	−221.5	−224.2	−254.4	−180.8	−243.1
Other Investment Liab., n.i.e.	78bi d									−58.9	−105.3	−83.8	−86.0	25.4	−21.9	217.3
Monetary Authorities	78bs d									.2	−.2	—	—	—	—	—
General Government	78bt d									48.6	−152.8	−103.5	−161.5	−129.5	−97.8	69.4
Banks	78bu d									−2.3	−10.2	−22.1	43.4	.3	−39.6	−15.0
Other Sectors	78bv d									−105.4	57.9	41.7	32.2	154.6	115.5	162.9
Net Errors and Omissions	78ca d									−45.3	−29.9	−22.0	−7.8	−51.4	−95.7	−83.8
Overall Balance	78cb d									8.4	−16.5	96.0	117.9	146.7	−89.3	13.1
Reserves and Related Items	79da d									−8.4	16.5	−96.0	−117.9	−146.7	89.3	−13.1
Reserve Assets	79db d									−18.2	6.8	−91.1	−117.8	−144.5	97.2	−11.2
Use of Fund Credit and Loans	79dc d									9.8	9.7	−4.9	—	−2.2	−8.0	−1.9
Exceptional Financing	79de d															
Government Finance															*Billions of Francs:*	
Deficit (-) or Surplus	80	....	....	....	−17.6	−15.5	−37.0	ⅈ−158.1	....	....	ⅈ−3.5	55.1	8.2	35.1	−16.3	3.1
Revenue	81	....	....	....	38.9	89.2	167.4	ⅈ189.1	....	....	ⅈ275.0	350.6	419.4	488.4	505.0	602.0
Grants Received	81z	....	....	....	—	—	—	ⅈ—	....	....	ⅈ—	3.2	3.8	—	4.4	4.8
Expenditure	82	....	....	....	54.9	98.9	195.4	ⅈ340.5	....	....	ⅈ276.9	330.3	415.6	451.0	516.3	594.9
Lending Minus Repayments	83	....	....	....	1.6	5.7	9.0	ⅈ6.7	....	....	ⅈ1.6	−31.6	−.6	2.3	9.4	8.8
Financing																	
Domestic	84a	....	....	....	1.7	−5.9	2.8	ⅈ22.8	....	....	....		−55.1	−8.1	−35.1	16.1	−2.8
Foreign	85a	....	....	....	15.9	21.4	34.2	ⅈ135.3	....	....	....	—	−.1	—	.2	−.3
National Accounts															*Billions of Francs*	
Gross Domestic Product (GDP)	99b	93.1	100.8	108.5	161.1	371.7	462.4	719.1	690.2	539.2	644.6	904.5	1,049.0	1,188.9	1,320.0	1,455.6
																Millions:	
Population	99z	.95	.96	.97	.98	.99	1.00	1.02	ⅈ1.00	1.02	1.04	ⅈ1.81	.84	.88	.91	.95

	1985	1986	1987	1988	1989	1990	1991	1992	1993	1994	1995	1996	1997	1998	1999	
Billions of Francs																**International Transactions**
Exports	876.70	440.00	387.00	356.10	509.60	600.00	632.70	551.10	649.80	1,304.90	1,354.40	1,628.70	1,765.20	....	....	70
Imports, c.i.f.	384.00	300.00	220.00	235.70	244.60	250.00	235.40	185.20	239.30	420.00	440.20	489.30	644.30	....	....	71
Imports, c.i.f., from DOTS	429.96	312.02	236.60	276.48	261.43	230.49	306.39	256.29	258.32	419.60	455.90	459.63	697.27	656.13	741.79	71y
Minus Sign Indicates Debit																**Balance of Payments**
Current Account, n.i.e.	−162.5	−1,057.4	−449.1	−615.5	−192.2	167.7	74.8	−168.1	−49.1	317.4	99.8	....	....			78al *d*
Goods: Exports f.o.b.	1,951.4	1,074.2	1,286.4	1,195.6	1,626.0	2,488.8	2,227.9	2,259.2	2,326.2	2,365.3	2,642.9					78aa *d*
Goods: Imports f.o.b.	−854.7	−979.1	−731.8	−791.2	−751.7	−805.1	−861.0	−886.3	−845.1	−776.7	−898.5					78ab *d*
Trade Balance	1,096.7	95.1	554.5	404.3	874.3	1,683.7	1,366.9	1,372.9	1,481.1	1,588.6	1,744.4					78ac *d*
Services: Credit	138.5	123.6	114.8	213.0	289.0	241.6	324.0	347.6	311.1	219.6	272.9					78ad *d*
Services: Debit	−1,058.3	−882.7	−752.3	−811.0	−900.8	−1,006.6	−881.6	−924.8	−1,022.7	−826.7	−949.4					78ae *d*
Balance on Goods & Services	176.8	−664.0	−83.0	−193.7	262.5	918.7	809.3	795.6	769.5	981.4	1,067.8					78af *d*
Income: Credit	29.2	18.1	16.0	15.1	19.0	20.1	28.0	47.2	32.1	11.9	13.4					78ag *d*
Income: Debit	−272.8	−264.7	−258.7	−292.7	−347.8	−636.7	−642.7	−868.9	−658.3	−509.9	−783.5					78ah *d*
Balance on Gds, Serv. & Inc.	−66.8	−910.6	−325.7	−471.2	−66.2	302.0	194.6	−26.1	143.4	483.4	297.7					78ai *d*
Current Transfers, n.i.e.: Credit	42.0	52.8	57.1	53.8	42.3	58.9	44.0	51.4	48.0	18.7	4.4					78aj *d*
Current Transfers: Debit	−137.7	−199.7	−180.5	−198.1	−168.3	−193.3	−163.8	−193.4	−240.5	−184.8	−202.3					78ak *d*
Capital Account, n.i.e.	—	—	—	—	—	—	—	—	—	—	—	....	....			78bc *d*
Capital Account, n.i.e.: Credit	—	—	—	—	—	—	—	—	—	—	....	....				78ba *d*
Capital Account: Debit	—	—	—	—	—	—	—	—	—	....	....					78bb *d*
Financial Account, n.i.e.	164.2	910.9	364.9	716.6	61.1	−398.3	−306.7	−218.7	−389.2	−745.0	−412.7	....	....			78bj *d*
Direct Investment Abroad	−4.1	−6.6	−7.7	−9.7	−8.0	−28.8	−14.9	−25.7	−2.5	—						78bd *d*
Dir. Invest. in Rep. Econ., n.i.e.	15.1	110.2	89.8	132.5	−30.5	73.5	−54.6	126.9	−113.7	−99.6	−113.4					78be *d*
Portfolio Investment Assets	—	—	—	—	—	—	—	—	....	....						78bf *d*
Equity Securities	—	—	—	—	—	—	—	—	....	....						78bk *d*
Debt Securities	—	—	—	—	—	—	—	—	....	....						78bl *d*
Portfolio Investment Liab., n.i.e.	—	—	—	—	—	—	—	—	....	....						78bg *d*
Equity Securities	—	—	—	—	—	—	—	—	....	....						78bm *d*
Debt Securities	—	—	—	—	—	—	—	—	....	....						78bn *d*
Financial Derivatives Assets										....	....					78bw *d*
Financial Derivatives Liabilities										....	....					78bx *d*
Other Investment Assets	−184.2	−45.5	−113.1	42.1	−278.3	−285.1	−14.2	−27.2	−7.8	−258.6	−5.4					78bh *d*
Monetary Authorities										....	....					78bo *d*
General Government	−5.8	−11.1	11.1	−6.1	−36.4	10.0	.7	6.8	4.6	−22.9	13.8					78bp *d*
Banks	−178.4	−34.3	−124.2	48.2	−241.9	−295.0	−14.9	−34.0	−12.4	−235.8	−19.2					78bq *d*
Other Sectors	337.3	852.7	395.8	551.7	378.0	−157.8	−223.0	−292.8	−265.2	−386.7	−293.9					78br *d*
Other Investment Liab., n.i.e.						−31.8	−2.9	1.9	−6.4	−203.9	33.7					78bi *d*
Monetary Authorities																78bs *d*
General Government	86.6	356.0	285.2	288.1	223.0	−187.7	−149.2	−236.1	−174.1	−133.1	−280.3					78bt *d*
Banks	58.5	26.4	−84.4	−32.6	16.6	29.0	11.3	−2.6	1.8	−54.9	34.3					78bu *d*
Other Sectors	192.2	470.3	195.1	296.3	138.4	32.6	−82.2	−55.9	−86.5	5.2	−81.5					78bv *d*
Net Errors and Omissions	−62.6	−48.9	−51.0	−101.9	35.0	−38.0	8.6	−55.1	−13.6	254.6	−108.2					78ca *d*
Overall Balance	−60.9	−195.4	−135.2	−.8	−96.1	−268.6	−223.3	−442.0	−451.9	−173.0	−421.2					78cb *d*
Reserves and Related Items	60.9	195.4	135.2	.8	96.1	268.6	223.3	442.0	451.9	173.0	421.2					79da *d*
Reserve Assets	60.9	99.3	115.6	−55.7	29.8	−219.3	−54.0	246.3	67.5	−173.8	27.1					79db *d*
Use of Fund Credit and Loans	—	33.1	19.7	74.6	5.0	−5.9	−19.4	−36.3	−35.9	40.9	5.0					79dc *d*
Exceptional Financing	—	63.0	−.1	−18.1	61.3	493.8	296.7	232.0	420.3	306.0	389.1					79de *d*
Year Ending December 31																**Government Finance**
Deficit (-) or Surplus	1.1	....	....	....	‡−64.1	51.0	−25.2	....	....	....						80
Revenue	643.4	....	....	....	‡282.6	373.4	441.7	....								81
Grants Received	5.0	....	....	....	‡6.0	5.0	6.0									81z
Expenditure	637.2	....	....	....	‡351.7	326.7	465.5									82
Lending Minus Repayments	10.1	....	....	....	‡1.0	.7	7.4									83
Financing																
Domestic	−3.8	....	....	....	‡60.5	−94.0	25.5									84a
Foreign	2.7	....	....	....	‡3.6	43.0	−.3									85a
Billions of Francs																**National Accounts**
Gross Domestic Product (GDP)	1,576.0	1,590.0	1,156.0	1,135.1	1,335.6	1,477.3	1,524.1	1,480.3	1,530.8	2,326.7	2,475.2	2,880.3	3,117.4	2,753.0	....	99b
Midyear Estimates																
Population	.99	1.02	1.05	.88	.91	.94	.96	.99	1.02	1.05	1.08	1.11	1.14	1.19	1.39	99z

(See notes in the back of the book.)

Gambia, The

		1970	1971	1972	1973	1974	1975	1976	1977	1978	1979	1980	1981	1982	1983	1984
Exchange Rates															*Dalasis per SDR:*	
Market Rate	aa	2.089	ɪ2.127	2.312	2.077	2.085	2.314	2.730	2.549	2.561	2.369	2.139	2.440	2.733	2.887	4.238
															Dalasis per US Dollar:	
Market Rate	ae	2.089	ɪ1.959	2.129	1.722	1.703	1.977	2.350	2.099	1.966	1.799	1.677	2.096	2.478	2.757	4.323
Market Rate	rf	2.083	2.055	2.001	1.702	1.711	1.808	2.226	2.293	2.086	1.888	1.721	1.990	2.290	2.639	3.584
														Index Numbers (1995=100):		
Market Rate	ahx	457.54	466.74	477.76	566.32	558.34	530.35	431.15	416.66	458.19	506.42	555.29	484.07	417.85	362.11	272.31
Nominal Effective Exchange Rate	nec	....	....	....	....	....	....	....	....	....	164.78	181.38	185.44	187.54	188.17	164.09
Real Effective Exchange Rate	rec	....	....	....	....	....	....	....	....	....	....	139.67	133.75	134.39	135.47	128.72
Fund Position															*Millions of SDRs:*	
Quota	2f.s	7.00	7.00	7.00	7.00	7.00	7.00	7.00	7.00	9.00	9.00	13.50	13.50	13.50	17.10	17.10
SDRs	1b.s	.84	1.59	2.18	2.10	2.02	2.01	2.00	.86	1.13	.69	—	.05	.12	.12	—
Reserve Position in the Fund	1c.s	.26	.27	.44	.52	.59	1.75	1.74	—	—	—	—	—	.04	.04	.04
Total Fund Cred.&Loans Outstg.	2tl	—	—	—	—	—	—	—	—	4.26	11.70	10.36	12.67	21.70	36.35	33.52	33.65
International Liquidity													*Millions of US Dollars Unless Otherwise Indicated:*			
Total Reserves minus Gold	1l.d	8.11	10.94	11.38	16.24	28.05	28.55	20.64	24.39	26.07	1.93	5.67	3.95	8.39	2.92	2.26
SDRs	1b.d	.84	1.73	2.37	2.53	2.47	2.35	2.32	1.04	1.47	.91	—	.06	.13	.13	—
Reserve Position in the Fund	1c.d	.26	.29	.48	.63	.72	2.05	2.02	—	—	—	—	—	.04	.04	.04
Foreign Exchange	1d.d	7.01	8.92	8.54	13.08	24.85	24.15	16.29	23.35	24.60	1.02	5.67	3.89	8.21	2.75	2.22
Other Official Inst. Assets	3b.d	3.62	7.79	12.39	2.03	.58	.32	.03	.02	.15	.05	....	....	....	....	....
Deposit Money Banks: Assets	7a.d	1.73	.18	.94	1.13	3.05	2.42	1.25	2.21	3.13	6.33	9.96	7.82	3.77	2.07	5.18
Liabilities	7b.d	2.01	3.11	—	.57	.72	.08	.37	2.13	2.63	6.63	20.87	17.55	12.82	10.47	1.33
Monetary Authorities															*Millions of Dalasis:*	
Foreign Assets	11	16.90	21.00	21.87	27.96	47.77	56.44	48.47	51.18	51.27	12.39	9.53	8.27	23.19	8.04	15.37
Claims on Central Government	12a	.03	.01	-.71	-1.08	.68	-2.34	3.64	20.59	ɪ16.96	41.92	15.02	60.01	33.85	79.96	95.54
Claims on Official Entities	12bx	—	—	—	—	—	—	—	—	3.09	3.09	9.09	21.34	39.33	76.16	94.12
Claims on Private Sector	12d	2.63	4.55	2.97	—	—	—	—	—	.30	.44	.58	.87	1.37	1.40	1.48
Claims on Deposit Money Banks	12e	7.68	5.88	7.00	23.56	24.71	29.90	32.55	11.81	33.62	46.95	86.41	110.48	129.61	132.18	131.81
Reserve Money	14	14.25	14.83	16.23	27.90	27.57	29.81	35.51	28.06	ɪ42.72	50.40	55.80	76.20	89.59	120.80	ɪ57.35
of which: Currency Outside DMBs	14a	12.12	12.73	14.94	25.21	24.06	27.15	32.08	19.79	34.53	36.53	36.76	42.62	55.92	57.18	58.38
Restricted Deposits	16b	—	—	—	20.38	41.82	52.39	33.34	29.34	12.77	.02	.29	—	.80	ɪ78.61	
Foreign Liabilities	16c	—	—	—	—	—	—	—	.63	11.42	30.54	25.65	27.82	55.12	112.49	151.25	343.78
Central Government Deposits	16d	8.10	9.10	7.17	1.71	2.05	1.51	8.33	10.72	ɪ3.51	2.26	4.13	28.55	4.86	17.25	ɪ13.67
Capital Accounts	17a	2.75	4.56	6.11	6.11	6.11	6.77	10.88	10.94	12.21	13.73	13.11	16.94	18.90	23.28	30.67
Other Items (Net)	17r	2.14	2.95	1.62	-5.66	-4.39	-6.48	-4.03	-6.90	3.50	12.73	19.48	24.16	1.51	-15.63	ɪ-185.76
of which: Valuation Adjustment	17rv				-7.18	-7.18	-6.62	-4.90	-7.19	4.15	1.82	9.49	5.48	-4.06	-21.49	-93.30
Deposit Money Banks															*Millions of Dalasis:*	
Reserves	20	2.05	2.05	1.30	2.78	2.77	2.66	3.43	8.31	7.16	5.56	21.17	35.16	43.17	61.01	-1.78
Foreign Assets	21	3.60	.35	1.81	1.95	5.20	4.79	2.93	4.63	6.16	11.39	16.70	16.39	9.34	5.72	22.41
Claims on Central Government	22a	—	—	.50	—	.75	.75	3.50	5.40	12.18	4.75	14.54	3.75	17.37	26.39	35.61
Claims on Official Entities	22bx	—	—	3.97	12.20	14.80	25.25	34.55	13.68	13.08	27.77	62.12	73.75	101.53	65.06	60.14
Claims on Private Sector	22d	15.22	15.37	12.50	20.94	24.08	22.96	39.12	53.74	75.40	83.06	98.46	104.44	102.91	137.59	158.17
Demand Deposits	24	4.33	3.63	7.84	6.59	8.97	10.19	17.34	20.01	ɪ22.93	20.06	23.95	33.50	30.34	41.43	40.45
Time and Savings Deposits	25	2.91	3.08	4.29	6.62	9.21	10.56	20.49	21.65	31.90	24.41	29.42	32.69	39.80	60.64	70.20
Restricted Deposits	26b	....	....	....	....	....	....	....	....	....	....	....	....	....	....	60.70
Foreign Liabilities	26c	4.19	5.96	—	.98	1.22	.16	.86	4.46	5.18	11.93	35.01	36.79	31.76	28.87	ɪ5.77
Central Government Deposits	26d	1.59	—	—	—	—	—	—	—	.09	.09	.09	.09	.09	.09	3.10
Credit from Monetary Authorities	26g	7.68	5.88	7.00	23.56	23.22	29.90	32.55	17.86	33.12	46.96	86.16	101.28	130.78	131.64	128.88
Capital Accounts	27a	.98	.98	1.26	1.41	1.85	4.39	8.41	12.03	16.60	19.26	22.84	25.61	30.34	21.07	20.24
Other Items (Net)	27r	-.82	-1.78	-.28	-1.33	3.12	1.20	3.87	9.75	4.16	9.84	15.52	3.53	11.21	12.03	ɪ-54.72
Monetary Survey															*Millions of Dalasis:*	
Foreign Assets (Net)	31n	16.31	15.39	23.68	28.93	51.75	61.07	49.91	39.93	21.72	-13.79	-36.60	-67.25	-111.72	-166.36	ɪ-311.77
Domestic Credit	32	8.19	10.83	12.06	30.35	38.26	45.11	72.48	82.69	ɪ117.41	158.68	195.59	235.52	291.41	369.22	ɪ428.29
Claims on Central Govt. (Net)	32an	-9.66	-9.09	-7.38	-2.79	-.62	-3.10	-1.19	15.27	ɪ25.54	44.32	25.34	35.12	46.27	89.01	ɪ114.38
Claims on Official Entities	32bx	—	—	3.97	12.20	14.80	25.25	34.55	13.68	16.17	30.86	71.21	95.09	140.86	141.22	154.26
Claims on Private Sector	32d	17.85	19.92	15.47	20.94	24.08	22.96	39.12	53.74	75.70	83.50	99.04	105.31	104.28	138.99	159.65
Money	34	16.45	16.36	22.78	31.80	33.03	37.34	49.42	39.80	ɪ57.78	57.78	61.28	76.97	87.22	100.32	99.58
Quasi-Money	35	2.91	3.08	4.29	6.62	9.21	10.56	20.49	21.65	31.90	24.41	29.42	32.69	39.80	60.64	70.20
Restricted Deposits	36b	—	—	—	20.38	41.82	52.39	33.34	29.34	12.77	.02	.29	—	—	.80	17.91
Capital Accounts	37a	3.73	5.54	7.37	7.52	7.96	11.16	19.29	22.97	28.81	32.99	35.95	42.55	49.24	44.35	50.91
Other Items (Net)	37r	1.40	1.22	1.33	-7.08	-2.02	-5.28	-.16	8.86	7.87	29.70	32.05	16.06	3.43	-3.24	ɪ-122.08
Money plus Quasi-Money	35l	19.36	19.44	27.07	38.42	42.24	47.90	69.91	61.45	ɪ89.68	82.19	90.70	109.66	127.02	160.96	169.78
Other Banking Institutions															*Millions of Dalasis:*	
Deposits	45	1.06	.96	1.03	.83	.79	.97	1.16	1.34	1.09	1.19	1.11	1.04	1.04ᵉ	.88	.80
Liquid Liabilities	55l	20.42	20.40	28.10	39.25	43.03	48.87	71.07	62.79	ɪ90.77	83.38	91.81	110.70	128.06	161.84	170.58
Interest Rates															*Percent Per Annum*	
Discount Rate (End of Period)	60	....	....	....	....	6.00	6.00	6.00	6.00	6.00	6.00	8.00	9.50	9.50	9.50	9.50
Deposit Rate	60l	....	....	....	....	....	....	....	....	....	5.00	5.00	8.50	8.50	8.50	9.00
Lending Rate	60p	....	....	....	....	....	....	....	....	15.00	15.00	15.00	18.00	18.00	18.00	18.00
Prices															*Index Numbers (1995=100):*	
Consumer Prices	64	5.5	5.7	6.2	6.6	ɪ7.2	9.1	10.6	11.9	13.0	13.8	14.7	15.6	17.3	19.1	23.4
															Number in Thousands:	
Labor Force	67d	....	....	....	....	....	....	....	....	....	....	....	....	....	....	....
Employment	67e	....	....	....	....	....	....	....	....	....	....	....	....	....	....	....

1985	1986	1987	1988	1989	1990	1991	1992	1993	1994	1995	1996	1997	1998	1999		
End of Period															**Exchange Rates**	
3.802	9.084	9.134	8.961	10.928	10.662	12.813	12.673	13.096	13.983	14.330	14.225	14.207	15.476	15.849	Market Rate	**aa**
End of Period (ae)	*Period Average (rf)*															
3.461	7.426	6.439	6.659	8.315	7.495	8.957	9.217	9.535	9.579	9.640	9.892	10.530	10.991	11.547	Market Rate	**ae**
3.894	6.938	7.074	6.709	7.585	7.883	8.803	8.888	9.129	9.576	9.546	9.789	10.200	10.643	11.395	Market Rate	**rf**
Period Averages																
247.55	139.82	135.14	142.62	126.56	121.49	109.37	107.15	104.67	99.66	100.00	97.55	93.64	89.72	83.83	Market Rate	**ahx**
165.92	82.84	74.90	82.10	86.24	88.31	85.02	87.49	99.80	104.75	100.00	100.72	104.61	103.47	98.26	Nominal Effective Exchange Rate	**nec**
138.01	99.20	104.58	114.22	109.70	104.75	100.21	102.45	110.94	103.11	100.00	99.06	103.56	101.98	99.60	Real Effective Exchange Rate	**rec**
End of Period															**Fund Position**	
17.10	17.10	17.10	17.10	17.10	17.10	17.10	17.10	22.90	22.90	22.90	22.90	22.90	22.90	31.10	Quota	**2f. s**
—	.59	3.24	.96	1.03	1.24	.54	.45	.23	.18	.09	.20	.09	.30	.49	SDRs	**1b. s**
.04	.05	.05	.05	.05	.03	.03	1.48	1.49	1.48	1.48	1.48	1.48	1.48	1.48	Reserve Position in the Fund	**1c. s**
30.36	24.13	26.65	25.69	28.67	31.55	30.61	28.39	26.68	23.94	19.84	14.71	9.58	8.91	9.26	Total Fund Cred.&Loans Outstg.	**2tl**
End of Period															**International Liquidity**	
1.73	13.56	25.76	19.05	20.59	55.39	67.62	94.03	....	98.02	106.15	102.13	96.04	106.36	111.25	Total Reserves minus Gold	**1l. d**
—	.72	4.60	1.29	1.35	1.76	.77	.62	.31	.26	.13	.29	.11	.42	.67	SDRs	**1b. d**
.04	.06	.07	.07	.07	.04	.04	2.04	2.04	2.04	2.17	2.21	2.14	2.00	2.09	2.04	Reserve Position in the Fund	**1c. d**
1.69	12.78	21.09	17.69	19.17	53.58	66.80	91.38	....	95.59	103.81	99.71	93.92	103.85	108.54	Foreign Exchange	**1d. d**
....	....	....	....	....	....	....	....	....	....	....	....	....	....	....	Other Official Inst. Assets	**3b. d**
5.37	3.66	5.10	4.59	2.86	4.50	4.33	12.47	2.81	3.59	5.64	3.43	10.68	6.54	10.92	Deposit Money Banks: Assets	**7a. d**
3.64	1.77	1.43	1.30	1.24	.37	.24	1.35	4.05	3.03	2.52	6.28	14.52	12.93	17.01	Liabilities	**7b. d**
End of Period															**Monetary Authorities**	
10.66	102.57	134.66	187.06	233.43	405.09	589.07	869.92	1,020.68	948.01	1,030.19	1,011.63	1,010.13	1,163.67	1,277.17	Foreign Assets	**11**
142.15	23.79	21.61	35.16	.89	29.99	21.60	258.76	270.72	297.93	253.65	259.73	240.84	239.90	239.39	Claims on Central Government	**12a**
113.39	109.00	46.85	43.73	22.73	—	—	—	—	—	—	—	—	—	—	Claims on Official Entities	**12bx**
1.57	1.68	2.64	2.97	6.13	9.18	11.56	13.97	15.02	17.02	20.45	21.54	21.08	20.86	21.91	Claims on Private Sector	**12d**
154.64	151.71	84.11	86.05	50.20	50.08	51.27	—	—	—	—	—	—	—	—	Claims on Deposit Money Banks	**12e**
103.57	101.63	121.21	150.55	192.35	204.62	278.28	287.44	319.64	307.08	385.02	386.85	490.42	525.60	601.65	Reserve Money	**14**
85.67	91.18	95.02	111.99	134.78	152.17	182.28	207.08	224.49	207.36	247.97	255.03	360.51	347.55	379.72	*of which: Currency Outside DMBs*	**14a**
124.24	110.97	97.06	81.81	32.38	14.67	14.67	—	—	—	—	—	—	—	—	Restricted Deposits	**16b**
354.69	566.12	497.07	430.05	451.72	449.15	530.31	453.55	407.04	354.07	284.26	209.19	136.05	137.85	146.82	Foreign Liabilities	**16c**
26.83	112.74	165.69	189.20	181.63	361.69	475.00	383.29	553.08	597.69	559.54	669.41	718.02	782.05	808.47	Central Government Deposits	**16d**
29.40	55.52	56.78	56.65	65.96	68.01	65.91	71.12	73.70	75.50	83.59	80.87	81.34	85.33	86.76	Capital Accounts	**17a**
-216.32	-558.23	-647.94	-553.29	-610.65	-603.80	-690.67	-52.75	-47.04	-71.38	-8.11	-53.42	-153.78	-106.39	-105.23	Other Items (Net)	**17r**
-72.55	-398.89	-450.50	-459.31	-532.64	-322.93	-482.57	250.37	199.18	217.07	249.70	231.01	129.79	154.75	390.50	*of which: Valuation Adjustment*	**17rv**
End of Period															**Deposit Money Banks**	
14.71	14.04	23.52	20.87	55.97	38.03	98.21	83.15	98.01	97.09	117.71	128.16	129.91	178.05	221.93	Reserves	**20**
18.59	27.21	32.86	30.55	23.81	33.73	38.83	114.93	26.80	34.41	54.36	33.94	112.47	71.90	126.06	Foreign Assets	**21**
37.26	57.41	71.78	83.06	127.39	134.29	132.80	168.52	135.74	100.50	228.00	355.70	447.25	516.62	587.86	Claims on Central Government	**22a**
51.74	95.78	48.42	61.44	13.55	11.91	12.45	1.54	3.81	.10	.18	.43	1.11	3.86	9.20	Claims on Official Entities	**22bx**
212.37	192.34	184.14	208.53	231.31	265.45	300.52	222.85	361.90	385.44	342.35	341.89	425.26	489.76	591.41	Claims on Private Sector	**22d**
74.98	73.14	100.32	97.86	120.03	137.90	211.30	228.09	236.89	200.17	223.50	198.46	268.90	279.02	336.32	Demand Deposits	**24**
94.85	109.15	145.70	180.67	215.93	219.90	255.16	303.15	371.17	393.49	443.45	514.30	560.66	685.01	754.26	Time and Savings Deposits	**25**
55.79	30.11	27.58	25.97	—	—	—	—	—	—	—	—	—	—	—	Restricted Deposits	**26b**
12.61	13.11	9.19	8.69	10.33	2.74	2.19	12.47	38.65	28.98	24.25	62.10	152.86	142.17	196.46	Foreign Liabilities	**26c**
4.09	4.05	4.05	4.05	4.05	3.99	4.05	3.96	3.96	3.96	3.96	3.96	3.96	3.96	3.96	Central Government Deposits	**26d**
149.73	140.94	85.30	84.80	57.78	53.18	53.18	—	—	—	—	—	—	—	—	Credit from Monetary Authorities	**26g**
15.10	36.67	51.75	49.57	55.37	108.42	111.41	49.71	68.77	72.28	77.98	88.13	113.08	126.34	188.41	Capital Accounts	**27a**
-72.48	-20.39	-63.17	-47.16	-11.46	-42.72	-54.48	-6.39	-93.18	-81.34	-30.54	-6.83	16.54	23.69	57.05	Other Items (Net)	**27r**
End of Period															**Monetary Survey**	
-338.05	-449.44	-338.74	-221.13	-204.80	-13.07	95.40	518.83	601.79	599.37	776.05	774.28	833.70	955.55	1,059.95	Foreign Assets (Net)	**31n**
527.56	363.21	205.70	241.64	216.32	85.14	-.12	278.39	230.15	199.34	281.13	305.92	413.56	484.99	637.34	Domestic Credit	**32**
148.49	-35.59	-76.35	-75.03	-57.40	-201.40	-324.65	40.03	-150.58	-203.22	-81.85	-57.94	-33.89	-29.49	14.82	Claims on Central Govt. (Net)	**32an**
165.13	204.78	95.27	105.17	36.28	11.91	12.45	1.54	3.81	.10	.18	.43	1.11	3.86	9.20	Claims on Official Entities	**32bx**
213.94	194.02	186.78	211.50	237.44	274.63	312.08	236.82	376.92	402.46	362.80	363.43	446.34	510.62	613.32	Claims on Private Sector	**32d**
162.10	166.49	197.83	213.52	260.25	296.19	393.58	435.17	461.38	407.53	471.47	453.49	629.41	626.57	716.04	Money	**34**
94.85	109.15	145.70	180.67	215.93	219.90	255.16	303.15	371.17	393.49	443.45	514.30	560.66	685.01	754.26	Quasi-Money	**35**
68.45	80.86	69.48	55.84	32.38	14.67	14.67	—	—	—	—	—	—	—	—	Restricted Deposits	**36b**
44.50	92.19	108.53	106.22	121.33	176.43	177.32	120.83	142.47	147.78	161.57	169.00	194.42	211.67	275.17	Capital Accounts	**37a**
-180.39	-534.93	-654.58	-535.74	-618.37	-635.12	-745.45	-61.93	-143.08	-150.09	-19.31	-56.59	-137.24	-82.70	-48.18	Other Items (Net)	**37r**
256.95	275.64	343.53	394.19	476.18	516.09	648.74	738.32	832.55	801.02	914.92	967.79	1,190.07	1,311.58	1,470.30	Money plus Quasi-Money	**35l**
End of Period															**Other Banking Institutions**	
.72	1.22	.99	1.22	1.03	.93	....	....	....	....	....	....	....	....	....	Deposits	**45**
257.67	276.86	344.52	395.41	477.21	517.02	....	....	....	....	....	....	....	....	....	Liquid Liabilities	**55l**
Percent Per Annum															**Interest Rates**	
15.00	20.00	21.00	19.00	15.00	16.50	15.50	17.50	13.50	13.50	14.00	14.00	14.00	12.00	10.50	Discount Rate *(End of Period)*	**60**
9.75	16.13	15.75	15.00	12.92	11.33	12.71	13.83	13.00	12.58	12.50	12.50	12.50	12.50	12.50	Deposit Rate	**60l**
14.48	28.00	27.92	29.54	26.83	26.50	26.50	26.75	26.08	25.00	25.04	25.50	25.50	25.38	24.00	Lending Rate	**60p**
Period Averages															**Prices**	
27.7	43.3	53.5	59.8	64.7	72.6	78.8	86.3	91.9	93.5	100.0	101.1	103.9	105.1	109.1	Consumer Prices	**64**
Period Averages																
....	....	....	....	....	....	....	....	325	....	....	....	....	....	....	Labor Force	**67d**
24	21	26	30	31	....	....	....	....	....	....	....	....	....	....	Employment	**67e**

Gambia, The

		1970	1971	1972	1973	1974	1975	1976	1977	1978	1979	1980	1981	1982	1983	1984
International Transactions															*Millions of Dalasis*	
Exports	70	35.12	27.70	37.38	39.98	72.21	77.00	74.67	110.19	82.91	109.82	54.26	51.46	98.53	126.90	162.57
Imports, c.i.f.	71	37.43	43.79	49.53	53.39	79.54	108.12	164.32	177.71	209.78	266.31	285.40	246.76	235.63	304.60	354.16
Balance of Payments															*Millions of US Dollars: F.Y. Ending*	
Current Account, n.i.e.	78al d	...	...					...	...	−47.00	−37.05	−90.58	−43.63	−21.45	−31.54	6.61
Goods: Exports f.o.b.	78aa d	...	...					...	...	42.11	56.89	50.31	39.77	55.74	51.32	74.30
Goods: Imports f.o.b.	78ab d	...	...					...	...	−85.12	−100.27	−143.46	−113.41	−89.86	−84.38	−81.42
Trade Balance	78ac d	...	...					...	...	−43.00	−43.39	−93.15	−73.64	−34.13	−33.06	−7.13
Services: Credit	78ad d	...	...					...	...	13.94	23.82	18.71	17.76	23.14	25.58	22.71
Services: Debit	78ae d	...	...					...	...	−27.48	−39.45	−43.31	−36.65	−34.42	−28.15	−21.19
Balance on Goods & Services	78af d	...	...					...	...	−56.54	−59.01	−117.75	−92.53	−45.40	−35.63	−5.62
Income: Credit	78ag d	...	...					...	...	2.03	2.03	—	—	.91	.20	—
Income: Debit	78ah d	...	...					...	...	−4.92	−4.68	−2.30	−2.40	−10.86	−16.61	—
Balance on Gds, Serv. & Inc.	78ai d	...	...					...	...	−59.42	−61.65	−120.04	−94.93	−55.35	−52.04	−5.62
Current Transfers, n.i.e.: Credit	78aj d	...	...					...	...	14.08	27.33	30.31	53.57	37.13	23.07	13.20
Current Transfers: Debit	78ak d	...	...					...	...	−1.65	−2.73	−.84	−2.28	−3.23	−2.57	−.97
Capital Account, n.i.e.	78bc d	...	...					...	...	.09	.24	—	—	.07	.51	—
Capital Account, n.i.e.: Credit	78ba d	...	...					...	...	.35	.49	—	—	.19	.70	—
Capital Account: Debit	78bb d	...	...					...	...	−.26	−.25	—	—	−.12	−.19	—
Financial Account, n.i.e.	78bj d	...	...					...	...	12.71	21.72	−2.12	37.04	10.17	−4.82	−17.58
Direct Investment Abroad	78bd d	...	...					...	...	—	—	—	—	—	—	—
Dir. Invest. in Rep. Econ., n.i.e.	78be d	...	...					...	...	2.10	12.36	—	2.01	—	—	—
Portfolio Investment Assets	78bf d	...	...					...	...	—	—	—	—	—	—	—
Equity Securities	78bk d	...	...					...	...	—	—	—	—	—	—	—
Debt Securities	78bl d	...	...					...	...	—	—	—	—	—	—	—
Portfolio Investment Liab., n.i.e.	78bg d	...	...					...	...	—	—	—	—	—	—	—
Equity Securities	78bm d	...	...					...	...	—	—	—	—	—	—	—
Debt Securities	78bn d	...	...					...	...	—	—	—	—	—	—	—
Financial Derivatives Assets	78bw d	...	...					...	...							...
Financial Derivatives Liabilities	78bx d	...	...					...	...							...
Other Investment Assets	78bh d	...	...					...	...	2.67	.72	−6.45	2.95	−7.26	4.76	1.82
Monetary Authorities	78bo d	...	...					...	...							...
General Government	78bp d	...	...					...	...	−.18	—	—	—	—	—	—
Banks	78bq d	...	...					...	...	2.83	−.41	−.56	−1.58	−4.38	2.35	1.82
Other Sectors	78br d	...	...					...	...	.02	1.13	−5.89	4.54	−2.88	2.41	—
Other Investment Liab., n.i.e.	78bi d	...	...					...	...	7.93	8.64	4.33	32.08	17.43	−9.58	−19.39
Monetary Authorities	78bs d	...	...					...	...	−.91	1.72	—	—	—	−.32	−.66
General Government	78bt d	...	...					...	...	8.40	6.89	5.49	10.48	16.91	−5.11	−8.30
Banks	78bu d	...	...					...	...	1.25	1.76	−1.16	21.60	.52	−4.15	−10.44
Other Sectors	78bv d	...	...					...	...	−.81	−1.74	—	—	—	—	—
Net Errors and Omissions	78ca d	...	...					...	...	16.68	−5.33	55.94	.77	−17.06	14.43	−5.40
Overall Balance	78cb d	...	...					...	...	−17.52	−20.41	−36.75	−5.81	−28.27	−21.42	−16.37
Reserves and Related Items	79da d	...	...					...	...	17.52	20.41	36.75	5.81	28.27	21.42	16.37
Reserve Assets	79db d	...	...					...	...	12.87	15.21	4.27	−16.57	15.83	1.81	−2.22
Use of Fund Credit and Loans	79dc d	...	...					...	...	2.41	3.47	6.79	9.46	7.84	6.84	.36
Exceptional Financing	79de d	...	...					...	...	2.24	1.73	25.69	12.92	4.60	12.77	18.24
Government Finance															*Millions of Dalasis:*	
Deficit (-) or Surplus	80	−1.41	−1.00	I −4.58	.30	−2.79	−6.61	−6.65	−26.49	−35.85	−38.42	−18.32	−50.10	−33.86	....	....
Revenue	81	17.47	26.70	I 22.70	22.80	26.91	32.28	45.61	64.59	83.03	75.40	95.78	76.52	87.05	103.10	122.97
Grants Received	81z	.08	—	I —	.09	.04	2.76	1.89	—	19.74	13.46	13.27	20.90	48.02	....	....
Expenditure	82	20.81	27.57	I 27.12	22.43	28.87	40.81	51.21	85.86	130.68	115.68	131.56	143.68	159.48	....	....
Lending Minus Repayments	83	−1.85	.13	I .16	.16	.87	.84	2.94	5.22	7.94	11.60	−4.19	3.84	9.45	....	16.74
Financing																
Domestic	84a	−1.08	1.40	I 1.17	−3.86	.12	1.35	1.39	20.48	8.47	18.41	13.44	14.09	−1.80	....	....
Foreign	85a	2.50	−.39	I 3.41	3.56	2.67	5.26	5.26	6.01	27.38	20.01	4.88	36.01	35.66	....	....
Debt: Domestic	88a	....	....	....	3.46	4.21	10.73	11.21	12.50	33.48	57.01	69.61	78.10	73.69	....	....
Foreign	89a	....	....	....	13.19	16.95	21.59	26.54	33.62	69.51	82.04	92.00	111.03	144.80	....	....
National Accounts															*Millions of Dalasis:*	
Gross Domestic Product (GDP)	99b	81.9	81.4	108.8	109.8	158.4	221.2	278.3	355.1	360.7	425.0	411.6	451.4	522.1	599.4	748.5
GDP Volume 1970 prices	99b.p	81.9	94.7	101.6	106.2	163.4	156.7	167.0	155.0	....	....	....	....	....	....	....
GDP Volume 1976 Prices	99b.p	....	....	....	....	....	....	....	336.0	365.4	371.1	169.9	372.8	423.1	432.1	439.0
GDP Volume (1995=100)	99bv p	30.1	34.8	37.3	39.0	60.0	57.5	....	56.0	60.9	61.8	28.3	62.1	70.5	72.0	73.1
GDP Deflator (1990=100)	99bi p	10.3	8.8	11.0	10.6	9.9	14.5	15.0	23.9	22.3	25.9	54.8	27.4	27.9	31.4	38.6
																Millions:
Population	99z	.46	.48	.49	.49	.51	.52	.54	.55	.57	.58	.60	.62	.64	.70	.72

1985	1986	1987	1988	1989	1990	1991	1992	1993	1994	1995	1996	1997	1998	1999		
Millions of Dalasis															**International Transactions**	
172.92	235.73	281.39	388.72	198.05	244.80	333.45	510.52	604.73	337.80	155.23	209.15	149.82	285.97	80.60	Exports	70
362.27	733.39	897.24	919.36	1,221.01	1,482.11	1,759.38	1,944.94	2,372.27	2,032.75	1,741.26	2,527.62	1,773.80	2,605.39	2,186.82	Imports, c.i.f.	71
June 30: Minus Sign Indicates Debit															**Balance of Payments**	
7.69	3.09	6.33	26.66	13.93	22.31	11.86	38.20	−5.16	8.11	−8.14	−47.12	−22.95	. . . .	. . . .	Current Account, n.i.e.	78al *d*
66.23	46.64	76.94	83.56	92.92	114.11	128.88	151.05	152.19	123.90	122.09	117.30	116.52			Goods: Exports f.o.b.	78aa *d*
−78.94	−60.80	−98.04	−106.56	−116.25	−144.94	−166.89	−182.73	−207.85	−180.06	−161.38	−214.46	−201.74			Goods: Imports f.o.b.	78ab *d*
−12.70	−14.16	−21.10	−23.00	−23.33	−30.83	−38.01	−31.67	−55.66	−56.16	−39.29	−97.15	−85.22			*Trade Balance*	78ac *d*
25.76	20.62	50.98	62.58	60.95	59.29	72.65	83.12	77.11	89.69	53.33	99.98	106.52			Services: Credit	78ad *d*
−20.35	−15.44	−45.76	−48.47	−46.93	−53.46	−65.16	−68.80	−72.26	−66.47	−68.76	−76.09	−72.74			Services: Debit	78ae *d*
−7.30	−8.98	−15.88	−8.88	−9.30	−25.00	−30.52	−17.36	−50.81	−32.94	−54.72	−73.27	−51.44			*Balance on Goods & Services*	78af *d*
		.84	1.45	1.86	1.64	3.41	4.98	5.64	4.82	4.34	5.94	3.63			Income: Credit	78ag *d*
−.05	−.62	−18.17	−13.32	−14.66	−13.45	−10.19	−7.52	−4.95	−5.10	−9.51	−9.17	−11.01			Income: Debit	78ah *d*
−7.35	−9.60	−33.22	−20.75	−22.11	−36.80	−37.30	−19.89	−50.12	−33.21	−59.89	−76.50	−58.82			*Balance on Gds, Serv. & Inc.*	78ai *d*
15.68	13.35	44.25	54.78	43.00	61.87	52.84	62.21	48.45	45.46	55.41	34.67	43.87			Current Transfers, n.i.e.: Credit	78aj *d*
−.65	−.67	−4.70	−7.37	−6.97	−2.76	−3.68	−4.11	−3.49	−4.14	−3.66	−5.29	−8.00			Current Transfers: Debit	78ak *d*
											8.41	5.59			Capital Account, n.i.e.	78bc *d*
—	—	—	—	—	—	—	—	—	—	—	8.41	5.59			Capital Account, n.i.e.: Credit	78ba *d*
											. . . .	. . . .			Capital Account: Debit	78bb *d*
−4.12	−6.71	−.62	9.69	8.79	−6.28	18.73	19.23	38.17	32.85	24.60	57.88	38.42			Financial Account, n.i.e.	78bj *d*
—	—	—	—	—	—	—	—	—	—	—					Direct Investment Abroad	78bd *d*
		1.53	1.18	13.71	—	9.20	6.33	10.72	9.72	7.73	10.66	11.67			Dir. Invest. in Rep. Econ., n.i.e.	78be *d*
—	—	—	—	—	—	—	—	—	—	. . . .	. . . .	. . . .			Portfolio Investment Assets	78bf *d*
—	—	—	—	—	—	—	—	—	—	. . . .	. . . .	. . . .			Equity Securities	78bk *d*
—	—	—	—	—	—	—	—	—	—	. . . .	. . . .	. . . .			Debt Securities	78bl *d*
—	—	—	—	—	—	—	—	—	—	. . . .	. . . .	. . . .			Portfolio Investment Liab., n.i.e.	78bg *d*
—	—	—	—	—	—	—	—	—	—	. . . .	. . . .	. . . .			Equity Securities	78bm *d*
—	—	—	—	—	—	—	—	—	—	. . . .	. . . .	. . . .			Debt Securities	78bn *d*
											. . . .	. . . .			Financial Derivatives Assets	78bw *d*
											. . . .	. . . .			Financial Derivatives Liabilities	78bx *d*
−6.89	3.06	−1.62	1.64	−2.24	−1.07	−.55	−1.56	1.36	3.75	−3.63	5.55	10.01			Other Investment Assets	78bh *d*
. . . .	. . . .										. . . .	. . . .			Monetary Authorities	78bo *d*
—	—	—	—	—	—	—	—	—	—	—	—	—			General Government	78bp *d*
−6.89	3.06	−1.62	1.64	−2.24	−1.07	−.55	−1.56	1.36	3.75	−3.63	4.65	6.95			Banks	78bq *d*
											.90	3.06			Other Sectors	78br *d*
2.77	−9.78	−.53	6.88	−2.68	−5.21	10.08	14.46	26.09	19.37	20.50	41.67	16.74			Other Investment Liab., n.i.e.	78bi *d*
−1.84	−1.15	−1.56									33.60	2.92			Monetary Authorities	78bs *d*
2.09	−7.03	1.66	6.43	−3.84	−5.01	10.50	14.21	22.41	17.64	22.44	3.07	10.22			General Government	78bt *d*
2.51	−1.59	−.47	1.02	1.29	.83	−.29	.48	3.68	1.73	−1.94	−.26	.12			Banks	78bu *d*
—	—	−.16	−.57	−.14	−1.04	−.13	−.23	—	—	. . . .	5.26	3.48			Other Sectors	78bv *d*
−9.93	−18.35	5.45	−11.36	−19.75	−11.98	−14.85	−37.66	−21.91	−34.79	−15.49	−4.79	−13.66			Net Errors and Omissions	78ca *d*
−6.36	−21.97	11.16	24.99	2.97	4.05	15.74	19.77	11.11	6.16	.97	14.38	7.39			*Overall Balance*	78cb *d*
6.36	21.97	−11.16	−24.99	−2.97	−4.05	−15.74	−19.77	−11.11	−6.16	−.97	−14.38	−7.39			Reserves and Related Items	79da *d*
3.89	.10	−11.98	−30.24	3.79	−2.92	−23.13	−36.33	−8.68	−3.27	4.20	−7.36	−.12			Reserve Assets	79db *d*
−5.08	−3.06	−5.82	2.39	3.52	4.13	−1.76	.28	−2.43	−2.89	−5.17	−7.02	−7.27			Use of Fund Credit and Loans	79dc *d*
7.55	24.94	6.64	2.86	−10.28	−5.26	9.14	16.29	—	—	. . . .	. . . .	. . . .			Exceptional Financing	79de *d*
Year Ending June 30															**Government Finance**	
. . . .	. . . .	. . . .	. . . .	.50	ɪ 23.18	ɪ −42.60	140.84 [P]	120.69 [P]	. . . .	. . . .	. . . .	. . . .			Deficit (-) or Surplus	80
146.04	203.67	. . . .	. . . .	434.60	ɪ 486.17	ɪ 562.80	644.46 [P]	791.77 [P]	. . . .	. . . .	. . . .	. . . .			Revenue	81
. . . .	14.46	23.97	. . . .	56.16	ɪ 66.07	ɪ 75.24	45.81 [P]	8.14 [P]	. . . .	. . . .	. . . .	. . . .			Grants Received	81z
. . . .	. . . .	. . . .	. . . .	496.67	ɪ 549.10	ɪ 684.71	563.60 [P]	695.14 [P]	. . . .	. . . .	. . . .	. . . .			Expenditure	82
1.17	47.08	. . . .	. . . .	−6.41	ɪ −20.04	ɪ −4.07	−14.17 [P]	−15.92 [P]	. . . .	. . . .	. . . .	. . . .			Lending Minus Repayments	83
															Financing	
. . . .	. . . .	. . . .	. . . .	−23.56	. . . .	ɪ −68.82	−280.05 [P]	−219.12 [P]	. . . .	. . . .	. . . .	. . . .			Domestic	84a
. . . .	. . . .	. . . .	. . . .	23.06	. . . .	ɪ 109.42	139.21 [P]	98.43 [P]	. . . .	. . . .	. . . .	. . . .			Foreign	85a
. . . .	. . . .	. . . .	. . . .	. . . .	. . . .	. . . .	. . . .	. . . .	. . . .	. . . .	. . . .	. . . .			Debt: Domestic	88a
															Foreign	89a
Year Ending June 30															**National Accounts**	
869.6	1,085.2	1,486.0	1,635.5	1,942.3	2,366.4	2,629.6	2,947.6	2,518.5	2,886.3	. . . .	. . . .	. . . .			Gross Domestic Product (GDP)	99b
456.7	469.4	476.6	498.4	526.2	535.1	564.3	566.8	604.0	626.1	600.4					GDP Volume 1970 prices	99b. *p*
															GDP Volume 1976 Prices	99b. *p*
76.1	78.2	79.4	83.0	87.6	89.1	94.0	94.4	100.6	104.3	100.0	. . . .	. . . .			GDP Volume (1995=100)	99bv *p*
43.1	52.3	70.5	74.2	83.5	100.0	105.4	117.6	94.3	104.3	. . . .	. . . .	. . . .			GDP Deflator (1990=100)	99bi *p*
Midyear Estimates																
.74	.77	.81	.85	.88	.92	.96	ɪ .88	1.03	1.07	1.11	1.15	1.19	1.23	1.27	**Population**	99z

(See notes in the back of the book.)

Georgia

	1970	1971	1972	1973	1974	1975	1976	1977	1978	1979	1980	1981	1982	1983	1984

Exchange Rates
Lari per SDR:

Official Rate .... aa ... ...

Lari per US Dollar:

Official Rate .... ae ... ...
Official Rate .... rf ... ...

Index Numbers (1995=100):

Nominal Effective Exchange Rate .... ne c ... ...
Real Effective Exchange Rate .... re c ... ...

Fund Position
Millions of SDRs:

Quota .... 2f. s ... ...
SDRs .... 1b. s ... ...
Reserve Position in the Fund ...... 1c. s ... ...
Total Fund Cred.& Loans Outstg. ... 2tl ... ...

International Liquidity
Millions of US Dollars Unless Otherwise Indicated:

Total Reserves minus Gold .... 1l. d ... ...
SDRs .... 1b. d ... ...
Reserve Position in the Fund ..... 1c. d ... ...
Foreign Exchange .... 1d. d ... ...
Gold(Millions Fine Troy Ounces) .... 1ad ... ...
Gold (National Valuation) .... 1an d ... ...
Monetary Authorities: Other Assets ...... 3.. d ... ...
Other Liab. .... 4.. d ... ...
Deposit Money Banks: Assets .... 7a. d ... ...
Liabilities .... 7b. d ... ...

Monetary Authorities
Millions of Lari:

Foreign Assets .... 11 ... ...
Claims on General Government .... 12a ... ...
Claims on Deposit Money Banks .... 12e ... ...
Claims on Other Resident Sectors .... 12d ... ...
Reserve Money .... 14 ... ...
of which: Currency Outside DMBs ...... 14a ... ...
Foreign Liabilities .... 16c ... ...
General Government Deposits .... 16d ... ...
Counterpart Funds .... 16e ... ...
Capital Accounts .... 17a ... ...
Other Items (Net) .... 17r ... ...

Deposit Money Banks
Millions of Lari:

Reserves .... 20 ... ...
Foreign Assets .... 21 ... ...
Claims on General Government .... 22a ... ...
of which: Claims on Local Govt. .... 22ab ... ...
Claims on Nonbank Fin. Insts. .... 22g ... ...
Claims on Other Resident Sectors .... 22d ... ...
Demand Deposits .... 24 ... ...
Time,Savings,& Fgn.Currency Dep. .... 25 ... ...
Foreign Liabilities .... 26c ... ...
General Government Deposits .... 26d ... ...
of which: Local Govt. Deposits .... 26db ... ...
Counterpart Funds .... 26e ... ...
Central Govt. Lending Funds .... 26f ... ...
Capital Accounts .... 27a ... ...
Other Items (Net) .... 27r ... ...

Monetary Survey
Millions of Lari:

Foreign Assets (Net) .... 31n ... ...
Domestic Credit .... 32 ... ...
Claims on General Govt. (Net) .... 32an ... ...
Claims on Nonbank Fin. Insts. .... 32g ... ...
Claims on Other Resident Sectors .... 32d ... ...
Money .... 34 ... ...
Quasi-Money .... 35 ... ...
Counterpart Funds .... 36e ... ...
Central Govt. Lending Funds .... 36f ... ...
Capital Accounts .... 37a ... ...
Other Items (Net) .... 37r ... ...
Money plus Quasi-Money .... 35l ... ...

Interest Rates
Percent Per Annum

Money Market Rate .... 60b ... ...
Deposit Rate .... 60l ... ...
Deposit Rate (Foreign Currency) .... 60l. f ... ...
Lending Rate .... 60p ... ...
Lending Rate (Foreign Currency) .... 60p. f ... ...

Prices
Index Numbers (1998=100):

Producer Prices .... 63 ... ...
Consumer Prices .... 64 ... ...

1985	1986	1987	1988	1989	1990	1991	1992	1993	1994	1995	1996	1997	1998	1999		
End of Period															**Exchange Rates**	
....	....	....	....	....	....	....	....	....	....	1.8284	1.8348	1.7594	2.5345	2.6489	Official Rate	aa
End of Period (ae) Period Average (rf)																
....	....	....	....	....	....	....	....	....	....	1.2300	1.2760	1.3040	1.8000	1.9300	Official Rate	ae
....	....	....	....	....	....	....	....	....	....	....	1.2628	1.2975	1.3898	2.0245	Official Rate	rf
Period Averages																
....	....	....	....	....	....	....	....	....	158.36	100.00	117.88	138.71	159.99	....	Nominal Effective Exchange Rate	ne c
....	....	....	....	....	....	....	....	....	44.73	100.00	129.37	136.48	135.73	....	Real Effective Exchange Rate	re c
End of Period															**Fund Position**	
....	....	....	....	....	....	....	111.00	111.00	111.00	111.00	111.00	111.00	111.00	150.30	Quota	2f. s
....	....	....	....	....	....	....	—	—	1.61	1.12	.05	.10	3.69	6.13	SDRs	1b. s
....	....	....	....	....	....	....	.01	.01	.01	.01	.01	.01	.01	.01	Reserve Position in the Fund	1c. s
....	....	....	....	....	....	....	—	—	27.75	77.70	133.20	188.70	215.76	233.33	Total Fund Cred.& Loans Outstg.	2tl
End of Period															**International Liquidity**	
....	....	....	....	....	....	....	....	....	....	194.01	188.91	199.80	122.99	132.39	Total Reserves minus Gold	1l. d
....	....	....	....	....	....	....	—	—	2.35	1.66	.07	.13	5.20	8.42	SDRs	1b. d
....	....	....	....	....	....	....	.01	.01	.01	.01	.01	.01	.01	.01	Reserve Position in the Fund	1c. d
....	....	....	....	....	....	....	....	....	....	192.33	188.83	199.66	117.78	123.96	Foreign Exchange	1d. d
....	....	....	....	....	....	....	....	....	....	.0021	.0021	.0021	.0021	.0021	Gold(Millions Fine Troy Ounces)	1ad
....	....	....	....	....	....	....	....	....	....	1.20	1.20	.50	.50	.54	Gold (National Valuation)	1an d
....	....	....	....	....	....	....	....	....	....	.11	—	—	—	—	Monetary Authorities: Other Assets	3.. d
....	....	....	....	....	....	....	....	....	....	.06	.06	27.75	36.68	41.18	Other Liab.	4.. d
....	....	....	....	....	....	....	....	....	....	26.88	33.88	39.10	46.41	48.57	Deposit Money Banks: Assets	7a. d
....	....	....	....	....	....	....	....	....	....	49.26	4.80	11.95	35.99	46.94	Liabilities	7b. d
End of Period															**Monetary Authorities**	
....	....	....	....	....	....	....	....	....	....	240.29	242.68	261.20	222.49	256.54	Foreign Assets	11
....	....	....	....	....	....	....	....	....	....	112.45	296.72	437.52	541.78	717.82	Claims on General Government	12a
....	....	....	....	....	....	....	....	....	....	3.66	14.30	5.26	6.56	1.86	Claims on Deposit Money Banks	12e
....	....	....	....	....	....	....	....	....	....	—	—	36.67	66.67	80.86	Claims on Other Resident Sectors	12d
....	....	....	....	....	....	....	....	....	....	153.28	208.96	277.07	259.72	308.47	Reserve Money	14
....	....	....	....	....	....	....	....	....	....	124.78	176.76	239.87	212.19	244.00	of which: Currency Outside DMBs	14a
....	....	....	....	....	....	....	....	....	....	142.14	244.47	368.19	612.84	697.55	Foreign Liabilities	16c
....	....	....	....	....	....	....	....	....	....	57.17	87.86	52.08	41.94	21.74	General Government Deposits	16d
....	....	....	....	....	....	....	....	....	....	—	—	—	4.41	.75	Counterpart Funds	16e
....	....	....	....	....	....	....	....	....	....	14.88	18.53	94.02	−14.88	182.32	Capital Accounts	17a
....	....	....	....	....	....	....	....	....	....	−11.08	−6.12	−50.71	−66.54	−153.75	Other Items (Net)	17r
End of Period															**Deposit Money Banks**	
....	....	....	....	....	....	....	....	....	....	38.00	30.39	41.15	45.68	58.06	Reserves	20
....	....	....	....	....	....	....	....	....	....	33.06	43.23	50.99	83.55	93.73	Foreign Assets	21
....	....	....	....	....	....	....	....	....	....	1.47	1.27	4.86	1.12	1.70	Claims on General Government	22a
....	....	....	....	....	....	....	....	....	....	1.42	1.26	1.09	1.12	—	of which: Claims on Local Govt.	22ab
....	....	....	....	....	....	....	....	....	....	.31	.06	—	—	—	Claims on Nonbank Fin. Insts.	22g
....	....	....	....	....	....	....	....	....	....	148.71	127.80	175.06	239.95	339.74	Claims on Other Resident Sectors	22d
....	....	....	....	....	....	....	....	....	....	30.68	35.90	38.75	38.47	31.62	Demand Deposits	24
....	....	....	....	....	....	....	....	....	....	28.51	46.69	94.82	118.63	171.44	Time,Savings,& Fgn.Currency Dep.	25
....	....	....	....	....	....	....	....	....	....	60.59	6.12	15.58	64.79	90.59	Foreign Liabilities	26c
....	....	....	....	....	....	....	....	....	....	13.61	18.18	9.01	15.52	10.60	General Government Deposits	26d
....	....	....	....	....	....	....	....	....	....	4.91	4.72	3.50	4.69	3.88	of which: Local Govt. Deposits	26db
....	....	....	....	....	....	....	....	....	....	—	10.26	10.37	8.10	1.33	Counterpart Funds	26e
....	....	....	....	....	....	....	....	....	....	—	—	—	—	3.52	Central Govt. Lending Funds	26f
....	....	....	....	....	....	....	....	....	....	61.09	90.82	145.14	200.17	280.27	Capital Accounts	27a
....	....	....	....	....	....	....	....	....	....	27.08	−5.22	−41.59	−75.38	−96.12	Other Items (Net)	27r
End of Period															**Monetary Survey**	
....	....	....	....	....	....	....	....	....	....	70.63	35.32	−71.59	−371.60	−437.86	Foreign Assets (Net)	31n
....	....	....	....	....	....	....	....	....	....	192.16	319.81	593.03	792.06	1,107.79	Domestic Credit	32
....	....	....	....	....	....	....	....	....	....	43.14	191.95	381.30	485.45	687.18	Claims on General Govt. (Net)	32an
....	....	....	....	....	....	....	....	....	....	.31	.06	—	—	—	Claims on Nonbank Fin. Insts.	32g
....	....	....	....	....	....	....	....	....	....	148.71	127.80	211.73	306.62	420.60	Claims on Other Resident Sectors	32d
....	....	....	....	....	....	....	....	....	....	155.46	212.66	278.62	250.67	275.62	Money	34
....	....	....	....	....	....	....	....	....	....	28.51	46.69	94.82	118.63	171.44	Quasi-Money	35
....	....	....	....	....	....	....	....	....	....	—	10.26	10.37	12.50	2.08	Counterpart Funds	36e
....	....	....	....	....	....	....	....	....	....	—	—	—	—	3.52	Central Govt. Lending Funds	36f
....	....	....	....	....	....	....	....	....	....	75.97	109.35	239.16	185.30	462.58	Capital Accounts	37a
....	....	....	....	....	....	....	....	....	....	2.84	−23.83	−101.51	−146.63	−245.32	Other Items (Net)	37r
....	....	....	....	....	....	....	....	....	....	183.97	259.34	373.44	369.29	447.06	Money plus Quasi-Money	35l
Percent Per Annum															**Interest Rates**	
....	....	....	....	....	....	....	....	....	....	....	43.39	26.58	43.26	34.61	Money Market Rate	60b
....	....	....	....	....	....	....	....	....	....	....	31.05	13.73	17.00	14.58	Deposit Rate	60l
....	....	....	....	....	....	....	....	....	....	....	24.55	19.11	15.75	14.58	Deposit Rate (Foreign Currency)	60l. f
....	....	....	....	....	....	....	....	....	....	....	58.24	50.64	46.00	33.42	Lending Rate	60p
....	....	....	....	....	....	....	....	....	....	....	51.92	54.16	46.75	42.92	Lending Rate (Foreign Currency)	60p. f
Period Averages															**Prices**	
....	....	....	....	....	....	....	....	....	....	....	....	....	100.0	....	Producer Prices	63
....	....	....	....	....	....	....	34.1	1,185.7	24.6	64.7	90.2	96.6	100.0	119.1	Consumer Prices	64

Georgia

		1970	1971	1972	1973	1974	1975	1976	1977	1978	1979	1980	1981	1982	1983	1984
International Transactions																*Millions of Lari*
Exports	70	...	...	...	...	...	...	...	...	...	...	...	...	...	...	...
Imports, c.i.f.	71	...	...	...	...	...	...	...	...	...	...	...	...	...	...	...
Imports, f.o.b.	71.v	...	...	...	...	...	...	...	...	...	...	...	...	...	...	...
Balance of Payments																*Millions of US Dollars:*
Current Account, n.i.e.	78al d	...	...	...	...	...	...	...	...	...	...	...	...	...	...	...
Goods: Exports f.o.b	78aa d	...	...	...	...	...	...	...	...	...	...	...	...	...	...	...
Goods: Imports f.o.b	78ab d	...	...	...	...	...	...	...	...	...	...	...	...	...	...	...
Trade Balance	78ac d	...	...	...	...	...	...	...	...	...	...	...	...	...	...	...
Services: Credit	78ad d	...	...	...	...	...	...	...	...	...	...	...	...	...	...	...
Services: Debit	78ae d	...	...	...	...	...	...	...	...	...	...	...	...	...	...	...
Balance on Goods & Services	78af d	...	...	...	...	...	...	...	...	...	...	...	...	...	...	...
Income: Credit	78ag d	...	...	...	...	...	...	...	...	...	...	...	...	...	...	...
Income: Debit	78ah d	...	...	...	...	...	...	...	...	...	...	...	...	...	...	...
Balance on Gds, Serv. & Inc.	78ai d	...	...	...	...	...	...	...	...	...	...	...	...	...	...	...
Current Transfers, n.i.e.: Credit	78aj d	...	...	...	...	...	...	...	...	...	...	...	...	...	...	...
Current Transfers: Debit	78ak d	...	...	...	...	...	...	...	...	...	...	...	...	...	...	...
Capital Account, n.i.e.	78bc d	...	...	...	...	...	...	...	...	...	...	...	...	...	...	...
Capital Account, n.i.e.: Credit	78ba d	...	...	...	...	...	...	...	...	...	...	...	...	...	...	...
Capital Account: Debit	78bb d	...	...	...	...	...	...	...	...	...	...	...	...	...	...	...
Financial Account, n.i.e.	78bj d	...	...	...	...	...	...	...	...	...	...	...	...	...	...	...
Direct Investment Abroad	78bd d	...	...	...	...	...	...	...	...	...	...	...	...	...	...	...
Dir. Invest. in Rep. Econ., n.i.e.	78be d	...	...	...	...	...	...	...	...	...	...	...	...	...	...	...
Portfolio Investment Assets	78bf d	...	...	...	...	...	...	...	...	...	...	...	...	...	...	...
Equity Securities	78bk d	...	...	...	...	...	...	...	...	...	...	...	...	...	...	...
Debt Securities	78bl d	...	...	...	...	...	...	...	...	...	...	...	...	...	...	...
Portfolio Investment Liab., n.i.e.	78bg d	...	...	...	...	...	...	...	...	...	...	...	...	...	...	...
Equity Securities	78bm d	...	...	...	...	...	...	...	...	...	...	...	...	...	...	...
Debt Securities	78bn d	...	...	...	...	...	...	...	...	...	...	...	...	...	...	...
Financial Derivatives Assets	78bw d	...	...	...	...	...	...	...	...	...	...	...	...	...	...	...
Financial Derivatives Liabilities	78bx d	...	...	...	...	...	...	...	...	...	...	...	...	...	...	...
Other Investment Assets	78bh d	...	...	...	...	...	...	...	...	...	...	...	...	...	...	...
Monetary Authorities	78bo d	...	...	...	...	...	...	...	...	...	...	...	...	...	...	...
General Government	78bp d	...	...	...	...	...	...	...	...	...	...	...	...	...	...	...
Banks	78bq d	...	...	...	...	...	...	...	...	...	...	...	...	...	...	...
Other Sectors	78br d	...	...	...	...	...	...	...	...	...	...	...	...	...	...	...
Other Investment Liab., n.i.e.	78bi d	...	...	...	...	...	...	...	...	...	...	...	...	...	...	...
Monetary Authorities	78bs d	...	...	...	...	...	...	...	...	...	...	...	...	...	...	...
General Government	78bt d	...	...	...	...	...	...	...	...	...	...	...	...	...	...	...
Banks	78bu d	...	...	...	...	...	...	...	...	...	...	...	...	...	...	...
Other Sectors	78bv d	...	...	...	...	...	...	...	...	...	...	...	...	...	...	...
Net Errors and Omissions	78ca d	...	...	...	...	...	...	...	...	...	...	...	...	...	...	...
Overall Balance	78cb d	...	...	...	...	...	...	...	...	...	...	...	...	...	...	...
Reserves and Related Items	79da d	...	...	...	...	...	...	...	...	...	...	...	...	...	...	...
Reserve Assets	79db d	...	...	...	...	...	...	...	...	...	...	...	...	...	...	...
Use of Fund Credit and Loans	79dc d	...	...	...	...	...	...	...	...	...	...	...	...	...	...	...
Exceptional Financing	79de d	...	...	...	...	...	...	...	...	...	...	...	...	...	...	...
Government Finance																*Millions of Lari:*
Deficit (-) or Surplus	80	...	...	...	...	...	...	...	...	...	...	...	...	...	...	...
Total Revenue and Grants	81y	...	...	...	...	...	...	...	...	...	...	...	...	...	...	...
Revenue	81	...	...	...	...	...	...	...	...	...	...	...	...	...	...	...
Grants	81z	...	...	...	...	...	...	...	...	...	...	...	...	...	...	...
Exp.& Lending Minus Repayments	82z	...	...	...	...	...	...	...	...	...	...	...	...	...	...	...
Expenditure	82	...	...	...	...	...	...	...	...	...	...	...	...	...	...	...
Lending Minus Repayments	83	...	...	...	...	...	...	...	...	...	...	...	...	...	...	...
Total Financing	80h	...	...	...	...	...	...	...	...	...	...	...	...	...	...	...
Domestic	84a	...	...	...	...	...	...	...	...	...	...	...	...	...	...	...
Foreign	85a	...	...	...	...	...	...	...	...	...	...	...	...	...	...	...
Total Debt by Residence	88	...	...	...	...	...	...	...	...	...	...	...	...	...	...	...
Domestic	88a	...	...	...	...	...	...	...	...	...	...	...	...	...	...	...
Foreign	89a	...	...	...	...	...	...	...	...	...	...	...	...	...	...	...
																Millions:
Population	99z	...	...	...	...	...	...	...	...	...	...	...	...	...	...	...

	1985	1986	1987	1988	1989	1990	1991	1992	1993	1994	1995	1996	1997	1998	1999		
Millions of Lari																**International Transactions**	
	...	...	...	...	...	...	...	...	...	163	194	251	312	269	...	Exports..	70
	...	...	...	...	...	...	...	...	...	288	507	868	1,225	1,230	...	Imports, c.i.f.	71
	...	...	...	...	...	...	...	...	...	259	456	781	1,103	1,107	...	Imports, f.o.b.	71.v
Minus Sign Indicates Debit																Balance of Payments	
	...	...	...	...	...	...	...	...	...	...	...	...	...	–416.4	...	Current Account, n.i.e.	78al *d*
	...	...	...	...	...	...	...	...	...	...	...	...	...	300.1	...	Goods: Exports f.o.b........................	78aa *d*
	...	...	...	...	...	...	...	...	...	...	...	...	...	–1,060.4	...	Goods: Imports f.o.b	78ab *d*
	...	...	...	...	...	...	...	...	...	...	...	...	...	–760.3	...	*Trade Balance*	78ac *d*
	...	...	...	...	...	...	...	...	...	...	...	...	...	289.9	...	Services: Credit	78ad *d*
	...	...	...	...	...	...	...	...	...	...	...	...	...	–345.1	...	Services: Debit	78ae *d*
	...	...	...	...	...	...	...	...	...	...	...	...	...	–815.5	...	*Balance on Goods & Services*	78af *d*
	...	...	...	...	...	...	...	...	...	...	...	...	...	243.3	...	Income: Credit	78ag *d*
	...	...	...	...	...	...	...	...	...	...	...	...	...	–52.4	...	Income: Debit	78ah *d*
	...	...	...	...	...	...	...	...	...	...	...	...	...	–624.6	...	*Balance on Gds, Serv. & Inc.*	78ai *d*
	...	...	...	...	...	...	...	...	...	...	...	...	...	220.1	...	Current Transfers, n.i.e.: Credit	78aj *d*
	...	...	...	...	...	...	...	...	...	...	...	...	...	–11.8	...	Current Transfers: Debit	78ak *d*
	...	...	...	...	...	...	...	...	...	...	...	...	...	–6.1	...	Capital Account, n.i.e.	78bc *d*
	...	...	...	...	...	...	...	...	...	...	...	...	...	—	...	Capital Account, n.i.e.: Credit	78ba *d*
	...	...	...	...	...	...	...	...	...	...	...	...	...	–6.1	...	Capital Account: Debit	78bb *d*
	...	...	...	...	...	...	...	...	...	...	...	...	...	348.8	...	Financial Account, n.i.e.	78bj *d*
	...	...	...	...	...	...	...	...	...	...	...	...	...	—	...	Direct Investment Abroad	78bd *d*
	...	...	...	...	...	...	...	...	...	...	...	...	...	265.3	...	Dir. Invest. in Rep. Econ., n.i.e.	78be *d*
	...	...	...	...	...	...	...	...	...	...	...	...	...	...	...	Portfolio Investment Assets	78bf *d*
	...	...	...	...	...	...	...	...	...	...	...	...	...	...	...	Equity Securities............................	78bk *d*
	...	...	...	...	...	...	...	...	...	...	...	...	...	...	...	Debt Securities..............................	78bl *d*
	...	...	...	...	...	...	...	...	...	...	...	...	...	...	...	Portfolio Investment Liab., n.i.e.	78bg *d*
	...	...	...	...	...	...	...	...	...	...	...	...	...	...	...	Equity Securities............................	78bm *d*
	...	...	...	...	...	...	...	...	...	...	...	...	...	...	...	Debt Securities..............................	78bn *d*
	...	...	...	...	...	...	...	...	...	...	...	...	...	...	...	Financial Derivatives Assets	78bw *d*
	...	...	...	...	...	...	...	...	...	...	...	...	...	...	...	Financial Derivatives Liabilities........	78bx *d*
	...	...	...	...	...	...	...	...	...	...	...	...	...	–86.8	...	Other Investment Assets	78bh *d*
	...	...	...	...	...	...	...	...	...	...	...	...	...	...	...	Monetary Authorities	78bo *d*
	...	...	...	...	...	...	...	...	...	...	...	...	...	–45.0	...	General Government	78bp *d*
	...	...	...	...	...	...	...	...	...	...	...	...	...	–23.2	...	Banks	78bq *d*
	...	...	...	...	...	...	...	...	...	...	...	...	...	–18.7	...	Other Sectors	78br *d*
	...	...	...	...	...	...	...	...	...	...	...	...	...	170.2	...	Other Investment Liab., n.i.e.	78bi *d*
	...	...	...	...	...	...	...	...	...	...	...	...	...	—	...	Monetary Authorities	78bs *d*
	...	...	...	...	...	...	...	...	...	...	...	...	...	141.4	...	General Government	78bt *d*
	...	...	...	...	...	...	...	...	...	...	...	...	...	37.3	...	Banks	78bu *d*
	...	...	...	...	...	...	...	...	...	...	...	...	...	–8.5	...	Other Sectors	78bv *d*
	...	...	...	...	...	...	...	...	...	...	...	...	...	5.9	...	Net Errors and Omissions	78ca *d*
	...	...	...	...	...	...	...	...	...	...	...	...	...	–67.8	...	*Overall Balance*	78cb *d*
	...	...	...	...	...	...	...	...	...	...	...	...	...	67.8	...	Reserves and Related Items	79da *d*
	...	...	...	...	...	...	...	...	...	...	...	...	...	31.9	...	Reserve Assets	79db *d*
	...	...	...	...	...	...	...	...	...	...	...	...	...	35.8	...	Use of Fund Credit and Loans..........	79dc *d*
	...	...	...	...	...	...	...	...	...	...	...	...	...	...	...	Exceptional Financing	79de *d*
Year Ending December 31																**Government Finance**	
	...	...	...	...	...	...	...	...	...	...	...	...	...	–137.71	...	Deficit (-) or Surplus	80
	...	...	...	...	...	...	...	...	...	...	...	...	...	627.31	...	Total Revenue and Grants	81y
	...	...	...	...	...	...	...	...	...	...	...	...	...	559.76	...	Revenue	81
	...	...	...	...	...	...	...	...	...	...	...	...	...	67.55	...	Grants	81z
	...	...	...	...	...	...	...	...	...	...	...	...	...	765.02	...	Exp.& Lending Minus Repayments	82z
	...	...	...	...	...	...	...	...	...	...	...	...	...	775.05	...	Expenditure	82
	...	...	...	...	...	...	...	...	...	...	...	...	...	–10.03	...	Lending Minus Repayments	83
	...	...	...	...	...	...	...	...	...	...	...	...	...	137.71	...	Total Financing	80h
	...	...	...	...	...	...	...	...	...	...	...	...	...	107.80	...	Domestic	84a
	...	...	...	...	...	...	...	...	...	...	...	...	...	29.91	...	Foreign	85a
	...	...	...	...	...	...	...	...	...	...	...	...	...	...	...	Total Debt by Residence..........................	88
	...	...	...	...	...	...	...	...	...	...	...	...	...	558.52	...	Domestic	88a
	...	...	...	...	...	...	...	...	...	...	...	...	...	...	...	Foreign	89a
Midyear Estimates																	
	...	...	...	...	...	...	5.46	5.45	5.44	5.43	5.42	5.41	...	...	...	**Population**...	99z

Germany

		1970	1971	1972	1973	1974	1975	1976	1977	1978	1979	1980	1981	1982	1983	1984
Exchange Rates											*Deutsche Mark per SDR through 1998,*					
Market Rate	aa	3.6480	3.5486	3.4759	3.2608	2.9501	3.0698	2.7448	2.5570	2.3815	2.2810	2.4985	2.6245	2.6215	2.8517	3.0857
												Deutsche Mark per US Dollar through 1998,					
Market Rate	ae	3.6480	3.2685	3.2015	2.7030	2.4095	2.6223	2.3625	2.1050	1.8280	1.7315	1.9590	2.2548	2.3765	2.7238	3.1480
Market Rate	rf	3.6600	3.5074	3.1886	2.6726	2.5878	2.4603	2.5180	2.3222	2.0086	1.8329	1.8177	2.2600	2.4266	2.5533	2.8459
												Deutsche Mark per ECU:					
ECU Rate	ea	....	....	....	....	....	....	....	....	....	2.4906	2.5656	2.4444	2.3001	2.2575	2.2318
ECU Rate	eb	....	....	....	....	....	....	2.8165	2.6485	2.5557	2.5108	2.5244	2.5147	2.3770	2.2705	2.2380
												Index Numbers (1995=100):					
Market Rate	ah x	39.3	83.5	44.9	54.0	55.4	58.3	56.9	61.7	71.4	78.2	78.9	63.6	59.1	56.2	50.5
Nominal Effective Exchange Rate	ne u	44.1	45.3	46.4	51.4	54.3	55.1	59.1	64.0	67.5	70.4	70.8	68.0	72.0	75.6	75.3
Real Effective Exchange Rate	re u	....	....	....	....	....	80.1	81.1	85.3	72.9	73.5	Ι72.1	66.6	68.3	70.2	68.8
Fund Position												*Millions of SDRs:*					
Quota	2f. s	1,600	1,600	1,600	1,600	1,600	1,600	1,600	1,600	2,156	2,156	3,234	3,234	3,234	5,404	5,404
SDRs	1b. s	258	454	822	1,388	1,440	1,451	1,747	1,177	1,379	1,576	1,443	1,383	1,862	1,541	1,390
Reserve Position in the Fund	1c. s	917	1,078	1,140	1,207	1,290	1,581	2,133	2,185	3,302	2,372	1,796	2,117	2,799	3,580	3,826
of which: Outstg.Fund Borrowing	2c	—	—	—	—	—	150	600	1,031	1,278	948	629	929	1,205	878	853
International Liquidity											*Millions of US Dollars Unless Otherwise Indicated:*						
Total Res.Min.Gold (Eurosys.Def)	1l. d	9,630	14,231	19,326	28,206	27,359	26,216	30,019	34,708	48,474	52,549	48,592	43,719	44,762	42,674	40,141
SDRs	1b. d	258	493	893	1,674	1,763	1,698	2,030	1,429	1,796	2,076	1,840	1,609	2,054	1,613	1,362
Reserve Position in the Fund	1c. d	917	1,171	1,238	1,456	1,580	1,851	2,478	2,654	4,302	3,125	2,291	2,465	3,088	3,748	3,750
Foreign Exchange	1d. d	8,455	12,567	17,195	25,076	24,016	22,666	25,511	30,625	42,376	47,348	44,461	39,645	39,620	37,313	35,028
o/w: Fin.Deriv.Rel.to Reserves	1dd d	....	....	....	....	....	....	....	....	....	....	....	....	....	....	....
Other Reserve Assets	1e. d	....	....	....	....	....	....	....	....	....	....	....	....	....	....	....
Gold (Million Fine Troy Ounces)	1ad	113.70	116.47	117.36	117.61	117.61	117.61	117.61	118.30	118.64	95.25	95.18	95.18	95.18	95.18	95.18
Gold (National Valuation)	1an d	3,994	4,494	4,364	5,179	5,810	5,339	5,926	6,684	9,344	7,906	6,988	6,071	5,761	5,026	4,349
Memo: Euro Cl. on Non-EA Res.	1dg d	....	....	....	....	....	....	....	....	....	....	....	....	....	....	....
Non-Euro Cl. on EA Res.	1dh d	....	....	....	....	....	....	....	....	....	....	....	....	....	....	....
Mon. Auth.: Other Foreign Assets	3.. d	689	771	772	919	1,511	1,442	1,569	1,683	1,360	1,433	1,274	1,114	1,042	913	794
Foreign Liabilities	4.. d	768	892	917	710	914	713	1,160	939	3,757	2,839	5,214	5,064	6,475	5,177	4,813
Banking Insts.: Foreign Assets	7a. d	14,270	16,053	15,410	21,139	29,433	38,321	48,229	58,271	73,206	82,558	85,171	84,535	81,729	74,756	75,232
Foreign Liab.	7b. d	9,139	11,417	12,093	15,759	18,572	21,912	30,201	38,371	57,927	76,697	72,093	66,795	64,692	57,923	58,224
Monetary Authorities											*Billions of Deutsche Mark through 1998;*					
Fgn. Assets (Cl.on Non-EA Ctys)	11	52.6	62.4	77.6	92.5	83.5	86.4	88.5	90.2	107.2	107.0	104.4	103.7	108.0	111.0	111.8
Claims on General Government	12a. u	....	....	....	....	....	....	....	....	....	....	....	....	....	....	....
o/w: Claims on Gen.Govt.in Cty	12a	15.2	15.2	13.9	16.7	15.5	22.4	15.9	16.4	19.6	18.1	22.4	24.9	23.6	25.9	24.3
Claims on Banking Institutions	12e. u	....	....	....	....	....	....	....	....	....	....	....	....	....	....	....
o/w: Claims on Bank.Inst.in Cty	12e	18.7	18.8	20.2	11.2	15.5	8.5	19.5	19.6	24.3	36.2	57.6	68.1	74.9	85.5	96.3
Claims on Other Resident Sectors	12d. u	....	....	....	....	....	....	....	....	....	....	....	....	....	....	....
o/w: Cl. on Oth.Res.Sect.in Cty	12d	....	....	....	....	....	....	....	....	....	....	....	....	....	....	....
Claims on ECB	12u	....	....	....	....	....	....	....	....	....	....	....	....	....	....	....
Currency in Circulation	14a	39.5	43.2	48.9	51.0	55.4	60.6	64.7	71.7	81.4	86.4	91.2	91.6	96.7	104.7	109.6
Liabilities to Banking Insts	14c. u	....	....	....	....	....	....	....	....	....	....	....	....	....	....	....
o/w: Liabs to Bank.Inst.in Cty	14c	27.9	34.3	49.1	54.4	48.7	46.6	53.4	55.9	62.9	65.4	55.0	52.1	54.8	55.3	56.3
Demand Dep. of Other Res.Sect.	14d. u	....	....	....	....	....	....	....	....	....	....	....	....	....	....	....
o/w: D.Dep.of Oth.Res.Sect.in Cty	14d	.4	.6	.6	.6	.6	.6	.6	.5	.6	.7	.7	.7	.7	.6	.8
Other Dep. of Other Res.Sect.	15.. u	....	....	....	....	....	....	....	....	....	....	....	....	....	....	....
o/w: O.Dep.of Oth.Res.Sect.in Cty	15	....	....	....	....	....	....	....	....	....	....	....	....	....	....	....
Money Market Instruments	16m. u	....	....	....	....	....	....	....	....	....	....	....	....	....	....	....
Bonds (Debt Securities)	16n. u	....	....	....	....	....	....	....	....	....	....	....	....	....	....	....
Foreign Liab. (to Non-EA Ctys)	16c	2.8	2.9	3.0	1.9	2.2	1.9	2.7	2.0	6.9	5.0	14.4	11.4	15.4	14.1	15.2
Central Government Deposits	16d. u	....	....	....	....	....	....	....	....	....	....	....	....	....	....	....
o/w: Cent.Govt.Dep. in Cty	16d	1.3	.9	2.8	2.8	.9	4.8	2.7	2.1	4.6	2.9	1.0	.7	1.2	2.1	.9
Liabilities to ECB	16u	....	....	....	....	....	....	....	....	....	....	....	....	....	....	....
Capital Accounts	17a	2.3	3.7	2.7	2.5	2.7	2.9	3.2	3.3	3.3	3.4	3.4	4.4	8.6	9.3	11.6
Other Items (Net)	17r	12.3	10.9	4.6	7.2	4.0	.1	−3.4	−9.2	−8.5	−2.4	18.8	35.8	29.1	36.3	38.1
Banking Institutions											*Billions of Deutsche Mark through 1998;*					
Claims on Monetary Authorities	20	31.0	38.7	53.5	60.5	55.5	54.3	59.4	62.9	72.3	78.8	70.4	66.5	69.0	69.5	75.6
Claims on Bk.Inst.in Oth.EA Ctys	20b. u	....	....	....	....	....	....	....	....	....	....	....	....	....	....	....
Fgn. Assets (Cl.on Non-EA Ctys)	21	52.2	51.7	49.7	56.4	70.9	100.5	113.9	122.7	133.8	143.0	166.9	190.6	194.2	203.6	236.8
Claims on General Government	22a. u	....	....	....	....	....	....	....	....	....	....	....	....	....	....	....
o/w: Claims on Gen.Govt.in Cty	22a	83.9	94.1	104.6	114.1	132.6	180.8	211.5	238.7	273.4	301.4	322.2	369.2	409.1	428.5	447.4
Claims on Other Resident Sectors	22d. u	....	....	....	....	....	....	....	....	....	....	....	....	....	....	....
o/w: Cl. on Oth.Res.Sect.in Cty	22d	469.0	535.9	621.7	694.8	742.1	780.0	854.2	934.1	1,031.1	1,157.4	1,270.9	1,365.6	1,439.5	1,538.6	1,634.1
Demand Deposits	24.. u	....	....	....	....	....	....	....	....	....	....	....	....	....	....	....
o/w: D.Dep.of Oth.Res.Sect.in Cty	24	66.3	76.0	87.1	87.7	98.2	114.6	116.2	130.6	150.7	153.6	158.8	154.7	167.4	181.1	194.2
Other Deposits	25.. u	....	....	....	....	....	....	....	....	....	....	....	....	....	....	....
o/w: O.Dep.of Oth.Res.Sect.in Cty	25	269.4	306.6	350.0	393.8	418.8	462.3	506.2	553.6	599.9	638.9	671.1	710.4	755.6	789.6	826.1
Money Market Instruments	26m. u	....	....	....	....	....	....	....	....	....	....	....	....	....	....	....
Bonds (Debt Securities)	26n	....	....	....	....	....	....	....	....	....	....	....	....	....	....	....
o/w: Bonds Held by Resid.of Cty	26n	112.4	133.3	169.0	213.8	240.7	277.5	322.1	355.1	397.5	467.4	524.3	600.5	634.1	687.8	739.6
Foreign Liab. (to Non-EA Ctys)	26c	33.5	36.8	39.0	42.1	44.8	57.5	71.4	80.8	105.9	132.8	141.2	150.6	153.7	157.8	183.3
Central Government Deposits	26d. u	....	....	....	....	....	....	....	....	....	....	....	....	....	....	....
o/w: Cent.Govt.Dep. in Cty	26d	94.6	100.0	107.1	115.8	119.2	125.8	128.5	131.5	134.7	138.8	149.3	161.3	164.4	171.0	176.9
Credit from Monetary Authorities	26g	18.7	18.8	20.2	11.2	15.5	8.5	19.5	19.6	24.3	36.2	57.6	68.1	74.9	85.5	96.3
Liab. to Bk.Inst.in Oth. EA Ctys	26h. u	....	....	....	....	....	....	....	....	....	....	....	....	....	....	....
Capital Accounts	27a	38.5	42.3	48.5	54.2	60.0	66.1	73.9	81.2	88.6	96.6	103.3	112.8	121.7	132.6	144.2
Other Items (Net)	27r	2.9	6.7	8.7	7.3	4.0	3.4	1.4	6.0	9.0	16.3	24.8	33.5	40.0	34.9	33.4

	1985	1986	1987	1988	1989	1990	1991	1992	1993	1994	1995	1996	1997	1998	1999		
																Exchange Rates	
Euros per SDR Thereafter: End of Period																	
	2.7035	2.3740	2.2436	2.3957	2.2312	2.1255	2.1685	2.2193	2.3712	2.2610	2.1309	2.2357	2.4180	2.3556	1.3662	Market Rate	aa
Euros per US Dollar Thereafter: End of Period (ae) Period Average (rf)																	
	2.4613	1.9408	1.5815	1.7803	1.6978	1.4940	1.5160	1.6140	1.7263	1.5488	1.4335	1.5548	1.7921	1.6730	.9954	Market Rate	ae
	2.9440	2.1715	1.7974	1.8800	1.6157	1.6595	1.5617	1.6533	1.6228	1.4331	1.5048	1.7341	1.7597	.9386	Market Rate	rf
End of Period (ea) Period Average (eb)																	
	2.1839	2.0761	2.0603	2.0778	2.0241	2.0420	2.0355	1.9556	1.9357	1.9053	1.8840	1.9465	1.9763	1.9558	....	ECU Rate	ea
	2.2263	2.1287	2.0715	2.0744	2.0700	2.0519	2.0507	2.0210	1.9368	1.9248	1.8736	1.9096	1.9642	1.9692	....	ECU Rate	eb
Period Averages																	
	49.0	66.2	79.8	81.7	76.2	88.8	86.6	91.9	86.6	88.4	100.0	95.2	82.7	81.5	....	Market Rate	ahx
	75.7	82.2	87.0	86.4	85.7	89.4	88.6	91.3	94.9	95.1	100.0	97.3	92.9	93.1	91.3	Nominal Effective Exchange Rate	neu
	69.0	74.7	79.1	79.2	78.3	82.6	81.6	84.5	90.2	93.1	100.0	98.7	92.1	89.5	....	Real Effective Exchange Rate	reu
End of Period																**Fund Position**	
	5,404	5,404	5,404	5,404	5,404	5,404	5,404	8,242	8,242	8,242	8,242	8,242	8,242	8,242	13,008	Quota	2f. s
	1,408	1,651	1,384	1,380	1,373	1,321	1,340	611	700	763	1,346	1,326	1,325	1,327	1,427	SDRs	1b. s
	3,467	3,146	2,749	2,487	2,315	2,148	2,494	3,083	2,877	2,760	3,505	3,803	4,407	5,698	4,677	Reserve Position in the Fund	1c. s
	723	424	173	—	—	—	—	—	—	—	—	—	—	—	530	of which: Outstg.Fund Borrowing	2c
End of Period																**International Liquidity**	
	44,380	51,734	78,756	58,528	60,709	67,902	63,001	90,967	77,640	77,363	85,005	83,178	77,587	74,024	‡61,039	Total Res.Min.Gold (Eurosys.Def)	1l. d
	1,547	2,020	1,964	1,857	1,804	1,880	1,917	841	962	1,114	2,001	1,907	1,788	1,868	1,959	SDRs	1b. d
	3,808	3,848	3,900	3,346	3,043	3,056	3,567	4,239	3,951	4,030	5,210	5,468	5,946	8,023	6,419	Reserve Position in the Fund	1c. d
	39,025	45,866	72,893	53,324	55,862	62,967	57,517	85,887	72,727	72,219	77,794	75,803	69,853	64,133	52,661	Foreign Exchange	1d. d
	....	....	....	....	....	....	....	....	....	....	....	....	....	....	—	o/w: Fin.Deriv.Rel.to Reserves	1dd d
	....	....	....	....	....	....	....	....	....	....	....	....	....	....	—	Other Reserve Assets	1e. d
	95.18	95.18	95.18	95.18	95.18	95.18	95.18	95.18	95.18	95.18	95.18	95.18	95.18	118.98	111.52	Gold (Million Fine Troy Ounces)	1ad
	5,562	7,054	8,656	7,690	8,062	9,162	9,029	8,481	7,929	8,838	9,549	8,804	7,638	10,227	32,436	Gold (National Valuation)	1an d
	....	....	....	....	....	....	....	....	....	....	....	....	....	....	9,191	Memo: Euro Cl. on Non-EA Res.	1dg d
																Non-Euro Cl. on EA Res.	1dh d
	1,003	1,263	1,542	1,372	1,434	1,623	1,715	1,637	1,548	1,539	1,371	944	559	680	‡9,204	Mon. Auth.: Other Foreign Assets	3.. d
	7,451	12,137	12,794	15,306	30,417	34,979	27,925	16,423	22,909	15,620	11,435	10,035	9,436	9,551	‡6,195	Foreign Liabilities	4.. d
	112,932	178,483	232,608	230,090	292,860	395,487	402,020	386,841	461,962	484,892	578,196	606,018	650,287	828,893	‡513,967	Banking Insts.: Foreign Assets	7a. d
	75,773	101,288	131,375	131,000	159,529	226,371	231,086	264,432	286,135	378,834	482,236	490,213	561,585	760,827	‡490,158	Foreign Liab.	7b. d
Billions of Euros Beginning 1999: End of Period																**Monetary Authorities**	
	108.7	110.4	140.7	113.6	114.9	117.5	109.1	152.0	134.5	128.7	132.9	132.2	129.7	135.1	102.2	Fgn. Assets (Cl.on Non-EA Ctys)	11
	....	....	....	....	....	....	....	....	....	....	....	....	....	....	4.4	Claims on General Government	12a. u
	22.2	26.5	24.2	25.4	25.5	26.3	27.0	33.2	27.7	26.6	24.7	24.0	24.2	24.3	4.4	o/w: Claims on Gen.Govt.in Cty	12a
	....	....	....	....	....	....	....	....	....	....	....	....	....	....	123.7	Claims on Banking Institutions	12e. u
	105.3	96.4	82.4	144.7	175.3	208.5	225.3	188.9	257.5	217.7	213.1	226.2	235.2	216.0	90.6	o/w: Claims on Bank.Inst.in Cty	12e
	....	....	....	....	....	....	....	....	....	....	....	....	....	....	—	Claims on Other Resident Sectors	12d. u
	....	....	....	....	....	....	....	....	....	....	....	....	....	....	—	o/w: Cl. on Oth.Res.Sect.in Cty	12d
	....	....	....	....	....	....	....	....	....	....	....	....	....	....	12.2	Claims on ECB	12u
	114.7	123.7	135.9	154.8	162.1	179.7	194.6	227.3	238.6	250.9	263.5	275.7	276.2	271.0	148.2	Currency in Circulation	14a
	....	....	....	....	....	....	....	....	....	....	....	....	....	....	43.4	Liabilities to Banking Insts	14c. u
	56.5	58.3	63.0	65.5	71.6	81.9	81.3	88.9	73.4	56.2	49.7	51.9	48.7	57.7	41.9	o/w: Liabs to Bank.Inst.in Cty	14c
	....	....	....	....	....	....	....	....	....	....	....	....	....	....	.5	Demand Dep. of Other Res.Sect.	14d. u
	.9	.9	.8	.8	.9	1.3	1.0	.8	.8	.7	.7	1.3	1.1	1.0	.5	o/w: D.Dep.of Oth.Res.Sect.in Cty	14d
	....	....	....	....	....	....	....	....	....	....	....	....	....	....	—	Other Dep. of Other Res.Sect.	15.. u
	....	....	....	....	....	....	....	....	....	....	....	....	....	....	—	o/w: O.Dep.of Oth.Res.Sect.in Cty	15
	....	....	....	....	....	....	....	....	....	....	....	....	....	....	—	Money Market Instruments	16m. u
	....	....	....	....	....	....	....	....	....	....	....	....	....	....	—	Bonds (Debt Securities)	16n. u
	18.3	23.6	20.2	27.3	51.6	52.3	42.3	26.5	23.2	19.6	16.4	15.6	16.9	16.0	6.2	Foreign Liab. (to Non-EA Ctys)	16c
	....	....	....	....	....	....	....	....	....	....	....	....	....	....	—	Central Government Deposits	16d. u
	2.2	1.1	4.6	3.5	6.1	19.0	12.7	.4	13.4	.2	.1	.4	.3	.2	—	o/w: Cent.Govt.Dep. in Cty	16d
	....	....	....	....	....	....	....	....	....	....	....	....	....	....	5.3	Liabilities to ECB	16u
	14.4	11.6	11.0	10.6	12.5	13.1	14.4	18.8	21.1	23.1	22.4	23.1	24.6	21.5	41.7	Capital Accounts	17a
	29.2	14.1	11.7	21.3	10.9	5.1	15.2	11.5	49.2	22.2	17.9	14.4	21.3	8.0	-2.8	Other Items (Net)	17r
Billions of Euros Beginning 1999: End of Period																**Banking Institutions**	
	‡78.3	80.2	83.6	89.0	96.8	117.7	112.8	115.0	102.0	86.5	87.0	88.6	89.5	92.1	45.6	Claims on Monetary Authorities	20
	....	....	....	....	....	....	....	....	....	....	....	....	....	....	203.1	Claims on Bk.Inst.in Oth.EA Ctys	20b. u
	‡278.0	346.4	367.9	409.6	497.2	590.9	609.5	624.4	797.5	751.0	828.8	942.2	1,165.4	1,386.7	511.6	Fgn. Assets (Cl.on Non-EA Ctys)	21
	....	....	....	....	....	....	....	....	....	....	....	....	....	....	735.7	Claims on General Government	22a. u
	‡467.6	472.2	501.3	543.6	550.7	608.0	635.2	746.2	849.3	937.4	1,078.7	1,161.4	1,223.7	1,251.8	632.1	o/w: Claims on Gen.Govt.in Cty	22a
	....	....	....	....	....	....	....	....	....	....	....	....	....	....	2,391.7	Claims on Other Resident Sectors	22d. u
	‡1,740.4	1,808.7	1,865.5	1,950.2	2,083.7	2,446.1	2,699.6	2,939.1	3,206.4	3,451.4	3,630.7	3,900.1	4,137.6	4,471.9	2,326.4	o/w: Cl. on Oth.Res.Sect.in Cty	22d
	....	....	....	....	....	....	....	....	....	....	....	....	....	....	426.0	Demand Deposits	24.. u
	‡209.7	227.2	240.8	265.0	282.9	392.0	402.3	439.6	484.8	505.3	545.4	631.8	650.0	747.7	419.5	o/w: D.Dep.of Oth.Res.Sect.in Cty	24
	....	....	....	....	....	....	....	....	....	....	....	....	....	....	1,541.7	Other Deposits	25.. u
	‡885.3	927.7	967.4	996.2	1,040.6	1,176.5	1,261.9	1,337.9	1,500.9	1,523.6	1,572.2	1,649.6	1,692.4	1,752.4	1,435.6	o/w: O.Dep.of Oth.Res.Sect.in Cty	25
	....	....	....	....	....	....	....	....	....	....	....	....	....	....	96.1	Money Market Instruments	26m. u
	....	....	....	....	....	....	....	....	....	....	....	....	....	....	1,274.0	Bonds (Debt Securities)	26n. u
	‡796.2	843.3	894.7	917.1	1,003.5	1,130.9	1,266.3	1,370.0	1,467.6	1,612.5	1,786.9	1,948.0	2,075.8	2,196.0	....	o/w: Bonds Held by Resid.of Cty	26n
	‡186.5	196.6	207.8	233.2	270.8	338.2	350.3	426.8	494.0	586.7	691.3	762.2	1,006.4	1,272.9	487.9	Foreign Liab. (to Non-EA Ctys)	26c
	....	....	....	....	....	....	....	....	....	....	....	....	....	....	46.6	Central Government Deposits	26d. u
	‡188.2	199.5	204.0	208.6	219.0	241.2	251.8	237.5	242.9	249.5	245.4	248.1	248.4	251.3	45.9	o/w: Cent.Govt.Dep. in Cty	26d
	105.3	96.4	82.4	144.7	175.3	208.5	225.3	188.9	257.5	217.7	213.1	226.2	235.2	216.0	92.1	Credit from Monetary Authorities	26g
	....	....	....	....	....	....	....	....	....	....	....	....	....	....	166.3	Liab. to Bk.Inst.in Oth. EA Ctys	26h. u
	‡161.2	176.7	191.0	198.5	211.0	265.0	312.7	352.1	391.6	410.1	438.1	463.9	507.0	544.9	237.0	Capital Accounts	27a
	‡31.7	40.1	30.2	29.1	25.0	10.3	-13.5	71.8	116.1	120.7	132.8	162.7	201.0	221.4	-480.0	Other Items (Net)	27r

Germany

	1970	1971	1972	1973	1974	1975	1976	1977	1978	1979	1980	1981	1982	1983	1984
Banking Survey (Nat'l Residency)											*Billions of Deutsche Mark through 1998;*				
Foreign Assets (Net) 31n	68.6	74.4	85.3	104.9	107.4	127.6	128.4	130.1	128.3	112.2	115.6	132.3	133.1	142.7	150.2
Domestic Credit 32	472.2	544.4	630.3	707.0	770.1	852.7	950.5	1,055.6	1,184.8	1,335.2	1,465.2	1,597.7	1,706.5	1,819.9	1,928.0
Claims on General Govt. (Net) 32an	3.2	8.5	8.6	12.2	28.0	72.7	96.3	121.5	153.7	177.8	194.3	232.1	267.0	281.3	294.0
Claims on Other Resident Sectors 32d	469.0	535.9	621.7	694.8	742.1	780.0	854.2	934.1	1,031.1	1,157.4	1,270.9	1,365.6	1,439.5	1,538.6	1,634.1
Currency in Circulation 34a.n	39.5	43.2	48.9	51.0	55.4	60.6	64.7	71.7	81.4	86.4	91.2	91.6	96.7	104.7	109.6
Demand Deposits 34b.n	66.8	76.6	87.7	88.2	98.7	115.2	116.7	131.1	151.3	154.3	159.4	155.4	168.1	181.8	195.0
Other Deposits .... 35..n	269.4	306.6	350.0	393.8	418.8	462.3	506.2	553.6	599.9	638.9	671.1	710.4	755.6	789.6	826.1
Money Market Instruments 36m	....	....	....	....											
Bonds (Debt Securities) 36n	112.4	133.3	169.0	213.8	240.7	277.5	322.1	355.1	397.5	467.4	524.3	600.5	634.1	687.8	739.6
o/w: Bonds Over Two Years 36na	....	....	....	....											
Capital Accounts 37a	40.8	46.1	51.1	56.7	62.7	69.0	77.2	84.5	92.0	100.0	106.8	117.2	130.4	142.0	155.9
Other Items (Net) 37r	12.0	13.2	8.9	8.4	1.2	–4.3	–8.1	–10.2	–8.9	.5	28.1	54.9	54.8	56.9	52.2
Banking Survey (EA-Wide Residency)											*Billions of Euros:*				
Foreign Assets (Net) 31n.u	....	....	....	....	....	....	....	....	....	....	....	....	....	....	....
Domestic Credit .... 32..u	....	....	....	....	....	....	....	....	....	....	....	....	....	....	....
Claims on General Govt. (Net) .... 32an u	....	....	....	....	....	....	....	....	....	....	....	....	....	....	....
Claims on Other Resident Sect. 32d.u	....	....	....	....	....	....	....	....	....	....	....	....	....	....	....
Currency in Circulation 34a.u	....	....	....	....	....	....	....	....	....	....	....	....	....	....	....
Demand Deposits 34b.u	....	....	....	....	....	....	....	....	....	....	....	....	....	....	....
Other Deposits .... 35..u	....	....	....	....	....	....	....	....	....	....	....	....	....	....	....
o/w: Other Dep. Over Two Yrs .... 35ab u	....	....	....	....	....	....	....	....	....	....	....	....	....	....	....
Money Market Instruments 36m.u	....	....	....	....	....	....	....	....	....	....	....	....	....	....	....
Bonds (Debt Securities) 36n.u	....	....	....	....	....	....	....	....	....	....	....	....	....	....	....
o/w: Bonds Over Two Years .... 36na u	....	....	....	....	....	....	....	....	....	....	....	....	....	....	....
Capital Accounts 37a	....	....	....	....	....	....	....	....	....	....	....	....	....	....	....
Other Items (Net) 37r.u	....	....	....	....	....	....	....	....	....	....	....	....	....	....	....
Money (National Definitions)											*Billions of Deutsche Mark:*				
Central Bank Money,Seas. Adj. .... 19m. c	41.3	44.8	50.0	54.7	58.2	63.5	69.1	75.3	80.7	87.2	91.7	94.2	97.6	105.4	110.9
M1, Seasonally Adjusted .... 39ma c	98.3	110.1	125.0	132.3	140.1	159.6	176.2	190.6	216.2	232.5	237.9	240.8	249.4	275.0	284.0
M2, Seasonally Adjusted .... 39mb c	158.8	180.3	206.1	243.1	262.2	260.9	275.1	298.3	333.5	369.2	403.8	446.1	476.1	489.9	506.6
M3, Seasonally Adjusted .... 39mc c	270.6	304.3	344.3	385.8	419.5	450.9	495.9	542.2	600.0	653.6	688.0	732.2	780.1	831.7	863.6
Extended Money M3,Seas.Adj. .... 39md c	....	....	....	....	456.7	489.2	535.0	584.5	645.5	707.3	753.7	816.6	876.5	934.0	975.4
Liquid Liabilities 551	413.7	469.9	537.0	591.4	636.8	709.3	766.1	841.3	923.6	977.1	1,025.0	1,066.4	1,133.9	1,193.8	1,247.2
Interest Rates											*Percent Per Annum*				
Discount Rate (End of Period) 60	6.00	4.00	4.50	7.00	6.00	3.50	3.50	3.00	3.00	6.00	7.50	7.50	5.00	4.00	4.50
Money Market Rate 60b	8.65	6.16	4.30	10.18	8.87	4.40	3.89	4.14	3.36	5.87	9.06	11.26	8.67	5.36	5.55
Treasury Bill Rate 60c	....	....	....	....	5.40	5.19	4.36	3.76	5.48	7.85	10.37	8.31	5.63	5.66	
Deposit Rate 60l	....	....	....	....	....	....	....	3.06	5.14	7.95	9.74	7.54	4.56	4.86	
Lending Rate 60p	....	....	....	....	....	....	....	7.33	8.63	12.04	14.69	13.50	10.05	9.82	
Government Bond Yield 61	8.30	8.00	7.90	9.30	10.40	8.50	7.80	6.20	5.80	7.40	8.50	10.38	8.95	7.89	7.78
Prices, Production, Labor											*Index Numbers (1995=100):*				
Share Prices 62	28.3	27.8	30.5	28.1	23.6	28.2	29.6	29.8	32.2	30.9	29.7	30.2	31.0	41.8	47.2
Producer Prices 63	46.5	48.4	49.7	53.0	60.1	62.9	65.2	67.0	67.8	71.1	76.4	82.4	87.2	88.5	91.1
Consumer Prices 64	40.4	42.5	44.8	47.9	51.3	54.3	56.7	58.8	60.3	62.8	66.2	70.4	74.1	76.6	78.4
Harmonized CPI 64h	....	....	....	....	....	....	....	....	....	....	....	....	....		
Wages: Hrly Earnings (1990=100) ... 65.. c	24.5	27.7	30.6	34.6	39.6	44.1	46.7	50.7	54.1	57.9	62.8	67.4	70.9	73.8	76.2
Industrial Production .... 66.. c	72.9	74.0	76.7	80.9	79.1	73.7	79.1	81.0	82.5	86.6	86.8	84.7	82.0	82.4	84.7
Investment Goods .... 66iy c	65.9	65.5	67.0	71.7	69.8	66.5	71.4	74.7	74.7	78.1	80.3	80.1	78.8	78.0	80.2
Other Prod. Goods .... 66jy c	....	....	....	....	....	....	....	....	....	....	....	....	....		
Consumer Goods .... 66hy c	85.0	87.9	92.7	94.4	89.9	85.1	91.1	94.0	94.2	97.2	96.0	90.3	85.9	87.3	89.3
Labor Force 67d	....	....	....	....	....	....	....	....	....	....	*Number in Thousands:*				
Employment 67e	....	....	....	....	....	....	....	....	....	....	....	....	....	....	....
Unemployment 67c	....	....	....	....	....	....	....	....	....	....	....	....	....	....	....
Unemployment Rate (%) 67r	....	....	....	....	....	....	....	....	....	....	....	....	....	....	....
International Transactions											*Billions of Deutsche Mark through 1998;*				
Exports 70	125.28	136.01	149.02	178.40	230.58	221.59	256.64	273.61	284.91	314.47	350.33	396.90	427.74	432.28	488.22
Imports, c.i.f. 71	109.61	120.12	128.74	145.42	179.73	184.31	222.17	235.18	243.71	292.04	341.38	369.18	376.46	390.19	434.26
Imports, f.o.b. 71.v	102.87	112.72	121.72	137.73	171.88	177.06	214.56	227.69	235.75	282.66	331.41	357.33	365.17	378.51	421.42
															1995=100
Volume of Exports 72	32.9	34.3	36.4	41.5	46.1	40.9	48.5	50.5	52.1	54.6	55.5	59.2	61.1	61.0	66.5
Volume of Imports 73	34.4	37.2	39.6	41.8	40.1	40.0	47.1	48.2	51.5	55.3	55.3	52.6	53.3	55.4	58.3
Unit Value of Exports........................ 74	53.5	55.6	57.3	60.1	70.1	75.8	74.0	75.9	76.6	80.7	88.4	93.9	98.0	99.3	102.8
Export Prices 76	48.4	50.0	51.0	54.3	63.5	66.0	68.6	69.8	70.9	74.2	78.8	83.4	87.0	88.5	91.6
Unit Value of Imports 75	51.3	52.0	52.3	56.1	72.0	74.1	75.8	78.5	76.2	84.8	99.2	112.9	113.6	113.2	119.9
Import Prices 76.x	52.5	52.7	52.4	59.1	76.0	74.7	79.3	80.5	77.5	86.5	99.5	113.1	115.6	115.3	122.2

Banking Survey (Nat'l Residency)

Billions of Euros Beginning 1999: End of Period

1985	1986	1987	1988	1989	1990	1991	1992	1993	1994	1995	1996	1997	1998	1999		
I 181.8	236.7	280.6	262.8	289.6	317.9	325.9	323.1	414.9	273.3	254.0	296.6	271.7	233.0	266.0	Foreign Assets (Net)	31n
I 2,039.9	2,106.8	2,182.4	2,307.0	2,434.7	2,820.1	3,097.3	3,480.6	3,827.2	4,165.6	4,488.6	4,837.1	5,137.0	5,496.5	2,917.1	Domestic Credit	32
I 299.5	298.2	316.9	356.8	351.1	374.1	397.7	541.6	620.7	714.2	857.8	937.0	999.4	1,024.6	590.6	Claims on General Govt. (Net)	32an
I 1,740.4	1,808.7	1,865.5	1,950.2	2,083.7	2,446.1	2,699.6	2,939.1	3,206.4	3,451.4	3,630.7	3,900.1	4,137.6	4,471.9	2,326.4	Claims on Other Resident Sectors	32d
114.7	123.7	135.9	154.8	162.1	179.7	194.6	227.3	238.6	250.9	263.5	275.7	276.2	271.0	148.2	Currency in Circulation	34a. n
I 210.6	228.1	241.6	265.7	283.8	393.3	403.3	440.4	485.6	506.1	546.2	633.0	651.1	748.7	420.0	Demand Deposits	34b. n
I 885.3	927.7	967.4	996.2	1,040.8	1,176.5	1,261.9	1,337.9	1,500.9	1,523.6	1,572.2	1,649.6	1,692.4	1,752.4	1,435.6	Other Deposits	35.. n
....	....	....	....	....	....	....	....	....	....	....	....	....	....	96.1	Money Market Instruments	36m
I 796.2	843.3	894.7	917.1	1,003.5	1,130.9	1,266.3	1,370.0	1,467.6	1,612.5	1,786.9	1,948.0	2,075.8	2,196.0	1,274.0	Bonds (Debt Securities)	36n
....	....	....	....	....	....	....	....	....	....	....	....	....	....	1,226.2	o/w: Bonds Over Two Years	36na
I 175.5	188.4	202.0	209.1	223.5	278.1	327.1	370.9	412.6	433.2	460.5	487.0	531.6	566.4	278.7	Capital Accounts	37a
I 39.2	32.2	21.3	26.9	10.6	−20.4	−29.9	57.2	136.7	112.7	113.3	140.3	181.5	194.9	−469.5	Other Items (Net)	37r

Banking Survey (EA-Wide Residency)

End of Period

1999		
119.7	Foreign Assets (Net)	31n.. u
3,085.2	Domestic Credit	32.. u
693.5	Claims on General Govt. (Net)	32an u
2,391.7	Claims on Other Resident Sect.	32d. u
148.2	Currency in Circulation	34a. u
426.5	Demand Deposits	34b. u
1,541.7	Other Deposits	35.. u
664.4	o/w: Other Dep. Over Two Yrs	35ab u
96.1	Money Market Instruments	36m. u
1,274.0	Bonds (Debt Securities)	36n. u
1,226.2	o/w: Bonds Over Two Years	36na u
278.7	Capital Accounts	37a
−560.3	Other Items (Net)	37r. u

Money (National Definitions)

End of Period

1985	1986	1987	1988	1989	1990	1991	1992	1993	1994	1995	1996	1997	1998	1999		
115.2	122.8	133.9	148.0	161.3	....	188.6	205.7	229.8	249.7	258.8	274.3	282.5	281.8	....	Central Bank Money,Seas. Adj.	19m. c
296.2	325.9	355.3	389.9	414.4	473.6	547.4	586.3	641.2	703.0	729.0	805.0	872.9	930.6	....	M1, Seasonally Adjusted	39ma c
529.3	568.5	606.5	644.7	703.2	837.2	991.5	1,108.9	1,204.4	1,279.2	1,206.5	1,224.6	1,265.7	1,322.1	....	M2, Seasonally Adjusted	39mb c
906.8	I 973.3	1,047.3	1,114.2	1,177.8	1,321.1	1,476.5	1,596.5	1,720.8	1,875.1	1,885.6	2,026.1	2,151.3	2,245.2	....	M3, Seasonally Adjusted	39mc c
1,022.6	1,108.4	1,184.3	1,264.2	1,370.3	I 1,461.6	1,649.2	1,802.0	1,986.0	2,179.7	2,215.8	2,341.6	2,460.5	2,569.4	....	Extended Money M3,Seas.Adj.	39md c
1,336.0	1,403.1	1,465.1	1,538.2	1,611.1	1,879.2	1,996.2	2,148.8	2,375.4	2,437.6	2,542.5	2,729.1	2,800.4	2,956.9	....	Liquid Liabilities	551

Interest Rates

Percent Per Annum

1985	1986	1987	1988	1989	1990	1991	1992	1993	1994	1995	1996	1997	1998	1999		
4.00	3.50	2.50	3.50	6.00	6.00	8.00	8.25	5.75	4.50	3.00	2.50	2.50	2.50	....	Discount Rate (End of Period)	60
5.19	4.57	3.72	4.01	6.59	7.92	8.84	9.42	7.49	5.35	4.50	3.27	3.18	3.41	2.73	Money Market Rate	60b
5.04	3.86	3.28	3.62	6.28	8.13	8.27	8.32	6.22	5.05	4.40	3.30	3.32	3.42	2.88	Treasury Bill Rate	60c
4.44	3.71	3.20	3.29	5.50	7.07	7.62	8.00	6.27	4.47	3.85	2.83	2.69	2.88	2.43	Deposit Rate	60l
9.53	8.75	8.36	8.33	9.94	11.59	12.46	13.59	12.85	11.48	10.94	10.02	9.13	9.02	8.81	Lending Rate	60p
6.87	5.92	5.84	6.10	7.09	8.88	8.63	7.96	6.28	6.67	6.50	5.63	5.08	4.39	4.26	Government Bond Yield	61

Prices, Production, Labor

Period Averages

1985	1986	1987	1988	1989	1990	1991	1992	1993	1994	1995	1996	1997	1998	1999		
65.3	89.1	76.4	65.3	83.8	96.8	88.6	84.5	90.6	102.7	100.0	114.1	156.3	200.0	207.3	Share Prices	62
93.3	90.9	88.7	89.8	92.6	94.2	I 96.2	97.6	97.7	98.3	100.0	99.6	100.7	I 100.3	99.3	Producer Prices	63
I 80.1	80.0	80.2	81.2	I 83.5	85.7	I 87.2	91.6	95.7	98.3	100.0	101.4	103.3	104.3	104.9	Consumer Prices	64
....	....	....	....	....	....	....	....	....	....	100.0	101.2	102.7	103.4	104.0	Harmonized CPI	64h
79.3	83.5	87.6	91.0	94.9	100.0	107.2	114.8	121.7	123.6	....	....	....	....	....	Wages: Hrly Earnings (1990=100)	65.. c
88.1	90.0	90.1	93.3	97.8	103.2	I 103.5	102.0	95.3	99.3	100.0	99.8	102.6	106.2	107.7	Industrial Production	66.. c
87.6	91.3	91.7	94.8	101.6	107.1	I 110.0	104.3	93.2	94.8	100.0	101.2	105.5	113.5	113.4	Investment Goods	66iy c
....	....	....	....	....	....	101.3	100.6	93.8	100.0	100.0	99.8	106.1	110.9	113.7	Other Prod. Goods	66jy c
90.3	92.0	92.9	95.7	99.2	106.6	I 110.2	107.8	100.4	101.8	100.0	100.8	101.4	103.4	105.6	Consumer Goods	66hy c

Period Averages

1985	1986	1987	1988	1989	1990	1991	1992	1993	1994	1995	1996	1997	1998	1999		
....	....	....	....	....	....	39,128	39,044	39,139	39,218	40,083	39,455	39,694	39,709	....	Labor Force	67d
....	....	....	....	....	....	37,445	36,940	36,380	I 36,075	36,048	35,982	35,805	35,860	....	Employment	67e
....	....	....	....	....	....	2,207	2,621	3,443	3,693	3,612	3,980	4,400	4,266	4,093	Unemployment	67c
....	....	....	....	....	....	....	....	9.8	10.6	10.4	11.5	12.7	12.3	11.7	Unemployment Rate (%)	67r

International Transactions

Billions of Euros Beginning 1999

1985	1986	1987	1988	1989	1990	1991	1992	1993	1994	1995	1996	1997	1998	1999		
537.16	526.36	527.38	567.65	641.04	I 660.72	666.17	658.47	632.22	694.69	749.54	788.94	888.64	954.67	I 508.32	Exports	70
463.81	413.74	409.64	439.61	506.47	I 556.08	645.41	628.19	571.91	622.92	664.23	690.40	772.33	828.29	I 443.50	Imports, c.i.f.	71
451.15	402.94	399.49	428.42	493.40	I 542.92	629.14	612.56	556.41	605.96	646.14	671.59	751.29	805.72	I 431.42	Imports, f.o.b.	71.v

1995=100

1985	1986	1987	1988	1989	1990	1991	1992	1993	1994	1995	1996	1997	1998	1999		
70.5	71.4	73.4	78.3	84.7	85.9	85.9	87.8	84.0	96.0	I 100.0	107.6	120.7	130.5	136.4	Volume of Exports	72
60.7	64.4	67.9	72.2	77.5	86.7	97.7	100.0	90.3	98.4	I 100.0	106.0	115.5	126.9	132.9	Volume of Imports	73
106.7	103.3	100.6	101.3	106.0	104.8	104.2	103.4	98.7	97.8	I 100.0	97.8	98.2	97.6	96.2	Unit Value of Exports	74
94.1	92.4	91.5	93.4	96.0	96.1	97.1	97.7	97.8	98.6	100.0	100.0	101.5	101.4	100.9	Export Prices	76
122.9	103.4	97.0	97.8	105.1	102.5	104.2	101.0	95.5	97.4	I 100.0	98.1	100.6	98.4	96.6	Unit Value of Imports	75
123.9	104.5	98.8	100.0	104.5	102.2	103.0	100.5	98.9	99.8	100.0	100.4	104.0	100.8	100.2	Import Prices	76.x

Germany

		1970	1971	1972	1973	1974	1975	1976	1977	1978	1979	1980	1981	1982	1983	1984
Balance of Payments															*Billions of US Dollars:*	
Current Account, n.i.e.	78al d	....	.10	.34	4.22	9.15	3.09	3.77	3.91	9.36	−5.45	−13.32	−3.50	4.86	4.60	9.57
Goods: Exports f.o.b.	78aa d	....	38.39	46.19	66.75	89.13	90.06	101.70	117.27	141.15	170.23	191.16	174.15	174.43	167.49	169.98
Goods: Imports f.o.b.	78ab d	....	−33.87	−40.19	−54.26	−70.54	−76.39	−86.41	−98.80	−117.88	−155.13	−183.22	−158.73	−150.29	−148.07	−148.48
Trade Balance	78ac d	....	4.52	5.99	12.49	18.59	13.67	15.29	18.47	23.27	15.10	7.94	15.42	24.14	19.42	21.51
Services: Credit	78ad d	....	5.83	6.74	8.64	10.14	12.59	17.46	19.51	24.82	28.57	33.06	31.37	32.09	30.43	29.53
Services: Debit	78ae d	....	−7.23	−8.56	−11.73	−13.58	−16.91	−21.65	−24.81	−30.67	−37.96	−42.38	−38.27	−38.09	−35.86	−33.30
Balance on Goods & Services	78af d	....	3.12	4.18	9.40	15.15	9.35	11.10	13.18	17.42	5.70	−1.38	8.52	18.15	13.99	17.73
Income: Credit	78ag d	....	2.67	3.15	4.39	5.37	5.50	5.98	6.47	9.47	12.07	13.96	13.67	14.00	14.31	15.16
Income: Debit	78ah d	....	−3.03	−3.53	−4.75	−6.03	−5.47	−5.64	−7.61	−8.06	−11.62	−13.04	−14.02	−15.98	−13.22	−12.15
Balance on Gds, Serv. & Inc.	78ai d	....	2.76	3.80	9.03	14.48	9.38	11.44	12.04	18.84	6.15	−.46	8.17	16.17	15.08	20.75
Current Transfers, n.i.e.: Credit	78aj d	....	1.37	1.65	2.54	2.95	2.98	3.50	5.16	7.13	7.65	8.01	6.99	6.68	7.32	7.13
Current Transfers: Debit	78ak d	....	−4.03	−5.11	−7.35	−8.29	−9.27	−11.17	−13.29	−16.61	−19.24	−20.87	−18.66	−17.99	−17.80	−18.30
Capital Account, n.i.e.	78bc d	....	−.01	−.03	−.03	−.03	−.02	—	.01	−.04	−.25	−.92	−.07	−.07	−.08	−.05
Capital Account, n.i.e.: Credit	78ba d	....	.07	.05	.07	.07	.09	.09	.13	.10	.15	.15	.12	.13	.15	.12
Capital Account: Debit	78bb d	....	−.08	−.08	−.10	−.10	−.11	−.09	−.12	−.14	−.40	−1.07	−.19	−.19	−.23	−.16
Financial Account, n.i.e.	78bj d	....	2.50	3.67	2.88	−10.82	−3.94	−.18	.75	5.76	4.49	5.65	1.00	.50	−6.35	−12.16
Direct Investment Abroad	78bd d	....	−1.20	−1.81	−1.96	−2.13	−2.18	−2.61	−2.42	−3.94	−5.02	−4.70	−4.48	−3.02	−3.67	−4.66
Dir. Invest. in Rep. Econ., n.i.e.	78be d	....	1.09	1.90	2.12	2.18	.69	1.32	.95	1.60	1.73	.33	.30	.75	1.72	.53
Portfolio Investment Assets	78bf d	....	.16	1.27	.12	−.42	−1.08	−.35	−2.36	−2.07	−1.82	−4.19	−2.67	−4.59	−4.20	−5.42
Equity Securities	78bk d	....	−.18	−.09	.06	−.16	−.51	.17	−.38	−.31	.41	−.21	.05	−.17	−1.87	−.04
Debt Securities	78bl d	....	.34	1.35	.06	−.26	−.58	−.52	−1.98	−1.76	−2.23	−3.98	−2.72	−4.42	−2.33	−5.38
Portfolio Investment Liab., n.i.e.	78bg d	....	.57	3.37	2.55	−.75	−.57	1.86	1.05	1.62	3.18	.45	.42	1.07	5.11	5.87
Equity Securities	78bm d	....	.11	.94	−.10	.02	.78	.65	.70	1.52	1.00	.32	1.06	.21	1.11	1.29
Debt Securities	78bn d	....	.47	2.43	2.65	−.77	−1.35	1.21	.35	.10	2.17	.13	−.65	.86	4.00	4.59
Financial Derivatives Assets	78bw d	....	—	—	—	—	—	—	—	—	—	—	—	—	—	—
Financial Derivatives Liabilities	78bx d	....	—	—	—	—	—	—	—	—	—	—	—	—	—	—
Other Investment Assets	78bh d	....	−.91	−1.18	−3.24	−14.68	−13.06	−11.94	−7.45	−11.43	−12.66	−19.41	−17.34	−4.62	−8.33	−18.83
Monetary Authorities	78bo d	....														
General Government	78bp d	....	−.12	−.39	−.77	−.82	−.62	−.70	−.53	−1.05	−.66	−.56	−1.77	−1.80	−2.54	−2.14
Banks	78bq d	....	.11	.16	−1.71	−5.73	−10.71	−5.19	−3.81	−5.67	−3.84	−8.55	−7.03	.66	−.41	−7.83
Other Sectors	78br d	....	−.89	−.95	−.76	−8.12	−1.74	−6.06	−3.10	−4.71	−8.15	−10.30	−8.54	−3.49	−5.37	−8.86
Other Investment Liab., n.i.e.	78bi d	....	2.78	.12	3.29	4.97	12.26	11.53	10.96	19.97	19.08	33.17	24.78	10.92	3.02	10.34
Monetary Authorities	78bs d	....	.08	.27	−.83	.04	1.24	.32	−.40	2.48	−1.16	5.40	−1.91	1.66	−.13	.20
General Government	78bt d	....	.03	.24	−.09	.51	1.76	1.88	.52	1.18	−.50	12.47	10.77	3.85	3.17	1.18
Banks	78bu d	....	1.50	.21	.96	1.45	4.97	6.19	5.53	14.19	15.96	3.18	3.51	−.06	−2.62	6.50
Other Sectors	78bv d	....	1.16	−.60	3.24	2.97	4.30	3.14	5.32	2.13	3.77	12.12	12.41	5.47	2.59	2.46
Net Errors and Omissions	78ca d	....	1.97	1.00	1.97	1.27	−.11	.20	−.20	−2.15	−2.23	−1.06	.09	−2.45	−.12	2.28
Overall Balance	78cb d	....	4.56	4.98	9.04	−.43	−.98	3.79	4.46	12.92	−3.44	−9.64	−2.48	2.84	−1.95	−.35
Reserves and Related Items	79da d	....	−4.56	−4.98	−9.04	.43	.98	−3.79	−4.46	−12.92	3.44	9.64	2.48	−2.84	1.95	.35
Reserve Assets	79db d	....	−4.56	−4.98	−9.04	.43	.98	−3.79	−4.46	−12.92	3.44	9.64	2.48	−2.84	1.95	.35
Use of Fund Credit and Loans	79dc d	....														
Exceptional Financing	79de d	....	....	....	....	....	....	....	....	....	....	....	....	....	....	....
International Investment Position															*Billions of US Dollars*	
Assets	79aa d											257.40	250.64	254.39	242.91	242.89
Direct Investment Abroad	79ab d											31.35	32.20	32.61	31.48	32.09
Portfolio Investment	79ac d											20.37	21.26	25.93	29.69	33.56
Equity Securities	79ad d											5.21	4.65	5.22	8.03	7.74
Debt Securities	79ae d											15.16	16.61	20.71	21.66	25.83
Financial Derivatives	79al d															
Other Investment	79af d											164.58	162.68	160.29	151.80	151.31
Monetary Authorities	79ag d											2.06	1.59	1.03	.90	.78
General Government	79ah d											18.61	18.32	19.70	20.09	19.78
Banks	79ai d											69.11	68.31	65.57	59.24	60.51
Other Sectors	79aj d											74.80	74.45	73.99	71.57	70.24
Reserve Assets	79ak d											41.10	34.51	35.55	29.94	25.93
Liabilities	79la d											224.02	221.48	223.93	210.31	200.99
Dir. Invest. in Rep. Economy	79lb d											25.34	21.61	20.73	19.44	17.43
Portfolio Investment	79lc d											37.56	42.79	46.89	53.77	54.32
Equity Securities	79ld d											10.09	9.69	10.55	13.74	13.93
Debt Securities	79le d											27.46	33.10	36.34	40.03	40.39
Financial Derivatives	79ll d															
Other investment	79lf d											161.13	157.07	156.30	137.09	129.23
Monetary Authorities	79lg d											13.84	10.07	10.78	8.68	7.99
General Government	79lh d											.49	1.80	2.25	1.23	.75
Banks	79li d											73.50	68.13	65.38	57.12	57.54
Other Sectors	79lj d											73.31	77.07	77.90	70.06	62.95
Government Finance																
Central Government														*Billions of Deutsche Mark through 1998:*		
Deficit (-) or Surplus	80	‡6.94	6.37	5.83	12.43	‡−6.43	‡−37.16	−31.21	−25.57	−26.49	−27.63	−26.91	−36.31	−32.02	−32.96	−32.31
Revenue	81	‡166.51	186.03	208.63	241.96	‡258.86	‡271.79	303.47	326.52	349.83	377.18	423.94	450.02	478.05	490.83	524.21
Grants Received	81z	‡1.86	2.27	2.26	1.92	‡2.00	‡2.23	2.35	3.39	3.78	3.15	2.52	2.18	2.68	3.16	3.00
Adj. to Cash-Revenue & Grants	81x	‡−2.15	−1.51	−2.55	−1.49	‡−.38	‡−.93	−3.27	−.54	−1.09	−2.59	−.63	−.50			
Expenditure	82	‡157.25	177.78	199.82	226.13	‡263.62	‡304.14	330.16	352.68	375.76	400.37	447.54	481.64	506.03	520.05	549.04
Lending Minus Repayments	83	‡2.03	2.64	2.69	3.83	‡3.29	‡6.11	3.60	2.26	3.25	5.00	5.20	5.92	5.56	7.04	8.09
Overall Cash Adjustment	80x	....						—	—	—	—	—	−.45	−1.16	.14	−2.39
Financing																
Net Borrowing	84						‡36.29	19.98	20.53	26.32	27.17	28.01	40.62	36.63	31.82	28.03
Domestic	84a						‡34.48	15.20	20.06	24.57	25.05	7.17	19.45	29.15	18.32	18.56
Foreign	85a						‡1.81	4.78	.47	1.75	2.12	20.84	21.17	7.48	13.50	9.47
Seigniorage	86d															
Pending Redemptions	87c															
Use of Cash Balances	87						‡.87	11.23	5.04	.17	.46	−1.10	−4.31	−4.61	1.14	4.28
Debt	88	‡47.32	48.76	55.30	61.36	‡72.14	‡103.32	128.88	153.58	179.94	205.60	235.77	277.99	314.44	347.27	373.91
Domestic	88a						‡97.85	118.62	142.83	164.85	188.39	197.72	218.77	247.73	267.08	284.25
Foreign	89a						‡5.47	10.26	10.75	15.09	17.21	38.05	59.22	66.71	80.19	89.66
Intragovernmental Debt	88s						‡11.79	6.23	2.09	2.18	2.19	2.50	2.82	2.80	2.86	2.57
Other Deficits(-)or Surpluses																
Equalization of Burden Fund	80.. i	.28	.23	.28	.47	‡1.53	‡1.29	.46	.98	.68	.16	....	....	....	....	....
Social Insurance System	80.r	2.99	4.51	5.35	5.92	‡1.52	‡−5.12	−5.97	−6.18	....	....	....	....	....	....	....
General Government															*As Percent of*	
Deficit (-) or Surplus	80g														....	....
Debt	88g														....	....

Balance of Payments

Minus Sign Indicates Debit

	1985	1986	1987	1988	1989	1990	1991	1992	1993	1994	1995	1996	1997	1998	1999		Code
Current Account, n.i.e.	17.58	40.91	46.44	50.35	57.00	48.30	-17.67	-19.14	-13.87	-20.94	-18.93	-7.97	-2.90	-4.56	-20.90		**78al** d
Goods: Exports f.o.b.	182.69	241.52	291.49	322.11	340.10	411.01	403.98	430.48	382.68	430.54	523.58	522.58	510.71	542.80	539.31		**78aa** d
Goods: Imports f.o.b.	-154.27	-186.84	-223.45	-245.76	-265.12	-342.50	-384.54	-402.28	-341.49	-379.63	-458.48	-453.20	-439.90	-463.91	-468.80		**78ab** d
Trade Balance	28.42	54.68	68.04	76.35	74.98	68.51	19.44	28.20	41.19	50.92	65.11	69.38	70.81	78.89	70.50		**78ac** d
Services: Credit	30.67	39.33	45.83	47.60	50.06	63.70	65.06	69.02	64.70	66.25	81.84	85.56	83.23	83.82	83.03		**78ad** d
Services: Debit	-33.64	-43.76	-53.70	-60.75	-62.62	-81.00	-86.24	-99.70	-97.76	-105.94	-127.20	-129.82	-125.15	-130.27	-134.39		**78ae** d
Balance on Goods & Services	25.45	50.25	60.18	63.19	62.42	51.22	-1.74	-2.47	8.14	11.22	19.75	25.12	28.89	32.45	19.14		**78af** d
Income: Credit	15.55	22.69	29.66	36.00	45.39	65.60	74.15	80.44	77.13	68.51	84.89	81.36	80.33	84.02	85.90		**78ag** d
Income: Debit	-12.75	-18.64	-26.33	-28.97	-31.10	-44.77	-52.46	-62.45	-63.85	-61.68	-84.59	-80.42	-81.76	-90.69	-98.61		**78ah** d
Balance on Gds, Serv. & Inc.	28.26	54.30	63.51	70.22	76.72	72.05	19.96	15.52	21.42	18.05	20.04	26.06	27.46	25.78	6.43		**78ai** d
Current Transfers, n.i.e.: Credit	7.02	10.77	12.15	11.68	10.48	13.07	13.42	14.90	13.38	13.89	16.87	17.89	16.46	16.46	17.01		**78aj** d
Current Transfers: Debit	-17.70	-24.16	-29.21	-31.55	-30.19	-36.82	-51.04	-49.56	-48.67	-52.88	-55.84	-51.92	-46.83	-46.80	-44.34		**78ak** d
Capital Account, n.i.e.	-.18	-.02	-.09	-.01	.09	-1.33	-.65	.60	.49	.15	-2.73	-2.18	—	.72	-.13		**78bc** d
Capital Account, n.i.e.: Credit	.11	.21	.19	.27	.40	.41	.77	1.12	1.38	1.56	1.68	2.76	2.83	3.31	3.01		**78ba** d
Capital Account: Debit	-.29	-.23	-.28	-.28	-.32	-1.73	-1.41	-.52	-.89	-1.42	-4.41	-4.94	-2.82	-2.59	-3.14		**78bb** d
Financial Account, n.i.e.	-18.30	-36.97	-24.00	-67.56	-59.07	-54.78	5.22	51.80	16.21	30.43	43.98	16.13	.50	8.38	-24.91		**78bj** d
Direct Investment Abroad	-5.30	-10.56	-9.76	-12.07	-15.26	-24.20	-23.72	-19.67	-15.26	-17.26	-39.10	-50.75	-41.68	-92.40	-98.84		**78bd** d
Dir. Invest. in Rep. Econ., n.i.e.	.49	1.02	1.82	1.02	7.15	2.53	4.11	2.64	1.95	1.94	11.99	6.43	11.66	20.14	52.23		**78be** d
Portfolio Investment Assets	-11.03	-9.73	-13.52	-40.52	-26.23	-13.99	-17.25	-44.72	-25.33	-41.48	-18.05	-30.89	-90.08	-141.10	-189.29		**78bf** d
Equity Securities	-1.57	-2.21	.12	-10.18	-4.97	1.06	-8.64	-40.45	-16.80	-20.97	.28	-17.52	-42.62	-74.00	-85.96		**78bk** d
Debt Securities	-9.46	-7.53	-13.64	-30.34	-21.26	-15.05	-8.61	-4.27	-8.53	-20.51	-18.33	-13.37	-47.46	-67.10	-103.33		**78bl** d
Portfolio Investment Liab., n.i.e.	12.85	33.15	18.01	4.18	23.80	12.29	41.19	76.93	145.72	10.64	53.15	93.90	90.86	144.79	173.64		**78bg** d
Equity Securities	2.11	6.82	-.79	3.02	12.08	-1.90	1.64	-2.80	7.54	3.92	-1.51	12.98	12.86	56.35	33.75		**78bm** d
Debt Securities	10.74	26.34	18.81	1.17	11.72	14.19	39.55	79.73	138.18	6.72	54.66	80.92	78.00	88.44	139.89		**78bn** d
Financial Derivatives Assets	—	—	-.24	-.30	-.40	-1.18	-.71	-3.35	-7.33	-10.71	—	—	—	—	—		**78bw** d
Financial Derivatives Liabilities	—	—	-.42	-.01	.60	1.15	1.06	3.07	6.67	11.25	-.66	-5.73	-8.82	-6.71	2.16		**78bx** d
Other Investment Assets	-22.92	-54.49	-24.01	-34.92	-90.85	-74.67	-24.28	-7.29	-131.42	-.62	-61.28	-39.77	-83.54	-85.11	-71.06		**78bh** d
Monetary Authorities	—	—	...	...	...	...	—	-.02	-.01	.17	.28	.35	.29	-.11	-51.70		**78bo** d
General Government	-1.57	-2.01	-2.67	-2.58	-4.58	-7.93	-5.17	-6.36	-7.07	2.46	-6.72	-.34	-2.33	-.63	8.47		**78bp** d
Banks	-15.73	-34.75	-16.13	-15.16	-47.13	-38.20	-2.19	3.63	-88.21	14.98	-55.18	-39.13	-80.40	-79.22	-48.33		**78bq** d
Other Sectors	-5.62	-17.73	-5.21	-17.18	-39.15	-28.54	-16.92	-4.54	-36.13	-18.23	.35	-.64	-1.10	-5.15	20.50		**78br** d
Other Investment Liab., n.i.e.	7.61	3.64	4.12	15.06	42.12	43.28	24.82	44.18	41.22	76.66	97.94	42.93	122.10	168.76	106.25		**78bi** d
Monetary Authorities	1.07	2.35	-2.03	3.62	12.91	.40	-5.81	-9.53	-1.57	-2.04	-2.65	-1.17	-.39	2.16	-2.21		**78bs** d
General Government	-.60	-2.32	-5.57	-5.80	-2.80	.24	-.55	-1.19	3.73	2.12	3.84	3.45	-7.75	-1.56	-12.17		**78bt** d
Banks	6.90	11.54	11.50	11.24	22.58	26.22	10.51	48.01	35.34	69.19	83.71	36.62	120.20	159.94	102.64		**78bu** d
Other Sectors	.23	-7.93	.23	6.01	9.43	16.42	20.67	6.88	3.72	7.39	13.04	4.03	10.04	8.21	17.99		**78bv** d
Net Errors and Omissions	3.13	1.50	-.86	1.62	4.84	15.06	6.91	3.92	-17.02	-11.68	-15.09	-7.17	-1.35	-.52	31.82		**78ca** d
Overall Balance	2.23	5.43	21.49	-15.60	2.86	7.25	-6.18	37.18	-14.20	-2.04	7.22	-1.20	-3.76	4.01	-14.11		**78cb** d
Reserves and Related Items	-2.23	-5.43	-21.49	15.60	-2.86	-7.25	6.18	-37.18	14.20	2.04	-7.22	1.20	3.76	-4.01	14.11		**79da** d
Reserve Assets	-2.23	-5.43	-21.49	15.60	-2.86	-7.25	6.18	-37.18	14.20	2.04	-7.22	1.20	3.76	-4.01	14.11		**79db** d
Use of Fund Credit and Loans															—		**79dc** d
Exceptional Financing															...		**79de** d

International Investment Position

Billions of US Dollars

	1985	1986	1987	1988	1989	1990	1991	1992	1993	1994	1995	1996	1997	1998	1999		Code
Assets	341.81	501.72	665.68	689.50	863.59	1,086.51	1,141.85	1,172.60	1,285.19	1,431.95	1,663.86	1,699.46	1,742.74	2,209.35	....		**79aa** d
Direct Investment Abroad	42.60	58.12	75.49	80.20	94.99	124.96	143.57	148.46	156.70	188.32	234.13	250.14	292.94	389.55	....		**79ab** d
Portfolio Investment	51.60	71.26	93.89	135.51	171.29	185.23	213.57	246.49	279.91	320.00	385.42	413.49	500.05	716.22	....		**79ac** d
Equity Securities	12.56	18.86	20.06	32.96	43.95	44.96	58.00	94.61	115.20	145.79	165.97	187.47	243.42	369.48	....		**79ad** d
Debt Securities	39.04	52.40	73.83	102.54	127.33	140.27	155.57	151.88	164.70	174.22	219.45	226.02	256.63	346.74	....		**79ae** d
Financial Derivatives															....		**79al** d
Other Investment	213.65	325.15	420.31	420.61	539.87	706.69	722.20	690.08	778.99	850.27	959.68	958.94	878.96	1,023.46	....		**79af** d
Monetary Authorities	1.00	1.26	1.54	1.37	1.43	1.62	1.71	1.62	1.52	1.52	1.36	.93	.54	.64	....		**79ag** d
General Government	26.89	35.85	46.64	44.17	50.16	32.79	39.04	43.37	48.60	52.34	62.62	59.52	55.32	61.53	....		**79ah** d
Banks	90.61	147.43	193.12	193.07	252.04	370.74	371.11	346.69	413.31	426.96	504.98	516.48	545.59	662.52	....		**79ai** d
Other Sectors	95.16	140.62	179.00	182.00	236.23	301.54	310.34	298.40	315.56	369.45	390.72	382.01	277.51	298.77	....		**79aj** d
Reserve Assets	33.95	47.19	76.00	53.19	57.44	69.63	62.50	37.57	68.58	73.35	84.62	76.90	70.79	80.11	....		**79ak** d
Liabilities	289.02	405.38	497.26	480.66	595.02	750.52	829.56	909.26	1,079.71	1,236.60	1,534.69	1,610.49	1,672.17	2,181.16	....		**79la** d
Dir. Invest. in Rep. Economy	22.84	32.35	40.37	39.81	44.10	75.45	79.08	75.48	71.17	85.72	101.48	101.73	181.95	213.56	....		**79lb** d
Portfolio Investment	98.52	161.35	188.89	176.16	225.39	207.58	261.02	326.07	486.93	493.72	635.81	703.91	753.10	1,019.83	....		**79lc** d
Equity Securities	34.09	51.72	39.69	48.32	81.04	80.70	83.38	69.46	93.61	99.51	110.78	140.29	187.09	287.66	....		**79ld** d
Debt Securities	64.43	109.63	149.19	127.84	144.36	126.88	177.64	256.61	393.32	394.21	525.04	563.62	566.00	732.17	....		**79le** d
Financial Derivatives															....		**79ll** d
Other investment	167.65	211.68	268.01	264.69	325.52	467.49	489.47	507.72	521.62	657.16	797.40	804.84	737.12	947.76	....		**79lf** d
Monetary Authorities	11.32	17.20	19.71	21.89	36.97	43.71	36.79	25.00	22.01	22.13	21.98	20.54	18.56	19.31	....		**79lg** d
General Government	.54	.31	.56	.76	1.08	30.76	29.84	26.82	28.17	33.51	46.24	45.54	32.27	33.06	....		**79lh** d
Banks	74.28	99.76	129.70	129.56	157.59	221.51	229.40	263.47	285.75	380.24	485.00	493.18	564.45	760.00	....		**79li** d
Other Sectors	81.52	94.42	118.04	112.48	129.88	171.51	193.44	192.43	185.69	221.29	244.18	245.59	121.85	135.39	....		**79lj** d

Government Finance

Central Government

Millions of Euros Beginning 1999: Year Ending December 31

	1985	1986	1987	1988	1989	1990	1991	1992	1993	1994	1995	1996	1997	1998	1999		Code
Deficit (-) or Surplus	-20.01	-17.56	-21.57	-35.54	-3.60	‡-39.55	-62.29	‡-73.39	-78.79	-44.85	-62.33	-76.29	-49.63P	-34.47P	....		**80**
Revenue	551.33	572.59	588.77	605.00	655.37	‡698.99	808.44	‡985.18	1,017.55	1,099.41	1,124.66	1,133.06	1,160.25P	1,188.14P	....		**81**
Grants Received	3.10	3.07	2.77	2.87	3.14	‡2.60	3.45	‡4.52	5.11	5.24	6.10	6.70	6.44P	6.31P	....		**81z**
Adj. to Cash-Revenue & Grants	—	—	—	—	—	‡—	—	‡—	—	—	—	—	—P	—P	....		**81x**
Expenditure	564.55	584.66	609.79	637.41	654.91	‡716.28	860.74	‡1045.45	1,084.30	1,142.81	1,188.04	1,213.20	1,214.65P	1,233.89P	....		**82**
Lending Minus Repayments	7.44	4.58	3.30	3.92	6.73	‡9.64	11.98	‡13.83	12.10	15.84	3.60	3.02	-3.01P	-17.98P	....		**83**
Overall Cash Adjustment	-2.45	-3.98	-.02	-2.08	-.47	‡-15.22	-1.46	-3.81	-5.05	9.15	-1.45	.17	-4.68P	-13.01P	....		**80x**
Financing																	
Net Borrowing	23.50	22.22	27.97	34.70	16.39	‡65.04	76.45	‡56.40	91.49	34.23	46.86	70.10	50.04P	34.74P	....		**84**
Domestic	5.42	-6.13	11.27	25.24	-2.81	‡51.73	31.40	‡1.78	-16.45	57.19	-11.61	15.82	-29.87P	-42.68P	....		**84a**
Foreign	18.08	28.35	16.70	9.46	19.20	‡13.31	45.05	‡54.62	107.94	-22.96	58.47	54.28	79.91P	77.42P	....		**85a**
Seigniorage	....	....	....	....	....	....	....	....	....	....	....	....	....	....	....		**86d**
Pending Redemptions															....		**87c**
Use of Cash Balances	-3.49	-4.66	-6.40	.84	-12.79	‡-25.49	-14.16	‡16.99	-12.70	10.62	15.47	6.19	-.41P	-.27P	....		**87**
Debt	399.15	421.99	446.56	481.26	497.66	‡599.14	680.87	‡801.86	902.71	1,004.15	1,289.81	1,373.07	1,423.68P	1,460.89P	....		**88**
Domestic	291.41	285.90	293.77	319.01	316.21	‡404.38	437.66	‡504.03	496.94	610.53	762.27	791.26	758.67P	718.44P	....		**88a**
Foreign	107.74	136.09	152.79	162.25	181.45	‡194.76	243.21	‡297.83	405.77	393.62	527.54	581.81	665.01P	742.45P	....		**89a**
Intragovernmental Debt	2.25	....															**88s**
Other Deficits(-)or Surpluses																	
Equalization of Burden Fund																	**80.. i**
Social Insurance System	....	....															**80.r**

General Government

	1985	1986	1987	1988	1989	1990	1991	1992	1993	1994	1995	1996	1997	1998	1999		Code
Deficit (-) or Surplus	....	....	....	....	....	-2.1	-3.1	-2.6	-3.2	-2.4	-3.3	-3.4	-2.6	-1.7	-1.2		**80g**
Debt	....	....	....	....	....	43.8	41.5	44.1	48.0	50.2	58.3	59.8	60.9	60.7	61.1		**88g**

Gross Domestic Product

Germany

		1970	1971	1972	1973	1974	1975	1976	1977	1978	1979	1980	1981	1982	1983	1984
National Accounts																*Billions of Deutsche Mark: through 1998;*
Househ.Cons.Expend.,incl.NPISHs	96f. c	368.9	409.0	452.0	495.6	533.6	583.5	631.9	682.1	725.9	781.3	837.0	883.5	916.1	959.3	1,001.2
Government Consumption Expend	91f. c	106.5	126.8	141.0	163.1	190.1	210.1	221.9	235.1	253.1	273.5	298.0	318.4	326.4	336.4	350.4
Gross Fixed Capital Formation	93e. c	172.1	196.1	209.2	219.3	212.7	209.4	225.7	242.4	264.9	301.3	332.1	331.3	323.5	340.8	350.7
Changes in Inventories	93i. c	14.2	4.5	4.3	12.4	3.7	−6.4	15.7	7.0	7.2	43.0	37.0	26.3	26.1	34.2	40.6
Exports of Goods and Services	90c. c	....	....	....	....	....	....	....	....	329.6	349.2	388.9	440.8	472.2	477.9	536.8
Imports of Goods & Services	98c. c	....	....	....	....	....	....	....	....	....	−359.9	−422.2	−464.8	−477.3	−481.6	−530.1
Gross Domestic Product (GDP)	99b. c	675.3	749.1	822.9	917.4	985.1	1,027.7	1,117.5	1,194.2	1,283.0	1,388.4	1,471.0	1,535.5	1,586.9	1,667.1	1,749.5
Net Primary Income from Abroad	98.n c	.4	.7	1.5	1.6	−.2	1.1	3.3	.3	5.9	5.4	6.5	4.1	3.4	8.6	13.7
Gross National Income (GNI)	99a. c	675.7	750.4	824.6	918.8	983.7	1,027.7	1,123.8	1,195.6	1,289.4	1,393.8	1,477.4	1,539.6	1,590.3	1,675.7	1,763.3
Net National Income	99e. c	530.4	586.2	643.5	720.4	769.7	800.6	878.2	933.7	1,007.2	1,084.0	1,139.6	1,179.8	1,214.2	1,278.1	1,347.1
Net Current Transf. from Abroad	98t. c	....	....	....	....	....	....	....	....	....	....	....	....	....	....	....
Gross Nat'l Disposable Inc(GNDI)	99i. c	....	....	....	....	....	....	....	....	....	....	....	....	....	....	....
Gross Savings	99s. c	....	....	....	....	....	....	....	....	....	....	....	....	....	....	....
GDP Volume 1991 Prices	99b. r	1,543.3	1,588.9	1,657.4	1,737.2	1,742.7	1,720.6	1,805.2	1,859.7	1,916.7	1,998.2	2,017.9	2,020.7	1,999.6	2,034.4	2,091.8
GDP Volume 1995 Prices	99b. r	....	....	....	....	....	....	....	....	....	....	....	....	....	....	....
GDP Volume (1995=100)	99bv r	51.4	52.9	55.2	57.8	58.0	57.3	60.1	61.9	63.8	66.5	67.2	67.3	66.6	67.7	69.6
GDP Deflator (1995=100)	99bi r	37.3	40.2	42.3	45.0	48.2	50.9	52.8	54.8	57.1	59.3	62.2	64.8	67.7	69.9	71.3
																Millions:
Population	99z	60.71	61.29	61.67	61.97	62.04	61.83	61.51	61.40	61.31	61.44	61.54	61.66	61.60	61.38	61.13

	1985	1986	1987	1988	1989	1990	1991	1992	1993	1994	1995	1996	1997	1998	1999	National Accounts	
Billions of Euros Beginning 1999:																	
	1,036.5	1,066.4	1,108.0	1,153.7	1,221.0	1,318.7	I 1,665.4	1,786.0	1,857.5	1,925.1	2,001.6	2,055.4	2,106.8	2,174.7	I 1,144.7	Househ.Cons.Expend.,incl.NPISHs	**96f.** *c*
	365.7	382.6	397.3	412.4	418.8	444.1	I 563.9	623.6	643.0	669.2	697.8	717.5	714.2	719.4	I 376.4	Government Consumption Expend	**91f.** *c*
	355.8	373.5	385.8	409.9	448.5	507.8	I 698.0	758.5	745.2	785.2	790.6	779.4	785.0	797.2	I 415.0	Gross Fixed Capital Formation	**93e.** *c*
	41.4	48.9	48.9	66.8	77.1	89.1	I 15.7	−7.0	−17.3	1.9	8.1	−5.6	7.1	29.6	I 24.1	Changes in Inventories	**93i.** *c*
	596.1	582.8	576.3	617.6	701.7	783.6	I 772.7	774.0	736.5	800.1	862.3	908.8	1,020.9	1,092.1	I 578.9	Exports of Goods and Services	**90c.** *c*
	−569.5	−526.3	−525.0	−566.1	−643.5	−713.8	I −777.6	−779.8	−729.5	−787.1	−837.4	−869.5	−967.3	−1,028.9	I −556.7	Imports of Goods & Services	**98c.** *c*
	1,826.0	1,927.9	1,991.2	2,094.3	2,223.5	2,431.2	I 2,938.0	3,155.2	3,235.4	3,394.4	3,523.0	3,586.0	3,666.6	3,784.2	I 1,982.3	Gross Domestic Product (GDP)	**99b.** *c*
	8.4	8.2	11.8	13.8	25.5	18.8	I 102.1	95.0	94.0	60.3	44.8	−15.9	−17.2	−30.2	I −19.2	Net Primary Income from Abroad	**98.n** *c*
	1,834.5	1,936.1	2,003.0	2,108.0	2,249.1	2,448.2	I 2,955.7	3,170.6	3,248.9	3,380.6	3,504.4	3,570.1	3,649.4	3,754.1	I 1,963.1	Gross National Income (GNI)	**99a.** *c*
	1,406.8	1,497.6	1,550.0	1,635.5	1,738.0	1,891.8	I 2,544.3	2,719.5	2,766.3	2,878.1	2,983.3	3,037.5	3,103.0	3,192.5	I 1,669.3	Net National Income	**99e.** *c*
	....	....	....	....	....	....	I −42.0	−31.7	−37.5	−39.7	−32.7	−33.7	−36.3	−39.5	I −19.5	Net Current Transf. from Abroad	**98t.** *c*
	....	....	....	....	....	....	2,913.7	3,138.9	3,211.4	3,340.9	3,471.7	3,536.3	3,613.1	3,714.6	I 1,943.7	Gross Nat'l Disposable Inc(GNDI)	**99i.** *c*
	....	....	....	....	....	....	684.4	729.3	710.9	746.6	772.3	763.4	792.1	820.4	I 422.6	Gross Savings	**99s.** *c*
	2,139.4	2,189.2	2,219.3	2,299.0	2,383.4	2,520.4	2,853.6	....	....	....	....	....	....	....	....	GDP Volume 1991 Prices	**99b.** *r*
	....	....	....	....	....	....	I 3,346.0	3,421.0	3,383.8	3,463.2	3,523.0	3,549.6	3,601.1	3,678.6	I 1,908.3	GDP Volume 1995 Prices	**99b.** *r*
	71.2	72.9	73.9	76.5	79.3	83.9	95.0	97.1	96.0	98.3	100.0	100.8	102.2	104.4	105.9	GDP Volume (1995=100)	**99bv** *r*
	72.8	75.1	76.5	77.7	79.6	82.3	I 87.8	92.2	95.6	98.0	100.0	101.0	101.8	102.9	103.9	GDP Deflator (1995=100)	**99bi** *r*
Midyear Estimates																	
	60.97	61.01	61.09	61.42	78.68	79.36	79.98	80.57	81.19	81.42	81.66	81.90	82.06	82.02	82.09	**Population**	**99z**

(See notes in the back of the book.)

Ghana

652		1970	1971	1972	1973	1974	1975	1976	1977	1978	1979	1980	1981	1982	1983	1984
Exchange Rates																*Cedis per SDR:*
Market Rate	**aa**	1.02	1.97	1.39	1.39	1.41	1.35	1.34	1.40	3.58	3.62	3.51	3.20	3.03	31.41	49.01
																Cedis per US Dollar:
Market Rate	**ae**	1.02	1.82	1.28	1.15	1.15	1.15	1.15	1.15	2.75	2.75	2.75	2.75	2.75	30.00	50.00
Market Rate	**rf**	1.02	1.03	1.33	1.17	1.15	1.15	1.15	1.15	1.76	2.75	2.75	2.75	2.75	8.83	35.99
																Index Numbers (1995=100):
Nominal Effective Exchange Rate	**ne c**	....	....	....	....	....	....	....	....	....	14,238.33	14,398.37	16,717.84	18,936.82	7,891.60	1,943.41
Real Effective Exchange Rate	**re c**	....	....	....	....	....	....	....	....	....	....	651.40	1,452.31	1,814.24	1,221.89	474.25
Fund Position																*Millions of SDRs:*
Quota	**2f. s**	87.0	87.0	87.0	87.0	87.0	87.0	87.0	87.0	106.0	106.0	159.0	159.0	159.0	204.5	204.5
SDRs	**1b. s**	—	3.1	10.0	9.7	9.6	7.5	6.7	10.1	9.5	13.7	—	.6	.2	2.1	.1
Reserve Position in the Fund	**1c. s**	—	—	—	5.9	10.6	—	—	—	—	—	—	—	—	—	—
Total Fund Cred.&Loans Outstg.	**2tl**	46.1	18.3	1.7	—	—	38.6	38.6	38.6	34.4	82.5	82.5	73.2	68.4	316.6	525.1
International Liquidity																*Millions of US Dollars Unless Otherwise Indicated:*
Total Reserves minus Gold	**1l. d**	36.6	36.1	93.7	176.1	71.5	124.7	91.7	148.6	277.2	289.1	180.4	145.6	138.9	144.8	301.6
SDRs	**1b. d**	—	3.3	10.9	11.7	11.8	8.8	7.7	12.3	12.4	18.0	—	.7	.2	2.2	.1
Reserve Position in the Fund	**1c. d**	—	—	—	7.2	13.0	—	—	—	—	—	—	—	—	—	—
Foreign Exchange	**1d. d**	36.6	32.8	82.8	157.2	46.7	115.9	84.0	136.3	264.8	271.1	180.4	144.9	138.7	142.6	301.5
Gold (Million Fine Troy Ounces)	**1ad**	.160	.160	.160	.160	.160	.160	.160	.200	.219	.219	.253	.309	.384	.384	.440
Gold (National Valuation)	**1an d**	5.6	5.6	5.6	5.6	5.6	5.6	5.6	7.2	8.1	8.1	19.0	48.2	68.8	72.5	91.7
Monetary Authorities: Other Assets	**3.. d**	15.7	5.5	7.6	6.1	15.3	18.5	5.9	6.8	2.3	2.5	16.2	2.4	3.5	1.2	11.5
Monetary Authorities: Other Liab.	**4.. d**	29.7	37.1	5.5	7.7	94.1	8.7	32.1	110.6	129.8	64.3	20.0	134.2	84.8	101.2	233.1
Deposit Money Banks: Assets	**7a. d**	4.2	4.7	1.4	12.2	.1	.1	8.9	6.3	2.1	.8	.8	3.2	3.7	30.7	9.2
Liabilities	**7b. d**	21.8	1.7	9.5	2.1	11.9	3.9	15.1	14.5	7.0	11.0	21.3	50.5	60.1	92.9	12.6
Monetary Authorities																*Millions of Cedis through 1985;*
Foreign Assets	**11**	75.1	97.1	147.5	229.5	144.9	212.8	129.3	247.2	783.7	816.6	588.0	512.1	580.5	6,519.8	19,661.1
Claims on Central Government	**12a**	254.6	349.2	304.8	339.5	573.8	881.3	1,513.5	2,527.5	4,286.8	4,413.2	5,723.6	9,494.2	10,165.1	24,342.8	35,053.5
Claims on Nonfin.Pub.Enterprises	**12c**	114.5	119.5	156.5	76.3	145.9	90.8	108.6	90.0	627.9	1,093.6	1,346.5	2,191.0	4,966.0	154.7	3,482.1
Claims on Deposit Money Banks	**12e**	—	—	10.9	—	—	3.0	4.5	6.0	6.1	6.0	6.0	6.0	6.0	6.0	6.0
Claims on Other Financial Insts	**12f**	7.2	11.8	18.7	48.8	67.5	72.2	77.2	85.3	79.3	73.6	73.0	99.3	128.6	199.6	997.3
Reserve Money	**14**	230.6	238.0	352.1	437.2	594.0	878.8	1,246.1	2,017.3	3,721.4	4,396.2	5,743.8	8,925.8	10,212.8	14,641.2	21,827.6
of which: Currency Outside DMBs	**14a**	150.6	158.8	239.2	245.0	336.0	485.6	706.9	1,157.1	2,121.6	2,458.5	3,521.3	6,049.5	6,957.2	10,389.0	17,631.2
Nonfin.Pub.Ent. Deps.	**14e**	4.4	3.1	3.4	27.8	41.4	28.5	40.1	118.3	219.4	348.7	475.7	55.7	199.6	853.2	439.9
Liabs. of Central Bank: Securities	**16ac**	....	....	....	....	....	....	....	....	....	....	....	....	....	....	....
Restricted Deposits	**16b**	1.2	88.9	193.7	147.1	126.6	149.7	154.0	259.7	489.9	648.3	458.4	698.9	1,817.3	3,536.1	5,735.4
Foreign Liabilities	**16c**	77.3	103.6	9.4	8.8	108.3	62.0	88.5	181.1	480.2	475.7	344.5	603.4	440.4	12,980.9	37,385.6
Central Government Deposits	**16d**	62.3	28.1	12.9	30.9	40.0	57.8	111.5	84.0	131.9	217.3	276.5	535.0	1,868.7	609.9	1,439.7
Counterpart Funds	**16e**	6.4	3.2	11.1	.1	.1	—	.2	—	1.0	.5	.2	29.2	20.9	1.8	—
Capital Accounts	**17a**	48.9	84.8	96.8	131.7	149.2	168.9	197.3	272.2	416.0	664.0	572.1	1,036.8	1,576.6	3,943.2	4,576.1
Other Items (Net)	**17r**	24.9	31.1	−37.6	−61.7	−86.1	−57.0	35.5	141.7	543.2	.9	341.8	473.6	−90.5	−4,490.2	−11,764.3
Deposit Money Banks																*Millions of Cedis through 1985;*
Reserves	**20**	88.0	78.9	114.0	171.1	214.9	375.3	510.5	714.3	1,423.0	1,667.7	1,854.4	2,801.8	3,365.9	4,340.7	8,757.3
Other Claims on Monetary Author.	**20c**	....	....	....	....	....	....	....	....	....	....	....	....	....	....	....
Foreign Assets	**21**	4.3	8.5	1.7	14.0	.2	.2	10.2	7.2	5.8	2.3	2.3	8.9	10.1	921.8	461.8
Claims on Central Government	**22a**	120.0	53.9	114.6	108.4	124.8	158.8	240.1	434.1	555.1	873.4	1,300.6	1,980.8	3,030.5	4,872.4	4,443.8
Claims on Nonfin.Pub.Enterprises	**22c**	.9	.9	11.1	I 154.5	192.0	204.5	284.5	332.8	484.7	540.5	615.9	1,202.6	1,117.0	1,181.9	806.1
Claims on Private Sector	**22d**	186.4	314.6	283.2	I 187.1	264.5	305.6	385.2	560.2	739.0	795.5	939.6	1,341.7	1,558.2	2,838.4	5,977.8
Demand Deposits	**24**	150.9	159.2	219.9	290.9	320.0	494.6	679.0	1,119.0	1,786.9	1,872.6	2,090.0	3,309.8	4,048.0	5,477.0	8,778.1
Time and Savings Deposits	**25**	121.2	153.6	205.1	229.8	307.7	377.5	474.0	651.2	1,005.0	1,262.3	1,863.6	2,615.5	3,634.5	4,086.3	5,113.0
Foreign Liabilities	**26c**	22.3	3.1	12.2	2.4	13.6	4.4	17.4	16.7	19.4	30.2	58.5	138.9	165.2	255.5	632.3
Central Government Deposits	**26d**	21.1	85.6	48.1	40.8	74.7	57.9	68.7	95.0	187.1	166.5	229.3	291.1	269.6	550.5	598.2
Credit from Monetary Authorities	**26g**	—	—	—	—	—	—	—	—	—	—	—	—	—	—	—
Capital Accounts	**27a**	18.8	24.3	28.6	32.2	35.0	39.9	44.5	55.3	77.2	114.2	144.4	253.5	409.6	852.2	1,297.5
Other Items (Net)	**27r**	65.2	30.9	10.7	39.1	45.5	70.1	147.0	111.4	131.9	433.6	327.0	726.9	554.7	2,933.7	4,027.7
Monetary Survey																*Millions of Cedis through 1985;*
Foreign Assets (Net)	**31n**	−20.2	−1.2	127.6	232.3	23.1	146.6	33.7	56.6	289.8	313.0	187.3	−221.2	−15.0	−5,794.7	−17,894.9
Domestic Credit	**32**	600.3	736.2	827.9	I 842.9	1,253.8	1,597.5	2,428.8	3,851.0	6,453.6	7,405.9	9,493.5	15,483.4	18,826.9	32,429.3	48,722.7
Claims on Central Govt. (Net)	**32an**	291.2	289.3	358.4	376.2	584.0	924.4	1,573.3	2,782.6	4,522.9	4,902.7	6,518.4	10,648.9	11,057.2	28,054.7	37,459.4
Claims on Nonfin.Pub.Enterprises	**32c**	115.4	120.4	167.6	I 230.8	337.9	295.3	393.1	422.8	1,112.5	1,634.1	1,962.5	3,393.6	6,083.0	1,336.6	4,288.2
Claims on Private Sector	**32d**	186.4	314.6	283.2	I 187.1	264.5	305.6	385.2	560.2	739.0	795.5	939.6	1,341.7	1,558.2	2,838.4	5,977.8
Claims on Other Financial Insts	**32f**	7.2	11.8	18.7	48.8	67.5	72.2	77.2	85.3	79.3	73.6	73.0	99.3	128.6	199.6	997.3
Money	**34**	305.9	321.1	462.6	563.8	697.4	1,008.6	1,426.0	2,394.4	4,127.9	4,679.8	6,087.0	9,415.0	11,204.7	16,719.2	26,849.2
Quasi-Money	**35**	121.2	153.6	205.1	229.8	307.7	377.5	474.0	651.2	1,005.0	1,262.3	1,863.6	2,615.5	3,634.5	4,086.3	5,113.0
Liabs. of Central Bank: Securities	**36ac**	....	....	....	....	....	....	....	....	....	....	....	....	....	....	....
Restricted Deposits	**36b**	1.2	88.9	193.7	147.1	126.6	149.7	154.0	259.7	489.9	648.3	458.4	698.9	1,817.3	3,536.1	5,735.4
Counterpart Funds	**36e**	6.4	3.2	11.1	.1	.1	—	.2	—	1.0	.5	.2	29.2	20.9	1.8	—
Capital Accounts	**37a**	67.7	109.1	125.4	163.8	184.2	208.8	241.8	327.5	493.2	778.2	716.5	1,290.3	1,986.2	4,795.4	5,873.6
Other Items (Net)	**37r**	77.7	59.3	−42.4	−29.3	−39.0	−.5	166.6	274.7	626.5	349.8	555.3	1,213.2	148.3	−2,504.3	−12,743.4
Money plus Quasi-Money	**35l**	427.1	474.7	667.7	793.5	1,005.0	1,386.1	1,899.9	3,045.7	5,132.8	5,942.1	7,950.6	12,030.6	14,839.2	20,805.5	31,962.2
Other Banking Institutions																*Billions of Cedis:*
Reserves	**40**	....	....	....	....	....	....	....	....	....	....	....	....	....	....	....
Other Claims on Monetary Author.	**40c**	....	....	....	....	....	....	....	....	....	....	....	....	....	....	....
Claims on Central Government	**42a**	....	....	....	....	....	....	....	....	....	....	....	....	....	....	....
Claims on Nonfin.Pub.Enterprises	**42c**	....	....	....	....	....	....	....	....	....	....	....	....	....	....	....
Claims on Deposit Money Banks	**42e**	....	....	....	....	....	....	....	....	....	....	....	....	....	....	....
Claims on Other Financial Insts	**42f**	....	....	....	....	....	....	....	....	....	....	....	....	....	....	....
Quasi-Monetary Liabilities	**45**	....	....	....	....	....	....	....	....	....	....	....	....	....	....	....
Money Market Instruments	**46aa**	....	....	....	....	....	....	....	....	....	....	....	....	....	....	....
Credit from Monetary Authorities	**46g**	....	....	....	....	....	....	....	....	....	....	....	....	....	....	....
Capital Accounts	**47a**	....	....	....	....	....	....	....	....	....	....	....	....	....	....	....
Other Items (Net)	**47r**	....	....	....	....	....	....	....	....	....	....	....	....	....	....	....
Banking Survey																*Billions of Cedis:*
Foreign Assets (Net)	**51n**	....	....	....	....	....	....	....	....	....	....	....	....	....	....	....
Domestic Credit	**52**	....	....	....	....	....	....	....	....	....	....	....	....	....	....	....
Claims on Central Govt. (Net)	**52an**	....	....	....	....	....	....	....	....	....	....	....	....	....	....	....
Claims on Nonfin.Pub.Enterprises	**52c**	....	....	....	....	....	....	....	....	....	....	....	....	....	....	....
Claims on Private Sector	**52d**	....	....	....	....	....	....	....	....	....	....	....	....	....	....	....
Claims on Other Financial Insts	**52f**	....	....	....	....	....	....	....	....	....	....	....	....	....	....	....

1985	1986	1987	1988	1989	1990	1991	1992	1993	1994	1995	1996	1997	1998	1999		
End of Period															**Exchange Rates**	
65.89	110.10	249.76	309.36	398.23	490.57	558.76	716.15[e]	1,125.87	1,536.68	2,154.33	2,522.74	3,066.48	3,274.49	4,732.79	Market Rate	aa
End of Period (ae) Period Average (rf)																
59.99	90.01	176.06	229.89	303.03	344.83	390.63	520.83[e]	819.67	1,052.63	1,449.28	1,754.39	2,272.73	2,325.58	3,448.28	Market Rate	ae
54.37	89.20	153.73	202.35	270.00	326.33	367.83	437.09[e]	649.06	956.71	1,200.43	1,637.23	2,050.17	2,314.15	2,647.32	Market Rate	rf
Period Averages																
1,417.93	711.88	424.21	350.00	309.68	269.85	255.47	227.08	178.75	130.72	100.00	75.43	64.10	59.08	53.58	Nominal Effective Exchange Rate	ne c
342.77	197.04	151.64	145.73	136.75	136.14	139.21	123.00	108.03	86.86	100.00	109.02	115.62	125.08	125.68	Real Effective Exchange Rate	re c
End of Period															**Fund Position**	
204.5	204.5	204.5	204.5	204.5	204.5	204.5	274.0	274.0	274.0	274.0	274.0	274.0	274.0	369.0	Quota	2f. s
17.2	1.6	11.2	.2	22.8	3.1	8.8	3.2	.4	2.9	1.6	1.6	2.5	42.4	13.3	SDRs	1b. s
—	—	—	—	—	—	—	17.4	17.4	17.4	17.4	17.4	17.4	17.4	41.1	Reserve Position in the Fund	1c. s
638.0	642.3	610.9	566.4	561.2	523.4	583.1	537.8	537.3	479.7	436.2	377.3	257.0	236.9	225.8	Total Fund Cred.&Loans Outstg.	2tl
End of Period															**International Liquidity**	
478.5	513.0	195.1	221.3	347.3	218.8	550.2	319.9	409.7	583.9	697.5	828.7	....	377.0	453.8	Total Reserves minus Gold	1l. d
18.9	2.0	15.9	.3	29.9	4.4	12.5	4.4	.5	4.2	2.4	2.2	3.4	59.7	18.2	SDRs	1b. d
—	—	—	—	—	—	—	23.9	23.9	25.4	25.8	25.0	23.4	24.5	56.5	Reserve Position in the Fund	1c. d
459.6	511.0	179.2	221.0	317.4	214.4	537.7	291.6	385.3	554.3	669.2	801.5	....	292.8	379.1	Foreign Exchange	1d. d
.225	.284	.282	.217	.221	.235	.266	.275	.275	.275	.275	.275	....	.277	.279	Gold (Million Fine Troy Ounces)	1ad
46.1	76.6	81.5	77.5	78.3	63.3	74.0	78.1	77.2	77.2	77.4	77.2	....	78.8	78.9	Gold (National Valuation)	1an d
7.4	15.1	50.5	....	....	....	....	....	....	....	....	....	....	....	....	Monetary Authorities: Other Assets	3.. d
354.4	832.0	180.7	283.4	519.8	445.2	59.1	67.6	56.3	96.5	34.8	45.4	126.7	52.0	105.0	Monetary Authorities: Other Liab.	4.. d
7.5	4.3	27.2	28.0	112.9	289.9	306.3	311.1	313.8	405.4	327.9	396.7	392.3	361.3	348.0	Deposit Money Banks: Assets	7a. d
38.3	28.5	49.2	56.6	105.8	110.1	132.2	115.9	161.4	225.4	265.2	364.9	400.1	432.2	619.8	Liabilities	7b. d
Billions of Cedis Beginning 1986: End of Period															**Monetary Authorities**	
31,921.2	I 91.8	57.5	77.1	141.3	113.4	I 269.6	192.2	380.0	663.2	1,079.9	1,182.1	1,337.6	1,372.3	1,624.7	Foreign Assets	11
45,017.6	I 78.6	161.7	160.2	134.0	166.8	I 344.2	482.6	850.6	893.0	1,405.5	1,553.3	2,001.7	2,000.1	2,256.2	Claims on Central Government	12a
12,543.6	I 15.9	15.1	1.2	25.1	5.8	I 20.3	3.8	44.8	148.8	151.9	135.8	71.9	9.9	10.0	Claims on Nonfin.Pub.Enterprises	12c
6.0	I —	—	—	—	1.6	I 8.1	4.2	6.8	6.7	8.3	9.4	33.0	11.1	11.1	Claims on Deposit Money Banks	12e
2,789.4	I 3.8	4.8	6.2	9.2	9.0	I —	—	—	—	37.2	10.7	4.6	.9	.9	Claims on Other Financial Insts	12f
29,569.5	I 47.2	67.0	103.0	126.5	129.8	I 130.5	245.8	257.9	461.3	623.1	902.2	1,203.1	1,403.5	1,583.9	Reserve Money	14
22,557.4	I 32.3	49.0	67.9	82.9	80.1	I 89.9	183.5	222.2	368.8	546.3	724.0	981.8	1,083.6	1,186.1	*of which: Currency Outside DMBs*	14a
2,510.3	I 5.1	10.0	21.7	10.3	15.7	I 13.1	2.2	3.3	3.5	6.3	7.9	6.3	3.2	2.8	*Nonfin.Pub.Ent. Deps.*	14e
....	....	....	....	....	....	101.9	148.1	334.5	479.5	722.4	518.2	182.6	1.1	—	Liabs. of Central Bank: Securities	16ac
8,312.9	I 12.9	15.7	5.9	1.3	—	I .9	.9	.9	.9	.9	.9	—	—	—	Restricted Deposits	16b
63,298.6	I 145.6	184.4	223.2	324.3	327.0	I 348.9	420.4	651.1	838.7	990.3	1,031.5	1,076.0	896.7	1,430.9	Foreign Liabilities	16c
1,160.8	I 6.9	8.9	14.1	17.5	33.9	I 11.0	5.0	47.4	65.0	106.1	180.6	217.1	431.8	74.0	Central Government Deposits	16d
—	I —	—	—	—	—	I 62.6	99.2	189.8	253.1	388.2	143.9	267.7	408.4	803.6	Counterpart Funds	16e
6,036.3	I 13.6	15.3	16.6	15.8	22.3	I 23.6	14.4	88.1	126.7	296.5	348.9	623.9	621.5	734.8	Capital Accounts	17a
–16,100.3	I –36.1	–52.2	–118.0	–175.9	–216.4	I –37.3	–251.1	–287.4	–513.6	–444.7	–235.0	–121.6	–368.7	–724.4	Other Items (Net)	17r
Billions of Cedis Beginning 1986: End of Period															**Deposit Money Banks**	
10,847.7	I 20.2	18.5	23.8	45.1	44.7	I 59.3	78.7	41.6	88.7	106.7	194.1	219.2	326.5	448.7	Reserves	20
....	....	....	....	....	....	79.5	56.7	263.1	369.4	564.1	475.3	153.3	.2	—	Other Claims on Monetary Author.	20c
449.3	I .4	4.8	6.4	34.2	100.0	I 119.7	162.0	257.2	426.8	475.3	695.9	891.7	840.2	1,199.9	Foreign Assets	21
5,179.3	I 6.2	5.9	5.1	6.4	3.0	I .9	.3	.3	.3	.3	74.1	737.0	1,417.8	2,270.9	Claims on Central Government	22a
3,775.0	I 4.3	5.0	6.9	16.0	24.1	I 34.9	68.5	43.0	29.5	44.5	57.4	144.0	184.2	483.8	Claims on Nonfin.Pub.Enterprises	22c
10,663.3	I 18.6	23.5	33.0	82.8	94.7	I 88.8	138.5	187.3	273.3	393.3	680.9	1,156.6	1,639.3	2,466.3	Claims on Private Sector	22d
13,240.1	I 17.7	25.2	32.4	93.2	110.7	I 132.0	174.8	235.3	320.9	371.1	482.1	776.5	982.5	939.2	Demand Deposits	24
8,410.2	I 14.0	21.8	33.0	53.4	65.2	I 109.7	165.2	203.3	275.2	434.4	586.9	856.3	1,234.1	1,714.4	Time and Savings Deposits	25
2,298.4	I 2.6	8.7	13.0	32.1	38.0	I 51.6	60.4	132.3	237.2	384.3	640.1	909.4	1,005.1	2,137.3	Foreign Liabilities	26c
984.4	I 1.3	1.8	3.0	13.0	16.5	I 17.7	22.5	63.5	69.2	76.0	105.4	37.9	55.0	52.1	Central Government Deposits	26d
—	I —	—	—	3.4	1.1	I 1.6	2.1	5.8	19.8	17.6	29.4	44.4	47.3	32.8	Credit from Monetary Authorities	26g
2,337.8	I 5.0	7.4	7.4	–2.4	48.0	I 76.0	90.2	131.9	249.9	270.2	359.0	525.0	596.5	863.3	Capital Accounts	27a
3,643.7	I 9.0	–7.0	–13.5	–8.1	–13.1	I –5.6	–10.6	20.4	15.8	30.6	–25.2	152.3	487.5	1,130.3	Other Items (Net)	27r
Billions of Cedis Beginning 1986: End of Period															**Monetary Survey**	
–33,226.5	I –56.0	–130.8	–152.6	–180.8	–151.5	I –11.3	–126.5	–146.2	14.0	180.6	206.4	243.9	310.7	–743.7	Foreign Assets (Net)	31n
77,823.0	I 119.1	205.4	195.5	243.0	252.8	I 460.3	666.1	1,015.2	1,210.6	1,850.6	2,226.2	3,860.9	4,765.3	7,361.9	Domestic Credit	32
48,051.7	I 76.6	156.9	148.2	109.9	119.3	I 316.3	455.4	740.1	759.1	1,223.7	1,341.4	2,483.7	2,931.1	4,400.9	Claims on Central Govt. (Net)	32an
16,318.6	I 20.2	20.1	8.1	41.1	29.9	I 55.3	72.3	87.8	178.3	196.4	193.2	215.9	194.1	493.8	Claims on Nonfin.Pub.Enterprises	32c
10,663.3	I 18.6	23.5	33.0	82.8	94.7	I 88.8	138.5	187.3	273.3	393.3	680.9	1,156.6	1,639.3	2,466.3	Claims on Private Sector	32d
2,789.4	I 3.8	4.8	6.2	9.2	9.0	I —	—	—	—	37.2	10.7	4.6	.9	.9	Claims on Other Financial Insts	32f
38,307.8	I 55.2	84.2	122.0	186.4	206.4	I 235.7	360.7	461.3	693.5	925.3	1,215.7	1,767.3	2,073.1	2,129.4	Money	34
8,410.2	I 14.0	21.8	33.0	53.4	65.2	I 109.7	165.2	203.3	275.2	434.4	586.9	856.3	1,234.1	1,714.4	Quasi-Money	35
....	....	....	....	....	....	22.4	91.5	71.4	110.1	158.4	43.0	29.3	1.0	—	Liabs. of Central Bank: Securities	36ac
8,312.9	I 12.9	15.7	5.9	1.3	—	I .9	.9	.9	.9	.9	.9	—	—	—	Restricted Deposits	36b
—	I —	—	—	—	—	I 62.6	99.2	189.8	253.1	388.2	143.9	267.7	408.4	803.6	Counterpart Funds	36e
8,374.1	I 18.5	22.6	24.0	13.5	70.3	I 99.6	104.6	219.9	376.6	566.7	707.9	1,148.9	1,217.9	1,598.1	Capital Accounts	37a
–18,808.5	I –37.4	–69.7	–141.9	–192.4	–240.7	I –82.0	–282.5	–277.7	–484.8	–442.6	–265.7	35.3	141.5	372.6	Other Items (Net)	37r
46,718.0	I 69.1	106.0	155.0	239.8	271.6	I 345.5	525.9	664.7	968.7	1,359.7	1,802.6	2,623.6	3,307.2	3,843.8	Money plus Quasi-Money	35l
End of Period															**Other Banking Institutions**	
....	....	....	....	....	....	....	.2	.5	.6	.3	.5	.5	.9	2.7	Reserves	40
....	....	....	....	....	....	....	26.0	30.8	41.1	50.7	36.9	44.5	19.6	41.3	Other Claims on Monetary Author.	40c
....	....	....	....	....	....	....	—	—	—	—	—	.1	41.5	46.1	Claims on Central Government	42a
....	....	....	....	....	....	....	7.2	1.2	—	—	—	—	—	—	Claims on Nonfin.Pub.Enterprises	42c
....	....	....	....	....	....	....	.2	2.3	.8	6.9	5.3	8.3	2.1	5.1	Claims on Deposit Money Banks	42e
....	....	....	....	....	....	....	.3	.1	.2	1.7	—	—	—	.2	Claims on Other Financial Insts	42f
....	....	....	....	....	....	....	32.1	30.8	37.7	23.0	35.1	44.5	67.6	60.3	Quasi-Monetary Liabilities	45
....	....	....	....	....	....	....	—	—	—	—	—	—	—	11.5	Money Market Instruments	46aa
....	....	....	....	....	....	....	2.9	—	—	33.4	10.7	3.7	.5	18.8	Credit from Monetary Authorities	46g
....	....	....	....	....	....	....	3.6	3.6	7.3	6.0	4.7	9.2	11.8	15.9	Capital Accounts	47a
....	....	....	....	....	....	....	–4.7	.4	–2.3	–2.8	–7.8	–4.1	–15.8	–11.0	Other Items (Net)	47r
End of Period															**Banking Survey**	
....	....	....	....	....	....	....	–126.5	–146.2	14.0	180.6	206.4	243.9	310.7	–743.7	Foreign Assets (Net)	51n
....	....	....	....	....	....	....	675.8	1,016.4	1,210.8	1,852.2	2,226.2	3,860.9	4,806.8	7,408.2	Domestic Credit	52
....	....	....	....	....	....	....	455.4	740.1	759.1	1,223.7	1,341.4	2,483.8	2,972.6	4,447.0	Claims on Central Govt. (Net)	52an
....	....	....	....	....	....	....	79.5	88.9	178.3	196.4	193.2	215.9	194.1	493.8	Claims on Nonfin.Pub.Enterprises	52c
....	....	....	....	....	....	....	138.5	187.3	273.3	393.3	680.9	1,156.6	1,639.3	2,466.3	Claims on Private Sector	52d
....	....	....	....	....	....	....	.3	.1	.2	38.9	10.7	4.6	.9	1.1	Claims on Other Financial Insts	52f

Ghana

		1970	1971	1972	1973	1974	1975	1976	1977	1978	1979	1980	1981	1982	1983	1984
Banking Survey (Cont.)																*Billions of Cedis:*
Liquid Liabilities	55l	...	...	...	...	...	...	...	...	...	...	...	...	...	...	...
Money Market Instruments	56aa	...	...	...	...	...	...	...	...	...	...	...	...	...	...	...
Liabs. of Central Bank: Securities	56ac	...	...	...	...	...	...	...	...	...	...	...	...	...	...	...
Restricted Deposits	56b	...	...	...	...	...	...	...	...	...	...	...	...	...	...	...
Counterpart Funds	56e	...	...	...	...	...	...	...	...	...	...	...	...	...	...	...
Capital Accounts	57a	...	...	...	...	...	...	...	...	...	...	...	...	...	...	...
Other Items (Net)	57r	...	...	...	...	...	...	...	...	...	...	...	...	...	...	...
Interest Rates																*Percent Per Annum*
Discount Rate *(End of Period)*	60	5.50	8.00	8.00	6.00	6.00	8.00	8.00	8.00	13.50	13.50	13.50	19.50	10.50	14.50	18.00
Treasury Bill Rate	60c	...	...	...	...	...	...	...	...	13.00	13.00	13.00	13.00	13.00	13.00	14.16
Deposit Rate	60l	...	...	...	...	...	...	...	...	11.50	11.50	11.50	11.50	11.50	11.50	15.00
Lending Rate	60p	...	...	...	...	...	...	...	...	19.00	19.00	19.00	19.00	19.00	19.00	21.17
Prices and Labor																*Index Numbers (1995=100):*
Consumer Prices	64	—	—	—	—	—	.1	.1	.2	.4	.6	.9	1.9	2.3	5.1	7.1
																Number in Thousands:
Employment	67e	...	...	...	...	...	...	...	...	...	...	...	...	...	...	...
Unemployment	67c	...	...	...	...	...	...	...	...	...	...	...	...	...	...	...
International Transactions																*Millions of Cedis through 1985;*
Exports	70	467	504	580	763	849	938	957	1,166	1,645	2,737	3,458	2,928	2,402	10,225	18,942
Cocoa Beans	70r	301	203	275	397	466	556	516	680	988	1,846	2,564	1,118	1,072	6,343	12,795
Imports, c.i.f.	71	419	443	393	526	944	909	992	1,193	1,682	2,344	3,104	3,041	1,939	11,022	21,887
Volume of Exports																*1995=100*
Cocoa Beans	72r	160.0	143.1	171.6	187.3	131.4	134.4	129.7	100.2	84.5	75.0	102.0	71.9	95.0	68.9	60.3
Export Prices																
Cocoa Beans (Unit Value)	74r	—	—	—	—	.1	.1	.1	.1	.3	.5	.6	.3	.3	2.0	4.6
Balance of Payments																*Millions of US Dollars:*
Current Account, n.i.e.	78al d	...	...	...	...	...	17.6	−74.0	−79.7	−45.9	123.5	30.2	−419.2	−107.3	−172.2	−38.8
Goods: Exports f.o.b.	78aa d	...	...	...	...	...	801.0	779.0	889.6	892.8	1,065.7	710.6	710.7	607.0	439.1	565.9
Goods: Imports f.o.b.	78ab d	...	...	...	...	...	−650.5	−690.3	−860.2	−780.3	−803.1	−908.3	−954.3	−588.7	−499.7	−533.0
Trade Balance	78ac d	...	...	...	...	...	150.4	88.8	29.4	112.5	262.6	195.3	−243.6	18.3	−60.6	32.9
Services: Credit	78ad d	...	...	...	...	...	90.0	112.4	128.3	103.3	97.0	106.7	119.1	103.9	38.2	43.8
Services: Debit	78ae d	...	...	...	...	...	−231.0	−260.3	−261.0	−292.6	−260.9	−269.9	−295.3	−228.2	−134.7	−163.0
Balance on Goods & Services	78af d	...	...	...	...	...	9.4	−59.0	−103.4	−76.8	98.7	32.1	−419.8	−106.0	−157.1	−86.3
Income: Credit	78ag d	...	...	...	...	...	4.4	2.5	2.5	1.3	1.9	2.8	2.0	.3	.3	2.0
Income: Debit	78ah d	...	...	...	...	...	−40.8	−44.3	−37.4	−28.7	−57.4	−85.3	−86.0	−88.2	−89.7	−116.8
Balance on Gds, Serv. & Inc.	78ai d	...	...	...	...	...	−26.9	−100.8	−138.3	−104.2	43.2	−50.4	−503.8	−191.3	−246.5	−201.1
Current Transfers, n.i.e.: Credit	78aj d	...	...	...	...	...	56.6	40.3	71.4	69.7	89.5	89.3	93.3	90.1	88.0	169.0
Current Transfers: Debit	78ak d	...	...	...	...	...	−12.1	−13.5	−12.9	−11.5	−9.2	−8.7	−8.7	−6.1	−13.7	−6.7
Capital Account, n.i.e.	78bc d	...	...	...	...	...	—	—	—	—	−1.5	−1.0	−1.6	−1.5	−1.9	—
Capital Account, n.i.e.: Credit	78ba d	...	...	...	...	...	—	—	—	—	—	—	—	—	—	—
Capital Account: Debit	78bb d	...	...	...	...	...	—	—	—	—	−1.5	−1.0	−1.6	−1.5	−1.9	—
Financial Account, n.i.e.	78bj d	...	...	...	...	...	82.4	−36.6	58.9	103.0	53.9	69.9	108.5	123.5	119.1	206.9
Direct Investment Abroad	78bd d	...	...	...	...	...	—	—	—	—	—	—	—	—	—	—
Dir. Invest. in Rep. Econ., n.i.e.	78be d	...	...	...	...	...	70.9	−18.3	19.2	9.7	−2.8	15.6	16.3	16.3	2.4	2.0
Portfolio Investment Assets	78bf d	...	...	...	...	...	—	—	—	—	—	—	—	—	—	—
Equity Securities	78bk d	...	...	...	...	...	—	—	—	—	—	—	—	—	—	—
Debt Securities	78bl d	...	...	...	...	...	—	—	—	—	—	—	—	—	—	—
Portfolio Investment Liab., n.i.e.	78bg d	...	...	...	...	...	—	—	—	—	—	—	—	—	—	—
Equity Securities	78bm d	...	...	...	...	...	—	—	—	—	—	—	—	—	—	—
Debt Securities	78bn d	...	...	...	...	...	—	—	—	—	—	—	—	—	—	—
Financial Derivatives Assets	78bw d	...	...	...	...	...	...	...	...	...	...	...	...	...	...	...
Financial Derivatives Liabilities	78bx d	...	...	...	...	...	...	...	...	...	...	...	...	...	...	...
Other Investment Assets	78bh d	...	...	...	...	...	−3.1	3.9	1.7	10.8	20.7	−6.3	14.9	−.3	−25.8	11.1
Monetary Authorities	78bo d	...	...	...	...	...	—	—	—	—	—	—	—	—	—	—
General Government	78bp d	...	...	...	...	...	−3.1	12.6	−1.0	4.6	−.3	−6.3	17.3	.2	1.1	−10.3
Banks	78bq d	...	...	...	...	...	—	−8.7	2.6	6.2	1.3	—	−2.4	−.5	−26.9	21.4
Other Sectors	78br d	...	...	...	...	...	—	—	—	—	19.7	—	—	—	—	—
Other Investment Liab., n.i.e.	78bi d	...	...	...	...	...	14.7	−22.2	38.1	82.5	36.0	60.6	77.3	107.5	142.5	193.8
Monetary Authorities	78bs d	...	...	...	...	...	−8.9	−.9	−1.4	2.7	−5.3	—	−.1	−12.2	−.1	—
General Government	78bt d	...	...	...	...	...	23.7	7.6	64.3	90.7	93.8	53.9	90.7	112.8	19.6	212.2
Banks	78bu d	...	...	...	...	...	−8.0	11.2	−.5	−7.5	4.0	10.3	29.2	9.6	32.8	−80.2
Other Sectors	78bv d	...	...	...	...	...	7.9	−40.2	−24.3	−3.5	−56.5	−3.6	−42.5	−2.7	90.2	61.8
Net Errors and Omissions	78ca d	...	...	...	...	...	6.3	−26.7	12.4	−119.4	−106.1	−100.4	24.0	−32.6	−126.0	−132.5
Overall Balance	78cb d	...	...	...	...	...	106.3	−137.3	−8.4	−62.4	69.8	−1.3	−288.3	−17.9	−180.9	35.6
Reserves and Related Items	79da d	...	...	...	...	...	−106.3	137.3	8.4	62.4	−69.8	1.3	288.3	17.9	180.9	−35.6
Reserve Assets	79db d	...	...	...	...	...	−45.6	59.3	−109.4	−80.2	3.1	124.1	47.2	6.6	−4.8	−146.7
Use of Fund Credit and Loans	79dc d	...	...	...	...	...	48.1	—	—	−5.3	62.1	.4	−10.9	−5.4	260.5	212.9
Exceptional Financing	79de d	...	...	...	...	...	−108.9	78.0	117.8	147.9	−135.0	−123.3	252.0	16.6	−74.7	−101.8

Banking Survey (Cont.)

End of Period

Item	1985	1986	1987	1988	1989	1990	1991	1992	1993	1994	1995	1996	1997	1998	1999	Code
Liquid Liabilities	…	…	…	…	…	…	…	557.9	695.0	1,005.8	1,382.4	1,837.2	2,667.6	3,373.9	3,901.4	55l
Money Market Instruments															11.5	56aa
Liabs. of Central Bank: Securities								65.5	40.6	69.0	107.6	6.1	—	—	—	56ac
Restricted Deposits								.9	.9	.9	.9	.9	—	—	—	56b
Counterpart Funds								99.2	189.8	253.1	388.2	143.9	267.7	408.4	803.6	56e
Capital Accounts								108.2	223.5	383.9	572.7	712.5	1,158.2	1,229.7	1,614.0	57a
Other Items (Net)								-282.4	-279.6	-487.9	-418.9	-268.1	11.4	105.5	334.0	57r

Interest Rates

Percent Per Annum

Item	1985	1986	1987	1988	1989	1990	1991	1992	1993	1994	1995	1996	1997	1998	1999	Code
Discount Rate *(End of Period)*	18.50	20.50	23.50	26.00	26.00	33.00	20.00	30.00	35.00	33.00	45.00	45.00	45.00	37.00	27.00	60
Treasury Bill Rate	17.13	18.47	21.71	19.76	19.84	21.78	29.23	19.38	30.95	27.72	35.38	41.64	42.77	34.33	26.37	60c
Deposit Rate	15.75	17.00	17.58	16.50	…	…	21.32	16.32	23.63	23.15	28.73	34.50	35.76	32.05	23.56	60l
Lending Rate	21.17	20.00	25.50	25.58	…	…	…	…	…	…	…	…	…	…	…	60p

Prices and Labor

Period Averages

Item	1985	1986	1987	1988	1989	1990	1991	1992	1993	1994	1995	1996	1997	1998	1999	Code
Consumer Prices	7.9	9.8	13.7	18.0	22.5	30.9	36.5	40.2	50.2	62.7	100.0	146.6	I187.4	214.8	241.5	64

Period Averages

Item	1985	1986	1987	1988	1989	1990	1991	1992	1993	1994	1995	1996	1997	1998	1999	Code
Employment	464	414	394	307	215	230	186	…	…	…	…	…	…	…	…	67e
Unemployment	24	26	…	29	27	30	31	31	39	37	41	…	…	…	…	67c

International Transactions

Billions of Cedis Beginning 1986

Item	1985	1986	1987	1988	1989	1990	1991	1992	1993	1994	1995	1996	1997	1998	1999	Code
Exports	33,185	I177	147	206	275	…	…	547	632	1,359	2,070	2,733	3,353	4,151	…	70
Cocoa Beans	18,323	I142	80	94	112	121	127	118	162	266	457	791	826	1,437	1,422	70r
Imports, c.i.f.	47,155	I193	175	186	347	…	388	951	2,439	2,029	2,289	3,452	4,769	5,932	9,347	71

Volume of Exports

1995=100

Item	1985	1986	1987	1988	1989	1990	1991	1992	1993	1994	1995	1996	1997	1998	1999	Code
Cocoa Beans	66.2	84.9	83.4	87.6	107.2	106.2	95.7	88.6	101.6	94.3	100.0	142.3	103.4	138.1	151.3	72r

Export Prices

Item	1985	1986	1987	1988	1989	1990	1991	1992	1993	1994	1995	1996	1997	1998	1999	Code
Cocoa Beans (Unit Value)	6.1	10.7	20.3	23.4	22.9	24.9	28.8	29.2	34.9	61.8	100.0	121.4	1,748.6	242.8	204.6	74r

Balance of Payments

Minus Sign Indicates Debit

Item	1985	1986	1987	1988	1989	1990	1991	1992	1993	1994	1995	1996	1997	1998	1999	Code
Current Account, n.i.e.	-133.9	-85.3	-97.9	-67.1	-93.9	-223.2	-252.1	-377.0	-559.8	-254.6	-144.6	-324.7	-549.7	-380.0	-766.0	78al d
Goods: Exports f.o.b.	632.4	749.3	826.8	881.0	808.2	896.8	997.7	986.3	1,063.6	1,237.7	1,431.2	1,570.1	1,489.9	2,090.8	2,116.6	78aa d
Goods: Imports f.o.b.	-668.7	-735.1	-933.9	-993.4	-1,011.6	-1,205.0	-1,318.7	-1,456.5	-1,728.0	-1,579.9	-1,687.8	-1,937.0	-2,128.2	-2,896.5	-3,228.1	78ab d
Trade Balance	-36.3	14.2	-107.1	-112.4	-203.4	-308.2	-321.0	-470.2	-664.4	-342.2	-256.6	-366.9	-638.3	-805.7	-1,111.5	78ac d
Services: Credit	38.0	54.8	78.7	76.7	80.9	86.4	102.8	118.4	144.7	147.5	150.6	156.8	164.9	440.9	467.8	78ad d
Services: Debit	-167.7	-240.8	-266.9	-268.0	-275.9	-300.5	-336.4	-389.3	-445.3	-420.8	-432.7	-456.4	-505.0	-612.8	-610.5	78ae d
Balance on Goods & Services	-166.0	-171.7	-295.3	-303.7	-398.4	-522.3	-554.6	-741.1	-965.0	-615.5	-538.7	-666.5	-978.4	-977.6	-1,254.2	78af d
Income: Credit	5.6	.6	.6	1.0	4.9	6.8	7.5	10.5	11.6	11.8	13.7	23.5	26.7	26.7	15.0	78ag d
Income: Debit	-115.9	-105.3	-127.0	-131.9	-122.7	-118.2	-126.9	-116.7	-123.9	-122.7	-142.9	-163.4	-158.1	-163.0	-146.8	78ah d
Balance on Gds, Serv. & Inc.	-276.3	-276.4	-421.7	-434.6	-516.2	-633.7	-674.0	-847.3	-1,077.3	-726.4	-667.9	-806.4	-1,109.8	-1,113.9	-1,386.0	78ai d
Current Transfers, n.i.e.: Credit	147.4	200.1	333.1	376.8	432.2	421.1	434.1	484.8	532.0	487.3	539.0	497.9	576.5	751.0	637.8	78aj d
Current Transfers: Debit	-5.0	-9.0	-9.3	-9.3	-9.9	-10.6	-12.2	-14.5	-14.5	-15.5	-15.7	-16.2	-16.4	-17.1	-17.8	78ak d
Capital Account, n.i.e.	-.3	-.5	-.6	-.7	-.8	—	-.9	-1.0	-1.0	-1.0	-1.0	-1.0	-1.0	-1.0	-1.0	78bc d
Capital Account, n.i.e.: Credit																78ba d
Capital Account: Debit	-.3	-.5	-.6	-.7	-.8	—	-.9	-1.0	-1.0	-1.0	-1.0	-1.0	-1.0	-1.0	-1.0	78bb d
Financial Account, n.i.e.	84.9	61.9	218.4	208.2	181.3	250.5	367.8	275.9	642.6	481.7	462.1	285.1	493.8	515.8	391.8	78bj d
Direct Investment Abroad																78bd d
Dir. Invest. in Rep. Econ., n.i.e.	5.6	4.3	4.7	5.0	15.0	14.8	20.0	22.5	125.0	233.0	106.5	120.0	82.6	55.7	17.0	78be d
Portfolio Investment Assets	—	—	—	—	—	—	—	—	—	—	—	—	—	—	—	78bf d
Equity Securities	—	—	—	—	—	—	—	—	—	—	—	—	—	—	—	78bk d
Debt Securities	—	—	—	—	—	—	—	—	—	—	—	—	—	—	—	78bl d
Portfolio Investment Liab., n.i.e.	—	—	—	—	—	—	—	—	—	—	—	—	—	—	—	78bg d
Equity Securities	—	—	—	—	—	—	—	—	—	—	—	—	—	—	—	78bm d
Debt Securities	—	—	—	—	—	—	—	—	—	—	—	—	—	—	—	78bn d
Financial Derivatives Assets																78bw d
Financial Derivatives Liabilities																78bx d
Other Investment Assets	5.8	-2.2	-31.5	-.4	-49.8	-94.2	26.2	-49.8	5.8	-119.6	-20.0	-179.4	33.1	87.9	183.1	78bh d
Monetary Authorities	…	-7.2	-6.8	.4	4.2	-11.8	-19.6	1.6	12.5	3.2	3.0	-.4	.2	-.1	-3.3	78bo d
General Government	4.1															78bp d
Banks	1.7	5.0	-24.7	-.8	-54.0	-64.7	18.3	-5.1	-1.2	-93.3	77.6	-72.0	34.4	83.7	200.3	78bq d
Other Sectors						-17.7	27.5	-46.3	-5.5	-29.5	-100.6	-107.0	-1.5	4.3	-13.9	78br d
Other Investment Liab., n.i.e.	73.5	59.8	245.2	203.6	216.1	329.9	321.6	303.2	511.8	368.3	375.6	344.5	378.1	372.2	191.7	78bi d
Monetary Authorities	11.2	-2.2	.4	7.4	21.6	22.5	-42.3	-33.4	32.2	-19.4	-39.1	—	—			78bs d
General Government	39.3	128.2	218.0	179.9	171.2	290.4	356.6	386.5	370.2	295.3	215.5	341.2	499.4	348.9	144.2	78bt d
Banks	25.6	-21.4	32.3	7.4	19.0	-4.0	-6.1	-16.2	44.8	64.8	-31.2	30.6				78bu d
Other Sectors	-2.6	-44.8	-5.5	8.9	4.3	21.0	13.4	-33.7	64.6	27.6	230.4	-27.3	-121.3	23.3	47.5	78bv d
Net Errors and Omissions	63.4	-36.9	20.2	40.7	70.0	78.0	21.9	-20.7	-28.5	-54.0	-65.7	20.2	83.7	-27.0	327.3	78ca d
Overall Balance	14.1	-60.8	140.1	181.1	156.6	105.3	136.7	-122.8	53.3	172.1	250.8	-20.4	26.7	107.8	-47.9	78cb d
Reserves and Related Items	-14.1	60.8	-140.1	-181.1	-156.6	-105.3	-136.7	122.8	-53.3	-172.1	-250.8	20.4	-26.7	-107.8	47.9	79da d
Reserve Assets	-183.4	13.0	-41.5	-48.9	-52.4	-17.5	-220.5	186.2	-52.2	-89.2	-185.6	105.7	139.0	-81.7	62.9	79db d
Use of Fund Credit and Loans	115.7	5.9	-36.7	-59.1	-8.8	-53.8	83.8	-63.4	-1.1	-82.9	-65.2	-85.3	-165.8	-26.1	-15.0	79dc d
Exceptional Financing	53.5	41.9	-61.9	-73.2	-95.4	-34.0	…	…	…	…	…	…	…	…	…	79de d

Ghana

Government Finance

Millions of Cedis through 1985; Billions of Cedis Beginning 1986:

		1970	1971	1972	1973	1974	1975	1976	1977	1978	1979	1980	1981	1982	1983	1984
Deficit (-) or Surplus	80	-49.9	-88.4	‡-161.2	-186.6	-196.1	-401.3	-736.2	-1,056.8	-1,896.7	-1,800.0	-1,808.0	-4,706.8	-4,848.0	‡-4933.3	-4,843.0
Revenue	81	437.3	450.7	‡418.7	391.1	578.9	809.0	869.8	1,140.9	1,392.1	2,600.0	2,951.0	3,234.1	4,804.0	‡10185.0	21,728.0
Grants Received	81z	...	...	‡3.2	.5	4.7	.9	—	30.3	1.0	—	—	45.0	52.0	‡56.6	914.0
Expenditure	82	467.9	523.8	‡543.1	548.5	754.1	1,146.2	1,484.0	2,136.6	3,164.8	4,295.7	4,668.0	7,719.3	9,530.0	‡14755.3	26,694.0
Lending Minus Repayments	83	19.3	15.3	‡40.0	29.7	25.6	65.0	122.0	91.4	125.0	104.3	91.0	266.6	174.0	‡419.6	791.0
Financing																
Domestic	84a	44.8	72.0	‡79.4	167.8	197.7	399.9	734.4	1,044.1	1,720.0	1,800.0	1,518.0	4,339.5	4,421.0	‡3,824.8	3,028.0
Foreign	85a	48.0	24.2	‡81.8	18.8	-1.6	1.4	1.8	12.7	67.2	—	290.0	367.3	389.0	‡970.1	1,815.0
Use of Cash Balances	87	-42.5	-7.8	....	—	—	....									
Unallocable Financing	87c	...	...	‡—	—	—				109.5	....	—	—	38.0	‡138.4	—
Debt: Domestic	88a	681.1	710.5	‡928.1	1,055.9	1,275.5	1,486.0	2,269.5	3,208.2	5,136.0	6,154.0	7,622.0	11,846.2	17,487.7	‡29315.5	32,908.0
Foreign	89a	487.6	509.3	‡228.3	261.4	263.9	482.2	482.2	....	....	2,741.7	3,104.8	3,588.6	4,083.0	‡5,052.5	6,869.0

National Accounts

Millions of Cedis through 1985:

		1970	1971	1972	1973	1974	1975	1976	1977	1978	1979	1980	1981	1982	1983	1984
Exports of Goods & Services	90c	523	443	648	820	956	1,023	1,025	1,171	1,754	3,169	3,629	3,454	2,886	10,225	20,161
Government Consumption	91f	290	324	355	382	569	689	799	1,409	2,371	2,903	4,784	6,384	5,603	10,787	19,641
Gross Fixed Capital Formation	93e	271	311	244	267	555	614	641	1,049	1,355	1,899	2,613	3,430	3,053	6,922	18,542
Increase/Decrease(-) in Stocks	93i	49	42	-44	48	53	59	-62	186	66	-54	-203	-109	-132	-21	65
Private Consumption	96f	1,664	1,917	2,096	2,619	3,588	3,873	5,171	8,638	17,473	23,455	35,953	63,333	77,619	167,147	233,023
Imports of Goods & Services	98c	-539	-536	-484	-635	-1,061	-974	-1,047	-1,289	-2,033	-3,150	-3,923	-3,966	-2,578	-11,022	-20,871
Gross Domestic Product (GDP)	99b	2,259	2,501	2,815	3,502	4,660	5,283	6,526	11,163	20,986	28,222	42,853	72,526	86,451	184,038	270,561
Net Factor Inc/Pmts(-) Abroad	98.n	-48	-52	-40	-30	-47	-42	-48	-40	-48	-98	-182	-232	-225	-1,640	-3,643
Gross National Income (GNI)	99a	2,211	2,449	2,775	3,472	4,613	5,241	6,478	11,123	20,938	28,124	42,671	72,294	86,225	182,398	266,918
Net National Income	99e	2,077	2,304	2,605	3,255	4,378	4,918	6,100	10,599	20,213	27,071	41,159	70,186	83,598	178,202	255,713
GDP Volume 1975 Prices	99b.p	4,943	5,218	5,088	5,864	6,063	5,283	5,097	5,212	5,654	5,475	5,475	5,377	4,990	5,025	5,158
GDP Volume (1995=100)	99bv p	57.9	61.1	59.6	68.7	71.0	61.9	59.7	61.1	66.2	64.1	64.1	63.0	58.5	58.9	60.4
GDP Deflator (1995=100)	99bi p	.1	.1	.1	.1	.1	.1	.1	.2	.4	.6	.9	1.5	1.9	4.0	5.8

Millions:

		1970	1971	1972	1973	1974	1975	1976	1977	1978	1979	1980	1981	1982	1983	1984
Population	99z	8.61	8.86	9.09	9.39	9.61	9.87	10.31	10.41	10.75	‡10.48	10.73	11.07	11.47	11.92	12.39

	1985	1986	1987	1988	1989	1990	1991	1992	1993	1994	1995	1996	1997	1998	1999		
																Government Finance	
Year Ending June 30 through 1982, Year Ending December 31 thereafter																	
	−7,579.0	⅂ .3	4.1	3.9	10.3	3.3	39.0	−144.4	−97.3	111.7	70.3	−335.5	−297.6	−1,048.8	....	Deficit (−) or Surplus	80
	38,691.0	⅂ 69.8	105.0	142.2	193.2	239.5	354.4	333.6	657.6	1,221.8	1,691.0	2,191.0	2,549.9	3,276.1	....	Revenue	81
	1,620.0	⅂ 3.9	6.0	11.6	21.3	27.8	36.3	32.7	66.6	39.5	93.8	77.5	66.6	161.9	....	Grants Received	81z
	45,763.0	⅂ 70.7	102.1	143.9	196.5	254.5	340.3	498.8	813.5	1,141.3	1,698.7	2,515.2	2,908.9	4,513.2	....	Expenditure	82
	2,127.0	⅂ 2.7	4.9	6.0	7.7	9.5	11.4	11.9	8.0	8.3	15.8	88.8	5.2	−26.4	....	Lending Minus Repayments	83
																Financing	
	4,043.0	⅂ 5.3	−2.9	−6.2	−15.3	−28.0	−51.7	144.1	45.4	−26.7	−27.7	531.1	728.0	672.6	....	Domestic	84a
	3,522.0	⅂ −5.6	−1.2	2.3	4.9	24.6	12.7	.3	51.9	−85.0	−42.6	−195.7	−430.3	376.2	....	Foreign	85a
	....	⅂		....											....	Use of Cash Balances	87
	14.0	⅂ —	—	—	—	—	—	—	—	—	—	—	—	—	....	Unallocable Financing	87c
	37,766.0	....	....	....	....	....	....	....	....	....	....	....	....	....	....	Debt: Domestic	88a
	9,839.0	....	....	....	....	....	....	....	....	....	....	....	....		....	Foreign	89a
																National Accounts	
Billions of Cedis Beginning 1986																	
	33,185	⅂ 82	158	218	292	313	405	483	693	1,172	1,899	2,827	2,795		....	Exports of Goods & Services	90c
	32,241	⅂ 57	75	105	145	222	294	400	568	714	936	1,366	1,744		....	Government Consumption	91f
	32,689	⅂ 48	77	114	191	248	326	386	921	1,175	1,638	2,332	3,338		....	Gross Fixed Capital Formation	93e
	139	⅂ —	1	1	1	1	2	2	−61	72	−86	102	127		....	Increase/Decrease(−) in Stocks	93i
	284,621	⅂ 415	610	834	1,187	1,736	2,012	2,338	3,049	3,835	5,910	8,629	11,267		....	Private Consumption	96f
	−39,826	⅂ −90	−175	−221	−399	−488	−611	−806	−1,298	−1,762	−2,544	−3,917	−5,158		....	Imports of Goods & Services	98c
	343,048	⅂ 511	746	1,051	1,417	2,032	2,428	2,803	3,873	5,205	7,753	11,339	14,113		....	Gross Domestic Product (GDP)	99b
	−5,769	⅂ −13	−21	−27	−28	−37	−44	−46	73	106	155	220	274		....	Net Factor Inc/Pmts(−) Abroad	98.n
	337,280	⅂ 499	725	1,025	1,389	1,995	2,384	2,756	3,800	5,099	7,598	11,119	13,840		....	Gross National Income (GNI)	99a
	320,941	⅂ 470	678	956	1,303	1,884	2,253	2,600	3,471	4,688	7,084	10,318	12,843		....	Net National Income	99e
	5,420	5,702	5,976	6,312	6,633	6,853	7,217	7,498	7,868	8,168	8,535	8,976	9,434		....	GDP Volume 1975 Prices	99b.*p*
	63.5	66.8	70.0	74.0	77.7	80.3	84.6	87.9	92.2	95.7	100.0	105.2	110.5		....	GDP Volume (1995=100)	99bv *p*
	7.0	9.9	13.7	18.3	23.5	32.6	37.0	41.2	54.2	70.2	100.0	139.1	164.7		....	GDP Deflator (1995=100)	99bi *p*
Midyear Estimates																	
	12.72	13.05	13.39	14.14	14.67	15.13	15.61	16.11	16.63	17.14	17.65	18.15	18.66	19.16	19.68	Population	99z

(See notes in the back of the book.)

Greece

		1970	1971	1972	1973	1974	1975	1976	1977	1978	1979	1980	1981	1982	1983	1984
Exchange Rates														*Drachmas per SDR:*		
Market Rate	aa	30.00	32.57	32.57	35.83	36.73	41.73	43.02	43.13	46.91	50.43	59.35	67.08	77.85	103.30	125.94
														Drachmas per US Dollar:		
Market Rate	ae	30.00	30.00	30.00	29.70	30.00	35.65	37.03	35.51	36.01	38.28	46.54	57.63	70.57	98.67	128.48
Market Rate	rf	30.00	30.00	30.00	29.63	30.00	32.05e	36.52	36.84	36.75	37.04	42.62	55.41	66.80	88.06	112.72
							Drachmas per ECU through 1998; Drachmas per Euro Beginning 1999:										
Euro Rate	ea	....	....	....	....	....	....	....	....	....	....	....	62.18	68.54	81.78	91.04
Euro Rate	eb	....	....	....	....	....	....	....	....	....	....	59.24	61.62	65.30	78.09	88.44
														Index Numbers (1995=100):		
Market Rate	ahx	771.8	459.0	771.8	781.9	771.8	725.6e	634.2	628.6	630.2	625.2	544.8	419.9	348.4	264.0	206.8
Nominal Effective Exchange Rate	neu	956.8	934.9	868.9	798.8	808.2	732.8	704.6	687.6	623.7	583.9	507.1	475.7	445.3	368.4	321.3
Real Effective Exchange Rate	reu	....	....	....	....	....	....	....	....	78.1	79.7	79.1	85.8	99.0	95.1	100.6
Fund Position														*Millions of SDRs:*		
Quota	2f.s	138.0	138.0	138.0	138.0	138.0	138.0	138.0	138.0	185.0	185.0	277.5	277.5	277.5	399.9	399.9
SDRs	1b.s	—	4.5	25.6	25.2	26.7	17.6	16.9	13.4	13.4	.8	.1	55.6	55.6	.6	1.1
Reserve Position in the Fund	1c.s	34.5	34.5	34.5	34.5	—	—	—	—	33.5	32.4	55.6	55.6	55.6	86.2	81.4
Total Fund Cred.&Loans Outstg.	2tl	—	—	—	—	36.2	189.8	247.8	176.5	185.2	147.3	78.5	13.9			
International Liquidity												*Millions of US Dollars Unless Otherwise Indicated:*					
Total Reserves Minus Gold	1l.d	193.6	412.4	898.8	898.9	781.7	‡963.6	880.6	1,048.3	1,305.0	1,342.8	1,345.9	1,022.0	861.1	900.5	954.2
SDRs	1b.d	—	4.9	27.8	30.4	32.7	20.6	19.6	16.3	17.4	1.1	—	.1		.6	1.1
Reserve Position in the Fund	1c.d	34.5	37.5	37.5	41.6					43.6	42.7	70.9	64.7	61.3	90.2	79.8
Foreign Exchange	1d.d	159.1	370.1	833.6	826.8	749.0	‡943.0	861.0	1,032.0	1,244.0	1,299.0	1,275.0	957.2	799.8	809.7	873.3
Gold (Million Fine Troy Ounces)	1ad	3.329	2.805	3.495	3.502	3.610	3.629	3.651	3.730	3.770	3.808	3.835	3.853	3.872	3.880	4.106
Gold (National Valuation)	1and	116.5	98.2	132.8	147.9	154.7	148.7	148.5	158.6	171.9	175.6	171.2	157.0	149.5	142.2	140.9
Deposit Money Banks: Assets	7a.d	103.2	112.7	159.6	253.0	236.9	280.4	348.7	445.2	407.1	738.9	1,187.9	1,666.2	1,408.0	1,386.0	1,598.0
Liabilities	7b.d	138.1	259.1	403.3	562.0	751.5	982.6	1,565.0	2,268.0	2,931.0	3,557.5	4,000.7	4,675.6	4,916.0	5,037.0	5,031.0
Other Banking Insts.: Liabilities	7f.d	....	....	....	211.0	243.0	271.0	378.0	542.0	768.5	978.8	1,150.1	1,247.1	1,394.5	1,558.2	1,564.6
Monetary Authorities														*Billions of Drachmas:*		
Foreign Assets	11	11.7	16.3	32.9	32.0	33.1	38.8	40.0	42.8	51.1	52.7	74.1	72.5	79.2	114.9	152.9
Claims on Central Government	12a	17.5	18.4	20.3	30.8	47.2	47.1	60.3	80.5	122.5	154.3	200.3	356.1	617.9	530.8	656.5
o/w: Cntrprt Gov.L/T.For.Liab.	12aeb	....	....	....	....	....	....	....	....	....	....	....	....	....	....	....
Claims on Deposit Money Banks	12e	2.5	1.2	.9	1.9	4.0	11.1	9.4	11.9	12.6	16.6	24.5	31.7	35.5	18.5	15.3
Claims on Other Banking Insts	12f	35.3	43.8	53.8	67.4	82.2	97.4	116.5	138.5	139.5	159.8	173.6	254.6	264.1	289.0	274.8
Reserve Money	14	47.7	57.3	68.7	81.9	99.3	121.0	145.9	177.1	213.7	237.8	304.0	440.4	563.4	617.8	806.3
of which: Currency Outside DMBs	14a	39.1	43.3	50.8	65.3	80.6	92.1	112.3	133.4	161.8	184.7	211.8	263.7	305.2	348.2	408.2
Private Sector Deposits	14d	4.2	6.6	5.8	6.8	8.4	11.2	11.9	13.8	17.6	22.2	21.1	24.3	29.1	55.0	56.9
Restricted Deposits	16b	14.6	16.4	22.8	28.6	33.9	39.9	46.6	64.3	73.7	86.9	92.5	106.5	127.2	174.5	170.7
Foreign Liabilities	16c	....	....	....	....	....	....	....	....	....	....	....	....	....	....	....
Long-Term Foreign Liabilities	16cl	....	....	....	....	....	....	....	....	....	....	....	....	....	....	....
Central Government Deposits	16d	5.3	4.5	12.8	13.2	19.5	19.3	26.9	28.2	34.4	24.7	38.1	85.4	179.8	70.3	104.9
Other Items (Net)	17r	7.0	7.6	14.6	23.2	40.2	74.7	72.2	62.3	70.4	100.9	208.9	347.2	524.2	808.1	1,247.5
Deposit Money Banks														*Billions of Drachmas:*		
Reserves	20	5.3	8.9	14.9	14.8	15.0	20.6	34.1	36.7	43.7	58.7	100.8	198.3	324.6	348.8	600.9
Foreign Assets	21	3.1	3.4	4.8	7.5	7.1	10.0	12.9	15.8	14.7	28.3	55.3	96.0	99.3	136.6	205.4
Claims on Central Government	22a	17.8	23.3	33.2	40.8	48.3	62.9	81.9	106.9	141.6	168.6	217.5	261.5	327.9	530.6	691.4
Claims on Official Entities	22bx	....	....	....	....	....	....	....	....	....	....	....	....	....	....	....
Claims on Private Sector	22d	62.5	76.8	96.7	108.7	131.6	173.8	227.5	285.0	355.8	422.3	516.8	671.7	831.3	933.5	1,143.1
Claims on Other Banking Insts	22f	....	....	....	....	....	....	....	....	....	....	....	....	....	....	....
Demand Deposits	24	11.3	13.8	19.3	21.6	23.2	27.2	35.4	39.4	48.8	58.6	75.9	89.4	124.8	122.4	165.8
Time, Savings, and Other Deposits	25	63.8	82.4	103.1	114.6	139.1	183.5	232.8	287.5	364.8	429.4	544.7	757.9	990.3	1,208.5	1,587.1
Restricted Deposits	26b	....	....	....	....	....	....	....	....	....	....	....	....	....	....	....
Foreign Liabilities	26c	4.1	7.8	12.1	16.7	22.5	35.0	57.7	80.2	105.5	136.2	186.2	269.5	346.9	497.0	646.4
Credit from Monetary Authorities	26g	2.5	1.2	1.0	2.0	4.2	11.2	10.7	12.8	16.2	34.0	46.3	68.4	78.1	115.5	177.1
Other Items (Net)	27r	7.0	7.2	14.1	16.8	13.1	10.3	19.8	24.6	20.4	19.7	37.3	42.5	42.8	6.4	64.4
Monetary Survey														*Billions of Drachmas:*		
Foreign Assets (Net)	31n	10.7	11.9	25.6	22.9	16.3	5.9	−15.5	−29.2	−48.5	−62.7	−61.4	−101.9	−168.4	−245.3	−288.1
Domestic Credit	32	132.9	162.9	195.5	243.5	300.3	374.2	472.9	598.6	737.1	895.0	1,091.5	1,485.0	1,877.9	2,225.0	2,671.7
Claims on Central Govt. (Net)	32an	30.0	37.2	40.6	58.3	76.1	90.7	115.2	159.1	229.7	298.2	379.8	532.2	765.9	991.2	1,243.0
Claims on Official Entities	32bx	....	....	....	....	....	....	....	....	....	....	....	....	....	....	....
Claims on Private Sector	32d	67.6	81.9	101.0	117.8	142.1	186.1	241.2	301.0	367.9	437.1	538.1	698.2	847.9	944.9	1,153.9
Claims on Other Banking Insts	32f	35.3	43.8	53.8	67.4	82.2	97.4	116.5	138.5	139.5	159.8	173.6	254.6	264.1	289.0	274.8
Money	34	54.6	63.6	75.9	93.7	112.2	130.6	159.6	186.6	228.2	265.4	308.8	377.4	459.1	525.6	630.9
Quasi-Money	35	78.4	98.8	125.9	143.3	173.0	223.3	279.5	351.8	438.5	516.3	637.2	864.4	1,117.5	1,383.0	1,757.8
Restricted Deposits	36b	....	....	....	....	....	....	....	....	....	....	....	....	....	....	....
Other Items (Net)	37r	18.1	18.6	30.3	44.1	57.8	86.6	83.8	89.2	88.4	117.6	255.0	406.1	530.8	788.4	1,224.9
Money plus Quasi-Money	35l	133.0	162.5	201.8	236.9	285.2	353.9	439.0	538.4	666.7	781.8	946.0	1,241.7	1,576.6	1,908.6	2,400.4
Other Banking Institutions														*Billions of Drachmas:*		
Cash	40	....	....	....	....	....	....	....	....	‡27.0	29.7	33.3	45.9	60.0	102.5	82.3
Claims on Central Government	42a	3.6	3.4	3.0	3.1	3.1	2.5	4.1	6.5	‡34.4	39.1	34.0	34.6	11.2	.5	35.0
Claims on Nonfin.Pub.Enterprises	42c	....	....	....	....	....	....	....	....	‡57.6	78.2	113.8	214.4	333.5	396.6	470.1
Claims on Private Sector	42d	46.6	58.2	72.9	90.3	111.4	135.3	165.2	205.5	‡271.0	318.0	372.3	445.0	560.8	690.6	827.1
Demand Deposits	44	....	....	....	....	....	....	....	....	‡12.5	14.7	16.3	23.7	32.6	47.6	57.0
Time, Savings,& Fgn.Currency Dep.	45	5.9	8.0	10.3	13.0	16.2	21.5	33.1	47.8	‡145.1	180.6	230.8	317.1	424.1	520.6	695.3
Bonds	46ab	....	....	....	....	....	....	....	....	‡8.1	10.4	17.2	30.6	48.3	77.1	127.4
Foreign Liabilities	46c	....	....	....	....	....	....	....	....	‡27.7	37.5	53.5	71.9	98.4	153.8	201.0
of which: Natls.Residing Abroad	46cx	....	....	....	....	....	....	....	....	‡21.6	27.2	33.2	42.7	58.2	84.8	114.6
Credit from Monetary Authorities	46j	....	....	....	....	....	....	....	....	‡144.5	164.5	180.1	260.3	272.0	294.0	278.4
Capital Accounts	47a	9.9	11.2	12.5	13.0	15.8	17.6	19.1	20.5	‡43.8	48.3	56.8	62.4	79.3	99.5	127.8
Other Items (Net)	47r	....	....	....	....	....	....	....	....	‡8.5	9.0	−1.4	−26.2	10.7	−2.3	−72.3
Liquid Liabilities	55l	139.0	170.5	212.1	250.0	301.4	375.4	472.2	586.2	‡797.3	947.4	1,159.8	1,536.7	1,973.5	2,374.3	3,070.3

	Code	1985	1986	1987	1988	1989	1990	1991	1992	1993	1994	1995	1996	1997	1998	1999
Exchange Rates																
End of Period																
Market Rate	aa	162.30	169.73	178.64	199.30	207.36	224.25	250.73	295.05	342.32	350.51	352.36	355.20	381.31	397.87	450.79
End of Period (ae) Period Average (rf)																
Market Rate	ae	147.76	138.76	125.93	148.10	157.79	157.63	175.28	214.58	249.22	240.10	237.04	247.02	282.61	282.57	328.44
Market Rate	rf	138.12	139.98	135.43	141.86	162.42	158.51	182.27	190.62	229.25	242.60	231.66	240.71	273.06	295.53	305.65
End of Period (ea) Period Average (eb)																
Euro Rate	ea	131.20	148.53	164.48	172.91	188.23	214.07	235.07	260.20	278.20	294.78	303.76	306.83	312.12	330.01	1.00
Euro Rate	eb	105.66	137.41	156.19	167.55	178.88	201.43	225.22	246.60	267.99	287.21	299.54	301.48	308.51	331.50	1.07
Period Averages																
Market Rate	ahx	168.1	165.6	171.0	163.6	142.7	146.2	127.6	121.9	101.2	95.4	100.0	96.2	84.9	78.5	75.7
Nominal Effective Exchange Rate	neu	273.8	209.7	187.0	174.1	161.6	146.5	130.2	119.9	110.6	103.1	100.0	98.3	96.3	90.5	90.1
Real Effective Exchange Rate	reu	98.3	83.5	79.7	86.5	93.0	94.8	92.7	92.0	91.8	93.9	100.0	103.6	107.3	103.5	. . . .
Fund Position																
End of Period																
Quota	2f.s	399.9	399.9	399.9	399.9	399.9	399.9	399.9	587.6	587.6	587.6	587.6	587.6	587.6	587.6	823.0
SDRs	1b.s	—	—	—	.2	.3	.2	.3	—	.1	.2	—	.4	.2	.3	3.8
Reserve Position in the Fund	1c.s	75.0	70.1	70.1	71.1	89.2	74.7	74.7	116.9	113.7	113.7	113.7	113.7	113.7	191.5	285.0
Total Fund Cred.&Loans Outstg.	2tl	—	—	—	—	—	—	—	—	—	—	—	—	—	—	—
International Liquidity																
End of Period																
Total Reserves Minus Gold	1l.d	868.0	I 1,518.7	2,681.4	3,619.4	3,223.5	3,412.1	5,188.9	4,793.6	7,790.3	14,487.9	14,780.0	17,501.4	12,594.8	17,458.4	18,122.3
SDRs	1b.d	—	—	—	.3	.4	.3	.4	—	.2	.3	—	.6	.3	.5	5.2
Reserve Position in the Fund	1c.d	82.4	85.8	99.5	95.7	117.2	106.3	106.9	160.7	156.2	166.0	169.0	163.5	153.4	269.6	391.1
Foreign Exchange	1d.d	785.6	I 1,432.9	2,581.9	3,523.4	3,105.8	3,305.5	5,081.6	4,632.9	7,634.0	14,321.6	14,611.0	17,337.3	12,441.1	17,188.3	17,726.0
Gold (Million Fine Troy Ounces)	1ad	4.123	3.308	3.342	3.395	3.395	3.400	3.425	3.433	3.443	3.448	3.461	3.469	3.644	3.623	4.237
Gold (National Valuation)	1and	I 862.8	841.3	1,057.2	925.0	902.1	834.4	807.2	746.5	856.3	850.9	871.7	833.2	684.5	685.3	781.8
Deposit Money Banks: Assets	7a.d	1,980.0	1,788.0	1,876.3	2,593.4	2,974.7	3,456.5	4,001.5	4,707.1	5,358.7	6,051.3	8,962.9	12,656.1	15,994.8	15,550.7	. . . .
Liabilities	7b.d	5,694.0	6,689.0	8,362.8	9,335.6	10,995.3	12,548.6	12,815.7	13,593.3	13,696.5	20,956.1	28,707.1	33,594.2	36,990.7	44,706.8	. . . .
Other Banking Insts.: Liabilities	7f.d	1,894.2	2,434.0	3,048.2	2,964.3	3,370.0	3,913.0	4,395.5	4,533.4	4,539.0	5,454.2	5,579.0	4,946.0	5,287.9	2,147.4	. . . .
Monetary Authorities																
End of Period																
Foreign Assets	11	265.1	331.8	I 483.1	696.0	695.2	811.8	1,351.0	1,736.7	2,975.5	4,463.9	4,333.9	5,253.9	4,020.3	5,414.0	6,434.2
Claims on Central Government	12a	747.9	787.6	I 2,012.2	2,271.2	2,632.4	3,189.2	3,721.4	4,555.9	I 7,966.2	7,352.3	7,059.4	6,457.6	6,012.1	5,757.9	5,911.7
o/w: Cntrprt Gov.L/T.For.Liab.	12aeb	. . . .	. . . .	1,012.9	1,160.0	1,319.9	1,451.2	1,819.7	2,440.9	3,596.3	3,294.5	2,750.2	2,129.6	1,578.8	1,082.8	1,029.4
Claims on Deposit Money Banks	12e	5.8	6.5	I 384.7	378.2	455.8	591.2	569.5	715.7	293.1	158.1	291.0	261.0	697.5	367.8	54.1
Claims on Other Banking Insts	12f	276.5	291.8	I 315.9	283.8	312.9	392.8	305.7	344.0	287.2	219.7	170.4	71.8	94.3	79.4	.3
Reserve Money	14	856.1	1,015.0	I 1,308.9	1,392.7	1,519.1	1,868.3	2,083.4	2,305.9	2,500.1	3,491.3	3,626.7	4,138.9	4,693.5	6,126.5	7,434.6
of which: Currency Outside DMBs	14a	513.5	550.1	I 641.4	754.9	988.7	1,190.2	1,293.3	1,444.9	1,542.5	1,725.9	1,904.4	1,995.1	2,239.2	2,284.3	2,810.0
Private Sector Deposits	14d	31.3	123.5	I 132.0	138.0	130.0	173.4	196.3	203.5	200.9	315.4	366.7	460.4	570.7	568.4	643.1
Restricted Deposits	16b	179.0	157.9	I 1,438.0	1,716.2	1,941.0	2,321.1	3,239.5	3,964.7	4,813.4	4,487.4	4,734.7	4,886.5	3,491.7	3,560.6	3,522.6
Foreign Liabilities	16c	. . . .	. . . .	39.8	41.4	229.1	307.2	102.8	226.4	182.3	186.7	203.9	196.5	377.7	251.0	240.9
Long-Term Foreign Liabilities	16cl	. . . .	. . . .	999.5	1,145.4	1,304.0	1,436.9	1,817.9	2,482.5	3,626.6	3,342.7	2,742.2	2,102.0	1,533.9	1,065.9	1,015.0
Central Government Deposits	16d	55.2	34.5	I 56.6	135.0	91.5	135.9	161.7	102.0	259.6	237.6	621.2	672.5	443.4	345.5	128.9
Other Items (Net)	17r	1,939.6	2,324.8	I –646.9	–801.5	–988.5	–1,084.3	–1,457.5	–1,729.2	140.1	448.3	–74.1	47.8	284.0	269.7	58.2
Deposit Money Banks																
End of Period																
Reserves	20	661.4	715.5	984.9	1,210.0	1,119.7	1,384.9	1,639.5	1,979.3	2,333.7	2,575.0	4,640.8	4,588.9	4,915.1	6,666.6	. . . .
Foreign Assets	21	292.6	248.1	I 236.3	384.1	469.4	544.8	701.4	1,010.0	1,335.5	1,452.9	2,124.6	3,126.3	4,520.3	4,394.2	. . . .
Claims on Central Government	22a	1,005.6	1,234.7	I 1,505.5	1,996.9	2,629.5	3,220.5	3,321.3	4,216.3	4,888.2	5,160.4	5,326.8	6,181.0	6,351.6	6,186.2	. . . .
Claims on Official Entities	22bx	. . . .	. . . .	413.5	515.3	620.6	526.9	674.7	415.0	478.3	527.7	589.1	707.6	746.6	938.9	. . . .
Claims on Private Sector	22d	1,355.4	1,670.9	I 1,507.0	1,734.4	2,120.8	2,406.6	2,770.5	3,274.2	3,870.0	4,530.1	5,822.5	6,810.5	8,067.3	10,614.3	. . . .
Claims on Other Banking Insts	22f	. . . .	. . . .	11.3	30.8	16.4	19.9	106.0	112.9	104.1	88.1	126.9	223.6	293.0	105.7	. . . .
Demand Deposits	24	198.5	222.5	I 284.2	312.8	367.8	484.6	608.0	728.6	901.0	1,344.6	1,568.7	1,879.4	2,221.5	2,708.5	. . . .
Time, Savings, and Other Deposits	25	2,031.6	2,483.3	I 3,101.7	3,841.2	4,705.3	5,228.7	5,618.7	5,946.7	6,250.1	7,712.0	8,594.3	9,747.3	10,581.9	11,098.9	. . . .
Restricted Deposits	26b	. . . .	. . . .	51.7	58.4	63.5	71.2	86.1	99.6	81.8	77.4	83.5	96.9	126.5	141.2	. . . .
Foreign Liabilities	26c	841.4	927.2	I 1,053.1	1,382.6	1,735.0	1,978.0	2,246.3	2,916.9	3,413.5	5,031.6	6,804.7	8,298.5	10,453.9	12,632.8	. . . .
Credit from Monetary Authorities	26g	249.7	248.5	I 188.5	77.8	30.8	36.4	449.1	1,037.3	1,942.9	322.5	380.6	337.6	732.3	1,691.7	. . . .
Other Items (Net)	27r	–6.2	–12.2	I –20.9	198.5	74.1	304.7	205.2	278.7	420.7	–153.9	1,198.9	1,278.1	777.8	632.8	. . . .
Monetary Survey																
End of Period																
Foreign Assets (Net)	31n	–283.6	–347.2	I –1373.0	–1,489.3	–2,103.5	–2,365.4	–2,114.7	–2,879.0	–2,911.3	–2,644.1	–3,292.4	–2,216.8	–3,824.9	–4,141.6	. . . .
Domestic Credit	32	3,342.6	3,963.3	I 5,715.4	6,704.4	8,250.4	9,628.7	10,745.3	12,820.6	I 17338.2	17,645.5	18,488.0	19,799.5	21,143.4	23,361.6	. . . .
Claims on Central Govt. (Net)	32an	1,698.2	1,987.8	I 3,461.1	4,133.1	5,170.5	6,273.8	6,881.1	8,670.2	I 12594.8	12,275.1	11,765.0	11,966.1	11,920.3	11,598.7	. . . .
Claims on Official Entities	32bx	. . . .	. . . .	413.7	515.4	620.6	526.9	674.7	415.0	478.3	527.7	589.1	707.6	746.6	938.9	. . . .
Claims on Private Sector	32d	1,368.0	1,683.6	I 1,513.4	1,741.3	2,129.9	2,415.3	2,777.9	3,278.5	3,873.8	4,534.9	5,836.6	6,830.4	8,089.2	10,638.9	. . . .
Claims on Other Banking Insts	32f	276.5	291.8	I 327.2	314.6	329.4	412.7	411.7	456.9	391.3	307.8	297.3	295.3	387.3	185.2	. . . .
Money	34	743.3	896.0	I 1,057.7	1,205.7	1,486.4	1,848.1	2,097.6	2,377.0	2,644.4	3,385.8	3,839.8	4,334.9	5,031.3	5,561.2	. . . .
Quasi-Money	35	2,210.6	2,641.2	I 3,101.7	3,841.2	4,705.3	5,228.7	5,618.7	5,946.7	6,250.1	7,712.0	8,594.3	9,747.3	10,581.9	11,098.9	. . . .
Restricted Deposits	36b	. . . .	. . . .	1,489.7	1,774.6	2,004.5	2,392.3	3,325.6	4,064.3	4,895.2	4,564.8	4,818.2	4,983.4	3,618.2	3,701.8	. . . .
Other Items (Net)	37r	1,839.9	2,193.2	I –1306.8	–1,606.6	–2,049.4	–2,205.8	–2,411.2	–2,446.4	637.3	–661.2	–2,056.7	–1,482.9	–1,913.0	–1,142.0	. . . .
Money plus Quasi-Money	35l	2,953.9	3,537.2	I 4,159.4	5,047.0	6,191.7	7,076.8	7,716.3	8,323.7	8,894.5	11,097.8	12,434.1	14,082.2	15,613.2	16,660.2	. . . .
Other Banking Institutions																
End of Period																
Cash	40	49.8	84.0	119.8	115.0	229.8	153.1	181.3	211.0	245.4	525.0	528.7	653.1	995.6	964.6	. . . .
Claims on Central Government	42a	56.5	50.6	135.2	249.8	335.6	794.2	785.7	1,773.9	2,852.9	3,195.2	3,877.3	3,685.8	3,970.8	3,714.4	. . . .
Claims on Nonfin.Pub.Enterprises	42c	569.8	703.2	691.1	822.1	982.1	801.1	939.8	634.5	737.9	639.5	655.6	507.7	496.5	514.7	. . . .
Claims on Private Sector	42d	1,032.0	1,209.9	1,500.9	1,733.4	2,113.7	2,416.8	2,848.2	3,081.9	2,774.9	3,001.5	3,320.4	3,560.7	3,834.8	3,107.2	. . . .
Demand Deposits	44	61.0	69.2	83.3	99.1	120.2	154.1	150.9	154.6	225.5	275.1	305.9	460.8	477.9	396.1	. . . .
Time, Savings,& Fgn.Currency Dep.	45	886.5	1,057.3	1,347.4	1,702.4	2,126.3	2,424.0	2,696.2	3,122.8	3,513.6	4,214.8	5,091.0	5,593.1	6,125.2	5,490.4	. . . .
Bonds	46ab	184.6	244.3	251.6	399.5	481.2	594.0	663.2	744.5	767.6	883.9	582.6	115.1	148.0	180.3	. . . .
Foreign Liabilities	46c	279.9	337.7	383.8	439.0	531.8	616.8	770.5	972.8	1,131.2	1,309.6	1,322.5	1,221.8	1,494.4	606.8	. . . .
of which: Natls.Residing Abroad	46cx	174.0	216.6	257.5	302.2	362.9	427.6	518.3	639.8	732.5	803.9	824.9	788.9	926.2	389.9	. . . .
Credit from Monetary Authorities	46j	278.5	300.1	277.3	208.4	226.6	216.9	221.6	213.4	229.1	170.5	238.7	185.9	272.2	166.4	. . . .
Capital Accounts	47a	159.7	219.7	263.9	347.4	423.2	543.6	711.2	774.7	908.5	777.8	938.6	1,046.2	984.4	1,122.7	. . . .
Other Items (Net)	47r	–142.2	–180.8	–160.4	–275.5	–248.0	–384.2	–458.4	–281.4	–164.4	–270.6	–97.2	–215.6	–204.5	338.3	. . . .
Liquid Liabilities	55l	3,851.6	4,579.7	5,470.3	6,733.5	8,208.4	9,501.8	10,382.0	11,390.1	12,388.1	15,062.7	17,302.2	19,482.9	21,220.7	21,582.0	. . . .

Greece

	1970	1971	1972	1973	1974	1975	1976	1977	1978	1979	1980	1981	1982	1983	1984
Interest Rates														*Percent Per Annum*	
Central Bank Rate 60	6.5	6.5	6.5	9.0	8.0	10.0	10.0	11.0	14.0	19.0	20.5	20.5	20.5	20.5	20.5
Treasury Bill Rate 60c	....	....	....	....	....	....	....	....	....	....	....	....	....	....	....
Deposit Rate 60l	5.80	5.80	5.80	5.80	9.83	9.58	8.92	8.50	9.96	11.88	14.50	14.50	14.50	14.50	15.42
Lending Rate 60p	8.00	8.00	8.00	9.00	11.83	11.88	11.50	12.00	13.46	16.71	21.25	21.33	20.50	20.50	20.50
Government Bond Yield 61	....	....	....	....	....	....	....	....	....	....	....	....	....	....	18.46
Prices, Production, Labor														*Index Numbers (1995=100):*	
Wholesale Prices 63	‡2.9	3.0	3.2	3.9	5.1	5.6	6.4	7.2	8.0	9.6	‡12.4	....	....	21.7	26.3
Home and Import Goods 63a	‡2.8	2.9	3.1	3.7	4.9	5.4	6.1	6.9	7.7	9.2	11.9	15.0	17.6	21.0	25.3
Consumer Prices 64	2.4	2.5	2.6	3.0	3.8	4.3	4.9	5.5	6.2	7.4	9.2	‡11.4	13.8	16.6	19.7
Harmonized CPI 64h	....	....	....	....	....	....	....	....	....	....	....	....	....	....	....
Wages: Hourly Earnings 65	1.3	1.4	1.5	1.8	2.2	2.8	3.6	4.3	5.4	6.5	8.2	10.5	14.0	16.7	21.1
Manufacturing Production 66ey	51.2	56.2	65.0	75.3	73.9	77.1	85.2	86.5	93.1	98.8	‡99.7	....	98.3	96.9	98.2
Industrial Employment 67ey	88.6	94.0	97.5	103.5	104.7	105.6	112.0	117.2	120.9	124.2	125.6	127.0	127.1	125.7	126.1
														Number in Thousands:	
Labor Force 67d	....	....	....	....	....	....	....	....	....	....	....	....	....	....	....
Employment 67e	....	....	....	....	....	....	....	....	....	....	....	....	....	....	....
Unemployment 67c	....	....	....	....	....	....	....	....	....	....	....	....	....	....	....
Unemployment Rate (%) 67r	....	....	....	....	....	....	....	....	....	....	....	....	....	....	....
International Transactions														*Millions of US Dollars*	
Exports .... 70..d	.6	.7	.9	1.5	2.0	2.3	2.6	2.8	3.4	3.9	5.2	4.2	4.3	4.4	4.8
Imports, c.i.f. .... 71..d	2.0	2.1	2.3	3.5	4.4	5.4	6.1	6.9	7.8	9.6	10.5	8.8	10.0	9.5	9.4
														1995=100	
Volume of Exports 72	15.1	15.6	19.7	24.7	27.1	29.5	34.1	‡33.5	38.8	40.9	45.1	38.0	38.1	43.5	52.8
Volume of Imports 73	18.9	20.2	23.2	29.3	26.7	26.1	28.2	‡29.8	31.3	34.1	31.6	31.6	35.0	38.3	38.5
Unit Value of Exp. 74	5.2	5.2	5.4	6.9	9.2	10.3	11.2	‡12.3	12.9	13.9	20.0	24.6	29.6	35.5	41.0
Unit Value of Imp. 75	4.6	4.8	5.2	6.2	9.1	10.7	12.0	‡12.5	13.4	16.5	22.5	26.0	32.4	37.4	46.6
Export Prices 76	3.2	3.3	3.6	5.3	‡6.3	6.5	7.7	9.2	9.7	12.2	15.4	19.3	20.8	‡24.9	32.3
Import Prices 76.x	2.1	2.3	2.6	3.2	‡4.4	4.9	5.6	6.3	7.1	8.5	10.9	14.3	‡16.5	20.0	24.8
Balance of Payments														*Millions of US Dollars:*	
Current Account, n.i.e. .... 78al d	....	....	....	....	....	....	−929	−1,075	−955	−1,886	−2,209	−2,408	−1,892	−1,878	−2,132
Goods: Exports f.o.b. .... 78aa d							2,258	2,583	3,036	3,991	4,175	4,884	4,273	4,179	4,426
Goods: Imports f.o.b. .... 78ab d							−4,997	−5,728	−6,530	−8,997	−9,717	−10,221	−8,972	−8,449	−8,648
Trade Balance .... 78ac d							−2,739	−3,145	−3,494	−5,006	−5,542	−5,337	−4,699	−4,270	−4,222
Services: Credit .... 78ad d							1,808	2,133	2,705	3,436	3,947	3,953	3,360	2,857	2,724
Services: Debit .... 78ae d							−677	−829	−985	−1,308	−1,428	−1,720	−1,562	−1,411	−1,309
Balance on Goods & Services .... 78af d							−1,608	−1,841	−1,774	−2,878	−3,023	−3,104	−2,901	−2,824	−2,807
Income: Credit .... 78ag d							136	118	164	253	252	346	258	130	183
Income: Debit .... 78ah d							−267	−275	−327	−426	−525	−887	−848	−951	−1,140
Balance on Gds, Serv. & Inc. .... 78ai d							−1,739	−1,998	−1,937	−3,051	−3,296	−3,645	−3,491	−3,645	−3,764
Current Transfers, n.i.e.: Credit .... 78aj d							812	926	985	1,169	1,091	1,241	1,603	1,771	1,636
Current Transfers: Debit .... 78ak d							−2	−3	−3	−4	−4	−4	−4	−4	−4
Capital Account, n.i.e. .... 78bc d	....	....	....	....	....	....	—	—	—	—	—	—	—	—	—
Capital Account, n.i.e.: Credit .... 78ba d							—	—	—	—	—	—	—	—	—
Capital Account: Debit .... 78bb d							—	—	—	—	—	—	—	—	—
Financial Account, n.i.e. .... 78bj d	....	....	....	....	....	....	922	1,313	1,419	1,424	2,468	1,769	1,283	2,391	2,172
Direct Investment Abroad .... 78bd d							—	—	—	—	—	—	—	—	—
Dir. Invest. in Rep. Econ., n.i.e. .... 78be d							305	387	428	613	672	520	436	439	485
Portfolio Investment Assets .... 78bf d							—	—	—	—	—	—	—	—	—
Equity Securities .... 78bk d							—	—	—	—	—	—	—	—	—
Debt Securities .... 78bl d							—	—	—	—	—	—	—	—	—
Portfolio Investment Liab., n.i.e. .... 78bg d							−1	−1	—	—	—	—	—	—	—
Equity Securities .... 78bm d							—	—	—	—	—	—	—	—	—
Debt Securities .... 78bn d							−1	−1	—	—	—	—	—	—	—
Financial Derivatives Assets .... 78bw d							....	....	....	....	....	....	....	....	....
Financial Derivatives Liabilities .... 78bx d							....	....	....	....	....	....	....	....	....
Other Investment Assets .... 78bh d							−4	−54	83	−332	−399	—	—	—	—
Monetary Authorities .... 78bo d							....	....	....	....	....	....	....	....	....
General Government .... 78bp d							65	44	46	—	—	—	—	—	—
Banks .... 78bq d							−69	−98	37	−332	−399	—	—	—	—
Other Sectors .... 78br d							....	....	....	....	....	....	....	....	....
Other Investment Liab., n.i.e. .... 78bi l							622	981	908	1,143	2,195	1,249	847	1,952	1,687
Monetary Authorities .... 78bs d							−91	113	178	8	690	243	367	499	430
General Government .... 78bt d							−28	−17	50	−33	−95	−13	−89	18	−17
Banks .... 78bu d							496	556	367	441	633	354	129	312	223
Other Sectors .... 78bv d							245	329	313	727	967	665	440	1,123	1,051
Net Errors and Omissions .... 78ca d	....	....	....	....	....	....	−127	−108	−270	470	−395	446	47	−313	−242
Overall Balance .... 78cb d							−134	130	194	8	−136	−193	−562	200	−202
Reserves and Related Items .... 79da d	....	....	....	....	....	....	134	−130	−194	−8	136	193	562	−200	202
Reserve Assets .... 79db d							5	−88	−144	92	227	234	128	−100	−131
Use of Fund Credit and Loans .... 79dc d							67	−83	10	−49	−90	−75	−16	—	—
Exceptional Financing .... 79de d							62	41	−60	−51	−1	35	450	−100	333

	1985	1986	1987	1988	1989	1990	1991	1992	1993	1994	1995	1996	1997	1998	1999		
Interest Rates																	
Percent Per Annum																	
Central Bank Rate	20.5	20.5	20.5	19.0	19.0	19.0	19.0	19.0	21.5	20.5	18.0	16.5	14.5	....	⅋11.8		60
Treasury Bill Rate		17.0	17.3	16.3	16.5	18.5	18.8	17.7	18.2	18.2	14.3	11.9	9.5	12.0	9.5		60c
Deposit Rate	15.50	15.50	15.33	⅋17.33	17.14	19.52	20.67	19.92	19.33	18.92	15.75	13.51	10.11	10.70	8.69		60l
Lending Rate	20.50	20.50	21.82	22.89	23.26	27.62	29.45	28.71	28.56	27.44	23.05	20.96	18.92	18.56	15.00		60p
Government Bond Yield	15.77	15.78	....	16.56	....	....	....	....	....	....	....	....	....	8.48	6.30		61
Prices, Production, Labor																	
Period Averages																	
Wholesale Prices	31.7	36.9	40.5	44.6	50.6	58.7	68.5	76.3	85.3	92.8	100.0	⅋106.1	109.6	113.9	116.3		63
Home and Import Goods	30.4	36.0	39.6	43.6	49.1	57.8	68.2	76.5	85.7	93.1	100.0	⅋106.2	109.8	114.3	117.3		63a
Consumer Prices	23.5	28.9	33.6	⅋38.2	43.4	52.3	62.4	72.3	82.8	⅋91.8	100.0	108.2	114.2	119.6	122.8		64
Harmonized CPI	....	....	....	....	....	....	....	....	....	....	100.0	107.9	113.7	118.9	121.4		64h
Wages: Hourly Earnings	25.3	28.5	31.2	37.0	44.6	53.2	62.1	70.7	78.1	88.3	100.0	108.6	118.3	123.9	....		65
Manufacturing Production	100.7	100.0	98.0	102.9	105.3	102.3	101.4	100.1	96.8	97.9	⅋100.0	100.2	102.2	106.5	107.2		66ey
Industrial Employment	124.6	124.8	123.1	124.4	124.7	122.8	115.2	109.5	103.0	99.9	100.0	99.4	96.2	95.3	....		67ey
Period Averages																	
Labor Force				3,953	....	....	3,873	4,034	4,112	4,189	4,245	4,314	4,293	....	....		67d
Employment	3,589	3,601	3,597	3,657	3,671	3,719	3,632	3,685	3,720	3,790	3,824	3,872	3,854	....	....		67e
Unemployment		287	286	303	296	281	301	350	398	404	425	446	440	....	....		67c
Unemployment Rate (%)		7.4	7.4	7.7	7.5	7.0	7.7	8.7	9.7	9.6	10.0	10.3	10.3	....	....		67r
International Transactions																	
Millions of US Dollars																	
Exports	4.5	5.6	6.5	5.4	7.5	8.1	8.7	9.8	8.4	9.4	11.0	9.5	8.6	....	....		70..d
Imports, c.i.f.	10.1	11.4	13.2	12.3	16.2	19.8	21.6	23.2	22.0	18.7	22.9	24.1	23.6	23.2	....		71..d
1995=100																	
Volume of Exports	⅋52.7	61.6	69.6	46.8	64.4	61.0	69.9	89.5	87.1	90.7	100.0	106.8	118.7	....	....		72
Volume of Imports	⅋43.7	44.3	54.0	40.5	54.6	61.4	69.2	79.8	87.5	92.2	100.0	109.0	110.7	....	....		73
Unit Value of Exp.	46.9	50.4	53.9	65.3	75.1	⅋81.8	89.0	86.9	89.2	99.3	100.0	105.2	100.7	....	....		74
Unit Value of Imp.	53.9	60.8	59.4	73.0	81.7	⅋89.4	97.7	98.4	99.6	98.4	100.0	105.4	112.3	....	....		75
Export Prices	39.4	43.0	46.3	52.9	60.5	63.6	70.5	75.0	83.5	90.7	100.0	⅋105.6	108.7	112.0	111.9		76
Import Prices	30.6	36.9	41.0	46.7	52.6	59.1	67.8	76.3	85.6	93.5	100.0	⅋101.6	103.8	109.4	110.0		76.x
Balance of Payments																	
Minus Sign Indicates Debit																	
Current Account, n.i.e.	-3,276	-1,676	-1,223	-958	-2,561	-3,537	-1,574	-2,140	-747	-146	-2,864	-4,554	-4,860	....	....		78al d
Goods: Exports f.o.b.	4,357	4,586	5,699	6,015	6,074	6,458	6,911	6,076	5,112	5,338	5,918	5,890	5,576	....	....		78aa d
Goods: Imports f.o.b.	-9,370	-8,961	-11,134	-12,042	-13,401	-16,564	-16,933	-17,637	-15,611	-16,611	-20,343	-21,395	-20,951	....	....		78ab d
Trade Balance	-5,013	-4,375	-5,435	-6,027	-7,327	-10,106	-10,022	-11,561	-10,499	-11,273	-14,425	-15,505	-15,375	....	....		78ac d
Services: Credit	2,600	3,213	4,332	5,094	4,828	6,560	7,222	8,697	8,214	9,213	9,605	9,348	9,287	....	....		78ad d
Services: Debit	-1,401	-1,574	-1,726	-2,164	-2,415	-3,000	-3,193	-3,701	-3,521	-3,774	-4,368	-4,238	-4,650	....	....		78ae d
Balance on Goods & Services	-3,814	-2,736	-2,829	-3,097	-4,914	-6,546	-5,993	-6,565	-5,806	-5,834	-9,188	-10,395	-10,738	....	....		78af d
Income: Credit	154	106	185	269	283	315	421	555	927	1,099	1,312	1,156	1,208	....	....		78ag d
Income: Debit	-1,282	-1,413	-1,614	-1,779	-1,913	-2,024	-2,185	-2,605	-2,367	-2,347	-2,996	-3,337	-2,840	....	....		78ah d
Balance on Gds, Serv. & Inc.	-4,942	-4,043	-4,258	-4,607	-6,544	-8,255	-7,757	-8,615	-7,246	-7,082	-10,872	-12,576	-12,370	....	....		78ai d
Current Transfers, n.i.e.: Credit	1,670	2,375	3,044	3,663	3,996	4,730	6,199	6,489	6,516	6,964	8,039	8,053	7,538	....	....		78aj d
Current Transfers: Debit	-4	-8	-9	-14	-13	-12	-16	-14	-17	-28	-31	-31	-28	....	....		78ak d
Capital Account, n.i.e.	—	—	—	—	—	—	—	—	—	—	—	—	—	....	....		78bc d
Capital Account, n.i.e.: Credit	—	—	—	—	—	—	—	—	—	—	—	—	—	....	....		78ba d
Capital Account: Debit	—	—	—	—	—	—	—	—	—	—	—	—	—	....	....		78bb d
Financial Account, n.i.e.	2,924	2,408	1,974	1,854	2,751	4,002	3,961	2,619	4,817	6,903	3,162	8,658	119	....	....		78bj d
Direct Investment Abroad	—	—	—	—	—	—	—	—	—	—	—	—	—	....	....		78bd d
Dir. Invest. in Rep. Econ., n.i.e.	447	471	683	907	752	1,005	1,135	1,144	977	981	1,053	1,058	984	....	....		78be d
Portfolio Investment Assets	—	—	—	—	—	—	—	—	—	—	—	—	—	....	....		78bf d
Equity Securities	—	—	—	—	—	—	—	—	—	—	—	—	—	....	....		78bk d
Debt Securities	—	—	—	—	—	—	—	—	—	—	—	—	—	....	....		78bl d
Portfolio Investment Liab., n.i.e.	—	—	—	—	—	—	—	—	—	—	—	—	—	....	....		78bg d
Equity Securities	—	—	—	—	—	—	—	—	—	—	—	—	—	....	....		78bm d
Debt Securities	—	—	—	—	—	—	—	—	—	—	—	—	—	....	....		78bn d
Financial Derivatives Assets	....	....	....	....	....	....	....	....	....	....	....	....	....	....	....		78bw d
Financial Derivatives Liabilities	....	....	....	....	....	....	....	....	....	....	....	....	....	....	....		78bx d
Other Investment Assets	....	....	....	....	....	....	....	....	....	....	....	....	980	....	....		78bh d
Monetary Authorities	....	....	....	....	....	....	....	....	....	....	....	....	....	....	....		78bo d
General Government	....	....	....	....	....	....	....	....	....	....	....	....	980	....	....		78bp d
Banks	—	—	—	—	—	—	—	—	—	—	—	—	—	....	....		78bq d
Other Sectors	—	—	—	—	—	—	—	—	—	—	—	—	—	....	....		78br d
Other Investment Liab., n.i.e.	2,477	1,937	1,291	947	1,999	2,997	2,826	1,475	3,840	5,922	2,109	7,600	-1,845	....	....		78bi d
Monetary Authorities	1,386	650	-92	288	736	367	710	1,460	2,584	-1,791	-2,385	-2,194	-2,570	....	....		78bs d
General Government	28	781	851	-145	255	936	688	-1,773	884	4,703	3,441	3,530	7,101	....	....		78bt d
Banks	227	190	321	143	503	581	175	-2	78	89	-2,110	-598	-3,348	....	....		78bu d
Other Sectors	836	316	211	661	505	1,113	1,253	1,790	294	2,921	3,163	6,862	-3,028	....	....		78bv d
Net Errors and Omissions	-44	-82	223	41	-538	-185	-183	-853	-631	-448	-321	111	226	....	....		78ca d
Overall Balance	-396	650	974	937	-348	280	2,204	-374	3,439	6,309	-23	4,215	-4,515	....	....		78cb d
Reserves and Related Items	396	-650	-974	-937	348	-280	-2,204	374	-3,439	-6,309	23	-4,215	4,515	....	....		79da d
Reserve Assets	141	-270	-806	-1,148	341	-40	-1,660	188	-3,019	-6,309	23	-4,215	4,515	....	....		79db d
Use of Fund Credit and Loans	—	—	—	—	—	—	—	—	—	—	—	—	—	....	....		79dc d
Exceptional Financing	255	-380	-168	211	7	-240	-544	186	-420	—	—	—	—	....	....		79de d

Greece

		1970	1971	1972	1973	1974	1975	1976	1977	1978	1979	1980	1981	1982	1983	1984
Government Finance																*Billions of Drachmas:*
Budgetary Central Government																
Deficit (-) or Surplus	**80**	-5.2	-6.4	-9.8	-11.0	-18.0	-26.3	-31.2	-35.8	-42.4	-51.5	-53.4	-176.8	-174.5	-283.3	-351.0
Revenue	**81**	54.3	59.4	69.4	83.9	100.8	134.2	170.4	205.2	242.0	306.2	341.3	404.2	590.4	721.0	936.5
Grants Received	**81z**	.2	.2	.9	1.4	1.7	.8	.8	.8	.6	.4	.6	8.3	7.7	5.7	7.5
Expenditure	**82**	59.7	66.0	80.1	96.4	120.6	161.3	202.4	241.7	285.0	358.2	395.4	589.3	772.6	1,010.0	1,295.0
Financing																
Net Borrowing	**84**	5.2	6.4	9.8	11.0	18.0	26.3	31.2	35.8	42.4	51.5	53.4	176.8	174.5	283.3	351.0
Borrowing: Domestic	**84c**	5.6	7.3	10.5	7.3	17.0	16.0	35.8	39.3	36.5	41.4	38.0	153.2	148.5	229.4	233.9
Foreign	**85c**	2.7	2.7	3.2	8.6	5.2	15.4	1.0	4.7	14.6	20.5	26.1	43.0	47.6	77.9	159.4
Amortization	**84y**	-3.2	-3.6	-3.9	-4.9	-4.2	-5.1	-5.6	-8.2	-8.6	-10.4	-10.6	-19.3	-21.7	-24.0	-42.2
National Accounts																*Billions of Drachmas*
Househ.Cons.Expend.,incl.NPISHs	**96f**	206.8	224.5	248.1	307.1	381.9	454.0	542.5	634.9	756.8	904.9	1,104.6	1,383.1	1,734.2	2,053.6	2,461.4
Government Consumption Expend.	**91f**	37.7	41.4	45.9	55.4	78.1	102.0	124.3	153.8	185.2	233.5	280.0	368.5	471.2	579.4	742.8
Gross Fixed Capital Formation	**93e**	70.7	83.3	104.8	135.7	125.5	139.9	175.0	221.4	278.0	369.2	413.7	456.4	513.5	624.0	702.9
Changes in Inventories	**93i**	13.3	9.0	6.8	37.5	39.9	41.4	41.7	33.3	43.4	61.6	75.7	64.3	29.8	49.2	60.4
Exports of Goods and Services	**90c**	30.0	34.1	44.3	68.9	90.8	113.3	145.1	162.3	204.4	249.6	357.7	422.4	473.0	609.5	824.6
Imports of Goods & Services	**98c**	-55.0	-60.9	-75.7	-122.1	-144.7	-180.6	-213.1	-243.3	-286.1	-360.8	-448.9	-556.1	-738.3	-925.4	-1,139.1
Gross Domestic Product (GDP)	**99b**	298.9	330.3	377.7	484.1	564.2	672.2	825.0	963.7	1,161.4	1,428.7	1,711.0	2,050.1	2,574.6	3,079.2	3,805.7
Gross National Income (GNI)	**99a**	304.4	338.2	387.3	497.2	582.1	691.4	849.9	994.0	1,193.8	1,472.2	1,767.6	2,109.1	2,632.4	3,109.6	3,807.6
GDP Volume 1970 Prices	**99b.** p	298.9	320.2	348.6	374.1	360.5	382.4	406.7	420.7	448.8	465.4	473.5	473.8	475.7	477.6	490.7
GDP Volume 1995 Prices	**99b.** p	....	....	....	....	....	....	....	....	....	....	....	....	....	....	....
GDP Volume (1995=100)	**99bv** p	51.0	54.6	59.5	63.8	61.5	65.3	69.4	71.8	76.6	79.4	80.8	80.9	81.2	81.5	83.7
GDP Deflator (1995=100)	**99bi** p	2.2	2.2	2.3	2.8	3.4	3.8	4.4	4.9	5.6	6.6	7.8	9.3	11.6	13.9	16.7
																Millions:
Population	**99z**	8.79	8.83	8.89	8.93	8.96	9.05	9.17	9.27	9.36	9.45	9.64	9.73	9.79	9.85	9.90

	1985	1986	1987	1988	1989	1990	1991	1992	1993	1994	1995	1996	1997	1998	1999		
Year Ending December 31																**Government Finance**	
																Budgetary Central Government	
	−586.6	−519.9	−703.3	−1,045.1	−1,553.1	−1,814.3	−1,775.0	−1,358.4	−2,431.7	−5,050.3	−3,252.2	−2,904.2	....	....	....	Deficit (-) or Surplus	80
	1,114.4	1,464.9	1,707.4	1,936.0	2,134.8	2,888.0	3,679.6	4,617.6	4,989.1	5,883.4	6,753.5	7,306.9	....	....	....	Revenue	81
	7.9	30.1	10.7	56.0	63.0	103.3	137.3	204.0	292.6	308.3	360.1	649.5	....	....	....	Grants Received	81z
	1,708.9	2,014.9	2,421.3	3,037.1	3,751.0	4,805.7	5,591.9	6,180.0	7,713.4	11,242.0	10,365.8	10,860.6	....	....	....	Expenditure	82
																Financing	
	586.6	519.9	703.3	1,045.1	1,553.1	1,814.3	1,775.0	1,358.4	2,431.7	5,050.3	3,252.2	2,904.2	....	....	....	Net Borrowing	84
	395.8	350.0	643.4	1,021.5	1,498.2	1,922.7	2,205.4	2,892.3	3,385.9	6,439.2	5,111.7	5,180.4	....	....	....	Borrowing: Domestic	84c
	257.1	292.7	320.7	175.6	260.0	230.3	490.8	649.0	649.8	1,138.0	914.0	1,362.0	....	....	....	Foreign	85c
	−66.2	−122.8	−260.8	−152.0	−205.1	−338.7	−921.1	−2,182.9	−1,604.0	−2,526.9	−2,773.5	−3,638.2	....	....	....	Amortization	84y
Billions of Drachmas																**National Accounts**	
	3,025.5	3,718.9	4,356.3	6,502.0	7,827.7	9,627.7	11,851.4	14,033.5	15,900.9	18,012.1	I 19907.6	22,050.8	23,905.7	25,541.6	26,860.8	Househ.Cons.Expend.,incl.NPISHs	96f
	942.0	1,067.2	1,224.8	1,311.0	1,654.5	2,007.0	2,337.9	2,613.9	3,063.3	3,345.4	I 4,174.1	4,348.0	4,976.6	5,520.5	5,698.4	Government Consumption Expend.	91f
	880.4	1,018.1	1,074.7	1,966.7	2,447.4	3,027.1	3,650.3	3,983.8	4,267.1	4,453.5	I 5,066.0	5,829.1	6,950.1	7,931.2	8,817.5	Gross Fixed Capital Formation	93e
	102.9	75.0	28.3	I 53.4	−24.1	−39.5	152.9	−60.4	−75.5	25.8	I 85.7	95.5	−138.1	−268.2	−297.6	Changes in Inventories	93i
	977.6	1,233.1	1,536.8	1,696.4	1,982.8	2,209.8	2,620.7	3,174.5	3,355.5	3,904.0	I 4,800.2	5,245.6	5,871.7	6,331.3	6,824.8	Exports of Goods and Services	90c
	−1,513.5	−1,703.3	−1,993.4	−2,360.5	−2,993.1	−3,689.0	−4,382.7	−4,979.2	−5,375.6	−5,757.2	I -6792.4	−7,633.9	−8,544.2	−9,145.8	−9,670.5	Imports of Goods & Services	98c
	4,617.8	5,514.7	6,271.9	I 9,169.0	10,895.2	13,143.1	16,230.5	18,766.1	21,135.7	23,983.6	I 27235.2	29,935.1	33,021.8	35,910.6	38,233.4	Gross Domestic Product (GDP)	99b
	4,584.0	5,446.9	6,208.6	I 9,151.7	10,865.9	13,248.2	16,427.0	19,015.9	21,273.5	24,195.7	I 28096.9	30,770.3	34,034.1	37,009.2	39,418.6	Gross National Income (GNI)	99a
	506.0	514.2	511.8	534.6	553.5	550.4	569.4	571.9	566.7	575.0	586.0	....	....	....	....	GDP Volume 1970 Prices	99b.p
	....	....	....	....	....	....	....	....	....	....	27,235.2	27,877.5	28,831.1	29,885.8	30,887.0	GDP Volume 1995 Prices	99b.p
	86.3	87.7	87.3	91.2	94.5	93.9	97.2	97.6	96.7	98.1	100.0	102.4	105.9	109.7	113.4	GDP Volume (1995=100)	99bv p
	19.6	23.1	26.4	I 36.9	42.4	51.4	61.3	70.6	80.2	89.7	I 100.0	107.4	114.5	120.2	123.8	GDP Deflator (1995=100)	99bi p
Midyear Estimates																	
	9.93	9.97	10.00	10.04	10.09	10.16	10.25	10.32	10.38	10.43	10.45	10.48	10.50	10.52	10.63	**Population**	99z

(See notes in the back of the book.)

Grenada

		1970	1971	1972	1973	1974	1975	1976	1977	1978	1979	1980	1981	1982	1983	1984
Exchange Rates														*E.Caribbean Dollars per SDR: End of Period (aa)*		
Official Rate	aa	2.0053	2.0417	2.2194	2.4925	2.5024	2.7770	3.1369	3.2797	3.5175	3.5568	3.4436	3.1427	2.9784	2.8268	2.6466
Official Rate	ae	2.0053	1.8805	2.0442	2.0661	2.0439	2.3721	2.7000	2.7000	2.7000	2.7000	2.7000	2.7000	2.7000	2.7000	2.7000
													Index Numbers (1995=100):			
Official Rate	ahx	134.8	137.3	140.7	137.9	131.6	125.0	100.0	100.0	100.0	100.0	100.0	100.0	100.0	100.0	100.0
Nominal Effective Exchange Rate	nec	....	....	....	....	....	....	....	....	....	50.3	49.0	52.9	56.4	59.4	63.8
Real Effective Exchange Rate	rec	....	....	....	....	....	....	....	....	....	88.0	91.5	105.8	112.3	118.4	126.3
Fund Position														*Millions of SDRs:*		
Quota	2f. s	....	....	....	....	....	2.00	2.00	2.00	3.00	3.00	4.50	4.50	4.50	6.00	6.00
SDRs	1b. s	....	....	....	....	....	.07	.09	.02	—	.01	—	—	.01	.14	.02
Reserve Position in the Fund	1c. s	....	....	....	....	....	—	—	—	—	—	—	—	—	—	—
Total Fund Cred.&Loans Outstg.	2tl	....	....	....	....	....	.81	1.21	1.42	2.03	2.40	2.21	7.10	6.27	7.32	6.30
International Liquidity											*Millions of US Dollars Unless Otherwise Indicated:*					
Total Reserves minus Gold	1l. d	5.32	5.82	5.60	5.00	5.36	‡5.04	8.11	7.65	9.70	12.22	12.91	16.10	9.23	14.14	14.23
SDRs	1b. d	—	—	—	—	—	.08	.10	.02	—	.01	—	—	.01	.15	.02
Reserve Position in the Fund	1c. d	—	—	—	—	—	—	—	—	—	—	—	—	—	—	—
Foreign Exchange	1d. d	5.32	5.82	5.60	5.00	5.36	‡4.95	8.01	7.63	9.70	12.21	12.91	16.10	9.22	14.00	14.21
Deposit Money Banks: Assets	7a. d	1.94	1.72	.68	1.40	4.33	6.03	5.26	4.99	5.44	11.08	10.89	12.71	6.49	7.47	8.04
Liabilities	7b. d	4.02	7.10	10.13	11.57	15.12	11.75	6.26	6.84	6.48	11.10	11.04	12.50	12.56	9.61	9.70
Monetary Authorities													*Millions of E. Caribbean Dollars:*			
Foreign Assets	11	10.63	10.72	10.32	10.34	10.96	‡11.95	21.91	20.66	26.20	32.99	34.85	43.46	24.93	38.18	38.43
Claims on Central Government	12a	.60	.70	.70	1.59	1.89	5.53	8.36	9.44	12.56	14.89	14.90	31.84	38.85	29.95	42.91
Claims on Deposit Money Banks	12e	—	—	—	—	—	—	—	—	—	—	—	—	—	—	—
Reserve Money	14	11.24	11.43	11.03	11.92	12.85	‡15.22	26.47	25.44	31.61	39.35	42.15	52.98	45.09	47.45	64.66
of which: Currency Outside DMBs	14a	6.09	6.90	8.28	8.39	9.71	12.65	15.32	18.33	23.67	28.50	32.58	37.41	39.95	41.36	20.58
Foreign Liabilities	16c	—	—	—	—	—	2.25	3.80	4.66	7.14	8.54	7.61	22.33	18.69	20.69	16.68
Central Government Deposits	16d	—	—	—	—	—	—	—	—	—	—	—	—	—	—	—
Other Items (Net)	17r	—	—	—	—	—	—	—	—	—	—	—	—	—	—	—
Deposit Money Banks													*Millions of E. Caribbean Dollars:*			
Reserves	20	4.55	3.88	1.96	2.64	2.38	‡2.57	11.15	7.11	7.95	10.85	9.57	15.56	5.14	6.08	43.27
Foreign Assets	21	3.88	3.17	1.39	2.89	8.86	‡14.30	14.20	13.48	14.70	29.93	29.39	34.32	17.52	20.17	21.71
Claims on Central Government	22a	7.97	9.77	13.43	12.13	15.33	15.45	13.26	13.14	13.34	10.12	12.42	12.05	23.53	32.57	28.53
Claims on Local Government	22b	—	—	—	—	—	—	—	—	—	—	—	—	—	—	—
Claims on Nonfin.Pub.Enterprises	22c	—	—	—	—	—	.50	.50	.50	.40	.76	1.53	2.25	10.51	8.77	7.40
Claims on Private Sector	22d	31.33	38.54	46.32	50.72	45.94	‡39.42	38.74	48.02	56.54	64.34	72.34	75.11	78.80	76.17	81.27
Claims on Nonbank Financial Insts	22g	.22	.12	.50	.50	.50	.50	.50	.49	.37	.27	.29	.50	.53	.45	1.76
Demand Deposits	24	4.72[e]	4.97[e]	6.03	7.23	6.07	6.73	11.38	11.18	14.37	17.15	15.87	15.91	19.62	16.74	30.13
Time, Savings,& Fgn.Currency Dep.	25	31.87[e]	33.54[e]	39.60	39.86	38.69	47.29	52.58	58.55	66.09	77.75	82.51	87.83	87.03	88.86	97.71
Foreign Liabilities	26c	8.05[e]	13.08[e]	20.70	23.90	30.90	‡27.88	16.91	18.48	17.48	29.98	29.80	33.75	33.90	25.95	26.20
Central Government Deposits	26d	—	—	—	—	—	—	.10	.10	.40	.71	3.31	2.28	1.12	2.49	4.73
Credit from Monetary Authorities	26g	—	—	—	—	—	—	—	—	—	—	—	—	2.54	6.41	—
Capital Accounts	27a	.85	.88	.93	.95	1.00	.98	1.12	1.20	1.30	.88	.70	3.03	3.10	9.54	17.87
Other Items (Net)	27r	2.45	3.02	–3.66	–3.07	–3.67	–10.15	–3.76	–6.78	–6.35	–10.21	–6.64	–3.01	–11.29	–5.78	7.29
Monetary Survey													*Millions of E. Caribbean Dollars:*			
Foreign Assets (Net)	31n	6.46	.82	–8.98	–10.67	–11.08	–3.89	15.40	11.00	16.27	‡24.40	26.84	21.71	–10.15	11.72	17.26
Domestic Credit	32	40.12	49.14	60.95	64.93	63.65	61.40	61.25	71.49	82.81	89.67	98.17	119.46	151.11	145.42	157.13
Claims on Central Govt. (Net)	32an	8.57	10.47	14.13	13.71	17.21	20.98	21.51	22.47	25.50	24.31	24.01	41.61	61.27	60.04	66.71
Claims on Local Government	32b	—	—	—	—	—	—	—	—	—	—	—	—	—	—	—
Claims on Nonfin.Pub.Enterprises	32c	—	—	—	—	—	.50	.50	.50	.40	.76	1.53	2.25	10.51	8.77	7.40
Claims on Private Sector	32d	31.33	38.54	46.32	50.72	45.94	39.42	38.74	48.02	56.54	64.34	72.34	75.11	78.80	76.17	81.27
Claims on Nonbank Financial Inst	32g	.22	.12	.50	.50	.50	.50	.50	.49	.37	.27	.29	.50	.53	.45	1.76
Money	34	10.81	11.87	14.31	15.62	15.79	19.38	26.70	29.51	38.04	45.65	48.45	53.32	59.57	58.10	50.71
Quasi-Money	35	31.87	33.54	39.60	39.86	38.69	47.29	52.58	58.55	66.09	77.75	82.51	87.83	87.03	88.86	97.71
Capital Accounts	37a	.85	.88	.93	.95	1.00	.98	1.12	1.20	1.30	1.98	2.83	5.95	5.87	12.17	20.33
Other Items (Net)	37r	3.05	3.66	–2.87	–2.18	–2.91	–10.15	–3.76	–6.78	–6.35	–11.31	–8.77	–5.93	–11.52	–1.99	5.64
Money plus Quasi-Money	35l	42.68	45.41	53.91	55.48	54.48	66.67	79.28	88.07	104.13	123.40	130.95	141.16	146.61	146.96	148.42
Interest Rates														*Percent Per Annum*		
Treasury Bill Rate	60c	....	....	....	....	....	....	....	....	....	....	6.5	6.5	6.5	6.5	6.5
Deposit Rate	60l	....	....	....	....	....	....	....	....	....	....	4.5	4.5	4.5	5.9	7.0
Lending Rate	60p	....	....	....	....	....	....	....	....	9.0	8.5	9.5	9.5	10.5	10.5	10.5
Prices														*Index Numbers (1995=100):*		
Consumer Prices	64	....	....	....	....	....	25.3	30.0	35.4	42.9	52.2	62.0	66.9	70.9	74.9	
International Transactions													*Millions of E. Caribbean Dollars*			
Exports	70	12.08	10.19	10.53	14.51	19.27	26.84	33.82	38.75	45.58	57.80	46.95	51.36	50.09	51.09	49.11
Imports, c.i.f.	71	44.63	46.05	42.81	42.49	37.08	52.63	66.25	87.29	96.45	117.98	135.57	146.71	152.43	154.48	151.10

	1985	1986	1987	1988	1989	1990	1991	1992	1993	1994	1995	1996	1997	1998	1999		
																Exchange Rates	
E.Caribbean Dollars per US Dollar: End of Period (ae)																	
	2.9657	3.3026	3.8304	3.6334	3.5482	3.8412	3.8622	3.7125	3.7086	3.9416	4.0135	3.8825	3.6430	3.8017	3.7058	Official Rate	aa
	2.7000	2.7000	2.7000	2.7000	2.7000	2.7000	2.7000	2.7000	2.7000	2.7000	2.7000	2.7000	2.7000	2.7000	2.7000	Official Rate	ae
Period Averages																	
	100.0	100.0	100.0	100.0	100.0	100.0	100.0	100.0	100.0	100.0	100.0	100.0	100.0	100.0	100.0	Official Rate	ah x
	65.5	62.7	59.4	58.0	61.1	63.4	68.6	74.4	88.4	101.1	100.0	102.2	106.3	107.9	110.3	Nominal Effective Exchange Rate	ne c
	126.4	117.8	105.9	102.9	107.5	99.8	99.0	98.1	103.5	103.5	100.0	101.2	103.9	105.1	105.6	Real Effective Exchange Rate	re c
																Fund Position	
End of Period																	
	6.00	6.00	6.00	6.00	6.00	6.00	6.00	8.50	8.50	8.50	8.50	8.50	8.50	8.50	11.70	Quota	2f. s
	.01	—	—	—	—	—	—	—	—	.02	.02	.04	—	.03	—	SDRs	1b. s
	—	—	—	—	—	—	—	—	—	—	—	—	—	—	—	Reserve Position in the Fund	1c. s
	3.83	2.13	1.47	.91	.35	.01	—	—	—	—	—	—	—	—	—	Total Fund Cred.&Loans Outstg.	2tl
																International Liquidity	
End of Period																	
	20.81	20.57	22.74	16.92	15.44	17.58	17.47	25.88	26.90	31.23	36.73	35.73	42.67	46.84	50.84	Total Reserves minus Gold	1l. d
	.01	—	—	—	—	—	—	—	—	.03	.02	.06	.01	.04	—	SDRs	1b. d
	—	—	—	—	—	—	—	—	—	—	—	—	—	—	—	Reserve Position in the Fund	1c. d
	20.80	20.57	22.74	16.92	15.44	17.58	17.47	25.88	26.90	31.20	36.71	35.67	42.66	46.80	50.84	Foreign Exchange	1d. d
	7.55	9.21	14.25	21.33	10.31	18.52	18.05	27.93	35.68	51.88	59.06	61.88	57.07	54.97	72.71	Deposit Money Banks: Assets	7a. d
	10.29	13.12	18.12	16.59	23.40	20.57	22.12	29.70	37.26	41.15	38.98	50.55	68.25	69.12	74.01	Liabilities	7b. d
																Monetary Authorities	
End of Period																	
	56.19	55.53	61.40	45.69	41.69	47.46	47.18	69.25	72.68	84.20	99.18	96.70	115.48	126.72	137.82	Foreign Assets	11
	37.62	33.78	32.19	33.28	36.16	36.52	37.71	35.02	28.34	24.30	21.70	20.60	18.40	18.39	15.85	Claims on Central Government	12a
	.86	.24	1.90	1.43	3.22	1.15	.85	.64	.48	.27	.09	.01	.02	.03	.02	Claims on Deposit Money Banks	12e
	83.30	82.50	89.86	77.10	79.84	85.09	85.74	104.91	100.79	107.24	116.31	116.76	131.28	139.70	148.04	Reserve Money	14
	25.07	30.69	33.07	35.13	31.40	38.05	40.35	46.68	46.56	52.96	53.83	53.18	58.35	64.08	64.75	*of which: Currency Outside DMBs*	14a
	11.37	7.04	5.63	3.31	1.24	.04	—	—	—	—	—	—	—	—	—	Foreign Liabilities	16c
	—	—	—	—	—	—	—	—	.71	1.54	4.66	.55	2.61	5.44	5.66	Central Government Deposits	16d
	—	—	—	—	—	—	—	—	—	—	—	—	—	—	—	Other Items (Net)	17r
																Deposit Money Banks	
End of Period																	
	44.69	49.72	53.80	44.15	54.19	45.53	43.15	55.55	53.14	56.10	56.87	59.35	73.43	76.10	92.36	Reserves	20
	20.39	24.85	38.49	57.60	27.83	50.00	48.74	75.42	96.33	140.08	159.47	167.09	154.08	148.42	196.32	Foreign Assets	21
	32.09	31.87	31.95	38.44	35.62	40.12	43.83	34.62	38.39	42.98	46.44	55.93	74.32	80.49	50.86	Claims on Central Government	22a
										.06	—	—	—	—	14.05	Claims on Local Government	22b
	7.38	7.88	9.55	10.57	14.49	12.83	11.04	9.38	9.74	6.71	6.12	16.07	20.92	25.88	26.13	Claims on Nonfin.Pub.Enterprises	22c
	109.67	152.02	188.60	212.70	272.99	270.74	287.52	315.02	413.64	414.60	437.29	495.26	587.95	684.68	767.87	Claims on Private Sector	22d
	.52	.51	.42	.30	.32	.36	.32	2.22	4.82	4.24	6.06	10.31	10.09	15.59	23.33	Claims on Nonbank Financial Insts	22g
	29.05	38.65	41.24	47.87	56.59	53.04	49.17	63.44	77.51	85.95	91.52	95.26	98.27	114.31	126.28	Demand Deposits	24
	123.09	157.61	179.24	216.63	234.26	263.32	283.35	290.62	364.42	409.15	455.19	504.59	564.27	627.50	722.76	Time, Savings,& Fgn.Currency Dep.	25
	27.80	35.41	48.93	44.80	63.18	55.54	59.72	80.19	100.60	111.11	105.24	136.50	184.29	186.63	199.83	Foreign Liabilities	26c
	2.65	1.25	4.80	10.35	14.89	13.08	6.98	17.03	20.35	24.37	30.55	41.02	42.04	56.74	71.04	Central Government Deposits	26d
	—	—	3.21	1.42	2.86	1.21	.83	.79	.58	.25	.07	.02	.02	2.72	.02	Credit from Monetary Authorities	26g
	19.43	22.38	27.18	28.32	30.94	35.18	43.33	47.02	64.73	68.28	71.07	72.39	79.56	86.15	97.22	Capital Accounts	27a
	12.72	11.55	18.20	14.38	2.71	−1.81	−8.78	−6.87	−12.14	−34.35	−41.39	−45.76	−47.65	−42.89	−46.22	Other Items (Net)	27r
																Monetary Survey	
End of Period																	
	37.42	37.92	45.33	55.18	5.10	41.88	36.19	64.48	68.41	113.17	153.41	127.29	85.28	88.51	134.32	Foreign Assets (Net)	31n
	184.63	224.81	257.91	284.96	344.69	347.48	373.44	379.23	473.86	466.97	482.40	556.60	667.03	762.84	821.40	Domestic Credit	32
	67.05	64.40	59.34	61.38	56.89	63.56	74.56	52.61	45.65	41.36	32.93	34.96	48.07	36.71	−9.99	Claims on Central Govt. (Net)	32an
										.06	—	—	—	—	14.05	Claims on Local Government	32b
	7.38	7.88	9.55	10.57	14.49	12.83	11.04	9.38	9.74	6.71	6.12	16.07	20.92	25.88	26.13	Claims on Nonfin.Pub.Enterprises	32c
	109.67	152.02	188.60	212.70	272.99	270.74	287.52	315.02	413.64	414.60	437.29	495.26	587.95	684.68	767.87	Claims on Private Sector	32d
	.52	.51	.42	.30	.32	.36	.32	2.22	4.82	4.24	6.06	10.31	10.09	15.59	23.33	Claims on Nonbank Financial Inst	32g
	54.12	69.34	74.31	83.00	87.99	91.09	89.50	110.12	124.07	139.05	145.60	148.46	156.64	178.38	191.03	Money	34
	123.09	157.61	179.24	216.63	234.26	263.32	283.35	290.62	364.42	409.15	455.19	504.59	564.27	627.50	722.76	Quasi-Money	35
	22.19	25.45	30.75	31.70	34.24	38.76	46.92	50.47	68.18	71.95	74.80	76.00	82.95	89.68	100.66	Capital Accounts	37a
	22.65	10.33	18.95	8.80	−6.70	−3.80	−10.14	−7.49	−14.41	−40.00	−39.78	−45.16	−51.55	−44.21	−58.74	Other Items (Net)	37r
	177.21	226.95	253.55	299.63	322.25	354.42	372.86	400.74	488.49	548.20	600.78	653.05	720.91	805.88	913.80	Money plus Quasi-Money	35l
																Interest Rates	
Percent Per Annum																	
	6.5	6.5	6.5	6.5	6.5	6.5	6.5	6.5	6.5	6.5	6.5	6.5	6.5	6.5	6.5	Treasury Bill Rate	60c
	7.0	6.5	6.1	5.5	5.0	6.5	6.2	5.5	5.0	4.2	4.0	4.1	4.5	4.6	5.2	Deposit Rate	60l
	11.7	11.5	11.4	10.5	10.7	10.5	10.6	10.5	10.5	10.5	10.5	10.5	10.5	10.5	10.5	Lending Rate	60p
																Prices	
Period Averages																	
	76.8	77.2	I 76.6	79.6	84.1	86.4	88.7	92.0	94.6	98.2	100.0	102.0	103.3	104.7	104.9	Consumer Prices	64
																International Transactions	
Millions of E. Caribbean Dollars																	
	61.33	84.36	86.10	88.50	75.40	71.60	61.50	58.20	58.10	66.40	62.60	56.70	. . . .	. . . .	. . . .	Exports	70
	187.00	225.72	239.17	248.80	267.90	283.80	327.00	287.80	388.80	322.40	349.70	411.10	. . . .	. . . .	. . . .	Imports, c.i.f.	71

Grenada

		1970	1971	1972	1973	1974	1975	1976	1977	1978	1979	1980	1981	1982	1983	1984
Balance of Payments																*Millions of US Dollars:*
Current Account, n.i.e.	78al d	...	...	...	...	...	...	...	1.31	1.05	−1.11	.24	−13.95	−17.71	−15.09	1.80
Goods: Exports f.o.b.	78aa d	...	...	...	...	...	...	...	14.26	16.90	21.40	17.40	19.00	18.50	19.30	18.20
Goods: Imports f.o.b.	78ab d	...	...	...	...	...	...	...	−28.54	−33.35	−42.64	−48.79	−56.07	−59.03	−57.88	−51.12
Trade Balance	78ac d								−14.28	−16.45	−21.24	−31.39	−37.07	−40.53	−38.58	−32.92
Services: Credit	78ad d								14.60	16.40	19.15	20.60	18.70	18.30	18.60	21.60
Services: Debit	78ae d								−4.35	−6.60	−12.42	−11.07	−13.39	−17.37	−15.82	−18.38
Balance on Goods & Services	78af d								−4.03	−6.65	−14.51	−21.86	−31.76	−39.60	−35.80	−29.70
Income: Credit	78ag d								.30	.30	.80	1.10	1.30	1.50	1.70	1.40
Income: Debit	78ah d								−.20	−.40	−.60	−3.20	−6.30	−6.50	−6.10	−2.90
Balance on Gds, Serv. & Inc.	78ai d								−3.93	−6.75	−14.31	−23.96	−36.76	−44.60	−40.20	−31.20
Current Transfers, n.i.e.: Credit	78aj d								5.24	7.80	14.90	26.10	25.11	30.19	29.61	37.20
Current Transfers: Debit	78ak d								—	—	−1.70	−1.90	−2.30	−3.30	−4.50	−4.20
Capital Account, n.i.e.	78bc d								—	—	—	—	—	—	—	—
Capital Account, n.i.e.: Credit	78ba d								—	—	—	—	—	—	—	—
Capital Account: Debit	78bb d								—	—	—	—	—	—	—	—
Financial Account, n.i.e.	78bj d								2.34	1.46	1.44	1.63	7.26	17.02	11.99	7.57
Direct Investment Abroad	78bd d								—	—	—	—	—	—	—	—
Dir. Invest. in Rep. Econ., n.i.e.	78be d								−.10	1.40	—	—	—	1.90	2.50	2.80
Portfolio Investment Assets	78bf d								—	—	—	—	—	—	—	—
Equity Securities	78bk d								—	—	—	—	—	—	—	—
Debt Securities	78bl d								—	—	—	—	—	—	—	—
Portfolio Investment Liab., n.i.e.	78bg d								—	—	—	—	—	—	—	—
Equity Securities	78bm d								—	—	—	—	—	—	—	—
Debt Securities	78bn d								—	—	—	—	—	—	—	—
Financial Derivatives Assets	78bw d								...	...	...	...	...	...	...	...
Financial Derivatives Liabilities	78bx d								...	...	...	...	...	...	...	...
Other Investment Assets	78bh d								.27	−.45	−5.40	.49	−1.83	6.22	−.98	−.57
Monetary Authorities	78bo d								...	...	...	...	...	...	...	...
General Government	78bp d								—	—	—	—	—	—	—	—
Banks	78bq d								.27	−.45	−5.40	.49	−1.83	6.22	−.98	−.57
Other Sectors	78br d								—	—	—	—	—	—	—	—
Other Investment Liab., n.i.e.	78bi d								2.17	.51	6.84	1.14	9.09	8.90	10.47	5.34
Monetary Authorities	78bs d								—	—	—	—	—	—	—	—
General Government	78bt d								1.49	.87	1.93	1.27	7.58	8.58	11.71	3.30
Banks	78bu d								.58	−.37	4.63	−.07	1.47	.06	−2.94	.09
Other Sectors	78bv d								.10	.01	.28	−.06	.03	.26	1.70	1.95
Net Errors and Omissions	78ca d								−4.02	−1.48	1.41	−.96	2.84	−1.31	2.76	−11.65
Overall Balance	78cb d								−.37	1.03	1.74	.91	−3.85	−2.00	−.34	−2.28
Reserves and Related Items	79da d								.37	−1.03	−1.74	−.91	3.85	2.00	.34	2.28
Reserve Assets	79db d								.13	−1.79	−2.22	−.69	−1.98	2.90	−1.25	.31
Use of Fund Credit and Loans	79dc d								.24	.76	.47	−.25	5.75	−.91	1.10	−1.03
Exceptional Financing	79de d								—	—	—	.03	.08	.01	.49	3.00
Government Finance														*Millions of E. Caribbean Dollars:*		
Deficit (-) or Surplus	80	...	...	...	...	...	−5.25	−5.08	−6.37	−1.66	I−10.60	−7.80	−4.60	...	...	...
Revenue	81						15.76	18.41	28.18	33.65	I44.80	55.10	59.10	...	...	...
Grants Received	81z						2.94	2.84	1.63	1.59	I1.60	34.40	29.60	...	...	...
Expenditure	82						22.79	24.52	34.43	34.77	I52.70	95.40	91.00	...	...	...
Lending Minus Repayments	83						1.16	1.81	1.75	2.13	I4.30	1.90	2.30	...	...	...
Financing																
Domestic	84a	...	...	...	...	...	3.05	6.22	5.57	1.12	I5.40	3.00	.40	...	...	...
Foreign	85a						2.20	−1.14	.80	.54	I5.20	4.80	4.20	...	...	...
National Accounts														*Millions of E. Caribbean Dollars*		
Exports of Goods & Services	90c	...	...	...	36.4	32.5	58.2	67.3	80.5	92.3	109.1	106.9	106.1	103.4	105.3	112.8
Government Consumption	91f				17.7	17.3	21.0	30.2	29.2	46.1	50.8	41.7	45.0	47.2	55.9	59.3
Gross Fixed Capital Formation	93e				15.2	13.6	6.3	13.7	14.8	13.8	31.3	52.7	91.1	107.2	106.8	80.0
Increase/Decrease(-) in Stocks	93i				...	...	—	1.6	6.2	.6	.7	3.2	4.9	−.1	−5.2	1.7
Private Consumption	96f				41.5	48.7	69.5	75.6	97.0	132.1	156.0	161.1	154.6	195.0	183.9	213.2
Imports of Goods & Services	98c				−42.5	−38.1	−58.8	−72.3	−93.4	−112.6	−145.3	−163.6	−185.0	−213.3	−193.8	−192.1
Gross Domestic Product (GDP)	99b				68.3	74.0	96.2	116.1	134.3	172.3	202.6	202.0	216.7	239.4	252.9	274.9
GDP Volume 1980 prices	99b.p				...	...	181.7	198.1	209.4	226.4	231.8	232.2	...	...	...	...
GDP Volume 1984 Prices	99b.p				...	...	...	...	...	...	...	I194.5	198.5	209.1	261.7	273.9
GDP Volume (1990=100)	99bv p				...	...	49.6	54.1	57.2	61.8	63.3	63.4	64.7	68.2	85.3	89.3
GDP Deflator (1990=100)	99bi p				21.9	23.8	32.5	36.0	39.3	46.7	53.6	53.4	56.1	58.8	49.7	51.6
																Millions:
Population	99z	.09	.10	.10	.10	.10	.11	.11	.11	.11	.09	.11	.09	.09	.09	.09

1985	1986	1987	1988	1989	1990	1991	1992	1993	1994	1995	1996	1997	1998	1999		
Minus Sign Indicates Debit															**Balance of Payments**	
2.22	−19.09	−29.19	−27.77	−36.32	−46.24	−46.58	−32.29	−43.54	−21.84	−35.22	−57.94	....	....	....	Current Account, n.i.e.	78al *d*
22.30	28.96	32.26	33.19	31.11	29.29	26.71	23.33	22.53	26.48	25.86	24.93				Goods: Exports f.o.b.	78aa *d*
−65.56	−80.89	−89.07	−92.19	−99.04	−106.26	−113.58	−103.18	−118.13	−115.60	−125.37	−147.50				Goods: Imports f.o.b.	78ab *d*
−43.26	−51.93	−56.81	−59.00	−67.93	−76.98	−86.87	−79.85	−95.59	−89.11	−99.51	−122.57				*Trade Balance*	78ac *d*
30.59	46.19	47.52	53.00	54.22	63.81	71.81	76.00	87.73	101.53	99.19	106.69				Services: Credit	78ad *d*
−21.07	−24.92	−26.02	−27.70	−29.59	−32.54	−35.54	−35.10	−41.01	−41.26	−38.54	−45.69				Services: Debit	78ae *d*
−33.74	−30.66	−35.31	−33.70	−43.30	−45.71	−50.59	−38.95	−48.87	−28.85	−38.86	−61.58				*Balance on Goods & Services*	78af *d*
1.39	1.82	1.73	2.73	2.43	2.51	2.48	3.41	2.80	3.61	4.91	4.33				Income: Credit	78ag *d*
−3.10	−7.37	−8.37	−9.00	−11.96	−14.38	−9.77	−8.74	−11.16	−12.43	−18.36	−20.04				Income: Debit	78ah *d*
−35.44	−36.21	−41.96	−39.98	−52.83	−57.58	−57.88	−44.29	−57.23	−37.67	−52.30	−77.29				*Balance on Gds, Serv. & Inc.*	78ai *d*
41.96	17.81	13.70	13.04	17.39	12.46	13.25	14.26	16.10	19.75	21.58	23.44				Current Transfers, n.i.e.: Credit	78aj *d*
−4.30	−.68	−.94	−.83	−.88	−1.11	−1.96	−2.25	−2.41	−3.92	−4.50	−4.09				Current Transfers: Debit	78ak *d*
—	15.84	10.22	12.93	9.87	22.10	17.51	13.43	16.89	21.67	25.84	29.37				Capital Account, n.i.e.	78bc *d*
—	24.44	19.33	20.85	10.69	23.36	18.51	14.80	18.27	23.04	27.28	30.89				Capital Account, n.i.e.: Credit	78ba *d*
—	−8.59	−9.11	−7.93	−.81	−1.26	−1.01	−1.38	−1.38	−1.38	−1.44	−1.52				Capital Account: Debit	78bb *d*
5.99	9.44	21.23	11.43	33.16	18.54	23.39	18.29	18.96	4.06	3.10	26.23				Financial Account, n.i.e.	78bj *d*
															Direct Investment Abroad	78bd *d*
4.11	4.48	14.72	14.98	10.48	12.87	15.27	22.58	20.20	19.31	19.98	17.90				Dir. Invest. in Rep. Econ., n.i.e.	78be *d*
—	—	—	—	—	—	—	—	—	—	—	—				Portfolio Investment Assets	78bf *d*
—	—	—	—	—	—	—	—	—	—	....	—				Equity Securities	78bk *d*
—	—	—	—	—	—	—	—	—	—	....	—				Debt Securities	78bl *d*
—	—		.15	—	.02	.05	−.16	.20	−.38	−.87	−.92				Portfolio Investment Liab., n.i.e.	78bg *d*
—	—		.15	—	.02	.05	−.16	.20	−.38	−.87	−.92				Equity Securities	78bm *d*
—	—														Debt Securities	78bn *d*
															Financial Derivatives Assets	78bw *d*
															Financial Derivatives Liabilities	78bx *d*
.49	1.19	−.01	−8.35	17.52	−11.48	2.02	−2.30	−.19	−12.31	−9.36	8.77				Other Investment Assets	78bh *d*
....	....	....	....	....	....	....	....	....	....	....	....				Monetary Authorities	78bo *d*
—	—	—	—	—	—	—	—	—	—	—	—				General Government	78bp *d*
.49	1.19	−.01	−8.35	17.52	−11.48	2.02	−2.30	−.19	−12.31	−9.36	8.77				Banks	78bq *d*
—	—	—	—	—	—	—	—	—	—	—	—				Other Sectors	78br *d*
1.39	3.78	6.52	4.65	5.16	17.13	6.04	−1.83	−1.26	−2.56	−6.66	.48				Other Investment Liab., n.i.e.	78bi *d*
—	—	—	—	—	—	—	—	—	—	—	—				Monetary Authorities	78bs *d*
.03	3.30	5.59	6.19	6.56	16.19	8.59	1.07	.31	3.77	−4.67	−.26				General Government	78bt *d*
.59															Banks	78bu *d*
.76	.48	.93	−1.54	−1.40	.94	−2.54	−2.89	−1.57	−6.33	−1.99	.74				Other Sectors	78bv *d*
−1.99	−4.25	1.55	−1.72	−7.55	8.12	8.15	8.67	8.73	.65	12.32	2.59				Net Errors and Omissions	78ca *d*
6.22	1.95	3.81	−5.14	−.84	2.53	2.46	8.10	1.04	4.54	6.03	.26				*Overall Balance*	78cb *d*
−6.22	−1.95	−3.81	5.14	.84	−2.53	−2.46	−8.10	−1.04	−4.54	−6.03	−.26				Reserves and Related Items	79da *d*
−6.76	.01	−2.96	5.89	1.56	−2.07	−2.44	−8.10	−1.04	−4.54	−6.03	−.26				Reserve Assets	79db *d*
−2.51	−1.97	−.85	−.75	−.72	−.46	−.01	—	—	—	—	—				Use of Fund Credit and Loans	79dc *d*
3.06	—	—	—	—	—	—									Exceptional Financing	79de *d*
Year Ending December 31															**Government Finance**	
....	....	....	....	....	....	I−12.23	1.18	−1.42	−7.86	16.79		....		....	Deficit (-) or Surplus	80
....	....	....	....	....	....	I165.55	165.59	178.27	194.26	205.00		....		....	Revenue	81
						I22.77	14.15	16.33	26.50	21.48				....	Grants Received	81z
						I200.55	178.56	196.02	228.62	209.69				....	Expenditure	82
						I—	—	—	—	—				....	Lending Minus Repayments	83
															Financing	
....	....	....	....	....	....	....	....	....	....	....	....	....		....	Domestic	84a
....	....	....	....	....	....	....	....	....	....	....	....	....		....	Foreign	85a
Millions of E. Caribbean Dollars															**National Accounts**	
149.0	204.9	215.4	232.7	224.6	252.8	260.8	258.3	288.9	346.7	339.6	351.3	385.9	439.1	....	Exports of Goods & Services	90c
68.9	88.2	92.0	94.1	129.1	128.8	137.1	127.5	123.7	126.6	123.7	130.3	137.5	145.0		Government Consumption	91f
97.1	117.1	141.6	160.5	181.4	210.5	226.2	187.4	197.6	239.6	227.3	268.4	297.2	349.9		Gross Fixed Capital Formation	93e
−5.2	−.6	8.4	7.4	15.0	17.0	20.9	12.1	12.9	14.2	12.0	12.0	14.0	14.0		Increase/Decrease(-) in Stocks	93i
264.2	207.4	309.1	330.4	373.6	370.8	416.5	475.2	470.7	406.5	391.6	549.6	577.7	503.0		Private Consumption	96f
−237.9	−288.1	−315.0	−326.8	−348.4	−383.9	−409.4	−383.1	−418.7	−424.7	−447.5	−516.1	−562.0	−625.1		Imports of Goods & Services	98c
346.2	388.8	451.5	498.2	575.3	596.9	652.2	677.4	675.1	708.9	646.0	795.6	850.2	905.9		Gross Domestic Product (GDP)	99b
....	....	....	....	....	....	....	....								GDP Volume 1980 prices	99b.*p*
296.3	307.9	262.1	275.9	291.5	306.7	315.7	317.5	....	....	....	....				GDP Volume 1984 Prices	99b.*p*
96.6	100.4	85.5	90.0	95.0	100.0	102.9	103.5	....	....	....	....				GDP Volume (1990=100)	99bv *p*
60.0	64.9	88.5	92.8	101.4	100.0	106.1	109.6	....	....	....	....				GDP Deflator (1990=100)	99bi *p*
Midyear Estimates																
.09	.10	.10	.09	.09	.09	.09	.09	.09	.09	.09	.10	.09	.09	.09	**Population**	99z

(See notes in the back of the book.)

Guatemala

258

		1970	1971	1972	1973	1974	1975	1976	1977	1978	1979	1980	1981	1982	1983	1984
Exchange Rates																*Quetzales per SDR:*
Market Rate......aa= ......wa		1.0000	1.0857	1.0857	1.2064	1.2244	1.1707	1.1618	1.2147	1.3028	1.3173	1.2754	1.1640	1.1031	1.0470	.9802
																Quetzales per US Dollar:
Market Rate......ae= ......we		1.0000	1.0000	1.0000	1.0000	1.0000	1.0000	1.0000	1.0000	1.0000	1.0000	1.0000	1.0000	1.0000	1.0000	1.0000
Market Rate......rf= ......wf		1.0000	1.0000	1.0000	1.0000	1.0000	1.0000	1.0000	1.0000	1.0000	1.0000	1.0000	1.0000	1.0000	1.0000	1.0000
Secondary Rate	xe	....	....	....	....	....	....	....	....	....	....	....	....	....	....	1.47
Secondary Rate	xf	....	....	....	....	....	....	....	....	....	....	....	....	....	....	....
Tertiary Rate	yf	....	....	....	....	....	....	....	....	....	....	....	....	....	....	....
Fund Position																*Millions of SDRs:*
Quota	2f. s	36.0	36.0	36.0	36.0	36.0	36.0	36.0	36.0	51.0	51.0	76.5	76.5	76.5	108.0	108.0
SDRs	1b. s	2.1	7.8	7.6	11.5	11.5	11.5	11.4	11.5	11.6	18.4	17.7	2.2	—	.6	2.0
Reserve Position in the Fund	1c. s	—	3.0	9.0	9.0	9.0	9.0	12.0	12.4	12.9	14.1	21.7	8.4	—	7.9	—
of which: Outstg.Fund Borrowing	2c	—	—	—	—	—	—	—	—	—	—	—	8.4	—	—	—
Total Fund Cred.&Loans Outstg.	2tl	—	—	—	—	—	—	—	—	—	—	—	95.6	95.6	133.9	153.0
International Liquidity														*Millions of US Dollars Unless Otherwise Indicated:*		
Total Reserves minus Gold	1l. d	60.8	74.7	116.2	191.3	181.3	283.8	491.0	668.9	741.5	696.3	444.7	149.7	112.2	210.0	274.4
SDRs	1b. d	2.1	8.5	8.3	11.5	14.1	13.4	13.3	14.0	15.1	24.2	22.6	2.6	—	.6	2.0
Reserve Position in the Fund	1c. d	—	3.3	9.8	10.9	11.0	10.5	13.9	15.0	16.8	18.6	27.7	9.7	—	8.2	—
Foreign Exchange	1d. d	58.7	62.9	98.2	166.6	156.2	259.8	463.8	639.9	709.6	653.5	394.4	137.4	112.2	201.2	272.4
Gold (Million Fine Troy Ounces)	1ad	.500	.495	.492	.492	.492	.492	.492	.507	.515	.522	.522	.522	.522	.522	.522
Gold (National Valuation)	1and	17.5	17.3	18.7	20.8	20.8	20.8	20.8	21.4	21.7	22.1	22.1	22.1	22.1	22.1	22.1
Monetary Authorities: Other Liab.	4.. d	27.1	24.1	22.2	19.2	24.2	50.1	69.8	101.5	111.4	104.6	183.7	296.5	361.7	784.1	1,124.2
Deposit Money Banks: Assets	7a. d	3.9	3.7	5.0	7.0	8.5	8.6	14.3	16.9	16.1	27.2	20.1	23.4	46.2	72.3	53.8
Liabilities	7b. d	9.5	13.0	9.2	11.7	9.8	12.7	23.5	26.4	27.5	51.6	53.6	49.3	73.8	137.1	149.0
Other Banking Insts.: Assets	7e. d	.3	—	.3	.3	2.9	.2	.3	1.4	.6	6.9	.3	.7	.6	.2	.2
Liabilities	7f. d	1.1	.8	.7	9.8	16.1	8.9	11.6	14.3	12.5	17.9	11.8	15.8	21.6	24.5	30.7
Monetary Authorities																*Millions of Quetzales:*
Foreign Assets	11	98.9	114.6	161.6	245.8	230.2	339.3	554.7	740.5	817.4	798.7	604.3	384.9	319.5	372.9	431.4
Claims on Central Government	12a	50.8	63.7	70.0	55.5	125.3	102.7	203.0	254.8	291.0	268.8	461.4	860.4	1,362.1	1,619.1	1,791.8
Claims on Local Government	12b	.4	2.0	4.6	1.6	3.7	3.1	3.3	3.3	3.4	3.4	3.8	2.7	3.9	8.5	7.7
Claims on Nonfin.Pub.Enterprises	12c	4.0	6.1	5.6	5.7	14.1	24.4	9.9	9.0	9.4	13.6	15.3	37.9	35.0	25.6	17.3
Claims on Private Sector	12d	—	—	—	—	—	—	—	—	—	—	—	—	—	—	—
Claims on Deposit Money Banks	12e	51.9	34.3	37.7	29.7	38.6	50.5	29.5	27.5	27.7	76.2	121.2	138.1	85.8	146.7	144.3
Claims on Other Banking Insts	12f	—	—	—	—	.1	.1	1.5	2.1	14.7	15.1	27.3	74.0	53.0	77.6	77.3
Reserve Money	14	158.5	167.8	213.6	252.0	291.5	344.1	527.5	595.2	652.4	681.7	680.4	720.1	838.3	773.7	805.6
of which: Currency Outside DMBs	14a	96.5	99.0	114.1	137.3	158.3	175.4	236.6	284.4	324.6	365.4	381.0	405.2	404.6	437.9	460.9
Time and Foreign Currency Deposits	15	—	—	—	—	—	—	—	—	—	—	—	—	—	—	—
Bonds	16ab	—	—	—	—	—	—	—	—	—	—	—	—	—	—	—
Foreign Liabilities	16c	5.5	4.4	5.6	8.9	15.9	13.3	9.6	33.5	32.8	30.7	53.8	152.9	154.3	464.3	730.6
Long-Term Foreign Liabilities	16cl	21.6	19.7	16.6	10.3	8.3	36.8	60.2	68.0	78.6	73.9	129.9	254.9	312.9	459.9	543.6
Central Government Deposits	16d	22.2	25.1	31.1	38.4	62.6	82.8	141.8	264.2	288.9	206.1	171.0	171.7	420.2	443.0	284.7
Liabilities to Other Banking Insts	16i	—	—	—	—	—	—	—	—	—	—	—	—	—	—	—
Capital Accounts	17a	14.5	18.4	23.2	24.6	24.7	25.9	46.3	56.1	62.6	76.7	124.2	149.0	138.1	123.9	122.1
Other Items (Net)	17r	−16.3	−14.7	−10.6	4.1	9.0	17.2	16.5	20.2	48.3	106.7	74.0	49.4	−4.5	−14.4	−16.8
Deposit Money Banks																*Millions of Quetzales:*
Reserves	20	61.3	66.8	95.7	108.4	125.1	160.5	271.6	284.4	278.3	266.7	245.5	265.5	370.7	274.5	365.1
Foreign Assets	21	3.9	3.7	5.0	7.0	8.5	8.6	14.3	16.9	16.1	27.2	20.1	23.4	46.2	72.3	53.8
Claims on Central Government	22a	11.2	20.8	53.6	84.6	53.0	94.5	91.9	99.3	64.9	41.5	55.2	74.6	123.6	56.1	47.8
Claims on Local Government	22b															
Claims on Nonfin.Pub.Enterprises	22c															
Claims on Private Sector	22d	218.1	238.6	261.3	296.0	386.2	433.1	502.8	651.1	826.9	998.4	1,222.2	1,374.4	1,476.4	1,670.3	1,867.8
Claims on Other Banking Insts	22f															
Demand Deposits	24	75.1	78.0	95.8	120.4	138.2	168.7	236.7	279.9	291.9	320.4	320.5	325.3	339.7	346.2	381.6
Time, Savings,& Fgn.Currency Dep.	25	170.9	204.4	262.5	315.5	362.9	454.9	558.0	655.0	759.6	802.3	939.6	1,128.9	1,404.1	1,321.3	1,529.7
Bonds	26ab	.3	.2	.2	.6	.4	.6	.4	—	—	—	—	—	—	—	—
Foreign Liabilities	26c	7.7	11.2	7.9	11.5	9.6	12.5	23.4	26.3	27.5	51.6	53.6	49.3	73.8	137.1	149.0
Long-Term Foreign Liabilities	26cl	1.8	1.8	1.3	.2	.2	.2	.1	.1	—	—	—	—	—	—	—
Central Government Deposits	26d	3.8	2.3	1.6	2.0	3.2	3.1	5.3	3.3	3.3	4.6	7.0	3.3	4.8	9.9	5.5
Credit from Monetary Authorities	26g	16.6	12.0	19.4	15.5	19.6	17.1	7.8	8.2	31.0	80.8	130.1	132.3	92.4	153.2	147.8
Liabilities to Other Banking Insts	26i												1.9			
Capital Accounts	27a	42.4	45.9	53.1	56.3	64.1	68.2	91.4	114.2	131.2	160.7	155.2	166.7	171.6	189.0	208.6
Other Items (Net)	27r	−24.1	−25.9	−26.2	−26.0	−25.4	−28.6	−42.5	−35.3	−58.3	−86.6	−63.0	−69.8	−69.5	−83.5	−87.7
Monetary Survey																*Millions of Quetzales:*
Foreign Assets (Net)	31n	89.6	102.7	153.1	232.4	213.2	322.1	536.0	697.6	773.2	743.6	517.0	206.1	137.6	−156.2	−394.4
Domestic Credit	32	258.5	303.8	362.4	403.0	516.6	572.0	665.3	752.1	918.1	1,130.1	1,607.2	2,249.0	2,629.0	3,004.3	3,519.5
Claims on Central Govt. (Net)	32an	36.0	57.1	90.9	99.7	112.5	111.3	147.8	86.6	63.7	99.6	338.6	760.0	1,060.7	1,222.3	1,549.4
Claims on Local Government	32b	.4	2.0	4.6	1.6	3.7	3.1	3.3	3.3	3.4	3.4	3.8	2.7	3.9	8.5	7.7
Claims on Nonfin.Pub.Enterprises	32c	4.0	6.1	5.6	5.7	14.1	24.4	9.9	9.0	9.4	13.6	15.3	37.9	35.0	25.6	17.3
Claims on Private Sector	32d	218.1	238.6	261.3	296.0	386.2	433.1	502.8	651.1	826.9	998.4	1,222.2	1,374.4	1,476.4	1,670.3	1,867.8
Claims on Other Banking Insts	32f	—	—	—	—	.1	.1	1.5	2.1	14.7	15.1	27.3	74.0	53.0	77.6	77.3
Money	34	172.8	178.9	214.4	264.3	305.4	353.6	493.8	594.1	664.0	734.9	752.8	775.9	786.6	833.8	869.4
Quasi-Money	35	170.9	204.4	262.5	315.5	362.9	454.9	558.0	655.0	759.6	802.3	939.6	1,128.9	1,404.1	1,321.3	1,529.7
Bonds	36ab	.3	.2	.2	.6	.4	.6	.4	—	—	—	—	—	—	—	—
Long-Term Foreign Liabilities	36cl	23.4	21.5	17.9	10.5	8.5	37.0	60.3	68.1	78.6	73.9	129.9	254.9	312.9	459.9	543.6
Liabilities to Other Banking Insts	36i												1.9			
Capital Accounts	37a	56.9	64.3	76.3	80.9	88.8	94.1	137.7	170.3	193.8	237.4	279.4	315.7	309.7	312.9	330.7
Other Items (Net)	37r	−76.2	−62.8	−55.8	−36.4	−36.2	−46.1	−48.9	−37.8	−4.7	25.2	22.5	−22.2	−46.7	−79.8	−148.3
Money plus Quasi-Money	35l	343.7	383.3	476.9	579.8	668.3	808.5	1,051.8	1,249.1	1,423.6	1,537.2	1,692.4	1,904.8	2,190.7	2,155.1	2,399.1

1985	1986	1987	1988	1989	1990	1991	1992	1993	1994	1995	1996	1997	1998	1999		
End of Period															**Exchange Rates**	
1.0984	3.0580	3.5467	3.6401	4.4681	7.1341	7.2142	7.2522	7.9876	8.2460	8.9810	8.5782	8.3342	9.6425	10.7342	Market Rate............aa= ....wa	wa
End of Period (we) Period Average (wf)																
1.0000	2.5000	2.5000	2.7050	3.4000	5.0146	5.0434	5.2743	5.8152	5.6485	6.0418	5.9656	6.1769	6.8482	7.8208	Market Rate............ae=	we
1.0000	1.8750	2.5000	2.6196	2.8161	4.4858	5.0289	5.1706	5.6354	5.7512	5.8103	6.0495	6.0653	6.3947	7.3856	Market Rate............rf=	wf
2.93	1.00	1.00	1.00	1.00	1.00	1.00	1.00	1.00	1.00	1.00	1.00	1.00	1.00	1.00	Secondary Rate	xe
2.77	1.80	1.00	1.00	1.00	1.00	1.00	1.00	1.00	1.00	1.00	1.00	1.00	1.00	1.00	Secondary Rate	xf
....	2.85	2.70	2.65	....	....	....	....	....	....	....	....	....	....	....	Tertiary Rate	yf
End of Period															**Fund Position**	
108.0	108.0	108.0	108.0	108.0	108.0	108.0	153.8	153.8	153.8	153.8	153.8	153.8	153.8	210.2	Quota	2f. s
—	—	1.2	.1	.6	—	—	11.4	11.4	11.4	10.6	10.2	9.4	8.7	8.4	SDRs	1b. s
—	—	—	—	—	—	—	—	—	—	—	—	—	—	—	Reserve Position in the Fund	1c. s
—	—	—	—	—	—	—	—	—	—	—	—	—	—	—	of which: Outstg.Fund Borrowing	2c
105.2	57.2	41.7	65.4	55.5	46.8	44.8	22.4	—	—	—	—	—	—	—	Total Fund Cred.&Loans Outstg.	2tl
End of Period															**International Liquidity**	
300.9	362.1	287.8	201.2	306.0	282.0	807.3	765.2	867.8	863.1	702.0	869.7	1,111.1	1,335.1	1,189.2	Total Reserves minus Gold	1l. d
—	—	1.7	.2	.7	—	—	15.6	15.7	16.6	15.8	14.6	12.7	12.2	11.5	SDRs	1b. d
—	—	—	—	—	—	—	—	—	—	—	—	—	—	—	Reserve Position in the Fund	1c. d
300.9	362.1	286.1	201.0	305.3	282.0	807.3	749.6	852.1	846.5	686.2	855.1	1,098.4	1,322.9	1,177.7	Foreign Exchange	1d. d
.522	.522	.523	.523	.542	.207	.208	.122	.209	.209	.210	.212	.213	.215	.215	Gold (Million Fine Troy Ounces)	1ad
22.1	22.1	22.1	22.1	22.9	8.8	8.8	5.1	8.8	8.8	8.9	8.9	9.0	9.1	9.1	Gold (National Valuation)	1an d
1,259.6	437.4	436.7	257.8	209.3	146.4	127.9	115.1	89.6	66.5	55.4	48.1	184.3	152.3	126.4	Monetary Authorities: Other Liab.	4.. d
76.7	18.5	30.0	17.9	12.7	4.3	4.6	6.8	8.6	17.7	66.3	81.2	72.6	65.6	84.1	Deposit Money Banks: Assets	7a. d
78.7	37.2	52.5	55.0	48.2	26.6	26.7	48.4	113.1	373.3	266.2	375.4	413.4	500.9	452.5	Liabilities	7b. d
.4	.1	.1	.1	.1	.1	.3	—	.1	4.1	4.3	4.5	1.8	12.1	4.3	Other Banking Insts.: Assets	7e. d
32.9	14.3	14.0	16.8	10.7	70.2	76.7	79.4	79.9	100.2	515.8	554.3	592.0	615.8	633.7	Liabilities	7f. d
End of Period															**Monetary Authorities**	
478.2	608.4	510.7	492.4	530.5	567.6	1,123.7	1,149.3	1,307.4	1,292.5	1,157.7	1,341.6	ℐ7,566.2	10,109.3	10,521.1	Foreign Assets	11
1,931.7	1,528.2	1,441.2	1,571.4	1,615.3	1,551.1	117.3	452.4	112.5	357.6	187.4	698.0	ℐ78.7	.2	.2	Claims on Central Government	12a
8.8	7.9	7.1	6.2	5.3	4.4	—	—	2.6	2.0	1.3	.6	ℐ.3	—	—	Claims on Local Government	12b
12.2	11.4	9.4	10.6	8.4	7.4	7.4	7.4	7.4	7.4	7.4	—	ℐ29.7	30.0	29.9	Claims on Nonfin.Pub.Enterprises	12c
											—	ℐ29.7	30.0	29.9	Claims on Private Sector	12d
121.1	133.9	122.0	156.2	162.4	159.4	154.6	184.6	184.8	61.3	123.3	97.5	ℐ81.9	228.5	652.6	Claims on Deposit Money Banks	12e
68.3	55.0	51.1	64.0	66.9	74.7	153.8	284.3	245.2	188.3	148.4	97.1	ℐ44.1	12.8	41.7	Claims on Other Banking Insts	12f
1,302.0	1,569.6	1,578.6	1,932.7	2,301.8	3,079.7	3,946.2	4,263.2	5,255.3	5,494.3	5,689.3	6,418.2	ℐ10746.6	10,323.0	10,608.5	Reserve Money	14
697.8	804.6	931.2	1,069.0	1,329.2	1,897.1	2,089.4	2,712.6	3,097.3	3,714.6	4,018.9	4,179.1	ℐ4,890.2	5,632.5	7,752.8	of which: Currency Outside DMBs	14a
							1,141.9	2,460.9	3,845.6	4,600.0	6,582.4	ℐ665.2	1,104.6	1,995.1	Time and Foreign Currency Deposits	15
			559.3	526.8	477.7	842.2	970.1	670.7	372.9	76.0	50.3	ℐ212.7	67.5	60.9	Bonds	16ab
735.1	669.0	639.9	303.7	230.7	637.3	623.1	506.1	323.5	338.3	352.6	359.5	ℐ13.4	9.2	8.4	Foreign Liabilities	16c
640.0	599.3	599.5	631.6	728.8	625.7	539.4	462.1	451.6	277.6	236.2	202.1	ℐ1,125.2	1,034.0	980.2	Long-Term Foreign Liabilities	16cl
355.4	568.5	683.7	746.7	694.7	687.6	1,416.3	1,555.4	1,421.5	1,566.3	1,439.6	1,872.3	ℐ5,293.5	7,586.1	6,405.8	Central Government Deposits	16d
												ℐ2.0	—	—	Liabilities to Other Banking Insts	16i
125.3	128.8	134.2	132.1	131.3	331.7	334.1	333.7	354.1	363.5	384.6	372.1	ℐ330.2	366.4	396.6	Capital Accounts	17a
-537.5	-1,190.4	-1,494.4	-2,005.3	-2,225.3	-3,475.1	-6,144.5	-7,154.6	-9,077.7	-10,349.5	-11,152.8	-13,622.2	ℐ-10587.9	-10,110.0	-9,210.0	Other Items (Net)	17r
End of Period															**Deposit Money Banks**	
583.0	770.3	756.4	1,048.3	1,118.7	1,450.3	2,306.2	2,346.5	2,815.2	2,175.5	4,019.2	4,794.7	ℐ5,731.3	4,823.0	3,121.7	Reserves	20
76.7	46.2	74.9	48.3	43.1	21.4	23.0	35.7	50.0	100.1	400.8	484.2	ℐ448.4	449.5	657.4	Foreign Assets	21
137.1	295.7	239.1	65.7	148.5	240.3	1,994.1	1,732.4	1,794.1	2,869.7	1,292.5	1,676.9	ℐ2,870.0	2,389.0	2,277.1	Claims on Central Government	22a
—	—	—	—	—	—	—	—	—	—	—	—	ℐ81.3	14.4	14.6	Claims on Local Government	22b
—	—	—	—	—	—	—	—	—	—	—	—	ℐ—	—	63.1	Claims on Nonfin.Pub.Enterprises	22c
2,037.1	2,242.1	2,711.2	3,109.2	3,427.1	4,299.9	5,010.6	6,624.8	7,434.4	9,156.9	13,898.6	15,446.7	ℐ16603.7	21,142.4	24,115.9	Claims on Private Sector	22d
—	—	—	—	—	—	—	—	—	—	—	—	ℐ2,116.8	2,482.6	2,034.7	Claims on Other Banking Insts	22f
614.5	748.6	807.9	915.6	1,065.6	1,341.5	1,752.8	1,475.4	1,928.0	3,336.2	3,728.4	4,617.5	ℐ6,856.2	7,866.9	7,614.1	Demand Deposits	24
1,846.4	2,266.7	2,402.2	2,976.0	3,362.8	4,054.8	7,022.1	8,912.8	8,893.9	7,450.0	8,900.3	8,802.5	ℐ10535.8	12,976.8	13,682.8	Time, Savings,& Fgn.Currency Dep.	25
—	—	—	—	—	—	—	—	—	—	—	—	ℐ5,139.9	4,480.2	4,266.1	Bonds	26ab
78.7	93.0	131.3	148.9	164.0	133.6	134.8	255.5	657.9	2,108.7	1,608.2	2,239.3	ℐ2,385.2	3,261.9	3,318.0	Foreign Liabilities	26c
—	—	—	—	—	—	—	—	—	—	—	—	ℐ168.4	168.6	221.0	Long-Term Foreign Liabilities	26cl
10.5	11.7	15.7	20.1	24.9	28.6	42.3	63.3	76.7	71.0	171.5	194.4	ℐ410.7	677.9	1,197.0	Central Government Deposits	26d
121.5	111.8	96.7	132.8	147.8	172.8	164.6	187.0	185.9	66.0	123.5	97.6	ℐ7.4	162.7	804.6	Credit from Monetary Authorities	26g
—	—	—	—	—	—	—	—	—	—	—	—	ℐ478.9	575.9	578.0	Liabilities to Other Banking Insts	26i
236.7	270.9	293.5	385.5	440.2	666.6	884.7	1,056.3	1,293.0	1,586.7	1,821.9	2,019.8	ℐ2,315.5	2,775.7	3,810.3	Capital Accounts	27a
-74.4	-148.4	34.3	-307.4	-467.9	-386.0	-667.4	-1,210.9	-941.7	-316.4	3,257.3	4,431.4	ℐ-446.5	-1,645.7	-3,207.4	Other Items (Net)	27r
End of Period															**Monetary Survey**	
-258.9	-107.4	-185.6	88.1	178.9	-181.9	388.8	423.4	376.0	-1,054.4	-402.3	-773.0	ℐ5,616.0	7,287.7	7,852.1	Foreign Assets (Net)	31n
3,829.3	3,560.1	3,759.7	4,060.3	4,551.9	5,461.6	5,824.6	7,482.6	8,098.0	10,944.6	13,924.5	15,852.6	ℐ16120.4	17,807.4	20,974.4	Domestic Credit	32
1,702.9	1,243.7	980.9	870.3	1,044.2	1,075.2	652.8	566.1	408.4	1,590.0	-131.2	308.2	ℐ-2755.5	-5,874.8	-5,325.5	Claims on Central Govt. (Net)	32an
8.8	7.9	7.1	6.2	5.3	4.4	—	—	2.6	2.0	1.3	.6	ℐ81.6	14.4	14.6	Claims on Local Government	32b
12.2	11.4	9.4	10.6	8.4	7.4	7.4	7.4	7.4	7.4	7.4	—	ℐ—	—	63.1	Claims on Nonfin.Pub.Enterprises	32c
2,037.1	2,242.1	2,711.2	3,109.2	3,427.1	4,299.9	5,010.6	6,624.8	7,434.4	9,156.9	13,898.6	15,446.7	ℐ16633.4	21,172.4	24,145.8	Claims on Private Sector	32d
68.3	55.0	51.1	64.0	66.9	74.7	153.8	284.3	245.2	188.3	148.4	97.1	ℐ2,160.9	2,495.4	2,076.4	Claims on Other Banking Insts	32f
1,346.5	1,608.4	1,765.6	2,019.0	2,437.8	3,241.5	3,843.4	4,193.2	5,048.1	7,073.6	7,771.8	8,822.4	ℐ11997.5	13,613.5	15,467.6	Money	34
1,846.4	2,266.7	2,402.2	2,976.0	3,362.8	4,054.8	7,022.1	10,054.7	11,354.8	11,295.6	13,500.3	15,384.9	ℐ11201.0	14,081.4	15,677.9	Quasi-Money	35
—	—	—	559.3	526.8	477.7	842.2	970.1	670.7	372.9	76.0	50.3	ℐ5,352.6	4,547.7	4,327.0	Bonds	36ab
640.0	599.3	599.5	631.6	728.8	625.7	539.4	462.1	451.6	277.6	236.2	202.1	ℐ1,293.6	1,202.6	1,201.2	Long-Term Foreign Liabilities	36cl
—	—	—	—	—	—	—	—	—	—	—	—	ℐ480.9	575.9	578.0	Liabilities to Other Banking Insts	36i
362.0	399.7	427.7	517.6	571.5	998.3	1,218.8	1,390.0	1,647.1	1,950.2	2,206.5	2,391.9	ℐ2,645.7	3,142.1	4,206.9	Capital Accounts	37a
-624.5	-1,421.4	-1,620.9	-2,555.1	-2,896.9	-4,118.3	-7,252.5	-9,164.2	-10,698.3	-11,079.8	-10,268.6	-11,772.1	ℐ-11234.9	-12,068.1	-12,632.1	Other Items (Net)	37r
3,192.9	3,875.1	4,167.8	4,995.0	5,800.6	7,296.3	10,865.5	14,247.9	16,402.9	18,369.2	21,272.1	24,207.3	ℐ23198.5	27,694.9	31,145.5	Money plus Quasi-Money	35l

Guatemala

		1970	1971	1972	1973	1974	1975	1976	1977	1978	1979	1980	1981	1982	1983	1984
Other Banking Institutions																*Millions of Quetzales:*
Reserves	40	1.6	2.4	4.9	7.3	9.9	10.7	21.9	31.2	49.1	50.7	53.0	47.2	44.5	51.9	29.9
Foreign Assets	41	.3	—	.3	.3	2.9	.2	.3	1.4	.6	6.9	.3	.7	.6	.2	.2
Claims on Central Government	42a	1.0	2.1	2.7	5.8	6.2	2.6	10.0	13.8	13.7	4.5	6.2	7.5	1.4	5.2	1.6
Claims on Nonfin.Pub.Enterprises	42c	....	....	....	....	....	....	....	....	....	....	....	....	....	....	....
Claims on Private Sector	42d	23.6	12.5	10.8	9.9	14.0	23.7	32.7	40.5	41.0	45.0	56.2	60.3	60.4	69.2	68.6
Claims on Deposit Money Banks	42e	....	....	....	....	....	....	....	....	....	....	....	....	....	....	....
Time, Savings,& Fgn.Currency Dep.	45	....	....	....	....	....	....	....	....	....	....	....	....	....	....	....
Bonds	46ab	—	—	—	—	—	—	—	—	—	—	—	—	—	9.8	—
Foreign Liabilities	46c	.3	.1	.2	9.3	15.7	8.5	11.2	14.3	.4	6.4	.9	.4	.3	.4	—
Long-Term Foreign Liabilities	46cl	.8	.7	.5	.5	.4	.4	.4	—	12.1	11.5	10.9	15.4	21.3	24.1	30.7
Credit from Monetary Authorities	46g	26.8	13.7	9.8	5.5	11.8	28.5	10.7	8.4	6.0	3.6	3.0	14.1	8.6	6.8	.6
Credit from Deposit Money Banks	46h	.1	.1	.1	—	—	—	—	—	1.0	—	—	—	—	—	—
Capital Accounts	47a	7.3	4.5	5.6	11.9	18.1	28.6	32.9	39.4	39.5	37.8	40.2	36.4	32.4	37.5	30.5
Other Items (Net)	47r	-8.8	-2.1	2.5	-3.9	-13.0	-28.8	9.7	24.8	45.4	47.8	60.7	49.4	44.3	47.9	38.5
Banking Survey																*Millions of Quetzales:*
Foreign Assets (Net)	51n	76.5	87.9	134.2	200.5	174.3	286.4	492.9	648.1	733.0	700.7	442.3	127.3	72.5	-221.8	-459.6
Domestic Credit	52	282.1	317.3	374.0	417.2	534.6	595.1	704.4	803.4	957.1	1,161.7	1,640.6	2,243.7	2,665.4	3,034.5	3,538.4
Claims on Central Govt. (Net)	52an	36.0	58.1	91.7	104.0	116.5	110.7	154.2	98.3	75.5	100.7	343.1	755.1	1,050.3	1,221.6	1,537.7
Claims on Local Government	52b	.4	2.0	4.6	1.6	3.7	3.1	3.3	3.3	3.4	3.4	3.8	2.7	3.9	8.5	7.7
Claims on Nonfin.Pub.Enterprises	52c	4.0	6.1	5.6	5.7	14.1	24.4	9.9	9.0	9.4	13.6	15.3	37.9	35.0	25.6	17.3
Claims on Private Sector	52d	241.7	251.1	272.1	305.9	400.3	456.9	537.0	692.8	868.8	1,044.0	1,278.4	1,448.0	1,576.2	1,778.8	1,975.7
Liquid Liabilities	55l	350.1	389.2	483.0	591.3	674.4	827.0	1,081.9	1,284.6	1,461.0	1,568.0	1,734.4	1,948.3	2,241.8	2,211.6	2,466.0
Bonds	56ab	.3	.2	.2	.6	.4	.6	.4	—	—	—	—	—	—	9.8	—
Long-Term Foreign Liabilities	56cl	24.2	22.2	18.4	11.0	8.9	37.4	60.7	68.1	90.7	85.4	140.8	270.3	334.2	484.0	574.3
Capital Accounts	57a	64.2	68.8	81.9	92.8	106.9	122.7	170.6	209.7	233.3	275.2	319.6	352.1	342.1	350.4	361.2
Other Items (Net)	57r	-80.2	-75.2	-75.3	-78.0	-81.7	-106.2	-116.3	-110.9	-94.9	-66.2	-111.9	-199.7	-180.2	-243.1	-322.7
Interest Rates																*Percent Per Annum*
Discount Rate *(End of Period)*	60	4.0	4.0	4.0	4.0	5.0	5.0	5.0	7.0	5.0	9.0	8.0	12.0	9.0	9.0	9.0
Money Market Rate	60b	....	....	....	....	....	....	....	....	....	....	....	....	....	....	....
Savings Rate	60k	....	....	....	....	....	....	....	....	....	....	....	....	....	....	....
Deposit Rate	60l	....	....	....	....	....	....	....	....	9.0	9.0	9.0	10.0	12.0	9.0	9.0
Lending Rate	60p	....	....	....	....	....	....	....	....	11.0	11.0	11.0	12.0	12.0	12.0	12.0
Prices and Labor																*Index Numbers (1995=100):*
Consumer Prices	64	5.3	5.3	5.3	6.0	7.0	I7.9	I8.8	9.9	10.7	11.9	13.2	14.7	14.8	15.4	16.0
																Number in Thousands:
Labor Force	67d	....	....	....	....	....	....	....	....	....	....	....	....	....	....	....
Employment	67e	....	....	....	....	....	....	....	....	....	....	....	....	....	....	....
Unemployment	67c	....	....	....	....	....	....	....	....	....	....	....	....	....	....	....
International Transactions																*Millions of US Dollars*
Exports	70..d	290.2	283.2	327.5	436.2	572.1	623.5	760.4	1,160.2	1,089.5	1,241.4	1,519.8	1,226.1	1,119.8	1,158.8	1,128.5
Imports, c.i.f.	71..d	284.3	296.6	324.0	431.0	700.5	732.7	838.9	1,052.5	1,285.7	1,503.9	1,598.2	1,688.3	1,388.0	1,126.1	1,278.5
Imports, f.o.b.	71.vd	261.0	278.1	289.5	389.0	624.1	669.8	766.8	926.5	1,178.9	1,395.4	1,472.6	1,539.9	1,284.2	1,054.6	1,180.3
Balance of Payments																*Millions of US Dollars:*
Current Account, n.i.e.	78ald	....	....	....	....	....	....	....	-35.3	-270.5	-205.6	-163.3	-572.7	-399.1	-223.9	-377.4
Goods: Exports f.o.b.	78aad	....	....	....	....	....	....	....	1,160.2	1,092.4	1,221.4	1,519.8	1,291.3	1,170.4	1,091.7	1,132.2
Goods: Imports f.o.b.	78abd	....	....	....	....	....	....	....	-1,087.0	-1,283.8	-1,401.7	-1,472.6	-1,540.0	-1,284.3	-1,056.0	-1,182.2
Trade Balance	78acd	....	....	....	....	....	....	....	73.2	-191.4	-180.3	47.2	-248.7	-113.9	35.7	-50.0
Services: Credit	78add	....	....	....	....	....	....	....	161.5	183.8	228.5	211.2	155.1	107.6	80.3	96.0
Services: Debit	78aed	....	....	....	....	....	....	....	-339.5	-361.0	-383.1	-487.4	-484.3	-341.9	-257.8	-245.5
Balance on Goods & Services	78afd	....	....	....	....	....	....	....	-104.8	-368.6	-334.9	-229.0	-577.9	-348.2	-141.8	-199.5
Income: Credit	78agd	....	....	....	....	....	....	....	47.9	72.9	102.1	103.0	79.5	34.2	33.0	33.0
Income: Debit	78ahd	....	....	....	....	....	....	....	-74.2	-90.4	-99.4	-147.1	-165.2	-147.8	-145.7	-239.6
Balance on Gds, Serv. & Inc.	78aid	....	....	....	....	....	....	....	-131.1	-386.1	-332.2	-273.1	-663.6	-461.8	-254.5	-406.1
Current Transfers, n.i.e.: Credit	78ajd	....	....	....	....	....	....	....	116.4	139.4	149.5	125.3	96.9	66.1	34.2	31.6
Current Transfers: Debit	78akd	....	....	....	....	....	....	....	-20.6	-23.8	-22.9	-15.5	-6.0	-3.4	-3.6	-2.9
Capital Account, n.i.e.	78bcd	....	....	....	....	....	....	....	—	—	—	—	—	—	—	—
Capital Account, n.i.e.: Credit	78bad	....	....	....	....	....	....	....	—	—	—	—	—	—	—	—
Capital Account: Debit	78bbd	....	....	....	....	....	....	....	—	—	—	—	—	—	—	—
Financial Account, n.i.e.	78bjd	....	....	....	....	....	....	....	222.4	377.2	205.5	-143.9	110.6	11.2	187.8	-115.4
Direct Investment Abroad	78bdd	....	....	....	....	....	....	....	—	—	—	—	—	—	—	—
Dir. Invest. in Rep. Econ., n.i.e.	78bed	....	....	....	....	....	....	....	97.5	127.2	117.0	110.7	127.1	77.1	45.0	38.0
Portfolio Investment Assets	78bfd	....	....	....	....	....	....	....	.5	2.3	8.0	4.2	-.4	—	-.1	.3
Equity Securities	78bkd	....	....	....	....	....	....	....	.5	2.3	8.0	4.2	-.4	—	-.1	.3
Debt Securities	78bld	....	....	....	....	....	....	....								
Portfolio Investment Liab., n.i.e.	78bgd	....	....	....	....	....	....	....	4.8	9.4	-2.7	-.3	.7	.5	—	-9.9
Equity Securities	78bmd	....	....	....	....	....	....	....	-1.0	1.4	-2.7	-.3	.7	.5	—	—
Debt Securities	78bnd	....	....	....	....	....	....	....	5.8	8.0						-9.9
Financial Derivatives Assets	78bwd	....	....	....	....	....	....	....	....	....	....	....	....	....	....	....
Financial Derivatives Liabilities	78bxd	....	....	....	....	....	....	....	....	....	....	....	....	....	....	....
Other Investment Assets	78bhd	....	....	....	....	....	....	....	14.6	21.3	-217.2	-311.3	-149.1	-10.4	—	4.7
Monetary Authorities	78bod	....	....	....	....	....	....	....	—	—	....	....	—	—	—	—
General Government	78bpd	....	....	....	....	....	....	....	—	—	—	—	—	-1.3	—	3.2
Banks	78bqd	....	....	....	....	....	....	....	—	—	—	—	—	—	—	—
Other Sectors	78brd	....	....	....	....	....	....	....	14.6	21.3	-217.2	-311.3	-149.1	-9.1	—	1.5
Other Investment Liab., n.i.e.	78bid	....	....	....	....	....	....	....	105.0	217.0	300.4	52.8	132.3	-56.0	142.9	-148.5
Monetary Authorities	78bsd	....	....	....	....	....	....	....	-1.9	6.6	.1	17.3	2.1	24.5	-25.8	-172.1
General Government	78btd	....	....	....	....	....	....	....	49.0	83.0	95.1	80.5	96.6	84.8	92.8	41.9
Banks	78bud	....	....	....	....	....	....	....	3.3	1.2	24.1	2.3	-6.9	13.6	71.0	9.1
Other Sectors	78bvd	....	....	....	....	....	....	....	54.6	126.2	181.1	-47.3	40.5	-178.9	4.9	-27.4
Net Errors and Omissions	78cad	....	....	....	....	....	....	....	-26.5	-58.6	-44.4	-18.1	4.3	-18.0	-37.1	15.5
Overall Balance	78cbd	....	....	....	....	....	....	....	160.6	48.1	-44.5	-325.3	-457.8	-405.9	-73.2	-477.3
Reserves and Related Items	79dad	....	....	....	....	....	....	....	-160.6	-48.1	44.5	325.3	457.8	405.9	73.2	477.3
Reserve Assets	79dbd	....	....	....	....	....	....	....	-181.7	-68.3	25.7	257.9	189.8	38.4	-91.1	-30.9
Use of Fund Credit and Loans	79dcd	....	....	....	....	....	....	....	—	—	—	—	111.5	—	40.1	20.2
Exceptional Financing	79ded	....	....	....	....	....	....	....	21.1	20.2	18.8	67.4	156.5	367.5	124.2	487.9

1985	1986	1987	1988	1989	1990	1991	1992	1993	1994	1995	1996	1997	1998	1999		
End of Period															**Other Banking Institutions**	
37.1	58.5	31.1	40.1	49.2	I 11.7	51.4	51.7	66.1	31.5	48.3	69.6	I 14.9	120.8	45.8	Reserves	40
.4	.2	.2	.3	.3	I .5	1.4	.2	.4	23.4	26.2	26.6	I 10.9	83.2	33.9	Foreign Assets	41
14.1	31.8	22.7	11.1	48.1	I 8.4	109.0	36.0	36.2	48.4	42.6	111.5	I 77.0	120.0	88.7	Claims on Central Government	42a
....	....	....	....	....	....	....	....	....	....	....	....	13.2	.2	.2	Claims on Nonfin.Pub.Enterprises	42c
97.5	108.5	214.3	236.0	255.7	I 565.5	641.3	1,188.9	1,489.9	2,055.3	2,512.4	2,655.5	I 3,388.5	4,310.1	3,859.8	Claims on Private Sector	42d
....	....	....	....	....	137.6	279.4	186.2	331.7	309.3	458.5	443.5	I 555.7	550.1	453.8	Claims on Deposit Money Banks	42e
....	....	....	....	....	—	—	—	—	—	—	—	I 3.8	201.4	4.5	Time, Savings,& Fgn.Currency Dep.	45
—	—	—	—	—	I 200.2	463.6	942.2	1,326.4	1,710.5	1,176.0	1,378.7	I 2,298.6	2,692.3	2,192.6	Bonds	46ab
.7	.1	.9	12.1	5.8	I 2.0	8.4	9.0	26.4	99.7	146.1	157.7	I —	—	—	Foreign Liabilities	46c
32.2	35.6	34.0	33.4	30.6	I 349.9	378.6	409.9	438.0	466.4	2,970.0	3,149.1	I 3,656.5	4,216.9	4,956.2	Long-Term Foreign Liabilities	46cl
.5	.5	26.1	28.8	26.6	I 94.1	170.4	295.6	259.3	195.4	144.2	102.3	I —	—	—	Credit from Monetary Authorities	46g
—	—	—	—	—	I 293.1	363.1	431.2	523.5	877.6	1,637.1	1,689.4	I 1,584.0	1,925.9	2,110.8	Credit from Deposit Money Banks	46h
47.4	51.6	55.7	58.8	65.2	I -73.3	-107.2	-107.0	-142.8	-107.4	-2,559.7	-2,667.4	I -2849.0	-3,329.4	-4,019.0	Capital Accounts	47a
68.3	111.2	151.6	154.4	225.1	I -142.3	-194.4	-517.9	-506.5	-774.3	-425.7	-503.1	I -633.7	-522.7	-762.9	Other Items (Net)	47r
End of Period															**Banking Survey**	
-334.6	-223.9	-305.9	-52.9	44.2	I -183.4	381.8	414.6	350.0	-1,130.7	-522.2	-904.1	I 5,626.9	7,370.9	7,886.0	Foreign Assets (Net)	51n
3,897.7	3,653.2	3,973.9	4,273.1	4,816.8	I 5,960.8	6,421.1	8,423.2	9,378.9	12,860.0	16,331.1	18,522.5	I 17438.2	19,743.0	22,853.3	Domestic Credit	52
1,702.8	1,244.0	992.6	871.8	1,081.0	I 1,083.6	761.8	602.1	444.6	1,638.4	-88.6	419.7	I -2678.5	-5,754.8	-5,236.8	Claims on Central Govt. (Net)	52an
8.8	7.9	7.1	6.2	5.3	4.4	—	—	2.6	2.0	1.3	.6	I 81.6	15.1	21.2	Claims on Local Government	52b
12.2	11.4	9.4	10.6	8.4	7.4	7.4	7.4	7.4	7.4	7.4	—	I 13.2	.2	63.3	Claims on Nonfin.Pub.Enterprises	52c
2,173.9	2,389.9	2,964.8	3,384.5	3,722.1	I 4,865.4	5,651.9	7,813.7	8,924.3	11,212.2	16,411.0	18,102.2	I 20021.9	25,482.5	28,005.6	Claims on Private Sector	52d
3,276.4	3,955.8	4,285.3	5,130.6	5,968.8	I 7,284.6	10,814.1	14,196.2	16,336.8	18,337.7	21,223.8	24,137.7	I 23186.8	27,913.5	31,097.0	Liquid Liabilities	55l
—	—	—	559.3	526.8	I 677.9	1,305.8	1,912.3	1,997.1	2,083.4	1,252.0	1,429.0	I 7,651.2	7,240.0	6,519.6	Bonds	56ab
672.2	634.9	633.5	665.0	759.4	I 975.6	918.0	872.0	889.6	744.0	3,206.2	3,351.2	I 4,950.1	5,419.5	6,157.4	Long-Term Foreign Liabilities	56cl
409.4	451.3	483.4	576.4	636.7	I 925.0	1,111.6	1,283.0	1,504.3	1,842.8	-353.2	-275.5	I -203.3	-187.3	187.9	Capital Accounts	57a
-794.9	-1,612.7	-1,734.2	-2,711.1	-3,030.7	I -4085.7	-7,346.6	-9,425.8	-10,998.9	-11,278.7	-9,519.9	-11,024.1	I -12519.7	-13,271.8	-13,222.6	Other Items (Net)	57r
Percent Per Annum															**Interest Rates**	
9.0	9.0	9.0	9.0	13.0	18.5	16.5	....	....	....	....	....	....	....	....	Discount Rate *(End of Period)*	60
....	....	....	....	....	....	....	....	....	....	....	....	7.8	6.6	9.2	Money Market Rate	60b
....	....	....	....	....	....	....	....	....	....	....	....	5.1	4.5	5.2	Savings Rate	60k
9.0	10.2	11.0	12.2	13.0	18.2	24.4	10.4	12.6	9.7	7.9	7.7	I 5.8	5.4	8.0	Deposit Rate	60l
12.0	13.2	14.0	15.2	16.0	23.3	34.1	19.5	24.7	22.9	21.2	22.7	I 18.6	16.6	19.5	Lending Rate	60p
Period Averages															**Prices and Labor**	
18.9	25.9	29.1	32.3	36.0	50.8	67.6	74.4	83.2	92.2	100.0	111.1	121.3	129.8	136.1	Consumer Prices	64
Period Averages																
....	....	....	....	2,688	....	....	....	....	2,326	....	....	....	....	3,489	Labor Force	67d
632	660	679	780	788	786	787	796	823	830	856	831	....	....	....	Employment	67e
3	3	2	2	2	2	2	2	1	1	1	....	....	....	....	Unemployment	67c
Millions of US Dollars															**International Transactions**	
1,057.0	1,043.8	987.3	1,021.7	1,108.0	1,163.0	1,202.2	1,295.3	1,340.4	1,521.5	2,155.5	2,030.7	2,344.1	2,581.6	2,397.5	Exports	70..d
1,174.8	958.5	1,447.2	1,557.0	1,653.8	1,648.8	1,851.3	2,531.5	2,599.3	2,781.4	3,292.5	3,146.1	3,851.9	4,651.1	4,381.7	Imports, c.i.f.	71..d
1,076.7	875.6	1,333.2	1,413.2	1,497.2	1,428.0	1,672.5	2,330.7	2,384.0	2,425.7	3,032.5	2,880.3	3,542.8	4,164.5	4,010.5	Imports, f.o.b.	71.vd
Minus Sign Indicates Debit															Balance of Payments	
-246.3	-17.6	-442.5	-414.0	-367.1	-232.9	-183.7	-705.9	-701.7	-625.3	-572.0	-451.5	-633.5	-1,039.1	-1,025.9	Current Account, n.i.e.	78ald
1,059.7	1,043.8	977.9	1,073.3	1,126.1	1,211.4	1,230.0	1,283.7	1,363.2	1,550.1	2,157.5	2,236.9	2,602.9	2,846.9	2,780.6	Goods: Exports f.o.b.	78aad
-1,076.7	-875.7	-1,333.2	-1,413.2	-1,484.4	-1,428.0	-1,673.0	-2,327.8	-2,384.0	-2,546.6	-3,032.6	-2,880.3	-3,542.7	-4,255.7	-4,225.7	Goods: Imports f.o.b.	78abd
-17.0	168.1	-355.3	-339.9	-358.3	-216.6	-443.0	-1,044.1	-1,020.8	-996.5	-875.1	-643.4	-939.8	-1,408.8	-1,445.1	*Trade Balance*	78acd
101.1	123.7	158.3	195.8	297.7	356.1	458.8	614.0	660.4	697.5	665.9	559.0	588.8	639.9	699.5	Services: Credit	78add
-180.0	-170.1	-259.5	-317.9	-376.9	-383.7	-356.4	-525.3	-586.1	-644.9	-694.9	-659.7	-650.5	-791.8	-790.7	Services: Debit	78aed
-95.9	121.7	-456.5	-462.0	-437.5	-244.2	-340.6	-955.4	-946.5	-943.9	-904.1	-744.1	-1,001.5	-1,560.7	-1,536.3	*Balance on Goods & Services*	78afd
30.5	35.7	31.1	31.6	31.0	20.9	63.9	69.1	61.1	63.6	46.6	40.2	72.4	91.4	76.2	Income: Credit	78agd
-200.6	-250.1	-210.4	-207.9	-210.4	-216.6	-166.7	-210.1	-179.5	-193.6	-205.7	-270.1	-311.1	-275.1	-280.7	Income: Debit	78ahd
-266.0	-92.7	-635.8	-638.3	-616.9	-439.9	-443.4	-1,096.4	-1,064.9	-1,073.9	-1,063.2	-974.0	-1,240.2	-1,744.4	-1,740.8	*Balance on Gds, Serv. & Inc.*	78aid
21.0	76.2	195.9	227.7	255.1	217.6	276.7	406.2	371.4	456.4	508.2	537.1	628.8	742.9	754.4	Current Transfers, n.i.e.: Credit	78ajd
-1.3	-1.1	-2.6	-3.4	-5.3	-10.6	-17.0	-15.7	-8.2	-7.8	-17.0	-14.6	-22.1	-37.6	-39.5	Current Transfers: Debit	78akd
—	—	—	—	—	—	—	—	—	—	61.6	65.0	85.0	71.0	68.4	Capital Account, n.i.e.	78bcd
—	—	—	—	—	—	—	—	—	—	61.6	65.0	85.0	71.0	68.4	Capital Account, n.i.e.: Credit	78bad
—	—	—	—	—	—	—	—	—	—	....	....	....	....	....	Capital Account: Debit	78bbd
-124.3	-329.0	187.7	78.0	228.3	-46.1	731.8	610.5	816.2	655.2	494.8	672.3	737.4	1,136.7	637.5	Financial Account, n.i.e.	78bjd
—	—	—	—	—	—	—	—	—	—	....	....	....	....	....	Direct Investment Abroad	78bdd
61.8	68.8	150.2	329.7	76.2	47.7	90.7	94.1	142.5	65.2	75.2	76.9	84.4	672.8	154.6	Dir. Invest. in Rep. Econ., n.i.e.	78bed
-1.1	-.2	—	—	—	-1.8	-.2	1.8	112.4	-9.8	-22.2	-11.5	-18.1	-11.6	-26.0	Portfolio Investment Assets	78bfd
-1.1	-.2	—	—	—	—	—	—	—	—	....	....	....	....	....	Equity Securities	78bkd
—	—	—	—	—	-1.8	-.2	1.8	112.4	-9.8	-22.2	-11.5	-18.1	-11.6	-26.0	Debt Securities	78bld
-26.5	-11.4	-16.0	-372.2	-63.9	-19.5	71.3	9.6	-27.0	7.1	5.9	-4.5	249.7	65.8	136.5	Portfolio Investment Liab., n.i.e.	78bgd
—	-1.2	—	—	—	—	—	—	—	—	....	....	....	....	....	Equity Securities	78bmd
-26.5	-10.2	-16.0	-372.2	-63.9	-19.5	71.3	9.6	-27.0	7.1	5.9	-4.5	249.7	65.8	136.5	Debt Securities	78bnd
....	....	....	....	....	....	....	....	....	—	....	....	....	....	....	Financial Derivatives Assets	78bwd
....	....	....	....	....	....	....	....	....	—	....	....	....	....	....	Financial Derivatives Liabilities	78bxd
—	—	—	29.4	98.7	-78.0	68.1	57.2	-3.0	116.8	125.1	199.2	221.2	241.7	199.9	Other Investment Assets	78bhd
....	....	....	....	....	....	....	....	....	—	....	....	....	....	....	Monetary Authorities	78bod
—	—	—	29.4	98.7	-90.7	—	—	-45.9	-49.2	....	....	....	....	....	General Government	78bpd
—	—	—	—	—	—	—	—	—	—	....	....	....	....	....	Banks	78bqd
—	—	—	—	—	12.7	68.1	57.2	42.9	166.0	125.1	199.2	221.2	241.7	199.9	Other Sectors	78brd
-158.5	-386.2	53.5	91.1	117.3	5.5	501.9	447.8	591.3	475.9	310.8	412.2	200.2	168.0	172.5	Other Investment Liab., n.i.e.	78bid
-321.5	-450.3	-246.3	-87.8	-93.9	-102.5	-66.1	.6	-44.1	-63.9	-78.3	-56.3	-108.6	-54.2	-25.6	Monetary Authorities	78bsd
44.9	-18.6	-17.0	31.6	60.6	3.6	-25.8	-16.3	-51.3	132.7	11.8	91.1	89.5	252.4	295.9	General Government	78btd
-64.0	13.0	38.7	16.9	-14.3	-17.0	-3.9	14.4	—	—	7.3	19.4	-4.6	3.2	23.0	Banks	78bud
182.1	69.7	278.1	130.4	164.9	121.4	597.7	449.1	686.7	407.1	370.0	358.0	223.9	-33.4	-120.8	Other Sectors	78bvd
43.6	67.3	-72.7	-2.4	54.7	36.1	83.3	81.8	85.2	-23.6	-136.2	-71.7	40.7	66.8	195.0	Net Errors and Omissions	78cad
-327.0	-279.3	-327.5	-338.5	-84.1	-242.9	631.4	-13.6	199.7	6.3	-151.8	214.1	229.6	235.4	-125.0	*Overall Balance*	78cbd
327.0	279.3	327.5	338.5	84.1	242.9	-631.4	13.6	-199.7	-6.3	151.8	-214.1	-229.6	-235.4	125.0	Reserves and Related Items	79dad
-62.6	-56.2	73.2	110.6	-59.0	41.8	-551.3	51.6	-120.5	-47.3	157.3	-199.0	-257.7	-263.0	125.0	Reserve Assets	79dbd
-48.6	-56.7	-20.1	30.8	-12.7	-11.9	-2.8	-31.7	-31.3	—	—	—	—	—	—	Use of Fund Credit and Loans	79dcd
438.2	392.2	274.5	197.0	155.8	213.0	-77.3	-6.4	-47.9	41.0	-5.5	-15.1	28.1	27.6	....	Exceptional Financing	79ded

Guatemala

		1970	1971	1972	1973	1974	1975	1976	1977	1978	1979	1980	1981	1982	1983	1984
Government Finance																*Millions of Quetzales:*
Deficit (-) or Surplus	80	−13.0	−30.1	−44.9	−37.2	−45.8	−6.7	−96.6	−40.6	6.6	−167.5	−362.6	−613.0	−360.4	−295.3	....
Revenue	81	165.3	173.4	186.6	214.7	282.1	351.3	428.0	603.0	734.9	682.2	753.7	748.7	749.1	742.9	
Grants Received	81z	....	....	....	....	....	....	....	....	....	....	....	....	....	....	
Exp. & Lending Minus Repay.	82z	....	....	....	....	....	....	....	....	....	....	....	....	....	....	
Expenditure	82	178.3	203.5	231.5	251.9	327.9	358.0	524.6	643.6	728.3	849.7	1,116.3	1,361.7	1,109.5	1,038.2	
Lending Minus Repayments	83	....	....	....	....	....	....	....	....	....	....	....	....	....	....	
Adjustment to Cash Basis	82x	....	....	....	....	....	....	....	....	....	....	....	....	....	....	
Financing (by Residence of Lender)																
Domestic	84a	....	....	....	....	....	....	....	....	....	....	....	....	....	....	
Foreign	85a	....	....	....	....	....	....	....	....	....	....	....	....	....	....	
Debt: Domestic	88a	....	....	....	....	....	....	....	....	....	....	....	....	....	....	
Foreign	89a	....	....	....	....	....	....	....	....	....	....	....	....	....	....	
Financing (by Currency)																
Net Borrowing: Quetzales	84b	−6.4	28.1	20.3	19.6	48.8	24.6	125.6	95.1	21.1	−37.1	222.1	409.4	440.4	250.9	....
Foreign Currency	85b	24.4	7.4	31.5	21.4	18.7	12.9	16.7	33.0	94.5	99.7	113.3	105.3	82.4	80.3	....
Use of Cash Balances	87	−5.0	−5.4	−6.9	−3.8	−21.7	−30.8	−45.7	−87.5	−122.2	104.9	27.2	98.3	−162.4	−35.9	....
National Accounts																*Millions of Quetzales*
Exports of Goods & Services	90c	354	343	397	537	708	792	942	1,340	1,304	1,474	1,748	1,471	1,289	1,176	1,256
Government Consumption	91f	151	139	157	167	207	250	297	354	435	488	627	680	676	688	726
Gross Fixed Capital Formation	93e	239	264	273	357	468	571	900	1,039	1,218	1,286	1,295	1,443	1,310	950	912
Increase/Decrease(-) in Stocks	93i	6	22	−18	−5	120	16	34	60	95	8	−44	23	−76	52	184
Private Consumption	96f	1,493	1,588	1,682	2,034	2,470	2,875	3,396	4,127	4,675	5,432	6,217	7,022	7,150	7,501	7,856
Imports of Goods & Services	98c	−338	−371	−389	−519	−811	−858	−1,204	−1,439	−1,655	−1,784	−1,963	−2,032	−1,629	−1,317	−1,464
Gross Domestic Product (GDP)	99b	1,904	1,985	2,102	2,569	3,162	3,646	4,365	5,481	6,071	6,903	7,879	8,608	8,717	9,050	9,470
Net Factor Inc/Pmts(-) Abroad	98.n	−42	−44	−48	−48	−50	−69	−74	−33	−26	−12	−71	−103	−121	−113	−207
Gross National Income (GNI)	99a	1,862	1,941	2,054	2,521	3,111	3,577	4,292	5,448	6,044	6,891	7,809	8,505	8,596	8,937	9,264
GDP Volume 1958 Prices	99b.p	1,793	1,893	2,032	2,169	2,308	2,353	2,527	2,724	2,860	2,995	3,107	3,128	3,017	2,940	2,954
GDP Volume (1995=100)	99bv p	42.9	45.3	48.6	51.9	55.2	56.3	60.4	65.2	68.4	71.6	74.3	74.8	72.2	70.3	70.7
GDP Deflator (1995=100)	99bi p	5.2	5.1	5.1	5.8	6.7	7.6	8.5	9.9	10.4	11.3	12.4	13.5	14.2	15.1	15.7
																Millions:
Population	99z	5.27	5.42	5.58	5.74	I 6.05	6.24	I 6.19	6.36	6.54	6.73	6.92	7.11	7.32	7.52	7.74

	1985	1986	1987	1988	1989	1990	1991	1992	1993	1994	1995	1996	1997	1998	1999		
Year Ending December 31																**Government Finance**	
	−214.8	−218.5	−182.7	−284.6	−754.2	−406.2	242.5	407.0	−1,064.5	‡−938.7	−218.4	−268.0	−2,244.3	−2,708.9	−3,805.2	Deficit (-) or Surplus	80
	845.4	1,460.7	1,875.6	2,299.3	2,382.3	2,777.6	4,301.1	5,575.0	5,645.8	‡5,712.3	7,227.7	8,605.1	9,730.3	12,714.0	14,734.7	Revenue	81
	....	....	....	....	....	....	....	....	....	‡74.3	39.1	53.0	55.1	94.2	188.2	Grants Received	81z
	....	....	....	....	....	....	....	....	....	‡6,725.3	7,485.2	8,926.1	12,029.7	15,517.1	18,728.1	Exp. & Lending Minus Repay.	82z
	1,060.2	1,679.2	2,058.3	2,583.9	3,136.5	3,183.8	4,058.6	5,168.0	6,710.3	‡6,592.2	7,512.4	8,378.5	11,408.0	15,517.1	18,728.1	Expenditure	82
	....	....	....	....	....	....	....	....	....	‡237.8	308.4	235.9	—	—	—	Lending Minus Repayments	83
	....	....	....	....	....	....	....	....	....	‡−104.7	−335.6	311.7	621.7	—	—	Adjustment to Cash Basis	82x
																Financing (by Residence of Lender)	
	....	....	....	....	....	....	....	....	....	‡−187.5	433.0	−54.7	92.9	1,306.7	1,541.9	Domestic	84a
	....	....	....	....	....	....	....	....	....	‡1,126.2	−214.6	322.7	2,151.4	1,402.2	2,262.3	Foreign	85a
	....	....	....	....	....	....	....	....	....	4,854.7	4,485.2	5,093.0	5,862.2	6,259.8	7,807.1	Debt: Domestic	88a
	....	....	....	....	....	....	....	....	....	887.8	1,203.5	1,308.2	1,491.3	1,693.8	2,034.4	Foreign	89a
																Financing (by Currency)	
	213.9	134.9	174.0	292.5	279.6	346.0	369.3	80.9	551.7	....	....	....	....	....	....	Net Borrowing: Quetzales	84b
	84.8	75.6	78.7	152.4	122.2	126.5	−21.7	−11.2	−84.9	....	....	....	....	....	....	Foreign Currency	85b
	−83.9	8.0	−70.0	−160.3	352.4	−66.3	−590.1	−476.7	597.7	....	....	....	....	....	....	Use of Cash Balances	87
Millions of Quetzales																**National Accounts**	
	2,068	2,542	2,807	3,309	4,099	6,776	8,349	9,483	11,613	13,170	16,400	17,005	19,370	22,532	25,103	Exports of Goods & Services	90c
	777	1,124	1,400	1,640	1,870	2,324	2,714	3,482	4,151	4,468	4,692	4,851	5,391	6,733	7,729	Government Consumption	91f
	1,225	1,593	2,188	2,747	3,255	4,455	5,760	8,445	10,335	10,622	12,360	12,727	16,302	20,785	23,801	Gross Fixed Capital Formation	93e
	61	43	275	67	−54	213	1,002	1,448	745	1,087	460	−614	−1,540	−1,424	−2,810	Increase/Decrease(-) in Stocks	93i
	9,296	12,847	14,989	17,289	19,837	28,692	39,693	45,899	54,165	63,893	72,899	83,072	93,804	105,119	114,769	Private Consumption	96f
	−2,247	−2,311	−3,949	−4,507	−5,323	−8,143	−10,216	−14,771	−16,765	−18,571	−21,656	−21,562	−25,454	−32,618	−35,015	Imports of Goods & Services	98c
	11,180	15,838	17,711	20,545	23,685	34,317	47,302	53,985	64,243	74,669	85,157	95,479	107,873	121,127	133,577	Gross Domestic Product (GDP)	99b
	−331	−436	−472	−471	−544	−828	−517	−426	−854	−856	926	−1,400	−1,451	−1,139	−1,513	Net Factor Inc/Pmts(-) Abroad	98.n
	10,849	15,402	17,239	20,074	23,141	33,489	43,786	53,560	63,389	73,813	84,231	94,079	106,422	119,988	132,064	Gross National Income (GNI)	99a
	2,936	2,940	3,044	3,163	3,288	3,390	3,514	3,684	3,829	3,983	4,180	4,303	4,491	4,722	4,885	GDP Volume 1958 Prices	99b.p
	70.2	70.3	72.8	75.7	78.7	81.1	84.1	88.1	91.6	95.3	100.0	102.9	107.4	113.0	116.9	GDP Volume (1995=100)	99bv p
	18.7	26.4	28.6	31.9	35.4	49.7	66.1	71.9	82.4	92.0	100.0	108.9	117.9	125.9	134.2	GDP Deflator (1995=100)	99bi p
Midyear Estimates																	
	7.96	8.19	8.43	8.68	8.94	8.75	8.98	9.22	9.47	9.72	9.98	10.24	10.52	10.80	11.09	**Population**	99z

(See notes in the back of the book.)

Guinea

		1970	1971	1972	1973	1974	1975	1976	1977	1978	1979	1980	1981	1982	1983	1984
Exchange Rates															*Francs per SDR:*	
Official Rate	aa	24.7	24.7	24.7	24.9	25.3	24.7	24.7	24.7	24.7	24.7	24.7	24.7	24.7	24.7	24.7
															Francs per US Dollar:	
Official Rate	ae	24.7	22.7	22.7	20.7	20.7	21.1	21.2	20.3	18.9	18.7	19.4	21.2	22.4	23.6	25.2
Official Rate	rf	24.7	24.6	22.7	20.7	20.6	20.7	21.4	21.1	19.7	19.1	19.0	20.9	22.4	23.1	24.1
Fund Position															*Millions of SDRs:*	
Quota	2f. s	24.00	24.00	24.00	24.00	24.00	24.00	24.00	24.00	30.00	30.00	45.00	45.00	45.00	57.90	57.90
SDRs	1b. s	.15	.11	2.88	1.43	3.41	3.14	2.86	2.17	—	—	—	—	.17	.02	.03
Reserve Position in the Fund	1c. s	—	—	—	—	—	—	—	—	—	—	—	.55	1.45	—	—
Total Fund Cred.&Loans Outstg.	2tl	3.45	2.95	2.95	1.02	9.51	7.11	7.11	18.38	19.98	26.16	27.45	23.67	34.95	34.28	32.29
International Liquidity													*Millions of US Dollars Unless Otherwise Indicated:*			
Total Reserves minus Gold	1l. d	....	....	....	....	....	....	....	....	....	....	....	....	....	....	....
SDRs	1b. d	.15	.12	3.13	1.73	4.18	3.68	3.32	2.64	—	—	—	—	.19	.02	.03
Reserve Position in the Fund	1c. d	—	—	—	—	—	—	—	—	—	—	—	.64	1.60	—	—
Foreign Exchange	1d. d	....	....	....	....	....	....	....	....	....	....	....	....	....	....	....
Monetary Authorities: Other Liab.	4.. d	....	....	....	....	....	....	....	....	....	....	....	....	....	....	....
Deposit Money Banks: Assets	7a. d	....	....	....	....	....	....	....	....	....	....	....	....	....	....	....
Liabilities	7b. d	....	....	....	....	....	....	....	....	....	....	....	....	....	....	....
Monetary Authorities															*Millions of Francs:*	
Foreign Assets	11	....	....	....	....	....	....	....	....	....	....	....	....	....	....	....
Claims on Central Government	12a	....	....	....	....	....	....	....	....	....	....	....	....	....	....	....
Claims on Nonfin.Pub.Enterprises	12c	....	....	....	....	....	....	....	....	....	....	....	....	....	....	....
Claims on Private Sector	12d	....	....	....	....	....	....	....	....	....	....	....	....	....	....	....
Claims on Deposit Money Banks	12e	....	....	....	....	....	....	....	....	....	....	....	....	....	....	....
Claims on Other Banking Insts	12f	....	....	....	....	....	....	....	....	....	....	....	....	....	....	....
Reserve Money	14	....	....	....	....	....	....	....	....	....	....	....	....	....	....	....
of which: Currency Outside DMBs	14a	....	....	....	....	....	....	....	....	....	....	....	....	....	....	....
Foreign Liabilities	16c	....	....	....	....	....	....	....	....	....	....	....	....	....	....	....
Central Government Deposits	16d	....	....	....	....	....	....	....	....	....	....	....	....	....	....	....
Capital Accounts	17a	....	....	....	....	....	....	....	....	....	....	....	....	....	....	....
Other Items (Net)	17r	....	....	....	....	....	....	....	....	....	....	....	....	....	....	....
Deposit Money Banks															*Millions of Francs:*	
Reserves	20	....	....	....	....	....	....	....	....	....	....	....	....	....	....	....
Foreign Assets	21	....	....	....	....	....	....	....	....	....	....	....	....	....	....	....
Claims on Central Government	22a	....	....	....	....	....	....	....	....	....	....	....	....	....	....	....
Claims on Nonfin.Pub.Enterprises	22c	....	....	....	....	....	....	....	....	....	....	....	....	....	....	....
Claims on Private Sector	22d	....	....	....	....	....	....	....	....	....	....	....	....	....	....	....
Demand Deposits	24	....	....	....	....	....	....	....	....	....	....	....	....	....	....	....
Time, Savings,& Fgn.Currency Dep.	25	....	....	....	....	....	....	....	....	....	....	....	....	....	....	....
Foreign Liabilities	26c	....	....	....	....	....	....	....	....	....	....	....	....	....	....	....
Central Government Deposits	26d	....	....	....	....	....	....	....	....	....	....	....	....	....	....	....
Credit from Monetary Authorities	26g	....	....	....	....	....	....	....	....	....	....	....	....	....	....	....
Capital Accounts	27a	....	....	....	....	....	....	....	....	....	....	....	....	....	....	....
Other Items (Net)	27r	....	....	....	....	....	....	....	....	....	....	....	....	....	....	....
Monetary Survey															*Millions of Francs:*	
Foreign Assets (Net)	31n	....	....	....	....	....	....	....	....	....	....	....	....	....	....	....
Domestic Credit	32	....	....	....	....	....	....	....	....	....	....	....	....	....	....	....
Claims on Central Govt. (Net)	32an	....	....	....	....	....	....	....	....	....	....	....	....	....	....	....
Claims on Nonfin.Pub.Enterprises	32c	....	....	....	....	....	....	....	....	....	....	....	....	....	....	....
Claims on Private Sector	32d	....	....	....	....	....	....	....	....	....	....	....	....	....	....	....
Claims on Other Banking Insts	32f	....	....	....	....	....	....	....	....	....	....	....	....	....	....	....
Money	34	....	....	....	....	....	....	....	....	....	....	....	....	....	....	....
Quasi-Money	35	....	....	....	....	....	....	....	....	....	....	....	....	....	....	....
Capital Accounts	37a	....	....	....	....	....	....	....	....	....	....	....	....	....	....	....
Other Items (Net)	37r	....	....	....	....	....	....	....	....	....	....	....	....	....	....	....
Money plus Quasi-Money	35l	....	....	....	....	....	....	....	....	....	....	....	....	....	....	....
Interest Rates															*Percent Per Annum*	
Refinancing Rate *(End of Period)*	60	....	....	....	....	....	....	....	....	....	....	....	....	....	....	....
Savings Rate	60k	....	....	....	....	....	....	....	....	....	....	....	....	....	....	....
Deposit Rate	60l	....	....	....	....	....	....	....	....	....	....	....	....	....	....	....
Lending Rate	60p	....	....	....	....	....	....	....	....	....	....	....	....	....	....	....

1985	1986	1987	1988	1989	1990	1991	1992	1993	1994	1995	1996	1997	1998	1999		
End of Period															**Exchange Rates**	
24.7	288.2	624.2	740.1	814.8	967.4	1,148.6	1,268.3	1,335.7	1,432.1	1,483.5	1,494.2	1,544.8	1,827.7	2,382.7	Official Rate	aa
End of Period (ae) Period Average (rf)																
22.5	235.6	440.0	550.0	620.0	680.0	803.0	922.4	972.4	981.0	998.0	1,039.1	1,145.0	1,298.0	1,736.0	Official Rate	ae
24.3	333.5	428.4	474.4	591.6	660.2	753.9	902.0	955.5	976.6	991.4	1,004.0	1,095.3	1,236.8	....	Official Rate	rf
End of Period															**Fund Position**	
57.90	57.90	57.90	57.90	57.90	57.90	57.90	78.70	78.70	78.70	78.70	78.70	78.70	78.70	107.10	Quota	2f. s
—	.32	.21	.18	—	.16	9.44	7.93	8.49	3.79	5.01	.54	1.97	1.02	.94	SDRs	1b. s
—	—	—	—	—	—	—	.03	.07	.07	.07	.08	.08	.08	.08	Reserve Position in the Fund	1c. s
28.35	32.93	40.09	36.08	46.65	36.17	38.39	46.32	44.00	48.64	63.11	57.32	73.39	90.05	92.71	Total Fund Cred.&Loans Outstg.	2tl
End of Period															**International Liquidity**	
....	....	....	....	....	....	80.05	86.96	132.12	87.85	86.76	87.34	121.63	....	....	Total Reserves minus Gold	1l. d
—	.39	.30	.24	—	.23	13.50	10.90	11.67	5.53	7.45	.77	2.66	1.43	1.29	SDRs	1b. d
—	—	—	—	—	—	—	.04	.09	.10	.10	.11	.10	.11	.10	Reserve Position in the Fund	1c. d
....	....	....	....	....	....	66.55	76.01	120.36	82.22	79.21	86.46	118.88	....	....	Foreign Exchange	1d. d
....	....	....	....	....	....	13.92	15.88	5.50	6.70	5.30	44.61	10.13	....	....	Monetary Authorities: Other Liab.	4..d
....	....	....	....	56.79	70.36	81.27	87.24	85.47	86.27	90.89	81.05	73.08	....	....	Deposit Money Banks: Assets	7a. d
....	....	....	....	45.42	48.79	51.31	45.68	46.81	52.39	79.93	70.17	53.86	....	....	Liabilities	7b. d
End of Period															**Monetary Authorities**	
....	....	....	....	....	....	112,302	147,595	188,247	164,098	197,253	206,368	258,071	....	....	Foreign Assets	11
....	....	....	....	....	....	131,239	163,336	178,636	226,365	333,304	422,249	516,452	....	....	Claims on Central Government	12a
....	....	....	....	....	....	2,428	2,359	2,352	3,059	3,685	4,063	4,659	....	....	Claims on Nonfin.Pub.Enterprises	12c
....	....	....	....	....	....	189	445	42	129	108	159	3,362	....	....	Claims on Private Sector	12d
....	....	....	....	....	....	15,403	9,890	8,211	8,587	8,632	8,196	26,227	....	....	Claims on Deposit Money Banks	12e
....	....	....	....	....	....	86			48	493			....	....	Claims on Other Banking Insts	12f
....	....	....	....	....	....	147,756	165,178	196,468	176,724	198,442	195,681	248,968	....	....	Reserve Money	14
....	....	....	....	....	....	119,409	133,028	166,609	154,748	167,144	154,420	191,635	....	....	*of which: Currency Outside DMBs*	14a
....	....	....	....	....	....	55,262	73,396	64,127	76,223	98,912	132,011	124,978	....	....	Foreign Liabilities	16c
....	....	....	....	....	....	77,036	93,479	129,003	151,170	249,942	313,926	444,141	....	....	Central Government Deposits	16d
....	....	....	....	....	....	31,512	41,609	51,848	57,608	55,460	51,645	52,291	....	....	Capital Accounts	17a
....	....	....	....	....	....	-49,918	-50,038	-63,958	-59,438	-59,278	-52,226	-61,607	....	....	Other Items (Net)	17r
End of Period															**Deposit Money Banks**	
....	....	....	....	3,599	7,407	13,978	17,591	20,458	15,380	28,310	31,930	46,130	....	....	Reserves	20
....	....	....	....	35,210	47,846	65,256	80,474	83,110	84,630	90,710	84,220	83,670	....	....	Foreign Assets	21
....	....	....	....	156	4	16	20	12,596	13,210	29,910	38,500	46,750	....	....	Claims on Central Government	22a
....	....	....	....	1	192	21	59	124	10	270	430	260	....	....	Claims on Nonfin.Pub.Enterprises	22c
....	....	....	....	53,138	71,648	79,397	106,487	130,322	144,410	181,410	188,270	184,070	....	....	Claims on Private Sector	22d
....	....	....	....	30,194	42,908	53,012	76,665	86,763	94,430	104,060	112,590	130,430	....	....	Demand Deposits	24
....	....	....	....	17,703	14,623	26,059	38,624	54,794	52,180	64,950	77,710	83,430	....	....	Time, Savings,& Fgn.Currency Dep.	25
....	....	....	....	28,163	33,175	41,199	42,135	45,523	51,400	79,770	72,920	61,670	....	....	Foreign Liabilities	26c
....	....	....	....	8,422	10,360	13,515	13,934	15,267	17,100	16,490	15,800	19,960	....	....	Central Government Deposits	26d
....	....	....	....	10,611	15,820	16,291	10,622	9,601	10,360	11,580	10,360	10,660	....	....	Credit from Monetary Authorities	26g
....	....	....	....	16,272	23,652	26,760	39,613	47,601	46,400	50,870	38,980	49,600	....	....	Capital Accounts	27a
....	....	....	....	-19,261	-13,441	-18,168	-16,962	-12,939	-14,230	2,920	14,960	5,120	....	....	Other Items (Net)	27r
End of Period															**Monetary Survey**	
....	....	....	....	....	....	81,098	112,537	161,707	121,105	109,282	85,657	155,094	....	....	Foreign Assets (Net)	31n
....	....	....	....	....	....	122,825	165,293	179,802	218,961	282,748	323,945	291,452	....	....	Domestic Credit	32
....	....	....	....	....	....	40,704	55,943	46,962	71,305	96,782	131,023	99,101	....	....	Claims on Central Govt. (Net)	32an
....	....	....	....	....	....	2,449	2,418	2,476	3,069	3,955	4,493	4,919	....	....	Claims on Nonfin.Pub.Enterprises	32c
....	....	....	....	....	....	79,586	106,932	130,364	144,539	181,518	188,429	187,432	....	....	Claims on Private Sector	32d
....	....	....	....	....	....	86			48	493			....	....	Claims on Other Banking Insts	32f
....	....	....	....	....	....	182,469	218,445	260,854	252,582	274,125	273,465	331,666	....	....	Money	34
....	....	....	....	17,703	14,623	26,059	38,624	54,794	52,180	64,950	77,710	83,430	....	....	Quasi-Money	35
....	....	....	....	....	....	58,272	81,222	99,449	104,008	106,330	90,625	101,891	....	....	Capital Accounts	37a
....	....	....	....	....	....	-62,877	-60,461	-73,588	-68,703	-53,343	-32,226	-70,452	....	....	Other Items (Net)	37r
....	....	....	....	....	....	208,528	257,069	315,648	304,762	339,075	351,175	415,096	....	....	Money plus Quasi-Money	35l
Percent Per Annum															**Interest Rates**	
....	9.00	10.00	10.00	13.00	15.00	19.00	19.00	17.00	17.00	18.00	18.00	15.00	....	....	Refinancing Rate *(End of Period)*	60
....	....	....	12.00	12.67	16.08	19.00	21.00	17.00	16.00	15.50	....	....	....	....	Savings Rate	60k
....	....	15.00	16.83	19.50	21.00	22.00	23.00	19.75	18.00	17.50	....	....	....	....	Deposit Rate	60l
....	....	15.00	15.00	17.25	21.17	24.50	27.00	24.50	22.00	21.50	....	....	....	....	Lending Rate	60p

Guinea

		1970	1971	1972	1973	1974	1975	1976	1977	1978	1979	1980	1981	1982	1983	1984
International Transactions															*Millions of Francs*	
Imports, c.i.f.	71	....	....	....	....	....	....	....	....	....	....	....	....	....	....	....
Balance of Payments															*Millions of US Dollars:*	
Current Account, n.i.e.	78al d	....	....	....			....		....		....	....	....	....	....	....
Goods: Exports f.o.b.	78aa d	....	....	....			....				....	....	....	....	....	....
Goods: Imports f.o.b.	78ab d	....	....	....			....				....	....	....	....	....	....
Trade Balance	78ac d	....	....	....			....				....	....	....	....	....	....
Services: Credit	78ad d	....	....	....			....				....	....	....	....	....	....
Services: Debit	78ae d	....	....	....			....				....	....	....	....	....	....
Balance on Goods & Services	78af d	....	....	....			....				....	....	....	....	....	....
Income: Credit	78ag d	....	....	....			....				....	....	....	....	....	....
Income: Debit	78ah d	....	....	....			....				....	....	....	....	....	....
Balance on Gds, Serv. & Inc.	78ai d	....	....	....			....				....	....	....	....	....	....
Current Transfers, n.i.e.: Credit	78aj d	....	....	....			....				....	....	....	....	....	....
Current Transfers: Debit	78ak d	....	....	....			....				....	....	....	....	....	....
Capital Account, n.i.e.	78bc d	....	....	....			....				....	....	....	....	....	....
Capital Account, n.i.e.: Credit	78ba d	....	....	....			....				....	....	....	....	....	....
Capital Account: Debit	78bb d	....	....	....			....				....	....	....	....	....	....
Financial Account, n.i.e.	78bj d	....	....	....			....				....	....	....	....	....	....
Direct Investment Abroad	78bd d	....	....	....			....				....	....	....	....	....	....
Dir. Invest. in Rep. Econ., n.i.e. ...	78be d	....	....	....			....				....	....	....	....	....	....
Portfolio Investment Assets	78bf d	....	....	....			....				....	....	....	....	....	....
Equity Securities	78bk d	....	....	....			....				....	....	....	....	....	....
Debt Securities	78bl d	....	....	....			....				....	....	....	....	....	....
Portfolio Investment Liab., n.i.e.	78bg d	....	....	....			....				....	....	....	....	....	....
Equity Securities	78bm d	....	....	....			....				....	....	....	....	....	....
Debt Securities	78bn d	....	....	....			....				....	....	....	....	....	....
Financial Derivatives Assets	78bw d	....	....	....			....				....	....	....	....	....	....
Financial Derivatives Liabilities	78bx d	....	....	....			....				....	....	....	....	....	....
Other Investment Assets	78bh d	....	....	....			....				....	....	....	....	....	....
Monetary Authorities	78bo d	....	....	....			....				....	....	....	....	....	....
General Government	78bp d	....	....	....			....				....	....	....	....	....	....
Banks	78bq d	....	....	....			....				....	....	....	....	....	....
Other Sectors	78br d	....	....	....			....				....	....	....	....	....	....
Other Investment Liab., n.i.e.	78bi d	....	....	....			....				....	....	....	....	....	....
Monetary Authorities	78bs d	....	....	....			....				....	....	....	....	....	....
General Government	78bt d	....	....	....			....				....	....	....	....	....	....
Banks	78bu d	....	....	....			....				....	....	....	....	....	....
Other Sectors	78bv d	....	....	....			....				....	....	....	....	....	....
Net Errors and Omissions	78ca d	....	....	....			....				....	....	....	....	....	....
Overall Balance	78cb d	....	....	....			....				....	....	....	....	....	....
Reserves and Related Items	79da d	....	....	....			....				....	....	....	....	....	....
Reserve Assets	79db d	....	....	....			....				....	....	....	....	....	....
Use of Fund Credit and Loans	79dc d	....	....	....			....				....	....	....	....	....	....
Exceptional Financing	79de d	....	....	....			....				....	....	....	....	....	....
Government Finance															*Millions of Francs:*	
Deficit (-) or Surplus	80	....	....		....										....	....
Revenue	81	....	....		....										....	....
Grants Received	81z	....	....		....										....	....
Expenditure	82	....	....		....										....	....
Lending Minus Repayments	83	....	....		....										....	....
Financing																
Domestic	84a	....	....		....										....	....
Foreign	85a	....	....		....										....	....
															Millions:	
Population	99z	3.92	4.02	4.11	....	....	4.34	4.43	I 5.06	5.17	5.29	5.41	4.55	4.64	I 4.41	4.53

	1985	1986	1987	1988	1989	1990	1991	1992	1993	1994	1995	1996	1997	1998	1999		
Millions of Francs																**International Transactions**	
	....	....	....	....	....	....	....	....	....	....	....	....	....	....	....	Imports, c.i.f.	71
Minus Sign Indicates Debit																Balance of Payments	
	....	−123.9	−38.3	−221.5	−179.7	−203.0	−288.8	−262.7	−56.8	−248.0	−216.5	−177.3	−91.1	−183.6	−151.6	Current Account, n.i.e.	78al *d*
	....	506.6	544.6	511.9	595.6	671.2	687.1	517.2	561.1	515.7	582.8	636.5	630.1	693.0	677.9	Goods: Exports f.o.b.	78aa *d*
	....	−422.7	−380.3	−510.6	−531.6	−585.8	−694.9	−608.4	−582.7	−685.4	−621.7	−525.3	−512.5	−572.0	−583.4	Goods: Imports f.o.b.	78ab *d*
	....	83.9	164.4	1.3	64.0	85.5	−7.8	−91.2	−21.6	−169.7	−39.0	111.2	117.6	121.0	94.5	*Trade Balance*	78ac *d*
	....	55.6	53.6	52.6	103.7	157.5	144.7	159.7	186.8	152.9	117.5	124.1	110.7	110.8	113.2	Services: Credit	78ad *d*
	....	−137.4	−154.0	−230.8	−259.8	−367.3	−347.8	−322.6	−334.8	−366.0	−389.3	−422.2	−321.6	−382.7	−342.1	Services: Debit	78ae *d*
	....	2.2	64.0	−177.0	−92.1	−124.3	−210.9	−254.0	−169.6	−382.9	−310.8	−186.8	−93.3	−150.9	−134.4	*Balance on Goods & Services*	78af *d*
	....	4.9	4.6	11.2	8.6	12.6	15.5	7.9	9.3	6.5	12.9	12.8	7.8	9.0	24.7	Income: Credit	78ag *d*
	....	−156.6	−128.8	−142.4	−178.5	−161.5	−181.4	−148.9	−92.6	−79.8	−97.5	−105.7	−121.3	−133.5	−106.9	Income: Debit	78ah *d*
	....	−149.6	−60.2	−308.1	−261.9	−273.2	−376.8	−395.0	−252.9	−456.1	−395.5	−279.8	−206.9	−275.5	−216.6	*Balance on Gds, Serv. & Inc.*	78ai *d*
	....	37.9	37.6	121.3	143.6	118.8	136.2	193.5	260.3	280.6	258.3	137.8	131.4	116.2	80.1	Current Transfers, n.i.e.: Credit	78aj *d*
	....	−12.3	−15.6	−34.7	−61.3	−48.6	−48.2	−61.2	−64.2	−72.5	−79.3	−35.3	−15.6	−24.3	−15.1	Current Transfers: Debit	78ak *d*
	....	....	....	....	198.7	—	—	8.0	5.0	—	—	—	—	—	—	Capital Account, n.i.e.	78bc *d*
	....	....	....	....	198.7	—	—	8.0	5.0	—	—	—	—	—	—	Capital Account, n.i.e.: Credit	78ba *d*
	....	....	....	....	....	....	....	....	....	....	....	....	....	....	....	Capital Account: Debit	78bb *d*
	....	−11.2	−49.5	34.8	−158.9	53.8	18.8	61.7	62.6	84.2	109.2	47.5	−89.3	8.0	117.2	Financial Account, n.i.e.	78bj *d*
	....	....	....	....	....	....	....	....	....	....	....	....	−.5		—	Direct Investment Abroad	78bd *d*
	....	8.4	12.9	15.7	12.3	17.9	38.8	19.7	2.7	.2	.8	23.8	17.3	17.8	63.4	Dir. Invest. in Rep. Econ., n.i.e.	78be *d*
	....	....	....	....	....	....	....	....	....	....	....	....	....	−82.7	−20.0	Portfolio Investment Assets	78bf *d*
	....	....	....	....	....	....	....	....	....	....	....	....	....	....	....	Equity Securities	78bk *d*
	....	....	....	....	....	....	....	....	....	....	....	....	....	−82.7	−20.0	Debt Securities.............................	78bl *d*
	....	....	....	....	....	....	....	....	....	....	....	....	....	....	....	Portfolio Investment Liab., n.i.e.	78bg *d*
	....	....	....	....	....	....	....	....	....	....	....	....	....	....	....	Equity Securities	78bm *d*
	....	....	....	....	....	....	....	....	....	....	....	....	....	....	....	Debt Securities.............................	78bn *d*
	....	....	....	....	....	....	....	....	....	....	....	....	....	....	....	Financial Derivatives Assets	78bw *d*
	....	....	....	....	....	....	....	....	....	....	....	....	....	....	....	Financial Derivatives Liabilities	78bx *d*
	....	−29.1	−15.8	−5.2	−39.1	−52.7	−47.0	−27.5	−20.1	−14.5	−73.7	−19.8	−99.1	−14.6	.7	Other Investment Assets	78bh *d*
	....	....	....	....	....	....	....	....	....	....	−6.5	9.0	6.0	2.4	1.2	−1.0	Monetary Authorities	78bo *d*
	....	....	−5.4	3.1	−.9	−10.6	−1.1	−4.1	2.2	....	....	....	....	....	....	General Government	78bp *d*
	....	−25.9	−23.8	6.6	−7.6	−12.5	−11.4	−5.0	—	−2.2	−4.6	9.0	9.3	−12.5	7.6	Banks...	78bq *d*
	....	−3.3	13.4	−15.0	−30.6	−29.6	−34.5	−18.4	−22.3	−5.8	−78.2	−34.7	−110.8	−3.3	−6.0	Other Sectors	78br *d*
	....	9.6	−46.5	24.4	−132.1	88.7	27.0	69.6	80.0	98.5	182.2	44.0	−7.5	87.5	73.1	Other Investment Liab., n.i.e.	78bi *d*
	....	−15.9	—	—	—		8.4	−5.7	−.1	.1	−.5	39.1	−35.3	−3.0	.2	Monetary Authorities	78bs *d*
	....	39.2	−38.3	−28.8	−153.8	54.3	−34.1	15.4	54.6	79.6	106.5	−14.4	48.2	37.6	84.2	General Government	78bt *d*
	....	−.5	10.2	23.7	−2.6	9.4	2.4	−6.5	.1	8.3	26.0	−9.8	−18.1	6.7	3.7	Banks...	78bu *d*
	....	−13.3	−18.4	29.5	24.2	25.0	50.3	66.4	25.4	10.5	50.2	29.0	−2.3	46.2	−15.1	Other Sectors	78bv *d*
	....	22.6	−9.3	65.6	−44.9	52.4	112.3	18.6	−107.5	39.8	34.8	69.9	49.8	17.8	−45.0	Net Errors and Omissions	78cad
	....	−112.5	−97.1	−121.1	−184.9	−96.7	−157.8	−174.4	−96.7	−124.1	−72.5	−59.9	−130.6	−157.8	−79.5	*Overall Balance*	78cb *d*
	....	112.5	97.1	121.1	184.9	96.7	157.8	174.4	96.7	124.1	72.5	59.9	130.6	157.8	79.5	Reserves and Related Items	79da *d*
	....	−24.5	−15.0	−35.4	−13.4	−3.4	10.5	1.6	−49.9	32.4	−43.8	−6.5	−20.3	60.7	64.2	Reserve Assets	79db *d*
	....	5.2	8.9	−5.4	13.9	−14.3	3.2	11.0	−3.2	7.0	22.1	−8.4	22.4	22.8	3.7	Use of Fund Credit and Loans........	79dc *d*
	....	131.8	103.2	162.0	184.3	114.4	144.1	161.8	149.9	84.7	94.2	74.9	128.5	74.3	11.5	Exceptional Financing	79de *d*
Year Ending December 31																**Government Finance**	
	....	....	....	....	−50,145	−61,090	−76,955	−83,585	....	....	....	....	....	−192,650	−116,310 [f]	Deficit (-) or Surplus..........................	80
	....	....	....	....	222,778	297,860	326,183	357,889	....	....	....	....	....	497,293	574,901 [f]	Revenue..	81
	....	....	....	....	52,500	68,300	82,500	117,300	....	....	....	....	....	106,481	320,500 [f]	Grants Received.............................	81z
	....	....	....	....	326,960	426,852	489,323	559,854	....	....	....	....	....	792,554	1,010,060 [f]	Expenditure...................................	82
	....	....	....	....	−1,537	398	−3,685	−1,080	....	....	....	....	....	3,870	1,650 [f]	Lending Minus Repayments	83
																Financing	
	....	....	....	....	−15,092	−14,654	478	−26,108	....	....	....	....	....	−2,610	8,250 [f]	Domestic	84a
	....	....	....	....	65,237	75,744	76,477	109,693	....	....	....	....	....	195,260	108,060 [f]	Foreign...	85a
Midyear Estimates																	
	4.66	4.79	4.93	5.07	5.54	5.76	6.03	6.34	6.66	6.94	7.15	7.28	7.33	7.34	7.36	**Population**...................................	99z

(See notes in the back of the book.)

Guinea-Bissau

	1970	1971	1972	1973	1974	1975	1976	1977	1978	1979	1980	1981	1982	1983	1984
Exchange Rates														*Francs per SDR:*	
Official Rate .... aa	.44	.46	.45	.48	.46	.49	.56	.64	.68	.68	.68	.68	.68	1.36	1.92
														Francs per US Dollar:	
Official Rate .... ae	.44	.42	.42	.40	.38	.42	.49	.53	.52	.51	.53	.58	.61	1.29	1.96
Official Rate .... rf	.44	.44	.42	.38	.39	.39	.47	.52	.54	.52	.52	.57	.61	.65	1.61
Fund Position														*Millions of SDRs:*	
Quota .... 2f. s	....		....			....		3.20	3.90	3.90	5.90	5.90	5.90	7.50	7.50
SDRs .... 1b. s	....		....			....		—	—	.09	—	.07	.01	.01	.09
Reserve Position in the Fund .... 1c. s	....		....			....		.80	—	—	.50	—	—	—	—
Total Fund Cred.&Loans Outstg. 2tl	....		....			....		—	—	1.10	1.10	2.95	2.68	2.26	3.73
International Liquidity												*Millions of US Dollars Unless Otherwise Indicated:*			
Total Reserves minus Gold .... 1l. d	....		....			....	....	....		....	....				
SDRs .... 1b. d	....		....			....	....	....		—	—	—			
Reserve Position in the Fund .... 1c. d	....		....			....	....	....	—	—	.12	—	.08	.01	.01	.09
Foreign Exchange .... 1d. d	....		....			....	....	....		—	—	—			
Monetary Authorities: Other Liab. .. 4.. d	....		....			....	....	....		....	....				
Deposit Money Banks: Assets .... 7a. d	....		....			....	....	....		....	....				
Liabilities .... 7b. d	....		....			....	....	....		....	....				
Monetary Authorities														*Millions of Francs:*	
Foreign Assets 11	....		....			....	....	....		....	....				
Claims on Central Government 12a	....		....			....	....	....		....	....				
Claims on Other Financial Insts. 12f	....		....			....	....	....		....	....				
Reserve Money 14	....		....			....	....	....		....	....				
of which: Currency Outside DMBs 14a	....		....			....	....	....		....	....				
Foreign Liabilities 16c	....		....			....	....	....		....	....				
Central Government Deposits 16d	....		....			....	....	....		....	....				
Other Items (Net) 17r	....		....			....	....	....		....	....				
Deposit Money Banks														*Millions of Francs:*	
Reserves 20	....		....			....	....	....		....	....				
Foreign Assets 21	....		....			....	....	....		....	....				
Claims on Central Government 22a	....		....			....	....	....		....	....				
Claims on Private Sector 22d	....		....			....	....	....		....	....				
Claims on Other Financial Insts. 22f	....		....			....	....	....		....	....				
Demand Deposits 24	....		....			....	....	....		....	....				
Time & Foreign Currency Deposits 25	....		....			....	....	....		....	....				
Foreign Liabilities 26c	....		....			....	....	....		....	....				
Long-Term Foreign Liabilities 26cl	....		....			....	....	....		....	....				
Central Government Deposits 26d	....		....			....	....	....		....	....				
Credit from Monetary Authorities 26g	....		....			....	....	....		....	....				
Other Items (Net) 27r	....		....			....	....	....		....	....				
Monetary Survey														*Millions of Francs:*	
Foreign Assets (Net) 31n	....		....			....	....	....		....	....				
Domestic Credit 32	....		....			....	....	....		....	....				
Claims on Central Govt. (Net) 32an	....		....			....	....	....		....	....				
Claims on Private Sector 32d	....		....			....	....	....		....	....				
Claims on Other Financial Insts. 32f	....		....			....	....	....		....	....				
Money 34	....		....			....	....	....		....	....				
Quasi-Money 35	....		....			....	....	....		....	....				
Long-Term Foriegn Liabilities 36cl	....		....			....	....	....		....	....				
Other Items (Net) 37r	....		....			....	....	....		....	....				
Money plus Quasi-Money 35l	....		....			....	....	....		....	....				
Interest Rates														*Percent Per Annum*	
Discount Rate *(End of Period)* 60	....		....			....		....		....	....				
Money Market Rate 60b	....		....			....	7.28	7.38	7.40	7.72	10.13	13.68	14.66	12.23	11.92
Deposit Rate 60l	....		....			....		....		....	....				
Lending Rate 60p	....		....			....		....		....	....				
Prices														*Index Numbers (1995=100):*	
Consumer Prices 64	....		....			....		....		....	....				
International Transactions														*Millions of Francs*	
Exports 70	....		....			....		....		....	....				
Imports, c.i.f. 71	....		....			....		....		....	....				
Imports, f.o.b. 71.v	....		....			....		....		....	....				

1985	1986	1987	1988	1989	1990	1991	1992	1993	1994	1995	1996	1997	1998	1999		
End of Period															**Exchange Rates**	
2.98	4.49	18.58	28.21	40.18	54.91	109.13	183.10	242.25	345.18	501.49	772.88	807.94	791.61	I896.19	Official Rate	aa
End of Period (ae) Period Average (rf)																
2.71	3.67	13.10	20.97	30.57	38.59	76.29	133.16	176.37	236.45	337.37	537.48	598.81	562.21	I652.95	Official Rate	ae
2.45	3.13	8.60	17.07	27.85	33.62	56.29	106.68	155.11	198.34	278.04	405.75	583.67	589.95	I615.70	Official Rate	rf
End of Period															**Fund Position**	
7.50	7.50	7.50	7.50	7.50	7.50	7.50	10.50	10.50	10.50	10.50	10.50	10.50	10.50	14.20	Quota	2f. s
—	—	.05	—	—	—	—	—	.01	—	.01	.01	.04	.02	.06	SDRs	1b. s
—	—	—	—	—	—	—	—	—	—	—	—	—	—	—	Reserve Position in the Fund	1c. s
2.80	1.87	3.14	2.20	3.75	3.75	3.75	3.75	3.45	3.15	3.98	5.33	9.04	10.95	12.63	Total Fund Cred.&Loans Outstg.	2tl
End of Period															**International Liquidity**	
....	-.63	10.31	15.97	20.84	18.22	14.58	17.75	14.17	18.43	20.27	11.53	33.70	35.76	35.28	Total Reserves minus Gold	1l. d
—	—	.07	—	—	—	—	—	.01	—	.01	.01	.06	.03	.08	SDRs	1b. d
—	—	—	—	—	—	—	—	—	—	—	—	—	—	—	Reserve Position in the Fund	1c. d
....	-.63	10.24	15.97	20.84	18.22	14.58	17.75	14.16	18.43	20.26	11.52	33.65	35.73	35.21	Foreign Exchange	1d. d
....	79.4	96.3	92.2	43.4	32.5	38.6	53.1	48.3	42.6	38.6	18.2	1.8	.7	1.4	Monetary Authorities: Other Liab.	4.. d
....	....	....	....	....	4.5	2.8	12.1	10.8	12.1	18.7	16.7	19.2	19.3	16.6	Deposit Money Banks: Assets	7a. d
....	....	....	....	....	1.0	.2	1.7	.7	7.2	6.9	7.5	11.7	12.9	11.1	Liabilities	7b. d
End of Period															**Monetary Authorities**	
....	-2	135	335	637	703	1,112	2,364	2,499	4,357	6,837	6,196	20,183	20,105	23,038	Foreign Assets	11
....	328	668	1,105	2,444	2,007	1,982	2,857	3,197	4,144	4,728	7,679	10,690	12,453	13,081	Claims on Central Government	12a
....	....	....	....	....	....	....	....	....	....	....	....	....	....	—	Claims on Other Financial Insts.	12f
....	133	258	475	647	794	1,831	3,031	4,005	5,300	6,998	9,709	21,922	19,011	25,561	Reserve Money	14
....	84	143	246	384	562	839	1,603	2,039	3,015	4,278	6,370	20,137	17,642	24,186	of which: Currency Outside DMBs	14a
....	302	1,405	2,114	1,676	1,461	3,354	7,752	9,360	11,157	15,012	13,878	8,359	9,055	12,251	Foreign Liabilities	16c
....	-8	306	592	1,474	1,905	2,286	2,487	2,642	4,915	7,722	9,080	6,110	8,148	2,994	Central Government Deposits	16d
....	-100	-1,167	-1,741	-717	-243	-2,097	-4,808	-5,985	-8,542	-13,840	-18,793	-5,518	-3,655	-4,686	Other Items (Net)	17r
End of Period															**Deposit Money Banks**	
...	...	...	...	...	230	949	1,484	2,052	2,420	3,362	2,614	4,392	2,728	2,728	Reserves	20
...	...	...	...	...	173	214	1,610	1,912	2,856	6,295	8,989	11,479	10,827	10,827	Foreign Assets	21
...	...	...	...	...	443	460	624	544	576	567	77	21	21	21	Claims on Central Government	22a
...	...	...	...	...	1,518	1,787	1,751	2,859	4,617	4,612	5,305	7,651	9,859	9,859	Claims on Private Sector	22d
...	—	—	...	—	—	—	—	—	—	—	—	—	—	—	Claims on Other Financial Insts.	22f
...	...	...	...	...	431	477	834	1,050	1,855	2,880	4,507	16,431	14,476	14,476	Demand Deposits	24
...	...	...	...	...	358	513	1,452	2,361	3,207	4,395	6,320	1,132	1,355	1,355	Time & Foreign Currency Deposits	25
...	...	...	...	...	39	16	228	114	1,700	2,330	3,999	6,984	7,220	7,220	Foreign Liabilities	26c
...	...	...	...	...	—	—	3	4	6	8	13	14	14	14	Long-Term Foreign Liabilities	26cl
...	...	...	...	...	2	7	232	132	47	14	561	820	1,014	1,014	Central Government Deposits	26d
...	...	...	...	...	1,208	2,272	3,223	4,328	4,328	4,328	97	—	—	—	Credit from Monetary Authorities	26g
...	...	...	...	...	324	124	-502	-622	-674	881	1,489	-1,838	-644	-644	Other Items (Net)	27r
End of Period															**Monetary Survey**	
....	-302	-1,184	-1,660	-839	-625	-2,044	-4,006	-5,064	-5,644	-4,211	-2,692	16,318	14,657	14,394	Foreign Assets (Net)	31n
....	310	446	692	1,739	6,355	1,935	2,514	3,825	4,374	2,171	3,420	11,432	13,172	18,954	Domestic Credit	32
....	164	196	217	692	4,550	6	62	-542	-2,302	-3,959	-3,923	331	613	9,095	Claims on Central Govt. (Net)	32an
....	145	250	475	1,047	1,805	1,930	2,452	4,368	6,677	6,129	7,343	11,101	12,559	9,859	Claims on Private Sector	32d
....	—	—	—	—	—	—	—	—	—	—	—	—	—	—	Claims on Other Financial Insts.	32f
....	133	265	489	638	5,291	1,332	2,440	3,105	4,910	7,211	10,891	36,625	32,194	39,420	Money	34
....	2	86	120	199	358	513	1,452	2,361	3,207	4,395	6,320	1,132	1,355	1,355	Quasi-Money	35
....	....	....	....	....	—	—	3	4	6	8	13	14	14	14	Long-Term Foriegn Liabilities	36cl
....	-100	-1,165	-1,739	-662	-113	-2,877	-6,775	-8,598	-11,538	-16,195	-19,639	-10,020	-5,733	-7,440	Other Items (Net)	37r
....	135	351	609	837	5,649	1,845	3,891	5,466	8,116	11,606	17,212	37,757	33,548	40,774	Money plus Quasi-Money	35l
Percent Per Annum															**Interest Rates**	
....	....	....	....	....	42.00	42.00	45.50	41.00	26.00	39.00	54.00	6.00	6.25	5.75	Discount Rate (End of Period)	60
10.66	8.58	8.37	8.72	10.07	10.98	10.94	11.45	....	....	....	....	....	4.81	4.95	Money Market Rate	60b
....	....	....	23.00	28.00	32.67	36.00	39.33	53.92	28.67	26.50	47.25	4.63	3.50	3.50	Deposit Rate	60l
....	18.00	18.00	30.00	38.33	45.75	47.00	50.33	63.58	36.33	32.92	51.75	....	....	....	Lending Rate	60p
Period Averages															**Prices**	
....	....	3.9	6.3	11.3	15.1	23.8	40.3	59.7	68.8	100.0	150.7	224.7	239.4	237.7	Consumer Prices	64
Millions of Francs															**International Transactions**	
....	....	....	271	395	648	1,150	690	4,360	16,580	12,310	11,030	28,300	15,800	30,300	Exports	70
....	....	....	1,131	2,159	2,882	4,272	10,181	9,541	32,530	36,990	35,240	51,800	37,200	58,300	Imports, c.i.f.	71
....	....	....	1,006	1,919	2,289	3,798	8,908	8,348	2,857	16,092	21,150	45,043	....	....	Imports, f.o.b.	71.v

Guinea-Bissau

654

		1970	1971	1972	1973	1974	1975	1976	1977	1978	1979	1980	1981	1982	1983	1984
Balance of Payments														*Millions of US Dollars:*		
Current Account, n.i.e.	78al d	...	...	...	...	...	...	...	...	...	...	...	...	−79.50	−72.00	−65.50
Goods: Exports f.o.b.	78aa d	...	...	...	...	...	...	...	...	...	...	...	...	11.80	8.60	17.40
Goods: Imports f.o.b.	78ab d	...	...	...	...	...	...	...	...	...	...	...	...	−61.50	−58.40	−60.10
Trade Balance	78ac d													−49.70	−49.80	−42.70
Services: Credit	78ad d	...	...	...	...	...	...	...	...	...	...	...	...	5.60	6.70	8.00
Services: Debit	78ae d													−13.60	−13.20	−21.20
Balance on Goods & Services	78af d													−57.70	−56.30	−55.90
Income: Credit	78ag d	...	...	...	...	...	...	...	...	...	...	...	...	—	—	—
Income: Debit	78ah d													−7.80	−4.80	−4.70
Balance on Gds, Serv. & Inc.	78ai d													−65.50	−61.10	−60.60
Current Transfers, n.i.e.: Credit	78aj d	...	...	...	...	...	...	...	...	...	...	...	...	—	—	—
Current Transfers: Debit	78ak d													−14.00	−10.90	−4.90
Capital Account, n.i.e.	78bc d	...	...	...	...	...	...	...	...	...	...	...	...	44.50	43.00	29.30
Capital Account, n.i.e.: Credit	78ba d													44.50	43.00	29.30
Capital Account: Debit	78bb d													—	—	—
Financial Account, n.i.e.	78bj d	...	...	...	...	...	...	...	...	...	...	...	...	23.80	16.66	36.63
Direct Investment Abroad	78bd d													—	—	—
Dir. Invest. in Rep. Econ., n.i.e.	78be d													—	—	—
Portfolio Investment Assets	78bf d													—	—	—
Equity Securities	78bk d													—	—	—
Debt Securities	78bl d													—	—	—
Portfolio Investment Liab., n.i.e.	78bg d													—	—	—
Equity Securities	78bm d													—	—	—
Debt Securities	78bn d													—	—	—
Financial Derivatives Assets	78bw d															...
Financial Derivatives Liabilities	78bx d															...
Other Investment Assets	78bh d													—	—	—
Monetary Authorities	78bo d															
General Government	78bp d													—	—	—
Banks	78bq d													—	—	—
Other Sectors	78br d													—	—	—
Other Investment Liab., n.i.e.	78bi d													23.80	16.66	36.63
Monetary Authorities	78bs d													—	—	—
General Government	78bt d													23.80	16.66	36.63
Banks	78bu d													—	—	—
Other Sectors	78bv d													—	—	—
Net Errors and Omissions	78ca d	...	...	...	...	...	...	...	...	...	...	...	...	−9.17	−5.35	−12.88
Overall Balance	78cb d													−20.37	−17.69	−12.45
Reserves and Related Items	79da d	...	...	...	...	...	...	...	...	...	...	...	...	20.37	17.69	12.45
Reserve Assets	79db d													16.17	13.50	2.60
Use of Fund Credit and Loans	79dc d													−.29	−.45	1.48
Exceptional Financing	79de d													4.50	4.64	8.37
Government Finance														*Millions of Francs:*		
Deficit (-) or Surplus	80														−34.1	−71.0
Revenue	81	...	...	...	...	...	...	...	...	...	...	...	...		15.6	30.6
Grants Received	81z														23.1	48.6
Expenditure	82														72.8	150.2
Lending Minus Repayments	83	...	...	...	...	...	...	...	...	...	...	...	...		—	—
Financing																
Domestic	84a														19.4	19.3
Foreign	85a														10.4	45.3
Unallocated Financing	84xx	...	...	...	...	...	...	...	...	...	...	...	...		4.3	6.4
National Accounts														*Millions of Francs*		
Exports of Goods & Services	90c	...	...	...	...	...	...	...	...	...	...	...	...			...
Government Consumption	91f															
Gross Fixed Capital Formation	93e															
Increase/Decrease(-) in Stocks	93i															
Private Consumption	96f															
Imports of Goods & Services	98c															
Gross Domestic Product (GDP)	99b															
Net Factor Inc/Pmts(-) Abroad	98.n															
Gross National Income (GNI)	99a															
GDP Volume 1986 Prices	99b.p	...	...	...	...	...	...	...	...	...	...	...	...			...
GDP Volume (1995=100)	99bv p															
GDP Deflator (1995=100)	99bi p	...	...	...	...	...	...	...	...	...	...	...	...			...
																Millions:
Population	99z	1.53	.54	.55	.57	.60	.63	.66	.70	.74	.78	.78	.80	.81	.83	.85

	1985	1986	1987	1988	1989	1990	1991	1992	1993	1994	1995	1996	1997	1998	1999		
Minus Sign Indicates Debit																**Balance of Payments**	
	−75.80	−62.50	−56.50	−68.40	−92.80	−60.49	−79.04	−104.18	−65.48	−47.63	−50.65	−60.43	−30.28	. . .	. . .	Current Account, n.i.e.	**78al** *d*
	11.60	9.70	15.40	15.90	14.20	19.26	20.44	6.47	15.96	33.21	23.90	21.61	48.86	. . .	. . .	Goods: Exports f.o.b.	**78aa** *d*
	−59.50	−51.20	−44.70	−58.90	−68.90	−68.07	−67.47	−83.51	−53.82	−53.80	−59.34	−56.80	−62.49	. . .	. . .	Goods: Imports f.o.b.	**78ab** *d*
	−47.90	−41.50	−29.30	−43.00	−54.70	−48.81	−47.03	−77.04	−37.86	−20.59	−35.44	−35.19	−13.63	. . .	. . .	*Trade Balance*	**78ac** *d*
	6.50	—	—	—	6.44	6.84	13.06	11.56	9.76	5.61	5.69	6.96	8.00	. . .	. . .	Services: Credit	**78ad** *d*
	−25.10	−14.40	−15.30	−17.10	−27.39	−20.10	−27.41	−27.56	−21.14	−27.11	−29.91	−29.25	−26.15	. . .	. . .	Services: Debit	**78ae** *d*
	−66.50	−55.90	−44.60	−60.10	−75.65	−62.07	−61.38	−93.04	−49.24	−42.09	−59.66	−57.48	−31.78	. . .	. . .	*Balance on Goods & Services*	**78af** *d*
	−5.90	−16.50	−17.90	−19.90	−28.05	−22.28	−32.91	−27.78	−28.98	−26.27	−21.09	−18.65	−14.30	. . .	. . .	Income: Credit	**78ag** *d*
	−72.40	−72.40	−62.50	−80.00	−103.70	−84.35	−94.29	−120.82	−78.22	−68.36	−80.75	−76.13	−46.08	. . .	. . .	Income: Debit	**78ah** *d*
	—	11.40	8.00	11.60	10.90	23.86	19.39	17.28	14.39	21.79	31.42	15.70	15.80	. . .	. . .	*Balance on Gds, Serv. & Inc.*	**78ai** *d*
	−3.40	−1.50	−2.00	—	—	—	−4.14	−.64	−1.65	−1.06	−1.32	—	—	. . .	. . .	Current Transfers, n.i.e.: Credit	**78aj** *d*
																Current Transfers: Debit	**78ak** *d*
	30.50	26.90	32.20	26.90	41.60	28.96	32.72	28.49	36.57	44.42	49.20	40.70	32.20	. . .	. . .	Capital Account, n.i.e.	**78bc** *d*
	30.50	26.90	32.20	26.90	41.60	28.96	32.72	28.49	36.57	44.42	49.20	40.70	32.20	. . .	. . .	Capital Account, n.i.e.: Credit	**78ba** *d*
																Capital Account: Debit	**78bb** *d*
	62.96	6.67	1.48	−3.44	−8.38	1.22	−12.50	2.13	−15.82	−26.98	−28.25	−12.30	2.03	. . .	. . .	Financial Account, n.i.e.	**78bj** *d*
	—	—	—	—	—	—	—	—	—	. . . .	. . . .	. . . .	. . . .			Direct Investment Abroad	**78bd** *d*
	—	—	—	—	—	—	—	—	—	. . . .	. . . .	. . . .	. . . .			Dir. Invest. in Rep. Econ., n.i.e.	**78be** *d*
	—	—	—	—	—	—	—	—	—	. . . .	. . . .	. . . .	. . . .			Portfolio Investment Assets	**78bf** *d*
	—	—	—	—	—	—	—	—	—	. . . .	. . . .	. . . .	. . . .			Equity Securities	**78bk** *d*
	—	—	—	—	—	—	—	—	—	. . . .	. . . .	. . . .	. . . .			Debt Securities	**78bl** *d*
	—	—	—	—	—	—	—	—	—	. . . .	. . . .	. . . .	. . . .			Portfolio Investment Liab., n.i.e.	**78bg** *d*
	—	—	—	—	—	—	—	—	—	. . . .	. . . .	. . . .	. . . .			Equity Securities	**78bm** *d*
	—	—	—	—	—	—	—	—	—	. . . .	. . . .	. . . .	. . . .			Debt Securities	**78bn** *d*
	. . . .	. . . .	. . . .	. . . .	. . . .	. . . .	. . . .	. . . .	. . . .	. . . .	. . . .	. . . .	. . . .			Financial Derivatives Assets	**78bw** *d*
	. . . .	. . . .	. . . .	. . . .	. . . .	. . . .	. . . .	. . . .	. . . .	. . . .	. . . .	. . . .	. . . .			Financial Derivatives Liabilities	**78bx** *d*
	—	—	—	—	—	—	—	—	—	—	—	—	−5.80			Other Investment Assets	**78bh** *d*
	—	—	—	—	—	—	—	—	—	—	—	—	—			Monetary Authorities	**78bo** *d*
	—	—	—	—	—	—	—	—	—	—	—	—	—			General Government	**78bp** *d*
	—	—	—	—	—	—	—	—	—	—	—	—	−5.80			Banks	**78bq** *d*
	—	—	—	—	—	—	—	—	—	—	—	—	—			Other Sectors	**78br** *d*
	62.96	6.67	1.48	−3.44	−8.38	1.22	−12.50	2.13	−15.82	−26.98	−28.25	−12.30	7.83			Other Investment Liab., n.i.e.	**78bi** *d*
					−1.38	—	−3.75	—	−2.27	—	−6.88	—	.43			Monetary Authorities	**78bs** *d*
	62.96	6.67	1.48	−3.44	−7.00	1.22	−8.75	2.13	−13.55	−26.98	−21.37	−12.30	7.40			General Government	**78bt** *d*
	—	—	—	—	—	—	—	—	—	. . . .	. . . .	. . . .	. . . .			Banks	**78bu** *d*
	—	—	—	—	—	—	—	—	—	—	—	—	—			Other Sectors	**78bv** *d*
	−9.64	−3.71	−7.70	3.50	−11.60	−1.38	−16.28	22.01	−15.97	−24.33	−10.90	−11.47	−19.19	. . .	. . .	Net Errors and Omissions	**78ca** *d*
	8.01	−32.65	−30.52	−41.44	−71.18	−31.69	−75.10	−51.55	−60.70	−54.52	−40.60	−43.50	−15.24			*Overall Balance*	**78cb** *d*
	−8.01	32.65	30.52	41.44	71.18	31.69	75.10	51.55	60.70	54.52	40.60	43.50	15.24			Reserves and Related Items	**79da** *d*
	−15.61	−3.10	−2.36	−11.83	6.70	−5.20	8.89	−5.10	9.02	6.24	−3.64	−8.90	−35.15			Reserve Assets	**79db** *d*
	−.94	−1.09	1.62	−1.26	1.97	—	—	—	—	−.42	−.43	1.19	1.94	5.11		Use of Fund Credit and Loans	**79dc** *d*
	8.54	36.83	31.26	54.53	62.51	36.89	66.21	56.65	52.10	48.72	43.05	50.46	45.28			Exceptional Financing	**79de** *d*
Year Ending December 31																**Government Finance**	
	−110.2	−115.8	⅂−52.6	−325.5	−536.9	−1,110.5	−1,759.1	−3,655.8 [P]	. . . .	. . . .	. . . .	. . . .	. . . .			Deficit (-) or Surplus	**80**
	45.2	58.9	⅂193.5	358.5	657.5	1,502.2	1,904.5	2,592.2 [P]	. . . .	. . . .	. . . .	. . . .	. . . .			Revenue	**81**
	84.2	118.1	⅂392.2	751.2	1,620.8	1,488.2	2,120.0	3,328.3 [P]	. . . .	. . . .	. . . .	. . . .	. . . .			Grants Received	**81z**
	223.4	295.9	⅂636.6	1,198.2	2,664.3	3,622.6	5,093.4	8,552.3 [P]	. . . .	. . . .	. . . .	. . . .	. . . .			Expenditure	**82**
	16.2	−3.0	⅂1.7	237.1	150.9	478.2	690.2	1,024.0 [P]	. . . .	. . . .	. . . .	. . . .	. . . .			Lending Minus Repayments	**83**
																Financing	
	27.1	. . . .	⅂−146.8	−201.8	−196.3	468.5	−412.5	452.2 [P]	. . . .	. . . .	. . . .	. . . .	. . . .			Domestic	**84a**
	75.6	. . . .	⅂226.2	498.5	824.3	884.3	2,001.4	3,203.2 [P]	. . . .	. . . .	. . . .	. . . .	. . . .			Foreign	**85a**
	7.5	. . . .	⅂−26.8	28.8	−91.1	−242.2	170.2	.6 [P]	. . . .	. . . .	. . . .	. . . .	. . . .			Unallocated Financing	**84xx**
Millions of Francs																**National Accounts**	
	. . . .	4,525	6,350	6,209	6,586	7,101	9,450	4,669	7,149	23,222	16,051	17,304	38,370	. . .	. . .	Exports of Goods & Services	**90c**
	. . . .	13,596	9,235	11,938	13,904	10,547	12,623	9,748	8,573	15,645	10,033	10,891	18,118	. . .	. . .	Government Consumption...................	**91f**
	. . . .	15,708	14,451	17,512	18,684	16,108	18,398	22,078	15,255	23,302	22,373	21,248	21,278	. . .	. . .	Gross Fixed Capital Formation	**93e**
	. . . .	3,153	283	532	1,579	−119	−446	3,694	1,182	−7,021	154	5,624	27			Increase/Decrease(-) in Stocks	**93i**
	. . . .	70,198	49,850	47,715	63,849	64,190	63,324	51,017	58,010	119,594	117,485	132,206	141,323	. . .	. . .	Private Consumption	**96f**
	. . . .	−28,232	−22,619	−27,356	−36,161	−27,140	−31,404	−32,537	−24,490	−48,871	−42,122	−47,932	−60,154			Imports of Goods & Services	**98c**
	. . . .	78,700	57,500	53,000	68,200	70,700	70,900	60,100	65,600	129,200	128,900	127,400	154,600			Gross Domestic Product (GDP)	**99b**
	. . . .	—	−7	−38	−113	340	−119	14	−131	. . . .	. . . .	. . . .	. . . .			Net Factor Inc/Pmts(-) Abroad	**98.n**
	. . . .	723	1,414	2,608	5,408	8,188	13,034	23,553	36,264	. . . .	. . . .	. . . .	. . . .			Gross National Income (GNI)	**99a**
	. . . .	78,700	79,900	82,000	85,800	91,000	94,500	96,200	98,600	103,500	107,300	112,500	117,900			GDP Volume 1986 Prices	**99b.** *p*
	. . . .	73.3	74.5	76.4	80.0	84.8	88.1	89.7	91.9	96.5	100.0	104.8	109.9			GDP Volume (1995=100)	**99bv** *p*
	. . . .	83.2	59.9	53.8	66.2	64.7	62.5	52.0	55.4	103.9	100.0	94.3	109.2			GDP Deflator (1995=100)	**99bi** *p*
Midyear Estimates																	
	.87	.89	.91	.93	.95	.97	.99	1.02	1.04	1.06	1.09	1.11	1.14	1.16	1.19	**Population**.......................................	**99z**

(See notes in the back of the book.)

Guyana

336		1970	1971	1972	1973	1974	1975	1976	1977	1978	1979	1980	1981	1982	1983	1984
Exchange Rates															*Guyana Dollars per SDR:*		
Market Rate	aa	2.0	2.2	2.4	2.7	2.7	3.0	3.0	3.1	3.3	3.4	3.3	3.5	3.3	3.1	4.1
														Guyana Dollars per US Dollar:		
Market Rate	ae	2.0	2.0	2.2	2.2	2.2	2.6	2.6	2.6	2.6	2.6	2.6	3.0	3.0	3.0	4.2
Market Rate	rf	2.0	2.0	2.1	2.1	2.2	2.4	2.6	2.6	2.6	2.6	2.6	2.8	3.0	3.0	3.8
													Index Numbers (1995=100):			
Market Rate	ah x	7,081.4	214.5	6,810.5	6,675.3	6,367.4	6,049.1	5,564.0	5,564.0	5,564.0	5,564.0	5,564.0	5,076.8	4,728.8	4,728.8	3,717.1
Nominal Effective Exchange Rate	ne c	....	....	....	....	....	....	....	....	....	1,644.3	1,672.7	1,695.4	1,749.5	1,954.5	1,774.8
Real Effective Exchange Rate	re c	....	....	....	....	....	....	....	....	....	....	523.8	567.4	641.8	754.3	772.2
Fund Position															*Millions of SDRs:*		
Quota	2f. s	20.00	20.00	20.00	20.00	20.00	20.00	20.00	20.00	25.00	25.00	37.50	37.50	37.50	49.20	49.20
SDRs	1b. s	.07	2.17	4.10	4.04	3.91	3.77	3.54	2.73	2.76	2.83	—	1.04	2.59	—	—
Reserve Position in the Fund	1c. s	1.81	—	.57	—	1.76	5.00	—	—	—	—	—	—	—	—	—
Total Fund Cred.&Loans Outstg.	2tl	—	2.06	—	3.87	5.00	—	17.25	17.25	30.27	40.49	67.40	85.31	89.07	85.01	84.01
International Liquidity												*Millions of US Dollars Unless Otherwise Indicated:*					
Total Reserves minus Gold	1l. d	20.40	26.16	36.75	13.97	62.57	100.50	27.28	22.98	58.27	17.53	12.70	6.91	10.56	6.49	5.85
SDRs	1b. d	.07	2.36	4.45	4.87	4.79	4.41	4.11	3.32	3.60	3.73	—	1.21	2.86	—	—
Reserve Position in the Fund	1c. d	1.81	—	.62	—	2.15	5.85	—	—	—	—	—	—	—	—	—
Foreign Exchange	1d. d	18.52	23.80	31.68	9.10	55.63	90.23	23.17	19.66	54.67	13.80	12.70	5.70	7.70	6.49	5.85
Monetary Authorities: Other Liab.	4..d	—	—	.05	—	14.99	30.20	30.47	43.71	44.02	37.93	80.35	79.46	127.69	210.79	286.19
Deposit Money Banks: Assets	7a. d	2.08	2.31	1.12	5.99	6.27	17.20	10.28	8.31	13.25	21.91	23.12	12.16	10.24	9.13	6.93
Liabilities	7b. d	4.90	5.15	4.13	3.75	6.94	14.39	8.33	10.58	19.47	28.45	27.49	22.53	25.46	22.16	15.58
Other Banking Insts.: Assets	7e. d	.52	.68	.70	.70	.78	.74	.81	.88	.97	.98	1.10	1.05	.60	.66	.52
Liabilities	7f. d	—	—	.01	.01	.02	.02	.02	.02	.03	.03	.26	.26	.24	.23	.09
Monetary Authorities														*Millions of Guyana Dollars:*		
Foreign Assets	11	40	57	74	28	138	256	70	60	149	45	32	21	32	19	21
Claims on Central Government	12a	21	20	29	89	29	44	254	346	396	589	828	934	1,467	2,026	2,421
Claims on Nonfin.Pub.Enterprises	12c	—	—	—	—	—	—	—	—	—	—	—	—	—	—	—
Reserve Money	14	50	55	72	75	86	127	143	183	259	268	293	377	588	749	960
of which: Currency Outside DMBs	14a	37	41	48	56	64	92	105	143	156	148	167	186	231	269	336
Time, Savings,& Fgn.Currency Dep.	15	—	—	—	—	—	—	—	—	—	—	—	—	—	—	—
Restricted Deposits	16b	—	—	—	—	—	—	—	—	—	—	—	—	—	—	—
Foreign Liabilities	16c	—	5	—	10	14	—	51	79	126	146	229	304	297	468	955
Long-Term Foreign Liabilities	16cl	—	—	—	—	33	77	78	86	87	87	195	232	380	431	575
Central Government Deposits	16d	—	—	6	1	—	42	2	2	4	41	2	8	13	400	26
Capital Accounts	17a	12	18	24	26	27	29	31	33	35	46	56	72	74	76	92
Other Items (Net)	17r	–1	–1	1	5	7	25	20	22	34	46	85	–40	146	–78	–165
Deposit Money Banks														*Millions of Guyana Dollars:*		
Reserves	20	11	13	22	16	18	29	29	35	101	114	126	187	361	482	617
Foreign Assets	21	4	5	2	13	14	44	26	21	34	56	59	36	31	27	29
Claims on Central Government	22a	21	38	59	66	64	146	136	187	213	199	216	249	418	578	630
Claims on Local Government	22b	1	1	1	2	3	2	3	4	4	4	5	6	5	4	5
Claims on Nonfin.Pub.Enterprises	22c	12	13	12	20	56	57	76	119	122	173	229	376	306	613	551
Claims on Private Sector	22d	79	84	85	101	106	118	120	113	122	163	196	263	314	377	463
Claims on Other Banking Insts	22f	3	2	1	2	2	1	4	1	2	2	2	4	3	5	2
Demand Deposits	24	22	26	32	34	60	102	97	127	127	122	136	144	184	219	251
Time, Savings,& Fgn.Currency Dep.	25	99	116	139	167	180	232	257	303	345	408	478	584	738	899	1,035
Restricted Deposits	26b	—	—	—	—	—	—	—	—	1	1	1	1	285	398	458
Foreign Liabilities	26c	10	10	8	8	15	37	21	27	50	73	70	68	76	66	65
Central Government Deposits	26d	—	—	—	4	4	7	9	9	11	17	25	34	32	32	35
Liabilities to Other Banking Insts	26i	7	10	12	14	10	17	23	19	28	24	59	63	95	125	166
Capital Accounts	27a	1	2	2	3	4	5	5	8	9	14	18	24	39	63	69
Other Items (Net)	27r	–7	–9	–10	–9	–11	–1	–17	–15	29	50	47	205	–12	284	217
Monetary Survey														*Millions of Guyana Dollars:*		
Foreign Assets (Net)	31n	35	46	68	23	123	263	23	–25	7	–118	–208	–314	–311	–488	–969
Domestic Credit	32	137	158	182	276	255	321	584	758	845	1,071	1,450	1,790	2,467	3,172	4,010
Claims on Central Govt. (Net)	32an	42	58	82	151	88	142	380	522	595	729	1,018	1,141	1,839	2,172	2,989
Claims on Local Government	32b	1	1	1	2	3	2	3	4	4	4	5	6	5	4	5
Claims on Nonfin.Pub.Enterprises	32c	12	13	12	20	56	57	76	119	122	173	229	376	306	613	551
Claims on Private Sector	32d	79	84	85	101	106	118	120	113	122	163	196	263	314	377	463
Claims on Other Banking Insts	32f	3	2	1	2	2	1	4	1	2	2	2	4	3	5	2
Money	34	61	69	83	93	127	199	207	276	290	277	309	336	421	494	594
Quasi-Money	35	99	116	139	167	180	232	257	303	345	408	478	584	738	899	1,035
Restricted Deposits	36b	—	—	—	—	—	—	—	—	1	1	1	1	285	398	458
Long-Term Foreign Liabilities	36cl	—	—	—	—	33	77	78	86	87	87	195	232	380	431	575
Liabilities to Other Banking Insts	36i	7	10	12	14	10	17	23	19	28	24	59	63	95	125	166
Capital Accounts	37a	13	20	26	29	31	35	36	41	44	60	75	97	113	138	161
Other Items (Net)	37r	–8	–10	–10	–4	–4	24	6	7	57	96	126	163	123	198	53
Money plus Quasi-Money	35l	160	185	222	260	307	431	465	579	635	686	787	920	1,159	1,393	1,629
Other Banking Institutions														*Millions of Guyana Dollars:*		
Cash	40	—	1	1	1	—	—	1	1	4	3	8	10	9	10	17
Foreign Assets	41	1	1	1	2	2	2	2	2	2	3	3	3	2	2	2
Claims on Central Government	42a	—	—	1	1	2	5	8	9	7	9	10	18	27	46	87
Claims on Local Government	42b	—	—	—	1	1	1	1	2	1	1	1	1	1	1	1
Claims on Private Sector	42d	9	10	12	15	18	22	27	36	44	51	74	86	111	117	115
Claims on Deposit Money Banks	42e	—	—	—	—	—	—	—	—	—	—	—	3	5	9	6
Time, Savings,& Fgn.Currency Dep.	45	10	12	14	19	22	28	37	48	58	65	92	114	144	173	220
Foreign Liabilities	46c	—	—	—	—	—	—	—	—	—	—	1	1	1	1	—
Capital Accounts	47a	1	1	1	1	2	2	2	2	3	3	4	5	5	6	7
Other Items (Net)	47r	—	—	—	—	—	—	–1	–1	–1	–1	—	5	5	6	2
Banking Survey														*Millions of Guyana Dollars:*		
Foreign Assets (Net)	51n	36	48	69	24	125	265	25	–23	9	–115	–206	–312	–310	–486	–968
Domestic Credit	52	144	166	193	291	274	347	616	804	896	1,129	1,534	1,891	2,604	3,331	4,212
Claims on Central Govt. (Net)	52an	42	58	83	152	90	147	388	531	602	738	1,028	1,159	1,866	2,218	3,076
Claims on Local Government	52b	1	1	1	3	4	3	4	5	5	6	6	6	7	5	6
Claims on Nonfin.Pub.Enterprises	52c	12	13	12	20	56	57	76	119	122	173	229	376	306	613	551
Claims on Private Sector	52d	88	94	97	116	125	139	147	149	166	214	271	349	425	494	578
Liquid Liabilities	55l	170	196	235	278	329	459	501	627	688	747	870	1,024	1,293	1,556	1,831
Restricted Deposits	56b	—	—	—	—	—	—	—	—	1	1	1	1	285	398	458
Long-Term Foreign Liabilities	56cl	—	—	—	—	33	77	78	86	87	87	195	232	380	431	575
Capital Accounts	57a	14	21	27	30	33	37	38	43	47	62	79	102	118	144	168
Other Items (Net)	57r	–5	–3	—	7	4	39	25	25	82	117	183	220	217	315	213

Guyana

336

1985	1986	1987	1988	1989	1990	1991	1992	1993	1994	1995	1996	1997	1998	1999		
End of Period															**Exchange Rates**	
4.6	5.4	14.2	13.5	43.4	64.0	174.5	173.3	179.6	208.0	208.9	203.1	194.3	228.5	247.7	Market Rate	aa
End of Period (ae) Period Average (rf)																
4.2	4.4	10.0	10.0	33.0	45.0	122.0	126.0	130.8	142.5	140.5	141.3	144.0	162.3	180.5	Market Rate	ae
4.3	4.3	9.8	10.0	27.2	39.5	111.8	125.0	126.7	138.3	142.0	140.4	142.4	150.5	178.0	Market Rate	rf
Period Averages																
3,340.4	3,321.8	1,467.6	1,418.7	678.2	366.7	139.2	113.0	112.0	102.7	100.0	101.1	99.4	94.5	79.8	Market Rate	ahx
1,767.3	1,674.0	733.8	749.7	410.8	207.8	94.5	89.5	102.7	104.9	100.0	103.7	108.0	105.9	90.6	Nominal Effective Exchange Rate	nec
798.0	757.3	389.3	170.9	136.3	96.6	82.5	90.6	98.9	98.2	100.0	108.0	113.9	114.5	103.8	Real Effective Exchange Rate	rec
End of Period															**Fund Position**	
49.20	49.20	49.20	49.20	49.20	49.20	49.20	67.20	67.20	67.20	67.20	67.20	67.20	67.20	90.90	Quota	2f.s
—	—	—	—	—	1.49	.99	.24	—	.05	.09	.07	.14	.17	.92	SDRs	1b.s
—	—	—	—	—	—	—	—	—	—	—	—	—	—	—	Reserve Position in the Fund	1c.s
83.01	82.45	81.74	81.74	80.91	79.38	104.46	122.17	128.60	122.25	115.60	117.11	116.44	109.50	102.15	Total Fund Cred.&Loans Outstg.	2tl
End of Period															**International Liquidity**	
6.47	9.00	8.43	4.04	13.35	28.68	124.42	188.08	247.45	247.13	268.94	329.68	315.51	276.60	268.28	Total Reserves minus Gold	1l.d
—	—	—	—	—	2.12	1.42	.33	—	.08	.14	.11	.20	.24	1.27	SDRs	1b.d
—	—	—	—	—	—	—	—	—	—	—	—	—	—	—	Reserve Position in the Fund	1c.d
6.47	9.00	8.43	4.04	13.35	26.56	123.00	187.75	247.45	247.05	268.80	329.57	315.31	276.36	267.01	Foreign Exchange	1d.d
357.70	384.77	418.61	427.85	605.64	711.78	727.42	729.66	715.25	656.62	725.00	448.57	286.86	222.56	187.68	Monetary Authorities: Other Liab.	4..d
8.19	9.17	16.05	16.42	23.06	53.38	19.74	29.83	24.40	24.88	27.03	26.55	24.29	23.91	40.13	Deposit Money Banks: Assets	7a.d
15.21	19.77	14.37	14.14	5.73	19.77	7.52	14.64	15.92	20.57	20.52	25.62	34.47	31.93	22.23	Liabilities	7b.d
.58	.55	.27	.40	.12	.12	.16	.57	.87	1.04	1.20	1.31	2.27	1.93	2.15	Other Banking Insts.: Assets	7e.d
.12	.23	.22	.23	—	—	—	—	.04	—	7.30	1.03	1.12	.69	.46	Liabilities	7f.d
End of Period															**Monetary Authorities**	
27	38	84	40	470	1,328	15,277	23,488	I 31,557	35,741	38,398	46,466	43,578	40,149	44,590	Foreign Assets	11
3,228	4,252	6,664	10,445	24,199	31,301	68,417	100,839	I 109,080	118,849	125,918	96,232	76,959	67,904	71,686	Claims on Central Government	12a
—	—	41	94	318	671	801	898	I 762	1,098	811	2,441	3,238	3,320	4,709	Claims on Nonfin.Pub.Enterprises	12c
1,052	1,298	3,111	3,695	3,399	4,016	10,316	15,647	I 12,523	16,453	19,603	20,760	24,314	27,179	26,128	Reserve Money	14
422	509	726	1,058	1,506	2,211	3,711	5,095	I 6,480	8,167	8,967	9,959	11,210	11,334	13,394	*of which: Currency Outside DMBs*	14a
—	8	—	—	8	53	108	278	I 378	335	561	489	749	694	1,219	Time, Savings,& Fgn.Currency Dep.	15
—	8	—	1	30	—	—	84	I —	—	—	—	—	—	—	Restricted Deposits	16b
1,281	1,524	3,948	3,978	18,854	27,312	79,613	86,008	I 89,751	91,358	95,914	63,243	44,406	45,418	46,547	Foreign Liabilities	16c
582	613	1,398	1,401	4,641	9,800	27,361	27,094	I 26,864	27,641	30,091	23,903	19,525	15,708	12,636	Long-Term Foreign Liabilities	16cl
5	8	7	–18	31	70	680	1,260	I 15,220	22,623	21,335	30,256	27,147	22,066	34,594	Central Government Deposits	16d
106	118	249	242	677	977	2,540	2,522	I –1,455	2,345	3,253	2,567	3,449	5,184	5,891	Capital Accounts	17a
229	714	–1,924	1,279	–2,654	–8,930	–36,124	–7,669	I –1,882	–5,068	–5,631	3,921	4,187	–4,875	–6,030	Other Items (Net)	17r
End of Period															**Deposit Money Banks**	
628	791	2,433	2,697	1,865	1,802	6,629	10,548	5,503	8,171	10,326	10,781	13,315	16,070	12,419	Reserves	20
34	40	161	164	761	2,402	2,409	3,759	3,190	3,546	3,798	3,750	3,497	3,880	7,243	Foreign Assets	21
823	1,086	352	731	2,686	4,111	7,227	12,282	20,064	15,651	14,847	17,251	18,028	15,851	13,346	Claims on Central Government	22a
4	3	6	4	10	2	2	28	36	—	36	1	4	500	48	Claims on Local Government	22b
838	323	356	552	652	755	359	835	471	188	410	254	216	410	683	Claims on Nonfin.Pub.Enterprises	22c
520	674	987	1,591	2,566	4,160	6,672	8,735	10,254	13,900	21,107	36,309	44,863	51,838	55,823	Claims on Private Sector	22d
3	7	6	5	7	1	62	5	28	13	73	183	118	195	569	Claims on Other Banking Insts	22f
286	337	558	934	1,165	1,918	3,126	3,897	4,902	4,941	6,336	7,565	8,064	7,639	9,949	Demand Deposits	24
1,270	1,507	2,173	2,733	4,479	6,742	12,003	21,483	25,271	28,764	36,661	44,708	49,032	53,981	57,049	Time, Savings,& Fgn.Currency Dep.	25
489	562	641	763	957	916	746	517	368	334	330	330	318	307	70	Restricted Deposits	26b
63	87	144	141	189	890	917	1,845	2,081	2,931	2,883	3,619	4,964	5,181	4,012	Foreign Liabilities	26c
60	154	194	248	356	515	1,064	1,612	3,161	3,246	2,071	2,920	5,662	5,782	3,857	Central Government Deposits	26d
155	129	356	676	975	1,437	2,840	3,200	2,895	1,356	1,827	2,757	3,778	5,898	5,796	Liabilities to Other Banking Insts	26i
93	132	170	247	388	797	1,397	4,045	3,660	3,968	5,392	13,712	15,054	19,385	21,477	Capital Accounts	27a
435	16	64	2	38	20	1,265	–409	–2,792	–4,072	–4,903	–7,079	–6,828	–9,429	–12,081	Other Items (Net)	27r
End of Period															**Monetary Survey**	
–1,283	–1,533	–3,846	–3,914	–17,812	–24,472	–62,845	–60,606	I –57,085	–55,003	–56,600	–16,646	–2,294	–6,570	1,274	Foreign Assets (Net)	31n
5,352	6,183	8,210	13,191	30,050	40,415	81,796	120,749	I 122,314	123,830	139,796	119,495	110,619	112,172	108,412	Domestic Credit	32
3,987	5,177	6,815	10,946	26,497	34,827	73,900	110,249	I 110,763	108,630	117,360	80,307	62,178	55,908	46,581	Claims on Central Govt. (Net)	32an
4	3	6	4	10	2	2	28	36	—	36	1	4	500	48	Claims on Local Government	32b
838	323	397	646	970	1,426	1,160	1,733	I 1,232	1,286	1,220	2,695	3,455	3,730	5,392	Claims on Nonfin.Pub.Enterprises	32c
520	674	987	1,591	2,566	4,160	6,672	8,735	10,254	13,900	21,107	36,309	44,863	51,838	55,823	Claims on Private Sector	32d
3	7	6	5	7	1	62	5	28	13	73	183	118	195	569	Claims on Other Banking Insts	32f
714	852	1,291	1,999	2,677	4,136	6,844	8,999	I 11,881	13,115	15,310	17,531	19,281	18,980	23,350	Money	34
1,270	1,515	2,173	2,733	4,487	6,795	12,112	21,762	I 25,649	29,100	37,222	45,197	49,780	54,675	58,268	Quasi-Money	35
489	570	642	764	987	916	746	601	I 368	334	330	330	318	307	70	Restricted Deposits	36b
582	613	1,398	1,401	4,641	9,800	27,361	27,094	I 26,864	27,641	30,091	23,903	19,525	15,708	12,636	Long-Term Foreign Liabilities	36cl
155	129	356	676	975	1,437	2,840	3,200	2,895	1,356	1,827	2,757	3,778	5,898	5,796	Liabilities to Other Banking Insts	36i
199	250	419	489	1,065	1,774	3,937	6,567	I 2,205	6,313	8,645	16,278	18,503	24,569	27,368	Capital Accounts	37a
660	721	–1,915	1,216	–2,594	–8,914	–34,889	–8,080	I –4,634	–9,032	–10,231	–3,146	–2,860	–14,536	–17,803	Other Items (Net)	37r
1,984	2,367	3,464	4,732	7,164	10,930	18,956	30,760	I 37,531	42,214	52,532	62,727	69,061	73,655	81,618	Money plus Quasi-Money	35l
End of Period															**Other Banking Institutions**	
3	2	21	73	61	95	133	73	165	91	372	202	142	188	357	Cash	40
2	2	3	4	4	6	20	71	113	148	168	185	327	313	387	Foreign Assets	41
161	260	316	339	483	743	1,326	2,146	2,611	3,444	3,410	4,339	5,055	5,226	4,705	Claims on Central Government	42a
1	9	9	9	10	12	12	12	18	17	17	—	—	—	—	Claims on Local Government	42b
135	152	204	286	357	479	626	1,300	2,102	2,446	3,615	5,335	6,609	8,718	10,914	Claims on Private Sector	42d
8	9	5	7	5	82	178	390	503	73	216	319	136	151	103	Claims on Deposit Money Banks	42e
303	428	538	662	904	1,063	1,633	3,435	4,339	5,254	6,360	8,450	10,477	12,065	13,352	Time, Savings,& Fgn.Currency Dep.	45
1	1	2	2	—	—	—	—	5	—	1,025	145	162	111	83	Foreign Liabilities	46c
10	16	33	54	45	66	130	259	389	616	890	1,723	1,698	2,049	2,477	Capital Accounts	47a
–3	–11	–15	—	–28	287	531	299	779	350	–477	62	–68	371	553	Other Items (Net)	47r
End of Period															**Banking Survey**	
–1,282	–1,531	–3,846	–3,913	–17,808	–24,466	–62,825	–60,535	I –56,976	–54,855	–57,457	–16,606	–2,129	–6,368	1,578	Foreign Assets (Net)	51n
5,645	6,598	8,733	13,820	30,893	41,648	83,698	124,202	I 127,017	129,724	146,764	128,986	122,165	125,921	123,463	Domestic Credit	52
4,148	5,437	7,131	11,284	26,980	35,570	75,226	112,395	I 113,374	112,074	120,769	84,646	67,234	61,134	51,286	Claims on Central Govt. (Net)	52an
5	13	15	14	20	14	14	40	55	17	53	1	4	500	48	Claims on Local Government	52b
838	323	397	646	970	1,426	1,160	1,733	I 1,232	1,286	1,220	2,695	3,455	3,730	5,392	Claims on Nonfin.Pub.Enterprises	52c
655	826	1,190	1,877	2,923	4,638	7,299	10,035	12,356	16,346	24,722	41,644	51,472	60,556	66,737	Claims on Private Sector	52d
2,284	2,793	3,981	5,321	8,007	11,899	20,456	34,122	I 41,705	47,377	58,519	70,975	79,396	85,532	94,614	Liquid Liabilities	55l
489	570	642	764	987	916	746	601	I 368	334	330	330	318	307	70	Restricted Deposits	56b
582	613	1,398	1,401	4,641	9,800	27,361	27,094	I 26,864	27,641	30,091	23,903	19,525	15,708	12,636	Long-Term Foreign Liabilities	56cl
209	266	452	543	1,110	1,840	4,067	6,826	I 2,594	6,930	9,535	18,001	20,201	26,618	29,845	Capital Accounts	57a
801	825	–1,585	1,880	–1,660	–7,274	–31,757	–4,976	I –1,490	–7,413	–9,169	–829	596	–8,612	–12,125	Other Items (Net)	57r

Guyana

		1970	1971	1972	1973	1974	1975	1976	1977	1978	1979	1980	1981	1982	1983	1984
Interest Rates														*Percent Per Annum*		
Discount Rate *(End of Period)*	60	6.5	6.5	6.5	6.5	6.5	6.5	6.5	6.5	8.5	10.5	12.5	12.5	14.0	14.0	14.0
Treasury Bill Rate	60c	....	....	5.9	5.9	5.9	5.9	5.9	5.9	7.0	9.1	10.7	11.6	12.3	12.8	12.8
Deposit Rate	60l	....	....	....	....	4.0	4.0	4.0	4.0	7.0	9.0	11.0	11.0	11.6	12.0	12.0
Lending Rate	60p	....	....	....	....	7.5	7.5	7.5	7.5	9.5	11.5	13.5	13.5	14.4	15.0	15.0
Prices														*Index Numbers (1995=100):*		
Consumer Prices	64	....	....	....	....	....	....	....	....	....	....	....	....	....	....	....
International Transactions														*Millions of Guyana Dollars*		
Exports	70	271.9	298.4	306.5	288.0	600.0	858.0	711.3	661.2	753.8	746.4	992.4	974.3	724.0	566.5	807.7
Imports, c.i.f.	71	268.2	267.6	297.9	372.6	567.0	810.6	927.4	800.3	711.1	809.8	1,010.4	1,207.6	842.4	738.3	811.5
															1995=100	
Volume of Exports	72	128	132	115	73	89	89	86	65	86	80	76	79	68	59	60
Balance of Payments														*Millions of US Dollars:*		
Current Account, n.i.e.	78al d	....	....	....	....	....	....	....	−97.5	−29.6	−82.9	−128.5	−184.5	−142.3	−157.5	−98.9
Goods: Exports f.o.b.	78aa d	....	....	....	....	....	....	....	259.3	295.6	292.7	388.9	346.4	241.4	193.3	216.9
Goods: Imports f.o.b.	78ab d	....	....	....	....	....	....	....	−286.7	−253.5	−288.8	−386.4	−399.6	−254.2	−225.7	−201.6
Trade Balance	78ac d	....	....	....	....	....	....	....	−27.4	42.1	3.9	2.4	−53.2	−12.7	−32.4	15.2
Services: Credit	78ad d	....	....	....	....	....	....	....	16.2	18.2	18.5	19.8	23.0	22.6	31.5	29.2
Services: Debit	78ae d	....	....	....	....	....	....	....	−60.7	−60.1	−71.4	−107.3	−98.9	−94.5	−98.1	−99.0
Balance on Goods & Services	78af d	....	....	....	....	....	....	....	−72.0	.2	−48.9	−85.1	−129.1	−84.6	−99.0	−54.6
Income: Credit	78ag d	....	....	....	....	....	....	....	—	—	3.7	1.9	3.1	.3	.3	.3
Income: Debit	78ah d	....	....	....	....	....	....	....	−21.6	−23.3	−38.1	−44.5	−57.6	−49.3	−57.8	−44.9
Balance on Gds, Serv. & Inc.	78ai d	....	....	....	....	....	....	....	−93.6	−23.1	−83.3	−127.7	−183.7	−133.5	−156.5	−99.3
Current Transfers, n.i.e.: Credit	78aj d	....	....	....	....	....	....	....	3.6	3.8	10.2	8.9	8.3	3.1	5.1	3.7
Current Transfers: Debit	78ak d	....	....	....	....	....	....	....	−7.5	−10.3	−9.8	−9.7	−9.1	−11.9	−6.1	−3.4
Capital Account, n.i.e.	78bc d	....	....	....	....	....	....	....	—	—	—	—	—	—	—	2.6
Capital Account, n.i.e.: Credit	78ba d	....	....	....	....	....	....	....	—	—	—	—	—	—	—	2.6
Capital Account: Debit	78bb d	....	....	....	....	....	....	....	—	—	—	—	—	—	—	—
Financial Account, n.i.e.	78bj d	....	....	....	....	....	....	....	30.7	34.7	29.2	22.4	−17.7	−61.6	−131.4	−28.6
Direct Investment Abroad	78bd d	....	....	....	....	....	....	....								
Dir. Invest. in Rep. Econ., n.i.e.	78be d	....	....	....	....	....	....	....	−1.8	—	.6	.6	−1.8	4.4	4.7	4.5
Portfolio Investment Assets	78bf d	....	....	....	....	....	....	....	−1.0	−1.5	3.5	2.5	—	—	—	—
Equity Securities	78bk d	....	....	....	....	....	....	....	—	—	—	—	—	—	—	—
Debt Securities	78bl d	....	....	....	....	....	....	....	−1.0	−1.5	3.5	2.5	—	—	—	—
Portfolio Investment Liab., n.i.e.	78bg d	....	....	....	....	....	....	....	—	—	—	—	—	—	—	—
Equity Securities	78bm d	....	....	....	....	....	....	....	—	—	—	—	—	—	—	—
Debt Securities	78bn d	....	....	....	....	....	....	....	—	—	—	—	—	—	—	—
Financial Derivatives Assets	78bw d	....	....	....	....	....	....	....	....	....	....	....	....	....	....	....
Financial Derivatives Liabilities	78bx d	....	....	....	....	....	....	....	....	....	....	....	....	....	....	....
Other Investment Assets	78bh d	....	....	....	....	....	....	....	−3.6	−12.7	−5.3	−1.1	9.8	−1.4	1.1	−.4
Monetary Authorities	78bo d	....	....	....	....	....	....	....	....	....	....	....	....	....	....	....
General Government	78bp d	....	....	....	....	....	....	....								
Banks	78bq d	....	....	....	....	....	....	....	2.0	−4.9	−8.7	−1.2	8.0	1.9	1.1	−.4
Other Sectors	78br d	....	....	....	....	....	....	....	−5.6	−7.7	3.4	.1	1.8	−3.4	—	—
Other Investment Liab., n.i.e.	78bi d	....	....	....	....	....	....	....	37.1	48.9	30.3	20.4	−25.8	−64.6	−137.3	−32.7
Monetary Authorities	78bs d	....	....	....	....	....	....	....	—	—	−6.3	−15.5	−64.3	−32.5	−72.3	—
General Government	78bt d	....	....	....	....	....	....	....	8.7	20.9	26.9	46.5	36.2	−40.4	−42.8	−32.5
Banks	78bu d	....	....	....	....	....	....	....	2.3	8.9	9.0	−1.0	−.9	2.9	−3.3	−.5
Other Sectors	78bv d	....	....	....	....	....	....	....	26.2	19.1	.7	−9.7	3.3	5.4	−18.9	.3
Net Errors and Omissions	78ca d	....	....	....	....	....	....	....	9.6	21.4	−8.0	.1	−10.8	43.4	58.1	−12.7
Overall Balance	78cb d	....	....	....	....	....	....	....	−57.3	26.6	−61.8	−106.0	−213.1	−160.5	−230.9	−137.6
Reserves and Related Items	79da d	....	....	....	....	....	....	....	57.3	−26.6	61.8	106.0	213.1	160.5	230.9	137.6
Reserve Assets	79db d	....	....	....	....	....	....	....	11.4	−32.9	44.0	8.2	10.6	−3.5	4.0	−22.9
Use of Fund Credit and Loans	79dc d	....	....	....	....	....	....	....	—	16.4	13.0	35.1	21.0	3.9	−4.4	−1.0
Exceptional Financing	79de d	....	....	....	....	....	....	....	45.8	−10.0	4.8	62.7	181.5	160.1	231.2	161.5
Government Finance														*Millions of Guyana Dollars:*		
Deficit (-) or Surplus	80	Ɪ−24	−33	−39	−105	−22	−78	−313	−133	−129	−232	−440	−589	−958	−592	−756
Total Revenue and Grants	81y	Ɪ144	141	163	180	323	503	399	381	404	481	540	647	627	631	701
Revenue	81	Ɪ143	137	163	176	322	503	399	378	404	465	527	644	624	630	651
Grants	81z	Ɪ1	4	—	3	1	—	—	2	1	16	13	3	3	1	51
Exp. & Lending Minus Repay.	82z	Ɪ168	174	203	285	345	581	712	514	533	713	980	1,236	1,585	1,223	1,457
Expenditure	82	Ɪ169	173	202	280	340	560	685	513	533	689	906	1,154	1,509	1,141	1,457
Lending Minus Repayments	83	Ɪ—	1	1	4	5	21	27	1	—	24	74	82	76	82	—
Total Financing	80h	Ɪ24	33	39	105	22	78	313	133	129	232	440	589	958	592	756
Total Net Borrowing	84	Ɪ24	44	39	147	17	160	351	167	183	225	440	659	835	440	1,066
Net Domestic	84a	Ɪ18	−20	33	106	−46	9	225	153	138	173	347	377	784	348	1,012
Net Foreign	85a	Ɪ7	64	7	41	63	152	126	14	45	52	93	282	51	91	54
Use of Cash Balances	87	Ɪ—	−11	—	−42	5	−83	−38	−34	−55	7	—	−70	122	153	−310
Total Debt	88	Ɪ153	240	286	451	603	892	1,211	1,414	1,599	1,892	3,676	4,046	4,801	5,914	7,142
Domestic	88a	Ɪ83	113	157	210	189	304	511	692	810	1,014	1,637	1,808	2,763	3,810	4,396
Foreign	89a	Ɪ70	127	129	241	414	588	700	722	789	879	2,039	2,238	2,038	2,104	2,746
National Accounts														*Millions of Guyana Dollars*		
Exports of Goods & Services	90c	265	287	300	288	595	830	711	661	750	746	992	974	775	565	831
Government Consumption	91f	87	98	117	159	180	247	330	298	335	348	436	470	435	465	790
Gross Fixed Capital Formation	93e	123	105	119	175	252	392	425	290	241	411	449	573	380	395	390
Private Consumption	96f	328	336	363	424	517	562	638	707	669	810	1,010	1,236	842	893	969
Imports of Goods & Services	98c	−266	−266	−298	−373	−567	−811	−927	−804	−711	−930	−1,215	−1,375	−1,037	−738	−812
Gross Domestic Product (GDP)	99b	533	561	598	644	943	1,179	1,117	1,120	1,246	1,326	1,508	1,597	1,446	1,455	1,700
Net Factor Inc/Pmts(-) Abroad	98.n	−43	−36	−22	−27	−38	−44	−60	−67	−53	−73	−83	−161	−156	−173	−182
Gross National Income (GNI)	99a	491	525	576	617	905	1,135	1,057	1,053	1,193	1,253	1,425	1,446	1,290	1,282	1,518
Net National Income	99e	457	492	543	581	865	1,088	1,003	993	1,123	1,168	1,330	1,343	1,172	1,162	1,393
GDP Volume 1977 Prices	99b.p	947	974	955	971	1,039	1,148	1,181	Ɪ1,120	1,105	976	992	989	886	804	....
GDP Volume 1988 Prices	99b.p	....	....	....	....	....	....	....	....	....	....	....	....	....	3,749	2,830
GDP Volume (1990=100)	99bv p	133.1	136.9	134.2	136.5	146.0	161.2	165.9	Ɪ158.0	155.3	137.1	139.4	138.9	124.5	113.0	85.3
GDP Deflator (1990=100)	99bi p	2.6	2.6	2.8	3.0	4.1	4.7	4.3	Ɪ4.5	5.1	6.2	6.9	7.3	7.4	8.2	12.7
																Millions:
Population	99z	.70	.73	.75	.76	.77	.78	.79	.81	.82	.85	.87	.77	.77	.78	.79

	1985	1986	1987	1988	1989	1990	1991	1992	1993	1994	1995	1996	1997	1998	1999		
Percent Per Annum																**Interest Rates**	
	14.0	14.0	14.0	14.0	35.0	30.0	32.5	24.3	17.0	20.3	17.3	12.0	11.0	11.3	13.3	Discount Rate *(End of Period)*	60
	12.8	12.8	11.3	11.0	15.2	30.0	30.9	25.7	16.8	17.7	17.5	11.4	8.9	8.3	11.3	Treasury Bill Rate	60c
	12.0	12.0	11.1	12.0	15.8	29.2	29.5	22.5	12.3	11.4	12.9	10.5	8.6	8.1	9.1	Deposit Rate	60l
	15.0	15.0	15.0	15.1	18.9	32.8	33.6	28.7	19.4	18.4	19.2	17.8	17.0	16.8	17.1	Lending Rate	60p
Period Averages																**Prices**	
	....	....	....	....	....	....	....	....	....	89.1	100.0	107.1	110.9	116.0	124.7	Consumer Prices	64
Millions of Guyana Dollars																**International Transactions**	
	705.6	953.2	2,596.3	2,295.6	6,123.2	10,207.7	28,107.2	36,567.2	52,506.9	63,389.8	64,581.3	72,597.9	91,808.7	73,336.3	....	Exports	70
	959.6	1,030.0	2,590.0	2,156.0	7,012.0	12,290.0	34,274.9	55,319.8	61,376.0	70,000.6	74,911.5	83,895.0	89,746.8	....	....	Imports, c.i.f.	71
1995=100																	
	62	62	59	45	52	44	45	70	81	88	100	70	102	98	106	Volume of Exports	72
Minus Sign Indicates Debit																Balance of Payments	
	-96.6	....	....	....	....	....	....	-138.5	-140.2	-124.9	-134.8	....	....	....	....	Current Account, n.i.e.	78al *d*
	214.0	....	....	....	....	....	....	381.7	415.5	463.4	495.7	....	....	....	....	Goods: Exports f.o.b.	78aa *d*
	-209.1	....	....	....	....	....	....	-442.7	-483.8	-504.0	-536.5	....	....	....	....	Goods: Imports f.o.b.	78ab *d*
	4.9	....	....	....	....	....	....	-61.0	-68.3	-40.6	-40.8	....	....	....	....	*Trade Balance*	78ac *d*
	48.0	....	....	....	....	....	....	105.9	115.3	120.7	133.5	....	....	....	....	Services: Credit	78ad *d*
	-104.0	....	....	....	....	....	....	-139.8	-148.1	-160.9	-171.8	....	....	....	....	Services: Debit	78ae *d*
	-51.1	....	....	....	....	....	....	-95.0	-101.1	-80.8	-79.2	....	....	....	....	*Balance on Goods & Services*	78af *d*
	—	....	....	....	....	....	....	4.9	5.1	8.7	12.2	....	....	....	....	Income: Credit	78ag *d*
	-40.3	....	....	....	....	....	....	-101.5	-106.8	-114.8	-129.9	....	....	....	....	Income: Debit	78ah *d*
	-91.4	....	....	....	....	....	....	-191.6	-202.9	-186.9	-196.8	....	....	....	....	*Balance on Gds, Serv. & Inc.*	78ai *d*
	2.3	....	....	....	....	....	....	62.9	70.0	68.1	67.4	....	....	....	....	Current Transfers, n.i.e.: Credit	78aj *d*
	-7.5	....	....	....	....	....	....	-9.9	-7.4	-6.2	-5.3	....	....	....	....	Current Transfers: Debit	78ak *d*
	—	....	....	....	....	....	....	1.6	4.4	8.3	9.5	....	....	....	....	Capital Account, n.i.e.	78bc *d*
	—	....	....	....	....	....	....	3.4	6.6	11.0	12.5	....	....	....	....	Capital Account, n.i.e.: Credit	78ba *d*
	—	....	....	....	....	....	....	-1.8	-2.2	-2.7	-3.0	....	....	....	....	Capital Account: Debit	78bb *d*
	-37.6	....	....	....	....	....	....	63.1	88.7	126.9	71.1	....	....	....	....	Financial Account, n.i.e.	78bj *d*
	—	....	....	....	....	....	....	....	....	....	....	....	....	....	....	Direct Investment Abroad	78bd *d*
	1.8	....	....	....	....	....	....	146.6	69.5	106.7	74.4	....	....	....	....	Dir. Invest. in Rep. Econ., n.i.e.	78be *d*
	—	....	....	....	....	....	....	....	....	....	....	....	....	....	....	Portfolio Investment Assets	78bf *d*
	—	....	....	....	....	....	....	....	....	....	....	....	....	....	....	Equity Securities	78bk *d*
	—	....	....	....	....	....	....	....	....	....	....	....	....	....	....	Debt Securities	78bl *d*
	—	....	....	....	....	....	....	2.8	3.6	15.8	3.2	....	....	....	....	Portfolio Investment Liab., n.i.e.	78bg *d*
	—	....	....	....	....	....	....	....	....	....	....	....	....	....	....	Equity Securities	78bm *d*
	—	....	....	....	....	....	....	2.8	3.6	15.8	3.2	....	....	....	....	Debt Securities	78bn *d*
	....	....	....	....	....	....	....	....	....	....	....	....	....	....	....	Financial Derivatives Assets	78bw *d*
	....	....	....	....	....	....	....	....	....	....	....	....	....	....	....	Financial Derivatives Liabilities	78bx *d*
	-1.2	....	....	....	....	....	....	-19.9	8.8	-5.8	-8.9	....	....	....	....	Other Investment Assets	78bh *d*
	....	....	....	....	....	....	....	....	....	....	....	....	....	....	....	Monetary Authorities	78bo *d*
	—	....	....	....	....	....	....	-3.4	1.4	1.3	-2.2	....	....	....	....	General Government	78bp *d*
	-1.2	....	....	....	....	....	....	-6.4	3.2	4.2	-2.8	....	....	....	....	Banks	78bq *d*
	—	....	....	....	....	....	....	-10.2	4.2	-11.2	-3.9	....	....	....	....	Other Sectors	78br *d*
	-38.2	....	....	....	....	....	....	-66.4	6.7	10.2	2.3	....	....	....	....	Other Investment Liab., n.i.e.	78bi *d*
	—	....	....	....	....	....	....	-4.7	-13.9	1.3	18.6	....	....	....	....	Monetary Authorities	78bs *d*
	-37.2	....	....	....	....	....	....	-73.6	27.3	-1.0	-5.4	....	....	....	....	General Government	78bt *d*
	-.4	....	....	....	....	....	....	-5.5	-4.9	-2.9	-.4	....	....	....	....	Banks	78bu *d*
	-.7	....	....	....	....	....	....	17.4	-1.8	12.9	-10.5	....	....	....	....	Other Sectors	78bv *d*
	-4.3	....	....	....	....	....	....	12.2	11.0	-16.3	11.2	....	....	....	....	Net Errors and Omissions	78ca *d*
	-138.6	....	....	....	....	....	....	-61.6	-36.1	-6.0	-43.0	....	....	....	....	*Overall Balance*	78cb *d*
	138.6	....	....	....	....	....	....	61.6	36.1	6.0	43.0	....	....	....	....	Reserves and Related Items	79da *d*
	-3.5	....	....	....	....	....	....	-67.1	-57.1	-21.8	.8	....	....	....	....	Reserve Assets	79db *d*
	-1.0	....	....	....	....	....	....	24.8	9.1	-8.8	-9.7	....	....	....	....	Use of Fund Credit and Loans	79dc *d*
	143.1	....	....	....	....	....	....	103.9	84.2	36.6	52.0	....	....	....	....	Exceptional Financing	79de *d*
Year Ending December 31																**Government Finance**	
	-740	-1,306	-1,425	-1,309	-719	-3,398	-9,166	-7,994	-4,001	-5,092	-2,886	-3,115	-6,611	....	....	Deficit (-) or Surplus	80
	812	1,047	1,291	1,790	4,241	7,536	13,545	19,464	23,901	29,133	32,428	37,180	39,071	....	....	Total Revenue and Grants	81y
	781	1,022	1,221	1,730	3,248	5,642	13,392	18,913	23,191	28,138	30,823	34,666	36,006	....	....	Revenue	81
	31	26	70	59	992	1,895	152	551	710	995	1,605	2,515	3,065	....	....	Grants	81z
	1,553	2,354	2,716	3,099	4,960	10,935	22,711	27,457	27,902	34,226	35,314	40,295	45,682	....	....	Exp. & Lending Minus Repay.	82z
	1,553	2,354	2,716	3,099	4,960	10,935	22,711	27,457	27,902	34,226	35,314	40,295	45,682	....	....	Expenditure	82
	—	—	—	—	—	—	—	—	—	—	—	—	—	....	....	Lending Minus Repayments	83
	740	1,306	1,425	1,309	719	3,398	9,166	7,994	4,001	5,092	2,886	3,115	6,611	....	....	Total Financing	80h
	1,036	1,706	4,307	1,139	2,836	3,468	6,357	4,715	-5,398	-699	2,826	-931	4,310	....	....	Total Net Borrowing	84
	996	1,600	4,210	1,384	2,549	737	233	1,183	-6,573	-4,394	1,627	-7,298	-162	....	....	Net Domestic	84a
	40	106	97	-245	287	2,731	6,124	3,532	1,175	3,695	1,199	6,367	4,473	....	....	Net Foreign	85a
	-296	-400	-2,882	170	-2,116	-70	2,809	3,278	9,399	5,791	60	4,046	2,301	....	....	Use of Cash Balances	87
	8,707	I 10,673	17,984	19,419	55,208	91,687	239,708	265,920	283,213	316,419	322,444	249,167	258,325	....	....	Total Debt	88
	5,293	6,117	6,810	7,084	9,275	9,782	11,958	18,053	27,793	31,490	33,252	37,478	35,888	....	....	Domestic	88a
	3,414	I 4,557	11,174	12,335	45,933	81,905	227,750	247,867	255,420	284,929	289,191	211,688	222,436	....	....	Foreign	89a
Millions of Guyana Dollars																**National Accounts**	
	869	920	2,406	2,123	6,452	8,630	29,870	47,689	52,518	59,185	70,315	82,155	84,375	....	....	Exports of Goods & Services	90c
	700	876	952	1,162	1,701	2,133	4,610	6,383	8,529	11,817	14,092	17,330	21,747	....	....	Government Consumption	91f
	410	586	1,123	890	3,536	6,624	13,746	25,113	30,745	34,348	40,077	43,436	47,099	....	....	Gross Fixed Capital Formation	93e
	1,071	1,000	1,715	2,279	5,987	9,537	21,504	23,525	29,134	36,131	40,897	44,224	47,147	....	....	Private Consumption	96f
	-960	-1,030	-2,619	-2,125	-7,012	-12,290	-34,275	-55,310	-64,370	-64,370	-74,912	-83,895	-91,749	....	....	Imports of Goods & Services	98c
	1,964	2,220	3,357	4,137	10,330	15,665	38,966	46,734	59,124	75,412	88,271	99,038	105,859	....	....	Gross Domestic Product (GDP)	99b
	-107	-283	-606	-869	-2,790	-4,239	-15,093	-13,800	-11,912	-11,473	-12,203	-7,319	-10,406	....	....	Net Factor Inc/Pmts(-) Abroad	98.n
	1,857	1,936	2,751	3,268	7,540	11,426	23,873	32,934	47,212	63,939	76,068	91,719	95,399	....	....	Gross National Income (GNI)	99a
	1,731	1,802	2,611	3,128	7,160	11,426	23,873	32,934	47,212	63,939	76,068	91,719	95,399	....	....	Net National Income	99e
	....	....	....	....	....	....	....	....	....	....	....	....	....	....	....	GDP Volume 1977 Prices	99b.*p*
	3,843	3,664	3,695	3,600	3,482	3,319	3,519	3,792	4,104	....	....	....	....	....	....	GDP Volume 1988 Prices	99b.*p*
	115.8	110.4	111.3	108.5	104.9	100.0	106.0	114.3	123.7	....	....	....	....	....	....	GDP Volume (1990=100)	99bv *p*
	10.8	12.8	19.2	24.3	62.9	100.0	234.6	261.1	305.2	....	....	....	....	....	....	GDP Deflator (1990=100)	99bi *p*
Midyear Estimates																	
	.79	.79	.79	.79	.79	.80	.80	.81	.82	.82	.83	.84	.85	.85	.86	**Population**	99z

(See notes in the back of the book.)

Haiti

		1970	1971	1972	1973	1974	1975	1976	1977	1978	1979	1980	1981	1982	1983	1984
Exchange Rates																*Gourdes per SDR:*
Market Rate	aa	4.999	5.428	5.428	6.031	6.121	5.852	5.808	6.072	6.513	6.585	6.376	5.819	5.515	5.234	4.900
																Gourdes per US Dollar:
Market Rate	ae	4.999	4.999	4.999	4.999	4.999	4.999	4.999	4.999	4.999	4.999	4.999	4.999	4.999	4.999	4.999
Market Rate	rf	5.000	5.000	5.000	5.000	5.000	5.000	5.000	5.000	5.000	5.000	5.000	5.000	5.000	5.000	5.000
Fund Position																*Millions of SDRs:*
Quota	2f. s	19.0	19.0	19.0	19.0	19.0	19.0	19.0	19.0	23.0	23.0	34.5	34.5	34.5	44.1	44.1
SDRs	1b. s	—	1.1	3.1	1.7	2.5	2.0	1.2	1.6	3.8	5.5	—	—	1.0	1.0	
Reserve Position in the Fund	1c. s	—	2.5	2.9	.2	—	—	—	—	2.4	4.4	—	—	.1	.1	.1
Total Fund Cred.&Loans Outstg.	2tl	2.2	.8	—	—	6.6	11.0	12.4	10.5	15.5	19.3	35.7	50.6	61.4	90.1	102.3
International Liquidity													*Millions of US Dollars Unless Otherwise Indicated:*			
Total Reserves minus Gold	1l. d	4.3	10.4	17.9	17.0	19.7	12.4	27.9	33.8	38.6	55.0	16.2	24.0	4.2	9.0	13.0
SDRs	1b. d	—	1.2	3.3	2.0	3.0	2.3	1.4	1.9	5.0	7.2	—	—	1.0	1.0	—
Reserve Position in the Fund	1c. d	—	2.7	3.2	.2	—	—	—	—	3.1	5.8	—	—	.1	.1	.1
Foreign Exchange	1d. d	4.3	6.5	11.4	14.8	16.7	10.1	26.5	31.9	30.6	42.0	16.2	24.0	3.1	7.9	12.9
Gold (Million Fine Troy Ounces)	1ad	....	....	....	....	.002	.002	.002	.006	.010	.018	.018	.018	.018	.018	.018
Monetary Authorities: Other Liab.	4..d	5.1	5.4	6.2	7.0	7.4	17.9	33.2	59.7	82.6	103.2	114.6	124.1	132.9	143.9	157.0
Deposit Money Banks: Assets	7a. d	.5	1.2	3.5	2.4	3.0	5.5	5.3	8.9	6.0	8.8	20.7	46.5	19.4	26.5	29.8
Liabilities	7b. d	.5	—	—	4.7	17.0	23.0	19.6	16.8	16.2	13.3	13.3	12.3	15.4	11.9	8.8
Monetary Authorities															*Millions of Gourdes:*	
Foreign Assets	11	20.1	49.5	92.1	84.5	98.8	62.6	140.0	171.1	193.1	295.0	149.4	190.3	116.4	133.3	145.8
Claims on Central Government	12a	201.2	212.9	216.0	242.5	306.3	446.1	534.1	754.6	739.2	793.4	1,094.1	1,382.3	1,549.0	2,183.1	2,204.3
Claims on Local Government	12b	—	—	—	—	—	—	—	—	—	—	—	—	—	—	—
Claims on Nonfin.Pub.Enterprises	12c	22.5	26.5	32.2	46.0	61.9	161.4	243.8	298.6	358.8	421.1	597.9	626.5	522.5	514.3	514.9
Claims on Private Sector	12d	34.7	41.3	57.8	84.8	111.3	149.2	184.6	226.9	370.6	315.7	346.0	394.1	374.5	266.6	314.5
Claims on Deposit Money Banks	12e	3.8	3.1	3.3	10.1	19.6	15.7	20.8	39.0	50.8	79.2	53.5	53.2	69.7	35.2	25.2
Claims on Other Banking Insts	12f	9.0	9.0	9.8	11.2	12.8	11.0	12.4	12.4	10.2	16.6	15.9	31.7	36.5	43.6	48.9
Claims on Nonbank Financial Insts	12g															
Reserve Money	14	183.3	210.6	256.5	305.0	319.0	396.7	548.8	649.5	717.7	804.6	994.3	1,157.0	1,169.7	1,153.1	1,397.9
of which: Currency Outside DMBs	14a	114.6	126.1	147.7	172.9	182.7	189.5	243.2	265.5	311.4	418.5	418.1	487.4	565.6	599.5	691.0
Time, Savings,& Fgn.Currency Dep.	15	23.8	31.6	41.2	55.1	74.1	82.2	107.1	135.1	168.6	168.9	175.2	208.4	223.4	260.9	277.9
Liabs. of Central Bank: Securities	16ac	....	....	....	....	....	....	....	....	....	....	....	....	....	....	....
Foreign Liabilities	16c	11.2	4.4	2.0	2.7	45.6	66.4	76.0	68.7	107.2	136.4	234.3	309.5	357.2	485.9	560.9
Long-Term Foreign Liabilities	16cl	25.5	27.1	28.8	32.1	32.2	87.3	161.9	293.2	406.7	507.1	565.8	605.2	646.0	704.9	725.3
Central Government Deposits	16d	16.4	13.8	14.2	14.6	59.0	141.7	174.4	259.1	295.6	268.6	190.6	226.3	186.3	203.2	218.3
Capital Accounts	17a	33.6	47.6	62.1	71.3	75.7	76.9	87.5	103.3	120.7	156.0	237.8	229.7	210.6	167.4	286.5
Other Items (Net)	17r	-2.4	7.3	6.4	-1.6	5.1	-5.2	-20.0	-6.3	-93.8	-120.7	-141.2	-57.9	-124.6	200.8	-213.1
Deposit Money Banks															*Millions of Gourdes:*	
Reserves	20	20.1	31.9	42.6	58.8	74.2	124.1	159.6	191.4	214.3	241.7	325.8	344.9	359.5	363.9	601.1
Other Claims on Monetary Author.	20c	....	....													
Foreign Assets	21	2.4	6.1	17.7	12.2	14.9	27.5	26.4	44.3	30.0	44.1	103.4	232.5	97.1	132.4	149.0
Claims on Central Government	22a	3.6	2.5	2.5	2.5	22.0	27.2	27.1	26.3	25.5	—	.5	3.0	2.5	48.0	40.9
Claims on Private Sector	22d	42.8	43.9	65.4	143.3	255.4	331.3	419.2	480.6	598.5	672.5	726.0	816.4	858.1	850.2	884.6
Demand Deposits	24	27.3	33.8	52.6	75.8	91.3	110.9	135.6	155.7	183.4	186.7	224.0	295.2	318.2	357.2	384.4
Time, Savings,& Fgn.Currency Dep.	25	34.2	43.8	69.1	99.4	167.1	250.1	358.5	452.6	545.1	602.9	817.6	800.1	859.4	912.0	990.7
Bonds	26ab															
Foreign Liabilities	26c	2.5	—	—	23.4	84.7	114.7	97.9	83.8	81.1	66.6	66.2	61.6	77.1	59.4	43.7
Central Government Deposits	26d	3.9	3.9	3.9	3.9	3.9	11.4	11.4	11.4	11.4	11.4	—	4.1	4.1	3.9	3.9
Credit from Monetary Authorities	26g	3.2	2.9	3.1	5.4	7.9	11.1	12.7	25.1	27.2	50.4	23.9	41.8	10.6	42.5	33.7
Capital Accounts	27a	7.7	7.7	6.8	18.5	24.1	28.9	29.4	30.9	40.4	31.5	33.5	290.1	305.5	293.8	339.2
Other Items (Net)	27r	-10.0	-7.7	-7.4	-9.7	-12.6	-17.1	-13.2	-16.7	-20.4	8.8	-9.7	-96.0	-257.6	-274.3	-120.0
Monetary Survey															*Millions of Gourdes:*	
Foreign Assets (Net)	31n	8.8	51.3	107.7	70.5	-16.6	-91.1	-7.5	63.0	34.8	136.1	-47.8	51.7	-220.7	-279.6	-309.8
Domestic Credit	32	293.5	318.4	365.7	511.8	706.8	976.2	1,237.6	1,530.3	1,796.2	1,939.8	2,590.2	3,024.2	3,153.2	3,699.1	3,786.0
Claims on Central Govt. (Net)	32an	184.5	197.7	200.4	226.5	265.4	320.1	375.5	510.4	457.7	513.4	904.0	1,154.9	1,361.1	2,024.0	2,023.0
Claims on Local Government	32b	—	—	—	—	—	3.2	2.2	1.4	.5	.5	.5	.5	.5	.5	....
Claims on Nonfin.Pub.Enterprises	32c	22.5	26.5	32.2	46.0	61.9	161.4	243.8	298.6	358.8	421.1	597.9	626.5	522.5	514.3	514.9
Claims on Private Sector	32d	77.5	85.2	123.2	228.1	366.7	480.5	603.8	707.6	969.0	988.2	1,071.9	1,210.6	1,232.6	1,116.7	1,199.1
Claims on Other Banking Insts	32f	9.0	9.0	9.8	11.2	12.8	11.0	12.4	12.4	10.2	16.6	15.9	31.7	36.5	43.6	48.9
Claims on Nonbank Financial Inst	32g															
Money	34	190.6	214.6	271.2	332.8	342.4	402.6	549.6	629.1	717.8	802.5	945.4	1,166.5	1,164.3	1,174.7	1,388.0
Quasi-Money	35	58.0	75.4	110.3	154.5	241.3	332.2	465.6	587.8	713.7	771.8	992.8	1,008.5	1,082.7	1,172.9	1,268.6
Bonds	36ab															
Long-Term Foreign Liabilities	36cl	25.6	27.2	28.9	32.2	32.3	87.4	161.9	293.2	406.7	507.1	565.8	605.2	646.0	704.9	725.3
Capital Accounts	37a	41.2	55.3	68.9	89.8	99.7	105.8	117.0	134.1	161.2	187.5	271.3	519.8	516.1	461.1	625.7
Other Items (Net)	37r	-13.3	-2.9	-6.0	-27.0	-25.5	-42.9	-64.0	-50.9	-168.3	-193.0	-232.9	-224.0	-476.6	-94.1	-531.4
Money plus Quasi-Money	35l	248.6	290.0	381.6	487.3	583.7	734.8	1,015.2	1,216.8	1,431.5	1,574.4	1,938.2	2,175.0	2,247.0	2,347.6	2,656.6
Other Banking Institutions															*Millions of Gourdes:*	
Cash	40	5.4	3.7	4.4	5.4	7.8	3.8	11.3	11.7	11.5	11.1	2.8	8.8	9.9	14.8	4.5
Claims on Private Sector	42d	21.1	24.3	23.7	25.6	26.7	31.1	32.4	57.0	44.6	52.9	72.3	96.3	68.9	85.6	105.5
Credit from Monetary Authorities	46g	9.0	8.3	8.7	8.5	11.7	12.5	14.0	14.6	12.4	14.3	17.8	32.5	50.8	60.9	55.5
Capital Accounts	47a	13.6	14.9	17.1	18.0	21.0	22.7	28.2	41.1	47.3	63.0	52.2	51.6	31.0	40.5	58.2
Other Items (Net)	47r	4.0	4.8	2.2	4.5	1.8	-.4	1.6	13.1	-3.6	-13.3	5.2	20.9	-3.0	-1.0	-3.7
Interest Rates															*Percent per Annum*	
Treasury Bill Rate	60c	....	....	....	....	....	....	....	....	....	....	....	....	....	....	....
Savings Rate	60k	....	....	....	....	....	....	....	....	....	....	....	....	....	....	....
Deposit Rate	60l	....	....	....	....	....	....	....	....	....	....	....	....	....	....	....
Lending Rate	60p	....	....	....	....	....	....	....	....	....	....	....	....	....	....	....
Prices															*Index Numbers (1995=100):*	
Consumer Prices	64	6.0	6.6	6.8	8.3	9.6	11.2	12.0	12.7	12.4	14.0	⌐16.5	18.3	19.6	21.7	23.0

	1985	1986	1987	1988	1989	1990	1991	1992	1993	1994	1995	1996	1997	1998	1999		
End of Period																**Exchange Rates**	
	5.491	6.115	7.092	6.727	6.570	7.112	I 11.787	15.060	17.588	18.900	24.022	21.703	23.357	23.239	24.658	Market Rate	aa
End of Period (ae) Period Average (rf)																	
	4.999	4.999	4.999	4.999	4.999	4.999	I 8.240	10.953	12.805	12.947	16.160	15.093	17.311	16.505	17.965	Market Rate	ae
	5.000	5.000	5.000	5.000	5.000	5.000	6.034	9.802	12.823	15.040	15.110	15.701	16.655	16.766	16.938	Market Rate	rf
End of Period																**Fund Position**	
	44.1	44.1	44.1	44.1	44.1	44.1	44.1	44.1	44.1	44.1	60.7	60.7	60.7	60.7	60.7	Quota	2f. s
	—	5.4	—	—	.1	—	—	—	—	—	.4	—	.1	.4	.6	SDRs	1b. s
	.1	.1	.1	.1	.1	.1	.1	.1	—	—	—	—	—	—	—	Reserve Position in the Fund	1c. s
	87.4	72.8	51.1	33.8	30.6	25.5	23.8	23.8	23.8	3.8	18.2	31.6	31.6	40.8	32.6	Total Fund Cred.&Loans Outstg.	2tl
End of Period																**International Liquidity**	
	6.4	15.9	17.0	13.0	12.6	3.2	17.3	....	....	30.9	105.8	107.9	77.1	....	....	Total Reserves minus Gold	1l. d
	—	6.6	—	—	.1	—	—	—	—	—	.5	.1	.1	.5	.9	SDRs	1b. d
	.1	.1	.1	.1	.1	.1	.1	.1	.1	.1	.1	.1	.1	.1	.1	Reserve Position in the Fund	1c. d
	6.3	9.2	16.9	12.9	12.4	3.1	17.2	....	....	30.9	105.2	107.8	77.0	....	....	Foreign Exchange	1d. d
	.018	.018	.018	.018	.018	.018	.018	.019	.019	.019	.019	.019	.020	.020	.001	Gold (Million Fine Troy Ounces)	1ad
	139.6	154.0	165.3	175.2	177.7	4.8	4.8	9.0	9.7	48.3	20.6	82.1	59.6	60.4	60.7	Monetary Authorities: Other Liab.	4.. d
	30.0	30.2	23.4	23.1	17.1	42.4	32.4	54.0	78.3	96.1	98.1	114.9	133.1	124.4	150.8	Deposit Money Banks: Assets	7a. d
	....	2.4	1.6	1.6	8.5	20.3	.5	—	—	.8	4.9	6.9	17.9	8.3	12.1	Liabilities	7b. d
End of Period																**Monetary Authorities**	
	104.2	180.1	182.0	162.5	209.6	100.1	75.9	152.9	236.8	834.0	3,073.7	3,988.0	I 4,757.2	5,308.4	5,916.0	Foreign Assets	11
	2,199.9	2,700.0	2,769.8	2,848.8	2,876.1	3,243.4	3,397.2	3,985.1	4,394.6	5,860.7	7,074.0	7,238.8	I 7,668.1	8,273.3	10,302.3	Claims on Central Government	12a
	—	—	—	—	—	—	—	—	—	—	—	12.9	I 8.5	5.0	1.7	Claims on Local Government	12b
	496.3	287.8	278.3	397.2	382.1	296.8	283.8	348.7	426.5	328.1	152.1	80.8	I 50.9	85.5	84.5	Claims on Nonfin.Pub.Enterprises	12c
	363.9	336.0	338.0	291.2	323.2	—	—	—	—	—	—	141.2	I 163.5	233.1	304.2	Claims on Private Sector	12d
	26.3	7.4	8.3	5.6	9.2	22.3	5.4	331.9	754.6	415.6	65.0	70.2	I 129.2	106.2	264.6	Claims on Deposit Money Banks	12e
	35.2	73.2	73.0	71.4	70.5	15.0	10.0	—	—	—	28.6	—	I —	—	—	Claims on Other Banking Insts	12f
	—	—	—	—	—	—	—	—	—	—	—	4.7	I 22.4	19.8	13.9	Claims on Nonbank Financial Insts	12g
	1,569.7	1,809.1	2,174.8	1,595.5	2,629.4	3,081.7	3,356.7	4,346.1	5,616.6	6,954.9	7,975.8	7,645.1	I 7,653.3	7,672.5	9,894.3	Reserve Money	14
	763.2	829.1	979.5	205.0	1,458.8	1,382.3	1,544.6	2,074.5	2,668.8	3,029.5	3,536.7	3,435.7	I 3,935.4	3,905.4	4,927.1	*of which: Currency Outside DMBs*	14a
	366.4	375.4	412.4	400.0	430.8	—	—	—	—	—	—	—	I 8.4	37.3	55.9	Time, Savings,& Fgn.Currency Dep.	15
	....	....	....	....	....	....	....	....	....	....	....	....	857.0	1,980.0	2,335.0	Liabs. of Central Bank: Securities	16ac
	479.9	445.0	395.0	284.2	246.0	205.1	320.6	456.9	543.7	136.0	555.9	1,595.1	I 737.5	954.0	802.6	Foreign Liabilities	16c
	697.9	769.9	793.7	818.9	843.0	—	—	—	—	560.6	212.8	—	I 1,030.9	990.4	1,091.0	Long-Term Foreign Liabilities	16cl
	462.8	586.0	427.5	586.6	212.6	407.7	428.0	457.3	481.3	892.7	1,983.0	1,617.2	I 1,514.2	1,647.6	1,895.3	Central Government Deposits	16d
	181.1	164.9	216.9	227.0	259.1	232.5	316.4	411.4	472.2	564.0	1,139.1	857.2	I 1,266.6	1,313.1	1,566.8	Capital Accounts	17a
	−531.9	−565.9	−770.8	−135.4	−750.3	−249.4	−649.4	−853.1	−1,301.3	−1,669.8	−1,473.3	−178.0	I −268.1	−563.7	−753.8	Other Items (Net)	17r
End of Period																**Deposit Money Banks**	
	610.8	637.4	808.1	751.3	865.9	1,517.0	1,736.9	2,420.8	3,059.1	3,718.1	3,608.0	3,979.8	I 3,323.6	3,411.0	4,394.1	Reserves	20
	....	....	....	....	....	....	....	....	....	....	....	....	857.0	1,980.0	2,335.0	Other Claims on Monetary Author.	20c
	150.0	151.0	117.0	115.6	85.3	212.2	266.6	592.0	1,002.7	1,243.6	1,584.9	1,734.2	I 2,303.9	2,053.8	2,709.8	Foreign Assets	21
	27.5	26.7	17.8	28.4	31.6	12.3	11.7	11.5	8.0	114.1	11.3	6.5	I 6.5	6.5	169.3	Claims on Central Government	22a
	885.4	886.0	957.1	1,250.5	1,503.3	1,800.6	1,862.2	2,100.2	2,516.3	3,253.2	5,072.4	5,825.0	I 8,511.2	9,156.2	10,128.9	Claims on Private Sector	22d
	512.6	544.2	658.6	715.7	767.2	920.2	1,062.5	1,199.9	1,429.6	1,578.0	2,372.7	2,211.1	I 2,435.2	2,544.2	3,241.5	Demand Deposits	24
	1,045.3	1,111.2	1,183.3	1,277.7	1,494.4	2,371.2	2,764.5	3,671.8	4,944.8	6,486.8	8,018.7	9,064.7	I 11499.7	13,209.8	16,078.8	Time, Savings,& Fgn.Currency Dep.	25
	....	....	....	....	....	....	....	....	....	....	....	....	46.1	44.9	21.9	Bonds	26ab
	51.4	11.8	8.2	7.9	42.5	101.5	3.8	.5	.3	10.7	78.6	104.5	I 310.3	136.4	218.2	Foreign Liabilities	26c
	3.9	3.9	3.9	—	—	50.9	31.0	26.3	27.0	27.6	37.5	54.5	I 514.7	475.1	402.8	Central Government Deposits	26d
	17.7	25.0	18.6	33.6	73.5	—	—	—	—	—	72.6	81.9	I 49.0	42.8	134.7	Credit from Monetary Authorities	26g
	325.5	314.1	344.7	460.9	515.1	221.3	199.1	269.7	320.9	395.7	525.7	946.2	I 1,373.9	1,692.9	1,811.2	Capital Accounts	27a
	−282.9	−309.0	−317.3	−350.1	−406.7	−123.0	−183.5	−43.7	−136.5	−169.8	−829.1	−917.4	I −1226.7	−1,538.6	−2,172.0	Other Items (Net)	27r
End of Period																**Monetary Survey**	
	−277.2	−125.6	−104.3	−14.1	6.4	5.7	18.1	287.5	695.5	1,930.9	4,024.1	4,022.6	I 6,013.4	6,271.8	7,604.9	Foreign Assets (Net)	31n
	3,541.5	3,719.8	4,002.7	4,301.0	4,974.2	4,909.5	5,105.9	5,961.9	6,837.1	8,440.9	10,317.9	11,638.2	I 14402.1	15,656.7	18,706.8	Domestic Credit	32
	1,760.7	2,136.8	2,356.3	2,290.6	2,695.1	2,797.1	2,949.9	3,513.0	3,894.3	4,861.4	5,064.8	5,573.6	I 5,645.7	6,157.1	8,173.6	Claims on Central Govt. (Net)	32an
	....	....	....	....	....	—	—	—	—	—	—	12.9	I 8.5	5.0	1.7	Claims on Local Government	32b
	496.3	287.8	278.3	397.2	382.1	296.8	283.8	348.7	426.5	326.3	152.1	80.8	I 50.9	85.5	84.5	Claims on Nonfin.Pub.Enterprises	32c
	1,249.3	1,222.0	1,295.2	1,541.7	1,826.5	1,800.6	1,862.2	2,100.2	2,516.3	3,253.2	5,072.4	5,966.2	I 8,674.6	9,389.3	10,433.0	Claims on Private Sector	32d
	35.2	73.2	73.0	71.4	70.5	15.0	10.0	—	—	—	28.6	—	I —	—	—	Claims on Other Banking Insts	32f
	—	—	—	—	—	—	—	—	—	—	—	4.7	I 22.4	19.8	13.9	Claims on Nonbank Financial Inst	32g
	1,588.7	1,789.9	2,097.9	1,635.2	2,633.6	2,302.5	2,464.4	3,150.1	3,866.4	5,095.5	6,703.9	5,823.9	I 6,633.5	6,650.9	8,423.0	Money	34
	1,411.7	1,486.7	1,595.7	1,677.7	1,925.3	2,371.2	2,764.5	3,671.8	4,944.8	6,486.8	8,018.7	9,064.7	I 11508.1	13,247.1	16,134.7	Quasi-Money	35
	....	....	....	....	....	....	....	....	....	....	....	....	46.1	44.9	21.9	Bonds	36ab
	697.9	769.9	793.7	818.9	843.0	—	—	—	—	560.6	212.8	—	I 1,030.9	990.4	1,091.0	Long-Term Foreign Liabilities	36cl
	506.6	479.0	561.6	687.9	774.2	453.8	515.5	681.1	793.1	959.7	1,664.7	1,803.4	I 2,640.5	3,006.0	3,378.0	Capital Accounts	37a
	−940.5	−931.3	−1,150.4	−532.8	−1,195.4	−212.3	−620.4	−1,253.6	−2,071.7	−2,730.8	−2,258.1	−1,031.3	I −1443.6	−2,010.8	−2,737.0	Other Items (Net)	37r
	3,000.4	3,276.5	3,693.6	3,312.9	4,558.8	4,673.7	5,228.9	6,821.9	8,811.2	11,582.3	14,722.5	14,888.6	I 18141.5	19,898.0	24,557.7	Money plus Quasi-Money	35l
End of Period																**Other Banking Institutions**	
	4.5	3.3	....	....	....	....	....	....	....	....	....	....	....	....	....	Cash	40
	....	....	....	....	....	....	....	....	....	....	....	....	....	....	....	Claims on Private Sector	42d
	54.8	58.2	....	....	....	....	....	....	....	....	....	....	....	....	....	Credit from Monetary Authorities	46g
	87.8	28.6	....	....	....	....	....	....	....	....	....	....	....	....	....	Capital Accounts	47a
	....	....	....	....	....	....	....	....	....	....	....	....	....	....	....	Other Items (Net)	47r
Percent per Annum																**Interest Rates**	
	....	....	....	....	....	....	....	....	....	....	....	....	14.13	16.21	7.71	Treasury Bill Rate	60c
	....	....	....	....	....	....	....	....	....	....	....	....	5.36	5.50	3.51	Savings Rate	60k
	....	....	....	....	....	....	....	....	....	....	....	....	10.74	13.06	7.39	Deposit Rate	60l
	....	....	....	....	....	....	....	....	....	....	....	....	21.00	23.62	22.88	Lending Rate	60p
Period Averages																**Prices**	
	25.5	26.3	23.3	24.3	26.0	31.5	I 36.3	I 43.4	56.2	78.4	100.0	120.6	145.4	160.8	174.8	Consumer Prices	64

Haiti

		1970	1971	1972	1973	1974	1975	1976	1977	1978	1979	1980	1981	1982	1983	1984
International Transactions															*Millions of Gourdes*	
Exports	70	201.8	236.6	220.0	263.6	357.7	398.8	621.7	742.8	776.7	926.9	1,131.0	757.5	888.4	830.0	896.0
Imports, c.i.f.	71	275.0	302.1	344.6	415.7	626.0	744.8	1,033.7	1,063.3	1,166.0	1,360.4	1,770.7	2,239.8	1,936.4	2,202.6	2,360.7
Balance of Payments															*Millions of US Dollars: F.Y. Ending*	
Current Account, n.i.e.	78al *d*	....	5.0	8.2	1.2	−21.0	−24.5	−12.5	−37.7	−44.9	−52.8	−101.1	−148.8	−98.5	−111.2	−103.0
Goods: Exports f.o.b.	78aa *d*	....	45.3	42.9	54.4	70.0	80.3	111.9	137.6	149.9	138.0	215.8	151.1	177.1	186.6	214.6
Goods: Imports f.o.b.	78ab *d*	....	−53.2	−57.6	−66.5	−96.5	−122.1	−158.7	−199.9	−207.5	−220.1	−319.0	−360.1	−301.9	−325.9	−337.9
Trade Balance	78ac *d*	....	−7.9	−14.7	−12.1	−26.5	−41.8	−46.7	−62.3	−57.5	−82.1	−103.2	−209.0	−124.8	−139.3	−123.3
Services: Credit	78ad *d*	....	18.8	21.0	21.6	21.8	25.6	28.8	36.4	61.3	74.9	89.9	90.4	97.7	103.3	104.5
Services: Debit	78ae *d*	....	−21.7	−22.2	−27.5	−34.2	−37.3	−52.8	−63.1	−101.6	−107.9	−162.0	−156.5	−169.1	−171.3	−189.1
Balance on Goods & Services	78af *d*	....	−10.8	−15.9	−18.0	−38.9	−53.5	−70.8	−89.0	−97.9	−115.0	−175.3	−275.1	−196.2	−207.4	−207.9
Income: Credit	78ag *d*	....	—	—	.2	—	.3	1.0	1.3	2.0	2.6	3.1	4.1	3.6	4.7	4.5
Income: Debit	78ah *d*	....	−4.0	−5.4	−6.6	−8.1	−7.4	−8.1	−13.4	−16.7	−16.0	−17.4	−17.2	−17.6	−18.9	−22.6
Balance on Gds, Serv. & Inc.	78ai *d*	....	−14.8	−21.3	−24.3	−46.7	−60.6	−77.9	−101.0	−112.5	−128.4	−189.6	−288.1	−210.2	−221.6	−226.0
Current Transfers, n.i.e.: Credit	78aj *d*	....	25.1	32.7	33.3	36.5	76.9	111.8	107.4	114.9	126.3	158.5	201.2	159.0	153.9	168.0
Current Transfers: Debit	78ak *d*	....	−5.3	−3.1	−7.9	−10.8	−40.8	−46.5	−44.1	−47.3	−50.7	−70.0	−61.8	−47.3	−43.5	−45.0
Capital Account, n.i.e.	78bc *d*	....	−.8	−1.0	−1.1	−1.0	−.3	−.4	—	—	—	—	—	—	—	—
Capital Account, n.i.e.: Credit	78ba *d*	....	—	—	—	—	—	—	—	—	—	—	—	—	—	—
Capital Account: Debit	78bb *d*	....	−.8	−1.0	−1.1	−1.0	−.3	−.4	—	—	—	—	—	—	—	—
Financial Account, n.i.e.	78bj *d*	....	1.9	10.0	7.4	21.1	33.8	26.5	67.3	36.4	59.8	76.0	109.8	90.5	91.2	112.7
Direct Investment Abroad	78bd *d*	....	—	—	—	—	—	—	—	—	—	—	—	—	—	—
Dir. Invest. in Rep. Econ., n.i.e.	78be *d*	....	3.4	4.1	7.0	7.9	2.6	7.8	8.0	10.0	12.0	13.0	8.3	7.1	8.4	4.5
Portfolio Investment Assets	78bf *d*	....	—	—	—	—	—	—	—	—	—	—	—	—	—	—
Equity Securities	78bk *d*	....	—	—	—	—	—	—	—	—	—	—	—	—	—	—
Debt Securities	78bl *d*	....	—	—	—	—	—	—	—	—	—	—	—	—	—	—
Portfolio Investment Liab., n.i.e.	78bg *d*	....	—	—	—	—	—	—	—	—	—	—	—	—	—	—
Equity Securities	78bm *d*	....	—	—	—	—	—	—	—	—	—	—	—	—	—	—
Debt Securities	78bn *d*	....	—	—	—	—	—	—	—	—	—	—	—	—	—	—
Financial Derivatives Assets	78bw *d*	....	....	....	....	....	....	....	....	....	....	....	....	....	....	....
Financial Derivatives Liabilities	78bx *d*	....	....	....	....	....	....	....	....	....	....	....	....	....	....	....
Other Investment Assets	78bh *d*	....	−1.0	−1.5	2.0	−1.8	−1.1	−2.7	.7	−3.0	3.5	−7.5	−3.4	6.7	−.1	6.1
Monetary Authorities	78bo *d*	....	....	....	....	....	....	....	....	....	....	....	....	....	....	....
General Government	78bp *d*	....	....	....	....	....	....	....	....	....	....	....	....	....	....	....
Banks	78bq *d*	....	−1.0	−1.5	2.0	−1.8	−1.1	−2.7	.7	−3.0	3.5	−7.5	−3.4	6.7	−.1	6.1
Other Sectors	78br *d*	....	....	....	....	....	....	....	....	....	....	....	....	....	....	....
Other Investment Liab., n.i.e.	78bi *d*	....	−.5	7.5	−1.6	14.9	32.3	21.4	58.6	29.4	44.3	70.5	104.9	76.7	82.9	102.1
Monetary Authorities	78bs *d*	....	—	—	.3	−.3	.4	−.2	.1	.3	.8	−1.7	—	—	.4	10.0
General Government	78bt *d*	....	−1.3	3.8	−2.9	−1.9	13.8	19.3	40.2	24.2	32.1	45.3	27.9	48.5	33.4	67.1
Banks	78bu *d*	....	.2	.1	.9	10.9	12.2	−4.5	−1.5	−.9	−5.7	4.9	2.1	−.8	5.6	6.2
Other Sectors	78bv *d*	....	.6	3.5	.1	6.3	5.9	6.8	19.8	5.9	17.1	22.1	74.9	29.0	43.5	18.9
Net Errors and Omissions	78ca *d*	....	−.1	−10.2	−9.1	−7.7	−21.7	−2.5	−19.9	15.1	−5.2	−12.2	.7	−11.6	−8.6	−29.9
Overall Balance	78cb *d*	....	6.0	7.0	−1.6	−8.5	−12.7	11.1	9.7	6.6	1.8	−37.2	−38.3	−19.6	−28.6	−20.1
Reserves and Related Items	79da *d*	....	−6.0	−7.0	1.6	8.5	12.7	−11.1	−9.7	−6.6	−1.8	37.2	38.3	19.6	28.6	20.1
Reserve Assets	79db *d*	....	−4.3	−5.7	1.6	4.8	3.0	−12.8	−7.6	−13.5	−5.7	31.9	23.6	−9.5	3.4	−1.0
Use of Fund Credit and Loans	79dc *d*	....	−1.7	−1.3	—	3.7	9.7	1.6	−2.3	6.7	3.6	5.0	14.7	29.1	24.9	20.3
Exceptional Financing	79de *d*	....	—	—	—	—	—	.1	.2	.2	.3	.3	—	—	.2	.8
Government Finance															*Millions of Gourdes:*	
Deficit (−) or Surplus	80	−3.9	−9.8	2.5	1.2	−10.4	−42.2	−64.2	−143.3	−168.2	−168.0	−327.7	−446.3	−380.6	−277.1	−572.7
Revenue	81	225.0	263.3	278.8	302.5	333.3	475.3	644.3	784.5	986.9	623.3	789.3	759.9	858.6	952.9	1,075.7
Grants Received	81z	....	....	....	....	....	....	....	....	....	....	151.0	157.7	593.0	640.8	341.9
Expenditure	82	228.9	273.1	276.3	301.3	343.7	517.5	708.5	927.8	1,155.1	791.3	1,268.0	1,363.9	1,832.2	1,870.8	1,990.3
Financing																
Net Domestic Borrowing	84a	6.3	15.4	2.8	5.0	20.7	54.5	31.8	45.0	36.1	68.2	165.2	367.8	157.7	129.3	431.6
Monetary Authorities	84aa	5.0	6.1	3.6	5.3	23.0	50.3	34.7	46.1	22.9	66.8	161.0	364.8	154.4	109.5	435.9
Other	84ac	1.3	9.3	−.8	−.3	−2.3	4.2	−2.9	−1.1	13.2	1.4	4.2	3.0	3.3	19.8	−4.3
Net Foreign Borrowing	85a	−5.9	−6.2	−6.7	−6.5	−9.0	−9.5	49.8	185.0	130.4	117.3	156.6	105.6	171.8	150.8	159.6
Use of Cash Balances	87	4.7	.9	1.4	.3	−2.3	−2.1	−17.3	−85.3	2.2	−17.5	5.9	−27.1	51.1	−3.0	−18.5
Adjustment to Financing	84x	−1.2	−.3	—	—	1.0	−.7	−.1	−1.4	−.5						
National Accounts															*Millions of Gourdes:*	
Exports of Goods & Services	90c	261	321	332	381	663	785	1,046	1,249	1,495	1,522	2,148	1,944	2,139	2,302	2,598
Gross Fixed Capital Formation	93e	161	186	207	258	‡410	533	678	748	857	938	1,238	1,252	1,230	1,331	1,441
Increase/Decrease(−) in Stocks	93i	12	13	13	17	‡19	23	26	28	—	—	—	—			
Gov't and Private Consumption	96f	1,964	2,142	2,160	3,013	2,604	3,149	4,101	4,592	4,690	5,245	6,835	7,535	7,202	7,835	
Imports of Goods & Services	98c	−343	−395	−400	−508	−868	−1,082	−1,430	−1,692	−1,982	−2,105	−3,302	−3,650	−3,186	−3,381	−3,636
Gross Domestic Product (GDP)	99b	2,055	2,262	2,312	3,129	‡2,828	3,408	4,395	4,897	5,060	5,600	6,919	7,081	7,370	8,120	9,080
Net Factor Inc/Pmts(−) Abroad	98.n	−15	−16	−20	‡−21	−28	−34	−36	−63	−76	−70	−72	−66	−72	−73	−92
Gross National Income (GNI)	99a	2,040	2,246	2,292	3,108	2,800	3,374	4,359	4,834	4,984	5,530	6,847	7,015	7,299	8,045	8,990
Net National Income	99e	1,993	2,190	2,241	3,062	2,739	3,300	4,251	4,715	4,847	5,380	6,650	6,815	7,102	7,833	8,760
GDP Volume 1976 Prices	99b.*p*	3,365	3,583	3,617	3,789	4,009	4,054	4,395	4,416	4,631	4,983	5,342	5,196	5,018	5,056	5,071
GDP Volume (1995=100)	99bv *p*	77.6	82.7	83.5	87.4	92.5	93.5	101.4	101.9	106.9	115.0	123.3	119.9	115.8	116.7	117.0
GDP Deflator (1995=100)	99bi *p*	7.5	7.8	7.9	10.1	‡8.7	10.3	12.3	13.6	13.4	13.8	15.9	16.7	18.1	19.7	22.0
															Millions:	
Population	99z	4.24	4.31	4.37	4.44	4.51	4.58	4.67	4.75	4.83	4.92	5.01	5.46	5.56	5.66	5.76

International Transactions

Millions of Gourdes

	1985	1986	1987	1988	1989	1990	1991	1992	1993	1994	1995	1996	1997	1998	1999	
Exports	842.0	922.2	1,067.7	896.4	720.3	801.3	1,005.2	719.4	1,029.3	1,236.7	1,666.5	1,413.9	1,995.4	2,925.9	3,325.8	70
Imports, c.i.f.	2,207.8	1,799.9	1,995.9	1,721.3	1,455.0	1,661.1	2,414.2	2,727.9	4,555.7	3,783.6	9,866.2	10,448.2	10,792.1	13,365.6	17,366.9	71

Balance of Payments

Sept 30; Minus Sign Indicates Debit

	1985	1986	1987	1988	1989	1990	1991	1992	1993	1994	1995	1996	1997	1998	1999	
Current Account, n.i.e.	-94.7	-44.9	-31.1	-40.4	-62.7	-21.9	-91.5	7.3	-11.8	-23.4	-87.1	-137.7	-47.7	-38.1	....	78al d
Goods: Exports f.o.b.	223.0	190.8	210.1	180.4	148.3	265.8	166.6	73.4	80.3	60.3	88.3	82.5	205.4	299.3	....	78aa d
Goods: Imports f.o.b.	-344.7	-303.2	-311.2	-283.9	-259.3	-442.6	-448.6	-212.5	-260.5	-171.5	-517.2	-498.6	-559.6	-640.7	....	78ab d
Trade Balance	-121.7	-112.5	-101.1	-103.5	-111.0	-176.8	-282.0	-139.1	-180.2	-111.2	-428.9	-416.1	-354.2	-341.4	....	78ac d
Services: Credit	114.2	101.3	110.3	94.5	88.5	52.2	57.6	38.5	35.8	6.7	104.1	109.1	173.7	180.0	....	78ad d
Services: Debit	-212.4	-170.2	-190.5	-197.1	-188.8	-72.0	-83.3	-35.2	-30.2	-63.9	-284.5	-283.3	-331.5	-380.6	....	78ae d
Balance on Goods & Services	-219.9	-181.4	-181.3	-206.1	-211.4	-196.6	-307.7	-135.8	-174.6	-168.4	-609.3	-590.3	-512.0	-542.0	....	78af d
Income: Credit	5.1	4.6	5.2	6.2	4.6	6.9	2.0	1.0	2.0							78ag d
Income: Debit	-24.9	-19.9	-26.1	-33.4	-30.2	-25.1	-20.0	-12.9	-12.6	-11.2	-30.6	-9.9	-13.6	-11.7	....	78ah d
Balance on Gds, Serv. & Inc.	-239.7	-196.8	-202.2	-233.2	-236.9	-214.8	-325.7	-147.7	-185.2	-179.6	-639.9	-600.2	-525.6	-553.7	....	78ai d
Current Transfers, n.i.e.: Credit	192.3	205.3	228.0	253.6	237.7	192.9	234.2	155.0	173.4	156.2	552.9	462.5	477.9	515.6	....	78aj d
Current Transfers: Debit	-47.2	-53.4	-56.9	-60.7	-63.5	—	—	—	—	—	—	....	....	....	....	78ak d
Capital Account, n.i.e.	—	—	—	—	—											78bc d
Capital Account, n.i.e.: Credit	—	—	—	—	—							....	....			78ba d
Capital Account: Debit	—	—	—	—	—						....	....	....			78bb d
Financial Account, n.i.e.	46.0	34.4	53.4	26.3	60.1	33.0	24.1	-22.8	-46.5	-15.8	99.2	67.9	61.5	193.1	....	78bj d
Direct Investment Abroad	—	—	—	—	—	8.0	13.6	—	—		....					78bi d
Dir. Invest. in Rep. Econ., n.i.e.	4.9	4.8	4.7	10.1	9.4	—	-1.8	-2.2	-2.8	—	7.4	4.1	4.0	10.8	....	78be d
Portfolio Investment Assets	—	—	—	—	—						....					78bf d
Equity Securities	—	—	—	—	—						....					78bk d
Debt Securities	—	—	—	—	—						....					78bl d
Portfolio Investment Liab., n.i.e.	—	—	—	—	—						....					78bg d
Equity Securities	—	—	—	—	—						....					78bm d
Debt Securities	—	—	—	—	—						....					78bn d
Financial Derivatives Assets											....					78bw d
Financial Derivatives Liabilities											....					78bx d
Other Investment Assets	-7.1	-1.1	-7.8	-3.1	21.5	-23.1	-16.2	-12.6	-30.6	-5.5	-11.2	-4.6	21.6	86.8	....	78bh d
Monetary Authorities											....					78bo d
General Government	—	—	—	—	—						....					78bp d
Banks	-7.1	-1.1	-7.8	-3.1	21.5	-23.1	-16.2	-12.6	-30.6	-5.5	-11.2	-4.6	3.6	2.8	....	78bq d
Other Sectors													18.0	84.0	....	78br d
Other Investment Liab., n.i.e.	48.2	30.6	56.5	19.3	29.3	48.1	28.5	-8.0	-13.1	-10.3	103.1	68.4	35.9	95.5	....	78bi d
Monetary Authorities	6.7	5.6	4.7	-2.1	-.4	-.6	—	2.9	2.2	2.1						78bs d
General Government	24.9	-.2	18.1	-4.5	2.3	48.7	28.5	-10.9	-15.3	-12.4	112.5	68.8	37.7	43.0	....	78bt d
Banks	-7.4	-9.3	-1.2	8.1	9.1	—	—	—	—	—	.4	-.4	12.3	-4.5	....	78bu d
Other Sectors	24.0	34.5	34.9	17.9	18.3	—	—	—	—	—	-9.8	.1	-14.1	57.0	....	78bv d
Net Errors and Omissions	46.6	14.9	-16.4	14.3	-10.7	-46.4	80.1	9.2	35.3	-10.5	124.9	19.4	16.0	-120.5	....	78ca d
Overall Balance	-2.1	4.4	5.9	.3	-13.2	-35.2	12.7	-6.3	-23.0	-49.7	137.1	-50.4	29.8	34.5	....	78cb d
Reserves and Related Items	2.1	-4.4	-5.9	-.3	13.2	35.2	-12.7	6.3	23.0	49.7	-137.1	50.4	-29.8	-34.5	....	79da d
Reserve Assets	6.8	-1.3	11.8	1.2	3.9	39.0	-20.0	-11.3	-19.1	12.8	-175.6	48.5	-50.6	-29.1	....	79db d
Use of Fund Credit and Loans	-12.1	-23.3	-17.7	-26.6	-5.6	-7.0	-4.5	—	—	—	-5.6	-2.6	20.8	-5.3	....	79dc d
Exceptional Financing	7.5	20.2	—	25.1	14.9	3.2	11.8	17.6	42.1	36.9	44.1	4.4	....	....	....	79de d

Government Finance

Year Ending September 30

	1985	1986	1987	1988	1989	1990	1991	1992	1993	1994	1995	1996	1997	1998	1999	
Deficit (-) or Surplus	-217.5	-236.6	-151.2	-424.1	-523.7	-577.5	-233.3	-590.2	-506.9	-947.1	-986.1	-329.5	-320.5	-776.5	-1,647.7	80
Revenue	1,279.4	1,339.8	1,287.9	1,235.3	1,265.4	1,214.7	1,425.1	1,234.7	1,284.2	874.8	2,456.0	3,436.1	4,781.8	5,330.0	6,211.2	81
Grants Received	515.8	385.9	564.6	146.5	16.2	7.6	45.9	14.0	1.1	2.2	696.7	354.3	694.6	644.7	47.0	81z
Expenditure	2,012.7	1,962.3	2,003.7	1,805.9	1,805.3	1,799.8	1,704.3	1,838.9	1,792.2	1,824.1	4,138.8	4,119.9	5,796.9	6,751.2	7,905.9	82
Financing																
Net Domestic Borrowing	351.8	109.7	56.3	93.5	175.1	333.5	116.0	625.4	516.9	1,109.6	885.7	650.4	223.7	431.5	1,900.1	84a
Monetary Authorities	356.6	111.7	60.0	110.5	172.4	328.4	109.9	618.7	516.9	1,109.6	885.7	650.4	223.7	591.5	1,799.6	84aa
Other	-4.8	-2.0	-3.7	-17.0	2.7	5.1	6.1	6.7	—	—	—	—	—	-160.0	100.5	84ac
Net Foreign Borrowing	33.6	229.8	134.4	88.7	51.3	30.2	92.9	1.1	—	—	1,031.3	-260.7	-272.0	-421.7	-577.5	85a
Use of Cash Balances	-167.9	35.3	-1.3	61.7	26.4	-110.7	-15.1	-32.2	39.1	-88.1	-975.8	-28.4	-327.3	85.5	-544.4	87
Adjustment to Financing	-138.2	-38.2	180.2	270.9	324.5	39.5	-4.1	-49.1	-74.4	44.9	-31.8	696.1	681.2	869.5		84x

National Accounts

Year Ending September 30

	1985	1986	1987	1988	1989	1990	1991	1992	1993	1994	1995	1996	1997	1998	1999	
Exports of Goods & Services	2,716	2,340	2,860	2,542	2,143	2,511	3,783	1,346	1,912	1,942	3,845	5,278	5,920	7,799	9,017	90c
Gross Fixed Capital Formation	1,673	1,620	1,545	1,500	1,791	1,136	2,201	1,375	1,487	1,857	4,867	6,279	6,432	7,596	8,924	93e
Increase/Decrease(-) in Stocks	—	—	—	—	—											93i
Gov't and Private Consumption	9,471	10,472	9,156	9,137	9,590	13,166	15,270	15,321	21,344	31,302	38,167	44,445	53,194	60,543	68,808	96f
Imports of Goods & Services	-3,813	-3,245	-3,767	-3,766	-2,688	-2,862	-5,336	-3,022	-4,849	-4,173	-11,634	-13,258	-13,968	-16,883	-19,460	98c
Gross Domestic Product (GDP)	10,050	11,190	10,800	11,130	12,520	14,910	18,500	19,350	22,410	27,880	35,265	42,744	51,578	59,055	67,288	99b
Net Factor Inc/Pmts(-) Abroad	-101	-100	-105	-135	-128	-125	-131	-153	-211	-584	....	....	....	....	....	98.n
Gross National Income (GNI)	9,946	11,079	9,937	9,773	10,368	11,617	14,624	14,871	....	....						99a
Net National Income	9,680	10,822	9,697	9,534	10,083	11,328										99e
GDP Volume 1976 Prices	5,085	5,134	5,122	5,110	5,091	5,100	5,342	4,638	4,525	4,149	4,331	4,452	4,502	4,634	4,762	99b.p
GDP Volume (1995=100)	117.3	118.5	118.2	117.9	117.5	117.7	123.3	107.0	104.4	95.8	100.0	102.7	104.1	107.3	109.9	99bv p
GDP Deflator (1995=100)	24.3	26.8	25.9	26.8	30.2	35.9	42.6	51.3	60.9	82.6	100.0	118.0	140.5	156.0	173.7	99bi p

Midyear Estimates

	1985	1986	1987	1988	1989	1990	1991	1992	1993	1994	1995	1996	1997	1998	1999	
Population	5.86	5.99	6.11	6.24	6.36	6.49	6.62	6.76	6.90	7.04	7.18	7.34	7.49	7.65	7.80	99z

(See notes in the back of the book.)

Honduras

		1970	1971	1972	1973	1974	1975	1976	1977	1978	1979	1980	1981	1982	1983	1984
Exchange Rates															*Lempiras per SDR:*	
Market Rate	aa	2.0000	2.1714	2.1714	2.4127	2.4487	2.3413	2.3237	2.4294	2.6056	2.6347	2.5508	2.3279	2.2062	2.0939	1.9604
															Lempiras per US Dollar:	
Market Rate	ae	2.0000	2.0000	2.0000	2.0000	2.0000	2.0000	2.0000	2.0000	2.0000	2.0000	2.0000	2.0000	2.0000	2.0000	2.0000
Market Rate	rf	2.0000	2.0000	2.0000	2.0000	2.0000	2.0000	2.0000	2.0000	2.0000	2.0000	2.0000	2.0000	2.0000	2.0000	2.0000
Fund Position															*Millions of SDRs:*	
Quota	2f. s	25.00	25.00	25.00	25.00	25.00	25.00	25.00	25.00	34.00	34.00	51.00	51.00	51.00	67.80	67.80
SDRs	1b. s	.19	2.85	5.45	5.41	5.27	3.98	2.66	3.55	2.95	7.68	.02	1.39	1.63	2.12	.16
Reserve Position in the Fund	1c. s	—	—	—	6.25	—	—	—	—	6.25	6.06	—	—	—	4.20	—
Total Fund Cred.&Loans Outstg.	2tl	—	—	—	—	16.78	16.78	16.78	4.29	—	7.58	25.73	46.46	108.16	154.06	152.47
International Liquidity											*Millions of US Dollars Unless Otherwise Indicated:*					
Total Reserves minus Gold	1l. d	20.13	21.77	35.09	41.66	44.30	96.97	130.83	179.77	184.44	209.17	149.83	101.02	112.23	113.62	128.16
SDRs	1b. d	.19	3.09	5.92	6.53	6.45	4.66	3.09	4.31	3.84	10.12	.03	1.62	1.80	2.22	.16
Reserve Position in the Fund	1c. d	—	—	—	7.54	—	—	—	—	8.14	7.98	—	—	—	4.40	—
Foreign Exchange	1d. d	19.94	18.68	29.17	27.59	37.85	92.31	127.74	175.46	172.45	191.07	149.80	99.40	110.43	107.00	128.00
Gold (Million Fine Troy Ounces)	1ad	.003	.003	.003	.003	.003	.003	.003	.014	.014	.014	.016	.016	.016	.016	.016
Gold (National Valuation)	1and	.10	.10	.10	.15	.15	.15	.15	.60	.60	.80	1.05	1.05	1.05	1.05	1.05
Monetary Authorities: Other Liab.	4.. d	1.70	1.30	1.50	3.75	26.95	111.00	121.10	134.50	129.20	161.30	180.90	223.95	266.10	230.75	276.15
Deposit Money Banks: Assets	7a. d	2.10	3.75	2.50	2.25	3.75	7.05	5.10	7.00	7.70	7.90	9.15	12.65	5.10	2.85	2.85
Liabilities	7b. d	10.30	17.70	20.35	27.75	29.75	32.50	43.50	67.05	52.40	67.25	46.95	19.50	13.45	19.75	23.45
Other Banking Insts.: Liabilities	7f. d	27.15	16.15	20.95	22.55	27.70	44.60	56.25	72.70	87.10	101.90	109.55	126.60	125.15	118.90	123.05
Monetary Authorities															*Millions of Lempiras:*	
Foreign Assets	11	42	46	75	89	95	201	277	381	390	440	324	237	258	265	297
Claims on Central Government	12a	43	58	60	62	79	77	86	60	144	200	276	455	509	442	593
Claims on Local Government	12b	4	7	11	12	15	17	16	21	32	62	66	66	61	65	69
Claims on Private Sector	12d	—	—	—	—	—	—	—	—	—	1	1	1	1	1	1
Claims on Deposit Money Banks	12e	20	20	19	30	47	68	62	75	80	97	140	152	161	162	237
Claims on Other Banking Insts	12f	17	17	17	24	35	50	56	51	68	71	95	147	193	234	279
Reserve Money	14	113	123	126	153	147	169	238	276	334	379	387	412	445	476	469
of which: Currency Outside DMBs	14a	77	80	90	112	109	115	173	193	215	270	275	302	314	362	384
Time, Savings,& Fgn.Currency Dep.	15	1	1	2	3	3	1	2	2	2	3	2	4	5	11	
Foreign Liabilities	16c	3	2	1	3	88	158	158	131	81	100	140	241	438	453	492
Long-Term Foreign Liabilities	16cl	1	—	2	4	7	103	123	148	178	243	287	315	333	331	359
Central Government Deposits	16d	17	22	55	47	57	42	60	72	121	167	132	155	164	35	177
Capital Accounts	17a	23	33	41	47	51	52	51	66	86	118	170	195	213	245	268
Other Items (Net)	17r	−32	−33	−44	−39	−82	−113	−137	−107	−87	−139	−217	−261	−414	−377	−302
Deposit Money Banks															*Millions of Lempiras:*	
Reserves	20	34	40	35	38	41	54	55	78	108	111	104	111	118	80	130
Foreign Assets	21	4	8	5	5	8	14	10	14	15	16	18	25	10	6	6
Claims on Central Government	22a	23	27	55	59	67	70	91	133	144	167	193	182	276	371	449
Claims on Local Government	22b	1	1	1	3	—	—	—	—	—	—	—	3	—	44	59
Claims on Private Sector	22d	234	279	305	378	427	504	637	774	859	931	945	992	1,095	1,253	1,414
Claims on Other Banking Insts	22f	1	1	2	3	3	8	9	11	12	13	13	17	33	32	36
Demand Deposits	24	80	88	101	125	132	144	184	214	257	270	323	328	380	431	444
Time, Savings,& Fgn.Currency Dep.	25	127	149	170	202	214	241	301	379	472	490	515	586	745	895	1,051
Bonds	26ab	4	8	11	14	17	12	25	37	51	52	31	28	23	26	31
Foreign Liabilities	26c	21	18	21	25	25	30	43	65	34	97	60	24	17	32	41
Long-Term Foreign Liabilities	26cl	—	17	20	31	34	35	44	69	71	38	34	15	10	8	6
Central Government Deposits	26d	1	2	2	2	9	13	16	25	29	33	37	54	65	70	73
Credit from Monetary Authorities	26g	19	19	19	30	45	67	64	79	79	100	180	166	174	177	255
Capital Accounts	27a	46	52	57	61	69	80	92	105	122	144	161	172	184	207	240
Other Items (Net)	27r	−1	2	—	−5	—	29	35	37	25	13	−65	−48	−66	−59	−47
Monetary Survey															*Millions of Lempiras:*	
Foreign Assets (Net)	31n	23	33	57	66	−11	28	86	198	291	259	143	−2	−187	−214	−231
Domestic Credit	32	305	366	393	491	561	671	818	953	1,109	1,243	1,422	1,650	1,938	2,338	2,649
Claims on Central Govt. (Net)	32an	47	61	58	71	79	91	100	96	139	167	300	428	555	709	791
Claims on Local Government	32b	5	8	12	15	15	17	16	21	32	62	69	66	61	109	128
Claims on Private Sector	32d	235	279	305	378	428	505	638	774	859	931	946	992	1,095	1,254	1,415
Claims on Other Banking Insts	32f	18	18	18	27	38	58	65	62	80	84	107	164	226	267	315
Money	34	160	170	193	240	243	266	370	417	491	548	611	638	724	823	843
Quasi-Money	35	128	151	172	205	217	242	302	381	474	493	517	589	749	901	1,062
Bonds	36ab	4	8	11	14	17	12	25	37	51	52	31	28	23	26	31
Long-Term Foreign Liabilities	36cl	1	17	22	35	41	139	167	217	248	281	322	330	343	339	365
Capital Accounts	37a	69	85	98	108	120	131	143	171	208	263	331	367	397	452	508
Other Items (Net)	37r	−34	−31	−46	−46	−89	−91	−103	−71	−72	−133	−247	−305	−485	−416	−390
Money plus Quasi-Money	35l	288	321	366	445	460	508	672	798	965	1,041	1,128	1,227	1,473	1,723	1,905
Other Banking Institutions															*Millions of Lempiras:*	
Reserves	40	4	3	5	6	6	8	15	14	20	16	18	19	30	36	29
Foreign Assets	41	1	1	1	1	1	1	3	3	5	5	3	4	2	1	5
Claims on Central Government	42a	1	—	1	1	2	6	9	22	11	12	17	11	12	52	59
Claims on Local Government	42b	2	2	1	1	3	4	6	12	10	18	25	41	45	54	62
Claims on Private Sector	42d	113	90	109	129	155	193	201	264	342	429	532	598	678	713	744
Claims on Deposit Money Banks	42e	1	1	1	2	12	25	26	16	18	18	13	6	7	11	14
Demand Deposits	44	6	5	6	8	7	8	6	8	6	10	9	5	7	7	9
Time, Savings,& Fgn.Currency Dep.	45	9	10	11	14	14	25	29	49	60	73	94	108	124	148	165
Bonds	46ab	3	—	4	11	15	20	8	17	27	50	38	40	44	49	58
Foreign Liabilities	46c	7	4	5	7	8	11	30	25	26	49	70	45	40	36	40
Long-Term Foreign Liabilities	46cl	47	28	37	38	48	78	82	120	148	155	149	208	210	202	206
Central Government Deposits	46d	—	5	7	5	12	20	22	11	20	36	64	78	85	101	105
Credit from Monetary Authorities	46g	18	17	17	25	35	51	56	51	62	64	92	150	211	250	290
Credit from Deposit Money Banks	46h	2	—	1	2	7	7	3	4	4	3	3	7	21	22	24
Capital Accounts	47a	56	55	63	68	78	101	121	131	143	160	153	181	302	303	312
Other Items (Net)	47r	−26	−27	−34	−37	−43	−82	−98	−86	−90	−102	−63	−143	−271	−250	−296

	1985	1986	1987	1988	1989	1990	1991	1992	1993	1994	1995	1996	1997	1998	1999		
																	Exchange Rates	
End of Period	2.1968	2.4464	2.8373	2.6914	2.6283	7.6212	7.7243	8.0163	9.9720	13.7227	15.3751	18.5057	17.6673	19.4415	19.9067	Market Rate	aa
End of Period (ae) Period Average (rf)																	
	2.0000	2.0000	2.0000	2.0000	2.0000	5.3570	5.4000	5.8300	7.2600	9.4001	10.3432	12.8694	13.0942	13.8076	14.5039	Market Rate	ae
	2.0000	2.0000	2.0000	2.0000	2.0000	4.1120	5.3167	5.4979	6.4716	8.4088	9.4710	11.7053	13.0035	13.3850	14.2132	Market Rate	rf
																Fund Position	
End of Period	67.80	67.80	67.80	67.80	67.80	67.80	67.80	95.00	95.00	95.00	95.00	95.00	95.00	95.00	129.50	Quota	2f. s
	—	—	—	—	—	.01	—	.11	.11	.15	.10	.06	.06	.05	.68	SDRs	1b. s
															8.63	Reserve Position in the Fund	1c. s
	133.72	89.54	54.37	27.29	26.96	22.66	23.55	81.35	86.01	74.81	66.36	40.28	33.90	80.04	153.33	Total Fund Cred.&Loans Outstg.	2tl
																International Liquidity	
End of Period	105.80	111.30	106.00	50.00	21.10	40.41	104.90	197.45	97.15	171.01	261.45	249.19	580.37	818.07	1,257.58	Total Reserves minus Gold	1l. d
	—	—	—	—	—	.01	—	.15	.15	.21	.15	.09	.07	.07	.94	SDRs	1b. d
															11.84	Reserve Position in the Fund	1c. d
	105.80	111.30	106.00	50.00	21.10	40.40	104.90	197.30	97.00	170.80	261.30	249.10	580.30	818.00	1,244.80	Foreign Exchange	1d. d
	.016	.016	.016	.016	.016	.016	.021	.021	.021	.021	.021	.021	.021	.021	.021	Gold (Million Fine Troy Ounces)	1ad
	1.05	1.05	1.05	1.05	1.05	1.05	7.78	7.79	8.47	8.30	8.41	8.03	6.43	6.25	6.28	Gold (National Valuation)	1an d
	392.80	479.30	546.96	570.73	617.12	662.67	616.98	588.14	560.88	599.86	595.09	509.27	334.26	249.30	232.99	Monetary Authorities: Other Liab.	4.. d
	3.30	4.60	4.30	9.55	14.95	24.62	29.11	66.52	75.65	84.32	123.47	209.97	228.00	275.70	379.81	Deposit Money Banks: Assets	7a. d
	31.20	33.10	51.90	45.15	24.40	16.33	17.28	16.95	28.71	68.89	103.20	154.84	271.39	344.95	297.64	Liabilities	7b. d
	122.85	119.85	128.60	120.05	111.90	112.99	17.69	17.51	13.93	15.80	16.49	13.01	15.80	17.19	9.84	Other Banking Insts.: Liabilities	7f. d
																Monetary Authorities	
End of Period	203	221	196	152	95	357	748	1,343	954	1,930	3,058	3,641	‡10,436	14,281	21,190	Foreign Assets	11
	681	643	881	1,299	1,428	1,905	1,360	1,555	2,023	1,512	1,284	1,220	‡1,462	1,534	1,014	Claims on Central Government	12a
	67	64	62	59	54	80	75	67	63	60	53	92	‡48	45	42	Claims on Local Government	12b
	1	1	3	18	27	29	32	42	59	58	64	58	‡1	1	1	Claims on Private Sector	12d
	425	517	476	481	542	543	653	665	665	678	616	721	‡136	99	60	Claims on Deposit Money Banks	12e
	302	329	450	443	483	509	468	532	547	569	572	555	‡157	108	108	Claims on Other Banking Insts	12f
	465	498	622	714	892	1,113	1,200	1,734	1,852	2,723	3,373	4,842	‡9,045	10,423	11,720	Reserve Money	14
	410	426	492	570	676	882	977	1,141	1,448	1,995	2,111	2,630	‡3,315	3,744	4,714	of which: Currency Outside DMBs	14a
	14	20	18	21	34	128	122	39	52	86	318	219	‡791	581	1,582	Time, Savings,& Fgn.Currency Dep.	15
	692	763	811	779	841	2,187	2,007	2,428	3,103	4,274	4,438	4,216	‡362	64	137	Foreign Liabilities	16c
	388	415	437	436	464	1,536	1,507	1,599	1,692	2,206	2,216	2,456	‡4,015	4,188	Long-Term Foreign Liabilities		16cl
	211	243	367	541	459	1,275	1,185	1,390	1,751	1,229	1,562	2,042	‡2,878	4,766	7,409	Central Government Deposits	16d
	337	361	347	411	486	639	782	891	1,116	1,422	1,762	1,930	‡1,287	537	566	Capital Accounts	17a
	−429	−525	−535	−451	−548	−3,456	−3,467	−3,876	−5,255	−7,133	−8,022	−9,420	‡−6,138	−4,604	−3,186	Other Items (Net)	17r
																Deposit Money Banks	
End of Period	129	129	125	197	279	274	463	648	423	668	1,118	1,968	‡5,021	6,018	6,374	Reserves	20
	7	9	9	19	30	132	157	388	549	793	1,277	2,702	‡2,985	3,807	5,509	Foreign Assets	21
	518	691	699	715	836	919	1,202	1,045	968	1,287	1,205	867	‡275	77	41	Claims on Central Government	22a
	14	16	35	64	60	47	40	5	2	1	10	15	‡54	147	125	Claims on Local Government	22b
	1,617	1,795	2,131	2,386	2,604	3,026	3,481	4,341	5,009	6,364	7,711	10,966	‡16,744	23,247	28,014	Claims on Private Sector	22d
	35	30	33	31	30	28	3	6	6	37	55	29	‡26	43	473	Claims on Other Banking Insts	22f
	424	490	581	625	774	903	1,138	1,276	1,313	1,761	2,368	3,074	‡4,287	4,841	5,666	Demand Deposits	24
	1,036	1,140	1,355	1,589	1,738	1,990	2,486	3,151	3,432	4,287	5,626	8,721	‡13,657	18,094	22,228	Time, Savings,& Fgn.Currency Dep.	25
	24	32	41	36	32	28	23	19	16	14	29	33	‡61	90	58	Bonds	26ab
	45	42	83	66	30	48	32	66	74	256	459	759	‡1,294	1,314	878	Foreign Liabilities	26c
	17	24	21	24	19	39	62	33	135	392	609	1,234	‡2,259	3,449	3,439	Long-Term Foreign Liabilities	26cl
	135	201	210	272	350	465	467	649	349	300	270	331	‡1,059	2,004	2,846	Central Government Deposits	26d
	429	522	479	497	554	545	656	679	704	691	619	760	‡156	90	60	Credit from Monetary Authorities	26g
	278	307	336	372	426	531	708	876	1,234	1,670	2,224	2,846	‡3,885	4,876	5,958	Capital Accounts	27a
	−68	−87	−74	−69	−85	−123	−225	−315	−302	−222	−829	−1,212	‡−1,553	−1,419	−598	Other Items (Net)	27r
																Monetary Survey	
End of Period	−527	−574	−689	−674	−747	−1,746	−1,133	−763	−1,673	−1,807	−562	1,368	‡11,765	16,710	25,683	Foreign Assets (Net)	31n
	2,889	3,125	3,716	4,201	4,712	4,803	5,009	5,554	6,577	8,359	9,122	11,427	‡14,830	18,432	19,563	Domestic Credit	32
	853	890	1,003	1,201	1,455	1,084	910	561	890	1,270	657	−287	‡−2,200	−5,158	−9,200	Claims on Central Govt. (Net)	32an
	81	80	97	123	114	127	114	72	66	61	63	107	‡102	192	168	Claims on Local Government	32b
	1,618	1,795	2,134	2,404	2,630	3,055	3,513	4,383	5,068	6,422	7,775	11,024	‡16,745	23,247	28,015	Claims on Private Sector	32d
	337	359	483	474	513	537	471	538	553	606	627	583	‡183	151	581	Claims on Other Banking Insts	32f
	816	882	1,117	1,250	1,501	1,855	2,060	2,523	2,825	3,845	4,678	6,053	‡8,294	9,344	11,050	Money	34
	1,051	1,159	1,373	1,610	1,773	2,118	2,609	3,190	3,485	4,374	5,945	8,941	‡14,448	18,675	23,810	Quasi-Money	35
	24	32	41	36	32	28	23	19	16	14	29	33	‡61	90	58	Bonds	36ab
	405	439	458	460	482	1,575	1,569	1,632	1,826	2,597	2,825	3,690	‡6,274	7,751	7,626	Long-Term Foreign Liabilities	36cl
	615	668	683	783	912	1,170	1,490	1,767	2,350	3,093	3,986	4,775	‡5,172	5,413	6,524	Capital Accounts	37a
	−549	−630	−645	−611	−735	−3,689	−3,874	−4,340	−5,599	−7,370	−8,902	−10,697	‡−7,654	−6,131	−3,822	Other Items (Net)	37r
	1,866	2,042	2,490	2,860	3,273	3,973	4,668	5,713	6,309	8,219	10,623	14,994	‡22,742	28,019	34,860	Money plus Quasi-Money	35l
																Other Banking Institutions	
End of Period	39	39	32	35	40	39	48	58	75	139	124	121	‡661	759	654	Reserves	40
	2	4	3	4	4	8	23	38	64	96	96	160	‡106	94	111	Foreign Assets	41
	55	70	82	83	82	89	79	76	79	110	137	156	‡294	79	54	Claims on Central Government	42a
	75	80	67	73	73	76	73	76	80	86	93	95	‡136	131	112	Claims on Local Government	42b
	811	832	890	785	834	842	785	981	1,094	1,261	1,529	1,507	‡3,044	3,337	3,969	Claims on Private Sector	42d
	18	8	13	25	19	21	8	7	20	27	38	34	‡881	1,462	2,597	Claims on Deposit Money Banks	42e
	14	9	14	25	22	21	17	17	19	21	19	20	‡26	18	40	Demand Deposits	44
	164	183	229	226	231	258	355	557	675	744	938	1,063	‡3,387	3,154	3,504	Time, Savings,& Fgn.Currency Dep.	45
	60	61	65	68	65	63	4	1	1	1	1	—	‡17	7	—	Bonds	46ab
	47	53	70	76	85	248	3	1	—	6	18	1	‡30	14	1	Foreign Liabilities	46c
	199	187	187	164	139	357	93	101	101	143	153	166	‡177	224	142	Long-Term Foreign Liabilities	46cl
	119	121	102	122	120	142	147	194	217	326	425	407	‡636	1,091	1,462	Central Government Deposits	46d
	350	403	469	450	492	537	637	589	579	647	586	584	‡177	110	112	Credit from Monetary Authorities	46g
	20	13	17	13	10	7	2	4	5	36	54	28	‡374	645	1,178	Credit from Deposit Money Banks	46h
	328	329	321	310	368	373	328	345	301	407	449	497	‡2,068	2,098	2,876	Capital Accounts	47a
	−300	−325	−387	−450	−478	−932	−570	−574	−487	−611	−623	−693	‡−1,771	−1,499	−1,818	Other Items (Net)	47r

Honduras

		1970	1971	1972	1973	1974	1975	1976	1977	1978	1979	1980	1981	1982	1983	1984
Banking Survey																*Millions of Lempiras:*
Foreign Assets (Net)	51n	17	30	53	60	−17	18	58	176	269	215	76	−43	−225	−249	−266
Domestic Credit	52	402	436	478	591	671	796	947	1,178	1,372	1,583	1,824	2,058	2,360	2,789	3,093
Claims on Central Govt. (Net)	52an	48	57	52	67	70	78	86	106	130	143	253	361	482	661	745
Claims on Local Government	52b	6	10	13	16	19	21	22	34	41	80	94	107	106	162	190
Claims on Private Sector	52d	347	369	414	508	582	697	839	1,038	1,201	1,360	1,477	1,590	1,773	1,966	2,159
Liquid Liabilities	55l	300	333	378	461	474	533	693	841	1,011	1,108	1,213	1,322	1,574	1,842	2,050
Bonds	56ab	7	8	15	25	32	31	32	54	78	102	69	68	67	75	89
Long-Term Foreign Liabilities	56cl	48	45	59	74	89	217	249	338	396	436	471	539	553	541	571
Capital Accounts	57a	125	139	161	176	198	232	264	302	350	422	484	548	699	755	819
Other Items (Net)	57r	−61	−60	−81	−85	−140	−199	−233	−181	−195	−270	−336	−461	−758	−672	−701
Money (National Definitions)																*Millions of Lempiras:*
Reserve Money (M0)	19ma	....	....	....	....	....	....	....	....	....	....	269	297	307	355	377
M1	59ma	....	....	....	....	....	....	....	....	....	....	605	632	699	799	832
M2	59mb	....	....	....	....	....	....	....	....	....	....	1,303	1,446	1,689	1,931	2,161
M3	59mc	....	....	....	....	....	....	....	....	....	....	1,368	1,504	1,748	1,985	2,206
M4	59md	....	....	....	....	....	....	....	....	....	....	1,385	1,548	1,824	2,110	2,388
Interest Rates																*Percent Per Annum*
Discount Rate (End of Period)	60									13.0	13.5	16.0	16.0	24.0	24.0	24.0
Savings Rate	60k													7.5	7.1	7.2
Savings Rate (Fgn.Currency)	60k. f															
Deposit Rate	60l													10.6	11.3	10.3
Deposit Rate (Fgn.Currency)	60l. f															
Lending Rate	60p													16.5	16.1	16.2
Lending Rate (Fgn.Currency)	60p. f															
Government Bond Yield	61														9.4	10.3
Prices and Labor																*Index Numbers (1995=100):*
Consumer Prices	64	8.6	8.8	9.1	9.5	10.8	11.7	12.2	13.3	I 14.0	15.7	18.6	20.3	22.2	24.0	25.1
																Number in Thousands:
Labor Force	67d	....	....	....	....	....	....	....	....	....	....	....	....	....	....	....
Employment	67e	....	....	....	....	....	....	....	....	....	....	....	....	....	....	....
Unemployment	67c	....	....	....	....	....	....	....	....	....	....	....	....	....	....	....
Unemployment Rate (%)	67r	....	....	....	....	....	....	....	....	....	....	....	....	....	....	....
International Transactions																*Millions of US Dollars:*
Exports	70..d	179.1	189.0	204.5	258.7	289.1	295.0	400.1	513.5	607.6	733.6	829.5	760.7	659.5	671.8	725.4
Imports, c.i.f.	71..d	220.7	193.7	193.3	262.3	382.2	400.1	455.9	574.7	693.0	825.9	1,008.7	949.1	700.5	802.6	893.4
Imports, f.o.b.	71.vd	199.1	172.4	171.3	235.2	348.0	364.5	414.3	520.6	628.9	748.8	912.3	860.5	636.6	722.7	810.7
																1995=100
Volume of Exports	72	77.5	93.0	93.5	96.7	74.6	98.2	116.3	133.5	136.5	161.1	162.0	156.8	154.2	146.8	142.1
Unit Value of Exports	74..d	....	....	....	....	....	45.4	56.3	81.4	74.1	70.9	84.4	76.5	74.0	74.6	79.0
Balance of Payments																*Millions of US Dollars:*
Current Account, n.i.e.	78ald	....	....	....	....	−103.9	−112.1	−104.8	−128.7	−157.2	−192.1	−316.8	−302.7	−228.3	−232.0	−374.3
Goods: Exports f.o.b.	78aad					303.9	313.1	415.5	534.4	631.2	763.8	860.1	793.0	685.1	707.2	746.2
Goods: Imports f.o.b.	78abd					−387.5	−372.4	−432.5	−550.1	−654.5	−783.5	−954.1	−898.6	−680.7	−756.3	−884.8
Trade Balance	78acd					−83.5	−59.3	−17.0	−15.7	−23.3	−19.7	−94.0	−105.7	4.4	−49.1	−138.6
Services: Credit	78add					27.9	31.3	38.2	46.3	56.2	74.3	81.5	90.6	81.9	93.8	101.2
Services: Debit	78aed					−68.3	−73.8	−82.2	−105.4	−123.1	−148.2	−174.0	−163.7	−144.3	−158.4	−183.2
Balance on Goods & Services	78afd					−123.9	−101.8	−60.9	−74.9	−90.2	−93.7	−186.4	−178.7	−58.0	−113.6	−220.6
Income: Credit	78agd					5.0	6.5	9.7	13.2	19.1	21.2	25.9	19.7	16.6	14.0	15.8
Income: Debit	78ahd					−17.5	−34.6	−66.8	−81.2	−103.4	−140.1	−177.8	−171.2	−216.8	−164.1	−191.7
Balance on Gds, Serv. & Inc.	78aid					−136.5	−129.8	−118.0	−142.8	−174.5	−212.6	−338.3	−330.2	−258.3	−263.7	−396.5
Current Transfers, n.i.e.: Credit	78ajd					37.4	23.2	19.5	20.6	25.4	35.5	37.7	38.1	40.0	42.9	33.7
Current Transfers: Debit	78akd					−4.9	−5.5	−6.2	−6.5	−8.1	−15.0	−16.2	−10.6	−10.0	−11.1	−11.5
Capital Account, n.i.e.	78bcd	....	....	....	....	—	—	—	—	—	—	—	—	—	—	—
Capital Account, n.i.e.: Credit	78bad					—	—	—	—	—	—	—	—	—	—	—
Capital Account: Debit	78bbd					—	—	—	—	—	—	—	—	—	—	—
Financial Account, n.i.e.	78bjd	....	....	....	....	91.7	118.8	135.7	185.0	136.5	208.0	237.4	229.5	153.3	102.1	284.5
Direct Investment Abroad	78bdd					—	—	—	—	−.6	−.1	−.1	−.3	−.2	.2	−1.9
Dir. Invest. in Rep. Econ., n.i.e.	78bed					−1.2	7.0	5.3	8.9	13.2	28.2	5.8	−3.6	13.8	21.0	20.5
Portfolio Investment Assets	78bfd					—	—	—	—	−.6	−.1	−.1	−.3	−.2	.2	−1.9
Equity Securities	78bkd					—	—	—	—	—	—	—	—	—	—	—
Debt Securities	78bld					—	—	—	—	−.6	−.1	−.1	−.3	−.2	.2	−1.9
Portfolio Investment Liab., n.i.e.	78bgd					—	—	—	—	—	—	—	—	—	—	—
Equity Securities	78bmd					—	—	—	—	—	—	—	—	—	—	—
Debt Securities	78bnd					—	—	—	—	—	—	—	—	—	—	—
Financial Derivatives Assets	78bwd	....	....	....	....	....	....	....	....	....	....	....	....	....	....	....
Financial Derivatives Liabilities	78bxd	....	....	....	....	....	....	....	....	....	....	....	....	....	....	....
Other Investment Assets	78bhd	....	....	....	....	−5.8	−7.7	−1.6	−12.0	−12.0	−13.2	−10.6	−18.1	−.9	−6.3	−2.5
Monetary Authorities	78bod															
General Government	78bpd					−2.0	−1.5	−1.6	−7.3	−3.7	−3.0	−10.3	−14.1	−10.0	−8.7	−2.5
Banks	78bqd					−1.4	−3.3	1.3	−1.5	−1.5	−.2	−.3	−4.1	9.1	2.4	—
Other Sectors	78brd					−2.4	−2.9	−1.3	−3.3	−6.8	−10.0					
Other Investment Liab., n.i.e.	78bid					98.6	119.4	132.0	188.1	135.9	193.1	242.2	251.4	140.6	87.2	268.4
Monetary Authorities	78bsd					.3	35.5	2.5	6.9	−9.2	8.8	−43.4	5.0	59.1	−39.7	53.2
General Government	78btd					22.8	42.6	46.1	28.1	39.1	26.2	57.8	60.1	32.6	42.0	60.0
Banks	78bud					4.1	6.0	14.4	24.2	−14.6	28.1	−6.5	−26.0	6.6	2.5	−10.5
Other Sectors	78bvd					71.5	35.5	69.1	129.1	120.6	130.1	234.3	212.3	42.3	82.5	165.6
Net Errors and Omissions	78cad					−4.8	−.4	−1.6	−6.4	12.7	−18.5	−38.9	−18.4	−.5	12.7	−8.6
Overall Balance	78cbd					−17.0	6.3	29.3	49.9	−8.0	−2.6	−118.4	−91.7	−75.5	−117.2	−98.4
Reserves and Related Items	79dad					17.0	−6.3	−29.3	−49.9	8.0	2.6	118.4	91.7	75.5	117.2	98.4
Reserve Assets	79dbd					−3.2	−53.4	−37.9	−51.8	−4.0	−20.1	62.2	47.5	7.6	−1.6	−8.9
Use of Fund Credit and Loans	79dcd					20.2	—	—	−14.6	−5.7	9.9	23.9	23.4	67.8	49.2	−1.6
Exceptional Financing	79ded					—	47.1	8.6	16.6	17.6	12.9	32.3	20.7	—	69.7	108.8

Banking Survey
End of Period

1985	1986	1987	1988	1989	1990	1991	1992	1993	1994	1995	1996	1997	1998	1999		
−572	−624	−756	−746	−828	−1,987	−1,112	−726	−1,610	−1,717	−484	1,527	‡11,841	16,790	25,793	Foreign Assets (Net)	51n
3,375	3,627	4,169	4,547	5,068	5,131	5,327	5,954	7,059	8,884	9,830	12,195	‡17,484	20,737	21,655	Domestic Credit	52
790	839	982	1,162	1,417	1,030	842	442	752	1,054	369	−537	‡−2,542	−6,171	−10,609	Claims on Central Govt. (Net)	52an
156	160	163	196	187	203	187	148	146	146	156	202	‡238	323	280	Claims on Local Government	52b
2,429	2,627	3,024	3,189	3,464	3,897	4,298	5,364	6,161	7,683	9,305	12,530	‡19,788	26,584	31,983	Claims on Private Sector	52d
2,005	2,195	2,701	3,076	3,486	4,213	4,993	6,229	6,928	8,845	11,455	15,956	‡25,494	30,432	37,749	Liquid Liabilities	55l
85	94	105	104	97	91	27	20	17	14	30	33	‡78	97	58	Bonds	56ab
604	626	645	624	622	1,932	1,662	1,733	1,927	2,740	2,977	3,856	‡6,451	7,974	7,768	Long-Term Foreign Liabilities	56cl
943	997	1,004	1,093	1,279	1,543	1,818	2,111	2,652	3,500	4,434	5,272	‡7,241	7,511	9,400	Capital Accounts	57a
−834	−908	−1,043	−1,097	−1,244	−4,635	−4,285	−4,865	−6,074	−7,932	−9,550	−11,396	‡−9,938	−8,488	−7,528	Other Items (Net)	57r

Money (National Definitions)
End of Period

1985	1986	1987	1988	1989	1990	1991	1992	1993	1994	1995	1996	1997	1998	1999		
404	418	483	561	666	869	960	1,121	1,425	1,966	2,078	2,595	3,274	3,699	4,663	*Reserve Money (M0)*	19ma
844	917	1,080	1,215	1,462	1,831	2,139	2,444	2,762	3,783	4,474	5,690	7,609	8,572	10,450	*M1*	59ma
2,241	2,456	2,915	3,322	3,752	4,582	5,113	6,270	6,822	8,537	10,224	12,560	20,344	23,984	28,728	*M2*	59mb
2,289	2,512	2,971	3,360	3,782	4,654	5,258	6,592	7,517	9,834	12,173	16,727	25,716	30,671	37,159	*M3*	59mc
2,669	2,726	3,209	3,641	4,168	5,085	5,491	6,805	7,768	10,053	12,489	17,300	26,952	....		*M4*	59md

Interest Rates
Percent Per Annum

1985	1986	1987	1988	1989	1990	1991	1992	1993	1994	1995	1996	1997	1998	1999		
24.0	24.0	24.0	24.0	24.0	28.2	30.1	26.1	....	....	....	....	....	....	12.0	Discount Rate (*End of Period*)	60
7.1	7.2	6.6	6.9	6.4	7.8	9.4	9.6	9.2	9.4	10.0	9.9	12.6	12.3	12.0	Savings Rate	60k
												4.7	4.5	4.0	Savings Rate (Fgn.Currency)	60k. f
9.9	9.7	9.6	8.6	8.6	8.8	11.5	12.3	11.6	11.6	12.0	16.7	21.3	18.6	20.0	Deposit Rate	60l
												9.9	9.5	9.1	Deposit Rate (Fgn.Currency)	60l. f
16.3	16.1	15.5	15.4	15.4	17.1	21.9	21.7	22.1	24.7	27.0	29.7	32.1	30.7	30.2	Lending Rate	60p
												12.9	12.5	12.6	Lending Rate (Fgn.Currency)	60p. f
10.4	10.4	10.4	10.4	10.4	10.4	10.4	10.4	10.4	23.1	27.2	35.6	29.6	20.3	16.0	Government Bond Yield	61

Prices and Labor
Period Averages

1985	1986	1987	1988	1989	1990	1991	1992	1993	1994	1995	1996	1997	1998	1999		
26.0	27.1	27.8	29.0	31.9	39.3	52.7	57.3	63.5	77.2	100.0	123.8	‡148.8	169.2	188.9	Consumer Prices	64

Period Averages

1985	1986	1987	1988	1989	1990	1991	1992	1993	1994	1995	1996	1997	1998	1999		
....	....	....	....	....	....	....	....	....	....	1,777	1,977	2,053	2,135	....	Labor Force	67d
281	406	391	1,354	1,394	1,213	1,494	1,675	....	....	1,806	1,985	2,088	2,135	....	Employment	67e
....	....	....	....	62	72	54	....	....	59	89	69	88		....	Unemployment	67c
....	....	....	4.8	4.6	3.1	....	....	3.2	4.3	3.2	3.9		....		Unemployment Rate (%)	67r

International Transactions
Millions of US Dollars

1985	1986	1987	1988	1989	1990	1991	1992	1993	1994	1995	1996	1997	1998	1999		
780.1	854.2	791.4	841.9	858.5	831.0	792.4	801.5	814.0	842.0	1,220.2	1,316.0	1,445.7	1,575.0	939.5	Exports	70..d
888.1	875.1	827.4	940.1	968.6	934.8	955.1	1,036.6	1,130.0	1,055.9	1,642.7	1,839.9	2,148.6	2,499.6	2,727.6	Imports, c.i.f.	71..d
803.7	791.9	748.8	801.6	789.2	796.8	796.2	938.1	1,022.6	955.6	1,486.6	1,665.1				Imports, f.o.b.	71.v d

1995=100

1985	1986	1987	1988	1989	1990	1991	1992	1993	1994	1995	1996	1997	1998	1999		
158.0	140.8	164.3	144.1	125.2	125.0	110.7	125.1	111.4	96.1	100.0	118.7	103.5	103.3	....	Volume of Exports	72
81.2	97.2	88.2	93.7	94.0	94.4	92.4	72.4	74.2	77.4	100.0	92.9	96.8	94.4	....	Unit Value of Exports	74..d

Balance of Payments
Minus Sign Indicates Debit

1985	1986	1987	1988	1989	1990	1991	1992	1993	1994	1995	1996	1997	1998	1999		
−308.6	−224.6	−245.2	−161.0	−180.3	−186.4	−213.4	−298.2	−308.7	−343.3	−200.9	−335.4	−272.2	−332.9	....	Current Account, n.i.e.	78al d
805.7	902.1	830.5	889.5	911.2	895.2	840.6	839.3	999.6	1,101.5	1,377.2	1,638.4	1,856.5	2,016.5	....	Goods: Exports f.o.b.	78aa d
−891.7	−879.5	−871.4	−923.4	−955.7	−907.0	−912.5	−990.2	−1,203.1	−1,351.1	−1,518.6	−1,925.8	−2,150.4	−2,339.6	....	Goods: Imports f.o.b.	78ab d
−86.1	22.6	−40.9	−34.0	−44.5	−11.8	−71.9	−150.9	−203.5	−249.6	−141.4	−287.4	−293.9	−323.1	....	*Trade Balance*	78ac d
103.8	109.6	119.7	136.4	149.7	137.3	175.0	202.0	223.9	242.4	257.6	283.3	334.9	370.0	....	Services: Credit	78ad d
−195.3	−198.6	−202.4	−217.5	−230.5	−219.8	−226.7	−243.2	−294.7	−311.0	−333.7	−327.8	−360.9	−396.0	....	Services: Debit	78ae d
−177.6	−66.4	−123.7	−115.1	−125.3	−94.3	−123.6	−192.1	−274.3	−318.2	−217.5	−331.9	−319.9	−349.1	....	*Balance on Goods & Services*	78af d
14.9	13.1	15.2	22.0	24.3	20.7	39.8	61.4	16.6	24.0	32.3	61.2	70.0	90.5	....	Income: Credit	78ag d
−203.0	−222.2	−247.9	−253.3	−261.9	−257.5	−285.9	−343.4	−215.3	−238.1	−258.2	−292.0	−281.8	−266.2	....	Income: Debit	78ah d
−365.7	−275.5	−356.4	−346.4	−362.9	−331.1	−369.7	−474.1	−473.0	−532.3	−443.4	−562.7	−531.7	−524.8	....	*Balance on Gds, Serv. & Inc.*	78ai d
69.0	63.4	124.2	198.4	194.6	156.2	166.3	186.1	165.5	190.2	243.7	271.7	306.8	268.6	....	Current Transfers, n.i.e.: Credit	78aj d
−11.9	−12.5	−13.0	−13.0	−12.0	−11.5	−10.0	−10.2	−1.2	−1.2	−1.2	−44.4	−24.9	−76.7	....	Current Transfers: Debit	78ak d
											28.5	14.6	47.6	....	Capital Account, n.i.e.	78bc d
											29.2	15.3	48.4	....	Capital Account, n.i.e.: Credit	78ba d
											−.7	−.7	−.8	....	Capital Account: Debit	78bb d
175.0	69.4	96.0	45.4	−48.6	−16.7	−98.3	22.0	22.8	157.5	114.6	70.2	243.3	260.7	....	Financial Account, n.i.e.	78bj d
—	—	—	—	—	—	—	—	—	—	—	—	—	—	....	Direct Investment Abroad	78bd d
27.5	30.0	38.7	48.3	51.0	43.5	52.1	47.6	26.7	34.8	50.0	90.9	121.5	84.0	....	Dir. Invest. in Rep. Econ., n.i.e.	78be d
1.2	−1.0	.6	−.2	.1	.1	.1	.1	—	—	—	16.0	—	....		Portfolio Investment Assets	78bf d
1.2	−1.0	.6	−.2	.1	.1	.1	.1	....	....	....	16.0	—	....		Equity Securities	78bk d
—	—	—	—	—	—	—	—	—	—	....	....	....	....		Debt Securities	78bl d
—	—	—	—	—	—	—	—	—	—	....	....	....	....		Portfolio Investment Liab., n.i.e.	78bg d
—	—	—	—	—	—	—	—	—	—	....	....	....	....		Equity Securities	78bm d
—	—	—	—	—	—	—	—	—	—	....	....	....	....		Debt Securities	78bn d
....	....	....	....	....	....	....	....	....	....	....	....	....			Financial Derivatives Assets	78bw d
....	....	....	....	....	....	....	....	....	....	....	....	....	−25.8		Financial Derivatives Liabilities	78bx d
−44.8	−41.2	−1.6	−12.5	−6.2	−39.5	−17.4	−63.4	−139.6	8.9	−12.8	−89.4	−53.4	−61.7	....	Other Investment Assets	78bh d
....	....	....	....	....	....	....	....	3.9	3.3	11.7	....	....	....		Monetary Authorities	78bo d
−44.6	−39.4	−2.1	−7.2	−.7	12.9	1.6	−26.3	−132.0	14.4	14.4	....	....	....	....	General Government	78bp d
−.2	−1.8	.5	−5.3	−5.5	−52.4	−19.0	−37.1	−11.5	−8.8	−38.9	−89.4	−53.4	−61.7	....	Banks	78bq d
															Other Sectors	78br d
191.1	81.5	58.4	9.8	−93.5	−20.8	−133.1	37.7	135.7	113.8	77.4	52.7	175.2	264.2	....	Other Investment Liab., n.i.e.	78bi d
54.8	59.2	31.3	−9.1	−12.4	−31.2	−125.4	−84.8	−73.6	−60.7	−73.1	−180.1	−24.1	7.5	....	Monetary Authorities	78bs d
47.2	68.4	55.7	68.5	−1.6	128.7	184.1	104.7	224.8	96.2	101.7	141.9	−48.4	63.1	....	General Government	78bt d
12.9	2.3	28.5	−6.1	−15.5	−24.6	−15.6	−7.3	1.7	−2.2	6.3	34.5	113.8	73.1	....	Banks	78bu d
76.3	−48.4	−57.1	−43.6	−64.1	−93.7	−176.2	25.1	−17.2	80.5	42.5	56.4	133.9	120.5	....	Other Sectors	78bv d
−38.6	3.2	−33.4	−93.1	−138.9	−107.4	152.0	29.2	−47.5	115.5	45.0	157.9	196.5	22.7	....	Net Errors and Omissions	78ca d
−172.2	−152.1	−182.6	−208.7	−367.7	−310.5	−159.7	−247.0	−333.4	−70.3	−41.3	−78.8	182.2	−1.9	....	*Overall Balance*	78cb d
172.2	152.1	182.6	208.7	367.7	310.5	159.7	247.0	333.4	70.3	41.3	78.8	−182.2	1.9	....	Reserves and Related Items	79da d
53.9	−7.9	−19.9	21.6	29.0	−20.1	−66.9	−92.0	99.6	−74.1	−90.3	12.7	−307.9	−237.5	....	Reserve Assets	79db d
−19.2	−51.9	−45.0	−36.0	−.4	−4.2	1.1	80.7	6.4	−16.1	−13.7	−38.0	−8.8	64.8	....	Use of Fund Credit and Loans	79dc d
137.5	212.0	247.4	223.1	339.2	334.8	225.5	258.3	227.4	160.4	145.3	104.1	134.5	174.6	....	Exceptional Financing	79de d

Honduras

	1970	1971	1972	1973	1974	1975	1976	1977	1978	1979	1980	1981	1982	1983	1984
Government Finance														*Millions of Lempiras:*	
Deficit (-) or Surplus **80**	−39.4	−44.6	−45.4	−16.0	−5.6	−48.0	−31.2	2.7	−29.7	−79.2	−140.2	−144.5	−379.6	−603.8	−678.6
Total Revenue and Grants **81y**	....	....	....	....	....	....	....	....	....	....	....	....	....	....	....
Revenue **81**	177.8	181.0	192.9	219.5	257.0	272.0	352.7	457.1	549.5	655.9	756.6	738.7	770.1	778.1	951.0
Grants **81z**	....	....	....	....	....	....	....	....	....	....	....	....	....	....	....
Exp. & Lending Minus Repay. **82z**	....	....	....	....	....	....	....	....	....	....	....	....	....	....	....
Expenditure **82**	217.2	225.6	238.3	235.5	262.6	320.0	383.9	454.4	579.2	735.1	896.8	883.2	1,149.7	1,381.9	1,629.6
Lending Minus Repayments **83**	....	....	....	....	....	....	....	....	....	....	....	....	....	....	....
Total Financing **80h**	....	....	....	....	....	....	....	....	....	....	....	....	....	....	....
Domestic **84a**	....	....	....	....	....	....	....	....	....	....	....	....	....	....	....
Foreign **85a**	....	....	....	....	....	....	....	....	....	....	....	....	....	....	....
Total Debt by Residence **88**	222.9	281.8	333.0	355.5	410.5	506.5	615.2	698.5	942.3	1,182.0	1,532.1	1,972.7	2,538.7	2,991.8	3,510.0
Domestic **88a**	86.1	105.3	136.0	141.3	153.2	162.4	198.8	218.0	296.9	347.2	451.0	649.3	817.5	1,101.6	1,250.5
Foreign **89a**	136.8	176.5	197.0	214.2	257.3	344.1	416.4	480.5	645.4	834.8	1,081.1	1,323.4	1,721.2	1,890.2	2,259.5
Memorandum Item:															
Intragovernmental Debt **88s**	8.8	6.8	6.0	8.9	14.0	23.7	43.7	61.0	65.4	77.3	93.7	93.2	129.3	160.9	186.0
National Accounts														*Millions of Lempiras*	
Exports of Goods & Services **90c**	395	426	461	579	656	680	898	1,149	1,366	1,649	1,860	1,784	1,549	1,610	1,706
Government Consumption **91f**	166	175	193	186	242	278	348	417	442	520	650	721	758	807	876
Gross Fixed Capital Formation **93e**	268	253	245	325	433	476	550	711	941	1,004	1,258	1,088	1,009	1,028	1,251
Increase/Decrease(-) in Stocks **93i**	34	−3	11	23	109	−50	−32	59	93	170	13	100	−190	−176	−95
Private Consumption **96f**	1,073	1,142	1,222	1,382	1,581	1,754	1,964	2,314	2,511	2,945	3,612	4,072	4,310	4,684	5,026
Imports of Goods & Services **98c**	−490	−442	−449	−600	−907	−890	−1,032	−1,311	−1,555	−1,863	−2,261	−2,126	−1,629	−1,799	−2,126
Gross Domestic Product (GDP) **99b**	1,446	1,551	1,683	1,895	2,114	2,248	2,696	3,339	3,798	4,425	5,132	5,639	5,807	6,154	6,638
Net Factor Inc/Pmts(-) Abroad **98.n**	−40	−45	−50	−62	−22	−50	−102	−124	−157	−210	−275	−319	−429	−338	−373
Gross National Income (GNI) **99a**	1,406	1,506	1,633	1,833	2,092	2,198	2,594	3,215	3,641	4,215	4,857	5,320	5,378	5,816	6,265
Net National Income **99e**	1,353	1,451	1,576	1,772	1,974	2,101	2,479	3,061	3,475	4,015	4,536	4,960	4,984	5,389	5,803
GDP Volume 1966 prices **99b.p**	1,297	1,367	1,422	1,502	1,500	1,455	....	....	....	....	....	....	....	....	....
GDP Volume 1978 Prices..................... **99b.p**	....	....	....	....	....	2,876	3,178	3,508	3,798	4,038	4,066	4,169	4,111	4,073	4,250
GDP Volume (1995=100) .... **99bv p**	41.7	44.0	45.7	48.3	48.2	46.8	51.7	57.1	61.8	65.7	66.1	67.8	66.9	66.2	69.1
GDP Deflator (1995=100) .... **99bi p**	9.2	9.4	9.8	10.5	11.7	12.8	13.9	15.6	16.4	18.0	20.7	22.2	23.2	24.8	25.6
															Millions:
Population **99z**	2.64	2.72	2.81	2.90	2.99	3.09	3.20	3.32	3.44	3.56	3.69	3.82	3.96	4.09	4.23

	1985	1986	1987	1988	1989	1990	1991	1992	1993	1994	1995	1996	1997	1998	1999		
Year Ending December 31																**Government Finance**	
	−653.6	−492.2	−298.7	−274.3	−339.2	−425.7	I−458.0	−860.6	−1,447.7	−1,458.6	−1,326.1	−1,516.1	−1,260.2	−383.7	....	Deficit (-) or Surplus	80
	....	....	....	....	....	....	I3,142.7	3,772.1	4,453.1	4,952.1	7,296.6	8,512.4	11,091.2	13,954.5	....	Total Revenue and Grants	81y
	1,064.1	1,151.8	1,290.0	1,377.8	1,534.4	2,059.1	I2,980.4	3,500.5	4,182.2	4,809.8	7,139.5	8,256.8	10,773.8	13,583.8	....	Revenue	81
	....	....	....	....	....	....	I162.3	271.6	270.9	142.3	157.1	255.6	317.4	370.7	....	Grants	81z
	....	....	....	....	....	....	I3,600.7	4,632.7	5,900.8	6,410.7	8,622.7	10,028.5	12,351.4	14,338.2	....	Exp. & Lending Minus Repay.	82z
	1,717.7	1,644.0	1,588.7	1,652.1	1,873.6	2,484.8	I3,331.5	4,414.6	5,888.7	6,030.7	7,780.4	9,778.8	12,727.6	14,601.0	....	Expenditure	82
	....	....	....	....	....	....	I269.2	218.1	12.1	380.0	842.3	249.7	−376.2	−262.8	....	Lending Minus Repayments	83
	....	....	....	....	....	....	I458.0	860.6	1,447.7	1,458.6	1,326.1	1,516.1	1,260.2	488.4	....	Total Financing	80h
	....	....	....	....	....	....	I234.3	−170.0	−322.8	505.2	−134.8	337.4	129.0	−458.5	....	Domestic	84a
	....	....	....	....	....	....	I223.7	1,030.6	1,770.5	953.4	1,460.9	1,178.7	1,131.2	946.9	....	Foreign	85a
	4,053.8	4,531.8	5,196.8	5,958.2	6,819.2	14,787.1	14,853.9	16,955.2	22,597.0	30,997.1	36,435.5	44,360.1	46,680.4	50,721.6	....	Total Debt by Residence	88
	1,438.0	1,640.6	2,043.3	2,433.8	3,017.4	3,427.1	3,176.9	3,065.8	3,460.8	3,570.3	3,711.7	3,875.5	4,424.1	3,970.4	....	Domestic	88a
	2,615.8	2,891.2	3,153.5	3,524.4	3,801.8	11,360.0	11,677.0	13,889.4	19,136.2	27,426.8	32,723.8	40,484.6	42,256.3	46,751.2	....	Foreign	89a
																Memorandum Item:	
	212.1	208.6	285.0	276.6	256.9	477.0	−187.3	−100.7	−67.3	−332.2	−347.8	−394.1	−304.4	−330.2	....	Intragovernmental Debt	88s
Millions of Lempiras																**National Accounts**	
	1,827	2,025	1,907	2,432	3,204	4,664	5,632	6,048	7,869	11,498	16,391	22,378	28,217	33,054	32,672	Exports of Goods & Services	90c
	953	1,087	1,181	1,308	1,475	1,621	1,769	2,171	2,405	2,780	3,495	4,556	5,118	7,086	8,766	Government Consumption	91f
	1,234	1,045	1,132	1,429	1,884	2,533	3,096	4,202	6,535	8,110	8,994	11,110	15,354	20,702	23,748	Gross Fixed Capital Formation	93e
	27	10	314	513	94	348	926	679	1,079	2,751	2,842	3,400	3,994	910	2,980	Increase/Decrease(-) in Stocks	93i
	5,412	5,606	5,916	6,245	7,226	8,379	11,021	12,520	14,717	18,114	23,819	31,127	40,528	45,781	51,609	Private Consumption	96f
	−2,174	−2,156	−2,145	−2,676	−3,549	−5,008	−6,130	−6,820	−9,916	−14,391	−18,033	−24,821	−31,775	−37,301	−43,212	Imports of Goods & Services	98c
	7,279	7,617	8,305	9,251	10,334	12,537	16,314	18,800	22,689	28,862	37,507	47,750	61,436	70,232	76,563	Gross Domestic Product (GDP)	99b
	−384	−420	−475	−570	−740	−1,136	−1,499	−1,859	−1,498	−1,825	−2,532	−3,069	−2,872	−2,854	−2,235	Net Factor Inc/Pmts(-) Abroad	98.n
	6,895	7,197	7,830	8,681	9,594	11,401	14,815	16,941	21,191	27,037	34,975	44,681	58,564	67,379	74,328	Gross National Income (GNI)	99a
	6,408	6,663	7,259	8,073	8,940	10,529	13,700	15,727	19,819	25,330	32,717	41,836	55,036	63,293	69,683	Net National Income	99e
	....	....	....	....	....	....	....	....	....	....	....	....	....	....	....	GDP Volume 1966 prices	99b, *p*
	4,428	4,460	4,729	4,947	5,161	5,166	5,334	5,634	5,985	5,907	6,148	6,371	6,693	6,890	6,760	GDP Volume 1978 Prices	99b, *p*
	72.0	72.5	76.9	80.5	83.9	84.0	86.8	91.6	97.3	96.1	100.0	103.6	108.9	112.1	110.0	GDP Volume (1995=100)	99bv *p*
	26.9	28.0	28.8	30.7	32.8	39.8	50.1	54.7	62.1	80.1	100.0	122.9	150.5	167.1	185.6	GDP Deflator (1995=100)	99bi *p*
Midyear Estimates																	
	4.37	4.51	4.66	4.80	4.60	4.76	4.92	5.08	5.25	5.42	5.60	5.79	5.98	6.18	6.39	**Population**	99z

(See notes in the back of the book.)

Hungary

944

944

		1970	1971	1972	1973	1974	1975	1976	1977	1978	1979	1980	1981	1982	1983	1984
Exchange Rates														*Forint per SDR:*		
Official Rate	aa	60.000	59.996	59.996	56.400	57.241	50.934	47.984	49.317	46.351	46.868	41.084	40.075	43.694	47.315	50.186
														Forint per US Dollar:		
Official Rate	ae	60.000	55.260	55.260	46.752	46.752	43.509	41.300	40.600	35.578	35.578	32.213	34.430	39.610	45.193	51.199
Official Rate	rf	60.000	59.822	55.260	48.966	46.752	43.971	41.575	40.961	37.911	35.578	32.532	34.314	36.631	42.671	48.042
Secondary Rate	xe	30.000	27.630	27.630	23.376	23.376	20.449	20.650	20.300	17.789	20.330	23.950	....			
Secondary Rate	xf	30.000	29.911	27.630	24.483	23.376	20.666	20.788	20.480	18.956	20.013	22.139	....			
														Index Numbers (1995=100):		
Official Rate	ahx	208.4	209.0	226.3	256.0	267.4	284.5	300.8	305.3	330.2	351.4	384.5	364.7	342.4	293.7	260.8
Nominal Effective Exchange Rate	nec	....	....	....	....	....	....	....	....	....	243.6	267.4	304.0	319.2	299.4	298.4
Real Effective Exchange Rate	rec	....	....	....	....	....	....	....	....	....			83.9	90.4	93.5	88.3	89.6
Fund Position														*Millions of SDRs:*		
Quota	2f.s	....										....		375	531	531
SDRs	1b.s	—	—	—	—	—	—	—	—	—	—	—	—	2	44	—
Reserve Position in the Fund	1c.s	....										....		—	39	—
Total Fund Cred.&Loans Outstg.	2tl	....										....		215	547	972
International Liquidity											*Millions of US Dollars Unless Otherwise Indicated:*					
Total Reserves minus Gold	1l.d	....													1,231	1,560
SDRs	1b.d	....												3	46	—
Reserve Position in the Fund	1c.d	....												—	41	—
Foreign Exchange	1d.d	....												....	1,144	1,560
Gold (Million Fine Troy Ounces)	1ad	....	1.446	1.671	1.820	1.330	.951	1.322	1.282	1.978	1.777	2.069	1.685	.646	1.532	2.063
Gold (National Valuation)	1and	....	61	71	77	56	67	66	70	249	402	468	381	146	346	466
Other Liabs.	4..d	....												8,689	9,002	8,922
Deposit Money Banks: Assets	7a.d	....												76	127	119
Liabilities	7b.d	....												1,128	1,148	1,015
Monetary Authorities														*Billions of Forint:*		
Foreign Assets	11	....												57.8	91.2	121.3
Claims on Consolidated Cent.Govt	12a	....												487.7	486.8	489.5
Other Claims on Residents	12d	....												276.2	283.2	299.7
Claims on Deposit Money Banks	12e	....												—	—	—
Reserve Money	14	....												360.9	324.2	289.2
of which: Currency Outside DMBs	14a	....												84.9	94.8	105.4
Time & Foreign Currency Deposits	15	....												51.4	44.4	44.3
Money Market Instruments	16aa	....												....	....	....
Bonds	16ab	....												—	—	—
Foreign Liabilities	16c	....												119.1	178.8	171.0
Long-Term Foreign Liabilities	16cl	....												234.4	253.9	334.6
Consolidated Centr.Govt.Deposits	16d	....												35.9	33.6	39.7
Capital Accounts	17a	....												10.4	10.5	16.9
Other Items (Net)	17r	....												9.5	15.7	14.9
of which: Valuation Changes	17rv	....												−37.8	−31.3	−40.9
Banking Institutions														*Billions of Forint:*		
Reserves	20	....												181.5	143.0	103.2
Foreign Assets	21	....												3.0	5.8	6.1
Claims on Consolidated Cent.Govt	22a	....												7.2	7.2	8.7
Claims on Local Government	22b	....												6.7	6.3	6.0
Other Claims on Residents	22d	....												133.6	154.3	179.6
Demand Deposits	24	....												8.2	11.0	14.9
Time, Savings,& Fgn.Currency Dep.	25	....												178.9	190.8	204.1
Bonds	26ab	....												8.2	11.6	26.9
Foreign Liabilities	26c	....												12.2	20.9	23.1
Long-Term Foreign Liabilities	26cl	....												32.5	31.0	28.9
Consolidated Centr.Govt.Deposits	26d	....												—	—	—
Credit from Monetary Authorities	26g	....												—	—	—
Capital Accounts	27a	....												3.8	4.1	5.2
Other Items (Net)	27r	....												88.2	47.2	.5
Banking Survey														*Billions of Forint*		
Foreign Assets (Net)	31n	....												−70.6	−102.8	−66.7
Domestic Credit	32	....												875.5	904.2	943.8
Claims on Cons.Cent.Govt.(Net)	32an	....												459.0	460.4	458.5
Claims on Local Government	32b	....												6.7	6.3	6.0
Other Claims on Residents	32d	....												409.8	437.5	479.3
Money	34	....												187.6	192.2	200.9
Quasi-Money	35	....												230.3	235.2	248.4
Money Market Instruments	36aa	....												—	—	—
Bonds	36ab	....												8.2	11.6	26.9
Long-Term Foreign Liabilities	36cl	....												266.8	284.9	363.5
Capital Accounts	37a	....												14.3	14.6	22.1
Other Items (Net)	37r	....												97.7	63.0	15.4
Money plus Quasi-Money	35l	....												417.9	427.4	449.3
Money (National Definition)														*Billions of Forint:*		
M1	39ma	....												....	....	....
M2	39mb	....												....	....	....
M3	39mc	....												....	....	....
M4	39md	....												....	....	....
Interest Rates														*Percent Per Annum*		
Discount Rate (End of Period)	60	....												....	....	....
Treasury Bill Rate	60c	....												....	....	....
Deposit Rate	60l	3.0	3.0	3.0	3.0	3.0	3.0	3.0	3.0	3.0	3.0	3.0	3.0	3.5	5.0	5.0
Lending Rate	60p	....												....	....	....

Hungary

1985	1986	1987	1988	1989	1990	1991	1992	1993	1994	1995	1996	1997	1998	1999		
Exchange Rates																
End of Period																
52.007	56.177	65.807	70.699	82.192	87.421	108.169	115.459	138.317	161.591	207.321	237.163	274.572	308.401	346.586	Official Rate	aa
End of Period (ae) Period Average (rf)																
47.347	45.927	46.387	52.537	62.543	61.449	75.620	83.970	100.700	110.690	139.470	164.930	203.500	219.030	252.520	Official Rate	ae
50.119	45.832	46.971	50.413	59.066	63.206	74.735	78.988	91.933	105.160	125.681	152.647	186.789	214.402	237.146	Official Rate	rf
....	....	....	....	....	....	....	....	....	....	....	....	....	....	....	Secondary Rate	xe
....	....	....	....	....	....	....	....	....	....	....	....	....	....	....	Secondary Rate	xf
Period Averages																
249.7	272.9	266.4	248.7	212.3	198.0	167.6	158.4	136.5	119.0	100.0	82.1	67.2	58.3	52.8	Official Rate	ahx
302.7	267.6	230.7	215.8	202.0	178.1	158.2	151.2	144.8	128.3	100.0	85.7	79.6	71.0	66.9	Nominal Effective Exchange Rate	nec
92.4	83.2	75.0	76.8	77.7	80.6	89.0	96.8	105.3	104.2	100.0	102.8	108.1	107.5	109.5	Real Effective Exchange Rate	rec
Fund Position																
End of Period																
531	531	531	531	531	531	531	755	755	755	755	755	755	755	1,038	Quota	2f.s
—	—	—	—	—	1	1	2	2	1	1	—	—	1	3	SDRs	1b.s
—	—	—	—	—	—	—	56	56	56	56	56	56	56	177	Reserve Position in the Fund	1c.s
884	843	570	471	347	232	880	876	896	782	259	119	119	—		Total Fund Cred.&Loans Outstg.	2tl
International Liquidity																
End of Period																
2,153	2,302	1,634	1,467	1,246	1,069	3,934	4,425	6,700	6,735	11,974	9,720	8,408	9,319	10,954	Total Reserves minus Gold	1l.d
—	—	—	—	—	1	1	3	3	2	1	—	—	1	4	SDRs	1b.d
—	—	—	—	—	—	—	77	77	82	83	81	76	79	243	Reserve Position in the Fund	1c.d
2,153	2,302	1,634	1,467	1,246	1,068	3,933	4,345	6,620	6,652	11,890	9,639	8,332	9,239	10,707	Foreign Exchange	1d.d
2.327	2.346	1.641	1.593	1.497	.300	.258	.102	.114	.110	.111	.101	.101	.101	.101	Gold (Million Fine Troy Ounces)	1ad
640	751	525	510	479	97	83	33	45	42	43	37	29	29	29	Gold (National Valuation)	1and
11,394	13,931	16,817	16,746	17,426	17,431	16,739	14,974	17,244	19,191	20,836	16,239	11,647	11,677	9,847	Other Liabs.	4..d
344	634	661	777	1,004	1,156	1,405	1,504	1,331	1,030	921	1,679	2,495	3,306	3,598	Deposit Money Banks: Assets	7a.d
1,197	1,725	1,766	1,839	2,045	1,689	1,813	1,831	1,783	2,379	2,878	3,092	4,702	5,574	5,931	Liabilities	7b.d
Monetary Authorities																
End of Period																
172.7	159.8	138.3	138.6	162.7	140.4	362.5	385.2	689.8	784.0	1,680.7	1,614.9	1,723.3	2,054.3	2,992.4	Foreign Assets	11
488.5	563.1	633.0	666.7	739.4	‡1,297.4	1,622.1	1,841.9	2,166.9	2,558.3	3,144.7	2,902.9	2,854.0	2,929.5	2,300.3	Claims on Consolidated Cent.Govt	12a
322.5	353.8	2.6	5.3	1.3	2.2	2.0	3.8	4.4	4.4	3.8	—	.1	.1	—	Other Claims on Residents	12d
—	—	253.8	225.4	252.5	354.0	417.4	293.4	368.8	405.8	302.6	231.4	185.3	178.4	126.6	Claims on Deposit Money Banks	12e
330.1	352.2	313.4	299.3	358.0	524.4	499.9	606.7	624.2	614.1	723.5	660.4	858.2	1,033.0	1,297.1	Reserve Money	14
116.8	130.9	153.8	164.5	180.6	209.8	260.2	322.3	371.2	410.7	443.9	497.7	562.6	667.0	845.3	*of which: Currency Outside DMBs*	14a
27.8	22.5	.6	.7	.7	‡181.0	290.8	282.2	398.5	555.7	745.8	581.9	530.8	724.9	565.8	Time & Foreign Currency Deposits	15
....	....	....	....	....	8.4	10.1	1.6	—	5.3	54.1	419.6	650.9	606.7	764.6	Money Market Instruments	16aa
....	....	....	....	....	....	....	5.6	7.6	6.4	5.2	3.5	2.3	—	—	Bonds	16ab
145.4	169.6	141.1	150.6	143.9	88.0	125.4	111.5	140.6	148.3	104.9	57.8	138.2	42.6	166.1	Foreign Liabilities	16c
440.1	517.5	676.5	762.5	974.5	1,003.4	1,235.6	1,247.0	1,719.9	2,102.3	2,854.7	2,648.7	2,264.7	2,515.1	2,320.5	Long-Term Foreign Liabilities	16cl
36.2	48.5	55.9	47.2	32.7	‡97.7	228.0	255.3	341.1	316.8	561.8	389.9	328.4	193.7	367.8	Consolidated Centr.Govt.Deposits	16d
18.4	19.2	18.8	19.8	21.6	24.9	26.8	39.5	46.1	31.6	55.2	59.3	72.7	128.2	74.0	Capital Accounts	17a
-14.2	-52.8	-178.7	-244.2	-375.4	54.3	-12.5	-25.1	-48.1	-28.0	26.5	-71.9	-83.6	-81.9	-136.7	Other Items (Net)	17r
-43.2	-106.2	-196.3	-249.5	-460.7	—	—	—	—	—	—	—	—	—	—	*of which: Valuation Changes*	17rv
Banking Institutions																
End of Period																
117.7	120.0	151.9	126.8	169.7	306.4	527.0	555.8	629.6	749.0	1,066.4	1,151.0	1,399.0	1,526.9	1,766.2	Reserves	20
16.3	29.1	30.7	40.8	62.8	71.0	106.3	126.3	134.1	114.0	128.5	276.9	507.7	724.0	908.4	Foreign Assets	21
8.7	8.7	13.6	12.9	28.7	25.1	160.7	269.2	608.2	663.1	747.7	930.2	976.9	1,173.6	1,083.5	Claims on Consolidated Cent.Govt	22a
6.7	7.3	10.9	15.7	13.4	15.7	13.6	13.0	22.6	47.6	49.9	38.5	30.3	44.4	50.0	Claims on Local Government	22b
208.6	240.6	648.7	668.9	804.7	965.1	967.2	973.7	997.5	1,139.5	1,248.1	1,500.9	‡2,044.7	2,393.3	2,921.7	Other Claims on Residents	22d
27.3	34.3	145.2	129.5	191.7	‡299.5	339.6	475.7	512.4	553.9	561.5	730.8	961.3	1,121.9	1,274.7	Demand Deposits	24
230.8	253.1	287.0	304.6	327.2	‡395.5	569.5	695.5	853.2	1,008.0	1,335.4	1,610.8	1,992.4	2,782.6	3,167.5	Time, Savings,& Fgn.Currency Dep.	25
30.6	34.8	53.1	58.7	67.5	93.9	186.8	237.0	250.2	284.7	377.1	494.9	483.0	29.6	52.5	Bonds	26ab
24.9	25.0	28.9	38.6	60.8	41.6	64.5	83.0	90.6	134.3	196.0	307.9	593.3	689.2	746.7	Foreign Liabilities	26c
31.8	54.2	53.1	58.0	67.1	62.1	72.6	70.8	89.0	129.1	205.4	202.1	363.6	531.7	751.1	Long-Term Foreign Liabilities	26cl
—	—	1.5	2.9	3.9	3.3	5.1	14.4	16.1	31.1	13.0	10.0	7.6	5.0	4.5	Consolidated Centr.Govt.Deposits	26d
—	—	253.8	225.4	252.5	354.0	417.4	293.4	368.8	405.8	302.6	231.4	185.3	178.4	126.6	Credit from Monetary Authorities	26g
9.0	11.6	40.4	59.0	118.8	184.4	247.3	277.5	174.0	230.8	316.7	382.9	559.8	597.0	685.6	Capital Accounts	27a
3.7	-7.2	-7.2	-11.7	-10.1	-51.1	-128.2	-209.2	37.6	-64.5	-67.0	-73.2	-187.8	-73.0	-79.4	Other Items (Net)	27r
Banking Survey																
End of Period																
18.7	-5.8	-1.0	-9.8	20.9	81.8	278.9	317.1	592.7	615.4	1,508.3	1,526.2	1,499.5	2,046.6	2,988.1	Foreign Assets (Net)	31n
998.9	1,125.1	1,251.3	1,319.3	1,550.9	‡2,204.4	2,532.4	2,831.8	3,442.3	4,064.9	4,619.4	4,972.7	‡5,570.0	6,342.3	5,983.1	Domestic Credit	32
461.0	523.4	589.2	629.4	731.5	‡1,221.4	1,549.6	1,841.4	2,417.8	2,873.5	3,317.6	3,433.3	3,494.9	3,904.5	3,011.4	Claims on Cons.Cent.Govt.(Net)	32an
6.7	7.3	10.9	15.7	13.4	15.7	13.6	13.0	22.6	47.6	49.9	38.5	30.3	44.4	50.0	Claims on Local Government	32b
531.1	594.4	651.2	674.2	806.0	967.3	969.2	977.4	1,001.9	1,143.8	1,251.9	1,501.0	‡2,044.8	2,393.4	2,921.7	Other Claims on Residents	32d
239.7	266.5	306.6	302.0	379.9	517.5	611.5	807.7	901.9	973.9	1,011.3	1,237.2	1,528.3	1,789.2	2,123.4	Money	34
258.6	275.5	287.6	305.3	327.8	‡396.8	571.5	698.1	856.7	1,014.1	1,342.7	1,615.3	1,997.4	2,800.8	3,180.2	Quasi-Money	35
....	....	....	....	....	8.4	10.1	1.6	—	5.3	54.1	419.6	650.9	606.7	764.6	Money Market Instruments	36aa
30.6	34.8	53.1	58.7	67.5	93.9	186.8	242.5	257.8	291.1	382.3	498.5	485.2	29.6	52.5	Bonds	36ab
471.8	571.7	729.6	820.5	1,041.7	1,065.5	1,308.2	1,317.8	1,808.9	2,231.3	3,060.1	2,850.9	2,628.3	3,046.7	3,071.6	Long-Term Foreign Liabilities	36cl
27.4	30.8	59.2	78.8	140.4	209.3	274.1	317.0	220.1	262.4	371.8	442.2	632.5	725.2	759.6	Capital Accounts	37a
-10.5	-60.0	-185.8	-255.9	-385.5	182.9	-150.9	-235.8	-10.5	-97.8	-94.7	-564.7	-853.4	-609.4	-980.7	Other Items (Net)	37r
498.3	542.0	594.3	607.3	707.7	914.3	1,183.0	1,505.8	1,758.7	1,988.0	2,354.0	2,852.5	3,525.7	4,577.3	5,292.1	Money plus Quasi-Money	35l
Money (National Definition)																
End of Period																
....	....	....	....	....	517.49	611.48	807.73	901.91	973.89	1,011.32	1,237.20	1,528.31	1,789.23	2,123.38	M1	39ma
....	....	....	....	....	914.28	1,182.96	1,505.82	1,758.65	1,987.97	2,354.01	2,852.45	3,525.73	....	....	M2	39mb
....	....	....	....	....	1,009.41	1,369.78	1,748.33	2,016.42	2,279.09	2,736.33	3,350.90	4,010.97	4,619.66	5,356.10	M3	39mc
....	....	....	....	....		1,415.42	1,820.07	2,223.48	2,628.14	3,285.51	4,170.24	5,287.90	6,347.82	7,536.66	M4	39md
Interest Rates																
Percent Per Annum																
11.5	10.5	10.5	14.0	17.0	22.0	22.0	21.0	22.0	25.0	28.0	23.0	20.5	17.0	14.5	Discount Rate (*End of Period*)	60
....	....	....	18.0	20.5	30.1	34.5	22.7	17.2	26.9	32.0	24.0	20.1	17.8	14.7	Treasury Bill Rate	60c
5.0	4.5	4.0	5.3	9.4	‡24.7	30.4	24.4	15.7	20.3	26.1	22.2	18.5	16.2	13.3	Deposit Rate	60l
....	....	....	....	20.3	28.8	35.1	33.1	25.4	27.4	32.6	27.3	21.8	19.3	16.3	Lending Rate	60p

Hungary

		1970	1971	1972	1973	1974	1975	1976	1977	1978	1979	1980	1981	1982	1983	1984
Prices, Production, Labor														*Index Numbers (1995=100):*		
Producer Prices: Industry	63	48.5	49.7	50.6	52.1	53.8	59.5	62.3	63.5	65.9	67.3	77.6	82.5	86.4	91.2	95.0
Consumer Prices	64	....	....	7.9	8.1	8.3	8.6	9.1	9.4	9.9	10.7	11.7	12.3	13.1	14.0	15.2
Wages: Avg. Earnings (1990=100)	65	20.5	21.5	22.5	24.2	26.2	27.8	29.5	31.9	34.7	36.6	38.9	41.7	44.3	46.5	49.7
Industrial Production	66	70.7	75.6	79.5	85.4	93.3	98.2	102.7	109.5	114.8	118.7	116.2	119.5	121.7	123.4	126.2
Industrial Employment (1990=100)	67	129.7	131.2	133.1	134.9	137.2	138.5	137.4	137.2	137.0	134.8	131.1	128.3	125.7	123.2	122.7
														Number in Thousands:		
Labor Force	67d	....	....	....	....	....	....	....	....	....	....	....	....	....	....	....
Employment	67e	....	....	....	....	....	....	....	....	....	....	....	....	....	....	....
Unemployment	67c	....	....	....	....	....	....	....	....	....	....	....	....	....	....	....
Unemployment Rate (%)	67r	....	....	....	....	....	....	....	....	....	....	....	....	....	....	....
International Transactions														*Billions of Forint*		
Exports	70	103.6	110.5	132.8	164.2	184.3	198.7	204.8	238.6	240.7	282.1	281.0	299.5	324.5	374.1	414.0
Imports, c.i.f.	71	112.6	134.5	130.2	147.8	208.2	237.5	230.1	267.3	300.9	308.9	299.9	314.3	324.8	365.0	390.5
Imports, f.o.b.	71.v	110.6	132.1	127.9	145.2	204.5	233.2	225.4	262.9	295.8	304.0	294.6	307.9	319.0	359.2	384.0
														1995=100		
Volume of Exports	72	34.7	36.9	43.5	50.3	51.2	53.7	58.0	65.3	66.3	74.6	75.4	77.3	79.8	85.1	91.1
Volume of Imports	73	43.8	51.3	48.6	50.9	58.9	61.9	64.3	69.8	78.5	75.9	75.1	75.2	72.2	72.9	73.6
Export Prices (1990=100)	76	47.6	47.7	48.6	52.0	57.4	59.0	56.3	58.2	57.9	60.3	59.5	61.7	62.4	65.7	68.7
Import Prices (1990=100)	76.x	36.0	36.8	37.5	40.7	49.6	53.8	50.2	53.8	53.8	57.0	56.1	58.7	60.7	65.5	70.1
Balance of Payments														*Millions of US Dollars:*		
Current Account, n.i.e.	78ald	....	....	....	....	....	....	....	....	....	....	....	....	−531	−181	39
Goods: Exports f.o.b.	78aad	....	....	....	....	....	....	....	....	....	....	....	....	9,038	8,978	9,090
Goods: Imports f.o.b.	78abd	....	....	....	....	....	....	....	....	....	....	....	....	−8,628	−8,544	−8,310
Trade Balance	78acd	....	....	....	....	....	....	....	....	....	....	....	....	410	434	780
Services: Credit	78add	....	....	....	....	....	....	....	....	....	....	....	....	633	589	595
Services: Debit	78aed	....	....	....	....	....	....	....	....	....	....	....	....	−524	−485	−552
Balance on Goods & Services	78afd	....	....	....	....	....	....	....	....	....	....	....	....	519	538	823
Income: Credit	78agd	....	....	....	....	....	....	....	....	....	....	....	....	109	117	139
Income: Debit	78ahd	....	....	....	....	....	....	....	....	....	....	....	....	−1,222	−892	−989
Balance on Gds, Serv. & Inc.	78aid	....	....	....	....	....	....	....	....	....	....	....	....	−594	−237	−27
Current Transfers, n.i.e.: Credit	78ajd	....	....	....	....	....	....	....	....	....	....	....	....	63	56	66
Current Transfers: Debit	78akd	....	....	....	....	....	....	....	....	....	....	....	....	—	—	—
Capital Account, n.i.e.	78bcd	....	....	....	....	....	....	....	....	....	....	....	....	—	—	—
Capital Account, n.i.e.: Credit	78bad	....	....	....	....	....	....	....	....	....	....	....	....	—	—	—
Capital Account: Debit	78bbd	....	....	....	....	....	....	....	....	....	....	....	....	—	—	—
Financial Account, n.i.e.	78bjd	....	....	....	....	....	....	....	....	....	....	....	....	−474	646	267
Direct Investment Abroad	78bdd	....	....	....	....	....	....	....	....	....	....	....	....	—	—	—
Dir. Invest. in Rep. Econ., n.i.e.	78bed	....	....	....	....	....	....	....	....	....	....	....	....	—	—	—
Portfolio Investment Assets	78bfd	....	....	....	....	....	....	....	....	....	....	....	....	—	—	—
Equity Securities	78bkd	....	....	....	....	....	....	....	....	....	....	....	....	—	—	—
Debt Securities	78bld	....	....	....	....	....	....	....	....	....	....	....	....	—	—	—
Portfolio Investment Liab., n.i.e.	78bgd	....	....	....	....	....	....	....	....	....	....	....	....	—	—	—
Equity Securities	78bmd	....	....	....	....	....	....	....	....	....	....	....	....	—	—	—
Debt Securities	78bnd	....	....	....	....	....	....	....	....	....	....	....	....	—	—	—
Financial Derivatives Assets	78bwd	....	....	....	....	....	....	....	....	....	....	....	....			
Financial Derivatives Liabilities	78bxd	....	....	....	....	....	....	....	....	....	....	....	....			
Other Investment Assets	78bhd	....	....	....	....	....	....	....	....	....	....	....	....	−880	−429	−251
Monetary Authorities	78bod	....	....	....	....	....	....	....	....	....	....	....	....	—	—	—
General Government	78bpd	....	....	....	....	....	....	....	....	....	....	....	....	−528	−177	−48
Banks	78bqd	....	....	....	....	....	....	....	....	....	....	....	....	−76	−51	8
Other Sectors	78brd	....	....	....	....	....	....	....	....	....	....	....	....	−276	−201	−211
Other Investment Liab., n.i.e.	78bid	....	....	....	....	....	....	....	....	....	....	....	....	406	1,075	518
Monetary Authorities	78bsd	....	....	....	....	....	....	....	....	....	....	....	....	−177	934	−710
General Government	78btd	....	....	....	....	....	....	....	....	....	....	....	....	583	121	1,361
Banks	78bud	....	....	....	....	....	....	....	....	....	....	....	....	—	20	−133
Other Sectors	78bvd	....	....	....	....	....	....	....	....	....	....	....	....	—	—	—
Net Errors and Omissions	78cad	....	....	....	....	....	....	....	....	....	....	....	....	465	−590	−240
Overall Balance	78cbd	....	....	....	....	....	....	....	....	....	....	....	....	−540	−125	66
Reserves and Related Items	79dad	....	....	....	....	....	....	....	....	....	....	....	....	540	125	−66
Reserve Assets	79dbd	....	....	....	....	....	....	....	....	....	....	....	....	305	−228	−501
Use of Fund Credit and Loans	79dcd	....	....	....	....	....	....	....	....	....	....	....	....	235	353	436
Exceptional Financing	79ded	....	....	....	....	....	....	....	....	....	....	....	....	....	....	....
International Investment Position														*Millions of US Dollars*		
Assets	79aad	....	....	....	....	....	....	....	....	....	....	....	....	....	....	....
Direct Investment Abroad	79abd	....	....	....	....	....	....	....	....	....	....	....	....	....	....	....
Portfolio Investment	79acd	....	....	....	....	....	....	....	....	....	....	....	....	....	....	....
Equity Securities	79add	....	....	....	....	....	....	....	....	....	....	....	....	....	....	....
Debt Securities	79aed	....	....	....	....	....	....	....	....	....	....	....	....	....	....	....
Financial Derivatives	79ald	....	....	....	....	....	....	....	....	....	....	....	....	....	....	....
Other Investment	79afd	....	....	....	....	....	....	....	....	....	....	....	....	....	....	....
Monetary Authorities	79agd	....	....	....	....	....	....	....	....	....	....	....	....	....	....	....
General Government	79ahd	....	....	....	....	....	....	....	....	....	....	....	....	....	....	....
Banks	79aid	....	....	....	....	....	....	....	....	....	....	....	....	....	....	....
Other Sectors	79ajd	....	....	....	....	....	....	....	....	....	....	....	....	....	....	....
Reserve Assets	79akd	....	....	....	....	....	....	....	....	....	....	....	....	....	....	....
Liabilities	79lad	....	....	....	....	....	....	....	....	....	....	....	....	....	....	....
Dir. Invest. in Rep. Economy	79lbd	....	....	....	....	....	....	....	....	....	....	....	....	....	....	....
Portfolio Investment	79lcd	....	....	....	....	....	....	....	....	....	....	....	....	....	....	....
Equity Securities	79ldd	....	....	....	....	....	....	....	....	....	....	....	....	....	....	....
Debt Securities	79led	....	....	....	....	....	....	....	....	....	....	....	....	....	....	....
Financial Derivatives	79lld	....	....	....	....	....	....	....	....	....	....	....	....	....	....	....
Other Investment	79lfd	....	....	....	....	....	....	....	....	....	....	....	....	....	....	....
Monetary Authorities	79lgd	....	....	....	....	....	....	....	....	....	....	....	....	....	....	....
General Government	79lhd	....	....	....	....	....	....	....	....	....	....	....	....	....	....	....
Banks	79lid	....	....	....	....	....	....	....	....	....	....	....	....	....	....	....
Other Sectors	79ljd	....	....	....	....	....	....	....	....	....	....	....	....	....	....	....

1985	1986	1987	1988	1989	1990	1991	1992	1993	1994	1995	1996	1997	1998	1999		
Period Averages															**Prices, Production, Labor**	
100.0	102.1	105.7	110.6	127.6	155.7	206.5	231.9	259.9	I 189.1	I 100.0	121.8	146.6	163.3	170.2	Producer Prices: Industry	63
I 16.2	17.1	18.6	21.5	25.2	32.4	43.6	I 53.5	65.6	77.9	100.0	123.5	146.1	167.1	184.3	Consumer Prices	64
54.8	59.0	64.2	70.7	84.5	I 100.0	124.0	150.5	180.5	226.5	....	....	....	....	....	Wages: Avg. Earnings (1990=100)	65
127.1	128.9	132.6	I 131.7	125.0	112.5	92.7	84.0	86.3	95.2	I 100.0	103.8	I 115.0	129.4	142.8	Industrial Production	66
121.4	120.6	117.6	114.3	109.7	I 100.0	86.6	72.4	65.4	61.0	....	....	....	....	....	Industrial Employment (1990=100)	67
Period Averages																
....	....	....	....	....	4,525	....	4,242	....	4,144	4,095	4,048	....	4,011	....	Labor Force	67d
....	....	....	....	....	....	....	4,083	3,827	3,752	3,679	3,648	3,646	3,698	....	Employment	67e
....	....	....	....	....	....	....	444	519	449	417	400	349	313	405	Unemployment	67c
....	....	....	....	....	....	....	9.8	11.9	10.7	10.2	9.9	8.7	7.8	....	Unemployment Rate (%)	67r
Billions of Forint															**International Transactions**	
424.6	420.3	450.1	504.1	571.3	603.6	764.3	843.6	819.9	1,128.7	1,576.1	1,936.4	3,498.9	4,927.4	5,938.5	Exports	70
410.1	439.7	463.1	472.5	518.7	544.9	855.6	878.6	1,158.1	1,518.3	1,894.4	2,426.4	3,877.3	5,494.7	6,645.6	Imports, c.i.f.	71
402.0	432.1	455.1	463.8	515.1	547.5	840.5	863.1	1,137.6	1,491.5	1,860.9	2,383.5	3,808.7	....	....	Imports, f.o.b.	71.v
1995=100																
95.8	93.7	96.9	103.4	103.8	99.6	94.7	95.6	83.1	I 94.3	I 100.0	104.6	I 135.8	165.9	192.5	Volume of Exports	72
79.1	81.2	83.0	82.9	83.6	79.3	83.6	78.1	94.5	I 104.4	I 100.0	105.5	I 133.4	166.5	192.4	Volume of Imports	73
70.7	71.6	73.8	78.6	90.9	I 100.0	130.7	142.9	159.9	188.8	....	....	....	....	....	Export Prices (1990=100)	76
72.8	76.4	78.0	81.2	91.3	I 100.0	145.9	160.3	175.4	202.6	....	....	....	....	....	Import Prices (1990=100)	76.x
Minus Sign Indicates Debit															Balance of Payments	
–455	–1,365	–676	–572	–588	379	403	352	–4,262	–4,054	–2,530	–1,689	–982	–2,304	–2,101	Current Account, n.i.e.	78al*d*
8,578	9,198	9,967	9,989	10,493	9,151	9,688	10,097	8,119	7,648	12,864	14,184	19,640	20,747	21,846	Goods: Exports f.o.b.	78aa*d*
–8,130	–9,663	–9,887	–9,406	–9,450	–8,617	–9,330	–10,108	–12,140	–11,364	–15,297	–16,836	–21,602	–23,101	–24,037	Goods: Imports f.o.b.	78ab*d*
448	–465	80	583	1,043	534	358	–11	–4,021	–3,716	–2,433	–2,652	–1,962	–2,354	–2,191	*Trade Balance*	78ac*d*
622	729	980	1,047	1,291	2,884	2,526	3,405	2,836	3,117	5,182	5,980	5,733	5,921	5,650	Services: Credit	78ad*d*
–723	–713	–814	–1,227	–1,658	–2,400	–1,991	–2,641	–2,620	–2,958	–3,616	–3,506	–3,465	–4,141	–4,266	Services: Debit	78ae*d*
347	–449	246	403	676	1,019	892	753	–3,805	–3,557	–867	–178	306	–574	–806	*Balance on Goods & Services*	78af*d*
195	261	247	240	231	280	322	424	465	676	798	1,202	1,382	1,111	775	Income: Credit	78ag*d*
–1,062	–1,252	–1,274	–1,332	–1,625	–1,707	–1,678	–1,684	–1,655	–2,082	–2,602	–2,658	–2,808	–2,990	–2,417	Income: Debit	78ah*d*
–520	–1,440	–781	–689	–718	–408	–464	–506	–4,995	–4,963	–2,671	–1,634	–1,120	–2,453	–2,448	*Balance on Gds, Serv. & Inc.*	78ai*d*
65	75	105	117	130	1,595	2,604	2,866	2,694	2,871	364	160	335	379	590	Current Transfers, n.i.e.: Credit	78aj*d*
—	—	—	—	—	–808	–1,737	–2,008	–1,961	–1,961	–222	–214	–197	–231	–243	Current Transfers: Debit	78ak*d*
—	—	—	—	—	—	—	—	—	—	59	156	117	189	29	Capital Account, n.i.e.	78bc*d*
—	—	—	—	—	—	—	—	—	—	80	266	266	408	509	Capital Account, n.i.e.: Credit	78ba*d*
—	—	—	—	—	—	—	—	—	—	–20	–110	–149	–219	–480	Capital Account: Debit	78bb*d*
1,066	1,388	235	680	901	–801	1,474	416	6,083	3,370	7,080	–687	658	3,017	4,667	Financial Account, n.i.e.	78bj*d*
—	—	—	—	—	—	—	—	–11	–49	–43	4	–433	–478	–250	Direct Investment Abroad	78bd*d*
—	—	—	—	—	—	1,462	1,479	2,350	1,144	4,519	2,274	2,167	2,037	1,951	Dir. Invest. in Rep. Econ., n.i.e.	78be*d*
—	—	—	—	—	—	—	—	–8	6	–1	–35	–134	–93	–75	Portfolio Investment Assets	78bf*d*
—	—	—	—	—	—	—	—	—	–10	....	–15	–32	–45	16	Equity Securities	78bk*d*
—	—	—	—	—	—	—	—	–8	16	–1	–20	–102	–48	–91	Debt Securities	78bl*d*
—	—	—	—	—	—	—	—	3,927	2,458	2,213	–396	–914	1,925	2,065	Portfolio Investment Liab., n.i.e.	78bg*d*
—	—	—	—	—	—	—	—	46	224	....	359	1,004	556	1,191	Equity Securities	78bm*d*
—	—	—	—	—	—	—	—	3,881	2,234	2,213	–754	–1,918	1,369	874	Debt Securities	78bn*d*
....	....	....	....	....	....	....	....	....	....	....	17	12	185	852	Financial Derivatives Assets	78bw*d*
....	....	....	....	....	....	....	....	....	....	....	–1	–4	–38	–899	Financial Derivatives Liabilities	78bx*d*
–424	180	–319	–83	–322	–524	–13	–421	881	362	592	–1,256	–584	–507	–1,151	Other Investment Assets	78bh*d*
....	....	....	....	....	....	....	....	....	....	–15	14	1	4	—	Monetary Authorities	78bo*d*
–225	–127	–153	–95	–95	–524	–136	–899	811	156	27	45	189	75	30	General Government	78bp*d*
–225	–290	–27	–116	–227	—	116	616	–127	191	125	–1,129	–789	–333	–430	Banks	78bq*d*
26	597	–139	128	—	—	6	–138	198	15	456	–185	15	–253	–750	Other Sectors	78br*d*
1,490	1,208	554	763	1,223	–278	25	–642	–1,055	–551	–199	–1,294	549	–13	2,176	Other Investment Liab., n.i.e.	78bi*d*
–612	–340	–573	173	–358	–570	–431	174	54	17	–904	–1,875	–659	–15	286	Monetary Authorities	78bs*d*
1,920	1,020	1,086	517	1,375	292	815	–787	–1,541	–1,761	–438	–331	–106	–288	235	General Government	78bt*d*
182	528	41	73	206	—	–359	–29	–69	365	321	394	1,123	619	522	Banks	78bu*d*
—	—	—	—	—	—	—	—	501	828	823	518	190	–329	1,133	Other Sectors	78bv*d*
–75	109	160	50	–141	10	–82	2	724	209	789	976	32	49	–261	Net Errors and Omissions	78ca*d*
536	132	–281	158	172	–413	1,795	770	2,545	–475	5,399	–1,244	–175	951	2,335	*Overall Balance*	78cb*d*
–536	–132	281	–158	–172	413	–1,795	–770	–2,545	475	–5,399	1,244	175	–951	–2,335	Reserves and Related Items	79da*d*
–441	–82	637	–25	–14	558	–2,700	–763	–2,574	640	–4,614	1,447	175	–790	–2,335	Reserve Assets	79db*d*
–95	–49	–356	–132	–158	–145	905	–7	30	–165	–785	–203	—	–160	—	Use of Fund Credit and Loans	79dc*d*
....	....	....	....	....	....	....	....	....	....	....	....	....	....	....	Exceptional Financing	79de*d*
Millions of US Dollars															International Investment Position	
....	....	....	....	....	....	....	....	....	....	....	....	13,335	15,651	19,336	Assets	79aa*d*
....	....	....	....	....	....	....	....	....	....	....	....	887	1,273	1,482	Direct Investment Abroad	79ab*d*
....	....	....	....	....	....	....	....	....	....	....	....	171	293	367	Portfolio Investment	79ac*d*
....	....	....	....	....	....	....	....	....	....	....	....	32	87	73	Equity Securities	79ad*d*
....	....	....	....	....	....	....	....	....	....	....	....	139	206	294	Debt Securities	79ae*d*
....	....	....	....	....	....	....	....	....	....	....	....	—	9	880	Financial Derivatives	79al*d*
....	....	....	....	....	....	....	....	....	....	....	....	3,841	4,730	5,623	Other Investment	79af*d*
....	....	....	....	....	....	....	....	....	....	....	....	32	23	20	Monetary Authorities	79ag*d*
....	....	....	....	....	....	....	....	....	....	....	....	593	505	468	General Government	79ah*d*
....	....	....	....	....	....	....	....	....	....	....	....	2,323	3,083	3,391	Banks	79ai*d*
....	....	....	....	....	....	....	....	....	....	....	....	893	1,118	1,744	Other Sectors	79aj*d*
....	....	....	....	....	....	....	....	....	....	....	....	8,437	9,348	10,983	Reserve Assets	79ak*d*
....	....	....	....	....	....	....	....	....	....	....	....	41,180	45,574	49,909	Liabilities	79la*d*
....	....	....	....	....	....	....	....	....	....	....	....	16,073	18,505	19,191	Dir. Invest. in Rep. Economy	79lb*d*
....	....	....	....	....	....	....	....	....	....	....	....	12,496	14,534	16,934	Portfolio Investment	79lc*d*
....	....	....	....	....	....	....	....	....	....	....	....	2,582	2,317	4,335	Equity Securities	79ld*d*
....	....	....	....	....	....	....	....	....	....	....	....	9,914	12,217	12,599	Debt Securities	79le*d*
....	....	....	....	....	....	....	....	....	....	....	....	450	11	164	Financial Derivatives	79ll*d*
....	....	....	....	....	....	....	....	....	....	....	....	12,161	12,524	13,621	Other Investment	79lf*d*
....	....	....	....	....	....	....	....	....	....	....	....	1,216	1,094	1,322	Monetary Authorities	79lg*d*
....	....	....	....	....	....	....	....	....	....	....	....	1,635	1,380	1,532	General Government	79lh*d*
....	....	....	....	....	....	....	....	....	....	....	....	4,290	5,185	5,297	Banks	79li*d*
....	....	....	....	....	....	....	....	....	....	....	....	5,019	4,866	5,470	Other Sectors	79lj*d*

Hungary

Government Finance

Billions of Forint:

	code	1970	1971	1972	1973	1974	1975	1976	1977	1978	1979	1980	1981	1982	1983	1984
Deficit (-) or Surplus	80	....	....	....	....	....	....	....	....	....	....	....	−22.1	−16.1	−6.4	15.7
Total Revenue and Grants	81y	....	....	....	....	....	....	....	....	....	....	....	418.1	438.7	485.5	535.2
Revenue	81	....	....	....	....	....	....	....	....	....	....	....	418.1	438.7	485.5	535.2
Grants	81z	....	....	....	....	....	....	....	....	....	....	....	—	—	—	—
Exp. & Lending Minus Repay.	82z	....	....	....	....	....	....	....	....	....	....	....	440.2	454.8	491.9	519.5
Expenditure	82	....	....	....	....	....	....	....	....	....	....	....	438.2	453.8	492.3	519.5
Lending Minus Repayments	83	....	....	....	....	....	....	....	....	....	....	....	2.0	1.0	−.4	—
Total Financing	80h	....	....	....	....	....	....	....	....	....	....	....	22.1	16.1	6.4	−15.7
Total Net Borrowing	84	....	....	....	....	....	....	....	....	....	....	....	16.3	17.8	7.6	−3.1
Net Domestic	84a	....	....	....	....	....	....	....	....	....	....	....	—	14.9	3.5	−4.4
Net Foreign	85a	....	....	....	....	....	....	....	....	....	....	....	16.3	2.9	4.1	1.3
Use of Cash Balances	87	....	....	....	....	....	....	....	....	....	....	....	5.8	−1.7	−1.2	−12.6
Total Debt by Residence	88	....	....	....	....	....	....	....	....	....	....	....	....	....	....	....
Domestic	88a	....	....	....	....	....	....	....	....	....	....	....	....	....	....	....
Foreign	89a	....	....	....	....	....	....	....	....	....	....	....	....	....	....	....
Memorandum Item:																
Privatization Receipts	83a	....	....	....	....	....	....	....	....	....	....	....	....	....	....	....

National Accounts

Billions of Forint

	code	1970	1971	1972	1973	1974	1975	1976	1977	1978	1979	1980	1981	1982	1983	1984
Exports of Goods & Services	90c	.1	.1	.1	.2	.2	.2	.2	.2	243.9	283.3	281.8	308.2	321.8	360.7	402.0
Government Consumption	91f	34.4	37.8	38.6	40.5	46.9	50.2	53.2	57.8	65.8	71.3	74.1	79.1	84.2	90.9	95.3
Gross Fixed Capital Formation	93e	113.1	116.8	123.1	139.2	161.0	161.0	168.2	197.7	214.4	220.8	207.7	206.7	213.9	220.0	225.4
Increase/Decrease(-) in Stocks	93i	11.4	22.8	7.3	4.1	21.3	21.4	21.5	18.8	45.5	11.3	13.6	24.6	27.9	17.1	26.4
Private Consumption	96f	194.1	209.6	223.5	241.7	261.4	286.1	307.3	334.0	361.7	401.2	441.2	477.7	515.1	551.2	600.5
Imports of Goods & Services	98c	−.1	−.1	−.1	−.1	−.2	−.2	−.2	−.3	−301.6	−305.6	−297.4	−316.4	−315.0	−343.6	−371.1
Gross Domestic Product (GDP)	99b	332.5	360.8	391.0	429.0	448.9	482.7	528.9	582.0	629.7	682.3	721.0	779.9	847.9	896.3	978.5
Net National Income	99e	295.9	320.6	347.8	382.9	398.8	427.8	467.1	513.4	553.6	598.9	628.3	683.6	746.8	793.5	868.6
GDP Volume 1976 prices	99b.*p*	373.8	397.1	421.5	450.4	476.8	506.4	528.9	564.5	589.6	605.4	606.7	....	....	....	....
GDP Volume 1981 prices	99b.*p*	....	....	....	....	....	....	....	....	....	....	751.0	779.9	794.5	800.3	821.5
GDP Volume 1988 prices	99b.*p*	....	....	....	....	....	....	....	....	....	....	....	....	....	....	....
GDP Volume 1991 Prices	99b.*p*	....	....	....	....	....	....	....	....	....	....	....	....	....	....	....
GDP Volume (1995=100)	99bv *p*	58.4	62.0	65.8	70.3	74.4	79.1	81.9	88.1	92.1	94.5	94.7	97.5	100.2	101.0	103.6
GDP Deflator (1995=100)	99bi *p*	10.2	10.5	10.7	11.0	10.8	11.0	11.6	11.9	12.3	13.0	13.7	14.4	15.2	16.0	17.0

Millions:

	code	1970	1971	1972	1973	1974	1975	1976	1977	1978	1979	1980	1981	1982	1983	1984
Population	99z	10.34	10.37	10.40	10.43	10.48	10.53	10.59	10.64	10.67	10.70	10.71	10.70	10.68	10.66	10.62

Government Finance

Year Ending December 31

1985	1986	1987	1988	1989	1990	1991	1992	1993	1994	1995	1996	1997	1998	1999		
-10.1	-30.9	-40.3	-3.2	-32.6	16.7	I-95.2	-214.6	-202.9	-310.8	-355.5	-213.1	-383.6	-631.5	-420.0	Deficit (-) or Surplus	80
539.0	606.8	660.4	789.9	926.6	1,105.9	I1,270.5	1,411.1	1,716.1	2,085.4	2,393.6	2,908.9	3,205.9	4,072.5	4,663.1	Total Revenue and Grants	81y
539.0	606.8	652.0	789.9	926.6	1,105.9	I1,270.5	1,411.1	1,716.1	2,085.2	2,393.4	2,908.5	3,205.3	4,065.5	4,649.9	Revenue	81
—	—	8.4				I	—	—	.2	.2	.4	.6	7.0	13.2	Grants	81z
549.1	637.7	700.7	793.1	959.2	1,089.2	I1,365.7	1,625.7	1,919.0	2,396.2	2,749.1	3,122.0	3,589.5	4,704.0	5,083.1	Exp. & Lending Minus Repay.	82z
549.8	636.5	700.1	792.0	957.8	1,088.8	I1,367.1	1,623.1	1,985.6	2,390.9	2,734.4	3,122.1	3,644.0	4,671.6	5,070.0	Expenditure	82
-.7	1.2	.6	1.1	1.4	.4	I-1.4	2.6	-66.6	5.3	14.7	-.1	-54.5	32.4	13.1	Lending Minus Repayments	83
10.1	30.9	40.3	3.2	32.6	-16.7	I95.1	214.6	203.0	310.8	355.5	213.2	....	....	....	Total Financing	80h
.1	31.2	40.3	4.4	32.0	-5.8	I110.8	218.4	221.8	203.9	204.4	380.6	....	....	....	Total Net Borrowing	84
1.2	39.8	47.9	14.9	42.3	4.9	I112.7	217.7	216.7	202.4	198.5	373.7	....	....	....	Net Domestic	84a
-1.1	-8.6	-7.6	-10.5	-10.3	-10.7	I-1.9	.7	5.1	1.5	5.9	6.9	....	....	....	Net Foreign	85a
10.0	-.3	—	-1.2	.6	-10.9	I-15.7	-3.8	-18.8	106.9	151.1	-167.4	....	....	....	Use of Cash Balances	87
....	....	....	....	....	....	I1,850.0	2,310.8	3,181.6	3,801.0	4,781.6	4,959.1	5,405.7	6,161.5	6,890.5	Total Debt by Residence	88
....	....	....	....	....	....	I1,731.2	2,176.9	2,978.9	3,564.5	4,461.7	4,669.2	5,055.4	5,867.3	5,940.0	Domestic	88a
....	....	....	....	....	....	I118.8	133.9	202.7	236.5	319.9	289.9	350.3	294.2	950.5	Foreign	89a

Memorandum Item:

1985	1986	1987	1988	1989	1990	1991	1992	1993	1994	1995	1996	1997	1998	1999		
						—	20.0	7.2	31.0	150.0	219.9	161.9	13.0	4.0	Privatization Receipts	83a

National Accounts

Billions of Forint

1985	1986	1987	1988	1989	1990	1991	1992	1993	1994	1995	1996	1997	1998	1999		
436.2	431.6	464.4	530.4	620.9	650.7	818.4	925.3	937.0	1,262.5	1,914.8	2,678.7	....	....	....	Exports of Goods & Services	90c
104.6	116.0	126.3	168.5	177.7	221.8	I264.7	336.4	491.4	527.1	629.5	694.8	....	....	....	Government Consumption	91f
232.1	261.2	303.5	310.8	372.5	402.4	I522.9	584.7	670.0	878.5	1,059.6	1,470.6	....	....	....	Gross Fixed Capital Formation	93e
26.3	31.6	23.9	53.9	85.6	128.0	I-12.0	-111.7	38.1	90.1	279.7	362.9	....	....	....	Increase/Decrease(-) in Stocks	93i
649.3	695.5	778.5	868.5	1,029.6	1,282.5	I1,746.9	2,141.1	2,639.9	3,151.7	3,715.0	4,392.0	....	....	....	Private Consumption	96f
-414.8	-447.0	-470.3	-491.7	-563.5	-596.1	-842.6	-933.2	-1,228.1	-1,545.1	-2,036.6	-2,753.6	....	....	....	Imports of Goods & Services	98c
1,033.7	1,088.8	1,226.4	1,440.4	1,722.8	2,089.3	I2,498.3	2,942.6	3,548.3	4,364.8	5,561.9	6,823.3	8,461.6	10,162.6	....	Gross Domestic Product (GDP)	99b
919.4	966.9	1,097.7	1,278.9	....	....	....	....	....	....	....	....				Net National Income	99e
															GDP Volume 1976 prices	99b.p
819.4	....	....													GDP Volume 1981 prices	99b.p
1,291.0	1,322.4	1,372.2	I1,440.4	1,458.9	1,407.9	1,240.4	....	....	....	....	....				GDP Volume 1988 prices	99b.p
....	....	....	....	....	....		2,498.3	2,421.8	2,407.8	2,478.8	2,515.7	....	....	....	GDP Volume 1991 Prices	99b.p
103.4	105.9	109.9	I115.9	116.8	112.7	99.3	96.3	95.7	98.5	100.0	....	....	....	....	GDP Volume (1995=100)	99bv p
18.0	18.5	20.1	I22.3	26.5	33.3	I45.2	55.0	66.7	79.6	100.0	....	....	....	....	GDP Deflator (1995=100)	99bi p

Midyear Estimates

1985	1986	1987	1988	1989	1990	1991	1992	1993	1994	1995	1996	1997	1998	1999		
10.58	10.53	10.49	10.44	10.40	10.36	10.35	10.32	10.29	10.26	10.23	10.19	10.15	10.11	10.07	**Population**	99z

(See notes in the back of the book.)

Iceland

		1970	1971	1972	1973	1974	1975	1976	1977	1978	1979	1980	1981	1982	1983	1984
Exchange Rates															*Kronur per SDR:*	
Official Rate	**aa**	.881	.949	1.063	1.013	⅄1.451	1.999	2.204	2.589	4.144	5.202	7.957	⅄9.513	18.339	30.016	39.743
															Kronur per US Dollar:	
Official Rate	**ae**	.881	.874	.979	.840	⅄1.185	1.708	1.897	2.131	3.181	3.949	6.239	⅄8.173	16.625	28.670	40.545
Official Rate	**rf**	.880	.880	.883	.901	1.000	1.537	1.822	1.989	2.711	3.526	4.798	7.224	12.352	24.843	31.694
															Index Numbers (1995=100):	
Official Rate	**ahx**	7,339.6	4,714.6	7,371.6	7,199.4	6,579.7	4,245.2	3,554.1	3,256.7	2,416.3	1,845.0	1,370.3	902.2	544.8	267.1	205.8
Nominal Effective Exchange Rate	**nec**	....	....	....	....	....	....	....	....	....	....	1,516.2	1,127.3	850.1	571.8	304.6	255.4
Real Effective Exchange Rate	**rec**	....	....	....	....	....	....	....	....	....	....	112.1	117.1	124.4	113.4	104.2	111.0
Fund Position															*Millions of SDRs:*	
Quota	**2f.s**	23.0	23.0	23.0	23.0	23.0	23.0	23.0	23.0	29.0	29.0	43.5	43.5	43.5	59.6	59.6
SDRs	**1b.s**	.5	3.0	6.4	6.3	6.3	4.8	1.8	2.7	1.8	.2	1.8	3.4	2.0	.2	.4
Reserve Position in the Fund	**1c.s**	—	5.7	5.8	5.8	—	—	—	—	—	5.4	9.0	9.0	—	4.0	4.0
Total Fund Cred.&Loans Outstg.	**2tl**	1.8	—	—	—	15.5	31.4	56.4	56.4	47.3	34.7	15.7	5.9	22.4	21.5	21.5
International Liquidity											*Millions of US Dollars Unless Otherwise Indicated:*					
Total Reserves minus Gold	**1l.d**	52.7	68.8	83.0	98.4	47.3	45.6	79.4	98.3	135.8	161.9	173.8	229.5	145.2	149.3	127.6
SDRs	**1b.d**	.5	3.2	6.9	7.6	7.7	5.6	2.1	3.2	2.3	.2	2.3	4.0	2.2	.2	.4
Reserve Position in the Fund	**1c.d**	—	6.2	6.2	6.9	—	—	—	—	—	7.1	11.5	10.5	—	4.2	4.0
Foreign Exchange	**1d.d**	52.2	59.4	69.9	83.8	39.6	40.0	77.3	95.1	133.5	154.6	160.0	215.0	143.0	144.9	123.3
Gold (Million Fine Troy Ounces)	**1ad**	.029	.029	.029	.029	.030	.030	.030	.039	.044	.049	.049	.049	.049	.049	.049
Gold (National Valuation)	**1and**	1.0	1.0	1.1	1.2	1.2	1.2	1.2	1.7	2.0	2.2	2.1	2.0	1.9	1.8	1.7
Monetary Authorities: Other Liab.	**4..d**	11.9	15.6	18.3	21.4	28.5	56.5	54.0	31.1	39.5	32.0	26.5	36.0	42.4	55.4	69.3
Deposit Money Banks: Assets	**7a.d**	2.2	1.9	3.4	4.8	10.9	11.7	11.3	13.4	14.8	17.4	25.0	20.2	24.5	26.7	27.6
Liabilities	**7b.d**	5.9	8.2	13.8	21.4	39.6	60.8	60.3	78.1	102.9	126.5	177.9	209.1	222.4	289.4	260.4
Monetary Authorities											*Thousands of Kronur through 1974;*					
Foreign Assets	**11**	47,387	61,171	82,483	84,902	57,448	⅄80	153	213	438	648	1,106	1,889	2,441	4,324	5,234
Claims on Central Government	**12a**	14,952	11,644	16,322	28,600	64,550	⅄137	163	201	347	411	463	545	599	2,022	2,754
Claims on Private Sector	**12d**	6,690	6,763	1,509	1,430	1,620	⅄1	2	3	4	4	15	30	48	92	44
Claims on Deposit Money Banks	**12e**	1,750	6,935	11,467	18,390	69,690	⅄56	85	68	62	95	113	197	1,579	2,018	3,447
Claims on Other Financial Insts	**12f**	5,496	9,175	12,478	13,430	13,270	⅄32	38	36	36	33	38	105	153	251	594
Reserve Money	**14**	56,793	65,226	78,702	115,390	147,220	⅄198	270	410	617	939	1,577	2,612	4,059	7,243	10,009
of which: Currency Outside DMBs	**14a**	14,120	17,194	21,436	27,000	34,530	⅄44	57	88	124	160	224	406	527	770	966
Foreign Liabilities	**16c**	12,033	13,698	18,012	19,940	56,298	⅄159	227	212	322	307	290	351	1,114	2,233	3,666
Central Government Deposits	**16d**	13,495	20,398	29,360	36,540	52,310	⅄43	64	103	237	346	380	660	979	1,862	2,080
Other Items (Net)	**17r**	11,369	16,877	25,025	16,182	32,980	⅄32	40	61	109	185	480	536	1,603	2,284	3,126
Deposit Money Banks											*Thousands of Kronur through 1974;*					
Reserves	**20**	28,990	34,590	44,060	63,530	79,130	⅄108	150	233	381	559	1,045	1,771	2,626	4,277	6,134
Foreign Assets	**21**	1,910	1,690	3,330	4,500	12,950	⅄20	21	29	47	69	156	165	407	765	1,119
Claims on Central Government	**22a**	2,280	2,550	3,780	4,670	6,030	⅄6	9	9	9	20	71	146	264	525	⅄421
Claims on Private Sector	**22d**	142,800	176,150	215,240	293,230	465,430	⅄615	785	1,103	1,646	2,599	4,294	7,313	14,261	26,034	⅄38,749
Claims on Other Financial Insts	**22f**	10,220	12,830	13,420	16,740	21,420	⅄29	37	50	64	74	109	152	265	581	963
Demand Deposits	**24**	32,360	39,450	47,580	68,840	90,150	⅄123	151	217	306	469	786	1,222	1,549	2,928	⅄3,715
Savings Deposits	**25**	126,240	151,980	177,740	230,970	295,680	⅄375	513	732	1,110	1,792	2,993	⅄3,371	6,437	11,634	15,291
Bonds	**26a**	....	....	....	....	....	....	....	....	....	....	....	....	....	....	....
Restricted Deposits	**26b**	1,700	1,940	2,260	3,930	5,100	⅄6	7	9	16	8	9	13	6	11	19
Foreign Liabilities	**26c**	5,220	7,190	13,580	19,890	46,890	⅄104	114	166	327	499	1,110	1,709	3,698	8,297	10,556
Credit from Monetary Authorities	**26g**	18,900	27,410	38,330	58,160	151,170	⅄182	242	333	460	658	994	1,507	4,463	6,939	10,251
Other Items (Net)	**27r**	8,470	7,510	9,390	14,340	16,420	⅄14	11	17	1	16	−7	219	−122	−779	⅄2,743
Monetary Survey											*Thousands of Kronur through 1974;*					
Foreign Assets (Net)	**31n**	32,044	41,973	54,221	49,572	−32,790	⅄−163	−167	−137	−164	−90	−138	−5	−1,964	−5,441	−7,869
Domestic Credit	**32**	168,483	198,254	233,389	321,560	520,010	⅄777	971	1,298	1,869	2,795	4,610	7,631	14,611	27,643	⅄41,445
Claims on Central Govt. (Net)	**32an**	3,277	−6,664	−9,258	−3,270	18,270	⅄100	108	106	118	84	154	31	−116	685	⅄1,095
Claims on Private Sector	**32d**	149,490	182,913	216,749	294,660	467,050	⅄616	788	1,106	1,650	2,604	4,309	7,343	14,309	26,126	⅄38,793
Claims on Other Financial Inst	**32f**	15,716	22,005	25,898	30,170	34,690	⅄61	76	86	100	107	147	257	418	832	1,557
Money	**34**	46,480	56,644	69,016	95,840	124,680	⅄167	208	305	430	629	1,010	1,628	2,076	3,698	⅄4,681
Quasi-Money	**35**	126,240	151,980	177,740	230,970	295,680	⅄375	513	732	1,110	1,792	2,993	3,371	6,437	11,634	15,291
Bonds	**36a**	....	....	....	....	....	....	....	....	....	....	....	....	....	....	—
Other Items (Net)	**37r**	51,663	59,570	76,744	99,082	⅄66,860	⅄72	83	124	156	284	469	758	1,791	2,754	15,601
Money plus Quasi-Money	**35l**	172,720	208,624	246,756	326,810	420,360	⅄542	720	1,038	1,540	2,421	4,003	4,999	8,513	15,332	⅄19,972
Interest Rates															*Percent Per Annum*	
Discount Rate *(End of Period)*	**60**	5.3	5.3	5.3	6.3	7.3	7.3	7.3	14.0	17.0	26.0	28.0	28.0	28.0	22.0	16.5
Money Market Rate	**60b**	....	....	....	....	....	....	....	....	....	....	....	....	....	....	36.90
Treasury Bill Rate	**60c**	....	....	....	....	....	....	....	....	....	....	....	....	....	....	....
Deposit Rate	**60l**	....	....	....	12.0	17.0	17.0	13.6	29.0	42.3	29.5	38.8	38.8	38.3	39.5	18.1
Housing Bond Rate	**60m**	....	....	....	....	....	....	....	....	....	....	....	....	....	....	....
Lending Rate	**60p**	....	....	....	....	....	....	....	....	33.0	42.5	45.0	40.0	46.0	42.8	22.8
Government Bond Yield	**61**	....	....	....	....	....	....	....	....	....	....	....	....	....	....	....
Prices, Production, Labor															*Index Numbers (1995=100):*	
Consumer Prices	**64**	.3	.3	.3	.4	.5	.8	⅄1.1	1.4	2.0	2.9	4.7	7.0	10.6	19.6	25.3
Wages, Hourly	**65**	.3	.3	.4	.5	.7	.9	⅄1.2	1.6	2.5	3.6	5.6	8.6	13.4	20.3	22.6
Total Fish Catch	**66al**	46.0	44.2	46.4	58.0	61.2	66.4	63.2	88.9	101.5	106.4	97.8	93.1	50.9	54.0	98.9
															Number in Thousands:	
Labor Force	**67d**	....	....	....	....	....	....	....	....	....	....	....	....	....	....	....
Employment	**67e**	....	....	....	....	....	....	....	....	....	....	....	....	....	....	....
Unemployment	**67c**	....	....	....	....	....	....	....	....	....	....	....	....	....	....	....
Unemployment Rate (%)	**67r**	....	....	....	....	....	....	....	....	....	....	....	....	....	....	....
International Transactions											*Thousands of Kronur through 1974;*					
Exports	**70**	129,000	131,800	167,000	260,200	328,800	⅄474	735	1,019	1,763	2,786	4,461	6,530	8,479	18,633	23,557
Fish	**70al**	61,700	71,400	78,100	107,600	146,700	⅄262	366	465	810	1,293	1,884	2,945	4,330	8,611	9,989
Fishmeal	**70z**	10,200	9,800	11,600	36,200	32,600	⅄39	55	121	218	269	361	423	235	335	1,547
Imports, c.i.f.	**71**	138,400	184,500	204,200	318,600	525,700	⅄751	857	1,210	1,843	2,913	4,802	7,485	11,647	20,596	26,780
															1995=100	
Volume of Exports	**72**	41	34	42	45	42	45	52	56	66	72	⅄77	75	64	72	74
Volume of Imports	**73**	47	57	60	71	77	65	66	74	81	81	⅄87	92	89	79	85
Unit Value of Exports	**74**	.2	.3	⅄.3	.4	.6	.8	1.1	1.4	2.1	3.1	⅄4.5	6.8	10.8	20.4	24.6
Unit Value of Imports	**75**	.3	.3	⅄.3	.4	.5	.9	1.1	1.3	1.9	3.0	⅄4.6	6.8	10.7	21.2	26.3

1985	1986	1987	1988	1989	1990	1991	1992	1993	1994	1995	1996	1997	1998	1999		
End of Period															**Exchange Rates**	
46.200	49.221	50.589	62.198	80.387	78.801	79.561	87.890	99.899	99.708	96.964	96.185	97.389	97.605	99.576	Official Rate	aa
End of Period (ae) Period Average (rf)																
42.060	40.240	35.660	46.220	61.170	55.390	55.620	63.920	72.730	68.300	65.230	66.890	72.180	69.320	72.550	Official Rate	ae
41.508	41.104	38.677	43.014	57.042	58.284	58.996	57.546	67.603	69.944	64.692	66.500	70.904	70.958	72.335	Official Rate	rf
Period Averages																
155.9	157.3	167.3	151.6	114.1	111.1	109.8	112.6	96.0	92.5	100.0	97.2	91.2	91.2	89.4	Official Rate	ahx
201.4	168.8	159.7	138.5	109.5	100.6	102.7	105.3	100.0	98.9	100.0	100.3	102.6	105.2	104.8	Nominal Effective Exchange Rate	nec
110.1	109.8	118.6	124.2	113.3	112.0	114.8	115.3	106.8	100.3	100.0	100.5	102.5	105.4	107.0	Real Effective Exchange Rate	rec
End of Period															**Fund Position**	
59.6	59.6	59.6	59.6	59.6	59.6	59.6	85.3	85.3	85.3	85.3	85.3	85.3	85.3	117.6	Quota	2f.s
.4	.2	1.9	1.0	—	.3	.1	—	—	.1	—	—	—	—	—	SDRs	1b.s
4.0	4.0	4.0	4.0	4.0	4.0	4.0	10.5	10.5	10.5	10.5	10.5	10.5	10.5	18.6	Reserve Position in the Fund	1c.s
21.5	10.8	—	—	—	—	—	—	—	—	—	—	—	—	—	Total Fund Cred.&Loans Outstg.	2tl
End of Period															**International Liquidity**	
205.5	309.8	311.3	290.7	337.3	436.1	449.5	498.3	426.4	292.9	308.1	453.7	383.7	426.4	478.4	Total Reserves minus Gold	1l.d
.4	.2	2.7	1.3	—	.4	.1	—	.1	.1	—	—	—	—	—	SDRs	1b.d
4.4	4.9	5.7	5.4	5.3	5.7	5.8	14.4	14.4	15.3	15.6	15.1	14.2	14.8	25.5	Reserve Position in the Fund	1c.d
200.7	304.7	302.9	284.0	332.0	430.0	443.6	483.9	412.0	277.5	292.5	438.6	369.5	411.6	452.9	Foreign Exchange	1d.d
.049	.049	.049	.049	.049	.049	.049	.049	.049	.049	.049	.049	.049	.056	.056	Gold (Million Fine Troy Ounces)	1ad
1.9	2.1	2.4	2.3	2.2	2.4	2.5	2.4	2.4	2.5	2.6	2.7	2.6	2.8	....	Gold (National Valuation)	1and
13.3	25.8	22.2	40.3	16.7	17.1	20.3	12.4	36.8	137.5	176.5	75.5	75.1	130.9	....	Monetary Authorities: Other Liab.	4..d
40.9	43.6	63.9	63.7	62.3	81.0	83.5	70.8	94.0	118.7	79.9	108.9	153.4	162.7	188.8	Deposit Money Banks: Assets	7a.d
422.0	418.5	629.8	754.1	696.0	705.4	714.8	682.4	593.0	464.1	419.4	639.0	875.8	1,477.8	1,989.9	Liabilities	7b.d
Millions of Kronur Beginning 1975: End of Period															**Monetary Authorities**	
8,723	12,532	11,167	13,563	20,797	24,261	25,248	32,017	31,318	24,347	25,961	36,151	33,274	35,136	....	Foreign Assets	11
4,830	3,264	6,017	10,707	10,800	5,112	10,882	6,751	12,865	24,546	18,476	10,534	12,852	5,011	....	Claims on Central Government	12a
49	128	357	445	922	672	412	380	330	408	413	487	142	113	....	Claims on Private Sector	12d
4,603	5,634	4,995	4,565	4,726	4,319	3,342	3,983	2,630	2,226	5,353	1,878	6,496	19,600	....	Claims on Deposit Money Banks	12e
670	859	1,091	1,196	873	1,866	603	531	639	4,490	3,380	3,443	3,472	7,770	....	Claims on Other Financial Insts	12f
12,362	15,463	16,489	19,087	23,550	21,097	21,637	22,328	20,333	20,949	17,164	21,691	24,153	24,690	....	Reserve Money	14
1,251	1,734	2,244	2,631	2,975	3,057	3,239	3,593	3,906	4,641	5,169	5,475	5,751	6,322	....	*of which: Currency Outside DMBs*	14a
1,553	1,567	792	1,862	1,019	950	1,127	792	2,678	9,389	11,513	5,049	5,418	9,073	....	Foreign Liabilities	16c
2,184	1,286	2,351	2,428	2,226	2,448	5,118	5,512	7,350	7,419	6,177	6,850	6,438	13,176	....	Central Government Deposits	16d
3,845	4,421	4,154	7,099	11,321	11,735	12,605	15,031	17,421	18,259	18,728	18,904	20,226	20,691	....	Other Items (Net)	17r
Millions of Kronur Beginning 1975: End of Period															**Deposit Money Banks**	
7,365	9,955	10,747	11,899	19,525	15,042	16,706	14,474	11,747	11,540	10,325	13,418	14,100	13,990	29,026	Reserves	20
1,719	1,753	2,277	2,943	3,810	4,488	4,644	4,524	6,835	8,105	5,213	7,285	11,076	11,276	13,699	Foreign Assets	21
482	458	1,813	2,644	8,022	18,416	18,848	20,577	26,746	19,168	11,432	13,241	10,578	6,287	7,271	Claims on Central Government	22a
51,266	59,970	84,854	116,711	147,389	157,123	175,155	187,675	193,643	196,262	208,982	236,720	348,883	376,127	461,004	Claims on Private Sector	22d
1,230	1,567	1,999	2,398	2,521	2,642	3,227	3,162	4,265	4,485	1,750	1,167	1,680	375	934	Claims on Other Financial Insts	22f
4,707	6,863	8,965	10,376	16,825	21,587	26,317	26,351	27,663	30,313	33,146	36,081	42,600	51,852	63,346	Demand Deposits	24
24,849	31,968	44,293	59,591	92,291	103,258	118,696	124,088	132,526	132,482	133,341	140,725	150,977	171,434	198,763	Savings Deposits	25
317	1,238	3,084	7,928	13,963	17,453	19,180	20,589	22,699	22,337	24,095	32,166	40,731	53,419	62,938	Bonds	26a
24	46	68	83	66	—	19	—	—	—	6	2	5	2	1	Restricted Deposits	26b
17,751	16,842	22,459	34,853	42,575	39,072	39,755	43,616	43,127	31,697	27,356	42,741	63,215	102,438	144,370	Foreign Liabilities	26c
5,656	6,035	5,038	4,578	4,737	3,625	3,335	2,520	1,600	4,833	4,860	1,954	6,480	21,000	30,797	Credit from Monetary Authorities	26g
2,829	1,472	5,384	7,155	7,291	8,437	9,282	11,210	13,689	15,563	15,018	18,287	18,198	8,053	11,718	Other Items (Net)	27r
Millions of Kronur Beginning 1975: End of Period															**Monetary Survey**	
-8,862	-4,124	-9,806	-20,208	-18,987	-11,272	-10,990	-7,867	-7,652	-8,635	-7,695	-4,354	-24,282	-65,099	....	Foreign Assets (Net)	31n
56,342	64,959	93,781	131,673	168,300	183,383	204,009	213,565	231,138	241,940	238,256	258,743	371,168	382,507	....	Domestic Credit	32
3,128	2,436	5,479	10,922	16,595	21,080	24,612	21,816	32,260	36,295	23,731	16,925	16,991	-1,878	....	Claims on Central Govt. (Net)	32an
51,315	60,098	85,211	117,156	148,311	157,795	175,567	188,055	193,973	196,670	209,395	237,207	349,025	376,240	....	Claims on Private Sector	32d
1,900	2,426	3,090	3,594	3,394	4,508	3,830	3,693	4,904	8,975	5,130	4,610	5,152	8,145	....	Claims on Other Financial Inst	32f
5,958	8,597	11,209	13,007	19,800	24,644	29,556	29,944	31,569	34,954	38,315	41,556	48,351	58,174	....	Money	34
24,849	31,968	44,293	59,591	92,291	103,258	118,696	124,088	132,526	132,482	133,341	140,725	150,977	171,434	198,763	Quasi-Money	35
317	1,238	3,084	7,928	13,963	17,453	19,180	20,589	22,699	22,337	24,095	32,166	40,731	53,419	62,938	Bonds	36a
11,497	10,114	13,148	18,907	19,739	22,476	23,592	29,039	34,760	41,197	34,930	40,067	42,715	34,524	....	Other Items (Net)	37r
30,807	40,565	55,502	72,598	112,091	127,902	148,252	154,032	164,095	167,436	171,656	182,281	199,328	229,608	....	Money plus Quasi-Money	35l
Percent Per Annum															**Interest Rates**	
30.0	21.0	49.2	24.1	38.4	21.0	21.0	I16.6	....	4.7	5.9	5.7	6.6	....	....	Discount Rate *(End of Period)*	60
....	....	31.52	34.49	21.58	12.73	14.85	12.38	8.61	4.96	6.58	6.96	7.38	8.12	9.24	Money Market Rate	60b
....	....	....	26.39	23.00	12.92	14.25	I11.30	8.35	4.95	7.22	6.97	7.04	7.40	8.61	Treasury Bill Rate	60c
24.7	12.2	15.5	17.4	12.3	4.3	4.9	1.4	....	....	I3.4	3.3	3.3	....	....	Deposit Rate	60l
....	....	....	....	....	....	....	....	....	5.75	5.80	5.78	5.30	4.71	4.78	Housing Bond Rate	60m
32.6	18.8	26.6	30.3	28.0	16.2	17.5	13.1	14.1	10.6	11.6	12.4	12.9	12.8	13.3	Lending Rate	60p
....	....	....	....	....	....	....	7.75	6.80	5.02	7.18	5.61	5.49	4.73	4.28	Government Bond Yield	61
Period Averages															**Prices, Production, Labor**	
33.3	40.6	47.8	60.1	72.6	83.8	89.5	93.1	96.9	98.4	100.0	102.3	104.1	105.9	109.3	Consumer Prices	64
29.9	37.5	62.6	79.4	90.0	I96.9	98.4	98.5	96.3	96.8	100.0	....	....	....	....	Wages, Hourly	65
107.2	105.1	102.3	110.5	88.6	96.7	64.3	99.6	109.0	93.7	100.0	127.6	145.0	99.4	93.6	Total Fish Catch	66al
Period Averages																
....	....	....	....	....	....	....	....	....	145	149	148	148	152	....	Labor Force	67d
....	....	....	....	....	....	137	137	137	138	142	142	142	148	154	Employment	67e
1	1	1	1	2	2	2	4	6	6	7	6	5	4	....	Unemployment	67c
.9	.7	.4	.6	1.7	1.8	1.5	3.0	4.3	4.7	4.9	4.4	3.9	2.8	....	Unemployment Rate (%)	67r
Millions of Kronur Beginning 1975															**International Transactions**	
33,826	45,093	53,053	61,674	79,131	92,624	91,560	87,833	94,711	113,279	116,613	108,977	131,228	145,008	145,132	Exports	70
15,330	19,557	24,190	25,941	33,695	43,895	49,189	42,599	45,754	54,644	50,535	46,030	46,712	54,722	60,028	Fish	70al
1,879	2,671	2,222	3,699	3,934	3,369	1,700	4,415	5,015	4,757	4,789	8,792	9,460	9,896	7,404	Fishmeal	70z
37,600	45,910	61,237	68,996	80,284	97,559	104,129	96,895	90,775	102,499	113,388	135,165	141,355	176,521	181,321	Imports, c.i.f.	71
1995=100																
82	90	94	93	97	95	88	87	91	102	100	109	111	108	....	Volume of Exports	72
92	99	124	117	104	105	110	101	87	94	100	116	124	154	....	Volume of Imports	73
32.7	40.2	45.8	52.1	64.2	78.6	91.0	88.3	91.3	95.4	100.0	98.4	99.6	....	....	Unit Value of Exports	74
34.6	39.2	42.4	50.3	66.0	79.2	83.9	83.3	90.9	96.1	100.0	102.7	103.4	....	....	Unit Value of Imports	75

Iceland

176		1970	1971	1972	1973	1974	1975	1976	1977	1978	1979	1980	1981	1982	1983	1984
Balance of Payments																*Millions of US Dollars:*
Current Account, n.i.e.	78al*d*	....	....	....	....	....	....	-24	-48	20	-19	-76	-148	-261	-56	-133
Goods: Exports f.o.b.	78aa*d*	....	....	....	....	....	....	402	513	640	780	920	896	686	742	743
Goods: Imports f.o.b.	78ab*d*	....	....	....	....	....	....	-428	-565	-618	-754	-900	-926	-838	-722	-757
Trade Balance	78ac*d*	....	....	....	....	....	....	-26	-52	22	26	20	-29	-152	20	-13
Services: Credit	78ad*d*	....	....	....	....	....	....	173	212	262	293	280	303	341	343	347
Services: Debit	78ae*d*	....	....	....	....	....	....	-117	-150	-192	-254	-263	-282	-309	-281	-311
Balance on Goods & Services	78af*d*	....	....	....	....	....	....	29	10	92	65	37	-8	-120	82	23
Income: Credit	78ag*d*	....	....	....	....	....	....	3	5	6	12	14	22	28	16	16
Income: Debit	78ah*d*	....	....	....	....	....	....	-56	-63	-78	-95	-126	-159	-166	-153	-171
Balance on Gds, Serv. & Inc.	78ai*d*	....	....	....	....	....	....	-23	-48	20	-18	-75	-145	-258	-55	-132
Current Transfers, n.i.e.: Credit	78aj*d*	....	....	....	....	....	....	—	1	1	1	1	1	1	1	2
Current Transfers: Debit	78ak*d*	....	....	....	....	....	....	-1	-1	-1	-2	-2	-4	-4	-3	-3
Capital Account, n.i.e.	78bc*d*	....	....	....	....	....	....	1	—	-1	-2	-3	—	-2	-1	1
Capital Account, n.i.e.: Credit	78ba*d*	....	....	....	....	....	....	1	1	1	1	1	2	1	1	6
Capital Account: Debit	78bb*d*	....	....	....	....	....	....	—	-1	-2	-3	-4	-3	-3	-2	-4
Financial Account, n.i.e.	78bj*d*	....	....	....	....	....	....	33	85	64	95	157	234	214	66	145
Direct Investment Abroad	78bd*d*	....	....	....	....	....	....	—	—	—	—	—	—	—	—	—
Dir. Invest. in Rep. Econ., n.i.e.	78be*d*	....	....	....	....	....	....	5	4	8	3	22	53	36	-23	14
Portfolio Investment Assets	78bf*d*	....	....	....	....	....	....	—	—	—	—	—	—	—	—	—
Equity Securities	78bk*d*	....	....	....	....	....	....	—	—	—	—	—	—	—	—	—
Debt Securities	78bl*d*	....	....	....	....	....	....	—	—	—	—	—	—	—	—	—
Portfolio Investment Liab., n.i.e.	78bg*d*	....	....	....	....	....	....	31	45	-5	—	—	—	—	—	—
Equity Securities	78bm*d*	....	....	....	....	....	....	—	—	—	—	—	—	—	—	—
Debt Securities	78bn*d*	....	....	....	....	....	....	31	45	-5	—	—	—	—	—	—
Financial Derivatives Assets	78bw*d*	....	....	....	....	....	....	....	....	....	....	....	....	....	....	....
Financial Derivatives Liabilities	78bx*d*	....	....	....	....	....	....	....	....	....	....	....	....	....	....	....
Other Investment Assets	78bh*d*	....	....	....	....	....	....	-11	-20	-28	-34	-56	-21	-1	-44	-26
Monetary Authorities	78bo*d*	....	....	....	....	....	....	....	....	....	....	....	....	....	....	....
General Government	78bp*d*	....	....	....	....	....	....	—	—	—	—	—	—	—	—	—
Banks	78bq*d*	....	....	....	....	....	....	-2	-1	1	-2	-12	2	-8	-1	-16
Other Sectors	78br*d*	....	....	....	....	....	....	-9	-19	-28	-32	-44	-23	7	-43	-10
Other Investment Liab., n.i.e.	78bi*d*	....	....	....	....	....	....	8	56	88	126	191	202	179	133	157
Monetary Authorities	78bs*d*	....	....	....	....	....	....	-12	-13	8	-5	-3	12	10	9	18
General Government	78bt*d*	....	....	....	....	....	....	34	44	51	80	73	98	170	117	135
Banks	78bu*d*	....	....	....	....	....	....	—	6	5	29	19	30	18	29	-7
Other Sectors	78bv*d*	....	....	....	....	....	....	-13	19	25	22	102	61	-19	-22	10
Net Errors and Omissions	78ca*d*	....	....	....	....	....	....	-6	-20	-32	-37	-44	-14	-47	2	-28
Overall Balance	78cb*d*	....	....	....	....	....	....	4	16	51	37	34	72	-96	11	-15
Reserves and Related Items	79da*d*	....	....	....	....	....	....	-4	-16	-51	-37	-34	-72	96	-11	15
Reserve Assets	79db*d*	....	....	....	....	....	....	-33	-16	-40	-20	-10	-60	78	-10	15
Use of Fund Credit and Loans	79dc*d*	....	....	....	....	....	....	29	—	-12	-16	-25	-12	18	-1	—
Exceptional Financing	79de*d*	....	....	....	....	....	....	....	....	....	....	....	....	....	....	....
International Investment Position																*Millions of US Dollars*
Assets	79aa*d*	....	....	....	....	....	....	....	....	....	....	....	....	....	....	....
Direct Investment Abroad	79ab*d*	....	....	....	....	....	....	....	....	....	....	....	....	....	....	....
Portfolio Investment	79ac*d*	....	....	....	....	....	....	....	....	....	....	....	....	....	....	....
Equity Securities	79ad*d*	....	....	....	....	....	....	....	....	....	....	....	....	....	....	....
Debt Securities	79ae*d*	....	....	....	....	....	....	....	....	....	....	....	....	....	....	....
Financial Derivatives	79al*d*	....	....	....	....	....	....	....	....	....	....	....	....	....	....	....
Other Investment	79af*d*	....	....	....	....	....	....	....	....	....	....	....	....	....	....	....
Monetary Authorities	79ag*d*	....	....	....	....	....	....	....	....	....	....	....	....	....	....	....
General Government	79ah*d*	....	....	....	....	....	....	....	....	....	....	....	....	....	....	....
Banks	79ai*d*	....	....	....	....	....	....	....	....	....	....	....	....	....	....	....
Other Sectors	79aj*d*	....	....	....	....	....	....	....	....	....	....	....	....	....	....	....
Reserve Assets	79ak*d*	....	....	....	....	....	....	....	....	....	....	....	....	....	....	....
Liabilities	79la*d*	....	....	....	....	....	....	....	....	....	....	....	....	....	....	....
Dir. Invest. in Rep. Economy	79lb*d*	....	....	....	....	....	....	....	....	....	....	....	....	....	....	....
Portfolio Investment	79lc*d*	....	....	....	....	....	....	....	....	....	....	....	....	....	....	....
Equity Securities	79ld*d*	....	....	....	....	....	....	....	....	....	....	....	....	....	....	....
Debt Securities	79le*d*	....	....	....	....	....	....	....	....	....	....	....	....	....	....	....
Financial Derivatives	79ll*d*	....	....	....	....	....	....	....	....	....	....	....	....	....	....	....
Other Investment	79lf*d*	....	....	....	....	....	....	....	....	....	....	....	....	....	....	....
Monetary Authorities	79lg*d*	....	....	....	....	....	....	....	....	....	....	....	....	....	....	....
General Government	79lh*d*	....	....	....	....	....	....	....	....	....	....	....	....	....	....	....
Banks	79li*d*	....	....	....	....	....	....	....	....	....	....	....	....	....	....	....
Other Sectors	79lj*d*	....	....	....	....	....	....	....	....	....	....	....	....	....	....	....
Government Finance																*Thousands of Kronur through 1974;*
Deficit (-) or Surplus	80	....	....	-17,950	-29,960	-66,330	I -122	-69	-173	-156	-193	-193	-172	-958	-1,998	-1,610
Revenue	81	....	....	193,400	271,940	410,500	I 586	773	1,071	1,719	2,629	4,090	6,621	10,767	17,510	23,628
Grants Received	81z	....	....	100	13,680	6,980	I 2	—	—	—	1	1	3	5	4	6
Expenditure	82	....	....	188,920	286,160	451,460	I 638	741	1,086	1,720	2,644	4,015	6,383	10,454	19,094	22,754
Lending Minus Repayments	83	....	....	22,530	29,420	32,350	I 72	100	159	155	179	268	413	1,276	417	2,490
Financing																
Domestic	84a	....	....	-1,780	14,480	49,250	I 84	15	51	115	47	76	-22	-63	733	-810
Foreign	85a	....	....	19,700	15,480	17,080	I 38	54	122	42	146	117	194	1,021	1,265	2,421
Debt: Domestic	88a	....	....	36,600	42,360	57,280	I 137	200	286	411	777	1,530	2,284	3,515	6,525	7,513
Foreign	89a	....	....	72,920	80,100	134,900	I 222	316	522	920	1,304	2,118	2,756	6,741	12,487	19,498
National Accounts																*Thousands of Kronur through 1974;*
Exports of Goods & Services	90c	208,100	220,300	259,000	369,300	474,750	I 718	1,048	1,443	2,482	3,810	5,746	8,724	12,466	26,683	33,765
Government Consumption	91f	56,840	74,750	104,170	141,600	229,200	I 335	449	653	1,074	1,638	2,546	4,195	6,942	12,050	14,701
Gross Fixed Capital Formation	93e	104,100	162,200	194,000	291,260	455,000	I 636	780	1,090	1,546	2,248	3,927	5,929	9,726	14,839	19,337
Increase/Decrease(-) in Stocks	93i	-3,000	14,130	-10,000	-3,000	25,340	I 37	-18	66	-39	51	80	253	913	-1,070	-661
Private Consumption	96f	268,950	341,000	419,000	556,830	845,400	I 1,188	1,626	2,342	3,656	5,501	8,937	14,361	23,864	41,016	55,872
Imports of Goods & Services	98c	-196,700	-253,900	-267,600	-383,850	-610,900	I -883	-1,019	-1,452	-2,242	-3,631	-5,648	-8,936	-14,329	-25,275	-33,871
Gross Domestic Product (GDP)	99b	438,000	558,000	698,000	972,000	1,418,000	I 2,031	2,866	4,142	6,477	9,617	15,588	24,526	39,582	68,243	89,143
Net Factor Inc/Pmts(-) Abroad	98.n	-4,801	-5,101	-8,902	-11,803	-19,205	I -49	-73	-88	-161	-244	-411	-811	-1,247	-2,671	-4,024
Gross National Income (GNI)	99a	433,000	553,000	689,000	960,000	1,399,000	I 1,982	2,793	4,054	6,316	9,373	15,177	23,715	38,335	65,572	85,119
Net National Income	99e	372,000	486,000	604,000	846,000	1,227,000	I 1,699	2,422	3,565	5,563	8,235	13,367	20,817	33,235	56,242	73,710
GDP Volume 1985 prices	99b.*p*	56,320	63,683	67,365	71,257	75,761	76,450	81,097	88,325	94,483	99,641	106,621	111,256	113,478	....	....
GDP Volume 1990 Prices	99b.*p*	....	....	....	....	....	....	....	....	....	....	....	....	295,794	289,609	301,394
GDP Volume (1995=100)	99bv*p*	39.0	44.1	46.6	49.3	52.4	52.9	56.1	61.1	65.4	69.0	73.8	77.0	78.6	76.9	80.0
GDP Deflator (1995=100)	99bi*p*	.2	.3	.3	.4	.6	.8	1.1	1.5	2.2	3.1	4.7	7.1	11.2	19.7	24.7
																Millions:
Population	99z	.21	.21	.21	.21	.22	.22	.22	.22	.22	.23	.23	.23	.23	.24	.24

544 INTERNATIONAL FINANCIAL STATISTICS YEARBOOK 2000

1985	1986	1987	1988	1989	1990	1991	1992	1993	1994	1995	1996	1997	1998	1999		
Minus Sign Indicates Debit															Balance of Payments	
–115	16	–188	–231	–102	–126	–273	–158	42	109	54	–117	–125	–560	–591	Current Account, n.i.e.	78al *d*
814	1,097	1,376	1,425	1,402	1,588	1,552	1,529	1,398	1,561	1,804	1,890	1,855	1,927	2,009	Goods: Exports f.o.b.	78aa *d*
–814	–1,000	–1,428	–1,439	–1,267	–1,509	–1,599	–1,527	–1,217	–1,288	–1,598	–1,871	–1,850	–2,279	–2,316	Goods: Imports f.o.b.	78ab *d*
—	97	–52	–14	134	79	–47	2	181	273	206	19	5	–352	–307	*Trade Balance*	78ac *d*
394	453	542	532	517	562	569	587	602	615	689	768	844	947	968	Services: Credit	78ad *d*
–363	–374	–510	–536	–495	–556	–605	–591	–594	–577	–641	–739	–800	–964	–1,044	Services: Debit	78ae *d*
31	176	–20	–18	156	85	–83	–2	189	311	254	48	49	–369	–383	*Balance on Goods & Services*	78af *d*
16	20	28	26	33	86	85	101	91	73	91	113	104	123	114	Income: Credit	78ag *d*
–163	–183	–198	–229	–270	–295	–266	–254	–235	–267	–286	–272	–273	–298	–313	Income: Debit	78ah *d*
–115	13	–190	–220	–81	–124	–264	–155	45	117	59	–111	–120	–544	–582	*Balance on Gds, Serv. & Inc.*	78ai *d*
3	6	7	9	11	26	13	19	18	12	15	10	17	4	5	Current Transfers, n.i.e.: Credit	78aj *d*
–2	–3	–5	–20	–32	–28	–22	–22	–21	–20	–20	–16	–22	–20	–14	Current Transfers: Debit	78ak *d*
—	1	–3	10	18	2	3	–2	1	–6	–3	–1	1	–5	—	Capital Account, n.i.e.	78bc *d*
3	6	10	18	26	17	15	11	12	6	13	10	11	9	18	Capital Account, n.i.e.: Credit	78ba *d*
–4	–5	–13	–9	–8	–15	–12	–13	–11	–12	–16	–11	–10	–14	–18	Capital Account: Debit	78bb *d*
233	100	232	227	125	240	264	242	–55	–293	–17	303	197	679	967	Financial Account, n.i.e.	78bj *d*
—	–2	–1	–1	–8	–13	–31	–10	–14	–23	–25	–62	–48	–74	–69	Direct Investment Abroad	78bd *d*
24	9	2	–15	–27	22	19	–11	–1	1	–10	80	144	150	90	Dir. Invest. in Rep. Econ., n.i.e.	78be *d*
—	—	—	—	1	—	–4	–4	–34	–73	–76	–64	–201	–302	–443	Portfolio Investment Assets	78bf *d*
—	—	—	—	—	....	–4	–4	–15	–25	–55	–81	–180	–253	–344	Equity Securities	78bk *d*
—	—	—	—	1	—	—	—	–19	–48	–21	17	–21	–49	–99	Debt Securities	78bl *d*
—	—	—	—	—	26	187	286	303	242	214	176	–38	66	1,035	Portfolio Investment Liab., n.i.e.	78bg *d*
—	—	—	—	—	....	....	....	....	....	—	1	–1	14	56	Equity Securities	78bm *d*
—	—	—	—	—	26	187	286	303	242	214	175	–37	52	979	Debt Securities	78bn *d*
....	....	....	....	....	—	—	7	....	–49	–17	–1	–1	–1	60	Financial Derivatives Assets	78bw *d*
....	....	....	....	....	....	....	–7	....	54	16	—	—	—	–57	Financial Derivatives Liabilities	78bx *d*
41	—	–55	–65	12	–47	4	30	–28	–31	22	–30	–162	3	–172	Other Investment Assets	78bh *d*
....	....	....	....	....	....	....	....	....	....	....	....	....	....	....	Monetary Authorities	78bo *d*
—	—	—	—	—	....	....	—	....	....	....	....	....	....	....	General Government	78bp *d*
6	—	–11	–7	3	–26	–3	13	–28	–16	47	–37	–86	28	–92	Banks	78bq *d*
35	—	–44	–58	9	–21	7	17	—	–15	–25	7	–76	–25	–80	Other Sectors	78br *d*
168	94	285	308	148	252	89	–49	–281	–414	–141	204	503	837	523	Other Investment Liab., n.i.e.	78bi *d*
–53	2	–16	20	–25	–1	2	1	23	39	21	–100	–1	55	–3	Monetary Authorities	78bs *d*
118	103	83	144	192	21	72	–117	–46	–76	58	–17	34	81	47	General Government	78bt *d*
15	9	76	74	63	–21	10	–9	–69	–158	–54	288	306	422	440	Banks	78bu *d*
89	–20	142	69	–82	253	5	76	–189	–219	–166	33	164	279	39	Other Sectors	78bv *d*
–53	–18	–59	–4	13	–42	15	–3	–47	40	–30	–32	–117	–82	–301	Net Errors and Omissions	78ca *d*
64	99	–18	1	55	74	9	79	–59	–150	4	153	–44	32	75	*Overall Balance*	78cb *d*
–64	–99	18	–1	–55	–74	–9	–79	59	150	–4	–153	44	–32	–75	Reserves and Related Items	79da *d*
–64	–86	32	–1	–55	–74	–9	–79	59	150	–4	–153	44	–32	–75	Reserve Assets	79db *d*
—	–13	–14	—	—	—	—	—	—	—	—	—	—	—	—	Use of Fund Credit and Loans	79dc *d*
....	....	....	....	....	....	....	....	....	....	....	....	....	....	....	Exceptional Financing	79de *d*
Millions of US Dollars															International Investment Position	
....	....	....	588	648	759	777	783	786	872	1,008	1,306	1,601	2,196	3,348	Assets	79aa *d*
....	....	....	57	58	75	101	99	114	149	180	242	275	340	413	Direct Investment Abroad	79ab *d*
....	—	—	—	—	—	4	9	41	118	198	264	488	967	1,919	Portfolio Investment	79ac *d*
....	—	—	—	—	—	4	9	22	48	103	183	398	830	1,715	Equity Securities	79ad *d*
....	—	—	—	—	—	—	—	19	71	95	81	90	137	205	Debt Securities	79ae *d*
....	—	—	—	—	12	13	4	4	59	81	81	76	78	16	Financial Derivatives	79al *d*
....	187	258	241	261	245	218	175	201	248	235	259	376	385	506	Other Investment	79af *d*
....	—	—	3	10	—	—	—	—	—	—	—	—	—	—	Monetary Authorities	79ag *d*
....	—	—	—	—	—	—	—	—	—	—	—	—	—	—	General Government	79ah *d*
....	37	54	59	57	90	80	61	94	119	80	115	164	142	184	Banks	79ai *d*
....	150	204	179	194	155	138	114	107	129	155	143	212	243	321	Other Sectors	79aj *d*
....	312	313	290	329	427	441	496	426	298	315	461	386	427	495	Reserve Assets	79ak *d*
....	....	....	3,142	3,266	3,771	4,089	4,135	4,123	4,245	4,478	4,719	5,008	6,344	7,579	Liabilities	79la *d*
....	....	....	95	109	147	166	124	117	127	129	199	332	458	499	Dir. Invest. in Rep. Economy	79lb *d*
....	—	—	—	—	844	1,028	1,251	1,550	1,882	2,129	2,213	2,039	2,200	3,121	Portfolio Investment	79lc *d*
....	—	—	—	—	—	—	—	—	—	—	1	—	14	66	Equity Securities	79ld *d*
....	—	—	—	—	844	1,028	1,251	1,550	1,882	2,128	2,212	2,039	2,186	3,054	Debt Securities	79le *d*
....	—	—	—	—	12	12	4	4	56	74	74	74	74	16	Financial Derivatives	79ll *d*
....	2,297	2,891	3,047	3,157	2,768	2,883	2,756	2,452	2,180	2,147	2,233	2,563	3,613	3,943	Other Investment	79lf *d*
....	40	23	41	17	6	12	12	32	82	103	2	1	57	51	Monetary Authorities	79lg *d*
....	756	879	904	1,004	347	468	395	333	287	377	334	345	446	438	General Government	79lh *d*
....	419	609	748	686	702	712	676	592	459	421	660	903	1,427	1,803	Banks	79li *d*
....	1,082	1,380	1,354	1,450	1,713	1,691	1,673	1,495	1,352	1,246	1,238	1,314	1,683	1,650	Other Sectors	79lj *d*
Millions of Kronur Beginning 1975: Year Ending December 31															**Government Finance**	
–4,719	–7,639	–4,278	–9,702	–7,962	–8,953	–17,342	–12,490	–16,844	–21,972	–20,270	–4,389	1,863	I 16,284	20,435	Deficit (-) or Surplus	80
31,249	41,938	54,330	71,782	92,993	107,612	117,438	122,284	122,285	129,409	135,715	150,816	155,200	I 166,529	194,250	Revenue	81
8	—	1,245	1,643	2,091	226	—	575	525	599	—	—	—	I 859	743	Grants Received	81z
33,551	48,381	60,199	82,334	105,933	117,531	132,473	133,466	135,537	142,756	146,826	156,454	152,990	I 159,651	177,964	Expenditure	82
2,424	1,196	–347	792	–2,888	–740	2,308	1,883	4,117	9,224	9,159	–1,248	347	I –8,547	–3,406	Lending Minus Repayments	83
															Financing	
1,508	3,859	3,678	4,878	2,912	6,281	9,633	2,118	13,866	10,493	5,185	–2,254	4,660	I 48	–19,586	Domestic	84a
3,211	3,780	600	4,823	5,050	2,672	7,709	10,371	2,979	11,479	15,085	6,643	–6,523	I –10,546	–1,105	Foreign	85a
10,348	15,122	22,071	28,068	38,671	53,005	59,703	66,139	78,725	83,473	86,314	93,459	99,483	I 92,938	74,480	Debt: Domestic	88a
25,631	29,304	29,955	40,205	58,512	59,779	67,953	87,273	102,305	113,633	127,261	132,218	126,628	I 116,082	116,213	Foreign	89a
Millions of Kronur Beginning 1975															**National Accounts**	
48,774	61,961	71,681	81,721	106,282	124,936	125,671	121,597	135,694	157,436	161,250	176,863	190,948	203,726	215,063	Exports of Goods & Services	90c
21,130	28,776	38,981	50,537	60,341	69,989	78,157	80,375	84,818	89,424	94,080	100,358	107,810	122,879	138,050	Government Consumption	91f
25,528	30,911	42,639	50,498	58,698	70,103	76,173	69,589	64,177	65,876	65,950	87,322	98,818	127,387	127,050	Gross Fixed Capital Formation	93e
–3,111	–3,748	–3,779	–3,080	–8,143	–4,247	–891	–486	1,016	–26	2,285	–1,202	–222	1,143	139	Increase/Decrease(-) in Stocks	93i
77,240	99,196	133,557	161,068	190,254	223,176	248,366	248,339	248,182	256,949	272,708	296,840	320,314	361,593	400,211	Private Consumption	96f
–48,663	–55,880	–73,965	–84,100	–99,240	–119,556	–130,491	–121,782	–122,466	–134,631	–144,725	–173,727	–187,717	–230,055	–242,901	Imports of Goods & Services	98c
120,898	161,216	209,114	256,644	308,192	364,401	396,985	397,632	411,421	435,028	451,548	486,454	529,951	586,673	637,628	Gross Domestic Product (GDP)	99b
–4,824	–5,302	–4,799	–6,506	–11,164	–12,481	–10,635	–8,915	–9,750	–13,677	–12,302	–10,661	–11,892	–12,722	–14,212	Net Factor Inc/Pmts(-) Abroad	98.n
116,074	155,914	204,315	250,138	297,028	351,920	386,350	388,717	401,671	421,351	439,246	475,793	518,059	573,951	623,416	Gross National Income (GNI)	99a
100,591	136,218	180,842	221,233	259,720	308,228	338,417	337,836	347,527	364,898	381,544	415,882	455,073	507,291	551,376	Net National Income	99e
....	....	....	....	....	....	....	....	....	....	....	....	....	....	....	GDP Volume 1985 prices	99b.*p*
311,329	331,277	359,590	359,263	360,174	364,401	368,413	356,087	359,610	372,732	376,551	398,011	413,684	433,007	452,238	GDP Volume 1990 Prices	99b.*p*
82.7	88.0	95.5	95.4	95.7	96.8	97.8	94.6	95.5	99.0	100.0	105.7	109.9	115.0	120.1	GDP Volume (1995=100)	99bv *p*
32.4	40.6	48.5	59.6	71.4	83.4	89.9	93.1	95.4	97.3	100.0	101.9	106.8	113.0	117.6	GDP Deflator (1995=100)	99bi *p*
Midyear Estimates																
.24	.24	.25	.25	.25	.25	.26	.26	.26	.27	.27	.27	.27	.27	.28	**Population**	99z

(See notes in the back of the book.)

India

		1970	1971	1972	1973	1974	1975	1976	1977	1978	1979	1980	1981	1982	1983	1984
Exchange Rates															*Rupees per SDR:*	
Market Rate	aa	7.576	7.903	8.773	9.896	ⅼ9.978	10.462	10.318	9.971	10.668	10.416	10.114	10.591	10.627	10.986	12.205
															Rupees per US Dollar:	
Market Rate	ae	7.576	7.279	8.080	8.203	ⅼ8.150	8.937	8.881	8.209	8.188	7.907	7.930	9.099	9.634	10.493	12.451
Market Rate	rf	7.500	7.492	7.594	7.742	8.102	8.376	8.960	8.739	8.193	8.126	7.863	8.659	9.455	10.099	11.363
Fund Position															*Millions of SDRs:*	
Quota	2f. s	940	940	940	940	940	940	940	940	1,145	1,145	1,718	1,718	1,718	2,208	2,208
SDRs	1b. s	44	148	246	245	240	212	189	149	226	371	377	468	339	105	338
Reserve Position in the Fund	1c. s	21	76	76	76	—	—	—	—	69	162	330	330	364	487	487
Total Fund Cred.&Loans Outstg.	2tl	10	—	—	—	497	698	406	125	—	—	791	1,095	2,595	4,062	4,529
International Liquidity												*Millions of US Dollars Unless Otherwise Indicated:*				
Total Reserves minus Gold	1l. d	763	942	916	849	1,028	1,089	2,792	4,872	6,426	7,432	6,944	4,693	4,315	4,937	5,842
SDRs	1b. d	44	161	268	296	294	248	220	181	294	489	480	545	374	110	331
Reserve Position in the Fund	1c. d	21	83	83	92	—	—	—	—	90	213	420	384	402	510	477
Foreign Exchange	1d. d	698	699	566	461	734	841	2,572	4,691	6,042	6,731	6,043	3,764	3,539	4,318	5,034
Gold (Million Fine Troy Ounces)	1ad	6.954	6.954	6.954	6.954	6.954	6.954	6.954	7.356	8.362	8.560	8.594	8.594	8.594	8.594	8.737
Gold (National Valuation)	1an d	241	251	226	222	228	204	205	235	268	284	284	248	234	215	184
Other Banking Insts.: Liabilities	7f. d	119	137	145	162	176	215	234	273	303	306	293	371	422	447	470
Monetary Authorities															*Billions of Rupees:*	
Foreign Assets	11	6.5	7.7	10.3	11.0	13.0	17.7	27.3	43.7	55.4	63.0	57.2	46.6	44.1	54.3	76.2
Claims on Central Government	12a	42.3	49.5	54.4	64.7	71.4	75.5	72.6	79.3	84.4	102.4	144.3	187.1	237.9	273.7	330.7
Claims on Deposit Money Banks	12e	6.2	5.3	3.6	6.7	7.5	11.4	15.9	10.9	10.3	13.9	10.9	13.6	8.3	8.7	16.5
Claims on Other Financial Insts	12f	1.0	1.7	1.3	1.9	3.4	4.6	6.3	7.9	10.4	13.6	15.9	18.4	29.9	33.9	49.0
Reserve Money	14	46.0	51.1	55.6	68.1	70.4	74.3	86.8	105.1	126.6	153.2	176.5	195.1	230.3	260.2	303.9
of which: Currency Outside DMBs	14a	41.6	45.6	49.1	57.8	61.4	64.4	73.2	84.2	94.6	108.0	126.3	137.4	157.4	181.3	218.1
Foreign Liabilities	16c	.1	—	—	—	5.0	7.3	4.2	1.2	—	—	2.7	6.0	22.0	38.8	48.8
Central Government Deposits	16d	2.9	2.0	.8	.6	.6	.7	1.1	.7	.5	.6	.8	.7	.6	18.9	30.7
Capital Accounts	17a	5.5	7.0	8.7	10.1	11.2	13.6	15.8	18.6	22.2	27.3	32.9	38.9	34.2	36.6	39.3
Other Items (Net)	17r	1.6	4.2	4.6	5.6	8.0	13.5	14.2	16.2	11.2	11.7	15.4	25.0	33.1	16.1	49.8
Deposit Money Banks															*Billions of Rupees:*	
Reserves	20	3.6	4.5	5.3	9.4	8.9	8.8	12.0	23.0	28.6	41.6	47.7	54.8	70.4	76.6	81.9
Claims on Central Government	22a	13.9	16.9	22.2	24.5	28.7	32.5	1.2	49.2	63.3	76.7	92.5	103.9	114.5	148.8	188.7
Claims on Private Sector	22d	52.6	62.6	71.4	88.0	102.5	127.3	13.3	160.5	217.3	258.9	302.1	366.7	438.5	515.3	612.4
Demand Deposits	24	25.4	30.2	36.5	42.9	49.4	57.3	78.7	93.6	ⅼ61.2	65.8	76.1	93.2	113.8	125.7	144.5
Time Deposits	25	4.5	5.5	6.8	8.4	10.1	13.4	5.1	5.9	ⅼ213.9	260.5	302.3	362.9	424.0	507.0	596.7
Credit from Monetary Authorities	26g	6.2	5.3	3.6	6.6	7.5	11.4	15.5	14.4	13.3	13.9	10.9	13.5	18.0	8.8	16.5
Other Items (Net)	27r	5.5	7.6	10.8	13.2	14.6	17.0	6.2	2.2	6.3	33.6	49.6	52.4	64.2	175.7	125.3
Monetary Survey															*Billions of Rupees:*	
Foreign Assets (Net)	31n	6.5	7.7	10.3	11.0	8.0	10.4	23.1	42.5	55.4	63.0	54.5	40.6	22.1	15.5	27.4
Domestic Credit	32	107.0	128.8	148.5	178.6	205.4	239.3	92.3	296.1	374.9	451.0	554.1	675.5	820.1	952.7	1,150.1
Claims on Central Govt. (Net)	32an	53.4	64.5	75.9	88.6	99.5	107.4	72.6	127.8	147.2	178.5	236.1	290.3	351.8	403.5	488.7
Claims on Private Sector	32d	52.6	62.6	71.4	88.0	102.5	127.3	13.3	160.5	217.3	258.9	302.1	366.7	438.5	515.3	612.4
Claims on Other Financial Insts	32f	1.0	1.7	1.3	1.9	3.4	4.6	6.3	7.9	10.4	13.6	15.9	18.4	29.9	33.9	49.0
Money	34	67.6	76.5	86.2	101.0	111.3	122.3	152.8	178.5	ⅼ157.6	176.9	204.6	232.5	273.7	308.6	365.6
Quasi-Money	35	4.5	5.5	6.8	8.4	10.1	13.4	5.1	5.9	ⅼ213.9	260.5	302.3	362.9	424.0	507.0	596.7
Other Items (Net)	37r	12.8	19.0	24.7	29.3	33.6	44.5	36.5	37.6	44.2	73.2	98.3	117.3	141.1	229.1	215.3
Money plus Quasi-Money	35l	100.1	117.1	135.2	161.5	181.3	206.7	257.4	306.7	371.5	434.4	503.5	592.0	692.8	809.2	954.8
Other Banking Institutions															*Billions of Rupees:*	
Claims on Private Sector	42d	6.39	7.36	8.20	9.35	11.57	14.03	17.57	21.72	27.37	34.51	42.81	55.58	68.35	85.02	102.69
Bonds	46ab	1.40	1.54	2.14	2.47	3.07	4.13	5.78	7.70	10.40	14.27	20.15	27.34	35.93	43.94	56.81
Long-Term Foreign Liabilities	46cl	.89	1.00	1.17	1.33	1.43	1.92	2.08	2.24	2.48	2.42	2.33	3.38	4.06	4.69	5.85
Central Govt. Lending Funds	46f	2.90	2.82	2.69	2.53	2.36	2.15	2.00	1.95	1.78	1.68	1.57	2.10	3.97	4.15	4.99
Capital Accounts	47a	.90	1.09	1.30	1.41	1.61	1.76	1.92	2.27	2.73	3.38	4.01	5.25	6.92	8.39	11.12
Other Items (Net)	47r	.31	.91	.90	1.61	3.10	4.06	5.79	7.57	9.98	12.75	14.75	17.52	17.47	23.86	23.92
Post Office: Savings Deposits	45.. i	9.12	9.88	10.37	11.31	11.62	11.66	14.34	15.23	16.78	18.53	20.83	22.68	23.20	24.86	26.14
Nonbank Financial Institutions															*Billions of Rupees:*	
Claims on Central Government	42a. s	11.51	13.16	14.92	16.88	19.26	21.81	24.68	28.55	32.33	36.64	43.11	50.14	57.25	65.71	....
Claims on Local Government	42b. s	.32	.37	.37	.37	.37	.35	.34	.33	.34	.43	.53	.62	.62	.57	....
Claims on Private Sector	42d. s	5.94	6.67	7.50	8.46	9.86	10.94	12.25	13.42	14.46	19.35	20.58	22.74	26.62	28.37	....
Incr.in Total Assets(Within Per.)	49z. s	2.09	2.50	3.06	3.66	3.61	4.05	5.21	5.80	6.78	7.56	9.14	9.77	10.34	11.54	....
Liquid Liabilities	55l	81.15	91.74	103.12	120.50	132.88	147.18	172.08	199.84	ⅼ385.92	455.88	527.71	618.01	720.95	840.44	988.40
Interest Rates															*Percent Per Annum:*	
Bank Rate (End of Period)	60	5.00	6.00	6.00	7.00	9.00	9.00	9.00	9.00	9.00	9.00	9.00	10.00	10.00	10.00	10.00
Money Market Rate	60b	5.68	6.30	4.69	6.64	13.52	10.40	11.28	10.18	8.05	8.47	7.24	8.61	7.27	8.30	9.95
Lending Rate	60p	....	....	....	....	....	....	....	....	13.50	14.50	16.50	16.50	16.50	16.50	16.50
Government Bond Yield	61	5.00	ⅼ5.64	5.65	5.65	6.04	6.35	6.29	6.32	6.37	6.45	6.71	7.15	7.59	7.99	8.65
Prices, Production, Labor															*Index Numbers (1995=100):*	
Share Prices	62	5.1	5.0	4.9	ⅼ5.4	6.0	4.9	5.2	5.3	6.2	7.1	7.7	9.4	9.2	9.7	ⅼ10.3
Wholesale Prices	63	12.2	12.8	13.9	16.2	20.9	21.7	21.2	22.9	22.8	25.5	30.6	34.3	35.1	ⅼ37.9	40.5
Consumer Prices	64	12.3	12.7	13.5	15.8	20.3	21.4	19.8	21.4	22.0	23.4	26.0	29.4	31.8	35.5	38.5
Industrial Production	66	24.3	25.3	26.8	27.2	27.8	29.1	32.0	33.6	35.9	36.4	36.6	ⅼ39.9	40.7	42.8	46.8
															Number in Thousands:	
Labor Force	67d	....	....	....	....	....	....	....	....	....	....	....	....	....	....	....
Employment	67e	....	....	....	....	....	....	....	....	....	....	....	....	....	....	....
Unemployment	67c	....	....	....	....	....	....	....	....	....	....	....	....	....	....	....
International Transactions															*Billions of Rupees:*	
Exports	70	15	15	19	23	32	36	50	56	55	63	68	72	88	92	107
Imports, c.i.f.	71	16	18	17	25	42	53	51	58	64	80	117	133	140	142	173
															1995=100	
Unit Value of Exports	74	9	9	ⅼ10	11	13	16	17	18	21	21	22	23	26	27	31
Unit Value of Imports	75	9	9	ⅼ9	10	14	24	28	27	25	28	32	37	38	39	36

1985	1986	1987	1988	1989	1990	1991	1992	1993	1994	1995	1996	1997	1998	1999		
End of Period															**Exchange Rates**	
13.363	16.051	18.268	20.117	22.387	25.712	36.953	36.025	43.102	45.810	52.295	51.666	52.999	59.813	59.690	Market Rate..	**aa**
End of Period (ae) Period Average (rf)																
12.166	13.122	12.877	14.949	17.035	18.073	25.834	26.200	31.380	31.380	35.180	35.930	39.280	42.480	43.490	Market Rate..	**ae**
12.369	12.611	12.962	13.917	16.226	17.504	22.742	25.918	30.493	31.374	32.427	35.433	36.313	41.259	43.055	Market Rate..	**rf**
End of Period															**Fund Position**	
2,208	2,208	2,208	2,208	2,208	2,208	2,208	3,056	3,056	3,056	3,056	3,056	3,056	3,056	4,158	Quota..	**2f. s**
306	291	112	71	86	222	32	3	73	1	93	85	57	59	3	SDRs...	**1b. s**
487	487	487	487	487	—	—	213	213	213	213	213	213	213	489	Reserve Position in the Fund	**1c. s**
4,354	3,918	3,175	2,282	1,440	804	2,426	3,260	3,585	2,763	1,967	1,085	590	285	39	Total Fund Cred.&Loans Outstg.	**2tl**
End of Period															**International Liquidity**	
6,420	6,396	6,454	4,899	3,859	1,521	3,627	5,757	10,199	19,698	17,922	20,170	24,688	27,341	32,667	Total Reserves minus Gold....................	**1l. d**
336	356	159	96	113	316	46	4	100	2	139	122	77	83	4	SDRs...	**1b. d**
535	596	691	656	640	—	—	292	292	310	316	306	287	300	671	Reserve Position in the Fund	**1c. d**
5,549	5,444	5,603	4,148	3,105	1,205	3,580	5,461	9,807	19,386	17,467	19,742	24,324	26,958	31,992	Foreign Exchange..................................	**1d. d**
9.397	10.449	10.449	10.449	10.449	10.692	11.282	11.348	11.457	11.800	12.780	12.781	12.740	11.487	11.502	Gold (Million Fine Troy Ounces)...........	**1ad**
203	209	213	183	161	3,667	3,168	2,908	3,325	3,355	3,669	3,614	2,880	2,492	2,403	Gold (National Valuation)	**1an d**
623	826	1,268	1,566	1,641	1,926	1,718	....	....	....	....	....	....	....	332	Other Banking Insts.: Liabilities	**7f. d**
Last Friday of Period															**Monetary Authorities**	
79.2	88.0	83.8	77.1	68.4	96.4	177.9	230.6	413.0	721.3	749.0	847.8	1,058.1	1,256.4	1,525.2	Foreign Assets	**11**
406.4	480.7	552.2	649.2	758.7	896.5	1,056.0	1,020.6	1,155.7	1,034.9	1,128.0	1,360.6	1,373.8	1,571.3	1,627.4	Claims on Central Government	**12a**
6.2	5.8	16.7	16.5	24.4	18.2	4.1	37.7	13.2	25.2	60.1	7.9	12.7	31.9	26.8	Claims on Deposit Money Banks	**12e**
52.7	56.5	65.4	76.4	86.4	91.6	97.8	105.4	103.8	120.7	125.2	124.0	134.9	146.2	158.6	Claims on Other Financial Insts	**12f**
375.3	436.5	516.0	599.9	712.1	809.7	961.1	1,042.2	1,268.0	1,543.8	1,737.8	1,903.2	2,116.1	2,378.7	2,645.9	Reserve Money	**14**
239.4	268.0	315.6	356.4	434.5	501.9	591.3	645.8	783.3	948.5	1,136.2	1,295.2	1,443.0	1,624.4	1,930.0	*of which: Currency Outside DMBs*	**14a**
51.1	56.1	52.2	41.6	29.8	20.6	89.7	117.5	154.5	126.6	102.8	56.1	31.3	17.0	2.3	Foreign Liabilities	**16c**
.7	.6	.6	1.6	.8	2.1	1.1	.6	.7	.7	.7	.6	.6	.6	1.4	Central Government Deposits	**16d**
42.3	46.8	51.2	57.0	63.8	135.3	148.7	148.1	152.9	154.8	159.2	158.8	166.8	167.4	164.3	Capital Accounts	**17a**
75.0	91.2	98.1	119.2	131.3	135.0	135.1	86.0	109.5	76.4	61.7	221.5	264.7	442.0	524.0	Other Items (Net)	**17r**
Last Friday of Period															**Deposit Money Banks**	
130.7	143.3	194.8	239.1	263.5	287.4	352.0	379.9	483.9	628.8	646.9	568.7	604.3	783.7	653.2	Reserves	**20**
194.2	245.0	308.4	366.1	422.3	508.0	617.1	761.2	922.1	1,223.3	1,291.1	1,545.9	1,896.4	2,237.7	2,703.9	Claims on Central Government	**22a**
698.9	821.4	918.5	1,085.2	1,311.6	1,435.5	1,577.6	1,880.0	2,087.7	2,429.9	2,713.9	3,264.2	3,640.0	4,196.4	4,638.1	Claims on Private Sector.......................	**22d**
170.1	207.8	224.1	272.7	307.0	337.4	445.8	466.4	530.6	710.8	686.2	808.5	933.1	1,039.1	1,171.1	Demand Deposits	**24**
712.3	847.7	999.6	1,192.2	1,365.1	1,576.7	1,829.3	2,239.4	2,601.5	3,034.0	3,366.2	4,084.4	4,914.7	5,963.3	6,744.0	Time Deposits	**25**
6.2	7.7	16.5	16.5	25.7	18.1	4.0	37.4	16.2	77.6	138.4	18.1	7.7	63.1	25.5	Credit from Monetary Authorities	**26g**
135.2	146.6	181.4	209.1	299.6	298.6	267.7	277.9	345.3	459.7	461.1	467.8	285.2	152.3	54.5	Other Items (Net)	**27r**
Last Friday of Period															**Monetary Survey**	
28.1	31.9	31.6	35.5	38.6	75.9	88.3	113.2	258.4	594.8	646.2	791.7	1,026.8	1,239.3	1,522.9	Foreign Assets (Net)	**31n**
1,351.4	1,603.0	1,843.8	2,175.4	2,578.2	2,929.5	3,347.4	3,766.6	4,268.6	4,808.2	5,257.5	6,294.0	7,044.4	8,151.0	9,126.6	Domestic Credit	**32**
599.9	725.0	859.9	1,013.7	1,180.2	1,402.4	1,672.0	1,781.2	2,077.1	2,257.6	2,418.4	2,905.9	3,269.6	3,808.4	4,329.9	Claims on Central Govt. (Net)	**32an**
698.9	821.4	918.5	1,085.2	1,311.6	1,435.5	1,577.6	1,880.0	2,087.7	2,429.9	2,713.9	3,264.2	3,640.0	4,196.4	4,638.1	Claims on Private Sector....................	**32d**
52.7	56.5	65.4	76.4	86.4	91.6	97.8	105.4	103.8	120.7	125.2	124.0	134.9	146.2	158.6	Claims on Other Financial Insts...........	**32f**
412.4	478.7	543.2	632.8	746.9	853.6	1,046.1	1,120.9	1,330.2	1,695.0	1,883.5	2,148.9	2,419.3	2,703.5	3,133.9	Money	**34**
712.3	847.7	999.6	1,192.2	1,365.1	1,576.7	1,829.3	2,239.4	2,601.5	3,034.0	3,366.2	4,084.4	4,914.7	5,963.3	6,744.0	Quasi-Money	**35**
254.8	308.7	332.7	385.9	504.7	575.1	560.2	519.5	595.3	673.9	653.9	852.4	737.3	723.6	771.5	Other Items (Net)	**37r**
1,116.1	1,316.9	1,531.4	1,810.9	2,095.9	2,413.0	2,856.1	3,338.3	3,913.9	4,711.1	5,249.7	6,209.1	7,307.8	8,635.5	9,843.8	Money plus Quasi-Money	**35l**
End of Period															**Other Banking Institutions**	
124.35	151.36	186.09	228.99	....	....	....	....	....	....	....	....	....	....	....	Claims on Private Sector.......................	**42d**
71.00	86.24	107.16	127.26	....	....	....									Bonds	**46ab**
7.58	10.84	16.33	23.41	27.95	34.80	44.39									Long-Term Foreign Liabilities	**46cl**
5.13	5.56	5.28	5.11	....	....	....									Central Govt. Lending Funds	**46f**
13.10	15.87	19.08	23.91	....	....	....									Capital Accounts	**47a**
27.54	32.86	38.25	49.15	....	....	....									Other Items (Net)	**47r**
27.76	29.62	32.63	34.02	37.36	39.92	42.45									Post Office: Savings Deposits ....**45.. *i***	
Year Beginning April 1															**Nonbank Financial Institutions**	
....	....	....	....												Claims on Central Government	**42a. s**
....	....	....	....												Claims on Local Government	**42b. s**
....	....	....	....												Claims on Private Sector.......................	**42d. s**
....	....	....	....												*Incr.in Total Assets(Within Per.)*...........**49z. s**	
1,152.48	1,346.51	1,564.04	1,844.95	2,133.28	2,452.97	2,898.59									Liquid Liabilities	**55l**
Percent Per Annum															**Interest Rates**	
10.00	10.00	10.00	10.00	10.00	10.00	12.00	12.00	12.00	12.00	12.00	12.00	9.00	9.00	8.00	Bank Rate *(End of Period)*......................	**60**
10.00	9.97	9.83	9.73	11.39	15.57	19.35	15.23	8.64	7.14	15.57	11.04	5.29	....	....	Money Market Rate...............................	**60b**
16.50	16.50	16.50	16.50	16.50	16.50	17.88	18.92	16.25	14.75	15.46	15.96	13.83	13.54	12.54	Lending Rate	**60p**
8.99	....	....	....	....	....	....									Government Bond Yield	**61**
Period Averages															**Prices, Production, Labor**	
15.4	18.7	17.2	17.7	26.7	37.0	49.9	91.6	75.1	119.3	100.0	91.3	84.5	76.8	....	Share Prices	**62**
42.4	44.8	47.9	52.1	55.6	60.6	68.8	77.0	82.7	91.5	100.0	105.9	111.4	119.1	123.3	Wholesale Prices	**63**
40.6	44.2	48.0	I 52.6	55.8	60.8	69.2	77.4	82.3	90.7	100.0	109.0	116.8	132.2	138.4	Consumer Prices....................................	**64**
51.1	54.5	60.6	65.0	68.6	76.2	77.4	79.6	81.1	88.7	I 100.0	108.6	114.5	118.4	126.8	Industrial Production	**66**
Period Averages																
....	....	....	....	....	302,204	....	....	....	....	....	....	....	....	....	Labor Force	**67d**
24,578	25,056	25,388	25,712	25,962	26,353	26,733	27,056	27,177	27,375	27,987	27,941	28,245	....	....	Employment	**67e**
24,861	28,261	30,542	I 30,050	32,776	34,632	36,300	I 36,758	36,276	36,692	36,742	37,430	39,140	40,090	....	Unemployment	**67c**
Billions of Rupees															**International Transactions**	
113	119	146	184	258	314	401	509	657	785	995	1,172	1,271	1,379	1,564	Exports	**70**
197	195	216	266	334	414	459	611	694	842	1,127	1,344	1,505	1,772	1,934	Imports, c.i.f.	**71**
1995=100																
35	35	37	48	57	61	76	87	98	102	100	104	122	....	....	Unit Value of Exports...........................	**74**
46	46	40	53	65	76	88	95	93	93	100	114	115	....	....	Unit Value of Imports...........................	**75**

India

	1970	1971	1972	1973	1974	1975	1976	1977	1978	1979	1980	1981	1982	1983	1984
Balance of Payments														*Millions of US Dollars:*	
Current Account, n.i.e. .... 78al d	....	....	....	....	....	−148	1,571	2,108	683	48	−1,785	−2,698	−2,524	−1,953	−2,343
Goods: Exports f.o.b. .... 78aa d	....	....	....	....	....	4,666	5,410	6,249	6,518	7,597	8,303	8,437	9,226	9,770	10,192
Goods: Imports f.o.b. .... 78ab d	....	....	....	....	....	−4,952	−4,623	−5,317	−7,402	−9,819	−13,947	−14,149	−14,046	−13,868	−14,216
Trade Balance .... 78ac d	....	....	....	....	....	−286	787	932	−884	−2,222	−5,644	−5,711	−4,820	−4,098	−4,025
Services: Credit .... 78ad d	....	....	....	....	....	841	1,056	1,316	1,607	2,083	2,971	2,797	2,933	3,290	3,232
Services: Debit .... 78ae d	....	....	....	....	....	−1,054	−1,140	−1,286	−1,555	−2,120	−2,981	−3,249	−3,471	−3,705	−3,641
Balance on Goods & Services .... 78af d	....	....	....	....	....	−500	703	962	−832	−2,258	−5,654	−6,163	−5,359	−4,513	−4,434
Income: Credit .... 78ag d	....	....	....	....	....	130	195	275	390	749	1,058	972	608	480	487
Income: Debit .... 78ah d	....	....	....	....	....	−388	−355	−425	−492	−485	−523	−513	−690	−982	−1,166
Balance on Gds. Serv. & Inc. .... 78ai d	....	....	....	....	....	−758	543	813	−935	−1,995	−5,119	−5,704	−5,441	−5,014	−5,113
Current Transfers, n.i.e.: Credit .... 78aj d	....	....	....	....	....	636	1,043	1,306	1,637	2,065	3,347	3,026	2,939	3,075	2,789
Current Transfers: Debit .... 78ak d	....	....	....	....	....	−26	−16	−11	−20	−23	−14	−21	−22	−13	−19
Capital Account, n.i.e. .... 78bc d	....	....	....	....	....	—	—	—	—	—	—	—	—	—	—
Capital Account, n.i.e.: Credit .... 78ba d	....	....	....	....	....	—	—	—	—	—	—	—	—	—	—
Capital Account: Debit .... 78bb d	....	....	....	....	....	—	—	—	—	—	—	—	—	—	—
Financial Account, n.i.e. .... 78bj d	....	....	....	....	....	944	930	430	806	483	483	845	456	2,051	3,044
Direct Investment Abroad .... 78bd d	....	....	....	....	....	—	—	—	—	—	—	—	—	—	—
Dir. Invest. in Rep. Econ., n.i.e. .... 78be d	....	....	....	....	....	−10	−8	—	—	—	—	—	—	—	—
Portfolio Investment Assets .... 78bf d	....	....	....	....	....	—	—	—	—	—	—	—	—	—	—
Equity Securities .... 78bk d	....	....	....	....	....	—	—	—	—	—	—	—	—	—	—
Debt Securities .... 78bl d	....	....	....	....	....	—	—	—	—	—	—	—	—	—	—
Portfolio Investment Liab., n.i.e. .... 78bg d	....	....	....	....	....	—	—	—	—	—	—	—	—	—	—
Equity Securities .... 78bm d	....	....	....	....	....	—	—	—	—	—	—	—	—	—	—
Debt Securities .... 78bn d	....	....	....	....	....	—	—	—	—	—	—	—	—	—	—
Financial Derivatives Assets .... 78bw d	....	....	....	....	....	....	....	....	....	....	....	....	....	....	....
Financial Derivatives Liabilities .... 78bx d	....	....	....	....	....	....	....	....	....	....	....	....	....	....	....
Other Investment Assets .... 78bh d	....	....	....	....	....	3	−51	−210	95	−19	−318	−47	−691	541	−254
Monetary Authorities .... 78bo d	....	....	....	....	....										
General Government .... 78bp d	....	....	....	....	....	19	−91	−138	1	29	42	−104	−591	496	−156
Banks .... 78bq d	....	....	....	....	....	−20	35	−72	102	−20	−342	61	−93	51	−89
Other Sectors .... 78br d	....	....	....	....	....	4	5	1	−7	−28	−18	−4	−7	−5	−9
Other Investment Liab., n.i.e. .... 78bi d	....	....	....	....	....	952	989	640	711	502	802	893	1,147	1,510	3,298
Monetary Authorities .... 78bs d	....	....	....	....	....	−8	−92	223	−55	89	−23	−68	−82	−54	308
General Government .... 78bt d	....	....	....	....	....	997	1,068	264	662	416	627	781	995	930	1,911
Banks .... 78bu d	....	....	....	....	....	18	43	96	58	13	135	68	92	5	188
Other Sectors .... 78bv d	....	....	....	....	....	−56	−31	57	46	−15	62	111	142	629	890
Net Errors and Omissions .... 78ca d	....	....	....	....	....	−439	−291	−456	431	301	−361	−325	369	−850	368
Overall Balance .... 78cb d	....	....	....	....	....	357	2,210	2,081	1,920	832	−1,663	−2,178	−1,698	−752	1,070
Reserves and Related Items .... 79da d	....	....	....	....	....	−357	−2,210	−2,081	−1,920	−832	1,663	2,178	1,698	752	−1,070
Reserve Assets .... 79db d	....	....	....	....	....	−597	−1,881	−2,090	−1,772	−835	624	1,824	43	−840	−1,595
Use of Fund Credit and Loans .... 79dc d	....	....	....	....	....	239	−337	−330	−158	—	1,039	354	1,656	1,576	494
Exceptional Financing .... 79de d	....	....	....	....	....	—	8	338	9	3	—	—	16	31	
Government Finance														*Billions of Rupees:*	
Deficit (-) or Surplus 80	−13.6	−16.0	−21.8	−17.0	⅃−23.6	−32.0	−36.9	−37.9	−50.8	−63.0	−88.6	−87.3	−107.3	−133.3	−175.8
Revenue 81	33.3	40.6	45.7	49.7	⅃75.3	91.7	102.6	113.5	129.6	144.0	161.1	195.9	225.1	255.2	296.1
Grants Received 81z	....	....	....	....	⅃1.0	2.8	2.7	3.2	2.7	3.9	4.4	3.8	4.0	3.3	4.8
Expenditure 82	39.3	49.3	55.2	58.1	⅃77.0	93.3	104.1	114.8	133.5	159.0	180.3	208.4	244.2	287.2	351.3
Lending Minus Repayments 83	7.6	7.2	12.3	8.6	⅃22.9	33.3	38.1	39.9	49.6	51.8	73.9	78.7	92.1	104.6	125.3
Financing															
Net Borrowing: Domestic 84a	....	....	....	....	⅃17.6	22.0	20.9	58.3	21.2	60.0	83.4	73.5	133.0	85.5	161.5
Rupees 84b	10.6	10.6	19.4	−3.3	....										
Foreign 85a	....	....	....	....	⅃6.5	14.7	11.2	3.8	4.5	5.0	7.0	9.2	11.9	12.9	13.8
Foreign Currency 85b	3.3	3.5	2.9	4.7	....										
Finance from Foreign Aid 86a	.4	.2	.3	16.7	....										
Use of Cash Balances 87	−.7	1.7	−.9	−1.1	⅃−.6	−4.8	4.7	−24.2	25.2	−2.1	−1.8	4.7	−37.6	34.9	.5
Debt: Domestic 88a	....	....	....	....	⅃174.0	201.3	221.6	281.1	305.8	367.8	453.4	527.7	673.6	746.8	887.8
Rupees 88b	133.8	145.9	168.2	184.0	....										
Foreign 89a	....	....	....	....	⅃64.2	76.0	86.1	89.9	93.8	99.6	107.6	117.9	131.4	145.8	161.0
Foreign Currency 89b	64.9	68.3	71.2	58.7	....										
National Accounts														*Billions of Rupees:*	
Househ.Cons.Expend.,incl.NPISHs 96f	325.5	351.0	386.9	434.3	565.1	578.2	600.8	691.8	752.4	817.0	992.9	1,137.7	1,251.7	1,459.7	1,614.6
Government Consumption Expend. 91f	38.4	44.6	47.3	51.6	62.4	73.0	82.3	87.6	97.2	111.7	130.8	153.6	182.7	211.4	243.5
Gross Fixed Capital Formation 93e	63.1	70.8	81.3	90.7	110.0	133.3	153.0	172.2	188.8	213.1	262.8	314.6	357.7	399.9	455.7
Changes in Inventories 93i	10.7	14.6	5.9	22.6	34.7	30.8	24.7	18.0	41.1	48.4	21.8	85.6	50.2	38.0	34.4
Exports of Goods and Services 90c	16.4	17.9	21.5	26.6	36.9	49.5	61.3	64.0	71.2	83.4	90.3	102.6	115.6	131.6	158.5
Imports of Goods & Services 98c	−18.2	−21.8	−20.5	−31.8	−47.8	−56.6	−56.1	−65.2	−74.2	−100.9	−136.0	−148.1	−157.4	−176.8	−194.8
Gross Domestic Product (GDP) 99b	431.6	462.6	510.1	620.1	732.4	787.6	848.9	960.7	1,041.9	1,143.6	1,360.1	1,597.6	1,781.3	2,075.9	2,313.4
Net Primary Income from Abroad 98.n	−2.8	−2.9	−3.1	−3.0	−2.5	−2.6	−2.3	−2.4	−1.6	1.5	3.5	.4	−6.3	−9.4	−14.2
Gross National Income (GNI) 99a	428.8	459.7	507.0	616.8	729.4	785.1	846.6	958.3	1,040.3	1,145.1	1,363.6	1,598.0	1,775.0	2,066.5	2,299.2
Gross Nat'l Diposable Inc.(gndi) 99i	....	....	....	....	....	....	....	....	....	....	....	....	....	....	....
Gross Savings 99s	....	....	....	....	....	....	....	....	....	....	....	....	....	....	....
GDP at factor cost 99ba	....	....	....	....	....	....	....	....	....	....	....	....	....	....	....
GDP Volume 1980/81 Prices 99b.p	1,013.6	1,032.0	1,025.7	1,056.0	1,068.5	1,166.8	1,187.5	1,272.9	1,346.4	1,275.7	1,360.1	1,449.0	1,503.8	1,615.5	1,674.9
GDP Volume 1993/94 Prices 99b.p	....	....	....	....	....	....	....	....	....	....	....	....	....	....	....
GDP Vol.,fact.cost,93/94 Prices .... 99ba p	....	....	....	....	....	....	....	....	....	....	....	....	....	....	....
GDP Volume (1995=100) .... 99bv p	32.9	33.5	33.3	34.2	34.6	37.8	38.5	41.3	43.6	41.4	44.1	47.0	48.8	52.4	54.3
GDP Deflator (1995=100) .... 99bi p	11.1	11.7	13.0	15.3	17.9	17.6	18.7	19.7	20.2	23.4	26.1	28.8	30.9	33.5	36.0
														Millions:	
Population 99z	539.08	551.23	563.53	575.89	588.30	600.76	613.27	625.82	⅃646.00	660.00	675.00	690.00	705.00	720.00	736.00

	1985	1986	1987	1988	1989	1990	1991	1992	1993	1994	1995	1996	1997	1998	1999	Code
Balance of Payments (*Minus Sign Indicates Debit*)																
Current Account, n.i.e.	-4,177	-4,598	-5,192	-7,172	-6,826	-7,037	-4,292	-4,485	-1,876	-1,676	-5,563	-5,956	-2,965	-6,903	-2,784	78ald
Goods: Exports f.o.b.	9,465	10,248	11,884	13,510	16,144	18,286	18,095	20,019	22,016	25,523	31,239	33,737	35,702	34,076	37,528	78aad
Goods: Imports f.o.b.	-15,081	-15,686	-17,661	-20,091	-22,254	-23,437	-21,087	-22,931	-24,108	-29,673	-37,957	-43,789	-45,730	-44,828	-45,556	78abd
Trade Balance	-5,616	-5,438	-5,777	-6,581	-6,110	-5,151	-2,992	-2,911	-2,093	-4,150	-6,719	-10,052	-10,028	-10,752	-8,029	78acd
Services: Credit	3,384	3,228	3,363	3,791	4,140	4,625	4,925	4,934	5,107	6,038	6,775	7,238	9,111	11,691	14,443	78add
Services: Debit	-3,903	-3,945	-4,629	-5,321	-5,874	-6,090	-5,945	-6,735	-6,497	-8,200	-10,268	-11,171	-12,443	-14,540	-17,411	78aed
Balance on Goods & Services	-6,135	-6,156	-7,043	-8,112	-7,844	-6,616	-4,012	-4,712	-3,482	-6,312	-10,212	-13,984	-13,360	-13,601	-10,997	78afd
Income: Credit	528	518	450	427	446	436	232	377	375	821	1,486	1,411	1,484	1,806	1,919	78agd
Income: Debit	-1,347	-1,581	-1,605	-2,211	-2,498	-3,693	-4,235	-4,289	-4,121	-4,370	-5,219	-4,667	-5,002	-5,443	-5,629	78ahd
Balance on Gds, Serv. & Inc.	-6,953	-7,219	-8,198	-9,895	-9,896	-9,873	-8,015	-8,624	-7,228	-9,861	-13,945	-17,240	-16,878	-17,238	-14,707	78aid
Current Transfers, n.i.e.: Credit	2,799	2,638	3,034	2,739	3,093	2,853	3,736	4,157	5,375	8,208	8,410	11,350	13,975	10,402	11,958	78ajd
Current Transfers: Debit	-23	-17	-28	-16	-23	-17	-13	-18	-23	-23	-27	-66	-62	-67	-35	78akd
Capital Account, n.i.e.	—	—	—	—	—	—	....	....	....	....	....	....	—	—	—	78bcd
Capital Account, n.i.e.: Credit	—	—	—	—	—	—	....	....	....	....	....	....	—	—	—	78bad
Capital Account: Debit	—	—	—	—	—	—	....	....	....	....	....	....	—	—	—	78bbd
Financial Account, n.i.e.	3,281	3,992	5,734	7,175	7,212	5,528	3,450	4,075	7,074	10,576	3,861	11,848	9,635	8,584	9,154	78bjd
Direct Investment Abroad	—	—	—	—	—	—	....	....	—	-83	-117	-239	-113	-48	-79	78bdd
Dir. Invest. in Rep. Econ., n.i.e.	—	—	—	—	—	—	74	277	550	973	2,144	2,426	3,577	2,635	2,169	78bed
Portfolio Investment Assets	—	—	—	—	—	—	....	....	....	....	....	....	—	—	—	78bfd
Equity Securities	—	—	—	—	—	—	....	....	....	....	....	....	—	—	—	78bkd
Debt Securities	—	—	—	—	—	—	....	....	....	....	....	....	—	—	—	78bld
Portfolio Investment Liab., n.i.e.	—	—	—	—	—	—	5	284	1,369	5,491	1,590	3,958	2,556	-601	2,317	78bgd
Equity Securities	—	—	—	—	—	—	5	284	1,369	5,491	1,590	3,958	2,556	-601	2,317	78bmd
Debt Securities	—	—	—	—	—	—	....	....	....	....	....	....	—	—	—	78bnd
Financial Derivatives Assets	....	....	....	....	....	....	....	....	....	....	....	....	—	—	....	78bwd
Financial Derivatives Liabilities	....	....	....	....	....	....	....	....	....	....	....	....	—	—	....	78bxd
Other Investment Assets	53	-250	125	276	114	-611	-808	929	1,830	1,170	-1,179	-4,710	-4,743	-3,239	-1,455	78bhd
Monetary Authorities	....	....	....	....	....	....	....	1	3	1	....	....	—	—	-496	78bod
General Government	2	-213	90	43	-186	-868	183	-791	309	9	-29	-5	67	11	33	78bpd
Banks	52	-37	31	240	310	333	-1,003	1,732	-148	-1,029	-92	-1,642	-2,156	-1,355	1,140	78bqd
Other Sectors	-2	—	3	-6	-10	-76	12	-13	1,667	2,189	-1,058	-3,063	-2,653	-1,896	-2,132	78brd
Other Investment Liab., n.i.e.	3,228	4,242	5,609	6,899	7,099	6,139	4,180	2,587	3,325	3,024	1,423	10,413	8,357	9,837	6,203	78bid
Monetary Authorities	-149	-217	1,163	1,296	1,344	1,867	-297	407	81	142	-65	45	233	122	1,344	78bsd
General Government	1,839	2,674	2,955	3,877	3,605	2,999	1,319	-1,345	141	92	1,483	1,698	397	-72	237	78btd
Banks	19	-51	-76	-297	-281	-450	69	1,947	2,045	1,307	266	2,989	1,098	1,739	2,458	78bud
Other Sectors	1,519	1,836	1,566	2,023	2,431	1,723	3,090	1,578	1,058	1,483	-261	5,680	6,629	8,047	2,164	78bvd
Net Errors and Omissions	500	197	-409	-18	-150	-432	607	1,482	-987	1,492	970	-1,934	-1,348	1,390	293	78cad
Overall Balance	-397	-409	133	-16	237	-1,941	-235	1,072	4,211	10,391	-733	3,958	5,321	3,071	6,664	78cbd
Reserves and Related Items	397	409	-133	16	-237	1,941	235	-1,072	-4,211	-10,391	733	-3,958	-5,321	-3,071	-6,664	79dad
Reserve Assets	538	891	800	1,184	836	2,798	-2,040	-2,253	-4,663	-9,238	1,956	-2,676	-4,637	-2,659	-6,327	79dbd
Use of Fund Credit and Loans	-177	-512	-954	-1,197	-1,086	-858	2,275	1,181	451	-1,153	-1,223	-1,282	-684	-412	-337	79dcd
Exceptional Financing	37	30	21	29	13	1	....	....	....	....	....	....	—	—	—	79ded
Government Finance (*Year Beginning April 1*)																
Deficit (-) or Surplus	-222.5	-272.0	-278.8	-320.6	-361.8	-434.6	-358.2	-399.0	-605.3	-567.5	-598.5	-668.8	-872.0[p]	-932.1[f]	....	80
Revenue	361.2	420.7	480.8	557.4	675.4	723.6	892.1	1,004.6	1,011.7	1,283.2	1,488.8	1,717.1	1,911.8[p]	2,161.7[f]	....	81
Grants Received	4.9	4.4	4.9	6.0	7.5	5.9	9.5	9.2	9.9	10.4	11.4	11.9	11.7[p]	10.5[f]	....	81z
Expenditure	430.7	518.1	597.1	694.9	818.3	924.6	1,050.5	1,189.3	1,363.7	1,540.6	1,763.1	2,010.6	2,339.4[p]	2,594.7[f]	....	82
Lending Minus Repayments	157.9	178.9	167.4	189.0	226.4	239.5	209.3	223.5	263.2	320.5	335.6	387.2	456.1[p]	509.7[f]	....	83
Financing																
Net Borrowing: Domestic	208.9	258.5	244.4	302.0	335.8	407.0	304.4	340.5	564.7	519.4	611.9	634.3	836.8[p]	908.8[f]	....	84a
Rupees	....	....	....	....	....	....	....	....	....	....	....	....	....	....	....	84b
Foreign	13.7	19.4	32.7	24.6	26.0	31.8	54.2	53.2	50.7	35.8	3.2	29.9	12.0[p]	23.4[f]	....	85a
Foreign Currency	....	....	....	....	....	....	....	....	....	....	....	....	....	....	....	85b
Finance from Foreign Aid	....	....	....	....	....	....	....	....	....	....	....	....	....	....	....	86a
Use of Cash Balances	—	-6.0	1.6	-6.0	—	-4.2	-.3	5.4	-10.2	12.3	-16.6	4.6	23.2[p]	—[f]	....	87
Debt: Domestic	1,083.6	1,315.4	1,532.9	1,830.4	2,202.6	2,610.4	2,942.5	3,359.0	4,060.7	4,586.9	5,213.0	5,835.2	6,718.3[p]	7,748.0[f]	....	88a
Rupees	....	....	....	....	....	....	....	....	....	....	....	....	....	....	....	88b
Foreign	181.5	203.0	232.2	257.5	283.4	315.3	369.5	422.7	473.5	509.3	512.5	542.4	552.4[p]	573.0[f]	....	89a
Foreign Currency	....	....	....	....	....	....	....	....	....	....	....	....	....	....	....	89b
National Accounts (*Year Beginning April 1*)																
Househ.Cons.Expend.,incl.NPISHs	1,768.5	1,986.0	2,225.5	2,574.2	2,882.4	3,303.7	3,818.9	4,301.8	5,718.6	6,561.2	7,530.0	8,923.9	9,721.4	11,160.6	....	96f
Government Consumption Expend.	291.7	346.3	408.4	473.3	542.0	617.8	694.6	786.0	977.3	1,086.3	1,287.2	1,456.1	1,715.2	2,163.6	....	91f
Gross Fixed Capital Formation	542.6	620.5	721.9	856.7	1,027.8	1,240.0	1,365.0	1,588.6	1,842.9	2,220.7	2,909.9	3,138.6	3,439.1	3,780.1	....	93e
Changes in Inventories	91.9	58.5	26.9	107.4	74.2	111.5	35.7	108.0	-16.7	157.5	222.3	-157.9	100.9	65.1	....	93i
Exports of Goods and Services	149.5	165.4	202.8	259.1	346.1	406.4	562.5	673.1	861.5	1,016.1	1,307.3	1,448.5	1,652.0	1,971.3	....	90c
Imports of Goods & Services	-217.5	-223.6	-252.6	-320.1	-402.1	-487.0	-562.5	-730.0	-860.0	-1,047.1	-1,449.5	-1,610.2	-1,843.3	-2,225.1	....	98c
Gross Domestic Product (GDP)	2,622.4	2,929.5	3,332.0	3,957.8	4,568.2	5,355.3	6,168.0	7,059.2	8,592.2	10,099.1	11,819.6	13,619.5	15,156.5	17,626.1	....	99b
Net Primary Income from Abroad	-14.3	-18.1	-26.2	-45.0	-57.3	-75.4	-100.8	-118.0	-120.8	-130.9	-134.8	-130.8	-132.1	-149.7	....	98.n
Gross National Income (GNI)	2,608.1	2,911.4	3,305.8	3,912.9	4,510.9	5,279.9	6,067.2	6,941.2	8,471.4	9,968.2	11,684.8	13,488.7	15,024.4	17,476.4	....	99a
Gross Nat'l Diposable Inc.(gndi)	....	....	3,007.4	3,562.1	4,092.4	4,795.1	5,530.3	6,292.6	7,803.0	9,242.2	10,734.0	12,581.9	13,956.8	16,249.9	....	99i
Gross Savings	....	....	696.3	846.7	1,023.7	1,300.0	1,412.5	1,552.3	1,936.2	2,520.8	3,009.6	3,175.7	3,744.2	3,936.0	....	99s
GDP at factor cost	....	....	....	3,527.1	4,086.1	4,778.1	5,527.7	6,307.7	7,813.5	9,141.9	10,672.2	12,372.9	13,844.5	16,123.8	....	99ba
GDP Volume 1980/81 Prices	1,766.5	1,852.5	1,940.9	2,133.5	2,273.7	2,402.4	2,412.6	2,543.3	2,669.3	....	....	....	....	....	....	99b.p
GDP Volume 1993/94 Prices	....	....	....	....	....	....	....	....	8,592.2	9,222.9	9,928.9	10,619.0	11,103.8	11,854.0	....	99b.p
GDP Vol.,fact.cost,93/94 Prices	....	....	....	....	....	....	....	....	7,813.5	8,358.6	8,969.9	9,643.9	10,128.2	10,818.3	....	99bap
GDP Volume (1995=100)	57.3	60.1	62.9	69.2	73.7	77.9	78.2	82.5	86.5	92.9	100.0	107.0	111.8	119.4	....	99bvp
GDP Deflator (1995=100)	38.7	41.3	44.8	48.4	52.4	58.2	66.7	72.4	84.0	92.0	100.0	107.7	114.7	124.9	....	99bip
Midyear Estimates																
Population	750.86	767.20	783.73	800.50	817.49	835.13	851.90	868.90	886.25	903.94	921.99	939.54	955.22	970.93	986.61	99z

(See notes in the back of the book.)

Indinesia

		1970	1971	1972	1973	1974	1975	1976	1977	1978	1979	1980	1981	1982	1983	1984
Exchange Rates															*Rupiah per SDR:*	
Market Rate	aa	378.0	450.6	450.6	500.6	508.1	485.8	482.2	504.1	814.2	826.0	799.4	749.6	763.9	1,040.7	1,052.7
															Rupiah per US Dollar:	
Market Rate	ae	378.0	415.0	415.0	415.0	415.0	415.0	415.0	415.0	625.0	627.0	626.8	644.0	692.5	994.0	1,074.0
Market Rate	rf	362.8	391.9	415.0	415.0	415.0	415.0	415.0	415.0	442.0	623.1	627.0	631.8	661.4	909.3	1,025.9
Fund Position															*Millions of SDRs:*	
Quota	2f. s	260	260	260	260	260	260	260	260	480	480	720	720	720	1,010	1,010
SDRs	1b. s	—	—	36	43	56	6	4	22	57	129	137	227	282	4	1
Reserve Position in the Fund	1c. s	—	—	—	—	29	—	—	—	—	—	—	—	—	72	72
Total Fund Cred.&Loans Outstg.	2tl	138	125	107	19	—	—	—	—	68	69	74	161	196	218	425	421
International Liquidity												*Millions of US Dollars Unless Otherwise Indicated:*					
Total Reserves minus Gold	1l. d	156	ɪ185	572	805	1,490	584	1,497	2,509	2,626	4,062	5,392	5,014	3,144	3,718	4,773
SDRs	1b. d	—	—	39	52	68	7	5	26	75	170	175	264	311	4	1
Reserve Position in the Fund	1c. d	—	—	—	—	35	—	—	83	90	97	205	228	241	76	71
Foreign Exchange	1d. d	156	ɪ185	533	753	1,386	577	1,492	2,400	2,461	3,795	5,012	4,521	2,593	3,639	4,702
Gold (Million Fine Troy Ounces)	1ad	.114	.057	.121	.057	.057	.057	.057	.169	.224	.280	2.394	3.104	3.104	3.104	3.104
Gold (National Valuation)	1an d	4	2	5	2	2	2	2	7	37	105	1,108	1,062	1,052	1,096	947
Monetary Authorities: Other Liab.	4.. d	17	—	—	—	—	301	468	70	73	2	—	—	—	1	—
Deposit Money Banks: Assets	7a. d	227	263	377	521	722	475	690	761	1,097	2,098	4,364	5,059	3,776	4,547	4,777
Liabilities	7b. d	221	285	323	610	622	612	650	663	710	687	618	676	966	973	713
Monetary Authorities															*Billions of Rupiah:*	
Foreign Assets	11	...	...	...	...	...	...	...	...	...	...	4,217	4,037	3,685	5,309	8,041
Claims on Central Government	12a	...	...	...	...	...	...	...	...	...	...	716	925	1,154	1,521	1,670
Claims on Official Entities	12bx	...	...	...	...	...	...	...	...	...	...	2,370	2,467	2,453	1,864	203
Claims on Private Sector	12d	...	...	...	...	...	...	...	...	...	...	69	107	409	444	652
Claims on Deposit Money Banks	12e	...	...	...	...	...	...	...	...	...	...	1,722	2,548	5,050	5,866	9,521
Claims on Nonbank Financial Insts	12g	...	...	...	...	...	...	...	...	...	...	44	117	215	366	518
Reserve Money	14	...	...	...	...	...	...	...	...	...	...	3,375	3,920	4,107	5,138	5,701
of which: Currency Outside DMBs	14a	...	...	...	...	...	...	...	...	...	...	2,169	2,546	2,934	3,340	3,712
Time & Foreign Currency Deposits	15	...	...	...	...	...	...	...	...	...	...	41	104	57	110	25
Liabs. of Central Bank: Securities	16ac	...	...	...	...	...	...	...	...	...	...					
Restricted Deposits	16b	...	...	...	...	...	...	...	...	...	...	119	134	46	74	33
Foreign Liabilities	16c	...	...	...	...	...	...	...	...	...	...	30	27	23	471	467
Central Government Deposits	16d	...	...	...	...	...	...	...	...	...	...	2,755	4,770	5,796	5,946	8,745
Capital Accounts	17a	...	...	...	...	...	...	...	...	...	...	1,182	1,040	601	596	1,179
Other Items (Net)	17r	...	...	...	...	...	...	...	...	...	...	1,636	206	2,336	3,034	4,455
Deposit Money Banks															*Billions of Rupiah:*	
Reserves	20	...	...	...	...	...	...	...	...	...	...	1,262	1,430	1,988	1,815	2,273
Other Claims on Monetary Author.	20c	...	...	...	...	...	...	...	...	...	...					
Foreign Assets	21	...	...	...	...	...	...	...	...	...	...	2,741	3,233	2,591	4,520	5,107
Claims on Central Government	22a	...	...	...	...	...	...	...	...	...	...	28	69	139	266	440
Claims on Prov. and Local Govts	22b	...	...	...	...	...	...	...	...	...	...					
Claims on Official Entities	22bx	...	...	...	...	...	...	...	...	...	...	1,359	1,791	2,427	2,819	4,515
Claims on Nonfin.Pub.Enterprises	22c	...	...	...	...	...	...	...	...	...	...					
Claims on Private Sector	22d	...	...	...	...	...	...	...	...	...	...	4,254	5,942	8,106	10,490	14,086
Claims on Other Banking Insts	22f	...	...	...	...	...	...	...	...	...	...					
Claims on Nonbank Financial Insts	22g	...	...	...	...	...	...	...	...	...	...	19	26	20	25	37
Demand Deposits	24	...	...	...	...	...	...	...	...	...	...	2,795	3,847	4,133	4,177	4,817
Time, Savings,& Fgn. Currency Dep.	25	...	...	...	...	...	...	...	...	...	...	2,654	3,127	3,897	6,983	9,331
Money Market Instruments	26aa	...	...	...	...	...	...	...	...	...	...					
Restricted Deposits	26b	...	...	...	...	...	...	...	...	...	...	366	298	300	242	218
Foreign Liabilities	26c	...	...	...	...	...	...	...	...	...	...	388	432	663	968	762
Central Government Deposits	26d	...	...	...	...	...	...	...	...	...	...	735	914	691	779	1,397
Central Govt. Lending Funds	26f	...	...	...	...	...	...	...	...	...	...					
Credit from Monetary Authorities	26g	...	...	...	...	...	...	...	...	...	...	1,636	2,596	3,890	4,264	7,045
Liab. to Nonbank Financial Insts	26j	...	...	...	...	...	...	...	...	...	...					
Capital Accounts	27a	...	...	...	...	...	...	...	...	...	...	803	1,014	1,268	1,630	2,211
Other Items (Net)	27r	...	...	...	...	...	...	...	...	...	...	285	262	427	893	677
Monetary Survey															*Billions of Rupiah:*	
Foreign Assets (Net)	31n	−43	−58	117	296	659	−345	525	1,061	1,844	3,483	6,540	6,811	5,590	8,391	11,919
Domestic Credit	32	378	517	ɪ633	1,086	1,388	2,803	3,283	3,299	4,522	4,616	5,369	5,759	8,434	11,069	11,978
Claims on Central Govt. (Net)	32an	29	37	−12	−32	−151	18	−279	−613	−878	−1,711	−2,746	−4,691	−5,195	−4,938	−8,031
Claims on Prov. and Local Govts	32b	...	...	...	...	...	...	...	...	...	...	...	...	...	...	...
Claims on Official Entities	32bx	55	69	105	70	146	125	84	84	140	133	3,729	4,258	4,879	4,682	4,717
Claims on Nonfin.Pub.Enterprises	32c	...	...	...	...	...	...	...	...	...	...					
Claims on Private Sector	32d	294	411	ɪ540	1,048	1,394	2,660	3,477	3,828	5,260	6,194	4,323	6,049	8,515	10,934	14,737
Claims on Other Banking Insts	32f	...	...	...	...	...	...	...	...	...	...					
Claims on Nonbank Financial Inst	32g	...	...	...	...	...	...	...	...	...	...	62	143	235	391	555
Money	34	241	313	471	669	940	1,250	1,601	2,006	2,488	3,379	5,011	6,474	7,120	7,576	8,581
Quasi-Money	35	80	145	190	319	515	747	1,019	1,125	1,320	1,837	2,696	3,231	3,954	7,093	9,356
Money Market Instruments	36aa	...	...	...	...	...	...	...	...	...	...					
Restricted Deposits	36b	...	...	...	...	...	...	...	...	...	...	484	432	346	316	251
Central Govt. Lending Funds	36f	...	...	...	...	...	...	...	...	...	...					
Liab. to Nonbank Financial Insts	36j	...	...	...	...	...	...	...	...	...	...					
Capital Accounts	37a	...	...	...	...	...	...	...	...	...	...	...	...	...	...	...
Other Items (Net)	37r	15	2	90	394	592	460	1,188	1,228	2,557	2,883	3,717	2,433	2,604	4,475	5,709
Money plus Quasi-Money	35l	321	458	661	988	1,455	1,997	2,620	3,131	3,808	5,216	7,707	9,705	11,074	14,670	17,937
Other Banking Institutions															*Billions of Rupiah:*	
Cash	40	1	1	1	2	6	8	10	16	22	30	42	61	75	101	130
Savings Deposits	45	1	1	1	2	3	5	8	13	17	20	36	46	54	75	98
Credit from Monetary Authorities	46g	1	1	1	1	—	3	5	6	6	11	44	122	222	389	523
Other Items (Net)	47r	−1	−1	−1	−1	3	—	−3	−3	—	−2	−38	−107	−200	−362	−492
Liquid Liabilities	55l	321	458	661	988	1,452	1,994	2,618	3,127	3,802	5,206	7,701	9,690	11,052	14,643	17,905
Interest Rates															*Percent Per Annum*	
Discount Rate (*End of Period*)	60	...	...	...	...	...	...	...	...	...	...	...	...	...	...	...
Money Market Rate	60b	...	...	...	...	11.42	13.41	14.17	7.23	7.29	13.23	12.87	16.26	17.24	13.17	18.63
Deposit Rate	60l	21.00	21.00	15.00	12.00	12.00	12.00	12.00	9.00	6.00	6.00	6.00	6.00	6.00	6.00	16.00
Lending Rate	60p	...	...	...	...	...	...	...	...	...	...	...	...	...	...	...

Indonesia

536

1985	1986	1987	1988	1989	1990	1991	1992	1993	1994	1995	1996	1997	1998	1999		
End of Period															**Exchange Rates**	
1,235.7	2,007.3	2,340.8	2,329.4	2,361.5	2,704.5	2,849.4	2,835.3	2,898.2	3,211.7	3,430.8	3,426.7	6,274.0	11,299.4	9,724.2	Market Rate	**aa**
End of Period (ae) Period Average (rf)																
1,125.0	1,641.0	1,650.0	1,731.0	1,797.0	1,901.0	1,992.0	2,062.0	2,110.0	2,200.0	2,308.0	2,383.0	4,650.0	8,025.0	7,085.0	Market Rate	**ae**
1,110.6	1,282.6	1,643.8	1,685.7	1,770.1	1,842.8	1,950.3	2,029.9	2,087.1	2,160.8	2,248.6	2,342.3	2,909.4	10,013.6	7,855.2	Market Rate	**rf**
End of Period															**Fund Position**	
1,010	1,010	1,010	1,010	1,010	1,010	1,010	1,498	1,498	1,498	1,498	1,498	1,498	1,498	2,079	Quota	**2f.s**
51	36	4	2	1	2	3	—	—	—	1	2	370	222	—	SDRs	**1b.s**
72	72	72	72	72	72	72	194	200	214	270	298	—	—	145	Reserve Position in the Fund	**1c.s**
42	42	505	463	463	347	116	—	—	—	—	—	2,201	6,456	7,467	Total Fund Cred.&Loans Outstg.	**2tl**
End of Period															**International Liquidity**	
4,974	4,051	5,592	5,048	5,454	7,459	9,258	10,449	11,263	12,133	13,708	18,251	16,587	22,713	26,445	Total Reserves minus Gold	**1l.d**
56	43	6	3	1	3	4	—	—	—	1	2	499	312	—	SDRs	**1b.d**
80	89	103	97	95	103	104	267	274	312	401	429	—	—	200	Reserve Position in the Fund	**1c.d**
4,838	3,919	5,483	4,948	5,357	7,353	9,151	10,181	10,988	11,820	13,306	17,820	16,088	22,401	26,245	Foreign Exchange	**1d.d**
3.104	3.104	3.104	3.104	3.107	3.111	3.111	3.101	3.101	3.101	3.101	3.101	3.101	3.101	3.101	Gold (Million Fine Troy Ounces)	**1ad**
906	1,360	1,319	1,158	1,044	1,061	992	946	1,092	1,067	1,079	1,030	809	803	812	Gold (National Valuation)	**1and**
—	—	—	—	—	28	24	26	22	20	21	21	419	3,356	3,517	Monetary Authorities: Other Liab.	**4..d**
5,546	4,993	4,731	4,815	5,985	6,223	5,589	6,337	5,374	5,852	7,407	8,737	10,067	14,412	16,967	Deposit Money Banks: Assets	**7a.d**
523	329	456	664	1,781	6,737	6,025	7,894	9,691	11,311	11,678	12,482	15,147	12,192	14,167	Liabilities	**7b.d**
End of Period															**Monetary Authorities**	
8,507	8,352	12,458	11,732	11,835	17,950	25,155	I 32,795	37,643	36,444	40,163	59,886	94,202	179,439	183,866	Foreign Assets	**11**
1,237	3,106	3,518	4,427	4,589	5,221	6,258	I 7,528	8,591	6,632	3,726	3,775	4,996	34,895	247,289	Claims on Central Government	**12a**
32	24	36	58	830	759	35	....	....	....	....	....	....	....	....	Claims on Official Entities	**12bx**
823	1,133	1,676	1,724	1,307	1,732	953	I —	—	—	—	—	—	—	—	Claims on Private Sector	**12d**
10,041	12,552	14,562	20,375	15,240	20,990	14,867	I 11,054	10,885	13,607	16,456	15,182	67,313	125,759	21,310	Claims on Deposit Money Banks	**12e**
729	877	978	950	988	992	1,012	I 6	—	—	—	—	—	41,294	23,117	Claims on Nonbank Financial Insts	**12g**
6,721	8,170	9,032	8,381	10,788	12,549	12,961	I 16,997	18,414	23,053	27,160	36,896	51,014	81,448	102,043	Reserve Money	**14**
4,460	5,338	5,802	6,245	7,908	9,094	9,346	I 11,465	14,430	18,634	20,807	22,487	28,424	41,394	58,353	*of which: Currency Outside DMBs*	**14a**
69	42	305	143	11	18	21	I —	—	—	—	—	—	—	—	Time & Foreign Currency Deposits	**15**
....	....	....	....	....	....	....	20,595	23,339	15,051	11,851	18,553	14,885	49,590	63,049	Liabs. of Central Bank: Securities	**16ac**
23	24	24	25	26	26	24	I 382	534	497	461	436	267	660	244	Restricted Deposits	**16b**
74	111	3,308	5,219	6,804	6,327	7,013	I 54	46	43	49	50	15,761	99,879	97,526	Foreign Liabilities	**16c**
8,970	10,643	9,713	10,435	10,545	13,460	14,509	I 11,206	13,016	13,536	15,558	16,856	33,472	35,438	83,990	Central Government Deposits	**16d**
1,192	2,409	3,715	3,624	3,825	3,587	4,594	I 3,157	2,475	2,575	2,891	3,408	4,397	9,693	17,794	Capital Accounts	**17a**
4,320	4,643	7,132	11,438	2,789	11,676	9,158	I –1,008	–705	1,928	2,375	2,645	46,715	104,678	110,936	Other Items (Net)	**17r**
End of Period															**Deposit Money Banks**	
2,940	2,935	3,433	5,151	5,615	4,893	12,300	I 4,112	4,591	5,051	7,371	14,896	24,172	48,090	59,290	Reserves	**20**
....	....	....	....	....	....	....	11,782	14,799	7,619	5,152	11,225	6,318	47,103	72,238	Other Claims on Monetary Author.	**20c**
6,239	8,193	7,807	8,397	10,731	11,681	11,076	I 13,009	11,340	12,874	17,096	20,820	46,810	115,657	120,209	Foreign Assets	**21**
530	683	1,093	1,069	960	933	1,027	I 3,541	4,004	2,843	4,165	5,727	8,571	10,230	274,551	Claims on Central Government	**22a**
....	....	....	....	....	....	....	1,032	256	113	276	290	292	319	214	Claims on Prov. and Local Govts	**22b**
4,981	5,080	4,782	6,292	7,730	6,950	9,671	....	....	....	....	....	....	....	....	Claims on Official Entities	**22bx**
....	....	....	....	....	....	....	6,000	6,492	6,866	8,423	9,248	11,036	15,128	11,854	Claims on Nonfin.Pub.Enterprises	**22c**
17,281	21,731	28,034	38,809	58,404	97,145	114,453	I 128,521	161,273	198,311	243,067	295,195	381,741	508,558	225,236	Claims on Private Sector	**22d**
....	....	....	....	....	....	....	97	190	236	312	370	364	277	100	Claims on Other Banking Insts	**22f**
41	25	115	170	246	345	590	I 1,934	1,276	2,329	2,785	4,897	6,353	5,763	1,998	Claims on Nonbank Financial Insts	**22g**
5,560	6,082	6,776	8,032	12,477	14,532	17,103	I 14,206	19,057	22,710	26,202	28,883	40,232	45,717	55,327	Demand Deposits	**24**
12,985	15,942	20,895	27,538	37,956	60,793	72,696	I 91,570	109,402	130,280	171,257	226,097	279,073	481,350	525,227	Time, Savings,& Fgn. Currency Dep.	**25**
....	....	....	....	....	....	....	1,730	2,435	2,437	4,162	3,353	4,306	3,223	2,986	Money Market Instruments	**26aa**
268	402	425	684	632	1,048	966	I 1,370	1,699	1,541	1,779	2,099	1,419	2,417	1,659	Restricted Deposits	**26b**
588	541	752	1,159	3,193	12,645	11,935	I 16,206	20,448	24,885	26,952	29,744	70,434	97,842	100,375	Foreign Liabilities	**26c**
1,884	1,687	1,779	2,227	3,943	4,719	5,487	I 7,442	11,683	10,344	11,844	13,858	16,929	23,169	23,336	Central Government Deposits	**26d**
....	....	....	....	....	....	....	—	3,307	3,801	3,871	5,029	1,653	1,416	4,508	Central Govt. Lending Funds	**26f**
7,039	7,747	8,100	11,711	12,936	11,144	11,692	I 10,554	16,237	11,432	10,394	11,622	23,008	112,947	33,360	Credit from Monetary Authorities	**26g**
....	....	....	....	....	....	....	10,974	1,153	1,326	1,564	2,533	7,536	39,332	14,725	Liab. to Nonbank Financial Insts	**26j**
2,541	3,049	3,650	4,464	7,376	11,255	9,075	I 15,196	21,973	26,775	36,506	42,523	53,408	–94,556	–17,346	Capital Accounts	**27a**
1,146	3,197	2,888	4,072	5,171	5,811	20,161	I 780	–3,173	711	–5,884	–3,073	–12,341	38,268	21,533	Other Items (Net)	**27r**
End of Period															**Monetary Survey**	
14,083	15,892	16,206	13,751	12,568	10,659	17,283	I 29,544	28,489	24,390	30,258	50,912	54,817	97,374	106,174	Foreign Assets (Net)	**31n**
14,799	20,329	28,739	40,835	60,564	95,898	114,002	I 130,030	157,396	193,458	235,356	288,788	362,952	557,857	677,033	Domestic Credit	**32**
–9,087	–8,541	–6,882	–7,167	–8,941	–12,024	–12,711	I –7,579	–12,104	–14,405	–19,511	–21,212	–36,834	–13,482	414,514	Claims on Central Govt. (Net)	**32an**
....	....	....	....	....	....	....	1,032	256	113	276	290	292	319	214	Claims on Prov. and Local Govts	**32b**
5,013	5,104	4,818	6,350	8,560	7,709	9,706	....	....	....	....	....	....	....	....	Claims on Official Entities	**32bx**
....	....	....	....	....	....	....	6,019	6,505	6,874	8,427	9,248	11,036	15,128	11,854	Claims on Nonfin.Pub.Enterprises	**32c**
18,104	22,864	29,710	40,532	59,711	98,877	115,406	I 128,521	161,273	198,311	243,067	295,195	381,741	508,558	225,236	Claims on Private Sector	**32d**
....	....	....	....	....	....	....	97	190	236	312	370	364	277	100	Claims on Other Banking Insts	**32f**
770	902	1,093	1,120	1,234	1,337	1,601	I 1,940	1,276	2,329	2,785	4,897	6,353	47,057	25,115	Claims on Nonbank Financial Inst	**32g**
10,124	11,631	12,705	14,392	20,559	23,819	26,693	I 27,485	33,739	41,462	47,135	51,652	68,785	87,301	114,562	Money	**34**
13,054	15,984	21,200	27,681	37,967	60,811	72,717	I 91,570	109,402	130,280	171,257	226,097	279,073	481,350	525,227	Quasi-Money	**35**
....	....	....	....	....	....	....	1,730	2,435	2,437	4,162	3,353	4,306	3,223	2,986	Money Market Instruments	**36aa**
291	426	449	709	658	1,074	990	I 1,752	2,233	2,038	2,240	2,535	1,686	3,077	1,903	Restricted Deposits	**36b**
....	....	....	....	....	....	....	—	3,307	3,801	3,871	5,029	1,653	1,416	4,508	Central Govt. Lending Funds	**36f**
....	....	....	....	....	....	....	10,974	1,153	1,326	1,564	2,533	7,536	39,332	14,725	Liab. to Nonbank Financial Insts	**36j**
....	....	....	....	....	....	....	18,353	24,448	29,350	39,397	45,931	57,805	–84,863	448	Capital Accounts	**37a**
5,414	8,180	10,592	11,806	13,948	20,852	30,885	I 7,710	9,168	7,154	–4,012	2,571	–3,075	124,395	118,848	Other Items (Net)	**37r**
23,177	27,615	33,904	42,073	58,526	84,630	99,410	I 119,055	143,141	171,742	218,392	277,749	347,858	568,651	639,789	Money plus Quasi-Money	**35l**
End of Period															**Other Banking Institutions**	
74	63	72	76	65	162	99	....	....	....	....	....	....	....	....	Cash	**40**
134	220	348	492	289	740	919	....	....	....	....	....	....	....	....	Savings Deposits	**45**
734	882	1,157	951	1,827	1,412	1,338	....	....	....	....	....	....	....	....	Credit from Monetary Authorities	**46g**
–793	–1,038	–1,433	–1,368	–2,051	–1,990	–2,158	....	....	....	....	....	....	....	....	Other Items (Net)	**47r**
23,237	27,772	34,181	42,489	58,750	85,208	100,230	....	....	....	....	....	....	....	....	Liquid Liabilities	**55l**
Percent Per Annum															**Interest Rates**	
....	....	....	....	....	18.83	18.47	13.50	8.82	12.44	13.99	12.80	20.00	38.44	12.51	Discount Rate *(End of Period)*	**60**
10.33	....	14.52	15.00	12.57	13.97	14.91	11.99	8.66	9.74	13.64	13.96	27.82	62.79	23.58	Money Market Rate	**60b**
18.00	15.39	16.78	17.72	18.63	I 17.53	23.32	19.60	14.55	12.53	16.72	17.26	20.01	39.07	25.74	Deposit Rate	**60l**
....	21.49	21.67	22.10	21.70	20.83	25.53	24.03	20.59	17.76	18.85	19.22	21.82	32.15	27.66	Lending Rate	**60p**

Indonesia

	1970	1971	1972	1973	1974	1975	1976	1977	1978	1979	1980	1981	1982	1983	1984
Prices, Production, Labor														*Index Numbers (1995=100):*	
Wholesale Prices: Incl. Petroleum **63**	....	4.4	5.0	6.9	10.3	10.9	12.5	14.3	‡15.6	23.4	29.7	32.9	35.4	‡41.7	46.3
Excl. Petroleum **63a**	....	4.8	5.4	7.3	9.4	10.4	12.3	14.0	‡15.4	20.6	24.4	26.8	29.1	34.8	39.4
Consumer Prices **64**	6.0	6.2	6.6	8.7	12.2	14.5	17.4	19.3	20.9	‡24.3	28.6	32.2	35.2	39.4	43.5
Crude Petroleum Production **66aa**	53.1	55.4	67.6	83.3	85.5	81.3	93.8	104.8	101.7	98.9	98.3	99.7	83.2	83.6	88.1
														Number in Thousands:	
Labor Force **67d**	....	....	....	....	....	....	....	....	....	....	....	....	....	....	....
Employment **67e**	....	....	....	....	....	....	....	....	....	....	....	....	....	....	....
Unemployment **67c**	....	....	....	....	....	....	....	....	....	....	....	....	....	....	....
Unemployment Rate (%) **67r**	....	....	....	....	....	....	....	....	....	....	....	....	....	....	....
International Transactions														*Millions of US Dollars*	
Exports .... **70..d**	1,108	1,234	1,777	3,211	7,426	7,102	8,547	10,853	11,643	15,591	21,909	25,165	22,328	21,146	21,888
Crude Petroleum & Products **70a.d**	446	565	913	1,609	5,211	5,311	6,004	7,298	7,439	8,871	12,850	14,390	14,861	13,478	12,097
Crude Petroleum .... **70aa d**	409	468	834	1,359	4,680	4,933	5,652	6,827	7,015	8,124	11,671	13,183	14,002	11,646	10,214
Imports, c.i.f. .... **71..d**	1,002	1,103	1,562	2,729	3,842	4,770	5,673	6,230	6,690	7,202	10,834	13,272	16,859	16,352	13,882
															1995=100
Volume of Exports **72**	22	‡26	31	38	39	40	46	53	56	54	51	42	40	48	48
Crude Petroleum **72aa**	77	81	101	124	128	128	147	167	171	149	122	127	105	123	115
Export Prices															*1995=100:*
Exports (Unit Value) .... **74..d**	‡15.6	15.4	18.6	27.0	59.0	62.4	65.6	73.2	74.2	104.3	152.4	152.6	148.9	132.1	130.6
Crude Petroleum (Unit Value) ..... **74aa d**	5.8	8.0	12.7	17.3	53.0	58.2	59.0	62.1	62.4	84.3	141.6	162.4	162.8	141.9	135.2
Crude Petroleum (Ofc.Price) .... **76aa d**	9.6	12.0	16.0	23.0	68.5	72.7	73.9	77.9	77.9	105.7	175.6	201.1	200.7	174.0	169.7
Balance of Payments														*Millions of US Dollars:*	
Current Account, n.i.e. .... **78al d**	....	....	....	....	....	....	....	....	....	....	....	−566	−5,324	−6,338	−1,856
Goods: Exports f.o.b. .... **78aa d**	....	....	....	....	....	....	....	....	....	....	....	23,348	19,747	18,689	20,754
Goods: Imports f.o.b. .... **78ab d**	....	....	....	....	....	....	....	....	....	....	....	−16,542	−17,854	−17,726	−15,047
Trade Balance .... **78ac d**	....	....	....	....	....	....	....	....	....	....	....	6,806	1,893	963	5,707
Services: Credit .... **78ad d**	....	....	....	....	....	....	....	....	....	....	....	449	504	546	570
Services: Debit .... **78ae d**	....	....	....	....	....	....	....	....	....	....	....	−4,998	−4,862	−4,311	−4,239
Balance on Goods & Services .... **78af d**	....	....	....	....	....	....	....	....	....	....	....	2,257	−2,465	−2,802	2,038
Income: Credit .... **78ag d**	....	....	....	....	....	....	....	....	....	....	....	1,081	1,023	631	828
Income: Debit .... **78ah d**	....	....	....	....	....	....	....	....	....	....	....	−4,154	−4,016	−4,281	−4,889
Balance on Gds, Serv. & Inc. .... **78ai d**	....	....	....	....	....	....	....	....	....	....	....	−816	−5,458	−6,452	−2,023
Current Transfers, n.i.e.: Credit .... **78aj d**	....	....	....	....	....	....	....	....	....	....	....	250	134	114	167
Current Transfers: Debit .... **78ak d**	....	....	....	....	....	....	....	....	....	....	....	—	—	—	—
Capital Account, n.i.e. .... **78bc d**	....	....	....	....	....	....	....	....	....	....	....	—	—	—	—
Capital Account, n.i.e.: Credit .... **78ba d**	....	....	....	....	....	....	....	....	....	....	....	—	—	—	—
Capital Account: Debit .... **78bb d**	....	....	....	....	....	....	....	....	....	....	....	—	—	—	—
Financial Account, n.i.e. .... **78bj d**	....	....	....	....	....	....	....	....	....	....	....	1,861	5,622	6,054	3,457
Direct Investment Abroad .... **78bd d**	....	....	....	....	....	....	....	....	....	....	....	—	—	—	—
Dir. Invest. in Rep. Econ., n.i.e. ...... **78be d**	....	....	....	....	....	....	....	....	....	....	....	133	225	292	222
Portfolio Investment Assets .... **78bf d**	....	....	....	....	....	....	....	....	....	....	....	—	—	—	—
Equity Securities............................. **78bk d**	....	....	....	....	....	....	....	....	....	....	....	—	—	—	—
Debt Securities .... **78bl d**	....	....	....	....	....	....	....	....	....	....	....	—	—	—	—
Portfolio Investment Liab., n.i.e. ...... **78bg d**	....	....	....	....	....	....	....	....	....	....	....	47	315	368	−10
Equity Securities............................. **78bm d**	....	....	....	....	....	....	....	....	....	....	....	—	—	—	—
Debt Securities .... **78bn d**	....	....	....	....	....	....	....	....	....	....	....	47	315	368	−10
Financial Derivatives Assets .... **78bw d**	....	....	....	....	....	....	....	....	....	....	....	....	....	....	....
Financial Derivatives Liabilities ..... **78bx d**	....	....	....	....	....	....	....	....	....	....	....	....	....	....	....
Other Investment Assets .... **78bh d**	....	....	....	....	....	....	....	....	....	....	....	—	—	—	—
Monetary Authorities .... **78bo d**	....	....	....	....	....	....	....	....	....	....	....	—	—	—	—
General Government .... **78bp d**	....	....	....	....	....	....	....	....	....	....	....	—	—	—	—
Banks .... **78bq d**	....	....	....	....	....	....	....	....	....	....	....	—	—	—	—
Other Sectors .... **78br d**	....	....	....	....	....	....	....	....	....	....	....	—	—	—	—
Other Investment Liab., n.i.e. .... **78bi d**	....	....	....	....	....	....	....	....	....	....	....	1,681	5,082	5,394	3,245
Monetary Authorities .... **78bs d**	....	....	....	....	....	....	....	....	....	....	....	—	—	—	—
General Government .... **78bt d**	....	....	....	....	....	....	....	....	....	....	....	1,666	3,668	3,860	2,918
Banks .... **78bu d**	....	....	....	....	....	....	....	....	....	....	....	—	—	—	—
Other Sectors .... **78bv d**	....	....	....	....	....	....	....	....	....	....	....	15	1,414	1,534	327
Net Errors and Omissions.................. **78ca d**	....	....	....	....	....	....	....	....	....	....	....	−1,669	−2,151	467	−620
Overall Balance .... **78cb d**	—	—	—	—	—	—	—	—	—	—	—	−374	−1,853	183	981
Reserves and Related Items .... **79da d**	—	—	—	—	—	—	—	—	—	—	—	374	1,853	−183	−981
Reserve Assets .... **79db d**	....	....	....	....	....	....	....	....	....	....	....	374	1,853	−633	−977
Use of Fund Credit and Loans .... **79dc d**	....	....	....	....	....	....	....	....	....	....	....	—	—	450	−4
Exceptional Financing .... **79de d**	....	....	....	....	....	....	....	....	....	....	....	....	....	....	....

1985	1986	1987	1988	1989	1990	1991	1992	1993	1994	1995	1996	1997	1998	1999		
															Prices, Production, Labor	
Period Averages																
48.6	49.7	59.2	62.2	67.5	74.3	78.1	82.1	85.2	89.8	100.0	107.9	117.5	237.2	....	Wholesale Prices: Incl. Petroleum	63
‡41.1	44.5	51.2	56.5	60.9	65.1	69.9	74.1	79.5	87.8	100.0	106.2	114.4	206.3	....	Excl. Petroleum	63a
45.5	48.2	52.6	56.9	60.5	65.3	71.4	‡76.8	84.2	91.4	100.0	‡108.0	115.2	181.7	218.9	Consumer Prices	64
82.5	86.5	81.7	83.8	87.6	90.9	99.1	93.9	95.1	100.3	100.0	99.5	73.7	96.9	....	Crude Petroleum Production	66aa
Period Averages																
....	....	....	....	....	....	....	....	....	....	....	88,187	89,603	94,735	....	Labor Force	67d
62,457	68,338	70,402	72,518	73,425	75,850	76,423	78,104	79,201	80,110	82,038	85,702	87,050	87,672	....	Employment	67e
1,369	1,855	1,843	2,106	2,083	1,952	2,032	2,199	2,246	3,738	....	3,625	4,197	5,063	....	Unemployment	67c
2.1	2.6	2.6	2.8	2.8	2.5	2.6	2.7	2.8	4.4	....	4.0	4.7	5.5	....	Unemployment Rate (%)	67r
															International Transactions	
Millions of US Dollars																
18,587	14,805	17,136	19,219	22,160	25,675	29,142	33,967	36,823	40,055	45,417	49,814	53,443	48,847	48,665	Exports	70..d
7,670	5,167	5,919	....	4,964	6,481	5,745	5,850	5,009	6,006	6,441	7,243	6,822	4,264	....	Crude Petroleum & Products	70a.d
7,217	4,721	4,590	4,396	4,349	5,313	4,999	4,648	4,259	5,072	5,146	5,712	5,479	3,349	....	Crude Petroleum	70aa d
10,259	10,718	12,370	13,249	16,360	21,837	25,869	27,280	28,328	31,983	40,630	42,929	41,694	27,337	24,004	Imports, c.i.f.	71..d
1995=100																
53	58	59	55	60	‡59	....	83	87	96	100	105	135	125	....	Volume of Exports	72
85	100	98	78	82	81	87	84	71	107	100	94	96	90	....	Crude Petroleum	72aa
															Export Prices	
Indices of Unit Values in US Dollars																
112.4	74.8	73.4	69.9	74.2	‡90.3	91.0	90.3	88.3	87.6	100.0	105.8	100.5	78.4	....	Exports (Unit Value)	74..d
128.5	83.1	77.9	72.9	76.0	129.9	113.2	110.0	104.8	91.8	100.0	117.6	113.5	72.2	....	Crude Petroleum (Unit Value)	74aa d
164.4	164.0	106.2	88.8	100.8	127.7	108.8	108.8	100.3	92.3	100.0	116.9	74.1	....	....	Crude Petroleum (Ofc.Price)	76aa d
															Balance of Payments	
Minus Sign Indicates Debit																
-1,923	-3,911	-2,098	-1,397	-1,108	-2,988	-4,260	-2,780	-2,106	-2,792	-6,431	-7,663	-4,889	4,096	....	Current Account, n.i.e.	78al d
18,527	14,396	17,206	19,509	22,974	26,807	29,635	33,796	36,607	40,223	47,454	50,188	56,298	50,371	....	Goods: Exports f.o.b.	78aa d
-12,705	-11,938	-12,532	-13,831	-16,310	-21,455	-24,834	-26,774	-28,376	-32,322	-40,921	-44,240	-46,223	-31,942	....	Goods: Imports f.o.b.	78ab d
5,822	2,458	4,674	5,678	6,664	5,352	4,801	7,022	8,231	7,901	6,533	5,948	10,075	18,429	....	*Trade Balance*	78ac d
844	844	1,065	1,369	1,875	2,488	2,822	3,391	3,959	4,797	5,469	6,599	6,941	4,479	....	Services: Credit	78ad d
-5,135	-4,256	-4,440	-4,606	-5,439	-6,056	-6,564	-8,100	-9,846	-11,416	-13,540	-15,139	-16,607	-11,961	....	Services: Debit	78ae d
1,531	-954	1,299	2,441	3,100	1,784	1,059	2,313	2,344	1,282	-1,538	-2,592	409	10,947	....	*Balance on Goods & Services*	78af d
768	732	561	492	562	409	917	818	1,028	1,048	1,306	1,210	1,855	1,910	....	Income: Credit	78ag d
-4,310	-3,948	-4,215	-4,584	-5,109	-5,599	-6,498	-6,482	-6,015	-5,741	-7,180	-7,218	-8,187	-10,099	....	Income: Debit	78ah d
-2,011	-4,170	-2,355	-1,651	-1,447	-3,406	-4,522	-3,351	-2,643	-3,411	-7,412	-8,600	-5,923	2,758	....	*Balance on Gds, Serv. & Inc.*	78ai d
88	259	257	254	339	418	262	571	537	619	981	937	1,034	1,338	....	Current Transfers, n.i.e.: Credit	78aj d
															Current Transfers: Debit	78ak d
—	—	—	—	—	—	—	—	—	—	—	—	—	—	....	Capital Account, n.i.e.	78bc d
—	—	—	—	—	—	—	—	—	—	—	—	—	—	....	Capital Account, n.i.e.: Credit	78ba d
—	—	—	—	—	—	—	—	—	—	—	—	—	—	....	Capital Account: Debit	78bb d
1,782	4,177	3,481	2,217	2,918	4,495	5,697	6,129	5,632	3,839	10,259	10,847	-603	-9,638	....	Financial Account, n.i.e.	78bj d
—	—	—	—	—	—	—	—	-356	-609	-603	-600	-178	-44	....	Direct Investment Abroad	78bd d
310	258	385	576	682	1,093	1,482	1,777	2,004	2,109	4,346	6,194	4,677	-356	....	Dir. Invest. in Rep. Econ., n.i.e.	78bn d
....	....	....	....	....	....	....	....	....	....	....	....	....	....	....	Portfolio Investment Assets	78bf d
—	—	—	—	—	—	—	—	—	—	....	....	....	—	....	Equity Securities	78bk d
....	....	....	....	....	....	....	....	....	....	....	....	....	....	....	Debt Securities	78bl d
-35	268	-88	-98	-173	-93	-12	-88	1,805	3,877	4,100	5,005	-2,632	-1,878	....	Portfolio Investment Liab., n.i.e.	78bg d
								1,805	1,900	1,493	1,819	-4,987	-4,371	....	Equity Securities	78bm d
-35	268	-88	-98	-173	-93	-12	-88	—	1,977	2,607	3,186	2,355	2,493	....	Debt Securities	78bn d
....	....	....	....	....	....	....	....	....	....	....	....	....	....	....	Financial Derivatives Assets	78bw d
....	....	....	....	....	....	....	....	....	....	....	....	....	....	....	Financial Derivatives Liabilities	78bx d
—	—	—	—	—	—	—	—	—	—	....	....	—	—	....	Other Investment Assets	78bh d
—	—	—	—	—	—	—	—	—	—			—	—	....	Monetary Authorities	78bo d
—	—	—	—	—	—	—	—	—	—	....	....	—	—	....	General Government	78bp d
....	....	....	....	....	....	....	....	....	....	....	....	....	....	....	Banks	78bq d
—	—	—	—	—	—	—	—	—	—			—	—	....	Other Sectors	78br d
1,507	3,651	3,184	1,739	2,409	3,495	4,227	4,440	2,179	-1,538	2,416	248	-2,470	-7,360	....	Other Investment Liab., n.i.e.	78bi d
—	—	—	—	—	—	—	—	—	—	—	—	—	—	....	Monetary Authorities	78bs d
1,747	2,618	2,021	1,908	2,777	474	1,299	858	552	137	6	-663	-265	4,209	....	General Government	78bt d
								1,357	527	1,953	-758	-276	-2,270	....	Banks	78bu d
-240	1,033	1,163	-169	-368	3,021	2,928	3,582	270	-2,202	457	1,669	-1,929	-9,299	....	Other Sectors	78bv d
651	-1,269	-753	-933	-1,315	744	91	-1,279	-2,932	-263	-2,255	1,319	-2,645	1,849	....	Net Errors and Omissions	78ca d
510	-1,003	630	-113	495	2,251	1,528	2,070	594	784	1,573	4,503	-8,137	-3,693	....	*Overall Balance*	78cb d
-510	1,003	-630	113	-495	-2,251	-1,528	-2,070	-594	-784	-1,573	-4,503	8,137	3,693	....	Reserves and Related Items	79da d
-126	1,003	-1,233	167	-495	-2,088	-1,210	-1,909	-594	-784	-1,573	-4,503	5,113	-2,090	....	Reserve Assets	79db d
-385	—	604	-54	—	-163	-319	-161	—	—	—	—	3,025	5,782	....	Use of Fund Credit and Loans	79dc d
....	....	....	....	....	....	....	....	....	....	....	....	....	....	....	Exceptional Financing	79de d

Indonesia

		1970	1971	1972	1973	1974	1975	1976	1977	1978	1979	1980	1981	1982	1983	1984
Government Finance															*Billions of Rupiah:*	
Deficit (-) or Surplus	80	−101	−91	‡−117	−163	−168	−468	−693	−393	−754	−764	−1,102	−1,172	−1,191	−1,862	1,219
Revenue	81	360	442	‡644	1,020	1,832	2,300	2,968	3,634	4,378	7,050	10,406	13,763	12,815	15,511	18,724
Grants Received	81z	....	....	—	—	—	—	—	—	—	—	—	—	—	—	—
Expenditure	82	461	534	‡718	1,103	1,857	2,592	3,375	3,707	4,870	7,284	10,827	14,246	13,568	16,359	16,803
Lending Minus Repayments	83	....	....	43	80	143	176	286	320	262	530	681	689	438	1,014	702
Financing																
Net Borrowing: Domestic	84a	5	5	‡5	−2	−15	28	−37	64	42	41	43	145	−155	960	−1,088
Foreign	85a	88	92	‡112	165	182	454	750	460	701	868	1,024	1,094	1,277	1,082	207
Use of Cash Balances	87	8	−5	‡—	—	—	−14	−20	−131	11	−145	35	−67	69	−180	−338
Debt: Domestic	88a	....	....	111	115	115	143	106	170	212	252	229	371	216	1,176	115
Foreign	89a	....	....	1,890	2,170	2,358	2,671	3,317	3,831	7,144	7,392	8,211	9,462	17,254	21,018	22,972
National Accounts															*Billions of Rupiah*	
Exports of Goods & Services	90c	429	530	754	1,354	3,105	2,851	3,430	4,466	4,935	9,629	13,849	16,177	15,103	19,847	22,999
Government Consumption	91f	293	341	414	716	841	1,254	1,591	2,077	2,659	3,733	4,688	6,452	7,229	8,077	9,122
Gross Capital Formation	93	455	580	857	1,208	1,797	2,572	3,205	3,826	4,671	6,704	9,485	17,324	17,406	22,261	23,543
Private Consumption	96f	2,693	2,833	3,402	4,791	7,259	8,745	10,464	12,458	13,850	19,514	27,503	32,293	37,924	47,063	54,067
Imports of Goods & Services	98c	−529	−611	−862	−1,316	−2,294	−2,778	−3,222	−3,817	−3,370	−7,555	−10,080	−14,119	−15,186	−19,626	−19,845
Gross Domestic Product (GDP)	99b	3,340	3,672	4,564	6,753	10,708	12,643	15,467	19,011	22,746	32,025	45,446	58,127	62,476	77,623	89,885
Net Factor Inc/Pmts(-) Abroad	98.n	−50	−67	−159	−246	−507	−556	−432	−679	−892	−1,484	−2,011	−1,930	−1,980	−3,283	−4,183
Gross National Income (GNI)	99a	3,290	3,605	4,405	6,508	10,201	12,087	15,035	18,332	21,854	30,541	43,435	56,197	60,496	74,340	85,702
Net National Income	99e	3,071	3,367	4,109	6,069	9,505	11,266	14,028	17,097	20,371	28,452	40,473	52,685	56,620	70,459	81,208
GDP Volume 1970 prices	99b.*p*	3,340	3,574	....	....	....	....	....	....	....	....	....	....	....	....	....
GDP Volume 1973 prices	99b.*p*	....	5,545	6,067	6,753	7,269	7,631	8,156	8,871	9,567	10,165	11,169	12,055	12,325	12,842	....
GDP Volume 1983 Prices	99b.*p*	....	....	....	....	....	....	....	....	....	....	....	....	....	77,623	83,037
GDP Volume 1993 Prices	99b.*p*	....	....	....	....	....	....	....	....	....	....	....	....	....	....	....
GDP Volume (1995=100)	99bv*p*	19.3	20.6	22.6	25.1	27.0	28.4	30.3	33.0	35.6	37.8	41.5	44.8	45.8	47.7	51.1
GDP Deflator (1995=100)	99bi*p*	3.8	3.9	4.5	5.9	8.7	9.8	11.2	12.7	14.1	18.6	24.1	28.5	30.0	35.8	38.7
															Millions:	
Population	99z	119.47	122.53	125.64	128.80	132.00	135.67	‡133.53	136.63	139.80	143.04	147.49	151.31	154.66	158.08	161.58

Year Beginning April 1

1985	1986	1987	1988	1989	1990	1991	1992	1993	1994	1995	1996	1997	1998	1999		
															Government Finance	
−948	−3,621	−1,037	−4,388	−3,362	798	982	−1,096	2,018	3,581	10,085	6,180	−4,211	−22,494 P	....	Deficit (-) or Surplus	**80**
20,347	21,324	24,781	24,088	29,093	39,566	42,415	50,645	56,318	69,402	80,427	90,298	113,882	158,148 P	....	Revenue	**81**
—	—	—	—	—	—	—	—		67				—P	....	Grants Received	**81z**
20,770	24,844	26,056	28,691	32,545	38,720	41,319	52,200	54,983	61,866	66,723	77,964	112,893	168,614 P	....	Expenditure	**82**
525	101	−238	−215	−90	48	114	−459	−683	4,022	3,619	6,154	5,200	12,028 P	....	Lending Minus Repayments	**83**
															Financing	
348	836	610	1,424	336	−147	594	−1,225	444	−4,295	....	−3,058	5,210	....	....	Net Borrowing: Domestic	**84a**
705	2,889	456	3,354	2,882	1,515	1,798	1,159	−451	−303	−1,677	−2,659	−4,674	44,346 P	....	Foreign	**85a**
−105	−104	−29	−390	144	−2,166	−3,374	1,162	−2,011	1,017	....	−463	3,676	....	....	Use of Cash Balances	**87**
462	1,298	1,908	3,343	3,686	3,578	4,172	5,449	4,861	939	3,229	83	....	....	....	Debt: Domestic	**88a**
30,747	52,298	63,297	76,902	74,817	85,891	87,435	105,546	118,797	138,841	136,781	127,324	....	....	....	Foreign	**89a**

Billions of Rupiah

1985	1986	1987	1988	1989	1990	1991	1992	1993	1994	1995	1996	1997	1998	1999		
															National Accounts	
21,867	21,486	30,837	36,493	45,764	55,852	68,452	83,050	I88,231	101,332	119,593	137,533	174,871	506,245	387,952	Exports of Goods & Services	**90c**
11,067	12,167	12,126	13,421	16,872	18,953	22,830	26,879	I29,757	31,014	35,584	40,299	42,952	54,416	72,631	Government Consumption	**91f**
27,630	31,236	40,247	46,993	63,122	76,196	88,671	101,194	I97,213	118,707	145,118	163,453	199,301	442,728	128,242	Gross Capital Formation	**93**
57,985	68,453	74,246	85,318	95,414	114,693	137,469	147,709	I192,958	228,119	279,876	332,094	387,171	663,460	818,933	Private Consumption	**96f**
−20,142	−22,645	−28,825	−32,830	−41,564	−54,827	−67,453	−76,438	I−78,383	−96,953	−125,657	−140,812	−176,600	−413,059	−300,467	Imports of Goods & Services	**98c**
98,406	110,697	128,630	149,395	179,608	210,866	249,969	282,395	I329,776	382,220	454,514	532,568	627,695	1,253,790	1,107,291	Gross Domestic Product (GDP)	**99b**
−3,941	−4,193	−6,022	−6,922	−8,074	−9,616	−10,899	−12,447	I−12,553	−10,248	−13,366	−14,272	−18,355	−53,894	−78,856	Net Factor Inc/Pmts(-) Abroad	**98.n**
94,465	106,504	122,607	142,472	171,533	201,249	239,069	269,947	I296,095	348,072	413,661	489,377	571,512	1,203,998	1,005,892	Gross National Income (GNI)	**99a**
88,206	93,356	112,554	135,367	163,168	191,465	227,689	256,902	I279,606	328,961	390,936	462,749	540,236	1,154,519	950,528	Net National Income	**99e**
....	....	....	....	....	....	....	....	....	....	....	....	....	....	....	GDP Volume 1970 prices	**99b.** *p*
....	....	....	....	....	....	....	....	....	....	....	....	....	....	....	GDP Volume 1973 prices	**99b.** *p*
85,082	90,081	94,518	99,981	107,437	115,217	123,225	131,185	139,707	....	....	....	....	....	....	GDP Volume 1983 Prices	**99b.** *p*
....	....	....	....	....	....	....	....	329,776	354,641	383,792	413,798	433,246	376,052	376,903	GDP Volume 1993 Prices	**99b.** *p*
52.3	55.4	58.1	61.5	66.1	70.9	75.8	80.7	85.9	92.4	100.0	107.8	112.9	98.0	98.2	GDP Volume (1995=100)	**99bv** *p*
41.4	44.0	48.7	53.5	59.8	65.5	72.6	77.0	I84.4	91.0	100.0	108.7	122.3	281.5	248.1	GDP Deflator (1995=100)	**99bi** *p*

Midyear Estimates

1985	1986	1987	1988	1989	1990	1991	1992	1993	1994	1995	1996	1997	1998	1999		
164.63	168.35	172.01	175.59	179.14	I179.48	181.39	184.49	187.59	190.68	194.75	196.81	199.87	I204.42	209.26	Population	**99z**

(See notes in the back of the book.)

Iran, I.R. of

		1970	1971	1972	1973	1974	1975	1976	1977	1978	1979	1980	1981	1982	1983	1984
Exchange Rates																*Rials per SDR:*
Official Rate	aa	76.38	82.93	82.93	81.58	82.80	81.10	82.05	85.61	91.81	92.84	92.30	92.30	92.30	92.30	92.30
																Rials per US Dollar:
Official Rate	ae	76.38	76.38	76.38	67.63	67.63	69.28	70.63	70.48	70.48	70.48	72.32	79.45	83.43	88.16	93.99
Official Rate	rf	75.75	75.75	75.75	68.88	67.63	67.64	70.22	70.62	70.48	70.48	70.61	78.33	83.60	86.36	90.03
																Rials per US Dollar:
Weighted Average	yf	....	....	....	....	....	....	....	....	....	....	....	....	....	....	....
																Index Numbers (1995=100):
Nominal Effective Exchange Rate	ne c	....	....	....	....	....	....	....	....	....	1,566.10	1,607.99	1,697.21	1,811.43	1,907.28	2,032.36
Real Effective Exchange Rate	re c	....	....	....	....	....	....	....	....	....	238.98	261.03	310.69	363.53	430.42	485.31
Fund Position																*Millions of SDRs:*
Quota	2f. s	192	192	192	192	192	192	192	192	660	660	660	660	660	660	660
SDRs	1b. s	1	1	34	37	45	56	64	70	96	167	240	291	300	309	320
Reserve Position in the Fund	1c. s	—	—	19	48	422	959	998	986	725	325	235	141	76	71	71
Total Fund Cred.&Loans Outstg.	2tl	—	—	—	—	—	—	—	—	—	—	—	—	—	—	—
International Liquidity															*Millions of US Dollars Unless Otherwise Indicated:*	
Total Reserves minus Gold	1l. d	77	479	818	1,078	8,223	8,744	8,681	12,106	11,977	15,210	10,223	1,605	5,701	....	....
SDRs	1b. d	1	1	37	45	55	65	75	85	125	220	307	339	331	324	314
Reserve Position in the Fund	1c. d	—	—	21	58	517	1,122	1,160	1,197	945	428	299	165	84	74	69
Foreign Exchange	1d. d	76	478	760	976	7,652	7,556	7,447	10,824	10,907	14,561	9,617	1,102	5,287	....	....
Gold (Million Fine Troy Ounces)	1ad	3.743	3.743	3.743	3.743	3.738	3.738	3.738	3.779	3.820	3.903	4.343	4.343	4.343	4.343	4.343
Gold (National Valuation)	1and	131	142	142	158	160	153	152	161	174	180	194	177	168	159	149
Monetary Authorities: Other Assets	3..d	17	35	33	48	28	27	51	58	....	209	203	185	176	1,143	....
Deposit Money Banks: Assets	7a. d	108	100	183	233	458	637	583	618	969	1,409	2,218	1,824	3,090	2,191	1,626
Liabilities	7b. d	71	102	161	321	639	1,069	1,419	1,830	1,500	653	693	743	798	730	622
Other Banking Insts.: Liabilities	7f. d	55	83	206	305	383	578	1,192	1,913	2,200	2,133	1,778	1,473	1,363	1,197	—
Monetary Authorities																*Billions of Rials:*
Foreign Assets	11	17	48	75	87	569	628	660	903	....	1,109	837	479	1,232	720	....
Claims on Central Government	12a	118	141	149	208	124	156	101	176	....	480	1,636	3,003	4,003	3,758	....
Claims on Official Entities	12bx	12	9	15	32	128	268	445	473	....	723	720	892	954	1,005	....
Claims on Deposit Money Banks	12e	17	15	20	38	37	82	101	80	....	80	100	127	110	120	116
Reserve Money	14	106	131	179	246	330	412	573	733	....	1,444	1,833	2,421	3,408	3,823	....
of which: Currency Outside DMBs	14a	37	42	56	70	102	148	206	252	....	769	1,108	1,248	1,465	1,757	....
Nonfin.Pub.Ent. Deps.	14e	23	34	57	82	96	77	102	139	....	220	169	167	329	335	....
Restricted Deposits	16b	11	15	25	46	147	131	124	151	....	163	201	185	201	335	....
Foreign Liabilities	16c	33	41	20	2	12	11	12	12	....	14	53	56	26	92	....
Central Government Deposits	16d	8	17	22	48	296	423	408	513	....	528	588	796	836	1,005	....
Capital Accounts	17a	6	8	12	12	14	39	54	61	....	106	112	117	178	218	....
Other Items (Net)	17r	–1	—	1	10	59	117	137	162	....	136	507	926	1,649	130	....
Deposit Money Banks																*Billions of Rials:*
Reserves	20	47	53	66	86	132	187	265	342	....	455	556	1,006	1,614	1,731	2,056
Foreign Assets	21	8	8	14	16	31	44	41	44	....	99	160	145	258	193	153
Claims on Central Government	22a	5	11	18	32	83	148	229	349	....	479	496	543	763	943	1,179
Claims on Private Sector	22d	174	205	266	369	480	738	1,041	1,223	....	1,639	2,006	2,104	2,199	2,703	2,730
Demand Deposits	24	69	79	101	126	183	233	360	431	....	700	981	1,222	1,499	1,830	2,296
Time and Savings Deposits	25	121	155	204	268	398	592	843	1,083	....	1,497	1,767	2,046	2,591	3,061	2,986
Foreign Liabilities	26c	5	8	12	22	43	74	100	129	....	46	50	59	67	64	59
Credit from Monetary Authorities	26g	17	15	20	38	37	82	101	80	....	80	100	127	110	120	116
Capital Accounts	27a	14	15	17	26	33	73	96	129	....	162	—	—	—	—	85
Other Items (Net)	27r	8	5	10	24	32	63	76	105	....	188	320	344	567	495	576
Monetary Survey																*Billions of Rials:*
Foreign Assets (Net)	31n	–13	7	57	79	544	587	590	805	....	1,147	895	509	1,397	756	....
Domestic Credit	32	304	348	427	594	520	838	1,368	1,661	....	2,724	4,236	5,689	7,132	7,141	....
Claims on Central Govt. (Net)	32an	115	135	146	193	–88	–168	–124	–44	....	352	1,504	2,688	3,916	3,414	....
Claims on Official Entities	32bx	14	9	15	32	128	268	450	482	....	732	726	898	1,017	1,024	....
Claims on Private Sector	32d	174	205	266	369	480	738	1,041	1,223	....	1,639	2,006	2,104	2,199	2,703	2,730
Money	34	128	155	214	278	381	458	668	822	1,078[e]	1,689	2,258	2,637	3,293	3,922	....
Quasi-Money	35	121	155	204	268	398	592	843	1,083	1,273	1,497	1,767	2,046	2,591	3,061	2,986
Restricted Deposits	36b	11	15	25	46	147	131	124	151	....	163	201	185	201	335	....
Other Items (Net)	37r	30	31	39	81	138	244	323	411	....	522	906	1,330	2,444	579	....
Money plus Quasi-Money	35l	250	310	419	546	779	1,050	1,511	1,905	2,351	3,186	4,025	4,683	5,884	6,983	....
Other Banking Institutions																*Billions of Rials:*
Cash	40	2	3	4	5	7	19	25	28	....	26	16	22	29	33	33
Claims on Central Government	42a	1	2	4	5	6	14	13	13	....	7	7	4	4	3	122
Claims on Official Entities	42bx	2	8	13	17	20	22	22	20	....	18	17	17	14	12	19
Claims on Private Sector	42d	47	54	68	83	134	233	360	497	....	697	896	1,014	1,174	1,403	1,594
Demand Deposits	44	9	10	11	14	35	45	51	50	....	50	54	74	83	111	103
Private Sector	44x	2	3	4	5	9	14	18	21	....	27	43	63	83	111	103
Official Entities	44y	6	7	7	9	26	32	33	30	....	23	11	11	—	—	—
Time and Savings Deposits	45	5	6	11	15	20	30	48	67	....	99	166	203	236	302	385
Foreign Liabilities	46c	4	6	16	21	26	40	84	135	....	150	129	117	114	106	—
Central Government Deposits	46d	5	14	20	26	31	64	75	83	....	78	109	139	83	139	269
Credit from Monetary Authorities	46g	3	2	1	2	11	23	42	95	....	163	214	299	365	336	332
Capital Accounts	47a	26	27	33	39	53	79	98	118	....	171	200	153	....	231	273
Other Items (Net)	47r	2	1	–1	–5	–8	7	21	11	....	37	65	72	....	228	404
Liquid Liabilities	55l	261	322	436	569	826	1,106	1,584	1,994	....	3,309	4,228	4,937	6,174	7,363	8,501
Interest Rates																*Percent Per Annum*
Discount Rate (End of Period)	60	8.00	7.00	7.50	9.00	9.00	8.00	8.00	8.00	10.00	9.00	....	....	....	....	....
Prices and Production																*Index Numbers (1995=100):*
Wholesale Prices	63	1.3	1.4	1.4	1.6	1.9	2.0	2.2	2.6	2.8	3.2	4.3	5.3	5.9	6.8	7.3
Home Goods	63a	1.2	1.3	1.4	1.5	1.8	2.0	2.2	2.6	2.8	3.3	4.4	5.5	6.3	7.3	7.9
Consumer Prices	64	1.6	1.7	1.8	2.0	2.2	2.5	2.8	3.6	4.0	4.4	5.3	6.6	7.8	9.4	10.6
Wages (1985=100)	65ey	3.4	4.1	5.0	6.3	8.3	ⲭ11.7	16.3	21.1	27.7	41.0	ⲭ55.5	60.2	66.0	76.9	88.1
Crude Petroleum Production	66aa	106.0	125.7	139.5	162.3	166.7	148.1	163.3	156.8	148.4	85.7	46.3	39.8	67.4	75.4	65.6

	1985	1986	1987	1988	1989	1990	1991	1992	1993	1994	1995	1996	1997	1998	1999		
Exchange Rates																	
End of Period																	
	92.30	92.30	92.30	92.30	92.30	92.30	92.30	92.30	2,415.49	2,534.26	2,597.64	2,515.19	2,366.94	2,465.36	2,405.04	Official Rate	aa
End of Period (ae) Period Average (rf)																	
	84.23	75.64	65.62	68.59	70.24	65.31	64.59	67.04	1,758.56	1,735.97	1,747.50	1,749.14	1,754.26	1,750.93	1,752.29	Official Rate	ae
	91.05	78.76	71.46	68.68	72.01	68.10	67.51	65.55	1,267.77	1,748.75	1,747.93	1,750.76	1,752.92	1,751.86	1,752.93	Official Rate	rf
Months Ending the 20th																	
	207.300	217.500	221.600	237.100	299.100	394.200	511.700	655.100		890.083	1,221.700	1,725.800	2,194.000	2,779.500	3,206.000	4,172.000	Weighted Average	yf
Period Averages																	
	1,218.48	726.53	607.08	570.16	515.62	360.12	304.80	271.31	183.04	105.13	100.00	111.42	126.52	133.92	139.13	Nominal Effective Exchange Rate	ne c
	288.10	192.79	202.17	232.78	245.51	166.37	150.11	151.99	111.20	74.38	100.00	135.34	170.84	206.04	250.07	Real Effective Exchange Rate	re c
Fund Position																	
End of Period																	
	660	660	660	660	660	660	660	1,079	1,079	1,079	1,079	1,079	1,079	1,079	1,497	Quota	2f. s
	328	335	342	116	305	310	216	7	105	98	90	240	245	1	101	SDRs	1b. s
	71	71	71	—	—	—	—	105	—	—	—	—	—	—	—	Reserve Position in the Fund	1c. s
	—	—	—	—	—	—	—	—	—	—	—	—	—	—	—	Total Fund Cred.&Loans Outstg.	2tl
International Liquidity																	
End of Period																	
	....	....	....	....	....	....	....	....	....	....	....	....	....	....	....	Total Reserves minus Gold	1l. d
	361	410	486	156	400	442	309	10	144	143	134	345	330	2	139	SDRs	1b. d
	78	87	100	—	—	—	—	144	—	—	—	—	—	—	—	Reserve Position in the Fund	1c. d
	....	....	....	....	....	....	....	....	....	....	....	....	....	....	....	Foreign Exchange	1d. d
	4.343	4.343	4.343	4.343	4.343	4.343	4.343	4.343	4.765	4.740	4.842	....	....	....	....	Gold (Million Fine Troy Ounces)	1ad
	167	186	216	205	200	216	217	209	229	242	252	....	....	....	....	Gold (National Valuation)	1an d
	....	....	....	....	....	....	....	....	....	....	....	....	....	....	....	Monetary Authorities: Other Assets	3.. d
	2,004	2,083	1,518	1,448	2,029	3,110	2,912	3,070	1,459	3,321	3,354	4,319	4,403	4,648	2,258	Deposit Money Banks: Assets	7a. d
	....	997	1,067	1,077	1,242	1,860	2,262	4,053	3,397	5,589	4,015	2,668	2,128	2,771	3,410	Liabilities	7b. d
	—	—	—	10	3	5	227	71	53	118	110	66	136	250		Other Banking Insts.: Liabilities	7f. d
Monetary Authorities																	
Year Ending December 20th																	
	....	569	758	602	731	696	1,238	1,349	7,916	9,681	14,413	19,454	15,669	9,827	11,413	Foreign Assets	11
	....	6,290	8,095	10,156	11,954	12,818	14,267	14,651	16,002	28,169	32,648	42,461	42,624	55,710	61,731	Claims on Central Government	12a
	....	942	1,036	1,072	1,137	1,651	2,384	2,520	3,792	5,549	10,704	18,826	15,618	18,842	19,794	Claims on Official Entities	12bx
	....	82	99	128	162	194	379	742	3,751	1,967	10,462	2,056	11,162	9,565	13,392	Claims on Deposit Money Banks	12e
	....	5,798	7,240	9,063	10,254	10,577	12,293	13,901	16,511	22,165	32,805	41,708	51,298	60,533	70,911	Reserve Money	14
	....	2,354	2,712	3,068	3,225	3,518	3,862	4,088	4,925	6,199	7,949	9,598	11,271	14,050	16,652	*of which: Currency Outside DMBs*	14a
	....	290	281	214	151	183	553	559	862	1,604	2,020	2,639	2,642	4,662	5,304	*Nonfin.Pub.Ent. Deps.*	14e
	....	241	364	289	377	611	568	352	1,158	4,004	7,085	8,764	6,789	3,810	4,066	Restricted Deposits	16b
	....	51	26	28	64	148	129	166	2,924	2,883	2,679	3,466	5,057	8,012	6,562	Foreign Liabilities	16c
	....	1,164	1,269	1,515	1,788	2,426	2,779	3,077	4,965	6,752	9,738	13,035	13,837	13,814	18,275	Central Government Deposits	16d
	....	244	261	261	265	275	281	294	801	903	989	1,004	1,003	1,012	1,097	Capital Accounts	17a
	....	385	828	800	1,236	1,322	2,220	1,472	5,104	8,658	14,929	14,820	7,089	6,763	5,420	Other Items (Net)	17r
Deposit Money Banks																	
Year Ending December 20th																	
	2,909	3,068	4,207	5,715	6,797	6,780	7,764	9,134	10,586	14,179	22,519	28,865	36,563	40,385	47,190	Reserves	20
	169	158	100	99	143	203	188	206	2,566	5,766	5,861	7,555	7,724	8,138	3,957	Foreign Assets	21
	1,194	1,194	1,249	1,247	1,347	1,346	1,338	1,343	1,236	1,232	1,827	1,823	1,821	1,521	7,494	Claims on Central Government	22a
	3,045	3,647	4,184	4,672	6,184	8,729	12,059	16,665	22,131	27,535	32,938	41,043	52,579	63,716	85,701	Claims on Private Sector	22d
	....	2,865	3,469	3,836	4,862	6,028	7,851	9,434	12,519	18,120	24,373	33,628	41,064	48,732	59,996	Demand Deposits	24
	....	4,339	5,283	6,988	9,045	10,663	13,342	17,770	23,181	29,377	37,599	49,426	62,881	74,438	90,435	Time and Savings Deposits	25
	....	75	70	74	87	122	146	272	5,973	9,703	7,016	4,667	3,734	4,851	5,975	Foreign Liabilities	26c
	....	82	99	128	162	194	379	742	3,751	1,967	10,462	2,056	11,162	9,565	13,392	Credit from Monetary Authorities	26g
	100	84	134	134	134	134	134	134	3,719	3,724	3,724	3,724	3,724	3,724	3,764	Capital Accounts	27a
	....	620	685	573	180	−83	−502	−1,003	−12,625	−14,180	−20,030	−14,215	−23,878	−27,250	−29,220	Other Items (Net)	27r
Monetary Survey																	
Year Ending December 20th																	
	....	600	762	599	723	629	1,152	1,118	1,585	2,860	10,578	18,876	14,603	5,102	2,833	Foreign Assets (Net)	31n
	....	10,874	13,414	15,807	19,199	22,751	28,030	33,915	43,385	59,484	74,426	101,566	115,511	151,740	187,227	Domestic Credit	32
	....	6,257	7,972	9,746	11,367	11,636	12,727	12,816	12,211	22,556	24,674	31,026	30,370	43,463	48,057	Claims on Central Govt. (Net)	32an
	28	971	1,258	1,389	1,647	2,386	3,244	4,434	9,043	9,393	16,814	29,498	32,562	44,561	53,469	Claims on Official Entities	32bx
	3,045	3,647	4,184	4,672	6,184	8,729	12,059	16,665	22,131	27,535	32,938	41,043	52,579	63,716	85,701	Claims on Private Sector	32d
	....	5,509	6,462	7,118	8,238	9,729	12,266	14,081	18,305	25,923	34,342	45,865	54,977	67,444	81,951	Money	34
	....	4,339	5,283	6,988	9,045	10,663	13,342	17,770	23,181	29,377	37,599	49,426	62,881	74,438	90,435	Quasi-Money	35
	....	241	364	289	377	611	568	352	1,158	4,004	7,085	8,764	6,789	3,810	4,066	Restricted Deposits	36b
	....	1,385	2,066	2,011	2,262	2,377	3,007	2,829	2,327	3,040	5,977	16,387	5,467	11,150	13,608	Other Items (Net)	37r
	....	9,848	11,745	14,106	17,283	20,392	25,607	31,851	41,486	55,299	71,941	95,291	117,858	141,883	172,386	Money plus Quasi-Money	35l
Other Banking Institutions																	
Year Ending December 20th																	
	37	40	46	75	93	109	132	147	166	218	361	671	912	1,549	1,901	Cash	40
	2	2	2	2	2	2	2	2	2	2	2	2	2	2	941	Claims on Central Government	42a
	13	16	17	16	21	67	75	58	113	141	90	163	591	1,002	195	Claims on Official Entities	42bx
	1,765	1,874	1,948	2,130	2,577	3,191	4,214	5,134	6,159	7,504	9,831	13,506	18,611	25,812	36,411	Claims on Private Sector	42d
	143	184	157	155	213	281	408	476	767	870	1,287	2,129	3,325	4,002	4,001	Demand Deposits	44
	143	184	157	155	213	281	408	476	767	870	1,287	2,129	3,325	4,002	4,001	Private Sector	44x
																Official Entities	44y
	345	336	342	408	484	549	682	729	914	1,409	2,367	3,327	5,591	9,157	12,584	Time and Savings Deposits	45
					1	—	—	15	125	91	207	192	116	238	438	Foreign Liabilities	46c
	160	118	177	148	144	65	95	138	139	114	124	175	158	106	69	Central Government Deposits	46d
	319	248	270	257	275	307	307	509	215	795	3,437	8,126	3,518	4,635	5,895	Credit from Monetary Authorities	46g
	270	212	259	260	260	280	300	567	870	1,928	1,928	1,940	1,940	1,940	1,940	Capital Accounts	47a
	582	835	807	995	1,316	1,888	2,632	2,907	3,409	2,658	935	−1,548	5,469	8,287	14,522	Other Items (Net)	47r
	11,416	10,327	12,198	14,594	17,887	21,112	26,565	32,908	43,002	57,360	75,232	100,077	125,862	153,493	187,070	Liquid Liabilities	55l
Interest Rates																	
Year Ending December 20																	
	....	....	....	....	....	....	....	....	....	....	....	....	....	....	....	Discount Rate (End of Period)	60
Prices and Production																	
Year Ending December 20																	
	‡7.7	9.2	12.1	14.8	17.9	‡21.5	27.1	36.0	45.3	62.3	100.0	132.9	147.1	164.7	196.3	Wholesale Prices	63
	‡8.3	9.8	12.6	15.3	18.7	‡22.5	27.7	37.8	47.4	65.1	100.0	130.8	146.3	171.1	205.2	Home Goods	63a
	‡11.0	13.1	16.8	21.6	26.5	28.5	‡33.4	41.9	50.8	66.8	100.0	128.9	151.0	180.3	218.2	Consumer Prices	64
	100.0	....	....	....	....	....	....	....	....	....	100.0	101.6	100.4	99.4	....	Wages (1985=100)	65ey
	69.3	60.2	68.1	70.8	81.6	88.6	92.6	95.2	99.5	101.0	100.0	101.6	100.4	99.4	97.0	Crude Petroleum Production	66aa

Iran, I.R. of

429	1970	1971	1972	1973	1974	1975	1976	1977	1978	1979	1980	1981	1982	1983	1984
International Transactions															*Millions of US Dollars*
Exports 70..d	2,403	3,824	1,799	2,669	8,401	7,963	8,935	9,216	8,560	8,310	I 7,109	I 3,947	12,968	19,378	12,422
Imports, c.i.f. 71..d	1,662	1,873	2,409	3,393	5,433	10,343	12,894	14,070	13,549	9,738	I 12,246	14,693	11,955	18,320	15,370
Imports, f.o.b. 71.vd	1,462	1,624	2,096	2,925	4,563	8,526	10,857	12,122	11,681	8,395	I 10,557	12,667	10,306	15,793	13,250
Volume of Exports															*1995=100:*
Petroleum 72a	141.3	164.4	183.2	208.8	212.1	187.4	201.9	188.9	174.1	98.7	I 43.3	I 27.2	64.9	68.1	62.3
Crude Petroleum 72aa	135.4	163.1	184.8	216.3	220.0	191.5	213.7	200.0	184.9	95.4	I 32.6	I 29.2	66.5	74.9	65.9
															1990=100
Export Prices 76	....	....	1.6	2.3	2.6	2.7	3.0	3.7	3.8	4.4	I 5.8	7.0	8.2	8.5	9.4
Import Prices 76.x	8.4	8.5	I 9.1	10.3	11.8	12.4	13.0	14.5	16.2	18.0	I 22.2	25.1	27.5	29.2	30.2
Balance of Payments															*Millions of US$: Year Beginning*
Current Account, n.i.e. 78ald	....	....	....	....	....	....	7,660	2,816	104	11,968	–2,438	–3,446	5,733	358	–414
Goods: Exports f.o.b. 78aad	....	....	....	....	....	....	24,719	24,076	17,675	24,171	12,338	11,831	20,452	21,507	17,087
Goods: Imports f.o.b. 78abd	....	....	....	....	....	....	–13,860	–16,718	–11,803	–8,521	–10,888	–13,138	–12,552	–18,027	–14,729
Trade Balance 78acd	....	....	....	....	....	....	10,859	7,358	5,872	15,650	1,450	–1,307	7,900	3,480	2,358
Services: Credit 78add	....	....	....	....	....	....	2,651	3,699	3,104	1,580	731	556	509	540	475
Services: Debit 78aed	....	....	....	....	....	....	–5,773	–8,201	–9,177	–5,690	–5,223	–3,315	–3,061	–4,273	–3,698
Balance on Goods & Services 78afd	....	....	....	....	....	....	7,737	2,856	–201	11,540	–3,042	–4,066	5,348	–253	–865
Income: Credit 78agd	....	....	....	....	....	....	610	769	1,100	1,240	1,004	895	612	795	594
Income: Debit 78ahd	....	....	....	....	....	....	–670	–684	–780	–797	–398	–275	–227	–184	–143
Balance on Gds, Serv. & Inc. 78aid	....	....	....	....	....	....	7,677	2,941	119	11,983	–2,436	–3,446	5,733	358	–414
Current Transfers, n.i.e.: Credit 78ajd	....	....	....	....	....	....	—	—	—	—	—	—	—	—	—
Current Transfers: Debit 78akd	....	....	....	....	....	....	–17	–125	–15	–15	–2	—	—	—	—
Capital Account, n.i.e. 78bcd	....	....	....	....	....	....	—	—	—	—	—	—	—	—	—
Capital Account, n.i.e.: Credit 78bad	....	....	....	....	....	....	—	—	—	—	—	—	—	—	—
Capital Account: Debit 78bbd	....	....	....	....	....	....	—	—	—	—	—	—	—	—	—
Financial Account, n.i.e. 78bjd	....	....	....	....	....	....	–4,957	–366	–165	–8,023	–8,238	1,441	–1,847	–2,474	–2,818
Direct Investment Abroad 78bdd	....	....	....	....	....	....	—	—	—	—	—	—	—	—	—
Dir. Invest. in Rep. Econ., n.i.e. 78bed	....	....	....	....	....	....	—	—	—	—	—	—	—	—	—
Portfolio Investment Assets 78bfd	....	....	....	....	....	....	—	—	—	—	—	—	—	—	—
Equity Securities 78bkd	....	....	....	....	....	....	—	—	—	—	—	—	—	—	—
Debt Securities 78bld	....	....	....	....	....	....	—	—	—	—	—	—	—	—	—
Portfolio Investment Liab., n.i.e. 78bgd	....	....	....	....	....	....	—	—	—	—	—	—	—	—	—
Equity Securities 78bmd	....	....	....	....	....	....	—	—	—	—	—	—	—	—	—
Debt Securities 78bnd	....	....	....	....	....	....	—	—	—	—	—	—	—	—	—
Financial Derivatives Assets 78bwd	....	....	....	....	....	....	....	....	....	....	....	....	....	....	....
Financial Derivatives Liabilities 78bxd	....	....	....	....	....	....	....	....	....	....	....	....	....	....	....
Other Investment Assets 78bhd	....	....	....	....	....	....	–5,623	–3,663	–879	–4,396	91	1,968	–157	–915	504
Monetary Authorities 78bod	....	....	....	....	....	....	....	....	....	....	....	....	....	....	....
General Government 78bpd	....	....	....	....	....	....	–1,254	–126	195	945	636	618	160	282	121
Banks 78bqd	....	....	....	....	....	....	48	–281	68	–999	–685	311	–200	–438	591
Other Sectors 78brd	....	....	....	....	....	....	–4,417	–3,256	–1,142	–4,342	140	1,039	–117	–759	–208
Other Investment Liab., n.i.e. 78bid	....	....	....	....	....	....	666	3,297	714	–3,627	–8,329	–527	–1,690	–1,559	–3,322
Monetary Authorities 78bsd	....	....	....	....	....	....	38	–20	51	130	212	–202	–468	752	–1,605
General Government 78btd	....	....	....	....	....	....	–151	822	15	–935	–5,882	–496	–2,027	–433	–427
Banks 78bud	....	....	....	....	....	....	893	754	220	–1,177	–342	135	–55	–45	–1,095
Other Sectors 78bvd	....	....	....	....	....	....	–114	1,741	428	–1,645	–2,317	36	860	–1,833	–195
Net Errors and Omissions 78cad	....	....	....	....	....	....	–198	–337	–519	–1,005	828	1,633	980	862	–904
Overall Balance 78cbd	....	....	....	....	....	....	2,505	2,113	–580	2,940	–9,848	–372	4,866	–1,254	–4,136
Reserves and Related Items 79dad	....	....	....	....	....	....	–2,505	–2,113	580	–2,940	9,848	372	–4,866	1,254	4,136
Reserve Assets 79dbd	....	....	....	....	....	....	–2,505	–2,113	580	–2,940	9,848	372	–4,866	1,254	4,136
Use of Fund Credit and Loans 79dcd	....	....	....	....	....	....	—	—	—	—	—	—	—	—	—
Exceptional Financing 79ded	....	....	....	....	....	....	....	....	....	....	....	....	....	....	....
Government Finance															*Billions of Rials:*
Deficit (-) or Surplus 80	–54	–26	–54	–13	140	12	–38	–262	–450	–231	–915	–841	–603	–842	–597
Revenue 81	187	275	323	491	1,427	1,627	1,896	2,193	1,736	1,781	1,430	1,923	2,698	2,994	2,989
Expenditure 82	241	301	378	504	1,287	1,615	1,933	2,455	2,286	2,104	2,368	2,814	3,317	3,857	3,598
Lending Minus Repayments 83	—	—	—	—	—	—	—	—	–100	–92	–23	–51	–16	–21	–12
Financing															
Domestic 84a	35	11	44	16	34	124	130	331	505	267	952	886	641	878	627
Foreign 85a	19	15	11	–3	–174	–136	–93	–69	–56	–35	–37	–45	–38	–36	–30
Debt: Domestic 88a	....	....	....	....	....	368	391	738	....	....	....	....	....	....	....
National Accounts															*Billions of Rials:*
Exports of Goods & Services 90c	154	241	299	642	1,478	1,440	1,787	1,751	1,189	1,762	883	945	1,726	1,878	1,570
Government Consumption 91f	141	189	243	313	639	818	1,004	1,134	1,245	1,223	1,380	1,676	1,910	2,151	2,190
Gross Fixed Capital Formation 93e	185	220	293	387	530	999	1,589	1,790	1,628	1,197	1,442	1,528	1,842	2,870	3,096
Increase/Decrease(-) in Stocks 93i	82	58	113	106	35	14	–251	–169	–479	99	520	295	–165	226	508
Private Consumption 96f	493	597	679	852	1,180	1,430	1,869	2,697	2,503	3,027	3,531	4,653	5,943	7,771	8,927
Imports of Goods & Services 98c	–158	–199	–251	–345	–676	–1,127	–1,295	–1,491	–1,103	–923	–1,089	–1,260	–1,251	–1,851	–1,605
Gross Domestic Product (GDP) 99b	771	969	1,208	1,764	3,090	3,512	4,697	5,948	5,179	5,970	6,632	8,009	10,540	13,376	14,804
Net Factor Inc/Pmts(-) Abroad 98.n	–40	–46	–29	–36	–11	–15	–5	–98	–186	56	26	33	—	–7	–11
Gross National Income (GNI) 99a	732	923	1,179	1,728	3,079	3,497	4,692	5,850	4,993	6,025	6,658	8,042	10,540	13,370	14,793
GDP Volume 1974 Prices 99b.p	2,001	2,248	2,614	2,838	3,090	3,176	3,758	4,043	3,191	2,895	2,491	....	....	....	....
GDP Volume 1982 Prices 99b.p	....	....	....	....	....	....	....	....	....	....	9,556	9,321	10,540	11,935	12,044
GDP Volume (1995=100) 99bvp	55.9	62.8	73.0	79.2	86.3	88.7	104.9	112.9	89.1	80.8	69.5	67.8	76.7	86.9	87.6
GDP Deflator (1995=100) 99bip	.8	.9	.9	1.2	2.0	2.2	2.5	2.9	3.2	4.1	5.3	6.6	7.7	8.6	9.4
															Millions:
Population 99z	28.66	29.61	30.41	31.23	32.50	33.38	33.71	34.69	36.11	37.20	39.30	40.85	42.48	44.08	45.80

	1985	1986	1987	1988	1989	1990	1991	1992	1993	1994	1995	1996	1997	1998	1999		
Millions of US Dollars																**International Transactions**	
	13,328	7,171	11,916	10,709	13,081	19,305	18,661	19,868	18,080	19,434	18,360	22,391	18,381	....	....	Exports	70..*d*
	11,635	10,521	9,570	9,454	14,794	20,322	27,927	25,860	21,427	13,774	13,882	16,274	14,165	....	....	Imports, c.i.f.	71..*d*
	10,030	9,070	8,250	8,150	12,753	17,519	24,075	22,293	18,472	11,874	12,774	14,973	....	....	....	Imports, f.o.b.	71.v*d*
Year Ending December 20																Volume of Exports	
	56.6	44.9	55.1	58.7	69.8	79.3	94.8	102.4	99.2	95.8	100.0	100.8	....	....	....	Petroleum	72a
	60.5	51.2	63.4	67.5	77.0	85.9	101.3	109.5	103.5	98.6	100.0	100.0	....	....	....	Crude Petroleum	72aa
1990=100																	
	11.3	33.4	76.1	90.5	93.6	100.0	154.0	174.8	180.4	....	....	....	....	....	....	Export Prices	76
	32.5	38.8	53.9	68.0	77.9	100.0	124.3	165.4	217.2	....	....	....	....	....	....	Import Prices	76.x
March 21:Minus Sign Indicates Debit																**Balance of Payments**	
	−476	−5,155	−2,090	−1,869	−191	327	−9,448	−6,504	−4,215	4,956	3,358	5,232	2,213	−1,897	....	Current Account, n.i.e.	78al *d*
	14,175	7,171	11,916	10,709	13,081	19,305	18,661	19,868	18,080	18,080	19,434	18,360	22,391	18,381	12,982	Goods: Exports f.o.b.	78aa *d*
	−12,006	−10,585	−12,005	−10,608	−13,448	−18,330	−25,190	−23,274	−19,287	−12,617	−12,774	−14,989	−14,123	−13,608	....	Goods: Imports f.o.b.	78ab *d*
	2,169	−3,414	−89	101	−367	975	−6,529	−3,406	−1,207	6,817	5,586	7,402	4,258	−626	....	*Trade Balance*	78ac *d*
	370	242	231	244	446	436	668	559	1,084	438	593	860	1,192	1,315	....	Services: Credit	78ad *d*
	−3,308	−2,282	−2,372	−2,355	−3,018	−3,962	−5,715	−5,783	−5,600	−3,226	−2,339	−3,083	−3,371	−2,581	....	Services: Debit	78ae *d*
	−769	−5,454	−2,230	−2,010	−2,939	−2,551	−11,576	−8,630	−5,723	4,029	3,840	5,179	2,079	−1,892	....	*Balance on Goods & Services*	78af *d*
	393	365	206	223	352	456	213	287	151	142	316	488	466	230	....	Income: Credit	78ag *d*
	−100	−66	−66	−82	−104	−78	−85	−157	−143	−413	−794	−898	−725	−732	....	Income: Debit	78ah *d*
	−476	−5,155	−2,090	−1,869	−2,691	−2,173	−11,448	−8,500	−5,715	3,758	3,362	4,769	1,820	−2,394	....	*Balance on Gds, Serv. & Inc.*	78ai *d*
	—	—	—	—	2,500	2,500	2,000	1,996	1,500	1,200	—	471	400	500	....	Current Transfers, n.i.e.: Credit	78aj *d*
	—	—	—	—	—	—	—	—	—	−2	−4	−8	−7	−3	....	Current Transfers: Debit	78ak *d*
	—	—	—	—	—	—	—	—	—	—	—	—	—	—	....	Capital Account, n.i.e.	78bc *d*
	—	—	—	—	—	—	—	—	—	—	—	—	—	—	....	Capital Account, n.i.e.: Credit	78ba *d*
	—	—	—	—	—	—	—	—	—	—	—	—	—	—	....	Capital Account: Debit	78bb *d*
	544	3,127	1,711	320	3,261	295	6,033	4,703	5,563	−346	−774	−5,508	−4,822	3,099	....	Financial Account, n.i.e.	78bj *d*
	—	—	—	—	—	—	—	—	—	—	—	—	—	—	....	Direct Investment Abroad	78bd *d*
	—	—	—	—	—	—	—	—	—	2	17	26	53	24	....	Dir. Invest. in Rep. Econ., n.i.e.	78be *d*
	—	—	—	—	—	—	—	—	—	—	—	—	—	—	....	Portfolio Investment Assets	78bf *d*
	—	—	—	—	—	—	—	—	—	—	—	—	—	—	....	Equity Securities	78bk *d*
	—	—	—	—	—	—	—	—	—	—	—	—	—	—	....	Debt Securities	78bl *d*
	—	—	—	—	—	—	—	—	—	—	—	—	—	—	....	Portfolio Investment Liab., n.i.e.	78bg *d*
	—	—	—	—	—	—	—	—	—	—	—	—	—	—	....	Equity Securities	78bm *d*
	—	—	—	—	—	—	—	—	—	—	—	—	—	—	....	Debt Securities	78bn *d*
	....	....	....	....	....	....	....	....	....	—	—	—	—	—	....	Financial Derivatives Assets	78bw *d*
	....	....	....	....	....	....	....	....	....	—	—	—	—	—	....	Financial Derivatives Liabilities	78bx *d*
	−334	1,164	1,248	10	539	−1,510	1,082	1,000	1,250	−1,258	−419	−1,305	2,293	2,779	....	Other Investment Assets	78bh *d*
	—	—	—	—	—	—	—	—	—	—	—	—	—	—	....	Monetary Authorities	78bo *d*
	205	1,030	899	140	1,099	142	910	342	44	−42	235	−48	−99	−22	....	General Government	78bp *d*
	−539	134	349	−130	−560	−1,652	172	658	1,206	−1,216	−654	−1,257	2,392	2,801	....	Banks	78bq *d*
	—	—	—	—	—	—	—	—	—	—	—	—	—	—	....	Other Sectors	78br *d*
	878	1,963	463	310	2,722	1,805	4,951	3,703	4,313	910	−372	−4,229	−7,168	296	....	Other Investment Liab., n.i.e.	78bi *d*
	−1,000	1,076	−192	117	501	387	−372	63	68	−252	−64	−283	179	93	....	Monetary Authorities	78bs *d*
	−320	−190	−142	−144	−71	−41	440	4,556	−1,358	10,447	1,684	−4,523	−4,035	−490	....	General Government	78bt *d*
	188	157	197	−29	344	1,101	489	—	—	—	—	—	—	—	....	Banks	78bu *d*
	2,010	920	600	366	1,948	358	4,394	−916	5,603	−9,285	−1,992	577	−3,312	693	....	Other Sectors	78bv *d*
	486	814	155	539	−770	−947	1,322	1,781	−1,263	−3,703	283	2,639	−1,088	−2,771	....	Net Errors and Omissions	78ca *d*
	554	−1,214	−224	−1,010	2,300	−325	−2,093	−20	85	907	2,867	2,363	−3,697	−1,569	....	*Overall Balance*	78cb *d*
	−554	1,214	224	1,010	−2,300	325	2,093	20	−85	−907	−2,867	−2,363	3,697	1,569	....	Reserves and Related Items	79da *d*
	−554	1,214	224	1,010	−2,300	325	2,093	20	−85	−907	−2,867	−2,363	3,697	1,569	....	Reserve Assets	79db *d*
	—	—	—	—	—	—	—	—	—	—	—	—	—	—	....	Use of Fund Credit and Loans	79dc *d*
	....	....	....	....	....	....	....	....	....	—	—	—	—	—	....	Exceptional Financing	79de *d*
Year Beginning March 21																**Government Finance**	
	−594	−1,353	−1,419	‡−2,041	−1,089	−665	−1,129	−964	−443	−262	2,637	313	−1,391	1,144 [f]	....	Deficit (-) or Surplus	80
	2,964	2,017	2,511	‡2,656	3,830	6,617	8,385	12,299	22,018	31,080	45,171	62,127	68,315	88,791 [f]	....	Revenue	81
	3,583	3,438	3,966	‡4,703	4,924	7,288	9,553	13,269	22,565	31,400	42,795	61,814	70,036	87,962 [f]	....	Expenditure	82
	−25	−68	−36	‡−6	−5	−6	−39	−6	−104	−58	−261	—	−330	−315 [f]	....	Lending Minus Repayments	83
																Financing	
	625	1,375	1,430	‡2,048	1,093	670	1,131	966	445	266	−2,637	−313	1,204	−1,500 [f]	....	Domestic	84a
	−31	−22	−11	‡−7	−4	−5	−2	−2	−2	−4	—	—	187	356 [f]	....	Foreign	85a
	....	....	....	....	....	....	....	....	....	....	....	....	....	....	....	Debt: Domestic	88a
Year Beginning March 21																**National Accounts**	
	1,251	553	837	1,514	2,773	5,395	7,439	9,864	22,617	31,909	36,747	43,535	36,374	27,144	53,964	Exports of Goods & Services	90c
	2,443	2,371	2,707	3,199	3,294	4,054	5,367	6,927	13,644	16,177	23,053	31,906	38,365	43,792	56,296	Government Consumption	91f
	2,759	2,494	2,662	2,957	3,709	5,663	10,844	14,640	20,657	29,853	41,511	60,534	69,232	72,446	92,619	Gross Fixed Capital Formation	93e
	562	1,099	2,417	1,296	2,891	4,827	5,806	8,867	6,499	1,265	−6,507	−11,254	−9,829	−412	−3,957	Increase/Decrease(-) in Stocks	93i
	9,627	10,439	12,226	14,906	18,448	24,071	31,677	41,187	51,623	71,963	108,922	140,514	172,350	212,784	265,498	Private Consumption	96f
	−1,266	−935	−950	−1,756	−3,594	−6,792	−9,749	−12,319	−21,431	−22,785	−24,851	−30,003	−28,661	−27,416	−46,252	Imports of Goods & Services	98c
	15,775	16,227	19,949	22,304	27,787	36,645	50,107	66,463	93,610	128,382	178,875	235,233	277,831	328,337	418,169	Gross Domestic Product (GDP)	99b
	−34	−19	−39	−116	−212	−263	463	−67	−2,485	−3,015	−1,809	−2,100	−1,762	−1,120	−1,198	Net Factor Inc/Pmts(-) Abroad	98.n
	15,742	16,208	19,910	22,188	27,575	36,381	50,570	66,396	91,125	128,367	177,066	233,133	276,069	327,217	416,971	Gross National Income (GNI)	99a
	....	....	....	....	....	....	....	....	....	....	....	....	....	....	....	GDP Volume 1974 Prices	99b.*p*
	12,072	10,249	10,368	9,468	9,782	10,930	12,181	12,879	13,084	13,181	13,741	14,661	15,203	15,479	....	GDP Volume 1982 Prices	99b.*p*
	87.9	74.6	75.5	68.9	71.2	79.5	88.6	93.7	95.2	95.9	100.0	106.7	110.6	112.6	....	GDP Volume (1995=100)	99bv *p*
	10.0	12.2	14.8	18.1	21.8	25.8	31.6	39.6	55.0	74.8	100.0	123.3	140.4	162.9	....	GDP Deflator (1995=100)	99bi *p*
Midyear Estimates																	
	47.82	49.44	50.66	51.91	53.19	54.50	55.84	56.66	57.49	58.33	59.19	60.06	60.94	61.84	62.75	**Population**	99z

(See notes in the back of the book.)

Iraq

		1970	1971	1972	1973	1974	1975	1976	1977	1978	1979	1980	1981	1982	1983	1984
Exchange Rates															*SDRs per Dinar:*		
Principal Rate	ac	2.7849	2.7307	2.7440	2.8070	2.7657	2.8926	2.9145	2.7877	2.5992	2.5705	2.6550	2.9092	2.9162	3.0726	3.2818
															US Dollars per Dinar:	
Principal Rate	ag	2.7849	2.9647	2.9792	3.3862	3.3862	3.3862	3.3862	3.3862	3.3862	3.3862	3.3862	3.3862	3.2169	3.2169	3.2169
Principal Rate	rh	2.8000	2.8305	3.0039	3.3064	3.3862	3.3862	3.3862	3.3862	3.3862	3.3862	3.3862	3.3862	3.3513	3.2169	3.2169
															Index Numbers (1995=100):	
Principal Rate	ahx	86.9	88.2	93.4	102.8	105.3	105.3	105.3	105.3	105.3	105.3	105.3	105.3	104.2	100.0	100.0
Nominal Effective Exchange Rate	ne c	....	....	....	....	....	....	....	....	....	56.9	58.0	67.4	75.7	77.6	85.2
Fund Position															*Millions of SDRs:*	
Quota	2f. s	109.0	109.0	109.0	109.0	109.0	109.0	109.0	109.0	141.0	141.0	234.1	234.1	234.1	234.1	504.0
SDRs	1b. s	—	11.7	23.2	20.1	23.0	23.0	28.0	34.2	45.5	82.2	87.2	113.7	74.2	8.6	.1
Reserve Position in the Fund	1c. s	—	—	17.3	27.3	27.3	27.3	27.3	27.5	27.7	47.8	111.9	111.9	111.9	—	—
Total Fund Cred.&Loans Outstg.	2tl	—	—	—	—	—	—	—	—	—	—	—	—	—	—	—
International Liquidity													*Millions of US Dollars Unless Otherwise Indicated:*			
Total Reserves minus Gold	1l. d	318.7	444.6	625.7	1,380.0	3,097.5	2,559.3	4,434.0	6,819.6	....	....	....	....	....	....	....
SDRs	1b. d	—	12.7	25.2	24.2	28.2	26.9	32.5	41.5	59.3	108.3	111.2	132.3	81.9	9.0	....
Reserve Position in the Fund	1c. d	—	—	18.7	32.9	33.4	31.9	31.7	33.4	36.0	63.0	142.7	130.3	123.5	—	—
Foreign Exchange	1d. d	318.7	431.9	581.8	1,322.9	3,035.9	2,500.5	4,369.8	6,744.7	....	....	....	....	....	....	....
Gold (Million Fine Troy Ounces)	1ad	4.099	4.099	4.099	4.099	4.099	4.099	4.099	4.144	....	....	....	....	....	....	....
Monetary Authorities: Other Assets	3..d	—	—	9.1	7.9	13.3	12.5	10.0	....	....	....	....	....	....	....	....
Other Liab.	4..d	31.7	34.4	49.6	176.0	284.3	43.4	1.4	....	....	....	....	....	....	....	....
Deposit Money Banks: Assets	7a.d	24.5	30.7	26.4	121.4	348.7	269.3	333.8	....	....	....	....	....	....	....	....
Liabilities	7b.d	3.2	5.3	2.4	4.5	47.1	42.0	54.6	....	....	....	....	....	....	....	....
Monetary Authorities															*Millions of Dinars:*	
Foreign Assets	11	165.1	197.5	260.1	462.1	993.9	805.7	1,356.8	....	....	....	....	....	....	....	....
Claims on Central Government	12a	138.5	120.9	110.7	69.5	90.0	130.5	64.2	....	....	....	....	....	....	....	....
Claims on Deposit Money Banks	12e	1.9	.5	.4	.1	—	295.7		....	....	....	....	....	....	....	....
Reserve Money	14	217.3	217.5	257.2	344.5	444.6	571.8	726.6	....	....	....	....	....	....	....	....
of which: Currency Outside DMBs	14a	173.0	179.4	206.9	252.2	358.2	472.6	565.9	....	....	....	....	....	....	....	....
Foreign Liabilities	16c	11.3	11.3	16.3	52.1	84.0	12.8	.4	....	....	....	....	....	....	....	....
Central Government Deposits	16d	32.1	38.8	43.8	73.7	393.9	480.6	486.5	....	....	....	....	....	....	....	....
Capital Accounts	17a	50.4	56.3	59.7	68.1	132.9	130.7	145.0	....	....	....	....	....	....	....	....
Other Items (Net)	17r	−5.5	−5.0	−5.9	−6.7	28.6	36.0	62.6	....	....	....	....	....	....	....	....
Deposit Money Banks															*Millions of Dinars:*	
Reserves	20	42.6	36.6	46.3	78.8	65.6	95.8	150.0	....	....	....	....	....	....	....	....
Foreign Assets	21	8.8	10.1	8.7	36.0	103.0	79.5	98.6	....	....	....	....	....	....	....	....
Claims on Central Government	22a	63.1	94.8	114.5	151.3	316.2	621.4	620.4	....	....	....	....	....	....	....	....
Claims on Private Sector	22d	87.2	85.4	82.5	81.1	102.5	118.2	132.8	....	....	....	....	....	....	....	....
Demand Deposits	24	43.5	46.4	50.5	64.3	92.7	149.5	184.9	....	....	....	....	....	....	....	....
Time and Savings Deposits	25	73.9	85.8	95.2	122.4	172.8	257.0	315.0	....	....	....	....	....	....	....	....
Central Government Deposits	26d	57.6	66.1	75.1	118.7	201.4	301.2	399.4	....	....	....	....	....	....	....	....
Credit from Monetary Authorities	26g	1.9	.5	.4	.1	—	130.5	—	....	....	....	....	....	....	....	....
Capital Accounts	27a	28.5	27.8	28.7	33.1	51.1	74.5	89.9	....	....	....	....	....	....	....	....
Other Items (Net)	27r	−3.8	.3	2.2	8.4	69.3	2.3	12.6	....	....	....	....	....	....	....	....
Monetary Survey															*Millions of Dinars:*	
Foreign Assets (Net)	31n	161.4	194.5	251.7	444.7	999.0	860.0	1,438.8	....	....	....	....	....	....	....	....
Domestic Credit	32	208.2	206.0	197.8	117.8	−74.4	107.8	−37.7	....	....	....	....	....	....	....	....
Claims on Central Govt. (Net)	32an	111.9	110.8	106.3	28.3	−189.1	−29.9	−201.3	....	....	....	....	....	....	....	....
Claims on Private Sector	32d	87.2	85.4	82.5	81.1	102.5	118.2	132.8	....	....	....	....	....	....	....	....
Claims on Other Banking Insts.	32f	9.1	9.7	9.0	8.3	12.3	19.5	30.8	....	....	....	....	....	....	....	....
Money	34	217.7	227.1	259.7	322.7	462.3	625.5	754.8	....	....	....	....	....	....	....	....
Quasi-Money	35	73.9	85.8	95.2	122.4	172.8	257.0	315.0	....	....	....	....	....	....	....	....
Other Items (Net)	37r	78.0	87.6	94.5	117.3	289.5	85.3	331.4	....	....	....	....	....	....	....	....
Money plus Quasi-Money	35l	291.6	312.9	354.9	445.1	635.1	882.6	1,069.8	....	....	....	....	....	....	....	....
Other Banking Institutions																	
Specialized Banks																*Millions of Dinars:*	
Cash	40	1.8	2.4	4.1	7.9	14.2	12.6	14.8	....	....	....	....	....	....	....	....
Claims on Private Sector	42d	71.8	79.0	84.1	96.6	122.0	150.9	189.5	....	....	....	....	....	....	....	....
Central Government Deposits	46d	29.8	34.5	38.2	44.4	52.3	64.2	79.4	....	....	....	....	....	....	....	....
Credit from Monetary Authorities	46g	4.0	4.2	3.2	1.9	1.2	2.9	10.5	....	....	....	....	....	....	....	....
Credit from Deposit Money Banks	46h	5.4	4.8	5.5	5.7	10.6	17.3	17.4	....	....	....	....	....	....	....	....
Capital Accounts	47a	37.3	40.2	43.4	52.7	70.7	74.5	87.7	....	....	....	....	....	....	....	....
Other Items (Net)	47r	−2.8	−2.4	−2.0	−.1	1.4	4.6	9.2	....	....	....	....	....	....	....	....
Post Office: Savings Deposits	45.. i	5.8	6.1	6.9	8.4	12.4	16.6	21.3	....	....	....	....	....	....	....	....
Nonbank Financial Institutions																*Millions of Dinars:*	
Cash	40.. s	1.37	1.50	1.60	2.04	2.68	3.80	4.61	....	....	....	....	....	....	....	....
Claims on Central Government	42a. s	.68	.68	1.11	1.09	.86	.86	.86	....	....	....	....	....	....	....	....
Claims on Private Sector	42d. s	.81	.87	.96	1.07	1.18	1.25	1.40	....	....	....	....	....	....	....	....
Incr.in Total Assets(Within Per.)	49z. s	.34	.39	.52	.58	.81	1.11	1.31	....	....	....	....	....	....	....	....
Production															*Index Numbers (1995=100):*	
Wholesale Prices (1975=100)	63	75.2	80.0	76.9	80.5	90.6	100.0	111.2	....	....	....	....	....	....	....	....
Crude Petroleum	66aa	76.5	83.8	73.2	100.6	98.1	112.6	120.5	114.4	130.9	171.9	132.2	44.7	45.9	50.1	60.1

	1985	1986	1987	1988	1989	1990	1991	1992	1993	1994	1995	1996	1997	1998	1999		
																Exchange Rates	
End of Period																Principal Rate	ac
	2.9287	2.6299	2.2676	2.3905	2.4479	2.2612	2.2489	2.3396	2.3420	2.2036	2.1641	2.2371	2.3842	2.2847	2.3438		
End of Period (ag) Period Average (rh)																Principal Rate	ag
	3.2169	3.2169	3.2169	3.2169	3.2169	3.2169	3.2169	3.2169	3.2169	3.2169	3.2169	3.2169	3.2169	3.2169	3.2169	Principal Rate	rh
	3.2169	3.2169	3.2169	3.2169	3.2169	3.2169	3.2169	3.2169	3.2169	3.2169	3.2169	3.2169	3.2169	3.2169	3.2169		
Period Averages																Principal Rate	ah x
	100.0	100.0	100.0	100.0	100.0	100.0	100.0	100.0	100.0	100.0	100.0	100.0	100.0	100.0	100.0	Nominal Effective Exchange Rate	ne c
	88.4	69.1	60.4	58.3	62.7	61.4	68.0	73.9	87.8	101.1	100.0	108.1	123.4	131.2	140.1		
																Fund Position	
End of Period																Quota	2f. s
	504.0	504.0	504.0	504.0	504.0	504.0	504.0	504.0	504.0	504.0	504.0	504.0	504.0	504.0	504.0	SDRs	1b. s
	—	—	5.1	—	—	—	—	—	—	—	—	—	—	—	—	Reserve Position in the Fund	1c. s
	—	—	—	—	—	—	—	—	—	—	—	—	—	—	—	Total Fund Cred.&Loans Outstg.	2tl
	—	—	—	—	—	—	—	—	—	—	—	—	—	—	—		
																International Liquidity	
End of Period																Total Reserves minus Gold	1l. d
	....	—	....	—	....	....	....	....	....	—	—	....	—	....	....	SDRs	1b. d
	—	—	7.2	—	—	—	—	—	—	—	—	—	—	—	—	Reserve Position in the Fund	1c. d
	—	—	—	—	—	—	—	—	—	—	—	—	—	—	—	Foreign Exchange	1d. d
	....	....	....	....	....	....	....	....	....	....	....	....	....	....	....	Gold (Million Fine Troy Ounces)	1ad
	....	....	....	....	....	....	....	....	....	....	....	....	....	....	....	Monetary Authorities: Other Assets	3.. d
	....	....	....	....	....	....	....	....	....	....	....	....	....	....	....	Other Liab.	4.. d
	....	....	....	....	....	....	....	....	....	....	....	....	....	....	....	Deposit Money Banks: Assets	7a. d
	....	....	....	....	....	....	....	....	....	....	....	....	....	....	....	Liabilities	7b. d
																Monetary Authorities	
End of Period																Foreign Assets	11
	....	....	....	....	....	....	....	....	....	....	....	....	....	....	....	Claims on Central Government	12a
	....	....	....	....	....	....	....	....	....	....	....	....	....	....	....	Claims on Deposit Money Banks	12e
	....	....	....	....	....	....	....	....	....	....	....	....	....	....	....	Reserve Money	14
	....	....	....	....	....	....	....	....	....	....	....	....	....	....	....	*of which: Currency Outside DMBs*	14a
	....	....	....	....	....	....	....	....	....	....	....	....	....	....	....	Foreign Liabilities	16c
	....	....	....	....	....	....	....	....	....	....	....	....	....	....	....	Central Government Deposits	16d
	....	....	....	....	....	....	....	....	....	....	....	....	....	....	....	Capital Accounts	17a
	....	....	....	....	....	....	....	....	....	....	....	....	....	....	....	Other Items (Net)	17r
																Deposit Money Banks	
End of Period																Reserves	20
	....	....	....	....	....	....	....	....	....	....	....	....	....	....	....	Foreign Assets	21
	....	....	....	....	....	....	....	....	....	....	....	....	....	....	....	Claims on Central Government	22a
	....	....	....	....	....	....	....	....	....	....	....	....	....	....	....	Claims on Private Sector	22d
	....	....	....	....	....	....	....	....	....	....	....	....	....	....	....	Demand Deposits	24
	....	....	....	....	....	....	....	....	....	....	....	....	....	....	....	Time and Savings Deposits	25
	....	....	....	....	....	....	....	....	....	....	....	....	....	....	....	Central Government Deposits	26d
	....	....	....	....	....	....	....	....	....	....	....	....	....	....	....	Credit from Monetary Authorities	26g
	....	....	....	....	....	....	....	....	....	....	....	....	....	....	....	Capital Accounts	27a
	....	....	....	....	....	....	....	....	....	....	....	....	....	....	....	Other Items (Net)	27r
																Monetary Survey	
End of Period																Foreign Assets (Net)	31n
	....	....	....	....	....	....	....	....	....	....	....	....	....	....	....	Domestic Credit	32
	....	....	....	....	....	....	....	....	....	....	....	....	....	....	....	Claims on Central Govt. (Net)	32an
	....	....	....	....	....	....	....	....	....	....	....	....	....	....	....	Claims on Private Sector	32d
	....	....	....	....	....	....	....	....	....	....	....	....	....	....	....	Claims on Other Banking Insts.	32f
	....	....	....	....	....	....	....	....	....	....	....	....	....	....	....	Money	34
	....	....	....	....	....	....	....	....	....	....	....	....	....	....	....	Quasi-Money	35
	....	....	....	....	....	....	....	....	....	....	....	....	....	....	....	Other Items (Net)	37r
	....	....	....	....	....	....	....	....	....	....	....	....	....	....	....	Money plus Quasi-Money	35l
																Other Banking Institutions	
																Specialized Banks	
End of Period																Cash	40
	....	....	....	....	....	....	....	....	....	....	....	....	....	....	....	Claims on Private Sector	42d
	....	....	....	....	....	....	....	....	....	....	....	....	....	....	....	Central Government Deposits	46d
	....	....	....	....	....	....	....	....	....	....	....	....	....	....	....	Credit from Monetary Authorities	46g
	....	....	....	....	....	....	....	....	....	....	....	....	....	....	....	Credit from Deposit Money Banks	46h
	....	....	....	....	....	....	....	....	....	....	....	....	....	....	....	Capital Accounts	47a
	....	....	....	....	....	....	....	....	....	....	....	....	....	....	....	Other Items (Net)	47r
	....	....	....	....	....	....	....	....	....	....	....	....	....	....	....	Post Office: Savings Deposits	45.. i
																Nonbank Financial Institutions	
End of Period																Cash	40.. s
	....	....	....	....	....	....	....	....	....	....	....	....	....	....	....	Claims on Central Government	42a. s
	....	....	....	....	....	....	....	....	....	....	....	....	....	....	....	Claims on Private Sector	42d. s
	....	....	....	....	....	....	....	....	....	....	....	....	....	....	....	*Incr.in Total Assets(Within Per.)*	49z. s
																Production	
Period Averages																Wholesale Prices (1975=100)	63
	....	....	....	....	....	....	....	....	....	....	....	....	....	....	....	Crude Petroleum	66aa
	71.4	84.1	103.5	130.5	140.6	100.0	14.9	21.9	29.9	29.9	29.9	31.3	60.5	105.4	124.7		

Iraq

		1970	1971	1972	1973	1974	1975	1976	1977	1978	1979	1980	1981	1982	1983	1984
International Transactions																*Millions of Dinars*
Exports	70	392.3	549.4	362.0	251.4	706.5	4,705.5	5,389.5	5,614.6	6,422.7	12,522.0	....	....			
Crude Petroleum	70aa	525.4	712.2	658.6	1,102.3	3,813.8	4,669.9	5,342.9	5,571.9	6,360.5	12,480.0	15,321.3	6,089.6	5,982.4	5,954.8	6,937.0
Imports, c.i.f.	71	181.6	247.9	234.6	270.3	700.1	1,244.7	1,150.9	1,323.2	1,244.1	1,738.9	2,208.1	2,333.8			
Imports, c.i.f., from DOTS	71y	....	....	....	....	....	....	....	....	....	....	....	6,013.0	6,309.0	3,086.2	3,032.4
Volume of Exports																*1985=100*
Crude Petroleum	72aa	108.6	118.5	103.1	142.4	138.7	149.8	166.7	161.0	184.2	241.7	187.7	62.9	64.6	70.4	84.5
Export Prices																*1985=100:*
Crude Petroleum	76aa *d*	5.2	6.5	7.3	9.8	35.6	38.1	40.7	44.7	44.6	65.9	107.2	125.5	118.4	104.4	100.7
Balance of Payments																*Millions of US Dollars:*
Current Account, n.i.e.	78al *d*	....	....	....	....	....	....	2,495	2,988	....	....	....	....	....	....	....
Goods: Exports f.o.b.	78aa *d*	....	....	....	....	....	....	7,854	10,838	....	....	....	....	....	....	....
Goods: Imports f.o.b.	78ab *d*	....	....	....	....	....	....	−4,269	−5,867	....	....	....	....	....	....	....
Trade Balance	78ac *d*	....	....	....	....	....	....	3,585	4,971	....	....	....	....	....	....	....
Services: Credit	78ad *d*	....	....	....	....	....	....	582	760	....	....	....	....	....	....	....
Services: Debit	78ae *d*	....	....	....	....	....	....	−1,540	−2,708	....	....	....	....	....	....	....
Balance on Goods & Services	78af *d*	....	....	....	....	....	....	2,627	3,023	....	....	....	....	....	....	....
Income: Credit	78ag *d*	....	....	....	....	....	....	....	....	....	....	....	....	....	....	....
Income: Debit	78ah *d*	....	....	....	....	....	....	....	....	....	....	....	....	....	....	....
Balance on Gds, Serv. & Inc.	78ai *d*	....	....	....	....	....	....	2,627	3,023	....	....	....	....	....	....	....
Current Transfers, n.i.e.: Credit	78aj *d*	....	....	....	....	....	....	....	....	....	....	....	....	....	....	....
Current Transfers: Debit	78ak *d*	....	....	....	....	....	....	−132	−35	....	....	....	....	....	....	....
Capital Account, n.i.e.	78bc *d*	....	....	....	....	....	....	—	—	....	....	....	....	....	....	....
Capital Account, n.i.e.: Credit	78ba *d*	....	....	....	....	....	....	—	—	....	....	....	....	....	....	....
Capital Account: Debit	78bb *d*	....	....	....	....	....	....	—	—	....	....	....	....	....	....	....
Financial Account, n.i.e.	78bj *d*	....	....	....	....	....	....	−1,053	−7	....	....	....	....	....	....	....
Direct Investment Abroad	78bd *d*	....	....	....	....	....	....	—	—	....	....	....	....	....	....	....
Dir. Invest. in Rep. Econ., n.i.e.	78be *d*	....	....	....	....	....	....	—	—	....	....	....	....	....	....	....
Portfolio Investment Assets	78bf *d*	....	....	....	....	....	....	—	—	....	....	....	....	....	....	....
Equity Securities	78bk *d*	....	....	....	....	....	....	—	—	....	....	....	....	....	....	....
Debt Securities	78bl *d*	....	....	....	....	....	....	—	—	....	....	....	....	....	....	....
Portfolio Investment Liab., n.i.e.	78bg *d*	....	....	....	....	....	....	—	—	....	....	....	....	....	....	....
Equity Securities	78bm *d*	....	....	....	....	....	....	—	—	....	....	....	....	....	....	....
Debt Securities	78bn *d*	....	....	....	....	....	....	—	—	....	....	....	....	....	....	....
Financial Derivatives Assets	78bw *d*	....	....	....	....	....	....	....	....	....	....	....	....	....	....	....
Financial Derivatives Liabilities	78bx *d*	....	....	....	....	....	....	....	....	....	....	....	....	....	....	....
Other Investment Assets	78bh *d*	....	....	....	....	....	....	−201	−152	....	....	....	....	....	....	....
Monetary Authorities	78bo *d*	....	....	....	....	....	....	....	....	....	....	....	....	....	....	....
General Government	78bp *d*	....	....	....	....	....	....	−137	−80	....	....	....	....	....	....	....
Banks	78bq *d*	....	....	....	....	....	....	−65	−72	....	....	....	....	....	....	....
Other Sectors	78br *d*	....	....	....	....	....	....	....	....	....	....	....	....	....	....	....
Other Investment Liab., n.i.e.	78bi *d*	....	....	....	....	....	....	−852	145	....	....	....	....	....	....	....
Monetary Authorities	78bs *d*	....	....	....	....	....	....	−41	12	....	....	....	....	....	....	....
General Government	78bt *d*	....	....	....	....	....	....	−231	−121	....	....	....	....	....	....	....
Banks	78bu *d*	....	....	....	....	....	....	—	57	....	....	....	....	....	....	....
Other Sectors	78bv *d*	....	....	....	....	....	....	−579	197	....	....	....	....	....	....	....
Net Errors and Omissions	78ca *d*	....	....	....	....	....	....	423	−508	....	....	....	....	....	....	....
Overall Balance	78cb *d*	....	....	....	....	....	....	1,865	2,473	....	....	....	....	....	....	....
Reserves and Related Items	79da *d*	....	....	....	....	....	....	−1,865	−2,473	....	....	....	....	....	....	....
Reserve Assets	79db *d*	....	....	....	....	....	....	−1,865	−2,473	....	....	....	....	....	....	....
Use of Fund Credit and Loans	79dc *d*	....	....	....	....	....	....	—	—	....	....	....	....	....	....	....
Exceptional Financing	79de *d*	....	....	....	....	....	....	....	....	....	....	....	....	....	....	....
National Accounts																*Millions of Dinars*
Exports of Goods & Services	90c	437.5	596.5	505.7	720.5	2,075.9	2,329.0	2,491.0	3,425.6	3,977.1	6,974.3	10,012.4	3,587.8	3,350.5	3,107.9	3,734.3
Government Consumption	91f	268.9	301.6	....	....	2,075.9	755.6	870.6	1,223.3	1,584.1	1,646.3	2,451.2	3,446.2	4,468.2	5,475.3	4,989.1
Gross Fixed Capital Formation	93e	185.1	194.7	217.1	288.6	628.6	1,067.9	1,336.4	1,478.6	1,993.0	2,714.3	3,807.1	5,708.1	6,536.5	5,513.2	4,433.4
Increase/Decrease(-) in Stocks	93i	17.7	14.7	56.2	70.6	320.2	150.8	−301.2	—	−537.4	564.3	1,053.3	1,313.6	833.6	−3,533.3	−1,733.2
Private Consumption	96f	609.9	633.2	956.1	929.4	1,427.1	2,266.7	2,611.9	3,669.9	2,628.9	2,971.8	3,601.9	4,156.2	6,035.6	6,848.9	7,815.2
Imports of Goods & Services	98c	−236.6	−314.2	−294.2	−382.7	−1,073.8	−1,792.0	−1,479.0	−2,532.0	−2,220.8	−3,480.1	−4,977.6	−7,068.3	−8,447.4	−4,156.3	−4,316.4
Gross Domestic Product (GDP)	99b	1,282.5	1,433.8	1,440.9	1,626.4	3,378.0	4,022.4	4,659.1	6,042.1	7,224.9	11,390.9	15,948.4	11,143.6	12,777.0	13,255.7	14,922.4
Net Factor Inc/Pmts(-) Abroad	98.n	−166.0	−214.9	−136.5	−82.0	−242.0	−115.0	37.7	80.7	139.0	90.4	474.2	−401.0	−729.1	−589.6	−470.5
Gross National Income (GNI)	99a	1,085.2	1,218.9	1,304.4	1,544.4	3,136.0	3,907.4	....	....	7,363.9	11,481.3	16,422.6	10,742.6	12,051.9	12,666.1	14,451.9
Net National Income	99e	1,011	1,140	1,219	1,451	3,033	3,802	....	....	....	....	....	....	....	....	....
																Millions:
Population	99z	9.44	9.75	10.07	10.41	10.77	11.12	11.51	12.03	12.41	12.82	13.24	13.67	14.11	14.59	15.08

	1985	1986	1987	1988	1989	1990	1991	1992	1993	1994	1995	1996	1997	1998	1999	
International Transactions																
Millions of Dinars																
Exports	....	....	....	....	....	....	....	....	....	....	....	....	....	....	....	70
Crude Petroleum	8,142.5	5,126.2	6,988.9	7,245.8	....	....	....	....	....	....	....	....	....	....	....	70aa
Imports, c.i.f.	....	....	....	....	....	....	....	....	....	....	....	....	....	....	....	71
Imports, c.i.f., from DOTS	3,285.7	2,773.0	2,268.7	2,888.8	3,077.1	2,028.5	131.5	187.3	165.6	155.0	203.6	175.9	283.1	418.0	318.3	71y
1985=100																
Volume of Exports — Crude Petroleum	100.0	117.7	143.5	180.5	197.2	....	....	....							....	72aa
Index of Prices in US Dollars																
Export Prices — Crude Petroleum	100.0	54.0	59.8	49.2	....	....	....									76aa *d*

Minus Sign Indicates Debit

Balance of Payments

	1985	1986	1987	1988	1989	1990	1991	1992	1993	1994	1995	1996	1997	1998	1999	
Current Account, n.i.e.	....	....	....	....	....	....	....	....	....	....	....	....	....	....	....	78al *d*
Goods: Exports f.o.b.	....	....	....	....	....	....	....	....	....	....	....	....	....	....	....	78aa *d*
Goods: Imports f.o.b.	....	....	....	....	....	....	....	....	....	....	....	....	....	....	....	78ab *d*
Trade Balance	....	....	....	....	....	....	....	....	....	....	....	....	....	....	....	78ac *d*
Services: Credit	....	....	....	....	....	....	....	....	....	....	....	....	....	....	....	78ad *d*
Services: Debit	....	....	....	....	....	....	....	....	....	....	....	....	....	....	....	78ae *d*
Balance on Goods & Services	....	....	....	....	....	....	....	....	....	....	....	....	....	....	....	78af *d*
Income: Credit	....	....	....	....	....	....	....	....	....	....	....	....	....	....	....	78ag *d*
Income: Debit	....	....	....	....	....	....	....	....	....	....	....	....	....	....	....	78ah *d*
Balance on Gds, Serv. & Inc.	....	....	....	....	....	....	....	....	....	....	....	....	....	....	....	78ai *d*
Current Transfers, n.i.e.: Credit	....	....	....	....	....	....	....	....	....	....	....	....	....	....	....	78aj *d*
Current Transfers: Debit	....	....	....	....	....	....	....	....	....	....	....	....	....	....	....	78ak *d*
Capital Account, n.i.e.	....	....	....	....	....	....	....	....	....	....	....	....	....	....	....	78bc *d*
Capital Account, n.i.e.: Credit	....	....	....	....	....	....	....	....	....	....	....	....	....	....	....	78ba *d*
Capital Account: Debit	....	....	....	....	....	....	....	....	....	....	....	....	....	....	....	78bb *d*
Financial Account, n.i.e.	....	....	....	....	....	....	....	....	....	....	....	....	....	....	....	78bj *d*
Direct Investment Abroad	....	....	....	....	....	....	....	....	....	....	....	....	....	....	....	78bd *d*
Dir. Invest. in Rep. Econ., n.i.e.	....	....	....	....	....	....	....	....	....	....	....	....	....	....	....	78be *d*
Portfolio Investment Assets	....	....	....	....	....	....	....	....	....	....	....	....	....	....	....	78bf *d*
Equity Securities	....	....	....	....	....	....	....	....	....	....	....	....	....	....	....	78bk *d*
Debt Securities	....	....	....	....	....	....	....	....	....	....	....	....	....	....	....	78bl *d*
Portfolio Investment Liab., n.i.e.	....	....	....	....	....	....	....	....	....	....	....	....	....	....	....	78bg *d*
Equity Securities	....	....	....	....	....	....	....	....	....	....	....	....	....	....	....	78bm *d*
Debt Securities	....	....	....	....	....	....	....	....	....	....	....	....	....	....	....	78bn *d*
Financial Derivatives Assets	....	....	....	....	....	....	....	....	....	....	....	....	....	....	....	78bw *d*
Financial Derivatives Liabilities	....	....	....	....	....	....	....	....	....	....	....	....	....	....	....	78bx *d*
Other Investment Assets	....	....	....	....	....	....	....	....	....	....	....	....	....	....	....	78bh *d*
Monetary Authorities	....	....	....	....	....	....	....	....	....	....	....	....	....	....	....	78bo *d*
General Government	....	....	....	....	....	....	....	....	....	....	....	....	....	....	....	78bp *d*
Banks	....	....	....	....	....	....	....	....	....	....	....	....	....	....	....	78bq *d*
Other Sectors	....	....	....	....	....	....	....	....	....	....	....	....	....	....	....	78br *d*
Other Investment Liab., n.i.e.	....	....	....	....	....	....	....	....	....	....	....	....	....	....	....	78bi *d*
Monetary Authorities	....	....	....	....	....	....	....	....	....	....	....	....	....	....	....	78bs *d*
General Government	....	....	....	....	....	....	....	....	....	....	....	....	....	....	....	78bt *d*
Banks	....	....	....	....	....	....	....	....	....	....	....	....	....	....	....	78bu *d*
Other Sectors	....	....	....	....	....	....	....	....	....	....	....	....	....	....	....	78bv *d*
Net Errors and Omissions	....	....	....	....	....	....	....	....	....	....	....	....	....	....	....	78ca *d*
Overall Balance	....	....	....	....	....	....	....	....	....	....	....	....	....	....	....	78cb *d*
Reserves and Related Items	....	....	....	....	....	....	....	....	....	....	....	....	....	....	....	79da *d*
Reserve Assets	....	....	....	....	....	....	....	....	....	....	....	....	....	....	....	79db *d*
Use of Fund Credit and Loans	....	....	....	....	....	....	....	....	....	....	....	....	....	....	....	79dc *d*
Exceptional Financing	....	....	....	....	....	....	....	....	....	....	....	....	....	....	....	79de *d*

National Accounts

Millions of Dinars

	1985	1986	1987	1988	1989	1990	1991	1992	1993	1994	1995	1996	1997	1998	1999	
Exports of Goods & Services	3,774.7	2,417.8	4,087.1	3,824.5	4,482.6	4,305.4	547.8	670.3	1,474.0	....	....	....	....	....	....	90c
Government Consumption	4,431.8	5,252.8	5,673.8	6,645.8	5,990.1	6,142.0	7,033.3	8,898.0	15,576.3	....	....	....	....	....	....	91f
Gross Fixed Capital Formation	4,301.2	3,859.2	3,657.5	2,899.2	6,305.5	6,220.0	3,289.1	10,782.0	16,258.7	....	....	....	....	....	....	93e
Increase/Decrease(-) in Stocks	-636.5	-990.9	-124.1	1,193.5	-2,317.5	-976.9	520.0	-2,379.0	1,102.0	....	....	....	....	....	....	93i
Private Consumption	8,098.7	8,397.7	9,204.4	10,101.4	11,232.4	11,760.5	9,611.1	40,929.8	81,106.0	....	....	....	....	....	....	96f
Imports of Goods & Services	-4,476.0	-3,873.6	-4,598.4	-5,038.1	-4,667.3	-4,154.2	-1,061.6	-1,540.6	-3,375.0	....	....	....	....	....	....	98c
Gross Domestic Product (GDP)	15,493.8	15,063.0	17,900.6	19,626.3	21,025.8	23,296.8	19,939.7	57,360.5	112,142.0	....	....	....	....	....	....	99b
Net Factor Inc/Pmts(-) Abroad	-558.8	-692.4	-704.7	-700.4	-678.2	....	....	....	....	....	....	....	....	....	....	98.n
Gross National Income (GNI)	14,935.0	14,370.6	17,195.9	19,332.1	19,331.6	....	....	....	....	....	....	....	....	....	....	99a
Net National Income	....	....	....	....	....	....	....	....	....	....	....	....	....	....	....	99e

Midyear Estimates

	1985	1986	1987	1988	1989	1990	1991	1992	1993	1994	1995	1996	1997	1998	1999	
Population	15.58	16.11	16.33	16.88	17.43	18.08	18.51	18.90	19.26	19.65	20.09	20.61	21.18	21.80	22.45	99z

Ireland

		1970	1971	1972	1973	1974	1975	1976	1977	1978	1979	1980	1981	1982	1983	1984
Exchange Rates															*SDRs per Pound through 1998,*	
Market Rate	ac	2.3937	2.3510	2.1627	1.9258	1.9182	1.7285	1.4653	1.5691	1.5616	1.6283	1.4878	1.3574	1.2660	1.0841	1.0115
															US Dollars per Pound through 1998,	
Market Rate	ag	2.3937	2.5525	2.3481	2.3232	2.3485	2.0235	1.7024	1.9060	2.0345	2.1450	1.8975	1.5800	1.3965	1.1350	.9915
Market Rate	rh	2.4000	2.4344	2.5018	2.4522	2.3390	2.2218	1.8062	1.7455	1.9195	2.0475	2.0580	1.6167	1.4222	1.2482	1.0871
															ECUs per Pound:	
ECU Rate	ec	....	....	....	....	....	....	....	....	....	1.4913	1.4537	1.4560	1.4432	1.3718	1.3986
ECU Rate	ed	....	....	....	....	....	....	....	....	1.5063	1.4938	1.4793	1.4470	1.4502	1.3996	1.3773
															Index Numbers (1995=100):	
Market Rate	ahx	149.4	152.4	156.0	152.9	145.8	138.5	112.6	108.8	119.7	127.7	128.3	100.8	88.7	77.8	67.8
Nominal Effective Exchange Rate	neu	164.20	164.25	159.13	146.45	143.12	134.15	120.99	116.60	117.01	117.21	114.64	105.02	103.84	100.17	96.45
Fund Position															*Millions of SDRs:*	
Quota	2f. s	121	121	121	121	121	121	121	121	155	155	233	233	233	343	343
SDRs	1b. s	13	26	39	39	41	41	45	46	48	71	71	91	96	65	89
Reserve Position in the Fund	1c. s	30	35	40	40	42	39	69	66	60	61	77	75	75	116	124
Total Fund Cred.&Loans Outstg.	2tl	—														
International Liquidity														*Millions of US Dollars Unless Otherwise Indicated:*		
Total Res.Min.Gold (Eurosys.Def)	1l. d	681	978	1,109	1,007	1,247	1,513	1,818	2,351	2,668	2,212	2,860	2,651	2,622	2,640	2,352
SDRs	1b. d	13	29	43	48	50	48	53	55	63	93	91	106	106	68	88
Reserve Position in the Fund	1c. d	30	38	44	49	52	46	80	80	78	80	98	87	83	121	122
Foreign Exchange	1d. d	637	911	1,023	911	1,146	1,419	1,686	2,216	2,528	2,039	2,672	2,458	2,433	2,450	2,143
o/w: Fin.Deriv.Rel.to Reserves	1dd d	....	....	....	....	....	....	....	....	....	....	....	....	....	....	....
Other Reserve Assets	1e. d	....	....	....	....	....	....	....	....	....	....	....	....	....	....	....
Gold (Million Fine Troy Ounces)	1ad	.457	.457	.457	.429	.447	.447	.447	.473	.447	.383	.357	.359	.360	.360	.360
Gold (National Valuation)	1an d	16	17	17	18	19	18	18	18	20	18	16	117	96	106	88
Memo: Euro Cl. on Non-EA Res.	1dg d	....	....	....	....	....	....	....	....	....	....	....	....	....	....	....
Non-Euro Cl. on EA Res.	1dh d	....	....	....	....	....	....	....	....	....	....	....	....	....	....	....
Mon. Auth.: Other Foreign Assets	3.. d															
Foreign Liabilities	4.. d	—	—	—	—	—	—	—	—	—	—	—	—	—	—	—
Banking Insts.: Foreign Assets	7a. d	954	⌐1,508	1,727	2,625	3,328	3,138	3,203	4,216	5,321	7,084	8,781	8,583	2,774	2,579	2,631
Foreign Liab.	7b. d	804	1,740	2,174	2,964	3,736	3,573	3,577	5,331	6,528	8,549	10,720	10,363	⌐5,075	5,116	5,127
Monetary Authorities														*Millions of Pounds through 1998;*		
Fgn. Assets (Cl.on Non-EA Ctys)	11	290	381	432	443	504	689	978	1,218	1,270	989	1,369	1,507	1,637	2,061	2,160
Claims on General Government	12a. u	....	....	....	....	....	....	....	....	....	....	....	....	....	....	....
o/w: Claims on Gen.Govt.in Cty	12a	47	27	33	61	63	114	108	111	136	278	342	334	398	412	513
Claims on Banking Institutions	12e. u	....	....	....	....	....	....	....	....	....	....	....	....	....	....	....
o/w: Claims on Bank.Inst.in Cty	12e	....	....	....	....	....	....	....	....	....	....	....	....	....	....	....
Claims on Other Resident Sectors	12d. u	....	....	....	....	....	....	....	....	....	....	....	....	....	....	....
o/w: Cl. on Oth.Res.Sect.in Cty	12d	—	—	—	—	—	67	10	26	15				55	—	4
Claims on ECB	12u	....														
Currency in Circulation	14a	173	186	205	240	268	321	369	422	512	633	721	797	879	985	1,035
Liabilities to Banking Insts	14c. u	....	....	....	....	....	....	....	....	....	....	....	....	....	....	....
o/w: Liabs to Bank.Inst.in Cty	14c	67	119	138	188	265	299	357	405	525	508	603	484	517	565	636
Demand Dep. of Other Res.Sect.	14d. u	....	....	....	....	....	....	....	....	....	....	....	....	....	....	....
o/w: D.Dep.of Oth.Res.Sect.in Cty	14d	....	....	....	....	....	....	....	....	....	....	....	....	....	....	....
Other Dep. of Other Res.Sect.	15.. u	....	....	....	....	....	....	....	....	....	....	....	....	....	....	....
o/w: O.Dep.of Oth.Res.Sect.in Cty	15	....	....	....	....	....	....	....	....	....	....	....	....	....	....	....
Money Market Instruments	16m. u	....	....	....	....	....	....	....	....	....	....	....	....	....	....	....
o/w: MMI Held by Resid.of Cty	16m	....	....	....	....	....	....	....	....	....	....	....	....	....	....	....
Bonds (Debt Securities)	16n. u	....	....	....	....	....	....	....	....	....	....	....	....	....	....	....
o/w: Bonds Held by Resid.of Cty	16n	....	....	....	....	....	....	....	....	....	....	....	....	....	....	....
Foreign Liab. (to Non-EA Ctys)	16c	—	—	—	—	—	—	—	—	—	—	—	—	—	—	—
Central Government Deposits	16d. u	....	....	....	....	....	....	....	....	....	....	....	....	....	....	....
o/w: Cent.Govt.Dep. in Cty	16d	30	58	85	40	28	135	232	297	193	117	138	130	186	222	198
Liabilities to ECB	16u	....														
Capital Accounts	17a	28	39	43	41	62	84	183	202	183	203	248	382	434	654	796
Other Items (Net)	17r	13	−23	−7	−4	−56	−37	12	15	19	−180	1	48	73	47	13
Banking Institutions														*Millions of Pounds through 1998;*		
Claims on Monetary Authorities	20	86e	⌐172	164	229	302	341	402	476	620	622	770	953	567	639	742
Claims on Bk.Inst.in Oth.EA Ctys	20b. u	....	....	....	....	....	....	....	....	....	....	....	....	....	....	....
Fgn. Assets (Cl.on Non-EA Ctys)	21	397e	⌐579	663	1,130	1,417	1,551	1,882	2,212	2,615	3,302	4,628	5,432	1,986	2,272	2,654
Claims on General Government	22a. u	....	....	....	....	....	....	....	....	....	....	....	....	....	....	....
o/w: Claims on Gen.Govt.in Cty	22a	170e	⌐259	293	348	488	656	722	879	930	1,056	1,275	1,443	1,844	2,161	2,740
Claims on Other Resident Sectors	22d. u	....	....	....	....	....	....	....	....	....	....	....	....	....	....	....
o/w: Cl. on Oth.Res.Sect.in Cty	22d	461e	⌐686	917	1,088	1,256	1,470	1,747	2,304	3,037	3,669	4,300	5,224	⌐6,423	7,229	7,891
Demand Deposits	24.. u	....	....	....	....	....	....	....	....	....	....	....	....	....	....	....
o/w: D.Dep.of Oth.Res.Sect.in Cty	24	234e	⌐414	512	645	757	894	1,025	1,214	1,673	1,988	2,407	3,064	⌐1,318	1,450	1,779
Other Deposits	25.. u	....	....	....	....	....	....	....	....	....	....	....	....	....	....	....
o/w: O.Dep.of Oth.Res.Sect.in Cty	25	541e	⌐598	654	824	1,042	1,280	1,417	1,693	2,047	2,400	2,993	3,439	⌐4,932	5,161	5,587
Money Market Instruments	26m. u	....	....	....	....	....	....	....	....	....	....	....	....	....	....	....
o/w: MMI Held by Resid.of Cty	26m	....	....	....	....	....	....	....	....	....	....	....	....	....	....	....
Bonds (Debt Securities)	26n. u	....	....	....	....	....	....	....	....	....	....	....	....	....	....	....
o/w: Bonds Held by Resid.of Cty	26n	....	....	....	....	....	....	....	....	....	....	....	....	....	....	....
Foreign Liab. (to Non-EA Ctys)	26c	335e	⌐668	834	1,276	1,591	1,766	2,101	2,797	3,209	3,986	5,650	6,559	⌐3,634	4,508	5,171
Central Government Deposits	26d. u	....	....	....	....	....	....	....	....	....	....	....	....	....	....	....
o/w: Cent.Govt.Dep. in Cty	26d	23e	⌐37	9	17	13	15	27	34	30	38	22	43	⌐46	60	84
Credit from Monetary Authorities	26g	....	....	....	....	....	....	....	....	....	....	....	....	105	70	143
Liab. to Bk.Inst.in Oth. EA Ctys	26h. u	....	....	....	....	....	....	....	....	....	....	....	....	....	....	....
Capital Accounts	27a	....	26	16	23	36	38	49	68	91	115	142	184	1,188	1,372	1,607
Other Items (Net)	27r	−19	⌐−49	9	—	25	26	32	66	152	123	−241	−238	⌐−403	−321	−345

1985	1986	1987	1988	1989	1990	1991	1992	1993	1994	1995	1996	1997	1998	1999		
															Exchange Rates	
SDRs per Euro Thereafter: End of Period																
1.1321	1.1441	1.1810	1.1202	1.1843	1.2480	1.2233	1.1850	1.0271	1.0598	1.0801	1.1691	1.0601	1.0563	.7319	Market Rate	ac
US Dollars per Euro Thereafter: End of Period (ag) Period Average (rh)																
1.2435	1.3995	1.6755	1.5075	1.5563	1.7755	1.7498	1.6294	1.4108	1.5471	1.6055	1.6811	1.4304	1.4873	1.0046	Market Rate	ag
1.0656	1.3415	1.4881	1.5261	1.4190	1.6585	1.6155	1.7053	1.4671	1.4978	1.6038	1.6006	1.5180	1.4257	1.0668	Market Rate	rh
End of Period (ec) Period Average (ed)																
1.4005	1.3075	1.2855	1.2846	1.3002	1.3024	1.3049	1.3456	1.2630	1.2578	1.2218	1.3417	1.2960	1.2697	....	ECU Rate	ec
1.3982	1.3661	1.2896	1.2892	1.2873	1.3026	1.3024	1.3146	1.2514	1.2604	1.2263	1.2611	1.3380	1.2717	....	ECU Rate	ed
Period Averages																
66.4	83.6	92.8	95.2	88.5	103.4	100.7	106.3	91.5	93.4	100.0	99.8	94.7	88.9	....	Market Rate	ahx
97.26	101.67	99.78	98.03	96.99	102.81	101.41	104.57	99.17	99.50	100.00	102.11	102.39	97.06	94.20	Nominal Effective Exchange Rate	neu
															Fund Position	
End of Period																
343	343	343	343	343	343	343	525	525	525	525	525	525	525	838	Quota	2f.s
99	113	126	134	145	158	170	90	97	101	107	115	123	137	29	SDRs	1b.s
121	131	131	134	125	105	124	171	155	152	197	226	252	414	303	Reserve Position in the Fund	1c.s
														—	Total Fund Cred.&Loans Outstg.	2tl
															International Liquidity	
End of Period																
2,940	3,236	4,796	5,087	4,057	5,223	5,740	3,440	5,925	6,115	8,630	8,205	6,526	9,397	‡5,346	Total Res.Min.Gold (Eurosys.Def)	1l.d
109	139	179	181	191	225	243	124	133	148	159	165	166	193	40	SDRs	1b.d
133	160	186	181	165	149	177	236	213	222	294	325	340	582	416	Reserve Position in the Fund	1c.d
2,698	2,938	4,431	4,725	3,702	4,849	5,320	3,080	5,579	5,745	8,178	7,715	6,020	8,622	4,890	Foreign Exchange	1d.d
....	....	....	....	....	....	....	....	....	....	....	....	....	....	—	o/w: Fin.Deriv.Rel.to Reserves	1dd d
														—	Other Reserve Assets	1e.d
.359	.359	.359	.359	.359	.359	.359	.360	.360	.360	.361	.361	.361	.451	.176	Gold (Million Fine Troy Ounces)	1ad
95	105	139	114	109	109	104	109	123	141	137	143	116	132	56	Gold (National Valuation)	1an d
....	....	....	....	....	....	....	....	....	....	....	....	....	....	23.17	Memo: Euro Cl. on Non-EA Res.	1dg d
														94.00	Non-Euro Cl. on EA Res.	1dh d
															Mon. Auth.: Other Foreign Assets	3..d
						1,167							—	‡1,389	Foreign Liabilities	4..d
3,213	3,829	5,862	6,103	9,704	13,445	14,338	18,428	21,381	30,088	46,679	70,324	101,447	142,089	‡78,106	Banking Insts.: Foreign Assets	7a.d
6,323	8,318	10,754	10,750	12,823	17,740	17,053	18,727	19,146	28,127	49,100	70,169	99,225	142,772	‡77,733	Foreign Liab.	7b.d
															Monetary Authorities	
Millions of Euros Beginning 1999: End of Period																
2,326	2,259	2,868	3,220	2,565	2,926	3,294	2,158	4,283	4,173	5,471	4,959	4,634	6,445	5,411	Fgn. Assets (Cl.on Non-EA Ctys)	11
														2,109	Claims on General Government	12a.u
454	442	439	492	484	496	361	361	315	254	183	132	132	132	279	o/w: Claims on Gen.Govt.in Cty	12a
														7,753	Claims on Banking Institutions	12e.u
														5,062	o/w: Claims on Bank.Inst.in Cty	12e
														—	Claims on Other Resident Sectors	12d.u
2	—	5	—	—	—	—	—	—	—	—	—	—	—	—	o/w: Cl. on Oth.Res.Sect. in Cty	12d
														909	Claims on ECB	12u
1,073	1,130	1,215	1,347	1,460	1,550	1,568	1,604	1,776	1,907	2,092	2,287	2,619	3,040	4,524	Currency in Circulation	14a
														4,228	Liabilities to Banking Insts	14c.u
727	731	843	774	764	912	679	457	709	685	1,188	1,030	1,326	2,258	2,074	o/w: Liabs to Bank.Inst.in Cty	14c
														—	Demand Dep. of Other Res.Sect.	14d.u
														—	o/w: D.Dep.of Oth.Res.Sect.in Cty	14d
														—	Other Dep. of Other Res.Sect.	15..u
														—	o/w: O.Dep.of Oth.Res.Sect.in Cty	15
														—	Money Market Instruments	16m.u
														—	o/w: MMI Held by Resid.of Cty	16m
														—	Bonds (Debt Securities)	16n.u
														—	o/w: Bonds Held by Resid.of Cty	16n
—	—	—	—	—	—	716	—	—	—	—	—	—	—	1,383	Foreign Liab. (to Non-EA Ctys)	16c
														3,546	Central Government Deposits	16d.u
193	274	648	883	1,133	979	1,248	639	1,426	836	1,082	1,178	1,191	1,674	3,546	o/w: Cent.Govt.Dep. in Cty	16d
														—	Liabilities to ECB	16u
793	824	864	863	933	807	822	999	1,366	1,416	1,264	841	1,265	1,248	2,593	Capital Accounts	17a
-5	-257	-258	-156	-1,241	-827	-662	-1,897	-679	-417	28	-245	-1,635	-1,642	-92	Other Items (Net)	17r
															Banking Institutions	
Millions of Euros Beginning 1999: End of Period																
827	833	946	906	910	1,138	857	642	775	675	1,436	1,348	1,686	2,706	2,486	Claims on Monetary Authorities	20
														34,495	Claims on Bk.Inst.in Oth.EA Ctys	20b.u
2,584	2,736	3,499	4,048	6,235	7,573	8,194	11,310	15,155	19,448	29,074	41,832	70,922	95,535	77,748	Fgn. Assets (Cl.on Non-EA Ctys)	21
														29,909	Claims on General Government	22a.u
2,939	3,045	3,237	2,966	2,695	2,773	2,786	3,260	3,196	3,581	4,637	4,049	4,220	4,676	6,335	o/w: Claims on Gen.Govt.in Cty	22a
														109,999	Claims on Other Resident Sectors	22d.u
8,197	8,805	9,222	10,551	12,199	13,615	13,276	14,321	14,835	16,571	29,106	33,978	44,058	54,020	91,795	o/w: Cl. on Oth.Res.Sect.in Cty	22d
														12,711	Demand Deposits	24..u
1,765	1,828	1,915	2,122	2,349	2,674	2,658	2,783	3,103	3,539	6,808	7,552	5,199	6,802	12,649	o/w: D.Dep.of Oth.Res.Sect.in Cty	24
														67,614	Other Deposits	25..u
6,026	5,794	6,584	6,930	7,089	8,405	9,031	9,744	12,693	13,848	20,494	24,324	32,890	38,108	59,223	o/w: O.Dep.of Oth.Res.Sect.in Cty	25
														—	Money Market Instruments	26m.u
															o/w: MMI Held by Resid.of Cty	26m
														24,237	Bonds (Debt Securities)	26n.u
															o/w: Bonds Held by Resid.of Cty	26n
5,085	5,943	6,418	7,131	8,240	9,991	9,746	11,493	13,571	18,180	30,582	41,740	69,369	95,994	77,377	Foreign Liab. (to Non-EA Ctys)	26c
														1,274	Central Government Deposits	26d.u
55	93	83	99	110	124	125	121	119	360	239	248	299	332	1,274	o/w: Cent.Govt.Dep. in Cty	26d
87	369	338	240	1,302	884	817	2,065	737	403	37	261	1,637	1,755	5,245	Credit from Monetary Authorities	26g
														44,248	Liab. to Bk.Inst.in Oth. EA Ctys	26h.u
1,686	1,584	1,768	2,293	3,130	3,390	3,509	3,934	4,322	4,854	6,486	7,249	10,280	12,881	22,091	Capital Accounts	27a
-157	-192	-202	-343	-180	-371	-774	-607	-584	-909	-394	-167	1,211	1,067	-158	Other Items (Net)	27r

Ireland

178

	1970	1971	1972	1973	1974	1975	1976	1977	1978	1979	1980	1981	1982	1983	1984
Banking Survey (Nat'l Residency)													*Millions of Pounds through 1998;*		
Foreign Assets (Net) **31n**	353	ℐ292	261	298	330	474	758	633	677	306	347	380	ℐ–11	–175	–358
Domestic Credit **32**	625	ℐ877	1,148	1,440	1,766	2,090	2,385	2,973	3,906	4,864	5,757	6,829	ℐ8,488	9,519	10,867
Claims on General Govt. (Net) **32an**	164	ℐ191	231	352	510	620	571	659	843	1,179	1,457	1,605	ℐ2,010	2,290	2,971
Claims on Other Resident Sectors **32d**	461	ℐ686	917	1,088	1,256	1,470	1,814	2,314	3,063	3,684	4,300	5,224	ℐ6,478	7,229	7,896
Currency in Circulation **34a.n**	173	186	205	240	268	321	369	422	512	633	721	797	879	985	1,035
Demand Deposits **34b.n**	234	ℐ414	512	645	757	894	1,025	1,214	1,673	1,988	2,407	3,064	ℐ1,318	1,450	1,779
Other Deposits .... **35..n**	541	ℐ598	654	824	1,042	1,280	1,417	1,693	2,047	2,400	2,993	3,439	ℐ4,932	5,161	5,587
Money Market Instruments **36m**	....	....	....	....	....	....	....	....	....	....	....	....	....	....	....
Bonds (Debt Securities) **36n**	....	....	....	....	....	....	....	....	....	....	....	....	....	....	....
o/w: Bonds Over Two Years **36na**	....	....	....	....	....	....	....	....	....	....	....	....	....	....	....
Capital Accounts **37a**	28	ℐ64	59	64	98	122	232	270	275	318	390	565	ℐ1,622	2,026	2,403
Other Items (Net) **37r**	–24	ℐ–125	–24	–45	–68	–52	–1	9	76	–170	–406	–659	ℐ–275	–278	–295
Banking Survey (EA-Wide Residency)													*Millions of Euros:*		
Foreign Assets (Net) **31n.u**	....	....	....	....	....	....	....	....	....	....	....	....	....	....	....
Domestic Credit .... **32..u**	....	....	....	....	....	....	....	....	....	....	....	....	....	....	....
Claims on General Govt. (Net) **32an.u**	....	....	....	....	....	....	....	....	....	....	....	....	....	....	....
Claims on Other Resident Sect. **32d.u**	....	....	....	....	....	....	....	....	....	....	....	....	....	....	....
Currency in Circulation **34a.u**	....	....	....	....	....	....	....	....	....	....	....	....	....	....	....
Demand Deposits **34b.u**	....	....	....	....	....	....	....	....	....	....	....	....	....	....	....
Other Deposits .... **35..u**	....	....	....	....	....	....	....	....	....	....	....	....	....	....	....
o/w: Other Dep. Over Two Yrs **35ab.u**	....	....	....	....	....	....	....	....	....	....	....	....	....	....	....
Money Market Instruments **36m.u**	....	....	....	....	....	....	....	....	....	....	....	....	....	....	....
Bonds (Debt Securities) **36n.u**	....	....	....	....	....	....	....	....	....	....	....	....	....	....	....
o/w: Bonds Over Two Years **36na.u**	....	....	....	....	....	....	....	....	....	....	....	....	....	....	....
Capital Accounts **37a**	....	....	....	....	....	....	....	....	....	....	....	....	....	....	....
Other Items (Net) **37r.u**	....	....	....	....	....	....	....	....	....	....	....	....	....	....	....
Nonbank Financial Institutions													*Millions of Pounds:*		
Cash .... **40..k**	6	5	7	9	13	26	28	30	38	74	91	111	ℐ300	319	402
Foreign Assets .... **41..k**	....	2	1	2	1	1	1	1	1	1	—	—	ℐ11	10	15
Claims on Central Government........... **42a.k**	8	226	270	306	363	444	544	721	868	1,024	1,155	1,285	ℐ923	980	1,560
Claims on Private Sector **42d.k**	436	116	152	191	218	266	354	458	585	776	987	1,264	ℐ2,357	2,680	3,021
Quasi-Monetary Liabilities .... **45..k**	....	313	386	458	535	673	847	1,108	1,357	1,699	2,061	2,442	ℐ2,794	3,163	3,697
Foreign Liabilities **46c.k**	....	13	16	18	29	24	29	34	44	38	36	33	ℐ460	487	528
Cred.from Deposit Money Banks **46h.k**	....	13	16	19	24	20	23	30	41	70	67	89	ℐ203	183	184
Capital Accounts **47a.k**	4	5	7	8	11	15	16	20	30	39	50	66	ℐ131	159	184
Other Items (Net) **47r.k**	....	4	5	5	–3	6	11	19	21	29	22	31	–11	–2	18
Liquid Liabilities **55l**	....	1,177	1,352	1,682	2,033	2,456	2,770	3,261	4,142	4,914	5,954	6,832	ℐ8,280	8,792	9,657
Interest Rates													*Percent Per Annum*		
Discount Rate (End of Period) **60**	7.31	4.81	8.00	12.75	12.00	10.00	14.75	6.75	11.85	ℐ16.50	14.00	16.50	14.00	12.25	14.00
Money Market Rate **60b**	....	4.81	8.75	12.12	13.81	10.71	14.94	8.27	12.44	16.11	16.39	16.20	17.65	14.45	12.93
Treasury Bill Rate **60c**	7.27	4.58	7.98	9.52	11.58	10.33	14.28	8.15	11.83	12.96	15.13	15.20	16.33	13.26	13.13
Deposit Rate **60l**	4.50	3.69	3.33	7.06	9.63	7.75	7.54	6.17	6.33	10.96	12.00	11.33	12.73	9.27	7.83
Lending Rate **60p**	....	....	....	....	....	11.25	13.25	9.65	13.00	15.50	15.96	15.50	17.04	14.13	12.92
Government Bond Yield **61**	9.86	8.48	9.46	12.33	16.86	14.64	15.49	11.30	12.83	15.07	15.35	17.26	17.06	13.90	14.62
Prices, Production, Labor													*Index Numbers (1995=100):*		
Share Prices **62**	8.9	8.7	12.8	ℐ15.1	10.1	10.0	10.4	13.1	19.8	21.2	20.9	21.7	17.7	22.0	29.2
Wholesale Prices **63**	15.3	16.1	17.8	21.0	23.8	ℐ29.6	35.4	41.5	45.2	50.7	56.1	65.8	73.2	77.7	83.6
Output Manufacturing Industry **63a**	14.8	15.6	17.2	20.4	22.8	ℐ28.5	33.8	39.8	43.4	48.5	53.8	62.8	70.2	74.8	80.3
Consumer Prices **64**	11.7	12.7	13.8	15.4	18.0	21.8	ℐ25.7	29.2	31.5	35.6	ℐ42.1	50.7	59.4	65.6	71.2
Harmonized CPI **64h**															
Wages: Weekly Earnings **65ey**	6.7	7.8	9.0	10.8	12.7	16.6	19.9	23.5	27.0	30.9	36.5	42.6	48.0	53.7	60.2
Industrial Production .... **66..c**	20.6	21.4	22.3	24.5	25.2	24.2	26.3	28.5	30.7	33.1	ℐ32.7	34.5	34.2	36.9	40.5
Manufacturing Employment **67ey**	93.3	92.9	93.3	97.8	99.4	93.3	93.0	95.9	97.8	107.2	107.4	104.3	101.1	95.0	92.2
Labor Force **67d**	....	....	....	....	....	....	....	....	....	....	....	....	*Number in Thousands:*		
Employment **67e**	....	....	....	....	....	....	....	....	....	....	....	....	....	....	1,103
Unemployment **67c**															214
Unemployment Rate (%) **67r**															16.4
International Transactions													*Millions of Pounds through 1998;*		
Exports **70**	467	539	645	869	1,136	1,447	1,859	2,518	2,963	3,483	4,082	4,778	5,691	6,944	8,898
Imports, c.i.f. **71**	676	755	843	1,137	1,627	1,704	2,341	3,091	3,713	4,828	5,421	6,578	6,816	7,367	8,912
													1995=100		
Volume of Exports **72**	10.5	11.3	11.9	12.5	14.0	ℐ15.0	15.6	18.4	20.6	22.2	23.4	24.0	25.5	28.6	33.7
Volume of Imports **73**	22.5	23.6	25.6	29.1	29.4	ℐ26.5	30.5	34.4	40.2	45.8	43.5	44.1	42.3	43.8	47.9
Unit Value of Exports **74**	15.9	17.1	19.6	24.9	29.1	ℐ34.6	42.7	49.2	51.6	56.4	62.7	72.0	80.1	86.9	94.7
Unit Value of Imports **75**	14.2	15.0	15.7	17.7	25.9	ℐ31.3	37.2	43.6	44.8	51.2	60.8	72.5	78.4	81.8	90.6

1985	1986	1987	1988	1989	1990	1991	1992	1993	1994	1995	1996	1997	1998	1999		
Millions of Euros Beginning 1999: End of Period															**Banking Survey (Nat'l Residency)**	
−174	−949	−51	137	560	507	1,742	1,258	5,867	5,440	3,963	5,051	6,187	5,986	31,539	Foreign Assets (Net)	**31n**
11,344	11,927	12,173	13,027	14,135	15,780	15,049	17,182	16,801	19,210	32,604	36,733	46,920	56,822	93,589	Domestic Credit	**32**
3,145	3,121	2,945	2,476	1,936	2,165	1,773	2,861	1,966	2,639	3,498	2,755	2,862	2,802	1,794	Claims on General Govt. (Net)..........	**32an**
8,199	8,805	9,227	10,551	12,199	13,615	13,276	14,321	14,835	16,571	29,106	33,978	44,058	54,020	91,795	Claims on Other Resident Sectors	**32d**
1,073	1,130	1,215	1,347	1,460	1,550	1,568	1,604	1,776	1,907	2,092	2,287	2,619	3,040	5,204	Currency in Circulation	**34a.n**
1,765	1,828	1,915	2,122	2,349	2,674	2,658	2,783	3,103	3,539	6,808	7,552	5,199	6,802	12,649	Demand Deposits	**34b.n**
6,026	5,794	6,584	6,930	7,089	8,405	9,031	9,744	12,693	13,848	20,494	24,324	32,890	38,108	59,223	Other Deposits......................................	**35..n**
....	....	....	....	....	....	....	....	....	....	....	....	....	....	—	Money Market Instruments	**36m**
....	....	....	....	....	....	....	....	....	....	....	....	....	....	24,237	Bonds (Debt Securities)..........................	**36n**
....	....	....	....	....	....	....	....	....	....	....	....	....	....	10,200	*o/w:* Bonds Over Two Years..............	**36na**
2,479	2,408	2,632	3,155	4,063	4,197	4,331	4,934	5,688	6,271	7,750	8,090	11,545	14,129	24,684	Capital Accounts	**37a**
−174	−182	−225	−390	−264	−540	−798	−625	−591	−914	−577	−469	853	732	−867	Other Items (Net)	**37r**
End of Period															**Banking Survey (EA-Wide Residency)**	
....	....	....	....	....	....	....	....	....	....	....	....	....	....	4,399	Foreign Assets (Net)	**31n.u**
....	....	....	....	....	....	....	....	....	....	....	....	....	....	137,197	Domestic Credit	**32..u**
....	....	....	....	....	....	....	....	....	....	....	....	....	....	27,198	Claims on General Govt. (Net).........	**32an u**
....	....	....	....	....	....	....	....	....	....	....	....	....	....	109,999	Claims on Other Resident Sect.	**32d.u**
....	....	....	....	....	....	....	....	....	....	....	....	....	....	5,204	Currency in Circulation	**34a.u**
....	....	....	....	....	....	....	....	....	....	....	....	....	....	12,711	Demand Deposits	**34b.u**
....	....	....	....	....	....	....	....	....	....	....	....	....	....	67,614	Other Deposits	**35..u**
....	....	....	....	....	....	....	....	....	....	....	....	....	....	7,633	*o/w:* Other Dep. Over Two Yrs........	**35ab u**
....	....	....	....	....	....	....	....	....	....	....	....	....	....	—	Money Market Instruments	**36m.u**
....	....	....	....	....	....	....	....	....	....	....	....	....	....	24,237	Bonds (Debt Securities)..........................	**36n.u**
....	....	....	....	....	....	....	....	....	....	....	....	....	....	10,200	*o/w:* Bonds Over Two Years............	**36na u**
....	....	....	....	....	....	....	....	....	....	....	....	....	....	24,684	Capital Accounts	**37a**
....	....	....	....	....	....	....	....	....	....	....	....	....	....	7,148	Other Items (Net)	**37r.u**
End of Period															**Nonbank Financial Institutions**	
463	437	632	607	676	679	830	915	1,559	1,676	Ɪ18	6	5	5	....	Cash	**40..k**
5	5	23	103	103	55	20	112	241	704	Ɪ2	5	8	11	....	Foreign Assets	**41..k**
1,383	1,344	1,498	1,598	1,592	1,882	2,022	2,147	1,801	1,777	Ɪ717	762	786	819	....	Claims on Central Government	**42a.k**
3,325	3,577	3,626	4,006	4,627	5,251	5,894	6,836	7,634	8,438	Ɪ644	703	878	1,051	....	Claims on Private Sector	**42d.k**
4,280	4,393	4,793	5,103	5,385	6,175	6,894	7,927	8,682	9,274	Ɪ917	1,039	1,154	1,237	....	Quasi-Monetary Liabilities	**45..k**
530	547	610	674	849	895	1,114	1,456	1,690	2,233	Ɪ2	5	8	10	....	Foreign Liabilities................................	**46c.k**
185	198	176	278	383	475	627	653	1,009	1,285	Ɪ394	339	448	564	....	Cred.from Deposit Money Banks	**46h.k**
209	268	282	334	382	426	495	607	795	928	Ɪ35	78	53	56	....	Capital Accounts	**47a.k**
−28	−43	−81	−75	—	−104	−365	−634	−941	−1,125	Ɪ33	15	15	18	....	Other Items (Net)	**47r.k**
10,311	8,955	10,250	10,326	10,595	12,730	12,849	12,679	17,137	19,744	30,141	44,906	....	....	....	Liquid Liabilities	**55l**
Percent Per Annum															**Interest Rates**	
10.25	13.25	9.25	8.00	12.00	11.25	10.75	....	7.00	6.25	6.50	6.25	6.75	4.06	....	Discount Rate *(End of Period)*...................	**60**
11.87	12.28	10.84	7.84	9.55	11.10	10.45	15.12	10.49	Ɪ5.75	5.45	5.74	6.43	3.23	3.14	Money Market Rate	**60b**
11.78	11.85	10.70	7.81	9.70	10.90	10.12	....	Ɪ9.06	5.87	6.19	5.36	6.03	5.37	....	Treasury Bill Rate	**60c**
6.98	6.50	6.21	3.63	4.54	6.29	5.21	5.42	2.27	.33	.44	.29	.46	.43	.10	Deposit Rate	**60l**
12.44	12.23	11.15	8.29	9.42	11.29	10.63	Ɪ12.66	9.93	6.13	6.56	5.85	6.57	6.22	3.34	Lending Rate	**60p**
12.64	11.07	11.27	9.49	8.95	10.08	9.17	9.11	7.72	8.19	8.30	7.48	6.49	4.99	....	Government Bond Yield	**61**
Period Averages															**Prices, Production, Labor**	
Ɪ31.2	49.0	70.7	69.4	Ɪ82.4	75.0	69.0	64.1	80.1	91.4	100.0	125.1	169.8	238.7	245.9	Share Prices	**62**
Ɪ86.3	84.4	84.9	88.4	93.3	90.7	91.8	92.6	97.0	98.0	100.0	100.4	100.0	101.6	102.0	Wholesale Prices...................................	**63**
Ɪ83.4	82.4	83.8	87.2	91.4	89.9	90.7	92.2	96.4	97.5	100.0	100.6	100.1	100.9	101.9	Output Manufacturing Industry	**63a**
Ɪ75.1	78.0	80.4	82.1	85.5	88.3	91.1	94.0	95.3	97.5	100.0	101.7	Ɪ103.2	105.7	107.4	Consumer Prices	**64**
										100.0	102.2	103.4	105.6	108.2	Harmonized CPI	**64h**
65.0	69.9	73.4	76.9	80.0	83.1	86.7	90.2	95.1	97.8	100.0	102.5	105.4	110.2	....	Wages: Weekly Earnings......................	**65ey**
41.9	42.8	46.6	53.0	59.4	62.1	63.8	70.1	74.0	83.3	100.0	108.0	125.4	146.1	....	Industrial Production	**66..c**
88.4	87.1	86.2	86.4	88.4	90.7	91.7	91.7	90.9	94.2	100.0	105.4	111.2	114.5	....	Manufacturing Employment	**67ey**
Period Averages																
										1,443	1,494	1,539	1,621	....	Labor Force	**67d**
1,076	1,095	1,111	1,111	1,111	1,160	1,156	1,165	1,183	1,221	Ɪ1,282	1,329	1,380	1,495	....	Employment...	**67e**
231	236	247	241	322	225	254	283	294	282	277	279	254	227	193	Unemployment	**67c**
17.7	18.1	18.8	18.4	17.9	17.2	19.0	16.3	16.7	15.1	14.1	....	....	....	....	Unemployment Rate (%)	**67r**
Millions of Euros Beginning 1999															**International Transactions**	
9,743	9,374	10,723	12,305	14,597	14,337	15,019	16,744	19,830	22,753	27,825	30,407	35,336	45,205	66,315	Exports...	**70**
9,428	8,621	9,155	10,215	12,284	12,469	12,851	13,195	14,885	17,283	20,619	22,429	25,882	31,266	43,614	Imports, c.i.f.	**71**
1995=100																
Ɪ35.4	36.9	42.1	45.0	Ɪ50.1	54.3	57.4	65.8	72.5	83.3	100.0	109.9	126.3	157.4	181.1	Volume of Exports	**72**
Ɪ49.5	51.0	54.1	56.7	Ɪ64.0	68.4	68.9	72.2	77.2	87.4	100.0	110.0	126.3	149.1	159.3	Volume of Imports	**73**
Ɪ98.7	91.5	91.5	98.0	104.5	Ɪ94.6	93.9	91.4	98.3	98.2	100.0	99.4	100.6	103.2	102.6	Unit Value of Exports...........................	**74**
Ɪ92.8	82.4	82.4	87.8	Ɪ93.4	88.7	90.8	88.9	93.5	95.9	100.0	98.8	99.4	101.7	104.7	Unit Value of Imports............................	**75**

Ireland

		1970	1971	1972	1973	1974	1975	1976	1977	1978	1979	1980	1981	1982	1983	1984
Balance of Payments															*Millions of US Dollars:*	
Current Account, n.i.e.	78ald	....	....	....	....	−688	−124	−428	−522	−849	−2,100	−2,132	−2,601	−1,935	−1,219	−1,038
Goods: Exports f.o.b.	78aad	....	....	....	....	2,479	3,032	3,326	4,229	5,604	6,949	8,229	7,696	7,933	8,438	9,421
Goods: Imports f.o.b.	78abd	....	....	....	....	−3,561	−3,518	−3,935	−5,049	−6,669	−9,269	−10,452	−9,950	−9,096	−8,690	−9,183
Trade Balance	78acd	....	....	....	....	−1,082	−486	−609	−820	−1,065	−2,320	−2,222	−2,255	−1,162	−252	237
Services: Credit	78add	....	....	....	....	508	568	561	715	896	1,169	1,381	1,209	1,219	1,174	1,166
Services: Debit	78aed	....	....	....	....	−407	−550	−572	−739	−1,024	−1,372	−1,593	−1,435	−1,375	−1,372	−1,435
Balance on Goods & Services	78afd	....	....	....	....	−982	−467	−620	−844	−1,193	−2,523	−2,434	−2,481	−1,318	−450	−32
Income: Credit	78agd	....	....	....	....	331	347	360	343	442	565	808	776	712	584	663
Income: Debit	78ahd	....	....	....	....	−342	−395	−485	−608	−984	−1,288	−1,710	−1,734	−2,162	−2,179	−2,468
Balance on Gds, Serv. & Inc.	78aid	....	....	....	....	−992	−515	−744	−1,109	−1,735	−3,246	−3,336	−3,439	−2,768	−2,045	−1,837
Current Transfers, n.i.e.: Credit	78ajd	....	....	....	....	335	468	431	736	1,039	1,336	1,442	1,064	1,082	1,113	1,075
Current Transfers: Debit	78akd	....	....	....	....	−31	−77	−114	−149	−153	−190	−238	−226	−248	−286	−276
Capital Account, n.i.e.	78bcd	....	....	....	....	—	—	—	—	—	—	—	—	—	—	4
Capital Account, n.i.e.: Credit	78bad	....	....	....	....	—	—	—	—	—	—	—	—	—	—	92
Capital Account: Debit	78bbd	....	....	....	....	—	—	—	—	—	—	—	—	—	—	−87
Financial Account, n.i.e.	78bjd	....	....	....	....	717	485	990	1,397	1,164	1,671	2,724	2,392	2,371	1,752	1,208
Direct Investment Abroad	78bdd	....	....	....	....											
Dir. Invest. in Rep. Econ., n.i.e.	78bed	....	....	....	....	51	158	173	136	375	337	286	203	242	170	121
Portfolio Investment Assets	78bfd	....	....	....	....	2	−1	9	56	−58	−32	−44	−116	−108	−90	−91
Equity Securities	78bkd	....	....	....	....											
Debt Securities	78bld	....	....	....	....	2	−1	9	56	−58	−32	−44	−116	−108	−90	−91
Portfolio Investment Liab., n.i.e.	78bgd	....	....	....	....	155	114	139	275	537	−86	224	605	279	467	1,268
Equity Securities	78bmd	....	....	....	....	—	—	—	—	—	—	—	—	—	—	—
Debt Securities	78bnd	....	....	....	....	155	114	139	275	537	−86	224	605	279	467	1,268
Financial Derivatives Assets	78bwd	....	....	....	....	....	....	....	....	....	....	....	....	....	....	....
Financial Derivatives Liabilities	78bxd	....	....	....	....	....	....	....	....	....	....	....	....	....	....	....
Other Investment Assets	78bhd	....	....	....	....	−519	−452	−9	−22	−301	−117	−500	−229	−649	−423	−634
Monetary Authorities	78bod	....	....	....	....											
General Government	78bpd	....	....	....	....						−9					
Banks	78bqd	....	....	....	....	−679	−319	−58	−295	−277	−336	−583	−530	−872	−423	−452
Other Sectors	78brd	....	....	....	....	159	−133	49	274	−16	220	83	301	223	—	−183
Other Investment Liab., n.i.e.	78bid	....	....	....	....	1,029	666	679	951	611	1,569	2,757	1,929	2,607	1,628	545
Monetary Authorities	78bsd	....	....	....	....											
General Government	78btd	....	....	....	....	170	248	401	111	123	851	945	1,299	1,471	448	−317
Banks	78bud	....	....	....	....	859	418	278	841	488	717	1,813	630	1,136	1,180	862
Other Sectors	78bvd	....	....	....	....											
Net Errors and Omissions	78cad	....	....	....	....	103	−12	−233	−467	−172	−157	120	201	−315	−345	−218
Overall Balance	78cbd	....	....	....	....	132	350	329	408	142	−586	712	−8	121	188	−43
Reserves and Related Items	79dad	....	....	....	....	−132	−350	−329	−408	−142	586	−712	8	−121	−188	43
Reserve Assets	79dbd	....	....	....	....	−132	−350	−329	−408	−142	586	−712	8	−121	−188	43
Use of Fund Credit and Loans	79dcd	....	....	....	....											
Exceptional Financing	79ded	....	....	....	....	....	....	....	....	....	....	....	....	....	....	....
Government Finance																
Central Government															*Millions of Pounds through 1998;*	
Deficit (-) or Surplus	80	−103.6	−100.5	−127.6	−170.5	−352.2	−499.4	−491.3	−555.6	−856.3	−1,055.2	−1,284.7	−1,789.1	−2,027.8	−1,835.3	−1,821.7
Revenue	81	427.0	581.7	634.0	758.6	911.7	1,295.5	1,550.9	1,779.3	2,076.1	2,483.6	3,256.2	4,064.2	5,158.7	5,878.2	6,138.7
Expenditure	82	530.6	682.2	761.6	929.1	1,263.9	1,794.9	2,042.2	2,334.9	2,932.4	3,538.8	4,540.9	5,853.3	7,186.5	7,713.5	7,960.4
Financing																
Net Borrowing	84	103.8	100.5	127.6	170.5	352.2	499.4	491.3	555.6	856.3	1,055.2	1,284.7	1,789.1	2,027.8	1,835.3	1,821.7
Use of Cash Balances	87	−.2	—	—	—	—	—	—	—	—	—	—	—	—	—	—
Total Debt *(Yr. Beg. April 1)*	88	1,105.9	1,251.4	1,421.1	1,622.2	1,957.9	2,743.8	3,612.0	4,208.2	....	....	....	....	....	....	....
General Government																
Deficit (-) or Surplus	80g	....	....	....	....	....	....	....	....	....	....	....	....	....	*As Percent of*	
Debt	88g	....	....	....	....	....	....	....	....	....	....	....	....	....	....	....
National Accounts															*Millions of Pounds through 1998;*	
Househ.Cons.Expend.,incl NPISH's	96f	1,116	1,261	1,455	1,738	2,045	2,434	3,004	3,661	4,309	5,170	6,158	7,490	8,001	8,950	9,801
Government Consumption	91f	237	283	342	422	512	703	838	970	1,156	1,431	1,860	2,260	2,646	2,857	3,067
Gross Fixed Capital Formation	93e	362	430	497	671	753	885	1,157	1,414	1,862	2,430	2,718	3,350	3,531	3,414	3,506
Changes in Inventories	93i	35	15	64	83	118	—	24	178	99	184	−114	−128	185	106	228
Exports of Goods & Services	90c	599	669	773	1,026	1,272	1,619	2,152	2,817	3,374	3,936	4,639	5,504	6,433	7,752	9,770
Imports of Goods & Services	98c	−728	−804	−893	−1,211	−1,708	−1,849	−2,522	−3,337	−4,043	−5,235	−5,900	−7,117	−7,414	−8,164	−9,815
Gross Domestic Product (GDP)	99b	1,621	1,853	2,238	2,729	2,991	3,792	4,653	5,703	6,757	7,917	9,361	11,359	13,382	14,916	16,556
Primary Income from Abroad	98.n	28	27	30	12	19	4	−36	−108	−228	−283	−358	−505	−928	−1,184	−1,639
Gross National Income (GNI)	99a	1,648	1,880	2,267	2,742	3,010	3,796	4,617	5,595	6,529	7,634	9,003	10,854	12,455	13,732	14,917
Net National Income	99e	1,514	1,724	2,083	2,527	2,751	3,493	4,223	5,095	5,872	6,835	7,969	9,690	11,089	12,203	13,320
GDP Volume 1975 prices	99b.p	3,042	3,146	3,351	3,560	....	....	....	....	....	....	....	....	....	....	....
GDP Volume 1980 prices	99b.p	....	....	....	7,034	7,319	7,491	7,596	8,220	8,810	9,081	9,361	....	....	....	....
GDP Volume 1990 prices	99b.p	....	....	....	....	....	....	....	....	....	....	....	19,139	19,572	19,525	20,372
GDP Volume 1995 Prices	99b.p	....	....	....	....	....	....	....	....	....	....	....	....	....	....	....
GDP Volume (1995=100)	99bvp	35.0	36.2	38.5	40.9	42.6	43.6	44.2	47.8	51.3	52.8	54.5	56.3	57.6	57.4	59.9
GDP Deflator (1995=100)	99bip	11.3	12.5	14.2	16.3	17.1	21.2	25.7	29.1	32.1	36.5	41.9	49.2	56.7	63.3	67.4
															Millions:	
Population	99z	2.95	2.98	3.02	3.07	3.12	3.18	3.23	3.27	3.31	3.37	3.40	3.44	3.48	3.50	3.53

1985	1986	1987	1988	1989	1990	1991	1992	1993	1994	1995	1996	1997	1998	1999		
Minus Sign Indicates Debit															**Balance of Payments**	
−736	−847	−76	−25	−581	−361	284	607	1,765	1,577	1,721	2,049	1,866	2,142	305	Current Account, n.i.e.	78ald
10,131	12,366	15,566	18,389	20,356	23,341	23,659	28,107	28,728	33,642	44,423	49,184	55,293	78,893	66,841	Goods: Exports f.o.b.	78aad
−9,500	−11,221	−12,952	−14,567	−16,352	−19,397	−19,366	−21,062	−20,553	−24,275	−30,866	−33,430	−36,668	−53,241	−42,835	Goods: Imports f.o.b.	78abd
631	1,145	2,614	3,822	4,003	3,944	4,294	7,045	8,175	9,366	13,557	15,754	18,625	25,653	24,006	*Trade Balance*	78acd
1,302	1,595	2,069	2,414	2,533	3,445	3,667	4,054	3,769	4,319	5,017	5,749	6,186	16,060	14,146	Services: Credit	78add
−1,547	−2,192	−3,015	−3,837	−4,342	−5,178	−5,662	−7,084	−6,760	−8,452	−11,303	−13,448	−15,195	−28,934	−26,184	Services: Debit	78aed
386	548	1,668	2,399	2,194	2,211	2,298	4,015	5,185	5,233	7,270	8,055	9,616	12,779	11,968	*Balance on Goods & Services*	78afd
756	934	1,085	1,411	1,795	3,280	3,259	3,282	2,780	3,513	5,110	5,576	7,353	25,429	25,224	Income: Credit	78agd
−2,878	−3,595	−4,152	−5,282	−6,075	−8,235	−7,858	−8,827	−8,116	−8,919	−12,435	−13,772	−17,059	−38,228	−37,386	Income: Debit	78ahd
−1,736	−2,112	−1,399	−1,473	−2,086	−2,745	−2,301	−1,530	−151	−173	−55	−141	−90	−20	−194	*Balance on Gds, Serv. & Inc.*	78aid
1,314	1,730	1,792	1,908	1,976	3,089	3,395	3,033	2,858	2,850	3,009	3,538	3,083	7,057	4,905	Current Transfers, n.i.e.: Credit	78ajd
−314	−465	−469	−460	−471	−705	−809	−896	−941	−1,100	−1,233	−1,349	−1,128	−4,895	−4,405	Current Transfers: Debit	78akd
55	42	−16	95	103	387	601	787	775	387	817	785	871	1,218	593	Capital Account, n.i.e.	78bcd
117	134	179	247	231	486	698	889	863	477	914	881	962	1,327	674	Capital Account, n.i.e.: Credit	78bad
−62	−93	−195	−152	−127	−99	−97	−102	−89	−90	−96	−96	−91	−108	−81	Capital Account: Debit	78bbd
1,127	1,790	632	200	−1,574	−2,009	−2,002	−3,962	−901	−3,963	−33	−2,780	−7,484	4,322	−2,970	Financial Account, n.i.e.	78bjd
					−365	−195	−215	−220	−438	−820	−727	−1,008	−4,955	−5,415	Direct Investment Abroad	78bdd
164	−40	89	92	85	627	1,357	1,442	1,121	838	1,447	2,618	2,743	10,671	18,454	Dir. Invest. in Rep. Econ., n.i.e.	78bed
−134	−239	−316	−485	−1,120	−465	−1,717	−439	−272	−1,019	−1,056	−183	−716	−82,698		Portfolio Investment Assets	78bfd
													−27,624	−36,175	Equity Securities	78bkd
−134	−239	−316	−485	−1,120	−465	−1,717	−439	−272	−1,019	−1,056	−183	−716	−39,114	−46,523	Debt Securities	78bld
1,104	1,986	109	1,475	1,770	266	648	−2,750	2,723	−379	771	982	−2,505	54,735	67,370	Portfolio Investment Liab., n.i.e.	78bgd
													47,948	52,041	Equity Securities	78bmd
1,104	1,986	109	1,475	1,770	266	648	−2,750	2,723	−379	771	982	−2,505	6,787	15,329	Debt Securities	78bnd
....	....	....	....	....	....	....	....	....	....	....	....	....	....	....	Financial Derivatives Assets	78bwd
....	....	....	....	....	....	....	....	....	....	....	....	....	....	....	Financial Derivatives Liabilities	78bxd
44	−443	−1,906	−1,941	−4,483	−5,284	−1,860	−8,489	−10,642	−4,483	−16,572	−22,162	−48,337	−25,211	−37,831	Other Investment Assets	78bhd
															Monetary Authorities	78bod
									−76	76	—	—			General Government	78bpd
197	−187	−1,158	−1,214	−2,942	−2,310	−662	−6,414	−9,486	−2,919	−14,083	−19,623	−43,421	....	....	Banks	78bqd
−153	−255	−748	−727	−1,541	−2,973	−1,197	−2,075	−1,157	−1,489	−2,565	−2,539	−4,916			Other Sectors	78brd
−50	526	2,655	1,060	2,175	3,212	−235	6,489	6,389	1,519	16,197	16,691	42,340	35,820	37,149	Other Investment Liab., n.i.e.	78bid
							1,376	−1,255							Monetary Authorities	78bsd
−145	−397	1,696	−615	−413	−195	−239	1,142	−580	−1,585	−808	−947	−812	....	....	General Government	78btd
95	924	960	1,675	2,588	3,406	4	3,972	8,224	3,103	17,005	17,639	43,152	....	....	Banks	78bud
															Other Sectors	78bvd
−399	−1,079	346	322	1,115	2,608	1,579	402	1,021	1,823	−167	−106	3,639	−4,675	−1,044	Net Errors and Omissions	78cad
48	−94	886	592	−937	626	463	−2,166	2,660	−176	2,339	−52	−1,109	3,007	−3,116	*Overall Balance*	78cbd
−48	94	−886	−592	937	−626	−463	2,166	−2,660	176	−2,339	52	1,109	−3,007	3,116	Reserves and Related Items	79dad
−48	94	−886	−592	937	−626	−463	2,166	−2,660	176	−2,339	52	1,109	−3,007	3,116	Reserve Assets	79dbd
															Use of Fund Credit and Loans	79dcd
....	....	....	....	....	....	....	....	....	....	....	....	....	....		Exceptional Financing	79ded

Government Finance

Central Government

1985	1986	1987	1988	1989	1990	1991	1992	1993	1994	1995	1996	1997	1998	1999		
Millions of Euros Beginning 1999: Year Ending December 31																
−2,129.1	−2,115.2	−1,803.4	−640.3	−484.7	−471.9	−235.4	−700.5	−260.4	−322.6	−259.5	102.0	289.7	1,226.2	....	Deficit (-) or Surplus	80
6,601.7	6,936.7	7,467.5	8,160.2	8,145.2	8,586.2	9,457.5	9,812.9	10,872.8	11,676.6	12,423.4	13,422.3	15,108.6	17,175.6	....	Revenue	81
8,730.8	9,051.9	9,270.9	8,800.5	8,629.9	9,058.1	9,692.9	10,513.4	11,133.2	11,999.2	12,682.9	13,320.3	14,818.9	15,949.4	....	Expenditure	82
															Financing	
2,129.1	2,192.1	2,042.2	1,045.5	737.8	347.0	527.3	−440.0	850.2	−18.6	535.0	164.5	−109.3	−881.8	....	Net Borrowing	84
—	−76.9	−238.8	−405.2	−253.1	124.9	−291.9	1,140.5	−589.8	341.2	−275.5	−266.5	−180.4	−344.4	....	Use of Cash Balances	87
															Total Debt *(Yr. Beg. April 1)*	88
Gross Domestic Product															*General Government*	
....	....	....	....	....	−2.3	−2.3	−2.5	−2.4	−1.7	−2.1	−.6	.8	2.1	2.0	Deficit (-) or Surplus	80g
					96.0	95.3	92.3	96.3	88.2	78.9	74.1	65.3	55.6	52.4	Debt	88g
Millions of Euros Beginning in 1999															**National Accounts**	
10,777	12,138	12,845	13,946	15,403	Ɪ17,227	18,017	19,085	20,063	21,509	22,934	25,059	27,555	30,689	....	Househ.Cons.Expend.,incl NPISH's	96f
3,301	3,542	3,575	3,540	3,683	Ɪ4,308	4,742	5,155	5,495	5,838	6,177	6,516	7,175	7,983	....	Government Consumption	91f
3,377	3,456	3,453	3,568	4,294	Ɪ5,287	5,072	5,211	5,259	6,043	7,124	8,563	10,684	13,399	....	Gross Fixed Capital Formation	93e
173	118	28	−47	262	Ɪ727	631	−87	−112	−135	428	427	649	788	....	Changes in Inventories	93i
10,738	10,377	11,855	13,634	16,137	Ɪ16,175	16,984	18,881	22,033	25,308	30,837	34,341	40,640	50,305	....	Exports of Goods & Services	90c
−10,397	−9,929	−10,681	−11,921	−14,360	Ɪ−14,891	−15,587	−16,597	−18,573	−21,891	−26,369	−29,367	−34,324	−43,326	....	Imports of Goods & Services	98c
17,969	19,703	21,075	22,718	25,418	Ɪ28,524	29,584	31,406	33,912	36,479	41,028	45,210	51,822	59,637	....	Gross Domestic Product (GDP)	99b
−1,966	−2,017	−2,112	−2,662	−3,233	Ɪ−2,933	−2,809	−3,225	−3,541	−3,594	−4,525	−5,064	−6,323	−7,454	....	Primary Income from Abroad	98.n
16,003	17,686	18,963	20,056	22,185	Ɪ25,591	26,775	28,181	30,370	32,885	36,503	40,146	45,499	52,183	....	Gross National Income (GNI)	99a
14,279	15,801	16,900	17,894	19,806	22,944	23,476	25,094	27,037	29,170	32,366	35,618	40,392	46,109	....	Net National Income	99e
....	....	....	....	....	....	....	....	....	....	....	....	....	....	....	GDP Volume 1975 prices	99b.p
21,004	21,777	22,793	23,765	25,219	27,190	....	....	....	....	....	....	....	....	....	GDP Volume 1980 prices	99b.p
....	....	....	....	....	32,803	33,414	34,517	35,427	37,468	41,028	44,201	48,931	53,303	....	GDP Volume 1990 prices	99b.p
															GDP Volume 1995 Prices	99b.p
61.8	64.0	67.0	69.9	74.2	80.0	81.4	84.1	86.3	91.3	100.0	107.7	119.3	129.9	....	GDP Volume (1995=100)	99bv p
70.9	75.0	76.6	79.2	83.5	Ɪ87.0	88.5	91.0	95.7	97.4	100.0	102.3	105.9	111.9	....	GDP Deflator (1995=100)	99bi p
Midyear Estimates																
3.54	3.54	3.54	3.54	3.51	3.50	3.53	3.55	3.57	3.59	3.60	3.63	3.67	3.70	3.75	**Population**	99z

(See notes in the back of the book.)

Israel

		1970	1971	1972	1973	1974	1975	1976	1977	1978	1979	1980	1981	1982	1983	1984
Exchange Rates											*New Sheqalim per Thousand SDRs through 1980*					
Market Rate	aa	.3496	.4555	.4555	.5061	.7338	.8303	1.0158	1.8672	2.4746	4.6517	9.6268	I.0182	.0371	.1128	.6261
											New Sheqalim per Thousand US Dollars through 1980					
Market Rate	ae	.3496	.4195	.4195	.4195	.5994	.7092	.8743	1.5372	1.8995	3.5311	7.5480	I.0156	.0337	.1078	.6387
Market Rate	rf	.3500	.4200	.4180	.4195	.4452	.6336	.7926	1.0445	1.7435	2.5406	5.1243	I.0114	.0243	.0562	.2932
													Index Numbers (1995=100):			
Nominal Effective Exchange Rate	ne c	....	....	....	....	....	....	....	....	....	*,***,***	60,531.99	30,650.05	15,931.25	7,755.53	1,895.64
Real Effective Exchange Rate	re c	....	....	....	....	....	....	....	....	....	90.42	92.31	93.78	98.17	106.83	100.39
Fund Position													*Millions of SDRs:*			
Quota	2f. s	130.0	130.0	130.0	130.0	130.0	130.0	130.0	130.0	205.0	205.0	307.5	307.5	307.5	446.6	446.6
SDRs	1b. s	—	13.1	29.2	27.9	2.5	2.0	8.7	22.2	21.0	4.8	8.8	.6	.5	1.6	.1
Reserve Position in the Fund	1c. s	—	—	—	32.5	—	—	—	—	—	31.6	25.6	—	—	34.8	—
Total Fund Cred.&Loans Outstg.	2tl	12.5	32.5	—	—	32.5	208.3	285.3	285.2	271.3	224.2	156.4	87.5	27.2	—	—
International Liquidity												*Millions of US Dollars Unless Otherwise Indicated:*				
Total Reserves minus Gold	1l. d	405.2	689.8	1,178.8	1,768.3	1,153.4	1,137.1	1,328.3	1,521.6	2,625.1	3,063.5	3,351.4	3,496.7	3,839.3	3,651.2	3,060.3
SDRs	1b. d	—	14.3	31.7	33.6	3.1	2.4	10.0	27.0	27.3	6.3	11.2	.7	.6	1.7	.1
Reserve Position in the Fund	1c. d	—	—	—	39.2	—	—	—	—	—	41.6	32.7	—	—	36.4	—
Foreign Exchange	1d. d	405.2	675.5	1,147.1	1,695.4	1,150.3	1,134.7	1,318.3	1,494.6	2,597.8	3,015.6	3,307.5	3,496.0	3,838.7	3,613.1	3,060.2
Gold (Million Fine Troy Ounces)	1ad	1.240	1.240	1.143	1.097	1.099	1.101	1.103	1.164	1.171	1.231	1.194	1.193	1.084	1.015	1.017
Gold (National Valuation)	1and	43.4	47.1	43.4	46.3	47.1	45.1	44.9	49.5	53.4	56.8	53.3	48.6	41.9	37.2	34.9
Monetary Authorities: Other Assets	3..d	28.6	47.6	95.2	119.0	100.1	84.6	228.8	214.7	279.0	36.8	90.1	6.4	218.4	70.0	1.6
Monetary Authorities: Other Liab.	4..d	62.9	150.0	150.0	116.7	133.5	145.2	209.3	214.7	7.9	25.2	17.2	17.2	14.6	13.5	17.4
Deposit Money Banks: Assets	7a. d	514.3	795.2	1,250.9	1,695.2	1,818.6	1,876.7	1,989.0	2,472.7	3,452.0	4,318.7	5,522.5	6,270.8	7,193.3	6,693.6	6,637.2
Liabilities	7b. d	562.9	897.6	1,357.1	1,876.2	2,230.7	2,638.1	2,917.8	3,190.3	4,679.2	6,215.6	7,593.4	8,662.5	10,965.1	10,631.4	10,308.9
Monetary Authorities												*Thousands of New Sheqalim through 1982;*				
Foreign Assets	11	168	331	570	826	778	902	1,416	2,784	5,673	11,332	26,625	55,386	136,370	I410	1,980
Claims on Central Government	12a	319	445	424	428	695	829	1,249	2,558	3,540	5,688	9,383	34,104	104,040	I493	3,104
Claims on Deposit Money Banks	12e	101	129	172	279	460	639	796	1,809	3,308	7,989	19,283	27,378	18,360	I83	294
Reserve Money	14	242	364	760	957	1,157	1,378	2,021	6,492	11,189	21,741	46,832	96,666	224,030	I832	4,596
of which: Currency Outside DMBs	14a	128	159	198	271	317	397	477	632	878	1,205	2,100	4,413	8,430	I25	123
Foreign Cur.Deps.	14cf	....	....	220	268	435	554	898	4,891	9,142	19,461	42,288	86,042	199,000	I775	4,288
Foreign Liabilities	16c	26	78	63	49	104	276	473	863	686	1,132	1,636	1,858	1,498	I1	11
Central Government Deposits	16d	19	21	48	103	30	32	46	223	644	1,040	2,334	4,281	14,870	I87	473
Other Items (Net)	17r	301	441	296	424	643	685	921	−426	2	1,096	4,490	14,063	18,372	I65	297
Deposit Money Banks												*Thousands of New Sheqalim through 1982;*				
Reserves	20	93	173	I825	1,021	1,472	1,721	2,743	5,822	10,321	20,540	44,756	96,171	228,692	I836	4,601
Foreign Assets	21	180	334	I48	61	143	124	141	1,143	1,863	5,294	12,617	97,851	242,053	I738	4,239
Claims on Central Government	22a	91	101	I225	506	1,220	2,233	3,388	6,502	10,730	24,402	64,203	173,753	456,180	I1,353	9,000
Claims on Other Banking Insts	22f	....	....	51	84	134	297	531	899	1,462	3,176	7,356	15,712	39,723	I119	777
Claims on Private Sector	22d	563	695	I1,027	1,424	2,254	3,172	4,260	7,379	15,313	33,051	79,029	164,099	409,170	I1,097	6,236
Demand Deposits	24	210	276	I359	470	554	666	871	1,240	1,818	2,343	4,879	8,101	17,880	I38	154
Time and Savings Deposits	25	627	851	I557	624	1,063	1,590	2,383	4,217	3,553	5,985	15,346	205,775	496,798	I1,554	9,640
Restricted Deposits	26b	....	....	459	904	1,786	2,905	4,632	7,932	13,010	29,072	76,059	175,826	435,335	I1,227	7,115
Foreign Liabilities	26c	197	377	I—	—	—	—	—	—	3,628	9,838	25,663	135,170	368,976	I1,146	6,584
Central Government Deposits	26d	4	5	I245	302	415	604	816	1,208	1,701	3,115	6,695	16,713	47,388	I149	922
Credit from Monetary Authorities	26g	....	....	138	243	421	623	795	1,834	3,341	7,964	19,181	26,716	33,340	I111	433
Other Items (Net)	27r	−111	−208	I418	552	985	1,160	1,566	5,314	12,638	28,147	60,056	−20,715	−23,900	I−83	5
Monetary Survey												*Thousands of New Sheqalim through 1982;*				
Foreign Assets (Net)	31n	125	210	I555	837	817	750	1,084	3,065	3,221	5,656	11,943	16,209	7,950	I1	−376
Domestic Credit	32	950	1,215	I1,434	2,037	3,859	5,895	8,567	15,907	28,700	62,163	150,861	366,674	946,854	I2,827	17,722
Claims on Central Govt. (Net)	32an	387	520	I356	529	1,471	2,426	3,776	7,629	11,925	25,935	64,477	186,864	497,961	I1,611	10,709
Claims on Other Banking Insts	32f	....	....	51	84	134	297	531	899	1,462	3,176	7,356	15,712	39,723	I119	777
Claims on Private Sector	32d	563	695	I1,027	1,424	2,254	3,172	4,260	7,379	15,313	33,051	79,029	164,099	409,170	I1,097	6,236
Money	34	338	435	I557	741	871	1,063	1,348	1,872	2,696	3,548	6,979	13,354	27,930	I67	304
Quasi-Money	35	627	851	I557	624	1,063	1,590	2,383	4,217	3,631	6,432	17,230	211,629	516,186	I1,602	9,884
Restricted Deposits	36b	....	....	459	904	1,786	2,905	4,632	7,932	13,010	29,072	76,059	175,826	435,335	I1,227	7,115
Other Items (Net)	37r	110	136	I418	604	957	1,089	1,287	4,951	12,585	28,768	62,536	−17,925	−24,647	I−70	42
Money plus Quasi-Money	35l	965	1,286	I1,114	1,366	1,935	2,652	3,732	6,089	6,327	9,979	24,210	224,983	544,116	I1,670	10,188
Interest Rates													*Percent Per Annum*			
Discount Rate	60	....	....	....	....	....	....	....	....	....	....	....	....	....	....	....
Treasury Bill Rate	60c	....	....	....	....	....	....	....	....	....	....	....	....	108.2	I311.0	690.3
Deposit Rate	60l	....	....	....	....	....	....	....	....	....	....	....	....	....	....	217.3
Lending Rate	60p	....	....	....	....	....	....	....	....	....	....	....	....	132.9	438.4	
Lending Rate	60p	....	....	....	....	....	....	....	....	....	89.2	176.9	170.6	140.2	186.2	823.0
Prices, Production, Labor													*Index Numbers (1995=100):*			
Share Prices	62	I—	—	—	—	—	—	—	—	—	—	I.1	I.1	I—	1	I2
Prices: Industrial Products	63	—	—	—	—	—	I—	—	—	—	—	.1	.2	.5	1.2	I6.1
Consumer Prices	64	—	—	—	—	—	I—	—	—	—	—	I.1	.2	.4	1.0	I4.7
Wages: Daily Earnings	65	—	—	—	—	—	—	—	—	I—	—	.1	.2	.3	I.9	4.3
Industrial Production	66..c	31.7	34.7	38.9	40.6	42.8	I44.1	45.8	48.0	51.5	54.2	52.5	55.9	56.5	58.7	61.2
Industrial Employment	67	68.6	71.2	75.2	76.0	78.1	78.7	80.7	82.3	I83.8	86.6	83.3	85.5	87.1	I88.6	89.5
													Number in Thousands:			
Labor Force	67d	....	....	....	....	....	....	....	....	....	....	....	....	....	....	....
Employment	67e	....	....	....	....	....	....	....	....	....	....	....	....	....	....	....
Unemployment	67c	....	....	....	....	....	....	....	....	....	....	....	....	....	....	....
Unemployment Rate (%)	67r	....	....	....	....	....	....	....	....	....	....	....	....	....	....	....
International Transactions													*Millions of US Dollars*			
Exports	70..d	779	958	1,147	1,449	1,825	1,941	2,415	3,082	3,921	4,546	5,538	5,670	5,255	5,108	5,807
Imports, c.i.f.	71..d	2,079	2,363	2,473	4,240	5,437	5,997	5,669	5,787	7,415	8,576	9,784	10,235	9,655	9,574	9,819
Imports,c.i.f.,excl. Military Gds	71.m d	1,462	1,833	1,987	2,987	4,215	4,173	4,140	4,807	5,843	7,511	7,995	7,960	8,071	8,599	8,413
														1995=100		
Volume of Exports	72	17.3	20.6	I22.7	23.1	24.7	25.2	30.9	33.8	33.8	34.7	I37.9	40.2	39.4	39.8	45.9
Volume of Imports	73	21.4	25.7	I26.9	31.7	32.5	30.9	31.2	33.6	35.0	36.6	I32.5	33.2	36.8	40.3	40.1
Unit Value of Exports(US$)	74..d	21.5	22.3	I24.3	30.3	35.4	37.0	I37.6	44.5	I58.8	I67.6	I76.1	I73.5	69.5	I67.8	I66.6
Unit Value of Imports(US$)	75..d	21.9	22.4	I23.9	30.8	41.8	43.7	I42.7	46.5	I57.1	I70.9	I87.1	I84.3	77.1	I73.6	I73.6

1985	1986	1987	1988	1989	1990	1991	1992	1993	1994	1995	1996	1997	1998	1999		
and per SDR thereafter: End of Period															**Exchange Rates**	
1.6471	1.8181	2.1828	2.2675	2.5797	2.9136	3.2657	3.8005	4.1015	4.4058	4.6601	4.6748	4.7709	5.8588	5.7000	Market Rate	**aa**
and per US Dollar thereafter: End of Period (ae) Period Average (rf)																
1.4995	1.4864	1.5386	1.6850	1.9630	2.0480	2.2830	2.7640	2.9860	3.0180	3.1350	3.2510	3.5360	4.1610	4.1530	Market Rate	**ae**
1.1788	1.4878	1.5946	1.5989	1.9164	2.0162	2.2791	2.4591	2.8301	3.0111	3.0113	3.1917	3.4494	3.8001	4.1397	Market Rate	**rf**
Period Averages																
414.71	247.80	207.18	201.58	177.34	155.61	139.12	125.48	115.24	106.52	100.00	97.35	97.57	91.32	84.29	Nominal Effective Exchange Rate	**ne c**
97.20	94.79	92.50	101.45	102.45	100.07	101.93	99.35	98.14	99.20	100.00	105.87	113.28	109.93	105.71	Real Effective Exchange Rate	**re c**
End of Period															**Fund Position**	
446.6	446.6	446.6	446.6	446.6	446.6	446.6	666.2	666.2	666.2	666.2	666.2	666.2	666.2	928.2	Quota	**2f. s**
.1	—	.1	.1	.1	.2	.3	.2	.4	.2	.4	1.0	—	.2	.1	SDRs	**1b. s**
—	—	—	—	—	—	—	—	—	—	—	—	—	—	65.5	Reserve Position in the Fund	**1c. s**
—	—	—	—	—	—	—	178.6	178.6	178.6	111.7	22.3	—	—	—	Total Fund Cred.&Loans Outstg.	**2tl**
End of Period															**International Liquidity**	
3,680.2	4,659.6	5,876.1	4,015.6	5,276.2	6,275.1	6,279.1	5,127.4	6,382.6	6,792.4	8,119.3	11,414.6	20,332.1	22,674.3	22,604.9	Total Reserves minus Gold	**1l. d**
.1	—	.1	.1	.1	.2	.4	.3	.5	.4	.6	1.4	—	.3	.2	SDRs	**1b. d**
—	—	—	—	—	—	—	—	—	—	—	—	—	—	89.9	Reserve Position in the Fund	**1c. d**
3,680.1	4,659.6	5,876.0	4,015.5	5,276.1	6,274.9	6,278.7	5,127.1	6,382.1	6,792.0	8,118.7	11,413.2	I 20332.0	22,674.0	22,514.8	Foreign Exchange	**1d. d**
1.017	1.017	1.017	1.018	1.017	.839	.421	.009	.009	.009	.009	.009	.009	—	—	Gold (Million Fine Troy Ounces)	**1ad**
39.1	43.5	50.5	47.9	46.8	41.8	21.1	.4	.4	.4	.5	.4	.4	—	—	Gold (National Valuation)	**1and**
1.3	161.5	—	—	—	—	—	—	—	—	—	—	—	....	....	Monetary Authorities: Other Assets	**3.. d**
17.3	19.5	29.2	36.2	32.6	28.8	28.9	37.7	38.5	37.8	38.6	38.1	30.0	21.9	17.8	Monetary Authorities: Other Liab.	**4.. d**
6,256.3	6,575.0	6,447.3	7,264.4	7,360.8	8,316.7	8,896.8	10,608.7	10,137.7	11,330.0	12,055.9	12,945.4	10,823.5	12,746.6	14,146.6	Deposit Money Banks: Assets	**7a. d**
10,038.0	10,313.0	10,264.4	10,676.4	9,982.2	11,024.5	11,480.4	12,093.0	12,159.1	13,098.9	14,514.4	15,113.4	16,738.3	18,334.0	20,452.2	Liabilities	**7b. d**
Millions of New Sheqalim Beginning 1983: End of Period															**Monetary Authorities**	
5,578	7,230	9,377	7,391	10,464	12,935	14,380	14,186	19,065	20,508	25,578	37,130	70,970	94,326	93,878	Foreign Assets	**11**
8,498	8,144	8,029	9,905	10,086	10,300	10,285	10,419	10,338	9,976	10,818	12,304	12,199	12,288	12,416	Claims on Central Government	**12a**
392	500	1,205	3,853	4,711	3,066	5,475	11,053	16,972	15,555	4,503	1,236	1,519	838	810	Claims on Deposit Money Banks	**12e**
11,366	11,926	14,128	15,059	16,530	18,815	20,488	21,901	28,051	26,166	19,157	25,838	56,659	64,802	80,218	Reserve Money	**14**
481	974	1,365	1,643	2,225	2,817	3,228	I 4,113	4,852	5,467	6,731	7,772	8,767	10,051	12,178	*of which: Currency Outside DMBs*	**14a**
9,158	8,978	9,919	11,796	12,700	14,442	15,364	15,893	20,203	16,413	10,119	7,982	7,633	7,931	10,741	*Foreign Cur.Deps.*	**14cf**
26	29	45	61	64	59	66	783	848	901	641	228	106	91	74	Foreign Liabilities	**16c**
1,369	2,620	3,469	5,025	7,503	6,108	8,383	11,694	16,165	17,456	19,325	23,013	26,509	39,407	32,242	Central Government Deposits	**16d**
1,707	1,299	969	1,004	1,164	1,319	1,203	1,280	1,311	1,516	1,775	1,591	1,414	3,152	–5,430	Other Items (Net)	**17r**
Millions of New Sheqalim Beginning 1983: End of Period															**Deposit Money Banks**	
11,107	11,227	13,026	13,313	14,223	15,911	17,053	I 17,854	23,223	20,743	12,425	18,085	48,103	54,578	68,029	Reserves	**20**
9,381	9,773	9,920	12,241	14,449	17,033	20,311	29,322	30,271	34,194	37,795	42,086	38,272	53,038	58,751	Foreign Assets	**21**
25,939	30,034	34,588	40,937	46,860	49,814	56,836	I 62,094	65,080	66,289	69,960	77,542	66,136	63,806	61,984	Claims on Central Government	**22a**
2,361	2,971	3,661	4,299	5,289	5,605	7,515	....	....	....	....	....	....	....	....	Claims on Other Banking Insts	**22f**
17,051	23,267	31,698	40,720	49,464	60,957	75,468	I 94,092	121,800	154,285	185,123	219,842	254,886	303,434	347,730	Claims on Private Sector	**22d**
508	1,203	1,922	2,012	3,079	4,133	4,680	I 6,324	8,526	8,946	9,870	12,227	13,502	14,937	17,933	Demand Deposits	**24**
24,243	27,989	34,595	45,136	52,273	60,780	71,643	I 89,564	104,678	139,899	171,485	217,117	251,747	306,960	352,796	Time and Savings Deposits	**25**
20,518	24,625	27,206	29,937	32,830	35,500	37,855	I 29,879	28,775	28,730	22,979	21,481	19,368	17,063	13,593	Restricted Deposits	**26b**
15,052	15,329	15,793	17,990	19,595	22,578	26,210	33,425	36,307	39,533	45,503	49,134	59,187	76,288	84,938	Foreign Liabilities	**26c**
2,661	3,974	4,781	5,648	6,606	8,145	12,149	I 15,147	19,604	23,211	26,684	27,590	28,190	24,286	24,300	Central Government Deposits	**26d**
665	832	1,546	3,828	4,685	3,056	5,453	I 11,053	16,896	15,569	4,212	1,186	1,506	835	814	Credit from Monetary Authorities	**26g**
2,192	3,321	7,051	6,960	11,215	15,127	19,194	I 17,972	25,587	19,621	24,570	28,821	33,895	34,486	42,119	Other Items (Net)	**27r**
Millions of New Sheqalim Beginning 1983: End of Period															**Monetary Survey**	
–119	1,645	3,459	1,581	5,254	7,331	8,415	9,300	12,181	14,268	17,229	29,854	49,949	70,986	67,617	Foreign Assets (Net)	**31n**
49,819	57,822	69,726	85,188	97,589	112,424	129,573	I 139,765	161,448	189,882	219,891	259,086	278,521	315,834	365,588	Domestic Credit	**32**
30,406	31,584	34,368	40,169	42,837	45,861	46,589	I 45,673	39,649	35,598	34,768	39,244	23,635	12,401	17,858	Claims on Central Govt. (Net)	**32an**
2,361	2,971	3,661	4,299	5,289	5,605	7,515	....	....	....	....	....	....	....	....	Claims on Other Banking Insts	**32f**
17,051	23,267	31,698	40,720	49,464	60,957	75,468	I 94,092	121,800	154,285	185,123	219,842	254,886	303,434	347,730	Claims on Private Sector	**32d**
1,052	2,238	3,346	3,723	5,376	7,022	7,988	I 10,541	13,486	14,523	16,716	20,131	22,401	25,145	30,263	Money	**34**
26,309	30,800	38,691	47,668	56,842	67,280	79,486	I 100,085	121,441	153,587	187,829	235,519	271,480	326,491	376,345	Quasi-Money	**35**
20,518	24,625	27,206	29,937	32,830	35,500	37,855	I 29,879	28,775	28,730	22,979	21,481	19,368	17,063	13,593	Restricted Deposits	**36b**
1,821	1,804	3,943	5,441	7,796	9,952	12,660	I 8,560	9,928	7,310	9,596	11,809	15,221	18,120	13,004	Other Items (Net)	**37r**
27,361	33,038	42,037	51,391	62,218	74,303	87,473	I 110,626	134,926	168,109	204,545	255,650	293,881	351,636	406,608	Money plus Quasi-Money	**35l**
Percent Per Annum															**Interest Rates**	
79.6	31.4	26.8	30.9	15.0	13.0	14.2	10.4	9.8	17.0	14.2	....	....	....	....	Discount Rate	**60**
210.1	19.9	20.0	16.0	12.9	15.1	14.5	11.8	10.5	11.8	14.4	15.5	13.9	12.2	....	Treasury Bill Rate	**60c**
178.8	18.6	19.4	14.5	14.1	14.4	13.9	11.3	10.4	12.2	14.1	14.5	13.1	11.0	11.3	Deposit Rate	**60l**
503.4	60.3	61.4	41.7	31.6	26.4	26.4	19.9	16.4	17.4	20.2	20.7	18.7	16.2	16.4	Lending Rate	**60p**
Period Averages															**Prices, Production, Labor**	
I 11	14	17	17	30	35	54	103	145	88	100	99	134	138	227	Share Prices	**62**
22.2	I 32.2	38.2	44.8	54.3	60.5	I 70.3	77.4	83.7	90.3	100.0	108.6	115.4	120.3	128.7	Prices: Industrial Products	**63**
I 18.8	I 27.9	33.4	38.8	46.7	54.7	65.1	72.9	I 80.9	I 90.9	100.0	111.3	121.3	127.9	134.5	Consumer Prices	**64**
15.3	24.7	32.4	39.4	I 47.7	I 56.0	63.2	71.5	78.8	87.1	100.0	113.9	130.8	143.9	155.4	Wages: Daily Earnings	**65**
63.2	65.3	68.5	66.3	I 65.4	69.6	74.8	81.0	86.1	I 92.7	100.0	105.1	107.2	110.1	111.6	Industrial Production	**66.. c**
89.2	90.0	91.8	88.6	I 83.1	82.4	85.8	89.3	93.1	I 96.4	100.0	101.6	100.5	99.6	98.2	Industrial Employment	**67**
Period Averages																
....	....	....	....	....	1,650	1,770	1,858	1,946	2,030	I 2,110	2,157	2,210	2,272	....	Labor Force	**67d**
1,349	1,368	1,404	1,453	1,461	1,492	1,583	1,650	1,751	1,871	I 1,965	2,013	2,040	2,077	2,137	Employment	**67e**
97	104	90	100	143	158	187	208	195	158	I 145	144	170	195	208	Unemployment	**67c**
6.7	7.1	6.1	6.4	8.9	9.6	10.6	11.2	10.0	7.8	I 6.9	6.7	7.7	8.6	8.9	Unemployment Rate (%)	**67r**
Millions of US Dollars															**International Transactions**	
6,260	7,154	8,454	8,198	10,738	11,576	11,921	10,019	14,826	16,884	19,046	20,610	22,503	22,993	25,794	Exports	**70.. d**
9,875	10,806	14,348	15,018	14,347	16,794	18,658	15,535	22,624	25,237	29,579	31,620	30,781	29,342	33,160	Imports, c.i.f.	**71.. d**
8,320	9,645	11,921	12,960	13,197	15,312	16,839	18,814	20,518	23,776	28,287	29,951	29,084	27,470	31,090	Imports,c.i.f.,excl. Military Gds	**71.m d**
1995=100																
50.0	55.4	61.4	63.4	66.2	I 66.6	65.3	71.5	80.4	92.9	100.0	108.3	119.8	127.2	138.0	Volume of Exports	**72**
40.9	47.7	53.5	53.6	51.2	I 55.1	64.0	71.1	80.2	91.0	100.0	106.6	108.4	108.5	122.1	Volume of Imports	**73**
65.9	68.1	72.5	82.7	88.0	I 95.3	95.7	96.4	96.8	95.4	100.0	99.9	99.1	96.1	97.3	Unit Value of Exports(US$)	**74.. d**
72.0	71.6	78.8	85.4	91.1	I 98.1	93.4	93.5	90.3	92.2	100.0	99.3	94.8	89.5	87.1	Unit Value of Imports(US$)	**75.. d**

Israel

	1970	1971	1972	1973	1974	1975	1976	1977	1978	1979	1980	1981	1982	1983	1984
Balance of Payments														*Millions of US Dollars:*	
Current Account, n.i.e. .... 78al *d*	−617	−545	−216	−525	−1,563	−1,822	−676	−356	−1,009	−920	−871	−1,361	−2,125	−2,099	−1,423
Goods: Exports f.o.b. .... 78aa *d*	814	1,012	1,227	1,571	2,029	2,192	2,688	3,422	4,104	4,841	5,946	6,095	5,733	5,718	6,375
Goods: Imports f.o.b. .... 78ab *d*	−1,944	−2,224	−2,307	−3,987	−5,060	−5,600	−5,345	−5,484	−6,814	−8,088	−9,201	−9,694	−8,986	−8,971	−8,959
Trade Balance .... 78ac *d*	−1,130	−1,212	−1,080	−2,416	−3,031	−3,408	−2,657	−2,062	−2,710	−3,247	−3,255	−3,599	−3,253	−3,253	−2,584
Services: Credit.............. 78ad *d*	496	702	727	848	1,140	1,126	1,338	1,606	1,954	2,318	2,722	2,724	2,572	2,697	2,788
Services: Debit.............. 78ae *d*	−453	−632	−634	−880	−1,092	−1,198	−1,365	−1,538	−1,851	−2,133	−2,310	−2,663	−2,980	−3,226	−3,221
Balance on Goods & Services . 78af *d*	−1,087	−1,142	−987	−2,448	−2,983	−3,480	−2,684	−1,994	−2,607	−3,062	−2,843	−3,538	−3,662	−3,781	−3,018
Income: Credit.............. 78ag *d*	92	160	166	278	394	370	371	431	561	916	1,190	1,735	1,897	1,588	1,362
Income: Debit.............. 78ah *d*	−217	−240	−278	−396	−604	−739	−756	−796	−1,047	−1,369	−1,947	−2,253	−2,683	−2,616	−2,925
Balance on Gds, Serv. & Inc. . 78ai *d*	−1,212	−1,222	−1,099	−2,566	−3,193	−3,849	−3,069	−2,359	−3,093	−3,515	−3,600	−4,056	−4,448	−4,809	−4,580
Current Transfers, n.i.e.: Credit ... 78aj *d*	628	691	933	2,101	1,651	2,065	2,492	2,103	2,212	2,733	2,864	2,894	2,547	2,957	3,376
Current Transfers: Debit .... 78ak *d*	−33	−14	−50	−60	−21	−38	−99	−100	−128	−138	−135	−199	−224	−247	−218
Capital Account, n.i.e. .... 78bc *d*	55	113	166	148	100	64	40	69	141	242	296	403	129	120	125
Capital Account, n.i.e.: Credit ... 78ba *d*	55	113	166	148	100	64	40	69	141	242	296	403	129	120	125
Capital Account: Debit .... 78bb *d*	—	—	—	—	—	—	—	—	—	—	—	—	—	—	—
Financial Account, n.i.e. .... 78bj *d*	691	363	581	1,111	908	1,728	418	381	1,331	1,668	1,082	2,277	3,219	1,809	1,448
Direct Investment Abroad ...... 78bd *d*	−9	−4	—	—	—	2	−6	−6	−7	−1	3	−114	−189	−100	−24
Dir. Invest. in Rep. Econ., n.i.e. . 78be *d*	49	57	114	149	84	45	47	81	39	11	51	114	51	88	53
Portfolio Investment Assets ...... 78bf *d*	−14	−7	—	−14	−9	14	−6	−2	−107	−149	−173	−155	−32	−269	144
Equity Securities .... 78bk *d*	−12	−10	−2	−6	−5	9	3	1	−64	−68	−58	−42	−4	−259	56
Debt Securities .... 78bl *d*	−2	3	2	−8	−4	5	−9	−3	−43	−81	−115	−113	−29	−11	88
Portfolio Investment Liab., n.i.e. . 78bg *d*	148	200	221	399	187	162	169	193	248	127	148	93	74	883	66
Equity Securities .... 78bm *d*	—	—	—	—	—	—	—	—	—	—	—	—	—	—	—
Debt Securities .... 78bn *d*	148	200	221	399	187	162	169	193	248	127	148	93	74	883	66
Financial Derivatives Assets ...... 78bw *d*	....	....	....	....	....	....	....	....	....	....	....	....	....	....	....
Financial Derivatives Liabilities ... 78bx *d*	....	....	....	....	....	....	....	....	....	....	....	....	....	....	....
Other Investment Assets .... 78bh *d*	−60	−240	−484	−301	−55	−301	−819	−1,122	−1,015	−1,607	−1,694	−347	−502	−244	215
Monetary Authorities............. 78bo *d*	....	....	....	....	....	....	....	....	....	....	....	....	....	....	....
General Government .... 78bp *d*	—	−5	15	59	60	163	−388	−452	49	−468	−177	398	152	−582	392
Banks .... 78bq *d*	−47	−164	−450	−327	90	−358	−224	−479	−851	−782	−1,198	−685	−717	348	−2
Other Sectors .... 78br *d*	−13	−71	−49	−33	−205	−106	−207	−191	−213	−357	−319	−59	63	−10	−175
Other Investment Liab., n.i.e. ... 78bi *d*	577	357	730	878	701	1,806	1,033	1,237	2,173	3,287	2,747	2,685	3,818	1,453	995
Monetary Authorities............. 78bs *d*	3	−40	—	—	—	—	—	—	—	—	—	1	−1	69	18
General Government .... 78bt *d*	412	283	215	276	413	948	913	758	719	912	1,280	1,211	1,113	1,094	961
Banks .... 78bu *d*	105	—	341	422	244	660	50	446	1,290	1,484	1,260	1,272	2,393	−331	−265
Other Sectors .... 78bv *d*	57	114	174	180	44	198	70	33	164	891	207	201	312	621	281
Net Errors and Omissions.......... 78ca *d*	−122	280	17	−186	−287	−126	402	120	482	−779	34	−768	−309	−330	−698
Overall Balance .... 78cb *d*	7	211	548	548	−842	−156	184	214	945	211	541	550	914	−500	−547
Reserves and Related Items .... 79da *d*	−7	−211	−548	−548	842	156	−184	−214	−945	−211	−541	−550	−914	500	547
Reserve Assets .... 79db *d*	3	−231	−513	−548	802	−57	−273	−214	−929	−151	−453	−468	−847	529	547
Use of Fund Credit and Loans ...... 79dc *d*	−10	20	−35	—	39	213	88	—	−16	−61	−89	−82	−67	−29	....
Exceptional Financing .... 79de *d*	....	....	....	....	....	....	....	....	....	....	....	....	....	....	....
Government Finance											*Thousands of New Sheqalim through 1982; Millions Beginning 1983:*				
Deficit (-) or Surplus.............. 80	−383	−437	I−463	−745	I−1,329	−1,561	−1,818	−2,798	−2,990	−6,730	−18,107	−58,218	−100,501	I−412	−1,440
Revenue 81	659	916	I1,018	1,442	I2,369	3,588	5,206	7,700	12,300	25,900	58,300	133,800	354,800	I954	4,490
Grants Received 81z	76	61	I22	500	I206	609	1,005	1,318	2,132	4,633	11,437	24,181	26,605	I154	1,301
Expenditure 82	996	1,274	I1,403	2,521	I3,611	5,251	7,356	10,900	16,055	34,037	81,229	198,568	443,100	I1,373	6,803
Lending Minus Repayments 83	122	140	I100	166	I293	507	673	916	1,367	3,226	6,615	17,631	38,806	I148	429
Financing															
Domestic 84a	209	255	I341	560	I700	896	1,500	1,900	1,600	2,800	9,000	46,900	48,400	I280	1,137
Foreign 85a	174	183	I178	236	I553	665	417	925	1,461	3,922	9,100	11,277	52,111	I132	302
Debt: Domestic 88a	....	....	2,500	3,700	5,300	7,600	10,500	16,774	26,100	51,700	190,000	491,400	884,500	I4,328	20,321
Foreign 89a	....	....	1,500	1,700	3,000	4,532	6,900	13,810	20,200	46,200	107,200	251,600	588,100	I2,396	13,838
National Accounts											*Thousands of New Sheqalim through 1982:*				
Househ.Cons.Expend.,incl.NPISHs 96f	1,132	1,328	1,669	2,182	3,264	4,628	6,192	8,795	14,576	27,956	I58,891	145,250	342,832	I910	4,160
Government Consumption Expend........ 91f	673	794	924	1,640	2,207	3,393	4,027	5,101	9,022	15,187	44,701	109,973	228,133	I545	2,919
Gross Fixed Capital Formation 93e	500	690	920	1,260	1,750	2,300	2,550	3,100	5,540	11,510	24,543	59,002	136,006	I360	1,568
Changes in Inventories 93i	40	50	50	30	20	190	140	320	660	750	840	−2,768	4,968	I5	100
Exports of Goods and Services 90c	508	720	939	1,165	1,683	2,551	3,851	6,413	11,771	21,104	I48,863	112,684	227,483	I546	3,099
Imports of Goods and Services 98c	−970	−1,244	−1,512	−2,182	−3,264	−5,262	−6,816	−9,431	−18,047	−31,813	I−66,226	−158,993	−343,990	I−824	−4,210
Gross Domestic Product (GDP) 99b	1,880	2,341	2,999	3,877	5,595	7,817	9,888	14,390	23,745	44,490	I111,612	265,148	596,306	I1,542	7,636
Net Primary Income from Abroad 98.n	−31	−38	−52	−115	−167	−284	−356	−361	−710	−1,758	−3,802	−6,350	−17,747	I−48	−333
Gross National Income (GNI) 99a	1,849	2,303	2,947	3,762	5,427	7,533	9,532	14,029	23,035	42,732	107,809	258,795	578,559	I1,494	7,303
Net National Income 99e	1,667	2,075	2,656	3,375	4,820	6,556	8,330	12,105	20,970	39,170	90,941	217,995	486,351	I1,261	6,093
GDP Volume 1970 prices .... 99b. *p*	40	40	40	60	60	70	....	....	....	....	....	....	....	....	....
GDP Volume 1975 prices .... 99b. *p*	....	....	....	....	....	270	280	220	250	310	320	....	....	....	....
GDP Volume 1980 prices(Thousands) . 99b. *p*	....	....	....	....	....	....	....	....	....	....	111,608	116,646	118,174	121,176	123,766
GDP Volume 1986 prices(Millions) ... 99b. *p*	....	....	....	....	....	....	....	....	....	....	....	....	....	....	....
GDP Volume 1990 Prices(Millions) ... 99b. *p*	....	....	....	....	....	....	....	....	....	....	....	....	....	....	....
GDP Vol.1995 Ref.,Chained(Millions) . 99b. *p*	....	....	....	....	....	....	....	....	....	....	....	....	....	....	....
GDP Volume (1995=100) .... 99bv *p*	25.6	25.6	25.6	38.5	38.5	44.9	46.5	36.6	41.6	51.5	53.2	55.6	56.3	57.8	59.0
GDP Deflator (1995=100) .... 99bi *p*	—	—	—	—	—	—	—	—	—	—	I.1	.2	.4	1.0	4.9
															Millions:
Population........................... 99z	2.97	3.07	3.15	3.28	3.38	3.46	3.53	3.61	3.69	3.79	3.88	3.95	4.03	4.11	4.16

Minus Sign Indicates Debit

1985	1986	1987	1988	1989	1990	1991	1992	1993	1994	1995	1996	1997	1998	1999		
															Balance of Payments	
1,157	1,497	-1,227	-638	213	161	-1,315	-979	-2,561	-3,387	-5,196	-5,434	-3,514	-842	-2,601	Current Account, n.i.e.	78al d
6,820	7,890	9,306	10,334	11,142	12,707	12,133	13,487	14,752	17,198	19,268	21,241	22,650	22,972	25,386	Goods: Exports f.o.b.	78aa d
-9,202	-9,735	-13,018	-13,241	-13,047	-15,307	-17,094	-18,389	-20,533	-22,753	-26,834	-28,426	-27,824	-26,197	-29,927	Goods: Imports f.o.b.	78ab d
-2,382	-1,845	-3,712	-2,907	-1,905	-2,599	-4,961	-4,902	-5,780	-5,555	-7,566	-7,185	-5,174	-3,226	-4,541	*Trade Balance*	78ac d
3,139	3,114	3,779	4,115	4,348	4,569	4,672	5,812	5,967	6,579	7,759	8,093	8,419	9,049	10,398	Services: Credit	78ad d
-2,752	-3,239	-4,093	-4,529	-4,276	-4,921	-5,178	-5,545	-6,398	-7,701	-8,382	-9,271	-9,382	-9,825	-11,015	Services: Debit	78ae d
-1,995	-1,970	-4,026	-3,320	-1,833	-2,952	-5,467	-4,636	-6,211	-6,677	-8,189	-8,363	-6,137	-4,001	-5,158	*Balance on Goods & Services*	78af d
1,023	939	975	1,132	1,376	1,596	1,689	1,615	1,261	1,219	1,739	1,839	2,119	2,985	2,805	Income: Credit	78ag d
-2,774	-2,568	-2,501	-2,690	-3,403	-3,571	-3,329	-3,651	-3,239	-3,575	-4,512	-5,182	-5,709	-5,969	-6,606	Income: Debit	78ah d
-3,746	-3,599	-5,552	-4,878	-3,860	-4,927	-7,107	-6,672	-8,188	-9,033	-10,963	-11,706	-9,727	-6,985	-8,958	*Balance on Gds, Serv. & Inc.*	78ai d
5,017	5,205	4,522	4,425	4,238	5,295	6,146	6,005	5,918	5,889	6,024	6,565	6,500	6,710	7,134	Current Transfers, n.i.e.: Credit	78aj d
-115	-110	-196	-185	-164	-207	-354	-312	-291	-244	-258	-293	-287	-567	-777	Current Transfers: Debit	78ak d
120	349	503	433	857	976	1,054	1,312	1,426	1,816	2,027	2,060	2,197	1,765	1,693	Capital Account, n.i.e.	78bc d
120	349	503	433	857	976	1,054	1,312	1,426	1,816	2,027	2,060	2,197	1,765	1,693	Capital Account, n.i.e.: Credit	78ba d
—	—	—	—	—	—	—	—	—	—	—	—	—	—	—	Capital Account: Debit	78bb d
447	133	1,739	-813	-990	311	442	-1,127	407	-628	2,905	3,309	7,243	-496	1,958	Financial Account, n.i.e.	78bj d
-55	-57	-80	-62	-109	-199	-331	-580	-615	-742	-733	-1,042	-834	-830	-702	Direct Investment Abroad	78bd d
99	137	233	235	146	129	301	577	596	432	1,337	1,382	1,622	1,850	2,256	Dir. Invest. in Rep. Econ., n.i.e.	78be d
118	131	68	-39	-102	-345	-262	-1,268	-727	-252	133	223	-105	-223	-831	Portfolio Investment Assets	78bf d
61	67	32	5	-3	14	-345	-926	80	303	16	160	17	65	248	Equity Securities	78bk d
57	64	36	-44	-99	-358	83	-341	-806	-555	117	63	-122	-288	-1,079	Debt Securities	78bl d
204	261	100	4,211	-24	-28	-9	-40	276	462	978	1,438	1,998	506	1,466	Portfolio Investment Liab., n.i.e.	78bg d
				-17	-18	17	-32	284	469	991	1,440	2,005	515	1,467	Equity Securities	78bm d
204	261	100	4,211	-7	-10	-26	-8	-7	-6	-13	-2	-7	-9	-1	Debt Securities	78bn d
				-27	-78	2	35	-136	-101	-42	92	89	199	-62	Financial Derivatives Assets	78bw d
....	....	....	....	....	....	....	....	....	....	....	....	....	....	....	Financial Derivatives Liabilities	78bx d
345	-954	854	-217	-1,282	-868	-693	-1,770	509	-2,016	-1,681	117	1,572	-2,900	-2,705	Other Investment Assets	78bh d
															Monetary Authorities	78bo d
-111	-684	710	497	-222	-190	-180	78	261	-28	-1,230	864	-19	-13	-188	General Government	78bp d
538	-145	430	-413	-538	-244	-604	-1,657	948	-1,728	-216	-1,165	1,686	-1,809	-728	Banks	78bq d
-83	-125	-285	-301	-523	-434	92	-191	-699	-261	-236	417	-94	-1,079	-1,788	Other Sectors	78br d
-262	616	564	-4,941	409	1,699	1,434	1,918	503	1,588	2,913	1,099	2,901	902	2,536	Other Investment Liab. n.i.e.	78bi d
2	-16	19	23	—	—	—	—	—	—	—	—	—	—	—	Monetary Authorities	78bs d
56	119	-110	-4,810	-713	102	403	905	225	-104	267	74	-268	-287	180	General Government	78bt d
-608	1	-411	-59	-2	389	177	692	280	1,000	1,219	612	2,352	1,525	2,387	Banks	78bu d
288	512	1,066	-96	1,144	1,207	854	321	-2	692	1,427	414	817	-335	-31	Other Sectors	78bv d
-1,325	-986	-354	-151	596	-794	-584	-704	350	46	693	1,245	1,269	-561	-830	Net Errors and Omissions	78ca d
399	993	661	-1,170	676	654	-403	-1,499	-378	-2,153	427	1,180	7,195	-134	221	*Overall Balance*	78cb d
-399	-993	-661	1,170	-676	-654	403	1,499	378	2,153	-427	-1,180	-7,195	134	-221	Reserves and Related Items	79da d
-399	-993	-661	1,170	-1,399	-519	173	1,466	-1,483	-82	-1,070	-3,389	-9,323	-1,858	-1,393	Reserve Assets	79db d
—	—	—	—	—	—	—	245	—	—	-101	-129	-31	—	—	Use of Fund Credit and Loans	79dc d
....	....	....	....	723	-136	230	-212	1,861	2,235	745	2,339	2,159	1,991	1,172	Exceptional Financing	79de d
															Government Finance	

Year Ending March 31 through 1991, Year Ending December 31 thereafter

1985	1986	1987	1988	1989	1990	1991	1992	1993	1994	1995	1996	1997	1998	1999		
-951	333	-2,000	-5,897	-3,677	-5,641	‡-9,160	‡-6,949	-4,675	-6,882	-13,106	-13,028	1,419	-4,628	....	Deficit (-) or Surplus	80
15,503	23,094	27,862	29,582	34,355	42,286	‡39,758	‡63,295	73,482	88,559	106,634	122,255	143,843	158,704	....	Revenue	81
5,446	6,010	5,193	5,020	5,816	6,941	‡6,458	‡9,074	8,229	7,927	5,126	12,986	11,386	12,572	....	Grants Received	81z
19,817	26,696	32,487	35,010	42,649	53,702	‡50,818	‡78,163	86,273	102,350	123,892	147,838	163,530	181,362	....	Expenditure	82
2,083	2,076	2,568	5,488	1,199	1,165	‡4,558	‡1,155	113	1,018	974	431	-9,720	-5,458	....	Lending Minus Repayments	83
															Financing	
807	-11	2,056	4,196	4,138	4,837	‡8,307	‡4,864	-273	655	12,615	7,430	-5,092	538	....	Domestic	84a
144	-322	-56	1,701	-461	804	‡853	‡2,085	4,948	6,227	491	5,598	3,673	4,090	....	Foreign	85a
47,205	58,138	68,827	87,275	103,729	123,837	147,861	168,248	188,706	211,726	240,333	277,034	292,401	318,398	....	Debt: Domestic	88a
25,314	27,992	26,701	32,655	35,659	41,362	42,638	54,742	64,112	71,069	75,083	83,673	92,523	114,261	....	Foreign	89a
															National Accounts	

Millions of New Sheqalim Beginning 1983

1985	1986	1987	1988	1989	1990	1991	1992	1993	1994	1995	1996	1997	1998	1999		
16,490	27,801	36,393	44,257	53,168	64,745	81,484	97,915	116,475	142,478	‡158,435	183,996	206,788	225,554	246,594	Househ.Cons.Expend.,incl.NPISHs	96f
10,313	13,641	19,214	22,199	25,108	31,745	40,015	45,783	53,188	62,634	‡78,376	92,270	101,675	110,342	121,364	Government Consumption Expend.	91f
5,338	8,051	11,294	12,776	14,554	20,234	32,280	38,068	42,485	52,014	‡62,706	71,203	74,043	75,367	81,667	Gross Fixed Capital Formation	93e
117	401	-204	113	258	422	1,960	2,138	4,505	2,220	‡4,614	4,005	803	-2,178	939	Changes in Inventories	93i
12,700	17,434	22,179	24,635	31,461	36,715	40,299	49,544	60,536	73,334	‡81,698	93,794	107,386	121,926	148,161	Exports of Goods and Services	90c
-16,570	-23,136	-32,302	-33,799	-39,078	-48,030	-61,183	-71,709	-90,613	-107,843	‡-121424	-137,282	-145,760	-154,905	-188,615	Imports of Goods and Services	98c
28,437	44,191	56,572	70,181	85,471	105,805	134,855	161,738	186,576	224,838	‡264,304	307,987	344,938	376,107	410,111	Gross Domestic Product (GDP)	99b
-1,119	-1,561	-1,804	-1,779	-2,204	-2,496	-2,490	-3,209	-2,952	-3,329	‡-4,595	-6,536	-8,887	-7,796	....	Net Primary Income from Abroad	98.n
27,318	42,630	54,768	68,402	83,267	103,335	132,365	158,529	183,624	221,509	‡259,709	301,451	336,051	368,311	....	Gross National Income (GNI)	99a
22,575	35,288	45,791	57,946	70,296	87,674	113,176	136,468	157,343	190,035	‡222,933	258,892	287,347	313,602	....	Net National Income	99e
....	....	....	....	....	....	....	....	....	....	....	....	....	....	....	GDP Volume 1970 prices	99b.p
....	....	....	....	....	....	....	....	....	....	....	....	....	....	....	GDP Volume 1975 prices	99b.p
128,726	134,052	....	....	....	....										GDP Volume 1980 prices(Thousands)	99b.p
....	44,561	47,299	48,758	49,372	52,217										GDP Volume 1986 prices(Millions)	99b.p
					105,805	111,787	119,157	122,965	131,280	140,540					GDP Volume 1990 Prices(Millions)	99b.p
										‡264,304	276,536	284,612	290,932	296,826	GDP Vol.1995 Ref.,Chained(Millions)	99b.p
61.4	63.9	67.8	69.9	70.8	74.9	79.5	84.8	87.5	93.4	100.0	104.6	107.7	110.1	112.3	GDP Volume (1995=100)	99bv p
17.5	26.2	31.6	38.0	45.7	53.5	64.1	72.2	80.7	91.1	‡100.0	111.4	121.2	129.3	138.2	GDP Deflator (1995=100)	99bi p

Midyear Estimates

1985	1986	1987	1988	1989	1990	1991	1992	1993	1994	1995	1996	1997	1998	1999		
4.23	4.30	4.37	4.44	4.52	4.66	4.95	5.12	5.26	5.40	5.54	5.70	5.83	5.97	6.10	**Population**	99z

(See notes in the back of the book.)

		1970	1971	1972	1973	1974	1975	1976	1977	1978	1979	1980	1981	1982	1983	1984
Exchange Rates															*Lire per SDR through 1998,*	
Market Rate	aa	623.0	644.9	632.4	733.4	795.1	800.2	1,016.6	1,058.7	1,081.0	1,059.1	1,186.8	1,396.8	1,511.3	1,737.4	1,897.6
														Lire per US Dollar through 1998,		
Market Rate	ae	623.0	594.0	582.5	607.9	649.4	683.6	875.0	871.6	829.8	804.0	930.5	1,200.0	1,370.0	1,659.5	1,935.9
Market Rate	rf	625.0	620.4	583.2	583.0	650.3	652.8	832.3	882.4	848.7	830.9	856.4	1,136.8	1,352.5	1,518.8	1,757.0
															Lire per ECU:	
ECU Rate	ea	....	....	....	....	....	....	....	....	....	1,157.2	1,215.0	1,303.6	1,325.7	1,372.0	1,371.1
ECU Rate	eb	....	....	....	....	....	....	929.8	1,006.9	1,080.6	1,138.5	1,189.1	1,263.1	1,323.6	1,349.7	1,376.0
														Index Numbers (1995=100):		
Market Rate	ahx	259.6	307.5	279.1	279.4	249.7	249.7	196.4	184.5	191.9	196.0	190.4	144.2	120.7	107.6	93.0
Nominal Effective Exchange Rate	neu	381.8	378.3	373.2	333.1	300.1	286.3	240.3	221.1	206.9	197.8	190.8	172.8	162.1	158.4	151.7
Real Effective Exchange Rate	reu	....	....	....	....	....	104.5	96.2	92.8	122.4	125.4	125.5	122.8	121.5	128.3	130.5
Fund Position															*Millions of SDRs:*	
Quota	2f. s	1,000	1,000	1,000	1,000	1,000	1,000	1,000	1,000	1,240	1,240	1,860	1,860	1,860	2,909	2,909
SDRs	1b. s	77	228	341	343	181	83	78	119	226	449	521	673	711	565	645
Reserve Position in the Fund	1c. s	276	349	330	297	—	—	—	—	243	237	646	631	631	945	1,096
of which: Outstg.Fund Borrowing	2c	—	—	—	—	—	—	—	—	—	—	—	—	—	—	—
Total Fund Cred.&Loans Outstg.	2tl	—	—	—	—	1,377	2,457	2,457	1,581	880	—	—	—	—	—	—
International Liquidity												*Millions of US Dollars Unless Otherwise Indicated:*				
Total Res.Min.Gold (Eurosys.Def)	1l. d	2,465	3,689	2,954	2,953	3,406	1,306	3,223	8,104	11,109	18,197	23,126	20,134	14,091	20,105	20,795
SDRs	1b. d	77	247	371	414	221	97	91	144	294	592	665	783	785	591	633
Reserve Position in the Fund	1c. d	276	378	359	359	—	—	—	—	316	312	823	734	696	990	1,074
Foreign Exchange	1d. d	2,113	3,063	2,225	2,181	3,185	1,209	3,132	7,960	10,499	17,294	21,638	18,617	12,611	18,524	19,088
o/w: Fin.Deriv.Rel.to Reserves	1dd d	....	....	....	....	....	....	....	....	....	....	....	....	....	....	....
Other Reserve Assets	1e. d	....	....	....	....	....	....	....	....	....	....	....	....	....	....	....
Gold (Million Fine Troy Ounces)	1ad	82.48	82.40	82.37	82.48	82.48	82.48	82.48	82.91	83.12	66.71	66.67	66.67	66.67	66.67	66.67
Gold (National Valuation)	1an d	2,887	2,884	3,130	3,482	3,482	3,482	9,321	11,260	14,334	20,125	36,722	28,993	23,685	26,152	21,637
Memo: Euro Cl. on Non-EA Res.	1dg d	....	....	....	....	....	....	....	....	....	....	....	....	....	....	....
Non-Euro Cl. on EA Res.	1dh d	....	....	....	....	....	....	....	....	....	....	....	....	....	....	....
Mon. Auth.: Other Foreign Assets	3.. d	....	....	....	....	....	....	....	....	....	....	....	....	....	....	....
Foreign Liabilities	4.. d	141	335	442	717	4,344	3,797	4,620	5,029	2,152	1,937	2,164	1,971	1,342	1,249	824
Banking Insts.: Foreign Assets	7a. d	11,518	14,800	22,418	30,767	20,724	22,336	19,063	21,385	28,586	33,830	35,087	39,385	36,484	36,354	40,138
Foreign Liab.	7b. d	11,110	14,712	22,196	30,246	22,520	22,790	22,769	29,298	36,152	42,598	51,411	54,282	52,006	55,508	61,811
Monetary Authorities												*Trillions of Lire through 1998;*				
Fgn. Assets (Cl.on Non-EA Ctys)	11	3.65	4.23	3.80	3.86	4.34	3.19	11.72	17.94	22.39	32.10	57.05	60.38	53.01	78.11	83.41
Claims on General Government	12a. u	....	....	....	....	....	....	....	....	....	....	....	....	....	....	....
o/w: Claims on Gen.Govt.in Cty	12a	3.38	3.33	4.12	5.22	22.19	29.87	39.88	36.04	40.81	41.48	53.43	66.34	78.23	83.93	91.83
Claims on Banking Institutions	12e. u	....	....	....	....	....	....	....	....	....	....	....	....	....	....	....
o/w: Claims on Bank.Inst.in Cty	12e	1.66	1.94	2.89	3.18	3.59	4.25	2.63	2.83	2.75	5.34	2.72	2.94	3.99	3.88	4.65
Claims on Other Resident Sectors	12d. u	....	....	....	....	....	....	....	....	....	....	....	....	....	....	....
o/w: Cl. on Oth.Res.Sect.in Cty	12d	—	—	—	—	—	—	—	—	—	—	—	—	—	—	—
Claims on ECB	12u															
Currency in Circulation	14a	6.84	7.51	9.00	10.30	11.45	13.23	14.94	16.91	20.10	23.23	27.01	31.41	35.07	39.36	44.22
Liabilities to Banking Insts	14c. u	....	....	....	....	....	....	....	....	....	....	....	....	....	....	....
o/w: Liabs to Bank.Inst.in Cty	14c	4.21	5.42	5.51	6.47	8.29	14.45	18.38	22.84	29.47	33.31	36.75	40.17	47.38	56.64	65.64
Demand Dep. of Other Res.Sect.	14d. u	....	....	....	....	....	....	....	....	....	....	....	....	....	....	....
o/w: D.Dep.of Oth.Res.Sect.in Cty	14d	....	....	....	....	....	....	....	....	....	....	....	....	....	....	....
Other Dep. of Other Res.Sect.	15.. u	....	....	....	....	....	....	....	....	....	....	....	....	....	....	....
o/w: O.Dep.of Oth.Res.Sect.in Cty	15	....	....	....	....	....	....	....	....	....	....	....	....	....	....	....
Money Market Instruments	16m. u	....	....	....	....	....	....	....	....	....	....	....	....	....	....	....
o/w: MMI Held by Resid.of Cty	16m	....	....	....	....	....	....	....	....	....	....	....	....	....	....	....
Bonds (Debt Securities)	16n. u	....	....	....	....	....	....	....	....	....	....	....	....	....	....	....
o/w: Bonds Held by Resid.of Cty	16n	.03	.03	.04	.05	.06	.08	.09	.11	.19	.27	.26	.33	.41	.40	.56
Foreign Liab. (to Non-EA Ctys)	16c	.09	.20	.26	.44	3.92	4.56	6.54	6.06	2.74	1.56	2.01	2.37	1.84	2.07	1.60
Central Government Deposits	16d. u	....	....	....	....	....	....	....	....	....	....	....	....	....	....	....
o/w: Cent.Govt.Dep. in Cty	16d	....	....	....	....	....	....	....	....	....	....	....	....	....	....	....
Liabilities to ECB	16u	—	—	—	—	—	—	—	—	—	—	—	—	—	—	—
Capital Accounts	17a	—	—	—	—	—	—	—	—	—	—	44.79	48.90	47.08	63.47	64.49
Other Items (Net)	17r	−2.47	−3.65	−4.00	−4.99	6.41	5.00	14.27	10.91	13.46	20.55	2.38	6.49	3.44	3.99	3.40
Banking Institutions												*Trillions of Lire through 1998;*				
Claims on Monetary Authorities	20	4.58	5.79	6.03	7.15	8.95	15.13	19.08	23.65	30.56	34.88	39.07	43.30	50.13	58.67	68.66
Claims on Bk.Inst.in Oth.EA Ctys	20b. u	....	....	....	....	....	....	....	....	....	....	....	....	....	....	....
Fgn. Assets (Cl.on Non-EA Ctys)	21	7.20	8.61	13.04	18.70	13.46	15.27	16.68	18.64	23.72	27.20	32.65	47.26	49.98	60.33	77.70
Claims on General Government	22a. u	....	....	....	....	....	....	....	....	....	....	....	....	....	....	....
o/w: Claims on Gen.Govt.in Cty	22a	6.84	8.51	10.66	13.78	18.58	26.59	25.46	42.67	56.38	64.50	69.83	73.80	103.65	129.84	141.94
Claims on Other Resident Sectors	22d. u	....	....	....	....	....	....	....	....	....	....	....	....	....	....	....
o/w: Cl. on Oth.Res.Sect.in Cty	22d	46.38	53.57	63.22	76.13	88.57	102.86	122.67	142.54	158.26	183.10	215.23	249.52	282.29	315.80	371.49
Demand Deposits	24.. u	....	....	....	....	....	....	....	....	....	....	....	....	....	....	....
o/w: D.Dep.of Oth.Res.Sect.in Cty	24	22.18	27.15	31.86	38.91	44.10	50.71	62.09	76.31	98.74	122.54	140.07	153.71	181.73	203.94	230.32
Other Deposits	25.. u	....	....	....	....	....	....	....	....	....	....	....	....	....	....	....
o/w: O.Dep.of Oth.Res.Sect.in Cty	25	23.10	26.76	31.94	38.64	39.60	54.71	65.81	80.47	95.95	109.90	122.04	136.36	168.90	192.41	215.14
Money Market Instruments	26m. u	....	....	....	....	....	....	....	....	....	....	....	....	....	....	....
o/w: MMI Held by Resid.of Cty	26m	....	....	....	....	....	....	....	....	....	....	....	....	....	....	....
Bonds (Debt Securities)	26n. u	....	....	....	....	....	....	....	....	....	....	....	....	....	....	....
o/w: Bonds Held by Resid.of Cty	26n	11.86	14.38	17.16	23.86	26.36	32.78	38.17	43.73	49.44	54.69	60.98	68.86	77.17	85.13	89.55
Foreign Liab. (to Non-EA Ctys)	26c	6.94	8.56	12.91	18.39	14.63	15.58	19.92	25.54	30.00	34.25	47.84	65.14	71.25	92.12	119.66
Central Government Deposits	26d. u	....	....	....	....	....	....	....	....	....	....	....	....	....	....	....
o/w: Cent.Govt.Dep. in Cty	26d	1.44	1.64	1.83	2.09	14.36	16.74	16.81	16.68	16.43	16.30	15.86	16.12	16.15	15.70	14.91
Credit from Monetary Authorities	26g	.86	.87	1.84	2.10	3.19	2.53	1.02	1.00	.31	3.60	.50	.97	2.02	4.79	1.24
Liab. to Bk.Inst.in Oth. EA Ctys	26h. u	....	....	....	....	....	....	....	....	....	....	....	....	....	....	....
Capital Accounts	27a	1.13	1.29	1.46	1.83	2.08	2.40	2.89	3.48	1.74	5.65	6.77	8.36	10.03	12.59	15.32
Other Items (Net)	27r	−2.53	−4.16	−6.05	−10.07	−14.75	−15.61	−22.83	−19.69	−23.68	−37.25	−37.28	−35.64	−41.20	−42.04	−26.35
Post Office: Checking Deposits	24.. i	.66	.72	1.06	.99	1.21	1.47	1.84	2.53	3.60	5.93	4.34	5.10	5.86	7.12	7.44
Post Office: Savings Deposits	25.. i	....	....	....	....	2.30	2.84	3.36	3.87	4.56	5.43	6.12	6.70	7.30	7.91	8.57
Savings Certif.	26ab i	3.12	4.15	5.16	6.23	6.45	7.62	9.04	10.29	12.51	15.11	17.13	17.80	19.00	20.86	24.73

1985	1986	1987	1988	1989	1990	1991	1992	1993	1994	1995	1996	1997	1998	1999		
Euros per SDR Thereafter: End of Period															**Exchange Rates**	
1,843.7	1,661.3	1,658.8	1,757.2	1,669.6	1,607.8	1,646.5	2,022.4	2,340.5	2,379.2	2,355.7	2,200.9	2,373.6	2,327.6	1.3662	Market Rate	aa
Euros per US Dollar Thereafter: End of Period (ae) Period Average (rf)																
1,678.5	1,358.1	1,169.3	1,305.8	1,270.5	1,130.2	1,151.1	1,470.9	1,704.0	1,629.7	1,584.7	1,530.6	1,759.2	1,653.1	.9954	Market Rate	ae
1,909.4	1,490.8	1,296.1	1,301.6	1,372.1	1,198.1	1,240.6	1,232.4	1,573.7	1,612.4	1,628.9	1,542.9	1,703.1	1,736.2	.9386	Market Rate	rf
End of Period (ea) Period Average (eb)																
1,489.9	1,446.2	1,521.7	1,531.1	1,517.6	1,540.3	1,542.4	1,787.4	1,908.4	1,997.5	2,082.7	1,913.7	1,940.7	1,936.3	....	ECU Rate	ea
1,430.7	1,462.1	1,494.7	1,537.3	1,510.7	1,521.9	1,533.3	1,587.5	1,841.6	1,913.9	2,131.3	1,958.6	1,929.7	1,943.7	....	ECU Rate	eb
Period Averages																
85.6	109.6	125.7	125.4	118.7	136.1	131.7	132.7	103.6	101.1	100.0	105.5	95.7	93.9	....	Market Rate	ah x
144.0	146.1	145.7	140.8	142.0	144.3	142.2	137.8	116.0	110.9	100.0	109.3	110.1	109.6	107.7	Nominal Effective Exchange Rate	ne u
126.4	127.9	128.9	127.6	133.1	137.1	138.3	136.5	115.0	108.1	100.0	111.9	115.1	115.6	....	Real Effective Exchange Rate	re u
End of Period															**Fund Position**	
2,909	2,909	2,909	2,909	2,909	2,909	2,909	4,591	4,591	4,591	4,591	4,591	4,591	4,591	7,056	Quota	2f. s
297	480	668	705	759	729	650	173	175	86	—	20	50	79	122	SDRs	1b. s
1,056	1,037	1,020	941	1,099	1,205	1,576	1,774	1,575	1,393	1,321	1,290	1,661	3,075	2,584	Reserve Position in the Fund	1c. s
														257	*of which:* Outstg.Fund Borrowing	2c
—	—	—	—	—	—	—	—	—	—	—	—	—	—	—	Total Fund Cred.&Loans Outstg.	2tl
End of Period															**International Liquidity**	
15,595	19,987	30,214	34,715	46,720	62,927	48,679	27,643	27,545	32,265	34,905	45,948	55,739	29,888	I 22,425	Total Res.Min.Gold (Eurosys.Def)	1l. d
326	587	948	949	998	1,037	930	238	241	125	—	29	67	111	168	SDRs	1b. d
1,160	1,268	1,447	1,266	1,444	1,714	2,255	2,439	2,164	2,033	1,963	1,855	2,241	4,330	3,546	Reserve Position in the Fund	1c. d
14,109	18,132	27,819	32,500	44,278	60,176	45,495	24,966	25,140	30,107	32,942	44,064	53,431	25,447	18,626	Foreign Exchange	1d. d
....	....	....	....	....	....	....	....	....	....	....	....	....	....	—	o/w: Fin.Deriv.Rel.to Reserves	1dd d
														85	Other Reserve Assets	1e. d
66.67	66.67	66.67	66.67	66.67	66.67	66.67	66.67	66.67	66.67	66.67	66.67	66.67	83.36	78.83	Gold (Million Fine Troy Ounces)	1ad
23,558	26,055	34,050	28,521	26,496	24,913	23,230	23,175	23,593	26,342	25,570	25,369	21,806	24,711	22,880	Gold (National Valuation)	1and d
....	....	....	....	....	....	....	....	....	....	....	....	....	....	1	Memo: Euro Cl. on Non-EA Res.	1dg d
....	....	....	....	....	....	....	....	....	....	....	....	....	....	3,620	Non-Euro Cl. on EA Res.	1dh d
															Mon. Auth.: Other Foreign Assets	3.. d
894	1,065	1,105	1,092	1,238	1,353	1,368	6,282	1,543	1,510	2,598	1,249	1,123	1,045	I 6,315	Foreign Liabilities	4.. d
50,444	60,532	68,514	66,859	86,872	102,731	108,509	112,306	134,425	123,919	145,842	193,215	177,149	193,743	I 91,399	Banking Insts.: Foreign Assets	7a. d
72,831	90,957	114,421	122,171	161,774	205,376	243,066	249,851	217,128	230,505	216,808	237,872	223,249	236,896	I 136,361	Foreign Liab.	7b. d
Billions of Euros Beginning 1999: End of Period															**Monetary Authorities**	
66.71	62.86	75.59	84.20	94.81	104.93	95.91	76.54	86.57	93.90	95.59	108.65	135.62	90.33	45.80	Fgn. Assets (Cl.on Non-EA Ctys)	11
....	....	....	....	....	....	....	....	....	....	....	....	....	....	60.12	Claims on General Government	12a. u
114.40	123.45	136.31	139.76	141.49	140.27	140.40	161.75	170.23	195.88	196.42	168.95	174.17	156.37	60.12	o/w: Claims on Gen.Govt.in Cty	12a
														43.90	Claims on Banking Institutions	12e. u
14.08	11.50	6.87	5.79	11.24	14.82	34.71	49.28	44.94	42.50	41.04	50.03	32.30	11.04	36.01	o/w: Claims on Bank.Inst.in Cty	12e
														7.36	Claims on Other Resident Sectors	12d. u
—	—	—	—	—	—	—	.10	4.35	.56	2.64	—	—	—	7.13	o/w: Cl. on Oth.Res.Sect.in Cty	12d
														7.45	Claims on ECB	12u
48.05	51.60	55.62	60.20	71.36	74.81	82.02	90.85	95.23	101.86	105.22	108.16	116.27	124.88	71.96	Currency in Circulation	14a
														22.97	Liabilities to Banking Insts	14c. u
80.67	87.38	96.29	105.23	113.84	122.35	128.38	127.97	104.19	87.54	72.30	73.69	79.08	13.78	9.23	o/w: Liabs to Bank.Inst.in Cty	14c
....	....	....	....	....	....	....	....	....	....	....	....	....	....	.39	Demand Dep. of Other Res.Sect.	14d. u
....	....	....	....	....	....	....	....	....	....	....	....	....	....	.39	o/w: D.Dep.of Oth.Res.Sect.in Cty	14d
														—	Other Dep. of Other Res.Sect.	15.. u
														—	o/w: O.Dep.of Oth.Res.Sect.in Cty	15
														—	Money Market Instruments	16m. u
....	....	....	....	....	....	....	....	....	....	....	....	....	....	—	o/w: MMI Held by Resid.of Cty	16m
														—	Bonds (Debt Securities)	16n. u
.67	.74	.77	.82	1.55	1.54	1.55	1.30	1.22	1.47	1.99	1.66	1.20	.92	—	o/w: Bonds Held by Resid.of Cty	16n
1.50	1.45	1.29	1.43	1.57	1.53	1.58	9.24	2.63	2.46	4.12	1.91	1.98	1.73	6.29	Foreign Liab. (to Non-EA Ctys)	16c
								30.67	63.94	72.13	54.76	57.78	42.21	29.08	Central Government Deposits	16d. u
								30.67	63.94	72.13	54.76	57.78	42.21	29.08	o/w: Cent.Govt.Dep. in Cty	16d
														1.87	Liabilities to ECB	16u
64.16	59.67	66.31	66.61	64.35	64.29	66.12	69.80	84.36	90.66	94.79	99.84	98.93	75.85	35.37	Capital Accounts	17a
.13	-3.04	-1.52	-4.53	-5.13	-4.50	-8.62	-11.51	-12.21	-15.09	-14.85	-12.39	-13.15	-1.61	-3.29	Other Items (Net)	17r
Billions of Euros Beginning 1999: End of Period															**Banking Institutions**	
83.73	90.79	100.11	108.56	I 119.08	129.97	134.15	133.29	109.65	93.29	79.31	81.70	87.81	23.65	9.90	Claims on Monetary Authorities	20
....	....	....	....	....	....	....	....	....	....	....	....	....	....	67.33	Claims on Bk.Inst.in Oth.EA Ctys	20b. u
84.67	82.21	80.11	87.30	I 110.37	116.10	124.90	165.19	229.06	201.96	231.12	295.73	311.64	320.28	90.98	Fgn. Assets (Cl.on Non-EA Ctys)	21
														243.30	Claims on General Government	22a. u
161.62	168.62	165.04	161.02	I 206.73	217.66	293.45	355.88	404.16	434.80	413.46	442.92	408.43	395.40	240.10	o/w: Claims on Gen.Govt.in Cty	22a
														812.18	Claims on Other Resident Sectors	22d. u
411.45	455.64	503.74	584.90	645.11	745.89	850.93	942.92	969.94	983.66	1,027.70	1,060.42	1,123.53	1,224.36	789.04	o/w: Cl. on Oth.Res.Sect.in Cty	22d
														386.95	Demand Deposits	24. u
254.23	285.29	308.00	334.81	I 353.67	385.62	430.80	426.20	454.92	471.38	471.06	498.87	531.72	601.15	384.91	o/w: D.Dep.of Oth.Res.Sect.in Cty	24
														194.71	Other Deposits	25.. u
237.78	250.09	265.13	294.07	I 321.74	363.97	389.56	430.86	469.88	458.91	476.50	469.39	359.51	287.75	190.60	o/w: O.Dep.of Oth.Res.Sect.in Cty	25
....	....	....	....	10.02	14.14	53.30	99.36	95.80	87.71	126.67	119.76	132.48	108.68	13.07	Money Market Instruments	26m. u
....	....	....	....	....	....	....	....	....	....	....	....	....	....	—	o/w: MMI Held by Resid.of Cty	26m
														271.50	Bonds (Debt Securities)	26n. u
95.02	102.19	113.68	121.24	129.64	135.87	153.17	166.41	194.11	215.68	215.29	280.21	377.74	435.32	....	o/w: Bonds Held by Resid.of Cty	26n
122.25	123.53	133.79	159.53	I 205.53	232.11	279.78	367.50	369.98	375.66	343.58	364.08	392.74	391.61	135.74	Foreign Liab. (to Non-EA Ctys)	26c. u
														7.96	Central Government Deposits	26d. u
14.39	14.84	15.41	15.22	11.43	11.06	11.22	10.73	13.40	13.23	9.29	11.15	12.73	13.40	7.92	o/w: Cent.Govt.Dep. in Cty	26d
6.91	3.55	3.88	4.47	I 12.69	16.27	34.71	49.28	44.94	42.50	41.04	50.03	32.30	11.04	33.29	Credit from Monetary Authorities	26g
														102.86	Liab. to Bk.Inst.in Oth. EA Ctys	26h. u
18.11	21.23	23.61	25.96	I 115.83	126.56	162.50	189.99	206.02	219.39	232.44	250.19	257.05	280.93	118.43	Capital Accounts	27a
-7.24	-3.46	-14.49	-13.50	I -79.28	-75.99	-111.62	-143.06	-136.25	-170.74	-164.29	-162.91	-164.86	-166.20	-40.82	Other Items (Net)	27r
8.76	9.44	10.21	7.70	9.39	7.83	7.02	9.34	9.48	8.16	8.49	7.28	6.67	1.66	....	Post Office: Checking Deposits	24.. i
9.51	11.05	13.43	16.37	19.73	23.59	26.92	29.06	30.86	39.15	43.94	46.26	52.00	58.33	....	Post Office: Savings Deposits	25.. i
28.57	33.82	40.13	46.54	52.10	57.22	61.87	66.58	72.16	87.05	97.77	110.61	117.35	121.65	....	Savings Certif.	26ab i

Italy

	1970	1971	1972	1973	1974	1975	1976	1977	1978	1979	1980	1981	1982	1983	1984
Banking Survey (Nat'l Residency)												*Trillions of Lire through 1998:*			
Foreign Assets (Net) 31n	3.82	4.09	3.67	3.74	−.74	−1.68	1.94	4.99	13.38	23.49	39.84	40.14	29.90	I44.25	39.86
Domestic Credit 32	58.94	68.64	82.39	100.25	I124.93	154.51	185.42	221.26	259.69	299.23	350.21	403.14	480.17	549.77	631.09
Claims on General Govt. (Net) 32an	12.56	15.08	19.17	12.90	I36.37	51.65	62.75	78.72	101.43	116.14	134.98	153.61	197.88	233.96	259.60
Claims on Other Resident Sectors 32d	46.38	53.57	63.22	76.13	88.57	102.86	122.67	142.54	158.26	183.10	215.23	249.52	282.29	315.80	371.49
Currency in Circulation 34a.n	7.50	8.23	10.06	11.29	12.66	14.70	16.78	19.44	23.70	29.16	31.34	36.51	40.94	46.48	51.66
Demand Deposits 34b.n	22.18	27.15	31.86	38.91	44.10	50.71	62.09	76.31	98.74	122.54	140.07	153.71	181.73	203.94	230.32
Other Deposits ...... 35..n	23.10	26.76	31.94	38.64	I41.90	57.55	69.17	84.33	100.51	115.33	128.16	143.06	176.19	200.32	223.70
Money Market Instruments 36m															
Bonds (Debt Securities) 36n	15.01	18.56	22.36	30.13	32.86	40.47	47.29	54.13	62.14	70.07	78.37	86.99	96.59	106.39	114.84
o/w: Bonds Over Two Years 36na															
Capital Accounts 37a	1.13	1.29	1.46	1.83	2.08	2.40	2.89	3.48	1.74	5.65	51.56	57.26	57.11	76.06	79.81
Other Items (Net) 37r	−6.16	−9.25	−11.62	−16.82	I−9.40	−13.01	−10.87	−11.44	−13.76	−20.01	−39.44	−34.25	−42.49	I−39.18	−29.39
Banking Survey (EA-Wide Residency)												*Billions of Euros:*			
Foreign Assets (Net) 31n.u	....	....	....	....	....	....	....	....	....	....	....	....	....	....	....
Domestic Credit ...... 32..u	....	....	....	....	....	....	....	....	....	....	....	....	....	....	....
Claims on General Govt. (Net) ...... 32an u	....	....	....	....	....	....	....	....	....	....	....	....	....	....	....
Claims on Other Resident Sect. 32d.u	....	....	....	....	....	....	....	....	....	....	....	....	....	....	....
Currency in Circulation 34a.u	....	....	....	....	....	....	....	....	....	....	....	....	....	....	....
Demand Deposits 34b.u	....	....	....	....	....	....	....	....	....	....	....	....	....	....	....
Other Deposits ...... 35..u	....	....	....	....	....	....	....	....	....	....	....	....	....	....	....
o/w: Other Dep. Over Two Yrs ...... 35ab u	....	....	....	....	....	....	....	....	....	....	....	....	....	....	....
Money Market Instruments 36m.u	....	....	....	....	....	....	....	....	....	....	....	....	....	....	....
Bonds (Debt Securities) 36n.u	....	....	....	....	....	....	....	....	....	....	....	....	....	....	....
o/w: Bonds Over Two Years ...... 36na u	....	....	....	....	....	....	....	....	....	....	....	....	....	....	....
Capital Accounts 37a	....	....	....	....	....	....	....	....	....	....	....	....	....	....	....
Other Items (Net) 37r.u	....	....	....	....	....	....	....	....	....	....	....	....	....	....	....
Money (National Definitions)												*Trillions of Lire:*			
M2 ...... 39m	....	....	....	....	94.61	118.13	142.63	173.56	214.95	258.48	290.05	321.54	378.50	429.84	479.85
Liquid Liabilities 55l	56.94	67.45	80.23	96.46	I106.73	132.73	159.71	193.40	238.91	285.96	321.12	356.07	423.33	477.48	535.92
Interest Rates												*Percent Per Annum:*			
Discount Rate (End of Period) 60	5.50	4.50	4.00	6.50	8.00	6.00	15.00	11.50	10.50	15.00	16.50	19.00	18.00	17.00	16.50
Money Market Rate 60b	7.38	5.76	5.18	6.93	14.57	10.64	15.68	14.03	11.49	11.86	17.17	19.60	20.16	18.44	17.27
Treasury Bill Rate 60c	....	....	....	....	....	....	....	12.34	11.99	12.51	15.92	19.70	19.44	17.89	15.37
Deposit Rate 60l	....	....	....	....	....	....	....	....	10.82	10.59	12.70	14.31	15.28	12.91	11.75
Lending Rate 60p	....	....	....	....	....	....	....	....	16.05	14.64	19.03	18.36	17.37	22.27	21.97
Govt Bond Yield (Long-Term) 61	9.01	8.34	7.47	7.42	9.87	11.54	13.08	14.62	13.70	14.05	16.11	20.56	20.90	18.02	14.95
Govt Bond Yield (Medium-Term) 61b	7.73	7.00	6.59	6.92	9.61	10.04	12.66	14.71	13.05	13.02	15.25	19.36	20.22	18.30	15.60
Prices, Production, Labor												*Index Numbers (1995=100):*			
Share Prices 62	16.6	12.9	12.3	15.8	14.5	I10.8	9.4	7.8	8.3	10.6	17.0	33.3	27.8	30.1	33.1
Producer Prices 63	....	....	....	....	....	....	....	....	....	....	....	46.6	52.7	58.5	64.5
Consumer Prices 64	8.5	9.0	9.5	10.5	12.5	14.6	17.1	20.0	22.5	25.8	31.2	36.8	42.8	49.1	54.4
Harmonized CPI 64h															
Wages: Contractual 65ey	4.7	5.2	5.7	7.0	8.4	10.8	13.0	16.6	19.4	23.0	28.1	34.8	40.9	47.0	52.3
Industrial Production ...... 66..c	58.1	58.1	60.6	66.5	69.5	63.1	70.9	71.7	73.1	77.9	82.2	80.9	78.4	75.9	78.5
Industrial Employment 67	121.8	123.5	121.6	121.9	125.1	125.1	123.2	124.4	123.0	123.3	123.9	122.6	119.9	116.6	111.6
												Number in Thousands:			
Labor Force 67d	....	....	....	....	....	....	....	....	....	....	....	....	....	....	....
Employment 67e	....	....	....	....	....	....	....	....	....	....	....	....	....	....	....
Unemployment 67c	....	....	....	....	....	....	....	....	....	....	....	....	....	....	....
Unemployment Rate (%) 67r	....	....	....	....	....	....	....	....	....	....	....	....	....	....	....
International Transactions												*Billions of Lire through 1998:*			
Exports 70	8,253	9,363	10,850	12,971	19,825	22,867	31,170	39,968	47,506	59,927	66,869	87,716	99,596	110,599	130,836
Imports, c.i.f. 71	9,359	9,902	11,265	16,225	26,715	25,199	36,730	42,430	47,867	64,598	86,215	106,574	117,802	121,078	149,469
												1995=100:			
Volume of Exports 72	I25.4	27.3	30.7	31.2	33.7	34.4	38.7	41.7	46.2	49.5	I45.6	48.5	47.8	49.4	53.3
Volume of Imports 73	I36.5	36.6	40.4	45.4	42.8	38.0	44.1	43.7	47.0	53.3	I54.5	52.2	51.2	50.1	55.6
Unit Value of Exports 74	I8.6	9.1	9.4	11.1	15.7	17.4	21.3	25.4	27.2	31.9	I38.5	47.4	54.7	58.7	64.3
Unit Value of Imports 75	I7.8	8.3	8.5	11.1	18.9	20.0	25.2	29.2	30.7	36.6	I47.2	61.0	68.7	72.0	80.1

	1985	1986	1987	1988	1989	1990	1991	1992	1993	1994	1995	1996	1997	1998	1999	
Billions of Euros Beginning 1999: End of Period																**Banking Survey (Nat'l Residency)**
	27.63	20.09	20.62	10.55	Ɫ−1.92	−12.61	−60.55	−135.01	−56.99	−82.27	−20.99	38.39	52.54	17.26	−14.84	Foreign Assets (Net) **31n**
	719.91	787.18	853.46	941.07	1,063.11	1,181.38	1,369.36	1,554.88	1,617.11	1,672.10	1,708.99	1,770.52	1,811.64	1,902.18	1,059.39	Domestic Credit **32**
	308.46	331.54	349.72	256.17	418.01	435.49	518.44	611.86	642.82	687.88	678.65	710.10	688.11	677.82	263.22	Claims on General Govt. (Net).......... **32an**
	411.45	455.64	503.74	584.90	645.11	745.89	850.93	943.01	974.29	984.22	1,030.34	1,060.42	1,123.53	1,224.36	796.17	Claims on Other Resident Sectors **32d**
	56.81	61.04	65.83	67.90	80.75	82.63	89.04	100.19	104.71	110.02	113.71	115.44	122.94	126.54	71.96	Currency in Circulation .... **34a.** *n*
	254.23	285.29	308.00	334.81	353.67	385.62	430.80	426.20	454.92	471.38	471.06	498.87	531.72	601.15	385.30	Demand Deposits .... **34b.** *n*
	247.29	261.13	278.56	310.45	341.48	387.56	416.49	459.92	500.75	498.06	520.44	515.65	411.52	346.08	190.60	Other Deposits............................ **35..** *n*
	....	....	....	....	10.02	14.14	53.30	99.36	95.80	87.71	126.67	119.76	132.48	108.68	13.07	Money Market Instruments **36m**
	124.26	136.75	154.58	168.60	183.29	194.63	216.58	234.29	267.50	304.20	315.05	392.48	496.29	557.89	271.50	Bonds (Debt Securities)........................ **36n**
															258.99	*o/w:* Bonds Over Two Years.............. **36na**
	82.28	80.90	89.92	92.57	Ɫ180.18	190.85	228.62	259.79	290.37	310.05	327.22	350.03	355.99	356.78	153.80	Capital Accounts **37a**
	−17.33	−17.84	−22.82	−22.69	Ɫ−88.19	−86.65	−126.01	−159.89	−153.92	−191.58	−186.14	−183.31	−186.74	−177.68	−41.68	Other Items (Net) **37r**
End of Period																**Banking Survey (EA-Wide Residency)**
	....	....	....	....	....	....	....	....	....	....	....	....	....	....	−5.24	Foreign Assets (Net) .... **31n.** *u*
	....	....	....	....	....	....	....	....	....	....	....	....	....	....	1,085.91	Domestic Credit .... **32..** *u*
	....	....	....	....	....	....	....	....	....	....	....	....	....	....	266.38	Claims on General Govt. (Net) **32an** *u*
	....	....	....	....	....	....	....	....	....	....	....	....	....	....	819.53	Claims on Other Resident Sect. .... **32d.** *u*
	....	....	....	....	....	....	....	....	....	....	....	....	....	....	71.96	Currency in Circulation .... **34a.** *u*
	....	....	....	....	....	....	....	....	....	....	....	....	....	....	387.33	Demand Deposits .... **34b.** *u*
	....	....	....	....	....	....	....	....	....	....	....	....	....	....	194.91	Other Deposits............................ **35..** *u*
	....	....	....	....	....	....	....	....	....	....	....	....	....	....	17.00	*o/w:* Other Dep. Over Two Yrs........ **35ab** *u*
	....	....	....	....	....	....	....	....	....	....	....	....	....	....	13.07	Money Market Instruments .... **36m.** *u*
	....	....	....	....	....	....	....	....	....	....	....	....	....	....	271.50	Bonds (Debt Securities)........................ **36n.** *u*
	....	....	....	....	....	....	....	....	....	....	....	....	....	....	258.99	*o/w:* Bonds Over Two Years............ **36na** *u*
	....	....	....	....	....	....	....	....	....	....	....	....	....	....	153.80	Capital Accounts **37a**
	....	....	....	....	....	....	....	....	....	....	....	....	....	....	−11.69	Other Items (Net) .... **37r.** *u*
End of Period																**Money (National Definitions)**
	530.74	575.96	618.61	654.29	711.48	759.41	807.84	814.20	841.32	847.42	834.15	863.29	930.99	975.34	....	M2 .... **39m**
	593.34	648.98	703.04	772.92	Ɫ844.01	931.22	1,019.40	1,076.88	....	....	....	....	....	....	....	Liquid Liabilities **55l**
Percent Per Annum																**Interest Rates**
	15.00	12.00	12.00	12.50	13.50	12.50	12.00	12.00	8.00	7.50	9.00	7.50	5.50	3.00	....	Discount Rate *(End of Period)*.................... **60**
	15.25	13.41	11.51	11.29	12.69	12.38	Ɫ12.21	14.02	10.20	8.51	10.46	8.82	6.88	4.99	2.95	Money Market Rate **60b**
	13.71	11.40	10.73	11.19	12.58	12.38	12.54	14.32	10.58	9.17	10.85	8.46	6.33	4.59	2.92	Treasury Bill Rate **60c**
	11.00	8.89	7.01	6.69	6.93	6.80	6.64	7.11	Ɫ7.79	6.20	6.45	6.49	4.83	3.16	1.61	Deposit Rate **60l**
	18.06	15.93	13.58	13.57	14.21	Ɫ14.09	13.90	15.76	13.87	11.22	12.47	12.06	9.75	7.88	5.58	Lending Rate **60p**
	13.00	10.52	9.68	10.16	10.72	11.51	Ɫ13.18	13.27	11.31	10.56	12.21	9.40	6.86	4.90	4.73	Govt Bond Yield (Long-Term)................. **61**
	13.71	10.47	10.58	10.54	11.61	11.87	Ɫ13.37	13.67	11.21	10.57	11.98	8.93	6.47	4.55	4.04	Govt Bond Yield (Medium-Term)........... **61b**
Period Averages																**Prices, Production, Labor**
	52.0	109.9	104.5	84.2	104.1	104.8	88.8	73.9	87.5	109.1	100.0	100.6	137.7	220.5	245.5	Share Prices **62**
	69.5	69.6	71.7	74.2	78.6	81.8	84.6	86.2	89.4	92.7	100.0	101.9	103.2	103.3	103.1	Producer Prices **63**
	59.4	62.8	65.8	69.2	73.5	78.3	83.2	87.4	91.3	95.0	Ɫ100.0	104.0	106.1	108.2	110.0	Consumer Prices **64**
	....	....	....	....	....	....	....	....	....	....	100.0	104.0	106.0	108.0	109.8	Harmonized CPI **64h**
	58.1	60.9	64.8	68.8	72.9	78.2	85.9	90.6	93.7	97.0	100.0	103.2	106.9	109.9	112.4	Wages: Contractual **65ey**
	79.4	82.2	85.4	90.5	93.4	93.5	92.6	92.4	90.2	94.9	100.0	99.1	102.4	104.3	104.4	Industrial Production .... **66..** *c*
	109.1	107.3	105.6	106.1	106.1	107.7	108.6	106.8	104.5	102.3	100.0	98.9	98.5	99.5	99.6	Industrial Employment **67**
Period Averages																
								24,245			22,680	22,734	22,849	22,889	....	Labor Force **67d**
	20,894	21,006	20,986	21,253	21,154	21,454	21,595	21,459	Ɫ20,427	20,119	20,010	20,088	20,087	....	....	Employment **67e**
	2,382	2,611	2,832	2,885	2,865	2,621	2,653	2,799	Ɫ2,360	2,541	2,725	2,763	2,805	....	....	Unemployment.................................... **67c**
	10.3	11.1	11.9	12.0	12.0	11.0	10.9	11.4	Ɫ10.2	11.3	12.0	12.1	12.3	....	....	Unemployment Rate (%) **67r**
Billions of Euros Beginning 1999																**International Transactions**
	145,888	144,460	150,880	166,380	192,797	203,515	209,731	219,435	266,213	308,045	381,175	388,885	409,128	426,182	Ɫ216	Exports **70**
	167,095	148,196	162,353	180,014	209,910	217,704	225,751	232,200	231,519	272,382	335,661	321,286	357,587	378,784	Ɫ204	Imports, c.i.f. **71**
1995=100																
	55.1	57.1	59.0	61.9	67.5	69.8	69.9	72.5	79.0	88.2	100.0	97.8	103.2	105.8	....	Volume of Exports **72**
	57.9	62.3	69.4	73.8	79.9	83.5	87.2	90.2	81.1	91.1	100.0	95.2	106.4	116.8	....	Volume of Imports **73**
	69.5	66.3	67.0	70.4	74.8	76.4	78.7	79.3	88.3	91.5	100.0	104.3	104.0	104.2	....	Unit Value of Exports **74**
	86.1	70.8	69.8	72.7	78.2	77.6	77.1	76.6	85.6	89.0	100.0	100.0	100.1	95.5	....	Unit Value of Imports............................ **75**

Italy

		1970	1971	1972	1973	1974	1975	1976	1977	1978	1979	1980	1981	1982	1983	1984
Balance of Payments															*Millions of US Dollars:*	
Current Account, n.i.e.	78al d	816	1,616	1,984	−2,841	−8,275	−635	−2,849	2,347	6,054	5,914	−10,587	−10,467	−7,380	699	−3,190
Goods: Exports f.o.b.	78aa d	13,218	15,117	18,635	22,261	30,495	34,998	37,269	45,312	56,050	72,218	78,106	77,071	73,791	72,877	74,564
Goods: Imports f.o.b.	78ab d	−13,464	−14,817	−18,392	−26,013	−38,556	−35,656	−41,011	−44,926	−52,595	−72,372	−94,016	−88,386	−81,771	−74,588	−79,696
Trade Balance	78ac d	−246	300	243	−3,752	−8,061	−658	−3,741	386	3,455	−155	−15,910	−11,315	−7,981	−1,711	−5,132
Services: Credit	78ad d	4,146	4,558	5,339	6,277	6,910	8,167	8,343	10,630	13,339	17,129	19,192	16,359	16,891	17,723	18,010
Services: Debit	78ae d	−3,792	−4,045	−4,613	−5,848	−6,736	−7,970	−7,323	−8,797	−10,615	−13,175	−16,249	−14,488	−14,598	−14,090	−14,726
Balance on Goods & Services	78af d	108	812	969	−3,323	−7,887	−461	−2,721	2,219	6,179	3,799	−12,967	−9,444	−5,688	1,922	−1,848
Income: Credit	78ag d	1,581	1,799	2,115	2,540	3,329	2,564	2,081	2,585	3,787	5,849	7,681	7,842	7,694	6,069	6,648
Income: Debit	78ah d	−1,032	−1,190	−1,470	−2,138	−3,632	−3,059	−2,594	−2,671	−3,429	−4,546	−6,402	−9,470	−10,148	−8,579	−9,196
Balance on Gds, Serv. & Inc.	78ai d	656	1,422	1,614	−2,922	−8,190	−956	−3,234	2,133	6,537	5,102	−11,689	−11,072	−8,142	−588	−4,396
Current Transfers, n.i.e.: Credit	78aj d	885	1,241	1,588	1,656	1,277	1,917	1,879	2,299	2,896	4,469	5,457	4,839	5,080	5,655	5,775
Current Transfers: Debit	78ak d	−725	−1,047	−1,218	−1,575	−1,362	−1,596	−1,494	−2,085	−3,379	−3,657	−4,356	−4,233	−4,317	−4,369	−4,570
Capital Account, n.i.e.	78bc d	10	−5	−31	−38	−83	−120	24	4	−19	−100	205	166	253	201	290
Capital Account, n.i.e.: Credit	78ba d	56	37	15	12	12	14	125	118	88	223	497	380	484	461	530
Capital Account: Debit	78bb d	−46	−42	−46	−50	−95	−133	−101	−113	−108	−323	−292	−214	−231	−260	−240
Financial Account, n.i.e.	78bj d	−327	−370	−2,298	3,275	7,054	−1,931	5,711	4,073	−2,858	−2,160	12,030	8,259	2,513	3,916	2,848
Direct Investment Abroad	78bd d	−114	−406	−221	−276	−203	−343	−159	−560	−160	−538	−740	−1,392	−969	−2,022	−1,882
Dir. Invest. in Rep. Econ., n.i.e.	78be d	624	550	674	664	596	645	109	1,128	476	415	577	1,127	617	1,190	1,321
Portfolio Investment Assets	78bf d	−521	−189	−706	−715	124	195	271	318	21	48	−410	−561	57	−163	−222
Equity Securities	78bk d	−180	−57	−74	−62	−24	26	28	48	−27	−96	−484	−535	−100	−322	−344
Debt Securities	78bl d	−342	−132	−633	−653	148	169	243	270	48	144	74	−26	157	158	122
Portfolio Investment Liab., n.i.e.	78bg d	5	111	53	−387	−174	−109	−133	22	−107	66	−526	159	−448	403	320
Equity Securities	78bm d	—	—	—	—	—	—	—	—	—	—	—	—	—	—	—
Debt Securities	78bn d	5	111	53	−387	−174	−109	−133	22	−107	66	−526	159	−448	403	320
Financial Derivatives Assets	78bw d	—	—	—	—	—	—	—	—	—	—	—	—	—	—	—
Financial Derivatives Liabilities	78bx d	—	—	—	—	—	—	—	—	—	—	—	—	—	—	—
Other Investment Assets	78bh d	−4,530	−3,868	−9,495	−7,657	7,050	−4,402	−2,475	−2,999	−9,319	−12,113	−8,218	−16,114	−1,582	−9,400	−9,669
Monetary Authorities	78bo d	....	....	....	....	....	....	....	....	....	....	....	....	....	....	....
General Government	78bp d	−17	−69	−11	−49	23	11	−19	−15	−74	−105	−224	−182	−541	−651	−765
Banks	78bq d	−2,841	−2,262	−6,638	−6,412	9,893	−2,733	−205	−2,555	−7,005	−6,180	−4,579	−12,313	−1,274	−5,972	−6,160
Other Sectors	78br d	−1,672	−1,537	−2,846	−1,195	−2,866	−1,680	−2,251	−430	−2,239	−5,828	−3,416	−3,619	232	−2,776	−2,744
Other Investment Liab., n.i.e.	78bi d	4,210	3,432	7,398	11,646	−339	2,082	8,098	6,164	6,230	9,962	21,347	25,041	4,839	13,908	12,980
Monetary Authorities	78bs d	−146	65	−6	307	3,587	−539	867	377	−2,945	−418	136	−220	−531	94	−348
General Government	78bt d	738	−8	−290	973	113	191	163	259	1,470	1,539	3,820	4,611	2,878	2,355	3,217
Banks	78bu d	2,897	2,453	7,035	6,438	−8,847	2,329	3,304	6,420	5,693	7,393	12,491	10,925	−971	9,443	9,167
Other Sectors	78bv d	720	922	659	3,928	4,807	102	3,764	−892	2,011	1,448	4,899	9,724	3,463	2,016	944
Net Errors and Omissions	78ca d	−262	−177	−495	−482	90	−396	−806	−200	859	−676	−851	1,083	−91	1,060	2,612
Overall Balance	78cb d	237	1,065	−840	−85	−1,214	−3,081	2,080	6,225	4,035	2,977	797	−958	−4,704	5,875	2,560
Reserves and Related Items	79da d	−237	−1,065	840	85	1,214	3,081	−2,080	−6,225	−4,035	−2,977	−797	958	4,704	−5,875	−2,560
Reserve Assets	79db d	−237	−1,065	840	85	−432	1,786	−2,080	−5,201	−3,151	−1,835	−797	958	4,704	−5,875	−2,560
Use of Fund Credit and Loans	79dc d	—	—	—	—	1,646	1,295	—	−1,024	−885	−1,142	—	—	—	—	—
Exceptional Financing	79de d	....	....	....	....	....	....	....	....	....	....	....	....	....	....	....
International Investment Position															*Millions of US Dollars*	
Assets	79aa d	....	....	53,258	59,141	47,781	47,706	52,663	65,237	85,761	113,821	135,630	126,887	111,658	122,178	125,716
Direct Investment Abroad	79ab d	....	....	3,373	3,247	3,574	3,359	3,408	4,478	5,141	6,236	7,319	7,718	8,424	8,743	13,099
Portfolio Investment	79ac d	....	....	3,224	3,839	3,934	3,720	2,691	3,381	4,891	5,091	5,222	4,183	4,129	3,890	4,646
Equity Securities	79ad d	....	....	707	707	707	683	574	704	1,103	999	2,199	2,187	2,318	2,219	3,153
Debt Securities	79ae d	....	....	2,517	3,132	3,227	3,037	2,118	2,677	3,788	4,092	3,023	1,997	1,812	1,670	1,494
Financial Derivatives	79ai d	....	....	—	—	—	—	—	—	—	—	—	—	—	—	—
Other Investment	79af d	....	....	40,369	45,807	33,770	36,111	33,301	36,914	48,853	62,670	61,869	64,754	60,513	62,611	65,029
Monetary Authorities	79ag d	....	....	—	—	—	—	—	—	—	—	—	—	—	—	—
General Government	79ah d	....	....	....	....	....	....	....	....	....	....	—	—	—	—	—
Banks	79ai d	....	....	....	....	....	....	....	....	....	....	31,378	37,341	35,072	35,930	37,513
Other Sectors	79aj d	....	....	20,427	20,467	19,978	20,159	20,296	21,061	25,194	31,927	29,884	26,511	24,368	....	24,284
Reserve Assets	79ak d	....	....	6,292	6,247	6,503	4,515	13,263	20,464	26,876	39,823	61,220	50,231	38,592	46,934	42,942
Liabilities	79la d	....	....	43,356	56,270	51,353	54,596	54,860	62,555	70,944	83,414	99,836	111,824	108,953	113,191	120,149
Dir. Invest. in Rep. Economy	79lb d	....	....	6,647	7,299	8,364	8,999	6,245	7,442	8,682	9,888	9,711	8,456	8,121	8,051	12,291
Portfolio Investment	79lc d	....	....	3,820	3,968	2,946	2,800	1,819	2,190	2,209	3,418	5,239	4,671	3,882	3,694	2,580
Equity Securities	79ld d	....	....	—	—	—	—	—	—	—	—	—	—	—	—	—
Debt Securities	79le d	....	....	3,820	3,968	2,946	2,800	1,819	2,190	2,209	3,418	5,239	4,671	3,882	3,694	2,580
Financial Derivatives	79ll d	....	....	—	—	—	—	—	—	—	—	—	—	—	—	—
Other investment	79lf d	....	....	32,889	45,003	40,043	42,797	46,796	52,923	60,053	70,108	84,886	98,698	96,950	101,445	105,279
Monetary Authorities	79lg d	....	....	....	....	....	....	....	....	....	....	1,430	1,153	566	514	136
General Government	79lh d	....	....	....	....	....	....	....	....	....	....	11,192	15,289	17,848	19,482	21,248
Banks	79li d	....	....	....	....	....	....	....	....	....	....	47,229	50,732	45,703	48,800	52,652
Other Sectors	79lj d	....	....	....	....	....	....	....	....	....	....	25,034	31,523	32,832	32,650	31,243

1985	1986	1987	1988	1989	1990	1991	1992	1993	1994	1995	1996	1997	1998	1999		

Minus Sign Indicates Debit / **Balance of Payments**

1985	1986	1987	1988	1989	1990	1991	1992	1993	1994	1995	1996	1997	1998	1999	Description	Code
−4,084	2,462	−2,635	−7,181	−12,812	−16,479	−24,463	−29,217	7,802	13,209	25,076	39,999	32,403	19,998	8,239	Current Account, n.i.e.	78al d
76,718	97,207	116,712	127,860	140,556	170,304	169,465	178,155	169,153	191,421	233,998	252,039	240,404	242,572	230,831	Goods: Exports f.o.b.	78aa d
−82,086	−92,159	−116,628	−128,784	−142,219	−171,778	−172,049	−178,355	−140,264	−159,854	−195,269	−197,921	−200,527	−206,941	−210,445	Goods: Imports f.o.b.	78ab d
−5,367	5,048	83	−924	−1,664	−1,474	−2,584	−200	28,889	31,568	38,729	54,118	39,878	35,631	20,385	*Trade Balance*	78ac d
19,818	23,645	29,715	30,187	31,790	49,666	46,911	58,545	52,284	53,681	61,619	65,660	66,991	67,549	61,177	Services: Credit	78ad d
−16,406	−20,189	−26,252	−29,060	−32,121	−46,795	−44,379	−58,134	−48,939	−48,238	−55,050	−57,605	−59,227	−63,379	−58,376	Services: Debit	78ae d
−1,955	8,503	3,546	203	−1,995	1,397	−52	211	32,235	37,011	45,299	62,173	47,642	39,801	23,186	*Balance on Goods & Services*	78af d
6,960	8,159	9,193	11,025	14,585	18,997	21,930	28,757	31,844	28,599	34,168	40,142	45,734	51,319	43,323	Income: Credit	78ag d
−9,692	−12,398	−14,108	−16,536	−21,906	−33,709	−39,477	−50,644	−49,062	−45,289	−49,812	−55,101	−56,936	−63,636	−53,786	Income: Debit	78ah d
−4,687	4,264	−1,370	−5,308	−9,315	−13,315	−17,598	−21,676	15,017	20,321	29,655	47,213	36,440	27,483	12,722	*Balance on Gds, Serv. & Inc.*	78ai d
5,398	6,739	8,872	10,394	11,214	12,562	13,743	14,198	12,925	12,254	14,287	14,320	15,552	14,402	18,918	Current Transfers, n.i.e.: Credit	78aj d
−4,795	−8,541	−10,138	−12,267	−14,710	−15,726	−20,607	−21,739	−20,140	−19,366	−18,866	−21,535	−19,588	−21,887	−23,402	Current Transfers: Debit	78ak d
244	−56	236	580	912	759	589	807	1,659	1,026	1,671	66	3,434	2,358	2,917	Capital Account, n.i.e.	78bc d
526	751	984	1,514	1,608	1,823	1,718	2,266	2,807	2,213	2,797	1,414	4,582	3,359	5,035	Capital Account, n.i.e.: Credit	78ba d
−282	−807	−749	−934	−696	−1,063	−1,129	−1,459	−1,149	−1,187	−1,125	−1,348	−1,148	−1,001	−2,118	Capital Account: Debit	78bb d
117	1,971	8,910	16,710	24,738	42,639	24,212	11,550	5,260	−14,207	−2,889	−7,982	−6,878	−18,074	−19,954	Financial Account, n.i.e.	78bj d
−1,736	−2,456	−2,094	−4,703	−2,160	−7,394	−7,534	−4,148	−7,329	−5,239	−7,024	−8,697	−10,414	−12,407	−2,985	Direct Investment Abroad	78bd d
1,072	−172	4,175	6,801	2,166	6,411	2,401	3,105	3,749	2,199	4,842	3,546	3,700	2,635	4,981	Dir. Invest. in Rep. Econ., n.i.e.	78be d
−780	−2,216	−3,642	−5,498	−9,062	−19,325	−23,490	−16,827	12,187	−37,718	−4,938	−25,598	−61,857	−109,064	−128,396	Portfolio Investment Assets	78bf d
−347	110	132	924	−4,742	−6,135	429	3,699	385	−3,360	1,014	−1,036	−15,116	−26,570	−62,591	Equity Securities	78bk d
−434	−2,327	−3,774	−6,422	−4,319	−13,190	−23,918	−20,526	11,802	−34,358	−5,952	−24,562	−46,741	−82,493	−65,805	Debt Securities	78bl d
1,029	1,118	−3,678	5,805	12,262	19,216	18,720	25,237	62,107	29,895	45,583	74,655	73,375	111,987	104,950	Portfolio Investment Liab., n.i.e.	78bg d
—	—	—	—	4,242	3,950	70	−432	4,133	−1,395	5,358	9,331	9,414	14,423	−5,162	Equity Securities	78bm d
1,029	1,118	−3,678	5,805	8,020	15,266	18,650	25,670	57,974	31,290	40,225	65,324	63,962	97,563	110,112	Debt Securities	78bn d
—	—	—	1	−7	39	−18	−148	−8	87	−852	−1,009	−1,118	−850	161	Financial Derivatives Assets	78bw d
—	—	2	4	−17	43	−18	−108	−221	628	1,079	1,272	1,273	1,041	1,709	Financial Derivatives Liabilities	78bx d
−5,810	−1,211	1,804	−10,938	−21,492	−13,894	−16,293	−28,863	−44,197	2,092	−28,947	−68,358	−25,541	−21,232	−32,512	Other Investment Assets	78bh d
														5,399	Monetary Authorities	78bo d
−912	−1,109	−1,421	−2,556	−1,365	−1,341	−1,772	−1,820	−1,539	−2,023	−2,148	−1,112	−62	−1,101	−247	General Government	78bp d
−5,060	198	3,343	−7,281	−16,818	−4,384	−5,831	−16,090	−33,300	22,599	−18,689	−45,046	−1,602	−7,052	−9,643	Banks	78bq d
163	−299	−118	−1,101	−3,310	−8,169	−8,691	−10,953	−9,358	−18,483	−8,110	−22,199	−23,877	−13,078	−28,021	Other Sectors	78br d
6,342	6,908	12,343	25,239	43,047	57,542	50,444	33,301	−21,027	−6,152	−12,632	16,206	13,703	9,816	32,139	Other Investment Liab., n.i.e.	78bi d
−9	67	−140	68	161	7	43	7,198	−4,602	−95	1,062	−1,269	−48	−128	915	Monetary Authorities	78bs d
3,128	2,797	5,729	3,870	2,318	5,814	87	1,423	765	−1,812	4,893	−2,583	−1,798	−5,739	−3,144	General Government	78bt d
1,956	3,928	1,104	15,350	27,906	23,589	38,167	17,005	−16,752	−1,527	−22,716	26,613	6,861	12,780	−4,279	Banks	78bu d
1,268	116	5,650	5,950	12,662	28,132	12,147	7,675	−439	−2,719	4,129	−6,555	8,688	2,903	38,647	Other Sectors	78bv d
−3,863	−2,030	−1,040	−1,693	−1,480	−15,296	−7,055	−7,132	−17,856	1,547	−21,054	−20,176	−15,810	−25,754	−54	Net Errors and Omissions	78ca d
−7,585	2,348	5,470	8,417	11,358	11,623	−6,718	−23,992	−3,135	1,575	2,804	11,907	13,150	−21,472	−8,852	*Overall Balance*	78cb d
7,585	−2,348	−5,470	−8,417	−11,358	−11,623	6,718	23,992	3,135	−1,575	−2,804	−11,907	−13,150	21,472	8,852	Reserves and Related Items	79da d
7,585	−2,348	−5,470	−8,417	−11,358	−11,623	6,718	23,992	3,135	−1,575	−2,804	−11,907	−13,150	21,472	8,852	Reserve Assets	79db d
—	—	—	—	—	—	—	—	—	—	—	—	—	—	—	Use of Fund Credit and Loans	79dc d
....	....	....	....	....	....	....	....	....	....	....	....	....	....	....	Exceptional Financing	79de d

Millions of US Dollars / **International Investment Position**

1985	1986	1987	1988	1989	1990	1991	1992	1993	1994	1995	1996	1997	1998	1999	Description	Code
143,474	182,393	230,042	238,415	296,776	380,737	424,365	410,960	450,985	516,329	597,810	727,498	809,597	1,002,865	....	Assets	79aa d
16,600	26,080	32,332	37,432	43,462	57,261	67,233	71,004	81,892	91,097	109,176	113,251	130,668	165,412	....	Direct Investment Abroad	79ab d
7,464	14,334	18,444	24,411	38,054	62,843	94,850	111,125	130,670	150,426	171,793	192,351	257,494	394,501	....	Portfolio Investment	79ac d
5,166	7,941	9,051	8,327	14,070	15,730	15,143	12,170	11,723	14,015	13,982	16,915	26,600	37,690	....	Equity Securities	79ad d
2,298	6,393	9,393	16,084	23,983	47,113	79,707	98,955	118,947	136,411	157,811	175,436	230,894	356,811	....	Debt Securities	79ae d
—	—	—	—	—	—	—	—	—	—	—	—	—	—	....	Financial Derivatives	79al d
79,944	95,967	114,838	112,179	140,633	167,787	178,953	176,794	187,620	217,192	256,520	350,907	344,344	388,310	....	Other Investment	79af d
—	—	—	—	—	—	—	—	—	—	—	—	—	—	....	Monetary Authorities	79ag d
—	—	—	—	—	—	—	—	—	—	—	—	—	—	....	General Government	79ah d
48,398	57,825	63,664	70,064	90,098	102,381	106,122	106,045	116,107	121,726	146,945	214,524	198,520	225,089	....	Banks	79ai d
27,203	31,982	42,535	34,084	39,720	52,608	58,529	57,294	57,872	79,006	90,034	114,606	125,644	140,653	....	Other Sectors	79aj d
39,466	46,012	64,428	64,394	74,627	92,845	83,329	52,037	50,803	57,615	60,321	70,989	77,091	54,642	....	Reserve Assets	79ak d
151,518	192,024	239,467	257,711	342,678	465,424	530,368	521,563	535,352	587,612	650,102	761,656	807,436	1,022,771	....	Liabilities	79la d
19,949	26,930	32,952	38,529	50,937	59,997	61,576	50,730	54,538	60,955	65,980	74,640	83,158	105,397	....	Dir. Invest. in Rep. Economy	79lb d
5,644	9,379	9,604	15,900	32,097	53,319	91,395	101,229	160,403	188,595	237,861	333,422	385,388	544,602	....	Portfolio Investment	79lc d
—	—	5	202	451	5,129	9,872	9,938	7,724	11,123	11,118	16,434	27,245	35,500	65,833	Equity Securities	79ld d
5,644	9,374	9,402	15,449	26,969	43,447	81,457	93,504	149,280	177,477	221,427	306,177	349,888	478,769	....	Debt Securities	79le d
—	—	—	—	—	—	—	—	—	—	—	—	—	—	....	Financial Derivatives	79ll d
125,924	155,716	196,912	203,282	259,644	352,107	377,396	369,604	320,411	338,063	346,261	353,593	338,891	372,772	....	Other investment	79lf d
122	210	109	147	315	354	363	5,316	578	485	1,554	239	175	56	....	Monetary Authorities	79lg d
28,371	35,602	48,145	30,705	37,702	47,179	25,542	21,579	21,506	21,551	26,328	22,187	21,470	15,595	....	General Government	79lh d
62,988	79,544	93,554	129,264	161,942	202,898	239,554	242,770	213,524	229,119	228,859	247,732	239,171	268,935	....	Banks	79li d
34,443	40,360	55,105	43,165	59,686	101,677	111,938	99,939	84,803	86,907	89,521	83,436	78,075	88,186	....	Other Sectors	79lj d

Italy

		1970	1971	1972	1973	1974	1975	1976	1977	1978	1979	1980	1981	1982	1983	1984
Government Finance																
Central Government															*Trillions of Lire through 1998;*	
Deficit (-) or Surplus	80	-3.24	-4.79	-5.90	-8.03	-9.07	-16.77	-14.74	-22.23	-34.28	-30.41	-37.02	-53.30	-72.80	-88.26	ǂ-94.01
Revenue	81	10.37	11.66	12.06	14.08	18.18	23.36	31.55	41.36	52.68	63.49	89.24	106.83	151.73	177.24	ǂ199.68
Expenditure	82	12.68	14.89	16.39	19.90	24.97	37.30	42.07	52.54	79.84	90.26	118.29	150.93	210.81	249.10	ǂ280.50
Lending Minus Repayments	83	.93	1.56	1.56	2.20	2.28	2.83	4.23	11.05	7.12	3.64	7.97	9.20	13.72	16.40	ǂ13.19
Financing																
Net Borrowing: Lire	84b	3.14	4.74	5.82	7.91	8.88	16.38	14.85	22.49	33.65	29.67	36.32	50.59	69.83	86.02	93.10
Net Borrowing: Foreign Currency	85b	.06	—	-.03	.13	.02	.03	.20	.08	.27	.58	.79	2.52	2.57	1.26	2.27
Monetary Operations	86c	.01	.01	.02	.02	.02	.03	.04	.05	.15	.09	.05	.06	.09	.09	.10
Debt: Lire & Foreign Currency	88	22.93	27.94	33.93	42.48	53.71	69.06	85.18	109.92	144.55	175.26	212.56	267.51	341.71	432.29	ǂ521.19
General Government															*As Percent of*	
Deficit (-) or Surplus	80g	....	....	....	....	....	....	....	....	....	....	....	....	....	....	....
Debt	88g	....	....	....	....	....	....	....	....	....	....	....	....	....	....	....
National Accounts															*Trillions of Lire through 1998;*	
Household Cons. Expenditure	96f. c	40.4	44.1	48.6	59.2	74.5	87.1	107.8	131.9	154.3	189.7	241.4	289.1	342.5	392.7	449.7
Gov.Cons.Expend.incl. NPISHs	91f. c	8.9	10.8	12.3	14.2	17.1	19.9	24.0	30.1	36.5	45.7	58.1	75.4	88.8	106.5	121.5
Gross Fixed Capital Formation	93e. c	16.5	17.5	18.5	24.1	31.7	34.6	41.8	50.3	57.7	70.8	94.1	110.7	121.7	134.7	152.8
Changes in Inventories	93i. c	1.9	.7	.7	2.2	5.2	-1.4	5.3	3.0	3.5	5.6	10.5	4.1	6.5	5.2	13.0
Exports of Goods and Services	90c. c	10.0	11.2	12.7	15.2	22.9	26.3	35.9	45.6	54.0	68.3	77.3	100.0	114.2	125.7	149.5
Imports of Goods and Services	98c. c	-10.5	-11.3	-13.0	-18.1	-29.1	-27.9	-39.9	-46.6	-52.5	-70.3	-93.5	-115.3	-128.6	-133.2	-163.7
Gross Domestic Product (GDP)	99b. c	67.2	73.0	79.8	96.7	122.2	138.6	174.9	214.4	253.5	309.8	387.7	464.0	545.1	631.6	722.8
Net Primary Income from Abroad	98.n	.3	.3	.3	.1	-.3	-.4	-.6	-.2	—	1.0	1.0	-2.0	-3.5	-4.1	-4.8
Gross National Income (GNI)	99a	67.4	73.3	80.1	96.7	121.7	138.1	174.0	212.5	251.0	308.8	386.3	459.1	538.6	627.6	718.0
Net National Income	99e	58.0	55.5	61.0	75.3	101.7	129.2	157.9	194.4	223.6	264.3	341.7	402.6	470.9	549.6	629.4
GDP Volume 1990 Prices	99b. r	738.4	752.4	774.4	825.1	863.8	845.2	900.2	926.2	960.7	1,015.2	1,051.0	1,056.0	1,060.9	1,073.8	1,101.4
GDP Volume 1995 Prices	99b. r	....	....	....	....	....	....	....	....	....	....	....	....	....	....	....
GDP Volume (1995=100)	99bv r	53.0	54.0	55.6	59.2	62.0	60.7	64.6	66.5	68.9	72.9	75.4	75.8	76.1	77.1	79.0
GDP Deflator (1995=100)	99bi r	7.1	7.6	8.0	9.1	11.0	12.8	15.1	18.0	20.6	23.8	28.8	34.3	40.1	45.9	51.2
																Millions:
Population	99z	53.66	54.01	54.41	54.80	55.10	55.40	55.70	55.93	56.13	56.29	56.43	56.51	56.64	56.84	57.00

1985	1986	1987	1988	1989	1990	1991	1992	1993	1994	1995	1996	1997	1998	1999		
															Government Finance	
Millions of Euros Beginning 1999: Year Ending December 31															*Central Government*	
−118.74	−107.58	−110.98	−121.73	−128.33	−138.62	−146.51	−162.78	I −157.79	−153.10	−122.60	−136.07	−31.13	−49.00	....	Deficit (-) or Surplus	80
221.55	253.80	281.42	311.87	353.55	406.46	445.41	499.08	I 470.09	476.46	522.84	548.82	620.74	596.19	....	Revenue	81
324.98	348.70	380.34	418.61	466.17	526.30	581.83	651.44	I 610.26	601.23	617.40	652.45	595.05	604.87	....	Expenditure	82
15.31	12.68	12.07	14.99	15.71	18.79	10.09	10.42	I 17.62	28.33	28.04	32.44	56.83	40.32	....	Lending Minus Repayments	83
															Financing	
118.76	110.39	108.25	121.57	124.68	129.18	145.55	....	150.31	147.52	100.93	129.89	....	....	....	Net Borrowing: Lire	84b
2.94	.86	6.07	4.23	8.40	14.92	5.51	.18	14.45	9.19	25.75	12.92	....	....	....	Net Borrowing: Foreign Currency	85b
.04	.02	.09	.08	.09	.09	.18	.10	.09	.11	.14	.06	....	....	....	Monetary Operations	86c
642.27	750.32	864.17	987.83	1,116.77	1,260.00	1,412.04	1,595.12	1,765.52	1,931.85	2,072.71	2,205.04	2,248.73	2,290.04	....	Debt: Lire & Foreign Currency	88
Gross Domestic Product															*General Government*	
....	....	....	....	....	−11.1	−10.1	−9.6	−9.5	−9.2	−7.7	−7.1	−2.7	−2.8	−1.9	Deficit (-) or Surplus	80g
....	....	....	....	....	98.0	101.5	108.7	119.1	124.9	125.3	122.1	119.8	116.3	114.9	Debt	88g
Billions of Euros Beginning 1999															**National Accounts**	
506.3	557.0	610.8	635.1	701.4	761.5	838.1	897.6	917.8	984.1	1,064.5	1,122.4	1,181.3	1,231.4	I 660.3	Household Cons. Expenditure	96f. c
137.2	150.0	168.0	218.5	236.6	272.7	298.8	311.0	318.6	323.5	326.9	352.0	369.5	381.6	I 204.3	Gov.Cons.Expend.incl. NPISHs	91f. c
167.6	177.5	193.7	232.6	255.4	283.3	303.1	310.7	288.2	297.6	327.9	348.8	359.6	381.2	I 208.0	Gross Fixed Capital Formation	93e. c
15.0	11.6	15.1	13.9	12.6	10.2	9.4	4.7	−1.1	8.1	17.8	6.4	15.4	25.7	I 15.6	Changes in Inventories	93i. c
168.7	166.1	174.9	191.2	222.1	244.3	247.1	263.9	316.2	359.4	442.2	449.8	478.7	499.4	I 255.4	Exports of Goods and Services	90c. c
−184.6	−164.0	−179.7	−198.4	−231.4	−251.2	−255.8	−270.3	−276.5	−319.3	−392.0	−377.2	−420.6	−451.6	I −244.4	Imports of Goods and Services	98c. c
810.1	898.3	982.8	1,092.8	1,196.8	1,320.8	1,440.6	1,517.6	1,563.3	1,653.4	1,787.3	1,896.0	1,974.6	2,057.7	I 1,099.1	Gross Domestic Product (GDP)	99b. c
−5.4	−6.6	−6.6	−6.9	−9.9	−17.3	−21.6	−26.8	−26.7	−26.6	−25.5	−23.1	−18.4	−19.9	....	Net Primary Income from Abroad	98.n
804.6	891.7	976.1	1,086.0	1,186.9	1,303.5	1,419.1	1,490.8	1,536.6	1,626.8	1,761.7	1,879.2	1,965.5	2,047.8	....	Gross National Income (GNI)	99a
704.5	783.7	859.3	936.3	1,022.7	1,122.0	1,220.3	1,277.8	1,310.3	1,388.2	1,507.1	1,611.2	1,685.0	1,755.3	....	Net National Income	99e
1,132.3	1,164.5	1,200.5	1,247.0	....	....	....	....	....	....	....	....	....	....	....	GDP Volume 1990 Prices	99b. r
....	....	....	1,599.5	1,645.4	1,677.9	1,701.2	1,714.1	1,699.0	1,736.5	1,787.3	1,802.7	1,829.5	1,853.9	I 978.4	GDP Volume 1995 Prices	99b. r
81.3	83.6	86.2	89.5	92.1	93.9	95.2	95.9	95.1	97.2	100.0	100.9	102.4	103.7	106.0	GDP Volume (1995=100)	99bv r
55.8	60.1	63.8	68.3	72.7	78.7	84.7	88.5	92.0	95.2	100.0	105.2	107.9	111.0	112.3	GDP Deflator (1995=100)	99bi r
Midyear Estimates																
57.14	57.25	57.34	57.44	57.54	57.66	56.75	56.86	57.05	57.20	57.30	57.38	57.52	57.59	I 57.34	**Population**	99z

(See notes in the back of the book.)

	1970	1971	1972	1973	1974	1975	1976	1977	1978	1979	1980	1981	1982	1983	1984
Exchange Rates												*Jamaica Dollars per SDR:*			
Market Rate................aa= ....**wa**	.836	.851	.925	1.097	1.113	1.064	1.056	1.104	2.208	2.347	2.272	2.074	1.965	3.432	4.832
												Jamaica Dollars per US Dollar:			
Market Rate................ae= ....**we**	.836	.784	.852	.909	.909	.909	.909	.909	1.695	1.781	1.781	1.781	1.781	3.278	4.930
Market Rate................rf= ....**wf**	.833	.833	.767	.902	.909	.909	.909	.909	1.413	1.765	1.781	1.781	1.781	1.932	3.943
Fund Position												*Millions of SDRs:*			
Quota...**2f. s**	53.0	53.0	53.0	53.0	53.0	53.0	53.0	53.0	74.0	74.0	111.0	111.0	111.0	111.0	145.5
SDRs..**1b. s**	6.4	12.8	6.9	6.4	5.1	4.3	.8	14.3	4.5	.4	—	1.1	.1	—	—
Reserve Position in the Fund...........**1c. s**	9.5	13.3										2.4	3.8	—	—
Total Fund Cred.&Loans Outstg............**2tl**	—	—	—	13.3	13.3	13.3	68.9	88.1	138.6	266.8	242.5	403.5	528.4	599.1	641.4
International Liquidity										*Millions of US Dollars Unless Otherwise Indicated:*					
Total Reserves minus Gold ....**1l. d**	139.2	179.1	159.7	127.4	190.4	125.6	32.4	47.8	58.8	63.8	105.0	85.2	109.0	63.2	96.9
SDRs.....................................**1b. d**	6.4	13.9	7.5	7.7	6.3	5.0	.9	17.4	5.8	.5	—	1.3	.1	—	—
Reserve Position in the Fund...........**1c. d**	9.5	14.4										2.8	4.1	—	—
Foreign Exchange........................**1d. d**	123.3	150.8	152.2	119.7	184.1	120.6	31.5	30.4	53.0	63.3	105.0	81.1	104.7	63.2	96.9
Other Official Insts.: Assets ....**3b. d**	1.8	2.1	2.8	5.3	14.1	33.5	1.4	.8	1.2	1.1	.8	10.8	14.5	—	37.1
Monetary Authorities: Other Liab. ....**4. d**					20.0	51.2	116.6	132.7	205.8	161.8	320.2	411.4	415.0	834.6	529.7
Deposit Money Banks: Assets ....**7a. d**	19.6	22.9	30.4	51.4	44.0	38.2	36.3	40.1	32.2	28.4	37.8	45.8	60.8	82.4	56.7
Liabilities ....**7b. d**	45.5	31.8	71.1	125.9	111.4	109.7	115.2	119.0	73.5	67.1	65.1	91.5	94.7	53.7	48.2
Other Banking Insts.: Assets ....**7e. d**	.7	.8	.6	.2	.8	.9	1.0	2.7	.8	1.9	.3	.4	.6	.4	.2
Liabilities ....**7f. d**	.9	13.2	22.6	24.5	45.1	63.3	49.5	38.9	31.4	31.3	8.0	12.8	12.6	4.7	.1
Monetary Authorities												*Millions of Jamaica Dollars:*			
Foreign Assets **11**	116	138	118	117	174	115	35	44	99	122	200	324	203	244	475
Claims on Central Government..............**12a**	7	11	33	51	72	204	505	469	616	1,347	1,539	1,989	2,235	3,164	3,919
Claims on Deposit Money Banks..........**12e**	6	7	10	32	46	11	16	6	10	18	64	10	15	—	49
Reserve Money..................................**14**	75	96	109	140	170	202	234	273	302	362	510	489	433	744	1,427
of which: Currency Outside DMBs.........**14a**	46	58	72	82	102	127	138	182	173	220	260	282	316	375	436
Foreign Liabilities..............................**16c**	—	—	—	15	33	61	179	218	655	914	1,121	1,570	1,778	4,792	5,711
Central Government Deposits **16d**	40	39	27	21	74	58	138	50	15	119	406	243	349	448	833
Capital Accounts **17a**	12	17	23	26	28	27	35	36	44	65	79	88	84	143	200
Other Items (Net)................................**17r**	2	4	3	−2	−12	−18	−30	−57	−290	27	−314	−66	−192	−2,719	−3,730
Deposit Money Banks												*Millions of Jamaica Dollars:*			
Reserves...**20**	30	39	40	58	70	70	95	93	198	156	392	302	59	372	1,015
Foreign Assets **21**	16	18	23	47	40	35	33	36	55	51	67	82	108	270	280
Claims on Central Government..............**22a**	63	76	79	74	77	107	133	288	355	384	378	553	705	794	744
Claims on Nonfin.Pub.Enterprises **22c**	—	—	—	35	33	47	58	92	105	129	195	274	330	368	380
Claims on Private Sector......................**22d**	280	326	416	471	549	641	622	544	654	775	904	1,231	1,683	2,123	2,483
Claims on Other Banking Insts..............**22f**	1	—	9	5	9	4	16	3	13	—		11	21	74	123
Demand Deposits................................**24**	80	102	101	Ⅰ136	156	195	200	292	397	410	457	492	560	691	882
Time and Savings Deposits..................**25**	252	311	356	Ⅰ359	428	506	558	570	665	793	996	1,422	1,897	2,461	2,878
Foreign Liabilities..............................**26c**	38	24	55	Ⅰ114	101	100	105	108	125	120	116	163	169	176	237
Central Government Deposits **26d**	5	4	3	9	10	10	13	13	17	32	35	45	44	88	200
Credit from Monetary Authorities **26g**	—	—	—	33	1	7	8	—	3	18	64	2	3	1	26
Capital Accounts **27a**	16	22	36	69	109	119	115	104	141	158	182	205	224	327	490
Other Items (Net)................................**27r**	−2	−3	16	−31	−27	−32	−42	−32	32	−36	87	123	10	256	409
Monetary Survey												*Millions of Jamaica Dollars:*			
Foreign Assets (Net)...........................**31n**	94	131	87	Ⅰ34	80	−11	−215	−246	−626	−861	−970	−1,327	−1,635	−4,454	−5,194
Domestic Credit **32**	307	373	511	610	667	950	1,201	1,348	1,735	2,527	2,649	3,797	4,605	6,012	6,736
Claims on Central Govt. (Net) **32an**	25	44	82	95	66	243	487	693	939	1,581	1,476	2,255	2,548	3,422	3,729
Claims on Local Government **32b**	—	—	—	—	1	3	3	3	3	10	6	2	7	6	5
Claims on Nonfin.Pub.Enterprises.......**32c**	—	—	—	35	33	47	58	92	105	129	195	274	330	368	380
Claims on Private Sector....................**32d**	281	329	420	475	558	650	630	552	663	785	914	1,241	1,692	2,135	2,494
Claims on Other Banking Insts **32f**	1	—	9	5	9	7	23	8	25	22	59	26	29	81	128
Money...**34**	127	160	173	Ⅰ218	258	322	339	474	570	629	717	775	876	1,066	1,319
Quasi-Money......................................**35**	252	311	356	Ⅰ359	428	506	558	570	665	793	996	1,422	1,897	2,461	2,878
Capital Accounts **37a**	28	39	59	95	136	146	149	139	185	223	261	293	308	471	690
Other Items (Net)................................**37r**	−6	−5	11	−28	−77	−35	−61	−82	−310	20	−293	−20	−111	−2,440	−3,346
Money plus Quasi-Money......................**35l**	379	471	528	Ⅰ578	687	828	897	1,044	1,235	1,422	1,712	2,197	2,773	3,527	4,197
Other Banking Institutions												*Millions of Jamaica Dollars:*			
Reserves...**40**	—	—	1	—	—	—	—	—	—	—	—	—	—	2	—
Foreign Assets **41**	1	1	—	—	1	1	1	2	1	3	—	1	1	1	1
Claims on Central Government..............**42a**	—	—	—	—	—	—	—	8	5	23	9	7	10	7	9
Claims on Private Sector......................**42d**	11	23	43	92	136	160	159	141	168	169	134	170	258	347	476
Claims on Deposit Money Banks..........**42e**	6	10	31	29	98	73	61	54	66	50	55	57	42	77	130
Demand Deposits................................**44**	—	—	—	7	95	—	—	—	—	—	1	3	—	10	12
Time and Savings Deposits..................**45**	14	21	53	81	86	135	133	101	119	116	129	158	242	362	483
Foreign Liabilities..............................**46c**	1	10	17	21	41	56	44	34	52	54	14	22	10	—	—
Long-Term Foreign Liabilities...............**46cl**	—	—	—	1	—	1	1	1	1	2	1	1	12	15	—
Credit from Deposit Money Banks..........**46h**	1	—	2	3	—	6	10	27	24	39	17	22	36	30	113
Capital Accounts **47a**	2	3	5	6	6	14	14	15	15	17	18	19	25	29	54
Other Items (Net)................................**47r**	—	—	−2	1	7	22	20	27	29	18	18	9	−14	−12	−46
Banking Survey												*Millions of Jamaica Dollars:*			
Foreign Assets (Net)...........................**51n**	94	122	70	Ⅰ13	39	−66	−259	−278	−676	−911	−983	−1,348	−1,645	−4,453	−5,193
Domestic Credit **52**	317	396	545	698	795	1,103	1,338	1,488	1,883	2,697	2,733	3,948	4,845	6,285	7,092
Claims on Central Govt. (Net) **52an**	25	44	82	95	66	243	487	701	944	1,604	1,485	2,262	2,558	3,429	3,737
Claims on Local Government **52b**	—	—	—	—	1	3	3	3	3	10	6	2	7	6	5
Claims on Nonfin.Pub.Enterprises.......**52c**	—	—	—	35	33	47	58	92	105	129	195	274	330	368	380
Claims on Private Sector....................**52d**	292	352	463	567	694	810	789	692	831	954	1,047	1,411	1,950	2,482	2,971
Liquid Liabilities.................................**55l**	393	492	581	Ⅰ667	868	962	1,030	1,145	1,353	1,538	1,842	2,358	3,015	3,897	4,692
Long-Term Foreign Liabilities...............**56cl**	—	—	—	1	—	1	1	1	1	2	1	1	12	15	—
Capital Accounts **57a**	30	41	64	101	142	161	163	154	200	240	279	312	333	500	744
Other Items (Net)................................**57r**	−12	−15	−30	−57	−176	−87	−115	−90	−348	5	−372	−71	−160	−2,580	−3,537

1985	1986	1987	1988	1989	1990	1991	1992	1993	1994	1995	1996	1997	1998	1999	
End of Period															**Exchange Rates**
6.019	6.703	7.803	7.374	8.516	11.435	30.744	30.504	44.606	48.469	58.889	50.135	49.033	52.174	56.672	Market Rate....................aa= .... wa
End of Period (we) Period Average (wf)															
5.480	5.480	5.500	5.480	6.480	8.038	21.493	22.185	32.475	33.202	39.616	34.865	36.341	37.055	41.291	Market Rate....................ae= .... we
5.559	5.478	5.487	5.489	5.745	7.184	12.116	22.960	24.949	33.086	35.142	37.120	35.404	36.550	39.044	Market Rate....................rf= .... wf
End of Period															**Fund Position**
145.5	145.5	145.5	145.5	145.5	145.5	145.5	200.9	200.9	200.9	200.9	200.9	200.9	200.9	273.5	Quota .... 2f. s
—	.3	1.0	—	—	.3	—	9.0	9.1	—	.3	—	.2	.5	.5	SDRs .... 1b. s
—	—	—	—	—	—	—	—	—	—	—	—	—	—	—	Reserve Position in the Fund .... 1c. s
631.1	554.4	478.2	358.8	291.8	250.7	273.6	259.7	244.2	217.6	161.7	112.2	87.1	74.7	60.8	Total Fund Cred.&Loans Outstg. 2tl
End of Period															**International Liquidity**
161.3	98.4	174.3	147.2	107.5	168.2[e]	106.1	324.1	417.0	735.9	681.3	880.0	682.1	709.5	554.5	Total Reserves minus Gold...................... 1l. d
—	.4	1.4	—	—	.5	.1	12.3	12.4	—	.5	.1	.2	.7	.7	SDRs .... 1b. d
—	—	—	—	—	—	—	—	—	—	—	—	—	—	—	Reserve Position in the Fund .... 1c. d
161.3	98.0	172.9	147.2	107.5	167.7[e]	106.0	311.8	404.6	735.9	680.8	879.9	681.9	708.8	553.8	Foreign Exchange .... 1d. d
37.6	49.4	54.1	59.7	52.9	....	....	14.9	17.5	8.3	7.7	8.0	1.1	1.0	3.2	Other Official Insts.: Assets.................... 3b. d
667.6	608.4	493.9	535.1	523.4	492.1	232.0	109.8	65.1	58.2	....	....	....	....	....	Monetary Authorities: Other Liab. .... 4.. d
59.9	62.1	66.1	99.0	122.2	113.0	236.2	307.0	292.6	449.5	489.0	464.6	542.0	457.9	573.3	Deposit Money Banks: Assets .... 7a. d
71.1	81.0	104.1	155.4	161.5	138.4	204.0	253.4	238.3	393.2	336.2	370.2	371.6	328.0	278.0	Liabilities........... 7b. d
.4	.5	—	2.3	2.4	2.9	2.6	7.6	1.8	34.1	7.0	9.1	16.7	23.8	33.7	Other Banking Insts.: Assets .... 7e. d
.1	—	—	.6	.3	3.5	.7	.1	3.9	53.8	47.0	43.5	11.7	6.4	5.4	Liabilities .... 7f. d
End of Period															**Monetary Authorities**
1,087	573	930	806	692	1,352	2,311	6,912	12,618	24,486	27,084	30,663	24,739	26,280	22,850	Foreign Assets 11
3,598	4,294	2,829	2,940	3,343	3,316	2,614	2,562	7,055	7,466	15,702	20,751	39,777	51,219	57,268	Claims on Central Government 12a
47	38	—	150	127	12	—	—	—	—	—	—	—	—	—	Claims on Deposit Money Banks 12e
1,926	2,285	2,736	3,752	4,604	5,321	6,820	12,859	18,588	24,969	32,381	33,668	38,770	47,324	45,343	Reserve Money 14
540	729	844	1,288	1,378	1,640	2,632	3,741	5,228	7,118	9,516	10,760	12,449	13,504	18,175	*of which: Currency Outside DMBs* 14a
7,457	7,050	6,448	5,578	5,876	6,822	13,398	10,357	13,007	12,480	8,077	2,136	1,588	1,345	906	Foreign Liabilities... 16c
1,349	1,855	2,261	3,707	4,452	6,410	9,188	12,682	17,255	26,512	28,948	37,755	41,571	45,837	48,058	Central Government Deposits 16d
248	276	321	303	350	468	1,252	1,243	1,815	1,972	2,395	2,060	2,015	2,143	2,325	Capital Accounts 17a
-6,249	-6,561	-8,007	-9,444	-11,121	-14,341	-25,734	-27,668	-30,993	-33,981	-29,015	-24,205	-19,427	-19,150	-16,515	Other Items (Net) 17r
End of Period															**Deposit Money Banks**
1,304	2,340	2,323	3,270	3,838	4,273	5,059	11,113	13,681	18,794	25,623	23,568	29,167	30,812	26,424	Reserves 20
328	340	364	543	792	908	5,076	6,810	9,501	14,924	19,373	16,197	19,697	16,966	23,672	Foreign Assets 21
1,069	1,920	2,049	1,977	1,150	1,539	1,843	8,134	7,580	16,967	13,716	22,281	23,898	23,280	30,299	Claims on Central Government 22a
558	157	276	285	423	335	222	159	730	1,016	2,081	1,902	3,326	3,462	3,357	Claims on Nonfin.Pub.Enterprises........... 22c
2,602	3,109	4,046	5,549	7,290	8,583	11,940	14,358	23,326	32,164	44,408	52,006	57,482	74,777	84,081	Claims on Private Sector......................... 22d
125	71	10	82	86	66	233	488	281	686	803	380	512	342	610	Claims on Other Banking Insts 22f
980	1,410	1,407	2,157	1,775	2,376	5,185	9,650	11,675	14,134	19,804	22,788	22,022	23,160	28,620	Demand Deposits 24
3,718	4,548	5,275	6,513	7,460	8,875	11,698	20,908	29,725	44,300	57,075	62,243	74,017	80,138	86,768	Time and Savings Deposits 25
390	444	572	852	1,046	1,113	4,384	5,622	7,740	13,055	13,319	12,905	13,504	12,153	11,478	Foreign Liabilities... 26c
141	139	206	262	366	378	563	1,814	2,304	6,529	6,945	6,690	8,086	5,736	8,128	Central Government Deposits 26d
23	42	21	145	148	108	8	442	38	283	3,721	8,120	5,239	101	242	Credit from Monetary Authorities 26g
522	788	958	1,232	1,560	1,876	2,510	3,902	5,139	8,615	10,613	14,140	16,469	33,180	33,323	Capital Accounts 27a
212	567	628	545	1,223	979	23	-1,275	-1,522	-2,363	-5,474	-10,554	-5,254	-4,830	-113	Other Items (Net) 27r
End of Period															**Monetary Survey**
-6,432	-6,580	-5,727	-5,081	-5,440	-5,675	-10,396	-2,257	1,372	13,876	25,061	31,818	29,345	29,748	34,139	Foreign Assets (Net) 31n
6,482	7,597	6,808	7,006	7,616	7,227	7,273	11,378	19,442	25,492	41,074	53,129	75,593	101,760	119,682	Domestic Credit 32
3,178	4,220	2,411	948	-325	-1,932	-5,294	-3,800	-4,924	-8,608	-6,475	-1,413	14,019	22,926	31,381	Claims on Central Govt. (Net) 32an
4	—	—	—	—	—	—	—	—	6	6	2	3	1	—	Claims on Local Government 32b
558	157	276	285	423	335	222	159	730	1,016	2,081	1,902	3,326	3,462	3,357	Claims on Nonfin.Pub.Enterprises 32c
2,613	3,146	4,046	5,689	7,430	8,756	12,113	14,531	23,355	32,391	44,660	52,258	57,734	75,029	84,333	Claims on Private Sector 32d
129	74	76	84	88	68	233	488	281	686	803	380	512	342	610	Claims on Other Banking Insts 32f
1,520	2,140	2,252	3,445	3,153	4,016	7,818	13,391	16,903	21,252	29,320	33,548	34,470	36,664	46,795	Money 34
3,718	4,548	5,275	6,513	7,460	8,875	11,698	20,908	29,725	44,300	57,075	62,243	74,017	80,138	86,768	Quasi-Money.. 35
771	1,064	1,279	1,535	1,910	2,344	3,763	5,145	6,954	10,587	13,009	16,200	18,484	35,323	35,648	Capital Accounts 37a
-5,958	-6,735	-7,724	-9,567	-10,346	-13,683	-26,401	-30,322	-32,768	-36,771	-33,269	-27,043	-22,033	-20,618	-15,391	Other Items (Net) 37r
5,238	6,687	7,527	9,958	10,612	12,891	19,516	34,299	46,628	65,552	86,396	95,791	108,487	116,803	133,563	Money plus Quasi-Money 35l
End of Period															**Other Banking Institutions**
12	45	71	187	196	257	406	870	1,396	1,276	1,287	1,390	1,233	1,279	765	Reserves 40
2	3	—	13	15	23	55	168	59	1,133	277	318	608	882	1,393	Foreign Assets 41
52	103	214	328	334	323	471	832	312	1,681	2,818	4,404	4,281	1,894	1,500	Claims on Central Government 42a
615	768	1,122	1,843	2,724	3,149	4,257	6,902	7,468	7,627	9,890	10,662	7,069	5,781	4,354	Claims on Private Sector.......................... 42d
96	103	100	115	153	409	332	1,019	686	1,148	932	865	1,442	379	299	Claims on Deposit Money Banks 42e
—	19	—	—	—	—	—	—	—	—	—	—	—	—	—	Demand Deposits 44
771	917	1,403	2,140	2,635	2,929	3,229	6,580	7,306	6,998	7,077	6,996	6,862	5,759	4,938	Time and Savings Deposits 45
—	—	—	—	—	—	—	—	—	—	—	—	15	24	—	Foreign Liabilities... 46c
—	—	—	3	2	28	16	2	127	1,786	1,863	1,516	410	213	224	Long-Term Foreign Liabilities 46cl
65	120	41	117	336	402	661	843	949	1,312	1,096	5,463	4,098	1,120	—	Credit from Deposit Money Banks 46h
67	90	125	198	202	252	491	1,189	1,738	2,521	2,924	3,013	1,688	2,946	4,259	Capital Accounts 47a
-127	-124	-62	29	246	550	1,124	1,177	-200	249	2,244	649	1,559	153	-1,111	Other Items (Net) 47r
End of Period															**Banking Survey**
-6,430	-6,578	-5,727	-5,068	-5,424	-5,651	-10,341	-2,090	1,432	15,009	25,339	32,136	29,937	30,606	35,532	Foreign Assets (Net) 51n
7,020	8,395	8,069	9,093	10,586	10,631	11,768	18,624	26,940	34,114	52,979	67,815	86,431	109,094	124,924	Domestic Credit 52
3,230	4,324	2,626	1,276	9	-1,609	-4,824	-2,968	-4,612	-6,927	-3,658	2,991	18,299	24,821	32,880	Claims on Central Govt. (Net) 52an
4	—	—	—	—	—	—	—	—	6	6	2	3	1	—	Claims on Local Government 52b
558	157	276	285	423	335	222	159	730	1,016	2,081	1,902	3,326	3,462	3,357	Claims on Nonfin.Pub.Enterprises 52c
3,228	3,914	5,167	7,532	10,154	11,904	16,370	21,433	30,823	40,018	54,550	62,920	64,803	80,810	88,687	Claims on Private Sector 52d
5,997	7,579	8,859	11,910	13,051	15,563	22,339	40,008	52,538	71,273	92,186	101,398	114,116	121,282	137,735	Liquid Liabilities 55l
—	—	—	3	2	28	16	2	127	1,786	1,863	1,516	410	213	224	Long-Term Foreign Liabilities 56cl
838	1,154	1,403	1,733	2,113	2,596	4,254	6,334	8,692	13,108	15,933	19,213	20,172	38,270	39,908	Capital Accounts 57a
-6,245	-6,916	-7,921	-9,621	-10,004	-13,208	-25,181	-29,810	-32,986	-37,044	-31,663	-22,175	-18,330	-20,065	-17,411	Other Items (Net) 57r

Jamaica

		1970	1971	1972	1973	1974	1975	1976	1977	1978	1979	1980	1981	1982	1983	1984
Interest Rates															*Percent Per Annum*	
Bank Rate *(End of Period)*	60	6.00	5.00	6.00	7.00	9.00	8.00	9.00	9.00	9.00	9.00	11.00	11.00	11.00	11.00	16.00
Treasury Bill Rate	60c	4.03	3.81	4.32	5.54	7.19	6.94	7.23	7.21	8.26	9.25	9.97	9.83	8.61	12.38	13.29
Deposit Rate	60l	....	....	....	....	....	....	10.78	7.08	5.68	8.28	9.53	10.55	10.71	13.60	15.86
Lending Rate	60p	....	....	....	....	....	....	13.76	13.86	13.68	13.81	15.63	16.07	16.44	16.97	18.53
Government Bond Yield	61	7.83	8.35	8.35	8.81	10.41	11.10	11.60	11.70	11.70	12.28	13.61	13.68	13.68	15.16	17.14
Prices, Production, Labor															*Index Numbers (1995=100)*	
Industrial Share Prices	62	.5	.5	.6	.6	.4	.4	.3	.2	.2	.3	.3	.7	1.0	1.3	2.1
Consumer Prices	64	.9	.9	1.0	1.2	1.5	1.7	1.9	2.1	2.9	3.7	4.7	5.3	5.7	6.3	8.1
Industrial Production	66	....	....	....	....	....	....	....	....	....	....	....	....	....	....	
															Number in Thousands:	
Labor Force	67d	....	....	....	....	....	....	....	....	....	....	....	....	....	....	
Employment	67e	....	....	....	....	....	....	....	....	....	....	....	....	....	....	
Unemployment	67c	....	....	....	....	....	....	....	....	....	....	....	....	....	....	
Unemployment Rate (%)	67r	....	....	....	....	....	....	....	....	....	....	....	....	....	....	
International Transactions															*Millions of Jamaica Dollars*	
Exports	70	285	283	300	355	549	690	573	699	1,143	1,446	1,715	1,735	1,367	1,392	2,733
Imports, c.i.f.	71	438	460	489	615	851	1,021	830	782	1,260	1,754	2,087	2,623	2,460	2,841	4,510
															1995=100	
Volume of Exports	72	107.4	107.4	113.9	104.0	49.2	97.5	77.5	87.5	89.0	86.3	88.8	91.1	65.8	70.8	65.1
Balance of Payments															*Millions of US Dollars*	
Current Account, n.i.e.	78al *d*	....	....	....	....	....	....	−263.8	−12.7	−21.7	−106.5	−136.1	−306.8	−383.3	−338.6	−315.2
Goods: Exports f.o.b.	78aa *d*	....	....	....	....	....	....	656.4	737.8	831.1	818.2	962.7	974.0	767.4	685.7	702.3
Goods: Imports f.o.b.	78ab *d*	....	....	....	....	....	....	−791.6	−666.7	−750.1	−882.5	−1,038.2	−1,296.7	−1,208.9	−1,124.2	−1,037.0
Trade Balance	78ac *d*	....	....	....	....	....	....	−135.2	71.1	81.0	−64.3	−75.5	−322.7	−441.5	−438.5	−334.7
Services: Credit	78ad *d*	....	....	....	....	....	....	232.7	217.2	285.4	351.8	400.7	430.9	493.0	540.1	566.3
Services: Debit	78ae *d*	....	....	....	....	....	....	−332.8	−257.0	−299.7	−339.5	−369.9	−407.1	−430.0	−403.3	−418.0
Balance on Goods & Services	78af *d*	....	....	....	....	....	....	−235.3	31.3	66.7	−52.0	−44.7	−298.9	−378.5	−301.7	−186.4
Income: Credit	78ag *d*	....	....	....	....	....	....	53.8	52.0	53.3	50.9	58.2	94.9	110.7	106.4	66.6
Income: Debit	78ah *d*	....	....	....	....	....	....	−127.0	−145.5	−195.8	−217.9	−270.2	−257.1	−285.9	−261.3	−332.9
Balance on Gds, Serv. & Inc.	78ai *d*	....	....	....	....	....	....	−308.5	−62.2	−75.8	−219.0	−256.7	−461.1	−553.7	−456.6	−452.7
Current Transfers, n.i.e.: Credit	78aj *d*	....	....	....	....	....	....	94.2	92.3	93.3	152.7	162.7	199.3	219.0	174.8	178.5
Current Transfers: Debit	78ak *d*	....	....	....	....	....	....	−49.5	−42.8	−39.2	−40.2	−42.1	−45.0	−48.6	−56.8	−41.0
Capital Account, n.i.e.	78bc *d*	....	....	....	....	....	....	−38.8	−29.4	−28.3	−32.4	−29.9	−30.0	−25.2	−20.0	−20.0
Capital Account, n.i.e.: Credit	78ba *d*	....	....	....	....	....	....	—	—	—	—	—	—	—	—	—
Capital Account: Debit	78bb *d*	....	....	....	....	....	....	−38.8	−29.4	−28.3	−32.4	−29.9	−30.0	−25.2	−20.0	−20.0
Financial Account, n.i.e.	78bj *d*	....	....	....	....	....	....	58.0	−6.7	−139.4	−14.1	117.9	95.0	199.7	−27.2	552.6
Direct Investment Abroad	78bd *d*	....	....	....	....	....	....	—	—	—	—	—	—	—	—	—
Dir. Invest. in Rep. Econ., n.i.e.	78be *d*	....	....	....	....	....	....	−.6	−9.7	−26.6	−26.4	27.7	−11.5	−15.8	−18.7	12.2
Portfolio Investment Assets	78bf *d*	....	....	....	....	....	....	3.8	—	—	—	—	—	—	—	—
Equity Securities	78bk *d*	....	....	....	....	....	....	—	—	—	—	—	—	—	—	—
Debt Securities	78bl *d*	....	....	....	....	....	....	3.8	—	—	—	—	—	—	—	—
Portfolio Investment Liab., n.i.e.	78bg *d*	....	....	....	....	....	....	—	—	—	—	—	—	—	—	—
Equity Securities	78bm *d*	....	....	....	....	....	....	—	—	—	—	—	—	—	—	—
Debt Securities	78bn *d*	....	....	....	....	....	....	—	—	—	—	—	—	—	—	—
Financial Derivatives Assets	78bw *d*	....	....	....	....	....	....	....	....	....	....	....	....	....	....	....
Financial Derivatives Liabilities	78bx *d*	....	....	....	....	....	....	....	....	....	....	....	....	....	....	....
Other Investment Assets	78bh *d*	....	....	....	....	....	....	13.1	.1	2.5	.1	−11.6	−16.7	−21.6	−14.7	−33.9
Monetary Authorities	78bo *d*	....	....	....	....	....	....	—	—	—	—	—	—	—	—	—
General Government	78bp *d*	....	....	....	....	....	....	−1.8	−1.1	−2.3	−2.6	−2.1	−8.7	−6.6	−7.0	−8.6
Banks	78bq *d*	....	....	....	....	....	....	3.9	−4.3	4.8	2.7	−9.5	−8.0	−15.0	−7.7	−25.3
Other Sectors	78br *d*	....	....	....	....	....	....	11.0	5.5	—	—	—	—	—	—	—
Other Investment Liab., n.i.e.	78bi *d*	....	....	....	....	....	....	41.7	2.9	−115.3	12.2	101.8	123.2	237.1	6.2	574.3
Monetary Authorities	78bs *d*	....	....	....	....	....	....	9.2	15.8	−8.4	−13.3	14.4	30.4	−73.8	59.2	109.1
General Government	78bt *d*	....	....	....	....	....	....	75.5	52.5	85.3	72.6	188.2	101.5	276.8	61.4	356.5
Banks	78bu *d*	....	....	....	....	....	....	1.0	4.2	—	—	−4.1	13.1	−13.3	−17.8	1.1
Other Sectors	78bv *d*	....	....	....	....	....	....	−44.0	−69.6	−192.2	−47.1	−96.7	−21.8	47.4	−96.6	107.6
Net Errors and Omissions	78ca *d*	....	....	....	....	....	....	43.5	−1.1	35.8	−4.2	−28.4	3.9	18.0	−.9	−64.0
Overall Balance	78cb *d*	....	....	....	....	....	....	−201.1	−49.9	−153.6	−157.2	−76.5	−237.8	−190.8	−386.7	153.3
Reserves and Related Items	79da *d*	....	....	....	....	....	....	201.1	49.9	153.6	157.2	76.5	237.8	190.8	386.7	−153.3
Reserve Assets	79db *d*	....	....	....	....	....	....	119.9	−8.4	−9.8	−.4	−41.6	25.1	−19.7	56.6	−65.9
Use of Fund Credit and Loans	79dc *d*	....	....	....	....	....	....	64.4	22.5	63.3	165.8	−31.0	190.3	137.3	76.6	44.3
Exceptional Financing	79de *d*	....	....	....	....	....	....	16.8	35.8	100.1	−8.2	149.1	22.4	73.3	253.5	−131.7
Government Finance															*Millions of Jamaica Dollars:*	
Deficit (-) or Surplus	80	....	....	....	....	....	−253.0	−394.9	−496.5	−514.1	−542.6	−739.3	−720.6	−893.3	−1,389.4	−547.0
Revenue	81	....	....	....	....	....	682.0	709.9	734.1	1,129.7	1,149.9	1,381.9	1,671.7	1,719.4	1,840.8	2,882.2
Grants Received	81z	....	....	....	....	....	....	....	....	....	....	....	....	....	....	....
Expenditure	82	....	....	....	....	....	805.6	946.2	1,064.5	1,427.7	1,426.4	1,980.9	2,116.6	2,263.2	2,847.3	3,168.2
Lending Minus Repayments	83	....	....	....	....	....	129.4	158.6	166.1	216.1	266.1	140.3	275.7	349.5	383.4	261.0
Debt: Domestic	88a	....	....	....	....	....	....	....	....	....	....	2,253.1	2,585.3	3,158.4	6,178.1	5,871.8
Foreign	89a	....	....	....	....	....	....	....	....	....	....	1,700.1	2,232.1	2,605.9	4,681.2	8,417.5
National Accounts															*Millions of Jamaica Dollars*	
Exports of Goods & Services	90c	389	434	472	543	770	917	783	928	1,575	2,065	2,426	2,510	2,240	2,621	4,956
Government Consumption	91f	137	159	197	280	386	477	562	612	750	825	966	1,095	1,288	1,406	1,548
Gross Fixed Capital Formation	93e	367	356	367	448	478	610	451	350	499	748	690	954	1,168	1,436	1,981
Increase/Decrease(-) in Stocks	93i	2	56	27	94	47	60	40	12	63	74	69	123	57	120	183
Private Consumption	96f	713	803	968	1,063	1,469	1,723	1,887	2,030	2,387	2,714	3,147	3,682	4,034	4,874	6,271
Imports of Goods & Services	98c	−438	−525	−591	−707	−991	−1,186	−1,022	−972	−1,525	−2,133	−2,525	−3,058	−2,919	−3,465	−5,580
Gross Domestic Product (GDP)	99b	1,171	1,282	1,439	1,720	2,159	2,600	2,696	2,954	3,737	4,297	4,773	5,307	5,867	6,993	9,359
Net Factor Inc/Pmts(-) Abroad	98.n	−51	−74	−25	−27	52	20	−69	−98	−152	−257	−318	−293	−289	−248	−902
Gross National Income (GNI)	99a	1,120	1,208	1,414	1,693	2,211	2,620	2,632	2,862	3,598	4,037	4,455	5,014	5,578	6,745	8,456
GDP Volume 1974 prices	99b.*p*	1,982.2	2,068.9	2,231.3	2,293.4	2,169.6	2,143.8	2,009.5	1,961.8	1,976.0	1,940.0	1,828.8	1,875.5	1,898.7	1,942.2	1,925.0
GDP Volume 1986 Prices	99b.*p*	....	....	....	....	....	....	....	....	....	....	....	....	....	....	....
GDP Volume (1995=100)	99bv *p*	80.5	84.0	90.6	93.2	88.1	87.1	81.6	79.7	80.3	78.8	74.3	76.2	77.1	78.9	78.2
GDP Deflator (1995=100)	99bi *p*	.9	.9	.9	1.1	1.4	1.8	1.9	2.2	2.7	3.2	3.8	4.1	4.5	5.2	7.0
															Millions:	
Population	99z	1.87	1.90	1.93	1.97	2.01	2.04	2.07	2.09	2.10	2.11	2.13	2.18	2.19	2.24	2.28

		1985	1986	1987	1988	1989	1990	1991	1992	1993	1994	1995	1996	1997	1998	1999
Interest Rates		*Percent Per Annum*														
Bank Rate *(End of Period)*	60	21.00	21.00	21.00	21.00	21.00	21.00	....	....	....	....	....	....	....	....	....
Treasury Bill Rate	60c	19.03	20.88	18.16	18.50	19.10	26.21	25.56	34.36	28.85	42.98	27.65	37.95	21.14	25.65	20.75
Deposit Rate	60l	19.58	18.76	15.64	15.80	15.95	23.88	24.67	33.63	27.59	36.41	23.21	25.16	13.95	15.61	13.48
Lending Rate	60p	24.92	27.34	25.45	25.19	25.22	30.50	31.51	44.81	43.71	49.46	43.58	39.83	32.86	31.59	27.01
Government Bond Yield	61	22.48	22.62	20.83	20.40	20.17	25.46	26.33	30.50	24.82	26.82	26.85	26.87	26.85	....	....
Prices, Production, Labor		*Period Averages*														
Industrial Share Prices	62	3.4	6.5	9.9	8.1	11.6	12.6	29.2	67.9	122.4	83.4	100.0	81.2	97.3	122.5	115.0
Consumer Prices	64	10.2	11.7	12.5	I 13.5	15.5	18.9	28.5	50.6	61.7	83.4	100.0	126.4	138.6	150.6	159.5
Industrial Production	66	....	75.2	80.2	80.1	93.0	100.0	....	....	....	....	....	....	....	....	....
		Period Averages														
Labor Force	67d	....	....	....	....	....	1,060	....	....	....	....	....	....	....	1,129	....
Employment	67e	782	821	845	872	881	896	908	906	906	923	963	960	956	954	....
Unemployment	67c	261	251	224	203	177	167	169	169	177	167	187	183	187	175	....
Unemployment Rate (%)	67r	25.0	23.6	21.0	18.9	16.8	15.7	15.7	15.4	16.3	15.4	16.2	16.0	....	....	....
International Transactions		*Millions of Jamaica Dollars*														
Exports	70	3,128	3,226	3,874	4,830	5,747	8,305	13,079	24,099	26,421	40,121	49,916	51,513	48,972	47,940	43,991
Imports, c.i.f.	71	6,147	5,322	6,791	7,983	10,668	13,923	20,830	38,267	53,737	73,631	99,418	109,687	110,952	109,537	100,802
		1995=100														
Volume of Exports	72	59.2	57.9	58.7	62.5	78.0	98.3	103.1	99.0	99.3	106.9	100.0	110.1	112.3	115.3	115.2
Balance of Payments		*Minus Sign Indicates Debit*														
Current Account, n.i.e.	78al*d*	–273.4	–17.9	–125.7	46.6	–282.6	–312.1	–240.1	28.5	–184.0	93.2	–74.1	–111.6	–312.3	–255.3	....
Goods: Exports f.o.b.	78aa*d*	568.6	589.5	725.2	898.4	1,028.9	1,190.6	1,196.7	1,116.5	1,105.4	1,548.0	1,796.0	1,721.0	1,700.3	1,613.4	....
Goods: Imports f.o.b.	78ab*d*	–1,004.2	–837.4	–1,077.3	–1,255.3	–1,618.7	–1,692.7	–1,588.3	–1,541.1	–1,920.5	–2,099.2	–2,625.3	–2,715.2	–2,832.6	–2,710.1	....
Trade Balance	78ac*d*	–435.6	–247.9	–352.1	–356.9	–589.8	–502.1	–391.6	–424.6	–815.1	–551.2	–829.3	–994.2	–1,132.3	–1,096.7	....
Services: Credit	78ad*d*	609.5	753.5	837.5	785.3	876.1	1,026.5	992.1	1,104.0	1,260.7	1,497.0	1,612.8	1,624.5	1,714.6	1,769.9	....
Services: Debit	78ae*d*	–414.9	–411.4	–455.0	–567.6	–720.8	–697.4	–670.3	–714.4	–823.5	–960.5	–1,093.9	–1,140.8	–1,225.8	–1,260.0	....
Balance on Goods & Services	78af*d*	–241.0	94.2	30.4	–139.2	–434.5	–173.0	–69.8	–35.0	–377.9	–14.7	–310.4	–510.5	–643.5	–586.8	....
Income: Credit	78ag*d*	88.1	68.0	71.5	88.0	104.0	107.6	59.7	75.0	117.0	104.6	146.6	141.8	147.3	156.3	....
Income: Debit	78ah*d*	–369.9	–348.7	–414.8	–423.2	–454.1	–537.6	–498.5	–368.9	–312.9	–456.6	–517.3	–366.5	–440.9	–459.8	....
Balance on Gds, Serv. & Inc.	78ai*d*	–522.8	–186.5	–312.9	–474.4	–784.6	–603.0	–508.6	–328.9	–573.8	–366.7	–681.1	–735.2	–937.1	–890.3	....
Current Transfers, n.i.e.: Credit	78aj*d*	294.4	209.4	217.7	587.8	523.8	314.9	294.8	387.2	415.9	504.2	669.6	709.3	705.7	732.1	....
Current Transfers: Debit	78ak*d*	–45.0	–40.8	–30.5	–66.8	–21.8	–24.0	–26.3	–29.8	–26.1	–44.3	–62.6	–85.7	–80.9	–97.1	....
Capital Account, n.i.e.	78bc*d*	–31.0	–22.3	–16.5	–15.4	–15.0	–15.9	–15.7	–17.6	–12.9	31.7	31.1	37.7	16.9	15.5	....
Capital Account, n.i.e.: Credit	78ba*d*	—	—	—	—	—	—	—	—	—	33.2	34.5	42.5	21.7	20.3	....
Capital Account: Debit	78bb*d*	–31.0	–22.3	–16.5	–15.4	–15.0	–15.9	–15.7	–17.6	–12.9	–1.5	–3.4	–4.8	–4.8	–4.8	....
Financial Account, n.i.e.	78bj*d*	216.5	–118.0	357.5	92.8	115.8	428.2	254.9	297.3	257.1	256.1	108.3	288.6	168.9	327.3	....
Direct Investment Abroad	78bd*d*	—	—	—	—	—	—	—	—	—	–52.7	–66.3	–93.3	–56.6	–82.0	....
Dir. Invest. in Rep. Econ., n.i.e.	78be*d*	–9.0	–4.6	53.4	–12.0	57.1	137.9	133.2	142.4	77.9	129.7	147.4	183.7	203.3	369.1	....
Portfolio Investment Assets	78bf*d*	—	—	—	—	—	—	—	—	—	....	....	....	....	–3.9	....
Equity Securities	78bk*d*	—	—	—	—	—	—	—	—	—	....	....	....	....	....	....
Debt Securities	78bl*d*	—	—	—	—	—	—	—	—	—	....	....	....	....	–3.9	....
Portfolio Investment Liab., n.i.e.	78bg*d*	—	—	—	—	—	—	—	—	—	....	....	....	5.7	10.9	....
Equity Securities	78bm*d*	—	—	—	—	—	—	—	—	—	....	....	....	....	....	....
Debt Securities	78bn*d*	—	—	—	—	—	—	—	—	—	....	....	....	5.7	10.9	....
Financial Derivatives Assets	78bw*d*	....	....	....	....	....	....	....	....	....	....	....	....	....	....	....
Financial Derivatives Liabilities	78bx*d*	....	....	....	....	....	....	....	....	....	....	....	....	....	....	....
Other Investment Assets	78bh*d*	–5.2	–8.4	1.6	1.3	12.0	–2.5	105.7	10.2	1.1	–141.3	–148.8	–13.8	–92.4	–38.6	....
Monetary Authorities	78bo*d*	....	....	....	....	....	....	....	....	....	—	—	—	—	....	....
General Government	78bp*d*	–9.1	–8.8	–5.5	–22.9	–6.1	–7.4	–8.0	–1.0	–1.4	—	—	—	—	....	....
Banks	78bq*d*	3.9	.4	7.1	24.2	18.1	4.9	113.7	11.2	2.5	–177.9	–199.2	–88.1	–166.1	–121.3	....
Other Sectors	78br*d*	—	—	—	—	—	—	—	—	—	36.6	50.4	74.3	73.7	82.7	....
Other Investment Liab., n.i.e.	78bi*d*	230.7	–105.0	302.5	103.5	46.7	292.8	16.0	144.7	178.1	320.4	176.0	212.0	108.9	71.8	....
Monetary Authorities	78bs*d*	7.2	–33.0	15.3	1.9	–1.3	.5	–55.3	–50.8	–35.9	—	—	—	—	—	....
General Government	78bt*d*	141.1	–126.7	198.4	61.3	216.8	94.7	94.9	–10.0	37.8	–127.4	–97.0	–144.7	43.1	–41.3	....
Banks	78bu*d*	13.4	8.0	–3.4	–28.8	–19.9	–21.7	–151.3	–46.4	–6.0	142.2	74.7	130.7	141.3	175.1	....
Other Sectors	78bv*d*	69.0	46.7	92.2	69.1	–148.9	219.3	127.7	251.9	182.2	305.6	198.3	226.0	–75.5	–62.0	....
Net Errors and Omissions	78ca*d*	17.0	80.0	84.6	–46.0	10.0	29.3	–20.4	–59.9	49.7	–23.3	–38.3	56.7	–43.9	–43.6	....
Overall Balance	78cb*d*	–70.8	–78.2	299.9	78.0	–171.8	129.5	–21.3	248.3	109.9	357.7	27.0	271.4	–170.4	43.9	....
Reserves and Related Items	79da*d*	70.8	78.2	–299.9	–78.0	171.8	–129.5	21.3	–248.3	–109.9	–357.7	–27.0	–271.4	170.4	–43.9	....
Reserve Assets	79db*d*	–18.7	–14.1	–69.3	25.2	39.9	–65.3	52.9	–192.2	–92.9	–321.0	55.8	–201.7	205.0	–26.9	....
Use of Fund Credit and Loans	79dc*d*	–10.5	–88.6	–96.5	–160.2	–86.0	–53.2	32.6	–19.4	–21.3	–38.2	–84.6	–71.9	–34.6	–17.0	....
Exceptional Financing	79de*d*	100.1	180.9	–134.1	57.0	217.9	–11.1	–64.2	–36.7	4.4	1.5	1.9	2.2	—	—	....
Government Finance		*Year Ending December 31*														
Deficit (-) or Surplus	80	–963.4	....	....	....	....	....	....	....	....	....	....	....	....	....	....
Revenue	81	3,740.8	....	....	....	....	....	....	....	....	....	....	....	....	....	....
Grants Received	81z	—	....	....	....	....	....	....	....	....	....	....	....	....	....	....
Expenditure	82	4,492.6	....	....	....	....	....	....	....	....	....	....	....	....	....	....
Lending Minus Repayments	83	211.6	....	....	....	....	....	....	....	....	....	....	....	....	....	....
Debt: Domestic	88a	6,831.0	....	....	....	....	....	....	....	....	....	....	....	....	....	....
Foreign	89a	10,404.4	....	....	....	....	....	....	....	....	....	....	....	....	....	....
National Accounts		*Millions of Jamaica Dollars*														
Exports of Goods & Services	90c	6,521	7,370	8,405	9,168	11,036	15,856	24,978	50,552	57,835	83,815	103,214	106,090	103,466	107,162	....
Government Consumption	91f	1,738	2,151	2,497	3,018	3,270	4,301	5,772	7,719	13,572	16,536	22,998	31,836	39,741	44,641	....
Gross Fixed Capital Formation	93e	2,581	2,432	3,545	4,865	6,538	8,362	11,825	23,953	33,781	43,499	57,901	70,022	76,494	72,519	....
Increase/Decrease(-) in Stocks	93i	256	134	151	123	164	140	231	215	740	344	659	372	605	425	....
Private Consumption	96f	8,247	8,744	10,387	12,329	15,651	18,956	27,975	45,879	69,392	92,288	123,528	143,289	154,946	167,030	....
Imports of Goods & Services	98c	–7,669	–6,924	–8,344	–10,041	–13,259	–17,115	–25,567	–51,319	–67,883	–93,908	–124,175	–133,943	–137,264	–140,655	....
Gross Domestic Product (GDP)	99b	11,674	13,898	16,640	19,458	23,400	30,518	45,217	73,253	99,843	132,377	170,133	203,109	220,556	251,122	....
Net Factor Inc/Pmts(-) Abroad	98.n	–1,488	–1,505	–1,904	–1,879	–2,022	–3,122	–5,080	–6,843	–4,689	–7,952	–8,575	–4,852	–4,655	–3,044	....
Gross National Income (GNI)	99a	10,186	12,401	14,736	17,584	21,378	27,379	40,134	70,156	102,746	134,620	175,551	212,815	233,332	248,079	....
GDP Volume 1974 prices	99b.*p*	1,836.1	1,867.2	....	....	....	....	....	....	....	....	....	....	....	....	....
GDP Volume 1986 Prices	99b.*p*	....	13,898	14,981	15,408	16,459	17,359	17,486	17,752	18,015	18,180	18,324	18,064	17,692	17,566	....
GDP Volume (1995=100)	99bv*p*	74.6	75.8	81.8	84.1	89.8	94.7	95.4	96.9	98.3	99.2	100.0	98.6	96.6	95.9	....
GDP Deflator (1995=100)	99bi*p*	9.2	10.8	12.0	13.6	15.3	18.9	27.9	44.4	59.7	78.4	100.0	121.1	134.3	154.0	....
		Midyear Estimates														
Population	99z	2.31	2.34	2.35	2.36	2.39	2.41	I 2.37	2.42	2.45	2.47	2.50	2.52	2.55	I 2.54	2.56

(See notes in the back of the book.)

		1970	1971	1972	1973	1974	1975	1976	1977	1978	1979	1980	1981	1982	1983	1984
Exchange Rates																*Yen per SDR:*
Market Rate	aa	357.65	341.78	327.88	337.78	368.47	357.23	340.18	291.53	253.52	315.76	258.91	255.95	259.23	243.10	246.13
																Yen per US Dollar:
Market Rate	ae	357.65	314.80	302.00	280.00	300.95	305.15	292.80	240.00	194.60	239.70	203.00	219.90	235.00	232.20	251.10
Market Rate	rf	360.00	350.68	303.17	271.70	292.08	296.79	296.55	268.51	210.44	219.14	226.74	220.54	249.08	237.51	237.52
																Index Numbers (1995=100):
Market Rate	ahx	26.1	67.9	30.8	34.5	32.0	31.5	31.5	34.9	44.8	42.8	41.4	42.5	37.7	39.4	39.4
Nominal Effective Exchange Rate	neu	28.8	29.2	32.6	34.7	32.4	31.4	32.7	36.1	44.3	41.1	39.5	44.2	41.4	45.3	47.8
Real Effective Exchange Rate	reu	....	....	....	....	....	88.0	87.1	93.3	67.4	59.1	Ɪ 52.7	56.7	50.3	54.0	55.8
Fund Position																*Millions of SDRs:*
Quota	2f. s	1,200	1,200	1,200	1,200	1,200	1,200	1,200	1,200	1,659	1,659	2,489	2,489	2,489	4,223	4,223
SDRs	1b. s	146	283	424	425	432	444	460	494	1,053	1,281	1,363	1,662	1,895	1,848	1,966
Reserve Position in the Fund	1c. s	973	490	571	529	603	686	1,143	1,329	1,642	1,121	1,044	1,339	1,878	2,199	2,264
of which: Outstg.Fund Borrowing	2c	440	—	—	—	—	—	—	339	369	236	381	641	825	839	793
International Liquidity														*Millions of US Dollars Unless Otherwise Indicated:*		
Total Reserves minus Gold	1l. d	4,308	14,622	17,564	11,355	12,614	11,950	15,746	22,341	32,407	19,522	24,636	28,208	23,334	24,602	26,429
SDRs	1b. d	146	307	461	513	529	520	535	600	1,372	1,688	1,738	1,934	2,091	1,935	1,927
Reserve Position in the Fund	1c. d	973	532	620	639	739	804	1,329	1,615	2,139	1,477	1,331	1,558	2,071	2,303	2,219
Foreign Exchange	1d. d	3,188	13,783	16,483	10,203	11,347	10,627	13,883	20,126	28,896	16,357	21,567	24,716	19,172	20,364	22,283
Gold (Million Fine Troy Ounces)	1ad	15.22	19.42	21.10	21.11	21.11	21.11	21.11	21.62	23.97	24.23	24.23	24.23	24.23	24.23	24.23
Gold (National Valuation)	1and	533	680	802	891	905	865	858	919	1,093	1,117	1,082	987	935	888	831
Deposit Money Banks: Assets	7a. d	6,599	6,020	8,864	Ɪ17,110	20,610	20,360	21,647	21,694	33,691	45,435	65,666	84,607	90,949	109,063	126,921
Liabilities	7b. d	5,539	7,491	8,356	Ɪ13,620	24,950	26,690	29,037	28,581	39,013	50,485	80,209	100,391	100,018	106,645	127,046
Monetary Authorities																*Trillions of Yen:*
Foreign Assets (Net)	11	Ɪ1.68	4.58	5.43	3.55	3.97	3.73	4.82	6.69	6.96	3.45	5.27	5.32	4.76	5.17	5.47
Claims on Central Government	12a	2.57	1.82	1.22	1.74	4.05	7.49	7.29	6.90	8.73	9.09	10.25	13.35	14.72	14.57	14.50
Claims on Deposit Money Banks	12e	2.25	.62	2.79	6.24	5.80	4.03	4.38	5.15	5.42	5.46	5.25	2.24	3.43	5.97	5.35
Reserve Money	14	6.20	7.10	9.15	12.29	14.28	14.86	16.13	17.48	20.08	21.58	22.96	23.57	25.03	26.39	28.63
of which: Currency Outside DMBs	14a	5.10	5.96	7.71	9.11	10.73	11.58	12.86	14.12	16.26	17.05	17.48	18.58	19.78	20.58	22.11
Central Government Deposits	16d	.23	.31	.68	1.27	.93	.66	.76	1.01	1.42	1.88	.95	1.49	1.37	3.48	1.33
Other Items (Net)	17r	Ɪ.08	−.38	−.40	−2.03	−1.38	−.27	−.40	.24	Ɪ−.40	−5.46	−3.14	−4.15	−3.50	−4.16	−4.63
Deposit Money Banks																*Trillions of Yen:*
Reserves	20	1.10	1.14	1.45	3.18	3.55	3.28	3.28	3.36	3.82	4.53	5.48	4.99	5.26	5.81	6.51
Foreign Assets	21	2.38	1.85	2.73	3.08	4.03	3.99	4.40	4.45	5.00	6.17	10.93	12.83	14.24	17.09	17.92
Claims on Central Government	22a	.63	1.11	2.61	1.99	1.50	3.84	8.53	12.50	18.49	20.08	20.24	21.27	22.05	25.08	26.12
Claims on Local Government	22b	1.31	1.65	2.16	2.78	3.99	4.79	5.27	6.59	8.20	9.65	10.33	11.22	10.89	10.56	10.45
Claims on Nonfin.Pub.Enterprises	22c	1.38	1.86	1.99	2.33	2.59	2.99	3.70	4.26	4.94	6.12	7.08	8.71	9.55	10.46	11.24
Claims on Private Sector	22d	56.83	69.40	87.24	103.25	116.12	130.04	145.04	157.78	173.74	187.49	203.02	221.84	241.72	262.70	287.37
Demand Deposits	24	16.26	21.74	26.82	31.20	34.22	38.37	43.32	46.66	52.67	53.97	52.10	57.93	61.12	60.23	64.26
Time Deposits	25	32.88	39.71	49.51	57.88	64.54	75.38	86.07	97.25	109.79	122.70	137.42	152.70	165.68	182.78	195.43
Certificates of Deposit	26aa	—	—	—	—	—	—	—	—	—	1.29	2.00	2.84	3.88	5.11	7.91
Bonds	26ab	3.93	4.45	6.12	7.22	8.45	10.89	13.51	15.26	17.28	18.69	20.19	22.03	24.40	27.72	31.26
Foreign Liabilities	26c	1.99	2.31	2.57	4.15	7.60	8.14	8.74	8.27	8.60	10.34	18.87	21.13	23.32	25.43	30.05
Credit from Monetary Authorities	26g	2.25	.62	2.79	6.24	5.80	4.03	4.38	5.15	5.42	5.46	5.25	2.24	3.43	5.97	5.35
Other Items (Net)	27r	6.31	8.19	10.37	9.92	11.18	12.12	14.20	16.35	20.42	21.58	21.26	21.99	21.85	24.45	25.33
Monetary Survey																*Trillions of Yen:*
Foreign Assets (Net)	31n	Ɪ2.06	4.13	5.59	2.49	.40	−.42	.48	2.86	3.36	−.72	−2.67	−2.99	−4.32	−3.18	−6.67
Domestic Credit	32	62.50	75.53	94.54	110.82	127.33	148.49	169.07	187.02	212.67	230.55	249.97	274.90	297.55	319.88	348.34
Claims on Central Govt. (Net)	32an	2.98	2.62	3.15	2.46	4.62	10.67	15.06	18.39	25.80	27.28	29.54	33.13	35.39	36.16	39.29
Claims on Local Government	32b	1.31	1.65	2.16	2.78	3.99	4.79	5.27	6.59	8.20	9.65	10.33	11.22	10.89	10.56	10.45
Claims on Nonfin.Pub.Enterprises	32c	1.38	1.86	1.99	2.33	2.59	2.99	3.70	4.26	4.94	6.12	7.08	8.71	9.55	10.46	11.24
Claims on Private Sector	32d	56.83	69.40	87.24	103.25	116.12	130.04	145.04	157.78	173.74	187.49	203.02	221.84	241.72	262.70	287.37
Money	34	21.36	27.69	34.53	40.31	44.95	49.95	56.18	60.79	68.93	71.02	69.57	76.51	80.90	80.80	86.38
Quasi-Money	35	32.88	39.71	49.51	57.88	64.54	75.38	86.07	97.25	109.79	122.70	137.42	152.70	165.68	182.78	195.43
Certificates of Deposit	36aa	—	—	—	—	—	—	—	—	—	1.29	2.00	2.84	3.88	5.11	7.91
Bonds	36ab	3.93	4.45	6.12	7.22	8.45	10.89	13.51	15.26	17.28	18.69	20.19	22.03	24.40	27.72	31.26
Other Items (Net)	37r	Ɪ6.39	7.82	9.98	7.89	9.79	11.85	13.80	16.59	Ɪ20.03	16.13	18.12	17.84	18.36	20.28	20.70
Money plus Quasi-Money	35l	54.24	67.40	84.04	98.19	109.49	125.33	142.25	158.03	178.72	193.72	206.99	229.21	246.58	263.59	281.81
Other Banking Institutions																*Trillions of Yen:*
Cash	40	3.73	4.32	5.43	5.35	6.93	8.40	9.66	12.06	15.17	16.60	16.46	18.20	20.40	24.06	28.32
Claims on Central Government	42a	2.42	3.46	5.59	5.72	5.68	7.24	10.05	15.55	20.73	25.52	32.09	36.51	44.59	53.03	60.71
Claims on Local Government	42b	3.93	4.61	5.59	7.31	9.23	11.44	14.39	16.90	19.78	23.54	27.44	31.15	35.65	39.59	43.55
Claims on Nonfin.Pub.Enterprises	42c	3.66	4.63	5.78	7.81	10.14	12.99	15.90	18.52	21.98	24.63	28.09	31.09	34.58	37.11	39.83
Claims on Private Sector	42d	20.27	24.31	28.82	36.72	43.52	50.90	59.02	65.64	71.19	80.99	91.32	100.67	110.84	118.62	125.01
Demand and Time Deposits	45a	23.42	29.04	36.47	45.16	54.01	65.92	78.68	93.24	108.75	124.52	141.38	159.59	177.56	195.66	211.15
Trust Funds	46ab	5.39	6.59	8.42	9.99	11.65	13.59	16.09	18.76	21.58	24.43	26.96	30.91	36.00	40.32	46.12
Insurance Reserves	47d	2.41	2.88	3.50	4.29	5.22	6.37	7.73	9.23	10.86	12.68	14.70	16.96	19.50	22.22	25.00
Other Items (Net)	47r	2.80	2.81	2.83	3.47	4.62	5.10	6.52	7.46	7.65	9.65	12.35	10.16	13.00	14.20	15.09
Nonbank Financial Institutions																*Trillions of Yen:*
Cash	40.. s	.74	.85	1.11	1.22	1.56	1.73	2.07	2.69	3.48	3.94	4.33	4.75	5.57	6.62	8.61
Claims on Central Government	42a. s	.02	.03	.05	.05	.03	.19	.44	.50	.88	1.02	1.00	1.34	1.76	2.64	3.09
Claims on Local Government	42b. s	.06	.06	.07	.08	.13	.20	.30	.49	.74	1.11	1.41	1.49	1.72	1.75	1.80
Claims on Nonfin.Pub.Enterprises	42c. s	.52	.54	.60	.64	.72	.83	.95	1.20	1.46	1.65	1.75	1.93	2.37	2.79	3.17
Claims on Private Sector	42d. s	Ɪ5.76	7.25	8.63	10.41	12.05	13.97	15.95	17.72	19.01	20.99	24.50	27.60	30.03	32.11	34.30
Insurance Reserves	47d. s	6.64	7.97	9.44	10.96	12.82	15.01	17.52	20.13	23.04	26.57	30.56	35.04	40.13	45.67	52.22
Other Items (Net)	47r. s	.46	.75	1.01	1.43	1.67	1.92	2.17	2.47	2.53	2.14	2.43	2.06	1.31	.24	−1.24

1985	1986	1987	1988	1989	1990	1991	1992	1993	1994	1995	1996	1997	1998	1999		
															Exchange Rates	
End of Period																
220.23	194.61	175.20	169.36	188.52	191.21	179.09	171.53	153.63	145.61	152.86	166.80	175.34	162.77	140.27	Market Rate	aa
End of Period (ae) Period Average (rf)																
200.50	159.10	123.50	125.85	143.45	134.40	125.20	124.75	111.85	99.74	102.83	116.00	129.95	115.60	102.20	Market Rate	ae
238.54	168.52	144.64	128.15	137.96	144.79	134.71	126.65	111.20	102.21	94.06	108.78	120.99	130.91	113.91	Market Rate	rf
Period Averages																
39.5	55.8	64.8	73.0	67.9	64.9	69.5	73.9	84.3	91.6	100.0	86.0	77.4	71.7	82.0	Market Rate	ahx
48.8	62.4	67.8	75.1	71.8	64.7	70.2	73.6	88.3	95.2	100.0	86.8	81.7	76.5	89.4	Nominal Effective Exchange Rate	neu
55.5	70.2	73.7	78.1	74.4	66.9	71.5	74.4	90.3	96.1	100.0	84.9	78.8	71.8	....	Real Effective Exchange Rate	reu
															Fund Position	
End of Period																
4,223	4,223	4,223	4,223	4,223	4,223	4,223	8,242	8,242	8,242	8,242	8,242	8,242	8,242	13,313	Quota	2f.s
1,926	1,813	1,736	2,182	1,862	2,138	1,803	795	1,123	1,427	1,821	1,837	1,955	1,891	1,935	SDRs	1b.s
2,071	1,947	2,011	2,436	2,677	4,197	5,398	6,284	6,015	5,912	5,449	4,639	6,777	6,813	4,774	Reserve Position in the Fund	1c.s
663	487	294	154	134	1,866	3,000	2,985	2,985	2,913	1,137	—	—	508		*of which:* Outstg.Fund Borrowing	2c
															International Liquidity	
End of Period																
26,719	42,257	80,973	96,728	83,957	78,501	72,059	71,623	98,524	125,860	183,250	216,648	219,648	215,471	286,916	Total Reserves minus Gold	1l.d
2,116	2,218	2,463	2,936	2,447	3,042	2,579	1,094	1,543	2,083	2,707	2,642	2,638	2,663	2,656	SDRs	1b.d
2,275	2,382	2,853	3,278	3,518	5,971	7,722	8,641	8,261	8,631	8,100	6,671	9,144	9,593	6,552	Reserve Position in the Fund	1c.d
22,328	37,657	75,657	90,514	77,992	69,487	61,758	61,888	88,720	115,146	172,443	207,335	207,866	203,215	277,708	Foreign Exchange	1d.d
24.23	24.23	24.23	24.23	24.23	24.23	24.23	24.23	24.23	24.23	24.23	24.23	24.23	24.23	24.23	Gold (Million Fine Troy Ounces)	1ad
931	1,037	1,203	1,141	1,114	1,206	1,213	1,166	1,165	1,238	1,260	1,219	1,144	1,194	1,164	Gold (National Valuation)	1and
194,620	345,327	576,828	733,688	842,055	950,578	942,431	879,191	918,559	1,007,605	1,217,867	1,123,529	....	....	....	Deposit Money Banks: Assets	7a.d
179,306	345,987	592,027	772,423	879,721	958,478	845,674	708,623	688,436	723,697	738,324	695,848	....	....	....	Liabilities	7b.d
															Monetary Authorities	
End of Period																
5.87	6.70	11.82	11.78	8.86	7.63	4.11	3.40	6.73	7.25	11.54	17.49	16.86	14.47	21.56	Foreign Assets (Net)	11
12.83	11.30	12.28	12.12	13.27	21.33	15.27	19.13	21.40	21.98	25.08	31.30	32.87	37.93	50.06	Claims on Central Government	12a
9.01	10.62	10.82	11.68	15.68	12.89	20.76	20.01	14.13	12.92	11.62	9.91	13.80	15.28	14.60	Claims on Deposit Money Banks	12e
29.71	32.12	34.92	39.46	44.57	47.86	47.19	45.40	48.03	49.44	53.32	57.84	62.09	64.42	89.59	Reserve Money	14
23.41	26.20	28.58	31.52	36.68	37.25	37.97	38.10	40.85	42.35	46.23	49.08	52.73	54.31	59.40	*of which:* Currency Outside DMBs	14a
2.52	1.41	6.07	5.03	2.25	2.02	3.14	5.61	1.97	5.03	5.85	7.64	3.79	7.65	8.08	Central Government Deposits	16d
-4.52	-4.90	-6.07	-8.92	-9.01	-8.03	-10.21	-8.47	-7.73	-12.31	-10.93	-6.77	-2.35	-4.40	-11.45	Other Items (Net)	17r
															Deposit Money Banks	
End of Period																
6.30	5.92	6.34	7.94	7.89	10.61	9.22	7.29	7.18	7.09	7.09	8.75	9.36	10.11	30.19	Reserves	20
25.33	36.02	48.35	63.79	81.62	96.68	86.51	77.99	102.29	98.89	110.01	104.51	128.73	109.07	77.75	Foreign Assets	21
27.91	31.12	34.26	38.71	41.48	40.02	36.74	40.25	42.89	40.14	38.50	37.04	37.68	44.39	67.07	Claims on Central Government	22a
10.51	10.47	10.54	10.26	10.75	10.73	10.98	12.01	14.95	17.38	19.78	20.72	21.39	23.75	24.79	Claims on Local Government	22b
11.71	13.09	13.69	13.95	13.88	14.12	14.04	13.58	13.47	12.55	11.57	10.06	9.01	8.34	8.06	Claims on Nonfin.Pub.Enterprises	22c
318.50	348.73	387.70	430.13	480.17	524.38	552.11	564.98	558.67	559.81	569.20	575.88	578.79	583.35	570.91	Claims on Private Sector	22d
65.57	72.02	74.39	80.32	77.79	82.37	93.07	98.04	104.77	109.31	125.11	139.06	151.55	160.09	180.13	Demand Deposits	24
217.82	237.09	269.72	297.53	343.15	375.38	376.48	370.66	372.57	382.44	377.04	373.00	374.11	387.86	383.27	Time Deposits	25
8.14	8.58	8.17	10.36	12.40	9.96	8.82	8.69	8.65	7.32	10.22	14.16	19.10	19.23	15.21	Certificates of Deposit	26aa
33.69	37.82	39.94	44.14	47.43	55.30	61.86	65.89	64.39	63.90	62.22	62.10	53.56	43.31	43.13	Bonds	26ab
40.89	59.60	80.04	97.18	116.31	134.83	108.48	89.01	77.24	71.58	75.53	80.07	92.26	80.18	54.54	Foreign Liabilities	26c
9.01	10.62	10.82	11.68	15.68	12.89	20.76	20.01	14.13	12.92	11.62	9.91	13.80	15.28	14.60	Credit from Monetary Authorities	26g
25.14	19.63	17.79	23.56	23.02	25.81	40.15	63.81	97.69	88.38	94.19	78.67	80.58	76.73	89.11	Other Items (Net)	27r
															Monetary Survey	
End of Period																
-9.70	-16.88	-19.88	-21.61	-25.83	-30.52	-17.86	-7.62	31.78	34.56	46.01	41.94	53.33	43.36	44.77	Foreign Assets (Net)	31n
378.94	413.31	452.40	500.13	557.29	608.57	626.01	644.34	649.41	646.82	658.28	667.36	675.96	690.11	712.82	Domestic Credit	32
38.22	41.02	40.48	45.80	52.50	59.34	48.88	53.77	62.32	57.09	57.73	60.70	66.76	74.67	109.06	Claims on Central Govt. (Net)	32an
10.51	10.47	10.54	10.26	10.75	10.73	10.98	12.01	14.95	17.38	19.78	20.72	21.39	23.75	24.79	Claims on Local Government	32b
11.71	13.09	13.69	13.95	13.88	14.12	14.04	13.58	13.47	12.55	11.57	10.06	9.01	8.34	8.06	Claims on Nonfin.Pub.Enterprises	32c
318.50	348.73	387.70	430.13	480.17	524.38	552.11	564.98	558.67	559.81	569.20	575.88	578.79	583.35	570.91	Claims on Private Sector	32d
88.98	98.21	102.97	111.84	114.47	119.63	131.04	136.14	145.61	151.67	171.54	188.15	204.28	214.40	239.54	Money	34
217.82	237.09	269.72	297.53	343.15	375.38	376.48	370.66	372.57	382.44	377.04	373.00	374.11	387.86	383.27	Quasi-Money	35
8.14	8.58	8.17	10.36	12.40	9.96	8.82	8.69	8.65	7.32	10.22	14.16	19.10	19.23	15.21	Certificates of Deposit	36aa
33.69	37.82	39.94	44.14	47.43	55.30	61.86	65.89	64.39	63.90	62.22	62.10	53.56	43.31	43.13	Bonds	36ab
20.61	14.72	11.72	14.65	14.01	17.78	29.94	55.34	89.96	76.07	83.27	71.90	78.23	72.34	77.66	Other Items (Net)	37r
306.80	335.31	372.70	409.38	457.62	495.01	507.53	506.79	518.19	534.10	548.59	561.14	578.39	602.26	622.80	Money plus Quasi-Money	35l
															Other Banking Institutions	
End of Period																
31.82	40.35	46.95	53.30	55.14	56.73	65.19	76.47	82.85	76.56	82.47	87.21	84.43	....	....	Cash	40
71.90	83.82	90.68	94.40	97.70	93.59	103.51	111.09	117.65	126.45	142.11	151.55	170.24	....	....	Claims on Central Government	42a
46.78	49.80	53.19	57.44	60.41	62.97	66.01	69.31	74.34	82.91	89.40	100.50	110.58	....	....	Claims on Local Government	42b
40.20	42.25	29.35	29.79	31.52	33.43	36.62	39.17	43.44	47.27	50.76	54.46	57.78	....	....	Claims on Nonfin.Pub.Enterprises	42c
132.22	143.79	177.81	204.74	226.60	249.06	265.12	289.22	307.76	324.62	327.79	339.87	332.09	....	....	Claims on Private Sector	42d
229.72	250.76	269.78	289.98	317.64	336.34	371.75	401.74	430.84	456.40	479.69	502.71	531.44	....	....	Demand and Time Deposits	45a
54.06	67.21	84.22	98.50	116.38	124.10	129.05	138.86	147.58	153.18	150.65	155.69	153.94	....	....	Trust Funds	46ab
27.98	31.29	35.31	39.93	44.78	49.94	55.56	62.81	71.34	79.86	88.88	88.16	95.68	....	....	Insurance Reserves	47d
11.16	10.75	8.68	11.26	-7.43	-14.79	-19.91	-18.16	-23.73	-31.64	-26.70	-12.97	-25.93	....	....	Other Items (Net)	47r
															Nonbank Financial Institutions	
End of Period																
11.34	10.29	11.03	11.95	12.36	19.45	22.14	24.62	27.30	30.88	33.05	27.86	33.77	....	....	Cash	40..s
3.86	5.20	5.60	7.13	6.86	5.36	6.14	10.39	14.86	20.86	29.58	29.72	31.36	....	....	Claims on Central Government	42a.s
1.79	2.07	2.35	2.02	1.89	2.08	2.09	2.19	2.98	4.44	6.78	7.90	8.79	....	....	Claims on Local Government	42b.s
3.46	4.07	3.38	2.56	2.78	3.30	3.42	4.38	3.62	4.42	4.44	4.83	5.20	....	....	Claims on Nonfin.Pub.Enterprises	42c.s
37.04	39.77	48.89	60.06	73.60	89.13	100.04	105.59	111.33	114.86	112.66	120.58	108.74	....	....	Claims on Private Sector	42d.s
60.69	73.50	87.58	106.50	126.94	144.16	157.62	171.50	186.38	199.49	210.48	226.01	230.02	....	....	Insurance Reserves	47d.s
-3.20	-12.11	-16.34	-22.78	-29.45	-24.85	-23.79	-24.34	-26.30	-24.04	-23.99	-35.12	-42.17	....	....	Other Items (Net)	47r.s

Japan

158		1970	1971	1972	1973	1974	1975	1976	1977	1978	1979	1980	1981	1982	1983	1984
Financial Survey																*Trillions of Yen:*
Foreign Assets (Net)	**51n**	2.06	4.13	5.59	2.49	.40	–.42	.48	2.86	3.36	–.72	–2.67	–2.99	–4.32	–3.18	–6.67
Domestic Credit	**52**	99.14	120.41	149.67	179.55	208.83	246.25	286.06	323.54	368.43	409.99	457.56	506.68	559.08	607.51	659.80
Claims on Central Govt. (Net)	**52an**	5.42	6.11	8.79	8.23	10.33	18.10	25.55	34.44	47.41	53.82	62.63	70.98	81.74	91.82	103.10
Claims on Local Government	**52b**	5.29	6.32	7.82	10.17	13.36	16.43	19.96	23.98	28.71	34.29	39.18	43.87	48.25	51.90	55.80
Claims on Nonfin.Pub.Enterprises	**52c**	5.56	7.03	8.37	10.77	13.46	16.81	20.55	23.98	28.37	32.40	36.92	41.73	46.50	50.36	54.23
Claims on Private Sector	**52d**	82.87	100.95	124.69	150.37	171.69	194.91	220.01	241.14	263.94	289.48	318.83	350.10	382.59	413.43	446.67
Liquid Liabilities	**55l**	74.89	92.74	115.73	139.02	158.67	185.19	213.63	242.07	275.57	306.50	337.43	376.89	411.56	443.74	477.58
Bonds and Trust Funds	**56ab**	9.32	11.04	14.53	17.21	20.09	24.48	29.60	34.03	38.86	43.12	47.15	52.95	60.41	68.04	77.38
Insurance Reserves	**57d**	9.05	10.85	12.93	15.25	18.04	21.38	25.24	29.35	33.90	39.25	45.26	52.00	59.63	67.89	77.22
Other Items (Net)	**57r**	7.94	9.91	12.06	10.55	12.44	14.79	18.07	20.97	23.46	20.41	25.06	21.86	23.16	24.65	20.91
Interest Rates																*Percent Per Annum*
Discount Rate *(End of Period)*	**60**	6.00	4.75	4.25	9.00	9.00	6.50	6.50	4.25	3.50	6.25	7.25	5.50	5.50	5.00	5.00
Money Market Rate	**60b**	8.28	6.41	4.72	7.16	12.54	10.67	6.98	5.68	4.36	5.86	10.93	7.43	6.94	6.39	6.10
Private Bill Rate	**60bs**	....	....	....	....	....	....	....	....	....	....	....	7.69	7.12	6.72	6.32
Deposit Rate	**60l**	4.00	4.00	3.88	4.00	5.33	5.33	4.50	3.83	2.69	3.31	5.50	4.44	3.75	3.75	3.50
Lending Rate	**60p**	7.66	7.59	7.05	7.19	9.11	9.10	8.26	7.56	6.42	6.37	8.35	7.86	7.31	7.13	6.75
Government Bond Yield	**61**	7.19	7.28	6.70	7.26	9.26	9.20	8.72	7.33	6.09	7.69	9.22	8.66	8.06	7.42	6.81
Prices, Production, Labor																*Index Numbers (1995=100):*
Share Prices	**62**	11.8	13.0	20.5	26.3	22.3	22.6	25.2	27.3	30.1	32.6	34.3	39.9	39.8	46.9	59.1
Wholesale Prices	**63**	58.1	57.7	58.2	67.4	88.5	91.2	95.9	97.7	95.2	102.1	120.3	121.9	124.1	121.4	121.1
Consumer Prices	**64**	I 32.3	34.3	36.0	40.2	49.5	55.3	60.5	65.5	68.2	70.8	76.3	80.0	82.2	83.8	85.7
Wages: Monthly Earnings	**65**	I 18.4	21.1	24.4	29.0	36.2	42.7	48.0	52.5	56.2	59.4	62.9	66.1	69.4	71.6	74.0
Industrial Production	**66..c**	47.7	49.0	52.5	60.4	58.1	51.6	57.3	59.7	63.5	68.2	71.4	72.1	72.4	74.5	81.5
Mfg. Employment	**67ey c**	104.1	104.8	102.8	103.1	102.7	97.3	95.3	94.5	92.4	91.9	I 92.9	93.8	94.3	94.0	95.1
																Number in Thousands:
Labor Force	**67d**	....	....	....	....	....	....	....	....	....	....	....	....	....	....	....
Employment	**67e**	....	....	....	....	....	....	....	....	....	....	....	....	....	....	....
Unemployment	**67c**	....	....	....	....	....	....	....	....	....	....	....	....	....	....	....
Unemployment Rate (%)	**67r**	....	....	....	....	....	....	....	....	....	....	....	....	....	....	....
International Transactions																*Billions of Yen*
Exports	**70**	6,954	8,393	8,806	10,031	16,220	16,572	19,930	21,648	20,526	22,532	29,382	33,469	34,433	34,910	40,325
Imports, c.i.f.	**71**	6,797	6,910	7,229	10,404	18,067	17,175	19,229	19,132	16,728	24,245	31,995	31,464	32,656	30,015	32,320
																1995=100
Volume of Exports	**72**	22.4	26.6	28.2	30.2	36.4	36.3	44.0	47.7	48.0	48.1	56.4	62.3	60.9	I 66.2	76.7
Volume of Imports	**73**	25.5	25.4	29.0	37.8	37.5	33.0	35.9	36.8	39.3	43.7	41.5	40.6	40.4	I 40.9	45.2
Unit Value of Exports	**74**	74.2	75.7	74.7	79.3	106.5	109.0	108.3	108.6	102.5	111.9	124.7	128.4	135.1	I 126.0	125.8
Unit Value of Imports	**75**	84.2	85.6	78.6	86.8	151.9	164.2	168.1	163.0	133.8	174.1	241.9	243.1	253.7	230.3	224.0
Export Prices	**76**	105.9	104.4	101.1	111.4	149.1	143.1	142.1	135.4	126.4	140.2	152.2	154.0	160.0	150.5	151.4
Import Prices	**76.x**	68.0	68.0	65.0	78.9	132.3	142.0	149.4	142.6	117.6	151.4	219.1	222.7	240.2	221.5	214.0
Balance of Payments																*Billions of US Dollars:*
Current Account, n.i.e.	**78al d**	....	....	....	....	....	....	....	10.91	16.53	–8.74	–10.75	4.77	6.85	20.80	35.00
Goods: Exports f.o.b.	**78aa d**	....	....	....	....	....	....	....	79.16	95.32	101.12	126.74	149.52	137.66	145.47	168.29
Goods: Imports f.o.b.	**78ab d**	....	....	....	....	....	....	....	–62.00	–71.02	–99.38	–124.61	–129.56	–119.58	–114.01	–124.03
Trade Balance	**78ac d**	....	....	....	....	....	....	....	17.16	24.30	1.74	2.13	19.96	18.08	31.46	44.26
Services: Credit	**78ad d**	....	....	....	....	....	....	....	11.77	13.55	16.01	20.24	23.83	22.56	21.81	23.12
Services: Debit	**78ae d**	....	....	....	....	....	....	....	–17.68	–21.51	–27.35	–32.36	–36.59	–34.01	–33.86	–35.02
Balance on Goods & Services	**78af d**	....	....	....	....	....	....	....	11.25	16.34	–9.60	–9.99	7.20	6.63	19.41	32.36
Income: Credit	**78ag d**	....	....	....	....	....	....	....	3.82	5.41	9.13	11.25	15.95	18.53	15.78	18.98
Income: Debit	**78ah d**	....	....	....	....	....	....	....	–3.76	–4.54	–7.15	–10.48	–16.76	–16.93	–12.84	–14.83
Balance on Gds, Serv. & Inc.	**78ai d**	....	....	....	....	....	....	....	11.31	17.21	–7.62	–9.22	6.39	8.23	22.35	36.51
Current Transfers, n.i.e.: Credit	**78aj d**	....	....	....	....	....	....	....	.26	.30	.37	.39	.44	.47	.48	.56
Current Transfers: Debit	**78ak d**	....	....	....	....	....	....	....	–.66	–.98	–1.49	–1.92	–2.06	–1.85	–2.03	–2.07
Capital Account, n.i.e.	**78bc d**	....	....	....	....	....	....	....	—	—	—	—	—	—	—	—
Capital Account, n.i.e.: Credit	**78ba d**	....	....	....	....	....	....	....	—	—	—	—	—	—	—	—
Capital Account: Debit	**78bb d**	....	....	....	....	....	....	....	—	—	—	—	—	—	—	—
Financial Account, n.i.e.	**78bj d**	....	....	....	....	....	....	....	–4.96	–6.70	–6.82	18.88	–1.56	–16.20	–21.32	–36.57
Direct Investment Abroad	**78bd d**	....	....	....	....	....	....	....	–1.65	–2.37	–2.90	–2.39	–4.90	–4.54	–3.61	–5.96
Dir. Invest. in Rep. Econ., n.i.e.	**78be d**	....	....	....	....	....	....	....	.02	.01	.24	.28	.19	.44	.41	–.01
Portfolio Investment Assets	**78bf d**	....	....	....	....	....	....	....	–1.72	–5.30	–5.87	–3.75	–8.77	–9.74	–16.02	–30.63
Equity Securities	**78bk d**	....	....	....	....	....	....	....	–.01	–.12	–.58	.21	–.24	–.15	–.66	–.05
Debt Securities	**78bl d**	....	....	....	....	....	....	....	–1.71	–5.18	–5.29	–3.96	–8.53	–9.59	–15.36	–30.58
Portfolio Investment Liab., n.i.e.	**78bg d**	....	....	....	....	....	....	....	2.36	2.49	4.28	13.11	13.22	11.86	14.15	7.03
Equity Securities	**78bm d**	....	....	....	....	....	....	....	–.78	–.81	.33	6.55	5.92	2.55	6.13	–3.61
Debt Securities	**78bn d**	....	....	....	....	....	....	....	3.14	3.30	3.95	6.56	7.30	9.31	8.02	10.64
Financial Derivatives Assets	**78bw d**	....	....	....	....	....	....	....	....	....	....	....	....	....	....	....
Financial Derivatives Liabilities	**78bx d**	....	....	....	....	....	....	....	....	....	....	....	....	....	....	....
Other Investment Assets	**78bh d**	....	....	....	....	....	....	....	–2.13	–13.65	–16.18	–20.14	–25.53	–14.64	–24.41	–29.33
Monetary Authorities	**78bo d**	....	....	....	....	....	....	....	....	....	....	....	....	....	....	....
General Government	**78bp d**	....	....	....	....	....	....	....	–1.78	–2.78	–2.71	–2.70	–3.66	–3.52	–3.61	–3.42
Banks	**78bq d**	....	....	....	....	....	....	....	1.41	–9.88	–12.44	–16.05	–17.46	–4.69	–15.64	–14.48
Other Sectors	**78br d**	....	....	....	....	....	....	....	–1.76	–.99	–1.03	–1.39	–4.41	–6.43	–5.16	–11.43
Other Investment Liab., n.i.e.	**78bi d**	....	....	....	....	....	....	....	–1.84	12.12	13.61	31.77	24.23	.42	8.16	22.33
Monetary Authorities	**78bs d**	....	....	....	....	....	....	....	.74	2.12	–.23	1.02	–.24	.21	.31	.79
General Government	**78bt d**	....	....	....	....	....	....	....	–.04	–.03	–1.04	–.04	–.04	–.03	–.03	–.02
Banks	**78bu d**	....	....	....	....	....	....	....	–1.50	8.40	12.13	28.81	22.18	1.34	7.90	23.33
Other Sectors	**78bv d**	....	....	....	....	....	....	....	–1.04	1.63	2.75	1.98	2.33	–1.10	–.02	–1.77
Net Errors and Omissions	**78ca d**	....	....	....	....	....	....	....	.54	.13	2.42	–3.10	.43	4.65	2.07	3.69
Overall Balance	**78cb d**	....	....	....	....	....	....	....	6.49	9.96	–13.14	5.03	3.64	–4.70	1.55	2.12
Reserves and Related Items	**79da d**	....	....	....	....	....	....	....	–6.49	–9.96	13.14	–5.03	–3.64	4.70	–1.55	–2.12
Reserve Assets	**79db d**	....	....	....	....	....	....	....	–6.49	–9.96	13.14	–5.03	–3.64	4.70	–1.55	–2.12
Use of Fund Credit and Loans	**79dc d**	....	....	....	....	....	....	....	—	—	—	—	—	—	—	—
Exceptional Financing	**79de d**	....	....	....	....	....	....	....	....	....	....	....	....	....	....	....

	1985	1986	1987	1988	1989	1990	1991	1992	1993	1994	1995	1996	1997	1998	1999		
End of Period																**Financial Survey**	
	-9.70	-16.88	-19.88	-21.61	-25.83	-30.52	-17.86	-7.62	31.78	34.56	46.01	41.94	53.33	43.36	44.77	Foreign Assets (Net)	51n
	716.19	784.07	863.64	958.27	1,058.65	1,147.49	1,208.95	1,275.67	1,325.38	1,372.64	1,421.79	1,476.78	1,500.72	....	....	Domestic Credit	52
	113.98	130.04	136.75	147.33	157.06	158.29	158.53	175.25	194.82	204.40	229.42	241.97	268.36	....	....	Claims on Central Govt. (Net)	52an
	59.08	62.34	66.08	69.73	73.04	75.78	79.08	83.51	92.27	104.72	115.95	129.13	140.75	....	....	Claims on Local Government	52b
	55.37	59.41	46.41	46.29	48.18	50.85	54.08	57.12	60.53	64.24	66.77	69.35	71.99	....	....	Claims on Nonfin.Pub.Enterprises	52c
	487.77	532.28	614.40	694.93	780.37	862.57	917.27	959.79	977.75	999.29	1,009.65	1,036.33	1,019.62	....	....	Claims on Private Sector	52d
	519.33	567.36	619.43	675.85	756.28	806.12	847.89	868.82	900.42	945.09	976.19	1,019.37	1,065.51	....	....	Liquid Liabilities	55l
	87.75	105.03	124.16	142.64	163.81	179.40	190.91	204.76	211.97	217.08	212.87	217.79	207.51	....	....	Bonds and Trust Funds	56ab
	88.66	104.79	122.89	146.43	171.72	194.10	213.18	234.31	257.73	279.35	299.37	314.17	325.70	....	....	Insurance Reserves	57d
	10.75	-9.99	-22.70	-28.26	-58.99	-62.65	-60.89	-39.84	-12.96	-34.33	-20.64	-32.62	-44.65	....	....	Other Items (Net)	57r
Percent Per Annum																**Interest Rates**	
	5.00	3.00	2.50	2.50	4.25	6.00	4.50	3.25	1.75	1.75	.50	.50	.50	.50	.50	Discount Rate *(End of Period)*	60
	6.46	4.79	3.51	3.62	4.87	I 7.24	7.46	4.58	I 3.06	2.20	1.21	.47	.48	.37	.06	Money Market Rate	60b
	6.70	4.99	3.88	4.08	5.37	7.67	I 7.31	4.40	2.97	2.24	1.22	.59	.62	.72	.15	Private Bill Rate	60bs
	3.50	2.32	1.76	1.76	1.97	3.56	I 4.14	I 3.35	2.14	1.70	.90	.30	.30	.27	.12	Deposit Rate	60l
	6.60	6.02	5.21	5.03	5.29	6.95	7.53	6.15	I 4.41	4.13	3.40	2.66	2.45	2.32	2.16	Lending Rate	60p
	6.34	4.94	4.21	4.27	5.05	7.36	6.53	4.94	3.69	3.71	2.53	2.23	1.69	1.10	I 1.77	Government Bond Yield	61
Period Averages																**Prices, Production, Labor**	
	72.2	95.9	141.8	154.4	186.1	158.0	133.4	98.8	110.4	115.8	100.0	116.3	101.0	85.4	100.4	Share Prices	62
	119.7	108.8	104.7	103.6	106.3	108.5	108.7	I 107.1	103.0	100.9	I 100.0	100.1	101.6	100.0	96.7	Wholesale Prices	63
	87.4	88.0	88.1	88.7	90.7	93.4	96.5	98.2	99.4	I 100.1	100.0	100.1	101.8	102.5	102.2	Consumer Prices	64
	76.4	78.6	80.2	83.0	85.6	88.9	91.9	93.9	95.7	97.9	100.0	101.9	103.4	103.1	103.6	Wages: Monthly Earnings	65
	84.6	84.4	87.2	95.6	101.2	105.3	107.2	100.6	96.1	96.7	100.0	102.9	I 107.3	99.7	100.1	Industrial Production	66..c
	I 96.6	97.2	95.9	96.9	99.1	101.7	104.2	104.9	104.2	101.8	100.0	97.7	96.9	95.6	93.1	Mfg. Employment	67ey c
Period Averages																	
	....	....	....	....	....	....	....	....	66,140	66,440	66,670	67,110	67,870	67,930	....	Labor Force	67d
	58,070	58,530	59,110	60,110	61,280	62,490	63,690	64,360	64,500	64,530	64,570	64,860	65,570	65,140	64,623	Employment	67e
	1,560	1,670	1,730	1,550	1,420	1,340	1,360	1,420	1,656	1,920	2,098	2,250	2,303	2,787	3,171	Unemployment	67c
	2.6	2.8	2.8	2.5	2.3	2.1	2.1	2.2	2.5	2.9	3.2	3.4	3.4	4.1	4.7	Unemployment Rate (%)	67r
Billions of Yen																**International Transactions**	
	41,959	35,291	33,316	33,928	37,823	41,457	42,359	43,011	40,200	40,470	41,532	44,729	50,938	50,644	47,549	Exports	70
	31,076	21,551	21,739	24,007	28,981	33,854	31,900	29,527	26,824	28,051	31,534	37,992	40,956	36,653	35,270	Imports, c.i.f.	71
1995=100																	
	80.9	80.5	I 80.7	85.5	89.2	93.8	96.2	97.6	95.2	96.9	100.0	100.6	I 110.2	108.7	111.1	Volume of Exports	72
	45.6	50.0	I 54.6	64.4	69.5	73.4	76.4	76.1	78.2	88.9	100.0	103.4	I 106.2	100.5	110.2	Volume of Imports	73
	124.9	105.7	I 99.3	95.6	102.2	106.3	106.0	106.0	101.6	100.7	100.0	107.0	I 111.3	112.1	103.1	Unit Value of Exports	74
	I 216.0	136.7	I 126.1	118.2	132.3	146.2	132.4	123.1	108.9	100.3	100.0	116.4	I 122.3	115.6	101.5	Unit Value of Imports	75
	149.2	I 126.7	120.3	117.6	122.7	125.3	118.6	114.3	105.2	102.2	I 100.0	104.8	106.7	108.2	97.2	Export Prices	76
	208.7	I 133.9	123.0	117.4	126.1	137.1	125.9	118.2	105.9	100.1	I 100.0	109.7	117.9	112.1	101.7	Import Prices	76.x
Minus Sign Indicates Debit																Balance of Payments	
	51.13	85.88	84.35	79.25	63.21	44.08	68.20	112.57	131.64	130.26	111.04	65.88	94.35	120.70	106.87	Current Account, n.i.e.	78al *d*
	175.46	206.42	225.51	260.88	270.99	282.31	308.17	332.56	352.66	385.70	428.72	400.28	409.24	374.04	403.69	Goods: Exports f.o.b.	78aa *d*
	-120.17	-115.23	-133.93	-168.64	-190.87	-213.02	-212.08	-207.79	-213.24	-241.51	-296.93	-316.72	-307.64	-251.66	-280.37	Goods: Imports f.o.b.	78ab *d*
	55.29	91.19	91.58	92.24	80.12	69.28	96.08	124.76	139.42	144.19	131.79	83.56	101.60	122.39	123.32	*Trade Balance*	78ac *d*
	21.65	23.25	28.94	35.37	40.26	41.38	44.84	49.07	53.22	58.30	65.27	67.72	69.30	62.41	61.00	Services: Credit	78ad *d*
	-31.25	-36.22	-49.33	-65.62	-76.96	-84.28	-86.63	-93.03	-96.30	-106.36	-122.63	-129.96	-123.45	-111.83	-115.16	Services: Debit	78ae *d*
	45.69	78.22	71.19	61.99	43.42	26.39	54.29	80.80	96.33	96.13	74.43	21.32	47.45	72.97	69.16	*Balance on Goods & Services*	78af *d*
	22.31	29.26	49.41	75.11	102.23	122.64	140.93	142.87	147.83	155.19	192.45	225.10	222.15	209.58	188.27	Income: Credit	78ag *d*
	-15.57	-19.93	-33.07	-54.49	-79.27	-100.15	-114.97	-107.27	-107.42	-114.96	-148.16	-171.55	-166.41	-153.01	-138.43	Income: Debit	78ah *d*
	52.43	87.55	87.53	82.61	66.39	48.88	80.24	116.41	136.74	136.36	118.72	74.88	103.19	129.54	119.00	*Balance on Gds, Serv. & Inc.*	78ai *d*
	.58	.56	.82	1.36	1.30	1.29	1.42	1.67	1.58	1.83	1.98	6.04	6.01	5.53	6.21	Current Transfers, n.i.e.: Credit	78aj *d*
	-1.88	-2.24	-4.00	-4.73	-4.47	-6.09	-13.46	-5.50	-6.68	-7.94	-9.66	-15.04	-14.84	-14.37	-18.35	Current Transfers: Debit	78ak *d*
	-.42	-.49	-.77	-1.01	-1.39	-1.06	-1.20	-1.30	-1.46	-1.85	-2.23	-3.29	-4.05	-14.45	-16.47	Capital Account, n.i.e.	78bc *d*
	—	—	—	—	—	—	—	—	—	—	.01	1.22	1.51	1.57	.75	Capital Account, n.i.e.: Credit	78ba *d*
	-.42	-.49	-.77	-1.01	-1.39	-1.06	-1.20	-1.30	-1.46	-1.85	-2.24	-4.51	-5.57	-16.02	-17.21	Capital Account: Debit	78bb *d*
	-55.20	-72.89	-41.36	-64.36	-53.31	-30.71	-67.66	-100.28	-102.21	-85.11	-63.98	-28.10	-118.05	-116.76	-31.11	Financial Account, n.i.e.	78bj *d*
	-6.49	-14.67	-20.30	-35.46	-46.02	-50.50	-31.62	-17.39	-13.83	-18.09	-22.51	-23.44	-26.06	-24.62	-22.27	Direct Investment Abroad	78bd *d*
	.64	.23	1.16	-.48	-1.04	1.78	1.29	2.76	.12	.91	.04	.20	3.20	3.27	12.31	Dir. Invest. in Rep. Econ., n.i.e.	78be *d*
	-60.68	-105.60	-95.74	-98.17	-114.21	-37.80	-81.63	-33.95	-63.74	-91.97	-86.05	-100.62	-47.06	-95.24	-154.41	Portfolio Investment Assets	78bf *d*
	-1.00	-7.07	-16.95	-2.98	-17.96	-6.24	-3.63	2.98	-15.28	-14.00	.07	-8.18	-13.73	-14.00	-32.40	Equity Securities	78bk *d*
	-59.68	-98.54	-78.80	-95.19	-96.25	-31.56	-78.00	-36.93	-48.46	-77.97	-86.11	-92.44	-33.34	-81.24	-122.01	Debt Securities	78bl *d*
	17.99	1.69	-11.38	21.81	97.00	46.68	127.34	9.57	-6.11	64.53	59.79	66.81	79.19	56.06	126.93	Portfolio Investment Liab., n.i.e.	78bg *d*
	-.67	-15.71	-43.55	6.82	6.95	-13.36	46.62	8.88	19.86	48.95	50.60	49.46	27.00	16.11	103.89	Equity Securities	78bm *d*
	18.66	17.39	32.18	14.99	90.06	60.04	80.72	.70	-25.97	15.58	9.19	17.35	52.19	39.95	23.04	Debt Securities	78bn *d*
	....	....	....	....	....	....	-.03	-.61	-.49	.43	-1.20	-13.96	-24.16	-18.49	-12.43	Financial Derivatives Assets	78bw *d*
	....	....	....	....	....	....	-1.29	-1.97	-.54	-.20	-9.12	6.63	20.77	17.64	17.53	Financial Derivatives Liabilities	78bx *d*
	—	—	—	—	—	—	26.46	46.56	15.07	-35.12	-102.24	5.22	-191.96	37.94	266.34	Other Investment Assets	78bh *d*
	....	....	....	....	....	....	....	....	....	....	....	....	....	....	....	Monetary Authorities	78bo *d*
	....	....	....	....	....	....	-12.56	-9.51	-7.80	-8.76	-8.66	-5.28	-9.12	-15.50	-11.56	General Government	78bp *d*
	....	....	....	....	....	....	37.03	49.64	27.73	-10.67	-85.62	75.56	-140.18	54.14	239.40	Banks	78bq *d*
	....	....	....	....	....	....	1.99	6.42	-4.85	-15.69	-7.96	-65.07	-42.66	-.70	38.50	Other Sectors	78br *d*
	-6.68	45.47	84.90	47.94	10.98	9.12	-108.19	-105.24	-32.70	-5.60	97.30	31.07	68.03	-93.33	-265.12	Other Investment Liab., n.i.e.	78bi *d*
	—	—	—	—	—	—	—	—	—	—	—	—	—	—	—	Monetary Authorities	78bs *d*
	....	....	....	....	....	....	-2.16	1.28	-.10	-2.00	1.18	-2.13	-.11	-1.30	.55	General Government	78bt *d*
	....	....	....	....	....	....	-126.97	-119.86	-37.90	4.87	17.27	-9.06	43.34	-23.75	-189.16	Banks	78bu *d*
	....	....	....	....	....	....	20.94	13.34	5.30	-8.47	78.86	42.26	24.80	-68.28	-76.50	Other Sectors	78bv *d*
	4.02	2.62	-4.17	3.68	-21.57	-21.40	-7.73	-10.38	-.50	-18.03	13.78	.64	34.31	4.36	16.97	Net Errors and Omissions	78ca *d*
	-.50	15.13	38.05	17.56	-13.05	-9.09	-8.39	.62	27.47	25.27	58.61	35.14	6.57	-6.16	76.26	*Overall Balance*	78cb *d*
	.50	-15.12	-38.05	-17.57	13.06	9.09	8.39	-.62	-27.47	-25.27	-58.61	-35.14	-6.57	6.16	-76.26	Reserves and Related Items	79da *d*
	.50	-15.12	-38.05	-17.57	13.06	9.09	8.39	-.62	-27.47	-25.27	-58.61	-35.14	-6.57	6.16	-76.26	Reserve Assets	79db *d*
	—	—	—	—	—	—	—	—	—	—	—	—	—	—	—	Use of Fund Credit and Loans	79dc *d*
	....	....	....	....	....	....	....	....	....	....	....	....	....	....	....	Exceptional Financing	79de *d*

Japan

		1970	1971	1972	1973	1974	1975	1976	1977	1978	1979	1980	1981	1982	1983	1984
International Investment Position																*Billions of US Dollars*
Assets	79aa d	...	...	...	...	...	...	...	...	...	...	159.65	210.06	228.50	271.78	341.04
Direct Investment Abroad	79ab d	...	...	...	...	...	...	...	...	...	...	19.61	24.51	28.97	32.18	37.92
Portfolio Investment	79ac d	...	...	...	...	...	...	...	...	...	...	21.44	31.54	40.07	56.12	87.58
Equity Securities	79ad d	...	...	...	...	...	...	...	...	...	...	...	...	...	...	...
Debt Securities	79ae d	...	...	...	...	...	...	...	...	...	...	...	...	...	...	...
Financial Derivatives	79al d	...	...	...	...	...	...	...	...	...	...	...	...	...	...	...
Other Investment	79af d	...	...	...	...	...	...	...	...	...	...	92.88	124.86	135.29	158.10	188.45
Monetary Authorities	79ag d	...	...	...	...	...	...	...	...	...	...	—	—	—	—	—
General Government	79ah d	...	...	...	...	...	...	...	...	...	...	21.38	27.82	29.43	32.86	37.24
Banks	79ai d	...	...	...	...	...	...	...	...	...	...	54.78	74.12	76.70	90.85	105.09
Other Sectors	79aj d	...	...	...	...	...	...	...	...	...	...	16.72	22.92	29.16	34.39	46.12
Reserve Assets	79ak d	...	...	...	...	...	...	...	...	...	...	25.72	29.15	24.17	25.38	27.09
Liabilities	79la d	...	...	...	...	...	...	...	...	...	...	147.13	197.30	202.03	233.76	265.99
Dir. Invest. in Rep. Economy	79lb d	...	...	...	...	...	...	...	...	...	...	3.27	3.92	4.00	4.36	4.46
Portfolio Investment	79lc d	...	...	...	...	...	...	...	...	...	...	42.55	68.27	73.91	97.48	107.67
Equity Securities	79ld d	...	...	...	...	...	...	...	...	...	...	14.18	27.77	29.81	47.42	48.03
Debt Securities	79le d	...	...	...	...	...	...	...	...	...	...	28.37	40.50	44.10	50.06	59.64
Financial Derivatives	79ll d	...	...	...	...	...	...	...	...	...	...	—	—	—	—	—
Other investment	79lf d	...	...	...	...	...	...	...	...	...	...	101.31	125.11	124.12	131.92	153.86
Monetary Authorities	79lg d	...	...	...	...	...	...	...	...	...	...	5.37	5.98	5.57	5.90	6.87
General Government	79lh d	...	...	...	...	...	...	...	...	...	...	.23	.18	.15	.13	.10
Banks	79li d	...	...	...	...	...	...	...	...	...	...	78.06	100.98	100.41	107.63	130.43
Other Sectors	79lj d	...	...	...	...	...	...	...	...	...	...	17.65	17.97	17.99	18.26	16.46
Government Finance																*Billions of Yen:*
Deficit (-) or Surplus	80	−319	−181	−1,457	−1,825	−1,798	Ⅰ−7,666	−9,417	−11,916	−15,236	−16,318	−16,872	−16,826	−17,583	−18,843	−17,290
Revenue	81	8,053	9,320	9,681	9,868	12,200	Ⅰ14,608	16,509	18,469	20,606	24,113	27,907	31,429	32,826	33,776	36,738
Grants Received	81z						Ⅰ93	146	124	134	157	198	212	212	139	97
Expenditure	82	8,372	9,501	11,138	11,693	13,997	Ⅰ21,827	25,534	29,841	35,207	39,728	44,137	47,619	49,831	52,012	53,148
Lending Minus Repayments	83	...	...	...	...	...	Ⅰ540	538	668	769	860	840	848	790	746	977
Financing																
Net Borrowing Yen	84b	318	307	1,457	1,570	2,009	...	...	...	...	...	...	...	...	...	...
Foreign Currency	85b	−5	−11	−4	−33	−4	...	...	...	...	...	...	...	...	...	...
Use of Cash Balances	87	6	−115	4	288	−207	...	...	...	...	...	...	...	...	...	...
Debt: Domestic	88a	...	...	...	...	...	Ⅰ23,448	33,542	46,932	63,098	78,367	97,528	113,209	127,646	144,679	159,356
Foreign	89a	...	...	...	...	...	Ⅰ517	528	587	518	408	621	691	735	704	925
National Accounts																*Billions of Yen*
Exports of Goods & Services	90c. c	7,926	9,452	9,779	11,291	18,258	18,982	22,582	24,308	22,729	25,627	32,887	37,977	39,391	39,275	45,066
Government Consumption	91f. c	5,455	6,422	7,537	9,336	12,240	14,890	16,417	18,243	19,753	21,486	23,568	25,585	26,796	27,996	29,449
Gross Fixed Capital Formation	93e. c	26,043	27,637	31,524	40,938	46,695	48,136	51,945	55,982	62,147	70,171	75,821	78,908	79,735	78,881	83,251
Increase/Decrease(-) in Stocks	93i. c	2,573	1,215	1,299	1,885	3,396	476	1,092	1,280	1,027	1,813	1,613	1,424	1,187	187	1,011
Private Consumption	96f. c	38,333	43,230	49,901	60,308	72,912	84,763	95,784	107,076	117,923	130,078	141,324	149,997	160,834	169,687	178,631
Imports of Goods & Services	98c. c	−6,985	−7,254	−7,645	−11,261	−19,257	−18,919	−21,247	−21,267	−19,174	−27,629	−35,036	−35,927	−37,341	−34,258	−36,866
Gross Domestic Product (GDP)	99b. c	73,345	80,701	92,394	112,498	134,244	148,327	166,573	185,622	204,404	221,547	240,176	257,963	270,601	281,767	300,543
Net Factor Inc/Pmts(-) Abroad	98.n c	−157	−109	6	21	−247	−157	−156	−92	70	278	−78	−546	69	311	505
Gross National Income (GNI)	99a. c	73,188	80,592	92,401	112,520	133,997	148,170	166,417	185,530	204,475	221,825	240,098	257,417	270,669	282,078	301,048
GDP Volume 1980 Prices	99b. r	152,535	158,984	172,309	185,882	183,620	188,393	197,406	207,845	218,449	229,785	...	...	...	...	...
GDP Volume 1985 Prices	99b. r	...	...	...	...	...	...	...	...	...	...	257,372	266,722	276,268	285,002	292,702	305,187
GDP Volume 1990 Prices	99b. r	...	...	...	...	...	...	...	...	...	...	...	...	...	...	...
GDP Volume (1995=100)	99bv r	39.9	41.5	45.0	48.6	48.0	49.2	51.6	54.3	57.1	Ⅰ60.0	62.2	64.5	66.5	68.3	71.2
GDP Deflator (1995=100)	99bi r	38.1	40.2	42.5	47.9	57.9	62.4	66.8	70.7	74.1	76.4	79.9	82.8	84.2	85.4	87.4
																Millions:
Population	99z	104.34	105.70	107.19	108.71	110.16	111.57	112.77	113.86	114.90	115.87	116.81	117.66	118.48	119.31	120.08

	1985	1986	1987	1988	1989	1990	1991	1992	1993	1994	1995	1996	1997	1998	1999		
Billions of US Dollars																**International Investment Position**	
	437.28	726.85	1,071.35	1,469.34	1,771.01	1,857.88	2,006.51	2,035.24	2,180.88	2,424.24	2,632.86	2,652.61	2,737.45	2,986.33	3,013.60	Assets	79aa *d*
	43.97	58.07	77.02	110.78	154.37	201.44	231.79	248.06	259.80	275.57	238.45	258.61	271.90	270.04	248.78	Direct Investment Abroad	79ab *d*
	145.75	257.93	354.55	449.31	561.85	595.84	679.18	715.45	771.11	858.69	855.07	933.20	902.26	1,056.49	1,242.37	Portfolio Investment	79ac *d*
	....	....	....	....	....	....	....	....	....	....	146.26	154.90	158.77	209.38	285.34	Equity Securities	79ad *d*
	....	....	....	....	....	....	....	....	....	....	708.81	778.30	743.49	847.11	957.04	Debt Securities	79ae *d*
											3.21	3.97	4.41	5.09	4.46	Financial Derivatives	79al *d*
	220.33	368.02	557.88	811.39	969.72	980.89	1,022.27	998.94	1,050.29	1,162.87	1,351.31	1,239.23	1,338.08	1,438.88	1,230.34	Other Investment	79af *d*
																Monetary Authorities	79ag *d*
	36.84	51.43	66.21	82.41	89.42	90.44	110.73	123.40	142.22	165.01	184.05	170.47	162.32	196.16	230.91	General Government	79ah *d*
	131.49	243.50	389.79	585.09	716.70	725.40	729.67	690.32	701.47	752.12	911.23	773.14	861.44	876.07	630.02	Banks	79ai *d*
	52.00	73.09	101.88	143.89	163.60	165.05	181.87	185.22	206.60	245.74	256.02	295.63	314.32	366.65	369.41	Other Sectors	79aj *d*
	27.23	42.83	81.90	97.86	85.07	79.71	73.27	72.79	99.68	127.10	184.82	217.61	220.81	215.83	287.66	Reserve Assets	79ak *d*
	306.90	545.87	829.63	1,176.41	1,476.62	1,528.52	1,622.17	1,520.39	1,568.84	1,733.92	1,815.26	1,761.59	1,778.72	1,832.69	2,184.48	Liabilities	79la *d*
	4.74	6.51	9.02	10.42	9.16	9.85	12.29	15.51	16.89	19.17	33.51	29.94	27.08	26.07	46.12	Dir. Invest. in Rep. Economy	79lb *d*
	117.81	186.04	229.46	317.73	431.88	395.97	527.69	513.10	545.32	630.67	545.42	556.25	582.48	632.76	1,165.44	Portfolio Investment	79lc *d*
	45.95	78.69	66.30	113.52	162.08	90.38	141.78	124.59	171.17	250.88	306.28	315.65	279.53	304.33	833.43	Equity Securities	79ld *d*
	71.86	107.35	163.16	204.21	269.80	305.59	385.91	388.51	374.15	379.79	239.14	240.60	302.95	328.43	332.01	Debt Securities	79le *d*
											2.85	2.72	4.10	4.54	3.10	Financial Derivatives	79ll *d*
	184.35	353.32	591.15	848.26	1,035.58	1,122.70	1,082.19	991.78	1,006.63	1,084.08	1,233.48	1,172.69	1,165.06	1,169.32	969.83	Other investment	79lf *d*
	7.59	11.68	10.38	13.81	25.03	35.74	50.11	54.72	65.52	99.85	—	—	—	—	—	Monetary Authorities	79lg *d*
	.08	.07	.05	.03	.01	—	—	—	—	—	14.96	11.35	10.12	9.65	11.62	General Government	79lh *d*
	161.27	322.50	532.13	766.93	897.88	904.41	812.82	696.71	673.58	694.94	745.42	701.56	714.28	751.47	570.71	Banks	79li *d*
	15.41	19.07	48.59	67.49	112.66	182.55	219.26	240.35	267.53	289.29	473.10	459.78	440.66	408.20	387.50	Other Sectors	79lj *d*
Year Beginning April 1																**Government Finance**	
	−15,603	−15,967	−12,195	−9,657	−11,645	−6,781	ɪ7,759	1,473 [P]	−7,318 [P]	....	....	....	....	....	....	Deficit (-) or Surplus	80
	40,262	41,683	47,176	52,082	55,762	62,146	ɪ104,462	99,412 [P]	99,866 [P]	....	....	....	....	....	....	Revenue	81
	99	108	134	148	160	166	ɪ2,883	3,278 [P]	3,498 [P]	....	....	....	....	....	....	Grants Received	81z
	55,214	56,962	58,641	60,863	66,695	67,533	ɪ97,478	100,642 [P]	112,655 [P]	....	....	....	....	....	....	Expenditure	82
	750	796	864	1,024	872	1,560	ɪ2,108	575 [P]	−1,973 [P]	....	....	....	....	....	....	Lending Minus Repayments	83
																Financing	
	....	....	....	....	....	....	....	....	....	....	....	....	....	....	....	Net Borrowing Yen	84b
																Foreign Currency	85b
	....	....	....	....	....	....	....	....	....	....	....	....	....	....	....	Use of Cash Balances	87
	173,660	196,148	210,407	220,644	231,008	238,746	ɪ187,605	196,194 [P]	212,474 [P]	....	....	....	....	....	....	Debt: Domestic	88a
	991	1,036	1,144	1,200	1,149	1,186	....	....	....	....	....	....	....	....	....	Foreign	89a
Billions of Yen																**National Accounts**	
	46,307	38,090	36,210	37,483	42,352	45,920	46,723	47,384	44,197	44,410	45,393	49,700	56,332	55,324	51,284	Exports of Goods & Services	90c. *c*
	30,685	32,388	32,975	34,184	36,275	38,807	41,356	43,262	44,771	45,743	47,419	48,423	49,555	50,676	50,985	Government Consumption	91f. *c*
	88,040	91,499	99,152	110,856	122,274	136,467	143,998	143,525	140,433	137,291	137,611	147,425	143,999	129,866	....	Gross Fixed Capital Formation	93e. *c*
	2,159	1,560	661	2,676	2,976	2,430	3,453	1,489	620	50	546	2,443	1,917	1,338	....	Increase/Decrease(-) in Stocks	93i. *c*
	188,759	196,712	205,956	217,839	232,890	249,288	261,891	272,294	278,703	286,154	290,524	299,341	305,907	304,766	306,790	Private Consumption	96f. *c*
	−35,532	−24,791	−25,195	−29,065	−36,768	−42,872	−39,121	−36,891	−33,343	−34,387	−38,272	−47,022	−50,316	−45,607	−43,183	Imports of Goods & Services	98c. *c*
	320,419	335,457	349,760	373,973	399,998	430,040	458,299	471,064	475,381	479,260	483,220	500,310	509,645	498,499	495,375	Gross Domestic Product (GDP)	99b. *c*
	1,137	381	719	−242	−952	−2,571	−3,812	−3,651	−5,028	−6,083	4,055	5,491	6,527	....	....	Net Factor Inc/Pmts(-) Abroad	98.n *c*
	321,556	335,838	350,479	373,731	399,046	427,469	454,487	467,413	470,353	473,177	....	....	....	....	....	Gross National Income (GNI)	99a. *c*
	320,397	328,816	342,315	363,567	380,709	399,043	....	....	....	....	....	....	....	....	....	GDP Volume 1980 Prices	99b. *r*
							....	....	....	....	....	....	....	....	....	GDP Volume 1985 Prices	99b. *r*
	....	....	....	....	....	429,986	446,315	450,924	452,282	455,197	461,893	485,219	492,142	478,051	....	GDP Volume 1990 Prices	99b. *r*
	74.7	76.7	79.9	84.8	88.8	ɪ93.1	96.6	97.6	97.9	98.6	100.0	105.1	106.5	103.5	....	GDP Volume (1995=100)	99bv *r*
	88.7	90.5	90.6	91.2	93.2	95.6	98.2	99.9	100.5	100.6	100.0	98.6	99.0	99.7	....	GDP Deflator (1995=100)	99bi *r*
Midyear Estimates																	
	120.84	121.49	122.09	122.58	123.07	123.48	123.96	124.42	124.83	125.18	125.47	125.76	126.07	126.41	126.51	**Population**	99z

(See notes in the back of the book.)

Jordan

		1970	1971	1972	1973	1974	1975	1976	1977	1978	1979	1980	1981	1982	1983	1984
Exchange Rates														*SDRs per Dinar:*		
Official Rate	ac	2.8000	2.5790	2.5790	2.5192	2.5929	2.5790	2.5790	2.5790	2.5790	2.5790	2.5790	2.5790	2.5790	2.5790	2.5790
														US Dollars per Dinar:		
Official Rate	ag	2.8000	2.8000	2.8000	3.0390	3.1746	3.0303	3.0211	3.1746	3.4130	3.3898	3.2415	2.9498	2.8450	2.6918	2.4691
Official Rate	rh	2.8000	2.8000	2.8000	3.0462	3.1113	3.1393	3.0122	3.0375	3.2733	3.3299	3.3543	3.0293	2.8384	2.7550	2.6036
Fund Position														*Millions of SDRs:*		
Quota	2f. s	23.0	23.0	23.0	23.0	23.0	23.0	23.0	23.0	30.0	30.0	45.0	45.0	45.0	73.9	73.9
SDRs	1b. s	2.7	5.1	7.6	7.5	7.4	7.4	7.4	7.4	7.4	11.0	11.7	15.5	16.5	17.4	15.8
Reserve Position in the Fund	1c. s	5.8	5.8	5.8	5.8	5.8	5.8	5.8	5.8	5.6	10.3	16.6	16.6	16.6	7.2	—
Total Fund Cred.&Loans Outstg.	2tl	—	4.5	4.5	1.6	—	—	—	—	—	—	—	—	—	—	—
International Liquidity												*Millions of US Dollars Unless Otherwise Indicated:*					
Total Reserves minus Gold	1l. d	227.7	222.9	241.0	270.7	312.8	458.9	471.5	643.1	885.6	1,166.1	1,142.8	1,086.7	884.1	824.2	515.0
SDRs	1b. d	2.7	5.6	8.2	9.1	9.1	8.7	8.6	9.0	9.6	14.4	14.9	18.0	18.2	18.2	15.5
Reserve Position in the Fund	1c. d	5.8	6.2	6.2	6.9	7.1	6.7	6.7	7.0	7.3	13.6	21.1	19.3	18.3	7.6	—
Foreign Exchange	1d. d	219.3	211.1	226.5	254.7	296.7	443.5	456.2	627.2	868.7	1,138.1	1,106.8	1,049.4	847.6	798.4	499.5
Gold (Million Fine Troy Ounces)	1ad	.797	.797	.797	.797	.797	.797	.797	.806	.811	.816	1.021	1.067	1.080	1.090	1.060
Gold (National Valuation)	1an d	27.9	27.9	30.3	33.6	34.3	32.8	79.7	80.6	81.1	81.6	204.2	213.4	216.0	199.5	172.2
Monetary Authorities: Other Liab.	4.. d	.4	.5	.5	1.2	1.8	1.5	.5	1.2	.8	11.2	1.3	3.6	1.5	.7	1.1
Deposit Money Banks: Assets	7a. d	17.0	8.6	9.5	20.4	25.3	37.7	58.1	116.6	254.7	271.4	665.2	688.2	726.6	819.3	816.1
Liabilities	7b. d	9.9	7.0	6.8	8.1	13.5	31.4	80.4	67.4	204.6	283.6	480.5	523.3	572.1	664.2	779.3
Other Banking Insts.: Liabilities	7f. d	10.0	10.4	10.4	11.9	13.2	14.9	12.8	42.6	34.3	48.1	53.1	56.4	59.0	57.0	71.0
Monetary Authorities														*Millions of Dinars:*		
Foreign Assets	11	91.3	89.6	96.9	100.4	110.2	162.3	182.2	229.1	286.1	370.8	416.9	433.7	372.9	380.3	278.3
Claims on Central Government	12a	10.8	19.5	11.5	28.8	30.4	27.2	44.9	58.9	56.5	60.3	126.7	150.3	195.4	200.4	181.1
Reserve Money	14	97.3	99.5	100.7	117.2	140.5	173.5	216.4	255.2	299.9	380.3	467.3	534.1	596.5	663.6	676.2
of which: Currency Outside DMBs	14a	82.4	83.0	81.5	97.5	115.5	139.0	161.5	188.2	219.5	275.4	351.6	412.3	470.0	516.0	530.5
Foreign Liabilities	16c	.2	1.9	1.9	1.0	.6	.5	.2	.4	.2	3.3	.4	1.2	.5	.3	.5
Central Government Deposits	16d	2.5	1.7	2.4	6.7	4.2	14.1	10.0	23.9	31.4	31.5	51.1	39.3	23.6	40.3	17.5
Other Items (Net)	17r	2.3	5.9	3.4	4.4	−4.6	1.2	.5	8.5	11.1	16.0	24.7	9.4	−52.3	−123.5	−234.7
Deposit Money Banks														*Millions of Dinars:*		
Reserves	20	14.8	16.4	19.2	18.8	24.5	35.9	54.2	67.6	81.7	101.6	116.6	115.1	118.5	134.0	136.2
Foreign Assets	21	6.1	3.1	3.4	6.6	8.0	12.5	19.2	36.7	74.6	80.1	205.2	233.3	255.4	304.4	330.5
Claims on Central Government	22a	3.3	8.6	16.2	16.9	14.9	24.5	23.0	32.9	68.6	73.8	59.8	80.8	102.8	147.2	208.5
Claims on Private Sector	22d	43.6	44.8	47.9	59.3	80.3	115.6	177.2	196.7	313.8	444.0	541.6	689.7	843.0	993.3	1,133.5
Demand Deposits	24	23.0	25.0	33.5	40.9	55.7	84.5	113.9	139.8	150.0	182.0	225.2	280.1	305.1	338.7	336.9
Time and Savings Deposits	25	23.4	26.5	31.1	36.6	47.3	63.6	99.1	135.1	226.8	298.2	386.4	476.8	614.5	745.2	877.4
Foreign Liabilities	26c	3.5	2.5	2.4	2.6	4.3	10.3	26.6	21.2	60.0	83.7	148.2	177.4	201.1	246.7	315.6
Central Government Deposits	26d	8.7	6.1	6.2	6.1	8.4	12.0	16.6	21.0	24.3	45.8	63.6	77.2	78.3	97.2	111.9
Capital Accounts	27a	8.0	8.0	8.0	8.0	11.6	14.9	21.0	32.7	54.7	67.9	76.8	91.7	131.2	140.3	152.9
Other Items (Net)	27r	1.2	4.8	5.3	7.4	.4	3.2	−3.6	−16.0	23.0	21.9	23.0	15.7	−10.5	10.7	14.1
Monetary Survey														*Millions of Dinars:*		
Foreign Assets (Net)	31n	93.7	88.2	95.9	103.4	113.3	163.8	174.7	244.2	300.6	363.9	473.4	488.4	426.7	437.7	292.8
Domestic Credit	32	49.4	68.4	71.4	98.1	122.0	152.6	240.0	275.7	425.2	545.9	666.7	883.9	1,162.1	1,360.4	1,587.7
Claims on Central Govt. (Net)	32an	3.0	20.2	19.1	32.9	32.8	25.5	41.3	46.8	69.4	56.7	71.8	114.6	196.3	210.1	260.2
Claims on Nonfin.Pub.Enterprises	32c	2.8	3.3	4.4	5.8	9.0	11.5	21.4	31.6	42.0	44.2	53.3	78.2	122.8	157.0	173.5
Claims on Private Sector	32d	43.6	44.9	47.9	59.3	80.3	115.6	177.2	197.3	313.8	445.0	541.6	691.1	843.0	993.3	1,133.5
Money	34	105.5	108.0	115.0	139.2	172.0	224.7	276.7	329.0	370.5	465.6	580.7	701.7	787.5	869.4	878.4
Quasi-Money	35	23.8	27.1	31.6	37.2	48.5	67.5	110.8	144.9	237.1	301.6	399.5	482.0	619.4	748.5	883.8
Other Items (Net)	37r	13.8	21.4	20.7	25.0	14.8	24.4	27.2	46.0	118.2	142.7	159.9	188.6	181.9	180.2	118.3
Money plus Quasi-Money	35l	129.3	135.1	146.6	176.4	220.5	292.1	387.5	473.9	607.6	767.2	980.3	1,183.6	1,406.9	1,617.9	1,762.2
Other Banking Institutions														*Millions of Dinars:*		
Cash	40	1.6	1.4	.8	1.3	1.3	.9	2.1	2.3	3.4	7.0	9.2	18.3	12.5	12.2	13.6
Claims on Private Sector	42d	14.1	14.9	16.2	17.5	21.5	25.1	30.5	36.0	43.4	50.0	59.9	71.5	95.9	119.9	128.0
Deposits	45	—	—	—	—	—	—	2.1	—	—	—	—	10.2	10.4	12.4	16.5
Foreign Liabilities	46c	3.6	3.7	3.7	3.8	4.2	4.9	4.2	13.4	10.0	14.2	16.4	19.1	20.6	25.3	28.8
Central Govt. Lending Funds	46f	1.9	1.8	1.8	1.7	1.6	1.7	1.7	1.5	1.5	1.5	1.3	1.2	2.1	2.0	2.1
Capital Accounts	47a	11.4	12.1	13.0	14.1	15.0	17.9	19.5	22.4	24.4	28.1	31.7	39.5	48.5	55.4	62.3
Other Items (Net)	47r	−1.1	−1.4	−1.5	−.8	2.0	1.5	5.1	1.0	10.9	13.2	19.7	19.8	26.7	37.0	31.8
Liquid Liabilities	55l	127.64	133.73	145.75	175.09	218.57	287.48	387.54	471.58	604.21	760.20	971.01	1,175.50	1,404.83	1,618.06	1,765.12
Interest Rates														*Percent Per Annum*		
Discount Rate (End of Period)	60	5.25	5.25	5.00	5.00	5.00	5.00	5.50	5.50	5.50	6.00	6.00	6.50	6.50	6.25	6.25
Deposit Rate (Period Average)	60l	....	....	....	....	....	....	....	....	....	....	....	....	....	....	....
Lending Rate (Period Average)	60p	....	....	....	....	....	....	....	....	....	....	....	....	....	....	....
Prices and Production														*Index Numbers (1995=100):*		
Wholesale Prices	63	....	....	....	....	27.0	30.8	32.9	34.7	36.9	42.4	46.3	47.7	49.6	50.5	
Consumer Prices	64	13.8	14.5	15.6	17.3	20.7	I 23.2	25.9	29.6	31.7	I 36.2	40.2	43.3	46.5	48.9	50.7
Industrial Production	66	10.8	12.8	15.7	17.3	18.0	I 19.3	24.1	25.0	30.8	36.8	44.0	51.3	53.0	55.6	63.7
International Transactions														*Millions of Dinars*		
Exports	70	12.2	11.4	17.0	24.0	49.8	48.9	68.7	82.1	90.9	120.9	171.4	242.6	264.5	210.6	290.7
Imports, c.i.f.	71	65.8	76.6	97.7	108.2	156.8	234.0	334.1	454.4	458.8	589.5	716.1	1,047.5	1,142.5	1,103.3	1,071.4
																1995=100
Volume of Exports	72	9.5	8.6	10.7	11.6	16.5	I 14.2	17.2	20.7	22.3	27.5	34.3	40.0	41.0	I 40.7	57.1
Volume of Imports	73	14.6	14.1	17.9	17.5	19.5	I 24.8	37.2	43.4	49.6	58.2	57.1	67.8	74.4	I 75.1	70.4
Export Prices	74	12.9	12.0	14.5	14.6	29.7	I 33.7	31.4	31.4	30.2	30.4	36.1	41.5	45.3	I 41.4	45.1
Unit Value of Imports	75	16.1	18.8	20.5	21.5	27.3	I 37.4	36.5	37.2	36.1	38.7	48.0	58.5	59.4	I 54.3	60.0

	1985	1986	1987	1988	1989	1990	1991	1992	1993	1994	1995	1996	1997	1998	1999		
End of Period																**Exchange Rates**	
	2.5790	2.5790	2.5790	1.5579	1.1743	1.0570	1.0357	1.0525	1.0341	.9772	.9488	.9809	1.0454	1.0017	1.0276	Official Rate	**ac**
End of Period (ag) Period Average (rh)																	
	2.7192	2.9061	3.0395	2.0964	1.5432	1.5038	1.4815	1.4472	1.4205	1.4265	1.4104	1.4104	1.4104	1.4104	1.4104	Official Rate	**ag**
	2.5379	2.8583	2.9522	2.6916	1.7532	1.5069	1.4689	1.4712	1.4434	1.4312	1.4276	1.4104	1.4104	1.4104	1.4104	Official Rate	**rh**
End of Period																**Fund Position**	
	73.9	73.9	73.9	73.9	73.9	73.9	73.9	121.7	121.7	121.7	121.7	121.7	121.7	121.7	170.5	Quota	**2f. s**
	21.9	19.6	8.5	—	8.4	.7	.8	.4	4.0	.5	.8	.6	.1	.6	.2	SDRs	**1b. s**
	—	—	—	—	—	—	—	12.0	—	—	—	—	—	—	—	Reserve Position in the Fund	**1c. s**
	57.4	57.4	57.4	35.9	73.4	66.2	66.2	81.2	59.2	98.9	169.2	236.1	316.6	333.4	362.9	Total Fund Cred.&Loans Outstg.	**2tl**
End of Period																**International Liquidity**	
	422.8	437.1	424.7	109.6	470.7	848.8	825.8	767.2	**I** 1,637.4	1,692.6	1,972.9	1,759.3	2,200.3	1,750.4	2,629.1	Total Reserves minus Gold	**1l. d**
	24.1	23.9	12.1	.1	11.0	1.0	1.1	.6	5.5	.7	1.2	.8	.2	.8	.3	SDRs	**1b. d**
	—	—	—	—	—	—	—	16.4	—	—	—	—	—	—	—	Reserve Position in the Fund	**1c. d**
	398.7	413.2	412.6	109.5	459.7	847.8	824.7	750.2	**I** 1,631.9	1,691.9	1,971.7	1,758.5	2,200.1	1,749.6	2,628.8	Foreign Exchange	**1d. d**
	1.061	1.064	1.002	.743	.748	.753	.789	.789	.791	.794	.793	.800	.812	.827	.486	Gold (Million Fine Troy Ounces)	**1ad**
	189.8	203.5	200.1	138.3	102.5	100.6	103.8	101.4	99.8	198.5	195.9	197.7	200.7	204.3	120.0	Gold (National Valuation)	**1and**
	1.0	1.0	176.2	25.5	15.4	10.6	.5	.8	1.8	....	....	....	....	....	....	Monetary Authorities: Other Liab.	**4.. d**
	1,046.6	1,172.1	1,374.0	1,200.4	976.0	986.9	1,922.5	2,137.9	2,216.3	2,399.3	2,655.3	2,845.0	3,077.5	3,607.1	4,101.5	Deposit Money Banks: Assets	**7a. d**
	917.9	1,011.6	1,160.0	1,157.8	779.2	691.5	1,367.1	2,310.5	2,166.6	2,518.5	2,926.5	3,100.7	3,084.7	3,079.7	3,286.3	Liabilities	**7b. d**
	81.0	101.0	110.0	77.0	61.0	75.0	86.0	98.0	112.3	120.6	130.3	117.0	126.0	124.7	....	Other Banking Insts.: Liabilities	**7f. d**
End of Period																**Monetary Authorities**	
	379.3	402.0	391.7	346.9	601.4	788.0	949.5	999.7	**I** 1,688.7	1,904.3	2,185.2	2,253.9	2,557.1	2,297.7	2,889.6	Foreign Assets	**11**
	204.7	225.9	351.6	663.7	741.3	747.5	685.9	688.9	772.5	905.3	867.1	930.9	989.4	1,033.4	1,007.5	Claims on Central Government	**12a**
	701.7	747.2	779.9	959.1	1,135.9	1,279.7	1,665.6	1,771.3	**I** 2,236.0	2,349.5	2,498.9	2,164.4	2,104.0	2,005.0	2,253.5	Reserve Money	**14**
	531.8	583.9	655.8	811.2	871.1	1,006.2	992.4	1,003.9	1,047.9	1,072.6	1,050.9	952.1	987.6	952.8	1,106.6	*of which: Currency Outside DMBs*	**14a**
	23.6	24.5	84.8	35.2	72.5	69.7	64.3	77.7	**I** 145.7	183.6	236.7	291.3	333.9	356.1	516.6	Foreign Liabilities	**16c**
	6.7	10.4	1.7	—	21.4	5.7	210.7	137.6	101.3	225.1	163.5	323.7	321.0	137.7	97.0	Central Government Deposits	**16d**
	−148.0	−154.1	−123.1	16.2	112.9	180.3	−305.2	−297.9	**I** −21.8	51.4	153.1	405.4	787.5	832.3	1,030.0	Other Items (Net)	**17r**
End of Period																**Deposit Money Banks**	
	161.9	180.6	181.0	248.8	456.4	566.6	1,318.2	1,584.9	1,477.1	1,576.9	1,799.6	1,854.9	2,163.8	2,015.9	2,389.2	Reserves	**20**
	384.9	403.3	452.0	572.6	632.4	656.3	1,297.7	1,477.3	1,560.3	1,681.9	1,882.6	2,017.1	2,182.0	2,557.5	2,907.9	Foreign Assets	**21**
	228.3	275.7	345.9	334.9	369.0	388.8	424.1	457.9	358.7	307.0	240.0	238.1	163.0	412.5	570.4	Claims on Central Government	**22a**
	1,193.4	1,291.5	1,349.9	1,461.5	1,565.0	1,716.1	1,841.0	2,013.7	2,310.5	2,763.4	3,192.5	3,354.9	3,526.5	3,803.2	3,998.6	Claims on Private Sector	**22d**
	308.4	310.7	322.8	353.7	425.4	413.8	640.3	685.9	**I** 669.6	666.0	664.7	578.1	636.1	648.8	659.8	Demand Deposits	**24**
	1,023.2	1,173.8	1,391.4	1,459.3	1,638.5	1,673.0	2,361.1	2,448.8	**I** 2,510.0	2,782.4	3,040.5	3,209.8	3,469.3	3,734.4	4,103.7	Time and Savings Deposits	**25**
	337.6	348.1	381.6	552.3	504.9	459.8	922.8	1,596.5	1,525.3	1,765.5	2,074.9	2,198.4	2,187.1	2,183.5	2,330.0	Foreign Liabilities	**26c**
	121.3	156.2	127.3	110.6	161.1	168.8	212.4	91.5	**I** 424.8	499.8	550.9	634.6	736.3	848.3	1,118.4	Central Government Deposits	**26d**
	164.4	177.5	185.6	194.4	204.2	79.7	88.7	348.5	492.6	582.8	701.7	771.0	1,047.1	1,181.3	1,316.6	Capital Accounts	**27a**
	13.6	−15.3	−80.0	−52.5	88.8	536.4	655.6	362.7	**I** 84.3	32.9	82.0	73.2	−41.3	193.2	338.5	Other Items (Net)	**27r**
End of Period																**Monetary Survey**	
	403.1	432.7	377.4	332.0	656.5	914.7	1,260.1	802.7	**I** 1,578.0	1,637.6	1,756.2	1,781.3	2,218.1	2,315.6	2,950.9	Foreign Assets (Net)	**31n**
	1,743.0	1,833.6	2,190.5	2,637.3	2,780.7	2,935.1	2,759.1	3,220.9	**I** 3,324.8	3,723.1	4,089.1	4,114.2	4,184.4	4,780.0	4,867.2	Domestic Credit	**32**
	305.0	335.0	568.5	888.0	927.7	961.7	686.9	917.8	**I** 605.1	487.4	392.7	210.8	95.1	460.0	362.5	Claims on Central Govt. (Net)	**32an**
	218.7	175.1	237.9	253.0	251.4	250.5	225.4	235.0	**I** 296.8	341.9	362.2	408.9	425.3	381.2	364.9	Claims on Nonfin.Pub.Enterprises	**32c**
	1,197.1	1,296.2	1,354.7	1,467.4	1,568.4	1,719.5	1,844.7	2,018.1	2,316.1	2,769.9	3,200.1	3,363.0	3,535.2	3,812.7	4,010.5	Claims on Private Sector	**32d**
	848.2	897.1	979.8	1,166.8	1,302.3	1,425.3	1,646.6	1,716.0	**I** 1,719.4	1,741.6	1,738.7	1,532.8	1,626.1	1,612.9	1,774.6	Money	**34**
	1,030.9	1,181.7	1,424.4	1,611.2	1,935.3	2,080.1	2,412.8	2,479.0	**I** 2,664.7	2,788.6	3,051.0	3,213.3	3,482.7	3,818.8	4,440.3	Quasi-Money	**35**
	267.0	187.6	163.7	191.3	199.5	344.4	−40.2	−171.4	**I** 518.8	830.1	1,055.6	1,149.4	1,293.6	1,664.2	1,603.9	Other Items (Net)	**37r**
	1,879.1	2,078.8	2,404.2	2,778.0	3,237.6	3,505.4	4,059.4	4,195.0	**I** 4,384.1	4,530.2	4,789.7	4,746.1	5,108.8	5,431.7	6,215.0	Money plus Quasi-Money	**35l**
End of Period																**Other Banking Institutions**	
	22.9	19.8	26.8	25.1	42.3	39.1	65.9	49.8	**I** 70.6	59.9	63.3	54.3	53.0	41.2	....	Cash	**40**
	138.4	144.0	191.2	213.0	210.5	209.8	219.8	256.2	**I** 294.9	284.8	306.2	315.0	334.9	349.3	....	Claims on Private Sector	**42d**
	18.6	28.7	35.9	29.4	32.2	35.4	58.9	44.9	**I** 66.5	47.4	32.7	24.5	17.0	11.8	....	Deposits	**45**
	30.0	34.6	36.3	36.8	39.8	50.0	57.8	67.5	**I** 79.0	84.6	92.4	83.0	89.3	88.4	....	Foreign Liabilities	**46c**
	2.2	2.3	2.2	3.0	2.8	2.9	3.1	.9	**I** 17.1	16.2	16.2	15.0	14.3	13.7	....	Central Govt. Lending Funds	**46f**
	63.9	69.1	70.7	76.6	80.9	88.1	78.5	104.0	**I** 90.9	91.6	111.5	132.0	153.2	164.5	....	Capital Accounts	**47a**
	46.7	29.1	73.0	92.4	97.1	72.9	87.4	88.7	**I** 111.9	104.9	116.8	114.9	114.2	112.0	....	Other Items (Net)	**47r**
	1,874.79	2,087.65	2,413.28	2,782.24	3,227.50	3,501.62	4,052.39	4,190.08	**I** 4379.98	4,517.76	4,759.07	4,716.33	5,072.73	5,402.30	....	Liquid Liabilities	**55l**
Percent Per Annum																**Interest Rates**	
	6.25	6.25	6.25	6.25	8.00	8.50	8.50	8.50	8.50	8.50	8.50	8.50	7.75	9.00	8.00	Discount Rate (End of Period)	**60**
	....	....	....	....	....	8.15	8.13	7.20	6.88	7.09	7.68	8.50	9.10	....	....	Deposit Rate (Period Average)	**60l**
	....	....	....	....	....	10.31	10.37	10.16	10.23	10.45	10.66	11.25	12.25	....	....	Lending Rate (Period Average)	**60p**
Period Averages																**Prices and Production**	
	51.2	51.1	51.6	56.4	75.4	86.3	90.7	**I** 94.5	97.7	102.5	100.0	102.0	103.6	104.3	99.9	Wholesale Prices	**63**
	I 52.3	52.3	52.2	55.6	69.9	81.2	87.8	**I** 91.4	94.4	97.7	100.0	106.5	109.7	114.6	115.3	Consumer Prices	**64**
	68.2	69.2	75.6	69.4	72.9	73.3	72.5	**I** 78.1	84.3	**I** 89.0	100.0	93.7	98.2	100.2	102.6	Industrial Production	**66**
Millions of Dinars																**International Transactions**	
	310.9	256.0	315.7	381.5	637.6	706.1	770.8	829.3	864.7	995.2	1,241.1	1,288.2	1,301.4	1,277.9	1,263.7	Exports	**70**
	1,074.4	850.2	915.6	1,022.5	1,230.0	1,725.8	1,710.5	2,214.0	2,453.6	2,362.6	2,590.3	3,043.6	2,908.1	2,714.4	2,643.3	Imports, c.i.f.	**71**
1995=100																	
	59.5	61.0	72.5	81.2	85.6	82.4	72.4	79.6	85.9	**I** 92.0	100.0	97.3	104.0	106.9	107.6	Volume of Exports	**72**
	72.1	75.7	78.6	82.9	68.8	71.7	70.8	97.1	105.9	**I** 103.2	100.0	107.1	105.3	99.5	98.4	Volume of Imports	**73**
	43.8	37.7	35.0	40.7	63.6	75.7	84.2	81.2	82.0	**I** 85.9	100.0	106.4	103.3	97.5	94.1	Export Prices	**74**
	58.5	44.0	45.7	48.3	70.2	94.4	94.7	89.4	90.9	**I** 88.3	100.0	109.1	106.7	105.8	103.5	Unit Value of Imports	**75**

Jordan

439		1970	1971	1972	1973	1974	1975	1976	1977	1978	1979	1980	1981	1982	1983	1984
Balance of Payments																*Millions of US Dollars:*
Current Account, n.i.e.	**78al d**	....	....	6.4	12.5	3.4	44.7	36.1	-16.5	-288.4	-6.5	373.9	-38.9	-332.7	-390.7	-264.7
Goods: Exports f.o.b.	**78aa d**	....	....	47.6	73.7	154.3	152.9	206.9	248.9	297.4	402.2	575.2	733.2	751.6	580.0	751.9
Goods: Imports f.o.b.	**78ab d**	....	....	-236.6	-291.9	-430.3	-648.2	-907.9	-1,225.2	-1,339.2	-1,743.2	-2,136.1	-2,815.3	-2,878.6	-2,700.1	-2,472.6
Trade Balance	**78ac d**	....	....	-189.0	-218.2	-276.0	-495.3	-700.9	-976.3	-1,041.8	-1,341.0	-1,560.9	-2,082.0	-2,127.0	-2,120.1	-1,720.7
Services: Credit	**78ad d**	....	....	65.0	96.2	98.1	226.4	344.3	442.5	572.4	731.3	1,002.9	1,160.0	1,112.1	1,124.5	1,131.0
Services: Debit	**78ae d**	....	....	-90.7	-122.0	-172.3	-293.3	-387.4	-426.0	-650.5	-1,001.7	-1,094.3	-1,386.1	-1,376.9	-1,159.5	-1,330.2
Balance on Goods & Services	**78af d**	....	....	-214.8	-244.1	-350.2	-562.2	-744.0	-959.8	-1,119.9	-1,611.3	-1,652.4	-2,308.2	-2,391.8	-2,155.1	-1,920.0
Income: Credit	**78ag d**	....	....	12.3	19.2	27.3	35.3	39.2	40.4	51.5	88.1	126.1	200.4	204.7	173.0	100.7
Income: Debit	**78ah d**	....	....	-2.8	-4.0	-6.5	-9.7	-14.2	-18.2	-24.7	-49.0	-78.9	-113.0	-112.0	-127.9	-161.4
Balance on Gds, Serv. & Inc.	**78ai d**	....	....	-205.2	-228.9	-329.4	-536.6	-719.0	-937.6	-1,093.1	-1,572.2	-1,605.1	-2,220.8	-2,299.1	-2,110.0	-1,980.6
Current Transfers, n.i.e.: Credit	**78aj d**	....	....	211.7	241.3	333.1	583.2	779.6	975.5	872.4	1,666.3	2,140.8	2,344.2	2,149.3	1,925.0	1,979.5
Current Transfers: Debit	**78ak d**	....	....	—	—	-.3	-1.9	-24.4	-54.4	-67.7	-100.6	-161.8	-162.3	-183.0	-205.7	-263.7
Capital Account, n.i.e.	**78bc d**	....	....	—	—	—	—	—	—	—	—	—	—	—	—	—
Capital Account, n.i.e.: Credit	**78ba d**	....	....	—	—	—	—	—	—	—	—	—	—	—	—	—
Capital Account: Debit	**78bb d**	....	....	—	—	—	—	—	—	—	—	—	—	—	—	—
Financial Account, n.i.e.	**78bj d**	....	....	17.4	23.1	39.4	164.5	16.0	134.8	426.5	268.2	328.2	299.5	385.5	483.7	123.7
Direct Investment Abroad	**78bd d**	....	....	-1.7	-5.5	-3.4	-6.3	-2.7	—	—	—	-3.1	7.0	-3.4	-4.8	-2.7
Dir. Invest. in Rep. Econ., n.i.e.	**78be d**	....	....	.6	2.1	6.8	25.6	-7.5	11.2	56.4	26.4	33.8	140.8	59.4	34.9	77.5
Portfolio Investment Assets	**78bf d**	....	....	—	—	—	—	—	—	—	—	—	—	—	—	—
Equity Securities	**78bk d**	....	....	—	—	—	—	—	—	—	—	—	—	—	—	—
Debt Securities	**78bl d**	....	....	—	—	—	—	—	—	—	—	—	—	—	—	—
Portfolio Investment Liab., n.i.e.	**78bg d**	....	....	—	—	—	—	—	—	—	—	—	—	—	—	—
Equity Securities	**78bm d**	....	....	—	—	—	—	—	—	—	—	—	—	—	—	—
Debt Securities	**78bn d**	....	....	—	—	—	—	—	—	—	—	—	—	—	—	—
Financial Derivatives Assets	**78bw d**	....	....	....	....	....	....	....	....	....	....	....	....	....	....	....
Financial Derivatives Liabilities	**78bx d**	....	....	....	....	....	....	....	....	....	....	....	....	....	....	....
Other Investment Assets	**78bh d**	....	....	.3	.3	.6	-1.9	.3	-7.8	-2.6	-38.0	-170.8	-244.4	-104.2	-198.1	-246.2
Monetary Authorities	**78bo d**	....	....	....	....	....	....	....	....	....	....	....	....	....	-76.6	-212.9
General Government	**78bp d**	....	....	.3	.3	.6	-1.9	.3	-7.8	-2.6	-38.0	-170.8	-244.4	-104.2	-121.6	-33.2
Banks	**78bq d**	....	....	—	—	—	—	—	—	—	—	—	—	—	—	—
Other Sectors	**78br d**	....	....	—	—	—	—	—	—	—	—	—	—	—	—	—
Other Investment Liab., n.i.e.	**78bi d**	....	....	18.2	26.2	35.4	147.0	25.9	131.4	372.6	279.8	468.3	396.1	433.7	651.7	295.0
Monetary Authorities	**78bs d**	....	....	—	2.7	.3	7.8	22.0	-11.2	2.7	-9.1	6.2	-3.3	-.3	—	-.5
General Government	**78bt d**	....	....	18.5	22.8	30.1	120.1	-34.3	148.4	239.5	209.4	246.5	313.4	367.9	524.0	122.5
Banks	**78bu d**	....	....	-.3	.6	5.0	19.1	38.3	-5.8	130.3	79.4	215.7	86.0	66.1	127.7	173.0
Other Sectors	**78bv d**	....	....	—	—	—	—	—	—	—	—	—	—	—	—	—
Net Errors and Omissions	**78ca d**	....	....	-5.1	3.8	-16.9	-36.3	-24.7	67.6	113.9	59.2	-257.3	-99.6	-152.3	-40.0	-47.9
Overall Balance	**78cb d**	....	....	18.7	39.4	26.0	172.9	27.4	185.9	251.9	320.9	444.8	161.0	-99.5	53.0	-189.0
Reserves and Related Items	**79da d**	....	....	-18.7	-39.4	-26.0	-172.9	-27.4	-185.9	-251.9	-320.9	-444.8	-161.0	99.5	-53.0	189.0
Reserve Assets	**79db d**	....	....	-18.7	-35.6	-24.1	-172.9	-27.4	-185.9	-251.9	-320.9	-444.8	-161.0	99.5	-53.0	189.0
Use of Fund Credit and Loans	**79dc d**	....	....	—	-3.8	-1.9	—	—	—	—	—	—	—	—	—	—
Exceptional Financing	**79de d**	....	....	—	—	—	—	—	—	—	—	—	—	—	—	—
International Investment Position																*Millions of US Dollars*
Assets	**79aa d**	....	....	....	....	....	....	....	....	....	....	....	....	....	....	....
Direct Investment Abroad	**79ab d**	....	....	....	....	....	....	....	....	....	....	....	....	....	....	....
Portfolio Investment	**79ac d**	....	....	....	....	....	....	....	....	....	....	....	....	....	....	....
Equity Securities	**79ad d**	....	....	....	....	....	....	....	....	....	....	....	....	....	....	....
Debt Securities	**79ae d**	....	....	....	....	....	....	....	....	....	....	....	....	....	....	....
Financial Derivatives	**79al d**	....	....	....	....	....	....	....	....	....	....	....	....	....	....	....
Other Investment	**79af d**	....	....	....	....	....	....	....	....	....	....	....	....	....	....	....
Monetary Authorities	**79ag d**	....	....	....	....	....	....	....	....	....	....	....	....	....	....	....
General Government	**79ah d**	....	....	....	....	....	....	....	....	....	....	....	....	....	....	....
Banks	**79ai d**	....	....	....	....	....	....	....	....	....	....	....	....	....	....	....
Other Sectors	**79aj d**	....	....	....	....	....	....	....	....	....	....	....	....	....	....	....
Reserve Assets	**79ak d**	....	....	....	....	....	....	....	....	....	....	2,016.6	1,967.6	1,787.6	....	....
Liabilities	**79la d**	....	....	....	....	....	....	....	....	....	....	....	....	....	....	....
Dir. Invest. in Rep. Economy	**79lb d**	....	....	....	....	....	....	....	....	....	....	....	....	....	....	....
Portfolio Investment	**79lc d**	....	....	....	....	....	....	....	....	....	....	....	....	....	....	....
Equity Securities	**79ld d**	....	....	....	....	....	....	....	....	....	....	....	....	....	....	....
Debt Securities	**79le d**	....	....	....	....	....	....	....	....	....	....	....	....	....	....	....
Financial Derivatives	**79ll d**	....	....	....	....	....	....	....	....	....	....	....	....	....	....	....
Other Investment	**79lf d**	....	....	....	....	....	....	....	....	....	....	....	....	....	....	....
Monetary Authorities	**79lg d**	....	....	....	....	....	....	....	....	....	....	....	....	....	....	....
General Government	**79lh d**	....	....	....	....	....	....	....	....	....	....	....	....	....	....	....
Banks	**79li d**	....	....	....	....	....	....	....	....	....	....	....	....	....	....	....
Other Sectors	**79lj d**	....	....	....	....	....	....	....	....	....	....	....	....	....	....	....
Government Finance																*Millions of Dinars:*
Deficit (-) or Surplus	**80**	-15.03	-15.10	21.99	-23.10	-15.13	-14.83	-81.41	-61.08	-110.80	-104.07	-103.93	-100.77	-113.00	-68.21	-141.99
Revenue	**81**	30.26	35.74	42.56	46.18	65.74	82.63	107.59	142.25	158.49	187.90	226.15	309.20	362.04	400.58	415.01
Grants Received	**81z**	35.42	35.12	45.56	43.57	57.65	97.11	66.24	122.20	81.70	210.30	209.30	206.31	199.58	197.01	106.11
Expenditure	**82**	80.40	85.68	66.08	112.65	138.23	183.62	243.98	307.93	340.10	475.37	512.54	576.17	643.65	630.04	640.64
Lending Minus Repayments	**83**	.31	.28	.05	.20	.29	10.95	11.26	17.60	10.89	26.90	26.84	40.11	30.97	35.76	22.47
Financing																
Net Borrowing: Dinars	**84b**	4.20	12.10	4.25	9.32	8.08	9.75	12.89	9.62	13.29	26.89	11.21	16.06	19.19	8.04	14.24
Foreign Currency	**85b**	1.45	3.58	3.94	8.22	9.36	9.25	12.76	51.58	82.89	29.69	54.60	54.73	55.50	60.38	85.38
Use of Cash Balances	**87**	9.38	-.58	-30.18	5.56	-2.31	-4.17	55.76	-.12	14.62	47.49	38.12	29.98	38.31	-.21	42.37
Debt: Domestic	**88a**	14.30	29.40	37.70	50.40	56.00	65.40	89.30	105.90	135.20	139.40	177.80	209.50	250.00	287.90	316.50
Foreign	**89a**	41.80	48.00	59.50	67.70	79.80	91.70	114.10	147.30	187.80	233.70	255.90	350.20	441.50	536.50	653.60
National Accounts																*Millions of Dinars*
Exports of Goods & Services	**90c**	17.6	17.8	37.0	52.4	80.3	118.9	192.1	242.0	264.3	339.5	448.0	588.5	670.2	I 639.6	746.3
Government Consumption	**91f**	58.7	60.4	68.3	80.0	97.7	110.1	155.9	156.6	190.0	235.3	342.7	455.5	477.9	473.4	534.6
Gross Fixed Capital Formation	**93e**	25.2	30.7	36.3	47.2	63.2	87.9	138.0	201.0	229.1	294.5	452.9	672.6	626.9	535.9	526.8
Increase/Decrease(-) in Stocks	**93i**	-3.1	4.5	6.0	-8.0	2.4	.9	12.2	5.5	-6.1	-14.5	11.0	28.4	23.9	I 53.9	44.4
Private Consumption	**96f**	152.8	161.7	177.4	183.1	199.8	261.9	325.5	412.8	517.4	736.8	858.3	1,074.5	1,457.9	I 1,579.1	1,648.4
Imports of Goods & Services	**98c**	-76.8	-88.9	-117.8	-136.4	-196.1	-301.1	-422.0	-540.3	-605.6	-824.5	-961.7	-1,392.7	-1,555.7	I -1453.2	-1,519.1
Gross Domestic Product (GDP)	**99b**	211.8	226.2	251.7	265.2	300.4	379.1	512.1	624.6	767.9	914.6	1,151.2	1,426.7	1,701.1	I 1,828.7	1,981.4
Net Factor Inc/Pmts(-) Abroad	**98.n**	12.6	13.2	13.8	23.2	32.0	63.9	140.8	145.9	148.8	168.3	32.4	57.5	64.4	I 49.2	13.6
Gross National Income (GNI)	**99a**	187.7	200.2	221.9	242.4	280.4	377.5	564.6	662.7	784.0	924.9	1,183.6	1,484.2	1,765.5	1,877.9	1,995.0
Net National Income	**99e**	177.1	189.3	210.7	231.0	268.7	360.2	545.0	639.1	754.0	882.8	1,096.3	1,371.2	1,608.1	1,699.2	1,795.3
GDP Volume 1985 Prices	**99b.p**	....	....	....	....	....	....	....	....	....	....	....	....	....	....	....
GDP Volume (1995=100)	**99bvp**	....	....	....	....	....	....	....	....	....	....	....	....	....	....	....
GDP Deflator (1995=100)	**99bip**	....	....	....	....	....	....	....	....	....	....	....	....	....	....	....
																Millions:
Population	**99z**	2.30	2.38	2.46	2.54	2.62	2.70	2.78	I 2.71	2.77	2.84	2.92	3.01	3.10	3.20	I 3.36

1985	1986	1987	1988	1989	1990	1991	1992	1993	1994	1995	1996	1997	1998	1999		
Minus Sign Indicates Debit															**Balance of Payments**	
−260.5	−39.8	−351.8	−293.7	384.9	−227.1	−393.5	−835.2	−629.1	−398.0	−258.6	−221.9	29.3	14.1	....	Current Account, n.i.e.	78al *d*
788.9	732.0	933.1	1,007.4	1,109.4	1,063.8	1,129.5	1,218.9	1,246.3	1,424.5	1,769.6	1,816.9	1,835.5	1,802.4	....	Goods: Exports f.o.b.	78aa *d*
−2,426.7	−2,158.4	−2,400.1	−2,418.7	−1,882.5	−2,300.7	−2,302.2	−2,998.7	−3,145.2	−3,003.8	−3,287.8	−3,818.1	−3,648.5	−3,403.9	....	Goods: Imports f.o.b.	78ab *d*
−1,637.9	−1,426.4	−1,467.0	−1,411.3	−773.1	−1,236.9	−1,172.7	−1,779.7	−1,898.8	−1,579.4	−1,518.2	−2,001.1	−1,813.0	−1,601.6	....	*Trade Balance*	78ac *d*
1,167.1	1,058.8	1,291.7	1,420.6	1,239.2	1,447.2	1,351.2	1,449.2	1,573.7	1,562.0	1,709.2	1,846.3	1,736.8	1,825.1	....	Services: Credit	78ad *d*
−1,286.9	−1,150.5	−1,298.3	−1,340.5	−1,063.3	−1,267.9	−1,122.5	−1,324.7	−1,347.2	−1,392.7	−1,614.9	−1,597.7	−1,537.2	−1,783.8	....	Services: Debit	78ae *d*
−1,757.7	−1,518.1	−1,473.6	−1,331.1	−597.1	−1,057.6	−944.0	−1,655.2	−1,672.3	−1,410.1	−1,424.0	−1,752.6	−1,613.4	−1,560.2	....	*Balance on Goods & Services*	78af *d*
101.1	100.1	58.3	40.6	39.0	67.3	114.3	112.4	99.0	72.7	115.7	111.7	248.2	306.9	....	Income: Credit	78ag *d*
−189.6	−240.4	−278.6	−354.8	−235.6	−281.8	−447.7	−460.0	−409.4	−387.5	−394.5	−412.7	−457.0	−445.0	....	Income: Debit	78ah *d*
−1,846.2	−1,658.4	−1,693.8	−1,645.2	−793.7	−1,272.1	−1,277.4	−2,002.8	−1,982.8	−1,724.9	−1,702.8	−2,053.6	−1,822.1	−1,698.3	....	*Balance on Gds, Serv. & Inc.*	78ai *d*
1,828.3	1,872.7	1,547.1	1,532.0	1,284.5	1,123.1	949.5	1,263.6	1,441.1	1,447.4	1,591.8	1,970.2	2,096.1	1,984.3	....	Current Transfers, n.i.e.: Credit	78aj *d*
−242.5	−254.1	−205.1	−180.5	−105.8	−78.2	−65.7	−96.1	−87.4	−120.5	−147.6	−138.5	−244.6	−271.9	....	Current Transfers: Debit	78ak *d*
—	—	—	—	—	—	—	—	—	—	197.2	157.7	163.8	81.1	....	Capital Account, n.i.e.	78bc *d*
—	—	—	—	—	—	—	—	—	—	197.2	157.7	163.8	81.1	....	Capital Account, n.i.e.: Credit	78ba *d*
—	—	—	—	—	—	—	—	—	—	—	—	—	—	....	Capital Account: Debit	78bb *d*
248.2	99.5	465.2	374.2	79.5	572.7	2,097.3	615.1	−530.0	188.9	230.0	233.9	242.3	−177.3	....	Financial Account, n.i.e.	78bj *d*
.7	−3.9	−1.2	.1	−16.7	31.5	−13.7	3.4	53.0	23.1	27.3	43.3	—	—	....	Direct Investment Abroad	78bd *d*
24.9	22.8	39.5	23.7	−1.3	37.6	−11.9	40.7	−33.5	2.9	13.3	15.5	360.9	310.0	....	Dir. Invest. in Rep. Econ., n.i.e.	78be *d*
—	—	—	—	—	—	—	—	—	—	....	....	....	....	....	Portfolio Investment Assets	78bf *d*
—	—	—	—	—	—	—	—	—	—	....	....	....	....	....	Equity Securities	78bk *d*
—	—	—	—	—	—	—	—	—	—	....	....	....	....	....	Debt Securities	78bl *d*
—	—	—	—	—	—	—	—	—	—	....	—	....	....	....	Portfolio Investment Liab., n.i.e.	78bg *d*
—	—	—	—	—	—	—	—	—	—	....	—	....	....	....	Equity Securities	78bm *d*
—	—	—	—	—	—	—	—	—	—	....	—	....	....	....	Debt Securities	78bn *d*
....	....	....	....	....	....	....	....	....	....	....	....	....	....	....	Financial Derivatives Assets	78bw *d*
....	....	....	....	....	....	....	....	....	....	....	....	....	....	....	Financial Derivatives Liabilities	78bx *d*
−190.2	−84.9	−9.0	—	—	222.2	561.5	609.2	384.8	62.5	−313.4	−5.9	16.4	−80.3	....	Other Investment Assets	78bh *d*
−112.4	−77.1	−13.8	—	—	110.1	−241.7	−113.6	−94.9	−163.5	−313.4	−5.9	16.4	−80.3	....	Monetary Authorities	78bo *d*
−77.8	−7.8	4.8	—	—	—	—	—	−.3	—	....	....	....	....	....	General Government	78bp *d*
—	—	—	—	—	—	—	—	—	—	....	....	....	....	....	Banks	78bq *d*
—	—	—	—	—	112.1	803.2	722.8	480.0	225.9	....	....	....	....	....	Other Sectors	78br *d*
412.7	165.6	435.9	350.4	97.6	281.4	1,561.4	−38.3	−934.3	100.4	502.8	181.0	−135.0	−407.1	....	Other Investment Liab., n.i.e.	78bi *d*
—	—	169.9	−133.2	5.2	.2	—	.6	.7	−8.7	−34.4	−11.0	−27.6	−11.0	....	Monetary Authorities	78bs *d*
355.2	135.5	183.4	13.4	202.6	353.2	296.5	−532.1	−675.8	−235.4	96.8	17.8	−91.4	−391.0	....	General Government	78bt *d*
57.5	30.0	100.0	457.2	−75.9	−66.7	1,267.9	495.1	−257.5	344.5	440.5	174.2	−15.9	−5.1	....	Banks	78bu *d*
—	—	−17.5	13.0	−34.3	−5.3	−3.1	−1.9	−1.7	—	—	—	—	—	....	Other Sectors	78bv *d*
−29.6	−17.2	27.9	123.4	.3	75.4	321.4	83.1	298.0	−55.8	−339.9	−357.9	−160.8	−454.0	....	Net Errors and Omissions	78ca *d*
−41.9	42.5	141.3	203.9	464.7	421.0	2,025.2	−137.1	−861.1	−264.9	−171.3	−188.2	274.6	−536.1	....	*Overall Balance*	78cb *d*
41.9	−42.5	−141.3	−203.9	−464.7	−421.0	−2,025.2	137.1	861.1	264.9	171.3	188.2	−274.6	536.1	....	Reserves and Related Items	79da *d*
−14.1	−42.5	−141.3	−175.2	−512.0	−411.5	−2,025.2	−432.0	402.9	−216.8	−371.5	−280.7	−677.1	−83.4	....	Reserve Assets	79db *d*
56.0	—	—	−28.7	47.2	−9.5	—	21.1	−31.0	57.6	106.5	97.6	110.3	22.4	....	Use of Fund Credit and Loans	79dc *d*
—	—	—	—	—	—	—	548.0	489.1	424.1	436.3	371.4	292.2	597.0	....	Exceptional Financing	79de *d*
Millions of US Dollars															**International Investment Position**	
....	....	....	....	....	....	....	....	....	....	....	7,826.9	8,854.4	6,892.9	....	Assets	79aa *d*
....	....	....	....	....	....	....	....	....	....	....	—	—	—	....	Direct Investment Abroad	79ab *d*
....	....	....	....	....	....	....	....	....	....	....	209.0	270.9	279.8	....	Portfolio Investment	79ac *d*
....	....	....	....	....	....	....	....	....	....	....	89.1	110.6	109.7	....	Equity Securities	79ad *d*
....	....	....	....	....	....	....	....	....	....	....	119.9	160.4	170.1	....	Debt Securities	79ae *d*
....	....	....	....	....	....	....	....	....	....	—	—	—	—	—	Financial Derivatives	79al *d*
....	....	....	....	....	....	....	....	....	....	....	5,660.8	6,257.0	6,407.9	....	Other Investment	79af *d*
....	....	....	....	....	....	....	....	....	....	....	2,890.1	3,323.4	2,946.0	....	Monetary Authorities	79ag *d*
....	....	....	....	....	....	....	....	....	....	....	—	—	—	....	General Government	79ah *d*
....	....	....	....	....	....	....	....	....	....	....	2,770.7	2,933.6	3,461.9	....	Banks	79ai *d*
....	....	....	....	....	....	....	....	....	....	....	—	—	—	....	Other Sectors	79aj *d*
....	....	....	....	....	....	....	....	....	....	....	1,957.1	2,326.5	205.2	....	Reserve Assets	79ak *d*
....	....	....	....	....	....	....	....	....	....	....	9,833.2	9,611.8	10,169.3	....	Liabilities	79la *d*
....	....	....	....	....	....	....	....	....	....	....	—	—	—	....	Dir. Invest. in Rep. Economy	79lb *d*
....	....	....	....	....	....	....	....	....	....	....	—	—	—	....	Portfolio Investment	79lc *d*
....	....	....	....	....	....	....	....	....	....	....	....	....	....	....	Equity Securities	79ld *d*
....	....	....	....	....	....	....	....	....	....	....	....	....	....	....	Debt Securities	79le *d*
....	....	....	....	....	....	....	....	....	....	—	—	—	—	—	Financial Derivatives	79ll *d*
....	....	....	....	....	....	....	....	....	....	....	9,833.2	9,611.8	10,169.3	....	Other Investment	79lf *d*
....	....	....	....	....	....	....	....	....	....	....	410.9	470.9	502.2	....	Monetary Authorities	79lg *d*
....	....	....	....	....	....	....	....	....	....	....	6,321.6	6,056.1	6,587.6	....	General Government	79lh *d*
....	....	....	....	....	....	....	....	....	....	....	3,100.7	3,084.8	3,079.6	....	Banks	79li *d*
....	....	....	....	....	....	....	....	....	....		—	—	—	....	Other Sectors	79lj *d*
Year Ending December 31															**Government Finance**	
−111.74	−153.13	−198.21	−204.57	−137.10	−94.42	12.42	181.00	69.70	105.00	15.20	75.90	−102.60	....	....	Deficit (-) or Surplus	80
440.81	514.39	531.53	544.34	565.40	744.07	828.78	1,168.90	1,191.50	1,306.40	1,389.10	1,518.00	1,425.70	....	....	Revenue	81
187.84	143.71	127.54	155.43	261.72	164.28	225.20	137.40	163.30	175.60	182.80	191.30	225.00	....	....	Grants Received	81z
713.44	770.13	825.71	910.87	947.92	1,000.92	1,077.35	1,140.54	1,306.40	1,396.60	1,561.90	1,648.30	1,763.30	....	....	Expenditure	82
26.95	41.10	31.57	−6.53	16.30	1.85	−35.79	−15.24	−21.30	−19.60	−5.20	−14.90	−10.00	....	....	Lending Minus Repayments	83
															Financing	
25.89	−8.90	95.13	115.32	22.32	14.42	−7.05	−51.20	−47.70	−15.50	−119.00	−15.20	−47.20	....	....	Net Borrowing: Dinars	84b
124.97	86.11	7.24	−10.91	96.01	129.73	211.39	208.60	−133.20	75.40	287.80	296.50	−2.60	....	....	Foreign Currency	85b
−39.12	75.92	95.84	100.16	18.77	−49.74	−216.76	−338.40	111.20	−164.90	−184.00	−357.20	152.40	....	....	Use of Cash Balances	87
370.20	416.80	630.80	926.30	1,038.03	1,076.16	1,085.31	1,078.40	1,174.58	1,225.25	1,067.85	....	....	....	....	Debt: Domestic	88a
727.20	836.30	898.20	3,814.20	3,453.65	4,340.65	4,264.99	3,839.96	3,556.96	3,792.95	3,798.20	....	....	....	....	Foreign	89a
Millions of Dinars															**National Accounts**	
781.5	634.1	756.2	1,020.8	1,359.5	1,652.1	1,697.6	1,819.9	1,962.1	2,093.4	2,438.5	2,597.2	2,532.8	2,515.7	....	Exports of Goods & Services	90c
531.7	566.5	586.7	604.3	618.8	663.9	742.0	790.6	857.9	985.6	1,111.3	1,204.1	1,316.8	1,365.0	....	Government Consumption	91f
384.8	409.3	448.5	513.4	554.1	694.0	678.0	1,049.2	1,303.5	1,391.0	1,395.1	1,445.3	1,325.1	1,182.9	....	Gross Fixed Capital Formation	93e
30.1	35.0	67.1	19.1	9.1	156.1	60.5	159.6	119.2	60.0	159.3	52.1	−3.3	35.6	....	Increase/Decrease(-) in Stocks	93i
1,794.8	1,718.2	1,669.8	1,626.5	1,635.1	1,976.5	2,052.8	2,692.5	2,767.7	2,824.5	2,891.8	3,252.2	3,451.1	3,689.5	....	Private Consumption	96f
−1,502.7	−1,199.5	−1,319.7	−1,519.7	−1,804.5	−2,474.3	−2,362.6	−2,974.7	−3,151.7	−3,107.6	−3,435.2	−3,839.9	−3,676.7	−3,608.7	....	Imports of Goods & Services	98c
2,020.2	2,163.6	2,208.6	2,264.4	2,372.1	2,668.3	2,868.3	3,537.1	3,858.7	4,246.9	4,560.8	4,711.0	4,945.8	5,180.0	....	Gross Domestic Product (GDP)	99b
−4.7	−17.3	−50.2	−88.5	−191.4	−239.5	−221.1	−186.2	−149.1	−151.4	−116.8	−112.3	−47.4	−5.8	....	Net Factor Inc/Pmts(-) Abroad	98.n
2,015.5	2,146.3	2,158.4	2,175.9	2,180.7	2,428.8	2,647.2	3,350.9	3,709.6	4,095.5	4,444.0	4,598.7	4,898.4	5,174.2	....	Gross National Income (GNI)	99a
1,809.0	1,949.1	1,955.1	1,955.3	1,942.5	2,195.4	2,344.5	3,027.1	3,357.2	3,705.1	4,010.2	4,081.8	4,336.7	4,578.4	....	Net National Income	99e
2,020.2	2,161.9	2,224.5	2,183.2	1,889.6	1,908.0	1,951.9	2,283.7	2,417.0	2,601.5	2,702.2	2,729.6	2,764.5	2,824.9	....	GDP Volume 1985 Prices	99b.*p*
74.8	80.0	82.3	80.8	69.9	70.6	72.2	84.5	89.4	96.3	100.0	101.0	102.3	104.5	....	GDP Volume (1995=100)	99bv *p*
59.2	59.3	58.8	61.5	74.4	82.9	87.1	91.8	94.6	96.7	100.0	102.3	106.0	108.6	....	GDP Deflator (1995=100)	99bi *p*
Midyear Estimates																
3.83	3.94	4.00	4.06	4.50	4.62	4.80	5.02	5.26	5.51	5.73	5.94	6.13	6.30	6.48	**Population**	99z

(See notes in the back of the book.)

Kazakhstan

		1970	1971	1972	1973	1974	1975	1976	1977	1978	1979	1980	1981	1982	1983	1984
Exchange Rates																*Tenge per SDR:*
Official Rate	aa	....	....	....	....	....	....	....	....	....	....	....	....	....	....	
																Tenge per US Dollar:
Official Rate	ae	....	....	....	....	....	....	....	....	....	....	....	....	....	....	
Official Rate	rf	....	....	....	....	....	....	....	....	....	....	....	....	....	....	
Fund Position																*Millions of SDRs:*
Quota	2f. s	....	....	....	....	....	....	....	....	....	....	....	....	....	....	
SDRs	1b. s	....	....	....	....	....	....	....	....	....	....	....	....	....	....	
Reserve Position in the Fund	1c. s	....	....	....	....	....	....	....	....	....	....	....	....	....	....	
Total Fund Cred.&Loans Outstg.	2tl	....	....	....	....	....	....	....	....	....	....	....	....	....	....	
International Liquidity												*Millions of US Dollars Unless Otherwise Indicated:*				
Total Reserves minus Gold	1l. d	....	....	....	....	....	....	....	....	....	....	....	....	....	....	
SDRs	1b. d	....	....	....	....	....	....	....	....	....	....	....	....	....	....	
Reserve Position in the Fund	1c. d	....	....	....	....	....	....	....	....	....	....	....	....	....	....	
Foreign Exchange	1d. d	....	....	....	....	....	....	....	....	....	....	....	....	....	....	
Gold (Million Fine Troy Ounces)	1ad	....	....	....	....	....	....	....	....	....	....	....	....	....	....	
Gold (National Valuation)	1an d	....	....	....	....	....	....	....	....	....	....	....	....	....	....	
Monetary Authorities: Other Assets	3..d	....	....	....	....	....	....	....	....	....	....	....	....	....	....	
Other liab.	4..d	....	....	....	....	....	....	....	....	....	....	....	....	....	....	
Deposit Money Banks: Assets	7a. d	....	....	....	....	....	....	....	....	....	....	....	....	....	....	
Liabilities	7b. d	....	....	....	....	....	....	....	....	....	....	....	....	....	....	
Monetary Authorities																*Millions of Tenge:*
Foreign Assets	11	....	....	....	....	....	....	....	....	....	....	....	....	....	....	
Claims on General Government	12a	....	....	....	....	....	....	....	....	....	....	....	....	....	....	
Claims on Rest of the Economy	12d	....	....	....	....	....	....	....	....	....	....	....	....	....	....	
Claims on Deposit Money Banks	12e	....	....	....	....	....	....	....	....	....	....	....	....	....	....	
Reserve Money	14	....	....	....	....	....	....	....	....	....	....	....	....	....	....	
of which: Currency Outside Banks	14a	....	....	....	....	....	....	....	....	....	....	....	....	....	....	
Other Deposits	15	....	....	....	....	....	....	....	....	....	....	....	....	....	....	
Bonds & Money Market Instr.	16a	....	....	....	....	....	....	....	....	....	....	....	....	....	....	
Foreign Liabilities	16c	....	....	....	....	....	....	....	....	....	....	....	....	....	....	
General Government Deposits	16d	....	....	....	....	....	....	....	....	....	....	....	....	....	....	
Capital Accounts	17a	....	....	....	....	....	....	....	....	....	....	....	....	....	....	
Other Items (Net)	17r	....	....	....	....	....	....	....	....	....	....	....	....	....	....	
Deposit Money Banks																*Millions of Tenge:*
Reserves	20	....	....	....	....	....	....	....	....	....	....	....	....	....	....	
Foreign Assets	21	....	....	....	....	....	....	....	....	....	....	....	....	....	....	
Claims on General Government	22a	....	....	....	....	....	....	....	....	....	....	....	....	....	....	
Claims on Rest of the Economy	22d	....	....	....	....	....	....	....	....	....	....	....	....	....	....	
Demand Deposits	24	....	....	....	....	....	....	....	....	....	....	....	....	....	....	
Other Deposits	25	....	....	....	....	....	....	....	....	....	....	....	....	....	....	
Bonds	26ab	....	....	....	....	....	....	....	....	....	....	....	....	....	....	
Foreign Liabilities	26c	....	....	....	....	....	....	....	....	....	....	....	....	....	....	
General Government Deposits	26d	....	....	....	....	....	....	....	....	....	....	....	....	....	....	
Credit from Central Bank	26g	....	....	....	....	....	....	....	....	....	....	....	....	....	....	
Capital Accounts	27a	....	....	....	....	....	....	....	....	....	....	....	....	....	....	
Other Items (Net)	27r	....	....	....	....	....	....	....	....	....	....	....	....	....	....	
Monetary Survey																*Millions of Tenge:*
Foreign Assets (Net)	31n	....	....	....	....	....	....	....	....	....	....	....	....	....	....	
Domestic Credit	32	....	....	....	....	....	....	....	....	....	....	....	....	....	....	
Claims on General Govt. (Net)	32an	....	....	....	....	....	....	....	....	....	....	....	....	....	....	
Claims on Rest of the Economy	32d	....	....	....	....	....	....	....	....	....	....	....	....	....	....	
Money	34	....	....	....	....	....	....	....	....	....	....	....	....	....	....	
Quasi-Money	35	....	....	....	....	....	....	....	....	....	....	....	....	....	....	
Bonds & Money Market Instr.	36a	....	....	....	....	....	....	....	....	....	....	....	....	....	....	
Capital Accounts	37a	....	....	....	....	....	....	....	....	....	....	....	....	....	....	
Other Items (Net)	37r	....	....	....	....	....	....	....	....	....	....	....	....	....	....	
Money plus Quasi-Money	35l	....	....	....	....	....	....	....	....	....	....	....	....	....	....	
Interest Rates																*Percent Per Annum*
Refinancing Rate (End of Per.)	60	....	....	....	....	....	....	....	....	....	....	....	....	....	....	
Treasury Bill Rate	60c	....	....	....	....	....	....	....	....	....	....	....	....	....	....	
Prices and Labor																*Index Numbers:*
Producer Prices	63	....	....	....	....	....	....	....	....	....	....	....	....	....	....	
Consumer Prices	64	....	....	....	....	....	....	....	....	....	....	....	....	....	....	
Wages: Monthly Earnings	65	....	....	....	....	....	....	....	....	....	....	....	....	....	....	
Total Employment	67	....	....	....	....	....	....	....	....	....	....	....	....	....	....	
																Number in Thousands:
Unemployment	67c	....	....	....	....	....	....	....	....	....	....	....	....	....	....	
Unemployment Rate (%)	67r	....	....	....	....	....	....	....	....	....	....	....	....	....	....	
International Transactions																*Millions of US Dollars*
Exports	70..d	....	....	....	....	....	....	....	....	....	....	....	....	....	....	
Imports, c.i.f.	71..d	....	....	....	....	....	....	....	....	....	....	....	....	....	....	

1985	1986	1987	1988	1989	1990	1991	1992	1993	1994	1995	1996	1997	1998	1999		
End of Period															**Exchange Rates**	
								8.67	79.21	95.06	105.40	101.94	117.99	189.68	Official Rate	aa
End of Period (ae) Period Average (rf)																
								6.31	54.26	63.95	73.30	75.55	83.80	138.20	Official Rate	ae
									35.54	60.95	67.30	75.44	78.30	119.52	Official Rate	rf
End of Period															**Fund Position**	
							247.50	247.50	247.50	247.50	247.50	247.50	247.50	365.70	Quota	2f. s
							—	13.98	69.54	154.87	240.19	327.15	275.08	164.24	SDRs	1b. s
							.01	.01	.01	.01	.01	.01	.01	.01	Reserve Position in the Fund	1c. s
							—	61.88	198.00	290.82	383.60	378.96	463.66	335.15	Total Fund Cred.&Loans Outstg.	2tl
End of Period															**International Liquidity**	
								455.7	837.5	1,135.6	1,294.7	1,697.1	1,461.2	1,479.2	Total Reserves minus Gold......................	1l. d
								19.2	101.5	230.2	345.4	441.4	387.3	225.4	SDRs	1b. d
							.01	.01	.01	.01	.01	.01	.01	.01	Reserve Position in the Fund	1c. d
								436.5	736.0	905.3	949.3	1,255.7	1,073.9	1,253.8	Foreign Exchange	1d. d
								.65	.99	1.36	1.80	1.81	1.75	1.80	Gold (Million Fine Troy Ounces)	1ad
								255.5	378.0	524.3	949.3	523.9	503.6	522.8	Gold (National Valuation)	1an d
								133.1	3.5	2.4					Monetary Authorities: Other Assets	3.. d
									26.3	60.9					Other liab.	4.. d
								345.6	271.9	440.9	330.1	273.8	344.6	580.6	Deposit Money Banks: Assets	7a. d
								563.5	1,195.8	414.2	138.1	207.5	390.5	237.0	Liabilities	7b. d
End of Period															**Monetary Authorities**	
								5,328	66,143	106,300	129,801	I172,971	164,663	276,712	Foreign Assets	11
								1,696	20,236	39,467	39,265	I77,078	87,931	109,229	Claims on General Government	12a
								197	760	332	16,906	I620	7,277	12,658	Claims on Rest of the Economy	12d
								6,095	13,355	10,487	9,059	I8,248	2,084	4,634	Claims on Deposit Money Banks	12e
								4,309	31,171	66,550	84,354	I115,389	81,427	125,139	Reserve Money	14
								2,273	20,255	47,998	62,811	I92,796	68,728	103,492	of which: Currency Outside Banks..........	14a
								127	738	445	3,068	I18	47	1,107	Other Deposits	15
												6,855	12,046	6,206	Bonds & Money Market Instr.	16a
								2,660	16,548	31,444	46,001	I42,409	56,354	66,068	Foreign Liabilities.................................	16c
								2,016	8,337	14,641	13,908	I53,647	59,766	95,504	General Government Deposits	16d
								2,744	47,653	62,822	64,993	I52,611	63,480	118,511	Capital Accounts	17a
								1,460	-3,953	-19,317	-17,293	I-12,012	-11,167	-9,301	Other Items (Net)	17r
End of Period															**Deposit Money Banks**	
								1,914	8,638	14,771	16,891	I22,361	12,144	26,257	Reserves	20
								2,181	14,755	28,197	24,196	I20,685	28,874	80,233	Foreign Assets	21
								514	426	5,104	8,691	I25,303	21,184	32,752	Claims on General Government	22a
								14,310	111,747	71,988	72,448	I85,866	107,099	162,841	Claims on Rest of the Economy	22d
								5,593	32,894	63,930	71,938	I57,998	49,511	99,662	Demand Deposits	24
												22,073	29,767	66,723	Other Deposits.....................................	25
								—	92	1,902	119	I30	—	42	Bonds	26ab
								3,556	64,883	26,485	10,120	I15,674	32,727	32,750	Foreign Liabilities	26c
								111	1,494	5,416	11,494	I26,484	10,986	14,909	General Government Deposits	26d
								6,049	14,204	5,883	11,482	I8,208	5,092	2,801	Credit from Central Bank	26g
								1,091	14,662	29,259	39,289	I40,183	59,735	89,090	Capital Accounts	27a
								2,521	7,338	-12,815	-22,216	I-16,436	-18,517	-3,895	Other Items (Net)	27r
End of Period															**Monetary Survey**	
								1,293	-533	76,568	97,876	I135,572	104,455	258,127	Foreign Assets (Net)	31n
								14,590	123,338	96,834	111,908	I108,737	152,739	207,067	Domestic Credit	32
								83	10,831	24,514	22,554	I22,250	38,363	31,568	Claims on General Govt. (Net)..........	32an
								14,507	112,507	72,320	89,354	I86,487	114,376	175,499	Claims on Rest of the Economy	32d
								8,198	55,417	115,384	139,452	I150,908	118,735	204,544	Money...	34
												22,091	29,815	67,830	Quasi-Money	35
								—	92	1,902	119	I6,885	12,046	6,248	Bonds & Money Market Instr.	36a
								3,835	62,315	92,081	104,282	I92,794	123,215	207,601	Capital Accounts	37a
								3,852	4,982	-35,966	-34,069	I-28,369	-26,617	-21,029	Other Items (Net)	37r
								8,198	55,417	115,384	139,452	I172,999	148,549	272,373	Money plus Quasi-Money	35l
Percent Per Annum															**Interest Rates**	
								170.00	230.00	I52.50	35.00	18.50	25.00	18.00	Refinancing Rate *(End of Per.)*................	60
									214.34	48.98	28.91	15.15	23.59	15.63	Treasury Bill Rate	60c
Period Averages															**Prices and Labor**	
										100.0	123.9	142.8	144.0	171.4	Producer Prices	63
								1.8	36.2	100.0	139.3	163.5	175.2	189.6	Consumer Prices	64
								2.7	36.1	100.0	142.9	178.5	202.3	229.5	Wages: Monthly Earnings	65
								112.6	105.3	100.0	87.7	72.7	61.5	54.9	Total Employment	67
Period Averages																
							34	41	70	140	282	258	252		Unemployment......................................	67c
							.4	.6	1.1	2.1	4.2	3.8	3.7		Unemployment Rate (%)	67r
Millions of US Dollars															**International Transactions**	
								3,277.0	3,230.8	5,250.2	5,911.0	6,497.0	5,435.8	5,592.2	Exports...	70.. d
								3,887.4	3,561.2	3,806.7	4,241.1	4,300.8	4,349.6	3,682.7	Imports, c.i.f.	71.. d

Kazakhstan

916

		1970	1971	1972	1973	1974	1975	1976	1977	1978	1979	1980	1981	1982	1983	1984
Balance of Payments																
																Millions of US Dollars:
Current Account, n.i.e.	78al *d*	....	....	....	....	....	....	....	....	....	....	....	....	....	....	....
Goods: Exports f.o.b.	78aa *d*	....	....	....	....	....	....	....	....	....	....	....	....	....	....	....
Goods: Imports f.o.b.	78ab *d*	....	....	....	....	....	....	....	....	....	....	....	....	....	....	....
Trade Balance	78ac *d*	....	....	....	....	....	....	....	....	....	....	....	....	....	....	....
Services: Credit	78ad *d*	....	....	....	....	....	....	....	....	....	....	....	....	....	....	....
Services: Debit	78ae *d*	....	....	....	....	....	....	....	....	....	....	....	....	....	....	....
Balance on Goods & Services	78af *d*	....	....	....	....	....	....	....	....	....	....	....	....	....	....	....
Income: Credit	78ag *d*	....	....	....	....	....	....	....	....	....	....	....	....	....	....	....
Income: Debit	78ah *d*	....	....	....	....	....	....	....	....	....	....	....	....	....	....	....
Balance on Gds, Serv. & Inc.	78ai *d*	....	....	....	....	....	....	....	....	....	....	....	....	....	....	....
Current Transfers, n.i.e.: Credit	78aj *d*	....	....	....	....	....	....	....	....	....	....	....	....	....	....	....
Current Transfers: Debit	78ak *d*	....	....	....	....	....	....	....	....	....	....	....	....	....	....	....
Capital Account, n.i.e.	78bc *d*	....	....	....	....	....	....	....	....	....	....	....	....	....	....	....
Capital Account, n.i.e.: Credit	78ba *d*	....	....	....	....	....	....	....	....	....	....	....	....	....	....	....
Capital Account: Debit	78bb *d*	....	....	....	....	....	....	....	....	....	....	....	....	....	....	....
Financial Account, n.i.e.	78bj *d*	....	....	....	....	....	....	....	....	....	....	....	....	....	....	....
Direct Investment Abroad	78bd *d*	....	....	....	....	....	....	....	....	....	....	....	....	....	....	....
Dir. Invest. in Rep. Econ., n.i.e.	78be *d*	....	....	....	....	....	....	....	....	....	....	....	....	....	....	....
Portfolio Investment Assets	78bf *d*	....	....	....	....	....	....	....	....	....	....	....	....	....	....	....
Equity Securities	78bk *d*	....	....	....	....	....	....	....	....	....	....	....	....	....	....	....
Debt Securities	78bl *d*	....	....	....	....	....	....	....	....	....	....	....	....	....	....	....
Portfolio Investment Liab., n.i.e.	78bg *d*	....	....	....	....	....	....	....	....	....	....	....	....	....	....	....
Equity Securities	78bm *d*	....	....	....	....	....	....	....	....	....	....	....	....	....	....	....
Debt Securities	78bn *d*	....	....	....	....	....	....	....	....	....	....	....	....	....	....	....
Financial Derivatives Assets	78bw *d*	....	....	....	....	....	....	....	....	....	....	....	....	....	....	....
Financial Derivatives Liabilities	78bx *d*	....	....	....	....	....	....	....	....	....	....	....	....	....	....	....
Other Investment Assets	78bh *d*	....	....	....	....	....	....	....	....	....	....	....	....	....	....	....
Monetary Authorities	78bo *d*	....	....	....	....	....	....	....	....	....	....	....	....	....	....	....
General Government	78bp *d*	....	....	....	....	....	....	....	....	....	....	....	....	....	....	....
Banks	78bq *d*	....	....	....	....	....	....	....	....	....	....	....	....	....	....	....
Other Sectors	78br *d*	....	....	....	....	....	....	....	....	....	....	....	....	....	....	....
Other Investment Liab., n.i.e.	78bi *d*	....	....	....	....	....	....	....	....	....	....	....	....	....	....	....
Monetary Authorities	78bs *d*	....	....	....	....	....	....	....	....	....	....	....	....	....	....	....
General Government	78bt *d*	....	....	....	....	....	....	....	....	....	....	....	....	....	....	....
Banks	78bu *d*	....	....	....	....	....	....	....	....	....	....	....	....	....	....	....
Other Sectors	78bv *d*	....	....	....	....	....	....	....	....	....	....	....	....	....	....	....
Net Errors and Omissions	78ca *d*	....	....	....	....	....	....	....	....	....	....	....	....	....	....	....
Overall Balance	78cb *d*	....	....	....	....	....	....	....	....	....	....	....	....	....	....	....
Reserves and Related Items	79da *d*	....	....	....	....	....	....	....	....	....	....	....	....	....	....	....
Reserve Assets	79db *d*	....	....	....	....	....	....	....	....	....	....	....	....	....	....	....
Use of Fund Credit and Loans	79dc *d*	....	....	....	....	....	....	....	....	....	....	....	....	....	....	....
Exceptional Financing	79de *d*	....	....	....	....	....	....	....	....	....	....	....	....	....	....	....
International Investment Position																
																Millions of US Dollars
Assets	79aa *d*	....	....	....	....	....	....	....	....	....	....	....	....	....	....	....
Direct Investment Abroad	79ab *d*	....	....	....	....	....	....	....	....	....	....	....	....	....	....	....
Portfolio Investment	79ac *d*	....	....	....	....	....	....	....	....	....	....	....	....	....	....	....
Equity Securities	79ad *d*	....	....	....	....	....	....	....	....	....	....	....	....	....	....	....
Debt Securities	79ae *d*	....	....	....	....	....	....	....	....	....	....	....	....	....	....	....
Financial Derivatives	79al *d*	....	....	....	....	....	....	....	....	....	....	....	....	....	....	....
Other Investment	79af *d*	....	....	....	....	....	....	....	....	....	....	....	....	....	....	....
Monetary Authorities	79ag *d*	....	....	....	....	....	....	....	....	....	....	....	....	....	....	....
General Government	79ah *d*	....	....	....	....	....	....	....	....	....	....	....	....	....	....	....
Banks	79ai *d*	....	....	....	....	....	....	....	....	....	....	....	....	....	....	....
Other Sectors	79aj *d*	....	....	....	....	....	....	....	....	....	....	....	....	....	....	....
Reserve Assets	79ak *d*	....	....	....	....	....	....	....	....	....	....	....	....	....	....	....
Liabilities	79la *d*	....	....	....	....	....	....	....	....	....	....	....	....	....	....	....
Dir. Invest. in Rep. Economy	79lb *d*	....	....	....	....	....	....	....	....	....	....	....	....	....	....	....
Portfolio Investment	79lc *d*	....	....	....	....	....	....	....	....	....	....	....	....	....	....	....
Equity Securities	79ld *d*	....	....	....	....	....	....	....	....	....	....	....	....	....	....	....
Debt Securities	79le *d*	....	....	....	....	....	....	....	....	....	....	....	....	....	....	....
Financial Derivatives	79ll *d*	....	....	....	....	....	....	....	....	....	....	....	....	....	....	....
Other Investment	79lf *d*	....	....	....	....	....	....	....	....	....	....	....	....	....	....	....
Monetary Authorities	79lg *d*	....	....	....	....	....	....	....	....	....	....	....	....	....	....	....
General Government	79lh *d*	....	....	....	....	....	....	....	....	....	....	....	....	....	....	....
Government Finance																
																Millions of Tenge:
Deficit (-) or Surplus	80	....	....	....	....	....	....	....	....	....	....	....	....	....	....	....
Total Revenue and Grants	81y	....	....	....	....	....	....	....	....	....	....	....	....	....	....	....
Revenue	81	....	....	....	....	....	....	....	....	....	....	....	....	....	....	....
Grants Received	81z	....	....	....	....	....	....	....	....	....	....	....	....	....	....	....
Exp. & Lending Minus Repay	82z	....	....	....	....	....	....	....	....	....	....	....	....	....	....	....
Expenditure	82	....	....	....	....	....	....	....	....	....	....	....	....	....	....	....
Lending Minus Repayments	83	....	....	....	....	....	....	....	....	....	....	....	....	....	....	....
Total Financing																
Domestic	84a	....	....	....	....	....	....	....	....	....	....	....	....	....	....	....
Foreign	85a	....	....	....	....	....	....	....	....	....	....	....	....	....	....	....
National Accounts																
																Billions of Tenge
Househ.Cons.Expend.,incl.NPISHs	96f	....	....	....	....	....	....	....	....	....	....	....	....	....	....	....
Government Consumption Expend.	91f	....	....	....	....	....	....	....	....	....	....	....	....	....	....	....
Gross Fixed Capital Formation	93e	....	....	....	....	....	....	....	....	....	....	....	....	....	....	....
Changes in Inventories	93i	....	....	....	....	....	....	....	....	....	....	....	....	....	....	....
Exports of Goods and Services	90c	....	....	....	....	....	....	....	....	....	....	....	....	....	....	....
Imports of Goods and Services	98c	....	....	....	....	....	....	....	....	....	....	....	....	....	....	....
Gross Domestic Product (GDP)	99b	....	....	....	....	....	....	....	....	....	....	....	....	....	....	....
Statistical Discrepancy	99bs	....	....	....	....	....	....	....	....	....	....	....	....	....	....	....
GDP, Production Based	99bp	....	....	....	....	....	....	....	....	....	....	....	....	....	....	....
Net Primary Income from Abroad	98.n	....	....	....	....	....	....	....	....	....	....	....	....	....	....	....
Gross National Income (GNI)	99a	....	....	....	....	....	....	....	....	....	....	....	....	....	....	....
Net Current Transf.from Abroad	98t	....	....	....	....	....	....	....	....	....	....	....	....	....	....	....
Gross Nat'l Disposable Inc.(GNDI)	99i	....	....	....	....	....	....	....	....	....	....	....	....	....	....	....
Gross Savings	99s	....	....	....	....	....	....	....	....	....	....	....	....	....	....	....
GDP Volume (1995=100)	99bv *p*	....	....	....	....	....	....	....	....	....	....	....	....	....	....	....
GDP Deflator (1995=100)	99bi *p*	....	....	....	....	....	....	....	....	....	....	....	....	....	....	....
																Millions:
Population	99z	....	....	....	....	....	....	....	....	....	....	....	....	....	....	....

	1985	1986	1987	1988	1989	1990	1991	1992	1993	1994	1995	1996	1997	1998	1999		
Minus Sign Indicates Debit																Balance of Payments	
	....	....	....	....	....	....	....	....	....	....	–213.1	–751.0	–799.3	–1,224.9	–171.0	Current Account, n.i.e.	78al *d*
	....	....	....	....	....	....	....	....	....	....	5,440.0	6,291.6	6,899.3	5,870.5	5,988.7	Goods: Exports f.o.b.	78aa *d*
	....	....	....	....	....	....	....	....	....	....	–5,325.9	–6,626.7	–7,175.7	–6,671.7	–5,645.0	Goods: Imports f.o.b.	78ab *d*
	....	....	....	....	....	....	....	....	....	....	114.1	–335.1	–276.4	–801.2	343.7	*Trade Balance*	78ac *d*
	....	....	....	....	....	....	....	....	....	....	535.1	674.4	841.9	904.3	932.5	Services: Credit	78ad *d*
	....	....	....	....	....	....	....	....	....	....	–775.8	–928.3	–1,124.4	–1,154.1	–1,104.2	Services: Debit	78ae *d*
	....	....	....	....	....	....	....	....	....	....	–126.6	–589.0	–558.9	–1,051.0	172.0	*Balance on Goods & Services*	78af *d*
	....	....	....	....	....	....	....	....	....	....	44.6	56.7	73.8	95.5	108.6	Income: Credit	78ag *d*
	....	....	....	....	....	....	....	....	....	....	–190.1	–277.1	–388.8	–391.8	–608.3	Income: Debit	78ah *d*
	....	....	....	....	....	....	....	....	....	....	–272.1	–809.4	–873.9	–1,347.3	–327.7	*Balance on Gds, Serv. & Inc.*	78ai *d*
	....	....	....	....	....	....	....	....	....	....	79.9	83.4	104.7	141.4	174.7	Current Transfers, n.i.e.: Credit	78aj *d*
	....	....	....	....	....	....	....	....	....	....	–20.9	–25.0	–30.1	–19.0	–18.0	Current Transfers: Debit	78ak *d*
	....	....	....	....	....	....	....	....	....	....	–380.6	–315.5	–439.8	–369.1	–234.0	Capital Account, n.i.e.	78bc *d*
	....	....	....	....	....	....	....	....	....	....	116.1	87.9	58.3	65.9	61.1	Capital Account, n.i.e.: Credit	78ba *d*
	....	....	....	....	....	....	....	....	....	....	–496.7	–403.4	–498.1	–435.0	–295.1	Capital Account: Debit	78bb *d*
	....	....	....	....	....	....	....	....	....	....	1,162.5	2,005.1	2,901.6	2,229.1	1,299.2	Financial Account, n.i.e.	78bj *d*
	....	....	....	....	....	....	....	....	....	....	–.3	....	–1.4	–8.1	–3.6	Direct Investment Abroad	78bd *d*
	....	....	....	....	....	....	....	....	....	....	964.2	1,137.0	1,321.4	1,151.4	1,587.0	Dir. Invest. in Rep. Econ., n.i.e.	78be *d*
	....	....	....	....	....	....	....	....	....	....	—	....	–1.2	–5.3	–5.6	Portfolio Investment Assets	78bf *d*
	....	....	....	....	....	....	....	....	....	....	....	....	–1.2	–.4	–1.8	Equity Securities	78bk *d*
	....	....	....	....	....	....	....	....	....	....	—	....	....	–4.9	–3.8	Debt Securities	78bl *d*
	....	....	....	....	....	....	....	....	....	....	7.2	223.5	405.4	66.2	–39.9	Portfolio Investment Liab., n.i.e.	78bg *d*
	....	....	....	....	....	....	....	....	....	....	....	....	....	....	....	Equity Securities	78bm *d*
	....	....	....	....	....	....	....	....	....	....	7.2	223.5	405.4	66.2	–39.9	Debt Securities	78bn *d*
	....	....	....	....	....	....	....	....	....	....	....	....	....	....	....	Financial Derivatives Assets	78bw *d*
	....	....	....	....	....	....	....	....	....	....	....	....	....	....	....	Financial Derivatives Liabilities	78bx *d*
	....	....	....	....	....	....	....	....	....	....	–657.4	243.8	–139.5	–220.5	–778.4	Other Investment Assets	78bh *d*
	....	....	....	....	....	....	....	....	....	....	21.3	2.1	....	....	–.3	Monetary Authorities	78bo *d*
	....	....	....	....	....	....	....	....	....	....	—	27.8	.3	–41.1	16.3	General Government	78bp *d*
	....	....	....	....	....	....	....	....	....	....	–152.3	174.4	–66.0	–67.9	–205.8	Banks	78bq *d*
	....	....	....	....	....	....	....	....	....	....	–526.4	39.5	–73.8	–111.5	–588.6	Other Sectors	78br *d*
	....	....	....	....	....	....	....	....	....	....	848.8	400.8	1,316.9	1,245.4	539.7	Other Investment Liab., n.i.e.	78bi *d*
	....	....	....	....	....	....	....	....	....	....	–4.9	12.1	–5.0	–37.7	—	Monetary Authorities	78bs *d*
	....	....	....	....	....	....	....	....	....	....	331.3	323.4	317.2	673.3	291.5	General Government	78bt *d*
	....	....	....	....	....	....	....	....	....	....	–251.5	–125.7	161.4	60.2	–20.2	Banks	78bu *d*
	....	....	....	....	....	....	....	....	....	....	773.9	191.0	843.3	549.6	268.4	Other Sectors	78bv *d*
	....	....	....	....	....	....	....	....	....	....	–270.1	–780.0	–1,114.1	–1,078.4	–641.6	Net Errors and Omissions	78ca *d*
	....	....	....	....	....	....	....	....	....	....	298.7	158.6	548.4	–443.3	252.6	*Overall Balance*	78cb *d*
	....	....	....	....	....	....	....	....	....	....	–298.7	–158.6	–548.4	443.3	–252.6	Reserves and Related Items	79da *d*
	....	....	....	....	....	....	....	....	....	....	–440.1	–293.7	–542.0	321.7	–77.1	Reserve Assets	79db *d*
	....	....	....	....	....	....	....	....	....	....	141.4	135.1	–6.4	121.6	–175.5	Use of Fund Credit and Loans	79dc *d*
	....	....	....	....	....	....	....	....	....	....	....	....	....	....	....	Exceptional Financing	79de *d*
Millions of US Dollars																International Investment Position	
	....	....	....	....	....	....	....	....	....	....	....	....	2,629.1	2,391.8	2,598.3	Assets	79aa *d*
	....	....	....	....	....	....	....	....	....	....	....	....	2.6	3.1	3.1	Direct Investment Abroad	79ab *d*
	....	....	....	....	....	....	....	....	....	....	....	....	2.0	4.2	1.0	Portfolio Investment	79ac *d*
	....	....	....	....	....	....	....	....	....	....	....	....	—	—	—	Equity Securities	79ad *d*
	....	....	....	....	....	....	....	....	....	....	....	....	2.0	4.2	1.0	Debt Securities	79ae *d*
	....	....	....	....	....	....	....	....	....	....	....	....	—	2.0	—	Financial Derivatives	79al *d*
	....	....	....	....	....	....	....	....	....	....	....	....	335.3	417.7	592.1	Other Investment	79af *d*
	....	....	....	....	....	....	....	....	....	....	....	....	.3	.1	....	Monetary Authorities	79ag *d*
	....	....	....	....	....	....	....	....	....	....	....	....	....	....	46.8	General Government	79ah *d*
	....	....	....	....	....	....	....	....	....	....	....	....	288.2	370.8	545.0	Banks	79ai *d*
	....	....	....	....	....	....	....	....	....	....	....	....	....	....	....	Other Sectors	79aj *d*
	....	....	....	....	....	....	....	....	....	....	....	....	2,289.2	1,964.8	2,002.1	Reserve Assets	79ak *d*
	....	....	....	....	....	....	....	....	....	....	....	....	2,597.7	3,592.6	3,658.6	Liabilities	79la *d*
	....	....	....	....	....	....	....	....	....	....	....	....	50.1	122.3	112.7	Dir. Invest. in Rep. Economy	79lb *d*
	....	....	....	....	....	....	....	....	....	....	....	....	623.9	663.4	617.2	Portfolio Investment	79lc *d*
	....	....	....	....	....	....	....	....	....	....	....	....	53.9	49.9	37.7	Equity Securities	79ld *d*
	....	....	....	....	....	....	....	....	....	....	....	....	570.0	613.5	579.5	Debt Securities	79le *d*
	....	....	....	....	....	....	....	....	....	....	....	....	—	—	—	Financial Derivatives	79ll *d*
	....	....	....	....	....	....	....	....	....	....	....	....	1,923.7	2,806.9	2,928.7	Other Investment	79lf *d*
	....	....	....	....	....	....	....	....	....	....	....	....	555.4	655.4	462.6	Monetary Authorities	79lg *d*
	....	....	....	....	....	....	....	....	....	....	....	....	....	....	....	General Government	79lh *d*
Year Ending December 31																**Government Finance**	
	....	....	....	....	....	....	....	....	....	–30,382	–25,181	–59,564	–63,998	–72,073	–66,607	Deficit (-) or Surplus	80
	....	....	....	....	....	....	....	....	....	79,474	178,347	306,943	405,624	379,521	395,586	Total Revenue and Grants	81y
	....	....	....	....	....	....	....	....	....	79,413	178,347	306,943	405,342	374,068	392,957	Revenue	81
	....	....	....	....	....	....	....	....	....	61	—	—	282	5,453	2,629	Grants Received	81z
	....	....	....	....	....	....	....	....	....	109,856	203,528	366,507	469,622	451,594	462,193	Exp. & Lending Minus Repay	82z
	....	....	....	....	....	....	....	....	....	109,672	210,603	381,602	439,476	426,142	444,257	Expenditure	82
	....	....	....	....	....	....	....	....	....	184	–7,075	–15,095	30,146	25,452	17,936	Lending Minus Repayments	83
																Total Financing	
	....	....	....	....	....	....	....	....	....	....	....	....	17,175	20,504	19,050	Domestic	84a
	....	....	....	....	....	....	....	....	....	....	....	....	46,823	51,569	47,557	Foreign	85a
Billions of Tenge																**National Accounts**	
	....	....	....	....	....	....	....	....	20,853	328,847	721,130	952,790	1,179,145	1,243,457	....	Househ.Cons.Expend.,incl.NPISHs	96f
	....	....	....	....	....	....	....	....	4,089	45,234	137,748	182,790	207,023	187,787	....	Government Consumption Expend.	91f
	....	....	....	....	....	....	....	....	8,211	110,655	233,812	243,876	271,765	296,205	....	Gross Fixed Capital Formation	93e
	....	....	....	....	....	....	....	....	–2,319	10,898	2,695	–15,281	–10,941	1,487	....	Changes in Inventories	93i
	....	....	....	....	....	....	....	....	11,150	156,958	395,269	499,318	583,860	525,945	....	Exports of Goods and Services	90c
	....	....	....	....	....	....	....	....	–13,752	–199,526	–441,665	–509,737	–626,095	–604,215	....	Imports of Goods and Services	98c
	....	....	....	....	....	....	....	....	28,232	453,065	1,048,989	1,353,755	1,604,756	1,650,666	....	Gross Domestic Product (GDP)	99b
	....	....	....	....	....	....	....	....	1,191	–29,597	–34,799	61,995	67,386	82,598	....	Statistical Discrepancy	99bs
	....	....	....	....	....	....	....	....	29,423	423,469	1,014,190	1,415,750	1,672,142	1,733,264	....	GDP, Production Based	99bp
	....	....	....	....	....	....	....	....	–71	–2,171	–9,110	–12,276	–23,379	–23,329	....	Net Primary Income from Abroad	98.n
	....	....	....	....	....	....	....	....	29,352	421,298	1,005,080	1,403,474	1,648,764	1,709,934	....	Gross National Income (GNI)	99a
	....	....	....	....	....	....	....	....	342	7,364	7,884	9,813	5,633	6,114	....	Net Current Transf.from Abroad	98t
	....	....	....	....	....	....	....	....	29,694	428,661	1,012,964	1,413,287	1,654,397	1,716,049	....	Gross Nat'l Disposable Inc.(GNDI)	99i
	....	....	....	....	....	....	....	....	4,752	54,580	154,085	277,707	268,230	284,804	....	Gross Savings	99s
	....	....	....	....	....	....	....	....	....	I 95.2	100.0	109.5	110.8	106.9	....	GDP Volume (1995=100)	99bv *p*
	....	....	....	....	....	....	....	....	....	I —	100.0	117.9	138.1	147.2	....	GDP Deflator (1995=100)	99bi *p*
Midyear Estimates																	
	....	....	....	....	....	....	....	16.52	16.48	16.30	16.07	15.58	15.33	15.07	14.94	**Population**	99z

(See notes in the back of the book.)

Kenya

		1970	1971	1972	1973	1974	1975	1976	1977	1978	1979	1980	1981	1982	1983	1984
Exchange Rates														*Shillings per SDR:*		
Principal Rate	aa	7.143	7.755	7.755	8.324	8.745	9.660	9.660	9.660	9.660	9.660	9.660	11.950	14.060	14.417	15.187
														Shillings per US Dollar:		
Principal Rate	ae	7.143	7.143	7.143	6.900	7.143	8.260	8.310	7.947	7.404	7.328	7.569	10.286	12.725	13.796	15.781
Principal Rate	rf	7.143	7.143	7.143	7.020	7.143	7.343	8.367	8.277	7.729	7.475	7.420	9.047	10.922	13.312	14.414
Fund Position														*Millions of SDRs:*		
Quota	2f. s	48.0	48.0	48.0	48.0	48.0	48.0	48.0	48.0	69.0	69.0	103.5	103.5	103.5	142.0	142.0
SDRs	1b. s	5.8	12.0	17.1	17.1	1.9	3.8	2.8	14.4	11.0	82.1	20.2	9.4	14.0	16.6	2.2
Reserve Position in the Fund	1c. s	12.0	12.0	12.0	12.3								.2			
Total Fund Cred.&Loans Outstg.	2tl	—	—	—	—	32.1	68.6	85.0	52.8	72.2	142.7	199.1	222.2	356.7	443.5	428.3
International Liquidity											*Millions of US Dollars Unless Otherwise Indicated:*						
Total Reserves minus Gold	1l. d	219.8	170.9	202.0	233.0	193.3	173.4	275.5	522.4	352.6	627.7	491.7	231.1	211.7	376.0	389.8
SDRs	1b. d	5.8	13.0	18.5	20.6	2.3	4.4	3.2	17.5	14.3	108.1	25.7	10.9	15.4	17.4	2.1
Reserve Position in the Fund	1c. d	12.0	13.1	13.1	14.8								.2	1.6	10.1	10.7
Foreign Exchange	1d. d	202.0	144.9	170.4	197.6	191.0	169.0	272.3	504.9	338.3	519.6	466.0	220.0	194.6	348.5	377.0
Gold (Million Fine Troy Ounces)	1ad	....	....	....	—	—	—	—	.021	.072	.080	.080	.080	.080	.080	.080
Gold (National Valuation)	1an d	....	....	....	—e	—	—	—	.9	9.4	9.7	9.4	18.6	17.4	16.6	13.6
Monetary Authorities: Other Liab.	4.. d	1.3	1.1	2.9	.8	1.3	10.5	2.8	7.6	9.0	13.4	6.0	4.2	14.4	4.7	.8
Deposit Money Banks: Assets	7a. d	25.2	22.0	16.4	32.1	42.6	40.7	48.3	42.0	50.4	68.8	70.4	67.5	49.3	44.2	40.1
Liabilities	7b. d	19.6	25.0	25.4	39.5	56.0	58.1	49.7	52.0	52.5	72.7	68.7	42.8	44.1	45.3	51.5
Other Banking Insts.: Liabilities	7f. d	3.6	2.3	1.9	2.7	7.5	6.2	8.3	8.7	11.1	11.3	17.8	14.5	11.1	9.9	7.5
Monetary Authorities													*Millions of Shillings:*			
Foreign Assets	11	1,586	1,230	1,416	1,603	1,347	1,427	2,301	4,259	2,732	4,780	3,784	2,577	2,957	5,459	6,444
Claims on Central Government	12a	75	158	194	237	526	1,169	834	1,217	1,639	1,783	2,663	4,955	8,725	7,028	7,089
Claims on Deposit Money Banks	12e	—	10	—	—	236	34	9	18	130	—	211	127	20	—	20
Reserve Money	14	1,248	1,143	1,264	1,395	1,789	1,613	2,001	3,233	3,466	4,325	4,422	4,605	5,787	5,659	6,304
of which: Currency Outside DMBs	14a	697	740	894	982	1,086	1,235	1,625	2,182	2,305	2,673	3,032	3,569	3,724	4,083	4,370
Foreign Liabilities	16c	9	8	21	6	289	750	845	570	763	1,476	1,967	2,704	5,190	6,470	6,637
Long-Term Foreign Liabilities	16cl	—	—	—	—	—	—	—	—	—	—	—	—	—	—	—
Central Government Deposits	16d	339	190	241	330	37	—	55	1,253	—	—	—	103	—	—	—
Counterpart Funds	16e															
Capital Accounts	17a	52	52	52	182	186	186	186	186	186	312	364	391	431	525	618
Other Items (Net)	17r	13	5	32	−73	−192	82	57	251	85	449	−96	−143	294	−167	−6
Deposit Money Banks													*Millions of Shillings:*			
Reserves	20	515	391	343	372	514	298	313	972	833	1,184	1,204	985	1,834	1,323	1,635
Foreign Assets	21	180	157	117	222	304	336	401	334	373	504	533	695	627	609	632
Claims on Central Government	22a	357	233	452	650	510	677	1,192	1,963	1,805	2,216	1,542	2,133	2,544	2,121	3,093
Claims on Local Government	22b	15	21	26	42	38	34	25	24	29	33	28	15	25	23	24
Claims on Nonfin.Pub.Enterprises	22c	86	152	157	188	185	269	190	235	182	207	337	333	540	1,138	1,526
Claims on Private Sector	22d	1,732	2,214	2,481	3,143	3,814	4,149	4,892	6,513	8,901	9,774	11,759	13,025	14,357	15,380	16,944
Claims on Other Financial Insts	22f						196	471	684	235	692	147	117	434	693	563
Demand Deposits	24	1,489	1,616	1,880	2,413	2,620	2,851	3,525	5,095	5,445	6,327	5,814	6,374	6,798	7,640	8,901
Time & Foreign Currency Deposits	25	1,279	1,398	1,492	1,907	2,064	2,672	3,335	5,193	6,277	6,833	7,702	8,872	10,735	10,953	12,198
Foreign Liabilities	26c	140	178	181	273	400	480	413	413	388	533	520	440	561	626	813
Central Government Deposits	26d	54	67	58	76	70	81	72	128	219	353	246	212	566	440	613
Credit from Monetary Authorities	26g	—	5	—	—	254	19	—	—	120	—	197	75	—	4	165
Credit from Other Financial Insts	26i															
Capital Accounts	27a	185	212	273	307	373	433	537	750	983	1,056	1,360	1,718	1,964	2,099	2,454
Other Items (Net)	27r	−261	−309	−308	−359	−416	−578	−398	−855	−1,074	−493	−289	−387	−263	−474	−727
Monetary Survey													*Millions of Shillings:*			
Foreign Assets (Net)	31n	1,617	1,200	1,331	1,546	962	534	1,446	3,610	1,954	3,275	1,830	128	−2,167	−1,027	−374
Domestic Credit	32	1,879	2,527	3,019	3,861	4,966	6,413	7,476	9,254	12,571	14,351	16,230	20,264	26,059	25,944	28,626
Claims on Central Govt. (Net)	32an	39	133	346	480	929	1,765	1,898	1,799	3,225	3,646	3,959	6,773	10,703	8,710	9,569
Claims on Local Government	32b	15	21	26	42	38	34	25	24	29	33	28	15	25	23	24
Claims on Nonfin.Pub.Enterprises	32c	86	152	157	188	185	269	190	235	182	207	337	333	540	1,138	1,526
Claims on Private Sector	32d	1,732	2,214	2,481	3,143	3,814	4,149	4,892	6,513	8,901	9,774	11,759	13,025	14,357	15,380	16,944
Claims on Other Financial Insts	32f	7	7	8	7	—	196	471	684	235	692	147	117	434	693	563
Money	34	2,226	2,371	2,804	3,449	3,755	4,143	5,120	7,333	7,879	9,178	8,434	9,409	10,635	11,473	13,095
Quasi-Money	35	1,279	1,398	1,492	1,907	2,064	2,672	3,335	5,193	6,277	6,833	7,702	8,872	10,735	10,953	12,198
Long-Term Foreign Liabilities	36cl	—	—	—	—	—	—	—	—	—	—	—	—	—	—	—
Counterpart Funds	36e															
Capital Accounts	37a	237	264	325	489	559	620	723	936	1,169	1,368	1,724	2,108	2,395	2,625	3,072
Other Items (Net)	37r	−247	−306	−270	−438	−450	−487	−256	−599	−799	248	200	3	126	−134	−113
Money plus Quasi-Money	35l	3,505	3,769	4,295	5,356	5,819	6,814	8,455	12,527	14,155	16,011	16,136	18,281	21,370	22,426	25,293
Other Banking Institutions													*Millions of Shillings:*			
Cash	40	....	....	....	40	44	163	206	458	527	682	847	642	1,390	1,281	2,065
Claims on Central Government	42a	....	....	....	131	173	166	166	191	257	286	577	854	1,073	2,340	2,464
Claims on Local Government	42b	....	....	....	2	2	—	13	—	—	—	—	1		1	
Claims on Nonfin.Pub.Enterprises	42c	....	....	....	33	17	16	1	13	13	39	34	35	118	79	70
Claims on Private Sector	42d	....	....	....	712	842	1,059	1,409	1,772	2,406	2,935	4,136	5,209	6,710	7,978	10,324
Claims on Deposit Money Banks	42e	....	....	....	....	....	....	....	....	....	....	....	....	....	....	....
Claims on Other Financial Insts	42f	....	....	....	19	20	3	31	124	153	193	169	320	714	683	1,714
Demand Deposits	44	....	....	....	14	3	105	35	450	307	376	104	324	323	488	919
Time and Savings Deposits	45	....	....	....	790	952	1,295	1,536	1,837	2,636	3,548	5,037	5,745	7,281	8,623	11,714
Foreign Liabilities	46c	....	....	....	19	54	51	69	69	82	83	134	149	141	137	119
Central Government Deposits	46d	....	....	....	22	63	73	116	118	220	172	166	169	185	229	238
Credit from Deposit Money Banks	46h	....	....	....	122	51	8	26	36	112	214	124	377	854	1,150	1,046
Capital Accounts	47a	....	....	....	91	90	117	136	171	233	293	455	589	742	878	1,003
Other Items (Net)	47r	....	....	....	−121	−115	−242	−92	−124	−235	−551	−258	−293	478	857	1,600

	1985	1986	1987	1988	1989	1990	1991	1992	1993	1994	1995	1996	1997	1998	1999		
Exchange Rates																	
End of Period																	
Principal Rate	17.738	19.135	23.429	25.029	28.387	34.263	40.158	49.797	93.626	65.458	83.153	79.118	84.568	87.165	100.098		aa
End of Period (ae) Period Average (rf)																	
Principal Rate	16.284	16.042	16.515	18.599	21.601	24.084	28.074	36.216	68.163	44.839	55.939	55.021	62.678	61.906	72.931		ae
Principal Rate	16.432	16.226	16.454	17.747	20.572	22.915	27.508	32.217	58.001	56.051	51.430	57.115	58.732	60.367	70.326		rf
Fund Position																	
End of Period																	
Quota	142.0	142.0	142.0	142.0	142.0	142.0	142.0	199.4	199.4	199.4	199.4	199.4	199.4	199.4	271.4		2f. s
SDRs	.8	9.9	11.4	.4	8.7	2.8	1.0	.6	.8	.5	.2	.5	.5	.4	1.7		1b. s
Reserve Position in the Fund	12.2	12.2	12.2	12.2	12.2	12.2	12.2	12.2	12.2	12.3	12.3	12.3	12.4	12.4	12.4		1c. s
Total Fund Cred.&Loans Outstg.	474.7	375.9	282.9	338.4	316.1	338.9	344.8	286.1	264.3	277.3	251.5	234.5	185.6	139.5	95.8		2tl
International Liquidity																	
End of Period																	
Total Reserves minus Gold	390.6	413.3	255.8	263.7	284.6	205.4	116.9	53.0[e]	405.6	557.6	353.4	746.5	787.9	783.1	791.6		1l. d
SDRs	.9	12.1	16.2	.6	11.5	3.9	1.4	.8	1.1	.7	.3	.8	.7	.6	2.4		1b. d
Reserve Position in the Fund	13.4	14.9	17.3	16.4	16.1	17.4	17.5	16.8	16.8	18.0	18.3	17.7	16.7	17.5	17.1		1c. d
Foreign Exchange	376.4	386.3	222.3	246.7	257.1	184.1	98.1	35.4[e]	387.7	538.9	334.8	728.0	770.6	765.0	772.2		1d. d
Gold (Million Fine Troy Ounces)	.080	.080	.080	.080	.080	.080	.080	.080	.080	.080	.080	.080	.080	—	—		1ad
Gold (National Valuation)	12.6	14.0	17.8	16.9	14.5	13.5	15.0	12.2	14.3	15.2	15.4	14.8	23.1	—	—		1an d
Monetary Authorities: Other Liab.	11.3	7.0	5.9	3.2	72.3	175.7	211.6	203.0	232.0	278.1	265.7	261.6	205.8	174.8	126.5		4.. d
Deposit Money Banks: Assets	39.3	45.9	39.8	46.1	64.8	68.7	70.4	108.2	348.9	425.4	439.6	444.2	594.2	501.6	313.6		7a. d
Liabilities	50.0	53.2	54.4	83.8	77.9	70.5	49.5	53.1	49.8	293.1	103.8	103.3	165.2	195.8	218.2		7b. d
Other Banking Insts.: Liabilities	8.7	7.9	17.1	14.5	19.8	15.3	16.5	13.4	10.2	11.0	8.7	7.0	18.9	1.2	.8		7f. d
Monetary Authorities																	
End of Period																	
Foreign Assets	6,807	7,115	4,753	5,558	7,310	6,630	5,339	6,315	34,527	28,227	25,683	47,266	44,499	47,103	57,816		11
Claims on Central Government	8,884	11,260	14,491	15,078	13,225	20,963	24,900	16,074	49,274	53,857	98,401	57,287	47,905	43,585	39,028		12a
Claims on Deposit Money Banks	—	—	—	223	1,019	208	864	12,717	11,484	10,072	9,766	9,056	9,124	1,140	904		12e
Reserve Money	7,257	10,132	12,093	12,342	14,434	17,585	20,341	31,230	47,628	58,472	76,610	82,903	84,621	84,269	89,341		14
of which: Currency Outside DMBs	5,038	6,371	7,688	8,536	9,655	10,829	12,761	17,205	21,355	24,817	28,887	30,390	36,178	38,713	42,963		14a
Foreign Liabilities	8,607	7,410	6,673	8,507	9,399	12,035	13,871	14,287	24,771	18,252	20,923	18,590	15,715	12,244	9,653		16c
Long-Term Foreign Liabilities	68	78	53	23	62	42	89	81	83	25	21	14	5	2	2		16cl
Central Government Deposits	—	—	—	—	—	—	—	—	38,289	32,920	55,239	27,349	11,698	17,172	18,922		16d
Counterpart Funds	34	33	38	46	49	42	58	73	73	127	6	—	—	—	—		16e
Capital Accounts	708	805	898	1,049	1,229	1,479	1,820	2,278	720	813	1,079	1,892	2,484	4,057	5,097		17a
Other Items (Net)	−982	−83	−510	−1,108	−3,619	−3,383	−5,075	−12,843	−16,279	−18,454	−20,028	−17,139	−12,995	−25,916	−25,267		17r
Deposit Money Banks																	
End of Period																	
Reserves	2,272	3,420	3,475	3,430	4,119	5,353	6,571	8,956	20,870	31,790	35,316	42,460	39,736	34,970	36,081		20
Foreign Assets	640	737	658	857	1,401	1,653	1,975	3,919	23,783	19,073	24,594	24,440	37,240	31,051	22,871		21
Claims on Central Government	2,407	5,252	7,046	5,383	7,737	9,548	11,562	18,010	21,136	38,088	26,417	42,576	46,121	70,550	68,415		22a
Claims on Local Government	25	33	49	80	50	62	64	148	219	249	304	358	582	595	895		22b
Claims on Nonfin.Pub.Enterprises	1,735	1,757	3,516	3,372	2,735	3,198	3,960	4,003	3,885	5,174	4,987	5,290	7,572	6,922	6,479		22c
Claims on Private Sector	19,491	22,684	24,154	28,064	32,759	36,648	44,752	58,587	61,705	78,809	117,351	145,926	182,253	182,976	202,657		22d
Claims on Other Financial Insts	560	1,000	1,507	2,638	2,725	3,036	3,907	4,809	3,793	6,835	11,347	14,620	16,255	32,507	50,317		22f
Demand Deposits	9,219	11,314	11,281	11,551	14,931	16,773	19,155	26,621	33,664	39,294	38,994	43,094	46,258	47,273	56,849		24
Time & Foreign Currency Deposits	13,976	18,172	20,750	23,696	26,746	30,571	37,804	50,003	64,332	95,755	133,520	175,401	210,888	215,615	218,788		25
Foreign Liabilities	814	854	898	1,558	1,682	1,698	1,388	1,922	3,392	13,144	5,807	5,681	10,356	12,122	15,914		26c
Central Government Deposits	928	961	1,624	2,086	3,470	3,098	5,323	3,078	4,790	4,950	5,531	3,822	4,226	9,592	8,754		26d
Credit from Monetary Authorities	165	1	—	183	864	25	1,342	4,921	252	—	—	—	448	4,335	1,614		26g
Credit from Other Financial Insts	—	—	6	—	—	—	—	—	—	—	2	—	—	—	—		26i
Capital Accounts	2,806	3,386	5,572	6,456	8,465	10,098	12,360	17,398	24,328	31,942	45,104	56,111	72,324	78,930	91,311		27a
Other Items (Net)	−779	196	275	−1,706	−4,633	−2,764	−4,583	−5,510	4,634	−5,068	−8,643	−8,439	−14,740	−8,298	−5,513		27r
Monetary Survey																	
End of Period																	
Foreign Assets (Net)	−1,975	−411	−2,159	−3,651	−2,370	−5,450	−7,945	−5,975	30,146	15,903	23,546	47,434	55,669	53,787	55,121		31n
Domestic Credit	32,173	41,025	49,139	52,529	55,761	70,356	83,821	98,554	96,934	145,142	198,876	236,037	285,817	311,661	341,495		32
Claims on Central Govt. (Net)	10,363	15,552	19,912	18,375	17,492	27,412	31,138	31,007	27,331	54,075	64,048	68,693	78,101	87,370	79,767		32an
Claims on Local Government	25	33	49	80	50	62	64	148	219	249	304	358	582	595	895		32b
Claims on Nonfin.Pub.Enterprises	1,735	1,757	3,516	3,372	2,735	3,198	3,960	4,003	3,885	5,174	4,987	5,290	7,572	6,922	6,479		32c
Claims on Private Sector	19,491	22,684	24,154	28,064	32,759	36,648	44,752	58,587	61,705	78,809	118,189	147,077	183,306	184,267	204,037		32d
Claims on Other Financial Insts	560	1,000	1,507	2,638	2,725	3,036	3,907	4,809	3,793	6,835	11,347	14,620	16,255	32,507	50,317		32f
Money	12,923	17,522	18,917	19,160	21,647	27,529	31,667	46,577	59,322	66,792	69,333	78,995	91,037	94,092	109,506		34
Quasi-Money	13,976	18,172	20,750	23,696	26,746	30,571	37,804	50,003	64,332	95,755	133,520	175,401	210,888	215,615	218,788		35
Long-Term Foreign Liabilities	68	78	53	23	62	42	89	81	83	25	21	14	5	2	2		36cl
Counterpart Funds	34	33	38	46	49	42	58	73	73	127	6	—	—	—	—		36e
Capital Accounts	3,514	4,191	6,469	7,504	9,694	11,577	14,180	19,675	25,048	32,756	46,183	58,004	74,808	82,987	96,408		37a
Other Items (Net)	−316	618	754	−1,551	−4,807	−4,854	−7,922	−23,830	−21,778	−34,409	−26,641	−28,941	−35,252	−27,248	−28,087		37r
Money plus Quasi-Money	26,898	35,694	39,667	42,856	48,393	58,099	69,471	96,579	123,654	162,547	202,853	254,395	301,924	309,707	328,293		35l
Other Banking Institutions																	
End of Period																	
Cash	1,978	2,470	1,325	2,287	2,845	4,033	4,196	5,502	5,781	8,762	12,988	11,937	5,148	6,900	4,920		40
Claims on Central Government	3,420	4,021	4,206	3,906	4,734	4,507	5,971	8,915	20,933	24,065	10,748	7,193	8,826	7,163	8,122		42a
Claims on Local Government	—	—	11	12	37	44	39	47	39	35	35	16	7	8	8		42b
Claims on Nonfin.Pub.Enterprises	71	152	184	314	133	583	601	434	348	1,031	48	34	10	6	6		42c
Claims on Private Sector	12,290	12,856	13,819	17,655	20,715	27,523	30,921	33,557	35,734	37,808	40,629	36,398	27,632	28,723	24,378		42d
Claims on Deposit Money Banks	....	....	67	133	83	82	68	92	150	446	27	423	—	—	4		42e
Claims on Other Financial Insts	1,506	1,980	1,139	671	1,212	1,375	1,336	2,083	578	1,024	541	151	124	106	96		42f
Demand Deposits	1,455	1,976	2,199	2,019	2,979	5,578	6,421	6,062	7,763	12,738	6,687	3,276	2,432	2,261	1,921		44
Time and Savings Deposits	13,112	14,779	15,111	17,476	20,266	25,111	28,355	32,764	37,939	43,266	42,335	36,447	22,385	24,752	23,335		45
Foreign Liabilities	142	126	282	269	428	368	462	484	697	494	487	384	1,185	75	58		46c
Central Government Deposits	258	280	388	412	441	937	724	511	403	908	572	459	667	661	775		46d
Credit from Deposit Money Banks	1,047	899	724	1,283	1,852	1,626	1,489	1,687	661	674	1,672	2,417	1,327	1,442	229		46h
Capital Accounts	1,082	1,350	1,525	1,988	2,308	2,996	3,393	4,154	6,315	7,773	7,148	6,423	4,347	4,278	4,410		47a
Other Items (Net)	2,171	2,068	520	1,531	1,484	1,532	2,288	4,968	9,785	7,318	6,114	6,744	9,405	9,437	6,806		47r

Kenya

		1970	1971	1972	1973	1974	1975	1976	1977	1978	1979	1980	1981	1982	1983	1984
Banking Survey																*Millions of Shillings:*
Foreign Assets (Net)	51n	....	....	....	1,531	911	483	1,377	3,541	1,871	3,193	1,695	−21	−2,308	−1,164	−492
Domestic Credit	52	....	....	....	4,733	5,957	7,584	8,981	11,235	15,181	17,633	20,981	26,513	34,489	36,796	42,962
Claims on Central Govt. (Net)	52an	....	....	....	589	1,040	1,858	1,949	1,872	3,263	3,760	4,370	7,458	11,591	10,821	11,796
Claims on Local Government	52b	....	....	....	43	40	35	38	24	30	33	28	16	25	24	25
Claims on Nonfin.Pub.Enterprises	52c	....	....	....	221	203	284	192	247	195	245	371	368	658	1,217	1,596
Claims on Private Sector	52d	....	....	....	3,855	4,655	5,208	6,301	8,285	11,306	12,709	15,895	18,234	21,067	23,358	27,268
Claims on Nonbank Financial Inst	52f	....	....	....	26	20	199	502	807	388	885	316	437	1,148	1,376	2,277
Liquid Liabilities	55l	....	....	....	6,120	6,731	8,051	9,820	14,355	16,571	19,253	20,431	23,708	27,585	30,256	35,862
Long-Term Foreign Liabilities	56cl	....	....	....	—	—	—	—	—	—	—	—	—	—	—	—
Counterpart Funds	56e	....	....	....	—	—	—	—	—	—	—	—	—	—	—	—
Capital Accounts	57a	....	....	....	580	649	737	859	1,108	1,402	1,661	2,179	2,697	3,137	3,503	4,075
Other Items (Net)	57r	....	....	....	−435	−511	−721	−322	−686	−921	−89	66	87	1,459	1,873	2,533
Interest Rates																*Percent Per Annum*
Discount Rate (End of Period)	60	6.50	6.50	6.50	6.50	6.50	7.00	7.00	6.50	7.50	7.50	8.00	12.50	15.00	15.00	12.50
Treasury Bill Rate	60c	2.00	1.42	3.45	1.92	4.63	6.08	5.54	2.13	4.29	6.01	5.26	7.61	12.58	14.15	13.24
Deposit Rate	60l	3.50	3.50	3.50	3.50	4.32	5.13	5.13	5.13	5.13	5.13	5.75	8.85	12.20	13.27	11.77
Lending Rate	60p	....	9.00	9.00	9.00	9.50	10.00	10.00	10.00	10.00	10.00	10.58	12.42	14.50	15.83	14.42
Prices, Production, Labor																*Index Numbers (1995=100):*
Consumer Prices	64	3.6	Ⅰ3.7	3.9	4.3	Ⅰ5.1	6.0	6.7	7.7	9.0	9.7	Ⅰ11.1	12.4	14.9	16.7	18.4
Industrial Production	66	15.0	16.5	17.4	19.9	21.0	Ⅰ20.9	24.9	28.9	32.6	35.0	36.9	38.7	39.0	40.8	42.5
Employment	67e	....	....	....	....	....	....	....	....	....	....	....	....	....	*Number in Thousands:*	
International Transactions																*Millions of Shillings*
Exports	70	2,179	2,244	2,567	3,335	4,305	4,464	6,610	9,824	7,914	8,144	9,248	10,248	11,146	11,579	15,415
Imports, c.i.f.	71	3,159	3,999	3,822	4,316	7,327	6,948	8,113	10,663	13,225	12,228	15,747	17,413	17,809	17,802	21,180
Volume of Exports	72	....	....	....	....	....	....	....	....	....	....	....	....	....	....	*1995=100*
Volume of Imports	73	84	99	86	83	94	Ⅰ70	68	82	96	78	Ⅰ90	70	60	47	55
Export Prices	74	5	4	5	5	7	Ⅰ8	11	16	13	14	Ⅰ17	19	20	25	29
Unit Value of Imports	75	2	3	3	3	5	Ⅰ7	8	8	9	10	Ⅰ13	17	19	25	26
Balance of Payments																*Millions of US Dollars:*
Current Account, n.i.e.	78ald	....	....	....	....	....	−220.2	−120.2	35.1	−661.0	−494.6	−877.7	−563.4	−307.9	−50.4	−129.8
Goods: Exports f.o.b.	78aad	....	....	....	....	....	688.0	811.4	1,222.5	1,056.4	1,120.2	1,430.7	1,192.7	1,045.7	984.0	1,081.7
Goods: Imports f.o.b.	78abd	....	....	....	....	....	−846.9	−809.7	−1,112.8	−1,631.8	−1,594.2	−2,344.8	−1,834.0	−1,467.7	−1,197.9	−1,348.2
Trade Balance	78acd	....	....	....	....	....	−158.9	1.7	109.7	−575.5	−474.0	−914.1	−641.3	−422.0	−214.0	−266.5
Services: Credit	78add	....	....	....	....	....	266.8	296.2	330.6	439.9	448.7	576.7	568.9	562.3	512.2	542.4
Services: Debit	78aed	....	....	....	....	....	−283.8	−294.6	−320.9	−428.4	−376.6	−501.6	−503.0	−398.4	−341.5	−377.0
Balance on Goods & Services	78afd	....	....	....	....	....	−175.9	3.2	119.4	−564.0	−401.9	−839.1	−575.4	−258.0	−43.3	−101.1
Income: Credit	78agd	....	....	....	....	....	56.4	35.4	40.8	47.4	60.5	53.9	37.0	21.9	28.7	39.0
Income: Debit	78ahd	....	....	....	....	....	−149.3	−177.4	−199.1	−234.9	−248.3	−248.2	−238.1	−201.4	−213.2	−240.8
Balance on Gds, Serv. & Inc.	78aid	....	....	....	....	....	−268.8	−138.8	−38.9	−751.5	−589.7	−1,033.4	−776.5	−437.5	−227.8	−302.9
Current Transfers, n.i.e.: Credit	78ajd	....	....	....	....	....	91.1	67.8	93.8	115.4	114.6	163.0	241.4	157.2	209.2	208.4
Current Transfers: Debit	78akd	....	....	....	....	....	−42.5	−49.2	−19.8	−24.8	−19.5	−7.3	−28.4	−27.6	−31.9	−35.3
Capital Account, n.i.e.	78bcd	....	....	....	....	....	−3.5	−5.7	−9.2	−1.3	−5.6	−9.7	3.2	3.2	2.3	3.5
Capital Account, n.i.e.: Credit	78bad	....	....	....	....	....	1.9	1.7	3.6	7.8	8.0	2.4	7.1	6.8	5.5	5.6
Capital Account: Debit	78bbd	....	....	....	....	....	−5.4	−7.4	−12.8	−9.1	−13.6	−12.1	−3.9	−3.6	−3.2	−2.1
Financial Account, n.i.e.	78bjd	....	....	....	....	....	197.3	209.3	240.2	435.4	566.9	506.6	185.9	99.6	130.7	179.1
Direct Investment Abroad	78bdd	....	....	....	....	....	−1.4	−4.3	−2.7	−2.3	−5.9	−1.1	−5.9	−9.6	−14.5	−6.9
Dir. Invest. in Rep. Econ., n.i.e.	78bed	....	....	....	....	....	17.2	46.4	56.5	34.4	84.0	79.0	14.1	13.0	23.7	10.8
Portfolio Investment Assets	78bfd	....	....	....	....	....	−2.2	—	—	—	—	—	—	—	—	—
Equity Securities	78bkd	....	....	....	....	....	.3	—	—	—	—	—	—	—	—	—
Debt Securities	78bld	....	....	....	....	....	−2.5	—	—	—	—	—	—	—	—	—
Portfolio Investment Liab., n.i.e.	78bgd	....	....	....	....	....	−.5	−4.3	.7	—	—	.8	—	—	—	—
Equity Securities	78bmd	....	....	....	....	....	.3	1.7	.7	—	—	.3	—	—	—	—
Debt Securities	78bnd	....	....	....	....	....	−.8	−6.0	—	—	—	.5	—	—	—	—
Financial Derivatives Assets	78bwd	....	....	....	....	....	....	....	....	....	....	....	....	....	....	....
Financial Derivatives Liabilities	78bxd	....	....	....	....	....	....	....	....	....	....	....	....	....	....	....
Other Investment Assets	78bhd	....	....	....	....	....	−13.9	−31.2	11.5	−18.8	−41.5	−15.4	−94.7	−77.7	−61.5	−64.1
Monetary Authorities	78bod	....	....	....	....	....	−1.9	−.5	—	—	—	—	—	—	—	—
General Government	78bpd	....	....	....	....	....	—	—	—	—	—	−.8	−5.7	−8.7	−5.0	−18.8
Banks	78bqd	....	....	....	....	....	−9.3	−4.2	8.8	−5.0	−19.3	−5.1	−16.7	7.2	1.3	−1.6
Other Sectors	78brd	....	....	....	....	....	−2.7	−26.5	2.7	−13.7	−22.2	−9.4	−72.3	−76.3	−57.7	−43.7
Other Investment Liab., n.i.e.	78bid	....	....	....	....	....	198.1	202.7	174.1	422.0	530.3	443.3	272.3	174.0	182.9	239.4
Monetary Authorities	78bsd	....	....	....	....	....	9.7	−7.8	4.8	1.3	4.3	−7.1	—	—	—	—
General Government	78btd	....	....	....	....	....	85.5	76.3	81.9	278.0	185.5	226.0	137.7	57.8	96.8	142.8
Banks	78bud	....	....	....	....	....	10.9	−8.0	—	−3.2	19.4	−1.8	−8.8	11.1	4.9	13.0
Other Sectors	78bvd	....	....	....	....	....	92.1	142.2	87.4	145.9	321.1	226.1	143.5	105.1	81.2	83.5
Net Errors and Omissions	78cad	....	....	....	....	....	−16.6	.6	3.0	6.8	4.8	9.4	68.4	45.2	15.0	8.6
Overall Balance	78cbd	....	....	....	....	....	−43.0	83.9	269.1	−220.2	71.6	−371.4	−305.9	−159.9	97.6	61.5
Reserves and Related Items	79dad	....	....	....	....	....	43.0	−83.9	−269.1	220.2	−71.6	371.4	305.9	159.9	−97.6	−61.5
Reserve Assets	79dbd	....	....	....	....	....	−6.3	−104.5	−233.2	194.3	−263.2	144.8	160.6	5.8	−194.0	−48.9
Use of Fund Credit and Loans	79dcd	....	....	....	....	....	44.0	18.8	−37.6	24.1	91.5	72.7	28.7	151.6	93.2	−15.5
Exceptional Financing	79ded	....	....	....	....	....	5.3	1.7	1.6	1.8	100.1	154.0	116.6	2.5	3.2	2.9

1985	1986	1987	1988	1989	1990	1991	1992	1993	1994	1995	1996	1997	1998	1999		
															Banking Survey	
End of Period																
-2,117	-537	-2,441	-3,919	-2,798	-5,817	-8,407	-6,458	29,449	15,411	23,067	47,060	54,493	53,771	55,064	Foreign Assets (Net)	51n
49,204	59,754	68,109	74,675	82,151	103,450	121,965	143,079	154,163	208,196	250,305	279,369	321,748	347,007	373,330	Domestic Credit	52
13,525	19,292	23,730	21,870	21,785	30,982	36,386	39,411	47,861	77,232	74,224	75,427	86,260	93,872	87,114	Claims on Central Govt. (Net)	52an
25	33	60	91	86	106	103	195	258	284	339	374	589	603	903	Claims on Local Government	52b
1,806	1,909	3,700	3,686	2,869	3,781	4,561	4,438	4,233	6,204	5,035	5,324	7,582	6,928	6,485	Claims on Nonfin.Pub.Enterprises	52c
31,781	35,540	37,973	45,719	53,475	64,171	75,673	92,144	97,440	116,617	158,818	183,475	210,938	212,990	228,415	Claims on Private Sector	52d
2,066	2,980	2,646	3,308	3,936	4,411	5,242	6,892	4,371	7,859	11,889	14,770	16,379	32,613	50,413	Claims on Nonbank Financial Inst	52f
39,488	49,979	55,653	60,064	68,794	84,755	100,051	129,903	163,575	209,789	238,888	282,181	321,592	329,821	348,628	Liquid Liabilities	55l
68	78	53	23	62	42	89	81	83	25	21	14	5	2	2	Long-Term Foreign Liabilities	56cl
34	33	38	46	49	42	58	73	73	127	6	—	—	—	—	Counterpart Funds	56e
4,596	5,541	7,994	9,492	12,001	14,573	17,573	23,830	31,364	40,529	53,331	64,427	79,155	87,265	100,818	Capital Accounts	57a
2,902	3,586	1,931	1,131	-1,553	-1,778	-4,212	-17,267	-11,481	-26,863	-18,874	-20,192	-24,511	-16,311	-21,054	Other Items (Net)	57r
															Interest Rates	
Percent Per Annum																
12.50	12.50	12.50	16.02	16.50	19.43	20.27	20.46	45.50	21.50	24.50	26.88	32.27	17.07	26.46	Discount Rate *(End of Period)*	60
13.90	13.23	12.86	13.48	13.86	14.78	16.59	16.53	49.80	23.32	18.29	22.25	22.87	22.83	13.87	Treasury Bill Rate	60c
11.25	11.25	10.31	10.33	12.00	13.67	....	....	....	....	13.60	17.59	16.72	18.40	9.55	Deposit Rate	60l
14.00	14.00	14.00	15.00	17.25	18.75	19.00	21.07	29.99	36.24	28.80	33.79	30.25	29.49	22.38	Lending Rate	60p
															Prices, Production, Labor	
Period Averages																
20.8	21.8	23.4	26.0	29.4	34.0	40.7	52.7	76.9	99.2	100.0	108.8	121.9	129.0	132.4	Consumer Prices	64
44.5	47.1	49.7	I 52.7	58.9	61.7	63.7	70.0	73.8	83.2	100.0	111.0	....	....	....	Industrial Production	66
Period Averages																
1,174	1,221	1,265	1,311	1,356	1,409	1,442	1,463	1,475	1,506	1,557	1,607	1,647	....	....	Employment	67e
															International Transactions	
Millions of Shillings																
15,725	19,459	15,790	18,934	19,510	23,697	30,386	43,756	77,919	87,142	97,284	118,226	119,960	121,252	....	Exports	70
23,589	26,163	28,618	35,303	44,779	50,913	52,918	59,097	101,128	115,080	155,168	168,486	190,674	193,032	....	Imports, c.i.f.	71
1995=100																
....	....	....	....	....	54	57	66	73	83	100	....	....	....	....	Volume of Exports	72
51	60	63	71	74	71	66	64	69	86	100	99	105	107	....	Volume of Imports	73
29	31	26	30	32	35	44	50	90	92	100	106	124	126	....	Export Prices	74
30	29	29	32	39	46	52	60	95	87	100	109	117	120	....	Unit Value of Imports	75
															Balance of Payments	
Minus Sign Indicates Debit																
-117.6	-46.8	-503.0	-472.1	-590.6	-527.1	-213.3	-180.2	71.2	97.9	-400.5	-73.5	-377.3	-363.0	....	Current Account, n.i.e.	78al d
991.0	1,219.4	962.5	1,072.7	1,001.5	1,090.2	1,185.3	1,108.5	1,262.6	1,537.0	1,923.7	2,083.3	2,062.6	2,013.1	....	Goods: Exports f.o.b.	78aa d
-1,269.8	-1,454.6	-1,622.6	-1,802.2	-1,963.4	-2,005.3	-1,697.3	-1,608.7	-1,509.6	-1,775.3	-2,673.9	-2,598.2	-2,948.4	-3,028.7	....	Goods: Imports f.o.b.	78ab d
-278.7	-235.2	-660.1	-729.5	-961.9	-915.2	-511.9	-500.2	-247.0	-238.4	-750.1	-514.8	-885.9	-1,015.6	....	*Trade Balance*	78ac d
577.3	646.0	738.7	798.9	921.4	1,138.3	1,014.4	1,042.2	1,063.5	1,117.3	1,024.5	936.2	914.3	837.6	....	Services: Credit	78ad d
-359.5	-415.2	-504.7	-530.0	-603.1	-699.7	-632.7	-563.7	-569.4	-686.8	-868.1	-854.0	-823.1	-665.9	....	Services: Debit	78ae d
-60.9	-4.4	-426.1	-460.5	-643.7	-476.5	-130.2	-21.7	247.0	192.2	-593.7	-432.6	-794.7	-843.9	....	*Balance on Goods & Services*	78af d
38.2	36.9	37.4	20.1	11.8	4.8	5.9	1.7	3.3	20.9	25.6	21.4	23.0	41.2	....	Income: Credit	78ag d
-281.8	-277.8	-319.9	-365.5	-330.1	-423.2	-434.7	-359.6	-392.2	-385.7	-350.5	-242.2	-254.9	-214.7	....	Income: Debit	78ah d
-304.5	-245.3	-708.6	-805.9	-962.0	-894.9	-559.0	-379.6	-141.8	-172.6	-918.6	-653.4	-1,026.6	-1,017.3	....	*Balance on Gds, Serv. & Inc.*	78ai d
214.4	232.0	246.1	372.9	420.6	422.9	396.7	392.9	276.0	333.7	563.6	585.4	649.3	654.4	....	Current Transfers, n.i.e.: Credit	78aj d
-27.4	-33.5	-40.4	-39.1	-49.1	-55.1	-51.1	-193.5	-63.0	-63.2	-45.5	-5.4	—	—	....	Current Transfers: Debit	78ak d
4.7	8.4	8.0	11.5	11.0	6.8	3.2	83.1	28.1	-.4	-.4	-.4	—	—	....	Capital Account, n.i.e.	78bc d
6.1	9.8	10.3	11.8	11.2	7.6	3.6	83.5	28.5	—	—	—	—	—	....	Capital Account, n.i.e.: Credit	78ba d
-1.5	-1.4	-2.2	-.3	-.2	-.8	-.4	-.4	-.4	-.4	-.4	-.4	—	—	....	Capital Account: Debit	78bb d
32.0	132.6	325.4	382.3	633.9	360.9	96.6	-270.1	55.1	-41.7	247.9	589.1	362.7	562.1	....	Financial Account, n.i.e.	78bj d
-5.4	-4.9	-30.8	-2.2	-1.4	—	—	—	—	—	—	.5	-2.1	—	....	Direct Investment Abroad	78bd d
28.8	32.7	39.4	.4	62.2	57.1	18.8	6.4	1.6	3.7	32.5	12.7	19.7	11.4	....	Dir. Invest. in Rep. Econ., n.i.e.	78be d
—	—	—	—	—	—	—	—	—	—	—	—	—	—	....	Portfolio Investment Assets	78bf d
—	—	—	—	—	—	—	—	—	—	—	—	—	—	....	Equity Securities	78bk d
—	—	—	—	—	—	—	—	—	—	—	—	—	—	....	Debt Securities	78bl d
—	—	—	—	—	—	—	—	—	—	6.0	7.5	34.2	1.3	....	Portfolio Investment Liab., n.i.e.	78bg d
—	—	—	—	—	—	—	—	—	—	6.0	7.5	26.9	1.3	....	Equity Securities	78bm d
—	—	—	—	—	—	—	—	—	—	—	—	7.3	—	....	Debt Securities	78bn d
														....	Financial Derivatives Assets	78bw d
														....	Financial Derivatives Liabilities	78bx d
-58.5	-83.1	-5.5	-14.4	-56.5	72.7	-77.5	-125.0	-31.4	171.1	277.1	628.2	549.3	678.4	....	Other Investment Assets	78bh d
												-4.7	—	....	Monetary Authorities	78bo d
3.1	-4.4	-6.0					-4.3							....	General Government	78bp d
—	-6.0	4.8	-11.2	-26.4	-7.8	-11.7	-117.5	-310.7	-61.2	—	—	-44.2	-44.4	....	Banks	78bq d
-61.6	-72.8	-4.3	-3.2	-30.1	80.5	-65.8	-3.2	279.3	232.3	277.1	628.2	598.2	722.8	....	Other Sectors	78br d
67.1	187.9	322.2	398.4	629.6	231.1	155.3	-151.5	85.0	-216.5	-67.7	-59.9	-238.3	-129.0	....	Other Investment Liab., n.i.e.	78bi d
4.9														....	Monetary Authorities	78bs d
-15.3	18.2	197.2	289.0	378.8	91.8	83.8	-64.8	152.7	-113.3	-5.7	5.0	-110.9	-109.4	....	General Government	78bt d
—	2.5	37.3	5.1	5.8	-3.5	-11.2	13.8	25.4	32.1	—	—	—	22.6	....	Banks	78bu d
77.4	167.2	87.7	104.4	245.0	142.8	82.7	-100.5	-93.0	-135.3	-61.9	-64.9	-127.4	-42.2	....	Other Sectors	78bv d
28.8	43.2	144.3	34.7	67.7	66.9	69.6	110.3	257.5	5.8	11.4	-128.2	134.8	-125.5	....	Net Errors and Omissions	78ca d
-52.1	137.4	-25.3	-43.6	121.9	-92.5	-43.9	-256.9	411.8	61.6	-141.6	387.0	120.2	73.7	....	*Overall Balance*	78cb d
52.1	-137.4	25.3	43.6	-121.9	92.5	43.9	256.9	-411.8	-61.6	141.6	-387.0	-120.2	-73.7	....	Reserves and Related Items	79da d
-.9	-23.0	145.1	-30.8	-92.9	58.8	36.9	-27.4	-477.3	-95.3	174.2	-378.1	-33.9	14.2	....	Reserve Assets	79db d
48.6	-116.2	-120.7	73.6	-29.2	33.7	7.0	-82.9	-30.6	19.3	-39.1	-24.6	-67.3	-62.8	....	Use of Fund Credit and Loans	79dc d
4.5	1.8	.9	.8	.2	—	—	367.1	96.2	14.4	6.5	15.8	-19.0	-25.2	....	Exceptional Financing	79de d

Kenya

		1970	1971	1972	1973	1974	1975	1976	1977	1978	1979	1980	1981	1982	1983	1984
Government Finance															*Millions of Shillings:*	
Deficit (-) or Surplus	80	−376	−335	−782	−696	−558	−1,259	−1,558	−1,020	−871	−2,411	−1,122	−3,897	−4,462	−1,597	−2,710
Total Revenue and Grants	81y	1,631	2,153	2,554	2,616	3,386	4,438	5,037	5,863	9,166	10,543	12,717	14,351	15,589	16,025	18,434
Revenue	81	1,623	2,143	2,539	2,612	3,380	4,438	5,037	5,863	9,166	10,376	12,508	13,853	15,137	15,706	17,844
Grants	81z	8	10	15	4	6	—	—	—	—	167	209	498	452	319	590
Exp. & Lending Minus Repay.	82z	....	....	....	....	....	....	....	....	....	....	....	....	....	....	....
Expenditure	82	2,007	2,488	3,336	3,312	3,944	5,697	6,595	6,883	10,037	12,954	13,839	18,248	20,051	17,622	21,144
Lending Minus Repayments	83	....	....	....	....	....	....	....	....	....	....	....	....	....	....	....
Statistical Discrepancy	80xx	....	....	....	....	....	....	....	....	....	....	....	....	....	....	....
Total Financing	80h	376	335	782	696	558	1,259	1,558	1,020	871	2,411	1,122	3,897	4,462	1,597	2,710
Domestic	84a	200	152	593	390	308	879	791	501	266	2,194	994	2,681	3,647	1,474	3,689
Foreign	85a	176	183	189	306	250	380	767	519	605	217	128	1,216	815	123	−979
Total Debt by Currency	88	....	....	....	....	....	....	....	....	....	....	....	....	....	....	....
National	88a	....	....	....	....	....	....	....	....	....	....	....	....	....	....	....
Foreign	89a	....	....	....	....	....	....	....	....	....	....	....	....	....	....	....
National Accounts															*Millions of Shillings*	
Exports of Goods & Services	90c	3,207	3,423	4,002	4,812	7,144	7,138	9,434	13,004	11,862	12,002	15,066	15,474	17,552	19,927	23,410
Government Consumption	91f	1,885	2,285	2,573	2,796	3,530	4,386	5,075	6,441	7,972	8,946	10,675	11,528	12,949	14,662	15,512
Gross Fixed Capital Formation	93e	2,254	2,884	3,302	3,645	4,075	4,837	5,808	7,800	10,280	10,809	12,451	14,508	13,364	14,349	16,143
Increase/Decrease(-) in Stocks	93i	268	360	−111	−304	1,715	−496	79	1,024	1,932	−484	3,333	2,663	1,990	2,237	2,372
Private Consumption	96f	7,292	8,153	9,003	10,848	12,554	16,240	17,908	20,680	24,977	28,896	32,178	37,203	44,612	48,734	56,481
Imports of Goods & Services	98c	−3,407	−4,259	−4,323	−5,036	−8,676	−8,260	−9,232	−11,752	−15,860	−14,732	−21,054	−20,914	−20,188	−20,284	−24,639
Gross Domestic Product (GDP)	99b	11,499	12,845	13,776	15,790	18,776	21,140	25,562	32,699	35,601	39,543	44,648	51,641	58,214	66,218	72,550
Net Factor Inc/Pmts(-) Abroad	98.n	−230	−187	−434	−879	−846	−1,271	−1,362	−1,574	−1,812	−1,672	−1,680	−1,942	−2,787	−2,544	−3,043
Gross National Income (GNI)	99a	11,269	12,658	14,013	15,882	19,496	22,575	27,710	35,623	39,351	43,765	50,969	58,520	68,085	73,860	86,170
GDP Volume 1976 Prices	99b.p	12,335	13,180	22,744	....	....										
GDP Volume 1982 Prices	99b.p	....	....	24,161	25,811	26,195	27,089	28,993	45,855	34,024	51,905	53,965	57,203	58,213	60,716	61,286
GDP Volume (1995=100)	99bv p	12.2	13.0	22.5	24.0	24.3	25.2	26.9	42.6	31.6	48.2	50.2	53.2	54.1	56.4	57.0
GDP Deflator (1995=100)	99bi p	20.3	21.2	13.2	14.1	16.6	18.0	20.4	16.5	24.2	17.6	19.1	20.9	23.1	25.2	27.4
																Millions:
Population	99z	11.23	11.67	12.07	12.48	12.91	13.41	13.85	14.35	14.88	15.33	16.67	17.34	18.04	18.77	19.54

	1985	1986	1987	1988	1989	1990	1991	1992	1993	1994	1995	1996	1997	1998	1999		
																Government Finance	
Year Ending June 30																	
	−3,775	−5,586	−9,841	−5,526	−6,574	−8,374	−11,171	−3,443	−14,931	−23,415	−6,172	6,228	Ⅰ−8,728	−5,304	−5,189	Deficit (-) or Surplus	80
	19,942	23,946	27,513	32,427	39,211	46,703	54,582	67,321	78,469	112,413	138,181	156,804	Ⅰ156,167	179,055	201,177	Total Revenue and Grants	81y
	19,428	22,956	26,585	30,898	36,770	41,547	49,474	58,580	69,661	103,250	125,312	145,558	Ⅰ150,384	173,783	196,257	Revenue	81
	514	990	928	1,529	2,441	5,156	5,108	8,741	8,808	9,163	12,869	11,246	5,783	5,272	4,920	Grants	81z
																Exp. & Lending Minus Repay.	82z
	23,717	29,532	37,354	37,953	45,785	55,077	65,753	70,764	93,400	135,828	144,353	150,576	Ⅰ164,895	184,359	206,366	Expenditure	82
	....	....	....	....	....	....	....	....	....	....	....	....	....	....	....	Lending Minus Repayments	83
												—	Ⅰ−5,925	66	10	Statistical Discrepancy	80xx
	3,775	5,585	9,841	5,526	6,574	8,374	11,171	3,443	14,931	23,415	6,172	−6,228	Ⅰ14,653	5,238	5,179	Total Financing	80h
	5,386	7,851	11,994	6,514	5,173	3,824	6,662	4,958	8,571	21,962	16,977	−5,437	Ⅰ21,287	12,439	11,016	Domestic	84a
	−1,611	−2,266	−2,153	−988	1,401	4,550	4,509	−1,515	6,360	1,453	−10,805	−791	−6,634	−7,201	−5,837	Foreign	85a
	....	....	....	....	....	....	....	....	....	....	....	....	....	....	....	Total Debt by Currency	88
	....	....	....	....	....	....	....	....	....	....	....	....	....	....	....	National	88a
	....	....	....	....	....	....	....	....	....	....	....	....	....	....	....	Foreign	89a
																National Accounts	
Millions of Shillings																	
	25,524	30,334	27,992	33,084	39,554	51,186	60,512	69,287	134,918	148,225	152,596	173,531	174,835	172,087	188,390	Exports of Goods & Services	90c
	17,602	21,518	24,354	27,293	30,769	36,620	37,606	41,475	48,307	60,719	69,057	81,960	100,770	112,365	125,276	Government Consumption	91f
	17,631	23,064	25,735	30,359	33,156	40,560	42,671	43,777	56,505	75,616	99,497	104,469	109,870	113,807	117,793	Gross Fixed Capital Formation	93e
	8,119	2,504	6,116	7,417	9,209	6,906	4,351	898	2,245	1,683	2,020	3,000	5,400	6,210	6,798	Increase/Decrease(-) in Stocks	93i
	58,435	70,385	81,654	94,127	111,149	121,655	139,437	178,571	210,596	250,098	322,622	360,177	450,664	520,404	537,483	Private Consumption	96f
	−26,540	−30,129	−34,682	−41,086	−52,247	−61,391	−63,327	−69,041	−118,958	−135,641	−180,139	−195,170	−220,596	−225,915	−238,511	Imports of Goods & Services	98c
	100,831	117,472	131,169	151,194	171,589	195,536	221,250	264,967	333,613	400,722	465,653	527,967	627,436	698,958	737,230	Gross Domestic Product (GDP)	99b
	−3,665	−4,183	−5,030	−6,412	−7,097	−10,179	−12,572	−12,548	−24,380	−23,074	−19,832	−15,837	−14,533	−11,134	−13,230	Net Factor Inc/Pmts(-) Abroad	98.n
	97,062	113,287	126,139	144,782	164,492	185,357	208,678	252,419	309,233	377,626	445,821	512,130	612,903	687,824	724,000	Gross National Income (GNI)	99a
	....	....	....	....	....	....	....	....	....	....	....	....	....	....	....	GDP Volume 1976 Prices	99b.*p*
	75,621	81,023	85,833	91,157	95,433	99,431	100,864	100,057	100,411	103,054	107,595	112,058	115,469	116,444	....	GDP Volume 1982 Prices	99b.*p*
	70.3	75.3	79.8	84.7	88.7	92.4	93.7	93.0	93.3	95.8	100.0	104.1	107.3	108.2	....	GDP Volume (1995=100)	99bv*p*
	30.8	33.5	35.3	38.3	41.5	45.4	50.7	61.2	76.8	89.8	100.0	108.9	125.6	138.7	....	GDP Deflator (1995=100)	99bi*p*
Midyear Estimates																	
	20.33	21.16	22.94	23.88	24.87	Ⅰ24.03	25.91	25.70	Ⅰ28.11	29.29	30.52	31.80	33.14	Ⅰ29.01	29.55	Population	99z

(See notes in the back of the book.)

Korea

		1970	1971	1972	1973	1974	1975	1976	1977	1978	1979	1980	1981	1982	1983	1984
Exchange Rates															*Won per SDR:*	
Market Rate	aa	316.65	405.30	433.09	479.52	592.59	566.60	562.33	587.92	630.55	637.59	841.64	815.35	826.01	832.85	811.03
															Won per US Dollar:	
Market Rate	ae	316.65	373.30	398.90	397.50	484.00	484.00	484.00	484.00	484.00	484.00	659.90	700.50	748.80	795.50	827.40
Market Rate	rf	310.56	347.15	392.89	398.32	404.47	484.00	484.00	484.00	484.00	484.00	607.43	681.03	731.08	775.75	805.98
Fund Position															*Millions of SDRs:*	
Quota	2f. s	50.0	80.0	80.0	80.0	80.0	80.0	80.0	80.0	160.0	160.0	255.9	255.9	255.9	462.8	462.8
SDRs	1b. s	10.3	17.6	26.1	26.1	1.4	3.4	6.8	10.0	11.4	18.9	9.9	54.1	57.8	60.2	30.9
Reserve Position in the Fund	1c. s	12.5	12.5	12.5	20.0	—	—	—	—	10.4	18.8	—	—	—	51.7	—
of which: Outstg.Fund Borrowing	2c	—	—	—	—	—	—	—	—	—	—	—	—	—	—	—
Total Fund Cred.&Loans Outstg.	2tl	—	—	—	—	110.0	217.3	301.7	280.4	201.8	104.4	535.4	1,070.6	1,141.7	1,292.8	1,598.9
International Liquidity												*Millions of US Dollars Unless Otherwise Indicated:*				
Total Reserves minus Gold	1l. d	606.3	433.5	523.0	884.8	277.2	781.3	1,970.0	2,967.1	2,763.9	2,959.2	2,924.9	2,681.7	2,807.3	2,346.7	2,753.6
SDRs	1b. d	10.3	19.1	28.3	31.5	1.7	3.9	7.9	12.2	14.9	24.9	12.6	63.0	63.7	63.0	30.3
Reserve Position in the Fund	1c. d	12.5	13.6	13.6	24.1	—	—	—	—	13.6	24.8	—	—	—	54.1	—
Foreign Exchange	1d. d	583.5	400.8	481.1	829.2	275.5	777.4	1,962.1	2,954.9	2,735.5	2,909.5	2,912.3	2,618.7	2,743.6	2,229.5	2,723.3
Gold (Million Fine Troy Ounces)	1ad	.097	.099	.107	.110	.110	.111	.112	.147	.275	.295	.299	.303	.303	.304	.309
Gold (National Valuation)	1an d	3.4	3.5	4.0	4.6	4.7	4.7	4.7	6.2	29.7	30.6	30.8	32.2	30.9	31.0	31.1
Monetary Authorities: Other Liab.	4.. d	29.1	11.1	11.4	11.4	114.5	218.4	247.4	182.8	49.7	54.2	52.1	52.9	59.7	59.8	62.5
Deposit Money Banks: Assets	7a. d	79.9	133.7	212.7	204.9	773.8	764.2	986.0	1,333.4	2,143.8	2,718.6	3,615.8	4,176.2	4,146.9	4,531.0	4,865.0
Liabilities	7b. d	233.1	387.2	447.0	376.4	1,073.1	1,514.0	1,740.7	2,295.7	3,217.1	5,106.8	7,145.9	9,288.9	11,976.0	10,751.0	14,188.0
Other Banking Insts.: Assets	7e. d	....	....	....	....	....	....	....	....	111.0	232.0	144.0	210.0	402.0	306.0	389.0
Liabilities	7f. d	....	....	....	....	....	....	....	....	1,255.0	2,375.0	2,821.0	3,636.0	4,628.0	5,353.0	6,322.0
Monetary Authorities															*Billions of Won:*	
Foreign Assets	11	171	150	135	268	102	367	927	1,514	1,320	1,447	1,939	1,897	2,162	1,869	2,288
Claims on Central Government	12a	51	47	189	208	409	682	818	925	1,191	1,177	1,176	1,712	1,922	2,217	2,176
Claims on Official Entities................	12bx	30	32	34	43	20	110	110	210	240	240	270	370	470	570	570
Claims on Deposit Money Banks	12e	90	112	179	280	667	686	686	849	1,493	2,339	2,917	3,627	4,193	5,244	7,095
Reserve Money	14	300	288	428	624	775	1,077	1,438	2,072	2,802	3,468	3,244	2,802	3,825	4,095	4,248
of which: Currency Outside DMBs	14a	134	162	218	311	411	507	677	953	1,364	1,604	1,856	2,025	2,574	2,874	3,109
Bonds	16ab	4	1	8	18	1	94	150	429	426	532	580	1,934	2,538	3,737	5,651
Foreign Liabilities........................	16c	9	4	5	5	121	229	289	253	151	93	485	910	988	1,124	1,348
Central Government Deposits	16d	42	38	88	104	154	217	388	711	914	902	780	544	627	764	1,121
Other Items (Net)	17r	−11	−18	−34	2	147	228	277	34	−49	208	1,213	1,416	769	180	−240
Deposit Money Banks															*Billions of Won:*	
Reserves	20	162	102	158	258	352	557	755	1,110	1,401	1,815	1,324	738	1,196	1,129	856
Central Bank Bonds	20r	5	26	52	79	65	284	327	571	447	493	936	1,987	2,409	2,836	4,126
Foreign Assets	21	25	44	163	195	483	698	767	1,313	1,427	1,657	3,074	3,601	3,659	4,336	4,861
Claims on Central Government.............	22a	5	3	4	28	47	104	228	371	518	632	1,030	1,407	2,229	2,395	2,897
Claims on Private Sector	22d	919	1,201	1,453	1,890	2,789	3,481	4,374	5,465	8,082	11,303	15,788	19,923	25,050	29,429	33,649
Demand Deposits	24	185	220	332	440	533	668	866	1,233	1,325	1,648	1,920	1,969	1,969	3,872	3,777
Time, Savings,& Fgn.Currency Dep.	25	589	725	929	1,245	1,506	1,965	2,660	3,699	5,211	6,603	8,727	11,688	14,105	16,154	17,885
Bonds	26ab	7	10	11	24	36	52	82	151	176	235	316	44	90	180	200
Restricted Deposits	26b	35	52	77	168	173	258	327	298	329	370	617	592	281	306	287
Foreign Liabilities........................	26c	74	145	178	150	519	733	842	1,111	1,557	2,472	4,716	6,507	8,968	9,956	11,739
Central Government Deposits	26d	1	5	2	1	13	31	57	—	—	33	23	4	321	569	521
Central Govt. Lending Funds	26f	93	102	116	127	168	209	299	394	531	738	882	1,130	1,434	1,742	1,928
Credit from Monetary Authorities	26g	90	112	179	280	666	673	686	849	1,496	2,340	2,918	3,627	4,197	5,245	7,098
Capital Accounts	27a	71	95	126	173	215	348	445	545	829	1,134	1,404	1,689	1,907	2,383	2,706
Other Items (Net)	27r	−28	−89	−121	−159	−93	187	185	551	419	327	629	406	−65	−281	249
Monetary Survey															*Billions of Won:*	
Foreign Assets (Net)	31n	114	46	114	309	−54	103	562	1,462	1,039	540	−188	−1,919	−4,134	−4,875	−5,939
Domestic Credit	32	962	1,240	1,600	2,074	3,171	4,201	5,165	6,395	9,295	12,605	17,719	23,215	29,044	33,683	38,087
Claims on Central Govt. (Net)	32an	13	6	103	131	289	538	602	586	795	874	1,403	2,572	3,204	3,279	3,431
Claims on Official Entities	32bx	30	32	34	43	20	110	110	210	240	240	270	370	470	570	570
Claims on Private Sector	32d	919	1,201	1,463	1,900	2,863	3,554	4,454	5,599	8,260	11,491	16,047	20,273	25,371	29,834	34,086
Money....................................	34	308	358	519	730	946	1,182	1,544	2,173	2,714	3,275	3,807	3,982	5,799	6,783	6,821
Quasi-Money	35	590	727	932	1,250	1,511	1,968	2,661	3,702	5,215	6,603	8,727	11,689	14,105	16,155	17,885
Bonds	36ab	9	−13	−24	−19	36	78	164	199	264	448	341	412	243	1,086	1,725
Restricted Deposits	36b	35	52	77	168	173	258	327	298	329	370	617	592	281	306	287
Central Govt. Lending Funds	36f	96	105	121	133	178	219	310	402	534	738	882	1,130	1,435	1,742	1,928
Other Items (Net)	37r	40	30	47	74	274	599	721	1,084	1,279	1,711	3,157	3,490	3,048	2,737	3,503
Money plus Quasi-Money..................	35l	898	1,085	1,452	1,980	2,457	3,150	4,205	5,874	7,929	9,878	12,534	15,671	19,904	22,938	24,706
Other Banking Institutions																
Development Institutions																*Billions of Won:*	
Claims on Private Sector	42d	185	215	311	386	502	723	918	1,249	1,743	2,470	3,620	4,449	5,311	6,049	6,699
Bonds	46ab	28	26	51	82	88	67	115	176	235	299	510	610	786	900	1,160
Counterpart Funds	46e	17	17	17	16	16	15	15	14	14	13	12	12	3	2	2
Central Govt. Lending Funds	46f	52	69	85	100	162	251	361	486	786	1,108	1,468	1,925	2,333	2,728	2,779
Credit from Deposit Money Banks	46h	25	38	40	40	34	36	23	35	29	32	31	39	12	20	9
Capital Accounts	47a	61	67	125	129	143	237	330	365	449	480	618	666	685	781	768
Other Items (Net)........................	47r	21	15	2	27	62	117	75	172	231	538	981	1,197	1,493	1,617	1,982
Trust Accounts of Coml. Banks																*Billions of Won:*	
Claims on Private Sector..................	42d. g	73	115	131	167	149	160	256	507	765	1,062	1,826	2,873	4,044	5,190	6,493
Claims on Deposit Money Banks	42e. g	10	5	18	5	21	27	46	23	7	24	36	28	117	120	100
Quasi-Monetary Liabilities..................	45.. g	79	125	158	183	191	186	251	355	429	588	1,043	1,448	1,581	1,721	2,236
Other Items (Net)	47r. g	4	−4	−9	−10	−20	—	51	175	344	498	819	1,453	2,580	3,589	4,356
Postal Savings Deposits....................	45.. h	15	16	25	32	40	47	62	35	30	41	85	93	282	439	586

1985	1986	1987	1988	1989	1990	1991	1992	1993	1994	1995	1996	1997	1998	1999		
															Exchange Rates	
977.81	1,053.66	1,124.00	920.59	893.10	1,019.19	1,088.27	1,084.05	1,109.97	1,151.38	1,151.58	1,213.93	2,286.98	1,695.27	1,561.92	Market Rate	aa

End of Period

End of Period (ae) Period Average (rf)

| 890.20 | 861.40 | 792.30 | 684.10 | 679.60 | 716.40 | 760.80 | 788.40 | 808.10 | 788.70 | 774.70 | 844.20 | 1,695.00 | 1,204.00 | 1,138.00 | Market Rate | ae |
| 870.02 | 881.45 | 822.57 | 731.47 | 671.46 | 707.76 | 733.35 | 780.65 | 802.67 | 803.45 | 771.27 | 804.45 | 951.29 | 1,401.44 | 1,188.82 | Market Rate | rf |

End of Period

															Fund Position	
462.8	462.8	462.8	462.8	462.8	462.8	462.8	799.6	799.6	799.6	799.6	799.6	799.6	799.6	1,633.6	Quota	2f.s
36.2	14.4	11.6	4.2	1.2	10.1	20.9	30.6	42.3	52.3	65.7	82.3	43.6	8.1	.5	SDRs	1b.s
.7	.7	.7	.7	178.2	224.5	255.4	319.1	339.2	363.6	438.5	474.3	443.7	.1	208.6	Reserve Position in the Fund	1c.s
—	—	—	—	—	—	—	—	—	—	—	—	—	—	—	of which: Outstg.Fund Borrowing	2c
1,373.0	1,266.3	369.8	—	—	—	—	—	—	—	—	—	8,200.0	12,000.0	4,462.5	Total Fund Cred.&Loans Outstg.	2tl

End of Period

															International Liquidity	
2,869.3	3,319.6	3,583.7	12,346.7	15,213.6	14,793.0	13,701.1	17,120.6	20,228.2	25,639.3	32,677.7	34,037.1	20,367.9	51,974.5	73,987.3	Total Reserves minus Gold	1l.d
39.8	17.7	16.4	5.7	1.6	14.4	29.8	42.0	58.1	76.3	97.7	118.4	58.8	11.4	.7	SDRs	1b.d
.7	.8	1.0	.9	234.2	319.4	365.3	438.7	465.9	530.8	651.8	682.0	598.7	.1	286.3	Reserve Position in the Fund	1c.d
2,828.8	3,301.1	3,566.3	12,340.1	14,977.8	14,459.2	13,306.0	16,639.9	19,704.2	25,032.1	31,928.2	33,236.7	19,710.4	51,963.0	73,700.3	Foreign Exchange	1d.d
.313	.317	.320	.320	.320	.320	.321	.323	.324	.325	.327	.327	.335	.435	.437	Gold (Million Fine Troy Ounces)	1ad
31.4	31.5	31.6	31.6	31.6	31.6	32.2	32.6	33.3	33.6	34.4	36.0	36.9	66.3	67.1	Gold (National Valuation)	1and
71.5	83.1	112.0	143.5	−77.0	166.1	178.6	46.4	95.4	442.4	158.6	381.1	140.1	1,670.7	1,588.5	Monetary Authorities: Other Liab.	4..d
4,848.0	4,692.0	5,578.0	‡8,513.0	7,868.0	9,532.0	10,705.0	12,905.0	16,211.0	20,938.0	27,806.0	33,136.0	32,749.0	34,310.0	34,748.0	Deposit Money Banks: Assets	7a.d
15,867.0	14,536.0	11,591.0	10,246.0	9,686.0	10,181.0	13,896.0	14,665.0	14,795.0	21,170.0	31,446.0	42,197.0	27,975.0	29,455.0	27,547.0	Liabilities	7b.d
385.0	179.0	150.0	357.0	659.0	1,064.0	1,788.0	1,963.0	5,365.0	7,897.0	4,136.0	7,144.0	10,761.0	10,027.0	8,975.0	Other Banking Insts.: Assets	7e.d
8,396.0	8,606.0	5,204.0	3,803.0	3,368.0	4,653.0	7,609.0	9,780.0	15,834.0	21,692.0	21,816.0	26,857.0	29,661.0	22,466.0	18,033.0	Liabilities	7f.d

End of Period

															Monetary Authorities	
2,481	2,806	2,802	8,458	10,360	10,820	10,712	13,684	16,672	20,880	25,390	28,173	29,227	64,832	85,342	Foreign Assets	11
2,188	2,193	2,312	2,841	2,738	2,237	2,498	2,333	2,659	2,628	1,951	2,235	5,562	5,961	6,382	Claims on Central Government	12a
570	572	572	570	570	570	570	570	570	570	570	370	2,370	8,640	2,370	Claims on Official Entities	12bx
9,078	10,849	14,890	15,958	16,144	19,553	21,122	25,571	29,169	28,971	28,076	24,378	62,442	37,830	26,003	Claims on Deposit Money Banks	12e
4,319	5,017	7,469	9,728	12,819	13,811	16,322	18,107	23,080	25,204	29,306	25,723	22,519	20,703	28,487	Reserve Money	14
3,286	3,679	4,443	5,133	6,140	7,011	7,913	8,581	12,109	13,127	15,061	15,453	15,448	13,670	19,475	of which: Currency Outside DMBs	14a
8,418	9,677	13,635	20,470	19,371	18,403	17,651	23,614	27,148	29,114	29,598	29,068	26,701	53,580	61,389	Bonds	16ab
1,406	1,406	504	98	−52	119	136	37	77	349	123	322	18,991	22,355	8,778	Foreign Liabilities	16c
1,187	1,447	3,408	5,766	7,276	7,424	5,770	4,524	5,059	6,477	6,917	6,684	5,410	5,917	9,126	Central Government Deposits	16d
−1,013	−1,128	−4,441	−8,236	−9,601	−6,577	−4,976	−4,124	−6,293	−8,095	−9,956	−6,640	25,980	14,708	12,318	Other Items (Net)	17r

End of Period

															Deposit Money Banks	
1,016	1,307	3,017	4,535	6,613	6,717	8,304	9,399	10,836	11,947	14,092	10,181	6,798	6,610	8,958	Reserves	20
5,558	5,023	4,474	4,606	3,296	2,761	4,052	7,068	8,865	12,700	15,775	18,419	20,996	29,559	27,375	Central Bank Bonds	20r
5,139	4,928	5,206	5,824	5,400	6,829	8,145	10,174	13,100	16,514	21,542	28,627	55,509	41,309	39,543	Foreign Assets	21
2,968	3,595	4,426	5,120	4,927	5,131	5,394	4,921	4,912	5,196	5,373	4,897	6,341	13,564	21,372	Claims on Central Government	22a
39,991	46,014	52,425	59,018	74,383	94,332	113,936	128,230	144,828	173,903	200,769	240,936	293,812	318,667	383,884	Claims on Private Sector	22d
4,302	5,223	5,829	7,112	8,419	9,218	14,009	16,182	17,344	19,593	23,672	24,221	19,331	21,569	25,139	Demand Deposits	24
21,001	25,023	30,172	36,786	44,308	52,800	61,984	71,660	83,178	100,668	115,072	138,769	168,482	222,926	284,916	Time, Savings,& Fgn.Currency Dep.	25
218	96	24	70	794	1,533	1,381	1,896	2,270	2,923	4,782	6,167	5,954	17,072	11,287	Bonds	26ab
359	725	1,305	1,694	1,286	1,052	1,723	1,693	635	792	904	988	1,214	772	803	Restricted Deposits	26b
14,124	12,521	9,184	7,009	6,647	7,294	10,495	11,552	11,957	16,697	24,361	36,454	47,418	35,464	31,348	Foreign Liabilities	26c
240	187	67	356	23	305	123	400	424	286	948	1,632	3,290	4,499	5,493	Central Government Deposits	26d
2,172	2,554	3,132	3,925	4,553	5,300	6,904	7,708	9,234	11,032	13,493	14,828	23,193	26,703	29,946	Central Govt. Lending Funds	26f
9,112	10,860	14,858	15,948	16,103	19,664	21,207	25,874	29,420	29,256	28,429	24,460	63,076	38,738	26,242	Credit from Monetary Authorities	26g
3,031	3,462	4,069	6,205	11,803	12,939	14,504	15,641	17,110	20,406	22,523	24,877	22,673	21,891	28,152	Capital Accounts	27a
113	216	908	−2	680	5,665	7,500	7,186	10,970	18,605	23,366	30,663	28,825	20,075	37,807	Other Items (Net)	27r

End of Period

															Monetary Survey	
−7,910	−6,193	−1,679	7,174	9,165	10,236	8,226	12,269	17,739	20,347	22,448	20,024	18,327	48,322	84,759	Foreign Assets (Net)	31n
44,847	51,384	59,767	66,685	81,732	102,194	125,074	139,463	157,358	186,520	213,688	255,240	314,581	351,179	412,126	Domestic Credit	32
3,729	4,153	3,262	1,839	367	−361	1,999	2,329	2,089	1,061	−541	−1,183	3,204	9,108	13,135	Claims on Central Govt. (Net)	32an
570	572	572	570	570	570	570	570	570	570	570	370	2,370	8,640	2,370	Claims on Official Entities	32bx
40,548	46,659	55,934	64,276	80,795	101,985	122,505	136,564	154,699	184,888	213,658	256,054	309,008	333,431	396,621	Claims on Private Sector	32d
7,558	8,809	10,107	12,152	14,328	15,905	21,752	24,586	29,041	32,511	38,873	39,542	35,036	35,583	44,375	Money	34
21,007	25,024	30,172	36,787	44,309	52,802	61,994	71,672	83,178	100,668	115,073	138,770	168,495	222,956	284,943	Quasi-Money	35
3,078	4,750	9,185	15,934	16,869	17,174	14,980	18,442	20,553	19,338	18,606	16,817	11,659	41,092	45,301	Bonds	36ab
359	725	1,305	1,694	1,286	1,052	1,723	1,693	635	792	904	988	1,214	772	803	Restricted Deposits	36b
2,173	2,554	3,133	3,925	4,553	5,300	6,906	7,713	9,234	11,032	13,493	14,828	23,193	26,703	29,946	Central Govt. Lending Funds	36f
2,763	3,329	4,185	3,368	9,550	20,196	25,945	27,625	32,455	42,526	49,187	64,320	93,311	72,396	91,518	Other Items (Net)	37r
28,565	33,833	40,280	48,939	58,637	68,708	83,746	96,259	112,219	133,179	153,946	178,312	203,532	258,538	329,317	Money plus Quasi-Money	35l

| | | | | | | | | | | | | | | | **Other Banking Institutions** | |
| | | | | | | | | | | | | | | | *Development Institutions* | |

End of Period

7,740	8,315	9,760	10,447	12,403	15,187	18,665	21,102	23,874	26,771	30,616	35,600	48,097	55,361	55,283	Claims on Private Sector	42d
1,710	2,229	2,688	2,896	3,404	4,612	7,974	10,412	13,921	16,617	19,639	23,764	34,782	36,096	34,666	Bonds	46ab
2	2	2	1	1	1	1	1	1	1	1	1	1	1	1	Counterpart Funds	46e
2,948	2,650	2,661	2,829	2,927	3,085	3,117	3,121	3,045	2,967	3,018	3,336	3,822	14,549	15,380	Central Govt. Lending Funds	46f
36	55	2,328	3,640	4,663	5,183	5,480	4,910	5,110	5,450	5,710	5,564	2,130	2,397	1,358	Credit from Deposit Money Banks	46h
786	825	946	1,023	1,059	1,242	1,387	1,285	1,382	1,615	1,614	1,814	2,909	4,486	6,247	Capital Accounts	47a
2,256	2,554	1,135	58	348	1,064	706	1,372	414	121	634	1,122	4,454	−2,168	−2,367	Other Items (Net)	47r

End of Period

															Trust Accounts of Coml. Banks	
9,425	13,358	18,008	27,344	38,990	47,578	56,964	79,724	112,416	143,539	182,319	216,569	253,305	307,920	273,872	Claims on Private Sector	42d.g
375	259	356	356	879	854	833	1,259	1,000	1,118	1,475	1,982	2,797	8,570	9,366	Claims on Deposit Money Banks	42e.g
3,928	5,095	8,741	13,453	22,119	29,175	36,619	53,022	71,319	93,415	124,891	151,093	171,456	138,941	115,360	Quasi-Monetary Liabilities	45..g
5,872	8,522	9,622	14,246	17,750	19,257	21,178	27,961	42,096	51,242	58,903	67,458	84,646	177,549	167,878	Other Items (Net)	47r..g
475	512	1,052	1,566	1,710	1,973	2,346	3,578	4,078	5,948	5,321	6,421	7,280	11,491	14,980	Postal Savings Deposits	45..h

Korea

		1970	1971	1972	1973	1974	1975	1976	1977	1978	1979	1980	1981	1982	1983	1984
Nonbank Financial Institutions																*Billions of Won:*
Cash	40..s	2	2	3	4	5	5	7	8	14	22	40	59	87	127	208
Claims on Central Government	42a.s	—	1	1	1	5	13	21	25	44	52	72	113	152	172	252
Claims on Private Sector	42d.s	8	12	16	29	39	50	70	137	227	494	728	1,061	1,519	2,356	3,447
Real Estate	42h.s	10	13	15	17	21	23	35	28	48	71	111	176	332	484	644
Incr.in Total Assets(Within Per.)	49z.s	5	8	8	17	22	25	38	70	141	314	322	479	817	1,138	1,455
Liquid Liabilities	551	990	1,224	1,632	2,191	2,682	3,379	4,511	6,256	8,374	10,484	13,622	17,153	21,680	24,972	27,320
Interest Rates																*Percent Per Annum*
Discount Rate *(End of Period)*	60	19.0	16.0	11.0	11.0	11.0	14.0	14.0	14.0	15.0	15.0	16.0	11.0	5.0	5.0	5.0
Money Market Rate	60b	....	....	....	....	....	....	....	18.1	19.3	18.9	22.9	18.1	14.2	13.0	11.4
Corporate Bond Rate	60bc	....	....	....	....	....	....	....	....	....	....	....	17.4	19.3	14.4	13.6
Deposit Rate	60l	22.8	20.4	12.0	12.0	15.0	15.0	16.2	14.4	18.6	18.6	19.5	16.2	8.0	8.0	9.2
Lending Rate	60p	....	....	....	....	....	....	....	....	....	....	18.0	17.4	11.8	10.0	10.0
Government Bond Yield	61	....	....	....	....	21.0	21.1	21.6	21.5	21.6	25.2	28.8	23.6	17.4	13.1	14.3
Prices, Production, Labor																*Index Numbers (1995=100):*
Share Prices	62	....	....	4.6	8.7	8.6	9.5	11.7	Ι12.3	15.6	13.1	11.8	13.7	13.3	13.2	14.3
Producer Prices	63	11.6	Ι12.6	14.3	15.3	21.8	27.6	Ι30.9	33.7	37.6	44.7	62.1	74.8	78.3	Ι78.4	78.9
Consumer Prices	64	8.9	10.2	11.3	11.7	14.5	18.2	Ι21.0	23.2	26.5	31.3	40.3	48.9	52.5	Ι54.3	55.5
Wages: Monthly Earnings	65ey	1.3	1.5	1.8	2.0	2.7	3.4	4.6	6.1	8.3	10.7	13.1	15.7	18.0	20.2	21.8
Industrial Production	66..c	4.0	4.6	5.2	7.0	8.9	10.6	13.8	16.5	20.3	22.7	22.3	25.1	26.4	Ι30.5	35.1
Manufacturing Employment	67ey	26.4	28.0	30.3	37.2	42.1	46.2	56.1	58.6	63.2	65.5	62.3	60.2	63.3	68.6	70.2
																Number in Thousands:
Labor Force	67d	....	....	....	....	....	....	....	....	....	....	....	....	....	....	....
Employment	67e	....	....	....	....	....	....	....	....	....	....	....	....	....	....	....
Unemployment	67c	....	....	....	....	....	....	....	....	....	....	....	....	....	....	....
Unemployment Rate (%)	67r	....	....	....	....	....	....	....	....	....	....	....	....	....	....	....
International Transactions																*Millions of US Dollars*
Exports	70..d	836	1,067	1,625	3,221	4,462	4,945	7,716	10,048	12,722	15,057	17,512	21,268	21,853	24,446	29,245
Imports, c.i.f.	71..d	1,984	2,394	2,522	4,240	6,852	7,274	8,774	10,811	14,972	20,339	22,292	26,131	24,251	26,192	30,631
																1995=100
Volume of Exports	72	2.2	2.8	4.2	6.6	7.2	8.9	12.1	14.4	16.5	16.3	18.2	21.3	22.8	26.4	30.6
Volume of Imports	73	5.3	6.4	6.6	8.5	8.7	9.0	11.1	13.4	17.5	19.5	17.7	19.7	19.9	22.6	26.1
Unit Value of Exports	74	12.4	13.7	15.7	20.1	25.8	28.7	32.1	35.1	38.8	46.4	60.8	70.4	73.0	74.5	80.1
Unit Value of Imports	75	11.1	12.4	14.2	19.2	30.4	37.4	36.6	37.4	39.5	48.3	72.9	86.2	85.7	86.6	91.1
Export Prices	76	....	16.3	18.2	20.9	22.5	26.9	30.3	32.5	36.9	43.3	56.4	65.5	67.7	69.8	73.9
Import Prices	76.x	....	11.7	14.1	18.0	25.4	29.5	30.3	30.7	31.9	40.5	64.3	75.4	76.8	77.9	81.0
Balance of Payments																*Millions of US Dollars*
Current Account, n.i.e.	78ald	....	....	....	....	....	....	−310	12	−1,085	−4,151	−5,312	−4,607	−2,551	−1,524	−1,293
Goods: Exports f.o.b.	78aad	....	....	....	....	....	....	7,814	10,046	12,711	14,705	17,245	20,747	20,934	23,272	26,486
Goods: Imports f.o.b.	78abd	....	....	....	....	....	....	−8,404	−10,523	−14,491	−19,100	−21,859	−24,596	−23,762	−25,120	−27,575
Trade Balance	78acd	....	....	....	....	....	....	−590	−477	−1,780	−4,395	−4,613	−3,849	−2,827	−1,849	−1,089
Services: Credit	78add	....	....	....	....	....	....	1,527	2,784	4,059	4,392	2,570	3,068	3,627	3,901	3,973
Services: Debit	78aed	....	....	....	....	....	....	−1,191	−2,025	−3,195	−3,503	−3,293	−3,554	−3,362	−3,507	−3,600
Balance on Goods & Services	78afd	....	....	....	....	....	....	−254	282	−916	−3,506	−5,336	−4,335	−2,562	−1,455	−716
Income: Credit	78agd	....	....	....	....	....	....	116	243	391	433	2,149	2,772	3,194	2,635	2,699
Income: Debit	78ahd	....	....	....	....	....	....	−518	−736	−1,031	−1,517	−2,660	−3,659	−3,839	−3,428	−3,963
Balance on Gds, Serv. & Inc.	78aid	....	....	....	....	....	....	−656	−211	−1,556	−4,590	−5,848	−5,222	−3,207	−2,248	−1,979
Current Transfers, n.i.e.: Credit	78ajd	....	....	....	....	....	....	461	388	574	560	720	770	795	822	790
Current Transfers: Debit	78akd	....	....	....	....	....	....	−115	−165	−103	−121	−185	−155	−139	−99	−104
Capital Account, n.i.e.	78bcd	....	....	....	....	....	....	—	—	—	—	4	−35	−97	−80	−82
Capital Account, n.i.e.: Credit	78bad	....	....	....	....	....	....	—	—	—	—	4	3	5	6	8
Capital Account: Debit	78bbd	....	....	....	....	....	....	—	—	—	—	—	−39	−101	−85	−90
Financial Account, n.i.e.	78bjd	....	....	....	....	....	....	1,866	1,390	2,129	5,353	5,925	4,720	3,950	2,311	2,822
Direct Investment Abroad	78bdd	....	....	....	....	....	....	−6	−21	−28	−19	−26	−48	−151	−130	−52
Dir. Invest. in Rep. Econ., n.i.e.	78bed	....	....	....	....	....	....	81	94	89	35	6	102	69	69	110
Portfolio Investment Assets	78bfd	....	....	....	....	....	....	—	—	—	—	—	—	—	—	—
Equity Securities	78bkd	....	....	....	....	....	....	—	—	—	—	—	—	—	—	—
Debt Securities	78bld	....	....	....	....	....	....	—	—	—	—	—	—	—	—	—
Portfolio Investment Liab., n.i.e.	78bgd	....	....	....	....	....	....	74	70	42	8	134	24	−15	546	836
Equity Securities	78bmd	....	....	....	....	....	....	—	—	—	—	—	—	—	—	—
Debt Securities	78bnd	....	....	....	....	....	....	74	70	42	8	134	24	−15	546	836
Financial Derivatives Assets	78bwd	....	....	....	....	....	....									
Financial Derivatives Liabilities	78bxd	....	....	....	....	....	....									
Other Investment Assets	78bhd	....	....	....	....	....	....	−289	−924	−175	−687	−492	−19	−794	−547	296
Monetary Authorities	78bod	....	....	....	....	....	....	....	....	....	....	−24	−12	−13	−7	−9
General Government	78bpd	....	....	....	....	....	....	−11	−14	−15	−8	....				
Banks	78bqd	....	....	....	....	....	....	−128	−377	265	−125	−108	−70	−474	66	56
Other Sectors	78brd	....	....	....	....	....	....	−150	−533	−425	−554	−361	64	−307	−606	250
Other Investment Liab., n.i.e.	78bid	....	....	....	....	....	....	2,006	2,171	2,201	6,016	6,303	4,660	4,840	2,374	1,632
Monetary Authorities	78bsd	....	....	....	....	....	....	6	10	9	5	16	4	5	2	8
General Government	78btd	....	....	....	....	....	....	608	388	326	1,497	1,223	1,269	1,355	852	669
Banks	78bud	....	....	....	....	....	....	263	479	1,002	1,967	2,228	1,989	3,211	48	1,073
Other Sectors	78bvd	....	....	....	....	....	....	1,129	1,294	864	2,547	2,836	1,399	269	1,472	−118
Net Errors and Omissions	78cad	....	....	....	....	....	....	−243	−32	−313	−328	−433	−328	−1,292	−831	−1,062
Overall Balance	78cbd	....	....	....	....	....	....	1,313	1,370	731	874	184	−250	10	−124	385
Reserves and Related Items	79dad	....	....	....	....	....	....	−1,313	−1,370	−731	−874	−184	250	−10	124	−385
Reserve Assets	79dbd	....	....	....	....	....	....	−1,410	−1,345	−630	−749	−747	−379	−94	−36	−703
Use of Fund Credit and Loans	79dcd	....	....	....	....	....	....	97	−25	−100	−125	564	629	84	160	318
Exceptional Financing	79ded	....	....	....	....	....	....	....	....	....	....	....	....	....	....	....

End of Period — **Nonbank Financial Institutions**

	1985	1986	1987	1988	1989	1990	1991	1992	1993	1994	1995	1996	1997	1998	1999	Code
Cash	328	549	870	1,324	1,850	2,304	3,247	4,496	3,186	3,633	5,984	8,310	12,071	7,906	5,836	40..s
Claims on Central Government	286	213	137	22	63	108	324	401	452	269	107	123	163	510	1,677	42a.s
Claims on Private Sector	4,575	5,653	7,937	10,608	14,411	19,279	24,337	28,656	33,091	38,931	43,207	51,210	55,510	43,442	42,937	42d.s
Real Estate	748	839	917	1,147	1,489	2,210	2,798	3,333	3,842	4,504	5,124	6,173	7,333	8,703	9,752	42h.s
Incr.in Total Assets(Within Per.)	1,703	1,901	3,163	3,933	5,223	7,657	8,196	6,528	5,607	7,230	10,951	13,101	12,461	357	15,997	49z.s
Liquid Liabilities	32,640	38,892	49,202	62,634	80,616	97,551	119,465	148,364	184,430	228,909	278,174	327,515	370,197	401,064	453,822	55l

Percent Per Annum — **Interest Rates**

	1985	1986	1987	1988	1989	1990	1991	1992	1993	1994	1995	1996	1997	1998	1999	Code
Discount Rate (End of Period)	5.0	7.0	7.0	8.0	7.0	7.0	7.0	7.0	5.0	5.0	5.0	5.0	5.0	3.0	3.0	60
Money Market Rate	9.4	9.7	8.9	9.6	13.3	14.0	17.0	14.3	12.1	12.5	12.6	12.4	13.2	15.0	5.0	60b
Corporate Bond Rate	13.4	13.3	12.9	12.8	15.7	13.3	13.4	16.0	12.6	12.9	13.8	11.9	13.4	15.1	8.9	60bc
Deposit Rate	10.0	10.0	10.0	10.0	10.0	10.0	10.0	10.0	8.6	8.5	8.8	7.5	I10.8	13.3	7.9	60l
Lending Rate	10.0	10.0	10.0	10.1	11.3	10.0	10.0	10.0	8.6	8.5	9.0	8.8	I11.9	15.3	9.4	60p
Government Bond Yield	13.6	11.6	12.4	13.0	14.7	15.0	16.5	15.1	12.1	12.3	12.4	10.9	11.7	12.8	8.7	61

Period Averages — **Prices, Production, Labor**

	1985	1986	1987	1988	1989	1990	1991	1992	1993	1994	1995	1996	1997	1998	1999	Code
Share Prices	15.1	24.7	45.3	75.3	99.7	81.1	71.4	63.8	79.7	105.1	100.0	90.3	70.9	44.4	87.0	62
Producer Prices	79.7	78.5	78.8	81.0	I82.2	85.6	89.6	91.6	93.0	95.5	I100.0	103.2	107.2	120.3	117.8	63
Consumer Prices	56.9	58.4	60.2	64.5	I68.2	74.1	80.9	I86.0	90.1	95.7	100.0	104.9	109.6	117.8	118.8	64
Wages: Monthly Earnings	24.0	26.2	29.2	35.0	43.7	52.6	61.4	71.1	78.8	91.0	100.0	112.2	118.0	114.4	131.2	65ey
Industrial Production	36.7	44.2	I52.2	59.2	61.1	66.5	72.8	I77.1	80.5	89.3	100.0	107.9	115.2	105.8	131.7	66..c
Manufacturing Employment	73.6	80.2	92.5	97.8	102.3	102.9	104.6	101.2	97.5	98.4	100.0	98.0	93.7	81.7	83.9	67ey

Period Averages

	1985	1986	1987	1988	1989	1990	1991	1992	1993	1994	1995	1996	1997	1998	1999	Code
Labor Force	....	....	....	....	....	....	....	....	....	20,326	20,798	21,188	21,604	21,390	....	67d
Employment	14,970	15,505	16,354	16,870	17,560	18,085	18,612	18,961	19,253	19,837	20,379	20,764	21,048	19,926	20,281	67e
Unemployment	622	611	519	435	463	454	436	465	550	489	419	425	557	1,463	1,353	67c
Unemployment Rate (%)	4.0	3.8	3.1	2.5	2.6	2.4	2.3	2.4	2.8	2.4	2.0	2.0	2.6	6.8	6.3	67r

Millions of US Dollars — **International Transactions**

	1985	1986	1987	1988	1989	1990	1991	1992	1993	1994	1995	1996	1997	1998	1999	Code
Exports	30,282	34,715	47,281	60,696	62,377	65,016	71,870	76,632	82,236	96,013	125,058	129,715	136,164	132,313	144,745	70..d
Imports, c.i.f.	31,136	31,585	41,020	51,811	61,465	69,844	81,525	81,775	83,800	102,348	135,119	150,339	144,616	93,282	119,750	71..d

1995=100

	1985	1986	1987	1988	1989	1990	1991	1992	1993	1994	1995	1996	1997	1998	1999	Code
Volume of Exports	32.9	36.9	45.7	I51.6	52.0	55.2	60.7	I65.8	70.2	80.7	100.0	119.8	149.6	174.9	179.6	72
Volume of Imports	27.6	29.8	36.1	I41.2	47.9	53.6	62.6	I63.8	67.9	82.5	100.0	112.6	114.3	90.3	113.9	73
Unit Value of Exports	83.2	86.1	88.5	89.4	83.5	86.4	90.0	94.3	97.4	99.2	100.0	90.3	89.8	114.6	94.8	74
Unit Value of Imports	94.2	89.6	89.8	88.3	82.7	88.5	91.7	96.1	95.0	95.6	100.0	103.1	115.5	136.2	114.8	75
Export Prices	77.8	81.5	83.3	86.9	85.5	87.9	91.3	93.7	I96.0	98.7	100.0	95.8	102.1	134.1	108.8	76
Import Prices	84.0	86.1	91.1	87.8	86.9	86.6	87.9	I91.0	94.6		100.0	100.6	110.2	141.4	124.2	76.x

Minus Sign Indicates Debit — **Balance of Payments**

	1985	1986	1987	1988	1989	1990	1991	1992	1993	1994	1995	1996	1997	1998	1999	Code
Current Account, n.i.e.	−795	4,709	10,058	14,505	5,361	−2,003	−8,317	−3,944	990	−3,867	−8,507	−23,006	−8,167	40,558	....	78ald
Goods: Exports f.o.b.	26,633	34,128	46,560	59,973	61,832	63,659	70,541	76,199	82,089	94,964	124,632	129,968	138,619	132,122	....	78aad
Goods: Imports f.o.b.	−26,653	−29,829	−39,031	−48,690	−57,471	−66,109	−77,344	−77,954	−79,771	−97,824	−129,076	−144,933	−141,798	−90,495	....	78abd
Trade Balance	−20	4,299	7,529	11,283	4,361	−2,450	−6,803	−1,755	2,319	−2,860	−4,444	−14,965	−3,179	41,627	....	78acd
Services: Credit	3,823	5,281	6,810	8,375	8,958	9,637	10,014	10,722	12,950	16,805	22,827	23,412	26,301	24,580	....	78add
Services: Debit	−3,364	−3,929	−4,533	−6,118	−8,514	−10,252	−12,167	−13,605	−15,076	−18,606	−25,806	−29,592	−29,502	−23,951	....	78aed
Balance on Goods & Services	438	5,651	9,806	13,540	4,805	−3,065	−8,956	−4,639	192	−4,661	−7,423	−21,144	−6,379	42,255	....	78afd
Income: Credit	1,907	1,725	1,992	1,745	2,387	2,895	2,911	2,450	2,509	2,836	3,486	3,666	3,878	3,271	....	78agd
Income: Debit	−3,993	−4,035	−3,578	−3,073	−2,964	−2,982	−3,075	−2,846	−2,900	−3,322	−4,787	−5,482	−6,333	−8,320	....	78ahd
Balance on Gds, Serv. & Inc.	−1,647	3,341	8,219	12,213	4,228	−3,152	−9,120	−5,035	−199	−5,147	−8,725	−22,960	−8,834	37,206	....	78aid
Current Transfers, n.i.e.: Credit	997	1,475	1,931	2,551	2,097	2,454	2,837	3,239	3,382	3,672	4,104	4,279	5,288	6,737	....	78ajd
Current Transfers: Debit	−145	−106	−92	−259	−964	−1,305	−2,034	−2,147	−2,194	−2,392	−3,886	−4,325	−4,621	−3,384	....	78akd
Capital Account, n.i.e.	−93	−96	−209	−353	−318	−331	−330	−407	−475	−437	−488	−598	−608	171	....	78bcd
Capital Account, n.i.e.: Credit	8	6	5	6	8	7	7	5	2	8	15	19	17	464	....	78bad
Capital Account: Debit	−101	−102	−215	−359	−327	−338	−336	−412	−477	−445	−502	−617	−624	−293	....	78bbd
Financial Account, n.i.e.	1,960	−3,994	−8,937	−4,222	−2,568	2,895	6,741	6,994	3,217	10,733	17,273	23,924	−9,195	−8,438	....	78bjd
Direct Investment Abroad	−591	−1,227	−515	−643	−598	−1,052	−1,489	−1,162	−1,340	−2,461	−3,552	−4,671	−4,449	−4,799	....	78bdd
Dir. Invest. in Rep. Econ., n.i.e.	234	460	616	1,014	1,118	788	1,180	728	589	810	1,776	2,326	2,844	5,415	....	78bed
Portfolio Investment Assets	—	—	—	−473	−709	−500	198	76	−986	−2,481	−2,907	−6,413	1,076	−1,999	....	78bfd
Equity Securities	—	—	—	−61	−105	−55	10	8	−204	−382	−238	−653	−320	42	....	78bkd
Debt Securities	—	—	—	−412	−603	−445	188	68	−781	−2,098	−2,669	−5,760	1,395	−2,041	....	78bld
Portfolio Investment Liab., n.i.e.	1,737	−333	−297	−607	−2	662	2,906	5,875	11,088	8,713	14,619	21,514	13,308	775	....	78bgd
Equity Securities	—	—	—	—	—	381	200	2,482	6,615	3,614	4,219	5,954	2,525	3,856	....	78bmd
Debt Securities	1,737	−333	−297	−607	−2	281	2,706	3,392	4,473	5,099	10,400	15,561	10,783	−3,081	....	78bnd
Financial Derivatives Assets	—	—	—	—	—	366	519	773	448	452	623	414	932	412	....	78bwd
Financial Derivatives Liabilities	—	—	—	—	—	−444	−568	−921	−535	−565	−744	−331	−1,021	−1,066	....	78bxd
Other Investment Assets	−1,108	−682	−112	−1,463	−963	−2,425	−3,006	−3,299	−4,592	−7,369	−13,991	−13,487	−13,568	6,693	....	78bhd
Monetary Authorities	−20	−15	−29	−27	−17	−26	−31	−24	−42	−72	−36	—	−86	−36	....	78bod
General Government	—	—	—	—	−82	49	−344	−213	−625	−296	−156	−543	−149	−46	....	78bpd
Banks	−49	−255	−307	−1,616	192	−2,244	−1,810	−3,291	−3,993	−5,061	−9,199	−8,173	−8,336	6,970	....	78bqd
Other Sectors	−1,040	−412	223	180	−1,056	−204	−822	228	68	−1,940	−4,600	−4,770	−4,996	−194	....	78brd
Other Investment Liab., n.i.e.	1,689	−2,213	−8,629	−2,050	−1,414	5,500	7,001	4,924	−1,455	13,632	21,450	24,571	−8,317	−13,868	....	78bid
Monetary Authorities	18	13	25	20	9	22	2	7	15	−2	−10	−29	23	25	....	78bsd
General Government	375	−214	−1,473	−1,256	−1,238	−817	−705	−700	−1,842	−335	−593	−493	4,671	4,628	....	78btd
Banks	946	−1,475	−2,731	−803	639	1,942	4,247	1,820	720	7,368	11,389	9,952	−9,785	−6,233	....	78bud
Other Sectors	350	−536	−4,450	−10	−824	4,353	3,458	3,798	−348	6,600	10,664	15,142	−3,226	−12,288	....	78bvd
Net Errors and Omissions	−862	−585	1,187	−603	1,164	−1,769	758	1,080	−722	−1,816	−1,240	1,095	−5,010	−6,361	....	78cad
Overall Balance	211	34	2,100	9,327	3,639	−1,208	−1,147	3,724	3,009	4,614	7,039	1,416	−22,979	25,930	....	78cbd
Reserves and Related Items	−211	−34	−2,100	−9,327	−3,639	1,208	1,147	−3,724	−3,009	−4,614	−7,039	−1,416	22,979	−25,930	....	79dad
Reserve Assets	22	93	−882	−8,837	−3,639	1,208	1,147	−3,724	−3,009	−4,614	−7,039	−1,416	11,875	−30,968	....	79dbd
Use of Fund Credit and Loans	−232	−127	−1,218	−490	—	—	—	—	—	—	—	—	—	11,104	5,038	79dcd
Exceptional Financing	....	....	....	....	....	....	....	....	....	....	....	....	....	....	....	79ded

		1970	1971	1972	1973	1974	1975	1976	1977	1978	1979	1980	1981	1982	1983	1984
International Investment Position																*Millions of US Dollars*
Assets	79aa d	....	....	....	....	....	....	....	....	....	....	8,891	9,285	9,861	9,751	10,432
Direct Investment Abroad	79ab d	....	....	....	....	....	....	....	....	....	....	142	184	329	455	492
Portfolio Investment	79ac d	....	....	....	....	....	....	....	....	....	....	—	—	—	—	—
Equity Securities	79ad d	....	....	....	....	....	....	....	....	....	....	—	—	—	—	—
Debt Securities	79ae d	....	....	....	....	....	....	....	....	....	....	—	—	—	—	—
Financial Derivatives	79al d	....	....	....	....	....	....	....	....	....	....					
Other Investment	79af d	....	....	....	....	....	....	....	....	....	....	2,145	2,178	2,522	2,363	2,266
Monetary Authorities	79ag d	....	....	....	....	....	....	....	....	....	....					
General Government	79ah d	....	....	....	....	....	....	....	....	....	....					
Banks	79ai d	....	....	....	....	....	....	....	....	....	....	497	536	922	860	849
Other Sectors	79aj d	....	....	....	....	....	....	....	....	....	....	1,648	1,642	1,600	1,503	1,417
Reserve Assets	79ak d	....	....	....	....	....	....	....	....	....	....	6,604	6,923	7,010	6,933	7,674
Liabilities	79la d	....	....	....	....	....	....	....	....	....	....	9,236	12,012	15,322	15,758	17,885
Dir. Invest. in Rep. Economy	79lb d	....	....	....	....	....	....	....	....	....	....	867	969	1,038	1,107	1,217
Portfolio Investment	79lc d	....	....	....	....	....	....	....	....	....	....	267	327	342	530	863
Equity Securities	79ld d	....	....	....	....	....	....	....	....	....	....	—	44	44	44	65
Debt Securities	79le d	....	....	....	....	....	....	....	....	....	....	267	283	298	486	798
Financial Derivatives	79ll d	....	....	....	....	....	....	....	....	....	....					
Other investment	79lf d	....	....	....	....	....	....	....	....	....	....	8,102	10,716	13,942	14,121	15,805
Monetary Authorities	79lg d	....	....	....	....	....	....	....	....	....	....	752	1,319	1,337	1,433	1,653
General Government	79lh d	....	....	....	....	....	....	....	....	....	....					
Banks	79li d	....	....	....	....	....	....	....	....	....	....	7,350	9,397	12,605	12,688	14,152
Other Sectors	79lj d	....	....	....	....	....	....	....	....	....	....	—	—	—	—	—
Government Finance																*Billions of Won:*
Deficit (-) or Surplus	80	I-21	-10	-161	-27	-164	-202	-192	-316	-300	-545	-849	-1,585	-1,656	-663	-841
Revenue	81	I419	514	558	679	1,026	1,549	2,325	2,958	4,108	5,446	6,834	8,605	9,983	11,538	12,604
Grants Received	81z	I29	24	27	16	13	15	2	—	—	—					
Expenditure	82	I443	542	751	707	1,065	1,601	2,294	2,804	3,781	5,225	6,563	8,045	10,115	10,682	11,875
Lending Minus Repayments	83	I26	7	-5	14	138	165	225	470	627	766	1,120	2,145	1,524	1,519	1,570
Financing																
Domestic	84a	I7	4	105	-38	69	46	-22	38	-65	272	524	1,046	974	260	527
Foreign	85a	I14	7	56	64	95	156	215	278	365	273	325	539	682	403	314
Net Borrowing	84	....	....	....	....	....	....	....	....	....	....	....	....	....	....	....
Use of Cash Balances	87	....	....	....	....	....	....	....	....	....	....	....	....	....	....	....
Debt	88	I280	409	647	775	1,107	1,505	1,867	2,347	2,980	3,530	5,328	7,346	9,343	10,715	11,614
Domestic	88a	I82	92	190	195	276	384	539	652	861	1,183	1,511	2,851	4,020	4,743	5,241
Foreign	89a	I198	317	456	580	831	1,121	1,328	1,695	2,119	2,347	3,817	4,495	5,323	5,972	6,373
National Accounts																*Billions of Won;*
Private Consumption	96f	2,041	2,548	3,055	3,705	5,323	7,248	9,235	11,250	14,786	19,367	24,585	30,633	34,554	38,892	43,443
Exports of Goods & Services	90c	376	510	815	1,561	2,074	2,785	4,281	5,560	7,010	8,399	42,373	16,613	18,467	21,539	24,969
Government Consumption	91f	249	320	411	444	724	1,114	1,517	1,929	2,534	3,132	4,428	5,582	6,352	6,976	7,392
Gross Fixed Capital Formation	93e	696	769	871	1,298	2,069	2,745	3,594	5,107	7,924	10,573	12,230	13,369	15,586	18,944	21,381
Increase/Decrease(-) in Stocks	93i	-2	91	22	80	380	191	167	51	110	684	-162	66	40	-340	794
Imports of Goods & Services	98c	-652	-866	-1,011	-1,725	-2,929	-3,652	-4,536	-5,681	-7,894	-10,581	-15,335	-19,182	-19,855	-22,234	-25,132
Statistical Discrepancy	99bs	23	3	-9	1	17	-26	-11	42	112	161	293	429	-64	931	1,215
Gross Domestic Product (GDP)	99b	2,725	3,379	4,172	5,378	7,597	10,228	13,998	17,946	24,233	31,036	37,789	47,383	54,431	63,858	73,004
Net Factor Inc/Pmts(-) Abroad	98.n	27	9	-8	-25	-20	-124	-131	-158	-114	-269	-756	-1,224	-1,292	-1,284	-1,672
Gross National Income (GNI)	99a	2,752	3,388	4,164	5,353	7,577	10,104	13,867	17,788	24,119	30,767	37,032	46,149	53,140	62,574	71,332
Net National Income	99e	2,564	3,147	3,862	4,927	6,982	9,351	12,797	16,393	22,342	28,339	34,002	42,251	48,197	56,585	64,228
GDP Volume 1975 prices	99b.p	6,315	....	....	....	....	....	....	....	....	....	....	....	....	....	....
GDP Volume 1995 Prices	99b.p	56,209	61,025	64,001	71,898	77,212	82,258	91,468	100,622	109,687	117,435	114,978	122,412	131,286	145,331	157,318
GDP Volume (1995=100)	99bv p	14.9	16.2	17.0	19.1	20.5	21.8	24.2	26.7	29.1	31.1	30.5	32.4	34.8	38.5	41.7
GDP Deflator (1995=100)	99bi p	4.8	5.5	6.5	7.5	9.8	12.4	15.3	17.8	22.1	26.4	32.9	38.7	41.5	43.9	46.4
																Millions:
Population	99z	32.24	32.88	33.51	34.10	34.69	35.28	35.85	36.41	36.97	37.53	38.12	38.72	39.33	39.91	40.41

Millions of US Dollars

International Investment Position

	1985	1986	1987	1988	1989	1990	1991	1992	1993	1994	1995	1996	1997	1998	1999	Code
Assets	10,779	11,300	13,075	24,093	26,915	28,639	30,369	38,068	46,762	60,612	....	....	....	....	....	79aa d
Direct Investment Abroad	526	636	819	970	1,275	2,095	3,452	4,499	5,555	7,630	....	....	....	....	....	79ab d
Portfolio Investment	—	—	—	22	80	168	206	225	522	992	....	....	....	....	....	79ac d
Equity Securities	—	—	—	—	—	—	—	—	—	—	....	....	....	....	....	79ad d
Debt Securities	—	—	—	22	80	168	206	225	522	992	....	....	....	....	....	79ae d
Financial Derivatives	—	—	—								....	....	....	....	....	79al d
Other Investment	2,479	2,685	3,038	10,723	10,315	11,552	12,979	16,192	20,423	26,317	....	....	....	....	....	79af d
Monetary Authorities							18				....	....	....	....	....	79ag d
General Government	—	—	—				—				....	....	....	....	....	79ah d
Banks	934	1,095	1,447	8,924	8,163	9,068	9,989	12,081	15,389	19,944	....	....	....	....	....	79ai d
Other Sectors	1,545	1,590	1,591	1,799	2,152	2,484	2,972	4,111	5,034	6,373	....	....	....	....	....	79aj d
Reserve Assets	7,774	7,979	9,218	12,378	15,245	14,824	13,732	17,152	20,262	25,673	....	....	....	....	....	79ak d
Liabilities	20,543	19,973	16,652	15,710	17,463	20,564	33,264	41,508	53,706	69,830	....	....	....	....	....	79la d
Dir. Invest. in Rep. Economy	1,451	1,886	2,487	3,358	4,116	4,831	5,947	6,482	6,984	7,715	....	....	....	....	....	79lb d
Portfolio Investment	1,845	2,146	2,033	1,573	1,602	2,501	5,655	11,416	22,438	29,714	....	....	....	....	....	79lc d
Equity Securities	186	225	263	292	322	702	702	3,030	9,316	11,796	....	....	....	....	....	79ld d
Debt Securities	1,659	1,921	1,770	1,281	1,280	1,799	4,953	8,386	13,122	17,918	....	....	....	....	....	79le d
Financial Derivatives	—	—	—								....	....	....	....	....	79ll d
Other investment	17,247	15,941	12,132	10,779	11,745	13,232	21,662	23,610	24,284	32,401	....	....	....	....	....	79lf d
Monetary Authorities	1,612	1,666	667	162	162	184	186	193	208	207	....	....	....	....	....	79lg d
General Government	—	—	—								....	....	....	....	....	79lh d
Banks	15,635	14,275	11,465	10,617	11,583	13,048	21,476	23,417	24,076	32,194	....	....	....	....	....	79li d
Other Sectors	—	—	—								....	....	....	....	....	79lj d

Year Ending December 31

Government Finance

	1985	1986	1987	1988	1989	1990	1991	1992	1993	1994	1995	1996	1997	1998	1999	Code
Deficit (-) or Surplus	−943	−86	478	2,009	285	−1,207	−3,494	−1,188	1,704	984	1,035	431	−5,747	−16,954	−22,406	80
Revenue	13,923	15,840	18,658	22,890	25,962	32,089	36,818	43,805	50,750	61,109	72,087	84,272	91,979	95,482	105,408	81
Grants Received																81z
Expenditure	13,336	14,948	16,944	19,454	23,776	29,004	35,619	40,776	45,010	53,887	62,320	72,600	79,004	87,995	99,848	82
Lending Minus Repayments	1,530	978	1,236	1,427	1,901	4,292	4,693	4,217	4,036	6,238	8,732	11,241	18,722	24,441	27,966	83
Financing																
Domestic	501	233	−489	−1,297	315	1,535	3,776	1,499	−1,257	−589	−678	−136	−1,214	11,420	22,465	84a
Foreign	442	−147	11	−712	−600	−328	−282	−311	−447	−395	−357	−295	6,961	5,534	−59	85a
Net Borrowing	....	....														84
Use of Cash Balances																87
Debt	12,751	13,576	14,417	13,516	14,144	14,927	24,837	27,737	28,998	30,466	31,537	33,687	47,045	68,409	....	88
Domestic	5,422	5,759	6,562	7,548	9,034	9,369	19,137	22,216	23,504	24,800	26,296	28,636	31,724	43,984	....	88a
Foreign	7,329	7,817	7,855	5,968	5,110	5,558	5,700	5,521	5,494	5,666	5,241	5,051	15,321	24,425	....	89a

National Accounts

	1985	1986	1987	1988	1989	1990	1991	1992	1993	1994	1995	1996	1997	1998	1999	Code
Private Consumption	48,027	52,822	59,031	67,963	79,424	93,505	113,226	130,028	148,264	175,970	206,407	233,644	254,987	250,349		96f
Exports of Goods & Services	26,744	34,825	43,972	49,853	47,556	52,020	59,226	67,942	76,423	89,986	113,972	123,468	157,413	219,380	203,633	90c
Government Consumption	8,383	9,688	11,000	12,877	15,588	18,702	22,691	26,506	29,250	32,857	36,434	42,477	45,660	48,782	48,837	91f
Gross Fixed Capital Formation	23,435	26,976	32,600	39,451	47,673	66,689	84,507	90,809	100,354	116,436	138,439	153,976	159,110	132,308	135,234	93e
Increase/Decrease(-) in Stocks	963	611	982	1,965	2,554	736	1,773	931	−1,804	1,636	1,826	4,793	−3,933	−38,253	−5,432	93i
Imports of Goods & Services	−26,135	−29,745	−35,726	−39,972	−44,295	−54,101	−65,741	−71,600	−76,278	−93,668	−119,534	−140,659	−162,031	−158,325	−170,643	98c
Statistical Discrepancy	1,184	1,111	922	1,859	1,989	1,245	830	1,084	1,287	190	−192	779	2,071	−922	2,499	99bs
Gross Domestic Product (GDP)	81,312	94,862	111,198	132,112	148,197	178,797	216,511	245,700	277,497	323,407	377,350	418,479	453,276	444,367	483,778	99b
Net Factor Inc/Pmts(-) Abroad	−2,142	−2,223	−1,610	−1,051	−427	−169	−208	−312	−389	−596	−1,033	−1,371	−2,423	−6,495	−5,527	98.n
Gross National Income (GNI)	79,170	92,638	109,588	131,061	147,770	178,628	216,303	245,388	277,108	322,812	376,316	417,108	450,853	437,871	478,251	99a
Net National Income	71,170	83,395	98,267	117,262	132,378	159,744	194,279	220,382	248,387	290,534	335,469	370,438	399,681	379,623	412,637	99e
GDP Volume 1975 prices	....	....														99b.p
GDP Volume 1995 Prices	167,502	185,869	206,287	227,864	241,726	263,431	287,738	303,384	320,044	346,448	377,350	402,821	423,007	394,711	436,799	99b.p
GDP Volume (1995=100)	44.4	49.3	54.7	60.4	64.1	69.8	76.3	80.4	84.8	91.8	100.0	106.8	112.1	104.6	115.8	99bv p
GDP Deflator (1995=100)	48.5	51.0	53.9	58.0	61.3	67.9	75.2	81.0	86.7	93.3	100.0	103.9	107.2	112.6	110.8	99bi p

Midyear Estimates

	1985	1986	1987	1988	1989	1990	1991	1992	1993	1994	1995	1996	1997	1998	1999	Code
Population	40.81	41.21	41.62	42.03	42.45	42.87	43.30	43.75	44.19	44.64	45.09	45.54	45.99	46.43	46.86	99z

(See notes in the back of the book.)

Kuwait

		1970	1971	1972	1973	1974	1975	1976	1977	1978	1979	1980	1981	1982	1983	1984
Exchange Rates																*SDRs per Dinar:*
Official Rate	ac	2.8000	2.8000	2.8102	2.7940	2.8199	2.9040	2.9995	2.9392	2.8241	2.7795	2.8901	3.0529	3.1400	3.2648	3.3508
																US Dollars per Dinar:
Official Rate	ag	2.8000	3.0400	3.0511	3.3705	3.4526	3.3996	3.4849	3.5703	3.6792	3.6615	3.6860	3.5535	3.4638	3.4181	3.2845
Official Rate	rh	2.8000	2.8085	3.0400	3.3770e	3.4115	3.4483	3.4203	3.4898	3.6362	3.6203	3.6993	3.5878	3.4737	3.4309	3.3785
Fund Position																*Millions of SDRs:*
Quota	2f. s	65.0	65.0	65.0	65.0	65.0	65.0	65.0	65.0	235.0	235.0	393.3	393.3	393.3	635.3	635.3
SDRs	1b. s	—	—	—	—	—	—	—	—	—	—	—	35.4	62.3	35.6	76.0
Reserve Position in the Fund	1c. s	21.3	20.7	20.7	19.7	255.8	573.6	742.7	722.2	588.4	389.7	410.5	476.9	409.7	461.0	716.4
of which: Outstg.Fund Borrowing	2c	—	—	—	—	225.0	523.9	685.0	676.2	543.9	339.6	313.0	287.4	291.2	358.7	362.1
International Liquidity													*Millions of US Dollars Unless Otherwise Indicated:*			
Total Reserves minus Gold	1l. d	117.1	193.7	269.0	380.8	1,249.2	1,491.5	1,701.8	2,883.1	2,500.4	2,870.1	3,928.5	4,067.5	5,913.2	5,192.1	4,590.2
SDRs	1b. d	—	—	—	—	—	—	—	—	—	—	—	41.2	68.7	37.3	74.5
Reserve Position in the Fund	1c. d	21.3	22.5	22.5	23.8	313.2	671.5	862.9	877.2	766.6	513.4	523.6	476.9	508.6	729.4	702.3
Foreign Exchange	1d. d	95.8	171.2	246.5	357.0	936.0	820.0	838.9	2,005.9	1,733.8	2,356.7	3,404.9	3,549.4	5,335.9	4,425.4	3,813.4
Gold (Million Fine Troy Ounces)	1ad	2.463	2.480	2.480	2.846	3.504	3.988	5.578	2.511	2.525	2.539	2.539	2.539	2.539	2.539	2.539
Gold (National Valuation)	1and	86.2	94.2	94.2	—	150.5	169.6	242.9	112.1	116.3	116.1	116.8	112.6	109.8	108.4	104.1
Deposit Money Banks: Assets	7a. d	1,230.9	1,452.8	1,560.7	1,618.0	1,938.3	2,088.7	2,352.0	2,936.2	4,468.0	5,154.3	6,930.0	8,923.9	8,765.1	9,267.5	9,810.5
Liabilities	7b. d	323.7	316.8	314.9	459.7	495.1	574.5	1,129.5	1,498.8	2,213.0	2,943.5	4,181.0	4,969.9	5,651.5	5,816.6	5,685.5
Other Financial Insts.: Assets	7e. d	....	....	....	....	....	....	695.6	980.0	1,322.7	1,571.9	2,010.3	2,681.8	2,916.2	3,514.5	3,299.9
Liab.	7f. d	....	....	....	....	....	....					1,360.1	2,170.5	2,626.3	2,965.2	2,195.0
Monetary Authorities																*Millions of Dinars:*
Foreign Assets	11	72.5	94.7	119.6	148.5	395.0	482.4	547.0	821.9	709.8	814.1	1,092.0	1,162.6	1,720.1	1,537.2	1,405.5
Claims on Central Government	12a	....	....	....	....	....		....								
Claims on Deposit Money Banks	12e	—	—	—	—	—	4.5	2.0	20.7	30.6	195.3	298.6	282.4	276.7	334.6	547.0
Reserve Money	14	51.1	59.0	71.0	95.8	129.2	169.2	224.8	431.5	318.7	379.2	506.2	679.3	1,097.7	841.0	743.9
of which: Currency Outside DMBs	14a	44.8	50.4	57.1	71.1	81.7	101.7	129.1	150.9	177.0	215.9	251.3	284.5	342.4	340.1	324.7
Central Government Deposits	16d	14.7	30.9	36.5	28.4	213.1	271.5	270.8	325.1	274.8	446.1	668.7	536.5	649.3	537.6	683.1
Capital Accounts	17a	5.0	5.0	5.0	5.0	5.0	5.0	5.0	8.0	27.9	27.9	30.0	32.8	33.7	138.2	188.7
Other Items (Net)	17r	1.7	−.2	7.1	19.2	47.7	41.2	48.4	78.0	119.0	156.3	185.7	196.5	216.1	354.9	336.9
Deposit Money Banks																*Millions of Dinars:*
Reserves	20	6.2	8.5	13.8	26.9	57.9	67.2	92.4	271.0	122.7	143.3	221.7	382.5	744.1	485.1	397.6
Foreign Assets	21	439.6	477.9	513.4	479.0	561.4	614.4	674.9	822.4	1,214.4	1,407.7	1,880.1	2,511.3	2,530.5	2,711.3	2,986.9
Claims on Central Government	22a	—	.1	.7	1.9	3.6	5.9	12.5	15.2	20.6	35.3	47.4	176.7	318.5	1,005.0	1,200.8
Claims on Private Sector	22d	137.1	146.9	175.7	247.6	351.7	500.8	921.8	1,221.5	1,543.5	2,088.3	2,629.1	3,663.3	4,484.5	4,367.0	4,653.4
Demand Deposits	24	54.2	57.3	84.9	101.3	113.9	188.6	264.6	339.8	459.4	453.5	469.5	1,002.1	940.0	874.3	667.9
Time and Savings Deposits	25	266.9	311.1	351.6	363.9	489.0	600.8	826.4	1,078.0	1,314.0	1,593.3	2,136.8	2,755.0	3,267.9	3,683.7	4,176.9
Foreign Liabilities	26c	115.6	104.2	103.6	136.1	143.4	169.0	324.1	419.8	601.5	803.9	1,134.3	1,398.6	1,631.6	1,701.7	1,731.0
Central Government Deposits	26d	80.9	83.1	71.2	58.2	83.7	87.3	71.0	114.9	99.2	139.9	164.9	444.4	653.4	613.5	638.0
Credit from Monetary Authorities	26g	—	—	—	—	10.0	10.5	8.1	28.7	34.1	188.8	277.0	292.4	287.0	344.6	571.9
Capital Accounts	27a	31.6	36.4	40.8	45.6	51.0	63.8	89.2	197.4	218.4	268.6	337.0	490.4	698.7	792.9	958.1
Other Items (Net)	27r	37.4	41.3	51.6	50.4	83.6	68.3	118.2	151.5	174.5	226.6	258.8	351.0	599.2	557.6	494.9
Monetary Survey																*Millions of Dinars:*
Foreign Assets (Net)	31n	396.5	468.4	529.4	491.4	813.0	927.8	897.8	1,224.5	1,322.7	1,417.9	1,837.8	2,275.3	2,619.0	2,546.8	2,661.4
Domestic Credit	32	41.5	33.0	68.7	162.9	58.5	147.9	592.5	796.7	1,190.1	1,537.6	1,842.9	2,859.1	3,500.4	4,220.9	4,533.1
Claims on Central Govt. (Net)	32an	−95.6	−113.9	−107.0	−84.7	−293.2	−352.9	−329.3	−424.8	−353.4	−550.7	−786.2	−804.2	−984.1	−146.1	−120.3
Claims on Private Sector	32d	137.1	146.9	175.7	247.6	351.7	500.8	921.8	1,221.5	1,543.5	2,088.3	2,629.1	3,663.3	4,484.5	4,367.0	4,653.4
Money	34	99.0	107.7	142.0	172.4	195.6	290.3	393.7	490.7	636.4	669.4	720.8	1,286.6	1,282.4	1,214.4	992.6
Quasi-Money	35	266.9	311.1	351.6	363.9	489.0	600.8	826.4	1,078.0	1,314.0	1,593.3	2,136.8	2,755.0	3,267.9	3,683.7	4,176.9
Other Items (Net)	37r	75.8	82.6	104.6	118.0	186.9	184.6	270.2	452.5	562.3	692.9	823.1	1,093.0	1,569.2	1,869.4	2,025.1
Money plus Quasi-Money	35l	365.9	418.8	493.6	536.3	684.6	891.1	1,220.1	1,568.7	1,950.4	2,262.7	2,857.6	4,041.6	4,550.3	4,898.1	5,169.5
Other Financial Institutions																*Millions of Dinars:*
Cash	40	....	....	....	....	....	....	34.4	63.4	75.0	22.3	39.1	35.4	40.9	50.0	54.7
Foreign Assets	41	....	....	....	....	....	....	199.6	274.5	359.5	429.3	545.4	754.7	841.9	1,028.2	1,004.7
Claims on Private Sector	42d	....	....	....	....	....	....	62.9	90.8	130.0	196.0	285.6	453.9	808.0	717.7	596.5
Foreign Liabilities	46c	....	....	....	....	....	....	—	—	—	—	369.0	610.8	758.2	867.5	668.3
Central Government Deposits	46d	....	....	....	....	....	....	51.0	67.7	111.3	126.8	99.8	99.9	169.5	150.6	276.1
Credit from Deposit Money Banks	46h	....	....	....	....	....	....	22.1	69.9	83.9	90.2	126.6	182.8	231.1	166.1	147.1
Capital Accounts	47a	....	....	....	....	....	....	76.9	87.8	103.2	155.4	162.0	222.0	458.2	425.3	325.5
Other Items (Net)	47r	....	....	....	....	....	....	82.9	72.6	48.4	20.1	112.7	128.5	75.7	186.3	238.8
Interest Rates																*Percent Per Annum:*
Discount Rate *(End of Period)*	60	....	....	....	....	....	5.50	5.50	5.50	5.50	6.00	6.00	6.00	6.00	6.00	6.00
Money Market Rate	60b	....	....	....	....	....	....	....	....	....	8.58	10.94	10.13	10.25	6.78	8.91
Treasury Bill Rate	60c	....	....	....	....	....	....	....	....	....	....	6.50	6.50	6.42	5.69	5.69
Deposit Rate	60l	....	....	....	....	....	....	....	....	....	....	....	4.50	9.21	7.13	7.73
Lending Rate	60p	....	....	....	....	....	....	....	....	....	6.30	6.80	9.28	9.39	8.35	8.58
Prices and Production																*Index Numbers (1995=100):*
Wholesale Prices	63	....	....	31.7	38.7	42.7	46.0	49.5	52.9	52.3	55.7	61.5	65.8	⊺66.5	67.7	67.3
Consumer Prices	64	....	....	31.4	34.0	38.4	41.6	43.8	48.1	⊺52.3	56.0	59.9	64.3	69.3	72.6	73.4
Crude Petroleum Production	66aa	146.4	149.9	161.4	148.0	124.8	102.1	105.4	96.4	104.3	122.4	81.5	55.2	40.3	51.6	57.0

	1985	1986	1987	1988	1989	1990	1991	1992	1993	1994	1995	1996	1997	1998	1999		
End of Period																**Exchange Rates**	
	3.1501	2.7965	2.6117	2.6294	2.6062	....	2.4593	2.4026	2.4396	2.2824	2.2504	2.3190	2.4308	2.3551	2.3953	Official Rate	ac
End of Period (ag)		*Period Average (rh)*															
	3.4601	3.4206	3.7051	3.5384	3.4250	....	3.5178	3.3036	3.3510	3.3320	3.3453	3.3346	3.2798	3.3161	3.2875	Official Rate	ag
	3.3261	3.4412	3.5896	3.5848	3.4049	....	....	3.4087	3.3147	3.3600	3.3509	3.3399	3.2966	3.2814	3.2850	Official Rate	rh
End of Period																**Fund Position**	
	635.3	635.3	635.3	635.3	635.3	635.3	635.3	635.3	995.2	995.2	995.2	995.2	995.2	995.2	1,381.1	Quota	2f. s
	104.3	128.4	148.8	166.8	97.8	113.9	128.3	130.4	49.1	55.0	61.3	68.2	74.1	82.5	53.7	SDRs	1b. s
	639.4	515.8	378.0	247.3	158.2	123.5	111.1	96.7	167.8	142.6	139.0	136.5	167.5	244.8	368.3	Reserve Position in the Fund	1c. s
	309.2	228.8	140.2	70.9	23.9	4.3	—	—	—	—	—	—	—	31.8		*of which:* Outstg.Fund Borrowing	2c
End of Period																**International Liquidity**	
	5,470.7	5,501.1	4,141.6	1,923.5	3,101.9	1,951.7	3,409.0	5,146.9	4,214.1	3,500.7	3,560.8	3,515.1	3,451.8	3,947.1	4,823.7	Total Reserves minus Gold	1l. d
	114.6	157.1	211.1	224.4	128.6	162.1	183.5	179.2	67.4	80.3	91.1	98.0	100.0	116.2	73.8	SDRs	1b. d
	702.3	631.0	536.2	332.8	207.9	175.7	158.9	132.9	230.5	208.2	206.6	196.3	226.1	346.6	505.5	Reserve Position in the Fund	1c. d
	4,653.8	4,713.1	3,394.3	1,366.3	2,765.4	1,613.9	3,066.6	4,834.8	3,916.3	3,212.2	3,263.2	3,220.8	3,125.7	3,486.3	4,244.4	Foreign Exchange	1d. d
	2.539	2.539	2.539	2.539	2.539	2.539	2.539	2.539	2.539	2.539	2.539	2.539	2.539	2.539	2.539	Gold (Million Fine Troy Ounces)	1ad
	109.7	108.4	117.5	112.2	108.6	....	111.5	104.7	106.2	105.6	106.0	105.7	104.0	105.1	104.2	Gold (National Valuation)	1an d
	9,537.1	9,385.4	10,451.7	10,893.0	11,839.9	....	7,082.0	5,449.0	5,946.6	6,419.1	7,127.7	7,230.3	6,945.2	5,928.5	5,873.2	Deposit Money Banks: Assets	7a. d
	5,258.3	4,633.9	5,005.6	5,163.6	5,730.7	....	1,303.7	1,936.9	1,803.2	2,377.0	2,239.0	2,536.6	4,009.2	3,595.3	3,871.1	Liabilities	7b. d
	3,055.6	2,615.0	3,123.8	4,206.4	5,027.6	....	4,436.3	4,115.3	3,772.2	3,706.5	3,666.7	3,556.0	4,339.1	5,498.4	5,997.8	Other Financial Insts.: Assets	7e. d
	2,193.7	1,638.5	1,520.6	1,875.7	2,255.7	....	2,288.7	2,381.2	1,790.8	1,533.7	1,584.6	1,592.9	2,330.6	3,504.4	3,693.2	Liab.	7f. d
End of Period																**Monetary Authorities**	
	1,579.6	1,564.4	1,059.1	511.8	917.6	....	1,017.7	1,564.5	1,151.4	1,168.2	1,124.1	1,112.0	1,108.7	1,186.3	1,476.1	Foreign Assets	11
	—	—	62.5	483.5	505.2	....	43.8	152.9	87.1	59.2	2.3	41.2	39.3	.1	45.1	Claims on Central Government	12a
	407.2	520.2	404.0	346.4	188.7	....	157.1	77.6	142.4	90.8	—	—	6.0	—	—	Claims on Deposit Money Banks	12e
	729.6	667.7	547.5	394.3	390.0	....	570.4	537.4	503.4	504.0	470.9	474.7	426.9	448.4	582.9	Reserve Money	14
	327.5	336.6	337.8	342.0	333.7	....	445.6	379.1	355.2	351.3	311.5	350.1	345.3	348.7	442.9	*of which:* Currency Outside DMBs	14a
	666.7	390.2	381.5	565.5	909.9	....	322.7	863.7	497.2	368.8	163.9	265.7	298.7	229.0	450.8	Central Government Deposits	16d
	194.6	188.1	194.5	194.0	198.5	....	204.1	208.0	210.3	209.7	193.7	188.5	189.6	186.1	186.5	Capital Accounts	17a
	396.0	838.7	402.1	188.0	113.2	....	121.3	186.0	170.0	236.1	298.0	224.2	238.9	322.9	301.0	Other Items (Net)	17r
End of Period																**Deposit Money Banks**	
	376.4	306.8	200.7	53.7	55.0	....	120.6	160.9	146.0	151.8	158.1	123.0	79.0	98.0	141.2	Reserves	20
	2,756.3	2,743.8	2,820.9	3,078.5	3,456.9	....	2,013.2	1,649.4	1,774.6	1,926.5	2,130.7	2,168.3	2,117.6	1,787.8	1,786.5	Foreign Assets	21
	1,209.9	1,200.5	1,740.8	2,042.3	2,275.9	....	6,815.3	7,111.6	5,989.9	5,881.7	5,760.3	4,901.3	4,782.8	4,641.5	4,667.3	Claims on Central Government	22a
	4,736.0	4,867.0	5,175.0	5,244.7	5,264.9	....	836.6	1,032.7	1,240.9	1,703.2	2,436.3	3,173.1	4,324.2	4,801.6	5,014.8	Claims on Private Sector	22d
	695.7	688.7	747.5	663.7	635.8	....	755.6	729.4	758.3	774.7	873.5	892.5	902.2	794.7	921.0	Demand Deposits	24
	4,066.6	4,085.2	4,155.0	4,594.0	4,897.7	....	4,815.5	4,950.0	5,282.5	5,616.9	6,189.8	6,088.3	6,368.5	6,413.1	6,306.6	Time and Savings Deposits	25
	1,519.7	1,354.7	1,351.0	1,459.3	1,673.2	....	370.6	586.3	538.1	713.4	669.3	760.7	1,222.4	1,084.2	1,177.5	Foreign Liabilities	26c
	748.6	629.7	642.8	520.9	520.8	....	563.9	613.5	555.9	421.3	459.4	374.1	343.6	256.8	195.0	Central Government Deposits	26d
	479.4	928.0	1,090.0	1,037.1	1,160.0	....	1,707.3	1,384.2	196.4	112.0	6.0	—	6.0	.7	—	Credit from Monetary Authorities	26g
	978.0	1,042.7	1,153.5	1,211.8	1,260.4	....	952.5	977.1	1,059.8	1,090.1	1,201.5	1,259.0	1,407.8	1,469.9	1,502.5	Capital Accounts	27a
	591.3	389.4	797.6	932.4	904.9	....	620.9	714.3	760.0	935.0	1,086.2	991.2	1,053.1	1,309.7	1,507.0	Other Items (Net)	27r
End of Period																**Monetary Survey**	
	2,816.2	2,953.5	2,529.0	2,131.0	2,701.3	....	2,660.3	2,627.6	2,387.9	2,381.3	2,585.5	2,519.6	2,003.9	1,889.9	2,085.1	Foreign Assets (Net)	31n
	4,530.6	5,047.6	5,954.0	6,684.1	6,615.3	....	6,809.1	6,820.0	6,264.8	6,854.0	7,575.6	7,475.8	8,504.0	8,957.4	9,081.4	Domestic Credit	32
	−205.4	180.6	779.0	1,439.4	1,350.4	....	5,972.5	5,787.3	5,023.9	5,150.8	5,139.3	4,302.7	4,179.8	4,155.8	4,066.6	Claims on Central Govt. (Net)	32an
	4,736.0	4,867.0	5,175.0	5,244.7	5,264.9	....	836.6	1,032.7	1,240.9	1,703.2	2,436.3	3,173.1	4,324.2	4,801.6	5,014.8	Claims on Private Sector	32d
	1,023.2	1,025.3	1,085.3	1,005.7	969.5	....	1,201.2	1,108.5	1,114.0	1,126.0	1,185.0	1,242.6	1,247.5	1,143.4	1,363.9	Money	34
	4,066.6	4,085.2	4,155.0	4,594.0	4,897.7	....	4,815.5	4,950.0	5,282.5	5,616.9	6,189.8	6,088.3	6,368.5	6,413.1	6,306.6	Quasi-Money	35
	2,257.8	2,891.0	3,242.7	3,215.5	3,449.6	....	3,453.2	3,389.4	2,256.3	2,493.0	2,786.7	2,664.5	2,892.0	3,291.0	3,495.8	Other Items (Net)	37r
	5,089.8	5,110.5	5,240.3	5,599.7	5,867.2	....	6,016.7	6,058.5	6,396.5	6,742.9	7,374.8	7,330.9	7,616.0	7,556.5	7,670.5	Money plus Quasi-Money	35l
End of Period																**Other Financial Institutions**	
	76.7	48.1	70.9	168.5	139.4	....	163.4	141.6	132.6	120.5	95.7	125.8	153.9	258.7	207.8	Cash	40
	883.1	764.5	843.1	1,188.8	1,467.9	....	1,261.1	1,245.7	1,125.7	1,112.4	1,096.1	1,066.4	1,323.0	1,658.1	1,824.4	Foreign Assets	41
	518.2	560.7	582.1	744.9	741.7	....	795.5	878.8	713.1	596.6	632.9	707.6	904.0	1,244.9	927.0	Claims on Private Sector	42d
	634.0	479.0	410.4	530.1	658.6	....	650.6	720.8	534.4	460.3	473.7	477.7	710.6	1,056.8	1,123.4	Foreign Liabilities	46c
	197.0	195.1	228.5	333.2	247.6	....	202.2	267.3	181.0	119.9	101.1	142.7	94.5	84.8	7.5	Central Government Deposits	46d
	145.6	88.5	102.7	136.6	157.1	....	245.9	230.7	186.5	134.7	185.5	158.5	206.9	296.1	207.7	Credit from Deposit Money Banks	46h
	282.6	248.4	304.9	550.3	661.8	....	522.8	594.0	609.7	686.0	769.1	861.6	1,018.3	1,325.5	1,252.8	Capital Accounts	47a
	218.8	362.3	449.6	551.9	623.8	....	598.5	453.3	460.0	428.5	295.3	259.4	350.8	398.6	367.8	Other Items (Net)	47r
Percent Per Annum																**Interest Rates**	
	6.00	6.00	6.00	7.50	7.50	....	7.50	7.50	5.75	7.00	7.25	7.25	7.50	7.00	6.75	Discount Rate *(End of Period)*	60
	7.59	7.52	6.08	6.12	8.70	....			7.43	6.31	7.43	6.98	7.05	7.24	6.32	Money Market Rate	60b
	5.69	5.69	5.48	6.01	8.28	....	....	....		6.32	7.35	6.93	6.98			Treasury Bill Rate	60c
	7.25	6.80	5.73	5.30	7.40	....	....	7.59	7.07	5.70	6.53	6.05	5.93	6.32	5.76	Deposit Rate	60l
	8.75	8.63	7.86	6.72	8.38	....		8.00	7.95	7.61	8.37	8.77	8.80	8.93	8.56	Lending Rate	60p
Period Averages																**Prices and Production**	
	66.4	66.8	69.0	72.2	78.5	81.5	96.6	97.1	98.8	98.6	100.0	105.2	103.8	102.1	100.8	Wholesale Prices	63
	74.5	75.2	75.7	76.9	79.4	87.2	95.1	94.6	95.0	97.4	100.0	103.6	104.2	104.4	....	Consumer Prices	64
	52.0	69.1	65.4	68.6	87.3	59.1	9.0	50.5	91.7	99.6	100.0	101.3	102.2	102.3	92.8	Crude Petroleum Production	66aa

Kuwait

		1970	1971	1972	1973	1974	1975	1976	1977	1978	1979	1980	1981	1982	1983	1984
International Transactions															*Millions of Dinars*	
Exports	70	604.7	808.6	841.3	1,129.7	3,214.8	2,663.0	2,874.4	2,792.6	2,864.1	5,088.5	5,368.9	4,530.8	3,156.4	3,373.6	3,632.4
Oil Exports	70a	578.3	774.2	791.7	1,059.9	3,098.0	2,492.6	2,658.7	2,557.1	2,628.7	4,781.0	4,960.8	3,969.2	2,611.5	2,938.2	3,256.9
Imports, c.i.f.	71	223.3	232.3	262.2	310.6	455.1	693.2	972.0	1,387.1	1,263.9	1,437.0	1,764.9	1,945.4	2,384.6	2,149.1	2,041.7
Balance of Payments															*Millions of US Dollars:*	
Current Account, n.i.e.	78ald	....	....	....	....	....	5,930	6,929	4,561	6,130	14,032	15,302	13,699	4,963	5,311	6,428
Goods: Exports f.o.b.	78aad						8,485	9,621	9,561	10,234	18,114	20,633	16,023	10,819	11,473	12,156
Goods: Imports f.o.b.	78abd						−2,400	−3,300	−4,735	−4,326	−4,870	−6,756	−6,736	−7,811	−6,889	−6,549
Trade Balance	78acd						6,086	6,320	4,826	5,908	13,243	13,877	9,287	3,008	4,584	5,607
Services: Credit	78add						521	612	625	702	1,183	1,225	1,392	941	868	888
Services: Debit	78aed						−759	−975	−1,406	−1,854	−2,265	−3,067	−2,905	−3,491	−3,620	−3,705
Balance on Goods & Services	78afd						5,848	5,958	4,044	4,755	12,161	12,035	7,773	458	1,832	2,790
Income: Credit	78agd						1,283	1,631	1,965	2,901	3,575	5,487	8,325	6,780	5,712	5,854
Income: Debit	78ahd						−131	−123	−199	−294	−416	−640	−739	−754	−683	−838
Balance on Gds, Serv. & Inc.	78aid						6,999	7,466	5,810	7,362	15,320	16,881	15,359	6,485	6,862	7,806
Current Transfers, n.i.e.: Credit	78ajd						—	—	—	—	—	—	—	—	—	—
Current Transfers: Debit	78akd						−1,069	−537	−1,249	−1,232	−1,288	−1,580	−1,661	−1,521	−1,551	−1,378
Capital Account, n.i.e.	78bcd	....	....	....	....	....	—	—	—	—	—	—	—	—	—	—
Capital Account, n.i.e.: Credit	78bad						—	—	—	—	—	—	—	—	—	—
Capital Account: Debit	78bbd						—	—	—	—	—	—	—	—	—	—
Financial Account, n.i.e.	78bjd	....	....	....	....	....	−6,648	−8,752	−4,030	−5,148	−9,929	−11,306	−8,300	−3,032	124	−7,451
Direct Investment Abroad	78bdd						−93	−109	−52	−95	188	−407	151	−108	−240	−95
Dir. Invest. in Rep. Econ., n.i.e.	78bed						—	—	—	—	—	—	—	—	—	—
Portfolio Investment Assets	78bfd						−90	−174	−157	−80	−586	−329	−140	—	−213	−7
Equity Securities	78bkd						—	—	—	—	—	—	—	—	—	—
Debt Securities	78bld						−90	−174	−157	−80	−586	−329	−140	—	−213	−7
Portfolio Investment Liab., n.i.e.	78bgd						—	—	—	15	—	—	14	184	—	216
Equity Securities	78bmd						—	—	—	—	—	—	—	—	—	—
Debt Securities	78bnd						—	—	—	15	—	—	14	184	—	216
Financial Derivatives Assets	78bwd						....	....	....	....	....	....	....	....	....	....
Financial Derivatives Liabilities	78bxd						....	....	....	....	....	....	....	....	....	....
Other Investment Assets	78bhd						−6,368	−8,920	−4,086	−5,526	−10,334	−12,198	−8,810	−4,088	628	−7,431
Monetary Authorities	78bod						−5,430	−7,333	−3,518	−4,112	−9,354	−10,377	−7,942	−4,435	1,431	−5,641
General Government	78bpd						−714	−1,413	−94	−276	−119	−118	538	483	−744	−476
Banks	78bqd						−183	−209	−516	−1,425	−738	−1,709	−1,309	−21	−172	−699
Other Sectors	78brd						−41	34	42	287	−123	7	−97	−115	113	−615
Other Investment Liab., n.i.e.	78bid						−97	451	265	538	803	1,628	484	979	−51	−135
Monetary Authorities	78bsd						—	—	—	—	—	—	—	—	—	—
General Government	78btd						—	—	—	—	—	—	—	—	—	—
Banks	78bud						90	530	335	662	731	1,221	466	910	69	34
Other Sectors	78bvd						−186	−79	−70	−124	72	407	18	69	−120	−169
Net Errors and Omissions	78cad						1,032	2,070	412	−1,424	−3,737	−2,950	−5,116	44	−4,432	1,140
Overall Balance	78cbd						315	247	943	−443	366	1,045	283	1,975	1,002	117
Reserves and Related Items	79dad						−315	−247	−943	443	−366	−1,045	−283	−1,975	−1,002	−117
Reserve Assets	79dbd						−315	−247	−943	443	−366	−1,045	−283	−1,975	−1,002	−117
Use of Fund Credit and Loans	79dcd						—	—	—	—	—	—	—	—	—	—
Exceptional Financing	79ded	....	....	....	....	....	....	....	....	....	....	....	....	....	....	....
Government Finance															*Millions of Dinars:*	
Deficit (-) or Surplus	80	60	67	Ɪ192	162	Ɪ529	2,393	1,911	924	1,093	2,938	3,035	1,240	377	−94	145
Total Revenue and Grants	81y	374	424	Ɪ609	696	Ɪ1,129	3,324	2,839	2,330	2,791	4,955	5,452	3,895	2,968	2,767	2,919
Revenue	81	374	424	Ɪ609	696	Ɪ1,129	3,324	2,839	2,330	2,791	4,955	5,452	3,895	2,968	2,767	2,919
Grants	81z	—	—	Ɪ—	—	Ɪ—	—	—	—	—	—	—	—	—	—	—
Exp. & Lending Minus Repay.	82z	314	357	Ɪ402	421	Ɪ600	931	927	1,406	1,698	2,017	2,417	2,655	2,591	2,860	2,774
Expenditure	82	303	347	Ɪ379	458	Ɪ600	931	927	1,406	1,698	2,017	2,417	2,655	2,591	2,860	2,774
Lending Minus Repayments	83	11	10	Ɪ38	76	Ɪ—	—	—	—	—	—	—	—	—	—	—
National Accounts															*Millions of Dinars*	
Exports of Goods & Services	90c	614	917	1,004	1,154	3,239	2,806	2,992	2,918	3,008	5,333	6,065	4,855	3,386	3,597	3,862
Government Consumption	91f	139	173	199	215	279	386	432	586	616	764	865	993	1,190	1,287	1,345
Gross Capital Formation	93	124	130	136	153	259	444	635	944	863	934	1,078	1,162	1,426	1,508	1,351
Gross Fixed Capital Formation	93e	126	127	127	146	222	418	563	815	794	790	973	1,073	1,297	1,527	1,359
Increase/Decrease(-) in Stocks	93i	−2	3	9	7	37	26	72	129	69	144	105	89	129	−19	−8
Private Consumption	96f	396	420	427	439	563	756	1,027	1,363	1,478	1,734	2,325	2,630	3,344	2,694	2,735
Imports of Goods & Services	98c	−248	−258	−303	−356	−528	−907	−1,250	−1,760	−1,700	−1,902	−2,577	−2,601	−3,132	−3,002	−2,868
Gross Domestic Product (GDP)	99b	1,026	1,382	1,464	1,604	3,812	3,485	3,837	4,052	4,264	6,862	7,755	7,039	6,214	6,083	6,425
Net Factor Inc/Pmts(-) Abroad	98.n	−175	−265	−362	−342	−281	224	441	506	717	873	1,310	2,137	1,709	1,466	1,485
Gross National Income (GNI)	99a	851	1,117	1,103	1,262	3,532	3,709	4,277	4,558	4,981	7,735	9,065	9,176	7,923	7,549	7,910
Net National Income	99e	808	1,053	1,032	1,186	3,451	3,616	4,170	4,428	4,812	7,518	8,802	8,886	7,586	7,202	7,486
GDP Volume 1984 Prices	99b.p	8,976	10,669	11,090	10,370	9,044	7,951	8,964	8,140	8,728	9,926	7,905	6,409	5,656	6,105	6,425
GDP Volume (1995=100)	99bvp	97.2	115.5	120.0	112.3	97.9	86.1	97.0	88.1	94.5	107.4	85.6	69.4	61.2	66.1	69.5
GDP Deflator (1995=100)	99bip	13.3	15.1	15.4	18.0	49.1	51.1	49.9	58.0	56.9	80.6	114.4	128.0	128.1	116.2	116.6
															Millions:	
Population	99z	.74	.79	.84	.89	.94	1.01	1.07	1.14	1.21	1.29	1.37	1.43	1.50	1.57	1.64

	1985	1986	1987	1988	1989	1990	1991	1992	1993	1994	1995	1996	1997	1998	1999	Code
International Transactions																
Millions of Dinars																
Exports	3,185.0	2,105.0	2,304.4	2,166.0	3,378.0	2,031.4	309.4	1,931.1	3,091.2	3,342.3	3,814.5	4,458.0	4,314.3	2,911.6	3,711.3	70
Oil Exports	2,843.0	1,853.4	2,096.7	1,908.4	3,064.9	1,842.0	248.6	1,824.9	2,929.6	3,112.7	3,597.1	4,231.3	4,085.4	2,581.8	3,348.0	70a
Imports, c.i.f.	1,806.0	1,661.2	1,530.7	1,714.2	1,849.4	1,145.7	1,353.3	2,129.2	2,123.8	1,988.2	2,323.1	2,507.2	2,501.6	2,626.2	2,318.3	71
Balance of Payments																
Minus Sign Indicates Debit																
Current Account, n.i.e.	4,798	5,616	4,561	4,602	9,136	3,886	−26,478	−450	2,498	3,227	5,016	7,107	7,935	2,215	5,062	78al d
Goods: Exports f.o.b.	10,374	7,216	8,221	7,709	11,396	6,989	1,080	6,548	10,264	11,284	12,833	14,946	14,281	9,618	12,276	78aa d
Goods: Imports f.o.b.	−5,719	−5,265	−4,938	−5,999	−6,410	−3,810	−5,073	−7,237	−6,941	−6,616	−7,254	−7,949	−7,747	−7,714	−6,705	78ab d
Trade Balance	4,655	1,951	3,284	1,709	4,987	3,179	−3,993	−689	3,323	4,669	5,579	6,997	6,534	1,903	5,571	78ac d
Services: Credit	1,137	1,053	1,030	1,158	1,345	1,279	992	1,494	1,242	1,415	1,401	1,520	1,760	1,762	1,688	78ad d
Services: Debit	−4,086	−3,861	−4,077	−4,204	−4,119	−3,359	−5,090	−4,590	−4,589	−4,531	−5,381	−5,100	−5,129	−5,542	−5,374	78ae d
Balance on Goods & Services	1,706	−857	237	−1,337	2,213	1,099	−8,091	−3,786	−23	1,553	1,598	3,417	3,165	−1,877	1,886	78af d
Income: Credit	5,330	8,352	6,129	7,863	9,211	8,584	6,093	5,907	4,489	4,174	6,125	6,409	7,744	7,163	6,205	78ag d
Income: Debit	−665	−613	−545	−606	−793	−846	−682	−662	−663	−1,004	−1,243	−1,229	−1,467	−1,296	−1,025	78ah d
Balance on Gds, Serv. & Inc.	6,371	6,882	5,821	5,921	10,630	8,837	−2,681	1,460	3,803	4,723	6,480	8,597	9,441	3,990	7,066	78ai d
Current Transfers, n.i.e.: Credit	—	—	....	....	....	—	—	17	109	94	54	53	79	98	99	78aj d
Current Transfers: Debit	−1,573	−1,266	−1,260	−1,319	−1,494	−4,951	−23,798	−1,927	−1,415	−1,590	−1,518	−1,543	−1,586	−1,874	−2,102	78ak d
Capital Account, n.i.e.	—	—	....	....	....	....	....	....	−205	−205	−194	−204	−96	79	506	78bc d
Capital Account, n.i.e.: Credit	—	—	....	....	....	....	....	....	....	....	....	3	115	289	716	78ba d
Capital Account: Debit	—	—	....	....	....	....	....	....	−205	−205	−194	−207	−211	−210	−210	78bb d
Financial Account, n.i.e.	−2,334	−7,505	−5,566	−7,340	−8,323	413	38,766	11,067	421	3,304	157	−7,632	−6,211	−2,920	−6,051	78bj d
Direct Investment Abroad	−70	−248	−775	−477	−994	−239	186	−1,211	−653	1,519	1,022	−1,740	969	1,867	−283	78bd d
Dir. Invest. in Rep. Econ., n.i.e.	....	....	....	....	....	....	....	....	13	....	7	347	20	59	72	78be d
Portfolio Investment Assets	−392	−506	−179	−720	−623	−919	−813	−3	−931	394	−2,064	−788	−6,926	−4,768	−2,598	78bf d
Equity Securities	....	....	....	....	....	....	....	....	....	....	....	....	....	....	....	78bk d
Debt Securities	−392	−506	−179	−720	−623	−919	−813	−3	−931	394	−2,064	−788	−6,926	−4,768	−2,598	78bl d
Portfolio Investment Liab., n.i.e.	47	21	219	280	24	537	211	276	....	....	−50	27	....	....	−23	78bg d
Equity Securities	....	....	....	....	....	....	....	....	....	....	....	....	....	....	....	78bm d
Debt Securities	47	21	219	280	24	537	211	276	....	....	−50	27	....	....	−23	78bn d
Financial Derivatives Assets																78bw d
Financial Derivatives Liabilities																78bx d
Other Investment Assets	−1,184	−6,235	−4,389	−6,042	−7,295	829	43,061	11,261	−669	529	−221	−745	3,356	646	−3,610	78bh d
Monetary Authorities	−1,902	−6,105	−3,865	−5,121	−5,647	−281	38,745	10,490	....	....	....	....	....	....	....	78bo d
General Government	−336	−496	−187	−434	−701	783	....	−634	−523	825	724	−1,122	2,993	−10	−3,502	78bp d
Banks	924	179	−370	−699	−1,236	55	3,785	1,385	−301	−401	−734	−23	260	929	−161	78bq d
Other Sectors	130	186	32	211	289	270	531	20	156	104	−211	401	102	−272	53	78br d
Other Investment Liab., n.i.e.	−735	−537	−441	−380	565	205	−3,880	743	2,660	862	1,464	−4,733	−3,629	−725	391	78bi d
Monetary Authorities	—	—	....	....	....	....	....	....	7	−3	−54	−17	3	−10	—	78bs d
General Government	....	....	....	....	....	....	....	....	3,429	525	1,541	−5,371	−6,290	−1,316	−115	78bt d
Banks	−665	−502	−29	201	742	205	−4,176	720	−159	589	−97	304	1,523	−456	302	78bu d
Other Sectors	−70	−34	−413	−581	−177	....	295	24	−616	−249	74	351	1,134	1,057	204	78bv d
Net Errors and Omissions	−1,919	1,806	−842	810	462	−5,196	−11,012	−8,765	−4,192	−6,273	−5,119	705	−1,621	886	1,401	78ca d
Overall Balance	545	−83	−1,847	−1,928	1,275	−897	1,276	1,851	−1,479	53	−140	−24	7	259	918	78cb d
Reserves and Related Items	−545	83	1,847	1,928	−1,275	897	−1,276	−1,851	1,479	−53	140	24	−7	−259	−918	79da d
Reserve Assets	−545	83	1,847	1,928	−1,275	897	−1,276	−1,851	1,479	−53	140	24	−7	−259	−918	79db d
Use of Fund Credit and Loans	—	—	....	....	....	—	—	—	—	—	—	—	—	—	—	79dc d
Exceptional Financing	....	....	....	....	....	....	....	....	....	....	....	....	....	....	....	79de d
Government Finance																
Year Ending December 31																
Deficit (-) or Surplus	−229	−939	159	−623	251	....	....	....	....	−977	−656	1,031	1,050	−456	385	80
Total Revenue and Grants	2,703	1,676	2,518	1,874	3,024	....	....	....	....	2,787	3,076	4,198	4,179	2,859	3,710	81y
Revenue	2,703	1,676	2,518	1,874	3,024	....	....	....	....	2,787	3,076	4,198	4,179	2,859	3,710	81
Grants	—	—	—	—	—	....	....	....	....	—	—	—	—	—	—	81z
Exp. & Lending Minus Repay.	2,932	2,614	2,359	2,497	2,773	....	....	....	....	3,763	3,732	3,167	3,129	3,315	3,325	82z
Expenditure	2,932	2,614	2,359	2,497	2,773	....	....	....	....	3,763	3,732	3,167	3,129	3,315	3,325	82
Lending Minus Repayments	—	—	—	—	—	....	....	....	....	—	—	—	—	—	—	83
National Accounts																
Millions of Dinars																
Exports of Goods & Services	3,462	2,403	3,275	2,746	3,743	2,385	529	2,358	3,454	3,753	4,248	4,930	4,866	3,468	4,240	90c
Government Consumption	1,445	1,403	1,374	1,517	1,814	2,056	6,294	3,237	2,593	2,503	2,612	2,571	2,452	2,412	2,465	91f
Gross Capital Formation	1,216	1,150	1,094	906	878	846	1,230	1,158	1,243	1,192	1,197	1,424	1,240	1,253	1,136	93
Gross Fixed Capital Formation	1,277	1,127	1,056	790	733	833	1,150	1,013	1,094	982	1,100	1,318	1,240	1,253	1,136	93e
Increase/Decrease(-) in Stocks	−61	23	37	116	145	13	80	145	149	210	97	106	....	....	....	93i
Private Consumption	3,084	2,744	2,805	3,083	3,662	3,123	2,920	2,233	3,143	3,055	3,272	4,073	4,194	4,309	4,529	96f
Imports of Goods & Services	−2,757	−2,498	−2,314	−2,479	−2,955	−3,082	−7,843	−3,159	−3,202	−3,098	−3,405	−3,695	−3,645	−3,723	−3,337	98c
Gross Domestic Product (GDP)	6,450	5,203	6,233	5,773	7,143	5,328	3,131	5,826	7,231	7,380	7,925	9,303	9,107	7,718	9,033	99b
Net Factor Inc/Pmts(-) Abroad	1,403	2,249	1,556	2,025	2,473	2,232	1,538	1,538	1,155	941	1,457	1,551	1,904	1,788	1,577	98.n
Gross National Income (GNI)	7,853	7,452	7,789	7,798	9,616	7,560	4,669	7,364	8,386	8,321	9,382	10,854	11,011	9,506	10,610	99a
Net National Income	7,377	6,965	7,270	7,244	9,043	7,027	4,172	6,832	7,815	7,681	8,671	10,183	10,310	8,894	9,955	99e
GDP Volume 1984 Prices	6,151	6,678	7,222	6,496	8,178	....	....	6,290	8,428	9,139	9,238	8,932	....	....	....	99b.p
GDP Volume (1995=100)	66.6	72.3	78.2	70.3	88.5	....	....	68.1	91.2	98.9	100.0	96.7	....	....	....	99bv p
GDP Deflator (1995=100)	122.2	90.8	100.6	103.6	101.8	....	....	108.0	100.0	94.1	100.0	121.4	....	....	....	99bi p
Midyear Estimates																
Population	1.72	1.80	1.88	1.97	2.05	2.14	I2.09	I1.42	1.46	1.62	1.80	1.89	1.98	2.03	2.11	99z

(See notes in the back of the book.)

Kyrgyz Republic

		1970	1971	1972	1973	1974	1975	1976	1977	1978	1979	1980	1981	1982	1983	1984
Exchange Rates															*Soms per SDR:*	
Official Rate	aa	....	....	....	....	....	....	....	....	....	....	....	....	....	....	....
															Soms per US Dollar:	
Official Rate	ae	....	....	....	....	....	....	....	....	....	....	....	....	....	....	....
Official Rate	rf	....	....	....	....	....	....	....	....	....	....	....	....	....	....	....
Fund Position															*Millions of SDRs:*	
Quota	2f. s	....	....	....	....	....	....	....	....	....	....	....	....	....	....	
SDRs	1b. s	....	....	....	....	....	....	....	....	....	....	....	....	....	....	
Reserve Position in the Fund	1c. s	....	....	....	....	....	....	....	....	....	....	....	....	....	....	
Total Fund Cred.&Loans Outstg.	2tl	....	....	....	....	....	....	....	....	....	....	....	....	....	....	
International Liquidity												*Millions of US Dollars Unless Otherwise Indicated:*				
Total Reserves minus Gold	1l. d	....	....	....	....	....	....	....	....	....	....	....	....	....	....	....
SDRs	1b. d	....	....	....	....	....	....	....	....	....	....	....	....	....	....	....
Reserve Position in the Fund	1c. d	....	....	....	....	....	....	....	....	....	....	....	....	....	....	....
Foreign Exchange	1d. d	....	....	....	....	....	....	....	....	....	....	....	....	....	....	....
Gold (Million Fine Troy Ounces)	1ad	....	....	....	....	....	....	....	....	....	....	....	....	....	....	....
Gold (National Valuation)	1and	....	....	....	....	....	....	....	....	....	....	....	....	....	....	....
Monetary Authorities: Other Liab	4.. d	....	....	....	....	....	....	....	....	....	....	....	....	....	....	....
Banking Institutions: Assets	7a. d	....	....	....	....	....	....	....	....	....	....	....	....	....	....	....
Liabilities	7b. d	....	....	....	....	....	....	....	....	....	....	....	....	....	....	....
Monetary Authorities															*Millions of Soms:*	
Foreign Assets	11	....	....	....	....	....	....	....	....	....	....	....	....	....	....	....
Claims on General Government	12a	....	....	....	....	....	....	....	....	....	....	....	....	....	....	....
Claims on Banking Institutions	12e	....	....	....	....	....	....	....	....	....	....	....	....	....	....	....
Reserve Money	14	....	....	....	....	....	....	....	....	....	....	....	....	....	....	....
of which: Currency Outside Banks	14a	....	....	....	....	....	....	....	....	....	....	....	....	....	....	....
Other Liabilities to DMBs	14n	....	....	....	....	....	....	....	....	....	....	....	....	....	....	....
Foreign Liabilities	16c	....	....	....	....	....	....	....	....	....	....	....	....	....	....	....
General Government Deposits	16d	....	....	....	....	....	....	....	....	....	....	....	....	....	....	....
Capital Accounts	17a	....	....	....	....	....	....	....	....	....	....	....	....	....	....	....
Other Items (Net)	17r	....	....	....	....	....	....	....	....	....	....	....	....	....	....	....
Banking Institutions															*Millions of Soms:*	
Reserves	20	....	....	....	....	....	....	....	....	....	....	....	....	....	....	....
Other Claims on Monetary Author.	20n	....	....	....	....	....	....	....	....	....	....	....	....	....	....	....
Foreign Assets	21	....	....	....	....	....	....	....	....	....	....	....	....	....	....	....
Claims on General Government	22a	....	....	....	....	....	....	....	....	....	....	....	....	....	....	....
Claims on Rest of the Economy	22d	....	....	....	....	....	....	....	....	....	....	....	....	....	....	....
Demand Deposits	24	....	....	....	....	....	....	....	....	....	....	....	....	....	....	....
Time & Foreign Currency Deposits	25	....	....	....	....	....	....	....	....	....	....	....	....	....	....	....
Foreign Liabilities	26c	....	....	....	....	....	....	....	....	....	....	....	....	....	....	....
General Government Deposits	26d	....	....	....	....	....	....	....	....	....	....	....	....	....	....	....
Credit from Monetary Authorities	26g	....	....	....	....	....	....	....	....	....	....	....	....	....	....	....
Capital Accounts	27a	....	....	....	....	....	....	....	....	....	....	....	....	....	....	....
Other Items (Net)	27r	....	....	....	....	....	....	....	....	....	....	....	....	....	....	....
Banking Survey															*Millions of Soms:*	
Foreign Assets (Net)	31n	....	....	....	....	....	....	....	....	....	....	....	....	....	....	....
Domestic Credit	32	....	....	....	....	....	....	....	....	....	....	....	....	....	....	....
Claims on General Govt. (Net)	32an	....	....	....	....	....	....	....	....	....	....	....	....	....	....	....
Claims on Rest of the Economy	32d	....	....	....	....	....	....	....	....	....	....	....	....	....	....	....
Money	34	....	....	....	....	....	....	....	....	....	....	....	....	....	....	....
Quasi-Money	35	....	....	....	....	....	....	....	....	....	....	....	....	....	....	....
Capital Accounts	37a	....	....	....	....	....	....	....	....	....	....	....	....	....	....	....
Other Items (Net)	37r	....	....	....	....	....	....	....	....	....	....	....	....	....	....	....
Money plus Quasi-Money	35l	....	....	....	....	....	....	....	....	....	....	....	....	....	....	....
Interest Rates															*Percent per Annum*	
Lombard Rate	60.a	....	....	....	....	....	....	....	....	....	....	....	....	....	....	....
Money Market Rate	60b	....	....	....	....	....	....	....	....	....	....	....	....	....	....	....
Treasury Bill Rate	60c	....	....	....	....	....	....	....	....	....	....	....	....	....	....	....
Deposit Rate	60l	....	....	....	....	....	....	....	....	....	....	....	....	....	....	....
Lending Rate	60p	....	....	....	....	....	....	....	....	....	....	....	....	....	....	....
Prices, Production, Labor															*Index Numbers (1995=100):*	
Producer Prices	63	....	....	....	....	....	....	....	....	....	....	....	....	....	....	....
Consumer Prices	64	....	....	....	....	....	....	....	....	....	....	....	....	....	....	....
Wages: Average Earnings	65	....	....	....	....	....	....	....	....	....	....	....	....	....	....	....
															Number in Thousands:	
Employment	67e	....	....	....	....	....	....	....	....	....	....	....	....	....	....	....
Unemployment	67c	....	....	....	....	....	....	....	....	....	....	....	....	....	....	....
International Transactions															*Millions of Soms*	
Exports	70.. d	....	....	....	....	....	....	....	....	....	....	....	....	....	....	....
Imports, c.i.f.	71.. d	....	....	....	....	....	....	....	....	....	....	....	....	....	....	....

	1985	1986	1987	1988	1989	1990	1991	1992	1993	1994	1995	1996	1997	1998	1999		
End of Period																**Exchange Rates**	
	....	....	....	....	....	....	....	....	11.030	15.547	16.649	24.014	23.443	41.362	62.352	Official Rate............	**aa**
End of Period (ae) Period Average (rf)																	
	....	....	....	....	....	....	....	....	8.030	10.650	11.200	16.700	17.375	29.376	45.429	Official Rate............	**ae**
	....	....	....	....	....	....	....	....	....	10.842	10.822	12.810	17.362	20.838	39.008	Official Rate............	**rf**
End of Period																**Fund Position**	
	....	....	....	....	....	....	....	64.5	64.5	64.5	64.5	64.5	64.5	64.5	88.8	Quota............	**2f. s**
	....	....	....	....	....	....	....	—	9.4	.7	9.6	5.1	.7	.2	3.7	SDRs............	**1b. s**
	....	....	....	....	....	....	....	—	—	—	—	—	—	—	—	Reserve Position in the Fund............	**1c. s**
	....	....	....	....	....	....	....	—	43.9	53.3	83.6	97.1	122.2	124.4	138.7	Total Fund Cred.&Loans Outstg.............	**2tl**
End of Period																**International Liquidity**	
	....	....	....	....	....	....	....	....	48.2	26.2	81.0	94.6	169.8	163.8	229.7	Total Reserves minus Gold............	**1l. d**
	....	....	....	....	....	....	....	....	12.9	1.0	14.3	7.4	.9	.3	5.1	SDRs............	**1b. d**
	....	....	....	....	....	....	....	....	—	—	—	—	—	—	—	Reserve Position in the Fund............	**1c. d**
	....	....	....	....	....	....	....	....	35.4	25.2	66.7	87.2	168.9	163.4	224.6	Foreign Exchange............	**1d. d**
	....	....	....	....	....	....	....	....	....	....	....	....	....	.0831	.0831	Gold (Million Fine Troy Ounces)............	**1ad**
	....	....	....	....	....	....	....	....	....	....	43.22	28.13	24.11	23.88	24.17	Gold (National Valuation)............	**1an d**
	....	....	....	....	....	....	....	....	....	....	73.5	65.8	59.2	39.7	50.1	Monetary Authorities: Other Liab	**4.. d**
	....	....	....	....	....	....	....	....	....	....	19.6	13.1	34.3	17.1	15.8	Banking Institutions: Assets............	**7a. d**
	....	....	....	....	....	....	....	....	....	....	2.8	1.8	13.1	8.3	1.8	Liabilities............	**7b. d**
End of Period																**Monetary Authorities**	
	....	....	....	....	....	....	....	....	....	....	1,393	2,035	3,368	5,517	11,338	Foreign Assets............	**11**
	....	....	....	....	....	....	....	....	....	....	2,049	3,911	4,473	4,940	5,787	Claims on General Government............	**12a**
	....	....	....	....	....	....	....	....	....	....	1,153	124	92	333	543	Claims on Banking Institutions............	**12e**
	....	....	....	....	....	....	....	....	....	....	2,044	2,533	3,069	3,303	4,317	Reserve Money............	**14**
	....	....	....	....	....	....	....	....	....	....	1,938	2,416	2,678	2,829	3,578	*of which: Currency Outside Banks*............	**14a**
	....	....	....	....	....	....	....	....	....	....	—	—	200	36	243	Other Liabilities to DMBs............	**14n**
	....	....	....	....	....	....	....	....	....	....	2,216	3,430	3,893	6,314	10,652	Foreign Liabilities............	**16c**
	....	....	....	....	....	....	....	....	....	....	28	174	305	322	1,239	General Government Deposits............	**16d**
	....	....	....	....	....	....	....	....	....	....	136	243	506	949	1,118	Capital Accounts............	**17a**
	....	....	....	....	....	....	....	....	....	....	171	−311	−40	−133	98	Other Items (Net)............	**17r**
End of Period																**Banking Institutions**	
	....	....	....	....	....	....	....	....	....	....	113	110	381	449	739	Reserves............	**20**
	....	....	....	....	....	....	....	....	....	....			162	107	172	Other Claims on Monetary Author.............	**20n**
	....	....	....	....	....	....	....	....	....	....	219	219	596	503	719	Foreign Assets............	**21**
	....	....	....	....	....	....	....	....	....	....	83	93	323	378	150	Claims on General Government............	**22a**
	....	....	....	....	....	....	....	....	....	....	2,024	2,026	1,047	1,804	2,448	Claims on Rest of the Economy............	**22d**
	....	....	....	....	....	....	....	....	....	....	545	478	442	379	624	Demand Deposits............	**24**
	....	....	....	....	....	....	....	....	....	....	295	295	1,095	1,745	2,418	Time & Foreign Currency Deposits............	**25**
	....	....	....	....	....	....	....	....	....	....	31	31	228	245	84	Foreign Liabilities............	**26c**
	....	....	....	....	....	....	....	....	....	....	—	—	30	45	64	General Government Deposits............	**26d**
	....	....	....	....	....	....	....	....	....	....	1,132	1,148	118	318	605	Credit from Monetary Authorities............	**26g**
	....	....	....	....	....	....	....	....	....	....	120	149	735	980	1,125	Capital Accounts............	**27a**
	....	....	....	....	....	....	....	....	....	....	317	347	−138	−471	−694	Other Items (Net)............	**27r**
End of Period																**Banking Survey**	
	....	....	....	....	....	....	....	....	....	....	−635	−1,207	−157	−539	1,321	Foreign Assets (Net)............	**31n**
	....	....	....	....	....	....	....	....	....	....	4,129	5,856	5,528	6,780	7,120	Domestic Credit............	**32**
	....	....	....	....	....	....	....	....	....	....	2,105	3,830	4,462	4,951	4,634	Claims on General Govt. (Net)............	**32an**
	....	....	....	....	....	....	....	....	....	....	2,024	2,026	1,066	1,828	2,487	Claims on Rest of the Economy............	**32d**
	....	....	....	....	....	....	....	....	....	....	2,482	2,893	3,119	3,208	4,203	Money............	**34**
	....	....	....	....	....	....	....	....	....	....	295	295	1,095	1,745	2,418	Quasi-Money............	**35**
	....	....	....	....	....	....	....	....	....	....	256	392	1,242	1,929	2,243	Capital Accounts............	**37a**
	....	....	....	....	....	....	....	....	....	....	461	1,069	−85	−641	−423	Other Items (Net)............	**37r**
	....	....	....	....	....	....	....	....	....	....	2,766	3,177	4,214	4,953	6,627	Money plus Quasi-Money............	**35l**
Percent per Annum																**Interest Rates**	
	....	....	....	....	....	....	....	....	265.5	94.1	64.1	43.1	43.2	54.0	51.6	Lombard Rate............	**60.a**
	....	....	....	....	....	....	....	....	....	....	....	....	....	44.0	43.7	Money Market Rate............	**60b**
	....	....	....	....	....	....	....	....	....	143.1	34.9	40.1	35.8	43.7	47.2	Treasury Bill Rate............	**60c**
	....	....	....	....	....	....	....	....	....	....	....	36.7	39.6	35.8	35.6	Deposit Rate............	**60l**
	....	....	....	....	....	....	....	....	....	....	....	65.0	49.4	73.4	60.9	Lending Rate............	**60p**
Period Averages																**Prices, Production, Labor**	
	....	....	....	....	....	....	....	....	26.0	82.1	100.0	123.0	155.3	167.6	257.6	Producer Prices............	**63**
	....	....	....	....	....	....	....	....	....	....	100.0	131.9	162.9	179.9	244.5	Consumer Prices............	**64**
	....	....	....	....	....	....	....	....	22.8	63.4	100.0	133.3	184.7	228.3	....	Wages: Average Earnings............	**65**
Period Averages																	
	....	....	....	....	....	....	....	1,836	1,681	1,645	1,642	1,652	1,689	1,705	....	Employment............	**67e**
	....	....	....	....	....	....	....	....	3	13	50	77	55	56	....	Unemployment............	**67c**
Millions of Soms																**International Transactions**	
	....	....	....	....	....	....	....	....	339.7	340.0	408.9	505.4	603.8	513.6	453.8	Exports............	**70.. d**
	....	....	....	....	....	....	....	418.00	429.50	315.90	522.33	837.69	709.31	841.50	599.70	Imports, c.i.f.............	**71.. d**

		1970	1971	1972	1973	1974	1975	1976	1977	1978	1979	1980	1981	1982	1983	1984
Balance of Payments																*Millions of US Dollars:*
Current Account, n.i.e.	78al *d*	....	....	....	....	....	....	....	....	....	....	....	....	....	....	....
Goods: Exports f.o.b.	78aa *d*	....	....	....	....	....	....	....	....	....	....	....	....	....	....	....
Goods: Imports f.o.b.	78ab *d*	....	....	....	....	....	....	....	....	....	....	....	....	....	....	....
Trade Balance	78ac *d*	....	....	....	....	....	....	....	....	....	....	....	....	....	....	....
Services: Credit	78ad *d*	....	....	....	....	....	....	....	....	....	....	....	....	....	....	....
Services: Debit	78ae *d*	....	....	....	....	....	....	....	....	....	....	....	....	....	....	....
Balance on Goods & Services	78af *d*	....	....	....	....	....	....	....	....	....	....	....	....	....	....	....
Income: Credit	78ag *d*	....	....	....	....	....	....	....	....	....	....	....	....	....	....	....
Income: Debit	78ah *d*	....	....	....	....	....	....	....	....	....	....	....	....	....	....	....
Balance on Gds, Serv. & Inc.	78ai *d*	....	....	....	....	....	....	....	....	....	....	....	....	....	....	....
Current Transfers, n.i.e.: Credit	78aj *d*	....	....	....	....	....	....	....	....	....	....	....	....	....	....	....
Current Transfers: Debit	78ak *d*	....	....	....	....	....	....	....	....	....	....	....	....	....	....	....
Capital Account, n.i.e.	78bc *d*	....	....	....	....	....	....	....	....	....	....	....	....	....	....	....
Capital Account, n.i.e.: Credit	78ba *d*	....	....	....	....	....	....	....	....	....	....	....	....	....	....	....
Capital Account: Debit	78bb *d*	....	....	....	....	....	....	....	....	....	....	....	....	....	....	....
Financial Account, n.i.e.	78bj *d*	....	....	....	....	....	....	....	....	....	....	....	....	....	....	....
Direct Investment Abroad	78bd *d*	....	....	....	....	....	....	....	....	....	....	....	....	....	....	....
Dir. Invest. in Rep. Econ., n.i.e.	78be *d*	....	....	....	....	....	....	....	....	....	....	....	....	....	....	....
Portfolio Investment Assets	78bf *d*	....	....	....	....	....	....	....	....	....	....	....	....	....	....	....
Equity Securities	78bk *d*	....	....	....	....	....	....	....	....	....	....	....	....	....	....	....
Debt Securities	78bl *d*	....	....	....	....	....	....	....	....	....	....	....	....	....	....	....
Portfolio Investment Liab., n.i.e.	78bg *d*	....	....	....	....	....	....	....	....	....	....	....	....	....	....	....
Equity Securities	78bm *d*	....	....	....	....	....	....	....	....	....	....	....	....	....	....	....
Debt Securities	78bn *d*	....	....	....	....	....	....	....	....	....	....	....	....	....	....	....
Financial Derivatives Assets	78bw *d*	....	....	....	....	....	....	....	....	....	....	....	....	....	....	....
Financial Derivatives Liabilities	78bx *d*	....	....	....	....	....	....	....	....	....	....	....	....	....	....	....
Other Investment Assets	78bh *d*	....	....	....	....	....	....	....	....	....	....	....	....	....	....	....
Monetary Authorities	78bo *d*	....	....	....	....	....	....	....	....	....	....	....	....	....	....	....
General Government	78bp *d*	....	....	....	....	....	....	....	....	....	....	....	....	....	....	....
Banks	78bq *d*	....	....	....	....	....	....	....	....	....	....	....	....	....	....	....
Other Sectors	78br *d*	....	....	....	....	....	....	....	....	....	....	....	....	....	....	....
Other Investment Liab., n.i.e.	78bi *d*	....	....	....	....	....	....	....	....	....	....	....	....	....	....	....
Monetary Authorities	78bs *d*	....	....	....	....	....	....	....	....	....	....	....	....	....	....	....
General Government	78bt *d*	....	....	....	....	....	....	....	....	....	....	....	....	....	....	....
Banks	78bu *d*	....	....	....	....	....	....	....	....	....	....	....	....	....	....	....
Other Sectors	78bv *d*	....	....	....	....	....	....	....	....	....	....	....	....	....	....	....
Net Errors and Omissions	78ca *d*	....	....	....	....	....	....	....	....	....	....	....	....	....	....	....
Overall Balance	78cb *d*	....	....	....	....	....	....	....	....	....	....	....	....	....	....	....
Reserves and Related Items	79da *d*	....	....	....	....	....	....	....	....	....	....	....	....	....	....	....
Reserve Assets	79db *d*	....	....	....	....	....	....	....	....	....	....	....	....	....	....	....
Use of Fund Credit and Loans	79dc *d*	....	....	....	....	....	....	....	....	....	....	....	....	....	....	....
Exceptional Financing	79de *d*	....	....	....	....	....	....	....	....	....	....	....	....	....	....	....
International Investment Position																*Millions of US Dollars*
Assets	79aa *d*	....	....	....	....	....	....	....	....	....	....	....	....	....	....	....
Direct Investment Abroad	79ab *d*	....	....	....	....	....	....	....	....	....	....	....	....	....	....	....
Portfolio Investment	79ac *d*	....	....	....	....	....	....	....	....	....	....	....	....	....	....	....
Equity Securities	79ad *d*	....	....	....	....	....	....	....	....	....	....	....	....	....	....	....
Debt Securities	79ae *d*	....	....	....	....	....	....	....	....	....	....	....	....	....	....	....
Financial Derivatives	79al *d*	....	....	....	....	....	....	....	....	....	....	....	....	....	....	....
Other Investment	79af *d*	....	....	....	....	....	....	....	....	....	....	....	....	....	....	....
Monetary Authorities	79ag *d*	....	....	....	....	....	....	....	....	....	....	....	....	....	....	....
General Government	79ah *d*	....	....	....	....	....	....	....	....	....	....	....	....	....	....	....
Banks	79ai *d*	....	....	....	....	....	....	....	....	....	....	....	....	....	....	....
Other Sectors	79aj *d*	....	....	....	....	....	....	....	....	....	....	....	....	....	....	....
Reserve Assets	79ak *d*	....	....	....	....	....	....	....	....	....	....	....	....	....	....	....
Liabilities	79la *d*	....	....	....	....	....	....	....	....	....	....	....	....	....	....	....
Dir. Invest. in Rep. Economy	79lb *d*	....	....	....	....	....	....	....	....	....	....	....	....	....	....	....
Portfolio Investment	79lc *d*	....	....	....	....	....	....	....	....	....	....	....	....	....	....	....
Equity Securities	79ld *d*	....	....	....	....	....	....	....	....	....	....	....	....	....	....	....
Debt Securities	79le *d*	....	....	....	....	....	....	....	....	....	....	....	....	....	....	....
Financial Derivatives	79ll *d*	....	....	....	....	....	....	....	....	....	....	....	....	....	....	....
Other Investment	79lf *d*	....	....	....	....	....	....	....	....	....	....	....	....	....	....	....
Monetary Authorities	79lg *d*	....	....	....	....	....	....	....	....	....	....	....	....	....	....	....
General Government	79lh *d*	....	....	....	....	....	....	....	....	....	....	....	....	....	....	....
Banks	79li *d*	....	....	....	....	....	....	....	....	....	....	....	....	....	....	....
Other Sectors	79lj *d*	....	....	....	....	....	....	....	....	....	....	....	....	....	....	....
Government Finance																*Millions of Soms:*
Deficit (-) or Surplus	80	....	....	....	....	....	....	....	....	....	....	....	....	....	....	....
Revenue	81	....	....	....	....	....	....	....	....	....	....	....	....	....	....	....
Expenditure	82	....	....	....	....	....	....	....	....	....	....	....	....	....	....	....
National Accounts																*Millions of Soms*
Househ.Cons.Expend.,Incl.NPISHs	96f	....	....	....	....	....	....	....	....	....	....	....	....	....	....	....
Government Consumption Expend.	91f	....	....	....	....	....	....	....	....	....	....	....	....	....	....	....
Gross Fixed Capital Formation	93e	....	....	....	....	....	....	....	....	....	....	....	....	....	....	....
Changes in Inventories	93i	....	....	....	....	....	....	....	....	....	....	....	....	....	....	....
Exports of Goods and Services	90c	....	....	....	....	....	....	....	....	....	....	....	....	....	....	....
Imports of Goods and Services	98c	....	....	....	....	....	....	....	....	....	....	....	....	....	....	....
Gross Domestic Product (GDP)	99b	....	....	....	....	....	....	....	....	....	....	....	....	....	....	....
Net Primary Income from Abroad	98.n	....	....	....	....	....	....	....	....	....	....	....	....	....	....	....
Gross National Income (GNI)	99a	....	....	....	....	....	....	....	....	....	....	....	....	....	....	....
GDP Volume 1995 Prices	99b.*p*	....	....	....	....	....	....	....	....	....	....	....	....	....	....	....
GDP Volume (1995=100)	99bv *p*	....	....	....	....	....	....	....	....	....	....	....	....	....	....	....
GDP Deflator (1995=100)	99bi *p*	....	....	....	....	....	....	....	....	....	....	....	....	....	....	....
																Millions:
Population	99z	....	....	....	....	....	....	....	....	....	....	....	....	....	....	....

Item	Code	1985	1986	1987	1988	1989	1990	1991	1992	1993	1994	1995	1996	1997	1998	1999
Minus Sign Indicates Debit — Balance of Payments																
Current Account, n.i.e.	78al *d*	....	....	....	....	....	....	....	....	–87.6	–84.0	–234.7	–424.8	–138.5	–370.9	....
Goods: Exports f.o.b.	78aa *d*	....	....	....	....	....	....	....	....	339.6	340.0	408.9	531.2	630.8	535.1	....
Goods: Imports f.o.b.	78ab *d*	....	....	....	....	....	....	....	....	–446.7	–426.1	–531.0	–782.9	–646.1	–755.7	....
Trade Balance	78ac *d*	....	....	....	....	....	....	....	....	–107.1	–86.1	–122.0	–251.7	–15.3	–220.7	....
Services: Credit	78ad *d*	....	....	....	....	....	....	....	....	8.7	32.7	39.2	31.5	45.0	62.8	....
Services: Debit	78ae *d*	....	....	....	....	....	....	....	....	–50.7	–71.1	–195.1	–249.0	–171.2	–180.4	....
Balance on Goods & Services	78af *d*	....	....	....	....	....	....	....	....	–149.1	–124.6	–278.0	–469.2	–141.4	–338.2	....
Income: Credit	78ag *d*	....	....	....	....	....	....	....	....	....	....	3.7	4.4	6.8	10.3	....
Income: Debit	78ah *d*	....	....	....	....	....	....	....	....	–5.7	–22.0	–39.2	–43.9	–71.4	–91.7	....
Balance on Gds, Serv. & Inc.	78ai *d*	....	....	....	....	....	....	....	....	–154.8	–146.6	–313.4	–508.7	–206.1	–419.6	....
Current Transfers, n.i.e.: Credit	78aj *d*	....	....	....	....	....	....	....	....	68.0	63.4	80.4	85.9	69.8	50.8	....
Current Transfers: Debit	78ak *d*	....	....	....	....	....	....	....	....	–.8	–.8	–1.7	–1.9	–2.2	–2.0	....
Capital Account, n.i.e.	78bc *d*	....	....	....	....	....	....	....	....	–107.1	–62.4	–29.0	–15.9	–8.4	–8.1	....
Capital Account, n.i.e.: Credit	78ba *d*	....	....	....	....	....	....	....	....	....	.3	2.2	9.0	6.2	3.9	....
Capital Account: Debit	78bb *d*	....	....	....	....	....	....	....	....	–107.1	–62.7	–31.3	–25.0	–14.6	–12.0	....
Financial Account, n.i.e.	78bj *d*	....	....	....	....	....	....	....	....	181.2	103.4	259.9	362.5	250.7	292.0	....
Direct Investment Abroad	78bd *d*	....	....	....	....	....	....	....	....	....	....	....	....	....	–.6	....
Dir. Invest. in Rep. Econ., n.i.e.	78be *d*	....	....	....	....	....	....	....	....	10.0	38.2	96.1	47.2	83.8	109.2	....
Portfolio Investment Assets	78bf *d*	....	....	....	....	....	....	....	....	....	....	–.1	.1	.6	–.2	....
Equity Securities	78bk *d*	....	....	....	....	....	....	....	....	....	....	....	....	....	....	....
Debt Securities	78bl *d*	....	....	....	....	....	....	....	....	....	....	–.1	.1	.6	–.2	....
Portfolio Investment Liab., n.i.e.	78bg *d*	....	....	....	....	....	....	....	....	....	....	1.8	–1.8	5.0	–4.1	....
Equity Securities	78bm *d*	....	....	....	....	....	....	....	....	....	....	....	....	....	....	....
Debt Securities	78bn *d*	....	....	....	....	....	....	....	....	....	....	1.8	–1.8	5.0	–4.1	....
Financial Derivatives Assets	78bw *d*	....	....	....	....	....	....	....	....	....	....	....	....	19.0	30.6	....
Financial Derivatives Liabilities	78bx *d*	....	....	....	....	....	....	....	....	....	....	....	....	....	....	....
Other Investment Assets	78bh *d*	....	....	....	....	....	....	....	....	–53.0	–43.2	11.9	1.9	–43.1	–98.6	....
Monetary Authorities	78bo *d*	....	....	....	....	....	....	....	....	....	....	–1.0	....	–3.0	....	....
General Government	78bp *d*	....	....	....	....	....	....	....	....	....	–1.7	–2.1	13.3	—	–2.4	....
Banks	78bq *d*	....	....	....	....	....	....	....	....	–13.4	1.3	–1.2	1.6	–18.7	9.6	....
Other Sectors	78br *d*	....	....	....	....	....	....	....	....	–39.6	–42.9	16.2	–13.0	–21.5	–105.9	....
Other Investment Liab., n.i.e.	78bi *d*	....	....	....	....	....	....	....	....	224.2	108.5	150.2	315.1	185.4	255.7	....
Monetary Authorities	78bs *d*	....	....	....	....	....	....	....	....	17.9	–17.7	.2	.2	—	–.1	....
General Government	78bt *d*	....	....	....	....	....	....	....	....	179.5	110.9	102.0	104.7	137.5	129.6	....
Banks	78bu *d*	....	....	....	....	....	....	....	....	5.7	3.6	–3.3	–2.1	14.0	1.0	....
Other Sectors	78bv *d*	....	....	....	....	....	....	....	....	21.1	11.7	51.2	212.2	33.9	125.2	....
Net Errors and Omissions	78ca *d*	....	....	....	....	....	....	....	....	–16.2	48.0	–76.9	58.4	–57.7	63.1	....
Overall Balance	78cb *d*	....	....	....	....	....	....	....	....	–29.6	5.0	–80.7	–19.8	46.2	–24.0	....
Reserves and Related Items	79da *d*	....	....	....	....	....	....	....	....	29.6	–5.0	80.7	19.8	–46.2	24.0	....
Reserve Assets	79db *d*	....	....	....	....	....	....	....	....	–35.5	–31.9	.1	–18.6	–82.8	5.9	....
Use of Fund Credit and Loans	79dc *d*	....	....	....	....	....	....	....	....	62.1	13.8	46.3	19.6	34.1	2.8	....
Exceptional Financing	79de *d*	....	....	....	....	....	....	....	....	3.0	13.1	34.4	18.8	2.6	15.3	....
Millions of US Dollars — International Investment Position																
Assets	79aa *d*	....	....	....	....	....	....	....	32.0	118.6	190.3	202.5	203.3	309.6	336.4	....
Direct Investment Abroad	79ab *d*	....	....	....	....	....	....	....	—	—	—	—	—	—	.6	....
Portfolio Investment	79ac *d*	....	....	....	....	....	....	....	—	—	—	.1	—	—	.2	....
Equity Securities	79ad *d*	....	....	....	....	....	....	....	—	—	—	—	—	—	.2	....
Debt Securities	79ae *d*	....	....	....	....	....	....	....	—	—	—	.1	—	—	—	....
Financial Derivatives	79al *d*	....	....	....	....	....	....	....	—	—	—	—	—	—	—	—
Other Investment	79af *d*	....	....	....	....	....	....	....	32.0	55.1	92.3	88.6	75.8	113.7	147.0	....
Monetary Authorities	79ag *d*	....	....	....	....	....	....	....	—	—	—	—	—	—	—	....
General Government	79ah *d*	....	....	....	....	....	....	....	—	—	1.7	4.8	6.4	42.7	69.1	....
Banks	79ai *d*	....	....	....	....	....	....	....	7.8	21.2	19.9	20.9	19.5	38.1	29.2	....
Other Sectors	79aj *d*	....	....	....	....	....	....	....	24.2	33.9	70.7	62.9	49.9	32.9	48.7	....
Reserve Assets	79ak *d*	....	....	....	....	....	....	....	—	63.5	98.0	113.8	127.5	195.9	188.6	....
Liabilities	79la *d*	....	....	....	....	....	....	....	34.1	193.2	370.7	713.8	1,069.7	1,450.1	1,721.3	....
Dir. Invest. in Rep. Economy	79lb *d*	....	....	....	....	....	....	....	—	10.0	48.2	144.3	191.0	274.0	383.3	....
Portfolio Investment	79lc *d*	....	....	....	....	....	....	....	—	—	—	1.8	—	5.1	1.0	....
Equity Securities	79ld *d*	....	....	....	....	....	....	....	—	—	—	—	—	1.1	1.1	....
Debt Securities	79le *d*	....	....	....	....	....	....	....	—	—	—	1.8	—	4.0	–.1	....
Financial Derivatives	79ll *d*	....	....	....	....	....	....	....	—	—	—	—	—	—	—	—
Other Investment	79lf *d*	....	....	....	....	....	....	....	34.1	183.2	322.5	567.7	878.7	1,171.0	1,337.0	....
Monetary Authorities	79lg *d*	....	....	....	....	....	....	....	—	60.2	77.8	124.3	139.6	164.9	175.2	....
General Government	79lh *d*	....	....	....	....	....	....	....	—	91.3	202.4	304.7	409.9	601.8	738.1	....
Banks	79li *d*	....	....	....	....	....	....	....	—	5.7	9.3	6.0	3.9	17.9	18.9	....
Other Sectors	79lj *d*	....	....	....	....	....	....	....	34.1	26.0	33.0	132.7	325.3	386.4	404.8	....
Year Ending December 31 — **Government Finance**																
Deficit (-) or Surplus	80	....	....	....	....	....	....	....	....	–377.8	–921.2	–1,864.6	–1,269.3	–1,445.0	–1,033.4	–1,213.5
Revenue	81	....	....	....	....	....	....	....	....	856.4	1,896.4	2,745.9	3,933.1	5,038.6	6,132.1	7,828.7
Expenditure	82	....	....	....	....	....	....	....	....	1,234.2	2,817.6	4,610.5	5,202.4	6,483.6	7,165.5	9,042.2
Millions of Soms — **National Accounts**																
Househ.Cons.Expend.,Incl.NPISHs	96f	....	....	....	....	....	....	59.3	524.3	I 4,053.1	9,421.8	12,110.6	19,211.8	21,150.9	30,163.0	....
Government Consumption Expend.	91f	....	....	....	....	....	....	20.2	158.4	I 1,086.2	2,272.1	3,154.5	4,333.1	5,307.3	6,103.0	....
Gross Fixed Capital Formation	93e	....	....	....	....	....	....	....	108.1	I 714.5	1,492.7	3,337.9	5,296.0	3,871.5	4,499.5	....
Changes in Inventories	93i	....	....	....	....	....	....	....	39.6	I –89.8	–409.4	–376.8	600.0	2,781.2	813.4	....
Exports of Goods and Services	90c	....	....	....	....	....	....	....	263.8	I 1,795.5	4,057.9	4,757.5	7,192.5	11,748.6	12,470.5	....
Imports of Goods and Services	98c	....	....	....	....	....	....	....	–352.9	I –2204.8	–4,815.9	–6,838.6	–13,234.1	–14,173.8	–19,834.1	....
Gross Domestic Product (GDP)	99b	....	....	....	....	....	....	....	741.3	I 5,354.7	12,019.2	16,145.1	22,467.7	30,685.7	34,181.4	....
Net Primary Income from Abroad	98.n	....	....	....	....	....	....	....	–4.1	I –68.3	–189.6	–200.2	–485.2	–1,003.9	–1,748.4	....
Gross National Income (GNI)	99a	....	....	....	....	....	....	....	737.1	I 5,286.0	11,829.6	15,944.9	22,914.1	29,681.8	32,433.0	....
GDP Volume 1995 Prices	99b.*p*	....	....	....	....	....	....	....	25,278.2	I 21360.1	17,066.7	16,145.1	17,288.9	19,003.3	19,402.4	....
GDP Volume (1995=100)	99bv *p*	....	....	....	....	....	....	....	156.6	I 132.3	105.7	100.0	107.1	117.7	120.2	....
GDP Deflator (1995=100)	99bi *p*	....	....	....	....	....	....	....	2.9	I 25.1	70.4	100.0	130.0	161.5	176.2	....
Midyear Estimates																
Population	99z	....	....	....	....	....	....	....	4.55	4.54	4.54	4.59	4.66	4.72	4.80	4.87

(See notes in the back of the book.)

Lao People's Dem.Rep

		1970	1971	1972	1973	1974	1975	1976	1977	1978	1979	1980	1981	1982	1983	1984
Exchange Rates																*Kip per SDR:*
Official Rate	aa	240.00	260.57	651.43	723.81	734.61	‡877.99	232.37	242.94	521.12	‡13.17	12.75	34.92	38.61	36.64	34.31
																Kip per US Dollar:
Official Rate	ae	240.00	240.00	600.00	600.00	600.00	‡750.00	200.00	200.00	400.00	‡10.00	10.00	30.00	35.00	35.00	35.00
Official Rate	rf	240.00	240.00	510.00	600.00	600.00	‡725.00	429.17	200.00	333.33	‡367.50	10.00	21.67	35.00	35.00	35.00
Fund Position																*Millions of SDRs:*
Quota	2f. s	13.00	13.00	13.00	13.00	13.00	13.00	13.00	13.00	16.00	16.00	24.00	24.00	24.00	24.00	29.30
SDRs	1b. s	.50	.90	1.34	1.29	1.25	1.63	1.46	1.54	1.02	.78	.01	.56	.04	.14	.02
Reserve Position in the Fund	1c. s	2.80	2.80	2.80	2.80	3.25	—	—	—	—	—	—	—	—	—	—
Total Fund Cred.&Loans Outstg.	2tl	—	—	—	—	—	3.25	6.50	6.50	15.89	18.30	21.22	25.64	25.64	25.64	19.88
International Liquidity												*Millions of US Dollars Unless Otherwise Indicated:*				
Total Reserves minus Gold	1l. d	....	....	....	....	....						....		....		
SDRs	1b. d	.50	.98	1.45	1.56	1.53	1.91	1.70	1.87	1.33	1.03	.01	.65	.04	.15	.02
Reserve Position in the Fund	1c. d	2.80	3.04	3.04	3.38	3.98	—	—	—	—	—	—	—	—	—	—
Foreign Exchange	1d. d	....	....	....	....	....	....	....	....	....	....	....	....	....	....	....
Gold (Million Fine Troy Ounces)	1ad	....	....	....	....	....	....	....	....	....	....	....	....	....	....	....
Gold (National Valuation)	1an d	....	....	....	....	....	....	....	....	....	....	....	....	....	....	....
Deposit Money Banks: Assets	7a. d	....	....	....	....	....	....	....	....	....	....	....	....	....	....	....
Liabilities	7b. d	....	....	....	....	....	....	....	....	....	....	....	....	....	....	....
Monetary Authorities																*Millions of Kip:*
Foreign Assets	11	....	....	....	....	....	....	....	....	....	....	....	....	....	....	....
Claims on Central Government	12a	....	....	....	....	....	....	....	....	....	....	....	....	....	....	....
Claims on Nonfin.Pub.Enterprises	12c	....	....	....	....	....	....	....	....	....	....	....	....	....	....	....
Claims on Private Sector	12d	....	....	....	....	....	....	....	....	....	....	....	....	....	....	....
Claims on Deposit Money Banks	12e	....	....	....	....	....	....	....	....	....	....	....	....	....	....	....
Reserve Money	14	....	....	....	....	....	....	....	....	....	....	....	....	....	....	....
of which: Currency Outside DMBs	14a	....	....	....	....	....	....	....	....	....	....	....	....	....	....	....
Foreign Liabilities	16c	....	....	....	....	....	....	....	....	....	....	....	....	....	....	....
Central Government Deposits	16d	....	....	....	....	....	....	....	....	....	....	....	....	....	....	....
Government Lending Funds	16f	....	....	....	....	....	....	....	....	....	....	....	....	....	....	....
Capital Accounts	17a	....	....	....	....	....	....	....	....	....	....	....	....	....	....	....
Other Items (Net)	17r	....	....	....	....	....	....	....	....	....	....	....	....	....	....	....
Deposit Money Banks																*Millions of Kip:*
Reserves	20	....	....	....	....	....	....	....	....	....	....	....	....	....	....	....
Foreign Assets	21	....	....	....	....	....	....	....	....	....	....	....	....	....	....	....
Claims on Central Government	22a	....	....	....	....	....	....	....	....	....	....	....	....	....	....	....
Claims on Nonfin.Pub.Enterprises	22c	....	....	....	....	....	....	....	....	....	....	....	....	....	....	....
Claims on Private Sector	22d	....	....	....	....	....	....	....	....	....	....	....	....	....	....	....
Demand Deposits	24	....	....	....	....	....	....	....	....	....	....	....	....	....	....	....
Time, Savings,& Fgn.Currency Dep.	25	....	....	....	....	....	....	....	....	....	....	....	....	....	....	....
Restricted Deposits	26b	....	....	....	....	....	....	....	....	....	....	....	....	....	....	....
Foreign Liabilities	26c	....	....	....	....	....	....	....	....	....	....	....	....	....	....	....
Central Government Deposits	26d	....	....	....	....	....	....	....	....	....	....	....	....	....	....	....
Credit from Monetary Authorities	26g	....	....	....	....	....	....	....	....	....	....	....	....	....	....	....
Capital Accounts	27a	....	....	....	....	....	....	....	....	....	....	....	....	....	....	....
Other Items (Net)	27r	....	....	....	....	....	....	....	....	....	....	....	....	....	....	....
Monetary Survey																*Millions of Kip:*
Foreign Assets (Net)	31n	....	....	....	....	....	....	....	....	....	....	....	....	....	....	....
Domestic Credit	32	....	....	....	....	....	....	....	....	....	....	....	....	....	....	....
Claims on Central Govt. (Net)	32an	....	....	....	....	....	....	....	....	....	....	....	....	....	....	....
Claims on Nonfin.Pub.Enterprises	32c	....	....	....	....	....	....	....	....	....	....	....	....	....	....	....
Claims on Private Sector	32d	....	....	....	....	....	....	....	....	....	....	....	....	....	....	....
Money	34	....	....	....	....	....	....	....	....	....	....	....	....	....	....	....
Quasi-Money	35	....	....	....	....	....	....	....	....	....	....	....	....	....	....	....
Other Items (Net)	37r	....	....	....	....	....	....	....	....	....	....	....	....	....	....	....
Money plus Quasi-Money	35l	....	....	....	....	....	....	....	....	....	....	....	....	....	....	....
Interest Rates																*Percent Per Annum*
Bank Rate *(End of Period)*	60	....	....	....	....	....	....	....	....	....	....	....	....	....	....	....
Treasury Bill Rate	60c	....	....	....	....	....	....	....	....	....	....	....	....	....	....	....
Deposit Rate	60l	....	....	....	....	....	....	....	....	....	....	....	....	....	....	....
Lending Rate	60p	....	....	....	....	....	....	....	....	....	....	....	....	....	....	....
Prices																*Index Numbers (1995=100):*
Consumer Prices	64	....	....	....	....	....	....	....	....	....	....	....	....	....	....	....

Exchange Rates

End of Period

1985	1986	1987	1988	1989	1990	1991	1992	1993	1994	1995	1996	1997	1998	1999		
104.35	116.20	549.73	608.93	937.65	989.46	1,017.75	985.88	986.22	1,049.63	I1372.03	1,344.49	3,554.60	6,017.92	10,431.08	Official Rate	aa

End of Period (ae) Period Average (rf)

1985	1986	1987	1988	1989	1990	1991	1992	1993	1994	1995	1996	1997	1998	1999		
95.00	95.00	387.50	452.50	713.50	695.50	711.50	717.00	718.00	719.00	I923.00	935.00	2,634.50	4,274.00	7,600.00	Official Rate	ae
55.00	95.00	187.50	400.37	591.50	707.75	702.08	716.08	716.25	717.67	I804.69	921.02	1,259.98	3,298.33	7,102.03	Official Rate	rf

Fund Position

End of Period

1985	1986	1987	1988	1989	1990	1991	1992	1993	1994	1995	1996	1997	1998	1999		
29.30	29.30	29.30	29.30	29.30	29.30	29.30	39.10	39.10	39.10	39.10	39.10	39.10	39.10	39.10	Quota	2f. s
.01	.17	—	—	.01	.01	.34	.57	1.90	7.46	9.49	7.17	9.31	4.32	.05	SDRs	1b. s
															Reserve Position in the Fund	1c. s
11.36	6.96	4.43	1.90	6.30	5.91	14.65	20.51	26.38	32.24	42.80	46.61	48.96	44.27	38.41	Total Fund Cred.&Loans Outstg.	2tl

International Liquidity

End of Period

1985	1986	1987	1988	1989	1990	1991	1992	1993	1994	1995	1996	1997	1998	1999		
....	....	....	....	1.42	1.78	28.65[e]	40.31[e]	62.96[e]	60.93[e]	92.11	165.00	112.18	116.82	101.19	Total Reserves minus Gold	1l. d
.01	.21	—	—	.01	.01	.49	.78	2.61	10.89	14.10	10.31	12.56	6.09	.07	SDRs	1b. d
															Reserve Position in the Fund	1c. d
....	....	....	....	1.41	1.76	28.16[e]	39.52[e]	60.34[e]	50.03[e]	78.01	154.69	99.62	110.73	101.12	Foreign Exchange	1d. d
....	....	....	....	.0171	.0171	.0171	.0171	.0171	.0171	.0171	.0171	.0171	.0171	.1171	Gold (Million Fine Troy Ounces)	1ad
—	—	—	—	.60	.60	.60	.60	.60	.60	.60	.60	.60	.60	4.10	Gold (National Valuation)	1an d
....	....	28.24	28.62	58.09	62.54	28.27	44.32	87.49	97.06	98.80	114.95	68.46	105.76	150.64	Deposit Money Banks: Assets	7a. d
....	....	27.51	25.97	23.81	26.52	4.34	5.53	12.92	29.92	43.07	50.13	29.32	39.62	36.75	Liabilities	7b. d

Monetary Authorities

End of Period

1985	1986	1987	1988	1989	1990	1991	1992	1993	1994	1995	1996	1997	1998	1999		
....	....	....	....	1,198	1,594	20,541	29,059	45,362	43,965	85,180	158,640	295,696	479,763	799,776	Foreign Assets	11
....	....	....	....	7,085	5,885	5,886	10,826	8,957	12,159	4,251	4,251	4,701	91,273	198,830	Claims on Central Government	12a
....	....	....	....	12,245	4,005	1,593	1,438	860	1,859	6,975	10,867	59,540	112,799	223,706	Claims on Nonfin.Pub.Enterprises	12c
....	....	....	....	3,008	1,724	410	1,145	3,011	6,825	10,399	13,901	38,223	72,051	143,250	Claims on Private Sector	12d
....	....	....	....	27,725	10,948	11,508	15,180	34,615	37,051	46,585	52,371	57,944	80,345	301,899	Claims on Deposit Money Banks	12e
....	....	....	....	20,382	22,091	26,255	36,903	60,697	74,232	84,172	104,373	150,094	281,745	481,753	Reserve Money	14
....	....	....	....	16,842	18,569	19,218	22,827	33,241	38,610	41,954	42,968	53,306	63,163	77,785	of which: Currency Outside DMBs	14a
....	....	....	....	5,919	5,848	14,910	20,220	26,011	33,840	58,721	62,670	174,037	266,428	400,668	Foreign Liabilities	16c
....	....	....	....	1,616	850	22	810	8,585	13,515	7,452	64,824	52,743	77,508	235,225	Central Government Deposits	16d
....	....	....	....	—	580	8,805	16,306	18,340	12,066	16,167	18,036	31,085	54,371	87,325	Government Lending Funds	16f
....	....	....	....	11,077	14,405	14,811	14,380	13,849	15,229	26,445	25,210	91,253	172,614	456,951	Capital Accounts	17a
....	....	....	....	12,267	-19,618	-24,865	-30,971	-34,678	-47,023	-39,565	-35,084	-43,107	-16,435	5,542	Other Items (Net)	17r

Deposit Money Banks

End of Period

1985	1986	1987	1988	1989	1990	1991	1992	1993	1994	1995	1996	1997	1998	1999		
....	....	....	....	1,226	2,815	5,965	13,748	30,661	36,445	44,161	59,241	77,702	212,415	416,080	Reserves	20
....	....	....	....	41,448	43,495	20,114	31,781	62,819	69,785	91,196	107,474	180,350	451,999	1,144,840	Foreign Assets	21
....	....	....	....	-552	—	—	—	—	26,812	19,382	39,179	40,775	37,858	11,501	Claims on Central Government	22a
....	....	....	....	24,402	35,725	18,828	16,400	17,465	15,571	20,691	26,063	60,877	110,748	221,588	Claims on Nonfin.Pub.Enterprises	22c
....	....	....	....	1,395	4,175	20,892	36,538	62,901	92,022	118,456	141,789	247,352	460,770	729,726	Claims on Private Sector	22d
....	....	....	....	6,552	5,961	8,565	12,051	18,993	22,728	25,218	32,585	26,622	105,816	139,107	Demand Deposits	24
....	....	8,894	9,475	15,756	19,106	23,087	41,318	73,609	104,690	126,089	169,371	326,065	696,950	1,328,472	Time, Savings,& Fgn.Currency Dep.	25
....	....	....	....	1,288	1,487	1,203	1,316	1,547	1,774	1,729	1,555	2,120	4,427	1,287	Restricted Deposits	26b
....	....	10,662	....	16,991	18,444	3,085	3,963	9,275	21,512	39,757	46,872	77,244	169,336	279,278	Foreign Liabilities	26c
....	....	....	....	19,133	19,467	6,617	9,322	9,792	12,691	15,405	21,602	36,338	103,462	245,649	Central Government Deposits	26d
....	....	....	....	27,721	10,564	6,277	10,839	29,574	35,044	41,925	49,115	51,461	81,672	314,629	Credit from Monetary Authorities	26g
....	....	....	....	3,575	6,164	7,784	14,797	33,831	47,445	56,548	66,514	126,783	215,970	463,560	Capital Accounts	27a
....	....	....	....	-23,099	5,013	9,182	4,860	-2,773	-5,248	-12,783	-13,868	-39,578	-103,843	-248,247	Other Items (Net)	27r

Monetary Survey

End of Period

1985	1986	1987	1988	1989	1990	1991	1992	1993	1994	1995	1996	1997	1998	1999		
....	....	....	....	19,736	20,797	22,660	36,657	72,894	58,398	77,898	156,571	224,765	495,998	1,264,670	Foreign Assets (Net)	31n
....	....	....	....	26,834	31,197	40,970	56,215	74,817	129,042	157,297	149,624	362,387	704,529	1,047,727	Domestic Credit	32
....	....	....	....	-14,216	-14,432	-753	694	-9,420	12,765	776	-42,996	-43,605	-51,839	-270,543	Claims on Central Govt. (Net)	32an
....	....	....	....	36,647	39,730	20,421	17,838	18,325	17,430	27,666	36,930	120,417	223,547	445,294	Claims on Nonfin.Pub.Enterprises	32c
....	....	....	....	4,403	5,899	21,302	37,683	65,912	98,847	128,855	155,690	285,575	532,821	872,976	Claims on Private Sector	32d
....	....	....	....	25,127	25,088	28,228	35,144	52,239	61,343	67,177	75,558	79,935	168,982	216,895	Money	34
....	....	8,954	9,555	15,987	19,251	23,087	41,318	73,609	104,690	126,089	169,371	326,065	696,950	1,328,472	Quasi-Money	35
....	....	....	....	5,454	7,651	12,316	16,409	21,865	21,408	41,933	61,266	181,152	334,595	767,033	Other Items (Net)	37r
....	....	....	....	41,114	44,339	51,315	76,462	125,848	166,033	193,266	244,929	406,000	865,932	1,545,367	Money plus Quasi-Money	35l

Interest Rates

Percent Per Annum

1985	1986	1987	1988	1989	1990	1991	1992	1993	1994	1995	1996	1997	1998	1999		
....	....	....	....				23.67	25.00	30.00	32.08	35.00	....	35.00	34.89	Bank Rate (*End of Period*)	60
....	....	....	....				....	....	....	20.46	....	....	23.66	30.00	Treasury Bill Rate	60c
....	....	....	....	30.00	30.00	I23.50	15.00	13.33	12.00	14.00	16.00	....	17.79	13.42	Deposit Rate	60l
....	....	....	....	....	....	26.00	26.00	I25.33	24.00	I25.67	27.00	....	29.28	32.00	Lending Rate	60p

Prices

Period Averages

1985	1986	1987	1988	1989	1990	1991	1992	1993	1994	1995	1996	1997	1998	1999		
....	....	....	27.0	43.6	59.1	67.1	73.7	78.3	83.6	100.0	I113.0	144.1	275.2	628.7	Consumer Prices	64

Lao People's Dem.Rep

		1970	1971	1972	1973	1974	1975	1976	1977	1978	1979	1980	1981	1982	1983	1984
International Transactions															*Millions of US Dollars*	
Exports	70..d	72.0	61.9	42.4	54.0	95.5	11.5	11.7	4.2	3.2	19.0	28.0	23.0	40.0	41.0	44.0
Imports, c.i.f.	71..d	113.9	82.3	63.0	57.2	64.8	45.1	44.6	13.8	16.3	70.0	92.0	110.0	132.0	150.0	162.0
Balance of Payments															*Millions of US Dollars:*	
Current Account, n.i.e.	78al d	....	....	....	....	....	....	....	....	....	....	....	....	....	....	−163.6
Goods: Exports f.o.b.	78aa d	....	....	....	....	....	....	....	....	....	....	....	....	....	....	43.8
Goods: Imports f.o.b.	78ab d	....	....	....	....	....	....	....	....	....	....	....	....	....	....	−161.9
Trade Balance	78ac d	....	....	....	....	....	....	....	....	....	....	....	....	....	....	−118.1
Services: Credit	78ad d	....	....	....	....	....	....	....	....	....	....	....	....	....	....	15.1
Services: Debit	78ae d	....	....	....	....	....	....	....	....	....	....	....	....	....	....	−57.5
Balance on Goods & Services	78af d	....	....	....	....	....	....	....	....	....	....	....	....	....	....	−160.5
Income: Credit	78ag d	....	....	....	....	....	....	....	....	....	....	....	....	....	....	—
Income: Debit	78ah d	....	....	....	....	....	....	....	....	....	....	....	....	....	....	−3.1
Balance on Gds, Serv. & Inc.	78ai d	....	....	....	....	....	....	....	....	....	....	....	....	....	....	−163.6
Current Transfers, n.i.e.: Credit	78aj d	....	....	....	....	....	....	....	....	....	....	....	....	....	....	—
Current Transfers: Debit	78ak d	....	....	....	....	....	....	....	....	....	....	....	....	....	....	—
Capital Account, n.i.e.	78bc d	....	....	....	....	....	....	....	....	....	....	....	....	....	....	2.8
Capital Account, n.i.e.: Credit	78ba d	....	....	....	....	....	....	....	....	....	....	....	....	....	....	2.8
Capital Account: Debit	78bb d	....	....	....	....	....	....	....	....	....	....	....	....	....	....	—
Financial Account, n.i.e.	78bj d	....	....	....	....	....	....	....	....	....	....	....	....	....	....	−4.4
Direct Investment Abroad	78bd d	....	....	....	....	....	....	....	....	....	....	....	....	....	....	—
Dir. Invest. in Rep. Econ., n.i.e.	78be d	....	....	....	....	....	....	....	....	....	....	....	....	....	....	—
Portfolio Investment Assets	78bf d	....	....	....	....	....	....	....	....	....	....	....	....	....	....	—
Equity Securities	78bk d	....	....	....	....	....	....	....	....	....	....	....	....	....	....	—
Debt Securities	78bl d	....	....	....	....	....	....	....	....	....	....	....	....	....	....	—
Portfolio Investment Liab., n.i.e.	78bg d	....	....	....	....	....	....	....	....	....	....	....	....	....	....	—
Equity Securities	78bm d	....	....	....	....	....	....	....	....	....	....	....	....	....	....	—
Debt Securities	78bn d	....	....	....	....	....	....	....	....	....	....	....	....	....	....	—
Financial Derivatives Assets	78bw d	....	....	....	....	....	....	....	....	....	....	....	....	....	....	—
Financial Derivatives Liabilities	78bx d	....	....	....	....	....	....	....	....	....	....	....	....	....	....	....
Other Investment Assets	78bh d	....	....	....	....	....	....	....	....	....	....	....	....	....	....	—
Monetary Authorities	78bo d	....	....	....	....	....	....	....	....	....	....	....	....	....	....	—
General Government	78bp d	....	....	....	....	....	....	....	....	....	....	....	....	....	....	—
Banks	78bq d	....	....	....	....	....	....	....	....	....	....	....	....	....	....	—
Other Sectors	78br d	....	....	....	....	....	....	....	....	....	....	....	....	....	....	—
Other Investment Liab., n.i.e.	78bi d	....	....	....	....	....	....	....	....	....	....	....	....	....	....	−4.4
Monetary Authorities	78bs d	....	....	....	....	....	....	....	....	....	....	....	....	....	....	—
General Government	78bt d	....	....	....	....	....	....	....	....	....	....	....	....	....	....	−10.0
Banks	78bu d	....	....	....	....	....	....	....	....	....	....	....	....	....	....	—
Other Sectors	78bv d	....	....	....	....	....	....	....	....	....	....	....	....	....	....	5.6
Net Errors and Omissions	78ca d	....	....	....	....	....	....	....	....	....	....	....	....	....	....	32.5
Overall Balance	78cb d	....	....	....	....	....	....	....	....	....	....	....	....	....	....	−132.7
Reserves and Related Items	79da d	....	....	....	....	....	....	....	....	....	....	....	....	....	....	132.7
Reserve Assets	79db d	....	....	....	....	....	....	....	....	....	....	....	....	....	....	8.4
Use of Fund Credit and Loans	79dc d	....	....	....	....	....	....	....	....	....	....	....	....	....	....	−5.9
Exceptional Financing	79de d	....	....	....	....	....	....	....	....	....	....	....	....	....	....	130.2
National Accounts															*Billions of Kip*	
Gross Domestic Product (GDP)	99b	....	....	....	....	....	....	....	....	....	....	....	....	11.0	20.0	29.0
GDP Volume 1990 Prices	99b. p	....	....	....	....	....	....	....	....	....	....	355.9	410.4	429.8	442.7	471.2
GDP Volume (1995=100)	99bv p	....	....	....	....	....	....	....	....	....	....	42.6	49.1	51.4	53.0	56.4
GDP Deflator (1995=100)	99bi p	....	....	....	....	....	....	....	....	....	....	....	....	1.5	2.7	3.6
																Millions:
Population	99z	2.96	3.03	3.11	3.18	3.26	‡3.43	3.48	3.53	3.58	‡3.16	3.21	3.26	3.33	3.41	3.50

	1985	1986	1987	1988	1989	1990	1991	1992	1993	1994	1995	1996	1997	1998	1999		
																International Transactions	
Millions of US Dollars																	
	54.0	55.1	64.1	58.0	63.3	78.7	96.6	132.6	241.0	300.5	311.0	322.8	359.0	369.5	310.8	Exports..	**70.** *d*
	193.0	186.0	216.0	149.0	194.0	185.0	170.0	270.0	432.0	564.1	588.8	689.6	706.0	552.8	524.8	Imports, c.i.f.	**71.** *d*
Minus Sign Indicates Debit																**Balance of Payments**	
	−163.6	−141.6	−165.1	−103.2	−136.5	−110.8	−115.1	−111.3	−139.2	−284.0	−346.2	−346.8	−305.5	−150.1	....	Current Account, n.i.e.	**78al** *d*
	53.6	55.0	64.3	57.8	63.3	78.7	96.6	132.6	247.9	305.5	310.9	322.8	318.3	342.1	....	Goods: Exports f.o.b.	**78aa** *d*
	−193.2	−185.7	−216.2	−149.4	−193.8	−185.5	−197.9	−232.8	−397.4	−519.2	−626.8	−643.7	−601.3	−506.8	....	Goods: Imports f.o.b.	**78ab** *d*
	−139.6	−130.7	−151.9	−91.6	−130.5	−106.8	−101.3	−100.2	−149.5	−213.7	−315.9	−320.9	−283.0	−164.7	....	*Trade Balance*	**78ac** *d*
	21.3	24.4	26.3	17.8	22.5	23.7	37.8	61.4	85.2	87.0	96.8	104.4	105.8	145.0	....	Services: Credit	**78ad** *d*
	−42.9	−33.8	−38.1	−26.7	−25.8	−26.4	−47.6	−71.3	−75.9	−152.1	−121.6	−126.0	−110.5	−95.5	....	Services: Debit	**78ae** *d*
	−161.2	−140.1	−163.7	−100.5	−133.8	−109.5	−111.1	−110.1	−140.2	−278.8	−340.7	−342.5	−287.7	−115.2	....	*Balance on Goods & Services*	**78af** *d*
	—	—	—	.4	.8	2.2	3.3	5.6	8.6	7.2	7.4	9.2	11.1	6.9	....	Income: Credit	**78ag** *d*
	−2.4	−1.5	−1.4	−2.5	−3.1	−3.2	−4.4	−4.6	−5.6	−9.2	−12.9	−13.5	−28.9	−41.8	....	Income: Debit	**78ah** *d*
	−163.6	−141.6	−165.1	−102.6	−136.1	−110.5	−112.2	−109.1	−137.2	−280.8	−346.2	−346.8	−305.5	−150.1	....	*Balance on Gds, Serv. & Inc.*	**78ai** *d*
	—	—	—	−.6	−.4	−.3	−2.9	−2.2	−2.0	−3.2	—	—	—	—	....	Current Transfers, n.i.e.: Credit	**78aj** *d*
	—	—	—	—	—	—	—	—	—	—	—	—	—	—	....	Current Transfers: Debit	**78ak** *d*
	3.5	3.7	3.5	6.7	8.3	10.9	10.4	8.6	9.5	9.5	13.2	35.0	33.4	43.1	....	Capital Account, n.i.e.	**78bc** *d*
	3.5	3.7	3.5	6.7	8.3	10.9	10.4	8.6	9.5	9.5	21.7	44.9	40.3	49.4	....	Capital Account, n.i.e.: Credit	**78ba** *d*
	—	—	—	—	—	—	—	—	—	—	−8.5	−9.9	−6.9	−6.3	....	Capital Account: Debit	**78bb** *d*
	−11.1	−6.7	−5.6	−25.2	−4.4	14.2	39.5	−3.0	−21.0	24.3	90.0	135.7	3.5	−43.4	....	Financial Account, n.i.e.	**78bj** *d*
												....			....	Direct Investment Abroad	**78bd** *d*
	—	—	—	2.0	4.0	6.0	6.9	7.8	29.9	59.2	95.1	159.8	—	—	....	Dir. Invest. in Rep. Econ., n.i.e.	**78be** *d*
	—	—	—	—	—	—	—	—	—	—	—	—	—	—	....	Portfolio Investment Assets	**78bf** *d*
	—	—	—	—	—	—	—	—	—	—	—	—	—	—	....	Equity Securities...........................	**78bk** *d*
	—	—	—	—	—	—	—	—	—	—	—	—	—	—	....	Debt Securities..............................	**78bl** *d*
	—	—	—	—	—	—	1.1	1.2	—	—	—	—	—	—	....	Portfolio Investment Liab., n.i.e.	**78bg** *d*
	—	—	—	—	—	—	1.1	1.2	—	—	—	—	—	—	....	Equity Securities...........................	**78bm** *d*
	—	—	—	—	—	—	—	—	—	—	—	—	—	—	....	Debt Securities..............................	**78bn** *d*
	....	....	....	....	....	....	....	....	....	....	....	....				Financial Derivatives Assets	**78bw** *d*
	....	....	....	....	....	....	....	....	....	....	....	....				Financial Derivatives Liabilities........	**78bx** *d*
	—	—	—	−28.7	−29.4	−4.5	34.2	−16.1	−43.2	−9.6	−1.5	−14.1	39.5	−22.8	....	Other Investment Assets	**78bh** *d*
	....	....	....	....	....	....	....	....	....	....	....	....				Monetary Authorities	**78bo** *d*
	—	—	—	—	—	—	—	—	—	—	—	—	—	—	....	General Government	**78bp** *d*
	—	—	—	−28.7	−29.4	−4.5	34.2	−16.1	−43.2	−9.6	−1.5	−14.1	39.5	−22.8	....	Banks	**78bq** *d*
	—	—	—	—	—	—	—	—	—	—	—	—	—	—	....	Other Sectors	**78br** *d*
	−11.1	−6.7	−5.6	1.5	21.0	12.7	−2.7	4.1	−7.7	−25.3	−3.6	−10.0	−36.0	−20.6	....	Other Investment Liab., n.i.e.	**78bi** *d*
	—	—	—	—	—	—	—	—	—	—	−15.4	−17.5	−18.2	−25.3	....	Monetary Authorities	**78bs** *d*
	−14.4	−10.3	−9.1	−9.2	−10.6	−7.3	−12.0	−9.0	−9.3	−8.3	—	—	—	—	....	General Government	**78bt** *d*
	—	—	—	1.5	−1.2	−.9	−.7	−1.2	−7.4	−17.0	11.8	7.5	−17.8	4.7	....	Banks	**78bu** *d*
	3.3	3.6	3.5	9.2	32.8	20.9	10.0	14.3	9.0	—	—	—	—	—	....	Other Sectors	**78bv** *d*
	35.7	15.0	15.1	17.4	−31.2	−40.2	−60.3	−16.3	13.2	71.8	92.4	17.7	−100.5	−103.8	....	Net Errors and Omissions	**78ca** *d*
	−135.5	−129.6	−152.1	−104.3	−163.8	−125.9	−125.5	−122.0	−137.5	−178.4	−150.6	−158.4	−369.1	−254.2	....	*Overall Balance*.................................	**78cb** *d*
	135.5	129.6	152.1	104.3	163.8	125.9	125.5	122.0	137.5	178.4	150.6	158.4	369.1	254.2	....	Reserves and Related Items	**79da** *d*
	−14.8	−6.6	11.4	−.7	−1.0	−.7	−27.0	−12.8	−24.1	−5.6	−73.0	−70.7	25.4	28.1	....	Reserve Assets	**79db** *d*
	−8.6	−5.1	−3.3	−3.4	5.4	−.5	11.8	8.1	8.3	8.1	15.6	5.5	3.3	−6.4	....	Use of Fund Credit and Loans..........	**79dc** *d*
	158.9	141.3	144.0	108.4	159.4	127.1	140.7	126.7	153.3	175.9	208.0	223.6	340.4	232.5	....	Exceptional Financing	**79de** *d*
																National Accounts	
Billions of Kip																	
	84.0	124.3	160.9	228.6	431.3	612.6	722.0	844.4	950.9	1,107.8	1,419.0	1,710.0	2,200.0	4,260.0	....	Gross Domestic Product (GDP)	**99b**
	514.2	539.0	533.8	522.6	574.2	612.7	637.2	681.8	712.8	780.7	835.6	893.3	955.0	992.9	....	GDP Volume 1990 Prices	**99b.** *p*
	61.5	64.5	63.9	62.5	68.7	73.3	76.3	81.6	85.3	93.4	100.0	106.9	114.3	118.8	....	GDP Volume (1995=100)	**99bv** *p*
	9.6	13.6	17.7	25.8	44.2	58.9	66.7	72.9	78.6	83.6	100.0	112.7	135.7	252.7	....	GDP Deflator (1995=100)	**99bi** *p*
Midyear Estimates																	
	3.59	3.70	3.82	3.94	4.03	4.15	4.27	4.40	4.52	4.65	4.77	4.90	5.03	5.16	5.30	**Population**..	**99z**

(See notes in the back of the book.)

Latvia

		1970	1971	1972	1973	1974	1975	1976	1977	1978	1979	1980	1981	1982	1983	1984

Exchange Rates — *Lats per SDR:*

Official Rate	aa	

Lats per US Dollar:

Official Rate	ae
Official Rate	rf

Fund Position — *Millions of SDRs:*

Quota	2f. s
SDRs	1b. s
Reserve Position in the Fund	1c. s
Total Fund Cred.&Loans Outstg.	2tl

International Liquidity — *Millions of US Dollars Unless Otherwise Indicated:*

Total Reserves minus Gold	1l. d
SDRs	1b. d
Reserve Position in the Fund	1c. d
Foreign Exchange	1d. d
Gold (Million Fine Troy Ounces)	1ad
Gold (National Valuation)	1an d
Monetary Authorities: Other Assets	3.. d
Other Liab.	4.. d
Deposit Money Banks: Assets	7a. d
Liabilities	7b. d

Monetary Authorities — *Millions of Lats:*

Foreign Assets	11
Claims on Central Government	12a
Claims on Banks	12e
Reserve Money	14
of which: Currency Outside Banks	14a
Foreign Liabilities	16c
Central Government Deposits	16d
Capital Accounts	17a
of which: Valuation Adjustment	17av
Other Items (Net)	17r

Banking Institutions — *Millions of Lats:*

Reserves	20
Foreign Assets	21
Claims on Central Government	22a
Claims on Local Government	22b
Claims on Nonfin.Pub.Enterprises	22c
o/w: Funded by Gvt.Lend.Fund	22c. a
Claims on Private Sector	22d
o/w: Funded by Gvt.Lend.Fund	22d. a
Demand Deposits	24
Time, Savings,& Fgn.Currency Dep.	25
Foreign Liabilities	26c
Central Government Deposits	26d
Government Lending Funds	26f
Credit from Central Bank	26g
Capital Accounts	27a
Other Items (Net)	27r

Banking Survey — *Millions of Lats:*

Foreign Assets (Net)	31n
Domestic Credit	32
Claims on Central Govt. (Net)	32an
Claims on Local Government	32b
Claims on Nonfin.Pub.Enterprises	32c
Claims on Private Sector	32d
Money	34
Quasi-Money	35
Government Lending Funds	36f
Other Items (Net)	37r
Money plus Quasi-Money	35l

Interest Rates — *Percent Per Annum*

Discount Rate (End of Period)	60
Money Market Rate	60b
Treasury Bill Rate	60c
Deposit Rate	60l
Lending Rate	60p

Prices, Production, Labor — *Index Numbers (1995=100):*

Producer Prices	63
Consumer Prices	64
Wages: Average Earnings	65
Industrial Employment	67

Number in Thousands:

Labor Force	67d
Employment	67e
Unemployment	67c
Unemployment Rate (%)	67r

International Transactions — *Millions of Lats*

Exports	70
Imports, c.i.f.	71
Imports, f.o.b.	71.v

(1995=100)

Volume of Exports	72
Unit Value of Exports	74

End of Period

1985	1986	1987	1988	1989	1990	1991	1992	1993	1994	1995	1996	1997	1998	1999		
															Exchange Rates	
							1.148	.817	.800	.798	.800	.796	.801	.800	Official Rate	**aa**

End of Period (ae) Period Average (rf)

1985	1986	1987	1988	1989	1990	1991	1992	1993	1994	1995	1996	1997	1998	1999		
							.835	.595	.548	.537	.556	.590	.569	.583	Official Rate	**ae**
							.736	.675	.560	.528	.551	.581	.590	.585	Official Rate	**rf**

End of Period

1985	1986	1987	1988	1989	1990	1991	1992	1993	1994	1995	1996	1997	1998	1999		
															Fund Position	
—	—	—	—	—	—	—	91.50	91.50	91.50	91.50	91.50	91.50	91.50	126.80	Quota	**2f. s**
—	—	—	—	—	—	—	19.33	71.10	.21	1.49	1.56	1.50	.21	2.24	SDRs	**1b. s**
—	—	—	—	—	—	—	.01	.01	.01	.01	.01	.01	.01	.01	Reserve Position in the Fund	**1c. s**
—	—	—	—	—	—	—	25.16	77.78	109.80	107.89	90.36	63.67	45.37	34.31	Total Fund Cred.&Loans Outstg.	**2tl**

End of Period

1985	1986	1987	1988	1989	1990	1991	1992	1993	1994	1995	1996	1997	1998	1999		
															International Liquidity	
								431.55	545.18	505.70	654.07	703.96	728.24	840.17	Total Reserves minus Gold	**1l. d**
—	—	—	—	—	—	—	26.58	97.66	.31	2.22	2.25	2.03	.29	3.07	SDRs	**1b. d**
—	—	—	—	—	—	—	.01	.01	.01	.01	.01	.01	.01	.01	Reserve Position in the Fund	**1c. d**
								333.88	544.86	503.47	651.81	701.93	727.94	837.09	Foreign Exchange	**1d. d**
							.0675	.2428	.2492	.2492	.2493	.2491	.2493	.2493	Gold (Million Fine Troy Ounces)	**1ad**
							20.20	72.80	74.80	74.77	74.78	74.11	76.91	72.41	Gold (National Valuation)	**1an d**
								.01	—	—	—	—	.01	.01	Monetary Authorities: Other Assets	**3. d**
								.01						.01	Other Liab.	**4. d**
								229.93	664.25	599.56	1,021.16	1,800.04	1,439.44	1,637.31	Deposit Money Banks: Assets	**7a. d**
								92.26	448.07	452.38	852.57	1,520.22	1,525.47	1,910.72	Liabilities	**7b. d**

End of Period

1985	1986	1987	1988	1989	1990	1991	1992	1993	1994	1995	1996	1997	1998	1999		
															Monetary Authorities	
								307.13	341.98	313.52	407.63	461.47	461.23	535.64	Foreign Assets	**11**
									6.59	39.38	22.33	72.88	81.00	57.70	Claims on Central Government	**12a**
								13.31	21.40	22.04	20.22	7.55	52.04	63.32	Claims on Banks	**12e**
								225.56	269.43	273.62	336.66	441.74	471.45	526.28	Reserve Money	**14**
								152.75	213.06	209.54	264.00	332.65	340.19	377.41	of which: Currency Outside Banks	**14a**
								67.11	88.46	86.56	72.55	51.17	36.66	31.54	Foreign Liabilities	**16c**
								3.08	10.78	3.62	35.40	24.91	42.03	79.03	Central Government Deposits	**16d**
								14.70	8.02	11.00	20.89	36.60	47.22	47.23	Capital Accounts	**17a**
								10.90		3.29	8.24	19.54	22.34	14.54	of which: Valuation Adjustment	**17av**
								10.00	−6.71	.15	−15.32	−12.52	−3.09	−27.40	Other Items (Net)	**17r**

End of Period

1985	1986	1987	1988	1989	1990	1991	1992	1993	1994	1995	1996	1997	1998	1999		
															Banking Institutions	
								69.31	57.29	64.15	71.69	107.23	129.93	144.46	Reserves	**20**
								136.81	364.01	321.96	567.77	1,062.03	819.04	954.55	Foreign Assets	**21**
								520.53	†97.14	120.81	140.09	113.01	71.41	114.01	Claims on Central Government	**22a**
								—	6.66	11.51	15.52	2.66	4.41	15.77	Claims on Local Government	**22b**
								16.94	39.59	24.99	17.71	28.15	23.82	30.61	Claims on Nonfin.Pub.Enterprises	**22c**
									22.10	15.14	5.80	3.80	.29		o/w: Funded by Gvt.Lend.Fund	**22c. a**
								253.97	335.67	184.13	202.99	344.28	533.10	612.18	Claims on Private Sector	**22d**
									38.96	23.94	15.38	13.60	14.15	18.68	o/w: Funded by Gvt.Lend.Fund	**22d. a**
								115.03	138.08	144.24	156.36	232.76	259.75	257.52	Demand Deposits	**24**
								196.49	346.82	195.06	230.50	331.56	357.60	398.73	Time, Savings,& Fgn.Currency Dep.	**25**
								54.90	245.54	242.93	474.03	896.93	867.99	1,113.95	Foreign Liabilities	**26c**
								520.57	†13.92	36.98	6.31	50.33	32.83	18.10	Central Government Deposits	**26d**
								16.94	61.43	39.68	22.00	19.66	16.73	22.48	Government Lending Funds	**26f**
								—	1.44	3.52	4.32	6.94	54.94	63.18	Credit from Central Bank	**26g**
								73.52	167.50	132.66	173.26	163.74	120.57	109.97	Capital Accounts	**27a**
								20.12	−74.35	−67.52	−51.01	−44.57	−128.71	−112.34	Other Items (Net)	**27r**

End of Period

1985	1986	1987	1988	1989	1990	1991	1992	1993	1994	1995	1996	1997	1998	1999		
															Banking Survey	
								321.94	371.98	306.00	428.82	575.40	375.62	344.71	Foreign Assets (Net)	**31n**
								267.79	†460.96	340.22	356.93	485.74	638.88	733.15	Domestic Credit	**32**
								−3.12	†79.04	119.59	120.71	110.66	77.55	74.60	Claims on Central Govt. (Net)	**32an**
								—	6.66	11.51	15.52	2.66	4.41	15.77	Claims on Local Government	**32b**
								16.94	39.59	24.99	17.71	28.15	23.82	30.61	Claims on Nonfin.Pub.Enterprises	**32c**
								253.97	335.67	184.13	202.99	344.28	533.10	612.18	Claims on Private Sector	**32d**
								267.78	351.13	353.78	425.65	567.27	601.27	639.34	Money	**34**
								196.49	346.82	195.06	230.50	331.56	357.60	398.73	Quasi-Money	**35**
								16.94	61.43	39.68	22.00	19.66	16.73	22.48	Government Lending Funds	**36f**
								108.53	73.57	57.70	107.60	142.64	38.90	17.31	Other Items (Net)	**37r**
								464.27	697.95	548.84	656.15	898.83	958.87	1,038.07	Money plus Quasi-Money	**35l**

Percent Per Annum

1985	1986	1987	1988	1989	1990	1991	1992	1993	1994	1995	1996	1997	1998	1999		
															Interest Rates	
								27.00	25.00	24.00	9.50	4.00	4.00	4.00	Discount Rate (End of Period)	**60**
									37.18	22.39	13.08	3.76	4.42	4.72	Money Market Rate	**60b**
										28.24	16.27	4.73	5.27	6.23	Treasury Bill Rate	**60c**
								34.78	31.68	14.79	11.71	5.90	5.33	5.04	Deposit Rate	**60l**
								86.36	55.86	34.56	25.78	15.25	14.29	14.20	Lending Rate	**60p**

Period Averages

1985	1986	1987	1988	1989	1990	1991	1992	1993	1994	1995	1996	1997	1998	1999		
															Prices, Production, Labor	
							35.2	76.5	89.4	100.0	113.7	118.4	120.6	115.7	Producer Prices	**63**
						8.2	†28.2	58.9	80.0	100.0	117.6	127.5	133.4	136.6	Consumer Prices	**64**
							23.8	50.4	80.6	100.0	114.9	139.7	148.9	154.8	Wages: Average Earnings	**65**
							153.1	129.8	106.0	100.0	94.0	97.5	89.6	88.3	Industrial Employment	**67**

Period Averages

1985	1986	1987	1988	1989	1990	1991	1992	1993	1994	1995	1996	1997	1998	1999		
							1,367	1,320	1,300	....	1,182	1,186	1,168	....	Labor Force	**67d**
							1,294	1,205	1,083	1,046	1,018	1,037	....	....	Employment	**67e**
							31	77	84	83	91	85	111	116	Unemployment	**67c**
							2.3	5.8	6.4	6.3	7.0	7.4	....	9.7	Unemployment Rate (%)	**67r**

Millions of Lats

1985	1986	1987	1988	1989	1990	1991	1992	1993	1994	1995	1996	1997	1998	1999		
															International Transactions	
							573	676	553	688	795	972	1,069	1,008	Exports	**70**
									960	1,278	1,582	1,881	1,724		Imports, c.i.f.	**71**
								639	695	923	1,223	1,513	1,796	1,652	Imports, f.o.b.	**71.v**

Period Averages

1985	1986	1987	1988	1989	1990	1991	1992	1993	1994	1995	1996	1997	1998	1999		
								129.7	87.9	100.0	108.0	143.2	144.9	147.7	Volume of Exports	**72**
								74.8	86.1	100.0	106.2	107.9	107.8	103.8	Unit Value of Exports	**74**

Latvia

941

		1970	1971	1972	1973	1974	1975	1976	1977	1978	1979	1980	1981	1982	1983	1984
Balance of Payments															*Millions of US Dollars:*	
Current Account, n.i.e.	78al *d*	...	...	...	...	...	...	...	...	...	...	...	...	...	...	...
Goods: Exports f.o.b.	78aa *d*	...	...	...	...	...	...	...	...	...	...	...	...	...	...	...
Goods: Imports f.o.b.	78ab *d*	...	...	...	...	...	...	...	...	...	...	...	...	...	...	...
Trade Balance	78ac *d*	...	...	...	...	...	...	...	...	...	...	...	...	...	...	...
Services: Credit	78ad *d*	...	...	...	...	...	...	...	...	...	...	...	...	...	...	...
Services: Debit	78ae *d*	...	...	...	...	...	...	...	...	...	...	...	...	...	...	...
Balance on Goods & Services	78af *d*	...	...	...	...	...	...	...	...	...	...	...	...	...	...	...
Income: Credit	78ag *d*	...	...	...	...	...	...	...	...	...	...	...	...	...	...	...
Income: Debit	78ah *d*	...	...	...	...	...	...	...	...	...	...	...	...	...	...	...
Balance on Gds, Serv. & Inc.	78ai *d*	...	...	...	...	...	...	...	...	...	...	...	...	...	...	...
Current Transfers, n.i.e.: Credit	78aj *d*	...	...	...	...	...	...	...	...	...	...	...	...	...	...	...
Current Transfers: Debit	78ak *d*	...	...	...	...	...	...	...	...	...	...	...	...	...	...	...
Capital Account, n.i.e.	78bc *d*	...	...	...	...	...	...	...	...	...	...	...	...	...	...	...
Capital Account, n.i.e.: Credit	78ba *d*	...	...	...	...	...	...	...	...	...	...	...	...	...	...	...
Capital Account: Debit	78bb *d*	...	...	...	...	...	...	...	...	...	...	...	...	...	...	...
Financial Account, n.i.e.	78bj *d*	...	...	...	...	...	...	...	...	...	...	...	...	...	...	...
Direct Investment Abroad	78bd *d*	...	...	...	...	...	...	...	...	...	...	...	...	...	...	...
Dir. Invest. in Rep. Econ., n.i.e.	78be *d*	...	...	...	...	...	...	...	...	...	...	...	...	...	...	...
Portfolio Investment Assets	78bf *d*	...	...	...	...	...	...	...	...	...	...	...	...	...	...	...
Equity Securities	78bk *d*	...	...	...	...	...	...	...	...	...	...	...	...	...	...	...
Debt Securities	78bl *d*	...	...	...	...	...	...	...	...	...	...	...	...	...	...	...
Portfolio Investment Liab., n.i.e.	78bg *d*	...	...	...	...	...	...	...	...	...	...	...	...	...	...	...
Equity Securities	78bm *d*	...	...	...	...	...	...	...	...	...	...	...	...	...	...	...
Debt Securities	78bn *d*	...	...	...	...	...	...	...	...	...	...	...	...	...	...	...
Financial Derivatives Assets	78bw *d*	...	...	...	...	...	...	...	...	...	...	...	...	...	...	...
Financial Derivatives Liabilities	78bx *d*	...	...	...	...	...	...	...	...	...	...	...	...	...	...	...
Other Investment Assets	78bh *d*	...	...	...	...	...	...	...	...	...	...	...	...	...	...	...
Monetary Authorities	78bo *d*	...	...	...	...	...	...	...	...	...	...	...	...	...	...	...
General Government	78bp *d*	...	...	...	...	...	...	...	...	...	...	...	...	...	...	...
Banks	78bq *d*	...	...	...	...	...	...	...	...	...	...	...	...	...	...	...
Other Sectors	78br *d*	...	...	...	...	...	...	...	...	...	...	...	...	...	...	...
Other Investment Liab., n.i.e.	78bi *d*	...	...	...	...	...	...	...	...	...	...	...	...	...	...	...
Monetary Authorities	78bs *d*	...	...	...	...	...	...	...	...	...	...	...	...	...	...	...
General Government	78bt *d*	...	...	...	...	...	...	...	...	...	...	...	...	...	...	...
Banks	78bu *d*	...	...	...	...	...	...	...	...	...	...	...	...	...	...	...
Other Sectors	78bv *d*	...	...	...	...	...	...	...	...	...	...	...	...	...	...	...
Net Errors and Omissions	78ca *d*	...	...	...	...	...	...	...	...	...	...	...	...	...	...	...
Overall Balance	78cb *d*	...	...	...	...	...	...	...	...	...	...	...	...	...	...	...
Reserves and Related Items	79da *d*	...	...	...	...	...	...	...	...	...	...	...	...	...	...	...
Reserve Assets	79db *d*	...	...	...	...	...	...	...	...	...	...	...	...	...	...	...
Use of Fund Credit and Loans	79dc *d*	...	...	...	...	...	...	...	...	...	...	...	...	...	...	...
Exceptional Financing	79de *d*	...	...	...	...	...	...	...	...	...	...	...	...	...	...	...
International Investment Position															*Millions of US Dollars*	
Assets	79aa *d*	...	...	...	...	...	...	...	...	...	...	...	...	...	...	...
Direct Investment Abroad	79ab *d*	...	...	...	...	...	...	...	...	...	...	...	...	...	...	...
Portfolio Investment	79ac *d*	...	...	...	...	...	...	...	...	...	...	...	...	...	...	...
Equity Securities	79ad *d*	...	...	...	...	...	...	...	...	...	...	...	...	...	...	...
Debt Securities	79ae *d*	...	...	...	...	...	...	...	...	...	...	...	...	...	...	...
Financial Derivatives	79al *d*	...	...	...	...	...	...	...	...	...	...	...	...	...	...	...
Other Investment	79af *d*	...	...	...	...	...	...	...	...	...	...	...	...	...	...	...
Monetary Authorities	79ag *d*	...	...	...	...	...	...	...	...	...	...	...	...	...	...	...
General Government	79ah *d*	...	...	...	...	...	...	...	...	...	...	...	...	...	...	...
Banks	79ai *d*	...	...	...	...	...	...	...	...	...	...	...	...	...	...	...
Other Sectors	79aj *d*	...	...	...	...	...	...	...	...	...	...	...	...	...	...	...
Reserve Assets	79ak *d*	...	...	...	...	...	...	...	...	...	...	...	...	...	...	...
Liabilities	79la *d*	...	...	...	...	...	...	...	...	...	...	...	...	...	...	...
Dir. Invest. in Rep. Economy	79lb *d*	...	...	...	...	...	...	...	...	...	...	...	...	...	...	...
Portfolio Investment	79lc *d*	...	...	...	...	...	...	...	...	...	...	...	...	...	...	...
Equity Securities	79ld *d*	...	...	...	...	...	...	...	...	...	...	...	...	...	...	...
Debt Securities	79le *d*	...	...	...	...	...	...	...	...	...	...	...	...	...	...	...
Financial Derivatives	79ll *d*	...	...	...	...	...	...	...	...	...	...	...	...	...	...	...
Other Investment	79lf *d*	...	...	...	...	...	...	...	...	...	...	...	...	...	...	...
Monetary Authorities	79lg *d*	...	...	...	...	...	...	...	...	...	...	...	...	...	...	...
General Government	79lh *d*	...	...	...	...	...	...	...	...	...	...	...	...	...	...	...
Banks	79li *d*	...	...	...	...	...	...	...	...	...	...	...	...	...	...	...
Other Sectors	79lj *d*	...	...	...	...	...	...	...	...	...	...	...	...	...	...	...

Minus Sign Indicates Debit

Balance of Payments

1985	1986	1987	1988	1989	1990	1991	1992	1993	1994	1995	1996	1997	1998	1999		
...	...	...	...	...	...	...	191	417	201	-16	-280	-345	-650	-641	Current Account, n.i.e.	78al d
...	...	...	...	...	...	...	800	1,054	1,022	1,368	1,488	1,838	2,011	1,889	Goods: Exports f.o.b.	78aa d
...	...	...	...	...	...	...	-840	-1,051	-1,322	-1,947	-2,286	-2,686	-3,141	-2,916	Goods: Imports f.o.b.	78ab d
...	...	...	...	...	...	...	-40	3	-301	-580	-798	-848	-1,130	-1,027	*Trade Balance*	78ac d
...	...	...	...	...	...	...	291	533	657	720	1,126	1,033	1,108	1,029	Services: Credit	78ad d
...	...	...	...	...	...	...	-156	-205	-297	-246	-742	-662	-806	-689	Services: Debit	78ae d
...	...	...	...	...	...	...	94	332	60	-106	-414	-477	-827	-686	*Balance on Goods & Services*	78af d
...	...	...	...	...	...	...	3	17	51	71	140	177	207	158	Income: Credit	78ag d
...	...	...	...	...	...	...	-1	-10	-42	-53	-99	-122	-154	-206	Income: Debit	78ah d
...	...	...	...	...	...	...	95	339	68	-87	-373	-422	-774	-734	*Balance on Gds, Serv. & Inc.*	78ai d
...	...	...	...	...	...	...	97	81	136	75	98	91	137	114	Current Transfers, n.i.e.: Credit	78aj d
...	...	...	...	...	...	...	-1	-3	-3	-5	-5	-14	-13	-21	Current Transfers: Debit	78ak d
							...	...	...	...	...	14	14	13	Capital Account, n.i.e.	78bc d
							...	...	...	...	...	14	14	13	Capital Account, n.i.e.: Credit	78ba d
							...	...	...	...	...	—	—	—	Capital Account: Debit	78bb d
...	...	...	...	...	...	...	-110	67	363	636	537	347	601	822	Financial Account, n.i.e.	78bj d
							-2	5	65	65	-3	-6	-54	—	Direct Investment Abroad	78bd d
							29	45	214	180	382	521	357	366	Dir. Invest. in Rep. Econ., n.i.e.	78be d
							—	—	-22	-37	-165	-539	-33	56	Portfolio Investment Assets	78bf d
							...	—	-12	-7	12	-113	7	75	Equity Securities	78bk d
							—	—	-10	-30	-177	-426	-40	-19	Debt Securities	78bl d
							...	...	...	—	24	-32	27	226	Portfolio Investment Liab., n.i.e.	78bg d
							...	...	...	—	-2	6	30	7	Equity Securities	78bm d
							...	...	...	...	26	-39	-3	219	Debt Securities	78bn d
							...	...	...	...	...	...	...	—	Financial Derivatives Assets	78bw d
							...	...	...	...	...	...	...	...	Financial Derivatives Liabilities	78bx d
							-371	-129	-387	-31	-214	-326	75	-204	Other Investment Assets	78bh d
							-24	39	5	1	-1	—	—	38	Monetary Authorities	78bo d
							3			...				—	General Government	78bp d
							-59	-119	-400	99	-261	-253	67	-275	Banks	78bq d
							-291	-50	8	-130	48	-73	9	33	Other Sectors	78br d
							234	146	493	458	513	730	229	378	Other Investment Liab., n.i.e.	78bi d
							10	-4	-5	—	—	—	—	6	Monetary Authorities	78bs d
							22	99	54	55	45	20	45	29	General Government	78bt d
							5	76	272	88	385	558	69	354	Banks	78bu d
							198	-25	172	315	84	152	115	-11	Other Sectors	78bv d
...	...	...	...	...	...	...	-44	-186	-508	-653	-46	87	97	-28	Net Errors and Omissions	78ca d
							37	298	57	-33	211	102	63	165	*Overall Balance*	78cb d
							-37	-298	-57	33	-211	-102	-63	-165	Reserves and Related Items	79da d
							-73	-371	-103	36	-186	-65	-38	-150	Reserve Assets	79db d
							36	74	47	-3	-25	-37	-25	-15	Use of Fund Credit and Loans	79dc d
...	...	...	...	...	...	...	...	...	...	...	...	...	...	...	Exceptional Financing	79de d

Millions of US Dollars

International Investment Position

1985	1986	1987	1988	1989	1990	1991	1992	1993	1994	1995	1996	1997	1998	1999		
...	...	...	...	...	...	...	...	...	...	1,851	2,366	3,244	3,050	3,262	Assets	79aa d
...	...	...	...	...	...	...	...	...	...	231	209	222	281	215	Direct Investment Abroad	79ab d
...	...	...	...	...	...	...	...	...	...	62	227	755	590	533	Portfolio Investment	79ac d
...	...	...	...	...	...	...	...	...	...	21	9	122	113	37	Equity Securities	79ad d
...	...	...	...	...	...	...	...	...	...	41	218	633	477	495	Debt Securities	79ae d
...	...	...	...	...	...	...	...	...	...	—	—	—	—	—	Financial Derivatives	79al d
...	...	...	...	...	...	...	...	...	...	972	1,158	1,442	1,298	1,602	Other Investment	79af d
...	...	...	...	...	...	...	...	...	...	2	3	2	1	36	Monetary Authorities	79ag d
...	...	...	...	...	...	...	...	...	...	—	—	—	—	—	General Government	79ah d
...	...	...	...	...	...	...	...	...	...	542	800	1,047	871	1,135	Banks	79ai d
...	...	...	...	...	...	...	...	...	...	429	356	392	426	431	Other Sectors	79aj d
...	...	...	...	...	...	...	...	...	...	586	772	825	881	913	Reserve Assets	79ak d
...	...	...	...	...	...	...	...	...	...	1,932	2,717	3,707	4,250	5,235	Liabilities	79la d
...	...	...	...	...	...	...	...	...	...	616	936	1,272	1,558	1,885	Dir. Invest. in Rep. Economy	79lb d
...	...	...	...	...	...	...	...	...	...	23	46	13	43	275	Portfolio Investment	79lc d
...	...	...	...	...	...	...	...	...	...	7	5	9	42	51	Equity Securities	79ld d
...	...	...	...	...	...	...	...	...	...	16	41	4	1	224	Debt Securities	79le d
...	...	...	...	...	...	...	...	...	...	—	—	—	—	—	Financial Derivatives	79ll d
...	...	...	...	...	...	...	...	...	...	1,294	1,735	2,422	2,650	3,076	Other Investment	79lf d
...	...	...	...	...	...	...	...	...	...	161	130	87	64	54	Monetary Authorities	79lg d
...	...	...	...	...	...	...	...	...	...	242	279	284	343	346	General Government	79lh d
...	...	...	...	...	...	...	...	...	...	399	782	1,332	1,278	1,618	Banks	79li d
...	...	...	...	...	...	...	...	...	...	492	544	719	965	1,058	Other Sectors	79lj d

Latvia

		1970	1971	1972	1973	1974	1975	1976	1977	1978	1979	1980	1981	1982	1983	1984
Government Finance																*Millions of Lats:*
Deficit (-) or Surplus	80	....	....	....	....	....	....	....	....	....	....	....	....	....	....	....
Total Revenue and Grants	81y	....	....	....	....	....	....	....	....	....	....	....	....	....	....	....
Revenue	81	....	....	....	....	....	....	....	....	....	....	....	....	....	....	....
Grants	81z	....	....	....	....	....	....	....	....	....	....	....	....	....	....	....
Exp. & Lending Minus Repay.	82z	....	....	....	....	....	....	....	....	....	....	....	....	....	....	....
Expenditure	82	....	....	....	....	....	....	....	....	....	....	....	....	....	....	....
Lending Minus Repayments	83	....	....	....	....	....	....	....	....	....	....	....	....	....	....	....
Total Financing	80h	....	....	....	....	....	....	....	....	....	....	....	....	....	....	....
Domestic	84a	....	....	....	....	....	....	....	....	....	....	....	....	....	....	....
Foreign	85a	....	....	....	....	....	....	....	....	....	....	....	....	....	....	....
National Accounts																*Millions of Lats*
Househ.Cons.Expend.,incl.NPISHs	96f	....	....	....	....	....	....	....	....	....	....	....	....	....	....	....
Government Consumption Expend.	91f	....	....	....	....	....	....	....	....	....	....	....	....	....	....	....
Gross Fixed Capital Formation	93e	....	....	....	....	....	....	....	....	....	....	....	....	....	....	....
Changes in Inventories	93i	....	....	....	....	....	....	....	....	....	....	....	....	....	....	....
Exports of Goods & Services	90c	....	....	....	....	....	....	....	....	....	....	....	....	....	....	....
Imports of Goods & Services	98c	....	....	....	....	....	....	....	....	....	....	....	....	....	....	....
Gross Domestic Product (GDP)	99b	....	....	....	....	....	....	....	....	....	....	....	....	....	....	....
Net Primary Income from Abroad	98.n	....	....	....	....	....	....	....	....	....	....	....	....	....	....	....
Gross National Income	99a	....	....	....	....	....	....	....	....	....	....	....	....	....	....	....
GDP Volume 1993 Prices	99b.p	....	....	....	....	....	....	....	....	....	....	....	....	....	....	....
GDP Volume (1995=100)	99bv p	....	....	....	....	....	....	....	....	....	....	....	....	....	....	....
GDP Deflator (1995=100)	99bi p	....	....	....	....	....	....	....	....	....	....	....	....	....	....	....
																Millions:
Population	99z	....	....	....	....	....	....	....	....	....	....	....	....	....	....	....

	1985	1986	1987	1988	1989	1990	1991	1992	1993	1994	1995	1996	1997	1998	1999		
Year Ending December 31																**Government Finance**	
	....	....	....	....	....	....	....	....	....	....	....	I−44.13	I23.34	I5.32	−140.15	Deficit (-) or Surplus	80
	....	....	....	....	....	....	....	....	....	....	357.10	I874.92	1,174.54	I1289.69	1,291.17	Total Revenue and Grants	81y
	....	....	....	....	....	....	....	....	....	....	....	....	....	....	....	Revenue	81
	....	....	....	....	....	....	....	....	....	....	....	....	....	....	....	Grants	81z
	....	....	....	....	....	....	....	....	....	....	....	I919.05	I1151.20	I1284.37	1,431.32	Exp. & Lending Minus Repay.	82z
	....	....	....	....	....	....	....	....	....	....	445.60	I907.14	I1116.81	I1283.65	1,419.29	Expenditure	82
	....	....	....	....	....	....	....	....	....	....	....	I11.91	34.39	I.72	12.03	Lending Minus Repayments	83
	....	....	....	....	....	....	....	....	....	....	....	I44.13	−23.34	I−5.32	140.15	Total Financing	80h
	....	....	....	....	....	....	....	....	....	....	....	I31.81	−41.06	I−18.38	13.28	Domestic	84a
	....	....	....	....	....	....	....	....	....	....	....	I12.32	17.72	I13.06	126.87	Foreign	85a
Millions of Lats																**National Accounts**	
	....	....	....	....	....	....	....	395.9	769.8	1,199.1	1,470.5	1,912.9	2,181.1	2,316.0	2,400.0	Househ.Cons.Expend.,incl.NPISHs	96f
	....	....	....	....	....	....	....	125.4	324.1	410.6	521.8	612.3	626.2	768.1	696.6	Government Consumption Expend.	91f
	....	....	....	....	....	....	....	112.3	201.8	303.9	354.9	512.8	613.7	979.5	914.5	Gross Fixed Capital Formation	93e
	....	....	....	....	....	....	....	301.9	−67.2	86.9	58.7	19.9	132.6	11.3	50.0	Changes in Inventories	93i
	....	....	....	....	....	....	....	803.1	1,074.4	948.8	1,101.0	1,440.1	1,669.1	1,841.4	1,711.1	Exports of Goods & Services	90c
	....	....	....	....	....	....	....	−734.0	−835.9	−906.8	−1,157.8	−1,668.8	−1,947.3	−2,326.8	−2,109.8	Imports of Goods & Services	98c
	....	....	....	....	....	....	....	1,004.6	1,467.0	2,042.6	2,349.2	2,829.1	3,275.5	3,589.5	3,662.3	Gross Domestic Product (GDP)	99b
	....	....	....	....	....	....	....	−1.1	1.3	4.0	−11.5	....	....	....	....	Net Primary Income from Abroad	98.n
	....	....	....	....	....	....	....	1,005.7	1,465.7	2,038.5	2,360.7	2,829.1	3,275.5	3,589.5	3,662.3	Gross National Income	99a
	....	....	....	....	....	....	....	2,764.2	2,353.2	2,368.4	2,349.2	2,427.7	2,636.8	2,739.1	2,741.0	GDP Volume 1993 Prices	99b.p
	....	....	....	....	....	....	....	117.7	100.2	100.8	100.0	103.3	112.2	116.6	116.7	GDP Volume (1995=100)	99bv p
	....	....	....	....	....	....	....	36.3	62.3	86.2	100.0	116.5	124.2	131.0	133.6	GDP Deflator (1995=100)	99bi p
Midyear Estimates																	
	....	....	....	....	....	....	....	2.63	2.59	2.55	2.51	2.49	2.47	2.45	2.43	Population	99z

(See notes in the back of the book.)

Lebanon

		1970	1971	1972	1973	1974	1975	1976	1977	1978	1979	1980	1981	1982	1983	1984
Exchange Rates															*Pounds per SDR:*	
Market Rate	aa	3.3	3.4	3.3	3.0	2.8	2.8	3.4	3.6	3.9	4.3	4.7	5.4	4.2	5.7	8.7
															Pounds per US Dollar:	
Market Rate	ae	3.3	3.2	3.0	2.5	2.3	2.4	2.9	3.0	3.0	3.3	3.6	4.6	3.8	5.5	8.9
Market Rate	rf	3.3	3.2	3.1	2.6	2.3	2.3[e]	2.9	3.1	3.0	3.2	3.4	4.3	4.3	4.5	6.5
															Index Numbers (1995=100):	
Market Rate	ahx	49,687.92	50,332.24	53,258.45	62,478.04	69,839.43	70,616.98[e]	57,236.80	52,932.74	54,967.03	50,131.55	47,314.24	37,857.06	34,465.79	36,312.94	25,471.03
Nominal Effective Exchange Rate	nec	....	....	....	....	....	....	....	....	....	35,017.78	33,082.87	31,202.85	31,990.65	36,263.01	27,922.17
Fund Position															*Millions of SDRs:*	
Quota	2f.s	9.0	9.0	9.0	9.0	9.0	9.0	9.0	9.0	12.0	12.0	27.9	27.9	27.9	78.7	78.7
SDRs	1b.s	—	—	—	—	—	—	—	—	—	1.3	—	1.9	2.0	—	.8
Reserve Position in the Fund	1c.s	2.3	2.3	2.3	2.3	2.3	2.3	2.3	2.3	2.3	2.1	6.1	6.1	6.1	18.8	18.8
Total Fund Cred.&Loans Outstg.	2tl	—	—	—	—	—	—	—	—	—	—	—	—	—	—	—
International Liquidity														*Millions of US Dollars Unless Otherwise Indicated:*		
Total Reserves minus Gold	1l.d	98.0	197.0	324.9	472.4	1,278.8	1,201.7	1,302.6	1,568.8	1,834.9	1,531.5	1,588.2	1,516.4	2,608.1	1,902.5	671.6
SDRs	1b.d	—	—	—	—	—	—	—	—	—	1.6	—	2.2	2.3	—	.8
Reserve Position in the Fund	1c.d	2.3	2.5	2.5	2.7	2.8	2.7	2.6	2.8	3.0	2.8	7.8	7.1	6.8	19.7	18.5
Foreign Exchange	1d.d	95.7	194.5	322.4	469.7	1,276.0	1,199.0	1,300.0	1,566.0	1,831.9	1,527.0	1,580.4	1,507.0	2,599.1	1,882.8	652.3
Gold (Million Fine Troy Ounces)	1ad	8.214	9.211	9.211	9.217	9.215	9.215	9.215	9.218	9.218	9.222	9.222	9.222	9.222	9.222	9.222
Gold (National Valuation)	1an.d	272.5	349.6	350.2	389.1	386.1	389.1	389.0	389.2	389.2	389.4	389.4	389.4	389.4	389.4	389.4
Monetary Authorities: Other Liab.	4..d	3.1	1.6	1.6	2.1	2.5	2.7	19.7	21.5	24.8	21.4	21.9	22.0	17.1	1.6	1.3
Deposit Money Banks: Assets	7a.d	642.4	825.0	1,056.0	1,443.8	1,730.5	2,103.8	1,544.2	1,923.9	2,017.6	2,879.3	3,673.9	4,336.7	3,695.9	3,284.8	2,948.0
Liabilities	7b.d	279.7	332.8	389.9	605.4	881.5	1,178.1	958.0	852.5	1,030.3	1,200.1	1,577.1	1,594.8	1,782.6	1,603.7	1,390.4
Monetary Authorities														*Millions of Pounds through 1985;*		
Foreign Assets	11	1,193.5	1,732.7	2,048.5	2,165.7	3,810.7	3,865.2	4,957.2	5,872.9	6,683.4	6,251.8	7,213.4	8,803.1	11,411.9	12,582.6	9,423.7
Claims on Central Government	12a	55.5	15.0	12.9	197.4	300.8	144.5	802.6	891.4	843.1	1,476.2	1,924.1	1,957.3	3,090.2	5,198.3	12,481.2
Claims on Private Sector	12d	65.6	57.2	52.4	50.7	37.6	44.8	45.4	32.9	76.4	110.3	128.7	147.6	267.3	323.1	515.6
Claims on Deposit Money Banks	12e	172.8	103.0	100.1	172.8	71.2	109.2	164.6	100.9	77.3	71.9	60.3	125.7	116.2	127.3	1,122.1
Reserve Money	14	1,198.6	1,461.8	1,643.1	1,877.1	3,131.3	3,171.6	4,228.7	4,751.1	5,384.2	5,208.9	6,197.3	7,156.4	10,147.0	11,583.5	13,169.8
of which: Currency Outside DMBs	14a	844.6	919.2	1,032.7	1,226.0	1,353.0	2,240.9	3,083.5	2,729.1	3,286.2	3,506.2	3,982.4	4,625.1	5,582.3	7,057.7	7,668.7
Foreign Liabilities	16c	10.0	5.0	4.8	5.2	5.7	6.5	57.8	64.4	74.4	69.8	79.8	101.8	65.3	8.8	11.4
Long-Term Foreign Liabilities	16cl	....	....	....	....	....	....	....	....	....	....	....	....	....	....	....
Central Government Deposits	16d	202.0	360.2	465.6	593.1	978.0	901.9	1,491.2	1,843.4	1,716.4	1,828.8	1,448.5	1,543.6	3,862.6	3,142.6	4,019.6
Capital Accounts	17a	34.1	41.4	41.4	58.7	58.7	126.0	161.2	212.8	212.8	278.1	369.6	494.0	665.2	858.5	858.5
Other Items (Net)	17r	42.6	39.5	59.1	52.6	46.4	−42.2	30.9	26.4	292.6	524.6	1,231.3	1,738.0	145.5	2,637.7	5,483.3
of which: Valuation Adjustment	17rv	....	....	....	....	....	....	....	....	....	....	604.0	1,430.0	−1,366.0	1,927.0	4,102.0
Deposit Money Banks														*Millions of Pounds through 1985;*		
Reserves	20	344.6	542.3	576.8	625.5	1,666.9	808.2	1,073.9	1,897.7	2,031.6	1,389.9	2,168.1	2,534.9	4,567.6	4,395.9	5,291.6
Foreign Assets	21	2,087.7	2,606.9	3,178.5	3,624.0	3,980.2	5,112.2	4,524.5	5,770.4	6,063.0	9,379.3	13,400.4	20,057.1	14,081.3	18,033.3	26,207.8
Claims on Central Government	22a	100.9	59.7	77.5	60.0	36.3	15.7	10.1	474.6	982.0	1,065.9	2,027.2	4,175.7	11,048.9	14,711.8	15,241.3
Claims on Private Sector	22d	2,144.6	2,672.5	3,272.0	4,671.1	5,733.3	6,854.9	7,247.1	8,031.3	10,009.0	13,030.3	16,165.9	21,292.0	25,728.9	33,604.1	43,267.8
Demand Deposits	24	830.0	1,080.0	1,239.3	1,389.9	1,642.2	1,587.7	1,803.6	2,299.6	2,838.0	3,151.7	3,668.4	4,359.7	5,467.8	5,867.7	6,089.0
Time & Foreign Currency Deposits	25	2,590.4	3,273.4	4,105.5	5,112.1	6,578.2	6,813.9	6,299.2	9,309.3	11,078.0	15,182.2	21,157.9	31,388.7	37,485.2	48,773.1	62,492.1
Foreign Liabilities	26c	908.9	1,051.8	1,173.5	1,519.5	2,027.4	2,862.8	2,806.8	2,557.6	3,096.0	3,909.3	5,752.4	7,376.1	6,791.8	8,804.5	12,360.7
Central Government Deposits	26d	14.9	111.4	176.4	259.3	344.0	406.8	418.6	490.1	517.0	584.8	585.6	803.1	826.1	733.7	745.3
Credit from Monetary Authorities	26g	172.8	103.0	100.1	172.8	71.2	109.2	164.6	100.9	77.3	71.9	60.3	125.7	116.2	127.3	1,122.1
Capital Accounts	27a	358.8	379.2	413.1	437.4	496.2	551.2	583.1	618.8	683.0	878.4	1,180.4	1,668.0	2,161.6	2,978.0	3,384.0
Other Items (Net)	27r	−198.0	−117.3	−103.2	89.7	257.8	459.5	779.6	797.7	796.7	1,087.5	1,356.5	2,338.4	2,578.0	3,460.8	3,815.3
Monetary Survey														*Millions of Pounds through 1985;*		
Foreign Assets (Net)	31n	2,362.3	3,282.8	4,048.7	4,265.0	5,757.8	6,108.1	6,617.1	9,021.3	9,576.0	11,652.0	14,781.6	21,382.3	18,636.1	21,802.4	23,259.4
Domestic Credit	32	2,149.7	2,332.8	2,772.8	4,126.8	4,786.0	5,751.2	6,195.4	7,096.7	9,677.1	13,269.1	18,211.8	25,225.9	35,446.6	49,961.0	66,741.0
Claims on Central Govt. (Net)	32an	−60.5	−396.9	−551.6	−595.0	−984.9	−1,148.5	−1,097.1	−967.5	−408.3	128.5	1,917.2	3,786.3	9,450.4	16,033.8	22,957.6
Claims on Private Sector	32d	2,210.2	2,729.7	3,324.4	4,721.8	5,770.9	6,899.7	7,292.5	8,064.2	10,085.4	13,140.6	16,294.6	21,439.6	25,996.2	33,927.2	43,783.4
Money	34	1,676.5	2,001.5	2,274.7	2,618.9	2,998.2	3,835.9	4,904.8	5,061.5	6,147.8	6,683.8	7,666.6	9,005.1	11,069.8	12,945.0	13,783.6
Quasi-Money	35	2,592.1	3,274.6	4,107.5	5,114.4	6,580.0	6,816.4	6,302.0	9,311.3	11,080.8	15,184.3	21,159.7	31,392.1	37,487.0	48,774.9	62,493.8
Other Items (Net)	37r	243.3	339.6	439.3	658.7	965.7	1,207.2	1,605.6	1,745.2	2,025.1	3,053.4	4,167.0	6,211.1	5,525.9	10,043.5	13,723.0
Money plus Quasi-Money	35l	4,268.6	5,276.1	6,382.2	7,733.3	9,578.2	10,652.3	11,206.8	14,372.8	17,228.6	21,868.1	28,826.3	40,397.2	48,556.8	61,719.9	76,277.4
Interest Rates														*Percent Per Annum*		
Discount Rate (End of Period)	60	3.00	3.00	3.00	5.00	7.00	7.00	6.00	6.00	6.00	8.50	10.00	13.00	12.00	12.00	12.00
Treasury Bill Rate	60c	....	....	....	....	....	....	....	....	....	9.50	10.40	14.00	14.02	9.52	13.08
Deposit Rate	60l	....	....	....	....	....	....	....	....	....	....	....	....	12.94	10.01	11.53
Lending Rate	60p	....	....	....	....	....	....	....	....	....	....	....	....	16.83	14.53	15.58
International Transactions														*Billions of US Dollars*		
Exports	70..d	190	245	377	921	1,636	1,233	546	760	830	850	955	920	800	760	378
Imports, c.i.f.	71..d	659	731	924	1,286	2,355	2,048	612	1,539	1,922	2,700	3,650	3,499	3,391	3,661	2,948
Government Finance														*Billions of Pounds:*		
Deficit (-) or Surplus	80	....	....	....	....	....	....	....	....	....	....	....	....	....	....	....
Revenue	81	....	....	....	....	....	....	....	....	....	....	....	....	....	....	....
Grants Received	81z	....	....	....	....	....	....	....	....	....	....	....	....	....	....	....
Expenditure	82	....	....	....	....	....	....	....	....	....	....	....	....	....	....	....
Lending Minus Repayments	83	....	....	....	....	....	....	....	....	....	....	....	....	....	....	....
Financing																
Domestic	84a	....	....	....	....	....	....	....	....	....	....	....	....	....	....	....
Foreign	85a	....	....	....	....	....	....	....	....	....	....	....	....	....	....	....
Adj. to Total Financing	84x	....	....	....	....	....	....	....	....	....	....	....	....	....	....	....
Debt: Domestic	88a	....	....	....	....	....	....	....	....	....	....	....	....	....	....	....
Foreign	89a	....	....	....	....	....	....	....	....	....	....	....	....	....	....	....
																Millions:
Population	99z	2.47	2.53	2.60	2.66	2.73	2.77	2.77	2.76	2.73	2.70	2.67	2.66	2.66	2.66	2.68

1985	1986	1987	1988	1989	1990	1991	1992	1993	1994	1995	1996	1997	1998	1999		
End of Period															**Exchange Rates**	
19.9	106.4	645.5	713.2	663.7	1,197.9	1,257.3	2,527.3	2,350.2	2,404.4	2,372.4	2,231.7	2,060.3	2,123.3	2,069.1	Market Rate	aa
End of Period (ae) Period Average (rf)																
18.1	87.0	455.0	530.0	505.0	842.0	879.0	1,838.0	1,711.0	1,647.0	1,596.0	1,552.0	1,527.0	1,508.0	1,507.5	Market Rate	ae
16.4	38.4	224.6	409.2	496.7	695.1	928.2	1,712.8	1,741.4	1,680.1	1,621.4	1,571.4	1,539.5	1,516.1	1,507.8	Market Rate	rf
Period Averages																
10,138.06	5,017.24	1,030.18	404.68	328.61	241.64	175.54	105.91	93.16	96.53	100.00	103.18	105.35	106.93	107.53	Market Rate	ahx
11,650.42	4,696.38	846.41	320.57	274.59	191.63	147.07	90.64	91.61	100.89	100.00	106.66	120.40	127.58	131.78	Nominal Effective Exchange Rate	nec
End of Period															**Fund Position**	
78.7	78.7	78.7	78.7	78.7	78.7	78.7	78.7	78.7	146.0	146.0	146.0	146.0	146.0	203.0	Quota	2f.s
1.8	2.6	3.4	4.2	5.4	6.9	8.3	9.5	10.5	11.4	12.3	13.3	14.3	15.4	16.4	SDRs	1b.s
18.8	18.8	18.8	18.8	18.8	18.8	18.8	18.8	18.8	18.8	18.8	18.8	18.8	18.8	18.8	Reserve Position in the Fund	1c.s
—	—	—	—	—	—	—	—	—	—	—	—	—	—	—	Total Fund Cred.&Loans Outstg.	2tl
End of Period															**International Liquidity**	
1,073.8	488.0	367.9	977.8	938.2	659.9	1,275.5	1,496.4	2,260.3	3,884.2	4,533.3	5,931.9	5,976.4	6,556.3	7,775.6	Total Reserves minus Gold	1l.d
1.9	3.2	4.8	5.7	7.1	9.8	11.8	13.0	14.4	16.6	18.3	19.2	19.3	21.7	22.5	SDRs	1b.d
20.7	23.0	26.7	25.3	24.7	26.8	26.9	25.9	25.9	27.5	28.0	27.1	25.4	26.5	25.8	Reserve Position in the Fund	1c.d
1,051.2	461.8	336.4	946.8	906.3	623.3	1,236.7	1,457.5	2,220.0	3,840.1	4,487.0	5,885.6	5,931.6	6,508.0	7,727.3	Foreign Exchange	1d.d
9.222	9.222	9.222	9.222	9.222	9.222	9.222	9.222	9.222	9.222	9.222	9.222	9.222	9.222	9.222	Gold (Million Fine Troy Ounces)	1ad
389.4	389.4	389.4	3,781.2	3,696.8	3,554.0	3,260.1	3,066.4	3,603.6	3,534.5	3,571.8	3,410.0	2,670.3	2,651.0	2,678.0	Gold (National Valuation)	1and
1.1	1.1	3.3	1.8	3.0	3.2	3.2	3.3	5.6	29.5	71.3	54.4	72.9	174.0	156.3	Monetary Authorities: Other Liab.	4..d
2,559.0	2,753.2	3,153.1	3,198.9	2,887.6	2,820.1	3,482.6	3,169.1	4,114.9	3,806.5	3,970.7	4,329.2	6,014.4	6,620.8	5,910.8	Deposit Money Banks: Assets	7a.d
1,019.0	745.6	899.9	943.0	887.5	901.3	1,019.1	950.5	1,198.6	1,579.7	2,063.4	2,989.5	4,189.3	5,908.2	6,392.5	Liabilities	7b.d
Billions of Pounds Beginning 1986: End of Period															**Monetary Authorities**	
26,450.4	I76.1	342.4	2,519.2	2,337.0	3,539.9	3,976.3	8,362.5	10,025.9	12,208.7	12,923.9	14,486.2	13,191.4	13,851.8	15,725.0	Foreign Assets	11
15,642.2	I34.8	119.0	98.1	151.0	589.1	252.5	236.3	427.8	31.6	57.2	63.6	354.8	113.0	147.5	Claims on Central Government	12a
371.0	I.5	1.0	1.2	6.8	17.9	20.1	95.1	44.4	73.1	120.0	338.7	587.7	640.3	578.7	Claims on Private Sector	12d
1,262.0	I1.4	1.5	2.0	93.3	169.1	189.2	163.9	187.1	166.8	289.9	105.1	96.8	346.1	405.9	Claims on Deposit Money Banks	12e
18,642.0	I25.1	57.7	196.0	332.0	509.1	800.1	1,521.9	2,159.8	3,816.7	4,624.5	5,604.4	8,404.0	7,944.3	8,378.2	Reserve Money	14
10,267.2	I14.7	39.2	116.2	192.4	332.9	484.6	798.0	714.7	938.8	1,046.2	1,160.7	1,210.1	1,241.3	1,369.3	*of which: Currency Outside DMBs*	14a
20.6	I.1	1.5	.9	1.5	2.7	2.8	6.0	9.6	48.6	113.8	84.4	111.3	262.3	235.6	Foreign Liabilities	16c
....	....	....	....	....	....	....	....	....	....	....	....	....	1,068.1	1,068.1	Long-Term Foreign Liabilities	16cl
9,561.0	I18.6	96.6	186.6	104.5	200.6	289.4	927.4	1,237.3	2,383.5	2,440.5	3,585.5	1,189.3	1,795.8	3,304.4	Central Government Deposits	16d
1,267.0	I1.7	2.7	14.5	14.5	26.7	60.1	79.9	95.7	88.5	134.1	312.7	328.1	796.7	883.1	Capital Accounts	17a
14,235.0	I67.1	305.3	2,222.5	2,135.6	3,576.8	3,285.8	6,322.6	7,182.8	6,142.7	6,078.2	5,406.6	4,197.8	3,084.2	2,987.8	Other Items (Net)	17r
12,278.0	I62.2	289.5	2,236.4	2,103.6	3,429.0	3,227.8	6,252.5	6,630.3	6,094.0	5,912.1	5,222.7	3,616.3	3,046.4	2,918.3	*of which:* Valuation Adjustment	17rv
Billions of Pounds Beginning 1986: End of Period															**Deposit Money Banks**	
8,847.8	I9.7	18.7	72.5	130.9	178.0	282.5	669.2	1,434.9	2,786.4	3,541.5	4,377.9	6,224.6	6,513.4	6,826.7	Reserves	20
46,317.3	I239.5	1,434.7	1,695.4	1,458.2	2,374.5	3,061.2	5,824.9	7,040.6	6,269.3	6,337.3	6,718.9	9,184.0	9,984.2	8,910.5	Foreign Assets	21
28,057.2	I37.1	51.8	302.3	558.3	688.4	1,309.4	3,098.4	4,013.3	6,908.6	7,948.9	12,060.3	13,234.2	17,942.1	21,840.8	Claims on Central Government	22a
57,707.0	I127.1	530.1	738.5	878.1	1,548.3	1,971.1	4,804.1	5,897.9	7,799.8	10,320.0	12,687.0	15,451.3	18,681.5	20,994.3	Claims on Private Sector	22d
9,852.0	I15.6	29.5	65.8	92.5	115.3	202.0	393.5	422.4	492.7	508.0	568.7	685.5	758.3	845.8	Demand Deposits	24
98,947.9	I293.6	1,402.4	1,991.8	2,178.0	3,372.4	4,810.1	10,574.9	13,986.8	18,193.7	21,297.8	26,935.9	32,621.4	38,067.1	42,458.0	Time & Foreign Currency Deposits	25
18,444.7	I64.9	409.4	499.8	448.2	758.9	895.7	1,746.9	2,050.9	2,601.7	3,293.1	4,639.8	6,397.1	8,909.6	9,636.7	Foreign Liabilities	26c
704.9	I.9	3.0	5.7	11.3	26.1	40.0	106.5	151.7	255.4	261.0	285.1	216.6	346.1	701.7	Central Government Deposits	26d
1,262.0	I1.4	1.5	2.0	93.3	169.1	189.2	163.9	187.1	166.8	289.9	105.1	96.8	346.1	405.9	Credit from Monetary Authorities	26g
3,782.6	I4.2	5.4	11.3	23.7	58.9	94.1	215.4	444.1	675.8	1,145.9	1,943.5	2,990.1	3,619.9	4,019.3	Capital Accounts	27a
7,935.2	I33.0	183.9	232.4	178.5	288.5	393.2	1,195.3	1,143.6	1,378.0	1,351.9	1,366.1	1,086.5	1,074.0	504.8	Other Items (Net)	27r
Billions of Pounds Beginning 1986: End of Period															**Monetary Survey**	
54,302.4	I250.6	1,366.1	3,714.0	3,345.6	5,152.8	6,139.0	12,434.4	15,006.0	15,827.6	15,854.3	16,481.0	15,866.9	13,596.1	13,695.1	Foreign Assets (Net)	31n
91,511.5	I180.0	602.2	947.7	1,478.4	2,616.8	3,223.7	7,199.9	8,994.3	12,174.1	15,744.6	21,279.0	28,222.0	35,235.0	39,555.2	Domestic Credit	32
33,433.5	I52.4	71.1	208.0	593.5	1,050.7	1,232.5	2,300.8	3,052.0	4,301.3	5,304.6	8,253.3	12,183.0	15,913.2	17,982.2	Claims on Central Govt. (Net)	32an
58,078.0	I127.6	531.1	739.7	884.9	1,566.1	1,991.2	4,899.2	5,942.3	7,872.9	10,440.0	13,025.7	16,039.0	19,321.8	21,573.0	Claims on Private Sector	32d
20,154.2	I30.3	68.9	182.9	287.2	449.9	689.4	1,199.4	1,143.2	1,436.8	1,560.6	1,753.4	1,929.4	2,051.5	2,260.8	Money	34
98,947.9	I293.6	1,402.4	1,991.8	2,178.0	3,372.4	4,810.1	10,576.4	14,535.2	18,214.5	21,322.7	27,161.6	32,640.2	38,087.2	42,564.3	Quasi-Money	35
26,711.8	I106.7	497.0	2,487.1	2,358.8	3,947.3	3,863.2	7,858.5	8,321.8	8,350.4	8,715.5	8,844.9	9,519.2	8,692.3	8,425.2	Other Items (Net)	37r
119,102.1	I323.9	1,471.3	2,174.6	2,465.2	3,822.3	5,499.5	11,775.8	15,678.5	19,651.3	22,883.3	28,915.1	34,569.6	40,138.8	44,825.1	Money plus Quasi-Money	35l
Percent Per Annum															**Interest Rates**	
19.70	21.85	21.85	21.84	21.84	21.84	18.04	16.00	20.22	16.49	19.01	25.00	30.00	30.00	25.00	Discount Rate *(End of Period)*	60
14.96	I18.67	26.91	25.17	18.84	18.84	17.47	22.40	18.27	15.09	19.40	15.19	13.42	12.70	11.57	Treasury Bill Rate	60c
13.24	16.42	21.18	21.96	17.54	16.86	16.76	17.09	15.56	14.80	16.30	15.54	13.37	13.61	12.50	Deposit Rate	60l
17.29	22.21	36.54	44.46	39.86	39.94	38.01	40.21	28.53	23.88	24.69	25.21	20.29	....	19.48	Lending Rate	60p
Billions of US Dollars															**International Transactions**	
288	550	650	780	485	494	539	560	452	470	656	736	643	662	677	Exports	70..d
2,203	2,203	1,880	2,457	2,235	2,525	3,743	4,202	I2,215	2,598	5,480	7,540	7,467	7,070	6,207	Imports, c.i.f.	71..d
Year Ending December 31															**Government Finance**	
....	....	....	....	....	....	....	....	-1,017.0	-2,631.0	-3,309.3	-4,198.3	-5,902.8	-3,944.6	....	Deficit (-) or Surplus	80
....	....	....	....	....	....	....	....	1,855.0	2,241.0	3,032.7	3,533.7	3,753.2	4,440.9	....	Revenue	81
....	....	....	....	....	....	....	....	197.0	507.0	—	—	72.0	—	....	Grants Received	81z
....	....	....	....	....	....	....	....	3,069.0	5,379.0	6,342.0	7,732.0	9,728.0	8,385.5	....	Expenditure	82
....	....	....	....	....	....	....	....	—	—	—	—	—	—	....	Lending Minus Repayments	83
															Financing	
....	....	....	....	....	....	....	....	868.0	1,946.0	2,452.3	3,334.3	5,022.9	1,162.8	....	Domestic	84a
....	....	....	....	....	....	....	....	149.0	685.0	857.0	864.0	744.5	2,470.0	....	Foreign	85a
....	....	....	....	....	....	....	....	—	—	—	—	135.4	311.8	....	Adj. to Total Financing	84x
....	....	....	....	....	....	....	....	6,089.4	9,347.5	11,997.2	17,228.8	19,787.1	21,685.7	....	Debt: Domestic	88a
....	....	....	....	....	....	....	....	563.6	1,286.0	2,157.8	2,960.6	3,713.3	6,282.6	....	Foreign	89a
Midyear Estimates																
2.67	2.64	2.60	2.56	2.54	2.56	2.61	2.70	2.81	2.91	3.01	3.08	3.14	3.19	3.24	Population	99z

(See notes in the back of the book.)

Lesotho

666

		1970	1971	1972	1973	1974	1975	1976	1977	1978	1979	1980	1981	1982	1983	1984
Exchange Rates																*Loti per SDR:*
Principal Rate	aa	.71723	.83085	.85000	.80966	.84435	1.01797	1.01029	1.05627	1.13286	1.08924	.95066	1.11341	1.18729	1.27926	1.94563
																Loti per US Dollar:
Principal Rate	ae	.71723	.76526	.78290	.67116	.68963	.86957	.86957	.86957	.86957	.82686	.74538	.95657	1.07631	1.22190	1.98491
Principal Rate	rf	.71429	.71522	.76873	.69396	.67948	.73951	.86957	.86957	.86957	.84202	.77883	.87753	1.08582	1.11410	1.47528
																Index Numbers (1995=100):
Principal Rate	ahx	506.2	306.4	469.7	523.6	533.9	495.5	417.1	417.1	417.1	430.8	466.2	416.7	335.3	326.1	252.2
Nominal Effective Exchange Rate	nec	....	....	....	....	....	....	....	....	....	....	147.3	147.7	148.1	147.3	146.6
Real Effective Exchange Rate	rec	....	....	....	....	....	....	....	....	....	....	100.3	102.3	100.2	98.3	101.9
Fund Position																*Millions of SDRs:*
Quota	2f. s	5.00	5.00	5.00	5.00	5.00	5.00	5.00	5.00	7.00	7.00	10.50	10.50	10.50	15.10	15.10
SDRs	1b. s	—	.44	.86	.66	.58	.54	.50	.45	.41	1.09	.85	1.41	1.10	1.04	.97
Reserve Position in the Fund	1c. s	.03	.13	.23	.43	.63	1.25	1.25	1.25	1.14	1.14	1.98	2.01	.08	1.24	1.25
Total Fund Cred.&Loans Outstg.	2tl	—	—	—	—	—	—	—	—	.54	2.08	3.59	4.87	4.89	4.89	4.75	4.33
International Liquidity														*Millions of US Dollars Unless Otherwise Indicated:*		
Total Reserves minus Gold	1l. d	....	.48	.93	.80	.71	.63	.58	.55	.53	....	50.27	43.40	47.54	66.68	48.58
SDRs	1b. d	—	.48	.93	.80	.71	.63	.58	.55	.53	1.44	1.08	1.64	1.21	1.09	.95
Reserve Position in the Fund	1c. d	.03	.14	.25	.52	.77	1.46	1.45	1.52	1.49	1.50	2.53	2.34	.09	1.30	1.23
Foreign Exchange	1d. d											46.66	39.41	46.23	64.29	46.40
Monetary Authorities: Other Liab.	4.. d	....	....	....	....	....	....	....	....	....	....	.08	21.17	23.52	13.22	1.42
Deposit Money Banks: Assets	7a. d	....	....	....	20.72	22.11	20.87	21.56	28.22	48.42	61.89	45.21	37.33	51.03	58.95	44.79
Liabilities	7b. d	....	....	....	6.68	1.83	.87	1.54	1.58	3.02	2.08	8.25	5.89	3.23	18.98	3.78
Monetary Authorities																*Millions of Maloti:*
Foreign Assets	11	....	....	....	....	....	....	....	....	....	....	41.23	45.58	52.62	83.40	100.20
Claims on Central Government	12a	....	....	....	....	....	....	....	....	....	....	4.63	26.45	34.60	24.94	13.82
Claims on Deposit Money Banks	12e	....	....	....	....	....	....	....	....	....	....	—	—	—	—	—
Reserve Money	14	....	....	....	....	....	....	....	....	....	....	40.20	42.59	46.07	72.57	85.35
of which: Currency Outside DMBs	14a	....	....	....	....	....	....	....	....	....	....	6.92	10.62	17.77	23.14	23.67
Foreign Liabilities	16c	....	....	....	....	....	....	....	....	....	....	4.69	25.69	31.12	22.22	11.25
Central Government Deposits	16d	....	....	....	....	....	....	....	....	....	....	.01	.74	5.38	6.09	2.33
Capital Accounts	17a	....	....	....	....	....	....	....	....	....	....	3.89	5.40	5.72	7.62	15.79
Other Items (Net)	17r	....	....	....	....	....	....	....	....	....	....	-2.92	-2.39	-1.07	-.15	-.70
Deposit Money Banks																*Millions of Maloti:*
Reserves	20	....	....	....	1.16	1.67	1.20	2.69	3.55	4.72	6.67	32.87	28.60	28.48	48.85	54.03
Foreign Assets	21	....	....	....	14.60	15.25	18.15	18.74	24.54	42.11	51.17	33.70	35.71	54.92	72.03	88.91
Claims on Central Government	22a	....	....	....	1.48	1.04	1.75	4.14	9.45	10.79	17.55	38.40	42.65	54.50	64.91	62.28
Claims on Official Entities	22bx	....	....	....	.95	1.57	1.40	2.34	4.29	10.21	8.55	9.24	10.44	10.92	14.30	13.38
Claims on Private Sector	22d	....	....	....	5.74	8.61	8.43	11.57	13.64	18.44	23.85	21.45	37.15	46.97	51.75	68.34
Claims on Other Banking Insts.	22f	....	....	....	....	....	....	....	....	....	....					
Demand Deposits	24	....	....	....	4.71	5.46	7.41	11.37	18.78	28.08	39.81	41.55	48.00	59.40	61.52	79.60
Time and Savings Deposits	25	....	....	....	13.39	14.73	18.70	23.24	29.24	47.83	55.77	68.17	85.58	108.24	132.36	147.04
Foreign Liabilities	26c	....	....	....	4.71	1.26	.76	1.34	1.38	2.62	1.72	6.15	5.63	3.48	23.20	7.51
Central Government Deposits	26d	....	....	....	2.70	7.18	2.56	2.67	3.16	7.09	9.36	15.57	12.41	12.47	13.14	12.43
Capital Accounts	27a	....	....	....	1.48	1.81	3.20	3.76	5.58	6.40	8.48	11.30	13.21	18.53	33.15	39.82
Other Items (Net)	27r	....	....	....	-3.06	-2.32	-1.69	-2.89	-2.66	-5.75	-7.35	-7.08	-10.29	-6.33	-11.54	.54
Monetary Survey																*Millions of Maloti:*
Foreign Assets (Net)	31n	....	....	....	....	....	....	....	....	....	....	64.09	49.96	72.94	110.01	170.35
Domestic Credit	32	....	....	....	....	....	....	....	....	....	....	58.13	103.54	129.14	136.67	143.07
Claims on Central Govt. (Net)	32an	....	....	....	....	....	....	....	....	....	....	27.44	55.95	71.25	70.62	61.34
Claims on Official Entities	32bx	....	....	....	....	....	....	....	....	....	....	9.24	10.44	10.92	14.30	13.38
Claims on Private Sector	32d	....	....	....	....	....	....	....	....	....	....	21.45	37.15	46.97	51.75	68.34
Claims on Other Banking Insts.	32f	....	....	....	....	....	....	....	....	....	....	—	—	—	—	—
Money	34	....	....	....	....	....	....	....	....	....	....	48.47	58.62	77.17	84.67	103.28
Quasi-Money	35	....	....	....	....	....	....	....	....	....	....	68.17	85.58	108.24	132.36	147.04
Capital Accounts	37a	....	....	....	....	....	....	....	....	....	....	15.18	18.61	24.25	40.77	55.61
Other Items (Net)	37r	....	....	....	....	....	....	....	....	....	....	-9.59	-9.31	-7.58	-11.12	7.49
Money plus Quasi-Money	35l	....	....	....	....	....	....	....	....	....	....	116.64	144.20	185.41	217.03	250.32
Other Banking Institutions																*Millions of Maloti:*
Cash	40	....	....	....	....	....	....	.33	.99	1.33	—	.52	.53	1.24	1.99
Claims on Private Sector	42d	....	....	....	....	....	....	.01	.50	1.79	6.61	7.99	8.08	7.93	11.68
Time and Savings Deposits	45	....	....	....	....	....	....	.01	.03	.58	1.97	1.96	2.26	4.37	3.18
Capital Accounts	47a	....	....	....	....	....	....	.25	1.25	2.25	3.52	5.29	5.44	5.44	6.97
Other Items (Net)	47r	....	....	....	....	....	....	.08	.20	.29	1.12	1.26	.92	-.64	3.51
Liquid Liabilities	55l	....	....	....	....	....	....	....	....	....	....	118.60	145.64	187.14	220.16	251.52
Interest Rates																*Percent Per Annum*
Discount Rate *(End of Period)*	60	....	....	....	....	....	....	....	....	....	....	8.00	12.00	12.00	12.00	15.00
Treasury Bill Rate	60c	....	....	....	....	....	....	....	....	....	....	....	7.00	10.67	18.00	18.42
Deposit Rate	60l	....	....	....	....	....	....	....	....	....	....	....	9.63	11.75	9.38	9.90
Lending Rate	60p	....	....	....	....	....	....	....	....	....	....	11.00	15.00	17.00	15.42	17.58
Prices																*Index Numbers (1995=100):*
Consumer Prices	64	....	....	....	6.0	6.8	7.8	8.7	10.1	I11.5	13.3	I15.5	17.4	19.5	22.9	25.4

	1985	1986	1987	1988	1989	1990	1991	1992	1993	1994	1995	1996	1997	1998	1999		
Exchange Rates																	
End of Period																	
Principal Rate	2.80926	2.67072	2.73793	3.19971	3.33272	3.64560	3.92372	4.19788	4.66667	5.17298	5.42197	6.73325	6.56747	8.25106	8.44711		**aa**
End of Period (ae) Period Average (rf)																	
Principal Rate	2.55754	2.18341	1.92994	2.37773	2.53601	2.56253	2.74303	3.05300	3.39750	3.54350	3.64750	4.68250	4.86750	5.86000	6.15450		**ae**
Principal Rate	2.22868	2.28503	2.03603	2.27347	2.62268	2.58732	2.76132	2.85201	3.26774	3.55080	3.62709	4.29935	4.60796	5.52828	6.10948		**rf**
Period Averages																	
Principal Rate	165.5	159.9	178.2	160.4	138.6	140.2	131.6	127.3	111.1	102.2	100.0	84.9	78.8	66.2	59.4		**ah x**
Nominal Effective Exchange Rate	144.1	142.5	142.4	141.6	141.2	136.2	130.5	125.5	115.1	105.8	100.0	86.4	84.2	72.3	66.3		**ne c**
Real Effective Exchange Rate	98.6	97.0	93.9	92.8	93.1	91.4	97.9	105.7	105.0	100.0	100.0	91.1	93.8	85.2	83.3		**re c**
Fund Position																	
End of Period																	
Quota	15.10	15.10	15.10	15.10	15.10	15.10	15.10	23.90	23.90	23.90	23.90	23.90	23.90	23.90	34.90		**2f. s**
SDRs	.99	.80	.62	.97	.74	.46	.20	.48	.41	.33	.24	.92	.89	.86	.85		**1b. s**
Reserve Position in the Fund	1.25	1.26	1.27	1.29	1.29	1.30	1.31	3.51	3.51	3.51	3.51	3.51	3.52	3.53	3.53		**1c. s**
Total Fund Cred.&Loans Outstg.	3.51	2.54	1.56	3.75	7.72	10.59	12.84	18.12	24.92	27.63	25.82	23.48	20.39	16.76	12.46		**2tl**
International Liquidity																	
End of Period																	
Total Reserves minus Gold	43.52	60.26	67.53	56.28	49.00	72.37	115.04	157.49	252.69	372.62	456.74	460.51	571.74	575.08	499.56		**1l. d**
SDRs	1.09	.98	.88	1.31	.97	.65	.29	.66	.56	.47	.35	1.33	1.20	1.22	1.17		**1b. d**
Reserve Position in the Fund	1.37	1.54	1.80	1.74	1.70	1.85	1.87	4.83	4.82	5.13	5.22	5.05	4.75	4.98	4.85		**1c. d**
Foreign Exchange	41.06	57.74	64.85	53.24	46.33	69.87	112.88	152.00	247.30	367.02	451.17	454.13	565.78	568.89	493.54		**1d. d**
Monetary Authorities: Other Liab.	.79	.95	1.13	1.02	.99	.73	2.11	1.80	1.63	1.85	1.56	1.33	1.29	1.14	1.08		**4.. d**
Deposit Money Banks: Assets	43.93	38.17	35.31	41.23	43.40	79.88	71.89	95.26	65.84	48.52	45.42	58.36	51.13	72.20	79.64		**7a. d**
Liabilities	3.09	4.54	6.85	13.78	16.36	9.60	11.34	7.99	9.64	10.29	12.11	12.83	8.50	8.05	6.48		**7b. d**
Monetary Authorities																	
End of Period																	
Foreign Assets	116.06	135.48	135.64	140.21	129.85	197.29	322.48	483.08	869.28	1,337.58	1,691.29	2,173.44	2,795.54	3,381.64	3,085.50		**11**
Claims on Central Government	36.15	44.33	92.18	262.71	294.02	295.68	601.72	169.01	326.53	332.42	246.16	281.16	134.55	134.66	107.92		**12a**
Claims on Deposit Money Banks	—	—	—	—	—	—	—	6.25	.39	.44	.64	.73	.71	—	—		**12e**
Reserve Money	110.61	137.09	161.05	236.47	222.20	208.59	245.81	191.77	233.68	249.15	311.86	336.50	380.58	526.95	702.32		**14**
of which: Currency Outside DMBs	25.23	32.55	33.19	41.87	53.36	59.79	37.01	39.86	43.75	52.57	74.76	84.82	89.92	134.50	122.66		**14a**
Foreign Liabilities	11.89	8.87	6.45	14.43	28.24	40.48	56.14	81.55	121.82	149.49	145.70	164.31	140.13	144.99	111.88		**16c**
Central Government Deposits	2.93	7.19	29.36	125.94	155.88	210.11	593.50	349.19	790.87	1,134.25	1,325.78	1,587.43	2,012.79	2,120.06	1,561.21		**16d**
Capital Accounts	27.28	20.82	21.62	23.35	24.69	54.14	53.10	54.30	77.86	82.34	70.80	80.08	82.51	94.89	96.47		**17a**
Other Items (Net)	−.50	5.85	9.34	2.72	−7.15	−20.35	−24.33	−18.48	−28.03	55.21	83.95	287.01	314.79	629.42	721.45		**17r**
Deposit Money Banks																	
End of Period																	
Reserves	77.94	97.55	118.47	189.37	161.57	136.40	189.68	135.95	179.47	180.45	165.33	245.58	244.10	489.20	573.72		**20**
Foreign Assets	112.36	83.34	68.15	98.04	110.05	204.69	197.19	290.84	223.69	171.94	165.66	273.27	248.88	423.09	490.15		**21**
Claims on Central Government	74.00	126.06	135.02	128.54	189.66	153.29	131.07	108.45	99.72	103.95	74.91	74.35	74.23	51.53	586.38		**22a**
Claims on Official Entities	11.26	11.07	7.61	24.05	24.62	26.24	35.86	28.91	29.31	30.92	80.53	141.33	123.30	225.53	105.28		**22bx**
Claims on Private Sector	89.16	90.47	112.70	145.32	170.85	208.78	273.79	316.37	502.61	699.24	739.16	668.42	732.35	784.90	811.70		**22d**
Claims on Other Banking Insts.	.17	.39	.80	.98	1.38	.14	.62	2.77	10.00	10.39	10.78	12.42	14.45	17.19	17.38		**22f**
Demand Deposits	107.91	122.09	123.62	178.01	191.82	204.43	275.77	311.29	389.43	434.02	445.91	548.00	672.46	836.92	821.27		**24**
Time and Savings Deposits	177.58	197.47	230.26	270.12	310.63	338.41	345.45	371.62	501.99	550.42	601.05	692.40	686.77	775.24	714.08		**25**
Foreign Liabilities	7.91	9.90	13.22	32.76	41.50	24.60	31.11	24.40	32.74	36.47	44.18	60.06	41.36	47.20	39.89		**26c**
Central Government Deposits	20.62	24.19	19.28	17.24	23.08	32.21	26.85	39.85	48.30	39.59	37.53	38.66	48.15	76.77	77.12		**26d**
Capital Accounts	53.87	62.22	63.82	79.94	91.61	122.24	143.55	160.67	189.51	233.51	226.32	245.03	193.04	145.42	760.66		**27a**
Other Items (Net)	−3.01	−7.01	−7.47	8.20	−.51	7.65	5.47	−24.54	−117.17	−97.12	−118.61	−168.79	−204.46	109.90	171.60		**27r**
Monetary Survey																	
End of Period																	
Foreign Assets (Net)	208.62	200.05	184.12	191.05	170.16	336.90	432.43	667.97	938.41	1,323.56	1,667.07	2,222.34	2,862.94	3,612.54	3,423.87		**31n**
Domestic Credit	187.19	240.93	299.65	418.40	501.57	441.81	422.70	236.47	129.00	3.08	−211.77	−448.42	−982.05	−983.01	−9.75		**32**
Claims on Central Govt. (Net)	86.60	139.01	178.55	248.06	304.72	206.66	112.44	−111.58	−412.92	−737.47	−1,042.23	−1,270.58	−1,852.16	−2,010.63	−944.11		**32an**
Claims on Official Entities	11.26	11.07	7.61	24.05	24.62	26.24	35.86	28.91	29.31	30.92	80.53	141.33	123.30	225.53	105.28		**32bx**
Claims on Private Sector	89.16	90.47	112.70	145.32	170.85	208.78	273.79	316.37	502.61	699.24	739.16	668.42	732.35	784.90	811.70		**32d**
Claims on Other Banking Insts.	.17	.39	.80	.98	1.38	.14	.62	2.77	10.00	10.39	10.78	12.42	14.45	17.19	17.38		**32f**
Money	133.14	154.64	156.81	219.88	245.18	264.22	312.78	351.15	433.18	486.59	520.67	632.82	762.39	971.41	943.93		**34**
Quasi-Money	177.58	197.47	230.26	270.12	310.63	338.41	345.45	371.62	501.99	550.42	601.05	692.40	686.77	775.24	714.08		**35**
Capital Accounts	81.16	83.04	85.44	103.29	116.30	176.38	196.64	214.97	267.37	315.85	297.12	325.11	275.55	240.31	857.13		**37a**
Other Items (Net)	3.94	5.84	11.25	16.16	−.39	−.30	.26	−33.31	−135.13	−26.22	36.47	123.60	156.18	642.56	898.98		**37r**
Money plus Quasi-Money	310.72	352.11	387.08	490.00	555.82	602.64	658.23	722.77	935.17	1,037.01	1,121.72	1,325.22	1,449.16	1,746.66	1,658.01		**35l**
Other Banking Institutions																	
End of Period																	
Cash	2.64	2.26	2.12	2.88	2.95	2.86	2.48	8.00	....	....	....	....	....	....	....		**40**
Claims on Private Sector	12.49	13.70	17.63	24.04	31.65	42.57	52.08	64.91	....	....	....	....	....	....	....		**42d**
Time and Savings Deposits	3.17	5.54	7.77	10.09	15.11	24.38	32.29	41.52	....	....	....	....	....	....	....		**45**
Capital Accounts	7.63	8.43	8.54	9.34	9.59	9.23	9.46	9.23	....	....	....	....	....	....	....		**47a**
Other Items (Net)	4.33	1.99	3.44	7.50	9.89	11.83	12.80	22.16	....	....	....	....	....	....	....		**47r**
Liquid Liabilities	311.25	355.39	392.73	497.21	567.98	624.16	688.04	756.29	....	....	....	....	....	....	....		**55l**
Interest Rates																	
Percent Per Annum																	
Discount Rate *(End of Period)*	12.00	9.50	9.00	15.50	17.00	15.75	18.00	15.00	13.50	13.50	15.50	17.00	15.60	19.50	19.00		**60**
Treasury Bill Rate	17.60	11.21	10.75	11.42	15.75	16.33	15.75	14.20	13.10	Ɪ9.44	12.40	13.89	14.83	15.47	12.45		**60c**
Deposit Rate	10.42	10.04	7.00	9.58	12.82	13.00	13.00	10.63	8.06	8.43	13.34	12.73	11.81	10.73	7.45		**60l**
Lending Rate	19.67	13.42	11.13	13.67	18.75	20.42	20.00	18.25	15.83	14.25	16.38	17.71	18.03	20.06	19.06		**60p**
Prices																	
Period Averages																	
Consumer Prices	28.8	34.0	38.0	42.3	48.5	54.2	63.8	74.7	84.6	91.5	100.0	109.3	....	....	Ɪ135.2		**64**

Lesotho

		1970	1971	1972	1973	1974	1975	1976	1977	1978	1979	1980	1981	1982	1983	1984
International Transactions																*Millions of Maloti*
Exports	70	4.2	3.0	6.1	8.8	9.8	9.2	14.6	12.2	28.7	38.9	46.6	44.6	40.6	34.6	41.8
Imports, c.i.f.	71	22.9	28.0	43.0	60.5	81.7	122.2	184.4	203.3	244.2	275.3	331.5	405.5	497.8	539.7	634.5
Balance of Payments																*Millions of US Dollars:*
Current Account, n.i.e.	78ald	....	....	....	....	....	−1.1	−34.2	−9.2	8.5	—	56.3	4.3	22.1	40.7	6.5
Goods: Exports f.o.b.	78aad						13.5	17.9	15.2	33.0	39.1	58.2	45.2	37.4	31.1	28.3
Goods: Imports f.o.b.	78abd						−151.5	−189.4	−210.8	−243.1	−316.7	−424.5	−448.6	−446.9	−482.5	−433.2
Trade Balance	78acd						−137.9	−171.5	−195.6	−210.1	−277.7	−366.3	−403.4	−409.6	−451.4	−404.9
Services: Credit	78add						12.0	12.0	14.1	16.8	18.6	32.2	34.3	26.2	27.9	24.4
Services: Debit	78aed						−19.1	−20.9	−24.8	−29.9	−35.3	−50.3	−55.2	−46.7	−50.2	−45.1
Balance on Goods & Services	78afd						−145.0	−180.4	−206.3	−223.2	−294.3	−384.4	−424.3	−430.0	−473.7	−425.6
Income: Credit	78agd						127.0	142.7	170.7	183.5	219.7	273.1	301.9	361.4	395.0	343.5
Income: Debit	78ahd						−4.5	−4.1	−5.1	−5.8	−6.1	−7.6	−9.1	−15.1	−12.4	−11.1
Balance on Gds, Serv. & Inc.	78aid						−22.4	−41.9	−40.7	−45.4	−80.6	−118.9	−131.5	−83.8	−91.2	−93.2
Current Transfers, n.i.e.: Credit	78ajd						21.4	16.2	31.5	53.9	80.8	222.1	184.8	163.1	192.8	147.5
Current Transfers: Debit	78akd						—	−8.5	—	—	−.1	−46.9	−49.0	−57.3	−60.9	−47.8
Capital Account, n.i.e.	78bcd						—	—	—	—	—	—	—	—	—	—
Capital Account, n.i.e.: Credit	78bad						—	—	—	—	—	—	—	—	—	—
Capital Account: Debit	78bbd						—	—	—	—	—	—	—	—	—	—
Financial Account, n.i.e.	78bjd	....	....	....	....	....	−.1	1.6	.2	3.1	8.3	−3.7	7.2	7.2	−1.7	−28.4
Direct Investment Abroad	78bdd						—	—	—	—	—	—	—	—	—	—
Dir. Invest. in Rep. Econ., n.i.e.	78bed						—	—	—	—	—	4.5	4.8	3.0	4.8	2.3
Portfolio Investment Assets	78bfd						—	—	—	—	—	—	—	—	—	—
Equity Securities	78bkd						—	—	—	—	—	—	—	—	—	—
Debt Securities	78bld						—	—	—	—	—	—	—	—	—	—
Portfolio Investment Liab., n.i.e.	78bgd						—	—	—	—	—	—	—	—	—	—
Equity Securities	78bmd						—	—	—	—	—	—	—	—	—	—
Debt Securities	78bnd						—	—	—	—	—	—	—	—	—	—
Financial Derivatives Assets	78bwd	....	....	....	....	....	....	....	....	....	....	....	....	....	....	....
Financial Derivatives Liabilities	78bxd	....	....	....	....	....	....	....	....	....	....	....	....	....	....	....
Other Investment Assets	78bhd	....	....	....	....	....	−3.8	−1.6	−9.7	−7.5	−13.7	−41.9	−53.4	−31.2	−53.0	−17.9
Monetary Authorities	78bod						....	....	....	....	....	....	....	....	....	....
General Government	78bpd						−.4	−.5	−.5	−.5	−.6	−68.1	−50.7	−15.8	−37.3	−5.2
Banks	78bqd						−3.4	−1.2	−9.2	−7.0	−13.1	26.2	−2.7	−15.4	−15.7	−12.7
Other Sectors	78brd						....	....	....	....	....	....	....	....	....	....
Other Investment Liab., n.i.e.	78bid	....	....	....	....	....	3.7	3.2	9.9	10.6	21.9	33.7	55.8	35.4	46.5	−12.8
Monetary Authorities	78bsd						—	—	—	—	—	—	—	—	—	—
General Government	78btd						4.3	2.5	9.9	9.1	23.0	30.0	54.7	37.4	28.8	−2.2
Banks	78bud						−.7	.7	—	1.5	−1.1	3.7	1.1	−2.0	17.7	−10.6
Other Sectors	78bvd						—	—	—	—	—	—	—	—	—	—
Net Errors and Omissions	78cad						1.9	32.5	8.3	−13.7	−11.1	−11.2	−10.9	−21.3	−12.9	30.5
Overall Balance	78cbd						.7	—	−.7	−2.1	−2.9	41.4	.6	8.0	26.1	8.6
Reserves and Related Items	79dad						−.7	—	.7	2.1	2.9	−41.4	−.6	−8.0	−26.1	−8.6
Reserve Assets	79dbd						−.7	—	.1	.2	.9	−43.1	−.6	−8.0	−26.0	−8.1
Use of Fund Credit and Loans	79dcd						—	—	.6	1.9	2.0	1.7	—	—	−.2	−.4
Exceptional Financing	79ded						....	....	....	....	....	....	....	....	....	....
Government Finance																*Millions of Maloti:*
Deficit (-) or Surplus	80	....	−.5	−.8	4.7	8.7	−8.7	−12.9	−3.0	....						
Revenue	81	....	10.3	11.2	20.4	28.5	28.4	38.1	60.2	....				135.8	167.9	216.4
Grants Received	81z	....	4.6	3.8	3.5	3.5	4.0	2.2	10.0	....						23.1
Exp. & Lending Minus Repay.	82z	....	15.4	15.8	19.2	23.3	41.1	53.2	73.1	....						....
Expenditure	82	....	15.3	15.9	19.2	23.1	40.6	53.2	71.2	....						....
Lending Minus Repayments	83	....	.2	−.1	—	.2	.5	—	2.0	....						....
Financing																
Domestic	84a	....	....	....	−6.7	2.3	10.4	−1.5	....				18.0	−6.1	6.6	
Foreign	85a	....	....	....	−2.0	6.4	2.5	4.5	....							
Debt: Domestic	88a															52.0
Foreign	89a															398.6
National Accounts																*Millions of Maloti:*
Exports of Goods & Services	90c	3.4	2.6	5.8	9.0	14.1	14.6	21.3	18.0	36.4	50.0	58.0	58.2	55.4	50.8	60.5
Government Consumption	91f	6.2	8.3	9.3	9.6	15.8	21.3	24.9	29.2	40.9	52.4	74.0	81.0	89.9	91.7	98.6
Gross Fixed Capital Formation	93e	5.0	6.6	6.0	10.4	14.5	20.7	45.5	40.3	51.0	73.7	115.8	133.2	186.8	130.9	184.7
Increase/Decrease(-) in Stocks	93i	—		1.2	5.6	2.8			.9	1.7	9.1	10.9	6.3	−2.9	.6	5.2
Private Consumption	96f	58.6	67.7	86.4	115.5	146.9	167.2	210.5	264.2	300.7	353.7	387.2	471.0	557.1	686.2	783.4
Imports of Goods & Services	98c	−24.3	−30.6	−46.5	−66.1	−91.6	−113.2	−174.7	−185.3	−206.3	−296.4	−350.2	−423.3	−513.4	−569.6	−676.8
Gross Domestic Product (GDP)	99b	49.1	54.7	62.2	84.1	102.5	110.6	128.4	168.1	231.8	244.3	287.0	328.4	372.9	390.6	455.5
Net Factor Inc/Pmts(-) Abroad	98.n	14.1	15.5	20.7	29.7	60.1	89.1	119.3	139.9	153.3	178.2	205.0	254.8	372.9	423.1	487.2
Gross National Income (GNI)	99a	63.1	70.2	82.9	113.8	162.6	199.7	247.7	308.0	385.1	422.5	492.0	583.2	745.8	813.7	942.6
Net National Income	99e	63.1	70.2	81.7	112.9	153.2	210.7	260.8	326.5	413.9	492.1	570.5	650.6	789.2	897.8	1,073.5
GDP Volume 1980 Prices	99b,p	....	....	....	....	....	....	....	....	....	....	287.0	289.8	300.2	274.4	297.6
GDP Volume (1995=100)	99bvp	....	....	....	....	....	....	....	....	....	....	55.4	56.0	58.0	53.0	57.5
GDP Deflator (1995=100)	99bip	....	....	....	....	....	....	....	....	....	....	15.3	17.3	19.0	21.8	23.4
																Millions:
Population	99z	1.06	1.09	1.11	1.14	1.16	1.19	1.21	1.24	1.28	1.31	1.34	1.37	1.41	1.43	1.47

	1985	1986	1987	1988	1989	1990	1991	1992	1993	1994	1995	1996	1997	1998	1999	
International Transactions																
Millions of Maloti																
Exports	50.0	58.0	94.7	144.9	173.0	153.0	186.0	310.0	438.0	509.0	581.0	812.0	904.0	1,071.0	....	70
Imports, c.i.f.	751.0	803.3	954.8	1,327.5	1,552.0	1,738.0	2,242.0	2,564.0	2,839.0	3,000.0	3,576.0	4,303.0	4,722.0	4,699.0	....	71
Balance of Payments																
Minus Sign Indicates Debit																
Current Account, n.i.e.	−12.1	−2.8	23.6	−24.6	10.4	65.0	83.1	37.6	29.3	108.1	−323.0	−302.5	−269.2	−280.2	....	78al d
Goods: Exports f.o.b.	22.4	25.4	46.5	63.7	66.4	59.5	67.2	109.2	134.0	143.5	160.0	186.9	196.1	193.4	....	78aa d
Goods: Imports f.o.b.	−324.0	−341.5	−451.5	−559.4	−592.6	−672.6	−803.5	−932.6	−868.1	−810.2	−985.2	−998.6	−1,024.4	−866.0	....	78ab d
Trade Balance	−301.6	−316.2	−405.0	−495.7	−526.2	−613.2	−736.4	−823.4	−734.1	−666.7	−825.2	−811.8	−828.3	−672.5	....	78ac d
Services: Credit	18.3	20.2	27.5	32.1	32.9	40.6	40.9	41.3	37.0	37.8	39.0	42.6	86.9	53.6	....	78ad d
Services: Debit	−35.5	−46.2	−60.7	−69.1	−70.9	−81.4	−83.9	−82.8	−70.5	−64.2	−61.1	−55.9	−67.6	−52.2	....	78ae d
Balance on Goods & Services	−318.8	−342.1	−438.2	−532.7	−564.2	−654.0	−779.5	−864.9	−767.6	−693.2	−847.3	−825.1	−809.0	−671.2	....	78af d
Income: Credit	242.0	268.6	364.8	384.9	380.0	455.0	476.8	496.3	444.5	369.6	471.6	453.0	447.4	357.7	....	78ag d
Income: Debit	−9.0	−10.3	−15.0	−14.9	−20.3	−21.8	−20.4	−32.6	−22.8	−39.4	−157.4	−119.5	−110.0	−123.6	....	78ah d
Balance on Gds, Serv. & Inc.	−85.8	−83.8	−88.4	−162.8	−204.5	−220.9	−323.1	−401.1	−345.9	−363.0	−533.2	−491.6	−471.6	−437.1	....	78ai d
Current Transfers, n.i.e.: Credit	104.4	116.9	160.8	197.0	281.7	362.3	492.8	542.1	376.5	472.1	211.3	190.2	202.9	158.0	....	78aj d
Current Transfers: Debit	−30.7	−35.8	−48.7	−58.8	−66.8	−76.4	−86.6	−103.3	−1.3	−.9	−1.2	−1.1	−.5	−1.2	....	78ak d
Capital Account, n.i.e.	—	—	—	—	—	—	—	—	—	—	43.7	45.5	44.5	22.9	....	78bc d
Capital Account, n.i.e.: Credit	—	—	—	—	—	—	—	—	—	—	43.7	45.5	44.5	22.9	....	78ba d
Capital Account: Debit	—	—	—	—	—	—	—	—	—	—	—	—	—	—	....	78bb d
Financial Account, n.i.e.	16.0	16.8	3.3	−8.0	−20.2	−45.0	−60.8	−67.0	55.2	33.0	349.1	350.6	323.7	316.1	....	78bj d
Direct Investment Abroad	—	—	—	−.1	—	—	—	—	—	—	....	....	....	....	....	78bd d
Dir. Invest. in Rep. Econ., n.i.e.	—	2.1	5.7	21.0	13.4	17.1	7.5	2.7	15.0	18.7	275.3	287.5	268.1	264.8	....	78be d
Portfolio Investment Assets	—	—	—	—	—	—	—	—	....	....	....	....	....	....	....	78bf d
Equity Securities	—	—	—	—	—	—	—	—	....	....	....	....	....	....	....	78bk d
Debt Securities	—	—	—	—	—	—	—	—	....	....	....	....	....	....	....	78bl d
Portfolio Investment Liab., n.i.e.	—	—	—	—	—	—	—	—	....	....	....	....	....	....	....	78bg d
Equity Securities	—	—	—	—	—	—	—	—	....	....	....	....	....	....	....	78bm d
Debt Securities	—	—	—	—	—	—	—	—	....	....	....	....	....	....	....	78bn d
Financial Derivatives Assets	....	....	....	....	....	....	....	....	....	....	....	....	....	....	....	78bw d
Financial Derivatives Liabilities	....	....	....	....	....	....	....	....	....	....	....	....	....	....	....	78bx d
Other Investment Assets	−9.0	−1.6	−39.0	−80.0	−64.8	−109.7	−103.6	−106.4	8.9	−13.4	18.8	−7.0	−5.0	−1.7	....	78bh d
Monetary Authorities	....	....	....	....	....	....	....	....	....	....	....	....	....	....	....	78bo d
General Government	1.9	−15.5	−45.5	−64.6	−61.4	−71.5	−105.1	−73.2	—	—	....	....	....	....	....	78bp d
Banks	−10.8	13.9	6.6	−15.4	−3.5	−38.2	1.5	−33.3	8.9	−13.4	18.8	−7.0	−5.0	−1.7	....	78bq d
Other Sectors	....	....	....	....	....	....	....	....	....	....	....	....	....	....	....	78br d
Other Investment Liab., n.i.e.	24.9	16.3	36.6	51.0	31.3	47.6	35.4	36.8	31.3	27.6	55.0	70.1	60.5	53.0	....	78bi d
Monetary Authorities	—	—	—	.1	—	6.0	1.4	−.1	—	.3	6.3	−.2	—	.1	....	78bs d
General Government	24.7	15.5	34.9	41.3	33.0	43.4	36.0	37.1	27.7	26.0	49.2	71.8	68.6	59.8	....	78bt d
Banks	.2	.9	1.7	12.8	−1.2	−2.6	−1.3	.5	1.5	1.9	—	—	−7.2	−6.7	....	78bu d
Other Sectors	—	—	—	−3.2	−.5	.8	−.7	−.7	2.1	−.5	−.5	−1.4	−.9	−.1	....	78bv d
Net Errors and Omissions	1.7	−1.4	−26.0	26.5	1.9	−2.8	20.1	79.2	17.8	−20.3	28.1	23.3	42.1	56.8	....	78ca d
Overall Balance	5.6	12.6	.9	−6.1	−7.9	17.2	42.4	49.9	102.3	120.9	97.8	116.9	141.0	115.6	....	78cb d
Reserves and Related Items	−5.6	−12.6	−.9	6.1	7.9	−17.2	−42.4	−49.9	−102.3	−120.9	−97.8	−116.9	−141.0	−115.6	....	79da d
Reserve Assets	−4.8	−11.5	.3	3.3	3.0	−21.0	−45.4	−57.3	−111.7	−124.6	−95.1	−113.5	−136.8	−110.7	....	79db d
Use of Fund Credit and Loans	−.8	−1.1	−1.2	2.8	4.9	3.8	3.0	7.5	9.5	3.8	−2.7	−3.4	−4.3	−4.9	....	79dc d
Exceptional Financing	....	....	....	....	....	....	....	....	....	....	....	....	....	....	....	79de d
Government Finance																
Year Beginning April 1																
Deficit (−) or Surplus	....	....	−160.5	−181.2	−103.4	−16.8	−9.9	81.5	147.2	149.3	108.6	137.4	88.8	−188.8	−360.6	80
Revenue	238.2	260.2	300.1	369.2	525.2	627.7	820.0	1,003.1	1,269.4	1,438.5	1,681.6	2,034.6	2,353.4	2,158.7	2,213.7	81
Grants Received	....	27.1	62.6	96.6	151.9	188.0	149.2	141.8	137.4	143.6	163.2	203.4	178.7	120.0	130.0	81z
Exp. & Lending Minus Repay.	....	....	523.2	647.1	780.5	832.5	979.0	1,063.4	1,259.6	1,432.8	1,736.2	2,100.6	2,443.3	2,467.5	2,704.3	82z
Expenditure	....	....	518.0	636.9	770.2	823.5	970.0	1,050.9	1,169.4	994.1	1,118.1	1,179.0	1,537.6	2,104.7	2,689.3	82
Lending Minus Repayments	....	....	5.2	10.2	10.3	9.0	9.1	12.6	90.2	438.7	618.1	921.6	905.7	362.8	15.0	83
Financing																
Domestic	33.2	50.1	90.2	110.0	−8.4	−110.6	−116.6	−253.6	−298.9	−252.5	−319.5	−537.3	−559.8	155.1	437.2	84a
Foreign	....	....	70.3	71.2	111.8	127.4	126.5	172.1	151.7	103.2	210.9	399.9	471.0	33.7	−76.6	85a
Debt: Domestic	....	....	271.7	381.4	372.8	262.2	....	....	....	....	....	....	....	....		88a
Foreign	....	....	522.6	685.3	815.0	978.1	1,113.8	1,345.7	....	1,704.4	1,861.5	2,255.1	2,568.8	3,180.8	3,457.3	89a
National Accounts																
Year Beginning April 1																
Exports of Goods & Services	70.1	80.4	141.7	217.5	256.5	267.6	299.1	430.7	559.6	642.8	720.4	994.1	1,301.9	1,320.7	....	90c
Government Consumption	135.9	159.3	163.9	208.9	215.6	224.0	295.8	346.4	403.6	486.5	607.2	658.6	800.0	969.7	....	91f
Gross Fixed Capital Formation	273.3	277.3	348.5	523.4	664.6	857.9	1,252.8	1,547.8	1,485.1	1,699.2	2,071.2	2,346.5	2,578.2	2,397.1	....	93e
Increase/Decrease(−) in Stocks	−.9	13.6	4.4	7.3	−17.6	−1.8	−14.3	22.2	−16.1	−44.6	−24.3	7.8	−47.1	−158.1	....	93i
Private Consumption	837.9	935.9	1,256.0	1,614.2	2,005.8	2,211.3	2,545.2	2,811.0	3,472.3	3,544.9	4,075.3	4,834.8	5,369.4	5,604.0	....	96f
Imports of Goods & Services	−765.2	−835.3	1,032.5	1,427.2	1,733.8	1,949.4	2,473.3	2,800.3	3,231.9	3,357.4	4,066.1	4,801.8	5,287.7	5,284.6	....	98c
Gross Domestic Product (GDP)	551.1	631.2	881.9	1,144.0	1,391.1	1,609.7	1,905.3	2,357.7	2,672.6	2,971.5	3,383.7	4,040.0	4,714.8	4,848.9	....	99b
Net Factor Inc/Pmts(−) Abroad	514.3	583.3	705.8	825.2	899.7	1,050.7	1,061.2	1,215.1	1,325.2	1,348.5	1,410.9	1,684.0	1,812.1	1,941.8	....	98.n
Gross National Income (GNI)	1,065.4	1,214.6	1,557.8	1,969.2	2,290.7	2,660.3	2,966.5	3,572.8	3,997.8	4,320.0	4,794.7	5,724.0	6,526.9	6,437.7	....	99a
Net National Income	1,230.3	1,366.1	1,603.7	2,092.1	2,525.8	3,025.5	3,078.4	3,697.6	4,079.9	4,671.8	5,236.5	6,219.1	....	....	....	99e
GDP Volume 1980 Prices	308.0	314.1	330.4	2,418.3	2,609.5	2,771.1	2,876.7	3,016.0	3,129.9	3,237.1	3,383.7	3,720.6	4,019.7	3,797.9	....	99b.p
GDP Volume (1995=100)	59.5	60.7	63.8	71.5	77.1	81.9	85.0	89.1	92.5	95.7	100.0	110.0	118.8	112.2	....	99bv p
GDP Deflator (1995=100)	27.4	30.7	40.8	47.3	53.3	58.1	66.2	78.2	85.4	91.8	100.0	108.6	117.3	127.7	....	99bi p
Midyear Estimates																
Population	1.50	1.58	1.62	1.69	1.70	1.72	1.76	1.80	1.84	1.88	1.93	1.97	2.02	2.06	2.11	99z

(See notes in the back of the book.)

Liberia

		1970	1971	1972	1973	1974	1975	1976	1977	1978	1979	1980	1981	1982	1983	1984
Exchange Rates															*Liberian Dollars per SDR*	
Market Rate	aa	1.0000	1.0857	1.0857	1.2064	1.2244	1.1707	1.1618	1.2147	1.3028	1.3173	1.2754	1.1640	1.1031	1.0470	.9802
														Liberian Dollars per US Dollar:		
Market Rate	ae	1.0000	1.0000	1.0000	1.0000	1.0000	1.0000	1.0000	1.0000	1.0000	1.0000	1.0000	1.0000	1.0000	1.0000	1.0000
Market Rate	rf	1.0000	1.0000	1.0000	1.0000	1.0000	1.0000	1.0000	1.0000	1.0000	1.0000	1.0000	1.0000	1.0000	1.0000	1.0000
Fund Position															*Millions of SDRs:*	
Quota	2f. s	29.00	29.00	29.00	29.00	29.00	29.00	29.00	29.00	37.00	37.00	55.50	55.50	55.50	71.30	71.30
SDRs	1b. s	1.03	.09	1.63	3.28	3.18	2.90	3.52	3.33	3.34	6.52	—	1.08	.01	—	.03
Reserve Position in the Fund	1c. s	—	—	.31	—	1.36	1.78	—	—	—	—	—	.01	—	—	—
Total Fund Cred.&Loans Outstg.	2tl	4.35	1.52	—	.06	—	—	—	3.11	12.02	50.98	69.78	115.27	176.82	223.75	237.25
International Liquidity															*Millions of US Dollars:*	
Total Reserves minus Gold	1l. d	....	....	....	....	18.72	19.19	17.17	27.34	18.02	54.98	5.45	8.34	6.47	20.40	3.48
SDRs	1b. d	1.03	.10	1.77	3.96	3.89	3.39	4.09	4.04	4.35	8.59	—	1.26	.01	—	.03
Reserve Position in the Fund	1c. d	—	—	.34	—	1.67	2.08	—	—	—	—	—	.01	—	—	—
Foreign Exchange	1d. d	....	....	....	....	13.16	13.71	13.08	23.30	13.67	46.39	5.45	7.07	6.46	20.40	3.45
Monetary Authorities: Other Liab.	4. d	....	....	....	....	—	.03	3.61	.94	5.03	27.67	25.63	13.44	7.53	16.69	.14
Deposit Money Banks: Assets	7a. d	11.16	9.44	11.86	16.80	33.68	33.98	54.98	38.77	35.36	49.34	24.27	15.53	26.37	24.50	11.66
Liabilities	7b. d	22.58	20.55	16.31	13.90	26.58	25.03	15.65	20.31	29.58	62.75	49.36	56.35	54.55	40.59	35.61
Monetary Authorities															*Millions of Liberian Dollars:*	
Foreign Assets	11	....	....	....	....	13.6	13.9	17.2	27.3	18.0	55.0	⅃5.5	8.3	6.5	20.4	3.5
Claims on Central Government	12a	....	....	....	....	21.3	21.0	27.9	30.7	75.4	118.4	⅃173.5	214.2	284.2	352.1	347.7
Claims on Nonfin.Pub.Enterprises	12c	....	....	....	....	....	....	....	....	....	....	2.3	4.2	4.4	5.6	5.3
Claims on Private Sector	12d	....	....	....	....	—	1.9	1.5	1.5	.3	.3	⅃.5	.5	.6	.7	1.8
Claims on Deposit Money Banks	12e	....	....	....	....	2.7	2.9	3.7	2.7	3.0	2.4	⅃1.7	1.1	1.2	2.3	.9
Claims on Other Financial Insts	12f	....	....	....	....	....	....	....	....	....	....	.5	1.6	2.0	2.1	2.0
Reserve Money	14	....	....	....	....	12.4	13.1	15.5	18.5	31.8	30.5	⅃42.7	41.1	57.4	71.8	86.9
of which: Currency Outside DMB	14a	....	....	....	....	8.5	8.0	8.4	9.2	10.2	11.0	11.3	11.6	15.7	19.8	28.6
Time Deposits	15	....	....	....	....	—	—	—	—	1.0	—	⅃—	.8	.5	—	.5
Foreign Liabilities	16c	....	....	....	....	—	—	3.6	4.7	20.7	94.8	⅃114.6	147.6	202.6	250.9	232.7
Central Government Deposits	16d	....	....	....	....	5.8	8.9	12.9	19.8	22.8	28.8	⅃25.5	25.3	28.3	25.8	7.7
Capital Accounts	17a	....	....	....	....	16.7	16.5	16.2	16.9	17.8	22.9	⅃30.0	36.0	43.9	51.2	65.8
Other Items (Net)	17r	....	....	....	....	2.6	1.1	2.0	2.3	2.6	-1.0	⅃-28.9	-20.1	-34.2	-16.9	-32.4
Deposit Money Banks															*Millions of Liberian Dollars:*	
Reserves	20	.5	.6	.7	1.1	3.5	4.7	6.2	9.1	19.1	14.4	29.6	27.7	39.9	53.3	57.2
Foreign Assets	21	11.2	9.4	11.9	16.8	33.7	34.0	55.0	38.8	35.4	49.3	24.3	15.5	26.4	24.5	11.7
Claims on Central Government	22a	19.5	18.8	17.4	8.3	4.0	2.2	1.0	4.8	9.4	2.8	2.9	3.9	4.1	2.8	3.5
Claims on Nonfin.Pub.Enterprises	22c	—	—	—	.8	.8	1.8	.7	1.1	11.3	38.0	40.9	33.1	42.4	44.4	47.9
Claims on Private Sector	22d	35.3	38.8	47.3	54.3	72.7	76.8	83.1	109.2	132.2	146.3	88.7	91.5	75.0	71.3	74.8
Claims on Other Financial Insts	22f	—	—	—	—	—	—	.5	.9	—	—	—	—	1.3	.2	.4
Demand Deposits	24	20.1	18.3	21.4	27.9	37.2	33.8	53.6	47.0	63.9	66.2	58.0	41.3	48.9	55.7	62.5
Time and Savings Deposits	25	13.7	19.0	28.4	31.0	30.1	35.0	49.6	69.1	77.5	82.2	48.9	51.1	64.2	68.6	54.5
Foreign Liabilities	26c	22.6	20.5	16.3	13.9	26.6	25.0	15.6	20.3	29.6	62.8	49.4	56.4	54.6	40.6	35.6
Central Government Deposits	26d	12.1	8.8	11.9	5.6	2.9	4.2	1.0	.8	—	.1	.1	.1	.1	1.5	6.3
Credit from Monetary Authorities	26g	—	—	—	—	2.5	2.4	3.1	2.1	1.4	1.5	.5	.5	.6	1.1	.5
Capital Accounts	27a	5.7	5.9	4.9	8.7	8.9	5.8	8.8	14.5	17.2	18.6	17.9	18.3	19.7	22.6	25.1
Other Items (Net)	27r	-7.6	-5.0	-5.6	-5.9	6.4	13.3	14.8	10.0	17.8	19.6	11.6	4.1	.9	6.5	11.0
Monetary Survey															*Millions of Liberian Dollars:*	
Foreign Assets (Net)	31n	....	....	....	....	19.9	22.9	52.9	41.1	3.1	-53.3	⅃-134.3	-180.1	-224.3	-246.6	-253.2
Domestic Credit	32	....	....	....	....	89.2	88.8	99.6	125.6	194.4	239.0	⅃283.7	323.6	385.4	452.0	469.5
Claims on Central Govt. (Net)	32an	....	....	....	....	16.5	10.1	15.0	14.9	62.0	92.4	⅃150.8	192.7	259.9	327.6	337.3
Claims on Nonfin.Pub.Enterprises	32c	....	....	....	....	....	....	....	....	....	....	43.3	37.3	46.8	50.0	53.2
Claims on Private Sector	32d	....	....	....	....	72.7	78.7	84.6	110.7	132.4	146.6	⅃89.2	92.0	75.5	72.0	76.6
Claims on Other Financial Insts	32f	....	....	....	....	....	....	....	....	....	....	.5	1.6	3.2	2.3	2.4
Money	34	....	....	....	....	44.9	39.0	59.3	53.2	72.5	72.6	⅃69.8	54.0	66.2	76.1	91.3
Quasi-Money	35	....	....	....	....	30.1	35.0	49.6	69.1	78.5	82.2	⅃48.9	51.1	65.0	69.1	55.0
Capital Accounts	37a	....	....	....	....	25.6	22.2	25.0	31.4	34.9	41.5	⅃47.9	54.3	63.6	73.8	90.9
Other Items (Net)	37r	....	....	....	....	8.5	15.5	18.7	13.0	11.6	-10.5	⅃-17.1	-15.8	-33.7	-13.6	-20.8
Money plus Quasi-Money	35l	....	....	....	....	75.0	73.9	108.9	122.3	151.0	154.7	⅃118.7	105.1	131.2	145.2	146.3
Interest Rates															*Percent Per Annum:*	
Savings Rate	60k	....						....		....		....	....	8.00	8.00	8.05
Deposit Rate	60l	....						....		....		10.30	11.50	10.21	10.25	9.81
Lending Rate	60p	....						....		....		18.40	21.50	18.23	20.69	20.63
Prices															*Index Numbers (1985=100):*	
Consumer Prices	64	33.0	32.8	34.1	40.8	48.5	55.3	58.4	62.0	66.6	74.3	85.2	91.7	97.1	99.8	101.0

	1985	1986	1987	1988	1989	1990	1991	1992	1993	1994	1995	1996	1997	1998	1999		
																Exchange Rates	
End of Period	1.0984	1.2232	1.4187	1.3457	1.3142	1.4227	1.4304	1.3750	1.3736	1.4599	1.4865	1.4380	1.3493	Ɪ60.8973	54.2141	Market Rate	aa
End of Period (ae) Period Average (rf)																	
	1.0000	1.0000	1.0000	1.0000	1.0000	1.0000	1.0000	1.0000	1.0000	1.0000	1.0000	1.0000	1.0000	Ɪ43.2500	39.5000	Market Rate	ae
	1.0000	1.0000	1.0000	1.0000	1.0000	1.0000	1.0000	1.0000	1.0000	1.0000	1.0000	1.0000	1.0000	41.5075	41.9025	Market Rate	rf
																Fund Position	
End of Period	71.30	71.30	71.30	71.30	71.30	71.30	71.30	71.30	71.30	71.30	71.30	71.30	71.30	71.30	71.30	Quota	2f. s
	—	—	—	—	—	—	—	—	—	—	—	—	—	—	—	SDRs	1b. s
	.02	.02	.03	.03	.03	.03	.03	.03	.03	.03	.03	.03	.03	.03	.03	Reserve Position in the Fund	1c. s
	230.40	230.40	230.40	229.36	227.20	226.52	226.52	226.52	226.52	225.83	225.74	225.74	225.70	225.26	224.82	Total Fund Cred.&Loans Outstg.	2tl
																International Liquidity	
End of Period	1.52	2.66	.51	.38	7.88	. . . .	1.31	.98	2.36	5.07	28.09	.38	.42	.62	.43	Total Reserves minus Gold	1l. d
	—	—	—	—	—	—	—	—	—	—	—	—	—	—	—	SDRs	1b. d
	.02	.02	.04	.04	.04	.04	.04	.04	.04	.04	.04	.04	.04	.04	.04	Reserve Position in the Fund	1c. d
	1.50	2.64	.47	.34	7.84	. . . .	1.27	.94	2.32	5.03	28.05	.34	.38	.58	.39	Foreign Exchange	1d. d
	11.50	35.57	65.05	87.51	115.77	. . . .	216.88	232.46	260.40	292.67	315.56	322.35	317.91	344.78	346.96	Monetary Authorities: Other Liab.	4.. d
	14.71	18.50	18.57	23.05	34.05	. . . .	17.53	13.78	49.05	9.46	12.04	9.49	15.59	10.36	16.71	Deposit Money Banks: Assets	7a. d
	46.22	34.45	39.32	39.47	43.17	. . . .	48.32	36.97	17.86	46.33	15.35	5.12	8.44	2.47	3.01	Liabilities	7b. d
																Monetary Authorities	
End of Period	1.5	2.7	.5	.4	7.9	. . . .	1.3	1.0	2.4	5.1	28.1	.4	.4	26.7	17.0	Foreign Assets	11
	428.0	477.0	563.0	733.8	841.1	. . . .	985.3	1,072.9	1,264.1	1,284.9	1,513.0	1,803.1	1,916.2	35,687.0	32,605.1	Claims on Central Government	12a
	1.0	—	—	—	4.1	. . . .	4.8	4.8	4.8	4.8	4.8	5.6	5.6	5.8	5.5	Claims on Nonfin.Pub.Enterprises	12c
	.7	.8	1.0	1.0	1.1	. . . .	11.0	12.0	17.8	15.5	15.4	20.5	20.2	25.5	24.6	Claims on Private Sector	12d
	.8	2.0	.9	1.9	2.5	. . . .	24.4	23.8	23.4	51.4	61.5	2.5	2.3	4.3	1.7	Claims on Deposit Money Banks	12e
	2.0	2.0	3.8	3.6	3.8	. . . .	3.8	3.8	3.8	.7	.7	—	.2	1.5	1.5	Claims on Other Financial Insts	12f
	121.6	169.1	217.2	259.2	337.5	. . . .	406.1	411.0	522.9	551.1	723.4	852.6	920.5	938.4	979.9	Reserve Money	14
	46.2	66.1	82.5	96.5	101.6	. . . .	189.3	154.9	274.1	302.9	485.8	568.4	576.6	565.5	556.9	*of which: Currency Outside DMB*	14a
	.9	.2	.7	1.1	1.5	. . . .	.4	1.4	2.2	2.1	2.7	3.9	4.8	3.0	1.7	Time Deposits	15
	264.6	317.4	391.9	396.2	414.3	. . . .	540.9	543.9	571.5	622.4	651.1	646.9	622.4	28,629.2	25,893.0	Foreign Liabilities	16c
	9.4	15.4	17.2	17.0	25.3	. . . .	15.9	7.8	71.6	74.2	15.1	18.6	20.0	137.4	71.0	Central Government Deposits	16d
	78.1	22.2	22.4	−7.2	83.0	. . . .	102.4	73.1	70.1	59.6	10.9	42.7	64.0	9,259.4	6,597.4	Capital Accounts	17a
	−40.4	−39.8	−80.2	74.5	−1.3	. . . .	−34.9	81.2	74.8	53.0	219.5	267.5	313.1	−3,216.6	−887.5	Other Items (Net)	17r
																Deposit Money Banks	
End of Period	70.6	79.2	106.4	126.1	190.1	. . . .	113.9	143.9	217.3	215.4	201.8	188.4	240.0	768.5	815.2	Reserves	20
	14.7	18.5	18.6	23.0	34.1	. . . .	17.5	13.8	49.1	9.5	12.0	9.5	15.6	447.9	660.2	Foreign Assets	21
	4.2	10.0	10.9	17.6	9.8	. . . .	7.2	3.1	8.8	5.4	5.1	3.5	—	306.2	358.1	Claims on Central Government	22a
	45.9	52.9	38.7	49.7	42.0	. . . .	47.9	55.6	82.7	63.1	21.0	5.7	7.9	12.2	44.5	Claims on Nonfin.Pub.Enterprises	22c
	77.5	74.3	89.9	74.4	123.3	. . . .	96.6	152.8	127.2	222.7	176.0	55.4	82.7	1,148.1	900.9	Claims on Private Sector	22d
	.4	1.4	.1	1.2	.3	. . . .	6.3	.3	.3	—	2.1	5.3	—	—	—	Claims on Other Financial Insts	22f
	68.5	83.4	94.6	93.8	135.0	. . . .	92.8	111.4	151.6	155.3	167.0	127.4	110.0	1,005.5	1,247.9	Demand Deposits	24
	56.2	53.7	56.7	66.4	73.9	. . . .	72.0	156.3	274.5	324.4	360.9	195.5	235.5	335.8	324.7	Time and Savings Deposits	25
	46.2	34.5	39.3	39.5	43.2	. . . .	48.3	37.0	17.9	46.3	15.3	5.1	8.4	106.9	119.0	Foreign Liabilities	26c
	10.6	18.8	13.1	20.3	26.0	. . . .	35.1	29.9	30.5	35.3	30.3	10.6	51.1	112.0	165.4	Central Government Deposits	26d
	1.9	.2	.6	1.1	1.2	. . . .	14.2	20.7	20.0	23.7	16.9	—	—	1.9	2.0	Credit from Monetary Authorities	26g
	22.0	25.0	29.8	35.0	48.7	. . . .	44.6	48.3	22.7	33.5	3.8	3.4	−5.5	36.3	685.6	Capital Accounts	27a
	7.9	20.8	30.3	35.9	71.6	. . . .	−17.7	−33.9	−31.7	−102.4	−176.5	−74.1	−53.4	1,084.5	234.3	Other Items (Net)	27r
																Monetary Survey	
End of Period	−294.6	−330.7	−412.2	−412.2	−415.6	. . . .	−570.4	−566.1	−538.0	−654.2	−626.3	−642.2	−614.9	−28,261.6	−25,334.9	Foreign Assets (Net)	31n
	539.8	584.4	677.0	844.1	974.4	. . . .	1,112.0	1,267.8	1,404.4	1,487.6	1,692.0	1,870.1	1,961.7	36,936.9	33,703.9	Domestic Credit	32
	412.2	452.8	543.5	714.1	799.6	. . . .	941.5	1,038.4	1,170.8	1,180.7	1,472.6	1,777.4	1,845.0	35,743.8	32,726.8	Claims on Central Govt. (Net)	32an
	46.9	52.9	38.7	49.7	46.2	. . . .	52.7	60.4	87.5	68.0	25.8	11.3	13.5	18.0	50.1	Claims on Nonfin.Pub.Enterprises	32c
	78.3	75.1	90.9	75.4	124.4	. . . .	107.6	164.9	145.1	238.2	191.5	75.8	102.9	1,173.6	925.5	Claims on Private Sector	32d
	2.4	3.5	3.9	4.8	4.2	. . . .	10.1	4.1	1.0	.7	2.1	5.5	.2	1.5	1.5	Claims on Other Financial Insts	32f
	115.2	150.4	177.5	190.4	236.7	. . . .	282.1	266.4	425.8	458.3	652.8	696.2	686.8	1,571.0	1,804.8	Money	34
	57.0	53.9	57.5	67.5	75.4	. . . .	72.4	157.7	276.7	326.5	363.6	199.4	240.3	338.8	326.4	Quasi-Money	35
	100.1	47.2	52.2	27.8	131.8	. . . .	147.0	121.4	92.8	93.0	14.8	46.0	58.5	9,295.8	7,283.0	Capital Accounts	37a
	−27.1	2.2	−22.3	146.2	114.8	. . . .	40.1	156.2	71.2	−44.4	34.5	286.2	361.3	−2,530.2	−1,045.1	Other Items (Net)	37r
	172.2	204.3	234.9	257.8	312.2	. . . .	354.5	424.1	702.5	784.8	1,016.4	895.6	927.0	1,909.8	2,131.2	Money plus Quasi-Money	35l
																Interest Rates	
Percent Per Annum	8.09	7.79	6.82	6.68	6.78	. . . .	. . . .	. . . .	. . . .	6.16	6.12	. . . .	6.08	6.00	6.02	Savings Rate	60k
	9.34	7.25	5.88	5.43	6.77	. . . .	. . . .	. . . .	. . . .	6.34	6.37	. . . .	6.43	6.22	6.25	Deposit Rate	60l
	19.34	14.45	13.63	13.36	13.82	. . . .	. . . .	. . . .	. . . .	14.53	15.57	. . . .	16.83	Ɪ21.74	16.72	Lending Rate	60p
																Prices	
Period Averages	100.0	104.0	109.2	119.8	130.6	. . . .	. . . .	. . . .	. . . .	. . . .	. . . .	. . . .	. . . .	. . . .	. . . .	Consumer Prices	64

Liberia

668		1970	1971	1972	1973	1974	1975	1976	1977	1978	1979	1980	1981	1982	1983	1984
International Transactions																*Millions of Liberian Dollars*
Exports	**70**	213.73	222.13	244.40	324.00	400.27	393.83	459.96	447.42	504.05	536.56	600.40	529.16	477.44	427.60	452.12
Imports, c.i.f.	**71**	149.70	157.37	178.68	193.45	288.44	331.20	399.22	463.53	480.87	506.55	534.62	447.38	428.32	411.58	363.21
																1985=100
Unit Value of Exports	**74**	38.5	I 42.8	42.8	47.5	62.5	I 81.8	84.2	98.1	88.3	103.9	121.1	I 100.6	109.1	101.9	100.5
Unit Value of Imports	**75**	....	33	37	42	62	I 67	64	79	81	94	109	I 98	104	99	108
Balance of Payments																*Millions of US Dollars:*
Current Account, n.i.e.	**78al *d***	....	....	....	....	....	....	....	....	....	16.2	46.0	75.1	2.5	–104.0	–2.1
Goods: Exports f.o.b.	**78aa *d***	....	....	....	....	....	....	....	....	....	536.6	600.4	529.2	477.4	420.8	446.7
Goods: Imports f.o.b.	**78ab *d***	....	....	....	....	....	....	....	....	....	–457.5	–478.0	–423.9	–390.2	–374.8	–325.4
Trade Balance	**78ac *d***	....	....	....	....	....	....	....	....	....	79.1	122.4	105.3	87.2	46.0	121.3
Services: Credit	**78ad *d***	....	....	....	....	....	....	....	....	....	17.0	13.1	11.5	32.7	38.5	36.9
Services: Debit	**78ae *d***	....	....	....	....	....	....	....	....	....	–68.9	–72.7	–58.7	–92.0	–108.7	–92.5
Balance on Goods & Services	**78af *d***	....	....	....	....	....	....	....	....	....	27.2	62.8	58.1	27.9	–24.2	65.7
Income: Credit	**78ag *d***	....	....	....	....	....	....	....	....	....	—	—	—	1.8	1.8	2.6
Income: Debit	**78ah *d***	....	....	....	....	....	....	....	....	....	–13.7	–24.0	–21.1	–74.1	–155.4	–129.4
Balance on Gds, Serv. & Inc.	**78ai *d***	....	....	....	....	....	....	....	....	....	13.5	38.8	37.0	–44.4	–177.8	–61.1
Current Transfers, n.i.e.: Credit	**78aj *d***	....	....	....	....	....	....	....	....	....	37.7	39.2	71.1	124.9	146.5	142.6
Current Transfers: Debit	**78ak *d***	....	....	....	....	....	....	....	....	....	–35.0	–32.0	–33.0	–78.0	–72.7	–83.6
Capital Account, n.i.e.	**78bc *d***	....	....	....	....	....	....	....	....	....	—	—	—	—	—	—
Capital Account, n.i.e.: Credit	**78ba *d***	....	....	....	....	....	....	....	....	....	—	—	—	—	—	—
Capital Account: Debit	**78bb *d***	....	....	....	....	....	....	....	....	....	—	—	—	—	—	—
Financial Account, n.i.e.	**78bj *d***	....	....	....	....	....	....	....	....	....	122.1	82.2	58.7	139.6	–16.6	–16.4
Direct Investment Abroad	**78bd *d***	....	....	....	....	....	....	....	....	....	—	—	—	—	—	—
Dir. Invest. in Rep. Econ., n.i.e.	**78be *d***	....	....	....	....	....	....	....	....	....	—	—	—	34.8	49.1	36.2
Portfolio Investment Assets	**78bf *d***	....	....	....	....	....	....	....	....	....	—	—	—	—	5.0	6.8
Equity Securities	**78bk *d***	....	....	....	....	....	....	....	....	....	—	—	—	—	—	—
Debt Securities	**78bl *d***	....	....	....	....	....	....	....	....	....	—	—	—	—	5.0	6.8
Portfolio Investment Liab., n.i.e.	**78bg *d***	....	....	....	....	....	....	....	....	....	—	—	—	—	—	—
Equity Securities	**78bm *d***	....	....	....	....	....	....	....	....	....	—	—	—	—	—	—
Debt Securities	**78bn *d***	....	....	....	....	....	....	....	....	....	—	—	—	—	—	—
Financial Derivatives Assets	**78bw *d***	....	....	....	....	....	....	....	....	....	....	....	....	....	....	....
Financial Derivatives Liabilities	**78bx *d***	....	....	....	....	....	....	....	....	....	....	....	....	....	....	....
Other Investment Assets	**78bh *d***	....	....	....	....	....	....	....	....	....	–14.0	25.1	8.7	10.8	–3.3	–28.7
Monetary Authorities	**78bo *d***	....	....	....	....	....	....	....	....	....	....	....	....	....	....	....
General Government	**78bp *d***	....	....	....	....	....	....	....	....	....	—	—	—	—	—	–4.3
Banks	**78bq *d***	....	....	....	....	....	....	....	....	....	–14.0	25.1	8.7	10.8	1.9	12.8
Other Sectors	**78br *d***	....	....	....	....	....	....	....	....	....	—	—	—	—	–5.2	–37.2
Other Investment Liab., n.i.e.	**78bi *d***	....	....	....	....	....	....	....	....	....	136.1	57.1	50.0	94.0	–67.4	–30.7
Monetary Authorities	**78bs *d***	....	....	....	....	....	....	....	....	....	—	—	–.9	—	–7.3	–16.7
General Government	**78bt *d***	....	....	....	....	....	....	....	....	....	102.9	70.5	43.9	86.3	74.5	19.3
Banks	**78bu *d***	....	....	....	....	....	....	....	....	....	33.2	–13.4	7.0	–1.8	–11.5	–3.2
Other Sectors	**78bv *d***	....	....	....	....	....	....	....	....	....	—	—	—	9.5	–123.2	–30.1
Net Errors and Omissions	**78ca *d***	....	....	....	....	....	....	....	....	....	–211.1	–175.0	–182.7	–265.8	–7.0	–134.3
Overall Balance	**78cb *d***	....	....	....	....	....	....	....	....	....	–72.8	–46.8	–48.9	–123.7	–127.6	–152.8
Reserves and Related Items	**79da *d***	....	....	....	....	....	....	....	....	....	72.8	46.8	48.9	123.7	127.6	152.8
Reserve Assets	**79db *d***	....	....	....	....	....	....	....	....	....	–.5	25.9	1.4	1.2	–14.2	16.9
Use of Fund Credit and Loans	**79dc *d***	....	....	....	....	....	....	....	....	....	50.7	24.4	53.0	67.1	50.1	14.1
Exceptional Financing	**79de *d***	....	....	....	....	....	....	....	....	....	22.6	–3.5	–5.5	55.5	91.6	121.8
Government Finance																*Millions of Liberian Dollars:*
Deficit (-) or Surplus	**80**	–6.2	10.4	13.2	10.5	6.8	3.4	–16.0	I –24.2	–56.2	–141.2	–88.3	–110.3	–116.6	–102.9	–61.0
Revenue	**81**	66.5	67.6	75.1	88.8	104.6	121.0	147.9	I 165.4	181.7	201.3	202.3	218.0	236.9	229.7	223.7
Grants Received	**81z**	10.8	13.2	11.3	11.0	12.3	11.3	16.0	I 16.0	16.0	23.0	23.0	24.5	41.4	33.0	36.0
Exp. & Lending Minus Repay.	**82z**	83.5	70.4	73.2	89.3	110.1	128.9	179.9	I 205.6	253.9	365.5	313.6	352.8	394.9	365.6	320.7
Expenditure	**82**	....	....	....	....	102.3	119.9	178.4	I 182.6	232.7	344.3	281.0	323.2	371.0	338.3	298.4
Lending Minus Repayments	**83**	....	....	....	....	7.8	9.0	1.5	I 23.0	21.2	21.2	32.6	29.6	23.9	27.3	22.3
Financing	**84x**	6.2	–10.4	–13.2	–10.5	–6.8	–3.4	16.0	I 24.2	56.2	141.2	88.3	110.3	116.6	102.9	61.0
Domestic	**84a**	....	....	....	....	–1.6	–5.7	....	I –13.5	41.3	30.8	58.0	48.9	75.6	63.2	41.1
Foreign	**85a**	....	....	....	....	–5.2	2.3	....	I 37.7	14.9	110.4	30.3	61.4	41.0	39.7	19.9
Debt: Domestic	**88a**	....	....	....	7.7	13.2	10.9	....	I 35.9	63.5	95.1	156.0	206.1	258.3	335.0	363.0
Foreign	**89a**	....	....	....	143.2	138.7	141.9	....	I 215.2	223.7	350.5	435.8	498.2	511.4	559.7	585.1
National Accounts																*Millions of Liberian Dollars*
Exports of Goods & Services	**90c**	240.1	251.8	274.8	329.9	407.2	403.7	467.1	459.0	500.0	553.6	613.5	540.7	487.4	466.1	489.0
Government Consumption	**91f**	45.1	53.1	55.4	56.9	64.5	73.2	89.3	120.0	139.0	156.6	182.0	229.5	231.1	197.0	152.2
Gross Fixed Capital Formation	**93e**	77.8	73.4	88.7	85.5	116.7	161.2	206.4	234.3	260.1	277.6	196.1	179.6	193.1	183.1	168.9
Increase/Decrease(-) in Stocks	**93i**	8.4	14.8	15.4	–13.9	5.1	85.8	33.4	51.7	20.4	43.9	109.0	18.5	42.9	47.2	25.7
Private Consumption	**96f**	152.4	166.8	176.4	197.1	245.8	257.6	281.7	363.1	402.8	436.2	430.0	647.2	650.4	723.0	710.2
Imports of Goods & Services	**98c**	–172.2	–187.4	–204.8	–240.9	–332.1	–371.9	–446.2	–521.9	–548.6	–587.4	–614.0	–560.9	–478.5	–479.2	–411.5
Gross Domestic Product (GDP)	**99b**	351.6	372.5	405.9	414.6	507.2	609.6	631.7	706.2	773.7	880.5	916.6	1,022.3	1,119.5	1,128.9	1,058.0
Net Factor Inc/Pmts(-) Abroad	**98.n**	–93.5	–91.0	–68.0	–92.0	–85.4	–122.8	–86.0	–80.0	–95.9	–87.7	–83.7	–125.2	–145.9	–153.6	–126.8
Gross National Income (GNI)	**99a**	258.1	281.5	337.9	322.6	421.8	486.8	545.7	626.2	677.8	792.8	832.9	942.1	973.6	975.3	931.2
GDP Volume 1971 prices	**99b.*p***	354.9	372.5	386.6	376.8	404.7	343.5	357.2	354.2	368.2	384.4	366.2	350.1	342.6	331.3	321.3
GDP Volume (1985=100)	**99bv*p***	100.6	105.6	109.6	106.8	114.7	97.4	101.2	100.4	104.4	109.0	103.8	106.1	103.1	102.3	101.4
GDP Deflator (1985=100)	**99bi*p***	32.7	33.0	34.6	36.3	41.4	58.6	58.4	65.8	69.3	75.6	82.6	90.1	101.6	103.2	97.6
																Millions:
Population	**99z**	1.37	1.38	1.42	1.47	1.50	1.55	1.61	1.67	1.72	1.78	1.85	1.91	1.98	2.04	2.11

1985	1986	1987	1988	1989	1990	1991	1992	1993	1994	1995	1996	1997	1998	1999		
Millions of Liberian Dollars															**International Transactions**	
435.60	408.37	382.20	396.33	460.11	....	....	....	....	....	....	....	....	....	....	Exports	70
284.40	259.04	307.60	272.32	....	....	....	....	....	....	....	....	....	....	....	Imports, c.i.f.	71
1985=100																
100.0	98.2	93.6	....	....	....	....	....	....	....	....	....	....	....	....	Unit Value of Exports	74
100	105	112	....	....	....	....	....	....	....	....	....	....	....	....	Unit Value of Imports	75
															Balance of Payments	
Minus Sign Indicates Debit																
55.3	−17.7	−145.1	....	....	....	....	....	....	....	....	....	....	....	....	Current Account, n.i.e.	78al d
430.4	407.9	374.9	....	....	....	....	....	....	....	....	....	....	....	....	Goods: Exports f.o.b.	78aa d
−263.8	−258.8	−311.7	....	....	....	....	....	....	....	....	....	....	....	....	Goods: Imports f.o.b.	78ab d
166.6	149.1	63.2	....	....	....	....	....	....	....	....	....	....	....	....	*Trade Balance*	78ac d
34.6	56.9	52.5	....	....	....	....	....	....	....	....	....	....	....	....	Services: Credit	78ad d
−80.2	−80.5	−74.2	....	....	....	....	....	....	....	....	....	....	....	....	Services: Debit	78ae d
121.0	125.5	41.5	....	....	....	....	....	....	....	....	....	....	....	....	*Balance on Goods & Services*	78af d
3.7	2.1	5.2	....	....	....	....	....	....	....	....	....	....	....	....	Income: Credit	78ag d
−131.8	−183.3	−188.3	....	....	....	....	....	....	....	....	....	....	....	....	Income: Debit	78ah d
−7.1	−55.7	−141.6	....	....	....	....	....	....	....	....	....	....	....	....	*Balance on Gds, Serv. & Inc.*	78ai d
130.0	97.9	50.0	....	....	....	....	....	....	....	....	....	....	....	....	Current Transfers, n.i.e.: Credit	78aj d
−67.6	−59.9	−53.5	....	....	....	....	....	....	....	....	....	....	....	....	Current Transfers: Debit	78ak d
—	—	—	....	....	....	....	....	....	....	....	....	....	....	....	Capital Account, n.i.e.	78bc d
—	—	—	....	....	....	....	....	....	....	....	....	....	....	....	Capital Account, n.i.e.: Credit	78ba d
—	—	—	....	....	....	....	....	....	....	....	....	....	....	....	Capital Account: Debit	78bb d
−150.0	−202.9	−185.3	....	....	....	....	....	....	....	....	....	....	....	....	Financial Account, n.i.e.	78bj d
			....	....	....	....	....	....	....	....	....	....	....	....	Direct Investment Abroad	78bd d
−16.2	−16.5	38.5	....	....	....	....	....	....	....	....	....	....	....	....	Dir. Invest. in Rep. Econ., n.i.e.	78be d
4.4	5.6	—	....	....	....	....	....	....	....	....	....	....	....	....	Portfolio Investment Assets	78bf d
			....	....	....	....	....	....	....	....	....	....	....	....	Equity Securities	78bk d
4.4	5.6	—	....	....	....	....	....	....	....	....	....	....	....	....	Debt Securities	78bl d
—	—	—	....	....	....	....	....	....	....	....	....	....	....	....	Portfolio Investment Liab., n.i.e.	78bg d
—	—	—	....	....	....	....	....	....	....	....	....	....	....	....	Equity Securities	78bm d
—	—	—	....	....	....	....	....	....	....	....	....	....	....	....	Debt Securities	78bn d
....	....	....	....	....	....	....	....	....	....	....	....	....	....	....	Financial Derivatives Assets	78bw d
			....	....	....	....	....	....	....	....	....	....	....	....	Financial Derivatives Liabilities	78bx d
−9.3	7.1	4.3	....	....	....	....	....	....	....	....	....	....	....	....	Other Investment Assets	78bh d
....	....	....	....	....	....	....	....	....	....	....	....	....	....	....	Monetary Authorities	78bo d
—	—	—	....	....	....	....	....	....	....	....	....	....	....	....	General Government	78bp d
−3.1	7.1	4.3	....	....	....	....	....	....	....	....	....	....	....	....	Banks	78bq d
−6.2	—	—	....	....	....	....	....	....	....	....	....	....	....	....	Other Sectors	78br d
−128.9	−199.1	−228.1	....	....	....	....	....	....	....	....	....	....	....	....	Other Investment Liab., n.i.e.	78bi d
−12.1	−2.6	−.7	....	....	....	....	....	....	....	....	....	....	....	....	Monetary Authorities	78bs d
−84.6	−91.3	−120.0	....	....	....	....	....	....	....	....	....	....	....	....	General Government	78bt d
12.3	1.7	.2	....	....	....	....	....	....	....	....	....	....	....	....	Banks	78bu d
−44.5	−107.0	−107.6	....	....	....	....	....	....	....	....	....	....	....	....	Other Sectors	78bv d
−108.7	−73.4	30.3	....	....	....	....	....	....	....	....	....	....	....	....	Net Errors and Omissions	78ca d
−203.4	−294.0	−300.1	....	....	....	....	....	....	....	....	....	....	....	....	*Overall Balance*	78cb d
203.4	294.0	300.1	....	....	....	....	....	....	....	....	....	....	....	....	Reserves and Related Items	79da d
2.0	2.6	.5	....	....	....	....	....	....	....	....	....	....	....	....	Reserve Assets	79db d
−7.0	—	—	....	....	....	....	....	....	....	....	....	....	....	....	Use of Fund Credit and Loans	79dc d
208.4	291.4	299.6	....	....	....	....	....	....	....	....	....	....	....	....	Exceptional Financing	79de d
Year Ending December 31															**Government Finance**	
−87.1	−90.9	−83.9	I−91.9	....	....	....	....	....	....	....	....	....	....	....	Deficit (-) or Surplus	80
206.8	180.7	180.6	I 212.8	....	....	....	....	....	....	....	....	....	....	....	Revenue	81
22.5	25.0	18.0	I —	....	....	....	....	....	....	....	....	....	....	....	Grants Received	81z
316.4	296.6	282.5	I 304.7	....	....	....	....	....	....	....	....	....	....	....	Exp. & Lending Minus Repay.	82z
291.0	273.9	263.5	I 283.4	....	....	....	....	....	....	....	....	....	....	....	Expenditure	82
25.4	22.7	19.0	I 21.3	....	....	....	....	....	....	....	....	....	....	....	Lending Minus Repayments	83
87.1	90.9	83.9	I 91.9	....	....	....	....	....	....	....	....	....	....	....	Financing	84x
34.8	22.1	42.3	I 71.9	....	....	....	....	....	....	....	....	....	....	....	Domestic	84a
52.3	68.8	41.6	I 20.0	....	....	....	....	....	....	....	....	....	....	....	Foreign	85a
378.5	412.6	459.4	I 507.0	....	....	....	....	....	....	....	....	....	....	....	Debt: Domestic	88a
982.1	1,121.0	1,306.4	I 1,427.1	....	....	....	....	....	....	....	....	....	....	....	Foreign	89a
Millions of Liberian Dollars															**National Accounts**	
470.2	462.2	427.4	448.9	521.9	....	....	....	....	....	....	....	....	....	....	Exports of Goods & Services	90c
149.9	131.0	163.2	142.8	160.0	....	....	....	....	....	....	....	....	....	....	Government Consumption	91f
126.5	115.0	120.4	115.3	96.8	....	....	....	....	....	....	....	....	....	....	Gross Fixed Capital Formation	93e
7.8	7.8	7.0	3.5	4.0	....	....	....	....	....	....	....	....	....	....	Increase/Decrease(-) in Stocks	93i
706.8	662.6	713.9	733.3	656.8	....	....	....	....	....	....	....	....	....	....	Private Consumption	96f
−322.8	−299.7	−356.8	−321.5	−275.2	....	....	....	....	....	....	....	....	....	....	Imports of Goods & Services	98c
1,069.2	1,051.2	1,120.9	1,174.4	1,182.8	....	....	....	....	....	....	....	....	....	....	Gross Domestic Product (GDP)	99b
−123.6	−180.5	−183.1	−193.8	−199.1	....	....	....	....	....	....	....	....	....	....	Net Factor Inc/Pmts(-) Abroad	98.n
945.6	820.7	937.8	980.6	983.8	....	....	....	....	....	....	....	....	....	....	Gross National Income (GNI)	99a
318.5	....	....	....	....	....	....	....	....	....	....	....	....	....	....	GDP Volume 1971 prices	99b. p
100.0	102.9	105.7	105.7	....	....	....	....	....	....	....	....	....	....	....	GDP Volume (1985=100)	99bv p
100.0	95.5	99.2	103.9	....	....	....	....	....	....	....	....	....	....	....	GDP Deflator (1985=100)	99bi p
Midyear Estimates																
2.16	2.22	2.28	2.34	2.40	2.46	2.52	2.58	2.64	2.70	2.76	2.81	2.88	I 2.67	2.93	**Population**	99z

(See notes in the back of the book.)

Libya

672		1970	1971	1972	1973	1974	1975	1976	1977	1978	1979	1980	1981	1982	1983	1984
Exchange Rates																*SDRs per Dinar: End of Period (ac)*
Official Rate	ac	2.8000	2.8000	2.8000	2.8000	2.7589	2.8854	2.9073	2.7807	2.5927	2.5641	2.6484	2.9020	3.0621	3.2263	3.4460
Official Rate	ag	2.8000	3.0400	3.0400	3.3778	3.3778	3.3778	3.3778	3.3778	3.3778	3.3778	3.3778	3.3778	3.3778	3.3778	3.3778
Fund Position																*Millions of SDRs:*
Quota	2f.s	24	24	24	24	24	24	24	24	185	185	298	298	298	298	516
SDRs	1b.s	—	—	—	—	—	—	—	—	—	31	47	104	129	158	133
Reserve Position in the Fund	1c.s	6	6	6	6	6	6	6	6	6	42	148	189	189	189	244
Total Fund Cred.&Loans Outstg.	2tl	—	—	—	—	—	—	—	—	—	—	—	—	—	—	—
International Liquidity																*Millions of US Dollars Unless Otherwise Indicated:*
Total Reserves minus Gold	1l.d	1,505	2,573	2,832	2,024	3,511	2,095	3,106	4,786	4,105	6,344	13,091	9,003	7,059	5,219	3,634
SDRs	1b.d	—	—	—	—	—	—	—	—	—	40	59	121	143	165	130
Reserve Position in the Fund	1c.d	6	7	7	7	7	7	7	7	8	56	189	220	209	198	239
Foreign Exchange	1d.d	1,499	2,566	2,826	2,017	3,504	2,088	3,099	4,779	4,097	6,248	12,842	8,662	6,708	4,856	3,266
Gold (Million Fine Troy Ounces)	1ad	2.437	2.437	2.437	2.437	2.438	2.438	2.438	2.448	2.448	2.464	3.078	3.578	3.578	3.578	3.648
Gold (National Valuation)	1and	88	94	95	107	103	103	103	103	103	104	130	151	151	151	154
Deposit Money Banks: Assets	7a.d	21	25	46	121	131	138	197	258	224	417	1,052	929	894	683	665
Liabilities	7b.d	5	7	19	40	15	82	52	148	156	120	113	256	239	203	146
Monetary Authorities																*Millions of Dinars:*
Foreign Assets	11	567.9	876.8	962.3	629.6	1,244.7	753.0	1,064.2	1,623.6	1,492.4	2,219.2	4,223.2	2,808.1	2,158.0	1,643.0	1,114.2
Claims on Central Government	12a	—	—	—	163.8	249.3	584.2	533.5	353.8	1,106.6	1,129.1	340.3	1,192.0	1,825.2	932.3	1,151.4
Claims on Nonfin.Pub.Enterprises	12c	16.1	20.1	53.1	152.8	368.7	421.6	443.1	501.4	789.7	1,161.4	1,594.8	2,365.0	1,816.7	1,541.4	1,640.7
Claims on Private Sector	12d	.4	.3	.3	.5	.7	.8	1.0	1.4	2.0	2.5	2.8	3.9	4.1	4.3	4.3
Claims on Deposit Money Banks	12e	.8	—	—	—	—	157.6	161.7	156.0	161.1	180.7	180.7	272.7	272.7	292.7	339.2
Reserve Money	14	199.4	314.5	347.4	378.9	590.0	650.1	829.4	1,051.2	1,355.7	1,793.5	2,296.8	2,166.0	2,260.5	1,798.9	1,717.9
of which: Currency Outside DMBs	14a	112.3	120.7	147.4	202.6	262.2	346.0	436.0	585.0	868.5	1,053.7	685.7	791.1	889.9	838.2	767.5
Nonfin.Pub.Enterp.Dep.	14e	52.3	102.5	112.3	133.0	180.6	185.8	210.5	265.9	260.0	488.7	783.1	833.4	748.0	377.6	308.1
Time & Foreign Currency Deposits	15	26.6	31.7	40.5	68.6	151.9	101.2	120.9	142.0	166.9	184.3	227.0	188.2	202.9	239.0	287.2
Restricted Deposits	16b	13.9	13.3	39.8	75.1	170.9	144.8	140.2	144.1	133.0	150.4	221.0	226.7	259.1	269.6	354.8
Foreign Liabilities	16c	.4	.4	.7	1.0	.5	1.5	.9	.6	1.1	2.6	2.9	3.2	7.1	—	—
Central Government Deposits	16d	278.8	480.0	520.8	325.7	376.3	308.3	321.6	312.1	423.4	490.0	847.3	716.9	681.1	653.7	648.4
Capital Accounts	17a	6.7	8.0	8.0	8.0	8.0	8.0	8.0	8.0	8.0	15.5	22.5	127.3	184.2	241.2	254.1
Other Items (Net)	17r	59.4	49.3	38.0	66.2	565.7	680.0	782.3	978.0	1,463.4	2,056.2	2,723.7	3,212.6	2,481.2	1,211.4	987.4
Deposit Money Banks																*Millions of Dinars:*
Reserves	20	27.1	124.5	135.0	97.9	148.7	157.1	186.5	225.9	234.0	291.7	875.6	563.2	597.6	595.0	632.3
Foreign Assets	21	7.5	8.1	15.1	35.8	38.7	40.7	58.3	76.5	66.2	123.5	311.4	275.1	264.6	202.2	196.9
Claims on Central Government	22a	—	—	—	—	3.0	10.4	95.7	219.2	183.1	455.2	828.5	535.5	325.1	561.5	1,097.5
Claims on Nonfin. Pub. Enterprises	22c	10.2	11.5	15.3	59.5	40.4	46.1	39.0	56.5	58.6	57.2	59.7	139.1	182.5	76.1	117.7
Claims on Private Sector	22d	85.3	96.0	132.7	216.8	411.9	599.2	705.0	800.4	880.1	1,004.9	1,087.1	2,048.9	1,395.4	2,143.6	2,053.3
Claims on Other Banking Insts	22f	....	....	....	....	....	....	....	....	....	....	....	....	....	....	....
Claims on Nonbank Financial Insts	22g	....	....	....	....	....	....	....	....	....	....	....	....	....	....	....
Demand Deposits	24	76.5	141.3	153.3	178.4	311.1	335.7	492.9	592.9	559.3	705.0	1,430.1	1,887.6	1,594.4	1,668.6	1,635.7
Time & Foreign Currency Deposits	25	28.7	34.7	64.6	90.2	146.9	134.9	173.0	212.9	211.4	375.6	428.9	413.9	354.4	475.6	606.8
Restricted Deposits	26b	10.5	18.8	30.7	63.0	110.8	112.0	121.5	185.3	174.6	242.3	328.8	305.9	256.8	258.2	215.2
Foreign Liabilities	26c	1.3	2.2	5.5	8.7	4.3	24.3	15.5	43.7	46.3	35.5	33.3	75.7	70.8	60.0	43.2
Central Government Deposits	26d	—	12.1	8.2	30.0	19.5	27.8	29.5	45.0	41.5	78.2	195.1	198.7	286.5	160.4	387.6
Credit from Monetary Authorities	26g	1.2	—	—	—	.9	157.6	161.7	156.0	161.1	181.4	180.7	272.7	272.7	293.4	339.2
Capital Accounts	27a	9.9	10.3	20.2	24.2	31.1	43.6	47.9	65.3	90.5	117.7	148.6	164.3	220.5	237.1	188.9
Other Items (Net)	27r	.8	20.7	13.1	12.4	12.1	22.2	41.7	79.6	141.8	210.6	417.2	243.0	-287.6	432.9	684.3
Monetary Survey																*Millions of Dinars:*
Foreign Assets (Net)	31n	573.8	882.4	971.1	655.6	1,278.6	768.0	1,106.1	1,655.8	1,511.2	2,304.6	4,498.4	3,004.3	2,344.8	1,785.2	1,267.8
Domestic Credit	32	-166.8	-364.1	-327.6	237.7	678.2	1,326.2	1,466.3	1,575.7	2,555.1	3,242.1	2,870.7	5,368.7	4,581.3	4,445.1	5,028.7
Claims on Central Govt. (Net)	32an	-278.8	-492.0	-529.0	-191.9	-143.5	258.5	278.2	216.0	824.8	1,016.1	126.4	811.9	1,182.7	679.7	1,212.7
Claims on Nonfin.Pub.Enterprises	32c	26.3	31.6	68.4	212.3	409.1	467.7	482.1	558.0	848.3	1,218.6	1,654.5	2,504.1	1,999.2	1,617.5	1,758.5
Claims on Private Sector	32d	85.7	96.3	133.0	217.3	412.6	600.0	706.0	801.8	882.0	1,007.4	1,089.9	2,052.7	1,399.4	2,147.9	2,057.5
Claims on Other Banking Insts	32f	....	....	....	....	....	....	....	....	....	....	....	....	....	....	....
Claims on Nonbank Fin. Insts	32g	....	....	....	....	....	....	....	....	....	....	....	....	....	....	....
Money	34	241.1	364.5	413.0	514.0	753.8	867.6	1,139.4	1,443.8	1,687.8	2,247.3	2,898.9	3,512.2	3,232.3	2,884.5	2,711.3
Quasi-Money	35	55.3	66.4	105.1	158.8	298.8	236.1	293.9	354.9	378.3	559.8	655.9	602.1	557.3	714.6	894.0
Restricted Deposits	36b	24.4	32.0	70.5	138.1	281.7	256.8	261.7	329.5	307.6	392.7	549.8	532.6	515.9	527.8	570.0
Capital Accounts	37a	16.6	18.3	28.2	32.2	39.1	51.6	55.9	73.3	98.5	133.2	171.1	291.5	404.7	478.3	442.9
Other Items (Net)	37r	68.5	37.0	24.1	47.1	577.4	686.6	820.7	1,032.3	1,598.7	2,227.3	3,093.8	3,434.8	2,219.2	1,633.2	1,681.7
Money plus Quasi-Money	35l	55.3	66.4	105.1	158.8	298.8	236.1	293.9	354.9	378.3	559.8	655.9	602.1	557.3	714.6	894.0
Other Banking Institutions																*Millions of Dinars:*
Cash	40	9.77	8.94	6.48	6.45	9.06	16.38	17.02	22.66	20.66	19.97	48.25	25.72	28.69	....	....
Claims on Private Sector	42d	11.38	16.18	22.11	25.26	29.50	30.54	32.24	38.66	40.62	45.17	38.25	46.00	46.09	....	....
Capital Accounts	47a	7.20	8.37	8.37	11.81	12.75	12.76	44.98	45.98	45.98	45.98	45.98	46.07	46.60	....	....
Other Items (Net)	47r	13.95	16.74	20.22	19.88	25.81	34.17	4.28	15.35	15.30	19.16	40.51	25.64	28.19	....	....
Interest Rates																*Percent Per Annum*
Discount Rate *(End of Period)*	60	5.0	5.0	5.0	5.0	5.0	5.0	5.0	5.0	5.0	5.0	5.0	5.0	5.0	5.0	5.0
Money Market Rate	60b	4.0	4.0	4.0	4.0	4.0	4.0	4.0	4.0	4.0	4.0	4.0	4.0	4.0	4.0	4.0
Deposit Rate	60l	4.0	4.0	4.0	4.0	4.0	4.0	4.0	4.0	4.0	4.0	5.1	5.5	5.5	5.5	5.5
Lending Rate	60p	7.0	7.0	7.0	7.0	7.0	7.0	7.0	7.0	7.0	7.0	7.0	7.0	7.0	7.0	7.0
Production																*Index Numbers (1995=100):*
Consumer Prices (1975=100)	64	81.7	79.2	79.0	85.3	91.6	100.0	105.5	112.1	145.0	136.3	....	....	....	....	....
Foodstuffs (1975=100)	64a	118.4	96.6	95.9	87.8	93.9	100.0	113.5	127.3	142.2	180.7	....	....	....	....	....
Crude Petroleum Production	66aa	238.7	198.6	161.5	155.8	109.5	106.5	139.6	148.4	142.3	148.2	129.0	79.8	82.7	77.4	77.4
International Transactions																*Millions of Dinars*
Exports	70	841.8	959.9	966.3	1,196.4	2,445.2	2,023.2	2,828.5	3,378.2	2,929.3	4,759.3	6,486.4	4,609.8	3,908.8	3,616.6	3,300.4
Crude Petroleum	70aa	841.1	956.9	949.2	1,161.7	2,388.3	1,925.3	2,711.2	3,189.7	2,719.5	4,419.2	6,287.3	4,384.3	3,718.0	3,370.7	3,020.8
Imports, c.i.f.	71	198.0	250.4	343.2	539.9	817.8	1,048.7	950.8	1,117.1	1,362.6	1,572.4	2,006.2	2,481.4	2,124.3	1,785.0	1,842.0
Imports, c.i.f., from DOTS	71y	....	....	....	....	....	....	....	....	....	....	....	2,481.4	2,548.4	2,287.1	2,148.6
																1995=100
Volume of Exports	72	....	....	....	....	....	....	....	....	....	....	....	....	76.6	76.1	74.6
Volume of Imports	73	....	....	....	....	....	....	....	....	....	....	....	....	125.8	123.7	132.6
Unit Value of Exports	74	....	....	....	....	....	....	....	....	....	....	....	....	170.5	156.8	145.4
Unit Value of Imports	75	....	....	....	....	....	....	....	....	....	....	....	....	81.6	76.5	72.4
Export Prices																*1985=100:*
Crude Petroleum	76aad	7.8	9.6	10.2	14.5	43.3	38.8	41.0	46.0	45.5	70.0	119.5	132.8	117.8	102.5	100.0

1985	1986	1987	1988	1989	1990	1991	1992	1993	1994	1995	1996	1997	1998	1999	Series	Code
US Dollars per Dinar: End of Period (ag)															**Exchange Rates**	
3.0751	2.6046	2.6046	2.6046	2.6046	2.6046	2.6046	2.4138e	2.2400	1.9048	1.9048	1.9048	1.9048	1.8765	1.5783	Official Rate	ac
3.3778	3.1860e	3.6951e	3.5051e	3.4229e	3.7055e	3.7258e	3.3190e	3.0768	2.7807	2.8314	2.7390	2.5700	2.6421	2.1662	Official Rate	ag
End of Period															**Fund Position**	
516	516	516	516	516	516	516	818	818	818	818	818	818	818	1,124	Quota	2f. s
156	178	198	219	249	287	323	278	303	325	350	374	398	426	373	SDRs	1b. s
244	244	244	244	244	244	244	319	319	319	319	319	319	319	396	Reserve Position in the Fund	1c. s
—	—	—	—	—	—	—	—	—	—	—	—	—	—	—	Total Fund Cred.&Loans Outstg.	2tl
End of Period															**International Liquidity**	
5,904	5,953e	5,838e	4,322e	4,333e	5,839e	5,695e	6,182e	....	....	....	....	....	7,270	6,995	Total Reserves minus Gold	1l. d
172	217	280	294	328	409	461	383	417	474	520	538	538	600	511	SDRs	1b. d
267	298	345	328	320	346	348	439	438	466	474	459	430	449	543	Reserve Position in the Fund	1c. d
5,465	5,438e	5,212e	3,699e	3,685e	5,084e	4,885e	5,361e	....	....	....	....	....	6,221	5,940	Foreign Exchange	1d. d
3.600	3.600	3.600	3.600	3.600	3.600	3.600	3.600	....	....	....	....	....	4.616	4.624	Gold (Million Fine Troy Ounces)	1ad
152	152	152	152	152	152	152	152	....	....	....	....	....	194	194	Gold (National Valuation)	1and
522	458	339	109	160	273	257	435	401	385	459	583	1,183	736	736	Deposit Money Banks: Assets	7a. d
1	171	46	540	906	1,017	1,103	694	171	169	109	207	3,581	2,576	1,836	Liabilities	7b. d
End of Period															**Monetary Authorities**	
1,897.4	1,978.6	1,696.5	1,358.5	1,475.7	1,872.4	1,745.1	2,037.8	1,435.5	1,674.7	2,414.5	2,740.3	3,580.3	3,583.1	3,813.0	Foreign Assets	11
828.2	686.4	650.8	625.1	3,728.8	4,216.0	4,630.9	4,726.5	4,740.0	4,815.0	5,064.6	5,107.4	5,406.7	5,927.2	5,320.1	Claims on Central Government	12a
1,228.4	960.5	926.7	798.1	879.6	1,147.5	1,545.3	1,168.0	1,230.0	1,890.1	2,208.3	2,336.3	1,671.4	1,559.2	1,704.0	Claims on Nonfin.Pub.Enterprises	12c
4.4	4.1	5.0	5.6	6.0	6.2	6.4	6.3	6.3	6.7	6.6	6.4	6.4	6.4	7.1	Claims on Private Sector	12d
319.2	317.4	352.2	352.2	304.7	298.8	298.8	298.8	298.8	283.5	283.5	200.0	144.4	144.4	144.4	Claims on Deposit Money Banks	12e
2,221.6	2,113.2	2,250.7	1,912.9	2,371.1	3,185.9	3,185.5	4,092.3	3,992.6	4,627.4	4,985.7	5,434.8	Ɪ 5,821.2	5,760.4	5,454.5	Reserve Money	14
985.0	1,023.7	1,068.2	899.6	1,131.6	1,461.0	1,620.8	1,982.2	2,216.8	1,989.8	2,035.4	2,419.8	2,534.2	2,698.6	2,657.5	*of which: Currency Outside DMBs*	14a
394.9	182.0	162.1	131.4	298.2	751.6	392.9	312.0	264.3	478.8	603.9	414.5	536.2	176.3	133.7	*Nonfin.Pub.Enterp.Dep.*	14e
297.6	289.1	288.2	333.5	520.8	462.1	337.4	419.8	529.5	615.0	701.4	522.8	Ɪ 62.6	65.3	20.3	Time & Foreign Currency Deposits	15
307.8	284.3	356.9	290.7	210.8	341.4	240.6	175.6	248.6	988.1	344.8	414.2	414.2	332.0	428.1	Restricted Deposits	16b
—	—	—	—	—	—	—	—	—	—	—	—	618.3	476.9	623.8	Foreign Liabilities	16c
641.6	639.0	662.2	665.6	681.2	696.1	887.0	694.1	676.6	678.2	708.3	741.2	Ɪ 3,368.6	3,696.4	4,450.6	Central Government Deposits	16d
270.1	280.6	312.6	332.6	347.6	352.6	352.6	354.3	356.2	360.9	360.9	360.9	Ɪ 1,207.9	1,244.0	1,076.5	Capital Accounts	17a
538.9	340.9	–239.4	–395.6	2,263.4	2,502.5	3,223.5	2,501.3	1,907.1	1,400.5	2,876.4	2,916.6	–683.3	–354.7	–1,065.3	Other Items (Net)	17r
End of Period															**Deposit Money Banks**	
851.9	902.7	1,025.4	846.9	944.7	1,073.1	1,232.2	1,786.3	1,506.6	2,204.6	2,336.6	2,606.1	2,705.8	2,776.1	2,428.4	Reserves	20
154.4	143.7	91.7	31.0	46.7	73.6	69.1	131.1	130.3	138.6	162.2	212.8	460.3	278.6	339.7	Foreign Assets	21
1,406.5	1,546.5	1,319.1	1,597.7	1,437.7	1,436.5	1,436.5	1,444.1	1,444.1	1,451.1	1,451.1	1,436.5	1,387.5	1,387.5	1,387.5	Claims on Central Government	22a
107.1	151.6	417.7	80.9	73.9	72.8	104.6	109.1	127.1	146.2	153.2	328.8	Ɪ 1,440.7	1,491.9	1,866.4	Claims on Nonfin. Pub. Enterprises	22c
1,942.7	1,894.0	2,021.2	2,252.3	2,391.4	2,484.8	2,546.4	2,737.3	3,001.2	3,223.6	3,468.1	2,878.4	3,109.1	3,123.4	3,989.1	Claims on Private Sector	22d
....	....	....	....	....	....	....	....	....	....	....	....	....	....	40.3	Claims on Other Banking Insts	22f
....	....	....	....	....	....	....	....	....	....	....	....	....	....	124.2	Claims on Nonbank Financial Insts	22g
2,112.3	1,835.7	2,208.3	1,980.6	2,091.6	2,239.6	2,279.1	2,693.0	2,728.2	3,417.3	3,612.1	3,489.4	3,556.5	3,753.4	4,162.8	Demand Deposits	24
790.6	956.8	689.2	866.9	645.1	662.7	886.2	1,019.3	1,069.4	1,260.5	1,550.4	1,744.0	1,555.2	1,838.0	Ɪ 1,121.3	Time & Foreign Currency Deposits	25
165.4	239.7	300.3	251.9	258.4	282.7	234.1	236.9	208.7	173.9	271.7	277.3	368.1	331.0	266.5	Restricted Deposits	26b
.3	53.6	12.4	154.1	202.8	202.2	296.0	209.0	55.7	60.8	38.5	75.7	Ɪ 1,393.3	975.0	847.4	Foreign Liabilities	26c
164.8	437.2	187.1	136.6	160.4	193.1	149.8	181.0	175.5	171.5	114.3	340.0	385.0	354.9	Ɪ 1,365.4	Central Government Deposits	26d
319.2	317.4	199.2	352.2	304.7	298.8	319.0	291.5	299.9	283.5	283.5	203.6	147.9	147.9	147.9	Credit from Monetary Authorities	26g
208.8	225.6	249.8	293.0	287.3	311.8	356.1	373.3	391.2	405.2	411.8	491.5	601.3	659.7	728.5	Capital Accounts	27a
704.8	574.2	861.7	842.8	881.8	877.6	868.5	1,204.0	1,280.6	1,391.7	1,289.9	841.1	1,096.3	997.9	1,535.8	Other Items (Net)	27r
End of Period															**Monetary Survey**	
2,051.6	2,068.7	1,775.8	1,235.5	1,319.6	1,743.8	1,518.2	1,960.0	1,510.1	1,752.5	2,538.2	2,877.4	2,029.0	2,409.8	2,681.5	Foreign Assets (Net)	31n
4,710.8	4,166.9	4,491.1	4,557.6	7,675.8	8,474.5	9,233.3	9,316.2	9,696.7	10,683.0	11,529.3	11,012.6	9,268.2	9,444.3	8,622.7	Domestic Credit	32
1,428.2	1,156.7	1,120.5	1,420.7	4,324.9	4,763.2	5,030.6	5,295.5	5,332.1	5,416.4	5,693.1	5,462.7	3,040.6	3,263.4	891.6	Claims on Central Govt. (Net)	32an
1,335.5	1,112.1	1,344.4	879.0	953.5	1,220.3	1,649.9	1,277.1	1,357.1	2,036.3	2,361.5	2,665.1	3,112.1	3,051.1	3,570.4	Claims on Nonfin.Pub.Enterprises	32c
1,947.1	1,898.1	2,026.2	2,257.9	2,397.4	2,491.0	2,552.8	2,743.7	3,007.5	3,230.3	3,474.7	2,884.8	3,115.5	3,129.8	3,996.2	Claims on Private Sector	32d
....	....	....	....	....	....	....	....	....	....	....	....	....	....	40.3	Claims on Other Banking Insts	32f
....	....	....	....	....	....	....	....	....	....	....	....	....	....	124.2	Claims on Nonbank Fin. Insts	32g
3,492.2	3,041.4	3,438.6	3,011.6	3,521.4	4,452.2	4,292.8	4,987.2	5,209.3	5,885.9	6,251.4	6,323.7	6,654.5	6,683.8	7,001.2	Money	34
1,088.2	1,246.0	977.3	1,200.3	1,165.8	1,124.8	1,223.6	1,439.0	1,598.9	1,875.5	2,251.8	2,266.8	1,617.8	1,903.3	1,141.6	Quasi-Money	35
473.2	524.0	657.2	542.6	469.2	624.1	474.8	412.5	457.3	1,162.0	616.5	691.5	782.3	663.0	694.6	Restricted Deposits	36b
478.9	506.2	562.4	625.5	634.9	664.3	708.6	727.6	747.4	766.1	772.7	852.4	1,809.2	1,903.7	1,805.0	Capital Accounts	37a
1,233.4	919.8	464.2	482.2	3,141.8	3,280.3	4,051.8	3,709.9	3,193.7	2,746.3	4,176.1	3,755.7	433.9	700.6	661.7	Other Items (Net)	37r
1,088.2	1,246.0	977.3	1,200.3	1,165.8	1,124.8	1,223.6	1,439.0	1,598.9	1,875.5	2,251.8	2,266.8	2,032.0	1,903.3	1,141.8	Money plus Quasi-Money	35l
End of Period															**Other Banking Institutions**	
....	....	....	....	....	....	....	....	....	....	....	....	....	....	....	Cash	40
....	....	....	....	....	....	....	....	....	....	....	....	....	....	....	Claims on Private Sector	42d
....	....	....	....	....	....	....	....	....	....	....	....	....	....	....	Capital Accounts	47a
....	....	....	....	....	....	....	....	....	....	....	....	....	....	....	Other Items (Net)	47r
Percent Per Annum															**Interest Rates**	
5.0	5.0	5.0	5.0	5.0	5.0	5.0	5.0	5.0	....	....	....	....	3.0	5.0	Discount Rate *(End of Period)*	60
4.0	4.0	4.0	4.0	4.0	4.0	4.0	4.0	4.0	....	....	....	....	4.0	4.0	Money Market Rate	60b
5.5	5.5	5.5	5.5	5.5	5.5	5.5	5.5	5.5	....	....	....	....	....	3.2	Deposit Rate	60l
7.0	7.0	7.0	7.0	7.0	7.0	7.0	7.0	7.0	....	....	....	....	....	7.0	Lending Rate	60p
Period Averages															**Production**	
....	....	....	....	....	....	....	....	....	....	....	....	....	....	....	Consumer Prices (1975=100)	64
....	....	....	....	....	....	....	....	....	....	....	....	....	....	....	Foodstuffs (1975=100)	64a
76.0	74.4	70.0	73.1	78.9	97.1	107.1	107.0	99.1	99.2	100.0	101.1	103.7	99.1	94.7	Crude Petroleum Production	66aa
Millions of Dinars															**International Transactions**	
3,645.6	2,432.0	2,372.0	1,907.0	2,407.0	3,745.0	3,154.0	....	....	2,873.0	3,107.2	3,581.6	3,684.2	2,620.6	....	Exports	70
3,184.3	1,572.0	....	....	....	....	....	....	....	....	....	....	....	....	....	Crude Petroleum	70aa
1,214.0	1,316.0	1,278.0	1,677.0	1,475.0	1,511.0	1,505.0	....	....	1,780.0	1,866.8	2,124.1	2,336.2	2,151.1	....	Imports, c.i.f.	71
1,658.9	1,121.8	1,279.7	1,689.0	1,316.1	1,603.6	1,498.9	1,470.1	1,638.9	1,337.8	1,711.1	1,854.3	2,053.1	2,203.8	2,248.0	Imports, c.i.f., from DOTS	71y
1995=100																
Ɪ 83.1	83.4	82.0	77.5	85.6	104.6	110.8	100.0	95.6	100.7	100.0	94.6	99.9	....	....	Volume of Exports	72
Ɪ 96.2	96.7	87.9	126.9	109.3	109.4	114.5	97.0	110.3	95.3	100.0	108.6	122.6	....	....	Volume of Imports	73
Ɪ 144.4	94.8	91.3	75.4	87.0	110.9	89.8	90.4	79.2	94.8	100.0	124.5	109.9	....	....	Unit Value of Exports	74
Ɪ 70.9	82.7	80.5	78.6	80.5	81.1	74.1	83.1	84.4	89.7	100.0	101.3	102.7	....	....	Unit Value of Imports	75
Index of Prices in US Dollars															Export Prices	
100.0	....	....	....	....	....	....	....	....	....	....	....	....	....	....	Crude Petroleum	76aa d

Libya

		1970	1971	1972	1973	1974	1975	1976	1977	1978	1979	1980	1981	1982	1983	1984
Balance of Payments																*Millions of US Dollars:*
Current Account, n.i.e.	78al d	....	....	....	....	....	....	....	2,159	738	3,771	8,214	–3,963	–1,560	–1,643	–1,456
Goods: Exports f.o.b.	78aa d	....	....	....	....	....	....	....	10,406	9,900	15,981	21,919	14,731	13,701	12,348	11,028
Goods: Imports f.o.b.	78ab d	....	....	....	....	....	....	....	–4,929	–5,764	–8,647	–10,368	–14,563	–10,976	–8,978	–8,464
Trade Balance	78ac d	....	....	....	....	....	....	....	5,476	4,136	7,334	11,551	168	2,725	3,370	2,564
Services: Credit	78ad d	....	....	....	....	....	....	....	136	153	143	164	163	163	161	170
Services: Debit	78ae d	....	....	....	....	....	....	....	–1,301	–1,448	–1,953	–2,303	–2,757	–2,265	–2,315	–2,202
Balance on Goods & Services	78af d	....	....	....	....	....	....	....	4,311	2,841	5,523	9,413	–2,427	624	1,216	532
Income: Credit	78ag d	....	....	....	....	....	....	....	244	317	424	1,282	1,627	868	676	550
Income: Debit	78ah d	....	....	....	....	....	....	....	–1,459	–1,370	–1,273	–1,347	–1,517	–1,376	–1,433	–1,218
Balance on Gds, Serv. & Inc.	78ai d	....	....	....	....	....	....	....	3,096	1,788	4,673	9,348	–2,317	115	459	–135
Current Transfers, n.i.e.: Credit	78aj d	....	....	....	....	....	....	....	15	17	18	20	26	32	29	14
Current Transfers: Debit	78ak d	....	....	....	....	....	....	....	–952	–1,067	–920	–1,154	–1,672	–1,706	–2,131	–1,335
Capital Account, n.i.e.	78bc d	....	....	....	....	....	....	....	—	—	—	—	—	—	—	—
Capital Account, n.i.e.: Credit	78ba d	....	....	....	....	....	....	....	—	—	—	—	—	—	—	—
Capital Account: Debit	78bb d	....	....	....	....	....	....	....	—	—	—	—	—	—	—	—
Financial Account, n.i.e.	78bj d	....	....	....	....	....	....	....	–518	–1,406	–1,298	–1,703	–511	–625	93	831
Direct Investment Abroad	78bd d								–60	–28	–21	–47	–25	–19	—	—
Dir. Invest. in Rep. Econ., n.i.e.	78be d								–451	–692	–588	–1,089	–744	–392	–327	–17
Portfolio Investment Assets	78bf d								–220	–146	–23	–113	–430	–255	–107	47
Equity Securities	78bk d								–220	–45	–23	–113	–421	–243	–98	47
Debt Securities	78bl d								—	–101	—	—	–9	–12	–8	—
Portfolio Investment Liab., n.i.e.	78bg d								—	—	—	—	—	—	—	—
Equity Securities	78bm d								—	—	—	—	—	—	—	—
Debt Securities	78bn d								—	—	—	—	—	—	—	—
Financial Derivatives Assets	78bw d								....	....						.....
Financial Derivatives Liabilities	78bx d								....	....						.....
Other Investment Assets	78bh d	....	....	....	....	....	....	....	–232	–716	–839	–1,275	52	–578	38	324
Monetary Authorities	78bo d								–7	–7	—	—	—	—	–49	100
General Government	78bp d								–326	–218	–298	–123	–514	372	–83	50
Banks	78bq d								–53	–3	–235	–623	153	49	207	21
Other Sectors	78br d								155	–488	–306	–530	412	–999	–37	153
Other Investment Liab., n.i.e.	78bi d								446	177	173	821	637	619	488	477
Monetary Authorities	78bs d								7	7	75	22	133	86	–49	100
General Government	78bt d								—	–78	—	—	—	—	—	—
Banks	78bu d								113	–4	8	–56	144	–22	315	–57
Other Sectors	78bv d								326	253	90	855	361	554	223	434
Net Errors and Omissions	78ca d	....	....	....	....	....	....	....	33	47	–253	–104	329	172	–236	–1,096
Overall Balance	78cb d	....	....	....	....	....	....	....	1,674	–621	2,220	6,407	–4,145	–2,013	–1,786	–1,721
Reserves and Related Items	79da d	....	....	....	....	....	....	....	–1,674	621	–2,220	–6,407	4,145	2,013	1,786	1,721
Reserve Assets	79db d	....	....	....	....	....	....	....	–1,674	621	–2,220	–6,407	4,145	2,013	1,786	1,721
Use of Fund Credit and Loans	79dc d	....	....	....	....	....	....	....	–1,674	621	–2,220	–6,407	4,145	2,013	1,786	1,721
Exceptional Financing																

		1970	1971	1972	1973	1974	1975	1976	1977	1978	1979	1980	1981	1982	1983	1984
National Accounts																*Millions of Dinars*
Exports of Goods & Services	90c	870	975	998	1,240	2,490	2,053	2,881	3,431	2,978	4,801	6,538	4,410	4,105	3,703	3,351
Government Consumption	91f	260	318	359	465	865	1,044	1,185	1,400	1,692	2,007	2,442	2,552	2,456	2,381	3,159
Gross Fixed Capital Formation	93e	243	288	437	636	979	1,055	1,226	1,383	1,532	1,855	2,757	2,660	2,772	2,524	2,128
Increase/Decrease(-) in Stocks	93i	4	13	14	28	50	100	–50	58	20	110	101	235	53	76	75
Private Consumption	96f	464	469	543	703	927	1,194	1,337	1,482	1,665	1,895	2,795	4,673	3,908	3,591	3,038
Imports of Goods & Services	98c	–403	–436	–552	–826	–1,428	–1,666	–1,671	–1,948	–2,199	–2,822	–3,752	–5,128	–3,920	–3,343	–3,386
Gross Domestic Product (GDP)	99b	1,426	1,627	1,798	2,246	3,883	3,780	4,907	5,763	5,688	7,846	10,882	9,401	9,373	8,932	8,364
Net Factor Inc/Pmts(-) Abroad	98.n	–216	–211	–275	–318	–439	–400	–517	–517	–505	....	....	....	....	....	....
Gross National Income (GNI)	99a	1,210	1,416	1,524	1,928	3,444	3,380	4,390	5,304	5,183	....	....	....	....	....	....
Net National Income	99e	1,101	1,316	1,412	1,816	3,296	3,214	4,198	5,096	4,946	7,030	9,908	8,570	7,790	....	....
GDP Volume 1964 prices	99b.p	1,099	1,041	1,136	1,158	1,415	1,472	....	....	....	....	....	....	....	....	....
GDP Volume 1975 Prices	99b.p	....	....	....	....	....	3,674	4,506	4,906	5,032	5,448	5,481	....	....		
GDP Volume (1980=100)	99bv p	50.0	47.4	51.7	52.7	64.4	67.0	82.2	89.5	91.8	99.4	100.0				
GDP Deflator (1980=100)	99bi p	26.2	31.5	31.9	39.1	55.4	51.8	54.9	59.2	56.9	72.5	100.0	....	....	....	....
																Millions:
Population	99z	1.98	2.07	2.15	2.24	2.33	2.43	2.56	2.67	2.79	2.91	2.76	2.87	2.99	3.11	3.24

Balance of Payments

Minus Sign Indicates Debit

1985	1986	1987	1988	1989	1990	1991	1992	1993	1994	1995	1996	1997	1998	1999		
1,906	−166	−1,043	−1,826	−1,026	2,201	−219	1,392	−1,362	29	1,998	1,477	1,875	−391	1,476	Current Account, n.i.e.	78al d
10,353	6,186	5,821	5,653	7,274	11,352	10,702	10,078	8,522	8,365	9,038	9,578	9,876	6,328	7,010	Goods: Exports f.o.b.	78aa d
−5,754	−4,718	−5,384	−5,762	−6,509	−7,575	−8,038	−7,461	−8,409	−7,339	−6,257	−7,059	−7,160	−5,857	−4,218	Goods: Imports f.o.b.	78ab d
4,599	1,468	437	−109	765	3,777	2,664	2,617	113	1,026	2,781	2,519	2,716	471	2,792	*Trade Balance*	78ac d
63	87	114	128	117	117	99	99	55	40	37	31	33	47	30	Services: Credit	78ad d
−1,775	−1,114	−1,436	−1,637	−1,481	−1,385	−2,696	−1,192	−1,171	−780	−716	−951	−920	−1,016	−1,051	Services: Debit	78ae d
2,887	442	−885	−1,617	−598	2,508	67	1,524	−1,003	286	2,102	1,599	1,829	−498	1,771	*Balance on Goods & Services*	78af d
463	582	730	762	447	666	651	767	569	487	526	573	640	633	215	Income: Credit	78ag d
−540	−629	−363	−437	−388	−493	−502	−447	−600	−438	−365	−356	−354	−259	−116	Income: Debit	78ah d
2,811	395	−518	−1,292	−539	2,682	215	1,844	−1,034	335	2,263	1,816	2,115	−124	1,870	*Balance on Gds, Serv. & Inc.*	78ai d
9	7	5	7	6	7	8	7	8	5	5	3	4	5	....	Current Transfers, n.i.e.: Credit	78aj d
−913	−567	−531	−541	−493	−488	−442	−460	−336	−311	−270	−342	−244	−272	−394	Current Transfers: Debit	78ak d
—	—	—	—	—	—	—	—	—	—	....	....	....	....	....	Capital Account, n.i.e.	78bc d
—	—	—	—	—	—	—	—	—	—	....	....	....	....	....	Capital Account, n.i.e.: Credit	78ba d
—	—	—	—	—	—	—	—	—	—	....	....	....	....	....	Capital Account: Debit	78bb d
784	−458	−127	163	1,188	−1,006	131	329	−201	160	−250	224	−884	−555	−214	Financial Account, n.i.e.	78bj d
—	—	−114	−56	−35	−105	−174	149	478	−28	−83	−63	−282	−304	2	Direct Investment Abroad	78bd d
119	−188	−98	98	125	159	92	98	58	−79	−107	−135	−82	−152	....	Dir. Invest. in Rep. Econ., n.i.e.	78be d
55	−72	−2,972	−222	−52	−115	297	−54	−62	−137	−128	—	−774	−212	....	Portfolio Investment Assets	78bf d
55	−72	−2,972	−222	−52	−115	297	−54	−62	−137	−128	—	−774	−212	....	Equity Securities	78bk d
—	—	—	—	—	—	—	—	—	—	—	—	—	—	....	Debt Securities	78bl d
....	....	....	....	....	....	....	....	....	....	....	....	....	....	....	Portfolio Investment Liab., n.i.e.	78bg d
....	....	....	....	....	....	....	....	....	....	....	....	....	....	....	Equity Securities	78bm d
....	....	....	....	....	....	....	....	....	....	....	....	....	....	....	Debt Securities	78bn d
....	....	....	....	....	....	....	....	....	....	....	....	....	....	....	Financial Derivatives Assets	78bw d
....	....	....	....	....	....	....	....	....	....	....	....	....	....	....	Financial Derivatives Liabilities	78bx d
505	−404	3,494	−670	320	−715	342	185	−485	−1,904	−1,646	−1,734	−1,040	−164	−100	Other Investment Assets	78bh d
−112	−6	....	....	....	—	16	2	241	−10	46	−33	46	−7	−100	Monetary Authorities	78bo d
29	12	91	−150	−109	−230	305	−35	−729	−1,876	−1,657	−1,540	−678	−591	....	General Government	78bp d
150	42	171	−26	186	−90	21	218	3	−18	−35	−161	−408	434	....	Banks	78bq d
438	−453	3,233	−494	242	−395	....	....	....	....	....	....	....	....	....	Other Sectors	78br d
105	206	−436	1,013	830	−230	−426	−49	−190	2,308	1,714	2,156	1,294	277	−116	Other Investment Liab., n.i.e.	78bi d
−112	−6	−137	196	598	−130	−159	−31	96	184	207	443	−219	−6	—	Monetary Authorities	78bs d
—	—	—	—	—	—	37	81	212	2,109	1,571	1,681	1,576	263	−116	General Government	78bt d
−145	180	−119	486	214	21	−304	−99	−498	15	−64	32	−63	20	....	Banks	78bu d
362	32	−181	331	18	−121	....	....	....	....	....	....	....	....	....	Other Sectors	78bv d
−328	847	172	271	130	−37	343	38	−148	106	299	−234	878	432	−575	Net Errors and Omissions	78ca d
2,362	224	−999	−1,392	292	1,158	255	1,759	−1,712	295	2,047	1,467	1,869	−513	687	*Overall Balance*	78cb d
−2,362	−224	999	1,392	−292	−1,158	−255	−1,759	1,712	−295	−2,047	−1,467	−1,869	513	−687	Reserves and Related Items	79da d
−2,362	−224	999	1,392	−292	−1,158	−255	−1,759	1,712	−295	−2,047	−1,467	−1,869	513	−687	Reserve Assets	79db d
—	—	—	—	—	—	—	—	—	—	—	—	—	—	—	Use of Fund Credit and Loans	79dc d
															Exceptional Financing	

National Accounts

Millions of Dinars

1985	1986	1987	1988	1989	1990	1991	1992	1993	1994	1995	1996	1997	1998	1999		
3,673	2,459	1,697	1,652	2,213	3,248	3,038	2,919	2,636	2,695	3,116	3,490	3,790	....	....	Exports of Goods & Services	90c
2,229	2,055	1,616	2,196	2,520	1,997	2,376	2,755	2,124	2,246	2,370	2,888	3,593	....	....	Government Consumption	91f
1,558	1,376	950	1,050	1,157	1,135	1,034	1,008	1,211	1,165	1,124	1,588	1,552	....	....	Gross Fixed Capital Formation	93e
30	129	126	218	128	388	143	152	15	6	54	248	87	....	....	Increase/Decrease(-) in Stocks	93i
3,224	3,009	3,873	3,789	3,913	3,874	5,059	4,865	6,105	5,936	5,962	6,640	7,352	....	....	Private Consumption	96f
−2,488	−1,896	−2,009	−2,114	−2,394	−2,547	−2,763	−2,430	−2,944	−2,603	−2,394	−2,910	−3,091	....	....	Imports of Goods & Services	98c
8,227	7,132	6,253	6,791	7,537	8,095	8,887	9,269	9,148	9,444	10,232	11,945	13,284	....	....	Gross Domestic Product (GDP)	99b
....	....	−133	−49	−143	−77	−73	−20	−109	−83	−37	−40	−21	....	....	Net Factor Inc/Pmts(-) Abroad	98.n
....	....	....	....	....	....	....	....	....	....	....	....	....	....	....	Gross National Income (GNI)	99a
....	....	....	....	....	....	....	....	....	....	....	....	....	....	....	Net National Income	99e
....	....	....	....	....	....	....	....	....	....	....	....	....	....	....	GDP Volume 1964 prices	99b.p
....	....	....	....	....	....	....	....	....	....	....	....	....	....	....	GDP Volume 1975 Prices	99b.p
....	....	....	....	....	....	....	....	....	....	....	....	....	....	....	GDP Volume (1980=100)	99bv p
....	....	....	....	....	....	....	....	....	....	....	....	....	....	....	GDP Deflator (1980=100)	99bi p

Midyear Estimates

1985	1986	1987	1988	1989	1990	1991	1992	1993	1994	1995	1996	1997	1998	1999		
3.37	3.52	3.67	3.82	3.98	4.15	4.33	4.51	4.70	4.90	‡5.41	5.59	5.78	‡5.34	5.47	Population	99z

(See notes in the back of the book.)

Lithuania

946		1970	1971	1972	1973	1974	1975	1976	1977	1978	1979	1980	1981	1982	1983	1984
Exchange Rates																*Litai per SDR:*
Official Rate	aa	....	....	....	....	....	....	....	....	....	....	....	....	....	....	....
																Litai per US Dollar:
Official Rate	ae	....	....	....	....	....	....	....	....	....	....	....	....	....	....	....
Official Rate	rf	....	....	....	....	....	....	....	....	....	....	....	....	....	....	....
Fund Position																*Millions of SDRs:*
Quota	2f. *s*	....	....	....	....	....	....	....	....	....	....	....	....	....	....	....
SDRs	1b. *s*	....	....	....	....	....	....	....	....	....	....	....	....	....	....	....
Reserve Position in the Fund	1c. *s*	....	....	....	....	....	....	....	....	....	....	....	....	....	....	....
Total Fund Cred.&Loans Outstg.	2tl	....	....	....	....	....	....	....	....	....	....	....	....	....	....	....
International Liquidity																*Millions of US Dollars Unless Otherwise Indicated:*
Total Reserves minus Gold	1l. *d*	....	....	....	....	....	....	....	....	....	....	....	....	....	....	....
SDRs	1b. *d*	....	....	....	....	....	....	....	....	....	....	....	....	....	....	....
Reserve Position in the Fund	1c. *d*	....	....	....	....	....	....	....	....	....	....	....	....	....	....	....
Foreign Exchange	1d. *d*	....	....	....	....	....	....	....	....	....	....	....	....	....	....	....
Gold (Million Fine Troy Ounces)	1ad	....	....	....	....	....	....	....	....	....	....	....	....	....	....	....
Gold (National Valuation)	1an *d*	....	....	....	....	....	....	....	....	....	....	....	....	....	....	....
Monetary Authorities: Other Liab.	4.. *d*	....	....	....	....	....	....	....	....	....	....	....	....	....	....	....
Banking Institutions: Assets	7a. *d*	....	....	....	....	....	....	....	....	....	....	....	....	....	....	....
Liabilities	7b. *d*	....	....	....	....	....	....	....	....	....	....	....	....	....	....	....
Monetary Authorities																*Millions of Litai:*
Foreign Assets	11	....	....	....	....	....	....	....	....	....	....	....	....	....	....	....
Claims on Central Government	12a	....	....	....	....	....	....	....	....	....	....	....	....	....	....	....
Claims on Private Sector	12d	....	....	....	....	....	....	....	....	....	....	....	....	....	....	....
Claims on Banking Institutions	12e	....	....	....	....	....	....	....	....	....	....	....	....	....	....	....
Claims on Nonbank Financial Insts.	12g	....	....	....	....	....	....	....	....	....	....	....	....	....	....	....
Reserve Money	14	....	....	....	....	....	....	....	....	....	....	....	....	....	....	....
of which: Currency Outside Banks	14a	....	....	....	....	....	....	....	....	....	....	....	....	....	....	....
Foreign Currency Deposits	15	....	....	....	....	....	....	....	....	....	....	....	....	....	....	....
Foreign Liabilities	16c	....	....	....	....	....	....	....	....	....	....	....	....	....	....	....
Central Government Deposits	16d	....	....	....	....	....	....	....	....	....	....	....	....	....	....	....
Counterpart Funds	16e	....	....	....	....	....	....	....	....	....	....	....	....	....	....	....
Central Government Lending Funds	16f	....	....	....	....	....	....	....	....	....	....	....	....	....	....	....
Capital Accounts	17a	....	....	....	....	....	....	....	....	....	....	....	....	....	....	....
Other Items (Net)	17r	....	....	....	....	....	....	....	....	....	....	....	....	....	....	....
Banking Institutions																*Millions of Litai:*
Reserves	20	....	....	....	....	....	....	....	....	....	....	....	....	....	....	....
Foreign Assets	21	....	....	....	....	....	....	....	....	....	....	....	....	....	....	....
Claims on Central Government	22a	....	....	....	....	....	....	....	....	....	....	....	....	....	....	....
Claims on State and Local Govts.	22b	....	....	....	....	....	....	....	....	....	....	....	....	....	....	....
Claims on Nonfin.Pub.Enterprises	22c	....	....	....	....	....	....	....	....	....	....	....	....	....	....	....
Claims on Private Sector	22d	....	....	....	....	....	....	....	....	....	....	....	....	....	....	....
Claims on Nonbank Financial Insts.	22g	....	....	....	....	....	....	....	....	....	....	....	....	....	....	....
Demand Deposits	24	....	....	....	....	....	....	....	....	....	....	....	....	....	....	....
Time, Savings,& Fgn.Currency Dep.	25	....	....	....	....	....	....	....	....	....	....	....	....	....	....	....
Foreign Liabilities	26c	....	....	....	....	....	....	....	....	....	....	....	....	....	....	....
Central Government Deposits	26d	....	....	....	....	....	....	....	....	....	....	....	....	....	....	....
Counterpart Funds	26e	....	....	....	....	....	....	....	....	....	....	....	....	....	....	....
Central Government Lending Funds	26f	....	....	....	....	....	....	....	....	....	....	....	....	....	....	....
Credit from Monetary Authorities	26g	....	....	....	....	....	....	....	....	....	....	....	....	....	....	....
Capital Accounts	27a	....	....	....	....	....	....	....	....	....	....	....	....	....	....	....
Other Items (Net)	27r	....	....	....	....	....	....	....	....	....	....	....	....	....	....	....
Banking Survey																*Millions of Litai:*
Foreign Assets (Net)	31n	....	....	....	....	....	....	....	....	....	....	....	....	....	....	....
Domestic Credit	32	....	....	....	....	....	....	....	....	....	....	....	....	....	....	....
Claims on Central Govt. (Net)	32an	....	....	....	....	....	....	....	....	....	....	....	....	....	....	....
Claims on State and Local Govts.	32b	....	....	....	....	....	....	....	....	....	....	....	....	....	....	....
Claims on Nonfin.Pub.Enterprises	32c	....	....	....	....	....	....	....	....	....	....	....	....	....	....	....
Claims on Private Sector	32d	....	....	....	....	....	....	....	....	....	....	....	....	....	....	....
Claims on Nonbank Fin. Insts.	32g	....	....	....	....	....	....	....	....	....	....	....	....	....	....	....
Money	34	....	....	....	....	....	....	....	....	....	....	....	....	....	....	....
Quasi-Money	35	....	....	....	....	....	....	....	....	....	....	....	....	....	....	....
of which: Fgn. Currency Deposits	35b	....	....	....	....	....	....	....	....	....	....	....	....	....	....	....
Counterpart Funds	36e	....	....	....	....	....	....	....	....	....	....	....	....	....	....	....
Central Government Lending Funds	36f	....	....	....	....	....	....	....	....	....	....	....	....	....	....	....
Capital Accounts	37a	....	....	....	....	....	....	....	....	....	....	....	....	....	....	....
Other Items (Net)	37r	....	....	....	....	....	....	....	....	....	....	....	....	....	....	....
Money plus Quasi-Money	35l	....	....	....	....	....	....	....	....	....	....	....	....	....	....	....
Interest Rates																*Percent Per Annum*
Money Market Rate	60b	....	....	....	....	....	....	....	....	....	....	....	....	....	....	....
Treasury Bill Rate	60c	....	....	....	....	....	....	....	....	....	....	....	....	....	....	....
Deposit Rate	60l	....	....	....	....	....	....	....	....	....	....	....	....	....	....	....
Lending Rate	60p	....	....	....	....	....	....	....	....	....	....	....	....	....	....	....
Prices, Production, Labor																*Index Numbers (1995=100):*
Producer Prices	63	....	....	....	....	....	....	....	....	....	....	....	....	....	....	....
Consumer Prices	64	....	....	....	....	....	....	....	....	....	....	....	....	....	....	....
Wages: Average Earnings	65	....	....	....	....	....	....	....	....	....	....	....	....	....	....	....
Manufacturing Production	66	....	....	....	....	....	....	....	....	....	....	....	....	....	....	....
Manufacturing Employment	67	....	....	....	....	....	....	....	....	....	....	....	....	....	....	....
																Number in Thousands:
Labor Force	67d	....	....	....	....	....	....	....	....	....	....	....	....	....	....	....
Employment	67e	....	....	....	....	....	....	....	....	....	....	....	....	....	....	....
Unemployment	67c	....	....	....	....	....	....	....	....	....	....	....	....	....	....	....
Unemployment Rate (%)	67r	....	....	....	....	....	....	....	....	....	....	....	....	....	....	....
International Transactions																*Millions of Litai*
Exports	70	....	....	....	....	....	....	....	....	....	....	....	....	....	....	....
Imports, c.i.f.	71	....	....	....	....	....	....	....	....	....	....	....	....	....	....	....

1985	1986	1987	1988	1989	1990	1991	1992	1993	1994	1995	1996	1997	1998	1999		
End of Period															**Exchange Rates**	
....	....	....	....	....	....	....	5.211	5.357	5.839	5.946	5.752	5.397	5.632	5.490	Official Rate	aa
End of Period (ae) Period Average (rf)																
....	....	....	....	....	....	....	3.790	3.900	4.000	4.000	4.000	4.000	4.000	4.000	Official Rate	ae
....	....	....	....	....	....	....	1.773	4.344	3.978	4.000	4.000	4.000	4.000	4.000	Official Rate	rf
End of Period															**Fund Position**	
....	....	....	....	....	....	....	103.50	103.50	103.50	103.50	103.50	103.50	103.50	144.20	Quota	2f. s
....	....	....	....	....	....	....	.94	54.71	10.38	12.22	7.09	7.95	11.50	3.19	SDRs	1b. s
....	....	....	....	....	....	....	.01	.01	.01	.01	.01	.01	.02	.02	Reserve Position in the Fund	1c. s
....	....	....	....	....	....	....	17.25	87.98	134.55	175.95	190.11	200.46	179.83	167.76	Total Fund Cred.&Loans Outstg.	2tl
End of Period															**International Liquidity**	
....	....	....	....	....	....	....	45.34	350.32	525.48	757.05	772.25	1,009.95	1,409.13	1,195.01	Total Reserves minus Gold	1l. d
....	....	....	....	....	....	....	1.29	75.14	15.15	18.16	10.20	10.73	16.19	4.38	SDRs	1b. d
....	....	....	....	....	....	....	.01	.01	.01	.01	.01	.01	.02	.02	Reserve Position in the Fund	1c. d
....	....	....	....	....	....	....	44.03	275.17	510.33	738.88	762.04	999.21	1,392.92	1,190.61	Foreign Exchange	1d. d
....	....	....	....	....	....	....	.1859	.1859	.1858	.1860	.1863	.1864	.1861	.1863	Gold (Million Fine Troy Ounces)	1ad
....	....	....	....	....	....	....	61.90	61.90	61.86	61.95	62.04	52.74	50.87	47.10	Gold (National Valuation)	1an d
....	....	....	....	....	....	....	....	28.05	26.38	.28	1.33	.35	.33	.25	Monetary Authorities: Other Liab.	4.. d
....	....	....	....	....	....	....	....	77.77	96.68	123.35	293.60	370.63	302.15	423.30	Banking Institutions: Assets	7a. d
....	....	....	....	....	....	....	....	9.54	82.70	88.45	195.83	292.48	438.15	522.70	Liabilities	7b. d
End of Period															**Monetary Authorities**	
....	....	....	....	....	....	....	....	1,904.6	2,618.1	3,284.7	3,345.3	4,258.5	5,847.8	4,976.2	Foreign Assets	11
....	....	....	....	....	....	....	....	—	19.2	—	—	—	—	6.8	Claims on Central Government	12a
....	....	....	....	....	....	....	....	1.4	5.9	12.1	9.9	7.6	6.9	6.1	Claims on Private Sector	12d
....	....	....	....	....	....	....	....	292.0	157.0	168.1	142.0	70.3	52.3	30.1	Claims on Banking Institutions	12e
....	....	....	....	....	....	....	....	—	—	.3	3.1	19.4	6.9	20.0	Claims on Nonbank Financial Insts.	12g
....	....	....	....	....	....	....	....	1,256.8	1,812.5	2,446.3	2,499.3	3,308.7	4,260.5	4,088.3	Reserve Money	14
....	....	....	....	....	....	....	....	791.3	1,334.3	1,907.0	1,899.3	2,535.5	2,800.5	2,738.7	of which: Currency Outside Banks	14a
....	....	....	....	....	....	....	....	—	1.9	43.8	19.8	8.2	6.5	1.5	Foreign Currency Deposits	15
....	....	....	....	....	....	....	....	580.7	891.2	1,047.3	1,098.8	1,083.3	1,014.1	922.0	Foreign Liabilities	16c
....	....	....	....	....	....	....	....	93.1	45.1	111.1	66.0	268.7	904.4	302.1	Central Government Deposits	16d
....	....	....	....	....	....	....	....	—	14.7	37.5	41.9	38.1	40.8	30.8	Counterpart Funds	16e
....	....	....	....	....	....	....	....	—	.6	.7	—	.6	1.5	—	Central Government Lending Funds	16f
....	....	....	....	....	....	....	....	1,029.6	54.8	−77.8	−48.4	−247.3	−111.8	−90.4	Capital Accounts	17a
....	....	....	....	....	....	....	....	−762.2	−39.8	−124.5	−177.1	−104.4	−202.1	−215.1	Other Items (Net)	17r
End of Period															**Banking Institutions**	
....	....	....	....	....	....	....	....	469.0	464.1	522.7	583.6	742.1	1,447.5	1,342.3	Reserves	20
....	....	....	....	....	....	....	....	303.3	386.7	493.4	1,174.4	1,482.5	1,208.6	1,693.2	Foreign Assets	21
....	....	....	....	....	....	....	....	—	240.8	505.2	860.7	1,850.0	1,886.3	1,506.0	Claims on Central Government	22a
....	....	....	....	....	....	....	....	—	2.0	7.7	37.1	51.9	123.8	212.3	Claims on State and Local Govts.	22b
....	....	....	....	....	....	....	....	409.3	398.6	237.5	134.4	149.4	351.9	436.8	Claims on Nonfin.Pub.Enterprises	22c
....	....	....	....	....	....	....	....	1,603.5	I 2,974.6	3,654.8	3,496.2	4,161.9	4,866.7	5,538.7	Claims on Private Sector	22d
....	....	....	....	....	....	....	....	—	1.3	2.2	32.8	59.1	95.5		Claims on Nonbank Financial Insts.	22g
....	....	....	....	....	....	....	....	954.4	1,134.8	1,566.5	1,694.3	2,543.1	2,757.9	2,528.9	Demand Deposits	24
....	....	....	....	....	....	....	....	926.8	1,879.5	2,086.2	1,793.3	2,153.8	2,750.0	3,695.5	Time, Savings,& Fgn.Currency Dep.	25
....	....	....	....	....	....	....	....	37.2	330.8	353.8	783.3	1,169.9	1,752.6	2,090.8	Foreign Liabilities	26c
....	....	....	....	....	....	....	....	122.5	357.6	683.7	779.3	1,008.1	792.0	778.4	Central Government Deposits	26d
....	....	....	....	....	....	....	....	16.4	28.2	52.6	59.3	50.7	22.8	19.5	Counterpart Funds	26e
....	....	....	....	....	....	....	....	174.5	337.7	480.3	473.3	615.4	754.1	555.5	Central Government Lending Funds	26f
....	....	....	....	....	....	....	....	285.5	157.0	168.1	142.0	70.3	52.3	30.2	Credit from Monetary Authorities	26g
....	....	....	....	....	....	....	....	467.7	936.1	996.7	1,448.1	2,021.4	2,690.4	2,849.7	Capital Accounts	27a
....	....	....	....	....	....	....	....	−199.9	I−694.9	−965.3	−884.3	−1,162.1	−1,628.2	−1,723.7	Other Items (Net)	27r
End of Period															**Banking Survey**	
....	....	....	....	....	....	....	....	1,590.0	1,782.8	2,377.0	2,637.6	3,487.9	4,289.7	3,656.6	Foreign Assets (Net)	31n
....	....	....	....	....	....	....	....	1,798.6	I 3,219.2	3,643.3	3,698.3	4,996.2	5,605.2	6,741.7	Domestic Credit	32
....	....	....	....	....	....	....	....	−215.6	−161.9	−270.4	15.4	573.2	189.9	432.3	Claims on Central Govt. (Net)	32an
....	....	....	....	....	....	....	....	—	2.0	7.7	37.1	51.9	123.8	212.3	Claims on State and Local Govts.	32b
....	....	....	....	....	....	....	....	409.3	398.6	237.5	134.4	149.4	351.9	436.8	Claims on Nonfin.Pub.Enterprises	32c
....	....	....	....	....	....	....	....	1,604.9	I 2,980.5	3,666.9	3,506.1	4,169.5	4,873.6	5,544.8	Claims on Private Sector	32d
....	....	....	....	....	....	....	....	—	1.6	5.3	52.2	66.0	115.5		Claims on Nonbank Fin. Insts.	32g
....	....	....	....	....	....	....	....	1,746.4	2,475.7	3,488.4	3,610.9	5,109.9	5,570.9	5,275.0	Money	34
....	....	....	....	....	....	....	....	926.8	1,881.4	2,130.0	1,813.1	2,162.0	2,756.5	3,697.0	Quasi-Money	35
....	....	....	....	....	....	....	....	681.4	1,169.6	1,462.9	1,325.4	1,539.0	2,006.8	2,724.6	of which: Fgn. Currency Deposits	35b
....	....	....	....	....	....	....	....	16.4	42.9	90.1	101.2	88.8	63.6	50.3	Counterpart Funds	36e
....	....	....	....	....	....	....	....	174.5	338.3	481.0	473.3	616.0	755.6	555.5	Central Government Lending Funds	36f
....	....	....	....	....	....	....	....	1,497.3	990.9	918.9	1,399.7	1,774.1	2,578.6	2,759.3	Capital Accounts	37a
....	....	....	....	....	....	....	....	−972.8	I−727.2	−1,088.1	−1,062.3	−1,266.7	−1,830.3	−1,938.8	Other Items (Net)	37r
....	....	....	....	....	....	....	....	2,673.2	4,357.1	5,618.4	5,424.0	7,271.9	8,327.4	8,972.0	Money plus Quasi-Money	35l
Percent Per Annum															**Interest Rates**	
....	....	....	....	....	....	....	....	....	69.48	26.73	20.26	9.55	6.12	6.26	Money Market Rate	60b
....	....	....	....	....	....	....	....	....	....	26.82	20.95	8.64	10.69	11.14	Treasury Bill Rate	60c
....	....	....	....	....	....	....	....	88.29	48.43	20.05	13.95	7.89	5.98	4.94	Deposit Rate	60l
....	....	....	....	....	....	....	....	91.84	62.30	27.08	21.56	14.39	12.21	13.09	Lending Rate	60p
Period Averages															**Prices, Production, Labor**	
....	....	....	....	....	....	....	10.9	53.8	77.9	100.0	117.3	122.2	114.1	117.6	Producer Prices	63
....	....	....	....	....	....	....	8.1	I 41.6	71.6	100.0	124.6	135.7	142.5	143.6	Consumer Prices	64
....	....	....	....	....	....	....	11.0	36.6	69.7	100.0	136.0	169.4	201.8	214.0	Wages: Average Earnings	65
....	....	....	....	....	....	....	216.0	141.0	99.1	I 100.0	103.5	111.8	122.2	112.5	Manufacturing Production	66
....	....	....	....	....	....	....	186.3	146.2	116.7	I 100.0	95.8	95.8	94.9	93.6	Manufacturing Employment	67
Period Averages																
....	....	....	....	....	....	....	1,879	1,859	1,741	1,753	1,784	1,774	1,835	....	Labor Force	67d
....	....	....	....	....	....	....	1,855	1,778	1,656	1,632	1,620	1,564	1,588	....	Employment	67e
....	....	....	....	....	....	5	24	81	66	109	125	104	114	....	Unemployment	67c
....	....	....	....	....	....	.3	1.3	4.4	3.6	6.1	7.1	5.9	6.4	....	Unemployment Rate (%)	67r
Millions of Litai															**International Transactions**	
....	....	....	....	....	....	....	....	8,707	8,077	10,820	13,420	15,441	14,842	12,178	Exports	70
....	....	....	....	....	....	....	....	9,798	9,355	14,594	18,235	22,577	23,174	19,567	Imports, c.i.f.	71

Lithuania

		1970	1971	1972	1973	1974	1975	1976	1977	1978	1979	1980	1981	1982	1983	1984

Balance of Payments *Millions of US Dollars:*

		1970	1971	1972	1973	1974	1975	1976	1977	1978	1979	1980	1981	1982	1983	1984
Current Account, n.i.e.	78ald	...	...	...	...	...	...	...	...	...	...	...	...	...	...	...
Goods: Exports f.o.b.	78aad	...	...	...	...	...	...	...	...	...	...	...	...	...	...	...
Goods: Imports f.o.b.	78abd	...	...	...	...	...	...	...	...	...	...	...	...	...	...	...
Trade Balance	78acd	...	...	...	...	...	...	...	...	...	...	...	...	...	...	...
Services: Credit	78add	...	...	...	...	...	...	...	...	...	...	...	...	...	...	...
Services: Debit	78aed	...	...	...	...	...	...	...	...	...	...	...	...	...	...	...
Balance on Goods & Services	78afd	...	...	...	...	...	...	...	...	...	...	...	...	...	...	...
Income: Credit	78agd	...	...	...	...	...	...	...	...	...	...	...	...	...	...	...
Income: Debit	78ahd	...	...	...	...	...	...	...	...	...	...	...	...	...	...	...
Balance on Gds, Serv. & Inc.	78aid	...	...	...	...	...	...	...	...	...	...	...	...	...	...	...
Current Transfers, n.i.e.: Credit	78ajd	...	...	...	...	...	...	...	...	...	...	...	...	...	...	...
Current Transfers: Debit	78akd	...	...	...	...	...	...	...	...	...	...	...	...	...	...	...
Capital Account, n.i.e.	78bcd	...	...	...	...	...	...	...	...	...	...	...	...	...	...	...
Capital Account, n.i.e.: Credit	78bad	...	...	...	...	...	...	...	...	...	...	...	...	...	...	...
Capital Account: Debit	78bbd	...	...	...	...	...	...	...	...	...	...	...	...	...	...	...
Financial Account, n.i.e.	78bjd	...	...	...	...	...	...	...	...	...	...	...	...	...	...	...
Direct Investment Abroad	78bdd	...	...	...	...	...	...	...	...	...	...	...	...	...	...	...
Dir. Invest. in Rep. Econ., n.i.e.	78bed	...	...	...	...	...	...	...	...	...	...	...	...	...	...	...
Portfolio Investment Assets	78bfd	...	...	...	...	...	...	...	...	...	...	...	...	...	...	...
Equity Securities	78bkd	...	...	...	...	...	...	...	...	...	...	...	...	...	...	...
Debt Securities	78bld	...	...	...	...	...	...	...	...	...	...	...	...	...	...	...
Portfolio Investment Liab., n.i.e.	78bgd	...	...	...	...	...	...	...	...	...	...	...	...	...	...	...
Equity Securities	78bmd	...	...	...	...	...	...	...	...	...	...	...	...	...	...	...
Debt Securities	78bnd	...	...	...	...	...	...	...	...	...	...	...	...	...	...	...
Financial Derivatives Assets	78bwd	...	...	...	...	...	...	...	...	...	...	...	...	...	...	...
Financial Derivatives Liabilities	78bxd	...	...	...	...	...	...	...	...	...	...	...	...	...	...	...
Other Investment Assets	78bhd	...	...	...	...	...	...	...	...	...	...	...	...	...	...	...
Monetary Authorities	78bod	...	...	...	...	...	...	...	...	...	...	...	...	...	...	...
General Government	78bpd	...	...	...	...	...	...	...	...	...	...	...	...	...	...	...
Banks	78bqd	...	...	...	...	...	...	...	...	...	...	...	...	...	...	...
Other Sectors	78brd	...	...	...	...	...	...	...	...	...	...	...	...	...	...	...
Other Investment Liab., n.i.e.	78bid	...	...	...	...	...	...	...	...	...	...	...	...	...	...	...
Monetary Authorities	78bsd	...	...	...	...	...	...	...	...	...	...	...	...	...	...	...
General Government	78btd	...	...	...	...	...	...	...	...	...	...	...	...	...	...	...
Banks	78bud	...	...	...	...	...	...	...	...	...	...	...	...	...	...	...
Other Sectors	78bvd	...	...	...	...	...	...	...	...	...	...	...	...	...	...	...
Net Errors and Omissions	78cad	...	...	...	...	...	...	...	...	...	...	...	...	...	...	...
Overall Balance	78cbd	...	...	...	...	...	...	...	...	...	...	...	...	...	...	...
Reserves and Related Items	79dad	...	...	...	...	...	...	...	...	...	...	...	...	...	...	...
Reserve Assets	79dbd	...	...	...	...	...	...	...	...	...	...	...	...	...	...	...
Use of Fund Credit and Loans	79dcd	...	...	...	...	...	...	...	...	...	...	...	...	...	...	...
Exceptional Financing	79ded	...	...	...	...	...	...	...	...	...	...	...	...	...	...	...

International Investment Position *Millions of US Dollars*

		1970	1971	1972	1973	1974	1975	1976	1977	1978	1979	1980	1981	1982	1983	1984
Assets	79aad	...	...	...	...	...	...	...	...	...	...	...	...	...	...	...
Direct Investment Abroad	79abd	...	...	...	...	...	...	...	...	...	...	...	...	...	...	...
Portfolio Investment	79acd	...	...	...	...	...	...	...	...	...	...	...	...	...	...	...
Equity Securities	79add	...	...	...	...	...	...	...	...	...	...	...	...	...	...	...
Debt Securities	79aed	...	...	...	...	...	...	...	...	...	...	...	...	...	...	...
Financial Derivatives	79ald	...	...	...	...	...	...	...	...	...	...	...	...	...	...	...
Other Investment	79afd	...	...	...	...	...	...	...	...	...	...	...	...	...	...	...
Monetary Authorities	79agd	...	...	...	...	...	...	...	...	...	...	...	...	...	...	...
General Government	79ahd	...	...	...	...	...	...	...	...	...	...	...	...	...	...	...
Banks	79aid	...	...	...	...	...	...	...	...	...	...	...	...	...	...	...
Other Sectors	79ajd	...	...	...	...	...	...	...	...	...	...	...	...	...	...	...
Reserve Assets	79akd	...	...	...	...	...	...	...	...	...	...	...	...	...	...	...
Liabilities	79lad	...	...	...	...	...	...	...	...	...	...	...	...	...	...	...
Dir. Invest. in Rep. Economy	79lbd	...	...	...	...	...	...	...	...	...	...	...	...	...	...	...
Portfolio Investment	79lcd	...	...	...	...	...	...	...	...	...	...	...	...	...	...	...
Equity Securities	79ldd	...	...	...	...	...	...	...	...	...	...	...	...	...	...	...
Debt Securities	79led	...	...	...	...	...	...	...	...	...	...	...	...	...	...	...
Financial Derivatives	79lld	...	...	...	...	...	...	...	...	...	...	...	...	...	...	...
Other investment	79lfd	...	...	...	...	...	...	...	...	...	...	...	...	...	...	...
Monetary Authorities	79lgd	...	...	...	...	...	...	...	...	...	...	...	...	...	...	...
General Government	79lhd	...	...	...	...	...	...	...	...	...	...	...	...	...	...	...
Banks	79lid	...	...	...	...	...	...	...	...	...	...	...	...	...	...	...
Other Sectors	79ljd	...	...	...	...	...	...	...	...	...	...	...	...	...	...	...

1985	1986	1987	1988	1989	1990	1991	1992	1993	1994	1995	1996	1997	1998	1999		
Minus Sign Indicates Debit															**Balance of Payments**	
....	....	....	....	....	....	....	....	−85.7	−94.0	−614.4	−722.6	−981.3	−1,298.2	−1,194.0	Current Account, n.i.e.	**78al** d
....	....	....	....	....	....	....	....	2,025.8	2,029.2	2,706.1	3,413.2	4,192.4	3,961.6	3,146.7	Goods: Exports f.o.b.	**78aa** d
....	....	....	....	....	....	....	....	−2,180.5	−2,234.1	−3,404.0	−4,309.3	−5,339.9	−5,479.9	−4,551.2	Goods: Imports f.o.b.	**78ab** d
....	....	....	....	....	....	....	....	−154.7	−204.9	−697.9	−896.2	−1,147.5	−1,518.3	−1,404.6	*Trade Balance*	**78ac** d
....	....	....	....	....	....	....	....	197.8	321.9	485.2	797.5	1,031.8	1,109.0	1,091.5	Services: Credit	**78ad** d
....	....	....	....	....	....	....	....	−252.9	−376.5	−498.1	−676.7	−897.4	−868.5	−786.1	Services: Debit	**78ae** d
....	....	....	....	....	....	....	....	−209.8	−259.4	−710.8	−775.4	−1,013.0	−1,277.8	−1,099.1	*Balance on Goods & Services*	**78af** d
....	....	....	....	....	....	....	....	12.5	21.4	50.9	52.0	80.4	124.6	114.8	Income: Credit	**78ag** d
....	....	....	....	....	....	....	....	−4.3	−12.8	−63.7	−143.0	−278.8	−380.0	−372.6	Income: Debit	**78ah** d
....	....	....	....	....	....	....	....	−201.5	−250.8	−723.7	−866.4	−1,211.4	−1,533.2	−1,356.8	*Balance on Gds, Serv. & Inc.*	**78ai** d
....	....	....	....	....	....	....	....	115.9	161.6	112.3	149.4	237.0	240.4	167.4	Current Transfers, n.i.e.: Credit	**78aj** d
....	....	....	....	....	....	....	....	—	−4.8	−3.0	−5.6	−7.0	−5.4	−4.6	Current Transfers: Debit	**78ak** d
....	....	....	....	....	....	....	....	—	12.9	−39.0	5.5	4.1	−1.7	−3.3	Capital Account, n.i.e.	**78bc** d
....	....	....	....	....	....	....	....	—	12.9	3.3	5.5	4.5	.9	2.7	Capital Account, n.i.e.: Credit	**78ba** d
....	....	....	....	....	....	....	....	—	—	−42.3	—	−.4	−2.6	−6.0	Capital Account: Debit	**78bb** d
....	....	....	....	....	....	....	....	301.5	240.9	534.4	645.6	1,005.6	1,443.9	1,060.7	Financial Account, n.i.e.	**78bj** d
....	....	....	....	....	....	....	....	....	....	−1.0	−.1	−26.9	−4.2	−8.6	Direct Investment Abroad	**78bd** d
....	....	....	....	....	....	....	....	30.2	31.3	72.6	152.4	354.5	925.5	486.5	Dir. Invest. in Rep. Econ., n.i.e.	**78be** d
....	....	....	....	....	....	....	....	−.9	−.2	−10.5	−26.9	7.7	−10.1	−1.9	Portfolio Investment Assets	**78bf** d
....	....	....	....	....	....	....	....	−.9	−.2	−3.0	.8	.1	−.3	−3.0	Equity Securities	**78bk** d
....	....	....	....	....	....	....	....	....	....	−7.5	−27.7	7.6	−9.8	1.1	Debt Securities	**78bl** d
....	....	....	....	....	....	....	....	.6	4.6	26.6	89.6	180.5	−42.7	507.5	Portfolio Investment Liab., n.i.e.	**78bg** d
....	....	....	....	....	....	....	....	.6	4.6	6.2	15.9	30.5	11.4	8.9	Equity Securities	**78bm** d
....	....	....	....	....	....	....	....	....	—	20.4	73.7	150.1	−54.1	498.6	Debt Securities	**78bn** d
....	....	....	....	....	....	....	....	....	....	....	....	....	—	—	Financial Derivatives Assets	**78bw** d
....	....	....	....	....	....	....	....	....	....	....	....	....	—	—	Financial Derivatives Liabilities	**78bx** d
....	....	....	....	....	....	....	....	95.3	−26.4	−36.1	−170.4	−219.3	−24.0	−182.5	Other Investment Assets	**78bh** d
....	....	....	....	....	....	....	....	....	....	67.0	.2	.1	—	—	Monetary Authorities	**78bo** d
....	....	....	....	....	....	....	....	....	....	....	....	....	—	—	General Government	**78bp** d
....	....	....	....	....	....	....	....	108.9	−17.3	−18.0	−139.5	−88.1	57.2	−125.7	Banks	**78bq** d
....	....	....	....	....	....	....	....	−13.6	−9.2	−85.0	−31.1	−131.3	−81.2	−56.7	Other Sectors	**78br** d
....	....	....	....	....	....	....	....	176.5	231.6	482.8	601.0	709.1	599.3	259.7	Other Investment Liab., n.i.e.	**78bi** d
....	....	....	....	....	....	....	....	—	−.9	−25.1	1.0	−1.0	—	−.1	Monetary Authorities	**78bs** d
....	....	....	....	....	....	....	....	255.7	85.5	178.5	228.5	42.9	129.3	212.0	General Government	**78bt** d
....	....	....	....	....	....	....	....	−62.9	75.8	10.8	108.5	104.3	177.9	99.9	Banks	**78bu** d
....	....	....	....	....	....	....	....	−16.3	71.2	318.5	263.1	562.8	292.1	−52.1	Other Sectors	**78bv** d
....	....	....	....	....	....	....	....	−7.4	−46.9	287.2	66.7	195.8	282.9	−42.1	Net Errors and Omissions	**78ca** d
....	....	....	....	....	....	....	....	208.5	112.8	168.3	−4.8	224.2	426.8	−178.7	*Overall Balance*	**78cb** d
....	....	....	....	....	....	....	....	−208.5	−112.8	−168.3	4.8	−224.2	−426.8	178.7	Reserves and Related Items	**79da** d
....	....	....	....	....	....	....	....	−308.0	−179.7	−231.3	−15.9	−238.2	−398.8	195.3	Reserve Assets	**79db** d
....	....	....	....	....	....	....	....	99.5	66.9	63.0	20.7	14.1	−28.0	−16.6	Use of Fund Credit and Loans	**79dc** d
....	....	....	....	....	....	....	....	....	—	—	—	—	—	—	Exceptional Financing	**79de** d
Millions of US Dollars															**International Investment Position**	
....	....	....	....	....	....	....	....	....	997.6	1,274.6	1,692.7	2,148.6	2,472.2	2,452.7	Assets	**79aa** d
....	....	....	....	....	....	....	....	....	.2	1.2	2.8	26.0	16.5	25.9	Direct Investment Abroad	**79ab** d
....	....	....	....	....	....	....	....	....	.6	11.1	38.1	29.7	38.0	32.5	Portfolio Investment	**79ac** d
....	....	....	....	....	....	....	....	....	.2	3.1	2.6	2.9	2.9	5.9	Equity Securities	**79ad** d
....	....	....	....	....	....	....	....	....	.5	7.9	35.5	26.8	35.1	26.7	Debt Securities	**79ae** d
....	....	....	....	....	....	....	....	....	....	....	....	....	....	....	Financial Derivatives	**79al** d
....	....	....	....	....	....	....	....	....	409.4	443.4	817.5	1,030.2	957.7	1,152.1	Other Investment	**79af** d
....	....	....	....	....	....	....	....	....	67.2	.2	.1	—	—	—	Monetary Authorities	**79ag** d
....	....	....	....	....	....	....	....	....	....	....	....	....	....	....	General Government	**79ah** d
....	....	....	....	....	....	....	....	....	103.3	119.2	243.3	331.3	273.7	390.5	Banks	**79ai** d
....	....	....	....	....	....	....	....	....	238.9	323.9	574.1	699.0	684.0	761.7	Other Sectors	**79aj** d
....	....	....	....	....	....	....	....	....	587.4	819.0	834.3	1,062.7	1,460.0	1,242.1	Reserve Assets	**79ak** d
....	....	....	....	....	....	....	....	....	1,115.8	1,795.8	2,813.2	3,964.8	4,928.8	6,114.1	Liabilities	**79la** d
....	....	....	....	....	....	....	....	....	262.2	353.9	700.3	1,040.6	1,625.3	2,063.0	Dir. Invest. in Rep. Economy	**79lb** d
....	....	....	....	....	....	....	....	....	12.9	40.5	306.8	416.1	368.2	833.6	Portfolio Investment	**79lc** d
....	....	....	....	....	....	....	....	....	5.8	12.4	31.5	61.3	67.1	62.0	Equity Securities	**79ld** d
....	....	....	....	....	....	....	....	....	7.2	28.1	275.3	354.7	301.1	771.6	Debt Securities	**79le** d
....	....	....	....	....	....	....	....	....	....	....	....	....	....	....	Financial Derivatives	**79ll** d
....	....	....	....	....	....	....	....	....	840.7	1,401.4	1,806.1	2,508.1	2,935.3	3,217.5	Other investment	**79lf** d
....	....	....	....	....	....	....	....	....	221.6	261.6	275.1	270.8	253.5	230.5	Monetary Authorities	**79lg** d
....	....	....	....	....	....	....	....	....	235.2	424.0	447.4	549.2	694.2	881.3	General Government	**79lh** d
....	....	....	....	....	....	....	....	....	86.1	99.2	182.3	282.8	463.3	539.8	Banks	**79li** d
....	....	....	....	....	....	....	....	....	297.8	616.7	901.3	1,405.4	1,524.3	1,566.0	Other Sectors	**79lj** d

Lithuania

		1970	1971	1972	1973	1974	1975	1976	1977	1978	1979	1980	1981	1982	1983	1984
Government Finance																*Millions of Litai:*
Deficit (-) or Surplus	80	...	...	...	...	...	...	...	...	...	...	...	...	...	...	...
Total Revenue and Grants	81y	...	...	...	...	...	...	...	...	...	...	...	...	...	...	...
Revenue	81	...	...	...	...	...	...	...	...	...	...	...	...	...	...	...
Grants	81z	...	...	...	...	...	...	...	...	...	...	...	...	...	...	...
Exp.& Lending Minus Repayments	82z	...	...	...	...	...	...	...	...	...	...	...	...	...	...	...
Expenditure	82	...	...	...	...	...	...	...	...	...	...	...	...	...	...	...
Lending Minus Repayments	83	...	...	...	...	...	...	...	...	...	...	...	...	...	...	...
Total Financing																
Domestic	84a	...	...	...	...	...	...	...	...	...	...	...	...	...	...	...
Foreign	85a	...	...	...	...	...	...	...	...	...	...	...	...	...	...	...
Total Debt by Currency	88z	...	...	...	...	...	...	...	...	...	...	...	...	...	...	...
National	88b	...	...	...	...	...	...	...	...	...	...	...	...	...	...	...
Foreign	89b	...	...	...	...	...	...	...	...	...	...	...	...	...	...	...
National Accounts																*Millions of Litai*
Househ.Cons.Expend.,incl.NPISHs	96f	...	...	...	...	...	...	...	...	...	...	...	...	...	...	...
Government Consumption Expend.	91f	...	...	...	...	...	...	...	...	...	...	...	...	...	...	...
Gross Fixed Capital Formation	93e	...	...	...	...	...	...	...	...	...	...	...	...	...	...	...
Changes in Inventories	93i	...	...	...	...	...	...	...	...	...	...	...	...	...	...	...
Exports of Goods and Services	90c	...	...	...	...	...	...	...	...	...	...	...	...	...	...	...
Imports of Goods and Services	98c	...	...	...	...	...	...	...	...	...	...	...	...	...	...	...
Gross Domestic Product (GDP)	99b	...	...	...	...	...	...	...	...	...	...	...	...	...	...	...
Net Primary Income from Abroad	98.n	...	...	...	...	...	...	...	...	...	...	...	...	...	...	...
Gross National Income (GNI)	99a	...	...	...	...	...	...	...	...	...	...	...	...	...	...	...
Net Current Transf.from Abroad	98t	...	...	...	...	...	...	...	...	...	...	...	...	...	...	...
Gross Nat'l Disposable Inc.(GNDI)	99i	...	...	...	...	...	...	...	...	...	...	...	...	...	...	...
Gross Savings	99s	...	...	...	...	...	...	...	...	...	...	...	...	...	...	...
GDP Volume 1993 Prices	99b.*p*	...	...	...	...	...	...	...	...	...	...	...	...	...	...	...
GDP Volume 1995 Prices	99b.*p*	...	...	...	...	...	...	...	...	...	...	...	...	...	...	...
GDP Volume (1995=100)	99bv *p*	...	...	...	...	...	...	...	...	...	...	...	...	...	...	...
GDP Deflator (1995=100)	99bi *p*	...	...	...	...	...	...	...	...	...	...	...	...	...	...	...
																Millions:
Population	99z	...	...	...	...	...	...	...	...	...	...	...	...	...	...	...

Year Ending December 31

1985	1986	1987	1988	1989	1990	1991	1992	1993	1994	1995	1996	1997	1998	1999	Government Finance	
....	....	....	....	....	....	5.8	....	−694.2	−797.0	−1,151.5	−1,145.1	I−735.8	−183.6	....	Deficit (-) or Surplus	80
....	....	....	....	....	....	133.8	....	2,693.6	4,034.1	5,661.1	7,157.3	I10198.6	11,474.9	....	Total Revenue and Grants	81y
....	....	....	....	....	....	133.3	....	2,688.1	4,031.9	5,661.1	7,128.8	I10198.3	11,474.9	....	Revenue	81
....	....	....	....	....	....	.5	....	5.5	2.2	—	28.5	.3	—	....	Grants	81z
....	....	....	....	....	....	128.0	....	3,387.8	4,831.1	6,812.6	8,302.4	I10934.4	11,658.5	....	Exp.& Lending Minus Repayments	82z
....	....	....	....	....	....	120.0	....	2,475.3	4,292.1	6,079.1	7,894.1	I10515.0	13,037.6	....	Expenditure	82
....	....	....	....	....	....	8.0	....	912.5	539.0	733.5	408.3	419.4	−1,379.1	....	Lending Minus Repayments	83
															Total Financing	
....	....	....	....	....	....	....	....	71.4	518.2	417.9	138.7	I451.6	−574.1	....	Domestic	84a
....	....	....	....	....	....	....	....	622.8	278.8	733.6	1,006.4	I284.2	757.7	....	Foreign	85a
....	....	....	....	....	....	....	....	1,749.4	2,639.1	4,470.6	4,749.9	8,077.4	9,613.6	12,069.3	Total Debt by Currency	88z
....	....	....	....	....	....	....	....	514.6	654.3	1,111.4	2,024.0	2,470.1	2,876.1	2,354.1	National	88b
....	....	....	....	....	....	....	....	1,234.8	1,984.8	3,359.2	2,725.9	5,607.3	6,737.5	9,715.2	Foreign	89b

Millions of Litai

1985	1986	1987	1988	1989	1990	1991	1992	1993	1994	1995	1996	1997	1998	1999	National Accounts	
....	....	....	....	....	76	233	2,309	8,474	11,489	16,240	20,973	24,939	27,126	27,618	Househ.Cons.Expend.,incl.NPISHs	96f
....	....	....	....	....	26	45	445	1,800	3,319	4,747	5,966	7,277	10,481	9,566	Government Consumption Expend.	91f
....	....	....	....	....	37	93	783	2,677	3,905	5,554	7,269	9,337	10,463	9,581	Gross Fixed Capital Formation	93e
....	....	....	....	....	7	8	−247	−455	−792	405	462	840	31	228	Changes in Inventories	93i
....	....	....	....	....	70	123	795	9,567	9,361	12,765	16,843	20,897	20,283	16,953	Exports of Goods and Services	90c
....	....	....	....	....	−81	−87	−679	−10,472	−10,378	−15,609	−19,944	−24,949	−25,393	−21,350	Imports of Goods and Services	98c
....	....	....	....	....	134	415	3,406	11,590	16,904	24,103	31,569	38,340	42,990	42,597	Gross Domestic Product (GDP)	99b
....	....	....	....	....	....	....	....	34	34	−52	−364	−794	−1,022	−1,031	Net Primary Income from Abroad	98.n
....	....	....	....	....	....	....	....	11,624	16,938	24,051	31,205	37,547	41,968	41,566	Gross National Income (GNI)	99a
....	....	....	....	....	....	....	....	508	624	437	575	920	940	651	Net Current Transf.from Abroad	98t
....	....	....	....	....	....	....	....	12,132	17,562	24,489	31,780	38,467	42,908	42,217	Gross Nat'l Disposable Inc.(GNDI)	99i
....	....	....	....	....	....	....	....	1,859	2,754	3,501	4,841	6,251	5,301	5,033	Gross Savings	99s
....	....	....	....	....	....	....	13,835	11,590	10,458	10,802	....	....			GDP Volume 1993 Prices	99b. p
....	....	....	....	....	....	....	....	....	....	24,103	25,238	27,075	28,459	27,283	GDP Volume 1995 Prices	99b. p
....	....	....	....	....	....	....	128.1	107.3	96.8	100.0	104.7	112.3	118.1	113.2	GDP Volume (1995=100)	99bv p
....	....	....	....	....	....	....	11.0	44.8	72.4	100.0	125.1	141.6	151.1	156.1	GDP Deflator (1995=100)	99bi p

Midyear Estimates

1985	1986	1987	1988	1989	1990	1991	1992	1993	1994	1995	1996	1997	1998	1999		
....	....	....	....	....	....	....	3.74	3.73	3.72	3.71	3.71	3.71	3.70	3.66	Population	99z

(See notes in the back of the book.)

Luxembourg

137	1970	1971	1972	1973	1974	1975	1976	1977	1978	1979	1980	1981	1982	1983	1984
Exchange Rates															*Francs per SDR through 1998,*
Market Rate .... aa	49.675	48.591	47.839	49.846	44.227	46.273	41.806	40.013	37.520	36.948	40.205	44.766	51.758	58.252	61.832
															Francs per US Dollar through 1998,
Market Rate .... ae	49.675	44.755	44.063	41.320	36.123	39.528	35.983	32.940	28.800	28.048	31.523	38.460	46.920	55.640	63.080
Market Rate .... rf	50.000	48.870	44.015	38.977	38.952	36.779	38.605	35.843	31.492	29.319	29.242	37.129	45.691	51.132	57.784
															Francs per ECU:
ECU Rate .... ea	....	....	....	....	....	....	....	....	....	40.318	41.335	41.747	45.321	46.097	44.717
ECU Rate .... eb	....	....	....	....	....	....	42.913	40.884	40.059	40.164	40.601	41.301	44.680	45.430	45.438
															Index Numbers (1995=100):
Market Rate .... ahx	59.3	120.9	66.9	75.8	75.7	80.3	76.4	82.2	93.6	100.5	100.8	79.7	64.8	57.8	51.1
Nominal Effective Exchange Rate .... nec	....	....	....	....	....	....	....	....	....	104.6	104.2	102.0	94.7	92.5	91.7
Real Effective Exchange Rate .... rec	....	....	....	....	....	....	....	....	....	105.8	103.3	100.6	94.6	94.7	94.5
Fund Position															*Millions of SDRs:*
Quota 2f.s	19.00	20.00	20.00	20.00	20.00	20.00	20.00	20.00	31.00	31.00	46.50	46.50	46.50	77.00	77.00
SDRs 1b.s	3.19	5.22	7.34	7.34	7.34	7.34	7.34	7.44	7.58	11.59	11.32	14.88	15.41	15.98	16.58
Reserve Position in the Fund 1c.s	4.02	4.27	5.01	5.01	5.01	5.01	9.01	8.72	9.57	9.42	12.19	12.20	12.21	12.21	12.21
of which: Outstg.Fund Borrowing 2c	—	—	—	—	—	—	—	—	—	—	—	—	—	—	—
International Liquidity															*Millions of US Dollars Unless Otherwise Indicated:*
Total Res.Min.Gold (Eurosys.Def) 1l.d	....	....	....	....	....	....	....	....	....	....	....	....	....	....	28.6
SDRs 1b.d	3.19	5.67	7.97	8.85	8.99	8.59	8.53	9.04	9.88	15.27	14.44	17.32	17.00	16.73	16.25
Reserve Position in the Fund 1c.d	4.02	4.64	5.44	6.04	6.13	5.87	10.47	10.59	12.47	12.41	15.55	14.20	13.47	12.78	11.97
Foreign Exchange 1d.d	....	....	....	....	....	....	....	....	....	....	....	....	....	....	.34
o/w: Fin.Deriv.Rel.to Reserves 1ddd	....	....	....	....	....	....	....	....	....	....	....	....	....	....	....
Other Reserve Assets 1e.d	....	....	....	....	....	....	....	....	....	....	....	....	....	....	....
Gold (Million Fine Troy Ounces) 1ad	.440	.442	.442	.442	.442	.442	.442	.451	.455	.455	.455	.455	.455	.455	.429
Gold (National Valuation) 1and	18.56	18.67	18.67	18.67	18.67	18.67	18.67	19.04	19.22	19.22	19.22	19.22	19.22	19.22	18.12
Memo: Euro Cl. on Non-EA Res. 1dgd	....	....	....	....	....	....	....	....	....	....	....	....	....	....	....
Non-Euro Cl. on EA Res. 1dhd	....	....	....	....	....	....	....	....	....	....	....	....	....	....	....
Mon. Auth.: Other Foreign Assets .... 3..d	....	....	....	....	....	....	....	....	....	....	....	....	....	....	....
Foreign Liabilities .... 4..d	....	....	....	....	....	....	....	....	....	....	....	....	....	—	—
Banking Insts.: Foreign Assets 7a.d	3,709	6,287	9,601	17,264	24,608	30,369	38,174	51,191	68,898	95,095	104,828	114,204	109,711	103,235	101,708
Foreign Liab. 7b.d	3,589	5,942	8,954	15,608	22,108	27,890	35,123	48,206	64,010	89,507	98,454	106,698	102,572	94,967	93,349
Monetary Authorities															*Billions of Francs through 1998;*
Fgn. Assets (Cl.on Non-EA Ctys) 11	....	....	....	....	....	....	....	....	....	....	....	....	....	2.4	3.2
Claims on General Government 12a.u	....	....	....	....	....	....	....	....	....	....	....	....	....	....	....
o/w: Claims on Gen.Govt.in Cty 12a	....	....	....	....	....	....	....	....	....	....	....	....	....	—	—
Claims on Banking Institutions 12e.u	....	....	....	....	....	....	....	....	....	....	....	....	....	....	....
o/w: Claims on Bank.Inst.in Cty 12e	....	....	....	....	....	....	....	....	....	....	....	....	....	.5	.5
Claims on Other Resident Sectors 12d.u	....	....	....	....	....	....	....	....	....	....	....	....	....	....	....
o/w: Cl. on Oth.Res.Sect.in Cty 12d	....	....	....	....	....	....	....	....	....	....	....	....	....	....	....
Claims on ECB 12u	....	....	....	....	....	....	....	....	....	....	....	....	....	....	....
Currency in Circulation 14a	....	....	....	....	....	....	....	....	....	....	....	....	....	....	—
Liabilities to Banking Insts 14c.u	....	....	....	....	....	....	....	....	....	....	....	....	....	....	....
o/w: Liabs to Bank.Inst.in Cty 14c	....	....	....	....	....	....	....	....	....	....	....	....	....	....	....
Demand Dep. of Other Res.Sect. 14d.u	....	....	....	....	....	....	....	....	....	....	....	....	....	....	....
o/w: D.Dep.of Oth.Res.Sect.in Cty 14d	....	....	....	....	....	....	....	....	....	....	....	....	....	....	....
Other Dep. of Other Res.Sect. .... 15..u	....	....	....	....	....	....	....	....	....	....	....	....	....	....	....
o/w: O.Dep.of Oth.Res.Sect.in Cty 15	....	....	....	....	....	....	....	....	....	....	....	....	....	....	....
Money Market Instruments 16m.u	....	....	....	....	....	....	....	....	....	....	....	....	....	....	....
o/w: MMI Held by Resid.of Cty 16m	....	....	....	....	....	....	....	....	....	....	....	....	....	....	....
Bonds (Debt Securities) 16n.u	....	....	....	....	....	....	....	....	....	....	....	....	....	....	....
o/w: Bonds Held by Resid.of Cty 16n	....	....	....	....	....	....	....	....	....	....	....	....	....	....	....
Foreign Liab. (to Non-EA Ctys) 16c	....	....	....	....	....	....	....	....	....	....	....	....	....	—	—
Central Government Deposits 16d.u	....	....	....	....	....	....	....	....	....	....	....	....	....	....	....
o/w: Cent.Govt.Dep. in Cty 16d	....	....	....	....	....	....	....	....	....	....	....	....	....	1.2	.7
Liabilities to ECB 16u	....	....	....	....	....	....	....	....	....	....	....	....	....	....	....
Capital Accounts 17a	....	....	....	....	....	....	....	....	....	....	....	....	....	1.7	2.5
Other Items (Net) 17r	....	....	....	....	....	....	....	....	....	....	....	....	....	.1	.6
Banking Institutions															*Billions of Francs through 1998;*
Claims on Monetary Authorities 20	.9	1.0	1.1	1.5	1.1	1.2	1.1	1.5	.9	1.1	1.1	1.1	1.2	1.5	1.7
Claims on Bk.Inst.in Oth.EA Ctys 20b.u	....	....	....	....	....	....	....	....	....	....	....	....	....	....	....
Fgn. Assets (Cl.on Non-EA Ctys) 21	183.9	280.0	428.2	692.9	879.9	1,192.0	1,362.2	I 1,686.2	1,984.3	2,667.2	3,304.5	4,392.3	5,147.7	5,744.0	6,415.8
Claims on General Government 22a.u	....	....	....	....	....	....	....	....	....	....	....	....	....	....	....
o/w: Claims on Gen.Govt.in Cty 22a	1.7	1.7	1.6	2.0	1.4	1.3	1.2	1.2	1.4	1.2	1.1	1.4	1.4	1.7	1.4
Claims on Other Resident Sectors 22d.u	....	....	....	....	....	....	....	....	....	....	....	....	....	....	....
o/w: Cl. on Oth.Res.Sect.in Cty 22d	33.6	34.6	38.6	48.1	64.8	74.3	86.3	I 58.0	117.2	135.9	160.8	180.4	202.5	204.5	218.4
Demand Deposits .... 24..u	....	....	....	....	....	....	....	....	....	....	....	....	....	....	....
o/w: D.Dep.of Oth.Res.Sect.in Cty 24	9.4	10.6	12.7	15.6	16.8	22.1	20.2	23.0	25.6	23.6	25.1	27.1	29.6	34.9	38.9
Other Deposits .... 25..u	....	....	....	....	....	....	....	....	....	....	....	....	....	....	....
o/w: O.Dep.of Oth.Res.Sect.in Cty 25	23.1	28.6	37.9	54.6	76.7	85.8	103.6	112.4	141.7	160.7	191.0	222.6	246.1	272.2	300.4
Money Market Instruments 26m.u	....	....	....	....	....	....	....	....	....	....	....	....	....	....	....
o/w: MMI Held by Resid.of Cty 26m	....	....	....	....	....	....	....	....	....	....	....	....	....	....	....
Bonds (Debt Securities) 26n.u	....	....	....	....	....	....	....	....	....	....	....	....	....	....	....
o/w: Bonds Held by Resid.of Cty 26n	....	....	....	....	....	....	....	....	....	....	....	....	....	....	....
Foreign Liab. (to Non-EA Ctys) 26c	179.4	266.3	401.3	629.5	798.6	1,102.4	1,263.8	1,587.9	1,843.5	2,510.5	3,103.6	4,103.6	4,812.7	5,284.0	5,888.4
Central Government Deposits 26d.u	....	....	....	....	....	....	....	....	....	....	....	....	....	....	....
o/w: Cent.Govt.Dep. in Cty 26d	....	....	....	....	....	....	....	....	....	....	....	....	....	....	....
Credit from Monetary Authorities 26g	....	....	....	....	....	....	....	....	....	....	....	....	....	....	....
Liab. to Bk.Inst.in Oth. EA Ctys 26h.u	....	....	....	....	....	....	....	....	....	....	....	....	....	....	....
Capital Accounts 27a	8.5	11.2	17.4	25.0	36.0	47.3	59.3	76.5	95.4	119.5	147.4	190.0	252.7	315.8	388.7
Other Items (Net) 27r	−.4	.5	.2	19.8	19.0	11.1	3.9	I −52.7	−2.4	−8.8	.4	32.0	11.7	44.8	20.8

1985	1986	1987	1988	1989	1990	1991	1992	1993	1994	1995	1996	1997	1998	1999		
															Exchange Rates	
Euros per SDR Thereafter: End of Period																
55.316	49.429	47.032	50.255	46.994	44.078	44.730	45.623	49.599	46.478	43.725	46.022	49.814	48.682	1.3662	Market Rate	aa
Euros per US Dollar Thereafter: End of Period (ae) Period Average (rf)																
50.360	40.410	33.153	37.345	35.760	30.983	31.270	33.180	36.110	31.838	29.415	32.005	36.920	34.575	.9954	Market Rate	ae
59.378	44.672	37.334	36.768	39.404	33.418	34.148	32.150	34.597	33.456	29.480	30.962	35.774	36.299	.9386	Market Rate	rf
End of Period (ea) Period Average (eb)																
44.645	43.233	43.154	43.576	42.592	42.184	41.931	40.178	40.266	39.161	38.697	40.102	40.781	40.340	....	ECU Rate	ea
44.913	43.803	43.039	43.427	43.378	42.506	42.222	41.604	40.468	39.661	38.548	39.295	40.529	40.621	....	ECU Rate	eb
Period Averages																
50.0	66.2	79.0	80.3	74.8	88.4	86.6	91.8	85.2	88.2	100.0	95.1	82.4	81.2	....	Market Rate	ahx
92.1	93.7	95.0	94.7	94.4	96.1	96.4	97.1	97.0	98.2	100.0	98.8	97.0	96.7	96.5	Nominal Effective Exchange Rate	nec
95.0	95.7	95.4	94.8	94.5	96.3	96.7	97.0	97.3	98.2	100.0	98.3	96.1	95.7	95.5	Real Effective Exchange Rate	rec
															Fund Position	
End of Period																
77.00	77.00	77.00	77.00	77.00	77.00	77.00	135.50	135.50	135.50	135.50	135.50	135.50	135.50	279.10	Quota	2f.s
17.08	17.54	17.96	18.41	19.05	19.86	20.60	6.62	6.98	7.22	7.46	7.75	8.04	8.72	1.78	SDRs	1b.s
12.21	12.23	12.23	12.23	12.25	12.25	12.27	25.85	23.58	23.61	22.94	23.56	21.75	59.37	54.37	Reserve Position in the Fund	1c.s
—	—	—	—	—	—	—	—	—	—	—	—	—	31.34	—	*of which:* Outstg.Fund Borrowing	2c
															International Liquidity	
End of Period																
32.7	36.4	42.8	41.2	75.2	80.5	80.4	74.1	67.4	75.7	75.0	73.7	64.1	....	Ɪ77.1	Total Res.Min.Gold (Eurosys.Def)	1l.d
18.76	21.45	25.48	24.77	25.03	28.25	29.47	9.10	9.59	10.54	11.09	11.14	10.85	12.28	2.45	SDRs	1b.d
13.41	14.96	17.35	16.46	16.10	17.43	17.55	35.54	32.38	34.46	34.10	33.87	29.35	83.60	74.62	Reserve Position in the Fund	1c.d
.53	.01	.01	.01	34.11	34.85	33.34	29.48	25.40	30.73	29.79	28.67	23.87	....	....	Foreign Exchange	1d.d
....	....	....	....	....	....	....	....	....	....	....	....	....	....	—	*o/w:* Fin.Deriv.Rel.to Reserves	1dd d
....	....	....	....	....	....	....	....	....	....	....	....	....	....	—	Other Reserve Assets	1e.d
.429	.429	.429	.429	Ɪ.343	.343	.343	.343	.305	.305	.305	.305	.305	.305	.076	Gold (Million Fine Troy Ounces)	1ad
18.12	18.11	18.11	18.11	Ɪ16.79	19.38	19.20	19.25	14.90	16.90	18.28	16.81	14.44	....	22.00	Gold (National Valuation)	1an d
														....	Memo: Euro Cl. on Non-EA Res.	1dg d
														....	Non-Euro Cl. on EA Res.	1dh d
														—	Mon. Auth.: Other Foreign Assets	3..d
—	—	—	—	34.12	34.86	33.26	26.22	25.48	30.78	29.58	28.43	24.11	....	Ɪ2171.95	Foreign Liabilities	4..d
130,949	171,691	226,519	232,010	280,189	355,119	358,711	376,499	....	451,135	504,838	496,510	471,904	....	Ɪ178,653	Banking Insts.: Foreign Assets	7a.d
117,205	151,901	197,771	199,238	241,426	308,087	309,656	320,644	....	386,770	434,105	415,569	389,816	....	Ɪ164,243	Foreign Liab.	7b.d
															Monetary Authorities	
Millions of Euros Beginning 1999: End of Period																
3.4	5.3	5.4	5.7	7.1	7.0	7.1	7.0	8.3	8.5	8.3	7.5	6.2	....	952	Fgn. Assets (Cl.on Non-EA Ctys)	11
														97	Claims on General Government	12a.u
2.3	2.5	2.8	3.0	3.0	3.5	3.4	3.2	5.5	5.5	4.9	4.8	4.7	....	....	*o/w:* Claims on Gen.Govt.in Cty	12a
														13,038	Claims on Banking Institutions	12e.u
.3	.3	.3	.3	.2	.2	.3	.3	.1	.1	.2	.0	2.6	....	9,000	*o/w:* Claims on Bank.Inst.in Cty	12e
														163	Claims on Other Resident Sectors	12d.u
....	....	....	....	....	....	....	....	....	....	....	....	....	....	—	*o/w:* Cl. on Oth.Res.Sect.in Cty	12d
														542	Claims on ECB	12u
2.3	2.5	2.8	3.0	3.0	3.5	3.4	3.2	5.5	5.5	4.9	5.7	5.7	....	585	Currency in Circulation	14a
														11,509	Liabilities to Banking Insts	14c.u
														4,183	*o/w:* Liabs to Bank.Inst.in Cty	14c
														18	Demand Dep. of Other Res.Sect.	14d.u
														3	*o/w:* D.Dep.of Oth.Res.Sect.in Cty	14d
														—	Other Dep. of Other Res.Sect.	15..u
														—	*o/w:* O.Dep.of Oth.Res.Sect.in Cty	15
														—	Money Market Instruments	16m.u
														—	*o/w:* MMI Held by Resid.of Cty	16m
														—	Bonds (Debt Securities)	16n.u
														—	*o/w:* Bonds Held by Resid.of Cty	16n
—	—	—	—	1.2	1.1	1.0	.9	.9	1.0	.9	.9	.9	....	2,162	Foreign Liab. (to Non-EA Ctys)	16c
														485	Central Government Deposits	16d.u
.7	2.7	2.7	2.7	2.7	2.7	2.8	2.9	3.2	3.4	3.4	3.3	3.4	....	485	*o/w:* Cent.Govt.Dep. in Cty	16d
														—	Liabilities to ECB	16u
2.5	2.4	2.4	2.6	2.8	2.8	3.1	3.3	4.1	4.2	4.2	4.3	4.5	....	199	Capital Accounts	17a
.4	.5	.6	.7	.6	.5	.6	.2	.2	.1	—	-.9	-1.1	....	-166	Other Items (Net)	17r
															Banking Institutions	
Millions of Euros Beginning 1999: End of Period																
1.9	2.1	2.4	2.4	.9	3.2	3.4	4.0	....	3.0	3.7	19.1	13.6	....	4,183	Claims on Monetary Authorities	20
														228,490	Claims on Bk.Inst.in Oth.EA Ctys	20b.u
6,594.6	6,938.0	7,509.7	8,664.4	10,019.5	11,002.5	11,216.9	12,492.3	....	14,363.0	14,849.8	15,890.8	17,422.7	....	177,835	Fgn. Assets (Cl.on Non-EA Ctys)	21
														53,469	Claims on General Government	22a.u
1.4	1.5	.7	.7	.6	1.0	.9	3.1	....	12.2	54.3	22.1	19.9	....	733	*o/w:* Claims on Gen.Govt.in Cty	22a
														82,554	Claims on Other Resident Sectors	22d.u
224.9	259.7	280.2	323.6	372.4	446.4	476.4	578.5	....	489.7	525.4	552.9	616.0	....	19,778	*o/w:* Cl. on Oth.Res.Sect.in Cty	22d
														42,610	Demand Deposits	24..u
38.4	45.1	60.9	83.5	96.6	106.9	98.1	101.8	....	78.5	72.7	79.5	81.5	....	26,687	*o/w:* D.Dep.of Oth.Res.Sect.in Cty	24
														89,947	Other Deposits	25..u
402.5	470.3	604.3	838.4	930.4	1,075.0	1,052.7	1,384.6	....	1,674.0	1,677.1	1,933.2	2,155.8	....	32,027	*o/w:* O.Dep.of Oth.Res.Sect.in Cty	25
														65,940	Money Market Instruments	26m.u
														38,771	*o/w:* MMI Held by Resid.of Cty	26m
								....	293.8	453.3	599.1	797.7	....		Bonds (Debt Securities)	26n.u
														—	*o/w:* Bonds Held by Resid.of Cty	26n
5,902.4	6,138.3	6,556.6	7,440.6	8,633.4	9,545.3	9,682.9	10,639.0	....	12,313.8	12,769.2	13,300.3	14,392.0	....	163,491	Foreign Liab. (to Non-EA Ctys)	26c
														4,595	Central Government Deposits	26d.u
								....	53.8	59.8	72.1	79.6	....	3,377	*o/w:* Cent.Govt.Dep. in Cty	26d
								....	3.8	35.5	3.8	4.6	....	9,000	Credit from Monetary Authorities	26g
														105,620	Liab. to Bk.Inst.in Oth. EA Ctys	26h.u
451.7	513.2	545.9	599.0	636.0	686.7	750.2	860.3	....	486.3	526.5	549.0	562.0	....	16,551	Capital Accounts	27a
27.7	34.4	25.3	29.6	97.2	39.3	113.7	92.2	....	Ɪ-36.2	-161.0	-51.9	-1.0	....	10,005	Other Items (Net)	27r

Luxembourg

		1970	1971	1972	1973	1974	1975	1976	1977	1978	1979	1980	1981	1982	1983	1984
Banking Survey (Nat'l Residency)															*Billions of Francs through 1998;*	
Foreign Assets (Net)	31n	...	...	...	...	...	...	...	...	...	...	...	...	...	462.5	530.6
Domestic Credit	32	...	...	...	...	...	...	...	...	...	...	...	...	...	205.1	219.1
Claims on General Govt. (Net)	32an	...	...	...	...	...	...	...	...	...	...	...	...	...	.6	.7
Claims on Other Resident Sectors	32d	...	...	...	...	...	...	...	...	...	...	...	...	...	204.5	218.4
Currency in Circulation	34a.n	...	...	...	...	...	...	...	...	...	...	...	...	...	—	—
Demand Deposits	34b.n	...	...	...	...	...	...	...	...	...	...	...	...	...	34.9	38.9
Other Deposits	35..n	...	...	...	...	...	...	...	...	...	...	...	...	...	272.2	300.4
Money Market Instruments	36m	...	...	...	...	...	...	...	...	...	...	...	...	...		
Bonds (Debt Securities)	36n	...	...	...	...	...	...	...	...	...	...	...	...	...	...	...
o/w: Bonds Over Two Years	36na	...	...	...	...	...	...	...	...	...	...	...	...	...	...	...
Capital Accounts	37a	...	...	...	...	...	...	...	...	...	...	...	...	...	317.5	391.2
Other Items (Net)	37r	...	...	...	...	...	...	...	...	...	...	...	...	...	42.9	19.2
Banking Survey (EA-Wide Residency)															*Millions of Euros:*	
Foreign Assets (Net)	31n.u	...	...	...	...	...	...	...	...	...	...	...	...	...	...	...
Domestic Credit	32..u	...	...	...	...	...	...	...	...	...	...	...	...	...	...	...
Claims on General Govt. (Net)	32an u	...	...	...	...	...	...	...	...	...	...	...	...	...	...	...
Claims on Other Resident Sect.	32d.u	...	...	...	...	...	...	...	...	...	...	...	...	...	...	...
Currency in Circulation	34a.u	...	...	...	...	...	...	...	...	...	...	...	...	...	...	...
Demand Deposits	34b.u	...	...	...	...	...	...	...	...	...	...	...	...	...	...	...
Other Deposits	35..u	...	...	...	...	...	...	...	...	...	...	...	...	...	...	...
o/w: Other Dep. Over Two Yrs	35ab u	...	...	...	...	...	...	...	...	...	...	...	...	...	...	...
Money Market Instruments	36m.u	...	...	...	...	...	...	...	...	...	...	...	...	...	...	...
Bonds (Debt Securities)	36n.u	...	...	...	...	...	...	...	...	...	...	...	...	...	...	...
o/w: Bonds Over Two Years	36na u	...	...	...	...	...	...	...	...	...	...	...	...	...	...	...
Capital Accounts	37a	...	...	...	...	...	...	...	...	...	...	...	...	...	...	...
Other Items (Net)	37r.u	...	...	...	...	...	...	...	...	...	...	...	...	...	...	...
Money (National Definitions)															*Billions of Francs:*	
Money	39ma	...	...	...	...	23.5	26.4	28.2	32.1	34.1	36.3	38.1	40.2	41.1	45.8	47.5
Quasi-Money	39mb					40.3	42.2	51.5	57.2	68.1	80.8	101.7	114.5	113.5	122.8	122.8
Broad Money	39mc	...	...	...	...	63.8	68.6	79.7	89.3	102.2	117.1	139.8	154.7	154.6	168.6	170.3
Interest Rates															*Percent Per Annum*	
Money Market Rate	60b	...	...	...	...	...	...	...	...	...	...	12.23	15.25	12.26	10.56	10.70
Deposit Rate	60l	...	...	...	...	...	...	...	...	...	...	6.50	6.75	7.50	7.17	7.00
Lending Rate	60p	...	...	...	...	...	...	...	...	...	...	9.25	9.63	10.00	9.38	9.25
Government Bond Yield	61	7.52	7.58	7.25	6.80	7.27	6.73	7.23	7.03[e]	‖6.64	6.78	7.50	8.68	10.50	9.83	10.22
Prices, Production, Labor															*Index Numbers (1995=100):*	
Share Prices	62	5.5	6.2	7.9	9.6	9.8	12.7	13.2	14.1	18.8	28.9	26.5	23.0	20.6	23.2	27.1
Producer Prices in Industry	63a	...	...	...	...	...	...	...	...	...	...	68.7	76.0	89.6	94.0	99.8
Consumer Prices	64	29.8	31.2	32.8	34.8	38.1	42.2	46.3	49.4	50.9	53.3	56.6	61.2	66.9	72.7	‖76.8
Harmonized CPI	64h	...	...	...	...	...	...	...	...	...	...	...	...	...	...	...
Industrial Production	66..b	64.4	63.5	66.2	74.1	76.6	59.8	61.2	61.5	64.5	66.6	64.4	60.8	61.3	64.6	73.2
Industrial Employment	67	82.3	‖85.1	87.7	90.2	93.7	94.1	92.2	90.9	89.7	90.5	91.2	90.6	89.6	87.6	86.5
															Number in Thousands:	
Labor Force	67d	...	...	...	...	...	...	...	...	...	...	...	...	...	...	...
Employment	67e	...	...	...	...	...	...	...	...	...	...	...	...	...	...	...
Unemployment	67c	...	...	...	...	...	...	...	...	...	...	...	...	...	...	...
Unemployment Rate (%)	67r	...	...	...	...	...	...	...	...	...	...	...	...	...	...	...
International Transactions															*Billions of Francs through 1998;*	
Exports	70	42.75	36.25	44.03	57.63	82.54	65.29	70.64	68.56	72.31	85.80	87.88	88.56	101.90	111.47	145.56
Imports, c.i.f.	71	37.37	33.99	42.26	51.95	67.51	66.85	71.84	73.01	79.57	91.20	105.62	111.33	124.64	136.22	160.06

	1985	1986	1987	1988	1989	1990	1991	1992	1993	1994	1995	1996	1997	1998	1999		
Millions of Euros Beginning 1999: End of Period																**Banking Survey (Nat'l Residency)**	
	695.6	805.1	958.5	1,229.5	1,392.0	1,463.1	1,540.0	1,859.4	....	2,056.7	2,088.0	2,597.1	3,036.0	....	177,387	Foreign Assets (Net)	31n
	227.8	261.0	281.0	324.6	373.2	448.2	477.9	581.9	....	I450.2	521.4	504.4	557.6	....	16,649	Domestic Credit	32
	2.9	1.3	.8	1.0	.8	1.8	1.5	3.4	....	−39.5	−4.0	−48.5	−58.4	....	−3,129	Claims on General Govt. (Net)	32an
	224.9	259.7	280.2	323.6	372.4	446.4	476.4	578.5	....	489.7	525.4	552.9	616.0	....	19,778	Claims on Other Resident Sectors	32d
	2.3	2.5	2.8	3.0	3.0	3.5	3.4	3.2	5.5	5.5	4.9	5.7	5.7	....	585	Currency in Circulation	34a.n
	38.4	45.1	60.9	83.5	96.6	106.9	98.1	101.8	....	78.5	72.7	79.5	81.5	....	26,690	Demand Deposits	34b.n
	402.5	470.3	604.3	838.4	930.4	1,075.0	1,052.7	1,384.6	....	1,674.0	1,677.1	1,933.2	2,155.8	....	32,027	Other Deposits	35..n
	....	....	....	....	....	....	....	....	....						65,941	Money Market Instruments	36m
									....	293.8	453.3	599.1	797.7	....	38,771	Bonds (Debt Securities)	36n
															31,161	o/w: Bonds Over Two Years	36na
	454.3	515.7	548.3	601.6	638.8	689.5	753.3	863.7	....	490.5	530.7	553.3	566.5	....	16,750	Capital Accounts	37a
	26.0	32.5	23.2	27.6	96.6	36.4	110.6	88.1	....	I−35.4	−129.4	−69.0	−13.7	....	13,272	Other Items (Net)	37r
End of Period																**Banking Survey (EA-Wide Residency)**	
	....	....	....	....	....	....	....	....	....	....	....	....	....	....	13,134	Foreign Assets (Net)	31n.u
	....	....	....	....	....	....	....	....	....	....	....	....	....	....	131,203	Domestic Credit	32..u
	....	....	....	....	....	....	....	....	....	....	....	....	....	....	48,486	Claims on General Govt. (Net)	32an u
	....	....	....	....	....	....	....	....	....	....	....	....	....	....	82,717	Claims on Other Resident Sect.	32d.u
	....	....	....	....	....	....	....	....	....	....	....	....	....	....	585	Currency in Circulation	34a.u
	....	....	....	....	....	....	....	....	....	....	....	....	....	....	42,628	Demand Deposits	34b.u
	....	....	....	....	....	....	....	....	....	....	....	....	....	....	89,947	Other Deposits	35..u
															6,926	o/w: Other Dep. Over Two Yrs	35ab u
															65,940	Money Market Instruments	36m.u
															38,771	Bonds (Debt Securities)	36n.u
															31,161	o/w: Bonds Over Two Years	36na u
															16,750	Capital Accounts	37a
															−110,285	Other Items (Net)	37r.u
End of Period																**Money (National Definitions)**	
	44.9	49.2	54.3	58.6	66.7	72.8	80.4	81.8	....	104.5	....	111.4	115.0	....	....	Money	39ma
	152.8	170.9	200.1	235.9	286.1	338.6	378.1	406.8	....	399.6	....	423.5	396.0	....	....	Quasi-Money	39mb
	197.7	220.1	254.4	294.5	352.8	411.4	458.5	488.6	....	504.1	....	534.9	511.0	....	....	Broad Money	39mc
Percent Per Annum																**Interest Rates**	
	9.26	7.30	6.71	7.16	10.02	9.67	9.10	8.93	8.09	5.16	4.26	3.29	3.36	3.48	....	Money Market Rate	60b
	6.50	5.50	4.94	4.46	5.04	6.00	6.00	6.00	5.33	5.00	5.00	3.54	3.46	3.31	....	Deposit Rate	60l
	8.75	7.75	7.19	6.71	7.25	8.23	8.25	8.75	7.65	6.58	6.50	5.50	5.50	5.27	....	Lending Rate	60p
	9.53	8.67	7.96	7.13	7.68	8.51	8.15	7.90	6.93	6.38	6.05	5.21	5.39	5.29	....	Government Bond Yield	61
Period Averages																**Prices, Production, Labor**	
	40.2	60.9	I55.4	55.3	66.8	61.5	58.7	55.7	78.3	110.4	100.0	117.5	152.5	194.2	....	Share Prices	62
	102.8	I100.2	93.7	96.1	103.4	101.4	98.8	96.1	94.8	I96.2	100.0	96.9	98.3	100.7	97.6	Producer Prices in Industry	63a
	79.9	80.2	80.1	81.3	84.0	I87.1	89.9	92.7	96.0	98.1	100.0	I101.4	102.8	103.8	104.8	Consumer Prices	64
											100.0	101.2	102.6	103.6	104.6	Harmonized CPI	64h
	78.1	80.3	80.7	90.3	97.1	97.5	97.1	96.3	93.7	99.1	100.0	100.7	106.2	114.1	118.1	Industrial Production	66..b
	87.4	89.2	90.2	93.7	96.2	100.0	95.7	....	....	....	....	....	....	....	....	Industrial Employment	67
Period Averages																	
	161	165	170	175	182	190	197	....	....	....	....	172	175	179	....	Labor Force	67d
																Employment	67e
	3	2	3	2	2	2	2	3	4	5	5	6	6	6	5	Unemployment	67c
	1.7	1.5	1.7	1.6	1.4	1.3	1.4	1.6	2.1	2.8	3.0	3.3	3.6	3.1	2.9	Unemployment Rate (%)	67r
Millions of Euros Beginning 1999																**International Transactions**	
	168.07	166.23	163.32	186.36	212.81	210.70	214.15	207.96	203.60	219.10	228.40	223.20	250.10	286.90	7.41	Exports	70
	186.70	188.81	195.60	213.73	244.70	253.83	274.68	264.31	265.90	280.00	287.30	299.20	335.70	268.20	10.27	Imports, c.i.f.	71

Luxembourg

137

		1970	1971	1972	1973	1974	1975	1976	1977	1978	1979	1980	1981	1982	1983	1984
Balance of Payments																*Millions of US Dollars:*
Current Account, n.i.e.	78ald	....	....	....	....	....	....	....	....	....	....	....	....	....	....	....
Goods: Exports f.o.b.	78aad	....	....	....	....	....	....	....	....	....	....	....	....	....	....	....
Goods: Imports f.o.b.	78abd	....	....	....	....	....	....	....	....	....	....	....	....	....	....	....
Trade Balance	78acd	....	....	....	....	....	....	....	....	....	....	....	....	....	....	....
Services: Credit	78add	....	....	....	....	....	....	....	....	....	....	....	....	....	....	....
Services: Debit	78aed	....	....	....	....	....	....	....	....	....	....	....	....	....	....	....
Balance on Goods & Services	78afd	....	....	....	....	....	....	....	....	....	....	....	....	....	....	....
Income: Credit	78agd	....	....	....	....	....	....	....	....	....	....	....	....	....	....	....
Income: Debit	78ahd	....	....	....	....	....	....	....	....	....	....	....	....	....	....	....
Balance on Gds, Serv. & Inc.	78aid	....	....	....	....	....	....	....	....	....	....	....	....	....	....	....
Current Transfers, n.i.e.: Credit	78ajd	....	....	....	....	....	....	....	....	....	....	....	....	....	....	....
Current Transfers: Debit	78akd	....	....	....	....	....	....	....	....	....	....	....	....	....	....	....
Capital Account, n.i.e.	78bcd	....	....	....	....	....	....	....	....	....	....	....	....	....	....	....
Capital Account, n.i.e.: Credit	78bad	....	....	....	....	....	....	....	....	....	....	....	....	....	....	....
Capital Account: Debit	78bbd	....	....	....	....	....	....	....	....	....	....	....	....	....	....	....
Financial Account, n.i.e.	78bjd	....	....	....	....	....	....	....	....	....	....	....	....	....	....	....
Direct Investment Abroad	78bdd	....	....	....	....	....	....	....	....	....	....	....	....	....	....	....
Dir. Invest. in Rep. Econ., n.i.e.	78bed	....	....	....	....	....	....	....	....	....	....	....	....	....	....	....
Portfolio Investment Assets	78bfd	....	....	....	....	....	....	....	....	....	....	....	....	....	....	....
Equity Securities	78bkd	....	....	....	....	....	....	....	....	....	....	....	....	....	....	....
Debt Securities	78bld	....	....	....	....	....	....	....	....	....	....	....	....	....	....	....
Portfolio Investment Liab., n.i.e.	78bgd	....	....	....	....	....	....	....	....	....	....	....	....	....	....	....
Equity Securities	78bmd	....	....	....	....	....	....	....	....	....	....	....	....	....	....	....
Debt Securities	78bnd	....	....	....	....	....	....	....	....	....	....	....	....	....	....	....
Financial Derivatives Assets	78bwd	....	....	....	....	....	....	....	....	....	....	....	....	....	....	....
Financial Derivatives Liabilities	78bxd	....	....	....	....	....	....	....	....	....	....	....	....	....	....	....
Other Investment Assets	78bhd	....	....	....	....	....	....	....	....	....	....	....	....	....	....	....
Monetary Authorities	78bod	....	....	....	....	....	....	....	....	....	....	....	....	....	....	....
General Government	78bpd	....	....	....	....	....	....	....	....	....	....	....	....	....	....	....
Banks	78bqd	....	....	....	....	....	....	....	....	....	....	....	....	....	....	....
Other Sectors	78brd	....	....	....	....	....	....	....	....	....	....	....	....	....	....	....
Other Investment Liab., n.i.e.	78bid	....	....	....	....	....	....	....	....	....	....	....	....	....	....	....
Monetary Authorities	78bsd	....	....	....	....	....	....	....	....	....	....	....	....	....	....	....
General Government	78btd	....	....	....	....	....	....	....	....	....	....	....	....	....	....	....
Banks	78bud	....	....	....	....	....	....	....	....	....	....	....	....	....	....	....
Other Sectors	78bvd	....	....	....	....	....	....	....	....	....	....	....	....	....	....	....
Net Errors and Omissions	78cad	....	....	....	....	....	....	....	....	....	....	....	....	....	....	....
Overall Balance	78cbd	....	....	....	....	....	....	....	....	....	....	....	....	....	....	....
Reserves and Related Items	79dad	....	....	....	....	....	....	....	....	....	....	....	....	....	....	....
Reserve Assets	79dbd	....	....	....	....	....	....	....	....	....	....	....	....	....	....	....
Use of Fund Credit and Loans	79dcd	....	....	....	....	....	....	....	....	....	....	....	....	....	....	....
Exceptional Financing	79ded	....	....	....	....	....	....	....	....	....	....	....	....	....	....	....
Government Finance																
Central Government																*Millions of Francs through 1998;*
Deficit (-) or Surplus	80	....	....	....	2,125	4,067	1,008	314	706	3,801	−294	1,673	−3,016	1,190	−3,538	10,279
Revenue	81	....	....	....	27,374	34,187	38,341	44,671	50,421	56,060	58,148	66,251	72,070	79,285	90,245	96,694
Grants Received	81z	....	....	....	140	170	222	115	111	89	102	101	161	314	144	366
Expenditure	82	....	....	....	25,077	29,439	36,761	43,137	47,958	51,058	56,921	64,818	70,985	81,389	88,971	92,095
Lending Minus Repayments	83	....	....	....	312	851	794	1,335	1,868	1,290	1,623	333	1,803	601	4,176	97
Adjustment for Complem. Period	80x	....	....	....	—	—	—	—	—	—	—	472	−2,459	3,581	−780	5,411
Financing																
Total Financing	84	....	....	....	−2,125	−4,067	−1,008	−314	−706	−3,801	294	−1,673	3,016	−1,190	3,538	−10,279
Domestic	84a	....	....	....	....	....	....	....	....	....	....	−1,591	3,103	−1,092	3,635	−10,940
Foreign	85a	....	....	....	....	....	....	....	....	....	....	−82	−87	−98	−97	661
Debt: Domestic	88a	....	....	....	8,496	8,007	8,571	8,718	8,798	8,322	8,155	9,340	10,774	12,834	14,089	
Foreign	89a	....	....	....	763	677	609	522	442	375	294	212	129	62	750	
General Government																*As Percent of*
Deficit (-) or Surplus	80g	....	....	....	....	....	....	....	....	....	....	....	....	....	....	....
Debt	88g	....	....	....	....	....	....	....	....	....	....	....	....	....	....	....
National Accounts																*Billions of Francs through 1998;*
Exports of Goods & Services	90c	48.9	49.4	52.4	68.6	96.1	80.2	87.9	89.1	94.0	111.0	117.7	122.8	141.3	157.6	195.8
Government Consumption	91f	5.8	6.6	7.4	8.7	10.7	13.0	14.7	16.3	17.6	19.5	22.2	24.7	26.1	27.6	29.8
Gross Fixed Capital Formation	93e	12.7	15.9	17.6	21.0	23.0	24.1	24.9	25.7	27.0	29.8	36.0	36.0	39.7	37.1	38.8
Increase/Decrease(-) in Stocks	93i	1.5	.7	.4	.2	−3.2	−4.2	−2.1	−4.8	1.0	−2.8	−2.5	−1.3	−.2	5.4	9.1
Private Consumption	96f	27.8	30.7	33.9	37.6	43.2	50.1	56.5	61.1	65.0	70.6	78.1	86.3	95.8	104.2	112.6
Imports of Goods & Services	98c	−41.7	−47.3	−48.5	−58.8	−76.2	−76.4	−82.1	−84.8	−92.3	−106.0	−118.5	−126.8	−143.8	−157.2	−192.3
Gross Domestic Product (GDP)	99b	55.0	56.1	63.2	76.8	93.6	86.7	99.8	102.6	112.2	122.1	132.9	141.7	158.8	174.7	193.7
Net Factor Inc/Pmts(-) Abroad	98.n	1.9	2.2	3.4	3.5	5.7	11.9	16.7	19.4	21.3	23.2	28.0	36.6	60.2	72.2	76.7
Gross National Income (GNI)	99a	57.0	58.3	66.6	80.3	99.3	98.6	116.5	122.0	133.5	145.3	160.9	178.3	218.9	246.9	270.4
Net National Income	99e	49.1	49.7	57.8	69.1	87.2	86.2	104.2	110.0	120.7	130.7	145.0	161.3	200.8	226.7	247.8
GDP Volume 1985 Prices	99b.p	140.45	144.19	153.71	166.48	173.50	162.09	166.20	168.81	175.69	179.61	181.32	180.32	182.36	187.82	199.44
GDP Volume (1990=100)	99bvp	54.5	56.0	59.7	64.6	67.4	62.9	64.5	65.5	68.2	69.7	70.4	70.0	70.8	72.9	77.4
GDP Deflator (1990=100)	99bip	28.1	27.9	29.5	33.1	38.7	38.4	43.1	43.6	45.8	48.8	52.6	56.4	62.5	66.7	69.7
																Millions:
Population	99z	.34	.34	.35	.35	.36	.36	.36	.36	.36	.36	.36	.37	.37	.37	.37

654   INTERNATIONAL FINANCIAL STATISTICS YEARBOOK   2000

Minus Sign Indicates Debit

Balance of Payments

1985	1986	1987	1988	1989	1990	1991	1992	1993	1994	1995	1996	1997	1998	1999		
										2,881	2,780	2,401	2,266	1,562	Current Account, n.i.e.	78al *d*
										9,244	8,477	8,473	9,010	8,889	Goods: Exports f.o.b.	78aa *d*
										-10,845	-10,211	-10,466	-11,009	-11,681	Goods: Imports f.o.b.	78ab *d*
										-1,601	-1,734	-1,993	-1,999	-2,793	*Trade Balance*	78ac *d*
										8,427	9,236	9,764	11,116	12,453	Services: Credit	78ad *d*
										-6,047	-6,718	-6,956	-8,045	-9,023	Services: Debit	78ae *d*
										779	784	815	1,072	637	*Balance on Goods & Services*	78af *d*
										49,367	40,130	38,140	42,548	42,409	Income: Credit	78ag *d*
										-46,638	-37,633	-36,043	-41,003	-41,092	Income: Debit	78ah *d*
										3,508	3,281	2,913	2,617	1,954	*Balance on Gds, Serv. & Inc.*	78ai *d*
										1,742	2,225	1,935	2,124	2,043	Current Transfers, n.i.e.: Credit	78aj *d*
										-2,369	-2,726	-2,446	-2,475	-2,434	Current Transfers: Debit	78ak *d*
															Capital Account, n.i.e.	78bc *d*
															Capital Account, n.i.e.: Credit	78ba *d*
															Capital Account: Debit	78bb *d*
															Financial Account, n.i.e.	78bj *d*
															Direct Investment Abroad	78bd *d*
															Dir. Invest. in Rep. Econ., n.i.e.	78be *d*
															Portfolio Investment Assets	78bf *d*
															Equity Securities	78bk *d*
															Debt Securities	78bl *d*
															Portfolio Investment Liab., n.i.e.	78bg *d*
															Equity Securities	78bm *d*
															Debt Securities	78bn *d*
															Financial Derivatives Assets	78bw *d*
															Financial Derivatives Liabilities	78bx *d*
															Other Investment Assets	78bh *d*
															Monetary Authorities	78bo *d*
															General Government	78bp *d*
															Banks	78bq *d*
															Other Sectors	78br *d*
															Other Investment Liab., n.i.e.	78bi *d*
															Monetary Authorities	78bs *d*
															General Government	78bt *d*
															Banks	78bu *d*
															Other Sectors	78bv *d*
															Net Errors and Omissions	78ca *d*
															Overall Balance	78cb *d*
															Reserves and Related Items	79da *d*
															Reserve Assets	79db *d*
															Use of Fund Credit and Loans	79dc *d*
															Exceptional Financing	79de *d*

Government Finance

Central Government

Millions of Euros Beginning 1999: Year Ending December 31

1985	1986	1987	1988	1989	1990	1991	1992	1993	1994	1995	1996	1997	1998	1999		
21,504	16,390	8,081	7,610	9,209	16,913	-37,189	....	....	2,656	12,573	25,846	12,609	....		Deficit (-) or Surplus	80
104,637	109,616	113,922	120,852	135,738	149,854	165,523	184,524	202,183	217,830	220,074	239,082	261,696			Revenue	81
543	417	253	264	1,403	954	613	525	944	596	797	507	7,037			Grants Received	81z
93,197	97,962	106,519	115,421	119,200	139,122	153,408	177,525	192,807	205,656	211,557	222,710	240,847			Expenditure	82
3,032	3,465	1,044	733	3,534	3,022	8,514	1,385	603	700	613	641	-5,563			Lending Minus Repayments	83
12,553	7,784	1,469	2,648	-5,198	8,249	-41,403	....	....	-9,414	3,872	9,608	-20,840			Adjustment for Complem. Period	80x

Financing

1985	1986	1987	1988	1989	1990	1991	1992	1993	1994	1995	1996	1997	1998	1999		
-21,504	-16,390	-8,081	-7,610	-9,209	-16,913	37,189	....	....	-2,656	-11,810	-25,846	-12,609			Total Financing	84
-21,470	-16,320	-6,490	-6,642	-8,675	-16,143	37,518	....	....	-2,300	-11,776	-25,598	-12,455			Domestic	84a
-34	-70	-1,591	-968	-534	-770	-329	....	....	-356	-34	-248	-154			Foreign	85a
14,110	15,469	14,739	13,035	11,774	9,473	8,190	12,181	15,473	....	....	....	24,616			Debt: Domestic	88a
750	4,997	3,316	2,402	1,951	1,289	1,053	902	512	....	....	....	6,311			Foreign	89a

General Government

Gross Domestic Product

1985	1986	1987	1988	1989	1990	1991	1992	1993	1994	1995	1996	1997	1998	1999		
....	....	....	....	....	5.0	1.9	.8	1.7	2.8	1.8	2.7	3.6	3.2	2.4	Deficit (-) or Surplus	80g
....	....	....	....	....	4.7	4.2	5.1	6.1	5.7	5.8	6.2	6.0	6.4	6.2	Debt	88g

National Accounts

Billions of Euros Beginning 1999

1985	1986	1987	1988	1989	1990	1991	1992	1993	1994	1995	1996	1997	1998	1999		
222.9	224.8	223.8	249.2	285.9	291.0	398.8	427.2	456.3	425.0	‡571.7	597.7	685.6	756.7	‡20.57	Exports of Goods & Services	90c
32.3	35.0	38.2	40.3	43.6	49.3	49.5	53.2	57.5	60.0	‡95.1	102.8	107.9	111.6	‡3.22	Government Consumption	91f
35.9	49.1	59.1	68.5	73.1	84.5	103.1	98.5	114.7	107.2	‡116.9	115.1	134.5	150.0	‡4.06	Gross Fixed Capital Formation	93e
2.4	—	.5	2.4	1.6	4.1	3.3	1.7	.5	1.9	‡-1.9	-.7	1.8	2.3	‡.07	Increase/Decrease(-) in Stocks	93i
120.5	126.2	134.7	143.7	154.6	166.5	234.5	240.2	254.4	269.7	‡257.8	273.7	289.0	300.6	‡7.87	Private Consumption	96f
-212.1	-215.0	-225.7	-250.7	-279.3	-291.3	-367.3	-361.8	-377.8	-383.4	‡-500.9	-524.3	-585.6	-633.2	‡-17.66	Imports of Goods & Services	98c
229.9	249.5	262.4	291.5	334.1	359.0	389.9	417.8	456.8	498.6	‡538.5	563.5	624.6	665.7	‡18.14	Gross Domestic Product (GDP)	99b
83.5	82.3	68.2	85.7	96.0	109.1	114.3	....	....	48.2	‡32.2	30.1	14.0	-24.0	....	Net Factor Inc/Pmts(-) Abroad	98.n
288.8	305.6	304.7	336.0	378.8	409.5	433.1	....	....	528.0	‡570.6	593.6	638.6	641.7	....	Gross National Income (GNI)	99a
264.8	280.5	278.3	308.2	348.5	377.8	399.1	....	....	....	‡491.1	510.2	554.6	554.6	....	Net National Income	99e
205.26	215.07	221.39	234.04	249.62	257.56	265.46	270.30	....	....	....	....	....	....	....	GDP Volume 1985 Prices	99b, *p*
79.7	83.5	86.0	90.9	96.9	100.0	103.1	104.9	....	....	....	....	....	....	....	GDP Volume (1990=100)	99bv *p*
80.3	83.2	85.0	89.3	96.0	100.0	105.4	110.9	....	....	....	....	....	....	....	GDP Deflator (1990=100)	99bi *p*

Midyear Estimates

1985	1986	1987	1988	1989	1990	1991	1992	1993	1994	1995	1996	1997	1998	1999		
.37	.37	.37	.37	.38	.38	.39	.39	.40	.40	.41	.42	.42	.43	.43	Population	99z

(See notes in the back of the book.)

		1970	1971	1972	1973	1974	1975	1976	1977	1978	1979	1980	1981	1982	1983	1984

Exchange Rates — *Denar per SDR:*

Market Rate	aa	....	....	....	....	....	....	....	....	....	....	....	....	....	....	....

Denar per US Dollar:

Market Rate	ae	....	....	....	....	....	....	....	....	....	....	....	....	....	....	....
Market Rate	rf															

Index Numbers (1995=100):

Nominal Effective Exchange Rate	ne c	....	....	....	....	....	....	....	....	....	....	....	....	....	....	....
Real Effective Exchange Rate	re c	....	....	....	....	....	....	....	....	....	....	....	....	....	....	....

Fund Position — *Millions of SDRs:*

Quota	2f. s	....	....	....	....	....	....	....	....	....	....	....	....	....	....	....
SDRs	1b. s	....	....	....	....	....	....	....	....	....	....	....	....	....	....	....
Reserve Position in the Fund	1c. s	....	....	....	....	....	....	....	....	....	....	....	....	....	....	....
Total Fund Cred.&Loans Outstg.	2tl	....	....	....	....	....	....	....	....	....	....	....	....	....	....	....

International Liquidity — *Millions of US Dollars Unless Otherwise Indicated:*

Total Reserves minus Gold	1l. d	....	....	....	....	....	....	....	....	....	....	....	....	....	....	....
SDRs	1b. d	....	....	....	....	....	....	....	....	....	....	....	....	....	....	....
Reserve Position in the Fund	1c. d	....	....	....	....	....	....	....	....	....	....	....	....	....	....	....
Foreign Exchange	1d. d	....	....	....	....	....	....	....	....	....	....	....	....	....	....	....
Gold (Million Fine Troy Ounces)	1ad	....	....	....	....	....	....	....	....	....	....	....	....	....	....	....
Gold (National Valuation)	1an d	....	....	....	....	....	....	....	....	....	....	....	....	....	....	....
Other Liab.	4.. d	....	....	....	....	....	....	....	....	....	....	....	....	....	....	....
Deposit Money Banks: Assets	7a. d	....	....	....	....	....	....	....	....	....	....	....	....	....	....	....
Liabilities	7b. d	....	....	....	....	....	....	....	....	....	....	....	....	....	....	....

Monetary Authorities — *Millions of Denar:*

Foreign Assets	11	....	....	....	....	....	....	....	....	....	....	....	....	....	....	....
Claims on Central Government	12a	....	....	....	....	....	....	....	....	....	....	....	....	....	....	....
Claims on Deposit Money Banks	12e	....	....	....	....	....	....	....	....	....	....	....	....	....	....	....
Reserve Money	14	....	....	....	....	....	....	....	....	....	....	....	....	....	....	....
of which: Currency Outside DMBs	14a	....	....	....	....	....	....	....	....	....	....	....	....	....	....	....
Restricted Deposits	16b	....	....	....	....	....	....	....	....	....	....	....	....	....	....	....
Foreign Liabilities	16c	....	....	....	....	....	....	....	....	....	....	....	....	....	....	....
Central Government Deposits	16d	....	....	....	....	....	....	....	....	....	....	....	....	....	....	....
Capital Accounts	17a	....	....	....	....	....	....	....	....	....	....	....	....	....	....	....
Other Items (Net)	17r	....	....	....	....	....	....	....	....	....	....	....	....	....	....	....

Deposit Money Banks — *Millions of Denar:*

Reserves	20	....	....	....	....	....	....	....	....	....	....	....	....	....	....	....
Foreign Assets	21	....	....	....	....	....	....	....	....	....	....	....	....	....	....	....
Claims on Central Government	22a	....	....	....	....	....	....	....	....	....	....	....	....	....	....	....
Claims on Local Government	22b	....	....	....	....	....	....	....	....	....	....	....	....	....	....	....
Claims on Nonfin.Pub.Enterprises	22c	....	....	....	....	....	....	....	....	....	....	....	....	....	....	....
Claims on Private Sector	22d	....	....	....	....	....	....	....	....	....	....	....	....	....	....	....
Demand Deposits	24	....	....	....	....	....	....	....	....	....	....	....	....	....	....	....
Time, Savings,& Fgn.Currency Dep.	25	....	....	....	....	....	....	....	....	....	....	....	....	....	....	....
Restricted Deposits	26b	....	....	....	....	....	....	....	....	....	....	....	....	....	....	....
Foreign Liabilities	26c	....	....	....	....	....	....	....	....	....	....	....	....	....	....	....
Central Government Deposits	26d	....	....	....	....	....	....	....	....	....	....	....	....	....	....	....
Credit from Monetary Authorities	26g	....	....	....	....	....	....	....	....	....	....	....	....	....	....	....
Capital Accounts	27a	....	....	....	....	....	....	....	....	....	....	....	....	....	....	....
Other Items (Net)	27r	....	....	....	....	....	....	....	....	....	....	....	....	....	....	....

Monetary Survey — *Millions of Denar:*

Foreign Assets (Net)	31n	....	....	....	....	....	....	....	....	....	....	....	....	....	....	....
Domestic Credit	32	....	....	....	....	....	....	....	....	....	....	....	....	....	....	....
Claims on Central Govt. (Net)	32an	....	....	....	....	....	....	....	....	....	....	....	....	....	....	....
Claims on Local Government	32b	....	....	....	....	....	....	....	....	....	....	....	....	....	....	....
Claims on Nonfin.Pub.Enterprises	32c	....	....	....	....	....	....	....	....	....	....	....	....	....	....	....
Claims on Private Sector	32d	....	....	....	....	....	....	....	....	....	....	....	....	....	....	....
Money	34	....	....	....	....	....	....	....	....	....	....	....	....	....	....	....
Quasi-Money	35	....	....	....	....	....	....	....	....	....	....	....	....	....	....	....
Restricted Deposits	36b	....	....	....	....	....	....	....	....	....	....	....	....	....	....	....
Capital Accounts	37a	....	....	....	....	....	....	....	....	....	....	....	....	....	....	....
Other Items (Net)	37r	....	....	....	....	....	....	....	....	....	....	....	....	....	....	....
Money plus Quasi-Money	35l	....	....	....	....	....	....	....	....	....	....	....	....	....	....	....

Interest Rates — *Percent Per Annum*

Bank Rate (End of Period)	60	....	....	....	....	....	....	....	....	....	....	....	....	....	....	....
Deposit Rate	60l	....	....	....	....	....	....	....	....	....	....	....	....	....	....	....
Lending Rate	60p	....	....	....	....	....	....	....	....	....	....	....	....	....	....	....

Prices, Production, Labor — *Index Numbers (1995=100):*

Consumer Prices	64	....	....	....	....	....	....	....	....	....	....	....	....	....	....	....
Wages: Average Monthly	65	....	....	....	....	....	....	....	....	....	....	....	....	....	....	....
Industrial Production	66	....	....	....	....	....	....	....	....	....	....	....	....	....	....	....

Number in Thousands:

Employment	67e	....	....	....	....	....	....	....	....	....	....	....	....	....	....	....
Unemployment	67c	....	....	....	....	....	....	....	....	....	....	....	....	....	....	....

International Transactions — *Millions of US Dollars*

Exports	70.. d	....	....	....	....	....	....	....	....	....	....	....	....	....	....	....
Imports, c.i.f.	71.. d	....	....	....	....	....	....	....	....	....	....	....	....	....	....	....

1985	1986	1987	1988	1989	1990	1991	1992	1993	1994	1995	1996	1997	1998	1999		Code
															Exchange Rates	
															End of Period	
....	....	....	....	....	....	....	....	61.062	59.264	56.456	59.547	74.776	72.987	82.816	Market Rate	aa
															End of Period (ae) Period Average (rf)	
....	....	....	....	....	....	....	....	44.456	40.596	37.980	41.411	55.421	51.836	60.339	Market Rate	ae
....	....	....	....	....	....	....	....	....	43.263	37.882	39.981	50.004	54.462	56.902	Market Rate	rf
															Period Averages	
....	....	....	....	....	....	....	765.24	129.54	81.49	100.00	117.74	163.38	161.70	182.79	Nominal Effective Exchange Rate	ne c
....	....	....	....	....	....	....	98.87	87.21	90.23	100.00	96.31	82.39	72.99	73.63	Real Effective Exchange Rate	re c
															Fund Position	
															End of Period	
....	....	....	....	....	....	....	—	49.6	49.6	49.6	49.6	49.6	49.6	68.9	Quota	2f. s
....	....	....	....	....	....	....	—	—	—	.2	—	.3	.8	.9	SDRs	1b. s
....	....	....	....	....	....	....	—	—	—	—	—	—	—	—	Reserve Position in the Fund	1c. s
....	....	....	....	....	....	....	—	2.8	14.0	38.1	47.4	65.3	72.7	74.1	Total Fund Cred.&Loans Outstg.	2tl
															International Liquidity	
															End of Period	
....	....	....	....	....	....	....		104.59	149.05	257.49	239.55	257.00	306.11	429.92	Total Reserves minus Gold	1l. d
....	....	....	....	....	....	....		—	—	.2	—	.4	1.1	1.2	SDRs	1b. d
....	....	....	....	....	....	....		—	—	—	—	—	—	—	Reserve Position in the Fund	1c. d
....	....	....	....	....	....	....		104.57	149.04	257.26	239.51	256.61	305.04	428.73	Foreign Exchange	1d. d
....	....	....	....	....	....	....	.021	.041	.045	.046	.076	.081	.100	.102	Gold (Million Fine Troy Ounces)	1ad
....	....	....	....	....	....	....	7.07	14.66	16.36	17.61	27.98	23.45	28.50	29.69	Gold (National Valuation)	1and
....	....	....	....	....	....	....	....								Other Liab.	4.. d
....	....	....	....	....	....	....	....	158.20	232.98	254.61	229.70	286.78	337.78	404.22	Deposit Money Banks: Assets	7a. d
....	....	....	....	....	....	....	....	579.43	528.30	85.47	138.37	185.72	250.00	262.28	Liabilities	7b. d
															Monetary Authorities	
															End of Period	
....	....	....	....	....	....	....	....	5,303	6,715	10,732	11,453	15,894	18,977	30,072	Foreign Assets	11
....	....	....	....	....	....	....	....	749	2,400	2,395	3,049	8,706	8,675	8,116	Claims on Central Government	12a
....	....	....	....	....	....	....	....	1,830	2,333	4,673	5,642	3,672	3,538	1,918	Claims on Deposit Money Banks	12e
....	....	....	....	....	....	....	....	3,705	6,360	‡8,306	8,044	9,872	10,421	13,508	Reserve Money	14
....	....	....	....	....	....	....	....	2,703	4,786	5,965	6,401	6,846	6,964	8,271	of which: Currency Outside DMBs	14a
....	....	....	....	....	....	....	....	—	—	114	136	9	56	271	Restricted Deposits	16b
....	....	....	....	....	....	....	....	172	831	2,150	2,822	4,882	5,308	6,137	Foreign Liabilities	16c
....	....	....	....	....	....	....	....	14	31	2,633	3,695	5,070	6,152	9,465	Central Government Deposits	16d
....	....	....	....	....	....	....	....	4,754	4,682	5,059	5,771	8,398	8,130	9,547	Capital Accounts	17a
....	....	....	....	....	....	....	....	−911	−360	−462	−325	41	1,123	1,178	Other Items (Net)	17r
															Deposit Money Banks	
															End of Period	
....	....	....	....	....	....	....	....	678	1,470	1,836	1,125	2,158	2,379	3,861	Reserves	20
....	....	....	....	....	....	....	....	7,033	9,458	9,670	9,512	15,897	17,509	24,390	Foreign Assets	21
....	....	....	....	....	....	....	....	52,503	48,954	5,624	6,311	1,782	1,288	1,289	Claims on Central Government	22a
....	....	....	....	....	....	....	....	—	—	2	12	27	20	14	Claims on Local Government	22b
....	....	....	....	....	....	....	....	—	—	528	121	208	293	237	Claims on Nonfin.Pub.Enterprises	22c
....	....	....	....	....	....	....	....	35,107	66,392	39,181	46,826	50,711	34,531	43,611	Claims on Private Sector	22d
....	....	....	....	....	....	....	....	2,853	5,080	5,567	4,854	6,281	7,336	10,458	Demand Deposits	24
....	....	....	....	....	....	....	....	38,138	9,726	8,417	8,652	11,537	13,573	17,846	Time, Savings,& Fgn.Currency Dep.	25
....	....	....	....	....	....	....	....	9,613	38,938	1,039	1,111	1,006	1,099	1,185	Restricted Deposits	26b
....	....	....	....	....	....	....	....	25,759	21,447	3,214	5,731	10,295	12,959	15,826	Foreign Liabilities	26c
....	....	....	....	....	....	....	....	445	2,411	1,481	1,345	1,678	2,181	2,904	Central Government Deposits	26d
....	....	....	....	....	....	....	....	1,310	1,961	4,016	4,395	2,388	2,303	1,287	Credit from Monetary Authorities	26g
....	....	....	....	....	....	....	....	10,520	15,567	17,483	23,799	23,157	23,651	29,046	Capital Accounts	27a
....	....	....	....	....	....	....	....	6,687	31,132	15,624	14,021	14,441	−7,082	−5,150	Other Items (Net)	27r
															Monetary Survey	
															End of Period	
....	....	....	....	....	....	....	....	−13,595	−6,106	15,038	12,412	16,614	18,219	32,499	Foreign Assets (Net)	31n
....	....	....	....	....	....	....	....	87,900	115,304	43,635	51,406	54,797	36,637	41,075	Domestic Credit	32
....	....	....	....	....	....	....	....	52,793	48,912	3,905	4,320	3,740	1,630	−2,964	Claims on Central Govt. (Net)	32an
....	....	....	....	....	....	....	....	—	—	2	12	27	20	14	Claims on Local Government	32b
....	....	....	....	....	....	....	....	—	—	528	121	208	293	237	Claims on Nonfin.Pub.Enterprises	32c
....	....	....	....	....	....	....	....	35,107	66,392	39,181	46,826	50,711	34,531	43,611	Claims on Private Sector	32d
....	....	....	....	....	....	....	....	5,590	9,965	‡12,223	11,788	13,702	14,952	19,795	Money	34
....	....	....	....	....	....	....	....	37,510	8,507	‡8,417	8,652	11,537	13,573	17,846	Quasi-Money	35
....	....	....	....	....	....	....	....	9,613	38,938	1,153	1,247	1,015	1,155	1,456	Restricted Deposits	36b
....	....	....	....	....	....	....	....	15,274	20,249	22,542	29,570	31,555	24,774	30,224	Capital Accounts	37a
....	....	....	....	....	....	....	....	6,174	31,624	14,338	12,561	13,602	402	4,253	Other Items (Net)	37r
....	....	....	....	....	....	....	....	43,100	18,472	‡20,640	20,440	25,239	28,525	37,641	Money plus Quasi-Money	35l
															Interest Rates	
															Percent Per Annum	
....	....	....	....	....	....	....	....	295.00	33.00	15.00	9.20	8.90	8.90	8.90	Bank Rate (*End of Period*)	60
....	....	....	....	....	....	....	....	....	117.56	24.07	12.75	11.64	11.68	11.40	Deposit Rate	60l
....	....	....	....	....	....	....	....	....	159.82	45.95	21.58	21.42	21.03	20.45	Lending Rate	60p
															Prices, Production, Labor	
															Period Averages	
....	....	....	....	....	....	....	....	37.9	85.9	100.0	102.7	103.8	104.4	103.0	Consumer Prices	64
....	....	....	....	....	....	....	....	....	90.6	100.0	102.8	....	....	....	Wages: Average Monthly	65
....	....	....	....	....	....	....	....	124.7	112.4	100.0	103.1	104.6	....	....	Industrial Production	66
															Period Averages	
....	....	....	....	517	507	468	446	421	396	357	340	319	310	....	Employment	67e
....	....	....	....	150	156	165	172	175	186	216	238	253	....	....	Unemployment	67c
															International Transactions	
															Millions of US Dollars	
....	....	....	....	....	....	....	....	1,055.3	1,086.3	1,204.0	....	....	....	....	Exports	70.. d
....	....	....	....	....	....	....	....	1,199.4	1,484.1	1,718.9	....	....	....	....	Imports, c.i.f.	71.. d

		1970	1971	1972	1973	1974	1975	1976	1977	1978	1979	1980	1981	1982	1983	1984
Balance of Payments																	*Millions of US Dollars:*
Current Account, n.i.e.	78al d	...	...	...	...	...	...	...	...	...	...	...	...	...	...	...
Goods: Exports f.o.b	78aa d	...	...	...	...	...	...	...	...	...	...	...	...	...	...	...
Goods: Imports f.o.b	78ab d	...	...	...	...	...	...	...	...	...	...	...	...	...	...	...
Trade Balance	78ac d	...	...	...	...	...	...	...	...	...	...	...	...	...	...	...
Services: Credit	78ad d	...	...	...	...	...	...	...	...	...	...	...	...	...	...	...
Services: Debit	78ae d	...	...	...	...	...	...	...	...	...	...	...	...	...	...	...
Balance on Goods & Services	78af d	...	...	...	...	...	...	...	...	...	...	...	...	...	...	...
Income: Credit	78ag d	...	...	...	...	...	...	...	...	...	...	...	...	...	...	...
Income: Debit	78ah d	...	...	...	...	...	...	...	...	...	...	...	...	...	...	...
Balance on Gds, Serv. & Inc.	78ai d	...	...	...	...	...	...	...	...	...	...	...	...	...	...	...
Current Transfers, n.i.e.: Credit	78aj d	...	...	...	...	...	...	...	...	...	...	...	...	...	...	...
Current Transfers: Debit	78ak d	...	...	...	...	...	...	...	...	...	...	...	...	...	...	...
Capital Account, n.i.e.	78bc d	...	...	...	...	...	...	...	...	...	...	...	...	...	...	...
Capital Account, n.i.e.: Credit	78ba d	...	...	...	...	...	...	...	...	...	...	...	...	...	...	...
Capital Account: Debit	78bb d	...	...	...	...	...	...	...	...	...	...	...	...	...	...	...
Financial Account, n.i.e.	78bj d	...	...	...	...	...	...	...	...	...	...	...	...	...	...	...
Direct Investment Abroad	78bd d	...	...	...	...	...	...	...	...	...	...	...	...	...	...	...
Dir. Invest. in Rep. Econ., n.i.e.	78be d	...	...	...	...	...	...	...	...	...	...	...	...	...	...	...
Portfolio Investment Assets	78bf d	...	...	...	...	...	...	...	...	...	...	...	...	...	...	...
Equity Securities	78bk d	...	...	...	...	...	...	...	...	...	...	...	...	...	...	...
Debt Securities	78bl d	...	...	...	...	...	...	...	...	...	...	...	...	...	...	...
Portfolio Investment Liab., n.i.e.	78bg d	...	...	...	...	...	...	...	...	...	...	...	...	...	...	...
Equity Securities	78bm d	...	...	...	...	...	...	...	...	...	...	...	...	...	...	...
Debt Securities	78bn d	...	...	...	...	...	...	...	...	...	...	...	...	...	...	...
Financial Derivatives Assets	78bw d	...	...	...	...	...	...	...	...	...	...	...	...	...	...	...
Financial Derivatives Liabilities	78bx d	...	...	...	...	...	...	...	...	...	...	...	...	...	...	...
Other Investment Assets	78bh d	...	...	...	...	...	...	...	...	...	...	...	...	...	...	...
Monetary Authorities	78bo d	...	...	...	...	...	...	...	...	...	...	...	...	...	...	...
General Government	78bp d	...	...	...	...	...	...	...	...	...	...	...	...	...	...	...
Banks	78bq d	...	...	...	...	...	...	...	...	...	...	...	...	...	...	...
Other Sectors	78br d	...	...	...	...	...	...	...	...	...	...	...	...	...	...	...
Other Investment Liab., n.i.e.	78bi d	...	...	...	...	...	...	...	...	...	...	...	...	...	...	...
Monetary Authorities	78bs d	...	...	...	...	...	...	...	...	...	...	...	...	...	...	...
General Government	78bt d	...	...	...	...	...	...	...	...	...	...	...	...	...	...	...
Banks	78bu d	...	...	...	...	...	...	...	...	...	...	...	...	...	...	...
Other Sectors	78bv d	...	...	...	...	...	...	...	...	...	...	...	...	...	...	...
Net Errors and Omissions	78ca d	...	...	...	...	...	...	...	...	...	...	...	...	...	...	...
Overall Balance	78cb d	...	...	...	...	...	...	...	...	...	...	...	...	...	...	...
Reserves and Related Items	79da d	...	...	...	...	...	...	...	...	...	...	...	...	...	...	...
Reserve Assets	79db d	...	...	...	...	...	...	...	...	...	...	...	...	...	...	...
Use of Fund Credit and Loans	79dc d	...	...	...	...	...	...	...	...	...	...	...	...	...	...	...
Exceptional Financing	79de d	...	...	...	...	...	...	...	...	...	...	...	...	...	...	...
International Investment Position																	*Millions of US Dollars*
Assets	79aa d	...	...	...	...	...	...	...	...	...	...	...	...	...	...	...
Direct Investment Abroad	79ab d	...	...	...	...	...	...	...	...	...	...	...	...	...	...	...
Portfolio Investment	79ac d	...	...	...	...	...	...	...	...	...	...	...	...	...	...	...
Equity Securities	79ad d	...	...	...	...	...	...	...	...	...	...	...	...	...	...	...
Debt Securities	79ae d	...	...	...	...	...	...	...	...	...	...	...	...	...	...	...
Financial Derivatives	79al d	...	...	...	...	...	...	...	...	...	...	...	...	...	...	...
Other Investment	79af d	...	...	...	...	...	...	...	...	...	...	...	...	...	...	...
Monetary Authorities	79ag d	...	...	...	...	...	...	...	...	...	...	...	...	...	...	...
General Government	79ah d	...	...	...	...	...	...	...	...	...	...	...	...	...	...	...
Banks	79ai d	...	...	...	...	...	...	...	...	...	...	...	...	...	...	...
Other Sectors	79aj d	...	...	...	...	...	...	...	...	...	...	...	...	...	...	...
Reserve Assets	79ak d	...	...	...	...	...	...	...	...	...	...	...	...	...	...	...
Liabilities	79la d	...	...	...	...	...	...	...	...	...	...	...	...	...	...	...
Dir. Invest. in Rep. Economy	79lb d	...	...	...	...	...	...	...	...	...	...	...	...	...	...	...
Portfolio Investment	79lc d	...	...	...	...	...	...	...	...	...	...	...	...	...	...	...
Equity Securities	79ld d	...	...	...	...	...	...	...	...	...	...	...	...	...	...	...
Debt Securities	79le d	...	...	...	...	...	...	...	...	...	...	...	...	...	...	...
Financial Derivatives	79ll d	...	...	...	...	...	...	...	...	...	...	...	...	...	...	...
Other Investment	79lf d	...	...	...	...	...	...	...	...	...	...	...	...	...	...	...
Monetary Authorities	79lg d	...	...	...	...	...	...	...	...	...	...	...	...	...	...	...
General Government	79lh d	...	...	...	...	...	...	...	...	...	...	...	...	...	...	...
Banks	79li d	...	...	...	...	...	...	...	...	...	...	...	...	...	...	...
Other Sectors	79lj d	...	...	...	...	...	...	...	...	...	...	...	...	...	...	...
Government Finance																	*Millions of Denar:*
Deficit (-) or Surplus	80	...	...	...	...	...	...	...	...	...	...	...	...	...	...	...
Total Revenue and Grants	81y	...	...	...	...	...	...	...	...	...	...	...	...	...	...	...
Revenue	81	...	...	...	...	...	...	...	...	...	...	...	...	...	...	...
Grants	81z	...	...	...	...	...	...	...	...	...	...	...	...	...	...	...
Exp. & Lending Minus Repay.	82z	...	...	...	...	...	...	...	...	...	...	...	...	...	...	...
Expenditure	82	...	...	...	...	...	...	...	...	...	...	...	...	...	...	...
Lending Minus Repayments	83	...	...	...	...	...	...	...	...	...	...	...	...	...	...	...
Total Financing	80h	...	...	...	...	...	...	...	...	...	...	...	...	...	...	...
Total Net Borrowing	84	...	...	...	...	...	...	...	...	...	...	...	...	...	...	...
Net Domestic	84a	...	...	...	...	...	...	...	...	...	...	...	...	...	...	...
Net Foreign	85a	...	...	...	...	...	...	...	...	...	...	...	...	...	...	...
Use of Cash Balances	87	...	...	...	...	...	...	...	...	...	...	...	...	...	...	...
National Accounts																	*Millions of Denar*
Househ.Cons.Expend.,incl.NPISHs	96f	...	...	...	...	...	...	...	...	...	...	...	...	...	...	...
Government Consumption Expend.	91f	...	...	...	...	...	...	...	...	...	...	...	...	...	...	...
Gross Fixed Capital Formation	93e	...	...	...	...	...	...	...	...	...	...	...	...	...	...	...
Changes in Inventories	93i	...	...	...	...	...	...	...	...	...	...	...	...	...	...	...
Exports of Goods and Services	90c	...	...	...	...	...	...	...	...	...	...	...	...	...	...	...
Imports of Goods and Services	98c	...	...	...	...	...	...	...	...	...	...	...	...	...	...	...
GDP, Production Based	99bp	...	...	...	...	...	...	...	...	...	...	...	...	...	...	...
Statistical Discrepancy	99bs	...	...	...	...	...	...	...	...	...	...	...	...	...	...	...
Population	99z	...	...	...	...	...	...	...	...	...	...	...	...	...	...	...	*Millions:*

Years columns: 1985 1986 1987 1988 1989 1990 1991 1992 1993 1994 1995 1996 1997 1998 1999

Balance of Payments

Minus Sign Indicates Debit

Item	1996	1997	1998	1999	Code
Current Account, n.i.e.	-288.1	-275.5	-311.7	-109.3	78al d
Goods: Exports f.o.b	1,147.4	1,201.4	1,292.9	1,192.1	78aa d
Goods: Imports f.o.b	-1,464.0	-1,589.1	-1,713.2	-1,602.2	78ab d
Trade Balance	-316.5	-387.6	-420.3	-410.1	78ac d
Services: Credit	154.3	128.3	131.3	248.4	78ad d
Services: Debit	-309.3	-272.9	-304.3	-323.8	78ae d
Balance on Goods & Services	-471.5	-532.2	-593.3	-485.5	78af d
Income: Credit	45.3	39.0	23.5	22.5	78ag d
Income: Debit	-75.0	-72.6	-68.4	-66.3	78ah d
Balance on Gds, Serv. & Inc.	-501.2	-565.8	-638.1	-529.4	78ai d
Current Transfers, n.i.e.: Credit	475.4	535.0	692.6	750.3	78aj d
Current Transfers: Debit	-262.3	-244.8	-366.2	-330.2	78ak d
Capital Account, n.i.e.			9.4	4.4	78bc d
Capital Account, n.i.e.: Credit			11.2	4.4	78ba d
Capital Account: Debit			-1.8	—	78bb d
Financial Account, n.i.e.	174.3	186.8	449.2	189.6	78bj d
Direct Investment Abroad	....	....	....	—	78bd d
Dir. Invest. in Rep. Econ., n.i.e.	11.2	15.7	117.7	30.1	78be d
Portfolio Investment Assets	-.5	-2.5	-.6	-.4	78bf d
Equity Securities	-.5	-2.5	-.6	-.4	78bk d
Debt Securities				—	78bl d
Portfolio Investment Liab., n.i.e.	.8	4.6	8.4	.5	78bg d
Equity Securities	.8	4.6	8.4	.5	78bm d
Debt Securities				—	78bn d
Financial Derivatives Assets			—	....	78bw d
Financial Derivatives Liabilities					78bx d
Other Investment Assets	-133.2	-73.0	-77.2	-81.0	78bh d
Monetary Authorities					78bo d
General Government				-14.6	78bp d
Banks	25.3	-57.5	-51.0	-66.4	78bq d
Other Sectors	-158.5	-15.6	-26.2	—	78br d
Other Investment Liab., n.i.e.	295.9	242.0	400.9	240.4	78bi d
Monetary Authorities					78bs z
General Government	59.9	-71.6	109.2	68.8	78bt d
Banks	-1.2	29.8	97.7	30.9	78bu d
Other Sectors	237.3	283.8	194.0	140.7	78bv d
Net Errors and Omissions	18.8	-29.9	-114.8	34.5	78ca d
Overall Balance	-95.1	-118.6	32.1	119.2	78cb d
Reserves and Related Items	95.1	118.6	-32.1	-119.2	79da d
Reserve Assets	7.6	-35.1	-42.0	-141.6	79db d
Use of Fund Credit and Loans	13.5	24.6	9.9	1.8	79dc d
Exceptional Financing	73.9	129.2	—	20.6	79de d

International Investment Position

Millions of US Dollars

Item	1996	1997	1998	1999	Code
Assets	496.8	567.2	672.3	863.8	79aa d
Direct Investment Abroad	—	—	—	—	79ab d
Portfolio Investment	—	—	—	—	79ac d
Equity Securities	—	—	—	—	79ad d
Debt Securities	—	—	—	—	79ae d
Financial Derivatives	—	—	—	—	79al d
Other Investment	229.3	286.8	337.8	404.2	79af d
Monetary Authorities					79ag d
General Government					79ah d
Banks	229.3	286.8	337.8	404.2	79ai d
Other Sectors	—	—	—	—	79aj d
Reserve Assets	267.5	280.4	334.6	459.6	79ak d
Liabilities	1,243.1	1,259.7	1,545.0	1,603.7	79la d
Dir. Invest. in Rep. Economy	—	—	—	—	79lb d
Portfolio Investment	—	—	—	—	79lc d
Equity Securities	—	—	—	—	79ld d
Debt Securities	—	—	—	—	79le d
Financial Derivatives	—	—	—	—	79ll d
Other Investment	1,243.1	1,259.7	1,545.0	1,603.7	79lf d
Monetary Authorities	68.2	88.1	102.4	101.7	79lg d
General Government	1,041.2	999.3	1,126.2	1,156.3	79lh d
Banks	121.3	156.3	289.7	321.2	79li d
Other Sectors	12.4	16.0	26.8	24.5	79lj d

Government Finance

Year Ending December 31

Item	1995	1996	Code
Deficit (-) or Surplus	2,267.6	175.3	80
Total Revenue and Grants	40,437.0	39,865.2	81y
Revenue	39,775.8	39,766.1	81
Grants	661.2	99.1	81z
Exp. & Lending Minus Repay.	38,169.4	39,689.9	82z
Expenditure	36,511.0	37,423.3	82
Lending Minus Repayments	1,658.4	2,266.6	83
Total Financing	-2,267.6	-175.3	80h
Total Net Borrowing	-3,445.2	-175.5	84
Net Domestic	-3,334.1	-1,200.0	84a
Net Foreign	-111.1	1,024.5	85a
Use of Cash Balances	1,177.6	.2	87

National Accounts

Millions of Denar

Item	1993	1994	1995	1996	1997	1998	Code
Househ.Cons.Expend.,incl.NPISHs	47,182	110,847	119,381	127,253	136,350	140,878	96f
Government Consumption Expend.	12,472	27,875	31,491	31,985	31,797	33,530	91f
Gross Fixed Capital Formation	10,994	22,461	28,027	30,654	32,189	33,982	93e
Changes in Inventories	-416	182	7,162	4,790	9,168	9,831	93i
Exports of Goods and Services	27,660	55,920	55,961	49,722	68,260	82,939	90c
Imports of Goods and Services	-32,360	-70,876	-72,501	-67,961	-92,783	-110,333	98c
GDP, Production Based	59,165	146,409	169,521	176,444	184,982	190,827	99bp
Statistical Discrepancy	-6,368	—	—	—	—	—	99bs

Midyear Estimates

Item	1993	1994	1995	1996	1997	1998	1999	Code
Population	2	2	2	2	2	2	2	99z

(See notes in the back of the book.)

Madagascar

		1970	1971	1972	1973	1974	1975	1976	1977	1978	1979	1980	1981	1982	1983	1984
Exchange Rates															*Francs per SDR:*	
Official Rate	aa	276.0	283.6	278.0	284.0	272.1	262.5	288.7	285.8	272.3	264.8	288.0	334.5	405.6	515.3	645.0
															Francs per US Dollar:	
Official Rate	ae	276.0	261.2	256.1	235.4	222.2	224.3	248.5	235.2	209.0	201.0	225.8	287.4	367.7	492.2	658.0
Official Rate	rf	277.7	276.9	252.0	222.9	240.7	214.3	238.9	245.7	225.7	212.7	211.3	271.7	349.7	430.4	576.6
Fund Position															*Millions of SDRs:*	
Quota	2f. s	26.0	26.0	26.0	26.0	26.0	26.0	26.0	26.0	34.0	34.0	51.0	51.0	51.0	66.4	66.4
SDRs	1b. s	3.2	6.0	8.7	8.7	.2	.9	1.9	6.9	8.7	—	—	.3	1.1	.1	1.5
Reserve Position in the Fund	1c. s	5.0	5.0	5.0	5.0	—	—	—	—	—	—	—	.3	1.2		
Total Fund Cred.&Loans Outstg.	2tl	—	—	—	—	3.5	14.3	14.3	15.7	24.2	20.7	68.2	100.2	152.0	158.1	173.8
International Liquidity													*Millions of US Dollars Unless Otherwise Indicated:*			
Total Reserves minus Gold	1l. d	37.1	46.3	52.2	67.9	49.4	35.6	42.2	68.9	59.2	5.0	9.1	26.5	20.0	29.2	58.9
SDRs	1b. d	3.2	6.5	9.5	10.5	.2	1.1	2.2	8.3	11.3	—	—	.3	1.3	.1	1.5
Reserve Position in the Fund	1c. d	5.0	5.5	5.5	6.1	—	—	—	—	—	—	—	.4	1.3		
Foreign Exchange	1d. d	28.9	34.4	37.3	51.3	49.2	34.5	40.0	60.6	47.9	5.0	9.1	25.8	17.4	29.1	57.4
Deposit Money Banks: Assets	7a. d	21.7	13.2	20.0	24.1	46.3	38.9	29.6	44.5	45.6	46.7	75.3	46.0	45.1	31.5	44.6
Liabilities	7b. d	10.2	8.7	8.8	11.2	6.5	7.1	4.1	5.7	6.2	67.4	111.5	103.6	68.8	42.5	33.5
Monetary Authorities															*Billions of Francs:*	
Foreign Assets	11	13.4	14.9	16.8	19.0	13.4	9.6	12.5	16.3	12.0	‡ .3	4.0	6.7	10.0	17.4	47.7
Claims on Central Government	12a	-3.1	-3.0	-1.8	-.7	10.2	17.1	26.7	46.9	82.8	‡ 139.5	215.1	278.8	361.7	460.1	572.2
Claims on Nonfin.Pub.Enterprises	12c	....	....	....	....	....	....	....	....	....	9.8	8.6	8.6	8.3	26.9	35.9
Claims on Deposit Money Banks	12e	17.2	19.5	18.0	14.5	19.1	18.9	12.0	12.4	8.3	‡ 9.0	2.3	1.5	—	8.2	8.9
Reserve Money	14	22.9	22.6	26.0	27.4	32.4	34.7	39.5	44.3	59.0	‡ 57.4	77.5	104.0	102.8	97.8	106.9
of which: Currency Outside DMBs	14a	22.5	22.2	25.4	27.0	31.9	34.0	35.5	42.1	48.2	‡ 53.5	70.2	83.1	90.4	75.8	89.9
Foreign Liabilities	16c	—	—	.4	.1	3.2	4.3	4.0	9.7	8.7	‡ 53.9	117.0	161.9	215.3	454.5	671.3
Central Government Deposits	16d	2.6	5.1	2.2	.5	2.2	2.1	2.1	17.7	32.6	‡ 43.1	31.3	42.9	82.4	116.2	169.3
Counterpart Funds	16e	....	....	....	....	....	....	....	....	....	....	.2	.6	1.3	1.5	.3
Capital Accounts	17a	2.4	3.4	4.2	5.0	6.0	5.8	6.0	5.7	5.3	‡ 6.2	7.2	8.2	8.2	8.2	8.2
Other Items (Net)	17r	2.3	5.4	2.5	.1	1.1	.8	1.7	15.9	30.1	‡ -2.1	-3.2	-21.9	-29.9	-165.5	-291.2
Deposit Money Banks															*Billions of Francs:*	
Reserves	20	.3	.3	.6	.4	.7	.6	2.0	2.7	10.8	‡ 3.8	7.3	20.5	12.0	20.8	14.8
Foreign Assets	21	6.0	3.4	5.1	5.6	10.3	8.6	7.4	10.5	9.5	‡ 9.4	17.0	13.2	16.6	15.5	29.4
Claims on Central Government	22a	2.6	3.4	5.4	5.7	8.5	9.7	9.7	9.9	10.0	‡ 13.2	12.4	17.0	16.8	9.0	9.4
Claims on Private Sector	22d	48.8	55.0	55.7	55.8	65.6	67.0	70.9	86.5	91.0	‡ 120.3	155.1	171.9	208.1	245.6	303.0
Demand Deposits	24	19.5	20.3	23.5	26.3	31.7	30.5	39.6	51.8	56.0	‡ 70.7	81.1	110.4	117.3	116.7	149.7
Time Deposits	25	9.0	11.6	12.1	10.7	14.2	14.4	17.4	16.5	23.5	‡ 16.4	18.3	16.4	20.9	14.3	16.3
Bonds	26ab	4.8	5.4	5.4	5.1	11.1	11.0	—	—		14.6	17.7	21.0	27.8	42.9	46.0
Foreign Liabilities	26c	2.8	2.2	2.2	2.6	1.5	1.6	1.0	1.3	1.3	‡ 10.6	14.0	15.1	9.3	6.4	10.3
Long-Term Foreign Liabilities	26cl	....	....	....	....	....	....	....	....	....	2.9	11.1	14.7	16.0	14.5	11.7
Central Government Deposits	26d	5.0	4.1	4.7	8.0	10.5	11.5	13.4	14.3	14.7	‡ 11.8	19.2	12.2	15.0	18.1	24.0
Central Govt. Lending Funds	26f	....	....	....	....	....	....	....	....	....	3.8	4.7	5.3	5.1	6.9	8.8
Credit from Monetary Authorities	26g	11.9	13.1	11.2	10.5	11.0	11.1	—	—	—	9.0	2.3	1.5	—	8.2	8.9
Capital Accounts	27a	3.1	3.3	3.7	3.8	5.2	5.4	5.7	12.5	13.5	‡ 15.4	23.7	27.4	33.3	47.0	64.1
Other Items (Net)	27r	18.3	20.5	20.6	16.1	21.9	22.6	12.8	13.2	12.4	‡ -8.5	-.5	-1.4	8.9	16.1	16.6
Treasury Claims: Private Sector	22d. i	4.1	4.7	3.8	3.9	4.4	5.5	5.3	4.9	5.1	4.7	5.6	....	....	....	....
Post Office: Checking Deposits	24.. i	2.0	2.0	2.0	2.2	1.9	2.1	2.2	2.4	3.0	3.9	3.8	....	....	....	....
Treasury: Checking Deposits	24.. r	2.1	2.4	2.6	1.8	2.5	2.8	2.4	3.8	5.7	10.1[e]	....	....	....	....	....
Monetary Survey															*Billions of Francs:*	
Foreign Assets (Net)	31n	16.6	16.0	19.3	21.8	19.0	12.2	14.8	15.7	11.5	‡ -54.9	-110.0	-157.1	-198.0	-427.9	-604.6
Domestic Credit	32	44.9	50.6	56.8	56.3	76.0	85.1	96.4	117.4	145.2	‡ 227.8	340.6	421.1	497.6	607.5	727.1
Claims on Central Govt. (Net)	32an	-7.9	-9.1	-2.7	-3.5	6.0	12.6	20.2	26.1	49.1	‡ 97.8	176.9	240.6	281.1	334.9	388.3
Claims on Private Sector	32d	52.8	59.7	59.5	59.8	70.0	72.5	76.2	91.3	96.1	‡ 130.1	163.7	180.5	216.5	272.6	338.8
Money	34	46.2	47.0	53.3	57.3	67.9	69.4	79.7	100.0	112.8	‡ 124.3	151.3	193.8	208.0	192.7	239.9
Quasi-Money	35	9.0	11.6	12.1	10.7	14.2	14.4	17.4	16.5	23.5	‡ 16.4	18.3	16.4	20.9	15.4	18.2
Bonds	36ab	4.8	5.4	5.4	5.1	11.1	11.0	—	—	—	14.6	17.7	21.0	27.8	42.9	46.0
Long-Term Foreign Liabilities	36cl	....	....	....	....	....	....	....	....	....	2.9	11.1	14.7	16.0	14.5	11.7
Other Items (Net)	37r	6.4	7.8	11.4	10.1	12.7	13.6	14.2	17.9	24.0	‡ 14.8	32.2	18.1	26.9	-86.0	-193.3
Money plus Quasi-Money	35l	55.2	58.6	65.4	68.0	82.2	83.7	97.1	116.4	136.3	‡ 140.7	169.6	210.2	228.9	208.1	258.1
Liquid Liabilities	55l	57.1	60.6	67.5	70.2	85.0	86.7	100.2	122.4	....	....	....	....	....		‡ 363.3
Interest Rates															*Percent Per Annum*	
Discount Rate *(End of Period)*	60	5.50	5.50	5.50	5.50	5.50	5.50	5.50	5.50	5.50	5.50	5.50	8.00	12.50	13.00	13.00
Base Rate *(End of Period)*	60a	....	....	....	....	....	....	....	....	....	....	....	....	....	....	....
Money Market Rate	60b	....	....	....	....	....	....	....	....	....	....	....	....	....	....	....
Deposit Rate	60l	....	....	....	....	....	....	....	....	....	....	....	....	....	....	....
Lending Rate	60p	....	....	....	....	....	....	....	....	....	....	....	....	....	....	....
Prices and Labor															*Index Numbers (1995=100):*	
Consumer Prices	64	2.9	3.0	3.2	3.4	4.1	4.5	4.7	4.8	5.2	5.9	7.0	9.1	12.0	14.3	15.7
															Number in Thousands:	
Labor Force	67d	....	....	....	....	....	....	....	....	....	....	....	....	....	....	....
Employment	67e	....	....	....	....	....	....	....	....	....	....	....	....	....	....	....
Unemployment	67c	....	....	....	....	....	....	....	....	....	....	....	....	....	....	....

	1985	1986	1987	1988	1989	1990	1991	1992	1993	1994	1995	1996	1997	1998	1999		
Exchange Rates																		
End of Period																Official Rate	aa
	698.4	941.6	1,751.0	2,054.1	2,014.0	2,085.4	2,621.5	2,626.5	2,695.8	5,651.2	5,088.2	6,224.2	7,130.3	7,606.5	8,980.6		
End of Period (ae) Period Average (rf)																Official Rate	ae
	635.8	769.8	1,234.3	1,526.4	1,532.5	1,465.8	1,832.7	1,910.2	1,962.7	3,871.1	3,423.0	4,328.5	5,284.7	5,402.2	6,543.2	Official Rate	rf
	662.5	676.3	1,069.2	1,407.1	1,603.4	1,494.1	1,835.4	1,864.0	1,913.8	3,067.3	4,265.6	4,061.3	5,090.9	5,441.4	6,283.8		
Fund Position																		
End of Period																Quota	2f. s
	66.4	66.4	66.4	66.4	66.4	66.4	66.4	90.4	90.4	90.4	90.4	90.4	90.4	90.4	122.2		
	—	—	—	.1	.1	.1	—	—	.1	—	—	—	—	—	.1	SDRs	1b. s
	—	—	—	—	—	—	—	—	—	—	—	—	—	—	—	Reserve Position in the Fund	1c. s
	167.6	166.0	167.7	141.4	125.8	101.0	88.7	77.1	67.0	58.6	48.9	50.8	51.5	41.2	45.8	Total Fund Cred.&Loans Outstg.	2tl
International Liquidity																		
End of Period																Total Reserves minus Gold	1l. d
	48.4	114.5	185.2	223.7	245.3	92.1	88.9	....	....	71.6	109.0	240.9	281.6	171.4	227.2		
	—	—	.1	.1	.1	.2	.1	—	.1	—	—	.1	.1	—	.1	SDRs	1b. d
	—	—	—	—	—	—	—	—	—	—	—	—	—	—	—	Reserve Position in the Fund	1c. d
	48.4	114.5	185.1	223.6	245.2	91.9	88.8	....	....	71.6	108.9	240.8	281.5	171.3	227.0	Foreign Exchange	1d. d
	46.9	52.0	58.6	61.6	79.5	93.0	97.0	102.8	126.7	157.7	176.6	137.9	151.7	142.0	140.5	Deposit Money Banks: Assets	7a. d
	27.8	31.3	21.0	22.7	20.8	48.3	26.6	22.9	22.2	38.6	33.5	37.3	32.0	40.0	50.9	Liabilities	7b. d
Monetary Authorities																		
End of Period																		
	31.3	87.8	236.7	342.4	379.0	136.3	163.0	159.8	156.8	238.1	374.6	1,043.6	1,492.9	926.8	1,487.2	Foreign Assets	11
	664.1	802.6	1,083.7	1,251.9	1,310.2	1,275.8	1,265.6	1,246.9	1,252.9	1,412.3	1,445.8	1,437.0	1,360.2	1,752.2	1,881.0	Claims on Central Government	12a
	32.4	29.7	32.7	26.7	26.6	21.2	22.2	9.3	8.1	7.0	12.6	14.1	15.1	15.9	15.8	Claims on Nonfin.Pub.Enterprises	12c
	4.8	.2	5.4	10.6	11.9	127.5	84.1	46.4	49.5	134.7	175.1	127.5	107.3	102.7	75.1	Claims on Deposit Money Banks	12e
	111.4	189.8	229.1	237.6	327.5	296.6	460.6	556.5	519.9	893.9	1,159.0	1,723.1	1,741.8	1,848.8	2,322.0	Reserve Money	14
	96.2	113.2	140.3	171.2	216.6	214.9	287.3	317.2	378.7	614.5	758.7	829.4	1,020.3	1,169.9	1,434.9	of which: Currency Outside DMBs	14a
	752.3	1,031.0	2,008.0	2,363.4	2,465.4	2,404.4	3,100.2	452.1	378.8	719.6	575.5	644.0	672.3	591.7	664.8	Foreign Liabilities	16c
	228.5	307.3	438.3	599.1	784.1	795.7	690.6	327.3	389.7	283.4	552.8	609.4	871.4	658.2	636.7	Central Government Deposits	16d
	.4	.1	.1	.1	.1	.1	.1	—	—	—	—	—	—	—	—	Counterpart Funds	16e
	9.2	9.2	9.2	9.2	9.2	9.2	9.2	42.7	42.2	43.8	122.6	33.5	93.9	94.1	107.2	Capital Accounts	17a
	−369.2	−617.2	−1,326.3	−1,577.9	−1,858.7	−1,945.2	−2,725.8	83.8	136.7	−148.6	−401.3	−387.7	−404.1	−395.0	−276.8	Other Items (Net)	17r
Deposit Money Banks																		
End of Period																		
	12.3	76.5	88.8	66.3	110.8	80.9	173.3	239.2	141.1	279.3	400.2	893.7	721.5	678.7	887.1	Reserves	20
	29.8	40.1	72.3	94.1	121.8	136.3	177.9	196.3	248.6	610.3	604.4	597.0	801.5	766.9	919.1	Foreign Assets	21
	9.8	10.7	10.7	15.0	78.6	61.1	25.9	19.0	220.1	250.6	174.0	206.3	356.5	436.4	481.0	Claims on Central Government	22a
	362.7	424.7	499.4	524.5	582.2	757.2	851.7	918.5	1,061.6	1,338.5	1,550.4	1,573.6	1,797.6	1,811.8	1,937.5	Claims on Private Sector	22d
	142.3	176.3	231.5	283.7	381.7	358.7	465.3	598.1	645.7	989.0	1,089.3	1,338.3	1,643.7	1,783.1	2,115.4	Demand Deposits	24
	51.0	77.7	63.2	77.6	113.7	169.5	222.8	277.1	456.8	656.1	770.6	875.8	1,012.0	950.2	1,100.6	Time Deposits	25
	52.8	61.1	71.4	80.0	89.2	59.7	37.3	36.5	39.7	42.6	58.5	95.5	70.4	129.8	151.8	Bonds	26ab
	9.6	18.4	18.6	29.8	28.5	69.7	47.6	37.4	37.4	128.1	94.9	136.7	135.7	191.0	262.9	Foreign Liabilities	26c
	8.1	5.7	7.3	4.9	3.4	1.1	1.1	6.3	6.3	21.2	19.9	24.9	33.3	25.1	70.2	Long-Term Foreign Liabilities	26cl
	28.7	33.4	45.3	43.8	69.4	111.5	125.4	137.9	155.5	141.3	123.9	160.4	157.5	141.2	134.9	Central Government Deposits	26d
	9.2	11.1	16.3	18.6	19.6	1.3	1.2	1.2	1.1	1.4	.9	2.9	2.4	.8	6.0	Central Govt. Lending Funds	26f
	4.8	.2	5.4	10.6	11.9	127.5	84.1	46.4	49.5	134.7	174.4	127.5	107.3	102.7	75.1	Credit from Monetary Authorities	26g
	86.6	131.3	152.1	144.9	149.5	174.1	198.0	226.9	106.6	97.6	207.0	535.6	645.9	399.5	445.8	Capital Accounts	27a
	21.5	36.8	60.0	6.0	26.6	−37.5	46.1	5.2	173.1	266.9	189.8	−27.0	−131.0	−29.6	−138.0	Other Items (Net)	27r
	....	3.5	5.9	6.8	8.3	11.8	5.6	9.2	10.0	10.2	14.0	13.3	1.4	.5	2.1	Treasury Claims: Private Sector	22d. i
	....	4.8	5.1	5.0	5.0	5.2	5.7	5.7	5.3	4.5	5.8	11.5	15.0	11.9	12.3	Post Office: Checking Deposits	24.. i
	....	9.7	9.7	9.7	9.7	9.7	9.7	9.7	9.7	9.7	9.7	9.7	9.7	9.7	9.7	Treasury: Checking Deposits	24.. r
Monetary Survey																		
End of Period																		
	−700.8	−921.5	−1,717.6	−1,956.7	−1,993.1	−2,201.5	−2,807.1	−133.5	−10.7	.8	308.6	859.9	1,486.4	911.0	1,478.7	Foreign Assets (Net)	31n
	811.8	927.0	1,142.7	1,175.2	1,144.1	1,208.2	1,349.5	1,728.4	1,997.5	2,583.7	2,506.2	2,461.3	2,500.4	3,216.9	3,543.7	Domestic Credit	32
	416.7	472.6	610.7	624.0	535.3	429.7	475.6	800.6	927.8	1,238.2	943.2	873.5	687.7	1,389.2	1,590.4	Claims on Central Govt. (Net)	32an
	395.1	454.4	532.1	551.2	608.8	778.4	873.9	927.8	1,069.7	1,345.5	1,563.0	1,587.8	1,812.7	1,827.6	1,953.3	Claims on Private Sector	32d
	238.6	289.6	371.8	455.0	598.3	574.5	752.6	915.3	1,024.4	1,603.5	1,848.0	2,167.7	2,663.9	2,953.2	3,550.2	Money	34
	53.7	77.7	63.2	77.6	113.7	169.5	222.8	277.1	456.8	656.1	770.6	875.8	1,012.0	950.2	1,100.6	Quasi-Money	35
	52.8	61.1	71.4	80.0	89.2	59.7	37.3	36.5	39.7	42.6	58.5	95.5	70.4	129.8	151.8	Bonds	36ab
	8.1	5.7	7.3	4.9	3.4	1.1	1.1	6.3	6.3	21.2	19.9	24.9	33.3	25.1	70.2	Long-Term Foreign Liabilities	36cl
	−242.2	−428.6	−1,088.6	−1,399.0	−1,653.6	−1,798.0	−2,471.2	359.8	459.6	261.0	118.3	157.3	207.2	69.9	145.3	Other Items (Net)	37r
	292.3	367.2	435.0	532.6	712.0	743.9	975.3	1,192.4	1,481.3	2,259.7	2,618.6	3,043.5	3,676.0	3,903.4	4,650.8	Money plus Quasi-Money	35l
	419.3	511.0	625.4	760.2	984.8	819.6	1,044.4	1,266.7	1,636.3	2,473.2	2,893.9	3,606.4	4,498.2	5,067.5	6,007.1	Liquid Liabilities	55l
Interest Rates																		
Percent Per Annum																		
	11.50	11.50	11.50	11.50	....	....	....	12.0	12.0	15.6	31.3	26.4	12.8	9.3	....	Discount Rate (End of Period)	60
	....	....	....	....	15.0	15.0	15.0	....	....	....	29.0	10.0	....	11.2	....	Base Rate (End of Period)	60a
	....	....	....	17.8	20.5	20.5	20.5	19.5	19.5	18.5	19.0	14.4	8.0	....		Money Market Rate	60b
	....	....	....	22.3	25.8	24.5	25.0	26.0	30.5	37.5	32.8	30.0	27.0	....		Deposit Rate	60l
																Lending Rate	60p
Prices and Labor																		
Period Averages																		
	17.3	19.9	22.8	29.0	31.6	35.3	38.3	43.9	48.3	67.1	100.0	119.8	125.1	132.9	146.1	Consumer Prices	64
Period Averages																		
	....	....	....	....	....	....	....	....	5,300	....	....	....	....	....	....	Labor Force	67d
	....	259	258	258	265	281	286	....	315	322	337	....	....	....	....	Employment	67e
	29	24	18	16	16	17	9	6	5	4	3	....	....	....	....	Unemployment	67c

Madagascar

		1970	1971	1972	1973	1974	1975	1976	1977	1978	1979	1980	1981	1982	1983	1984
International Transactions																*Billions of Francs*
Exports	70	40	41	42	45	59	65	66	83	87	84	85	86	108	113	192
Imports, c.i.f.	71	47	59	52	45	67	78	68	85	100	135	127	148	149	167	214
Balance of Payments																*Millions of US Dollars:*
Current Account, n.i.e.	78al d	...	...	...	...	−40	−56	−28	−15	−79	−426	−556	−363	−299	−247	−193
Goods: Exports f.o.b.	78aa d	...	...	...	...	240	320	289	351	405	414	436	332	327	310	337
Goods: Imports f.o.b.	78ab d	...	...	...	...	−238	−332	−262	−312	−404	−662	−764	−511	−452	−378	−360
Trade Balance	78ac d	...	...	...	...	2	−12	27	39	1	−249	−328	−179	−124	−68	−23
Services: Credit	78ad d	...	...	...	...	40	62	41	35	35	74	79	62	49	45	53
Services: Debit	78ae d	...	...	...	...	−107	−148	−132	−136	−169	−267	−311	−224	−200	−172	−155
Balance on Goods & Services	78af d	...	...	...	...	−65	−98	−63	−63	−133	−441	−559	−341	−275	−195	−125
Income: Credit	78ag d	...	...	...	...	7	5	4	2	5	2	2	4	6	3	5
Income: Debit	78ah d	...	...	...	...	−25	−22	−21	−8	−12	−30	−46	−92	−101	−121	−151
Balance on Gds, Serv. & Inc.	78ai d	...	...	...	...	−83	−115	−80	−68	−140	−469	−603	−430	−370	−313	−271
Current Transfers, n.i.e.: Credit	78aj d	...	...	...	...	64	99	87	81	94	76	86	103	102	89	95
Current Transfers: Debit	78ak d	...	...	...	...	−20	−39	−34	−28	−33	−34	−39	−36	−31	−23	−18
Capital Account, n.i.e.	78bc d	...	...	...	...	—	—	—	−1	−1	−1	—	—	—	—	—
Capital Account, n.i.e.: Credit	78ba d	...	...	...	...	—	—	—	—	—	—	—	—	—	—	—
Capital Account: Debit	78bb d	...	...	...	...	—	—	—	−1	−1	−1	—	—	—	—	—
Financial Account, n.i.e.	78bj d	...	...	...	...	11	30	20	28	1	300	381	196	2	−21	−23
Direct Investment Abroad	78bd d	...	...	...	...	—	—	—	—	—	—	—	—	—	—	—
Dir. Invest. in Rep. Econ., n.i.e.	78be d	...	...	...	...	14	5	1	−3	−4	−7	—	—	—	—	—
Portfolio Investment Assets	78bf d	...	...	...	...	—	—	—	—	—	—	—	—	—	—	—
Equity Securities	78bk d	...	...	...	...	—	—	—	—	—	—	—	—	—	—	—
Debt Securities	78bl d	...	...	...	...	—	—	—	—	—	—	—	—	—	—	—
Portfolio Investment Liab., n.i.e.	78bg d	...	...	...	...	—	—	—	—	—	—	—	—	—	—	—
Equity Securities	78bm d	...	...	...	...	—	—	—	—	—	—	—	—	—	—	—
Debt Securities	78bn d	...	...	...	...	—	—	—	—	—	—	—	—	—	—	—
Financial Derivatives Assets	78bw d	...	...	...	...	...	...	...	...	...	...	...	...	...	...	...
Financial Derivatives Liabilities	78bx d	...	...	...	...	...	...	...	...	...	...	...	...	...	...	...
Other Investment Assets	78bh d	...	...	...	...	−18	7	3	−15	3	—	7	−21	−2	8	10
Monetary Authorities	78bo d	...	...	...	...	...	...	...	...	...	...	...	...	...	...	...
General Government	78bp d	...	...	...	...	—	—	—	−1	−1	—	—	—	—	—	...
Banks	78bq d	...	...	...	...	—	—	—	−1	−1	—	—	—	—	—	...
Other Sectors	78br d	...	...	...	...	−18	7	3	−14	4	1	7	−21	−2	8	10
Other Investment Liab., n.i.e.	78bi d	...	...	...	...	16	19	15	46	2	307	375	217	5	−29	−33
Monetary Authorities	78bs d	...	...	...	...	9	−8	2	22	−18	75	—	—	—	—	—
General Government	78bt d	...	...	...	...	14	31	20	19	23	145	375	217	29	−21	−34
Banks	78bu d	...	...	...	...	−5	1	−2	−4	−2	2	—	—	−24	−8	—
Other Sectors	78bv d	...	...	...	...	−3	−5	−4	10	−1	85	—	—	—	—	—
Net Errors and Omissions	78ca d	...	...	...	...	−4	−8	11	−7	49	71	−73	3	88	−1	13
Overall Balance	78cb d	...	...	...	...	−33	−34	3	6	−29	−56	−248	−165	−209	−269	−204
Reserves and Related Items	79da d	...	...	...	...	33	34	−3	−6	29	56	248	165	209	269	204
Reserve Assets	79db d	...	...	...	...	29	20	−3	−8	19	60	−100	−6	−10	13	−40
Use of Fund Credit and Loans	79dc d	...	...	...	...	4	13	—	2	10	−5	63	38	56	7	16
Exceptional Financing	79de d	...	...	...	...	—	—	—	—	—	—	285	133	163	249	228
Government Finance																*Billions of Francs:*
Deficit (-) or Surplus	80	−6.4	...	‡ −6.7	−7.3	−9.0	...	...	...	...	...	...	...	...	...	...
Revenue	81	51.3	...	‡ 48.7	54.2	58.2	...	...	...	129.9	168.4	133.0	...	...	...	...
Grants Received	81z	...	...	‡ 1.2	—	—	...	...	...	...	...	...	...	...	...	...
Expenditure	82	55.9	...	‡ 55.2	59.5	63.2	...	...	...	—	—	—	...	...	...	...
Lending Minus Repayments	83	1.8	...	‡ 1.3	2.1	4.1	...	...	...	...	...	...	...	...	...	...
Adjustment to Cash Basis	80x	...	...	...	...	...	...	...	...	...	...	...	...	...	...	...
Financing																
Domestic	84a	1.6	...	‡ 5.0	3.3	5.7	...	...	...	...	...	...	...	...	...	...
Foreign	85a	4.8	...	‡ 1.8	4.0	3.4	...	...	...	...	...	...	...	...	...	...
Debt: Domestic	88a	...	8.9	‡ 10.0	15.2	15.8	...	...	...	...	...	...	...	...	...	...
Foreign	89a	...	18.7	‡ 20.5	24.5	27.9	...	...	...	...	...	...	...	...	...	...
National Accounts																*Billions of Francs*
Exports of Goods & Services	90c	43.5	46.1	46.3	42.2	65.8	74.5	73.9	97.6	96.1	95.3	96.8	96.4	125.7	139.7	225.1
Government Consumption	91f	50.3	56.1	52.6	51.0	59.0	60.4	66.6	72.8	81.6	103.0	117.8	129.1	149.5	165.3	166.8
Gross Capital Formation	93	38.9	48.4	37.9	42.6	50.8	50.6	53.9	60.2	70.4	150.8	162.4	142.5	133.0	160.7	182.4
Gross Fixed Capital Formation	93e	36.4	42.7	36.0	39.7	47.0	49.4	54.1	58.0	64.8	...	157.6	148.3	129.4	160.7	146.1
Increase/Decrease(-) in Stocks	93i	2.5	4.7	1.9	5.8	6.8	2.2	1.8	2.2	5.0	...	4.8	−5.8	3.6	...	...
Private Consumption	96f	169.6	181.4	191.7	206.7	277.7	301.1	305.2	343.1	360.6	444.3	526.1	604.6	799.0	973.4	1,460.5
Imports of Goods & Services	98c	−52.5	−62.5	−55.4	−47.7	−83.4	−91.4	−81.7	−105.6	−122.1	−198.3	−213.3	−183.6	−218.0	−303.6
Gross Domestic Product (GDP)	99b	249.4	268.5	273.1	297.6	372.9	395.2	419.9	468.1	486.6	595.1	689.8	789.0	996.1	1,221.1	1,695.0
Net Factor Inc/Pmts(-) Abroad	98.n	−6.3	−6.6	−2.8	−1.9	−3.7	−3.2	−1.9	−.6	−.6	−.9	...	...	...	...	...
Gross National Income (GNI)	99a	243.1	261.9	270.3	295.7	369.2	392.0	418.0	467.5	486.0	594.2	...	...	...	...	...
GDP Volume 1970 prices	99b.p	249.4	255.3	247.1	242.1	250.0	257.4	247.1	255.4	248.7	273.1	275.3	251.5	246.9	248.9	254.4
GDP Volume 1984 Prices	99b.p	...	...	...	...	...	...	...	...	...	...	...	...	...	...	1,695.0
GDP Volume (1995=100)	99bv p	86.0	88.1	85.2	83.5	86.2	88.8	85.2	88.1	85.8	94.2	95.0	86.8	85.2	85.9	87.8
GDP Deflator (1995=100)	99bi p	2.2	2.3	2.4	2.6	3.2	3.3	3.7	3.9	4.2	4.7	5.4	6.7	8.7	10.6	14.3
Population	99z	6.80	6.96	7.13	7.30	7.49	‡ 7.60	7.81	8.02	8.24	8.47	8.78	8.96	9.34	9.40	‡ 10.29

Millions: (Population)

International Transactions

Billions of Francs

1985	1986	1987	1988	1989	1990	1991	1992	1993	1994	1995	1996	1997	1998	1999		Code
182	213	354	385	515	477	559	517	499	1,247	1,569	1,216	1,139	1,310	....	Exports	70
266	238	323	538	596	970	786	834	896	1,409	2,334	2,056	2,392	2,790	....	Imports, c.i.f.	71

Balance of Payments

Minus Sign Indicates Debit

1985	1986	1987	1988	1989	1990	1991	1992	1993	1994	1995	1996	1997	1998	1999		Code
−184	−143	−141	−150	−84	−265	−230	−198	−258	−277	−276	−291	−266	−301	....	Current Account, n.i.e.	78ald
291	323	327	284	321	318	335	327	335	450	507	509	516	538	....	Goods: Exports f.o.b.	78aa d
−336	−331	−315	−319	−320	−566	−446	−471	−514	−546	−628	−629	−694	−693	....	Goods: Imports f.o.b.	78ab d
−44	−8	11	−34	1	−249	−111	−144	−180	−96	−122	−120	−178	−154	....	*Trade Balance*	78ac d
59	75	96	118	132	153	148	174	187	206	242	293	272	291	....	Services: Credit	78ad d
−167	−205	−226	−250	−229	−242	−233	−260	−302	−328	−359	−373	−386	−436	....	Services: Debit	78ae d
−153	−138	−119	−166	−96	−338	−196	−230	−295	−218	−238	−200	−292	−299	....	*Balance on Goods & Services*	78af d
4	5	9	13	18	15	4	6	3	2	7	6	20	25	....	Income: Credit	78ag d
−133	−160	−184	−193	−208	−176	−166	−153	−154	−158	−174	−169	−115	−103	....	Income: Debit	78ah d
−282	−293	−294	−345	−285	−499	−357	−377	−446	−374	−405	−363	−387	−377	....	*Balance on Gds, Serv. & Inc.*	78ai d
124	183	179	225	230	270	142	197	202	114	141	94	156	109	....	Current Transfers, n.i.e.: Credit	78aj d
−25	−32	−26	−30	−29	−36	−15	−17	−14	−17	−12	−23	−35	−33	....	Current Transfers: Debit	78ak d
—	2	1	1	2	3	49	50	78	62	45	5	115	103	....	Capital Account, n.i.e.	78bc d
—	2	1	1	2	3	49	50	78	62	45	5	115	103	....	Capital Account, n.i.e.: Credit	78ba d
														....	Capital Account: Debit	78bb d
6	21	−11	−21	−36	−18	−59	−100	−158	−122	−198	133	110	−76	....	Financial Account, n.i.e.	78bj d
															Direct Investment Abroad	78bd d
—	—	—	—	13	22	14	21	15	6	10	10	14	17		Dir. Invest. in Rep. Econ., n.i.e.	78be d
															Portfolio Investment Assets	78bf d
															Equity Securities	78bk d
															Debt Securities	78bl d
															Portfolio Investment Liab., n.i.e.	78bg d
															Equity Securities	78bm d
															Debt Securities	78bn d
															Financial Derivatives Assets	78bw d
															Financial Derivatives Liabilities	78bx d
42	27	37	9	−18	−7	−27	−3	−47	19	−62	37	135	−68	....	Other Investment Assets	78bh d
....	....	....	....	....	....	−25	9	−19	38	−45	....	157	−84	....	Monetary Authorities	78bo d
—	—	—	—	—	—										General Government	78bp d
42	27	37	9	−18	−7	−3	−13	−28	−18	−12	37	−22	16	....	Banks	78bq d
....	....	....	....	....	....	....	....	....	−1	−5	....	....	....	....	Other Sectors	78br d
−36	−6	−48	−30	−31	−33	−45	−117	−126	−147	−145	86	−39	−25	....	Other Investment Liab., n.i.e.	78bi d
—	−1	—	1	13	—	−204	−238	−254	−235	−230	—	—	—	....	Monetary Authorities	78bs d
−11	26	−8	−1	−29	−59	180	124	123	79	91	−167	−28	−26	....	General Government	78bt d
−25	−31	−40	−29	−15	26	−21	−3	5	6	−8	....	−4	9	....	Banks	78bu d
—	—	—	—	—	—	....	....	—	3	3	253	−8	−7	....	Other Sectors	78bv d
10	4	−11	53	−42	2	−52	−31	4	61	98	59	25	−25	....	Net Errors and Omissions	78ca d
−167	−116	−162	−117	−161	−278	−292	−278	−334	−276	−330	−94	−16	−299	....	*Overall Balance*	78cb d
167	116	162	117	161	278	292	278	334	276	330	94	16	299	....	Reserves and Related Items	79da d
28	−59	−51	−42	−26	167	28	−8	23	−14	−2	−137	−214	205	....	Reserve Assets	79db d
−6	−2	3	−35	−20	−34	−16	−16	−14	−12	−15	3	1	−14	....	Use of Fund Credit and Loans	79dc d
146	177	211	195	207	145	280	303	326	303	347	228	229	108	....	Exceptional Financing	79de d

Government Finance

Year Ending December 31

1985	1986	1987	1988	1989	1990	1991	1992	1993	1994	1995	1996	1997	1998	1999		Code
....	....	....	I−120.5	−166.2	−39.8	−251.3	−346.4	−307.5	−367.6	−212.8	−217.5	....	....	....	Deficit (-) or Surplus	80
....	....	....	I448.5	455.2	538.4	425.2	557.2	633.6	762.0	1,149.6	1,407.2	....	....	....	Revenue	81
....	....	....	I24.5	164.0	202.2	103.8	195.4	225.4	274.0	392.1	683.4	....	....	....	Grants Received	81z
....	....	....	I519.5	716.2	737.3	743.5	1,049.7	1,267.6	1,734.3	2,344.2	2,799.1	....	....	....	Expenditure	82
....	....	....	I68.1	66.3	34.7	57.9	71.1	55.2	44.3	29.7	73.1	....	....	....	Lending Minus Repayments	83
....	....	....	I−5.9	−2.9	−8.4	21.1	21.8	156.3	375.0	619.4	564.1	....	....	....	Adjustment to Cash Basis	80x
															Financing	
....	....	....	I−14.1	−19.1	−57.4	60.6	194.9	121.8	213.3	−38.1	−15.0	....	....	....	Domestic	84a
....	....	....	I134.6	185.3	97.2	190.7	151.5	185.7	154.3	250.9	232.5	....	....	....	Foreign	85a
....	....	....	....	....	806.5	373.0	805.5	934.8	1,124.0	1,076.7	895.4	....	....	....	Debt: Domestic	88a
....	....	....	....	....	4,230.9	6,441.0	6,610.6	7,169.1	15,646.3	15,072.4	....	....	....	....	Foreign	89a

National Accounts

Billions of Francs

1985	1986	1987	1988	1989	1990	1991	1992	1993	1994	1995	1996	1997	1998	1999		Code
231.8	267.7	454.4	560.2	738.9	764.8	881.8	923.5	988.1	2,011.8	3,418.0	3,324.8	3,937.3	4,358.8	5,710.9	Exports of Goods & Services	90c
184.8	194.9	250.5	279.6	350.9	367.3	422.0	463.4	506.5	628.8	904.2	985.7	1,378.1	1,524.9	1,841.9	Government Consumption	91f
217.7[e]	....	....	....	....	....	....	....	....	....	....	....	....	....	....	Gross Capital Formation	93
161.8	199.2	277.2	456.9	536.3	781.4	401.4	631.9	738.5	995.6	1,474.9	1,888.0	2,156.9	2,558.3	3,127.4	Gross Fixed Capital Formation	93e
—															Increase/Decrease(-) in Stocks	93i
1,703.1	1,884.5	2,378.4	2,934.0	3,271.3	3,981.4	4,508.0	4,964.9	5,805.7	8,215.7	11,955.8	14,236.7	16,081.7	18,026.1	20,104.7	Private Consumption	96f
−388.3	−342.6	−617.4	−793.9	−892.0	−1,290.4	−1,299.6	−1,390.6	−1,587.9	−2,720.9	−4,274.3	−4,219.1	−5,476.8	−6,078.7	−7,716.3	Imports of Goods & Services	98c
1,893.2	2,203.7	2,743.1	3,436.8	4,005.4	4,604.1	4,913.7	5,593.1	6,450.9	9,131.1	13,478.7	16,216.2	18,077.8	20,389.4	23,068.7	Gross Domestic Product (GDP)	99b
....	....	....	....	....	....	....	....	....	....	....	....	....	....	....	Net Factor Inc/Pmts(-) Abroad	98.n
....	....	....	....	....	....	....	....	....	....	....	....	....	....	....	Gross National Income (GNI)	99a
....	....	....	....	....	....	....	....	....	....	....	....	....	....	....	GDP Volume 1970 prices	99b.p
1,714.6	1,748.2	1,768.8	1,829.0	1,903.6	1,963.1	1,839.3	1,861.1	1,900.1	1,898.8	1,931.3	1,972.8	2,045.7	2,126.2	2,222.6	GDP Volume 1984 Prices	99b.p
88.8	90.5	91.6	94.7	98.6	101.6	95.2	96.4	98.4	98.3	100.0	102.1	105.9	110.1	115.1	GDP Volume (1995=100)	99bv p
15.8	18.1	22.2	26.9	30.1	33.6	38.3	43.1	48.6	68.9	100.0	117.8	126.6	137.4	148.7	GDP Deflator (1995=100)	99bi p

Midyear Estimates

1985	1986	1987	1988	1989	1990	1991	1992	1993	1994	1995	1996	1997	1998	1999		Code
9.98	10.99	11.37	11.82	12.28	I11.20	11.49	I12.43	12.86	13.30	13.74	14.18	14.62	15.06	15.50	**Population**	99z

(See notes in the back of the book.)

Malawi

676

		1970	1971	1972	1973	1974	1975	1976	1977	1978	1979	1980	1981	1982	1983	1984
Exchange Rates														*Kwacha per SDR:*		
Official Rate	aa	.8333	.8334	.9280	1.0224	1.0291	1.0541	1.0541	1.0541	1.0541	1.0541	1.0541	1.0541	1.2122	1.3577	1.5339
														Kwacha per US Dollar:		
Official Rate	ae	.8333	.7676	.8547	.8475	.8405	.8998	.9074	.8678	.8091	.7996	.8258	.9074	1.0970	1.2992	1.5649
Official Rate	rf	.8333	.8309	.8016	.8193	.8412	.8638	.9130	.9029	.8437	.8169	.8121	.8953	1.0555	1.1748	1.4134
														Index Numbers (1995=100):		
Official Rate	ahx	1,834.0	205.3	1,905.4	1,867.1	1,816.9	1,770.9	1,674.6	1,692.8	1,812.4	1,871.1	1,882.4	1,709.3	1,457.7	1,305.8	1,084.8
Nominal Effective Exchange Rate	ne c	....	....	....	....	....	....	....	....	....	566.4	570.6	589.2	574.6	572.1	557.8
Real Effective Exchange Rate	re c	....	....	....	....	....	....	....	....	....	....	182.8	182.7	175.9	179.1	177.6
Fund Position														*Millions of SDRs:*		
Quota	2f. s	15.00	15.00	15.00	15.00	15.00	15.00	15.00	15.00	19.00	19.00	28.50	28.50	28.50	37.20	37.20
SDRs	1b. s	1.89	3.49	4.60	4.60	4.59	4.56	4.31	3.87	3.29	3.05	.03	5.66	3.59	.83	2.85
Reserve Position in the Fund	1c. s	1.40	1.41	1.90	3.75	3.75							3.76	.01	2.18	2.20
Total Fund Cred.&Loans Outstg.	2tl	—	—	—	—	—	2.37	3.73	10.77	11.75	37.70	62.49	89.94	88.24	111.76	127.92
International Liquidity												*Millions of US Dollars Unless Otherwise Indicated:*					
Total Reserves minus Gold	1l. d	29.20	31.92	36.24	66.64	81.79	61.46	26.22	87.49	74.80	69.51	68.39	49.05	22.66	15.40	56.60
SDRs	1b. d	1.89	3.79	4.99	5.55	5.62	5.34	5.01	4.70	4.29	4.02	.04	6.59	3.96	.87	2.79
Reserve Position in the Fund	1c. d	1.40	1.53	2.06	4.52	4.59							4.38	.01	2.28	2.16
Foreign Exchange	1d. d	25.91	26.60	29.18	56.57	71.58	56.12	21.21	82.79	70.51	65.49	68.35	38.09	18.69	12.25	51.65
Gold (Million Fine Troy Ounces)	1ad	....	....	....	....	....	....	.006	.010	.013	.013	.013	.013	.013	.013	.013
Gold (National Valuation)	1and	....	....	....	....	....	....	.27	.44	.59	.57	.52	.50	.49	.30
Monetary Authorities: Other Liab.	4.. d	.08	.14	.30	.18	.21	27.87	30.28	32.55	42.39	56.52	36.75	50.72	57.42	40.64	.01
Deposit Money Banks: Assets	7a. d	.80	2.46	3.44	4.07	2.58	5.80	6.27	6.53	13.36	8.30	6.84	7.18	8.23	10.51	6.06
Liabilities	7b. d	5.51	6.99	6.94	9.26	8.23	12.59	24.71	36.61	39.81	69.18	56.39	32.69	29.85	29.85	32.75
Monetary Authorities														*Millions of Kwacha:*		
Foreign Assets	11	24.34	24.50	28.43	56.47	72.59	55.30	23.79	76.18	60.87	51.57	56.46	44.50	24.87	20.01	92.37
Claims on Central Government	12a	2.62	1.88	6.57	6.66	7.99	22.55	27.08	14.33	17.24	48.64	67.25	152.21	223.73	282.18	240.01
Claims on Nonfin.Pub.Enterprises	12c	—	—	—	—	—	25.43	27.73	28.18	33.79	30.68	34.52	39.33	36.35	40.12	50.63
Claims on Deposit Money Banks	12e	.38	2.80	1.54	2.00	2.24	—	—	3.48	—	6.00	17.68	8.85	—	1.00	—
Reserve Money	14	16.57	18.71	21.68	45.42	59.16	52.50	34.58	63.65	41.70	38.55	53.31	71.79	84.80	89.63	158.06
of which: Currency Outside DMBs	14a	13.28	14.80	17.30	21.31	28.31	27.84	23.07	24.58	29.80	32.29	35.34	39.36	49.47	50.03	56.85
Restricted Deposits	16b	—	—	—	—	—	—	—	—	—	—	—	—	—	8.12	10.00
Foreign Liabilities	16c	.07	.11	.23	.16	.17	27.58	31.41	39.60	46.69	84.91	96.16	141.02	169.77	204.81	196.24
Central Government Deposits	16d	4.28	2.70	3.40	5.24	5.37	8.22	2.72	5.75	7.69	8.40	.29	.78	26.84	36.59	31.87
Capital Accounts	17a	3.85	5.24	6.63	6.79	8.81	9.20	9.31	9.40	9.68	13.46	16.04	18.68	20.42	22.01	22.62
Other Items (Net)	17r	2.57	2.42	4.60	7.52	9.30	5.79	4.05	.29	12.15	3.26	1.28	3.76	−16.90	−17.86	−35.79
Deposit Money Banks														*Millions of Kwacha:*		
Reserves	20	3.26	2.86	3.80	22.16	26.62	20.67	5.13	17.47	9.86	4.81	17.63	30.94	34.43	33.44	91.55
Foreign Assets	21	.67	1.89	2.64	3.45	2.17	5.22	5.69	5.67	10.81	6.64	5.65	6.51	9.03	13.66	9.48
Claims on Central Government	22a	4.02	4.20	7.12	12.20	14.50	20.07	21.17	26.29	37.01	29.90	25.27	24.68	24.69	27.92	86.67
Claims on Nonfin.Pub.Enterprises	22c	.45	1.23	1.37	.71	2.48	7.35	14.68	19.76	16.91	25.77	22.39	22.70	29.12	24.38	32.02
Claims on Private Sector	22d	26.44	35.13	35.62	32.96	49.44	56.09	76.55	87.79	122.38	170.99	184.23	191.97	219.11	254.72	228.80
Demand Deposits	24	19.37	22.96	22.73	31.85	40.88	41.56	43.34	53.88	62.07	56.83	61.45	73.87	80.44	71.56	87.74
Time, Savings,& Fgn. Currency Dep.	25	14.44	17.84	22.32	29.68	42.45	48.73	48.22	60.86	74.77	79.50	94.33	126.66	145.57	165.02	234.04
Foreign Liabilities	26c	4.59	5.36	5.33	7.84	6.92	11.33	22.42	31.77	32.21	55.32	46.56	29.66	32.74	48.11	51.24
Central Government Deposits	26d															
Credit from Monetary Authorities	26g	.38	1.00	1.54	2.00	2.24	—	3.48	—	6.00	17.68	8.92	—	—	—	—
Capital Accounts	27a		2.08	2.23	2.87	5.05	6.17	9.09	16.35	20.29	21.95	25.85	24.94	32.40	36.24	41.27
Other Items (Net)	27r	−3.95	−3.94	−3.60	−2.76	−2.33	1.61	−3.34	−5.90	1.63	6.83	18.07	21.67	25.23	33.19	34.22
Monetary Survey														*Millions of Kwacha:*		
Foreign Assets (Net)	31n	20.35	20.91	25.51	51.92	67.66	21.61	−24.36	10.47	−7.23	−82.01	−80.62	−119.67	−168.61	−219.25	−145.63
Domestic Credit	32	29.25	39.74	47.28	47.30	69.04	123.28	164.48	170.60	219.65	297.58	333.37	430.12	506.15	592.73	606.25
Claims on Central Govt. (Net)	32an	2.36	3.38	10.29	13.62	17.12	34.40	45.52	34.87	46.57	70.14	92.23	176.12	221.57	273.51	294.81
Claims on Nonfin.Pub.Enterprises	32c	.45	1.23	1.37	.71	2.48	32.79	42.41	47.93	50.70	56.45	56.91	62.03	65.46	64.50	82.64
Claims on Private Sector	32d	26.44	35.13	35.62	32.96	49.44	56.09	76.55	87.79	122.38	170.99	184.23	191.97	219.11	254.72	228.80
Money	34	32.68	38.81	40.61	55.12	73.43	73.63	72.80	100.06	93.79	90.59	97.20	114.75	130.81	127.76	154.25
Quasi-Money	35	14.47	17.92	22.33	29.71	42.46	48.73	48.24	60.94	74.77	79.50	94.33	126.66	145.57	165.02	234.04
Restricted Deposits	36b	—	—	—	—	—	—	—	—	—	—	—	—	—	8.12	10.00
Capital Accounts	37a	3.85	7.32	8.86	9.66	13.86	15.37	18.41	25.75	29.97	35.41	41.89	43.62	52.81	58.25	63.89
Other Items (Net)	37r	−1.40	−3.39	.99	4.74	6.95	7.15	.68	−5.68	13.90	10.06	19.35	25.41	8.33	14.32	−1.56
Money plus Quasi-Money	35l	47.15	56.73	62.94	84.82	115.89	122.36	121.04	161.00	168.55	170.09	191.52	241.41	276.38	292.78	388.29
Other Banking Institutions														*Millions of Kwacha:*		
Cash	40	.10	.11	.11	.14	.31	.25	.47	.37	.72	1.62	1.36	4.00	2.38	2.00	7.08
Claims on Central Government	42a	6.10	7.40	8.45	2.14	1.25	1.95	1.84	2.75	2.50	2.08	2.40	2.82	5.93	7.69	7.47
Claims on Private Sector	42d	3.15	3.30	3.58	5.55	8.35	8.82	10.95	12.20	16.44	17.67	23.50	27.00	30.87	33.16	33.36
Shares, Time and Savings Deposits	45	9.21	10.48	11.72	8.63	10.26	11.18	14.19	16.94	18.77	22.66	26.70	32.71	37.42	42.86	47.38
Other Items (Net)	47r	.14	.33	.42	−.80	−.36	−.16	−.92	−1.62	.90	−1.29	.55	1.10	1.76	−.01	.53
Nonbank Financial Institutions														*Millions of Kwacha:*		
Claims on Central Government	42a. s	1.68	2.03	3.92	4.88	6.03	7.17	7.16	6.61	6.88	8.23	10.11	8.29	10.63	14.69	23.58
Claims on Private Sector	42d. s	.64	1.07	1.09	1.31	2.24	3.32	4.31	7.28	7.88	8.96	11.31	10.67	14.36	19.40	23.09
of which: Policy Loans	42dx s	.17	.21	.25	.44	.94	1.54	1.85	2.70	2.75	2.42	2.88	2.16	1.08	4.61	7.08
Incr.in Total Assets(Within Per.)	49z. s	1.14	.79	3.31	2.15	2.79	2.32	2.49	5.12	4.46	4.62	14.23	−2.57	−5.84	25.40	22.33
Liquid Liabilities	55l	56.26	67.10	74.55	93.31	125.85	133.29	134.75	177.57	186.59	191.13	216.86	270.12	311.42	333.64	428.60

	1985	1986	1987	1988	1989	1990	1991	1992	1993	1994	1995	1996	1997	1998	1999	
End of Period																**Exchange Rates**	
	1.8445	2.3882	2.9136	3.4120	3.5204	3.7656	3.8104	6.0442	6.1733	22.3337	22.7479	22.0340	28.6416	61.7894	63.7362	Official Rate	aa
End of Period (ae) *Period Average (rf)*																	
	1.6792	1.9524	2.0538	2.5355	2.6788	2.6469	2.6638	4.3958	4.4944	15.2986	15.3031	15.3231	21.2278	43.8836	46.4377	Official Rate	ae
	1.7191	1.8611	2.2087	2.5613	2.7595	2.7289	2.8033	3.6033	4.4028	8.7364	15.2837	15.3085	16.4442	31.0727	44.0881	Official Rate	rf
Period Averages																	
	895.8	823.6	693.8	598.0	554.1	560.9	546.1	436.0	346.6	199.3	100.0	99.8	93.5	52.5	34.7	Official Rate	ahx
	538.8	460.8	366.1	334.5	359.2	382.2	406.2	347.4	326.1	207.2	100.0	104.0	104.7	62.3	43.6	Nominal Effective Exchange Rate	ne c
	177.8	159.6	148.2	158.0	167.1	165.8	171.6	158.1	161.4	114.6	100.0	137.7	152.9	111.2	111.7	Real Effective Exchange Rate	re c
End of Period																**Fund Position**	
	37.20	37.20	37.20	37.20	37.20	37.20	37.20	50.90	50.90	50.90	50.90	50.90	50.90	50.90	69.40	Quota	2f. s
	.02	.37	—	2.38	.28	2.23	.18	.06	.17	4.25	.59	.94	.07	4.84	.29	SDRs	1b. s
	2.20	2.20	2.20	2.20	2.21	2.22	2.22	2.22	2.22	2.22	2.22	2.22	2.22	2.24	2.24	Reserve Position in the Fund	1c. s
	132.47	108.96	82.43	78.55	76.45	80.83	80.45	66.86	62.62	76.90	78.02	83.06	78.42	72.57	63.79	Total Fund Cred.&Loans Outstg.	2tl
End of Period																**International Liquidity**	
	44.95	24.60	51.83	145.57	100.31	137.16	153.20	39.95	56.88	42.79	110.01	225.73	162.24	269.73	250.61	Total Reserves minus Gold	1l. d
	.02	.45	—	3.20	.37	3.17	.26	.08	.23	6.20	.88	1.36	.09	6.82	.39	SDRs	1b. d
	2.42	2.69	3.12	2.96	2.90	3.16	3.18	3.05	3.05	3.25	3.31	3.20	3.15	3.07	Reserve Position in the Fund	1c. d
	42.51	21.46	48.71	139.41	97.04	130.83	149.77	36.82	53.59	33.35	105.82	221.17	159.15	259.77	247.15	Foreign Exchange	1d. d
	.013	.013	.013	.013	.013	.013	.013	.013	.013	.013	.013	.013	.013	.013	.013	Gold (Million Fine Troy Ounces)	1ad
	.53	.56	.42	.50	.48	.55	.54	.54	.54	.55	.54	.54	.54	.55	.54	Gold (National Valuation)	1and
	11.50	36.65	35.34	35.18	34.35	46.34	52.09	91.23	72.58	58.30	32.37	24.36	15.90	9.22	3.91	Monetary Authorities: Other Liab.	4..d
	7.76	5.31	3.07	5.83	8.28	11.33	4.56	10.06	17.34	25.61	29.39	36.17	41.63	60.00	47.28	Deposit Money Banks: Assets	7a. d
	40.85	50.86	27.89	17.96	18.57	21.59	19.97	29.15	24.47	27.22	9.80	10.37	10.67	13.75	16.03	Liabilities	7b. d
End of Period																**Monetary Authorities**	
	76.85	42.24	106.49	370.32	277.12	367.92	399.84	215.75	255.63	613.64	1,669.97	3,387.66	3,342.41	11,327.88	11,468.61	Foreign Assets	11
	297.73	383.69	498.33	417.33	491.00	440.48	459.19	803.27	958.66	1,309.48	1,266.17	710.81	876.99	3,727.89	2,559.27	Claims on Central Government	12a
	63.45	72.21	78.11	83.35	86.81	81.26	131.82	119.72	117.51	115.47	127.02	159.25	187.46	191.41	274.60	Claims on Nonfin.Pub.Enterprises	12c
	—	—	—	—	—	—	—	—	—	36.64	28.16	13.44	150.51	9.83	9.42	Claims on Deposit Money Banks	12e
	165.97	286.42	445.33	495.67	447.50	374.50	462.12	541.75	880.71	1,244.79	2,360.57	3,269.68	3,277.01	4,542.58	6,001.42	Reserve Money	14
	65.99	79.30	107.62	134.62	156.60	159.38	222.69	289.79	414.17	624.74	987.52	1,223.77	1,375.33	1,999.39	2,992.02	*of which: Currency Outside DMBs*	14a
	19.55	15.43	10.40	6.57	6.57	2.74	2.74	—	—	—	—	—	—	—	—	Restricted Deposits	16b
	263.65	331.76	313.06	357.22	361.15	427.03	445.31	805.13	712.77	2,609.31	2,270.20	2,203.41	2,583.48	4,888.49	4,247.57	Foreign Liabilities	16c
	33.23	18.91	82.20	167.50	222.92	290.14	351.24	234.99	351.72	349.54	591.77	883.33	291.29	4,564.55	3,035.28	Central Government Deposits	16d
	22.54	29.90	29.90	40.63	47.55	57.19	66.55	92.15	151.92	191.42	280.66	478.84	653.87	1,049.41	1,094.70	Capital Accounts	17a
	−66.90	−184.28	−197.95	−196.59	−230.76	−261.94	−337.11	−535.28	−728.68	−2,328.32	−2,426.60	−2,427.03	−2,388.96	211.57	−68.31	Other Items (Net)	17r
End of Period																**Deposit Money Banks**	
	96.42	189.72	303.76	288.21	225.61	221.66	174.33	209.46	380.18	591.37	1,311.74	1,814.51	1,803.58	2,176.44	2,761.90	Reserves	20
	13.03	10.37	6.31	14.79	22.18	29.99	12.14	44.24	77.95	391.74	449.81	554.19	883.72	2,633.01	2,195.59	Foreign Assets	21
	97.86	97.49	94.02	93.25	82.88	80.84	71.38	153.47	335.28	387.86	867.29	1,746.29	1,206.70	1,484.40	2,347.30	Claims on Central Government	22a
	46.78	41.09	53.44	23.79	30.50	45.57	84.15	22.54	154.34	47.63	182.97	398.03	413.57	185.80	1,442.87	Claims on Nonfin.Pub.Enterprises	22c
	212.67	236.33	205.09	262.38	383.16	519.05	662.63	888.56	785.11	1,207.90	1,263.76	1,414.95	1,620.91	3,208.69	3,392.69	Claims on Private Sector	22d
	97.51	124.07	156.46	230.96	230.88	284.25	346.00	444.90	560.15	895.94	1,218.14	1,518.01	1,824.45	2,771.19	3,641.75	Demand Deposits	24
	217.50	268.03	370.44	376.57	408.98	475.00	566.73	633.51	924.45	1,119.48	1,936.43	3,048.13	2,712.42	4,463.28	5,323.24	Time, Savings,& Fgn. Currency Dep.	25
	68.59	99.30	57.29	45.53	49.75	57.15	53.19	128.14	110.00	416.48	150.01	158.84	226.44	603.48	744.41	Foreign Liabilities	26c
	—	—	—	—	—	.45	.01	4.79	1.22	2.65	471.85	469.65	557.21	890.96	1,121.55	Central Government Deposits	26d
	—	—	.57	—	—	—	—	3.21	6.02	6.82	9.50	7.71	3.92	2.95	—	Credit from Monetary Authorities	26g
	46.36	58.67	62.93	67.43	99.29	102.50	146.30	184.50	214.20	410.50	598.16	845.24	1,113.35	1,413.43	2,152.79	Capital Accounts	27a
	36.81	24.94	14.93	−38.06	−44.56	−22.23	−107.61	−80.79	−83.17	−225.37	−308.52	−119.62	−509.29	−456.93	−843.39	Other Items (Net)	27r
End of Period																**Monetary Survey**	
	−242.35	−378.45	−257.55	−17.64	−111.59	−86.26	−86.51	−673.29	−489.19	−2,020.41	−300.43	1,579.60	1,416.21	8,468.92	8,672.22	Foreign Assets (Net)	31n
	685.27	811.91	846.79	712.61	851.43	876.61	1,057.92	1,747.78	1,997.96	2,716.15	2,643.59	3,076.34	3,457.14	3,342.68	5,859.90	Domestic Credit	32
	362.37	462.28	510.15	343.09	350.96	230.73	179.32	716.96	941.00	1,345.15	1,069.85	1,104.12	1,235.19	−243.22	749.74	Claims on Central Govt. (Net)	32an
	110.23	113.30	131.55	107.14	117.31	126.83	215.97	142.26	271.85	163.10	309.99	557.28	601.03	377.21	1,717.47	Claims on Nonfin.Pub.Enterprises	32c
	212.67	236.33	205.09	262.38	383.16	519.05	662.63	888.56	785.11	1,207.90	1,263.76	1,414.95	1,620.91	3,208.69	3,392.69	Claims on Private Sector	32d
	166.93	220.78	298.02	435.92	452.71	482.12	633.86	756.70	1,019.90	1,535.43	2,211.21	2,742.66	3,200.64	4,999.24	6,651.05	Money	34
	217.50	268.03	370.44	376.57	408.98	475.00	566.73	633.51	924.45	1,119.48	1,936.43	3,048.13	2,712.42	4,463.28	5,323.24	Quasi-Money	35
	19.55	15.43	10.40	6.57	6.57	2.74	2.74	—	—	—	—	—	—	—	—	Restricted Deposits	36b
	68.89	88.56	92.83	108.06	146.84	159.69	212.85	276.65	366.12	601.92	878.82	1,324.08	1,767.22	2,462.84	3,247.49	Capital Accounts	37a
	−29.97	−159.35	−182.45	−232.15	−275.26	−329.20	−444.78	−592.37	−801.69	−2,561.09	−2,683.30	−2,458.92	−2,806.93	−113.74	−689.76	Other Items (Net)	37r
	384.43	488.81	668.47	812.49	861.69	957.12	1,200.59	1,390.22	1,944.34	2,654.90	4,147.64	5,790.79	5,913.05	9,462.51	11,974.39	Money plus Quasi-Money	35l
End of Period																**Other Banking Institutions**	
	2.40	1.50	7.75	I 14.99	14.84	4.11	3.74	32.57	79.11	98.87	184.06	315.90	122.78	99.02	371.19	Cash	40
	11.74	11.07	15.20	I 26.13	26.64	24.22	23.79	23.74	29.23	8.88	5.40	26.38	112.23	90.71	161.66	Claims on Central Government	42a
	41.42	47.91	51.53	I 57.19	75.66	109.88	167.40	248.90	324.66	394.85	480.72	558.21	811.96	1,116.26	1,131.40	Claims on Private Sector	42d
	54.92	58.93	71.28	I 97.04	110.84	129.25	200.54	278.47	379.50	457.64	568.48	813.40	944.46	1,128.99	1,537.42	Shares, Time and Savings Deposits	45
	.64	1.55	3.20	I 1.27	6.31	8.96	−5.60	26.75	53.51	44.96	101.70	87.10	102.51	177.00	126.83	Other Items (Net)	47r
End of Period																**Nonbank Financial Institutions**	
	36.53	45.15	42.81	57.80	63.25	69.12	60.92	84.91	71.06	93.51	172.57	216.19	....	....	....	Claims on Central Government	42a. s
	26.28	32.73	35.06	44.60	46.67	80.71	112.26	138.82	208.70	269.01	377.83	584.02	....	....	....	Claims on Private Sector	42d. s
	7.63	10.09	8.97	9.40	7.47	8.69	10.19	12.34	11.05	12.48	15.25	16.38	....	....	....	*of which: Policy Loans*	42dx s
	9.92	27.57	14.09	38.10	41.94	68.70	−43.13	45.49	70.20	103.28	242.14	296.06	....	....	....	*Incr.in Total Assets(Within Per.)*	49z. s
	436.96	546.24	732.00	I 894.54	957.68	1,082.25	1,397.39	1,636.11	2,244.73	3,013.67	4,532.06	6,288.29	6,734.73	10,492.48	13,140.62	Liquid Liabilities	55l

Malawi

		1970	1971	1972	1973	1974	1975	1976	1977	1978	1979	1980	1981	1982	1983	1984
Interest Rates																*Percent Per Annum*
Discount Rate (*End of Period*)	60	6.00	6.00	6.00	6.00	6.00	6.00	7.00	7.00	7.00	8.00	10.00	10.00	10.00	10.00	10.00
Treasury Bill Rate	60c	....	....	....	....	....	....	....	....	....	....	....	9.00	9.00	11.00	11.00
Deposit Rate	60l	....	....	....	....	....	....	....	....	....	....	7.92	9.75	9.75	9.92	11.75
Lending Rate	60p	....	....	....	....	....	....	....	....	....	....	16.67	18.50	18.50	18.33	16.50
Government Bond Yield	61	....	....	....	....	....	....	....	....	....	....	9.25	9.75	9.73	10.27	10.58
Prices, Production, Labor														*Index Numbers (1995=100):*		
Consumer Prices	64	....	....	....	....	....	....	....	....	....	....	5.3	6.0	6.5	7.4	8.9
Industrial Production	66	31.3	34.6	38.2	46.2	48.8	56.4	55.8	62.4	68.9	69.1	70.1	77.3	72.7	83.4	82.5
Employment	67e	....	....	....	....	....	....	....	....	....	....	....	....	....	*Number in Thousands:*	
International Transactions														*Millions of Kwacha*		
Exports	70	50	59	64	80	101	122	152	180	156	190	239	256	257	271	446
Imports, c.i.f.	71	82	90	103	115	158	219	188	212	285	326	356	321	322	364	382
Imports, f.o.b.	71.v	71	78	90	101	139	192	165	186	251	289	313	283	283	319	340
															1985=100	
Volume of Exports	72	45.6	50.6	58.0	61.6	59.6	61.5	68.7	75.0	71.4	94.7	I105.5	83.6	86.9	115.2	83.8
Volume of Imports	73	76.7	80.7	89.5	83.2	87.7	98.7	75.8	84.3	112.1	113.9	I101.2	75.1	75.9	77.8	83.3
Export Prices	74	26.9	29.2	27.8	31.1	39.4	46.2	51.7	68.1	61.3	55.2	I57.1	80.0	87.7	89.5	110.7
Unit Value of Imports	75	15.3	16.3	17.0	19.8	26.7	32.5	37.1	41.3	41.5	47.3	I57.6	66.0	71.6	79.7	94.5
Balance of Payments														*Millions of US Dollars:*		
Current Account, n.i.e.	78ald	....	....	....	....	....	....	....	−61.8	−175.1	−265.6	−259.9	−146.8	−112.7	−131.8	−42.6
Goods: Exports f.o.b.	78aad								199.8	184.5	222.4	280.8	272.5	239.7	246.2	311.8
Goods: Imports f.o.b.	78abd								−183.0	−263.9	−317.6	−308.0	−244.3	−214.0	−216.2	−162.0
Trade Balance	78acd								16.8	−79.4	−95.1	−27.2	28.3	25.7	30.0	149.8
Services: Credit	78add								13.4	25.6	34.8	31.8	43.7	27.9	28.8	27.0
Services: Debit	78aed								−117.5	−119.3	−133.2	−178.6	−146.8	−123.0	−127.8	−141.6
Balance on Goods & Services	78afd								−87.3	−173.2	−193.5	−174.0	−74.8	−69.4	−69.0	35.2
Income: Credit	78agd								—	1.1	1.3	2.2	1.3	1.5	1.1	2.6
Income: Debit	78ahd								—	−49.4	−127.2	−151.3	−131.5	−92.9	−101.6	−116.3
Balance on Gds, Serv. & Inc.	78aid								−87.3	−221.5	−319.4	−323.1	−205.0	−160.9	−169.6	−78.5
Current Transfers, n.i.e.: Credit	78ajd								26.0	60.2	71.4	82.6	74.7	64.6	54.6	53.6
Current Transfers: Debit	78akd								−.6	−13.7	−17.6	−19.5	−16.5	−16.5	−16.8	−17.6
Capital Account, n.i.e.	78bcd								—	—	—	—	—	—	—	—
Capital Account, n.i.e.: Credit	78bad								—	—	—	—	—	—	—	—
Capital Account: Debit	78bbd								—	—	—	—	—	—	—	—
Financial Account, n.i.e.	78bjd								69.0	126.9	132.2	152.0	31.5	−8.7	35.2	45.3
Direct Investment Abroad	78bdd								—	—	—	—	—	—	—	—
Dir. Invest. in Rep. Econ., n.i.e.	78bed								5.5	9.1	−1.2	9.5	1.1	—	2.6	—
Portfolio Investment Assets	78bfd								—	—	—	—	—	—	—	—
Equity Securities	78bkd								—	—	—	—	—	—	—	—
Debt Securities	78bld								—	—	—	—	—	—	—	—
Portfolio Investment Liab., n.i.e.	78bgd								—	16.5	19.8	.5	1.9	3.3	.4	1.0
Equity Securities	78bmd								—	16.5	19.8	.5	1.9	3.3	.4	1.0
Debt Securities	78bnd								—	—	—	—	—	—	—	—
Financial Derivatives Assets	78bwd								....	....	....	....	....	....	....	....
Financial Derivatives Liabilities	78bxd								....	....	....	....	....	....	....	....
Other Investment Assets	78bhd								—	28.3	5.1	1.5	−.9	−2.4	−1.9	−4.4
Monetary Authorities	78bod								....	....	....	....	....	....	....	....
General Government	78bpd								—	—	—	—	—	—	—	—
Banks	78bqd								—	26.3	5.1	1.1	−.9	−2.4	−1.9	−4.4
Other Sectors	78brd								—	2.0	—	.4	—	—	—	—
Other Investment Liab., n.i.e.	78bid								63.5	73.0	108.5	140.5	29.4	−9.7	34.0	48.7
Monetary Authorities	78bsd								.9	—	—	—	—	—	—	—
General Government	78btd								32.8	47.1	58.0	147.3	35.5	3.8	23.8	53.2
Banks	78bud								10.4	.5	28.3	−30.8	−18.9	2.9	—	—
Other Sectors	78bvd								19.4	25.5	22.2	24.0	12.7	−16.4	10.2	−4.5
Net Errors and Omissions	78cad								42.3	35.4	50.3	86.0	88.7	83.5	−1.4	.8
Overall Balance	78cbd								49.5	−12.7	−83.1	−22.0	−26.5	−37.9	−98.0	3.5
Reserves and Related Items	79dad								−49.5	12.7	83.1	22.0	26.5	37.9	98.0	−3.5
Reserve Assets	79dbd								−57.7	11.6	49.4	−10.4	−6.1	20.5	12.5	−44.4
Use of Fund Credit and Loans	79dcd								8.2	1.1	33.7	32.1	31.4	−2.3	25.4	16.5
Exceptional Financing	79ded								—	—	—	.3	1.2	19.7	60.1	24.4
Government Finance														*Millions of Kwacha*		
Deficit (−) or Surplus	80	−25.5	I−24.9	−20.0	−20.6	−29.5	−48.6	−37.6	−45.2	−74.3	−75.5	−160.3	−137.7	−95.0	−101.8	−88.3
Revenue	81	38.6	I48.0	51.8	59.9	70.7	81.3	87.7	109.1	142.4	176.2	192.2	214.1	232.0	276.5	339.7
Grants Received	81z	9.4	I3.2	3.4	2.6	2.3	12.4	10.0	16.5	26.9	35.4	43.9	43.5	39.8	34.4	41.0
Exp. & Lending Minus Repay.	82z	73.5	I76.1	75.3	83.1	102.5	142.3	135.3	170.7	243.7	287.1	396.4	395.3	366.8	412.7	469.1
Expenditure	82	73.5	I67.9	71.1	79.6	103.9	140.5	129.2	159.8	214.8	279.6	347.7	393.4	359.8	415.4	473.4
Lending Minus Repayments	83	—	I8.2	4.1	3.5	−1.5	1.8	6.1	10.9	28.9	7.5	48.7	1.9	7.0	−2.7	−4.3
Financing																
Net Borrowing: Domestic	84a	−2.7	I4.2	6.0	5.5	11.8	13.4	.5	14.3	2.2	30.9	58.0	80.8	−6.6	56.4	73.5
Foreign	85a	30.9	I20.1	16.8	15.5	19.9	33.3	24.1	41.8	60.1	40.1	83.6	33.6	62.6	95.0	56.1
Other Financing	86c	—	....	....	....	....	....	....	....	....	....	....	....	....	....	....
Use of Cash Balances	87	−2.7	I.6	−2.9	−.4	−2.2	1.9	13.0	−10.9	12.0	4.5	18.7	23.4	39.1	−49.7	−41.3
Debt: Domestic	88a	....	I37.8	40.4	47.4	53.4	67.1	81.7	92.0	....	....	....	....	....	....	408.5
Debt: Foreign	89a	....	I105.4	127.7	157.6	179.0	218.6	241.5	251.6	195.1	274.0	366.7	426.9	630.0	798.7	915.3
National Accounts														*Millions of Kwacha*		
Exports of Goods & Services	90c	60.5	72.7	79.4	100.6	126.2	155.4	185.6	218.4	168.9	200.5	249.7	284.4	280.2	298.2	484.4
Government Consumption	91f	41.0	46.6	46.8	48.7	65.7	74.7	86.3	98.6	134.2	164.2	193.9	198.0	218.3	235.9	268.0
Gross Fixed Capital Formation	93e	61.1	54.4	72.4	74.3	87.3	131.8	135.3	161.6	247.1	231.9	223.1	167.8	181.7	197.3	222.7
Increase/Decrease(−) in Stocks	93i	8.5	10.6	16.4	7.2	41.0	48.6	10.9	18.0	60.7	95.4	97.3	90.3	112.2	193.8	−2.8
Private Consumption	96f	190.5	257.1	268.4	270.0	320.2	365.2	416.6	483.4	502.2	525.6	631.2	716.2	812.0	918.8	1,186.3
Imports of Goods & Services	98c	−94.5	−106.5	−124.3	−136.8	−178.9	−246.0	−222.7	−252.0	−312.4	−353.1	−390.1	−348.6	−359.3	−407.1	−451.2
Gross Domestic Product (GDP)	99b	267.1	334.9	359.1	364.0	461.5	529.7	612.0	728.0	800.7	864.5	1,005.1	1,108.1	1,245.1	1,436.9	1,707.4
Net Factor Inc/Pmts(−) Abroad	98.n	−6.1	−3.2	−3.7	.8	12.4	10.7	−17.5	−23.0	−4.0	−34.8	−81.1	−74.3	−101.3	−139.0	−78.8
Gross National Income (GNI)	99a	261.0	331.7	355.4	364.8	473.9	540.4	594.5	705.0	796.7	829.7	924.0	1,033.8	1,143.8	1,297.9	1,628.6
GDP Volume 1978 Prices	99b.p	....	....	....	545.5	586.1	618.5	657.0	685.5	742.5	767.3	764.4	724.4	744.9	771.2	805.5
GDP Volume (1995=100)	99bvp	....	....	....	52.6	56.5	59.6	63.3	66.0	71.5	73.9	73.6	69.8	71.8	74.3	77.6
GDP Deflator (1995=100)	99bip	....	....	....	3.0	3.6	3.9	4.2	4.8	4.9	5.1	6.0	7.0	7.6	8.5	9.6
																Millions:
Population	99z	4.44	4.55	4.67	4.79	5.10	5.24	5.37	5.54	5.68	5.86	6.05	6.23	6.45	6.62	6.84

	1985	1986	1987	1988	1989	1990	1991	1992	1993	1994	1995	1996	1997	1998	1999		
Percent Per Annum																**Interest Rates**	
	11.00	11.00	14.00	11.00	11.00	14.00	13.00	20.00	25.00	40.00	50.00	27.00	23.00	43.00	47.00	Discount Rate *(End of Period)*	60
	12.31	12.75	14.25	15.75	15.75	12.92	11.50	15.62	23.54	27.68	46.30	30.83	18.31	32.98	42.85	Treasury Bill Rate	60c
	12.50	12.75	14.25	13.50	12.75	12.10	12.50	16.50	21.75	25.00	37.27	26.33	10.21	19.06	33.21	Deposit Rate	60l
	18.38	19.00	19.50	22.25	23.00	21.00	20.00	22.00	29.50	31.00	47.33	45.33	28.25	37.67	53.58	Lending Rate	60p
	11.50	11.50	11.50	11.50	11.50	11.50	11.50	....	....	23.50	38.58	42.67	39.25	....	....	Government Bond Yield	61
Period Averages																**Prices, Production, Labor**	
	9.9	11.2	14.1	18.8	21.2	23.7	I26.7	33.0	40.5	54.5	100.0	137.6	150.2	194.9	282.4	Consumer Prices	64
	82.8	84.0	I81.0	85.6	93.1	105.8	111.3	110.0	103.0	99.1	100.0	103.6	102.7	106.3	90.3	Industrial Production	66
Period Averages																	
	415	432	412	427	435	468	559	546	583	653	701	....	....	....	....	Employment	67e
Millions of Kwacha																**International Transactions**	
	422	462	615	752	743	1,124	1,326	1,489	1,411	2,954	6,193	7,359	8,827	16,639	....	Exports	70
	506	478	654	1,080	1,399	1,572	1,976	2,654	2,405	2,528	4,353	5,727	12,848	11,875	....	Imports, c.i.f.	71
	304	287	392	648	839	943	1,185	1,592	1,440	2,793	4,353	5,727	7,709	11,875	....	Imports, f.o.b.	71.v
1985=100																	
	100.0	104.3	109.9	109.3	86.8	....	....	....	....	....	....	....	....	....	....	Volume of Exports	72
	100.0	73.2	96.7	76.4	109.1	....	....	....	....	....	....	....	....	....	....	Volume of Imports	73
	100.0	111.9	146.5	176.1	206.3	....	....	....	....	....	....	....	....	....	....	Export Prices	74
	100.0	128.5	174.3	216.5	248.5	....	....	....	....	....	....	....	....	....	....	Unit Value of Imports	75
Minus Sign Indicates Debit																Balance of Payments	
	-127.1	-85.3	-60.8	-87.0	-51.2	-86.2	-227.7	-284.9	-165.6	-449.6	....	....	....	....	....	Current Account, n.i.e.	78al*d*
	245.5	248.4	277.6	293.5	268.8	406.4	475.5	399.9	317.5	362.6	....	....	....	....	....	Goods: Exports f.o.b.	78aa*d*
	-176.7	-154.1	-177.6	-253.0	-204.8	-280.3	-415.8	-415.0	-340.2	-639.0	....	....	....	....	....	Goods: Imports f.o.b.	78ab*d*
	68.8	94.3	100.0	40.4	64.0	126.1	59.7	-15.0	-22.8	-276.4	....	....	....	....	....	*Trade Balance*	78ac*d*
	25.9	20.1	28.4	38.5	30.5	36.6	38.5	28.5	30.0	22.2	....	....	....	....	....	Services: Credit	78ad*d*
	-143.3	-130.5	-143.6	-197.9	-231.3	-268.4	-356.5	-338.8	-260.1	-233.7	....	....	....	....	....	Services: Debit	78ae*d*
	-48.5	-16.1	-15.3	-119.0	-136.8	-105.6	-258.3	-325.4	-252.9	-488.0	....	....	....	....	....	*Balance on Goods & Services*	78af*d*
	4.7	3.3	3.3	9.6	10.5	9.3	7.4	6.3	2.2	1.9	....	....	....	....	....	Income: Credit	78ag*d*
	-118.9	-114.9	-92.7	-108.3	-99.2	-88.9	-92.9	-83.4	-70.9	-87.8	....	....	....	....	....	Income: Debit	78ah*d*
	-162.7	-127.7	-104.7	-217.7	-225.4	-185.2	-343.8	-402.5	-321.6	-573.9	....	....	....	....	....	*Balance on Gds, Serv. & Inc.*	78ai*d*
	47.9	57.2	70.8	169.2	208.0	134.1	159.0	155.2	167.9	139.7	....	....	....	....	....	Current Transfers, n.i.e.: Credit	78aj*d*
	-12.3	-14.9	-26.9	-38.6	-33.9	-35.1	-42.9	-37.7	-11.9	-15.4	....	....	....	....	....	Current Transfers: Debit	78ak*d*
	—	—	—	—	—	—	—	—	—	—	....	....	....	....	....	Capital Account, n.i.e.	78bc*d*
	—	—	—	—	—	—	—	—	—	—	....	....	....	....	....	Capital Account, n.i.e.: Credit	78ba*d*
	—	—	—	—	—	—	—	—	—	—	....	....	....	....	....	Capital Account: Debit	78bb*d*
	-3.7	45.8	59.5	68.9	92.0	128.6	104.3	93.6	188.9	122.0	....	....	....	....	....	Financial Account, n.i.e.	78bj*d*
	—	—	—	—	—	—	—	—	—	—	....	....	....	....	....	Direct Investment Abroad	78bd*d*
	.5	—	.1	—	—	—	—	—	—	—	....	....	....	....	....	Dir. Invest. in Rep. Econ., n.i.e.	78be*d*
	—	—	—	—	—	—	—	—	—	—	....	....	....	....	....	Portfolio Investment Assets	78bf*d*
	—	—	—	—	—	—	—	—	—	—	....	....	....	....	....	Equity Securities	78bk*d*
	—	—	—	—	—	—	—	—	—	—	....	....	....	....	....	Debt Securities	78bl*d*
	.4	1.3	4.2	.8	2.6	.8	—	—	—	—	....	....	....	....	....	Portfolio Investment Liab., n.i.e.	78bg*d*
	.4	1.3	4.2	.8	2.6	.8	—	—	—	—	....	....	....	....	....	Equity Securities	78bm*d*
	—	—	—	—	—	—	—	—	—	—	....	....	....	....	....	Debt Securities	78bn*d*
	....	....	....	....	....	....	....	....	....	....	....	....	....	....	....	Financial Derivatives Assets	78bw*d*
	....	....	....	....	....	....	....	....	....	....	....	....	....	....	....	Financial Derivatives Liabilities	78bx*d*
	-2.6	13.8	6.6	6.7	42.8	33.9	-5.8	11.9	-11.8	—	....	....	....	....	....	Other Investment Assets	78bh*d*
	....	....	....	....	....	....	....	....	....	....	....	....	....	....	....	Monetary Authorities	78bo*d*
	—	—	—	—	—	—	—	—	—	—	....	....	....	....	....	General Government	78bp*d*
	-2.6	13.8	6.6	6.7	42.8	33.9	-5.8	11.9	-11.8	—	....	....	....	....	....	Banks	78bq*d*
	—	—	—	—	—	—	—	—	—	—	....	....	....	....	....	Other Sectors	78br*d*
	-2.0	30.7	48.6	61.4	46.7	93.9	110.0	81.7	200.6	122.0	....	....	....	....	....	Other Investment Liab., n.i.e.	78bi*d*
	—	—	—	—	—	—	—	—	—	—	....	....	....	....	....	Monetary Authorities	78bs*d*
	7.7	36.6	43.6	44.8	38.7	68.9	62.7	41.4	150.9	98.5	....	....	....	....	....	General Government	78bt*d*
	—	—	—	—	—	—	—	—	—	—	....	....	....	....	....	Banks	78bu*d*
	-9.7	-5.9	5.0	16.6	8.0	25.0	47.3	40.3	49.7	23.5	....	....	....	....	....	Other Sectors	78bv*d*
	105.1	38.9	46.8	78.3	-92.5	-13.7	139.2	144.8	.7	292.6	....	....	....	....	....	Net Errors and Omissions	78ca*d*
	-25.6	-.6	45.4	60.2	-51.7	28.7	15.7	-46.5	24.0	-35.1	....	....	....	....	....	*Overall Balance*	78cb*d*
	25.6	.6	-45.4	-60.2	51.7	-28.7	-15.7	46.5	-24.0	35.1	....	....	....	....	....	Reserves and Related Items	79da*d*
	13.0	25.0	-33.6	-102.1	36.7	-34.3	-15.8	65.7	-18.1	14.3	....	....	....	....	....	Reserve Assets	79db*d*
	5.1	-27.7	-34.6	-5.4	-2.6	5.6	.1	-19.2	-5.9	20.8	....	....	....	....	....	Use of Fund Credit and Loans	79dc*d*
	7.5	3.3	22.8	47.4	17.7	—	—	—	—	—	....	....	....	....	....	Exceptional Financing	79de*d*
Year Beginning April 1																**Government Finance**	
	-162.6	-217.7	-226.1	-204.7	-118.7	-81.4	....	....	....	....	....	....	....	....	....	Deficit (-) or Surplus	80
	431.6	479.2	542.8	722.9	945.5	1,018.5	....	....	....	....	....	....	....	....	....	Revenue	81
	29.8	52.1	83.7	82.3	91.5	204.3	....	....	....	....	....	....	....	....	....	Grants Received	81z
	623.9	749.1	852.5	1,010.0	1,155.7	1,304.1	....	....	....	....	....	....	....	....	....	Exp. & Lending Minus Repay.	82z
	608.5	742.6	841.5	1,006.5	1,159.4	1,306.1	....	....	....	....	....	....	....	....	....	Expenditure	82
	15.4	6.5	11.1	3.5	-3.8	-2.0	....	....	....	....	....	....	....	....	....	Lending Minus Repayments	83
																Financing	
	96.0	-30.9	81.6	....	....	....	....	....	....	....	....	....	....	....	....	Net Borrowing: Domestic	84a
	68.9	165.5	184.1	....	....	....	....	....	....	....	....	....	....	....	....	Foreign	85a
	....	....	....	....	....	....	....	....	....	....	....	....	....	....	....	Other Financing	86c
	-2.3	83.1	-39.6	....	....	....	....	....	....	....	....	....	....	....	....	Use of Cash Balances	87
	433.8	514.8	741.5	....	....	....	....	....	....	....	....	....	....	....	....	Debt: Domestic	88a
	1,196.8	1,918.4	2,266.6	....	....	....	....	....	....	....	....	....	....	....	....	Debt: Foreign	89a
Millions of Kwacha																**National Accounts**	
	470.5	504.7	665.1	824.3	824.1	1,220.6	1,437.2	1,504.3	1,470.7	3,059.5	7,047.6	7,743.8	9,619.3	15,468.0	....	Exports of Goods & Services	90c
	344.0	433.8	499.2	555.3	716.8	772.9	852.4	1,240.9	1,423.5	3,257.9	4,068.1	4,634.2	5,241.5	7,426.2	....	Government Consumption	91f
	259.5	264.1	352.9	524.0	699.6	820.0	1,030.0	1,077.0	890.0	2,764.3	3,164.7	3,404.5	4,079.7	5,973.3	....	Gross Fixed Capital Formation	93e
	102.2	5.3	49.2	116.5	189.0	150.0	200.0	180.0	200.0	240.0	550.0	900.0	1,000.0	1,288.6	....	Increase/Decrease(-) in Stocks	93i
	1,350.2	1,541.5	1,774.3	2,548.0	3,284.4	3,821.7	4,770.8	5,340.4	7,785.6	6,517.6	17,540.5	31,175.9	35,934.8	44,456.5	....	Private Consumption	96f
	-581.5	-551.8	-726.7	-1,150.2	-1,514.7	-1,715.3	-2,184.8	-2,648.8	-2,900.9	-5,211.5	-8,391.8	-11,895.6	-14,314.5	-22,207.7	....	Imports of Goods & Services	98c
	1,944.9	2,197.6	2,614.0	3,417.9	4,199.2	5,069.9	6,105.5	6,693.8	8,868.9	10,324.7	22,821.9	35,535.6	41,558.8	52,404.9	....	Gross Domestic Product (GDP)	99b
	-90.9	-112.9	-125.7	-137.9	-137.6	-118.2	-130.4	-140.5	-184.0	-375.3	-725.1	-596.7	-589.7	-1,171.3	....	Net Factor Inc/Pmts(-) Abroad	98.n
	1,854.0	2,084.7	2,488.3	3,280.0	4,061.6	4,951.7	5,975.1	6,553.3	8,684.9	9,949.4	22,096.8	34,938.9	40,969.1	51,233.6	....	Gross National Income (GNI)	99a
	841.4	850.6	868.7	898.3	934.6	979.4	1,055.7	972.1	1,077.1	952.1	1,038.0	1,136.8	1,209.5	1,285.6	....	GDP Volume 1978 Prices	99b.*p*
	81.1	81.9	83.7	86.5	90.0	94.4	101.7	93.7	103.8	91.7	100.0	109.5	116.5	123.9	....	GDP Volume (1995=100)	99bv*p*
	10.5	11.8	13.7	17.3	20.4	23.5	26.3	31.3	37.5	49.3	100.0	142.2	156.3	185.4	....	GDP Deflator (1995=100)	99bi*p*
Midyear Estimates																	
	7.06	7.28	7.50	7.75	8.02	8.29	8.56	8.82	9.13	9.46	9.79	10.14	10.44	10.35	10.64	**Population**	99z

(See notes in the back of the book.)

Malaysia

		1970	1971	1972	1973	1974	1975	1976	1977	1978	1979	1980	1981	1982	1983	1984
Exchange Rates															*Ringgit per SDR:*	
Official Rate	aa	3.0775	3.1334	3.0584	2.9580	2.8317	3.0300	2.9452	2.8734	2.8740	2.8836	2.8345	2.6099	2.5606	2.4481	2.3770
															Ringgit per US Dollar:	
Official Rate	ae	3.0775	2.8860	2.8170	2.4520	2.3128	2.5883	2.5350	2.3655	2.2060	2.1890	2.2224	2.2423	2.3213	2.3383	2.4250
Official Rate	rf	3.0612	3.0523	2.8196	2.4433	2.4071	2.3938	2.5416	2.4613	2.3160	2.1884	2.1769	2.3041	2.3354	2.3213	2.3436
														Index Numbers (1995=100):		
Official Rate	ahx	81.4	82.1	89.4	103.0	104.2	105.1	98.7	101.9	108.4	114.6	115.3	109.0	107.4	108.1	107.0
Nominal Effective Exchange Rate	nec	....	....	....	....	....	....	....	....	....	106.4	107.5	107.5	114.3	120.1	125.0
Real Effective Exchange Rate	rec	....	....	....	....	....	....	....	....	....	134.5	129.6	130.1	138.3	144.9	150.5
Fund Position															*Millions of SDRs:*	
Quota	2f.s	186	186	186	186	186	186	186	186	253	253	380	380	380	551	551
SDRs	1b.s	23	43	63	61	62	62	65	27	39	87	98	126	118	103	99
Reserve Position in the Fund	1c.s	51	39	39	47	50	54	54	52	54	67	116	117	117	159	159
of which: Outstg.Fund Borrowing	2c	—	—	—	—	—	—	—	—	—	—	—	—	—	—	—
Total Fund Cred.&Loans Outstg.	2tl	—	7	7	—	—	—	93	—	—	—	—	190	248	315	263
International Liquidity											*Millions of US Dollars Unless Otherwise Indicated:*					
Total Reserves minus Gold	1l.d	616	755	907	1,275	1,547	1,456	2,404	2,784	3,243	3,915	4,387	4,098	3,768	3,784	3,723
SDRs	1b.d	23	47	69	73	75	72	76	32	50	115	125	146	130	108	97
Reserve Position in the Fund	1c.d	51	43	43	56	61	63	62	64	70	89	149	136	129	167	156
Foreign Exchange	1d.d	542	665	796	1,146	1,411	1,321	2,266	2,688	3,123	3,711	4,114	3,816	3,509	3,509	3,470
Gold (Million Fine Troy Ounces)	1ad	1.370	1.660	1.660	1.660	1.660	1.660	1.660	1.740	1.890	2.130	2.320	2.330	2.330	2.330	2.330
Gold (National Valuation)	1and	48	63	63	70	71	68	68	74	86	98	104	95	90	85	80
Monetary Authorities: Other Liab.	4..d	5.3	9.1	1.5	4.6	2.5	4.8	9.1	13.3	18.3	9.3	1.6	4.9	3.1	5.5	11.0
Deposit Money Banks: Assets	7a.d	121	128	164	235	250	258	444	436	460	774	873	893	1,240	2,312	1,081
Liabilities	7b.d	94	123	154	326	378	330	543	626	771	826	1,303	1,606	1,690	2,965	2,470
Other Banking Insts.: Assets	7e.d	11.4	8.2	6.0	2.0	15.2	13.6	13.8	8.1	8.7	9.5	1.0	1.1	1.0	.7	.1
Liabilities	7f.d	.3	.7	.4	—	11.5	4.5	39.8	33.1	28.6	43.6	39.5	11.0	26.2	57.3	56.5
Monetary Authorities															*Millions of Ringgit:*	
Foreign Assets	11	2,034	2,307	2,735	3,319	3,763	3,943	6,272	6,772	7,404	9,247	10,316	9,805	9,338	9,456	9,655
Claims on Central Government	12a	124	128	171	277	253	445	325	422	386	742	1,681	708	2,001	3,525	4,809
Claims on Private Sector	12d	....	....	....	....	....	....	....	....	....	....	....	....	....	....	....
Claims on Deposit Money Banks	12e	....	....	....	....	....	....	....	....	....	....	....	....	....	....	....
Claims on Nonbank Financial Insts	12g	....	....	....	....	....	....	....	....	....	....	....	....	....	....	....
Reserve Money	14	1,349	1,456	1,903	2,582	2,931	3,004	3,567	4,126	4,755	5,498	6,493	7,164	8,360	8,718	9,038
of which: Currency Outside DMBs	14a	1,000	1,061	1,269	1,718	2,030	2,239	2,628	3,112	3,578	4,094	4,758	5,100	5,727	6,025	5,974
Time and Savings Deposits	15	8	8	98	107	123	111	130	154	116	86	1,130	16	5	6	2
Liabs. of Central Bank: Securities	16ac	....	....	....	....	....	....	....	....	....	....	....	....	....	....	....
Foreign Liabilities	16c	16	48	26	12	6	13	297	33	40	20	4	506	643	784	652
Central Government Deposits	16d	553	692	649	647	529	792	1,924	2,064	1,703	3,386	2,426	1,494	1,962	2,580	2,892
Capital Accounts	17a	165	251	312	339	373	415	481	477	661	738	1,119	1,333	1,326	1,616	1,741
Other Items (Net)	17r	67	−19	−82	−90	55	54	198	341	513	262	826	1	−957	−723	140
Deposit Money Banks															*Millions of Ringgit:*	
Reserves	20	285	300	575	750	858	731	869	938	1,049	1,246	1,587	1,834	2,323	2,451	2,816
Other Claims on Monetary Author.	20c	....	....	....	....	....	....	....	....	....	....	....	....	....	....	....
Foreign Assets	21	370	361	462	597	579	669	1,126	1,032	1,014	1,695	1,940	2,003	2,880	5,390	2,451
Claims on Central Government	22a	833	1,045	1,186	1,375	1,746	2,148	3,036	3,583	3,379	3,843	3,972	5,552	6,301	7,588	8,333
Claims on State & Local Govts	22b	....	....	....	....	....	....	....	....	....	....	....	....	....	....	....
Claims on Nonfin.Pub.Enterprises	22c	....	....	....	....	....	....	....	....	....	....	....	....	....	....	....
Claims on Private Sector	22d	2,245	2,572	3,014	4,586	5,278	6,084	7,471	8,970	11,627	14,641	20,353	24,976	29,197	35,403	41,976
Claims on Other Banking Insts	22f	....	....	....	....	....	....	....	....	....	....	1,473	2,452	2,912	3,016	3,755
Claims on Nonbank Financial Insts	22g	....	....	....	....	....	....	....	....	....	....	....	....	....	....	....
Demand Deposits	24	1,007	1,018	1,393	1,928	1,982	2,083	2,572	2,953	3,548	4,251	4,875	5,714	6,479	7,216	7,210
Time, Savings,& Fgn.Currency Dep.	25	2,050	2,485	2,957	3,731	4,551	5,541	7,384	8,580	10,162	13,166	16,549	21,309	25,136	27,725	32,500
Money Market Instruments	26aa	....	....	....	....	....	....	....	....	....	....	....	....	....	....	....
Bonds	26ab	....	....	....	....	....	....	....	....	....	....	....	....	....	....	....
Foreign Liabilities	26c	287	347	433	826	874	855	1,378	1,481	1,700	1,808	2,896	3,601	3,924	6,924	5,968
Central Government Deposits	26d	343	340	271	440	512	495	574	729	1,045	1,899	2,678	2,475	2,358	5,100	6,104
Credit from Central Bank	26g	....	....	....	....	....	....	....	....	....	....	....	....	....	....	....
Liabilities to Other Banking Insts	26i	....	....	....	....	....	....	....	....	....	....	....	....	....	....	....
Capital Accounts	27a	141	192	209	252	255	337	375	556	613	714	965	1,595	1,997	2,995	3,588
Other Items (Net)	27r	−95	−104	−26	132	287	320	219	225	2	−411	ⅼ1,361	2,123	3,719	3,887	3,960
Monetary Survey															*Millions of Ringgit:*	
Foreign Assets (Net)	31n	2,101	2,274	2,738	3,078	3,462	3,745	5,723	6,290	6,678	9,114	9,357	7,701	7,651	7,138	5,486
Domestic Credit	32	2,307	2,714	3,451	5,152	6,237	7,390	8,333	10,183	12,644	13,942	ⅼ22,375	29,719	36,090	41,851	49,877
Claims on Central Govt. (Net)	32an	62	142	437	566	959	1,306	862	1,213	1,017	−699	549	2,291	3,982	3,433	4,146
Claims on State & Local Govts	32b	—	—	—	—	—	—	—	—	—	—	—	—	—	—	—
Claims on Nonfin.Pub.Enterprises	32c	....	....	....	....	....	....	....	....	....	....	....	....	....	....	....
Claims on Private Sector	32d	2,245	2,572	3,014	4,586	5,278	6,084	7,471	8,970	11,627	14,641	20,353	24,976	29,197	35,403	41,976
Claims on Other Banking Insts	32f	....	....	....	....	....	....	....	....	....	....	1,473	2,452	2,912	3,016	3,755
Claims on Nonbank Financial Inst	32g	....	....	....	....	....	....	....	....	....	....	....	....	....	....	....
Money	34	2,071	2,172	2,715	3,735	4,055	4,349	5,257	6,127	7,243	8,486	9,757	11,015	12,477	13,432	13,357
Quasi-Money	35	2,058	2,493	3,055	3,838	4,674	5,652	7,514	8,734	10,278	13,252	17,680	21,325	25,141	27,731	32,502
Money Market Instruments	36aa	....	....	....	....	....	....	....	....	....	....	....	....	....	....	....
Bonds	36ab	....	....	....	....	....	....	....	....	....	....	....	....	....	....	....
Liabs. of Central Bank: Securities	36ac	....	....	....	....	....	....	....	....	....	....	....	....	....	....	....
Liabilities to Other Banking Insts	36i	....	....	....	....	....	....	....	....	....	....	....	....	....	....	....
Capital Accounts	37a	306	443	520	591	627	752	856	1,033	1,274	1,451	2,084	2,927	3,323	4,611	5,329
Other Items (Net)	37r	−28	−122	−102	66	342	381	430	579	526	−133	ⅼ2,211	2,153	2,800	3,215	4,175
Money plus Quasi-Money	35l	4,130	4,666	5,771	7,573	8,729	10,001	12,771	14,861	17,521	21,738	27,436	32,339	37,618	41,163	45,858

1985	1986	1987	1988	1989	1990	1991	1992	1993	1994	1995	1996	1997	1998	1999		
End of Period															**Exchange Rates**	
2.6653	3.1840	3.5364	3.6540	3.5526	3.8433	3.8965	3.5915	3.7107	3.7372	3.7787	3.6366	5.2511	5.3505	5.2155	Official Rate	**aa**
End of Period (ae) Period Average (rf)																
2.4265	2.6030	2.4928	2.7153	2.7033	2.7015	2.7240	2.6120	2.7015	2.5600	2.5420	2.5290	3.8919	3.8000	3.8000	Official Rate	**ae**
2.4830	2.5814	2.5196	2.6188	2.7088	2.7049	2.7501	2.5474	2.5741	2.6243	2.5044	2.5159	2.8132	3.9244	3.8000	Official Rate	**rf**
Period Averages																
101.0	97.2	99.5	95.8	92.6	92.7	91.2	98.5	97.4	95.6	100.0	99.7	91.0	64.1	66.0	Official Rate	**ahx**
122.0	103.2	99.3	91.9	91.5	90.7	89.9	97.1	100.8	100.0	100.0	103.1	100.3	77.1	78.0	Nominal Effective Exchange Rate	**nec**
143.0	120.0	113.8	103.9	102.1	97.1	94.5	101.0	102.1	99.4	100.0	104.3	101.8	80.9	83.2	Real Effective Exchange Rate	**rec**
End of Period															**Fund Position**	
551	551	551	551	551	551	551	833	833	833	833	833	833	833	1,487	Quota	**2f.s**
105	111	115	120	127	136	145	82	88	93	102	115	130	146	61	SDRs	**1b.s**
159	159	153	172	170	164	180	240	229	274	456	478	445	445	608	Reserve Position in the Fund	**1c.s**
—	—	—	—	—	—	—	—	—	—	—	—	—	—	—	*of which:* Outstg.Fund Borrowing	**2c**
107	—	—	—	—	—	—	—	—	—	—	—	—	—	—	Total Fund Cred.&Loans Outstg.	**2tl**
End of Period															**International Liquidity**	
4,912	6,027	7,435	6,527	7,783	9,754	10,886	17,228	27,249	25,423	23,774	27,009	20,788	25,559	30,588	Total Reserves minus Gold	**1l.d**
116	135	163	161	167	194	207	113	121	135	151	166	175	205	83	SDRs	**1b.d**
175	195	217	231	223	233	257	330	315	400	678	688	600	626	835	Reserve Position in the Fund	**1c.d**
4,621	5,697	7,055	6,134	7,393	9,327	10,421	16,784	26,814	24,888	22,945	26,156	20,013	24,728	29,670	Foreign Exchange	**1d.d**
2.340	2.340	2.350	2.350	2.370	2.350	2.350	2.390	2.390	2.390	2.390	2.390	2.350	2.350	1.180	Gold (Million Fine Troy Ounces)	**1ad**
90	100	117	111	109	117	118	115	115	122	124	120	111	116	57	Gold (National Valuation)	**1and**
7.5	12.9	33.5	3.8	8.7	7.3	5.6	8.5	14.5	11.7	10.5	6.3	.7	.8	.5	Monetary Authorities: Other Liab.	**4..d**
1,247	1,487	2,009	2,802	2,938	2,804	2,366	2,009	3,893	4,168	4,178	4,357	6,003	5,517	6,519	Deposit Money Banks: Assets	**7a.d**
2,633	2,371	1,999	1,874	2,783	3,500	4,957	7,153	13,956	8,161	8,242	11,241	12,339	9,161	7,296	Liabilities	**7b.d**
.1	.7	.8	.7	.7	—	.7	49.5	50.8	65.4	82.1	147.0	274.6	266.9	245.4	Other Banking Insts.: Assets	**7e.d**
48.4	37.7	10.1	30.1	....	....	—	—	—	11.9	24.3	346.0	445.7	348.6	244.6	Liabilities	**7f.d**
End of Period															**Monetary Authorities**	
12,479	16,358	19,516	18,340	21,673	27,040	30,463	47,233	76,485	68,200	63,790	I 70,737	60,369	99,427	117,255	Foreign Assets	**11**
2,468	2,058	1,961	2,164	1,529	2,681	1,611	I 561	454	980	2,155	I 7,113	7,153	3,926	2,377	Claims on Central Government	**12a**
....	....	....	....	....	....	....	410	1,296	601	566	I 8,270	9,843	16,018	22,517	Claims on Private Sector	**12d**
....	....	....	....	....	....	....	-11,566	3,597	3,443	3,250	I 3,676	27,451	2,512	2,135	Claims on Deposit Money Banks	**12e**
....	....	....	....	....	....	....	698	1,104	2,718	3,505	I 634	508	2,114	2,282	Claims on Nonbank Financial Insts	**12g**
9,729	10,134	10,664	11,894	14,783	18,145	20,771	I 25,306	28,253	38,482	47,970	I 70,596	89,926	55,192	91,827	Reserve Money	**14**
6,773	7,146	7,965	9,031	9,904	11,224	12,070	I 12,124	13,506	15,884	17,433	I 18,979	21,360	18,162	24,757	*of which: Currency Outside DMBs*	**14a**
2	1	8	1	1	1	1	I 5	25	16	5	I 5,790	2,320	9,079	2,043	Time and Savings Deposits	**15**
....	....	....	....	....	....	....	—	—	—	—	I 4,968	909	4	379	Liabs. of Central Bank: Securities	**16ac**
304	34	84	10	23	20	15	22	39	30	27	I 16	3	3	2	Foreign Liabilities	**16c**
989	601	1,053	1,112	1,068	5,233	5,989	I 5,679	2,912	8,469	8,379	I 11,401	10,545	25,281	18,514	Central Government Deposits	**16d**
1,935	2,177	3,248	3,416	3,578	3,892	4,100	4,155	4,172	3,507	3,513	I 3,633	4,085	4,099	31,413	Capital Accounts	**17a**
1,988	5,470	6,421	4,070	3,748	2,430	1,198	I 2,168	47,535	25,438	13,374	I -5,974	-2,466	30,339	2,389	Other Items (Net)	**17r**
End of Period															**Deposit Money Banks**	
2,552	2,440	2,472	2,598	4,204	6,205	7,807	I 8,604	9,242	15,810	20,459	I 32,911	45,197	30,814	58,148	Reserves	**20**
....	....	....	....	....	....	....	—	—	—	—	I 3,096	—	—	9	Other Claims on Monetary Author.	**20c**
2,995	3,821	4,863	7,267	6,841	6,672	5,500	I 5,247	10,482	10,542	10,320	I 11,020	23,364	20,966	24,772	Foreign Assets	**21**
7,823	7,644	10,544	10,384	11,811	11,851	12,376	I 11,324	10,683	11,127	10,182	I 10,270	12,605	17,719	15,292	Claims on Central Government	**22a**
....	....	....	....	....	....	....	—	—	—	—	I 556	744	721	552	Claims on State & Local Govts	**22b**
....	....	....	....	....	....	....	—	—	—	—	I 864	4,008	4,416	4,839	Claims on Nonfin.Pub.Enterprises	**22c**
47,849	51,275	51,308	55,763	68,219	82,657	99,668	I 110,418	122,344	141,965	185,472	I 224,084	276,381	284,692	293,064	Claims on Private Sector	**22d**
3,941	4,137	4,228	4,047	3,459	3,563	5,242	I 8,252	8,770	14,463	18,631	I 29,358	43,220	25,383	12,887	Claims on Other Banking Insts	**22f**
....	....	....	....	....	....	....	....	....	....	....	8,921	16,051	23,672	21,227	Claims on Nonbank Financial Insts	**22g**
7,088	7,003	8,342	9,627	11,979	14,106	15,758	I 18,931	29,128	31,724	36,191	I 40,406	41,970	36,032	46,841	Demand Deposits	**24**
34,786	39,779	39,970	41,404	47,314	51,255	61,670	I 73,682	90,184	99,776	124,935	I 154,338	189,878	203,465	239,207	Time, Savings,& Fgn.Currency Dep.	**25**
....	....	....	....	....	....	....	21,741	23,196	35,731	48,266	I 39,026	50,121	50,465	28,565	Money Market Instruments	**26aa**
....	....	....	....	....	....	....	....	....	....	....	561	1,878	1,267	1,704	Bonds	**26ab**
6,358	6,157	4,981	5,084	6,317	8,129	11,755	I 18,684	31,488	17,000	15,873	I 28,428	48,024	34,810	27,726	Foreign Liabilities	**26c**
7,934	6,300	6,491	7,552	7,576	5,415	6,137	I 1,495	1,903	2,795	4,149	I 5,887	7,182	10,069	12,238	Central Government Deposits	**26d**
....	....	....	....	....	....	....	-12,943	-40,080	-18,079	-10,190	I 1,710	18,055	12	4	Credit from Central Bank	**26g**
....	....	....	....	....	....	....	435	742	2,116	2,813	I 6,723	15,148	8,474	9,386	Liabilities to Other Banking Insts	**26i**
4,143	4,431	5,344	5,713	6,163	6,916	7,670	I 14,843	16,884	23,813	29,478	I 35,933	52,930	63,061	64,329	Capital Accounts	**27a**
4,851	5,648	8,288	10,679	15,186	25,127	27,602	I 6,976	8,076	-970	-6,452	I 8,067	-3,615	729	791	Other Items (Net)	**27r**
End of Period															**Monetary Survey**	
8,812	13,989	19,315	20,513	22,174	25,563	24,192	I 33,773	55,440	61,712	58,210	I 53,313	35,706	85,579	114,299	Foreign Assets (Net)	**31n**
53,158	58,213	60,497	63,694	76,375	90,103	106,771	I 124,488	139,837	160,591	207,985	I 272,780	352,785	343,313	344,285	Domestic Credit	**32**
1,368	2,801	4,961	3,884	4,696	3,883	1,861	I 4,710	6,323	844	-190	I 93	2,031	-13,705	-13,083	Claims on Central Govt. (Net)	**32an**
—	—	—	—	—	—	—	I —	—	—	—	I 556	744	721	552	Claims on State & Local Govts	**32b**
....	....	....	....	....	....	....	—	—	—	—	I 864	4,008	4,416	4,839	Claims on Nonfin.Pub.Enterprises	**32c**
47,849	51,275	51,308	55,763	68,219	82,657	99,668	I 110,828	123,640	142,566	186,038	I 232,353	286,224	300,711	315,581	Claims on Private Sector	**32d**
3,941	4,137	4,228	4,047	3,459	3,563	5,242	I 8,252	8,770	14,463	18,631	I 29,358	43,220	25,383	12,887	Claims on Other Banking Insts	**32f**
....	....	....	....	....	....	....	698	1,104	2,718	3,505	I 9,555	16,559	25,786	23,509	Claims on Nonbank Financial Inst	**32g**
14,132	14,523	16,375	18,730	21,978	25,405	27,928	I 35,544	48,077	56,175	63,594	I 74,182	82,840	58,522	75,602	Money	**34**
34,788	39,779	39,977	41,405	47,315	51,256	61,671	I 73,687	90,209	99,791	124,940	I 160,127	192,198	212,544	241,249	Quasi-Money	**35**
....	....	....	....	....	....	....	21,741	23,196	35,731	48,266	I 39,026	50,121	50,465	28,565	Money Market Instruments	**36aa**
....	....	....	....	....	....	....	....	....	....	....	561	1,878	1,267	1,704	Bonds	**36ab**
....	....	....	....	....	....	....	—	—	—	—	I 1,872	909	4	370	Liabs. of Central Bank: Securities	**36ac**
....	....	....	....	....	....	....	435	742	2,116	2,813	I 6,723	15,148	8,474	9,386	Liabilities to Other Banking Insts	**36i**
6,078	6,609	8,592	9,129	9,742	10,808	11,770	I 18,998	21,056	27,321	32,991	I 39,565	57,016	67,161	95,741	Capital Accounts	**37a**
6,972	11,291	14,868	14,942	19,514	28,197	29,594	I 7,856	11,996	1,168	-6,409	I 4,036	-11,617	30,455	5,966	Other Items (Net)	**37r**
48,920	54,302	56,352	60,136	69,294	76,661	89,599	I 109,231	138,286	155,966	188,533	I 234,309	275,038	271,066	316,852	Money plus Quasi-Money	**35l**

Malaysia

		1970	1971	1972	1973	1974	1975	1976	1977	1978	1979	1980	1981	1982	1983	1984
Other Banking Institutions															*Millions of Ringgit:*	
Reserves	40	186	⟨272	228	368	⟨671	674	802	943	1,183	1,209	1,678	2,150	2,746	3,111	4,053
Other Claims on Monetary Author.	40c	....	....	....	....	....	....	....	....	....	....	....	....	....	....	....
Foreign Assets	41	35	23	17	5	⟨35	35	35	19	19	21	2	3	2	2	—
Claims on Central Government	42a	273	⟨304	416	512	⟨4,086	4,651	5,410	6,398	7,430	8,747	9,881	11,507	13,677	15,831	18,654
Claims on State & Local Govts	42b	....	....	....	....	....	....	....	....	....	....	....	....	....	....	....
Claims on Nonfin.Pub.Enterprises	42c	....	....	....	....	....	....	....	....	....	....	....	....	....	....	....
Claims on Private Sector	42d	273	⟨351	433	617	⟨1,176	1,579	2,073	2,615	3,222	4,614	6,253	8,302	....	13,856	17,599
Claims on Deposit Money Banks	42e	....	....	....	....	....	....	....	....	....	....	....	....	....	....	....
Claims on Nonbank Financial Insts	42g	....	....	....	....	....	....	....	....	....	....	....	....	....	....	....
Time, Savings,& Fgn.Currency Dep.	45	709	⟨867	1,021	1,401	⟨4,951	5,905	7,259	8,335	10,232	12,560	15,552	19,183	....	28,683	35,366
Money Market Instruments	46aa	....	....	....	....	....	....	....	....	....	....	....	....	....	....	....
Bonds	46ab	....	....	....	....	....	....	....	....	....	....	....	....	....	....	....
Foreign Liabilities	46c	1	2	1	—	27	12	101	78	63	95	88	25	61	134	137
Central Government Deposits	46d	....	....	....	....	—	—	—	—	—	—	—	—	—	—	—
Credit from Monetary Authorities	46g	....	....	....	....	53	95	213	345	263	569	401	1,154	1,523	1,538	2,145
Credit from Deposit Money Banks	46h	....	....	....	....	....	....	....	....	....	....	....	....	....	....	....
Capital Accounts	47a	54	68	75	98	⟨141	166	198	223	257	344	411	490	642	869	1,111
Other Items (Net)	47r	3	⟨13	–3	3	⟨796	763	550	994	1,038	1,023	1,362	1,110	....	1,576	1,548
Banking Survey															*Millions of Ringgit:*	
Foreign Assets (Net)	51n	2,135	2,295	2,754	3,083	⟨3,471	3,768	5,657	6,231	6,633	9,040	9,271	7,679	7,593	7,005	5,350
Domestic Credit	52	2,853	3,369	4,300	6,281	⟨11,499	13,620	15,817	19,196	23,295	27,303	37,035	47,076	....	68,522	82,374
Claims on Central Govt. (Net)	52an	335	446	853	1,078	⟨5,044	5,957	6,273	7,611	8,447	8,048	10,429	13,797	17,658	19,263	22,799
Claims on State & Local Govts	52b	—	—	—	—	—	—	—	—	—	—	—	—	....	....	....
Claims on Nonfin.Pub.Enterprises	52c	....	....	....	....	....	....	....	....	....	....	....	....	....	....	....
Claims on Private Sector	52d	2,518	2,923	3,447	5,203	⟨6,454	7,663	9,544	11,585	14,849	19,256	26,606	33,278	....	49,259	59,575
Claims on Nonbank Financial Inst	52g	....	....	....	....	....	....	....	....	....	....	....	....	....	....	....
Liquid Liabilities	55l	4,654	⟨5,261	6,563	8,606	⟨13,010	15,232	19,227	22,253	26,570	33,088	41,310	49,372	....	66,735	77,171
Money Market Instruments	56aa	....	....	....	....	....	....	....	....	....	....	....	....	....	....	....
Bonds	56ab	....	....	....	....	....	....	....	....	....	....	....	....	....	....	....
Liabs. of Central Bank: Securities	56ac	....	....	....	....	....	....	....	....	....	....	....	....	....	....	....
Capital Accounts	57a	360	511	595	689	⟨768	918	1,054	1,256	1,531	1,795	2,495	3,417	3,964	5,480	6,440
Other Items (Net)	57r	–25	–109	–104	69	⟨1,191	1,238	1,192	1,918	1,827	1,459	⟨2,501	1,965	....	3,313	4,113
Nonbank Financial Institutions															*Millions of Ringgit:*	
Claims on Central Government	42a. *s*	48.9	69.4	104.6	123.6	136.6	159.5	187.8	222.7	244.8	279.0	327.8	398.2	442.9	421.4	450.9
Claims on Private Sector	42d. *s*	163.2	181.3	216.9	251.9	273.5	302.7	326.2	361.4	404.1	508.2	601.2	720.9	1,022.5	1,184.2	1,602.0
Real Estate	42h. *s*	27.6	30.0	31.0	36.7	40.0	45.0	52.2	56.4	64.8	70.0	76.7	85.5	105.4	124.5	166.8
Interest Rates															*Percent Per Annum*	
Discount Rate *(End of Period)*	60	5.13	4.25	3.75	3.78	4.89	4.97	4.38	3.56	4.21	3.47	4.46	4.50	5.12	5.20	5.06
Money Market Rate	60b	3.81	3.30	3.20	2.80	2.70	4.20	2.60	4.83	2.47	4.37	3.31	3.47	7.90	8.97	8.96
Treasury Bill Rate	60c	....	....	....	....	4.56	4.77	4.75	3.31	4.13	3.36	4.05	4.49	4.96	5.12	5.10
Deposit Rate	60l	....	....	....	....	....	....	5.50	5.21	5.13	5.50	6.23	9.67	9.75	8.02	9.54
Lending Rate	60p	....	....	....	....	....	....	8.50	7.92	7.50	7.50	7.75	8.50	8.79	11.08	11.35
Prices, Production, Labor															*Index Numbers (1995=100):*	
Producer Prices	63	....	....	....	....	....	....	....	....	....	....	....	....	....	....	80.9
Consumer Prices	64	33.2	33.8	34.9	38.6	45.2	47.3	48.5	50.8	53.3	55.3	⟨58.9	64.7	68.4	71.0	73.7
Industrial Production	66	11.3	11.5	12.6	14.4	16.0	16.0	18.5	20.0	22.0	23.9	25.3	⟨26.1	27.5	31.0	35.9
Total Employment	67	....	....	....	....	....	....	....	....	....	....	60.3	63.1	65.4	67.7	69.4
															Number in Thousands:	
Labor Force	67d	....	....	....	....	....	....	....	....	....	....	....	....	....	....	....
Employment	67e	....	....	....	....	....	....	....	....	....	....	....	....	....	....	....
Unemployment	67c	....	....	....	....	....	....	....	....	....	....	....	....	....	....	....
Unemployment Rate (%)	67r	....	....	....	....	....	....	....	....	....	....	....	....	....	....	....
International Transactions															*Millions of Ringgit*	
Exports	70	5,163	5,017	4,854	7,372	10,195	9,231	13,442	14,959	17,074	24,222	28,172	27,109	28,108	32,771	38,647
Rubber	70l	1,724	1,460	1,298	2,507	2,887	2,026	3,117	3,380	3,601	4,482	4,618	3,713	2,655	3,664	3,672
Palm Oil	70dg	264	380	368	467	1,086	1,320	1,155	1,680	1,871	2,471	2,603	2,836	2,742	2,995	4,547
Tin	70q	1,006	901	924	897	1,515	1,206	1,527	1,704	2,022	2,316	2,505	2,138	1,484	1,718	1,162
Imports, c.i.f.	71	4,288	4,416	4,543	5,934	9,891	8,530	9,713	11,165	13,646	17,161	23,451	26,604	29,023	30,795	32,926
Volume of Exports															*1995=100*	
Rubber	72l	133	137	135	162	155	144	160	163	159	163	151	147	136	154	157
Palm Oil	72dg	6	9	11	12	14	18	19	20	23	29	34	38	42	44	45
Tin	72q	263	248	255	235	242	221	232	189	199	205	197	189	138	162	113
Export Prices																
Rubber (Wholesale Price)	76l	31	26	23	42	45	34	50	51	58	70	78	65	50	62	56
Palm Oil (Unit Value)	74dg	43	43	34	38	79	74	60	84	81	85	75	74	63	66	99
Tin (Unit Value)	76q	71	67	67	73	121	103	122	170	186	209	231	209	194	195	188
Unit Value of Imports (1985=100)	75	36	38	40	46	66	69	71	72	74	80	95	109	109	104	101

Other Banking Institutions

End of Period

	1985	1986	1987	1988	1989	1990	1991	1992	1993	1994	1995	1996	1997	1998	1999		Code
Reserves	4,080	4,335	3,637	2,816	....	....	....	I4,436	8,421	10,394	12,259	I14,978	19,713	6,403	9,716	Reserves	40
												I539			—	Other Claims on Monetary Author.	40c
	—	2	2	2	2	—	2	I129	137	167	209	I372	1,069	1,014	933	Foreign Assets	41
	22,204	25,793	30,846	35,945	....	....	....	I4,209	3,703	3,010	2,997	I4,239	3,003	5,747	6,437	Claims on Central Government	42a
												I36	55	42	17	Claims on State & Local Govts	42b
												I79	593	828	660	Claims on Nonfin.Pub.Enterprises	42c
	20,460	21,368	21,325	24,102	....	....	....	I52,706	59,678	70,911	90,750	I113,372	140,765	129,147	116,908	Claims on Private Sector	42d
								5,482	7,020	9,136	9,149	I5,599	10,740	9,681	10,231	Claims on Deposit Money Banks	42e
												3,820	3,698	3,102	2,024	Claims on Nonbank Financial Insts	42g
	40,276	46,475	46,648	51,706	....	....	....	I44,801	56,353	61,072	68,712	I85,518	93,802	98,003	101,224	Time, Savings,& Fgn.Currency Dep.	45
								7,685	7,343	10,883	16,166	I2,625	5,548	5,890	226	Money Market Instruments	46aa
												212	1,022	892	820	Bonds	46ab
	117	98	25	82	....	....	—	I—	—	31	62	I875	1,735	1,325	929	Foreign Liabilities	46c
	—	13	37	64	73	....	38	I453	722	707	1,213	I2,365	1,711	2,274	2,167	Central Government Deposits	46d
	1,799	1,593	2,753	2,809	1,546	....	1,612	I—	—	—	—	I510	11,788	989	553	Credit from Monetary Authorities	46g
								6,085	6,981	13,267	19,094	I31,981	43,720	22,470	19,126	Credit from Deposit Money Banks	46h
	1,349	1,577	1,678	2,087	2,264	....	3,222	I5,934	6,834	8,588	10,746	I14,721	19,572	20,446	20,523	Capital Accounts	47a
	3,202	1,742	4,668	6,119	....	....	....	I2,006	726	-930	-630	I4,225	739	3,675	1,360	Other Items (Net)	47r

Banking Survey

End of Period

	1985	1986	1987	1988	1989	1990	1991	1992	1993	1994	1995	1996	1997	1998	1999		Code
	8,695	13,893	19,291	20,434	....	....	24,194	I33,902	55,577	61,849	58,357	I52,809	35,040	85,269	114,303	Foreign Assets (Net)	51n
	91,881	101,224	108,403	119,630	....	....	....	I172,698	193,725	219,341	281,887	I362,602	455,970	454,521	455,278	Domestic Credit	52
	23,572	28,581	35,769	39,765	....	....	....	I8,466	9,304	3,146	1,594	I1,967	3,323	-10,232	-8,812	Claims on Central Govt. (Net)	52an
	—	—	—	—	—	—	....	I—	—	—	—	I593	799	763	569	Claims on State & Local Govts	52b
												I943	4,602	5,244	5,499	Claims on Nonfin.Pub.Enterprises	52c
	68,309	72,644	72,633	79,865	....	....	....	I163,534	183,317	213,477	276,788	I345,725	426,989	429,857	432,489	Claims on Private Sector	52d
								698	1,104	2,718	3,505	I13,375	20,257	28,889	25,533	Claims on Nonbank Financial Inst	52g
	85,116	96,442	99,363	109,025	....	....	....	I149,596	186,218	206,644	244,986	I304,850	349,127	362,665	408,359	Liquid Liabilities	55l
								29,426	30,539	46,614	64,432	I41,651	55,669	56,356	28,792	Money Market Instruments	56aa
												773	2,900	2,159	2,523	Bonds	56ab
												I1,334	909	4	370	Liabs. of Central Bank: Securities	56ac
	7,427	8,186	10,270	11,216	12,006	....	14,992	I24,932	27,890	35,908	43,737	I54,287	76,587	87,607	116,264	Capital Accounts	57a
	8,032	10,489	18,061	19,822	....	....	....	I2,647	4,655	-7,976	-12,911	I12,517	5,818	30,999	13,273	Other Items (Net)	57r

Nonbank Financial Institutions

End of Period

	1985	1986	1987	1988	1989	1990	1991	1992	1993	1994	1995	1996	1997	1998	1999		Code
	580.5	541.6	1,293.9	949.9	1,816.3	2,041.5	3,438.1	3,170.2	4,546.6	6,050.1	....	....	....			Claims on Central Government	42a. s
	1,859.7	2,216.9	2,078.4	2,624.8	2,032.2	2,414.2	3,558.6	3,527.9	4,108.5	6,555.5	....	....	....			Claims on Private Sector	42d. s
	188.0	206.6	253.8	221.8	236.7	279.9	451.0	372.8	382.4	834.7	....	....	....			Real Estate	42h. s

Interest Rates

Percent Per Annum

	1985	1986	1987	1988	1989	1990	1991	1992	1993	1994	1995	1996	1997	1998	1999		Code
	4.13	3.89	3.20	4.12	4.89	7.23	7.70	7.10	5.24	4.51	6.47	7.28	....	....	....	Discount Rate (End of Period)	60
	6.76	4.19	3.12	4.11	4.72	6.81	7.83	8.01	6.53	4.65	5.78	I6.98	7.61	8.46	3.38	Money Market Rate	60b
	4.74	4.12	2.68	3.49	5.29	6.12	7.27	7.66	6.48	3.68	5.50	6.41	6.41	6.86	3.53	Treasury Bill Rate	60c
	8.81	7.17	3.00	3.19	4.60	5.90	7.18	7.97	7.04	4.94	5.93	I7.09	7.78	8.51	4.12	Deposit Rate	60l
	11.54	10.69	8.19	7.25	7.00	7.17	8.13	9.31	9.05	7.61	7.63	I8.89	9.53	10.61	7.29	Lending Rate	60p

Prices, Production, Labor

Period Averages

	1985	1986	1987	1988	1989	1990	1991	1992	1993	1994	1995	1996	1997	1998	1999		Code
	79.3	74.3	77.1	82.7	85.9	86.6	90.2	91.1	I92.5	96.1	100.0	102.3	....	116.3	....	Producer Prices	63
	74.0	74.5	74.7	76.7	78.8	I80.9	84.4	88.4	91.6	I95.0	100.0	103.5	106.2	111.8	114.9	Consumer Prices	64
	35.0	38.4	41.6	I47.5	53.1	59.6	66.3	72.0	78.9	88.4	100.0	I110.4	122.3	113.5	123.5	Industrial Production	66
	70.1	71.1	73.3	75.9	79.6	83.3	85.9	88.4	92.2	94.9	100.0	104.9	107.2	106.7	....	Total Employment	67

Period Averages

	1985	1986	1987	1988	1989	1990	1991	1992	1993	1994	1995	1996	1997	1998	1999		Code
													8,354	8,884	....	Labor Force	67d
	5,653	5,760	5,984	6,176	6,391	6,685	....	7,048	7,383	....	7,645	8,400	8,569	8,600	....	Employment	67e
	....	516	I473	482	389	315	314	271	317	231	248	217	215	284	....	Unemployment	67c
	....	8.3	7.3	7.2	6.3	5.1	4.3	3.7	3.0	2.9	2.8	2.5	2.5	3.3	....	Unemployment Rate (%)	67r

International Transactions

Millions of Ringgit

	1985	1986	1987	1988	1989	1990	1991	1992	1993	1994	1995	1996	1997	1998	1999		Code
	38,017	35,319	45,225	55,260	67,824	79,646	94,497	103,657	121,238	153,921	184,987	197,026	220,890	286,756	320,929	Exports	70
	2,872	3,183	3,915	5,256	3,949	3,027	2,690	2,357	2,132	2,927	4,038	3,510	2,971	2,829	....	Rubber	70l
	3,963	3,020	3,292	4,540	4,691	4,411	5,045	5,437	5,797	8,365	10,169	9,266	10,810	....	....	Palm Oil	70dg
	1,648	650	839	910	1,161	902	684	121	489	507	545	533	479	....	....	Tin	70q
	30,438	27,921	31,934	43,293	60,858	79,119	100,831	101,441	117,405	155,921	194,345	197,280	220,936	228,309	246,870	Imports, c.i.f.	71

Volume of Exports

1995=100

	1985	1986	1987	1988	1989	1990	1991	1992	1993	1994	1995	1996	1997	1998	1999		Code
	148	150	160	159	147	130	112	102	93	100	100	97	101	98	....	Rubber	72l
	49	65	62	63	75	86	84	84	89	100	100	110	115	113	....	Palm Oil	72dg
	163	115	141	139	141	150	121	128	101	105	100	98	90	64	....	Tin	72q

Export Prices

	1985	1986	1987	1988	1989	1990	1991	1992	1993	1994	1995	1996	1997	1998	1999		Code
	47	52	62	78	67	57	60	57	57	72	100	90	73	72	....	Rubber (Wholesale Price)	76l
	80	45	52	71	62	51	59	64	64	83	100	82	93	....	....	Palm Oil (Unit Value)	74dg
	192	99	109	119	152	111	104	103	89	89	100	100	97	136	....	Tin (Unit Value)	76q
	100	88	89	....	....	....	....	....	....	....	....	....	....	....	....	Unit Value of Imports (1985=100)	75

		1970	1971	1972	1973	1974	1975	1976	1977	1978	1979	1980	1981	1982	1983	1984
Balance of Payments																*Millions of US Dollars:*
Current Account, n.i.e.	78al d	....	....	....	....	−538	−491	586	447	127	941	−266	−2,469	−3,585	−3,482	−1,657
Goods: Exports f.o.b.	78aa d	....	....	....	....	4,199	3,826	5,293	6,093	7,380	11,074	12,963	11,771	12,070	13,804	16,521
Goods: Imports f.o.b.	78ab d	....	....	....	....	−3,959	−3,551	−3,812	−4,552	−5,760	−7,914	−10,569	−11,886	−12,801	−13,366	−13,590
Trade Balance	78ac d	....	....	....	....	241	275	1,481	1,541	1,620	3,160	2,393	−115	−731	438	2,931
Services: Credit	78ad d	....	....	....	....	372	410	398	491	628	790	1,135	1,315	1,579	1,851	1,932
Services: Debit	78ae d	....	....	....	....	−698	−848	−832	−1,050	−1,359	−2,108	−2,957	−2,856	−3,269	−3,964	−4,254
Balance on Goods & Services	78af d	....	....	....	....	−86	−163	1,047	982	889	1,842	572	−1,655	−2,421	−1,675	609
Income: Credit	78ag d	....	....	....	....	162	156	175	257	378	555	739	792	650	562	614
Income: Debit	78ah d	....	....	....	....	−576	−456	−602	−771	−1,114	−1,460	−1,575	−1,589	−1,797	−2,375	−2,856
Balance on Gds, Serv. & Inc.	78ai d	....	....	....	....	−500	−463	619	468	152	937	−264	−2,452	−3,569	−3,488	−1,633
Current Transfers, n.i.e.: Credit	78aj d	....	....	....	....	47	59	58	70	76	75	73	74	79	77	70
Current Transfers: Debit	78ak d	....	....	....	....	−86	−87	−91	−91	−101	−71	−75	−91	−95	−72	−94
Capital Account, n.i.e.	78bc d	....	....	....	....	−5	−5	−6	−11	−19	−12	−19	−17	−15	−15	−15
Capital Account, n.i.e.: Credit	78ba d	....	....	....	....	—	—	—	—	—	—	—	—	—	—	—
Capital Account: Debit	78bb d	....	....	....	....	−5	−5	−6	−11	−19	−12	−19	−17	−15	−15	−15
Financial Account, n.i.e.	78bj d	....	....	....	....	818	660	516	256	630	192	1,431	2,616	3,743	3,855	3,026
Direct Investment Abroad	78bd d	....	....	....	....	—	—	—	—	—	—	—	—	—	—	—
Dir. Invest. in Rep. Econ., n.i.e.	78be d	....	....	....	....	571	350	381	406	500	573	934	1,265	1,397	1,261	797
Portfolio Investment Assets	78bf d	....	....	....	....	—	—	—	—	—	—	—	—	—	—	—
Equity Securities	78bk d	....	....	....	....	—	—	—	—	—	—	—	—	—	—	—
Debt Securities	78bl d	....	....	....	....	—	—	—	—	—	—	—	—	—	—	—
Portfolio Investment Liab., n.i.e.	78bg d	....	....	....	....	12	268	52	63	79	194	−11	1,131	601	668	1,108
Equity Securities	78bm d	....	....	....	....	—	—	—	—	—	—	—	—	—	—	—
Debt Securities	78bn d	....	....	....	....	12	268	52	63	79	194	−11	1,131	601	668	1,108
Financial Derivatives Assets	78bw d	....	....	....	....	....	....	....	....	....	....	....	....	....	....	....
Financial Derivatives Liabilities	78bx d	....	....	....	....	....	....	....	....	....	....	....	....	....	....	....
Other Investment Assets	78bh d	....	....	....	....	130	−82	−282	−449	−166	−777	−101	−276	−136	−1,471	262
Monetary Authorities	78bo d	....	....	....	....	—	—	—	—	—	—	—	—	—	—	—
General Government	78bp d	....	....	....	....	−2	−24	19	−9	−9	−9	−10	−11	−137	−65	−23
Banks	78bq d	....	....	....	....	7	−37	−180	38	7	−496	71	−27	−377	−1,085	831
Other Sectors	78br d	....	....	....	....	125	−21	−121	−479	−165	−272	−161	−237	378	−321	−546
Other Investment Liab., n.i.e.	78bi d	....	....	....	....	105	124	365	237	218	202	609	496	1,881	3,398	859
Monetary Authorities	78bs d	....	....	....	....	−2	3	4	3	3	−9	−4	—	−2	3	6
General Government	78bt d	....	....	....	....	80	113	96	155	154	116	153	132	1,429	1,229	265
Banks	78bu d	....	....	....	....	20	−8	206	42	95	44	505	306	138	1,292	−408
Other Sectors	78bv d	....	....	....	....	7	16	59	37	−35	51	−45	58	315	874	996
Net Errors and Omissions	78ca d	....	....	....	....	−79	−96	−293	−381	−455	−329	−682	−582	−406	−371	−863
Overall Balance	78cb d	....	....	....	....	195	68	803	311	283	792	464	−452	−264	−13	492
Reserves and Related Items	79da d	....	....	....	....	−195	−68	−803	−311	−283	−792	−464	452	264	13	−492
Reserve Assets	79db d	....	....	....	....	−195	−68	−909	−204	−282	−792	−464	235	199	−60	−438
Use of Fund Credit and Loans	79dc d	....	....	....	....	—	—	107	−108	—	—	—	217	64	73	−54
Exceptional Financing	79de d	....	....	....	....	....	....	....	....	....	....	....	....	....	....	....
International Investment Position																*Millions of US Dollars*
Assets	79aa d	....	....	....	....	....	....	....	....	....	....	6,302	9,603	8,583	9,019	8,859
Direct Investment Abroad	79ab d	....	....	....	....	....	....	....	....	....	....	305	475	817	1,168	281
Portfolio Investment	79ac d	....	....	....	....	....	....	....	....	....	....	512	545	714	634	633
Equity Securities	79ad d	....	....	....	....	....	....	....	....	....	....	106	112	457	381	381
Debt Securities	79ae d	....	....	....	....	....	....	....	....	....	....	406	433	257	254	252
Financial Derivatives	79al d	....	....	....	....	....	....	....	....	....	....	—	—	—	—	—
Other Investment	79af d	....	....	....	....	....	....	....	....	....	....	1,052	4,445	2,995	3,140	3,599
Monetary Authorities	79ag d	....	....	....	....	....	....	....	....	....	....	—	—	—	—	—
General Government	79ah d	....	....	....	....	....	....	....	....	....	....	—	—	—	—	—
Banks	79ai d	....	....	....	....	....	....	....	....	....	....	1,047	906	1,254	2,326	1,038
Other Sectors	79aj d	....	....	....	....	....	....	....	....	....	....	5	3,539	1,741	814	2,561
Reserve Assets	79ak d	....	....	....	....	....	....	....	....	....	....	4,433	4,139	4,057	4,076	4,345
Liabilities	79la d	....	....	....	....	....	....	....	....	....	....	10,831	15,300	18,711	22,567	24,203
Dir. Invest. in Rep. Economy	79lb d	....	....	....	....	....	....	....	....	....	....	5,169	5,369	6,066	6,322	6,510
Portfolio Investment	79lc d	....	....	....	....	....	....	....	....	....	....	1,572	2,955	4,911	6,551	7,553
Equity Securities	79ld d	....	....	....	....	....	....	....	....	....	....	586	816	1,034	1,304	1,511
Debt Securities	79le d	....	....	....	....	....	....	....	....	....	....	986	2,139	3,877	5,248	6,042
Financial Derivatives	79ll d	....	....	....	....	....	....	....	....	....	....	—	—	—	—	—
Other investment	79lf d	....	....	....	....	....	....	....	....	....	....	4,091	6,975	7,734	9,694	10,140
Monetary Authorities	79lg d	....	....	....	....	....	....	....	....	....	....	—	221	274	330	258
General Government	79lh d	....	....	....	....	....	....	....	....	....	....	1,201	1,552	1,791	2,334	2,555
Banks	79li d	....	....	....	....	....	....	....	....	....	....	1,521	1,746	2,088	3,299	2,809
Other Sectors	79lj d	....	....	....	....	....	....	....	....	....	....	1,368	3,456	3,581	3,731	4,518

	1985	1986	1987	1988	1989	1990	1991	1992	1993	1994	1995	1996	1997	1998	1999		
Minus Sign Indicates Debit																**Balance of Payments**	
	−600	−101	2,575	1,867	315	−870	−4,183	−2,167	−2,991	−4,520	−8,469	−4,596	−4,792	....	....	Current Account, n.i.e.	78al *d*
	15,251	13,655	17,877	20,980	24,776	28,806	33,712	39,823	46,238	56,897	71,767	76,881	77,881	....	....	Goods: Exports f.o.b.	78aa *d*
	−11,677	−10,441	−12,093	−15,553	−20,498	−26,280	−33,321	−36,673	−43,201	−55,320	−71,871	−73,055	−74,005	....	....	Goods: Imports f.o.b.	78ab *d*
	3,573	3,214	5,783	5,427	4,277	2,525	391	3,150	3,037	1,577	−103	3,826	3,876	....	....	*Trade Balance*	78ac *d*
	1,934	1,981	2,273	2,379	2,870	3,859	4,374	4,989	6,412	9,320	11,602	14,510	15,016	....	....	Services: Credit	78ad *d*
	−3,927	−3,575	−3,595	−4,205	−4,792	−5,485	−6,564	−7,336	−9,516	−12,052	−14,981	−17,308	−17,516	....	....	Services: Debit	78ae *d*
	1,581	1,621	4,461	3,600	2,356	900	−1,799	804	−68	−1,155	−3,483	1,028	1,376	....	....	*Balance on Goods & Services*	78af *d*
	591	548	834	1,090	1,172	1,849	1,425	1,609	2,007	2,308	2,623	2,675	2,490	....	....	Income: Credit	78ag *d*
	−2,779	−2,329	−2,797	−3,032	−3,351	−3,721	−3,898	−4,752	−5,218	−5,903	−6,767	−7,371	−7,563	....	....	Income: Debit	78ah *d*
	−607	−160	2,498	1,659	177	−972	−4,271	−2,339	−3,278	−4,750	−7,626	−3,668	−3,698	....	....	*Balance on Gds, Serv. & Inc.*	78ai *d*
	93	149	173	288	212	249	215	296	469	411	700	758	762	....	....	Current Transfers, n.i.e.: Credit	78aj *d*
	−86	−91	−96	−80	−74	−147	−126	−124	−181	−182	−1,543	−1,686	−1,856	....	....	Current Transfers: Debit	78ak *d*
	−13	−21	−33	−58	−57	−48	−51	−40	−88	−82	−174	−252	−239	....	....	Capital Account, n.i.e.	78bc *d*
														....	....	Capital Account, n.i.e.: Credit	78ba *d*
	−13	−21	−33	−58	−57	−48	−51	−40	−88	−82	−174	−252	−239	....	....	Capital Account: Debit	78bb *d*
	1,929	1,108	−1,517	−2,001	1,335	1,784	5,621	8,746	10,805	1,288	7,639	9,479	2,742	....	....	Financial Account, n.i.e.	78bj *d*
														....	....	Direct Investment Abroad	78bd *d*
	695	489	423	719	1,668	2,332	3,998	5,183	5,006	4,342	4,178	5,078	5,106	....	....	Dir. Invest. in Rep. Econ., n.i.e.	78be *d*
	—	—	—	—	—	—	—	—	—	—	—	—	—	....	....	Portfolio Investment Assets	78bf *d*
	—	—	—	—	—	—	—	—	—	—	—	—	—	....	....	Equity Securities	78bk *d*
	—	—	—	—	—	—	—	—	—	—	—	—	—	....	....	Debt Securities	78bl *d*
	1,942	30	140	−448	−107	−255	170	−1,122	−709	−1,649	−436	−268	−248	....	....	Portfolio Investment Liab., n.i.e.	78bg *d*
														....	....	Equity Securities	78bm *d*
	1,942	30	140	−448	−107	−255	170	−1,122	−709	−1,649	−436	−268	−248	....	....	Debt Securities	78bn *d*
	....	....	....	....	....	....	....	....	....	....	....	....	....	....	....	Financial Derivatives Assets	78bw *d*
	....	....	....	....	....	....	....	....	....	....	....	....	....	....	....	Financial Derivatives Liabilities	78bx *d*
	155	58	−529	−1,083	32	−205	957	1,502	−934	504	−783	62	−989	....	....	Other Investment Assets	78bh *d*
														....	....	Monetary Authorities	78bo *d*
	−39	−1	−6	−4	72	4	−13	−42	−64	−52	1	35	2	....	....	General Government	78bp *d*
	−222	−329	−454	−920	−196	135	414	481	−2,057	−1,281	−440	364	−1,786	....	....	Banks	78bq *d*
	416	389	−68	−159	157	−344	556	1,063	1,187	1,837	−344	−338	795	....	....	Other Sectors	78br *d*
	−862	531	−1,551	−1,189	−258	−89	496	3,183	7,441	−1,909	4,679	4,607	−1,126	....	....	Other Investment Liab., n.i.e.	78bi *d*
	−4	6	20	−28	5	−1	−1	3	7	−3	—	—	—	....	....	Monetary Authorities	78bs *d*
	−1,402	594	−1,107	−734	−276	−36	−132	−122	−509	−163	−216	−597	−350	....	....	General Government	78bt *d*
	156	−77	−466	330	616	712	898	3,150	6,282	−3,789	468	2,974	807	....	....	Banks	78bu *d*
	387	8	3	−758	−602	−763	−269	153	1,662	2,047	4,428	2,231	−1,583	....	....	Other Sectors	78bv *d*
	−168	476	114	−267	−358	1,085	−151	79	3,624	154	−762	−2,116	−1,571	....	....	Net Errors and Omissions	78ca *d*
	1,148	1,461	1,139	−458	1,235	1,951	1,236	6,618	11,350	−3,160	−1,767	2,516	−3,859	....	....	*Overall Balance*	78cb *d*
	−1,148	−1,461	−1,139	458	−1,235	−1,951	−1,236	−6,618	−11,350	3,160	1,767	−2,516	3,859	....	....	Reserves and Related Items	79da *d*
	−987	−1,340	−1,139	458	−1,235	−1,951	−1,236	−6,618	−11,350	3,160	1,767	−2,516	3,859	....	....	Reserve Assets	79db *d*
	−161	−121	—	—	—	—	—	—	—	—	....	....	....	....	....	Use of Fund Credit and Loans	79dc *d*
	....	....	....	....	....	....	....	....	....	....	....	....	....	....	....	Exceptional Financing	79de *d*
Millions of US Dollars																**International Investment Position**	
	9,419	12,528	13,984	11,032	14,967	14,000	14,817	21,600	34,063	34,122	....	....	....	....	....	Assets	79aa *d*
	413	535	716	1,146	967	753	763	1,058	1,437	2,635	....	....	....	....	....	Direct Investment Abroad	79ab *d*
	425	383	373	356	999	393	429	429	391	650	....	....	....	....	....	Portfolio Investment	79ac *d*
	340	309	315	356	371	393	429	429	391	650	....	....	....	....	....	Equity Securities	79ad *d*
	85	73	58	—	628	—	—	—	—	—	....	....	....	....	....	Debt Securities	79ae *d*
											....	....	....	....	....	Financial Derivatives	79al *d*
	3,199	5,210	5,023	2,732	4,945	2,807	2,407	1,999	3,892	4,164	....	....	....	....	....	Other Investment	79af *d*
	—	—	—	—	—	—	—	—	—	—	....	....	....	....	....	Monetary Authorities	79ag *d*
	—	—	—	—	—	—	—	—	—	—	....	....	....	....	....	General Government	79ah *d*
	1,283	1,472	2,011	2,732	2,946	2,807	2,393	1,999	3,892	4,164	....	....	....	....	....	Banks	79ai *d*
	1,916	3,738	3,012	—	1,999	—	14	—	—	—	....	....	....	....	....	Other Sectors	79aj *d*
	5,382	6,400	7,872	6,798	8,056	10,047	11,218	18,115	28,343	26,673	....	....	....	....	....	Reserve Assets	79ak *d*
	27,325	28,819	29,693	20,494	25,674	25,008	32,059	35,247	42,898	39,757	....	....	....	....	....	Liabilities	79la *d*
	7,388	6,111	6,806	7,054	8,096	10,318	12,440	16,860	20,591	22,916	....	....	....	....	....	Dir. Invest. in Rep. Economy	79lb *d*
	8,435	9,460	9,533	8,335	8,151	8,504	8,808	8,136	7,777	7,238	....	....	....	....	....	Portfolio Investment	79lc *d*
	1,718	1,657	1,936	1,976	2,094	2,514	2,680	3,223	3,485	4,300	....	....	....	....	....	Equity Securities	79ld *d*
	6,717	7,803	7,598	6,358	6,057	5,990	6,128	4,913	4,292	2,938	....	....	....	....	....	Debt Securities	79le *d*
											....	....	....	....	....	Financial Derivatives	79ll *d*
	11,502	13,247	13,354	5,105	9,427	6,185	10,810	10,252	14,530	9,604	....	....	....	....	....	Other investment	79lf *d*
	118	—	—	—	—	—	—	—	—	—	....	....	....	....	....	Monetary Authorities	79lg *d*
	2,790	3,073	3,485	3,188	2,888	3,163	3,203	3,097	2,875	2,956	....	....	....	....	....	General Government	79lh *d*
	3,051	3,079	2,672	1,917	2,811	3,023	4,788	7,155	11,656	6,647	....	....	....	....	....	Banks	79li *d*
	5,542	7,095	7,197	—	3,728	—	2,819	—	—	—	....	....	....	....	....	Other Sectors	79lj *d*

Malaysia

		1970	1971	1972	1973	1974	1975	1976	1977	1978	1979	1980	1981	1982	1983	1984
Government Finance															*Millions of Ringgit:*	
Deficit (-) or Surplus	**80**	ɪ−475	−1,050	−1,371	−1,049	−1,381	−1,901	−1,705	−2,476	−2,249	−1,535	−3,704	−9,015	−10,421	−6,933	−4,775
Revenue	**81**	ɪ2,400	2,418	2,920	3,399	4,791	5,117	6,157	7,760	8,841	10,505	13,926	15,806	16,690	18,608	20,805
Expenditure	**82**	ɪ2,875	3,468	4,291	4,448	6,172	7,018	7,862	10,236	11,090	12,040	17,630	24,821	27,111	25,541	25,580
Lending Minus Repayments	**83**	....	....	....	....	....	....	....	....	....	....	....	....	....	....	....
Financing																
Net Borrowing: Domestic	**84a**	ɪ365	728	836	877	832	1,210	1,636	1,887	1,165	2,507	2,311	4,091	6,084	4,466	3,153
Foreign	**85a**	ɪ−2	372	354	69	223	912	638	269	541	679	310	3,419	4,893	4,569	3,093
Special Receipts	**86**	ɪ17	42	66	13	8	8	9	11	4	3	1	236	2	4	46
Use of Cash Balances	**87**	ɪ95	−92	115	90	318	−229	−578	309	539	−1,654	1,082	1,269	−558	−2,106	−1,517
Debt: Domestic	**88b**	ɪ4,272	5,000	5,835	6,712	7,544	8,755	10,391	12,277	13,783	16,281	18,578	22,851	28,711	33,955	37,075
Foreign	**89b**	ɪ745	1,089	1,396	1,295	1,497	2,424	2,806	3,352	3,859	4,543	4,861	8,278	13,158	17,728	20,848
National Accounts															*Millions of Ringgit*	
Exports of Goods & Services	**90c**	5,602	5,208	5,083	7,738	11,004	10,150	14,474	16,216	18,585	26,004	30,676	30,154	31,846	35,795	43,171
Government Consumption	**91f**	1,997	2,170	2,738	2,934	3,516	3,924	4,301	5,388	6,090	6,475	8,811	10,425	11,469	11,015	11,741
Gross Fixed Capital Formation	**93e**	2,152	2,701	3,211	4,219	5,798	5,602	6,206	7,465	9,381	12,250	16,597	20,759	22,745	25,213	25,391
Increase/Decrease(-) in Stocks	**93i**	315	2	−179	206	974	101	192	247	723	1,173	−380	−602	593	1,253	1,306
Private Consumption	**96f**	7,486	7,911	8,613	10,308	12,776	13,086	14,715	16,812	19,584	22,406	26,946	30,594	33,226	36,458	39,594
Imports of Goods & Services	**98c**	−5,397	−5,037	−5,246	−6,682	−11,210	−10,531	−11,803	−13,788	−16,477	−21,884	−29,342	−33,717	−37,300	−39,943	−41,653
Gross Domestic Product (GDP)	**99b**	12,155	12,955	14,220	18,723	22,858	22,332	28,085	32,340	37,886	46,424	53,308	57,613	62,579	69,941	79,550
Net Factor Inc/Pmts(-) Abroad	**98.n**	−355	−363	−378	−659	−997	−727	−1,097	−1,276	−1,700	−2,070	−1,918	−2,011	−2,889	−4,411	−5,368
Gross National Income (GNI)	**99a**	11,800	12,592	13,842	18,064	21,861	21,605	26,988	31,064	36,186	44,354	51,390	55,602	59,690	65,530	74,182
GDP Volume 1978 Prices	**99b.p**	20,129	22,149	24,228	27,063	29,315	29,550	32,966	35,522	37,886	41,428	44,511	47,600	50,446	53,584	57,743
GDP Volume 1987 Prices	**99b.p**	....	....	....	....	....	....	....	....	....	....	....	....	....	....	....
GDP Volume (1995=100)	**99bv p**	16.2	17.9	19.5	21.8	23.6	23.8	26.6	28.7	ɪ30.6	33.4	35.9	38.4	40.7	43.2	46.6
GDP Deflator (1995=100)	**99bi p**	33.6	32.6	32.7	38.6	43.5	42.1	47.5	50.7	55.7	62.4	66.7	67.4	69.1	72.7	76.8
																Millions:
Population	**99z**	10.39	10.70	11.00	11.31	11.65	11.90	12.30	12.58	12.91	13.45	13.70	14.11	14.51	14.89	15.27

1985	1986	1987	1988	1989	1990	1991	1992	1993	1994	1995	1996	1997	1998	1999		
															Government Finance	
Year Ending December 31																
-4,407	-7,506	-6,153	-3,290	-3,410	-3,437	-2,640	-1,243	354	4,408	1,861	1,815	6,627	-5,002	-9,488	Deficit (-) or Surplus	**80**
21,115	19,518	18,143	21,967	25,273	29,521	34,053	39,250	41,691	49,446	50,954	58,279	65,736	56,710	58,675	Revenue	**81**
25,522	27,024	24,296	25,257	28,683	32,958	36,693	40,493	41,337	45,038	49,093	56,464	59,109	60,371	68,210	Expenditure	**82**
....	....	....	....	....	....	....	....	....	....	....	....	....	1,341	-47	Lending Minus Repayments	**83**
															Financing	
3,591	4,929	8,693	7,857	2,368	3,798	....	1,480	375	1,751	—	1,291	-2,048	11,040	5,423	Net Borrowing: Domestic	**84a**
956	1,348	-2,438	-3,094	-1,038	-787	....	-3,170	-3,134	-4,757	-1,635	-2,177	-1,682	1,819	2,923	Foreign	**85a**
12	111	—	291	238	52	....	201	126	519	166	475	....	....	....	Special Receipts	**86**
-152	1,118	-102	-1,764	1,842	374	....	2,732	2,279	-1,921	-392	-1,404	‡-2,897	-7,857	1,142	Use of Cash Balances	**87**
40,812	45,698	54,796	63,097	65,763	69,988	73,655	76,083	76,536	78,260	78,038	79,211	76,968	88,197	93,750	Debt: Domestic	**88b**
23,070	28,310	27,629	25,922	24,182	24,182	25,145	20,922	19,362	14,818	13,331	10,471	12,951	14,924	18,369	Foreign	**89b**
Millions of Ringgit															**National Accounts**	
42,537	40,305	‡50,998	61,348	75,112	88,675	105,161	114,494	135,896	174,255	209,323	232,359	262,713	325,325	364,106	Exports of Goods & Services	**90c**
11,844	12,127	‡12,060	13,148	14,798	16,426	18,505	19,605	21,750	23,973	27,527	28,179	30,679	28,455	33,467	Government Consumption	**91f**
23,124	18,865	‡17,904	22,726	30,599	39,348	49,126	55,191	66,936	78,663	96,967	107,825	121,383	76,275	66,683	Gross Fixed Capital Formation	**93e**
-1,757	-261	‡812	1,624	835	-813	1,937	-1,906	535	1,871	120	-2,580	-447	-362	339	Increase/Decrease(-) in Stocks	**93i**
40,360	36,499	‡39,063	45,444	52,619	61,687	70,500	75,749	83,143	94,089	106,612	116,794	127,650	118,098	124,761	Private Consumption	**96f**
-38,561	-35,941	‡-39,752	-51,920	-68,730	-86,241	-110,107	-112,450	-136,068	-177,389	-218,077	-228,842	-260,093	-263,319	-290,163	Imports of Goods & Services	**98c**
77,547	71,594	‡81,085	92,370	105,223	119,081	135,123	150,681	172,193	195,460	222,472	253,732	281,889	284,474	299,193	Gross Domestic Product (GDP)	**99b**
-5,508	-4,780	‡-4,982	-5,084	-5,903	-5,064	-6,800	-8,006	-8,265	-9,412	-10,377	-11,801	-15,095	-15,336	-19,351	Net Factor Inc/Pmts(-) Abroad	**98.n**
72,039	66,814	‡76,104	87,286	99,330	114,017	128,324	142,676	163,928	186,049	212,096	241,931	266,700	269,136	279,842	Gross National Income (GNI)	**99a**
57,093	57,750	60,863	....	....	....	....	....	....	....	....	....	....	....	....	GDP Volume 1978 Prices	**99b.** *p*
....	....	81,805	89,143	97,218	105,977	116,093	126,408	138,916	151,713	166,625	183,292	196,714	182,221	192,506	GDP Volume 1987 Prices	**99b.** *p*
46.1	46.6	‡49.1	53.5	58.3	63.6	69.7	75.9	83.4	91.1	100.0	110.0	118.1	109.4	115.5	GDP Volume (1995=100)	**99bv** *p*
75.7	69.1	‡74.2	77.6	81.1	84.2	87.2	89.3	92.8	96.5	100.0	103.7	107.3	116.9	116.4	GDP Deflator (1995=100)	**99bi** *p*
Midyear Estimates																
15.68	16.11	16.53	16.94	17.66	18.10	18.55	19.04	19.56	20.11	20.67	21.17	21.66	22.18	22.71	**Population**	**99z**

(See notes in the back of the book.)

Maldives

		1970	1971	1972	1973	1974	1975	1976	1977	1978	1979	1980	1981	1982	1983	1984
Exchange Rates														*Rufiyaa per SDR:*		
Market Rate	aa	4.750	4.750	4.750	4.741	4.812	7.170	10.021	10.841	11.237	9.946	9.629	8.788	7.777	7.381	6.910
														Rufiyaa per US Dollar:		
Market Rate	ae	4.750	4.375	4.375	3.930	3.930	6.125	8.625	8.925	8.625	7.550	7.550	7.550	7.050	7.050	7.050
Market Rate	rf	4.750[e]	4.734[e]	4.375[e]	3.986[e]	3.930[e]	5.765[e]	8.365[e]	8.767[e]	8.969[e]	7.489	7.550	7.550	7.174	7.050	7.050
Fund Position														*Millions of SDRs:*		
Quota	2f. s	...	...	...	...	...	...	...	...	.9	.9	1.4	1.4	1.4	2.0	2.0
SDRs	1b. s	...	...	...	...	...	...	...	...	—	.1	.1	.2	.2	—	—
Reserve Position in the Fund	1c. s	...	...	...	...	...	...	...	...	.2	.2	.3	.3	.3	.5	—
Total Fund Cred.&Loans Outstg.	2tl	...	...	...	...	...	...	...	...	—	—	—	—	—	—	—
International Liquidity												*Millions of US Dollars Unless Otherwise Indicated:*					
Total Reserves minus Gold	1l.d	...	...	...	...	...	...	.01	.08	.57	.71	.95	1.15	8.41	4.54	5.13
SDRs	1b.d	...	...	...	...	...	...	...	...	—	.12	.08	.19	.17	—	.01
Reserve Position in the Fund	1c.d	...	...	...	...	...	...	...	...	.22	.22	.38	.35	.33	.47	—
Foreign Exchange	1d.d	...	...	...	...	...	...	.01	.08	.35	.37	.49	.61	7.91	4.07	5.12
Gold (Million Fine Troy Ounces)	1ad	...	...	...	...	...	...	...	...	...	...	...	...			
Gold (National Valuation)	1and	...	...	...	...	...	...	...	...	...	...	...	.055	.042	.042	.042
Monetary Authorities: Other Liab.	4..d	...	...	...	...	...	...	—	—	—	—	—	.23	8.20	7.71	7.21
Deposit Money Banks: Assets	7a.d	...	...	...	...	...	...	.23	.27	2.38	1.81	2.44	2.75	1.94	1.72	3.56
Liabilities	7b.d	...	...	...	...	...	...	.06	.93	.54	.24	1.58	10.43	14.31	18.32	25.55
Monetary Authorities														*Millions of Rufiyaa:*		
Foreign Assets	11	...	...	...	...	...	...	.02	.31	2.41	2.96	3.88	↕6.03	63.39	36.38	36.27
Claims on Central Government	12a	...	...	...	...	...	...	111.29	121.52	90.70	111.16	142.95	↕152.95	156.21	167.39	185.21
Claims on Nonfin.Pub.Enterprises	12c	...	...	...	...	...	...	...	...	...	...	...	...	...	...	...
Claims on Deposit Money Banks	12e	...	...	...	...	...	...	—	.01	2.57	2.24	3.32	1.96	1.15	.15	.40
Reserve Money	14	...	...	...	...	...	...	57.44	53.71	37.72	63.10	99.87	↕106.33	96.49	117.25	155.45
of which: Currency Outside DMBs	14a	...	...	...	...	...	...	13.22	14.18	17.53	23.12	27.46	32.37	41.70	50.31	56.77
Foreign Currency Deposits	15	...	...	...	...	...	...	...	...	...	...	...	.44	.69	.09	.24
Foreign Liabilities	16c	—	—	—	—	—	—	—	—	—	—	—	1.76	57.79	54.33	50.86
Central Government Deposits	16d	...	...	...	...	...	...	53.87	68.14	57.96	51.97	48.47	45.82	26.74	22.37	30.32
Capital Accounts	17a	...	...	...	...	...	...	—	—	—	.45	1.86	2.34	7.18	6.06	9.62
Other Items (Net)	17r	...	...	...	...	...	...	—	—	—	.84	−.05	↕4.26	31.86	3.82	−24.61
Deposit Money Banks														*Millions of Rufiyaa:*		
Reserves	20	...	...	...	...	...	...	23.71	22.68	4.25	12.08	10.31	3.87	20.05	47.29	71.24
Foreign Assets	21	...	...	...	...	...	...	1.97	2.42	20.56	13.64	18.43	20.80	13.71	12.13	25.12
Claims on Central Government	22a	...	...	...	...	...	...	—	—	—	—	—	22.83	34.40	20.14	—
Claims on Nonfin.Pub.Enterprises	22c	...	...	...	...	...	...	—	2.10	—	3.02	40.66	38.58	13.61	42.63	65.70
Claims on Private Sector	22d	...	...	...	...	...	...	2.20	16.43	13.66	17.55	16.47	51.16	97.92	126.51	187.07
Demand Deposits	24	...	...	...	...	...	...	16.16	18.16	3.91	6.23	7.29	6.31	14.28	18.60	29.37
Time, Savings,& Fgn. Currency Dep.	25	...	...	...	...	...	...	8.05	16.98	29.28	37.01	62.16	48.02	47.13	49.27	68.67
Foreign Liabilities	26c	...	...	...	...	...	...	.54	8.27	4.69	1.80	11.90	78.78	100.86	129.18	180.11
Central Government Deposits	26d	...	...	...	...	...	...	—	—	—	—	—	.16	.63	6.55	13.99
Credit from Monetary Authorities	26g	...	...	...	...	...	...	...	...	...	...	...	3.78	1.23	.14	.40
Capital Accounts	27a	...	...	...	...	...	...	—	—	.84	.14	.39	.47	5.63	26.61	26.83
Other Items (Net)	27r	...	...	...	...	...	...	3.12	.21	−.26	1.13	4.12	↕−.30	9.93	18.36	29.77
Monetary Survey														*Millions of Rufiyaa:*		
Foreign Assets (Net)	31n	...	...	...	...	...	...	1.45	−5.55	18.28	14.81	10.41	↕−53.72	−81.55	−135.00	−169.58
Domestic Credit	32	...	...	...	...	...	...	59.62	71.91	46.40	79.76	151.61	↕219.55	274.77	327.75	393.67
Claims on Central Govt. (Net)	32an	...	...	...	...	...	...	57.42	53.38	32.74	59.19	94.48	↕129.80	163.24	158.61	140.90
Claims on Nonfin.Pub.Enterprises	32c	...	...	...	...	...	...	—	2.10	—	3.02	40.66	38.58	13.61	42.63	65.70
Claims on Private Sector	32d	...	...	...	...	...	...	2.20	16.43	13.66	17.55	16.47	51.16	97.92	126.51	187.07
Money	34	...	...	...	...	...	...	53.76	46.19	37.52	53.41	80.75	↕109.33	92.74	88.80	113.90
Quasi-Money	35	...	...	...	...	...	...	8.05	16.98	29.28	37.01	62.16	48.47	47.82	49.35	68.91
Capital Accounts	37a	...	...	...	...	...	...	—	—	.84	.59	2.24	2.81	12.81	32.66	36.45
Other Items (Net)	37r	...	...	...	...	...	...	−.75	3.19	−2.96	3.56	16.87	↕5.22	39.85	21.94	4.84
Money plus Quasi-Money	35l	...	...	...	...	...	...	61.82	63.17	66.81	90.42	142.91	↕157.79	140.56	138.16	182.81
Interest Rates														*Percent Per Annum*		
Money Market Rate	60b	...	...	...	...	...	...	...	...	...	...	...	...	...	...	11.00
Prices and Production														*Index Numbers (1995=100):*		
Consumer Prices	64	...	...	...	...	...	...	...	17.2	19.4	24.7	30.6	37.9	46.2	—	—
Total Fish Catch	66al	...	...	...	...	...	...	...	25.2	24.7	26.5	33.1	33.4	29.0	36.9	52.7
Tourist Bed Night Index	66.t	...	...	...	...	...	...	...	4.8	7.5	7.9	11.0	16.3	21.8	23.7	29.1
International Transactions														*Millions of US Dollars*		
Exports	70..d	3.9	4.3	3.5	3.5	4.0	2.5	3.0	3.4	4.1	4.6	7.8	8.6	9.8	13.4	17.6
Imports, c.i.f.	71..d	2.4	3.5	5.4	7.5	7.5	7.4	6.0	10.0	14.4	21.5	28.6	30.6	43.2	56.9	53.3
Imports, f.o.b.	71.vd	2.2	3.2	4.9	6.8	6.8	6.8	5.5	9.1	13.1	19.5	26.0	27.9	39.3	51.7	48.5

	1985	1986	1987	1988	1989	1990	1991	1992	1993	1994	1995	1996	1997	1998	1999	
Exchange Rates																
End of Period																
Market Rate	7.830	8.861	13.328	11.472	12.097	13.686	14.762	14.486	15.253	17.182	17.496	16.925	15.881	16.573	16.154	aa
End of Period (ae) Period Average (rf)																
Market Rate	7.129	7.244	9.395	8.525	9.205	9.620	10.320	10.535	11.105	11.770	11.770	11.770	11.770	11.770	11.770	ae
Market Rate	7.098	7.151	9.223	8.785	9.041	9.552	10.253	10.569	10.957	11.586	11.770	11.770	11.770	11.770	11.770	rf
Fund Position																
End of Period																
Quota	2.0	2.0	2.0	2.0	2.0	2.0	2.0	5.5	5.5	5.5	5.5	5.5	5.5	5.5	8.2	2f. s
SDRs	—	—	—	—	—	—	—	—	—	—	—	.1	.1	.1	.1	1b. s
Reserve Position in the Fund	—	—	—	—	—	—	—	.9	.9	.9	.9	.9	.9	.9	1.6	1c. s
Total Fund Cred.&Loans Outstg.	—	—	—	—	—	—	—	—	—	—	—	—	—	—	—	2tl
International Liquidity																
End of Period																
Total Reserves minus Gold	4.59	6.91	8.19	21.59	24.77	24.38	23.47	28.19	26.15	31.22	47.95	76.17	98.31	118.54	127.12	1l. d
SDRs	.02	.02	.01	.03	.03	.03	.03	—	.03	.05	.07	.09	.11	.14	.19	1b. d
Reserve Position in the Fund	—	—	—	—	—	—	—	1.21	1.21	1.28	1.31	1.26	1.19	1.24	2.13	1c. d
Foreign Exchange	4.57	6.89	8.18	21.56	24.74	24.35	23.44	26.97	24.92	29.89	46.57	74.81	97.01	117.15	124.80	1d. d
Gold (Million Fine Troy Ounces)	.042	.042	.042	.042	.042	.042	.042	.042	.042	.042	....	....	....	....	—	1ad
Gold (National Valuation)	3.48	1.87	.13	.20	.19	.18	.17	.17	15.39	16.13	16.21	16.20	....	....	....	1an d
Monetary Authorities: Other Liab.	3.48	1.87	.13	.20	.19	.18	.17	.17	15.39	16.13	16.21	16.20	.86	.86	.86	4.. d
Deposit Money Banks: Assets	2.24	2.30	7.22	5.60	8.62	10.66	12.84	14.62	10.30	10.23	14.02	22.35	11.50	23.65	19.09	7a. d
Liabilities	30.66	24.84	21.29	19.08	28.83	27.95	17.81	22.08	18.37	13.61	19.03	12.83	12.20	15.06	26.90	7b. d
Monetary Authorities																
End of Period																
Foreign Assets	33.77	51.45	78.45	187.13	226.53	230.39	237.17	292.60	293.92	376.86	580.10	912.94	1,173.55	1,411.67	1,512.69	11
Claims on Central Government	ⱡ244.78	286.44	297.26	228.24	288.13	318.43	448.23	618.97	910.65	999.33	1,076.06	987.57	920.12	1,024.38	1,156.15	12a
Claims on Nonfin.Pub.Enterprises	9.10	3.36	11.92	14.84	20.06	4.45	40.68	8.86	9.75	6.16	8.42	7.86	—	3.20	2.48	12c
Claims on Deposit Money Banks	.17	.23	.95	.54	4.06	9.14	9.56	8.80	7.91	6.57	5.62	1.37	1.41	1.42	1.43	12e
Reserve Money	209.90	239.68	245.79	300.50	357.95	445.16	543.28	730.74	869.86	993.09	1,008.87	1,187.93	1,371.25	1,520.08	1,624.79	14
of which: Currency Outside DMBs	68.52	91.97	116.54	140.08	158.32	206.73	253.46	300.91	330.38	382.27	405.83	425.85	489.68	524.92	593.34	14a
Foreign Currency Deposits	.08	.08	.69	.76	.58	.64	.72	1.63	.63	5.50	17.00	26.64	32.70	20.69	26.51	15
Foreign Liabilities	ⱡ24.80	13.54	1.27	1.70	1.71	1.70	1.80	1.81	170.90	189.90	190.76	190.65	10.10	10.13	10.15	16c
Central Government Deposits	29.63	61.39	98.89	89.70	112.07	45.60	95.13	93.65	70.28	66.47	180.22	148.50	163.00	225.18	235.02	16d
Capital Accounts	11.22	13.16	26.58	17.81	36.72	42.23	51.57	46.63	74.49	90.52	62.70	105.57	130.40	105.37	118.27	17a
Other Items (Net)	12.19	13.62	15.36	20.28	29.76	27.08	43.14	54.77	36.07	43.44	210.65	250.45	387.63	559.22	658.01	17r
Deposit Money Banks																
End of Period																
Reserves	72.38	91.08	98.56	135.98	161.75	199.35	252.79	383.00	454.02	498.55	612.78	859.80	1,173.97	1,346.56	1,553.30	20
Foreign Assets	15.99	16.68	67.82	47.75	79.33	102.54	132.52	154.02	114.43	120.46	165.04	263.03	135.34	278.39	224.66	21
Claims on Central Government	4.80	2.32	2.97	1.62	2.44	5.60	8.73	9.95	4.21	—	—	—	—	—	—	22a
Claims on Nonfin.Pub.Enterprises	84.64	88.42	101.61	106.91	191.47	155.09	161.55	154.31	177.04	137.24	160.98	147.32	103.78	161.89	193.80	22c
Claims on Private Sector	184.00	181.51	180.59	159.15	195.55	255.30	247.80	256.75	398.53	507.38	655.09	717.40	996.79	1,253.18	1,302.81	22d
Demand Deposits	26.23	39.45	51.24	57.27	66.95	68.21	112.98	117.02	281.13	356.06	393.70	552.92	619.23	725.45	935.95	24
Time, Savings,& Fgn. Currency Dep.	72.39	107.05	132.17	156.26	189.75	224.67	269.48	293.80	340.13	429.26	569.91	785.77	1,075.30	1,423.72	1,318.10	25
Foreign Liabilities	ⱡ218.54	179.98	199.99	162.68	265.41	268.85	183.76	232.62	203.95	160.22	224.00	150.98	143.65	177.25	316.60	26c
Central Government Deposits	1.73	1.09	1.89	3.90	11.04	13.27	21.31	51.06	60.40	31.52	58.43	90.24	93.48	126.08	160.95	26d
Credit from Monetary Authorities	.19	.27	.85	.47	.21	8.99	9.59	8.67	7.64	6.63	5.15	1.34	.89	.89	.14	26g
Capital Accounts	27.81	32.57	43.76	44.14	38.66	48.04	62.15	91.72	122.32	143.77	157.69	281.00	358.92	486.96	496.18	27a
Other Items (Net)	14.92	19.61	21.64	26.69	58.53	85.83	144.12	163.14	132.66	136.17	185.01	125.30	118.41	99.67	46.65	27r
Monetary Survey																
End of Period																
Foreign Assets (Net)	ⱡ−193.58	−125.38	−54.99	70.50	38.74	62.38	184.13	212.19	33.50	147.20	330.38	834.34	1,155.14	1,502.68	1,410.60	31n
Domestic Credit	ⱡ495.95	499.56	493.57	417.15	574.54	679.99	790.55	904.13	1,369.50	1,552.12	1,661.90	1,621.41	1,764.21	2,091.39	2,259.27	32
Claims on Central Govt. (Net)	ⱡ218.21	226.27	199.45	136.25	167.46	265.16	340.52	484.21	784.18	901.34	837.41	748.83	663.64	673.12	760.18	32an
Claims on Nonfin.Pub.Enterprises	93.74	91.78	113.53	121.75	211.53	159.54	202.23	163.17	186.79	143.40	169.40	155.18	103.78	165.09	196.28	32c
Claims on Private Sector	184.00	181.51	180.59	159.15	195.55	255.30	247.80	256.75	398.53	507.38	655.09	717.40	996.79	1,253.18	1,302.81	32d
Money	163.69	188.80	198.45	221.67	263.14	312.86	402.05	463.88	694.54	850.87	899.06	1,059.35	1,195.60	1,384.24	1,585.18	34
Quasi-Money	72.47	107.12	132.86	157.01	190.33	225.31	270.20	295.43	340.76	434.76	586.91	812.41	1,108.00	1,444.41	1,344.61	35
Capital Accounts	39.03	45.73	70.34	61.95	75.38	90.27	113.72	138.35	196.81	234.29	220.39	386.57	489.32	592.33	614.45	37a
Other Items (Net)	27.18	32.52	36.93	47.02	84.44	113.92	188.71	218.66	170.89	179.40	285.92	197.42	126.43	173.09	125.63	37r
Money plus Quasi-Money	236.15	295.92	331.31	378.68	453.47	538.17	672.25	759.31	1,035.30	1,285.63	1,485.97	1,871.76	2,303.60	2,828.65	2,929.79	35l
Interest Rates																
Percent Per Annum																
Money Market Rate	9.00	9.00	8.67	8.50	7.33	7.00	7.00	7.00	5.00	5.00	6.80	6.80	6.80	6.80	6.80	60b
Prices and Production																
Period Averages																
Consumer Prices	—	—	—	51.3	ⱡ55.0	57.0	65.3	ⱡ76.3	91.7	94.8	100.0	106.3	114.3	112.7	116.0	64
Total Fish Catch	59.2	56.7	54.4	68.4	68.1	73.0	77.2	78.5	86.0	99.5	100.0	100.8	97.3	110.1	117.9	66al
Tourist Bed Night Index	38.6	37.9	46.5	61.0	53.7	61.7	63.3	72.5	76.8	86.3	100.0	111.5	120.0	127.2	136.4	66.t
International Transactions																
Millions of US Dollars																
Exports	23.0	24.5	30.8	40.2	44.7	52.1	53.7	40.0	34.6	45.9	49.5	59.3	73.2	74.3	63.7	70.. d
Imports, c.i.f.	53.0	45.0	81.0	90.0	112.6	137.8	161.2	189.3	191.3	221.7	267.9	301.8	348.9	354.0	402.2	71.. d
Imports, f.o.b.	47.9	40.5	73.7	81.9	95.7	117.1	137.0	166.6	168.3	195.1	235.6	265.6	307.0	311.5	353.9	71.v d

Maldives

	1970	1971	1972	1973	1974	1975	1976	1977	1978	1979	1980	1981	1982	1983	1984
Balance of Payments														*Millions of US Dollars:*	
Current Account, n.i.e. .... 78al *d*	....	....	....	....	....	....	....	—	1.6	−4.8	−22.2	−20.2	−19.1	−24.2	−16.3
Goods: Exports f.o.b. .... 78aa *d*	....	....	....	....	....	....	....	5.0	7.2	10.7	12.8	15.8	17.3	19.8	23.1
Goods: Imports f.o.b. .... 78ab *d*	....	....	....	....	....	....	....	−9.9	−14.8	−21.7	−44.0	−41.7	−46.0	−57.6	−61.0
Trade Balance .... 78ac *d*	....	....	....	....	....	....	....	−4.9	−7.6	−11.0	−31.2	−25.9	−28.7	−37.8	−37.9
Services: Credit .... 78ad *d*	....	....	....	....	....	....	....	5.0	5.6	31.1	52.4	58.7	59.3	56.9	61.4
Services: Debit .... 78ae *d*	....	....	....	....	....	....	....	−1.0	−1.4	−25.0	−43.1	−51.9	−47.7	−38.9	−34.2
Balance on Goods & Services .... 78af *d*	....	....	....	....	....	....	....	−.9	−3.4	−4.9	−21.9	−19.1	−17.1	−19.8	−10.7
Income: Credit .... 78ag *d*	....	....	....	....	....	....	....	—	—	—	—	—	.4	.6	.4
Income: Debit .... 78ah *d*	....	....	....	....	....	....	....	—	—	−1.6	−2.7	−3.5	−5.7	−10.1	−12.6
Balance on Gds, Serv. & Inc. .... 78ai *d*	....	....	....	....	....	....	....	−.9	−3.4	−6.5	−24.6	−22.6	−22.4	−29.3	−22.9
Current Transfers, n.i.e.: Credit .... 78aj *d*	....	....	....	....	....	....	....	.9	5.0	1.7	2.6	2.7	4.6	7.1	10.0
Current Transfers: Debit .... 78ak *d*	....	....	....	....	....	....	....	—	—	—	−.2	−.3	−1.3	−2.0	−3.4
Capital Account, n.i.e. .... 78bc *d*	....	....	....	....	....	....	....	—	—	—	—	—	—	—	—
Capital Account, n.i.e.: Credit .... 78ba *d*	....	....	....	....	....	....	....	—	—	—	—	—	—	—	—
Capital Account: Debit .... 78bb *d*	....	....	....	....	....	....	....	—	—	—	—	—	—	—	—
Financial Account, n.i.e. .... 78bj *d*	....	....	....	....	....	....	....	2.5	−.1	7.9	15.9	22.0	17.0	6.7	1.5
Direct Investment Abroad .... 78bd *d*	....	....	....	....	....	....	....	—	—	—	—	—	—	—	—
Dir. Invest. in Rep. Econ., n.i.e. .... 78be *d*	....	....	....	....	....	....	....	—	—	—	—	—	—	—	—
Portfolio Investment Assets .... 78bf *d*	....	....	....	....	....	....	....	—	—	—	—	—	—	—	—
Equity Securities .... 78bk *d*	....	....	....	....	....	....	....	—	—	—	—	—	—	—	—
Debt Securities .... 78bl *d*	....	....	....	....	....	....	....	—	—	—	—	—	—	—	—
Portfolio Investment Liab., n.i.e. .... 78bg *d*	....	....	....	....	....	....	....	—	—	—	—	—	—	—	—
Equity Securities .... 78bm *d*	....	....	....	....	....	....	....	—	—	—	—	—	—	—	—
Debt Securities .... 78bn *d*	....	....	....	....	....	....	....	....	....	....	....	....	....	....	....
Financial Derivatives Assets .... 78bw *d*	....	....	....	....	....	....	....	....	....	....	....	....	....	....	....
Financial Derivatives Liabilities .... 78bx *d*	....	....	....	....	....	....	....	....	....	....	....	....	....	....	....
Other Investment Assets .... 78bh *d*	....	....	....	....	....	....	....	—	−2.1	.6	−.6	−.3	.8	.2	−1.9
Monetary Authorities .... 78bo *d*	....	....	....	....	....	....	....	....	....	....	....	....	....	....	....
General Government .... 78bp *d*	....	....	....	....	....	....	....	—	—	—	—	—	—	—	—
Banks .... 78bq *d*	....	....	....	....	....	....	....	—	−2.1	.6	−.6	−.3	.8	.2	−1.9
Other Sectors .... 78br *d*	....	....	....	....	....	....	....	—	—	—	—	—	—	—	—
Other Investment Liab., n.i.e. .... 78bi *d*	....	....	....	....	....	....	....	2.5	2.0	7.3	16.5	22.3	16.2	6.5	3.4
Monetary Authorities .... 78bs *d*	....	....	....	....	....	....	....	—	—	4.8	−3.0	1.9	7.8	−.4	−.6
General Government .... 78bt *d*	....	....	....	....	....	....	....	1.6	2.4	2.8	18.1	11.5	4.5	2.9	−3.2
Banks .... 78bu *d*	....	....	....	....	....	....	....	.9	−.4	−.3	1.4	8.9	3.9	4.0	7.2
Other Sectors .... 78bv *d*	....	....	....	....	....	....	....	—	—	—	—	—	—	—	—
Net Errors and Omissions .... 78ca *d*	....	....	....	....	....	....	....	−2.4	−1.3	−3.1	6.3	−2.9	8.2	13.7	9.5
Overall Balance .... 78cb *d*	....	....	....	....	....	....	....	.1	.2	—	—	−1.1	6.1	−3.8	−5.3
Reserves and Related Items .... 79da *d*	....	....	....	....	....	....	....	−.1	−.2	—	—	1.1	−6.1	3.8	5.3
Reserve Assets .... 79db *d*	....	....	....	....	....	....	....	−.1	−.2	—	—	−.2	−6.9	3.8	−.5
Use of Fund Credit and Loans .... 79dc *d*	....	....	....	....	....	....	....	—	—	—	—	—	—	—	—
Exceptional Financing .... 79de *d*	....	....	....	....	....	....	....	....	....	....	....	1.3	.8	—	5.8
Government Finance														*Millions of Rufiyaa:*	
Deficit (-) or Surplus 80	....	....	....	....	....	....	....	....	....	−27.9	−76.4	−26.4	−19.6	−72.8	−25.1
Revenue 81	....	....	....	....	....	....	....	....	....	16.5	46.3	74.5	96.4	109.5	128.5
Grants Received 81z	....	....	....	....	....	....	....	....	....	7.9	11.5	8.3	23.4	12.4	35.2
Expenditure 82	....	....	....	....	....	....	....	....	....	48.6	102.9	108.4	138.8	192.9	192.7
Lending Minus Repayments 83	....	....	....	....	....	....	....	....	....	3.7	31.3	.8	.6	1.8	−3.9
Financing															
Domestic 84a	....	....	....	....	....	....	....	....	....	16.4	6.0	−9.9	2.7	42.6	27.3
Foreign 85a	....	....	....	....	....	....	....	....	....	11.5	70.4	36.3	16.9	30.2	−2.2
Debt: Domestic 88a	....	....	....	....	....	....	....	....	....	....	....	155.5	154.3	184.1	206.7
Foreign 89a	....	....	....	....	....	....	....	....	....	23.2	93.6	130.2	246.4	272.8	259.1
National Accounts														*Millions of Rufiyaa*	
Exports of Goods & Services 90c	....	....	....	....	....	....	....	....	....	....	59	65	74	101	124
Government Consumption 91f	....	....	....	....	....	....	....	....	....	....	39	50	61	76	99
Gross Fixed Capital Formation 93e	....	....	....	....	....	....	....	....	....	....	76	99	106	115	165
Private Consumption 96f	....	....	....	....	....	....	....	....	....	....	267	344	366	385	336
Imports of Goods & Services 98c	....	....	....	....	....	....	....	....	....	....	−186	−195	−275	−362	−364
Gross Domestic Product (GDP) 99b	....	....	....	....	....	....	....	142	170	224	321	376	432	466	502
GDP Volume 1984 prices 99b.*p*	....	....	....	....	191.9	187.9	237.1	275.3	316.7	349.3	379.4	368.0	348.0	415.0	528.0
GDP Volume 1985 Prices 99b.*p*	....	....	....	....	....	....	....	....	....	....	....	....	....	....	....
GDP Volume (1995=100) .... 99bv *p*	....	....	....	....	14.1	13.8	17.5	20.3	23.3	25.7	27.9	27.1	26.3	30.6	38.8
GDP Deflator (1995=100) .... 99bi *p*	....	....	....	....	....	....	....	22.0	22.8	27.2	35.9	43.4	51.4	47.8	40.5
														Millions:	
Population 99z	.11	.11	.11	.12	.13	.13	.13	.14	.15	.15	.15	.16	.16	.17	.18

Minus Sign Indicates Debit

1985	1986	1987	1988	1989	1990	1991	1992	1993	1994	1995	1996	1997	1998	1999	Balance of Payments	
−5.5	−.3	8.0	8.9	10.6	9.9	−9.1	−19.6	−53.9	−11.2	−18.1	−7.5	−36.5	−25.6	−59.9	Current Account, n.i.e.	78al *d*
25.5	26.9	34.9	44.6	63.7	78.0	76.2	65.1	52.7	75.4	85.0	79.9	92.6	95.6	88.6	Goods: Exports f.o.b.	78aa *d*
−58.0	−63.0	−66.5	−87.3	−111.3	−121.2	−141.8	−167.9	−177.8	−195.1	−235.8	−265.5	−307.0	−311.5	−354.1	Goods: Imports f.o.b.	78ab *d*
−32.5	−36.1	−31.6	−42.7	−47.6	−43.2	−65.6	−102.8	−125.1	−119.7	−150.8	−185.6	−214.4	−215.9	−265.5	*Trade Balance*	78ac *d*
65.6	69.7	76.3	83.3	86.4	101.1	108.0	154.3	160.7	197.4	232.9	289.0	310.1	329.3	353.8	Services: Credit	78ad *d*
−27.0	−23.2	−28.4	−28.5	−28.9	−38.0	−42.1	−49.4	−57.2	−62.8	−76.7	−87.9	−94.3	−98.6	−106.3	Services: Debit	78ae *d*
6.1	10.4	16.3	12.1	9.9	19.9	.3	2.1	−21.7	14.9	5.4	15.5	1.4	14.8	−18.0	*Balance on Goods & Services*	78af *d*
.3	1.4	1.3	2.0	3.8	4.7	3.8	2.9	3.0	3.8	4.5	5.9	7.5	8.3	8.9	Income: Credit	78ag *d*
−13.5	−19.9	−16.9	−11.7	−16.3	−18.5	−18.7	−20.0	−22.0	−24.0	−24.4	−27.8	−34.7	−36.4	−36.7	Income: Debit	78ah *d*
−7.1	−8.1	.7	2.4	−2.6	6.1	−14.6	−15.0	−40.7	−5.3	−14.5	−6.4	−25.8	−13.3	−45.8	*Balance on Gds, Serv. & Inc.*	78ai *d*
3.6	9.3	9.7	11.5	18.3	11.2	22.1	14.3	13.3	16.3	23.0	26.2	17.2	18.3	19.3	Current Transfers, n.i.e.: Credit	78aj *d*
−2.0	−1.5	−2.4	−5.0	−5.1	−7.4	−16.6	−18.9	−26.5	−22.2	−26.6	−27.3	−27.9	−30.6	−33.4	Current Transfers: Debit	78ak *d*
—	—	—	—	—	—	—	—	—	—	—	—	—	—	—	Capital Account, n.i.e.	78bc *d*
—	—	—	—	—	—	—	—	—	—	—	—	—	—	—	Capital Account, n.i.e.: Credit	78ba *d*
—	—	—	—	—	—	—	—	—	—	—	—	—	—	—	Capital Account: Debit	78bb *d*
−4.3	−5.5	−5.4	−1.5	11.8	8.1	5.7	44.6	46.3	27.5	67.5	52.2	61.5	72.5	75.8	Financial Account, n.i.e.	78bj *d*
															Direct Investment Abroad	78bd *d*
—	5.4	5.1	1.2	4.4	5.6	6.5	6.6	6.9	8.7	7.2	9.3	11.4	11.5	11.5	Dir. Invest. in Rep. Econ., n.i.e.	78be *d*
—	—	—	—	—	—	—	—	—	—	—	—	—	—	—	Portfolio Investment Assets	78bf *d*
—	—	—	—	—	—	—	—	—	—	—	—	—	—	—	Equity Securities	78bk *d*
—	—	—	—	—	—	—	—	—	—	—	—	—	—	—	Debt Securities	78bl *d*
—	—	—	—	—	—	—	—	—	—	—	—	—	—	—	Portfolio Investment Liab., n.i.e.	78bg *d*
—	—	—	—	—	—	—	—	—	—	—	—	—	—	—	Equity Securities	78bm *d*
—	—	—	—	—	—	—	—	—	—	—	—	—	—	—	Debt Securities	78bn *d*
....	....	....	....	....	....	....	....	....	....	....	....	....	....	....	Financial Derivatives Assets	78bw *d*
....	....	....	....	....	....	....	....	....	....	....	....	....	....	....	Financial Derivatives Liabilities	78bx *d*
1.4	−.1	−4.9	1.6	−2.9	−2.2	−2.2	15.7	25.0	13.2	29.8	32.7	53.7	35.7	47.5	Other Investment Assets	78bh *d*
....	....	....	....	....	....	....	....	....	....	....	....	....	....	....	Monetary Authorities	78bo *d*
—	—	—	—	—	—	—	—	—	—	—	—	—	2.0	—	General Government	78bp *d*
1.4	−.1	−4.9	1.6	−2.9	−2.2	−2.2	−1.8	4.3	.1	−3.8	−8.3	10.8	−10.2	4.6	Banks	78bq *d*
							17.5	20.7	13.1	33.6	41.0	42.9	43.9	42.9	Other Sectors	78br *d*
−5.7	−10.8	−5.6	−4.3	10.3	4.7	1.4	22.3	14.4	5.6	30.5	10.2	−3.6	25.3	16.8	Other Investment Liab., n.i.e.	78bi *d*
−3.5	−1.6	−1.7	.1	—	—	—	—	15.2	.8	.1	—	−15.3	1.0	—	Monetary Authorities	78bs *d*
−3.2	−3.4	−.3	−2.2	1.0	5.1	11.5	17.1	3.8	8.2	24.7	17.3	12.5	17.0	5.6	General Government	78bt *d*
1.0	−5.8	−3.6	−2.2	9.3	−.4	−10.1	5.2	−4.6	−3.4	5.7	−7.1	−.8	5.3	11.2	Banks	78bu *d*
—	—	—	—	—	—	—	—	—	—	—	—	—	2.0	....	Other Sectors	78bv *d*
11.3	1.6	−1.4	6.2	−20.1	−18.3	2.4	−20.2	7.5	−10.8	−32.1	−16.4	−2.8	−26.7	−6.3	Net Errors and Omissions	78ca *d*
1.5	−4.2	1.2	13.6	2.3	−.3	−1.0	4.8	−.1	5.5	17.3	28.3	22.1	20.2	9.6	*Overall Balance*	78cb *d*
−1.5	4.2	−1.2	−13.6	−2.3	.3	1.0	−4.8	.1	−5.5	−17.3	−28.3	−22.1	−20.2	−9.6	Reserves and Related Items	79da *d*
−3.0	−2.3	−1.2	−13.6	−2.3	.3	1.0	−4.8	.1	−5.5	−17.3	−28.3	−22.1	−20.2	−9.6	Reserve Assets	79db *d*
—	—	—	—	—	—	—	—	—	—	—	—	—	—	—	Use of Fund Credit and Loans	79dc *d*
1.5	6.5	—	—	—	—	—	—	—	—	—	—	—	—	....	Exceptional Financing	79de *d*

Year Ending December 31

1985	1986	1987	1988	1989	1990	1991	1992	1993	1994	1995	1996	1997	1998	1999	Government Finance	
−30.6	−83.7	19.1	25.6	−42.7	−170.8	−238.5	−356.9	−412.6	−206.6	−300.1	−133.8	−81.3	−123.1	−303.6 [f]	Deficit (−) or Surplus	80
155.9	179.8	273.6	315.0	406.8	460.3	568.9	684.2	765.2	981.7	1,209.5	1,324.9	1,656.5	1,765.7	2,013.2 [f]	Revenue	81
9.7	66.3	89.5	101.3	165.7	85.0	226.2	151.4	153.3	162.6	199.2	242.9	168.2	164.5	151.7 [f]	Grants Received	81z
187.0	312.3	327.0	377.8	600.7	699.5	1,014.4	1,166.9	1,317.4	1,357.5	1,717.8	1,692.6	1,936.9	2,113.9	2,455.0 [f]	Expenditure	82
9.2	17.5	17.0	12.9	14.5	16.6	19.2	25.6	13.7	−6.6	−9.0	9.0	−30.9	−60.6	13.5 [f]	Lending Minus Repayments	83
															Financing	
32.3	52.9	−20.2	−21.7	2.6	97.3	111.0	189.9	377.0	106.4	2.1	−29.2	−90.9	−6.2	263.3 [f]	Domestic	84a
−1.7	30.8	1.1	−3.9	40.1	73.5	127.5	167.0	35.6	100.2	298.0	163.0	172.2	129.3	40.3 [f]	Foreign	85a
237.4	246.6	245.0	178.2	183.0	200.1	331.5	526.1	846.5	960.9	1,063.0	957.6	877.1	980.3	1,101.1 [f]	Debt: Domestic	88a
253.7	276.7	321.0	325.8	358.7	432.2	559.9	726.9	762.5	862.7	1,160.7	1,323.7	1,495.9	1,625.2	1,665.5 [f]	Foreign	89a

1985	1986	1987	1988	1989	1990	1991	1992	1993	1994	1995	1996	1997	1998	1999	National Accounts	
164	179	289	351	401	503	544	417	377	555	586	....	....	....	....	Exports of Goods & Services	90c
111	137	230	263	347	422	....	....	....	....	....	....	....	....	....	Government Consumption	91f
234	253	511	545	685	755	....	....	....	....	....	....	....	....	....	Gross Fixed Capital Formation	93e
498	546	528	523	613	621	....	....	....	....	....	....	....	....	....	Private Consumption	96f
−340	−302	−726	−843	−1,020	−1,315	−1,654	−2,002	−2,097	−2,571	−3,153	....	....	....	....	Imports of Goods & Services	98c
600	674	845	988	1,148	1,393	1,687	2,029	2,380	2,790	3,195	3,550	3,990	4,440	4,625	Gross Domestic Product (GDP)	99b
600.0	652.0	710.0	772.0	843.0	934.0	....	....	....	....	....	....	....	....	....	GDP Volume 1984 prices	99b. *p*
....	....	....	....	....	980.0	1,054.8	1,121.1	1,190.2	1,268.6	1,359.4	1,466.5	1,600.4	1,746.0	1,895.2	GDP Volume 1985 Prices	99b. *p*
44.2	48.0	52.2	56.8	62.0	72.1	77.6	82.5	87.6	93.3	100.0	107.9	117.7	128.4	139.4	GDP Volume (1995=100)	99bv *p*
42.6	44.0	50.6	54.5	57.9	60.5	68.0	77.0	85.1	93.6	100.0	103.0	106.1	108.2	103.8	GDP Deflator (1995=100)	99bi *p*

Midyear Estimates

1985	1986	1987	1988	1989	1990	1991	1992	1993	1994	1995	1996	1997	1998	1999		
.18	.19	.20	.20	.21	.22	.22	.23	.24	.25	.25	.26	.27	.27	.28	**Population**	99z

(See notes in the back of the book.)

Mali

		1970	1971	1972	1973	1974	1975	1976	1977	1978	1979	1980	1981	1982	1983	1984
Exchange Rates															*Francs per SDR:*	
Official Rate	aa	276.02	283.61	278.00	284.00	272.08	262.55	288.70	285.76	272.28	264.78	287.99	334.52	370.92	436.97	470.11
															Francs per US Dollar:	
Official Rate	ae	276.02	261.22	256.05	235.42	222.22	224.27	248.49	235.25	209.00	201.00	225.80	287.40	336.25	417.37	479.60
Official Rate	rf	276.40	275.59	252.03	222.89	240.70	214.31	238.95	245.68	225.66	212.72	211.28	271.73	328.61	381.07	436.96
Fund Position															*Millions of SDRs:*	
Quota	2f. s	22.0	22.0	22.0	22.0	22.0	22.0	22.0	22.0	27.0	27.0	40.5	40.5	40.5	50.8	50.8
SDRs	1b. s	—	1.3	2.4	2.3	3.0	2.7	2.8	2.7	2.6	1.3	—	.2	.5	.1	1.7
Reserve Position in the Fund	1c. s	—	—	—	—	—	—	—	—	—	—	5.4	7.6	8.7	8.7	8.7
Total Fund Cred.&Loans Outstg.	2tl	8.6	7.5	8.3	7.3	10.4	10.6	12.7	11.2	19.2	22.1	30.3	28.2	52.5	65.3	84.3
International Liquidity												*Millions of US Dollars Unless Otherwise Indicated:*					
Total Reserves minus Gold	1l. d	.9	2.1	3.7	4.2	6.1	4.2	6.9	5.4	8.2	6.0	14.5	17.4	16.7	16.2	26.6
SDRs	1b. d	—	1.4	2.6	2.7	3.7	3.2	3.2	3.3	3.4	1.7	—	.2	.6	.1	1.7
Reserve Position in the Fund	1c. d	—	—	—	—	—	—	—	—	—	—	6.8	8.8	9.6	9.1	8.5
Foreign Exchange	1d. d	.9	.7	1.1	1.5	2.4	1.0	3.7	2.1	4.8	4.3	7.7	8.4	6.6	7.0	16.5
Gold (Million Fine Troy Ounces)	1ad	....	....	....	....	....	....	....	.010	.014	.019	.019	.019	.019	.019	.019
Gold (National Valuation)	1an d	....	....	....	....	....	....	....	.4	.6	.9	.9	7.9	8.0	7.3	6.3
Monetary Authorities: Other Liab.	4. d	49.0	58.2	64.4	88.2	127.0								—	—	3.9
Deposit Money Banks: Assets	7a. d	7.7	6.2	9.9	10.3	14.3	12.1	12.7	21.6	11.2	10.9	9.7	10.9	13.4	19.0	24.3
Liabilities	7b. d	12.0	11.4	17.4	19.5	24.6	21.6	22.6	33.1	23.6	33.9	34.4	27.4	26.4	23.9	33.5
Monetary Authorities															*Billions of Francs:*	
Foreign Assets	11	.2	.5	1.0	1.0	1.4	‡.9	1.7	1.4	1.8	1.8	3.5	4.8	5.8	6.8	‡12.8
Claims on Central Government	12a	19.4	20.7	21.6	24.2	27.2	‡31.6	34.9	46.4	50.4	53.8	55.3	60.9	78.3	93.1	‡47.2
Claims on Deposit Money Banks	12e	6.5	7.3	9.3	11.7	21.0	‡32.4	40.9	29.4	36.4	47.7	48.4	50.0	54.1	54.3	‡12.5
Claims on Other Financial Insts	12f	—	—	—	—	—	—	—	—	—	—	—	—	—	—	—
Reserve Money	14	9.0	9.8	10.8	11.5	15.3	‡18.7	22.5	22.5	27.4	30.7	38.2	40.6	40.9	45.0	‡63.6
of which: Currency Outside DMBs	14a	8.9	9.7	10.5	11.1	15.1	‡18.7	22.5	22.5	27.4	30.7	38.2	40.6	40.9	45.0	‡50.5
Foreign Liabilities	16c	15.9	17.0	18.8	22.3	31.0	‡2.8	3.7	3.2	5.2	5.8	8.7	9.4	19.5	28.5	‡49.9
Central Government Deposits	16d	.2	.1	—	.4	—	‡.7	.3	.3	1.1	.1	.9	.8	3.9	3.3	‡5.9
Other Items (Net)	17r	1.0	1.7	2.4	2.5	3.2	‡42.7	51.1	46.3	51.6	59.1	57.0	64.5	69.9	72.1	‡−46.9
Deposit Money Banks															*Billions of Francs:*	
Reserves	20	.1	.1	.2	.3	.3	.4	.7	.5	1.3	‡.6	.5	.4	1.4	.9	‡10.9
Foreign Assets	21	2.1	1.6	2.5	2.4	3.2	2.7	3.2	5.1	2.4	‡2.2	2.2	3.1	4.5	7.9	11.7
Claims on Central Government	22a	1.8	1.7	1.8	1.6	1.8	1.2	.8	.6	1.1	1.9	1.1	1.1	1.1	1.2	2.6
Claims on Private Sector	22d	11.7	13.8	17.0	21.6	34.1	51.1	61.3	53.3	65.8	‡76.1	82.0	87.4	95.0	101.6	‡70.3
Claims on Other Financial Insts	22f	....	....	....	....	....	....	....	....	....	....	....	....	....	....	....
Demand Deposits	24	4.1	4.3	5.1	5.6	11.3	12.5	12.6	12.8	17.3	‡18.1	18.5	18.9	22.9	30.7	53.4
Time Deposits	25	.2	.2	.4	.3	.1	.6	.6	1.2	3.0	‡3.3	3.3	4.5	4.0	6.0	10.3
Foreign Liabilities	26c	1.4	1.5	1.7	2.9	3.2	4.6	4.3	5.8	6.6	‡4.3	5.3	5.4	5.7	6.7	‡12.6
Long-Term Foreign Liabilities	26cl	1.2	1.3	1.9	2.1	2.3	2.1	2.5	2.7	2.6	‡2.5	2.5	2.5	3.1	3.3	3.5
Central Government Deposits	26d															6.0
Credit from Monetary Authorities	26g	6.5	7.3	9.3	11.7	21.0	32.3	40.8	29.3	36.4	‡47.7	48.4	50.0	54.1	54.3	6.9
Other Items (Net)	27r	2.4	2.6	3.1	3.3	1.5	3.3	5.1	7.7	4.7	‡3.8	7.8	10.8	12.1	10.7	2.8
Treasury Claims: Private Sector	22d. i	—	—	—	—	—	—	—	—	—	—	—	—	—	—	.3
Post Office: Checking Deposits	24.. i						.5	.5	.5	.5	.5	.4	.4	.4	.4	3.2
Monetary Survey															*Billions of Francs:*	
Foreign Assets (Net)	31n	−14.9	−16.4	−17.0	−21.9	−29.7	−42.7	−50.3	−46.4	−51.9	‡−6.1	−8.4	−6.9	−14.9	−20.6	‡−38.1
Domestic Credit	32	33.2	36.7	40.8	47.8	63.8	84.0	97.3	100.5	116.7	131.1	137.9	148.0	170.9	193.0	‡111.4
Claims on Central Govt. (Net)	32an	21.0	22.3	23.5	26.2	29.6	32.9	36.0	47.2	50.9	‡55.0	55.9	60.6	75.9	91.4	‡40.8
Claims on Private Sector	32d	11.7	13.8	17.0	21.6	34.1	51.1	61.3	53.3	65.8	76.1	82.0	87.4	95.0	101.6	‡70.6
Claims on Other Financial Insts	32f	....	....	....	....	....	....	....	....	....	....	....	....	....	....	....
Money	34	13.4	14.4	16.0	17.5	27.0	32.0	35.6	40.7	48.5	56.8	59.5	60.2	68.3	81.2	‡107.1
Quasi-Money	35	.2	.2	.4	.3	.1	.6	.6	1.2	3.0	‡3.3	3.3	4.5	4.0	6.0	‡10.3
Long-Term Foreign Liabilities	36cl	1.2	1.3	1.9	2.1	2.3	2.1	2.5	2.7	2.6	‡2.5	2.5	2.5	3.1	3.3	‡3.5
Other Items (Net)	37r	3.5	4.3	5.5	5.9	4.6	6.6	8.3	9.6	10.7	‡62.4	64.3	73.9	80.6	81.9	‡−47.6
Money plus Quasi-Money	35l	13.6	14.7	16.4	17.9	27.1	32.5	36.3	41.8	51.5	‡60.1	62.8	64.7	72.3	87.3	117.4
Other Banking Institutions															*Billions of Francs:*	
Savings Deposits	45	.3	.3	.3	.3	.4	.5	.5	.5	.5	.5	.4	.4	....	....	....
Liquid Liabilities	55l	13.9	15.0	16.7	18.2	27.5	33.0	36.7	42.3	52.0	‡60.6	63.2	65.1	....	....	....
Interest Rates															*Percent Per Annum:*	
Discount Rate (End of Period)	60	3.50	3.50	3.50	5.50	5.50	8.00	8.00	8.00	8.00	8.00	10.50	10.50	12.50	10.50	10.50
Money Market Rate	60b	....	....	....	....	....	....	7.28	7.38	7.40	7.72	10.13	13.68	14.66	12.23	11.84
Deposit Rate	60l	3.00	3.00	3.00	5.75	5.75	5.88	6.00	6.00	6.00	6.00	6.19	6.25	7.75	7.50	7.25
Lending Rate	60p	....	....	....	....	....	....	....	12.00	12.00	12.00	14.50	14.50	16.00	14.50	14.50

	1985	1986	1987	1988	1989	1990	1991	1992	1993	1994	1995	1996	1997	1998	1999		
End of Period																**Exchange Rates**	
	415.26	394.78	378.78	407.68	380.32	364.84	370.48	378.57	404.89	ɪ780.44	728.38	753.06	807.94	791.61	ɪ896.19	Official Rate...............	aa
End of Period (ae) Period Average (rf)																	
	378.05	322.75	267.00	302.95	289.40	256.45	259.00	275.32	294.77	ɪ534.60	490.00	523.70	598.81	562.21	ɪ652.95	Official Rate...............	ae
	449.26	346.31	300.54	297.85	319.01	272.26	282.11	264.69	283.16	ɪ555.20	499.15	511.55	583.67	589.95	ɪ615.70	Official Rate...............	rf
End of Period																**Fund Position**	
	50.8	50.8	50.8	50.8	50.8	50.8	50.8	68.9	68.9	68.9	68.9	68.9	68.9	68.9	93.3	Quota...............	2f. s
	1.7	—	.2	.2	.1	.3	.3	.1	.1	.1	.3	.2	—	.1	.4	SDRs...............	1b. s
	8.7	8.7	8.7	8.7	8.7	8.7	8.7	8.7	8.7	8.7	8.7	8.8	8.8	8.8	8.8	Reserve Position in the Fund...............	1c. s
	89.2	80.8	60.0	54.9	41.9	48.7	42.0	47.5	51.4	74.1	99.0	114.6	130.2	132.4	140.9	Total Fund Cred.&Loans Outstg.............	2tl
End of Period																**International Liquidity**	
	22.5	12.3	15.8	36.0	115.8	190.5	319.3	307.9	332.4	221.4	323.0	431.5	414.9	402.9	349.7	Total Reserves minus Gold...............	1l. d
	1.8	—	.3	.2	.2	.5	.4	.1	.1	.2	.5	.3	.1	.1	.6	SDRs...............	1b. d
	9.5	10.6	12.3	11.7	11.4	12.4	12.4	11.9	12.0	12.7	13.0	12.6	11.8	12.4	12.1	Reserve Position in the Fund...............	1c. d
	11.2	1.7	3.3	24.1	104.2	177.7	306.5	295.9	320.3	208.5	309.5	418.6	403.0	390.4	337.0	Foreign Exchange...............	1d. d
	.019	.019	.019	.019	.019	.019	.019	.019	.019	.019	.019	.019	.019	.019	.019	Gold (Million Fine Troy Ounces)...........	1ad
	6.1	7.6	8.9	7.8	7.3	7.1	6.7	6.5	7.0	7.0	7.3	7.1	5.8	5.5	5.6	Gold (National Valuation)...............	1an d
	2.7	34.3	51.9	6.9	7.6	4.9	16.2	2.5	6.0	9.7	1.9	-6.9	3.7	1.8	3.1	Monetary Authorities: Other Liab.......	4.. d
	15.4	24.8	27.2	19.4	63.7	72.1	60.8	40.4	26.3	118.7	163.6	136.7	117.6	125.2	116.6	Deposit Money Banks: Assets...............	7a. d
	51.2	72.6	87.4	87.0	93.1	113.0	78.4	47.3	42.2	34.3	102.1	70.0	28.2	49.1	87.9	Liabilities...........	7b. d
End of Period																**Monetary Authorities**	
	8.5	4.0	4.2	10.9	33.5	48.9	82.7	84.8	98.0	118.4	158.2	226.0	248.4	226.5	228.3	Foreign Assets...............	11
	51.2	48.8	46.8	52.1	42.1	34.1	34.5	37.2	41.0	58.7	65.1	77.0	99.8	105.9	112.9	Claims on Central Government...............	12a
	20.6	38.1	32.2	30.4	23.9	23.9	23.9	23.9	23.9	—	—	—	—	—	—	Claims on Deposit Money Banks...........	12e
	—	—	—	—	—	—	—	—	—	—	—	—	—	—	—	Claims on Other Financial Insts...............	12f
	71.7	80.7	78.1	86.4	98.9	100.3	132.0	131.7	143.8	115.9	127.7	151.1	162.8	153.7	173.1	Reserve Money...............	14
	59.8	66.9	60.8	62.2	54.8	46.9	60.0	60.9	65.1	91.1	107.5	120.3	129.5	135.3	123.4	*of which: Currency Outside DMBs*........	14a
	45.4	47.6	39.4	25.7	18.5	19.1	19.8	18.7	22.6	63.0	73.1	82.7	107.5	105.9	128.4	Foreign Liabilities...............	16c
	3.7	.5	1.0	12.3	6.1	8.9	3.1	5.9	5.5	12.8	27.1	63.0	70.6	63.7	41.5	Central Government Deposits...............	16d
	-40.5	-37.9	-35.2	-31.0	-23.9	-21.4	-13.6	-10.4	-9.1	-14.6	-4.6	6.2	7.4	9.2	-1.8	Other Items (Net)...............	17r
End of Period																**Deposit Money Banks**	
	12.8	14.0	17.3	24.6	43.8	54.0	71.8	70.5	79.4	25.3	17.1	29.5	32.1	16.5	47.7	Reserves...............	20
	5.8	8.0	7.3	5.9	18.4	18.5	15.8	11.1	7.8	63.4	80.2	71.6	70.4	70.4	76.2	Foreign Assets...............	21
	2.6	3.4	2.8	4.2	2.5	3.8	2.6	3.4	3.4	28.0	19.4	24.0	21.1	13.6	14.0	Claims on Central Government...............	22a
	83.2	99.5	95.2	70.2	84.1	84.1	86.2	91.9	93.8	84.9	130.3	171.2	195.9	251.0	286.5	Claims on Private Sector...............	22d
	—	—	—	—	—	—	—	—	—	—	—	—	—	—	—	Claims on Other Financial Insts...............	22f
	49.7	47.5	45.0	48.9	47.8	47.3	47.4	47.4	52.7	83.0	90.5	119.5	126.2	131.8	142.3	Demand Deposits...............	24
	13.8	17.8	20.6	26.0	31.6	36.6	45.4	49.0	52.6	63.1	56.4	76.4	89.0	91.9	97.0	Time Deposits...............	25
	17.0	19.8	18.1	19.0	19.6	21.2	14.0	8.7	8.8	11.5	45.3	30.5	5.9	19.5	50.3	Foreign Liabilities...............	26c
	2.4	3.7	5.3	7.4	7.3	7.8	6.3	4.3	3.6	6.9	4.7	6.1	10.9	8.1	7.1	Long-Term Foreign Liabilities...............	26cl
	10.5	9.9	11.1	16.9	21.4	27.2	32.7	37.1	33.0	39.3	50.8	71.5	68.2	78.0	102.3	Central Government Deposits...............	26d
	20.7	38.3	32.9	30.5	24.4	24.4	24.2	24.1	23.9	—	.1	—	—	—	—	Credit from Monetary Authorities.........	26g
	-9.7	-12.1	-10.3	-43.9	-3.3	-4.0	6.4	6.3	9.8	-2.1	-.7	-8.0	19.3	22.2	25.3	Other Items (Net)...............	27r
	.3	.3	.4	.2	.2	.3	.1	.7	1.5	2.1	1.5	2.0	4.5	3.9	5.2	Treasury Claims: Private Sector........22d. *i*	
	4.3	3.1	3.6	3.5	7.8	4.3										Post Office: Checking Deposits..........24.. *i*	
End of Period																**Monetary Survey**	
	-48.1	-55.4	-46.0	-27.9	13.9	27.1	64.8	68.5	74.3	107.3	120.0	184.3	205.5	171.5	125.9	Foreign Assets (Net)...............	31n
	127.2	144.4	136.4	100.8	109.0	90.2	87.5	89.4	99.7	119.5	136.9	137.6	178.0	228.8	269.5	Domestic Credit...............	32
	43.6	44.6	40.8	30.4	24.7	5.8	1.2	-3.2	4.4	32.6	5.1	-35.6	-22.4	-26.1	-22.2	Claims on Central Govt. (Net)...........	32an
	83.5	99.8	95.6	70.4	84.3	84.4	86.4	92.6	95.3	86.9	131.8	173.2	200.4	254.9	291.7	Claims on Private Sector...............	32d
	—	—	—	—	—	—	—	—	—	—	—	—	—	—	—	Claims on Other Financial Insts...........	32f
	113.8	117.5	109.3	114.6	110.4	98.5	107.4	108.3	117.8	174.2	198.2	240.4	256.0	267.6	266.0	Money...............	34
	13.8	17.8	20.6	26.0	31.6	36.6	45.4	49.0	52.6	63.1	56.4	76.4	89.0	91.9	97.0	Quasi-Money...............	35
	2.4	3.7	5.3	7.4	7.3	7.8	6.3	4.3	3.6	6.9	4.7	6.1	10.9	8.1	7.1	Long-Term Foreign Liabilities...............	36cl
	-50.9	-50.0	-44.8	-75.1	-26.4	-25.6	-6.8	-3.7	—	-17.3	-2.4	-1.0	27.5	32.8	25.2	Other Items (Net)...............	37r
	127.6	135.3	129.9	140.6	142.0	135.0	152.7	157.2	170.4	237.2	254.6	316.8	345.0	359.5	363.1	Money plus Quasi-Money...............	35l
End of Period																**Other Banking Institutions**	
	. . . .	. . . .	. . . .	. . . .	. . . .	. . . .	. . . .	. . . .	. . . .	. . . .	. . . .	—	—	—	—	Savings Deposits...............	45
	. . . .	. . . .	. . . .	. . . .	. . . .	. . . .	. . . .	. . . .	. . . .	. . . .	. . . .	316.8	345.0	359.5	363.1	Liquid Liabilities...............	55l
Percent Per Annum																**Interest Rates**	
	10.50	8.50	8.50	9.50	11.00	11.00	11.00	12.50	10.50	10.00	7.50	6.50	6.00	6.25	5.75	Discount Rate *(End of Period)*...............	60
	10.66	8.58	8.37	8.72	10.07	10.98	10.94	11.44	. . . .	. . . .	. . . .	. . . .	. . . .	4.81	4.95	Money Market Rate...............	60b
	7.25	6.08	5.25	5.25	6.42	7.00	7.00	7.75	. . . .	. . . .	. . . .	. . . .	. . . .	3.50	3.50	Deposit Rate...............	60l
	14.50	13.50	13.50	13.58	15.08	16.00	16.00	16.75	. . . .	. . . .	. . . .	. . . .	. . . .	. . . .	. . . .	Lending Rate...............	60p

Mali

	1970	1971	1972	1973	1974	1975	1976	1977	1978	1979	1980	1981	1982	1983	1984
Prices														*Index Numbers (1995=100):*	
Consumer Prices 64	....	....	....	....	....	....	....	....	....	....	....	....	....	....	....
International Transactions															
Exports 70	9.65	10.00	10.53	11.65	15.41	11.49	20.56	30.61	25.20	31.35	43.31	41.92	47.90	62.90	57.97
Imports, c.i.f. 71	9.47	16.47	19.81	28.13	43.04	37.71	36.85	39.00	64.30	76.45	93.05	104.75	109.20	134.60	121.69
Balance of Payments														*Millions of US Dollars:*	
Current Account, n.i.e. .... 78al *d*	....	....	....	....	....	−61.1	−42.2	5.2	−146.3	−113.6	−129.9	−143.0	−115.3	−113.2	−121.5
Goods: Exports f.o.b. .... 78aa *d*	....	....	....	....	....	71.9	94.4	124.6	94.2	145.7	204.9	154.2	145.8	166.8	192.0
Goods: Imports f.o.b. .... 78ab *d*	....	....	....	....	....	−136.2	−111.3	−111.1	−199.4	−270.3	−308.4	−269.0	−232.6	−240.9	−257.8
Trade Balance .... 78ac *d*	....	....	....	....	....	−64.3	−16.9	13.5	−105.2	−124.6	−103.4	−114.8	−86.9	−74.1	−65.8
Services: Credit .... 78ad *d*	....	....	....	....	....	22.9	17.8	23.9	37.2	45.6	57.7	46.2	44.4	42.0	40.7
Services: Debit .... 78ae *d*	....	....	....	....	....	−102.5	−78.7	−95.4	−150.7	−163.8	−211.8	−168.9	−162.7	−166.9	−172.9
Balance on Goods & Services ...... 78af *d*	....	....	....	....	....	−143.9	−77.8	−58.1	−218.7	−242.8	−257.5	−237.6	−205.1	−199.0	−198.0
Income: Credit .... 78ag *d*	....	....	....	....	....	—	—	—	—	—	—	—	—	—	—
Income: Debit .... 78ah *d*	....	....	....	....	....	−21.7	−16.6	−19.8	−13.3	−11.8	−16.9	−32.6	−24.2	−27.5	−19.2
Balance on Gds, Serv. & Inc. ... 78ai *d*	....	....	....	....	....	−165.6	−94.4	−77.9	−232.0	−254.6	−274.4	−270.1	−229.3	−226.5	−217.2
Current Transfers, n.i.e.: Credit .. 78aj *d*	....	....	....	....	....	119.9	62.6	91.3	101.0	165.6	169.3	147.2	133.7	131.7	111.9
Current Transfers: Debit .... 78ak *d*	....	....	....	....	....	−15.5	−10.5	−8.3	−15.3	−24.7	−24.8	−20.1	−19.6	−18.4	−16.2
Capital Account, n.i.e. .... 78bc *d*	....	....	....	....	....	4.5	—	—	47.2	—	—	—	—	—	52.9
Capital Account, n.i.e.: Credit ..... 78ba *d*	....	....	....	....	....	4.5	—	—	47.2	—	—	—	—	—	52.9
Capital Account: Debit .... 78bb *d*	....	....	....	....	....	—	—	—	—	—	—	—	—	—	—
Financial Account, n.i.e. .... 78bj *d*	....	....	....	....	....	4.3	6.7	22.9	49.8	120.8	127.9	107.8	76.7	88.7	68.4
Direct Investment Abroad .... 78bd *d*	....	....	....	....	....	−.6	−7.6	−8.0	−8.9	3.1	—	—	—	—	—
Dir. Invest. in Rep. Econ., n.i.e. .. 78be *d*	....	....	....	....	....	2.6	2.6	3.1	−.9	—	2.4	3.7	1.5	3.1	10.1
Portfolio Investment Assets ..... 78bf *d*	....	....	....	....	....	—	—	—	—	—	—	—	—	—	—
Equity Securities .... 78bk *d*	....	....	....	....	....	—	—	—	—	—	—	—	—	—	—
Debt Securities .... 78bl *d*	....	....	....	....	....	—	—	—	—	—	—	—	—	—	—
Portfolio Investment Liab., n.i.e. .... 78bg *d*	....	....	....	....	....	—	—	—	—	—	—	—	—	—	—
Equity Securities .... 78bm *d*	....	....	....	....	....	—	—	—	—	—	—	—	—	—	—
Debt Securities .... 78bn *d*	....	....	....	....	....	—	—	—	—	—	—	—	—	—	—
Financial Derivatives Assets .... 78bw *d*	....	....	....	....	....	....	....	....	....	....	....	....	....	....	....
Financial Derivatives Liabilities ... 78bx *d*	....	....	....	....	....	....	....	....	....	....	....	....	....	....	....
Other Investment Assets .... 78bh *d*	....	....	....	....	....	−13.6	−12.8	−7.5	5.8	26.7	6.2	4.2	—	—	−8.6
Monetary Authorities .... 78bo *d*	....	....	....	....	....	—	—	—	—	—	—	—	—	—	—
General Government .... 78bp *d*	....	....	....	....	....	−2.2	−.2	—	—	7.8	—	—	—	—	—
Banks .... 78bq *d*	....	....	....	....	....	—	—	—	—	—	—	—	—	—	−8.6
Other Sectors .... 78br *d*	....	....	....	....	....	−11.4	−12.6	−7.5	5.8	19.0	6.2	4.2	—	—	—
Other Investment Liab., n.i.e. ...... 78bi *d*	....	....	....	....	....	15.9	24.5	35.4	53.8	91.0	119.4	99.8	75.2	85.5	66.9
Monetary Authorities .... 78bs *d*	....	....	....	....	....	—	—	—	—	—	—	—	—	—	—
General Government .... 78bt *d*	....	....	....	....	....	18.2	16.6	47.7	56.9	81.6	103.5	87.5	77.1	83.0	53.4
Banks .... 78bu *d*	....	....	....	....	....	4.5	1.9	−6.2	2.2	5.9	11.1	7.9	1.1	2.5	13.5
Other Sectors .... 78bv *d*	....	....	....	....	....	−6.8	6.0	−6.1	−5.3	3.5	4.7	4.4	−3.0	—	—
Net Errors and Omissions .... 78ca *d*	....	....	....	....	....	−9.9	−7.5	−13.0	31.6	−27.2	−30.8	22.7	12.6	−7.3	.7
Overall Balance .... 78cb *d*	....	....	....	....	....	−62.1	−43.0	15.0	−17.7	−20.1	−32.8	−12.6	−26.0	−31.9	.5
Reserves and Related Items .... 79da *d*	....	....	....	....	....	62.1	43.0	−15.0	17.7	20.1	32.8	12.6	26.0	31.9	−.5
Reserve Assets .... 79db *d*	....	....	....	....	....	7.6	−4.6	.4	5.5	−1.2	4.7	9.5	−1.1	−1.5	−33.7
Use of Fund Credit and Loans .... 79dc *d*	....	....	....	....	....	.3	2.4	−1.8	9.9	3.8	10.6	−2.6	27.0	13.5	19.3
Exceptional Financing .... 79de *d*	....	....	....	....	....	54.1	45.2	−13.7	2.3	17.5	17.6	5.7	.1	19.8	13.9
Government Finance														*Billions of Francs;*	
Deficit (-) or Surplus 80	....	....	....	....	....	....	—	.2	−4.0	−9.1	Ɪ−16.0	−14.7	Ɪ−31.6	−34.5	−35.0
Total Revenue and Grants 81y	....	....	....	....	....	24.2	27.1	34.7	35.2	36.0	Ɪ61.4	72.0	Ɪ83.2	95.1	107.9
Revenue 81	....	....	....	....	....	18.4	24.4	32.1	33.1	32.8	Ɪ37.5	43.7	Ɪ52.6	54.6	66.1
Grants 81z	....	....	....	....	....	5.8	2.7	2.6	2.1	3.2	Ɪ23.9	28.3	Ɪ30.6	40.5	41.8
Exp.& Lending Minus Repay 82z	....	....	....	....	....	....	27.1	34.5	39.2	45.1	Ɪ77.4	86.7	Ɪ114.8	129.7	142.9
Expenditure 82	....	....	....	....	....	....	27.1	34.5	39.2	45.1	Ɪ73.4	86.8	Ɪ114.8	129.5	142.8
Lending Minus Repay 83	....	....	....	....	....	....	—	—	—	—	Ɪ4.0	−.1	Ɪ—	.1	.1
Statistical Discrepancy 80xx	....	....	....	....	....	....	....	....	....	....	....	....	....	....	....
Total Financing 80h	....	....	....	....	....	....	—	−.2	4.0	9.1	Ɪ16.0	14.7	Ɪ31.6	34.5	35.0
Domestic 84a	....	....	....	....	....	....	.4	.3	....	....	Ɪ1.3	−1.4	Ɪ3.3	4.7	2.5
Foreign 85a	....	....	....	....	....	....	−.4	−.6	....	....	Ɪ14.7	16.1	Ɪ28.3	29.9	32.5
Total Debt 88	....	....	....	....	....	....	....	....	....	....	Ɪ163.7	....	Ɪ308.2	334.1	....
Domestic 88a	....	....	....	....	....	....	....	....	....	....	Ɪ26.5	28.2	Ɪ43.2	44.4	....
Foreign 89a	....	....	....	....	....	....	....	....	....	....	Ɪ137.2	....	Ɪ264.9	289.6	....
National Accounts														*Billions of Francs*	
Exports of Goods & Services 90c	....	....	....	....	....	....	30.4	39.2	30.0	37.2	50.3	55.6	62.6	78.8	112.2
Government Consumption 91f	....	....	....	....	....	....	6.5	8.3	9.4	11.3	12.6	36.6	39.6	69.0	69.1
Gross Fixed Capital Formation 93e	....	....	....	....	....	....	....	....	....	....	....	93.0	71.4	90.7	69.8
Increase/Decrease(-) in Stocks 93i	....	....	....	....	....	....	....	....	....	....	....	—	−.4	2.5	12.6
Private Consumption 96f	....	....	....	....	....	135.4	149.9	172.8	213.6	246.5	315.6	360.4	374.7	452.4
Imports of Goods & Services 98c	....	....	....	....	....	....	−46.2	−51.3	−65.4	−76.9	−90.0	−120.6	−130.0	−145.5	−175.7
Gross Domestic Product (GDP) 99b	76.3	83.5	88.4	92.1	97.7	129.5	178.6	204.5	217.8	259.6	300.5	380.2	403.6	470.2	540.4
														Millions:	
Population 99z	5.05	5.14	5.26	5.38	5.66	Ɪ6.29	6.32	Ɪ6.51	6.70	6.90	7.10	7.29	7.51	7.74	7.97

	1985	1986	1987	1988	1989	1990	1991	1992	1993	1994	1995	1996	1997	1998	1999		
Period Averages																**Prices**	
	....	....	....	74.8	74.7	75.2	76.5	71.8	71.6	88.2	100.0	106.8	‡106.4	110.7	109.4	Consumer Prices	64
Billions of Francs																**International Transactions**	
	55.56	73.34	53.79	63.89	78.78	97.68	88.06	90.72	135.30	185.95	220.50	221.40	327.70	328.10	330.20	Exports	70
	134.54	153.71	112.44	150.23	108.47	164.02	129.90	160.81	179.43	327.22	395.20	431.20	443.80	449.80	462.60	Imports, c.i.f.	71
Minus Sign Indicates Debit																**Balance of Payments**	
	-209.7	-254.1	-219.2	-242.8	-155.1	-221.1	-172.5	-240.5	-188.6	-162.6	-283.8	-273.2	-178.4	....	....	Current Account, n.i.e.	78ald
	176.1	205.6	255.9	247.1	268.5	334.9	370.6	364.0	371.9	334.9	441.8	433.5	561.6	....	....	Goods: Exports f.o.b.	78aa d
	-328.4	-339.0	-335.4	-387.2	-362.1	-455.4	-516.9	-526.8	-492.4	-449.2	-556.8	-551.5	-551.9	....	....	Goods: Imports f.o.b.	78ab d
	-152.4	-133.4	-79.5	-140.1	-93.6	-120.5	-146.3	-162.8	-120.4	-114.3	-115.0	-118.0	9.7	....	....	Trade Balance	78ac d
	57.3	68.1	82.5	69.2	76.5	84.9	71.0	78.3	74.8	69.0	87.6	87.6	82.1	....	....	Services: Credit	78ad d
	-263.7	-306.7	-327.1	-312.2	-270.7	-374.1	-334.6	-428.6	-360.8	-317.0	-434.5	-382.8	-345.6	....	....	Services: Debit	78ae d
	-358.8	-371.9	-324.1	-383.1	-287.8	-409.8	-409.8	-513.0	-406.4	-362.3	-461.9	-413.2	-253.8	....	....	*Balance on Goods & Services*	78af d
	4.9	3.2	3.1	4.9	7.8	22.6	24.7	27.8	30.2	9.3	8.3	10.9	10.6	....	....	Income: Credit	78ag d
	-18.7	-24.8	-28.0	-37.4	-38.7	-59.3	-48.8	-56.1	-43.2	-49.7	-48.9	-67.1	-61.7	....	....	Income: Debit	78ah d
	-372.6	-393.6	-349.0	-415.7	-318.7	-446.5	-434.0	-541.2	-419.4	-402.7	-502.6	-469.3	-304.8	....	....	*Balance on Gds, Serv. & Inc.*	78ai d
	207.5	198.4	209.3	221.1	211.2	282.2	320.1	380.0	294.6	281.3	266.8	246.1	170.0	....	....	Current Transfers, n.i.e.: Credit	78aj d
	-44.5	-58.9	-79.5	-48.2	-47.7	-56.8	-58.6	-79.3	-63.7	-41.2	-48.0	-50.0	-43.5	....	....	Current Transfers: Debit	78ak d
	80.8	92.7	116.8	142.0	102.5	105.8	137.5	143.6	111.9	99.1	126.2	136.4	108.6	....	....	Capital Account, n.i.e.	78bc d
	80.8	92.7	116.8	142.0	102.5	105.8	137.5	143.6	111.9	99.1	126.2	136.4	108.6	....	....	Capital Account, n.i.e.: Credit	78ba d
	—	—	—	—	—	—	—	—	—	—	—	—	—			Capital Account: Debit	78bb d
	120.6	127.4	86.6	135.7	79.6	57.8	34.3	-5.6	-14.5	-7.0	118.6	174.6	52.7	....	....	Financial Account, n.i.e.	78bj d
											....	....	....			Direct Investment Abroad	78bd d
	2.9	-8.4	-6.0	7.1	6.4	5.7	1.2	-21.9	4.1	17.4	111.4	84.1	39.4	....	....	Dir. Invest. in Rep. Econ., n.i.e.	78be d
	—	—	—	—	—	—	—	—	—	—	....	....	....			Portfolio Investment Assets	78bf d
	—	—	—	—	—	—	—	—	—	—	....	....	....			Equity Securities	78bk d
	—	—	—	—	—	—	—	—	—	—	....	....	....			Debt Securities	78bl d
	—	—	—	—	—	—	—	—	—	—	....	....	....			Portfolio Investment Liab., n.i.e.	78bg d
	—	—	—	—	—	—	—	—	—	—	....	....	....			Equity Securities	78bm d
	—	—	—	—	—	—	—	—	—	—	....	....	....			Debt Securities	78bn d
	....	....	....	....	....	....	....	....	....	....	....	....	....			Financial Derivatives Assets	78bw d
	....	....	....	....	....	....	....	....	....	....	....	....	....			Financial Derivatives Liabilities	78bx d
	13.0	-6.2	2.4	-24.6	-61.6	-30.2	-28.7	5.8	-21.4	-104.0	-52.3	4.1	-12.4	....	....	Other Investment Assets	78bh d
	....	....	....	....	....	....	....	....	....	....	....	....	....			Monetary Authorities	78bo d
	—	—	—	—	—	—	—	—	—	—	....	....	....			General Government	78bp d
	13.0	-6.2	2.4	4.6	-39.4	-.1	9.6	17.5	11.9	-100.3	-33.2	16.8	2.0	....	....	Banks	78bq d
	—	—	—	-29.2	-22.2	-30.0	-38.4	-11.7	-33.3	-3.7	-19.2	-12.7	-14.4	....	....	Other Sectors	78br d
	104.7	142.0	90.2	153.2	134.8	82.2	61.9	10.5	2.8	79.6	59.6	86.4	25.7	....	....	Other Investment Liab., n.i.e.	78bi d
											....	....	....			Monetary Authorities	78bs d
	95.0	134.0	95.8	122.5	121.3	82.6	65.2	12.8	-18.0	33.1	89.8	80.5	57.7	....	....	General Government	78bt d
	9.7	8.1	-5.6	6.9	-.1	1.7	-25.6	-19.8	.4	11.9	-1.4	-10.6	6.7	....	....	Banks	78bu d
	—	—	—	23.8	13.6	-2.2	22.2	17.4	20.4	34.5	-28.7	16.5	-38.7	....	....	Other Sectors	78bv d
	-18.4	-15.6	1.5	-16.5	-26.1	-7.4	30.5	-35.3	-6.0	5.6	-13.0	-8.8	7.9	....	....	Net Errors and Omissions	78ca d
	-26.6	-49.5	-14.3	18.4	.8	-65.0	29.8	-137.9	-97.2	-65.0	-52.0	29.0	-9.2	....	....	*Overall Balance*	78cb d
	26.6	49.5	14.3	-18.4	-.8	65.0	-29.8	137.9	97.2	65.0	52.0	-29.0	9.2	....	....	Reserves and Related Items	79da d
	3.5	47.2	7.5	-34.6	-60.1	-55.3	-120.6	-7.2	-45.8	-37.6	-80.2	-131.6	-38.3	....	....	Reserve Assets	79db d
	5.1	-9.8	-26.8	-7.6	-16.6	8.3	-9.2	8.4	5.6	32.7	38.4	22.4	21.3	....	....	Use of Fund Credit and Loans	79dc d
	18.0	12.1	33.6	23.9	75.9	112.0	100.0	136.8	137.4	69.9	93.8	80.1	26.2	....	....	Exceptional Financing	79de d
Year Ending December 31																**Government Finance**	
	-46.5	-43.2	-30.9	-27.6	‡-28.4	-18.0	-26.5	-29.1	-30.6	-43.4	-36.7	-13.8	-29.9	‡-38.7	-61.7P	Deficit (-) or Surplus	80
	119.3	116.7	127.2	149.8	‡143.0	155.7	165.8	154.3	146.7	236.7	269.7	313.3	320.5	‡344.8	355.9P	Total Revenue and Grants	81y
	79.7	87.6	89.4	114.3	‡109.6	116.1	109.6	100.7	104.7	138.9	177.3	216.8	236.3	‡254.9	272.5P	Revenue	81
	39.6	29.1	37.8	35.5	‡33.4	39.6	56.2	53.6	42.0	97.8	92.4	96.5	84.2	‡89.9	83.4P	Grants	81z
	165.8	159.9	158.1	177.4										‡383.3	417.6P	Exp.& Lending Minus Repay	82z
	165.7	159.6	157.9	174.8	‡171.4	173.7	192.3	183.4	177.3	280.1	306.4	327.1	350.4	‡387.1	419.8P	Expenditure	82
	.1	.3	.2	2.6										‡-3.6	-2.2P	Lending Minus Repay	83
	....	....	6.2	—	-36.1	-4.8	-3.6	4.9	8.1	-29.7	-14.0	-18.8	-8.4	-10.0	6.2P	Statistical Discrepancy	80xx
	46.5	45.2	24.7	27.6	64.5	22.8	30.1	24.2	22.5	73.1	50.7	32.6	38.3	48.7	55.5P	Total Financing	80h
	5.4	1.4	-5.1	4.7	-11.7	-17.3	-12.1	-8.6	-3.0	-3.6	-40.2	-49.5	-10.7	-9.3	-4.8P	Domestic	84a
	41.1	43.8	29.8	22.9	76.2	40.1	42.2	32.8	25.5	76.7	90.9	82.1	49.0	58.0	60.3P	Foreign	85a
	....	570.4	....	....	....	....	....	....	....	....	....	....	....	....	....	Total Debt	88
	....	23.6	....	....	....	....	....	....	....	....	....	....	....	....	....	Domestic	88a
	....	546.8	604.0	726.8	....	673.8	700.9	730.3	773.9	1,576.6	1,595.2	1,498.4	1,641.6	1,684.3	1,542.5P	Foreign	89a
Billions of Francs																**National Accounts**	
	104.0	87.4	94.3	95.1	106.6	114.8	120.0	110.0	118.5	260.8	264.2	267.6	349.2	385.2	....	Exports of Goods & Services	90c
	78.6	86.9	88.2	91.2	98.5	95.6	118.1	130.2	123.4	185.1	204.5	210.6	216.8	228.9	....	Government Consumption	91f
	90.8	122.2	121.5	116.9	132.7	128.3	141.9	143.7	144.7	249.1	299.6	316.4	345.2	372.2	....	Gross Fixed Capital Formation	93e
	-10.5	-15.5	5.1	2.7	15.9	11.2	-10.2	12.6	-21.1	-10.9	-14.5	-41.5	-29.8	12.3	....	Increase/Decrease(-) in Stocks	93i
	522.2	519.2	464.7	472.6	497.6	536.1	541.6	546.3	560.5	751.1	930.0	1,059.6	1,065.4	1,104.3	....	Private Consumption	96f
	-227.2	-207.2	-183.3	-192.3	-206.4	-218.3	-226.9	-228.1	-267.7	-456.6	-494.8	-472.7	-489.4	-552.6	....	Imports of Goods & Services	98c
	554.5	593.0	590.5	589.1	642.4	666.2	685.6	713.9	712.2	958.0	1,154.6	1,292.5	1,431.9	1,550.3	....	Gross Domestic Product (GDP)	99b
Midyear Estimates																	
	8.21	‡7.57	7.70	7.83	7.96	8.16	‡9.05	9.26	9.48	9.71	9.94	10.19	10.44	10.69	10.96	Population	99z

(See notes in the back of the book.)

Malta

		1970	1971	1972	1973	1974	1975	1976	1977	1978	1979	1980	1981	1982	1983	1984
Exchange Rates																*SDRs per Lira:*
Official Rate	ac	2.4000	2.4110	2.3220	2.1437	2.1754	2.1161	2.0175	2.0864	2.1105	2.2076	2.2140	2.2185	2.1821	2.1440	2.0744
																US Dollars per Lira:
Official Rate	ag	2.4000	2.6176	2.5210	2.5860	2.6635	2.4772	2.3440	2.5344	2.7495	2.9082	2.8237	2.5823	2.4071	2.2447	2.0333
Official Rate	rh	2.4000	2.4496	2.6095	2.7232	2.5947	2.6202	2.3534	2.3688	2.5974	2.7911	2.8962	2.5894	2.4282	2.3135	2.1718
															Index Numbers (1995=100):	
Official Rate	ahx	84.7	114.5	92.1	96.1	91.6	92.5	83.1	83.6	91.7	98.5	102.2	91.4	85.7	81.7	76.7
Nominal Effective Exchange Rate	nec	....	....	....	....	....	....	....	....	....	....	85.9	87.9	94.5	100.5	105.0	109.8
Real Effective Exchange Rate	rec	....	....	....	....	....	....	....	....	....	....	115.8	122.0	131.9	136.4	132.8	131.1
Fund Position																*Millions of SDRs:*
Quota	2f.s	16.0	16.0	16.0	16.0	16.0	16.0	16.0	16.0	20.0	20.0	30.0	30.0	30.0	45.1	45.1
SDRs	1b.s	1.7	3.4	5.1	5.1	5.1	5.1	5.2	5.5	5.8	9.4	11.3	14.6	21.2	31.0	35.7
Reserve Position in the Fund	1c.s	4.0	4.0	4.0	4.0	4.0	7.8	13.8	12.2	13.2	13.3	15.8	23.7	25.8	28.8	30.9
International Liquidity												*Millions of US Dollars Unless Otherwise Indicated:*					
Total Reserves minus Gold	1l.d	148.2	184.7	261.7	310.4	386.7	485.8	607.8	719.6	925.1	1,012.7	990.1	1,073.8	1,083.6	1,112.3	990.2
SDRs	1b.d	1.7	3.7	5.5	6.1	6.2	6.0	6.0	6.7	7.6	12.4	14.5	17.0	23.4	32.4	35.0
Reserve Position in the Fund	1c.d	4.0	4.4	4.4	4.9	4.9	9.1	16.0	14.8	17.2	17.5	20.1	27.6	28.4	30.2	30.3
Foreign Exchange	1d.d	142.5	176.7	251.8	299.4	375.5	470.7	585.8	698.1	900.4	982.8	955.5	1,029.3	1,031.8	1,049.7	925.0
Gold (Million Fine Troy Ounces)	1ad	.277	.353	.353	.353	.353	.353	.353	.360	.360	.366	.434	.456	.462	.472	.466
Gold (National Valuation)	1and	9.7	12.3	12.3	12.3	12.3	12.3	12.3	12.6	12.7	12.8	51.4	62.9	62.9	66.7	64.5
Monetary Authorities: Other Assets	3..d	....	....	....	....	....	....	....	....	....	....	....	45.7	47.8	62.4	75.4
Other Official Insts.: Assets	3b.d	2.7	.3e	.2	....	9.3	.1	....	.1	4.9	5.4	6.1	39.3	33.5	40.2	37.4
Deposit Money Banks: Assets	7a.d	76.7	94.7	70.6	95.9	102.8	102.0	117.7	130.7	134.6	162.2	158.9	145.1	140.6	125.0	118.2
Liabilities	7b.d	8.0	7.6	15.2	2.9	1.5	4.7	8.7	13.9	17.6	18.3	19.0	24.6	25.4	30.3	26.5
Other Banking Insts.: Assets	7e.d	28.6	32.5	26.0	16.4	15.5	14.8	5.4	3.2	3.1	3.7	3.7	3.5	3.6	2.7	2.7
Liabilities	7f.d	.3	.4	.1	.1	.1	.1	.1	.1	.1	.2	.1	—	—	—	—
Monetary Authorities																*Millions of Liri:*
Foreign Assets	11	65.77	74.32	103.14	118.32	131.08	183.93	238.61	271.51	322.59	342.74	370.66	416.41	444.09	489.92	529.57
Claims on Central Government	12a	7.17	5.22	2.05	.23	.37	.06	8.77	.04	.04	.02	.16	.18	.23	.62	.67
Reserve Money	14	62.74	73.30	98.66	95.07	110.32	158.04	200.86	222.03	267.66	297.45	302.84	338.76	347.23	369.75	409.77
of which: Currency Outside DMBs	14a	45.89	55.69	62.27	72.69	79.57	98.88	119.64	137.83	155.02	176.25	206.08	239.16	259.73	279.63	283.69
Central Government Deposits	16d	4.38	.48	.56	11.31	3.25	3.34	3.22	6.25	16.15	19.52	28.43	35.34	31.82	37.42	35.44
Other Items (Net)	17r	5.85	5.78	5.98	12.19	17.90	22.61	43.30	43.26	38.83	25.79	39.54	42.50	65.27	83.38	85.03
Deposit Money Banks																*Millions of Liri:*
Reserves	20	16.82	16.76	30.82	18.24	24.13	51.75	74.90	77.78	100.15	96.08	76.52	76.76	70.21	75.17	114.32
Foreign Assets	21	31.96	35.44	26.43	37.09	38.61	41.19	50.20	51.57	48.95	55.77	56.29	56.18	58.43	55.69	58.13
Claims on Central Government	22a	8.18	10.22	9.41	8.83	8.49	6.22	6.22	6.23	6.23	6.23	6.23	6.23	6.23	6.23	18.74
Claims on Private Sector	22d	45.72	49.88	52.97	50.74	55.15	52.41	55.60	56.62	60.92	74.15	104.51	121.32	144.67	164.39	187.45
Demand Deposits	24	11.05	10.84	12.01	10.29	13.00	17.51	22.73	21.35	27.05	30.58	32.62	31.94	29.60	30.39	30.93
Time and Savings Deposits	25	78.63	89.99	94.70	94.45	99.13	116.02	139.12	146.31	162.32	173.05	180.07	195.03	209.65	230.88	303.57
Foreign Liabilities	26c	3.33	2.84	5.67	1.12	.57	1.90	3.71	5.47	6.41	6.29	6.72	9.51	10.54	13.50	13.06
Other Items (Net)	27r	9.67	8.62	7.25	9.03	13.67	16.15	21.37	19.07	20.47	22.30	24.13	24.01	29.74	26.70	31.07
Monetary Survey																*Millions of Liri:*
Foreign Assets (Net)	31n	95.12	107.44	124.10	154.29	169.12	223.22	285.11	317.61	365.14	392.22	420.22	463.08	491.97	532.12	574.64
Domestic Credit	32	56.41	64.48	63.71	48.43	60.31	54.97	67.37	56.64	50.90	60.82	82.41	92.25	119.16	133.69	171.24
Claims on Central Govt. (Net)	32an	10.69	14.60	10.74	-2.31	5.16	2.57	11.77	.02	-10.02	-13.33	-22.10	-29.07	-25.51	-30.70	-16.21
Claims on Private Sector	32d	45.72	49.88	52.97	50.74	55.15	52.41	55.60	56.62	60.92	74.15	104.51	121.32	144.67	164.39	187.45
Money	34	57.73	67.90	80.08	87.16	99.04	123.75	148.34	165.64	194.57	231.64	258.80	293.73	306.28	324.63	325.92
Quasi-Money	35	78.63	89.99	94.70	99.49	106.17	123.06	157.07	170.31	187.32	198.05	205.07	220.03	238.65	262.88	303.57
Other Items (Net)	37r	15.19	14.05	13.05	16.08	24.23	31.38	47.07	38.29	34.15	23.35	38.75	41.58	66.20	78.30	116.38
Money plus Quasi-Money	35l	136.36	157.89	174.77	186.65	205.21	246.81	305.42	335.95	381.89	429.69	463.88	513.76	544.93	587.51	629.49
Other Banking Institutions																*Millions of Liri:*
Foreign Assets	41	11.93	12.19	9.74	6.35	5.83	5.98	2.29	1.25	1.13	1.27	1.30	1.34	1.49	1.20	1.33
Claims on Private Sector	42d	4.14	4.72	4.86	4.47	4.74	6.45	7.01	8.15	9.09	10.97	12.93	17.89	24.10	40.06	42.82
Claims on Deposit Money Banks	42e	1.26	.81	.61	.54	.62	.87	1.20	1.56	1.94	.29	.26	.24	5.28	.27	.35
Foreign Liabilities	46c	.14	.14	.05	.04	.04	.04	.02	.04	.04	.09	.03	.01	.01	.01	.03
Credit from Deposit Money Banks	46h	2.19	3.02	3.23	2.36	4.06	5.74	6.15	4.33	5.15	7.03	8.40	12.85	18.62	28.07	33.01
Other Items (Net)	47r	15.00	14.55	11.93	8.96	7.09	7.52	4.32	6.60	6.97	5.41	6.06	6.60	12.26	13.44	11.46
Banking Survey																*Millions of Liri:*
Foreign Assets (Net)	51n	106.91	119.48	133.79	160.60	174.91	229.16	287.37	318.82	366.23	393.40	421.49	464.40	493.46	533.31	575.94
Domestic Credit	52	62.37	73.32	72.40	60.16	72.81	71.79	84.75	75.16	70.58	82.51	106.75	122.47	156.01	186.54	214.70
Claims on Central Govt. (Net)	52an	12.51	18.72	14.57	4.95	12.92	12.94	22.14	10.39	.57	-2.61	-10.69	-16.74	-12.77	-17.91	-15.57
Claims on Private Sector	52d	49.86	54.60	57.83	55.21	59.89	58.86	62.61	64.77	70.01	85.12	117.44	139.20	168.78	204.45	230.26
Liquid Liabilities	55l	152.06	174.35	189.54	202.46	220.40	264.46	319.02	349.12	395.28	441.10	475.73	526.57	562.78	601.96	631.35
Other Items (Net)	57r	17.24	18.48	16.67	18.32	27.34	36.50	53.11	44.86	41.53	34.81	52.52	60.30	86.69	117.89	159.29
Interest Rates																*Percent Per Annum*
Discount Rate (End of Period)	60	5.5	5.5	5.5	5.5	5.5	5.5	5.5	5.5	5.5	5.5	5.5	5.5	6.5	6.5	6.5
Treasury Bill Rate	60c	....	....	....	....	....	....	....	....	....	....	....	....	....	....	....
Deposit Rate	60l	....	....	....	....	....	....	5.0	5.0	5.0	5.0	5.0	5.0	5.0	5.0	5.0
Lending Rate	60p	....	....	....	....	....	8.0	8.0	8.0	8.0	8.0	8.0	8.0	8.0	8.0	8.0
Prices and Labor																*Index Numbers (1995=100):*
Consumer Prices	64	35.7	36.5	37.8	40.7	I43.6	47.5	47.7	52.5	55.0	58.9	68.2	76.0	80.5	I79.7	79.4
Industrial Production (1990=100)	66	....	....	....	....	....	29.0	33.6	39.8	41.7	44.4	52.8	53.7	56.3	57.9	I62.4
																Number in Thousands:
Labor Force	67d	....	....	....	....	....	....	....	....	....	....	....	....	....	....	....
Employment	67e	....	....	....	....	....	....	....	....	....	....	....	....	....	....	....
Unemployment	67c	....	....	....	....	....	....	....	....	....	....	....	....	....	....	....
Unemployment Rate (%)	67r	....	....	....	....	....	....	....	....	....	....	....	....	....	....	....
International Transactions																*Millions of Liri*
Exports	70	16.07	18.82	25.72	35.96	51.58	63.90	97.41	121.79	131.95	152.17	166.72	173.73	169.04	156.75	181.36
Imports, c.i.f.	71	67.12	65.38	67.21	88.10	138.97	144.45	179.92	217.68	221.50	271.96	323.74	332.27	325.07	316.63	330.49
																1985=100
Volume of Exports	72	17.4	22.3	28.6	38.3	40.2	44.8	63.9	80.1	83.0	89.7	I93.6	92.3	85.3	85.5	97.7
Volume of Imports	73	63.7	60.4	56.8	59.9	69.3	67.4	77.3	86.0	82.4	89.7	I98.8	88.8	88.8	86.5	92.0
Unit Value of Exports	74	40.9	40.2	44.7	49.4	62.7	66.7	74.3	77.1	83.8	90.5	I94.5	101.3	104.3	98.0	99.7
Unit Value of Imports	75	29.7	30.6	33.3	41.5	56.7	60.5	65.7	71.5	75.9	85.6	I92.5	102.2	103.3	103.3	101.4

1985	1986	1987	1988	1989	1990	1991	1992	1993	1994	1995	1996	1997	1998	1999		
End of Period															**Exchange Rates**	
2.1479	2.2147	2.2614	2.2373	2.2589	2.3371	2.2877	1.9436	1.8426	1.8609	1.9090	1.9338	1.8969	1.8818	1.7681	Official Rate	ac
End of Period (ag) Period Average (rh)																
2.3593	2.7090	3.2081	3.0107	2.9686	3.3249	3.2724	2.6725	2.5309	2.7166	2.8377	2.7807	2.5594	2.6496	2.4268	Official Rate	ag
2.1385	2.5481	2.8981	3.0251	2.8712	3.1527	3.1002	3.1462	2.6171	2.6486	2.8333	2.7745	2.5924	2.5743	2.5039	Official Rate	rh
Period Averages																
75.5	89.9	102.3	106.8	101.3	111.3	109.4	111.0	92.4	93.5	100.0	97.9	91.5	90.9	88.4	Official Rate	ahx
112.0	106.5	105.3	106.1	107.4	105.8	106.0	104.7	98.3	98.8	100.0	98.8	100.3	101.4	101.4	Nominal Effective Exchange Rate	nec
127.1	120.3	116.5	114.9	111.9	107.6	105.7	101.8	96.3	97.9	100.0	98.8	101.3	103.1	104.0	Real Effective Exchange Rate	rec
End of Period															**Fund Position**	
45.1	45.1	45.1	45.1	45.1	45.1	45.1	67.5	67.5	67.5	67.5	67.5	67.5	67.5	102.0	Quota	2f.s
39.6	43.1	46.6	50.1	53.6	59.1	64.2	33.1	35.3	35.6	37.6	39.7	41.9	44.4	22.5	SDRs	1b.s
29.7	32.4	31.2	27.3	23.5	19.6	20.8	25.3	25.3	25.4	27.3	30.7	31.6	31.6	40.3	Reserve Position in the Fund	1c.s
End of Period															**International Liquidity**	
986.9	1,145.4	1,414.6	1,364.7	1,355.1	1,431.8	1,333.3	1,268.3	1,362.4	1,849.6	1,604.5	1,619.8	....	1,662.7	1,879.9	Total Reserves minus Gold	1l.d
43.5	52.8	66.1	67.5	70.4	84.1	91.8	45.5	48.4	52.0	56.0	57.2	56.6	62.5	30.9	SDRs	1b.d
32.6	39.6	44.3	36.7	30.9	27.9	29.8	34.8	34.7	37.1	40.5	44.1	42.7	44.5	55.3	Reserve Position in the Fund	1c.d
910.9	1,053.0	1,304.2	1,260.5	1,253.8	1,319.8	1,211.7	1,188.0	1,279.3	1,760.5	1,508.0	1,518.6	....	1,555.7	1,793.8	Foreign Exchange	1d.d
.466	.466	.466	.466	.226	.157	.117	.120	.100	.105	.041	.044	.011	.006	.006	Gold (Million Fine Troy Ounces)	1ad
134.8	163.9	163.9	200.0	93.7	59.4	42.4	40.3	38.5	40.0	15.9	7.2	3.3	1.8	1.8	Gold (National Valuation)	1and
90.1	84.8	84.4	80.4	78.5	30.5	33.4	29.6	26.8	27.2	.1	.1	—	.1	....	Monetary Authorities: Other Assets	3..d
52.7	65.5	84.4	80.4	78.5	30.5	33.4	29.6	26.8	27.2	.1	.1	—	.1	—	Other Official Insts.: Assets	3b.d
157.3	198.7	260.0	308.3	425.1	657.6	806.6	860.1	939.9	1,116.1	I2,224.5	2,866.4	3,397.0	5,831.4	6,799.1	Deposit Money Banks: Assets	7a.d
42.1	49.2	76.5	103.2	124.3	219.8	301.4	164.1	262.6	255.2	I1,576.0	2,333.9	2,972.8	5,242.4	6,338.5	Liabilities	7b.d
52.4	51.0	110.9	181.8	220.0	298.5	321.0	303.1	294.0	13.7	11.0	9.1	18.0	18.6	15.9	Other Banking Insts.: Assets	7e.d
25.3	15.8	65.9	151.4	197.1	271.3	273.0	467.8	496.3	366.3	—	—	—	—	.5	Liabilities	7f.d
End of Period															**Monetary Authorities**	
513.86	514.57	529.59	534.00	509.97	452.63	423.81	494.46	559.11	698.01	593.74	568.12	575.53	639.77	740.30	Foreign Assets	11
.25	.30	4.12	1.85	2.88	22.21	58.17	62.30	18.08	39.22	67.73	74.28	59.16	24.32	6.15	Claims on Central Government	12a
413.36	417.22	429.05	430.10	412.82	389.84	416.51	442.60	443.58	584.20	512.98	491.66	498.99	514.05	549.32	Reserve Money	14
273.34	273.79	300.24	314.31	319.41	330.32	344.34	337.64	353.26	365.91	352.47	362.97	364.42	368.97	385.57	*of which: Currency Outside DMBs*	14a
56.91	32.86	33.73	47.25	25.98	22.96	16.74	17.00	21.04	22.25	42.01	33.53	35.70	47.61	96.21	Central Government Deposits	16d
43.84	64.79	70.94	58.50	74.05	62.04	48.73	97.17	112.56	130.78	106.48	117.22	100.01	102.44	100.92	Other Items (Net)	17r
End of Period															**Deposit Money Banks**	
127.18	127.55	113.21	103.61	86.40	58.35	62.79	93.82	83.25	194.50	I101.17	97.72	126.05	141.41	171.80	Reserves	20
66.67	73.34	81.04	102.39	143.19	197.79	246.50	321.83	371.36	410.85	I783.92	1,030.82	1,327.26	2,200.88	2,801.73	Foreign Assets	21
19.42	19.47	43.70	70.38	79.23	88.68	79.50	78.25	142.65	135.88	I149.66	196.36	296.17	385.93	458.46	Claims on Central Government	22a
212.81	244.69	276.42	311.23	376.12	470.85	548.04	608.20	697.77	782.02	I950.06	1,108.90	1,208.29	1,341.95	1,519.71	Claims on Private Sector	22d
35.48	36.66	39.01	38.62	42.04	49.75	53.22	57.43	59.42	72.15	I80.93	87.31	111.39	146.77	190.52	Demand Deposits	24
341.32	377.60	416.04	473.85	555.48	642.83	723.33	827.13	940.86	1,105.35	I1253.02	1,413.02	1,565.85	1,693.15	1,854.93	Time and Savings Deposits	25
17.83	18.15	23.86	34.28	41.87	66.11	92.11	61.41	103.75	93.94	I555.36	839.34	1,161.54	1,978.55	2,611.93	Foreign Liabilities	26c
31.46	32.64	35.45	40.86	45.57	56.98	68.18	156.12	190.99	251.81	I95.49	94.13	118.99	251.70	294.33	Other Items (Net)	27r
End of Period															**Monetary Survey**	
562.70	569.76	586.77	602.11	611.29	584.31	578.20	754.88	826.72	1,014.92	I822.30	759.60	741.25	862.10	930.10	Foreign Assets (Net)	31n
175.39	231.46	290.37	336.07	431.10	556.97	667.58	729.79	835.10	932.65	I1118.69	1,337.07	1,517.92	1,692.75	1,873.25	Domestic Credit	32
-37.42	-13.23	13.95	24.84	54.98	86.12	119.54	121.59	137.33	150.63	I168.63	228.17	309.63	350.80	353.54	Claims on Central Govt. (Net)	32an
212.81	244.69	276.42	311.23	376.12	470.85	548.04	608.20	697.77	782.02	I950.06	1,108.90	1,208.29	1,341.95	1,519.71	Claims on Private Sector	32d
321.21	323.25	354.59	363.95	368.64	384.63	406.70	408.56	425.07	463.55	I498.91	489.66	489.63	525.09	580.70	Money	34
341.32	377.60	416.04	473.85	555.48	642.83	723.33	827.13	940.86	1,105.35	I1253.02	1,413.02	1,565.85	1,693.15	1,854.93	Quasi-Money	35
75.56	100.37	106.51	100.39	118.27	113.82	115.75	248.98	295.88	378.67	I189.06	193.99	203.69	336.62	367.72	Other Items (Net)	37r
662.53	700.85	770.63	837.80	924.12	1,027.46	1,130.03	1,235.69	1,365.93	1,568.90	I1751.93	1,902.68	2,055.48	2,218.23	2,435.63	Money plus Quasi-Money	35l
End of Period															**Other Banking Institutions**	
22.21	18.81	34.58	60.39	74.11	89.77	98.10	113.40	116.16	5.04	3.86	3.29	7.04	7.02	6.54	Foreign Assets	41
49.49	54.13	63.24	77.58	88.66	104.54	138.21	164.00	181.76	203.49	147.04	152.43	142.17	150.31	139.22	Claims on Private Sector	42d
.22	.21	.24	.73	1.01	.70	.01	79.26	96.77	134.83	—	—	—	—	—	Claims on Deposit Money Banks	42e
10.72	5.82	20.55	50.30	66.41	81.59	83.44	175.06	196.11	134.84	—	—	—	—	.20	Foreign Liabilities	46c
44.85	50.26	59.02	67.39	75.96	87.00	62.17	88.93	106.32	121.85	122.39	125.60	117.88	124.58	110.37	Credit from Deposit Money Banks	46h
16.35	17.07	18.50	21.01	21.42	26.43	90.71	92.68	92.26	86.67	28.51	30.12	31.33	32.76	35.19	Other Items (Net)	47r
End of Period															**Banking Survey**	
574.19	582.75	600.80	612.20	618.99	592.49	592.87	693.22	746.77	885.12	I826.16	762.89	748.29	869.13	936.44	Foreign Assets (Net)	51n
225.54	286.24	354.97	417.07	523.05	666.57	805.79	893.80	1,016.85	1,136.14	I1265.87	1,489.64	1,660.93	1,848.85	2,017.02	Domestic Credit	52
-36.76	-12.57	15.31	28.26	58.27	91.18	119.54	121.59	137.33	150.63	I168.77	228.31	310.47	356.59	358.09	Claims on Central Govt. (Net)	52an
262.30	298.82	339.66	388.81	464.78	575.39	686.25	772.21	879.53	985.51	I1097.10	1,261.33	1,350.46	1,492.26	1,658.93	Claims on Private Sector	52d
664.54	702.87	773.78	844.25	930.60	1,035.92	1,130.02	1,235.68	1,365.92	1,568.90	I1753.37	1,903.67	2,056.63	2,223.72	2,440.98	Liquid Liabilities	55l
135.19	166.13	182.00	185.02	211.43	223.14	268.63	351.34	397.70	452.35	I338.66	348.87	352.59	494.26	512.48	Other Items (Net)	57r
Percent Per Annum															**Interest Rates**	
6.0	6.0	5.5	5.5	5.5	5.5	5.5	5.5	5.5	5.5	5.5	5.5	5.5	5.5	4.8	Discount Rate *(End of Period)*	60
....	....	4.50	4.24	4.24	4.25	4.46	4.58	4.60	4.29	4.65	4.99	5.08	5.41	5.15	Treasury Bill Rate	60c
5.0	4.5	4.5	4.5	4.5	4.5	4.5	4.5	4.5	4.5	4.5	4.5	4.6	4.6	4.7	Deposit Rate	60l
8.0	8.0	8.0	8.5	8.5	8.5	8.5	8.5	8.5	8.5	I7.4	7.8	8.0	8.1	7.7	Lending Rate	60p
Period Averages															**Prices and Labor**	
79.2	80.8	81.2	81.9	82.6	85.1	I87.3	I88.7	92.4	96.2	100.0	102.5	105.7	108.2	110.5	Consumer Prices	64
63.7	67.0	69.6	75.4	88.6	100.0	112.9	128.4	132.8	149.7	....	....	....	....	....	Industrial Production (1990=100)	66
Period Averages																
....	....	....	....	....	132	....	....	....	....	140	140	142	143	....	Labor Force	67d
113	115	122	125	126	127	130	132	132	134	149	140	137	137	....	Employment	67e
10	9	6	5	5	5	5	6	6	6	5	6	7	7	....	Unemployment	67c
8.1	6.8	4.4	4.0	3.7	3.9	3.6	4.0	4.2	4.2	3.5	3.7	3.8	....	....	Unemployment Rate (%)	67r
Millions of Liri															**International Transactions**	
187.10	194.67	208.59	235.92	294.41	357.90	405.50	490.90	518.30	592.40	674.90	624.10	632.80	706.90	793.30	Exports	70
354.14	348.11	392.88	447.40	515.80	620.50	684.00	747.80	830.90	918.80	1,037.70	1,007.80	985.30	1,042.00	1,141.90	Imports, c.i.f.	71
1985=100																
100.0	104.4	105.4	108.4	130.4	....	....	....	....	....	....	....	....	....	....	Volume of Exports	72
100.0	102.1	114.6	129.1	144.2	....	....	....	....	....	....	....	....	....	....	Volume of Imports	73
100.0	102.5	107.4	118.8	124.3	....	....	....	....	....	....	....	....	....	....	Unit Value of Exports	74
100.0	96.2	96.8	97.9	101.0	....	....	....	....	....	....	....	....	....	....	Unit Value of Imports	75

Malta

		1970	1971	1972	1973	1974	1975	1976	1977	1978	1979	1980	1981	1982	1983	1984
Balance of Payments																*Millions of US Dollars:*
Current Account, n.i.e.	78al d	....	1.2	22.5	30.4	5.2	59.3	55.0	40.0	72.7	46.6	38.8	86.4	12.4	−4.9	8.2
Goods: Exports f.o.b.	78aa d	....	51.3	81.5	113.9	171.0	199.3	254.7	319.0	362.2	462.2	537.6	499.9	445.5	406.1	426.4
Goods: Imports f.o.b.	78ab d	....	−142.0	−155.9	−212.9	−313.6	−332.4	−376.6	−456.8	−507.3	−674.3	−884.7	−778.1	−709.2	−659.5	−639.2
Trade Balance	78ac d	....	−90.6	−74.4	−99.0	−142.7	−133.1	−121.8	−137.8	−145.1	−212.0	−347.1	−278.3	−263.7	−253.4	−212.8
Services: Credit	78ad d	....	81.8	90.4	133.7	151.0	188.9	178.8	197.0	264.2	344.8	481.1	411.9	306.0	282.6	250.5
Services: Debit	78ae d	....	−41.8	−44.6	−51.8	−73.2	−80.0	−85.9	−114.8	−140.1	−184.1	−242.9	−243.6	−246.0	−207.2	−209.7
Balance on Goods & Services	78af d	....	−50.6	−28.6	−17.1	−64.9	−24.2	−28.9	−55.6	−21.0	−51.3	−108.9	−109.9	−203.8	−178.1	−172.0
Income: Credit	78ag d	....	28.5	32.2	35.0	48.0	63.7	61.6	70.1	78.9	102.1	153.1	161.6	174.0	133.0	138.6
Income: Debit	78ah d	....	−10.1	−10.7	−13.3	−15.0	−14.6	−16.0	−19.7	−31.7	−61.4	−57.6	−50.9	−28.6	−22.9	−20.0
Balance on Gds, Serv. & Inc.	78ai d	....	−32.2	−7.1	4.6	−31.9	24.9	16.7	−5.2	26.2	−10.6	−13.3	.8	−58.5	−68.0	−53.4
Current Transfers, n.i.e.: Credit	78aj d	....	37.8	34.9	31.5	41.2	39.0	44.0	49.0	52.7	64.7	60.5	93.9	76.7	68.2	68.5
Current Transfers: Debit	78ak d	....	−4.4	−5.2	−5.7	−4.2	−4.7	−5.6	−3.8	−6.2	−7.5	−8.4	−8.3	−5.8	−5.1	−6.9
Capital Account, n.i.e.	78bc d	....	4.7	2.6	6.2	7.5	6.8	7.5	6.4	7.0	6.1	5.8	4.7	3.9	3.2	3.0
Capital Account, n.i.e.: Credit	78ba d	....	4.7	2.6	6.2	7.5	6.8	7.5	6.4	7.0	6.1	5.8	4.7	3.9	3.2	3.0
Capital Account: Debit	78bb d	....	—	—	—	—	—	—	—	—	—	—	—	—	—	—
Financial Account, n.i.e.	78bj d	....	2.9	45.3	−3.3	27.2	34.8	41.2	18.2	50.9	−.8	24.9	41.9	24.3	88.8	22.1
Direct Investment Abroad	78bd d	....	....	....	....	....	....	....	....	....	....	....	....	....	....	....
Dir. Invest. in Rep. Econ., n.i.e.	78be d	....	11.5	4.5	5.2	10.6	15.9	14.1	18.5	21.5	16.2	26.6	39.0	20.9	24.5	26.2
Portfolio Investment Assets	78bf d	....	−30.2	14.9	22.2	7.3	−9.1	−1.9	−13.7	−18.9	−30.4	−8.7	3.9	−3.4	−27.1	.9
Equity Securities	78bk d	....	....	....	....	....	....	....	....	....	....	−9.8	....	.7	−18.5	—
Debt Securities	78bl d	....	−30.2	14.9	22.2	7.3	−9.1	−1.9	−13.7	−18.9	−30.4	1.2	3.9	−4.1	−8.6	.9
Portfolio Investment Liab., n.i.e.	78bg d	....	....	....	....	....	....	....	....	....	....	....	....	....	....	....
Equity Securities	78bm d	....	....	....	....	....	....	....	....	....	....	....	....	....	....	....
Debt Securities	78bn d	....	....	....	....	....	....	....	....	....	....	....	....	....	....	....
Financial Derivatives Assets	78bw d	....	....	....	....	....	....	....	....	....	....	....	....	....	....	....
Financial Derivatives Liabilities	78bx d	....	....	....	....	....	....	....	....	....	....	....	....	....	....	....
Other Investment Assets	78bh d	....	22.6	12.8	−32.0	−13.5	1.8	−15.5	4.3	18.9	.8	−13.6	−17.3	−21.6	−13.6	3.7
Monetary Authorities	78bo d	....	....	....	....	....	....	....	....	....	....	....	....	....	....	....
General Government	78bp d	....	—	—	—	—	—	—	—	—	—	—	—	—	—	—
Banks	78bq d	....	22.4	13.6	−29.6	−14.0	−10.1	−14.8	9.0	19.2	3.3	−2.6	−16.0	−12.9	−16.0	10.4
Other Sectors	78br d	....	.2	−.8	−2.4	.5	12.0	−.7	−4.7	−.3	−2.5	−11.0	−1.3	−8.7	2.3	−6.7
Other Investment Liab., n.i.e.	78bi d	....	−1.0	13.1	1.4	22.8	26.2	44.5	9.2	29.3	12.6	20.6	16.3	28.4	105.0	−8.7
Monetary Authorities	78bs d	....	....	....	....	....	....	....	....	....	....	....	....	....	....	....
General Government	78bt d	....	−7.1	−.8	4.6	3.9	2.6	12.2	1.4	3.6	4.5	11.9	8.8	2.2	22.7	7.4
Banks	78bu d	....	−3.7	5.8	−17.1	−1.6	3.4	4.0	.7	5.4	.8	5.2	4.9	22.8	27.1	−2.0
Other Sectors	78bv d	....	9.8	8.1	13.8	20.5	20.3	28.2	7.1	20.2	7.3	3.5	2.6	3.4	55.3	−14.1
Net Errors and Omissions	78ca d	....	8.4	1.6	6.0	2.1	12.0	−9.5	−4.6	−5.3	3.5	−18.1	14.9	11.6	17.0	−1.5
Overall Balance	78cb d	....	17.2	72.1	39.3	42.0	112.8	94.2	60.1	125.2	55.4	51.4	147.8	52.1	104.2	31.9
Reserves and Related Items	79da d	....	−17.2	−72.1	−39.3	−42.0	−112.8	−94.2	−60.1	−125.2	−55.4	−51.4	−147.8	−52.1	−104.2	−31.9
Reserve Assets	79db d	....	−17.2	−72.1	−39.3	−42.0	−112.8	−94.2	−60.1	−125.2	−55.4	−51.4	−147.8	−52.1	−104.2	−31.9
Use of Fund Credit and Loans	79dc d	....	—	—	—	—	—	—	—	—	—	—	—	—	—	—
Exceptional Financing	79de d	....	....	....	....	....	....	....	....	....	....	....	....	....	....	....
Government Finance																*Millions of Liri:*
Deficit (−) or Surplus	80	−6.31	10.11	−4.76	3.07	4.83	−6.22	4.50	3.47	11.75	....	**I** 4.29	5.55	−7.63	7.33	2.06
Total Revenue and Grants	81y	42.33	53.33	40.85	57.60	74.25	92.23	105.10	105.56	125.54	....	**I** 143.37	183.15	193.38	199.66	193.78
Revenue	81	33.83	50.74	37.75	57.35	74.08	91.79	104.78	105.24	125.29	....	**I** 139.92	167.40	186.35	192.88	186.83
Grants	81z	8.50	2.59	3.10	.25	.17	.44	.32	.32	.25	....	**I** 3.45	15.75	7.03	6.78	6.95
Exp. & Lending Minus Repay.	82z	48.64	43.22	45.61	54.53	69.42	98.45	100.60	102.09	113.79	....	**I** 139.08	177.60	201.01	192.33	191.72
Expenditure	82	48.16	43.04	43.42	47.19	67.57	83.35	92.46	96.30	106.44	....	**I** 131.29	155.54	175.02	180.31	187.40
Lending Minus Repayments	83	.48	.18	2.19	7.34	1.85	15.10	8.14	5.79	7.35	....	**I** 7.79	22.06	25.99	12.02	4.32
Total Financing	80h	6.31	−10.11	4.76	−3.07	−4.83	6.22	−4.50	−3.47	−11.75	....	**I** −4.29	−5.55	7.63	−7.33	−2.06
Total Net Borrowing	84	....	....	.62	.09	.65	7.51	2.41	−1.02	2.53	....	**I** 7.70	1.76	.96	10.02	2.26
Net Domestic	84b	....	....	−1.78	−.49	−.57	−.61	−.64	−.58	−1.21	....	**I** —	.01	—	—	—
Net Foreign	85b	....	....	2.40	.58	1.22	8.12	3.05	−.44	3.74	....	**I** 7.70	1.75	.96	10.02	2.26
Use of Cash Balances	87	....	....	4.14	−3.16	−5.48	−6.91	−2.45	−14.28	....	**I** −11.99	−7.31	6.67	−17.35	−4.32
Total Debt by Residence	88	33.93	37.42	36.37	36.90	37.90	43.96	46.52	46.38	50.52	....	**I** 58.27	57.91	57.80	67.64	70.55
Domestic	88a	20.90	30.34	27.46	27.46	27.46	27.46	27.46	27.46	27.46	....	**I** 25.21	25.22	25.24	25.23	25.24
Foreign	89a	13.03	7.08	8.91	9.44	10.44	16.50	19.06	18.92	23.06	....	**I** 33.06	32.69	32.56	42.41	45.31
National Accounts																*Millions of Liri*
Exports of Goods & Services	90c	47.1	50.0	53.5	75.3	110.4	137.3	172.7	207.4	229.6	290.8	356.6	355.9	319.8	307.6	323.5
Government Consumption	91f	18.3	19.5	19.8	22.8	26.9	30.5	35.9	39.7	46.1	53.7	63.4	75.4	85.2	82.3	80.3
Gross Fixed Capital Formation	93e	27.8	25.5	22.5	22.3	31.2	37.5	54.1	60.0	60.3	78.2	87.1	105.6	120.1	131.6	126.5
Increase/Decrease(−) in Stocks	93i	3.2	2.9	3.0	3.3	4.5	1.5	1.9	2.3	4.8	4.8	9.4	12.6	25.5	5.5	6.8
Private Consumption	96f	73.9	75.1	80.4	90.1	107.0	118.7	135.7	172.4	186.4	206.0	253.5	279.4	305.7	306.7	317.5
Imports of Goods & Services	98c	−75.5	−75.2	−76.9	−98.0	−148.4	−159.7	−196.6	−242.0	−249.5	−307.7	−378.0	−392.5	−394.6	−376.1	−393.5
Gross Domestic Product (GDP)	99b	94.8	97.9	102.2	115.7	131.6	165.8	203.7	239.8	277.6	325.8	392.0	436.5	461.8	457.6	461.1
Net Factor Inc/Pmts(−) Abroad	98.n	7.3	7.5	8.3	7.5	12.5	18.3	18.1	19.1	16.9	13.0	30.6	41.2	52.0	38.1	45.5
Gross National Income (GNI)	99a	102.1	105.3	110.5	123.2	144.0	184.0	221.9	258.9	294.6	338.7	422.5	477.7	513.8	495.7	506.5
Net National Income	99e	99.2	101.9	106.8	119.2	139.4	178.6	215.0	250.4	284.4	327.6	409.6	463.3	498.1	475.9	485.5
GDP Volume 1954 prices	99b.p	65	67	71	78	....	....	....	....	....	....	....	....	....	....	....
GDP Volume 1973 prices	99b.p	....	....	....	115.7	127.3	152.2	178.1	199.8	222.1	245.4	262.7	271.4	277.6	275.9	278.5
GDP Volume 1995 prices	99b.p	....	....	....	....	....	....	....	....	....	....	....	....	....	....	....
GDP Volume (1995=100)	99bv p	19.3	19.8	21.0	23.0	25.3	30.3	35.4	39.7	44.2	48.8	52.2	54.0	55.2	54.9	55.4
GDP Deflator (1995=100)	99bi p	42.8	43.1	42.6	43.9	45.4	47.8	50.2	52.7	54.9	58.3	65.5	70.6	73.0	72.8	72.7
																Millions:
Population	99z	.30	.30	.30	.30	.30	**I** .33	.33	.33	.34	**I** .32	.32	.32	.32	.33	.33

1985	1986	1987	1988	1989	1990	1991	1992	1993	1994	1995	1996	1997	1998	1999	Balance of Payments	
Minus Sign Indicates Debit																
−25.8	6.9	22.6	61.1	−9.5	−55.8	−7.4	30.2	−84.3	−131.5	−352.3	−352.3	−201.4	−199.9	−127.6	Current Account, n.i.e.	78al d
435.5	534.1	653.0	780.1	891.3	1,198.1	1,330.7	1,609.8	1,408.1	1,618.5	1,944.8	1,770.0	1,661.4	1,824.3	2,015.0	Goods: Exports f.o.b.	78aa d
−672.1	−786.5	−1,024.6	−1,222.3	−1,327.7	−1,769.2	−1,913.1	−2,122.9	−1,976.4	−2,221.0	−2,673.1	−2,536.2	−2,320.7	−2,417.0	−2,588.6	Goods: Imports f.o.b.	78ab d
−236.6	−252.4	−371.6	−442.2	−436.5	−571.1	−582.4	−513.0	−568.3	−602.5	−728.2	−766.2	−659.3	−592.7	−573.7	*Trade Balance*	78ac d
273.7	370.5	557.2	653.2	644.5	752.0	814.0	883.8	912.4	994.6	1,083.7	1,116.5	1,166.0	1,241.8	1,303.4	Services: Credit	78ad d
−218.5	−280.4	−358.9	−412.3	−433.3	−514.3	−528.9	−588.6	−604.2	−686.5	−808.2	−820.2	−791.8	−851.3	−912.3	Services: Debit	78ae d
−181.4	−162.3	−173.4	−201.3	−225.3	−333.3	−297.2	−217.8	−260.2	−294.5	−452.7	−469.9	−285.1	−202.2	−182.6	*Balance on Goods & Services*	78af d
126.6	146.3	139.5	156.6	190.5	269.0	268.3	271.2	241.8	219.4	287.7	309.7	360.4	510.8	1,237.5	Income: Credit	78ag d
−22.8	−44.0	−25.8	−53.5	−73.2	−78.9	−93.9	−116.9	−126.8	−150.6	−239.8	−290.5	−343.1	−578.4	−1,240.6	Income: Debit	78ah d
−77.6	−60.1	−59.6	−98.2	−107.9	−143.2	−122.9	−63.5	−145.2	−225.7	−404.8	−450.6	−267.9	−269.8	−185.7	*Balance on Gds, Serv. & Inc.*	78ai d
57.1	73.5	91.2	170.5	114.5	110.6	120.6	98.6	64.9	101.2	65.8	113.1	106.3	94.1	88.4	Current Transfers, n.i.e.: Credit	78aj d
−5.3	−6.6	−9.0	−11.2	−16.1	−23.1	−5.1	−4.8	−4.1	−7.1	−13.3	−14.7	−39.8	−24.3	−30.4	Current Transfers, n.i.e.: Debit	78ak d
3.0	4.3	4.3	7.0	6.0	—	—	—	13.1	—	—	—	—	—	—	Capital Account, n.i.e.	78bc d
3.0	4.3	4.3	7.0	6.0	—	—	—	13.1	—	—	—	—	—	—	Capital Account, n.i.e.: Credit	78ba d
—	—	—	—	—	—	—	—	—	—	—	—	—	—	—	Capital Account: Debit	78bb d
−24.7	−18.3	−2.6	17.2	−46.8	−43.1	13.3	27.0	188.7	480.9	33.2	215.6	121.3	298.6	366.6	Financial Account, n.i.e.	78bj d
									−.9	1.0	−55.5	−100.6	−14.6	−22.0	Direct Investment Abroad	78bd d
19.0	21.9	19.4	40.8	51.7	45.8	77.0	39.5	56.4	151.7	182.2	325.2	164.9	273.3	811.5	Dir. Invest. in Rep. Econ., n.i.e.	78be d
−32.8	44.0	−7.5	−38.4	−57.7	−1.9	−245.2	−214.1	−266.6	304.4	−460.8	−116.7	110.1	−140.1	−536.4	Portfolio Investment Assets	78bf d
—	2.3	.3	−5.4	—	.7	4.0	4.7	13.2	247.2	—	−.9	−10.1	6.3	−11.7	Equity Securities	78bk d
−32.8	41.7	−7.8	−32.9	−57.7	−2.6	−249.3	−218.8	−279.8	57.2	−460.8	−115.9	120.1	−146.4	−524.6	Debt Securities	78bl d
—	—	—	—	—	—	—	—	—	—	3.0	3.1	.3	58.9	−33.0	Portfolio Investment Liab., n.i.e.	78bg d
—	—	—	—	—	—	—	—	—	—	−4.2	3.1	.3	−1.5	−7.5	Equity Securities	78bm d
—	—	—	—	—	—	—	—	—	—	7.2	—	—	60.5	−25.5	Debt Securities	78bn d
—	—	—	—	—	—	—	—	—	—	1.1	−3.6	−2.4	−1.2	−1.8	Financial Derivatives Assets	78bw d
—	—	—	—	—	—	—	—	—	—	−1.4	—	—	—	—	Financial Derivatives Liabilities	78bx d
−1.1	−59.0	−62.5	−105.5	−100.1	−242.6	67.5	−96.1	131.1	103.4	−277.5	−609.3	−988.7	−2,047.8	−1,269.8	Other Investment Assets	78bh d
—	—	—	—	—	—	—	—	—	—	—	—	—	—	—	Monetary Authorities	78bo d
—	—	—	—	—	—	—	—	—	−.5	—	—	—	—	—	General Government	78bp d
1.7	−49.9	−59.6	−111.5	−98.1	−218.4	77.8	−99.7	146.4	79.6	−280.5	−581.5	−934.3	−2,077.4	−1,316.9	Banks	78bq d
−2.8	−9.2	−2.9	6.0	−2.0	−24.1	−10.3	3.6	−15.3	24.4	3.0	−27.9	−54.4	29.6	47.1	Other Sectors	78br d
−9.8	−25.2	48.0	120.3	59.4	155.6	114.0	297.7	268.7	−79.7	642.0	671.1	937.8	2,170.2	1,418.1	Other Investment Liab., n.i.e.	78bi d
—	—	—	—	—	—	—	—	—	—	—	—	—	—	—	Monetary Authorities	78bs d
5.1	−9.4	3.5	−4.5	4.0	38.6	26.6	102.8	35.3	6.0	−40.8	51.8	−26.3	−9.4	−41.7	General Government	78bt d
−7.9	−11.7	47.2	94.6	39.3	53.2	25.8	48.5	111.2	−274.6	680.6	597.5	903.4	2,183.7	1,500.3	Banks	78bu d
−7.0	−4.1	−2.6	30.2	16.1	63.7	61.6	146.4	122.2	188.8	2.2	21.7	60.7	−4.1	−40.5	Other Sectors	78bv d
−19.6	2.6	−28.8	−50.4	64.4	2.5	−84.7	−12.7	17.4	33.4	12.0	51.8	86.9	92.2	−.1	Net Errors and Omissions	78ca d
−67.1	−4.6	−4.5	34.8	14.2	−96.3	−78.8	44.6	134.8	382.8	−307.1	−84.9	6.8	190.9	239.0	*Overall Balance*	78cb d
67.1	4.6	4.5	−34.8	−14.2	96.3	78.8	−44.6	−134.8	−382.8	307.1	84.9	−6.8	−190.9	−239.0	Reserves and Related Items	79da d
67.1	4.6	4.5	−34.8	−14.2	96.3	78.8	−44.6	−134.8	−382.8	307.1	84.9	−6.8	−190.9	−239.0	Reserve Assets	79db d
—	—	—	—	—	—	—	—	—	—	—	—	—	—	—	Use of Fund Credit and Loans	79dc d
—	—	—	—	—	—	—	—	—	—	—	—	—	—	—	Exceptional Financing	79de d

1985	1986	1987	1988	1989	1990	1991	1992	1993	1994	1995	1996	1997	1998	1999	Government Finance	
Year Ending December 31																
−19.21	−19.50	−36.68	−.18	−31.13	−38.06	−40.76	−27.19	−27.56	−37.57	−30.87	−92.92	−125.99	. . . .	. . . .	Deficit (-) or Surplus	80
197.06	189.88	188.87	234.07	238.95	288.22	319.18	309.30	335.53	358.31	406.84	407.43	450.75	. . . .	. . . .	Total Revenue and Grants	81y
196.81	189.59	188.87	219.82	230.76	280.54	302.81	292.91	327.10	345.46	402.32	386.63	440.94	. . . .	. . . .	Revenue	81
.25	.29	—	14.25	8.19	7.68	16.37	16.39	8.43	12.85	4.52	20.80	9.81	. . . .	. . . .	Grants	81z
216.27	209.38	225.55	234.25	270.08	326.28	359.94	336.49	363.09	395.88	437.71	500.35	576.74	. . . .	. . . .	Exp. & Lending Minus Repay.	82z
190.77	204.00	223.71	229.85	274.41	327.20	360.38	333.79	367.78	402.47	447.46	500.00	535.42	. . . .	. . . .	Expenditure	82
25.50	5.38	1.84	4.40	−4.33	−.92	−.44	2.70	−4.69	−6.59	−9.75	.35	41.32	. . . .	. . . .	Lending Minus Repayments	83
19.21	19.50	36.68	.18	31.13	38.06	40.76	27.19	27.56	37.57	30.87	92.92	125.99	. . . .	. . . .	Total Financing	80h
−.09	−3.79	26.32	23.06	8.79	61.95	37.05	25.72	28.17	35.61	32.89	104.04	145.16	. . . .	. . . .	Total Net Borrowing	84
—	—	29.28	25.57	10.35	50.21	30.40	29.78	28.66	28.70	35.44	105.44	146.55	. . . .	. . . .	Net Domestic	84b
−.09	−3.79	−2.96	−2.51	−1.56	11.74	6.65	−4.06	−.49	6.91	−2.55	−1.40	−1.39	. . . .	. . . .	Net Foreign	85b
19.30	23.29	10.36	−22.88	22.34	−23.89	3.71	1.47	−.61	1.96	−2.02	−11.12	−19.17	. . . .	. . . .	Use of Cash Balances	87
67.78	60.69	84.73	108.54	117.84	163.03	201.99	235.33	296.30	339.59	410.79	514.47	661.35	. . . .	. . . .	Total Debt by Residence	88
25.26	25.25	54.89	80.40	90.95	125.54	157.28	186.93	245.82	283.33	357.36	462.68	610.90	. . . .	. . . .	Domestic	88a
42.52	35.44	29.84	28.14	26.89	37.49	44.71	48.40	50.48	56.26	53.43	51.79	50.45	. . . .	. . . .	Foreign	89a

1985	1986	1987	1988	1989	1990	1991	1992	1993	1994	1995	1996	1997	1998	1999	National Accounts	
Millions of Liri																
345.2	370.2	429.6	480.0	543.5	626.4	701.9	804.1	896.3	994.4	1,074.7	1,045.6	1,095.8	1,192.9	1,329.7	Exports of Goods & Services	90c
84.3	89.5	98.2	105.2	119.6	129.2	147.1	164.3	188.9	209.5	235.2	259.8	264.1	269.5	270.2	Government Consumption	91f
125.9	122.3	153.5	166.4	188.4	232.6	239.1	240.9	276.8	305.4	365.2	345.3	326.4	326.8	329.1	Gross Fixed Capital Formation	93e
7.9	8.2	−2.4	8.2	9.9	12.7	15.6	.1	3.7	10.0	1.2	−1.4	3.0	−10.7	10.8	Increase/Decrease(-) in Stocks	93i
333.2	343.4	351.2	387.6	425.5	460.8	494.5	531.4	561.5	608.3	700.4	764.9	803.5	846.0	908.0	Private Consumption	96f
−420.5	−421.7	−480.9	−540.9	−616.8	−726.9	−791.2	−866.0	−987.2	−1,099.0	−1,231.2	−1,212.8	−1,204.6	−1,270.3	−1,401.1	Imports of Goods & Services	98c
476.0	511.9	549.2	606.5	670.1	734.7	806.9	874.8	940.0	1,028.5	1,145.5	1,201.3	1,288.2	1,362.3	1,446.7	Gross Domestic Product (GDP)	99b
38.8	28.1	30.7	28.3	35.8	55.0	49.7	41.7	35.5	19.3	12.0	3.2	4.1	27.4	2.3	Net Factor Inc/Pmts(-) Abroad	98.n
514.8	539.9	579.8	634.8	705.9	789.8	856.5	916.4	975.5	1,047.9	1,157.5	1,204.5	1,292.3	1,334.9	1,444.4	Gross National Income (GNI)	99a
493.4	516.7	553.8	605.9	673.9	754.5	818.8	874.2	922.1	983.0	1,080.0	1,128.5	1,211.5	. . . .	. . . .	Net National Income	99e
										. . . .	. . . .	. . . .	. . . .	. . . .	GDP Volume 1954 prices	99b.p
285.7	296.8	309.0	335.0	362.4	385.2	409.3	428.5	447.7	473.3	502.8	. . . .	. . . .	. . . .	. . . .	GDP Volume 1973 prices	99b.p
										1,145.5	1,191.2	1,249.0	1,291.1	1,350.6	GDP Volume 1995 prices	99b.p
56.8	59.0	61.5	66.6	72.1	76.6	81.4	85.2	89.0	94.1	100.0	104.0	109.0	112.7	117.9	GDP Volume (1995=100)	99bv p
73.1	75.7	78.0	79.5	81.2	83.7	86.5	89.6	92.2	95.4	100.0	100.8	103.1	105.5	107.1	GDP Deflator (1995=100)	99bi p
Midyear Estimates																
.34	.34	.34	.35	.35	.35	.36	.36	.36	.36	.37	.37	.38	.38	.39	Population	99z

(See notes in the back of the book.)

Mauritania

		1970	1971	1972	1973	1974	1975	1976	1977	1978	1979	1980	1981	1982	1983	1984
Exchange Rates															*Ouguiyas per SDR:*	
Official Rate	aa	55.205	56.723	55.599	I 56.801	53.014	52.855	50.702	55.937	60.130	60.393	58.707	56.964	58.421	59.708	65.958
															Ouguiyas per US Dollar	
Official Rate	ae	55.205	52.245	51.210	I 47.085	43.300	45.150	43.640	46.050	46.155	45.845	46.030	48.940	52.960	57.030	67.290
Official Rate	rf	55.542	55.426	50.405	44.578	45.333e	43.104e	45.022e	45.587	46.163	45.893	45.914	48.296	51.769	54.812	63.803
Fund Position															*Millions of SDRs:*	
Quota	2f. s	13.0	13.0	13.0	13.0	13.0	13.0	13.0	13.0	17.0	17.0	25.5	25.5	25.5	33.9	33.9
SDRs	1b. s	1.7	.9	2.2	2.1	2.0	1.7	1.2	.6	.7	1.3	—	1.1	—	.7	—
Reserve Position in the Fund	1c. s	1.5	.6	.8	.9	—	—	—	—	—	—	—	—	—	—	—
Total Fund Cred.&Loans Outstg.	2tl	—	—	—	—	—	—	11.8	17.9	22.0	25.1	39.1	42.5	56.4	51.7	41.4
International Liquidity														*Millions of US Dollars Unless Otherwise Indicated:*		
Total Reserves minus Gold	1l. d	3.2	7.5	13.5	42.2	103.8	47.7	82.0	50.0	79.5	113.7	139.9	161.8	139.1	105.9	77.5
SDRs	1b. d	1.7	1.0	2.3	2.6	2.4	2.0	1.4	.7	.9	1.7	—	1.3	—	.7	—
Reserve Position in the Fund	1c. d	1.5	.7	.8	1.1	—	—	—	—	—	—	—	—	—	—	—
Foreign Exchange	1d. d	—	5.8	10.3	38.6	101.4	45.7	80.6	49.3	78.6	112.0	139.9	160.5	139.1	105.2	77.5
Gold (Million Fine Troy Ounces)	1ad	....	....	....	....	....	....	.006	.008	.008	.011	.011	.011	.011	.011	.011
Gold (National Valuation)	1an d	....	....	....	....	....	....	.2	.2	.2	1.7	6.9	4.5	4.1	4.5	3.6
Monetary Authorities: Other Liab.	4. d	.7	—	—	19.8	35.9	36.8	55.9	57.5	81.0	88.1	79.2	98.2	93.9	88.5	89.3
Deposit Money Banks: Assets	7a. d	.5	2.4	.6	1.1	1.0	.4	18.5	21.9	11.5	3.1	9.2	14.5	4.4	4.8	1.5
Liabilities	7b. d	3.9	6.6	5.5	7.9	24.1	11.4	29.5	40.0	67.7	70.1	81.3	79.3	98.0	78.7	93.4
Monetary Authorities															*Millions of Ouguiyas:*	
Foreign Assets	11	164	393	691	1,948	4,500	2,159	3,582	2,519	3,655	5,330	6,953	8,650	6,545	5,018	4,929
Claims on Central Government	12a	—	6	10	334	25	749	369	1,749	1,459	1,752	1,965	2,726	4,515	4,535	5,052
Claims on Nonfin.Pub.Enterprises	12c	....	....	....	....	....	....	....	....	....	....	....	....	....	....	....
Claims on Private Sector	12d	....	—	—	—	—	921	788	766	766	766	926	926	926	926	926
Claims on Deposit Money Banks	12e	491	346	280	822	490	1,348	1,428	2,255	2,103	1,781	1,770	1,679	1,952	3,105	4,029
Claims on Nonbank Financial Insts	12g	....	....	....	....	....	....	....	....	....	....	....	....	....	....	....
Reserve Money	14	475	480	662	788	1,833	1,653	1,796	2,038	2,210	2,963	3,163	4,178	4,138	4,023	4,045
of which: Currency Outside DMBs	14a	445	461	618	630	954	1,214	1,464	1,529	1,729	2,311	2,376	2,678	2,950	3,024	3,658
Restricted Deposits	16b	....	....	....	....	....	....	....	....	....	....	....	....	....	....	....
Foreign Liabilities	16c	4	2	—	933	1,555	1,663	3,040	3,574	4,738	4,990	5,195	6,500	7,528	7,394	8,009
Long-Term Foreign Liabilities	16cl	....	....	....	....	....	....	....	....	....	....	....	....	....	....	....
Central Government Deposits	16d	82	89	62	512	599	1,161	320	153	128	177	277	135	155	164	167
Capital Accounts	17a	—	171	247	454	506	552	751	869	871	1,131	1,818	2,230	2,708	3,130	3,380
Other Items (Net)	17r	94	3	10	417	522	148	260	654	38	367	1,162	939	−591	−1,126	−663
Deposit Money Banks															*Millions of Ouguiyas:*	
Reserves	20	32	38	432	1,106	7,964	3,202	344	504	476	638	719	890	697	999	627
Foreign Assets	21	25	122	29	50	44	19	808	1,008	533	142	424	708	235	276	100
Claims on Central Government	22a	17	6	116	20	74	48	111	26	59	57	31	24	85	17	50
Claims on Nonfin.Pub.Enterprises	22c	....	....	....	....	....	....	....	....	....	....	....	....	....	....	....
Claims on Private Sector	22d	1,526	1,544	1,789	2,740	3,041	4,616	5,488	7,112	7,712	7,835	8,869	10,051	11,425	12,735	13,855
Claims on Nonbank Financial Insts	22g	....	....	....	....	....	....	....	....	....	....	....	....	....	....	....
Demand Deposits	24	600	598	708	778	1,407	1,564	2,068	2,386	2,226	2,598	2,990	4,845	4,049	4,941	5,891
Time Deposits	25	143	125	160	531	694	1,052	1,131	964	1,025	1,212	1,403	1,777	2,437	1,995	1,682
Foreign Liabilities	26c	213	346	281	370	1,045	513	1,225	1,783	2,242	2,610	3,326	3,681	5,114	4,374	6,187
Long-Term Foreign Liabilities	26cl	....	....	....	....	....	....	62	57	882	604	414	201	74	116	100
Central Government Deposits	26d	90	159	317	89	162	277	267	217	143	75	115	25	491	89	105
Central Govt. Lending Funds	26f	....	....	....	....	....	....	....	....	....	69	1,162	1,223	605	820	1,448
Credit from Monetary Authorities	26g	491	347	281	822	161	1,296	1,428	2,255	2,109	1,781	1,770	1,574	2,036	2,406	3,784
Capital Accounts	27a	136	172	204	367	562	626	752	832	855	888	908	924	957	1,023	1,405
Other Items (Net)	27r	−73	−37	414	960	7,092	2,557	−182	157	−701	−1,164	−2,045	−2,575	−3,322	−1,737	−5,970
Monetary Survey															*Millions of Ouguiyas:*	
Foreign Assets (Net)	31n	−28	167	439	695	1,944	1	63	−1,888	−3,674	−2,732	−1,558	−1,025	−5,937	−6,590	−9,267
Domestic Credit	32	1,436	1,381	1,638	2,580	2,470	5,043	6,320	9,464	9,907	10,330	11,711	13,699	16,441	18,085	19,703
Claims on Central Govt. (Net)	32an	−117	−224	−216	−279	−709	−719	−241	1,394	1,052	1,443	1,630	2,436	3,683	4,216	4,715
Claims on Nonfin.Pub.Enterprises	32c	....	....	....	....	....	....	....	....	....	....	....	....	....	....	....
Claims on Private Sector	32d	1,553	1,605	1,854	2,858	3,179	5,762	6,561	8,071	8,855	8,887	10,081	11,263	12,758	13,869	14,989
Claims on Nonbank Financial Inst	32g	....	....	....	....	....	....	....	....	....	....	....	....	....	....	....
Money	34	1,110	1,132	1,428	1,494	2,451	2,926	3,683	4,095	4,134	5,081	5,677	7,653	7,135	8,090	9,641
Quasi-Money	35	143	125	160	531	694	1,052	1,131	964	1,025	1,212	1,403	1,777	2,437	1,995	1,682
Restricted Deposits	36b	....	....	....	....	....	....	....	....	....	....	....	....	....	....	....
Central Govt. Lending Funds	36f	—	—	—	—	—	—	—	—	—	69	1,162	1,223	605	820	1,448
Other Items (Net)	37r	155	291	489	1,250	1,268	1,066	1,569	2,518	1,073	1,236	1,911	2,021	327	590	−2,334
Money plus Quasi-Money	35l	1,252	1,257	1,588	2,024	3,145	3,979	4,964	5,239	5,340	6,465	7,392	9,560	9,708	10,209	11,414

Exchange Rates

End of Period

1985	1986	1987	1988	1989	1990	1991	1992	1993	1994	1995	1996	1997	1998	1999		Code
84.655	90.614	101.576	101.910	109.798	110.740	111.316	158.263	170.541	187.401	203.813	204.837	227.146	289.744	308.815	Official Rate	aa

End of Period (ae) Period Average (rf)

1985	1986	1987	1988	1989	1990	1991	1992	1993	1994	1995	1996	1997	1998	1999		Code
77.070	74.080	71.600	75.730	83.550	77.840	77.820	115.100	124.160	128.370	137.110	142.450	168.350	205.780	225.000	Official Rate	ae
77.085	74.375	73.878	75.261	83.051	80.609	81.946	87.027	120.806	123.575	129.768	137.222	151.853	188.476	209.514	Official Rate	rf

Fund Position

End of Period

1985	1986	1987	1988	1989	1990	1991	1992	1993	1994	1995	1996	1997	1998	1999		Code
33.9	33.9	33.9	33.9	33.9	33.9	33.9	47.5	47.5	47.5	47.5	47.5	47.5	47.5	64.4	Quota	2f. s
3.9	2.6	12.1	.1	.1	.6	.1	.1	.1	—	—	1.0	.3	—	—	SDRs	1b. s
—	—	—	—	—	—	—	—	—	—	—	—	—	—	—	Reserve Position in the Fund	1c. s
36.5	42.7	54.1	52.5	52.3	49.2	39.5	42.0	46.1	58.8	67.1	74.6	83.4	78.3	77.6	Total Fund Cred.&Loans Outstg.	2tl

International Liquidity

End of Period

1985	1986	1987	1988	1989	1990	1991	1992	1993	1994	1995	1996	1997	1998	1999		Code
59.2	48.2	71.8	55.6	82.4	54.1	67.6	61.2	44.6	39.7	85.5	141.2	200.8	202.9	224.3	Total Reserves minus Gold	1l. d
4.3	3.1	17.2	.1	.1	.8	.1	.1	.1	—	.1	1.4	.4	—	—	SDRs	1b. d
—	—	—	—	—	—	—	—	—	—	—	—	—	—	—	Reserve Position in the Fund	1c. d
54.9	45.1	54.6	55.5	82.3	53.3	67.5	61.1	44.4	39.7	85.4	139.8	200.4	202.8	224.3	Foreign Exchange	1d. d
.011	.012	.012	.012	.012	.012	.012	.012	.012	.012	.012	.012	.012	.012	.012	Gold (Million Fine Troy Ounces)	1ad
3.7	4.5	5.7	4.8	4.6	4.4	4.2	3.8	4.5	4.3	4.4	4.2	3.3	3.3	3.3	Gold (National Valuation)	1and
89.6	89.9	94.2	91.1	95.1	110.4	168.4	216.0	187.1	199.2	212.0	205.3	209.7	209.6	202.0	Monetary Authorities: Other Liab.	4..d
3.3	11.0	23.0	32.6	30.0	28.7	14.1	15.7	25.8	27.7	25.9	27.0	24.7	24.1	22.1	Deposit Money Banks: Assets	7a. d
56.8	77.5	79.9	87.6	106.0	120.6	181.8	110.0	106.4	105.8	67.4	35.5	26.4	15.0	13.6	Liabilities	7b. d

Monetary Authorities

End of Period

1985	1986	1987	1988	1989	1990	1991	1992	1993	1994	1995	1996	1997	1998	1999		Code
3,954	3,714	5,461	4,616	I7,386	4,136	5,308	7,598	6,218	5,746	12,425	21,030	34,425	42,546	51,335	Foreign Assets	11
3,839	4,476	4,811	4,779	I10,779	11,474	12,990	14,057	18,979	17,949	17,109	17,109	17,102	17,012	16,912	Claims on Central Government	12a
....	....	....	....	60	60	60	60	60	60	60	60	60	60	60	Claims on Nonfin.Pub.Enterprises	12c
925	—	—	—	I306	339	398	450	516	581	695	755	1,023	1,003	1,065	Claims on Private Sector	12d
6,471	4,303	5,122	6,396	I3,269	3,682	2,858	5,980	2,353	2,571	1,872	2,334	2,793	2,789	2,232	Claims on Deposit Money Banks	12e
....	....	....	....	49	49	49	49	49	49	49	49	49	49	49	Claims on Nonbank Financial Insts	12g
5,636	5,386	6,615	7,537	I9,356	8,961	12,102	14,706	22,810	21,966	20,724	10,462	9,089	8,406	8,788	Reserve Money	14
4,700	4,418	5,648	5,845	I6,040	6,139	7,335	7,898	9,097	8,598	7,383	5,093	5,854	5,801	5,963	*of which: Currency Outside DMBs*	14a
....	....	....	....	92	5	39	86	29	91	147	91	82	55	154	Restricted Deposits	16b
9,236	9,951	11,842	12,081	I6,054	5,559	4,767	13,533	10,813	12,093	14,649	15,543	19,232	23,096	23,968	Foreign Liabilities	16c
....	....	....	....	7,028	6,975	11,222	15,031	15,663	16,342	16,702	15,160	17,069	20,923	22,108	Long-Term Foreign Liabilities	16cl
191	425	191	366	I1,645	1,767	2,760	4,200	7,573	8,024	13,342	30,844	42,765	51,300	55,512	Central Government Deposits	16d
3,403	3,813	3,574	3,663	I4,475	4,149	4,177	4,496	4,946	4,888	4,415	4,059	4,821	5,161	5,594	Capital Accounts	17a
-3,277	-7,081	-6,829	-7,855	I-6,801	-7,676	-13,404	-23,858	-33,659	-36,448	-37,769	-34,822	-37,606	-46,075	-44,471	Other Items (Net)	17r

Deposit Money Banks

End of Period

1985	1986	1987	1988	1989	1990	1991	1992	1993	1994	1995	1996	1997	1998	1999		Code
1,226	938	1,412	728	I2,845	2,291	4,031	5,191	10,799	12,775	12,486	5,355	3,083	2,390	2,984	Reserves	20
256	815	1,643	2,465	I2,503	2,232	1,100	1,809	3,201	3,561	3,556	3,853	4,165	4,962	4,964	Foreign Assets	21
154	213	130	166	I252	198	152	193	1,083	916	782	2,742	4,302	4,202	4,637	Claims on Central Government	22a
														—	Claims on Nonfin.Pub.Enterprises	22c
15,519	17,202	18,959	20,598	I31,202	35,411	39,316	40,101	41,191	42,500	30,722	34,634	37,279	39,633	46,942	Claims on Private Sector	22d
....	....	....	....	....	....	....	....	....	....	....	....	....	....	....	Claims on Nonbank Financial Insts	22g
7,376	6,853	7,630	8,068	I10,813	11,178	11,646	11,986	11,508	11,145	10,674	11,015	11,629	17,321	13,697	Demand Deposits	24
1,674	3,471	4,244	3,971	I3,947	5,769	6,181	7,187	6,635	7,612	7,817	8,476	9,101	4,428	8,708	Time Deposits	25
4,321	5,662	5,623	6,070	I8,858	9,387	14,145	12,656	13,216	13,583	9,246	5,054	4,451	3,078	3,058	Foreign Liabilities	26c
55	78	99	563	I—	—	—	—	—	—	—	—	—	—	—	Long-Term Foreign Liabilities	26cl
130	160	254	273	I580	778	815	1,093	1,330	1,552	3,198	3,428	4,058	6,285	13,596	Central Government Deposits	26d
608	159	1,159	1,789	I617	719	978	1,179	1,208	1,208	—	—	—	—	—	Central Govt. Lending Funds	26f
4,879	5,331	6,384	5,855	I2,417	2,668	1,801	4,380	3,351	3,358	7	7	7	7	7	Credit from Monetary Authorities	26g
1,759	1,960	1,758	4,294	I12,226	12,597	13,905	14,018	20,802	21,972	20,709	22,359	23,260	24,203	25,169	Capital Accounts	27a
-3,648	-4,505	-5,006	-6,927	I-2,656	-2,964	-4,872	-5,204	-1,776	-678	-4,105	-3,755	-3,677	-4,135	-4,708	Other Items (Net)	27r

Monetary Survey

End of Period

1985	1986	1987	1988	1989	1990	1991	1992	1993	1994	1995	1996	1997	1998	1999		Code
-9,402	-11,162	-10,460	-11,633	I-12,051	-15,553	-23,726	-31,813	-30,273	-32,711	-24,616	-10,874	-2,162	411	7,165	Foreign Assets (Net)	31n
20,212	21,428	23,574	25,022	I40,423	44,986	49,390	49,617	52,975	52,479	32,877	21,077	12,992	4,374	557	Domestic Credit	32
3,561	3,966	4,355	4,165	I8,806	9,127	9,567	8,957	11,159	9,289	1,351	-14,421	-25,419	-36,371	-47,559	Claims on Central Govt. (Net)	32an
....	....	....	....	60	60	60	60	60	60	60	60	60	60	60	Claims on Nonfin.Pub.Enterprises	32c
16,651	17,462	19,219	20,858	I31,508	35,750	39,714	40,551	41,707	43,081	31,417	35,389	38,302	40,636	48,007	Claims on Private Sector	32d
....	....	....	....	49	49	49	49	49	49	49	49	49	49	49	Claims on Nonbank Financial Inst	32g
12,173	11,393	13,397	14,032	I17,028	17,622	19,376	20,202	20,938	19,816	18,202	16,227	17,579	23,358	19,675	Money	34
1,674	3,471	4,244	3,971	I3,947	5,769	6,181	7,187	6,635	7,612	7,817	8,476	9,101	4,428	8,708	Quasi-Money	35
....	....	....	....	92	5	39	86	29	91	147	91	82	55	154	Restricted Deposits	36b
608	159	1,159	1,789	I617	719	978	1,179	1,208	1,208	—	—	—	—	—	Central Govt. Lending Funds	36f
-3,645	-4,757	-5,686	-6,403	I6,688	5,318	-910	-10,849	-6,108	-8,959	-17,905	-14,591	-15,932	-23,649	-20,815	Other Items (Net)	37r
13,944	14,985	17,761	18,122	I20,975	23,391	25,557	27,389	27,573	27,428	26,019	24,703	26,680	27,786	28,383	Money plus Quasi-Money	35l

Mauritania

		1970	1971	1972	1973	1974	1975	1976	1977	1978	1979	1980	1981	1982	1983	1984
Interest Rates															*Percent Per Annum*	
Discount Rate *(End of Period)*	60	3.50	3.50	3.50	5.50	5.50	5.00	5.00	5.00	5.00	5.00	6.00	6.00	6.00	6.00	6.00
Deposit Rate	60l	....	....	....	....	....	....	....	....	....	....		5.50	5.50	5.50	5.50
Lending Rate	60p	....	....	....	....	....	....	....	....	....	....	12.00	12.00	12.00	12.00	12.00
Prices														Index Numbers (1995=100):		
Consumer Prices	64			....	....									....	....	....
International Transactions															*Millions of Ouguiyas*	
Exports	70	4,936	5,026	5,991	6,918	8,175	7,527	8,013	7,156	5,692	6,733	8,916	12,622	12,050	15,982	18,715
Imports, c.i.f.	71	3,103	3,156	3,475	5,692	5,453	6,934	8,049	9,414	8,361	11,869	13,118	12,793	14,213	12,411	13,201
Balance of Payments															*Millions of US Dollars:*	
Current Account, n.i.e.	78al d	....	....	....	....	....	−63.2	−86.0	−122.5	−78.5	−114.7	−133.6	−147.5	−277.0	−213.6	−111.2
Goods: Exports f.o.b.	78aa d						167.3	181.9	157.2	118.6	147.2	196.3	269.9	240.0	315.4	293.8
Goods: Imports f.o.b.	78ab d						−208.5	−272.0	−295.5	−267.1	−286.0	−321.3	−386.2	−426.6	−378.2	−302.1
Trade Balance	78ac d						−41.2	−90.2	−138.3	−148.5	−138.8	−125.0	−116.3	−186.5	−62.9	−8.3
Services: Credit	78ad d						18.0	19.5	21.5	33.9	45.5	56.5	48.9	47.2	30.2	28.0
Services: Debit	78ae d						−69.2	−80.9	−67.2	−75.3	−83.2	−127.8	−128.1	−157.5	−177.2	−177.8
Balance on Goods & Services	78af d						−92.3	−151.6	−184.0	−189.9	−176.6	−196.3	−195.5	−296.8	−209.8	−158.1
Income: Credit	78ag d						5.0	4.4	4.3	3.1	11.4	17.0	20.1	18.5	9.1	8.5
Income: Debit	78ah d						−35.1	−62.9	−47.7	−30.2	−42.8	−43.8	−70.7	−64.1	−71.4	−47.6
Balance on Gds, Serv. & Inc.	78ai d						−122.4	−210.2	−227.4	−217.0	−208.0	−223.1	−246.1	−342.4	−272.1	−197.2
Current Transfers, n.i.e.: Credit	78aj d						87.5	159.1	130.3	163.2	131.6	132.4	125.8	101.4	89.6	111.9
Current Transfers: Debit	78ak d						−28.3	−35.0	−25.5	−24.8	−38.3	−42.8	−27.2	−35.9	−31.1	−25.9
Capital Account, n.i.e.	78bc d	....	....	....	....	....	—	—	—	—	—	—	—	—	—	—
Capital Account, n.i.e.: Credit	78ba d						—	—	—	—	—	—	—	—	—	—
Capital Account: Debit	78bb d						—	—	—	—	—	—	—	—	—	—
Financial Account, n.i.e.	78bj d	....	....	....	....	....	10.2	100.6	63.4	113.3	148.4	151.4	147.9	219.5	166.2	97.9
Direct Investment Abroad	78bd d						—	—	—	—	—	—	—	—	—	—
Dir. Invest. in Rep. Econ., n.i.e.	78be d						−122.7	1.6	4.1	2.9	63.2	27.1	12.4	15.0	1.4	8.5
Portfolio Investment Assets	78bf d						—	—	—	—	—	—	—	—	—	—
Equity Securities	78bk d						—	—	—	—	—	—	—	—	—	—
Debt Securities	78bl d						—	—	—	—	—	—	—	—	—	—
Portfolio Investment Liab., n.i.e.	78bg d						—	—	—	—	—	—	—	—	—	—
Equity Securities	78bm d						—	—	—	—	—	—	—	—	—	—
Debt Securities	78bn d						—	—	—	—	—	—	—	—	—	—
Financial Derivatives Assets	78bw d						....	....	....	....	....	....	....	....	....	....
Financial Derivatives Liabilities	78bx d						....	....	....	....	....	....	....	....	....	....
Other Investment Assets	78bh d	....	....	....	....	....	−2.7	.9	−4.5	9.1	16.6	−24.4	−13.8	7.4	1.7	−7.9
Monetary Authorities	78bo d						....									
General Government	78bp d						−2.2	−3.3	−1.9	−5.0	−1.3	−5.7	—	−7.3	−.5	−.3
Banks	78bq d						−.2	−.2	.1	−.5	7.8	−19.1	−7.3	5.2	3.5	.7
Other Sectors	78br d						−.4	4.4	−2.7	14.6	10.0	.3	−6.5	9.4	−1.3	−8.4
Other Investment Liab., n.i.e.	78bi d						135.6	98.2	63.7	101.4	68.6	148.7	149.3	197.1	163.1	97.4
Monetary Authorities	78bs d						−.3	8.2	4.9	15.6	2.7	26.5	25.0	−5.6	8.4	19.4
General Government	78bt d						28.7	149.1	45.7	71.7	58.0	113.4	73.7	81.7	68.3	54.7
Banks	78bu d						1.2	.9	4.6	10.6	1.2	8.0	−6.3	33.2	−7.6	5.1
Other Sectors	78bv d						106.1	−60.0	8.5	3.5	6.7	.8	56.9	87.9	94.0	18.2
Net Errors and Omissions	78ca d						−2.5	1.0	14.5	−9.9	−26.5	−32.2	−.7	−4.6	12.7	−.8
Overall Balance	78cb d						−55.6	15.7	−44.7	24.9	7.2	−14.3	−.2	−62.1	−34.7	−14.1
Reserves and Related Items	79da d						55.6	−15.7	44.7	−24.9	−7.2	14.3	.2	62.1	34.7	14.1
Reserve Assets	79db d						55.3	−29.6	34.9	−30.7	−29.0	−19.0	−27.5	17.3	24.6	18.7
Use of Fund Credit and Loans	79dc d						—	13.7	7.1	5.1	4.0	18.6	3.6	15.7	−5.1	−10.5
Exceptional Financing	79de d						.3	.3	2.7	.7	17.8	14.7	24.1	29.2	15.2	5.9
Government Finance															*Billions of Ouguiyas:*	
Deficit (−) or Surplus	80	....	....	....	....	....	−.53	−2.32	−1.69	Ⅰ−.87	−1.46	....	....	....	....	....
Revenue	81	....	....	....	....	....	4.10	5.66	5.54	Ⅰ6.43	6.48	....	....	....	....	....
Grants Received	81z	....	....	....	....	....	3.54	6.40	3.86	Ⅰ3.34	3.18	....	....	....	....	....
Exp. & Lending Minus Repay.	82z	....	....	....	....	....	8.17	14.38	11.09	Ⅰ10.64	11.13	....	....	....	....	....
Financing																
Domestic	84a	....	....	....	....	....	−.08	.27	1.74	Ⅰ−.18	.43	....	....	....	....	....
Foreign	85a	....	....	....	....	....	.61	2.05	−.06	Ⅰ1.05	1.04	....	....	....	....	....
Debt: Foreign	89a	....	....	....	....	....	....	....	28.71	....	....	....	....			
National Accounts															*Millions of Ouguiyas*	
Exports of Goods & Services	90c	4,760	5,077	8,390	6,457	9,270	7,986	9,065	8,150	7,421	8,821	9,250	12,128	15,434	18,820	18,821
Government Consumption	91f	1,620	1,810	2,349	2,900	3,301	5,060	7,704	8,784	9,370	9,523	8,888	9,224	9,885	10,127	10,189
Gross Fixed Capital Formation	93e	2,339	2,563	4,023	4,780	6,480	7,016	10,744	9,793	4,040	5,906	7,800	9,572	10,600	11,365	14,700
Increase/Decrease(−) in Stocks	93i	220	310	362	−1,205	993	2,128	1,500	1,131	2,673	2,172	2,400	6,353	8,108	8,317	1,580
Private Consumption	96f	6,110	6,477	6,472	6,770	9,077	11,652	13,245	14,213	17,407	22,126	22,890	32,381	30,733	32,214	33,180
Imports of Goods & Services	98c	−3,840	−4,097	−8,712	−6,733	−11,204	−13,232	−18,247	−17,073	−16,003	−17,648	−19,500	−26,419	−32,091	−34,922	−33,970
Gross Domestic Product (GDP)	99b	11,209	12,140	12,884	12,919	16,660	20,595	24,105	24,998	24,908	30,853	31,728	36,125	38,838	43,014	46,068
																Millions:
Population	99z	1.25	1.28	1.31	1.35	1.38	1.42	1.46	1.50	1.54	1.51	1.55	1.59	1.63	1.68	1.72

	1985	1986	1987	1988	1989	1990	1991	1992	1993	1994	1995	1996	1997	1998	1999		
Percent Per Annum																**Interest Rates**	
	6.50	6.50	6.50	6.50	7.00	7.00	7.00	7.00	....	....	....	....	....	....	....	Discount Rate *(End of Period)*	60
	7.17	6.58	6.00	6.00	5.00	5.00	5.00	5.00	....	....	....	....	....	....	....	Deposit Rate	60l
	12.00	12.00	12.00	12.00	10.00	10.00	10.00	10.00	....	....	....	....	....	....	....	Lending Rate	60p
Period Averages																**Prices**	
	70.6	75.8	82.0	83.1	93.8	Ӿ100.0	105.6	116.3	127.2	132.5	141.2	147.8	154.6	167.0	173.8	Consumer Prices	64
Millions of Ouguiyas																**International Transactions**	
	28,887	25,956	31,608	26,655	36,332	....	....	....	....	....	....	....	....	....	....	Exports	70
	17,806	16,429	17,392	18,029	18,462	....	....	....	....	....	....	....	....	....	....	Imports, c.i.f.	71
Minus Sign Indicates Debit																Balance of Payments	
	-116.5	-194.6	-147.4	-96.0	-18.6	-9.6	-29.9	-118.3	-174.0	-69.9	22.1	91.3	47.8	77.2	....	Current Account, n.i.e.	78al d
	371.5	418.8	402.4	437.6	447.9	443.9	435.8	406.8	403.0	399.7	476.4	480.0	423.6	358.6	....	Goods: Exports f.o.b.	78aa d
	-333.9	-401.2	-359.2	-348.9	-349.3	-382.9	-399.1	-461.3	-400.4	-352.3	-292.6	-346.1	-316.5	-318.7	....	Goods: Imports f.o.b.	78ab d
	37.6	17.6	43.2	88.8	98.6	61.0	36.7	-54.5	2.6	47.4	183.8	133.9	107.2	40.0	....	*Trade Balance*	78ac d
	27.1	23.7	34.5	35.3	33.6	26.8	31.2	20.2	21.4	26.0	27.9	31.6	34.9	34.0	....	Services: Credit	78ad d
	-201.8	-211.1	-214.5	-217.0	-196.0	-136.8	-151.0	-179.1	-184.9	-181.1	-217.0	-231.3	-200.0	-152.5	....	Services: Debit	78ae d
	-137.1	-169.9	-136.8	-93.0	-63.9	-49.1	-83.1	-213.4	-160.9	-107.7	-5.3	-65.8	-57.9	-78.6	....	*Balance on Goods & Services*	78af d
	4.0	2.3	2.5	4.1	5.6	3.8	2.0	1.1	.8	1.1	1.3	.9	1.4	2.5	....	Income: Credit	78ag d
	-96.1	-118.6	-91.7	-89.7	-55.6	-50.2	-34.9	-29.9	-97.6	-47.7	-49.5	-45.9	-40.3	-34.0	....	Income: Debit	78ah d
	-229.2	-286.1	-226.0	-178.6	-113.9	-95.5	-115.9	-242.2	-257.8	-154.3	-53.5	-110.8	-96.8	-110.2	....	*Balance on Gds, Serv. & Inc.*	78ai d
	140.1	128.9	115.8	123.3	130.0	120.2	118.9	157.4	110.3	113.3	94.7	217.5	157.9	198.3	....	Current Transfers, n.i.e.: Credit	78aj d
	-27.4	-37.3	-37.2	-40.8	-34.7	-34.3	-32.8	-33.4	-26.5	-28.9	-19.2	-15.5	-13.3	-10.8	....	Current Transfers: Debit	78ak d
	....	....	....	....	....	....	....	....	....	....	....	....	....	....	....	Capital Account, n.i.e.	78bc d
	—	—	—	—	—	—	—	—	—	—	—	—	—	—	....	Capital Account, n.i.e.: Credit	78ba d
	—	—	—	—	—	—	—	—	—	—	—	—	—	—	....	Capital Account: Debit	78bb d
	91.5	171.0	117.0	48.9	16.3	-.5	26.7	77.9	-134.8	-11.4	-10.2	-86.1	-17.3	-25.9	....	Financial Account, n.i.e.	78bj d
		-1.4	-.2	-.9											....	Direct Investment Abroad	78bd d
	7.0	4.5	1.7	1.9	3.5	6.7	2.3	7.5	16.1	2.1	7.0	—	—	.1	....	Dir. Invest. in Rep. Econ., n.i.e.	78be d
	—	—	—	—	—	—	—	—	—	—	—	—	—	—	....	Portfolio Investment Assets	78bf d
	—	—	—	—	—	—	—	—	—	—	—	—	—	—	....	Equity Securities	78bk d
	—	—	—	—	—	—	—	—	—	—	—	—	—	—	....	Debt Securities	78bl d
	—	—	—	—	—	—	—	—	-.1	-.2	-.5	-.4		-.4	....	Portfolio Investment Liab., n.i.e.	78bg d
	—	—	—	—	—	—	—	—	—	—	—	—	—	—	....	Equity Securities	78bm d
	—	—	—	—	—	—	—	—	-.1	-.2	-.5	-.4		-.4	....	Debt Securities	78bn d
															....	Financial Derivatives Assets	78bw d
															....	Financial Derivatives Liabilities	78bx d
	-6.8	-7.5	8.1	2.2	-9.9	205.8	194.0	168.7	170.5	169.3	211.5	236.0	191.1	190.1	....	Other Investment Assets	78bh d
	....	....	....	....	....	....	....	....	....	....	....	....	....	....	....	Monetary Authorities	78bo d
	-.4	-3.9	-.3	-.1		—	—	—	-.8	-2.2	-.4	-.2		—	....	General Government	78bp d
	.4	6.7	-8.1	11.4	-6.5	—	—	—	—	—	—	—	—	—	....	Banks	78bq d
	-6.8	-10.3	16.5	-9.0	-3.4	205.8	194.0	168.7	171.3	171.5	211.9	236.2	191.1	190.1	....	Other Sectors	78br d
	91.2	175.4	107.5	45.7	22.7	-213.0	-169.6	-98.3	-321.3	-182.6	-228.2	-321.6	-208.4	-215.7	....	Other Investment Liab., n.i.e.	78bi d
	.6	-10.8	25.5	9.4	-.6	-1.6	2.4								....	Monetary Authorities	78bs d
	76.0	144.5	76.0	-8.9	29.0	-36.2	34.7	35.6	-137.6	-7.0	.2	-.2	5.3	.7	....	General Government	78bt d
	-2.5	-3.3	-3.9	5.0	5.8	-.6	-1.5	-.8	-18.8	—	—	—	—	—	....	Banks	78bu d
	17.1	45.0	9.9	40.1	-11.5	-174.5	-205.1	-133.1	-164.9	-175.5	-228.4	-321.4	-213.7	-216.4	....	Other Sectors	78bv d
	-5.6	-5.7	-101.5	-16.0	-3.5	-62.3	19.5	57.4	26.7	-23.5	-18.1	-1.0	-3.0	-8.1	....	Net Errors and Omissions	78ca d
	-30.6	-29.2	-131.8	-63.2	-5.9	-72.5	16.3	17.0	-282.1	-104.7	-6.2	4.2	27.6	43.2	....	*Overall Balance*	78cb d
	30.6	29.2	131.8	63.2	5.9	72.5	-16.3	-17.0	282.1	104.7	6.2	-4.2	-27.6	-43.2	....	Reserves and Related Items	79da d
	27.8	11.0	-12.8	10.6	-16.8	40.6	-3.1	-20.4	69.0	46.9	-42.9	-58.3	-58.8	-46.3	....	Reserve Assets	79db d
	-4.8	7.8	15.4	-1.9	-.7	-4.6	-13.2	3.4	5.6	17.9	12.2	10.9	12.0	-6.9	....	Use of Fund Credit and Loans	79dc d
	7.7	10.4	129.2	54.5	23.3	36.4	—	—	207.5	40.0	36.9	43.3	19.3	10.0	....	Exceptional Financing	79de d
Year Ending December 31																**Government Finance**	
	....	....	....	....	Ӿ-4.26	-4.68	-2.85	-8.86	-3.19	1.58	11.26	....	....	....	....	Deficit (-) or Surplus	80
	....	....	....	....	Ӿ20.23	20.56	20.15	29.32	29.46	33.21	44.72	....	....	....	....	Revenue	81
	....	....	....	....	Ӿ1.75	1.54	2.73	3.72	2.55	2.75	3.28	....	....	....	....	Grants Received	81z
	....	....	....	....	Ӿ26.24	26.78	25.73	41.90	35.20	34.38	36.74	....	....	....	....	Exp. & Lending Minus Repay.	82z
																Financing	
	....	....	....	....	Ӿ1.35	.86	-1.35	3.24	-1.47	-7.52	-15.81	....	....	....	....	Domestic	84a
	....	....	....	....	Ӿ2.91	3.82	4.22	5.62	4.66	5.94	4.55	....	....	....	....	Foreign	85a
	....	....	....	....	....	....	....	....	....	....	....	....	....	....	....	Debt: Foreign	89a
Millions of Ouguiyas																**National Accounts**	
	....	....	....	....	....	39,078	38,021	51,167	52,479	65,306	70,066	67,477	52,795		....	Exports of Goods & Services	90c
	....	....	....	....	....	15,473	17,545	24,814	25,883	30,072	31,111	32,456	23,525		....	Government Consumption	91f
	....	....	....	....	....	13,756	18,080	17,314	20,147	23,684	17,326	25,094	....		....	Gross Fixed Capital Formation	93e
	....	....	....	....	....	3,652	6,170	3,963	3,590	4,308	9,015	2,626	....		....	Increase/Decrease(-) in Stocks	93i
	....	....	....	....	....	67,402	76,200	87,887	87,863	79,984	99,913	111,297	113,422		....	Private Consumption	96f
	....	....	....	....	....	-49,596	-59,425	-70,601	-65,800	-66,015	-79,113	-78,332	-46,562		....	Imports of Goods & Services	98c
	53,230	62,699	69,171	72,053	81,517	84,615	89,765	96,591	114,544	124,162	137,339	148,318	160,618	....		Gross Domestic Product (GDP)	99b
Midyear Estimates																	
	1.77	1.81	1.86	1.90	1.97	2.03	2.04	2.14	2.15	2.21	2.28	2.35	2.46	2.53	2.60	**Population**	99z

(See notes in the back of the book.)

Mauritius

		1970	1971	1972	1973	1974	1975	1976	1977	1978	1979	1980	1981	1982	1983	1984
Exchange Rates															*Rupees per SDR:*	
Market Rate	aa	5.570	5.671	6.165	6.923	6.951	7.714	7.714	7.714	7.714	I 10.000	10.000	12.000	12.000	13.321	15.295
															Rupees per US Dollar:	
Market Rate	ae	5.570	5.224	5.678	5.739	5.677	I 6.589	6.639	6.350	5.921	7.586	7.835	10.329	10.861	12.723	15.603
Market Rate	rf	5.556	5.486	5.339	5.442	5.703	6.027	6.682[e]	6.607[e]	6.163[e]	6.308[e]	7.684[e]	8.937[e]	10.873[e]	11.706	13.800
Fund Position															*Millions of SDRs:*	
Quota	2f. s	22.0	22.0	22.0	22.0	22.0	22.0	22.0	22.0	27.0	27.0	40.5	40.5	40.5	53.6	53.6
SDRs	1b. s	2.6	5.0	7.3	7.3	2.8	2.6	2.7	2.3	1.6	.6	—	5.6	1.7	.1	.1
Reserve Position in the Fund	1c. s	1.8	2.5	2.5	2.5	—	5.5	5.5								
Total Fund Cred.&Loans Outstg.	2tl	—	—	—	—	—	—	—	11.0	20.3	48.4	79.9	136.9	159.4	172.8	164.2
International Liquidity												*Millions of US Dollars Unless Otherwise Indicated:*				
Total Reserves minus Gold	1l. d	46.2	51.7	70.1	66.8	131.1	166.0	89.5	66.3	45.8	29.2	90.7	35.1	38.0	17.9	23.6
SDRs	1b. d	2.6	5.4	7.9	8.8	3.4	3.0	3.1	2.8	2.1	.8	—	6.5	1.9	.1	.1
Reserve Position in the Fund	1c. d	1.8	2.7	2.7	3.0	—	6.4	6.4								
Foreign Exchange	1d. d	41.7	43.6	59.5	55.0	127.7	156.5	80.0	63.5	43.7	28.4	90.7	28.6	36.1	17.8	23.5
Gold (Million Fine Troy Ounces)	1ad	....	....	....	....	....	....	....	.009	.033	.038	.038	.038	.038	.038	.038
Gold (National Valuation)	1and	....	....	....	....	....	....	....	1.6	5.8	4.8	4.7	4.3	4.1	3.5	2.8
Government Assets	3ba d	2.7	1.4[e]	.7	.8	.3	1.4	.5	.7	1.1	1.6	.9	.1	.1		
Deposit Money Banks: Assets	7a. d	6.3	3.5	3.3	4.4	6.3	8.2	5.3	6.9	8.3	8.4	13.3	12.5	13.5	15.3	18.1
Liabilities	7b. d	1.9	2.8	1.5	2.0	1.7	1.8	1.4	15.8	15.4	16.1	19.7	16.4	2.6	6.3	8.4
Monetary Authorities															*Millions of Rupees:*	
Foreign Assets	11	256.6	264.8	393.4	383.4	743.6	1,093.5	594.2	431.1	305.5	257.9	747.0	406.1	456.3	271.5	411.9
Claims on Central Government	12a	5.2	2.9	33.4	13.7	17.6	−26.0	338.7	823.0	1,111.8	1,541.5	1,577.3	2,943.5	3,311.1	4,059.6	4,496.4
Claims on Deposit Money Banks	12e	1.4	31.7	31.6	66.4	10.9	3.0	42.9	34.8	42.0	80.0	55.0	64.5	20.1	15.0	54.2
Reserve Money	14	144.8	145.6	217.3	258.3	475.5	653.1	774.1	917.5	1,077.8	1,041.6	1,155.0	1,203.1	1,334.5	1,417.8	1,512.5
of which: Currency Outside DMBs	14a	104.7	126.3	156.3	200.7	314.2	438.1	587.9	693.6	824.1	724.8	735.0	791.3	875.2	922.4	958.2
Money Market Instruments	16aa	—	—	—	—	—	—	—	—	—	—	—	—	—	—	—
Foreign Liabilities	16c								84.9	156.5	498.9	798.0	1,645.5	1,909.1	2,454.8	2,621.0
Central Government Deposits	16d	29.2	34.1	132.2	73.3	86.4	118.7	.5	.6	1.9	3.1	3.4	1.7	1.0	2.3	.6
Capital Accounts	17a	24.4	42.5	57.5	70.7	75.9	84.9	89.8	89.9	89.9	134.7	162.8	222.2	221.6	242.7	273.7
Other Items (Net)	17r	64.8	77.3	51.4	61.2	134.3	213.9	111.3	196.1	133.2	201.0	260.1	341.6	321.4	228.6	554.7
Deposit Money Banks															*Millions of Rupees:*	
Reserves	20	39.1	18.4	42.9	56.7	160.6	190.1	182.0	213.0	243.2	294.4	388.0	400.9	454.9	458.3	536.2
Foreign Assets	21	34.8	18.0	17.1	25.3	35.8	54.3	34.9	43.9	49.4	63.6	104.4	129.6	146.9	194.8	282.6
Claims on Central Government	22a	50.1	78.5	127.6	145.4	479.4	518.7	247.0	338.6	502.7	637.0	989.9	717.8	1,161.2	1,225.1	1,412.0
Claims on Private Sector	22d	209.9	311.1	356.5	545.4	594.3	746.6	1,157.2	1,352.2	1,508.1	1,721.6	1,881.1	2,259.1	2,460.9	2,796.9	3,407.3
Claims on Other Banking Insts	22f															
Demand Deposits	24	123.8	134.4	201.9	265.0	468.8	530.2	506.5	525.3	615.5	683.8	953.3	731.2	861.5	844.3	1,074.0
Time, Savings,& Fgn.Currency Dep.	25	171.1	203.2	259.3	375.9	755.5	892.8	964.5	1,124.9	1,410.0	1,687.4	2,116.9	2,458.8	3,185.4	3,622.3	4,145.0
Foreign Liabilities	26c	10.6	14.3	7.9	11.5	9.7	11.8	9.1	100.4	91.3	122.1	154.3	169.9	28.5	79.6	130.4
Central Government Deposits	26d	2.5	3.7	2.4	6.1	9.7	10.1	4.5	5.2	4.5	3.1	9.6	16.5	34.9	28.0	45.2
Credit from Monetary Authorities	26g	1.4	31.7	31.6	66.4	10.9	3.0	25.6	33.2	35.4	71.5	45.3	56.8	10.0	9.3	34.5
Capital Accounts	27a	17.8	30.7	31.9	40.0	45.1	53.1	71.4	111.8	154.7	166.8	198.4	217.0	235.3	289.9	307.4
Other Items (Net)	27r	6.7	8.0	9.1	7.9	−29.6	8.7	39.5	46.9	−8.0	−18.1	−114.4	−142.8	−131.7	−198.3	−98.4
Monetary Survey															*Millions of Rupees:*	
Foreign Assets (Net)	31n	280.8	268.5	402.6	397.2	769.7	1,136.0	620.0	289.7	107.1	−299.5	−100.9	−1,279.6	−1,334.4	−2,068.0	−2,056.9
Domestic Credit	32	233.5	354.7	382.9	625.1	995.2	1,110.5	1,737.9	2,508.0	3,116.2	3,893.9	4,435.3	5,902.2	6,897.3	8,051.3	9,269.9
Claims on Central Govt. (Net)	32an	23.6	43.6	26.4	79.7	400.9	363.9	580.7	1,155.8	1,608.1	2,172.3	2,554.2	3,643.1	4,436.4	5,254.4	5,862.6
Claims on Private Sector	32d	209.9	311.1	356.5	545.4	594.3	746.6	1,157.2	1,352.2	1,508.1	1,721.6	1,881.1	2,259.1	2,460.9	2,796.9	3,407.3
Claims on Other Banking Insts	32f															
Money	34	229.6	261.6	376.3	466.6	783.7	993.2	1,098.6	1,219.2	1,449.2	1,426.2	1,720.3	1,533.4	1,741.1	1,803.8	2,050.3
Quasi-Money	35	231.6	273.8	301.2	413.9	802.0	953.4	985.3	1,132.4	1,412.3	1,687.4	2,116.9	2,458.8	3,185.4	3,622.3	4,145.0
Money Market Instruments	36aa															
Capital Accounts	37a	42.2	73.2	89.4	110.7	121.0	138.0	161.2	201.7	244.6	301.5	361.2	439.2	456.9	532.6	581.1
Other Items (Net)	37r	10.9	14.7	18.6	31.1	58.2	162.0	112.7	244.5	117.2	179.2	136.0	191.1	179.6	24.6	436.6
Money plus Quasi-Money	35l	461.2	535.4	677.5	880.5	1,585.7	1,946.6	2,083.9	2,351.6	2,861.5	3,113.6	3,837.2	3,992.2	4,926.5	5,426.1	6,195.3
Other Banking Institutions															*Millions of Rupees:*	
Deposits	45	27.7	30.4	35.3	40.8	48.6	62.1	78.9	93.6	106.9	104.7	101.5	101.0	121.4	129.8	146.5
Liquid Liabilities	55l	488.9	565.8	712.8	921.3	1,634.3	2,008.7	2,162.8	2,445.2	2,968.4	3,218.3	3,938.7	4,093.2	5,047.9	5,555.9	6,341.8
Interest Rates															*Percent Per Annum*	
Discount Rate *(End of Period)*	60	6.00	6.00	6.00	6.00	6.00	6.00	6.00	7.00	9.00	10.50	10.50	12.00	12.00	11.00	11.00
Money Market Rate	60b	....	....	....	....	....	....	....	....	7.90	9.98	9.90	9.90	9.90	10.82	11.00
Deposit Rate	60l	....	....	....	....	....	....	....	....	....	....	....	9.25	11.15	12.06	10.29
Lending Rate	60p	....	....	....	....	....	....	....	....	....	....	....	12.19	13.38	15.08	13.25
Prices and Labor															*Index Numbers (1995=100):*	
Share Prices	62	....	....	....	....	....	....	....	....	....	....	....	....	....	....	....
Consumer Prices	64	8.3	8.4	8.8	10.0	12.9	I 14.8	16.8	18.3	19.9	22.7	32.3	I 36.9	41.2	43.5	46.7
Labor Force	67d	....	....	....	....	....	....	....	....	....	....	....	....	....	*Number in Thousands:*	....
Employment	67e	....	....	....	....	....	....	....	....	....	....	....	....	....	....	....
Unemployment	67c	....	....	....	....	....	....	....	....	....	....	....	....	....	....	....
International Transactions															*Millions of Rupees:*	
Exports	70	383	361	574	748	1,788	1,839	1,770	2,042	1,987	2,433	3,341	2,999	3,989	4,311	5,180
Imports, c.i.f.	71	420	462	636	916	1,760	1,995	2,409	2,951	3,076	3,634	4,721	4,977	5,048	5,175	6,494
Imports, f.o.b.	71.v	360	392	536	787	1,533	1,688	2,046	2,459	2,572	3,004	3,902	4,260	4,319	4,473	5,662
															1995=100	
Unit Value of Exports	74	4.7	5.1	I 6.0	7.1	17.6	23.1	19.0	18.6	18.2	20.6	I 28.4	30.7	34.0	36.4	40.4
Unit Value of Imports	75	6.3	6.9	I 7.3	9.5	15.5	17.6	19.7	21.4	22.8	27.3	I 39.9	42.6	52.8	51.7	58.1

1985	1986	1987	1988	1989	1990	1991	1992	1993	1994	1995	1996	1997	1998	1999		
End of Period															**Exchange Rates**	
15.718	16.069	17.272	18.616	19.707	20.375	21.162	23.372	25.625	26.077	26.258	25.842	30.041	34.896	34.955	Market Rate	aa
End of Period (ae) Period Average (rf)																
14.310	13.137	12.175	13.834	14.996	14.322	14.794	16.998	18.656	17.863	17.664	17.972	22.265	24.784	25.468	Market Rate	ae
15.442	13.466	12.878	13.438	15.250	14.863	15.652	15.563	17.648	17.960	17.386	17.948	21.057	23.993	25.186	Market Rate	rf
End of Period															**Fund Position**	
53.6	53.6	53.6	53.6	53.6	53.6	53.6	73.3	73.3	73.3	73.3	73.3	73.3	73.3	101.6	Quota	2f.s
—	.5	4.1	3.7	5.0	10.3	18.0	17.6	21.0	21.3	21.7	22.2	22.5	22.8	16.1	SDRs	1b.s
—	—	—	—	—	.1	1.3	6.2	7.3	7.3	7.3	7.4	7.4	7.4	14.5	Reserve Position in the Fund	1c.s
150.1	132.1	106.9	76.5	47.6	15.5	—	—	—	—	—	—	—	—	—	Total Fund Cred.&Loans Outstg.	2tl
End of Period															**International Liquidity**	
29.9	136.0	343.5	442.0	517.8	737.6	893.2	820.1	757.0	747.6	863.3	896.1	693.3	559.0	731.0	Total Reserves minus Gold	1l.d
—	.6	5.9	5.0	6.6	14.6	25.7	24.3	28.9	31.2	32.2	31.9	30.3	32.2	22.1	SDRs	1b.d
—	—	.1	.1	.1	.1	1.8	8.6	10.1	10.7	10.9	10.6	9.9	10.4	19.9	Reserve Position in the Fund	1c.d
29.9	135.4	337.5	437.0	511.2	722.9	865.8	787.3	718.1	705.7	820.2	853.7	653.0	516.5	689.1	Foreign Exchange	1d.d
.038	.038	.038	.052	.061	.061	.061	.061	.062	.062	.062	.062	.062	.062	.062	Gold (Million Fine Troy Ounces)	1ad
3.1	3.3	3.6	4.4	4.8	5.0	4.9	4.2	3.9	4.0	4.1	4.0	6.1	11.9	12.3	Gold (National Valuation)	1and
—	.1	.3	.3	—	—	.1	.1	.1	.1	....	....	....	....	....	Government Assets	3bad
41.1	49.2	80.0	89.0	101.7	121.9	135.8	124.2	160.4	178.3	264.2	263.6	327.4	361.0	383.8	Deposit Money Banks: Assets	7a.d
6.0	2.7	5.4	8.3	9.0	12.8	9.9	3.3	28.2	39.8	67.5	59.5	38.4	127.9	104.3	Liabilities	7b.d
End of Period															**Monetary Authorities**	
472.5	1,830.9	4,225.8	6,174.7	7,837.0	10,635.6	13,286.3	14,011.5	14,194.9	13,425.7	15,322.0	16,176.8	15,571.8	14,150.3	18,930.9	Foreign Assets	11
3,868.6	2,732.0	1,085.6	272.5	289.5	301.8	3,108.2	1,351.4	1,021.4	1,741.8	654.6	914.4	1,662.4	4,994.8	2,223.4	Claims on Central Government	12a
48.1	31.9	76.5	120.5	173.5	172.2	301.8	411.2	523.5	291.0	672.8	446.2	410.8	707.8	375.1	Claims on Deposit Money Banks	12e
1,787.1	2,152.6	2,729.0	3,387.4	4,054.3	4,816.3	11,260.0	10,207.5	9,510.3	8,837.1	10,119.2	11,360.4	9,113.6	9,759.6	10,522.3	Reserve Money	14
1,095.7	1,304.9	1,663.4	2,008.7	2,403.6	2,848.7	3,407.5	3,820.1	4,230.9	4,412.2	4,847.2	5,050.7	5,410.4	5,832.9	6,126.7	*of which: Currency Outside DMBs*	14a
—	—	—	—	—	—	1,057.0	448.6	61.3	—	159.0	717.7	240.0	—	—	Money Market Instruments	16aa
2,488.7	2,161.7	1,890.3	1,427.5	944.6	322.7	76.0	74.7	11.1	33.2	12.1	19.9	20.7	14.8	5.7	Foreign Liabilities	16c
2.2	6.0	3.0	571.1	1,553.8	2,886.9	21.3	17.5	12.0	6.2	452.7	251.2	3.1	13.6	3.4	Central Government Deposits	16d
280.4	285.9	304.9	326.0	343.2	353.7	366.1	400.9	436.3	443.4	446.3	439.8	505.8	582.3	583.2	Capital Accounts	17a
–169.2	–11.5	460.7	855.7	1,404.1	2,730.0	3,916.0	4,624.9	5,708.8	6,138.6	5,460.1	4,748.5	7,761.8	9,482.6	10,414.7	Other Items (Net)	17r
End of Period															**Deposit Money Banks**	
648.5	839.9	1,056.9	1,366.4	1,639.5	1,954.8	7,846.3	6,381.7	5,275.5	4,416.4	5,231.8	6,304.6	3,697.1	3,899.8	4,365.3	Reserves	20
588.1	645.9	974.0	1,230.9	1,525.1	1,745.8	2,008.3	2,110.8	2,991.6	3,185.7	4,667.7	4,736.9	7,289.0	8,947.3	9,775.5	Foreign Assets	21
1,616.7	2,795.0	3,611.5	5,149.5	5,858.5	7,361.6	3,956.7	6,451.2	8,329.5	10,344.5	14,623.7	14,219.6	17,025.7	13,318.5	15,759.0	Claims on Central Government	22a
4,615.5	5,441.8	7,033.0	8,940.3	10,850.7	13,043.4	15,234.2	18,684.9	23,923.9	28,714.4	32,878.6	34,467.6	43,360.3	56,653.0	62,520.7	Claims on Private Sector	22d
—	—	—	—	—	78.4	147.3	304.9	238.0	146.5	132.3	163.1	160.5	424.6	1,766.2	Claims on Other Banking Insts	22f
900.2	1,119.5	1,631.6	1,799.2	2,096.1	2,716.3	3,262.8	3,383.4	3,188.3	4,443.3	4,685.4	4,774.0	5,194.5	5,730.2	5,844.8	Demand Deposits	24
6,109.1	8,084.6	10,350.5	13,748.4	15,764.8	18,990.0	23,278.1	27,501.1	33,198.5	36,754.5	44,574.4	48,406.8	57,201.3	63,819.9	74,851.6	Time, Savings,& Fgn.Currency Dep.	25
85.3	35.1	65.5	114.4	135.6	183.9	147.1	56.7	525.7	710.7	1,192.9	1,068.8	855.5	3,169.0	2,655.5	Foreign Liabilities	26c
16.7	15.4	107.5	170.8	166.1	189.4	200.5	224.8	277.9	84.2	1,468.0	319.6	277.0	132.0	264.4	Central Government Deposits	26d
25.0	15.0	66.4	116.2	108.6	87.7	157.0	267.5	329.0	156.2	550.0	—	250.0	475.0	250.0	Credit from Monetary Authorities	26g
411.9	469.0	658.7	885.0	1,576.9	1,859.1	2,356.6	3,439.0	4,758.6	5,144.4	5,447.8	6,620.4	7,842.4	9,092.1	10,848.6	Capital Accounts	27a
–79.4	–16.0	–204.8	–146.9	25.7	157.6	–209.3	–939.0	–1,519.5	–485.8	–384.4	–1,297.8	–88.1	825.0	–528.2	Other Items (Net)	27r
End of Period															**Monetary Survey**	
–1,513.4	280.0	3,244.0	5,863.7	8,282.0	11,874.7	15,071.5	15,990.9	16,649.7	15,867.5	18,784.7	19,825.0	21,984.6	19,913.8	26,045.2	Foreign Assets (Net)	31n
10,081.9	10,947.4	11,619.6	13,620.4	15,278.8	17,708.9	22,224.6	26,550.1	33,222.9	40,856.8	46,368.5	49,193.9	61,928.8	75,245.3	82,001.5	Domestic Credit	32
5,466.4	5,505.6	4,586.6	4,680.1	4,428.1	4,587.1	6,843.1	7,560.3	9,061.0	11,995.9	13,357.6	14,563.2	18,408.0	18,167.7	17,714.6	Claims on Central Govt. (Net)	32an
4,615.5	5,441.8	7,033.0	8,940.3	10,850.7	13,043.4	15,234.2	18,684.9	23,923.9	28,714.4	32,878.6	34,467.6	43,360.3	56,653.0	62,520.7	Claims on Private Sector	32d
—	—	—	—	—	78.4	147.3	304.9	238.0	146.5	132.3	163.1	160.5	424.6	1,766.2	Claims on Other Banking Insts	32f
2,038.8	2,432.2	3,303.7	3,820.2	4,510.9	5,577.8	6,676.5	7,209.2	7,423.2	8,864.0	9,572.8	9,829.8	10,611.0	11,590.0	12,001.8	Money	34
6,109.1	8,084.6	10,350.5	13,748.4	15,764.8	18,990.0	23,278.1	27,501.1	33,198.5	36,754.5	44,574.4	48,406.8	57,201.3	63,819.9	74,851.6	Quasi-Money	35
—	—	—	—	—	—	1,057.0	448.6	61.3	—	159.0	717.7	240.0	—	—	Money Market Instruments	36aa
692.3	754.9	963.6	1,211.0	1,920.1	2,212.8	2,722.7	3,839.9	5,194.9	5,587.8	5,894.1	7,060.2	8,348.2	9,674.4	11,431.8	Capital Accounts	37a
–271.7	–44.4	245.8	704.5	1,364.9	2,803.1	3,561.9	3,542.2	3,994.7	5,518.0	4,952.9	3,004.5	7,512.9	10,074.8	9,761.4	Other Items (Net)	37r
8,147.9	10,516.8	13,654.2	17,568.6	20,275.7	24,567.8	29,954.6	34,710.3	40,621.7	45,618.5	54,147.2	58,236.6	67,812.3	75,409.9	86,853.4	Money plus Quasi-Money	35l
End of Period															**Other Banking Institutions**	
167.4	188.8	196.9	228.4	266.2	295.5	311.7	346.3	373.8	397.0	420.4	448.2	494.8	557.3	611.0	Deposits	45
8,315.3	10,705.6	13,851.1	17,797.0	20,541.9	24,863.3	30,266.3	35,056.6	40,995.5	46,015.5	54,567.6	58,684.8	68,307.1	75,967.2	87,464.4	Liquid Liabilities	55l
Percent Per Annum															**Interest Rates**	
11.00	11.00	10.00	10.00	12.00	12.00	11.30	8.30	8.30	13.80	11.40	11.82	10.46	17.19	....	Discount Rate *(End of Period)*	60
11.17	11.05	10.29	10.71	11.98	13.26	12.24	9.05	7.73	10.23	10.35	9.96	9.43	8.99	10.01	Money Market Rate	60b
9.46	9.50	9.38	10.00	11.06	12.56	12.31	10.07	8.40	11.04	12.23	10.77	9.08	9.28	10.92	Deposit Rate	60l
13.83	14.33	14.13	14.96	16.13	18.00	17.75	17.13	16.58	18.92	20.81	20.81	18.92	19.92	21.63	Lending Rate	60p
Period Averages															**Prices and Labor**	
....	....	....	....	30.7	40.1	40.9	43.0	68.2	103.9	100.0	88.1	100.0	119.3	109.7	Share Prices	62
I 49.8	50.6	50.9	55.5	62.6	71.0	I 76.0	79.5	87.9	94.3	100.0	106.6	I 113.8	121.6	130.0	Consumer Prices	64
Period Averages																
....	....	....	....	....	....	....	474	485	499	481	....	....	....	....	Labor Force	67d
204	223	245	268	271	I 281	285	292	290	292	290	....	....	....	....	Employment	67e
65	55	47	28	18	13	11	8	7	7	8	10	11	11	....	Unemployment	67c
Millions of Rupees															**International Transactions**	
6,729	9,062	11,336	13,455	15,049	17,677	18,700	20,244	22,992	24,097	26,756	32,312	33,694	39,634	....	Exports	70
8,119	9,199	13,037	17,242	20,217	24,019	24,383	25,280	30,319	34,548	34,363	41,082	46,093	49,811	....	Imports, c.i.f.	71
6,988	8,294	11,701	15,628	18,295	21,921	22,212	22,931	27,507	31,601	31,508	38,073	42,570	46,015	....	Imports, f.o.b.	71.v
1995=100																
46.2	48.9	54.7	I 58.1	69.3	72.6	77.3	I 82.6	90.1	94.2	100.0	111.2	114.9	130.0	....	Unit Value of Exports	74
63.9	51.8	53.6	I 58.5	69.6	74.2	77.8	I 79.4	88.1	94.4	100.0	106.9	109.5	110.1	....	Unit Value of Imports	75

Mauritius

		1970	1971	1972	1973	1974	1975	1976	1977	1978	1979	1980	1981	1982	1983	1984
Balance of Payments																*Millions of US Dollars:*
Current Account, n.i.e.	78al *d*	....	....	....	....	....	....	−35.2	−77.9	−117.1	−145.7	−117.1	−147.7	−42.0	−20.2	−52.1
Goods: Exports f.o.b.	78aa *d*	....	....	....	....	....	....	264.6	307.2	319.6	384.7	433.6	334.2	366.5	371.3	376.9
Goods: Imports f.o.b.	78ab *d*	....	....	....	....	....	....	−307.4	−367.8	−418.4	−484.3	−515.9	−475.9	−396.7	−385.8	−415.0
Trade Balance	78ac *d*	....	....	....	....	....	....	−42.8	−60.5	−98.8	−99.6	−82.2	−141.7	−30.2	−14.5	−38.1
Services: Credit	78ad *d*	....	....	....	....	....	....	61.2	92.8	117.8	130.1	139.9	172.5	140.7	137.3	129.6
Services: Debit	78ae *d*	....	....	....	....	....	....	−66.6	−120.6	−143.8	−173.0	−174.0	−149.9	−140.9	−126.7	−126.3
Balance on Goods & Services	78af *d*	....	....	....	....	....	....	−48.2	−88.4	−124.8	−142.4	−116.3	−119.1	−30.4	−3.9	−34.9
Income: Credit	78ag *d*	....	....	....	....	....	....	14.7	5.0	5.7	3.8	5.1	7.0	4.0	2.5	2.9
Income: Debit	78ah *d*	....	....	....	....	....	....	−8.8	−7.9	−13.5	−20.6	−28.2	−52.6	−49.8	−43.9	−48.3
Balance on Gds, Serv. & Inc.	78ai *d*	....	....	....	....	....	....	−42.4	−91.3	−132.6	−159.2	−139.5	−164.6	−76.2	−45.4	−80.2
Current Transfers, n.i.e.: Credit	78aj *d*	....	....	....	....	....	....	10.0	16.5	18.7	19.8	28.8	22.7	38.1	30.9	32.8
Current Transfers: Debit	78ak *d*	....	....	....	....	....	....	−2.8	−3.2	−3.2	−6.3	−6.4	−5.8	−4.0	−5.7	−4.6
Capital Account, n.i.e.	78bc *d*	....	....	....	....	....	....	−.9	−.9	−1.6	−1.1	−1.6	−1.3	−.9	−1.1	−.8
Capital Account, n.i.e.: Credit	78ba *d*	....	....	....	....	....	....	—	—	—	—	—	—	—	—	—
Capital Account: Debit	78bb *d*	....	....	....	....	....	....	−.9	−.9	−1.6	−1.1	−1.6	−1.3	−.9	−1.1	−.8
Financial Account, n.i.e.	78bj *d*	....	....	....	....	....	....	−44.8	29.8	37.3	48.5	66.4	9.3	−10.9	−20.0	−12.2
Direct Investment Abroad	78bd *d*	....	....	....	....	....	....	.4	.8	.2	2.5	—	—	—	—	—
Dir. Invest. in Rep. Econ., n.i.e.	78be *d*	....	....	....	....	....	....	3.1	2.3	4.4	1.7	1.2	.7	1.7	1.6	4.9
Portfolio Investment Assets	78bf *d*	....	....	....	....	....	....	—	—	—	—	—	—	—	—	—
Equity Securities	78bk *d*	....	....	....	....	....	....	—	—	—	—	—	—	—	—	—
Debt Securities	78bl *d*	....	....	....	....	....	....	—	—	—	—	—	—	—	—	—
Portfolio Investment Liab., n.i.e.	78bg *d*	....	....	....	....	....	....	—	—	—	—	—	—	—	—	—
Equity Securities	78bm *d*	....	....	....	....	....	....	—	—	—	—	—	—	—	—	—
Debt Securities	78bn *d*	....	....	....	....	....	....	—	—	—	—	—	—	—	—	—
Financial Derivatives Assets	78bw *d*	....	....	....	....	....	....	....	....	....	....	....	....	....	....	....
Financial Derivatives Liabilities	78bx *d*	....	....	....	....	....	....	....	....	....	....	....	....	....	....	....
Other Investment Assets	78bh *d*	....	....	....	....	....	....	−29.9	−5.0	11.7	3.6	25.0	−17.7	−8.0	−13.1	−6.7
Monetary Authorities	78bo *d*	....	....	....	....	....	....	....	....	....	....	....	....	....	....	....
General Government	78bp *d*	....	....	....	....	....	....	....	....	....	....	....	....	....	....	....
Banks	78bq *d*	....	....	....	....	....	....	3.0	−1.4	−1.0	−2.2	−5.3	−2.8	−1.6	−4.1	−6.4
Other Sectors	78br *d*	....	....	....	....	....	....	−32.9	−3.6	12.7	5.9	30.3	−14.9	−6.4	−9.0	−.4
Other Investment Liab., n.i.e.	78bi *d*	....	....	....	....	....	....	−18.4	31.8	21.1	40.6	40.2	26.3	−4.6	−8.5	−10.4
Monetary Authorities	78bs *d*	....	....	....	....	....	....	—	—	—	−7.1	−2.0	—	—	13.1	−3.1
General Government	78bt *d*	....	....	....	....	....	....	3.3	6.8	16.9	25.0	18.1	31.4	7.8	−20.5	−21.4
Banks	78bu *d*	....	....	....	....	....	....	−.3	13.3	−3.7	4.8	4.2	1.7	−13.1	4.4	3.7
Other Sectors	78bv *d*	....	....	....	....	....	....	−21.4	11.7	8.0	17.9	19.9	−6.8	.6	−5.5	10.5
Net Errors and Omissions	78ca *d*	....	....	....	....	....	....	5.1	11.0	11.8	3.6	24.4	10.0	−6.3	9.9	21.5
Overall Balance	78cb *d*	....	....	....	....	....	....	−75.8	−38.0	−69.7	−94.6	−27.9	−129.7	−60.1	−31.4	−43.6
Reserves and Related Items	79da *d*	....	....	....	....	....	....	75.8	38.0	69.7	94.6	27.9	129.7	60.1	31.4	43.6
Reserve Assets	79db *d*	....	....	....	....	....	....	75.8	25.1	19.9	10.3	−59.6	43.0	−4.3	15.9	−10.2
Use of Fund Credit and Loans	79dc *d*	....	....	....	....	....	....	—	12.9	11.5	36.7	41.4	68.5	24.6	14.5	−8.4
Exceptional Financing	79de *d*	....	....	....	....	....	....	—	—	38.3	47.6	46.1	18.2	39.8	1.0	62.2
International Investment Position																*Millions of US Dollars*
Assets	79aa *d*	....	....	....	....	....	....	....	....	....	....	....	57.8	67.6	55.1	59.9
Direct Investment Abroad	79ab *d*	....	....	....	....	....	....	....	....	....	....	—	—	—	—	—
Portfolio Investment	79ac *d*	....	....	....	....	....	....	....	....	....	....	—	—	—	—	—
Equity Securities	79ad *d*	....	....	....	....	....	....	....	....	....	....	....	....	....	....	....
Debt Securities	79ae *d*	....	....	....	....	....	....	....	....	....	....	....	....	....	....	....
Financial Derivatives	79al *d*	....	....	....	....	....	....	....	....	....	....	—				
Other Investment	79af *d*	....	....	....	....	....	....	....	....	....	....	....	17.9	25.0	33.4	33.2
Monetary Authorities	79ag *d*	....	....	....	....	....	....	....	....	....	....	—	—	—	—	—
General Government	79ah *d*	....	....	....	....	....	....	....	....	....	....					
Banks	79ai *d*	....	....	....	....	....	....	....	....	....	....		12.6	13.5	15.3	18.1
Other Sectors	79aj *d*	....	....	....	....	....	....	....	....	....	....		5.3	11.5	18.1	15.1
Reserve Assets	79ak *d*	....	....	....	....	....	....	....	....	....	....	96.9	39.9	42.6	21.7	26.7
Liabilities	79la *d*	....	....	....	....	....	....	....	....	....	....	420.3	535.8	577.7	551.2	556.9
Dir. Invest. in Rep. Economy	79lb *d*	....	....	....	....	....	....	....	....	....	....	—	—	—	—	—
Portfolio Investment	79lc *d*	....	....	....	....	....	....	....	....	....	....	—	—	—	—	—
Equity Securities	79ld *d*	....	....	....	....	....	....	....	....	....	....	....	....	....	....	....
Debt Securities	79le *d*	....	....	....	....	....	....	....	....	....	....	....	....	....	....	....
Financial Derivatives	79ll *d*	....	....	....	....	....	....	....	....	....	....	—				
Other Investment	79lf *d*	....	....	....	....	....	....	....	....	....	....	420.3	535.8	577.7	551.2	556.9
Monetary Authorities	79lg *d*	....	....	....	....	....	....	....	....	....	....		159.3	175.8	193.0	168.0
General Government	79lh *d*	....	....	....	....	....	....	....	....	....	....		286.8	330.0	292.5	316.1
Banks	79li *d*	....	....	....	....	....	....	....	....	....	....		16.5	2.7	6.3	8.3
Other Sectors	79lj *d*	....	....	....	....	....	....	....	....	....	....		73.3	69.2	59.5	64.5

Balance of Payments

Minus Sign Indicates Debit

1985	1986	1987	1988	1989	1990	1991	1992	1993	1994	1995	1996	1997	1998	1999	
-30.4	93.6	64.8	-56.4	-103.5	-119.3	-16.6	-.1	-92.0	-232.1	-21.9	34.0	-88.9	3.3	-52.3	Current Account, n.i.e. .... 78al d
453.5	698.5	925.8	1,030.2	1,025.3	1,238.1	1,253.4	1,334.7	1,334.4	1,376.9	1,571.7	1,810.6	1,600.1	1,669.3	1,589.3	Goods: Exports f.o.b. .... 78aa d
-465.3	-622.1	-925.4	-1,177.8	-1,217.7	-1,494.8	-1,438.5	-1,493.9	-1,576.0	-1,773.9	-1,812.2	-2,136.3	-2,036.1	-1,933.3	-2,136.5	Goods: Imports f.o.b. .... 78ab d
-11.8	76.4	.4	-147.6	-192.4	-256.7	-185.1	-159.2	-241.6	-397.0	-240.5	-325.7	-436.0	-264.0	-547.2	*Trade Balance* .... 78ac d
121.2	185.5	285.3	348.8	372.7	483.9	528.3	577.5	566.2	632.7	777.7	960.8	893.7	916.9	1,070.3	Services: Credit .... 78ad d
-130.5	-164.6	-247.0	-307.1	-340.3	-421.0	-448.4	-522.8	-521.7	-546.4	-641.3	-672.9	-656.3	-718.0	-660.7	Services: Debit .... 78ae d
-21.0	97.4	38.7	-105.9	-160.0	-193.8	-105.2	-104.5	-197.1	-310.6	-104.2	-37.9	-198.6	-65.1	-137.7	*Balance on Goods & Services* ... 78af d
1.9	5.6	14.0	26.6	51.1	55.9	82.5	91.0	70.0	31.7	52.2	31.1	47.0	47.8	34.9	Income: Credit .... 78ag d
-47.3	-59.8	-55.4	-70.7	-70.9	-78.7	-76.9	-80.1	-66.5	-56.4	-71.3	-75.1	-64.6	-74.4	-53.4	Income: Debit .... 78ah d
-66.4	43.2	-2.7	-150.0	-179.8	-216.6	-99.5	-93.6	-193.6	-335.3	-123.3	-81.8	-216.3	-91.7	-156.2	*Balance on Gds, Serv. & Inc.* ... 78ai d
40.1	55.5	74.9	103.3	84.9	108.5	98.6	109.9	115.9	129.6	146.8	182.8	206.4	186.8	196.6	Current Transfers, n.i.e.: Credit .... 78aj d
-4.1	-5.2	-7.4	-9.7	-8.7	-11.2	-15.7	-16.4	-14.4	-26.3	-45.4	-67.0	-79.0	-91.8	-92.7	Current Transfers: Debit ..... 78ak d
-.8	-1.1	-1.8	-1.1	-.9	-.6	-1.6	-1.4	-1.5	-1.3	-1.1	-.8	-.5	-.8	-.5	Capital Account, n.i.e. .... 78bc d
—	—	—	—	—	—	—	—	—	—	—	—	—	—	—	Capital Account, n.i.e.: Credit .... 78ba d
-.8	-1.1	-1.8	-1.1	-.9	-.6	-1.6	-1.4	-1.5	-1.3	-1.1	-.8	-.5	-.8	-.5	Capital Account: Debit .... 78bb d
-23.7	-3.6	59.3	121.2	50.2	138.6	40.2	-14.8	19.3	41.4	25.1	91.9	-18.6	-26.0	60.9	Financial Account, n.i.e. .... 78bj d
—	—	—	-.1	-.6	-.6	-10.9	-43.3	-33.2	-1.1	-3.6	-2.7	-3.2	-13.7	-6.4	Direct Investment Abroad .... 78bd d
8.0	7.4	17.2	23.7	35.8	41.0	17.4	14.7	14.7	20.0	18.7	36.7	55.3	12.2	49.4	Dir. Invest. in Rep. Econ., n.i.e. .... 78be d
—	—	—	—	—	-2.2	-.4	—	—	-2.2	-.3	-2.0	-96.8	43.6	38.4	Portfolio Investment Assets .... 78bf d
—	—	—	—	—	—	—	—	—	—	—	—	—	-3.3	38.4	Equity Securities .... 78bk d
—	—	—	—	—	-2.2	-.4	—	—	-2.2	-.3	-2.0	-96.8	46.9	—	Debt Securities .... 78bl d
—	—	—	—	—	—	—	—	—	2.1	175.9	36.8	30.6	-28.7	-15.3	Portfolio Investment Liab., n.i.e. . 78bg d
—	—	—	—	—	—	—	—	—	2.1	22.0	36.8	30.6	5.0	-15.3	Equity Securities .... 78bm d
—	—	—	—	—	—	—	—	—	—	154.0	—	—	-33.7	—	Debt Securities .... 78bn d
....	....	....	....	....	....	....	....	....	....	....	....	....	....	....	Financial Derivatives Assets .... 78bw d
....	....	....	....	....	....	....	....	....	....	....	....	....	....	....	Financial Derivatives Liabilities .... 78bx d
-24.1	-14.7	-23.6	-33.7	-49.4	-7.1	-36.2	14.3	-26.7	-64.6	-136.4	17.9	-115.7	-66.7	-9.9	Other Investment Assets .... 78bh d
....	....	....	....	....	....	....	....	....	....	....	....	....	....	....	Monetary Authorities .... 78bo d
—	—	—	—	-2.2	—	—	—	—	—	—	—	—	—	—	General Government .... 78bp d
-19.8	-4.3	-25.5	-19.1	-19.3	-14.9	-16.8	33.0	-49.0	-11.5	-85.2	-3.9	-121.2	-69.1	-32.9	Banks .... 78bq d
-4.3	-10.4	1.9	-14.6	-27.9	7.7	-19.4	-18.7	22.3	-53.1	-51.2	21.8	5.5	2.4	23.0	Other Sectors .... 78br d
-7.6	3.6	65.8	131.3	64.4	107.4	70.4	-.5	66.6	85.2	-29.5	5.1	111.2	27.3	4.8	Other Investment Liab., n.i.e. .... 78bi d
-.6	-7.4	—	—	—	—	—	—	—	—	—	—	—	—	—	Monetary Authorities .... 78bs d
-8.4	.1	22.5	-15.4	1.6	-5.3	-22.0	-34.7	1.4	-14.1	-18.8	-20.4	9.0	-14.2	-12.5	General Government .... 78bt d
3.6	-11.1	2.4	3.6	1.4	3.3	-2.4	-5.8	26.6	9.2	27.7	-6.9	-10.1	96.4	-20.4	Banks .... 78bu d
-2.1	22.1	40.8	143.0	61.4	109.5	94.7	40.0	38.6	90.1	-38.5	32.5	112.3	-54.9	37.7	Other Sectors .... 78bv d
52.3	32.7	96.4	121.2	199.8	213.2	168.8	59.6	81.2	148.5	106.7	-76.8	73.4	-41.9	181.6	Net Errors and Omissions .... 78ca d
-2.6	121.5	218.8	184.8	145.6	231.9	190.8	43.3	7.0	-43.5	108.8	48.3	-34.6	-65.4	189.7	*Overall Balance* .... 78cb d
2.6	-121.5	-218.8	-184.8	-145.6	-231.9	-190.8	-43.3	-7.0	43.5	-108.8	-48.3	34.6	65.4	-189.7	Reserves and Related Items .... 79da d
-4.0	-100.8	-186.2	-144.0	-108.5	-188.3	-168.9	-43.3	-7.0	43.5	-108.8	-48.3	34.6	65.4	-189.7	Reserve Assets .... 79db d
-14.6	-21.2	-32.8	-41.0	-37.1	-43.6	-21.9	—	—	—	—	—	—	—	—	Use of Fund Credit and Loans .... 79dc d
21.2	.5	.2	.2	—	—	—	—	—	—	—	—	—	—	—	Exceptional Financing .... 79de d

International Investment Position

Millions of US Dollars

1985	1986	1987	1988	1989	1990	1991	1992	1993	1994	1995	1996	1997	1998	1999	
95.8	222.9	462.6	580.2	696.1	929.3	1,117.2	1,001.9	947.9	994.8	1,232.3	1,243.1	1,085.6	965.7	1,162.4	Assets .... 79aa d
—	—	—	—	—	—	—	—	—	—	—	—	—	—	—	Direct Investment Abroad .... 79ab d
—	—	—	—	—	—	—	—	—	—	—	—	—	—	—	Portfolio Investment .... 79ac d
....	....	....	....	....	....	....	....	....	....	....	....	....	....	....	Equity Securities .... 79ad d
....	....	....	....	....	....	....	....	....	....	....	....	....	....	....	Debt Securities .... 79ae d
—	—	—	—	—	—	—	—	—	—	—	—	—	—	—	Financial Derivatives .... 79al d
62.3	83.0	114.5	133.5	173.5	186.7	219.0	177.5	187.0	243.0	364.8	342.9	386.1	394.7	419.0	Other Investment .... 79af d
—	—	—	—	—	—	—	—	—	—	—	—	—	—	—	Monetary Authorities .... 79ag d
—	—	—	—	2.3	—	—	—	—	—	—	—	—	—	—	General Government .... 79ah d
41.1	49.2	80.0	89.0	101.7	121.9	135.7	87.9	126.4	142.5	227.9	228.4	298.8	335.1	383.9	Banks .... 79ai d
21.2	33.8	34.5	44.5	69.6	64.8	83.3	89.6	60.6	100.5	136.9	114.6	87.3	59.6	35.2	Other Sectors .... 79aj d
33.5	140.0	348.1	446.7	522.6	742.6	898.2	824.4	760.9	751.8	867.5	900.2	699.5	571.0	743.3	Reserve Assets .... 79ak d
609.9	600.3	726.5	780.9	810.2	923.5	970.9	922.5	937.5	1,128.3	1,345.6	1,427.1	1,318.1	1,320.0	1,275.3	Liabilities .... 79la d
—	—	—	—	—	—	—	—	—	—	—	—	—	—	—	Dir. Invest. in Rep. Economy .... 79lb d
—	—	—	—	—	—	—	—	—	—	—	—	—	—	—	Portfolio Investment .... 79lc d
....	....	....	....	....	....	....	....	....	....	....	....	....	....	....	Equity Securities .... 79ld d
....	....	....	....	....	....	....	....	....	....	....	....	....	....	....	Debt Securities .... 79le d
—	—	—	—	—	—	—	—	—	—	—	—	—	—	—	Financial Derivatives .... 79ll d
609.9	600.3	726.5	780.9	810.2	923.5	970.9	922.5	937.5	1,128.3	1,345.6	1,427.1	1,318.1	1,320.0	1,275.3	Other Investment .... 79lf d
171.9	161.6	151.7	103.0	62.5	22.1	—	—	—	—	—	—	—	—	—	Monetary Authorities .... 79lg d
356.4	350.5	409.8	380.6	377.2	389.0	376.8	316.2	316.6	324.8	484.7	519.7	451.0	411.8	392.6	General Government .... 79lh d
13.0	2.7	5.4	8.2	9.1	12.8	9.9	3.4	28.2	39.8	67.5	59.5	38.4	127.9	104.3	Banks .... 79li d
68.6	85.4	159.6	289.1	361.4	499.7	584.2	603.0	592.7	763.7	793.4	847.9	828.7	780.3	778.4	Other Sectors .... 79lj d

Mauritius

		1970	1971	1972	1973	1974	1975	1976	1977	1978	1979	1980	1981	1982	1983	1984
Government Finance																*Millions of Rupees:*
Deficit (-) or Surplus	80	−6.6	−20.2	−45.1	‡−27.1	−201.7	−186.0	−208.9	−456.8	−727.2	−882.2	−896.6	−1,293.3	−1,388.4	‡−977.6	−648.7
Revenue	81	235.4	259.9	284.7	‡341.6	456.1	715.6	1,062.3	1,168.2	1,232.2	1,417.0	1,810.7	2,059.1	2,220.9	‡2,962.3	3,241.9
Grants Received	81z	....	....	....	‡13.8	4.1	7.4	3.0	5.0	1.9	1.0	2.0	13.9	67.8	‡22.6	53.2
Expenditure	82	240.7	287.9	320.6	‡355.8	588.9	840.1	1,181.0	1,525.5	1,784.6	2,135.4	2,369.9	2,953.7	3,336.2	‡3,560.2	3,707.1
Lending Minus Repayments	83	1.3	−7.8	9.2	‡26.7	73.0	68.9	93.2	104.5	176.7	164.8	339.4	412.6	340.9	‡402.3	236.7
Financing																
Net Borrowing: Domestic	84a	6.9	37.8	76.2	‡95.3	200.4	249.5	164.4	427.5	397.4	543.8	656.7	588.7	730.8	‡1,132.3	721.6
Foreign	85a	−6.8	−22.6	3.2	‡10.7	30.4	44.0	16.6	69.4	284.2	316.2	218.5	701.0	794.1	‡−176.0	−140.0
Use of Cash Balances	87	6.4	5.0	−34.3	‡−78.9	−29.1	−107.5	27.9	−40.1	45.6	22.2	21.4	3.6	−136.5	‡17.4	68.2
Unallocated Financing	87c	....	....	....	‡—	—	—	—	—	—	—	—	—	—	‡3.9	−1.1
Debt: Domestic	88a	....	....	317.1	‡415.6	537.6	794.3	966.2	1,322.2	1,724.9	2,246.1	2,932.5	3,593.8	4,452.7	‡5,208.0	5,848.6
Foreign	89a	....	....	168.1	‡139.4	208.0	247.1	262.9	323.0	630.3	910.6	1,431.7	2,218.4	3,540.0	‡3,462.7	3,944.7
National Accounts																*Millions of Rupees*
Exports of Goods & Services	90c	518	599	777	1,052	2,324	2,184	2,388	2,656	2,705	3,260	4,450	4,566	5,529	5,953	6,989
Government Consumption	91f	166	182	219	235	360	443	586	798	933	1,009	1,224	1,422	1,624	1,706	1,835
Gross Fixed Capital Formation	93e	145	184	229	480	750	1,138	1,450	1,510	1,770	1,965	2,028	2,240	2,100	2,300	2,595
Increase/Decrease(-) in Stocks	93i	—	—	—	—	—	—	213	120	153	420	−225	338	30	−71	570
Private Consumption	96f	734	783	929	1,122	1,684	1,878	2,178	3,593	4,174	5,144	6,562	7,277	8,301	8,874	9,841
Imports of Goods & Services	98c	−515	−587	−722	−1,037	−1,902	−2,227	−2,712	−3,235	−3,477	−4,158	−5,342	−5,634	−5,859	−5,999	−7,470
Gross Domestic Product (GDP)	99b	1,048	1,161	1,432	1,852	3,216	3,416	4,103	5,442	6,258	7,640	8,697	10,209	11,725	12,763	14,360
Net Factor Inc/Pmts(-) Abroad	98.n	7	7	2	16	10	17	47	−17	−48	−106	−178	−408	−498	−485	−626
Gross National Income (GNI)	99a	1,055	1,168	1,434	1,868	3,226	3,433	4,150	5,425	6,210	7,534	8,519	9,801	11,227	12,278	13,734
GDP Volume 1987 Prices	99b.p	....	....	....	....	....	....	....	....	....	....	....	....	....	....	....
GDP Volume 1992 Prices	99b.p	....	....	....	....	....	....	....	....	....	....	....	....	....	....	....
GDP Volume (1995=100)	99bv p	26.1	27.3	29.5	32.9	35.6	36.0	42.0	44.8	46.5	48.2	43.3	45.9	48.4	48.6	50.9
GDP Deflator (1990=100)	99bi p	5.8	6.2	7.0	8.1	13.1	13.7	14.1	17.6	19.5	23.0	29.1	32.2	35.1	38.0	40.9
																Millions:
Population	99z	.81	.82	.83	.84	.85	.86	.87	.88	.90	.91	.94	.95	.96	.97	.98

1985	1986	1987	1988	1989	1990	1991	1992	1993	1994	1995	1996	1997	1998	1999		
Year Ending June 30															**Government Finance**	
−580.4	−346.5	54.1	I 87.3	I −468.1	−157.5	1.9	I −358.4	I 18.7	I −167.0	−813.7	−3,083.6	−3,427.2 P	....	....	Deficit (-) or Surplus	80
3,592.5	4,128.3	5,202.6	I 6,466.8	I 7,630.5	8,884.8	10,114.9	I 11378.0	I 12363.2	I 14076.0	14,396.4	14,468.6	18,276.4 P	....	....	Revenue	81
165.9	233.0	187.7	I 214.4	I 67.6	116.4	61.4	I 25.2	I 78.0	I 130.2	261.6	220.5	62.8 P	....	....	Grants Received	81z
4,229.2	4,444.9	5,125.0	I 6,376.7	I 7,482.8	8,879.9	9,943.5	I 11517.6	I 12147.8	I 14271.4	15,502.2	17,279.6	20,260.0 P	....	....	Expenditure	82
109.6	262.9	211.2	I 217.2	I 683.4	278.8	230.9	I 244.0	I 274.7	I 101.8	−30.5	493.1	1,506.4 P	....	....	Lending Minus Repayments	83
															Financing	
−117.8	524.7	−1.8	I 71.4	I 2,317.7	1,606.6	2,151.8	I −2738.8	I 724.9	I 1,737.6	2,058.7	1,543.4	3,228.0 P	....	....	Net Borrowing: Domestic	84a
720.8	−116.5	147.7	I 602.2	I −461.1	−165.8	−284.2	I −330.6	I −312.8	I −112.7	−370.7	2,374.4	197.9 P	....	....	Foreign	85a
−28.1	−61.7	−200.0	I −760.9	I −1388.5	−1,283.3	−1,869.5	I 3,427.8	I −430.8	I −1457.9	−874.3	−834.2	1.3 P	....	....	Use of Cash Balances	87
5.5	—	—	I —	I —	—	—	I —	I —	I —	—	—	— P	....	....	Unallocated Financing	87c
5,964.0	6,250.9	6,100.3	I 5,998.6	I 8,375.6	9,770.0	11,889.2	I 10559.9	I 11695.5	I 14149.0	17,310.8	19,214.6	21,921.0 P	....	....	Debt: Domestic	88a
5,207.3	4,632.5	4,843.8	I 5,801.1	I 5,735.5	5,868.1	5,964.0	I 5,475.6	I 5,712.1	I 5,765.6	5,778.3	9,159.1	9,666.3 P	....	....	Foreign	89a
Millions of Rupees															**National Accounts**	
8,895	11,919	15,639	18,565	21,363	25,619	27,861	29,759	33,515	36,249	41,205	50,281	54,357	65,711	68,235	Exports of Goods & Services	90c
1,915	2,068	2,835	3,644	4,078	4,617	5,190	5,695	6,822	7,862	8,343	9,453	10,428	11,413	12,555	Government Consumption	91f
3,100	3,890	5,175	8,090	8,680	12,030	12,680	13,810	16,065	19,350	16,750	20,125	23,430	23,075	30,100	Gross Fixed Capital Formation	93e
800	430	1,024	807	1,674	97	35	756	1,273	948	1,061	−915	1,888	1,958	46	Increase/Decrease(-) in Stocks	93i
11,118	12,000	14,690	17,565	21,280	25,370	28,085	30,999	35,915	40,482	44,631	49,325	54,865	62,104	69,527	Private Consumption	96f
−9,210	−10,607	−15,141	−19,988	−23,801	−28,458	−29,535	−31,386	−37,020	−41,848	−42,908	−50,959	−58,540	−66,543	−74,084	Imports of Goods & Services	98c
16,618	19,700	24,222	28,683	33,274	39,275	44,316	49,633	56,570	63,043	69,082	77,310	86,428	97,718	106,379	Gross Domestic Product (GDP)	99b
−700	−729	−593	−593	−303	−339	89	171	63	−443	−332	−789	−374	−637	−468	Net Factor Inc/Pmts(-) Abroad	98.n
15,918	18,971	23,689	28,090	32,971	38,936	44,405	49,804	56,633	62,600	68,750	76,521	86,054	97,081	105,911	Gross National Income (GNI)	99a
....	....	24,222	25,867	27,022	28,964	30,197	32,071	....	....	....	60,038	63,840	67,523	69,836	GDP Volume 1987 Prices	99b.p
....	....	....	....	....	....	....	49,633	52,407	54,471	57,022	60,038	63,840	67,523	69,836	GDP Volume 1992 Prices	99b.p
54.4	59.7	65.7	70.2	73.3	78.6	82.0	87.0	91.9	95.5	100.0	105.3	112.0	118.4	122.5	GDP Volume (1995=100)	99bv p
44.2	47.8	53.3	59.1	65.7	72.3	78.3	82.5	89.1	95.5	100.0	106.3	111.7	119.5	125.7	GDP Deflator (1990=100)	99bi p
Midyear Estimates																
.99	.99	1.00	1.01	1.02	1.03	1.04	1.05	1.06	1.08	1.09	1.13	1.15	1.16	1.17	**Population**	99z

(See notes in the back of the book.)

		1970	1971	1972	1973	1974	1975	1976	1977	1978	1979	1980	1981	1982	1983	1984
Exchange Rates														*Pesos per Thousand SDRs through 1985*		
Market Rate................aa= ....**wa**		12.50	13.57	13.57	15.08	15.30	14.63	23.18	27.62	29.60	30.04	29.66	30.53	106.43	150.69	188.75
												Pesos per Thousand US Dollars through 1985				
Market Rate................ae= ....**we**		12.50	12.50	12.50	12.50	12.50	12.50	19.95	22.74	22.72	22.80	23.26	26.23	96.48	143.93	192.56
Market Rate................rf= ....**wf**		12.50	12.50	12.50	12.50	12.50	12.50	15.43	22.57	22.77	22.81	22.95	24.51	56.40	120.09	167.83
Fund Position															*Millions of SDRs:*	
Quota...**2f.** *s*		370	370	370	370	370	370	370	370	535	535	803	803	803	1,166	1,166
SDRs..**1b.** *s*		48	88	128	128	129	86	1	47	43	152	113	153	5	22	3
Reserve Position in the Fund ....**1c.** *s*		135	98	98	98	98	98	—	—	—	—	100	161	—	91	—
Total Fund Cred.&Loans Outstg. **2tl**		—	—	—	—	—	—	319	419	229	103	—	—	201	1,204	2,408
International Liquidity												*Millions of US Dollars Unless Otherwise Indicated:*				
Total Reserves minus Gold ....**1l.** *d*		568	752	976	1,160	1,238	1,383	1,188	1,649	1,842	2,072	2,960	4,074	834	3,913	7,272
SDRs..**1b.** *d*		48	96	139	154	158	101	1	57	56	201	144	178	6	23	3
Reserve Position in the Fund ....**1c.** *d*		135	106	106	118	120	114	—	—	—	—	128	187	—	95	—
Foreign Exchange...........................**1d.** *d*		385	550	731	888	960	1,168	1,187	1,592	1,786	1,871	2,688	3,709	828	3,795	7,269
Gold (Million Fine Troy Ounces) **1ad**		5.029	5.257	4.943	4.629	3.663	3.660	1.602	1.755	1.893	1.984	2.062	2.256	2.065	2.308	2.422
Monetary Authorities: Other Liab. ....**4..** *d*		—	—	—	—	—	—	—	48	57	13	9	42	—		
Deposit Money Banks: Assets ....**7a.** *d*		....	....	....	....	....	....	....	299	414	710	1,320	984	1,433	2,179	1,912
Liabilities ....**7b.** *d*									1,817	2,663	3,872	7,174	10,156	9,221	10,751	10,284
Other Banking Insts.: Assets ....**7e.** *d*		....	....	....	....	....	....	....	31	31	31	47	38	156	341	386
Liabilities ....**7f.** *d*									10,950	11,259	12,810	13,755	21,231	22,991	23,137	23,715
Monetary Authorities												*Thousands of Pesos through 1976;*				
Foreign Assets **11**		10,330	12,860	16,800	17,980	18,180	20,150	28,160	I46	54	72	96	135	191	733	1,599
Claims on Central Government **12a**		17,760	14,620	38,430	60,950	95,790	127,470	133,990	I286	351	459	611	900	2,496	3,192	4,128
Claims on Nonbank Pub.Fin.Insts. **12cg**									....	....	....	....	99	153	219
Claims on Deposit Money Banks **12e**		110	950	180	440	320	1,150	18,940	I15	9	9	16	12	235	53	54
Claims on Other Banking Insts **12f**		2,270	2,840	1,720	2,690	3,850	4,680	11,970	I5	9	12	29	35	73	73	130
Reserve Money **14**		29,300	33,440	57,580	75,210	105,320	140,840	130,950	I296	381	513	722	1,045	2,068	3,225	4,879
of which: Currency Outside DMBs **14a**		20,210	21,890	26,880	34,310	42,900	52,510	80,230	I89	115	150	195	283	505	681	1,122
Time & Foreign Currency Deposits **15**		820	760	680	1,770	1,380	1,750	11,740	I13	12	16	15	23	48	198	376
Foreign Liabilities **16c**			—		—	—	—	7,400	I13	8	3	—	—	25	181	453
Central Government Deposits **16d**		....	....	....	....	....	....	....	I2	2	2	—	7	458	15	8
Liab. to Nonbank Pub.Fin.Insts **16dg**		....	....	....	....	....	....	....	I2	2	2	7	8	14	166	296
Capital Accounts **17a**									I4	4	6	7	9	31	44	55
Other Items (Net).................................**17r**		350	–2,930	–1,130	5,080	11,440	10,860	42,970	I24	14	10	—	–9	450	375	63
Deposit Money Banks												*Thousands of Pesos through 1976;*				
Reserves **20**		7,830	7,580	17,830	26,240	32,910	40,700	37,480	I202	261	355	515	746	1,480	2,514	3,801
Foreign Assets **21**									I7	9	16	31	26	138	313	367
Claims on Central Government.............**22a**		7,530	9,420	1,950	2,290	5,500	4,480	25,780	I8	8	18	22	57	I483	707	974
Claims on State and Local Govts **22b**		—	—	—	—	—	—	—	I2	4	5	4	5	I24	20	73
Claims on Nonfin.Pub.Enterprises **22c**									I15	21	24	37	76	228	578	1,011
Claims on Nonbank Pub.Fin.Insts. **22cg**									....	....	....	....	....	3	9	11
Claims on Private Sector **22d**		28,310	30,610	33,930	36,650	42,680	52,600	63,040	I247	353	487	696	1,015	I1,253	1,800	3,323
Claims on Other Banking Insts **22f**		4,450	4,680	5,450	7,660	7,690	9,700	13,510	I15	15	22	27	40	71	162	213
Claims on Nonbank Financial Insts **22g**		....	....	....	....	....	....	....	....	....	....	....	....	16	22	53
Demand Deposits..................................**24**		30,380	32,650	37,900	45,720	56,300	68,560	76,900	I106	143	197	260	315	I455	676	1,075
Time, Savings,& Fgn.Currency Dep. **25**		16,940	18,270	21,310	28,640	31,630	35,680	51,360	I305	418	574	806	1,282	I1,976	3,300	5,640
Money Market Instruments **26aa**		....	....	....	....	....	....	....	....	....	....	....	....	8	21	149
Foreign Liabilities **26c**									....	....	....	....	....	71	104	140
Long-Term Foreign Liabilities...............**26cl**									I41	61	88	167	266	I817	1,440	1,834
Central Government Deposits **26d**		....	....	....	....	....	....	....	....	....	....	....	....	8	15	24
Liab. to Nonbank Pub.Fin.Insts **26dg**									I22	35	48	60	101	202	329	519
Credit from Monetary Authorities **26g**									I14	8	7	15	8	22	38	83
Liabilities to Other Banking Insts **26i**									....	....	....	....	....	33	70	122
Liab. to Nonbank Financial Insts **26j**									I—	—	—	—	—			
Capital Accounts **27a**									I16	19	27	39	52	68	96	169
Other Items (Net)..................................**27r**		800	1,370	–50	–1,520	850	3,240	11,550	I–9	–12	–14	–15	–60	I36	36	71
Monetary Survey												*Thousands of Pesos through 1976;*				
Foreign Assets (Net)..............................**31n**		11,440	13,930	17,470	18,330	18,790	20,830	22,060	I41	52	83	125	160	I233	761	1,373
Domestic Credit **32**		60,030	62,220	80,990	108,830	155,160	197,150	239,300	I577	762	1,028	1,429	2,126	I4,180	6,528	9,879
Claims on Central Govt. (Net) **32an**		24,680	23,520	39,530	61,490	100,060	129,780	150,360	I292	357	475	633	950	I2,513	3,869	5,070
Claims on State and Local Govts **32b**		—	—	—	—	—	—	—	I2	4	5	4	5	I24	20	73
Claims on Nonfin.Pub.Enterprises **32c**									I15	21	24	37	76	228	578	1,011
Claims on Private Sector **32d**		28,630	31,180	34,290	36,990	43,560	52,990	63,460	I248	356	490	699	1,020	I1,255	1,804	3,329
Claims on Other Banking Insts **32f**		6,720	7,520	7,170	10,350	11,540	14,380	25,480	I20	24	34	56	75	144	235	343
Claims on Nonbank Financial Inst. **32g**		....	....	....	....	....	....	....	....	....	....	....	....	16	22	53
Money..**34**		53,800	57,890	68,240	83,520	100,770	122,360	157,970	I212	270	363	481	643	I1,031	1,447	2,315
Quasi-Money **35**		18,200	19,640	22,910	31,570	38,390	41,740	85,020	I317	429	588	820	1,298	I2,024	3,498	6,016
Money Market Instruments **36aa**									....	....	....	....	....	8	21	149
Long-Term Foreign Liabilities...............**36cl**									I41	61	88	167	266	I817	1,440	1,834
Liabilities to Other Banking Insts **36i**									....	....	....	....	....	33	70	122
Liab. to Nonbank Financial Insts **36j**									I—	—	—	—	—			
Capital Accounts **37a**		....	....	....	....	....	....	....	I20	23	33	46	61	99	140	224
Other Items (Net)..................................**37r**		–530	–1,380	7,310	12,070	34,790	53,880	18,370	I28	32	39	40	17	401	673	592
Money plus Quasi-Money........................**35l**		72,000	77,530	91,150	115,090	139,160	164,100	242,990	I525	699	949	1,297	1,933	I3,055	4,945	8,331

1985	1986	1987	1988	1989	1990	1991	1992	1993	1994	1995	1996	1997	1998	1999		
															Exchange Rates	
and per SDR thereafter: End of Period																
408.28	I1.13	3.13	3.07	4.19	4.39	4.28	4.27	7.77	11.36	11.29	10.91	13.89	13.06		Market Rate......aa= ......wa	
and per US Dollar thereafter: End of Period (we) Period Average (wf)																
371.70	I.92	2.21	2.28	2.64	2.95	3.07	3.12	3.11	5.33	7.64	7.85	8.08	9.87	9.51	Market Rate......ae=	we
256.87	I.61	1.38	2.27	2.46	2.81	3.02	3.09	3.12	3.38	6.42	7.60	7.92	9.14	9.56	Market Rate......rf=	wf
															Fund Position	
End of Period																
1,166	1,166	1,166	1,166	1,166	1,166	1,166	1,753	1,753	1,753	1,753	1,753	1,753	1,753	2,586	Quota	2f. s
—	7	498	293	292	293	409	399	163	121	1,074	179	490	240	575	SDRs	1b. s
—	—	—	—	—	—	—	—	—	—	—	—	—	—	—	Reserve Position in the Fund	1c. s
2,703	3,319	3,639	3,570	3,874	4,605	4,730	4,327	3,485	2,644	10,648	9,234	6,735	5,952	3,259	Total Fund Cred.&Loans Outstg.	2tl
															International Liquidity	
End of Period																
4,906	5,670	12,464	5,279	6,329	9,863	17,726	18,942	25,110	6,278	16,847	19,433	28,797	31,799	31,782	Total Reserves minus Gold	1l. d
—	9	706	394	383	417	586	548	223	177	1,597	257	661	337	790	SDRs	1b. d
—	—	—	—	—	—	—	—	—	—	—	—	—	—	—	Reserve Position in the Fund	1c. d
4,906	5,661	11,758	4,885	5,946	9,446	17,140	18,394	24,886	6,101	15,250	19,176	28,136	31,461	30,992	Foreign Exchange	1d. d
2.362	2.568	2.536	2.555	1.025	.919	.923	.688	.484	.426	.514	.255	.190	.223	.159	Gold (Million Fine Troy Ounces)	1ad
3	1	1	3	254	78	4	94	75	66	91	84	560	552	377	Monetary Authorities: Other Liab.	4..d
940	833	784	1,257	1,062	1,413	1,238	843	760	435	953	816	2,630	4,687	5,743	Deposit Money Banks: Assets	7a. d
2,203	2,106	336	1,060	1,251	1,340	2,291	4,410	5,410	6,771	7,948	5,414	6,909	5,462	4,147	Liabilities	7b. d
383	484	377	463	412	336	628	1,164	961	2,394	3,135	4,008	2,274	2,749	2,335	Other Banking Insts.: Assets	7e. d
25,342	27,310	29,635	28,214	26,881	20,926	22,987	25,795	31,170	37,029	36,408	32,615	28,292	28,487	26,995	Liabilities	7f. d
															Monetary Authorities	
Millions of Pesos Beginning 1977: End of Period																
2,248	6,437	30,856	15,558	18,744	30,979	56,333	60,940	79,710	34,490	122,814	140,217	I239,472	323,607	310,242	Foreign Assets	11
6,300	10,235	13,173	32,657	39,001	44,293	34,668	30,123	9,864	-54,067	13,211	10,488	I—			Claims on Central Government	12a
309	481	937	1,783	3,156	5,798	9,875	14,623	21,227	38,043	78,001	70,327	I81,067	93,796	99,926	Claims on Nonbank Pub.Fin.Insts	12cg
45	51	52	171	42	37	46	13	810	97,732	43,132	11,501	I1,877	428	96,169	Claims on Deposit Money Banks	12e
79	93	126	853	142	558	1,224	2,405	2,831	4,368	1,889	382	I553	270	157	Claims on Other Banking Insts	12f
5,706	8,444	14,402	20,874	23,012	31,135	39,797	45,535	50,274	60,923	81,274	100,069	I150,907	192,511	276,315	Reserve Money	14
1,738	3,067	7,339	13,201	18,030	24,689	32,513	38,116	43,351	52,035	60,839	74,338	I94,340	116,083	164,424	of which: Currency Outside DMBs	14a
565	373	1,350	1,193	643	834	383	528	592	10	6	12	I4,766	3,721	7,222	Time & Foreign Currency Deposits	15
1,094	3,716	11,411	10,966	14,115	19,307	21,019	18,826	15,101	20,906	121,665	104,910	I77,835	88,390	46,072	Foreign Liabilities	16c
		1,958	—	304	3,389	12,871	14,145	18,678	15,203	26,195	16,124	I82,330	95,005	185,941	Central Government Deposits	16d
735	2,023	5,275	7,277	7,838	8,763	5,628	3,484	5,801	8,884	23,420	18,732	I21,189	27,382	15,886	Liab. to Nonbank Pub.Fin.Insts	16dg
165	373	957	938	1,055	1,263	1,322	1,313	1,309	2,327	3,367	3,346	I30,030	49,767	35,949	Capital Accounts	17a
715	2,368	9,790	9,774	14,118	16,974	21,126	24,273	22,686	12,313	3,120	-10,279	I-44,089	-38,673	-60,890	Other Items (Net)	17r
															Deposit Money Banks	
Millions of Pesos Beginning 1977: End of Period																
3,927	5,184	6,739	7,390	5,710	6,637	7,433	7,824	6,293	9,268	114,111	230,487	I51,911	71,426	114,882	Reserves	20
346	762	1,733	2,868	2,804	4,161	3,803	2,625	2,359	2,315	7,287	6,409	I21,395	46,238	54,561	Foreign Assets	21
2,551	8,754	22,102	26,899	28,009	36,877	55,500	21,531	2,645	6,325	17,094	8,191	I331,020	361,813	428,933	Claims on Central Government	22a
73	83	227	299	1,499	2,689	3,900	4,912	9,027	14,912	5,398	4,024	I8,996	13,691	13,729	Claims on State and Local Govts	22b
397	544	604	831	2,208	961	1,241	1,078	1,525	1,817	1,208	1,310	I1,606	5,264	2,180	Claims on Nonfin.Pub.Enterprises	22c
6	13	41	53	551	572	1,045	281	123	176	64,872	192,496	I280,407	390,203	556,456	Claims on Nonbank Pub.Fin.Insts	22cg
4,591	7,383	17,798	33,574	70,682	113,321	178,954	288,066	362,508	496,078	464,075	394,723	I569,258	672,385	667,422	Claims on Private Sector	22d
177	538	1,705	869	659	307	1,637	1,936	6,544	13,835	16,309	10,697	I28,580	21,529	37,095	Claims on Other Banking Insts	22f
70	148	464	518	1,300	7,097	12,692	17,460	19,348	24,174	25,947	16,845	I66,634	37,896	59,014	Claims on Nonbank Financial Insts	22g
1,611	2,468	4,930	7,130	10,279	21,847	72,772	82,604	98,725	91,106	85,783	128,600	I169,337	190,036	229,128	Demand Deposits	24
7,730	14,094	34,907	16,813	58,336	111,961	131,668	172,687	195,852	260,570	384,294	464,112	I625,373	762,267	797,754	Time, Savings,& Fgn.Currency Dep.	25
417	2,218	4,671	35,348	22,637	6,327	4,933	4,253	4,705	7,055	7,176	3,180	I187,462	210,533	272,003	Money Market Instruments	26aa
128	259	419	1,400	716	774	1,001	832	731	1,525	2,525	4,237	I5,219	4,449	5,745	Foreign Liabilities	26c
683	1,668	323	1,018	2,588	3,172	6,034	12,906	16,072	34,530	58,215	38,270	I50,993	49,431	33,656	Long-Term Foreign Liabilities	26cl
20	63	81	156	210	441	685	956	1,188	2,024	2,190	3,894	I12,984	5,264	6,570	Central Government Deposits	26d
913	1,801	3,845	7,252	9,639	10,206	14,049	19,332	24,045	36,626	72,530	115,657	I231,254	331,201	339,177	Liab. to Nonbank Pub.Fin.Insts	26dg
35	61	73	198	277	241	699	712	4,208	39,697	42,129	12,185	I2,652	1,020	96,700	Credit from Monetary Authorities	26g
164	316	564	735	2,210	7,945	17,771	27,613	37,735	59,452	53,277	52,219	I64,569	66,274	59,299	Liabilities to Other Banking Insts	26i
												I31	25	22	Liab. to Nonbank Financial Insts	26j
274	588	1,937	3,783	5,789	8,450	11,334	17,990	23,515	31,575	9,921	8,916	I4,067	8,638	2,647	Capital Accounts	27a
163	-127	-337	-532	741	1,258	5,259	5,828	3,596	4,740	-1,739	33,912	I5,865	-8,430	91,571	Other Items (Net)	27r
															Monetary Survey	
Millions of Pesos Beginning 1977: End of Period																
1,372	3,224	20,759	6,060	6,717	15,059	38,116	43,907	66,237	14,374	5,911	37,479	I177,812	277,007	312,986	Foreign Assets (Net)	31n
14,228	27,731	54,197	96,415	143,081	202,410	276,557	352,789	394,876	490,215	516,746	426,642	I911,333	1,012,842	1,016,018	Domestic Credit	32
8,831	18,926	33,236	59,400	66,496	77,340	76,612	36,553	-7,357	-64,969	1,920	-1,339	I235,706	261,808	236,422	Claims on Central Govt. (Net)	32an
73	83	227	299	1,499	2,689	3,900	4,912	9,027	14,912	5,398	4,024	I8,996	13,691	13,729	Claims on State and Local Govts	32b
397	544	604	831	2,208	961	1,241	1,078	1,525	1,817	1,208	1,310	I1,606	5,264	2,180	Claims on Nonfin.Pub.Enterprises	32c
4,601	7,399	17,835	33,645	70,777	113,458	179,251	288,445	362,958	496,078	464,075	394,723	I569,258	672,385	667,422	Claims on Private Sector	32d
256	631	1,831	1,722	801	865	2,861	4,341	9,375	18,203	18,198	11,079	I29,133	21,799	37,252	Claims on Other Banking Insts	32f
70	148	464	518	1,300	7,097	12,692	17,460	19,348	24,174	25,947	16,845	I66,634	37,896	59,014	Claims on Nonbank Financial Inst	32g
3,463	5,790	12,629	21,191	29,087	47,439	106,227	122,220	143,902	145,429	150,572	206,180	I267,113	308,135	395,475	Money	34
8,295	14,467	36,257	18,006	58,979	112,795	132,051	173,215	196,444	260,580	384,300	464,124	I630,139	765,988	804,976	Quasi-Money	35
417	2,218	4,671	35,348	22,637	6,327	4,933	4,253	4,705	7,055	7,176	3,180	I187,462	210,533	272,003	Money Market Instruments	36aa
683	1,668	323	1,018	2,588	3,172	6,034	12,906	16,072	34,530	58,215	38,270	I50,993	49,431	33,656	Long-Term Foreign Liabilities	36cl
164	316	564	735	2,210	7,945	17,771	27,613	37,735	59,452	53,277	52,219	I64,569	66,274	59,299	Liabilities to Other Banking Insts	36i
												I31	25	22	Liab. to Nonbank Financial Insts	36j
439	961	2,894	4,721	6,844	9,713	12,656	19,303	24,824	33,902	13,288	12,262	I34,097	58,404	38,596	Capital Accounts	37a
2,138	5,535	17,617	21,456	27,453	30,078	35,001	37,186	37,430	-36,359	-144,171	-312,115	I-145258	-168,942	-275,022	Other Items (Net)	37r
11,758	20,257	48,886	39,197	88,066	160,234	238,278	295,435	340,346	406,009	534,872	670,304	I897,252	1,074,123	1,200,451	Money plus Quasi-Money	35l

		1970	1971	1972	1973	1974	1975	1976	1977	1978	1979	1980	1981	1982	1983	1984
Other Banking Institutions													*Thousands of Pesos through 1976;*			
Reserves	40	4,000	6,920	14,950	18,800	34,500	54,280	23,790	I 16	9	15	21	40	77	92	111
Foreign Assets	41	....	....	....	....	....	....	....	I 1	1	1	1	1	15	49	74
Claims on Central Government	42a	21,960	27,870	24,940	22,160	17,400	28,450	66,490	I 83	70	88	108	307	I 1,055	1,595	2,248
Claims on State and Local Govts	42b	—	—	—	—	—	—	—	I 4	4	9	14	25	128	133	240
Claims on Nonfin.Pub.Enterprises	42c	....	....	....	....	....	....	....	I 168	186	226	295	424	1,016	1,394	1,922
Claims on Nonbank Pub.Fin.Insts	42cg	....	....	....	....	....	....	....	....	....	....	....	....	77	98	134
Claims on Private Sector	42d	117,900	136,700	156,380	181,010	215,620	267,810	379,070	I 76	98	123	167	178	I 247	447	838
Claims on Deposit Money Banks	42e	....	....	....	....	....	....	....	I 6	12	15	17	43	41	96	130
Claims on Nonbank Financial Insts	42g	....	....	....	....	....	....	....	....	....	....	....	....	1	1	1
Demand Deposits	44	....	....	....	....	....	....	....	I 3	5	7	8	16	I 21	28	61
Time, Savings,& Fgn.Currency Dep.	45	66,890	79,210	91,930	112,960	140,240	185,810	310,790	I 38	55	73	121	192	I 254	470	793
Money Market Instruments	46aa	62,000	73,660	82,390	85,700	100,390	131,200	136,830	I 17	16	15	12	20	I 24	36	80
Foreign Liabilities	46c	....	....	....	....	....	....	....	....	....	....	....	....	5	1	5
Long-Term Foreign Liabilities	46cl	—	—	—	—	—	—	—	I 249	256	292	320	557	I 2,209	3,322	4,547
Central Government Deposits	46d	....	....	....	....	....	....	....	....	....	....	....	....	180	266	384
Liab. to Nonbank Pub.Fin.Insts	46dg	....	....	....	....	....	....	....	....	....	....	....	....	39	68	46
Credit from Monetary Authorities	46g	1,570	2,180	1,560	2,370	3,630	4,020	11,780	I 5	9	12	29	35	106	102	154
Credit from Deposit Money Banks	46h	7,960	9,540	13,200	18,610	24,910	32,340	37,420	I 15	15	22	26	40	181	163	247
Liab. to Nonbank Financial Insts	46j	....	....	....	....	....	....	....	....	....	....	....	....	....	....	....
Capital Accounts	47a	10,840	14,220	17,000	19,730	22,060	19,740	22,000	I 13	16	18	19	38	86	127	234
Other Items (Net)	47r	−5,400	−7,320	−9,810	−17,400	−23,710	−22,570	−49,470	I 13	9	39	87	119	I −448	−678	−853
Banking Survey													*Thousands of Pesos through 1976;*			
Foreign Assets (Net)	51n	11,440	13,930	17,470	18,330	18,790	20,830	22,060	I 42	53	84	126	161	I 243	809	1,442
Domestic Credit	52	193,170	219,270	255,140	301,650	376,640	479,030	659,380	I 887	1,097	1,439	1,956	2,985	I 6,303	9,597	14,401
Claims on Central Govt. (Net)	52an	46,640	51,390	64,470	83,650	117,460	158,230	216,850	I 375	427	563	741	1,257	I 3,388	5,198	6,934
Claims on State and Local Govts	52b	—	—	—	—	—	—	—	I 6	8	13	18	30	I 152	153	313
Claims on Nonfin.Pub.Enterprises	52c	....	....	....	....	....	....	....	I 183	207	250	332	500	1,244	1,972	2,933
Claims on Private Sector	52d	146,530	167,880	190,670	218,000	259,180	320,800	442,530	I 323	454	613	866	1,198	I 1,502	2,251	4,167
Claims on Nonbank Financial Inst	52g	....	....	....	....	....	....	....	....	....	....	....	....	17	23	54
Liquid Liabilities	55l	134,890	149,820	168,130	209,250	244,900	295,630	529,990	I 554	750	1,016	1,409	2,109	I 3,253	5,351	9,074
Money Market Instruments	56aa	62,000	73,660	82,390	85,700	100,390	131,200	136,830	I 17	16	15	12	20	I 32	57	229
Long-Term Foreign Liabilities	56cl	—	—	—	—	—	—	—	I 290	316	380	487	823	I 3,026	4,762	6,381
Liab. to Nonbank Financial Insts	56j	....	....	....	....	....	....	....	....	....	....	....	....	....	....	....
Capital Accounts	57a	10,840	14,220	17,000	19,730	22,060	19,740	22,000	I 33	39	51	65	99	185	267	458
Other Items (Net)	57r	−3,120	−4,500	5,090	5,300	28,080	53,290	−7,380	I 35	28	62	110	95	I 50	−31	−299
Money (National Definitions)													*Millions of Pesos:*			
Reserve Money	19ma	....	....	....	....	....	....	....	....	....	....	....	....	....	....	....
M1	59ma	....	....	....	....	....	....	....	....	....	....	....	....	....	....	....
M2	59mb	....	....	....	....	....	....	....	....	....	....	....	....	....	....	....
M3	59mc	....	....	....	....	....	....	....	....	....	....	....	....	....	....	....
M4	59md	....	....	....	....	....	....	....	....	....	....	....	....	....	....	....
M4a	59md a	....	....	....	....	....	....	....	....	....	....	....	....	....	....	....
M4 National Currency	59md n	....	....	....	....	....	....	....	....	....	....	....	....	....	....	....
M4 Foreign Currency	59md f	....	....	....	....	....	....	....	....	....	....	....	....	....	....	....
Interest Rates													*Percent Per Annum*			
Money Market Rate	60b	....	....	....	....	....	....	....	....	....	....	....	....	45.86	57.51	49.94
Treasury Bill Rate	60c	....	....	....	....	....	....	....	....	10.53	15.02	22.46	30.77	45.75	59.07	49.32
Savings Rate	60k	....	....	....	....	....	....	....	....	....	....	....	....	....	....	....
Deposit Rate	60l	....	....	....	....	....	....	....	....	8.00	11.00	16.17	25.20	25.28	45.83	57.36	48.84
Average Cost of Funds	60n	....	....	....	....	....	....	....	11.92	11.83	12.88	15.13	16.35	20.71	28.62	40.40	56.65	51.08
Lending Rate	60p	....	....	....	....	....	....	....	....	....	....	....	....	....	....	....
Government Bond Yield	61	....	....	....	....	....	....	....	....	....	....	....	....	....	....	....
Prices, Production, Labor													*Index Numbers (1995=100):*			
Share Prices	62	....	....	....	....	....	....	....	....	....	....	....	—	—	.1	.2
Wholesale Prices	63	.1	.1	.1	.1	.1	.1	.1	.2	I .2	.3	.3	.4	.6	1.3	2.2
Consumer Prices	64	.1	.1	.1	.1	.1	.1	.1	.2	.2	.2	.3	.4	.6	1.2	2.0
Wages, Monthly	65	.1	.1	.1	.1	.1	.2	.2	.3	.3	.3	.4	.6	.9	1.4	2.1
Industrial Production	66	41.1	42.0	46.2	50.9	54.6	I 57.2	58.8	60.8	66.9	I 73.7	81.0	88.1	86.4	79.3	82.2
Manufacturing Production	66ey	42.6	43.8	48.0	52.4	56.0	I 58.3	59.9	62.1	67.7	I 73.9	79.7	85.6	82.2	76.1	79.9
Mining Production	66zx	48.0	46.4	48.6	51.7	57.2	I 54.1	57.3	57.7	59.0	I 61.7	75.5	87.0	96.3	92.4	93.6
Crude Petroleum	66aa	....	....	....	....	....	....	....	....	....	53.2	70.6	83.8	98.0	94.6	95.2
														Number in Thousands:		
Labor Force	67d	....	....	....	....	....	....	....	....	....	....	....	....	....	....	....
Employment	67e	....	....	....	....	....	....	....	....	....	....	....	....	....	....	....
Unemployment	67c	....	....	....	....	....	....	....	....	....	....	....	....	....	....	....
Unemployment Rate (%)	67r	....	....	....	....	....	....	....	....	....	....	....	....	....	....	....
International Transactions													*Millions of US Dollars*			
Excluding Maquiladoras																
Exports	70n.d	1,373	1,474	1,674	2,070	2,850	2,861	3,319	4,416	5,823	8,877	15,243	19,379	20,929	21,423	24,069
Imports, f.o.b.	71nv d	2,344	2,293	2,589	3,632	5,768	6,267	5,730	5,213	7,708	11,510	19,342	25,360	14,412	9,409	12,181
Including Maquiladoras																
Exports	70..d	1,402	1,504	1,694	2,250	2,958	2,904	3,417	4,167	6,005	8,982	I 18,031	23,307	24,055	25,953	29,101
Imports, f.o.b.	71.v d	....	....	....	....	....	....	....	....	....	....	21,089	27,184	17,011	11,848	15,916

Other Banking Institutions

Millions of Pesos Beginning 1977: End of Period

	1985	1986	1987	1988	1989	1990	1991	1992	1993	1994	1995	1996	1997	1998	1999	
Reserves	142	264	632	783	875	628	670	787	1,386	1,611	3,262	10,911	I921	595	337	40
Foreign Assets	141	443	834	1,057	1,089	989	1,930	3,626	2,985	12,750	23,963	31,468	I18,504	27,119	22,186	41
Claims on Central Government	4,823	13,354	40,304	45,395	50,898	47,524	49,551	52,568	54,014	99,942	167,942	168,102	I172,089	217,707	220,195	42a
Claims on State and Local Govts	280	155	239	493	531	1,178	2,592	4,816	5,593	8,861	11,176	9,008	I11,016	10,341	11,768	42b
Claims on Nonfin.Pub.Enterprises	3,226	7,208	13,282	11,251	8,969	7,241	3,540	3,341	3,125	6,266	7,660	6,319	I9,438	7,794	8,451	42c
Claims on Nonbank Pub.Fin.Insts	317	745	2,630	3,303	3,174	2,081	1,989	1,394	1,718	3,212	4,374	17,980	I40,209	58,772	69,915	42cg
Claims on Private Sector	1,577	2,937	7,190	12,694	14,713	15,635	19,654	27,444	36,011	54,126	73,536	80,034	I78,307	74,043	81,622	42d
Claims on Deposit Money Banks	183	418	1,017	2,277	3,630	11,581	19,906	25,334	42,268	69,769	75,053	69,538	I65,244	72,285	90,908	42e
Claims on Nonbank Financial Insts	—	2	2	31	100	447	1,453	6,538	14,065	20,918	22,008	8,342	I43,542	38,469	22,990	42g
Demand Deposits	78	87	167	255	348	437	1,088	1,360	1,824	1,974	1,912	3,132	I3,316	3,183	3,539	44
Time, Savings,& Fgn.Currency Dep.	1,241	2,226	5,732	9,014	4,455	8,274	11,132	12,485	18,975	26,757	43,972	66,898	I84,703	97,103	133,408	45
Money Market Instruments	197	482	166	319	4,409	2,855	3,307	10,806	19,766	23,961	44,032	49,537	I42,316	43,288	47,904	46aa
Foreign Liabilities	5	46	18	112	1	—	1	—	6	7	49	95	I1,727	1,475	1,463	46c
Long-Term Foreign Liabilities	9,326	24,945	65,466	64,245	70,991	61,636	70,593	80,351	96,805	197,173	278,197	255,959	I228,454	279,546	254,993	46cl
Central Government Deposits	674	430	1,932	7,521	4,127	3,330	1,434	1,445	1,712	2,299	4,045	3,311	I9,576	12,550	2,884	46d
Liab. to Nonbank Pub.Fin.Insts	92	201	560	1,274	1,417	874	1,602	2,780	3,277	2,882	3,510	4,018	I6,702	5,005	5,633	46dg
Credit from Monetary Authorities	228	483	1,429	816	355	119	247	1,537	1,665	6,526	6,055	4,584	I4,738	5,291	5,024	46g
Credit from Deposit Money Banks	367	626	1,046	1,557	2,377	903	949	814	894	1,510	986	2,459	I23,976	31,354	30,448	46h
Liab. to Nonbank Financial Insts													I—		—	46j
Capital Accounts	329	541	932	3,664	7,930	8,259	8,000	11,426	11,404	12,439	11,990	12,054	I23,569	24,493	29,107	47a
Other Items (Net)	-1,848	-4,541	-11,318	-11,493	-12,431	617	2,932	2,844	4,837	1,927	-5,774	-345	I10,190	3,838	13,968	47r

Banking Survey

Millions of Pesos Beginning 1977: End of Period

	1985	1986	1987	1988	1989	1990	1991	1992	1993	1994	1995	1996	1997	1998	1999	
Foreign Assets (Net)	1,508	3,621	21,575	7,005	7,805	16,048	40,045	47,533	69,216	27,117	29,825	68,852	I194,589	302,651	333,709	51n
Domestic Credit	23,204	50,326	111,451	157,036	213,364	270,240	349,052	441,710	496,597	659,826	776,825	684,057	I1187015	1,372,576	1,320,908	52
Claims on Central Govt. (Net)	12,980	31,850	71,608	97,274	113,267	121,534	124,729	87,676	44,945	32,674	165,817	163,452	I398,218	512,694	453,733	52an
Claims on State and Local Govts	353	238	466	792	2,030	3,867	6,492	9,728	14,620	23,773	16,574	13,032	20,012	24,031	25,497	52b
Claims on Nonfin.Pub.Enterprises	3,623	7,752	13,886	12,082	11,177	8,202	4,781	4,419	4,650	8,868	7,629	11,044	13,058	10,631		52c
Claims on Private Sector	6,178	10,336	25,025	46,339	85,490	129,093	198,905	315,889	398,969	550,204	537,611	474,757	I647,565	746,428	749,044	52d
Claims on Nonbank Financial Inst	70	150	466	549	1,400	7,544	14,145	23,998	33,413	45,092	47,955	25,187	I110,176	76,365	82,003	52g
Liquid Liabilities	12,935	22,306	54,153	47,683	91,994	168,317	249,828	308,493	359,759	433,129	577,494	729,423	I984,350	1,175,364	1,337,061	55l
Money Market Instruments	614	2,700	4,837	35,667	27,046	9,182	8,240	15,059	24,471	31,016	51,208	52,717	I229,778	253,822	319,907	56aa
Long-Term Foreign Liabilities	10,009	26,613	65,789	65,263	73,579	64,808	76,627	93,257	112,877	231,703	336,412	294,229	I279,447	328,976	288,648	56cl
Liab. to Nonbank Financial Insts	—	—	—	—	—	—	—	—	—	—	—	—	I31	25	22	56j
Capital Accounts	768	1,502	3,826	8,385	14,774	17,972	20,656	30,729	36,228	46,341	25,278	24,316	I57,666	82,897	67,703	57a
Other Items (Net)	385	826	4,420	7,043	13,776	26,009	33,746	41,705	32,477	-55,246	-183,742	-347,777	I-169668	-165,857	-358,726	57r

Money (National Definitions)

End of Period

	1985	1986	1987	1988	1989	1990	1991	1992	1993	1994	1995	1996	1997	1998	1999	
Reserve Money	2,741	5,424	11,031	17,514	22,225	30,121	38,581	43,972	47,193	56,935	66,809	83,991	108,891	131,528	188,718	19ma
M1	3,447	5,691	12,759	21,433	30,835	50,958	113,634	131,732	157,044	163,828	171,638	245,260	325,391	387,897	489,136	59ma
M2	15,370	31,911	79,841	121,603	190,782	271,244	339,051	380,487	469,768	554,930	754,407	995,167	1,295,084	1,656,128	2,007,165	59mb
M3	15,484	32,133	80,276	122,459	191,640	277,790	357,973	426,852	540,875	657,103	784,495	1,025,836	1,325,560	1,683,152	2,034,756	59mc
M4	15,730	32,973	84,050	127,750	200,085	293,688	386,715	458,384	580,375	724,242	869,279	1,116,205	1,405,392	1,769,041	2,108,451	59md
M4a	16,267	34,083	88,100	131,519	204,894	301,314	395,152	468,036	590,428	737,647	898,185	1,183,382	1,526,928	1,897,194	2,265,818	59md a
M4 National Currency	15,050	30,907	76,804	110,933	179,967	263,719	345,762	417,073	527,247	530,328	754,710	985,568	1,283,497	1,627,038	1,964,246	59md n
M4 Foreign Currency	680	2,066	7,246	16,816	20,119	29,968	40,952	41,311	53,128	193,914	114,568	130,637	121,895	142,004	144,204	59md f

Interest Rates

Percent Per Annum

	1985	1986	1987	1988	1989	1990	1991	1992	1993	1994	1995	1996	1997	1998	1999	
Money Market Rate	62.44	88.01	95.59	69.01	I47.43	37.36	23.58	18.87	17.39	16.47	I60.92	33.61	21.91	26.89	24.10	60b
Treasury Bill Rate	63.20	....	103.07	I69.15	44.99	34.76	19.28	15.62	14.99	14.10	48.44	31.39	19.80	24.76	21.41	60c
Savings Rate	....	....	....	....	....	....	....	....	8.41	5.38	6.67	6.58	7.57	6.38	5.85	60k
Deposit Rate	55.23	75.91	92.44	52.70	30.85	27.88	16.57	14.48	15.06	13.32	38.12	24.70	14.66	13.75	9.61	60l
Average Cost of Funds	56.07	80.88	94.64	67.64	44.61	37.07	22.56	18.78	18.56	15.50	45.12	30.71	19.12	21.09	19.73	60n
Lending Rate	....	....	....	....	....	....	....	....	22.04	20.38	58.59	36.89	24.55	28.70	25.87	60p
Government Bond Yield	....	....	....	....	....	....	....	....	....	....	51.74	32.81	21.44	....	....	61

Prices, Production, Labor

Period Averages

	1985	1986	1987	1988	1989	1990	1991	1992	1993	1994	1995	1996	1997	1998	1999	
Share Prices	.3	1.1	7.3	8.5	14.8	25.7	48.8	74.8	83.6	113.6	100.0	142.5	200.2	191.1	240.3	62
Wholesale Prices	3.4	6.5	15.2	31.6	36.7	45.2	54.5	61.8	67.3	71.9	100.0	136.3	161.6	184.0	211.0	63
Consumer Prices	3.2	5.9	13.7	29.3	35.2	44.5	54.6	I63.1	69.3	74.1	100.0	134.4	162.1	187.9	219.1	64
Wages, Monthly	3.4	6.0	14.1	I29.8	39.9	52.1	67.2	78.9	85.7	90.9	100.0	....	156.6	....	....	65
Industrial Production	86.5	I81.9	85.3	87.2	91.7	96.8	100.8	103.9	I103.5	108.4	100.0	110.5	120.2	128.2	....	66
Manufacturing Production	85.2	I81.1	84.3	86.3	91.9	96.6	100.3	103.0	I101.0	105.0	100.0	111.0	121.7	130.7	....	66ey
Mining Production	94.4	I90.4	93.9	94.3	93.9	97.7	98.2	99.2	I100.2	102.7	100.0	108.3	112.9	116.8	....	66zx
Crude Petroleum	94.1	I90.0	94.1	94.1	94.8	97.6	101.5	101.1	I101.2	101.6	100.0	109.6	....	....	....	66aa

Period Averages

	1985	1986	1987	1988	1989	1990	1991	1992	1993	1994	1995	1996	1997	1998	1999	
Labor Force	....	....	....	....	....	....	....	....	....	....	34,309	35,444	37,217	39,507	....	67d
Employment	....	....	....	28,128	....	....	30,534	....	32,833	....	33,881	35,226	37,391	38,618	....	67e
Unemployment	....	....	....	724	....	....	695	....	819	....	1,677	1,355	985	890	....	67c
Unemployment Rate (%)	....	....	....	2.5	....	....	2.2	....	2.4	....	4.7	3.7	2.6	2.3	....	67r

International Transactions

Millions of US Dollars

Excluding Maquiladoras

	1985	1986	1987	1988	1989	1990	1991	1992	1993	1994	1995	1996	1997	1998	1999	
Exports	21,846	16,037	20,527	20,449	22,701	26,830	27,098	27,529	30,003	34,318	46,864	59,084	65,266	64,376	72,954	70n.d
Imports, f.o.b.	14,528	12,436	13,207	20,068	25,362	31,221	38,146	48,180	49,054	58,362	44,893	58,961	73,475	82,816	91,655	71nv d

Including Maquiladoras

	1985	1986	1987	1988	1989	1990	1991	1992	1993	1994	1995	1996	1997	1998	1999	
Exports	26,757	21,804	27,600	30,691	35,171	40,711	42,688	46,196	51,886	60,882	79,542	96,000	110,431	117,460	136,703	70..d
Imports, f.o.b.	18,359	16,784	18,812	28,082	34,766	41,594	49,967	62,129	65,367	79,346	72,453	89,469	109,808	125,373	142,064	71.v d

	1970	1971	1972	1973	1974	1975	1976	1977	1978	1979	1980	1981	1982	1983	1984
Balance of Payments														*Millions of US Dollars:*	
Current Account, n.i.e. ...... 78al d	…	…	…	…	…	…	…	…	…	−5,409	−10,422	−16,240	−5,889	5,866	4,183
Goods: Exports f.o.b. ...... 78aa d	…	…	…	…	…	…	…	…	…	11,512	18,031	23,307	24,056	25,953	29,101
Goods: Imports f.o.b. ...... 78ab d	…	…	…	…	…	…	…	…	…	−13,654	−21,087	−27,184	−17,009	−11,848	−15,915
Trade Balance ...... 78ac d	…	…	…	…	…	…	…	…	…	−2,142	−3,056	−3,877	7,047	14,105	13,186
Services: Credit ...... 78ad d	…	…	…	…	…	…	…	…	…	5,192	4,591	4,983	4,136	4,087	4,839
Services: Debit ...... 78ae d	…	…	…	…	…	…	…	…	…	−4,901	−6,514	−8,489	−6,066	−4,477	−5,235
Balance on Goods & Services ...... 78af d	…	…	…	…	…	…	…	…	…	−1,851	−4,979	−7,383	5,117	13,715	12,790
Income: Credit ...... 78ag d	…	…	…	…	…	…	…	…	…	872	1,365	1,746	1,709	1,686	2,507
Income: Debit ...... 78ah d	…	…	…	…	…	…	…	…	…	−4,655	−7,642	−11,621	−13,758	−10,710	−12,474
Balance on Gds, Serv. & Inc. ...... 78ai d	…	…	…	…	…	…	…	…	…	−5,634	−11,256	−17,258	−6,932	4,691	2,823
Current Transfers, n.i.e.: Credit ...... 78aj d	…	…	…	…	…	…	…	…	…	257	877	1,076	1,072	1,206	1,384
Current Transfers: Debit ...... 78ak d	…	…	…	…	…	…	…	…	…	−32	−43	−58	−29	−31	−24
Capital Account, n.i.e. ...... 78bc d	…	…	…	…	…	…	…	…	…	—	—	—	—	—	—
Capital Account, n.i.e.: Credit ...... 78ba d	…	…	…	…	…	…	…	…	…	—	—	—	—	—	—
Capital Account: Debit ...... 78bb d	…	…	…	…	…	…	…	…	…	—	—	—	—	—	—
Financial Account, n.i.e. ...... 78bj d	…	…	…	…	…	…	…	…	…	5,120	11,508	26,601	2,923	−3,275	81
Direct Investment Abroad ...... 78bd d	…	…	…	…	…	…	…	…	…	—	—	—	—	—	—
Dir. Invest. in Rep. Econ., n.i.e. ...... 78be d	…	…	…	…	…	…	…	…	…	1,332	2,090	3,078	1,901	2,192	1,542
Portfolio Investment Assets ...... 78bf d	…	…	…	…	…	…	…	…	…	−51	−17	165	275	−134	−320
Equity Securities ...... 78bk d	…	…	…	…	…	…	…	…	…	—	—	—	—	—	—
Debt Securities ...... 78bl d	…	…	…	…	…	…	…	…	…	−51	−17	165	275	−134	−320
Portfolio Investment Liab., n.i.e. ...... 78bg d	…	…	…	…	…	…	…	…	…	−342	60	996	645	−519	−435
Equity Securities ...... 78bm d	…	…	…	…	…	…	…	…	…	—	—	—	—	—	—
Debt Securities ...... 78bn d	…	…	…	…	…	…	…	…	…	−342	60	996	645	−519	−435
Financial Derivatives Assets ...... 78bw d	…	…	…	…	…	…	…	…	…	…	…	…	…	…	…
Financial Derivatives Liabilities ...... 78bx d	…	…	…	…	…	…	…	…	…	…	…	…	…	…	…
Other Investment Assets ...... 78bh d	…	…	…	…	…	…	…	…	…	−1,751	−1,229	−4,425	−1,101	−3,551	−1,580
Monetary Authorities ...... 78bo d	…	…	…	…	…	…	…	…	…						
General Government ...... 78bp d	…	…	…	…	…	…	…	…	…						
Banks ...... 78bq d	…	…	…	…	…	…	…	…	…	—	−179	−1,204	1,228	−1,091	95
Other Sectors ...... 78br d	…	…	…	…	…	…	…	…	…	−1,751	−1,050	−3,221	−2,329	−2,460	−1,675
Other Investment Liab., n.i.e. ...... 78bi d	…	…	…	…	…	…	…	…	…	5,932	10,604	26,787	1,203	−1,263	874
Monetary Authorities ...... 78bs d	…	…	…	…	…	…	…	…	…				1,217	−1,217	
General Government ...... 78bt d	…	…	…	…	…	…	…	…	…	−180	768	1,881	2,319	12,251	8,800
Banks ...... 78bu d	…	…	…	…	…	…	…	…	…	2,324	3,778	13,141	−813	1,769	658
Other Sectors ...... 78bv d	…	…	…	…	…	…	…	…	…	3,788	6,058	11,765	−1,520	−14,066	−8,584
Net Errors and Omissions ...... 78ca d	…	…	…	…	…	…	…	…	…	604	−269	−9,087	−7,454	−3,116	−2,115
Overall Balance ...... 78cb d	…	…	…	…	…	…	…	…	…	315	817	1,274	−10,420	−525	2,149
Reserves and Related Items ...... 79da d	…	…	…	…	…	…	…	…	…	−315	−817	−1,274	10,420	525	−2,149
Reserve Assets ...... 79db d	…	…	…	…	…	…	…	…	…	−155	−684	−1,274	3,354	−3,102	−3,390
Use of Fund Credit and Loans ...... 79dc d	…	…	…	…	…	…	…	…	…	−160	−133	—	219	1,069	1,241
Exceptional Financing ...... 79de d	…	…	…	…	…	…	…	…	…	—	—	—	6,846	2,558	—
Government Finance													*Thousands of Pesos through 1976;*		
Deficit (-) or Surplus 80	…	…	…	…	…	…	…	…	…	…	−136	−401	−1,168	−1,453	−2,112
Total Revenue and Grants 81y	…	…	…	…	…	…	…	…	…	…	674	911	1,523	3,014	4,608
Revenue 81	…	…	…	…	…	…	…	…	…	…	674	911	1,523	3,014	4,608
Grants 81z	…	…	…	…	…	…	…	…	…	…					
Exp.& Lending Minus Repayments 82z	…	…	…	…	…	…	…	…	…	…	810	1,312	2,691	4,467	6,720
Expenditure 82	…	…	…	…	…	…	…	…	…	…	798	1,302	2,679	4,437	6,686
Lending Minus Repayments 83	…	…	…	…	…	…	…	…	…	…	12	10	12	30	34
Total Financing 80h	…	…	…	…	…	…	…	…	…	…	136	401	1,168	1,453	2,112
Domestic 84a	…	…	…	…	…	…	…	…	…	…	153	610	1,254	828	1,624
Foreign 85a	…	…	…	…	…	…	…	…	…	…	−17	−209	−86	625	488
Total Debt by Residence 88	71,120	71,480	88,510	116,690	156,940	217,680	372,650	…	…	…	…	…	3,861	6,303	10,289
Domestic 88a	58,840	58,860	74,580	99,000	127,300	177,260	282,380	…	…	…	…	…	2,768	3,719	5,335
Foreign 89a	12,280	12,620	13,930	17,690	29,640	40,420	90,270	…	…	…	…	…	1,093	2,584	4,954
National Accounts													*Thousands of Pesos through 1976;*		
Househ.Cons.Expend.,incl.NPISHs ...... 96f. c	319,500	358,800	405,600	487,000	628,300	755,900	933,400	I1,226	1,544	1,976	2,909	3,945	6,036	10,882	18,590
Government Consumption Expend ...... 91f. c	32,200	37,300	48,700	63,400	82,300	113,500	150,900	I199	255	334	449	660	1,026	1,574	2,722
Gross Fixed Capital Formation ...... 93e. c	88,700	88,100	107,100	133,300	178,900	235,600	288,400	I363	492	719	1,214	1,617	2,249	3,137	5,287
Changes in Inventories ...... 93i. c	12,300	11,100	7,600	14,400	29,700	25,000	17,200	I59	59	78	107	70	−33	577	496
Exports of Goods and Services ...... 90c. c	34,500	37,400	45,500	58,100	75,700	75,800	116,400	I191	245	343	479	638	1,502	3,397	5,122
Imports of Goods and Services ...... 98c. c	−42,900	−42,700	−49,800	−65,400	−95,200	−105,800	−135,300	I−189	−258	−382	−580	−793	−1,011	−1,684	−2,815
Gross Domestic Product (GDP) ...... 99b. c	444,300	490,100	564,700	690,900	899,700	1,100,100	1,371,000	I1,849	2,337	3,068	4,470	6,137	9,770	17,882	29,402
Net Primary Income from Abroad ...... 98.n c	−5,600	−6,500	−7,400	−10,000	−15,000	−17,900	−29,000	I−43	−53	−77	−129	−217	−558	−1,055	−1,618
Gross National Income (GNI) ...... 99a. c	438,700	483,500	557,300	680,900	884,700	1,082,100	1,342,000	I1,806	2,285	2,990	4,341	5,911	9,240	16,824	27,854
GDP Volume 1970 Prices (Millions) ...... 99b. r	444.30	462.80	502.10	544.30	577.60	610.00	635.80	657.70	712.00	777.20	841.90				
GDP Volume 1993 Prices (Billions) ...... 99b. r	…	…	…	…	…	…	…	…	…	…	948	1,029	1,023	988	1,021
GDP Volume (1995=100) ...... 99bv r	I40.6	42.3	45.9	49.8	52.8	55.8	58.2	60.2	65.1	71.1	I77.0	83.6	83.1	80.2	83.0
GDP Deflator (1995=100) ...... 99bi r	.1	.1	.1	.1	.1	.1	.1	.2	.2	.2	.3	.4	.6	1.2	1.9
														Millions:	
Population 99z	50.69	52.45	54.27	56.16	58.12	60.15	61.98	63.81	65.66	67.52	69.66	71.35	73.02	74.67	76.31

1985	1986	1987	1988	1989	1990	1991	1992	1993	1994	1995	1996	1997	1998	1999	Balance of Payments	
Minus Sign Indicates Debit																
800	−1,377	4,247	−2,374	−5,825	−7,451	−14,888	−24,442	−23,400	−29,662	−1,576	−2,328	−7,454	−15,725	−14,016	Current Account, n.i.e.	78al d
26,758	21,803	27,599	30,692	35,171	40,711	42,687	46,196	51,885	60,882	79,542	96,000	110,431	117,459	136,703	Goods: Exports f.o.b.	78aa d
−18,359	−16,784	−18,813	−28,081	−34,766	−41,592	−49,966	−62,130	−65,366	−79,346	−72,453	−89,469	−109,808	−125,374	−142,063	Goods: Imports f.o.b.	78ab d
8,399	5,019	8,786	2,611	405	−881	−7,279	−15,934	−13,481	−18,464	7,089	6,531	623	−7,915	−5,360	*Trade Balance*	78ac d
4,808	4,591	5,437	6,084	7,208	8,094	8,869	9,275	9,517	10,321	9,780	10,899	11,400	12,064	11,957	Services: Credit	78ad d
−5,524	−5,194	−5,310	−6,281	−7,880	−10,323	−10,959	−11,959	−12,046	−13,043	−9,715	−10,816	−12,616	−13,067	−14,218	Services: Debit	78ae d
7,683	4,416	8,913	2,414	−267	−3,110	−9,369	−18,618	−16,010	−21,185	7,153	6,614	−593	−8,918	−7,621	*Balance on Goods & Services*	78af d
2,281	1,943	2,397	3,049	3,160	3,273	3,523	2,789	2,694	3,347	3,713	4,033	4,430	4,911	4,890	Income: Credit	78ag d
−11,148	−9,310	−8,982	−10,092	−11,261	−11,589	−11,788	−11,998	−13,724	−15,605	−16,402	−17,505	−16,538	−17,732	−17,601	Income: Debit	78ah d
−1,184	−2,951	2,328	−4,629	−8,368	−11,426	−17,634	−27,827	−27,040	−33,444	−5,536	−6,858	−12,701	−21,739	−20,332	*Balance on Gds, Serv. & Inc.*	78ai d
2,012	1,589	1,937	2,270	2,559	3,990	2,765	3,404	3,656	3,822	3,995	4,560	5,272	6,042	6,341	Current Transfers, n.i.e.: Credit	78aj d
−28	−15	−18	−15	−16	−15	−19	−19	−16	−40	−35	−30	−25	−28	−25	Current Transfers: Debit	78ak d
—	—	—	—	—	—	—	—	—	....	....	....	....	....	....	Capital Account, n.i.e.	78bc d
—	—	—	—	—	—	—	—	—	....	....	....	....	....	....	Capital Account, n.i.e.: Credit	78ba d
—	—	—	—	—	—	—	—	—	....	....	....	....	....	....	Capital Account: Debit	78bb d
−612	1,634	−3,067	−4,495	1,110	8,441	25,139	27,039	33,760	15,787	−10,487	6,132	19,253	18,540	17,826	Financial Account, n.i.e.	78bj d
															Direct Investment Abroad	78bd d
1,984	2,036	1,184	2,011	2,785	2,549	4,742	4,393	4,389	10,973	9,526	9,186	12,831	11,312	11,567	Dir. Invest. in Rep. Econ., n.i.e.	78be d
−389	−709	−397	−880	−56	−7,354	−603	1,165	−564	−767	−662	544	−708	−768	−836	Portfolio Investment Assets	78bf d
															Equity Securities	78bk d
−389	−709	−397	−880	−56	−7,354	−603	1,165	−564	−767	−662	544	−708	−768	−836	Debt Securities	78bl d
−595	−517	−1,002	1,001	354	3,369	12,741	18,041	28,919	8,182	−9,715	13,417	5,038	−578	10,791	Portfolio Investment Liab., n.i.e.	78bg d
				494	1,995	6,331	4,783	10,716	4,084	519	2,801	3,215	−665	3,769	Equity Securities	78bm d
−595	−517	−1,002	1,001	−140	1,374	6,410	13,258	18,203	4,099	−10,234	10,616	1,823	87	7,022	Debt Securities	78bn d
....	....	....	....	....	....	....	....	....	....	....	....	....	....	....	Financial Derivatives Assets	78bw d
....	....	....	....	....	....	....	....	....	....	....	....	....	....	....	Financial Derivatives Liabilities	78bx d
−989	874	−4,401	−874	−1,114	−1,345	−395	4,387	−3,038	−4,903	−6,694	−6,885	7,425	1,201	−1,804	Other Investment Assets	78bh d
....	....	....	....	....	....	....	....	—	−1,400	−3,619	−228	2,734	740	−557	Monetary Authorities	78bo d
															General Government	78bp d
−57	−363	−1,073	−338	−719	−749	−1,097	22	−1,683	−885	−1,510	−812	2,435	−1,923	−1,337	Banks	78bq d
−932	1,237	−3,328	−536	−395	−596	702	4,365	−1,355	−2,618	−1,565	−5,846	2,256	2,384	90	Other Sectors	78bs d
−623	−50	1,549	−5,753	−859	11,222	8,654	−947	4,054	2,302	−2,942	−10,130	−5,333	7,373	−1,892	Other Investment Liab., n.i.e.	78bi d
										−788	−1,459				Monetary Authorities	78bs d
11,586	8,568	3,881	−4,112	−104	1,657	−1,454	−5,867	−1,136	−986	210	−8,595	−3,994	1,356	−4,294	General Government	78bt d
123	846	814	320	680	9,061	7,845	1,626	3,622	2,799	−5,297	−2,966	−2,999	97	−2,134	Banks	78bu d
−12,332	−9,464	−3,146	−1,961	−1,435	504	2,263	3,294	1,568	488	2,933	2,891	1,660	5,920	4,536	Other Sectors	78bv d
−2,917	−738	2,954	−3,193	4,504	1,228	−2,278	−852	−3,128	−3,323	−4,248	58	2,198	378	468	Net Errors and Omissions	78ca d
−2,729	−481	4,134	−10,062	−211	2,218	7,973	1,745	7,232	−17,199	−16,312	3,863	13,997	3,193	4,278	*Overall Balance*	78cb d
2,729	481	−4,134	10,062	211	−2,218	−7,973	−1,745	−7,232	17,199	16,312	−3,863	−13,997	−3,193	−4,278	Reserves and Related Items	79da d
2,434	−595	−5,986	6,721	−542	−3,261	−8,154	−1,173	−6,057	18,398	−9,648	−1,806	−10,513	−2,118	−598	Reserve Assets	79db d
295	712	401	−84	364	958	161	−572	−1,175	−1,199	11,950	−2,057	−3,485	−1,075	−3,681	Use of Fund Credit and Loans	79dc d
	364	1,450	3,424	389	85	20	—	—	—	14,010					Exceptional Financing	79de d
Millions of Pesos Beginning 1977: Year Ending December 31															**Government Finance**	
−3,559	−10,333	−27,422	−37,007	−25,082	−18,672	27,694	46,921	6,451	−386	−9,784	−5,546	−34,161	−55,591	....	Deficit (-) or Surplus	80
7,559	11,990	31,476	62,170	86,939	113,317	140,636	174,278	186,644	211,434	278,626	379,573	459,047	488,959	....	Total Revenue and Grants	81y
7,559	11,990	31,476	62,170	86,939	113,317	140,636	174,278	186,644	211,434	278,626	379,573	459,047	488,959	....	Revenue	81
—	—	—	—	—	—	—	—	—	—	—	—	—	—	....	Grants	81z
11,118	22,323	58,898	99,177	112,021	131,989	112,942	127,357	180,193	211,820	288,410	385,119	493,208	544,550	....	Exp.& Lending Minus Repayments	82z
11,086	22,178	58,705	99,122	111,503	131,306	144,023	158,189	183,876	217,249	285,147	382,499	505,902	556,079	....	Expenditure	82
32	145	193	55	518	683	−31,081	−30,832	−3,683	−5,429	3,263	2,620	−12,694	−11,529	....	Lending Minus Repayments	83
3,559	10,333	27,422	37,007	25,082	18,672	−27,694	−46,921	−6,451	386	9,784	5,546	34,161	55,591	....	Total Financing	80h
3,463	11,077	23,580	32,485	24,436	16,644	−28,934	−42,888	−1,397	−1,397	−90,101	24,233	56,387	35,073	....	Domestic	84a
96	−744	3,842	4,522	646	2,028	1,240	−4,033	−5,054	−4,548	99,885	−18,687	−22,226	20,518	....	Foreign	85a
19,630	51,480	133,537	197,839	257,004	342,742	361,157	316,514	317,977	417,115	751,601	787,822	821,777	1,073,220	....	Total Debt by Residence	88
9,773	23,756	61,556	108,947	137,601	165,418	159,107	133,478	134,769	178,960	155,360	192,162	273,656	378,256	....	Domestic	88a
9,857	27,724	71,981	88,892	119,403	177,324	202,050	183,036	183,208	238,155	596,241	595,660	548,121	694,964	....	Foreign	89a
Millions of Pesos Beginning 1977															**National Accounts**	
30,575	54,209	127,268	281,569	377,907	514,117	669,159	808,120	‡903,174	1,016,129	1,232,003	1,624,278	2,038,235	2,585,196	3,145,433	Househ.Cons.Expend.,incl.NPISHs	96f. c
4,374	7,208	16,995	35,028	45,383	61,949	86,163	111,753	‡138,565	164,161	191,981	243,706	314,622	357,130	462,907	Government Consumption Expend	91f. c
9,048	15,415	35,667	77,110	94,670	132,113	177,044	220,545	‡233,179	274,861	296,708	449,949	619,494	807,077	971,168	Gross Fixed Capital Formation	93e. c
762	−1,139	1,416	16,812	31,254	38,879	44,379	41,563	‡30,597	33,538	67,391	132,477	208,275	116,088	103,231	Changes in Inventories	93i. c
7,305	13,732	37,692	82,962	104,266	137,441	155,327	171,476	‡191,540	238,966	558,798	812,854	963,938	1,184,600	1,421,565	Exports of Goods and Services	90c. c
−4,897	−10,639	−25,877	−77,174	−104,622	−145,603	−182,924	−228,123	‡−240859	−307,494	−509,862	−759,451	−965,611	1,258,900	1,481,515	Imports of Goods and Services	98c. c
47,168	78,787	193,162	416,305	548,858	738,898	949,148	1,125,334	‡1256196	1,420,159	1,837,019	2,503,813	3,178,954	3,791,191	4,622,789	Gross Domestic Product (GDP)	99b. c
−2,122	−4,255	−8,849	−16,174	−20,190	−23,927	−25,683	−18,979	−24,700	−29,856	−58,698	−66,843	....	....	....	Net Primary Income from Abroad	98.n c
45,270	74,936	184,462	400,131	528,668	714,971	923,465	1,106,355	1,231,496	1,390,303	1,778,321	2,436,970	....	....	....	Gross National Income (GNI)	99a. c
1,044	1,011	1,029	1,042	1,086	1,141	1,189	1,232	1,256	1,312	1,231	1,294	1,381	1,448	1,501	GDP Volume 1970 Prices (Millions)	99b. r
															GDP Volume 1993 Prices (Billions)	99b. r
84.8	82.2	83.6	84.7	88.2	92.7	96.6	100.1	102.1	106.6	100.0	105.2	112.2	117.6	122.0	GDP Volume (1995=100)	99bv r
3.0	5.2	12.6	26.8	33.9	43.4	53.5	61.2	‡67.0	72.5	100.0	129.6	154.2	175.4	206.3	GDP Deflator (1995=100)	99bi r
Midyear Estimates																
77.94	79.57	81.20	82.72	81.66	83.23	84.80	86.39	87.98	89.56	90.49	92.72	94.28	95.83	97.37	**Population**	99z

(See notes in the back of the book.)

Moldova

921

Exchange Rates

Lei per SDR:

	1970	1971	1972	1973	1974	1975	1976	1977	1978	1979	1980	1981	1982	1983	1984
Official Rate .... aa	...	...	...	...	...	...	...	...	...	...	...	...	...	...	...

Lei per US Dollar:

Official Rate .... ae	...	...	...	...	...	...	...	...	...	...	...	...	...	...	...
Official Rate .... rf	...	...	...	...	...	...	...	...	...	...	...	...	...	...	...

Index Numbers (1995=100):

Nominal Effective Exchange Rate .... ne c	...	...	...	...	...	...	...	...	...	...	...	...	...	...	...
Real Effective Exchange Rate .... re c	...	...	...	...	...	...	...	...	...	...	...	...	...	...	...

Fund Position

Millions of SDRs:

Quota .... 2f. s	...	...	...	...	...	...	...	...	...	...	...	...	...	...	...
SDRs .... 1b. s	...	...	...	...	...	...	...	...	...	...	...	...	...	...	...
Reserve Position in the Fund .... 1c. s	...	...	...	...	...	...	...	...	...	...	...	...	...	...	...
Total Fund Cred.&Loans Outstg. 2tl	...	...	...	...	...	...	...	...	...	...	...	...	...	...	...

International Liquidity

Millions of US Dollars Unless Otherwise Indicated:

Total Reserves minus Gold .... 1l. d	...	...	...	...	...	...	...	...	...	...	...	...	...	...	...
SDRs .... 1b. d	...	...	...	...	...	...	...	...	...	...	...	...	...	...	...
Reserve Position in the Fund .... 1c. d	...	...	...	...	...	...	...	...	...	...	...	...	...	...	...
Foreign Exchange .... 1d. d	...	...	...	...	...	...	...	...	...	...	...	...	...	...	...
Gold (Million Fine Troy Ounces) 1ad	...	...	...	...	...	...	...	...	...	...	...	...	...	...	...
Gold (National Valuation) .... 1an d	...	...	...	...	...	...	...	...	...	...	...	...	...	...	...
Monetary Authorities: Other Liab. ...... 4.. d	...	...	...	...	...	...	...	...	...	...	...	...	...	...	...
Dep.Money Banks: Assets Conv. ... 7ax d	...	...	...	...	...	...	...	...	...	...	...	...	...	...	...
Assets Nonconv .... 7ay d	...	...	...	...	...	...	...	...	...	...	...	...	...	...	...
Dep.Money Banks: Liab. Conv. .... 7bx d	...	...	...	...	...	...	...	...	...	...	...	...	...	...	...
Liab. Nonconv. ... 7by d	...	...	...	...	...	...	...	...	...	...	...	...	...	...	...

Monetary Authorities

Millions of Lei:

Foreign Assets 11	...	...	...	...	...	...	...	...	...	...	...	...	...	...	...
Claims on Central Government 12a	...	...	...	...	...	...	...	...	...	...	...	...	...	...	...
Claims on Private Sector 12d	...	...	...	...	...	...	...	...	...	...	...	...	...	...	...
Claims on Deposit Money Banks 12e	...	...	...	...	...	...	...	...	...	...	...	...	...	...	...
Reserve Money 14	...	...	...	...	...	...	...	...	...	...	...	...	...	...	...
of which: Currency Outside DMB 14a	...	...	...	...	...	...	...	...	...	...	...	...	...	...	...
Foreign Liabilities 16c	...	...	...	...	...	...	...	...	...	...	...	...	...	...	...
Central Government Deposits 16d	...	...	...	...	...	...	...	...	...	...	...	...	...	...	...
Capital Accounts 17a	...	...	...	...	...	...	...	...	...	...	...	...	...	...	...
Other Items (Net) 17r	...	...	...	...	...	...	...	...	...	...	...	...	...	...	...

Deposit Money Banks

Millions of Lei:

Reserves 20	...	...	...	...	...	...	...	...	...	...	...	...	...	...	...
Foreign Assets 21	...	...	...	...	...	...	...	...	...	...	...	...	...	...	...
Claims on Central Government 22a	...	...	...	...	...	...	...	...	...	...	...	...	...	...	...
Claims on Local Government 22b	...	...	...	...	...	...	...	...	...	...	...	...	...	...	...
Claims on Nonfin.Pub.Enterprises 22c	...	...	...	...	...	...	...	...	...	...	...	...	...	...	...
Claims on Private Sector 22d	...	...	...	...	...	...	...	...	...	...	...	...	...	...	...
Claims on Nonbank Financial Insts 22g	...	...	...	...	...	...	...	...	...	...	...	...	...	...	...
Demand Deposits 24	...	...	...	...	...	...	...	...	...	...	...	...	...	...	...
Time, Savings,& Fgn.Currency Dep. 25	...	...	...	...	...	...	...	...	...	...	...	...	...	...	...
Money Market Instruments 26aa	...	...	...	...	...	...	...	...	...	...	...	...	...	...	...
Foreign Liabilities 26c	...	...	...	...	...	...	...	...	...	...	...	...	...	...	...
Central Government Deposits 26d	...	...	...	...	...	...	...	...	...	...	...	...	...	...	...
Credit from Monetary Authorities 26g	...	...	...	...	...	...	...	...	...	...	...	...	...	...	...
Liabs. to Nonbank Financial Insts 26j	...	...	...	...	...	...	...	...	...	...	...	...	...	...	...
Capital Accounts 27a	...	...	...	...	...	...	...	...	...	...	...	...	...	...	...
Other Items (Net) 27r	...	...	...	...	...	...	...	...	...	...	...	...	...	...	...

Monetary Survey

Millions of Lei:

Foreign Assets (Net) 31n	...	...	...	...	...	...	...	...	...	...	...	...	...	...	...
Domestic Credit 32	...	...	...	...	...	...	...	...	...	...	...	...	...	...	...
Claims on Central Govt. (Net) 32an	...	...	...	...	...	...	...	...	...	...	...	...	...	...	...
Claims on Local Government 32b	...	...	...	...	...	...	...	...	...	...	...	...	...	...	...
Claims on Nonfin.Pub.Enterprises 32c	...	...	...	...	...	...	...	...	...	...	...	...	...	...	...
Claims on Private Sector 32d	...	...	...	...	...	...	...	...	...	...	...	...	...	...	...
Claims on Nonbank Financial Inst 32g	...	...	...	...	...	...	...	...	...	...	...	...	...	...	...
Money 34	...	...	...	...	...	...	...	...	...	...	...	...	...	...	...
Quasi-Money 35	...	...	...	...	...	...	...	...	...	...	...	...	...	...	...
Money Market Instruments 36aa	...	...	...	...	...	...	...	...	...	...	...	...	...	...	...
Liabs. to Nonbank Financial Insts 36j	...	...	...	...	...	...	...	...	...	...	...	...	...	...	...
Capital Accounts 37a	...	...	...	...	...	...	...	...	...	...	...	...	...	...	...
Other Items (Net) 37r	...	...	...	...	...	...	...	...	...	...	...	...	...	...	...
Money plus Quasi-Money 35l	...	...	...	...	...	...	...	...	...	...	...	...	...	...	...

Interest Rates

Percent Per Annum

Refinancing Rate 60a	...	...	...	...	...	...	...	...	...	...	...	...	...	...	...
Money Market Rate 60b	...	...	...	...	...	...	...	...	...	...	...	...	...	...	...
Money Market Rate (Fgn. Cur.) ...... 60b. f	...	...	...	...	...	...	...	...	...	...	...	...	...	...	...
Treasury Bill Rate 60c	...	...	...	...	...	...	...	...	...	...	...	...	...	...	...
Deposit Rate 60l	...	...	...	...	...	...	...	...	...	...	...	...	...	...	...
Deposit Rate (Foreign Currency) .... 60l. f	...	...	...	...	...	...	...	...	...	...	...	...	...	...	...
Lending Rate 60p	...	...	...	...	...	...	...	...	...	...	...	...	...	...	...
Lending Rate (Foreign Currency) .... 60p. f	...	...	...	...	...	...	...	...	...	...	...	...	...	...	...

Prices and Labor

Index Numbers (1995=100):

Consumer Prices 64	...	...	...	...	...	...	...	...	...	...	...	...	...	...	...

Number in Thousands:

Labor Force 67d	...	...	...	...	...	...	...	...	...	...	...	...	...	...	...
Employment 67e	...	...	...	...	...	...	...	...	...	...	...	...	...	...	...
Unemployment 67c	...	...	...	...	...	...	...	...	...	...	...	...	...	...	...
Unemployment Rate (%) 67r	...	...	...	...	...	...	...	...	...	...	...	...	...	...	...

1985	1986	1987	1988	1989	1990	1991	1992	1993	1994	1995	1996	1997	1998	1999	Description	Code
															Exchange Rates	
End of Period																
....	....	....	....	....	....	.0024	.5698	I4.9998	6.2336	6.6877	6.7215	6.2882	11.7185	15.9077	Official Rate	aa
End of Period (ae) Period Average (rf)																
....	....	....	....	....	....	.0017	.4144	I3.6400	4.2700	4.4990	4.6743	4.6605	8.3226	11.5902	Official Rate	ae
										4.4958	4.6045	4.6236	5.3707	10.5158	Official Rate	rf
Period Averages																
....	....	....	....	....	....	....	....		56.51	100.00	117.37	154.98	183.52	192.89	Nominal Effective Exchange Rate	ne c
....	....	....	....	....	....	....	....		115.61	100.00	97.83	105.70	107.07	100.08	Real Effective Exchange Rate	re c
End of Period																
															Fund Position	
....	....	....	....	....	....	....	90.00	90.00	90.00	90.00	90.00	90.00	90.00	123.20	Quota	2f. s
....	....	....	....	....	....	....	—	25.05	14.62	8.81	5.45	.89	.50	.23	SDRs	1b. s
....	....	....	....	....	....	....	.01	.01	.01	.01	.01	.01	.01	.01	Reserve Position in the Fund	1c. s
....	....	....	....	....	....	....	—	63.00	112.45	154.85	172.29	172.73	125.56	127.69	Total Fund Cred.&Loans Outstg.	2tl
End of Period																
															International Liquidity	
....	....	....	....	....	....	—	2.45	76.34	179.92	257.01	311.96	365.99	143.56	185.70	Total Reserves minus Gold	1l. d
							—	34.41	21.34	13.10	7.84	1.21	.70	.32	SDRs	1b. d
								.01	.01	.01	.01	.01	.01	.01	Reserve Position in the Fund	1c. d
....	....	....	....	....	....	—	2.44	41.92	158.57	243.90	304.11	364.77	142.85	185.37	Foreign Exchange	1d. d
									—	—	—	—	—	—	Gold (Million Fine Troy Ounces)	1ad
							—	—	—	—	—	—	—	—	Gold (National Valuation)	1an d
....	....	....	....	....	....	—	138.12	12.02	10.10	7.42	4.94	4.00	2.77	10.06	Monetary Authorities: Other Liab.	4.. d
....	....	....	....	....	....		2.02	2.19	14.92	32.77	37.41	23.78	32.33	53.42	Dep.Money Banks: Assets Conv.	7ax d
							.20	2.14	7.79	5.24	5.55	9.25	3.44	2.23	Assets Nonconv	7ay d
							—	.51	1.42	10.60	50.70	58.10	67.27	41.78	Dep.Money Banks: Liab. Conv.	7bx d
								1.51	.41	3.10	1.55	4.91	7.62	3.33	Liab. Nonconv.	7by d
End of Period																
															Monetary Authorities	
....	....	....	....	....	....	—	49.32	345.41	825.14	1,198.42	I1486.91	1,716.60	1,199.82	2,207.49	Foreign Assets	11
....	....	....	....	....	....	.48	52.24	236.21	284.01	452.92	I496.12	524.83	1,409.21	1,737.46	Claims on Central Government	12a
										1.79	I2.88	3.92	5.10	6.03	Claims on Private Sector	12d
....	....	....	....	....	....	1.14	3.37	98.68	274.67	366.55	I362.63	286.02	233.02	130.27	Claims on Deposit Money Banks	12e
....	....	....	....	....	....	7.74	49.04	241.14	551.94	779.85	I854.28	1,138.64	1,063.45	1,506.63	Reserve Money	14
....	....	....	....	....	....	1.83	9.75	119.45	345.55	640.15	I731.06	972.10	I855.45	1,122.07	of which: Currency Outside DMB	14a
....	....	....	....	....	....	—	57.25	358.73	744.09	1,068.96	I1181.13	1,104.75	1,494.36	2,147.89	Foreign Liabilities	16c
....	....	....	....	....	....	—	.20	90.12	17.45	21.38	I126.37	9.99	60.00	85.72	Central Government Deposits	16d
....	....	....	....	....	....	.08	.06	1.72	24.72	79.11	I95.26	91.92	161.36	215.21	Capital Accounts	17a
....	....	....	....	....	....	-6.20	-1.62	-11.40	45.63	70.37	I91.49	186.07	67.97	125.81	Other Items (Net)	17r
End of Period																
															Deposit Money Banks	
....	....	....	....	....	....	1.48	10.60	48.87	52.44	54.38	36.54	52.05	I200.66	360.92	Reserves	20
....	....	....	....	....	....	—	.99	62.11	113.76	171.03	200.79	153.90	I297.69	644.99	Foreign Assets	21
....	....	....	....	....	....	9.46	28.16	122.13	31.56	10.31	13.68	67.58	I184.46	267.81	Claims on Central Government	22a
....	....	....	....	....	....	—	4.03	10.21	22.82	2.59	13.19	23.68	I33.01	14.98	Claims on Local Government	22b
....	....	....	....	....	....	6.79	32.81	243.28	493.91	692.37	852.27	1,120.82	I144.17	146.32	Claims on Nonfin.Pub.Enterprises	22c
....	....	....	....	....	....	1.52	11.23	91.06	174.79	433.62	600.88	617.05	I1265.65	1,453.15	Claims on Private Sector	22d
													I23.06	37.30	Claims on Nonbank Financial Insts	22g
....	....	....	....	....	....	7.21	49.94	121.24	173.69	244.57	263.13	326.49	I210.00	357.76	Demand Deposits	24
....	....	....	....	....	....	9.17	23.61	106.02	228.68	358.18	435.57	624.02	I698.48	1,040.18	Time, Savings,& Fgn.Currency Dep.	25
													I1.21	2.10	Money Market Instruments	26aa
....	....	....	....	....	....			7.36	7.80	61.64	244.21	293.67	I623.24	522.87	Foreign Liabilities	26c
....	....	....	....	....	....	2.07	21.67	149.65	56.54	35.81	27.84	33.55	I13.51	44.72	Central Government Deposits	26d
....	....	....	....	....	....	2.78	6.47	104.70	292.23	389.12	368.12	285.91	I229.83	130.27	Credit from Monetary Authorities	26g
													I.77	1.55	Liabs. to Nonbank Financial Insts	26j
....	....	....	....	....	....	1.21	9.57	136.65	333.05	569.03	731.41	839.27	I756.20	1,242.83	Capital Accounts	27a
....	....	....	....	....	....	-3.18	-23.44	-47.96	-202.72	-294.04	-352.93	-367.84	I-384.56	-416.81	Other Items (Net)	27r
End of Period																
															Monetary Survey	
....	....	....	....	....	....	—	-6.94	41.44	187.01	238.85	I262.37	472.08	I-620.10	181.71	Foreign Assets (Net)	31n
....	....	....	....	....	....	16.27	107.39	463.12	933.10	1,536.40	I1824.80	2,314.34	I2991.14	3,532.62	Domestic Credit	32
....	....	....	....	....	....	7.87	58.53	118.57	241.58	406.04	I355.59	548.88	I1520.10	1,874.84	Claims on Central Govt. (Net)	32an
....	....	....	....	....	....	—	4.03	10.21	22.82	2.59	13.19	23.68	I33.01	14.98	Claims on Local Government	32b
....	....	....	....	....	....	6.88	33.60	243.28	493.91	692.37	I852.27	1,120.82	I144.17	146.32	Claims on Nonfin.Pub.Enterprises	32c
....	....	....	....	....	....	1.52	11.23	91.06	174.79	435.41	I603.76	620.97	I1270.75	1,459.19	Claims on Private Sector	32d
													I23.06	37.30	Claims on Nonbank Financial Inst	32g
....	....	....	....	....	....	9.04	59.79	242.07	524.20	885.04	I994.51	1,298.83	I1065.46	1,479.84	Money	34
....	....	....	....	....	....	9.17	23.61	107.17	229.01	360.18	I435.57	624.02	I698.48	1,040.18	Quasi-Money	35
													I1.21	2.10	Money Market Instruments	36aa
													I.77	1.55	Liabs. to Nonbank Financial Insts	36j
....	....	....	....	....	....	1.29	9.63	138.37	357.77	648.15	I826.67	931.20	I917.56	1,458.04	Capital Accounts	37a
....	....	....	....	....	....	-3.23	7.42	16.94	9.13	-118.10	I-169.58	-67.63	I-312.44	-267.37	Other Items (Net)	37r
....	....	....	....	....	....	18.21	83.39	349.24	753.21	1,245.22	I1430.08	1,922.86	I1763.94	2,520.02	Money plus Quasi-Money	35l
Percent Per Annum																
															Interest Rates	
....	....	....	....	....	....	....	....	....	143.9	28.3	20.2	19.0	....	....	Refinancing Rate	60a
....	....	....	....	....	....	....	....	....				28.1	30.9	32.6	Money Market Rate	60b
														11.9	Money Market Rate (Fgn. Cur.)	60b. f
....	....	....	....	....	....	....	....	....		52.9	39.0	23.6	30.5	28.5	Treasury Bill Rate	60c
....	....	....	....	....	....	....	....	....			25.4	23.5	21.7	27.5	Deposit Rate	60l
													9.9	5.3	Deposit Rate (Foreign Currency)	60l. f
....	....	....	....	....	....	....	....	....			36.7	33.3	30.8	35.5	Lending Rate	60p
													22.0	20.4	Lending Rate (Foreign Currency)	60p. f
Period Averages																
															Prices and Labor	
....	....	....	....	....	....	....	....		89.2	100.0	120.9	130.6	139.2	203.2	Consumer Prices	64
Period Averages																
....	....	....	....	....	....	....	2,065	....	....	....	1,686	....	1,659	....	Labor Force	67d
....	....	....	....	2,091	2,071	2,070	2,050	1,688	1,681	1,673	1,660	1,646	1,642	....	Employment	67e
....	....	....	....	....	....	....	15	14	21	25	23	28	32	....	Unemployment	67c
....	....	....	....	....	....	....	.7	.7	1.1	1.0	....	....	....	....	Unemployment Rate (%)	67r

Moldova

921		1970	1971	1972	1973	1974	1975	1976	1977	1978	1979	1980	1981	1982	1983	1984
International Transactions																*Millions of US Dollars*
Exports	**70..*d***	....	....	....	....	....	....	....	....	....	....	....	....	....	....	....
Imports, c.i.f.	**71..*d***	....	....	....	....	....	....	....	....	....	....	....	....	....	....	....
Imports, f.o.b.	**71.v*d***	....	....	....	....	....	....	....	....	....	....	....	....	....	....	....
Balance of Payments																*Millions of US Dollars:*
Current Account, n.i.e.	**78al*d***	....	....	....	....	....	....	....	....	....	....	....	....	....	....	....
Goods: Exports f.o.b.	**78aa*d***	....	....	....	....	....	....	....	....	....	....	....	....	....	....	....
Goods: Imports f.o.b.	**78ab*d***	....	....	....	....	....	....	....	....	....	....	....	....	....	....	....
Trade Balance	**78ac*d***	....	....	....	....	....	....	....	....	....	....	....	....	....	....	....
Services: Credit	**78ad*d***	....	....	....	....	....	....	....	....	....	....	....	....	....	....	....
Services: Debit	**78ae*d***	....	....	....	....	....	....	....	....	....	....	....	....	....	....	....
Balance on Goods & Services	**78af*d***	....	....	....	....	....	....	....	....	....	....	....	....	....	....	....
Income: Credit	**78ag*d***	....	....	....	....	....	....	....	....	....	....	....	....	....	....	....
Income: Debit	**78ah*d***	....	....	....	....	....	....	....	....	....	....	....	....	....	....	....
Balance on Gds, Serv. & Inc.	**78ai*d***	....	....	....	....	....	....	....	....	....	....	....	....	....	....	....
Current Transfers, n.i.e.: Credit	**78aj*d***	....	....	....	....	....	....	....	....	....	....	....	....	....	....	....
Current Transfers: Debit	**78ak*d***	....	....	....	....	....	....	....	....	....	....	....	....	....	....	....
Capital Account, n.i.e.	**78bc*d***	....	....	....	....	....	....	....	....	....	....	....	....	....	....	....
Capital Account, n.i.e.: Credit	**78ba*d***	....	....	....	....	....	....	....	....	....	....	....	....	....	....	....
Capital Account: Debit	**78bb*d***	....	....	....	....	....	....	....	....	....	....	....	....	....	....	....
Financial Account, n.i.e.	**78bj*d***	....	....	....	....	....	....	....	....	....	....	....	....	....	....	....
Direct Investment Abroad	**78bd*d***	....	....	....	....	....	....	....	....	....	....	....	....	....	....	....
Dir. Invest. in Rep. Econ., n.i.e.	**78be*d***	....	....	....	....	....	....	....	....	....	....	....	....	....	....	....
Portfolio Investment Assets	**78bf*d***	....	....	....	....	....	....	....	....	....	....	....	....	....	....	....
Equity Securities	**78bk*d***	....	....	....	....	....	....	....	....	....	....	....	....	....	....	....
Debt Securities	**78bl*d***	....	....	....	....	....	....	....	....	....	....	....	....	....	....	....
Portfolio Investment Liab., n.i.e.	**78bg*d***	....	....	....	....	....	....	....	....	....	....	....	....	....	....	....
Equity Securities	**78bm*d***	....	....	....	....	....	....	....	....	....	....	....	....	....	....	....
Debt Securities	**78bn*d***	....	....	....	....	....	....	....	....	....	....	....	....	....	....	....
Financial Derivatives Assets	**78bw*d***	....	....	....	....	....	....	....	....	....	....	....	....	....	....	....
Financial Derivatives Liabilities	**78bx*d***	....	....	....	....	....	....	....	....	....	....	....	....	....	....	....
Other Investment Assets	**78bh*d***	....	....	....	....	....	....	....	....	....	....	....	....	....	....	....
Monetary Authorities	**78bo*d***	....	....	....	....	....	....	....	....	....	....	....	....	....	....	....
General Government	**78bp*d***	....	....	....	....	....	....	....	....	....	....	....	....	....	....	....
Banks	**78bq*d***	....	....	....	....	....	....	....	....	....	....	....	....	....	....	....
Other Sectors	**78br*d***	....	....	....	....	....	....	....	....	....	....	....	....	....	....	....
Other Investment Liab., n.i.e.	**78bi*d***	....	....	....	....	....	....	....	....	....	....	....	....	....	....	....
Monetary Authorities	**78bs*d***	....	....	....	....	....	....	....	....	....	....	....	....	....	....	....
General Government	**78bt*d***	....	....	....	....	....	....	....	....	....	....	....	....	....	....	....
Banks	**78bu*d***	....	....	....	....	....	....	....	....	....	....	....	....	....	....	....
Other Sectors	**78bv*d***	....	....	....	....	....	....	....	....	....	....	....	....	....	....	....
Net Errors and Omissions	**78ca*d***	....	....	....	....	....	....	....	....	....	....	....	....	....	....	....
Overall Balance	**78cb*d***	....	....	....	....	....	....	....	....	....	....	....	....	....	....	....
Reserves and Related Items	**79da*d***	....	....	....	....	....	....	....	....	....	....	....	....	....	....	....
Reserve Assets	**79db*d***	....	....	....	....	....	....	....	....	....	....	....	....	....	....	....
Use of Fund Credit and Loans	**79dc*d***	....	....	....	....	....	....	....	....	....	....	....	....	....	....	....
Exceptional Financing	**79de*d***	....	....	....	....	....	....	....	....	....	....	....	....	....	....	....
International Investment Position																*Millions of US Dollars*
Assets	**79aa*d***	....	....	....	....	....	....	....	....	....	....	....	....	....	....	....
Direct Investment Abroad	**79ab*d***	....	....	....	....	....	....	....	....	....	....	....	....	....	....	....
Portfolio Investment	**79ac*d***	....	....	....	....	....	....	....	....	....	....	....	....	....	....	....
Equity Securities	**79ad*d***	....	....	....	....	....	....	....	....	....	....	....	....	....	....	....
Debt Securities	**79ae*d***	....	....	....	....	....	....	....	....	....	....	....	....	....	....	....
Financial Derivatives	**79al*d***	....	....	....	....	....	....	....	....	....	....	....	....	....	....	....
Other Investment	**79af*d***	....	....	....	....	....	....	....	....	....	....	....	....	....	....	....
Monetary Authorities	**79ag*d***	....	....	....	....	....	....	....	....	....	....	....	....	....	....	....
General Government	**79ah*d***	....	....	....	....	....	....	....	....	....	....	....	....	....	....	....
Banks	**79ai*d***	....	....	....	....	....	....	....	....	....	....	....	....	....	....	....
Other Sectors	**79aj*d***	....	....	....	....	....	....	....	....	....	....	....	....	....	....	....
Reserve Assets	**79ak*d***	....	....	....	....	....	....	....	....	....	....	....	....	....	....	....
Liabilities	**79la*d***	....	....	....	....	....	....	....	....	....	....	....	....	....	....	....
Dir. Invest. in Rep. Economy	**79lb*d***	....	....	....	....	....	....	....	....	....	....	....	....	....	....	....
Portfolio Investment	**79lc*d***	....	....	....	....	....	....	....	....	....	....	....	....	....	....	....
Equity Securities	**79ld*d***	....	....	....	....	....	....	....	....	....	....	....	....	....	....	....
Debt Securities	**79le*d***	....	....	....	....	....	....	....	....	....	....	....	....	....	....	....
Financial Derivatives	**79ll*d***	....	....	....	....	....	....	....	....	....	....	....	....	....	....	....
Other Investment	**79lf*d***	....	....	....	....	....	....	....	....	....	....	....	....	....	....	....
Monetary Authorities	**79lg*d***	....	....	....	....	....	....	....	....	....	....	....	....	....	....	....
General Government	**79lh*d***	....	....	....	....	....	....	....	....	....	....	....	....	....	....	....
Banks	**79li*d***	....	....	....	....	....	....	....	....	....	....	....	....	....	....	....
Other Sectors	**79lj*d***	....	....	....	....	....	....	....	....	....	....	....	....	....	....	....
National Accounts																*Millions of Lei*
Househ.Cons.Expend.,incl.NPISHs	**96f**	....	....	....	....	....	....	....	....	....	....	....	....	....	....	....
Government Consumption Expend.	**91f**	....	....	....	....	....	....	....	....	....	....	....	....	....	....	....
Gross Fixed Capital Formation	**93e**	....	....	....	....	....	....	....	....	....	....	....	....	....	....	....
Changes in Inventories	**93i**	....	....	....	....	....	....	....	....	....	....	....	....	....	....	....
Exports (Net)	**90n**	....	....	....	....	....	....	....	....	....	....	....	....	....	....	....
Gross Domestic Product (GDP)	**99b**	....	....	....	....	....	....	....	....	....	....	....	....	....	....	....
																Millions:
Population	**99z**	....	....	....	....	....	....	....	....	....	....	....	....	....	....	....

1985	1986	1987	1988	1989	1990	1991	1992	1993	1994	1995	1996	1997	1998	1999		
Millions of US Dollars															**International Transactions**	
....	....	....	....	....	....	....	470	483	619	739	805	890	644	....	Exports	70..d
....	....	....	....	....	....	....	640	628	703	841	1,079	1,200	1,018	....	Imports, c.i.f.	71..d
									672	794	1,077	1,238	1,032		Imports, f.o.b.	71.v d
Minus Sign Indicates Debit															Balance of Payments	
....	....	....	....	....	....	....	....	....	−82.0	−98.4	−201.2	−285.5	−347.3	−33.5	Current Account, n.i.e.	78al d
....	....	....	....	....	....	....	....	....	618.5	738.9	822.9	889.6	643.3	469.2	Goods: Exports f.o.b.	78aa d
....	....	....	....	....	....	....	....	....	−672.4	−809.2	−1,082.5	−1,237.8	−1,031.7	−592.2	Goods: Imports f.o.b.	78ab d
....	....	....	....	....	....	....	....	....	−53.9	−70.3	−259.6	−348.2	−388.4	−123.1	*Trade Balance*	78ac d
....	....	....	....	....	....	....	....	....	32.8	145.0	113.7	135.1	121.6	110.7	Services: Credit	78ad d
....	....	....	....	....	....	....	....	....	−79.0	−207.4	−180.6	−196.1	−196.1	−159.5	Services: Debit	78ae d
....	....	....	....	....	....	....	....	....	−100.0	−132.7	−326.5	−409.2	−462.9	−171.9	*Balance on Goods & Services*	78af d
....	....	....	....	....	....	....	....	....	10.8	14.1	99.1	132.6	136.9	120.4	Income: Credit	78ag d
....	....	....	....	....	....	....	....	....	−26.1	−32.3	−44.1	−85.2	−104.1	−81.4	Income: Debit	78ah d
....	....	....	....	....	....	....	....	....	−115.4	−150.9	−271.5	−361.8	−430.1	−132.9	*Balance on Gds, Serv. & Inc.*	78ai d
....	....	....	....	....	....	....	....	....	36.9	66.6	73.1	98.1	101.0	120.0	Current Transfers, n.i.e.: Credit	78aj d
....	....	....	....	....	....	....	....	....	−3.6	−14.1	−2.8	−21.8	−18.2	−20.5	Current Transfers: Debit	78ak d
....	....	....	....	....	....	....	....	....	−1.0	−.4	—	−.3	−.3	−.2	Capital Account, n.i.e.	78bc d
....	....	....	....	....	....	....	....	....	—	—	.1	.1	2.1	.2	Capital Account, n.i.e.: Credit	78ba d
....	....	....	....	....	....	....	....	....	−1.0	−.4	−.1	−.4	−2.4	−.4	Capital Account: Debit	78bb d
....	....	....	....	....	....	....	....	....	211.1	−57.9	45.0	99.9	−6.8	−85.8	Financial Account, n.i.e.	78bj d
....	....	....	....	....	....	....	....	....	....	−.5	−.6	−.5	.3	−.8	Direct Investment Abroad	78bd d
....	....	....	....	....	....	....	....	....	11.6	25.8	23.6	75.7	85.9	33.5	Dir. Invest. in Rep. Econ., n.i.e.	78be d
....	....	....	....	....	....	....	....	....	−.4	—	—	—	—	....	Portfolio Investment Assets	78bf d
....	....	....	....	....	....	....	....	....	−.4	—	—	—	—	....	Equity Securities	78bk d
....	....	....	....	....	....	....	....	....	....	—	—	—	—	....	Debt Securities	78bl d
....	....	....	....	....	....	....	....	....	.6	−.5	30.8	25.6	−53.8	−8.2	Portfolio Investment Liab., n.i.e.	78bg d
....	....	....	....	....	....	....	....	....	.6	−.6	.8	3.7	11.8	4.3	Equity Securities	78bm d
....	....	....	....	....	....	....	....	....	....	.1	30.0	21.9	−65.6	−12.5	Debt Securities	78bn d
....	....	....	....	....	....	....	....	....	....	—	—	—	—	....	Financial Derivatives Assets	78bw d
....	....	....	....	....	....	....	....	....	....	—	—	—	—	....	Financial Derivatives Liabilities	78bx d
....	....	....	....	....	....	....	....	....	−81.7	−116.3	−51.4	5.0	−52.6	−125.5	Other Investment Assets	78bh d
....	....	....	....	....	....	....	....	....	−1.3	2.8	.2	3.7	2.9	....	Monetary Authorities	78bo d
....	....	....	....	....	....	....	....	....	−4.1	11.9	12.3	4.7	2.6	....	General Government	78bp d
....	....	....	....	....	....	....	....	....	−10.1	−13.5	−6.5	10.5	−11.0	−15.4	Banks	78bq d
....	....	....	....	....	....	....	....	....	−66.2	−117.5	−57.4	−13.9	−47.1	−110.1	Other Sectors	78br d
....	....	....	....	....	....	....	....	....	281.0	33.6	42.6	−5.9	13.4	15.2	Other Investment Liab., n.i.e.	78bi d
....	....	....	....	....	....	....	....	....	3.1	1.9	−2.0	−2.7	5.1	−2.4	Monetary Authorities	78bs d
....	....	....	....	....	....	....	....	....	147.0	−19.4	—	−56.5	14.9	−15.1	General Government	78bt d
....	....	....	....	....	....	....	....	....	−.8	11.4	22.0	12.3	−2.7	−20.5	Banks	78bu d
....	....	....	....	....	....	....	....	....	131.6	39.7	22.6	41.0	−3.9	53.1	Other Sectors	78bv d
....	....	....	....	....	....	....	....	....	−115.2	−18.3	11.0	3.8	12.8	−2.5	Net Errors and Omissions	78ca d
....	....	....	....	....	....	....	....	....	12.9	−175.0	−145.2	−182.1	−341.6	−122.0	*Overall Balance*	78cb d
....	....	....	....	....	....	....	....	....	−12.9	175.0	145.2	182.1	341.6	122.0	Reserves and Related Items	79da d
....	....	....	....	....	....	....	....	....	−103.1	−76.8	−56.8	−52.5	222.5	−53.1	Reserve Assets	79db d
....	....	....	....	....	....	....	....	....	71.5	64.8	25.2	.8	−64.4	4.0	Use of Fund Credit and Loans	79dc d
....	....	....	....	....	....	....	....	....	18.7	187.0	176.8	233.9	183.5	171.0	Exceptional Financing	79de d
Millions of US Dollars															**International Investment Position**	
....	....	....	....	....	....	....	....	....	303.2	500.7	610.5	655.9	432.6	582.5	Assets	79aa d
....	....	....	....	....	....	....	....	....	17.8	18.3	18.9	19.3	19.0	19.8	Direct Investment Abroad	79ab d
....	....	....	....	....	....	....	....	....	.4	.4	.4	.4	.4	.4	Portfolio Investment	79ac d
....	....	....	....	....	....	....	....	....	.4	.4	.4	.4	.4	.4	Equity Securities	79ad d
....	....	....	....	....	....	....	....	....	—	—	—	—	—	—	Debt Securities	79ae d
....	....	....	....	....	....	....	....	....	—	—	—	—	—	—	Financial Derivatives	79al d
....	....	....	....	....	....	....	....	....	105.3	225.0	277.7	270.5	269.8	372.0	Other Investment	79af d
....	....	....	....	....	....	....	....	....	9.9	7.1	6.8	—	.1	—	Monetary Authorities	79ag d
....	....	....	....	....	....	....	....	....	31.7	19.9	7.6	6.0	.4	.4	General Government	79ah d
....	....	....	....	....	....	....	....	....	27.4	40.8	47.3	36.7	44.9	58.1	Banks	79ai d
....	....	....	....	....	....	....	....	....	36.3	157.2	215.9	227.9	224.5	313.6	Other Sectors	79aj d
....	....	....	....	....	....	....	....	....	179.8	257.0	313.6	365.7	143.4	190.3	Reserve Assets	79ak d
....	....	....	....	....	....	....	....	....	687.7	1,004.7	1,280.9	1,616.5	1,797.3	1,890.3	Liabilities	79la d
....	....	....	....	....	....	....	....	....	27.6	94.5	118.2	193.9	275.3	334.8	Dir. Invest. in Rep. Economy	79lb d
....	....	....	....	....	....	....	....	....	.7	.2	62.0	296.0	233.9	91.5	Portfolio Investment	79lc d
....	....	....	....	....	....	....	....	....	.7	.2	2.1	5.7	12.0	16.4	Equity Securities	79ld d
....	....	....	....	....	....	....	....	....	—	.1	59.9	290.3	221.9	75.1	Debt Securities	79le d
....	....	....	....	....	....	....	....	....							Financial Derivatives	79ll d
....	....	....	....	....	....	....	....	....	659.4	910.0	1,100.7	1,126.6	1,288.1	1,464.0	Other Investment	79lf d
....	....	....	....	....	....	....	....	....	164.2	230.2	247.7	233.0	176.8	175.3	Monetary Authorities	79lg d
....	....	....	....	....	....	....	....	....	349.4	435.8	491.9	485.0	588.2	642.2	General Government	79lh d
....	....	....	....	....	....	....	....	....	1.1	12.4	34.2	46.1	50.6	29.6	Banks	79li d
....	....	....	....	....	....	....	....	....	144.8	231.6	326.9	362.4	472.5	617.0	Other Sectors	79lj d
Millions of Lei															**National Accounts**	
....	....	....	....	....	....	14	80	735	2,508	3,692	5,350	5,943	....	....	Househ.Cons.Expend.,incl.NPISHs	96f
....	....	....	....	....	....	5	31	283	1,065	1,678	1,987	2,349	....	....	Government Consumption Expend.	91f
....	....	....	....	....	....	4	31	283	914	1,034	1,517	1,714	....	....	Gross Fixed Capital Formation	93e
....	....	....	....	....	....	3	84	734	451	578	351	397	....	....	Changes in Inventories	93i
....	....	....	....	....	....	—	−33	−213	−202	−503	−1,547	−1,748	....	....	Exports (Net)	90n
....	....	....	....	....	....	26	192	1,821	4,737	6,480	7,658	8,655	....	....	Gross Domestic Product (GDP)	99b
Midyear Estimates																
....	....	....	....	....	....	4.36	4.35	4.35	4.35	4.35	4.33	I 3.65	3.65	4.38	**Population**	99z

(See notes in the back of the book.)

Mongolia

948

		1970	1971	1972	1973	1974	1975	1976	1977	1978	1979	1980	1981	1982	1983	1984
Exchange Rates																*Togrogs per SDR:*
Market Rate	aa	....	....	....	....	....	....	....	....	....	....	....	....			
																Togrogs per US Dollar:
Market Rate	ae	....	....	....	....	....	....	....	....	....	....	....	....			
Market Rate	rf	....	....	....	....	....	....	....	....	....	....	....	....			
Fund Position																*Millions of SDRs:*
Quota	2f. *s*	....	....	....	....	....	....	....	....	....	....	....	....			
SDRs	1b. *s*	....	....	....	....	....	....	....	....	....	....	....	....			
Reserve Position in the Fund	1c. *s*	....	....	....	....	....	....	....	....	....	....	....	....			
Total Fund Cred.&Loans Outstg.	2tl	....	....	....	....	....	....	....	....	....	....	....	....			
International Liquidity												*Millions of US Dollars Unless Otherwise Indicated:*				
Total Reserves Minus Gold	1l. *d*	....	....	....	....	....	....	....	....	....	....	....	....	....	....	....
SDRs	1b. *d*	....	....	....	....	....	....	....	....	....	....	....	....	....	....	....
Reserve Position in the Fund	1c. *d*	....	....	....	....	....	....	....	....	....	....	....	....	....	....	....
Foreign Exchange	1d. *d*	....	....	....	....	....	....	....	....	....	....	....	....	....	....	....
Gold (Million Fine Troy Ounces)	1ad	....	....	....	....	....	....	....	....	....	....	.04	.05	.04	.04	.04
Gold (National Valuation)	1an *d*	....	....	....	....	....	....	....	....	....	....	11.00	12.60	13.10	13.50	12.90
Monetary Authorities: Other Liab.	4.. *d*	....	....	....	....	....	....	....	....	....	....	....	....	....	....	....
Deposit Money Banks: Assets	7a. *d*	....	....	....	....	....	....	....	....	....	....	....	....	....	....	....
Liabilities	7b. *d*	....	....	....	....	....	....	....	....	....	....	....	....	....	....	....
Monetary Authorities																*Millions of Togrogs:*
Foreign Assets	11	....	....	....	....	....	....	....	....	....	....	....	....	....	....	....
Claims on Central Government	12a	....	....	....	....	....	....	....	....	....	....	....	....	....	....	....
Claims on Deposit Money Banks	12e	....	....	....	....	....	....	....	....	....	....	....	....	....	....	....
Reserve Money	14	....	....	....	....	....	....	....	....	....	....	....	....	....	....	....
of which: Currency Outside DMBs	14a	....	....	....	....	....	....	....	....	....	....	....	....	....	....	....
Liabs. of Central Bank: Securities	16ac	....	....	....	....	....	....	....	....	....	....	....	....	....	....	....
Foreign Liabilities	16c	....	....	....	....	....	....	....	....	....	....	....	....	....	....	....
Central Government Deposits	16d	....	....	....	....	....	....	....	....	....	....	....	....	....	....	....
Capital Accounts	17a	....	....	....	....	....	....	....	....	....	....	....	....	....	....	....
Other Items (Net)	17r	....	....	....	....	....	....	....	....	....	....	....	....	....	....	....
Deposit Money Banks																*Millions of Togrogs:*
Reserves	20	....	....	....	....	....	....	....	....	....	....	....	....	....	....	....
Other Claims on Monetary Author.	20c	....	....	....	....	....	....	....	....	....	....	....	....	....	....	....
Foreign Assets	21	....	....	....	....	....	....	....	....	....	....	....	....	....	....	....
Claims on Central Government	22a	....	....	....	....	....	....	....	....	....	....	....	....	....	....	....
Claims on Nonfin.Pub.Enterprises	22c	....	....	....	....	....	....	....	....	....	....	....	....	....	....	....
Claims on Private Sector	22d	....	....	....	....	....	....	....	....	....	....	....	....	....	....	....
Demand Deposits	24	....	....	....	....	....	....	....	....	....	....	....	....	....	....	....
Time, Savings,& Fgn.Currency Dep.	25	....	....	....	....	....	....	....	....	....	....	....	....	....	....	....
Money Market Instruments	26aa	....	....	....	....	....	....	....	....	....	....	....	....	....	....	....
Restricted Deposits	26b	....	....	....	....	....	....	....	....	....	....	....	....	....	....	....
Foreign Liabilities	26c	....	....	....	....	....	....	....	....	....	....	....	....	....	....	....
Central Government Deposits	26d	....	....	....	....	....	....	....	....	....	....	....	....	....	....	....
Credit from Monetary Authorities	26g	....	....	....	....	....	....	....	....	....	....	....	....	....	....	....
Capital Accounts	27a	....	....	....	....	....	....	....	....	....	....	....	....	....	....	....
Other Items (Net)	27r	....	....	....	....	....	....	....	....	....	....	....	....	....	....	....
Monetary Survey																*Millions of Togrogs:*
Foreign Assets (Net)	31n	....	....	....	....	....	....	....	....	....	....	....	....	....	....	....
Domestic Credit	32	....	....	....	....	....	....	....	....	....	....	....	....	....	....	....
Claims on Central Govt. (Net)	32an	....	....	....	....	....	....	....	....	....	....	....	....	....	....	....
Claims on Nonfin.Pub.Enterprises	32c	....	....	....	....	....	....	....	....	....	....	....	....	....	....	....
Claims on Private Sector	32d	....	....	....	....	....	....	....	....	....	....	....	....	....	....	....
Money	34	....	....	....	....	....	....	....	....	....	....	....	....	....	....	....
Quasi-Money	35	....	....	....	....	....	....	....	....	....	....	....	....	....	....	....
Money Market Instruments	36aa	....	....	....	....	....	....	....	....	....	....	....	....	....	....	....
Liabs. of Central Bank: Securities	36ac	....	....	....	....	....	....	....	....	....	....	....	....	....	....	....
Restricted Deposits	36b	....	....	....	....	....	....	....	....	....	....	....	....	....	....	....
Capital Accounts	37a	....	....	....	....	....	....	....	....	....	....	....	....	....	....	....
Other Items (Net)	37r	....	....	....	....	....	....	....	....	....	....	....	....	....	....	....
Money plus Quasi-Money	35l	....	....	....	....	....	....	....	....	....	....	....	....	....	....	....
Interest Rates																*Percent per Annum*
Bank Rate *(End of Period)*	60	....	....	....	....	....	....	....	....	....	....	....	....	....	....	....
Deposit Rate *(End of Period)*	60l	....	....	....	....	....	....	....	....	....	....	....	....	....	....	....
Lending Rate *(End of Period)*	60p	....	....	....	....	....	....	....	....	....	....	....	....	....	....	....
Prices, Production, Labor																*Index Numbers (1995=100):*
Consumer Prices	64	....	....	....	....	....	....	....	....	....	....	....	....	....	....	....
Wages: Avg. Earnings ('90=100)	65	....	....	....	....	....	....	....	....	....	....	....	....	....	....	....
Industrial Production ('90=100)	66	....	....	....	....	....	....	....	....	....	....	....	....	....	....	....
Industrial Employment ('90=100)	67	....	....	....	....	....	....	....	....	....	....	....	....	....	....	....
International Transactions																*Millions of US Dollars*
Exports	70.. *d*	....	....	....	....	....	....	....	....	....	....	402.8	468.8	561.7	609.8	674.4
Imports, c.i.f.	71.. *d*	....	....	....	....	....	....	....	....	....	....	547.8	703.7	790.8	928.1	975.2

	1985	1986	1987	1988	1989	1990	1991	1992	1993	1994	1995	1996	1997	1998	1999		
Exchange Rates																	
End of Period																Market Rate	aa
	....	....	....	....	....	19.92	56.36	144.47	I544.63	604.51	704.03	997.24	1,097.16	1,270.04	1,471.84	Market Rate	aa
End of Period (ae) Period Average (rf)																	
	....	....	....	....	....	14.00	39.40	105.07	I396.51	414.09	473.62	693.51	813.16	902.00	1,072.37	Market Rate	ae
							9.52	42.56	....	I412.72	448.61	548.40	789.99	840.83	1,021.87	Market Rate	rf
Fund Position																	
End of Period																	
	....	....	....	....	....		25.00	37.10	37.10	37.10	37.10	37.10	37.10	37.10	51.10	Quota	2f. s
	....	....	....	....	....		.03	.01	.02	1.98	1.70	.30	.52	.34	.12	SDRs	1b. s
	....	....	....	....	....			.01	.01						.02	Reserve Position in the Fund	1c. s
	....	....	....	....	....		11.25	13.75	23.03	37.87	31.62	30.31	35.25	34.32	37.47	Total Fund Cred.&Loans Outstg.	2tl
International Liquidity																	
End of Period																	
	....	....	....	....	....		....	16.35	59.74	81.39	117.03	107.44	175.71	94.09	136.49	Total Reserves Minus Gold	1l. d
	....	....	....	....	....		.04	.01	.03	2.89	2.52	.43	.70	.48	.16	SDRs	1b. d
	....	....	....	....	....			.01	.01	.01	.01	.01	.01	.01	.03	Reserve Position in the Fund	1c. d
	....	....	....	....	....		....	16.33	59.70	78.49	114.50	107.00	175.00	93.60	136.30	Foreign Exchange	1d. d
	.05	.03	.03	.03	.03	.04	.14	.02	.02	.03	.10	.15	.08	.03	—	Gold (Million Fine Troy Ounces)	1ad
	18.00	18.00	18.50	19.70	19.00	22.90	49.70	24.20	5.31	11.00	34.50	53.60	24.60	9.10	.40	Gold (National Valuation)	1an d
	....	....	....	....	....		.27	.13	26.13	28.77	30.17	16.04	4.50	—	5.30	Monetary Authorities: Other Liab.	4.. d
	....	....	....	....	....		81.59	19.90	41.17	41.71	53.66	60.86	81.68	28.95	38.90	Deposit Money Banks: Assets	7a. d
	....	....	....	....	....		169.52	62.02	11.67	11.90	14.06	12.38	15.06	22.14	9.13	Liabilities	7b. d
Monetary Authorities																	
End of Period																	
	....	....	....	....	....		1,991	2,672	25,622	45,440	63,288	67,814	114,083	133,293	186,895	Foreign Assets	11
	....	....	....	....	....		714	1,985	7,477	13,661	4,520	38,953	23,980	26,111	24,136	Claims on Central Government	12a
	....	....	....	....	....		1,529	6,153	6,637	10,375	7,740	1,712	3,093	5,631	6,651	Claims on Deposit Money Banks	12e
	....	....	....	....	....		2,067	5,015	14,266	29,081	37,508	51,167	62,967	74,491	112,062	Reserve Money	14
	....	....	....	....	....		1,694	1,839	8,751	18,946	25,591	40,136	49,768	56,446	87,281	of which: Currency Outside DMBs	14a
	....	....	....	....	....				1,500	2,106	830	—	19,296	11,715	21,200	Liabs. of Central Bank: Securities	16ac
	....	....	....	....	....		645	2,000	22,899	34,804	36,548	41,343	42,328	43,585	60,832	Foreign Liabilities	16c
	....	....	....	....	....		784	1,202	580	2,465	9,500	8,388	12,984	24,010	17,215	Central Government Deposits	16d
	....	....	....	....	....		3,285	5,339	2,972	4,998	7,998	24,004	37,082	41,049	37,921	Capital Accounts	17a
	....	....	....	....	....		-2,548	-2,747	-2,481	-3,978	-16,837	-16,422	-33,502	-29,815	-31,548	Other Items (Net)	17r
Deposit Money Banks																	
End of Period																	
	....	....	....	....	....		345	3,023	5,690	10,319	12,531	17,848	13,457	17,921	24,171	Reserves	20
	....	....	....	....	....				1,500	2,106	830	—	19,055	11,697	21,200	Other Claims on Monetary Author.	20c
	....	....	....	....	....		3,215	2,091	16,325	17,272	25,412	42,207	66,416	26,116	41,711	Foreign Assets	21
	....	....	....	....	....		1,358	2,793	513	737	643	10,472	35,451	38,328	39,269	Claims on Central Government	22a
	....	....	....	....	....		9,501	11,789	16,938	12,193	10,883	8,660	7,963	10,151	4,661	Claims on Nonfin.Pub.Enterprises	22c
	....	....	....	....	....		3,351	7,340	14,675	40,763	51,838	59,763	44,256	77,293	75,821	Claims on Private Sector	22d
	....	....	....	....	....		5,592	5,790	9,756	14,104	17,045	20,702	26,341	26,136	27,544	Demand Deposits	24
	....	....	....	....	....		2,601	5,412	24,216	43,906	59,408	58,757	93,957	84,668	105,341	Time, Savings,& Fgn.Currency Dep.	25
	....	....	....	....	....		—	—	—	—	—	287	26	24		Money Market Instruments	26aa
	....	....	....	....	....		—	—	—	—	—	15,821	6,430	6,938	3,604	Restricted Deposits	26b
	....	....	....	....	....		6,679	6,517	4,629	4,926	6,660	8,585	12,246	19,973	9,794	Foreign Liabilities	26c
	....	....	....	....	....		1,186	1,950	7,498	8,451	16,655	21,768	33,258	20,081	24,126	Central Government Deposits	26d
	....	....	....	....	....		1,523	6,288	5,391	10,152	7,402	18,574	763	4,459	1,900	Credit from Monetary Authorities	26g
	....	....	....	....	....		2,139	3,782	11,460	15,892	18,725	4,789	28,518	34,167	41,568	Capital Accounts	27a
	....	....	....	....	....		-1,950	-2,702	-7,307	-14,041	-23,758	-10,334	-14,944	-14,943	-7,070	Other Items (Net)	27r
Monetary Survey																	
End of Period																	
	....	....	....	....	....		-2,119	-3,755	14,419	22,981	45,492	60,093	125,923	95,851	157,980	Foreign Assets (Net)	31n
	....	....	....	....	....		12,957	20,757	31,535	56,446	41,730	93,206	69,315	116,752	107,111	Domestic Credit	32
	....	....	....	....	....		102	1,627	-87	3,483	-20,992	19,270	13,189	20,348	22,064	Claims on Central Govt. (Net)	32an
	....	....	....	....	....		9,501	11,789	16,938	12,193	10,883	8,660	7,963	10,151	4,661	Claims on Nonfin.Pub.Enterprises	32c
	....	....	....	....	....		3,354	7,341	14,684	40,770	51,839	65,277	48,164	86,253	80,386	Claims on Private Sector	32d
	....	....	....	....	....		7,314	7,641	18,547	33,050	42,637	60,838	76,109	82,582	114,826	Money	34
	....	....	....	....	....		2,601	5,412	24,216	43,906	59,408	58,757	93,957	84,668	105,341	Quasi-Money	35
	....	....	....	....	....		—	—	—	—	—	287	29	26	24	Money Market Instruments	36aa
	....	....	....	....	....		—	—	—	—	—	—	241	18	—	Liabs. of Central Bank: Securities	36ac
	....	....	....	....	....		—	—	—	—	—	15,821	6,430	6,938	3,604	Restricted Deposits	36b
	....	....	....	....	....		5,424	9,122	14,432	20,891	26,723	28,794	65,599	75,216	79,489	Capital Accounts	37a
	....	....	....	....	....		-4,501	-5,172	-11,241	-18,420	-41,546	-11,198	-47,125	-36,846	-38,194	Other Items (Net)	37r
	....	....	....	....	....		9,915	13,053	42,763	76,956	102,045	119,595	170,066	167,250	220,167	Money plus Quasi-Money	35l
Interest Rates																	
Percent per Annum																	
	....						....	....	628.8	180.0	150.0	109.0	45.5	23.3	11.4	Bank Rate (End of Period)	60
	....	300.0	300.0	300.0	300.0	300.0	400.0	500.0	125.2	101.1	60.1	36.4	37.9	24.3	19.8	Deposit Rate (End of Period)	60l
	....	....					....	....	300.0	233.6	114.9	91.9	74.8	40.0	37.7	Lending Rate (End of Period)	60p
Prices, Production, Labor																	
Period Averages																	
							....	9.2	34.0	63.8	100.0	I149.3	203.9	223.0	239.9	Consumer Prices	64
	93.9	94.2	94.2	95.3	99.4	100.0	228.9	348.7	....	....	....	....	....	....	....	Wages: Avg. Earnings ('90=100)	65
	88.8	95.8	99.8	103.3	106.0	100.0	84.9	72.4	63.0	65.3	....	....	....	....	....	Industrial Production ('90=100)	66
	85.9	90.2	95.1	101.3	101.3	100.0	98.4	97.9	....	....	....	....	....	....	....	Industrial Employment ('90=100)	67
International Transactions																	
Millions of US Dollars																	
	689.1	716.1	717.9	739.1	721.5	660.7	348.0	388.5	382.6	356.1	473.3	424.3	451.5	345.2	763.2	Exports	70.. d
	1,095.5	1,839.7	1,104.6	1,113.6	963.0	924.0	360.9	418.3	379.0	258.4	415.3	450.9	468.3	503.3	1,010.1	Imports, c.i.f.	71. d

Mongolia

948

		1970	1971	1972	1973	1974	1975	1976	1977	1978	1979	1980	1981	1982	1983	1984
Balance of Payments															_Millions of US Dollars:_	
Current Account, n.i.e.	78al _d_	....	....	....	....	....	....	....	....	....	....	....	−807.5	−845.5	−824.1	−740.0
Goods: Exports f.o.b.	78aa _d_	....	....	....	....	....	....	....	....	....	....	....	438.1	518.6	556.8	596.2
Goods: Imports f.o.b.	78ab _d_	....	....	....	....	....	....	....	....	....	....	....	−1,240.7	−1,352.5	−1,362.3	−1,308.8
Trade Balance	78ac _d_												−802.6	−833.9	−805.5	−712.6
Services: Credit	78ad _d_	....	....	....	....	....	....	....	....	....	....	....	37.3	48.5	55.3	52.6
Services: Debit	78ae _d_	....	....	....	....	....	....	....	....	....	....	....	−31.2	−39.6	−42.7	−40.6
Balance on Goods & Services	78af _d_												−796.5	−825.0	−792.9	−700.6
Income: Credit	78ag _d_	....	....	....	....	....	....	....	....	....	....	....	.2	.2	—	.1
Income: Debit	78ah _d_	....	....	....	....	....	....	....	....	....	....	....	−11.1	−20.6	−31.1	−39.1
Balance on Gds, Serv. & Inc.	78ai _d_												−807.4	−845.4	−824.0	−739.6
Current Transfers, n.i.e.: Credit	78aj _d_	....	....	....	....	....	....	....	....	....	....	....				
Current Transfers: Debit	78ak _d_	....	....	....	....	....	....	....	....	....	....	....	−.1	−.1	−.1	−.4
Capital Account, n.i.e.	78bc _d_	....	....	....	....	....	....	....	....	....	....	....	—	—	—	—
Capital Account, n.i.e.: Credit	78ba _d_	....	....	....	....	....	....	....	....	....	....	....	—	—	—	—
Capital Account: Debit	78bb _d_	....	....	....	....	....	....	....	....	....	....	....	—	—	—	—
Financial Account, n.i.e.	78bj _d_	....	....	....	....	....	....	....	....	....	....	....	807.5	867.3	739.3	742.9
Direct Investment Abroad	78bd _d_	....	....	....	....	....	....	....	....	....	....	....	—	—	—	—
Dir. Invest. in Rep. Econ., n.i.e.	78be _d_	....	....	....	....	....	....	....	....	....	....	....	—	—	—	—
Portfolio Investment Assets	78bf _d_	....	....	....	....	....	....	....	....	....	....	....	—	—	—	—
Equity Securities	78bk _d_	....	....	....	....	....	....	....	....	....	....	....	—	—	—	—
Debt Securities	78bl _d_	....	....	....	....	....	....	....	....	....	....	....	—	—	—	—
Portfolio Investment Liab., n.i.e.	78bg _d_	....	....	....	....	....	....	....	....	....	....	....	—	—	—	—
Equity Securities	78bm _d_	....	....	....	....	....	....	....	....	....	....	....	—	—	—	—
Debt Securities	78bn _d_	....	....	....	....	....	....	....	....	....	....	....	—	—	—	—
Financial Derivatives Assets	78bw _d_	....	....	....	....	....	....	....	....	....	....	....	....	....	....	....
Financial Derivatives Liabilities	78bx _d_	....	....	....	....	....	....	....	....	....	....	....	....	....	....	....
Other Investment Assets	78bh _d_	....	....	....	....	....	....	....	....	....	....	....	—	—	—	—
Monetary Authorities	78bo _d_	....	....	....	....	....	....	....	....	....	....	....	—	—	—	—
General Government	78bp _d_	....	....	....	....	....	....	....	....	....	....	....	—	—	—	—
Banks	78bq _d_	....	....	....	....	....	....	....	....	....	....	....	—	—	—	—
Other Sectors	78br _d_	....	....	....	....	....	....	....	....	....	....	....	—	—	—	—
Other Investment Liab., n.i.e.	78bi _d_	....	....	....	....	....	....	....	....	....	....	....	807.5	867.3	739.3	742.9
Monetary Authorities	78bs _d_	....	....	....	....	....	....	....	....	....	....	....	.6	8.0	−1.3	−3.1
General Government	78bt _d_	....	....	....	....	....	....	....	....	....	....	....	806.9	859.3	740.6	746.0
Banks	78bu _d_	....	....	....	....	....	....	....	....	....	....	....	—	—	—	—
Other Sectors	78bv _d_	....	....	....	....	....	....	....	....	....	....	....	—	—	—	—
Net Errors and Omissions	78ca _d_	....	....	....	....	....	....	....	....	....	....	....	−1.2	−19.9	80.4	10.7
Overall Balance	78cb _d_												−1.2	1.9	−4.4	13.6
Reserves and Related Items	79da _d_	....	....	....	....	....	....	....	....	....	....	....	1.2	−1.9	4.4	−13.6
Reserve Assets	79db _d_	....	....	....	....	....	....	....	....	....	....	....	1.2	−1.9	4.4	−13.6
Use of Fund Credit and Loans	79dc _d_	....	....	....	....	....	....	....	....	....	....	....	—	—	—	—
Exceptional Financing	79de _d_	....	....	....	....	....	....	....	....	....	....	....	....	....	—	—
Government Finance															_Millions of Togrogs:_	
Deficit (−) or Surplus	80	....	....	....	....	....	....	....	....	....	....	....	....	....	....	....
Total Revenue and Grants	81y	....	....	....	....	....	....	....	....	....	....	....	....	....	....	....
Revenue	81	....	....	....	....	....	....	....	....	....	....	....	....	....	....	....
Grants	81z	....	....	....	....	....	....	....	....	....	....	....	....	....	....	....
Exp. & Lending Minus Repay.	82z	....	....	....	....	....	....	....	....	....	....	....	....	....	....	....
Expenditure	82	....	....	....	....	....	....	....	....	....	....	....	....	....	....	....
Lending Minus Repayments	83	....	....	....	....	....	....	....	....	....	....	....	....	....	....	....
Total Financing	80h	....	....	....	....	....	....	....	....	....	....	....	....	....	....	....
Domestic	84a	....	....	....	....	....	....	....	....	....	....	....	....	....	....	....
Foreign	85a	....	....	....	....	....	....	....	....	....	....	....	....	....	....	....
Total Debt by Residence	88	....	....	....	....	....	....	....	....	....	....	....	....	....	....	....
Domestic	88a	....	....	....	....	....	....	....	....	....	....	....	....	....	....	....
Foreign	89a	....	....	....	....	....	....	....	....	....	....	....	....	....	....	....
National Accounts															_Millions of Togrogs:_	
Gross Domestic Product (GDP)	99b	....	....	....	....	....	....	....	....	....	....	6,755	7,426	8,205	8,762	8,996
GDP Volume 1993 prices	99b._p_	....	....	....	....	....	....	....	....	....	....	....	....	....	....	....
GDP Volume 1995 Prices	99b._p_	....	....	....	....	....	....	....	....	....	....	....	....	....	....	....
GDP Volume (1995=100)	99bv _p_	....	....	....	....	....	....	....	....	....	....	68.7	74.4	80.6	85.3	90.4
GDP Deflator (1995=100)	99bi _p_	....	....	....	....	....	....	....	....	....	....	2.3	2.3	2.4	2.4	2.3
																Millions:	
Population	99z	1.25	1.28	1.32	1.36	1.40	1.44	1.47	1.51	1.55	1.60	1.66	1.70	1.75	1.79	1.83

	1985	1986	1987	1988	1989	1990	1991	1992	1993	1994	1995	1996	1997	1998	1999	
Minus Sign Indicates Debit																**Balance of Payments**
	-813.5	-1,060.6	-990.6	-1,033.3	-1,228.7	-639.5	-104.2	-55.7	31.1	46.4	38.9	-100.5	55.2	-128.5	-112.2	Current Account, n.i.e. .... **78al** *d*
	566.9	740.9	817.1	829.1	795.8	444.8	346.5	355.8	365.8	367.0	451.0	423.4	568.5	462.4	454.3	Goods: Exports f.o.b. .... **78aa** *d*
	-1,365.7	-1,692.0	-1,681.4	-1,701.9	-1,758.9	-941.7	-447.6	-384.9	-344.5	-333.3	-425.7	-459.7	-453.1	-524.2	-510.7	Goods: Imports f.o.b. .... **78ab** *d*
	-798.8	-951.1	-864.3	-872.8	-963.1	-496.9	-101.1	-29.1	21.3	33.7	25.3	-36.3	115.4	-61.8	-56.4	*Trade Balance* .... **78ac** *d*
	70.1	84.2	89.0	94.3	36.4	48.1	26.5	34.8	26.0	45.4	57.3	55.7	52.7	77.8	75.8	Services: Credit .... **78ad** *d*
	-39.7	-191.8	-203.7	-220.3	-257.0	-154.5	-66.3	-69.7	-66.9	-91.2	-95.4	-112.8	-105.1	-146.8	-145.7	Services: Debit .... **78ae** *d*
	-768.4	-1,058.7	-979.0	-998.8	-1,183.7	-603.3	-140.9	-64.0	-19.6	-12.1	-12.8	-93.4	63.0	-130.8	-126.3	*Balance on Goods & Services* .... **78af** *d*
	.1	.1	.2	.2	7.5	5.1	—	.2	.8	3.2	3.0	13.4	6.1	10.1	6.7	Income: Credit .... **78ag** *d*
	-45.1	-1.8	-11.5	-34.4	-56.4	-48.7	-4.9	-27.1	-21.0	-22.5	-28.4	-26.7	-18.1	-9.7	-6.6	Income: Debit .... **78ah** *d*
	-813.4	-1,060.4	-990.3	-1,033.0	-1,232.6	-646.9	-145.8	-90.9	-39.8	-31.4	-38.2	-106.7	51.0	-130.4	-126.2	*Balance on Gds, Serv. & Inc.* .... **78ai** *d*
	—	—	—	—	3.9	7.4	41.6	38.7	66.7	77.8	77.1	6.2	4.2	5.5	17.6	Current Transfers, n.i.e.: Credit .... **78aj** *d*
	-.1	-.2	-.3	-.3	—	—	—	-3.5	4.2	—	—	—	—	-3.6	-3.6	Current Transfers: Debit .... **78ak** *d*
	—	—	—	—	—	—	—	—	—	—	—	—	—	—	—	Capital Account, n.i.e. .... **78bc** *d*
	—	—	—	—	—	—	—	—	—	—	—	—	—	—	—	Capital Account, n.i.e.: Credit .... **78ba** *d*
	—	—	—	—	—	—	—	—	—	—	—	—	—	—	—	Capital Account: Debit .... **78bj** *d*
	754.5	1,086.6	1,143.4	1,019.4	1,313.0	541.0	10.8	-44.0	-11.8	-39.0	-15.9	41.3	27.0	126.2	69.6	Financial Account, n.i.e. .... **78bj** *d*
	—	—	—	—	—	—	—	—	—	—	—	—	—	—	—	Direct Investment Abroad .... **78bd** *d*
	—	—	—	—	—	—	—	2.0	7.7	6.9	9.8	15.9	25.0	18.9	30.4	Dir. Invest. in Rep. Econ., n.i.e. .... **78be** *d*
	—	—	—	—	—	—	—	—	—	—	—	—	—	—	....	Portfolio Investment Assets .... **78bf** *d*
	—	—	—	—	—	—	—	—	—	—	—	—	—	—	....	Equity Securities .... **78bk** *d*
	—	—	—	—	—	—	—	—	—	—	—	—	—	—	....	Debt Securities .... **78bl** *d*
	—	—	—	—	—	—	—	—	—	—	1.0	—	—	—	....	Portfolio Investment Liab., n.i.e. ...... **78bg** *d*
	—	—	—	—	—	—	—	—	—	—	—	—	—	—	....	Equity Securities .... **78bm** *d*
	—	—	—	—	—	—	—	—	—	—	1.0	—	—	—	....	Debt Securities .... **78bn** *d*
	....	....	....	....	....	....	....	....	....	....	....	....	....	....	....	Financial Derivatives Assets .... **78bw** *d*
	....	....	....	....	....	....	....	....	....	....	....	....	....	....	....	Financial Derivatives Liabilities .... **78bx** *d*
	—	—	—	—	—	-2.0	—	-64.0	-35.4	-51.0	-49.2	-76.4	-108.1	-54.8	-51.8	Other Investment Assets .... **78bh** *d*
	—	—	—	—	—	—	—	—	—	—	—	—	—	—	....	Monetary Authorities .... **78bo** *d*
	—	—	—	—	—	-2.0	—	—	—	—	—	—	—	—	....	General Government .... **78bp** *d*
	—	—	—	—	—	—	—	-11.6	-24.9	-15.3	-15.3	-9.3	-18.1	—	-14.8	Banks .... **78bq** *d*
	—	—	—	—	—	—	—	-52.4	-10.5	-35.7	-33.9	-67.1	-90.0	-54.8	-37.0	Other Sectors .... **78br** *d*
	754.5	1,086.6	1,143.4	1,019.4	1,313.0	543.0	10.8	18.0	15.9	5.1	22.5	101.8	110.1	162.1	91.0	Other Investment Liab., n.i.e. .... **78bi** *d*
	.6	29.8	24.9	-89.1	84.6	26.3	-32.8	-69.8	-11.2	—	—	—	—	-5.2	—	Monetary Authorities .... **78bs** *d*
	753.9	1,056.8	1,118.5	1,108.5	1,228.4	516.7	36.2	45.6	32.5	7.9	22.5	56.1	79.3	80.8	91.4	General Government .... **78bt** *d*
	—	—	—	—	—	—	—	—	3.6	—	—	—	—	40.0	-4.8	Banks .... **78bu** *d*
	—	—	—	—	—	—	7.4	42.2	-9.0	-2.8	—	45.7	30.8	46.5	4.4	Other Sectors .... **78bv** *d*
	83.6	-11.3	-76.5	14.6	45.4	-3.1	-36.4	17.4	-4.8	-1.0	9.1	-28.1	-75.6	-50.2	23.6	Net Errors and Omissions .... **78ca** *d*
	24.6	14.7	76.3	.7	129.7	-101.6	-129.8	-82.3	14.5	6.4	32.1	-87.3	6.6	-52.5	-19.0	*Overall Balance* .... **78cb** *d*
	-24.6	-14.7	-76.3	-.7	-129.7	101.6	129.8	82.3	-14.5	-6.4	-32.1	87.3	-6.6	52.5	19.0	Reserves and Related Items .... **79da** *d*
	-24.6	-14.7	-76.3	-.7	-129.7	101.6	51.2	72.3	-23.5	-27.4	-22.6	19.6	-61.2	-6.3	-40.6	Reserve Assets .... **79db** *d*
	—	—	—	—	—	—	15.3	3.5	13.1	21.1	-9.5	-1.8	6.7	-1.3	4.2	Use of Fund Credit and Loans .... **79dc** *d*
	—	—	—	—	—	—	63.3	6.5	-4.1	—	—	69.5	47.9	60.2	55.5	Exceptional Financing .... **79de** *d*
Year Ending December 31																**Government Finance**
	-783	-1,696	-1,868	-2,061	-1,807	-1,449	-1,774	I-2,840	-27,706	-26,018	-29,185	-49,679	I-65,908	-94,914	....	Deficit (-) or Surplus **80**
	4,918	4,360	4,540	4,681	5,255	5,363	7,155	I9,896	48,637	66,870	113,568	126,725	I176,153	192,102	....	Total Revenue and Grants **81y**
	4,918	4,360	4,540	4,681	5,243	5,329	6,065	I8,672	45,610	63,605	108,483	122,316	I171,744	183,552	....	Revenue **81**
	—	—	—	—	12	34	1,090	I1,224	3,027	3,265	5,085	4,409	I4,409	8,550	....	Grants **81z**
	5,701	6,056	6,408	6,742	7,062	6,812	8,929	I12,736	76,343	92,888	142,753	176,404	I242,061	287,016	....	Exp. & Lending Minus Repay. **82z**
	5,701	6,056	6,408	6,742	7,062	6,812	8,929	I10,187	42,468	61,238	97,656	121,233	I176,436	201,278	....	Expenditure **82**
	—	—	—	—	—	—	—	I2,549	33,875	31,650	45,097	55,171	I65,625	85,738	....	Lending Minus Repayments **83**
	783	1,696	1,868	2,061	1,807	1,449	1,774	I2,840	27,707	26,018	29,185	49,679	I65,909	94,913	....	Total Financing **80h**
	-40	-292	-46	223	159	858	-647	I-470	-4,650	1,268	5,271	14,804	I-24,989	26,319	....	Domestic **84a**
	823	1,988	1,914	1,838	1,648	591	2,421	I3,310	32,357	24,750	23,914	34,875	I90,898	68,594	....	Foreign **85a**
	....	....	....	....	....	....	....	2,840	27,707	161,558	211,894	363,278	I494,049	644,940	....	Total Debt by Residence **88**
	....	....	....	....	....	....	....	-470	-4,650	5,280	233	30,393	I56,244	84,076	....	Domestic **88a**
	....	....	....	....	....	....	....	3,310	32,357	156,278	211,661	332,885	I437,805	560,864	....	Foreign **89a**
Millions of Togrogs																**National Accounts**
	9,372	9,310	9,710	10,301	10,731	10,465	18,910	47,298	166,219	283,263	429,207	586,529	758,927	875,859	....	Gross Domestic Product (GDP) **99b**
	....	188,929	195,461	205,440	214,028	208,642	....	....	406,865	394,646	403,723	429,207	439,350	457,063	472,963	GDP Volume 1993 prices .... **99b.** *p*
	....	....	....	....	....	495,368	449,563	406,865	394,646	403,723	429,207	439,350	457,063	472,963	....	GDP Volume 1995 Prices .... **99b.** *p*
	95.6	104.5	108.1	113.6	118.4	115.4	104.7	94.8	91.9	94.1	100.0	102.4	106.5	110.2	....	GDP Volume (1995=100) .... **99bv** *p*
	2.3	2.1	2.1	2.1	2.1	2.1	4.2	11.6	42.1	70.2	100.0	133.5	166.0	185.2	....	GDP Deflator (1995=100) .... **99bi** *p*
Midyear																
	1.88	1.93	1.97	2.02	2.07	2.12	2.17	2.20	2.23	2.27	2.30	2.34	2.37	2.40	2.62	**Population** **99z**

(See notes in the back of the book.)

Morocco

	1970	1971	1972	1973	1974	1975	1976	1977	1978	1979	1980	1981	1982	1983	1984
Exchange Rates														*Dirhams per SDR:*	
Official Rate ... **aa**	5.029	5.168	5.066	5.175	5.087	4.898	5.210	5.256	5.063	4.925	5.528	6.208	6.914	8.439	9.362
														Dirhams per US Dollar:	
Official Rate ... **ae**	5.029	4.760	4.666	4.290	4.155	4.184	4.484	4.327	3.886	3.739	4.334	5.333	6.268	8.061	9.551
Official Rate ... **rf**	5.060	5.050	4.592	4.107	4.370	4.052	4.419	4.503	4.167	3.899	3.937	5.172	6.023	7.111	8.811
														Index Numbers (1995=100):	
Official Rate ... **ahx**	169.5	170.0	185.9	208.3	195.4	210.8	193.3	189.6	205.2	219.0	217.2	165.9	142.1	121.0	97.2
Nominal Effective Exchange Rate ... **nec**	....	....	....	....	....	....	....	....	....	....	103.9	105.2	97.3	94.3	87.1
Real Effective Exchange Rate ... **rec**	....	....	....	....	....	....	....	....	....	....	139.9	128.1	126.2	117.9	111.4
Fund Position														*Millions of SDRs:*	
Quota ... **2f.s**	113	113	113	113	113	113	113	113	150	150	225	225	225	307	307
SDRs ... **1b.s**	—	2	17	16	16	15	10	9	13	15	—	1	1	1	1
Reserve Position in the Fund ... **1c.s**	—	—	28	28	28	28	—	—	—	—	—	—	—	—	—
Total Fund Cred.&Loans Outstg. ... **2tl**	28	—	—	—	—	—	115	128	220	232	358	497	898	985	1,107
International Liquidity											*Millions of US Dollars Unless Otherwise Indicated:*				
Total Reserves minus Gold ... **1l.d**	119	151	214	241	391	352	467	505	618	557	399	230	218	107	49
SDRs ... **1b.d**	—	3	18	20	19	17	12	10	16	20	1	2	1	1	1
Reserve Position in the Fund ... **1c.d**	—	—	31	34	35	33	—	—	—	—	—	—	—	—	—
Foreign Exchange ... **1d.d**	119	148	165	187	337	302	455	495	602	537	398	228	217	106	48
Gold (Million Fine Troy Ounces) ... **1ad**	.600	.600	.600	.600	.608	.608	.608	.632	.680	.704	.704	.704	.704	.704	.704
Gold (National Valuation) ... **1and**	21	....	....	26	26	26	24	26	31	33	29	23	20	15	13
Monetary Authorities: Other Assets ... **3..d**	15	22	13	27	16	25	17	9	15	5	4	3	3	2	2
Monetary Authorities: Other Liab. ... **4..d**	16	12	5	1	10	13	29	23	−7	−56	−84	−52	−85	−33	−79
Deposit Money Banks: Assets ... **7a.d**	39	43	59	75	91	86	88	97	127	215	246	326	282	266	255
Liabilities ... **7b.d**	17	15	21	18	23	23	27	39	41	83	69	68	35	38	34
Other Banking Insts.: Liabilities ... **7f.d**	39	54	63	79	94	166	263	466	647	680	623	586	477	457	439
Monetary Authorities														*Millions of Dirhams:*	
Foreign Assets ... **11**	796	919	1,162	1,241	1,795	1,714	2,276	2,340	2,584	2,226	1,871	1,366	1,507	1,001	612
Claims on Central Government ... **12a**	1,563	1,474	1,724	1,919	2,184	3,019	3,727	5,209	6,389	7,266	‡9,516	12,062	13,676	17,211	18,548
Claims on Private Sector ... **12d**	480	493	546	670	536	655	824	627	827	1,237	‡601	542	809	1,189	1,380
Claims on Deposit Money Banks ... **12e**	207	280	284	411	769	592	1,153	1,200	1,160	1,931	1,631	2,662	2,870	3,041	4,123
Reserve Money ... **14**	2,527	2,801	3,326	3,815	4,607	5,298	6,450	7,450	8,595	10,013	10,532	11,952	12,777	14,472	16,137
of which: Currency Outside DMBs ... **14a**	2,261	2,461	2,944	3,411	4,063	4,650	5,732	6,650	7,676	9,020	9,807	11,133	12,022	13,636	14,770
Foreign Liabilities ... **16c**	308	81	31	26	94	75	735	850	1,335	1,382	2,399	3,688	6,443	8,967	10,519
Central Government Deposits ... **16d**	36	42	47	48	63	72	68	137	95	113	125	151	171	184	220
Capital Accounts ... **17a**	....	....	....	....	....	....	....	....	....	....	....	....	....	....	....
Other Items (Net) ... **17r**	176	242	313	351	520	535	727	939	934	1,152	562	841	−529	−1,181	−2,214
Deposit Money Banks														*Millions of Dirhams:*	
Reserves ... **20**	185	234	246	272	334	434	511	571	674	733	389	474	417	434	816
Foreign Assets ... **21**	195	199	276	315	380	358	394	421	492	803	1,066	1,737	‡1,769	2,148	2,432
Claims on Central Government ... **22a**	896	1,011	1,181	1,406	1,986	2,496	2,761	3,335	5,410	6,040	7,165	8,077	8,577	12,144	12,496
Claims on Private Sector ... **22d**	2,119	2,441	2,798	3,406	4,537	5,668	6,869	8,116	8,785	9,753	11,038	13,066	‡16,264	18,654	21,385
Claims on Other Financial Insts ... **22f**	....	....	....	....	....	....	....	....	....	....	....	....	689	392	142
Demand Deposits ... **24**	2,634	3,042	3,544	4,313	5,346	6,881	7,772	9,362	10,750	11,741	12,970	15,062	‡15,021	18,064	19,366
Time Deposits ... **25**	393	476	547	620	1,017	1,437	1,756	2,179	2,959	3,681	4,649	5,872	‡8,691	11,412	13,491
Foreign Liabilities ... **26c**	86	69	100	77	96	96	120	170	160	309	300	360	‡217	303	323
Credit from Monetary Authorities ... **26g**	207	280	284	411	769	592	1,153	1,200	1,160	1,931	1,661	2,674	2,870	3,041	3,734
Capital Accounts ... **27a**	....	....	....	....	....	....	....	....	....	....	....	....	....	....	....
Other Items (Net) ... **27r**	76	17	26	−23	9	−51	−266	−467	332	−334	78	−614	916	955	357
Post Office: Checking Deposits ... **24..i**	288	324	362	361	547	636	687	853	912	1,118	1,169	1,371	1,468	959	1,010
Treasury: Checking Deposits ... **24..r**	251	260	363	359	708	479	705	918	1,182	1,211	1,042	1,127	1,278	1,182	1,075
Monetary Survey														*Millions of Dirhams:*	
Foreign Assets (Net) ... **31n**	598	969	1,307	1,452	1,985	1,901	1,815	1,741	1,580	1,337	239	−946	‡−3,385	−6,121	−7,798
Domestic Credit ... **32**	5,561	5,960	6,927	8,072	10,434	12,881	15,505	18,921	23,409	26,512	‡31,215	36,939	43,719	52,321	56,759
Claims on Central Govt. (Net) ... **32an**	2,962	3,026	3,583	3,997	5,361	6,558	7,812	10,178	13,798	15,522	‡18,766	22,486	24,827	31,312	32,909
Claims on Private Sector ... **32d**	2,599	2,934	3,344	4,076	5,073	6,323	7,693	8,743	9,612	10,990	12,449	14,453	‡17,073	19,843	22,765
Claims on Other Financial Insts ... **32f**	....	....	....	....	....	....	....	....	....	....	....	....	1,818	1,166	1,086
Money ... **34**	5,514	6,193	7,336	8,572	10,869	12,838	15,102	18,002	20,785	23,352	25,312	29,016	‡30,064	34,197	36,779
Quasi-Money ... **35**	393	476	547	620	1,017	1,437	1,756	2,179	2,959	3,681	4,649	5,872	‡8,691	11,412	13,491
Other Items (Net) ... **37r**	252	260	352	333	534	507	461	481	1,245	816	1,493	1,106	1,579	593	−1,309
Money plus Quasi-Money ... **35l**	5,908	6,669	7,883	9,192	11,886	14,274	16,858	20,181	23,744	27,033	29,961	34,888	‡38,755	45,608	50,270
Other Banking Institutions														*Millions of Dirhams:*	
Reserves ... **40**	81	79	88	200	201	303	293	488	663	405	378	369	359	622	576
Claims on Central Government ... **42a**	200	213	257	292	260	322	385	515	600	844	1,062	1,138	1,726	1,827	1,683
Claims on Official Entities ... **42bx**	80	85	101	105	163	215	243	292	280	326	392	408	387	418	462
Claims on Private Sector ... **42d**	1,185	1,392	1,699	1,809	2,236	2,966	3,815	4,853	5,981	6,769	7,578	8,782	10,024	11,418	13,267
Time Deposits ... **45**	683	757	882	1,006	1,190	1,450	1,588	2,039	2,589	3,049	3,625	3,967	4,609	5,659	6,508
Bonds ... **46ab**	84	117	138	206	320	436	421	480	651	822	1,038	1,617	2,251	3,179	3,556
Long-Term Foreign Liabilities ... **46cl**	198	252	293	333	389	696	1,180	2,015	2,516	2,542	2,702	3,128	2,990	3,684	4,196
Central Govt. Lending Funds ... **46f**	148	157	160	139	173	270	390	358	347	375	373	404	399	424	608
Credit from Monetary Authorities ... **46g**	300	294	351	375	396	469	563	632	543	719	780	834	1,123	796	944
Credit from Deposit Money Banks ... **46h**	—	—	86	76	52	71	124	151	134	110	123	337	690	392	142
Capital Accounts ... **47a**	183	195	240	310	364	439	502	591	700	751	855	882	1,104	1,087	1,366
Other Items (Net) ... **47r**	−50	−3	−5	−39	−24	−25	−32	−118	44	−24	−86	−472	−670	−936	−1,332
Liquid Liabilities ... **55l**	6,510	7,347	8,677	9,998	12,875	15,421	18,153	21,732	25,670	29,677	33,208	38,486	‡43,364	51,267	56,778
Interest Rates														*Percent Per Annum*	
Discount Rate *(End of Period)* ... **60**	3.50	3.50	3.50	3.50	3.75	4.50	4.50	4.50	4.50	4.50	4.88	6.00	6.75	7.00	7.00
Money Market Rate ... **60b**	....	....	....	....	....	....	....	....	....	....	9.00	9.00	10.92	....	....
Deposit Rate ... **60l**	....	....	....	....	....	....	....	....	4.5	4.5	4.9	6.0	6.4	6.5	6.5
Lending Rate ... **60p**	....	....	....	....	....	....	....	....	7.0	7.0	7.0	7.0	7.0	7.0	7.0
Govt.Bond Yield: Long-Term ... **61**	....	....	....	....	....	....	....	....	....	....	....	....	....	....	....
Med.-Term ... **61a**	....	....	....	....	....	....	....	....	....	....	....	....	....	....	....

1985	1986	1987	1988	1989	1990	1991	1992	1993	1994	1995	1996	1997	1998	1999		
															Exchange Rates	
End of Period																
10.568	10.656	11.066	11.049	10.673	11.442	11.658	12.442	13.257	13.080	12.589	12.653	13.107	13.031	13.845	Official Rate	aa
End of Period (ae) Period Average (rf)																
9.621	8.712	7.800	8.211	8.122	8.043	8.150	9.049	9.651	8.960	8.469	8.800	9.714	9.255	10.087	Official Rate	ae
10.062	9.104	8.359	8.209	8.488	8.242	8.707	8.538	9.299	9.203	8.540	8.716	9.527	9.604	9.804	Official Rate	rf
Period Averages																
84.9	93.8	102.2	104.1	100.6	103.7	98.3	100.1	91.8	92.9	100.0	98.0	89.7	88.9	87.1	Official Rate	ahx
82.5	76.4	75.9	78.6	84.8	84.5	85.3	87.5	92.5	98.6	100.0	100.7	102.6	103.8	105.5	Nominal Effective Exchange Rate	nec
104.1	99.4	96.1	94.7	94.8	89.4	91.5	92.1	94.7	96.9	100.0	101.7	102.6	105.0	106.1	Real Effective Exchange Rate	rec
															Fund Position	
End of Period																
307	307	307	307	307	307	307	428	428	428	428	428	428	428	588	Quota	2f. s
—	16	3	—	—	1	103	56	25	18	17	5	1	2	62	SDRs	1b. s
							30	30	30	30	30	30	30	70	Reserve Position in the Fund	1c. s
1,161	894	789	711	647	527	402	319	207	101	35	2	—	—	—	Total Fund Cred.&Loans Outstg.	2tl
															International Liquidity	
End of Period																
115	211	411	547	488	2,066	3,100	3,584	3,655	4,352	3,601	3,794	3,993	4,435	5,689	Total Reserves minus Gold	1l. d
—	19	4	—	—	1	147	77	34	26	26	7	1	3	85	SDRs	1b. d
							42	42	44	45	44	41	43	97	Reserve Position in the Fund	1c. d
115	192	407	547	488	2,065	2,953	3,465	3,579	4,281	3,530	3,743	3,951	4,389	5,507	Foreign Exchange	1d. d
.704	.704	.704	.704	.704	.704	.704	.704	.704	.704	.704	.704	.704	.704	.704	Gold (Million Fine Troy Ounces)	1ad
13	14	16	15	15	16	15	14	202	218	230	222	201	211	193	Gold (National Valuation)	1and
-13	....	....	....	....	....	....	....	....	....	....	....	....	....	....	Monetary Authorities: Other Assets	3..d
-44	-15	23	44	38	44	144	139	53	47	41	62	84	78	82	Monetary Authorities: Other Liab.	4..d
322	388	439	495	569	781	690	598	518	755	653	665	I381	496	477	Deposit Money Banks: Assets	7a. d
49	85	70	103	127	226	267	354	386	672	442	520	I351	462	457	Liabilities	7b. d
594	891	1,170	1,171	1,187	1,448	1,585	1,523	1,450	1,534	1,589	1,452	....	....	....	Other Banking Insts.: Liabilities	7f. d
															Monetary Authorities	
End of Period																
1,247	1,987	3,351	4,639	4,111	I16,760	25,410	32,570	37,243	41,001	32,509	35,402	I40,808	43,070	59,392	Foreign Assets	11
18,766	15,584	13,224	13,881	13,693	I13,435	16,994	9,861	8,752	8,305	18,389	19,179	I27,860	27,459	21,129	Claims on Central Government	12a
3,383	7,663	8,606	8,901	8,814	I7,661	7,535	7,611	8,803	8,416	9,129	9,075	I1,250	3,495	1,393	Claims on Private Sector	12d
3,753	5,315	5,577	5,969	10,948	I2,118	2,699	1,828	599	512	500	1,250	I—	—	—	Claims on Deposit Money Banks	12e
17,351	21,471	22,636	26,200	30,839	I38,341	47,847	44,023	47,796	50,746	53,384	57,467	I62,557	66,999	75,911	Reserve Money	14
16,192	18,694	20,003	21,914	24,814	I29,543	34,298	35,745	37,202	41,107	43,261	46,581	I48,662	50,644	56,713	of which: Currency Outside DMBs	14a
12,664	9,994	9,284	8,388	7,248	I6,381	5,853	5,227	3,256	1,745	787	577	I817	725	826	Foreign Liabilities	16c
482	560	424	481	407	I482	517	498	523	605	633	816	I786	826	533	Central Government Deposits	16d
												4,799	4,877	4,977	Capital Accounts	17a
-3,348	-1,476	-1,586	-1,679	-928	I-5,230	-1,579	2,122	3,822	5,139	5,722	6,046	I959	597	-332	Other Items (Net)	17r
															Deposit Money Banks	
End of Period																
695	2,269	2,050	3,497	5,007	I8,086	12,633	7,109	8,671	8,293	9,018	9,419	I11,936	13,380	17,100	Reserves	20
3,100	3,378	3,428	4,068	4,618	I6,281	5,621	5,408	5,002	6,765	5,533	5,855	I3,703	4,592	4,812	Foreign Assets	21
16,977	24,646	28,810	30,428	34,453	I29,766	28,293	39,545	44,652	50,746	49,633	50,048	I58,616	58,614	54,917	Claims on Central Government	22a
22,920	....	....	....	....	I34,095	48,500	56,581	62,351	70,408	81,777	90,545	I151,203	167,602	183,569	Claims on Private Sector	22d
242	....	....	....	....	I1,101	1,011	994	355	1,409	1,637	627	I25,580	29,834	33,017	Claims on Other Financial Insts	22f
21,378	25,978	28,390	32,128	34,732	I54,171	61,757	66,636	70,033	79,099	84,606	87,323	I116,054	126,767	140,895	Demand Deposits	24
16,592	18,819	21,056	24,627	28,458	I24,143	30,383	36,425	42,687	45,958	50,552	54,962	I64,121	65,114	69,389	Time Deposits	25
472	740	549	842	1,028	I1,819	2,179	3,205	3,729	6,020	3,745	4,579	I3,409	4,276	4,605	Foreign Liabilities	26c
3,753	7,490	7,682	8,244	12,492	I5,862	8,398	2,566	965	1,108	1,232	2,508	I1,209	3,381	1,346	Credit from Monetary Authorities	26g
												38,743	44,973	47,759	Capital Accounts	27a
1,739	....	....	....	....	I-6,666	-6,659	805	3,617	5,436	7,463	7,122	I27,502	29,511	29,421	Other Items (Net)	27r
951	1,001	1,129	1,207	1,406	1,420	1,777	1,520	1,625	1,833	1,701	1,721	1,871	....	....	Post Office: Checking Deposits	24.. i
1,319	1,523	1,979	3,468	4,077	4,417	4,693	5,041	4,906	4,950	5,088	6,311	6,202	....	....	Treasury: Checking Deposits	24.. r
															Monetary Survey	
End of Period																
-8,789	-5,369	-3,054	-523	453	I14,841	22,999	29,546	35,260	40,002	33,509	36,101	I40,285	42,661	58,773	Foreign Assets (Net)	31n
64,938	72,114	77,243	84,026	92,644	I91,413	108,782	120,655	130,921	145,462	166,721	176,690	I263,723	286,178	293,492	Domestic Credit	32
37,531	42,194	44,718	48,503	53,222	I48,556	51,240	55,469	59,412	65,229	74,178	76,443	I85,690	85,247	75,513	Claims on Central Govt. (Net)	32an
26,303	....	....	....	....	I41,756	56,035	64,192	71,154	78,824	90,906	99,620	I153,279	171,990	187,203	Claims on Private Sector	32d
1,104	....	....	....	....	I1,101	1,507	994	355	1,409	1,637	627	I24,754	28,941	30,776	Claims on Other Financial Insts	32f
40,289	47,675	52,035	59,578	66,046	I90,659	103,709	110,082	115,458	128,284	135,964	143,818	I166,843	179,795	200,597	Money	34
16,592	18,819	21,056	24,627	28,458	I24,143	30,383	36,425	42,687	45,958	50,552	54,962	I64,121	65,114	69,389	Quasi-Money	35
-724	259	1,098	-702	-1,407	I-8,548	-2,311	3,694	8,036	11,222	13,714	14,011	I73,044	83,930	82,279	Other Items (Net)	37r
56,881	66,494	73,091	84,205	94,504	I114,802	134,092	146,507	158,145	174,242	186,516	198,780	I230,964	244,909	269,986	Money plus Quasi-Money	35l
															Other Banking Institutions	
End of Period																
397	781	464	709	474	594	899	1,428	1,938	1,383	1,301	1,469	....	....	106.1	Reserves	40
2,081	2,516	2,662	3,545	5,421	5,881	6,567	7,191	7,980	10,966	13,063	16,164	....	....		Claims on Central Government	42a
552	800	204	262	162	42	1	—	—	—	—	—	....	....		Claims on Official Entities	42bx
15,702	18,096	21,281	23,786	26,408	30,674	34,525	37,601	39,365	41,311	44,167	47,249	....	....		Claims on Private Sector	42d
7,342	8,597	9,294	10,890	12,978	15,014	17,410	19,670	21,836	24,606	28,574	32,745	....	....		Time Deposits	45
4,219	5,138	5,281	6,302	7,476	8,432	8,164	9,663	10,134	10,628	10,987	11,848	....	....		Bonds	46ab
5,712	7,763	9,124	9,613	9,641	11,643	12,917	13,779	13,997	13,744	13,461	12,776	....	....		Long-Term Foreign Liabilities	46cl
606	589	594	610	274	143	216	617	547	393	277	271	....	....		Central Govt. Lending Funds	46f
936	—	—	—	145	53	554	14	5	8	—		....	....		Credit from Monetary Authorities	46g
242	303	436	484	377	269	988	515	508	604	623	683	....	....		Credit from Deposit Money Banks	46h
1,539	2,066	2,715	2,903	3,978	4,713	5,271	5,958	6,911	8,093	9,122	10,068	....	....		Capital Accounts	47a
-1,864	-2,263	-2,833	-2,500	-2,404	-3,076	-3,528	-3,996	-4,655	-4,416	-4,513	-3,509	....	....		Other Items (Net)	47r
64,223	75,091	82,385	95,095	107,482	I129,816	151,502	166,177	179,981	198,848	215,090	231,525	....	....		Liquid Liabilities	55l
															Interest Rates	
Percent Per Annum																
8.13	8.50	8.50	8.50	....	....	....	....	....	7.17	....	....	....	6.04	5.42	Discount Rate (End of Period)	60
9.41	9.44	....	....	....	....	....	....	....	12.29	10.06	8.42	7.89	6.30	5.64	Money Market Rate	60b
8.0	8.5	8.5	8.5	8.5	8.5	8.5	....	....	....	....	....	....	7.3	6.4	Deposit Rate	60l
7.8	8.8	9.0	9.0	9.0	9.0	9.0	....	....	10.0	....	....	....	13.5	13.5	Lending Rate	60p
....	....	....	....	....	....	....	....	....	....	....	....	....	....	....	Govt.Bond Yield: Long-Term	61
....	....	....	....	....	....	....	....	....	....	....	....	....	....	....	Med.-Term	61a

Morocco

		1970	1971	1972	1973	1974	1975	1976	1977	1978	1979	1980	1981	1982	1983	1984
Prices, Production, Labor															*Index Numbers (1995=100):*	
Wholesale Prices	63	15.2	15.8	16.1	18.9	23.3	24.2	25.3	I28.9	....	34.1	37.0	43.5	48.7	52.3	59.5
Consumer Prices	64	16.3	17.0	17.6	I18.4	21.6	23.3	25.3	28.5	31.2	33.8	37.0	41.6	46.0	48.9	55.0
Manufacturing Production	66ey	38.6	41.1	42.7	47.4	48.7	51.4	55.0	58.7	I63.0	66.0	67.4	67.2	69.1	72.1	71.9
Mining Production	66zx	56.1	....	64.1	72.4	81.8	67.7	65.5	74.5	I80.7	84.8	80.3	78.1	81.5	88.6	92.2
Energy Production	66ze	....	....	....	....	....	....	....	....	....	....	....	....	....	....	....
															Number in Thousands:	
Labor Force	67d	....	....	....	....	....	....	....	....	....	....	....	....	....	....	....
Employment	67e	....	....	....	....	....	....	....	....	....	....	....	....	....	....	....
Unemployment	67c	....	....	....	....	....	....	....	....	....	....	....	....	....	....	....
Unemployment Rate (%)	67r	....	....	....	....	....	....	....	....	....	....	....	....	....	....	....
International Transactions															*Millions of Dirhams:*	
Exports	70	2,471	2,533	2,953	3,746	7,440	6,238	5,579	5,858	6,261	7,622	9,645	12,354	12,461	14,324	19,110
Imports, c.i.f.	71	3,463	3,537	3,577	4,683	8,292	10,398	11,555	14,400	12,361	14,328	16,793	22,692	25,983	25,542	34,397
Imports, f.o.b.	71.v	3,158	3,216	3,256	4,261	7,297	9,148	10,168	12,671	10,878	12,609	14,781	19,760	22,866	22,497	31,300
															1995=100	
Volume of Exports	72	32	34	I39	47	45	35	I40	44	37	46	46	48	48	53	56
Volume of Imports	73	21	20	I19	22	27	33	37	59	61	I64	61	64	71	61	67
Unit Value of Imports	75	15	16	I17	19	28	28	I28	22	24	32	40	51	53	61	74
Balance of Payments															*Millions of US Dollars:*	
Current Account, n.i.e.	78ald	....	....	....	....	....	−504	−1,368	−1,825	−1,311	−1,502	−1,407	−1,828	−1,867	−886	−984
Goods: Exports f.o.b.	78aad	....	....	....	....	....	1,539	1,262	1,301	1,503	1,955	2,450	2,321	2,070	2,075	2,170
Goods: Imports f.o.b.	78abd	....	....	....	....	....	−2,252	−2,287	−2,800	−2,614	−3,244	−3,771	−3,840	−3,816	−3,302	−3,571
Trade Balance	78acd						−712	−1,025	−1,498	−1,112	−1,289	−1,321	−1,520	−1,746	−1,227	−1,401
Services: Credit	78add	....	....	....	....	....	459	434	539	636	717	783	727	849	845	830
Services: Debit	78aed	....	....	....	....	....	−710	−1,192	−1,276	−1,322	−1,473	−1,436	−1,435	−1,333	−876	−781
Balance on Goods & Services	78afd						−963	−1,783	−2,236	−1,799	−2,044	−1,975	−2,228	−2,230	−1,257	−1,352
Income: Credit	78agd	....	....	....	....	....	28	24	31	26	39	38	36	25	11	16
Income: Debit	78ahd	....	....	....	....	....	−94	−123	−189	−310	−448	−600	−738	−675	−631	−592
Balance on Gds, Serv. & Inc.	78aid						−1,030	−1,882	−2,394	−2,082	−2,453	−2,537	−2,930	−2,880	−1,878	−1,927
Current Transfers, n.i.e.: Credit	78ajd	....	....	....	....	....	607	618	677	881	1,081	1,236	1,194	1,091	1,069	1,007
Current Transfers: Debit	78akd	....	....	....	....	....	−81	−105	−108	−110	−130	−106	−91	−78	−77	−64
Capital Account, n.i.e.	78bcd	....	....	....	....	....	−10	−10	−9	−11	−13	−12	−12	−8	−3	−2
Capital Account, n.i.e.: Credit	78bad	....	....	....	....	....	—	—	1	1	1	—	—	—	1	2
Capital Account: Debit	78bbd	....	....	....	....	....	−10	−10	−9	−12	−13	−12	−12	−9	−4	−4
Financial Account, n.i.e.	78bjd	....	....	....	....	....	828	2,400	3,019	2,153	1,396	1,101	1,491	1,451	697	726
Direct Investment Abroad	78bdd	....	....	....	....	....	—	—	—	—	—	—	—	—	—	—
Dir. Invest. in Rep. Econ., n.i.e.	78bed	....	....	....	....	....	—	38	8	12	7	89	59	80	46	47
Portfolio Investment Assets	78bfd	....	....	....	....	....	—	—	—	—	—	—	—	—	—	—
Equity Securities	78bkd	....	....	....	....	....	—	—	—	—	—	—	—	—	—	—
Debt Securities	78bld	....	....	....	....	....	—	—	—	—	—	—	—	—	—	—
Portfolio Investment Liab., n.i.e.	78bgd	....	....	....	....	....	—	—	—	—	—	—	—	—	—	—
Equity Securities	78bmd	....	....	....	....	....	—	—	—	—	—	—	—	—	—	—
Debt Securities	78bnd	....	....	....	....	....	—	—	—	—	—	—	—	—	—	—
Financial Derivatives Assets	78bwd	....	....	....	....	....	....	....	....	....	....	....	....	....	....	....
Financial Derivatives Liabilities	78bxd	....	....	....	....	....	....	....	....	....	....	....	....	....	....	....
Other Investment Assets	78bhd	....	....	....	....	....	81	26	−44	−64	−141	−14	−146	−99	−163	−173
Monetary Authorities	78bod	....	....	....	....	....	—	—	—	—	—	—	—	—	—	—
General Government	78bpd	....	....	....	....	....	−94	−6	−6	−14	−39	−54	−144	−122	−22	−37
Banks	78bqd	....	....	....	....	....	22	−6	1	−1	−35	−19	−25	−34	−53	−32
Other Sectors	78brd	....	....	....	....	....	153	38	−38	−49	−66	59	22	57	−88	−104
Other Investment Liab., n.i.e.	78bid	....	....	....	....	....	747	2,335	3,055	2,206	1,529	1,025	1,579	1,471	814	852
Monetary Authorities	78bsd	....	....	....	....	....	−7	13	10	10	−6	15	30	−29	58	−56
General Government	78btd	....	....	....	....	....	670	2,129	2,499	1,707	1,038	1,024	1,187	1,182	622	712
Banks	78bud	....	....	....	....	....	5	11	11	−6	39	−3	8	31	15	—
Other Sectors	78bvd	....	....	....	....	....	79	183	534	495	458	−10	353	287	120	197
Net Errors and Omissions	78cad	....	....	....	....	....	−341	−1,024	−1,191	−893	87	45	64	7	26	97
Overall Balance	78cbd						−27	−2	−6	−62	−32	−273	−284	−417	−166	−163
Reserves and Related Items	79dad	....	....	....	....	....	27	2	6	62	32	273	284	417	166	163
Reserve Assets	79dbd	....	....	....	....	....	27	−131	−8	−55	17	110	116	−24	71	35
Use of Fund Credit and Loans	79dcd	....	....	....	....	....	—	133	14	116	15	163	168	441	95	128
Exceptional Financing	79ded	....	....	....	....	....	—	—	—	—	—	—	—	—	—	—
Government Finance															*Millions of Dirhams:*	
Deficit (-) or Surplus	80	I−619	−658	−897	−526	−1,348	−3,341	−7,217	−7,647	−5,773	−6,039	−7,184	−10,557	−10,630	−7,680	−6,762
Revenue	81	I3,862	3,890	4,335	5,164	8,468	9,529	9,601	12,333	13,346	15,803	17,502	20,418	24,388	24,516	26,684
Expenditure	82	I4,490	4,544	5,265	5,630	9,879	12,399	16,495	19,904	18,986	21,673	24,520	30,903	34,822	32,043	33,399
Lending Minus Repayments	83	I−9	4	−33	60	−63	471	323	76	133	169	166	72	196	153	47
Financing																
Net Borrowing: Domestic	84a	I342	91	521	475	779	1,474	2,197	2,210	2,528	1,759	3,426	4,131	3,230	7,129	3,063
Foreign	85a	I277	321	296	−2	185	1,350	4,474	5,195	3,365	4,014	3,910	7,116	6,471	3,290	5,319
Use of Cash Balances	87	I—	246	80	53	384	517	546	242	−120	266	−152	−690	929	−2,739	−1,620
Debt: Domestic	88a	I1,878	2,056	2,349	2,641	3,172	3,770	5,245	5,908	7,360	8,611	10,197	11,632	13,519	17,166	19,003
Foreign	89a	I3,622	4,026	4,338	4,177	4,341	5,168	7,881	11,438	13,722	16,071	20,697	30,557	40,704	55,387	75,368
National Accounts															*Billions of Dirhams:*	
Exports of Goods & Services	90c	3.54	3.76	4.37	5.41	9.42	8.43	7.89	8.83	9.36	10.83	11.13	14.02	15.44	17.64	22.47
Government Consumption	91f	2.44	2.71	2.96	2.99	4.04	5.92	9.21	10.25	11.47	13.23	13.59	15.08	17.00	16.63	17.48
Gross Fixed Capital Formation	93e	2.99	3.27	3.18	3.47	4.93	9.04	12.18	15.90	13.73	14.88	16.48	20.51	25.38	24.23	25.95
Increase/Decrease(-) in Stocks	93i	.09	.06	−.33	.13	1.99	.13	−.64	1.13	.46	.32	1.45	.13	.84	−.45	2.45
Private Consumption	96f	14.53	15.81	16.88	18.40	22.45	24.81	27.66	31.81	36.28	40.81	50.93	55.32	63.57	69.30	81.15
Imports of Goods & Services	98c	−4.15	−4.22	−4.36	−5.50	−9.23	−11.93	−15.28	−18.16	−16.14	−18.02	−19.49	−26.02	−29.33	−28.21	−37.15
Gross Domestic Product (GDP)	99b	19.43	21.38	22.68	24.92	33.60	36.39	41.01	49.76	55.15	62.04	74.09	79.03	92.90	99.14	112.34
Net Factor Inc/Pmts(-) Abroad	98.n	.04	.18	.24	.63	1.08	1.45	1.74	1.39	1.38	1.41	1.63	1.23	.89	1.77	2.64
Gross National Income (GNI)	99a	19.47	21.57	22.93	25.54	34.68	37.86	42.75	51.15	56.53	63.46	75.72	80.26	93.79	100.91	114.98
Net National Income	99e	18.97	20.96	22.43	24.70	33.50	36.22	42.10	44.00	54.00	60.60	67.40	72.61	85.24	89.59	....
GDP Volume 1969 prices	99b.p	18.89	19.99	20.41	21.19	24.22	23.92	26.99	28.94	29.58	31.00	32.13				
GDP Volume 1980 Prices	99b.p											74.09	72.04	78.97	78.53	81.94
GDP Volume (1995=100)	99bvp	38.5	40.7	41.6	43.2	49.3	48.7	55.0	59.0	60.3	63.2	65.5	63.7	69.8	69.4	72.4
GDP Deflator (1995=100)	99bip	17.9	18.6	19.4	20.5	24.2	26.5	26.5	30.0	32.5	34.9	40.2	44.1	47.3	50.7	55.1
															Millions:	
Population	99z	15.31	15.38	15.70	16.31	16.80	17.31	17.83	18.36	18.91	19.47	20.05	20.65	I20.31	20.91	21.33

	1985	1986	1987	1988	1989	1990	1991	1992	1993	1994	1995	1996	1997	1998	1999	
Period Averages																**Prices, Production, Labor**
Wholesale Prices	65.1	70.2	70.9	74.0	76.8	80.3	85.4	87.8	91.8	93.9	100.0	104.4	102.7	106.3	107.2	63
Consumer Prices	59.2	64.4	66.1	67.7	69.8	74.6	‡80.6	85.2	89.6	94.2	100.0	103.0	103.9	106.9	107.7	64
Manufacturing Production	‡72.4	75.3	‡77.2	83.8	85.5	92.7	94.9	96.5	‡95.0	100.6	100.0	104.1	107.5	110.2	112.7	66ey
Mining Production	92.2	90.4	‡100.7	115.4	86.8	101.4	88.9	90.5	‡92.1	99.2	100.0	102.5	111.6	111.1	107.5	66zx
Energy Production			70.3	76.2	81.2	86.3	83.1	90.8	‡92.6	101.1	100.0	100.0	106.4	105.8	112.6	66ze
Period Averages																
Labor Force	…	…	…	…	…	3,804	…	…	…	…	4,863	…	…	5,138	…	67d
Employment	…	…	…	…	3,141	3,294	3,400	3,494	3,660	…	3,870	4,034	…	…	…	67e
Unemployment	…	…	…	…	…	601	695	650	681	…	1,112	871	…	…	…	67c
Unemployment Rate (%)	…	…	14.7	13.9	16.3	15.4	17.0	16.0	15.7	…	22.3	17.8	…	…	…	67r
Millions of Dirhams																**International Transactions**
Exports	21,740	22,103	23,390	29,751	28,271	35,135	37,283	33,960	28,446	50,965	58,673	60,013	67,057	68,608	72,283	70
Imports, c.i.f.	38,675	34,604	35,271	39,133	46,594	57,021	59,720	62,805	62,606	76,059	85,493	84,612	90,712	98,676	97,454	71
Imports, f.o.b.	35,194	31,493	32,097	35,604	42,401	51,890	50,859	57,146	60,579	60,168	78,654	77,843	83,455	90,546	95,577	71.v
1995=100																
Volume of Exports	56	59	63	73	‡72	87	95	89	92	‡101	100	97	104	107	…	72
Volume of Imports	65	65	71	77	‡83	92	103	118	111	‡89	100	93	101	124	…	73
Unit Value of Imports	82	73	72	73	‡82	90	86	82	90	‡102	100	106	102	89	…	75
Minus Sign Indicates Debit																**Balance of Payments**
Current Account, n.i.e.	-891	-209	182	473	-787	-196	-413	-433	-521	-723	-1,296	-58	-169	-236	…	78al d
Goods: Exports f.o.b.	2,162	2,428	2,798	3,624	3,331	4,229	5,094	5,010	4,936	5,541	6,871	6,886	7,039	7,144	…	78aa d
Goods: Imports f.o.b.	-3,515	-3,481	-3,864	-4,384	-5,027	-6,338	-6,858	-7,473	-7,001	-7,648	-9,353	-9,080	-8,903	-9,463	…	78ab d
Trade Balance	-1,353	-1,053	-1,066	-760	-1,697	-2,108	-1,764	-2,463	-2,065	-2,107	-2,482	-2,193	-1,864	-2,319	…	78ac d
Services: Credit	983	1,133	1,379	1,764	1,650	2,009	1,618	2,125	2,050	2,014	2,173	2,743	2,471	2,827	…	78ad d
Services: Debit	-829	-1,156	-1,141	-1,106	-1,204	-1,445	-1,427	-1,571	-1,593	-1,730	-1,890	-1,782	-1,724	-1,895	…	78ae d
Balance on Goods & Services	-1,199	-1,076	-828	-102	-1,251	-1,544	-1,573	-1,909	-1,608	-1,822	-2,199	-1,233	-1,117	-1,387	…	78af d
Income: Credit	15	15	16	18	32	83	199	292	224	224	251	189	172	194	…	78ag d
Income: Debit	-781	-704	-782	-1,055	-1,191	-1,071	-1,315	-1,349	-1,431	-1,394	-1,569	-1,498	-1,348	-1,295	…	78ah d
Balance on Gds, Serv. & Inc.	-1,965	-1,765	-1,595	-1,139	-2,411	-2,532	-2,688	-2,966	-2,816	-2,992	-3,516	-2,541	-2,292	-2,489	…	78ai d
Current Transfers, n.i.e.: Credit	1,121	1,602	1,822	1,663	1,669	2,383	2,356	2,614	2,361	2,355	2,298	2,565	2,204	2,347	…	78aj d
Current Transfers, n.i.e.: Debit	-47	-45	-46	-51	-46	-47	-81	-81	-66	-86	-78	-82	-81	-95	…	78ak d
Capital Account, n.i.e.	2	-2	-6	-6	-3	-5	-5	-6	-3	-3	-6	73	-5	-10	…	78bc d
Capital Account, n.i.e.: Credit	5	1	2	1	—	—	—	—	—	—	—	78	1	—	…	78ba d
Capital Account: Debit	-4	-3	-8	-7	-3	-5	-5	-6	-3	-4	-6	-5	-5	-10	…	78bb d
Financial Account, n.i.e.	815	579	84	-226	822	1,889	1,371	1,239	966	1,248	-984	-897	-990	-653	…	78bj d
Direct Investment Abroad	—	—	—	—	—	—	-23	-32	-23	-24	-15	-30	-9	-20	…	78bd d
Dir. Invest. in Rep. Econ., n.i.e.	20	1	60	85	167	165	317	422	491	551	92	76	4	12	…	78be d
Portfolio Investment Assets	—	—	—	—	—	—	—	—	—	—	—	—	—	—	…	78bf d
Equity Securities	—	—	—	—	—	—	—	—	—	—	—	—	—	—	…	78bk d
Debt Securities	—	—	—	—	—	—	—	—	—	—	—	—	—	—	…	78bl d
Portfolio Investment Liab., n.i.e.	—	—	—	—	—	—	2	1	24	238	20	142	38	24	…	78bg d
Equity Securities	—	—	—	—	—	—	—	—	24	238	20	142	38	24	…	78bm d
Debt Securities	—	—	—	—	—	—	2	1	1						…	78bn d
Financial Derivatives Assets															…	78bw d
Financial Derivatives Liabilities															…	78bx d
Other Investment Assets	-16	-212	-105	-376	-94	-267	—	—	—	344	—	—	—	—	…	78bh d
Monetary Authorities	…	…	…	…	…	…									…	78bo d
General Government	-11	-4	-11	-10	-18	-11	—	—	—	—	—	—	—	—	…	78bp d
Banks	-66	-31	-6	-78	-65	-202	—	—	—	—	—	—	—	—	…	78bq d
Other Sectors	61	-177	-88	-287	-11	-54	—	—	—	344	—	—	—	—	…	78br d
Other Investment Liab., n.i.e.	811	790	129	65	749	1,991	1,074	848	473	139	-1,083	-1,085	-1,022	-669	…	78bi d
Monetary Authorities	—	1	—	—	—	—	-7	-11	-7	19	—	—	—	—	…	78bs d
General Government	564	299	153	339	336	1,002	648	157	59	-421	-967	-867	-1,232	-954	…	78bt d
Banks	17	30	-27	35	25	101	—	—	—	-48	-132	-167	-123	-205	…	78bu d
Other Sectors	230	461	3	-308	388	887	433	702	422	588	16	-50	333	491	…	78bv d
Net Errors and Omissions	42	-38	38	22	-11	9	3	-10	-5	-39	391	209	175	181	…	78ca d
Overall Balance	-32	331	298	264	21	1,697	956	791	436	483	-1,895	-673	-988	-719	…	78cb d
Reserves and Related Items	32	-331	-298	-264	-21	-1,697	-956	-791	-436	-483	1,895	673	988	719	…	79da d
Reserve Assets	-17	-19	-165	-158	63	-1,537	-785	-675	-280	-362	984	-274	-553	-248	…	79db d
Use of Fund Credit and Loans	49	-311	-133	-105	-83	-161	-171	-116	-156	-152	-101	-47	-3	—	…	79dc d
Exceptional Financing	—	-1	—	—	—	—	—	—	—	31	1,013	995	1,544	967	…	79de d
Year Ending December 31																**Government Finance**
Deficit (-) or Surplus	-9,424	-11,872	-7,025	-5,841	-9,951	-4,760	-5,083	-3,368	-6,509	-8,915	-12,365	…	…	…	…	80
Revenue	30,213	32,884	37,089	45,454	49,238	56,635	62,437	69,907	78,653	81,442	82,018	…	…	…	…	81
Expenditure	39,336	44,752	44,163	51,300	59,121	61,342	67,400	73,000	84,832	90,072	93,889	…	…	…	…	82
Lending Minus Repayments	301	4	-49	-5	68	53	120	267	330	285	494	…	…	…	…	83
Financing																
Net Borrowing: Domestic	6,686	7,787	3,813	…	5,719	-2,725	427	5,816	5,682	13,949	14,843	…	…	…	…	84a
Net Borrowing: Foreign	4,506	-225	1,001	3,588	3,650	8,258	4,588	-445	-958	-4,428	-2,111	…	…	…	…	85a
Use of Cash Balances	-1,768	4,310	2,211	…	582	-773	68	-2,003	1,785	-606	-367	…	…	…	…	87
Debt: Domestic	26,009	…	…	51,571	58,987	57,501	58,920	67,225	76,847	93,843	93,843	…	…	…	…	88a
Debt: Foreign	84,835	…	…	156,786	161,608	159,404	115,549	136,952	141,345	134,952	129,766	…	…	…	…	89a
Billions of Dirhams																**National Accounts**
Exports of Goods & Services	25.81	26.03	27.46	35.37	33.74	41.25	44.34	42.38	44.55	58.20	77.63	69.64	73.59	78.11	…	90c
Government Consumption	20.52	23.75	24.63	28.04	30.41	32.98	37.69	40.85	45.05	47.85	48.99	53.82	56.61	62.00	…	91f
Gross Fixed Capital Formation	29.93	32.99	31.63	37.23	44.17	51.00	53.86	54.36	56.72	57.90	60.39	61.94	65.79	76.69	…	93e
Increase/Decrease(-) in Stocks	5.20	2.28	1.41	1.03	1.76	2.58	.96	2.01	-.74	1.72	-1.99	.60	.10	.52	…	93i
Private Consumption	89.83	110.51	111.84	123.91	134.67	138.70	168.97	170.14	170.67	197.17	201.35	227.34	218.59	229.36	…	96f
Imports of Goods & Services	-41.77	-40.84	-40.27	-43.35	-50.82	-63.55	-63.46	-69.30	-69.69	-86.30	-96.02	-82.02	-85.55	-92.92	…	98c
Gross Domestic Product (GDP)	129.51	154.73	156.70	182.23	193.93	213.99	242.36	242.91	249.22	279.32	281.70	319.34	318.35	341.38	…	99b
Net Factor Inc/Pmts(-) Abroad	2.56	7.60	8.04	4.38	3.52	10.45	9.27	11.94	9.06	10.11	6.70	12.68	11.13	13.60	…	98.n
Gross National Income (GNI)	132.07	162.33	164.73	186.61	197.46	223.27	251.63	254.85	258.29	289.44	290.40	332.02	329.48	354.99	…	99a
Net National Income	…	…	…	…	…	…	…	…	…	…	…	…	…	…	…	99e
GDP Volume 1969 prices																99b.p
GDP Volume 1980 Prices	87.12	94.35	91.94	101.50	103.93	106.12	115.58	110.92	109.80	121.17	113.18	127.03	124.17	132.27	132.15	99b.p
GDP Volume (1995=100)	77.0	83.4	81.2	89.7	91.8	93.8	102.1	98.0	97.0	107.1	100.0	112.2	109.7	116.9	116.8	99bv p
GDP Deflator (1995=100)	59.7	65.9	68.5	72.1	75.0	81.0	84.2	88.0	91.2	92.6	100.0	101.0	103.0	103.7	…	99bi p
Midyear Estimates																
Population	21.84	22.35	22.88	23.23	23.70	24.18	24.65	25.12	25.58	25.93	26.39	26.85	27.31	27.78	28.24	99z

(See notes in the back of the book.)

Mozambique

	1970	1971	1972	1973	1974	1975	1976	1977	1978	1979	1980	1981	1982	1983	1984
Exchange Rates															*Meticais per SDR:*
Market Rate ..... aa	28.7	29.9	29.3	31.2	30.1	32.2	36.7	39.5	42.2	42.5	41.8	41.6	42.1	43.1	42.7
											Meticais per US Dollar: End of Period (ae)				
Market Rate ..... ae	28.7	27.6	27.0	25.8	24.6	27.5	31.5	32.6	32.4	32.3	32.8	35.8	38.2	41.2	43.5
Market Rate ..... rf	28.8	29.6	27.1	24.5	25.4	25.6	30.2	33.0	33.0	32.6	32.4	35.3	37.8	40.2	42.4
Fund Position															*Millions of SDRs:*
Quota ..... 2f. s	....	....	....	....	....	....	....	....	....	....	....	....	....	....	61.00
SDRs ..... 1b. s	....	....	....	....	....	....	....	....	....	....	....	....	....	....	—
Reserve Position in the Fund ..... 1c. s	....	....	....	....	....	....	....	....	....	....	....	....	....	....	—
Total Fund Cred.&Loans Outstg. 2tl	....	....	....	....	....	....	....	....	....	....	....	....	....	....	—
International Liquidity															*Millions of US Dollars Unless Otherwise Indicated:*
Total Reserves minus Gold ..... 1l. d	....	....	....	....	....	....	....	....	....	....	....	....	....	....	55.29
SDRs ..... 1b. d	....	....	....	....	....	....	....	....	....	....	....	....	....	....	—
Reserve Position in the Fund ..... 1c. d	....	....	....	....	....	....	....	....	....	....	....	....	....	....	—
Foreign Exchange ..... 1d. d	....	....	....	....	....	....	....	....	....	....	....	....	....	....	55.29
Monetary Authorities: Other Liab. ..... 4.. d	....	....	....	....	....	....	....	....	....	....	....	....	....	....	694.79
Banking Institutions: Assets ..... 7a. d	....	....	....	....	....	....	....	....	....	....	....	....	....	....	1.26
Liabilities ..... 7b. d	....	....	....	....	....	....	....	....	....	....	....	....	....	....	
Monetary Authorities															*Billions of Meticais:*
Foreign Assets 11	....	....	....	....	....	....	....	....	....	....	....	....	....	....	4.0
Claims on Central Government 12a															72.1
Claims on Local Government 12b															—
Claims on Nonfin.Pub.Enterprises 12c															—
Claims on Private Sector 12d															78.7
Claims on Banking Institutions 12e															1.8
Reserve Money 14															62.9
of which: Currency Outside Banks 14a															27.0
Time & Foreign Currency Deposits 15															3.6
Liabs. of Central Bank: Securities 16ac															....
Foreign Liabilities 16c															3.0
Long-Term Foreign Liabilities 16cl															27.2
Central Government Deposits 16d															49.5
o/w: Cent.Govt.Earmarked Funds 16df															—
Capital Accounts 17a															9.5
Other Items (Net) 17r															.8
of which: Valuation Adjustment 17rv															
Banking Institutions															*Billions of Meticais:*
Reserves 20															7.7
Other Claims on Monetary Author. 20c	....	....	....	....	....	....	....	....	....	....	....	....	....	....	
Foreign Assets 21	....	....	....	....	....	....	....	....	....	....	....	....	....	....	.1
Claims on Central Government 22a															7.9
Claims on Local Government 22b															—
Claims on Nonfin.Pub.Enterprises 22c															16.3
Claims on Private Sector 22d															6.9
Claims on Nonbank Financial Insts 22g															—
Demand Deposits 24															25.8
Time & Foreign Currency Deposits 25															3.5
Foreign Liabilities 26c															—
Long-Term Foreign Liabilities 26cl															—
Central Government Deposits 26d															8.2
o/w: Cent.Govt.Earmarked Funds 26df															—
Credit from Central Bank 26g															.6
Capital Accounts 27a															2.1
Other Items (Net) 27r	....	....	....	....	....	....	....	....	....	....	....	....	....	....	−1.2
Banking Survey															*Billions of Meticais:*
Foreign Assets (Net) 31n	....	....	....	....	....	....	....	....	....	....	....	....	....	....	−26.2
Domestic Credit 32	....	....	....	....	....	....	....	....	....	....	....	....	....	....	124.2
Claims on Central Govt.(Net) 32an	....	....	....	....	....	....	....	....	....	....	....	....	....	....	22.3
Claims on Local Government 32b	....	....	....	....	....	....	....	....	....	....	....	....	....	....	—
Claims on Nonfin.Pub.Enterprises 32c	....	....	....	....	....	....	....	....	....	....	....	....	....	....	16.3
Claims on Private Sector 32d	....	....	....	....	....	....	....	....	....	....	....	....	....	....	85.7
Claims on Nonbank Financial Inst 32g	....	....	....	....	....	....	....	....	....	....	....	....	....	....	—
Money 34	....	....	....	....	....	....	....	....	....	....	....	....	....	....	80.8
Quasi-Money 35	....	....	....	....	....	....	....	....	....	....	....	....	....	....	7.1
Capital Accounts 37a	....	....	....	....	....	....	....	....	....	....	....	....	....	....	11.6
Other Items (Net) 37r	....	....	....	....	....	....	....	....	....	....	....	....	....	....	−1.5
Money plus Quasi-Money 35l	....	....	....	....	....	....	....	....	....	....	....	....	....	....	88.0
Prices															*Index Numbers (1995=100):*
Consumer Prices 64														....	....
															Number in Thousands:
Employment 67e	....	....	....	....	....	....	....	....	....	....	....	....	....	....	....

1985	1986	1987	1988	1989	1990	1991	1992	1993	1994	1995	1996	1997	1998	1999		
															Exchange Rates	
End of Period																
45.2	48.1	573.1	842.7	1,077.2	1,476.9	2,639.7	I4,058.2	7,339.2	9,709.5	16,187.9	16,359.7	15,574.4	17,411.7	18,254.4	Market Rate	aa
Period Average (rf)																
41.2	39.3	404.0	626.2	819.7	1,038.1	1,845.4	I2,951.4	5,343.2	6,651.0	10,890.0	11,377.0	11,543.0	12,366.0	13,300.0	Market Rate	ae
43.2	40.4	290.7	524.6	744.9	929.1	1,434.5	2,516.5	3,874.2	6,038.6	9,024.3	11,293.8	11,543.6	11,874.6	12,775.1	Market Rate	rf
															Fund Position	
End of Period																
61.00	61.00	61.00	61.00	61.00	61.00	61.00	84.00	84.00	84.00	84.00	84.00	84.00	84.00	113.60	Quota	2f. s
—	—	.02	.02	.02	.02	.03	.03	.03	.03	.03	.04	.04	.04	.05	SDRs	1b. s
—	.01	.01	.01	.01	.01	.01	.01	.01	.01	.01	.01	.01	.01	.01	Reserve Position in the Fund	1c. s
—	—	12.20	30.50	42.70	51.85	82.35	126.88	137.86	145.24	135.79	125.89	140.11	147.24	145.42	Total Fund Cred.&Loans Outstg.	2tl
															International Liquidity	
End of Period																
45.89	56.75	118.02	173.60	203.50	231.75	239.70	233.37	187.24	177.51	195.32	344.06	517.35	608.50	654.01	Total Reserves minus Gold	1l. d
—	—	.03	.03	.03	.03	.04	.04	.04	.04	.05	.05	.05	.06	.06	SDRs	1b. d
—	.01	.01	.01	.01	.01	.01	.01	.01	.01	.01	.01	.01	.01	.01	Reserve Position in the Fund	1c. d
45.89	56.74	117.98	173.56	203.46	231.70	239.64	233.31	187.19	177.45	195.26	344.00	517.29	608.43	653.93	Foreign Exchange	1d. d
886.94	1,057.18	1,116.50	1,070.35	1,066.29	1,073.14	1,207.99	1,058.99	1,185.63	645.60	551.40	537.91	591.66	593.36	587.88	Monetary Authorities: Other Liab.	4.. d
1.43	1.50	.21	.21	.66	5.94	14.09	96.80	148.34	220.79	274.47	250.19	242.10	204.66	192.08	Banking Institutions: Assets	7a. d
.02	.03	.01	.01	.38	5.26	37.07	41.78	55.25	44.94	69.05	58.05	87.56	65.51	33.52	Liabilities	7b. d
															Monetary Authorities	
End of Period																
2.8	3.3	61.0	126.1	189.3	267.9	I486.6	769.6	1,175.2	1,367.2	2,424.4	4,359.3	6,359.0	7,928.0	9,089.9	Foreign Assets	11
74.4	82.4	89.6	129.9	173.9	190.5	I244.1	250.1	545.5	578.4	663.2	496.9	369.8	82.7	6.9	Claims on Central Government	12a
—	—	—	—	2.5	9.7	I9.8	3.8	.3	.3	.2	1.5	.2	.2	.2	Claims on Local Government	12b
—	—	—	—	—	1.6	I—	—	—	.5	50.5	34.0	.5	.5	.5	Claims on Nonfin.Pub.Enterprises	12c
91.9	104.7	136.4	183.5	242.2	315.2	I—	—	.9	2.2	.9	14.3	54.7	74.7	73.9	Claims on Private Sector	12d
1.5	.9	.9	2.7	3.0	2.6	I27.9	94.0	478.1	781.5	734.9	768.6	566.7	589.5	552.8	Claims on Banking Institutions	12e
73.8	88.1	140.1	216.5	I312.6	383.5	I292.2	506.4	890.1	1,481.4	1,951.1	2,469.5	2,866.6	2,760.2	3,244.5	Reserve Money	14
29.8	33.5	36.6	61.4	90.9	139.3	I173.3	257.5	469.5	762.4	1,130.2	1,394.4	1,544.1	1,649.7	2,174.2	of which: Currency Outside Banks	14a
3.8	6.4	17.0	29.4	61.4	85.0	I—	.1	30.7	27.9	84.3	14.8	52.0	72.2	66.0	Time & Foreign Currency Deposits	15
....	....	....	....	....	....	....	....	....	....	....	....	....	135.0	145.0	Liabs. of Central Bank: Securities	16ac
2.3	3.0	45.1	84.9	I118.7	173.1	I217.4	514.9	1,011.8	1,410.2	2,198.1	2,059.5	2,182.1	2,563.7	2,654.6	Foreign Liabilities	16c
34.2	38.6	412.9	611.0	801.3	1,017.6	I2,229.2	3,125.5	6,335.0	4,293.9	6,004.8	6,119.8	6,829.6	7,337.5	7,818.8	Long-Term Foreign Liabilities	16cl
47.8	47.9	38.1	103.6	I206.2	262.3	I333.6	548.0	1,105.4	1,295.4	1,844.7	3,121.1	4,313.1	5,161.9	5,278.8	Central Government Deposits	16d
—	—	—	41.0	90.2	127.1	I191.1	467.8	907.9	960.6	1,258.2	2,265.6	3,068.7	3,987.7	4,345.6	o/w: Cent.Govt.Earmarked Funds	16df
10.5	12.0	25.9	26.0	51.0	125.4	I404.8	346.1	579.0	896.8	969.7	1,201.4	1,294.0	1,363.9	1,581.6	Capital Accounts	17a
-1.8	-4.8	-391.3	-629.3	-940.4	-1,259.1	I-2708.8	-3,923.5	-7,752.0	-6,675.5	-9,178.5	-9,311.4	-10,186.5	-10,718.8	-11,065.1	Other Items (Net)	17r
....	....	....	-563.0	-760.8	-1,051.0	I-1122.2	-1,621.2	-3,257.9	-5,663.9	-8,339.7	-8,683.2	-8,762.3	-9,192.1	-9,675.9	of which: Valuation Adjustment	17rv
															Banking Institutions	
End of Period																
13.6	15.8	29.2	44.7	80.1	102.5	I101.4	278.6	433.1	744.6	838.6	1,111.4	1,389.9	1,310.0	1,013.1	Reserves	20
....	....	....	....	....	....	....	....	....	....	....	....	....	135.0	145.0	Other Claims on Monetary Author.	20c
.1	.1	.1	.1	.5	6.2	I26.0	285.7	792.6	1,468.5	2,989.0	2,846.4	2,794.5	2,530.8	2,554.7	Foreign Assets	21
8.4	8.4	9.0	12.1	12.2	10.2	I12.7	42.7	6.6	—	.1	65.2	.1	8.3	232.7	Claims on Central Government	22a
—	—	—	—	—	.1	I—	19.7	—	.6	1.1	1.2	103.9	1.9	149.7	Claims on Local Government	22b
18.2	19.9	23.8	33.6	50.9	55.0	I63.8	42.2	121.2	170.4	111.0	65.0	223.0	181.1	46.2	Claims on Nonfin.Pub.Enterprises	22c
7.1	8.9	10.0	25.4	69.2	95.3	I591.0	856.2	971.3	1,538.2	2,373.3	3,440.3	5,114.8	6,467.0	8,552.7	Claims on Private Sector	22d
—	—	—	6.7	8.4	12.5	I—	—	—	—	.7	11.4	12.5	1.3	46.4	Claims on Nonbank Financial Insts	22g
32.8	38.9	40.2	71.8	129.3	178.2	I515.6	794.9	1,132.2	1,653.2	2,130.4	2,486.7	3,283.0	3,894.7	4,693.0	Demand Deposits	24
4.8	5.4	8.9	16.9	23.6	37.1	I164.5	465.8	906.9	1,380.6	2,296.8	2,791.2	3,376.6	4,132.6	5,880.9	Time & Foreign Currency Deposits	25
—	—	—	—	.3	5.3	I68.2	123.3	295.2	298.9	752.0	660.4	730.8	748.3	368.9	Foreign Liabilities	26c
—	—	—	—	—	.2	I.2	—	—	—	—	—	279.9	61.8	77.0	Long-Term Foreign Liabilities	26cl
8.0	8.0	21.7	34.2	62.0	64.1	I86.1	179.5	241.4	304.0	468.7	475.1	462.2	511.2	486.6	Central Government Deposits	26d
—	—	.7	7.2	22.9	23.7	I23.8	23.6	25.7	97.8	235.0	248.3	208.1	290.8	221.6	o/w: Cent.Govt.Earmarked Funds	26df
.6	.1	.1	.2	.1	.1	I.1	92.5	.8	581.2	667.9	686.5	555.0	471.9	452.3	Credit from Central Bank	26g
2.3	2.4	2.8	4.1	7.4	10.9	I16.7	302.4	555.2	770.4	1,415.7	1,934.5	2,723.9	3,146.1	3,809.9	Capital Accounts	27a
-1.2	-1.7	-1.6	-4.5	-1.4	-14.1	I-56.5	-433.3	-806.9	-1,066.0	-1,417.7	-1,493.5	-1,772.7	-2,331.2	-3,028.0	Other Items (Net)	27r
															Banking Survey	
End of Period																
-33.6	-38.2	-397.0	-569.7	I-730.5	-922.0	I-2002.4	-2,708.4	-5,674.2	-3,167.3	-3,541.4	-1,633.9	-869.0	-252.5	725.3	Foreign Assets (Net)	31n
144.2	168.4	209.0	253.4	I291.2	363.9	I501.7	487.2	299.6	691.2	887.6	533.5	1,104.3	1,144.6	3,343.8	Domestic Credit	32
27.0	34.9	38.8	4.2	I-82.0	-125.6	I-162.9	-434.7	-794.7	-1,021.0	-1,650.1	-3,034.2	-4,405.4	-5,582.1	-5,525.8	Claims on Central Govt.(Net)	32an
—	—	—	—	2.6	9.9	I9.8	23.5	.3	.9	1.3	2.7	104.1	2.1	149.9	Claims on Local Government	32b
18.2	19.9	23.8	33.6	50.9	56.6	I63.8	42.2	121.2	170.9	161.5	99.0	223.6	181.6	46.8	Claims on Nonfin.Pub.Enterprises	32c
99.0	113.6	146.4	208.9	311.4	410.5	I591.0	856.2	972.5	1,540.4	2,374.2	3,454.6	5,169.5	6,541.6	8,626.6	Claims on Private Sector	32d
—	—	—	6.7	8.4	12.5	I—	—	.6	—	.7	11.4	12.5	1.3	46.4	Claims on Nonbank Financial Inst	32g
92.6	109.6	152.8	244.4	I365.2	495.8	I727.0	1,056.6	1,606.1	2,417.9	3,264.0	3,917.2	4,901.7	5,613.0	6,994.4	Money	34
8.6	11.8	25.9	46.3	85.1	122.1	I164.5	465.9	937.6	1,408.5	2,381.1	2,806.0	3,428.6	4,204.7	5,946.9	Quasi-Money	35
12.7	14.4	28.6	30.1	58.4	136.3	I421.5	648.5	1,134.2	1,667.2	2,385.4	3,135.9	4,017.9	4,510.0	5,391.4	Capital Accounts	37a
-3.4	-5.6	-395.2	I-637.1	-948.0	-1,312.2	I-2813.7	-4,392.2	-9,052.5	-7,969.7	-10,684.3	-10,959.5	-12,112.9	-13,435.6	-14,263.6	Other Items (Net)	37r
101.2	121.4	178.6	290.7	I450.2	617.8	I891.5	1,522.5	2,543.7	3,826.4	5,645.1	6,723.2	8,330.3	9,817.7	12,941.3	Money plus Quasi-Money	35l
															Prices	
Period Averages																
1.3	....	4.7	7.0	9.8	I14.4	19.2	27.9	39.7	64.8	I100.0	146.9	156.3	157.1	160.3	Consumer Prices	64
Period Averages																
....	....	193	202	....	....	....	....	....	....	....	....	....	....	....	Employment	67e

Mozambique

		1970	1971	1972	1973	1974	1975	1976	1977	1978	1979	1980	1981	1982	1983	1984
International Transactions															*Billions of Meticais*	
Exports	70	...	...	...	...	...	...	...	...	...	...	...	...	...	...	...
Imports, c.i.f.	71	...	...	...	...	...	...	...	...	...	...	...	...	...	...	...
Balance of Payments															*Millions of US Dollars:*	
Current Account, n.i.e.	78al *d*	...	...	...	...	...	...	...	...	...	...	−367.0	−407.1	−496.5	−415.3	−308.4
Goods: Exports f.o.b.	78aa *d*	...	...	...	...	...	...	...	...	...	...	280.8	280.8	229.2	131.6	95.7
Goods: Imports f.o.b.	78ab *d*	...	...	...	...	...	...	...	...	...	...	−720.1	−721.0	−752.3	−572.8	−485.7
Trade Balance	78ac *d*	...	...	...	...	...	...	...	...	...	...	−439.3	−440.2	−523.1	−441.2	−390.0
Services: Credit	78ad *d*	...	...	...	...	...	...	...	...	...	...	117.9	114.0	107.8	90.6	61.0
Services: Debit	78ae *d*	...	...	...	...	...	...	...	...	...	...	−123.5	−137.5	−140.2	−121.4	−97.6
Balance on Goods & Services	78af *d*	...	...	...	...	...	...	...	...	...	...	−444.9	−463.7	−555.5	−472.0	−426.6
Income: Credit	78ag *d*	...	...	...	...	...	...	...	...	...	...	53.4	64.5	63.5	75.2	57.0
Income: Debit	78ah *d*	...	...	...	...	...	...	...	...	...	...	−31.4	−65.3	−83.9	−108.1	−106.6
Balance on Gds, Serv. & Inc.	78ai *d*	...	...	...	...	...	...	...	...	...	...	−422.9	−464.5	−575.9	−504.9	−476.2
Current Transfers, n.i.e.: Credit	78aj *d*	...	...	...	...	...	...	...	...	...	...	55.9	57.4	79.4	89.6	167.8
Current Transfers: Debit	78ak *d*	...	...	...	...	...	...	...	...	...	...					
Capital Account, n.i.e.	78bc *d*	...	...	...	...	...	...	...	...	...	...	—	—	—	—	—
Capital Account, n.i.e.: Credit	78ba *d*	...	...	...	...	...	...	...	...	...	...	—	—	—	—	—
Capital Account: Debit	78bb *d*	...	...	...	...	...	...	...	...	...	...	—	—	—	—	—
Financial Account, n.i.e.	78bj *d*	...	...	...	...	...	...	...	...	...	...	364.2	410.5	398.2	105.6	−113.1
Direct Investment Abroad	78bd *d*	...	...	...	...	...	...	...	...	...	...	—	—	—	—	—
Dir. Invest. in Rep. Econ., n.i.e.	78be *d*	...	...	...	...	...	...	...	...	...	...	—	—	—	—	—
Portfolio Investment Assets	78bf *d*	...	...	...	...	...	...	...	...	...	...	—	—	—	—	—
Equity Securities	78bk *d*	...	...	...	...	...	...	...	...	...	...	—	—	—	—	—
Debt Securities	78bl *d*	...	...	...	...	...	...	...	...	...	...	—	—	—	—	—
Portfolio Investment Liab., n.i.e.	78bg *d*	...	...	...	...	...	...	...	...	...	...	—	—	—	—	—
Equity Securities	78bm *d*	...	...	...	...	...	...	...	...	...	...	—	—	—	—	—
Debt Securities	78bn *d*	...	...	...	...	...	...	...	...	...	...	—	—	—	—	—
Financial Derivatives Assets	78bw *d*	...	...	...	...	...	...	...	...	...	...	...	...	...	...	...
Financial Derivatives Liabilities	78bx *d*	...	...	...	...	...	...	...	...	...	...	...	...	...	...	...
Other Investment Assets	78bh *d*	...	...	...	...	...	...	...	...	...	...	—	−2.2	−5.8	−3.3	−9.1
Monetary Authorities	78bo *d*	...	...	...	...	...	...	...	...	...	...	—	−2.2	−5.8	−3.3	−7.8
General Government	78bp *d*	...	...	...	...	...	...	...	...	...	...	—	—	—	—	—
Banks	78bq *d*	...	...	...	...	...	...	...	...	...	...	—	—	—	—	−1.3
Other Sectors	78br *d*	...	...	...	...	...	...	...	...	...	...	—	—	—	—	—
Other Investment Liab., n.i.e.	78bi *d*	...	...	...	...	...	...	...	...	...	...	364.2	412.7	404.0	108.9	−104.0
Monetary Authorities	78bs *d*	...	...	...	...	...	...	...	...	...	...	—	3.7	8.7	66.1	−31.0
General Government	78bt *d*	...	...	...	...	...	...	...	...	...	...	364.2	409.0	395.3	42.8	−73.0
Banks	78bu *d*	...	...	...	...	...	...	...	...	...	...	—	—	—	—	—
Other Sectors	78bv *d*	...	...	...	...	...	...	...	...	...	...	—	—	—	—	—
Net Errors and Omissions	78ca *d*	...	...	...	...	...	...	...	...	...	...	−29.6	−70.1	−42.3	9.0	25.8
Overall Balance	78cb *d*	...	...	...	...	...	...	...	...	...	...	−32.4	−66.7	−140.6	−300.7	−395.7
Reserves and Related Items	79da *d*	...	...	...	...	...	...	...	...	...	...	32.4	66.7	140.6	300.7	395.7
Reserve Assets	79db *d*	...	...	...	...	...	...	...	...	...	...	32.4	66.7	140.6	15.4	−23.0
Use of Fund Credit and Loans	79dc *d*	...	...	...	...	...	...	...	...	...	...	—	—	—	—	—
Exceptional Financing	79de *d*	...	...	...	...	...	...	...	...	...	...	—	—	—	285.3	418.7
National Accounts															*Billions of Meticais*	
Househ.Cons.Expend.,incl.NPISHs	96f	...	...	...	...	...	...	...	...	...	...	64	65	62	57	61
Government Consumption Expend.	91f	...	...	...	...	...	...	...	...	...	...	14	17	19	22	21
Gross Fixed Capital Formation	93e	...	...	...	...	...	...	...	...	...	...	15	16	18	15	18
Increase/Decrease(-) in Stocks	93i	...	...	...	...	...	...	...	...	...	...	—	—	—	—	—
Exports of Goods and Services	90c	...	...	...	...	...	...	...	...	...	...	...	...	18	9	7
Imports of Goods & Services	98c	...	...	...	...	...	...	...	...	...	...	...	...	−34	−28	−25
Gross Domestic Product (GDP)	99b	...	...	...	...	...	...	...	...	...	...	78	82	79	75	82
Gross National Income (GNI)	99a	...	...	...	...	...	...	...	...	...	...	79	81	91	77	87
GDP Volume (1995=100)	99bv *p*	...	...	...	...	...	...	...	...	...	...	...	...	...	...	71.0
GDP Deflator (1995=100)	99bi *p*	...	...	...	...	...	...	...	...	...	...	...	...	...	...	.6
																Millions:
Population	99z	8.14	8.36	8.52	...	...	9.72	10.16	10.66	11.17	11.66	12.13	12.45	12.78	13.11	13.51

1985	1986	1987	1988	1989	1990	1991	1992	1993	1994	1995	1996	1997	1998	1999		
															International Transactions	
Billions of Meticais																
....	....	....	....	....	....	....	....	....	979.3	1,573.2	2,509.2	2,614.4	2,783.1	3,429.0	Exports	70
....	....	....	....	....	....	....	....	....	3,279.0	6,527.1	8,733.7	8,704.7	9,575.9	14,859.3	Imports, c.i.f.	71
															Balance of Payments	
Minus Sign Indicates Debit																
−301.1	−409.3	−388.8	−358.5	−460.2	−415.3	−344.3	−352.3	−446.3	−467.2	−444.7	−420.5	−295.6	−429.3	....	Current Account, n.i.e.	78al *d*
76.6	79.1	97.0	103.0	104.8	126.4	162.3	139.3	131.8	149.5	168.9	226.1	230.0	244.6	....	Goods: Exports f.o.b.	78aa *d*
−381.4	−488.4	−577.8	−662.0	−726.9	−789.7	−808.8	−769.5	−859.2	−916.7	−705.2	−704.4	−684.0	−735.6	....	Goods: Imports f.o.b.	78ab *d*
−304.8	−409.3	−480.8	−559.0	−622.1	−663.3	−646.5	−630.2	−727.4	−767.2	−536.3	−478.3	−454.0	−491.0	....	*Trade Balance*	78ac *d*
66.3	62.9	79.0	85.0	95.4	103.0	147.2	164.6	180.2	191.1	242.4	253.2	278.7	286.2	....	Services: Credit	78ad *d*
−100.1	−154.3	−175.8	−190.9	−195.5	−206.0	−236.8	−246.4	−270.6	−323.3	−350.0	−319.0	−328.6	−396.2	....	Services: Debit	78ae *d*
−338.6	−500.7	−577.6	−664.9	−722.2	−766.3	−736.1	−712.0	−817.8	−899.4	−643.9	−544.1	−503.9	−601.0	....	*Balance on Goods & Services*	78af *d*
40.8	50.0	58.0	71.6	71.3	70.4	55.6	58.0	59.6	54.8	59.1	61.0	63.6	46.3	....	Income: Credit	78ag *d*
−142.3	−177.7	−173.4	−142.0	−196.8	−167.8	−165.5	−197.7	−191.4	−187.2	−199.1	−162.1	−168.2	−187.8	....	Income: Debit	78ah *d*
−440.1	−628.4	−693.0	−735.3	−847.7	−863.7	−846.0	−851.7	−949.6	−1,031.8	−783.9	−645.2	−608.5	−742.5	....	*Balance on Gds, Serv. & Inc.*	78ai *d*
139.0	219.1	304.2	376.8	387.5	448.4	501.7	499.4	503.3	564.6	339.2	224.7	312.9	313.2	....	Current Transfers, n.i.e.: Credit	78aj *d*
—	—	—	—	—	—	—	—	—	—	—	—	—	—	....	Current Transfers: Debit	78ak *d*
—	—	—	—	—	—	—	—	—	—	—	—	—	—	....	Capital Account, n.i.e.	78bc *d*
—	—	—	—	—	—	—	—	—	—	—	—	—	—	....	Capital Account, n.i.e.: Credit	78ba *d*
—	—	—	—	—	—	—	—	—	—	—	—	—	—	....	Capital Account: Debit	78bb *d*
−52.4	−20.2	−76.7	−126.0	−54.9	−83.4	160.9	513.7	246.9	344.4	366.7	235.0	182.2	300.4	....	Financial Account, n.i.e.	78bj *d*
—	—	—	—	—	—	—	—	—	—	—	—	—	—	....	Direct Investment Abroad	78bd *d*
	1.5	6.2	4.5	3.4	9.2	22.5	25.3	32.0	35.0	45.0	72.5	64.4	212.7	....	Dir. Invest. in Rep. Econ., n.i.e.	78be *d*
—	—	—	—	—	—	—	—	—	—	—	—	—	—	....	Portfolio Investment Assets	78bf *d*
—	—	—	—	—	—	—	—	—	—	—	—	—	—	....	Equity Securities	78bk *d*
—	—	—	—	—	—	—	—	—	—	—	—	—	—	....	Debt Securities	78bl *d*
—	—	—	—	—	—	—	—	—	—	—	—	—	—	....	Portfolio Investment Liab., n.i.e.	78bg *d*
—	—	—	—	—	—	—	—	—	—	—	—	—	—	....	Equity Securities	78bm *d*
—	—	—	—	—	—	—	—	—	—	—	—	—	—	....	Debt Securities	78bn *d*
															Financial Derivatives Assets	78bw *d*
....	....					....						....		....	Financial Derivatives Liabilities	78bx *d*
1.9	4.5	—	—	—	—	—	—	—	—	—	—	—	19.0	....	Other Investment Assets	78bh *d*
2.0	4.6	—	—	—	—	—	—	—	—	—	—	—	1.3	....	Monetary Authorities	78bo *d*
		—	—	—	—	—	—	—	—	—	—	—	—	....	General Government	78bp *d*
−.1	−.1	—	—	—	—	—	—	—	—	—	—	—	17.7	....	Banks	78bq *d*
		—	—	—	—	—	—	—	—	—	—	—	—	....	Other Sectors	78br *d*
−54.3	−26.2	−82.9	−130.5	−58.3	−92.6	138.4	488.4	214.9	309.4	321.7	162.5	117.8	68.7	....	Other Investment Liab., n.i.e.	78bi *d*
−14.6	24.8	—	—	—	—	—	—	—	—	—	—	—	−.8	....	Monetary Authorities	78bs *d*
−39.7	−51.0	−82.9	−130.5	−58.3	−92.6	138.4	488.4	214.9	309.4	321.7	86.2	48.8	−.8	....	General Government	78bt *d*
											76.3	69.0	69.5	....	Banks	78bu *d*
—	—	15.7	25.3	15.9	12.0	41.2	62.5	15.4	10.4	16.4				....	Other Sectors	78bv *d*
−12.8	457.6	−583.1	113.0	114.7	100.5	−274.5	−684.2	−447.4	−443.2	−308.6	−238.3	−364.8	−263.8	....	Net Errors and Omissions	78ca *d*
−366.3	28.1	−1,048.6	−371.5	−400.4	−398.2	−457.9	−522.8	−646.8	−566.0	−386.6	−423.8	−478.2	−392.7	....	*Overall Balance*	78cb *d*
366.3	−28.1	1,048.6	371.5	400.4	398.2	457.9	522.8	646.8	566.0	386.6	423.8	478.2	392.7	....	Reserves and Related Items	79da *d*
20.5	−28.1	−58.2	−50.5	−13.0	−17.9	−53.9	13.9	63.6	−12.0	16.4	161.0	162.3	91.5	....	Reserve Assets	79db *d*
—	—	15.7	25.3	15.9	12.0	41.2	62.5	15.4	10.4	10.4	−14.4	−14.4	19.9	9.6	....	Use of Fund Credit and Loans	79dc *d*
345.8	—	1,091.1	396.7	397.5	404.1	470.6	446.4	567.8	567.6	384.6	277.1	296.0	291.6	....	Exceptional Financing	79de *d*
															National Accounts	
Billions of Meticais																
83	90	298	482	742	947	4,040	5,223	8,078	12,648	20,473	30,510	36,659	38,865	41,117	Househ.Cons.Expend.,incl.NPISHs	96f
23	27	68	115	195	271	427	669	1,059	2,061	2,011	2,875	3,648	4,539	5,788	Government Consumption Expend.	91f
19	23	179	362	557	791	626	952	1,537	2,608	4,931	6,357	7,222	10,389	....	Gross Fixed Capital Formation	93e
—	—	—	—	—	—	140	199	316	402	810	487	91	−19	....	Increase/Decrease(-) in Stocks	93i
6	6	51	99	149	213	320	486	714	1,514	2,582	3,901	4,422	4,758	5,537	Exports of Goods and Services	90c
−21	−24	−202	−427	−652	−881	−1,609	−2,475	−3,692	−5,913	−10,129	−11,412	−11,438	−12,429	−20,333	Imports of Goods & Services	98c
111	122	393	631	991	1,341	3,943	5,053	8,011	13,319	20,678	32,719	40,603	46,203	51,560	Gross Domestic Product (GDP)	99b
113	123	432	810	1,214	1,713	2,473	4,164	7,136	11,665	16,128	....	....	....	....	Gross National Income (GNI)	99a
71.9	70.2	80.5	87.5	91.8	90.9	Ɪ92.7	84.7	90.5	96.8	100.0	106.8	118.8	133.1	145.0	GDP Volume (1995=100)	99bv *p*
.7	.8	2.4	3.5	5.2	7.1	20.6	28.8	42.8	66.5	100.0	148.2	165.3	167.9	171.9	GDP Deflator (1995=100)	99bi *p*
Midyear Estimates																
13.87	14.16	14.12	13.95	13.96	14.15	14.47	14.80	15.13	15.47	15.82	16.18	16.54	16.92	17.30	**Population**	99z

(See notes in the back of the book.)

Myanmar

		1970	1971	1972	1973	1974	1975	1976	1977	1978	1979	1980	1981	1982	1983	1984
Exchange Rates																*Kyats per SDR:*
Official Rate	aa	4.8020	5.9377	5.8650	5.8653	5.8891	7.7429	7.7429	8.5085	8.5085	8.5085	8.5085	8.5085	8.5085	8.5085	8.5085
																Kyats per US Dollar:
Official Rate	ae	4.8020	5.4690	5.4020	4.8620	4.8100	6.6777	6.7324	7.0873	6.6028	6.5186	6.7572	7.3970	7.7775	8.2231	8.7512
Official Rate	rf	4.7619	4.7648	5.4565	4.9283	4.8598	6.3676	6.7673	7.1194	6.8844	6.6538	6.5983	7.2807	7.7903	8.0355	8.3855
Fund Position																*Millions of SDRs:*
Quota	2f. s	60.0	60.0	60.0	60.0	60.0	60.0	60.0	60.0	73.0	73.0	109.5	109.5	109.5	137.0	137.0
SDRs	1b. s	—	—	5.6	9.7	9.5	8.0	7.6	7.5	2.9	4.7	5.4	2.4	1.1	.2	.1
Reserve Position in the Fund	1c. s	—	—	—	—	—	—	—	—	—	—	—	9.0	13.0	6.9	6.9
Total Fund Cred.&Loans Outstg.	2tl	16.5	18.0	8.0	15.0	36.5	40.5	34.5	58.1	85.3	97.0	87.7	107.6	130.3	141.5	129.7
International Liquidity												*Millions of US Dollars Unless Otherwise Indicated:*				
Total Reserves minus Gold	1l. d	I 31.4	48.8	40.2	91.9	182.4	132.8	118.3	103.3	96.4	203.3	260.6	229.0	104.3	89.4	62.1
SDRs	1b. d	—	—	6.1	11.7	11.7	9.4	8.8	9.1	3.8	6.2	6.9	2.7	1.2	.2	.1
Reserve Position in the Fund	1c. d	—	—	—	—	—	—	—	—	—	—	—	10.5	14.3	7.2	6.7
Foreign Exchange	1d. d	I 31.4	48.8	34.1	80.2	170.7	123.4	109.5	94.2	92.6	197.1	253.7	215.8	88.8	82.0	55.3
Gold (Million Fine Troy Ounces)	1ad	1.791	.617	.320	.200	.200	.200	.200	.226	.238	.251	.251	.251	.251	.251	.251
Gold (National Valuation)	1and	62.7	23.4	12.2	8.4	8.5	8.2	8.1	9.6	10.9	11.6	11.2	10.2	9.7	9.2	8.6
Monetary Authorities: Other Assets	3.. d	....	....	....	....	....	....	10.5	25.5	21.4	47.9	75.2	47.9	45.7	19.1	26.4
Monetary Authorities: Other Liab.	4.. d	5.3	2.3	6.7	7.0	10.1	9.3	9.6	17.0	57.1	50.6	53.2	48.4	43.8	46.1	42.7
Deposit Money Banks: Assets	7a. d	—	—	—	—	—	—	.1	.1	.3	.3	.7	1.9	1.4	1.6	1.4
Liabilities	7b. d	68.7	62.8	91.5	138.8	157.7	135.2	151.8	167.3	158.6	309.6	393.8	515.6	514.7	605.0	604.9
Monetary Authorities																*Millions of Kyats:*
Foreign Assets	11	I 477	442	366	541	1,066	1,132	841	864	908	1,705	2,201	2,125	1,242	968	850
Claims on Central Government	12a	2,241	2,655	3,399	3,553	4,608	5,720	5,500	5,083	3,883	2,846	1,123	-1,525	-3,549	-5,451	-7,878
Claims on Deposit Money Banks	12e	242	117	162	309	106	191	181	621	3,165	4,933	7,012	12,273	13,554	17,887	21,846
Reserve Money	14	I 1,812	1,874	2,322	2,947	3,620	4,538	5,981	5,712	6,403	7,671	8,561	10,291	9,753	10,823	12,361
of which: Currency Outside DMBs	14a	I 1,742	1,786	2,222	2,840	3,647	4,448	4,945	5,146	5,783	6,448	7,289	8,410	9,045	10,165	11,768
Other Liabilities to DMBs	14n															
Foreign Liabilities	16c	104	138	91	137	268	378	668	1,319	1,108	1,984	1,266	1,200	1,295	1,540	1,429
Capital Accounts	17a	300	354	414	452	490	562	414	414	451	548	650	770	783	783	784
Other Items (Net)	17r	743	849	1,105	877	1,401	1,564	I -538	-876	-7	-720	-142	611	368	258	243
Deposit Money Banks																*Millions of Kyats:*
Reserves	20	42	40	817	1,272	1,173	923	1,466	1,029	1,097	2,334	2,419	2,740	1,290	1,196	1,055
Other Claims on Monetary Author.	20n	....	....	....	....	....	....									
Foreign Assets	21	....	....	....	....	....	....	1	1	2	2	5	14	11	13	12
Claims on Central Govt. (Net)	22an	I 491	402	482	360	582	979	I -298	2,406	2,796	2,421	1,496	2,539	3,020	2,906	3,530
Claims on Local Government	22b	....	....	....	....	....	....			20	48	87	118	152	169	186
Claims on Nonfin.Pub.Enterprises	22c	2	21	440	618	1,033	1,151	I 117	758	2,855	5,274	8,489	13,025	17,843	22,798	28,241
Claims on Private Sector	22d	I 482	488	685	773	580	790	1,336	1,743	2,363	2,009	2,131	2,540	2,470	2,628	2,396
Demand Deposits	24	I 167	196	233	253	305	388	442	439	515	555	611	696	751	894	1,002
Time, Savings,& Fgn.Currency Dep.	25	I 567	590	631	626	609	607	642	708	990	1,500	2,047	2,866	3,752	4,603	5,659
Restricted Deposits	26b															
Foreign Liabilities	26c	327	336	489	668	758	903	1,022	1,186	1,047	2,018	2,661	3,814	4,003	4,975	5,294
Credit from Monetary Authorities	26g	242	117	162	309	106	191	181	621	3,165	4,933	7,012	12,273	13,554	17,887	21,846
Capital Accounts	27a	134	143	142	148	148	151	358	399	433	494	531	579	633	706	835
Other Items (Net)	27r	....	....	....	....	....	....	-23	2,584	2,983	2,588	1,765	748	2,093	645	784
Monetary Survey																*Millions of Kyats:*
Foreign Assets (Net)	31n	373	-32	-214	-264	39	-149	-849	-1,641	-1,248	-2,297	-1,726	-2,889	-4,056	-5,548	-5,873
Domestic Credit	32	3,516	3,848	5,203	5,388	6,825	8,675	7,571	10,193	12,676	12,707	14,692	18,532	20,850	25,656	28,487
Claims on Central Govt. (Net)	32an	I 2,731	3,058	3,881	3,913	5,190	6,698	6,108	7,685	7,453	5,422	4,071	2,966	536	229	-2,150
Claims on Local Government	32b	....	....	....	....	....	....	—	—	20	48	87	118	152	169	186
Claims on Nonfin.Pub.Enterprises	32c	303	302	637	703	1,056	1,187	127	765	2,860	5,276	8,490	13,026	17,844	22,799	28,241
Claims on Private Sector	32d	I 482	488	685	773	580	790	1,336	1,743	2,363	2,009	2,131	2,540	2,470	2,628	2,396
Money	34	1,937	2,030	2,494	3,143	3,997	4,859	5,397	5,592	6,298	7,003	7,900	9,112	9,803	11,067	12,777
Quasi-Money	35	I 567	590	631	626	609	607	642	708	990	1,500	2,047	2,866	3,752	4,603	5,659
Restricted Deposits	36b															
Capital Accounts	37a	434	496	556	600	638	712	769	813	884	1,042	1,181	1,349	1,416	1,489	1,619
Other Items (Net)	37r	I 951	699	1,308	755	1,621	2,348	-86	1,439	3,256	864	1,837	2,316	1,822	2,949	2,560
Money plus Quasi-Money	35l	I 2,504	2,620	3,125	3,769	4,606	5,466	6,039	6,300	7,288	8,503	9,947	11,978	13,555	15,670	18,436
Interest Rates																*Percent Per Annum*
Central Bank Rate (End of Per.)	60	....		....		....		....								
Deposit Rate	601	.75	.75	.75	.75	.75	.75	.75	.88	1.50	1.50	1.50	1.50	1.50	1.50	1.50
Lending Rate	60p	....		....		....		6.00	6.33	8.00	8.00	8.00	8.00	8.00	8.00	8.00
Government Bond Yield	61	....		....		....										
Prices and Labor														*Index Numbers (1995=100):*		
Consumer Prices	64	3.7	3.8	4.1	5.1	6.4	8.5	10.4	10.2	9.6	10.2	10.2	I 10.3	10.8e	11.4	I 12.0
														Number in Thousands:		
Employment	67e														....	....
Unemployment	67c	....		....		....									....	....
International Transactions																*Millions of Kyats*
Exports	70	513.0	594.6	653.5	640.4	911.8	1,102.0	1,394.9	1,516.7	1,665.9	2,547.7	3,122.7	3,352.7	3,040.0	3,039.4	2,512.0
Imports, c.i.f.	71	738.0	805.1	723.1	522.2	855.4	1,245.0	1,198.3	1,704.6	2,114.0	2,116.1	2,337.3	2,702.5	3,178.1	2,150.8	2,016.2

1985	1986	1987	1988	1989	1990	1991	1992	1993	1994	1995	1996	1997	1998	1999		
															Exchange Rates	
End of Period																
8.5085	8.5085	8.5085	8.5085	8.5085	8.5085	8.5085	8.5085	8.5085	8.5085	8.5085	8.5085	8.5085	8.5085	8.5085	Official Rate	aa
End of Period (ae)	*Period Average (rf)*															
7.8420	7.0395	6.1097	6.4104	6.4942	6.0804	6.0137	6.2411	6.2456	5.9030	5.7810	5.9877	6.3627	6.1087	6.2683	Official Rate	ae
8.4749	7.3304	6.6535	6.3945	6.7049	6.3386	6.2837	6.1045	6.1570	5.9749	5.6670	5.9176	6.2418	6.3432	6.2858	Official Rate	rf
															Fund Position	
End of Period																
137.0	137.0	137.0	137.0	137.0	137.0	137.0	184.9	184.9	184.9	184.9	184.9	184.9	184.9	258.4	Quota	2f.s
—	—	.1	.1	.4	.6	.1	—	.2	.1	.1	.1	.1	.2	.1	SDRs	1b.s
—	—	—	—	—	—	—	—	—	—	—	—	—	—	—	Reserve Position in the Fund	1c.s
106.4	68.0	28.9	8.0	2.0	.2	—	—	—	—	—	—	—	—	—	Total Fund Cred.&Loans Outstg.	2tl
															International Liquidity	
End of Period																
33.9	33.1	27.2	77.4	263.4	312.8	258.4	280.1	302.9	422.0	561.1	229.2	249.8	314.9	265.5	Total Reserves minus Gold	1l.d
—	—	.1	.1	.6	.8	.2	—	.3	.1	.1	.1	.1	.3	.2	SDRs	1b.d
—	—	—	—	—	—	—	—	—	—	—	—	—	—	—	Reserve Position in the Fund	1c.d
33.9	33.1	27.1	77.3	262.8	312.0	258.2	280.1	302.6	421.9	561.1	229.1	249.7	314.6	265.3	Foreign Exchange	1d.d
.251	.251	.251	.251	.251	.251	.251	.251	.251	.251	.231	.231	.231	.231	.231	Gold (Million Fine Troy Ounces)	1ad
9.7	10.8	12.5	11.8	11.6	12.5	12.6	12.1	12.1	12.8	12.0	11.6	10.9	11.4	11.1	Gold (National Valuation)	1and
30.0	13.0	....	....	....	....	....	....	....	....	....	....	....	....	....	Monetary Authorities: Other Assets	3..d
68.4	84.6	114.3	120.8	352.5	341.7	421.5	376.2	403.0	431.0	398.5	396.1	389.1	406.3	399.8	Monetary Authorities: Other Liab.	4..d
1.5	2.6	2.5	2.0	3.4	26.8	71.5	113.0	128.9	162.8	189.6	119.4	140.5	238.5	221.9	Deposit Money Banks: Assets	7a.d
795.6	1,155.2	1,469.0	1,609.9	58.7	455.7	98.4	167.1	1,884.2	2,208.2	2,414.5	2,402.6	1,940.4	1,941.2	1,916.0	Liabilities	7b.d
															Monetary Authorities	
End of Period																
577	400	363	659	1,537	1,796	2,976	3,841	3,998	5,255	6,283	4,616	3,428	4,901	4,201	Foreign Assets	11
-9,608	-5,949	-10,366	-10,650	42,740	51,811	I60,870	74,710	91,399	116,131	142,023	182,431	214,392	281,383	331,425	Claims on Central Government	12a
28,533	29,481	31,227	37,564	11,208	10,607	I12,543	14,138	10,375	3,639	5,191	5,923	23,785	15,553	19,602	Claims on Deposit Money Banks	12e
11,042	15,627	8,718	15,319	42,281	51,387	I50,358	65,698	79,275	97,584	124,675	164,513	213,025	270,104	320,579	Reserve Money	14
10,504	15,218	8,299	14,659	19,926	29,211	39,289	54,429	68,663	90,659	119,207	159,608	205,509	256,605	296,471	*of which:* Currency Outside DMBs	14a
						23,469	24,380	24,630	25,919	26,980	25,401	24,362	25,673	25,109	Other Liabilities to DMBs	14n
1,439	1,183	1,004	841	I2,416	2,080	I2,148	1,942	2,050	2,056	1,843	1,965	2,121	2,117	2,098	Foreign Liabilities	16c
787	786	788	787	787	636	634	666	787	788	1,086	1,082	1,681	2,882	4,874	Capital Accounts	17a
6,234	6,336	10,713	10,625	10,001	10,111	I-220	3	-969	-1,317	-1,086	9	414	1,062	2,559	Other Items (Net)	17r
															Deposit Money Banks	
End of Period																
879	I645	659	1,148	23,340	22,962	7,183	2,201	5,298	7,802	14,259	23,105	25,033	51,083	64,112	Reserves	20
....	....	....	....	....	....	23,469	24,380	24,630	25,919	26,980	25,401	24,362	25,673	25,109	Other Claims on Monetary Author.	20n
12	18	15	13	22	163	I111	176	166	310	456	326	505	1,044	1,346	Foreign Assets	21
2,322	1,951	-388	-365	I-8,373	-10,240	I5,625	3,425	2,820	-528	80	-1,525	2,745	-29,785	12,370	Claims on Central Govt. (Net)	22an
202	238	305	331	360	438	444	545	449	511	310	184	61	61	—	Claims on Local Government	22b
32,903	37,728	41,894	46,281	560	638	I4,010	4,571	6,459	11,343	8,351	10,631	11,419	46,688	53,960	Claims on Nonfin.Pub.Enterprises	22c
2,762	3,009	2,998	2,801	3,262	7,208	I12,406	19,173	23,076	28,262	45,956	75,346	115,505	155,761	188,649	Claims on Private Sector	22d
1,040	1,112	1,175	1,009	1,391	1,376	I4,725	4,963	5,827	9,183	11,241	14,961	25,600	44,782	72,707	Demand Deposits	24
6,558	7,447	8,446	7,615	9,467	11,789	I13,939	18,120	24,024	33,942	54,572	82,786	102,944	151,363	216,459	Time, Savings,& Fgn.Currency Dep.	25
						23	44	99	68	130	334	375	372	646	Restricted Deposits	26b
6,239	8,132	8,975	10,320	10,538	12,472	10,641	11,177	11,768	13,035	13,958	14,386	12,346	11,858	12,010	Foreign Liabilities	26c
28,533	29,481	31,227	37,564	11,208	10,607	I24,506	22,327	27,281	36,218	53,714	36,987	40,151	49,051	13,908	Credit from Monetary Authorities	26g
978	1,152	1,347	1,638	2,000	2,106	1,830	2,074	2,402	3,228	4,128	7,790	10,733	12,546	17,908	Capital Accounts	27a
-4,268	-3,735	-5,687	-7,937	-15,397	-17,181	I-2,418	-4,233	-8,523	-22,053	-41,349	-23,777	-12,519	-19,452	11,908	Other Items (Net)	27r
															Monetary Survey	
End of Period																
-7,101	-8,915	-9,616	-10,502	I-11,396	-12,593	I-9,702	-9,102	-9,654	-9,526	-9,063	-11,409	-10,534	-8,030	-8,561	Foreign Assets (Net)	31n
32,435	42,103	42,014	47,443	38,549	49,855	I83,355	102,424	124,203	155,719	196,720	267,068	344,122	454,108	586,404	Domestic Credit	32
-3,230	1,366	-2,878	-1,639	I34,367	41,571	I66,495	78,135	94,219	115,603	142,103	180,906	217,137	251,598	343,795	Claims on Central Govt. (Net)	32an
202	238	305	331	360	438	444	545	449	511	310	184	61	61	—	Claims on Local Government	32b
32,903	37,728	41,894	46,281	560	638	4,010	4,571	6,459	11,343	8,351	10,631	11,419	46,688	53,960	Claims on Nonfin.Pub.Enterprises	32c
2,762	3,009	2,998	2,801	3,262	7,208	I12,406	19,173	23,076	28,262	45,956	75,346	115,505	155,761	188,649	Claims on Private Sector	32d
11,551	16,337	9,474	15,668	21,317	30,587	I43,495	58,688	73,459	98,288	125,957	167,971	220,006	282,177	345,809	Money	34
6,558	7,447	8,446	7,615	9,467	11,789	I13,939	18,120	24,024	33,942	54,572	82,786	102,944	151,363	216,459	Quasi-Money	35
						23	44	99	68	130	334	375	372	646	Restricted Deposits	36b
1,765	1,938	2,135	2,425	2,787	2,742	2,464	2,740	3,189	4,016	5,213	8,871	12,413	15,428	22,782	Capital Accounts	37a
5,460	7,466	12,343	11,233	I-6,418	-7,857	13,730	13,730	13,759	9,885	1,788	-4,305	-2,154	-3,266	-7,862	Other Items (Net)	37r
18,109	23,784	17,920	23,283	30,784	42,376	I57,434	76,808	97,483	132,230	180,528	250,757	322,950	433,541	562,268	Money plus Quasi-Money	35l
															Interest Rates	
Percent Per Annum																
....	....	....	....	....	11.00	11.00	11.00	11.00	12.50	15.00	15.00	15.00	12.00		Central Bank Rate *(End of Per.)*	60
1.50	1.50	1.50	1.50	1.50	5.88	9.00	9.00	9.00	9.00	9.75	12.50	12.50	12.50	11.00	Deposit Rate	60l
8.00	8.00	8.00	8.00	8.00	8.00	....	8.00	....	16.50	16.50	16.50	16.50	16.50	16.13	Lending Rate	60p
....	....	....	....	....	....	....	....	....	10.50	10.50	13.13	14.00	14.00	....	Government Bond Yield	61
															Prices and Labor	
Period Averages																
12.8	14.0	17.4	20.2	25.7	30.3	40.0	48.8	64.4	79.9	100.0	116.3	150.8	228.5	270.5	Consumer Prices	64
Period Averages																
14,792	15,130	15,505	15,813	16,036	15,221	....	15,737	16,469	16,817	....	....	17,964	....	....	Employment	67e
338	354	331	313	486	555	559	503	518	541	....	....	535	....	....	Unemployment	67c
															International Transactions	
Millions of Kyats																
2,575.9	2,116.5	1,449.8	1,051.4	1,410.4	2,037.0	2,633.0	3,241.1	3,609.4	4,776.7	4,825.8	4,419.5	5,415.8	6,737.2	7,073.5	Exports	70
2,401.5	2,245.2	1,785.6	1,538.0	1,280.5	1,709.4	4,058.8	3,971.0	5,007.0	5,285.9	7,564.2	8,032.0	12,735.9	16,920.7	14,463.9	Imports, c.i.f.	71

		1970	1971	1972	1973	1974	1975	1976	1977	1978	1979	1980	1981	1982	1983	1984
Balance of Payments																*Millions of US Dollars:*
Current Account, n.i.e.	78ald	....	....	....	....	....	....	−33.8	−100.4	−215.1	−358.5	−347.1	−314.0	−498.7	−349.8	−217.8
Goods: Exports f.o.b.	78aad	....	....	....	....	....	....	172.7	206.3	272.3	362.6	428.6	533.2	422.8	375.2	364.1
Goods: Imports f.o.b.	78abd	....	....	....	....	....	....	−212.7	−307.4	−495.4	−731.7	−788.2	−863.1	−913.0	−728.2	−564.5
Trade Balance	78acd	....	....	....	....	....	....	−40.0	−101.2	−223.1	−369.1	−359.6	−329.9	−490.2	−353.0	−200.4
Services: Credit	78add	....	....	....	....	....	....	27.3	35.8	25.9	40.5	52.2	73.1	82.0	64.1	61.5
Services: Debit	78aed	....	....	....	....	....	....	−22.8	−31.2	−27.0	−59.0	−73.3	−91.5	−105.6	−75.1	−70.6
Balance on Goods & Services	78afd	....	....	....	....	....	....	−35.6	−96.6	−224.2	−387.6	−380.7	−348.3	−513.8	−364.0	−209.5
Income: Credit	78agd	....	....	....	....	....	....	3.5	3.8	4.8	8.7	14.0	20.1	13.3	4.0	4.9
Income: Debit	78ahd	....	....	....	....	....	....	−18.0	−18.6	−23.3	−37.6	−61.0	−69.8	−64.4	−72.1	−81.1
Balance on Gds, Serv. & Inc.	78aid	....	....	....	....	....	....	−50.1	−111.4	−242.7	−416.4	−427.8	−397.9	−564.9	−432.0	−285.7
Current Transfers, n.i.e.: Credit	78ajd	....	....	....	....	....	....	17.6	11.9	28.5	59.7	81.3	85.3	66.5	82.4	68.1
Current Transfers: Debit	78akd	....	....	....	....	....	....	−1.4	−.9	−.8	−1.7	−.6	−1.3	−.3	−.3	−.2
Capital Account, n.i.e.	78bcd	....	....	....	....	....	....	—	—	—	—	—	—	—	—	—
Capital Account, n.i.e.: Credit	78bad	....	....	....	....	....	....	—	—	—	—	—	—	—	—	—
Capital Account: Debit	78bbd	....	....	....	....	....	....	—	—	—	—	—	—	—	—	—
Financial Account, n.i.e.	78bjd	....	....	....	....	....	....	15.8	55.7	183.6	429.1	370.8	317.7	340.2	245.6	193.8
Direct Investment Abroad	78bdd	....	....	....	....	....	....	—	—	—	—	—	—	—	—	—
Dir. Invest. in Rep. Econ., n.i.e.	78bed	....	....	....	....	....	....	—	—	—	—	—	—	—	—	—
Portfolio Investment Assets	78bfd	....	....	....	....	....	....	—	—	—	—	—	—	—	—	—
Equity Securities	78bkd	....	....	....	....	....	....	—	—	—	—	—	—	—	—	—
Debt Securities	78bld	....	....	....	....	....	....	—	—	—	—	—	—	—	—	—
Portfolio Investment Liab., n.i.e.	78bgd	....	....	....	....	....	....	—	—	—	—	—	—	—	—	—
Equity Securities	78bmd	....	....	....	....	....	....	—	—	—	—	—	—	—	—	—
Debt Securities	78bnd	....	....	....	....	....	....	—	—	—	—	—	—	—	—	—
Financial Derivatives Assets	78bwd	....	....	....	....	....	....	....	....	....	....	....	....	....	....	....
Financial Derivatives Liabilities	78bxd	....	....	....	....	....	....	....	....	....	....	....	....	....	....	....
Other Investment Assets	78bhd	....	....	....	....	....	....	2.2	—	—	—	—	—	—	—	—
Monetary Authorities	78bod	....	....	....	....	....	....	—	—	—	—	—	—	—	—	—
General Government	78bpd	....	....	....	....	....	....	—	—	—	—	—	—	—	—	—
Banks	78bqd	....	....	....	....	....	....	—	—	—	—	—	—	—	—	—
Other Sectors	78brd	....	....	....	....	....	....	2.2	—	—	—	—	—	—	—	—
Other Investment Liab., n.i.e.	78bid	....	....	....	....	....	....	13.6	55.7	183.6	429.1	370.8	317.7	340.2	245.6	193.8
Monetary Authorities	78bsd	....	....	....	....	....	....	−.2	2.0	2.7	1.1	−.3	3.7	11.3	32.2	.2
General Government	78btd	....	....	....	....	....	....	13.9	53.8	180.9	428.0	371.1	314.0	328.9	213.4	193.5
Banks	78bud	....	....	....	....	....	....	—	—	—	—	—	—	—	—	—
Other Sectors	78bvd	....	....	....	....	....	....	—	—	—	—	—	—	—	—	—
Net Errors and Omissions	78cad	....	....	....	....	....	....	2.8	−6.1	−32.3	−13.3	7.7	−32.6	30.3	79.9	15.3
Overall Balance	78cbd	....	....	....	....	....	....	−15.2	−50.7	−63.8	57.3	31.3	−28.9	−128.3	−24.4	−8.8
Reserves and Related Items	79dad	....	....	....	....	....	....	15.2	50.7	63.8	−57.3	−31.3	28.9	128.3	24.4	8.8
Reserve Assets	79dbd	....	....	....	....	....	....	22.1	15.4	7.0	−95.9	−39.6	6.1	103.4	13.0	20.8
Use of Fund Credit and Loans	79dcd	....	....	....	....	....	....	−6.9	27.8	33.7	15.1	−11.7	22.8	24.8	11.4	−12.1
Exceptional Financing	79ded	....	....	....	....	....	....	—	7.5	23.1	23.6	20.0	—	—	—	—
Government Finance																*Millions of Kyats:*
Deficit (-) or Surplus	80	....	....	....	‡−855	‡−572	−678	−129	196	196	851	473	709	338	307	−93
Revenue	81	....	....	....	‡1,453	‡1,934	2,172	3,277	4,266	4,755	5,690	6,176	7,303	7,445	7,640	7,741
Grants Received	81z	....	....	....	73	‡110	149	141	86	248	326	415	269	658	405	404
Expenditure	82	....	....	....	‡2,349	‡2,601	2,990	3,533	4,147	4,787	5,194	6,119	7,046	7,898	7,936	8,509
Lending Minus Repayments	83	....	....	....	32	‡15	9	14	9	20	−29	−1	−183	−133	−198	−271
Financing																
Domestic	84a	....	....	....	941	‡626	669	123	−769	−467	−1,200	−941	−1,136	−886	−779	−485
Foreign	85a	....	....	....	−86	‡−54	9	6	573	271	349	468	427	548	472	578
National Accounts																*Millions of Kyats:*
Exports of Goods & Services	90c	585	664	680	953	‡912	‡1,192	1,414	1,729	1,842	2,679	3,177	3,432	3,003	3,373	3,133
Gross Fixed Capital Formation	93e	1,056	1,184	1,111	1,146	‡1,525	1,681	2,320	3,753	5,364	7,389	7,228	8,635	10,044	9,057	8,476
Increase/Decrease(-) in Stocks	93i	175	133	156	352	‡475	659	515	92	414	486	1,065	1,205	331	−95	−367
Govt. and Private Consumption	96f	9,474	9,712	10,493	12,824	‡17,452	21,389	24,805	26,132	27,404	28,980	31,774	35,218	39,747	42,685	47,396
Imports of Goods & Services	98c	−852	−921	−704	−575	‡−1,016	−1,443	−1,628	−2,087	−3,224	−4,201	−4,635	−5,611	−6,314	−5,197	−5,041
Gross Domestic Product (GDP)	99b	10,437	10,772	11,735	14,700	‡19,348	23,477	27,427	29,618	31,800	35,333	38,609	42,879	46,811	49,823	53,597
Net Factor Inc/Pmts(-) Abroad	98.n	....	....	....	....	....	−7	−18	−61	−92	−146	−160	−168	−347	−510	−517
Gross National Income (GNI)	99a	....	....	....	....	....	23,470	27,409	29,557	31,708	35,187	38,449	42,711	46,464	49,313	53,080
GDP Volume 1985/86 Prices	99b.p	....	....	....	....	....	....	35,120	39,692	39,261	41,112	44,362	47,157	49,714	51,878	54,437
GDP Volume (1995=100)	99bvp	....	....	....	....	....	....	52.6	59.5	58.8	61.6	66.5	70.7	74.5	77.7	81.6
GDP Deflator (1995=100)	99bip	4.7	4.6	4.7	5.1	‡6.3	8.0	8.6	8.2	8.9	9.5	9.6	10.0	10.4	10.6	10.9
Population	99z	27.03	27.64	28.26	28.89	29.52	30.17	30.83	31.51	32.21	32.91	33.64	35.09	35.91	36.75	37.61

(*Millions:* — Population units)

Minus Sign Indicates Debit

	Code	1985	1986	1987	1988	1989	1990	1991	1992	1993	1994	1995	1996	1997	1998	1999
Balance of Payments																
Current Account, n.i.e.	78al d	-205.5	-294.0	-180.0	-175.9	-68.0	-431.3	-267.4	-114.4	-227.8	-129.9	-258.5	-279.8	-412.0	-494.5	-222.1
Goods: Exports f.o.b.	78aa d	310.8	330.7	219.6	165.7	222.8	222.6	248.2	531.3	630.9	857.4	933.2	937.9	974.5	1,065.1	1,125.2
Goods: Imports f.o.b.	78ab d	-512.9	-620.9	-452.7	-370.2	-304.3	-524.3	-301.5	-636.2	-1,260.8	-1,466.7	-1,756.3	-1,869.1	-2,106.6	-2,451.2	-2,115.9
Trade Balance	78ac d	-202.1	-290.2	-233.1	-204.5	-81.5	-301.7	-53.3	-104.9	-629.9	-609.4	-823.0	-931.2	-1,132.1	-1,386.1	-990.7
Services: Credit	78ad d	66.8	66.4	69.1	46.9	56.6	93.5	56.0	112.4	246.6	270.7	360.9	427.7	521.7	626.1	482.1
Services: Debit	78ae d	-81.8	-56.8	-46.8	-34.5	-44.3	-72.3	-54.3	-42.4	-130.2	-128.9	-243.8	-302.0	-443.4	-364.8	-240.8
Balance on Goods & Services	78af d	-217.1	-280.6	-210.8	-192.0	-69.2	-280.6	-51.6	-34.9	-513.6	-467.6	-705.9	-805.4	-1,053.8	-1,124.7	-749.4
Income: Credit	78ag d	2.2	4.2	6.3	2.7	2.7	2.4	1.0	3.4	4.7	7.1	15.4	9.1	6.5	10.9	50.6
Income: Debit	78ah d	-71.1	-110.9	-82.5	-79.1	-57.1	-192.1	-272.2	-151.4	-63.0	-74.1	-124.2	-53.1	-20.3	-11.3	-54.0
Balance on Gds, Serv, & Inc.	78ai d	-286.0	-387.3	-287.1	-268.4	-123.6	-470.3	-322.8	-182.9	-571.9	-534.5	-814.7	-849.4	-1,067.5	-1,125.1	-752.8
Current Transfers, n.i.e.: Credit	78aj d	81.8	96.7	107.4	93.1	55.6	39.0	55.5	70.3	344.6	405.2	564.2	598.4	685.1	630.9	531.0
Current Transfers: Debit	78ak d	-1.3	-3.5	-.2	-.5	—	—	-.1	-1.8	-.5	-.6	-8.0	-28.8	-29.7	-.3	-.3
Capital Account, n.i.e.	78bc d	—	—	—	—	84.0	232.9	—	—	—	—	—	—	—	....	....
Capital Account, n.i.e.: Credit	78ba d	—	—	—	—	84.0	232.9	—	—	—	—	—	—	—	....	....
Capital Account: Debit	78bb d	—	—	—	—	—	—	—	—	—	—	—	—	—	....	....
Financial Account, n.i.e.	78bj d	148.7	274.0	202.9	139.7	82.0	185.8	275.0	191.0	160.8	185.2	242.8	266.8	469.1	535.1	211.9
Direct Investment Abroad	78bd d	—	—	—	—	—	—	—	—	—	—	—	....	....	....	....
Dir. Invest. in Rep. Econ., n.i.e.	78be d	—	—	—	—	7.8	161.1	238.1	171.6	104.7	126.1	277.2	310.4	387.2	314.5	216.3
Portfolio Investment Assets	78bf d	—	—	—	—	—	—	....	....	....	....	....	....	....	....	....
Equity Securities	78bk d	—	—	—	—	—	—	....	....	....	....	....	....	....	....	....
Debt Securities	78bl d	—	—	—	—	—	—	....	....	....	....	....	....	....	....	....
Portfolio Investment Liab., n.i.e.	78bg d	—	—	—	—	—	—	....	....	....	....	....	....	....	....	....
Equity Securities	78bm d	—	—	—	—	—	—	....	....	....	....	....	....	....	....	....
Debt Securities	78bn d	—	—	—	—	—	—	....	....	....	....	....	....	....	....	....
Financial Derivatives Assets	78bw d	....	....	....	....	....	....	....	....	....	....	....	....	....	....	....
Financial Derivatives Liabilities	78bx d	....	....	....	....	....	....	....	....	....	....	....	....	....	....	....
Other Investment Assets	78bh d	—	—	—	—	—	—	....	....	....	....	....	....	....	....	....
Monetary Authorities	78bo d	—	—	—	—	—	—	....	....	....	....	....	....	....	....	....
General Government	78bp d	—	—	—	—	—	—	....	....	....	....	....	....	....	....	....
Banks	78bq d	—	—	—	—	—	—	....	....	....	....	....	....	....	....	....
Other Sectors	78br d	—	—	—	—	—	—	....	....	....	....	....	....	....	....	....
Other Investment Liab., n.i.e.	78bi d	148.7	274.0	202.9	139.7	74.2	24.6	37.0	19.4	56.1	59.1	-34.4	-43.6	81.9	220.7	-4.3
Monetary Authorities	78bs d	1.5	2.3	-1.2	-3.3	-.6	-1.8	-2.8	-.7	—	2.6	2.3	-3.1	-5.6	-2.6	1.1
General Government	78bt d	147.2	271.7	204.1	143.0	74.8	26.4	39.8	20.2	56.1	56.5	-36.7	-40.6	87.5	226.9	-4.1
Banks	78bu d	—	—	—	—	—	—	....	....	....	....	....	....	....	-3.6	-1.3
Other Sectors	78bv d	—	—	—	—	—	—	....	....	....	....	....	....	....	....	....
Net Errors and Omissions	78ca d	41.7	69.3	14.7	116.7	52.6	21.4	-53.9	17.7	-10.0	-10.3	-16.2	-11.7	-26.0	19.1	-34.2
Overall Balance	78cb d	-15.0	49.3	37.7	80.5	150.6	8.7	-46.3	94.3	-77.0	45.0	-31.8	-24.7	31.0	59.7	-44.4
Reserves and Related Items	79da d	15.0	-49.3	-37.7	-80.5	-150.6	-8.7	46.3	-94.3	77.0	-45.0	31.8	24.7	-31.0	-59.7	44.4
Reserve Assets	79db d	38.7	-4.4	12.8	-52.4	-142.9	-6.3	46.6	-94.3	77.0	-45.0	31.8	24.7	-31.0	-59.7	44.4
Use of Fund Credit and Loans	79dc d	-23.6	-44.9	-50.4	-28.1	-7.7	-2.4	-.3	....	....	....	....	....	....	—	—
Exceptional Financing	79de d	—	—	—	—	—	—	....	....	....	....	....	....	....	....	—
Government Finance																
Year Beginning April 1																
Deficit (-) or Surplus	80	-443	-1,482	-1,515	-2,300	-5,189	-7,789	-8,993	Ɩ-7,054	-7,761	-15,757	-24,924	Ɩ-25,007	-20,448	8,176	-1,580
Revenue	81	7,620	7,320	7,201	6,463	11,842	16,048	18,039	Ɩ20,313	27,329	32,029	39,429	Ɩ54,580	71,502	79,739	90,599
Grants Received	81z	587	564	566	347	152	140	300	Ɩ358	456	429	744	Ɩ421	763	643	852
Expenditure	82	9,015	9,790	9,621	9,443	17,566	24,349	27,621	Ɩ27,931	35,696	48,021	64,884	Ɩ79,929	92,628	72,097	92,880
Lending Minus Repayments	83	-365	-424	-339	-333	-383	-372	-289	Ɩ-206	-150	194	213	Ɩ79	85	109	151
Financing																
Domestic	84a	-214	690	960	2,125	5,200	7,763	9,001	Ɩ7,038	7,738	15,749	25,201	Ɩ25,185	20,726	-8,125	1,260
Foreign	85a	657	792	555	175	-11	26	-8	Ɩ16	23	8	-277	Ɩ-178	-278	-51	320
National Accounts																
Year Beginning April 1																
Exports of Goods & Services	90c	2,566	2,418	1,655	2,169	2,834	2,953	2,926	3,590	4,228	5,405	5,033	5,488	6,290	7,700	....
Gross Fixed Capital Formation	93e	8,649	8,618	8,683	7,296	11,827	22,318	27,571	31,184	37,466	54,596	82,582	118,313	150,240	206,912	....
Increase/Decrease(-) in Stocks	93i	44	-1,139	-742	2,467	-325	-1,995	1,032	2,601	7,360	3,875	3,540	-21,262	-10,276	-7,604	....
Govt. and Private Consumption	96f	49,532	53,067	63,168	67,754	113,726	134,188	160,610	217,384	319,191	417,230	523,876	701,220	987,513	1,419,709	....
Imports of Goods & Services	98c	-4,802	-3,936	-4,066	-3,443	-3,395	-5,523	-5,337	-5,365	-7,923	-8,332	-10,302	-11,779	-14,258	-16,941	....
Gross Domestic Product (GDP)	99b	55,989	59,028	68,698	76,243	124,666	151,941	186,802	249,395	360,321	472,774	604,729	791,980	1,119,509	1,609,776	....
Net Factor Inc/Pmts(-) Abroad	98.n	-581	-658	-520	-261	-304	47	-291	-153	-429	-396	-689	-116	-69	34	....
Gross National Income (GNI)	99a	55,408	58,370	68,178	75,982	124,362	151,988	186,512	249,242	359,892	472,378	604,040	791,864	1,119,440	1,609,810	....
GDP Volume 1985/86 Prices	99b.p	55,989	55,397	53,178	47,141	48,883	50,260	49,933	54,757	58,064	62,406	66,742	71,042	75,123	79,460	....
GDP Volume (1995=100)	99bv p	83.9	83.0	79.7	70.6	73.2	75.3	74.8	82.0	87.0	93.5	100.0	106.4	112.6	119.1	....
GDP Deflator (1995=100)	99bi p	11.0	11.8	14.3	17.9	28.1	33.4	41.3	50.3	68.5	83.6	100.0	123.0	164.5	223.6	204.9
Population	99z															
Midyear Estimates		38.54	39.41	Ɩ39.19	39.84	40.60	41.35	Ɩ41.55	42.33	43.12	43.92	Ɩ45.11	45.92	46.40	44.5	45.06

(See notes in the back of the book.)

Namibia

728

		1970	1971	1972	1973	1974	1975	1976	1977	1978	1979	1980	1981	1982	1983	1984
Exchange Rates														*Namibia Dollars per SDR:*		
Market Rate	aa	.71723	.83085	.85000	.80966	.84435	1.01797	1.01029	1.05627	1.13286	1.08924	.95066	1.11341	1.18729	1.27926	1.94563
													Namibia Dollars per US Dollar:			
Market Rate	ae	.71723	.76526	.78290	.67116	.68963	.86957	.86957	.86957	.86957	.82686	.74538	.95657	1.07631	1.22190	1.98491
Market Rate	rf	.71641	.71305	.77283	.69411	.67948	.73951	.86957	.86957	.86957	.84202	.77883	.87758	1.08582	1.11410	1.47528
Fund Position														*Millions of SDRs:*		
Quota	2f. s	…	…	…	…	…	…	…	…	…	…	…	…	…	…	…
SDRs	1b. s	…	…	…	…	…	…	…	…	…	…	…	…	…	…	…
Reserve Position in the Fund	1c. s	…	…	…	…	…	…	…	…	…	…	…	…	…	…	…
Total Fund Cred.&Loans Outstg.	2tl	…	…	…	…	…	…	…	…	…	…	…	…	…	…	…
International Liquidity												*Millions of US Dollars Unless Otherwise Indicated:*				
Total Reserves minus Gold	1l. d	…	…	…	…	…	…	…	…	…	…	…	…	…	…	…
SDRs	1b. d	…	…	…	…	…	…	…	…	…	…	…	…	…	…	…
Reserve Position in the Fund	1c. d	…	…	…	…	…	…	…	…	…	…	…	…	…	…	…
Foreign Exchange	1d. d	…	…	…	…	…	…	…	…	…	…	…	…	…	…	…
Gold (Million Fine Troy Ounces)	1ad	…	…	…	…	…	…	…	…	…	…	…	…	…	…	…
Gold (National Valuation)	1an d	…	…	…	…	…	…	…	…	…	…	…	…	…	…	…
Monetary Authorities: Other Liab.	4.. d	…	…	…	…	…	…	…	…	…	…	…	…	…	…	…
Deposit Money Banks: Assets	7a. d	…	…	…	…	…	…	…	…	…	…	…	…	…	…	…
Liabilities	7b. d	…	…	…	…	…	…	…	…	…	…	…	…	…	…	…
Other Banking Insts.: Liabilities	7f. d	…	…	…	…	…	…	…	…	…	…	…	…	…	…	…
Monetary Authorities														*Millions of Namibia Dollars:*		
Foreign Assets	11	…	…	…	…	…	…	…	…	…	…	…	…	…	…	…
Claims on Central Government	12a	…	…	…	…	…	…	…	…	…	…	…	…	…	…	…
Reserve Money	14	…	…	…	…	…	…	…	…	…	…	…	…	…	…	…
Foreign Liabilities	16c	…	…	…	…	…	…	…	…	…	…	…	…	…	…	…
Central Government Deposits	16d	…	…	…	…	…	…	…	…	…	…	…	…	…	…	…
Capital Accounts	17a	…	…	…	…	…	…	…	…	…	…	…	…	…	…	…
Other Items (Net)	17r	…	…	…	…	…	…	…	…	…	…	…	…	…	…	…
Deposit Money Banks														*Millions of Namibia Dollars:*		
Reserves	20	…	…	…	…	…	…	…	…	…	…	…	…	…	…	…
Foreign Assets	21	…	…	…	…	…	…	…	…	…	…	…	…	…	…	…
Claims on Central Government	22a	…	…	…	…	…	…	…	…	…	…	…	…	…	…	…
Claims on Local Government	22b	…	…	…	…	…	…	…	…	…	…	…	…	…	…	…
Claims on Nonfin.Pub.Enterprises	22c	…	…	…	…	…	…	…	…	…	…	…	…	…	…	…
Claims on Private Sector	22d	…	…	…	…	…	…	…	…	…	…	…	…	…	…	…
Claims on Other Banking Insts	22f	…	…	…	…	…	…	…	…	…	…	…	…	…	…	…
Claims on Nonbank Financial Insts	22g	…	…	…	…	…	…	…	…	…	…	…	…	…	…	…
Demand Deposits	24	…	…	…	…	…	…	…	…	…	…	…	…	…	…	…
Time, Savings,& Fgn.Currency Dep.	25	…	…	…	…	…	…	…	…	…	…	…	…	…	…	…
Bonds	26ab	…	…	…	…	…	…	…	…	…	…	…	…	…	…	…
Foreign Liabilities	26c	…	…	…	…	…	…	…	…	…	…	…	…	…	…	…
Central Government Deposits	26d	…	…	…	…	…	…	…	…	…	…	…	…	…	…	…
Liabilities to Other Banking Insts	26i	…	…	…	…	…	…	…	…	…	…	…	…	…	…	…
Capital Accounts	27a	…	…	…	…	…	…	…	…	…	…	…	…	…	…	…
Other Items (Net)	27r	…	…	…	…	…	…	…	…	…	…	…	…	…	…	…
Monetary Survey														*Millions of Namibia Dollars:*		
Foreign Assets (Net)	31n	…	…	…	…	…	…	…	…	…	…	…	…	…	…	…
Domestic Credit	32	…	…	…	…	…	…	…	…	…	…	…	…	…	…	…
Claims on Central Govt. (Net)	32an	…	…	…	…	…	…	…	…	…	…	…	…	…	…	…
Claims on Local Government	32b	…	…	…	…	…	…	…	…	…	…	…	…	…	…	…
Claims on Nonfin.Pub.Enterprises	32c	…	…	…	…	…	…	…	…	…	…	…	…	…	…	…
Claims on Private Sector	32d	…	…	…	…	…	…	…	…	…	…	…	…	…	…	…
Claims on Other Banking Insts	32f	…	…	…	…	…	…	…	…	…	…	…	…	…	…	…
Claims on Nonbank Financial Inst	32g	…	…	…	…	…	…	…	…	…	…	…	…	…	…	…
Money	34	…	…	…	…	…	…	…	…	…	…	…	…	…	…	…
Quasi-Money	35	…	…	…	…	…	…	…	…	…	…	…	…	…	…	…
Bonds	36ab	…	…	…	…	…	…	…	…	…	…	…	…	…	…	…
Liabilities to Other Banking Insts	36i	…	…	…	…	…	…	…	…	…	…	…	…	…	…	…
Capital Accounts	37a	…	…	…	…	…	…	…	…	…	…	…	…	…	…	…
Other Items (Net)	37r	…	…	…	…	…	…	…	…	…	…	…	…	…	…	…
Money plus Quasi-Money	35l	…	…	…	…	…	…	…	…	…	…	…	…	…	…	…
Other Banking Institutions														*Millions of Namibia Dollars:*		
Reserves	40	…	…	…	…	…	…	…	…	…	…	…	…	…	…	…
Claims on Central Government	42a	…	…	…	…	…	…	…	…	…	…	…	…	…	…	…
Claims on Local Government	42b	…	…	…	…	…	…	…	…	…	…	…	…	…	…	…
Claims on Nonfin.Pub.Enterprises	42c	…	…	…	…	…	…	…	…	…	…	…	…	…	…	…
Claims on Private Sector	42d	…	…	…	…	…	…	…	…	…	…	…	…	…	…	…
Claims on Deposit Money Banks	42e	…	…	…	…	…	…	…	…	…	…	…	…	…	…	…
Claims on Nonbank Financial Insts	42g	…	…	…	…	…	…	…	…	…	…	…	…	…	…	…
Time, Savings,& Fgn.Currency Dep.	45	…	…	…	…	…	…	…	…	…	…	…	…	…	…	…
Money Market Instruments	46aa	…	…	…	…	…	…	…	…	…	…	…	…	…	…	…
Foreign Liabilities	46c	…	…	…	…	…	…	…	…	…	…	…	…	…	…	…
Central Government Deposits	46d	…	…	…	…	…	…	…	…	…	…	…	…	…	…	…
Credit from Deposit Money Banks	46h	…	…	…	…	…	…	…	…	…	…	…	…	…	…	…
Capital Accounts	47a	…	…	…	…	…	…	…	…	…	…	…	…	…	…	…
Other Items (Net)	47r	…	…	…	…	…	…	…	…	…	…	…	…	…	…	…

	1985	1986	1987	1988	1989	1990	1991	1992	1993	1994	1995	1996	1997	1998	1999		
Exchange Rates																	
End of Period																	
	2.80926	2.67072	2.73793	3.19971	3.33272	3.64557	3.92371	4.19788	4.66667	5.17298	5.42197	6.73325	6.56747	8.25106	8.44711	Market Rate	aa
End of Period (ae) Period Average (rf)																	
	2.55754	2.18341	1.92994	2.37773	2.53601	2.56250	2.74303	3.05300	3.39750	3.54350	3.64750	4.68250	4.86750	5.86000	6.15450	Market Rate	ae
	2.22868	2.28503	2.03603	2.27347	2.62268	2.58732	2.76132	2.85201	3.26774	3.55080	3.62709	4.29935	4.60796	5.52828	6.10948	Market Rate	rf
Fund Position																	
End of Period																	
	....	....	....	....	....	70	70	100	100	100	100	100	100	100	137	Quota	2f. s
	....	....	....	....	....	—	—	—	—	—	—	—	—	—	—	SDRs	1b. s
	....	....	....	....	....	—	—	—	—	—	—	—	—	—	—	Reserve Position in the Fund	1c. s
	....	....	....	....	....	—	—	—	—	—	—	—	—	—	—	Total Fund Cred.&Loans Outstg.	2tl
International Liquidity																	
End of Period																	
	....	....	....	....	....	....	....	49.72	133.70	202.62	220.98	193.87	250.53	260.25	305.49	Total Reserves minus Gold	1l. d
	....	....	....	....	....	—	.01	.01	.02	.02	.02	.02	.02	.02	.02	SDRs	1b. d
	....	....	....	....	....	—	.01	.01	.01	.01	.03	.04	.04	.05	.05	Reserve Position in the Fund	1c. d
	....	....	....	....	....	....	....	49.69	133.67	202.59	220.94	193.81	250.47	260.18	305.42	Foreign Exchange	1d. d
	....	....	....	....	....	—	—	—	—	—	—	—	—	—	—	Gold (Million Fine Troy Ounces)	1ad
	....	....	....	....	....	—	—	—	—	—	—	—	—	—	—	Gold (National Valuation)	1an d
	....	....	....	....	....	.03	.03	166.66	179.93	200.87	212.20	181.89	4.96	6.63	7.70	Monetary Authorities: Other Liab.	4.. d
	....	....	....	....	....	145.97	213.45	123.05	57.38	54.87	38.58	74.70	110.33	93.58	142.63	Deposit Money Banks: Assets	7a. d
	....	....	....	....	....	107.55	46.09	32.53	47.35	110.49	137.26	63.00	172.31	116.20	67.99	Liabilities	7b. d
	....	....	....	....	....	....	....	2.80	3.01	5.15	2.80	2.11	3.07	4.01	4.17	Other Banking Insts.: Liabilities	7f. d
Monetary Authorities																	
End of Period																	
	....	....	....	....	....	243.0	226.0	346.8	465.9	725.8	818.1	918.0	1,236.0	1,550.1	1,885.6	Foreign Assets	11
	....	....	....	....	....	—	—	510.3	619.6	720.0	783.7	856.9	—	—	—	Claims on Central Government	12a
	....	....	....	....	....	90.0	97.1	221.8	233.3	373.6	415.6	508.3	609.3	631.4	906.7	Reserve Money	14
	....	....	....	....	....	.1	.1	508.8	611.3	711.8	774.0	851.7	24.1	38.8	47.4	Foreign Liabilities	16c
	....	....	....	....	....	150.4	123.1	143.5	221.7	291.2	280.8	162.4	374.4	416.1	471.8	Central Government Deposits	16d
	....	....	....	....	....	10.0	21.8	31.9	40.6	71.2	119.5	303.8	316.5	513.4	562.9	Capital Accounts	17a
	....	....	....	....	....	-7.5	-16.2	-48.9	-21.4	-2.0	11.9	-51.3	-88.4	-49.8	-103.2	Other Items (Net)	17r
Deposit Money Banks																	
End of Period																	
	....	....	....	....	....	81.3	84.7	83.4	99.5	156.2	175.4	226.4	275.7	265.7	510.5	Reserves	20
	....	....	....	....	....	374.1	585.5	375.7	195.0	194.4	140.7	349.8	537.0	548.4	877.8	Foreign Assets	21
	....	....	....	....	....	40.0	40.8	171.6	279.2	238.8	256.2	460.9	659.8	701.7	1,020.0	Claims on Central Government	22a
	....	....	....	....	....	2.2	9.3	15.2	15.0	17.2	19.2	18.6	17.4	18.8	16.3	Claims on Local Government	22b
	....	....	....	....	....	4.0	50.1	42.1	42.2	42.1	72.1	72.2	148.8	142.7	136.6	Claims on Nonfin.Pub.Enterprises	22c
	....	....	....	....	....	1,372.6	1,599.9	2,079.2	2,705.5	3,542.6	4,742.8	5,663.2	6,553.5	7,129.3	7,434.2	Claims on Private Sector	22d
	....	....	....	....	....	47.6	13.0	21.0	10.1	95.1	74.6	7.0	23.6	14.6	.6	Claims on Other Banking Insts	22f
	....	....	....	....	....							10.1			10.1	Claims on Nonbank Financial Insts	22g
	....	....	....	....	....	605.6	809.5	1,002.4	1,333.1	1,465.3	1,581.9	2,516.7	2,562.5	3,315.9	4,073.6	Demand Deposits	24
	....	....	....	....	....	863.1	1,103.1	1,375.1	1,521.9	2,081.0	2,851.6	3,229.9	3,535.8	3,479.6	3,979.9	Time, Savings,& Fgn.Currency Dep.	25
	....	....	....	....	....	—	4.0	2.4	3.9	4.1	4.1	8.9	7.0	5.5	—	Bonds	26ab
	....	....	....	....	....	275.6	126.4	99.3	160.9	391.5	500.6	295.0	838.7	680.9	418.4	Foreign Liabilities	26c
	....	....	....	....	....	82.3	232.6	109.9	113.3	83.1	73.5	77.9	217.6	173.2	89.2	Central Government Deposits	26d
	....	....	....	....	....	....	....	45.1	7.6	5.1	74.0	20.9	67.2	45.2	56.8	Liabilities to Other Banking Insts	26i
	....	....	....	....	....	87.9	162.8	204.5	273.2	293.8	432.5	644.0	782.7	919.0	1,080.7	Capital Accounts	27a
	....	....	....	....	....	7.3	-55.2	-50.5	-67.4	-37.5	-37.2	14.8	204.4	201.7	307.6	Other Items (Net)	27r
Monetary Survey																	
End of Period																	
	....	....	....	....	....	341.4	685.0	114.3	-111.3	-183.0	-315.8	121.1	910.1	1,378.7	2,297.7	Foreign Assets (Net)	31n
	....	....	....	....	....	1,233.6	1,357.5	2,586.3	3,336.9	4,282.1	5,595.0	6,849.1	6,811.9	7,418.2	8,057.5	Domestic Credit	32
	....	....	....	....	....	-192.7	-314.9	428.5	563.8	584.5	685.6	1,077.4	67.8	112.3	459.0	Claims on Central Govt. (Net)	32an
	....	....	....	....	....	2.2	9.3	15.2	15.0	17.2	19.2	18.6	17.5	18.8	16.3	Claims on Local Government	32b
	....	....	....	....	....	4.0	50.1	42.1	42.2	42.1	72.1	72.2	148.8	142.7	136.6	Claims on Nonfin.Pub.Enterprises	32c
	....	....	....	....	....	1,372.6	1,599.9	2,079.2	2,705.5	3,542.6	4,742.8	5,663.2	6,553.5	7,129.3	7,434.2	Claims on Private Sector	32d
	....	....	....	....	....	47.6	13.1	21.3	10.5	95.6	75.3	7.7	24.3	15.1	1.3	Claims on Other Banking Insts	32f
	....	....	....	....	....							10.1			10.1	Claims on Nonbank Financial Inst	32g
	....	....	....	....	....	614.3	821.9	1,002.4	1,466.8	1,682.8	1,822.2	2,799.5	2,898.1	3,680.9	4,496.3	Money	34
	....	....	....	....	....	863.1	1,103.1	1,375.1	1,521.9	2,081.0	2,851.6	3,229.9	3,535.8	3,479.6	3,979.9	Quasi-Money	35
	....	....	....	....	....	—	4.0	2.4	3.9	4.1	4.1	8.9	7.0	5.5	—	Bonds	36ab
	....	....	....	....	....	....	....	45.1	7.6	5.1	74.0	20.9	67.2	45.2	56.8	Liabilities to Other Banking Insts	36i
	....	....	....	....	....	97.9	184.6	236.4	313.8	365.0	552.0	947.8	1,099.3	1,432.4	1,643.6	Capital Accounts	37a
	....	....	....	....	....	-.2	-71.2	39.3	-88.4	-39.0	-24.5	-36.7	114.6	153.3	178.6	Other Items (Net)	37r
	....	....	....	....	....	1,477.4	1,925.0	2,377.5	2,988.8	3,763.8	4,673.7	6,029.4	6,433.9	7,160.5	8,476.2	Money plus Quasi-Money	35l
Other Banking Institutions																	
End of Period																	
	....	....	....	....	....	....	....	138.4	43.1	.6	6.9	1.1	1.2	1.4	1.9	Reserves	40
	....	....	....	....	....	....	....	3.0	6.0	31.0	5.1	140.0	166.4	151.9	209.5	Claims on Central Government	42a
	....	....	....	....	....	....	....	5.8	6.1	5.5	5.3	5.3	5.2	5.1	5.0	Claims on Local Government	42b
	....	....	....	....	....	....	....	2.4	7.7	16.7	7.8	4.6	4.7	7.5	8.6	Claims on Nonfin.Pub.Enterprises	42c
	....	....	....	....	....	....	....	1,003.8	1,148.7	1,374.3	1,519.6	1,352.9	1,402.5	1,623.6	1,799.5	Claims on Private Sector	42d
	....	....	....	....	....	....	....	—	95.8	116.8	164.1	91.3	160.6	118.8	167.6	Claims on Deposit Money Banks	42e
	....	....	....	....	....	....	....	7.0	16.6	8.7	9.7	8.0	17.7	18.1	14.6	Claims on Nonbank Financial Insts	42g
	....	....	....	....	....	....	....	479.8	499.4	701.7	795.1	718.1	845.4	868.8	1,123.3	Time, Savings,& Fgn.Currency Dep.	45
	....	....	....	....	....	....	....	153.1	223.8	190.9	180.3	234.6	197.8	182.5	45.8	Money Market Instruments	46aa
	....	....	....	....	....	....	....	8.6	10.2	18.3	10.2	9.9	15.0	23.5	25.7	Foreign Liabilities	46c
	....	....	....	....	....	....	....	10.9	21.8	16.4	18.0	7.1	3.4	3.7	3.6	Central Government Deposits	46d
	....	....	....	....	....	....	....	21.0	20.0	24.0	68.5	35.6	36.3	41.0	38.0	Credit from Deposit Money Banks	46h
	....	....	....	....	....	....	....	563.2	634.2	763.1	821.2	792.2	894.7	960.2	1,099.9	Capital Accounts	47a
	....	....	....	....	....	....	....	-76.3	-85.6	-160.8	-174.9	-194.4	-234.3	-153.3	-129.5	Other Items (Net)	47r

Namibia

		1970	1971	1972	1973	1974	1975	1976	1977	1978	1979	1980	1981	1982	1983	1984
Banking Survey														*Millions of Namibia Dollars:*		
Foreign Assets (Net)	51n	...	...	...	...	...	...	...	...	...	...	...	...	...	...	...
Domestic Credit	52	...	...	...	...	...	...	...	...	...	...	...	...	...	...	...
Claims on Central Govt. (Net)	52an	...	...	...	...	...	...	...	...	...	...	...	...	...	...	...
Claims on Local Government	52b	...	...	...	...	...	...	...	...	...	...	...	...	...	...	...
Claims on Nonfin.Pub.Enterprises	52c	...	...	...	...	...	...	...	...	...	...	...	...	...	...	...
Claims on Private Sector	52d	...	...	...	...	...	...	...	...	...	...	...	...	...	...	...
Claims on Nonbank Financial Inst	52g	...	...	...	...	...	...	...	...	...	...	...	...	...	...	...
Liquid Liabilities	55l	...	...	...	...	...	...	...	...	...	...	...	...	...	...	...
Money Market Instruments	56aa	...	...	...	...	...	...	...	...	...	...	...	...	...	...	...
Bonds	56ab	...	...	...	...	...	...	...	...	...	...	...	...	...	...	...
Capital Accounts	57a	...	...	...	...	...	...	...	...	...	...	...	...	...	...	...
Other Items (Net)	57r	...	...	...	...	...	...	...	...	...	...	...	...	...	...	...
Interest Rates														*Percent Per Annum*		
BoN Overdraft Rate	60	...	...	...	...	...	...	...	...	...	...	...	...	...	...	...
Treasury Bill Rate	60c	...	...	...	...	...	...	...	...	...	...	...	...	...	...	...
Deposit Rate	60l	...	...	...	...	...	...	...	...	...	...	...	...	...	...	...
Lending Rate	60p	...	...	...	...	...	...	...	...	...	...	...	...	...	...	...
Government Bond Yield	61	...	...	...	...	...	...	...	...	...	...	...	...	...	...	...
Prices														*Index Numbers (1995=100):*		
Consumer Prices	64	...	...	...	...	...	...	...	...	...	...	17.0	19.5	22.6	25.3	27.6
International Transactions														*Millions of Namibia Dollars*		
Exports	70	...	...	...	...	...	...	...	...	...	...	...	...	...	...	...
Imports, c.i.f.	71	...	...	...	...	...	...	...	...	...	...	...	...	...	...	...
Imports, f.o.b.	71.v	...	...	...	...	...	...	...	...	...	...	...	...	...	...	...
Balance of Payments														*Millions of US Dollars:*		
Current Account, n.i.e.	78ald	...	...	...	...	...	...	...	...	...	...	...	...	...	...	...
Goods: Exports f.o.b.	78aad	...	...	...	...	...	...	...	...	...	...	...	...	...	...	...
Goods: Imports f.o.b.	78abd	...	...	...	...	...	...	...	...	...	...	...	...	...	...	...
Trade Balance	78acd	...	...	...	...	...	...	...	...	...	...	...	...	...	...	...
Services: Credit	78add	...	...	...	...	...	...	...	...	...	...	...	...	...	...	...
Services: Debit	78aed	...	...	...	...	...	...	...	...	...	...	...	...	...	...	...
Balance on Goods & Services	78afd	...	...	...	...	...	...	...	...	...	...	...	...	...	...	...
Income: Credit	78agd	...	...	...	...	...	...	...	...	...	...	...	...	...	...	...
Income: Debit	78ahd	...	...	...	...	...	...	...	...	...	...	...	...	...	...	...
Balance on Gds, Serv. & Inc.	78aid	...	...	...	...	...	...	...	...	...	...	...	...	...	...	...
Current Transfers, n.i.e.: Credit	78ajd	...	...	...	...	...	...	...	...	...	...	...	...	...	...	...
Current Transfers: Debit	78akd	...	...	...	...	...	...	...	...	...	...	...	...	...	...	...
Capital Account, n.i.e.	78bcd	...	...	...	...	...	...	...	...	...	...	...	...	...	...	...
Capital Account, n.i.e.: Credit	78bad	...	...	...	...	...	...	...	...	...	...	...	...	...	...	...
Capital Account: Debit	78bbd	...	...	...	...	...	...	...	...	...	...	...	...	...	...	...
Financial Account, n.i.e.	78bjd	...	...	...	...	...	...	...	...	...	...	...	...	...	...	...
Direct Investment Abroad	78bdd	...	...	...	...	...	...	...	...	...	...	...	...	...	...	...
Dir. Invest. in Rep. Econ., n.i.e.	78bed	...	...	...	...	...	...	...	...	...	...	...	...	...	...	...
Portfolio Investment Assets	78bfd	...	...	...	...	...	...	...	...	...	...	...	...	...	...	...
Equity Securities	78bkd	...	...	...	...	...	...	...	...	...	...	...	...	...	...	...
Debt Securities	78bld	...	...	...	...	...	...	...	...	...	...	...	...	...	...	...
Portfolio Investment Liab., n.i.e.	78bgd	...	...	...	...	...	...	...	...	...	...	...	...	...	...	...
Equity Securities	78bmd	...	...	...	...	...	...	...	...	...	...	...	...	...	...	...
Debt Securities	78bnd	...	...	...	...	...	...	...	...	...	...	...	...	...	...	...
Financial Derivatives Assets	78bwd	...	...	...	...	...	...	...	...	...	...	...	...	...	...	...
Financial Derivatives Liabilities	78bxd	...	...	...	...	...	...	...	...	...	...	...	...	...	...	...
Other Investment Assets	78bhd	...	...	...	...	...	...	...	...	...	...	...	...	...	...	...
Monetary Authorities	78bod	...	...	...	...	...	...	...	...	...	...	...	...	...	...	...
General Government	78bpd	...	...	...	...	...	...	...	...	...	...	...	...	...	...	...
Banks	78bqd	...	...	...	...	...	...	...	...	...	...	...	...	...	...	...
Other Sectors	78brd	...	...	...	...	...	...	...	...	...	...	...	...	...	...	...
Other Investment Liab., n.i.e.	78bid	...	...	...	...	...	...	...	...	...	...	...	...	...	...	...
Monetary Authorities	78bsd	...	...	...	...	...	...	...	...	...	...	...	...	...	...	...
General Government	78btd	...	...	...	...	...	...	...	...	...	...	...	...	...	...	...
Banks	78bud	...	...	...	...	...	...	...	...	...	...	...	...	...	...	...
Other Sectors	78bvd	...	...	...	...	...	...	...	...	...	...	...	...	...	...	...
Net Errors and Omissions	78cad	...	...	...	...	...	...	...	...	...	...	...	...	...	...	...
Overall Balance	78cbd	...	...	...	...	...	...	...	...	...	...	...	...	...	...	...
Reserves and Related Items	79dad	...	...	...	...	...	...	...	...	...	...	...	...	...	...	...
Reserve Assets	79dbd	...	...	...	...	...	...	...	...	...	...	...	...	...	...	...
Use of Fund Credit and Loans	79dcd	...	...	...	...	...	...	...	...	...	...	...	...	...	...	...
Exceptional Financing	79ded	...	...	...	...	...	...	...	...	...	...	...	...	...	...	...

	1985	1986	1987	1988	1989	1990	1991	1992	1993	1994	1995	1996	1997	1998	1999		
Banking Survey																	
End of Period																	
Foreign Assets (Net)	....	....	....	....	....	....	....	106.4	−120.8	−200.7	−325.5	111.2	895.2	1,355.2	2,272.0	Foreign Assets (Net)	51n
Domestic Credit	....	....	....	....	....	....	....	3,576.0	4,489.6	5,606.2	7,049.1	8,345.1	8,380.8	9,205.5	10,089.8	Domestic Credit	52
Claims on Central Govt. (Net)	....	....	....	....	....	....	....	420.6	548.0	599.1	672.7	1,210.3	230.8	260.5	664.8	Claims on Central Govt. (Net)	52an
Claims on Local Government	....	....	....	....	....	....	....	20.9	21.1	22.7	24.5	23.9	22.6	23.9	21.3	Claims on Local Government	52b
Claims on Nonfin.Pub.Enterprises	....	....	....	....	....	....	....	44.5	49.8	58.8	79.9	76.7	153.6	150.2	145.2	Claims on Nonfin.Pub.Enterprises	52c
Claims on Private Sector	....	....	....	....	....	....	....	3,082.9	3,854.2	4,917.0	6,262.4	7,016.1	7,956.1	8,752.8	9,233.8	Claims on Private Sector	52d
Claims on Nonbank Financial Inst	....	....	....	....	....	....	....	7.0	16.6	8.7	9.7	18.1	17.7	18.1	24.7	Claims on Nonbank Financial Inst	52g
Liquid Liabilities	....	....	....	....	....	....	....	2,718.9	3,445.1	4,464.9	5,461.9	6,746.4	7,278.2	8,027.9	9,597.6	Liquid Liabilities	55l
Money Market Instruments	....	....	....	....	....	....	....	153.1	223.8	190.9	180.3	234.6	197.8	182.5	45.8	Money Market Instruments	56aa
Bonds	....	....	....	....	....	....	....	2.4	3.9	4.1	4.1	8.9	7.0	5.5	—	Bonds	56ab
Capital Accounts	....	....	....	....	....	....	....	799.6	948.0	1,128.1	1,373.2	1,740.0	1,994.0	2,392.6	2,743.5	Capital Accounts	57a
Other Items (Net)	....	....	....	....	....	....	....	8.4	−252.0	−382.5	−295.9	−273.5	−201.0	−47.7	−25.1	Other Items (Net)	57r
Interest Rates																	
Percent Per Annum																	
BoN Overdraft Rate	....	....	....	....	....	....	20.50	16.50	14.50	15.50	17.50	17.75	16.00	18.75	11.50	BoN Overdraft Rate	60
Treasury Bill Rate	....	....	....	....	....	....	....	13.88	12.16	11.35	13.91	15.25	15.69	17.24	13.28	Treasury Bill Rate	60c
Deposit Rate	....	....	....	....	....	12.77	11.36	9.61	9.18	10.84	12.56	12.70	12.94	10.82		Deposit Rate	60l
Lending Rate	....	....	....	....	....	23.36	20.21	18.02	17.05	18.51	19.16	20.18	20.72	18.48		Lending Rate	60p
Government Bond Yield	....	....	....	....	....	....	15.44	13.94	14.63	16.11	15.48	14.70	15.10	14.96		Government Bond Yield	61
Prices																	
Period Averages																	
Consumer Prices	30.9	35.0	39.4	44.5	51.2	57.4	64.2	75.6	82.1	90.9	100.0	108.0	117.5	124.8	135.5	Consumer Prices	64
International Transactions																	
Millions of Namibia Dollars																	
Exports	....	....	....	2,400	2,943	2,809	3,351	3,826	4,214	4,692	....	....	....	....	....	Exports	70
Imports, c.i.f.	....	....	....	....	....	3,010	3,172	3,659	3,883	4,248	....	....	....	....	....	Imports, c.i.f.	71
Imports, f.o.b.	....	....	1,937	2,447	2,897	3,094	3,551	3,694	....	....	....	....	....	....	....	Imports, f.o.b.	71.v
																Balance of Payments	
Minus Sign Indicates Debit																	
Current Account, n.i.e.	....	....	....	....	....	27.6	105.1	49.8	110.2	85.3	175.9	115.8	90.4	161.8	....	Current Account, n.i.e.	78al d
Goods: Exports f.o.b.	....	....	....	....	....	1,088.3	1,179.2	1,311.3	1,293.1	1,320.4	1,418.4	1,403.7	1,343.3	1,278.3	....	Goods: Exports f.o.b.	78aa d
Goods: Imports f.o.b.	....	....	....	....	....	−1,230.2	−1,228.4	−1,389.1	−1,335.0	−1,406.3	−1,548.2	−1,530.9	−1,615.0	−1,450.9	....	Goods: Imports f.o.b.	78ab d
Trade Balance	....	....	....	....	....	−141.9	−49.1	−77.8	−41.8	−85.8	−129.7	−127.1	−271.7	−172.6	....	*Trade Balance*	78ac d
Services: Credit	....	....	....	....	....	131.8	144.6	169.8	228.1	259.0	315.3	337.4	380.1	327.0	....	Services: Credit	78ad d
Services: Debit	....	....	....	....	....	−354.2	−462.3	−510.5	−485.4	−468.3	−551.5	−580.9	−533.7	−456.9	....	Services: Debit	78ae d
Balance on Goods & Services	....	....	....	....	....	−364.2	−366.8	−418.4	−299.0	−295.1	−365.9	−370.7	−425.2	−302.4	....	*Balance on Goods & Services*	78af d
Income: Credit	....	....	....	....	....	183.3	243.0	201.9	212.7	213.8	374.0	319.2	252.0	226.7	....	Income: Credit	78ag d
Income: Debit	....	....	....	....	....	−145.8	−146.4	−185.4	−154.7	−159.8	−235.1	−249.0	−180.6	−165.9	....	Income: Debit	78ah d
Balance on Gds, Serv. & Inc.	....	....	....	....	....	−326.7	−270.2	−402.0	−241.1	−241.1	−227.1	−300.5	−353.8	−241.6	....	*Balance on Gds, Serv. & Inc.*	78ai d
Current Transfers, n.i.e.: Credit	....	....	....	....	....	375.0	398.1	476.6	373.2	349.2	426.9	437.3	462.2	418.2	....	Current Transfers, n.i.e.: Credit	78aj d
Current Transfers: Debit	....	....	....	....	....	−20.7	−22.8	−24.9	−21.9	−22.7	−23.9	−21.0	−18.0	−14.7	....	Current Transfers: Debit	78ak d
Capital Account, n.i.e.	....	....	....	....	....	42.2	28.9	32.0	27.0	43.2	40.1	42.1	33.5	23.8	....	Capital Account, n.i.e.	78bc d
Capital Account, n.i.e.: Credit	....	....	....	....	....	46.9	33.2	32.7	27.6	43.8	40.7	42.5	33.9	24.2	....	Capital Account, n.i.e.: Credit	78ba d
Capital Account: Debit	....	....	....	....	....	−4.6	−4.3	−.7	−.6	−.6	−.6	−.5	−.4	−.4	....	Capital Account: Debit	78bb d
Financial Account, n.i.e.	....	....	....	....	....	−202.8	−171.6	−121.2	−62.1	−102.1	−205.3	−174.0	−71.4	−145.6	....	Financial Account, n.i.e.	78bj d
Direct Investment Abroad	....	....	....	....	....	−1.4	−6.4	1.6	−8.7	6.1	3.5	21.7	−.7	2.2	....	Direct Investment Abroad	78bd d
Dir. Invest. in Rep. Econ., n.i.e.	....	....	....	....	....	29.6	120.4	118.2	55.3	98.0	153.0	128.7	91.0	96.2	....	Dir. Invest. in Rep. Econ., n.i.e.	78be d
Portfolio Investment Assets	....	....	....	....	....	−4.6	−10.8	.9	15.5	−17.0	−5.1	−8.1	−14.6	−11.1	....	Portfolio Investment Assets	78bf d
Equity Securities	....	....	....	....	....	−8.9	−12.4	−6.9	−4.9	−5.0	−3.8	−7.9	−14.6	−7.4	....	Equity Securities	78bk d
Debt Securities	....	....	....	....	....	4.4	1.6	7.8	20.4	−12.0	−1.3	−.3	—	−3.6	....	Debt Securities	78bl d
Portfolio Investment Liab., n.i.e.	....	....	....	....	....	15.5	−15.0	15.1	60.0	64.2	82.2	31.2	26.0	−4.4	....	Portfolio Investment Liab., n.i.e.	78bg d
Equity Securities	....	....	....	....	....	—	−4.1	6.0	1.1	37.5	45.7	51.2	28.8	18.1	....	Equity Securities	78bm d
Debt Securities	....	....	....	....	....	15.5	−10.9	9.0	58.9	26.7	36.5	−20.0	−2.8	−22.4	....	Debt Securities	78bn d
Financial Derivatives Assets	....	....	....	....	....	....	....	....	....	....	....	....	....	....	....	Financial Derivatives Assets	78bw d
Financial Derivatives Liabilities	....	....	....	....	....	....	....	....	....	....	....	....	....	....	....	Financial Derivatives Liabilities	78bx d
Other Investment Assets	....	....	....	....	....	−328.4	−257.6	−231.9	−180.9	−301.0	−428.0	−411.2	−289.9	−175.5	....	Other Investment Assets	78bh d
Monetary Authorities	....	....	....	....	....	....	....	....	....	....	....	....	....	....	....	Monetary Authorities	78bo d
General Government	....	....	....	....	....	−105.6	94.7	−6.0	−9.4	9.5	−1.4	−1.2	−1.1	−.9	....	General Government	78bp d
Banks	....	....	....	....	....	−7.6	−75.5	76.4	56.5	.1	14.8	−48.6	−40.6	−2.1	....	Banks	78bq d
Other Sectors	....	....	....	....	....	−215.2	−276.8	−302.3	−228.0	−310.7	−441.5	−361.4	−248.2	−172.6	....	Other Sectors	78br d
Other Investment Liab., n.i.e.	....	....	....	....	....	86.5	−2.4	−25.0	−3.3	47.6	−10.9	63.8	116.7	−53.1	....	Other Investment Liab., n.i.e.	78bi d
Monetary Authorities	....	....	....	....	....	....	....	....	....	....	....	....	....	....	....	Monetary Authorities	78bs d
General Government	....	....	....	....	....	38.4	39.8	3.5	18.5	4.9	21.8	27.7	17.4	16.9	....	General Government	78bt d
Banks	....	....	....	....	....	30.0	−61.9	−14.5	18.4	66.8	4.9	−49.0	116.5	−28.5	....	Banks	78bu d
Other Sectors	....	....	....	....	....	18.1	19.7	−14.0	−40.2	−24.1	−37.7	85.0	−17.1	−41.4	....	Other Sectors	78bv d
Net Errors and Omissions	....	....	....	....	....	169.8	25.2	32.8	16.2	48.5	13.4	39.1	15.3	15.7	....	Net Errors and Omissions	78ca d
Overall Balance	....	....	....	....	....	36.8	−12.4	−6.6	91.3	75.0	24.2	22.9	67.8	55.8	....	*Overall Balance*	78cb d
Reserves and Related Items	....	....	....	....	....	−36.8	12.4	6.6	−91.3	−75.0	−24.2	−22.9	−67.8	−55.8	....	Reserves and Related Items	79da d
Reserve Assets	....	....	....	....	....	−36.8	12.4	6.6	−91.3	−75.0	−24.2	−22.9	−67.8	−55.8	....	Reserve Assets	79db d
Use of Fund Credit and Loans	....	....	....	....	....	—	—	—	—	—	—	—	—	—	....	Use of Fund Credit and Loans	79dc d
Exceptional Financing	....	....	....	....	....	....	....	....	....	....	....	....	....	....	....	Exceptional Financing	79de d

	1970	1971	1972	1973	1974	1975	1976	1977	1978	1979	1980	1981	1982	1983	1984
International Investment Position														*Millions of US Dollars*	
Assets .... 79aa *d*	....	....	....	....	....	....	....	....	....	....	....	....	....	....	....
Direct Investment Abroad .... 79ab *d*	....	....	....	....	....	....	....	....	....	....	....	....	....	....	....
Portfolio Investment .... 79ac *d*	....	....	....	....	....	....	....	....	....	....	....	....	....	....	....
Equity Securities .... 79ad *d*	....	....	....	....	....	....	....	....	....	....	....	....	....	....	....
Debt Securities .... 79ae *d*	....	....	....	....	....	....	....	....	....	....	....	....	....	....	....
Financial Derivatives........................ 79al *d*	....	....	....	....	....	....	....	....	....	....	....	....	....	....	....
Other Investment .... 79af *d*	....	....	....	....	....	....	....	....	....	....	....	....	....	....	....
Monetary Authorities .... 79ag *d*	....	....	....	....	....	....	....	....	....	....	....	....	....	....	....
General Government...................... 79ah *d*	....	....	....	....	....	....	....	....	....	....	....	....	....	....	....
Banks .... 79ai *d*	....	....	....	....	....	....	....	....	....	....	....	....	....	....	....
Other Sectors .... 79aj *d*	....	....	....	....	....	....	....	....	....	....	....	....	....	....	....
Reserve Assets .... 79ak *d*	....	....	....	....	....	....	....	....	....	....	....	....	....	....	....
Liabilities .... 79la *d*	....	....	....	....	....	....	....	....	....	....	....	....	....	....	....
Dir. Invest. in Rep. Economy............ 79lb *d*	....	....	....	....	....	....	....	....	....	....	....	....	....	....	....
Portfolio Investment .... 79lc *d*	....	....	....	....	....	....	....	....	....	....	....	....	....	....	....
Equity Securities .... 79ld *d*	....	....	....	....	....	....	....	....	....	....	....	....	....	....	....
Debt Securities .... 79le *d*	....	....	....	....	....	....	....	....	....	....	....	....	....	....	....
Financial Derivatives .... 79ll *d*	....	....	....	....	....	....	....	....	....	....	....	....	....	....	....
Other investment .... 79lf *d*	....	....	....	....	....	....	....	....	....	....	....	....	....	....	....
Monetary Authorities.................... 79lg *d*	....	....	....	....	....	....	....	....	....	....	....	....	....	....	....
General Government...................... 79lh *d*	....	....	....	....	....	....	....	....	....	....	....	....	....	....	....
Banks .... 79li *d*	....	....	....	....	....	....	....	....	....	....	....	....	....	....	....
Other Sectors............................... 79lj *d*	....	....	....	....	....	....	....	....	....	....	....	....	....	....	....
Government Finance														*Millions of Namibia Dollars:*	
Deficit (-) or Surplus...................... 80	....	....	....	....	....	....	....	....	....	....	....	....	....	....	....
Revenue 81	....	....	....	....	....	....	....	....	....	....	....	....	....	....	....
Grants Received 81z	....	....	....	....	....	....	....	....	....	....	....	....	....	....	....
Expenditure 82	....	....	....	....	....	....	....	....	....	....	....	....	....	....	....
Lending Minus Repayments 83	....	....	....	....	....	....	....	....	....	....	....	....	....	....	....
Financing															
Domestic 84a	....	....	....	....	....	....	....	....	....	....	....	....	....	....	....
Foreign 85a	....	....	....	....	....	....	....	....	....	....	....	....	....	....	....
National Accounts														*Millions of Namibia Dollars*	
Exports of Goods & Services 90c	....	....	....	....	....	....	....	....	....	....	....	....	....	....	....
Government Consumption 91f	....	....	....	....	....	....	....	....	....	....	....	....	....	....	....
Gross Fixed Capital Formation 93e	....	....	....	....	....	....	....	....	....	....	....	....	....	....	....
Increase/Decrease(-) in Stocks 93i	....	....	....	....	....	....	....	....	....	....	....	....	....	....	....
Private Consumption 96f	....	....	....	....	....	....	....	....	....	....	....	....	....	....	....
Imports of Goods & Services 98c	....	....	....	....	....	....	....	....	....	....	....	....	....	....	....
Gross Domestic Product (GDP) 99b	....	....	....	....	....	....	....	....	....	....	....	....	....	....	....
Net Factor Inc/Pmts(-) Abroad 98.n	....	....	....	....	....	....	....	....	....	....	....	....	....	....	....
Gross National Income (GNI) 99a	....	....	....	....	....	....	....	....	....	....	....	....	....	....	....
GDP Volume 1985 Prices.................... 99b. *p*	....	....	....	....	....	....	....	....	....	....	....	....	....	....	....
GDP Volume 1990 Prices.................... 99b. *p*	....	....	....	....	....	....	....	....	....	....	....	....	....	....	....
GDP Volume (1995=100) .... 99bv *p*	....	....	....	....	....	....	....	....	....	....	....	....	....	....	....
GDP Deflator (1995=100).................. 99bi *p*	....	....	....	....	....	....	....	....	....	....	....	....	....	....	....
														Millions:	
Population................................... 99z	....	....	....	....	....	....	....	....	....	....	....	....	....	1.16	1.15

International Investment Position

Millions of US Dollars

Item	Code	1985	1986	1987	1988	1989	1990	1991	1992	1993	1994	1995	1996	1997	1998	1999
Assets	79aa d					1,772.9	2,107.3	2,348.2	2,264.7	2,579.9	2,788.0	2,692.6	2,095.9			
Direct Investment Abroad	79ab d					64.3	79.6	98.1	81.6	79.2	15.8	14.8	13.0			
Portfolio Investment	79ac d					160.9	161.2	167.3	145.1	117.4	165.1	164.8	128.8			
Equity Securities	79ad d					23.7	29.7	45.2	43.6	45.6	85.2	90.2	72.8			
Debt Securities	79ae d					137.2	131.5	122.1	101.5	71.8	79.9	74.6	56.0			
Financial Derivatives	79al d															
Other Investment	79af d					1,504.3	1,786.5	2,020.4	1,988.2	2,249.6	2,404.1	2,291.4	1,760.6			
Monetary Authorities	79ag d					—										
General Government	79ah d					—	106.5	4.4	9.5	17.7	7.3	8.5	7.7			
Banks	79ai d					129.7	128.4	208.2	106.8	46.8	38.1	29.9	67.5			
Other Sectors	79aj d					1,374.6	1,551.6	1,807.9	1,871.9	2,185.1	2,358.7	2,253.1	1,685.4			
Reserve Assets	79ak d					43.4	80.0	62.4	49.8	133.7	202.9	221.6	193.5			
Liabilities	79la d					2,667.6	2,845.7	2,824.2	2,811.0	2,201.0	2,420.2	2,685.1	2,355.2			
Dir. Invest. in Rep. Economy	79lb d					1,957.8	2,046.8	2,114.8	2,141.8	1,490.8	1,601.2	1,707.7	1,492.2			
Portfolio Investment	79lc d					213.3	220.5	182.6	183.8	221.3	289.8	390.4	334.9			
Equity Securities	79ld d					33.1	26.5	12.4	22.6	19.1	69.1	119.0	141.8			
Debt Securities	79le d					180.2	194.0	170.2	161.2	202.2	220.7	271.4	193.1			
Financial Derivatives	79ll d															
Other investment	79lf d					496.4	578.3	526.8	485.4	488.9	529.1	587.0	528.1			
Monetary Authorities	79lg d							—	164.4	181.9	203.2	214.9	183.0			
General Government	79lh d					85.2	124.9	159.7	8.5	25.3	29.9	51.5	46.8			
Banks	79li d					137.6	166.2	89.3	70.8	82.7	143.9	134.1	136.0			
Other Sectors	79lj d					273.7	287.2	277.8	241.7	199.0	152.1	186.4	162.3			

Government Finance

Year Beginning April 1

Item	Code	1985	1986	1987	1988	1989	1990	1991	1992	1993	1994	1995	1996	1997	1998	1999
Deficit (-) or Surplus	80		200.8	-141.9	2.1	324.7	I-71.7	-189.0	-435.0 [p]	-402.7 [f]						
Revenue	81		1,107.8	1,219.8	1,478.0	2,011.8	I1,905.9	2,534.6	2,833.7 [p]	2,958.5 [f]						
Grants Received	81z		499.6	308.0	317.2	280.9	I101.1	67.8	73.5 [p]	70.0 [f]						
Expenditure	82		1,408.4	1,666.4	1,800.2	1,970.8	I2,027.4	2,778.9	3,311.9 [p]	3,407.5 [f]						
Lending Minus Repayments	83		-1.8	3.3	-7.1	-2.8	I51.3	12.5	30.3 [p]	23.7 [f]						
Financing Domestic	84a		-162.2	131.8	43.9	-248.1	I-38.8	-.9	297.8 [p]	391.9 [f]						
Foreign	85a		-38.6	10.1	-46.0	-76.6	I110.5	189.9	137.2 [p]	10.8 [f]						

National Accounts

Millions of Namibia Dollars

Item	Code	1985	1986	1987	1988	1989	1990	1991	1992	1993	1994	1995	1996	1997	1998	1999
Exports of Goods & Services	90c	1,882	2,368	2,194	2,636	3,244	I3,188	3,787	4,317	4,972	5,724	6,244	7,348	7,954		
Government Consumption	91f	795	959	1,164	1,330	1,442	I1,862	2,305	2,868	3,009	3,307	3,758	4,292	4,728		
Gross Fixed Capital Formation	93e	380	426	504	659	829	I1,290	1,107	1,689	1,923	2,298	2,619	3,222	3,126		
Increase/Decrease(-) in Stocks	93i	5	-7	15	198	5	I441	183	80	-486	-115	227	-137	-141		
Private Consumption	96f	1,328	1,632	2,203	2,357	3,009	I3,351	4,157	4,476	5,059	5,762	6,790	7,565	8,240		
Imports of Goods & Services	98c	-1,537	-2,038	-2,566	-2,702	-3,286	I-3,808	-4,419	-5,071	-5,556	-6,398	-7,197	-8,578	-8,793		
Gross Domestic Product (GDP)	99b	2,854	3,340	3,515	4,478	5,242	I6,323	7,119	8,358	8,921	10,919	12,099	13,712	15,115		
Net Factor Inc/Pmts(-) Abroad	98.n	-629	-562	-218	-595	-342	I85	258	42	210	231	474	317	247		
Gross National Income (GNI)	99a	2,226	2,778	3,297	3,884	4,900	I6,408	7,377	8,400	9,131	11,150	12,573	14,029	15,362		
GDP Volume 1985 Prices	99b.p	2,854	2,959	3,026	3,294											
GDP Volume 1990 Prices	99b.p				5,814	5,938	I6,409	6,775	7,274	7,128	7,600	7,988	8,226			
GDP Volume (1995=100)	99bv p	63.1	65.4	66.9	72.8	74.3	I80.2	84.8	91.1	89.2	95.1	100.0	103.0			
GDP Deflator (1995=100)	99bi p	36.9	41.7	42.9	50.2	57.5	I65.1	69.4	75.9	82.6	94.9	100.0	110.1			

Midyear Estimates

Item	Code	1985	1986	1987	1988	1989	1990	1991	1992	1993	1994	1995	1996	1997	1998	1999
Population	99z	1.18	1.21	1.24	1.28	1.32	1.35	1.39	1.42	1.46	1.50	1.54	1.58	1.61	1.66	1.70

(See notes in the back of the book.)

Nepal

		1970	1971	1972	1973	1974	1975	1976	1977	1978	1979	1980	1981	1982	1983	1984
Exchange Rates																*Rupees per SDR:*
Market Rate	aa	10.125	10.993	10.993	12.739	12.929	14.633	14.523	15.184	15.633	15.808	15.305	15.364	15.774	15.914	17.644
																Rupees per US Dollar:
Market Rate	ae	10.125	10.125	10.125	10.560	10.560	12.500	12.500	12.500	12.000	12.000	12.000	13.200	14.300	15.200	18.000
Market Rate	rf	10.125	10.125	10.125	10.472	10.560	11.003	12.500	12.500	12.111	12.000	12.000	12.336	13.244	14.545	16.459
Fund Position																*Millions of SDRs:*
Quota	2f. s	10.0	10.8	11.6	12.4	12.4	12.4	12.4	12.4	19.0	19.0	28.5	28.5	28.5	37.3	37.3
SDRs	1b. s	—	1.1	2.2	2.2	2.2	2.2	2.1	1.9	1.2	1.7	.1	—	.8	.2	.1
Reserve Position in the Fund	1c. s	2.5	2.7	2.9	3.1	3.1	3.1	—	—	2.4	2.3	5.2	5.7	5.7	5.7	5.7
Total Fund Cred.&Loans Outstg.	2tl	—	—	—	—	—	—	4.5	6.0	15.3	18.6	32.6	32.5	27.7	22.4	15.8
International Liquidity														*Millions of US Dollars Unless Otherwise Indicated:*		
Total Reserves minus Gold	1l. d	88.7	96.1	98.4	117.5	121.3	95.7	ⅼ127.5	139.5	145.1	159.2	182.8	201.9	199.2	133.3	82.0
SDRs	1b. d	—	1.2	2.4	2.7	2.7	2.6	2.5	2.3	1.6	2.3	.1	—	.9	.2	.1
Reserve Position in the Fund	1c. d	2.5	2.9	3.2	3.8	3.8	3.6	—	—	3.1	3.1	6.6	6.6	6.3	6.0	5.6
Foreign Exchange	1d. d	86.2	92.0	92.8	111.1	114.8	89.5	ⅼ125.1	137.2	140.4	153.8	176.0	195.3	192.1	127.2	76.3
Gold (Million Fine Troy Ounces)	1ad	.147	.142	.136	.130	.130	.130	.130	.133	.146	.149	.151	.151	.151	.151	.151
Gold (National Valuation)	1and	5.2	5.0	5.2	5.5	5.5	5.5	5.5	5.6	6.2	6.3	6.4	6.4	6.4	6.4	6.4
Monetary Authorities: Other Assets	3..d	....	....	....	....	....	....	1.8	2.7	2.3	4.9	6.4	3.2	2.3	1.4	.4
Monetary Authorities: Other Liab.	4..d	7.5	4.4	4.7	6.1	14.4	12.6	4.0	6.0	5.6	10.4	11.5	15.8	15.1	3.1	3.7
Deposit Money Banks: Assets	7a. d	9.1	8.9	17.6	17.2	18.8	26.6	34.1	45.3	52.2	55.5	59.3	71.8	57.9	81.5	71.8
Liabilities	7b. d	1.6	1.4	1.7	1.7	6.3	5.1	16.3	22.5	16.4	11.8	6.3	8.7	7.4	12.6	16.1
Monetary Authorities																*Millions of Rupees:*
Foreign Assets	11	940	1,000	1,014	1,250	1,269	1,240	1,678	1,839	1,827	2,027	2,364	2,773	2,743	2,113	2,224
Claims on Central Government	12a	110	143	173	389	529	724	892	1,105	1,454	1,708	1,896	2,611	3,312	4,626	5,696
Claims on Private Sector	12d	11	11	8	19	21	21	17	18	20	34	41	53	55	64	113
Claims on Deposit Money Banks	12e	4	1	3	3	61	164	3	2	134	87	131	264	113	10	226
Claims on Other Financial Insts	12f	13	27	37	49	56	134	123	211	314	353	373	398	428	501	557
Reserve Money	14	ⅼ645	697	792	1,020	1,063	1,162	1,497	1,627	1,913	2,156	2,379	2,722	3,394	3,927	4,555
of which: Currency Outside DMBs	14a	526	549	596	747	882	882	996	1,212	1,379	1,627	1,814	2,147	2,408	2,783	3,302
Private Sector Deposits	14d	ⅼ42	69	44	77	82	98	127	142	164	184	229	154	270	306	351
Foreign Liabilities	16c	76	45	47	64	153	157	115	166	306	418	637	707	653	403	345
Central Government Deposits	16d	181	230	194	409	479	514	571	744	735	858	926	1,471	1,491	1,663	1,898
Capital Accounts	17a	82	107	189	230	250	405	411	497	572	681	738	890	919	1,154	2,308
Other Items (Net)	17r	10	54	35	10	14	72	156	179	223	100	140	278	195	166	−290
Deposit Money Banks																*Millions of Rupees:*
Reserves	20	75	131	135	207	120	163	353	348	325	406	369	518	611	614	650
Foreign Assets	21	93	90	179	181	199	332	426	567	626	666	712	948	827	1,239	1,293
Claims on Central Government	22a	17	36	70	100	100	101	320	640	418	347	387	355	796	1,422	1,654
Claims on Nonfin.Pub.Enterprises	22c	21	10	23	41	222	380	307	270	604	715	780	946	874	1,075	940
Claims on Private Sector	22d	240	332	356	459	605	710	614	810	1,106	1,393	1,961	2,456	2,620	2,670	3,230
Claims on Other Financial Insts	22f	....	....	....	....	....	....	....	....	....	....	....	....	86	130	157
Demand Deposits	24	131	167	202	267	326	353	513	579	657	723	821	904	1,027	1,278	1,289
Time and Savings Deposits	25	232	324	451	573	658	847	1,175	1,468	1,870	2,178	2,661	3,375	4,283	5,228	5,899
Foreign Liabilities	26c	16	14	17	18	66	63	204	281	197	142	76	115	106	191	290
Credit from Monetary Authorities	26g	4	1	3	3	61	164	3	2	134	87	131	264	113	10	226
Other Items (Net)	27r	63	94	88	127	134	258	126	304	221	397	520	564	286	442	220
Monetary Survey																*Millions of Rupees:*
Foreign Assets (Net)	31n	ⅼ941	1,032	1,128	1,349	1,249	1,352	1,785	1,958	1,949	2,132	2,362	2,898	2,812	2,758	2,883
Domestic Credit	32	123	227	460	620	1,036	1,514	1,648	2,183	3,024	3,692	4,513	5,348	6,685	8,828	10,453
Claims on Central Govt. (Net)	32an	−79	−93	36	52	133	269	587	875	981	1,198	1,357	1,495	2,617	4,385	5,452
Claims on Nonfin.Pub.Enterprises	32c	21	10	23	41	222	380	307	270	604	715	780	946	879	1,080	945
Claims on Private Sector	32d	252	343	365	478	626	731	631	827	1,126	1,426	2,002	2,510	2,675	2,733	3,343
Claims on Other Financial Insts	32f	....	....	....	....	....	....	....	....	....	....	....	....	514	629	713
Money	34	ⅼ699	784	842	1,090	1,290	1,334	1,636	1,933	2,200	2,534	2,864	3,205	3,705	4,366	4,942
Quasi-Money	35	232	324	451	573	658	847	1,175	1,468	1,870	2,178	2,661	3,375	4,283	5,228	5,899
Other Items (Net)	37r	132	161	316	328	360	712	659	779	904	1,117	1,364	1,636	1,510	1,992	2,495
Money plus Quasi-Money	35l	ⅼ931	1,108	1,293	1,663	1,948	2,180	2,811	3,401	4,070	4,712	5,526	6,580	7,987	9,594	10,841
Interest Rates																*Percent Per Annum:*
Discount Rate	60	....	....	....	....	....	....	12.00	12.00	12.00	12.00	12.00	12.00	15.00	15.00	15.00
Treasury Bill Rate	60c	....	....	....	....	....	....							5.00	5.00	5.00
Deposit Rate	60l	....	....	....	....	....	13.63	14.58	12.17	12.00	12.00	12.00	12.00	12.29	12.50	12.50
Lending Rate	60p	....	....	....	....	....	12.00	13.00	14.00	14.00	14.00	14.00	14.00	15.50	17.00	17.00
Government Bond Yield	61	....	....	....	....	....	....	....	....	....	....	....	10.50	10.50	10.50	10.50
Prices															*Index Numbers (1995=100):*	
Consumer Prices	64	10.8	10.6	11.5	12.8	ⅼ15.4	16.5	16.0	17.6	18.9	19.6	22.5	25.0	27.9	31.3	32.2
International Transactions																*Millions of Rupees*
Exports	70	430	483	587	659	698	1,097	1,229	1,007	1,100	1,306	964	1,731	1,161	1,361	2,109
Imports, c.i.f.	71	764	856	862	1,086	1,419	1,885	2,035	2,104	2,677	3,053	4,107	4,549	5,237	6,746	6,847

1985	1986	1987	1988	1989	1990	1991	1992	1993	1994	1995	1996	1997	1998	1999		
															Exchange Rates	
End of Period																
22.737	26.910	30.643	33.912	37.585	43.249	61.079	59.400	67.634	72.817	83.243	82.007	85.408	95.288	94.326	Market Rate	aa
End of Period (ae) Period Average (rf)																
20.700	22.000	21.600	25.200	28.600	30.400	42.700	43.200	49.240	49.880	56.000	57.030	63.300	67.675	68.725	Market Rate	ae
18.246	21.230	21.819	23.289	27.189	29.369	37.255	42.718	48.607	49.398	51.890	56.692	58.010	65.976	68.239		rf
															Fund Position	
End of Period																
37.3	37.3	37.3	37.3	37.3	37.3	37.3	52.0	52.0	52.0	52.0	52.0	52.0	52.0	71.3	Quota	2f. s
—	.1	.1	.1	.1	.1	.1	.1	—	.1	—	—	.1	—	.2	SDRs	1b. s
5.7	5.7	5.7	5.7	5.7	5.7	5.7	5.7	5.7	5.7	5.7	5.7	5.7	5.7	5.7	Reserve Position in the Fund	1c. s
19.8	19.2	30.3	39.2	39.9	30.9	26.9	31.7	35.8	37.7	32.5	27.2	22.0	17.2	12.9	Total Fund Cred.&Loans Outstg.	2tl
															International Liquidity	
Data as of Middle of December																
56.0	86.7	178.2	220.3	211.6	295.3	397.0	467.4	640.2	693.6	586.4	571.4	626.2	756.3	843.1	Total Reserves minus Gold	1l. d
—	.1	.1	.1	.2	.2	.1	.2	—	.1	—	—	.1	—	.3	SDRs	1b. d
6.3	7.0	8.1	7.7	7.5	8.1	8.2	7.9	7.9	8.4	8.5	8.2	7.7	8.1	7.9	Reserve Position in the Fund	1c. d
49.7	79.7	170.0	212.5	203.9	287.0	388.7	459.4	632.3	685.1	577.9	563.1	618.4	748.2	834.9	Foreign Exchange	1d. d
.151	.151	.151	.152	.153	.153	.153	.153	.153	.153	.153	.153	.153	.153	.153	Gold (Million Fine Troy Ounces)	1ad
6.4	6.4	6.4	6.4	6.4	6.5	6.5	6.5	6.5	6.5	6.5	6.6	6.6	48.3	48.1	Gold (National Valuation)	1and
—	—	....	....	....	....	....	....	....	....	....	....	....	....	....	Monetary Authorities: Other Assets	3.. d
10.8	8.7	31.4	18.0	38.3	39.7	32.2	51.6	55.3	62.1	54.0	45.0	32.9	27.8	19.5	Monetary Authorities: Other Liab.	4.. d
83.5	65.3	90.1	96.8	97.1	128.9	123.1	151.0	129.9	161.6	208.9	218.1	246.1	299.0	345.3	Deposit Money Banks: Assets	7a. d
24.4	24.8	26.0	29.4	30.7	32.8	35.8	57.8	68.6	66.1	67.4	87.7	111.3	149.7	174.9	Liabilities	7b. d
															Monetary Authorities	
Data as of Middle of December																
1,299	1,839	3,830	5,816	7,492	10,329	17,894	21,320	32,721	35,627	33,960	33,883	39,767	52,331	59,155	Foreign Assets	11
7,040	8,468	8,835	9,956	12,871	14,097	15,276	17,907	19,032	19,439	24,001	24,714	27,151	29,805	30,539	Claims on Central Government	12a
254	185	194	167	205	349	494	501	544	503	547	895	1,145	1,356	1,460	Claims on Private Sector	12d
364	497	341	155	—	42	34	49	39	21	12	646	6	6	6	Claims on Deposit Money Banks	12e
706	749	876	916	818	761	837	690	499	484	844	1,122	1,477	1,631	1,613	Claims on Other Financial Insts	12f
5,152	6,549	7,745	8,917	10,917	13,372	17,138	19,817	25,783	28,792	31,266	34,368	39,477	50,203	55,371	Reserve Money	14
3,797	4,787	5,827	6,671	7,905	9,818	12,465	14,201	17,390	21,005	23,230	25,428	27,905	32,244	36,929	*of which:* Currency Outside DMBs	14a
332	391	547	580	572	540	864	897	1,307	1,097	1,396	1,358	1,601	2,287	4,346	Private Sector Deposits	14d
675	708	1,607	1,782	2,593	2,543	3,018	3,780	4,389	4,617	4,327	3,422	2,525	2,024	1,338	Foreign Liabilities	16c
2,250	2,685	3,302	3,863	4,777	4,661	7,073	7,845	7,870	7,782	7,459	7,447	9,255	10,474	11,473	Central Government Deposits	16d
2,489	2,925	3,207	3,998	4,383	5,774	8,344	8,259	10,633	12,076	15,982	16,127	18,580	21,545	21,728	Capital Accounts	17a
-904	-1,129	-1,786	-1,549	-1,285	-773	-1,036	766	4,160	2,806	329	-104	-292	884	2,864	Other Items (Net)	17r
															Deposit Money Banks	
Data as of Middle of December																
914	1,047	1,364	1,364	2,451	2,943	2,999	3,943	5,837	7,321	8,488	7,583	9,972	15,673	14,096	Reserves	20
1,728	1,437	1,946	2,440	2,778	3,918	5,256	6,525	6,397	8,060	11,698	12,438	15,577	20,238	23,729	Foreign Assets	21
2,073	2,001	3,024	3,819	4,046	4,395	8,238	9,677	10,734	8,776	6,497	7,610	8,621	8,957	13,330	Claims on Central Government	22a
1,296	1,662	1,859	1,921	1,644	2,005	1,310	1,144	1,954	1,621	1,721	1,713	1,459	993	1,438	Claims on Nonfin.Pub.Enterprises	22c
4,336	5,712	6,481	8,897	11,443	12,897	16,038	19,991	25,059	36,462	49,494	56,848	65,541	84,875	97,306	Claims on Private Sector	22d
155	116	105	29	28	28	29	29	29	29	211	4,023	4,668	530	5,915	Claims on Other Financial Insts	22f
1,487	1,773	2,309	2,575	3,243	3,847	4,286	5,331	6,622	8,422	8,927	8,758	9,090	10,979	13,832	Demand Deposits	24
7,398	8,592	10,343	13,394	16,386	19,098	23,240	28,888	36,218	42,172	50,490	58,744	70,555	89,850	109,521	Time and Savings Deposits	25
505	546	561	742	878	997	1,529	2,498	3,380	3,297	3,776	5,003	7,048	10,134	12,020	Foreign Liabilities	26c
364	497	341	155	—	42	34	49	39	21	12	646	6	6	6	Credit from Monetary Authorities	26g
746	567	1,228	1,604	1,883	2,202	4,781	4,543	3,749	8,356	14,906	17,063	19,138	20,297	20,435	Other Items (Net)	27r
															Monetary Survey	
Data as of Middle of December																
1,847	2,023	3,609	5,733	6,799	10,707	18,603	21,566	31,349	35,772	37,555	37,896	45,770	60,411	69,527	Foreign Assets (Net)	31n
13,613	16,212	18,077	21,849	26,286	29,879	35,157	42,101	49,986	59,539	75,863	89,486	100,814	117,680	140,135	Domestic Credit	32
6,863	7,785	8,557	9,912	12,139	13,831	16,442	19,739	21,895	20,433	23,039	24,877	26,517	28,287	32,396	Claims on Central Govt. (Net)	32an
1,301	1,667	1,864	1,928	1,652	2,012	1,317	1,152	1,961	1,628	1,729	1,720	1,466	1,000	1,446	Claims on Nonfin.Pub.Enterprises	32c
4,590	5,897	6,675	9,064	11,648	13,246	16,532	20,492	25,602	36,965	50,041	57,742	66,685	86,231	98,766	Claims on Private Sector	32d
860	864	981	945	846	789	866	719	527	513	1,054	5,145	6,145	2,161	7,528	Claims on Other Financial Insts	32f
5,616	6,951	8,682	9,826	11,720	14,205	17,614	20,428	25,320	30,524	33,553	35,544	38,596	45,509	55,107	Money	34
7,398	8,592	10,343	13,394	16,386	19,098	23,240	28,888	36,218	42,172	50,490	58,744	70,555	89,850	109,521	Quasi-Money	35
2,446	2,691	2,662	4,362	4,978	7,282	12,907	14,351	19,797	22,615	29,376	33,093	37,433	42,732	45,034	Other Items (Net)	37r
13,014	15,543	19,024	23,219	28,106	33,304	40,855	49,316	61,538	72,696	84,043	94,288	109,151	135,359	164,628	Money plus Quasi-Money	35l
															Interest Rates	
Data as of Middle of December																
15.00	11.00	11.00	11.00	11.00	11.00	13.00	13.00	11.00	11.00	11.00	11.00	9.00	9.00	9.00	Discount Rate	60
5.00	5.00	5.00	5.00	5.62	7.93	8.80	9.00	4.50	6.50	9.90	11.51	2.52	3.70	4.30	Treasury Bill Rate	60c
12.50	12.50	12.50	12.50	12.50	11.92	....	....	....	8.75	....	9.63	9.79	8.92	7.31	Deposit Rate	60l
17.00	15.67	15.00	15.00	15.00	14.42	....	....	....	....	....	12.88	14.54	14.00	11.33	Lending Rate	60p
I 13.00	13.00	13.00	13.17	13.54	....	13.33	....	9.00	....	....	9.00	9.00	9.00	8.75	Government Bond Yield	61
															Prices	
Period Averages																
34.8	41.4	45.9	I 50.0	54.4	58.9	68.1	79.8	85.8	92.9	100.0	109.2	113.6	125.0	135.1	Consumer Prices	64
															International Transactions	
Millions of Rupees																
2,915	3,005	3,290	4,433	4,312	5,996	9,615	15,706	18,676	17,896	17,895	21,830	23,555	31,288	41,088	Exports	70
8,267	9,751	12,444	15,821	15,780	19,729	27,217	33,157	43,267	57,072	69,028	79,247	97,974	81,901	97,057	Imports, c.i.f.	71

	1970	1971	1972	1973	1974	1975	1976	1977	1978	1979	1980	1981	1982	1983	1984
Balance of Payments														*Millions of US Dollars:*	
Current Account, n.i.e. .... 78al *d*	....	....	....	....	....	....	18.5	−1.6	−25.7	−11.4	−38.9	−19.1	−85.4	−145.6	−95.2
Goods: Exports f.o.b. .... 78aa *d*	....	....	....	....	....	....	102.1	81.2	89.4	110.3	102.1	144.2	87.6	101.5	130.1
Goods: Imports f.o.b. .... 78ab *d*	....	....	....	....	....	....	−154.1	−165.7	−220.5	−251.4	−328.0	−362.4	−406.3	−468.3	−402.9
Trade Balance .... 78ac *d*	....	....	....	....	....	....	−52.0	−84.5	−131.1	−141.1	−225.9	−218.2	−318.7	−366.8	−272.8
Services: Credit .... 78ad *d*	....	....	....	....	....	....	61.4	72.2	99.1	111.5	155.0	155.5	160.2	171.0	159.2
Services: Debit .... 78ae *d*	....	....	....	....	....	....	−42.8	−46.0	−57.1	−74.3	−87.7	−94.0	−85.1	−88.0	−99.5
Balance on Goods & Services .... 78af *d*	....	....	....	....	....	....	−33.5	−58.3	−89.1	−103.8	−158.6	−156.6	−243.7	−283.8	−213.2
Income: Credit .... 78ag *d*	....	....	....	....	....	....	6.7	8.9	6.8	14.2	14.5	14.2	18.0	8.1	5.2
Income: Debit .... 78ah *d*	....	....	....	....	....	....	−1.6	−.8	−1.2	−2.9	−2.9	−3.2	−2.3	−2.4	−4.9
Balance on Gds, Serv. & Inc. .... 78ai *d*	....	....	....	....	....	....	−28.4	−50.3	−83.6	−92.6	−147.0	−145.7	−228.0	−278.1	−212.9
Current Transfers, n.i.e.: Credit .... 78aj *d*	....	....	....	....	....	....	48.3	50.4	59.0	82.4	109.5	127.6	144.9	135.3	119.7
Current Transfers: Debit .... 78ak *d*	....	....	....	....	....	....	−1.4	−1.7	−1.2	−1.2	−1.4	−1.0	−2.4	−2.8	−2.0
Capital Account, n.i.e. .... 78bc *d*	....	....	....	....	....	....	—	—	—	—	—	—	—	—	—
Capital Account, n.i.e.: Credit .... 78ba *d*	....	....	....	....	....	....	—	—	—	—	—	—	—	—	—
Capital Account: Debit .... 78bb *d*	....	....	....	....	....	....	—	—	—	—	—	—	—	—	—
Financial Account, n.i.e. .... 78bj *d*	....	....	....	....	....	....	14.2	22.7	−9.0	34.1	22.2	60.9	62.7	107.8	61.5
Direct Investment Abroad .... 78bd *d*	....	....	....	....	....	....	—	—	—	—	—	—	—	—	—
Dir. Invest. in Rep. Econ., n.i.e. .... 78be *d*	....	....	....	....	....	....	—	—	—	—	—	—	—	—	—
Portfolio Investment Assets .... 78bf *d*	....	....	....	....	....	....									
Equity Securities .... 78bk *d*	....	....	....	....	....	....									
Debt Securities .... 78bl *d*	....	....	....	....	....	....									
Portfolio Investment Liab., n.i.e. .... 78bg *d*	....	....	....	....	....	....									
Equity Securities .... 78bm *d*	....	....	....	....	....	....									
Debt Securities .... 78bn *d*	....	....	....	....	....	....									
Financial Derivatives Assets .... 78bw *d*	....	....	....	....	....	....	....	....	....	....	....	....	....	....	....
Financial Derivatives Liabilities .... 78bx *d*	....	....	....	....	....	....	....	....	....	....	....	....	....	....	....
Other Investment Assets .... 78bh *d*	....	....	....	....	....	....	1.5	−15.3	−20.4	3.3	−18.7	−8.1	10.1	42.3	−11.8
Monetary Authorities .... 78bo *d*	....	....	....	....	....	....									
General Government .... 78bp *d*	....	....	....	....	....	....									
Banks .... 78bq *d*	....	....	....	....	....	....	—	—	—	—	—	—	—	—	—
Other Sectors .... 78br *d*	....	....	....	....	....	....	1.5	−15.3	−20.4	3.3	−18.7	−8.1	10.1	42.3	−11.8
Other Investment Liab., n.i.e. .... 78bi *d*	....	....	....	....	....	....	12.6	38.0	11.4	30.8	40.8	69.0	52.6	65.5	73.3
Monetary Authorities .... 78bs *d*	....	....	....	....	....	....	−5.9	4.4	1.6	6.4	3.3	3.6	−8.4	−3.4	.1
General Government .... 78bt *d*	....	....	....	....	....	....	6.0	24.3	15.6	29.6	40.5	58.9	56.7	61.5	68.9
Banks .... 78bu *d*	....	....	....	....	....	....	11.4	7.2	−7.1	−5.6	−3.6	3.9	.4	6.6	—
Other Sectors .... 78bv *d*	....	....	....	....	....	....	1.2	2.2	1.3	.4	.6	2.7	3.9	.8	4.3
Net Errors and Omissions .... 78ca *d*	....	....	....	....	....	....	−4.1	−.7	10.5	4.8	3.5	9.2	24.4	30.1	12.8
Overall Balance .... 78cb *d*	....	....	....	....	....	....	28.6	20.4	−24.2	27.5	−13.1	51.0	1.6	−7.6	−20.9
Reserves and Related Items .... 79da *d*	....	....	....	....	....	....	−28.6	−20.4	24.2	−27.5	13.1	−51.0	−1.6	7.6	20.9
Reserve Assets .... 79db *d*	....	....	....	....	....	....	−33.7	−22.1	12.5	−31.7	−5.3	−50.9	3.0	13.3	27.6
Use of Fund Credit and Loans .... 79dc *d*	....	....	....	....	....	....	5.2	1.7	11.7	4.2	18.5	−.2	−5.3	−5.6	−6.8
Exceptional Financing .... 79de *d*	....	....	....	....	....	....	—	—	—	—	—	—	.8	—	—
Government Finance														*Millions of Rupees:*	
Deficit (-) or Surplus 80	24	−39	I−126	−223	−248	−236	−422	−576	−582	I−588	−705	−728	−1,591	−2,954	−2,985
Revenue 81	464	460	I 541	602	752	995	1,088	1,291	1,522	I 1,758	1,829	2,375	2,639	2,778	3,310
Grants Received 81z	244	271	I 242	180	223	283	360	393	467	I 564	791	859	988	1,089	877
Expenditure 82	684	770	I 880	966	1,191	1,488	1,884	2,269	2,586	I 2,928	3,340	3,967	5,221	6,852	7,238
Lending Minus Repayments 83			I 29	39	31	25	−14	−10	−15	I−17	−15	−5	−4	−31	−67
Financing															
Net Borrowing: Domestic 84a	14	32	I 87	127	162	112	212	417	230	I 241	252	161	1,180	2,006	1,370
Foreign 85a	8	33	I 39	47	86	95	137	153	364	I 352	432	472	339	948	1,615
Use of Cash Balances 87	−45	−25	I —	48	−1	29	73	6	−12	I−5	21	95	72	—	—
Debt: Domestic 88a	....	190	272	359	476	605	743	1,014	1,225	I 1,395	1,503	1,444	1,900	2,878	4,337
Foreign 89a	....	....	....	....	310	378	513	665	1,029	....	....	....	....		
National Accounts														*Millions of Rupees:*	
Exports of Goods & Services 90c	....	....	....	....	....	1,475	1,874	2,037	2,086	2,618	2,695	3,523	3,592	3,455	4,196
Government Consumption 91f	....	....	....	....	....	1,257	1,294	1,260	1,471	1,565	1,889	1,922	2,638	3,416	3,644
Gross Fixed Capital Formation 93e	....	....	....	....	....	2,223	2,443	2,580	3,294	3,263	3,681	4,299	5,465	6,576	6,907
Increase/Decrease(-) in Stocks 93i	....	....	....	....	....	179	189	188	213	251	589	509	−151	52	444
Private Consumption 96f	....	....	....	....	....	13,652	14,060	13,689	15,721	17,741	19,195	22,411	25,272	27,458	31,860
Imports of Goods & Services 98c	....	....	....	....	....	−2,215	−2,466	−2,474	−3,053	−3,547	−4,374	−5,357	−5,828	−7,196	−7,661
Gross Domestic Product (GDP) 99b	8,768	8,938	10,369	9,969	12,808	I 16,571	17,394	17,280	19,732	22,215	23,351	27,307	30,988	33,761	39,390
GDP Volume 1965 prices 99b.*p*	6,367	6,291	6,487	6,456	6,865	6,965	....	....	....	....	....	....	....	....	....
GDP Volume 1975 prices 99b.*p*	....	....	....	....	....	16,571	17,300	17,822	18,607	19,048	18,606	20,158	20,920	20,297	22,262
GDP Volume 1985 Prices 99b.*p*	....	....	....	....	....	....	....	....	....	....	....	....	....	....	....
GDP Volume (1995=100) .... 99bv *p*	41.7	41.2	42.4	42.2	44.9	45.6	47.6	49.0	51.2	52.4	51.2	55.4	57.5	55.8	61.2
GDP Deflator (1995=100) .... 99bi *p*	9.6	9.9	11.1	10.8	13.0	I 16.6	16.7	16.1	17.6	19.3	20.8	22.5	24.6	27.6	29.4
														Millions:	
Population 99z	I 11.42	11.56	11.81	12.06	12.32	12.59	12.86	13.14	13.42	13.71	14.01	15.02	15.42	15.83	16.25

1985	1986	1987	1988	1989	1990	1991	1992	1993	1994	1995	1996	1997	1998	1999		
Minus Sign Indicates Debit															**Balance of Payments**	
−121.6	−119.2	−123.3	−271.5	−243.3	−289.2	−304.4	−181.3	−222.5	−351.9	−356.4	−326.6	−388.1	−67.2	10.6	Current Account, n.i.e.	78al *d*
161.3	142.6	162.2	193.8	161.2	217.9	274.5	376.3	397.0	368.7	349.9	388.7	413.8	482.0	708.8	Goods: Exports f.o.b.	78aa *d*
−444.0	−436.5	−512.4	−664.9	−568.1	−666.6	−756.9	−752.1	−858.6	−1,158.9	−1,310.8	−1,494.7	−1,691.9	−1,239.1	−1,589.5	Goods: Imports f.o.b.	78ab *d*
−282.8	−293.9	−350.2	−471.1	−407.0	−448.7	−482.4	−375.8	−461.6	−790.3	−961.0	−1,105.9	−1,278.1	−757.1	−880.7	Trade Balance	78ac *d*
157.4	176.6	217.7	223.8	203.1	204.4	239.8	273.8	333.2	579.2	679.0	757.5	865.7	565.1	499.5	Services: Credit	78ad *d*
−115.7	−113.7	−131.2	−150.8	−147.7	−167.3	−183.9	−225.0	−251.8	−296.6	−313.3	−242.8	−224.5	−196.2	−212.5	Services: Debit	78ae *d*
−241.1	−231.0	−263.7	−398.1	−351.6	−411.7	−426.4	−327.0	−380.2	−507.6	−595.2	−591.3	−637.0	−388.1	−593.7	*Balance on Goods & Services*	78af *d*
4.7	4.4	6.8	16.2	21.2	25.1	27.0	33.5	28.9	34.6	43.6	33.1	31.9	45.4	55.8	Income: Credit	78ag *d*
−3.9	−3.7	−6.7	−14.4	−10.5	−11.2	−16.2	−16.8	−23.7	−30.8	−34.9	−32.0	−28.6	−26.5	−28.4	Income: Debit	78ah *d*
−240.3	−230.3	−263.6	−396.3	−340.9	−397.8	−415.6	−310.3	−375.0	−503.9	−586.5	−590.2	−633.7	−369.2	−566.3	*Balance on Gds, Serv. & Inc.*	78ai *d*
122.2	115.7	143.6	130.5	109.2	115.7	121.3	133.6	155.5	160.7	239.2	281.6	267.4	326.0	603.8	Current Transfers, n.i.e.: Credit	78aj *d*
−3.4	−4.6	−3.3	−5.6	−11.6	−7.1	−10.1	−4.6	−3.0	−8.7	−9.1	−18.0	−21.8	−24.1	−26.9	Current Transfers: Debit	78ak *d*
—	—	—	—	—	—	—	—	—	—	—	—	—	—	111.2	Capital Account, n.i.e.	78bc *d*
—	—	—	—	—	—	—	—	—	—	—	—	—	—	111.2	Capital Account, n.i.e.: Credit	78ba *d*
—	—	—	—	—	—	—	—	—	—	—	—	—	—	—	Capital Account: Debit	78bb *d*
25.8	87.4	190.7	252.7	196.1	304.5	457.1	335.9	283.5	407.3	368.5	275.2	340.3	212.9	33.8	Financial Account, n.i.e.	78bj *d*
—	—	—	—	—	—	—	—	—	—	—	—	—	—	—	Direct Investment Abroad	78bd *d*
—	—	—	—	—	—	—	—	—	—	—	19.2	23.1	12.0	4.4	Dir. Invest. in Rep. Econ., n.i.e.	78be *d*
—	—	—	—	—	—	—	—	—	—	—	—	—	—	—	Portfolio Investment Assets	78bf *d*
—	—	—	—	—	—	—	—	—	—	—	—	—	—	—	Equity Securities	78bk *d*
—	—	—	—	—	—	—	—	—	—	—	—	—	—	—	Debt Securities	78bl *d*
—	—	—	—	—	—	—	—	—	—	—	—	—	—	—	Portfolio Investment Liab., n.i.e.	78bg *d*
—	—	—	—	—	—	—	—	—	—	—	—	—	—	—	Equity Securities	78bm *d*
—	—	—	—	—	—	—	—	—	—	—	—	—	—	—	Debt Securities	78bn *d*
....	....	....	....	....	....	....	....	....	....	....	....	....	....	....	Financial Derivatives Assets	78bw *d*
....	....	....	....	....	....	....	....	....	....	....	....	....	....	....	Financial Derivatives Liabilities	78bx *d*
−96.0	.8	59.8	38.5	−19.0	116.2	220.0	182.3	149.6	159.2	264.4	91.6	89.4	90.8	−83.6	Other Investment Assets	78bh *d*
—	—	—	—	—	—	—	—	—	—	—	—	—	—	—	Monetary Authorities	78bo *d*
—	—	—	—	—	—	—	—	—	—	—	—	—	—	—	General Government	78bp *d*
—	—	—	—	—	—	—	—	—	—	—	—	—	—	—	Banks	78bq *d*
−96.0	.8	59.8	38.5	−19.0	116.2	220.0	182.3	149.6	159.2	264.4	91.6	89.4	90.8	−83.6	Other Sectors	78br *d*
121.8	86.7	130.9	214.2	215.1	188.3	237.1	153.7	133.9	248.0	104.1	164.5	227.8	110.0	113.1	Other Investment Liab., n.i.e.	78bi *d*
13.0	−5.9	13.2	−10.5	2.5	2.3	.3	1.5	−4.0	4.3	.1	−3.3	1.0	.4	−2.0	Monetary Authorities	78bs *d*
85.2	94.2	116.4	196.8	210.3	175.7	214.6	130.1	125.7	237.5	106.8	128.4	165.9	151.8	113.5	General Government	78bt *d*
14.7	−5.7	−10.1	10.8	.6	6.8	12.5	22.1	11.7	5.4	−4.5	38.2	68.8	17.0	8.2	Banks	78bu *d*
9.0	4.0	11.4	17.0	1.7	3.6	9.8	—	.4	.8	1.7	1.2	−7.8	−59.1	−6.6	Other Sectors	78bv *d*
2.3	−.8	−3.6	12.5	5.2	4.9	10.7	.8	4.6	7.1	2.8	82.3	216.6	134.0	−25.4	Net Errors and Omissions	78ca *d*
−93.5	−32.5	63.8	−6.3	−42.1	20.2	163.4	155.4	65.6	62.5	15.0	30.9	168.8	279.7	130.2	*Overall Balance*	78cb *d*
93.5	32.5	−63.8	6.3	42.1	−20.2	−163.4	−155.4	−65.6	−62.5	−15.0	−30.9	−168.8	−279.7	−130.2	Reserves and Related Items	79da *d*
88.5	33.1	−78.1	−5.7	41.2	−8.1	−157.9	−162.3	−71.4	−65.0	−7.0	−23.4	−161.7	−273.0	−170.2	Reserve Assets	79db *d*
4.9	−.6	14.3	12.0	.9	−12.2	−5.4	6.9	5.8	2.5	−8.0	−7.5	−7.2	−6.6	−5.9	Use of Fund Credit and Loans	79dc *d*
....	....	....	....	....	....	....	....	....	....	....	....	....	....	45.9	Exceptional Financing	79de *d*
Year Ending July 15															**Government Finance**	
−3,380	−3,637	−3,902	−4,280	−8,014	−7,013	I −9,915	−10,054	−10,359	−7,463	−7,894	−10,981	−10,909	−13,846	−15,864	Deficit (−) or Surplus	80
3,855	4,508	5,780	7,140	7,540	8,767	I 10,413	13,012	14,316	18,862	23,206	26,641	29,344	31,492	34,812	Revenue	81
917	1,173	1,285	2,077	1,681	1,829	I 2,165	1,644	3,793	2,394	3,937	4,825	5,988	5,403	5,886	Grants Received	81z
8,209	9,445	11,110	13,644	17,405	17,811	I 22,748	25,134	29,180	29,309	36,242	43,519	47,073	51,964	58,391	Expenditure	82
−56	−128	−142	−148	−170	−202	I −255	−424	−712	−590	−1,205	−1,072	−832	−1,223	−1,829	Lending Minus Repayments	83
....	....														Financing	
....	....	1,545	1,030	2,731	1,433	I 4,248	4,179	4,691	−233	2,410	3,500	3,968	5,572	4,453	Net Borrowing: Domestic	84a
....	....	2,455	3,518	5,282	5,580	I 5,667	5,875	5,668	7,696	5,484	7,481	6,941	8,274	11,411	Foreign	85a
....	....	−98	−268	—	—	I —	—	—	—	—	—	—	—	—	Use of Cash Balances	87
6,032	....	10,017	11,047	13,778	15,428	I 20,856	23,235	24,456	30,631	32,058	34,242	35,891	38,407	49,670	Debt: Domestic	88a
8,516	....	15,172	20,826	29,217	38,990	I 59,505	70,924	87,421	101,967	113,000	128,044	132,087	161,208	173,861	Foreign.............................	89a
Year Ending July 15															**National Accounts**	
5,372	6,506	7,555	8,717	9,897	10,887	14,226	23,909	30,948	47,548	53,084	55,405	73,853	68,613	74,010	Exports of Goods & Services	90c
4,371	5,065	5,797	6,895	8,947	8,959	11,085	11,908	14,900	15,987	20,267	23,018	24,987	27,481	32,584	Government Consumption	91f
9,386	9,431	11,825	13,414	16,392	17,002	22,780	29,276	37,278	42,032	48,370	56,081	60,794	62,755	67,254	Gross Fixed Capital Formation	93e
798	1,168	1,073	1,823	3,023	2,074	2,294	2,342	2,375	2,612	6,261	11,936	10,290	−1,402	−9,302	Increase/Decrease(−) in Stocks	93i
35,977	44,782	50,746	62,407	70,172	86,314	97,771	121,370	133,314	154,009	166,443	191,469	216,364	240,844	266,781	Private Consumption	96f
−9,317	−11,218	−13,132	−16,350	−19,162	−21,820	−27,785	−39,321	−47,429	−62,972	−75,850	−88,996	−105,775	−101,744	−96,604	Imports of Goods & Services	98c
I 46,587	55,734	63,864	76,906	89,269	103,416	120,371	149,487	171,474	199,272	219,175	248,913	280,513	296,547	334,723	Gross Domestic Product (GDP)	99b
....	....	....	....	....	....	....	....	....	....	....	....	....	....	....	GDP Volume 1965 prices	99b. *p*
23,630															GDP Volume 1975 prices	99b. *p*
46,587	48,714	49,540	53,353	55,662	58,243	61,952	64,496	66,684	71,447	71,685	75,773	79,388	81,551	84,315	GDP Volume 1985 Prices	99b. *p*
65.0	68.0	69.1	74.4	77.6	81.2	86.4	90.0	93.0	99.7	100.0	105.7	110.7	113.8	117.6	GDP Volume (1995=100)	99bv *p*
I 32.7	37.4	42.2	47.1	52.5	58.1	63.5	75.8	84.1	91.2	100.0	107.4	115.6	118.9	129.8	GDP Deflator (1995=100)	99bi *p*
Midyear Estimates																
16.69	17.13	17.56	17.37	17.74	18.11	18.49	18.94	19.39	19.86	20.34	20.83	21.33	21.84	22.37	**Population**.................................	99z

(See notes in the back of the book.)

Netherlands

		1970	1971	1972	1973	1974	1975	1976	1977	1978	1979	1980	1981	1982	1983	1984
Exchange Rates															*Guilders per SDR through 1998,*	
Market Rate	aa	3.5970	3.5374	3.5030	3.4073	3.0688	3.1473	2.8546	2.7695	2.5652	2.5102	2.7160	2.8732	2.8951	3.2084	3.4793
													Guilders per US Dollar through 1998,			
Market Rate	ae	3.5970	3.2581	3.2265	2.8245	2.5065	2.6885	2.4570	2.2800	1.9690	1.9055	2.1295	2.4685	2.6245	3.0645	3.5495
Market Rate	rf	3.6200	3.5171	3.2095	2.7956	2.6884	2.5290	2.6439	2.4543	2.1636	2.0060	1.9881	2.4952	2.6702	2.8541	3.2087
														Guilders per ECU:		
ECU Rate	ea	....	....	....	....	....	....	....	....	....	2.7460	2.7901	2.6831	2.5421	2.5371	2.5185
ECU Rate	eb	....	....	....	....	....	2.9570	2.7998	2.7535	2.7481	2.7606	2.7758	2.6153	2.5372	2.5233	
												Index Numbers (1995=100):				
Market Rate	ahx	44.4	93.9	50.0	57.7	59.8	63.6	60.7	65.4	74.3	80.0	80.8	64.6	60.1	56.4	50.2
Nominal Effective Exchange Rate	neu	60.3	60.8	61.8	64.2	67.7	69.5	71.7	75.5	77.4	78.3	78.3	75.1	79.0	80.8	79.8
Real Effective Exchange Rate	reu	....	....	....	....	....	131.3	133.1	133.9	135.7	131.3	Ɪ121.7	108.9	109.5	108.0	101.8
Fund Position															*Millions of SDRs:*	
Quota	2f.s	700	700	700	700	700	700	700	700	948	948	1,422	1,422	1,422	2,265	2,265
SDRs	1b.s	144	570	650	475	486	520	531	564	244	394	439	592	772	502	525
Reserve Position in the Fund	1c.s	539	644	554	309	442	747	900	954	632	458	510	498	561	901	963
of which: Outstg.Fund Borrowing	2c	130	—	—	—	87	325	350	416	294	126	101	77	74	99	93
International Liquidity													*Millions of US Dollars Unless Otherwise Indicated:*			
Total Res.Min.Gold (Eurosys.Def)	1l.d	1,454	1,724	2,726	4,253	4,630	4,884	5,178	5,742	5,088	7,591	11,645	9,339	10,132	10,171	9,237
SDRs	1b.d	144	619	705	573	595	609	617	685	318	519	561	689	851	525	515
Reserve Position in the Fund	1c.d	539	699	601	373	541	874	1,045	1,158	823	603	651	579	619	943	944
Foreign Exchange	1d.d	771	406	1,420	3,306	3,495	3,401	3,515	3,899	3,947	6,469	10,434	8,071	8,662	8,702	7,778
o/w: Fin.Deriv.Rel.to Reserves	1dd d	....	....	....	....	....	....	....	....	....	....	....	....	....	....	....
Other Reserve Assets	1e.d	....	....	....	....	....	....	....	....	....	....	....	....	....	....	....
Gold (Million Fine Troy Ounces)	1ad	51.06	54.53	54.17	54.33	54.33	54.33	54.33	54.63	54.78	43.97	43.94	43.94	43.94	43.94	43.94
Gold (National Valuation)	1and	1,790	2,110	2,117	2,425	2,732	2,548	2,788	3,021	6,490	5,383	4,814	5,204	4,895	4,192	8,702
Memo: Euro Cl. on Non-EA Res.	1dg d	....	....	....	....	....	....	....	....	....	....	....	....	....	....	....
Non-Euro Cl. on EA Res.	1dh d	....	....	....	....	....	....	....	....	....	....	....	....	....	....	....
Mon. Auth.: Other Foreign Assets	3..d	....	....	....	....	....	....	....	....	....	....	....	....	....	....	....
Foreign Liabilities	4.,d	14	39	104	705	63	69	47	270	511	114	182	111	109	133	76
Banking Insts.: Foreign Assets	7a.d	5,279	6,928	8,389	12,344	15,903	20,145	25,503	33,377	46,684	57,250	62,625	66,352	63,922	58,862	57,520
Foreign Liab.	7b.d	5,058	6,087	7,353	11,078	14,379	17,504	22,625	31,075	44,688	56,305	64,353	65,181	62,733	56,217	53,052
Monetary Authorities													*Billions of Guilders through 1998;*			
Fgn. Assets (Cl.on Non-EA Ctys)	11	11.70	12.46	15.61	18.85	18.92	20.45	20.07	20.47	23.04	24.99	35.30	36.25	39.78	44.34	64.57
Claims on General Government	12a.u	....	....	....	....	....	....	....	....	....	....	....	....	....	....	....
o/w: Claims on Gen.Govt.in Cty	12a	.85	.97	.98	.96	1.03	.96	1.07	1.30	1.45	1.58	1.87	2.11	2.20	2.37	2.88
Claims on Banking Institutions	12e.u	....	....	....	....	....	....	....	....	....	....	....	....	....	....	....
o/w: Claims on Bank.Inst.in Cty	12e	.05	.19	.53	1.15	1.26	1.84	1.65	2.20	5.21	5.17	5.80	8.08	4.70	7.54	5.80
Claims on Other Resident Sectors	12d.u	....	....	....	....	....	....	....	....	....	....	....	....	....	....	....
o/w: Cl. on Oth.Res.Sect.in Cty	12d	.08	.09	.14	.21	.23	.26	.28	.24	.29	.59	.42	.68	.92	.79	1.18
Claims on ECB	12u															
Currency in Circulation	14a	10.40	10.98	11.98	12.59	13.61	15.26	16.67	18.23	19.62	21.04	22.95	23.27	25.00	28.01	29.73
Liabilities to Banking Insts	14c.u	....	....	....	....	....	....	....	....	....	....	....	....	....	....	....
o/w: Liabs to Bank.Inst.in Cty	14c	.10	.04	.05	.03	.04	.10	.04	.05	.03	.04	.01	.04	.03	.03	.02
Demand Dep. of Other Res.Sect.	14d.u	....	....	....	....	....	....	....	....	....	....	....	....	....	....	....
o/w: D.Dep.of Oth.Res.Sect.in Cty	14d	.04	.04	.03	.03	.04	.03	.07	.05	.07	.25	.05	.14	.20	.15	.09
Other Dep. of Other Res.Sect.	15..u	....	....	....	....	....	....	....	....	....	....	....	....	....	....	....
o/w: O.Dep.of Oth.Res.Sect.in Cty	15	....	....	....	....	....	....	....	....	....	....	....	....	....	....	....
Money Market Instruments	16m.u	....	....	....	....	....	....	....	....	....	....	....	....	....	....	....
o/w: MMI Held by Resid.of Cty	16m	....	....	....	....	....	....	....	....	....	....	....	....	....	....	....
Bonds (Debt Securities)	16n.u	....	....	....	....	....	....	....	....	....	....	....	....	....	....	....
o/w: Bonds Held by Resid.of Cty	16n	....	....	....	....	....	....	....	....	....	....	....	....	....	....	....
Foreign Liab. (to Non-EA Ctys)	16c	.05	.13	.34	1.96	.16	.19	.12	.62	1.01	.22	.39	.27	.29	.41	.27
Central Government Deposits	16d.u	....	....	....	....	....	....	....	....	....	....	....	....	....	....	....
o/w: Cent.Govt.Dep. in Cty	16d	2.84	3.32	3.87	5.14	6.78	5.69	5.37	5.22	4.64	2.38	3.85	3.38	3.42	3.36	1.73
Liabilities to ECB	16u															
Capital Accounts	17a	.60	.93	1.46	1.46	1.51	1.54	1.58	1.65	4.70	8.70	16.54	19.84	18.56	23.67	43.75
Other Items (Net)	17r	−1.36	−1.73	−.47	−.04	−.71	.70	−.78	−1.58	−.09	−.26	−.43	.21	.13	−.61	−1.17
Banking Institutions													*Billions of Guilders through 1998;*			
Claims on Monetary Authorities	20	.67	.48	.58	.67	.71	.74	.81	.77	.91	1.05	1.03	.95	Ɪ1.57	1.64	1.91
Claims on Bk.Inst.in Oth.EA Ctys	20b.u	....	....	....	....	....	....	....	....	....	....	....	....	....	....	....
Fgn. Assets (Cl.on Non-EA Ctys)	21	19.11	22.48	27.22	34.33	39.86	54.16	62.66	76.10	91.92	109.09	133.36	163.79	Ɪ167.76	180.38	204.17
Claims on General Government	22a.u	....	....	....	....	....	....	....	....	....	....	....	....	....	....	....
o/w: Claims on Gen.Govt.in Cty	22a	20.59	22.06	24.10	23.88	25.45	28.06	30.37	31.60	34.74	39.49	45.40	50.07	Ɪ60.11	66.29	70.76
Claims on Other Resident Sectors	22d.u	....	....	....	....	....	....	....	....	....	....	....	....	....	....	....
o/w: Cl. on Oth.Res.Sect.in Cty	22d	42.19	48.34	57.19	71.96	85.75	97.02	117.06	147.34	178.58	204.79	224.76	236.84	Ɪ242.42	250.45	259.46
Demand Deposits	24..u	....	....	....	....	....	....	....	....	....	....	....	....	....	....	....
o/w: D.Dep.of Oth.Res.Sect.in Cty	24	15.96	19.32	23.68	23.19	26.54	32.67	35.09	40.30	41.40	41.65	43.54	41.56	Ɪ48.71	53.16	57.11
Other Deposits	25..u	....	....	....	....	....	....	....	....	....	....	....	....	....	....	....
o/w: O.Dep.of Oth.Res.Sect.in Cty	25	45.35	51.23	57.30	70.99	82.11	90.30	108.64	122.70	141.28	161.73	170.65	190.48	Ɪ195.83	201.65	214.70
Money Market Instruments	26m.u	....	....	....	....	....	....	....	....	....	....	....	....	....	....	....
o/w: MMI Held by Resid.of Cty	26m	....	....	....	....	....	....	....	....	....	....	....	....	....	....	....
Bonds (Debt Securities)	26n.u	....	....	....	....	....	....	....	....	....	....	....	....	....	....	....
o/w: Bonds Held by Resid.of Cty	26n	.87	.93	.97	1.46	1.67	2.63	2.93	12.11	19.43	25.79	31.47	31.01	Ɪ31.16	33.08	33.90
Foreign Liab. (to Non-EA Ctys)	26c	18.31	19.75	23.86	30.81	36.04	47.06	55.59	70.85	87.99	107.29	137.04	160.90	Ɪ164.64	172.28	188.31
Central Government Deposits	26d.u	....	....	....	....	....	....	....	....	....	....	....	....	....	....	....
o/w: Cent.Govt.Dep. in Cty	26d	.39	.43	.55	.56	.64	.70	.66	.75	.98	.82	.93	.85	Ɪ.78	.64	.59
Credit from Monetary Authorities	26g	.05	.25	.41	1.10	1.24	1.79	1.75	2.31	5.13	5.27	5.95	8.69	Ɪ5.26	7.03	5.85
Liab. to Bk.Inst.in Oth. EA Ctys	26h.u	....	....	....	....	....	....	....	....	....	....	....	....	....	....	....
Capital Accounts	27a	3.83	4.29	4.88	5.87	6.84	8.42	9.60	7.95	9.54	11.16	12.23	14.20	Ɪ20.23	22.24	24.35
Other Items (Net)	27r	−2.20	−2.84	−2.55	−3.14	−3.31	−3.59	−3.35	−1.16	.40	.80	2.75	3.97	Ɪ5.31	8.69	11.71

1985	1986	1987	1988	1989	1990	1991	1992	1993	1994	1995	1996	1997	1998	1999		
															Exchange Rates	
Euros per SDR Thereafter: End of Period																
3.0448	2.6812	2.5217	2.6907	2.5173	2.4043	2.4466	2.4944	2.6659	2.5330	2.3849	2.5072	2.7217	2.6595	1.3662	Market Rate	aa
Euros per US Dollar Thereafter: End of Period (ae) Period Average (rf)																
2.7720	2.1920	1.7775	1.9995	1.9155	1.6900	1.7104	1.8141	1.9409	1.7351	1.6044	1.7436	2.0172	1.8888	.9954	Market Rate	ae
3.3214	2.4500	2.0257	1.9766	2.1207	1.8209	1.8697	1.7585	1.8573	1.8200	1.6057	1.6859	1.9513	1.9837	.9386	Market Rate	rf
End of Period (ea) Period Average (eb)																
2.4585	2.3440	2.3160	2.3440	2.2730	2.3125	2.2885	2.1925	2.1670	2.1280	2.0554	2.1665	2.2280	2.2037	....	ECU Rate	ea
2.5111	2.4015	2.3340	2.3343	2.3335	2.3162	2.3127	2.2725	2.1723	2.1528	2.0774	2.1113	2.2048	2.2227	....	ECU Rate	eb
Period Averages																
48.7	65.8	79.3	81.3	75.7	88.3	86.1	91.4	86.4	88.3	100.0	95.2	82.3	81.0	....	Market Rate	ahx
79.9	85.7	89.7	89.2	88.4	91.5	90.9	92.9	95.8	96.2	100.0	98.1	93.5	93.4	92.1	Nominal Effective Exchange Rate	neu
99.1	104.8	107.8	103.6	98.6	98.6	96.1	97.8	99.3	99.1	100.0	96.4	90.9	88.3	....	Real Effective Exchange Rate	reu
															Fund Position	
End of Period																
2,265	2,265	2,265	2,265	2,265	2,265	2,265	3,444	3,444	3,444	3,444	3,444	3,444	3,444	5,162	Quota	2f.s
569	598	637	576	590	504	530	403	424	442	616	566	586	644	742	SDRs	1b.s
898	717	652	563	537	519	559	834	795	802	1,169	1,275	1,625	2,113	1,880	Reserve Position in the Fund	1c.s
79	59	36	15	5	—	—	—	—	—	—	—	—	193	—	of which: Outstg.Fund Borrowing	2c
															International Liquidity	
End of Period																
10,782	11,191	16,003	16,075	16,508	17,484	17,798	21,937	31,344	34,532	33,714	26,767	24,865	21,418	‡10,098	Total Res.Min.Gold (Eurosys.Def)	1l.d
625	731	903	776	776	718	758	554	583	645	916	814	791	907	1,019	SDRs	1b.d
987	877	926	757	706	738	800	1,147	1,092	1,171	1,738	1,834	2,193	2,975	2,580	Reserve Position in the Fund	1c.d
9,170	9,583	14,174	14,542	15,027	16,028	16,240	20,237	29,669	32,716	31,060	24,119	21,881	17,536	6,499	Foreign Exchange	1d.d
....	....	....	....	....	....	....	....	....	....	....	....	....	....		o/w: Fin.Deriv.Rel.to Reserves	1dd d
														—	Other Reserve Assets	1e.d
43.94	43.94	43.94	43.94	43.94	43.94	43.94	43.94	35.05	34.77	34.77	34.77	27.07	33.83	31.57	Gold (Million Fine Troy Ounces)	1ad
11,143	14,091	15,532	13,807	14,413	14,719	14,543	13,712	7,639	8,477	9,168	8,622	5,801	7,299	9,183	Gold (National Valuation)	1an
														817	Memo: Euro Cl. on Non-EA Res.	1dg d
														986	Non-Euro Cl. on EA Res.	1dh d
....	....	....	....	....	....	....	....	....	....	....	....	....	....		Mon. Auth.: Other Foreign Assets	3..d
110	235	94	26	87	85	245	38	152	263	141	79	64	725	‡542	Foreign Liabilities	4..d
72,876	91,099	115,975	120,572	146,271	185,921	189,048	190,591	195,752	200,374	234,141	238,726	263,592	....	‡147,416	Banking Insts.: Foreign Assets	7a.d
65,677	83,456	108,672	109,884	121,329	153,434	157,364	165,530	169,204	186,977	220,964	245,746	290,784	....	‡185,983	Foreign Liab.	7b.d
															Monetary Authorities	
Billions of Euros Beginning 1999: End of Period																
61.66	56.41	56.90	60.66	60.10	55.27	56.20	65.61	76.24	75.69	69.77	62.72	62.96	55.75	20.63	Fgn. Assets (Cl.on Non-EA Ctys)	11
														7.58	Claims on General Government	12a.u
2.64	2.99	3.06	4.21	6.20	6.04	6.38	6.15	4.14	4.12	4.20	4.47	4.74	4.90	1.73	o/w: Claims on Gen.Govt.in Cty	12a
														16.96	Claims on Banking Institutions	12e.u
6.75	10.91	6.84	6.45	6.39	9.18	3.06	5.35	4.46	8.26	9.97	16.05	11.37	18.68	9.88	o/w: Claims on Bank.Inst.in Cty	12e
														.31	Claims on Other Resident Sectors	12d.u
.84	1.54	1.45	1.50	1.74	1.75	2.14	1.25	.60	.35	.35	.28	.22	.22	.12	o/w: Cl. on Oth.Res.Sect.in Cty	12d
														5.81	Claims on ECB	12u
30.75	31.92	35.42	36.89	38.65	39.42	39.91	39.89	40.41	40.93	41.30	41.67	42.10	40.90	18.98	Currency in Circulation	14a
														20.70	Liabilities to Banking Insts	14c.u
.11	.05	.08	1.83	6.11	6.62	.12	12.52	15.82	18.74	11.09	8.39	13.06	17.16	7.52	o/w: Liabs to Bank.Inst.in Cty	14c
														—	Demand Dep. of Other Res.Sect.	14d.u
.17	.19	.30	.59	.60	.83	.35	.08	.13	.10	.02	.06	.06	.14		o/w: D.Dep.of Oth.Res.Sect.in Cty	14d
														—	Other Dep. of Other Res.Sect.	15..u
															o/w: O.Dep.of Oth.Res.Sect.in Cty	15
														—	Money Market Instruments	16m.u
															o/w: MMI Held by Resid.of Cty	16m
														—	Bonds (Debt Securities)	16n.u
															o/w: Bonds Held by Resid.of Cty	16n
.31	.52	.17	.05	.17	.14	.42	.07	.30	.46	.23	.14	.13	1.37	.54	Foreign Liab. (to Non-EA Ctys)	16c
														.01	Central Government Deposits	16d.u
3.39	5.80	3.40	3.09	.03	1.36	3.27	3.13	7.99	9.61	14.84	14.44	.09	5.10	.01	o/w: Cent.Govt.Dep. in Cty	16d
														—	Liabilities to ECB	16u
38.47	34.14	29.36	30.51	29.26	24.08	24.40	23.53	21.79	20.06	17.21	19.65	24.96	17.09	12.99	Capital Accounts	17a
-1.30	-.75	-.47	-.39	-.13	-.20	-.69	-.85	-1.00	-1.47	-.39	-.83	-1.10	-2.21	-1.95	Other Items (Net)	17r
															Banking Institutions	
Billions of Euros Beginning 1999: End of Period																
2.10	2.09	2.06	2.23	2.62	2.87	2.87	2.88	2.81	2.80	3.09	3.38	3.36	....	6.84	Claims on Monetary Authorities	20
														61.80	Claims on Bk.Inst.in Oth.EA Ctys	20b.u
202.01	199.69	206.15	241.08	280.18	314.21	323.35	345.75	379.94	347.67	375.66	416.24	531.72	....	146.74	Fgn. Assets (Cl.on Non-EA Ctys)	21
														105.60	Claims on General Government	22a.u
78.33	88.84	87.29	124.99	119.98	122.26	119.37	119.36	124.93	129.20	133.64	136.46	140.36	....	62.60	o/w: Claims on Gen.Govt.in Cty	22a
														475.19	Claims on Other Resident Sectors	22d.u
270.93	290.74	306.38	375.09	399.91	427.18	460.32	485.59	518.79	559.34	626.83	698.86	788.56	....	463.71	o/w: Cl. on Oth.Res.Sect.in Cty	22d
														113.59	Demand Deposits	24..u
62.00	67.25	70.56	76.10	82.42	86.63	92.00	98.00	111.92	114.04	134.71	155.58	170.49	....	111.01	o/w: D.Dep.of Oth.Res.Sect.in Cty	24
														232.77	Other Deposits	25..u
229.33	239.98	239.76	257.45	287.29	310.49	325.65	342.32	355.15	353.92	363.23	372.14	395.16	....	219.26	o/w: O.Dep.of Oth.Res.Sect.in Cty	25
														—	Money Market Instruments	26m.u
															o/w: MMI Held by Resid.of Cty	26m
														148.47	Bonds (Debt Securities)	26n.u
35.55	43.84	50.54	138.29	143.91	149.18	150.93	150.11	154.41	169.53	187.19	193.55	196.41	....		o/w: Bonds Held by Resid.of Cty	26n
182.06	182.94	193.17	219.71	232.41	259.30	269.16	300.29	328.41	324.42	354.51	428.48	586.57	....	185.13	Foreign Liab. (to Non-EA Ctys)	26c
														1.85	Central Government Deposits	26d.u
.67	.95	1.31	1.50	1.11	.87	1.92	1.14	1.32	.79	1.02	1.51	1.82	....	1.84	o/w: Cent.Govt.Dep. in Cty	26d
5.67	10.70	7.36	6.14	4.89	9.33	3.08	6.65	4.06	7.92	10.15	13.10	14.69	....	9.70	Credit from Monetary Authorities	26g
														51.13	Liab. to Bk.Inst.in Oth. EA Ctys	26h.u
23.57	26.79	30.50	35.06	38.22	42.97	46.39	48.84	54.30	57.52	61.65	78.17	86.89	....	45.53	Capital Accounts	27a
14.54	8.91	8.67	9.14	12.44	7.74	16.79	6.24	16.90	10.88	26.74	12.40	11.97	....	8.00	Other Items (Net)	27r

	1970	1971	1972	1973	1974	1975	1976	1977	1978	1979	1980	1981	1982	1983	1984
Banking Survey (Nat'l Residency)													*Billions of Guilders through 1998;*		
Foreign Assets (Net) **31n**	12.45	15.07	18.63	20.41	22.58	27.36	27.03	25.11	25.96	26.58	31.23	38.87	Ɩ42.62	52.04	80.16
Domestic Credit **32**	60.48	67.71	78.00	91.31	105.03	119.90	142.76	174.51	209.44	243.25	267.67	285.48	Ɩ301.45	315.89	331.96
Claims on General Govt. (Net) **32an**	18.22	19.27	20.67	19.14	19.05	22.63	25.42	26.93	30.58	37.87	42.59	47.95	Ɩ58.12	64.66	71.32
Claims on Other Resident Sectors **32d**	42.27	48.43	57.33	72.17	85.98	97.28	117.34	147.58	178.87	205.38	225.18	237.52	Ɩ243.34	251.24	260.65
Currency in Circulation **34a.n**	10.40	10.98	11.98	12.59	13.61	15.26	16.67	18.23	19.62	21.04	22.95	23.27	25.00	28.01	29.73
Demand Deposits **34b.n**	16.00	19.36	23.71	23.22	26.58	32.70	35.16	40.35	41.47	41.90	43.59	41.70	48.91	53.31	57.20
Other Deposits .... **35..n**	45.35	51.23	57.30	70.99	82.11	90.30	108.64	122.70	141.28	161.73	170.65	190.48	195.83	201.65	214.70
Money Market Instruments **36m**															
Bonds (Debt Securities) **36n**	.87	.93	.97	1.46	1.67	2.63	2.93	12.11	19.43	25.79	31.47	31.01	Ɩ31.16	33.08	33.90
o/w: Bonds Over Two Years **36na**															
Capital Accounts **37a**	4.43	5.22	6.33	7.32	8.35	9.96	11.18	9.60	14.24	19.86	28.77	34.04	38.79	45.91	68.10
Other Items (Net) **37r**	−4.13	−4.94	−3.66	−3.87	−4.72	−3.58	−4.79	−3.38	−.64	−.40	1.47	3.86	Ɩ4.45	5.96	8.70
Banking Survey (EA-Wide Residency)													*Billions of Euros:*		
Foreign Assets (Net) **31n.u**	....	....	....	....	....	....	....	....	....	....	....	....	....	....	....
Domestic Credit .... **32..u**	....	....	....	....	....	....	....	....	....	....	....	....	....	....	....
Claims on General Govt. (Net) **32an.u**	....	....	....	....	....	....	....	....	....	....	....	....	....	....	....
Claims on Other Resident Sect. **32d.u**	....	....	....	....	....	....	....	....	....	....	....	....	....	....	....
Currency in Circulation **34a.u**	....	....	....	....	....	....	....	....	....	....	....	....	....	....	....
Demand Deposits **34b.u**	....	....	....	....	....	....	....	....	....	....	....	....	....	....	....
Other Deposits .... **35..u**	....	....	....	....	....	....	....	....	....	....	....	....	....	....	....
o/w: Other Dep. Over Two Yrs **35ab.u**	....	....	....	....	....	....	....	....	....	....	....	....	....	....	....
Money Market Instruments **36m.u**	....	....	....	....	....	....	....	....	....	....	....	....	....	....	....
Bonds (Debt Securities) **36n.u**	....	....	....	....	....	....	....	....	....	....	....	....	....	....	....
o/w: Bonds Over Two Years **36na.u**	....	....	....	....	....	....	....	....	....	....	....	....	....	....	....
Capital Accounts **37a**	....	....	....	....	....	....	....	....	....	....	....	....	....	....	....
Other Items (Net) **37r.u**	....	....	....	....	....	....	....	....	....	....	....	....	....	....	....
Money (National Definitions)													*Billions of Guilders:*		
M3H **39m**	38.46	41.91	46.90	57.19	68.66	72.58	90.74	92.29	95.71	102.88	106.82	112.46	Ɩ217.95	228.96	242.23
M3H, Seasonally Adjusted **39m.c**	38.91	42.20	49.83	57.34	66.28	72.64	88.76	94.11	98.86	105.45	109.45	116.90	Ɩ221.45	233.07	247.57
Nonbank Financial Institutions													*Billions of Guilders:*		
Cash .... **40..l**	.34	.37	.33	.61	.94	1.33	2.40	2.09	1.18	1.50	1.37	2.07	1.78	2.03	1.82
Foreign Assets .... **41..l**	1.93	2.46	2.98	3.29	3.80	4.07	4.50	4.48	4.53	4.97	5.81	6.64	9.02	12.76	15.77
Claims on Central Government **42a.l**	12.84	14.28	16.29	18.25	20.79	24.18	28.62	33.36	38.38	43.11	50.22	58.42	65.32	76.24	88.96
Claims on Local Government **42b.l**	8.37	9.22	9.58	10.83	13.55	15.24	17.72	20.18	22.17	25.55	30.11	36.61	43.88	48.86	54.17
Claims on Private Sector **42d.l**	24.83	27.88	32.77	37.53	44.93	51.79	58.64	66.34	78.58	87.33	95.53	100.79	108.58	116.41	123.12
Real Estate **42h.l**	5.74	6.59	7.74	8.81	10.41	12.36	14.07	15.72	17.89	19.88	23.34	26.28	30.23	31.93	34.51
Capital Accounts **47a.l**	54.24	60.86	69.78	79.82	94.53	109.96	126.86	143.73	164.58	185.92	210.34	233.97	262.43	293.15	323.80
Other Items (Net) **47r.l**	−.19	−.06	−.11	−.50	−.12	−1.00	−.90	−1.57	−1.85	−3.58	−3.96	−3.16	−3.63	−4.91	−5.45
Interest Rates													*Percent Per Annum*		
Discount Rate *(End of Period)* **60**	6.00	5.00	4.00	8.00	7.00	4.50	6.00	4.50	6.50	9.50	8.00	9.00	5.00	5.00	5.00
Rate on Advances **60a**	....	....	....	....	....	....	....	....	....	....	....	....	....	....	....
Money Market Rate **60b**	7.96	Ɩ4.85	1.93	6.44	9.20	4.17	7.28	3.80	6.24	9.03	10.13	11.01	8.06	5.28	5.78
Treasury Bill Rate **60c**	....	....	....	....	....	....	5.84	4.50	9.39	13.80	10.13	10.68	8.12	5.48	5.97
Deposit Rate **60l**	....	....	....	....	....	....	....	....	5.04	5.54	5.96	6.06	5.88	4.03	4.10
Lending Rate **60p**	....	....	....	....	....	....	....	....	13.25	16.50	13.50	14.25	11.17	8.46	8.88
Government Bond Yield **61**	8.22	7.35	6.88	Ɩ7.92	9.83	8.79	8.95	8.10	7.74	8.78	10.21	11.55	10.10	8.61	8.33
Prices, Production, Labor													*Index Numbers (1995=100):*		
Share Prices: General **62**	Ɩ21.8	20.6	23.7	25.3	19.4	19.8	20.7	19.8	19.9	19.6	18.4	19.4	19.7	28.5	36.2
Manufacturing **62a**	Ɩ47.6	45.1	54.2	59.8	46.3	46.0	44.0	39.7	39.5	35.7	30.6	32.4	33.9	51.3	63.3
Prices: Final Products **63**	44.5	Ɩ46.5	48.7	51.7	56.4	59.8	63.9	67.4	68.4	70.2	75.3	81.9	86.6	87.8	91.7
Consumer Prices **64**	33.9	36.4	39.3	42.4	46.5	51.2	55.9	59.5	61.9	64.5	Ɩ68.7	73.4	77.7	79.9	82.5
Harmonized CPI **64h**															
Wages: Hourly Rates **65**	26.1	29.2	Ɩ32.9	37.2	43.6	49.5	53.9	57.7	61.0	63.7	66.5	68.7	73.4	75.3	76.2
Industrial Production .... **66..c**	57.7	61.6	64.0	69.5	72.7	71.9	76.6	76.6	76.6	79.8	Ɩ79.0	77.3	74.0	76.7	79.8
Industrial Employment **67**	145.8	144.1	139.9	136.0	134.4	130.1	125.9	121.7	118.1	Ɩ116.1	Ɩ115.0	111.7	95.5	103.6	102.5
													Number in Thousands:		
Labor Force **67d**	....	....	....	....	....	....	....	....	....	....	....	....	....	....	....
Employment **67e**	....	....	....	....	....	....	....	....	....	....	....	....	....	....	....
Unemployment **67c**	....	....	....	....	....	....	....	....	....	....	....	....	....	....	....
Unemployment Rate (%) **67r**	....	....	....	....	....	....	....	....	....	....	....	....	....	....	....
International Transactions													*Millions of Guilders through 1998;*		
Exports **70**	48,345	55,366	61,490	76,039	100,322	100,761	121,662	122,914	124,292	147,395	168,850	195,259	201,921	209,954	240,081
Imports, c.i.f. **71**	56,791	62,763	66,343	79,774	104,386	103,258	123,209	129,777	132,304	154,964	175,732	188,916	193,088	194,733	221,657
															1995=100
Volume of Exports **72**	26	28	31	35	39	38	42	42	43	47	Ɩ47	48	47	50	Ɩ53
Volume of Imports **73**	34	35	36	40	43	41	46	47	50	53	Ɩ52	48	48	50	Ɩ53
Unit Value of Exports **74**	Ɩ50	51	52	55	71	Ɩ74	79	81	Ɩ80	87	Ɩ98	114	118	118	127
Unit Value of Imports **75**	Ɩ49	51	50	54	73	Ɩ76	81	83	Ɩ82	91	Ɩ105	121	123	125	131

Billions of Euros Beginning 1999: End of Period

Banking Survey (Nat'l Residency)

1985	1986	1987	1988	1989	1990	1991	1992	1993	1994	1995	1996	1997	1998	1999		
81.31	72.65	69.71	81.97	107.71	110.03	109.97	111.01	127.48	98.48	90.68	50.34	7.98	....	41.76	Foreign Assets (Net)	31n
348.69	377.36	393.46	501.21	526.69	555.00	583.02	608.08	639.15	682.62	749.16	824.11	931.97	....	526.31	Domestic Credit	32
76.91	85.08	85.64	124.62	125.05	126.07	120.57	121.24	119.75	122.92	121.98	124.98	143.19	....	62.49	Claims on General Govt. (Net)	32an
271.78	292.28	307.83	376.59	401.64	428.93	462.45	486.84	519.40	559.69	627.18	699.13	788.78	....	463.83	Claims on Other Resident Sectors	32d
30.75	31.92	35.42	36.89	38.65	39.42	39.91	39.89	40.41	40.93	41.30	41.67	42.10	40.90	18.98	Currency in Circulation	34a.n
62.17	67.44	70.86	76.70	83.02	87.46	92.34	98.08	112.05	114.14	134.74	155.65	170.55	....	111.01	Demand Deposits	34b.n
229.33	239.98	239.76	257.45	287.29	310.49	325.65	342.32	355.15	353.92	363.23	372.14	395.16	....	219.26	Other Deposits	35..n
														—	Money Market Instruments	36m
35.55	43.84	50.54	138.29	143.91	149.18	150.93	150.11	154.41	169.53	187.19	193.55	196.41	....	148.47	Bonds (Debt Securities)	36n
														129.42	o/w: Bonds Over Two Years	36na
62.04	60.93	59.86	65.57	67.48	67.05	70.79	72.37	76.09	77.58	78.86	97.82	111.85	17.09	58.52	Capital Accounts	37a
10.16	5.89	6.73	8.29	14.03	11.42	13.36	16.33	28.51	25.01	34.52	13.62	23.88	....	11.83	Other Items (Net)	37r

End of Period

Banking Survey (EA-Wide Residency)

1999		
-18.30	Foreign Assets (Net)	31n.u
586.81	Domestic Credit	32..u
111.32	Claims on General Govt. (Net)	32an u
475.49	Claims on Other Resident Sect.	32d.u
18.98	Currency in Circulation	34a.u
113.59	Demand Deposits	34b.u
232.77	Other Deposits	35..u
55.33	o/w: Other Dep. Over Two Yrs	35ab u
—	Money Market Instruments	36m.u
148.47	Bonds (Debt Securities)	36n.u
129.42	o/w: Bonds Over Two Years	36na u
58.52	Capital Accounts	37a
-3.82	Other Items (Net)	37r.u

End of Period

Money (National Definitions)

1985	1986	1987	1988	1989	1990	1991	1992	1993	1994	1995	1996	1997	1998	1999		
264.13	282.73	294.21	319.81	359.72	386.02	407.19	432.15	465.08	466.02	486.57	514.99	553.24	....	....	M3H	39m
267.88	283.90	291.96	325.80	369.59	387.24	408.98	434.02	474.64	469.75	489.45	515.51	553.72	....	....	M3H, Seasonally Adjusted	39m.c

End of Period

Nonbank Financial Institutions

1985	1986	1987	1988	1989	1990	1991	1992	1993	1994	1995	1996	1997	1998	1999		
4.23	3.39	2.85	4.13	6.38	8.87	9.73	10.06	13.77	10.87	10.99	11.58	11.90	11.81	....	Cash	40..l
I28.52	37.78	41.06	49.05	55.38	57.16	69.33	83.26	108.54	115.34	145.81	188.36	271.83	380.97	....	Foreign Assets	41..l
I107.71	113.71	118.01	124.01	131.04	138.87	147.12	151.57	153.09	161.40	175.66	190.88	192.82	181.40	....	Claims on Central Government	42a.l
I62.15	69.10	76.88	25.03	25.18	26.04	27.28	28.49	30.88	31.81	31.55	30.19	27.52	25.53	....	Claims on Local Government	42b.l
I147.59	158.36	165.15	234.57	254.30	261.42	276.86	291.20	326.30	346.67	369.32	411.29	457.37	501.60	....	Claims on Private Sector	42d.l
I38.41	40.33	42.22	45.50	47.79	50.64	54.86	58.34	59.45	59.78	60.40	63.96	64.18	66.41	....	Real Estate	42h.l
I376.77	408.04	433.48	468.80	506.41	526.30	566.29	604.65	673.25	702.32	767.87	871.78	994.43	1,138.09	....	Capital Accounts	47a.l
11.82	14.63	12.70	13.49	13.66	16.69	18.88	18.27	18.79	23.56	25.85	24.49	31.19	29.64	....	Other Items (Net)	47r.l

Percent Per Annum

Interest Rates

1985	1986	1987	1988	1989	1990	1991	1992	1993	1994	1995	1996	1997	1998	1999		
5.00	4.50	3.75	4.50	7.00	7.25	8.50	7.75	5.00	....	....	....	....	....	....	Discount Rate (End of Period)	60
5.50	5.00	4.27	5.01	7.75	8.00	8.94	8.33	5.52	4.50	2.98	2.00	2.75	2.75	....	Rate on Advances	60a
6.30	5.83	5.16	4.48	6.99	8.29	9.01	9.27	7.10	5.14	4.22	2.89	3.07	3.21	....	Money Market Rate	60b
6.23	5.49	5.18	4.34	6.80	....	....	....	....	....	....	....	....	....	....	Treasury Bill Rate	60c
4.10	3.93	3.55	3.48	3.49	3.31	3.18	3.20	3.11	I4.70	4.40	3.54	3.18	3.10	2.74	Deposit Rate	601
9.25	8.63	8.15	7.77	10.75	11.75	12.40	12.75	10.40	8.29	7.21	5.90	6.13	6.50	I3.46	Lending Rate	60p
7.34	6.32	6.40	6.42	7.22	8.92	8.74	8.10	6.51	7.20	7.20	6.49	5.81	4.87	4.92	Government Bond Yield	61

Period Averages

Prices, Production, Labor

1985	1986	1987	1988	1989	1990	1991	1992	1993	1994	1995	1996	1997	1998	1999		
I46.8	53.8	56.0	50.7	64.1	62.5	64.2	67.3	78.1	92.5	100.0	134.4	195.3	261.6	284.6	Share Prices: General	62
47.6	60.9	54.3	49.6	63.9	61.7	61.7	66.0	77.3	93.9	100.0	125.9	192.1	242.5	264.4	Manufacturing	62a
93.1	90.6	89.5	89.9	93.1	96.1	I96.2	97.9	98.0	I98.5	100.0	102.0	103.8	103.6	104.7	Prices: Final Products	63
84.3	84.4	83.8	84.4	85.3	I87.4	90.2	93.0	95.4	98.1	I100.0	102.0	104.2	106.3	108.6	Consumer Prices	64
....	....	....	....	....	....	....	....	....	....	100.0	101.4	103.3	105.1	107.3	Harmonized CPI	64h
79.9	81.2	82.3	83.4	84.5	87.0	I90.2	94.1	97.1	I98.9	100.0	101.7	104.8	108.1	....	Wages: Hourly Rates	65
83.1	83.1	84.0	86.5	89.8	91.5	I94.0	93.8	92.7	I97.2	100.0	103.8	106.6	107.7	107.7	Industrial Production	66..c
103.6	105.7	106.7	106.7	108.5	110.9	I111.1	110.0	106.7	102.2	100.0	98.9	100.0	....	....	Industrial Employment	67

Period Averages

1985	1986	1987	1988	1989	1990	1991	1992	1993	1994	1995	1996	1997	1998	1999		
....	....	....	....	....	....	....	....	....	7,185	7,359	7,460	7,616	7,735	....	Labor Force	67d
5,145	....	I5,864	6,032	6,155	6,356	6,521	I6,597	6,448	6,692	6,835	6,971	7,194	7,398	....	Employment	67e
....	711	I686	I433	390	346	319	336	415	486	464	440	375	286	222	Unemployment	67c
....	12.0	I11.5	I6.5	5.8	5.0	4.5	5.3	6.5	7.6	I7.0	6.6	5.5	4.1	3.2	Unemployment Rate (%)	67r

Millions of Euros Beginning 1999

International Transactions

1985	1986	1987	1988	1989	1990	1991	1992	1993	1994	1995	1996	1997	1998	1999		
257,267	I197,285	188,016	203,730	228,544	239,181	249,051	246,541	258,343	282,209	314,693	332,920	380,018	398,686	I188,046	Exports	70
241,587	I185,053	184,844	196,347	220,987	229,708	237,118	236,597	231,637	256,442	283,538	304,559	347,286	371,760	I176,115	Imports, c.i.f.	71

1995=100

1985	1986	1987	1988	1989	1990	1991	1992	1993	1994	1995	1996	1997	1998	1999		
55	56	60	65	68	72	I75	78	83	I92	100	105	....	....	....	Volume of Exports	72
57	59	63	67	70	74	I77	78	81	I89	100	105	....	....	....	Volume of Imports	73
129	110	100	100	107	106	I105	101	98	I98	100	100	....	....	....	Unit Value of Exports	74
133	109	103	102	112	109	I109	106	100	I100	100	101	....	....	....	Unit Value of Imports	75

Netherlands

		1970	1971	1972	1973	1974	1975	1976	1977	1978	1979	1980	1981	1982	1983	1984
Balance of Payments															*Millions of US Dollars:*	
Current Account, n.i.e.	78al d	193	524	2,101	3,224	3,040	2,394	3,587	1,413	–904	350	–855	3,826	5,025	5,089	6,380
Goods: Exports f.o.b.	78aa d	11,607	13,485	16,793	23,605	33,283	34,962	39,468	43,021	49,122	63,398	73,230	68,588	66,804	64,534	65,666
Goods: Imports f.o.b.	78ab d	–12,386	–13,898	–16,135	–22,314	–31,897	–33,274	–37,240	–42,510	–49,945	–64,003	–73,474	–62,912	–60,546	–58,982	–59,027
Trade Balance	78ac d	–778	–413	658	1,290	1,386	1,688	2,228	510	–823	–605	–245	5,676	6,258	5,553	6,639
Services: Credit	78ad d	2,503	3,823	4,463	5,914	7,403	8,918	9,329	10,597	12,976	14,391	17,150	15,283	15,271	13,559	13,451
Services: Debit	78ae d	–2,332	–3,584	–3,897	–5,237	–6,841	–7,851	–8,610	–9,985	–12,454	–14,966	–18,148	–16,061	–15,579	–14,157	–14,003
Balance on Goods & Services	78af d	–607	–173	1,225	1,967	1,949	2,754	2,947	1,122	–300	–1,180	–1,242	4,899	5,951	4,955	6,088
Income: Credit	78ag d	1,964	2,234	2,464	3,547	4,454	3,885	4,371	4,871	5,567	10,240	12,763	12,672	12,365	11,189	11,807
Income: Debit	78ah d	–1,127	–1,452	–1,431	–2,151	–3,009	–3,548	–3,382	–3,962	–5,330	–7,958	–11,228	–12,304	–11,986	–10,076	–10,457
Balance on Gds, Serv. & Inc.	78ai d	229	609	2,258	3,364	3,394	3,091	3,936	2,031	–63	1,102	293	5,267	6,330	6,068	7,438
Current Transfers: Credit	78aj d	218	479	528	983	860	973	1,387	1,759	2,244	2,881	2,746	1,887	1,919	2,050	2,042
Current Transfers: Debit	78ak d	–254	–564	–685	–1,123	–1,213	–1,670	–1,736	–2,376	–3,086	–3,634	–3,894	–3,328	–3,224	–3,030	–3,100
Capital Account, n.i.e.	78bc d	–6	25	27	49	–5	–6	–124	–219	–317	–216	–250	–227	–310	–148	–76
Capital Account, n.i.e.: Credit	78ba d	56	77	103	105	116	111	90	114	110	149	129	166	213	129	126
Capital Account: Debit	78bb d	–62	–52	–76	–56	–122	–117	–214	–333	–427	–366	–379	–393	–523	–278	–201
Financial Account, n.i.e.	78bj d	110	–476	–1,431	–2,463	–2,688	–2,796	–3,061	–436	793	–816	2,411	–4,287	–2,803	–4,896	–7,559
Direct Investment Abroad	78bd d	–1,317	–1,319	–1,640	–2,117	–2,789	–2,519	–2,353	–3,038	–3,386	–6,282	–5,918	–4,527	–3,263	–3,835	–4,844
Dir. Invest. in Rep. Econ., n.i.e.	78be d	633	753	755	1,119	1,103	1,232	581	605	1,082	1,715	2,278	1,799	1,227	1,358	1,717
Portfolio Investment Assets	78bf d	–246	–403	–681	–877	–394	–565	12	–24	–322	481	176	–352	–1,470	–1,530	–1,073
Equity Securities	78bk d	–259	–337	–562	–692	–398	–472	211	179	21	523	484	268	31	–60	589
Debt Securities	78bl d	13	–66	–119	–185	4	–93	–199	–203	–342	–42	–308	–620	–1,501	–1,470	–1,662
Portfolio Investment Liab., n.i.e.	78bg d	668	717	280	–100	128	600	–168	1,802	1,413	2,075	3,026	1,184	1,069	1,393	1,000
Equity Securities	78bm d	60	150	214	–74	–300	27	–131	274	303	297	495	225	392	533	–81
Debt Securities	78bn d	608	567	66	–26	428	574	–37	1,528	1,110	1,778	2,531	959	678	860	1,080
Financial Derivatives Assets	78bw d	....	—	—	—	—	–1	2	—	2	18	–54	–52	–11	–28	22
Financial Derivatives Liabilities	78bx d	....														
Other Investment Assets	78bh d	–1,862	–1,296	–1,710	–3,211	–2,957	–5,836	–5,886	–5,498	–8,942	–11,137	–9,649	–7,966	–1,747	–289	–4,479
Monetary Authorities	78bo d	—	—	—	—	—	—	—	—	—	—	—	—	—		
General Government	78bp d	–89	–46	–121	–142	–332	–168	–205	–273	–156	–685	–375	–577	–411	–52	–227
Banks	78bq d	–1,737	–1,301	–1,452	–2,911	–2,481	–5,339	–4,717	–4,527	–8,453	–10,251	–8,437	–6,869	–46	901	–3,007
Other Sectors	78br d	–35	50	–138	–157	–143	–329	–963	–698	–333	–201	–837	–520	–1,290	–1,138	–1,245
Other Investment Liab., n.i.e.	78bi d	2,233	1,073	1,566	2,722	2,220	4,292	4,752	5,717	10,945	12,314	12,551	5,627	1,391	–1,966	99
Monetary Authorities	78bs d	1	24	65	12	–678	–3	–34	208	148	–392	83	–64	13	70	–50
General Government	78bt d	8	29	–16	8	35	49	–21	49	–41	206	–73	31	290	–103	–47
Banks	78bu d	1,796	764	1,433	2,970	2,325	4,073	4,955	5,376	10,042	12,053	11,952	5,333	591	–2,807	475
Other Sectors	78bv d	428	256	85	–269	538	163	–148	84	797	446	589	326	497	875	–279
Net Errors and Omissions	78ca d	325	111	232	–75	–42	731	–108	–251	–341	–297	–43	–202	–118	–202	1,243
Overall Balance	78cb d	622	185	929	735	306	323	295	507	–770	–980	1,264	–891	1,795	–157	–12
Reserves and Related Items	79da d	–622	–185	–929	–735	–306	–323	–295	–507	770	980	–1,264	891	–1,795	157	12
Reserve Assets	79db d	–622	–185	–929	–735	–306	–323	–295	–507	770	980	–1,264	891	–1,795	157	12
Use of Fund Credit and Loans	79dc d	—	—	—	—	—	—	—	—	—	—	—	—	—	—	—
Exceptional Financing	79de d	....	....													
International Investment Position															*Millions of US Dollars*	
Assets	79aa d	683	1,318	1,306	947	1,135	1,483	1,663	1,843	1,141	1,122	58,680	54,889	131,631	136,268	139,709
Direct Investment Abroad	79ab d	....	....	....	....	....	....	....	....	....	....	42,135	40,236	39,737	39,121	39,944
Portfolio Investment	79ac d	....	....	....	....	....	....	....	....	....	....			11,681	13,499	14,108
Equity Securities	79ad d	....	....	....	....	....	....	....	....	....	....			6,419	7,452	7,049
Debt Securities	79ae d	....	....	....	....	....	....	....	....	....	....			5,263	6,047	7,060
Financial Derivatives	79al d	....	....	....	....	....	....	....	....	....	....	—	—			
Other Investment	79af d	....	....	....	....	....	....	....	....	....	....	—	—	65,090	69,210	67,496
Monetary Authorities	79ag d	....	....	....	....	....	....	....	....	....	....	—	—	—	—	—
General Government	79ah d	....	....	....	....	....	....	....	....	....	....	—	—	3,050	2,905	2,818
Banks	79ai d	....	....	....	....	....	....	....	....	....	....	—	—	62,040	57,314	56,488
Other Sectors	79aj d	....	....	....	....	....	....	....	....	....	....			—	8,991	8,191
Reserve Assets	79ak d	683	1,318	1,306	947	1,135	1,483	1,663	1,843	1,141	1,122	16,544	14,654	15,122	14,438	18,161
Liabilities	79la d	—	—	—	—	—	—	—	—	—	—	27,868	26,865	107,811	102,860	101,007
Dir. Invest. in Rep. Economy	79lb d	....	....	....	....	....	....	....	....	....	....	19,167	18,405	17,975	16,924	18,196
Portfolio Investment	79lc d	....	....	....	....	....	....	....	....	....	....	8,518	8,349	22,812	26,027	27,011
Equity Securities	79ld d	....	....	....	....	....	....	....	....	....	....			11,643	15,715	16,611
Debt Securities	79le d	....	....	....	....	....	....	....	....	....	....	8,518	8,349	11,169	10,312	10,400
Financial Derivatives	79ll d	....	....	....	....	....	....	....	....	....	....	—	—			
Other investment	79lf d	....	....	....	....	....	....	....	....	....	....	182	111	67,024	59,909	55,800
Monetary Authorities	79lg d	—	—	—	—	—	—	—	—	—	—	182	111	109	432	346
General Government	79lh d	....	....	....	....	....	....	....	....	....	....	406	—	—	—	—
Banks	79li d	....	....	....	....	....	....	....	....	....	....			62,678	55,429	52,695
Other Sectors	79lj d	....	....	....	....	....	....	....	....	....	....			3,831	4,048	2,760
Government Finance																
Central Government															*Millions of Guilders through 1998;*	
Deficit (-) or Surplus	80	–1,319	–1,651	–92	467	–1,084	–6,406	–8,723	–8,068	I –9,255	–13,075	–15,282	–20,334	–26,903	–30,323	–30,045
Total Revenue and Grants	81y	31,657	37,551	43,896	50,291	57,749	66,908	76,961	87,200	99,803	105,834	115,362	121,101	126,104	127,433	134,130
Revenue	81	....	....	....	....	....	....	....	....	....	....	....	....	....	....	....
Grants	81z	....	....	....	....	....	....	....	....	....	....	....	....	....	....	....
Exp. & Lending Minus Repay.	82z	32,976	39,202	43,988	49,824	58,833	73,314	85,684	95,268	I 109,058	118,909	130,644	141,435	153,007	157,756	164,175
Expenditure	82	31,100	37,095	41,024	46,782	55,790	70,423	82,056	91,919	105,501	115,988	126,486	135,204	147,583	153,073	159,047
Lending Minus Repayments	83	1,876	2,107	2,964	3,042	3,043	2,891	3,628	3,349	I 3,557	2,921	4,158	6,231	5,424	4,683	5,128
Total Financing	80h	1,321	1,649	92	–467	1,084	6,406	8,723	8,068	9,255	13,075	15,282	20,334	26,903	30,323	30,045
Total Net Borrowing	84	1,809	1,860	1,069	2,800	2,810	6,195	7,615	8,016	8,958	10,596	16,863	19,786	27,223	30,115	28,362
Net Domestic	84a	1,819	1,884	1,083	2,821	2,826	6,206	7,627	8,016	8,958	10,596	16,863	20,387	27,364	30,329	28,968
Net Foreign	85a	–10	–24	–14	–21	–16	–11	–12	—	—	—	—	–601	–141	–214	–606
Use of Cash Balances	87	–488	–211	–977	–3,267	–1,726	211	1,108	52	297	2,479	–1,581	548	–320	208	1,683
Total Debt by Currency	88z	32,948	35,119	36,548	38,774	41,301	46,735	54,996	61,704	72,529	84,394	99,518	118,457	144,653	174,795	203,100
National	88b	32,850	35,045	36,488	38,735	41,278	46,723	54,996	61,704	72,529	84,394	99,518	118,457	144,653	174,795	203,100
Foreign	89b	98	74	60	39	23	12	—	—	—	—	—	—	—	—	—
General Government															*As Percent of*	
Deficit (-) or Surplus	80g	....	....	....	....	....	....	....	....	....	....	....	....	....	....	....
Debt	88g	....	....	....	....	....	....	....	....	....	....	....	....	....	....	....

1985	1986	1987	1988	1989	1990	1991	1992	1993	1994	1995	1996	1997	1998	1999		
Minus Sign Indicates Debit															Balance of Payments	
4,248	4,318	4,187	7,132	10,039	9,221	7,841	7,423	13,594	17,873	24,144	21,637	27,449	25,585	22,597	Current Account, n.i.e.	**78al *d***
68,294	78,662	92,146	103,389	108,155	130,002	130,759	137,332	127,876	141,810	175,315	175,266	166,967	171,088	167,994	Goods: Exports f.o.b.	**78aa *d***
-61,590	-71,254	-85,894	-93,317	-98,330	-117,944	-118,780	-125,024	-110,972	-123,124	-153,213	-154,885	-148,026	-153,068	-151,802	Goods: Imports f.o.b.	**78ab *d***
6,704	7,408	6,252	10,072	9,825	12,058	11,979	12,309	16,904	18,686	22,102	20,381	18,942	18,020	16,191	*Trade Balance*	**78ac *d***
13,796	17,135	20,673	22,318	24,745	30,444	33,121	38,716	38,681	42,714	48,025	49,717	51,643	53,674	55,360	Services: Credit	**78ad *d***
-14,948	-18,346	-22,013	-24,505	-25,413	-29,708	-33,814	-38,451	-38,004	-41,303	-45,760	-45,830	-45,912	-47,829	-48,470	Services: Debit	**78ae *d***
5,553	6,196	4,912	7,885	9,156	12,795	11,285	12,573	17,581	20,096	24,368	24,268	24,672	23,865	23,081	*Balance on Goods & Services*	**78af *d***
9,465	12,708	15,840	18,365	23,602	26,265	27,807	27,615	28,120	29,100	35,119	36,544	41,978	47,267	43,368	Income: Credit	**78ag *d***
-9,701	-12,900	-14,514	-17,247	-20,781	-26,895	-27,121	-28,410	-27,607	-26,046	-28,911	-32,408	-33,081	-38,361	-37,851	Income: Debit	**78ah *d***
5,317	6,004	6,239	9,003	11,978	12,164	11,971	11,778	18,094	23,150	30,576	28,404	33,569	32,770	28,599	*Balance on Gds, Serv. & Inc.*	**78ai *d***
2,102	2,994	4,051	5,592	5,142	4,478	4,603	4,642	4,359	4,197	4,725	4,318	4,345	3,789	4,530	Current Transfers, n.i.e.: Credit	**78aj *d***
-3,172	-4,680	-6,103	-7,464	-7,081	-7,421	-8,733	-8,997	-8,860	-9,474	-11,157	-11,085	-10,465	-10,974	-10,531	Current Transfers: Debit	**78ak *d***
-47	-198	-233	-198	-314	-301	-282	-631	-715	-1,006	-1,096	-2,026	-1,289	-372	-533	Capital Account, n.i.e.	**78bc *d***
151	201	312	293	299	314	343	369	579	564	857	1,265	1,100	1,035	1,140	Capital Account, n.i.e.: Credit	**78ba *d***
-199	-399	-545	-490	-613	-615	-625	-1,000	-1,294	-1,569	-1,954	-3,291	-2,388	-1,408	-1,672	Capital Account: Debit	**78bb *d***
-2,373	-2,101	-1,283	-668	-8,249	-4,910	-5,772	-7,416	-10,773	-9,353	-17,506	-6,019	-16,473	-20,224	-18,875	Financial Account, n.i.e.	**78bj *d***
-2,705	-4,093	-8,658	-7,117	-14,859	-15,395	-13,563	-14,413	-12,043	-17,662	-20,133	-31,057	-29,380	-52,217	-42,708	Direct Investment Abroad	**78bd *d***
1,505	3,129	3,029	4,781	8,559	12,352	6,351	7,823	8,469	7,206	12,104	15,009	14,525	42,729	32,060	Dir. Invest. in Rep. Econ., n.i.e.	**78be *d***
-2,770	-8,000	-4,013	-6,947	-662	-3,547	-4,807	-13,398	-10,702	-9,570	-16,496	-25,013	-38,924	-67,542	-82,250	Portfolio Investment Assets	**78bf *d***
-186	-2,681	-1,264	-1,642	-2,326	-2,521	-3,789	-2,703	-4,235	-6,595	-8,729	-2,894	-12,122	-19,889	-33,548	Equity Securities	**78bk *d***
-2,584	-5,320	-2,749	-5,305	1,664	-1,026	-1,018	-10,696	-6,467	-2,975	-7,767	-22,119	-26,802	-47,652	-48,702	Debt Securities	**78bl *d***
2,710	2,132	6,667	10,340	8,307	-1,378	4,096	3,825	12,355	-886	6,088	13,468	17,704	35,318	76,426	Portfolio Investment Liab., n.i.e.	**78bg *d***
1,084	924	-245	832	2,211	-2,736	-1,336	-1,512	3,503	-1,385	-743	3,279	681	9,125	27,258	Equity Securities	**78bm *d***
1,626	1,208	6,913	9,508	6,096	1,358	5,432	5,337	8,852	499	6,831	10,189	17,023	26,193	49,169	Debt Securities	**78bn *d***
-24	-69	6	-24	-68	-41	15	-32	265	300	-627	-605	-957	-8	3,870	Financial Derivatives Assets	**78bw *d***
....	....	....	....	....	....	....	....	....	....	....	....	....	....	....	Financial Derivatives Liabilities	**78bx *d***
-5,171	-6,638	-12,389	-14,054	-28,750	-24,353	-6,009	-7,189	-12,305	6,884	-6,965	1,522	-36,692	-55,536	-33,682	Other Investment Assets	**78bh *d***
—	—	—	—	-1	—	-1	—	—	—	—	—	—	—	-18,783	Monetary Authorities	**78bo *d***
-154	-813	-384	-983	-658	-368	265	-324	-189	-44	10	-271	148	-54	-3,518	General Government	**78bp *d***
-3,816	-3,501	-9,742	-11,337	-27,160	-22,212	-4,637	-4,200	-7,884	9,437	-3,471	2,928	-31,243	-49,383	-1,780	Banks	**78bq *d***
-1,201	-2,325	-2,263	-1,734	-932	-1,773	-1,637	-2,665	-4,232	-2,510	-3,503	-1,135	-5,597	-6,098	-9,601	Other Sectors	**78br *d***
4,082	11,439	14,075	12,352	19,224	27,452	8,145	15,968	3,189	4,374	8,524	20,658	57,251	77,031	27,409	Other Investment Liab., n.i.e.	**78bi *d***
21	55	-167	-59	57	-9	430	-309	99	91	-135	-43	42	933	20,897	Monetary Authorities	**78bs *d***
66	230	87	239	209	-20	-185	-183	166	1,151	24	-132	-536	279	271	General Government	**78bt *d***
3,700	9,765	11,125	10,962	12,984	20,914	3,940	17,023	3,122	-493	4,172	15,697	52,197	59,531	12,209	Banks	**78bu *d***
295	1,389	3,031	1,210	5,973	6,568	3,960	-562	-199	3,626	4,463	5,136	5,549	16,288	-5,969	Other Sectors	**78bv *d***
-1,056	-2,350	22	-4,698	-969	-3,743	-1,281	6,742	4,535	-7,013	-7,454	-19,286	-12,394	-7,327	-8,283	Net Errors and Omissions	**78ca *d***
771	-330	2,693	1,568	507	268	506	6,118	6,641	500	-1,912	-5,694	-2,707	-2,339	-5,094	*Overall Balance*	**78cb *d***
-771	330	-2,693	-1,568	-507	-268	-506	-6,118	-6,641	-500	1,912	5,694	2,707	2,339	5,094	Reserves and Related Items	**79da *d***
-771	330	-2,693	-1,568	-507	-268	-506	-6,118	-6,641	-500	1,912	5,694	2,707	2,339	5,094	Reserve Assets	**79db *d***
—	—	—	—	—	—	—	—	—	—	—	—	—	—	—	Use of Fund Credit and Loans	**79dc *d***
....	....	....	....	....	....	....	....	....	....	....	....	....	....	....	Exceptional Financing	**79de *d***
Millions of US Dollars															International Investment Position	
178,433	234,170	297,944	301,811	352,039	417,924	451,954	456,628	492,662	540,789	642,677	690,726	739,455	3,881	3,599	Assets	**79aa *d***
47,772	59,352	75,123	76,586	92,266	113,438	124,900	129,870	130,665	155,284	185,787	208,534	214,704	....	....	Direct Investment Abroad	**79ab *d***
22,671	36,921	47,068	54,275	61,169	64,205	78,038	84,501	106,470	119,466	164,013	204,757	244,160	....	....	Portfolio Investment	**79ac *d***
10,473	18,111	21,772	25,856	34,038	33,254	42,095	44,209	59,663	67,258	91,748	107,708	127,315	....	....	Equity Securities	**79ad *d***
12,198	18,809	25,296	28,419	27,131	30,951	35,943	40,292	46,807	52,207	72,265	97,049	116,845	....	....	Debt Securities	**79ae *d***
—	—	—	—	—	—	—	—	—	—	—	—	—	....	....	Financial Derivatives	**79al *d***
85,787	109,159	137,983	136,463	164,099	205,226	215,308	205,329	210,799	218,134	245,695	237,843	247,876	....	....	Other Investment	**79af *d***
—	—	—	—	—	—	—	—	—	—	—	—	—	....	....	Monetary Authorities	**79ag *d***
3,948	10,085	14,875	15,553	17,536	19,424	22,113	20,804	20,493	22,441	23,983	23,124	21,255	....	....	General Government	**79ah *d***
69,871	82,635	100,408	98,930	123,878	158,062	164,176	154,180	158,774	159,051	179,829	174,049	184,680	....	....	Banks	**79ai *d***
11,968	16,438	22,699	21,979	22,684	27,740	29,019	30,345	31,532	36,643	41,884	40,670	41,940	....	....	Other Sectors	**79aj *d***
22,203	28,739	37,771	34,487	34,504	35,054	33,708	36,928	44,729	47,904	47,182	39,592	32,716	3,881	3,599	Reserve Assets	**79ak *d***
136,545	186,668	239,095	241,512	292,266	354,124	385,581	401,448	433,944	482,768	582,524	651,759	718,935	—	—	Liabilities	**79la *d***
24,952	35,213	46,566	45,882	56,536	75,581	80,423	83,500	85,185	106,292	128,503	134,607	130,527	....	....	Dir. Invest. in Rep. Economy	**79lb *d***
42,963	56,577	70,349	77,163	99,783	102,484	120,912	132,134	164,631	176,409	225,267	276,532	322,676	....	....	Portfolio Investment	**79lc *d***
27,430	37,181	37,075	42,661	57,478	55,976	66,476	65,818	92,380	105,239	129,955	179,628	223,676	....	....	Equity Securities	**79ld *d***
15,533	19,396	33,275	34,502	42,305	46,508	54,436	66,317	72,252	71,171	95,312	96,904	99,000	....	....	Debt Securities	**79le *d***
—	—	—	—	—	—	—	—	—	—	—	—	—	....	....	Financial Derivatives	**79ll *d***
68,630	94,879	122,180	118,467	135,947	176,059	184,246	185,814	184,128	200,066	228,753	240,620	265,731	—	—	Other investment	**79lf *d***
554	235	94	26	87	85	245	38	152	263	141	79	64	—	—	Monetary Authorities	**79lg *d***
—	4,286	6,313	5,806	7,492	7,918	10,490	9,299	9,504	10,865	11,535	10,988	9,942	....	....	General Government	**79lh *d***
64,537	82,084	103,710	101,895	112,330	143,889	145,823	151,031	149,026	158,186	184,128	195,870	222,399	....	....	Banks	**79li *d***
3,539	8,274	12,062	10,740	16,038	24,167	27,688	25,446	25,446	30,752	32,949	33,683	33,326	....	....	Other Sectors	**79lj *d***
															Government Finance	
Millions of Euros Beginning 1999: Year Ending December 31															*Central Government*	
-23,028	-6,718	-15,013	-20,346	-20,141	-20,177	-18,564	-19,352	-7,818	1,095	-23,155	-9,169	-10,805	-5,029	938	Deficit (-) or Surplus	**80**
145,605	166,488	161,921	152,559	151,530	166,056	182,929	182,839	204,097	198,951	204,753	188,387	197,168	209,808	106,151	Total Revenue and Grants	**81y**
....	166,467	161,909	152,526	151,482	166,015	182,918	182,837	204,075	198,942	204,733	188,373	196,853	209,517	106,078	Revenue	**81**
....	21	12	33	48	41	11	2	22	9	20	14	315	291	73	Grants	**81z**
168,633	173,206	176,934	172,905	171,671	186,233	201,493	202,191	211,915	197,856	227,908	197,556	207,973	214,837	105,213	Exp. & Lending Minus Repay.	**82z**
166,351	184,565	187,054	175,016	173,604	186,491	201,196	201,853	222,579	218,364	254,827	197,556	209,287	218,446	....	Expenditure	**82**
2,282	-11,359	-10,120	-2,111	-1,933	-258	297	338	-10,664	-20,508	-26,919	—	-1,314	-3,609	....	Lending Minus Repayments	**83**
23,028	6,718	15,013	20,346	20,141	20,177	18,564	19,352	7,818	-1,095	23,155	9,169	10,805	5,029	-938	Total Financing	**80h**
24,768	9,170	12,545	20,663	17,038	21,198	21,232	18,600	12,693	-17	28,966	9,431	-4,179	15,198	-4,496	Total Net Borrowing	**84**
24,811	9,852	12,995	22,469	19,752	22,961	21,780	20,091	13,220	-1,687	28,824	9,888	-4,076	13,353	2,165	Net Domestic	**84a**
-43	-682	-450	-1,806	-2,714	-1,763	-548	-1,491	-527	1,670	142	-457	-103	1,845	-6,661	Net Foreign	**85a**
-1,740	-2,452	2,468	-317	3,103	-1,021	-2,668	752	-4,875	-1,078	-5,811	-262	14,984	-10,169	3,558	Use of Cash Balances	**87**
228,283	238,735	251,157	274,473	293,842	317,666	338,535	358,007	371,209	374,645	399,825	410,989	417,467	431,383	200,984	Total Debt by Currency	**88z**
228,283	238,735	251,157	274,473	293,842	317,666	338,535	358,007	371,209	374,645	399,825	410,989	417,467	431,383	200,984	National	**88b**
—	—	—	—	—	—	—	—	—	—	—	—	—	—	—	Foreign	**89b**
Gross Domestic Product															*General Government*	
....	....	....	....	....	-5.1	-2.9	-3.9	-3.2	-3.8	-4.0	-1.8	-1.2	-.8	.5	Deficit (-) or Surplus	**80g**
....	....	....	....	....	79.1	78.9	79.9	81.1	77.9	79.0	75.3	70.3	67.0	63.8	Debt	**88g**

Netherlands

		1970	1971	1972	1973	1974	1975	1976	1977	1978	1979	1980	1981	1982	1983	1984
National Accounts															*Billions of Guilders through 1998;*
Househ.Cons.Expend.,incl.NPISHs	**96f.** *c*	70.8	78.9	88.5	99.8	113.4	129.0	148.0	164.3	179.2	192.4	205.8	213.2	221.8	229.9	236.8
Government Consumption Expend	**91f.** *c*	18.7	21.9	24.4	27.4	32.5	38.3	43.5	47.9	52.6	57.2	60.3	62.8	65.1	66.6	66.4
Gross Fixed Capital Formation	**93e.** *c*	31.4	34.6	36.4	40.7	43.9	46.3	49.0	57.9	63.3	66.5	70.8	67.6	67.2	69.5	74.3
Changes in Inventories	**93i.** *c*	2.5	1.5	.7	2.5	4.6	−.9	3.0	1.5	1.8	1.5	1.7	−3.1	−1.0	.6	2.0
Exports of Goods & Services	**90c.** *c*	54.3	62.0	69.4	83.4	107.8	109.7	128.5	130.7	133.3	155.1	176.8	204.6	212.6	219.8	248.6
Imports of Goods & Services	**98c.** *c*	−56.4	−62.4	−65.2	−77.8	−102.3	−102.3	−119.9	−127.4	−133.2	−156.7	−178.6	−192.2	−196.8	−205.2	−227.8
Gross Domestic Product (GDP)	**99b.** *c*	121.2	136.5	154.3	176.0	199.8	220.0	251.9	274.9	297.0	316.0	336.7	352.9	368.9	381.0	400.3
Net Primary Income from Abroad	**98.n**	.6	.4	.7	1.3	1.7	—	.1	.2	−1.0	−1.1	−1.6	−1.9	−1.7	−.2	−.6
Gross National Income (GNI)	**99a**	121.7	136.9	155.0	177.3	201.5	219.9	252.1	279.0	293.6	318.8	340.4	356.3	374.9	387.0	404.1
GDP Volume 1995 Ref., Chained	**99b.** *r*	355.9	369.4	378.4	396.6	411.8	412.9	431.4	444.0	455.8	455.2	469.9	462.6	457.6	465.9	479.2
GDP Volume (1995=100)	**99bv** *r*	55.6	57.8	59.2	62.0	64.4	64.6	67.4	69.4	71.3	71.2	73.5	72.3	71.5	72.8	74.9
GDP Deflator (1995=100)	**99bi** *r*	34.1	36.9	40.8	44.4	48.5	53.3	58.4	61.9	65.2	69.4	71.7	76.3	80.6	81.8	83.5
																Millions:
Population	**99z**	13.03	13.19	13.33	13.44	13.54	13.65	13.77	13.85	13.94	14.03	14.14	14.25	14.31	14.36	14.42

	1985	1986	1987	1988	1989	1990	1991	1992	1993	1994	1995	1996	1997	1998	1999	National Accounts
Billions of Euros Beginning 1999:																
	252.9	260.2	267.9	271.6	284.5	303.1	322.5	340.9	352.0	368.1	379.6	398.5	419.4	445.3	‖185.2	Househ.Cons.Expend.,incl.NPISHs .... **96f.** *c*
	66.9	67.7	69.8	70.2	71.8	74.8	77.9	83.0	84.7	86.5	89.1	92.4	97.4	102.2	‖85.5	Government Consumption Expend .... **91f.** *c*
	83.7	89.4	91.6	97.4	104.1	107.9	110.8	113.3	111.7	117.3	124.8	131.6	142.4	149.9	‖82.3	Gross Fixed Capital Formation .... **93e.** *c*
	1.4	3.8	–.4	.3	5.4	6.5	5.2	3.1	–2.4	4.3	3.8	–3.5	1.0	2.0	‖–1.0	Changes in Inventories .... **93i.** *c*
	258.7	222.0	219.3	240.3	267.7	279.7	293.1	294.9	292.7	312.1	336.3	354.9	384.7	414.7	‖223.8	Exports of Goods & Services................. **90c.** *c*
	–238.3	–205.4	–207.6	–222.4	–248.8	–255.8	–267.4	–269.2	–259.7	–279.8	–298.9	–318.7	–346.5	–364.4	‖–206.3	Imports of Goods & Services .... **98c.** *c*
	425.4	437.7	440.6	457.4	484.7	516.3	542.2	566.1	579.0	608.4	639.7	661.8	703.4	750.6	‖369.5	Gross Domestic Product (GDP)........... **99b.** *c*
	–.8	–.7	–1.2	–3.5	–.2	–.9	–.9	–2.3	–.6	1.7	8.0	3.5	13.1	8.6	‖3.0	Net Primary Income from Abroad **98.n**
	425.5	437.2	439.7	454.2	484.8	515.6	541.6	563.8	580.9	616.0	674.0	697.8	748.0	784.8	‖372.5	Gross National Income (GNI) **99a**
	494.8	510.1	517.2	530.3	555.2	577.4	590.3	601.9	605.8	625.0	639.7	659.6	683.7	708.9	‖347.0	GDP Volume 1995 Ref., Chained......... **99b.** *r*
	77.4	79.7	80.9	82.9	86.8	90.3	92.3	94.1	94.7	97.7	100.0	103.1	106.9	110.8	119.6	GDP Volume (1995=100).................... **99bv** *r*
	85.9	85.8	85.2	86.2	87.3	89.4	91.9	94.0	95.6	97.3	100.0	100.3	102.9	105.9	106.5	GDP Deflator (1995=100) .... **99bi** *r*
Midyear Estimates																
	14.48	14.56	14.66	14.76	14.85	14.95	15.07	15.18	15.29	15.38	15.46	15.53	15.60	15.71	15.81	**Population**.. **99z**

(See notes in the back of the book.)

Netherlands Antilles

		1970	1971	1972	1973	1974	1975	1976	1977	1978	1979	1980	1981	1982	1983	1984
Exchange Rates														*Guilders per SDR: End of Period (aa)*		
Official Rate	aa	1.874	1.954	1.954	2.171	2.204	2.107	2.091	2.186	2.345	2.371	2.296	2.095	1.986	1.885	1.764
Official Rate	ae	1.874	1.800	1.800	1.800	1.800	1.800	1.800	1.800	1.800	1.800	1.800	1.800	1.800	1.800	1.800
														Index Numbers (1995=100):		
Official Rate	ahx	95.5	95.4	99.4	99.4	99.4	99.4	99.4	99.4	99.4	99.4	99.4	99.4	99.4	99.4	99.4
Nominal Effective Exchange Rate	nec	....	....	....	....	....	....	....	....	....	....	57.7	57.6	60.3	61.6	64.1	68.5
Real Effective Exchange Rate	rec	....	....	....	....	....	....	....	....	....	101.7	102.4	108.7	110.5	113.8	118.0
International Liquidity												*Millions of US Dollars Unless Otherwise Indicated:*				
Total Reserves minus Gold	1l.d	25	36	50	50	62	71	93	101	67	73	95	135	187	164	118
Foreign Exchange	1d.d	25	36	50	50	62	71	93	101	67	73	95	135	187	164	118
Gold (Million Fine Troy Ounces)	1ad	.558	.548	.548	.548	.548	.548	.548	.548	.548	.548	.548	.548	.548	.548	.548
Gold (National Valuation)	1and	19	19	21e	23e	23	23	23	23	23	23	23	23	23	23	23
Monetary Authorities: Other Liab.	4..d	1		2	2	3	3	3	1	8	1		—		—	
Deposit Money Banks: Assets	7a.d	118	143	148	125	118	125	318	584	887	1,529	2,634	3,055	3,341	2,459	1,331
Liabilities	7b.d	115	137	152	122	115	113	289	570	881	1,526	2,631	3,043	3,322	2,443	1,303
OBU: Assets	7k.d	....	....	....	....	....	....	1,228	1,799	2,283	3,588	4,759	7,513	8,512	7,788	6,377
Liabilities	7m.d	....	....	....	....	....	....	1,154	1,706	2,099	3,360	4,503	7,207	8,097	7,435	5,886
Monetary Authorities															*Millions of Guilders*	
Foreign Assets	11	78.3	105.0	125.7	127.8	149.2	168.1	206.9	217.3	161.1	172.5	211.2	285.9	375.5	337.3	253.4
Claims on Central Government	12a	3.7	6.3	14.3	26.1	56.5	94.7	96.9	93.2	134.4	131.4	111.1	101.5	100.4	111.0	119.7
Reserve Money	14	69.8	95.5	109.9	118.0	127.6	162.7	175.2	201.2	199.8	228.1	247.5	251.6	269.8	247.1	220.6
of which: Currency Outside DMBs	14a	52.6	56.1	60.4	62.8	76.8	88.0	94.7	104.9	125.8	137.7	139.2	161.6	167.0	162.6	167.8
Time Deposits	15	—	—	—	—	23.0	44.0	55.0	38.0	12.0	—	—	26.5	86.4	81.4	32.4
Foreign Liabilities	16c	1.2	—	3.1	3.5	6.0	6.0	6.0	2.0	14.5	1.4	.4	.1	.1	.6	.4
Central Government Deposits	16d	—	.7	8.0	8.6	15.0	13.7	26.2	29.1	25.0	28.7	26.7	39.7	31.4	44.2	43.2
Capital Accounts	17a	9.7	12.6	15.0	23.1	27.1	35.2	35.4	37.2	39.9	42.3	45.9	52.1	63.8	63.8	63.8
Other Items (Net)	17r	1.3	2.5	3.9	.7	7.0	1.2	6.0	3.0	4.3	3.4	1.9	17.4	24.4	11.1	12.7
Deposit Money Banks															*Millions of Guilders:*	
Reserves	20	17.6	38.7	37.4	55.0	39.2	70.0	77.2	81.4	51.7	76.8	84.8	73.8	91.7	63.8	41.7
Foreign Assets	21	221.8	256.2	264.6	223.9	211.7	224.9	572.9	1,052.0	1,596.5	2,752.6	4,741.4	5,499.1	6,014.2	4,425.8	2,396.5
Claims on Local Government	22b	5.7	3.0	2.5	9.1	4.9	2.6	2.7	6.1	15.3	18.4	13.3	10.9	5.2	4.3	12.7
Claims on Private Sector	22d	226.5	244.3	305.5	327.8	379.1	374.5	409.4	492.6	624.1	658.5	746.8	895.5	979.4	1,112.1	1,112.5
Demand Deposits	24	59.1	72.8	91.7	98.5	98.9	115.7	135.3	159.6	197.7	192.6	197.6	221.0	269.1	280.8	251.1
Time and Savings Deposits	25a	124.3	154.1	180.1	205.4	250.3	275.6	310.1	340.4	397.7	427.5	504.1	595.9	699.6	744.2	754.0
Foreign Currency Deposits	25b	32.0	31.0	34.0	37.7	44.7	45.5	50.4	65.2	62.2	77.1	90.0	110.5	98.2	117.3	133.9
Foreign Liabilities	26c	216.5	244.6	271.5	218.5	207.8	202.5	519.7	1,026.3	1,586.1	2,746.9	4,735.8	5,476.9	5,979.9	4,398.0	2,345.5
Central Government Deposits	26d	4.3	6.4	4.2	5.4	4.2	4.2	4.8	5.2	5.1	4.8	7.5	5.7	7.2	7.0	6.8
Capital Accounts	27a	29.0	29.8	31.9	33.2	29.1	34.8	44.4	47.7	53.9	70.1	81.1	95.2	105.8	116.9	135.0
Other Items (Net)	27r	6.4	3.5	−3.4	17.1	−.1	−6.1	−3.2	−12.3	−15.1	−12.7	−29.8	−26.1	−69.3	−58.2	−62.9
Girosystem Curacao																
Private Sector Deposits	24.. i	5.0	6.3	11.1	11.3	11.1	15.5	14.6	30.4	28.0	25.5	26.2	24.2	27.6	28.8	36.7
Central Government Deposits	26d. i	2.0	2.0	6.0	2.8	6.4	5.8	3.7	3.6	8.0	41.6	37.0	32.8	31.9	32.1	32.3
Monetary Survey															*Millions of Guilders*	
Foreign Assets (Net)	31n	82.4	116.6	115.7	129.7	147.1	184.5	254.1	241.0	157.0	176.8	216.4	308.0	409.7	364.5	304.0
Domestic Credit	32	238.1	255.4	323.0	366.2	436.7	473.8	496.3	608.1	804.4	840.5	914.9	1,050.6	1,180.8	1,302.8	1,324.6
Claims on Central Govt. (Net)	32an	−2.6	−2.8	−3.7	9.6	31.0	71.2	62.6	71.6	125.3	93.6	90.2	86.0	135.6	124.5	129.5
Claims on Local Government	32b	12.7	11.3	19.6	23.6	22.6	24.2	21.0	40.6	51.8	86.0	76.9	68.3	65.1	65.5	82.0
Claims on Private Sector	32d	228.0	246.9	307.1	333.0	383.1	378.4	412.7	495.9	627.3	660.9	747.8	896.3	980.1	1,112.8	1,113.1
Money	34	117.2	135.8	173.7	173.9	198.3	223.6	247.9	309.8	373.8	369.4	386.5	423.0	474.8	493.0	466.7
Quasi-Money	35	156.3	185.1	214.1	243.1	318.0	365.1	415.5	443.6	471.9	504.6	594.1	732.9	884.2	942.9	920.3
Other Items (Net)	37r	47.0	51.1	50.8	78.9	67.5	69.8	86.3	95.7	115.7	143.3	150.8	202.5	231.5	231.3	241.6
Money plus Quasi-Money	35l	273.5	320.9	387.8	417.0	516.3	588.7	663.4	753.4	845.7	874.0	980.6	1,155.9	1,359.0	1,435.9	1,387.0
Interest Rates															*Percent Per Annum*	
Discount Rate (End of Period)	60	....	....	....	....	....	....	....	....	....	....	9.00	9.00	9.00	8.00	8.00
Treasury Bill Rate	60c	....	....	....	....	....	....	....	....	....	....	....	....	7.50	7.25	7.35
Deposit Rate	60l	....	....	....	....	....	....	....	....	....	....	....	....	5.10	5.20
Lending Rate	60p	....	....	....	....	9.25	9.13	9.75	9.75	11.40	11.88	11.88	11.40	11.00	11.20
Government Bond Yield	61	....	....	....	....	....	....	....	....	....	....	....	....	....	10.65	10.63
Prices and Labor															*Index Numbers (1995=100):*	
Consumer Prices	64	〽25.0	25.6	26.6	28.8	34.4	〽39.7	41.8	44.1	47.7	53.1	60.9	68.3	72.5	〽74.5	76.1
															Number in Thousands:	
Labor Force	67d	....	....	....	....	....	....	....	....	....	....	....	....	....	....	....
Employment	67e	....	....	....	....	....	....	....	....	....	....	....	....	....	....	....
Unemployment	67c	....	....	....	....	....	....	....	....	....	....	....	....	....	....	....
Unemployment Rate (%)	67r	....	....	....	....	....	....	....	....	....	....	....	....	....	....	....

	1985	1986	1987	1988	1989	1990	1991	1992	1993	1994	1995	1996	1997	1998	1999		
Guilders per US Dollar: End of Period (ae)																**Exchange Rates**	
	1.977	2.202	2.554	2.422	2.352	2.547	2.560	2.461	2.459	2.613	2.661	2.574	2.415	2.520	2.457	Official Rate..............................	**aa**
	1.800	1.800	1.800	1.800	1.790	1.790	1.790	1.790	1.790	1.790	1.790	1.790	1.790	1.790	1.790	Official Rate..............................	**ae**
Period Averages																	
	99.4	99.4	99.4	99.4	99.8	100.0	100.0	100.0	100.0	100.0	100.0	100.0	100.0	100.0	100.0	Official Rate	**ah x**
	70.5	67.9	69.9	70.2	79.5	81.8	85.5	87.5	95.9	101.4	100.0	105.5	112.4	115.5	117.8	Nominal Effective Exchange Rate	**ne c**
	116.7	110.3	111.2	107.2	111.7	107.1	107.5	103.2	106.3	104.5	100.0	103.4	109.1	110.0	107.7	Real Effective Exchange Rate	**re c**
End of Period																**International Liquidity**	
	176	239	217	263	207	215	177	220	234	179	203	189	214	248	265	Total Reserves minus Gold.....................	**1l.d**
	176	239	217	263	207	215	177	220	234	179	203	189	214	248	265	Foreign Exchange	**1d.d**
	.548	.548	.548	.548	.548	.548	.548	.548	.548	.548	.548	.548	.548	.548	.548	Gold (Million Fine Troy Ounces)...........	**1ad**
	23	38	38	38	38	38	38	38	38	38	117	106	106	100	100	Gold (National Valuation)	**1an d**
	1	1	—	—	—	—	1	—	2	26	32	10	8	1	1	Monetary Authorities: Other Liab.	**4..d**
	1,197	361	399	571	880	555	681	749	825	748	442	400	396	471	473	Deposit Money Banks: Assets	**7a.d**
	1,155	294	354	532	840	548	660	722	780	720	391	402	392	421	455	Liabilities...........	**7b.d**
	5,417	5,610	6,548	8,011	13,047	15,881	20,327	I 22,952	29,155	29,152	26,085	28,106	31,393	36,430	....	OBU: Assets	**7k.d**
	4,922	4,990	5,907	7,280	12,418	15,199	19,401	I 21,717	27,619	28,315	15,256	26,263	29,437	33,772	....	Liabilities.....................................	**7m.d**
End of Period																**Monetary Authorities**	
	367.6	501.4	459.3	538.2	445.2	454.0	385.1	461.8	490.1	435.2	683.3	546.5	591.5	625.9	655.1	Foreign Assets	**11**
	188.9	130.0	124.0	131.0	91.5	75.4	75.3	71.0	66.2	59.9	69.2	68.6	82.0	79.1	117.5	Claims on Central Government	**12a**
	385.2	469.0	426.1	434.5	302.0	355.6	294.3	380.2	401.0	375.0	449.6	385.2	445.2	489.1	460.0	Reserve Money	**14**
	137.5	122.2	124.4	128.0	144.6	160.8	168.2	178.6	184.5	198.2	209.6	195.6	188.0	186.6	197.0	*of which: Currency Outside DMBs*	**14a**
	2.0	2.1	2.3	59.2	17.5	17.6	26.8	2.9	11.0	13.2	30.3	—	—	—	—	Time Deposits	**15**
	1.3	2.3	.5	.6	.4	.8	1.2	.7	3.1	47.0	58.0	18.7	15.1	2.5	.9	Foreign Liabilities..............................	**16c**
	78.1	77.8	62.1	77.5	91.0	47.4	44.7	40.0	71.2	13.0	46.0	38.7	45.1	55.5	164.7	Central Government Deposits	**16d**
	63.8	44.6	54.7	63.5	63.5	66.4	66.4	65.8	65.8	65.8	201.6	185.4	185.4	182.4	182.4	Capital Accounts	**17a**
	26.1	35.4	37.7	33.8	62.3	41.6	27.0	43.2	4.2	–18.9	–33.0	–12.9	–17.3	–24.5	–35.4	Other Items (Net)	**17r**
End of Period																**Deposit Money Banks**	
	155.9	265.8	216.7	234.1	127.7	138.4	74.9	122.2	176.9	128.5	209.7	164.4	232.1	263.0	251.3	Reserves	**20**
	2,155.0	649.2	718.5	1,027.7	1,575.5	993.0	1,219.3	1,339.9	1,476.6	1,339.5	791.7	715.9	709.7	843.6	846.0	Foreign Assets	**21**
	9.5	3.0	4.1	5.2	1.5	9.8	72.1	94.7	125.1	126.5	103.1	158.5	142.8	121.5	126.9	Claims on Local Government	**22b**
	1,041.1	777.8	982.6	1,126.5	1,371.4	1,549.5	1,679.6	1,716.6	1,796.9	2,034.4	2,130.2	2,275.8	2,262.8	2,299.8	2,529.3	Claims on Private Sector	**22d**
	260.8	271.4	317.1	333.7	354.6	384.0	413.6	424.8	501.8	560.7	653.6	702.9	710.7	721.7	770.3	Demand Deposits	**24**
	741.8	663.5	697.5	784.6	789.9	869.1	912.8	1,018.6	1,136.5	1,201.7	1,231.4	1,266.4	1,325.7	1,417.1	1,484.6	Time and Savings Deposits	**25a**
	149.0	154.1	183.3	220.4	263.1	275.8	330.8	350.8	375.5	399.7	470.4	413.5	409.4	399.5	456.7	Foreign Currency Deposits	**25b**
	2,079.5	529.2	637.4	958.1	1,503.1	981.8	1,181.1	1,292.9	1,396.8	1,289.6	699.0	719.1	701.5	752.9	813.6	Foreign Liabilities...............................	**26c**
	9.0	14.1	11.9	11.1	19.6	36.9	50.9	47.5	39.0	36.0	22.6	36.5	45.7	46.2	30.0	Central Government Deposits	**26d**
	147.3	137.0	135.4	140.0	168.8	227.6	242.8	236.6	249.9	274.4	245.7	301.5	301.0	318.4	332.5	Capital Accounts	**27a**
	–25.8	–73.3	–70.6	–54.3	–23.2	–84.2	–86.1	–80.0	–124.0	–137.7	–88.0	–125.3	–146.6	–127.9	–134.2	Other Items (Net)	**27r**
																Girosystem Curacao	
	39.0	38.9	42.6	44.3	40.5	42.0	45.7	55.5	60.1	87.1	71.4	....	....	....	....	Private Sector Deposits	**24.. i**
	34.4	32.9	39.4	34.0	35.1	33.6	34.2	34.5	34.3	34.9	1.5	....	....	....	....	Central Government Deposits...............	**26d. i**
End of Period																**Monetary Survey**	
	441.8	619.1	539.9	607.2	517.2	464.4	422.1	508.1	566.8	438.1	718.0	524.6	584.6	714.1	686.6	Foreign Assets (Net)	**31n**
	1,243.5	939.4	1,147.8	1,291.1	1,462.9	1,676.7	1,845.2	1,944.5	2,055.9	2,382.0	2,423.3	2,510.7	2,485.9	2,503.4	2,664.6	Domestic Credit	**32**
	118.6	86.1	78.4	85.8	13.8	25.6	7.6	41.2	39.0	90.6	87.0	76.4	80.1	67.1	–6.6	Claims on Central Govt. (Net)	**32an**
	83.2	75.0	86.3	83.6	77.2	101.1	157.5	186.2	219.5	256.5	206.0	158.5	142.8	136.5	141.9	Claims on Local Government	**32b**
	1,041.7	778.3	983.1	1,126.7	1,371.9	1,550.0	1,680.1	1,717.1	1,797.4	2,034.9	2,130.3	2,275.8	2,263.0	2,299.8	2,529.3	Claims on Private Sector	**32d**
	527.7	513.5	569.1	578.4	569.4	643.2	678.7	738.3	786.0	894.3	964.9	923.7	923.8	947.8	979.0	Money	**34**
	892.8	819.7	883.1	1,064.2	1,070.5	1,162.5	1,270.4	1,372.3	1,523.0	1,614.6	1,732.1	1,679.9	1,735.1	1,816.6	1,941.3	Quasi-Money	**35**
	264.9	225.3	235.7	260.7	340.0	335.7	318.2	359.8	313.7	306.7	444.3	431.7	411.6	453.1	430.9	Other Items (Net)	**37r**
	1,420.5	1,333.2	1,452.2	1,642.6	1,639.9	1,805.7	1,949.1	2,110.6	2,309.0	2,508.9	2,697.0	2,603.6	2,658.9	2,764.4	2,920.3	Money plus Quasi-Money	**35l**
Percent Per Annum																**Interest Rates**	
	8.00	8.00	6.00	6.00	6.00	6.00	6.00	6.00	5.00	5.00	6.00	6.00	6.00	6.00	6.00	Discount Rate (*End of Period*)..................	**60**
	7.21	7.34	6.36	5.79	5.96	6.10	....	....	4.83	4.48	5.46	5.66	5.77	5.82	6.15	Treasury Bill Rate	**60c**
	5.20	5.19	4.82	4.63	4.71	4.97	....	....	4.33	4.05	3.75	3.67	3.66	3.58	3.59	Deposit Rate	**60l**
	11.46	11.59	11.37	11.24	11.23	9.25	....	....	12.59	12.73	12.93	13.21	13.29	13.58	13.60	Lending Rate	**60p**
	9.46	9.29	10.36	10.74	10.63	10.74	....	....	8.14	7.48	8.02	8.25	8.67	8.60		Government Bond Yield	**61**
Period Averages																**Prices and Labor**	
	76.4	77.4	80.3	82.4	85.6	I 88.8	92.4	93.7	95.6	97.3	100.0	I 103.6	107.0	108.2	....	Consumer Prices....................................	**64**
Period Averages																	
	....	....	....	....	57	....	....	....	....	....	62	66	66	65	....	Labor Force	**67d**
	60	59	53	41	44	48	50	51	52	55	54	57	56	54	....	Employment..	**67e**
	....	....	....	13	11	10	9	8	8	8	8	9	10	11	....	Unemployment......................................	**67c**
	....	....	....	23.2	20.1	17.0	14.6	13.9	13.6	12.8	13.1	14.0	15.3	16.7	....	Unemployment Rate (%)	**67r**

Netherlands Antilles

353

		1970	1971	1972	1973	1974	1975	1976	1977	1978	1979	1980	1981	1982	1983	1984
International Transactions																*Millions of Guilders*
Exports	70	1,275	1,366	1,364	2,465	5,815	4,315	4,544	4,764	5,357	7,139	9,292	9,750	8,803	7,937	6,719
Imports, c.i.f.	71	1,504	1,661	1,565	2,868	6,536	5,088	6,601	5,631	6,284	7,911	10,216	10,551	9,157	8,148	7,258
Crude Petroleum	71aa	948	1,079	988	1,977	5,409	3,490	5,207	4,129	....	....	....	....	....	....	....
Imports, f.o.b.	71.v	1,327	1,411	1,338	2,452	5,588	4,350	5,894	5,029	5,612	7,065	9,123	9,422	8,178	7,276	6,480
Balance of Payments																*Millions of US Dollars:*
Current Account, n.i.e.	78al d	....	....	....	....	....	....	−83.0	56.6	−24.8	23.8	.6	52.9	178.0	87.6	175.4
Goods: Exports f.o.b.	78aa d	....	....	....	....	....	....	2,905.9	3,209.7	3,165.8	4,602.2	6,380.6	6,173.1	5,265.1	4,794.9	3,949.1
Goods: Imports f.o.b.	78ab d	....	....	....	....	....	....	−3,058.3	−3,312.7	−3,330.6	−4,459.4	−6,503.9	−6,360.2	−5,481.3	−4,966.1	−4,248.8
Trade Balance	78ac d							−152.4	−102.9	−164.7	142.8	−123.3	−187.1	−216.2	−171.1	−299.8
Services: Credit	78ad d							405.2	516.7	565.3	690.0	878.3	1,010.9	964.8	733.6	697.7
Services: Debit	78ae d							−289.7	−316.6	−330.0	−413.3	−529.1	−564.0	−557.6	−520.2	−454.7
Balance on Goods & Services	78af d							−36.9	97.1	70.6	419.5	225.9	259.8	191.0	42.3	−56.8
Income: Credit	78ag d							20.2	39.4	44.8	63.9	13.9	25.5	24.1	18.5	72.8
Income: Debit	78ah d							−104.5	−109.9	−192.8	−507.9	−343.1	−286.8	−118.8	−103.8	4.9
Balance on Gds, Serv. & Inc.	78ai d							−121.3	26.6	−77.4	−24.6	−103.3	−1.5	96.3	−43.0	20.9
Current Transfers, n.i.e.: Credit	78aj d							51.7	48.9	72.8	71.7	129.4	121.1	152.2	213.3	253.9
Current Transfers: Debit	78ak d							−13.4	−18.9	−20.2	−23.3	−25.6	−66.7	−70.6	−82.8	−99.4
Capital Account, n.i.e.	78bc d							−2.3	−3.5	−2.7	−5.0	−6.1	−3.6	−5.6	−6.3	−8.0
Capital Account, n.i.e.: Credit	78ba d							.6	.6	1.7	1.1	.6	1.2	1.3	.8	1.1
Capital Account: Debit	78bb d							−2.8	−4.1	−4.4	−6.1	−6.7	−4.7	−6.9	−7.1	−9.1
Financial Account, n.i.e.	78bj d							115.0	−52.2	−23.9	−23.3	20.0	−6.6	−129.3	−129.1	−193.2
Direct Investment Abroad	78bd d							−1.1	−1.1	−2.8	−3.9	−.6	−.7	−.6	−.9	−1.7
Dir. Invest. in Rep. Econ., n.i.e.	78be d							1.1	4.4	13.3	278.3	35.0	15.1	−153.9	−95.6	3.4
Portfolio Investment Assets	78bf d							−2.2	−3.9	−15.0	−14.4	−10.0	−28.7	−19.5	−31.3	−37.3
Equity Securities	78bk d							—	—	—	—	—	—	—	—	—
Debt Securities	78bl d							−2.2	−3.9	−15.0	−14.4	−10.0	−28.7	−19.5	−31.3	−37.3
Portfolio Investment Liab., n.i.e.	78bg d							.6	—	—	1.7	.6	−3.3	−2.4	−1.6	1.0
Equity Securities	78bm d							—	—	—	—	—	—	—	—	—
Debt Securities	78bn d							.6	—	—	1.7	.6	−3.3	−2.4	−1.6	1.0
Financial Derivatives Assets	78bw d							....	....	....	....	....	....	....	....	....
Financial Derivatives Liabilities	78bx d							....	....	....	....	....	....	....	....	....
Other Investment Assets	78bh d							−110.6	−337.2	−196.1	−842.2	−1,106.7	−411.8	62.6	−42.9	−117.6
Monetary Authorities	78bo d							....	....	....	....	....	....	....	....	....
General Government	78bp d							.6	3.9	10.0	.6	−7.8	7.9	−3.9	4.8	−1.7
Banks	78bq d							−180.6	−272.8	−316.1	−641.1	−1,097.2	−409.4	28.2	−23.3	−24.3
Other Sectors	78br d							69.4	−68.3	110.0	−201.7	−1.7	−10.3	38.3	−24.4	−91.7
Other Investment Liab., n.i.e.	78bi d							227.2	285.6	176.7	557.2	1,101.7	422.8	−15.5	43.2	−40.9
Monetary Authorities	78bs d							....	....	....	....	....	....	....	....	....
General Government	78bt d							13.9	8.9	—	10.6	25.0	21.7	14.3	23.3	23.7
Banks	78bu d							180.6	281.1	310.6	645.0	1,105.0	412.2	−34.3	18.8	19.3
Other Sectors	78bv d							32.8	−4.4	−133.9	−98.3	−28.3	−11.1	4.4	1.1	−83.9
Net Errors and Omissions	78ca d							4.9	−1.9	7.3	11.6	.3	10.3	7.8	21.6	−13.1
Overall Balance	78cb d							34.7	−1.1	−44.2	7.1	14.8	53.2	50.8	−26.3	−38.9
Reserves and Related Items	79da d							−34.7	1.1	44.2	−7.1	−14.8	−53.2	−50.8	26.3	38.9
Reserve Assets	79db d							−34.7	1.1	44.2	−7.1	−14.8	−53.2	−50.8	26.3	38.9
Use of Fund Credit and Loans	79dc d							—	—	—	—	—	—	—	—	—
Exceptional Financing	79de d							....	....	....	....	....	....	....	....	....
Government Finance																*Millions of Guilders:*
Deficit (-) or Surplus	80	....	....	....	−28.6	−35.5	−55.2	−21.4	−27.6	−71.3	−71.4	I−76.2	−100.8	−106.6	−87.9	−75.0
Revenue	81				119.1	112.9	85.1	125.8	138.4	177.6	213.3	I253.4	275.4	343.3	345.5	355.5
Grants Received	81z				19.6	16.9	27.2	27.0	21.5	26.7	33.4	I137.7	89.0	93.9	149.8	151.6
Expenditure	82				167.3	163.9	159.5	140.7	171.5	245.6	255.8	I465.2	459.6	540.8	556.9	570.4
Lending Minus Repayments	83				—	1.4	8.0	33.5	16.0	30.0	62.3	I2.1	5.6	3.0	26.3	11.7
Financing																
Domestic	84a	....	....	....	8.3	20.0	41.4	−4.2	11.0	58.3	50.0	I75.5	100.7	77.4	68.5	31.3
Foreign	85a				20.3	15.5	13.8	25.6	16.6	13.0	21.4	I.7	.1	29.2	19.4	43.7
Debt: Domestic	88a				3.7	3.4	3.1	2.8	24.6	65.8	105.2	I238.8	296.3	282.6	311.3	416.5
Foreign	89a				282.3	335.6	326.4	385.9	446.3	495.0	538.0	I525.8	499.6	449.9	542.4	403.0
																Millions:
Population	99z	.22	.23	.23	.23	.24	.24	I.24	.24	.23	.23	.19	.19	.18	.17	.18

Millions of Guilders

1985	1986	1987	1988	1989	1990	1991	1992	1993	1994	1995	1996	1997	1998	1999		
															International Transactions	
1,856	‡1,664	2,354	2,041	2,608	3,204	2,862	2,790	2,297	2,462	....	....	....	....	....	Exports	70
2,498	‡2,002	2,703	2,526	2,888	3,833	3,828	3,344	3,485	3,146	....	....	....	....	....	Imports, c.i.f.	71
....	....	....	....	....	....	....	....	....	....	....	....	....	....	....	Crude Petroleum	71aa
2,230	‡1,788	2,413	2,255	2,579	3,422	3,418	2,986	3,112	2,809	....	....	....	....	....	Imports, f.o.b.	71.v

Minus Sign Indicates Debit

1985	1986	1987	1988	1989	1990	1991	1992	1993	1994	1995	1996	1997	1998	1999		
															Balance of Payments	
403.1	50.7	-49.4	75.2	38.1	-44.0	-6.2	9.9	1.2	-97.9	86.5	....	....	....	....	Current Account, n.i.e.	78al d
1,810.8	155.0	157.2	225.8	313.4	302.7	301.8	332.3	306.0	351.1	354.2	....	....	....	....	Goods: Exports f.o.b.	78aa d
-2,132.3	-675.6	-771.7	-879.4	-1,017.8	-1,112.3	-1,118.9	-1,168.4	-1,143.8	-1,271.6	-1,318.7	....	....	....	....	Goods: Imports f.o.b.	78ab d
-321.5	-520.6	-614.4	-653.6	-704.4	-809.7	-817.2	-836.1	-837.8	-920.5	-964.4	....	....	....	....	*Trade Balance*	78ac d
674.2	646.3	671.1	892.6	960.8	1,161.4	1,227.9	1,339.6	1,346.0	1,414.2	1,686.8	....	....	....	....	Services: Credit	78ad d
-452.3	-284.4	-299.4	-378.2	-407.5	-518.2	-544.2	-606.9	-596.0	-670.5	-724.9	....	....	....	....	Services: Debit	78ae d
-99.6	-158.7	-242.8	-139.1	-151.1	-166.5	-133.5	-103.5	-87.8	-176.8	-2.6	....	....	....	....	*Balance on Goods & Services*	78af d
49.3	76.7	77.2	80.9	108.9	126.1	126.8	158.1	122.7	133.7	122.7	....	....	....	....	Income: Credit	78ag d
-19.5	-56.1	-41.1	-41.3	-73.0	-109.6	-109.6	-146.6	-140.3	-99.4	-130.9	....	....	....	....	Income: Debit	78ah d
-69.7	-138.2	-206.7	-99.5	-115.2	-149.9	-116.3	-92.0	-105.4	-142.5	-10.8	....	....	....	....	*Balance on Gds, Serv. & Inc.*	78ai d
565.6	277.2	241.1	268.7	260.9	213.1	228.7	217.4	250.3	217.9	245.9	....	....	....	....	Current Transfers, n.i.e.: Credit	78aj d
-92.8	-88.3	-83.9	-94.1	-107.6	-107.3	-118.6	-115.5	-143.7	-173.3	-148.5	....	....	....	....	Current Transfers: Debit	78ak d
-11.8	-6.1	-2.8	-2.9	-3.2	-1.7	-.7	-.6	-.8	-.7	-.8	....	....	....	....	Capital Account, n.i.e.	78bc d
.5	.6	.6	.4	.1	.5	.9	1.7	.8	1.0	1.4	....	....	....	....	Capital Account, n.i.e.: Credit	78ba d
-12.3	-6.7	-3.3	-3.3	-3.3	-2.2	-1.7	-2.3	-1.7	-1.7	-2.2	....	....	....	....	Capital Account: Debit	78bb d
-324.1	86.7	-12.1	-58.3	-93.7	9.4	-41.5	41.7	32.2	-2.3	31.1	....	....	....	....	Financial Account, n.i.e.	78bj d
3.3	-.8	-.1	-2.8	-4.8	-2.4	-1.1	-1.5	2.2	-1.0	-.7	....	....	....	....	Direct Investment Abroad	78bd d
-281.7	115.8	2.5	6.7	17.4	8.1	33.4	40.1	11.0	21.5	9.8	....	....	....	....	Dir. Invest. in Rep. Econ., n.i.e.	78be d
-48.6	-47.2	16.7	-55.1	-76.9	-50.3	-29.2	-21.6	-13.9	-69.1	-24.7	....	....	....	....	Portfolio Investment Assets	78bf d
—	—	—	—	—	—	—	—	—	—	—	....	....	....	....	Equity Securities	78bk d
-48.6	-47.2	16.7	-55.1	-76.9	-50.3	-29.2	-21.6	-13.9	-69.1	-24.7	....	....	....	....	Debt Securities	78bl d
6.1	-2.2	-2.8	-2.1	1.1	1.2	-1.5	2.8	1.5	10.9	1.7	....	....	....	....	Portfolio Investment Liab., n.i.e.	78bg d
—	—	—	—	—	—	—	—	—	—	—	....	....	....	....	Equity Securities	78bm d
6.1	-2.2	-2.8	-2.1	1.1	1.2	-1.5	2.8	1.5	10.9	1.7	....	....	....	....	Debt Securities	78bn d
....	....	....	....	....	....	....	....	....	....	....	....	....	....	....	Financial Derivatives Assets	78bw d
....	....	....	....	....	....	....	....	....	....	....	....	....	....	....	Financial Derivatives Liabilities	78bx d
76.0	-87.1	-73.6	-194.2	-335.5	-249.4	-165.8	-68.7	-38.4	15.3	83.6	....	....	....	....	Other Investment Assets	78bh d
....	....	....	....	....	....	....	....	....	....	....	....	....	....	....	Monetary Authorities	78bo d
6.3	7.8	-1.1	.7	-13.0	24.1	-40.5	—				....	....	....	....	General Government	78bp d
80.2	-111.0	-45.8	-182.1	-297.9	-290.8	-120.1	-61.0	-46.9	-55.8	-10.1	....	....	....	....	Banks	78bq d
-10.6	16.1	-26.7	-12.8	-24.6	17.4	-5.3	-7.7	8.5	71.1	93.7	....	....	....	....	Other Sectors	78br d
-79.2	108.2	45.3	189.1	305.0	302.1	122.7	90.6	69.8	20.1	-38.7	....	....	....	....	Other Investment Liab., n.i.e.	78bi d
....	....	....	....	....	....	....	....	....	....	....	....	....	....	....	Monetary Authorities	78bs d
20.4	18.9	12.8	6.3	14.3	-3.3	-7.9	.4	-9.5	-38.3	-17.6	....	....	....	....	General Government	78bt d
-84.1	110.4	59.7	177.6	303.9	290.1	114.6	60.6	59.7	59.7	4.4	....	....	....	....	Banks	78bu d
-15.6	-21.1	-27.2	5.2	-13.2	15.3	16.0	29.7	19.6	-1.3	-25.4	....	....	....	....	Other Sectors	78bv d
4.8	-33.4	34.7	19.5	14.6	6.5	6.2	8.2	11.5	24.9	22.5	....	....	....	....	Net Errors and Omissions	78ca d
71.9	97.9	-29.6	33.4	-44.2	-29.8	-42.2	59.2	44.0	-75.9	139.3	....	....	....	....	*Overall Balance*	78cb d
-71.9	-97.9	29.6	-33.4	44.2	29.8	42.2	-59.2	-44.0	75.9	-139.3	....	....	....	....	Reserves and Related Items	79da d
-71.9	-97.9	29.6	-33.4	44.2	29.8	42.2	-59.2	-44.0	75.9	-139.3	....	....	....	....	Reserve Assets	79db d
....	—	....	—	—	—	—	—	—	—	....	....	....	....	....	Use of Fund Credit and Loans	79dc d
											....	....	....	....	Exceptional Financing	79de d

Year Ending December 31

1985	1986	1987	1988	1989	1990	1991	1992	1993	1994	1995	1996	1997	1998	1999		
															Government Finance	
-20.8	‡-57.5	-55.6	-11.1	-60.1	-51.3	-44.9	-62.0	-25.2	-40.6[p]	‡-100.2	....	....	....	....	Deficit (-) or Surplus	80
356.4	‡320.2	334.1	365.2	337.7	438.0	463.1	517.0	587.8	663.3[p]	‡462.2	....	....	....	....	Revenue	81
200.5	‡112.0	149.0	145.9	77.3	56.2	78.3	67.0	105.0	91.9[p]	‡92.8	....	....	....	....	Grants Received	81z
552.6	‡488.5	536.9	521.4	475.1	536.0	586.7	638.0	719.4	795.4[p]	‡655.1	....	....	....	....	Expenditure	82
25.1	‡1.2	1.8	.8	—	9.5	-.4	8.0	-1.4	.4[p]	‡.1	....	....	....	....	Lending Minus Repayments	83
															Financing	
21.7	‡11.1	6.0	-24.4	75.1	-19.0	106.4	62.0	25.2	40.6[p]	‡100.2	....	....	....	....	Domestic	84a
-.9	‡46.4	49.6	35.5	-15.0	70.3	-61.5			—[p]	‡—	....	....	....	....	Foreign	85a
217.7	‡417.3	432.0	451.7	447.6	424.0	431.7	458.4	616.3	618.5[p]	‡704.6	....	....	....	....	Debt: Domestic	88a
541.1	‡215.5	260.0	248.9	235.4	307.0	208.5	187.8	170.9	—[p]	‡—	....	....	....	....	Foreign	89a

Midyear Estimates

1985	1986	1987	1988	1989	1990	1991	1992	1993	1994	1995	1996	1997	1998	1999		
.18	.18	.19	.19	.19	.19	.19	.19	.19	.20	.20	.21	.21	.21	.22	Population	99z

(See notes in the back of the book.)

New Zealand

		1970	1971	1972	1973	1974	1975	1976	1977	1978	1979	1980	1981	1982	1983	1984
Exchange Rates															SDRs per New Zealand Dollar:	
Market Rate	ac	1.1161	1.1008	1.1008	1.1841	1.0744	.8915	.8177	.8395	.8187	.7486	.7545	.7083	.6640	.6252	.4872
													US Dollars per New Zealand Dollar:			
Market Rate	ag	1.1161	1.1952	1.1952	1.4284	1.3155	1.0437	.9500	1.0197	1.0666	.9862	.9623	.8244	.7325	.6546	.4776
Market Rate	rh	1.1200	1.1361	1.1952	1.3615	1.4004	1.2157	.9963	.9708	1.0378	1.0229	.9742	.8700	.7519	.6688	.5785
													Index Numbers (1995=100):			
Market Rate	ahx	170.5	173.9	182.1	207.4	213.3	185.2	151.8	147.9	158.1	155.8	148.4	132.5	114.5	101.9	88.1
Nominal Effective Exchange Rate	nec	....	....	....	....	....	....	....	....	....	151.9	143.5	138.2	132.1	124.9	114.1
Real Effective Exchange Rate	rec	....	....	....	....	....	....	....	....	....	91.2	90.4	91.7	94.5	91.1	84.7
Fund Position															Millions of SDRs:	
Quota	2f. s	202	202	202	202	202	202	202	202	232	232	348	348	348	462	462
SDRs	1b. s	—	28	58	58	1	1	8	34	46	9	—	20	2	3	7
Reserve Position in the Fund	1c. s	51	51	51	51	—	—	—	—	23	—	28	28	—	28	—
Total Fund Cred.&Loans Outstg.	2tl	—	—	—	—	86	242	390	388	361	270	132	34	3	—	—
International Liquidity												Millions of US Dollars Unless Otherwise Indicated:				
Total Reserves minus Gold	1l. d	257	492	832	1,045	639	427	491	443	451	451	352	674	636	778	1,787
SDRs	1b. d	—	30	63	70	1	1	10	42	60	12	—	23	2	3	7
Reserve Position in the Fund	1c. d	51	55	55	61	—	—	—	—	30	—	35	32	—	30	—
Foreign Exchange	1d. d	206	407	714	914	638	426	481	401	361	439	317	619	634	745	1,780
Monetary Authorities	1da d	74	229	459	619	331	193	212	121	172	134	68	367	178	128	1,304
Government	1db d	132	178	255	295	307	233	269	280	189	305	249	252	456	617	476
Gold (Million Fine Troy Ounces)	1ad	.023	.023	.023	.023	.023	.023	.023	.044	.066	.045	.022	.022	.022	.022	.022
Gold (National Valuation)	1an d	1	1	1	1	1	1	1	2	3	2	1	1	1	1	1
Monetary Authorities: Other Liab.	4..d	10	4	1	—	51	199	278	345	373	381	573	1,012	1,071	866	776
Banking Institutions: Assets	7a. d	83	85	117	118	163	183	185	263	321	349	435	414	402	457	338
Liabilities	7b. d	18	26	74	80	140	142	106	137	140	152	182	159	208	346	318
Monetary Authorities															Millions of New Zealand Dollars:	
Foreign Assets	11	229	405	685	740	488	426	555	431	378	573	381	817	873	1,240	3,762
Claims on Central Government	12a	164	85	48	141	511	621	897	1,102	1,041	1,091	1,057	1,413	1,454	1,369	2,435
Claims on Banking Institutions	12e	30	8	—	—	15	—	3	5	186	22	31	34	54	51	12
Reserve Money	14	308	309	509	749	785	637	669	729	880	956	852	972	1,048	1,172	1,263
of which: Currency Outside DMBs	14a	195	212	242	290	336	352	418	460	536	590	577	683	714	739	867
Liabs.of Central Bank: Securities	16ac	....	....	....	....	....	....	....	....	....	....	....	....	....	....	....
Foreign Liabilities	16c	9	3	—	—	118	462	770	801	791	747	771	1,275	1,466	1,323	1,626
Central Government Deposits	16d	216	269	398	377	348	304	343	359	366	484	419	637	1,081	1,326	4,990
Capital Accounts	17a	44	66	86	86	117	102	113	118	132	179	215	267	287	323	402
Other Items (Net)	17r	−153	−148	−260	−331	−354	−457	−438	−469	−563	−679	−787	−886	−1,501	−1,485	−2,071
Banking Institutions															Millions of New Zealand Dollars:	
Reserves	20	96	81	228	335	286	112	131	118	128	118	93	109	116	140	87
Other Claims on Monetary Author.	20c	....	....	....	....	....	....	....	....	....	....	....	....	....	....	....
Foreign Assets	21	74	70	96	87	124	175	195	258	301	354	452	503	549	699	707
Claims on Central Government	22a	176	307	540	509	213	601	646	757	1,209	1,354	1,385	1,203	1,701	2,012	2,849
Claims on Private Sector	22d	688	726	789	1,227	1,555	1,679	2,073	2,458	3,001	3,635	4,230	5,305	6,002	6,569	7,843
Demand Deposits	24	654	724	956	1,151	1,115	1,245	1,385	1,370	1,637	1,741	1,876	2,129	2,259	2,629	2,855
Time, Savings,Fgn.Currency Dep.	25	307	410	630	930	1,022	1,155	1,526	1,995	2,537	3,369	3,829	4,481	5,419	5,581	7,079
of which: Fgn Currency Deposits	25b	....	....	....	....	....	....	....	....	....	....	....	....	....	....	....
Foreign Liabilities	26c	11	13	37	29	62	86	84	116	109	129	157	164	249	488	597
Central Government Deposits	26d	11	11	12	12	22	38	25	20	26	33	99	55	40	56	53
Capital Accounts	27a	....	....	....	....	....	....	....	....	....	....	....	....	....	....	....
Other Items (Net)	27r	52	26	17	37	−42	43	25	91	330	188	198	289	401	666	901
Banking Survey															Millions of New Zealand Dollars:	
Foreign Assets (Net)	31n	284	458	743	798	432	53	−104	−227	−220	50	−96	−119	−293	128	2,246
Domestic Credit	32	949	980	1,181	1,733	2,233	2,948	3,669	4,418	5,416	6,199	6,853	7,943	9,173	9,807	9,384
Claims on Central Govt. (Net)	32an	113	112	178	261	354	880	1,176	1,480	1,858	1,929	1,924	1,923	2,033	1,998	241
Claims on Local Government	32b	....	....	....	....	....	....	....	....	....	....	....	....	....	....	....
Claims on Private Sector	32d	836	867	1,003	1,472	1,879	2,068	2,493	2,938	3,558	4,271	4,929	6,020	7,140	7,809	9,143
Money	34	861	949	1,219	1,545	1,601	1,749	1,910	1,946	2,378	2,458	2,535	2,926	3,030	3,426	3,761
Quasi-Money	35	307	410	630	930	1,022	1,155	1,526	1,995	2,537	3,369	3,829	4,481	5,419	5,581	7,079
Capital Accounts	37a	44	66	86	86	117	102	113	118	132	179	215	267	287	323	402
Other Items (Net)	37r	21	14	−11	−30	−74	−5	16	131	149	243	178	150	145	605	388
Money plus Quasi-Money	35l	1,167	1,359	1,850	2,474	2,623	2,905	3,436	3,941	4,915	5,827	6,364	7,407	8,448	9,007	10,840
Money (National Definitions)																
M1	39ma	....	....	....	....	....	....	....	....	....	....	....	....	....	....	....
M2	39mb	....	....	....	....	....	....	....	....	....	....	....	....	....	....	....
M3R	39mc	....	....	....	....	....	....	....	....	....	....	....	....	....	....	....
M3	39md	....	....	....	....	....	....	....	....	....	....	....	16,009	18,066	20,669	25,020
Unused Overdrafts	39b	326	380	529	638	556	740	931	933	1,286	1,228	1,743	2,165	2,395	3,111	3,628
Other Banking Institutions															Millions of New Zealand Dollars:	
Claims on Central Government	42a. g	11.4	16.5	17.2	19.6	16.1	24.5	36.2	54.8	62.1	90.3	130.0	145.6	168.1	318.1	591.9
Claims on Private Sector	42d. g	144.8	192.0	249.8	334.5	317.4	378.8	546.9	826.7	954.5	1,187.5	1,497.7	1,974.7	2,591.2	3,135.7	3,995.4
Time Dep. Debentures & Notes	45.. g	122.0	169.9	204.9	240.2	203.8	270.2	466.8	693.5	812.6	1,048.9	1,332.0	1,762.4	2,326.0	2,974.9	3,974.4
Foreign Liabilities	46c. g	4.9	8.4	23.6	30.4	44.3	49.8	27.5	18.1	22.9	25.3	31.9	28.4	34.6	40.5	68.9
Cred.from Deposit Money Banks	46h. g	8.8	7.8	10.6	33.5	26.4	25.8	26.5	28.4	27.7	34.8	27.2	34.0	40.1	30.5	38.8
Capital Accounts	47a. g	27.0	37.5	47.8	65.0	67.1	70.7	88.2	131.2	150.5	158.2	206.9	241.5	292.3	352.4	425.5
Other Items (Net)	47r. g	−6.5	−15.1	−19.9	−14.9	−8.1	−13.2	−25.9	10.3	2.9	10.6	29.7	54.0	66.3	55.5	79.7
Post Office: Savings Deposits	45.. i	936.8	947.3	1,015.4	1,118.3	1,170.8	1,242.3	1,308.7	1,417.0	1,567.9	1,686.0	1,792.4	1,948.9	2,050.4	2,347.9	2,592.7
Trustee Savings Banks: Deposits	45.. k	476.1	510.2	590.2	707.5	758.3	850.0	944.9	1,075.7	1,357.1	1,567.6	1,872.5	2,242.1	2,493.3	2,989.5	3,399.4
Nonbank Financial Institutions															Millions of New Zealand Dollars:	
Claims on Central Government	42a. s	287.0	312.9	349.8	391.8	406.1	445.7	485.2	504.2	549.9	616.8	687.4	776.2	860.6	988.9	1,303.2
Claims on Local Government	42b. s	100.8	113.5	124.8	142.9	160.0	184.7	215.9	255.7	284.6	316.0	344.8	378.1	467.2	511.4	575.6
Claims on Private Sector	42d. s	800.7	850.9	918.8	989.0	1,080.7	1,153.1	1,251.2	1,359.5	1,462.3	1,584.9	1,776.9	1,997.6	2,240.0	2,517.1	2,789.6
Real Estate	42h. s	147.9	186.0	219.4	263.1	324.1	371.1	422.2	479.0	545.4	608.1	674.2	727.8	797.3	880.4	958.1
Incr.in Total Assets(Within Per.)	49z. s	134.1	126.2	154.4	174.5	188.2	185.0	218.6	233.5	258.5	295.6	343.7	419.3	477.8	585.0	770.1
Liquid Liabilities	55l	3,066.3	3,351.1	4,059.8	5,010.8	5,235.9	5,832.8	6,792.5	7,807.2	9,506.0	11,107.6	12,400.1	14,456.3	16,253.8	18,147.4	21,477.7

1985	1986	1987	1988	1989	1990	1991	1992	1993	1994	1995	1996	1997	1998	1999		
End of Period															**Exchange Rates**	
.4538	.4280	.4635	.4669	.4544	.4132	.3783	.3740	.4068	.4401	.4395	.4910	.4311	.3742	.3793	Market Rate	ac
End of Period (ag)			*Period Average (rh)*													
.4985	.5235	.6575	.6283	.5972	.5878	.5411	.5143	.5588	.6425	.6533	.7060	.5817	.5269	.5206	Market Rate	ag
.4984	.5239	.5922	.6560	.5985	.5970	.5792	.5381	.5407	.5937	.6564	.6876	.6630	.5367	.5295	Market Rate	rh
Period Averages																
75.9	79.8	90.2	99.9	91.2	90.9	88.2	82.0	82.4	90.4	100.0	104.8	101.0	81.8	80.7	Market Rate	ah x
105.0	97.0	100.0	104.9	99.1	95.1	92.3	84.5	89.1	95.2	100.0	107.4	110.9	95.0	92.5	Nominal Effective Exchange Rate	ne c
86.2	87.2	100.7	108.0	102.5	99.1	94.8	85.1	88.3	94.4	100.0	107.4	110.3	94.4	90.9	Real Effective Exchange Rate	re c
End of Period															**Fund Position**	
462	462	462	462	462	462	462	650	650	650	650	650	650	650	895	Quota	2f. s
6	9	1	1	—	—	—	—	—	—	1	—	—	1	5	SDRs	1b. s
—	—	—	8	40	40	54	109	104	101	110	127	132	253	309	Reserve Position in the Fund	1c. s
														—	Total Fund Cred.&Loans Outstg.	2tl
End of Period															**International Liquidity**	
1,596	3,771	3,260	2,836	3,027	4,129	2,950	3,079	3,337	3,709	4,410	5,953	4,451	4,204	4,455	Total Reserves minus Gold	1l. d
7	11	1	1	1	1	1	—	—	—	1	—	—	2	7	SDRs	1b. d
—	—	—	11	52	57	77	150	142	147	164	182	178	356	424	Reserve Position in the Fund	1c. d
1,589	3,760	3,258	2,824	2,974	4,071	2,872	2,929	3,195	3,561	4,245	5,771	4,273	3,846	4,025	Foreign Exchange	1d. d
984	2,834	1,369	908	2,422	2,473	2,522	2,366	2,378	2,351	2,575	2,714	2,751	2,461	2,804	Monetary Authorities	1da d
605	926	1,889	1,916	552	1,598	350	563	817	1,210	1,670	3,057	1,522	1,385	1,221	Government	1db d
.022	.022	.022	.022	.001	.001	.001	.001	—	—	—	—	—	—	—	Gold (Million Fine Troy Ounces)	1ad
1	1	1	1	1	—	—	—	—	—	—	—	—	—	—	Gold (National Valuation)	1an d
614	2,738	1,159	ɪ82	60	6	20	100	96	—	178	299	461	383	379	Monetary Authorities: Other Liab.	4.. d
474	579	915	ɪ1,785	933	1,821	1,305	1,190	1,159	1,559	1,955	3,552	1,915	2,829	4,786	Banking Institutions: Assets	7a. d
447	833	1,294	ɪ6,963	5,792	7,564	6,944	8,838	9,249	12,319	14,439	17,197	17,024	20,031	25,261	Liabilities	7b. d
End of Period															**Monetary Authorities**	
2,936	7,375	4,999	ɪ4,545	5,083	6,979	5,454	5,967	5,974	5,772	7,024	8,856	8,544	8,799	9,077	Foreign Assets	11
1,066	1,648	2,216	ɪ3,231	3,638	2,928	2,837	2,142	2,271	2,918	3,065	3,118	3,097	3,119	1,892	Claims on Central Government	12a
5	4	2	ɪ26	28	313	236	789	796	301	476	1,305	1,079	451	2,178	Claims on Banking Institutions	12e
1,409	1,227	1,488	ɪ1,690	1,655	1,646	1,613	1,648	1,695	1,891	2,026	1,972	2,068	2,198	3,870	Reserve Money	14
940	1,006	1,059	ɪ969	1,110	1,007	1,118	1,173	1,199	1,367	1,489	1,497	1,633	1,724	2,077	*of which: Currency Outside DMBs*	14a
....	....	....	1,278	1,166	1,226	1,208	1,056	1,149	1,185	1,218	1,242	1,250	1,076	—	Liabs.of Central Bank: Securities	16ac
1,232	5,231	1,763	ɪ131	100	11	37	194	172	—	273	424	793	726	728	Foreign Liabilities	16c
2,143	2,926	3,414	ɪ4,373	5,156	6,649	4,896	5,297	5,342	5,219	6,319	8,959	7,871	7,574	7,751	Central Government Deposits	16d
483	562	584	ɪ626	661	815	870	783	734	748	769	745	801	853	843	Capital Accounts	17a
−1,260	−919	−33	ɪ−296	11	−128	−97	−80	−52	−53	−39	−62	−63	−58	−45	Other Items (Net)	17r
End of Period															**Banking Institutions**	
182	97	316	ɪ425	480	558	471	506	491	467	606	532	409	448	1,592	Reserves	20
....	....	....	1,278	1,166	1,226	1,208	1,056	1,149	1,185	1,218	1,242	1,250	1,076	—	Other Claims on Monetary Author.	20c
950	1,107	1,392	ɪ2,841	1,562	3,099	2,411	2,314	2,074	2,427	2,993	5,031	3,292	5,369	9,194	Foreign Assets	21
4,496	4,565	4,941	ɪ6,876	5,703	7,123	7,203	8,448	7,079	5,932	4,249	3,302	3,572	4,384	6,921	Claims on Central Government	22a
10,020	14,230	18,315	ɪ48,214	53,482	55,583	58,222	63,842	67,549	74,588	85,150	94,647	105,190	112,124	121,884	Claims on Private Sector	22d
3,135	3,634	5,579	ɪ6,870	8,209	8,448	8,530	8,538	9,287	9,591	10,047	9,531	10,119	10,633	12,528	Demand Deposits	24
10,267	13,286	14,448	ɪ37,479	40,710	46,811	47,030	48,430	51,715	55,986	61,667	74,020	77,726	78,762	81,042	Time, Savings,Fgn.Currency Dep.	25
....	....	....	1,499	1,798	3,100	2,660	1,970	2,535	1,849	2,030	3,764	2,806	4,198	2,521	*of which: Fgn Currency Deposits*	25b
773	1,120	1,555	ɪ11,082	9,698	12,868	12,834	17,184	16,552	19,174	22,101	24,359	29,267	38,016	48,523	Foreign Liabilities	26c
52	64	59	ɪ—	—	47	26	14	3	10	19	26	33	30	61	Central Government Deposits	26d
....	....	....	6,758	5,125	5,019	5,350	6,111	5,255	5,158	5,798	5,547	7,262	8,224	9,348	Capital Accounts	27a
1,421	1,895	3,321	ɪ−2,554	−1,349	−5,604	−4,254	−4,110	−4,470	−5,320	−5,418	−8,727	−10,693	−12,263	−11,910	Other Items (Net)	27r
End of Period															**Banking Survey**	
1,882	2,131	3,072	ɪ−3,827	−3,153	−2,801	−5,005	−9,097	−8,676	−10,976	−12,357	−10,896	−18,224	−24,575	−30,980	Foreign Assets (Net)	31n
14,708	18,379	22,054	ɪ53,948	57,672	58,937	63,340	69,122	71,554	78,209	86,125	92,084	103,955	112,023	122,884	Domestic Credit	32
3,367	3,224	3,683	ɪ5,734	4,185	3,355	5,118	5,279	4,005	3,621	976	−2,564	−1,235	−101	1,001	Claims on Central Govt. (Net)	32an
....	....	....	....	5	....	....	....	....	....	....	....	....	....	....	Claims on Local Government	32b
11,341	15,156	18,370	ɪ48,214	53,482	55,583	58,222	63,842	67,549	74,588	85,150	94,647	105,190	112,124	121,884	Claims on Private Sector	32d
4,104	4,668	6,667	ɪ8,137	9,357	9,495	9,688	9,769	10,549	11,030	11,580	11,056	11,776	12,378	14,649	Money	34
10,267	13,286	14,448	ɪ37,479	40,710	46,811	47,030	48,430	51,715	55,986	61,667	74,020	77,726	78,762	81,042	Quasi-Money	35
483	562	584	ɪ7,383	5,786	5,834	6,219	6,893	5,990	5,906	6,567	6,292	8,062	9,076	10,190	Capital Accounts	37a
1,735	1,995	3,427	ɪ−2,878	−1,334	−6,004	−4,603	−5,069	−5,376	−5,688	−6,045	−10,180	−11,834	−12,767	−13,976	Other Items (Net)	37r
14,371	17,953	21,115	ɪ45,616	50,067	56,306	56,718	58,200	62,264	67,016	73,247	85,076	89,503	91,139	95,691	Money plus Quasi-Money	35l
End of Period															**Money (National Definitions)**	
....	....	....	....	....	....	....	....	....	10,948	11,516	11,003	11,718	12,887	14,880	*M1*	39ma
									27,840	31,977	32,765	33,162	37,991	40,964	*M2*	39mb
										58,385	65,461	73,318	78,263	78,523	84,669	*M3R*	39mc
31,397	37,807	42,932	44,418	46,137	52,832	56,489	64,239	65,873	67,948	77,800	87,568	91,023	92,120	98,748	*M3*	39md
4,121	4,269	....	....	....	....	....	....	....	....	....	....	....	....	....	*Unused Overdrafts*	39b
End of Period															**Other Banking Institutions**	
458.8ᶜ	432.4	....													Claims on Central Government	42a. g
5,389.9	5,978.9	....													Claims on Private Sector	42d. g
5,088.3	5,289.3	....													Time Dep. Debentures & Notes	45.. g
123.7	470.8	....													Foreign Liabilities	46c. g
48.1	61.5	....													Cred.from Deposit Money Banks	46h. g
492.0	640.3	....													Capital Accounts	47a. g
96.6	−50.6	....													Other Items (Net)	47r. g
2,827.3	3,084.6	....													Post Office: Savings Deposits	45.. i
3,750.3	4,202.6	....													Trustee Savings Banks: Deposits	45..k
End of Period															**Nonbank Financial Institutions**	
1,626.4	1,923.1	2,116.9	2,172.0	1,659.5	1,398.1	1,954.3	2,349.7	2,328.6	2,435.4	....	....	....	....	....	Claims on Central Government	42a. s
562.3	471.5	452.7	607.8	706.9	906.9	864.1	738.6	782.3	546.4	526.9	624.7	551.3	....	....	Claims on Local Government	42b. s
3,007.6	4,566.1	3,602.8	3,301.1	4,412.7	3,427.8	3,848.1	4,545.8	5,369.7	4,507.9	986.8	934.2	636.5	....	....	Claims on Private Sector	42d. s
1,113.0	1,745.6	2,725.3	2,746.4	3,091.8	2,580.0	2,061.4	1,740.6	1,488.7	1,590.9	....	....	....	....	....	Real Estate	42h. s
921.6	3,528.4	833.6	391.3	1,432.7	−1,559.2	522.9	765.3	2,178.4	−618.4	....	....	....	....	....	*Incr.in Total Assets(Within Per.)*	49z. s
26,601.3	31,018.5	....	....	....	....	....	....	....	....	....	....	....	....	....	Liquid Liabilities	55l

New Zealand

	1970	1971	1972	1973	1974	1975	1976	1977	1978	1979	1980	1981	1982	1983	1984
Interest Rates														*Percent Per Annum*	
Discount Rate *(End of Period)* 60	7.00	7.00	6.00	6.00	7.00	7.00	8.50	10.00	10.50	13.00	14.00	13.00	13.00	7.50	13.50
Treasury Bill Rate 60c	....	....	....	....	....	....	....	....	8.25	10.75	11.25	11.25	11.25	10.13	9.23
Deposit Rate 60l	....	....	....	....	....	....	....	....	....	....	....	11.00	10.79	9.75	10.46
Lending Rate 60p	....	....	....	....	....	....	....	8.16	9.65	10.26	12.63	13.50	13.73	13.83	12.53
Government Bond Yield 61	5.51	5.52	5.52	5.80	6.09	6.33	8.34	9.23	9.97	12.04	13.29	12.83	12.91	12.18	12.57
Prices, Production, Labor													*Index Numbers (1995=100):*		
Share Prices 62	13.1	11.6	12.1	14.5	12.1	11.2	12.2	10.7	10.9	11.9	15.4	22.0	21.5	28.4	40.5
Input Prices: All Industry 63	10.8	11.6	12.4	14.0	15.1	17.1	20.9	⅄24.4	27.2	32.0	39.3	45.9	⅄52.9	55.8	59.8
Consumer Prices 64	⅄10.0	11.0	11.8	12.8	14.2	16.3	19.0	21.8	24.4	27.7	32.4	37.4	43.4	46.6	49.5
Wages: Weekly Rates (1990=100) 65	12.1	14.5	15.8	17.7	19.8	22.5	25.5	⅄28.8	32.2	37.2	44.1	52.6	58.8	59.0	60.4
Labor Cost Index (Q492=100) 65a	....	....	....	....	....	....	....	....	....	....	....	....	....	....	....
Manufacturing Prod., Seas.Adj. .. 66ey c	....	....	....	....	....	....	....	76.9	75.3	80.2	79.9	83.6	87.6	85.6	97.3
Manufacturing Employment 67ey	....	82.3	81.9	85.6	89.3	87.9	89.3	90.4	86.7	89.4[e]	89.8	88.0	89.9	85.3	88.0
													Number in Thousands:		
Labor Force 67d	....	....	....	....	....	....	....	....	....	....	....	....	....	....	....
Employment 67e	....	....	....	....	....	....	....	....	....	....	....	....	....	....	....
Unemployment 67c	....	....	....	....	....	....	....	....	....	....	....	....	....	....	....
Unemployment Rate (%) 67r	....	....	....	....	....	....	....	....	....	....	....	....	....	....	....
International Transactions													*Millions of New Zealand Dollars:*		
Exports 70	1,091.6	1,199.8	1,499.5	1,913.2	1,733.9	1,796.3	2,815.5	3,294.9	⅄3,603.5	4,606.7	5,568.5	6,471.2	7,414.4	8,110.0	9,584.1
Butter 70fl	101.8	132.7	163.8	137.3	119.4	166.8	227.5	254.6	257.0	318.6	354.1	489.4	683.9	545.3	567.8
Imports, c.i.f. 71	1,112.0	1,186.1	1,274.0	1,591.5	2,615.0	2,613.5	3,270.8	3,464.0	⅄3,359.4	4,466.1	5,615.9	6,635.5	7,699.0	7,991.9	10,939.0
Imports, f.o.b. 71.v	1,038.28	1,102.32	1,189.54	1,480.47	2,396.88	2,386.76	3,028.52	3,189.69	⅄3110.56	4,052.72	5,171.18	5,587.30	7,044.80	6,928.20	8,197.90
													1995=100		
Volume of Exports 72	39	40	42	41	38	39	46	47	48	52	54	55	57	60	63
Butter 72fl	78	77	75	82	74	77	89	84	76	91	91	85	103	78	82
Volume of Imports 73	38	39	40	47	61	47	48	46	42	50	48	50	53	49	59
Unit Value of Exports 74	14	15	18	23	22	22	29	34	36	43	50	57	63	66	75
Butter (Unit Value) 74fl	16	22	27	21	20	26	31	37	41	43	50	73	86	91	89
Butter (Wholesale Price) 76fl	12	17	18	13	15	24	31	35	42	51	62	65	69	67	66
Unit Value of Imports 75	14	15	15	16	20	27	33	37	38	43	56	63	71	77	87
Balance of Payments													*Millions of US Dollars:*		
Current Account, n.i.e. .... 78al d	....	....	153	−149	−1,847	−1,222	−794	−661	−438	−802	−973	−1,045	−1,694	−960	−3,031
Goods: Exports f.o.b. .... 78aa d	....	....	1,955	2,511	2,277	2,449	3,009	3,225	4,020	4,988	5,394	5,603	5,323	5,328	5,385
Goods: Imports f.o.b. .... 78ab d	....	....	−1,457	−2,148	−3,595	−3,095	−3,129	−3,116	−3,418	−4,698	−5,091	−5,346	−5,603	−4,991	−5,837
Trade Balance .... 78ac d	....	....	498	362	−1,318	−646	−119	110	602	290	303	257	−280	337	−452
Services: Credit .... 78ad d	....	....	327	491	653	729	698	787	852	1,036	1,009	1,249	1,270	1,383	1,487
Services: Debit .... 78ae d	....	....	−549	−837	−1,060	−1,008	−962	−1,144	−1,339	−1,677	−1,843	−2,001	−2,034	−1,867	−1,860
Balance on Goods & Services ...... 78af d	....	....	277	16	−1,725	−925	−384	−247	116	−351	−531	−495	−1,043	−146	−825
Income: Credit .... 78ag d	....	....	75	122	122	105	103	119	116	132	159	216	283	247	205
Income: Debit .... 78ah d	....	....	−225	−308	−239	−401	−523	−554	−701	−649	−697	−860	−1,024	−1,144	−2,503
Balance on Gds, Serv. & Inc. .... 78ai d	....	....	128	−170	−1,842	−1,222	−804	−682	−469	−868	−1,069	−1,139	−1,785	−1,043	−3,123
Current Transfers, n.i.e.: Credit .. 78aj d	....	....	76	90	95	109	105	126	139	181	226	220	226	222	215
Current Transfers: Debit .... 78ak d	....	....	−51	−69	−99	−109	−96	−105	−108	−115	−130	−126	−136	−139	−123
Capital Account, n.i.e. .... 78bc d	....	....	11	27	4	2	−24	−28	−51	−41	−38	−71	−3	2	−10
Capital Account, n.i.e.: Credit ...... 78ba d	....	....	42	77	77	62	37	32	33	48	55	63	75	80	61
Capital Account: Debit .... 78bb d	....	....	−31	−50	−73	−60	−61	−60	−84	−89	−93	−133	−79	−79	−71
Financial Account, n.i.e. .... 78bj d	....	....	143	214	503	155	60	−199	−130	−12	−644	−710	343	48	296
Direct Investment Abroad .... 78bd d	....	....	−4	−19	−21	−22	−36	−32	−56	−75	−107	−104	−69	−75	−422
Dir. Invest. in Rep. Econ., n.i.e. .. 78be d	....	....	127	208	252	138	278	154	274	351	178	275	328	175	1,263
Portfolio Investment Assets .... 78bf d	....	....	—	—	—	—	—	—	—	—	—	—	—	—	—
Equity Securities .... 78bk d	....	....	—	—	—	—	—	—	—	—	—	—	—	—	—
Debt Securities .... 78bl d	....	....	—	—	—	—	—	—	—	—	—	—	—	—	—
Portfolio Investment Liab., n.i.e. ... 78bg d	....	....	—	—	—	—	—	—	—	—	—	—	—	—	—
Equity Securities .... 78bm d	....	....	—	—	—	—	—	—	—	—	—	—	—	—	—
Debt Securities .... 78bn d	....	....	—	—	—	—	—	—	—	—	—	—	—	—	—
Financial Derivatives Assets .... 78bw d	....	....	....	....	....	....	....	....	....	....	....	....	....	....	....
Financial Derivatives Liabilities ...... 78bx d	....	....	....	....	....	....	....	....	....	....	....	....	....	....	....
Other Investment Assets .... 78bh d	....	....	8	—	−42	−65	−26	−46	−40	3	−114	−34	−77	−100	26
Monetary Authorities .... 78bo d	....	....	....	....	....	....	....	....	....	....	....	....	....	....	....
General Government .... 78bp d	....	....	−2	−11	−14	−12	−7	—	−1	−3	−6	−4	−1	—	—
Banks .... 78bq d	....	....	—	—	−18	−44	−19	−23	−55	−56	−146	−48	−38	−103	21
Other Sectors .... 78br d	....	....	11	11	−10	−8	—	−22	16	62	38	18	−38	3	5
Other Investment Liab., n.i.e. ...... 78bi d	....	....	12	26	315	103	−156	−276	−307	−291	−601	−846	161	48	−571
Monetary Authorities .... 78bs d	....	....	—	—	—	—	—	−1	—	1	3	2	1	—	—
General Government .... 78bt d	....	....	−96	−81	−32	−251	−301	−352	−317	−378	−697	−1,079	−1,293	−964	−1,351
Banks .... 78bu d	....	....	—	—	—	—	—	—	—	—	28	—	66	163	27
Other Sectors .... 78bv d	....	....	108	107	347	354	144	78	10	86	65	231	1,388	848	753
Net Errors and Omissions .... 78ca d	....	....	145	−65	244	66	30	216	−265	−111	230	−277	−859	−204	1,199
Overall Balance .... 78cb d	....	....	452	27	−1,095	−999	−728	−672	−883	−966	−1,424	−2,102	−2,214	−1,114	−1,546
Reserves and Related Items .... 79da d	....	....	−452	−27	1,095	999	728	672	883	966	1,424	2,102	2,214	1,114	1,546
Reserve Assets .... 79db d	....	....	−488	−30	390	−34	15	−201	235	245	314	−344	31	−209	−1,027
Use of Fund Credit and Loans .... 79dc d	....	....	—	—	103	188	171	−2	−34	−118	−179	−116	−34	−3	—
Exceptional Financing .... 79de d	....	....	36	3	602	845	542	875	682	839	1,289	2,562	2,217	1,325	2,574

1985	1986	1987	1988	1989	1990	1991	1992	1993	1994	1995	1996	1997	1998	1999		
Percent Per Annum															**Interest Rates**	
19.80	24.60	18.55	15.10	15.00	13.25	8.30	9.15	5.70	9.75	9.80	8.80	9.70	5.60	5.00	Discount Rate *(End of Period)*	60
....	19.97	20.50	14.72	13.51	13.78	9.74	6.72	6.21	6.69	8.82	9.09	7.53	7.10	4.58	Treasury Bill Rate	60c
14.71	16.32	....	I13.41	10.92	I11.65	8.93	6.58	6.24	6.38	8.49	8.49	7.26	6.78	4.56	Deposit Rate	60l
....	....	I20.84	17.17	15.78	16.01	14.01	11.39	10.34	9.69	12.16	12.27	11.35	11.22	8.49	Lending Rate	60p
17.71	16.52	I16.35	13.45	12.78	12.46	10.00	7.87	6.69	7.48	7.94	8.04	7.21	6.47	6.13	Government Bond Yield	61
Period Averages															**Prices, Production, Labor**	
47.9	81.3	I95.0	58.8	64.5	56.8	49.9	57.1	74.9	94.8	100.0	112.3	130.7	153.3	136.4	Share Prices	62
68.9	72.9	78.7	82.8	I88.6	92.8	93.6	95.5	97.9	99.2	100.0	100.5	100.9	101.6	102.5	Input Prices: All Industry	63
I57.2	64.7	74.9	79.7	85.6	90.4	91.9	92.8	94.1	I96.4	100.0	102.3	103.5	104.8	104.7	Consumer Prices	64
I65.1	75.7	85.7	92.2	95.8	100.0	102.6	103.5	....	....	....	....	....	....	....	Wages: Weekly Rates (1990=100)	65
....	....	....	....	....	....	....	....	97.5	98.5	100.0	101.9	104.3	106.2	107.8	Labor Cost Index (Q492=100)	65a
95.5	94.1	93.5	89.1	88.9	85.4	81.7	85.1	90.8	96.5	100.0	100.6	102.4	99.8	101.6	Manufacturing Prod., Seas.Adj.	66ey c
89.0	106.5	100.9	92.2	86.7	83.7	80.9	86.4	86.4	96.3	100.0	98.7	94.8	97.1	93.3	Manufacturing Employment	67ey
Period Averages																
....	1,608	1,623	1,597	1,581	1,606	1,628	1,636	1,653	1,698	1,742	1,797	I1,817	1,864	....	Labor Force	67d
....	1,544	1,557	1,508	1,468	1,481	1,461	1,467	1,496	1,559	1,633	1,688	I1,693	1,725	....	Employment	67e
....	64	66	89	113	125	167	169	157	138	110	110	I123	139	....	Unemployment	67c
....	4.0	4.1	5.6	7.1	7.8	10.3	10.3	9.5	8.2	6.3	6.1	I6.6	7.5	....	Unemployment Rate (%)	67r
Millions of New Zealand Dollars															**International Transactions**	
11,603.2	11,225.1	12,149.7	13,488.2	14,820.0	15,760.0	16,671.0	18,208.0	19,492.0	20,519.0	20,787.0	20,966.0	21,230.0	22,493.0	23,535.0	Exports	70
670.6	498.8	517.7	554.9	560.4	654.2	733.7	677.3	828.4	790.5	777.9	907.7	945.9	1,073.7	972.4	Butter	70fl
12,075.5	11,622.1	12,242.5	11,216.9	14,710.1	15,895.5	14,526.8	17,132.0	17,781.0	19,981.0	21,252.4	21,400.0	21,963.0	23,349.0	27,118.0	Imports, c.i.f.	71
10,966.80	10,646.50	11,221.80	10,273.20	13,438.90	14,566.20	13,280.50	15,804.00	16,372.00	18,491.00	19,718.10	19,847.00	20,440.00	21,682.00	25,437.00	Imports, f.o.b.	71.v
1995=100																
I69	68	70	73	71	75	83	85	88	97	100	105	110	110	111	Volume of Exports	72
107	89	93	102	72	87	105	77	107	108	100	118	141	128	133	Butter	72fl
I59	58	64	59	72	77	70	77	81	94	100	103	107	110	125	Volume of Imports	73
I81	79	84	89	101	100	96	103	106	102	100	97	94	98	100	Unit Value of Exports	74
I86	77	71	73	94	97	95	111	108	98	100	99	89	107	95	Butter (Unit Value)	74fl
82	88	77	86	99	99	97	112	104	95	100	....	89	108	100	Butter (Wholesale Price)	76fl
I96	94	90	89	96	97	98	104	104	104	100	100	97	96	102	Unit Value of Imports	75
Minus Sign Indicates Debit															**Balance of Payments**	
−2,657	−2,826	−2,910	−1,863	−1,525	−1,453	−1,159	−1,071	−746	−2,384	−3,069	−3,935	−4,308	−2,596	−4,334	Current Account, n.i.e.	78ald
5,595	5,836	7,245	8,831	8,846	9,190	9,555	9,735	10,468	12,176	13,478	14,342	14,242	12,272	12,610	Goods: Exports f.o.b.	78aad
−5,656	−5,734	−6,656	−6,658	−7,873	−8,375	−7,485	−8,108	−8,749	−10,769	−12,584	−13,814	−13,380	−11,334	−13,031	Goods: Imports f.o.b.	78abd
−61	103	590	2,173	973	815	2,070	1,627	1,719	1,408	895	528	862	937	−421	*Trade Balance*	78acd
1,458	1,714	2,191	2,549	2,395	2,494	2,579	2,634	2,854	3,667	4,482	4,630	4,309	3,746	4,305	Services: Credit	78add
−1,814	−2,184	−2,658	−3,153	−3,167	−3,324	−3,414	−3,582	−3,505	−4,101	−4,694	−4,932	−4,949	−4,524	−4,568	Services: Debit	78aed
−417	−367	123	1,569	201	−15	1,235	679	1,068	973	682	226	221	159	−684	*Balance on Goods & Services*	78afd
252	356	542	451	661	719	33	117	394	358	917	360	396	457	48	Income: Credit	78agd
−2,586	−2,950	−3,719	−4,033	−2,545	−2,295	−2,566	−1,995	−2,340	−4,045	−4,900	−5,064	−5,248	−3,550	−3,942	Income: Debit	78ahd
−2,752	−2,961	−3,053	−2,014	−1,684	−1,591	−1,298	−1,199	−877	−2,713	−3,301	−4,478	−4,631	−2,934	−4,578	*Balance on Gds, Serv. & Inc.*	78aid
211	246	278	309	314	317	321	310	310	638	558	900	710	692	616	Current Transfers, n.i.e.: Credit	78ajd
−116	−111	−134	−159	−156	−179	−182	−182	−178	−309	−326	−358	−387	−354	−372	Current Transfers: Debit	78akd
−25	−42	−46	−49	47	213	252	292	542	617	1,224	1,335	236	73	−42	Capital Account, n.i.e.	78bcd
58	81	137	228	331	507	586	602	833	995	1,652	1,838	777	517	435	Capital Account, n.i.e.: Credit	78bad
−83	−123	−182	−277	−284	−294	−334	−311	−291	−379	−427	−502	−541	−444	−477	Capital Account: Debit	78bbd
−250	1	10	−1,790	−740	875	−709	3,229	2,825	2,220	4,664	3,570	4,046	825	....	Financial Account, n.i.e.	78bjd
−309	−592	−435	−373	−1,896	−1,594	−690	806	−1,276	−1,725	336	1,534	46	−752	....	Direct Investment Abroad	78bdd
1,266	1,214	1,284	1,717	1,627	1,735	1,290	2,095	2,350	2,543	3,659	2,231	2,623	745	....	Dir. Invest. in Rep. Econ., n.i.e.	78bed
—	—	—	—	−40	−111	−68	−7	−283	−72	−284	−430	−1,612	−837	....	Portfolio Investment Assets	78bfd
—	—	—	—	−50	−97	−53	−11	−187	−152	−215	−339	−924	−232	....	Equity Securities	78bkd
—	—	—	—	10	−14	−15	4	−97	81	−68	−91	−687	−605	....	Debt Securities	78bld
—	—	—	—	70	282	−83	−135	1,940	614	96	−104	403	395	....	Portfolio Investment Liab., n.i.e.	78bgd
—	—	—	—	12	146	129	53	116	23	−100	176	88	22	....	Equity Securities	78bmd
—	—	—	—	58	136	−212	−188	1,823	591	196	−279	315	373	....	Debt Securities	78bnd
....	....	....	....	....	....	....	....	....	....	....	....	....	....	....	Financial Derivatives Assets	78bwd
....	....	....	....	....	....	....	....	....	....	....	....	....	....	....	Financial Derivatives Liabilities	78bxd
31	−47	−85	628	−254	−81	−207	328	−739	−78	−393	−921	991	−307	....	Other Investment Assets	78bhd
....	....	....	....	....	....	....	....	....	....	....	....	....	....	....	Monetary Authorities	78bod
—	—	—	—	−24	−45	−47	−11	−62	−82	−58	−95	238	55	....	General Government	78bpd
72	−47	−85	628	−411	−42	31	124	−747	66	−346	−933	818	−289	....	Banks	78bqd
−40	—	—	—	181	6	−191	215	71	−61	10	106	−65	−73	....	Other Sectors	78brd
−1,237	−574	−754	−3,762	−247	644	−952	142	833	937	1,251	1,260	1,595	1,580	....	Other Investment Liab., n.i.e.	78bid
....	....	....	....	....	....	....	....	....	....	....	....	....	....	....	Monetary Authorities	78bsd
−1,489	−1,576	−3,239	−2,673	−1,231	−832	−1,239	222	−117	−290	−143	−135	−73	68	....	General Government	78btd
12	258	228	95	−397	−58	−23	1,365	573	767	1,095	964	1,131	1,568	....	Banks	78bud
240	744	2,257	−1,183	1,381	1,534	310	−1,445	377	460	298	432	537	−56	....	Other Sectors	78bvd
895	255	697	782	1,000	544	104	−2,319	−2,695	281	−2,436	803	−1,417	1,214	....	Net Errors and Omissions	78cad
−2,037	−2,612	−2,248	−2,921	−1,217	179	−1,511	131	−74	733	384	1,772	−1,442	−484	....	*Overall Balance*	78cbd
2,037	2,612	2,248	2,921	1,217	−179	1,511	−131	74	−733	−384	−1,772	1,442	484	−167	Reserves and Related Items	79dad
389	−2,044	389	735	−248	−1,014	1,319	−131	74	−733	−384	−1,772	1,442	484	−167	Reserve Assets	79dbd
—	—	—	—	—	—	—	....	....	....	....	....	....	....	....	Use of Fund Credit and Loans	79dcd
1,649	4,656	1,860	2,186	1,466	835	192	....	....	....	....	....	....	....	....	Exceptional Financing	79ded

New Zealand

		1970	1971	1972	1973	1974	1975	1976	1977	1978	1979	1980	1981	1982	1983	1984
IIP: End-March Stocks																*Millions of US Dollars*
Assets	79aa d	...	...	...	...	...	...	...	...	...	...	...	...	...	...	...
Direct Investment Abroad	79ab d	...	...	...	...	...	...	...	...	...	...	...	...	...	...	...
Portfolio Investment	79ac d	...	...	...	...	...	...	...	...	...	...	...	...	...	...	...
Equity Securities	79ad d	...	...	...	...	...	...	...	...	...	...	...	...	...	...	...
Debt Securities	79ae d	...	...	...	...	...	...	...	...	...	...	...	...	...	...	...
Financial Derivatives	79al d	...	...	...	...	...	...	...	...	...	...	...	...	...	...	...
Other Investment	79af d	...	...	...	...	...	...	...	...	...	...	...	...	...	...	...
Monetary Authorities	79ag d	...	...	...	...	...	...	...	...	...	...	...	...	...	...	...
General Government	79ah d	...	...	...	...	...	...	...	...	...	...	...	...	...	...	...
Banks	79ai d	...	...	...	...	...	...	...	...	...	...	...	...	...	...	...
Other Sectors	79aj d	...	...	...	...	...	...	...	...	...	...	...	...	...	...	...
Reserve Assets	79ak d	...	...	...	...	...	...	...	...	...	...	...	...	...	...	...
Liabilities	79la d	...	...	...	...	...	...	...	...	...	...	...	...	...	...	...
Dir. Invest. in Rep. Economy	79lb d	...	...	...	...	...	...	...	...	...	...	...	...	...	...	...
Portfolio Investment	79lc d	...	...	...	...	...	...	...	...	...	...	...	...	...	...	...
Equity Securities	79ld d	...	...	...	...	...	...	...	...	...	...	...	...	...	...	...
Debt Securities	79le d	...	...	...	...	...	...	...	...	...	...	...	...	...	...	...
Financial Derivatives	79ll d	...	...	...	...	...	...	...	...	...	...	...	...	...	...	...
Other investment	79lf d	...	...	...	...	...	...	...	...	...	...	...	...	...	...	...
Monetary Authorities	79lg d	...	...	...	...	...	...	...	...	...	...	...	...	...	...	...
General Government	79lh d	...	...	...	...	...	...	...	...	...	...	...	...	...	...	...
Banks	79li d	...	...	...	...	...	...	...	...	...	...	...	...	...	...	...
Other Sectors	79lj d	...	...	...	...	...	...	...	...	...	...	...	...	...	...	...
Government Finance																*Millions of New Zealand Dollars:*
Deficit (-) or Surplus	80	ɪ−108	−93	−298	−225	−416	−1,194	−614	−789	−1,502	−1,127	−1,541	−2,111	−2,389	−3,209	−3,234
Revenue	81	ɪ1,620	1,908	2,146	2,632	3,124	3,503	4,283	5,153	5,651	6,827	7,877	9,753	11,207	11,724	13,705
Expenditure	82	ɪ1,571	1,821	2,231	2,614	3,107	3,873	4,276	5,232	6,404	7,338	8,802	11,075	12,880	14,108	16,155
Lending Minus Repayments	83	ɪ157	180	213	243	433	824	621	710	749	616	616	789	716	825	784
Financing																
Domestic	84a	ɪ71	100	409	341	68	755	382	576	837	919	523	1,451	2,085	2,612	1,653
Foreign	85a	ɪ51	72	−49	−58	301	422	226	483	340	399	816	799	1,322	823	1,839
Use of Cash Balances	87a	ɪ−14	−79	−62	−58	47	17	6	−270	325	−191	202	−139	−1,018	−226	−258
Debt: Domestic	88a	ɪ2,445	2,546	2,956	3,295	3,365	4,121	4,478	5,061	5,917	6,806	7,399	8,858	11,004	13,701	15,875
Foreign	89a	ɪ576	654	564	465	863	1,463	1,827	2,447	2,920	3,568	4,236	5,549	7,765	8,227	12,409
Financing (by Currency)																
Use of Cash Balances	87	...	...	...	...	...	...	...	...	...	...	...	...	...	...	...
Debt: New Zealand Dollars	88b	...	...	...	...	...	...	...	...	...	...	...	...	...	...	...
National Accounts													*Millions of New Zealand Dollars; Year Beginning April 1*			
Exports of Goods & Services	90c. c	1,296	1,560	1,946	2,241	2,117	2,666	3,765	4,125	4,687	5,996	7,003	8,249	9,266	10,507	13,229
Government Consumption	91f. c	770	886	1,023	1,176	1,443	1,732	1,937	2,363	2,882	3,314	4,134	4,989	5,566	5,858	6,334
Gross Fixed Capital Formation	93e. c	1,214	1,420	1,778	2,091	2,695	3,246	3,538	3,545	3,880	4,067	4,754	6,597	7,774	8,612	9,994
Increase/Decrease(-) in Stocks	93i. c	204	306	154	452	1,036	459	810	133	−246	470	−33	165	248	375	1,111
Private Consumption	96f. c	3,742	4,210	4,764	5,488	6,206	7,098	8,162	9,149	10,324	12,053	14,169	16,633	19,018	20,718	23,582
Imports of Goods & Services	98c. c	−1,456	−1,505	−1,710	−2,233	−3,344	−3,430	−4,057	−4,378	−4,647	−6,256	−7,272	−9,168	−10,318	−11,063	−14,539
Gross Domestic Product (GDP)	99b. c	5,832	6,874	7,901	9,199	10,095	11,668	14,101	14,970	16,958	19,795	22,992	27,891	31,409	34,839	39,346
Net Factor Inc/Pmts(-) Abroad	98.n c	−41	−46	−54	−37	−82	−165	−265	−336	−409	−460	−511	−615	−858	−1,275	−2,002
Gross National Income (GNI)	99a. c	5,791	6,828	7,847	9,162	10,013	11,503	13,836	14,634	16,549	19,335	22,481	27,276	30,551	33,564	37,344
Net National Income	99e. c	5,268	6,276	7,234	8,470	9,216	10,563	12,758	13,379	15,117	17,774	20,934	25,486	28,567	31,209	34,293
GDP Volume 1965 Prices	99b. r	4,439	4,552	4,753	5,094	5,300	5,389	5,397	5,249							
GDP Volume 1991/92 Prices	99b. r	...	...	...	...	...	...	...	28,582	60,000	61,531	62,192	65,248	63,105	66,746	70,237
GDP Volume (1995=100)	99bv r	59.0	60.5	63.1	67.7	70.4	71.6	71.7	69.7	71.6	73.4	74.2	77.9	75.3	79.7	83.8
GDP Deflator (1995=100)	99bi r	10.8	12.4	13.7	14.9	15.7	17.8	21.5	23.5	25.9	29.5	33.9	39.2	45.6	47.8	51.3
																Millions:
Population	99z	2.81	2.85	2.90	2.96	3.01	3.07	3.09	3.11	3.11	3.10	3.11	3.12	3.16	3.20	3.23

Millions of US Dollars

	1985	1986	1987	1988	1989	1990	1991	1992	1993	1994	1995	1996	1997	1998	1999	IIP: End-March Stocks	
	....	....	....	....	4,434	8,687	12,554	12,325	10,125	13,205	16,195	23,566	23,013	19,248	21,406	Assets	79aa d
	....	....	....	....	534	3,269	5,951	6,282	4,234	5,163	7,630	8,928	6,749	5,775	7,187	Direct Investment Abroad	79ab d
	....	....	....	....	—	148	298	882	952	1,362	1,707	5,815	6,434	6,476	6,755	Portfolio Investment	79ac d
	....	....	....	....	....	143	270	503	602	834	1,226	4,407	4,895	4,620	4,428	Equity Securities	79ad d
	....	....	....	....	....	5	28	380	350	529	481	1,408	1,539	1,855	2,327	Debt Securities	79ae d
	....	....	....	....	....	....	....	....	....	....	....	....	....	....	....	Financial Derivatives	79al d
	....	....	....	....	1,416	2,022	2,428	1,989	1,644	2,793	2,898	4,245	5,314	2,804	3,606	Other Investment	79af d
	....	....	....	....	....	....	....	....	....	....	....	....	....	....	....	Monetary Authorities	79ag d
	....	....	....	....	....	....	....	....	....	....	....	....	....	....	....	General Government	79ah d
	....	....	....	....	....	....	....	....	....	....	....	....	....	....	....	Banks	79ai d
	....	....	....	....	....	....	....	....	....	....	....	....	....	....	....	Other Sectors	79aj d
	....	....	....	....	2,484	3,248	3,876	3,172	3,295	3,886	3,960	4,577	4,516	4,194	3,858	Reserve Assets	79ak d
	....	....	....	....	31,619	46,936	52,728	40,971	44,241	51,100	62,338	71,629	78,547	68,752	67,087	Liabilities	79la d
	....	....	....	....	5,964	7,938	10,761	12,545	14,849	19,315	25,574	33,381	37,491	34,889	33,217	Dir. Invest. in Rep. Economy	79lb d
	....	....	....	....	—	11,941	12,642	14,273	15,290	17,595	19,809	19,360	20,167	17,581	17,440	Portfolio Investment	79lc d
	....	....	....	....	....	903	1,036	468	1,320	816	1,483	288	1,045	208	224	Equity Securities	79ld d
	....	....	....	....	....	11,037	11,607	13,805	13,970	16,779	18,327	19,072	19,122	17,373	17,216	Debt Securities	79le d
	....	....	....	....	....	....	....	....	....	....	....	....	....	....	....	Financial Derivatives	79ll d
	....	....	....	....	25,655	27,057	29,325	14,153	14,101	14,189	16,955	18,888	20,890	16,282	16,430	Other investment	79lf d
	....	....	....	....	....	....	....	....	....	....	....	....	....	....	....	Monetary Authorities	79lg d
	....	....	....	....	....	....	....	....	....	....	....	....	....	....	....	General Government	79lh d
	....	....	....	....	....	....	....	....	....	....	....	....	....	....	....	Banks	79li d
	....	....	....	....	....	....	....	....	....	....	....	....	....	....	....	Other Sectors	79lj d

Government Finance

Fiscal Year (see note)

	1985	1986	1987	1988	1989	1990	1991	1992	1993	1994	1995	1996	1997	1998	1999		
	-2,082	-1,990	642	1,354	....	I2,894	1,419	-1,677	84	679	396	4,932	3,913	484	....	Deficit (-) or Surplus	80
	16,933	20,843	26,668	27,160	....	I30,866	28,457	26,616	26,742	30,236	32,861	33,975	33,285	33,827	....	Revenue	81
	18,330	22,711	27,815	28,492	....	I31,758	30,084	28,598	28,440	29,662	29,954	30,593	31,465	33,005	....	Expenditure	82
	685	122	-1,789	-2,686	....	I-3,786	-3,046	-305	-1,782	-105	2,511	-1,550	-2,093	338	....	Lending Minus Repayments	83
																Financing	
	1,167	I2,357	....	....												Domestic	84a
	946	I-367	....													Foreign	85a
	-31	....														Use of Cash Balances	87a
	17,276	20,744	21,855	23,008	....	I20,452	20,981									Debt: Domestic	88a
	14,726	21,735	17,257	16,593	....	I23,897	22,952									Foreign	89a
																Financing (by Currency)	
	....	....	....	....	....	....	....	....	....	....	....	....	....	....	....	Use of Cash Balances	87
	....	....	....	....	....	....	....	....	....	....	....	....	....	....	....	Debt: New Zealand Dollars	88b

National Accounts

	1985	1986	1987	1988	1989	1990	1991	1992	1993	1994	1995	1996	1997	1998	1999		
	13,947	15,122	16,663	18,060	19,151	19,960	21,680	23,889	25,311	27,173	27,423	27,540	28,459	30,328	....	Exports of Goods & Services	90c. c
	7,348	8,930	10,128	11,023	11,733	12,291	12,269	12,682	12,578	12,535	13,218	13,805	14,769	15,139	....	Government Consumption	91f. c
	11,978	12,363	13,382	12,892	14,303	13,795	11,536	12,280	14,768	17,607	19,251	20,236	19,821	18,984	....	Gross Fixed Capital Formation	93e. c
	-154	588	-381	-62	1,406	-116	85	757	1,729	1,438	1,161	689	885	-148	....	Increase/Decrease(-) in Stocks	93i. c
	27,869	32,962	37,432	40,523	43,455	45,760	45,810	46,680	49,026	52,943	56,576	59,625	62,124	64,274	....	Private Consumption	96f. c
	-15,311	-15,240	-15,635	-15,582	-18,938	-19,441	-19,104	-21,709	-22,588	-25,139	-26,169	-26,745	-27,805	-29,677	....	Imports of Goods & Services	98c. c
	45,282	54,725	61,641	66,454	70,773	72,248	72,277	74,578	80,824	86,556	91,461	94,940	98,025	98,913	....	Gross Domestic Product (GDP)	99b. c
	-2,520	-2,767	-3,270	-3,318	-4,770	-4,243	-4,424	-3,064	-3,957	-4,737	-5,847	-7,929	-6,807	-7,611	....	Net Factor Inc/Pmts(-) Abroad	98.n c
	42,762	51,958	58,371	63,136	66,003	68,005	67,853	71,514	76,867	81,819	85,614	87,011	91,218	91,302	....	Gross National Income (GNI)	99a. c
	39,125	47,745	53,374	57,579	60,079	61,605	61,085	64,199	69,438	73,814	77,039	78,530	81,992	81,517	....	Net National Income	99e. c
	....	....	....	....	....	....	....	....	....	....	....	....	....	....	....	GDP Volume 1965 Prices	99b. r
	70,083	72,390	72,965	73,792	73,696	73,080	72,278	72,849	77,389	81,469	83,799	86,077	88,638	87,987	....	GDP Volume 1991/92 Prices	99b. r
	83.6	86.4	87.1	88.1	87.9	87.2	86.3	86.9	92.4	97.2	100.0	102.7	105.8	105.0	....	GDP Volume (1995=100)	99bv r
	59.2	69.3	77.4	82.5	88.0	90.6	91.6	93.8	95.7	97.3	100.0	101.1	101.3	103.0	....	GDP Deflator (1995=100)	99bi r

Midyear Estimates

	1985	1986	1987	1988	1989	1990	1991	1992	1993	1994	1995	1996	1997	1998	1999		
	3.25	3.28	3.30	3.32	3.33	3.36	3.48	3.51	3.55	3.60	3.66	3.71	3.76	3.79	3.81	Population	99z

(See notes in the back of the book.)

		1970	1971	1972	1973	1974	1975	1976	1977	1978	1979	1980	1981	1982	1983	1984
Exchange Rates									*Gold Córdobas per Bill. SDRs through 1987, per Million SDRs in 1988, per*							
Principal Rate	aa	1.41	1.53	1.53	1.70	1.72	1.65	1.63	1.71	1.83	2.65	2.56	2.34	2.22	2.10	1.97
									Gold Córd.per Bill.US$ through 1987, per Mill.US$ in 1988,per Thous.US$							
Principal Rate	ae	1.41	1.41	1.41	1.41	1.41	1.41	1.41	1.41	1.41	2.01	2.01	2.01	2.01	2.01	2.01
Principal Rate	rf	2.06	2.06	2.06	2.06	2.06	2.06	2.06	2.06	2.06	2.79	2.95	2.95	2.95	2.95	2.95
													Index Numbers (1995=100):			
Principal Rate	ahx	....	....	....	....	....	....	....	....	....	....	....	....	....	....	....
Nominal Effective Exchange Rate	ne c	....	....	....	....	....	....	....	....	....	....	....	....	....	....	....
Real Effective Exchange Rate	re c	....	....	....	....	....	....	....	....	....	....	....	....	....	....	....
Fund Position														*Millions of SDRs:*		
Quota	2f. s	27.00	27.00	27.00	27.00	27.00	27.00	27.00	27.00	34.00	34.00	51.00	51.00	51.00	51.00	68.20
SDRs	1b. s	.96	3.68	6.22	5.71	5.80	4.57	3.47	3.77	4.34	.02	—	.06	.88	—	—
Reserve Position in the Fund	1c. s															
Total Fund Cred.&Loans Outstg.	2tl	8.00	10.99	8.25	12.24	10.06	15.50	8.74	2.00	2.01	43.51	38.67	21.19	17.54	13.29	9.04
International Liquidity											*Millions of US Dollars Unless Otherwise Indicated:*					
Total Reserves minus Gold	1l. d	48.59	58.11	80.11	116.26	104.49	121.59	146.05	148.33	50.77	146.62	64.52	111.43	171.17	174.70	....
SDRs	1b. d	.96	4.00	6.75	6.89	7.10	5.35	4.03	4.58	5.65	.03	—	.07	.97	—	....
Reserve Position in the Fund	1c. d															
Foreign Exchange	1d. d	47.63	54.11	73.36	109.37	97.39	116.24	142.02	143.75	45.12	146.59	64.52	111.36	170.20	174.70	....
Gold (Million Fine Troy Ounces)	1ad	.017	.018	.009	.015	.019	.018	.017	.026	.027	.018	.018	.018	.018	.120	....
Gold (National Valuation)	1an d	.60	.63	.34	.63	.80	.76	.72	1.10	1.14	.76	.76	.76	.76	5.07	....
Monetary Authorities: Other Liab.	4.. d	.26	−.30	.74	6.35	23.56	47.24	49.42	57.99	139.05	215.29	399.74	789.78	1,099.85	1,721.93	2,351.35
Deposit Money Banks: Assets	7a. d	5.67	8.19	11.04	16.61	10.28	14.32	17.80	16.71	31.01	24.06	23.76	46.87	58.45	38.03	13.32
Liabilities	7b. d	76.80	82.27	74.14	85.03	94.25	113.97	95.87	150.19	198.68	166.00	270.54	109.00	104.28	132.92	98.25
Monetary Authorities										*Thousandths (.000) of Gold Córdobas through 1985; Gold Córd. 1986-87;*						
Foreign Assets	11	69	82	111	164	147	172	205	209	72	244	92	254	266	‡369	915
Claims on Central Government	12a	38	39	40	74	63	75	79	85	244	364	772	991	1,594	‡3,852	5,625
Claims on Nonfin.Pub.Enterprises	12c	—	—	—	—	—	—	—	—	—	—	—	—	—	70	108
Claims on Private Sector	12d	...	...	...	...	...	...	...	...	...	...	...	...	...	‡	
Claims on Deposit Money Banks	12e	19	19	17	38	122	100	81	79	137	268	663	1,076	1,247	‡761	840
Claims on Nonbank Financial Insts	12g														84	316
Reserve Money	14	88	91	106	150	166	171	217	230	207	472	440	691	910	‡1,611	3,021
of which: Currency Outside DMBs	14a	50	50	66	82	90	89	127	138	177	314	393	475	617	‡1,085	2,268
Time, Savings,& Fgn.Currency Dep.	15	1	1	3	2	4	5	7	5	16	5	3	2	14	‡297	453
Liabs. of Central Bank: Securities	16ac															
Foreign Liabilities	16c	11	16	14	27	48	67	46	44	145	305	532	883	1,128	‡1,042	1,548
Long-Term Foreign Liabilities	16cl	—	—	—	3	3	25	38	41	54	243	371	754	1,121	‡2,447	3,196
Central Government Deposits	16d	7	7	16	53	68	40	31	29	20	152	216	45	130	‡34	167
Counterpart Funds	16e															
Liab. to Nonbank Financial Insts	16j														50	87
Capital Accounts	17a	10	14	19	21	21	21	20	21	21	38	48	57	56	‡54	52
Other Items (Net)	17r	9	11	10	20	22	18	6	3	−10	−339	−83	−111	−252	‡−400	−722
of which: Valuation Adjustment	17rv															
Deposit Money Banks										*Thousandths (.000) of Gold Córdobas through 1985; Gold Córd. 1986-87;*						
Reserves	20	39	42	41	68	78	84	90	95	77	82	86	200	293	‡571	961
Other Claims on Monetary Author.	20c															
Foreign Assets	21	8	11	15	23	14	20	25	23	44	46	48	94	117	‡76	27
Claims on Central Government	22a	—	—	7	6	17	7	5	16	7	65	622	117	65	‡27	60
Claims on Local Government	22b														59	82
Claims on Nonfin.Pub.Enterprises	22c														1,825	2,609
Claims on Private Sector	22d	249	273	293	398	531	532	594	708	775	1,393	2,010	2,573	3,132	‡1,844	1,581
Demand Deposits	24	65	73	83	147	172	162	195	200	183	305	427	531	664	‡1,170	1,873
Time, Savings,& Fgn.Currency Dep.	25	49	65	93	115	137	150	210	226	198	262	326	542	656	‡1,063	1,673
Money Market Instruments	26aa															
Foreign Liabilities	26c	49	42	24	30	43	75	59	147	227	335	443	115	124	‡125	59
Long-Term Foreign Liabilities	26cl	59	73	79	89	89	85	75	64	52	77	101	104	86	‡142	139
Central Government Deposits	26d	8	7	14	33	58	32	30	33	30	80	129	503	580	‡400	229
Credit from Monetary Authorities	26g	18	18	16	37	121	98	75	73	134	436	737	1,073	1,243	‡754	853
Liab. to Nonbank Financial Insts	26j														234	272
Capital Accounts	27a	60	66	70	76	80	92	99	102	112	142	171	112	495	‡665	781
Other Items (Net)	27r	−13	−19	−22	−32	−60	−51	−29	−1	−32	−51	432	4	−240	‡−151	−559
Monetary Survey										*Thousandths (.000) of Gold Córdobas through 1985; Gold Córd. 1986-87;*						
Foreign Assets (Net)	31n	16	35	88	130	71	50	125	41	−256	−349	−834	−650	−869	‡−3,311	−4,000
Domestic Credit	32	272	298	310	391	486	541	618	748	977	1,590	3,058	3,133	4,080	‡7,340	9,997
Claims on Central Govt. (Net)	32an	22	25	17	−6	−45	9	24	40	202	197	1,048	560	948	‡3,445	5,289
Claims on Local Government	32b														59	82
Claims on Nonfin.Pub.Enterprises	32c														1,895	2,717
Claims on Private Sector	32d	249	273	293	398	531	532	594	708	775	1,393	2,010	2,573	3,132	‡1,844	1,581
Claims on Nonbank Financial Inst	32g														97	329
Money	34	116	124	150	229	263	251	323	340	316	620	820	1,041	1,309	‡2,271	4,169
Quasi-Money	35	50	66	95	118	141	155	217	231	215	267	329	544	670	‡1,360	2,126
Money Market Instruments	36aa															
Liabs. of Central Bank: Securities	36ac															
Counterpart Funds	36e															
Liab. to Nonbank Financial Insts	36j														284	359
Capital Accounts	37a	70	80	89	97	101	113	119	122	133	180	219	169	551	‡718	834
Other Items (Net)	37r	52	63	64	77	52	72	84	96	57	174	855	729	682	‡−604	−1,491
Money plus Quasi-Money	35l	166	190	245	347	403	406	540	571	530	886	1,149	1,585	1,979	‡3,632	6,295

1985	1986	1987	1988	1989	1990	1991	1992	1993	1994	1995	1996	1997	1998	1999		
															Exchange Rates	

Thousand SDRs in 1989-90, per SDR thereafter: End of Period

1985	1986	1987	1988	1989	1990	1991	1992	1993	1994	1995	1996	1997	1998	1999		
6.15	17.12	19.86	I247.61	I10.03	853.60	I7.15	6.88	8.72	10.38	11.84	12.83	13.49	15.76	16.91	Principal Rate	aa

in 1989-90, per US$ thereafter: End of Period (ae) Period Average (rf)

1985	1986	1987	1988	1989	1990	1991	1992	1993	1994	1995	1996	1997	1998	1999		
5.60	14.00	14.00	I184.00	I7.63	600.00	I5.00	5.00	6.35	7.11	7.97	8.92	10.00	11.19	12.32	Principal Rate	ae
7.77	19.50	20.53	I53.95	I3.13	140.92	I4.27	5.00	5.62	6.72	7.55	8.44	9.45	10.58	11.81	Principal Rate	rf

Period Averages

1985	1986	1987	1988	1989	1990	1991	1992	1993	1994	1995	1996	1997	1998	1999		
....	....	....	....	515,859.5	35,093.7	282.6	150.0	142.1	111.7	100.0	89.0	79.2	71.0	63.5	Principal Rate	ahx
....	....	....	....	44,667.4	4,102.5	101.3	106.5	106.1	112.0	100.0	92.4	88.7	82.8	76.7	Nominal Effective Exchange Rate	ne c
....	....	....	31.8	17.5	53.9	99.4	114.5	116.1	108.8	100.0	98.3	100.7	103.6	104.3	Real Effective Exchange Rate	re c
															Fund Position	

End of Period

1985	1986	1987	1988	1989	1990	1991	1992	1993	1994	1995	1996	1997	1998	1999		
68.20	68.20	68.20	68.20	68.20	68.20	68.20	96.10	96.10	96.10	96.10	96.10	96.10	96.10	130.00	Quota	2f. s
—	—	.01	—	—	.02	.02	.06	.03	.01	—	.02	.03	.15	.16	SDRs	1b. s
—	—	—	—	—	—	—	—	—	—	—	—	—	—	—	Reserve Position in the Fund	1c. s
.01	—	—	—	—	—	17.03	17.03	17.03	34.92	26.41	20.02	20.02	36.84	113.15	Total Fund Cred.&Loans Outstg.	2tl
															International Liquidity	

End of Period

1985	1986	1987	1988	1989	1990	1991	1992	1993	1994	1995	1996	1997	1998	1999		
....	....	17.41	38.10	115.80	106.63	134.13	130.48	55.04	141.01	136.20	197.32	377.94	350.41	509.71	Total Reserves minus Gold	1l. d
....	....	.01	—	—	.03	.03	.08	.04	.01	—	.02	.04	.21	.21	SDRs	1b. d
—	—	—	—	—	—	—	—	—	—	—	—	—	—	—	Reserve Position in the Fund	1c. d
....	....	17.40	38.10	115.80	106.60	134.10	130.40	55.00	141.00	136.20	197.30	377.90	350.20	509.50	Foreign Exchange	1d. d
....	....	.198	.312	.120	.153	.100	.475	.010	.013	.015	.015	.015	.015	.015	Gold (Million Fine Troy Ounces)	1ad
....	....	9.60	12.80	4.80	5.90	3.60	17.10	.42	.55	.63	.63	.63	.63	.63	Gold (National Valuation)	1an d
2,720.96	2,819.85	3,237.13	3,637.93	3,560.99	3,809.93	4,120.70	4,340.22	3,586.21	3,470.70	2,936.22	2,113.12	2,086.84	2,045.55	1,990.79	Monetary Authorities: Other Liab.	4.. d
11.56	2.77	2.28	2.98	5.45	32.80	43.30	47.36	53.56	45.00	146.65	211.27	162.15	143.98		Deposit Money Banks: Assets	7a. d
98.39	20.97	30.94	1.09	.97	2.20	20.54	24.38	18.74	31.62	31.34	44.61	54.65	55.09	109.86	Liabilities	7b. d
															Monetary Authorities	

Thousands 1988-89; Millions Beginning 1990: End of Period

1985	1986	1987	1988	1989	1990	1991	1992	1993	1994	1995	1996	1997	1998	1999		
2,602	I4	4	I11	893	I45	840	896	558	1,227	1,284	I2,199	4,036	4,190	6,429	Foreign Assets	11
11,704	I26	119	I15	77	I52	1,080	20,498	21,646	23,257	22,469	I18,132	21,451	23,769	26,884	Claims on Central Government	12a
206	I—	1	I—	17	I6	135	170	169	381	468	I98	101	113	124	Claims on Nonfin.Pub.Enterprises	12c
	I—	—	I—	—	I—	—	—	—	—	13	I206	260	315	303	Claims on Private Sector	12d
1,271	I4	70	I23	328	I61	1,101	767	798	824	743	I152	806	99	327	Claims on Deposit Money Banks	12e
1,962	I6	27	I3	51	I51	834	1,107	1,705	1,206	1,151	I3,168	3,004	4,028	4,203	Claims on Nonbank Financial Insts	12g
8,564	I29	201	I23	604	I63	883	933	1,006	1,533	1,895	I2,546	3,373	4,038	4,268	Reserve Money	14
5,712	I20	146	I13	324	I29	401	468	509	688	771	I864	1,096	1,340	1,735	of which: Currency Outside DMBs	14a
779	I2	3	I—	—	I—	—	50	18	18	12	I46	48	60	67	Time, Savings,& Fgn.Currency Dep.	15
											436	3,643	2,250	2,303	Liabs. of Central Bank: Securities	16ac
6,548	I13	16	I234	11,522	I1,023	10,514	10,625	9,704	14,019	12,631	I12,327	12,701	13,180	19,568	Foreign Liabilities	16c
8,690	I26	30	I435	15,648	I1,263	10,212	11,193	13,216	11,026	11,069	I6,788	8,427	10,298	6,868	Long-Term Foreign Liabilities	16cl
470	I2	21	I3	37	I13	207	1,253	397	330	1,069	I242	175	591	1,673	Central Government Deposits	16d
											35	15	155	22	Counterpart Funds	16e
573	I1	2	I1	4	I1	29	29	44	184	122	I119	13	—	—	Liab. to Nonbank Financial Insts	16j
126	I—	—	I3	123	I13	187	183	188	213	299	I1,494	1,838	2,498	4,304	Capital Accounts	17a
-8,004	I-33	-53	I-646	-26,571	I-2,162	-18,043	-828	302	-428	-97	I-76	-575	-555	-801	Other Items (Net)	17r
-7,324	I-26	-576	I-576	-23,413	I-1,923	-12,718	—	—	—	—	I—	—	—	—	of which: Valuation Adjustment	17rv
															Deposit Money Banks	

Thousands 1988-89; Millions Beginning 1990: End of Period

1985	1986	1987	1988	1989	1990	1991	1992	1993	1994	1995	1996	1997	1998	1999		
2,740	I7	53	I16	249	I33	496	463	491	774	1,112	I1,681	2,324	2,753	2,627	Reserves	20
											158	1,365	1,367	1,506	Other Claims on Monetary Author.	20c
65	I—	—	I—	23	I3	164	217	301	381	358	I1,309	2,112	1,815	1,774	Foreign Assets	21
247	I—	1	I—	—	I—	—	—	3	—	—	I514	426	357	1,107	Claims on Central Government	22a
77	I—	—	I—	—	I—	—	2	8	5	—	I35	16	7	210	Claims on Local Government	22b
4,684	I12	116	I27	1,035	I104	728	17	12	41	10	I24	24	5	26	Claims on Nonfin.Pub.Enterprises	22c
3,737	I14	71	I10	345	I57	1,119	2,035	3,050	4,076	5,159	I4,676	6,626	9,716	13,271	Claims on Private Sector	22d
5,151	I18	138	I19	451	I21	324	373	295	408	471	I787	1,079	1,196	1,406	Demand Deposits	24
3,387	I10	38	I8	325	I37	691	846	1,356	2,501	3,630	I5,748	9,270	12,404	14,622	Time, Savings,& Fgn.Currency Dep.	25
											365	509	360	320	Money Market Instruments	26aa
162	I—	—	I—	7	I1	101	114	89	201	223	I310	443	485	1,120	Foreign Liabilities	26c
389	I—	—	I—	—	I—	1	8	30	24	26	I89	103	132	233	Long-Term Foreign Liabilities	26cl
1,102	I3	17	I2	56	I2	35	268	421	540	655	I756	957	798	1,662	Central Government Deposits	26d
1,215	I4	70	I29	885	I75	1,054	698	759	779	752	I36	743	35	28	Credit from Monetary Authorities	26g
314	I1	5	I—	7	I1	116	267	714	1,198	1,390	I274	484	676	879	Liab. to Nonbank Financial Insts	26j
788	I1	—	I7	69	I48	—	—	503	406	649	I825	222	1,201	1,999	Capital Accounts	27a
-960	I-4	-27	I-12	-149	I12	183	163	-307	-1,022	-914	I-792	-918	-1,268	-1,748	Other Items (Net)	27r
															Monetary Survey	

Thousands 1988-89; Millions Beginning 1990: End of Period

1985	1986	1987	1988	1989	1990	1991	1992	1993	1994	1995	1996	1997	1998	1999		
-13,121	I-36	-42	I-658	-26,262	I-2,239	-19,824	-20,828	-22,180	-23,663	-22,307	I-16,005	-15,526	-18,089	-19,587	Foreign Assets (Net)	31n
21,044	I54	298	I50	1,432	I255	3,653	22,312	25,770	28,096	28,417	I25,855	30,776	36,921	42,794	Domestic Credit	32
10,378	I21	82	I10	-16	I37	838	18,980	20,828	22,387	21,616	I17,648	20,745	22,737	24,656	Claims on Central Govt. (Net)	32an
77	I—	—	I—	—	I—	—	2	8	5	—	I35	16	7	210	Claims on Local Government	32b
4,890	I12	117	I27	1,052	I110	862	188	180	422	478	I122	125	119	150	Claims on Nonfin.Pub.Enterprises	32c
3,737	I14	71	I10	345	I57	1,119	2,035	3,050	4,076	5,172	I4,882	6,886	10,030	13,574	Claims on Private Sector	32d
1,962	I6	27	I3	51	I51	834	1,107	1,705	1,206	1,151	I3,168	3,004	4,028	4,203	Claims on Nonbank Financial Inst	32g
10,955	I39	284	I33	826	I53	758	845	806	1,097	1,242	I1,655	2,185	2,551	3,151	Money	34
4,166	I12	41	I8	325	I37	691	896	1,374	2,518	3,641	I5,794	9,319	12,464	14,689	Quasi-Money	35
											365	509	360	320	Money Market Instruments	36aa
....	....	....	....	....	....	....	....	....	....		278	2,278	883	797	Liabs. of Central Bank: Securities	36ac
....	....	....	....	....	....	....	....	....	....		35	15	155	22	Counterpart Funds	36e
887	I2	7	I1	11	I2	146	295	759	1,382	1,512	I392	497	676	879	Liab. to Nonbank Financial Insts	36j
914	I1	—	I10	192	I61	187	183	691	862	705	I2,319	2,061	3,699	6,302	Capital Accounts	37a
-8,999	I-36	-78	I-659	-26,184	I-2,137	-17,954	-735	-39	-1,426	-991	I-988	-1,614	-1,958	-2,953	Other Items (Net)	37r
15,121	I51	326	I41	1,151	I90	1,450	1,741	2,179	3,616	4,884	I7,449	11,504	15,015	17,840	Money plus Quasi-Money	35l

Nicaragua

		1970	1971	1972	1973	1974	1975	1976	1977	1978	1979	1980	1981	1982	1983	1984
Nonbank Financial Institutions														*Thousands of Gold Córdobas through 1989;*		
Reserves	40	...	...	...	...	...	...	...	...	...	...	...	...	...	...	...
Foreign Assets	41	...	...	...	...	...	...	...	...	...	...	...	...	...	...	...
Claims on Central Government	42a	...	...	...	...	...	...	...	...	...	...	...	...	...	...	...
Claims on Private Sector	42d	...	...	...	...	...	...	...	...	...	...	...	...	...	...	...
Claims on Deposit Money Banks	42e	...	...	...	...	...	...	...	...	...	...	...	...	...	...	...
Foreign Liabilities	46c	...	...	...	...	...	...	...	...	...	...	...	...	...	...	...
Central Government Deposits	46d	...	...	...	...	...	...	...	...	...	...	...	...	...	...	...
Credit from Monetary Authorities	46g	...	...	...	...	...	...	...	...	...	...	...	...	...	...	...
Capital Accounts	47a	...	...	...	...	...	...	...	...	...	...	...	...	...	...	...
Other Items (Net)	47r	...	...	...	...	...	...	...	...	...	...	...	...	...	...	...
Financial Survey														*Thousands of Gold Córdobas through 1989;*		
Foreign Assets (Net)	51n	...	...	...	...	...	...	...	...	...	...	...	...	...	...	...
Domestic Credit	52	...	...	...	...	...	...	...	...	...	...	...	...	...	...	...
Claims on Central Govt. (Net)	52an	...	...	...	...	...	...	...	...	...	...	...	...	...	...	...
Claims on Local Government	52b	...	...	...	...	...	...	...	...	...	...	...	...	...	...	...
Claims on Nonfin.Pub.Enterprises	52c	...	...	...	...	...	...	...	...	...	...	...	...	...	...	...
Claims on Private Sector	52d	...	...	...	...	...	...	...	...	...	...	...	...	...	...	...
Liquid Liabilities	55l	...	...	...	...	...	...	...	...	...	...	...	...	...	...	...
Money Market Instruments	56aa	...	...	...	...	...	...	...	...	...	...	...	...	...	...	...
Liabs. of Central Bank: Securities	56ac	...	...	...	...	...	...	...	...	...	...	...	...	...	...	...
Counterpart Funds	56e	...	...	...	...	...	...	...	...	...	...	...	...	...	...	...
Capital Accounts	57a	...	...	...	...	...	...	...	...	...	...	...	...	...	...	...
Other Items (Net)	57r	...	...	...	...	...	...	...	...	...	...	...	...	...	...	...
Interest Rates														*Percent Per Annum*		
Discount Rate (*End of period*)	60	...	...	...	...	...	...	...	...	...	...	...	...	...	...	...
Savings Rate	60k	...	...	...	...	...	...	...	...	...	...	...	...	...	...	...
Deposit Rate	60l	...	...	...	...	...	...	...	...	...	...	...	...	...	...	...
Lending Rate	60p	...	...	...	...	...	...	...	...	...	...	...	...	...	...	...
Prices and Labor														*Index Numbers (1995=100):*		
Consumer Prices (1995=10 Billions)	64.a	...	...	19	24	27	29	30	34	35	52	71	87	109	143	194
Consumer Prices (1995=100,000)	64.b	...	...	...	...	...	...	...	...	...	...	...	...	...	...	...
Consumer Prices	64.c	...	...	...	...	...	...	...	...	...	...	...	...	...	...	...
															Number in Thousands:	
Labor Force	67d	...	...	...	...	...	...	...	...	...	...	...	...	...	...	...
Employment	67e	...	...	...	...	...	...	...	...	...	...	...	...	...	...	...
Unemployment	67c	...	...	...	...	...	...	...	...	...	...	...	...	...	...	...
Unemployment Rate (%)	67r	...	...	...	...	...	...	...	...	...	...	...	...	...	...	...
International Transactions														*Millions of US Dollars*		
Exports	70..d	178.6	187.2	249.4	277.9	380.9	375.2	541.9	636.8	646.0	566.6	450.6	508.2	405.6	428.8	385.7
Imports, c.i.f.	71..d	198.8	210.4	218.5	327.0	561.7	516.9	532.1	762.0	596.0	360.2	887.2	999.4	775.6	825.6	848.4
Imports, f.o.b.	71.vd	178.7	190.4	197.2	299.4	504.7	466.1	481.9	659.4	540.4	335.5	822.3	932.5	723.6	778.1	799.6
Balance of Payments														*Millions of US Dollars:*		
Current Account, n.i.e.	78ald	...	...	...	...	...	...	...	-181.9	-24.9	180.2	-411.4	-591.6	-513.9	-507.4	-597.1
Goods: Exports f.o.b.	78aad	...	...	...	...	...	...	...	636.2	646.0	615.9	450.4	508.2	406.0	451.9	412.4
Goods: Imports f.o.b.	78abd	...	...	...	...	...	...	...	-704.2	-553.3	-388.9	-802.9	-922.4	-723.5	-742.3	-735.3
Trade Balance	78acd	...	...	...	...	...	...	...	-68.0	92.7	227.0	-352.5	-414.2	-317.5	-290.4	-322.9
Services: Credit	78add	...	...	...	...	...	...	...	83.1	74.2	56.3	44.4	45.1	40.8	46.1	48.4
Services: Debit	78aed	...	...	...	...	...	...	...	-139.2	-106.6	-123.6	-103.7	-110.2	-103.5	-128.2	-149.0
Balance on Goods & Services	78afd	...	...	...	...	...	...	...	-124.1	60.3	159.7	-411.8	-479.3	-380.2	-372.5	-423.5
Income: Credit	78agd	...	...	...	...	...	...	...	13.6	11.7	11.0	19.2	28.3	8.7	6.5	4.6
Income: Debit	78ahd	...	...	...	...	...	...	...	-82.6	-106.4	-82.1	-142.7	-210.9	-193.9	-220.7	-268.0
Balance on Gds, Serv. & Inc.	78aid	...	...	...	...	...	...	...	-193.1	-34.4	88.6	-535.3	-661.9	-565.4	-586.7	-686.9
Current Transfers, n.i.e.: Credit	78ajd	...	...	...	...	...	...	...	12.7	10.8	92.1	124.0	70.4	51.6	79.3	89.8
Current Transfers: Debit	78akd	...	...	...	...	...	...	...	-1.5	-1.3	-.5	-.1	-.1	-.1		
Capital Account, n.i.e.	78bcd	...	...	...	...	...	...	...								
Capital Account, n.i.e.: Credit	78bad	...	...	...	...	...	...	...	—	—	—	—	—	—	—	—
Capital Account: Debit	78bbd	...	...	...	...	...	...	...	—	—	—	—	—	—	—	—
Financial Account, n.i.e.	78bjd	...	...	...	...	...	...	...	192.1	-104.1	-144.4	42.7	426.7	360.9	-93.0	183.6
Direct Investment Abroad	78bdd	...	...	...	...	...	...	...								
Dir. Invest. in Rep. Econ., n.i.e.	78bed	...	...	...	...	...	...	...	10.0	7.0	2.8	—	—	—	—	—
Portfolio Investment Assets	78bfd	...	...	...	...	...	...	...	—	—	—	—	—	—	—	—
Equity Securities	78bkd	...	...	...	...	...	...	...	—	—	—	—	—	—	—	—
Debt Securities	78bld	...	...	...	...	...	...	...	—	—	—	—	—	—	—	—
Portfolio Investment Liab., n.i.e.	78bgd	...	...	...	...	...	...	...	—	—	—	—	—	—	—	—
Equity Securities	78bmd	...	...	...	...	...	...	...	—	—	—	—	—	—	—	—
Debt Securities	78bnd	...	...	...	...	...	...	...	—	—	—	—	—	—	—	—
Financial Derivatives Assets	78bwd	...	...	...	...	...	...	...	...	...						
Financial Derivatives Liabilities	78bxd	...	...	...	...	...	...	...	...	...						
Other Investment Assets	78bhd	...	...	...	...	...	...	...	-115.7	-296.0	—	—	—	—	—	—
Monetary Authorities	78bod	...	...	...	...	...	...	...								
General Government	78bpd	...	...	...	...	...	...	...	-4.4	-5.7	—	—	—	—	—	—
Banks	78bqd	...	...	...	...	...	...	...								
Other Sectors	78brd	...	...	...	...	...	...	...	-111.3	-290.3	—	—	—	—	—	—
Other Investment Liab., n.i.e.	78bid	...	...	...	...	...	...	...	297.8	184.9	-147.2	42.7	426.7	360.9	-93.0	183.6
Monetary Authorities	78bsd	...	...	...	...	...	...	...	9.4	26.3	55.1	108.8	395.0	211.9	-260.1	62.6
General Government	78btd	...	...	...	...	...	...	...	140.5	34.1	13.8	83.5	132.3	210.0	154.4	108.0
Banks	78bud	...	...	...	...	...	...	...	54.6	48.6	56.1	5.5	-65.0	18.1	11.8	-9.5
Other Sectors	78bvd	...	...	...	...	...	...	...	93.3	75.9	-272.2	-155.1	-35.6	-79.1	.9	22.5
Net Errors and Omissions	78cad	...	...	...	...	...	...	...	-3.9	-10.5	-38.5	-74.7	15.8	10.8	-106.0	-38.7
Overall Balance	78cbd	...	...	...	...	...	...	...	6.3	-139.5	-2.7	-443.4	-149.1	-142.2	-706.3	-452.3
Reserves and Related Items	79dad	...	...	...	...	...	...	...	-6.3	139.5	2.7	443.4	149.1	142.2	706.3	452.3
Reserve Assets	79dbd	...	...	...	...	...	...	...	-1.0	84.4	-50.6	207.7	-64.8	-31.3	-13.7	-244.4
Use of Fund Credit and Loans	79dcd	...	...	...	...	...	...	...	-7.9	—	53.3	-6.2	-21.4	-4.1	-4.6	-4.4
Exceptional Financing	79ded	...	...	...	...	...	...	...	2.6	55.1	—	241.9	235.4	177.6	724.5	701.0

Millions of Gold Córdobas Beginning 1990: End of Period

	1985	1986	1987	1988	1989	1990	1991	1992	1993	1994	1995	1996	1997	1998	1999	
Nonbank Financial Institutions																
Reserves	....	....	....	—	5	I1	21	24	39	182	122	I122	4	—	—	40
Foreign Assets	....	....	....	—	4	I—	3	13	20	40	15	I2	2	—	—	41
Claims on Central Government												319	367	—	—	42a
Claims on Private Sector	....	....	....	3	55	I119	1,011	1,014	1,285	....	—	I442	504	690	906	42d
Claims on Deposit Money Banks					4	I1	113	354	742	1,199	1,391	I4	113	14	32	42e
Foreign Liabilities						I—	—	—	—		—	I303	367	1	111	46c
Central Government Deposits													—	19	125	46d
Credit from Monetary Authorities	....	....	....	3	60	I87	1,064	1,086	1,705	1,206	1,151	I90	100	80	48	46g
Capital Accounts					-53	I30	-122	117	23	134	160	I517	563	579	668	47a
Other Items (Net)	....	....	....	1	62	I3	206	201	359	81	217	I-21	-40	25	-13	47r

Millions of Gold Córdobas Beginning 1990: End of Period

	1985	1986	1987	1988	1989	1990	1991	1992	1993	1994	1995	1996	1997	1998	1999	
Financial Survey																
Foreign Assets (Net)	....	....	....	-658	-26,257	I-2,239	-19,821	-20,816	-22,161	-23,622	-22,292	I-16,305	-15,892	-18,090	-19,697	51n
Domestic Credit	....	....	....	51	1,436	I323	3,830	22,219	25,351	26,890	27,266	I23,448	28,643	33,563	39,372	52
Claims on Central Govt. (Net)	....	....	....	10	-16	I37	838	18,980	20,828	22,387	21,616	I17,968	21,112	22,718	24,531	52an
Claims on Local Government					—	I—	—	2	8	5		35	16	7	210	52b
Claims on Nonfin.Pub.Enterprises	....	....	....	27	1,052	I110	862	188	180	422	478	122	125	119	150	52c
Claims on Private Sector				13	400	I176	2,130	3,049	4,335	4,076	5,172	I5,323	7,390	10,720	14,480	52d
Liquid Liabilities				41	1,146	I89	1,428	1,717	2,140	3,434	4,762	I7,326	11,500	15,015	17,840	55l
Money Market Instruments												365	509	360	320	56aa
Liabs. of Central Bank: Securities												278	2,278	883	797	56ac
Counterpart Funds												35	15	155	22	56e
Capital Accounts	....	....	....	10	139	I92	66	300	714	995	865	I2,837	2,624	4,278	6,970	57a
Other Items (Net)				-658	-26,106	I-2,096	-17,485	-613	336	-1,162	-653	I-3,698	-4,174	-5,218	-6,274	57r

Percent Per Annum

	1985	1986	1987	1988	1989	1990	1991	1992	1993	1994	1995	1996	1997	1998	1999	
Interest Rates																
Discount Rate (End of period)			....	12,874.6	311.0	10.0	15.0	15.0	11.8	10.5	....	....	8.9	....	8.5	60
Savings Rate				2,229.8	125.2	7.0	7.8	8.1	8.5	8.8	8.9	9.0	9.0	8.9	8.6	60k
Deposit Rate			....	107,379.1	1,585.9	9.5	11.6	12.0	11.6	11.7	11.1	12.3	12.4	10.8	10.3	60l
Lending Rate			....	121,906.0	558.0	22.0	17.9	19.3	20.2	20.1	19.9	20.7	21.0	21.6	22.1	60p

Period Averages

	1985	1986	1987	1988	1989	1990	1991	1992	1993	1994	1995	1996	1997	1998	1999	
Prices and Labor																
Consumer Prices (1995=10 Billions)	619	4,836	48,936	5,042,905	....	....	....	....	....	....	....	....	....	....	....	64.a
Consumer Prices (1995=100,000)			....	50	2,456	186,299	....	....	....	....	....	....	....	....	....	64.b
Consumer Prices						2	57	70	84	90	100	112	122	138	153	64.c

Period Averages

	1985	1986	1987	1988	1989	1990	1991	1992	1993	1994	1995	1996	1997	1998	1999	
Labor Force							1,299	....	....	....	1,385	1,441	....	1,630	....	67d
Employment	290	303	312	296	261	258	229	215	207	203	208	221	234	260	....	67e
Unemployment	35	52	67	72	107	146	194	....	....	....	245	225	208	216	....	67c
Unemployment Rate (%)	3.2	4.7	5.8	6.0	8.4	11.1	14.0	....	....	....	16.9	14.9	13.3	13.3	....	67r

Millions of US Dollars

	1985	1986	1987	1988	1989	1990	1991	1992	1993	1994	1995	1996	1997	1998	1999	
International Transactions																
Exports	301.5	247.2	272.8	232.7	310.7	330.6	272.4	223.1	267.0	351.7	526.3	670.6	703.6	573.1	543.9	70..d
Imports, c.i.f.	964.3	856.8	826.8	805.2	614.9	637.5	751.4	855.1	744.0	874.7	961.7	1,141.9	1,532.1	1,492.1	1,845.5	71..d
Imports, f.o.b.	878.2	782.0	734.4	716.6	547.3	567.3	668.7	770.9	669.6	784.7	790.1	1,033.1	1,450.4	1,383.6	1,683.1	71.vd

Minus Sign Indicates Debit

	1985	1986	1987	1988	1989	1990	1991	1992	1993	1994	1995	1996	1997	1998	1999	
Balance of Payments																
Current Account, n.i.e.	-770.9	-690.5	-690.4	-715.4	-361.7	-385.2	-534.2	-834.0	-644.3	-698.8	-563.5	-500.2	-556.2	-498.2	-652.2	78al d
Goods: Exports f.o.b.	305.1	257.8	295.1	235.7	318.7	332.4	268.1	223.1	267.0	339.2	448.4	489.8	630.9	579.4	550.0	78aa d
Goods: Imports f.o.b.	-794.1	-677.4	-734.4	-718.3	-547.3	-569.7	-688.0	-770.8	-659.4	-769.7	-850.0	-940.8	-1,329.3	-1,383.1	-1,683.2	78ab d
Trade Balance	-489.0	-419.6	-439.3	-482.6	-228.6	-237.3	-419.9	-547.7	-392.4	-430.5	-401.6	-451.0	-698.4	-803.7	-1,133.2	78ac d
Services: Credit	39.3	29.5	29.5	37.4	22.0	59.8	70.2	86.2	100.2	125.1	141.8	173.8	216.6	251.1	288.7	78ad d
Services: Debit	-129.6	-159.1	-160.5	-138.1	-119.2	-112.3	-136.2	-148.3	-156.6	-169.6	-217.2	-248.9	-237.1	-271.9	-327.7	78ae d
Balance on Goods & Services	-579.3	-549.2	-570.3	-583.3	-325.8	-289.8	-485.9	-609.8	-448.8	-475.0	-477.0	-526.1	-718.9	-824.5	-1,172.2	78af d
Income: Credit	1.5	.7	1.4	2.1	6.8	11.8	9.7	7.5	5.4	6.7	7.2	10.5	14.7	19.5	27.0	78ag d
Income: Debit	-274.8	-254.3	-245.3	-264.2	-211.6	-228.8	-373.0	-502.3	-434.5	-478.9	-379.2	-334.8	-279.4	-211.2	-227.0	78ah d
Balance on Gds, Serv. & Inc.	-852.6	-802.8	-814.2	-845.4	-530.6	-506.8	-849.2	-1,104.6	-877.9	-947.2	-849.0	-850.4	-983.6	-1,016.2	-1,372.2	78ai d
Current Transfers, n.i.e.: Credit	81.7	112.3	123.8	130.0	168.9	121.6	315.0	270.6	233.6	248.4	285.5	350.2	427.4	518.0	720.0	78aj d
Current Transfers: Debit																78ak d
Capital Account, n.i.e.	—	—	—	—	—	—	—	—	—	—	—	—	—	—	—	78bc d
Capital Account, n.i.e.: Credit	—	—	—	—	—	—	—	—	—	—	—	—	—	—	—	78ba d
Capital Account: Debit	—	—	—	—	—	—	—	—	—	—	—	—	—	—	—	78bb d
Financial Account, n.i.e.	361.7	-194.2	112.2	243.0	-89.3	-161.1	-615.7	-538.3	-502.8	-901.9	-601.8	-378.2	-61.0	83.6	391.9	78bj d
Direct Investment Abroad	—	—	—	—	—	—	—	—	—	—	—	—	—	—	—	78bd d
Dir. Invest. in Rep. Econ., n.i.e.	—	—	—	—	—	—	—	15.0	38.8	40.0	75.4	97.0	173.1	183.7	300.0	78be d
Portfolio Investment Assets								....	....	....	....	....	....	....	....	78bf d
Equity Securities								....	....	....	....	....	....	....	....	78bk d
Debt Securities								....	....	....	....	....	....	....	....	78bl d
Portfolio Investment Liab., n.i.e.								....	....	....	....	....	....	....	....	78bg d
Equity Securities								....	....	....	....	....	....	....	....	78bm d
Debt Securities								....	....	....	....	....	....	....	....	78bn d
Financial Derivatives Assets																78bw d
Financial Derivatives Liabilities																78bx d
Other Investment Assets	—	—	—	—	—	—	-21.1	-5.9	-10.1	-1.3	-32.0	-54.3	-70.8	55.2	22.2	78bh d
Monetary Authorities	—	—	—	—	—	....										78bo d
General Government	—	—	—	—	—	—	-8.0									78bp d
Banks	—	—	—	—	—	—	-13.1	-6.4	-10.1	-1.3	-32.0	-54.3	-70.8	55.2	22.2	78bq d
Other Sectors								.5								78br d
Other Investment Liab., n.i.e.	361.7	-194.2	112.2	243.0	-89.3	-161.1	-594.6	-547.4	-531.5	-940.6	-645.2	-420.9	-163.3	-155.3	69.7	78bi d
Monetary Authorities	98.8	-104.1	-119.3	131.4	-20.1	-78.4	-131.4	-88.0	-94.9	-544.3	-221.7	-126.1	-106.0	-18.1	58.9	78bs d
General Government	304.2	-74.7	230.0	132.9	-67.2	-57.9	-380.6	-459.7	-390.7	-418.7	-439.4	-295.4	-103.1	-154.8	-62.5	78bt d
Banks	2.4	.5	6.8	-10.2	-5.3	-16.9	4.2	-1.7	-16.6	14.3	5.9	6.0	25.1	.3	63.6	78bu d
Other Sectors	-43.7	-15.9	-5.3	-11.1	3.3	-7.9	-86.8	2.0	-29.3	8.1	10.0	-5.4	20.7	17.3	9.7	78bv d
Net Errors and Omissions	-186.8	-183.6	-78.9	51.9	-54.7	-149.2	17.2	60.2	128.1	72.1	64.2	79.5	322.6	13.8	-192.8	78ca d
Overall Balance	-596.0	-1,068.3	-657.1	-420.5	-505.7	-695.5	-1,132.7	-1,312.0	-1,019.0	-1,528.6	-1,101.1	-798.9	-294.6	-400.8	-453.1	78cb d
Reserves and Related Items	596.0	1,068.3	657.1	420.5	505.7	695.5	1,132.7	1,312.0	1,019.0	1,528.6	1,101.1	798.9	294.6	400.8	453.1	79da d
Reserve Assets	-7.8	211.3	-6.2	-43.9	-78.6	7.3	-41.7	-.5	79.4	-84.6	11.5	-53.1	-173.2	30.3	-156.5	79db d
Use of Fund Credit and Loans	-8.9	....	....	....	....	....	23.1	....	....	26.1	-12.9	-9.3	—	22.6	105.3	79dc d
Exceptional Financing	612.7	857.0	663.3	464.4	584.3	688.2	1,151.3	1,312.5	939.6	1,587.1	1,102.5	861.3	467.8	347.9	504.3	79de d

Nicaragua

		1970	1971	1972	1973	1974	1975	1976	1977	1978	1979	1980	1981	1982	1983	1984
Government Finance											*Thousandths (.000) of Gold Córdobas through 1985; Gold Córd. 1986-87;*					
Deficit (-) or Surplus	80	−15	−30	−43	−41	−117	−129	−102	−209	−230	−192	−348	−390	−654	−1,308	−2,043
Revenue	81	116	130	130	187	273	265	305	359	320	382	922	1,192	1,456	2,057	3,169
Grants Received	81z	—	—	—	—	—	—	—	1	—	—	26	45	49	123	69
Expenditure	82	131	160	174	229	390	394	408	569	552	557	1,296	1,627	2,159	3,488	5,281
Lending Minus Repayments	83	—	—	—	—	—	—	—	−1	−1	17					
Financing																
Domestic	84a	....	....	....	....	−9	24	63	88	218	164	186	286	533	971	1,790
Foreign	85a	....	....	....	....	126	105	38	122	13	28	161	102	121	336	252
Debt: Cordobas	88b	....	....	....	....	....	....	....	....	....	....	66	102	146	648	568
Foreign Currency	89b	....	....	....	....	....	....	....	....	....	....	41	20	40	9	111
National Accounts											*Thousandths (.000) of Gold Córdobas through 1985; Gold Córd. 1986-87;*					
Exports of Goods & Services	90c	290.6	304.4	435.2	432.0	619.0	624.4	853.6	1,006.4	1,032.0	1,220.0	1,007.8	1,094.0	906.0	1,277.4	1,480.7
Government Consumption	91f	103.9	112.3	115.5	124.3	164.0	200.9	241.0	278.5	351.5	516.8	818.4	1,071.3	1,325.6	2,064.6	3,174.1
Gross Fixed Capital Formation	93e	....	....	....	....	....	....	....	....	....	....	....	....	....	....	1,740.2
Increase/Decrease(-) in Stocks	93i															249.1
Private Consumption	96f	809.1	867.2	869.0	1,173.6	1,584.9	1,725.0	1,778.5	2,051.4	2,030.2	2,151.8	3,439.6	3,625.5	3,854.6	3,738.0	5,002.3
Imports of Goods & Services	98c	−317.5	−330.3	−365.8	−579.0	−907.6	−822.7	−824.1	−1,174.1	−937.6	−816.9	−1,800.6	−2,046.7	−1,477.8	−1,975.6	−2,653.5
Gross Domestic Product (GDP)	99b	1,085.7	1,155.6	1,210.3	1,513.5	2,126.0	2,187.7	2,515.3	2,944.7	2,849.2	2,898.7	4,154.0	4,889.8	5,662.1	6,574.8	8,993.4
Net Factor Inc/Pmts(-) Abroad	98.n	....	....	....	....	....	....	....	....	....	....	....	....	....	....	....
Gross National Income (GNI)	99a	....	....	....	....	....	....	....	....	....	....	....	....	....	....	....
Net National Income	99e	....	....	....	....	....	....	....	....	....	....	....	....	....	....	....
GDP Volume 1958 Prices(Millions)	99b.p	4.7	4.9	5.1	5.3	6.0	6.1	6.5	6.8	6.4	....	....	....	....	....	....
GDP Volume 1980 Prices(Thousands)	99b.p	4.0	4.2	14.2	4.5	5.2	5.1	5.4	5.9	5.4	4.0	4.2	4.4	4.3	4.5	4.5
GDP Volume (1995=100)	99bv p	102.9	106.3	108.7	115.6	132.1	131.9	138.7	150.3	138.5	101.9	106.6	112.3	111.4	116.5	114.7
GDP Deflator (1995=1 trillion)	99bi p	74.1	76.3	78.2	91.9	113.0	....	....	....	....	....	....	....	....	....	....
GDP Deflator (1995=10 billions)	99bi p	....	....	....	....	1	1	1	1	1	2	3	3	4	4	6
GDP Deflator (1995=100)	99bi p	....	....	....	....											
																Millions:
Population	99z	1.83	1.89	1.95	2.01	2.08	2.15	2.24	2.32	2.41	2.64	2.73	2.86	2.96	3.06	3.16

Government Finance

Thousands 1988-89; Millions Beg. 1990: Year Ending December 31

1985	1986	1987	1988	1989	1990	1991	1992	1993	1994	1995	1996	1997	1998	1999		
-5,023	I-14	-87	I-16	-106	I-293	305	-322	-6	-637	-69	-254	-243	-414 P	-1,209 P	Deficit (-) or Surplus	80
7,461	I28	149	I13	705	I229	1,447	1,893	2,222	2,530	3,136	3,654	4,660	5,906 P	6,739 P	Revenue	81
135	I1	3	I—	103	I23	861	399	806	601	1,191	1,149	822	675 P	1,935 P	Grants Received	81z
12,619	I43	240	I30	914	I545	1,936	2,596	3,009	3,689	4,246	5,055	5,719	6,995 P	9,701 P	Expenditure	82
I—			I—		I—	67	18	25	79	150	2	6	—P	182 P	Lending Minus Repayments	83
															Financing	
4,999	I14	88	I16	-3	I166	-342	-549	2	-153	101	-598	-22	-1,266 P	-1,377 P	Domestic	84a
23	I—	—	I—	109	I126	37	870	3	790	-32	852	265	1,680 P	2,586 P	Foreign	85a
....	....	....	....	....	....	....	....	....	....	....	....	....	....	....	Debt: Cordobas	88b
....	....	....	....	....	....	....	....	....	....	....	....	....	....	....	Foreign Currency	89b

National Accounts

Thousands 1988-89; Millions Beginning 1990

1985	1986	1987	1988	1989	1990	1991	1992	1993	1994	1995	1996	1997	1998	1999		
3,408.1	I11.1	65.0	I11.9	1,020.4	I390.0	1,575.9	1,546.5	2,178.7	3,030.3	4,241.3	5,249.9	7,434.4	8,056.7	9,004.4	Exports of Goods & Services	90c
8,224.9	I30.7	189.2	I21.4	837.2	I508.3	1,483.9	1,763.4	1,890.7	1,968.2	2,170.9	2,731.6	3,176.1	3,656.9	4,927.6	Government Consumption	91f
4,780.6	I12.1	72.8	I18.6	881.1	I319.3	1,358.8	1,797.8	2,089.2	2,702.3	3,408.7	4,313.5	5,787.6	7,300.8	11,385.6	Gross Fixed Capital Formation	93e
536.6	I2.5	14.5	I-.9	-16.8	I-17.7	145.5	-16.1	-39.5	54.4	60.0	11.8	48.8	141.9	78.9	Increase/Decrease(-) in Stocks	93i
11,143.9	I48.7	287.1	I54.0	2,498.3	I1,043.3	6,652.4	8,721.9	10,021.2	10,865.9	12,402.6	14,467.1	17,484.1	20,862.4	25,131.4	Private Consumption	96f
-5,039.7	I-18.2	-76.0	I-38.7	-2,044.5	I-678.9	-3,791.7	-4,596.0	-5,086.9	-6,310.5	-8,036.6	-10,112.6	-14,804.6	-17,519.2	-23,745.8	Imports of Goods & Services	98c
23,048.6	I87.0	552.6	I66.3	3,175.7	I1,565.0	7,424.6	9,217.2	11,053.1	12,310.6	14,246.8	16,661.4	19,126.5	22,499.5	26,782.1	Gross Domestic Product (GDP)	99b
			I-.5	-11.7	I-215.9	-1,687.1	-2,477.0	-2,642.0	-3,173.2	-2,801.7	-2,756.6	-2,500.8	-2,029.6	-2,357.1	Net Factor Inc/Pmts(-) Abroad	98.n
			I60.8	3,553.0	I1,348.8	5,737.5	6,740.2	8,411.1	9,137.4	11,445.1	13,904.9	16,625.7	20,469.9	24,425.0	Gross National Income (GNI)	99a
			I58.4	3,409.7	....	....	....	....	....	....	....	....	....	....	Net National Income	99e
....	....	....	....	....	....	....	....	....	....	....	....	....	....	....	GDP Volume 1958 Prices(Millions)	99b.p
4.3	4.3	4.2	3.7	3.6	3.6	3.6	3.6	3.6	3.7	3.9	4.1	4.3	4.6	4.8	GDP Volume 1980 Prices(Thousands)	99b.p
110.0	108.9	108.1	94.6	93.0	93.0	92.8	93.1	92.8	95.9	100.0	104.7	110.1	116.8	122.7	GDP Volume (1995=100)	99bv p
....	....	....	....	....	....	....	....	....	....	....	....	....	....	....	GDP Deflator (1995=1 trillion)	99bi p
15	56	359	49,196	2,397,128	....	....	....	....	....	....	....	....	....	....	GDP Deflator (1995=10 billions)	99bi p
				.02	11.82	56.17	69.47	83.63	90.14	100.00	111.70	121.98	135.19	153.26	GDP Deflator (1995=100)	99bi p

Midyear Estimates

1985	1986	1987	1988	1989	1990	1991	1992	1993	1994	1995	1996	1997	1998	1999		
3.27	3.38	3.50	3.62	3.74	3.87	4.00	4.13	4.26	4.40	4.54	4.55	4.68	4.81	4.94	Population	99z

(See notes in the back of the book.)

Niger

		1970	1971	1972	1973	1974	1975	1976	1977	1978	1979	1980	1981	1982	1983	1984
Exchange Rates															*Francs per SDR:*	
Official Rate	aa	276.02	283.61	278.00	284.00	272.08	262.55	288.70	285.76	272.28	264.78	287.99	334.52	370.92	436.97	470.11
															Francs per US Dollar:	
Official Rate	ae	276.02	261.22	256.05	235.42	222.22	224.27	248.49	235.25	209.00	201.00	225.80	287.40	336.25	417.37	479.60
Official Rate	rf	276.40	275.59	252.03	222.89	240.70	214.31	238.95	245.68	225.66	212.72	211.28	271.73	328.61	381.07	436.96
Fund Position															*Millions of SDRs:*	
Quota	2f. s	13.0	13.0	13.0	13.0	13.0	13.0	13.0	13.0	16.0	16.0	24.0	24.0	24.0	33.7	33.7
SDRs	1b. s	1.7	3.1	4.4	4.4	4.4	4.4	4.4	4.4	4.4	6.0	5.8	7.5	7.5	4.6	2.2
Reserve Position in the Fund	1c. s	2.1	2.1	2.1	2.1	2.1	2.1	2.1	3.1	5.0	5.0	6.0	6.0	6.0	8.6	8.6
Total Fund Cred.&Loans Outstg.	2tl	—	—	—	—	—	—	—	—	—	5.4	5.4	12.7	12.7	43.5	56.8
International Liquidity													*Millions of US Dollars Unless Otherwise Indicated:*			
Total Reserves minus Gold	1l. d	18.7	33.6	41.3	50.8	45.5	50.3	82.5	101.1	128.3	131.7	125.9	105.3	29.6	53.2	88.7
SDRs	1b. d	1.7	3.3	4.8	5.3	5.4	5.1	5.1	5.3	5.7	8.0	7.4	8.8	8.2	4.8	2.2
Reserve Position in the Fund	1c. d	2.1	2.3	2.3	2.5	2.6	2.5	2.5	3.8	6.6	6.6	7.7	7.0	6.8	9.0	8.4
Foreign Exchange	1d. d	15.0	28.0	34.3	42.9	37.5	42.6	74.9	92.0	116.1	117.1	110.8	89.6	14.6	39.4	78.1
Gold (Million Fine Troy Ounces)	1ad	....	....	....	....	....	....	—	.006	.008	.011	.011	.011	.011	.011	.011
Gold (National Valuation)	1and	....	....	....	....	....	....	—	.2	.4	.5	.5	4.7	4.7	4.3	3.7
Monetary Authorities: Other Liab.	4.. d	.4	—	.1	.4	.6	1.1	6.1	3.9	3.7	5.0	4.7	1.1	3.5	12.9	7.8
Deposit Money Banks: Assets	7a. d	1.0	4.4	5.7	7.0	9.6	6.8	11.5	23.2	17.3	36.2	17.9	15.4	8.8	16.4	9.9
Liabilities	7b. d	7.9	9.9	9.4	11.1	11.8	12.0	16.7	24.5	45.5	79.9	126.9	99.3	155.5	130.7	103.6
Monetary Authorities															*Billions of Francs:*	
Foreign Assets	11	5.2	8.6	10.6	11.7	10.1	11.3	20.5	23.8	26.8	26.5	28.4	30.3	10.0	22.2	42.5
Claims on Central Government	12a	—	—	—	—	—	—	—	.6	4.4	4.6	10.9	12.2	15.9	27.9	31.1
Claims on Deposit Money Banks	12e	1.4	—	.1	.2	4.4	6.2	1.2	1.0	6.4	13.6	13.5	22.3	30.7	33.3	20.8
Claims on Other Financial Insts	12f	—	—	—	—	—	—	.2	.2	.2	.3	.4	.4	.4	.2	.1
Reserve Money	14	5.0	6.3	6.5	7.4	10.5	10.1	14.2	17.2	26.5	30.0	34.8	41.1	41.7	38.3	48.7
of which: Currency Outside DMBs	14a	4.9	6.0	6.2	6.7	9.4	9.4	13.4	14.8	19.7	27.3	31.1	34.8	35.3	31.5	30.7
Foreign Liabilities	16c	.1	—	—	.1	.1	.2	1.5	.9	3.7	3.9	8.2	8.0	9.4	27.9	33.6
Central Government Deposits	16d	1.0	1.4	2.8	3.0	2.5	6.0	4.9	6.2	7.4	10.9	10.7	16.6	6.8	19.8	16.7
Other Items (Net)	17r	.5	.9	1.4	1.3	1.3	1.1	1.4	1.3	.3	.2	-.5	-.5	-.9	-2.4	-4.5
Deposit Money Banks															*Billions of Francs:*	
Reserves	20	.2	.4	.2	.5	.9	.6	.7	2.2	6.8	2.5	3.8	6.3	4.6	6.8	17.7
Foreign Assets	21	.3	1.1	1.5	1.6	2.1	1.5	2.9	5.5	3.6	7.3	4.0	4.4	3.0	6.8	4.8
Claims on Central Government	22a	.4	.4	.8	1.0	1.2	3.2	4.4	4.8	5.2	5.3	10.4	19.0	23.7	23.9	23.4
Claims on Private Sector	22d	9.6	9.4	10.3	12.2	20.7	28.1	27.5	31.3	52.5	74.2	89.1	102.6	111.3	118.3	108.3
Claims on Other Financial Insts	22f										.6	.6	.6	.7	.5	.3
Demand Deposits	24	3.6	4.1	4.7	6.4	7.6	10.1	10.7	16.6	25.9	29.0	32.3	38.8	34.5	33.8	45.9
Time Deposits	25	.8	1.6	1.5	1.9	2.7	2.2	4.5	5.3	7.8	7.2	13.3	19.3	12.0	16.1	22.6
Foreign Liabilities	26c	.9	1.1	1.0	1.3	1.4	1.5	3.1	4.9	8.1	12.6	19.2	12.0	32.3	24.6	21.7
Long-Term Foreign Liabilities	26cl	1.3	1.5	1.4	1.3	1.2	1.2	1.0	.9	1.4	3.5	9.5	16.6	20.0	28.1	28.0
Central Government Deposits	26d	1.1	1.4	1.4	1.6	6.2	8.8	11.7	15.4	13.3	17.2	17.8	17.1	15.3	15.3	17.4
Credit from Monetary Authorities	26g	1.4	—	.1	.2	4.4	6.3	1.2	1.0	6.4	13.6	13.5	22.4	30.7	33.3	20.9
Other Items (Net)	27r	1.5	1.6	2.7	2.7	1.5	3.4	3.3	-.2	5.1	6.8	2.4	6.8	-1.6	3.3	-2.2
Treasury Claims: Private Sector	22d. i	.4	.4	.4	.3	.3	.5	.8	1.1	1.5	1.2	1.6	1.6	2.3	—	.1
Post Office: Checking Deposits	24.. i	.4	.5	.5	.5	.7	.6	.7	.9	.7	1.0	1.3	1.1	1.1	1.2	1.8
Monetary Survey															*Billions of Francs:*	
Foreign Assets (Net)	31n	4.5	8.6	11.0	11.9	10.7	11.0	18.7	23.4	18.6	17.3	5.1	14.7	-28.7	-25.3	-8.0
Domestic Credit	32	8.4	7.4	7.3	9.2	13.8	17.1	16.2	16.3	42.4	57.9	84.2	102.3	131.1	136.9	130.8
Claims on Central Govt. (Net)	32an	-1.6	-2.3	-3.4	-3.3	-7.2	-11.5	-12.3	-16.4	-11.9	-18.4	-7.5	-3.0	16.3	17.9	22.0
Claims on Private Sector	32d	10.0	9.7	10.7	12.5	21.0	28.5	28.3	32.4	54.0	75.4	90.7	104.2	113.6	118.3	108.4
Claims on Other Financial Insts	32f	—	—	—	—	—	—	.2	.2	.2	.9	1.0	1.1	1.1	.7	.4
Money	34	8.8	10.6	11.4	13.6	17.6	20.1	24.8	32.3	46.4	57.3	64.6	74.8	70.9	66.5	78.4
Quasi-Money	35	.8	1.5	1.5	1.9	2.7	2.2	4.5	5.3	7.8	7.2	13.3	19.3	12.0	16.1	22.6
Long-Term Foreign Liabilities	36cl	1.3	1.5	1.4	1.3	1.2	1.2	1.0	.9	1.4	3.5	9.5	16.6	20.0	28.1	28.0
Other Items (Net)	37r	2.0	2.4	4.1	4.3	3.0	4.6	4.6	1.2	5.4	7.2	1.9	6.3	-.7	.9	-6.3
Money plus Quasi-Money	35l	9.6	12.1	12.9	15.5	20.3	22.3	29.2	37.6	54.2	64.5	77.9	94.1	83.0	82.7	101.0
Other Banking Institutions															*Billions of Francs:*	
Savings Deposits	45	.10	.11	.11	.12	.14	.17	.19	.23	.28	.38	.55	.67	.76	.89	1.00
Liquid Liabilities	55l	9.7	12.2	13.0	15.6	20.5	22.5	29.4	37.9	54.5	64.9	78.5	94.7	83.7	83.6	102.0
Interest Rates															*Percent Per Annum*	
Discount Rate (End of Period)	60	3.50	3.50	3.50	5.50	5.50	8.00	8.00	8.00	8.00	8.00	10.50	10.50	12.50	10.50	10.50
Money Market Rate	60b	....	....	....	....	....	....	7.28	7.40	7.38	7.72	10.13	13.35	14.66	12.23	11.84
Deposit Rate	60l	3.00	3.00	3.00	5.75	5.75	5.88	6.00	6.00	6.00	6.00	6.19	6.25	7.75	7.50	7.25
Lending Rate	60p	....	....	....	....	....	....	....	12.00	12.00	12.00	14.50	14.50	16.00	14.50	14.50

1985	1986	1987	1988	1989	1990	1991	1992	1993	1994	1995	1996	1997	1998	1999		
End of Period															**Exchange Rates**	
415.26	394.78	378.78	407.68	380.32	364.84	370.48	378.57	404.89	I780.44	728.38	753.06	807.94	791.61	I896.19	Official Rate	aa
End of Period (ae) Period Average (rf)																
378.05	322.75	267.00	302.95	289.40	256.45	259.00	275.32	294.77	I534.60	490.00	523.70	598.81	562.21	I652.95	Official Rate	ae
449.26	346.31	300.54	297.85	319.01	272.26	282.11	264.69	283.16	I555.20	499.15	511.55	583.67	589.95	I615.70	Official Rate	rf
End of Period															**Fund Position**	
33.7	33.7	33.7	33.7	33.7	33.7	33.7	48.3	48.3	48.3	48.3	48.3	48.3	48.3	65.8	Quota	2f.s
—	1.0	.2	.1	.9	—	.3	—	.4	.3	.2	1.3	.1	.1	1.0	SDRs	1b.s
8.6	8.6	8.6	8.6	8.6	8.6	8.6	8.6	8.6	8.6	8.6	8.6	8.6	8.6	8.6	Reserve Position in the Fund	1c.s
71.3	86.8	86.3	70.3	64.4	59.7	51.3	44.6	37.7	41.8	35.0	36.6	45.0	54.1	49.6	Total Fund Cred.&Loans Outstg.	2tl
End of Period															**International Liquidity**	
136.4	189.2	248.5	232.1	212.3	222.2	202.8	225.0	192.0	110.3	94.7	78.5	53.3	53.1	39.2	Total Reserves minus Gold	1l.d
—	1.2	.2	.2	1.2	—	.4	—	.6	.4	.3	1.9	.2	.2	1.3	SDRs	1b.d
9.4	10.5	12.1	11.5	11.2	12.2	12.2	11.8	11.8	12.5	12.7	12.3	11.6	12.1	11.7	Reserve Position in the Fund	1c.d
127.0	177.6	236.1	220.4	199.8	210.0	190.1	213.2	179.7	97.4	81.7	64.3	41.5	40.8	26.1	Foreign Exchange	1d.d
.011	.011	.011	.011	.011	.011	.011	.011	.011	.011	.011	.011	.011	.011	.011	Gold (Million Fine Troy Ounces)	1ad
3.6	4.5	5.2	4.6	4.3	4.2	3.9	3.8	4.1	4.1	4.3	4.2	3.4	3.3	3.3	Gold (National Valuation)	1and
10.9	14.7	15.6	14.2	16.8	14.7	13.1	45.7	49.8	2.9	1.5	2.2	.4	1.1	2.2	Monetary Authorities: Other Liab.	4..d
6.5	11.9	11.2	19.7	18.7	20.5	25.0	26.7	23.8	40.6	41.5	35.1	40.9	37.9	44.2	Deposit Money Banks: Assets	7a.d
114.7	124.4	143.8	121.5	125.9	120.3	134.9	130.0	55.5	49.9	44.9	41.7	32.9	30.5	39.5	Liabilities	7b.d
End of Period															**Monetary Authorities**	
51.6	61.1	66.3	70.3	61.4	57.0	52.5	61.9	56.6	58.9	46.4	41.1	31.9	29.8	25.6	Foreign Assets	11
38.9	47.7	41.9	37.3	37.9	33.5	32.6	31.0	33.0	47.3	52.5	57.2	67.7	74.3	69.5	Claims on Central Government	12a
20.3	26.3	30.4	29.1	25.8	27.1	27.1	27.0	27.0	1.1	4.9	4.6	3.2	3.9	1.2	Claims on Deposit Money Banks	12e
—	—	—	—	—	—	—	—	—	—	—	—	—	—	—	Claims on Other Financial Insts	12f
58.3	63.7	65.1	79.4	80.4	82.8	81.3	83.2	79.6	60.5	68.4	64.4	50.7	32.5	43.0	Reserve Money	14
33.3	40.5	35.6	42.3	41.8	37.6	41.0	39.5	48.3	48.7	59.6	57.7	41.7	24.5	34.1	*of which: Currency Outside DMBs*	14a
36.6	42.3	39.0	34.1	30.0	25.6	22.4	29.4	30.0	34.2	26.3	28.7	36.6	43.4	45.9	Foreign Liabilities	16c
16.5	28.4	31.7	21.1	11.7	3.8	3.2	3.0	3.3	15.6	8.3	8.1	8.5	16.4	4.1	Central Government Deposits	16d
−.6	.8	2.9	2.0	3.1	5.5	5.3	4.2	3.6	−3.0	.9	1.7	7.1	15.7	3.3	Other Items (Net)	17r
End of Period															**Deposit Money Banks**	
24.9	23.1	29.2	38.1	38.2	44.8	40.6	43.5	29.9	9.7	8.3	5.9	8.1	7.7	8.8	Reserves	20
2.4	3.9	3.0	6.0	5.4	5.3	6.5	7.3	7.0	21.7	20.3	18.4	24.5	21.3	28.9	Foreign Assets	21
21.7	20.7	19.5	18.6	17.1	16.1	16.4	16.0	2.9	13.4	12.4	14.1	16.7	12.9	12.1	Claims on Central Government	22a
101.2	114.0	108.3	107.0	90.1	83.0	75.3	72.4	64.9	71.4	42.0	43.3	35.5	49.4	47.7	Claims on Private Sector	22d
.1	.1	—	—	—	—	—	—	—	—	—	—	—	—	—	Claims on Other Financial Insts	22f
45.6	41.1	35.9	38.3	44.6	38.4	34.7	30.5	28.8	40.3	38.4	30.2	28.8	32.0	33.9	Demand Deposits	24
27.5	38.1	41.3	49.7	51.3	55.9	42.0	49.2	41.4	37.2	33.6	34.3	25.3	20.6	23.8	Time Deposits	25
16.6	13.9	13.8	12.8	13.4	10.6	10.8	12.2	10.0	23.3	18.4	18.5	19.7	17.2	25.8	Foreign Liabilities	26c
26.7	26.3	24.6	24.0	23.0	20.3	24.2	23.6	6.4	3.3	3.6	3.3	—	—	—	Long-Term Foreign Liabilities	26cl
19.1	21.8	20.0	23.4	20.8	21.5	27.4	24.1	21.5	21.0	19.3	19.8	3.9	9.8	8.8	Central Government Deposits	26d
20.6	26.4	30.6	29.4	27.6	26.3	27.1	27.0	27.0	27.8	4.9	4.6	2.0	3.9	1.2	Credit from Monetary Authorities	26g
−5.8	−5.7	−6.2	−7.9	−29.9	−23.8	−27.3	−27.4	−30.3	−36.8	−35.1	−29.0	5.2	7.7	4.0	Other Items (Net)	27r
—	.6	—	.2	—	—	—	—	.1	—	—	—	—	—	—	Treasury Claims: Private Sector	22d.i
1.7	1.5	1.7	1.5	1.8	1.8	4.3	1.5	1.9	2.1	1.8	2.6	2.5	2.7	.3	Post Office: Checking Deposits	24..i
End of Period															**Monetary Survey**	
.8	8.7	16.5	29.3	23.5	26.1	25.8	27.6	23.7	23.2	22.1	12.2	—	−9.4	−17.2	Foreign Assets (Net)	31n
127.9	133.8	119.6	119.9	114.4	109.2	98.0	93.8	77.9	97.6	81.2	89.3	110.1	113.1	116.6	Domestic Credit	32
26.6	19.1	11.4	12.7	24.2	26.2	22.7	21.4	12.9	26.1	39.2	46.0	74.5	63.7	68.9	Claims on Central Govt. (Net)	32an
101.2	114.6	108.3	107.2	90.1	83.0	75.3	72.4	64.9	71.4	42.0	43.3	35.6	49.4	47.7	Claims on Private Sector	32d
.1	.1	—	—	—	—	—	—	—	—	—	—	—	—	—	Claims on Other Financial Insts	32f
80.6	83.0	73.1	82.1	88.2	77.9	79.9	71.6	79.5	91.8	100.2	90.7	73.1	59.6	68.8	Money	34
27.5	38.1	41.3	49.7	51.3	55.9	42.0	49.2	41.4	37.2	33.6	34.3	25.3	20.6	23.8	Quasi-Money	35
26.7	26.3	24.6	24.0	23.0	20.3	24.2	23.6	6.4	3.3	3.6	3.3	—	—	—	Long-Term Foreign Liabilities	36cl
−6.2	−4.8	−2.9	−6.5	−24.6	−18.7	−22.3	−23.0	−25.7	−11.6	−34.1	−26.8	11.7	23.4	6.9	Other Items (Net)	37r
108.1	121.1	114.4	131.8	139.5	133.8	122.0	120.8	120.9	129.0	133.8	125.0	98.4	80.2	92.6	Money plus Quasi-Money	35l
End of Period															**Other Banking Institutions**	
1.25	1.61	2.15	2.65	3.10	....	....	....	....	....	....	—	—	—	—	Savings Deposits	45
109.4	122.7	116.6	134.5	142.6	....	....	....	....	....	....	125.0	98.4	80.2	92.6	Liquid Liabilities	55l
Percent Per Annum															**Interest Rates**	
10.50	8.50	8.50	8.50	11.00	11.00	11.00	12.50	10.50	10.00	7.50	6.50	6.00	6.25	5.75	Discount Rate (End of Period)	60
10.66	8.58	8.37	8.72	10.07	10.98	10.94	11.44	....	....	....	....	....	4.81	4.95	Money Market Rate	60b
7.25	6.08	5.25	5.25	6.42	7.00	7.00	7.75	....	....	....	....	....	3.50	3.50	Deposit Rate	60l
14.50	13.50	13.50	13.58	15.13	16.00	16.00	16.75	....	....	....	....	....	....	....	Lending Rate	60p

Niger

		1970	1971	1972	1973	1974	1975	1976	1977	1978	1979	1980	1981	1982	1983	1984
Prices														*Index Numbers (1995=100):*		
Consumer Prices	64	21.7	22.6	24.8	27.7	28.6	31.2	38.6	47.6	52.4	56.2	62.0	76.2	85.0	82.9	89.9
														Number in Thousands:		
Employment	67e	....	....	....	....	....	....	....	....	....	....	....	....	....	....	....
Unemployment	67c	....	....	....	....	....	....	....	....	....	....	....	....	....	....	....
International Transactions														*Millions of Francs*		
Exports	70	8,795	10,670	13,712	13,817	12,621	19,556	31,979	39,335	63,706	95,241	119,523	123,589	109,124	113,896	113,030
Imports, c.i.f.	71	16,214	14,975	16,576	19,098	23,144	21,889	30,383	48,221	68,896	98,058	125,426	138,512	153,214	123,287	126,034
Balance of Payments														*Millions of US Dollars:*		
Current Account, n.i.e.	78ald	....	....	....	....	-40.0	-39.4	-39.6	-103.5	-218.7	-143.5	-277.3	-192.6	-233.2	-63.6	-6.8
Goods: Exports f.o.b.	78aad					81.5	138.5	171.6	196.6	287.7	484.9	576.1	484.6	381.3	335.2	303.3
Goods: Imports f.o.b.	78abd					-144.9	-148.0	-198.4	-241.3	-410.6	-527.0	-677.4	-591.8	-515.3	-331.6	-269.9
Trade Balance	78acd					-63.4	-9.4	-26.7	-44.7	-123.0	-42.1	-101.3	-107.2	-134.0	3.7	33.4
Services: Credit	78add					17.9	23.9	23.4	26.0	31.5	35.7	40.6	39.8	41.8	40.3	31.4
Services: Debit	78aed					-77.1	-87.0	-103.7	-129.3	-163.4	-242.3	-279.0	-194.1	-213.0	-153.7	-124.2
Balance on Goods & Services	78afd					-122.6	-72.5	-107.0	-148.0	-254.8	-248.7	-339.7	-261.4	-305.1	-109.8	-59.5
Income: Credit	78agd					8.2	9.7	8.1	9.0	9.3	12.4	27.0	18.2	17.6	11.9	13.5
Income: Debit	78ahd					8.2	11.1	-11.8	-9.1	-39.1	7.4	-59.9	-46.9	-42.1	-50.6	-55.2
Balance on Gds, Serv. & Inc.	78aid					-106.2	-51.7	-110.8	-148.1	-284.6	-228.9	-372.6	-290.2	-329.7	-148.4	-101.2
Current Transfers, n.i.e.: Credit	78ajd					88.7	40.3	99.4	74.6	112.7	148.2	165.0	161.2	158.4	140.5	144.2
Current Transfers: Debit	78akd					-22.6	-27.9	-28.2	-29.9	-46.8	-62.8	-69.7	-63.7	-61.8	-55.7	-49.7
Capital Account, n.i.e.	78bcd					—	—	—	—	—	—	—	—	—	—	—
Capital Account, n.i.e.: Credit	78bad					—	—	—	—	—	—	—	—	—	—	—
Capital Account: Debit	78bbd					—	—	—	—	—	—	—	—	—	—	—
Financial Account, n.i.e.	78bjd					23.4	38.7	49.8	114.4	222.5	209.9	307.0	208.2	176.8	57.9	-38.7
Direct Investment Abroad	78bdd					-.3	-6.3	1.4	3.7	6.8	-11.2	4.2	.6	-3.3	-1.8	-.3
Dir. Invest. in Rep. Econ., n.i.e.	78bed					6.9	22.6	9.9	12.9	42.7	46.8	49.1	-6.1	28.2	1.2	1.4
Portfolio Investment Assets	78bfd					—	—	—	-1.4	-3.9	—	-.3	-.4	—	—	—
Equity Securities	78bkd					—	—	—	-1.4	-3.9	—	-.9	-.4	—	—	—
Debt Securities	78bld					—	—	—	—	—	—	.6	—	—	—	—
Portfolio Investment Liab., n.i.e.	78bgd					—	—	—	—	—	—	—	—	—	—	—
Equity Securities	78bmd					—	—	—	—	—	—	—	—	—	—	—
Debt Securities	78bnd					—	—	—	—	—	—	—	—	—	—	—
Financial Derivatives Assets	78bwd					....	....	....	....	....	....	....	....	....	....	....
Financial Derivatives Liabilities	78bxd					....	....	....	....	....	....	....	....	....	....	....
Other Investment Assets	78bhd					.7	-4.0	-32.8	-3.6	-10.5	-29.0	-.5	-13.0	12.8	-15.4	-1.1
Monetary Authorities	78bod					.4	-1.2	-10.5	5.4	-8.0	.5	-1.9	4.8	-6.7	-2.8	-1.9
General Government	78bpd					-2.6	2.1	-6.9	-9.4	7.2	-18.9	14.6	-3.2	5.6	-5.3	-2.4
Banks	78bqd					2.9	-4.8	-15.4	.4	-9.7	-10.6	-13.2	-14.6	13.9	-7.3	3.2
Other Sectors	78brd					16.1	26.4	71.3	102.8	187.4	203.3	254.4	227.2	139.1	73.9	-38.9
Other Investment Liab., n.i.e.	78bid					—	—	—	—	—	—	—	—	—	—	—
Monetary Authorities	78bsd					11.9	19.4	25.3	25.2	44.8	47.2	60.8	140.7	61.1	67.5	-5.1
General Government	78btd					.2	2.0	12.3	8.1	18.7	28.3	62.3	.2	75.7	2.6	-12.5
Banks	78bud					4.0	4.9	33.7	69.5	123.9	127.8	131.3	86.3	2.3	3.8	-21.3
Other Sectors	78bvd															
Net Errors and Omissions	78cad					-2.0	-45.0	7.9	-5.3	-14.5	-75.8	-35.1	-24.0	-7.3	-7.9	14.2
Overall Balance	78cbd					-18.6	-45.7	18.1	5.5	-10.7	-9.5	-5.4	-8.4	-63.7	-13.6	-31.3
Reserves and Related Items	79dad					18.6	45.7	-18.1	-5.5	10.7	9.5	5.4	8.4	63.7	13.6	31.3
Reserve Assets	79dbd					6.4	-5.7	-37.8	-13.4	-13.8	3.5	-5.8	-2.8	63.3	-29.8	-45.7
Use of Fund Credit and Loans	79dcd					—	—	—	—	6.7	—	9.6	.1	—	32.7	13.3
Exceptional Financing	79ded					12.2	51.4	19.6	7.9	17.7	5.9	1.6	11.2	.3	10.7	63.7
Government Finance														*Millions of Francs:*		
Deficit (-) or Surplus	80	....	....	....	....	....	....	-5,468	-5,261	-12,622	-12,105	-25,241	....	....	....	....
Revenue	81							29,276	36,957	48,794	62,190	77,436				
Grants Received	81z							1,213	698	1,595	369	—				
Expenditure	82							35,388	42,511	58,552	70,819	98,727				
Lending Minus Repayments	83							569	405	4,459	3,845	3,950				
Financing																
Net Borrowing: Domestic	84a							4,420	2,941	4,271	1,008	8,256				
Foreign	85a							5,813	6,307	9,925	14,278	21,616				
Use of Cash Balances	87							-4,765	-3,987	-1,574	-3,181	-4,631				
National Accounts														*Billions of Francs*		
Exports of Goods & Services	90c	13.2	20.4	23.0	28.2	26.2	I34.6	47.1	53.7	71.2	109.7	128.8	141.9	139.8	143.7	147.3
Government Consumption	91f	13.5	13.6	15.0	15.7	17.4	23.6	28.1	31.0	34.0	41.0	54.0	70.2	81.0	87.5	89.7
Gross Fixed Capital Formation	93e	7.5	8.4	8.8	15.0	18.0	36.7	43.6	65.9	90.7	112.8	136.7	163.9	155.2	119.4	55.0
Increase/Decrease(-) in Stocks	93i	3.0	.4	3.5	3.8	4.1	6.3	19.1	17.7	22.9	28.2	32.4	4.5	26.0	-12.4	-21.7
Private Consumption	96f	94.9	98.3	114.9	103.5	147.6	138.6	170.7	206.6	264.6	311.1	381.7	410.7	483.2	522.8	524.6
Imports of Goods & Services	98c	-24.7	-22.6	-29.2	-38.0	-54.3	I-59.5	-70.7	-86.1	-124.2	-159.6	-197.4	-189.5	-222.2	-173.9	-156.5
Gross Domestic Product (GDP)	99b	111.1	118.5	136.0	128.2	159.0	180.4	237.9	288.8	359.2	443.2	536.2	601.5	663.0	687.1	638.4
GDP Volume 1987 Prices	99b.p	....	....	....	....	....	....	....	....	....	....	....	....	....	....	....
GDP Volume (1995=100)	99bvp	....	....	....	....	....	....	....	....	....	....	....	....	....	....	....
GDP Deflator (1995=100)	99bip	....	....	....	....	....	....	....	....	....	....	....	....	....	....	....
															Millions:	
Population	99z	4.02	4.13	4.21	4.30	4.48	4.60	4.73	4.86	4.99	5.17	5.31	5.78	5.98	6.18	6.40

	1985	1986	1987	1988	1989	1990	1991	1992	1993	1994	1995	1996	1997	1998	1999		
Period Averages																**Prices**	
	89.0	86.2	80.4	79.3	77.0	76.4	Ⅰ70.5	67.3	66.5	90.4	100.0	105.3	Ⅰ108.4	113.3	110.7	Consumer Prices.......................................	64
Period Averages																**International Transactions**	
	23	26	28	26	28	25	24	....	....	....	....	....	....	....	....	Employment	67e
	29	28	27	26	25	21	21	....	....	....	....	....	....	....	....	Unemployment	67c
Millions of Francs																	
	116,538	109,645	93,863	85,941	77,710	76,939	86,626	88,200	81,200	125,100	143,024	166,300	158,500	175,600	169,800	Exports	70
	165,935	127,559	93,387	115,193	115,822	105,851	100,235	126,684	106,123	182,097	186,501	229,271	228,404	244,200	244,100	Imports, c.i.f.	71
Minus Sign Indicates Debit																Balance of Payments	
	−68.5	−155.9	−176.8	−230.5	−256.9	−235.9	−176.2	−159.2	−97.2	−126.1	−151.7	....	....	....	....	Current Account, n.i.e.	78al d
	259.4	352.0	477.4	426.3	390.8	488.4	351.5	347.3	300.4	226.8	288.1	....	....	....	....	Goods: Exports f.o.b.	78aa d
	−345.6	−379.9	−448.4	−459.3	−414.8	−501.7	−417.9	−396.5	−312.1	−271.3	−305.6	....	....	....	....	Goods: Imports f.o.b.	78ab d
	−86.2	−27.9	29.0	−33.0	−24.0	−13.3	−66.3	−49.2	−11.7	−44.5	−17.6	....	....	....	....	*Trade Balance*	78ac d
	38.6	46.5	54.1	40.7	31.7	44.4	49.6	57.7	36.5	30.4	33.3	....	....	....	....	Services: Credit	78ad d
	−127.5	−135.6	−193.0	−208.0	−202.2	−226.8	−203.2	−201.0	−185.6	−149.1	−151.8	....	....	....	....	Services: Debit	78ae d
	−175.1	−117.0	−109.8	−200.2	−194.5	−195.7	−220.0	−192.6	−160.9	−163.2	−136.0	....	....	....	....	*Balance on Goods & Services*	78af d
	18.4	22.9	15.7	16.7	18.0	20.4	20.1	19.7	19.3	15.6	5.8	....	....	....	....	Income: Credit	78ag d
	−60.7	−60.1	−79.1	−82.4	−59.0	−74.4	−33.7	−54.1	−30.2	−45.2	−52.9	....	....	....	....	Income: Debit	78ah d
	−217.4	−154.2	−173.3	−265.9	−235.5	−249.7	−233.6	−227.0	−171.7	−192.8	−183.2	....	....	....	....	*Balance on Gds, Serv. & Inc.*	78ai d
	213.1	68.3	59.8	103.3	37.2	81.4	122.2	133.6	139.5	115.1	60.6	....	....	....	....	Current Transfers, n.i.e.: Credit	78aj d
	−64.3	−70.1	−63.3	−67.9	−58.6	−67.6	−64.8	−65.7	−65.0	−48.5	−29.1	....	....	....	....	Current Transfers: Debit	78ak d
	—	134.1	132.1	116.4	149.1	117.4	103.5	109.0	109.3	88.2	65.3	....	....	....	....	Capital Account, n.i.e.	78bc d
	—	134.1	132.1	116.4	149.1	117.4	103.5	109.0	109.3	88.2	65.3	....	....	....	....	Capital Account, n.i.e.: Credit	78ba d
	—	....	....	....	....	....	....	....	....	....	....	....	....	....	....	Capital Account: Debit	78bb d
	−8.2	−27.5	33.3	35.9	10.3	46.5	−122.9	50.8	−123.3	29.9	−46.1	....	....	....	....	Financial Account, n.i.e.	78bj d
	−1.9	−29.4	−10.2	−4.7	−1.6	—	−2.6	−40.7	−5.8	1.8	−7.1	....	....	....	....	Direct Investment Abroad	78bd d
	−9.4	17.6	14.8	6.9	.8	40.8	15.2	56.4	−34.4	−11.3	7.2	....	....	....	....	Dir. Invest. in Rep. Econ., n.i.e.	78be d
	—	....	....	....	....	....	....	....	....	....	....	....	....	....	....	Portfolio Investment Assets	78bf d
	—	....	....	....	....	....	....	....	....	....	....	....	....	....	....	Equity Securities.............................	78bk d
	—	....	....	....	....	....	....	....	....	....	....	....	....	....	....	Debt Securities...............................	78bl d
	—	....	....	....	....	....	....	....	....	....	....	....	....	....	....	Portfolio Investment Liab., n.i.e.	78bg d
	—	....	....	....	....	....	....	....	....	....	....	....	....	....	....	Equity Securities.............................	78bm d
	—	....	....	....	....	....	....	....	....	....	....	....	....	....	....	Debt Securities...............................	78bn d
	....	....	....	....	....	....	....	....	....	....	....	....	....	....	....	Financial Derivatives Assets	78bw d
	....	....	....	....	....	....	....	....	....	....	....	....	....	....	....	Financial Derivatives Liabilities	78bx d
	5.6	−4.2	.9	−35.7	−13.7	−1.8	−43.0	10.4	11.2	22.3	−18.4	....	....	....	....	Other Investment Assets	78bh d
	....	....	....	....	....	....	....	....	....	....	....	....	....	....	....	Monetary Authorities	78bo d
	−.4	1.5	.6	.7	1.2	.6	.7	.1	.1	.3	—	....	....	....	....	General Government	78bp d
	5.2	....	....	....	....	....	....	....	....	....	....	....	....	....	....	Banks.......................................	78bq d
	.8	−5.7	.3	−36.4	−14.9	−2.4	−43.7	10.2	11.1	22.0	−18.4	....	....	....	....	Other Sectors	78br d
	−2.4	−11.6	27.8	69.3	24.8	7.5	−92.4	24.8	−94.4	17.1	−27.8	....	....	....	....	Other Investment Liab., n.i.e.	78bi d
	—	2.0	−2.0	1.4	1.2	−4.3	−1.3	34.6	7.7	−22.3	−2.3	....	....	....	....	Monetary Authorities	78bs d
	27.9	16.6	40.3	60.1	31.1	28.6	−18.5	31.4	−10.8	6.7	−14.8	....	....	....	....	General Government........................	78bt d
	−14.0	−9.6	−.4	−14.7	−5.3	−4.4	17.0	6.2	−65.0	19.4	−10.8	....	....	....	....	Banks.......................................	78bu d
	−16.3	−20.5	−10.1	22.6	−2.2	−12.3	−89.7	−47.4	−26.3	13.3	.1	....	....	....	....	Other Sectors	78bv d
	26.6	−70.8	−66.8	11.2	86.6	−18.4	135.8	−95.5	87.2	−67.8	114.4	....	....	....	....	Net Errors and Omissions	78ca d
	−50.2	−120.2	−78.1	−67.0	−10.8	−90.3	−59.8	−94.9	−23.9	−75.8	−18.1	....	....	....	....	*Overall Balance*	78cb d
	50.2	120.2	78.1	67.0	10.8	90.3	59.8	94.9	23.9	75.8	18.1	....	....	....	....	Reserves and Related Items	79da d
	−19.1	29.3	19.5	25.5	−29.2	−10.1	−6.4	31.0	−19.9	28.7	−25.8	....	....	....	....	Reserve Assets	79db d
	15.0	18.6	.6	−21.4	−7.8	−6.1	−11.4	−9.4	−9.6	5.4	−10.2	....	....	....	....	Use of Fund Credit and Loans..........	79dc d
	54.3	72.4	58.0	61.0	47.9	106.5	77.6	73.3	53.3	41.7	54.1	....	....	....	....	Exceptional Financing	79de d
Year Ending September 30																**Government Finance**	
	....	....	....	....	....	....	....	....	....	....	....	....	....	....	....	Deficit (-) or Surplus	80
	....	....	....	....	....	....	....	....	....	....	....	....	....	....	....	Revenue...	81
	....	....	....	....	....	....	....	....	....	....	....	....	....	....	....	Grants Received..............................	81z
	....	....	....	....	....	....	....	....	....	....	....	....	....	....	....	Expenditure.....................................	82
	....	....	....	....	....	....	....	....	....	....	....	....	....	....	....	Lending Minus Repayments	83
																Financing	
	....	....	....	....	....	....	....	....	....	....	....	....	....	....	....	Net Borrowing: Domestic	84a
	....	....	....	....	....	....	....	....	....	....	....	....	....	....	....	Foreign	85a
	....	....	....	....	....	....	....	....	....	....	....	....	....	....	....	Use of Cash Balances	87
Billions of Francs																**National Accounts**	
	116.5	130.9	160.4	138.9	135.3	99.3	111.6	83.3	84.3	141.4	138.1	161.6	174.7	....	....	Exports of Goods & Services	90c
	97.2	102.3	102.5	105.5	110.5	111.7	95.6	108.5	99.3	145.6	137.4	143.6	147.9	....	....	Government Consumption	91f
	92.4	84.1	92.4	89.3	95.8	112.2	51.4	36.1	38.3	91.2	85.8	92.7	104.4	....	....	Gross Fixed Capital Formation	93e
	6.6	3.5	−25.7	17.2	−6.4	−3.0	8.9	−2.3	−2.3	14.5	24.5	—	....	....	....	Increase/Decrease(-) in Stocks	93i
	510.2	505.3	510.0	514.7	524.9	506.2	511.5	505.7	523.0	690.7	622.2	684.0	759.0	....	....	Private Consumption	96f
	−165.9	−166.5	−193.2	−197.8	−195.6	−151.3	−122.5	−110.7	−113.8	−215.6	−184.3	−221.6	−263.9	....	....	Imports of Goods & Services	98c
	647.1	647.5	646.4	667.8	664.5	677.2	672.7	659.0	647.3	787.1	809.6	649.4	889.6	992.5	....	Gross Domestic Product (GDP)	99b
	....	653.6	646.4	688.7	683.7	681.5	746.5	752.3	745.1	722.4	741.6	766.3	763.1	830.5	....	GDP Volume 1987 Prices	99b. p
	....	88.1	87.2	92.9	92.2	91.9	100.7	101.4	100.5	97.4	100.0	103.3	102.9	112.0	....	GDP Volume (1995=100)	99bv p
	86.6	90.7	91.6	88.8	89.0	91.0	82.5	80.2	79.6	99.8	100.0	77.6	106.8	109.5	....	GDP Deflator (1995=100)	99bi p
Midyear Estimates																	
	6.61	6.82	7.04	7.26	7.49	7.73	7.99	8.26	8.36	8.85	9.15	9.45	9.76	10.08	10.40	**Population**...	99z

(See notes in the back of the book.)

		1970	1971	1972	1973	1974	1975	1976	1977	1978	1979	1980	1981	1982	1983	1984
Exchange Rates																*Naira per SDR:*
Principal Rate	aa	.714	.714	.714	.794	.754	.734	.733	.791	.844	.738	.694	.741	.739	.784	.792
																Naira per US Dollar:
Principal Rate	ae	.714	.658	.658	.658	.616	.627	.631	.651	.648	.561	.544	.637	.670	.749	.808
Principal Rate	rf	.714	.713	.658	.658	.630	.616	.627	.645	.635	.604	.547	.618	.673	.724	.767
																Index Numbers (1995=100):
Principal Rate	ahx	3,065.2	3,071.8	3,327.9	3,327.9	3,482.1	3,557.4	3,494.2	3,396.8	3,447.2	3,632.5	4,006.1	3,567.0	3,252.2	3,026.4	2,864.8
Nominal Effective Exchange Rate	ne c	....	....	....	....	....	....	....	....	....	3,233.2	3,591.7	3,713.0	3,884.7	4,035.1	4,324.2
Real Effective Exchange Rate	re c	....	....	....	....	....	....	....	....	....	....	....	287.5	319.2	327.5	387.6	535.8
Fund Position															*Millions of SDRs:*	
Quota	2f. s	135	135	135	135	135	135	135	135	360	360	540	540	540	850	850
SDRs	1b. s	17	31	46	46	48	57	61	66	67	108	133	239	40	26	11
Reserve Position in the Fund	1c. s	11	11	13	33	34	212	334	340	366	295	371	446	—	—	—
of which: Outstg.Fund Borrowing	2c						178	300	296	272	203	179	133	—	—	—
Total Fund Cred.&Loans Outstg.	2tl	—	—	—	—	—										
International Liquidity										*Millions of US Dollars Unless Otherwise Indicated:*						
Total Reserves minus Gold	1l. d	202	408	355	559	5,602	5,586	5,180	4,232	1,887	5,548	10,235	3,895	1,613	990	1,462
SDRs	1b. d	17	34	49	55	58	67	71	80	87	142	169	278	45	27	10
Reserve Position in the Fund	1c. d	11	12	14	40	41	248	388	413	477	389	473	519	—	—	—
Foreign Exchange	1d. d	174	362	292	464	5,503	5,270	4,721	3,739	1,323	5,017	9,593	3,098	1,568	963	1,452
Gold (Million Fine Troy Ounces)	1ad	.571	.543	.543	.571	.571	.571	.571	.629	.629	.687	.687	.687	.687	.687	.687
Gold (National Valuation)	1an d	20	....	....	24	26	25	25	25	28	34	35	30	28	25	24
Other Official Insts.: Assets	3b. d	28	32	38	39	44	34	35	20e	....	....	....	....	3	2	....
Monetary Authorities: Other Liab.	4..d	1	2	2	—	2	19	2	6	3	11	60	46	24	40	14
Deposit Money Banks: Assets	7a.d	9	24	19	59	104	170	253	346	275	422	458	407	368	459	510
Liabilities	7b.d	14	24	23	14	26	20	74	39	99	119	162	206	345	351	115
Other Banking Insts.: Assets	7e.d	—	—	—	—	—	7	2	12	18	37	54	83	149	123	130
Monetary Authorities															*Millions of Naira:*	
Foreign Assets	11	158	281	248	385	3,452	3,584	3,218	2,693	1,308	3,065	5,479	2,457	1,058	757	1,115
Claims on Central Government	12a	177	250	157	175	20	314	512	1,827	3,197	2,521	2,861	6,053	8,148	11,871	11,068
Claims on State & Local Govts.	12b	—	—	—	—	—	—	—	—	—	—	—	—	—	—	—
Claims on Nonfin.Pub.Enterprises	12c	....	....	....												
Claims on Private Sector	12d	95	61	76	10	15	89	118	171	102	96	100	106	112	91	91
Claims on Deposit Money Banks	12e	—	—	—	—	—	—	—	—	—	—	—	—	—	—	—
Claims on Nonbank Financial Insts	12g	34	32	65	98	180	169	172	244	439	638	656	804	807	972	1,213
Reserve Money	14	400	423	454	561	1,409	2,169	2,773	3,430	3,312	3,847	6,495	6,278	6,803	7,055	7,267
of which: Currency Outside DMBs	14a	342	355	385	436	570	1,031	1,351	1,941	2,157	2,351	3,186	3,862	4,223	4,843	4,884
Foreign Liabilities	16c	—	—	1	1	—	1	12	1	3	2	6	22	18	6	20
Long-Term Foreign Liabilities	16cl	—	—	—	—	—	—	—	1	1	—	11	11	10	10	9
Central Government Deposits	16d	17	17	24	19	2,098	1,732	1,088	649	820	1,442	1,885	1,459	576	1,343	1,659
Capital Accounts	17a	19	30	41	45	49	53	60	72	82	115	151	208	225	252	286
Other Items (Net)	17r	28	153	26	43	109	189	97	780	830	910	533	1,446	2,504	5,011	4,262
Deposit Money Banks															*Millions of Naira:*	
Reserves	20	47	38	44	66	331	862	1,237	1,438	1,114	923	1,552	1,396	2,023	1,285	1,051
Foreign Assets	21	6	16	12	39	64	107	160	225	178	236	249	259	246	344	413
Claims on Central Government	22a	506	300	385	388	768	787	1,197	1,418	1,118	2,439	2,987	2,186	3,193	5,514	9,060
Claims on State & Local Govts.	22b	1	3	8	13	25	32	45	60	110	144	132	259	382	517	518
Claims on Private Sector	22d	346	498	601	731	907	1,475	2,063	2,934	3,861	4,362	6,046	7,977	9,503	9,765	10,302
Demand Deposits	24	289	285	337	I293	583	1,124	2,050	2,842	2,530	3,061	4,422	4,702	4,938	5,620	6,051
Time, Savings,& Fgn.Currency Dep.	25	337	372	457	I582	973	1,572	1,979	2,255	2,420	3,702	5,163	5,494	6,645	7,752	9,039
Money Market Instruments	26aa	—	—	—	—	—	—	3	2	76	31	43	34	116	108	48
Bonds	26ab	—	1	—	6	8	3	—	—	—	—	11	8	9	65	69
Foreign Liabilities	26c	10	16	15	10	16	13	47	25	64	67	88	131	231	263	93
Central Government Deposits	26d	—	—	—	138	138	142	136	138	352	205	424	481	437	567	646
Credit from Monetary Authorities	26g	—	—	4	—	—	—	—	—	—	—	—	—	—	—	—
Capital Accounts	27a	58	69	77	80	92	124	157	202	267	328	378	490	659	780	898
Other Items (Net)	27r	213	112	161	129	285	283	330	611	671	710	437	737	2,314	2,271	4,500
Monetary Survey															*Millions of Naira:*	
Foreign Assets (Net)	31n	154	280	244	414	3,498	3,665	3,330	2,890	1,421	3,229	5,618	2,567	1,067	817	1,432
Domestic Credit	32	1,142	1,127	1,274	1,261	−314	1,018	2,940	5,946	7,782	8,693	10,732	15,781	21,527	27,708	30,471
Claims on Central Govt. (Net)	32an	666	532	518	407	−1,448	−774	486	2,458	3,143	3,313	3,539	6,299	10,328	15,475	17,823
Claims on State & Local Govts.	32b	1	3	8	13	25	32	45	60	110	144	132	259	382	517	518
Claims on Nonfin.Pub.Enterprises	32c	....	....	....												
Claims on Private Sector	32d	441	559	678	741	921	1,564	2,180	3,105	3,963	4,458	6,147	8,083	9,615	9,856	10,393
Claims on Nonbank Fin. Insts.	32g	34	32	65	98	180	169	172	244	439	638	656	804	807	972	1,213
Money	34	643	670	747	I788	1,619	2,463	3,728	5,420	5,101	6,147	9,227	9,745	10,049	11,283	12,204
Quasi-Money	35	337	372	457	I582	973	1,572	1,979	2,255	2,420	3,702	5,163	5,494	6,645	7,752	9,039
Money Market Instruments	36aa	—	—	—	—	—	—	3	2	76	31	43	34	116	108	48
Bonds	36ab	—	1	—	6	8	3	—	—	—	—	11	8	9	65	69
Long-Term Foreign Liabilities	36cl	—	—	—	—	—	—	—	1	1	—	11	11	10	10	9
Capital Accounts	37a	76	99	117	126	141	178	217	274	349	443	529	697	884	1,032	1,186
Other Items (Net)	37r	240	265	196	173	443	468	342	885	1,256	1,599	1,366	2,359	4,881	8,276	9,348
Money plus Quasi-Money	35l	979	1,042	1,204	I 1,370	2,592	4,035	5,708	7,675	7,521	9,849	14,390	15,239	16,694	19,034	21,243
Other Banking Institutions															*Millions of Naira:*	
Reserves	40.m	—	—	1	2	5	16	20	53	59	61	94	152	306	325	152
Foreign Assets	41.m	—	—	—	—	—	4	1	8	12	21	30	53	100	92	105
Claims on Central Government	42a.m	4	3	6	8	12	13	14	32	14	60	59	69	175	386	894
Claims on Private Sector	42d.m	2	8	14	14	26	84	81	110	164	199	362	586	888	1,066	1,276
Demand Deposits	44.m	1	1	2	6	3	9	3	4	12	54	67	122	272	485	511
Time and Savings Deposits	45.m	3	6	9	9	19	55	59	82	111	117	220	328	691	794	971
Foreign Liabilities	46c.m	—	—	—	—	—	—	—	—	1	1	2	12	2	27	7
Cred.from Deposit Money Banks	46h.m	—	1	5	5	15	38	37	52	38	50	110	177	76	−50	24
Capital Accounts	47a.m	2	2	2	2	7	11	10	11	14	19	26	37	63	85	132
Other Items (Net)	47r.m	1	2	4	2	—	5	9	53	73	101	120	183	365	529	783
Liquid Liabilities	55l	989	1,054	1,219	I 1,387	2,614	4,089	5,756	7,716	7,593	9,967	14,589	15,545	17,351	19,988	22,572
Interest Rates															*Percent Per Annum*	
Discount Rate (End of Period)	60	4.50	4.50	4.50	4.50	4.50	3.50	3.50	4.00	5.00	5.00	6.00	6.00	8.00	8.00	10.00
Treasury Bill Rate	60c	....	....	....	....	....										
Deposit Rate	60l	3.00	3.00	3.04	3.00	3.00	3.00	2.67	2.83	4.15	4.47	5.27	5.72	7.60	7.41	8.25
Lending Rate	60p	7.00	7.00	7.00	7.00	7.00	6.25	6.50	6.00	6.75	7.79	8.43	8.92	9.54	9.98	10.24

1985	1986	1987	1988	1989	1990	1991	1992	1993	1994	1995	1996	1997	1998	1999		
End of Period															**Exchange Rates**	
1.098	4.057	5.874	7.204	10.055	12.805	14.107	27.014	30.056	32.113	32.534	31.471	29.530	30.816	134.437	Principal Rate	aa
End of Period (ae) Period Average (rf)																
1.000	3.317	4.141	5.353	7.651	9.001	9.862	19.646	21.882	21.997	21.887	21.886	21.886	21.886	97.950	Principal Rate	ae
.894	1.755	4.016	4.537	7.365	8.038	9.909	17.298	22.065	21.996	21.895	21.884	21.886	21.886	92.338	Principal Rate	rf
Period Averages																
2,453.4	1,625.7	546.4	488.4	297.6	272.6	222.0	134.2	99.3	99.6	100.0	100.0	100.0	100.0	24.1	Principal Rate	ahx
3,964.0	2,211.4	666.5	546.5	366.0	367.7	301.8	192.3	146.6	192.9	100.0	96.5	104.3	106.1	51.0	Nominal Effective Exchange Rate	nec
568.7	310.5	99.0	99.5	88.6	82.3	70.0	58.0	63.6	118.0	100.0	123.7	142.0	155.7	78.9	Real Effective Exchange Rate	rec
End of Period															**Fund Position**	
850	850	850	850	850	850	850	1,282	1,282	1,282	1,282	1,282	1,282	1,282	1,753	Quota	2f.s
1	—	—	—	—	1	—	—	—	—	—	—	—	1	—	SDRs	1b.s
—	—	—	—	—	—	—	—	—	—	—	—	—	—	—	Reserve Position in the Fund	1c.s
—	—	—	—	—	—	—	—	—	—	—	—	—	—	—	*of which:* Outstg.Fund Borrowing	2c
—	—	—	—	—	—	—	—	—	—	—	—	—	—	—	Total Fund Cred.&Loans Outstg.	2tl
End of Period															**International Liquidity**	
1,667	1,081	1,165	651	1,766	3,864	4,435	967	1,372	1,386	1,443	4,075	....	....	....	Total Reserves minus Gold	1l.d
1	—	—	—	—	1	—	—	—	—	1	1	1	1	—	SDRs	1b.d
—	—	—	—	—	—	—	—	—	—	—	—	—	—	—	Reserve Position in the Fund	1c.d
1,666	1,081	1,165	651	1,765	3,863	4,435	967	1,372	1,386	1,443	4,075	....	....	....	Foreign Exchange	1d.d
.687	.687	.687	.687	.687	.687	.687	.687	.687	.687	.687	.687	....	....	....	Gold (Million Fine Troy Ounces)	1ad
19	6	5	4	2	2	2	1	1	1	1	1	....	....	....	Gold (National Valuation)	1and
....	....	....	....	....	....	....	....	....	....	....	....	....	....	....	Other Official Insts.: Assets	3b.d
15	19	10	9	6	5	4	2,993	2,539	2,747	2,450	1,852	2,866	2,244	172	Monetary Authorities: Other Liab.	4..d
415	525	755	948	979	737	1,081	1,424	1,539	1,157	3,490	2,899	3,180	4,395	1,651	Deposit Money Banks: Assets	7a.d
260	247	213	64	112	28	84	122	64	130	137	148	137	299	56	Liabilities	7b.d
136	342	311	517	495	423	532	437	....	....	....	....	....	....	....	Other Banking Insts.: Assets	7e.d
End of Period															**Monetary Authorities**	
1,676	3,606	4,661	3,290	11,705	34,972	44,267	I 43,162	32,045	33,596	42,338	93,830	179,201	588,379	510,591	Foreign Assets	11
11,522	17,722	19,197	28,087	35,378	48,720	83,102	I 139,764	210,734	309,876	439,610	309,827	403,774	438,761	532,292	Claims on Central Government	12a
—	—	—	—	—	159	3	I 94	12	124	25	2	7	7	7	Claims on State & Local Govts.	12b
....	....	....	....	....	....	....	2,344	2,743	1,878	1,468	2,929	2,526	18,739	692	Claims on Nonfin.Pub.Enterprises	12c
91	92	97	176	198	47	1,468	I 570	850	763	604	966	777	517	884	Claims on Private Sector	12d
—	—	54	467	313	399	—	I 3,855	7,802	12,896	24,131	27,606	20,576	20,705	22,070	Claims on Deposit Money Banks	12e
1,332	1,534	1,767	1,775	792	796	862	I 1,469	3,100	2,941	3,160	3,267	5,916	5,178	4,568	Claims on Nonbank Financial Insts	12g
7,785	8,292	9,853	13,982	19,195	24,570	34,892	I 75,706	111,404	149,072	179,946	192,446	204,132	240,119	287,893	Reserve Money	14
4,910	5,178	6,299	9,414	12,124	14,951	23,121	I 36,555	56,168	90,315	106,411	108,975	123,645	156,734	186,456	*of which: Currency Outside DMBs*	14a
8	23	4	6	–11	2	—	I 33,150	953	189	7,067	5,042	23,842	17,385	567	Foreign Liabilities	16c
8	41	37	42	56	40	43	I 25,652	54,611	60,230	46,558	35,499	38,881	31,728	16,304	Long-Term Foreign Liabilities	16cl
2,680	2,903	4,904	6,319	18,311	25,885	55,794	I 45,041	56,991	63,713	194,209	242,638	384,139	615,283	516,967	Central Government Deposits	16d
372	873	1,196	1,466	1,914	2,658	4,210	I 34,589	67,471	80,058	82,367	73,561	72,478	173,910	259,538	Capital Accounts	17a
3,770	10,823	9,781	11,980	8,921	31,936	34,762	I –22,879	–34,143	8,812	1,187	–110,758	–110,696	–6,138	–10,164	Other Items (Net)	17r
End of Period															**Deposit Money Banks**	
824	1,506	2,202	2,355	2,741	4,777	13,736	I 32,141	44,488	53,441	60,281	64,343	64,903	65,895	120,585	Reserves	20
415	1,740	3,128	5,077	7,489	6,634	10,663	I 27,968	33,680	25,449	76,390	63,440	69,590	96,184	161,754	Foreign Assets	21
10,730	5,009	8,253	7,945	3,777	9,107	7,030	I 6,908	39,292	47,829	22,894	56,469	46,187	58,881	202,253	Claims on Central Government	22a
470	474	501	544	755	935	937	I 1,419	1,532	2,117	2,909	3,528	1,475	935	2,095	Claims on State & Local Govts.	22b
11,253	14,916	16,059	18,969	20,920	24,475	29,458	I 54,753	64,133	113,965	172,024	212,547	265,789	331,788	446,959	Claims on Private Sector	22d
6,396	6,194	7,708	9,882	9,738	15,000	20,180	I 36,567	55,592	74,398	85,564	104,017	131,887	150,977	209,899	Demand Deposits	24
9,926	10,942	13,989	16,960	16,707	23,014	30,360	I 49,812	74,058	88,505	111,255	134,756	154,633	198,337	298,908	Time, Savings,& Fgn.Currency Dep.	25
20	50	102	72	194	213	136	I 489	653	329	283	692	130	285	74	Money Market Instruments	26aa
65	68	72	87	64	100	195	I 290	302	3,030	9,002	9,899	14,488	10,929	18,100	Bonds	26ab
260	820	882	345	853	248	832	I 2,393	1,409	2,860	2,988	3,229	3,009	6,540	5,474	Foreign Liabilities	26c
1,275	1,001	1,389	2,223	737	762	1,870	I 1,360	2,055	1,834	3,773	6,098	11,143	13,521	40,773	Central Government Deposits	26d
—	4	7	83	1,263	96	79	I 233	825	10,526	15,172	17,377	8,434	7,762	6,554	Credit from Monetary Authorities	26g
1,064	1,231	1,473	1,845	2,628	3,613	4,106	I 36,800	42,611	44,163	59,697	77,951	92,275	135,296	222,146	Capital Accounts	27a
4,686	3,335	4,520	3,393	3,498	2,884	4,069	I –4,753	5,621	17,158	46,766	46,308	31,946	30,038	131,719	Other Items (Net)	27r
End of Period															**Monetary Survey**	
1,824	4,504	6,902	8,016	18,352	41,357	54,098	I 35,587	63,363	55,997	108,673	148,999	221,939	660,637	666,303	Foreign Assets (Net)	31n
31,920	36,459	40,311	50,752	46,021	61,665	70,609	I 160,921	263,350	413,946	444,710	340,800	331,169	226,003	632,010	Domestic Credit	32
18,297	18,827	21,157	27,488	20,107	31,180	32,469	I 100,273	190,980	292,159	264,521	117,560	54,680	–131,161	176,805	Claims on Central Govt. (Net)	32an
470	474	501	544	755	1,094	940	I 1,513	1,544	2,241	2,934	3,530	1,482	941	2,102	Claims on State & Local Govts.	32b
....	....	....	....	....	....	....	2,344	2,743	1,878	1,468	2,929	2,526	18,739	692	Claims on Nonfin.Pub.Enterprises	32c
11,345	15,008	16,156	19,145	21,118	24,522	30,926	I 55,323	64,983	114,728	172,628	213,514	266,566	332,306	447,843	Claims on Private Sector	32d
1,332	1,534	1,767	1,775	792	796	862	I 1,469	3,100	2,941	3,160	3,267	5,916	5,178	4,568	Claims on Nonbank Fin. Insts.	32g
13,227	12,663	14,906	21,446	26,664	34,540	48,708	I 77,654	120,446	175,781	204,415	234,006	276,564	333,082	400,826	Money	34
9,926	10,942	13,989	16,960	16,707	23,014	30,360	I 49,812	74,058	88,505	111,255	134,756	154,633	198,337	298,908	Quasi-Money	35
20	50	102	72	194	213	136	I 489	653	329	283	692	130	285	74	Money Market Instruments	36aa
65	68	72	87	64	100	195	I 290	302	3,030	9,002	9,899	14,488	10,929	18,100	Bonds	36ab
8	41	37	42	56	40	43	I 25,652	54,611	60,230	46,558	35,499	38,881	31,728	16,304	Long-Term Foreign Liabilities	36cl
1,435	2,104	2,669	3,312	4,543	6,272	8,316	I 71,388	110,082	124,221	142,064	151,513	164,752	309,206	481,683	Capital Accounts	37a
9,062	15,096	15,437	16,849	16,145	38,844	36,950	I –28,777	–33,439	17,847	39,807	–76,565	–96,340	3,074	82,418	Other Items (Net)	37r
23,153	23,605	28,895	38,406	43,371	57,554	79,067	I 127,466	194,504	264,286	315,670	368,762	431,197	531,419	699,734	Money plus Quasi-Money	35l
End of Period															**Other Banking Institutions**	
133	178	697	2,644	1,154	1,248	2,479	....	....	....	....	....	....	....	....	Reserves	40.m
136	1,135	1,289	2,766	3,789	3,811	5,250	....	....	....	....	....	....	....	....	Foreign Assets	41.m
1,132	148	285	168	187	518	809	....	....	....	....	....	....	....	....	Claims on Central Government	42a.m
1,460	2,320	3,403	4,520	6,402	9,609	10,022	....	....	....	....	....	....	....	....	Claims on Private Sector	42d.m
531	602	560	835	1,294	989	2,022	....	....	....	....	....	....	....	....	Demand Deposits	44.m
1,318	1,740	2,823	3,983	2,515	4,104	5,046	....	....	....	....	....	....	....	....	Time and Savings Deposits	45.m
12	1	60	222	597	177	335	....	....	....	....	....	....	....	....	Foreign Liabilities	46c.m
27	132	–157	1,672	4,058	4,859	6,369	....	....	....	....	....	....	....	....	Cred.from Deposit Money Banks	46h.m
164	192	253	471	853	1,484	2,186	....	....	....	....	....	....	....	....	Capital Accounts	47a.m
809	1,114	2,136	2,916	2,214	3,573	2,601	....	....	....	....	....	....	....	....	Other Items (Net)	47r.m
24,869	25,769	31,581	40,580	46,027	61,399	83,657	....	....	....	....	....	....	....	....	Liquid Liabilities	55l
Percent Per Annum															**Interest Rates**	
10.00	10.00	12.75	12.75	18.50	18.50	15.50	17.50	26.00	13.50	13.50	13.50	13.50	13.50	18.00	Discount Rate *(End of Period)*	60
....	....	....	....	....	....	....	17.89	24.50	12.87	12.50	12.25	12.00	12.26	17.82	Treasury Bill Rate	60c
9.12	9.24	13.09	12.95	14.68	19.78	14.92	18.04	23.24	13.09	13.53	13.06	7.17	10.11	12.81	Deposit Rate	60l
9.43	9.96	13.96	16.62	20.44	25.30	20.04	24.76	31.65	20.48	20.23	19.84	17.80	18.18	20.29	Lending Rate	60p

Nigeria

694

	1970	1971	1972	1973	1974	1975	1976	1977	1978	1979	1980	1981	1982	1983	1984
Prices and Production													*Index Numbers (1995=100):*		
Consumer Prices 64	.5	.6	.6	.6	.7	I1.0	1.2	I1.4	1.7	1.8	2.0	2.5	2.6	3.3	I4.5
Industrial Production 66	I27.8	37.0	41.9	48.5	51.3	48.2	57.4	59.9	60.2	80.8	80.0	77.7	82.6	69.6	61.8
Crude Petroleum Production 66aa	58.2	82.1	97.7	110.3	121.0	95.8	111.3	112.4	102.4	123.8	110.9	77.2	68.9	66.2	74.3
Manufacturing Production 66ey	I18.3	20.8	22.1	27.1	26.6	33.0	40.4	43.0	46.8	72.7	76.5	87.7	99.0	100.9	83.5
International Transactions													*Millions of US Dollars*		
Exports .... 70..d	1,240	1,815	2,180	3,462	9,205	7,834	10,566	11,839	9,938	17,334	25,946	18,231	12,196	10,298	11,843
Crude Petroleum (Naira) 70aa	510	953	1,176	1,894	5,366	4,630	6,196	7,083	5,654	9,706	13,632	10,681	8,003	7,201	8,843
Imports, c.i.f. .... 71..d	1,059	1,514	1,505	1,862	2,772	6,041	8,213	11,095	12,821	10,218	16,660	20,877	16,061	12,254	9,364
Volume of Exports														*1985=100*	
Crude Petroleum 72aa	66	92	113	126	139	109	127	131	118	141	121	78	63	59	69
Balance of Payments													*Millions of US Dollars:*		
Current Account, n.i.e. .... 78al d	....	....	....	....	....	....	....	−1,016	−3,754	1,671	5,178	−6,474	−7,282	−4,332	123
Goods: Exports f.o.b. .... 78aa d								12,373	10,441	16,733	25,945	18,845	12,149	10,356	11,856
Goods: Imports f.o.b. .... 78ab d								−9,680	−11,608	−11,819	−14,728	−18,985	−14,874	−11,436	−8,856
Trade Balance .... 78ac d								2,693	−1,166	4,914	11,217	−1,140	−2,725	−1,079	3,001
Services: Credit .... 78ad d								563	877	1,026	1,127	926	508	402	433
Services: Debit .... 78ae d								−3,552	−2,967	−3,434	−5,285	−5,025	−3,446	−2,384	−1,799
Balance on Goods & Services .... 78af d								−296	−3,257	2,507	7,058	−5,239	−5,663	−3,062	1,635
Income: Credit .... 78ag d								351	290	263	688	701	226	108	57
Income: Debit .... 78ah d								−887	−518	−712	−1,992	−1,374	−1,415	−983	−1,238
Balance on Gds, Serv. & Inc. .... 78ai d								−833	−3,485	2,058	5,754	−5,912	−6,853	−3,937	454
Current Transfers, n.i.e.: Credit .... 78aj d								42	11	23	33	32	28	18	16
Current Transfers: Debit .... 78ak d								−225	−280	−411	−609	−594	−457	−413	−347
Capital Account, n.i.e. .... 78bc d															
Capital Account, n.i.e.: Credit .... 78ba d								—	—	—	—	—	—	—	—
Capital Account: Debit .... 78bb d								—	—	—	—	—	—	—	—
Financial Account, n.i.e. .... 78bj d								239	1,480	1,245	−60	1,565	1,659	1,321	−1,361
Direct Investment Abroad .... 78bd d								—	—	−5	—	—	—	—	—
Dir. Invest. in Rep. Econ., n.i.e. .... 78be d								441	211	310	−739	542	431	364	189
Portfolio Investment Assets .... 78bf d								—	—	—	—	—	—	—	—
Equity Securities .... 78bk d								—	—	—	—	—	—	—	—
Debt Securities .... 78bl d								—	—	—	—	—	—	—	—
Portfolio Investment Liab., n.i.e. .... 78bg d								—	—	—	—	—	—	—	—
Equity Securities .... 78bm d								—	—	—	—	—	—	—	—
Debt Securities .... 78bn d								—	—	—	—	—	—	—	—
Financial Derivatives Assets .... 78bw d								....	....	....	....	....	....	....	....
Financial Derivatives Liabilities .... 78bx d								....	....	....	....	....	....	....	....
Other Investment Assets .... 78bh d								−149	−209	−61	−27	146	−15	−444	−686
Monetary Authorities .... 78bo d															
General Government .... 78bp d								−47	−24	45	−18	−2		−237	—
Banks .... 78bq d								−102	74	−98	−24	−16	19	−137	−90
Other Sectors .... 78br d								—	−260	−8	15	164	−34	−70	−596
Other Investment Liab., n.i.e. .... 78bi d								−53	1,478	1,002	706	877	1,243	1,401	−864
Monetary Authorities .... 78bs d								5	6	10	—	—	—	—	—
General Government .... 78bt d								14	1,417	930	620	777	1,071	1,332	−965
Banks .... 78bu d								−26	61	5	40	70	148	44	−222
Other Sectors .... 78bv d								−45	−6	56	46	31	24	25	324
Net Errors and Omissions .... 78ca d								−46	179	233	−735	−127	4	124	267
Overall Balance .... 78cb d								−823	−2,096	3,148	4,382	−5,036	−5,619	−2,887	−971
Reserves and Related Items .... 79da d								823	2,096	−3,148	−4,382	5,036	5,619	2,887	971
Reserve Assets .... 79db d								823	2,096	−3,148	−4,382	4,976	2,085	431	−478
Use of Fund Credit and Loans .... 79dc d								—	—	—	—	—	—	—	—
Exceptional Financing .... 79de d								—	—	—	—	60	3,534	2,456	1,448
Government Finance													*Millions of Naira:*		
Deficit (-) or Surplus 80	−119	36	37	404	1,487	....	−1,130	1,135	2,122	2,871	9,184	2,055	−6,559	−5,392	−2,614
Revenue 81	463	969	1,023	1,769	4,190	4,712	5,523	6,263	5,645	8,609	11,628	7,050	5,819	6,272	6,939
Grants Received 81z								—	—	—	—				
Expenditure 82	573	834	898	1,207	2,684	....	6,580	5,255	3,769	5,448	2,351	4,134	12,378	11,664	9,553
Lending Minus Repayments 83	8	98	88	158	19	459	72	−127	−246	290	93	861	—	—	—
Financing															
Net Borrowing: Domestic 84a	195	204	−107	−114	....	....	....	....	....	....	....		3,402	7,376	3,450
Foreign 85a	−7	66	−11	5	....	....	....	....	....	....	....		263	1,107	1,184
Use of Cash Balances 87	−70	−306	81	−295	....	....	−222	−687	....	....	....		2,894	−3,091	−2,019
Debt: Domestic 88a	1,003	822	987	1,057	1,262	1,674	2,630	3,408	5,980	7,217	7,919	11,446	14,848	22,224	25,674
Central Bank 88aa	232	343	194	175	20	314	512	457	3,197	2,484	2,859	6,047	8,023	11,347	10,701
Commercial Banks 88ab	459	328	387	388	766	801	1,197	1,683	1,196	2,542	2,979	2,155	3,169	5,460	8,998
Other 88ac	312	152	406	494	477	559	922	1,269	1,587	2,192	2,080	3,244	3,657	5,417	5,975
Debt: Foreign 89a	175	179	263	277	322	350	376	364	1,252	1,614	1,867	3,024	2,595	10,577	14,537
National Accounts													*Millions of Naira*		
Exports of Goods & Services 90c	954	1,422	1,522	2,467	6,244	5,318	6,593	8,370	6,882	10,990	14,308	11,478	9,561	7,963	9,548
Government Consumption 91f	578	631	798	976	1,312	2,237	2,585	3,827	4,999	4,882	5,051	6,619	6,816	7,489	6,925
Gross Capital Formation 93	883	1,283	1,401	2,615	3,167	5,513	8,577	9,922	9,594		11,431	11,594	9,734	7,479	4,257
Private Consumption 96f	4,143	5,090	5,267	6,903	10,962	13,689	16,297	19,061	24,341	25,928	31,695	34,563	36,284	41,457	47,962
Imports of Goods & Services 98c	−937	−1,328	−1,286	−1,762	−2,874	−4,978	−6,480	−8,433	−10,024	−8,243	−11,636	−13,505	−10,686	−7,246	−5,084
Gross Domestic Product (GDP) 99b	8,962	10,375	11,035	12,252	19,604	22,945	28,611	33,585	36,053	42,912	50,270	50,751	51,953	57,144	63,608
Net Factor Inc/Pmts(-) Abroad 98.n	−496	−245	−570	−621	−435	−220	−274	−475	−474	−616	−1,090	−910	−1,162	−974	−1,599
Gross National Income (GNI) 99a	5,125	6,853	7,133	10,578	18,376	21,559	27,298	32,272	35,610	42,535	49,759	49,839	50,547	56,168	62,009
GDP Volume 1987 Prices 99b.p	78,540	89,723	92,741	97,742	108,651	102,971	112,282	119,046	112,184	119,767	124,803	108,419	108,165	102,438	97,502
GDP Volume (1995=100) .... 99bv p	50.4	57.5	59.5	62.7	69.7	66.0	72.0	76.3	71.9	76.8	80.0	69.5	69.4	65.7	62.5
GDP Deflator (1995=100) .... 99bi p	.9	.9	.9	1.0	1.4	1.8	2.0	2.2	2.5	2.8	3.2	3.7	3.8	4.4	5.1
														Millions:	
Population 99z	66.18	67.84	69.56	71.33	73.11	74.88	76.55	78.33	80.27	82.39	84.73	87.31	83.62	86.29	I93.33

1985	1986	1987	1988	1989	1990	1991	1992	1993	1994	1995	1996	1997	1998	1999		
Period Averages															**Prices and Production**	
4.9	5.2	5.7	8.9	13.4	14.3	16.2	23.4	36.9	57.9	100.0	129.3	139.9	154.3	164.6	Consumer Prices	64
70.6	70.2	‡82.2	86.1	98.9	103.4	111.2	110.8	106.7	101.0	100.0	104.1	105.5	106.3	104.6	Industrial Production	66
80.3	78.5	71.0	77.8	92.1	97.1	101.5	102.4	103.2	99.9	100.0	109.9	109.5	109.2	108.1	Crude Petroleum Production	66aa
74.3	71.8	‡96.0	99.2	113.2	119.5	130.7	132.7	119.2	106.7	100.0	101.0	101.7	97.5	100.8	Manufacturing Production	66ey
Millions of US Dollars															**International Transactions**	
12,537	5,923	7,344	6,916	7,876	13,596	12,264	11,886	9,908	9,415	‡11,725	16,153	15,213	9,729	....	Exports	70..d
10,891	8,368	28,209	28,436	55,017	106,627	116,857	201,384	213,779	200,936	‡716,206	1,286,248	1,212,499	773,252	....	Crude Petroleum (Naira)	70aa
8,877	4,034	3,912	4,717	4,187	5,627	8,986	8,275	5,537	7,438	‡7,912	6,932	10,330	10,002	....	Imports, c.i.f.	71..d
1985=100															Volume of Exports	
79	75	68	75	91	95	100	105	102	101	100	113	117	135		Crude Petroleum	72aa
Minus Sign Indicates Debit															**Balance of Payments**	
2,604	211	−73	−296	1,090	4,988	1,203	2,268	−780	−2,128	−2,578	3,507	552	−4,244	506	Current Account, n.i.e.	78ald
13,114	5,085	7,560	6,875	7,871	13,585	12,254	11,791	9,910	9,459	11,734	16,117	15,207	8,971	12,876	Goods: Exports f.o.b.	78aad
−7,447	−3,138	−4,082	−4,355	−3,693	−4,932	−7,813	−7,181	−6,662	−6,511	−8,222	−6,438	−9,501	−9,211	−8,588	Goods: Imports f.o.b.	78abd
5,667	1,947	3,478	2,520	4,178	8,653	4,441	4,611	3,248	2,948	3,513	9,679	5,706	−240	4,288	*Trade Balance*	78acd
316	250	224	364	552	965	886	1,053	1,163	371	608	733	786	884	980	Services: Credit	78add
−1,656	−1,106	−872	−804	−1,375	−1,976	−2,448	−1,810	−2,726	−3,007	−4,619	−4,827	−4,712	−4,166	−3,476	Services: Debit	78aed
4,327	1,091	2,831	2,080	3,355	7,642	2,879	3,853	1,685	312	−499	5,584	1,781	−3,522	1,792	*Balance on Goods & Services*	78afd
81	56	46	41	152	211	211	156	58	49	101	115	258	333	240	Income: Credit	78agd
−1,544	−799	−2,926	−2,405	−2,544	−2,949	−2,631	−2,494	−3,335	−2,986	−2,979	−3,137	−3,404	−2,624	−2,818	Income: Debit	78ahd
2,863	348	−49	−285	963	4,904	458	1,515	−1,593	−2,626	−3,377	2,562	−1,365	−5,813	−786	*Balance on Gds, Serv. & Inc.*	78aid
31	14	4	28	157	167	877	817	857	550	804	947	1,920	1,574	1,301	Current Transfers, n.i.e.: Credit	78ajd
−291	−152	−28	−40	−31	−82	−132	−64	−44	−52	−5	−2	−4	−5	−9	Current Transfers: Debit	78akd
—	—	—	—	—	—	—	—	—	—	−66	−68	−49	−54	−48	Capital Account, n.i.e.	78bcd
—	—	—	—	—	—	—	—	—	—	—	—	—	—		Capital Account, n.i.e.: Credit	78bad
—	—	—	—	—	—	—	—	—	—	−66	−68	−49	−54	−48	Capital Account: Debit	78bbd
−3,678	−1,087	−4,159	−4,611	−3,649	−4,182	−2,633	−7,784	−1,043	329	−46	−4,155	−425	1,502	−4,002	Financial Account, n.i.e.	78bjd
—	—	—	—	—	—	—	—	—	—	—	—	—	—		Direct Investment Abroad	78bdd
486	193	611	379	1,884	588	712	897	1,345	1,959	1,079	1,593	1,539	1,051	1,005	Dir. Invest. in Rep. Econ., n.i.e.	78bed
—	—	—	—	—	—	—	—	—	—	—	—	9	51	50	Portfolio Investment Assets	78bfd
—	—	—	—	—	—	—	—	—	—	—	—				Equity Securities	78bkd
—	—	—	—	—	—	—	—	—	—	—	—	9	51	50	Debt Securities	78bld
		−551	−69	−220	−197	−61	1,884	−18	−27	−82	−173	−76	−59	−39	Portfolio Investment Liab., n.i.e.	78bgd
															Equity Securities	78bmd
		−551	−69	−220	−197	−61	1,884	−18	−27	−82	−173	−76	−59	−39	Debt Securities	78bnd
															Financial Derivatives Assets	78bwd
															Financial Derivatives Liabilities	78bxd
−2,636	−388	−1,851	−1,121	−2,534	−2,886	−2,487	−5,840	−1,345	−1,286	−3,295	−4,320	−2,183	−332	−3,319	Other Investment Assets	78bhd
															Monetary Authorities	78bod
1,697	1,183	−336	−174	−2,397	−2,086	−771	−2,168	−1,087	−969	−1,030	—				General Government	78bpd
73	−259	−48	−187	−123	−3	−171	−746	−249	320	−560	138	−80	−284	−651	Banks	78bqd
−4,406	−1,313	−1,468	−760	−15	−797	−1,545	−2,926	−8	−637	−1,705	−4,458	−2,103	−48	−2,668	Other Sectors	78brd
−1,527	−893	−2,368	−3,799	−2,779	−1,687	−797	−4,725	−1,026	−317	2,251	−1,256	286	792	−1,699	Other Investment Liab., n.i.e.	78bid
—	89	−393	−113	—	49	—	—	—	—	—	—	—	—		Monetary Authorities	78bsd
−1,823	−979	−3,508	−3,448	−2,817	−1,644	−3,088	−5,180	−1,736	−1,885	−1,535	−3,039	−2,883	−1,637	−1,659	General Government	78btd
125	−14	−34	−148	36	−79	53	33	−28	−1	—	−4	1	21	34	Banks	78bud
170	11	1,567	−90	2	−13	2,238	423	738	1,570	3,787	1,787	3,167	2,407	−74	Other Sectors	78bvd
−135	−182	−306	−221	−107	235	−93	−122	−88	−139	−83	−45	−62	−77	7	Net Errors and Omissions	78cad
−1,209	−1,059	−4,539	−5,129	−2,667	1,041	−1,523	−5,638	−1,911	−1,938	−2,774	−761	15	−2,873	−3,538	*Overall Balance*	78cbd
1,209	1,059	4,539	5,129	2,667	−1,041	1,523	5,638	1,911	1,938	2,774	761	−15	2,873	3,538	Reserves and Related Items	79dad
−506	454	−39	506	−1,186	−2,478	−640	3,727	−611	−327	217	−2,634	−3,507	481	1,650	Reserve Assets	79dbd
															Use of Fund Credit and Loans	79dcd
1,715	605	4,578	4,623	3,853	1,437	2,163	1,911	2,522	2,265	2,557	3,395	3,491	2,392	1,887	Exceptional Financing	79ded
Year Ending December 31															**Government Finance**	
−3,040	−8,254	−5,889	−12,224	−15,135	−22,116	−35,755	−39,532	−107,735	−70,270	1,000	37,049	−5,000	−133,389	....	Deficit (-) or Surplus	80
9,640	7,969	16,129	15,525	25,893	38,152	30,829	53,265	83,494	90,623	249,768	325,144	351,262	310,174	....	Revenue	81
															Grants Received	81z
12,680	16,223	22,018	27,749	41,028	60,268	66,584	92,797	191,229	160,893	248,768	288,095	356,262	443,563	....	Expenditure	82
—	—	—	—	—	—	—	—	—	—	—	—	—	—		Lending Minus Repayments	83
															Financing	
2,277	499	8,339	10,240	10,020	27,042	32,107	46,716	91,136	60,248	7,102	−143,190	−60,637	103,886	....	Net Borrowing: Domestic	84a
1,046	708	832	1,919	5,719	1,564	278	−11,860	16,964	8,391	22,455	7,825	13,383	16,605	....	Foreign	85a
−283	7,047	−3,283	65	−604	−6,490	3,370	4,676	−364	1,632	−30,558	98,315	52,254	12,898	....	Use of Cash Balances	87
27,982	28,451	36,790	47,030	57,050	74,093	116,200	161,900	261,093	299,361	248,774	343,674	359,028	537,489	....	Debt: Domestic	88a
11,522	17,722	19,197	27,682	38,391	56,564	89,413	122,028	189,773	199,662	187,509	247,461	264,229	435,131	....	Central Bank	88aa
10,699	4,968	8,400	7,896	3,768	9,273	7,526	6,908	38,798	47,829	20,113	45,107	41,450	54,114	....	Commercial Banks	88ab
5,761	5,761	9,193	11,452	14,891	8,256	19,261	32,964	32,522	51,870	41,152	51,106	53,349	48,244	....	Other	88ac
17,290	41,452	100,787	133,956	240,033	298,614	328,051	544,264	633,144	648,813	716,775	617,320	595,932	633,017	....	Debt: Foreign	89a
Millions of Naira															**National Accounts**	
12,083	9,427	30,013	31,955	94,959	129,910	129,691	196,904	191,980	214,220	....	....	....	....	....	Exports of Goods & Services	90c
7,342	7,488	7,395	9,253	10,076	11,469	12,690	20,432	27,583	88,510	....	....	....	....	....	Government Consumption	91f
5,126	7,734	9,605	9,392	18,424	31,127	35,620	58,940	81,398	85,310	....	....	....	....	....	Gross Capital Formation	93
54,066	56,204	78,329	113,073	138,828	146,420	222,270	404,182	569,790	738,030	....	....	....	....	....	Private Consumption	96f
−6,262	−7,791	−16,457	−18,430	−37,490	−58,289	−76,260	−130,650	−173,661	−211,110	....	....	....	....	....	Imports of Goods & Services	98c
72,355	73,062	108,885	145,243	224,797	260,637	328,115	620,077	967,280	1,237,122	....	....	....	....	....	Gross Domestic Product (GDP)	99b
−1,623	−4,380	−11,660	−12,740	−17,619	−22,013	−24,500	−64,400	−73,210	−66,700	....	....	....	....	....	Net Factor Inc/Pmts(-) Abroad	98.n
70,732	68,682	97,225	132,503	207,173	238,624	299,511	485,408	623,528	848,626	....	....	....	....	....	Gross National Income (GNI)	99a
106,964	109,653	108,885	119,664	128,280	138,794	145,395	149,638	152,929	151,984	155,924	165,894	172,404	....	....	GDP Volume 1987 Prices	99b.p
68.6	70.3	69.8	76.7	82.3	89.0	93.2	96.0	98.1	97.5	100.0	106.4	110.6	....	....	GDP Volume (1995=100)	99bvp
5.3	5.3	7.9	9.6	13.8	14.8	17.8	32.7	49.9	64.2	100.0	....	....	....	....	GDP Deflator (1995=100)	99bip
Midyear Estimates																
95.69	98.17	101.41	104.96	84.72	87.03	89.36	91.72	94.11	96.52	98.95	101.41	103.90	106.41	108.95	Population	99z

(See notes in the back of the book.)

Norway

142

		1970	1971	1972	1973	1974	1975	1976	1977	1978	1979	1980	1981	1982	1983	1984
Exchange Rates																*Kroner per SDR:*
Official Rate	aa	7.1400	7.2851	I 7.2091	6.9094	6.3727	6.5381	6.0241	6.2430	6.5433	6.4892	6.6066	6.7597	7.7813	8.0847	8.9072
																Kroner per US Dollar:
Official Rate	ae	7.1400	6.7100	I 6.6400	5.7275	5.2050	5.5850	5.1850	5.1395	5.0225	4.9260	5.1800	5.8075	7.0540	7.7222	9.0870
Official Rate	rf	7.1429	7.0559	6.5882	5.7658	5.5397	5.2269	5.4565	5.3235	5.2423	5.0641	4.9392	5.7395	6.4540	7.2964	8.1615
													Kroner per ECU through 1998; Kroner per Euro Beginning 1999;			
Euro Rate	ea	....	....	....	....	....	....	....	....	....	....	....	....	....	....	....
Euro Rate	eb	....	....	....	....	....	....	....	....	....	....	....	....	....	....	....
														Index Numbers (1995=100):		
Official Rate	ahx	88.6	121.2	96.1	110.2	114.6	121.5	116.1	119.0	120.9	125.0	128.2	110.6	98.7	86.8	77.9
Nominal Effective Exchange Rate	neu	105.1	104.4	104.8	109.5	115.6	118.5	121.8	123.7	116.3	113.7	115.5	118.0	119.4	116.9	115.2
Real Effective Exchange Rate	reu	....	....	....	....	....	94.7	101.8	106.0	92.4	86.4	I 85.9	88.6	91.8	92.5	93.7
Fund Position																*Millions of SDRs:*
Quota	2f. s	240.0	240.0	240.0	240.0	240.0	240.0	240.0	240.0	295.0	295.0	442.5	442.5	442.5	699.0	699.0
SDRs	1b. s	27.2	54.9	87.9	88.0	88.2	89.0	89.5	92.8	96.3	139.7	157.6	195.3	284.3	257.3	262.2
Reserve Position in the Fund	1c. s	118.8	61.6	69.0	63.4	68.9	111.8	247.4	234.7	205.7	188.1	201.4	213.8	246.4	411.0	470.4
of which: Outstg.Fund Borrowing	2c	—	—	—	—	—	29.1	100.0	97.4	82.9	66.0	51.3	31.7	8.1	—	—
International Liquidity													*Millions of US Dollars Unless Otherwise Indicated:*			
Total Reserves minus Gold	1l. d	787.9	1,118.4	1,287.8	1,533.5	1,886.6	2,196.5	2,189.4	2,195.6	2,860.7	4,215.2	6,048.0	6,252.9	6,873.5	6,629.2	9,365.0
SDRs	1b. d	27.2	59.6	95.4	106.1	108.0	104.2	103.9	112.8	125.4	184.1	201.1	227.3	313.7	269.3	257.0
Reserve Position in the Fund	1c. d	118.8	66.9	74.9	76.5	84.4	130.9	287.4	285.0	268.0	247.8	256.8	248.8	271.9	430.3	461.1
Foreign Exchange	1d. d	641.9	991.9	1,117.5	1,350.8	1,694.2	1,961.4	1,798.1	1,797.8	2,467.2	3,783.4	5,590.1	5,776.8	6,288.0	5,929.5	8,647.0
Gold (Million Fine Troy Ounces)	1ad	.670	.947	.978	.979	.979	.979	.979	1.081	1.133	1.184	1.184	1.184	1.184	1.184	1.184
Gold (National Valuation)	1and	23.4	36.0e	37.2e	41.3	45.1	42.1	45.3	50.6	54.2	57.9	55.0	49.1	40.4	36.9	31.4
Deposit Money Banks: Assets	7a. d	396.2	293.4	308.5	410.8	507.2	422.6	520.7	823.8	664.4	634.4	626.8	1,882.0	2,346.5	2,539.7	2,996.5
Liabilities	7b. d	295.4	359.6	365.7	437.1	605.2	472.7	685.4	585.1	752.8	1,279.5	2,738.4	3,438.8	3,979.4	4,335.6	5,540.1
Other Banking Insts.: Liabilities	7f. d	....	....	....	....	....	....	....	1,135.5	2,049.6	3,364.0	3,311.0	2,950.3	2,674.2	2,386.0	1,955.0
Monetary Authorities																*Billions of Kroner:*
Foreign Assets	11	5.81	7.69	8.82	8.99	9.98	12.49	I 11.63	11.58	14.63	21.02	31.45	36.72	48.89	51.40	85.53
Claims on Central Government	12a	6.44	6.08	6.22	6.52	6.45	7.72	9.44	12.83	13.04	14.77	9.83	11.12	5.66	11.76	7.67
Claims on Deposit Money Banks	12e	.06	.30	1.01	1.32	1.92	1.22	1.39	5.53	2.31	1.49	.97	2.96	2.80	4.62	2.19
Reserve Money	14	8.22	9.17	9.60	10.23	11.64	13.66	I 15.37	17.20	19.44	21.19	23.01	22.86	24.36	25.36	29.36
of which: Currency Outside DMBs	14a	7.28	7.99	8.75	9.44	10.77	12.39	14.26	16.08	17.06	17.73	18.82	20.16	20.93	21.75	22.78
Central Government Deposits	16d	2.17	2.86	4.25	5.50	5.48	6.09	5.54	7.03	6.07	8.34	10.18	11.96	8.02	19.45	35.42
Other Items (Net)	17r	1.91	2.04	2.21	1.09	1.23	1.68	I 1.55	5.71	4.46	7.76	9.06	15.98	24.96	22.98	30.61
Deposit Money Banks																*Billions of Kroner:*
Reserves	20	1.27	1.42	1.33	1.40	1.44	1.30	I 1.46	1.17	1.82	5.30	2.65	1.60	2.00	3.68	4.22
Foreign Assets	21	2.83	1.95	2.05	2.34	2.64	2.36	I 2.70	4.23	3.34	3.13	3.25	10.93	16.55	19.61	27.23
Claims on Central Government	22a	4.43	5.96	7.26	8.31	7.98	7.49	I 20.00	23.01	28.26	37.61	48.42	48.04	47.81	49.81	67.74
Claims on Local Government	22b	....	....	....	....	....	....	5.21	5.89	6.46	7.10	8.29	9.50	8.90	8.85	10.30
Claims on Nonfin.Pub.Enterprises	22c	....	....	....	....	....	....	1.36	1.58	1.54	1.49	1.74	2.38	7.49	9.25	11.25
Claims on Private Sector	22d	29.65	33.74	38.18	43.23	49.10	57.05	I 60.06	70.04	76.00	84.61	96.79	112.13	127.26	145.63	184.37
Claims on Other Financial Insts	22f	....	....	....	....	....	....	11.05	14.72	15.67	16.33	19.14	22.57	25.44	31.09	32.07
Demand Deposits	24	7.99	9.12	10.59	12.09	13.70	15.26	I 17.96	20.73	22.09	24.67	25.48	31.13	36.69	42.84	57.71
Time, Savings,& Fgn.Currency Dep.	25	26.09	29.58	32.90	37.41	41.62	48.06	I 61.10	72.77	82.79	96.33	109.07	122.80	135.71	149.03	173.67
Foreign Liabilities	26c	2.11	2.39	2.43	2.49	3.15	2.64	I 3.55	3.01	3.78	6.30	14.19	19.97	28.07	33.48	50.34
Central Government Deposits	26d	....	....	....	....	....	....	7.87	7.19	9.57	10.67	12.75	11.74	11.11	11.69	15.18
Credit from Bank of Norway	26g	....	....	....	....	....	....	1.36	5.53	2.68	2.95	3.82	3.05	2.70	4.35	5.35
Other Items (Net)	27r	1.99	1.97	2.89	3.33	2.73	2.25	I 9.97	11.38	12.16	14.63	14.95	18.44	21.17	26.53	34.93
Monetary Survey																*Billions of Kroner:*
Foreign Assets (Net)	31n	6.38	7.12	8.29	8.67	9.21	12.01	I 10.59	9.91	13.99	17.54	20.25	27.44	36.91	36.78	62.04
Domestic Credit	32	44.28	49.94	56.31	63.50	70.33	81.22	I 94.18	114.31	125.84	143.37	161.72	182.48	204.01	225.76	263.29
Claims on Central Govt. (Net)	32an	12.03	13.12	14.53	16.00	15.94	18.00	I 16.03	21.61	25.65	33.38	35.33	35.46	34.34	30.43	24.81
Claims on Local Government	32b	1.71	2.17	2.70	3.29	4.08	4.52	I 5.24	5.92	6.49	7.12	8.31	9.52	8.91	8.87	10.31
Claims on Nonfin.Pub.Enterprises	32c	....	....	....	....	....	....	1.40	1.62	1.58	1.55	1.80	2.43	7.54	9.30	11.30
Claims on Private Sector	32d	30.54	34.65	39.08	44.21	50.31	58.70	I 60.18	70.19	76.23	84.81	96.99	112.37	127.66	145.97	184.71
Claims on Other Financial Insts	32f	....	....	....	....	....	....	11.32	14.97	15.89	16.52	19.29	22.71	25.57	31.20	32.17
Money	34	17.20	19.21	22.39	25.81	28.88	33.65	I 32.42	37.00	40.19	43.25	45.56	52.38	58.81	65.92	82.00
Quasi-Money	35	29.50	33.72	37.18	41.81	46.22	52.95	I 61.29	72.91	82.85	96.42	109.17	122.88	135.79	149.72	174.99
Other Items (Net)	37r	3.97	4.13	5.02	4.59	4.48	6.62	I 11.04	14.29	16.78	21.22	27.23	34.66	46.32	46.90	68.29
Money plus Quasi-Money	35l	46.70	52.93	59.56	67.62	75.10	86.60	I 93.71	109.91	123.04	139.67	154.73	175.26	194.60	215.63	256.99
Money (National Definitions)																*Billions of Kroner:*
Broad Money	39m	49.6	55.7	62.2	69.2	76.9	88.6	103.9	120.5	133.6	152.2	171.0	190.8	210.9	230.7	276.2
Broad Money, Seasonally Adj.	39m. c	48.6	54.7	61.2	68.1	75.7	87.2	102.2	118.5	131.3	149.5	167.8	187.0	206.4	225.6	270.5
Other Banking Institutions																
State Lending Institutions																*Billions of Kroner:*
Claims on State and Local Govts	42b	....	....	....	....	....	....	....	10.22	13.51	19.21	22.05	23.77	16.69	18.01	19.14
Claims on Private Sector	42d	18.10	21.08	24.77	28.51	32.25	37.97	45.43	I 42.14	50.32	57.08	63.97	70.60	77.05	82.01	89.26
Bonds (Net)	46ab	1.00	1.44	2.21	2.72	3.15	5.41	7.45	I 6.11	7.42	7.97	8.89	10.48	12.03	11.96	12.71
Foreign Liabilities	46c	....	....	....	....	....	....	....	5.84	10.29	16.19	16.68	16.67	18.41	17.97	17.28
Central Govt. Lending Funds	46f	16.27	18.85	21.91	25.11	28.52	32.12	37.11	I 43.21	49.02	55.50	62.66	67.73	73.77	79.72	87.52
Capital Accounts	47a	1.37	1.54	1.73	1.80	2.11	2.31	2.65	I 3.65	4.56	4.97	5.97	6.58	7.07	7.29	8.06
Other Items (Net)	47r	-.55	-.77	-1.10	-1.12	-1.53	-1.85	-1.77	I -6.45	-7.46	-8.33	-8.17	-7.09	-17.54	-16.92	-17.18

1985	1986	1987	1988	1989	1990	1991	1992	1993	1994	1995	1996	1997	1998	1999		
															Exchange Rates	
End of Period																
8.3288	9.0516	8.8418	8.8412	8.6932	8.4044	8.5440	9.5212	10.3264	9.8715	9.3931	9.2641	9.8707	10.7010	11.0343	Official Rate	aa
End of Period (ae) Period Average (rf)																
7.5825	7.4000	6.2325	6.5700	6.6150	5.9075	5.9730	6.9245	7.5180	6.7620	6.3190	6.4425	7.3157	7.6000	8.0395	Official Rate	ae
8.5972	7.3947	6.7375	6.5170	6.9045	6.2597	6.4829	6.2145	7.0941	7.0576	6.3352	6.4498	7.0734	7.5451	7.7992	Official Rate	rf
End of Period (ea) Period Average (eb)																
....	....	....	....	....	8.0230	8.0164	8.3848	8.3878	8.3175	8.3067	8.0615	8.0867	8.8708	1.0046	Euro Rate	ea
....	....	....	....	....	....	8.0186	8.0398	8.3505	8.3760	8.2859	8.1971	8.0131	8.4541	1.0668	Euro Rate	eb
Period Averages																
74.0	85.7	94.1	97.3	91.8	101.3	98.0	102.1	89.1	89.8	100.0	98.2	89.7	83.9	81.2	Official Rate	ah x
112.9	105.8	101.5	101.4	101.5	100.9	99.2	100.3	98.9	97.6	100.0	99.7	100.3	95.8	95.0	Nominal Effective Exchange Rate	ne u
94.8	92.7	96.5	98.5	97.0	95.6	94.0	93.2	92.4	93.4	100.0	103.9	108.2	107.2	....	Real Effective Exchange Rate	re u
															Fund Position	
End of Period																
699.0	699.0	699.0	699.0	699.0	699.0	699.0	1,104.6	1,104.6	1,104.6	1,104.6	1,104.6	1,104.6	1,104.6	1,671.7	Quota	2f. s
258.0	318.2	311.2	362.3	345.2	315.5	315.9	139.1	288.4	266.7	311.5	247.2	257.9	294.1	298.0	SDRs	1b. s
463.7	481.8	498.1	451.3	441.9	407.8	399.0	471.4	425.5	440.9	636.2	643.8	725.5	899.1	621.2	Reserve Position in the Fund	1c. s
—	—	—	—	—	—	—	—	—	—	—	—	—	—	35.3	of which: Outstg.Fund Borrowing	2c
															International Liquidity	
End of Period																
13,916.7	12,524.6	14,276.5	13,267.7	13,784.8	15,332.3	13,232.0	11,940.4	19,622.4	19,025.5	22,517.8	26,516.7	23,400.3	18,606.7	20,400.4	Total Reserves minus Gold	1l. d
283.4	389.2	441.5	487.5	453.7	448.9	451.9	191.2	396.2	389.4	463.0	355.5	347.9	414.1	409.0	SDRs	1b. d
509.3	589.4	706.6	607.4	580.7	580.2	570.8	648.1	584.4	643.7	945.6	925.8	978.9	1,266.0	852.6	Reserve Position in the Fund	1c. d
13,124.0	11,546.0	13,128.4	12,172.9	12,750.5	14,303.2	12,209.4	11,101.0	18,641.8	17,992.4	21,109.2	25,235.5	22,073.5	16,926.7	19,138.7	Foreign Exchange	1d. d
1.184	1.184	1.184	1.184	1.184	1.184	1.184	1.184	1.184	1.184	1.184	1.184	1.184	1.184	1.184	Gold (Million Fine Troy Ounces)	1ad
37.6	38.5	45.7	43.4	43.1	48.2	47.7	41.2	37.9	42.1	45.1	44.2	38.8	37.5	274.5	Gold (National Valuation)	1an d
3,643.9	6,799.7	8,507.3	6,326.0	6,428.1	7,816.8	8,954.1	11,398.8	6,597.1	7,267.4	7,473.0	9,087.8	9,781.4	12,324.9	12,418.4	Deposit Money Banks: Assets	7a. d
9,163.5	13,324.2	19,971.6	19,047.0	20,514.0	22,173.5	16,383.4	11,049.5	9,637.4	9,241.3	9,617.3	19,885.4	25,617.0	29,849.7	31,457.6	Liabilities	7b. d
2,137.0	2,309.0	2,512.0	5,531.8	5,942.9	7,725.9	7,270.6	5,946.3	5,731.3	6,040.1	6,434.6	6,198.7	7,081.2	8,179.1	8,774.8	Other Banking Insts.: Liabilities	7f. d
															Monetary Authorities	
End of Period																
107.47	93.05	89.62	87.52	91.83	90.92	78.75	82.50	151.43	143.58	142.78	225.37	284.17	312.96	408.32	Foreign Assets	11
19.21	47.74	23.93	18.24	24.05	12.56	7.98	12.58	29.25	13.69	18.06	12.41	10.65	9.43	10.77	Claims on Central Government	12a
8.27	71.46	77.27	79.83	70.77	69.04	66.25	55.40	17.48	5.86	10.09	.23	7.50	16.47	25.63	Claims on Deposit Money Banks	12e
31.44	31.07	33.39	32.56	34.45	34.12	36.73	38.52	42.66	44.09	46.39	70.96	62.79	55.89	83.95	Reserve Money	14
25.05	26.58	28.16	28.52	29.20	29.88	31.79	32.45	35.74	37.95	39.08	39.87	42.22	42.14	43.37	of which: Currency Outside DMBs	14a
81.38	144.65	119.27	116.75	121.09	109.01	85.00	67.62	106.76	87.24	98.39	131.24	201.16	222.73	290.18	Central Government Deposits	16d
22.13	36.53	38.17	36.30	31.11	29.39	31.25	44.40	48.75	31.80	26.15	35.81	38.37	60.24	70.59	Other Items (Net)	17r
															Deposit Money Banks	
End of Period																
4.31	3.60	4.31	3.10	3.27	3.00	3.34	4.57	2.88	4.32	5.15	28.06	17.28	14.07	38.36	Reserves	20
27.63	50.32	53.02	41.56	42.52	46.18	53.48	78.93	49.60	49.14	47.22	58.55	71.56	93.67	99.84	Foreign Assets	21
74.22	84.66	78.15	83.13	83.72	85.46	74.66	76.98	87.32	73.87	70.56	78.49	60.79	87.04	45.42	Claims on Central Government	22a
10.58	10.18	14.19	16.74	16.84	14.77	10.87	9.84	11.62	11.31	12.78	15.16	15.71	26.89	17.38	Claims on Local Government	22b
12.79	10.63	12.71	10.31	10.08	8.18	7.19	6.31	9.05	9.24	5.80	8.04	9.19	12.03	11.21	Claims on Nonfin.Pub.Enterprises	22c
241.34	309.05	378.46	406.09	441.17	461.68	441.38	447.36	457.14	479.68	527.46	599.82	708.01	801.58	848.09	Claims on Private Sector	22d
39.43	45.55	71.74	58.45	51.67	43.58	41.82	44.52	34.92	37.11	34.04	40.46	50.13	75.74	72.54	Claims on Other Financial Insts	22f
71.84	73.80	122.95	157.28	186.66	206.37	222.16	288.79	300.43	314.80	316.29	349.70	371.96	453.20	479.34	Demand Deposits	24
195.31	198.55	205.66	189.31	190.70	194.49	189.18	159.95	139.95	149.24	164.57	166.71	150.52	157.80	141.03	Time, Savings,& Fgn.Currency Dep.	25
69.48	98.60	124.47	125.14	135.70	130.99	97.86	76.51	72.45	62.49	60.77	128.11	187.41	226.86	252.90	Foreign Liabilities	26c
20.79	22.25	26.56	30.44	31.78	30.55	27.74	31.67	36.55	33.02	34.00	37.62	32.09	57.40	25.92	Central Government Deposits	26d
9.88	73.55	75.93	77.31	61.03	59.95	60.73	56.08	17.03	5.30	10.47	.45	7.88	18.79	25.92	Credit from Bank of Norway	26g
32.84	36.18	57.02	39.92	43.41	40.49	35.08	55.82	86.13	99.57	115.92	145.98	182.80	196.97	207.74	Other Items (Net)	27r
															Monetary Survey	
End of Period																
65.26	44.24	17.74	3.12	-1.78	5.89	34.11	80.32	123.14	123.81	125.01	142.13	159.34	169.03	227.89	Foreign Assets (Net)	31n
295.87	341.53	433.82	446.30	475.59	487.34	473.64	499.07	486.63	505.25	536.90	586.05	621.74	735.92	689.88	Domestic Credit	32
-8.74	-34.49	-43.75	-45.81	-45.10	-41.54	-30.09	-9.72	-26.74	-32.71	-43.77	-77.96	-161.81	-183.66	-259.90	Claims on Central Govt. (Net)	32an
10.59	10.19	14.20	16.75	16.85	14.77	10.87	9.84	11.62	11.31	12.78	15.16	15.71	26.89	17.38	Claims on Local Government	32b
12.85	10.69	12.79	10.32	10.08	8.18	7.19	6.31	9.05	9.24	5.80	8.04	9.19	12.03	11.21	Claims on Nonfin.Pub.Enterprises	32c
241.66	309.37	378.80	406.56	442.00	462.33	442.02	448.01	457.77	480.30	528.05	600.35	708.52	802.11	848.09	Claims on Private Sector	32d
39.51	45.78	71.79	58.49	51.76	43.60	43.66	44.63	34.92	37.11	34.04	40.46	50.13	78.55	72.54	Claims on Other Financial Insts	32f
98.65	101.76	152.63	187.15	218.30	237.63	255.80	323.33	340.12	354.96	358.71	392.72	416.99	497.51	525.30	Money	34
196.82	200.12	207.11	190.30	191.50	195.07	189.48	160.02	139.99	149.27	164.59	166.73	150.53	157.81	141.01	Quasi-Money	35
55.46	72.82	91.74	71.75	64.02	60.30	62.62	96.39	129.66	124.58	137.62	168.72	213.56	249.62	251.44	Other Items (Net)	37r
295.47	301.88	359.74	377.45	409.79	432.70	445.28	483.35	480.11	504.23	523.30	559.45	567.52	655.32	666.33	Money plus Quasi-Money	35l
															Money (National Definitions)	
End of Period																
317.9	332.4	382.5	404.5	435.0	460.4	509.8	546.9	550.0	586.0	616.0	653.2	674.6	709.9	787.3	*Broad Money*	39m
312.2	327.7	378.5	400.9	431.8	457.4	505.7	535.9	538.0	580.0	619.0	652.0	673.5	709.5	788.6	*Broad Money, Seasonally Adj.*	39m. c
															Other Banking Institutions	
															State Lending Institutions	
End of Period																
20.18	21.61	23.21	24.90	26.71	27.82	30.79	33.41	34.53	35.40	36.68	37.90	41.84	42.36	46.17	Claims on State and Local Govts	42b
94.13	100.11	107.43	115.53	123.46	131.54	140.95	149.31	145.34	139.53	138.56	135.69	131.73	140.96	146.46	Claims on Private Sector	42d
13.05	12.61	12.82	13.44	14.71	18.72	18.32	20.81	21.39	16.68	10.39	11.81	16.01	20.16	28.65	Bonds (Net)	46ab
15.77	16.64	15.20	13.21	11.09	8.23	6.41	5.27	3.69	1.81	1.14	1.17	.33	1.39	—	Foreign Liabilities	46c
93.87	101.28	112.21	122.54	133.06	140.88	152.07	162.13	160.22	155.32	154.28	153.78	152.38	158.75	162.43	Central Govt. Lending Funds	46f
8.26	8.15	8.04	7.74	8.27	7.87	8.10	9.00	12.23	10.30	10.39	8.61	8.45	8.25	6.74	Capital Accounts	47a
-16.64	-16.97	-17.64	-16.48	-16.94	-16.33	-13.15	-14.50	-17.66	-9.17	-.94	-1.78	-3.61	-5.22	-5.18	Other Items (Net)	47r

		1970	1971	1972	1973	1974	1975	1976	1977	1978	1979	1980	1981	1982	1983	1984
Mortgage Institutions																*Billions of Kroner:*
Foreign Assets	41.. *l*	....	....	....	....	....	....	....	....	....	....	....	....	....	....	....
Claims on Central Government	42a. *l*	....	....	....	....	....	....	....	....	....	....	....	....	....	....	....
Claims on State and Local Govt.	42b. *l*	....	....	....	....	....	....	....	....	....	....	....	....	....	....	....
Claims on Nonfin.Pub.Enterprises	42c. *l*	....	....	....	....	....	....	....	....	....	....	....	....	....	....	....
Claims on Private Sector	42d. *l*	5.44	6.40	7.18	8.29	9.48	81.49	81.40	81.29	81.18	81.03	81.11	80.94	80.83	80.62	80.89
Credit Market Instruments	46aa *l*	....	....	....	....	....	....	....	....	....	....	....	....	....	....	....
Bonds (net)	46ab *l*	5.13	6.04	6.93	8.10	9.37	69.94	69.94	69.95	69.95	69.95	69.95	69.82	69.94	69.98	69.98
Foreign Liabilities	46c. *l*	....	....	....	....	....	....	....	....	....	....	....	....	....	....	....
Capital Accounts	47a. *l*	....	....	....	....	....	....	....	....	....	....	....	....	....	....	....
Other Items (Net)	47r. *l*	....	....	....	....	....	....	....	....	....	....	....	....	....	....	....
Nonbank Financial Institutions																*Billions of Kroner:*
Claims on Central Government	42a. *s*	1.72	1.73	1.74	1.78	1.79	1.76	1.75	1.53	2.69	4.30	5.34	4.74	5.01	6.46	7.62
Claims on Local Government	42b. *s*	1.42	1.51	1.72	1.88	2.17	2.47	2.82	3.06	3.24	3.34	4.04	5.37	6.89	8.73	9.74
Claims on Private Sector	42d. *s*	6.38	6.89	7.39	8.02	8.76	9.62	10.66	11.56	12.03	12.58	13.61	15.32	17.13	19.79	23.16
Claims on Other Financial Insts	42f. *s*	1.40	1.61	1.89	2.23	2.56	3.05	3.80	5.27	5.81	6.37	7.27	9.10	11.08	12.79	14.59
Incr.in Total Assets(Within Per.)	49z. *s*	.83	.85	1.01	1.19	1.41	1.64	2.22	2.39	2.89	3.00	3.93	5.04	6.10	7.14	8.89
Interest Rates																*Percent Per Annum*
Discount Rate *(End of Period)*	60	4.50	4.50	4.50	4.50	5.50	5.00	6.00	6.00	7.00	9.00	9.00	9.00	I 9.20	10.00	10.20
Avg.Cost for Centr.Bank Funding	60.a	....	....	....	....	....	....	....	....	....	....	....	....	....	....	....
Deposit Rate	60l	....	....	....	....	....	....	....	....	....	5.10	5.00	5.10	5.10	5.30	5.30
Lending Rate	60p	....	....	....	....	....	....	....	....	....	12.23	12.63	13.90	14.33	14.35	13.69
Three Month Interbank Rate	60zb	....	....	....	....	....	....	....	....	....	....	....	....	15.37	13.30	13.02
Government Bond Yield	61	6.29	6.40	6.27	6.19	7.10	7.29	7.25	7.39	8.45	8.59	10.27	12.31	13.20	12.86	12.16
Prices, Production, Labor																*Index Numbers (1995=100):*
Industrial Share Prices	62	10	10	9	14	13	10	10	8	6	9	11	11	I 10	16	22
Producer Prices	63	....	....	....	....	....	....	....	46.0	47.8	51.3	58.1	64.2	69.7	74.2	79.4
Consumer Prices	64	19.1	20.2	21.7	23.3	25.5	28.5	31.1	33.9	36.7	38.4	42.6	48.5	54.0	58.5	62.2
Wages: Hourly Earnings	65	12.3	13.8	15.1	16.6	19.5	I 23.4	27.0	30.0	32.4	33.4	36.5	40.3	44.3	48.0	52.1
Industrial Production	66.. c	31.8	I 33.2	35.7	37.7	39.4	41.5	43.9	43.5	48.1	51.8	I 55.1	56.7	56.4	61.6	66.4
Crude Petroleum Production	66aa	—	.2	1.2	1.1	1.2	6.7	9.8	9.8	12.3	13.5	17.5	16.9	17.7	22.0	25.2
Employment	67	79.8	80.2	82.9	83.1	83.4	85.1	86.1	87.7	89.2	90.0	92.1	92.9	93.6	94.1	94.7
																Number in Thousands:
Labor Force	67d	....	....	....	....	....	....	....	....		....	....	....	....	....	....
Employment	67e	....	....	....	....	....	....	....	....	....	....	....	....	....	....	....
Unemployment	67c	....	....	....	....	....	....	....	....	....	....	....	....	....	....	....
Unemployment Rate (%)	67r	....	....	....	....	....	....	....	....	....	....	....	....	....	....	....
International Transactions																*Millions of Kroner*
Exports	70	17,549	18,003	21,625	27,085	34,732	37,922	43,330	47,263	57,084	68,527	91,672	104,265	113,236	131,397	154,035
Imports, c.i.f.	71	26,443	28,714	28,808	36,041	46,556	50,545	60,533	68,579	60,169	69,339	83,602	89,688	99,747	98,408	113,102
																1995=100
Volume of Exports	72	I 22.9	23.6	26.4	29.1	28.9	30.1	34.6	33.5	41.3	43.6	I 46.1	I 45.2	45.8	49.2	53.7
Volume of Imports	73	I 37.4	37.8	37.8	42.7	46.4	46.4	51.7	55.8	49.4	52.0	I 57.7	55.4	57.7	55.4	62.9
Unit Value of Exports	74	I 32.3	33.5	33.2	36.4	47.7	51.9	53.2	56.8	60.0	70.3	I 91.6	106.2	113.6	117.5	129.1
Unit Value of Imports	75	I 31.2	32.7	33.1	35.2	44.3	47.1	50.2	54.3	57.1	63.0	I 70.8	75.7	79.3	83.0	84.6
Balance of Payments																*Millions of US Dollars:*
Current Account, n.i.e.	78al *d*	....	....	....	....	....	–2,478	–3,746	–5,053	–2,118	–1,047	1,079	2,131	640	1,962	2,886
Goods: Exports f.o.b.	78aa *d*	....	....	....	....	....	7,270	8,047	9,152	11,033	13,747	18,649	18,494	17,664	18,055	19,115
Goods: Imports f.o.b.	78ab *d*	....	....	....	....	....	–10,141	–11,608	–13,205	–11,545	–13,601	–16,753	–15,459	–15,278	–13,704	–13,957
Trade Balance	78ac *d*	....	....	....	....	....	–2,871	–3,561	–4,053	–512	146	1,896	3,035	2,386	4,351	5,158
Services: Credit	78ad *d*	....	....	....	....	....	4,542	4,779	5,109	5,582	7,054	8,615	8,753	7,927	7,109	7,097
Services: Debit	78ae *d*	....	....	....	....	....	–3,641	–4,228	–4,918	–5,437	–5,977	–6,996	–7,283	–7,132	–7,148	–7,253
Balance on Goods & Services	78af *d*	....	....	....	....	....	–1,969	–3,010	–3,862	–367	1,223	3,516	4,505	3,181	4,312	5,002
Income: Credit	78ag *d*	....	....	....	....	....	313	288	304	407	597	988	1,443	1,629	1,378	1,616
Income: Debit	78ah *d*	....	....	....	....	....	–662	–826	–1,181	–1,775	–2,427	–2,909	–3,286	–3,587	–3,125	–3,193
Balance on Gds, Serv. & Inc.	78ai *d*	....	....	....	....	....	–2,319	–3,548	–4,740	–1,734	–607	1,594	2,662	1,223	2,565	3,425
Current Transfers, n.i.e.: Credit	78aj *d*	....	....	....	....	....	101	97	50	55	63	78	75	98	97	87
Current Transfers: Debit	78ak *d*	....	....	....	....	....	–260	–295	–363	–438	–504	–593	–606	–682	–699	–626
Capital Account, n.i.e.	78bc *d*	....	....	....	....	....	—	—	19	15	3	19	45	23	24	33
Capital Account, n.i.e.: Credit	78ba *d*	....	....	....	....	....	—	—	52	51	54	76	102	80	79	78
Capital Account: Debit	78bb *d*	....	....	....	....	....	—	—	–33	–36	–50	–56	–56	–58	–55	–45
Financial Account, n.i.e.	78bj *d*	....	....	....	....	....	2,618	3,499	4,521	2,213	1,727	–133	–1,732	148	–2,455	488
Direct Investment Abroad	78bd *d*	....	....	....	....	....	–172	–193	–125	–66	–44	–253	–173	–306	–355	–601
Dir. Invest. in Rep. Econ., n.i.e.	78be *d*	....	....	....	....	....	220	371	768	490	401	60	672	442	328	–180
Portfolio Investment Assets	78bf *d*	....	....	....	....	....	2	–17	5	—	–14	–88	15	11	–33	143
Equity Securities	78bk *d*	....	....	....	....	....	—	—	—	—	—	—	22	30	22	49
Debt Securities	78bl *d*	....	....	....	....	....	2	–17	5	—	–14	–88	–8	–18	–54	94
Portfolio Investment Liab., n.i.e.	78bg *d*	....	....	....	....	....	610	1,346	2,062	2,458	2,066	–54	–714	–679	–867	667
Equity Securities	78bm *d*	....	....	....	....	....	—	—	—	—	—	—	16	61	144	322
Debt Securities	78bn *d*	....	....	....	....	....	610	1,346	2,062	2,458	2,066	–54	–730	–740	–1,011	345
Financial Derivatives Assets	78bw *d*	....	....	....	....	....	....	....	....	....	....	....	....	....	....	....
Financial Derivatives Liabilities	78bx *d*	....	....	....	....	....	....	....	....	....	....	....	....	....	....	....
Other Investment Assets	78bh *d*	....	....	....	....	....	–328	–93	–572	–890	–1,590	–1,777	–1,707	–1,942	–1,279	–949
Monetary Authorities	78bo *d*	....	....	....	....	....	....	....	....	....	....	....	....	....	....	....
General Government	78bp *d*	....	....	....	....	....	5	1	–103	–271	60	–250	63	–27	–3	66
Banks	78bq *d*	....	....	....	....	....	–37	–29	–281	184	29	–69	–1,365	–1,231	–561	–1,309
Other Sectors	78br *d*	....	....	....	....	....	–296	–65	–188	–803	–1,679	–1,459	–405	–684	–715	295
Other Investment Liab., n.i.e.	78bi *d*	....	....	....	....	....	2,285	2,084	2,383	221	908	1,980	176	2,620	–249	1,408
Monetary Authorities	78bs *d*	....	....	....	....	....	–26	–1	519	–423	21	152	–17	56	71	–82
General Government	78bt *d*	....	....	....	....	....	495	104	141	425	4	–8	–239	–304	–369	–154
Banks	78bu *d*	....	....	....	....	....	26	124	–112	137	506	1,636	780	1,262	529	1,579
Other Sectors	78bv *d*	....	....	....	....	....	1,790	1,857	1,835	82	376	200	–348	1,606	–479	65
Net Errors and Omissions	78ca *d*	....	....	....	....	....	201	219	391	527	601	917	–14	–102	370	–340
Overall Balance	78cb *d*	....	....	....	....	....	340	–28	–121	637	1,285	1,882	431	708	–98	3,068
Reserves and Related Items	79da *d*	....	....	....	....	....	–340	28	121	–637	–1,285	–1,882	–431	–708	98	–3,068
Reserve Assets	79db *d*	....	....	....	....	....	–340	28	121	–637	–1,285	–1,882	–431	–708	98	–3,068
Use of Fund Credit and Loans	79dc *d*	....	....	....	....	....	—	—	—	—	—	—	—	—	—	—
Exceptional Financing	79de *d*	....	....	....	....	....	....	....	....	....	....	....	....	....	....	....

1985	1986	1987	1988	1989	1990	1991	1992	1993	1994	1995	1996	1997	1998	1999		
End of Period															Mortgage Institutions	
....	....	....	21.49	19.88	20.44	21.92	23.61	19.67	23.95	24.02	22.11	19.36	29.99	33.39	Foreign Assets	41.. *l*
....	....	....	2.00	1.01	.85	1.05	1.37	2.85	1.48	1.94	1.55	1.22	1.53	1.09	Claims on Central Government	42a. *l*
....	....	....	3.12	4.56	4.32	3.18	1.82	2.00	1.91	2.64	4.33	5.60	5.55	8.08	Claims on State and Local Govt.	42b. *l*
....	....	....	3.57	3.77	4.00	3.38	2.11	1.65	1.32	1.34	1.70	1.37	1.90	4.68	Claims on Nonfin.Pub.Enterprises	42c. *l*
81.31	85.61	123.65	121.50	136.96	138.74	117.00	80.73	72.15	62.34	60.05	55.55	66.33	88.87	82.04	Claims on Private Sector	42d. *l*
....	....	....	9.24	6.08	5.74	6.67	3.77	5.45	6.97	7.40	5.49	3.70	3.13	8.21	Credit Market Instruments	46aa *l*
69.98	69.98	87.29	94.01	115.24	114.40	100.25	55.87	42.16	35.01	36.46	37.21	33.14	36.46	36.62	Bonds (net)	46ab *l*
....	....	....	23.13	28.23	37.41	37.02	35.91	39.40	39.04	39.52	38.76	51.47	60.77	70.55	Foreign Liabilities	46c. *l*
....	....	....	4.60	5.39	5.62	4.03	6.38	8.00	7.76	7.59	6.64	6.51	8.31	8.73	Capital Accounts	47a. *l*
....	....	....	20.69	11.24	5.16	–3.27	7.60	2.86	2.23	–1.09	–2.96	–.93	19.17	5.17	Other Items (Net)	47r. *l*
End of Period															**Nonbank Financial Institutions**	
9.37	10.92	7.15	3.86	6.38	5.55	12.53	18.16	32.36	40.47	42.34	42.83	49.16	35.95	....	Claims on Central Government	42a. *s*
11.15	12.99	14.79	18.85	23.00	29.23	28.97	30.54	31.29	32.27	30.85	29.55	27.42	28.61	....	Claims on Local Government	42b. *s*
28.04	35.86	43.57	45.88	45.81	48.10	63.10	73.54	75.78	65.71	73.90	77.07	71.55	75.08	....	Claims on Private Sector	42d. *s*
16.83	21.24	28.33	38.01	44.73	44.43	32.75	28.44	24.30	28.05	32.58	38.85	42.54	48.10	....	Claims on Other Financial Insts	42f. *s*
11.85	13.64	12.78	12.80	14.56	8.87	9.08	12.61	14.67	7.94	10.92	6.91	3.02	–.86	....	*Incr.in Total Assets(Within Per.)*	49z. *s*
Percent Per Annum															**Interest Rates**	
10.70	14.80	13.80	12.00	11.00	10.50	10.00	11.00	7.00	6.75	6.75	6.00	5.50	10.00	7.50	Discount Rate *(End of Period)*	60
....	....	....	14.28	11.50	11.85	10.93	7.65	5.70	6.46	5.40	4.96	4.80	6.18	6.86	Avg.Cost for Centr.Bank Funding	60.a
10.06	10.97	12.03	11.49	9.63	9.68	9.60	10.69	5.51	5.21	4.95	4.15	3.63	7.24	5.38	Deposit Rate	60l
13.46	14.37	16.31	16.60	14.88	14.26	14.31	14.16	10.97	8.40	7.78	7.10	5.95	7.91	8.16	Lending Rate	60p
12.53	14.39	14.70	13.51	11.39	11.54	10.56	11.83	7.27	5.85	5.48	4.90	3.73	5.79	6.54	Three Month Interbank Rate	60zb
12.58	13.47	13.56	12.97	10.84	10.72	9.87	9.78	6.52	7.13	6.82	5.94	5.13	5.35	5.38	Government Bond Yield	61
Period Averages															**Prices, Production, Labor**	
29	31	38	33	53	66	61	57	73	94	100	120	170	167	171	Industrial Share Prices	62
83.2	80.4	83.2	87.1	91.7	95.4	97.7	97.2	96.3	97.5	100.0	102.2	103.6	104.2	107.4	Producer Prices	63
65.7	70.4	76.6	81.7	85.4	88.9	92.0	94.1	96.3	97.6	100.0	101.3	103.9	I106.2	108.7	Consumer Prices	64
56.4	62.1	72.2	76.0	79.7	84.3	88.7	91.5	93.9	96.6	100.0	104.2	....	....	....	Wages: Hourly Earnings	65
68.7	71.1	75.7	77.6	85.2	86.5	I88.5	89.6	92.1	97.2	100.0	102.5	106.0	108.8	....	Industrial Production	66.. c
27.6	30.5	35.7	40.7	53.8	58.8	67.1	76.7	82.2	92.9	100.0	112.6	....	....	....	Crude Petroleum Production	66aa
96.9	100.3	102.3	101.7	98.5	97.7	96.7	96.4	96.5	97.9	100.0	102.8	....	....	....	Employment	67
Period Averages																
....	....	....	....	....	....	....	....	2,131	....	2,186	2,246	2,285	2,317	....	Labor Force	67d
2,014	I2,086	2,126	I2,114	2,049	2,030	2,010	2,004	2,004	2,035	2,079	2,137	2,192	2,242	....	Employment	67e
53	42	45	69	106	112	116	126	127	116	107	108	93	75	....	Unemployment	67c
2.6	2.0	2.1	3.2	4.9	5.2	5.5	5.9	6.0	5.4	4.9	4.9	4.1	....	....	Unemployment Rate (%)	67r
Millions of Kroner															**International Transactions**	
170,733	133,847	144,543	146,166	187,146	211,579	220,316	218,474	225,714	243,809	265,883	320,130	342,421	298,968	350,582	Exports	70
132,563	150,052	152,041	151,101	163,380	169,998	165,181	160,821	170,069	192,073	208,627	229,720	252,232	272,970	265,696	Imports, c.i.f.	71
1995=100																
55.4	53.1	57.6	56.5	65.0	69.5	74.0	80.2	84.3	94.6	100.0	112.9	117.9	118.8	124.0	Volume of Exports	72
70.3	80.7	I79.3	71.4	67.9	74.6	76.4	79.3	79.6	92.9	100.0	110.0	119.3	131.4	128.8	Volume of Imports	73
134.2	100.8	I97.3	97.6	109.3	114.1	109.3	100.5	100.5	97.1	100.0	108.0	110.2	97.6	108.8	Unit Value of Exports	74
90.1	89.9	I92.4	95.2	101.0	101.7	100.0	98.1	98.8	99.0	100.0	99.5	98.6	100.0	97.9	Unit Value of Imports	75
Minus Sign Indicates Debit															Balance of Payments	
3,038	–4,551	–4,102	–3,896	212	3,992	5,032	4,471	3,522	3,760	4,854	10,240	8,017	–2,161	....	Current Account, n.i.e.	78al *d*
20,059	18,143	21,191	23,075	27,171	34,313	34,212	35,459	32,278	35,016	42,312	49,968	48,737	40,636	....	Goods: Exports f.o.b.	78aa *d*
–15,331	–20,257	–21,951	–23,284	–23,401	–26,552	–25,516	–27,205	–25,312	–27,520	–33,741	–37,037	–37,585	–39,070	....	Goods: Imports f.o.b.	78ab *d*
4,728	–2,115	–759	–209	3,770	7,761	8,696	8,254	6,966	7,496	8,571	12,931	11,152	1,566	....	*Trade Balance*	78ac *d*
7,456	8,142	8,545	9,729	10,770	12,765	13,330	12,692	12,159	12,247	13,347	14,171	14,624	14,132	....	Services: Credit	78ad *d*
–7,515	–8,608	–9,623	–10,270	–10,623	–12,358	–12,701	–12,210	–11,472	–12,065	–13,131	–13,545	–14,776	–15,370	....	Services: Debit	78ae *d*
4,670	–2,581	–1,837	–750	3,916	8,168	9,326	8,736	7,653	7,678	8,788	13,556	11,001	328	....	*Balance on Goods & Services*	78af *d*
2,099	2,723	3,039	3,265	3,425	3,896	3,540	2,689	2,380	3,415	4,541	5,088	5,501	6,487	....	Income: Credit	78ag *d*
–3,152	–3,883	–4,325	–5,274	–5,995	–6,596	–6,293	–5,501	–5,167	–5,589	–6,412	–6,893	–7,067	–7,385	....	Income: Debit	78ah *d*
3,617	–3,741	–3,122	–2,759	1,346	5,468	6,573	5,924	4,866	5,504	6,917	11,751	9,435	–569	....	*Balance on Gds, Serv. & Inc.*	78ai *d*
85	95	123	168	164	217	239	1,678	1,533	1,291	1,276	1,325	1,234	1,262	....	Current Transfers, n.i.e.: Credit	78aj *d*
–664	–906	–1,103	–1,305	–1,299	–1,693	–1,780	–3,131	–2,877	–3,035	–3,339	–2,835	–2,652	–2,853	....	Current Transfers: Debit	78ak *d*
14	6	–2	8	2	31	17	–172	–31	–157	–170	–127	–183	–101	....	Capital Account, n.i.e.	78bc *d*
81	81	104	107	101	109	118	143	306	93	86	65	29	41	....	Capital Account, n.i.e.: Credit	78ba *d*
–67	–76	–106	–99	–99	–78	–101	–315	–337	–250	–255	–192	–212	–141	....	Capital Account: Debit	78bb *d*
1,459	2,961	5,233	4,900	2,056	–761	–7,581	–1,044	6,568	–1,363	–640	–1,701	–7,413	–107	....	Financial Account, n.i.e.	78bj *d*
–1,304	–1,600	–873	–978	–1,358	–1,470	–1,782	120	–718	–2,166	–2,865	–5,880	–5,008	–2,521	....	Direct Investment Abroad	78bd *d*
–426	1,017	187	279	1,519	1,003	–398	–668	992	2,736	2,393	3,179	3,572	3,597	....	Dir. Invest. in Rep. Econ., n.i.e.	78be *d*
126	–373	–1,009	–392	–563	–987	–2,523	–1,972	2,088	992	–3,525	–9,839	–12,611	–11,528	....	Portfolio Investment Assets	78bf *d*
31	–116	–255	28	–310	–569	–298	–446	–124	213	–374	–1,182	–2,817	–9,417	....	Equity Securities	78bk *d*
95	–257	–755	–420	–252	–418	–2,224	–1,526	2,212	780	–3,151	–8,657	–9,794	–2,111	....	Debt Securities	78bl *d*
1,650	4,656	3,292	4,618	3,606	1,548	–585	865	–1,175	–518	655	100	2,298	7,114	....	Portfolio Investment Liab., n.i.e.	78bg *d*
–31	318	274	336	1,035	644	159	782	385	654	636	–237	–1,210	136	....	Equity Securities	78bm *d*
1,681	4,338	3,018	4,282	2,571	904	–743	83	–1,560	–1,172	19	337	3,508	6,978	....	Debt Securities	78bn *d*
....	....	....	....	....	....	....	....	....	....	....	–43	–52	–190	....	Financial Derivatives Assets	78bw *d*
....	....	....	....	....	....	....	....	....	....	....	101	124	75	....	Financial Derivatives Liabilities	78bx *d*
–790	–2,341	–1,171	643	–274	–1,502	–326	369	6,198	154	904	–189	–1,512	–1,591	....	Other Investment Assets	78bh *d*
....	....	....	....	....	....	....	....	....	....	....	....	....	....	....	Monetary Authorities	78bo *d*
–82	–131	–411	–159	76	170	207	–46	–65	–13	–156	71	–171	–156	....	General Government	78bp *d*
121	–2,598	207	1,343	–222	–223	–1,549	–741	3,997	–638	435	–1,216	–1,437	–1,087	....	Banks	78bq *d*
–829	388	–966	–542	–129	–1,448	1,016	1,156	2,266	804	625	955	95	–348	....	Other Sectors	78br *d*
2,204	1,602	4,808	730	–874	648	–1,968	242	–816	–2,562	1,798	10,870	5,777	4,939	....	Other Investment Liab., n.i.e.	78bi *d*
–18	70	–55	124	–58	3	56	1,282	217	139	–624	1,505	–829	1,375	....	Monetary Authorities	78bs *d*
–4	–18	113	–93	–2	35	3	–15	–7	–164	3	—	—	—	....	General Government	78bt *d*
1,932	1,045	4,497	–1,101	–817	–740	–4,174	–3,622	–302	–604	247	8,677	4,126	–710	....	Banks	78bu *d*
295	504	253	1,801	3	1,350	2,147	2,597	–724	–1,933	2,173	689	2,480	4,274	....	Other Sectors	78bv *d*
–1,059	–1,626	–1,349	–1,149	–1,305	–2,848	–219	–3,986	–1,806	–1,987	–3,470	–1,942	–1,619	–4,016	....	Net Errors and Omissions	78ca *d*
3,452	–3,211	–220	–138	965	414	–2,751	–732	8,253	253	575	6,470	–1,198	–6,385	....	*Overall Balance*	78cb *d*
–3,452	3,211	220	138	–965	–414	2,751	732	–8,253	–253	–575	–6,470	1,198	6,385	....	Reserves and Related Items	79da *d*
–3,452	3,211	220	138	–965	–414	2,751	732	–8,253	–253	–575	–6,470	1,198	6,385	....	Reserve Assets	79db *d*
—	—	—	—	—	—	—	—	—	—	—	—	—	—	....	Use of Fund Credit and Loans	79dc *d*
....	....	....	....	....	....	....	....	....	....	....	....	....	....	....	Exceptional Financing	79de *d*

	1970	1971	1972	1973	1974	1975	1976	1977	1978	1979	1980	1981	1982	1983	1984
International Investment Position														*Millions of US Dollars*	
Assets .... 79aa d	....	....	....	....	....	....	....	....	....	....	....	....	....	....	....
Direct Investment Abroad .... 79ab d	....	....	....	....	....	....	....	....	....	....	561	581	619	647	667
Portfolio Investment .... 79ac d	....	....	....	....	....	....	....	....	....	....	....	....	....	....	....
Equity Securities .... 79ad d	....	....	....	....	....	....	....	....	....	....	....	....	....	....	....
Debt Securities .... 79ae d	....	....	....	....	....	....	....	....	....	....	....	....	....	....	....
Financial Derivatives .... 79al d	....	....	....	....	....	....	....	....	....	....	....	....	....	....	....
Other Investment .... 79af d	....	....	....	....	....	....	....	....	....	....	9,008	9,815	9,864	9,772	9,853
Monetary Authorities .... 79ag d	....	....	....	....	....	....	....	....	....	....	—	—	—	—	—
General Government .... 79ah d	....	....	....	....	....	....	....	....	....	....					
Banks .... 79ai d	....	....	....	....	....	....	....	....	....	....	494	1,734	2,207	2,256	2,588
Other Sectors .... 79aj d	....	....	....	....	....	....	....	....	....	....	....	....	....	....	....
Reserve Assets .... 79ak d	....	....	....	....	....	....	....	....	....	....	6,044	6,309	6,910	6,640	9,401
Liabilities .... 79la d	....	....	....	....	....	....	....	....	....	....	....	....	....	....	....
Dir. Invest. in Rep. Economy .... 79lb d	....	....	....	....	....	....	....	....	....	....	775	735	686	681	699
Portfolio Investment .... 79lc d	....	....	....	....	....	....	....	....	....	....	....	....	....	....	....
Equity Securities .... 79ld d	....	....	....	....	....	....	....	....	....	....	....	....	....	....	....
Debt Securities .... 79le d	....	....	....	....	....	....	....	....	....	....	....	....	....	....	....
Financial Derivatives .... 79ll d	....	....	....	....	....	....	....	....	....	....	....	....	....	....	....
Other investment .... 79lf d	....	....	....	....	....	....	....	....	....	....	22,220	21,786	22,549	21,739	21,745
Monetary Authorities .... 79lg d	....	....	....	....	....	....	....	....	....	....	43	58	102	98	42
General Government .... 79lh d	....	....	....	....	....	....	....	....	....	....	....	....	....	....	....
Banks .... 79li d	....	....	....	....	....	....	....	....	....	....	2,618	3,191	3,731	3,873	4,714
Other Sectors .... 79lj d	....	....	....	....	....	....	....	....	....	....	....	....	....	....	....
Government Finance														*Millions of Kroner:*	
Deficit (-) or Surplus 80	−2,491	−2,331	I−1,438	−1,026	−1,761	−4,716	−10,005	−13,133	−14,472	−14,994	−5,400	6,817	3,894	9,443	8,963
Revenue 81	17,203	20,597	I35,992	41,305	47,165	53,648	63,842	73,155	81,596	91,919	116,849	140,094	153,404	176,023	193,630
Grants Received 81z	....	....	I1,333	1,605	1,861	2,086	2,281	700	1,092	965	998	1,186	1,376	1,529	1,559
Expenditure 82	17,549	20,385	I34,086	38,392	44,554	52,113	63,936	73,354	84,824	93,364	108,111	123,585	139,064	154,340	168,126
Lending Minus Repayments 83	2,145	2,543	I4,677	5,544	6,233	8,337	12,192	13,634	12,336	14,514	15,136	10,878	11,822	13,769	18,100
Financing															
Domestic 84a	....	....	I1,499	1,358	1,876	324	5,865	6,178	3,232	10,259	7,623	−3,171	711	2,744	−4,191
Foreign 85a	....	....	I−61	−332	−115	4,392	4,140	6,955	11,240	4,735	−2,223	−3,646	−4,605	−12,187	−4,535
Debt: Domestic 88a	....	I23,007	26,038	28,658	31,004	32,581	37,763	46,681	53,992	68,407	75,490	78,931	74,729	86,386	105,252
Foreign 89a	....	I1,684	1,621	1,290	1,179	5,587	9,708	16,666	27,923	32,125	29,886	26,233	21,629	9,440	4,853
Financing (by Currency)															
Net Borrowing: Kroner 84b	3,346	3,269	....	....	....	....	....	....	....	....	....	....	....	....	....
Foreign Currency 85b	−149	−161	....	....	....	....	....	....	....	....	....	....	....	....	....
Use of Cash Balances 87	−706	−777	....	....	....	....	....	....	....	....	....	....	....	....	....
Debt: Kroner 88b	16,892	....	....	....	....	....	....	....	....	....	....	....	....	....	....
Foreign Currency 89b	1,987	....	....	....	....	....	....	....	....	....	....	....	....	....	....
National Accounts														*Billions of Kroner*	
Househ.Cons.Expend.,incl.NPISHs 96f	43.05	47.90	52.56	58.29	66.11	77.62	89.49	103.92	I119.89	131.48	146.66	165.79	186.19	205.62	225.60
Government Consumption Expend. 91f	13.53	15.98	17.86	20.39	23.76	28.70	34.09	38.62	I47.32	50.82	56.85	67.98	76.33	84.54	90.76
Gross Fixed Capital Formation 93e	21.19	26.45	27.30	32.75	39.60	50.79	62.00	71.07	I74.60	78.91	84.41	96.62	107.62	121.82	129.96
Changes in Inventories 93i	3.13	1.71	−.08	.97	4.02	1.54	1.38	−1.58	I−4.08	−3.77	4.16	.01	3.82	−10.08	1.35
Exports of Goods and Services 90c	33.40	35.81	40.05	48.73	60.01	62.19	70.17	76.26	I87.36	105.15	135.49	155.41	164.67	184.52	213.02
Imports of Goods and Services 98c	−34.43	−38.74	−39.29	−49.27	−63.78	−72.14	−86.41	−96.77	I−85.65	−98.74	−116.14	−128.88	−143.93	−149.17	−168.41
Gross Domestic Product (GDP) 99b	79.88	89.11	98.41	111.85	129.73	148.70	170.71	191.53	I239.45	263.85	313.24	356.93	394.69	437.24	492.30
Net Primary Income from Abroad 98.n	−.62	−.75	−1.03	−1.19	−1.85	−1.92	−3.05	−4.73	I−7.44	−9.40	−9.63	−11.00	−12.88	−13.18	−13.38
Gross National Income (GNI) 99a	89.70	88.36	97.38	110.67	127.88	146.79	167.66	186.80	I232.00	254.45	303.61	345.93	381.82	424.07	478.92
Net Current Transf.from Abroad 98t	....	....	....	....	....	....	....	....	I−1.84	−2.21	−2.44	−3.07	−4.46	−4.33	−4.48
Gross Nat'l Disposable Inc.(GNDI) 99i	....	....	....	....	....	....	....	....	I230.16	252.24	301.17	342.86	377.36	419.74	474.44
Gross Savings 99s	....	....	....	....	....	....	....	....	I62.95	69.94	95.86	109.09	114.84	129.58	158.08
GDP Volume 1995 Ref., Chained 99b.p	....	....	....	....	....	....	....	....	....	....	....	....	....	....	....
GDP Volume 1997 Ref., Chained 99b.p	....	....	....	....	....	....	....	....	....	600	626	657	664	665	688	729
GDP Volume (1995=100) .... 99bv p	41.4	43.2	45.5	47.4	49.8	51.9	55.4	57.4	60.1	62.7	65.8	66.5	66.6	68.9	73.0
GDP Deflator (1995=100) .... 99bi p	20.8	22.2	23.3	25.4	28.0	30.9	33.2	35.9	I42.9	45.3	51.2	57.8	63.8	68.3	72.6
														Millions:	
Population 99z	3.88	3.90	3.93	3.96	3.99	4.01	4.03	4.04	4.06	4.07	4.09	4.10	4.11	4.13	4.14

1985	1986	1987	1988	1989	1990	1991	1992	1993	1994	1995	1996	1997	1998	1999		

Millions of US Dollars — **International Investment Position**

1985	1986	1987	1988	1989	1990	1991	1992	1993	1994	1995	1996	1997	1998	1999		
....	....	....	38,309	40,826	49,691	50,170	48,393	46,433	...	....	....	....	....	....	Assets	79aa *d*
1,093	1,609	2,455	2,757	3,506	4,403	5,170	4,234	5,080	...					....	Direct Investment Abroad	79ab *d*
....	....	....	1,626	1,565	2,320	3,403	5,607	5,762						....	Portfolio Investment	79ac *d*
															Equity Securities	79ad *d*
....	....	....	1,626	1,565	2,320	3,403	5,607	5,762							Debt Securities	79ae *d*
															Financial Derivatives	79al *d*
12,942	16,644	22,277	20,733	21,785	27,426	28,420	26,673	19,910							Other Investment	79af *d*
—	—	—	1,595	1,599	1,912	1,542	1,697	1,868							Monetary Authorities	79ag *d*
3,178	5,581	6,551	5,300	5,494	6,857	8,358	9,325	5,813							General Government	79ah *d*
....	....	....	13,837	14,691	18,657	18,520	15,651	12,228							Banks	79ai *d*
13,903	12,287	14,376	13,193	13,971	15,541	13,177	11,880	15,680							Other Sectors	79aj *d*
....	....	....	57,367	61,414	67,329	63,639	58,399	57,536							Reserve Assets	79ak *d*
															Liabilities	79la *d*
993	1,315	2,271	2,450	3,157	4,066	4,570	3,969	3,880							Dir. Invest. in Rep. Economy	79lb *d*
....	....	....	21,620	24,031	26,722	26,176	24,400	22,449							Portfolio Investment	79lc *d*
															Equity Securities	79ld *d*
....	....	....	21,620	24,031	26,722	26,176	24,400	22,449							Debt Securities	79le *d*
															Financial Derivatives	79ll *d*
25,424	28,336	35,965	33,297	34,226	36,541	32,893	30,030	31,207							Other investment	79lf *d*
45	81	67	125	61	29	72	705	101							Monetary Authorities	79lg *d*
....	....	....	690	703	995	1,047	1,692	2,238							General Government	79lh *d*
7,807	9,571	15,930	13,081	12,873	13,510	9,581	5,902	6,179							Banks	79li *d*
....	....	....	19,400	20,590	22,007	22,193	21,732	22,688							Other Sectors	79lj *d*

Year Ending December 31 — **Government Finance**

1985	1986	1987	1988	1989	1990	1991	1992	1993	1994	1995	1996	1997	1998	1999		
18,279	17,414	−385	−999	−5,118	3,863	−22,161	−51,912	−45,556	−14,774	14,487	6,524	7,771	....	....	Deficit (-) or Surplus	80
222,953	244,633	255,360	266,960	277,773	306,881	319,827	318,151	326,507	348,841	383,106	425,506	469,157	....	....	Revenue	81
1,531	900	1,621	4,780	6,347	5,674	3,488	1,892	1,490	1,423	1,345	1,299	1,323	....	....	Grants Received	81z
184,112	204,711	230,455	251,327	273,356	298,813	320,384	339,451	347,962	357,877	361,579	375,265	387,336	....	....	Expenditure	82
22,093	23,408	26,911	21,412	15,882	9,879	25,092	32,504	25,591	7,161	8,385	45,016	75,373	....	....	Lending Minus Repayments	83
															Financing	
−20,110	−23,808	−2,913	−4,796	2,220	311	12,505	28,073	25,189	20,459	−18,296	11,271	15,561	....	....	Domestic	84a
1,831	6,393	3,298	5,794	2,899	−4,174	9,656	23,839	20,368	−5,684	3,809	−17,795	−23,332	....	....	Foreign	85a
129,625	172,562	137,591	131,171	134,538	126,287	115,769	127,348	189,953	201,763	198,384	186,071	196,423	....	....	Debt: Domestic	88a
6,650	12,949	16,289	22,113	25,026	22,538	31,142	54,320	80,018	74,157	77,901	62,527	42,400	....	....	Foreign	89a
															Financing (by Currency)	
....	....	....	....	....	....	....	....	....	....	....	....	....	....	....	Net Borrowing: Kroner	84b
....	....	....	....	....	....	....	....	....	....	....	....	....	....	....	Foreign Currency	85b
....	....	....	....	....	....	....	....	....	....	....	....	....	....	....	Use of Cash Balances	87
....	....	....	....	....	....	....	....	....	....	....	....	....	....	....	Debt: Kroner	88b
....	....	....	....	....	....	....	....	....	....	....	....	....	....	....	Foreign Currency	89b

Billions of Kroner — **National Accounts**

1985	1986	1987	1988	1989	1990	1991	1992	1993	1994	1995	1996	1997	1998	1999		
261.24	292.66	312.87	ɪ325.17	338.78	357.10	376.28	394.95	411.64	433.10	458.49	486.68	515.75	545.97	578.33	Househ.Cons.Expend.,incl.NPISHs	96f
98.91	108.25	124.22	ɪ130.75	139.02	150.10	161.97	173.58	179.94	186.58	194.53	206.87	218.81	236.81	252.52	Government Consumption Expend.	91f
134.92	155.39	170.92	ɪ181.43	175.06	156.21	157.43	156.34	168.20	179.37	192.52	216.50	249.93	277.22	265.21	Gross Fixed Capital Formation	93e
8.97	22.08	15.45	ɪ5.62	4.30	11.90	6.07	5.77	9.63	14.50	27.44	22.22	23.74	31.08	25.00	Changes in Inventories	93i
235.05	194.07	199.79	ɪ213.86	262.66	293.75	308.05	300.09	315.96	333.20	353.43	414.27	447.58	412.22	465.51	Exports of Goods and Services	90c
−194.10	−213.29	−213.19	ɪ−217.23	−237.46	−246.36	−246.37	−245.81	−261.67	−279.18	−297.65	−326.49	−371.02	−402.53	−393.76	Imports of Goods and Services	98c
544.99	559.15	610.05	ɪ639.59	682.35	722.71	763.41	784.93	823.70	867.56	928.75	1,020.05	1,084.79	1,100.77	1,192.83	Gross Domestic Product (GDP)	99b
−9.89	−9.37	−9.38	ɪ−16.39	−19.24	−21.51	−25.33	−17.47	−19.77	−15.42	−11.87	−9.52	−9.69	−6.10	....	Net Primary Income from Abroad	98.n
535.10	549.78	600.66	ɪ623.20	663.11	701.20	738.08	767.46	803.93	852.14	916.88	1,010.53	1,075.10	1,094.67	1,180.54	Gross National Income (GNI)	99a
−4.95	−6.08	−6.55	ɪ−6.44	−6.61	−7.46	−7.94	−9.03	−9.53	−12.23	−13.05	−9.69	−10.10	−12.29	....	Net Current Transf.from Abroad	98t
530.15	543.70	594.12	ɪ616.76	656.50	693.73	730.15	758.43	794.40	839.92	903.83	1,000.84	1,065.01	1,082.38	....	Gross Nat'l Disposable Inc.(GNDI)	99i
169.99	142.79	157.03	ɪ160.84	178.71	186.53	191.90	189.90	202.82	220.24	250.81	307.29	330.45	299.60	337.11	Gross Savings	99s
....	738.9	753.9	753.0	760.0	775.0	799.1	825.2	847.8	894.3	928.7	979.6	1,013.3	1,033.4	....	GDP Volume 1995 Ref., Chained	99b.*p*
767	794	810	809	817	833	859	887	911	961	998	1,047	1,096	1,118	1,128	GDP Volume 1997 Ref., Chained	99b.*p*
76.8	79.6	81.2	81.1	81.8	83.4	86.0	88.9	91.3	96.3	100.0	104.9	109.8	112.0	113.0	GDP Volume (1995=100)	99bv *p*
76.4	75.7	80.9	ɪ84.9	89.8	93.3	95.5	95.1	97.2	97.0	100.0	104.7	106.4	105.8	113.7	GDP Deflator (1995=100)	99bi *p*

Midyear Estimates

1985	1986	1987	1988	1989	1990	1991	1992	1993	1994	1995	1996	1997	1998	1999		
4.15	4.17	4.19	4.21	4.23	4.24	4.26	4.29	4.31	4.32	4.36	4.38	4.41	4.43	....	Population	99z

(See notes in the back of the book.)

Oman

		1970	1971	1972	1973	1974	1975	1976	1977	1978	1979	1980	1981	1982	1983	1984
Exchange Rates												*Rials Omani per SDR: End of Period (aa)*					
Official Rate	aa	.4167	.4167	.4167	.4167	.4229	.4043	.4013	.4196	.4500	.4550	.4405	.4020	.3810	.3616	.3386
Official Rate	ae	.4167	.3838	.3838	.3454	.3454	.3454	.3454	.3454	.3454	.3454	.3454	.3454	.3454	.3454	.3454
												Index Numbers (1995=100):					
Official Rate	ahx	92.3	83.1	100.2	109.8	111.3	111.3	111.3	111.3	111.3	111.3	111.3	111.3	111.3	111.3	111.3
Nominal Effective Exchange Rate	ne c	....	....	....	....	....	....	....	....	....	122.9	121.7	133.2	147.8	154.9	165.6
Fund Position												*Millions of SDRs:*					
Quota	2f. s	....	7.0	7.0	7.0	7.0	7.0	7.0	7.0	20.0	20.0	20.0	30.0	30.0	63.1	63.1
SDRs	1b. s	....	—	.7	.7	.7	.7	.7	.7	.7	2.8	5.1	5.2	7.9	11.1	9.4
Reserve Position in the Fund	1c. s	....	1.8	1.8	1.8	15.3	24.4	25.0	19.4	13.9	12.8	14.9	16.5	20.8	30.5	33.2
of which: Outstg.Fund Borrowing	2c	....	—	—	—	11.6	19.7	20.2	16.4	11.0	8.3	4.8	1.2	.1	—	—
International Liquidity											*Millions of US Dollars Unless Otherwise Indicated:*						
Total Reserves minus Gold	1l. d	10.3	24.4	36.4	47.1	92.9	161.3	219.6	289.6	254.1	415.6	581.4	744.3	872.4	762.6	900.2
SDRs	1b. d	....	—	.8	.9	.9	.9	.9	.9	1.0	3.7	6.5	6.0	8.7	11.6	9.2
Reserve Position in the Fund	1c. d	....	1.9	1.9	2.1	18.8	28.6	29.1	23.6	18.2	16.8	19.0	19.2	22.9	31.9	32.5
Foreign Exchange	1d. d	10.3	22.5	33.7	44.1	73.3	131.9	189.7	265.1	234.9	395.1	555.9	719.1	840.8	719.1	858.4
Gold (Million Fine Troy Ounces)	1ad	.064	.014	.014	.014	.030	.030	.046	.101	.186	.187	.209	.274	.279	.288	.289
Gold (National Valuation)	1an d	.5	.5	.5	.6	3.3	2.9	4.5	12.5	27.6	27.7	40.0	70.2	71.9	75.6	76.0
Monetary Authorities: Other Assets	3.. d	....	....	....	....	....	....	....	....	....	....	120.2	237.3	332.4	550.1	620.6
Other Liab.	4.. d	—	....	—	—	—	2.8	22.5	24.4	105.3	30.8	12.4	9.2	14.9	10.6	7.0
Deposit Money Banks: Assets	7a. d	....	....	58.1	42.8	65.4	66.6	44.3	96.4	106.5	196.4	402.6	466.8	556.9	826.5	902.8
Liabilities	7b. d	....	....	13.8	9.3	163.0	208.5	260.6	195.7	200.9	230.2	320.1	246.7	268.9	271.1	263.1
Monetary Authorities													*Millions of Rials Omani:*			
Foreign Assets	11	4.5	9.5	14.2	17.0	34.6	56.7	76.8	105.5	97.3	153.3	256.2	363.3	441.0	479.5	551.6
Claims on Central Government	12a	—	—	—	—	—	7.1	18.4	8.4	49.3	.2	—	—	33.6	14.2	5.9
Reserve Money	14	5.1	9.4	13.9	16.3	31.9	49.0	64.3	80.0	88.5	109.7	144.9	221.8	276.8	210.5	254.4
of which: Currency Outside DMBs	14a	....	....	12.3	15.2	28.9	38.5	47.8	55.1	64.4	74.3	94.8	116.2	129.8	140.4	150.0
Foreign Liabilities	16c	—	—	—	—	—	1.0	7.8	8.4	36.4	10.7	4.3	3.2	5.2	3.7	2.4
Central Government Deposits	16d	—	—	—	—	—	8.6	11.3	12.1	2.8	5.3	66.1	83.6	116.3	190.4	214.4
Capital Accounts	17a	.1	.3	.5	1.3	1.2	7.6	7.9	14.8	19.5	28.5	46.8	67.2	74.5	83.3	92.0
Other Items (Net)	17r	—	−.3	−.2	−.6	1.5	−2.4	3.8	−1.5	−.6	−.6	−5.9	−12.5	1.8	5.9	−5.7
Deposit Money Banks													*Millions of Rials Omani:*			
Reserves	20	....	....	1.6	1.1	3.0	10.6	16.7	25.6	24.2	32.3	50.0	107.6	144.6	67.1	104.6
Foreign Assets	21	....	....	22.3	14.8	22.6	23.0	15.3	33.3	36.8	‖67.8	139.1	161.2	192.3	285.5	311.8
Claims on Central Government	22a	....	....	7.2	6.6	56.5	62.1	89.5	56.0	20.6	4.0	3.2	.6	.3	5.3	16.8
Claims on Nonfin.Pub.Enterprises	22c	....	....	....	....	....	....	....	....	....	....	....	....	8.3	11.8	....
Claims on Private Sector	22d	....	....	6.6	18.9	65.8	86.0	120.2	167.1	198.4	222.6	283.2	334.8	377.2	468.9	566.5
Demand Deposits	24	....	....	6.7	9.8	19.5	33.1	54.4	56.2	49.9	48.9	59.9	96.5	119.0	158.7	134.0
Quasi-Monetary Deposits	25	....	....	25.8	21.7	36.8	46.3	62.5	95.3	116.3	123.1	170.3	238.0	322.1	405.5	490.1
Foreign Liabilities	26c	....	....	5.3	3.2	56.3	72.0	90.0	67.6	69.4	‖79.5	110.6	85.2	92.9	93.6	90.9
Central Government Deposits	26d	....	....	.4	3.1	15.6	24.9	28.0	59.4	39.7	62.8	84.2	111.9	107.2	87.9	155.5
Capital Accounts	27a	....	....	....	....	....	4.2	6.3	8.9	10.8	13.7	23.5	46.0	71.1	90.6	110.6
Other Items (Net)	27r	....	....	−.3	3.7	19.7	1.1	.6	−5.5	−6.2	−1.3	27.1	26.6	10.4	2.4	18.6
Monetary Survey													*Millions of Rials Omani:*			
Foreign Assets (Net)	31n	....	....	31.2	28.6	.9	6.8	−5.7	62.8	28.3	‖131.0	280.5	436.2	535.3	667.7	770.1
Domestic Credit	32	....	....	13.5	22.3	106.7	121.6	188.7	159.9	225.8	158.7	136.1	139.8	195.9	221.9	219.3
Claims on Central Govt. (Net)	32an	....	....	6.8	3.5	40.9	35.6	68.5	−7.2	27.4	−63.9	−147.1	−194.9	−189.6	−258.8	−347.2
Claims on Nonfin.Pub.Enterprises	32c	....	....	....	....	....	....	....	....	....	....	....	....	8.3	11.8	....
Claims on Private Sector	32d	....	....	6.6	18.9	65.8	86.0	120.2	167.1	198.4	222.6	283.2	334.8	377.2	468.9	566.5
Money	34	....	....	19.0	24.9	48.4	71.6	102.1	111.2	114.3	123.1	154.7	212.7	248.8	299.1	283.9
Quasi-Money	35	....	....	25.8	21.7	36.8	46.3	62.5	95.3	116.3	123.1	170.3	238.0	322.1	405.5	490.1
Other Items (Net)	37r	....	....	—	4.4	22.4	10.5	18.4	16.1	23.5	43.4	91.6	125.3	160.3	185.0	215.4
Money plus Quasi-Money	35l	....	....	44.8	46.6	85.2	118.0	164.6	206.6	230.6	246.2	325.0	450.7	570.9	704.6	774.0
Interest Rates														*Percent Per Annum*		
Deposit Rate	60l	....	....	....	....	....	....	....	....	....	....	....	....	....	....	9.03
Lending Rate	60p	....	....	....	....	....	....	....	....	....	....	....	....	....	....	10.35
Prices and Production														*Index Numbers (1995=100):*		
Consumer Prices	64	....	....	....	....	....	....	....	....	....	....	....	....	....	....	....
Crude Petroleum	66aa	38.9	34.0	33.1	34.3	34.0	39.8	42.9	39.8	36.7	31.7	33.1	38.4	39.3	45.4	50.2
International Transactions														*Millions of Rials Omani*		
Exports	70	59.5	63.8	64.2	83.7	284.2	360.6	391.6	393.4	378.7	542.3	824.5	1,109.3	1,035.6	1,061.9	1,059.6
Crude Petroleum	70aa	47.6	51.1	51.4	66.9	228.7	289.8	314.5	315.8	302.6	433.3	660.6	886.4	825.3	846.2	910.4
Imports, c.i.f.	71	7.6	13.8	18.7	40.7	135.6	264.3	250.5	302.1	327.2	430.5	598.2	790.3	926.5	860.9	949.2
Refined Petroleum	71ab	....	....	....	....	....	38.6	40.3	29.5	33.2	52.5	81.7	101.2	94.0	12.2	13.5
Volume of Exports															*1995=100*		
Crude Petroleum	72aa	42.7	37.4	36.3	37.6	37.4	44.9	47.2	42.9	40.6	37.8	35.8	42.4	41.7	48.5	47.4
Export Prices															*1985=100:*		
Crude Petroleum	76aa d	9.9	12.1	13.6	18.6	65.2	68.6	71.0	78.5	79.3	121.8	196.5	223.2	210.5	185.0	174.5

	1985	1986	1987	1988	1989	1990	1991	1992	1993	1994	1995	1996	1997	1998	1999		
Exchange Rates																	
Rials Omani per US Dollar: End of Period (ae)																	
Official Rate	.3794	.4703	.5455	.5174	.5053	.5470	.5500	.5287	.5281	.5613	.5716	.5529	.5188	.5414	.5277	Official Rate	aa
Official Rate	.3454	.3845	.3845	.3845	.3845	.3845	.3845	.3845	.3845	.3845	.3845	.3845	.3845	.3845	.3845	Official Rate	ae
Period Averages																	
	111.3	100.7	100.0	100.0	100.0	100.0	100.0	100.0	100.0	100.0	100.0	100.0	100.0	100.0	100.0	Official Rate	ah x
	170.3	126.3	111.8	105.4	111.6	105.7	105.8	103.6	109.0	105.9	100.0	104.5	109.8	113.0	111.7	Nominal Effective Exchange Rate	ne c
Fund Position																	
End of Period																	
Quota	63.1	63.1	63.1	63.1	63.1	63.1	63.1	119.4	119.4	119.4	119.4	119.4	119.4	119.4	194.0	Quota	2f. s
SDRs	10.9	11.4	7.2	8.7	10.9	13.4	15.5	3.4	5.0	6.2	7.5	8.8	10.1	11.5	1.3	SDRs	1b. s
Reserve Position	32.1	32.1	32.1	28.7	27.7	25.2	22.7	39.4	37.8	36.0	34.5	34.0	31.1	31.1	49.8	Reserve Position in the Fund	1c. s
	—	—	—	—	—	—	—	—	—	—	—	—	—	—	—	of which: Outstg. Fund Borrowing	2c
International Liquidity																	
End of Period																	
Total Reserves minus Gold	1,090.2	967.9	1,402.2	1,054.2	1,354.3	1,672.4	1,663.3	1,983.5	908.1	979.4	1,138.3	1,389.4	1,548.8	1,064.1	1,593.0	Total Reserves minus Gold	1l. d
SDRs	12.0	13.9	10.2	11.7	14.3	19.0	22.2	4.7	6.8	9.0	11.1	12.7	13.6	16.2	1.8	SDRs	1b. d
Reserve Position	35.2	39.2	45.5	38.6	36.4	35.8	32.5	54.1	52.0	52.5	51.2	48.8	42.0	43.9	68.3	Reserve Position in the Fund	1c. d
Foreign Exchange	1,043.0	914.8	1,346.5	1,003.8	1,303.6	1,617.6	1,608.6	1,924.7	849.3	917.9	1,075.9	1,327.8	1,493.1	1,004.1	1,522.8	Foreign Exchange	1d. d
Gold (Million Fine Troy Ounces)	.289	.289	.289	.289	.289	.289	.289	.289	.289	.289	.291	.291	.291	.291	.291	Gold (Million Fine Troy Ounces)	1ad
Gold (National Valuation)	76.0	68.3	68.3	68.3	68.3	68.3	68.3	68.3	68.3	68.3	68.3	68.3	68.3	68.3	68.3	Gold (National Valuation)	1an d
Monetary Authorities: Other Assets	532.3	337.2	312.9	321.0	323.6	484.5	872.5	662.3	162.2	38.4	....	80.6	120.3	147.8	555.9	Monetary Authorities: Other Assets	3.. d
Other Liab.	10.9	4.3	4.7	3.9	.9	1.0	1.0	1.0	1.0	1.2	1.7	1.0	1.7	1.2	1.1	Other Liab.	4.. d
Deposit Money Banks: Assets	680.9	596.6	609.9	726.4	755.2	758.7	699.7	532.4	780.1	863.5	999.1	944.1	1,776.8	1,222.7	992.3	Deposit Money Banks: Assets	7a. d
Liabilities	249.2	337.7	278.6	313.2	267.8	203.0	104.3	105.8	167.1	239.5	441.4	652.4	1,326.5	1,522.2	1,662.4	Liabilities	7b. d
Monetary Authorities																	
End of Period																	
Foreign Assets	586.6	528.8	687.6	555.8	672.3	856.7	1,002.6	920.5	720.1	635.0	730.4	780.8	822.4	771.6	1,090.4	Foreign Assets	11
Claims on Central Government	—	116.9	—	121.6	51.0	—	32.3	38.9	49.3	97.0	89.4	47.0	32.7	159.6	4.1	Claims on Central Government	12a
Reserve Money	264.0	280.8	239.7	242.0	295.2	300.6	309.8	299.1	284.7	296.3	306.9	326.5	354.3	379.5	375.3	Reserve Money	14
of which: Currency Outside DMBs	178.5	168.8	180.4	176.3	183.6	214.1	215.9	226.7	232.9	245.5	235.9	231.2	242.2	244.2	273.5	of which: Currency Outside DMBs	14a
Foreign Liabilities	3.8	1.7	1.8	1.5	.4	.4	.4	.4	.4	.5	.6	.4	.6	.5	.4	Foreign Liabilities	16c
Central Government Deposits	184.4	129.9	122.4	123.8	124.6	187.6	336.2	255.0	62.4	14.8	41.0	31.1	46.6	57.0	242.6	Central Government Deposits	16d
Capital Accounts	104.3	121.8	135.2	144.2	156.9	188.0	202.0	213.7	219.9	235.2	251.9	268.3	283.1	297.9	312.4	Capital Accounts	17a
Other Items (Net)	30.0	111.6	188.4	165.8	146.3	180.1	186.5	191.2	201.9	185.3	219.5	201.5	170.4	196.3	163.8	Other Items (Net)	17r
Deposit Money Banks																	
End of Period																	
Reserves	86.1	111.4	57.8	70.1	110.7	88.2	85.0	72.3	49.4	51.6	67.8	86.9	116.0	132.2	99.2	Reserves	20
Foreign Assets	235.2	229.4	234.5	279.3	290.4	291.7	269.0	204.7	299.9	332.0	384.2	363.0	683.2	470.1	381.5	Foreign Assets	21
Claims on Central Government	52.8	41.0	84.5	32.8	23.6	48.7	124.8	190.7	154.1	97.9	91.9	175.8	157.4	198.0	334.7	Claims on Central Government	22a
Claims on Nonfin.Pub.Enterprises	13.1	12.3	8.6	5.1	12.9	16.7	9.8	8.4	16.8	3.0	3.1	4.8	.6	—	4.1	Claims on Nonfin.Pub.Enterprises	22c
Claims on Private Sector	675.2	674.5	688.5	764.8	823.9	926.1	935.0	1,029.9	1,088.0	1,227.3	1,357.5	1,564.9	2,170.9	2,563.1	2,783.9	Claims on Private Sector	22d
Demand Deposits	150.1	144.0	154.8	139.0	161.9	176.6	189.8	206.3	218.7	227.4	235.4	272.1	307.5	261.6	237.7	Demand Deposits	24
Quasi-Monetary Deposits	608.4	560.6	584.3	658.8	720.3	781.3	830.2	841.1	863.9	931.1	1,040.5	1,130.5	1,484.5	1,625.4	1,756.2	Quasi-Monetary Deposits	25
Foreign Liabilities	86.1	129.8	107.1	120.4	103.0	78.0	40.1	40.7	64.2	92.1	169.7	250.9	510.0	585.3	639.2	Foreign Liabilities	26c
Central Government Deposits	84.9	88.0	82.4	84.6	99.0	130.0	147.8	138.6	153.4	148.9	140.7	211.3	289.8	292.4	316.1	Central Government Deposits	26d
Capital Accounts	125.4	138.8	104.6	107.2	104.0	116.5	121.7	129.0	165.8	167.6	174.9	193.8	304.2	425.6	454.2	Capital Accounts	27a
Other Items (Net)	7.5	7.4	40.7	42.1	73.3	88.9	94.0	150.3	142.3	144.7	143.3	136.9	232.0	173.1	200.0	Other Items (Net)	27r
Monetary Survey																	
End of Period																	
Foreign Assets (Net)	731.9	626.7	813.2	713.1	859.4	1,070.0	1,231.1	1,084.1	955.4	874.5	944.2	892.6	994.9	656.0	832.3	Foreign Assets (Net)	31n
Domestic Credit	471.7	626.9	576.8	716.0	687.8	673.9	617.9	874.4	1,092.3	1,261.5	1,360.3	1,550.2	2,025.2	2,571.2	2,568.1	Domestic Credit	32
Claims on Central Govt. (Net)	-216.6	-60.0	-120.3	-54.0	-149.0	-268.9	-327.0	-164.0	-12.5	31.2	-.4	-19.6	-146.3	8.1	-219.9	Claims on Central Govt. (Net)	32an
Claims on Nonfin.Pub.Enterprises	13.1	12.3	8.6	5.1	12.9	16.7	9.8	8.4	16.8	3.0	3.1	4.8	.6	—	4.1	Claims on Nonfin.Pub.Enterprises	32c
Claims on Private Sector	675.2	674.5	688.5	764.8	823.9	926.1	935.0	1,029.9	1,088.0	1,227.3	1,357.5	1,564.9	2,170.9	2,563.1	2,783.9	Claims on Private Sector	32d
Money	328.6	312.8	335.2	315.3	345.4	390.8	405.7	433.0	451.5	472.9	471.3	503.4	549.7	505.8	511.2	Money	34
Quasi-Money	608.4	560.6	584.3	658.8	720.3	781.3	830.2	841.1	863.9	931.1	1,040.5	1,130.5	1,484.5	1,625.4	1,756.2	Quasi-Money	35
Other Items (Net)	266.6	380.1	470.5	455.0	481.4	571.9	613.0	684.4	732.3	731.9	792.7	808.9	985.9	1,096.0	1,132.9	Other Items (Net)	37r
Money plus Quasi-Money	937.0	873.4	919.5	974.1	1,065.8	1,172.0	1,235.9	1,274.1	1,315.5	1,404.1	1,511.8	1,633.9	2,034.2	2,131.2	2,267.5	Money plus Quasi-Money	35l
Interest Rates																	
Percent Per Annum																	
Deposit Rate	9.04	8.33	7.48	7.57	8.66	8.32	7.06	6.29	4.17	4.34	6.53	6.85	7.30	8.46	8.12	Deposit Rate	60l
Lending Rate	10.24	9.65	9.10	9.40	10.01	9.68	9.50	9.24	8.49	8.57	9.38	9.23	9.30	10.09	10.32	Lending Rate	60p
Prices and Production																	
Period Averages																	
Consumer Prices	....	....	....	....	....	95.4	99.9	100.8	101.7	101.3	100.0	100.1	100.2	99.4	99.8	Consumer Prices	64
Crude Petroleum	59.1	65.4	68.1	72.6	73.9	78.8	82.9	86.8	91.2	94.7	100.0	104.3	105.2	104.0	105.2	Crude Petroleum	66aa
International Transactions																	
Millions of Rials Omani																	
Exports	1,360.2	698.0	957.9	951.9	1,564.0	2,118.0	1,873.9	2,135.3	2,064.9	2,132.0	2,333.2	2,824.5	2,933.8	2,118.0	....	Exports	70
Crude Petroleum	1,253.0	553.6	762.1	642.4	....	....	....	1,018.7	935.0	921.5	1,042.7	1,283.9	1,276.1	801.3	1,206.0	Crude Petroleum	70aa
Imports, c.i.f.	1,088.9	916.7	700.7	846.5	867.9	1,031.0	1,228.0	1,449.3	1,581.8	1,505.3	1,633.2	1,760.1	1,932.5	2,184.6	1,797.1	Imports, c.i.f.	71
Refined Petroleum	....	....	....	....	....	....	....	....	....	....	....	....	....	....	....	Refined Petroleum	71ab
Volume of Exports																Volume of Exports	
Crude Petroleum	58.3	65.9	69.3	74.5	75.9	80.6	82.5	88.7	94.0	95.0	100.0	103.5	107.4	105.5	108.4	Crude Petroleum	72aa
Export Prices																Export Prices	
Index of Prices in US Dollars																	
Crude Petroleum	164.7	82.0	105.3	82.5	....	....	....	109.8	95.2	92.8	100.0	118.5	113.6	72.7	105.8	Crude Petroleum	76aa d

Oman

449

		1970	1971	1972	1973	1974	1975	1976	1977	1978	1979	1980	1981	1982	1983	1984
Balance of Payments														*Millions of US Dollars:*		
Current Account, n.i.e.	78al d	....	....	....	....	179	57	36	277	–50	549	942	1,237	489	494	303
Goods: Exports f.o.b.	78aa d					1,212	1,416	1,596	1,620	1,598	2,280	3,748	4,696	4,423	4,256	4,421
Goods: Imports f.o.b.	78ab d					–552	–908	–1,000	–1,044	–1,157	–1,285	–1,780	–2,296	–2,583	–2,360	–2,640
Trade Balance	78ac d					661	508	596	576	441	994	1,968	2,400	1,840	1,895	1,781
Services: Credit	78ad d					—	—	—	—	8	8	9	9	12	14	14
Services: Debit	78ae d					–104	–155	–177	–186	–193	–235	–518	–620	–701	–688	–673
Balance on Goods & Services	78af d					557	354	419	390	256	767	1,459	1,788	1,151	1,222	1,123
Income: Credit	78ag d					19	17	6	—	5	—	96	177	318	307	345
Income: Debit	78ah d					–310	–312	–220	–160	–118	–149	–352	–415	–471	–490	–560
Balance on Gds, Serv. & Inc.	78ai d					266	58	204	230	142	618	1,202	1,549	998	1,039	908
Current Transfers, n.i.e.: Credit	78aj d					24	207	52	268	49	212	137	185	87	191	255
Current Transfers: Debit	78ak d					–111	–208	–220	–222	–241	–281	–397	–498	–596	–735	–860
Capital Account, n.i.e.	78bc d	....	....	....	....	—	—	—	—	—	—	—	–3	–3	–3	–3
Capital Account, n.i.e.: Credit	78ba d					—	—	—	—	—	—	—	—	—	—	—
Capital Account: Debit	78bb d					—	—	—	—	—	—	—	–3	–3	–3	–3
Financial Account, n.i.e.	78bj d	....	....	....	....	–10	155	389	35	151	–136	–85	37	192	325	439
Direct Investment Abroad	78bd d					—	—	—	—	—	—	—	—	—	—	—
Dir. Invest. in Rep. Econ., n.i.e.	78be d					–61	106	81	48	86	118	98	63	182	155	158
Portfolio Investment Assets	78bf d					—	—	—	—	—	—	—	—	—	—	—
Equity Securities	78bk d					—	—	—	—	—	—	—	—	—	—	—
Debt Securities	78bl d					—	—	—	—	—	—	—	—	—	—	—
Portfolio Investment Liab., n.i.e.	78bg d					—	—	—	—	—	—	—	—	—	—	—
Equity Securities	78bm d					—	—	—	—	—	—	—	—	—	—	—
Debt Securities	78bn d					—	—	—	—	—	—	—	—	—	—	—
Financial Derivatives Assets	78bw d	....	....	....	....	....	....	....	....	....	....	....	....	....	....	....
Financial Derivatives Liabilities	78bx d	....	....	....	....	....	....	....	....	....	....	....	....	....	....	....
Other Investment Assets	78bh d	....	....	....	....	–27	–91	91	–33	6	–110	–257	–96	–139	–299	–146
Monetary Authorities	78bo d	....	....	....	....											
General Government	78bp d					—	—	—	—	–4	–28	–43	14	–55	–98	–17
Banks	78bq d					131	15	22	–52	–9	–31	–206	–64	–90	–270	–76
Other Sectors	78br d					–158	–106	69	19	18	–50	–8	–47	6	69	–52
Other Investment Liab., n.i.e.	78bi d					78	139	217	20	60	–144	74	71	149	470	427
Monetary Authorities	78bs d					—	—	—	—	—	—	—	—	—	—	—
General Government	78bt d					78	139	165	85	54	–115	–16	144	124	468	435
Banks	78bu d					—	—	52	–64	6	–29	90	–74	24	2	–8
Other Sectors	78bv d					—	—	—	—	—	—	—	—	—	—	—
Net Errors and Omissions	78ca d	....	....	....	....	–118	–146	–369	–240	–150	–257	–62	–24	67	–466	–421
Overall Balance	78cb d					50	66	57	72	–49	155	796	1,247	744	351	319
Reserves and Related Items	79da d	....	....	....	....	–50	–66	–57	–72	49	–155	–796	–1,247	–744	–351	–319
Reserve Assets	79db d					–50	–66	–57	–72	49	–155	–796	–1,247	–744	–351	–319
Use of Fund Credit and Loans	79dc d					—	—	—	—	—	—	—	—	—	—	—
Exceptional Financing	79de d					....	....	....	....	....	....	....	....	....	....	....
Government Finance														*Millions of Rials Omani:*		
Deficit (-) or Surplus	80	....	4.1	–17.1	–23.5	–56.4	–37.7	–84.7	58.1	–75.3	85.0	9.1	48.5	–222.8	–242.3	–346.8
Revenue	81	....	50.1	53.0	65.0	303.2	358.7	457.3	483.4	440.9	590.6	793.9	1,075.9	986.5	1,073.7	1,141.6
Grants Received	81z	....	—	—	3.5	8.3	71.6	18.0	92.7	6.7	61.9	35.2	50.0	14.7	50.7	72.8
Expenditure	82	....	46.0	69.4	91.7	329.3	466.5	551.0	497.7	498.7	548.8	794.9	1,028.0	1,176.5	1,308.1	1,501.0
Lending Minus Repayments	83	....	—	.7	.3	38.6	1.5	9.0	20.3	24.2	18.7	25.1	49.4	47.5	58.6	60.2
Financing																
Domestic	84a	....	–4.1	17.1	–12.5	28.6	–18.1	32.7	–88.8	83.4	–72.8	64.3	–137.7	181.1	–9.3	48.4
Foreign	85a	....	—	—	36.0	27.8	55.8	52.0	30.7	–8.1	–12.2	–73.4	89.2	41.7	251.6	298.4
Debt: Domestic	88a	....	.7	15.0	12.2	49.7	41.9	69.7	16.1	43.7	4.2	.8	.4			
Foreign	89a	....			10.9	46.2	102.0	154.0	184.7	176.6	164.4	169.1	219.5	261.2	424.0	574.7
National Accounts														*Millions of Rials Omani*		
Exports of Goods & Services	90c	79	82	84	115	419	489	551	559	552	787	1,295	1,625	1,532	1,475	1,532
Government Consumption	91f	14	26	42	63	197	229	241	269	272	355	499	656	715	591	701
Gross Capital Formation	93	15	36	42	44	174	258	317	290	274	335	466	584	707	710	804
Private Consumption	96f	21	21	35	41	50	115	182	246	310	337	577	591	795	1,210	1,340
Imports of Goods & Services	98c	–21	–40	–62	–94	–272	–367	–407	–417	–461	–525	–789	–964	–1,134	–1,053	–1,144
Gross Domestic Product (GDP)	99b	107	125	141	169	569	724	884	947	947	1,290	2,047	2,492	2,615	2,933	3,232
Net Factor Inc/Pmts(-) Abroad	98.n	–18	–20	–29	–63	–152	–135	–148	–130	–111	–137	–212	–235	–238	–297	–350
Gross National Income (GNI)	99a	89	105	112	107	417	589	736	817	836	1,153	1,835	2,257	2,377	2,444	2,698
GDP Volume 1972 Prices	99b.p	128	129	141	121	155	200	232	....	....	....	....	....	....	....	....
GDP Volume 1978 Prices	99b.p							684.1	804.8	946.9	990.5	1,047.2	1,225.6	1,367.1	1,585.3	1,850.6
GDP Volume 1988 Prices	99b.p	....	....	....	....	....	....	....	....	....	....	....	....	....	....	....
GDP Volume (1995=100)	99bv p	11.7	11.8	12.9	11.1	14.2	18.3	21.2	25.0	29.4	30.7	32.5	38.0	42.4	49.2	57.4
GDP Deflator (1995=100)	99bi p	17.2	20.0	20.6	28.8	75.3	74.6	78.5	71.5	60.7	79.1	118.8	123.5	116.2	112.4	106.1
																Millions:
Population	99z	.65	.67	.70	.72	.74	.77	.79	.84	.88	.93	.98	1.03	1.09	1.15	1.21

Balance of Payments

Minus Sign Indicates Debit

	1985	1986	1987	1988	1989	1990	1991	1992	1993	1994	1995	1996	1997	1998	1999	code
Current Account, n.i.e.	-10	-1,040	784	-309	305	1,106	-251	-598	-1,190	-805	-801	180	-40	-2,970	....	78al d
Goods: Exports f.o.b.	4,971	2,861	3,805	3,342	4,068	5,508	4,871	5,555	5,365	5,542	6,065	7,339	7,631	5,508	....	78aa d
Goods: Imports f.o.b.	-3,028	-2,309	-1,769	-2,107	-2,225	-2,623	-3,112	-3,627	-4,030	-3,693	-4,050	-4,385	-4,649	-5,217	....	78ab d
Trade Balance	1,943	552	2,036	1,235	1,842	2,885	1,759	1,928	1,336	1,849	2,015	2,954	2,982	291	....	78ac d
Services: Credit	14	13	13	13	59	68	61	13	13	13	13	18	18	18	....	78ad d
Services: Debit	-713	-689	-481	-523	-570	-719	-961	-932	-906	-900	-985	-975	-1,166	-1,303	....	78ae d
Balance on Goods & Services	1,245	-123	1,568	726	1,331	2,235	860	1,009	442	962	1,043	1,997	1,834	-993	....	78af d
Income: Credit	362	597	520	257	338	375	359	328	421	257	325	218	346	299	....	78ag d
Income: Debit	-688	-668	-610	-572	-588	-629	-596	-739	-688	-724	-699	-715	-789	-842	....	78ah d
Balance on Gds, Serv. & Inc.	919	-194	1,479	411	1,080	1,980	623	598	175	495	669	1,501	1,391	-1,537	....	78ai d
Current Transfers, n.i.e.: Credit	43	39	47	81	55	39	39	39	57	65	68	49	70	39	....	78aj d
Current Transfers: Debit	-973	-885	-741	-801	-830	-913	-913	-1,235	-1,423	-1,365	-1,537	-1,371	-1,501	-1,472	....	78ak d
Capital Account, n.i.e.	-3	—	—	—	—	—	—	—	—	—	—	—	—	—	....	78bc d
Capital Account, n.i.e.: Credit	—	—	—	—	—	—	—	—	—	—	—	—	—	—	....	78ba d
Capital Account: Debit	-3	—	—	—	—	—	—	—	—	—	—	—	—	—	....	78bb d
Financial Account, n.i.e.	458	1,015	-190	221	-15	-498	510	497	-79	230	-19	275	92	1,464	....	78bj d
Direct Investment Abroad	—	—	—	—	—	—	—	—	—	—	—	—	—	—	....	78bd d
Dir. Invest. in Rep. Econ., n.i.e.	161	140	35	92	112	142	135	104	142	76	46	75	53	106	....	78be d
Portfolio Investment Assets	—	—	—	—	—	—	—	—	....	....	....	....	....	....	....	78bf d
Equity Securities	—	—	—	—	—	—	—	—	....	....	....	....	....	....	....	78bk d
Debt Securities	—	—	—	—	—	—	—	—	....	....	....	....	....	....	....	78bl d
Portfolio Investment Liab., n.i.e.	—	—	—	—	—	—	—	—	....	....	....	....	....	....	....	78bg d
Equity Securities	—	—	—	—	—	—	—	—	....	....	....	....	....	....	....	78bm d
Debt Securities	—	—	—	—	—	—	—	—	....	....	....	....	....	....	....	78bn d
Financial Derivatives Assets																78bw d
Financial Derivatives Liabilities																78bx d
Other Investment Assets	97	198	-31	-88	-179	-270	146	120	-187	-174	-52	-23	-39	837	....	78bh d
Monetary Authorities	—	—	—	—	—	—	—	—	—	—	—	—	—	—	....	78bo d
General Government	-64	-13	—	-5	-39	-10	—	—	-31	-104	-88	-104	-81	-68	....	78bp d
Banks	222	57	-13	-117	-75	-49	-55	169	-187	-10	62	268	-156	749	....	78bq d
Other Sectors	-61	154	-18	34	-65	-211	200	-49	31	-60	-26	-187	198	156	....	78br d
Other Investment Liab., n.i.e.	199	676	-194	217	52	-369	229	273	-34	328	-13	224	78	520	....	78bi d
Monetary Authorities	—	—	—	—	—	—	—	—	—	—	—	—	—	—	....	78bs d
General Government	212	560	-135	186	52	-372	226	260	-91	325	-18	138	-179	-81	....	78bt d
Banks	-12	116	-59	31	—	3	3	13	57	3	5	10	34	23	....	78bu d
Other Sectors	—	—	—	—	—	—	—	—	—	....	....	75	224	577	....	78bv d
Net Errors and Omissions	-323	-588	-486	-379	33	-474	284	401	211	-86	388	-267	485	736	....	78ca d
Overall Balance	122	-613	108	-467	324	135	543	300	-1,058	-661	-432	189	537	-770	....	78cb d
Reserves and Related Items	-122	613	-108	467	-324	-135	-543	-300	1,058	661	432	-189	-537	770	....	79da d
Reserve Assets	-122	613	-108	467	-324	-135	-543	-300	1,058	661	432	-189	-537	770	....	79db d
Use of Fund Credit and Loans	—	—	—	—	—	—	—	—	—	—	—	—	—	—	....	79dc d
Exceptional Financing																79de d

Government Finance

Year Ending December 31

	1985	1986	1987	1988	1989	1990	1991	1992	1993	1994	1995	1996	1997	1998	1999	code
Deficit (-) or Surplus	-364.2	-700.2	-146.2	-346.7	-289.5	-32.8	-284.3	-584.5	-511.1	-485.9	-468.1	-259.7	-28.3	....	....	80
Revenue	1,337.8	848.6	1,185.1	999.6	1,125.4	1,580.1	1,261.4	1,338.1	1,357.7	1,386.7	1,487.9	1,602.8	1,867.4	....	....	81
Grants Received	59.8	46.4	14.3	30.5	27.9	6.6	23.0	.9	19.2	29.9	13.2	10.8	20.7	....	....	81z
Expenditure	1,731.1	1,587.2	1,330.1	1,364.3	1,425.5	1,601.0	1,575.1	1,900.3	1,871.4	1,912.7	1,971.2	1,879.4	1,848.0	....	....	82
Lending Minus Repayments	30.7	8.0	15.5	12.5	17.3	18.5	-6.4	23.2	16.6	-10.2	-2.0	-6.1	68.4	....	....	83
Financing																
Domestic	-9.5	105.6	54.0	149.5	243.6	191.1	201.6	413.5	211.2	141.8	46.4	-250.6	35.5	....	....	84a
Foreign	373.7	594.6	92.2	197.2	45.9	-158.3	82.7	171.0	299.9	344.1	421.7	510.3	-7.2	....	....	85a
Debt: Domestic	—	—	—	—	—	32.6	252.9	410.2	291.0	313.9	306.7	325.2	314.1	....	....	88a
Foreign	648.1	940.2	887.7	959.7	994.4	847.1	932.1	1,036.3	1,020.8	1,148.8	1,148.0	1,201.1	1,132.5	....	....	89a

National Accounts

Millions of Rials Omani

	1985	1986	1987	1988	1989	1990	1991	1992	1993	1994	1995	1996	1997	1998	1999	code
Exports of Goods & Services	1,722	1,098	1,468	1,290	1,568	2,122	‡1,878	2,141	2,068	2,136	2,337	2,829	2,941	2,125	2,782	90c
Government Consumption	796	880	908	956	1,035	1,195	‡1,150	1,303	1,333	1,429	1,462	1,446	1,415	1,402	1,434	91f
Gross Capital Formation	900	820	519	490	507	555	‡655	783	842	782	795	805	1,075	1,309	948	93
Private Consumption	1,457	1,491	1,288	1,500	1,527	1,861	‡2,193	2,263	1,289	2,347	2,600	2,798	2,895	3,116	2,909	96f
Imports of Goods & Services	-1,284	-1,145	-865	-1,011	-1,034	-1,240	‡-1,515	-1,702	-1,828	-1,543	-1,887	-2,003	-2,236	-2,507	....	98c
Gross Domestic Product (GDP)	3,591	3,143	3,318	3,225	3,604	4,493	‡4,361	4,788	4,804	4,967	5,307	5,874	6,090	5,445	6,011	99b
Net Factor Inc/Pmts(-) Abroad	-399	-336	-281	-406	-406	-419	‡-423	-608	-634	-683	-713	-695	-752	-788	-791	98.n
Gross National Income (GNI)	3,055	2,464	2,722	2,520	2,825	3,632	‡3,938	4,180	4,170	4,284	4,594	5,179	5,363	4,693	5,220	99a
GDP Volume 1972 Prices	....	....	....	....	....	....	....	....	....	....	....	....	....	....	....	99b.p
GDP Volume 1978 Prices	2,105.2	....														99b.p
GDP Volume 1988 Prices	3,124	3,191	3,064	3,225	3,321	3,599	3,816	4,141	4,395	4,564	4,784	4,923	5,238	5,381	....	99b.p
GDP Volume (1995=100)	65.3	66.7	64.0	67.4	69.4	75.2	79.8	86.5	91.9	95.4	100.0	102.9	109.5	112.5	....	99bv p
GDP Deflator (1995=100)	103.6	88.8	97.6	90.1	97.8	112.5	‡103.0	104.2	‡98.5	98.1	100.0	107.6	104.8	91.2	....	99bi p

Midyear Estimates

	1985	1986	1987	1988	1989	1990	1991	1992	1993	1994	1995	1996	1997	1998	1999	code
Population	‡2.00	‡1.46	1.53	1.63	156.00	1.63	1.76	1.88	2.00	2.05	2.13	2.21	2.26	2.29	2.46	99z

(See notes in the back of the book.)

		1970	1971	1972	1973	1974	1975	1976	1977	1978	1979	1980	1981	1982	1983	1984
Exchange Rates																*Rupees per SDR:*
Market Rate	aa	4.791	5.191	11.947	11.913	12.091	11.561	11.473	11.996	12.865	13.009	12.595	11.494	14.129	14.099	15.018
																Rupees per US Dollar:
Market Rate	ae	4.791	4.781	11.003	9.875	9.875	9.875	9.875	9.875	9.875	9.875	9.875	9.875	12.808	13.466	15.322
Market Rate	rf	4.762	4.762	8.648	9.947	9.853	9.853	9.853	9.853	9.853	9.853	9.853	9.853	11.792	13.055	13.980
																Index Numbers (1995=100):
Nominal Effective Exchange Rate	ne c	....	....	....	....	....	....	....	....	....	207.59	210.99	236.66	220.64	212.94	217.53
Real Effective Exchange Rate	re c	....	....	....	....	....	....	....	....	....	....	177.45	200.88	184.03	177.72	181.13
Fund Position																*Millions of SDRs:*
Quota	2f. s	235	235	235	235	235	235	235	235	285	285	428	428	428	546	546
SDRs	1b. s	10	13	19	27	20	25	32	29	30	34	23	49	46	1	37
Reserve Position in the Fund	1c. s	—	—	—	—	—	—	—	—	—	—	—	—	59	89	89
Total Fund Cred.&Loans Outstg.	2tl	45	43	111	130	239	374	440	463	492	435	528	880	1,286	1,540	1,469
International Liquidity														*Millions of US Dollars Unless Otherwise Indicated:*		
Total Reserves minus Gold	1l. d	136	129	221	412	392	340	466	449	408	213	496	721	969	1,973	1,035
SDRs	1b. d	10	14	21	32	24	29	37	35	40	45	29	56	51	1	37
Reserve Position in the Fund	1c. d	—	—	—	—	—	—	—	—	—	—	—	—	65	93	87
Foreign Exchange	1d. d	126	115	200	380	368	311	429	414	368	168	467	665	853	1,879	912
Gold (Million Fine Troy Ounces)	1ad	1.561	1.583	1.588	1.588	1.588	1.588	1.618	1.618	1.718	1.818	1.818	1.846	1.848	1.862	1.865
Gold (National Valuation)	1an d	54	55	....	....	67	67	68	68	333	730	1,191	788	559	757	635
Monetary Authorities: Other Liab.	4..d	3	3	1	1	4	7	8	8	48	69	348	347	343	341	329
Deposit Money Banks: Assets	7a. d	121	90	71	126	230	222	199	235	350	386	310	323	333	464	550
Liabilities	7b. d	192	202	140	145	123	143	198	212	204	215	215	317	291	444	839
Monetary Authorities																*Millions of Rupees:*
Foreign Assets	11	1,185	1,159	3,765	5,415	5,191	4,569	5,756	5,543	7,751	9,853	17,208	15,412	20,155	37,387	25,925
Claims on General Government	12a	7,985	9,661	10,770	9,958	9,087	12,450	13,771	19,750	25,334	32,528	35,325	39,962	49,731	51,774	66,901
of which: Provincial Government	12ax	241	503	387	419	415	393	195	443	88	183	134	25	25	25	26
Claims on Deposit Money Banks	12e	2,182	1,412	1,847	3,102	5,197	5,727	6,688	6,341	6,589	8,646	12,553	17,498	17,141	20,682	20,576
Reserve Money	14	9,512	10,544	12,380	13,861	13,956	15,326	18,358	22,525	26,483	33,564	39,157	42,369	49,859	56,719	66,002
of which: Currency Outside DMBs	14a	8,065	8,156	9,350	10,990	11,427	11,884	13,853	17,349	21,040	26,447	32,482	34,488	41,153	46,425	52,003
Restricted Deposits	16b	....	....	....	....	....	....	....	....	....	....	....	....	....	....	....
Foreign Liabilities	16c	230	233	1,337	1,564	2,931	4,399	5,119	5,630	6,813	6,333	10,092	13,535	22,571	26,309	27,109
General Government Deposits	16d	485	492	628	597	282	127	315	558	471	409	305	6,719	5,934	13,420	7,772
Counterpart Funds	16e	820	926	1,030	1,278	1,502	1,626	1,574	1,894	1,657	2,070	2,077	1,868	1,502	1,729	1,182
Other Items (Net)	17r	303	37	1,009	1,177	811	1,278	861	1,041	4,265	8,664	13,455	8,382	7,163	11,666	11,338
Deposit Money Banks																*Millions of Rupees:*
Reserves	20	1,156	1,441	1,599	2,062	1,862	2,775	3,738	4,529	5,031	6,742	6,167	7,451	8,207	10,101	13,809
Foreign Assets	21	575	427	785	1,247	2,277	2,193	933	1,070	1,733	2,112	3,060	3,190	4,262	6,243	8,426
Claims on General Government	22a	3,606	4,636	5,361	6,876	6,732	8,861	12,849	12,535	16,997	17,878	23,714	29,527	34,665	47,011	34,240
of which: Provincial Government	22ax	1,388	1,479	1,278	1,634	2,249	2,632	4,285	3,982	3,979	4,384	5,836	8,256	10,646	12,598	9,365
Claims on Private Sector	22d	11,948	12,273	14,658	17,074	17,289	20,632	28,435	33,958	38,071	45,853	51,903	61,313	73,076	88,431	103,071
Demand Deposits	24	5,765	7,592	9,427	10,588	10,614	13,107	19,519	21,926	25,887	29,981	33,698	37,227	45,641	53,685	53,035
Time Deposits	25	6,737	7,122	7,796	9,368	8,665	12,177	15,924	18,969	23,436	27,288	30,650	36,252	44,892	59,316	61,532
Foreign Liabilities	26c	308	315	405	371	452	623	1,050	1,228	1,144	1,290	1,229	2,259	2,493	4,576	10,745
Long-Term Foreign Liabilities	26cl	606	648	1,137	1,062	760	791	906	868	873	834	894	868	1,229	1,403	2,106
General Government Deposits	26d	722	748	980	1,339	1,410	1,248	2,282	1,669	2,162	2,567	3,472	3,749	2,799	2,927	948
Counterpart Funds	26e	395	409	420	399	410	428	447	466	487	523	566	637	701	782	
Credit from Monetary Authorities	26g	2,098	1,412	1,847	3,102	5,197	5,727	6,688	6,341	6,374	8,431	12,338	15,424	14,776	18,182	17,948
Other Items (Net)	27r	655	532	392	1,029	653	361	−860	624	1,468	1,670	1,997	5,094	7,743	10,996	12,450
Monetary Survey																*Millions of Rupees:*
Foreign Assets (Net)	31n	1,222	1,039	2,808	4,727	4,085	1,741	520	−244	1,527	4,343	8,947	2,809	−647	12,744	−3,503
Domestic Credit	32	22,535	25,553	29,577	32,228	31,676	41,163	53,756	65,981	80,219	96,526	111,483	126,945	157,046	179,863	206,596
Claims on General Govt. (Net)	32an	10,383	13,057	14,524	14,898	14,127	19,935	24,022	30,058	39,698	47,430	55,262	59,021	75,663	82,437	92,422
Claims on Private Sector	32d	12,152	12,496	15,054	17,329	17,549	21,228	29,733	35,923	40,522	49,097	56,220	67,924	81,383	97,426	114,174
Money	34	14,016	16,488	19,939	22,194	22,517	25,621	34,044	39,966	47,194	56,830	66,671	72,285	87,341	100,566	105,780
Quasi-Money	35	6,737	7,122	7,796	9,368	8,665	12,177	15,924	18,969	23,436	27,288	30,650	36,252	44,892	59,316	61,532
Restricted Deposits	36b	....	....	....	....	....	....	....	....	....	....	....	....	....	....	....
Long-Term Foreign Liabilities	36cl	606	648	1,137	1,062	760	791	906	868	873	834	894	868	1,229	1,403	2,106
Counterpart Funds	36e	1,215	1,335	1,450	1,676	1,912	2,054	2,020	2,360	2,144	2,593	2,643	2,475	2,139	2,430	1,964
Other Items (Net)	37r	1,184	999	2,065	2,654	1,914	2,271	1,394	3,586	8,115	13,337	19,571	17,874	20,799	28,894	31,711
Money plus Quasi-Money	35l	20,752	23,610	27,734	31,562	31,182	37,798	49,967	58,935	70,629	84,118	97,322	108,538	132,233	159,882	167,312
Other Banking Institutions																*Millions of Rupees:*
Post Office: Savings Deposits	45.. i	775	974	1,165	1,385	1,418	1,405	1,317	1,360	1,318	1,235	1,194	1,038	1,347	1,560	1,634
Liquid Liabilities	55l	21,527	24,584	28,899	32,947	32,600	39,202	51,285	60,295	71,947	85,352	98,515	109,575	133,580	161,442	168,946
Interest Rates																*Percent Per Annum*
Discount Rate (End of Period)	60	5.00	5.00	6.00	8.00	9.00	9.00	9.00	10.00	10.00	10.00	10.00	10.00	10.00	10.00	10.00
Money Market Rate	60b	5.50	6.60	5.34	6.51	10.33	9.87	9.37	10.87	10.41	8.83	8.63	9.27	9.51	8.15	8.97
Treasury Bill Rate	60c	....	....	....	....	....	....	....	....	....	....	....	....	....	....	....
Government Bond Yield	61	5.50	5.76	5.76	5.76	5.77	5.77	9.04	9.27	9.48	9.75	11.20	9.40	9.36	9.31	9.25
Prices, Production, Labor																*Index Numbers (1995=100):*
Share Prices	62	36.6	30.9	....	28.4	24.4	31.1	31.6	ⅰ40.3	45.7	52.7	48.7	48.2	ⅰ52.8	68.1	89.4
Wholesale Prices	63	8.1	8.4	8.9	10.5	13.3	16.9	18.5	20.4	22.0	23.5	26.4	29.9	32.5	34.3	37.7
Consumer Prices	64	9.5	ⅰ10.0	10.5	12.9	16.4	19.8	21.2	ⅰ23.4	24.8	26.8	30.0	33.6	ⅰ35.6	37.9	40.2
Manufacturing Production	66ey	24.3	24.5	23.7	26.6	ⅰ27.6	27.0	26.7	27.3	29.7	31.9	ⅰ35.4	ⅰ40.6	46.9	50.0	53.9
																Number in Thousands:
Labor Force	67d	....	....	....	....	....	....	....	....	....	....	....	....	....	....	....
Employment	67e	....	....	....	....	....	....	....	....	....	....	....	....	....	....	....
Unemployment	67c	....	....	....	....	....	....	....	....	....	....	....	....	....	....	....
Unemployment Rate (%)	67r	....	....	....	....	....	....	....	....	....	....	....	....	....	....	....
International Transactions																*Millions of Rupees*
Exports	70	1,892	2,225	ⅰ5,776	9,533	10,970	10,416	11,552	11,766	14,605	20,355	25,923	28,538	28,275	40,320	35,994
Imports, c.i.f.	71	3,483	3,229	ⅰ5,938	9,698	17,118	21,361	21,588	24,217	32,523	40,158	52,968	55,749	64,712	69,855	82,038
																1995=100
Volume of Exports	72	13.3ᵉ	18.6	26.6	27.4	24.7	27.1	29.7	ⅰ28.8	32.7	45.0	43.8	52.3	ⅰ41.9	58.8	48.3
Volume of Imports	73	13.8ᵉ	16.2	21.3	27.9	33.3	32.9	38.2	ⅰ43.2	52.9	62.0	61.9	65.8	ⅰ61.3	61.4	63.9
Unit Value of Exports	74	4.1	3.9	7.3	12.8	16.5	14.6	15.9	ⅰ19.1	21.8	25.2	26.9	27.9	ⅰ30.6	32.8	36.6
Unit Value of Imports	75	3.3	3.6	6.2	8.7	14.9	16.8	16.1	ⅰ16.7	17.6	19.9	24.8	28.5	ⅰ32.2	32.4	35.5

1985	1986	1987	1988	1989	1990	1991	1992	1993	1994	1995	1996	1997	1998	1999		
End of Period (aa)															**Exchange Rates**	
17.509	21.047	24.694	25.035	28.079	31.079	35.272	35.249	41.268	44.851	50.785	57.547	59.286	64.608	I 71.075	Market Rate	aa
End of Period (ae) Period Average (rf)																
15.940	17.207	17.406	18.603	21.367	21.845	24.658	25.636	30.045	30.723	34.165	40.020	43.940	45.885	I 51.785	Market Rate	ae
15.853	16.569	17.317	17.919	20.445	21.605	23.689	24.965	27.975	30.423	31.494	35.909	40.918	44.943	49.118	Market Rate	rf
Period Averages																
204.90	169.92	150.32	146.18	139.77	133.11	124.81	119.39	116.05	108.93	100.00	91.22	86.15	79.50	72.48	Nominal Effective Exchange Rate	ne c
169.53	139.92	123.74	121.82	114.01	106.55	104.63	103.18	102.89	100.68	100.00	98.22	101.40	97.95	92.44	Real Effective Exchange Rate	re c
End of Period															**Fund Position**	
546	546	546	546	546	546	546	758	758	758	758	758	758	758	1,034	Quota	2f. s
24	11	11	5	1	1	5	—	1	—	10	9	8	1	—	SDRs	1b. s
—	—	—	—	—	—	—	—	—	—	—	—	—	—	—	Reserve Position in the Fund	1c. s
1,289	973	647	411	710	587	746	820	817	1,097	1,115	1,001	980	996	1,271	Total Fund Cred.&Loans Outstg.	2tl
Last Thursday of Period															**International Liquidity**	
807	709	502	395	521	296	527	850	1,197	2,929	1,733	548	1,195	1,028	1,511	Total Reserves minus Gold	1l. d
26	13	16	7	1	1	7	—	1	—	15	13	11	1	—	SDRs	1b. d
—	—	—	—	—	—	—	—	—	—	—	—	—	—	—	Reserve Position in the Fund	1c. d
781	696	486	388	519	295	519	850	1,196	2,929	1,718	535	1,184	1,027	1,511	Foreign Exchange	1d. d
1.902	1.934	1.940	1.945	1.949	1.949	1.961	2.021	2.044	2.052	2.055	2.056	2.066	2.077	2.088	Gold (Million Fine Troy Ounces)	1ad
607	655	865	822	718	691	712	682	694	794	722	691	637	618	543	Gold (National Valuation)	1and
345	304	225	354	418	372	322	691	554	272	227	691	617	856	890	Monetary Authorities: Other Liab.	4.. d
564	689	799	827	936	1,459	1,581	1,387	1,408	1,586	1,609	1,550	1,410	1,281	1,365	Deposit Money Banks: Assets	7a. d
1,098	1,464	1,813	2,003	2,355	2,735	3,575	4,442	2,931	2,784	3,362	3,676	2,600	2,345	1,836	Liabilities	7b. d
Last Thursday of Period															**Monetary Authorities**	
23,126	24,081	24,295	23,200	27,048	20,406	30,366	39,544	56,923	115,577	86,700	61,804	93,158	77,768	104,870	Foreign Assets	11
70,063	84,218	93,720	96,648	116,547	137,171	162,941	180,966	209,953	202,151	254,211	303,209	274,647	347,900	502,118	Claims on General Government	12a
26	26	26	26	25	5,451	4,295	8,136	5,524	2,258	5,184	15,931	12,700	12,657	8,050	*of which: Provincial Government*	12ax
24,142	29,368	38,426	43,055	48,826	52,858	62,322	71,593	78,137	89,110	98,220	67,864	119,962	171,286	192,862	Claims on Deposit Money Banks	12e
71,690	85,893	102,617	113,734	133,146	154,362	196,554	213,817	244,175	282,541	333,207	321,058	367,082	414,627	468,491	Reserve Money	14
58,678	71,578	81,765	92,168	105,225	125,806	144,530	162,316	177,856	195,827	234,011	252,069	272,052	301,146	341,024	*of which: Currency Outside DMBs*	14a
....	....	....	....	....	....	....	....	....	....	....	....	....	....	8,115	Restricted Deposits	16b
28,053	25,707	19,900	16,891	28,859	26,384	34,261	46,625	50,331	48,479	54,104	73,602	66,453	75,892	103,921	Foreign Liabilities	16c
6,611	17,014	20,930	16,915	18,418	18,343	11,623	15,355	37,304	37,682	34,365	28,502	30,603	63,742	138,006	General Government Deposits	16d
918	564	302	350	445	540	542	539	671	614	644	686	644	585	660	Counterpart Funds	16e
10,059	8,488	12,692	15,012	11,553	10,807	12,648	15,766	12,532	37,524	16,812	9,029	22,984	42,110	80,659	Other Items (Net)	17r
Last Thursday of Period															**Deposit Money Banks**	
13,871	15,103	21,994	23,661	29,874	28,931	50,592	51,207	68,030	93,268	109,689	80,122	100,518	119,696	145,480	Reserves	20
8,988	11,848	13,903	15,391	20,008	31,872	38,974	35,563	42,306	48,721	54,958	62,022	61,940	58,800	70,682	Foreign Assets	21
34,926	44,970	75,978	75,544	78,001	81,079	114,904	191,287	208,114	251,172	263,013	333,162	396,083	395,218	321,548	Claims on General Government	22a
3,006	5,057	7,688	5,111	7,336	10,594	7,878	10,395	10,870	11,488	13,387	11,657	13,081	16,355	19,846	*of which: Provincial Government*	22ax
132,590	155,298	160,908	181,571	195,274	210,491	232,651	290,851	337,082	385,463	464,913	538,370	613,944	686,932	761,793	Claims on Private Sector	22d
63,668	72,785	90,403	96,563	110,909	127,379	156,588	203,653	191,613	235,265	253,189	269,947	420,823	423,091	447,919	Demand Deposits	24
68,925	77,592	86,380	89,543	83,028	80,372	92,475	143,406	230,515	278,960	322,037	448,144	470,719	530,230	521,619	Time Deposits	25
14,931	21,827	26,756	30,346	42,042	50,873	78,115	101,680	74,987	73,295	102,995	135,309	102,617	95,936	83,579	Foreign Liabilities	26c
2,572	3,358	4,801	6,915	8,280	8,870	10,041	12,198	13,074	12,235	11,853	11,788	11,634	11,676	11,493	Long-Term Foreign Liabilities	26cl
1,858	1,636	971	966	1,022	1,748	6,613	4,378	19,224	41,168	47,719	47,800	47,799	66,536	96,763	General Government Deposits	26d
815	837	1,329	131	–12	–24	–238	–20	–196	–181	–8	—	—	—	—	Counterpart Funds	26e
21,417	26,284	31,359	35,667	40,483	44,313	52,856	61,263	66,564	77,758	86,766	57,795	108,583	126,448	148,604	Credit from Monetary Authorities	26g
16,188	22,900	30,785	36,036	37,405	38,842	40,673	42,350	59,751	60,123	68,023	42,896	10,310	6,729	–10,474	Other Items (Net)	27r
Last Thursday of Period															**Monetary Survey**	
–10,870	–11,605	–8,458	–8,646	–23,845	–24,979	–43,036	–73,197	–26,089	42,524	–15,440	–85,086	–13,973	–35,260	–11,948	Foreign Assets (Net)	31n
242,712	282,857	328,778	357,681	394,726	435,355	520,254	673,872	731,696	797,049	941,642	1,140,656	1,246,673	1,349,909	1,411,041	Domestic Credit	32
96,520	110,537	147,798	154,310	175,107	198,159	259,609	352,520	361,539	374,473	435,140	560,069	592,328	612,840	588,897	Claims on General Govt. (Net)	32an
146,193	172,321	180,980	203,370	219,619	237,196	260,645	321,352	370,157	422,576	506,502	580,587	654,345	737,069	822,144	Claims on Private Sector	32d
123,060	145,251	173,016	189,834	217,027	254,620	305,978	371,796	378,111	435,388	490,961	528,011	699,806	732,291	795,370	Money	34
68,925	77,592	86,380	89,543	83,028	80,372	92,475	143,406	230,515	278,960	322,037	448,144	470,719	530,230	521,619	Quasi-Money	35
....	....	....	....	....	....	....	....	....	....	....	....	....	....	8,115	Restricted Deposits	36b
2,572	3,358	4,801	6,915	8,280	8,870	10,041	12,198	13,074	12,235	11,853	11,788	11,634	11,676	11,493	Long-Term Foreign Liabilities	36cl
1,733	1,401	1,631	481	433	517	304	520	475	433	636	686	644	585	660	Counterpart Funds	36e
35,552	43,651	54,492	62,261	62,115	65,999	68,421	72,755	83,432	112,558	100,716	66,945	49,897	39,869	61,838	Other Items (Net)	37r
191,985	222,842	259,396	279,378	300,054	334,991	398,453	515,202	608,626	714,348	812,998	976,155	1,170,525	1,262,521	1,316,989	Money plus Quasi-Money	35l
Last Thursday of Period															**Other Banking Institutions**	
1,838	2,109	3,102	3,814	5,462	5,361	7,028	8,612	8,586	9,891	12,370	14,189	18,622	22,473	27,603	Post Office: Savings Deposits	45.. i
193,823	224,951	262,498	283,191	305,516	340,352	405,481	523,814	617,212	724,239	825,368	990,344	1,189,147	1,284,994	1,344,592	Liquid Liabilities	55l
Percent Per Annum															**Interest Rates**	
10.00	10.00	10.00	10.00	10.00	10.00	10.00	10.00	10.00	I 15.00	17.00	20.00	18.00	16.50	13.00	Discount Rate *(End of Period)*	60
8.13	6.59	6.25	6.32	6.30	7.29	7.64	7.51	11.00	8.36	11.52	11.40	12.10	10.76	9.04	Money Market Rate	60b
....	....	....	....	....	....	....	12.47	13.03	11.26	12.49	13.61	I 15.74	....	....	Treasury Bill Rate	60c
9.19	8.77	8.26	8.32	8.18	8.05	7.88	7.67	7.40	7.07	6.63	6.06	5.43	4.79	4.16	Government Bond Yield	61
Period Averages															**Prices, Production, Labor**	
87.3	90.6	112.5	131.0	140.1	I 148.9	169.5	87.6	86.4	140.6	100.0	82.1	76.6	55.3	54.5	Share Prices	62
39.7	41.5	43.6	48.0	52.6	56.4	63.0	69.0	74.1	86.2	100.0	111.1	125.6	133.8	142.3	Wholesale Prices	63
42.4	43.9	46.0	50.0	54.0	58.8	65.8	I 72.0	79.2	89.0	100.0	110.4	122.9	130.6	136.0	Consumer Prices	64
58.2	62.4	66.9	72.7	74.4	79.6	85.2	90.6	93.6	96.1	100.0	99.4	98.9	105.9	113.7	Manufacturing Production	66ey
Period Averages																
....	....	....	....	....	....	....	....	34,726	33,324	33,191	....	36,407	....	....	Labor Force	67d
26,961	27,033	28,703	28,995	29,053	29,797	28,681	29,694	30,534	31,288	31,407	32,188	34,180	....	....	Employment	67e
....	1,018	903	937	939	963	1,922	1,845	1,516	1,591	1,783	1,827	2,227	....	....	Unemployment	67c
3.7	3.6	3.1	3.1	3.1	3.1	6.3	5.9	4.7	4.8	5.4	5.4	6.1	....	....	Unemployment Rate (%)	67r
Millions of Rupees															**International Transactions**	
43,645	56,336	72,583	81,348	96,646	121,345	155,398	183,599	187,787	225,200	252,714	335,313	359,046	382,477	417,322	Exports	70
93,793	89,297	101,310	118,681	146,444	160,134	201,409	235,296	265,142	271,744	362,686	437,769	476,346	419,311	505,451	Imports, c.i.f.	71
1995=100																
60.5	105.9	86.2	86.4	91.1	91.0	103.0	112.5	102.2	126.2	100.0	118.6	111.7	86.8	59.9	Volume of Exports	72
72.8	73.1	73.4	77.3	80.7	77.3	80.8	94.6	95.6	92.4	100.0	97.9	100.8	85.9	81.9	Volume of Imports	73
36.5	44.3	48.7	49.4	53.4	58.5	60.6	62.2	67.8	79.4	100.0	110.7	126.9	104.5	76.9	Unit Value of Exports	74
37.1	35.3	42.8	47.6	56.0	64.3	69.0	70.7	75.6	88.5	100.0	110.5	127.7	91.6	65.6	Unit Value of Imports	75

Pakistan

		1970	1971	1972	1973	1974	1975	1976	1977	1978	1979	1980	1981	1982	1983	1984
Balance of Payments															*Millions of US Dollars:*	
Current Account, n.i.e.	78al d	....	....	....	....	....	....	−783	−737	−722	−1,118	−925	−917	−805	27	−1,200
Goods: Exports f.o.b.	78aa d	....	....	....	....	....	....	1,172	1,127	1,404	1,957	2,581	2,743	2,352	2,890	2,492
Goods: Imports f.o.b.	78ab d	....	....	....	....	....	....	−2,202	−2,499	−3,236	−4,309	−5,470	−5,683	−5,771	−5,618	−6,263
Trade Balance	78ac d	....	....	....	....	....	....	−1,030	−1,373	−1,833	−2,352	−2,889	−2,939	−3,419	−2,728	−3,771
Services: Credit	78ad d	....	....	....	....	....	....	278	312	402	547	652	646	803	772	794
Services: Debit	78ae d	....	....	....	....	....	....	−442	−494	−619	−792	−877	−919	−951	−989	−1,092
Balance on Goods & Services	78af d	....	....	....	....	....	....	−1,194	−1,555	−2,050	−2,597	−3,115	−3,212	−3,567	−2,945	−4,069
Income: Credit	78ag d	....	....	....	....	....	....	32	34	40	38	86	112	128	160	192
Income: Debit	78ah d	....	....	....	....	....	....	−168	−223	−240	−313	−359	−378	−534	−580	−665
Balance on Gds, Serv. & Inc.	78ai d	....	....	....	....	....	....	−1,330	−1,745	−2,250	−2,872	−3,388	−3,479	−3,974	−3,365	−4,542
Current Transfers, n.i.e.: Credit	78aj d	....	....	....	....	....	....	565	1,011	1,542	1,757	2,467	2,564	3,175	3,397	3,349
Current Transfers: Debit	78ak d	....	....	....	....	....	....	−18	−4	−13	−3	−4	−3	−6	−5	−7
Capital Account, n.i.e.	78bc d	....	....	....	....	....	....	—	−1	—	−1	−1	−1	−1	−2	—
Capital Account, n.i.e.: Credit	78ba d	....	....	....	....	....	....	—	−1	—	—	—	—	—	—	—
Capital Account: Debit	78bb d	....	....	....	....	....	....	—	−1	—	−1	−1	−1	−1	−2	—
Financial Account, n.i.e.	78bj d	....	....	....	....	....	....	507	625	643	589	647	664	532	535	335
Direct Investment Abroad	78bd d	....	....	....	....	....	....	—	—	—	—	—	—	—	—	5
Dir. Invest. in Rep. Econ., n.i.e.	78be d	....	....	....	....	....	....	8	15	32	58	64	108	64	29	56
Portfolio Investment Assets	78bf d	....	....	....	....	....	....	—	—	—	—	—	—	—	—	—
Equity Securities	78bk d	....	....	....	....	....	....	—	—	—	—	—	—	—	—	—
Debt Securities	78bl d	....	....	....	....	....	....	—	—	—	—	—	—	—	—	—
Portfolio Investment Liab., n.i.e.	78bg d	....	....	....	....	....	....	—	—	—	—	—	—	—	—	9
Equity Securities	78bm d	....	....	....	....	....	....	—	—	—	—	—	—	—	—	7
Debt Securities	78bn d	....	....	....	....	....	....	—	—	—	—	—	—	—	—	2
Financial Derivatives Assets	78bw d	....	....	....	....	....	....	....	....	....	....	....	....	....	....	....
Financial Derivatives Liabilities	78bx d	....	....	....	....	....	....	....	....	....	....	....	....	....	....	....
Other Investment Assets	78bh d	....	....	....	....	....	....	−14	−21	23	−80	−17	12	−13	−10	−103
Monetary Authorities	78bo d	....	....	....	....	....	....									
General Government	78bp d	....	....	....	....	....	....	−14	−21	23	−80	−17	12	−13	−10	1
Banks	78bq d	....	....	....	....	....	....	—	—	—	—	—	—	—	—	−104
Other Sectors	78br d	....	....	....	....	....	....									
Other Investment Liab., n.i.e.	78bi d	....	....	....	....	....	....	513	631	588	611	600	543	481	516	369
Monetary Authorities	78bs d	....	....	....	....	....	....	—	—	2	—	11	−10	1	−15	−1
General Government	78bt d	....	....	....	....	....	....	331	504	504	551	506	343	165	216	295
Banks	78bu d	....	....	....	....	....	....	41	26	−10	−11	−7	20	58	53	−62
Other Sectors	78bv d	....	....	....	....	....	....	142	102	93	71	90	190	258	261	136
Net Errors and Omissions	78ca d	....	....	....	....	....	....	−76	12	−15	54	73	−6	35	−15	−97
Overall Balance	78cb d	....	....	....	....	....	....	−352	−100	−94	−476	−206	−261	−239	546	−963
Reserves and Related Items	79da d	....	....	....	....	....	....	352	100	94	476	206	261	239	−546	963
Reserve Assets	79db d	....	....	....	....	....	....	−114	16	28	208	−313	−233	−280	−1,107	874
Use of Fund Credit and Loans	79dc d	....	....	....	....	....	....	75	27	34	−74	120	414	452	276	−72
Exceptional Financing	79de d	....	....	....	....	....	....	391	58	32	342	400	80	66	285	161
Government Finance															*Millions of Rupees:*	
Deficit (-) or Surplus	80	−3,945	−3,069	−2,583	‡−4,554	−5,145	−11,466	−12,239	−12,580	−13,247	−17,997	−13,344	−16,138	−15,351	−24,784	−25,928
Revenue	81	8,007	7,342	7,053	‡8,256	11,794	14,259	17,737	20,439	25,171	29,502	38,102	45,359	50,370	57,750	71,042
Grants Received	81z	208	327	239	‡486	566	378	1,050	1,092	1,082	848	1,826	2,598	2,560	2,189	1,957
Expenditure	82	7,904	7,987	8,784	‡11,128	14,520	19,525	22,390	24,564	30,793	36,241	41,084	53,392	55,355	70,560	82,627
Lending Minus Repayments	83	4,256	2,751	1,091	‡2,168	2,985	6,578	8,636	9,547	8,707	12,106	12,188	10,703	12,926	14,163	16,300
Financing																
Domestic	84a	2,328	1,000	1,897	‡1,074	1,884	4,071	5,148	5,201	‡7,954	11,513	8,022	9,814	11,318	20,617	22,610
Foreign	85a	1,749	1,719	863	‡3,301	2,976	7,796	6,488	5,153	‡5,293	6,484	5,322	6,324	4,033	4,167	3,318
Use of Cash Balances	87	−131	348	−176	‡179	285	−401	603	2,226	....	....	....	....	....	....	....
Debt	88	‡22,852	26,096	49,271	50,147	55,475	59,102	74,148	86,279	97,965	117,354	127,492	134,012	177,828	198,582	227,794
Domestic	88a	11,426	12,873	16,667	17,818	17,426	21,245	27,420	32,700	38,530	49,371	56,754	60,088	76,656	87,856	106,554
Foreign	89a	11,426	13,223	32,604	32,329	38,049	37,857	46,728	53,579	59,435	67,983	70,738	73,924	101,172	110,726	121,240
Held by: State Bank	88aa	6,518	7,492	8,597	8,812	7,875	9,273	12,053	15,529	16,112	24,342	25,269	25,740	34,756	27,127	35,598
Deposit Money Banks	88ab	2,211	2,247	3,627	4,998	4,465	5,415	8,080	9,479	12,678	14,450	19,000	19,457	20,812	25,928	23,152
Other Financial Inst.	88ac	330	340	325	395	480	489	744	1,015	1,166	1,449	1,666	2,514	3,162	4,007	4,327
International Inst.	88ca	1,996	2,130	5,535	5,624	5,968	6,250	6,977	7,956	10,324	11,503	12,477	13,800	19,407	28,100	33,529
Foreign Govts. & Bks.	88cb	9,430	11,093	27,069	26,705	32,081	31,607	39,751	45,623	49,111	56,480	58,261	60,124	81,765	82,626	87,711
Others	88d	2,367	2,794	4,118	3,613	4,606	6,068	6,543	6,677	8,574	9,130	10,819	12,377	17,926	30,794	43,475
Intragovernmental Debt	88s	796	721	631	923	1,024	1,062	1,362	1,538	1,686	1,848	2,277	2,456	2,662	2,921	2,935
National Accounts															*Billions of Rupees:*	
Exports of Goods & Services	90c	3.64	3.92	3.92	9.96	11.96	12.99	13.88	13.99	16.63	21.53	29.49	35.71	33.03	44.40	47.84
Government Consumption	91f	4.85	5.27	6.48	7.72	8.54	11.95	15.17	16.71	19.12	20.34	23.54	28.28	33.52	41.61	50.74
Gross Fixed Capital Formation	93e	6.84	7.05	6.81	7.65	10.61	16.22	24.06	27.86	30.51	33.13	41.35	47.71	54.59	61.76	69.21
Increase/Decrease(-) in Stocks	93i	.71	.85	.85	1.00	1.00	2.00	—	1.00	1.00	1.75	2.00	4.50	7.86	6.70	7.49
Private Consumption	96f	36.67	38.73	40.72	50.14	69.94	91.04	101.12	116.93	141.68	160.70	192.39	224.14	263.66	291.94	336.75
Imports of Goods & Services	98c	−4.94	−5.32	−4.73	−9.60	−15.20	−23.02	−23.85	−26.74	−32.60	−42.53	−54.58	−62.13	−68.50	−82.02	−92.22
Gross Domestic Product (GDP)	99b	47.75	50.49	54.06	66.87	86.85	111.18	130.36	149.75	176.33	194.92	234.18	278.20	324.16	364.39	419.80
Net Factor Inc/Pmts(-) Abroad	98.n	—	.08	.10	.46	.62	1.15	2.99	5.48	12.14	14.53	18.28	22.69	25.35	39.40	39.60
Gross National Income (GNI)	99a	47.75	50.41	54.16	67.34	87.47	112.33	133.36	155.23	188.47	209.45	252.46	300.89	349.51	403.78	459.40
Net National Income	99e	44.66	47.22	50.78	63.19	82.00	106.04	126.03	146.85	178.65	198.60	239.41	284.76	330.59	381.89	433.83
GDP Volume 1960 prices	99b.p	35.7	35.9	36.1	38.6	40.7	42.6	44.5	46.2	49.9	52.3	56.9	60.8	....	....	....
GDP Volume 1981 Prices	99b.p	....	....	....	....	....	....	....	....	....	....	....	278.2	296.4	316.5	332.5
GDP Volume (1995=100)	99bv p	27.2	27.4	27.5	29.4	31.0	32.4	33.9	35.2	38.1	39.9	43.3	46.4	49.4	52.7	55.4
GDP Deflator (1995=100)	99bi p	9.3	9.8	10.4	12.1	14.9	18.2	20.4	22.6	24.6	26.0	28.7	31.9	34.9	36.7	40.3
																Millions:
Population	99z	114.18	116.62	‡64.30	66.84	68.84	70.90	‡73.21	75.44	77.75	80.13	82.58	85.12	87.76	90.48	93.29

	1985	1986	1987	1988	1989	1990	1991	1992	1993	1994	1995	1996	1997	1998	1999	
Minus Sign Indicates Debit																
Balance of Payments																
Current Account, n.i.e.	-1,083	-648	-563	-1,430	-1,340	-1,662	-1,403	-1,877	-2,901	-1,812	-3,349	-4,436	-1,712	....	....	78al *d*
Goods: Exports f.o.b.	2,661	3,206	3,956	4,426	4,818	5,405	6,411	6,913	6,793	7,117	8,356	8,507	8,351	....	....	78aa *d*
Goods: Imports f.o.b.	-5,906	-5,999	-6,283	-7,131	-7,401	-8,133	-8,683	-9,717	-9,380	-9,355	-11,248	-12,164	-10,750	....	....	78ab *d*
Trade Balance	-3,245	-2,793	-2,327	-2,705	-2,583	-2,727	-2,272	-2,803	-2,586	-2,239	-2,891	-3,656	-2,399	....	....	78ac *d*
Services: Credit	849	830	972	857	1,187	1,429	1,531	1,559	1,573	1,753	1,857	2,016	1,625	....	....	78ad *d*
Services: Debit	-1,184	-1,201	-1,288	-1,493	-1,712	-2,073	-2,314	-2,683	-2,639	-2,529	-2,938	-3,459	-2,658	....	....	78ae *d*
Balance on Goods & Services	-3,581	-3,164	-2,643	-3,341	-3,107	-3,371	-3,056	-3,927	-3,652	-3,015	-3,972	-5,099	-3,433	....	....	78af *d*
Income: Credit	112	107	116	94	142	96	73	73	63	149	187	175	147	....	....	78ag *d*
Income: Debit	-695	-757	-909	-912	-1,109	-1,181	-1,261	-1,485	-1,610	-1,830	-2,125	-2,198	-2,366	....	....	78ah *d*
Balance on Gds, Serv. & Inc.	-4,164	-3,814	-3,436	-4,159	-4,075	-4,455	-4,244	-5,339	-5,199	-4,695	-5,910	-7,121	-5,652	....	....	78ai *d*
Current Transfers, n.i.e.: Credit	3,095	3,185	2,899	2,760	2,770	2,834	2,890	3,502	2,337	2,919	2,611	2,739	3,981	....	....	78aj *d*
Current Transfers: Debit	-15	-18	-26	-30	-36	-40	-49	-40	-38	-35	-49	-54	-40	....	....	78ak *d*
Capital Account, n.i.e.	-2	-1	-1	-1	-1	-1	-1	-1	—	—	—	—	—	....	....	78bc *d*
Capital Account, n.i.e.: Credit	—	—	—	—	—	—	—	—	—	—	—	—	—	....	....	78ba *d*
Capital Account: Debit	-2	-1	-1	-1	-1	-1	-1	-1	—	—	—	—	—	....	....	78bb *d*
Financial Account, n.i.e.	634	885	630	1,670	1,389	1,453	1,326	2,147	3,334	2,977	2,449	3,496	2,321	....	....	78bj *d*
Direct Investment Abroad	8	1	-19	-13	-43	-2	4	12	2	-1	—	-7	24	....	....	78bd *d*
Dir. Invest. in Rep. Econ., n.i.e.	131	106	129	186	211	245	258	336	349	421	723	922	716	....	....	78be *d*
Portfolio Investment Assets	—	—	—	—	—	—	—	—	—	—	—	—	—	....	....	78bf *d*
Equity Securities	—	—	—	—	—	—	—	—	—	—	—	—	—	....	....	78bk *d*
Debt Securities	—	—	—	—	—	—	—	—	....	—	—	—	—	....	....	78bl *d*
Portfolio Investment Liab., n.i.e.	110	83	132	127	16	87	92	372	293	1,471	4	261	279	....	....	78bg *d*
Equity Securities	18	3	36	6	-1	—	43	241	225	1,254	10	285	330	....	....	78bm *d*
Debt Securities	93	80	96	121	17	87	50	131	68	217	-6	-24	-51	....	....	78bn *d*
Financial Derivatives Assets	....	....	....	....	....	....	....	....	....	....	....	....	....	....	....	78bw *d*
Financial Derivatives Liabilities	....	....	....	....	....	....	....	....	....	....	....	....	....	....	....	78bx *d*
Other Investment Assets	-79	-199	-167	-188	-200	-365	-310	-568	-286	-283	-196	-164	-21	....	....	78bh *d*
Monetary Authorities	....	....	....	....	....	....	....	....	....	....	....	....	....	....	....	78bo *d*
General Government	-13	8	1	-27	1	-11	-14	-456	46	-19	6	116	96	....	....	78bp *d*
Banks	-66	-158	-140	-62	-125	-609	-303	173	-86	-108	-116	8	-40	....	....	78bq *d*
Other Sectors	—	-50	-28	-100	-76	255	6	-285	-246	-157	-85	-288	-77	....	....	78br *d*
Other Investment Liab., n.i.e.	463	895	554	1,557	1,406	1,486	1,282	1,995	2,976	1,369	1,919	2,484	1,323	....	....	78bi *d*
Monetary Authorities	54	31	-16	258	74	50	-61	383	-140	-282	-50	474	-71	....	....	78bs *d*
General Government	198	366	178	1,007	978	955	501	1,292	1,260	1,132	1,034	700	1,878	....	....	78bt *d*
Banks	24	356	358	196	321	340	500	-360	613	313	613	310	-1,044	....	....	78bu *d*
Other Sectors	187	141	34	97	33	141	342	680	1,244	205	321	1,000	559	....	....	78bv *d*
Net Errors and Omissions	32	-44	15	22	-242	-105	-78	122	-6	178	-304	160	-72	....	....	78ca *d*
Overall Balance	-419	193	80	261	-194	-314	-155	392	428	1,343	-1,204	-780	538	....	....	78cb *d*
Reserves and Related Items	419	-193	-80	-261	194	314	155	-392	-428	-1,343	1,204	780	-538	....	....	79da *d*
Reserve Assets	309	157	326	40	-215	471	-217	-496	-426	-1,744	1,180	946	-511	....	....	79db *d*
Use of Fund Credit and Loans	-187	-371	-422	-317	398	-165	227	100	-4	401	23	-166	-27	....	....	79dc *d*
Exceptional Financing	297	21	16	16	11	9	145	5	2	—	—	—	—	....	....	79de *d*
Year Ending June 30																
Government Finance																
Deficit (-) or Surplus	-33,783	-46,917	-48,783	-42,426	-56,982	-46,232	-77,105	-95,418	-118,999	-113,462	-123,742	-169,477	-189,788	-172,015	-113,173P	80
Revenue	76,351	89,716	98,976	119,844	143,370	163,825	170,642	216,586	242,812	273,238	321,323	370,510	384,263	433,636	501,927P	81
Grants Received	2,717	4,510	3,350	5,372	7,831	7,159	10,544	7,511	—	5,665	5,513	4,804	—	—	4,603P	81z
Expenditure	93,613	120,114	127,822	158,122	191,463	192,079	237,388	294,370	330,509	362,891	425,418	515,219	547,768	535,573	540,419P	82
Lending Minus Repayments	19,238	21,029	23,287	9,520	16,720	25,137	20,903	25,145	31,302	29,474	25,160	29,572	26,283	70,078	79,284P	83
Financing																
Domestic	31,851	43,108	40,805	30,515	38,352	26,475	61,297	73,110	86,815	78,040	82,235	128,717	142,159	129,385	47,298P	84a
Foreign	1,932	3,809	7,978	11,911	18,630	19,757	15,808	22,308	32,184	35,422	41,507	40,760	47,629	42,630	65,875P	85a
Use of Cash Balances	....	....	....	....	....	....	....	....	....	....	....	....	....	....	....	87
Debt	284,085	360,388	412,276	492,236	581,192	674,248	776,583	902,828	1,058,682	1,219,863	1,400,547	1,573,338	1,863,329	2,094,051	....	88
Domestic	143,930	193,385	225,246	284,492	327,534	376,596	441,580	527,595	612,642	695,972	800,464	915,180	1,050,221	1,159,667	....	88a
Foreign	140,155	167,003	187,030	207,744	253,658	297,652	335,003	375,233	446,040	523,891	600,083	658,158	813,108	934,384	....	89a
Held by: State Bank	54,704	59,827	55,694	81,957	90,038	110,774	132,845	....	....	....	....	....	....	....	....	88aa
Deposit Money Banks	30,292	38,979	45,597	63,281	61,037	51,177	83,354	....	....	....	....	....	....	....	....	88ab
Other Financial Inst.	4,103	5,055	8,630	9,194	10,527	10,593	14,810	....	....	....	....	....	....	....	....	88ac
International Inst.	41,555	49,649	57,326	69,786	92,533	108,635	137,985	....	....	....	....	....	....	....	....	88ca
Foreign Govts. & Bks.	98,600	117,354	129,704	137,958	161,125	189,017	197,018	....	....	....	....	....	....	....	....	88cb
Others	54,831	89,524	115,325	130,060	165,932	204,052	223,571	....	....	....	....	....	....	....	....	88d
Intragovernmental Debt	3,897	4,125	5,298	3,130	3,647	4,243	4,989	....	....	....	....	....	....	....	....	88s
Year Ending June 30																
National Accounts																
Exports of Goods & Services	49.89	63.27	79.06	93.60	108.32	126.58	172.81	209.22	217.37	254.18	311.80	358.37	390.50	441.40	455.90	90c
Government Consumption	57.13	65.66	77.48	104.75	129.20	129.56	145.58	155.57	174.68	189.10	219.12	268.10	288.81	301.61	335.80	91f
Gross Fixed Capital Formation	77.93	87.55	100.04	111.27	133.17	148.08	177.65	225.36	256.64	280.88	318.31	369.08	397.80	396.60	400.50	93e
Increase/Decrease(-) in Stocks	8.60	9.00	9.50	10.40	12.40	14.00	15.80	18.70	21.10	24.60	28.20	34.34	38.28	71.38	46.34	93i
Private Consumption	385.35	392.53	415.67	486.57	543.30	611.02	697.45	849.95	970.98	1,121.64	1,367.06	1,566.20	1,846.43	1,998.27	2,233.30	96f
Imports of Goods & Services	-106.73	-103.48	-109.27	-131.20	-156.64	-173.29	-188.68	-247.41	-299.15	-297.30	-362.41	-454.29	-504.40	-469.30	-476.10	98c
Gross Domestic Product (GDP)	472.16	514.53	572.48	675.39	769.75	855.94	1,020.60	1,211.38	1,341.63	1,573.10	1,882.07	2,141.80	2,457.40	2,736.90	3,025.70	99b
Net Factor Inc/Pmts(-) Abroad	38.31	41.36	36.38	29.10	28.01	36.90	23.91	12.54	9.96	4.00	14.04	-7.14	-19.40	-24.70	-28.60	98.n
Gross National Income (GNI)	510.47	555.89	608.86	704.48	797.75	892.84	1,044.51	1,223.92	1,351.59	1,577.05	1,896.11	2,134.70	2,438.00	2,712.30	2,997.10	99a
Net National Income	481.75	524.37	574.12	665.24	753.98	842.97	983.87	1,148.86	1,123.36	1,315.48	1,581.75	1,807.10	2,075.70	2,332.80	2,552.80	99e
GDP Volume 1960 prices	....	....	....	....	....	....	....	....	....	....	....	....	....	....	....	99b. *p*
GDP Volume 1981 Prices	357.7	377.4	401.8	432.4	453.9	474.1	500.0	539.1	549.5	570.9	600.2	630.2	637.9	658.9	684.7	99b. *p*
GDP Volume (1995=100)	59.6	62.9	66.9	72.0	75.6	79.0	83.3	89.8	91.5	95.1	100.0	105.0	106.3	109.8	114.1	99bv *p*
GDP Deflator (1995=100)	42.1	43.5	45.4	49.8	54.1	57.6	65.1	71.7	77.9	87.9	100.0	108.4	122.9	132.5	140.9	99bi *p*
Midyear Estimates																
Population	96.18	99.54	102.70	105.97	109.14	112.40	115.77	119.23	122.79	126.47	130.25	134.15	138.16	I131.51	134.51	99z

(See notes in the back of the book.)

Panama

		1970	1971	1972	1973	1974	1975	1976	1977	1978	1979	1980	1981	1982	1983	1984
Exchange Rates															Balboas per SDR:	
Official Rate	aa	1.0000	1.0857	1.0857	1.2064	1.2244	1.1707	1.1618	1.2147	1.3028	1.3173	1.2754	1.1640	1.1031	1.0470	.9802
															Balboas per US Dollar:	
Official Rate	ae	1.0000	1.0000	1.0000	1.0000	1.0000	1.0000	1.0000	1.0000	1.0000	1.0000	1.0000	1.0000	1.0000	1.0000	1.0000
Fund Position															Millions of SDRs:	
Quota	2f. s	36.0	36.0	36.0	36.0	36.0	36.0	36.0	36.0	45.0	45.0	67.5	67.5	67.5	102.2	102.2
SDRs	1b. s	3.2	2.6	2.7	2.6	2.3	6.4	5.2	4.5	4.0	3.9	1.1	2.8	3.8	.4	—
Reserve Position in the Fund	1c. s	1.0	4.4	8.0	8.0	—	—	—	—	3.7	2.5	8.1	—	—	8.7	—
Total Fund Cred.&Loans Outstg.	2tl	—	—	—	—	7.4	17.5	42.6	42.2	40.3	31.5	18.1	80.5	76.1	184.1	276.6
International Liquidity												Millions of US Dollars Unless Otherwise Indicated:				
Total Reserves minus Gold	1l. d	15.8	21.0	43.1	41.7	39.3	34.4	78.9	70.9	150.4	118.7	117.4	119.9	101.0	206.7	215.6
SDRs	1b. d	3.2	2.9	3.0	3.1	2.8	7.4	6.0	5.5	5.2	5.2	1.4	3.2	4.2	.4	—
Reserve Position in the Fund	1c. d	1.0	4.8	8.7	9.6	—	—	—	—	4.9	3.2	10.3	—	—	9.1	—
Foreign Exchange	1d. d	11.5	13.4	31.5	29.0	36.5	27.0	72.9	65.4	140.4	110.3	105.7	116.7	96.8	197.2	215.6
Gold (National Valuation)	1an d	—	—	—	—	—	—	—	—	—	3.7	3.7	—	—	—	—
Monetary Authorities: Other Liab.	4.. d	18	28	30	32	69	93	120	105	107	138	186	221	281	338	352
Deposit Money Banks: Assets	7a. d	287	454	898	2,260	4,795	6,483	7,697	9,970	13,382	19,446	18,970	24,675	27,102	24,649	22,229
Liabilities	7b. d	364	588	1,097	2,588	5,340	7,116	8,372	10,634	13,846	20,315	19,508	25,234	26,965	24,791	22,380
Monetary Authorities															Millions of Balboas:	
Foreign Assets	11	15.7	21.0	43.1	41.7	39.3	34.4	78.9	70.9	150.4	122.4	121.1	119.9	101.0	206.7	215.6
Claims on Central Government	12a	26.6	26.7	39.2	35.8	60.1	89.8	168.5	155.4	129.7	170.4	172.3	343.1	346.4	480.0	638.0
Claims on Official Entities	12bx	—	—	—	2.5	2.1	8.2	25.6	12.3	33.7	78.5	32.8	59.4	96.5	96.1	93.7
Claims on Private Sector	12d	53.4	67.6	86.6	114.5	130.4	140.7	124.4	121.8	175.5	216.3	268.0	283.5	339.9	335.9	336.0
Claims on Deposit Money Banks	12e	5.5	9.3	30.4	17.6	25.4	41.1	25.2	51.5	54.1	40.9	81.5	123.7	125.8	111.9	70.2
Bankers Deposits	14c	17.6	19.3	32.9	31.3	32.7	52.0	79.5	88.0	61.5	146.4	155.9	221.5	207.5	207.5	210.2
Demand Deposits	14d	15.4	17.1	34.3	29.9	23.5	23.9	26.2	28.2	32.0	38.7	42.0	40.7	48.8	45.7	46.7
Time, Savings,& Fgn.Currency Dep.	15	15.1	17.3	22.5	22.3	23.4	25.4	30.5	37.8	45.8	49.3	63.2	83.7	99.7	128.8	157.3
Foreign Liabilities	16c	14.6	19.0	10.4	17.3	71.7	104.3	157.6	144.0	147.5	165.8	144.7	196.5	149.6	271.7	348.2
Long-Term Foreign Liabilities	16cl	3.4	8.7	20.0	14.8	6.6	9.1	11.6	12.6	12.3	13.8	63.9	117.8	215.1	259.4	275.3
Central Government Deposits	16d	25.3	29.7	48.3	59.2	63.4	68.9	103.0	109.5	205.2	147.5	144.0	210.3	218.6	243.4	223.7
Capital Accounts	17a	18.2	23.7	28.8	32.5	30.9	32.5	32.8	36.5	45.6	52.1	71.9	82.4	94.0	102.7	101.2
Other Items (Net)	17r	–8.4	–10.2	2.1	4.8	5.0	–1.8	–18.5	–44.8	–6.5	14.9	–9.9	–23.3	–23.7	–28.5	–9.1
Deposit Money Banks															Millions of Balboas:	
Foreign Assets	21	287.1	454.2	898.3	2,259.9	4,795.4	6,482.5	7,696.7	9,969.9	13,382.2	19,445.6	18,970.3	24,674.5	27,102.1	24,649.2	22,229.3
Claims on Central Government	22a	9.1	9.9	11.5	19.9	53.9	195.3	224.8	262.5	215.4	165.9	213.8	207.0	297.6	348.5	377.2
Claims on Private Sector	22d	329.4	441.5	596.0	758.2	1,052.6	1,060.6	1,092.0	1,148.7	1,250.0	1,496.3	1,803.2	2,185.8	2,195.2	2,177.4	2,200.5
Demand Deposits	24	85.1	88.3	119.3	131.2	172.8	149.2	163.8	185.0	214.0	262.6	293.3	319.0	330.5	326.9	334.3
Time and Savings Deposits	25	140.7	179.5	216.8	261.1	310.5	349.3	357.5	421.5	540.9	692.9	917.2	1,117.4	1,270.1	1,246.8	1,324.6
Foreign Liabilities	26c	364.0	588.0	1,097.0	2,588.0	5,340.0	7,116.1	8,372.3	10,633.8	13,845.7	20,315.4	19,508.4	25,233.6	26,965.2	24,791.1	22,380.0
Capital Accounts	27a	15.8	45.5	53.7	105.9	132.8	181.2	158.9	249.6	287.3	385.9	597.3	682.4	1,202.0	988.0	979.7
Other Items (Net)	27r	20.0	4.3	19.0	–48.2	–54.2	–57.4	–39.0	–108.8	–40.3	–549.0	–328.9	–285.1	–173.0	–177.7	–211.6
Monetary Survey															Millions of Balboas:	
Foreign Assets (Net)	31n	–75.8	–131.8	–166.0	–303.7	–577.0	–703.5	–754.3	–737.0	–460.6	–913.2	–561.7	–635.7	88.2	–206.9	–283.3
Domestic Credit	32	393.2	516.0	685.0	871.7	1,235.7	1,425.7	1,532.3	1,591.2	1,599.1	1,979.9	2,346.1	2,868.5	3,057.0	3,194.5	3,421.7
Claims on Central Govt. (Net)	32an	10.4	6.9	2.4	–3.5	50.6	216.2	290.3	308.4	139.9	188.8	242.1	339.8	425.4	585.1	791.5
Claims on Private Sector	32d	382.8	509.1	682.6	872.7	1,183.0	1,201.3	1,216.4	1,270.5	1,425.5	1,712.6	2,071.2	2,469.3	2,535.1	2,513.3	2,536.5
Deposit Money	34	100.5	105.4	153.6	161.1	196.3	173.1	190.0	213.2	246.0	301.3	335.3	359.7	379.3	372.6	381.0
Quasi-Money	35	155.8	196.8	239.3	283.4	333.9	374.7	388.0	459.3	586.7	742.2	980.4	1,201.1	1,369.8	1,375.6	1,481.9
Long-Term Foreign Liabilities	36cl	3.4	8.7	20.0	14.8	6.6	9.1	11.6	12.6	12.3	13.8	63.9	117.8	215.1	259.4	275.3
Capital Accounts	37a	34.0	69.2	82.5	138.4	163.7	213.7	191.7	286.1	332.9	438.0	669.2	764.8	1,296.0	1,090.7	1,080.9
Other Items (Net)	37r	23.8	4.1	23.6	–29.7	–41.9	–48.3	–3.2	–117.1	–39.4	–428.6	–264.4	–210.6	–115.0	–110.6	–80.7
Money plus Quasi-Money	35l	256.3	302.2	392.9	444.5	530.2	547.8	578.0	672.5	832.7	1,043.5	1,315.7	1,560.8	1,749.1	1,748.2	1,862.9
Other Banking Institutions															Millions of Balboas:	
Claims on Private Sector	42d	....	....	....	....	....	85.7	88.9	98.2	111.2	126.2	143.1	154.8	164.4	186.2	207.4
Claims on Deposit Money Banks	42e	....	....	....	....	....	—	—	—	—	—	.5	.5	3.2	5.2	6.6
Time and Savings Deposits	45	....	....	....	....	....	87.8	105.5	122.3	115.7	124.3	144.2	165.1	202.3	225.9	249.1
Capital Accounts	47a	....	....	....	....	....	6.9	7.0	7.0	7.3	7.5	7.7	7.9	8.2	8.6	8.8
Other Items (Net)	47r	....	....	....	....	....	–9.0	–23.6	–31.1	–11.8	–5.6	–8.3	–17.7	–42.9	–43.1	–43.9
Liquid Liabilities	55l	....	....	....	....	....	634.6	682.4	793.7	946.8	1,166.3	1,458.3	1,723.8	1,949.1	1,970.8	2,108.9
Interest Rates															Percent Per Annum:	
Deposit Rate	60l	....	....	....	....	....	....	....	....	....	....	....	....	....	....	....
Lending Rate	60p	....	....	....	....	....	....	....	....	....	....	....	....	....	....	....
Prices, Production and Labor															Index Numbers (1995=100):	
Wholesale Prices	63	31.8	33.5	36.4	40.2	52.3	59.7	64.3	69.0	72.7	82.9	95.6	105.2	113.9	109.5	110.6
Consumer Prices	64	40.1	40.8	43.0	46.0	53.5	56.6	58.8	61.5	64.1	69.3	78.8	84.6	88.2	90.0	91.4
Manufacturing production	66ey	....	....	....	....	....	....	....	....	....	....	....	....	....	....	....
															Number in Thousands:	
Labor Force	67d	....	....	....	....	....	....	....	....	....	....	....	....	....	....	....
Employment	67e	....	....	....	....	....	....	....	....	....	....	....	....	....	....	....
Unemployment	67c	....	....	....	....	....	....	....	....	....	....	....	....	....	....	....
Unemployment Rate (%)	67r	....	....	....	....	....	....	....	....	....	....	....	....	....	....	....
International Transactions															Millions of Balboas:	
Exports	70	109.5	116.5	122.6	137.8	210.5	286.4	238.2	251.0	256.4	302.9	360.5	328.1	375.0	320.5	276.0
Imports, c.i.f.	71	357.0	395.8	440.5	502.2	822.4	892.0	848.3	861.2	942.4	1,183.8	1,449.2	1,540.1	1,570.2	1,411.9	1,423.1
Imports, f.o.b.	71.v	326.4	359.0	401.1	454.0	755.7	815.6	779.7	777.8	844.9	1,062.9	1,288.9	1,393.0	1,406.7	1,267.2	1,276.3
															1990=100	
Volume of Exports	72	58	63	60	62	59	69	73	84	87	92	92	87	90	94	83
Unit Value of Exports (1990=100)	74	77	74	77	79	89	100	99	91	90	97	104	104	97	105	104

	1985	1986	1987	1988	1989	1990	1991	1992	1993	1994	1995	1996	1997	1998	1999		
																Exchange Rates	
End of Period																	
	1.0984	1.2232	1.4187	1.3457	1.3142	1.4227	1.4304	1.3750	1.3736	1.4599	1.4865	1.4380	1.3493	1.4080	1.3725	Official Rate	aa
End of Period																	
	1.0000	1.0000	1.0000	1.0000	1.0000	1.0000	1.0000	1.0000	1.0000	1.0000	1.0000	1.0000	1.0000	1.0000	1.0000	Official Rate	ae
End of Period																**Fund Position**	
	102.2	102.2	102.2	102.2	102.2	102.2	102.2	149.6	149.6	149.6	149.6	149.6	149.6	149.6	206.6	Quota	2f. s
	11.7	1.4	—	—	—	19.4	8.1	3.3	.1	—	.6	—	.4	.1	1.2	SDRs	1b. s
	—	—	—	—	—	—	—	11.9	11.9	11.9	11.9	11.9	11.9	11.9	11.9	Reserve Position in the Fund	1c. s
	283.4	288.6	243.9	243.8	243.2	191.3	150.7	79.8	82.3	91.3	74.4	91.0	105.4	125.5	108.3	Total Fund Cred.&Loans Outstg.	2tl
End of Period																**International Liquidity**	
	98.0	170.2	77.8	72.2	119.4	343.5	499.1	504.4	597.4	704.3	781.4	866.5	1,147.8	954.5	822.9	Total Reserves minus Gold	1l. d
	12.9	1.8	—	—	—	27.6	11.6	4.6	.1	—	.8	—	.5	.1	1.6	SDRs	1b. d
	—	—	—	—	—	—	—	16.3	16.3	17.3	17.6	17.1	16.0	16.7	16.3	Reserve Position in the Fund	1c. d
	85.1	168.4	77.8	72.2	119.4	315.9	487.4	483.5	581.0	686.9	762.9	849.4	1,131.3	937.7	805.0	Foreign Exchange	1d. d
	—	—	—	—	—	—	—	—	—	—	—	—	—	—	—	Gold (National Valuation)	1an d
	358	333	351	345	356	345	337	352	334	292	343	158	149	123	118	Monetary Authorities: Other Liab.	4.. d
	22,555	24,459	16,137	6,595	6,287	6,857	8,668	9,714	12,735	16,617	15,664	15,484	16,595	13,209	12,362	Deposit Money Banks: Assets	7a. d
	22,385	24,204	16,185	6,923	6,509	6,533	7,860	8,522	11,336	14,846	13,930	13,954	14,825	11,745	11,845	Liabilities	7b. d
End of Period																**Monetary Authorities**	
	98.0	170.2	77.8	72.2	119.4	343.5	499.1	504.4	597.4	704.3	781.4	866.5	1,147.8	954.5	822.9	Foreign Assets	11
	737.3	713.8	795.6	988.1	1,150.0	1,115.7	1,033.7	1,019.4	1,050.1	1,014.0	945.6	1,280.9	1,080.7	1,099.7	1,047.3	Claims on Central Government	12a
	92.3	102.0	105.6	106.8	106.8	106.8	106.8	106.8	—	—	—	—	—	—	—	Claims on Official Entities	12bx
	322.6	324.3	301.0	300.5	298.8	247.6	234.0	288.0	322.8	300.6	318.8	301.0	292.7	403.2	583.8	Claims on Private Sector	12d
	136.2	134.0	94.4	52.8	21.2	298.9	439.1	464.3	633.0	732.8	948.8	615.4	765.2	949.4	999.8	Claims on Deposit Money Banks	12e
	198.0	223.3	135.5	116.7	104.1	164.6	237.5	175.6	184.4	167.4	172.7	266.0	252.7	272.6	284.1	Bankers Deposits	14c
	50.0	55.7	46.2	28.6	37.9	52.8	57.9	62.1	63.0	75.4	77.0	83.0	105.8	97.8	80.6	Demand Deposits	14d
	154.4	201.9	179.3	141.2	137.3	148.4	164.7	172.9	187.3	192.5	205.0	227.2	240.8	283.4	296.5	Time, Savings,& Fgn.Currency Dep.	15
	406.1	425.8	479.4	456.1	451.4	390.4	327.0	254.8	244.7	225.5	182.2	195.1	207.2	224.8	195.1	Foreign Liabilities	16c
	263.5	259.8	217.7	216.7	224.0	226.8	225.2	207.1	202.3	199.5	271.5	93.8	84.5	74.8	71.4	Long-Term Foreign Liabilities	16cl
	266.6	305.9	323.1	516.0	686.0	1,060.6	1,262.7	1,358.8	1,550.6	1,716.2	1,857.8	1,871.5	2,025.2	2,039.7	2,094.5	Central Government Deposits	16d
	108.6	113.6	120.6	124.1	127.0	76.5	49.2	157.7	196.0	228.3	297.7	424.9	471.5	543.9	536.1	Capital Accounts	17a
	−60.9	−141.8	−127.4	−79.0	−71.5	−7.6	−11.4	−6.1	−24.9	−53.2	−69.4	−97.7	−101.4	−130.1	−104.5	Other Items (Net)	17r
End of Period																**Deposit Money Banks**	
	22,555.2	24,458.6	16,136.6	6,594.5	6,287.4	6,857.4	8,668.2	9,713.6	12,735.2	16,616.6	15,663.9	15,483.8	16,595.2	13,208.7	12,362.1	Foreign Assets	21
	351.4	365.7	201.4	169.4	159.5	157.5	157.5	165.8	104.8	74.3	62.3	79.4	73.2	54.6	111.9	Claims on Central Government	22a
	2,277.1	2,655.9	2,732.1	2,171.9	2,169.0	2,233.5	2,782.5	3,458.9	4,332.5	5,118.6	5,852.4	6,347.6	7,294.0	9,041.9	10,538.2	Claims on Private Sector	22d
	359.5	393.8	395.9	275.2	269.0	380.0	499.0	577.1	645.2	728.6	737.7	758.3	889.7	1,027.5	1,062.2	Demand Deposits	24
	1,388.6	1,708.5	1,657.1	1,203.5	1,156.0	1,604.0	2,141.0	2,765.4	3,296.0	3,845.5	4,204.2	4,476.5	5,138.6	5,795.3	6,376.7	Time and Savings Deposits	25
	22,385.2	24,204.1	16,184.7	6,922.9	6,509.0	6,533.1	7,860.0	8,521.8	11,336.5	14,845.9	13,929.8	13,954.3	14,825.0	11,744.7	11,844.5	Foreign Liabilities	26c
	1,050.2	1,193.6	1,034.2	671.0	636.0	656.0	736.0	898.0	1,008.0	1,321.3	1,431.8	1,660.8	1,945.1	2,171.5	2,257.8	Capital Accounts	27a
	.2	−19.8	−201.8	−136.8	45.9	75.3	372.2	576.0	886.9	1,068.2	1,275.1	1,060.9	1,164.1	1,566.2	1,471.0	Other Items (Net)	27r
End of Period																**Monetary Survey**	
	−138.2	−1.2	−449.7	−712.3	−553.6	277.4	980.3	1,441.4	1,751.5	2,249.5	2,333.2	2,200.8	2,710.8	2,193.7	1,145.4	Foreign Assets (Net)	31n
	3,514.1	3,855.8	3,812.6	3,220.7	3,198.1	2,800.5	3,051.9	3,680.1	4,259.6	4,791.5	5,321.3	6,137.3	6,715.5	8,559.7	10,186.7	Domestic Credit	32
	822.1	773.6	673.9	641.5	623.5	212.6	−71.4	−173.6	−395.7	−627.9	−849.9	−511.3	−871.2	−885.4	−935.3	Claims on Central Govt. (Net)	32an
	2,599.7	2,980.2	3,033.1	2,472.4	2,467.8	2,481.1	3,016.5	3,746.9	4,655.3	5,419.2	6,171.2	6,648.6	7,586.7	9,445.1	11,122.0	Claims on Private Sector	32d
	409.5	449.5	442.1	303.8	306.9	432.8	556.9	639.2	708.2	804.1	814.7	841.3	995.5	1,125.2	1,142.7	Deposit Money	34
	1,543.0	1,910.4	1,836.4	1,344.7	1,293.3	1,752.0	2,305.7	2,938.3	3,483.3	4,038.0	4,409.2	4,703.7	5,379.4	6,078.7	6,673.2	Quasi-Money	35
	263.5	259.8	217.7	216.7	224.0	226.8	225.2	207.1	202.3	199.5	271.5	93.8	84.5	74.8	71.4	Long-Term Foreign Liabilities	36cl
	1,158.8	1,307.2	1,154.8	795.1	763.0	732.5	785.2	1,055.7	1,203.9	1,549.6	1,729.5	2,085.7	2,416.6	2,715.4	2,793.9	Capital Accounts	37a
	1.1	−72.3	−288.1	−151.9	57.3	−66.6	159.1	281.2	413.4	449.6	429.6	613.7	550.3	759.2	650.8	Other Items (Net)	37r
	1,952.5	2,359.9	2,278.5	1,648.5	1,600.2	2,185.2	2,862.5	3,577.5	4,191.5	4,842.1	5,223.9	5,544.9	6,374.9	7,203.9	7,815.9	Money plus Quasi-Money	35l
End of Period																**Other Banking Institutions**	
	230.6	....	....	....	....	....	....	....	....	....	....	....	....	....	....	Claims on Private Sector	42d
	5.1	....	....	....	....	....	....	....	....	....	....	....	....	....	....	Claims on Deposit Money Banks	42e
	250.0	....	....	....	....	....	....	....	....	....	....	....	....	....	....	Time and Savings Deposits	45
	9.1	....	....	....	....	....	....	....	....	....	....	....	....	....	....	Capital Accounts	47a
	−23.4	....	....	....	....	....	....	....	....	....	....	....	....	....	....	Other Items (Net)	47r
	2,194.9	....	....	....	....	....	....	....	....	....	....	....	....	....	....	Liquid Liabilities	55l
Percent Per Annum																**Interest Rates**	
	....	6.50	6.59	7.54	8.49	8.40	7.73	I 5.67	5.90	6.11	7.18	7.20	7.03	6.76	6.92	Deposit Rate	60l
	....	12.36	12.60	12.47	12.92	I 11.98	11.79	10.61	10.06	10.15	11.10	10.62	10.63	10.82	10.05	Lending Rate	60p
Period Averages																**Prices, Production and Labor**	
	110.2	92.6	94.0	87.6	I 89.7	93.2	93.7	95.4	95.2	97.1	100.0	102.1	99.8	95.9	98.5	Wholesale Prices	63
	92.4	92.3	93.2	I 93.6	93.7	94.4	95.6	97.3	98.0	99.0	100.0	101.3	102.5	103.2	104.5	Consumer Prices	64
								90.1	96.1	99.3	100.0	99.9	105.6	109.8	105.3	Manufacturing production	66ey
Period Averages																	
	....	....	....	....	....	828	859	....	940	967	1,008	....	1,049	1,049	....	Labor Force	67d
	627	644	678	654	686	....	715	782	816	832	867	867	909	903	....	Employment	67e
	88	76	91	128	134	....	138	134	125	135	141	145	140	146	....	Unemployment	67c
	12.3	10.5	11.8	16.3	16.3	....	16.1	14.7	13.3	14.0	14.0	14.3	13.4	13.9	....	Unemployment Rate (%)	67r
Millions of Balboas																**International Transactions**	
	336.2	348.6	357.7	306.9	317.9	340.1	358.4	501.5	553.2	583.3	625.2	....	722.8	784.1	821.4	Exports	70
	1,391.8	1,229.2	1,306.2	751.0	985.9	1,538.6	1,695.0	2,023.6	2,187.8	2,404.1	2,510.7	2,779.9	3,002.0	3,073.5	3,515.8	Imports, c.i.f.	71
	1,238.8	1,103.8	1,165.2	673.4	867.5	1,339.2	1,523.5	1,830.6	1,979.6	2,177.5	2,280.2	2,548.1	2,738.5	2,806.4	3,214.7	Imports, f.o.b.	71.v
1990=100																	
	91	96	93	76	91	100	93	94	90	....	....	....	....	103	76	Volume of Exports	72
	103	94	103	114	159	100	101	....	....	....	....	....	....	....	....	Unit Value of Exports (1990=100)	74

Panama

283		1970	1971	1972	1973	1974	1975	1976	1977	1978	1979	1980	1981	1982	1983	1984
Balance of Payments																*Millions of US Dollars:*
Current Account, n.i.e.	78al*d*	....	....	....	....	....	....	....	–155.4	–207.7	–311.0	–328.7	–535.0	–194.1	198.7	–202.3
Goods: Exports f.o.b.	78aa*d*	....	....	....	....	....	....	....	401.0	385.7	453.2	2,519.3	2,774.2	2,579.6	1,840.0	1,889.7
Goods: Imports f.o.b.	78ab*d*	....	....	....	....	....	....	....	–790.4	–862.1	–1,085.7	–2,806.0	–3,118.1	–2,883.4	–2,217.6	–2,378.2
Trade Balance	78ac*d*	....	....	....	....	....	....	....	–389.4	–476.4	–632.5	–286.7	–343.9	–303.8	–377.6	–488.5
Services: Credit	78ad*d*	....	....	....	....	....	....	....	401.2	442.5	559.5	902.4	932.7	993.9	1,131.5	1,066.0
Services: Debit	78ae*d*	....	....	....	....	....	....	....	–205.0	–238.8	–287.7	–587.9	–668.1	–630.7	–550.4	–597.0
Balance on Goods & Services	78af*d*	....	....	....	....	....	....	....	–193.2	–272.7	–360.7	27.8	–79.3	59.4	203.5	–19.5
Income: Credit	78ag*d*	....	....	....	....	....	....	....	585.9	915.4	1,570.7	4,431.4	5,403.1	5,907.0	4,407.7	3,672.0
Income: Debit	78ah*d*	....	....	....	....	....	....	....	–545.7	–848.3	–1,533.3	–4,828.1	–5,919.9	–6,231.4	–4,492.7	–3,977.3
Balance on Gds, Serv. & Inc.	78ai*d*	....	....	....	....	....	....	....	–153.0	–205.6	–323.3	–368.9	–596.1	–265.0	118.5	–324.8
Current Transfers, n.i.e.: Credit	78aj*d*	....	....	....	....	....	....	....	32.4	36.6	57.0	81.7	97.7	111.7	126.9	161.2
Current Transfers: Debit	78ak*d*	....	....	....	....	....	....	....	–34.8	–38.7	–44.7	–41.5	–36.6	–40.8	–46.7	–38.7
Capital Account, n.i.e.	78bc*d*	....	....	....	....	....	....	....	—	—	—	....	....	....	....	....
Capital Account, n.i.e.: Credit	78ba*d*	....	....	....	....	....	....	....	—	—	—	....	....	....	....	....
Capital Account: Debit	78bb*d*	....	....	....	....	....	....	....	—	—	—	....	....	....	....	....
Financial Account, n.i.e.	78bj*d*	....	....	....	....	....	....	....	218.2	295.5	705.3	–283.2	393.5	385.1	56.4	–55.4
Direct Investment Abroad	78bd*d*	....	....	....	....	....	....	....	—	—	—	....	....	....	....	....
Dir. Invest. in Rep. Econ., n.i.e.	78be*d*	....	....	....	....	....	....	....	10.9	–2.5	49.8	218.5	303.2	366.6	79.4	–135.5
Portfolio Investment Assets	78bf*d*	....	....	....	....	....	....	....	—	—	—	–735.7	–66.1	–31.6	213.2	70.8
Equity Securities	78bk*d*	....	....	....	....	....	....	....	—	—	—	–.1	1.0	.4	.4	....
Debt Securities	78bl*d*	....	....	....	....	....	....	....	—	—	—	–735.6	–67.1	–32.0	212.8	70.8
Portfolio Investment Liab., n.i.e.	78bg*d*	....	....	....	....	....	....	....	12.6	70.4	203.9	16.3	25.3	–9.7	–35.9	–17.7
Equity Securities	78bm*d*	....	....	....	....	....	....	....	–.6	1.0	–.2	....	....	....	....	....
Debt Securities	78bn*d*	....	....	....	....	....	....	....	13.2	69.4	204.1	16.3	25.3	–9.7	–35.9	–17.7
Financial Derivatives Assets	78bw*d*	....	....	....	....	....	....	....	....	....	....	....	....	....	....	....
Financial Derivatives Liabilities	78bx*d*	....	....	....	....	....	....	....	....	....	....	....	....	....	....	....
Other Investment Assets	78bh*d*	....	....	....	....	....	....	....	–2,328.9	–3,408.0	–6,092.3	–1,111.0	–6,918.9	–2,380.2	5,939.3	4,892.8
Monetary Authorities	78bo*d*	....	....	....	....	....	....	....	....	....	....	....	....	....	....	....
General Government	78bp*d*	....	....	....	....	....	....	....	–1.4	—	—	–3.3	–1.6	–1.6	....	–5.7
Banks	78bq*d*	....	....	....	....	....	....	....	–2,273.0	–3,407.7	–6,046.8	–1,059.1	–6,802.1	–2,344.1	5,943.5	4,851.5
Other Sectors	78br*d*	....	....	....	....	....	....	....	–54.5	–.3	–45.5	–48.6	–115.2	–34.5	–4.2	47.0
Other Investment Liab., n.i.e.	78bi*d*	....	....	....	....	....	....	....	2,523.6	3,635.6	6,543.9	1,328.7	7,050.0	2,440.0	–6,139.6	–4,865.8
Monetary Authorities	78bs*d*	....	....	....	....	....	....	....	–407.7	–28.3	41.4	4.5	29.1	46.7	165.0	12.1
General Government	78bt*d*	....	....	....	....	....	....	....	91.6	341.3	112.6	218.9	68.0	362.8	106.2	78.7
Banks	78bu*d*	....	....	....	....	....	....	....	2,650.4	3,245.7	6,479.7	1,245.9	6,743.9	1,840.5	–6,279.7	–5,001.9
Other Sectors	78bv*d*	....	....	....	....	....	....	....	189.3	76.9	–89.8	–140.6	209.0	190.0	–131.1	45.3
Net Errors and Omissions	78ca*d*	....	....	....	....	....	....	....	–70.1	–1.6	–421.4	622.8	59.7	–208.9	–312.2	139.6
Overall Balance	78cb*d*	....	....	....	....	....	....	....	–7.3	86.2	–27.1	10.9	–81.8	–17.9	–57.1	–118.1
Reserves and Related Items	79da*d*	....	....	....	....	....	....	....	7.3	–86.2	27.1	–10.9	81.8	17.9	57.1	118.1
Reserve Assets	79db*d*	....	....	....	....	....	....	....	7.8	–84.0	38.7	6.2	2.5	19.2	–103.7	–8.4
Use of Fund Credit and Loans	79dc*d*	....	....	....	....	....	....	....	–.6	–2.3	–11.5	–17.3	70.9	–4.8	114.7	94.7
Exceptional Financing	79de*d*	....	....	....	....	....	....	....	—	—	—	.3	8.5	3.5	46.1	31.8
International Investment Position																*Millions of US Dollars*
Assets	79aa*d*	....	....	....	....	....	....	....	....	....	....	....	....	....	....	....
Direct Investment Abroad	79ab*d*	....	....	....	....	....	....	....	....	....	....	....	....	....	....	....
Portfolio Investment	79ac*d*	....	....	....	....	....	....	....	....	....	....	....	....	....	....	....
Equity Securities	79ad*d*	....	....	....	....	....	....	....	....	....	....	....	....	....	....	....
Debt Securities	79ae*d*	....	....	....	....	....	....	....	....	....	....	....	....	....	....	....
Financial Derivatives	79al*d*	....	....	....	....	....	....	....	....	....	....	....	....	....	....	....
Other Investment	79af*d*	....	....	....	....	....	....	....	....	....	....	....	....	....	....	....
Monetary Authorities	79ag*d*	....	....	....	....	....	....	....	....	....	....	....	....	....	....	....
General Government	79ah*d*	....	....	....	....	....	....	....	....	....	....	....	....	....	....	....
Banks	79ai*d*	....	....	....	....	....	....	....	....	....	....	....	....	....	....	....
Other Sectors	79aj*d*	....	....	....	....	....	....	....	....	....	....	....	....	....	....	....
Reserve Assets	79ak*d*	....	....	....	....	....	....	....	....	....	....	....	....	....	....	....
Liabilities	79la*d*	....	....	....	....	....	....	....	....	....	....	....	....	....	....	....
Dir. Invest. in Rep. Economy	79lb*d*	....	....	....	....	....	....	....	....	....	....	....	....	....	....	....
Portfolio Investement	79lc*d*	....	....	....	....	....	....	....	....	....	....	....	....	....	....	....
Equity Securities	79ld*d*	....	....	....	....	....	....	....	....	....	....	....	....	....	....	....
Debt Securities	79le*d*	....	....	....	....	....	....	....	....	....	....	....	....	....	....	....
Financial Derivatives	79ll*d*	....	....	....	....	....	....	....	....	....	....	....	....	....	....	....
Other Investment	79lf*d*	....	....	....	....	....	....	....	....	....	....	....	....	....	....	....
Monetary Authorities	79lg*d*	....	....	....	....	....	....	....	....	....	....	....	....	....	....	....
General Government	79lh*d*	....	....	....	....	....	....	....	....	....	....	....	....	....	....	....
Banks	79li*d*	....	....	....	....	....	....	....	....	....	....	....	....	....	....	....
Other Sectors	79lj*d*	....	....	....	....	....	....	....	....	....	....	....	....	....	....	....
Government Finance																*Millions of Balboas:*
Deficit (-) or Surplus	80	–49.1	–32.3	–105.7	I –91.0	–119.4	–149.5	–202.7	–119.0	–159.6	–371.8	–197.6	–334.6	–482.6	–272.5	–340.0
Revenue	81	....	....	....	I 306.1	385.5	437.4	425.4	536.8	591.6	690.1	965.0	1,029.8	1,203.8	1,324.3	1,344.1
Grants Received	81z	....	....	....	I —	6.0	14.3	14.8	9.6	6.0	6.5	1.1	—	—	—	30.0
Expenditure	82	209.3	213.5	303.5	I 387.0	503.7	581.7	626.5	649.8	736.7	1,066.0	1,163.4	1,322.1	1,612.0	1,512.4	1,653.3
Lending Minus Repayments	83	....	....	....	I 10.1	7.2	19.5	16.4	15.6	20.5	2.4	.3	42.3	74.4	84.4	60.8
Financing																
Total Financing	84	21.4	....	....	I 91.0	119.4	149.5	202.7	119.0	159.6	371.8	197.6	334.6	482.6	272.5	340.0
Domestic	84a	....	....	....	I 19.1	54.6	46.3	89.9	40.3	37.2	59.4	–8.9	133.2	95.1	49.4	158.6
Foreign	85a	....	....	....	I 71.9	64.8	103.2	112.8	78.7	122.4	312.4	206.5	201.4	387.5	223.1	181.4
Debt: Domestic	88a	144.9	155.0	190.4	I 180.0	231.5	294.6	332.7	330.5	374.8	404.8	484.4	691.6	728.4	897.1	957.5
Foreign	89a	140.6	173.4	214.9	I 296.9	358.9	427.4	510.2	614.0	1,025.6	1,344.0	1,578.6	1,689.8	2,049.8	2,175.1	2,263.9
National Accounts																*Millions of Balboas*
Exports of Goods & Services	90c	388.0	426.4	460.7	528.1	761.8	865.4	837.8	921.1	986.4	1,124.8	3,446.6	3,777.2	3,687.6	3,070.4	3,100.1
Government Consumption	91f	152.0	180.2	226.5	250.1	299.3	353.3	386.1	412.1	482.9	567.2	670.6	734.5	911.6	912.6	1,010.0
Gross Fixed Capital Formation	93e	261.9	306.3	372.2	434.8	465.0	535.5	608.6	445.9	606.3	661.2	875.5	1,103.7	1,215.2	945.0	772.1
Increase/Decrease(-) in Stocks	93i	22.0	43.6	30.3	50.9	91.1	31.9	10.2	45.0	45.4	124.5	195.5	119.4	67.2	–70.0	–15.0
Private Consumption	96f	619.0	665.2	698.3	767.6	954.0	1,054.1	1,088.8	1,242.6	1,431.7	1,693.8	2,038.9	2,271.1	2,168.6	2,702.2	3,151.1
Imports of Goods & Services	98c	–422.0	–469.8	–523.1	–584.9	–917.1	–999.4	–975.2	–996.9	–1,100.2	–1,371.3	–3,682.3	–4,014.0	–3,823.6	–3,119.6	–3,323.8
Gross Domestic Product (GDP)	99b	1,016.3	1,146.7	1,260.0	1,441.2	1,647.1	1,844.8	1,959.3	2,077.4	2,463.0	2,819.1	3,810.3	4,312.7	4,764.7	4,891.9	5,106.3
Net Factor Inc/Pmts(-) Abroad	98.n	–26.5	–29.6	–31.9	–39.1	–54.4	–19.5	–55.5	–63.1	–57.4	–102.8	–434.1	–152.3	–279.3	–259.7	–386.4
Gross National Income (GNI)	99a	995.0	1,122.3	1,233.0	1,407.5	1,599.7	1,821.3	1,900.8	2,006.7	2,395.1	2,697.4	3,110.7	3,839.6	3,947.3	4,180.9	4,308.1
Net National Income	99e	942.0	1,062.4	1,165.5	1,334.3	1,519.2	1,729.5	1,800.4	1,895.1	2,260.2	2,540.1	3,230.5	3,563.1	3,864.8	4,090.3	3,959.4
GDP Volume 1970 prices	99b.*p*	1,016.3	1,113.9	1,165.3	1,228.3	1,258.1	1,278.2	1,299.1	1,313.6	1,442.4	1,736.4	1,736.4	....	....	....	....
GDP Volume 1982 Prices	99b.*p*	....	....	....	....	....	....	....	....	....	....	4,141.5	4,522.8	4,764.7	4,550.7	4,674.0
GDP Volume (1995=100)	99bv*p*	39.1	42.9	44.8	47.3	48.4	49.2	50.0	50.5	55.5	66.8	66.8	73.0	76.9	73.4	75.4
GDP Deflator (1995=100)	99bi*p*	32.9	33.8	35.5	38.6	43.0	47.4	49.6	52.0	56.1	53.4	72.1	74.8	78.4	84.3	85.6
																Millions:
Population	99z	1.43	1.48	1.52	1.57	1.62	1.68	1.72	1.77	1.81	1.85	1.96	2.00	2.04	2.09	2.13

1985	1986	1987	1988	1989	1990	1991	1992	1993	1994	1995	1996	1997	1998	1999	Item	Code
Minus Sign Indicates Debit															Balance of Payments	
75.1	−98.9	544.9	721.4	111.5	209.1	−241.1	−267.2	−95.7	15.8	−369.1	−301.9	−603.5	−1,211.6	−1,332.6	Current Account, n.i.e.	**78al *d***
2,132.9	2,490.7	2,650.6	2,505.9	2,742.1	3,346.2	4,191.8	5,104.2	5,416.9	6,044.8	6,090.9	5,822.9	6,655.4	6,325.2	5,198.2	Goods: Exports f.o.b.	**78aa *d***
−2,570.2	−2,669.5	−2,843.5	−2,349.1	−2,865.9	−3,503.9	−4,591.4	−5,479.7	−5,751.1	−6,294.9	−6,679.8	−6,467.0	−7,355.7	−7,696.2	−6,595.9	Goods: Imports f.o.b.	**78ab *d***
−437.3	−178.8	−192.9	156.8	−123.8	−157.7	−399.6	−375.5	−334.2	−250.1	−588.9	−644.1	−700.3	−1,371.0	−1,397.7	*Trade Balance*	**78ac *d***
1,180.1	1,159.1	1,150.1	1,062.2	981.2	1,092.1	1,216.4	1,225.4	1,297.4	1,403.7	1,519.4	1,558.6	1,648.4	1,697.4	1,689.2	Services: Credit	**78ad *d***
−657.2	−796.8	−706.7	−518.0	−575.2	−689.2	−847.9	−917.1	−976.4	−1,064.3	−1,087.8	−1,034.0	−1,290.6	−1,172.5	−1,103.9	Services: Debit	**78ae *d***
85.6	183.5	250.5	701.0	282.2	245.2	−31.1	−67.2	−13.2	89.3	−157.3	−119.5	−342.5	−846.1	−812.4	*Balance on Goods & Services*	**78af *d***
3,089.4	2,550.0	2,232.7	976.3	976.2	1,139.1	1,078.8	1,138.9	1,054.7	1,202.9	1,644.1	1,422.1	1,436.0	1,725.2	1,565.1	Income: Credit	**78ag *d***
−3,240.9	−2,965.6	−2,056.1	−1,064.2	−1,242.6	−1,394.5	−1,511.2	−1,539.9	−1,340.3	−1,425.3	−2,008.5	−1,739.2	−1,847.6	−2,249.7	−2,249.5	Income: Debit	**78ah *d***
−65.9	−232.1	427.1	613.1	15.8	−10.2	−463.5	−468.2	−298.8	−133.1	−521.7	−436.6	−754.1	−1,370.6	−1,496.8	*Balance on Gds, Serv. & Inc.*	**78ai *d***
180.0	166.9	165.8	153.6	139.8	248.7	249.8	230.0	236.5	185.5	184.1	167.7	185.2	195.2	202.7	Current Transfers, n.i.e.: Credit	**78aj *d***
−39.0	−33.7	−48.0	−45.3	−44.1	−29.4	−27.4	−29.0	−33.4	−36.6	−31.5	−33.0	−34.6	−36.2	−38.5	Current Transfers: Debit	**78ak *d***
....	....	....	....	....	....	....	130.0	....	....	8.5	2.5	72.7	50.9	3.0	Capital Account, n.i.e.	**78bc *d***
....	....	....	....	....	....	....	130.0	....	....	8.5	2.5	72.7	50.9	3.0	Capital Account, n.i.e.: Credit	**78ba *d***
....	....	....	....	....	....	....	....	....	....	....	....	....	....	....	Capital Account: Debit	**78bb *d***
−82.7	−48.2	−690.2	−980.2	−648.8	−207.6	−697.9	−440.1	−521.4	−297.2	159.3	533.0	788.3	878.5	1,118.4	Financial Account, n.i.e.	**78bj *d***
....	....	....	....	....	....	....	....	....	....	....	....	....	....	....	Direct Investment Abroad	**78bd *d***
67.3	20.3	−556.5	−595.1	51.5	135.5	108.5	144.5	169.6	392.5	266.7	410.4	1,255.8	1,206.1	22.3	Dir. Invest. in Rep. Econ., n.i.e.	**78be *d***
−171.1	−985.0	−228.8	2,218.3	−438.2	−200.0	−222.6	−46.3	−754.6	−48.4	318.5	488.0	−1,036.3	437.7	−542.1	Portfolio Investment Assets	**78bf *d***
−1.4	1.2	....	....	....	....	....	....	....	....	.2	−10.2	−.8	−9.7	....	Equity Securities	**78bk *d***
−169.7	−986.2	−228.8	2,218.3	−438.2	−200.0	−222.6	−46.3	−754.6	−48.4	318.3	498.2	−1,035.5	447.4	−542.1	Debt Securities	**78bl *d***
−22.2	−31.3	−41.0	−64.1	−29.9	−35.8	−24.1	−71.1	−54.7	−.4	−.3	−67.1	−80.3	−65.6	−99.2	Portfolio Investment Liab., n.i.e.	**78bg *d***
....	....	−.7	.7	....	−1.0	1.8	−1.4	−.1	.4	.2	−.1	−.1	−.1	....	Equity Securities	**78bm *d***
−22.2	−31.3	−40.3	−64.8	−29.9	−34.8	−25.9	−69.7	−54.6	−.8	−.5	−67.0	−80.2	−65.5	−99.2	Debt Securities	**78bn *d***
....	....	....	....	....	....	....	....	....	....	....	....	....	....	....	Financial Derivatives Assets	**78bw *d***
....	....	....	....	....	....	....	....	....	....	....	....	....	....	....	Financial Derivatives Liabilities	**78bx *d***
−557.5	233.5	8,904.1	12,828.1	−434.8	−1,421.8	−1,383.2	−1,491.8	−1,281.4	−5,277.7	−371.3	394.1	−616.2	645.1	2,272.1	Other Investment Assets	**78bh *d***
....	....	....	....	....	....	....	....	....	....	....	....	....	....	−.2	Monetary Authorities	**78bo *d***
....	−2.4	....	−164.8	−135.2	299.1	−.9	−.9	−.9	....	−1.0	−38.2	−158.7	−497.7	249.1	General Government	**78bp *d***
−586.5	403.0	8,640.2	13,170.4	−153.0	−1,923.3	−1,259.5	−1,442.9	−1,186.6	−5,254.4	−176.3	521.0	−257.2	1,286.3	1,987.1	Banks	**78bq *d***
29.0	−167.1	263.9	−177.5	−146.6	202.4	−122.8	−48.0	−93.9	−23.3	−194.0	−88.7	−200.3	−143.5	36.1	Other Sectors	**78br *d***
600.8	714.3	−8,768.0	−15,367.4	202.6	1,314.5	823.5	1,024.6	1,399.7	4,636.8	−54.3	−692.4	1,265.3	−1,344.8	−534.7	Other Investment Liab., n.i.e.	**78bi *d***
−18.1	−3.2	−36.8	−96.3	15.0	−3.5	−2.0	11.2	.8	−1.3	54.6	−1.7	6.8	−.9	−.7	Monetary Authorities	**78bs *d***
32.5	48.7	−318.9	−346.6	−279.5	−144.8	−174.9	−155.8	−117.5	−198.8	−36.1	−50.5	130.4	85.6	33.7	General Government	**78bt *d***
583.7	579.8	−8,181.2	−14,840.1	541.4	1,516.0	945.8	1,199.7	1,606.7	4,915.5	−122.8	−804.8	1,029.9	−1,446.8	−510.6	Banks	**78bu *d***
2.7	89.0	−231.1	−84.4	−74.3	−53.2	54.6	−30.5	−90.3	−78.6	50.0	164.6	98.2	17.3	−57.1	Other Sectors	**78bv *d***
−120.9	141.2	−385.8	−745.4	−295.0	−137.4	610.9	390.2	309.0	−80.4	−130.0	33.2	85.8	−181.0	63.4	Net Errors and Omissions	**78ca *d***
−128.5	−5.9	−531.1	−1,004.2	−832.3	−135.9	−328.1	−187.1	−308.1	−361.8	−331.3	266.8	343.3	−463.2	−147.8	*Overall Balance*	**78cb *d***
128.5	5.9	531.1	1,004.2	832.3	135.9	328.1	187.1	308.1	361.8	331.3	−266.8	−343.3	463.2	147.8	Reserves and Related Items	**79da *d***
109.9	−66.3	95.5	5.5	−47.9	−355.7	−148.4	116.2	−93.0	−105.7	−77.7	−297.7	−611.1	103.3	−184.4	Reserve Assets	**79db *d***
8.0	6.7	−57.9	−.1	−.8	−70.7	−55.7	−98.6	3.4	12.5	−25.9	24.2	19.6	27.3	−23.5	Use of Fund Credit and Loans	**79dc *d***
10.6	65.5	493.5	998.8	881.0	562.3	532.3	169.5	397.7	454.9	434.9	6.8	248.2	332.6	355.7	Exceptional Financing	**79de *d***
Millions of US Dollars															International Investment Position	
....	....	....	....	....	....	....	....	....	....	....	24,916.3	27,247.6	26,062.1	24,516.0	Assets	**79aa *d***
....	....	....	....	....	....	....	....	....	....	....	—	—	—	—	Direct Investment Abroad	**79ab *d***
....	....	....	....	....	....	....	....	....	....	....	1,401.4	2,437.7	2,000.0	2,542.1	Portfolio Investment	**79ac *d***
....	....	....	....	....	....	....	....	....	....	....	17.8	18.6	28.3	28.3	Equity Securities	**79ad *d***
....	....	....	....	....	....	....	....	....	....	....	1,383.6	2,419.1	1,971.7	2,513.8	Debt Securities	**79ae *d***
....	....	....	....	....	....	....	....	....	....	....	—	—	—	—	Financial Derivatives	**79al *d***
....	....	....	....	....	....	....	....	....	....	....	22,436.3	23,052.5	22,407.4	20,135.3	Other Investment	**79af *d***
....	....	....	....	....	....	....	....	....	....	....	—	—	—	.2	Monetary Authorities	**79ag *d***
....	....	....	....	....	....	....	....	....	....	....	63.9	222.6	720.3	471.2	General Government	**79ah *d***
....	....	....	....	....	....	....	....	....	....	....	20,247.8	20,505.0	19,218.7	17,231.6	Banks	**79ai *d***
....	....	....	....	....	....	....	....	....	....	....	2,124.6	2,324.9	2,468.4	2,432.3	Other Sectors	**79aj *d***
....	....	....	....	....	....	....	....	....	....	....	1,078.6	1,757.4	1,654.7	1,838.6	Reserve Assets	**79ak *d***
....	....	....	....	....	....	....	....	....	....	....	30,101.5	32,521.9	32,634.4	32,320.8	Liabilities	**79la *d***
....	....	....	....	....	....	....	....	....	....	....	3,655.0	4,910.8	6,136.8	6,159.1	Dir. Invest. in Rep. Economy	**79lb *d***
....	....	....	....	....	....	....	....	....	....	....	3,593.9	3,528.5	3,734.1	3,948.2	Portfolio Investement	**79lc *d***
....	....	....	....	....	....	....	....	....	....	....	—	—	—	—	Equity Securities	**79ld *d***
....	....	....	....	....	....	....	....	....	....	....	3,593.9	3,528.5	3,734.1	3,948.2	Debt Securities	**79le *d***
....	....	....	....	....	....	....	....	....	....	....	—	—	—	—	Financial Derivatives	**79ll *d***
....	....	....	....	....	....	....	....	....	....	....	22,852.6	24,082.6	22,763.5	22,213.5	Other Investment	**79lf *d***
....	....	....	....	....	....	....	....	....	....	....	290.1	309.9	343.6	314.8	Monetary Authorities	**79lg *d***
....	....	....	....	....	....	....	....	....	....	....	1,086.8	1,178.0	1,339.3	1,398.1	General Government	**79lh *d***
....	....	....	....	....	....	....	....	....	....	....	19,905.6	20,935.5	19,488.7	18,978.1	Banks	**79li *d***
....	....	....	....	....	....	....	....	....	....	....	1,570.1	1,659.2	1,591.9	1,522.5	Other Sectors	**79lj *d***
Year Ending December 31															**Government Finance**	
−155.0	−220.7	−227.9	−108.1	−133.7	160.8	307.9	321.2	284.7	146.0	230.5	−60.9	....	....	....	Deficit (-) or Surplus	**80**
1,382.8	1,484.6	1,537.0	1,205.4	1,079.4	1,360.5	1,642.8	1,692.8	1,950.8	2,010.5	2,065.1	2,140.3	....	....	....	Revenue	**81**
20.1	8.2	7.1	2.4	—	4.9	71.6	26.1	27.8	15.5	8.5	4.6	....	....	....	Grants Received	**81z**
1,504.0	1,620.8	1,702.4	1,237.0	1,177.8	1,259.1	1,390.1	1,657.8	1,768.6	1,958.7	1,953.3	2,255.3	....	....	....	Expenditure	**82**
53.9	92.7	69.6	78.9	35.3	−54.5	16.4	−260.1	−74.7	−78.7	−110.2	−49.5	....	....	....	Lending Minus Repayments	**83**
															Financing	
155.0	220.7	227.9	108.1	133.7	−160.8	−307.9	−321.2	−284.7	−146.0	−230.5	60.9	....	....	....	Total Financing	**84**
152.3	37.5	247.7	281.1	....	21.2	−222.4	−277.6	−226.2	−135.2	−253.2	3.7	....	....	....	Domestic	**84a**
2.7	183.2	−19.8	−173.0	....	−182.0	−85.5	−43.6	−58.5	−10.8	22.7	57.2	....	....	....	Foreign	**85a**
1,055.2	1,191.6	1,143.4	1,088.3	1,208.1	937.4	851.5	999.5	1,810.1	1,805.6	1,681.4	1,794.2	1,737.5	1,737.6	2,108.8	Debt: Domestic	**88a**
2,265.5	2,372.5	2,399.1	2,443.5	2,457.7	2,450.4	2,432.9	2,624.9	2,600.2	2,812.9	3,001.5	4,542.2	4,659.6	5,042.5	5,457.6	Foreign	**89a**
Millions of Balboas															**National Accounts**	
3,706.3	3,992.8	4,032.0	3,665.8	3,856.4	4,610.9	5,655.4	6,642.1	7,037.9	7,711.6	7,979.4	7,580.3	8,494.6	8,210.0	....	Exports of Goods & Services	**90c**
1,056.8	1,152.3	1,241.9	1,019.4	943.7	962.3	1,025.3	1,055.9	1,098.3	1,144.8	1,194.1	1,270.5	1,402.6	1,507.6	....	Government Consumption	**91f**
834.1	955.7	1,087.0	428.4	318.2	454.0	873.5	1,227.9	1,681.3	1,828.8	2,057.9	2,059.2	2,295.0	2,624.9	....	Gross Fixed Capital Formation	**93e**
−11.9	11.8	−50.5	−62.1	−17.4	440.1	247.6	345.3	111.9	244.8	336.3	428.2	396.1	372.3	....	Increase/Decrease(-) in Stocks	**93i**
3,033.1	2,953.6	2,865.2	2,679.9	3,218.5	3,022.2	3,470.2	3,759.6	4,040.2	4,150.7	4,090.0	4,296.6	4,699.1	5,280.2	....	Private Consumption	**96f**
−3,216.4	−3,452.5	−3,537.3	−2,856.9	−3,431.9	−4,176.3	−5,429.7	−6,389.4	−6,716.9	−7,346.8	−7,751.6	−7,483.7	−8,629.9	−8,851.2	....	Imports of Goods & Services	**98c**
5,402.0	5,613.7	5,638.3	4,874.5	4,887.5	5,313.2	5,842.3	6,641.4	7,252.7	7,733.9	7,906.1	8,151.1	8,657.5	9,143.8	....	Gross Domestic Product (GDP)	**99b**
−195.8	−455.2	144.0	−100.7	−282.2	−289.1	−421.0	−439.4	−354.8	−272.3	−421.5	−360.5	−451.4	−563.3	....	Net Factor Inc/Pmts(-) Abroad	**98.n**
5,206.2	5,158.5	5,782.3	4,773.8	4,605.3	5,024.1	5,421.3	6,202.0	6,897.9	7,461.6	7,484.6	7,790.6	8,206.1	8,580.5	....	Gross National Income (GNI)	**99a**
4,837.8	4,767.2	5,376.2	4,415.0	4,259.5	4,647.5	4,997.5	5,826.7	6,400.9	6,928.3	6,925.7	7,213.9	7,605.0	7,939.4	....	Net National Income	**99e**
....	....	....	....	....	....	....	....	....	....	....	....	....	....	....	GDP Volume 1970 prices	**99b.*p***
4,905.0	5,080.0	4,988.1	4,320.7	4,388.2	4,743.6	5,190.4	5,616.1	5,922.5	6,091.3	6,198.0	6,372.2	6,657.5	6,932.9	7,157.7	GDP Volume 1982 Prices	**99b.*p***
79.1	82.0	80.5	69.7	70.8	76.5	83.7	90.6	95.6	98.3	100.0	102.8	107.4	111.9	115.5	GDP Volume (1995=100)	**99bv *p***
86.3	86.6	88.6	88.4	87.3	87.8	88.2	92.7	96.0	99.5	100.0	100.3	101.9	103.4	....	GDP Deflator (1995=100)	**99bi *p***
Midyear Estimates																
2.17	2.21	2.26	2.30	2.35	2.40	2.44	2.49	2.53	2.58	2.63	2.67	2.72	2.76	2.81	**Population**	**99z**

(See notes in the back of the book.)

Papua New Guinea

853

	code	1970	1971	1972	1973	1974	1975	1976	1977	1978	1979	1980	1981	1982	1983	1984
Exchange Rates																*SDRs per Kina:*
Official Rate	ac	1.1150	1.0970	1.1743	1.2335	1.0838	1.0738	1.0599	1.0867	1.1153	1.0998	1.2177	1.2625	1.2121	1.0910	1.0837
																US Dollars per Kina:
Official Rate	ag	1.1150	1.1910	1.2750	1.4880	1.3270	1.2571	1.2314	1.3200	1.4530	1.4488	1.5531	1.4695	1.3371	1.1422	1.0623
Official Rate	rh	1.1200	1.1331	1.1923	1.4227	1.4394	1.3102	1.2621	1.2640	1.4117	1.4053	1.4916	1.4871	1.3559	1.1989	1.1183
																Index Numbers (1995=100):
Official Rate	ahx	142.1	113.5	152.2	181.2	183.5	167.2	161.1	161.3	180.2	179.3	190.4	189.8	173.1	153.0	142.7
Nominal Effective Exchange Rate	nec	...	...	...	...	...	...	...	...	...	87.8	95.0	99.8	101.3	97.8	99.6
Real Effective Exchange Rate	rec	...	...	...	...	...	...	...	...	...	...	142.9	146.4	144.0	139.5	141.0
Fund Position																*Millions of SDRs:*
Quota	2f. s	...	...	...	...	...	20.00	20.00	20.00	30.00	30.00	45.00	45.00	45.00	65.90	65.90
SDRs	1b. s	...	...	...	...	...	—	1.68	.19	.42	.81		33.07	31.00	16.95	4.99
Reserve Position in the Fund	1c. s	...	...	...	...	...				.01	2.37	3.78	.05	.07	5.31	5.35
Total Fund Cred.&Loans Outstg.	2tl	...	...	...	...	...	—	24.80	24.80	23.09	18.10	24.28	64.55	64.55	64.55	34.59
International Liquidity													*Millions of US Dollars Unless Otherwise Indicated:*			
Total Reserves minus Gold	1l. d	...	...	...	31.26	32.45	179.67	257.20	426.63	404.72	503.55	423.43	396.17	452.88	440.07	435.23
SDRs	1b. d	...	...	...	...	...	—	1.95	.23	.55	1.07		38.49	34.20	17.75	4.89
Reserve Position in the Fund	1c. d	...	...	...	...	...				.01	3.12	4.82	.05	.08	5.56	5.24
Foreign Exchange	1d. d	...	...	...	31.26	32.45	179.67	255.25	426.40	404.16	499.36	418.61	357.63	418.61	416.76	425.09
Gold (Million Fine Troy Ounces)	1ad	...	...	...	...	...	...	...	.029	.044	.053	.058	.062	.062	.063	.063
Gold (National Valuation)	1an d	...	...	...	...	...	...	—	3.55	7.93	11.09	14.74	15.91	14.54	12.53	11.71
Monetary Authorities: Other Liab.	4.. d	...	...	...	6.21	5.79	4.04	35.36	60.33	25.31	15.90	13.23	64.18	57.78	49.08	17.48
Deposit Money Banks: Assets	7a. d	...	...	...	72.06	162.74	.27	10.14	80.18	35.93	21.13	16.02	18.28	7.15	10.59	14.28
Liabilities	7b. d	...	...	...	.05	1.59	20.54	22.86	46.00	52.33	22.93	9.88	38.30	26.76	33.63	54.61
Monetary Authorities																*Millions of Kina:*
Foreign Assets	11	...	...	...	99.37	114.48	194.32	208.77	327.51	297.22	372.94	293.56	290.19	269.84	395.45	416.78
Claims on Central Government	12a	...	...	...	3.24	3.24	7.57	22.21	11.55	12.75	30.14	39.39	52.76	72.88	27.51	12.52
Claims on Deposit Money Banks	12e												8.61		17.85	22.51
Reserve Money	14	...	...	...	64.13	81.62	142.19	168.13	203.51	194.10	235.72	99.46	88.82	90.46	138.04	128.25
of which: Currency Outside DMBs	14a	...	...	...	57.37	76.61	85.21	47.51	56.66	61.55	67.89	70.49	73.39	72.41	79.95	88.90
Time Deposits	15	...	...	...	—	—	—	—	49.73	68.37	95.38	102.27	90.60	90.73	83.30	80.15
Foreign Liabilities	16c	...	...	...	4.18	4.36	3.21	52.12	68.52	38.12	27.43	28.46	94.80	96.47	102.14	48.38
Central Government Deposits	16d	...	...	...	32.50	27.71	53.74	24.73	34.70	18.36	24.06	91.79	80.05	55.99	71.50	103.83
Capital Accounts	17a	...	...	...	5.01	5.53	6.26	16.18	10.23	4.19	17.86	2.44	19.39	49.93	98.80	96.86
Other Items (Net)	17r	...	...	...	-3.20	-1.50	-3.51	-30.17	-27.62	-13.18	2.63	8.53	-30.71	-32.25	-52.96	-5.65
Deposit Money Banks																*Millions of Kina:*
Reserves	20	...	...	...	6.25	5.09	54.95	116.81	141.57	126.99	160.26	26.09	18.35	16.07	56.02	35.67
Foreign Assets	21	...	...	...	48.44	122.64	.22	8.24	60.74	24.73	14.59	10.32	12.44	5.34	9.27	13.44
Claims on Central Government	22a	...	...	...	22.70	35.25	28.27	32.54	44.78	37.75	58.47	88.13	92.29	78.74	91.92	108.72
Claims on Local Governments	22b	...	...	...	—	.25	.39	.72	.97	.73	1.44	2.00	2.07	1.89	2.35	1.43
Claims on Nonfin.Pub.Enterprises	22c	...	...	...	—	.11	.92	7.46	13.76	6.88	20.07	23.70	18.48	17.20	28.44	
Claims on Private Sector	22d	...	...	...	137.16	152.04	163.31	156.62	169.00	173.74	204.39	277.61	330.31	361.22	417.89	502.98
Demand Deposits	24	...	...	...	41.53	63.22	63.55	83.87	107.44	111.87	119.94	128.18	120.71	114.25	124.42	156.12
Time, Savings,& Fgn. Currency Dep.	25	...	...	...	96.24	179.61	94.66	142.80	209.35	201.67	280.92	249.32	269.77	288.49	360.78	418.88
Foreign Liabilities	26c	...	...	...	.03	1.20	16.34	18.56	34.85	36.02	15.83	6.36	26.06	20.02	29.44	51.41
Central Government Deposits	26d	...	...	...	15.02	5.92	12.86	12.00	18.33	18.62	30.30	22.71	26.05	27.21	45.93	24.25
Credit from Monetary Authorities	26g	...	...	...	—	—	—	—	—	—	—	—	8.61		17.01	19.30
Capital Accounts	27a	...	...	...	49.53	69.30	71.14	76.14	77.41	29.93	30.07	41.54	48.68	45.36	56.44	47.00
Other Items (Net)	27r	...	...	...	12.21	-3.86	-10.51	-11.00	-16.56	-27.30	-17.86	-20.27	-17.33	-23.47	-28.15	-54.72
Monetary Survey																*Millions of Kina:*
Foreign Assets (Net)	31n	...	...	...	143.60	231.56	174.99	146.33	284.88	247.81	344.27	269.06	181.76	158.70	273.14	330.44
Domestic Credit	32	...	...	...	115.58	157.65	134.01	185.07	192.30	208.00	263.90	318.87	390.81	449.74	456.43	499.76
Claims on Central Govt. (Net)	32an	...	...	...	-21.58	4.86	-30.76	18.01	3.31	13.52	34.25	13.01	38.96	68.42	2.00	-6.85
Claims on Local Government	32b	...	...	...	—	.25	.39	.72	.97	.73	1.44	2.00	2.07	1.89	2.35	1.43
Claims on Nonfin.Pub.Enterprises	32c	...	...	...	—	.11	.92	7.46	13.76	6.88	20.07	23.70	18.48	17.20	28.44	
Claims on Private Sector	32d	...	...	...	137.16	152.04	163.31	156.62	169.00	173.74	204.39	277.61	330.31	361.22	417.89	502.98
Claims on Other Financial Insts	32f	...	...	...	—	.39	.15	2.27	5.27	13.14	3.77	2.54	.99	1.01	5.74	2.20
Money	34	...	...	...	99.40	140.43	150.80	135.02	169.38	178.99	195.41	201.56	194.36	188.64	205.97	248.99
Quasi-Money	35	...	...	...	96.24	179.61	94.66	142.80	259.08	270.05	376.30	351.59	360.37	379.22	444.08	499.03
Capital Accounts	37a	...	...	...	54.53	74.82	77.40	92.32	87.64	34.12	47.93	43.98	68.07	95.29	155.26	143.86
Other Items (Net)	37r	...	...	...	9.01	-5.66	-13.87	-38.74	-38.91	-27.35	-11.47	-9.20	-50.24	-54.71	-75.73	-61.68
Money plus Quasi-Money	35l	...	...	...	195.64	320.04	245.46	277.82	428.46	449.03	571.71	553.15	554.74	567.85	650.04	748.02
Interest Rates																*Percent Per Annum*
Discount Rate (End of Period)	60	...	...	...	...	...	...	...	...	...	...	...	...		8.75	8.75
Treasury Bill Rate	60c	...	...	...	...	8.18	8.27	7.73	6.38	5.78	6.03	7.16	11.56	13.80	10.92	9.28
Deposit Rate	60l	...	...	...	...	...	...	...	...	...	...	6.90	10.00	8.00	9.54	8.13
Lending Rate	60p	...	...	...	...	...	...	...	...	...	...	11.15	14.40	12.25	11.58	10.64
Prices and Labor																*Index Numbers (1995=100):*
Consumer Prices	64	...	18.2	19.3	20.9	25.8	28.5	30.7	I32.1	33.9	35.9	40.2	43.5	45.9	49.5	53.2
Total Employment	67	...	...	...	...	...	...	...	...	84.6	87.8	95.7	98.5	88.9	86.6	88.0

1985	1986	1987	1988	1989	1990	1991	1992	1993	1994	1995	1996	1997	1998	1999		
End of Period															**Exchange Rates**	
.8992	.8506	.8024	.8992	.8852	.7376	.7339	.7365	.7419	.5812	.5039	.5164	.4232	.3388	.2703	Official Rate	ac
End of Period (ag) Period Average (rh)																
.9877	1.0404	1.1384	1.2100	1.1633	1.0493	1.0498	1.0127	1.0190	.8485	.7490	.7425	.5710	.4770	.3710	Official Rate	ag
1.0000	1.0296	1.1012	1.1538	1.1685	1.0467	1.0504	1.0367	1.0221	.9950	.7835	.7588	.6975	.4859	.3939	Official Rate	rh
Period Averages																
127.6	131.4	140.5	147.3	149.1	133.6	134.1	132.3	130.5	127.0	100.0	96.8	89.0	62.0	50.3	Official Rate	ahx
99.3	94.5	96.3	99.0	108.8	104.3	109.9	115.0	127.3	131.3	100.0	98.6	97.1	74.8	60.0	Nominal Effective Exchange Rate	ne c
135.1	127.7	126.0	125.4	129.6	114.9	118.9	118.9	124.5	117.7	100.0	107.6	108.3	92.4	84.2	Real Effective Exchange Rate	re c
End of Period															**Fund Position**	
65.90	65.90	65.90	65.90	65.90	65.90	65.90	95.30	95.30	95.30	95.30	95.30	95.30	95.30	131.60	Quota	2f. s
5.89	2.61	3.31	3.04	2.67	—	.02	.10	.03	.07	.47	.04	.06	.04	.53	SDRs	1b. s
5.38	5.42	6.94	6.95	6.98	—	—	.04	.05	.05	.05	.05	.05	.05	.05	Reserve Position in the Fund	1c. s
26.33	12.34	8.44	4.55	2.31	42.91	42.84	42.84	32.13	10.71	33.34	35.34	35.34	32.35	15.68	Total Fund Cred.&Loans Outstg.	2tl
Approximately End of Period															**International Liquidity**	
442.57	425.46	436.83	393.49	384.38	403.04	323.05	238.58	141.45	96.06	261.35	583.89	362.68	192.88	205.14	Total Reserves minus Gold	1l. d
6.47	3.19	4.70	4.09	3.51	—	.03	.14	.05	.11	.69	.06	.08	.05	.72	SDRs	1b. d
5.91	6.63	9.85	9.35	9.17	—	—	.06	.07	.08	.08	.08	.07	.07	.07	Reserve Position in the Fund	1c. d
430.19	415.64	422.29	380.05	371.70	403.04	323.02	238.39	141.34	95.88	260.58	583.75	362.53	192.76	204.35	Foreign Exchange	1d. d
.063	.063	.063	.063	.063	.063	.063	.063	.063	.063	.014	.063	.063	.063	.063	Gold (Million Fine Troy Ounces)	1ad
10.93	11.08	11.08	11.09	11.09	11.09	11.09	11.09	11.09	11.09	2.40	28.30	28.30	28.30	27.90	Gold (National Valuation)	1an d
19.40	12.09	−.30	−.39	2.23	62.80	55.71	60.01	46.41	100.02	111.84	54.21	44.33	31.68	2.76	Monetary Authorities: Other Liab.	4.. d
16.21	10.06	24.27	29.92	22.32	20.65	39.72	61.61	160.59	175.61	100.11	119.12	117.38	136.34	103.23	Deposit Money Banks: Assets	7a. d
56.23	43.55	68.21	109.35	143.31	113.17	150.27	118.34	88.07	120.46	41.39	23.07	7.99	54.53	37.44	Liabilities	7b. d
Last Wednesday of Period															**Monetary Authorities**	
460.51	455.06	446.14	396.23	342.42	376.53	306.44	242.31	138.61	112.51	357.55	789.20	666.07	391.06	552.92	Foreign Assets	11
60.99	53.22	78.53	107.24	174.14	227.01	251.35	284.20	421.02	776.65	592.62	587.28	880.81	1,284.96	599.66	Claims on Central Government	12a
26.90	14.86	19.42	32.00	46.89	42.83	70.91	127.74	239.43	282.50	233.80	228.94	216.27	121.10	53.63	Claims on Deposit Money Banks	12e
130.53	125.56	134.16	141.91	152.24	176.04	164.64	168.93	199.20	221.65	255.66	488.98	321.12	387.47	671.55	Reserve Money	14
94.26	95.74	106.35	115.20	122.03	134.77	137.36	141.17	160.70	179.00	194.21	216.40	234.85	278.09	357.49	of which: Currency Outside DMBs	14a
80.55	89.15	64.97	12.69	2.64	1.39	1.15	.50	.50	.50	.50	.50	.50	.50	.50	Time Deposits	15
48.92	26.13	10.25	4.74	4.52	118.03	111.44	117.42	88.86	136.31	215.49	141.45	161.15	161.90	65.45	Foreign Liabilities	16c
96.33	120.67	172.96	172.98	196.02	171.18	171.79	221.02	366.60	655.95	623.61	842.32	964.72	883.44	46.11	Central Government Deposits	16d
156.01	146.15	168.76	180.29	204.14	224.63	227.61	218.31	204.45	140.20	122.57	122.13	245.05	254.78	261.74	Capital Accounts	17a
36.07	15.48	−7.02	22.85	3.88	−44.91	−47.93	−71.93	−60.55	17.05	−33.87	10.04	70.61	109.01	160.85	Other Items (Net)	17r
Last Wednesday of Period															**Deposit Money Banks**	
22.57	29.02	24.76	23.78	23.21	35.33	22.52	24.61	36.68	40.67	56.20	116.43	67.21	106.03	310.37	Reserves	20
16.41	9.67	21.32	24.73	19.19	19.68	37.84	60.84	157.59	206.97	133.66	160.44	205.57	285.83	278.26	Foreign Assets	21
80.79	130.42	105.59	140.10	110.36	121.92	232.60	364.57	502.65	446.27	727.57	1,105.13	1,107.80	888.60	791.57	Claims on Central Government	22a
3.66	4.08	3.83	2.45	1.08	3.79	1.17	3.96	6.22	5.95	1.58	1.91	1.29	5.05	5.46	Claims on Local Governments	22b
—	—	29.32	21.32	49.75	72.77	140.35	233.52	294.69	374.70	329.25	315.00	297.71	202.94	153.06	Claims on Nonfin.Pub.Enterprises	22c
563.78	668.22	709.26	802.21	887.97	878.38	940.98	890.55	820.27	897.99	900.78	908.93	1,223.08	1,577.98	1,554.88	Claims on Private Sector	22d
146.22	160.16	172.24	200.32	215.48	203.12	275.03	293.10	431.77	433.46	501.18	692.31	752.74	829.35	982.38	Demand Deposits	24
495.42	583.13	597.00	649.99	690.36	736.38	854.16	993.78	1,091.68	1,049.85	1,192.55	1,410.43	1,659.12	1,620.62	1,638.32	Time, Savings,& Fgn. Currency Dep.	25
56.93	41.86	59.92	90.37	123.19	107.85	143.14	116.85	86.43	141.97	55.26	31.07	14.00	114.33	100.91	Foreign Liabilities	26c
20.20	18.55	17.72	18.71	18.75	33.22	39.78	43.46	51.45	73.13	122.48	167.22	170.65	287.49	211.71	Central Government Deposits	26d
16.90	14.86	17.81	40.73	46.51	42.83	70.91	127.74	239.43	282.50	233.80	228.94	216.28	121.10	53.63	Credit from Monetary Authorities	26g
49.35	66.44	79.70	93.27	66.56	68.88	64.45	65.21	60.63	78.36	92.65	114.78	139.25	212.80	332.05	Capital Accounts	27a
−97.81	−43.59	−50.30	−78.81	−69.28	−60.42	−72.01	−62.10	−143.29	−86.72	−48.88	−36.92	−49.39	−119.26	−225.40	Other Items (Net)	27r
Last Wednesday of Period															**Monetary Survey**	
371.08	396.75	397.29	325.85	233.89	170.32	89.70	68.87	120.91	41.20	220.46	777.11	696.49	400.65	664.80	Foreign Assets (Net)	31n
594.69	718.66	740.48	884.81	1,012.70	1,101.72	1,357.22	1,521.24	1,633.63	1,772.48	1,805.70	1,908.71	2,375.32	2,788.59	2,846.80	Domestic Credit	32
25.26	44.42	−6.55	55.64	69.73	144.53	272.38	384.29	505.61	493.84	574.09	682.87	853.23	1,002.62	1,133.40	Claims on Central Govt. (Net)	32an
3.66	4.08	3.83	2.45	1.08	3.79	1.17	3.96	6.22	5.95	1.58	1.91	1.29	5.05	5.46	Claims on Local Government	32b
—	—	29.32	21.32	49.75	72.77	140.35	233.52	294.69	374.70	329.25	315.00	297.71	202.94	153.06	Claims on Nonfin.Pub.Enterprises	32c
563.78	668.22	709.26	802.21	887.97	878.38	940.98	890.55	820.27	897.99	900.78	908.93	1,223.08	1,577.98	1,554.88	Claims on Private Sector	32d
2.00	1.95	4.63	3.20	4.17	2.25	2.35	8.91	6.84							Claims on Other Financial Insts.	32f
244.15	256.68	281.33	322.17	344.50	343.84	417.16	437.42	594.29	614.48	700.64	1,064.87	1,006.66	1,110.79	1,343.56	Money	34
575.97	672.28	661.96	662.68	693.00	737.77	855.31	994.28	1,092.18	1,050.35	1,193.05	1,410.93	1,659.62	1,621.12	1,638.82	Quasi-Money	35
205.37	212.60	248.46	273.56	270.70	293.51	292.06	283.52	265.09	218.56	215.22	236.91	384.30	467.58	593.78	Capital Accounts	37a
−59.72	−26.15	−53.99	−47.75	−61.61	−103.07	−117.60	−125.12	−197.01	−69.72	−82.75	−26.88	21.22	−10.25	−64.55	Other Items (Net)	37r
820.12	928.96	943.29	984.85	1,037.50	1,081.61	1,272.46	1,431.70	1,686.46	1,664.83	1,893.69	2,475.80	2,666.29	2,731.91	2,982.37	Money plus Quasi-Money	35l
Percent Per Annum															**Interest Rates**	
9.75	11.40	8.80	10.80	9.55	9.30	9.30	7.12	16.39	....	....	....	....	....	....	Discount Rate (End of Period)	60
10.40	12.32	10.44	10.12	10.50	11.40	10.33	8.88	6.25	6.85	17.40	14.44	9.94	21.18	22.70	Treasury Bill Rate	60c
9.49	11.49	9.60	9.28	8.23	8.67	9.06	7.85	5.03	5.09	12.18	12.19	7.31	13.73	15.46	Deposit Rate	60l
11.54	12.33	11.94	12.68	14.62	15.52	14.17	14.53	11.29	9.16	13.14	13.30	10.45	17.70	18.90	Lending Rate	60p
Period Averages															**Prices and Labor**	
55.1	58.1	60.1	63.3	66.2	70.8	75.7	79.0	82.9	85.3	100.0	111.6	116.0	131.8	151.5	Consumer Prices	64
90.9	93.2	95.3	98.8	106.3	101.2	97.4	100.6	97.8	104.9	100.0	107.5	107.3	103.1	....	Total Employment	67

Papua New Guinea

		1970	1971	1972	1973	1974	1975	1976	1977	1978	1979	1980	1981	1982	1983	1984
International Transactions															*Millions of Kina*	
Exports	70	92.8	106.3	184.4	359.7	451.3	335.9	435.5	539.8	504.0	686.9	691.7	564.4	570.9	687.5	822.1
Imports, c.i.f.	71	270.0	313.7	277.1	250.1	363.5	451.8	397.7	507.4	545.2	643.0	786.8	848.9	864.4	937.1	996.9
Imports, f.o.b.	71.v	238.5	274.4	244.7	214.4	301.4	368.5	351.5	448.3	478.3	561.6	684.2	738.2	771.7	821.7	844.7
															1995=100	
Volume of Exports	72	....	....	....	....	....	....	....	....	....	....	38.3	43.2	47.5	48.7	52.2
Unit Value of Exports	74	....	....	....	21.0	I 32.2	23.8	29.2	38.8	34.3	46.5	I 48.3	37.7	37.3	43.5	48.0
Balance of Payments															*Millions of US Dollars*	
Current Account, n.i.e.	78al d	....	....	....	....	....	....	50.8	114.3	−32.2	107.0	−288.7	−484.3	−444.8	−337.4	−289.5
Goods: Exports f.o.b.	78aa d	....	....	....	....	....	....	550.4	683.1	713.4	1,010.3	985.5	840.1	768.8	820.3	915.3
Goods: Imports f.o.b.	78ab d	....	....	....	....	....	....	−434.2	−559.9	−688.4	−783.3	−1,020.5	−1,096.4	−1,017.6	−974.8	−962.8
Trade Balance	78ac d	....	....	....	....	....	....	116.2	123.3	25.1	226.9	−35.0	−256.3	−248.8	−154.5	−47.5
Services: Credit	78ad d	....	....	....	....	....	....	68.9	38.0	35.7	41.8	43.3	84.7	95.4	75.7	64.4
Services: Debit	78ae d	....	....	....	....	....	....	−175.6	−183.7	−217.2	−237.8	−301.6	−342.1	−347.8	−333.4	−356.1
Balance on Goods & Services	78af d	....	....	....	....	....	....	9.5	−22.4	−156.4	31.0	−293.3	−513.7	−501.2	−412.2	−339.2
Income: Credit	78ag d	....	....	....	....	....	....	19.8	30.3	38.3	49.4	59.8	47.4	59.6	58.3	50.6
Income: Debit	78ah d	....	....	....	....	....	....	−75.2	−81.3	−103.4	−158.1	−239.0	−209.2	−180.9	−180.3	−199.2
Balance on Gds, Serv. & Inc.	78ai d	....	....	....	....	....	....	−45.9	−73.4	−221.5	−77.8	−472.5	−675.4	−622.4	−534.2	−487.7
Current Transfers, n.i.e.: Credit	78aj d	....	....	....	....	....	....	159.5	245.5	270.5	268.3	283.9	300.8	293.6	293.8	291.1
Current Transfers: Debit	78ak d	....	....	....	....	....	....	−62.8	−57.8	−81.2	−83.5	−100.2	−109.8	−115.9	−97.1	−92.9
Capital Account, n.i.e.	78bc d	....	....	....	....	....	....	−10.5	−15.7	−23.2	−28.3	−22.8	−36.7	−39.6	−37.4	−31.3
Capital Account, n.i.e.: Credit	78ba d	....	....	....	....	....	....	14.0	8.7	9.2	9.1	5.4	4.7	6.1	4.3	5.4
Capital Account: Debit	78bb d	....	....	....	....	....	....	−24.5	−24.4	−32.4	−37.5	−28.2	−41.4	−45.7	−41.8	−36.7
Financial Account, n.i.e.	78bj d	....	....	....	....	....	....	30.0	35.3	−10.1	35.4	96.0	417.4	479.7	352.0	258.1
Direct Investment Abroad	78bd d	....	....	....	....	....	....	1.9	−1.8	−4.9	−3.2	−15.7	−.6	−1.8	−1.1	−2.3
Dir. Invest. in Rep. Econ., n.i.e.	78be d	....	....	....	....	....	....	20.8	19.8	38.9	44.2	75.5	86.2	85.9	138.9	115.7
Portfolio Investment Assets	78bf d	....	....	....	....	....	....	−3.1	−.9	−5.1	−2.9	—	−1.6	—	—	—
Equity Securities	78bk d	....	....	....	....	....	....	—	—	—	—	—	—	—	—	—
Debt Securities	78bl d	....	....	....	....	....	....	−3.1	−.9	−5.1	−2.9	—	−1.6	—	—	—
Portfolio Investment Liab., n.i.e.	78bg d	....	....	....	....	....	....	−3.3	−3.5	−8.4	—	—	—	—	—	—
Equity Securities	78bm d	....	....	....	....	....	....	—	—	—	—	—	—	—	—	—
Debt Securities	78bn d	....	....	....	....	....	....	−3.3	−3.5	−8.4	—	—	—	—	—	—
Financial Derivatives Assets	78bw d	....	....	....	....	....	....	....	....	....	....	....	....	....	....	....
Financial Derivatives Liabilities	78bx d	....	....	....	....	....	....	....	....	....	....	....	....	....	....	....
Other Investment Assets	78bh d	....	....	....	....	....	....	−10.8	−67.0	48.2	14.5	7.1	—	—	—	—
Monetary Authorities	78bo d	....	....	....	....	....	....	....	....	....	....	....	....	....	....	....
General Government	78bp d	....	....	....	....	....	....	....	....	....	....	....	....	....	....	....
Banks	78bq d	....	....	....	....	....	....	−10.8	−67.0	48.2	14.5	7.1	—	—	—	—
Other Sectors	78br d	....	....	....	....	....	....	—	—	—	—	—	—	—	—	—
Other Investment Liab., n.i.e.	78bi d	....	....	....	....	....	....	24.5	88.6	−78.9	−17.2	29.1	333.4	395.6	214.2	144.6
Monetary Authorities	78bs d	....	....	....	....	....	....	−3.8	17.6	−23.9	.4	−.2	—	—	—	—
General Government	78bt d	....	....	....	....	....	....	22.2	29.7	5.1	36.9	70.6	114.8	98.4	43.8	15.1
Banks	78bu d	....	....	....	....	....	....	4.1	19.4	.2	−28.7	−11.4	25.2	−1.7	6.4	19.2
Other Sectors	78bv d	....	....	....	....	....	....	1.9	21.9	−60.3	−25.8	−30.0	193.4	298.9	164.1	110.3
Net Errors and Omissions	78ca d	....	....	....	....	....	....	−28.5	25.9	37.8	−5.1	131.8	52.5	−31.2	120.0	111.6
Overall Balance	78cb d	....	....	....	....	....	....	41.7	159.8	−27.7	108.9	−83.7	−51.1	−35.9	97.2	48.8
Reserves and Related Items	79da d	....	....	....	....	....	....	−41.7	−159.8	27.7	−108.9	83.7	51.1	35.9	−97.2	−48.8
Reserve Assets	79db d	....	....	....	....	....	....	−70.3	−159.8	29.6	−105.8	75.4	4.2	35.9	−97.2	−18.1
Use of Fund Credit and Loans	79dc d	....	....	....	....	....	....	28.6	—	−2.0	—	−6.4	8.3	46.9	—	−30.7
Exceptional Financing	79de d	....	....	....	....	....	....	....	....	....	3.2	.1	−.1	—	—	
Government Finance															*Millions of Kina:*	
Deficit (-) or Surplus	80	....	....	....	....	....	−56.96	−26.80	−19.36	I −21.48	−62.80	−33.02	−107.72	−97.18	−94.57	−21.13
Total Revenue and Grants	81y	....	....	....	....	....	330.26	353.59	389.02	I 431.37	458.82	566.94	556.18	556.49	617.18	728.33
Revenue	81	....	....	....	....	....	173.98	234.20	214.09	I 259.41	283.99	392.34	371.85	369.79	404.09	496.37
Grants	81z	....	....	....	....	....	156.28	119.39	174.93	I 171.96	174.83	174.60	184.33	186.70	213.09	231.96
Exp. & Lending Minus Repay.	82z	....	....	....	....	....	387.22	380.39	408.38	I 452.85	521.62	599.96	663.90	653.67	711.75	749.46
Expenditure	82	....	....	....	....	....	365.73	368.57	400.80	I 448.95	511.48	587.56	649.52	633.91	679.26	733.56
Lending Minus Repayments	83	....	....	....	....	....	21.49	11.82	7.58	I 3.90	10.14	12.40	14.38	19.76	32.49	15.90
Total Financing	80h	....	....	....	....	....	56.96	26.80	19.36	I 21.48	62.80	33.02	107.72	97.18	94.57	21.13
Domestic	84a	....	....	....	....	....	25.97	15.85	9.39	I 19.30	39.76	−8.87	33.85	20.62	−22.28	−27.45
Foreign	85a	....	....	....	....	....	30.99	10.95	9.97	I 2.18	23.04	41.89	73.87	76.56	116.85	48.58
Total Debt by Residence	88	....	....	....	....	....	269.82	313.88	315.92	I 326.03	430.59	502.50	541.81	640.01	812.58	919.62
Domestic	88a	....	....	....	....	....	58.39	81.74	78.01	I 75.06	139.34	174.32	151.96	158.44	143.80	179.48
Foreign	89a	....	....	....	....	....	211.43	232.14	237.91	I 250.97	291.25	328.18	389.85	481.57	668.78	740.14
National Accounts															*Millions of Kina*	
Exports of Goods & Services	90c	99	114	157	290	531	428	400	I 591	586	752	747	651	652	776	800
Government Consumption	91f	164	183	207	228	270	328	367	I 358	374	393	436	481	496	499	502
Gross Fixed Capital Formation	93e	182	276	242	128	130	187	164	I 241	270	329	397	454	581	637	513
Increase/Decrease(-) in Stocks	93i	6	16	9	19	4	35	30	I 41	28	57	36	7	−14	−6	64
Private Consumption	96f	347	387	407	428	446	521	591	I 770	876	990	1,168	1,227	1,242	1,386	1,370
Imports of Goods & Services	98c	−268	−354	−384	−308	−329	−486	−471	I −609	−636	−755	−923	−1,001	−1,073	−1,145	−1,125
Gross Domestic Product (GDP)	99b	531	622	645	786	1,040	1,004	1,069	I 1,410	1,535	1,773	1,855	1,826	1,900	2,145	2,124
Net Factor Inc/Pmts(-) Abroad	98.n	9	27	35	37	79	72	39	I 27	19	40	59	60	73	119	73
Gross National Income (GNI)	99a	531	622	645	789	1,041	1,004	1,107	I 1,437	1,554	1,813	1,914	1,886	1,972	2,265	2,355
Net National Income	99e	500	566	574	695	895	862	952	I 1,187	1,290	1,486	1,525	1,483	1,527	1,973	2,064
GDP Volume 1973 prices	99b.p	....	....	....	786	816	824	810	775						....	....
GDP Volume 1977 prices	99b.p	....	....	....				....	1,410	1,531	1,559	1,523	1,540		....	....
GDP Volume 1981 prices	99b.p	....	....	....									1,826	1,841	1,905	....
GDP Volume 1983 Prices	99b.p	....	....	....											2,145	2,124
GDP Volume (1990=100)	99bv p	....	....	....	81.2	84.4	85.1	83.7	80.1	87.0	88.6	86.5	87.5	88.2	91.3	90.4
GDP Deflator (1990=100)	99bi p	....	....	....	31.5	40.1	38.4	41.5	I 57.2	57.4	65.1	69.7	67.8	70.0	76.4	76.4
																Millions:
Population	99z	2.42	2.52	2.58	2.59	2.64	2.69	2.75	2.81	2.87	2.93	2.98	3.04	3.11	3.19	3.26

	1985	1986	1987	1988	1989	1990	1991	1992	1993	1994	1995	1996	1997	1998	1999		
Millions of Kina																**International Transactions**	
	926.2	1,000.8	1,123.2	1,256.1	1,111.6	1,122.4	1,390.5	1,862.6	2,527.3	2,662.0	3,400.0	3,334.0	3,079.0	3,714.1	4,882.4	Exports	70
	1,005.7	1,048.9	1,055.8	1,205.3	1,314.7	1,138.6	1,535.9	1,431.2	1,270.5	1,534.1	1,862.9	2,296.0	2,428.9	2,549.6	3,059.1	Imports, c.i.f.	71
	874.8	902.1	995.6	1,199.0	1,152.0	1,056.5	1,336.5	1,275.0	1,110.4	1,336.0	1,620.0	1,996.0	2,128.5	2,229.8	2,631.9	Imports, f.o.b.	71.v
1995=100																	
	62.0	70.1	71.9	69.9	73.1	67.3	89.2	102.7	103.9	103.8	100.0	93.4	83.8	....	....	Volume of Exports	72
	49.5	48.8	53.3	61.9	51.9	54.2	53.7	54.7	61.1	71.3	100.0	98.6	109.2	125.3	....	Unit Value of Exports	74
Minus Sign Indicates Debit																**Balance of Payments**	
	-121.8	-98.1	-197.9	-296.4	-312.7	-75.7	-475.3	-159.9	474.1	402.1	491.9	188.9	-192.2	-28.9	94.7	Current Account, n.i.e.	78al *d*
	926.3	1,030.7	1,243.9	1,475.3	1,318.5	1,175.2	1,482.1	1,947.7	2,604.4	2,651.0	2,670.4	2,529.8	2,160.1	1,773.3	1,927.4	Goods: Exports f.o.b.	78aa *d*
	-874.8	-928.8	-1,129.6	-1,384.5	-1,341.3	-1,105.9	-1,403.9	-1,322.9	-1,134.7	-1,324.9	-1,262.4	-1,513.3	-1,483.3	-1,078.3	-1,071.4	Goods: Imports f.o.b.	78ab *d*
	51.5	101.8	114.3	90.8	-22.8	69.2	78.1	624.9	1,469.7	1,326.1	1,408.0	1,016.6	676.8	695.0	856.0	*Trade Balance*	78ac *d*
	64.0	72.5	97.3	122.3	167.9	205.7	266.8	329.2	306.7	235.4	321.3	432.2	396.9	318.0	247.8	Services: Credit	78ad *d*
	-288.5	-302.7	-377.6	-435.1	-408.8	-402.9	-543.3	-685.8	-804.6	-608.0	-642.1	-778.5	-923.6	-793.8	-728.1	Services: Debit	78ae *d*
	-173.0	-128.3	-166.0	-222.0	-263.7	-128.0	-198.3	268.2	971.8	953.5	1,087.2	670.2	150.1	219.2	375.6	*Balance on Goods & Services*	78af *d*
	55.5	91.5	57.9	118.6	87.0	106.6	107.1	59.7	31.3	22.4	22.5	32.1	35.1	20.9	18.6	Income: Credit	78ag *d*
	-161.8	-227.2	-219.4	-326.2	-265.2	-209.9	-320.4	-425.3	-400.2	-423.4	-510.7	-461.2	-344.8	-279.7	-291.1	Income: Debit	78ah *d*
	-279.2	-264.0	-327.5	-429.6	-441.9	-231.2	-411.6	-97.5	603.0	552.5	599.1	241.1	-159.5	-39.6	103.1	*Balance on Gds, Serv. & Inc.*	78ai *d*
	247.3	248.8	238.4	249.4	256.3	273.7	42.5	48.6	49.0	58.8	66.7	252.1	69.9	82.4	60.3	Current Transfers, n.i.e.: Credit	78aj *d*
	-89.8	-82.9	-108.8	-116.2	-127.2	-118.1	-106.2	-111.1	-178.0	-209.3	-173.9	-304.2	-102.6	-71.6	-68.7	Current Transfers: Debit	78ak *d*
	-27.9	-31.9	-29.8	-40.1	-42.6	-37.3	—	—	—	—	—	—	—	—	—	Capital Account, n.i.e.	78bc *d*
	5.6	7.0	13.4	10.0	7.2	5.4	21.0	20.7	20.4	19.9	15.7	15.2	13.9	9.7	7.8	Capital Account, n.i.e.: Credit	78ba *d*
	-33.5	-38.9	-43.3	-50.1	-49.8	-42.7	-21.0	-20.7	-20.4	-19.9	-15.7	-15.2	-13.9	-9.7	-7.8	Capital Account: Debit	78bb *d*
	124.0	134.5	177.1	245.1	265.0	214.4	61.9	-149.0	-716.2	-609.2	-444.7	46.6	8.0	-179.7	16.0	Financial Account, n.i.e.	78bj *d*
	-.9	8.7	22.2	-33.8	17.9	—	—	—	—	—	—	—	—	—	—	Direct Investment Abroad	78bd *d*
	83.3	90.8	93.2	153.5	203.4	155.4	116.7	104.3	62.0	57.0	454.6	111.3	28.6	109.6	296.5	Dir. Invest. in Rep. Econ., n.i.e.	78be *d*
	—	—	—	—	—	—	-755.2	-1,256.4	-686.9	-839.1	-1,114.9	69.9	-25.5	87.0	89.0	Portfolio Investment Assets	78bf *d*
	—	—	—	—	—	—	—	—	—	—	—	—	—	—	....	Equity Securities	78bk *d*
	—	—	—	—	—	—	-755.2	-1,256.4	-686.9	-839.1	-1,114.9	69.9	-25.5	87.0	89.0	Debt Securities	78bl *d*
	—	—	—	—	—	—	658.8	1,274.9	636.0	837.1	1,066.2	—	—	—	—	Portfolio Investment Liab., n.i.e.	78bg *d*
	—	—	—	—	—	—	—	—	—	—	—	....	....	....	....	Equity Securities	78bm *d*
	—	—	—	—	—	—	658.8	1,274.9	636.0	837.1	1,066.2	—	—	—	—	Debt Securities	78bn *d*
																Financial Derivatives Assets	78bw *d*
																Financial Derivatives Liabilities	78bx *d*
	—	—	—	—	—	—	-64.3	7.0	17.3	58.8	-283.8	180.0	29.6	-55.0	10.7	Other Investment Assets	78bh *d*
																Monetary Authorities	78bo *d*
															-2.1	General Government	78bp *d*
																Banks	78bq *d*
	—	—	—	—	—	—	-64.3	7.0	17.3	58.8	-283.8	180.0	29.6	-55.0	12.8	Other Sectors	78br *d*
	41.6	35.0	61.7	125.4	43.7	59.0	105.9	-278.8	-744.5	-722.9	-566.8	-314.6	-24.7	-321.2	-380.2	Other Investment Liab., n.i.e.	78bi *d*
												-68.2				Monetary Authorities	78bs *d*
	44.9	35.5	54.8	27.2	-18.4	88.1	-38.6	59.6	66.5	-102.1	-23.5	10.0	-62.7	-44.2	39.4	General Government	78bt *d*
	3.3	-9.3	9.4	34.6	13.0	-23.4	—	-36.1	-110.3	-26.9	27.4	-34.0	-42.3	16.4	—	Banks	78bu *d*
	-6.7	8.8	-2.4	63.6	49.1	-5.6	144.4	-302.3	-700.8	-593.9	-570.7	-222.4	80.3	-293.4	-419.6	Other Sectors	78bv *d*
	24.3	-1.3	52.5	37.9	31.6	-79.7	4.0	-17.2	-11.3	37.1	-86.6	-33.1	7.3	-12.5	14.3	Net Errors and Omissions	78ca *d*
	-1.4	3.3	2.0	-53.5	-58.7	21.7	-409.4	-326.1	-253.4	-170.1	-39.5	202.5	-177.0	-221.0	125.0	*Overall Balance*	78cb *d*
	1.4	-3.3	-2.0	53.5	58.7	-21.7	409.4	326.1	253.4	170.1	39.5	-202.5	177.0	221.0	-125.0	Reserves and Related Items	79da *d*
	9.3	13.2	3.0	58.7	61.6	-75.2	85.3	71.1	96.6	33.8	-177.4	-329.7	83.7	149.1	-49.7	Reserve Assets	79db *d*
	-8.0	-16.5	-4.9	-5.2	-2.9	53.5	-.1	—	-15.0	-30.6	35.0	2.9	—	-4.2	-22.8	Use of Fund Credit and Loans	79dc *d*
	—	—	—	—	—	—	324.2	255.0	171.8	166.8	181.9	124.4	93.2	76.1	-52.5	Exceptional Financing	79de *d*
Year Ending December 31																**Government Finance**	
	I-55.54	-80.07	-38.79	I-32.60	-35.07	-106.65	-68.01	-220.38	-283.55	-124.90	-33.50	37.00	15.40	-137.40	-143.70	Deficit (-) or Surplus	80
	I707.12	755.52	821.84	I900.98	999.37	999.67	1,213.18	1,117.64	1,310.65	1,445.50	1,721.50	1,897.70	2,024.00	1,991.20	2,216.40	Total Revenue and Grants	81y
	I490.77	550.84	637.59	I711.11	809.65	777.58	901.47	921.32	1,128.95	1,282.20	1,484.80	1,727.60	1,891.00	1,877.70	2,090.60	Revenue	81
	I216.35	204.68	184.25	I189.87	189.72	222.09	311.71	196.32	181.70	163.30	236.70	170.10	133.00	113.50	125.80	Grants	81z
	I762.66	835.59	860.63	I933.58	1,034.44	1,106.32	1,281.19	1,338.02	1,594.20	1,570.40	1,755.00	1,860.70	2,008.60	2,128.60	2,360.10	Exp. & Lending Minus Repay.	82z
	I752.88	795.65	828.90	I890.00	987.84	1,066.52	1,273.56	1,348.69	1,588.71	1,570.60	1,753.80	1,864.70	2,011.30	2,133.50	2,364.70	Expenditure	82
	I9.78	39.94	31.73	I43.58	46.60	39.80	7.63	-10.67	5.49	-.20	1.20	-4.00	-2.70	-4.90	-4.60	Lending Minus Repayments	83
	I55.54	80.07	38.79	I32.60	35.07	106.65	68.01	220.38	283.55	124.90	33.50	-37.00	-15.40	137.40	143.70	Total Financing	80h
	I40.00	20.32	30.03	I42.90	30.41	93.15	125.17	181.52	237.83	243.40	77.10	-47.10	57.90	253.70	19.30	Domestic	84a
	I15.54	59.75	8.76	I-10.30	4.66	13.50	-57.16	38.86	45.72	-118.50	-43.60	10.10	-73.30	-116.30	124.40	Foreign	85a
	I1045.22	1,153.44	1,294.32	I1168.55	1,249.37	1,505.90	1,680.60	1,894.62	2,157.40	2,961.20	3,324.20	3,780.80	4,344.40	5,159.00	5,440.71	Total Debt by Residence	88
	I192.44	201.50	259.54	I286.80	374.02	412.38	564.39	676.41	1,036.60	1,424.30	1,605.70	1,969.50	2,251.70	2,473.00	2,019.71	Domestic	88a
	I852.78	951.94	1,034.78	I881.75	875.35	1,093.52	1,116.21	1,218.21	1,120.80	1,536.90	1,718.50	1,811.30	2,092.70	2,686.00	3,421.00	Foreign	89a
Millions of Kina																**National Accounts**	
	898	1,006	996	1,371	1,238	1,250	1,524	2,021	2,605	....	....	....	....	....	....	Exports of Goods & Services	90c
	520	511	527	663	745	764	853	1,005	1,199	....	....	....	....	....	....	Government Consumption	91f
	390	459	453	737	791	773	1,010	914	893	....	....	....	....	....	....	Gross Fixed Capital Formation	93e
	24	-24	25	126	-83	-21	-22	70	-50	....	....	....	....	....	....	Increase/Decrease(-) in Stocks	93i
	1,469	1,452	1,500	1,919	1,962	1,816	2,121	2,144	2,195	....	....	....	....	....	....	Private Consumption	96f
	-1,102	-1,079	-1,111	-1,646	-1,607	-1,506	-1,881	-1,930	-1,920	....	....	....	....	....	....	Imports of Goods & Services	98c
	2,200	2,325	2,389	3,170	3,046	3,076	3,606	4,223	5,016	5,531	6,442	6,948	6,651	7,161	....	Gross Domestic Product (GDP)	99b
	89	72	131	122	115	118	205	336	323	....	....	....	....	....	....	Net Factor Inc/Pmts(-) Abroad	98.n
	2,491	2,645	2,985	3,292	2,931	2,958	3,400	3,887	4,599	....	....	....	....	....	....	Gross National Income (GNI)	99a
	2,179	2,259	2,462	2,769	2,615	2,619	2,983	3,550	4,118	....	....	....	....	....	....	Net National Income	99e
	....	....	....	....	....	....	....	....	....							GDP Volume 1973 prices	99b.*p*
	....	....	....	....	....	....	....	....	....							GDP Volume 1977 prices	99b.*p*
	....	....	....	....	....	....	....	....	....							GDP Volume 1981 prices	99b.*p*
	2,200	2,325	2,389	2,458	2,423	2,351	2,575	2,931	3,323	....	....	....	....	....	....	GDP Volume 1983 Prices	99b.*p*
	93.6	98.9	101.6	104.6	103.1	100.0	109.5	124.7	141.3	....	....	....	....	....	....	GDP Volume (1990=100)	99bv *p*
	76.4	76.4	76.4	98.5	96.0	100.0	107.0	110.1	115.4	....	....	....	....	....	....	GDP Deflator (1990=100)	99bi *p*
Midyear Estimates																	
	3.34	3.41	3.48	3.56	3.63	3.70	3.77	3.85	3.92	4.00	4.07	4.40	I4.21	4.60	4.70	Population	99z

(See notes in the back of the book.)

Paraguay

		1970	1971	1972	1973	1974	1975	1976	1977	1978	1979	1980	1981	1982	1983	1984
Exchange Rates																*Guaranies per SDR:*
Market Rate..............aa= ....**wa**		126.0	136.8	136.8	152.0	154.3	147.5	146.4	153.1	164.2	166.0	160.7	146.7	139.0	131.9	235.3
														Guaranies per US Dollar:		
Market Rate..............ae= ....**we**		126.0	126.0	126.0	126.0	126.0	126.0	126.0	126.0	126.0	126.0	126.0	126.0	126.0	126.0	240.0
Market Rate..............rf= ....**wf**		126.0	126.0	126.0	126.0	126.0	126.0	126.0	126.0	126.0	126.0	126.0	126.0	126.0	126.0	201.0
Secondary Rate ....**xf**		....	....	....	....	136.4	138.3	138.6	134.0	138.6	139.3	136.1	148.4	160.5	160.0	321.8
Tertiary Rate ....**yf**		....	....	....	....									....	315.2	224.3
														Index Numbers (1995=100):		
Market Rate ....**ahx**		1,558.0	1,558.0	1,558.0	1,558.0	1,558.0	1,558.0	1,558.0	1,558.0	1,558.0	1,558.0	1,558.0	1,558.0	1,558.0	1,558.0	1,043.5
Nominal Effective Exchange Rate ....**ne c**		....	....	....	....	....	....	....	....	....	.3	.4	.6	.7	1.0	1.5
Real Effective Exchange Rate ....**re c**		....	....	....	....	....	....	....	....	....	....	171.4	187.9	164.3	156.5	153.9
Fund Position															*Millions of SDRs:*	
Quota ....**2f. s**		19.00	19.00	19.00	19.00	19.00	19.00	19.00	19.00	23.00	23.00	34.50	34.50	34.50	48.40	48.40
SDRs ....**1b. s**		2.52	4.55	6.57	6.57	6.57	6.57	6.57	6.58	6.64	9.41	11.05	15.09	23.67	30.41	35.03
Reserve Position in the Fund .....**1c. s**		4.77	4.77	4.77	4.77	4.77	4.77	5.77	6.62	6.48	8.19	14.88	25.16	27.64	32.25	32.25
Total Fund Cred.&Loans Outstg. **2tl**		—	—	—	—	—	—	—	—	—	—	—	—	—	—	—
International Liquidity												*Millions of US Dollars Unless Otherwise Indicated:*				
Total Reserves minus Gold ....**1l. d**		17.52	21.04	31.39	57.01	87.13	115.02	157.51	267.84	448.73	609.09	761.85	805.70	739.00	680.19	666.27
SDRs ....**1b. d**		2.52	4.94	7.13	7.93	8.04	7.69	7.63	7.99	8.65	12.40	14.09	17.56	26.11	31.84	34.34
Reserve Position in the Fund ....**1c. d**		4.77	5.18	5.18	5.75	5.84	5.58	6.70	8.04	8.44	10.79	18.98	29.29	30.49	33.76	31.61
Foreign Exchange ....**1d. d**		10.23	10.92	19.08	43.33	73.25	101.74	143.17	251.81	431.64	585.90	728.78	758.85	682.40	614.59	600.32
of which: US Dollars ....**1dx d**		7.55	2.73	13.86	16.14	47.53	93.99	116.26	111.67	226.32	288.89	404.33	456.22	453.02	334.72	482.86
Gold (Million Fine Troy Ounces) **1ad**		.002	.002	.002	.002	.002	.002	.002	.006	.011	.035	.035	.035	.035	.035	.035
Gold (National Valuation) **1and**		.08	.08	.09	.10	.10	.10	.10	.26	.45	4.36	4.62	4.30	4.05	3.88	2.96
Monetary Authorities: Other Assets .....**3. d**		.73	.91	.05	.03											
Other Liab. ..**4. d**		1.08	1.44	1.27	4.46	4.45	4.38	5.73	7.91	11.23	20.16	21.09	32.41	39.70	69.77	132.94
Deposit Money Banks: Assets ....**7a. d**		2.15	2.49	3.09	4.30	12.06	12.47	16.49	18.96	17.09	35.32	53.75	94.20	80.68	111.43	71.86
Liabilities ....**7b. d**		19.78	19.52	20.86	20.57	18.68	14.26	7.10	14.22	21.21	30.02	34.13	67.48	52.69	98.14	60.20
Other Banking Insts.: Assets ....**7e. d**		—	-.03	—	-.13	-.35	-.27	-.34	-.22	-.06	-.23	-.19	-.27	-.21	-.20	
Liabilities ....**7f. d**		40.98	45.19	52.50	59.96	69.91	81.89	84.46	93.19	103.22	116.98	131.34	136.20	164.48	173.98	107.86
Monetary Authorities															*Billions of Guaranies:*	
Foreign Assets **11**		2.33	2.78	4.00	7.20	10.99	14.51	19.85	33.78	56.60	77.29	96.58	102.06	86.54	85.98	109.41
Claims on Central Government **12a**		2.75	3.17	4.21	4.43	3.18	2.97	2.67	2.92	4.29	4.38	3.85	3.96	3.54	20.33	28.89
Claims on Local Government **12b**		....	....	....	....	....	....	....	....	....	....	....	....	....	....	....
Claims on Nonfin.Pub.Enterprises **12c**		2.79	2.60	2.89	2.58	3.02	3.64	3.17	2.69	2.79	2.97	7.65	8.25	9.19	9.31	12.87
Claims on Private Sector **12d**		1.81	1.85	1.84	1.85	1.91	1.87	1.99	2.02	2.02	2.01	2.08	2.19	2.24	2.78	2.74
Claims on Deposit Money Banks **12e**		.34	.35	.26	.52	.84	.64	.53	.76	2.27	3.74	6.76	9.62	7.81	11.84	22.19
Claims on Other Banking Insts...............**12f**		.49	1.28	1.54	1.98	2.78	3.26	4.03	3.68	3.09	3.37	3.03	3.75	10.06	11.09	13.34
Reserve Money **14**		8.61	9.71	11.84	15.04	17.69	21.74	26.24	34.47	45.89	56.16	71.59	84.24	84.75	111.03	130.02
of which: Currency Outside DMBs ..**14a**		4.02	4.41	5.14	6.49	7.55	8.90	10.29	13.34	18.69	24.31	31.18	31.15	33.17	38.47	48.60
Quasi-Monetary Deposits **15**		.13	.13	.15	.17	.20	.68	.69	.64	1.08	3.92	6.62	11.62	17.03	18.43	20.05
Restricted Deposits **16b**		.40	.31	.27	.45	.53	.46	.65	1.07	1.72	2.19	2.14	1.90	.87	.19	.25
Foreign Liabilities **16c**		.14	.18	.16	.56	.56	.55	.72	1.00	1.42	2.54	2.66	4.08	5.00	8.79	31.90
Long-Term Foreign Liabilities...............**16cl**		....	....	....	....	....	....	....	....	....	....	....	....	....	....	....
Central Government Deposits **16d**		.81	.92	1.00	1.24	1.89	2.12	2.18	5.37	12.15	19.04	21.18	9.23	5.47	5.08	5.78
Capital Accounts **17a**		.38	.64	.98	1.11	1.25	1.69	2.04	2.54	3.37	5.01	9.64	16.13	18.86	18.27	19.68
Other Items (Net)......................**17r**		.06	.14	.33	-.02	.62	-.37	-.30	.76	5.43	4.90	6.11	2.63	-12.60	-20.46	-18.24
Deposit Money Banks															*Billions of Guaranies:*	
Reserves **20**		4.23	5.12	6.45	8.17	9.86	12.50	15.75	20.77	26.64	30.47	38.66	52.83	50.75	69.74	78.27
Foreign Assets **21**		.27	.31	.39	.54	1.52	1.57	2.08	2.39	2.15	4.45	6.77	11.87	10.17	14.04	17.25
Claims on Central Government **22a**		—	—	—	—	—	—		.55	.97	.84	1.02	1.54	2.16	1.81	1.35
Claims on Local Government **22b**		....	....	....	....	....	....	....	....	....	....	....	....	....	....	....
Claims on Nonfin.Pub.Enterprises **22c**		....	....	....	....	....	....	....	....	....	....	....	....	....	....	....
Claims on Private Sector **22d**		7.99	9.11	9.85	12.45	14.56	17.78	21.72	28.05	40.66	53.88	77.34	89.50	94.41	99.68	116.59
Claims on Other Banking Insts...............**22f**		....	....	....	....	....	....	....	....	....	....	....	....	....	....	....
Demand Deposits **24**		2.93	3.21	4.04	5.60	7.28	8.55	11.03	14.69	20.30	23.29	28.57	29.28	25.70	34.92	44.76
Quasi-Monetary Liabilities......................**25**		6.08	7.27	9.27	11.64	14.06	18.58	23.47	30.94	37.60	44.04	62.27	82.73	88.46	99.41	108.08
Bonds **26ab**		....	....	....	....	....	....	....	....	....	....	....	....	....	....	....
Foreign Liabilities......................**26c**		2.30	1.83	1.54	1.92	1.89	1.54	.71	1.24	2.27	3.26	3.82	7.76	5.39	11.76	13.88
Long-Term Foreign Liabilities...............**26cl**		.19	.63	1.09	.67	.46	.25	.19	.55	.40	.52	.48	.74	1.25	.61	.57
Central Government Deposits **26d**		.01	.01	.03	.05	.04	.05	.07	.09	.11	.16	.20	.18	.13	.13	.15
Credit from Monetary Authorities **26g**		.42	.47	.29	.57	.90	.67	.54	.75	2.24	3.71	6.75	9.25	7.41	13.51	24.94
Liabilities to Other Banking Insts **26i**		....	....	....	....	....	....	....	....	....	....	....	....	....	....	....
Capital Accounts **27a**		2.10	2.55	2.56	2.78	3.90	4.92	5.68	7.19	9.91	16.13	21.29	26.77	30.36	30.54	32.79
Other Items (Net)......................**27r**		-1.53	-1.42	-2.13	-2.06	-2.60	-2.71	-2.13	-3.70	-2.40	-1.47	.42	-.96	-1.23	-5.61	-11.70
Monetary Survey															*Billions of Guaranies:*	
Foreign Assets (Net) **31n**		.16	1.08	2.69	5.26	10.06	13.99	20.49	33.93	55.07	75.94	96.87	102.09	86.31	79.47	80.87
Domestic Credit **32**		15.01	17.08	19.31	22.00	23.52	27.33	31.33	34.45	41.55	48.24	73.59	99.80	116.00	139.77	169.86
Claims on Central Govt. (Net) **32an**		1.93	2.24	3.19	3.14	1.25	.79	.42	-1.99	-7.00	-13.98	-16.51	-3.89	.10	16.92	24.31
Claims on Local Government **32b**		....	....	....	....	....	....	....	....	....	....	....	....	....	....	....
Claims on Nonfin.Pub.Enterprises **32c**		2.79	2.60	2.89	2.58	3.02	3.64	3.17	2.69	2.79	2.97	7.65	8.25	9.19	9.31	12.87
Claims on Private Sector.....................**32d**		9.80	10.96	11.68	14.30	16.47	19.64	23.71	30.07	42.67	55.88	79.42	91.69	96.65	102.45	119.33
Claims on Other Banking Insts **32f**		.49	1.28	1.54	1.98	2.78	3.26	4.03	3.68	3.09	3.37	3.03	3.75	10.06	11.09	13.34
Money **34**		7.31	7.85	9.42	12.49	15.12	17.83	21.59	28.57	39.81	49.54	62.36	62.43	60.20	75.59	97.81
Quasi-Money **35**		6.20	7.39	9.42	11.81	14.26	19.26	24.16	31.58	38.68	47.95	68.89	94.35	105.49	117.84	128.13
Bonds **36ab**		....	....	....	....	....	....	....	....	....	....	....	....	....	....	....
Restricted Deposits **36b**		.40	.31	.27	.45	.53	.46	.65	1.07	1.72	2.19	2.14	1.90	.87	.19	.25
Long-Term Foreign Liabilities...............**36cl**		.19	.63	1.09	.67	.46	.25	.19	.55	.40	.52	.48	.74	1.25	.61	.57
Liabilities to Other Banking Insts **36i**		....	....	....	....	....	....	....	....	....	....	....	....	....	....	....
Capital Accounts **37a**		2.48	3.19	3.54	3.90	5.15	6.61	7.72	9.73	13.28	21.14	30.93	42.90	49.22	48.81	52.46
Other Items (Net)......................**37r**		-1.40	-1.21	-1.75	-2.06	-1.94	-3.09	-2.49	-3.12	2.72	2.84	5.65	-.44	-14.72	-23.78	-28.48
Money plus Quasi-Money......................**35l**		13.51	15.24	18.84	24.30	29.38	37.09	45.75	60.15	78.49	97.49	131.26	156.79	165.69	193.43	225.94

Paraguay

288

1985	1986	1987	1988	1989	1990	1991	1992	1993	1994	1995	1996	1997	1998	1999		
															Exchange Rates	
End of Period																
351.5	672.8	780.3	740.1	1,600.6	1,789.7	1,974.0	2,241.3	2,582.3	2,809.8	2,942.7	3,033.6	3,184.2	3,999.1	4,568.9	Market Rate....................aa=	wa
End of Period (we) Period Average (wf)																
320.0	550.0	550.0	550.0	1,218.0	1,258.0	1,380.0	1,630.0	1,880.0	1,924.7	1,979.7	2,109.7	2,360.0	2,840.2	3,328.9	Market Rate....................ae=	we
306.7	339.2	550.0	550.0	1,056.2	1,229.8	1,325.2	1,500.3	1,744.3	1,904.8	1,963.0	2,056.8	2,177.9	2,726.5	3,119.1	Market Rate....................rf=	wf
602.8	700.3	....	....	....	....	....	....	....	....	....	....	....	....	....	Secondary Rate	xf
226.7	253.3	400.0	400.0	....	....	....	....	....	....	....	....	....	....	....	Tertiary Rate	yf
Period Averages																
647.5	592.0	356.9	356.9	201.7	159.7	149.0	127.4	112.7	103.1	100.0	95.5	90.2	72.2	63.2	Market Rate	ahx
2.1	2.5	2.8	6.1	13.4	32.2	40.5	49.6	67.3	98.4	100.0	99.7	101.1	85.1	78.7	Nominal Effective Exchange Rate	nec
133.0	133.1	105.7	113.2	84.3	85.0	95.5	92.9	94.2	98.5	100.0	104.1	109.4	100.4	97.7	Real Effective Exchange Rate	rec
															Fund Position	
End of Period																
48.40	48.40	48.40	48.40	48.40	48.40	48.40	72.10	72.10	72.10	72.10	72.10	72.10	72.10	99.90	Quota	2f.s
38.80	42.08	44.78	47.38	50.83	54.93	58.76	62.12	65.08	67.63	70.58	73.30	76.08	79.14	74.81	SDRs	1b.s
31.58	24.86	19.57	14.97	12.48	11.02	11.02	16.94	16.48	14.53	14.53	14.53	14.53	14.53	21.48	Reserve Position in the Fund	1c.s
—	—	—	—	—	—	—	—	—	—	—	—	—	—	—	Total Fund Cred.&Loans Outstg.	2tl
															International Liquidity	
End of Period																
533.62	446.67	497.02	323.66	432.55	661.42	962.12	561.53	631.18	1,030.73	1,092.91	1,049.29	835.67	864.74	987.26	Total Reserves minus Gold	1l.d
42.62	51.47	63.53	63.76	66.80	78.15	84.05	85.42	89.39	98.73	104.92	105.40	102.65	111.44	102.68	SDRs	1b.d
34.69	30.41	27.76	20.15	16.40	15.68	15.76	23.29	22.63	21.20	21.59	20.89	19.60	20.45	29.48	Reserve Position in the Fund	1c.d
456.31	364.79	405.73	239.76	349.35	567.60	862.30	452.82	519.16	910.80	966.40	923.00	713.42	732.85	855.10	Foreign Exchange	1d.d
336.89	268.20	106.23	81.13	50.27	382.15	462.70	329.34	416.00	583.80	602.40	415.53	521.25	561.87	745.50	*of which: US Dollars*	1dxd
.035	.035	.035	.035	.035	.035	.035	.035	.035	.035	.035	.035	.349	.035	.035	Gold (Million Fine Troy Ounces)	1ad
11.68	13.82	17.01	14.31	13.98	13.97	12.79	11.60	13.70	13.40	13.50	12.90	10.10	10.03	10.15	Gold (National Valuation)	1and
32.80	15.00	12.50	—	2.22	—	—	....	....	3.98	3.44	3.44	3.44	7.07	7.07	Monetary Authorities: Other Assets	3..d
48.59	32.68	47.80	51.48	24.51	24.36	59.49	61.66	63.21	58.84	113.17	86.37	91.16	61.87	37.42	Other Liab.	4..d
43.12	31.49	31.37	59.12	134.84	158.15	152.70	240.30	300.39	298.21	428.59	353.03	281.83	369.09	370.22	Deposit Money Banks: Assets	7a.d
44.18	18.39	9.02	34.56	20.91	23.29	48.47	89.18	147.37	124.57	385.53	190.24	225.54	216.07	103.40	Liabilities	7b.d
—	—	—	—	—	—	—	—	—	—	.34	.66	6.88	8.14	5.55	Other Banking Insts.: Assets	7e.d
94.78	62.35	70.60	64.44	41.65	46.38	52.18	41.51	36.40	32.78	30.70	31.97	29.03	29.92	27.09	Liabilities	7f.d
															Monetary Authorities	
End of Period																
100.01	167.05	168.56	I 135.19	537.60	853.59	1,292.09	993.43	1,289.15	2,016.58	2,346.36	2,346.75	2,107.75	2,590.13	3,352.45	Foreign Assets	11
32.52	39.03	49.25	I 27.38	103.34	230.46	76.98	794.81	916.73	1,047.15	1,038.99	1,086.17	1,193.56	880.19	1,061.62	Claims on Central Government	12a
....	....	....	1.11	1.08	.94	.89	.83	.82	.82	.67	.62	.62	.62	.62	Claims on Local Government	12b
25.51	35.25	65.51	I 106.49	176.53	142.32	185.73	242.74	266.79	222.35	239.15	268.00	284.18	305.64	313.56	Claims on Nonfin.Pub.Enterprises	12c
2.63	4.14	4.39	I 1.58	2.79	5.39	6.55	6.30	6.29	6.58	7.17	11.83	14.73	18.39	22.27	Claims on Private Sector	12d
20.52	51.60	45.91	I 93.26	111.10	117.11	112.10	170.29	102.77	98.07	761.72	920.26	1,211.57	1,092.19	1,025.71	Claims on Deposit Money Banks	12e
11.55	22.34	22.67	I 10.58	17.40	18.70	21.53	16.53	16.21	15.65	44.45	45.06	200.81	221.94	209.88	Claims on Other Banking Insts	12f
154.65	209.17	293.37	I 379.06	506.43	644.79	863.55	1,185.63	1,422.54	1,803.48	2,155.13	2,230.77	2,446.94	2,808.23	3,167.47	Reserve Money	14
62.61	84.48	119.57	I 149.10	216.19	300.52	379.92	531.26	635.77	800.46	956.00	961.77	1,122.90	1,264.08	1,398.68	*of which: Currency Outside DMBs*	14a
31.85	38.09	34.47	I —	—	32.74	80.60	50.75	75.70	66.43	238.65	381.37	356.92	425.64	94.27	Quasi-Monetary Deposits	15
.17	.15	.37	I 3.92	3.96	5.51	8.13	10.12	17.11	26.47	26.01	51.75	54.55	58.21	72.21	Restricted Deposits	16b
15.55	17.97	26.29	I 19.42	26.35	26.95	2.76	7.49	17.36	16.21	131.12	89.76	118.03	70.09	11.72	Foreign Liabilities	16c
....	....	....	1.17	3.01	3.02	75.58	92.09	98.31	96.99	93.52	92.39	94.37	105.63	112.33	Long-Term Foreign Liabilities	16cl
8.96	13.54	23.43	I 51.82	224.25	382.06	288.49	228.31	134.37	414.23	574.41	566.73	462.99	545.86	1,318.07	Central Government Deposits	16d
22.22	28.35	35.91	I 40.02	59.82	100.88	169.11	286.93	304.13	331.91	376.46	375.96	1,356.45	842.81	1,198.82	Capital Accounts	17a
-40.66	12.15	-57.55	I -119.83	126.02	172.59	207.63	363.63	529.23	651.47	843.21	889.96	122.95	252.63	11.23	Other Items (Net)	17r
															Deposit Money Banks	
End of Period																
84.28	117.09	174.02	I 209.06	264.24	301.07	411.01	588.19	752.52	948.78	1,201.54	1,399.29	1,454.64	1,612.62	1,686.44	Reserves	20
13.80	17.32	17.25	I 23.65	164.50	198.01	208.44	388.08	549.71	573.75	850.75	744.53	656.67	1,048.20	1,227.29	Foreign Assets	21
.81	.64	1.32	I .07	1.58	.33	.18	—	.18	—	40.95	85.82	174.63	272.54	429.76	Claims on Central Government	22a
....	....	....	—	—	.02	.02	.30	.55	.01	—	.69	2.97	1.94	1.23	Claims on Local Government	22b
....	....	....	.38	.34	1.71	1.88	1.79	1.45	1.46	—	—	—	.79	1.27	Claims on Nonfin.Pub.Enterprises	22c
128.66	170.19	215.12	I 350.06	492.99	768.44	1,226.37	1,705.83	2,315.36	3,164.92	3,742.70	4,596.49	5,159.90	5,015.15	5,545.98	Claims on Private Sector	22d
....	....	....	1.71	2.30	2.96	4.73	4.93	11.08	11.58	54.31	28.63	54.56	43.33	55.17	Claims on Other Banking Insts	22f
56.25	67.44	113.73	I 163.52	188.97	215.27	288.88	306.57	367.48	499.43	648.95	681.21	701.84	682.36	733.47	Demand Deposits	24
115.88	150.89	191.20	I 192.80	405.69	690.94	1,077.61	1,628.79	2,170.28	2,663.58	2,989.99	3,794.04	4,177.95	4,569.29	5,534.31	Quasi-Monetary Liabilities	25
....	....	....	2.76	1.53	3.10	7.00	2.21	4.00	3.76	3.69	1.23	—	1.97	8.81	Bonds	26ab
13.70	9.55	4.34	I 8.38	11.97	19.61	26.74	71.07	149.61	211.29	711.49	351.27	519.92	590.80	314.53	Foreign Liabilities	26c
.44	.56	.62	I 5.44	13.55	9.56	39.42	72.96	120.08	28.39	53.79	49.95	5.58	22.83	28.24	Long-Term Foreign Liabilities	26cl
.35	.64	.98	I 19.27	35.79	50.91	63.99	97.40	209.98	432.74	690.79	1,084.58	919.99	737.07	743.48	Central Government Deposits	26d
20.87	51.94	46.01	I 92.14	114.08	116.51	111.34	169.18	102.45	94.01	156.36	346.59	321.61	33.27	68.68	Credit from Monetary Authorities	26g
....	....	....	6.32	11.94	2.63	5.39	2.85	.86	.01	8.42	1.75	—	—	—	Liabilities to Other Banking Insts	26i
35.88	39.13	47.36	I 86.50	131.12	188.84	256.33	342.21	483.01	719.50	839.75	1,032.01	1,237.78	1,325.44	1,267.23	Capital Accounts	27a
-15.80	-14.92	3.48	I 7.80	11.32	-24.82	-24.07	-4.12	23.11	47.82	-212.98	-487.19	-381.31	31.56	248.40	Other Items (Net)	27r
															Monetary Survey	
End of Period																
84.55	156.84	155.18	I 131.03	663.79	1,005.04	1,471.02	1,302.95	1,671.89	2,362.84	2,354.49	2,650.25	2,126.47	2,977.45	4,253.50	Foreign Assets (Net)	31n
192.38	257.42	333.85	I 428.28	538.31	738.31	1,172.38	2,448.35	3,191.11	3,623.54	3,903.17	4,471.99	5,702.96	5,477.60	5,579.82	Domestic Credit	32
24.03	25.49	26.16	I -43.64	-155.12	-202.18	-275.31	469.10	572.56	200.17	-185.27	-479.33	-14.79	-130.19	-570.16	Claims on Central Govt. (Net)	32an
....	....	....	1.11	1.08	.96	.91	1.13	1.37	.83	.67	1.31	3.58	2.56	1.85	Claims on Local Government	32b
25.51	35.25	65.51	I 106.87	176.88	144.03	187.61	244.53	268.23	223.81	239.15	268.00	284.18	306.43	314.83	Claims on Nonfin.Pub.Enterprises	32c
131.30	174.33	219.51	I 351.64	495.78	773.83	1,232.92	1,712.14	2,321.65	3,171.50	3,749.87	4,608.32	5,174.62	5,033.54	5,568.25	Claims on Private Sector	32d
11.55	22.34	22.67	I 12.29	19.69	21.66	26.26	21.46	27.29	27.23	98.76	73.69	255.36	265.27	265.06	Claims on Other Banking Insts	32f
125.20	158.67	243.67	I 330.16	434.89	558.06	738.91	905.03	1,054.01	1,370.31	1,756.64	1,715.58	1,900.87	2,020.46	2,206.86	Money	34
147.73	188.98	225.67	I 192.80	405.69	723.67	1,158.21	1,679.54	2,245.98	2,730.01	3,228.64	4,175.41	4,534.87	4,994.93	5,628.57	Quasi-Money	35
....	....	....	2.76	1.53	3.10	7.00	2.21	4.00	3.76	3.69	1.23	—	1.97	8.81	Bonds	36ab
.17	.15	.37	I 3.92	3.96	5.51	8.13	10.12	17.11	26.47	26.01	51.75	54.55	58.21	72.21	Restricted Deposits	36b
.44	.56	.62	I 6.61	16.56	12.57	115.00	165.05	218.39	125.38	147.30	142.34	99.95	128.46	140.57	Long-Term Foreign Liabilities	36cl
....	....	....	6.32	11.94	2.63	5.39	2.85	.86	.01	8.42	1.75	—	—	—	Liabilities to Other Banking Insts	36i
58.09	67.48	83.26	I 126.52	190.93	289.71	425.44	629.13	787.14	1,051.41	1,216.21	1,407.97	2,594.23	2,168.25	2,466.05	Capital Accounts	37a
-54.70	-1.58	-64.55	I -109.78	136.59	148.09	185.32	357.37	535.53	679.04	-129.23	-373.80	-1,355.04	-917.22	-689.76	Other Items (Net)	37r
272.94	347.65	469.34	I 522.96	840.58	1,281.73	1,897.12	2,584.57	3,299.99	4,100.32	4,985.28	5,890.99	6,435.74	7,015.39	7,835.43	Money plus Quasi-Money	35l

Paraguay

		1970	1971	1972	1973	1974	1975	1976	1977	1978	1979	1980	1981	1982	1983	1984
Other Banking Institutions																*Billions of Guaranies:*
Reserves	40	—	—	—	—	—	—	—	—	—	—	—	.01	—	—	—
Foreign Assets	41	—	—	—	—	—	—	—	—	—	—	—	—	—	—	—
Claims on Central Government	42a	—	—	—	—	—	—	—	—	—	—	—	—	—	—	—
Claims on Local Government	42b	....	....	....	....	....	....	....	....	....	....	....	....	....	....	....
Claims on Nonfin.Pub.Enterprises	42c	....	....	....	....	....	....	....	....	....	....	....	....	....	....	....
Claims on Private Sector	42d	7.33	8.03	9.51	11.22	13.40	14.78	16.65	19.88	19.96	24.34	26.54	33.19	40.23	41.81	50.27
Claims on Deposit Money Banks	42e	.01	.01	.01	.01	—	.03	.01	.01	.01	.01	.01	—	.01	—	.02
Time, Savings,& Fgn.Currency Dep.	45	—	—	—	—	—	—	—	—	—	—	—	—	—	—	—
Bonds	46ab	—	—	—	—	—	—	—	—	—	—	—	—	—	—	—
Foreign Liabilities	46c	.14	.05	.19	.12	.01	.10	—	—	—	—	—	—	—	—	—
Long-Term Foreign Liabilities	46cl	5.02	5.65	6.43	7.44	8.80	10.22	10.64	11.74	13.01	14.74	16.55	17.16	20.72	21.92	25.89
Credit from Monetary Authorities	46g	.45	1.09	1.50	1.83	2.48	2.95	3.64	3.66	3.09	3.32	3.01	2.22	10.04	10.90	12.43
Credit from Deposit Money Banks	46h	—	—	.01	—	—	—	.01	.02	.02	.03	.03	.03	.01	—	—
Capital Accounts	47a	1.70	2.06	2.20	2.43	2.49	2.48	3.18	4.23	5.24	5.98	6.87	8.81	9.99	12.04	13.80
Other Items (Net)	47r	.02	−.81	−.79	−.60	−.37	−.93	−.81	.25	−1.38	.28	.09	4.98	−.51	−3.05	−1.83
Banking Survey																*Billions of Guaranies:*
Foreign Assets (Net)	51n	.02	1.03	2.50	5.13	10.01	13.85	20.45	33.90	55.06	75.91	96.85	102.05	86.29	79.44	80.87
Domestic Credit	52	21.70	23.62	27.07	31.04	33.92	38.62	43.35	50.65	58.42	69.20	97.10	129.24	146.17	170.49	206.79
Claims on Central Govt. (Net)	52an	1.78	2.04	2.98	2.94	1.02	.56	−.17	−1.99	−7.00	−13.98	−16.51	−3.89	.10	16.92	24.31
Claims on Local Government	52b	....	....	....	....	....	....	....	....	....	....	....	....	....	....	....
Claims on Nonfin.Pub.Enterprises	52c	2.79	2.60	2.89	2.58	3.02	3.64	3.17	2.69	2.79	2.97	7.65	8.25	9.19	9.31	12.87
Claims on Private Sector	52d	17.13	18.99	21.20	25.52	29.87	34.42	40.35	49.95	62.63	80.22	105.96	124.88	136.89	144.26	169.60
Liquid Liabilities	55l	13.51	15.25	18.84	24.30	29.38	37.09	45.75	60.15	78.50	97.49	131.25	156.78	165.69	193.42	225.94
Bonds	56ab	....	....	....	....	....	....	....	....	....	....	....	....	....	....	....
Restricted Deposits	56b	.40	.31	.27	.45	.53	.46	.65	1.07	1.72	2.19	2.14	1.90	.87	.19	.25
Long-Term Foreign Liabilities	56cl	5.21	6.28	7.52	8.11	9.27	10.47	10.83	12.29	13.41	15.26	17.03	17.90	21.97	22.53	26.45
Capital Accounts	57a	4.18	5.26	5.74	6.33	7.63	9.09	10.90	13.96	18.53	27.12	37.80	51.71	59.21	60.86	66.27
Other Items (Net)	57r	−1.58	−2.44	−2.80	−3.03	−2.88	−4.63	−4.33	−2.92	1.31	3.06	5.72	3.00	−15.29	−27.06	−31.25
Money (National Definitions)																*Millions of Pesos:*
Reserve Money	19ma	....	....	....	....	....	....	....	....	....	....	....	....	....	....	....
M1	59ma	....	....	....	....	....	....	....	....	....	....	....	....	....	....	....
M2	59mb	....	....	....	....	....	....	....	....	....	....	....	....	....	....	....
M3	59mc	....	....	....	....	....	....	....	....	....	....	....	....	....	....	....
M4	59md	....	....	....	....	....	....	....	....	....	....	....	....	....	....	....
M5	59me	....	....	....	....	....	....	....	....	....	....	....	....	....	....	....
Interest Rates																*Percent Per Annum*
Discount Rate *(End of Period)*	60	....	....	....	....	....	....	....	....	....	....	....	....	....	....	....
Money Market Rate	60b	....	....	....	....	....	....	....	....	....	....	....	....	....	....	....
Savings Rate	60k	....	....	....	....	....	....	....	....	....	....	....	....	....	....	....
Savings Rate (Fgn.Currency)	60k. *f*	....	....	....	....	....	....	....	....	....	....	....	....	....	....	....
Deposit Rate	60l	....	....	....	....	....	....	....	....	....	....	....	....	....	....	....
Deposit Rate (Fgn.Currency)	60l. *f*	....	....	....	....	....	....	....	....	....	....	....	....	....	....	....
Lending Rate	60p	....	....	....	....	....	....	....	....	....	....	....	....	....	....	....
Lending Rate (Fgn.Currency)	60p. *f*	....	....	....	....	....	....	....	....	....	....	....	....	....	....	....
Prices and Labor																*Index Numbers (1995=100):*
Producer Prices (1996=100)	63	....	....	....	....	....	....	....	....	....	....	....	....	....	....	....
Consumer Prices	64	1.8	1.9	2.0	2.3	2.9	3.0	3.2	3.5	3.9	4.9	6.1	6.9	7.4	8.4	10.0
																Number in Thousands:
Labor Force	67d	....	....	....	....	....	....	....	....	....	....	....	....	....	....	....
Employment	67e	....	....	....	....	....	....	....	....	....	....	....	....	....	....	....
Unemployment	67c	....	....	....	....	....	....	....	....	....	....	....	....	....	....	....
Unemployment Rate (%)	67r	....	....	....	....	....	....	....	....	....	....	....	....	....	....	....
International Transactions																*Millions of U.S. Dollars*
Exports	70.*d*	63.0	64.0	84.6	124.2	166.5	176.3	181.2	278.9	257.0	305.2	310.2	295.6	329.8	269.2	334.5
Imports, c.i.f.	71.*d*	76.2	83.2	82.6	122.3	198.3	205.6	220.2	308.3	383.0	521.1	614.7	599.6	672.0	545.9	586.0
Imports, f.o.b.	71.v*d*	63.8	70.3	69.9	104.8	171.4	178.4	180.2	255.4	317.7	437.7	517.1	506.1	581.5	478.3	513.1
																1990=100
Volume of Exports	72	60.7	58.1	67.0	11.0	17.5	17.5	30.1	37.1	33.6	51.6	40.6	37.9	68.5	66.5	67.8
																1985=100:
Unit Value of Exports	74	39.9	40.6	44.9	56.3	396.7	444.9	219.4	350.9	349.3	666.7	1,033.0	595.2	779.6	402.2	692.7

	1985	1986	1987	1988	1989	1990	1991	1992	1993	1994	1995	1996	1997	1998	1999		
Other Banking Institutions																	
End of Period																	
Reserves	—	—	—	‖16.58	21.25	12.13	13.57	26.85	30.25	51.64	78.45	97.43	99.37	93.47	93.93	Reserves	40
Foreign Assets	—	—	—	‖—	—	—	—	—	—	—	.68	1.39	16.03	23.11	18.39	Foreign Assets	41
Claims on Central Government	—	—	—	‖—	—	—	—	—	—	—	—	—	—	.10	2.87	Claims on Central Government	42a
Claims on Local Government	....	....	....	.29	1.99	—	—	—	—	—	—	—	—	—	.11	Claims on Local Government	42b
Claims on Nonfin.Pub.Enterprises	....	....	....	.01	—	—	—	—	—	—	—	—	—	—	—	Claims on Nonfin.Pub.Enterprises	42c
Claims on Private Sector	55.39	73.34	84.58	‖133.44	172.92	249.42	335.32	432.03	600.11	858.31	1,051.61	1,234.66	1,546.13	1,482.22	1,502.91	Claims on Private Sector	42d
Claims on Deposit Money Banks	.02	—	—	‖8.25	15.16	27.70	76.48	59.07	68.59	122.40	139.44	150.92	83.58	79.97	83.74	Claims on Deposit Money Banks	42e
Time, Savings,& Fgn.Currency Dep.	—	—	—	‖63.30	79.15	117.44	174.25	179.67	201.09	270.97	338.67	427.93	559.17	288.35	288.81	Time, Savings,& Fgn.Currency Dep.	45
Bonds	....	....	....	15.50	21.13	10.74	14.04	58.71	119.50	222.27	331.84	323.50	322.36	312.38	275.21	Bonds	46ab
Foreign Liabilities	—	—	—	‖—	—	—	—	—	—	—	—	—	—	6.01	1.93	Foreign Liabilities	46c
Long-Term Foreign Liabilities	30.33	34.29	38.83	‖25.78	50.81	58.07	71.22	67.03	66.62	63.06	60.94	67.43	67.65	78.97	87.88	Long-Term Foreign Liabilities	46cl
Credit from Monetary Authorities	11.50	18.74	22.57	‖10.38	16.31	15.67	12.57	11.57	11.57	11.89	23.15	22.74	92.27	104.91	99.07	Credit from Monetary Authorities	46g
Credit from Deposit Money Banks	.02	—	—	‖.43	.49	1.74	4.08	1.41	2.31	1.77	3.62	1.64	4.23	2.30	58.04	Credit from Deposit Money Banks	46h
Capital Accounts	14.38	19.59	29.42	‖47.92	50.70	93.32	165.24	234.45	273.00	422.30	604.62	754.00	851.61	956.89	989.84	Capital Accounts	47a
Other Items (Net)	−.81	.72	−6.23	‖−4.74	−7.25	−7.72	−16.03	−34.89	24.87	40.09	−92.67	−112.84	−152.19	−70.94	−98.80	Other Items (Net)	47r
Banking Survey																	
End of Period																	
Foreign Assets (Net)	84.55	156.84	155.18	‖131.03	663.79	1,005.04	1,471.02	1,302.95	1,671.89	2,362.84	2,355.18	2,651.64	2,142.49	2,994.55	4,269.97	Foreign Assets (Net)	51n
Domestic Credit	236.23	308.42	395.76	‖549.72	693.53	966.06	1,481.44	2,858.92	3,763.93	4,454.62	4,856.02	5,632.95	6,993.72	6,694.65	6,820.66	Domestic Credit	52
Claims on Central Govt. (Net)	24.03	25.49	26.16	‖−43.64	−155.12	−202.18	−275.31	469.10	572.56	200.17	−185.27	−479.33	−14.79	−130.10	−567.29	Claims on Central Govt. (Net)	52an
Claims on Local Government	....	....	....	1.40	3.07	.96	.91	1.13	1.37	.83	.67	1.31	3.58	2.56	1.96	Claims on Local Government	52b
Claims on Nonfin.Pub.Enterprises	25.51	35.25	65.51	‖106.88	176.88	144.03	187.61	244.53	268.23	223.81	239.15	268.00	284.18	306.43	314.83	Claims on Nonfin.Pub.Enterprises	52c
Claims on Private Sector	186.69	247.67	304.09	‖485.08	668.70	1,023.25	1,568.24	2,144.16	2,921.76	4,029.80	4,801.48	5,842.98	6,720.75	6,515.76	7,071.16	Claims on Private Sector	52d
Liquid Liabilities	272.94	347.65	469.34	‖569.68	898.48	1,387.03	2,057.80	2,737.39	3,470.82	4,319.65	5,245.50	6,221.49	6,895.54	7,210.27	8,030.31	Liquid Liabilities	55l
Bonds	....	....	....	18.25	22.66	13.84	21.04	60.92	123.49	226.03	335.53	324.73	322.36	314.34	284.02	Bonds	56ab
Restricted Deposits	.17	.15	.37	‖3.92	3.96	5.51	8.13	10.12	17.11	26.47	26.01	51.75	54.55	58.21	72.21	Restricted Deposits	56b
Long-Term Foreign Liabilities	30.77	34.86	39.45	‖32.39	67.37	70.64	186.22	232.08	285.01	188.44	208.24	209.77	167.60	207.43	228.45	Long-Term Foreign Liabilities	56cl
Capital Accounts	72.47	87.07	112.68	‖174.43	241.63	383.03	590.68	863.58	1,060.14	1,473.72	1,820.83	2,161.97	3,445.83	3,125.14	3,455.89	Capital Accounts	57a
Other Items (Net)	−55.56	−4.46	−70.89	‖−117.92	123.22	111.05	88.59	257.78	479.25	583.15	−424.91	−685.12	−1,749.67	−1,226.19	−980.25	Other Items (Net)	57r
Money (National Definitions)																	
End of Period																	
Reserve Money	143.50	201.11	286.90	354.31	450.74	547.12	687.58	901.98	1,053.31	1,342.25	1,650.91	1,703.49	1,831.80	1,987.33	2,138.55	*Reserve Money*	19ma
M1	114.83	146.61	211.92	262.57	374.50	490.57	625.17	803.58	958.33	1,272.60	1,539.36	1,570.67	1,789.14	1,922.27	2,103.85	*M1*	59ma
M2	215.43	275.63	349.41	421.97	593.31	780.80	1,056.90	1,356.55	1,563.47	2,166.15	2,827.35	3,204.72	3,437.43	3,341.82	3,706.11	*M2*	59mb
M3	223.93	290.33	366.02	439.95	768.49	1,071.34	1,511.25	2,112.67	2,720.04	3,499.99	4,201.08	5,121.65	5,848.77	6,383.03	7,532.20	*M3*	59mc
M4	....	....	....	....	....	1,074.44	1,518.25	2,114.88	2,725.30	3,503.75	4,204.77	5,122.88	5,848.77	6,385.00	7,541.01	*M4*	59md
M5	....	....	....	....	....	1,164.68	1,684.19	2,320.51	2,970.03	3,693.60	4,381.96	5,262.52	5,849.76	6,385.00	7,541.01	*M5*	59me
Interest Rates																	
Percent Per Annum																	
Discount Rate (*End of Period*)	....	....	....	10.00	21.00	‖33.00	19.75	24.00	27.17	19.15	20.50	15.00	20.00	20.00	20.00	Discount Rate (*End of Period*)	60
Money Market Rate	....	....	....	....	....	....	12.39	21.59	22.55	18.64	20.18	16.35	12.48	20.74	17.26	Money Market Rate	60b
Savings Rate	....	....	....	....	....	10.50	12.04	10.37	10.60	‖12.00	11.53	9.92	6.93	5.12	6.06	Savings Rate	60k
Savings Rate (Fgn.Currency)	....	....	....	....	....	....	....	....	....	4.27	4.68	4.08	3.22	2.74	2.40	Savings Rate (Fgn.Currency)	60k. f
Deposit Rate	....	....	....	....	....	22.92	22.53	20.15	22.10	23.12	21.16	17.16	13.00	15.95	‖19.75	Deposit Rate	60l
Deposit Rate (Fgn.Currency)	....	....	....	....	....	....	....	....	....	....	....	....	....	8.01	7.27	Deposit Rate (Fgn.Currency)	60l. f
Lending Rate	....	....	....	....	....	31.00	34.94	27.96	30.78	‖35.47	33.94	31.88	27.79	30.49	30.21	Lending Rate	60p
Lending Rate (Fgn.Currency)	....	....	....	....	....	....	....	....	....	12.68	14.03	14.35	13.53	13.03	12.17	Lending Rate (Fgn.Currency)	60p. f
Prices and Labor																	
Period Averages																	
Producer Prices (1996=100)	....	....	....	....	....	....	....	....	....	....	....	100.0	101.2	116.2	122.4	Producer Prices (1996=100)	63
Consumer Prices	12.6	16.6	20.2	24.8	31.3	‖43.2	53.7	61.9	73.1	88.2	100.0	109.8	117.5	131.0	139.9	Consumer Prices	64
Period Averages																	
Labor Force	....	....	....	....	....	....	515	....	587	‖1,053	....	....	....	....	....	Labor Force	67d
Employment	407	412	426	448	490	486	495	522	570	‖1,050	....	1,190	....	....	....	Employment	67e
Unemployment	22	27	25	22	32	34	27	29	30	‖48	....	106	....	....	....	Unemployment	67c
Unemployment Rate (%)	5.1	6.1	5.5	4.7	6.1	6.6	5.1	5.3	5.1	‖4.4	....	8.2	....	....	....	Unemployment Rate (%)	67r
International Transactions																	
Millions of U.S. Dollars																	
Exports	303.9	233.5	353.4	509.9	1,005.9	958.7	737.1	656.6	725.2	816.8	919.2	1,043.5	1,088.6	....	....	Exports	70..d
Imports, c.i.f.	501.5	578.1	595.3	573.9	759.7	1,352.0	1,460.3	1,421.6	1,688.8	2,370.2	3,143.8	3,203.9	3,403.0	....	....	Imports, c.i.f.	71..d
Imports, f.o.b.	442.3	509.4	517.5	494.8	660.8	1,193.4	1,275.4	1,237.2	1,477.5	2,140.4	2,782.2	2,850.5	2,957.1	....	....	Imports, f.o.b.	71.v d
1990=100																	
Volume of Exports	100.0	91.3	142.4	166.6	245.1	243.0	149.1	128.3	182.6	161.8	....	....	....	....	....	Volume of Exports	72
Indexes of Unit Values in Guaranies																	
Unit Value of Exports	100.0	74.3	183.4	246.1	527.1	....	....	....	....	....	....	....	....	....	....	Unit Value of Exports	74

		1970	1971	1972	1973	1974	1975	1976	1977	1978	1979	1980	1981	1982	1983	1984
Balance of Payments																*Millions of US Dollars:*
Current Account, n.i.e.	78ald	....	....	....	....	....	-72.2	-68.5	-58.6	-112.9	-205.9	-277.0	-373.5	-374.8	-247.9	-317.4
Goods: Exports f.o.b.	78aad	....	....	....	....	....	188.0	202.1	327.1	356.1	384.5	400.3	398.5	396.2	326.0	361.3
Goods: Imports f.o.b.	78abd	....	....	....	....	....	-227.3	-236.4	-360.0	-432.0	-577.1	-675.3	-772.4	-711.3	-551.4	-649.1
Trade Balance	78acd	....	....	....	....	....	-39.3	-34.3	-32.9	-75.9	-192.6	-275.0	-373.9	-315.1	-225.4	-287.8
Services: Credit	78add	....	....	....	....	....	34.1	39.9	62.9	78.2	129.1	164.0	156.2	120.4	138.0	210.8
Services: Debit	78aed	....	....	....	....	....	-55.1	-57.8	-72.1	-95.6	-154.2	-165.1	-203.9	-250.3	-157.4	-211.9
Balance on Goods & Services	78afd	....	....	....	....	....	-60.3	-52.2	-42.1	-93.3	-217.7	-276.1	-421.6	-445.0	-244.8	-288.9
Income: Credit	78agd	....	....	....	....	....	11.7	15.8	29.6	54.8	80.1	126.8	163.8	162.7	96.0	93.9
Income: Debit	78ahd	....	....	....	....	....	-37.6	-36.3	-47.3	-80.2	-75.7	-132.3	-121.5	-97.5	-105.3	-131.7
Balance on Gds, Serv. & Inc.	78aid	....	....	....	....	....	-86.2	-72.7	-59.8	-118.7	-213.3	-281.6	-379.3	-379.8	-254.1	-326.7
Current Transfers, n.i.e.: Credit	78ajd	....	....	....	....	....	16.0	7.1	3.8	8.5	10.0	8.7	8.5	5.9	6.8	9.8
Current Transfers: Debit	78akd	....	....	....	....	....	-2.0	-2.9	-2.6	-2.7	-2.6	-4.1	-2.7	-.9	-.6	-.5
Capital Account, n.i.e.	78bcd	....	....	....	....	....	—	—	—	—	—	—	—	—	—	—
Capital Account, n.i.e.: Credit	78bad	....	....	....	....	....	—	—	—	—	—	—	—	—	—	—
Capital Account: Debit	78bbd	....	....	....	....	....	—	—	—	—	—	—	—	—	—	—
Financial Account, n.i.e.	78bjd	....	....	....	....	....	96.9	111.3	191.0	274.2	358.7	447.6	430.1	338.2	287.3	286.0
Direct Investment Abroad	78bdd	....	....	....	....	....		-25.0		-5.0						
Dir. Invest. in Rep. Econ., n.i.e.	78bed	....	....	....	....	....	24.4	22.0	21.7	24.6	50.2	31.7	31.9	36.6	4.9	5.2
Portfolio Investment Assets	78bfd	....	....	....	....	....	—	—	—	—	—	—	—	—	—	—
Equity Securities	78bkd	....	....	....	....	....	—	—	—	—	—	—	—	—	—	—
Debt Securities	78bld	....	....	....	....	....	—	—	—	—	—	—	—	—	—	—
Portfolio Investment Liab., n.i.e.	78bgd	....	....	....	....	....	—	—	—	—	—	—	5.9	-7.5	3.3	—
Equity Securities	78bmd	....	....	....	....	....	—	—	—	—	—	—	5.9	-7.5	3.3	—
Debt Securities	78bnd	....	....	....	....	....	—	—	—	—	—	—	—	—	—	—
Financial Derivatives Assets	78bwd	....	....	....	....	....										
Financial Derivatives Liabilities	78bxd	....	....	....	....	....										
Other Investment Assets	78bhd	....	....	....	....	....	22.2	9.4	74.0	106.4	130.7	191.2	182.6	175.5	131.6	97.0
Monetary Authorities	78bod	....	....	....	....	....										
General Government	78bpd	....	....	....	....	....										
Banks	78bqd	....	....	....	....	....	-.4	-4.0	-.6	.3	-17.4	-18.7	-40.9	15.5	-14.8	11.8
Other Sectors	78brd	....	....	....	....	....	22.6	13.4	74.6	106.1	148.1	209.9	223.5	160.0	146.4	85.2
Other Investment Liab., n.i.e.	78bid	....	....	....	....	....	50.3	104.9	95.3	148.2	177.8	224.7	209.7	133.6	147.5	183.8
Monetary Authorities	78bsd	....	....	....	....	....	-2.9	-.9	3.5	7.2	14.8	3.3	11.8	10.5	22.9	97.4
General Government	78btd	....	....	....	....	....	19.5	35.9	30.7	56.1	9.9	85.8	39.3	60.5	138.7	126.9
Banks	78bud	....	....	....	....	....	4.5	-9.7	4.4	8.5	11.2	5.4	38.2	-4.3	36.9	14.7
Other Sectors	78bvd	....	....	....	....	....	29.2	79.6	56.7	76.4	141.9	130.2	120.4	66.9	-51.0	-55.2
Net Errors and Omissions	78cad	....	....	....	....	....	3.9	-.4	-20.6	17.1	8.9	-20.1	-13.1	-25.7	-92.3	17.6
Overall Balance	78cbd	....	....	....	....	....	28.6	42.4	111.8	178.4	161.7	150.5	43.5	-62.3	-52.9	-13.8
Reserves and Related Items	79dad	....	....	....	....	....	-28.6	-42.4	-111.8	-178.4	-161.7	-150.5	-43.5	62.3	52.9	13.8
Reserve Assets	79dbd	....	....	....	....	....	-28.6	-42.4	-111.8	-178.4	-161.7	-150.5	-43.5	62.3	52.9	13.8
Use of Fund Credit and Loans	79dcd	....	....	....	....	....										
Exceptional Financing	79ded	....	....	....	....	....										
Government Finance																*Billions of Guaranies:*
Deficit (-) or Surplus	80	.2	-.3	‡-1.6	—	1.7	-.6	-2.2	1.6	3.1	4.3	1.8	-10.6	3.0	-7.7	-20.4
Revenue	81	8.8	9.0	‡11.0	13.5	18.4	21.2	23.9	31.4	40.5	51.2	62.0	72.7	85.8	84.0	102.2
Grants Received	81z	....	....	‡—						.3		.2	.1	.1		.3
Expenditure	82	8.7	9.3	‡12.4	13.3	16.3	21.2	25.3	29.2	37.7	45.5	56.8	75.6	86.7	87.3	115.4
Lending Minus Repayments	83			‡.2	.2	.4	.6	.9	.5	.1	1.4	3.5	7.8	-3.8	4.4	5.6
Exch.Rate Adj.to Overall Def./Sur	80x			‡—	—	—	—	—	—	—	—	—	—	—	—	-1.9
Financing																
Net Borrowing	84	—	.4	....	....											
Net Borrowing: Domestic	84a	....	....	‡1.1	.3	-1.3	-.1	-.3	.4	1.1	1.6	-.4	-1.8	-.9	-6.1	2.0
Foreign	85a	....	....	‡1.7	.1	.5	2.0	4.7	3.2	5.7	2.9	12.8	4.9	.6	13.9	18.4
Use of Cash Balances	87	-.1	-.1	‡-1.1	-.3	-.9	-1.4	-2.2	-5.2	-9.9	-8.8	-14.3	7.5	-2.7	....	....
Debt: Domestic	88a	....	....	....	4.2	2.8	2.5	2.5	3.0	4.4	5.9	4.3	4.4	4.0	....	....
Foreign	89a	....	....	....	7.3	7.5	9.2	13.5	16.3	22.0	24.9	37.8	42.8	43.5	....	....
National Accounts																*Billions of Guaranies:*
Exports of Goods & Services	90c	11.2	11.2	13.3	18.8	26.1	29.3	31.4	51.3	59.4	69.1	77.6	79.1	89.5	70.1	170.0
Government Consumption	91f	6.8	7.1	7.8	8.2	9.2	12.0	13.4	16.4	21.5	24.7	34.7	48.6	52.3	58.0	69.3
Gross Fixed Capital Formation	93e	10.9	11.8	13.3	20.4	30.9	39.5	48.8	62.9	81.3	116.1	152.7	194.2	176.9	164.5	231.2
Increase/Decrease(-) in Stocks	93i	.2	.4	1.3	3.5	4.4	6.4	4.0	2.2	6.5	6.8	8.6	10.1	12.1	10.7	14.3
Private Consumption	96f	58.0	66.6	74.6	92.5	126.3	141.1	155.2	190.1	225.2	306.5	399.4	504.1	552.0	642.2	822.0
Imports of Goods & Services	98c	-12.1	-13.4	-13.4	-17.9	-28.8	-37.8	-38.6	-59.2	-71.3	-92.8	-112.4	-127.4	-145.6	-127.4	-236.3
Gross Domestic Product (GDP)	99b	74.9	83.7	96.9	125.4	168.0	190.4	214.1	263.6	322.5	430.5	560.5	708.7	737.0	818.1	1,070.4
Net Factor Inc/Pmts(-) Abroad	98.n	-1.8	-1.6	-2.0	-2.1	-2.0	-1.5	-1.1	.4	1.8	1.3	5.3	8.8	8.3	5.0	-2.4
Gross National Income (GNI)	99a	73.1	82.1	95.0	123.3	166.0	188.9	213.0	264.0	324.3	431.8	565.7	717.5	745.3	823.1	1,068.0
Net National Income	99e	69.1	77.9	89.9	116.8	158.4	179.1	199.0	239.4	292.1	382.6	507.1	639.8	671.0	750.9	960.1
GDP Volume 1982 Prices	99b.p	295.3	312.2	333.1	358.0	388.5	416.5	446.7	495.5	551.7	614.4	684.7	744.4	737.0	714.9	736.9
GDP Volume (1995=100)	99bvp	27.2	28.7	30.6	32.9	35.7	38.3	41.1	45.6	50.7	56.5	63.0	68.5	67.8	65.7	67.8
GDP Deflator (1995=100)	99bip	1.6	1.6	1.8	2.2	2.7	2.8	2.9	3.3	3.6	4.3	5.0	5.8	6.1	7.0	8.9
																Millions:
Population	99z	2.30	2.36	2.43	2.50	2.57	2.69	2.78	2.87	2.95	3.05	3.15	3.25	3.36	3.47	3.58

Minus Sign Indicates Debit

1985	1986	1987	1988	1989	1990	1991	1992	1993	1994	1995	1996	1997	1998	1999	Balance of Payments	
−251.7	−364.9	−489.8	−210.2	255.6	390.1	85.1	−57.3	59.1	−274.1	−279.2	−495.1	−238.2	−106.4	....	Current Account, n.i.e.	78al *d*
465.6	575.8	597.4	871.0	1,180.0	2,096.2	1,997.1	1,997.1	2,859.0	3,360.1	4,295.5	3,880.3	3,980.0	3,824.1	....	Goods: Exports f.o.b.	78aa *d*
−659.3	−864.2	−918.7	−1,030.1	−1,015.9	−1,734.8	−1,920.5	−1,988.0	−2,779.6	−3,603.5	−4,489.1	−4,383.2	−4,186.8	−3,938.0	....	Goods: Imports f.o.b.	78ab *d*
−193.7	−288.4	−321.3	−159.1	164.1	361.4	76.6	9.1	79.4	−243.4	−193.6	−502.9	−206.8	−113.9	....	*Trade Balance*	78ac *d*
152.7	183.8	172.1	295.9	394.9	418.2	433.3	364.6	438.6	426.2	502.4	506.0	525.4	489.2	....	Services: Credit	78ad *d*
−180.3	−224.9	−256.3	−300.8	−303.5	−434.2	−460.3	−464.5	−592.8	−593.4	−735.9	−646.4	−644.4	−562.0	....	Services: Debit	78ae *d*
−221.3	−329.5	−405.5	−164.0	255.5	345.4	49.6	−90.8	−74.8	−410.6	−427.1	−643.3	−325.8	−186.7	....	*Balance on Goods & Services*	78af *d*
68.5	70.5	50.3	56.7	88.7	116.3	115.6	157.4	198.3	247.9	299.1	298.2	292.1	256.9	....	Income: Credit	78ag *d*
−106.8	−117.0	−161.5	−138.0	−112.1	−114.6	−125.3	−185.7	−142.6	−134.1	−211.6	−195.3	−244.2	−211.3	....	Income: Debit	78ah *d*
−259.6	−376.0	−516.7	−245.3	232.1	347.1	39.9	−119.1	−19.1	−296.8	−339.6	−540.4	−277.9	−141.1	....	*Balance on Gds, Serv. & Inc.*	78ai *d*
9.2	11.9	28.6	37.7	24.3	43.3	46.6	62.1	78.6	25.6	64.8	46.1	41.0	35.7	....	Current Transfers, n.i.e.: Credit	78aj *d*
−1.3	−.8	−1.7	−2.6	−.8	−.3	−1.4	−.3	−.4	−2.9	−4.4	−.8	−1.3	−1.0	....	Current Transfers: Debit	78ak *d*
−.4	—	.1	.1	.4	12.6	9.8	10.4	22.1	8.8	11.8	14.7	8.6	5.4	....	Capital Account, n.i.e.	78bc *d*
.1	—	.1	.2	.4	12.6	9.8	10.4	22.1	8.8	11.8	14.7	8.6	5.4	....	Capital Account, n.i.e.: Credit	78ba *d*
−.5	—	—	−.1	....	....	....	....	....	....	....	....	....	....	....	Capital Account: Debit	78bb *d*
38.6	114.7	78.1	−216.5	−173.9	−147.5	22.2	16.1	8.5	212.9	131.5	−39.7	623.6	375.6	....	Financial Account, n.i.e.	78bj *d*
—														....	Direct Investment Abroad	78bd *d*
.7	.6	5.3	8.4	12.8	76.9	86.1	117.5	75.0	137.1	155.4	245.7	269.5	256.3	....	Dir. Invest. in Rep. Econ., n.i.e.	78be *d*
										−.8	−3.6	4.1	−10.5	....	Portfolio Investment Assets	78bf *d*
										−.8	−3.6	4.1	−10.5	....	Equity Securities	78bk *d*
														....	Debt Securities	78bl *d*
														....	Portfolio Investment Liab., n.i.e.	78bg *d*
														....	Equity Securities	78bm *d*
														....	Debt Securities	78bn *d*
															Financial Derivatives Assets	78bw *d*
															Financial Derivatives Liabilities	78bx *d*
69.5	2.5	68.4	−49.0	−63.5	−49.7	−28.1	−48.4	−65.4	−89.8	21.4	2.0	114.7	−63.0	....	Other Investment Assets	78bh *d*
				−2.5	−2.7	1.6	....	.1	.5				−3.6		Monetary Authorities	78bo *d*
—	−15.0	2.5	−52.4	−54.8	−22.8	−21.3	27.6	1.6	23.1	−49.4	−64.5	−3.2	50.2		General Government	78bp *d*
18.5	−27.8	.3	3.4	−8.7	−24.4	3.5	−85.2	−75.2	−1.5	−86.3	19.7	126.8	−68.9		Banks	78bq *d*
51.0	45.3	65.6			−7.6	7.6	8.2	−111.5	156.6	46.8	−8.9	−40.7			Other Sectors	78br *d*
−31.6	111.6	4.4	−175.9	−123.2	−174.7	−35.8	−53.0	−1.1	165.6	−44.5	−283.8	235.3	192.8	....	Other Investment Liab., n.i.e.	78bi *d*
−47.7	−22.4	4.5	−53.3	6.1	−8.8	50.9	1.8	2.1	−1.6	−8.7	−3.5	−5.0	−4.3	....	Monetary Authorities	78bs *d*
97.1	110.5	−12.8	−11.5	−71.9	−46.7	−51.8	−4.1	−2.6	29.8	68.0	89.2	82.4	74.7	....	General Government	78bt *d*
33.6	−20.1	1.4	−5.4	−10.9	.3	46.9	20.5	−94.2	97.3	−42.5	−311.1	144.2	−8.5	....	Banks	78bu *d*
−114.6	43.6	11.3	−105.7	−46.5	−119.5	−81.8	−71.2	93.6	40.1	−61.3	−58.4	13.7	130.9	....	Other Sectors	78bv *d*
73.7	43.8	338.3	198.3	−90.6	−138.5	115.7	11.9	−46.4	353.0	197.3	380.0	−590.4	−174.3	....	Net Errors and Omissions	78ca *d*
−139.8	−206.4	−73.3	−228.3	−8.5	116.7	232.8	−18.9	43.3	300.6	61.4	−140.1	−196.4	100.3	....	*Overall Balance*	78cb *d*
139.8	206.4	73.3	228.3	8.5	−116.7	−232.8	18.9	−43.3	−300.6	−61.4	140.1	196.4	−100.3	....	Reserves and Related Items	79da *d*
97.8	139.8	−37.8	168.2	−145.2	−220.3	−299.3	360.2	−87.2	−339.3	−60.3	40.0	208.6	−23.4	....	Reserve Assets	79db *d*
														....	Use of Fund Credit and Loans	79dc *d*
42.0	66.6	111.1	60.1	153.7	103.6	66.5	−341.3	43.9	38.7	−1.1	100.1	−12.2	−76.9	....	Exceptional Financing	79de *d*

Year Ending December 31

1985	1986	1987	1988	1989	1990	1991	1992	1993	1994	1995	1996	1997	1998	1999	Government Finance	
−6.9	.5	−1.0	21.7	Ɪ112.5	189.6	−12.9	77.7	138.7	....	....	....	....	....	....	Deficit (−) or Surplus	80
135.3	178.6	253.0	323.1	Ɪ524.4	796.3	979.7	1,391.6	1,688.0	....	....	....	....	....	....	Revenue	81
.2	.1	.3	.6	Ɪ1.7	1.1	1.6	3.0	4.0	....	....	....	....	....	....	Grants Received	81z
126.7	148.3	224.7	295.4	Ɪ412.2	608.8	991.5	1,307.4	1,559.4	....	....	....	....	....	....	Expenditure	82
6.1	5.2	7.8	6.6	Ɪ1.4	−1.0	2.7	9.4	−6.0	....	....	....	....	....	....	Lending Minus Repayments	83
−9.6	−24.7	−21.8	—	Ɪ—	—	—	—	—	....	....	....	....	....	....	Exch.Rate Adj.to Overall Def./Sur	80x
															Financing	
....	....								....	....	....	....	....	....	Net Borrowing	84
−8.0	−5.7	−3.2	−16.1	Ɪ−2.1	2.0	−151.2	−2.1	−2.0	....	....	....	....	....	....	Net Borrowing: Domestic	84a
14.9	5.2	4.1	−5.6	Ɪ−6.2	−55.1	10.5	20.3	−96.2	....	....	....	....	....	....	Foreign	85a
....	....	....	....	Ɪ−104.2	−136.5	153.6	−95.9	−40.5	....	....	....	....	....	....	Use of Cash Balances	87
18.4	23.6	21.1	32.9	21.7	167.5	53.3	45.4	100.0	....	....	....	....	....	....	Debt: Domestic	88a
111.8	....	....	342.0	978.8	913.4	948.5	1,182.9	1,430.1	....	....	....	....	....	....	Foreign	89a

Billions of Guaranies

1985	1986	1987	1988	1989	1990	1991	1992	1993	1994	1995	1996	1997	1998	1999	National Accounts	
308.0	485.7	657.2	1,142.6	1,645.2	2,152.6	2,498.4	2,714.6	4,428.6	5,120.9	6,163.8	5,707.7	5,696.2	6,613.4	....	Exports of Goods & Services	90c
90.2	121.8	176.6	209.1	306.7	401.9	546.5	629.1	801.9	1,012.5	1,275.9	1,528.5	1,693.0	1,928.3	....	Government Consumption	91f
288.0	431.8	591.4	768.2	1,045.6	1,425.4	1,961.8	2,117.4	2,642.1	3,366.5	4,082.8	4,478.4	4,749.1	5,184.2	....	Gross Fixed Capital Formation	93e
18.5	27.1	34.4	40.6	53.2	55.0	93.9	97.6	109.6	127.7	151.8	156.7	181.0	205.6	....	Increase/Decrease(−) in Stocks	93i
1,056.1	1,353.7	1,904.8	2,383.9	3,033.9	4,996.5	6,344.6	7,843.3	9,749.8	13,231.8	15,089.2	16,853.3	17,704.3	20,101.4	....	Private Consumption	96f
−367.0	−586.3	−870.8	−1,225.2	−1,476.3	−2,557.0	−3,164.5	−3,731.1	−5,740.2	−7,899.3	−9,064.9	−8,919.8	−9,089.3	−10,580.0	....	Imports of Goods & Services	98c
1,393.9	1,833.8	2,493.6	3,319.1	4,608.4	6,474.4	8,280.8	9,670.8	11,991.7	14,960.1	17,698.6	19,804.8	20,934.3	23,436.9	....	Gross Domestic Product (GDP)	99b
−13.0	−21.1	−68.2	−8.8	92.5	143.6	114.8	22.1	43.0	78.8	158.8	145.1	221.7	304.5	....	Net Factor Inc/Pmts(−) Abroad	98.n
1,380.9	1,812.7	2,425.4	3,310.3	4,700.9	6,618.0	8,395.6	9,692.9	12,034.7	15,039.0	17,857.4	19,949.9	21,156.0	23,741.5	....	Gross National Income (GNI)	99a
1,235.6	1,616.2	2,136.3	2,954.7	4,241.7	5,924.1	7,705.3	8,923.8	11,104.0	13,878.0	16,479.3	18,400.0	19,516.8	21,906.5	....	Net National Income	99e
766.2	766.2	799.4	850.2	899.5	927.3	950.2	967.3	1,007.4	1,038.5	1,087.4	1,101.2	1,129.7	1,125.0	1,130.7	GDP Volume 1982 Prices	99b.*p*
70.5	70.5	73.5	78.2	82.7	85.3	87.4	89.0	92.6	95.5	100.0	101.3	103.9	103.5	104.0	GDP Volume (1995=100)	99bv *p*
11.2	14.7	19.2	24.0	31.5	42.9	53.5	61.4	73.1	88.5	100.0	110.5	113.9	128.0	....	GDP Deflator (1995=100)	99bi *p*

Midyear Estimates

1985	1986	1987	1988	1989	1990	1991	1992	1993	1994	1995	1996	1997	1998	1999		
3.61	3.72	3.84	3.96	4.09	4.22	4.33	4.45	4.57	4.70	4.83	4.96	5.09	5.22	5.36	**Population**	99z

(See notes in the back of the book.)

Peru

293

		1970	1971	1972	1973	1974	1975	1976	1977	1978	1979	1980	1981	1982	1983	1984
Exchange Rates									*Nuev.Soles per Billion SDRs through 1987, per Million SDRs 1988-89,*							
Market Rate	aa	38.7	42.0	42.0	46.7	47.4	52.7	80.6	158.4	255.6	329.5	435.8	590.1	1,091.7	2,377.8	5,583.3
									Nuev.Soles per Billion US$ through 1987, per Million US$ 1988-89,							
Market Rate	ae	38.7	38.7	38.7	38.7	38.7	45.0	69.4	130.4	196.2	250.1	341.7	507.0	989.7	2,271.2	5,696.0
Market Rate	rf	38.7	38.7	38.7	38.7	38.7	40.4	55.8	84.2	156.3	224.7	288.9	422.3	697.6	1,628.6	3,466.9
Fund Position														*Millions of SDRs:*		
Quota	2f. s	123.0	123.0	123.0	123.0	123.0	123.0	123.0	123.0	164.0	164.0	246.0	246.0	246.0	246.0	330.9
SDRs	1b. s	14.3	28.4	41.0	37.3	37.2	37.1	3.3	2.7	4.8	81.3	9.7	9.8	29.9	.6	22.9
Reserve Position in the Fund	1c. s	—	—	—	30.8	30.8	30.8									
Total Fund Cred.&Loans Outstg.	2tl	9.9	3.3	30.8	13.6	—		158.8	168.8	256.1	373.1	371.6	332.9	588.8	666.3	688.3
International Liquidity									*Millions of US Dollars Unless Otherwise Indicated:*							
Total Reserves minus Gold	1l. d	‡296.3	380.9	442.5	526.1	925.2	425.5	289.3	356.8	389.7	1,520.7	1,979.8	1,199.5	1,349.6	1,365.7	1,630.5
SDRs	1b. d	14.3	30.9	44.5	45.0	45.6	43.4	3.8	3.3	6.3	107.1	12.3	11.4	32.9	.6	22.4
Reserve Position in the Fund	1c. d				37.1	37.6	36.0									
Foreign Exchange	1d. d	‡282.0	350.0	398.0	444.0	842.0	346.1	285.5	353.5	383.4	1,413.6	1,967.5	1,188.1	1,316.7	1,365.1	1,608.1
Gold (Million Fine Troy Ounces)	1ad	1.134	1.131	1.089	1.003	1.003	1.003	1.003	1.003	1.004	1.158	1.398	1.398	1.398	1.398	1.398
Gold (National Valuation)	1an d	39.7	39.6	41.4	42.3	42.3	42.3	42.3	42.3	42.4	106.4	281.0	400.3	400.3	400.3	400.3
Monetary Authorities: Other Liab.	4.. d	.8	1.9	13.4	17.2	—	20.0	263.7	651.8	688.1	346.0	196.9	32.7	39.7	107.0	116.7
Deposit Money Banks: Assets	7a. d	126.6	118.9	2.6	2.6	165.4	48.9	61.5	48.2	138.4	582.8	387.3	568.1	388.4	312.8	330.7
Liabilities	7b. d	25.8	77.5	69.8	219.6	410.9	537.8	810.8	786.4	644.7	505.0	624.2	763.3	446.9	433.2	362.0
Other Banking Insts.: Liabilities	7f. d	46.5	49.1	38.8	69.8	98.2	111.1	133.8	146.4	164.2	152.0	190.0	217.6	345.7	299.4	212.5
Monetary Authorities									*Thousandths(.000) Nuev.Soles through 1976; Nuev.Soles from 1977 to 1987;*							
Foreign Assets	11	15,500	14,100	22,600	25,836	35,557	24,120	24,500	‡50	104	342	764	657	1,653	4,060	10,746
Claims on Central Government	12a	9,500	9,600	9,900	9,800	9,700	9,700	10,000	‡10	23	33	186	351	518	2,867	3,220
Claims on Deposit Money Banks	12e	1,200	3,900	3,800	2,700	3,200	15,900	52,300	‡74	106	140	45	174	35	281	1,753
Claims on Other Banking Insts	12f	2,200	2,800	4,900	6,900	10,400	14,400	28,900	‡44	72	86	122	209	378	966	2,039
Reserve Money	14	24,200	25,500	33,500	35,700	50,400	53,300	79,100	‡98	153	347	734	1,139	1,787	3,845	9,327
of which: Currency Outside DMBs	14a	16,300	18,900	21,900	27,200	33,500	42,600	49,500	‡61	91	162	273	437	622	1,116	2,502
Time, Savings,& Fgn.Currency Dep.	15	—	—	—	—	—	—	—	‡—	—	1	1	2	5	28	87
Restricted Deposits	16b	100	100	100	—	—	100	—	‡—	—	5	9	1	14	25	124
Foreign Liabilities	16c	412	210	1,810	1,303	—	900	29,127	‡94	194	208	226	209	654	1,800	4,115
Long-Term Foreign Liabilities	16cl	2,700	2,900	4,400	4,500	5,000	5,900	8,900	‡11	27	43	76	104	200	851	1,375
Central Government Deposits	16d	100	100	—	—	600	400	100	‡—	—	—	2	11	12	41	58
Capital Accounts	17a	1,453	2,053	2,601	2,990	3,518	3,832	4,463	‡11	21	39	38	57	105	269	743
Other Items (Net)	17r	−565	−463	−1,211	742	−661	−313	−5,990	‡−36	−91	−42	30	−132	−192	1,315	1,929
Deposit Money Banks									*Thousandths(.000) Nuev.Soles through 1976; Nuev.Soles from 1977 to 1987;*							
Reserves	20	7,400	6,200	10,500	7,700	15,700	9,500	26,900	‡36	58	158	360	560	1,088	2,469	6,314
Foreign Assets	21	4,900	4,600	100	100	6,400	2,200	4,000	‡5	26	145	131	283	369	700	1,720
Claims on Central Government	22a	13,300	14,900	20,500	28,200	29,700	47,700	87,700	‡126	189	215	189	320	551	1,259	4,132
Claims on Local Government	22b	200	600	1,000	1,400	1,300	1,400	1,100	‡1	1	1	1	22	25	6	1
Claims on Official Entities	22bx	3,700	4,400	4,500	10,000	25,700	40,200	59,200	‡83	139	118	129	237	229	380	1,257
Claims on Private Sector	22d	24,700	30,200	36,700	44,900	49,300	63,700	76,400	‡87	119	220	469	1,063	1,756	3,779	7,324
Claims on Other Banking Insts	22f	2,100	1,800	2,200	4,200	4,600	5,200	3,200	‡4	6	7	8	5	31	99	496
Demand Deposits	24	26,600	27,400	37,600	47,900	71,300	80,100	103,500	‡122	177	268	367	519	822	1,639	3,211
Time, Savings,& Fgn.Currency Dep.	25	14,100	15,500	16,700	19,100	21,200	23,400	26,900	‡40	92	233	545	1,076	2,186	4,532	10,952
Bonds	26ab	1,100	1,600	2,400	3,200	3,800	4,700	5,300	‡4	4	6	10	28	34	42	78
Foreign Liabilities	26c	900	2,200	1,700	4,800	10,600	14,900	41,100	‡72	105	105	172	310	263	616	1,537
Long-Term Foreign Liabilities	26cl	100	800	1,000	3,700	5,300	9,300	11,600	‡14	18	21	38	70	161	353	345
Central Government Deposits	26d	11,800	8,800	9,600	10,900	14,200	19,100	16,300	‡16	25	75	81	197	189	608	1,598
Credit from Monetary Authorities	26g	1,700	3,900	3,900	2,700	3,300	16,000	52,300	‡74	106	141	49	174	62	281	1,762
Capital Accounts	27a	6,900	7,600	8,700	10,400	13,100	16,000	20,500	‡27	43	84	144	254	450	975	3,579
Other Items (Net)	27r	−6,900	−5,400	−6,100	−6,200	−10,100	−13,600	−19,000	‡−27	−29	−69	−120	−139	−117	−355	−1,818
Monetary Survey									*Thousandths(.000) Nuev.Soles through 1976; Nuev.Soles from 1977 to 1987;*							
Foreign Assets (Net)	31n	19,088	16,290	19,190	19,832	31,357	10,520	−41,727	‡−111	−169	174	496	421	1,105	2,344	6,813
Domestic Credit	32	43,800	55,100	70,100	94,500	115,900	162,800	250,100	‡340	523	604	1,020	1,998	3,291	8,717	16,845
Claims on Central Govt. (Net)	32an	10,900	15,600	20,800	27,100	24,600	37,900	81,300	‡120	186	173	291	462	869	3,477	5,696
Claims on Local Government	32b	200	600	1,000	1,400	1,300	1,400	1,100	‡1	1	1	1	22	25	6	1
Claims on Official Entities	32bx	3,700	4,400	4,500	10,000	25,700	40,200	59,200	‡83	139	118	129	237	229	380	1,257
Claims on Private Sector	32d	24,700	30,200	36,700	44,900	49,300	63,700	76,400	‡87	119	220	469	1,064	1,759	3,790	7,355
Claims on Other Banking Insts	32f	4,300	4,600	7,100	11,100	15,000	19,600	32,100	‡49	78	93	130	214	409	1,064	2,536
Money	34	43,300	46,600	60,300	75,700	105,500	123,300	155,000	‡185	270	461	730	1,075	1,509	2,965	6,059
Quasi-Money	35	14,100	15,500	16,700	19,100	21,200	23,400	26,900	‡40	92	235	546	1,077	2,191	4,560	11,039
Bonds	36ab	1,100	1,600	2,400	3,200	3,800	4,700	5,300	‡4	4	6	10	28	34	42	78
Restricted Deposits	36b	100	100	100	—	—	100	—	‡—	—	5	9	1	14	25	124
Long-Term Foreign Liabilities	36cl	2,800	3,700	5,400	8,200	10,300	15,200	20,500	‡25	44	63	114	174	361	1,204	1,720
Capital Accounts	37a	8,353	9,653	11,301	13,390	16,618	19,832	24,963	‡38	64	123	182	311	555	1,244	4,322
Other Items (Net)	37r	−6,865	−5,763	−6,911	−5,258	−10,161	−13,213	−24,290	‡−63	−119	−114	−74	−246	−268	1,021	317
Money plus Quasi-Money	35l	57,400	62,100	77,000	94,800	126,700	146,700	181,900	‡225	362	695	1,276	2,152	3,701	7,525	17,098
Other Banking Institutions									*Thousandths(.000) Nuev.Soles through 1976; Nuev.Soles from 1977 to 1987;*							
Reserves	40	600	600	900	800	1,200	1,100	1,900	‡2	4	32	86	124	62	175	241
Foreign Assets	41	200	100	200	100	—	100	600	‡1	1	6	7	12	58	160	171
Claims on Central Government	42a	1,400	4,000	4,900	5,900	7,700	10,000	10,800	‡18	39	34	28	132	155	72	53
Claims on Official Entities	42bx	—	200	500	3,600	4,400	4,600	7,000	‡10	11	11	14	13	31	81	139
Claims on Private Sector	42d	15,400	18,200	23,200	29,800	36,600	46,800	60,300	‡82	118	171	301	570	1,265	2,639	6,483
Claims on Deposit Money Banks	42e	3,900	2,500	3,400	3,200	3,800	3,900	4,100	‡4	7	11	24	42	110	229	138
Demand Deposits	44	1,300	1,400	2,300	2,100	2,400	2,700	6,000	‡7	11	23	36	62	83	145	307
Time, Savings,& Fgn.Currency Dep.	45	700	900	1,100	1,200	1,500	1,900	1,500	‡4	12	18	26	58	124	369	1,143
Bonds	46ab	6,900	9,100	11,800	15,100	18,000	22,000	22,700	‡27	34	61	106	229	310	403	521
Foreign Liabilities	46c	400	400	—	—	—	—	—	‡—	1	2	11	18	104	216	118
Long-Term Foreign Liabilities	46cl	1,400	1,500	1,500	2,700	3,800	5,000	8,700	‡16	30	36	54	91	224	454	988
Central Government Deposits	46d	100	200	100	100	300	100	100	‡—	—	—	—	1	10	17	55
Credit from Monetary Authorities	46g	2,200	2,800	4,900	6,900	10,300	14,400	25,700	‡39	64	76	108	189	348	880	1,889
Credit from Deposit Money Banks	46h	1,900	2,000	2,200	4,200	4,800	5,300	3,400	‡4	6	11	9	11	37	51	529
Capital Accounts	47a	5,600	6,600	6,900	8,200	9,400	11,900	16,700	‡22	33	62	112	187	313	450	1,256
Other Items (Net)	47r	1,000	700	2,300	2,900	3,200	3,200	−100	‡−4	−11	−23	−1	48	129	371	419

1985	1986	1987	1988	1989	1990	1991	1992	1993	1994	1995	1996	1997	1998	1999		
per Thousand SDRs thereafter: End of Period															**Exchange Rates**	
15,317.5	17,063.5	46,815.8	I 672.9	6,914.3	I 735.4	1,373.2	2,241.3	2,966.9	3,182.5	3,433.8	3,738.7	3,683.5	4,449.4	4,817.5	Market Rate	aa
per Thousand US$ thereafter: End of Period (ae) Period Average (rf)																
13,945.0	13,950.0	33,000.0	I 500.0	5,261.4	I 516.9	960.0	1,630.0	2,160.0	2,180.0	2,310.0	2,600.0	2,730.0	3,160.0	3,510.0	Market Rate	ae
10,974.9	13,947.5	16,835.8	I 128.8	2,666.2	I 187.9	772.5	1,245.8	1,988.3	2,195.0	2,253.3	2,453.3	2,664.2	2,930.0	3,383.3	Market Rate	rf
End of Period															**Fund Position**	
330.9	330.9	330.9	330.9	330.9	330.9	330.9	330.9	466.1	466.1	466.1	466.1	466.1	466.1	638.4	Quota	2f. s
—	—	—	—	—	—	—	—	.7	.3	.5	.2	.2	1.5	.3	SDRs	1b. s
—	—	—	—	—	—	—	—	—	—	—	—	—	—	—	Reserve Position in the Fund	1c. s
639.0	595.5	595.4	595.4	577.0	530.5	493.4	458.7	642.7	642.7	642.7	642.7	749.6	642.5	535.4	Total Fund Cred.&Loans Outstg.	2tl
End of Period															**International Liquidity**	
1,842.0	1,407.2	645.8	511.0	808.4	1,039.8	2,443.0	2,849.0	3,407.9	6,992.4	8,221.7	10,578.3	10,982.2	9,565.5	8,730.5	Total Reserves minus Gold	1l. d
—	—	—	—	—	—	—	—	.9	.4	.7	.3	.2	2.1	.4	SDRs	1b. d
—	—	—	—	—	—	—	—	—	—	—	—	—	—	—	Reserve Position in the Fund	1c. d
1,842.0	1,407.2	645.8	511.0	808.4	1,039.8	2,443.0	2,849.0	3,407.0	6,992.0	8,221.0	10,578.0	10,982.0	9,563.4	8,730.1	Foreign Exchange	1d. d
1.954	2.137	1.497	1.712	1.967	2.210	1.831	1.822	1.305	1.116	1.116	1.115	1.115	1.100	1.100	Gold (Million Fine Troy Ounces)	1ad
419.6	458.9	513.4	587.1	671.6	728.9	556.5	515.6	434.0	362.9	366.6	349.7	272.0	268.8	270.9	Gold (National Valuation)	1an d
22.6	136.8	260.4	752.0	543.4	716.1	1,121.4	976.2	608.9	665.4	676.4	512.2	291.2	190.4	355.8	Monetary Authorities: Other Liab.	4..d
241.1	320.1	365.1	399.7	589.7	527.9	1,052.6	991.2	871.8	1,183.8	1,544.9	2,047.2	1,215.7	1,245.8	1,447.6	Deposit Money Banks: Assets	7a. d
298.2	268.0	262.8	282.0	308.4	250.2	275.9	396.9	415.3	765.8	1,566.1	1,812.4	3,473.6	3,291.0	2,286.2	Liabilities	7b. d
136.9	140.6	100.1	91.1	79.7	108.0	108.5	108.7	107.3	71.0	71.0	71.1	71.0	10.3	—	Other Banking Insts.: Liabilities	7f. d
Thousands from 1988 to 1989;Millions Beginning 1990: End of Period															**Monetary Authorities**	
33,009	28,953	34,118	I 527	7,649	I 920	2,681	5,461	9,335	16,001	19,093	25,933	31,208	32,399	33,548	Foreign Assets	11
2,986	5,003	32,514	I 55	404	I 5	117	90	55	614	614	614	614	614	538	Claims on Central Government	12a
3,507	5,694	13,274	I 151	3,079	I 109	152	197	149	64	4	107	—	203	263	Claims on Deposit Money Banks	12e
3,754	8,964	23,039	I 121	3,446	I 104	108	173	209	—	—	—	—	—	—	Claims on Other Banking Insts	12f
29,372	40,966	86,248	I 576	8,857	I 698	1,831	3,586	5,715	7,487	9,823	13,536	18,773	19,847	22,952	Reserve Money	14
8,145	16,435	41,945	I 261	5,372	I 273	643	1,101	1,591	2,385	3,043	3,245	3,827	3,950	4,609	*of which: Currency Outside DMBs*	14a
129	61	176	I 6	56	I 25	101	194	194	202	78	118	77	83	75	Time, Savings,& Fgn.Currency Dep.	15
188	179	962	I 71	701	I 21	5	7	1	1	1	1	1	—	1	Restricted Deposits	16b
10,102	12,061	30,998	I 777	6,460	I 733	1,424	2,114	2,103	2,317	2,445	2,450	2,199	2,052	1,393	Foreign Liabilities	16c
4,421	5,507	6,599	I 35	828	I 27	330	505	1,104	1,179	1,325	1,285	1,344	1,398	2,435	Long-Term Foreign Liabilities	16cl
619	551	602	I 6	26	I 1	3	55	96	3,684	5,384	8,498	7,989	7,558	4,057	Central Government Deposits	16d
1,441	1,628	4,492	I 64	680	I 91	137	224	254	377	457	592	735	867	871	Capital Accounts	17a
–3,014	–12,339	–27,131	I –681	–3,030	I –458	–773	–765	280	1,433	199	174	703	1,412	2,565	Other Items (Net)	17r
Thousands from 1988 to 1989;Millions Beginning 1990: End of Period															**Deposit Money Banks**	
19,081	22,548	37,298	I 260	3,391	I 267	852	2,040	3,519	5,326	6,846	10,240	12,135	11,126	11,897	Reserves	20
3,362	4,462	10,240	I 200	2,927	I 273	1,011	1,616	1,874	2,581	3,569	5,323	3,307	3,924	5,081	Foreign Assets	21
9,120	16,483	35,377	I 217	4,697	I 497	854	1,422	1,913	1,607	1,028	924	2,437	3,764	4,793	Claims on Central Government	22a
27	25	77	I 2	13	I 1	5	19	35	50	31	170	244	94	381	Claims on Local Government	22b
2,774	3,989	8,277	I 153	1,321	I 95	343	331	369	270	204	264	376	968	399	Claims on Official Entities	22bx
16,096	25,682	46,300	I 340	7,451	I 437	1,857	4,076	7,694	13,095	19,090	28,512	37,812	45,835	49,220	Claims on Private Sector	22d
1,621	2,726	4,482	I 53	676	I 9	19	7	7	3	3	3	—	—	—	Claims on Other Banking Insts	22f
13,063	24,940	48,967	I 285	4,738	I 275	656	1,298	2,142	3,193	4,357	5,633	7,950	10,174	11,038	Demand Deposits	24
20,637	24,070	42,930	I 407	9,865	I 584	2,641	5,148	9,528	13,501	17,362	25,136	29,510	33,269	37,763	Time, Savings,& Fgn.Currency Dep.	25
177	404	943	I 4	124	I 3	11	12	55	102	251	539	806	933	969	Bonds	26ab
3,417	3,573	7,101	I 130	1,482	I 127	232	590	796	1,462	3,127	4,023	8,196	9,160	6,539	Foreign Liabilities	26c
741	163	269	I 11	49	I 2	33	57	97	208	490	690	1,252	1,206	1,485	Long-Term Foreign Liabilities	26cl
4,923	7,768	14,874	I 79	983	I 159	764	1,041	1,248	2,367	1,561	4,808	3,710	3,849	3,718	Central Government Deposits	26d
3,511	5,694	13,692	I 156	3,150	I 119	153	207	149	64	4	107	—	203	263	Credit from Monetary Authorities	26g
9,908	12,694	31,457	I 459	7,492	I 565	1,269	2,096	3,181	4,792	6,261	8,514	11,045	14,309	18,944	Capital Accounts	27a
–4,297	–3,392	–18,184	I –305	–7,406	I –257	–816	–939	–1,785	–2,757	–2,643	–4,013	–6,157	–7,392	–8,949	Other Items (Net)	27r
Thousands from 1988 to 1989;Millions Beginning 1990: End of Period															**Monetary Survey**	
22,852	17,780	6,258	I –180	2,634	I 333	2,035	4,372	8,311	14,802	17,089	24,784	24,119	25,111	30,697	Foreign Assets (Net)	31n
30,973	54,721	134,821	I 859	17,040	I 988	2,544	5,029	8,947	9,588	14,025	17,181	29,784	39,869	47,556	Domestic Credit	32
6,565	13,167	52,415	I 188	4,092	I 342	204	416	625	–3,830	–5,303	–11,768	–8,648	–7,028	–2,444	Claims on Central Govt. (Net)	32an
27	25	77	I 2	13	I 1	5	19	35	50	31	170	244	94	381	Claims on Local Government	32b
2,774	3,990	8,287	I 153	1,321	I 95	343	331	369	270	204	264	376	968	399	Claims on Official Entities	32bx
16,232	25,849	46,522	I 342	7,491	I 438	1,864	4,083	7,702	13,095	19,090	28,512	37,812	45,835	49,220	Claims on Private Sector	32d
5,375	11,690	27,521	I 174	4,122	I 112	127	179	216	3	3	3	—	—	—	Claims on Other Banking Insts	32f
23,098	43,410	96,376	I 593	10,364	I 707	1,607	2,843	4,337	5,589	7,498	8,972	15,175	19,165	22,294	Money	34
20,766	24,131	43,106	I 413	9,922	I 608	2,742	5,341	9,722	13,703	17,440	25,254	29,587	33,352	37,838	Quasi-Money	35
177	404	943	I 4	124	I 3	11	12	55	102	251	539	806	933	969	Bonds	36ab
188	179	962	I 71	701	I 21	5	7	1	1	1	1	1	—	1	Restricted Deposits	36b
5,162	5,670	6,868	I 46	877	I 29	362	562	1,201	1,386	1,815	1,975	2,596	2,604	3,921	Long-Term Foreign Liabilities	36cl
11,349	14,323	35,949	I 523	8,171	I 656	1,406	2,320	3,435	5,169	6,718	9,106	11,780	15,176	19,815	Capital Accounts	37a
–6,915	–15,615	–43,124	I –970	–10,484	I –705	–1,554	–1,684	–1,495	–1,560	–2,609	–3,881	–6,041	–6,251	–6,584	Other Items (Net)	37r
43,864	67,541	139,481	I 1,006	20,286	I 1,316	4,349	8,184	14,060	19,292	24,938	34,226	44,762	52,518	60,132	Money plus Quasi-Money	35l
Thousands from 1988 to 1989;Millions Beginning 1990: End of Period															**Other Banking Institutions**	
1,245	897	3,151	I 33	273	I 11	33	5	4	—	—	—	—	—	—	Reserves	40
397	257	1,239	I 23	280	I 30	18	27	24	28	29	33	35	3	—	Foreign Assets	41
811	666	957	I 35	361	I 17	35	49	54	55	58	65	69	—	—	Claims on Central Government	42a
373	958	3,047	I 18	198	I 4	40	45	20	20	21	24	25	—	—	Claims on Official Entities	42bx
12,195	21,127	47,500	I 242	3,744	I 204	607	769	743	718	744	803	828	910	809	Claims on Private Sector	42d
330	964	2,283	I 7	76	I 6	23	11	1	2	2	2	2	—	—	Claims on Deposit Money Banks	42e
987	1,151	3,820	I 19	349	I 13	37	32	9	9	9	9	9	21	21	Demand Deposits	44
2,135	2,202	3,696	I 23	622	I 34	102	78	44	42	43	46	47	37	10	Time, Savings,& Fgn.Currency Dep.	45
1,182	2,724	4,768	I 15	487	I 8	28	17	11	6	6	6	6	—	—	Bonds	46ab
338	301	1,389	I 29	239	I 39	74	125	162	85	90	101	106	—	—	Foreign Liabilities	46c
1,571	1,659	1,420	I 16	156	I 17	31	52	69	70	74	84	87	33	—	Long-Term Foreign Liabilities	46cl
130	77	312	I —	5	I 1	5	5	5	5	6	6	6	—	—	Central Government Deposits	46d
3,495	8,563	22,764	I 122	3,499	I 106	108	168	209	—	—	—	—	—	—	Credit from Monetary Authorities	46g
1,653	2,710	4,687	I 54	656	I 13	18	14	13	4	4	5	5	—	—	Credit from Deposit Money Banks	46h
2,838	2,838	10,580	I 105	1,249	I 190	388	506	709	671	698	757	782	865	939	Capital Accounts	47a
1,023	2,645	4,740	I –26	–2,330	I –148	–35	–91	–385	–70	–76	–87	–92	–42	–160	Other Items (Net)	47r

		1970	1971	1972	1973	1974	1975	1976	1977	1978	1979	1980	1981	1982	1983	1984
Banking Survey									*Thousandths(.000) Nuev.Soles through 1976; Nuev.Soles from 1977 to 1987;*							
Foreign Assets (Net)	51n	18,888	15,990	19,390	19,932	31,357	10,620	−41,127	ⱅ−111	−169	179	492	416	1,059	2,287	6,867
Domestic Credit	52	56,200	72,700	91,500	122,600	149,300	204,500	296,000	ⱅ401	614	727	1,233	2,499	4,324	10,428	20,929
Claims on Central Govt. (Net)	52an	12,200	19,400	25,600	32,900	32,000	47,800	92,000	ⱅ138	226	207	320	593	1,014	3,532	5,694
Claims on Local Government	52b	200	600	1,000	1,400	1,300	1,400	1,100	ⱅ1	1	1	1	22	25	7	1
Claims on Official Entities	52bx	3,700	4,300	5,000	13,600	30,100	44,800	66,200	ⱅ93	151	128	143	250	261	460	1,396
Claims on Private Sector	52d	40,100	48,400	59,900	74,700	85,900	110,500	136,700	ⱅ170	237	391	769	1,634	3,024	6,429	13,838
Liquid Liabilities	55l	58,800	63,800	79,500	97,300	129,400	150,200	187,500	ⱅ234	382	705	1,251	2,148	3,845	7,865	18,308
Bonds	56ab	8,000	10,700	14,200	18,300	21,800	26,700	28,000	ⱅ31	38	66	116	257	343	444	599
Restricted Deposits	56b	100	100	100	—	—	100	—	ⱅ—	—	5	9	1	14	25	124
Long-Term Foreign Liabilities	56cl	4,200	5,200	6,900	10,900	14,100	20,200	29,200	ⱅ41	75	99	168	265	585	1,658	2,708
Capital Accounts	57a	13,953	16,253	18,201	21,590	26,018	31,732	41,663	ⱅ60	96	185	294	498	868	1,693	5,578
Other Items (Net)	57r	−9,965	−7,363	−8,011	−5,558	−10,661	−13,813	−31,490	ⱅ−76	−145	−154	−112	−254	−272	1,030	480
Interest Rates														*Percent Per Annum*		
Discount Rate *(End of Period)*	60	9.5	9.5	9.5	9.5	9.5	9.5	12.5	14.5	28.5	29.5	29.5	44.5	44.5	60.0	60.0
Deposit Rate	60l	....	....	....	....	....	....	....	....	....	....	....	....	....	....	....
Lending Rate	60p	....	....	....	....	....	....	....	....	....	....	....	....	....	....	....
Prices, Production, Labor														*Index Numbers (1995=100):*		
Share Prices	62	....	....	....	....	....	....	....	....	....	....	....	....	....	....	....
Wholesale Prices (1995=100,000)	63.a	....	....	....	....	....	....	....	....	....	....	.01	.01	.02	.04	.09
Wholesale Prices	63	....	....	....	....	....	....	....	....	....	....	....	....	....	....	....
Consumer Prices(1995=100 millions)	64.a	.2	.2	.2	.2	.3	.3	.4	.6	.9	1.5	2.4	4.3	7.0	14.9	31.2
Consumer Prices(1990=100,000)	64.b	....	....	....	....	....	....	....	....	....	....	....	....	....	....	....
Consumer Prices	64	....	....	....	....	....	....	....	....	....	....	....	....	....	....	....
Manufacturing Production	66ey	....	....	....	....	....	....	....	....	....	89.0	96.7	97.4	92.6	75.5	81.2
Industrial Employment	67	....	....	....	....	....	....	....	....	....	....	163.1	164.9	162.6	154.0	137.8
															Number in Thousands:		
Labor Force	67d	....	....	....	....	....	....	....	....	....	....	....	....	....	....	....
Employment	67e	....	....	....	....	....	....	....	....	....	....	....	....	....	....	....
Unemployment	67c	....	....	....	....	....	....	....	....	....	....	....	....	....	....	....
Unemployment Rate (%)	67r	....	....	....	....	....	....	....	....	....	....	....	....	....	....	....
International Transactions														*Millions of US Dollars*		
Exports	70..d	1,047.9	892.9	944.4	1,111.8	1,503.3	ⱅ1,290.9	1,359.6	1,725.6	1,940.7	3,490.9	3,898.3	3,255.0	3,258.9	3,015.2	3,147.1
Imports, c.i.f.	71..d	622.9	763.0	796.5	1,018.6	1,530.5	ⱅ2,550.0	2,037.3	1,910.9	1,174.7	1,820.1	2,499.5	3,481.6	3,600.7	2,547.9	2,212.0
Imports, f.o.b.	71.vd	499.0	611.2	638.0	815.3	1,275.7	ⱅ2,124.8	1,697.7	1,592.4	978.9	1,516.7	2,082.9	2,901.3	3,000.6	2,123.3	1,843.3
															1995=100		
Volume of Exports	72	71.9	66.1	70.7	50.1	52.7	47.3	51.5	63.0	69.4	80.1	72.6	70.1	77.3	69.0	75.5
															1995=100:		
Unit Value of Exports	74..d	29	27	28	42	111	ⱅ62	67	75	75	129	174	151	132	130	121
Balance of Payments														*Millions of US Dollars:*		
Current Account, n.i.e.	78ald	....	....	....	....	....	....	....	−923	−193	730	−101	−1,733	−1,612	−875	−235
Goods: Exports f.o.b.	78aad								1,726	1,941	3,491	3,916	3,249	3,293	3,015	3,147
Goods: Imports f.o.b.	78abd								−2,164	−1,601	−1,951	−3,090	−3,802	−3,721	−2,722	−2,140
Trade Balance	78acd								−438	340	1,540	826	−553	−428	293	1,007
Services: Credit	78add								406	459	594	715	770	784	711	670
Services: Debit	78aed								−523	−470	−560	−880	−1,087	−1,098	−965	−891
Balance on Goods & Services	78afd								−556	330	1,573	661	−870	−742	39	786
Income: Credit	78agd								13	16	58	202	204	109	116	157
Income: Debit	78ahd								−436	−594	−1,025	−1,111	−1,223	−1,143	−1,246	−1,334
Balance on Gds, Serv. & Inc.	78aid								−979	−248	607	−248	−1,889	−1,776	−1,091	−391
Current Transfers, n.i.e.: Credit	78ajd								60	59	126	147	156	164	216	156
Current Transfers: Debit	78akd								−3	−4	−4	—	—	—	—	—
Capital Account, n.i.e.	78bcd								—	—	—	—	—	—	—	—
Capital Account, n.i.e.: Credit	78bad								—	—	—	—	—	—	—	—
Capital Account: Debit	78bbd								—	—	—	—	—	—	—	—
Financial Account, n.i.e.	78bjd								669	−175	−296	−33	377	1,818	−306	−770
Direct Investment Abroad	78bdd								—	—	—	—	—	—	—	—
Dir. Invest. in Rep. Econ., n.i.e.	78bed								54	25	71	27	125	48	38	−89
Portfolio Investment Assets	78bfd								—	—	—	—	—	—	—	—
Equity Securities	78bkd								—	—	—	—	—	—	—	—
Debt Securities	78bld								—	—	—	—	—	—	—	—
Portfolio Investment Liab., n.i.e.	78bgd								—	—	—	—	—	—	—	—
Equity Securities	78bmd								—	—	—	—	—	—	—	—
Debt Securities	78bnd								—	—	—	—	—	—	—	—
Financial Derivatives Assets	78bwd								....	....	....	....	....	....	....	....
Financial Derivatives Liabilities	78bxd								....	....	....	....	....	....	....	....
Other Investment Assets	78bhd								—	—	—	—	—	—	—	—
Monetary Authorities	78bod								—	—	—	—	—	—	—	—
General Government	78bpd								—	—	—	—	—	—	—	—
Banks	78bqd								—	—	—	—	—	—	—	—
Other Sectors	78brd								—	—	—	—	—	—	—	—
Other Investment Liab., n.i.e.	78bid								615	−200	−367	−60	252	1,770	−344	−681
Monetary Authorities	78bsd								22	4	−198	−171	−209	−58	−147	—
General Government	78btd								576	−106	−64	−10	278	934	620	−358
Banks	78bud								−3	−114	−130	88	39	−279	55	−9
Other Sectors	78bvd								19	16	26	32	144	1,173	−872	−314
Net Errors and Omissions	78cad								−111	53	112	414	582	−402	120	−566
Overall Balance	78cbd								−365	−315	546	279	−774	−196	−1,061	−1,571
Reserves and Related Items	79dad								365	315	−546	−279	774	196	1,061	1,571
Reserve Assets	79dbd								−80	−134	−1,236	−650	735	−198	−50	−274
Use of Fund Credit and Loans	79dcd								12	111	151	−1	−46	281	84	24
Exceptional Financing	79ded								433	338	539	372	85	112	1,027	1,821

1985	1986	1987	1988	1989	1990	1991	1992	1993	1994	1995	1996	1997	1998	1999		
Thousands from 1988 to 1989;Millions Beginning 1990: End of Period															**Banking Survey**	
22,911	17,737	6,108	‡−186	2,675	‡323	1,979	4,273	8,173	14,745	17,028	24,716	24,048	25,115	30,697	Foreign Assets (Net)	**51n**
38,847	65,705	158,492	‡980	17,216	‡1,100	3,094	5,708	9,543	10,373	14,840	18,063	30,698	40,778	48,365	Domestic Credit	**52**
7,246	13,757	53,060	‡222	4,448	‡358	235	459	674	−3,780	−5,250	−11,708	−8,586	−7,028	−2,444	Claims on Central Govt. (Net)	**52an**
27	25	77	‡2	13	‡1	5	19	35	50	31	170	244	94	381	Claims on Local Government	**52b**
3,147	4,947	11,333	‡171	1,519	‡99	383	377	389	290	225	287	400	968	399	Claims on Official Entities	**52bx**
28,427	46,976	94,022	‡585	11,236	‡642	2,471	4,852	8,445	13,812	19,834	29,314	38,640	46,745	50,029	Claims on Private Sector	**52d**
45,741	69,997	143,847	‡1,015	20,983	‡1,351	4,455	8,289	14,108	19,343	24,990	34,281	44,818	52,575	60,163	Liquid Liabilities	**55l**
1,359	3,128	5,711	‡18	610	‡11	38	29	66	108	257	545	812	933	969	Bonds	**56ab**
188	179	962	‡71	701	‡21	5	7	1	1	1	1	1	—	1	Restricted Deposits	**56b**
6,732	7,329	8,288	‡62	1,033	‡46	393	614	1,270	1,456	1,889	2,058	2,683	2,637	3,921	Long-Term Foreign Liabilities	**56cl**
14,187	17,160	46,529	‡628	9,420	‡845	1,794	2,826	4,144	5,840	7,416	9,863	12,562	16,041	20,753	Capital Accounts	**57a**
−6,449	−14,351	−40,736	‡−1,001	−12,857	‡−852	−1,612	−1,784	−1,875	−1,630	−2,684	−3,968	−6,129	−6,293	−6,744	Other Items (Net)	**57r**
Percent Per Annum															**Interest Rates**	
42.6	36.1	29.8	748.0	865.6	289.6	67.7	48.5	28.6	16.1	18.4	18.2	15.9	18.7	17.8	Discount Rate *(End of Period)*	**60**
....	....	....	161.8	1,135.6	2,439.6	170.5	59.7	44.1	22.3	15.7	14.9	15.0	15.1	16.3	Deposit Rate	**60l**
....	40.5	35.7	174.3	1,515.9	4,774.5	751.5	173.8	97.4	53.6	27.2	26.1	30.0	30.8	30.8	Lending Rate	**60p**
Period Averages															**Prices, Production, Labor**	
....	....	....	....	—	.9	4.0	13.2	51.9	95.1	100.0	105.5	143.6	119.8	127.2	Share Prices	**62**
.26	.41	.63	4.56	119.11	....	....	....	....	....	....	....	....	....	....	Wholesale Prices (1995=100,000)	**63.a**
....	....	....	....	.1	8.1	33.1	52.0	76.7	90.5	100.0	109.4	117.5	126.1	132.3	Wholesale Prices	**63**
82.3	146.4	272.1	2,086.9	....	....	....	....	....	....	....	....	....	....	....	Consumer Prices(1995=100 millions)	**64.a**
....	....	....	2	73	5,536	28,206	48,946	72,723	....	....	....	....	....	....	Consumer Prices(1990=100,000)	**64.b**
....	....	....	....	....	....	....	....	72.7	90.0	100.0	111.5	121.1	129.9	134.4	Consumer Prices	**64**
86.2	101.7	115.9	101.0	81.5	75.6	80.7	78.4	82.1	95.0	100.0	101.8	108.5	105.5	113.5	Manufacturing Production	**66ey**
136.0	144.2	156.3	153.0	‡136.2	132.6	125.9	113.1	103.9	102.6	100.0	97.7	98.9	97.0	91.7	Industrial Employment	**67**
Period Averages																
....	....	....	....	....	....	2,513	....	....	2,930	3,103	....	....	7,407	....	Labor Force	**67d**
....	1,988	2,061	....	2,170	....	2,377	2,411	2,610	2,682	2,901	....	....	....	....	Employment	**67e**
....	112	104	....	187	....	146	251	286	263	221	‡462	565	573	....	Unemployment	**67c**
....	5.3	4.8	....	7.9	....	5.8	9.4	9.9	8.9	7.1	‡7.0	7.7	7.7	....	Unemployment Rate (%)	**67r**
Millions of US Dollars															**International Transactions**	
2,978.5	2,530.6	2,660.8	2,701.0	3,488.0	3,230.9	3,329.1	3,484.4	3,514.5	4,554.6	5,575.1	5,897.1	6,841.4	5,735.0	6,114.0	Exports	**70..d**
1,835.0	2,908.8	3,562.3	3,348.0	2,749.2	3,469.8	4,194.7	4,861.3	4,859.2	6,690.7	9,224.0	9,472.6	10,264.2	....	....	Imports, c.i.f.	**71..d**
1,529.2	2,424.0	2,968.6	2,790.0	2,291.0	2,891.5	3,495.6	4,051.1	4,049.3	5,575.6	7,686.7	7,893.8	8,553.5	8,199.8	6,713.9	Imports, f.o.b.	**71.v d**
1995=100																
79.4	75.8	73.6	63.4	73.2	73.0	77.1	81.9	89.9	100.3	100.0	105.7	115.3	98.8	111.2	Volume of Exports	**72**
Indexes of Unit Values in US Dollars																
107	75	95	94	104	104	84	85	74	84	100	106	103	80	85	Unit Value of Exports	**74..d**
Minus Sign Indicates Debit															**Balance of Payments**	
102	−1,393	−2,065	−1,819	−570	−1,384	−1,558	−2,116	−2,327	−2,667	−4,314	−3,643	−3,282	−3,800	....	Current Account, n.i.e.	**78ald**
3,049	2,576	2,715	2,731	3,533	3,321	3,406	3,661	3,516	4,598	5,588	5,899	6,832	5,735	....	Goods: Exports f.o.b.	**78aa d**
−1,830	−2,649	−3,215	−2,865	−2,287	−2,922	−3,595	−4,002	−4,123	−5,596	−7,756	−7,885	−8,553	−8,200	....	Goods: Imports f.o.b.	**78ab d**
1,219	−73	−500	−134	1,246	399	−189	−341	−607	−997	−2,168	−1,986	−1,721	−2,465	....	*Trade Balance*	**78ac d**
695	681	793	831	836	799	826	836	837	1,064	1,132	1,413	1,541	1,753	....	Services: Credit	**78ad d**
−934	−1,013	−1,164	−1,164	−1,143	−1,164	−1,239	−1,411	−1,412	−1,565	−1,898	−2,097	−2,308	−2,294	....	Services: Debit	**78ae d**
980	−405	−871	−466	939	33	−602	−916	−1,181	−1,499	−2,934	−2,670	−2,488	−3,006	....	*Balance on Goods & Services*	**78af d**
221	154	120	123	196	195	224	204	209	343	582	615	725	780	....	Income: Credit	**78ag d**
−1,195	−1,254	−1,433	−1,638	−1,881	−1,928	−1,591	−1,836	−1,824	−2,143	−2,582	−2,253	−2,191	−2,264	....	Income: Debit	**78ah d**
6	−1,505	−2,184	−1,981	−746	−1,700	−1,969	−2,548	−2,797	−3,299	−4,934	−4,308	−3,954	−4,490	....	*Balance on Gds, Serv. & Inc.*	**78ai d**
101	114	123	163	176	316	411	440	476	639	625	673	680	699	....	Current Transfers, n.i.e.: Credit	**78aj d**
−5	−2	−5	....	....	....	....	−8	−6	−7	−5	−8	−8	−9	....	Current Transfers: Debit	**78ak d**
8	13	36	4	−20	−25	−52	−50	−78	−93	41	14	−75	−107	....	Capital Account, n.i.e.	**78bc d**
32	46	57	50	39	50	56	40	48	31	66	52	25	20	....	Capital Account, n.i.e.: Credit	**78ba d**
−24	−33	−21	−46	−59	−75	−108	−90	−125	−124	−25	−38	−100	−127	....	Capital Account: Debit	**78bb d**
−200	−1,240	−1,620	−1,573	−1,853	−831	−902	451	−259	3,320	2,308	2,943	4,064	1,333	....	Financial Account, n.i.e.	**78bj d**
										48	16	−84	—	....	Direct Investment Abroad	**78bd d**
1	22	32	26	59	41	−7	136	670	3,084	2,000	3,226	1,785	1,930	....	Dir. Invest. in Rep. Econ., n.i.e.	**78be d**
											—	−133	18	....	Portfolio Investment Assets	**78bf d**
												−133	18	....	Equity Securities	**78bk d**
														....	Debt Securities	**78bl d**
—								228	572	163	181	295	−348	....	Portfolio Investment Liab., n.i.e.	**78bg d**
—								222	465	171	188	45	−483	....	Equity Securities	**78bm d**
—								6	108	−8	−7	250	135	....	Debt Securities	**78bn d**
														....	Financial Derivatives Assets	**78bw d**
														....	Financial Derivatives Liabilities	**78bx d**
105	−232	−412	−461	−666	432	−289	318	269	−263	−572	−632	795	−126	....	Other Investment Assets	**78bh d**
														....	Monetary Authorities	**78bo d**
....	....	....	....	....	....	....	....	....	....	....	....	....	....	....	General Government	**78bp d**
105	−57	−93	−13	−181	63	−476	84	119	−272	−429	−461	1,042	6	....	Banks	**78bq d**
....	−175	−319	−448	−485	369	187	234	150	9	−143	−171	−247	−132	....	Other Sectors	**78br d**
−306	−1,030	−1,240	−1,138	−1,246	−1,304	−606	−3	−1,426	−73	669	152	1,406	−141	....	Other Investment Liab., n.i.e.	**78bi d**
74	230	264	523	−204	109	68	−65	−670	37	−23	−87	−8	−38	....	Monetary Authorities	**78bs d**
−109	−1,403	−1,478	−1,471	−1,207	−1,262	−1,035	−777	−957	−962	−859	−878	−837	−859	....	General Government	**78bt d**
−107	16	25	8	6	−88	19	176	152	−241	801	226	1,669	−220	....	Banks	**78bu d**
−164	127	−51	−198	159	−63	343	663	49	1,093	750	891	582	976	....	Other Sectors	**78bv d**
−1,504	−125	−218	332	−167	−215	1,114	417	1,232	267	652	992	−307	423	....	Net Errors and Omissions	**78ca d**
−1,594	−2,746	−3,867	−3,056	−2,610	−2,455	−1,397	−1,299	−1,432	827	−1,312	306	400	−2,151	....	*Overall Balance*	**78cb d**
1,594	2,746	3,867	3,056	2,610	2,455	1,397	1,299	1,432	−827	1,312	−306	−400	2,151	....	Reserves and Related Items	**79da d**
−422	476	1,094	149	−242	−212	−899	−554	−667	−3,068	−911	−1,784	−1,493	1,142	....	Reserve Assets	**79db d**
−49	−51	—	—	−24	−63	−51	−49	254	—	—	—	149	−145	....	Use of Fund Credit and Loans	**79dc d**
2,065	2,321	2,773	2,907	2,876	2,731	2,347	1,901	1,845	2,241	2,223	1,478	944	1,154	....	Exceptional Financing	**79de d**

Peru

		1970	1971	1972	1973	1974	1975	1976	1977	1978	1979	1980	1981	1982	1983	1984
International Investment Position																*Millions of US Dollars*
Assets	79aa d	....	....	....	....	....	....	....	....	....	....	....	....	....	....	....
Direct Investment Abroad	79ab d	....	....	....	....	....	....	....	....	....	....	....	....	....	....	....
Portfolio Investment	79ac d	....	....	....	....	....	....	....	....	....	....	....	....	....	....	....
Equity Securities	79ad d	....	....	....	....	....	....	....	....	....	....	....	....	....	....	....
Debt Securities	79ae d	....	....	....	....	....	....	....	....	....	....	....	....	....	....	....
Financial Derivatives	79al d	....	....	....	....	....	....	....	....	....	....	—	—	—	—	—
Other Investment	79af d	....	....	....	....	....	....	....	....	....	....	....	....	....	....	....
Monetary Authorities	79ag d	....	....	....	....	....	....	....	....	....	....	....	....	....	....	....
General Government	79ah d	....	....	....	....	....	....	....	....	....	....	....	....	....	....	....
Banks	79ai d	....	....	....	....	....	....	....	....	....	....	....	....	....	....	....
Other Sectors	79aj d	....	....	....	....	....	....	....	....	....	....	....	....	....	....	....
Reserve Assets	79ak d	....	....	....	....	....	....	....	....	....	....	2,366	1,766	1,964	2,014	2,287
Liabilities	79la d	....	....	....	....	....	....	....	....	....	....	....	....	....	....	....
Dir. Invest. in Rep. Economy	79lb d	....	....	....	....	....	....	....	....	....	....	....	....	....	....	....
Portfolio Investment	79lc d	....	....	....	....	....	....	....	....	....	....	....	....	....	....	....
Equity Securities	79ld d	....	....	....	....	....	....	....	....	....	....	....	....	....	....	....
Debt Securities	79le d	....	....	....	....	....	....	....	....	....	....	....	....	....	....	....
Financial Derivatives	79ll d	....	....	....	....	....	....	....	....	....	....	....	....	....	....	....
Other investment	79lf d	....	....	....	....	....	....	....	....	....	....	....	10,727	12,339	13,929	12,976
Monetary Authorities	79lg d	....	....	....	....	....	....	....	....	....	....	1,209	866	1,396	1,809	675
General Government	79lh d	....	....	....	....	....	....	....	....	....	....	....	....	....	....	....
Banks	79li d	....	....	....	....	....	....	....	....	....	....	1,074	1,220	625	688	640
Other Sectors	79lj d	....	....	....	....	....	....	....	....	....	....	....	....	....	....	....
Government Finance												*Thousandths(.000) Nuev.Soles through 1976; Nuev.Soles from 1977 to 1987;*				
Deficit (-) or Surplus	80	–3,300	–8,100	–10,800	–14,100	–14,100	–30,600	–48,400	‡–79	–80	–18	–140	–416	–557	–2,351	‡–3,064
Revenue	81	38,800	41,400	45,600	53,300	68,600	87,900	111,400	‡154	264	552	1,019	1,523	2,493	3,732	‡9,646
Grants Received	81z								‡—		—	—	—	—	—	‡—
Expenditure	82	42,100	49,500	56,400	67,400	82,700	118,500	159,800	‡233	344	570	1,159	1,938	3,050	6,083	‡12,710
Lending Minus Repayments	83	—	—	—	—	—	—	—	‡—	—	—	—	—	—	—	‡—
Financing																
Domestic	84a	1,800	9,100	8,900	7,100	3,100	13,800	32,600	‡45	72	49	125	283	133	1,177	‡708
Foreign	85a	1,500	–1,000	1,900	7,000	11,000	16,800	15,800	‡35	8	–31	15	133	424	1,174	‡2,356
National Accounts												*Thousandths(.000) Nuev.Soles through 1976; Nuev.Soles from 1977 to 1987;*				
Exports of Goods & Services	90c	47,500	42,100	45,500	53,100	72,100	71,700	95,700	‡176	375	957	1,337	1,697	2,861	6,140	13,190
Government Consumption	91f	29,000	33,000	38,400	45,400	54,700	75,500	101,000	‡157	209	301	628	1,096	1,908	3,486	6,682
Gross Fixed Capital Formation	93e	29,900	33,300	37,800	45,400	68,000	96,800	127,800	‡154	230	720	1,497	3,041	5,150	7,389	14,034
Increase/Decrease(-) in Stocks	93i	1,200	6,400	4,000	10,800	16,500	12,400	9,200	‡5	9	33	239	575	664	172	–130
Private Consumption	96f	‡170,000	190,000	210,000	260,000	330,000	420,000	570,000	‡780	1,170	2,031	3,470	6,230	10,120	20,030	46,600
Imports of Goods & Services	98c	–37,700	–39,900	–43,200	–54,900	–96,400	–126,100	–139,100	‡–214	–320	–559	–1,159	–2,077	–3,383	–6,074	–10,891
Gross Domestic Product (GDP)	99b	240,700	264,400	294,700	359,200	447,500	550,200	764,500	‡1,058	1,678	‡3,490	6,010	10,540	17,310	31,160	68,800
Net Factor Inc/Pmts(-) Abroad	98.n	—	—	—	—	—	–10,000	–10,000	‡–20	–70	–140	–140	–420	–680	–1,770	–3,980
Gross National Income (GNI)	99a	237,300	262,500	292,200	355,200	444,100	545,200	752,800	‡1,035	1,609	2,977	4,830	10,125	16,632	29,387	64,823
Net National Income	99e	222,000	245,000	273,000	336,000	422,000	521,900	715,000	‡981	1,517	2,829	4,602	7,871	13,029	23,802	54,955
GDP Volume 1979 Prices	99b.p	2,519	2,624	2,699	2,844	3,107	3,213	3,276	3,289	3,299	3,490	3,655	3,856	3,757	3,384	3,559
GDP Volume (1995=100)	99bv p	57.1	59.5	61.2	64.5	70.5	72.9	74.3	74.6	74.8	79.1	82.9	87.4	85.2	76.7	80.7
GDP Deflator (1995=1 trillion)	99bi p	3,162.7	3,334.7	3,613.2	4,179.3	4,765.9	5,667.0	7,722.6	10,643.5	16,829.8	....	....	....	....	....	....
GDP Deflator (1995=10 billions)	99bi p	....	....	....	....	....	....	....	....	168	‡331	544	905	1,525	3,047	6,397
GDP Deflator (1995=100)	99bi p	....	....	....	....	....	....	....	....	....	....	....	....	....	....	....
																Millions:
Population	99z	13.45	13.59	13.95	14.35	14.75	15.16	15.57	15.99	16.41	16.85	17.30	17.75	18.14	18.57	18.99

International Investment Position

Millions of US Dollars

	1985	1986	1987	1988	1989	1990	1991	1992	1993	1994	1995	1996	1997	1998	1999	
Assets	....	4,329	3,856	4,168	5,279	5,123	6,235	6,432	6,814	10,670	12,341	14,856	15,896	14,813	....	79aa d
Direct Investment Abroad	....												137	239	239	....	79ab d
Portfolio Investment	....	—	—	—	—	—	—	—	—	—	—	—	46	219	201	....	79ac d
Equity Securities	....	....	....	....	....	....	....	....	....	....	....	....					79ad d
Debt Securities	....												46	219	201		79ae d
Financial Derivatives	....																79al d
Other Investment	....	2,524	2,791	3,105	3,826	3,385	3,662	3,339	3,061	3,854	4,606	5,155	4,427	4,504	....	79af d
Monetary Authorities	....																79ag d
General Government	....	248	341	354	535	472	948	864	745	1,017	1,446	1,907	865	859		79ah d
Banks	....	2,276	2,450	2,751	3,291	2,913	2,714	2,475	2,316	2,837	3,160	3,248	3,562	3,645		79ai d
Other Sectors	....																79aj d
Reserve Assets	2,599	1,805	1,065	1,063	1,453	1,738	2,573	3,093	3,753	6,816	7,735	9,518	11,011	9,869		79ak d
Liabilities	....	16,663	20,414	21,625	22,762	24,166	26,786	28,109	29,763	36,271	40,967	43,611	40,563	41,398		79la d
Dir. Invest. in Rep. Economy	....	1,152	1,173	1,258	1,287	1,330	1,370	1,501	1,663	4,462	5,991	6,703	7,742	8,051		79lb d
Portfolio Investment								27	695	1,661	1,680	3,184	8,174	7,314		79lc d
Equity Securities	....	....						27	689	1,547	1,599	3,111	3,721	2,726		79ld d
Debt Securities									6	114	81	73	4,453	4,588		79le d
Financial Derivatives																79ll d
Other investment	13,143	15,484	19,241	20,367	21,475	22,836	25,416	26,581	27,404	30,148	33,295	33,724	24,647	26,033		79lf d
Monetary Authorities	702	908	1,062	1,451	1,121	1,249	1,305	1,124	1,045	1,137	1,131	1,013	1,092	948		79lg d
General Government	....	12,704	16,248	17,188	18,466	19,982	22,135	22,637	23,319	25,055	26,825	25,196	14,657	15,432		79lh d
Banks	504	724	803	811	817	689	708	884	1,036	797	1,598	1,824	3,494	3,272		79li d
Other Sectors	....	1,148	1,128	917	1,071	917	1,270	1,938	2,006	3,159	3,741	5,691	5,404	6,381		79lj d

Government Finance

Thousands from 1988 to 1989; Millions Beginning 1990: Year Ending Dec. 31

	1985	1986	1987	1988	1989	1990	1991	1992	1993	1994	1995	1996	1997	1998	1999	
Deficit (-) or Surplus	-4,563	-14,734	-44,988	I-155	-5,956	I-434	-596	I-1,589	-2,172	2,061	-1,786	3,540	900	-276	....	80
Revenue	28,235	45,331	66,424	I403	7,499	I682	3,674	I6,861	10,529	16,349	20,479	24,494	27,869	29,637	....	81
Grants Received				I—		I—	32	I5	49	11					....	81z
Expenditure	32,798	60,065	111,412	I558	13,455	I1,116	4,254	I8,346	12,617	18,125	22,991	24,718	27,282	30,130	....	82
Lending Minus Repayments	—	—	—	I—	—	I—	48	I109	133	-3,826	-726	-3,764	-313	-217	....	83
Financing																
Domestic	-931	8,453	35,971	I64	4,131	I142	-358	I163	31	-4,514	-1,092	-4,621	-562	-273	....	84a
Foreign	5,494	6,281	9,017	I91	1,825	I292	954	I1,426	2,141	2,453	2,878	1,081	-338	549	....	85a

National Accounts

Thousands from 1988 to 1989; Millions Beginning 1990

	1985	1986	1987	1988	1989	1990	1991	1992	1993	1994	1995	1996	1997	1998	1999	
Exports of Goods & Services	43,737	48,491	76,631	I564	15,180	I827	3,232	5,648	8,654	12,416	15,121	17,918	22,265	21,994	26,373	90c
Government Consumption	17,940	34,623	70,175	I314	7,300	I386	1,905	3,508	5,421	5,211	11,079	12,331	14,804	16,274	17,426	91f
Gross Fixed Capital Formation	34,952	66,860	128,330	I859	18,000	I940	4,716	7,943	13,723	23,156	31,663	33,618	42,905	45,200	41,666	93e
Increase/Decrease(-) in Stocks	40	6,140	23,050	I101	1,000	I57	752	701	1,494	964	821	1,150	-588	-540	315	93i
Private Consumption	124,490	258,460	507,990	I3,183	76,000	I4,903	26,161	41,009	63,689	81,404	96,348	109,019	123,198	131,628	137,585	96f
Imports of Goods & Services	-30,522	-53,490	-88,210	I-678	-12,000	I-741	-3,846	-6,804	-11,083	-15,739	-21,775	-24,533	-28,934	-30,716	-30,029	98c
Gross Domestic Product (GDP)	189,140	361,270	718,160	I4,343	105,000	I6,372	32,921	52,005	81,898	110,412	133,258	149,504	173,689	183,841	193,336	99b
Net Factor Inc/Pmts(-) Abroad	-10,010	-10,460	-9,850	I-107	-1,616	I-160	-773	-1,083	-1,930	....						98.n
Gross National Income (GNI)	178,374	349,088	712,178	I4,199	113,499	I6,630	32,164	50,977	78,598	....						99a
Net National Income	144,608	....	690,734	I4,476	105,681	I6,199	30,734	47,806	72,585							99e
GDP Volume 1979 Prices	3,659	4,026	4,350	3,970	3,505	3,377	3,485	3,414	3,643	4,108	4,410	4,514	4,828	4,842	5,027	99b.p
GDP Volume (1995=100)	83.0	91.3	98.6	90.0	79.5	76.6	79.0	77.4	82.6	93.2	100.0	102.4	109.5	109.8	114.0	99bv p
GDP Deflator (1995=1 trillion)															....	99bi p
GDP Deflator (1995=10 billions)	17,107	29,696	54,636	362,018	9,913,947										....	99bi p
GDP Deflator (1995=100)					.1	6.2	31.3	50.4	74.4	88.9	100.0	109.6	119.1	125.7	127.3	99bi p

Midyear Estimates

	1985	1986	1987	1988	1989	1990	1991	1992	1993	1994	1995	1996	1997	1998	1999	
Population	19.42	19.84	20.26	20.68	21.11	21.57	22.00	22.45	22.74	23.13	23.53	23.95	24.37	24.80	25.23	99z

(See notes in the back of the book.)

Philippines

		1970	1971	1972	1973	1974	1975	1976	1977	1978	1979	1980	1981	1982	1983	1984
Exchange Rates																*Pesos per SDR:*
Market Rate	**aa**	‖6.435	6.987	7.362	8.119	8.650	8.778	8.630	8.952	9.608	9.768	9.693	9.544	10.117	14.659	19.369
																Pesos per US Dollar:
Market Rate	**ae**	‖6.435	6.435	6.781	6.730	7.065	7.498	7.428	7.370	7.375	7.415	7.600	8.200	9.171	14.002	19.760
Market Rate	**rf**	5.904	6.432	6.675	6.756	6.788	7.248	7.440	7.403	7.366	7.378	7.511	7.900	8.540	11.113	16.699
																Index Numbers (1995=100):
Market Rate	**ahx**	447.1	399.9	385.6	380.7	379.1	355.2	345.4	347.3	348.5	348.2	342.1	325.3	301.1	236.3	157.4
Nominal Effective Exchange Rate	**nec**	....	....	....	....	....	....	....	....	....	319.0	316.9	315.8	314.7	251.4	172.9
Real Effective Exchange Rate	**rec**	....	....	....	....	....	....	....	....	....	122.9	129.4	133.5	138.6	116.6	115.5
Fund Position																*Millions of SDRs:*
Quota	**2f.s**	155	155	155	155	155	155	155	155	210	210	315	315	315	440	440
SDRs	**1b.s**	—	—	22	24	28	23	14	19	13	26	—	2	3	1	20
Reserve Position in the Fund	**1c.s**	—	—	—	—	—	—	—	—	—	—	—	—	—	—	9
Total Fund Cred.&Loans Outstg.	**2tl**	69	90	95	76	68	165	348	435	506	618	820	975	906	1,046	903
International Liquidity															*Millions of US Dollars Unless Otherwise Indicated:*	
Total Reserves minus Gold	**1l.d**	195	309	480	993	1,459	1,314	1,597	1,479	1,763	2,250	2,846	2,066	888	747	602
SDRs	**1b.d**	—	—	24	29	34	27	16	23	17	34	—	—	2	3	1	19
Reserve Position in the Fund	**1c.d**	—	—	—	—	—	—	—	—	—	—	—	—	—	—	9
Foreign Exchange	**1d.d**	195	309	456	964	1,425	1,287	1,581	1,456	1,746	2,216	2,846	2,064	885	746	574
Gold (Million Fine Troy Ounces)	**1ad**	1.600	1.914	1.857	1.057	1.056	1.056	1.056	1.056	1.513	1.702	1.920	1.659	1.866	.289	.786
Gold (National Valuation)	**1and**	56	67	71	45	45	45	45	45	118	166	294	508	823	117	288
Monetary Authorities: Other Liab.	**4..d**	212	233	157	187	282	577	595	49	881	1,562	2,500	2,802	4,308	4,288	4,575
Deposit Money Banks: Assets	**7a.d**	162	187	355	675	1,004	1,121	716	639	1,033	1,436	2,170	2,322	2,629	1,873	2,171
Liabilities	**7b.d**	155	260	484	716	1,087	1,176	1,209	1,480	2,606	3,721	4,846	4,609	4,843	3,157	3,044
Other Banking Insts.: Liabilities	**7f.d**	....	....	....	....	163	160	271	516	582	731	986	1,253	1,643	1,646	1,701
OBU: Foreign Assets	**7k.d**	....	....	....	....	....	....	....	366	719	819	995	1,035	1,253	887	676
Foreign Liabilities	**7m.d**	....	....	....	....	....	....	....	359	1,248	1,998	2,916	3,798	4,321	4,164	3,809
Monetary Authorities																*Billions of Pesos:*
Foreign Assets	**11**	1.18	1.78	2.77	7.05	10.63	10.20	12.54	11.86	14.57	18.68	24.73	22.43	24.49	‖12.11	17.63
Claims on Central Government	**12a**	2.03	2.14	2.91	3.36	4.47	3.32	3.84	4.46	5.98	6.91	7.79	12.47	19.07	‖28.65	33.95
Claims on Local Government	**12b**	.50	.44	.46	.26	.27	.35	.72	.81	.74	.68	.56	.46	.43	‖—	
Claims on Nonfin.Pub.Enterprises	**12c**	....	....	....	....	....	....	....	....	....	....	....	.01	.08	‖1.81	.42
Claims on Deposit Money Banks	**12e**	1.15	1.03	1.24	1.04	2.23	6.27	4.28	2.90	5.86	9.74	14.09	16.88	18.50	‖18.06	19.86
Claims on Other Financial Insts	**12f**	.71	.84	.96	.57	.84	1.52	2.27	2.66	3.83	5.11	6.88	10.17	12.53	‖19.83	27.52
Reserve Money	**14**	3.24	3.57	4.47	5.03	6.27	7.12	8.01	9.90	12.30	15.08	16.95	18.64	19.67	‖28.85	34.62
of which: Currency Outside DMBs	**14a**	2.41	2.65	3.43	3.45	4.31	4.75	5.65	6.73	8.14	9.18	10.18	11.63	12.71	‖19.59	21.76
Restricted Deposits	**16b**														21.60	46.99
Foreign Liabilities	**16c**	1.81	2.12	1.76	1.98	3.39	6.99	8.65	5.67	9.62	15.81	25.22	29.98	43.21	‖73.22	105.35
o/w: Med.&Long-Term Fgn Liabs	**16cl**	....	....	....	....	....	....	....	....	....	....	....	....	....	36.95	53.79
Central Government Deposits	**16d**	.22	.29	.74	1.91	3.40	1.26	.97	1.49	2.63	2.30	2.33	2.46	2.41	‖6.17	13.00
Capital Accounts	**17a**	.27	.29	.34	.31	.33	.34	.37	.42	.41	.68	.50	.53	.52	‖1.99	2.63
Other Items (Net)	**17r**	.02	−.05	1.02	3.05	5.06	5.95	5.64	5.21	6.02	7.24	9.03	10.81	9.29	−52.37	−103.20
Deposit Money Banks																*Billions of Pesos:*
Reserves	**20**	.83	.92	1.03	1.58	1.96	2.26	2.30	3.09	3.96	5.45	6.02	6.17	5.94	‖8.37	11.87
Nonreserve Claims on Mon. Auths	**20r**	—	.29	.45	1.80	2.25	3.51	3.92	5.23	6.91	7.11	6.17	5.58	4.37	‖18.77	31.43
Foreign Assets	**21**	1.04	1.21	2.41	4.54	7.10	8.40	‖5.32	4.71	7.62	10.65	16.49	19.04	24.11	26.22	42.90
Claims on Central Government	**22a**	.90	.91	.83	1.53	1.38	1.25	1.68	3.27	3.93	4.45	4.98	6.13	9.42	‖13.03	15.44
Claims on Local Government	**22b**	1.58	1.47	1.36	1.09	1.70	4.58	5.87	6.05	6.43	7.38	8.68	7.39	10.02	‖1.22	.21
Claims on Nonfin.Pub.Enterprises	**22c**	....	....	....	....	....	....	....	....	....	....	....	....	....	15.37	21.19
Claims on Private Sector	**22d**	8.06	9.52	11.65	15.63	23.34	26.98	‖32.36	38.61	49.23	63.32	76.64	92.50	106.00	136.23	128.35
Claims on Other Financial Insts	**22f**	....	....	....	....	....	....	....	....	....	....	....	....	....	2.38	4.45
Demand Deposits	**24**	1.90	2.36	3.03	3.81	4.70	5.57	6.42	8.21	8.81	9.66	12.36	11.90	10.82	‖13.07	11.69
Time, Savings,& Fgn.Currency Dep.	**25**	5.48	6.32	6.45	8.69	9.55	10.80	14.96	19.82	26.24	29.71	36.02	45.24	57.95	‖90.87	111.49
Money Market Instruments	**26a**	—	.99	1.29	4.04	7.47	9.63	10.87	11.40	11.49	11.95	12.37	16.45	16.57	‖20.00	14.59
Foreign Liabilities	**26c**	1.00	1.67	3.28	4.82	7.68	8.82	8.98	10.90	19.22	27.59	36.83	37.79	53.28	‖44.20	60.16
Central Government Deposits	**26d**	.73	.69	.92	1.89	2.46	2.39	2.23	2.11	2.55	4.17	4.13	4.50	4.29	‖11.53	12.29
Credit from Monetary Authorities	**26g**	1.15	1.03	1.24	1.04	2.23	6.12	4.41	3.13	4.02	7.00	10.09	12.98	13.67	‖16.33	20.36
Capital Accounts	**27a**	1.52	1.72	2.06	2.77	3.64	5.05	5.67	6.73	7.76	8.90	10.47	13.79	16.16	‖22.43	27.41
Other Items (Net)	**27r**	.63	−.46	−.55	−.88	—	−1.40	−2.08	−1.34	−2.02	−.63	−3.31	−5.84	−12.67	2.16	−2.14
Monetary Survey																*Billions of Pesos:*
Foreign Assets (Net)	**31n**	−.58	−.81	.13	4.80	6.65	2.80	‖.23	—	−6.65	−14.09	−20.83	−26.30	−47.89	‖−79.10	−104.97
Domestic Credit	**32**	12.81	14.34	16.50	18.65	26.15	34.34	‖43.55	52.26	64.96	81.38	99.05	122.14	150.98	‖198.83	206.25
Claims on Central Govt. (Net)	**32an**	1.97	2.07	2.08	1.09	−.01	.91	2.32	4.13	4.74	4.89	6.30	11.63	22.00	‖23.98	24.11
Claims on Local Government	**32b**	2.08	1.91	1.82	1.35	1.97	4.93	6.59	6.85	7.17	8.06	9.24	7.85	10.45	‖1.22	.21
Claims on Nonfin.Pub.Enterprises	**32c**	....	....	....	....	....	....	....	....	....	....	....	....	....	16.19	21.61
Claims on Private Sector	**32d**	8.06	9.52	11.65	15.63	23.34	26.98	‖32.36	38.61	49.23	63.32	76.64	92.50	106.00	136.23	128.35
Claims on Other Financial Insts	**32f**	.71	.84	.96	.57	.84	1.52	2.27	2.66	3.83	5.11	6.88	10.17	12.53	‖22.21	31.97
Money	**34**	4.31	5.01	6.47	7.27	9.01	10.31	12.07	14.94	16.95	18.84	22.54	23.52	23.52	‖33.55	34.44
Quasi-Money	**35**	5.48	6.32	6.45	8.69	9.55	10.80	14.96	19.82	26.24	29.71	36.02	45.24	57.95	‖90.87	111.49
Money Market Instruments	**36a**	—	.99	1.29	4.04	7.47	9.63	10.87	11.40	11.49	11.95	12.37	16.45	16.57	‖20.00	14.59
Other Items (Net)	**37r**	2.44	1.21	2.42	3.45	6.77	6.40	5.87	6.10	3.64	6.79	7.29	10.62	5.04	‖−24.69	−59.24
Money plus Quasi-Money	**35l**	12.50	14.47	16.49	20.37	23.69	26.96	34.53	44.38	55.14	62.00	74.78	87.81	104.04	‖124.42	145.93

Philippines

Exchange Rates

End of Period

1985	1986	1987	1988	1989	1990	1991	1992	1993	1994	1995	1996	1997	1998	1999		
20.905	25.112	29.508	28.711	29.490	39.834	38.121	34.507	38.046	35.647	38.967	37.801	53.936	54.996	55.330	Market Rate	aa

End of Period (ae) Period Average (rf)

1985	1986	1987	1988	1989	1990	1991	1992	1993	1994	1995	1996	1997	1998	1999		
19.032	20.530	20.800	21.335	22.440	28.000	26.650	25.096	27.699	24.418	26.214	26.288	39.975	39.059	40.313	Market Rate	ae
18.607	20.386	20.568	21.095	21.737	24.311	27.479	25.512	27.120	26.417	25.714	26.216	29.471	40.893	39.089	Market Rate	rf

Period Averages

1985	1986	1987	1988	1989	1990	1991	1992	1993	1994	1995	1996	1997	1998	1999		
138.3	126.3	124.9	121.9	118.4	106.5	93.6	100.9	95.1	97.6	100.0	98.1	88.7	63.0	65.8	Market Rate	ahx
156.3	123.1	111.8	103.6	103.4	94.5	85.4	93.9	94.5	101.1	100.0	102.1	98.4	74.8	76.7	Nominal Effective Exchange Rate	ne c
126.3	98.6	90.7	88.7	89.1	84.1	83.8	93.2	92.9	97.4	100.0	109.3	108.8	88.7	96.4	Real Effective Exchange Rate	re c

Fund Position

End of Period

1985	1986	1987	1988	1989	1990	1991	1992	1993	1994	1995	1996	1997	1998	1999		
440	440	440	440	440	440	440	633	633	633	633	633	633	633	880	Quota	2f. s
35	5	—	—	1	1	3	—	7	17	5	2	1	1	5	SDRs	1b. s
24	39	39	39	39	39	39	87	87	87	87	87	87	87	87	Reserve Position in the Fund	1c. s
1,049	1,035	888	813	895	641	759	800	881	729	489	282	634	1,114	1,328	Total Fund Cred.&Loans Outstg.	2tl

International Liquidity

End of Period

1985	1986	1987	1988	1989	1990	1991	1992	1993	1994	1995	1996	1997	1998	1999		
615	1,728	968	1,003	1,417	924	3,246	4,403	4,676	6,017	6,372	10,030	7,266	9,226	13,230	Total Reserves minus Gold	1l. d
39	6	—	—	1	1	1	4	1	10	24	8	2	2	7	SDRs	1b. d
26	47	55	52	51	55	56	120	120	127	129	125	118	123	120	Reserve Position in the Fund	1c. d
550	1,675	913	951	1,365	868	3,186	4,283	4,546	5,866	6,235	9,902	7,147	9,101	13,103	Foreign Exchange	1d. d
1.478	2.259	2.776	2.841	2.447	2.888	3.366	2.798	3.221	2.892	3.580	4.651	4.988	5.432	6.199	Gold (Million Fine Troy Ounces)	1ad
501	799	1,046	1,108	959	1,124	1,280	935	1,245	1,104	1,403	1,715	1,472	1,555	1,782	Gold (National Valuation)	1an d
6,253	7,825	7,178	6,744	6,027	6,162	6,063	4,531	2,653	2,295	2,523	2,489	2,578	3,272	4,423	Monetary Authorities: Other Liab.	4..d
2,158	2,158	2,640	3,259	3,539	3,910	3,947	4,691	4,778	6,036	6,402	8,185	8,878	9,975	10,637	Deposit Money Banks: Assets	7a. d
2,500	1,827	1,940	2,099	2,024	2,378	2,059	2,995	2,913	4,640	6,420	14,364	15,406	13,263	11,978	Liabilities	7b. d
1,203	5	5	6	16	67	213	480	911	963	1,080	49	62	64	46	Other Banking Insts.: Liabilities	7f. d
643	441	505	549	518	508	357	483	508	485	283	174	203	123	121	OBU: Foreign Assets	7k. d
3,751	3,473	2,946	2,513	2,265	1,950	1,524	1,418	1,055	1,674	1,545	1,647	1,826	1,296	1,167	Foreign Liabilities	7m. d

Monetary Authorities

End of Period

1985	1986	1987	1988	1989	1990	1991	1992	1993	1994	1995	1996	1997	1998	1999		
20.68	51.42	41.88	45.04	53.23	57.60	122.40	133.46	‡164.01	173.78	203.60	308.76	349.29	422.13	605.18	Foreign Assets	11
33.34	58.67	45.72	40.92	40.03	39.80	32.14	76.24	‡293.48	233.87	227.85	240.26	226.57	194.18	237.91	Claims on Central Government	12a
								‡						—	Claims on Local Government	12b
4.49	4.09	4.38	5.05	5.97	6.29	5.99	3.45	‡2.31	1.97	1.93	1.82	2.98	4.26	17.76	Claims on Nonfin.Pub.Enterprises	12c
27.78	16.00	19.01	20.54	22.49	28.00	29.14	15.38	‡7.27	6.17	7.31	7.68	26.43	18.20	12.69	Claims on Deposit Money Banks	12e
27.79	9.29	8.72	8.18	8.01	7.62	6.80	6.45	‡5.91	4.60	6.26	6.48	8.02	13.51	14.18	Claims on Other Financial Insts	12f
39.48	52.13	59.42	69.10	96.00	112.98	135.68	153.36	‡182.27	191.56	224.43	257.02	277.22	245.62	325.94	Reserve Money	14
24.03	29.26	35.37	40.64	52.94	61.92	69.39	74.30	‡84.08	95.68	110.89	122.95	143.64	146.06	218.47	*of which: Currency Outside DMBs*	14a
58.17	48.98	30.40	31.09	29.56	34.26	80.60	94.72	‡60.97	45.43	36.09	102.09	43.01	87.98	127.37	Restricted Deposits	16b
138.72	184.73	174.14	166.62	161.50	198.04	190.51	141.32	‡107.00	82.01	85.22	76.10	137.26	189.08	251.76	Foreign Liabilities	16c
85.16	116.96	120.00	113.58	111.81	142.41	127.26	53.38	‡42.84	37.47	37.15	31.13	54.79	80.42	124.57	*o/w: Med.&Long-Term Fgn Liabs*	16cl
8.70	17.13	47.55	64.38	79.23	81.78	96.73	168.23	‡120.22	108.67	99.21	127.42	91.07	66.89	111.71	Central Government Deposits	16d
3.08	3.61	4.15	4.13	4.31	6.56	6.55	6.61	‡21.06	26.49	30.15	30.08	71.98	88.15	100.25	Capital Accounts	17a
-134.06	-167.11	-195.94	-215.59	-240.88	-294.30	-313.60	-329.25	‡-18.56	-33.76	-28.16	-27.71	-7.24	-25.44	-29.30	Other Items (Net)	17r

Deposit Money Banks

End of Period

1985	1986	1987	1988	1989	1990	1991	1992	1993	1994	1995	1996	1997	1998	1999		
14.42	21.77	22.37	26.65	40.05	46.80	59.97	70.54	87.66	86.74	101.84	120.30	122.82	93.77	103.25	Reserves	20
37.19	32.84	29.95	32.29	30.52	37.76	57.21	35.39	29.20	37.50	22.16	22.62	38.32	74.48	87.77	Nonreserve Claims on Mon. Auths	20r
41.08	44.31	54.92	69.54	79.42	109.49	105.18	117.73	132.35	147.38	167.83	215.16	354.90	389.62	428.82	Foreign Assets	21
13.65	21.44	24.21	38.69	54.84	59.70	61.33	84.34	98.89	147.56	177.21	237.53	304.31	300.34	332.42	Claims on Central Government	22a
.26	.25	.20	.17	.17	.16	.16	.36	.80	2.37	4.68	6.95	9.07	10.34	12.20	Claims on Local Government	22b
20.97	13.63	13.29	13.15	14.83	19.27	19.87	21.50	22.84	17.07	14.87	16.37	25.60	40.51	47.67	Claims on Nonfin.Pub.Enterprises	22c
115.03	90.45	109.08	128.85	159.87	206.56	221.64	276.30	388.87	491.98	715.32	1,063.80	1,370.07	1,277.76	1,246.64	Claims on Private Sector	22d
3.51	2.74	3.52	3.62	3.23	5.45	7.91	10.17	11.50	24.61	27.09	60.26	76.61	117.98	130.68	Claims on Other Financial Insts	22f
11.70	12.81	16.75	18.74	25.21	26.76	31.98	34.72	49.10	55.08	72.04	96.41	111.92	134.09	172.87	Demand Deposits	24
123.27	119.68	130.77	168.86	218.09	273.91	322.67	371.44	477.63	613.16	765.20	949.71	1,225.32	1,332.79	1,483.42	Time, Savings,& Fgn.Currency Dep.	25
11.03	7.83	6.76	5.38	6.88	14.56	7.35	7.39	8.86	8.03	9.79	9.63	15.34	13.16	11.22	Money Market Instruments	26a
47.58	37.52	40.34	44.77	45.42	66.59	54.87	75.17	80.70	113.29	168.29	377.59	615.86	518.03	482.86	Foreign Liabilities	26c
15.25	17.29	13.26	16.70	17.09	13.78	16.23	26.55	41.76	26.62	39.41	51.73	38.90	32.43	39.86	Central Government Deposits	26d
29.20	16.17	20.31	25.46	25.27	32.58	35.77	22.58	23.82	17.41	17.47	15.80	15.87	11.39	9.60	Credit from Monetary Authorities	26g
24.77	31.85	35.51	42.28	47.34	61.65	76.32	91.07	107.10	132.36	184.71	243.17	327.28	376.53	440.89	Capital Accounts	27a
-16.68	-15.71	-6.19	-9.24	-2.35	-4.65	-11.94	-12.57	-16.86	-10.75	-25.90	-1.05	-48.80	-113.61	-251.27	Other Items (Net)	27r

Monetary Survey

End of Period

1985	1986	1987	1988	1989	1990	1991	1992	1993	1994	1995	1996	1997	1998	1999		
-124.55	-126.51	-117.68	-96.81	-74.27	-97.55	-17.80	34.70	‡108.66	125.86	117.92	70.23	-48.93	104.63	299.38	Foreign Assets (Net)	31n
195.11	166.15	148.32	157.55	191.41	250.27	243.86	286.82	‡663.21	789.29	1,036.60	1,454.32	1,893.28	1,859.57	1,887.89	Domestic Credit	32
23.05	45.69	9.13	-1.48	-1.45	3.94	-19.50	-34.20	‡230.39	246.14	266.43	298.65	400.92	395.20	418.76	Claims on Central Govt. (Net)	32an
.26	.25	.20	.17	.17	.16	.16	.36	‡.80	2.37	4.68	6.95	9.07	10.34	12.20	Claims on Local Government	32b
25.46	17.73	17.67	18.19	20.80	25.55	25.86	24.96	25.14	19.04	16.80	18.19	28.58	44.77	65.43	Claims on Nonfin.Pub.Enterprises	32c
115.03	90.46	109.08	128.85	160.65	207.54	222.63	279.08	‡389.47	492.53	715.34	1,063.80	1,370.08	1,277.76	1,246.64	Claims on Private Sector	32d
31.31	12.03	12.24	11.81	11.24	13.07	14.71	16.62	‡17.41	29.21	33.35	66.73	84.63	131.49	144.86	Claims on Other Financial Insts	32f
36.76	43.17	53.80	61.20	81.28	92.94	107.69	117.54	‡143.71	159.90	194.63	233.12	266.33	285.95	395.56	Money	34
123.27	119.68	130.77	168.86	218.09	273.91	322.67	371.44	‡477.63	613.16	765.20	949.71	1,225.32	1,332.79	1,483.42	Quasi-Money	35
11.03	7.83	6.76	5.38	6.88	14.56	7.35	7.39	‡8.86	8.03	9.79	9.63	15.34	13.16	11.22	Money Market Instruments	36a
-100.49	-131.03	-160.70	-174.70	-189.10	-228.68	-211.65	-174.84	‡141.67	134.06	184.90	332.09	337.36	332.30	297.07	Other Items (Net)	37r
160.02	162.85	184.58	230.05	299.37	366.85	430.36	488.97	‡621.34	773.06	959.83	1,182.83	1,491.64	1,618.74	1,878.97	Money plus Quasi-Money	35l

		1970	1971	1972	1973	1974	1975	1976	1977	1978	1979	1980	1981	1982	1983	1984
Other Banking Institutions																*Billions of Pesos:*
Claims on Central Government	42a	.11	.22	.59	.41	.74	1.39	2.00	2.10	2.50	2.62	2.69	3.19	2.99	2.54	2.93
Claims on Private Sector	42d	3.26	4.03	4.49	5.26	5.55	7.12	10.19	13.35	15.76	20.11	26.23	36.03	42.29	54.17	56.31
Time and Savings Deposits	45	.94	1.15	1.24	1.63	2.21	4.73	5.56	6.18	7.91	9.93	12.36	14.44	16.04	14.49	9.78
Bonds	46ab	1.13	1.12	1.11	.54	.64	.55	.46	.30	1.81	2.25	2.65	3.23	4.78	6.03	6.53
Foreign Liabilities	46c	....	....	....	....	1.15	1.20	2.01	3.80	4.29	5.42	7.49	10.27	15.07	23.05	33.61
Capital Accounts	47a	.78	.82	.87	2.21	2.31	2.54	3.11	3.61	4.00	4.65	5.82	6.57	7.72	8.37	7.46
Other Items (Net)	47r	.52	1.16	1.86	1.28	-.07	-.56	1.02	1.56	.25	.49	.60	4.71	1.67	4.77	1.87
Liquid Liabilities	55l	10.73	12.48	14.16	17.58	20.76	25.84	32.60	40.94	51.09	58.48	70.92	83.20	97.52	138.91	155.71
Interest Rates																*Percent Per Annum*
Discount Rate *(End of Period)*	60	10.000	10.000	10.000	10.000	6.000	6.000	6.000	6.000	4.000	11.000	4.541	6.692	6.304	8.050	12.108
Treasury Bill Rate	60c	....	....	....	....	....	....	10.186	10.885	10.880	12.255	12.136	12.547	13.780	14.231	28.529
Deposit Rate	60l	....	....	....	....	....	....	8.500	8.500	8.500	8.667	12.250	13.717	13.742	13.581	21.172
Lending Rate	60p	....	....	....	....	....	....	12.000	12.000	12.000	14.000	14.000	15.335	18.120	19.238	28.195
Prices, Production, Labor																*Index Numbers (1995=100):*
Share Prices	62	25.1	15.2	11.7	16.5	14.0	10.2	10.3	8.2	10.5	10.3	7.7	6.7	5.5	5.5	4.9
Mining(1980=100)	62a	548.4	307.4	191.2	297.0	218.0	138.6	130.7	91.5	109.2	147.6	100.0	77.2	....	....	....
Sugar(1980=100)	62b	142.6	110.6	88.1	90.9	112.1	135.1	175.7	129.4	108.7	101.9	100.0	110.2	....	....	....
Wholesale Prices	63	4.0	4.6	5.1	6.3	9.3	9.8	11.2	12.0	12.6	15.0	17.7	20.3	22.4	26.0	43.5
Consumer Prices	64	4.6	5.6	6.1	7.1	9.5	10.2	11.1	12.2	13.1	15.4	18.2	20.6	22.5	23.7	34.7
Manufacturing Production	66ey	....	....	....	....	....	....	....	....	....	....	....	14.3	14.6	17.0	24.2
Manufacturing Empl. (1990=100)	67ey	....	....	....	....	....	....	....	....	....	....	....	111.6	103.6	101.5	95.8
																Number in Thousands:
Labor Force	67d	....	....	....	....	....	....	....	....	....	....	....	....	....	....	....
Employment	67e	....	....	....	....	....	....	....	....	....	....	....	....	....	....	19,368
Unemployment	67c	....	....	....	....	....	....	....	....	....	....	....	....	....	....	....
Unemployment Rate (%)	67r	....	....	....	....	....	....	....	....	....	....	....	....	....	....	....
International Transactions																*Millions of Pesos:*
Exports	70	6,183	7,064	7,351	12,735	18,505	16,607	19,005	23,148	25,051	33,696	43,142	44,620	42,411	54,641	88,339
Sugar	70i															
Coconut Oil	70ai	564	665	562	1,015	2,483	1,669	2,222	2,950	4,293	5,462	4,258	4,214	3,422	5,666	9,677
Imports, c.i.f.	71	7,299	8,523	9,474	12,156	23,556	27,226	29,328	31,606	37,885	48,786	62,308	66,984	70,569	88,657	107,670
Imports, f.o.b.	71.v	6,570	7,594	8,504	10,846	21,346	24,937	26,954	28,983	34,856	45,310	57,698	62,773	65,322	83,207	99,246
Volume of Exports																*1995=100*
Sugar	72i	801	878	790	962	1,007	635	957	1,594	758	817	1,133	798	814	639	624
Coconut Oil	72ai	25	30	35	32	31	46	64	56	73	60	68	78	69	71	44
Volume of Imports	73	37	40	40	38	44	47	49	48	57	62	63	58	66	63	45
Unit Value of Exports																
Sugar (Wholesale Price)	76i	7	8	10	11	21	21	17	13	13	13	17	18	24	26	47
Coconut Oil (W'sale price)	76ai	11	9	8	19	42	17	18	26	31	41	26	25	22	40	96
Unit Value of Imports	75	7	7	8	10	17	19	19	21	22	26	32	38	35	46	78
Balance of Payments																*Millions of US Dollars:*
Current Account, n.i.e.	78ald	....	....	....	....	....	....	....	-754	-1,094	-1,496	-1,917	-2,096	-3,212	-2,771	-1,294
Goods: Exports f.o.b.	78aad	....	....	....	....	....	....	....	3,151	3,425	4,601	5,788	5,722	5,021	5,005	5,391
Goods: Imports f.o.b.	78abd	....	....	....	....	....	....	....	-3,915	-4,732	-6,142	-7,727	-7,946	-7,667	-7,487	-6,070
Trade Balance	78acd	....	....	....	....	....	....	....	-764	-1,307	-1,541	-1,939	-2,224	-2,646	-2,482	-679
Services: Credit	78add	....	....	....	....	....	....	....	733	1,013	1,076	1,447	1,791	1,804	1,808	1,642
Services: Debit	78aed	....	....	....	....	....	....	....	-856	-1,000	-1,180	-1,439	-1,632	-1,823	-1,733	-1,194
Balance on Goods & Services	78afd	....	....	....	....	....	....	....	-887	-1,294	-1,645	-1,931	-2,065	-2,665	-2,407	-231
Income: Credit	78agd	....	....	....	....	....	....	....	352	472	578	762	1,070	1,179	1,319	984
Income: Debit	78ahd	....	....	....	....	....	....	....	-477	-590	-784	-1,182	-1,573	-2,200	-2,155	-2,433
Balance on Gds, Serv. & Inc.	78aid	....	....	....	....	....	....	....	-1,012	-1,412	-1,851	-2,351	-2,568	-3,686	-3,243	-1,680
Current Transfers, n.i.e.: Credit	78ajd	....	....	....	....	....	....	....	272	328	369	451	485	486	483	387
Current Transfers: Debit	78akd	....	....	....	....	....	....	....	-14	-10	-14	-17	-13	-12	-11	-1
Capital Account, n.i.e.	78bcd	....	....	....	....	....	....	....	1	1	—	—	—	—	—	—
Capital Account, n.i.e.: Credit	78bad	....	....	....	....	....	....	....	1	1	—	—	—	—	—	—
Capital Account: Debit	78bbd	....	....	....	....	....	....	....	—	—	—	—	—	—	—	—
Financial Account, n.i.e.	78bjd	....	....	....	....	....	....	....	497	1,741	1,563	2,684	2,018	2,847	-389	781
Direct Investment Abroad	78bdd	....	....	....	....	....	....	....								
Dir. Invest. in Rep. Econ., n.i.e.	78bed	....	....	....	....	....	....	....	210	101	7	-106	172	16	105	9
Portfolio Investment Assets	78bfd	....	....	....	....	....	....	....	-3	-5	-1	-1	-2			-3
Equity Securities	78bkd	....	....	....	....	....	....	....	—	—	—	—	—			—
Debt Securities	78bld	....	....	....	....	....	....	....	-3	-5	-1	-1	-2			-3
Portfolio Investment Liab., n.i.e.	78bgd	....	....	....	....	....	....	....	9	4	14	5	5	1	7	—
Equity Securities	78bmd	....	....	....	....	....	....	....	—	—	—	—	—			—
Debt Securities	78bnd	....	....	....	....	....	....	....	9	4	14	5	5	1	7	—
Financial Derivatives Assets	78bwd	....	....	....	....	....	....	....	....	....	....	....	....	....	....	....
Financial Derivatives Liabilities	78bxd	....	....	....	....	....	....	....	....	....	....	....	....	....	....	....
Other Investment Assets	78bhd	....	....	....	....	....	....	....	-337	-343	-889	-389	-713	-355	108	100
Monetary Authorities	78bod	....	....	....	....	....	....	....								
General Government	78bpd	....	....	....	....	....	....	....	—	—	—	—	—	—	—	—
Banks	78bqd	....	....	....	....	....	....	....	—	—	—	—	—	—	—	—
Other Sectors	78brd	....	....	....	....	....	....	....	-337	-343	-889	-389	-713	-355	108	100
Other Investment Liab., n.i.e.	78bid	....	....	....	....	....	....	....	618	1,984	2,432	3,175	2,556	3,185	-609	675
Monetary Authorities	78bsd	....	....	....	....	....	....	....	-109	13	377	781	-192	58	-69	-41
General Government	78btd	....	....	....	....	....	....	....	-45	525	972	477	1,072	1,957	176	629
Banks	78bud	....	....	....	....	....	....	....	337	934	626	708	496	460	-375	-249
Other Sectors	78bvd	....	....	....	....	....	....	....	435	512	457	1,209	1,180	710	-341	336
Net Errors and Omissions	78cad	....	....	....	....	....	....	....	210	112	249	124	-487	-364	-336	65
Overall Balance	78cbd	....	....	....	....	....	....	....	-46	760	316	891	-565	-729	-3,496	-448
Reserves and Related Items	79dad	....	....	....	....	....	....	....	46	-760	-316	-891	565	729	3,496	448
Reserve Assets	79dbd	....	....	....	....	....	....	....	-56	-898	-462	-1,163	151	792	1,886	-49
Use of Fund Credit and Loans	79dcd	....	....	....	....	....	....	....	102	90	146	259	182	-75	155	-149
Exceptional Financing	79ded	....	....	....	....	....	....	....	—	47	—	13	232	12	1,455	647

1985	1986	1987	1988	1989	1990	1991	1992	1993	1994	1995	1996	1997	1998	1999		
End of Period															**Other Banking Institutions**	
6.85	2.78	5.06	5.28	3.65	5.95	7.92	11.41	10.82	12.93	19.09	3.38	3.95	2.35	1.74	Claims on Central Government	42a
39.36	15.63	17.69	21.36	29.05	33.07	45.95	61.24	82.32	115.93	143.41	127.55	139.92	144.74	145.55	Claims on Private Sector	42d
13.52	13.32	15.49	20.14	24.84	29.60	40.72	51.30	63.19	69.09	93.73	106.89	120.70	119.08	120.58	Time and Savings Deposits	45
5.96	1.45	1.09	.48	.33	.19	—	—	.15	2.28	3.65	4.22	5.39	6.38	6.29	Bonds	46ab
22.90	.09	.10	.14	.36	1.87	5.69	12.04	25.23	23.51	28.31	1.29	2.49	2.49	1.87	Foreign Liabilities	46c
7.88	6.50	7.23	8.88	11.08	12.17	13.13	16.11	18.97	27.08	32.99	27.33	35.93	40.73	48.63	Capital Accounts	47a
-4.05	-2.96	-1.16	-2.99	-3.91	-4.81	-5.67	-6.79	-14.39	6.90	3.81	-8.79	-20.65	-21.60	-30.08	Other Items (Net)	47r
173.54	176.17	200.07	250.19	324.21	396.45	471.08	540.28	684.53	842.14	1,053.56	1,289.71	1,612.34	1,737.82	1,999.55	Liquid Liabilities	55l
Percent Per Annum															**Interest Rates**	
I 12.750	10.000	10.000	10.000	12.000	14.000	14.000	14.300	9.400	8.300	10.830	11.700	14.640	12.400	7.894	Discount Rate *(End of Period)*	60
26.725	16.081	11.509	14.667	18.646	23.672	21.478	16.018	12.448	12.714	11.761	12.338	12.893	15.004	9.996	Treasury Bill Rate	60c
18.914	11.253	8.202	11.315	14.126	19.538	18.802	14.275	9.606	10.539	8.392	9.683	10.194	12.106	8.167	Deposit Rate	60l
28.612	17.534	13.338	15.921	19.270	24.118	23.074	19.479	14.683	15.057	14.682	14.840	16.276	16.777	11.776	Lending Rate	60p
Period Averages															**Prices, Production, Labor**	
4.3	20.3	46.9	49.0	70.1	61.4	64.4	75.5	89.6	112.2	100.0	97.4	84.9	56.4	87.1	Share Prices	62
....	....	....	....	....	....	....	....	....	....	....	....	....	....	....	Mining(1980=100)	62a
....	....	....	....	....	....	....	....	....	....	....	....	....	....	....	Sugar(1980=100)	62b
51.4	50.6	55.2	62.6	69.3	76.3	86.6	90.5	89.5	96.8	I 100.0	108.9	109.5	122.2	129.3	Wholesale Prices	63
42.7	42.6	43.9	49.3	54.9	62.1	73.6	79.9	85.4	92.6	100.0	109.0	115.5	126.7	135.2	Consumer Prices	64
24.8	24.7	30.5	37.5	45.1	49.4	60.9	63.7	74.7	84.6	100.0	108.6	118.2	115.7	125.1	Manufacturing Production	66ey
88.4	82.8	88.5	97.6	102.3	100.0	91.5	88.3	87.0	85.8	....	....	....	....	....	Manufacturing Empl. (1990=100)	67ey
Period Averages																
....	....	....	....	....	....	25,241	26,180	26,816	27,478	28,039	29,637	30,265	31,278	....	Labor Force	67d
20,327	20,926	I 20,795	21,497	21,849	22,532	22,979	23,917	24,443	25,031	25,698	27,442	27,888	28,262	....	Employment	67e
....	1,438	I 2,085	1,954	2,009	1,993	2,267	I 2,263	2,379	2,317	2,342	2,195	2,377	3,016	....	Unemployment	67c
....	6.4	I 9.1	8.3	8.4	8.1	9.0	I 9.8	9.3	9.5	9.5	....	....	....	....	Unemployment Rate (%)	67r
Millions of Pesos															**International Transactions**	
85,283	97,375	116,237	148,204	168,928	197,962	241,612	248,359	302,998	350,078	450,487	535,054	738,415	1,206,197	1,432,595	Exports	70
....	....	....	....	....	2,555	3,169	2,225	2,740	2,758	1,713	3,544	2,270	3,102	3,219	Sugar	70i
6,460	6,727	7,827	8,608	8,190	8,770	8,203	12,275	9,698	12,552	21,242	14,960	19,846	28,857	13,497	Coconut Oil	70ai
101,518	107,324	147,875	184,246	243,013	317,977	353,191	393,723	511,311	596,611	729,960	894,665	1,139,830	1,290,274	1,272,176	Imports, c.i.f.	71
93,396	102,897	138,605	172,174	226,643	297,657	331,079	369,635	479,296	562,163	679,701	835,863	1,060,815	1,213,859	1,200,873	Imports, f.o.b.	71.v
1995=100																
															Volume of Exports	
373	145	106	93	137	161	179	136	212	119	100	207	129	121	93	Sugar	72i
49	92	77	59	57	85	63	66	64	63	100	59	81	88	36	Coconut Oil	72ai
41	49	64	78	93	100	102	....	....	....	....	....	....	....	....	Volume of Imports	73
															Unit Value of Exports	
62	58	64	85	91	93	96	95	76	82	100	100	84	6	53	Sugar (Wholesale Price)	76i
53	31	55	76	71	48	61	87	70	90	100	121	118	146	184	Coconut Oil (W'sale price)	76ai
81	73	74	76	83	100	108	....	....	....	....	....	....	....	....	Unit Value of Imports	75
Minus Sign Indicates Debit															Balance of Payments	
-36	952	-444	-390	-1,456	-2,695	-1,034	-1,000	-3,016	-2,950	-1,980	-3,953	-4,351	1,546	7,912	Current Account, n.i.e.	78al *d*
4,629	4,842	5,720	7,074	7,821	8,186	8,840	9,824	11,375	13,483	17,447	20,543	25,228	29,496	34,207	Goods: Exports f.o.b.	78aa *d*
-5,111	-5,044	-6,737	-8,159	-10,419	-12,206	-12,051	-14,519	-17,597	-21,333	-26,391	-31,885	-36,355	-29,524	-29,245	Goods: Imports f.o.b.	78ab *d*
-482	-202	-1,017	-1,085	-2,598	-4,020	-3,211	-4,695	-6,222	-7,850	-8,944	-11,342	-11,127	-28	4,962	*Trade Balance*	78ac *d*
2,235	2,860	2,345	2,413	3,225	3,244	3,654	4,742	4,673	6,768	9,348	12,947	15,137	7,477	4,802	Services: Credit	78ad *d*
-867	-844	-1,155	-1,308	-1,564	-1,761	-1,804	-2,308	-3,090	-4,654	-6,926	-9,429	-14,122	-10,107	-7,515	Services: Debit	78ae *d*
886	1,814	173	20	-937	-2,537	-1,361	-2,261	-4,639	-5,736	-6,522	-7,824	-10,112	-2,658	2,249	*Balance on Goods & Services*	78af *d*
1,053	931	1,109	1,179	1,361	1,598	1,969	2,755	2,824	3,782	6,067	6,059	7,698	6,440	8,081	Income: Credit	78ag *d*
-2,353	-2,232	-2,299	-2,364	-2,710	-2,470	-2,469	-2,310	-1,900	-1,932	-2,405	-2,777	-3,017	-2,671	-2,910	Income: Debit	78ah *d*
-414	513	-1,017	-1,165	-2,286	-3,409	-1,861	-1,816	-3,715	-3,886	-2,860	-4,542	-5,431	1,111	7,420	*Balance on Gds, Serv. & Inc.*	78ai *d*
387	443	575	778	832	717	828	825	746	1,041	1,147	1,185	1,670	758	610	Current Transfers, n.i.e.: Credit	78aj *d*
-9	-4	-2	-3	-2	-3	-1	-9	-47	-105	-267	-596	-590	-323	-118	Current Transfers: Debit	78ak *d*
1	2	—	—	—	—	—	1	—	—	—	—	—	—	-9	Capital Account, n.i.e.	78bc *d*
1	2	—	—	—	—	—	1	—	—	—	—	—	—	44	Capital Account, n.i.e.: Credit	78ba *d*
—	—	—	—	—	—	—	—	—	—	—	—	—	—	-53	Capital Account: Debit	78bb *d*
328	146	318	571	1,354	2,057	2,927	3,208	3,267	5,120	5,309	11,277	6,498	483	-1,190	Financial Account, n.i.e.	78bj *d*
—	—	—	—	—	—	—	—	-374	-302	-399	-182	-136	-160	-128	Direct Investment Abroad	78bd *d*
12	127	307	936	563	530	544	228	1,238	1,591	1,478	1,517	1,222	2,287	564	Dir. Invest. in Rep. Econ., n.i.e.	78be *d*
-12	—	-2	-1	-14	—	-15	-115	-949	-632	-1,429	191	-9	-603	-275	Portfolio Investment Assets	78bf *d*
—	—	—	—	—	—	—	—	....	....	....	21	30	-184	-51	Equity Securities	78bk *d*
-12	—	-2	-1	-14	—	-15	-115	-949	-632	-1,429	170	-39	-419	-224	Debt Securities	78bl *d*
17	13	21	51	294	-50	125	155	897	901	2,619	5,126	600	-325	5,088	Portfolio Investment Liab., n.i.e.	78bg *d*
—	—	—	—	—	—	—	—	....	....	....	2,101	-406	264	506	Equity Securities	78bm *d*
17	13	21	51	294	-50	125	155	897	901	2,619	3,025	1,006	-589	4,582	Debt Securities	78bn *d*
....	....	....	....	....	....	....	....	....	....	....	....	....	....	....	Financial Derivatives Assets	78bw *d*
....	....	....	....	....	....	....	....	....	....	....	....	....	....	....	Financial Derivatives Liabilities	78bx *d*
—	—	—	—	—	—	—	—	—	—	—	-1,745	425	809	-5,998	Other Investment Assets	78bh *d*
....	....	....	....	....	....	....	....	....	....	....	....	....	—	—	Monetary Authorities	78bo *d*
—	—	—	—	—	—	—	—	....	....	....	....	....	—	—	General Government	78bp *d*
—	—	—	—	—	—	—	—	....	....	....	-1,745	425	809	-1,278	Banks	78bq *d*
—	—	—	—	—	—	—	—	....	....	....	—	—	—	-4,720	Other Sectors	78br *d*
311	6	-8	-415	511	1,577	2,273	2,940	2,455	3,562	3,040	6,370	4,396	-1,525	-441	Other Investment Liab., n.i.e.	78bi *d*
-969	—	—	—	—	—	—	—	—	—	—	199	-98	5	75	Monetary Authorities	78bs *d*
2,565	1,277	-462	-68	108	875	375	2,731	1,065	-1,121	-408	-808	-218	-207	181	General Government	78bt *d*
-939	-250	402	321	370	307	473	1,921	-229	1,694	1,648	5,036	1,668	-1,118	-1,069	Banks	78bu *d*
-346	-1,021	52	-668	33	395	1,425	-1,712	1,619	2,989	1,800	1,943	3,044	-205	372	Other Sectors	78bv *d*
545	34	68	493	402	593	-138	-520	85	157	-2,094	-2,986	-5,241	-750	-3,054	Net Errors and Omissions	78ca *d*
838	1,134	-58	674	300	-45	1,755	1,689	336	2,327	1,235	4,338	-3,094	1,279	3,659	*Overall Balance*	78cb *d*
-838	-1,134	58	-674	-300	45	-1,755	-1,689	-336	-2,327	-1,235	-4,338	3,094	-1,279	-3,659	Reserves and Related Items	79da *d*
98	-1,124	249	-570	-408	388	-1,937	-1,746	-447	-2,107	-873	-4,037	2,610	-1,938	-3,947	Reserve Assets	79db *d*
164	-10	-190	-104	108	-343	182	58	111	-220	-362	-301	485	659	288	Use of Fund Credit and Loans	79dc *d*
-1,100	—	—	—	—	—	—	—	—	—	—	—	—	—	....	Exceptional Financing	79de *d*

Philippines

	1970	1971	1972	1973	1974	1975	1976	1977	1978	1979	1980	1981	1982	1983	1984
Government Finance														*Millions of Pesos:*	
Deficit (-) or Surplus............... **80**	59	−183	Ɪ−1,101	−843	445	−1,360	Ɪ−2,352	−2,807	−2,171	−349	−3,385	−12,154	−14,414	−7,468	−9,957
Revenue......................... **81**	4,849	5,869	Ɪ6,950	9,430	11,919	16,657	Ɪ17,895	19,782	23,826	29,095	34,151	35,478	37,710	45,290	56,467
Grants Received **81z**	....	....	Ɪ22	69	238	181	Ɪ405	177	181	224	222	258	283	316	359
Expenditure **82**	4,790	6,052	Ɪ7,507	10,060	9,968	17,276	Ɪ18,706	20,542	23,502	25,417	32,561	38,880	40,821	44,942	52,753
Lending Minus Repayments **83**	....	....	Ɪ566	282	1,744	922	Ɪ1,946	2,224	2,676	4,251	5,197	9,010	11,586	8,132	14,030
Financing															
Net Borrowing.................... **84**	....	216	....	....											
Domestic......................... **84a**	....	....	Ɪ695	594	−631	1,106	Ɪ2,302	2,561	362	−2,762	1,152	6,180	9,735	2,048	8,123
Foreign........................ **85a**	....	....	Ɪ406	249	186	254	Ɪ50	246	1,809	3,111	2,233	5,974	4,679	5,420	1,834
Use of Cash Balances **87**	....	−38	....	....	....	....	....	....	....	....	....	....	....	....	....
Debt: Domestic **88a**	4,019	4,287	Ɪ4,627	6,356	9,379	11,414	Ɪ13,171	15,301	15,571	16,191	18,534	23,227	31,772	42,639	61,350
Foreign **89a**	1,105	1,388	Ɪ1,536	1,272	3,071	4,937	Ɪ6,210	8,517	12,266	20,829	22,569	29,992	40,118	41,784	97,996
National Accounts														*Billions of Pesos*	
Exports of Goods & Services **90c**	8.1	9.3	9.9	8.1	22.3	21.3	23.2	28.9	32.4	41.5	57.5	67.1	64.5	78.8	126.0
Government Consumption **91f**	3.5	4.3	5.3	6.2	8.9	11.1	13.2	14.3	16.1	18.3	22.1	24.7	28.9	30.6	36.9
Gross Fixed Capital Formation..... **93e**	6.7	8.2	8.8	11.4	18.4	27.1	33.7	36.4	42.3	56.3	66.4	78.1	87.3	110.2	121.0
Increase/Decrease(-) in Stocks **93i**	2.3	2.3	2.7	3.2	6.6	6.7	8.3	7.9	9.0	11.4	4.5	−.8	1.1	−.9	−14.3
Private Consumption **96f**	29.6	35.6	39.9	48.2	67.2	76.2	87.1	102.6	118.8	146.6	156.8	181.5	208.1	237.5	362.3
Imports of Goods & Services....... **98c**	−8.2	−9.6	−10.3	−8.2	−25.4	−29.1	−31.8	−34.8	−41.3	−53.6	−69.4	−76.5	−82.9	−103.6	−131.5
Gross Domestic Product (GDP) **99b**	42.4	50.1	56.1	72.3	99.5	114.7	135.3	154.2	177.7	217.5	243.7	281.6	317.2	369.1	524.5
Net Factor Inc/Pmts(-) Abroad **98.n**	−.7	−.5	−.5	−.1	.4	−.3	−1.1	−1.0	−.6	.5	−.5	−1.1	−3.6	−5.8	−16.0
Gross National Income (GNI) **99a**	41.8	49.6	55.5	72.2	99.9	114.4	134.2	153.3	177.0	218.0	243.3	280.5	313.5	363.3	508.5
Net National Income **99e**	38.0	44.9	50.2	65.2	91.4	103.1	121.3	138.7	160.3	197.5	240.0	273.0	300.8	340.4	472.5
GDP Volume 1985 Prices............ **99b.p**	343.2	361.8	381.5	415.5	430.3	454.3	494.3	522.0	549.0	579.9	609.8	630.6	653.5	665.7	617.0
GDP Volume (1995=100) .... **99bv p**	42.8	45.1	47.6	51.8	53.6	56.6	61.6	65.1	68.4	72.3	76.0	78.6	81.5	83.0	76.9
GDP Deflator (1995=100) .... **99bi p**	5.2	5.8	6.2	7.3	9.7	10.6	11.5	12.4	13.6	15.8	16.8	18.8	20.4	23.3	35.8
															Millions:
Population............................. **99z**	36.85	37.90	38.99	40.12	41.30	42.07	43.41	44.58	45.79	47.04	48.32	49.54	50.78	52.06	53.35

	1985	1986	1987	1988	1989	1990	1991	1992	1993	1994	1995	1996	1997	1998	1999		
Year Ending December 31																**Government Finance**	
	−11,158	−30,648	−16,728	−23,244	−19,568	−37,194	−26,349	−15,965	−21,891	18,114	11,074	6,256	1,564	−49,981	−111,658	Deficit (-) or Surplus	80
	68,577	78,714	101,495	111,086	150,709	178,346	217,598	240,570	258,855	334,488	360,232	409,880	470,087	462,119	478,210	Revenue	81
	380	531	1,719	1,775	1,701	2,556	3,189	2,145	1,550	739	988	569	1,756	396	292	Grants Received	81z
	64,084	82,409	108,451	128,867	166,205	211,184	239,470	265,629	272,391	309,942	341,726	401,017	466,690	511,078	585,425	Expenditure	82
	16,031	27,484	11,491	7,238	5,773	6,912	7,666	−6,949	9,905	7,171	8,420	3,176	3,589	1,418	4,735	Lending Minus Repayments	83
																Financing	
	....	....	....	....	....	....	....	....	....	....	....	....	....	....	....	Net Borrowing	84
	11,308	27,068	9,947	19,002	11,358	33,068	19,469	1,576	8,979	−4,408	2,272	−348	5,254	37,635	28,858	Domestic	84a
	−150	3,580	6,781	4,242	8,210	4,126	6,880	14,390	12,912	−13,706	−13,346	−5,908	−6,818	12,346	82,800	Foreign	85a
	....	....	....	....	....	....	....	....	....	....	....	....	....	....	....	Use of Cash Balances	87
	79,940	116,236	224,697	260,359	284,073	293,821	330,380	435,110	640,867	638,025	....	....	....	....	....	Debt: Domestic	88a
	107,992	123,540	155,308	165,539	176,037	258,820	289,858	278,150	348,955	317,068	....	....	....	....	....	Foreign	89a
Billions of Pesos																**National Accounts**	
	137.3	160.3	181.9	226.9	260.2	296.4	369.4	393.7	462.4	572.6	693.0	879.8	1,188.0	1,389.9	1,533.0	Exports of Goods & Services	90c
	43.5	48.4	57.3	72.2	88.2	108.8	123.9	130.5	149.1	182.8	217.0	259.5	319.9	355.0	387.5	Government Consumption	91f
	94.2	97.7	112.7	142.2	192.7	249.0	250.1	282.8	350.5	400.1	423.2	508.7	593.3	561.7	566.8	Gross Fixed Capital Formation	93e
	−12.1	−4.9	6.8	7.0	7.2	11.2	2.2	5.6	3.1	7.2	4.7	12.9	8.7	−20.5	−6.0	Increase/Decrease(-) in Stocks	93i
	420.8	444.5	482.3	558.8	649.3	767.1	916.4	1,019.2	1,122.5	1,258.8	1,411.9	1,595.3	1,762.0	1,980.1	2,165.3	Private Consumption	96f
	−125.2	−136.2	−179.0	−215.3	−280.1	−358.5	−406.7	−459.9	−586.9	−679.4	−842.1	−1,070.6	−1,438.9	−1,566.6	−1,520.5	Imports of Goods & Services	98c
	571.9	608.9	682.8	799.2	925.4	1,077.2	1,248.0	1,351.6	1,474.5	1,692.9	1,906.0	2,171.9	2,421.3	2,667.1	2,989.1	Gross Domestic Product (GDP)	99b
	−15.8	−12.6	−11.9	−7.2	−13.4	−5.8	6.6	23.3	25.8	43.5	52.6	89.4	101.6	127.0	148.9	Net Factor Inc/Pmts(-) Abroad	98.n
	556.1	596.3	670.8	792.0	912.0	1,071.4	1,254.6	1,374.8	1,500.3	1,736.4	1,958.6	2,261.3	2,522.9	2,794.1	3,137.9	Gross National Income (GNI)	99a
	530.5	543.0	625.7	743.2	841.8	994.0	1,246.4	1,262.2	1,369.6	1,556.4	1,786.6	2,070.8	....	....	....	Net National Income	99e
	571.9	591.4	616.9	658.6	699.4	720.7	716.6	718.9	734.2	766.4	802.2	849.1	892.9	888.1	916.8	GDP Volume 1985 Prices	99b.p
	71.3	73.7	76.9	82.1	87.2	89.8	89.3	89.6	91.5	95.5	100.0	105.8	111.3	110.7	114.3	GDP Volume (1995=100)	99bvp
	42.1	43.3	46.6	51.1	55.7	62.9	73.3	79.1	84.5	93.0	100.0	107.7	114.1	126.4	137.2	GDP Deflator (1995=100)	99bip
Midyear Estimates																	
	54.67	56.00	57.36	58.72	60.10	61.48	ᵻ63.69	65.34	66.98	68.62	70.27	71.90	73.53	75.15	74.75	**Population**	99z

(See notes in the back of the book.)

Poland

		1970	1971	1972	1973	1974	1975	1976	1977	1978	1979	1980	1981	1982	1983	1984
Exchange Rates										*Zlotys per Million SDRs through 1977, per Thousand SDRs in 1978-89,*						
Market Rate	aa	400.00	399.54	399.54	400.51	406.48	388.66	385.73	403.28	‡4.33	5.14	5.87	6.50	9.54	10.30	12.37
											Zlotys per Millions US$ through 1977, per Thousand US$ in 1978-89,						
Market Rate	ae	400.00	368.00	368.00	332.00	332.00	332.00	332.00	332.00	‡3.32	3.90	4.61	5.58	8.65	9.84	12.62
Market Rate	rf	400.00	389.33	368.00	335.00	332.00	332.00	332.00	332.00	....	4.02	4.42	5.12	8.48	9.16	11.32
											Index Numbers (1995=100):						
Market Rate	ah x	606,035.9	623,602.1	658,734.6	724,211.3	730,163.7	730,163.7	730,163.7	730,163.7	....	60,362.1	54,836.8	47,685.1	28,597.7	26,564.9	21,560.8
Nominal Effective Exchange Rate	ne c	....	....	....	....	....	....	....	....	....	33,575.5	33,441.9	34,338.7	23,365.7	24,018.5	22,014.9
Real Effective Exchange Rate	re c	....	....	....	....	....	....	....	....	....		74.2	82.3	102.3	123.2	120.7
Fund Position											*Millions of SDRs:*						
Quota	2f. s									....	....	....	....	....	....	....
SDRs	1b. s									....	....	....	....	....	....	....
Reserve Position in the Fund	1c. s									....	....	....	....	....	....	....
Total Fund Cred.&Loans Outstg.	2tl									....	....	....	....	....	....	....
International Liquidity											*Millions of US Dollars Unless Otherwise Indicated:*						
Total Reserves minus Gold	1l. d	....	....	....	....	....	....	....	....	....	565.1	127.6	277.8	646.8	765.2	1,106.0
SDRs	1b. d	....	....	....	....	....	....	....	....	....						
Reserve Position in the Fund	1c. d	....	....	....	....	....	....	....	....	....						
Foreign Exchange	1d. d	....	....	....	....	....	....	....	....	....	565.1	127.6	277.8	646.8	765.2	1,106.0
Gold (Million Fine Troy Ounces)	1ad	....	....	....	....	....	....	....	....	....	1.285	.758	.470	.471	.472	.472
Gold (National Valuation)	1an d	....	....	....	....	....	....	....	....	....	267.3	303.0	188.0	188.5	188.8	188.8
Monetary Authorities: Other Liab.	4.. d	....	....	....	....	....	....	....	....	....	510.1	427.8	428.0	387.5	668.9	640.1
Deposit Money Banks: Assets	7a. d	....	....	....	....	....	....	....	....	....	1,576.5	1,476.7	2,034.4	1,713.1	1,639.7	1,895.6
Liabilities	7b. d	....	....	....	....	....	....	....	....	....	23,476.0	25,318.1	27,593.1	25,544.2	24,039.8	23,394.3
Monetary Authorities											*Millions of Zlotys:*						
Foreign Assets	11	....	....	....	....	....	....	....	....	....	3	2	‡3	7	10	17
Claims on General Government	12a	....	....	....	....	....	....	....	....	....	—	3	‡20	23	39	52
Claims on Nonfin.Pub.Enterprises	12c	....	....	....	....	....	....	....	....	....	....	....				
Claims on Private Sector	12d	....	....	....	....	....	....	....	....	....						
Claims on Deposit Money Banks	12e	....	....	....	....	....	....	....	....	....	180	200	‡189	197	207	202
Reserve Money	14	....	....	....	....	....	....	....	....	....	109	142	‡168	190	207	219
of which: Currency Outside DMBs	14a	....	....	....	....	....	....	....	....	....	24	29	‡40	61	72	82
Nonreserve Liabilities to Banks	16b	....	....	....	....	....	....	....	....	....						
Foreign Liabilities	16c	....	....	....	....	....	....	....	....	....	2	2	‡2	3	7	8
General Government Deposits	16d	....	....	....	....	....	....	....	....	....	68	56	‡37	25	32	47
Capital Accounts	17a	....	....	....	....	....	....	....	....	....	4	4	‡4	4	4	4
Other Items (Net)	17r	....	....	....	....	....	....	....	....	....	—	1	‡1	5	6	–7
Deposit Money Banks											*Millions of Zlotys:*						
Reserves	20	....	....	....	....	....	....	....	....	....	85	113	‡128	130	135	136
Nonreserve Claims on Mon. Auths	20c	....	....	....	....	....	....	....	....	....	—	—	—	—	—	—
Foreign Assets	21	....	....	....	....	....	....	....	....	....	6	7	‡11	15	16	24
Claims on General Government	22a	....	....	....	....	....	....	....	....	....	8	11	‡13	18	15	16
Claims on Nonfin.Pub.Enterprises	22c	....	....	....	....	....	....	....	....	....	283	308	‡331	379	415	454
Claims on Private Sector	22d	....	....	....	....	....	....	....	....	....	15	16	‡16	23	29	36
Demand Deposits	24	....	....	....	....	....	....	....	....	....	55	59	‡67	90	93	108
Time, Savings,& Fgn.Currency Dep.	25	....	....	....	....	....	....	....	....	....	56	64	‡80	107	129	158
Foreign Liabilities	26c	....	....	....	....	....	....	....	....	....	17	25	‡27	36	40	58
General Government Deposits	26d	....	....	....	....	....	....	....	....	....	7	5	‡4	14	10	10
of which: Local Govt. Dep.	26db	....	....	....	....	....	....	....	....	....	4	3	‡4	9	10	10
Credit from Monetary Authorities	26g	....	....	....	....	....	....	....	....	....	180	200	‡189	197	207	202
Capital Accounts	27a	....	....	....	....	....	....	....	....	....	3	3	‡3	3	5	6
Other Items (Net)	27r	....	....	....	....	....	....	....	....	....	80	98	‡129	118	126	124
Monetary Survey											*Millions of Zlotys:*						
Foreign Assets (Net)	31n	....	....	....	....	....	....	....	....	....	–10	–18	‡–15	–17	–20	–25
Domestic Credit	32	....	....	....	....	....	....	....	....	....	232	276	‡339	404	455	501
Claims on General Govt. (Net)	32an	....	....	....	....	....	....	....	....	....	–66	–48	‡–8	2	11	10
Claims on Nonfin.Pub.Enterprises	32c	....	....	....	....	....	....	....	....	....	283	308	‡331	379	415	454
Claims on Private Sector	32d	....	....	....	....	....	....	....	....	....	15	16	‡16	23	29	36
Money	34	....	....	....	....	....	....	....	....	....	78	88	‡107	150	165	190
Quasi-Money	35	....	....	....	....	....	....	....	....	....	56	64	‡80	107	129	158
Capital Accounts	37a	....	....	....	....	....	....	....	....	....	7	7	‡7	7	9	10
Other Items (Net)	37r	....	....	....	....	....	....	....	....	....	81	99	‡130	122	132	118
Money plus Quasi-Money	35l	....	....	....	....	....	....	....	....	....	134	152	‡187	257	294	348
Interest Rates											*Percent Per Annum*						
Discount Rate (End of Period)	60	....	....	....	....	....	....	....	....	....	....	....	....	....	3.0	4.0
Money Market Rate	60b	....	....	....	....	....	....	....	....	....	....	....	....	....	....	....
Treasury Bill Rate	60c	....	....	....	....	....	....	....	....	....	....	....	....	....	....	....
Deposit Rate	60l	....	....	....	....	....	....	....	....	....	....	....	....	....	....	....
Lending Rate	60p	....	....	....	....	....	....	....	....	....	8.0	8.0	8.0	9.0	9.0	9.0
Prices, Production, Labor											*Index Numbers (1995=100):*						
Share Prices	62	....	....	....	....	....	....	....	....	....	....	....	....	....	....	....
Producer Prices: Industry	63	....	....	....	....	....	....	....	.1	.1	.1	.1	.1	.3	.3	.4
Consumer Prices	64	.1	.1	.1	.1	.1	.1	.1	‡.1	.1	.1	.1	.1	.2	.2	.3
Wages: Average Earnings	65	....	....	....	....	....	....	....	.1	.1	.1	.1	.1	.2	.2	.3
Industrial Production	66	....	....	....	....	....	....	103.4	107.1		109.1	108.0	93.3	90.5	98.2	103.2
Industrial Employment	67	....	....	....	....	....	155.1	155.7	158.9	158.7	158.4	157.9	157.1	149.1	147.7	146.7
											Number in Thousands:						
Labor Force	67d	....	....	....	....	....	....	....	....	....	....	....	....	....	....	....
Employment	67e	....	....	....	....	....	....	....	....	....	....	....	....	....	....	....
Unemployment	67c	....	....	....	....	....	....	....	....	....	....	....	....	....	....	....
Unemployment Rate (%)	67r	....	....	....	....	....	....	....	....	....	....	....	....	....	....	....
International Transactions											*Millions of Zlotys*						
Exports	70	1	2	2	3	3	42	41	46	50	57	63	55	‡95	106	134
Imports, c.i.f.	71	....	....	....	....	....	56	56	58	61	65	74	65	‡90	100	125
Imports, f.o.b.	71.v	....	....	....	....	....	54	54	56	58	62	71	62	‡87	97	121
											1995=100						
Volume of Exports	72	....	....	....	....	....	44.3	46.9	50.8	53.7	57.4	54.9	44.5	48.1	53.4	58.4
Volume of Imports	73	....	....	....	....	....	46.9	51.7	51.1	51.9	51.3	50.3	41.8	36.1	37.9	41.2
Export Prices	76	....	....	....	....	....	.2	.2	.2	.2	.2	.2	.2	.4	.4	.5
Import Prices	76.x	....	....	....	....	....	.6	.5	.5	.6	.6	.7	.8	1.2	1.3	1.5

1985	1986	1987	1988	1989	1990	1991	1992	1993	1994	1995	1996	1997	1998	1999		
per SDR thereafter: End of Period															**Exchange Rates**	
16.24	24.17	44.76	67.63	854.20	I 1.35	1.57	2.17	2.93	3.56	3.67	4.13	4.75	4.93	5.69	Market Rate	aa
per US$ thereafter: End of Period (ae) Period Average (rf)																
14.79	19.76	31.55	50.26	650.00	I .95	1.10	1.58	2.13	2.44	2.47	2.88	3.52	3.50	4.15	Market Rate	ae
14.71	17.53	26.51	43.05	143.92	I .95	1.06	1.36	1.81	2.27	2.42	2.70	3.28	3.48	3.97	Market Rate	rf
Period Averages																
16,519.5	13,970.6	9,300.0	5,722.8	2,772.7	255.2	230.6	179.2	135.1	106.8	100.0	90.1	74.2	69.8	61.2	Market Rate	ahx
18,286.5	12,956.5	7,813.2	4,899.0	2,643.1	235.7	221.3	172.6	143.7	114.4	100.0	93.7	86.6	83.7	75.8	Nominal Effective Exchange Rate	nec
103.6	81.3	59.1	54.1	61.0	51.3	80.3	85.4	91.6	92.4	100.0	108.8	111.4	117.7	112.3	Real Effective Exchange Rate	rec
End of Period															**Fund Position**	
....	680	680	680	680	680	680	989	989	989	989	989	989	989	1,369	Quota	2f.s
....	—	—	—	—	1	5	1	1	1	2	3	4	5	8	SDRs	1b.s
....	—	—	—	—	—	—	77	77	77	77	77	77	77	172	Reserve Position in the Fund	1c.s
....	—	—	—	—	358	597	597	498	919	—	—	—	—	—	Total Fund Cred.&Loans Outstg.	2tl
End of Period															**International Liquidity**	
870.4	697.8	1,494.7	2,055.3	2,314.3	4,492.1	3,632.6	4,099.1	4,091.9	5,841.8	14,774.1	17,844.0	20,407.2	26,432.3	24,534.6	Total Reserves minus Gold	1l.d
....	.1	.1	.1	.1	.8	7.7	1.1	.7	1.5	2.2	4.4	5.4	7.1	11.2	SDRs	1b.d
....	—	—	—	—	—	—	106.1	105.9	112.6	114.6	110.9	104.1	108.6	236.4	Reserve Position in the Fund	1c.d
870.4	697.7	1,494.6	2,055.2	2,314.2	4,491.3	3,624.9	3,992.0	3,985.3	5,727.7	14,657.2	17,728.7	20,297.7	26,316.6	24,287.0	Foreign Exchange	1d.d
.472	.472	.472	.472	.472	.472	.473	.473	.473	.473	.473	.473	.904	3.305	3.306	Gold (Million Fine Troy Ounces)	1ad
188.8	188.9	189.0	189.0	189.0	189.0	189.1	189.0	189.0	189.0	189.0	189.0	262.4	950.0	959.4	Gold (National Valuation)	1and
771.6	700.3	680.4	503.0	664.3	939.9	397.9	423.5	446.2	355.6	363.5	246.4	914.3	1,028.2	1,939.3	Monetary Authorities: Other Liab.	4..d
2,295.1	2,373.2	2,782.5	2,794.7	2,773.1	6,091.2	5,306.4	6,648.3	5,925.5	7,742.2	7,154.4	6,132.1	7,275.5	5,405.3	7,874.7	Deposit Money Banks: Assets	7a.d
26,681.1	30,876.9	35,014.6	33,198.1	32,811.4	1,923.0	1,580.9	1,921.0	1,469.8	1,543.2	2,070.1	2,746.5	4,284.0	5,213.8	6,745.7	Liabilities	7b.d
End of Period															**Monetary Authorities**	
17	24	60	127	1,719	4,717	I 5,080	7,912	10,113	15,475	37,532	52,498	75,500	99,213	113,910	Foreign Assets	11
68	72	84	137	595	601	I 4,365	12,170	15,729	19,530	11,534	12,761	16,792	17,765	18,803	Claims on General Government	12a
....	....	....	....	....	....	15	8	6	3	3	35	39	34	42	Claims on Nonfin.Pub.Enterprises	12c
....	....	....	....	....	....	5	15	21	20	19	24	27	26	28	Claims on Private Sector	12d
216	227	208	483	2,691	7,613	I 7,512	4,848	6,362	7,450	8,244	11,246	9,710	8,044	7,394	Claims on Deposit Money Banks	12e
233	244	246	570	3,275	8,535	I 10,943	14,860	15,993	19,615	28,441	34,262	45,919	53,656	52,957	Reserve Money	14
101	117	131	252	988	3,934	I 5,618	7,798	9,982	12,274	19,530	23,563	27,256	30,225	38,083	*of which: Currency Outside DMBs*	14a
—	—	—	—	—	55	I 841	757	1,406	3,462	9,465	14,660	15,662	28,576	24,694	Nonreserve Liabilities to Banks	16b
11	14	21	25	432	1,376	I 1,371	1,961	2,411	4,135	897	708	3,216	3,603	8,045	Foreign Liabilities	16c
64	72	78	116	146	1,369	I 1,109	1,285	2,272	2,773	3,440	6,127	4,285	4,010	7,040	General Government Deposits	16d
4	4	5	7	15	82	I 100	150	210	300	400	400	400	1,548	1,548	Capital Accounts	17a
−11	−11	1	29	1,137	1,515	I 2,614	5,939	9,939	12,193	14,689	20,407	32,586	33,688	45,894	Other Items (Net)	17r
End of Period															**Deposit Money Banks**	
131	127	115	318	1,889	3,909	I 4,749	5,816	6,045	7,343	8,806	10,633	15,049	23,336	14,867	Reserves	20
—	—	—	—	—	9	I 860	757	1,406	2,877	8,113	13,757	15,216	28,321	24,539	Nonreserve Claims on Mon. Auths	20c
34	47	88	140	1,803	5,787	I 5,814	10,482	12,647	18,869	17,657	17,633	25,595	18,940	32,666	Foreign Assets	21
28	25	44	108	403	1,321	I 7,445	12,037	19,278	27,402	39,299	49,548	52,609	59,989	67,004	Claims on General Government	22a
529	629	721	1,002	3,061	10,105	I 10,379	11,770	14,252	16,751	20,342	24,123	28,756	31,426	31,920	Claims on Nonfin.Pub.Enterprises	22c
46	58	74	110	199	1,719	I 8,979	13,111	19,022	25,165	36,700	57,586	80,395	108,076	145,292	Claims on Private Sector	22d
128	163	220	280	864	5,411	I 5,113	7,096	9,654	15,175	17,817	28,702	34,425	41,438	49,970	Demand Deposits	24
192	253	363	636	5,078	9,022	I 14,609	25,041	36,268	49,844	66,913	84,186	111,084	149,104	175,302	Time, Savings,& Fgn.Currency Dep.	25
70	82	111	174	2,053	1,679	I 1,732	3,029	3,137	3,761	5,109	7,898	15,071	18,269	27,983	Foreign Liabilities	26c
17	21	31	49	264	1,472	I 1,870	3,921	2,706	3,688	5,506	7,942	9,857	12,515	14,113	General Government Deposits	26d
16	21	27	43	54	490	I 857	860	1,149	1,503	2,523	3,401	4,395	5,551	7,146	*of which:* Local Govt. Dep.	26db
216	227	208	483	2,691	7,613	I 7,512	4,848	6,338	7,020	7,788	10,685	9,180	7,565	7,010	Credit from Monetary Authorities	26g
6	7	9	14	107	1,503	I 3,374	4,323	7,129	9,990	12,999	18,534	24,715	30,049	34,294	Capital Accounts	27a
141	133	100	42	−3,703	−3,852	I 4,015	5,715	7,419	8,928	14,785	15,333	13,287	11,148	7,617	Other Items (Net)	27r
End of Period															**Monetary Survey**	
−31	−25	15	68	1,037	7,448	I 7,791	13,405	17,212	26,448	49,183	61,524	82,808	96,281	110,548	Foreign Assets (Net)	31n
591	691	814	1,192	3,847	10,905	I 28,210	43,904	63,330	82,410	98,951	130,008	164,476	200,791	241,937	Domestic Credit	32
16	4	19	80	587	−919	I 8,832	19,001	30,029	40,471	41,887	48,240	55,259	61,229	64,654	Claims on General Govt. (Net)	32an
529	629	721	1,002	3,061	10,105	I 10,394	11,778	14,258	16,754	20,345	24,158	28,795	31,460	31,963	Claims on Nonfin.Pub.Enterprises	32c
46	58	74	110	199	1,719	I 8,984	13,125	19,043	25,185	36,719	57,610	80,422	108,101	145,321	Claims on Private Sector	32d
229	279	352	532	1,881	9,426	I 10,783	14,963	19,646	27,450	37,439	52,331	61,686	71,670	88,201	Money	34
192	253	363	636	5,446	9,633	I 15,319	26,145	36,278	49,852	66,913	84,331	114,705	149,110	175,307	Quasi-Money	35
10	11	14	21	122	1,585	I 3,474	4,473	7,339	10,290	13,399	18,934	25,115	31,598	35,842	Capital Accounts	37a
129	122	100	71	−2,566	−2,291	I 6,424	11,727	17,278	21,266	30,383	35,938	45,777	44,694	53,135	Other Items (Net)	37r
421	533	715	1,168	7,327	19,060	I 26,102	41,108	55,924	77,302	104,352	136,662	176,392	220,780	263,508	Money plus Quasi-Money	35l
Percent Per Annum															**Interest Rates**	
4.0	4.0	4.0	6.0	I 104.0	48.0	36.0	32.0	29.0	28.0	25.0	22.0	24.5	18.3	19.0	Discount Rate *(End of Period)*	60
....	....	....	....	....	....	49.9	I 29.5	24.5	23.3	25.8	20.6	22.4	20.6	13.6	Money Market Rate	60b
....	....	....	....	....	....	....	44.0	33.2	28.8	25.6	20.3	21.6	19.1	13.1	Treasury Bill Rate	60c
....	....	....	....	100.0	41.7	I 53.5	37.8	34.0	I 33.4	26.8	20.0	19.4	18.2	11.2	Deposit Rate	60l
12.0	12.0	12.0	16.7	64.0	504.2	54.6	39.0	35.3	32.8	I 33.5	26.1	25.0	24.5	17.0	Lending Rate	60p
Period Averages															**Prices, Production, Labor**	
....	....	....	....	....	....	....	....	....	....	100.0	168.9	....	....	....	Share Prices	62
.5	.5	.7	1.1	3.4	24.1	I 36.3	46.3	61.2	79.7	100.0	I 113.2	127.0	136.2	143.7	Producer Prices: Industry	63
.3	.4	.5	.7	2.6	16.8	I 29.8	43.2	59.2	78.9	100.0	120.2	139.3	155.6	167.0	Consumer Prices	64
.3	.4	.5	.9	3.6	I 16.8	28.0	38.3	53.7	70.7	100.0	126.3	151.6	174.2	189.9	Wages: Average Earnings	65
106.9	111.7	115.5	121.0	117.5	87.6	I 73.6	I 76.5	80.2	91.4	100.0	....	....	....	....	Industrial Production	66
145.9	146.2	145.5	143.1	138.8	I 121.3	110.5	106.3	100.8	99.1	100.0	98.7	98.2	97.2	92.8	Industrial Employment	67
Period Averages																
....	....	....	....	....	....	....	17,526	17,368	17,004	17,076	....	17,101	17,162	....	Labor Force	67d
18,531	18,595	18,596	18,474	18,220	17,321	16,285	15,462	I 14,894	14,658	14,791	14,969	15,177	15,356	....	Employment	67e
....	....	....	....	....	1,126	2,156	2,509	I 2,890	2,838	2,629	2,360	1,826	1,831	2,155	Unemployment	67c
....	....	....	....	....	6.3	11.8	13.6	I 15.0	16.5	15.2	14.3	11.5	10.0	....	Unemployment Rate (%)	67r
Millions of Zlotys															**International Transactions**	
169	212	324	601	1,948	13,606	I 15,772	17,969	25,757	39,246	55,515	65,819	84,480	95,015	108,706	Exports	70
165	202	297	547	1,542	9,292	I 16,674	21,995	34,018	49,072	70,502	100,231	138,898	162,458	182,362	Imports, c.i.f.	71
159	196	288	527	1,486	9,051	I 16,426	19,126	29,581	42,287	61,306	87,157	120,781	141,268	....	Imports, f.o.b.	71.v
1995=100																
59.2	62.1	65.1	71.0	71.2	I 77.0	75.1	73.2	72.4	85.7	100.0	109.7	124.7	133.2	141.1	Volume of Exports	72
44.5	46.7	48.8	53.3	54.2	I 39.4	54.2	61.8	73.2	83.0	100.0	128.0	156.1	186.3	193.5	Volume of Imports	73
.6	.7	1.0	1.7	5.5	I 33.7	40.0	51.0	64.1	82.5	100.0	108.0	122.0	131.2	140.4	Export Prices	76
1.8	2.1	3.0	4.9	13.6	39.4	51.2	59.7	69.5	88.5	100.0	117.2	133.1	140.1	149.3	Import Prices	76.x

Poland

964		1970	1971	1972	1973	1974	1975	1976	1977	1978	1979	1980	1981	1982	1983	1984
Balance of Payments																*Millions of US Dollars:*
Current Account, n.i.e.	78al *d*	....	....	....	....	....	....	–2,793	–2,392	–2,545	–3,365	–3,417	–3,986	–1,941	–1,581	–1,083
Goods: Exports f.o.b.	78aa *d*	....	....	....	....	....	....	9,506	10,506	11,967	13,276	14,043	10,542	11,547	11,615	11,654
Goods: Imports f.o.b.	78ab *d*	....	....	....	....	....	....	–12,263	–12,724	–14,259	–15,660	–15,819	–12,723	–11,631	–11,312	–10,995
Trade Balance	78ac *d*	....	....	....	....	....	....	–2,757	–2,218	–2,292	–2,384	–1,776	–2,181	–84	303	659
Services: Credit	78ad *d*	....	....	....	....	....	....	1,180	1,385	1,586	1,874	2,018	1,913	1,842	1,990	2,017
Services: Debit	78ae *d*	....	....	....	....	....	....	–1,144	–1,309	–1,521	–1,863	–2,023	–1,727	–1,467	–1,783	–1,853
Balance on Goods & Services	78af *d*	....	....	....	....	....	....	–2,721	–2,142	–2,227	–2,373	–1,781	–1,995	291	510	823
Income: Credit	78ag *d*	....	....	....	....	....	....	37	36	40	71	139	171	93	184	195
Income: Debit	78ah *d*	....	....	....	....	....	....	–688	–924	–1,244	–1,738	–2,496	–3,395	–3,156	–2,978	–2,833
Balance on Gds, Serv. & Inc.	78ai *d*	....	....	....	....	....	....	–3,372	–3,030	–3,431	–4,040	–4,138	–5,219	–2,772	–2,284	–1,815
Current Transfers, n.i.e.: Credit	78aj *d*	....	....	....	....	....	....	597	660	909	953	1,234	1,878	926	942	1,106
Current Transfers: Debit	78ak *d*	....	....	....	....	....	....	–18	–22	–23	–278	–513	–645	–95	–239	–374
Capital Account, n.i.e.	78bc *d*	....	....	....	....	....	....	—	—	—	—	—	—	—	—	—
Capital Account, n.i.e.: Credit	78ba *d*	....	....	....	....	....	....	—	—	—	—	—	—	—	—	—
Capital Account: Debit	78bb *d*	....	....	....	....	....	....	—	—	—	—	—	—	—	—	—
Financial Account, n.i.e.	78bj *d*	....	....	....	....	....	....	3,145	2,282	2,927	3,479	2,870	–1,486	–5,006	–3,681	–3,520
Direct Investment Abroad	78bd *d*	....	....	....	....	....	....	–12	–17	–16	–13	–21	–3	–4	–1	–12
Dir. Invest. in Rep. Econ., n.i.e.	78be *d*	....	....	....	....	....	....	6	5	25	30	10	18	14	16	28
Portfolio Investment Assets	78bf *d*	....	....	....	....	....	....	—	—	—	—	—	—	—	—	—
Equity Securities	78bk *d*	....	....	....	....	....	....	—	—	—	—	—	—	—	—	—
Debt Securities	78bl *d*	....	....	....	....	....	....	—	—	—	—	—	—	—	—	—
Portfolio Investment Liab., n.i.e.	78bg *d*	....	....	....	....	....	....	—	—	—	—	—	—	—	—	—
Equity Securities	78bm *d*	....	....	....	....	....	....	—	—	—	—	—	—	—	—	—
Debt Securities	78bn *d*	....	....	....	....	....	....	—	—	—	—	—	—	—	—	—
Financial Derivatives Assets	78bw *d*	....	....	....	....	....	....	....	....	....	....	....	....	....	....	....
Financial Derivatives Liabilities	78bx *d*	....	....	....	....	....	....	....	....	....	....	....	....	....	....	....
Other Investment Assets	78bh *d*	....	....	....	....	....	....	–338	–378	–195	–252	–182	–711	–543	–336	–767
Monetary Authorities	78bo *d*	....	....	....	....	....	....	....	....	....	....	....	....	....	....	....
General Government	78bp *d*	....	....	....	....	....	....	–243	–180	–106	–28	–30	8	68	28	27
Banks	78bq *d*	....	....	....	....	....	....	–35	–86	–61	–35	–4	–41	–657	–190	–126
Other Sectors	78br *d*	....	....	....	....	....	....	–60	–112	–28	–189	–148	–678	46	–174	–668
Other Investment Liab., n.i.e.	78bi *d*	....	....	....	....	....	....	3,489	2,672	3,113	3,714	3,063	–790	–4,473	–3,360	–2,769
Monetary Authorities	78bs *d*	....	....	....	....	....	....	—	—	—	—	—	—	—	—	—
General Government	78bt *d*	....	....	....	....	....	....	–52	–56	85	111	89	–1,702	–2,684	–1,441	–1,149
Banks	78bu *d*	....	....	....	....	....	....	3,512	2,637	2,899	3,448	3,105	971	–1,994	–1,767	–1,569
Other Sectors	78bv *d*	....	....	....	....	....	....	29	91	129	155	–131	–59	205	–152	–51
Net Errors and Omissions	78ca *d*	....	....	....	....	....	....	–167	–261	–253	161	–90	–206	–217	344	333
Overall Balance	78cb *d*	....	....	....	....	....	....	185	–371	129	275	–637	–5,678	–7,164	–4,918	–4,270
Reserves and Related Items	79da *d*	....	....	....	....	....	....	–185	371	–129	–275	637	5,678	7,164	4,918	4,270
Reserve Assets	79db *d*	....	....	....	....	....	....	–185	371	–129	–275	637	–35	–370	–118	–341
Use of Fund Credit and Loans	79dc *d*	....	....	....	....	....	....	—	—	—	—	—	—	—	—	—
Exceptional Financing	79de *d*	....	....	....	....	....	....	—	—	—	—	—	5,713	7,534	5,036	4,611
International Investment Position																*Millions of US Dollars*
Assets	79aa *d*	....	....	....	....	....	....	....	....	....	....	....	....	....	....	....
Direct Investment Abroad	79ab *d*	....	....	....	....	....	....	....	....	....	....	....	....	....	....	....
Portfolio Investment	79ac *d*	....	....	....	....	....	....	....	....	....	....	....	....	....	....	....
Equity Securities	79ad *d*	....	....	....	....	....	....	....	....	....	....	....	....	....	....	....
Debt Securities	79ae *d*	....	....	....	....	....	....	....	....	....	....	....	....	....	....	....
Financial Derivatives	79al *d*	....	....	....	....	....	....	....	....	....	....	....	....	....	....	....
Other Investment	79af *d*	....	....	....	....	....	....	....	....	....	....	....	....	....	....	....
Monetary Authorities	79ag *d*	....	....	....	....	....	....	....	....	....	....	....	....	....	....	....
General Government	79ah *d*	....	....	....	....	....	....	....	....	....	....	....	....	....	....	....
Banks	79ai *d*	....	....	....	....	....	....	....	....	....	....	....	....	....	....	....
Other Sectors	79aj *d*	....	....	....	....	....	....	....	....	....	....	....	....	....	....	....
Reserve Assets	79ak *d*	....	....	....	....	....	....	....	....	....	....	....	....	....	....	....
Liabilities	79la *d*	....	....	....	....	....	....	....	....	....	....	....	....	....	....	....
Dir. Invest. in Rep. Economy	79lb *d*	....	....	....	....	....	....	....	....	....	....	....	....	....	....	....
Portfolio Investment	79lc *d*	....	....	....	....	....	....	....	....	....	....	....	....	....	....	....
Equity Securities	79ld *d*	....	....	....	....	....	....	....	....	....	....	....	....	....	....	....
Debt Securities	79le *d*	....	....	....	....	....	....	....	....	....	....	....	....	....	....	....
Financial Derivatives	79ll *d*	....	....	....	....	....	....	....	....	....	....	....	....	....	....	....
Other Investment	79lf *d*	....	....	....	....	....	....	....	....	....	....	....	....	....	....	....
Monetary Authorities	79lg *d*	....	....	....	....	....	....	....	....	....	....	....	....	....	....	....
General Government	79lh *d*	....	....	....	....	....	....	....	....	....	....	....	....	....	....	....
Banks	79li *d*	....	....	....	....	....	....	....	....	....	....	....	....	....	....	....
Other Sectors	79lj *d*	....	....	....	....	....	....	....	....	....	....	....	....	....	....	....
Government Finance																*Millions of Zlotys:*
Deficit (-) or Surplus	80	....	....	....	....	....	....	....	....	....	....	....	....	....	....	–4
Total Revenue and Grants	81y	....	....	....	....	....	....	....	....	....	....	....	....	....	....	375
Revenue	81	....	....	....	....	....	....	....	....	....	....	....	....	....	....	375
Grants	81z	....	....	....	....	....	....	....	....	....	....	....	....	....	....	—
Exp. & Lending Minus Repay.	82z	....	....	....	....	....	....	....	....	....	....	....	....	....	....	379
Expenditure	82	....	....	....	....	....	....	....	....	....	....	....	....	....	....	380
Lending Minus Repayments	83	....	....	....	....	....	....	....	....	....	....	....	....	....	....	—
Total Financing	80h	....	....	....	....	....	....	....	....	....	....	....	....	....	....	4
Domestic	84a	....	....	....	....	....	....	....	....	....	....	....	....	....	....	—
Foreign	85a	....	....	....	....	....	....	....	....	....	....	....	....	....	....	4
Total Debt by Residence	88	....	....	....	....	....	....	....	....	....	....	....	....	....	....	....
Domestic	88a	....	....	....	....	....	....	....	....	....	....	....	....	....	....	....
Foreign	89a	....	....	....	....	....	....	....	....	....	....	....	....	....	....	....
National Accounts																*Millions of Zlotys*
Househ.Cons.Expend.,incl.NPISHs	96f	....	....	....	....	....	....	....	....	....	....	168	204	348	449	543
Government Consumption Expend.	91f	....	....	....	....	....	....	....	....	....	....	23	26	45	61	80
Gross Fixed Capital Formation	93e	....	....	....	....	....	....	....	....	....	....	62	51	112	139	178
Changes in Inventories	93i	....	....	....	....	....	....	....	....	....	....	4	–1	43	34	48
Exports of Goods and Services	90c	....	....	....	....	....	....	....	....	....	....	71	64	108	119	152
Imports of Goods and Services	98c	....	....	....	....	....	....	....	....	....	....	–78	–70	–96	–107	–135
Gross Domestic Product (GDP)	99b	....	....	....	....	....	....	....	....	....	....	251	275	555	692	858
GDP Volume 1987 Prices	99b.*p*	....	....	....	....	....	....	....	....	....	....	I 1,584	1,426	1,358	1,433	1,514
GDP Volume 1990 Prices	99b.*p*	....	....	....	....	....	....	....	....	....	....	....	....	....	....	....
GDP Volume (1995=100)	99bv *p*	....	....	....	....	....	....	....	....	....	....	90.7	81.7	77.8	82.1	86.7
GDP Deflator (1995=10,000)	99bi *p*	....	....	....	....	....	....	....	....	....	....	9.0	10.9	23.1	27.4	32.1
GDP Deflator (1995=100)	99bi *p*	....	....	....	....	....	....	....	....	....	....	....	....	....	....	....
																Millions:
Population	99z	32.53	32.80	33.07	33.36	33.69	34.02	34.36	34.70	35.01	35.26	35.58	35.90	36.23	36.57	36.91

		1985	1986	1987	1988	1989	1990	1991	1992	1993	1994	1995	1996	1997	1998	1999
Balance of Payments *(Minus Sign Indicates Debit)*																
Current Account, n.i.e.	78al d	-982	-1,106	-379	-107	-1,409	3,067	-2,146	-3,104	-5,788	954	854	-3,264	-5,744	-6,901	....
Goods: Exports f.o.b.	78aa d	10,945	11,926	12,026	13,846	12,869	15,837	14,393	13,929	13,582	18,355	25,041	27,557	30,731	32,467	....
Goods: Imports f.o.b.	78ab d	-10,598	-11,459	-11,236	-12,757	-12,822	-12,248	-15,104	-14,060	-17,087	-18,930	-26,687	-34,844	-40,553	-45,303	....
Trade Balance	78ac d	347	467	790	1,089	47	3,589	-711	-131	-3,505	-575	-1,646	-7,287	-9,822	-12,836	....
Services: Credit	78ad d	2,104	2,015	2,216	2,472	3,201	3,200	3,687	4,773	4,201	6,699	10,675	9,833	8,986	10,920	....
Services: Debit	78ae d	-1,846	-2,012	-2,028	-2,404	-3,053	-2,847	-2,994	-4,045	-3,631	-3,859	-7,138	-6,429	-5,814	-6,704	....
Balance on Goods & Services	78af d	605	470	978	1,157	195	3,942	-18	597	-2,935	2,265	1,891	-3,883	-6,650	-8,620	....
Income: Credit	78ag d	173	188	217	271	410	603	573	728	579	546	1,089	1,527	1,467	2,226	....
Income: Debit	78ah d	-2,730	-2,861	-3,132	-3,226	-3,623	-3,989	-3,469	-4,895	-4,192	-3,109	-3,084	-2,602	-2,596	-3,404	....
Balance on Gds, Serv. & Inc.	78ai d	-1,952	-2,203	-1,937	-1,798	-3,018	556	-2,914	-3,570	-6,548	-298	-104	-4,958	-7,779	-9,798	....
Current Transfers, n.i.e.: Credit	78aj d	1,351	1,483	2,154	2,777	4,246	6,865	6,707	6,214	5,840	2,174	2,459	2,825	2,700	3,520	....
Current Transfers: Debit	78ak d	-381	-386	-596	-1,086	-2,637	-4,354	-5,939	-5,748	-5,080	-922	-1,501	-1,131	-665	-623	....
Capital Account, n.i.e.	78bc d	—	—	—	—	—	—	—	—	—	9,215	285	94	66	63	....
Capital Account, n.i.e.: Credit	78ba d	—	—	—	—	—	—	—	—	—	9,215	285	5,833	91	117	....
Capital Account: Debit	78bb d	—	—	—	—	—	—	—	—	—	—	—	-5,739	-25	-54	....
Financial Account, n.i.e.	78bj d	-1,476	-4,826	-3,318	-10,661	-1,796	-8,731	-4,183	-1,045	2,341	-9,065	9,260	6,486	7,957	13,053	....
Direct Investment Abroad	78bd d	-1	-22	-8	-22	-18	—	7	-13	-18	-29	-42	-53	-45	-316	....
Dir. Invest. in Rep. Econ., n.i.e.	78be d	15	16	12	15	11	89	291	678	1,715	1,875	3,659	4,498	4,908	6,365	....
Portfolio Investment Assets	78bf d	—	—	—	—	—	—	—	—	—	-624	1	282	815	-130	....
Equity Securities	78bk d	—	—	—	—	—	—	—	—	—	—	127	-17	56	1	....
Debt Securities	78bl d	—	—	—	—	—	—	—	—	—	-624	-126	299	759	-131	....
Portfolio Investment Liab., n.i.e.	78bg d	—	—	—	—	—	—	—	—	—	—	1,176	22	1,295	1,827	....
Equity Securities	78bm d	—	—	—	—	—	—	—	—	—	—	219	749	599	1,734	....
Debt Securities	78bn d	—	—	—	—	—	—	—	—	—	—	957	-727	696	93	....
Financial Derivatives Assets	78bw d	....	....	....	....	....	....	....	....	....	—	—	—	—	—	....
Financial Derivatives Liabilities	78bx d	....	....	....	....	....	....	....	....	....	—	—	-3	-12	—	....
Other Investment Assets	78bh d	-39	-1,128	-1,415	-1,226	-155	-4,504	-1,497	-958	848	-1,841	3,356	6,191	-754	2,107	....
Monetary Authorities	78bo d	....	....	....	....	....	....	....	....	....	194	65	37	—	1	....
General Government	78bp d	17	-140	-188	-161	-137	46	27	26	16	34	46	5,767	41	53	....
Banks	78bq d	-213	-585	-461	-26	111	-4,096	-980	-823	649	-1,718	1,057	453	-1,076	2,207	....
Other Sectors	78br d	157	-403	-766	-1,039	-129	-454	-544	-161	183	-351	2,188	-66	281	-154	....
Other Investment Liab., n.i.e.	78bi d	-1,451	-3,692	-1,907	-9,428	-1,634	-4,316	-2,984	-752	-204	-8,446	1,110	-4,451	1,750	3,200	....
Monetary Authorities	78bs d	—	—	—	—	—	—	—	—	—	15	14	-85	-14	-30	....
General Government	78bt d	-844	-681	-2,175	-285	-1,034	-3,936	-3,418	-1,439	-570	-8,709	-3	-6,033	-52	-370	....
Banks	78bu d	-584	-3,436	-232	-9,744	-601	-827	-227	437	114	170	575	314	719	1,483	....
Other Sectors	78bv d	-23	425	500	601	1	447	661	250	252	78	524	1,353	1,097	2,117	....
Net Errors and Omissions	78ca d	118	731	91	-267	-110	162	-745	-181	219	-98	-564	321	1,309	-520	....
Overall Balance	78cb d	-2,340	-5,201	-3,606	-11,035	-3,315	-5,502	-7,074	-4,330	-3,228	1,006	9,835	3,637	3,588	5,695	....
Reserves and Related Items	79da d	2,340	5,201	3,606	11,035	3,315	5,502	7,074	4,330	3,228	-1,006	-9,835	-3,637	-3,588	-5,695	....
Reserve Assets	79db d	236	173	-797	-561	-259	-2,418	830	-616	-100	-1,514	-8,431	-3,641	-3,591	-5,697	....
Use of Fund Credit and Loans	79dc d	—	—	—	—	—	479	323	—	-138	603	-1,408	—	—	—	....
Exceptional Financing	79de d	2,104	5,028	4,403	11,596	3,574	7,440	5,921	4,946	3,466	-96	4	4	3	2	....
International Investment Position *(Millions of US Dollars)*																
Assets	79aa d	....	....	....	....	....	....	....	....	....	....	....	28,556	31,175	36,986	....
Direct Investment Abroad	79ab d	....	....	....	....	....	....	....	....	....	....	....	735	678	1,165	....
Portfolio Investment	79ac d	....	....	....	....	....	....	....	....	....	....	....	1,338	839	1,093	....
Equity Securities	79ad d	....	....	....	....	....	....	....	....	....	....	....	38	2	9	....
Debt Securities	79ae d	....	....	....	....	....	....	....	....	....	....	....	1,300	837	1,084	....
Financial Derivatives	79al d	....	....	....	....	....	....	....	....	....	....	....	—	—	—	....
Other Investment	79af d	....	....	....	....	....	....	....	....	....	....	....	8,450	8,988	7,346	....
Monetary Authorities	79ag d	....	....	....	....	....	....	....	....	....	....	....	150	5	4	....
General Government	79ah d	....	....	....	....	....	....	....	....	....	....	....	799	829	802	....
Banks	79ai d	....	....	....	....	....	....	....	....	....	....	....	4,992	6,161	4,419	....
Other Sectors	79aj d	....	....	....	....	....	....	....	....	....	....	....	2,509	1,993	2,121	....
Reserve Assets	79ak d	....	....	....	....	....	....	....	....	....	....	....	18,033	20,670	27,382	....
Liabilities	79la d	....	....	....	....	....	....	....	....	....	....	....	58,328	61,706	77,877	....
Dir. Invest. in Rep. Economy	79lb d	....	....	....	....	....	....	....	....	....	....	....	11,463	14,587	22,479	....
Portfolio Investment	79lc d	....	....	....	....	....	....	....	....	....	....	....	10,148	11,325	13,658	....
Equity Securities	79ld d	....	....	....	....	....	....	....	....	....	....	....	2,279	2,672	4,969	....
Debt Securities	79le d	....	....	....	....	....	....	....	....	....	....	....	7,869	8,653	8,689	....
Financial Derivatives	79ll d	....	....	....	....	....	....	....	....	....	....	....	—	—	—	....
Other Investment	79lf d	....	....	....	....	....	....	....	....	....	....	....	36,717	35,794	41,740	....
Monetary Authorities	79lg d	....	....	....	....	....	....	....	....	....	....	....	78	58	32	....
General Government	79lh d	....	....	....	....	....	....	....	....	....	....	....	28,709	26,584	27,061	....
Banks	79li d	....	....	....	....	....	....	....	....	....	....	....	2,231	3,054	4,735	....
Other Sectors	79lj d	....	....	....	....	....	....	....	....	....	....	....	5,699	6,098	9,912	....
Government Finance *(Year Ending December 31)*																
Deficit (-) or Surplus	80	-18	-4	-24	-68	....	....	....	....	....	-4,812	-5,762	-7,826	-6,162	-5,561	....
Total Revenue and Grants	81y	454	542	660	1,101	....	....	....	....	....	88,153	117,946	144,462	172,519	196,964	....
Revenue	81	454	532	657	1,097	....	....	....	....	....	88,153	117,946	144,454	172,507	196,952	....
Grants	81z	—	10	3	4	....	....	....	....	....	—	—	8	12	12	....
Exp. & Lending Minus Repay.	82z	472	546	684	1,169	....	....	....	....	....	92,965	123,708	152,288	178,681	202,525	....
Expenditure	82	472	542	675	1,146	....	....	....	....	....	93,039	124,322	153,047	183,289	207,549	....
Lending Minus Repayments	83	—	4	9	23	....	....	....	....	....	-74	-614	-759	-4,608	-5,024	....
Total Financing	80h	18	4	24	67	....	....	....	....	....	4,812	5,762	7,826	6,162	5,561	....
Domestic	84a	13	-8	19	74	....	....	....	....	....	5,855	2,604	8,695	6,251	4,558	....
Foreign	85a	5	12	5	-7	....	....	....	....	....	-1,043	3,158	-869	-89	1,003	....
Total Debt by Residence	88	....	....	....	....	....	....	....	....	....	152,238	167,267	185,603	221,650	237,402	....
Domestic	88a	....	....	....	....	....	....	....	....	....	55,611	63,083	76,919	98,611	110,648	....
Foreign	89a	....	....	....	....	....	....	....	....	....	96,627	104,184	108,684	123,039	126,754	....
National Accounts *(Millions of Zlotys)*																
Househ.Cons.Expend.,incl.NPISHs	96f	I 551	679	874	1,460	6,076	I 27,187	48,643	71,925	99,627	142,746	188,416	245,560	301,069	352,063	....
Government Consumption Expend.	91f	I 189	230	294	474	707	I 10,488	17,691	23,819	30,407	37,853	51,747	63,480	75,653	85,497	....
Gross Fixed Capital Formation	93e	I 221	284	382	666	1,935	I 11,761	15,775	19,297	24,749	40,385	57,405	80,390	110,853	139,205	....
Changes in Inventories	93i	I 68	90	106	299	2,618	I 2,590	328	-1,860	-520	-715	3,300	4,428	5,150	5,801	....
Exports of Goods and Services	90c	I 190	236	363	674	2,257	I 16,051	19,026	27,242	35,733	53,218	78,172	94,192	120,408	155,874	....
Imports of Goods and Services	98c	I -176	-217	-322	-593	-1,761	I -12,050	-20,579	-25,479	-34,215	-48,389	-70,935	-100,224	-140,782	-184,879	....
Gross Domestic Product (GDP)	99b	I 1,045	1,295	1,694	2,963	11,832	I 56,027	80,883	114,944	155,780	225,098	308,104	387,827	472,350	553,560	....
GDP Volume 1987 Prices	99b.p	1,592	1,659	1,694	1,762	1,767	1,565	....	....	....	....	....	....	....	....	....
GDP Volume 1990 Prices	99b.p	....	....	....	....	....	56,027	52,121	53,489	55,516	....	....	....	....	....	....
GDP Volume (1995=100)	99bv p	91.2	95.0	97.0	100.9	101.2	89.6	83.4	85.6	88.8	93.4	100.0	106.0	113.3	118.8	....
GDP Deflator (1995=10,000)	99bi p	I 37.2	44.3	56.7	95.3	379.4	....	....	....	....	....	....	....	....	....	....
GDP Deflator (1995=100)	99bi p	....	....	....	....	3.8	I 20.3	31.5	43.6	56.9	78.2	100.0	118.7	135.4	151.3	....
Midyear Estimates																
Population	99z	37.20	37.46	37.66	37.86	37.96	38.12	38.24	38.37	38.46	38.54	38.59	38.62	38.65	38.67	38.65

(See notes in the back of the book.)

		1970	1971	1972	1973	1974	1975	1976	1977	1978	1979	1980	1981	1982	1983	1984
Exchange Rates															*Escudos per SDR through 1998,*	
Market Rate	aa	28.75	29.92	29.31	31.18	30.11	32.16	36.65	48.41	59.94	65.58	67.65	75.95	98.25	137.62	165.93
															Escudos per US Dollar through 1998,	
Market Rate	ae	28.75	27.56	27.00	25.85	24.60	27.47	31.55	39.86	46.01	49.78	53.04	65.25	89.06	131.45	169.28
Market Rate	rf	28.75	28.36	27.05	24.52	25.41	25.55	30.23	38.28	43.94	48.92	50.06	61.55	79.47	110.78	146.39
															Escudos per ECU:	
ECU Rate	ea	....	....	....	....	....	....	....	....	....	....	....	....	....	....	....
ECU Rate	eb	....	....	....	....	....	....	....	....	....	....	....	....	....	....	....
															Index Numbers (1995=100):	
Market Rate	ahx	527.5	602.6	558.1	617.7	594.6	592.4	500.8	396.7	344.7	308.8	301.8	246.5	192.6	138.9	103.8
Nominal Effective Exchange Rate	nec	....	....	....	....	....	....	....	....	....	281.7	273.7	266.7	235.1	186.5	154.5
Real Effective Exchange Rate	rec	....	....	....	....	....	....	....	....	....	78.5	79.8	84.3	83.8	77.8	79.1
Fund Position															*Millions of SDRs:*	
Quota	2f.s	75	117	117	117	117	117	117	117	172	172	258	258	258	377	377
SDRs	1b.s	—	—	—	—	—	7	8	4	—	1	—	9	2	1	13
Reserve Position in the Fund	1c.s	19	29	29	29	29	—	—	—	—	—	35	49	49	30	30
Total Fund Cred.&Loans Outstg.	2tl	—	—	—	—	—	—	173	245	203	172	94	47	10	355	572
International Liquidity												*Millions of US Dollars Unless Otherwise Indicated:*				
Total Res.Min.Gold (Eurosys.Def)	1l.d	602	945	1,291	1,676	1,161	398	176	366	871	931	795	534	447	385	516
SDRs	1b.d						8	10	5	—	1	—	10	2	1	12
Reserve Position in the Fund	1c.d	19	32	32	35	36	—	—	—	—	—	44	57	54	31	29
Foreign Exchange	1d.d	583	913	1,259	1,641	1,125	390	166	361	871	930	751	467	391	353	475
o/w: Fin.Deriv.Rel.to Reserves	1dd.d	....	....	....	....	....	....	....	....	....	....	....	....	....	....	....
Other Reserve Assets	1e.d	....	....	....	....	....	....	....	....	....	....	....	....	....	....	....
Gold (Million Fine Troy Ounces)	1ad	25.77	26.31	26.88	27.54	27.84	27.72	27.67	24.11	22.13	22.13	22.17	22.14	22.09	20.43	20.30
Gold (National Valuation)	1and	902	1,000	1,021	1,163	1,193	1,136	1,125	1,025	1,009	1,020	5,652	5,644	5,631	5,209	5,174
Memo: Euro Cl. on Non-EA Res.	1dgd	....	....	....	....	....	....	....	....	....	....	....	....	....	....	....
Non-Euro Cl. on EA Res.	1dhd	....	....	....	....	....	....	....	....	....	....	....	....	....	....	....
Mon. Auth.: Other Foreign Assets	3..d	....	....	....	....	....	....	....	....	....	....	....	....	....	....	....
Foreign Liabilities	4..d	4	4	4	4	4	34	I 969	1,169	878	I 1,564	1,087	947	826	1,168	1,053
Banking Insts.: Foreign Assets	7a.d	299	281	298	304	412	347	702	881	996	1,065	1,135	868	813	970	1,112
Foreign Liab.	7b.d	41	61	69	85	114	94	253	1,246	2,999	I 938	808	896	1,366	1,684	1,766
Monetary Authorities												*Billions of Escudos through 1998;*				
Fgn. Assets (Cl.on Non-EA Ctys)	11	43.5	52.5	62.4	70.4	54.7	40.1	I 40.6	54.1	81.6	I 85.7	334.6	399.7	540.9	730.8	953.0
Claims on General Government	12a.u	....	....	....	....	....	....	....	....	....	....					
o/w: Claims on Gen.Govt.in Cty	12a	2.7	2.7	3.2	3.5	10.7	34.9	I 71.7	134.4	169.4	I 265.6	190.6	293.7	422.7	562.3	787.7
Claims on Banking Institutions	12e.u	....	....	....	....	....	....	....	....	....	....					
o/w: Claims on Bank.Inst.in Cty	12e	2.2	1.9	2.0	2.2	3.7	2.3	I 99.7	92.4	73.8	I 24.4	13.6	28.1	18.5	42.7	31.9
Claims on Other Resident Sectors	12d.u	....	....	....	....	....	....	....	....	....	....					
o/w: Cl. on Oth.Res.Sect.in Cty	12d	—	—	—	—	.1	.2	I .2	.1	—	I 18.3	19.7	20.7	26.9	35.8	41.1
Claims on ECB	12u	....	....	....	....	....	....	....	....	....	....					
Currency in Circulation	14a	30.3	52.6	36.8	39.0	71.1	112.0	I 80.9	85.2	118.3	I 142.1	165.2	188.4	219.5	240.1	267.3
Liabilities to Banking Insts	14c.u	....	....	....	....	....	....	....	....	....	....					
o/w: Liabs to Bank.Inst.in Cty	14c							31.1	35.9	50.6	I 83.2	109.0	186.4	264.2	309.8	306.7
Demand Dep. of Other Res.Sect.	14d.u	....	....	....	....	....	....	....	....	....	....					
o/w: D.Dep.of Oth.Res.Sect.in Cty	14d							1.3	.3	.6	I 2.8	1.6	1.7	3.8	2.8	3.6
Other Dep. of Other Res.Sect.	15..u	....	....	....	....	....	....	....	....	....	....					
o/w: O.Dep.of Oth.Res.Sect.in Cty	15															
Money Market Instruments	16m.u	....	....	....	....	....	....	....	....	....	....					
o/w: MMI Held by Resid.of Cty	16m															
Bonds (Debt Securities)	16n.u	....	....	....	....	....	....	....	....	....	....					
o/w: Bonds Held by Resid.of Cty	16n															
Foreign Liab. (to Non-EA Ctys)	16c							36.9	58.4	52.6	I 89.1	64.0	65.4	74.6	202.4	273.1
Central Government Deposits	16d.u	....	....	....	....	....	....	....	....	....	....					
o/w: Cent.Govt.Dep. in Cty	16d	4.7	5.8	4.1	6.0	3.8	1.0	I 12.2	22.2	10.9	I 22.7	32.4	48.9	36.5	70.7	60.4
Liabilities to ECB	16u															
Capital Accounts	17a							29.7	36.6	43.9	I 34.2	101.0	106.1	110.0	144.6	107.3
Other Items (Net)	17r	13.3	18.8	26.6	31.1	−5.7	−35.6	I 20.1	42.3	47.9	I 19.8	85.3	145.3	300.5	401.1	795.3
Banking Institutions												*Billions of Escudos through 1998;*				
Claims on Monetary Authorities	20	15.8	20.0	25.8	31.7	23.8	18.9	I 29.2	33.7	47.5	I 93.2	171.3	262.3	362.3	395.6	681.8
Claims on Bk.Inst.in Oth.EA Ctys	20b.u	....	....	....	....	....	....	....	....	....	....					
Fgn. Assets (Cl.on Non-EA Ctys)	21	8.6	7.7	8.1	7.7	10.1	9.5	I 22.2	35.1	45.8	I 53.0	60.2	56.6	72.4	127.5	188.3
Claims on General Government	22a.u	....	....	....	....	....	....	....	....	....	....					
o/w: Claims on Gen.Govt.in Cty	22a	13.7	14.6	20.8	21.6	26.1	32.0	I 50.8	51.6	56.8	I 69.5	86.2	155.1	210.2	270.1	313.1
Claims on Other Resident Sectors	22d.u	....	....	....	....	....	....	....	....	....	....					
o/w: Cl. on Oth.Res.Sect.in Cty	22d	116.6	144.2	178.1	238.3	250.1	312.9	I 406.4	515.4	609.1	I 845.0	1,074.1	1,356.0	1,706.4	2,155.1	2,620.0
Demand Deposits	24..u	....	....	....	....	....	....	....	....	....	....					
o/w: D.Dep.of Oth.Res.Sect.in Cty	24	62.5	72.4	85.6	126.7	111.4	115.5	I 141.5	168.4	199.1	I 262.0	323.7	347.3	402.6	434.0	513.2
Other Deposits	25..u	....	....	....	....	....	....	....	....	....	....					
o/w: O.Dep.of Oth.Res.Sect.in Cty	25	63.1	84.1	112.5	135.7	159.8	158.2	I 209.9	258.7	331.5	I 600.8	863.3	1,204.2	1,581.8	1,977.6	2,604.5
Money Market Instruments	26m.u	....	....	....	....	....	....	....	....	....	....					
o/w: MMI Held by Resid.of Cty	26m															
Bonds (Debt Securities)	26n.u	....	....	....	....	....	....	....	....	....	....					
o/w: Bonds Held by Resid.of Cty	26n							.4	.3	.3	I .2	.2	1.1	1.1	2.9	2.0
Foreign Liab. (to Non-EA Ctys)	26c	1.2	1.7	1.9	2.2	2.8	2.6	I 18.9	85.5	138.0	I 46.7	42.9	58.5	121.7	221.4	298.9
Central Government Deposits	26d.u	....	....	....	....	....	....	....	....	....	....					
o/w: Cent.Govt.Dep. in Cty	26d	14.3	16.2	17.9	20.2	24.0	32.5	I 29.2	33.4	39.4	I 54.9	65.8	74.3	95.5	105.9	135.7
Credit from Monetary Authorities	26g							99.7	92.4	73.8	I 29.4	16.5	34.1	27.2	55.1	51.7
Liab. to Bk.Inst.in Oth. EA Ctys	26h.u	....	....	....	....	....	....	....	....	....	....					
Capital Accounts	27a	12.2	14.1	18.8	22.4	23.7	24.2	I 35.2	34.8	42.3	I 48.9	65.3	84.8	117.4	117.4	157.1
Other Items (Net)	27r	1.4	−2.1	−3.7	−7.9	−11.6	40.4	I −29.7	−36.8	−65.7	I 17.6	14.0	25.7	4.0	33.9	40.1
Banking Survey (Nat'l Residency)												*Billions of Escudos through 1998;*				
Foreign Assets (Net)	31n	49.8	58.4	68.6	75.9	62.0	38.8	I 6.9	−54.7	−63.1	I 2.9	287.9	332.4	417.1	434.5	569.2
Domestic Credit	32	123.3	148.8	189.9	248.8	303.4	434.5	I 487.8	645.8	785.1	I 1,120.7	1,272.4	1,702.3	2,234.2	2,846.6	3,565.7
Claims on General Govt. (Net)	32an	15.0	−4.7	2.0	−1.2	9.0	33.4	I 81.1	130.4	175.9	I 257.5	178.6	325.6	500.9	655.7	904.7
Claims on Other Resident Sectors	32d	126.4	153.5	187.9	250.0	294.4	401.1	I 406.6	515.5	609.2	I 863.3	1,093.8	1,376.7	1,733.3	2,190.9	2,661.0
Currency in Circulation	34a.n	30.3	32.6	36.8	39.0	71.1	112.0	I 109.2	113.3	121.4	I 142.1	165.2	188.4	219.5	240.1	267.3
Demand Deposits	34b.n	70.2	72.4	85.6	126.7	111.4	115.5	I 142.6	168.4	199.5	I 264.8	325.3	349.1	406.6	436.9	516.7
Other Deposits	35..n	66.1	84.1	112.5	135.7	159.8	158.2	I 209.9	258.7	331.5	I 600.8	863.3	1,204.2	1,581.8	1,977.6	2,604.5
Money Market Instruments	36m	....	....	....	....	....	....	....	....	....	....					
Bonds (Debt Securities)	36n							.4	.3	.3	I .2	.2	1.1	1.1	2.9	2.0
o/w: Bonds Over Two Years	36na	....	....	....	....	....	....	....	....	....	....					
Capital Accounts	37a							64.9	71.4	86.2	I 83.1	166.3	190.9	227.4	262.1	264.4
Other Items (Net)	37r	12.4	4.2	4.9	.9	−.7	63.6	I −4.3	6.9	−14.1	I 32.5	39.9	101.1	215.0	361.6	480.0

1985	1986	1987	1988	1989	1990	1991	1992	1993	1994	1995	1996	1997	1998	1999	Item	Code
Euros per SDR Thereafter: End of Period															**Exchange Rates**	
172.99	178.73	184.23	196.97	196.92	190.07	191.94	201.79	242.86	232.25	222.10	224.88	247.35	241.94	1.3662	Market Rate	aa
Euros per US Dollar Thereafter: End of Period (ae) Period Average (rf)																
157.49	146.12	129.87	146.37	149.84	133.60	134.18	146.76	176.81	159.09	149.41	156.38	183.33	171.83	.9954	Market Rate	ae
170.39	149.59	140.88	143.95	157.46	142.55	144.48	135.00	160.80	165.99	151.11	154.24	175.31	180.10	.9386	Market Rate	rf
End of Period (ea) Period Average (eb)																
140.28	156.39	169.39	171.69	177.90	183.20	179.31	177.35	197.20	195.17	191.58	194.27	202.13	201.22	....	ECU Rate	ea
....	148.84	162.49	169.19	173.32	181.43	178.83	174.44	187.80	196.37	194.12	193.18	197.96	201.99	....	ECU Rate	eb
Period Averages																
88.8	101.0	107.2	105.1	96.0	106.2	104.8	112.1	94.3	91.2	100.0	97.9	86.3	84.0	....	Market Rate	ahx
137.0	124.4	115.1	108.9	105.6	103.8	104.3	108.0	101.8	98.3	100.0	100.2	98.1	97.1	95.7	Nominal Effective Exchange Rate	nec
80.0	79.3	78.2	78.7	82.2	87.2	93.5	101.3	98.4	97.2	100.0	100.9	99.1	99.3	98.9	Real Effective Exchange Rate	rec
End of Period															**Fund Position**	
377	377	377	377	377	377	377	558	558	558	558	558	558	558	867	Quota	2f.s
16	54	56	3	1	40	68	34	42	48	57	68	79	96	32	SDRs	1b.s
30	30	30	30	95	124	189	228	219	231	303	320	313	442	275	Reserve Position in the Fund	1c.s
572	572	373	—	—	—	—	—	—	—	—	—	—	—	—	Total Fund Cred.&Loans Outstg.	2tl
End of Period															**International Liquidity**	
1,395	1,456	3,327	5,127	9,952	14,485	20,629	19,129	15,840	15,513	15,850	15,918	15,660	15,825	I 8,848	Total Res.Min.Gold (Eurosys.Def)	1l.d
17	66	80	4	2	57	98	46	58	71	85	98	107	135	44	SDRs	1b.d
33	36	42	40	125	176	270	314	301	337	450	461	423	623	377	Reserve Position in the Fund	1c.d
1,345	1,354	3,205	5,083	9,826	14,252	20,261	18,769	15,481	15,106	15,315	15,359	15,130	15,067	8,006	Foreign Exchange	1d.d
....	....	....	....	....	....	....	....	....	....	....	....	....	....	111.00	o/w: Fin.Deriv.Rel.to Reserves	1ddd
														421	Other Reserve Assets	1e.d
20.23	20.16	20.06	16.07	16.05	15.83	15.87	16.06	16.06	16.07	16.07	16.07	16.07	20.09	19.51	Gold (Million Fine Troy Ounces)	1ad
5,159[e]	5,139	5,114	5,190	5,184	5,113	5,125	5,188	5,189	5,185	5,189	4,993	3,265	3,389	5,673	Gold (National Valuation)	1and
....	....	....	....	....	....	....	....	....	....	....	....	....	....	2,795	Memo: Euro Cl. on Non-EA Res.	1dgd
....	....	....	....	....	....	....	....	....	....	....	....	....	....	871	Non-Euro Cl. on EA Res.	1dhd
....	....	....	....	....	....	....	....	....	....	....	....	....	....	3,666	Mon. Auth.: Other Foreign Assets	3..d
862	853	602	10	21	24	12	20	18	122	48	44	144	6	I 3,737	Foreign Liabilities	4..d
1,428	1,418	1,976	3,063	3,377	6,161	8,810	13,903	20,042	28,500	35,922	37,500	47,451	54,669	I 25,148	Banking Insts.: Foreign Assets	7a.d
1,636	1,516	1,770	2,059	3,360	5,782	9,730	12,270	13,875	21,527	32,432	36,975	48,282	60,976	I 31,351	Foreign Liab.	7b.d
Billions of Euros Beginning 1999: End of Period															**Monetary Authorities**	
1,023.4	956.3	1,098.8	1,517.5	2,283.0	2,622.3	3,449.3	3,568.2	3,706.7	3,294.8	3,142.8	3,250.5	3,469.8	3,324.6	16.70	Fgn. Assets (Cl.on Non-EA Ctys)	11
....	....	....	....	....	....	....	....	....	....	....	....	....	....	3.48	Claims on General Government	12a.u
1,057.0	1,202.4	1,186.6	1,100.9	1,099.4	993.1	304.2	336.2	313.0	289.9	267.6	248.2	217.6	94.6	.39	o/w: Claims on Gen.Govt.in Cty	12a
....	....	....	....	....	....	....	....	....	....	....	....	....	....	10.51	Claims on Banking Institutions	12e.u
56.0	72.8	52.0	19.1	112.0	10.9	150.6	9.7	266.3	560.1	631.9	261.8	112.5	246.4	2.58	o/w: Claims on Bank.Inst.in Cty	12e
....	....	....	....	....	....	....	....	....	....	....	....	....	....	.30	Claims on Other Resident Sectors	12d.u
38.8	33.9	15.1	12.2	9.3	20.4	24.0	35.0	36.3	45.7	38.2	39.8	41.0	42.6	.22	o/w: Cl. on Oth.Res.Sect.in Cty	12d
....	....	....	....	....	....	....	....	....	....	....	....	....	....	1.42	Claims on ECB	12u
319.0	399.3	457.7	509.5	577.3	623.9	683.1	708.2	752.9	795.8	841.0	880.9	776.1	923.6	7.25	Currency in Circulation	14a
....	....	....	....	....	....	....	....	....	....	....	....	....	....	10.92	Liabilities to Banking Insts	14c.u
287.5	285.1	412.9	473.0	1,313.3	1,428.1	1,830.4	2,071.5	2,277.0	432.3	376.8	473.5	558.8	421.1	4.02	o/w: Liabs to Bank.Inst.in Cty	14c
....	....	....	....	....	....	....	....	....	....	....	....	....	....	—	Demand Dep. of Other Res.Sect.	14d.u
3.0	11.7	5.0	7.7	4.4	.6	1.7	2.0	1.1	21.6	.6	.2	1.9	.4	—	o/w: D.Dep.of Oth.Res.Sect.in Cty	14d
....	....	....	....	....	....	....	....	....	....	....	....	....	....	—	Other Dep. of Other Res.Sect.	15..u
....	....	....	....	....	....	....	....	....	....	....	....	....	....	—	o/w: O.Dep.of Oth.Res.Sect.in Cty	15
....	....	....	....	....	....	....	....	....	....	....	....	....	....	—	Money Market Instruments	16m.u
....	....	....	....	....	....	....	....	....	....	....	....	....	....	....	o/w: MMI Held by Resid.of Cty	16m
....	....	....	....	....	....	....	....	....	....	....	....	....	....	4.57	Bonds (Debt Securities)	16n.u
....	....	....	....	....	....	....	....	....	....	....	....	....	....	....	o/w: Bonds Held by Resid.of Cty	16n
234.7	226.8	146.9	1.5	3.2	3.3	1.6	2.9	3.1	19.4	7.2	6.9	26.4	1.1	3.72	Foreign Liab. (to Non-EA Ctys)	16c
....	....	....	....	....	....	....	....	....	....	....	....	....	....	2.24	Central Government Deposits	16d.u
101.1	12.5	91.6	146.8	252.9	356.1	848.4	573.9	539.8	510.6	693.0	524.0	486.7	465.1	2.24	o/w: Cent.Govt.Dep. in Cty	16d
....	....	....	....	....	....	....	....	....	....	....	....	....	....	—	Liabilities to ECB	16u
263.7	398.0	395.4	482.0	474.9	385.6	267.3	184.0	493.9	446.7	303.7	310.3	693.0	588.3	3.85	Capital Accounts	17a
966.2	932.0	842.9	1,029.0	877.6	849.1	295.7	406.6	254.5	1,964.1	1,858.4	1,604.5	1,299.0	1,308.6	–.16	Other Items (Net)	17r
Billions of Euros Beginning 1999: End of Period															**Banking Institutions**	
1,060.3	1,294.0	1,392.5	1,395.1	2,091.6	2,227.0	2,019.0	2,325.8	2,188.6	2,158.1	2,090.4	1,891.3	1,648.1	1,617.9	8.26	Claims on Monetary Authorities	20
....	....	....	....	....	....	....	....	....	....	....	....	....	....	18.39	Claims on Bk.Inst.in Oth.EA Ctys	20b.u
224.9	207.3	256.6	448.4	506.0	823.1	1,182.2	2,040.3	3,543.7	4,534.1	5,367.2	5,864.5	8,698.9	9,393.7	25.03	Fgn. Assets (Cl.on Non-EA Ctys)	21
....	....	....	....	....	....	....	....	....	....	....	....	....	....	9.53	Claims on General Government	22a.u
509.4	633.9	982.6	1,394.1	1,474.2	1,860.4	3,440.1	3,387.7	3,548.4	4,126.9	4,194.3	3,983.1	3,139.5	2,383.9	8.37	o/w: Claims on Gen.Govt.in Cty	22a
....	....	....	....	....	....	....	....	....	....	....	....	....	....	133.71	Claims on Other Resident Sectors	22d.u
2,873.3	3,201.9	3,445.0	3,908.6	4,347.2	4,983.9	6,315.4	7,599.2	8,465.2	9,369.0	11,137.5	13,084.8	15,771.6	19,705.1	129.39	o/w: Cl. on Oth.Res.Sect.in Cty	22d
....	....	....	....	....	....	....	....	....	....	....	....	....	....	39.92	Demand Deposits	24..u
671.3	953.6	1,180.4	1,478.3	1,688.2	1,766.6	2,072.8	2,556.7	2,861.6	3,038.7	3,435.0	3,914.6	4,637.9	5,411.6	39.58	o/w: D.Dep.of Oth.Res.Sect.in Cty	24
....	....	....	....	....	....	....	....	....	....	....	....	....	....	71.37	Other Deposits	25..u
3,225.6	3,596.1	3,997.9	4,584.3	5,146.1	5,709.1	7,248.6	8,503.4	9,414.9	10,360.4	11,116.5	11,465.1	11,956.0	12,064.7	67.64	o/w: O.Dep.of Oth.Res.Sect.in Cty	25
....	....	....	....	....	....	....	....	....	....	....	....	....	....	—	Money Market Instruments	26m.u
....	....	....	....	....	....	....	....	....	....	....	....	....	....	....	o/w: MMI Held by Resid.of Cty	26m
....	....	....	....	....	....	....	....	....	....	....	....	....	....	16.91	Bonds (Debt Securities)	26n.u
4.3	2.4	40.7	38.5	39.0	69.0	84.5	106.7	197.1	169.0	125.7	257.7	331.5	599.5	....	o/w: Bonds Held by Resid.of Cty	26n
257.7	221.5	229.8	301.3	503.5	772.5	1,305.6	1,800.7	2,453.2	3,424.8	4,845.8	5,782.4	8,851.3	10,477.5	31.21	Foreign Liab. (to Non-EA Ctys)	26c
....	....	....	....	....	....	....	....	....	....	....	....	....	....	5.08	Central Government Deposits	26d.u
216.5	274.7	221.6	285.4	359.5	430.6	519.1	451.8	454.4	541.2	701.2	800.3	906.7	1,017.4	5.07	o/w: Cent.Govt.Dep. in Cty	26d
69.9	101.5	112.5	69.5	156.2	65.6	190.2	50.8	296.0	560.3	631.9	261.8	112.5	246.4	2.58	Credit from Monetary Authorities	26g
....	....	....	....	....	....	....	....	....	....	....	....	....	....	22.35	Liab. to Bk.Inst.in Oth. EA Ctys	26h.u
198.1	291.1	434.8	652.4	837.7	1,167.4	1,568.8	1,945.7	2,251.7	2,430.8	2,500.8	2,782.6	2,978.4	4,117.9	20.23	Capital Accounts	27a
24.5	–103.7	–140.9	–263.6	–311.1	–87.1	–33.7	–65.3	–183.6	–338.0	–573.1	–443.1	–515.9	–834.3	–14.72	Other Items (Net)	27r
Billions of Euros Beginning 1999: End of Period															**Banking Survey (Nat'l Residency)**	
755.8	715.2	978.6	1,663.0	2,282.4	2,669.6	3,324.3	3,804.9	4,794.2	4,384.7	3,657.0	3,325.6	3,291.0	2,239.7	10.83	Foreign Assets (Net)	31n
4,161.0	4,785.0	5,316.0	5,983.5	6,317.7	7,071.1	8,716.2	10,332.5	11,368.7	12,779.7	14,243.5	16,031.6	17,776.3	20,743.7	131.06	Domestic Credit	32
1,248.9	1,549.2	1,856.0	2,062.8	1,961.2	2,066.9	2,376.8	2,698.3	2,867.2	3,365.0	3,067.8	2,907.0	1,963.7	996.0	1.45	Claims on General Govt. (Net)	32an
2,912.1	3,235.8	3,460.1	3,920.8	4,356.5	5,004.2	6,339.5	7,634.3	8,501.5	9,414.7	11,175.7	13,124.6	15,812.6	19,747.7	129.61	Claims on Other Resident Sectors	32d
319.0	399.3	457.7	509.5	577.3	623.9	683.1	708.2	752.9	795.8	841.0	880.9	776.1	923.6	7.25	Currency in Circulation	34a.n
674.3	965.3	1,185.3	1,486.0	1,692.6	1,767.2	2,074.5	2,558.7	2,862.7	3,060.2	3,435.5	3,914.7	4,639.7	5,412.0	39.58	Demand Deposits	34b.n
3,225.6	3,596.1	3,997.9	4,584.3	5,146.1	5,709.1	7,248.6	8,503.4	9,414.9	10,360.4	11,116.5	11,465.1	11,956.0	12,064.7	67.64	Other Deposits	35..n
....	....	....	....	....	....	....	....	....	....	....	....	....	....	—	Money Market Instruments	36m
4.3	2.4	40.7	38.5	39.0	69.0	84.5	106.7	197.1	169.0	125.7	257.7	331.5	599.5	21.49	Bonds (Debt Securities)	36n
														19.87	o/w: Bonds Over Two Years	36na
461.8	689.1	830.3	1,134.5	1,312.6	1,553.0	1,836.1	2,129.7	2,745.6	2,877.5	2,804.5	3,093.0	3,671.4	4,706.2	24.08	Capital Accounts	37a
231.8	–151.9	–217.1	–106.3	–167.6	17.8	113.0	128.1	189.1	–99.4	–428.4	–256.4	–306.3	–722.4	–18.15	Other Items (Net)	37r

Portugal

		1970	1971	1972	1973	1974	1975	1976	1977	1978	1979	1980	1981	1982	1983	1984
Banking Survey (EA-Wide Residency)															*Billions of Euros:*	
Foreign Assets (Net)	31n.*u*	....	....	....	....	....	....	....	....	....	....	....	....	....	....	....
Domestic Credit	32..*u*	....	....	....	....	....	....	....	....	....	....	....	....	....	....	....
Claims on General Govt. (Net)	32an*u*	....	....	....	....	....	....	....	....	....	....	....	....	....	....	....
Claims on Other Resident Sect.	32d.*u*	....	....	....	....	....	....	....	....	....	....	....	....	....	....	....
Currency in Circulation	34a.*u*	....	....	....	....	....	....	....	....	....	....	....	....	....	....	....
Demand Deposits	34b.*u*	....	....	....	....	....	....	....	....	....	....	....	....	....	....	....
Other Deposits	35..*u*	....	....	....	....	....	....	....	....	....	....	....	....	....	....	....
o/w: Other Dep. Over Two Yrs	35ab*u*	....	....	....	....	....	....	....	....	....	....	....	....	....	....	....
Money Market Instruments	36m.*u*	....	....	....	....	....	....	....	....	....	....	....	....	....	....	....
Bonds (Debt Securities)	36n.*u*	....	....	....	....	....	....	....	....	....	....	....	....	....	....	....
o/w: Bonds Over Two Years	36na*u*	....	....	....	....	....	....	....	....	....	....	....	....	....	....	....
Capital Accounts	37a	....	....	....	....	....	....	....	....	....	....	....	....	....	....	....
Other Items (Net)	37r.*u*	....	....	....	....	....	....	....	....	....	....	....	....	....	....	....
Money (National Definitions)															*Billions of Escudos:*	
M1	39ma	....	....	....	....	....	....	....	....	....	392.6	473.6	518.1	602.5	654.7	757.3
M2	39mb	....	....	....	....	....	....	....	....	....	847.6	1,088.1	1,349.1	1,674.2	1,956.2	2,442.1
L	39mc	....	....	....	....	....	....	....	....	....	....	936.0	1,212.9	1,508.9	1,807.3	2,174.1
Interest Rates															*Percent Per Annum*	
Banco de Portugal Rate(End of Per)	60	3.50	3.75	4.00	5.00	7.50	6.50	6.50	13.00	18.00	18.00	18.00	18.00	19.00	25.00	25.00
Money Market Rate	60b	....	....	....	....	....	....	....	....	18.42	14.87	9.95	9.24	12.42	18.24	21.27
Treasury Bill Rate	60c	....	....	....	....	....	....	....	....	....	....	12.37	13.48	14.37	18.14	21.15
Deposit Rate	60l	....	....	....	....	....	....	9.50	12.54	17.67	19.00	19.00	19.25	21.00	26.08	28.00
Lending Rate	60p	....	....	....	....	....	....	8.75	12.50	17.58	18.75	18.75	20.13	23.00	27.88	29.42
Government Bond Yield	61	5.28	5.69	6.01	5.50	....	....	9.74	10.80	16.17	16.68	16.68	16.71	16.79	19.22	21.50
Prices, Production, Labor															*Index Numbers (1995=100):*	
Share Prices	62	....	....	....	....	....	....	....	....	....	....	....	....	....	....	....
Prices: Home & Import Goods('85=100)	63	7.4	7.5	7.9	8.8	11.4	12.9	15.3	19.7	25.9	33.6	35.8	43.5	55.5	64.7	82.5
Home Goods (1985=100)	63a	7.9	8.0	8.7	9.7	12.2	13.1	15.8	20.4	28.7	37.9	36.4	45.0	53.5	65.2	83.3
Consumer Prices	64	2.7	3.0	3.2	3.5	4.5	5.5	6.5	8.2	10.1	12.5	14.5	17.4	21.4	126.8	34.6
Harmonized CPI	64h	....	....	....	....	....	....	....	....	....	....	....	....	....	....	....
Wages: Daily Earnings (Mfg.)	65ey	....	....	....	....	....	....	....	....	....	15.5	19.5	23.4	32.7	38.0	45.8
Industrial Production	66	....	....	....	....	....	....	....	....	....	....	64.7	69.7	71.9	74.1	
															Number in Thousands:	
Labor Force	67d	....	....	....	....	....	....	....	....	....	....	....	....	....	....	....
Employment	67e	....	....	....	....	....	....	....	....	....	....	....	....	....	....	....
Unemployment	67c	....	....	....	....	....	....	....	....	....	....	....	....	....	....	....
Unemployment Rate (%)	67r	....	....	....	....	....	....	....	....	....	....	....	....	....	....	....
International Transactions															*Billions of Escudos through 1998;*	
Exports	70	27.2	29.7	35.1	44.8	57.5	49.3	54.7	75.7	106.5	170.5	232.2	254.9	331.7	508.6	760.6
Imports, c.i.f.	71	44.7	50.9	59.6	73.2	113.3	97.5	127.8	182.7	230.1	320.1	465.8	599.7	754.0	899.4	1,160.6
Imports, f.o.b.	71.v	39.9	45.5	53.2	65.7	102.6	88.4	115.1	165.6	208.6	290.2	422.2	543.6	683.4	817.3	1,052.3
															1990=100	
Volume of Exports	72	....	....	....	....	....	....	....	....	....	....	....	....	....	44.4	50.9
Volume of Imports	73	....	....	....	....	....	....	....	....	....	....	....	....	....	43.2	40.7
Export Prices	76	....	....	....	....	....	....	....	....	....	....	....	....	....	49.1	64.1
Import Prices	76.x	6.9	7.0	7.2	8.2	10.7	12.0	14.3	19.8	23.7	28.8	33.7	38.9	45.7	159.7	80.6
Balance of Payments															*Millions of US Dollars:*	
Current Account, n.i.e.	78al *d*	....	....	....	....	....	−755	−1,282	−957	−463	−54	−1,064	−4,686	−3,258	−1,632	−623
Goods: Exports f.o.b.	78aa *d*						1,942	1,825	2,564	2,782	3,608	4,668	4,185	4,194	4,646	5,246
Goods: Imports f.o.b.	78ab *d*						−3,544	−3,960	−4,528	−4,783	−6,183	−8,611	−11,132	−8,953	−7,631	−7,297
Trade Balance	78ac *d*						−1,603	−2,136	−1,964	−2,001	−2,575	−3,943	−6,948	−4,759	−2,985	−2,051
Services: Credit	78ad *d*						941	756	840	1,076	1,592	2,006	1,946	1,536	1,478	1,656
Services: Debit	78ae *d*						−1,110	−730	−785	−849	−1,128	−1,525	−1,639	−1,462	−1,254	−1,244
Balance on Goods & Services	78af *d*						−1,772	−2,110	−1,909	−1,774	−2,110	−3,462	−6,640	−4,685	−2,761	−1,638
Income: Credit	78ag *d*						115	47	67	87	133	173	206	153	167	195
Income: Debit	78ah *d*						−139	−184	−249	−410	−553	−781	−1,141	−1,405	−1,212	−1,355
Balance on Gds, Serv. & Inc.	78ai *d*						−1,796	−2,247	−2,090	−2,098	−2,531	−4,070	−7,575	−5,937	−3,806	−2,798
Current Transfers, n.i.e.: Credit	78aj *d*						1,103	1,007	1,222	1,718	2,536	3,047	2,918	2,718	2,245	2,257
Current Transfers: Debit	78ak *d*						−62	−42	−89	−83	−59	−41	−29	−40	−71	−82
Capital Account, n.i.e.	78bc *d*						—	—	—	—	—	—	—	—	—	—
Capital Account, n.i.e.: Credit	78ba *d*						—	—	—	—	—	—	—	—	—	—
Capital Account: Debit	78bb *d*						—	—	—	—	—	—	—	—	—	—
Financial Account, n.i.e.	78bj *d*	....	....	....	....	....	180	820	1,114	1,256	−477	−159	2,867	3,144	591	559
Direct Investment Abroad	78bd *d*						−8	−5	−3	−6	8	−14	−16	−8	−17	−7
Dir. Invest. in Rep. Econ., n.i.e.	78be *d*						115	63	58	66	78	157	174	144	146	195
Portfolio Investment Assets	78bf *d*						−1	1	1	1	1	2	8	1	1	—
Equity Securities	78bk *d*						—	—	—	—	—	1	6	1	1	—
Debt Securities	78bl *d*						−1	1	1	1	1		2	1		—
Portfolio Investment Liab., n.i.e.	78bg *d*						−5	7	1	−4	−4	−9	−3	153	140	149
Equity Securities	78bm *d*						—	—	—	—		−1	−1	2	8	1
Debt Securities	78bn *d*						−5	7	1	−4	−4	−8	−2	151	132	149
Financial Derivatives Assets	78bw *d*						....	....	....							
Financial Derivatives Liabilities	78bx *d*						....	....	....							
Other Investment Assets	78bh *d*						−15	−157	−231	−218	−503	−259	1,017	671	−946	−572
Monetary Authorities	78bo *d*						−27	−20	−6	5	−18	−5	5	—		
General Government	78bp *d*						−5	−46	−53	−91	4	−31	−47	−38	−32	−41
Banks	78bq *d*						21	−88	−183	−141	−505	−225	145	—	−300	−288
Other Sectors	78br *d*						−4	−4	12	9	16	2	915	709	−614	−242
Other Investment Liab., n.i.e.	78bi *d*						93	911	1,288	1,417	−58	−35	1,687	2,184	1,267	795
Monetary Authorities	78bs *d*						312	684	486	767	93	84	529	454	552	193
General Government	78bt *d*						−70	40	111	533	—	—	—	—	—	—
Banks	78bu *d*						−29	239	750	−60	−248	−222	84	484	271	95
Other Sectors	78bv *d*						−119	−53	−59	177	97	102	1,073	1,246	445	507
Net Errors and Omissions	78ca *d*						−150	58	−70	−293	597	1,218	1,707	100	−11	−31
Overall Balance	78cb *d*						−725	−404	87	500	66	−5	−113	−14	−1,053	−95
Reserves and Related Items	79da *d*						725	404	−87	−500	−66	5	113	14	1,053	95
Reserve Assets	79db *d*						725	168	−171	−474	−25	107	167	56	687	−127
Use of Fund Credit and Loans	79dc *d*						—	201	84	−54	−40	−102	−55	−42	366	221
Exceptional Financing	79de *d*						—	35	—	28	—	—	—	—	—	—

Banking Survey (EA-Wide Residency)

End of Period

1999	Item	Code
6.81	Foreign Assets (Net)	31n.u
139.70	Domestic Credit	32..u
5.70	Claims on General Govt. (Net)	32an.u
134.00	Claims on Other Resident Sect.	32d.u
7.25	Currency in Circulation	34b.u
39.93	Demand Deposits	34b.u
71.37	Other Deposits	35..u
4.72	o/w: Other Dep. Over Two Yrs	35ab u
—	Money Market Instruments	36m.u
21.49	Bonds (Debt Securities)	36n.u
19.87	o/w: Bonds Over Two Years	36na u
24.08	Capital Accounts	37a
-17.60	Other Items (Net)	37r.u

Money (National Definitions)

End of Period

	1985	1986	1987	1988	1989	1990	1991	1992	1993	1994	1995	1996	1997	1998	1999	Code
M1	964.1	1,315.5	1,585.3	1,916.4	2,192.6	2,312.6	2,653.0	3,116.4	3,354.5	3,589.4	3,901.2	4,302.2	4,882.1	5,757.4	....	39ma
M2	3,036.2	3,636.3	4,255.7	5,034.0	5,692.0	6,201.6	7,738.6	9,054.3	9,701.9	10,586.2	11,434.5	12,468.2	13,316.2	14,401.3	....	39mb
L	2,772.5	3,533.1	4,360.1	5,139.1	5,852.3	6,509.0	7,389.7	8,601.4	9,376.2	10,020.3	11,102.1	11,907.3	12,825.5	13,667.5	....	39mc

Interest Rates

Percent Per Annum

	1985	1986	1987	1988	1989	1990	1991	1992	1993	1994	1995	1996	1997	1998	1999	Code
Banco de Portugal Rate (End of Per)	19.00	16.00	14.50	13.50	14.50	14.50	‡20.00	21.96	11.00	8.88	8.50	6.70	5.31	3.00	....	60
Money Market Rate	20.17	‡14.52	13.69	12.31	12.68	13.12	15.50	‡17.48	13.25	10.62	8.91	7.38	5.78	4.34	2.71	60b
Treasury Bill Rate	20.90	‡15.56	13.89	12.97	....	13.51	14.20	12.88	....	....	7.75	5.75	4.43	....	....	60c
Deposit Rate	25.08	17.13	14.46	13.21	13.00	13.99	14.80	14.59	11.06	8.37	8.38	6.32	4.56	3.37	2.40	60l
Lending Rate	27.29	19.63	‡18.92	‡17.53	19.59	21.78	‡25.02	20.43	16.48	15.01	13.80	11.73	9.15	7.24	5.19	60p
Government Bond Yield	20.75	15.54	15.02	13.87	15.63	18.55	18.27	15.38	12.45	10.83	10.34	7.25	5.48	4.09	....	61

Prices, Production, Labor

Period Averages

	1985	1986	1987	1988	1989	1990	1991	1992	1993	1994	1995	1996	1997	1998	1999	Code
Share Prices	....	....	....	89.3	93.0	89.7	76.3	67.3	79.3	104.1	100.0	117.3	183.4	287.7	....	62
Prices: Home & Import Goods('85=100)	100.0	109.2	....	....	....	....	....	....	....	....	....	....	....	....	....	63
Home Goods (1985=100)	100.0	109.1	....	....	....	....	....	....	....	....	....	....	....	....	....	63a
Consumer Prices	41.3	46.2	50.5	55.3	62.3	70.7	‡78.7	85.7	91.5	96.0	100.0	103.1	‡105.3	108.3	110.8	64
Harmonized CPI	....	....	....	....	....	....	....	....	....	....	100.0	102.9	104.9	107.2	109.5	64h
Wages: Daily Earnings (Mfg.)	54.2	63.6	72.4	76.0	86.2	100.0	113.5	....	....	....	....	....	....	....	....	65ey
Industrial Production	‡74.9	79.7	83.4	86.5	91.9	‡100.6	102.0	100.1	96.5	95.4	100.0	101.4	103.9	‡107.9	....	66

Period Averages

	1985	1986	1987	1988	1989	1990	1991	1992	1993	1994	1995	1996	1997	1998	1999	Code
Labor Force	....	....	....	....	....	....	....	....	4,708	4,799	4,777	4,809	4,868	5,000	....	67d
Employment	4,279	4,287	4,403	4,517	4,613	4,718	4,857	‡4,587	4,493	4,482	4,442	4,467	4,546	‡4,752	....	67e
Unemployment	397	393	329	....	243	231	208	‡194	257	324	338	344	324	‡248	....	67c
Unemployment Rate (%)	8.5	8.3	7.0	....	5.0	4.7	4.1	‡4.2	5.6	6.9	7.2	7.3	6.8	....	....	67r

International Transactions

Millions of Euros Beginning 1999

	1985	1986	1987	1988	1989	1990	1991	1992	1993	1994	1995	1996	1997	1998	1999	Code
Exports	967.4	1,082.3	1,311.0	1,582.0	2,015.7	2,336.5	2,354.1	2,475.2	2,474.4	2,975.6	3,501.8	3,795.9	4,195.1	4,461.0	‡22433.9	70
Imports, c.i.f.	1,302.8	1,442.5	1,965.3	2,581.0	3,003.2	3,589.7	3,811.1	4,087.6	3,883.8	4,514.3	5,028.7	5,427.1	6,139.7	6,914.8	‡36220.2	71
Imports, f.o.b.	1,181.1	1,307.8	1,781.8	2,340.0	2,722.8	3,254.5	3,455.2	3,705.9	3,521.1	4,092.7	4,559.1	4,920.3	....	....	....	71.v

1990=100

	1985	1986	1987	1988	1989	1990	1991	1992	1993	1994	1995	1996	1997	1998	1999	Code
Volume of Exports	56.3	60.7	67.8	74.1	89.1	‡100.0	100.6	107.0	....	....	....	....	....	....	....	72
Volume of Imports	43.4	51.7	66.2	80.8	87.7	‡100.0	106.0	118.6	....	....	....	....	....	....	....	73
Export Prices	74.1	76.6	83.0	91.6	97.1	‡100.0	100.2	98.1	....	....	....	....	....	....	....	76
Import Prices	86.3	78.9	83.8	89.7	96.6	‡100.0	100.2	95.2	....	....	....	....	....	....	....	76.x

Balance of Payments

Minus Sign Indicates Debit

	1985	1986	1987	1988	1989	1990	1991	1992	1993	1994	1995	1996	1997	1998	1999	Code
Current Account, n.i.e.	380	1,166	435	-1,066	153	-181	-716	-184	233	-2,196	-132	-4,528	-5,527	-7,250	-9,004	78al d
Goods: Exports f.o.b.	5,749	7,265	9,335	11,015	12,843	16,458	16,391	18,348	15,931	18,645	24,024	25,519	24,806	26,016	25,673	78aa d
Goods: Imports f.o.b.	-7,179	-8,876	-12,847	-16,392	-17,585	-23,141	-24,079	-27,735	-23,981	-26,966	-32,934	-34,880	-34,847	-38,292	-39,830	78ab d
Trade Balance	-1,430	-1,611	-3,513	-5,377	-4,742	-6,684	-7,688	-9,387	-8,050	-8,321	-8,910	-9,360	-10,041	-12,277	-14,157	78ac d
Services: Credit	1,931	2,425	3,165	3,418	3,789	5,096	5,231	5,497	6,846	6,755	8,236	7,951	7,605	8,606	8,373	78ad d
Services: Debit	-1,269	-1,585	-2,157	-2,668	-2,830	-4,005	-4,420	-4,732	-5,481	-5,486	-6,611	-6,556	-6,306	-7,031	-6,782	78ae d
Balance on Goods & Services	-768	-772	-2,505	-4,627	-3,784	-5,592	-6,877	-8,621	-6,685	-7,052	-7,285	-7,945	-8,741	-10,702	-12,566	78af d
Income: Credit	277	300	414	477	719	1,360	1,550	2,067	2,455	2,232	4,095	4,403	4,481	4,558	4,255	78ag d
Income: Debit	-1,373	-1,276	-1,245	-1,238	-1,322	-1,457	-1,364	-1,456	-2,236	-2,797	-4,074	-5,410	-4,941	-5,138	-4,630	78ah d
Balance on Gds, Serv. & Inc.	-1,864	-1,748	-3,336	-5,387	-4,387	-5,689	-6,691	-8,010	-6,466	-7,616	-7,264	-8,952	-9,201	-11,281	-12,941	78ai d
Current Transfers, n.i.e.: Credit	2,329	3,306	4,365	4,946	5,227	6,433	7,237	9,344	8,395	7,410	9,046	6,806	5,652	6,098	6,080	78aj d
Current Transfers: Debit	-85	-392	-594	-624	-687	-926	-1,263	-1,518	-1,696	-1,989	-1,914	-2,381	-1,977	-2,067	-2,144	78ak d
Capital Account, n.i.e.	—	—	—	—	—	—	—	—	—	—	—	2,239	2,694	2,588	2,435	78bc d
Capital Account, n.i.e.: Credit												2,342	2,796	2,808	2,625	78ba d
Capital Account: Debit												-103	-102	-221	-190	78bb d
Financial Account, n.i.e.	580	-1,432	689	293	4,005	2,563	4,537	-950	-3,032	1,052	3,025	4,404	6,258	6,532	9,632	78bj d
Direct Investment Abroad	-22	—	10	-80	-84	-163	-463	-687	-147	-287	-688	-777	-1,926	-2,947	-2,679	78bd d
Dir. Invest. in Rep. Econ., n.i.e.	274	238	466	922	1,737	2,610	2,448	1,873	1,534	1,270	685	1,367	2,534	1,783	551	78be d
Portfolio Investment Assets	1	—	—	-27	—	—	—	-379	-2,382	-3,456	-3,148	-5,799	-6,428	-6,068	-4,585	78bf d
Equity Securities	—	—	—	-1	—	—	—	-9	-168	-66	-159	-1,036	-838	-891	-1,744	78bk d
Debt Securities	1	—	—	-27	—	—	—	-370	-2,214	-3,390	-2,989	-4,763	-5,590	-5,177	-2,841	78bl d
Portfolio Investment Liab., n.i.e.	123	404	816	1,841	1,050	961	1,895	-2,685	4,214	3,934	2,066	4,321	8,387	6,228	11,438	78bg d
Equity Securities	-1	1	243	220	605	508	215	570	579	562	-179	1,895	2,557	2,138	691	78bm d
Debt Securities	124	402	573	1,622	445	453	1,681	-3,255	3,634	3,372	2,244	2,427	5,830	4,090	10,747	78bn d
Financial Derivatives Assets	....	....	....	....	....	....	....	....	-5	—	—	44	215	964	2,682	78bw d
Financial Derivatives Liabilities												-74	-239	-852	-2,485	78bx d
Other Investment Assets	-385	-1,095	-87	-1,145	-7	-2,442	-1,511	-1,923	-8,424	-7,098	-7,568	-1,693	-8,020	-5,866	-1,813	78bh d
Monetary Authorities	-1	—	—	—	—	—	—	—	9	—	-26	-5	1	-94	-1,519	78bo d
General Government	-39	-49	-58	-108	-114	-137	-98	-40	....	....	....	-10	11	—	-13	78bp d
Banks	-93	186	-412	-1,256	-584	-1,786	-1,250	-2,207	-7,024	-4,741	-6,679	-745	-7,043	-3,807	1,017	78bq d
Other Sectors	-253	-1,231	383	219	690	-520	-163	324	-1,409	-2,358	-863	-933	-988	-1,966	-1,297	78br d
Other Investment Liab., n.i.e.	589	-979	-517	-1,218	1,310	1,598	2,168	2,851	2,178	6,689	11,678	7,014	11,735	13,289	6,524	78bi d
Monetary Authorities	126	-476	-118	-1,402	-470	-518	-385	-24	-32	299	-99	169	1,645	837	487	78bs d
General Government	-1	—	-1	—	—	—	—	—	-146	-139	144	-375	105	—	-45	78bt d
Banks	-232	-254	10	233	1,241	1,329	2,376	1,757	1,327	7,069	11,189	7,034	9,501	12,354	6,900	78bu d
Other Sectors	697	-249	-409	-49	538	786	176	1,117	1,028	-540	444	186	485	182	-818	78bv d
Net Errors and Omissions	-253	156	653	1,640	497	1,160	1,893	978	-48	-287	-3,193	-1,392	-2,180	-1,362	-2,861	78ca d
Overall Balance	707	-111	1,777	867	4,654	3,542	5,713	-156	-2,848	-1,430	-300	723	1,246	508	202	78cb d
Reserves and Related Items	-707	111	-1,777	-867	-4,654	-3,542	-5,713	156	2,848	1,430	300	-723	-1,246	-508	-202	78da d
Reserve Assets	-707	111	-1,521	-365	-4,654	-3,542	-5,713	156	2,848	1,430	300	-723	-1,246	-508	-202	78db d
Use of Fund Credit and Loans	—	—	-256	-502	—	—	—	....	....	....	....	....	....	....	....	78dc d
Exceptional Financing	—	—	—	—	—	—	—	....	....	....	....	....	....	....	....	78de d

Portugal

		1970	1971	1972	1973	1974	1975	1976	1977	1978	1979	1980	1981	1982	1983	1984
International Investment Position																*Millions of US Dollars*
Assets	79aa d	....	....	....	....	....	....	....	....	....	....	....	....	....	....	....
Direct Investment Abroad	79ab d	....	....	....	....	....	....	....	....	....	....	....	....	....	....	....
Portfolio Investment	79ac d	....	....	....	....	....	....	....	....	....	....	....	....	....	....	....
Equity Securities	79ad d	....	....	....	....	....	....	....	....	....	....	....	....	....	....	....
Debt Securities	79ae d	....	....	....	....	....	....	....	....	....	....	....	....	....	....	....
Financial Derivatives	79al d	....	....	....	....	....	....	....	....	....	....	....	....	....	....	....
Other Investment	79af d	....	....	....	....	....	....	....	....	....	....	....	....	....	....	....
Monetary Authorities	79ag d	....	....	....	....	....	....	....	....	....	....	....	....	....	....	....
General Government	79ah d	....	....	....	....	....	....	....	....	....	....	....	....	....	....	....
Banks	79ai d	....	....	....	....	....	....	....	....	....	....	....	....	....	....	....
Other Sectors	79aj d	....	....	....	....	....	....	....	....	....	....	....	....	....	....	....
Reserve Assets	79ak d	....	....	....	....	....	....	....	....	....	....	6,447	6,178	6,078	5,594	5,690
Liabilities	79la d	....	....	....	....	....	....	....	....	....	....	....	....	....	....	....
Dir. Invest. in Rep. Economy	79lb d	....	....	....	....	....	....	....	....	....	....	....	....	....	....	....
Portfolio Investment	79lc d	....	....	....	....	....	....	....	....	....	....	....	....	....	....	....
Equity Securities	79ld d	....	....	....	....	....	....	....	....	....	....	....	....	....	....	....
Debt Securities	79le d	....	....	....	....	....	....	....	....	....	....	....	....	....	....	....
Financial Derivatives	79ll d	....	....	....	....	....	....	....	....	....	....	....	....	....	....	....
Other Investment	79lf d	....	....	....	....	....	....	....	....	....	....	....	11,050	13,608	14,854	15,538
Monetary Authorities	79lg d	....	....	....	....	....	....	....	....	....	....	....	55	11	371	561
General Government	79lh d	....	....	....	....	....	....	....	....	....	....	....	....	....	....	....
Banks	79li d	....	....	....	....	....	....	....	....	....	....	....	843	1,336	1,643	1,677
Other Sectors	79lj d	....	....	....	....	....	....	....	....	....	....	....	....	....	....	....
Government Finance																
Central Government																*Billions of Escudos through 1998;*
Deficit (-) or Surplus	80	−3.1	−2.2	−5.6	−3.6	−8.9	𝟙−31.8	−54.0	−40.9	−92.8	−100.5	−121.5	−179.6	−195.0	−219.7	−272.4
Revenue	81	27.8	30.0	33.8	39.9	47.2	𝟙96.0	127.4	176.7	217.4	272.1	377.2	480.9	603.5	809.8	951.4
Grants Received	81z						𝟙—	.1	1.5	.6	1.0	2.9	1.5	1.2	1.9	3.9
Expenditure	82	27.4	30.6	33.8	41.3	55.4	𝟙123.5	172.8	210.0	283.8	352.8	475.9	620.2	751.0	974.1	1,141.7
Lending Minus Repayments	83	1.4	1.6	1.5	1.3	1.4	𝟙4.3	8.7	9.1	27.0	20.8	25.7	41.8	48.7	57.3	86.0
Unclass. Transactions (Net)	83x	2.0	−.1	4.1	.9	−.7	....	....	....	....	....	....	....	....	....	....
Financing																
Domestic	84a	2.5	1.2	3.5	3.9	6.2	𝟙32.3	52.9	41.3	73.1	95.1	93.8	141.8	141.9	143.2	174.8
Foreign	85a	.6	.8	−.3	.2	−.2	𝟙−.6	1.2	−.4	19.7	5.4	27.7	37.8	53.1	76.5	97.6
Use of Cash Balances	87	−.1	.1	2.5	−.5	2.9	....	....	....	....	....	....	....	....	....	....
Debt: Escudos	88b	13.10	12.42	15.32	39.62	48.91	90.09	147.18	....	....	....	....	....	....	....	....
Held By: Bk of Portugal	88ba	1.69	1.63	1.54	1.74	8.73	44.08	68.79	....	....	....	....	....	....	....	....
Commercial Banks	88bb	4.10	3.87	4.84	8.82	8.49	7.88	14.23	....	....	....	....	....	....	....	....
Savings Banks	88bc	2.62	2.59	3.53	6.36	6.10	5.40	8.20	....	....	....	....	....	....	....	....
Others	88bd	4.69	4.33	5.41	22.70	25.59	32.73	55.96	....	....	....	....	....	....	....	....
Intragovernmental Debt	88s	12.16	13.64	13.48	13.22	13.14	9.58	3.48	....	....	....	....	....	....	....	....
Held by: Social Insur. System	88sz	11.23	12.81	12.80	12.62	12.62	9.12	3.12	....	....	....	....	....	....	....	....
General Government																*As Percent of*
Deficit (-) or Surplus	80g	....	....	....	....	....	....	....	....	....	....	....	....	....	....	....
Debt	88g	....	....	....	....	....	....	....	....	....	....	....	....	....	....	....
National Accounts																*Billions of Escudos*
Exports of Goods & Services	90c	41	48	57	75	91	77	82	105	139	232	298	339	432	645	934
Government Consumption	91f	25	28	32	36	48	57	64	90	112	144	187	231	282	360	433
Gross Fixed Capital Formation	93e	44	52	67	76	88	98	118	166	220	264	359	463	575	672	664
Increase/Decrease(-) in Stocks	93i	4	4	2	7	9	−21	−2	16	23	52	73	116	112	−1	−38
Private Consumption	96f	119	132	148	183	247	291	352	452	540	665	849	1,012	1,258	1,610	2,056
Imports of Goods & Services	98c	−53	−61	−71	−95	−143	−124	−145	−203	−247	−362	−510	−660	−808	−984	−1,233
Gross Domestic Product (GDP)	99b	180	202	235	282	339	377	469	626	787	995	1,256	1,501	1,850	2,302	2,816
Net Factor Inc/Pmts(-) Abroad	98.n	1	—	1	2	4	—	−5	−8	16	−22	−33	−61	−103	−120	−177
Gross National Income (GNI)	99a	181	202	236	285	343	377	464	618	772	972	1,225	1,440	1,747	2,182	2,638
Net National Income	99e	172	192	223	271	328	359	449	592	736	928	1,170	1,377	1,665	2,061	2,507
GDP Volume 1990 prices	99b.p	4,541	4,842	5,230	5,816	5,882	5,627	6,015	6,352	6,531	6,899	7,216	7,332	7,489	7,476	7,335
GDP Volume 1995 Prices	99b.p	....	....	....	....	....	....	....	....	....	....	....	....	....	....	....
GDP Volume (1995=100)	99bv p	42.3	45.1	48.7	54.1	54.7	52.4	56.0	59.1	60.8	64.2	67.2	68.2	69.7	69.6	68.3
GDP Deflator (1995=100)	99bi p	2.7	2.8	3.1	3.3	3.9	4.6	5.3	6.7	8.2	9.8	11.8	13.9	16.8	20.9	26.1
																Millions:
Population	99z	9.04	8.99	8.97	8.98	8.99	9.43	9.67	9.74	9.80	𝟙9.66	9.77	9.86	9.86	9.88	9.90

International Investment Position

Millions of US Dollars

1985	1986	1987	1988	1989	1990	1991	1992	1993	1994	1995	1996	1997	1998	1999		Code
								45,989	54,212	59,764	86,425	99,344	122,007	....	Assets	79aa d
										—	4,726	5,932	9,846	....	Direct Investment Abroad	79ab d
										—	17,502	20,368	30,057	....	Portfolio Investment	79ac d
											4,997	4,765	6,441	....	Equity Securities	79ad d
											12,505	15,602	23,616	....	Debt Securities	79ae d
											422	381	290	....	Financial Derivatives	79al d
								24,170	32,543	37,810	42,030	52,341	60,228	....	Other Investment	79af d
										—	47	28	127	....	Monetary Authorities	79ag d
								15	15	28	80	78	81	....	General Government	79ah d
								18,016	25,149	30,288	29,900	38,718	44,331	....	Banks	79ai d
								6,139	7,379	7,494	12,003	13,516	15,688	....	Other Sectors	79aj d
6,554	6,595	8,441	10,317	15,136	19,598	25,754	24,317	21,819	21,669	21,954	21,745	20,321	21,586	....	Reserve Assets	79ak d
								38,073	50,922	65,961	93,951	113,075	142,926	....	Liabilities	79la d
											18,947	18,605	21,693	....	Dir. Invest. in Rep. Economy	79lb d
								8,907	13,656	16,430	21,327	36,207	46,766	....	Portfolio Investment	79lc d
								2,929	3,597	3,651	6,573	12,663	18,955	....	Equity Securities	79ld d
								5,978	10,059	12,779	14,755	23,544	27,811	....	Debt Securities	79le d
											—			....	Financial Derivatives	79ll d
17,310	16,987							29,166	37,266	49,532	53,677	58,263	74,467	....	Other Investment	79lf d
628	700							48	362	278	440	2,084	2,931	....	Monetary Authorities	79lg d
								2,099	1,973	2,229	1,676	1,614	1,637	....	General Government	79lh d
1,429	1,213							13,875	21,527	32,432	36,320	42,261	56,844	....	Banks	79li d
								13,144	13,403	14,592	15,241	12,305	13,055	....	Other Sectors	79lj d

Government Finance

Central Government

Millions of Euros Beginning 1999: Year Ending December 31

1985	1986	1987	1988	1989	1990	1991	1992	1993	1994	1995	1996	1997	1998	1999		Code
-522.0	-543.2	-538.8	-523.0	-287.1	-449.6	-666.8	-289.8	-932.7	-708.1	-795.8	-379.9	-372.2		....	Deficit (-) or Surplus	80
1,182.3	1,553.9	1,768.5	2,030.5	2,726.4	3,215.9	3,869.5	4,594.7	4,624.9	5,016.5	5,456.7	5,759.9	6,391.8		....	Revenue	81
5.1	56.6	94.3	105.9	140.7	153.4	259.1	429.8	446.6	411.6	525.6	662.2	649.9		....	Grants Received	81z
1,626.6	2,033.5	2,245.0	2,492.9	3,146.2	3,828.9	4,722.6	5,527.0	6,012.0	6,137.9	6,613.6	6,974.5	7,242.2		....	Expenditure	82
82.8	120.2	156.6	166.5	8.0	-10.0	72.8	-212.7	-7.8	-1.7	164.5	-172.5	171.7		....	Lending Minus Repayments	83
														....	Unclass. Transactions (Net)	83x

Financing

1985	1986	1987	1988	1989	1990	1991	1992	1993	1994	1995	1996	1997	1998	1999		Code
465.5	589.2	466.3	546.4	457.7	582.0	806.3	296.5	656.5	659.0	218.2	2.7	-12.1		....	Domestic	84a
56.5	-46.0	72.5	-23.4	-170.6	-132.4	-139.5	-6.7	276.2	49.1	577.6	377.2	384.3		....	Foreign	85a
														....	Use of Cash Balances	87
														....	Debt: Escudos	88b
														....	Held By: Bk of Portugal	88ba
														....	Commercial Banks	88bb
														....	Savings Banks	88bc
														....	Others	88bd
														....	Intragovernmental Debt	88s
														....	Held by: Social Insur. System	88sz

General Government

1985	1986	1987	1988	1989	1990	1991	1992	1993	1994	1995	1996	1997	1998	1999		Code
					-5.1	-6.0	-3.0	-6.1	-6.0	-5.7	-3.8	-2.6	-2.1	-2.0	Deficit (-) or Surplus	80g
					65.3	67.3	60.1	63.1	63.8	65.9	63.6	60.3	56.5	56.8	Debt	88g

Gross Domestic Product (left-column label)

National Accounts

Billions of Escudos

1985	1986	1987	1988	1989	1990	1991	1992	1993	1994	1995	1996	1997	1998	1999		Code
1,159	1,298	1,567	1,906	2,400	2,779	2,851	2,960	3,050	3,583	4,168	4,482	4,895	5,301	....	Exports of Goods & Services	90c
559	762	880	1,083	1,320	1,603	2,043	2,322	2,533	2,781	3,019	3,298	3,555	3,896	....	Government Consumption	91f
768	1,225	1,591	2,026	2,317	2,718	2,964	3,191	3,140	3,439	3,743	4,005	4,516	4,992	....	Gross Fixed Capital Formation	93e
-41	-49	39	141	101	102	60	112	-18	57	115	95	101	108	....	Increase/Decrease(-) in Stocks	93i
2,491	3,416	4,001	4,755	5,542	6,577	7,636	8,659	9,216	9,870	10,456	11,052	11,668	12,646	....	Private Consumption	96f
-1,412	-1,592	-2,150	-2,827	-3,307	-3,923	-4,240	-4,485	-4,458	-5,111	-5,698	-6,123	-6,876	-7,698	....	Imports of Goods & Services	98c
3,524	5,060	5,928	7,084	8,372	9,855	11,315	12,759	13,463	14,617	15,802	16,809	17,859	19,246	....	Gross Domestic Product (GDP)	99b
-196	-152	-131	-126	-113	-34	11	82							....	Net Factor Inc/Pmts(-) Abroad	98.n
3,328	4,269	5,044	5,877	7,064	8,527	9,948	11,425							....	Gross National Income (GNI)	99a
3,177														....	Net National Income	99e
7,541	7,854	8,355	8,981	....	....	....	....							....	GDP Volume 1990 prices	99b. p
			13,208	13,922	14,584	14,925	15,214	15,000	15,353	15,802	16,306	16,871	17,460	....	GDP Volume 1995 Prices	99b. p
70.2	73.1	77.8	83.6	88.1	92.3	94.5	96.3	94.9	97.2	100.0	103.2	106.8	110.5	....	GDP Volume (1995=100)	99bv p
31.8	43.8	48.2	53.6	60.1	67.6	75.8	83.9	89.8	95.2	100.0	103.1	105.9	110.2	....	GDP Deflator (1995=100)	99bi p

Midyear Estimates

1985	1986	1987	1988	1989	1990	1991	1992	1993	1994	1995	1996	1997	1998	1999		Code
9.91	10.01	9.99	9.97	9.94	9.90	9.87	9.87	9.88	9.90	9.92	9.93	9.94	9.97	9.96	Population	99z

(See notes in the back of the book.)

Qatar

		1970	1971	1972	1973	1974	1975	1976	1977	1978	1979	1980	1981	1982	1983	1984
Exchange Rates																*Riyals per SDR:*
Official Rate	aa	4.7619	4.7619	4.7619	4.7619	4.8330	4.6679	4.5989	4.8100	5.0008	4.8807	4.6425	4.2368	4.0153	3.8109	3.5680
																Riyals per US Dollar:
Official Rate	ae	4.7619	4.3860	4.3860	3.9474	3.9474	3.9874	3.9583	3.9598	3.8385	3.7050	3.6400	3.6400	3.6400	3.6400	3.6400
Official Rate	rf	4.7619	4.7480	4.3860	3.9963	3.9474	3.9307e	3.9634	3.9590	3.8769	3.7733	3.6570	3.6400	3.6400	3.6400	3.6400
															Index Numbers (1995=100):	
Official Rate	ahx	76.4	76.7	83.0	91.1	92.2	92.6e	91.8	91.9	93.9	96.5	99.5	100.0	100.0	100.0	100.0
Nominal Effective Exchange Rate	nec	....	....	....	....	....	....	....	....	....	82.4	84.2	94.1	104.5	110.2	118.6
Fund Position																*Millions of SDRs:*
Quota	2f.s	....	....	20.0	20.0	20.0	20.0	20.0	20.0	40.0	40.0	66.2	66.2	66.2	114.9	114.9
SDRs	1b.s	....	....	—	—	—	—	—	—	—	4.2	2.7	8.6	14.0	8.7	16.2
Reserve Position in the Fund	1c.s	....	....	5.0	5.0	5.0	13.1	16.2	14.5	14.7	13.6	18.1	18.1	19.4	37.2	38.4
International Liquidity												*Millions of US Dollars Unless Otherwise Indicated:*					
Total Reserves minus Gold	1l.d	30.5	38.4	53.4	67.7	63.7	96.7	129.3	161.7	210.7	288.0	343.4	365.8	386.6	384.1	380.0
SDRs	1b.d										5.5	3.5	10.0	15.4	9.1	15.9
Reserve Position in the Fund	1c.d	....	....	5.4	6.0	6.1	15.3	18.8	17.6	19.2	17.9	23.1	21.1	21.4	38.9	37.6
Foreign Exchange	1d.d	30.5	38.4	48.0	61.7	57.6	81.4	110.5	144.1	191.5	264.6	316.8	334.7	349.8	336.1	326.5
Gold (Million Fine Troy Ounces)	1ad	.185	.186	.186	.186	.186	.189	.192	.183	.252	.269	.474	.713	.897	1.066	1.205
Gold (National Valuation)	1and	6.5	7.0	7.0	7.8	7.8	7.7	7.8	7.8	11.5	12.4	21.2	29.0	34.6	39.0	41.3
Deposit Money Banks: Assets	7a.d	44.9	64.0	72.9	82.5	143.1	278.0	381.8	456.7	576.5	681.3	732.7	1,204.5	1,271.0	1,059.1	1,726.2
Liabilities	7b.d	8.3	5.9	.6	7.9	26.2	56.4	87.4	120.8	166.0	270.0	174.4	200.0	245.0	311.5	234.2
Monetary Authorities																*Millions of Riyals:*
Foreign Assets	11	85	94	126	164	282	416	542	671	853	1,113	1,327	1,437	1,533	1,540	1,534
Claims on Central Government	12a	....	....	....	....	....	....	....	....	....	....	....	....	....	....	....
Claims on Deposit Money Banks	12e	—	—	4	—	—	—	16	51	88	96	8	—	25	6	18
Reserve Money	14	61	70	93	129	188	298	428	582	774	988	1,159	1,193	1,325	1,335	1,350
of which: Currency Outside DMBs	14a	54	60	77	111	158	240	376	505	573	715	808	992	1,151	1,068	1,186
Central Government Deposits	16d	11	9	—	6	24	48	72	32	52	113	103	234	238	225	308
Capital Accounts	17a	15	17	16	16	26	30	30	30	30	50	69	84	81	79	76
Other Items (Net)	17r	–2	–2	21	13	44	40	28	78	85	57	4	–75	–87	–93	–182
Deposit Money Banks																*Millions of Riyals:*
Reserves	20	7	9	16	18	30	58	52	77	213	276	335	196	185	278	170
Foreign Assets	21	214	281	320	326	565	1,109	1,511	1,809	2,213	2,524	2,667	4,384	4,626	3,855	6,283
Claims on Central Government	22a	....	....	....	....	....	....	....	....	....	....	....	....	....	....	....
Claims on Nonfin.Pub.Enterprises	22c	....	....	....	....	....	....	....	....	....	....	....	....	....	....	....
Claims on Private Sector	22d	215	262	333	503	752	1,126	1,559	2,464	2,889	3,278	3,693	4,507	5,576	6,056	5,440
Demand Deposits	24	143	177	269	302	406	765	1,200	1,582	1,733	1,776	1,466	2,412	2,644	2,556	2,948
Time, Savings,& Fgn.Currency Dep.	25	187	226	319	364	485	744	1,129	1,480	1,809	2,020	3,003	4,072	4,772	4,863	6,220
Foreign Liabilities	26c	40	26	3	31	104	225	346	478	637	1,000	635	728	892	1,134	853
Central Government Deposits	26d	12	56	20	39	127	229	120	252	448	434	592	549	437	456	419
Credit from Monetary Authorities	26g	—	—	—	—	—	—	—	63	82	39	—	—	25	5	—
Capital Accounts	27a	53	67	67	95	169	252	210	232	284	386	563	572	700	859	1,040
Other Items (Net)	27r	—	2	–9	15	57	77	118	263	322	423	437	755	918	317	413
Monetary Survey																*Millions of Riyals:*
Foreign Assets (Net)	31n	259	349	443	458	744	1,300	1,708	2,002	2,429	2,637	3,359	5,093	5,268	4,261	6,964
Domestic Credit	32	192	198	312	458	601	848	1,367	2,181	2,389	2,731	2,998	3,724	4,901	5,376	4,713
Claims on Central Govt. (Net)	32an	–23	–65	–20	–45	–151	–277	–192	–283	–500	–547	–695	–783	–675	–681	–727
Claims on Nonfin.Pub.Enterprises	32c	....	....	....	....	....	....	....	....	....	....	....	....	....	....	....
Claims on Private Sector	32d	215	262	333	503	752	1,126	1,559	2,464	2,889	3,278	3,693	4,507	5,576	6,056	5,440
Money	34	198	237	345	413	564	1,005	1,576	2,087	2,307	2,492	2,274	3,403	3,795	3,625	4,135
Quasi-Money	35	187	226	319	364	485	744	1,129	1,480	1,809	2,020	3,003	4,072	4,772	4,863	6,220
Other Items (Net)	37r	66	84	92	139	296	399	370	615	703	857	1,080	1,342	1,601	1,149	1,323
Money plus Quasi-Money	35l	385	463	664	777	1,049	1,749	2,705	3,567	4,116	4,511	5,277	7,475	8,567	8,488	10,354
Interest Rates																*Percent Per Annum*
Deposit Rate	60l	....	....	....	....	....	....	....	....	....	6.0	6.0	6.0	6.0	6.0	6.0
Lending Rate	60p	....	....	....	....	....	....	....	....	....	....	9.5	9.5	9.5	9.5	9.5
Prices and Production																*Index Numbers (1995=100):*
Consumer Prices	64	....	....	....	....	....	....	....	....	....	59.7	63.7	69.2	73.1	75.1	75.9
Crude Petroleum	66aa	80.7	95.9	105.9	123.0	113.4	97.7	108.9	97.3	107.5	112.9	105.5	90.3	73.2	65.6	95.6
International Transactions																*Millions of Riyals*
Exports	70	1,142	1,496	1,740	2,511	7,954	7,094	8,757	8,205	9,268	14,120	20,768	20,696	15,802	12,221	....
Crude Petroleum	70aa	1,099	1,441	1,673	2,444	7,811	6,893	8,470	8,134	8,955	13,398	19,728	19,331	14,840	11,132	15,943
Imports, c.i.f.	71	306	516	616	778	1,070	1,622	3,237	4,850	4,590	5,378	5,203	5,525	7,088	5,299	4,230
Volume of Exports																*1985=100*
Crude Petroleum	72aa	115.6	136.4	154.1	181.9	162.9	137.1	158.9	132.1	152.9	159.7	148.8	125.2	102.9	89.3	130.1
Export Prices																*1985=100:*
Crude Petroleum	76aad	6.0	6.7	7.4	10.1	36.4	38.4	40.3	44.9	44.9	67.2	108.6	127.1	118.7	102.6	100.9
Government Finance																*Millions of Riyals:*
Deficit (-) or Surplus	80	75	255	272	178	3,565	1,832	3,118	837	1,752	3,820	8,066	4,500	815	....	....
Revenue	81	579	945	1,230	1,720	5,497	7,135	8,927	8,155	8,225	12,090	19,003	19,243	13,434	....	....
Expenditure	82	505	690	959	1,542	1,931	5,302	5,809	7,318	6,473	8,270	10,937	14,743	12,619	....	....
Financing																	
Use of Cash Balances	87	–75	–255	–272	–178	–3,565	–1,832	–3,118	–837	–1,752	–3,820	–8,066	–4,500	–815	....	....
National Accounts																*Millions of Riyals*
Exports of Goods & Services	90c	....	....	....	....	....	....	....	....	....	....	21,127	21,468	16,753	12,753	13,450
Government Consumption	91f	....	....	....	....	....	....	....	....	....	....	5,622	8,143	7,236	8,203	9,021
Gross Fixed Capital Formation	93e	....	....	....	....	....	....	....	....	....	....	4,766	5,312	7,391	5,720	4,302
Increase/Decrease(-) in Stocks	93i	....	....	....	....	....	....	....	....	....	....	117	284	215	–544	–155
Private Consumption	96f	....	....	....	....	....	....	....	....	....	....	4,509	5,424	5,921	5,769	5,927
Imports of Goods & Services	98c	....	....	....	....	....	....	....	....	....	....	–7,478	–9,063	–9,811	–8,296	–7,537
Gross Domestic Product (GDP)	99b	1,313	1,850	2,172	2,615	7,895	9,877	13,017	14,322	15,709	21,783	28,663	31,568	27,705	23,605	25,008
																Millions:
Population	99z	.11	.12	.13	.15	.16	.17	.18	.19	.20	.22	.23	.24	.26	.31	.33

	1985	1986	1987	1988	1989	1990	1991	1992	1993	1994	1995	1996	1997	1998	1999		
Exchange Rates																	
End of Period																	
	3.9982	4.4524	5.1639	4.8983	4.7835	5.1785	5.2068	5.0050	4.9998	5.3139	5.4108	5.2342	4.9113	5.1252	4.9959	Official Rate	aa
End of Period (ae) Period Average (rf)																	
	3.6400	3.6400	3.6400	3.6400	3.6400	3.6400	3.6400	3.6400	3.6400	3.6400	3.6400	3.6400	3.6400	3.6400	3.6400	Official Rate	ae
	3.6400	3.6400	3.6400	3.6400	3.6400	3.6400	3.6400	3.6400	3.6400	3.6400	3.6400	3.6400	3.6400	3.6400	3.6400	Official Rate	rf
Period Averages																	
	100.0	100.0	100.0	100.0	100.0	100.0	100.0	100.0	100.0	100.0	100.0	100.0	100.0	100.0	100.0	Official Rate	ahx
	121.8	99.5	88.8	84.3	89.5	87.8	91.0	92.5	101.5	104.8	100.0	103.8	111.7	116.6	116.2	Nominal Effective Exchange Rate	nec
Fund Position																	
End of Period																	
	114.9	114.9	114.9	114.9	114.9	114.9	114.9	190.5	190.5	190.5	190.5	190.5	190.5	190.5	263.8	Quota	2f.s
	18.9	21.1	24.7	26.4	28.7	31.3	33.8	17.1	18.7	19.9	21.2	22.5	23.8	25.1	10.7	SDRs	1b.s
	35.8	30.7	27.8	21.1	19.5	17.3	18.7	36.4	33.8	30.7	29.7	29.2	26.4	26.4	44.7	Reserve Position in the Fund	1c.s
International Liquidity																	
End of Period																	
	446.1	571.9	618.4	474.5	533.4	631.1	667.7	683.3	693.7	657.7	....	....	....	....	14.6	Total Reserves minus Gold	1l.d
	20.7	25.8	35.0	35.6	37.7	44.6	48.3	23.4	25.6	29.0	31.5	32.4	32.1	35.3	14.6	SDRs	1b.d
	39.3	37.6	39.5	28.4	25.7	24.6	26.8	50.1	46.4	44.7	44.2	42.0	35.6	37.2	61.4	Reserve Position in the Fund	1c.d
	386.2	508.5	543.9	410.5	470.0	561.9	592.6	609.8	621.7	584.0	....	....	....	....		Foreign Exchange	1d.d
	1.075	.966	.833	.880	.901	.833	.828	.861	.862	.814	.268	.268	.054	.054	.019	Gold (Million Fine Troy Ounces)	1ad
	41.3	41.3	41.3	41.5	41.5	41.5	41.5	41.5	41.5	41.6	....	....	....	....		Gold (National Valuation)	1and
	1,918.7	1,982.8	2,499.2	2,701.7	2,081.4	2,273.6	2,537.6	2,195.0	I2,264.3	2,648.0	3,093.7	2,396.3	2,643.4	2,324.3	2,455.5	Deposit Money Banks: Assets	7a.d
	246.6	430.6	734.1	977.5	409.7	578.7	1,192.7	58.2	I1,370.4	1,381.3	1,768.2	1,026.6	1,274.4	1,497.6	1,605.5	Liabilities	7b.d
Monetary Authorities																	
End of Period																	
	1,774	2,232	2,401	1,878	2,093	2,448	2,581	2,638	I2,686	2,546	2,859	2,649	3,044	3,854	4,767	Foreign Assets	11
	....	....	....	....	....	....	....	....	....	....	437	546	437	—	1,467	Claims on Central Government	12a
	5	4	5	24	106	155	150	151	I150	260	205	212	194	1,589	82	Claims on Deposit Money Banks	12e
	1,307	1,699	1,692	1,542	1,761	1,917	1,934	2,086	2,181	2,030	2,131	2,261	2,481	2,557	2,868	Reserve Money	14
	1,120	1,288	1,249	1,178	1,245	1,350	1,275	1,321	1,350	1,350	1,407	1,404	1,555	1,499	1,714	of which: Currency Outside DMBs	14a
	418	285	164	137	84	175	249	138	I33	42	381	116	120	145	30	Central Government Deposits	16d
	81	87	96	93	91	96	97	94	I576	705	1,178	1,242	1,339	1,466	1,536	Capital Accounts	17a
	−26	165	455	130	262	414	451	470	I46	30	−188	−212	−265	1,275	1,881	Other Items (Net)	17r
Deposit Money Banks																	
End of Period																	
	192	421	449	374	519	581	662	768	830	680	739	852	919	1,064	1,169	Reserves	20
	6,984	7,217	9,097	9,834	7,576	8,276	9,237	7,990	I8,242	9,639	11,261	8,723	9,622	8,460	8,938	Foreign Assets	21
	....	....	....	....	....	....	....	....	9,031	10,050	10,028	11,873	12,863	16,151	19,064	Claims on Central Government	22a
	....	....	....	....	....	....	....	....	....	228	384	728	878	609	537	Claims on Nonfin.Pub.Enterprises	22c
	6,445	8,031	8,743	9,265	10,553	9,906	13,344	18,113	I10,948	9,544	10,267	10,251	12,548	14,451	15,664	Claims on Private Sector	22d
	2,897	3,199	3,530	2,221	2,158	2,705	2,353	2,669	I2,904	2,561	2,313	2,481	2,575	2,717	2,465	Demand Deposits	24
	7,289	8,082	8,872	9,109	10,847	9,544	10,290	11,036	I12,635	14,509	14,901	15,772	17,466	19,117	21,804	Time, Savings,& Fgn.Currency Dep.	25
	898	1,567	2,672	3,558	1,491	2,107	4,342	212	I4,988	5,028	6,436	3,737	4,639	5,451	5,844	Foreign Liabilities	26c
	486	312	331	1,003	282	817	2,425	5,020	I3,394	1,903	2,671	3,795	4,601	5,248	6,540	Central Government Deposits	26d
	—	—	—	23	2	—	—	43	18	91	69	60	140	72	94	Credit from Monetary Authorities	26g
	1,129	1,416	1,522	1,750	1,990	2,271	2,525	2,762	I4,659	5,049	5,473	5,702	6,249	6,821	7,467	Capital Accounts	27a
	923	1,093	1,363	1,808	1,878	1,319	1,308	5,129	I685	1,001	815	880	1,160	1,309	1,157	Other Items (Net)	27r
Monetary Survey																	
End of Period																	
	7,861	7,882	8,826	8,154	8,177	8,617	7,476	10,416	I5,940	7,156	7,682	7,635	8,026	6,862	7,861	Foreign Assets (Net)	31n
	5,541	7,434	8,248	8,124	10,187	8,913	10,670	12,955	I16,785	17,879	18,064	19,488	22,007	25,819	30,162	Domestic Credit	32
	−904	−597	−495	−1,141	−366	−993	−2,673	−5,158	I5,604	8,105	7,413	8,508	8,579	10,757	13,960	Claims on Central Govt. (Net)	32an
	....	....	....	....	....	....	....	....	232	228	384	728	878	609	537	Claims on Nonfin.Pub.Enterprises	32c
	6,445	8,031	8,743	9,265	10,553	9,906	13,344	18,113	I10,949	9,545	10,268	10,252	12,550	14,453	15,665	Claims on Private Sector	32d
	4,017	4,487	4,778	3,399	3,403	4,055	3,629	3,990	I4,254	3,910	3,720	3,885	4,131	4,216	4,179	Money	34
	7,289	8,082	8,872	9,109	10,847	9,544	10,290	11,036	I12,635	14,509	14,901	15,772	17,466	19,117	21,804	Quasi-Money	35
	2,097	2,747	3,425	3,771	4,114	3,932	4,228	8,345	I5,836	6,616	7,125	7,467	8,437	9,348	12,041	Other Items (Net)	37r
	11,305	12,569	13,650	12,507	14,250	13,599	13,918	15,026	I16,889	18,419	18,622	19,657	21,596	23,333	25,982	Money plus Quasi-Money	35l
Interest Rates																	
Percent Per Annum																	
	6.0	6.0	6.0	6.0	6.0	6.0	6.0	4.8	4.1	4.8	6.2	6.5	6.6	6.6	6.5	Deposit Rate	60l
	9.5	9.5	9.5	9.5	9.5	9.5	9.5	8.1	7.2	8.9	....	....	....	....	....	Lending Rate	60p
Prices and Production																	
Period Averages																	
	77.4	I78.6	80.7	84.5	87.2	89.9	93.8	96.7	95.9	97.1	100.0	107.4	110.4	....	....	Consumer Prices	64
	73.5	79.8	68.6	70.2	87.2	85.9	84.7	88.5	92.2	90.6	100.0	106.3	137.5	147.3	146.9	Crude Petroleum	66aa
International Transactions																	
Millions of Riyals																	
	....	....	....	....	....	....	....	....	....	....	....	....	....			Exports	70
	12,147	....	....	....	....	....	....	....	....	....	....	....	....			Crude Petroleum	70aa
	4,147	4,000	4,128	4,613	4,827	6,169	6,261	7,336	6,882	7,016	12,369	10,441	12,091			Imports, c.i.f.	71
Volume of Exports																	
1985=100																	
	100.0	108.7	....													Crude Petroleum	72aa
Export Prices																	
Index of Prices in US Dollars																	
	100.0	....														Crude Petroleum	76aa d
Government Finance																	
Lunar Years																	
	....															Deficit (-) or Surplus	80
	....															Revenue	81
	....															Expenditure	82
Financing																	
	....															Use of Cash Balances	87
National Accounts																	
Millions of Riyals																	
	11,502	7,330	8,188	8,239	9,986	14,323	11,886	14,203	12,011	12,046	13,134	14,419	14,850	....	....	Exports of Goods & Services	90c
	7,882	8,384	8,776	9,983	9,165	8,802	8,934	9,258	9,370	9,250	9,436	10,886	11,150	....	....	Government Consumption	91f
	3,968	3,402	2,984	3,323	3,375	4,551	4,365	5,159	4,849	6,575	8,895	11,532	12,594	....	....	Gross Fixed Capital Formation	93e
	30	7	−126	191	237	263	415	583	300	8	1,495	262	450	....	....	Increase/Decrease(-) in Stocks	93i
	5,626	5,437	6,362	6,428	7,597	7,456	7,860	8,519	8,557	8,030	9,497	8,996	9,170	....	....	Private Consumption	96f
	−6,610	−6,167	−6,359	−6,185	−6,744	−8,603	−8,404	−9,890	−9,037	−9,066	−12,835	−13,119	−14,750	....	....	Imports of Goods & Services	98c
	22,398	18,393	19,825	21,979	23,616	26,792	25,056	27,832	26,050	26,843	29,622	32,976	33,464	....	....	Gross Domestic Product (GDP)	99b
Midyear Estimates																	
	.36	.39	.41	.43	.46	.49	.50	.53	.56	.59	I.55	.56	.57	.54	.59	Population	99z

(See notes in the back of the book.)

Romania

968

		1970	1971	1972	1973	1974	1975	1976	1977	1978	1979	1980	1981	1982	1983	1984
Exchange Rates															*Lei per SDR:*	
Market Rate	aa	6.0	6.0	6.0	24.1	24.5	23.4	23.2	24.3	23.5	23.7	23.0	17.5	16.5	19.2	17.4
															Lei per US Dollar:	
Market Rate	ae	6.0	5.5	5.5	20.0	20.0	20.0	20.0	20.0	18.0	18.0	18.0	15.0	15.0	18.3	17.8
Market Rate	rf	6.0	6.0	5.5	20.3	20.0	20.0	20.0	20.0	18.4	18.0	18.0	15.0	15.0	17.2	21.3
															Index Numbers (1990=100):	
Nominal Effective Exchange Rate	ne c	....	....	....	....	....	....	....	....	....	74.06	75.86	107.83	122.00	117.51	107.93
Real Effective Exchange Rate	re c	....	....	....	....	....	....	....	....	....	....	121.34[e]	158.26[e]	189.64[e]	178.41[e]	152.56[e]
Fund Position															*Millions of SDRs:*	
Quota	2f. s	....	....	190	190	190	190	190	190	245	245	368	368	368	523	523
SDRs	1b. s	....	....	—	6	5	8	13	7	—	1	—	1	12	—	—
Reserve Position in the Fund	1c. s	....	....	48	—	—	—	—	—	—	—	—	—	—	—	—
Total Fund Cred.&Loans Outstg.	2tl	....	....	—	48	48	88	238	270	256	247	257	507	782	905	956
International Liquidity													*Millions of US Dollars Unless Otherwise Indicated:*			
Total Reserves minus Gold	1l. d	....	....	....	215	241	539	562	256	376	525	323	404	450	525	709
SDRs	1b. d	....	....	—	7	7	9	15	8	—	1	—	1	13	—	—
Reserve Position in the Fund	1c. d	....	....	52	—	—	—	—	—	—	—	—	—	—	—	—
Foreign Exchange	1d. d	....	....	....	208	234	530	547	248	376	524	323	403	437	525	709
o/w: Held by Dep.Money Banks	1e. d	....	....	....	....	....	....	....	....	....	....	....	....	....	....	....
Gold (Million Fine Troy Ounces)	1ad	....	....	....	2.275	2.447	2.597	2.749	3.057	3.347	3.535	3.712	3.591	3.553	3.620	3.731
Gold (National Valuation)	1an d	....	....	....	96	105	106	112	130	153	141	43	50	49	41	44
Deposit Money Banks: Assets	7a. d	....	....	....	105	220	248	98	161	264	123	260	187	254	353	317
Liabilities	7b. d	....	....	....	290	460	610	2,320	2,984	4,143	6,534	8,381	9,056	8,034	7,603	6,460
Monetary Authorities															*Billions of Lei:*	
Foreign Assets	11	....	....	....	1	1	1	1	1	2	4	3	19	11	13	13
Claims on Government	12a	....	....	....	....	....	....	....	....	....	....	....	....	....	....	....
Claims on Private Sector	12d	....	....	....	75	99	111	123	111	119	133	152	168	188	194	209
Claims on Deposit Money Banks	12e	....	....	....	28	23	28	33	45	65	74	149	157	170	190	222
Reserve Money	14	....	....	....	38	57	74	78	77	96	121	167	183	188	178	158
of which: Currency Outside DMBs	14a	....	....	....	18	18	21	24	27	28	34	39	41	45	45	49
Transit Accounts	14x	....	....	....	....	....	....	....	....	....	....	....	....	....	....	....
Foreign Liabilities	16c	....	....	....	—	—	2	2	2	3	8	15	18	24	22	
Central Government Deposits	16d	....	....	....	38	30	20	22	17	16	7	14	13	31	52	101
Other Items (Net)	17r	....	....	....	17	22	29	33	15	10	9	10	5	3	—	2
Deposit Money Banks															*Billions of Lei:*	
Reserves	20	....	....	....	6	11	24	22	14	34	53	81	86	78	68	44
Foreign Assets	21	....	....	....	2	3	4	13	8	11	8	9	9	10	16	18
Claims on Central Government	22a	....	....	....	....	....	....	....	....	....	....	....	....	....	....	....
Claims on Nonfin.Pub.Enterprises	22c	....	....	....	....	....	....	....	....	....	....	....	....	....	....	....
Claims on Private Sector	22d	....	....	....	128	153	165	201	231	276	286	309	1293	316	350	381
Claims on Nonbank Financial Insts	22g	....	....	....	10	13	17	22	46	62	71	105	119	128	144	160
Demand Deposits	24	....	....	....	12	14	15	20	21	33	33	62	139	58	46	47
Transit Accounts	24x	....	....	....	....	....	....	....	....	....	....	....	....	....	....	....
Savings Deposits	25	....	....	....	36	41	47	55	64	80	90	101	115	118	128	139
Other Term Deposits	25a	....	....	....	....	....	....	....	....	....	....	....	....	....	....	....
Foreign Currency Deposits	25b	....	....	....	—	—	1	1	1	2	2	3	4	3	3	
Foreign Liabilities	26c	....	....	....	6	9	12	46	60	75	118	151	136	121	139	115
Government Deposits	26d	....	....	....	....	....	....	....	....	....	....	....	....	....	....	....
Credit from Monetary Authorities	26g	....	....	....	28	23	28	33	45	65	74	149	157	170	190	218
Capital Accounts	27a	....	....	....	....	....	....	....	....	....	....	....	....	....	....	....
Other Items (Net)	27r	....	....	....	64	92	107	103	108	129	102	39	57	62	71	79
Monetary Survey															*Billions of Lei:*	
Foreign Assets (Net)	31n	....	....	....	–4	–6	–8	–34	–54	–65	–108	–147	–133	–118	–134	–106
Domestic Credit	32	....	....	....	203	252	277	324	343	395	419	1428	459	504	544	589
Claims on Central Govt. (Net)	32an	....	....	....	....	....	....	....	....	....	....	....	....	....	....	....
Claims on Nonfin.Pub.Enterprises	32c	....	....	....	....	....	....	....	....	....	....	....	....	....	....	....
Claims on Private Sector	32d	....	....	....	....	....	....	....	....	....	....	....	....	....	....	....
Claims on Nonbank Financial Inst	32g	....	....	....	10	13	17	22	46	62	71	105	119	128	144	160
Money	34	....	....	....	45	61	66	76	84	95	102	1115	136	167	156	162
Transit Accounts	34x	....	....	....	....	....	....	....	....	....	....	....	....	....	....	....
Quasi-Money	35	....	....	....	36	41	48	56	66	81	92	104	118	122	131	143
Other Liquid Liabilities	36x	....	....	....	9	11	12	14	16	18	21	24	27	30	33	36
Other Items (Net)	37r	....	....	....	119	144	155	158	139	155	117	121	18	23	24	26
Money plus Quasi-Money	35l	....	....	....	80	102	113	132	150	176	194	1218	253	289	287	305
Interest Rates															*Percent Per Annum*	
Bank Rate (End of Period)	60a	....	....	....	....	....	....	....	....	....	....	....	....	....	....	....
Treasury Bill Rate	60c	....	....	....	....	....	....	....	....	....	....	....	....	....	....	....
Prices, Production, Labor															*Index Numbers (1995=100):*	
Producer Prices	63	....	....	....	....	....	....	....	....	....	....	....	....	....	....	....
Consumer Prices	64	....	....	....	....	....	....	....	....	....	....	....	....	....	....	....
Wages: Avg. Earnings	65	....	....	....	.6	.7	.7	.8	....	....	....	1.1	1.1	1.2	1.2	1.3
Industrial Production	66	....	....	....	63.4	72.6	81.4	90.8	102.2	....	....	128.2	130.3	133.0	139.3	148.6
Industrial Employment (1990=100)	67	....	....	....	64.4	68.9	72.6	75.3	78.4	80.5	83.7	86.1	87.8	89.8	94.4	91.2
															Number in Thousands:	
Labor Force	67d	....	....	....	....	....	....	....	....	....	....	....	....	....	....	....
Employment	67e	....	....	....	....	....	....	....	....	....	....	....	....	....	....	....
Unemployment	67c	....	....	....	....	....	....	....	....	....	....	....	....	....	....	....
Unemployment Rate (%)	67r	....	....	....	....	....	....	....	....	....	....	....	....	....	....	....
International Transactions															*Millions of US Dollars*	
Exports	70.d	1,850.8	2,107.3	2,601.0	3,691.0	4,874.5	5,341.5	6,137.7	7,021.0	8,086.4	9,724.2	11,209.0	12,610.0	11,559.0	11,512.0	12,646.0
Imports, c.i.f.	71..d	2,117.0	2,277.7	2,827.0	3,737.7	5,554.9	5,769.0	6,583.0	7,579.3	9,638.1	11,788.7	13,843.4	13,453.6	10,524.6	10,414.4	11,160.7
Imports, f.o.b.	71.v d	....	....	....	....	....	....	....	....	....	....	12,818.0	12,457.0	9,745.0	9,643.0	10,334.0

Note: † indicates a break in the series.

1985	1986	1987	1988	1989	1990	1991	1992	1993	1994	1995	1996	1997	1998	1999		Code
															Exchange Rates	

End of Period

1985	1986	1987	1988	1989	1990	1991	1992	1993	1994	1995	1996	1997	1998	1999	Item	Code
17.3	18.7	19.5	19.3	19.0	49.4	†270.4	632.5	1,752.7	2,579.6	3,832.2	5,802.2	10,825.0	15,419.3	25,055.2	Market Rate	aa

End of Period (ae) Period Average (rf)

1985	1986	1987	1988	1989	1990	1991	1992	1993	1994	1995	1996	1997	1998	1999	Item	Code
15.7	15.3	13.7	14.4	14.4	34.7	†189.0	460.0	1,276.0	1,767.0	2,578.0	4,035.0	8,023.0	10,951.0	18,255.0	Market Rate	ae
17.1	16.2	14.6	14.3	14.9	22.4	76.4	†308.0	760.1	1,655.1	2,033.3	3,084.2	7,167.9	8,875.6	15,332.8	Market Rate	rf

Period Averages

1985	1986	1987	1988	1989	1990	1991	1992	1993	1994	1995	1996	1997	1998	1999	Item	Code
143.25	128.09	129.13	135.23	143.96	100.00	38.98	8.03	3.45	1.53	1.20	.83	.40	.33	.20	Nominal Effective Exchange Rate	ne c
187.68e	160.56e	154.91e	153.43e	148.10e	100.00	93.10	57.56	79.82	85.77	83.90	75.84	88.37	114.89	97.81	Real Effective Exchange Rate	re c

Fund Position

End of Period

1985	1986	1987	1988	1989	1990	1991	1992	1993	1994	1995	1996	1997	1998	1999	Item	Code
523	523	523	523	523	523	523	754	754	754	754	754	754	754	1,030	Quota	2f.s
—	—	—	—	76	—	40	8	1	38	38	3	77	1	7	SDRs	1b.s
—	—	—	—	—	—	—	—	—	—	—	—	—	—	—	Reserve Position in the Fund	1c.s
783	584	358	107	—	—	566	751	751	906	698	453	475	383	334	Total Fund Cred.&Loans Outstg.	2tl

International Liquidity

End of Period

1985	1986	1987	1988	1989	1990	1991	1992	1993	1994	1995	1996	1997	1998	1999	Item	Code
199	582	1,402	780	1,859	524	695	826	995	2,086	1,579	2,103	3,803	2,867	2,687	Total Reserves minus Gold	1l.d
—	—	—	—	100	—	58	11	2	56	56	4	104	1	10	SDRs	1b.d
—	—	—	—	—	—	—	—	—	—	—	—	—	—	—	Reserve Position in the Fund	1c.d
199	582	1,402	780	1,759	524	637	815	994	2,031	1,523	2,099	3,700	2,866	2,677	Foreign Exchange	1d.d
						480	730								o/w: Held by Dep.Money Banks	1e.d
3.818	3.247	1.364	1.449	2.174	2.208	2.247	2.307	2.370	2.625	2.703	2.818	3.019	3.224	3.323	Gold (Million Fine Troy Ounces)	1ad
50	44	21	1,236	1,845	780	666	780	924	965	780	520	458	358	967	Gold (National Valuation)	1and
1,000	507	570	1,021	799	682	261	132	223	129	73	72	79	87	91	Deposit Money Banks: Assets	7a.d
6,046	5,948	5,896	1,972	512	1,723	724	461	560	687	823	1,238	1,148	933	611	Liabilities	7b.d

Monetary Authorities

End of Period

1985	1986	1987	1988	1989	1990	1991	1992	1993	1994	1995	1996	1997	1998	1999	Item	Code
†3	4	1	18	28	†28	171	405	†1,234	2,796	2,942	6,432	24,849	25,182	45,581	Foreign Assets	11
					4	41	263	†336	1,771	3,562	—	3,271	9,142	21,412	Claims on Government	12a
†227	227	261	266	332											Claims on Private Sector	12d
†284	322	357	444	409	†362	390	353	†1,880	2,395	4,724	8,822	3,367	3,618	2,433	Claims on Deposit Money Banks	12e
†128	146	155	181	252	†324	397	859	†2,031	3,809	5,952	9,008	21,305	25,738	49,520	Reserve Money	14
†55	60	61	65	75	†98	194	460	1,049	2,201	3,764	5,383	9,200	11,525	17,372	of which: Currency Outside DMBs	14a
				49	95	-36	27	21	14				27	264	Transit Accounts	14x
†4	4	2	2	—	†—	198	475	†1,317	2,444	3,502	7,810	15,167	17,639	15,885	Foreign Liabilities	16c
†145	173	226	281	228	†—	42	163	†496	1,354	2,660	-275	701	163	5,947	Central Government Deposits	16d
†55	26	12	25	22	†20	-131	-441	†-421	-666	-899	-1,290	-5,686	-5,624	-2,190	Other Items (Net)	17r

Deposit Money Banks

End of Period

1985	1986	1987	1988	1989	1990	1991	1992	1993	1994	1995	1996	1997	1998	1999	Item	Code
†36	8	—	—	—	†9	†177	443	†1,462	2,416	3,293	3,632	5,347	13,050	35,014	Reserves	20
†20	25	27	26	38	†141	105	298	†1,312	2,746	3,723	6,554	13,551	17,301	22,904	Foreign Assets	21
						†—		398	584	1,839	5,469	11,099	18,833	29,850	Claims on Central Government	22a
						1,375	1,912	4,902	9,485	16,099	13,202	12,749	11,734	9,223	Claims on Nonfin.Pub.Enterprises	22c
†439	470	513	547	479	684			†—	—	—	12,516	21,146	43,180	44,031	Claims on Private Sector	22d
†181	203	222	240	267	222				—	—	1,124	1,986	4,172	4,511	Claims on Nonbank Financial Insts	22g
†38	33	34	37	49	†141	555	600	1,018	2,094	3,007	5,366	8,742	9,590	11,059	Demand Deposits	24
		†—				3	245	153	159	212	354	615	110	328	364	Transit Accounts	24x
†153	167	176	186	202	†194	188	376	890	3,605	6,939	11,901	25,625	40,219	53,973	Savings Deposits	25
		†—				71	71	121	219	390	444	580	898	994	1,238	Other Term Deposits	25a
†4	4	5	4	4	†15	40	281	1,296	2,358	3,953	7,086	17,681	30,202	50,473	Foreign Currency Deposits	25b
†95	91	81	28	7	†60	137	212	715	1,213	2,121	4,996	9,213	10,213	11,158	Foreign Liabilities	26c
		†—				12	62	237	885	1,303	1,810	1,135	2,167	5,749	5,638	Government Deposits	26d
†274	311	347	434	409	†362	390	343	1,568	2,316	3,179	8,024	632	556	1,930	Credit from Monetary Authorities	26g
		†—					565	896	2,505	5,064	9,681	10,888	17,549		Capital Accounts	27a
†—	—	—	—	-153	†11	-20	154	†758	843	643	-2,270	-8,869	-477	-7,849	Other Items (Net)	27r

Monetary Survey

End of Period

1985	1986	1987	1988	1989	1990	1991	1992	1993	1994	1995	1996	1997	1998	1999	Item	Code
†-77	-66	-55	14	59	†9	-59	15	†514	1,884	1,043	181	14,020	14,632	41,442	Foreign Assets (Net)	31n
†666	697	774	813	810	†684	1,375	1,912	4,255	9,183	17,030	31,450	47,384	81,150	97,442	Domestic Credit	32
								-647	-301	931	4,609	11,503	22,063	39,677	Claims on Central Govt. (Net)	32an
						1,375	1,912	4,902	9,485	16,099	13,202	12,749	11,734	9,223	Claims on Nonfin.Pub.Enterprises	32c
						—	—	—			12,516	21,146	43,180	44,031	Claims on Private Sector	32d
											1,124	1,986	4,172	4,511	Claims on Nonbank Financial Inst	32g
181	203															
†156	168	171	199	204	†238	749	1,060	2,067	4,294	6,771	10,749	17,942	21,115	28,431	Money	34
		†52				340	117	185	233	368	615	110	355	628	Transit Accounts	34x
†157	171	182	190	206	†280	300	778	2,405	6,353	11,336	19,567	44,203	71,415	105,684	Quasi-Money	35
†39	43	48	53	58											Other Liquid Liabilities	36x
†60	58	58	80	151	†123	-73	-28	†111	187	-403	700	-852	2,888	4,141	Other Items (Net)	37r
†313	340	353	389	410	†518	1,048	1,838	4,472	10,648	18,107	30,316	62,145	92,530	134,114	Money plus Quasi-Money	35l

Interest Rates

Percent Per Annum

1985	1986	1987	1988	1989	1990	1991	1992	1993	1994	1995	1996	1997	1998	1999	Item	Code
									66.9	41.3	35.1	45.0	37.9	35.0	Bank Rate (End of Period)	60a
											51.1	85.7	64.0	74.2	Treasury Bill Rate	60c

Prices, Production, Labor

Period Averages

1985	1986	1987	1988	1989	1990	1991	1992	1993	1994	1995	1996	1997	1998	1999	Item	Code
					1.1	3.8	†11.6	†30.8	74.0	100.0	149.9	†384.5	512.2	728.1	Producer Prices	63
						2.9	9.0	31.9	75.6	100.0	138.8	353.7	562.7	820.4	Consumer Prices	64
1.3	1.3	1.3	1.4	1.4	1.6	3.5	9.4	28.3	64.9	100.0	149.0	295.0	502.9	719.6	Wages: Avg. Earnings	65
157.7	165.3	169.4	175.1	171.1	140.6	113.1	88.1	†88.6	91.4	100.0	†109.9	102.7	85.1	77.7	Industrial Production	66
97.4	94.2	95.7	95.7	98.3	100.0	88.3	78.2								Industrial Employment (1990=100)	67

Period Averages

1985	1986	1987	1988	1989	1990	1991	1992	1993	1994	1995	1996	1997	1998	1999	Item	Code
										12,089	11,726	11,756	11,577		Labor Force	67d
10,586	10,670	10,719	10,805	10,946	10,840	10,786	†10,458	10,062	†10,914	11,152	10,936	11,050	10,845		Employment	67e
						337	929	1,165	†1,224	998	658	881	1,025	1,131	Unemployment	67c
						3.0	8.2	10.4	†11.0	10.0	7.8	7.5	9.3		Unemployment Rate (%)	67r

International Transactions

Millions of US Dollars

1985	1986	1987	1988	1989	1990	1991	1992	1993	1994	1995	1996	1997	1998	1999	Item	Code
12,167.0	9,763.1	10,491.8	11,392.4	10,487.3	5,775.4	4,265.7	4,363.4	4,892.2	6,151.3	7,910.0	8,084.5	8,431.1	8,299.6	8,504.7	Exports	70..d
11,266.6	11,437.2	8,977.7	8,254.0	9,122.4	9,843.4	5,793.4	6,259.6	6,521.7	7,109.0	10,277.9	11,435.3	11,279.7	11,821.0	10,392.1	Imports, c.i.f.	71..d
10,432.0	10,590.0	8,312.7	7,642.6	8,437.7	9,202.5	5,372.0	5,784.1	6,020.1	6,562.4	9,486.7	10,555.0	10,411.4	10,911.0	9,592.1	Imports, f.o.b.	71.vd

Romania

		1970	1971	1972	1973	1974	1975	1976	1977	1978	1979	1980	1981	1982	1983	1984
Balance of Payments																*Millions of US Dollars:*
Current Account, n.i.e.	78al d	....	−23	−47	149	−359	−135	−16	−304	−759	−1,653	−2,420	−833	1,040	1,160	1,719
Goods: Exports f.o.b.	78aa d	....	2,102	2,599	3,667	4,858	5,341	6,134	6,859	8,022	9,303	11,024	12,367	11,559	11,512	12,646
Goods: Imports f.o.b.	78ab d	....	−2,102	−2,616	−3,425	−5,049	−5,342	−6,087	−7,002	−8,628	−10,519	−12,685	−12,264	−9,745	−9,643	−10,334
Trade Balance	78ac d	....	—	−17	242	−191	−1	47	−143	−606	−1,216	−1,661	103	1,814	1,869	2,312
Services: Credit	78ad d	....	280	265	338	419	471	508	498	706	830	1,063	1,095	825	727	840
Services: Debit	78ae d	....	−303	−295	−373	−518	−516	−453	−527	−691	−909	−1,045	−1,014	−748	−726	−774
Balance on Goods & Services	78af d	....	−23	−47	207	−290	−46	102	−172	−591	−1,295	−1,643	184	1,891	1,870	2,378
Income: Credit	78ag d	....	—	—	16	18	25	37	50	56	77	73	113	119	97	117
Income: Debit	78ah d	....	—	—	−74	−87	−114	−155	−182	−224	−435	−850	−1,130	−970	−807	−776
Balance on Gds, Serv. & Inc.	78ai d	....	−23	−47	149	−359	−135	−16	−304	−759	−1,653	−2,420	−833	1,040	1,160	1,719
Current Transfers, n.i.e.: Credit	78aj d	....	—	—	—	—	—	—	—	—	—	—	—	—	—	—
Current Transfers: Debit	78ak d	....	—	—	—	—	—	—	—	—	—	—	—	—	—	—
Capital Account, n.i.e.	78bc d	....	—	—	—	—	—	—	—	—	—	—	—	—	—	—
Capital Account, n.i.e.: Credit	78ba d	....	—	—	—	—	—	—	—	—	—	—	—	—	—	—
Capital Account: Debit	78bb d	....	—	—	—	—	—	—	—	—	—	—	—	—	—	—
Financial Account, n.i.e.	78bj d	....	−15	42	−266	366	90	−113	−31	925	1,864	2,175	−555	−233	−1,148	−1,691
Direct Investment Abroad	78bd d	....	—	—	—	—	—	—	—	—	—	—	—	—	—	—
Dir. Invest. in Rep. Econ., n.i.e.	78be d	....	—	—	—	—	—	—	—	—	—	—	—	—	—	—
Portfolio Investment Assets	78bf d	....	—	—	—	—	—	—	—	—	—	—	—	—	—	—
Equity Securities	78bk d	....	—	—	—	—	—	—	—	—	—	—	—	—	—	—
Debt Securities	78bl d	....	—	—	—	—	—	—	—	—	—	—	—	—	—	—
Portfolio Investment Liab., n.i.e.	78bg d	....	—	—	—	—	—	—	—	—	—	—	—	—	—	—
Equity Securities	78bm d	....	—	—	—	—	—	—	—	—	—	—	—	—	—	—
Debt Securities	78bn d	....	—	—	—	—	—	—	—	—	—	—	—	—	—	—
Financial Derivatives Assets	78bw d	....	....	....	....	....	....	....	....	....	....	....	....	....	....	....
Financial Derivatives Liabilities	78bx d	....	....	....	....	....	....	....	....	....	....	....	....	....	....	....
Other Investment Assets	78bh d	....	—	—	−43	−141	−198	−296	−151	−302	−418	−137	−153	−625	−659	−701
Monetary Authorities	78bo d	....														
General Government	78bp d	....	—	—	−12	12	44	163	101	—	—	—	—	—	—	−48
Banks	78bq d	....	—	—	−31	−153	−242	−459	−252	−302	−418	−137	−153	−625	−659	−653
Other Sectors	78br d	....														
Other Investment Liab., n.i.e.	78bi d	....	−15	42	−223	507	288	183	120	1,227	2,282	2,312	−402	392	−489	−990
Monetary Authorities	78bs d	....	—	—	—	—	—	—	—	—	103	96	−47	−22	−44	−78
General Government	78bt d	....	—	—	—	—	—	—	—	—	—	—	—	—	—	—
Banks	78bu d	....	−15	42	−223	507	288	183	120	1,124	2,186	2,359	−380	436	−411	−990
Other Sectors	78bv d	....	—	—	—	—	—	—	—	—	—	—	—	—	—	—
Net Errors and Omissions	78ca d	....	—	10	−9	—	13	9	1	−16	−73	−1	7	—	−2	100
Overall Balance	78cb d	....	−38	5	−126	7	−32	−120	−334	150	138	−246	−1,381	807	10	128
Reserves and Related Items	79da d	....	38	−5	126	−7	32	120	334	−150	−138	246	1,381	−807	−10	−128
Reserve Assets	79db d	....	38	−5	69	−7	−15	−52	297	−132	−126	232	−46	−353	245	−184
Use of Fund Credit and Loans	79dc d	....	—	—	57	—	47	173	37	−19	−12	15	284	301	133	56
Exceptional Financing	79de d	....	—	—	—	—	—	—	—	—	—	—	1,143	−755	−388	—
International Investment Position																*Millions of US Dollars:*
Assets	79aa d	....	....	....	....	....	....	....	....	....	....	....	....	....	....	....
Direct Investment Abroad	79ab d	....	....	....	....	....	....	....	....	....	....	....	....	....	....	....
Portfolio Investment	79ac d	....	....	....	....	....	....	....	....	....	....	....	....	....	....	....
Equity Securities	79ad d	....	....	....	....	....	....	....	....	....	....	....	....	....	....	....
Debt Securities	79ae d	....	....	....	....	....	....	....	....	....	....	....	....	....	....	....
Financial Derivatives	79al d	....	....	....	....	....	....	....	....	....	....	....	....	....	....	....
Other Investment	79af d	....	....	....	....	....	....	....	....	....	....	....	....	....	....	....
Monetary Authorities	79ag d	....	....	....	....	....	....	....	....	....	....	....	....	....	....	....
General Government	79ah d	....	....	....	....	....	....	....	....	....	....	....	....	....	....	....
Banks	79ai d	....	....	....	....	....	....	....	....	....	....	....	....	....	....	....
Other Sectors	79aj d	....	....	....	....	....	....	....	....	....	....	....	....	....	....	....
Reserve Assets	79ak d	....	....	....	....	....	....	....	....	....	....	....	....	....	....	....
Liabilities	79la d	....	....	....	....	....	....	....	....	....	....	....	....	....	....	....
Dir. Invest. in Rep. Economy	79lb d	....	....	....	....	....	....	....	....	....	....	....	....	....	....	....
Portfolio Investment	79lc d	....	....	....	....	....	....	....	....	....	....	....	....	....	....	....
Equity Securities	79ld d	....	....	....	....	....	....	....	....	....	....	....	....	....	....	....
Debt Securities	79le d	....	....	....	....	....	....	....	....	....	....	....	....	....	....	....
Financial Derivatives	79ll d	....	....	....	....	....	....	....	....	....	....	....	....	....	....	....
Other Investment	79lf d	....	....	....	....	....	....	....	....	....	....	....	....	....	....	....
Monetary Authorities	79lg d	....	....	....	....	....	....	....	....	....	....	....	....	....	....	....
General Government	79lh d	....	....	....	....	....	....	....	....	....	....	....	....	....	....	....
Banks	79li d	....	....	....	....	....	....	....	....	....	....	....	....	....	....	....
Other Sectors	79lj d	....	....	....	....	....	....	....	....	....	....	....	....	....	....	....
Government Finance																*Billions of Lei:*
Deficit (-) or Surplus	80	1.2	3.2	6.6	6.9	1.7	1.1	2.8	.9	.9	1.2	3.0	10.4	21.9	24.7	52.9
Revenue	81	116.0	119.1	130.3	152.0	186.2	216.9	230.3	260.2	277.8	317.5	279.3	260.4	255.5	236.8	288.8
Expenditure	82	114.8	115.9	123.7	145.1	184.5	215.8	227.5	259.4	276.9	316.3	276.3	250.0	233.6	212.0	235.9
Lending Minus Repayments	83	—	—	—	—	—	—	—	—	—	—	—	—	—	—	—
Financing																
Domestic	84a	....	....	....	....	....	....	....	....	....	....	....	....	....	....	....
Foreign	85a	....	....	....	....	....	....	....	....	....	....	....	....	....	....	....
National Accounts																*Billions of Lei:*
Househ.Cons.Expend.,incl.NPISHs	96f											357	380	438	433	463
Government Consumption expend.	91f											31	32	30	31	31
Gross Fixed Capital Formation	93e											213	209	216	231	245
Changes in Inventories	93i											33	17	29	31	34
Exports of Goods & Services	90c											139	174	173	204	227
Imports of Goods & Services	98c											137	157	134	143	164
Gross Domestic Product (GDP)	99b											617	624	727	769	816
GDP Volume 1995 Prices	99b. p											75,287	75,377	78,347	83,079	88,033
GDP Volume (1995=100)	99bv p											104.4	104.5	108.6	115.2	122.0
GDP Deflator (1995=100)	99bi p											.8	.8	.9	.9	.9
Population	99z	20.25	20.47	20.66	20.83	21.03	21.24	21.45	21.66	21.85	22.05	22.20	22.35	22.48	22.55	22.62 (*Millions:*)

Minus Sign Indicates Debit

1985	1986	1987	1988	1989	1990	1991	1992	1993	1994	1995	1996	1997	1998	1999	Balance of Payments	
1,381	1,395	2,043	3,922	2,514	-3,254	-1,012	-1,506	-1,231	-455	-1,780	-2,579	-2,137	-2,918	-1,303	Current Account, n.i.e.	78al d
10,174	9,763	10,491	11,392	10,487	5,770	4,266	4,364	4,892	6,151	7,910	8,085	8,431	8,302	8,505	Goods: Exports f.o.b.	78aa d
-8,402	-8,083	-8,313	-7,642	-8,437	-9,114	-5,372	-5,558	-6,020	-6,562	-9,487	-10,555	-10,411	-10,927	-9,592	Goods: Imports f.o.b.	78ab d
1,772	1,680	2,178	3,750	2,050	-3,344	-1,106	-1,194	-1,128	-411	-1,577	-2,470	-1,980	-2,625	-1,087	*Trade Balance*	78ac d
746	681	770	850	834	610	680	659	799	1,044	1,494	1,563	1,524	1,217	1,357	Services: Credit	78ad d
-524	-424	-515	-480	-450	-787	-819	-946	-914	-1,215	-1,819	-1,948	-1,938	-1,871	-1,766	Services: Debit	78ae d
1,994	1,937	2,433	4,120	2,434	-3,521	-1,245	-1,481	-1,243	-582	-1,902	-2,855	-2,394	-3,279	-1,496	*Balance on Goods & Services*	78af d
116	120	138	173	181	175	104	54	63	116	81	78	204	313	146	Income: Credit	78ag d
-729	-662	-528	-371	-101	-14	-89	-144	-208	-245	-322	-387	-526	-705	-521	Income: Debit	78ah d
1,381	1,395	2,043	3,922	2,514	-3,360	-1,230	-1,571	-1,388	-711	-2,143	-3,164	-2,716	-3,671	-1,871	*Balance on Gds, Serv. & Inc.*	78ai d
—	—	—	—	—	138	277	136	174	317	473	667	731	886	758	Current Transfers, n.i.e.: Credit	78aj d
—	—	—	—	—	-32	-59	-71	-17	-61	-110	-82	-152	-133	-190	Current Transfers: Debit	78ak d
—	—	—	—	—	—	—	—	—	—	32	152	43	39	—	Capital Account, n.i.e.	78bc d
—	—	—	—	—	—	—	—	—	—	32	152	43	39	—	Capital Account, n.i.e.: Credit	78ba d
—	—	—	—	—	—	—	—	—	—	—	—	—	—	—	Capital Account: Debit	78bb d
-1,580	-791	-1,083	-4,223	-1,376	1,613	320	1,380	640	535	812	1,486	2,458	2,042	422	Financial Account, n.i.e.	78bj d
—	—	—	—	—	-18	-3	-4	-7	—	-2	—	9	9	-12	Direct Investment Abroad	78bd d
—	—	—	—	—	—	40	77	94	341	419	263	1,215	2,031	961	Dir. Invest. in Rep. Econ., n.i.e.	78be d
—	—	—	—	—	—	—	—	-73	75	-22	—	-6	1	21	Portfolio Investment Assets	78bf d
—	—	—	—	—	—	—	—	—	—	-4	—	-6	1	21	Equity Securities	78bk d
—	—	—	—	—	—	—	—	-73	75	-18	—	—	—	—	Debt Securities	78bl d
—	—	—	—	—	—	—	—	—	—	54	193	540	129	-727	Portfolio Investment Liab., n.i.e.	78bg d
—	—	—	—	—	—	—	—	—	—	—	—	195	95	68	Equity Securities	78bm d
—	—	—	—	—	—	—	—	—	—	54	193	345	34	-795	Debt Securities	78bn d
....	....	....	....	....	....	....	....	....	....	—	—	—	—	—	Financial Derivatives Assets	78bw d
....	....	....	....	....	....	....	....	....	....	—	—	—	—	—	Financial Derivatives Liabilities	78bx d
-578	-1	191	-765	98	562	-86	94	-45	-671	186	-271	-6	208	288	Other Investment Assets	78bh d
—	—	—	—	—	—	—	—	—	—	—	—	—	—	—	Monetary Authorities	78bo d
-266	65	29	-400	169	529	162	112	-49	-24	-62	-9	10	-10	13	General Government	78bp d
-312	-66	162	-365	-71	33	-37	—	-168	-621	254	-315	-140	179	270	Banks	78bq d
—	—	—	—	—	—	-211	-18	172	-26	-6	53	124	39	5	Other Sectors	78br d
-1,002	-790	-1,274	-3,458	-1,474	1,069	369	1,213	671	790	177	1,301	706	-336	-109	Other Investment Liab., n.i.e.	78bi d
—	—	—	—	—	—	-533	-159	—	—	—	-150	—	—	79	Monetary Authorities	78bs d
—	—	—	—	—	—	—	812	68	75	-27	209	547	-7	41	General Government	78bt d
-1,002	-790	-1,274	-3,458	-1,474	1,069	149	-73	19	190	-57	536	-132	-260	-92	Banks	78bu d
—	—	—	—	—	—	753	633	584	525	261	706	291	-69	-137	Other Sectors	78bv d
-118	8	81	16	114	147	15	-12	152	91	456	359	1,095	194	1,115	Net Errors and Omissions	78ca d
-317	612	1,041	-285	1,252	-1,494	-677	-138	-439	171	-480	-582	1,459	-643	234	*Overall Balance*	78cb d
317	-612	-1,041	285	-1,252	1,494	677	138	439	-171	480	582	-1,459	643	-234	Reserves and Related Items	79da d
492	-376	-749	622	-1,111	1,494	-93	-124	54	-616	259	-218	-1,664	844	-168	Reserve Assets	79db d
-175	-236	-292	-337	-141	—	770	262	—	217	-316	-356	29	-126	-66	Use of Fund Credit and Loans	79dc d
—	—	—	—	—	—	—	—	385	228	536	1,157	176	-75	—	Exceptional Financing	79de d

Millions of US Dollars

1985	1986	1987	1988	1989	1990	1991	1992	1993	1994	1995	1996	1997	1998	1999	International Investment Position	
....	....	....	....	....	6,254	6,355	7,249	7,483	8,847	8,492	9,084	10,164	9,300	9,206	Assets	79aa d
....	....	....	....	....	66	87	79	104	107	121	120	114	122	133	Direct Investment Abroad	79ab d
....	....	....	....	....	808	817	1,124	1,208	1,179	1,224	1,252	1,115	1,170	1,112	Portfolio Investment	79ac d
....	....	....	....	....	807	817	1,113	1,124	1,176	1,211	1,239	1,103	1,147	1,108	Equity Securities	79ad d
....	....	....	....	....	—	—	11	84	3	13	13	11	23	4	Debt Securities	79ae d
....	....	....	....	....											Financial Derivatives	79al d
....	....	....	....	....	4,504	4,441	5,187	5,215	5,964	5,768	6,120	5,874	5,709	5,468	Other Investment	79af d
....	....	....	....	....	—	—	—	—	—	—	—	—	—	—	Monetary Authorities	79ag d
....	....	....	....	....	2,399	2,471	2,929	2,990	3,004	3,006	3,133	2,950	2,915	3,704	General Government	79ah d
....	....	....	....	....	502	490	730	871	1,491	1,244	1,556	1,637	1,469	1,163	Banks	79ai d
....	....	....	....	....	1,603	1,481	1,529	1,355	1,468	1,517	1,432	1,288	1,325	601	Other Sectors	79aj d
....	....	....	....	....	877	1,010	858	956	1,598	1,380	1,592	3,061	2,299	2,493	Reserve Assets	79ak d
....	....	....	....	....	3,499	3,973	5,276	6,196	7,500	7,976	11,468	13,691	15,695	15,731	Liabilities	79la d
....	....	....	....	....	—	45	122	216	401	418	1,081	2,305	4,335	5,296	Dir. Invest. in Rep. Economy	79lb d
....	....	....	....	....	766	726	943	858	719	785	2,408	3,069	3,328	2,521	Portfolio Investment	79lc d
....	....	....	....	....	766	726	943	858	719	732	1,178	1,312	1,450	1,436	Equity Securities	79ld d
....	....	....	....	....	—	—	—	—	—	54	1,229	1,757	1,878	1,085	Debt Securities	79le d
....	....	....	....	....											Financial Derivatives	79ll d
....	....	....	....	....	2,733	3,203	4,212	5,123	6,380	6,773	7,979	8,317	8,032	7,914	Other Investment	79lf d
....	....	....	....	....	—	809	1,032	1,031	1,383	1,358	941	858	580	565	Monetary Authorities	79lg d
....	....	....	....	....	1,754	1,237	1,944	2,388	2,298	2,335	2,484	2,881	2,954	2,883	General Government	79lh d
....	....	....	....	....	163	240	447	504	682	743	1,268	1,040	706	559	Banks	79li d
....	....	....	....	....	817	916	789	1,200	2,018	2,337	3,286	3,538	3,792	3,907	Other Sectors	79lj d

Year Ending December 31

1985	1986	1987	1988	1989	1990	1991	1992	1993	1994	1995	1996	1997	1998	1999	Government Finance	
20.9	36.0	60.1	50.0	65.8	8.0	42.8	-282.3	-93.9	-1,248.5	-2,132.9	-4,377.4	-9,755.0	....	....	Deficit (-) or Surplus	80
360.9	392.3	403.9	364.1	386.3	297.9	822.8	2,200.5	6,389.2	14,884.3	21,327.0	30,194.3	68,394.0	....	....	Revenue	81
340.0	356.3	343.8	314.1	320.6	289.9	780.0	2,406.0	6,311.8	15,913.1	22,927.2	34,033.1	79,734.0	....	....	Expenditure	82
—	—	—	—	—	—	—	76.7	171.3	219.7	532.7	538.5	-1,585.0	....	....	Lending Minus Repayments	83
															Financing	
....	....	....	....	....	-8.0	-42.8	282.3	93.9	1,248.5	2,133.0	4,377.0	9,755.0	....	....	Domestic	84a
....	....	....	....	....	—	—	—	—	....	....	....	....	....	....	Foreign	85a

Billions of Lei

1985	1986	1987	1988	1989	1990	1991	1992	1993	1994	1995	1996	1997	1998	1999	National Accounts	
460	467	489	501	‡470	566	1,339	3,782	12,762	31,601	48,785	75,666	189,481	267,873	363,285	Househ.Cons.Expend.,incl.NPISHs	96f
32	30	28	31	‡93	114	334	861	2,473	6,852	9,877	14,274	24,292	51,437	76,436	Government Consumption expend.	91f
246	249	245	240	‡239	170	317	1,157	3,584	10,096	15,425	24,999	55,074	71,350	96,309	Gross Fixed Capital Formation	93e
24	39	23	‡3	‡-25	90	301	737	2,212	2,253	2,085	3,161	-501	7,604	7,569	Changes in Inventories	93i
236	227	225	219	‡167	143	388	1,676	4,612	12,394	19,921	30,651	73,796	87,105	157,087	Exports of Goods & Services	90c
163	152	150	135	‡145	225	475	2,182	5,608	13,424	23,958	39,831	91,661	117,108	178,951	Imports of Goods & Services	98c
817	839	845	857	‡800	858	2,204	6,029	20,036	49,773	72,136	108,391	250,480	368,261	521,736	Gross Domestic Product (GDP)	99b
87,947	90,011	90,769	90,315	85,096	80,313	69,938	63,807	64,782	67,329	72,136	74,984	72,043	66,760	....	GDP Volume 1995 Prices	99b. p
121.9	124.8	125.8	125.2	118.0	111.3	97.0	88.5	89.8	93.3	100.0	103.9	99.9	92.5	....	GDP Volume (1995=100)	99bv p
.9	.9	.9	.9	‡.9	1.1	3.2	9.4	30.9	73.9	100.0	144.6	347.7	551.6	....	GDP Deflator (1995=100)	99bi p

Midyear Estimates

1985	1986	1987	1988	1989	1990	1991	1992	1993	1994	1995	1996	1997	1998	1999		
22.72	22.82	22.94	23.05	23.15	23.21	23.19	22.79	22.76	22.73	22.68	22.61	22.55	22.50	22.46	Population	99z

(See notes in the back of the book.)

Russia

		1970	1971	1972	1973	1974	1975	1976	1977	1978	1979	1980	1981	1982	1983	1984
Exchange Rates																*Rubles per SDR:*
Official Rate	aa	…	…	…	…	…	…	…	…	…	…	…	…	…	…	…
																Rubles per US Dollar:
Official Rate	ae	…	…	…	…	…	…	…	…	…	…	…	…	…	…	…
Official Rate	rf	…	…	…	…	…	…	…	…	…	…	…	…	…	…	…
														Index Numbers (1995=100):		
Nominal Effective Exchange Rate	ne c	…	…	…	…	…	…	…	…	…	…	…	…	…	…	…
Real Effective Exchange Rate	re c	…	…	…	…	…	…	…	…	…	…	…	…	…	…	…
Fund Position																*Millions of SDRs:*
Quota	2f. s	…	…	…	…	…	…	…	…	…	…	…	…	…	…	…
SDRs	1b. s	…	…	…	…	…	…	…	…	…	…	…	…	…	…	…
Reserve Position in the Fund	1c. s	…	…	…	…	…	…	…	…	…	…	…	…	…	…	…
Total Fund Cred.&Loans Outstg.	2tl	…	…	…	…	…	…	…	…	…	…	…	…	…	…	…
International Liquidity								*Millions of US Dollars Unless Otherwise Indicated:*								
Total Reserves minus Gold	1l. d	…	…	…	…	…	…	…	…	…	…	…	…	…	…	…
SDRs	1b. d	…	…	…	…	…	…	…	…	…	…	…	…	…	…	…
Reserve Position in the Fund	1c. d	…	…	…	…	…	…	…	…	…	…	…	…	…	…	…
Foreign Exchange	1d. d	…	…	…	…	…	…	…	…	…	…	…	…	…	…	…
Gold (Million Fine Troy Ounces)	1ad	…	…	…	…	…	…	…	…	…	…	…	…	…	…	…
Gold (National Valuation)	1an d	…	…	…	…	…	…	…	…	…	…	…	…	…	…	…
Monetary Authorities: Other Assets	3.. d	…	…	…	…	…	…	…	…	…	…	…	…	…	…	…
Other Liab.	4.. d	…	…	…	…	…	…	…	…	…	…	…	…	…	…	…
Deposit Money Banks: Assets	7a. d	…	…	…	…	…	…	…	…	…	…	…	…	…	…	…
Liabilities	7b. d	…	…	…	…	…	…	…	…	…	…	…	…	…	…	…
Monetary Authorities																*Millions of Rubles:*
Foreign Assets	11	…	…	…	…	…	…	…	…	…	…	…	…	…	…	…
Claims on General Government	12a	…	…	…	…	…	…	…	…	…	…	…	…	…	…	…
Claims on Nonfin.Pub.Enterprises	12c	…	…	…	…	…	…	…	…	…	…	…	…	…	…	…
Claims on Private Sector	12d	…	…	…	…	…	…	…	…	…	…	…	…	…	…	…
Claims on Deposit Money Banks	12e	…	…	…	…	…	…	…	…	…	…	…	…	…	…	…
Reserve Money	14	…	…	…	…	…	…	…	…	…	…	…	…	…	…	…
of which: Currency Outside DMBs	14a	…	…	…	…	…	…	…	…	…	…	…	…	…	…	…
Time & Foreign Currency Deposits	15	…	…	…	…	…	…	…	…	…	…	…	…	…	…	…
Foreign Liabilities	16c	…	…	…	…	…	…	…	…	…	…	…	…	…	…	…
General Government Deposits	16d	…	…	…	…	…	…	…	…	…	…	…	…	…	…	…
of which: Local Govt. Deposits	16db	…	…	…	…	…	…	…	…	…	…	…	…	…	…	…
Capital Accounts	17a	…	…	…	…	…	…	…	…	…	…	…	…	…	…	…
Other Items (Net)	17r	…	…	…	…	…	…	…	…	…	…	…	…	…	…	…
Deposit Money Banks																*Millions of Rubles:*
Reserves	20	…	…	…	…	…	…	…	…	…	…	…	…	…	…	…
Foreign Assets	21	…	…	…	…	…	…	…	…	…	…	…	…	…	…	…
Claims on General Government	22a	…	…	…	…	…	…	…	…	…	…	…	…	…	…	…
of which: Claims on Local Govts	22ab	…	…	…	…	…	…	…	…	…	…	…	…	…	…	…
Claims on Nonfin.Pub.Enterprises	22c	…	…	…	…	…	…	…	…	…	…	…	…	…	…	…
Claims on Private Sector	22d	…	…	…	…	…	…	…	…	…	…	…	…	…	…	…
Claims on Other Financial Insts	22f	…	…	…	…	…	…	…	…	…	…	…	…	…	…	…
Demand Deposits	24	…	…	…	…	…	…	…	…	…	…	…	…	…	…	…
Time, Savings,& Fgn.Currency Dep.	25	…	…	…	…	…	…	…	…	…	…	…	…	…	…	…
of which: Fgn. Currency Deposits	25b	…	…	…	…	…	…	…	…	…	…	…	…	…	…	…
Money Market Instruments	26aa	…	…	…	…	…	…	…	…	…	…	…	…	…	…	…
Restricted Deposits	26b	…	…	…	…	…	…	…	…	…	…	…	…	…	…	…
Foreign Liabilities	26c	…	…	…	…	…	…	…	…	…	…	…	…	…	…	…
General Government Deposits	26d	…	…	…	…	…	…	…	…	…	…	…	…	…	…	…
of which: Local Govt. Deposits	26db	…	…	…	…	…	…	…	…	…	…	…	…	…	…	…
Credit from Monetary Authorities	26g	…	…	…	…	…	…	…	…	…	…	…	…	…	…	…
Capital Accounts	27a	…	…	…	…	…	…	…	…	…	…	…	…	…	…	…
Other Items (Net)	27r	…	…	…	…	…	…	…	…	…	…	…	…	…	…	…
Monetary Survey																*Millions of Rubles:*
Foreign Assets (Net)	31n	…	…	…	…	…	…	…	…	…	…	…	…	…	…	…
Domestic Credit	32	…	…	…	…	…	…	…	…	…	…	…	…	…	…	…
Claims on General Govt. (Net)	32an	…	…	…	…	…	…	…	…	…	…	…	…	…	…	…
Claims on Nonfin.Pub.Enterprises	32c	…	…	…	…	…	…	…	…	…	…	…	…	…	…	…
Claims on Private Sector	32d	…	…	…	…	…	…	…	…	…	…	…	…	…	…	…
Claims on Other Financial Insts	32f	…	…	…	…	…	…	…	…	…	…	…	…	…	…	…
Money	34	…	…	…	…	…	…	…	…	…	…	…	…	…	…	…
Quasi-Money	35	…	…	…	…	…	…	…	…	…	…	…	…	…	…	…
Money Market Instruments	36aa	…	…	…	…	…	…	…	…	…	…	…	…	…	…	…
Restricted Deposits	36b	…	…	…	…	…	…	…	…	…	…	…	…	…	…	…
Capital Accounts	37a	…	…	…	…	…	…	…	…	…	…	…	…	…	…	…
Other Items (Net)	37r	…	…	…	…	…	…	…	…	…	…	…	…	…	…	…
Money plus Quasi-Money	35l	…	…	…	…	…	…	…	…	…	…	…	…	…	…	…
Interest Rates																*Percent Per Annum*
Refinancing Rate *(End of Period)*	60	…	…	…	…	…	…	…	…	…	…	…	…	…	…	…
Money Market Rate	60b	…	…	…	…	…	…	…	…	…	…	…	…	…	…	…
Treasury Bill Rate	60c	…	…	…	…	…	…	…	…	…	…	…	…	…	…	…
Deposit Rate	60l	…	…	…	…	…	…	…	…	…	…	…	…	…	…	…
Lending Rate	60p	…	…	…	…	…	…	…	…	…	…	…	…	…	…	…
Prices, Production, Labor																*Percent Change over*
Producer Prices	63.xx	…	…	…	…	…	…	…	…	…	…	…	…	…	…	…
Consumer Prices	64.xx	…	…	…	…	…	…	…	…	…	…	…	…	…	…	…
Wages	65.xx	…	…	…	…	…	…	…	…	…	…	…	…	…	…	…
														Index Numbers (1995=100):		
Industrial Employment	67	…	…	…	…	…	…	…	…	…	…	…	…	…	…	…
														Number in Thousands:		
Labor Force	67d	…	…	…	…	…	…	…	…	…	…	…	…	…	…	…
Employment	67e	…	…	…	…	…	…	…	…	…	…	…	…	…	…	…
Unemployment	67c	…	…	…	…	…	…	…	…	…	…	…	…	…	…	…
Unemployment Rate (%)	67r	…	…	…	…	…	…	…	…	…	…	…	…	…	…	…
International Transactions																*Millions of US Dollars*
Exports	70.. d	…	…	…	…	…	…	…	…	…	…	…	…	…	…	…
Imports, c.i.f.	71.. d	…	…	…	…	…	…	…	…	…	…	…	…	…	…	…

	1985	1986	1987	1988	1989	1990	1991	1992	1993	1994	1995	1996	1997	1998	1999		
End of Period																**Exchange Rates**	
	....	....	....	....	....	....	....	.5706	1.7128	5.1825	6.8973	7.9951	8.0415	I 29.0758	37.0578	Official Rate	aa
End of Period (ae) Period Average (rf)																	
	....	....	....	....	....	....	....	.4150	1.2470	3.5500	4.6400	5.5600	5.9600	I 20.6500	27.0000	Official Rate	ae
	....	....	....	....	....	....	....	....	.9917	2.1908	4.5592	5.1208	5.7848	9.7051	24.6199	Official Rate	rf
Period Averages																	
	....	....	....	....	....	....	....	....	....	162.95	100.00	97.06	98.89	80.31	32.57	Nominal Effective Exchange Rate	ne *c*
	....	....	....	....	....	....	....	....	....	91.12	100.00	122.07	128.92	114.16	80.90	Real Effective Exchange Rate	re *c*
End of Period																**Fund Position**	
	....	....	....	....	....	....	....	4,313.1	4,313.1	4,313.1	4,313.1	4,313.1	4,313.1	4,313.1	5,945.4	Quota	2f. *s*
	....	....	....	....	....	....	....	.6	3.7	2.1	78.5	3.1	90.7	.1	.4	SDRs	1b. *s*
	....	....	....	....	....	....	....	.5	1.0	.8	.8	.9	.9	.9	.9	Reserve Position in the Fund	1c. *s*
	....	....	....	....	....	....	....	719.0	1,797.3	2,875.6	6,469.8	8,698.2	9,805.9	13,732.0	11,102.3	Total Fund Cred.&Loans Outstg.	2tl
End of Period																**International Liquidity**	
	....	....	....	....	....	....	....	....	5,835.0	3,980.4	14,382.8	11,276.4	12,894.7	7,801.4	8,457.2	Total Reserves minus Gold	1l. *d*
	....	....	....	....	....	....	....	.8	5.0	3.1	116.7	4.5	122.4	.1	.6	SDRs	1b. *d*
	....	....	....	....	....	....	....	.7	1.4	1.2	1.1	1.3	1.2	1.3	1.3	Reserve Position in the Fund	1c. *d*
	....	....	....	....	....	....	....	....	5,828.6	3,976.1	14,264.9	11,270.6	12,771.1	7,800.0	8,455.4	Foreign Exchange	1d. *d*
	....	....	....	....	....	....	....	....	10.195	8.417	9.414	13.490	16.297	14.738	13.326	Gold (Million Fine Troy Ounces)	1ad
	....	....	....	....	....	....	....	....	3,058.5	2,525.1	2,824.1	4,047.1	4,889.2	4,421.6	3,998.3	Gold (National Valuation)	1an *d*
	....	....	....	....	....	....	....	....	9,074.6	5,768.2	3,458.8	3,176.8	2,911.2	1,642.6	1,743.0	Monetary Authorities: Other Assets	3.. *d*
	....	....	....	....	....	....	....	....	943.1	477.3	303.0	311.2	149.2	110.5	473.1	Other Liab.	4.. *d*
	....	....	....	....	....	....	....	....	12,669.3	13,891.6	9,946.0	13,107.0	12,200.9	10,634.0	13,727.8	Deposit Money Banks: Assets	7a. *d*
	....	....	....	....	....	....	....	....	3,773.4	4,076.8	6,459.0	10,592.2	17,482.8	9,837.1	8,245.4	Liabilities	7b. *d*
End of Period																**Monetary Authorities**	
	....	....	....	....	....	....	....	....	21,737	41,082	95,890	102,861	123,344	286,324	383,359	Foreign Assets	11
	....	....	....	....	....	....	....	....	16,802	84,498	138,578	187,365	226,049	525,374	572,030	Claims on General Government	12a
	....	....	....	....	....	....	....	....	123	251	85	67	46	150	114	Claims on Nonfin.Pub.Enterprises	12c
	....	....	....	....	....	....	....	....	21	72	237	813	281	412	316	Claims on Private Sector	12d
	....	....	....	....	....	....	....	....	8,889	16,177	17,450	11,377	11,119	76,438	203,484	Claims on Deposit Money Banks	12e
	....	....	....	....	....	....	....	....	20,544	62,357	129,601	164,929	210,450	263,675	439,743	Reserve Money	14
	....	....	....	....	....	....	....	....	10,730	34,493	80,815	103,824	130,540	187,843	266,544	*of which: Currency Outside DMBs*	14a
	....	....	....	....	....	....	....	....	1	4	17	23	240	1,828	1,575	Time & Foreign Currency Deposits	15
	....	....	....	....	....	....	....	....	4,254	16,538	46,030	71,272	79,744	401,551	424,201	Foreign Liabilities	16c
	....	....	....	....	....	....	....	....	7,003	17,096	24,898	15,062	21,313	41,863	75,871	General Government Deposits	16d
	....	....	....	....	....	....	....	....	847	3,273	2,117	2,068	3,564	2,863	10,515	*of which:* Local Govt. Deposits	16db
	....	....	....	....	....	....	....	....	638	17,014	27,530	54,179	69,552	118,113	151,844	Capital Accounts	17a
	....	....	....	....	....	....	....	....	15,132	29,071	24,164	–2,982	–20,460	61,669	66,070	Other Items (Net)	17r
End of Period																**Deposit Money Banks**	
	....	....	....	....	....	....	....	....	7,914	24,151	36,712	47,124	72,975	67,763	160,018	Reserves	20
	....	....	....	....	....	....	....	....	15,798	49,316	46,150	72,875	72,717	219,593	370,651	Foreign Assets	21
	....	....	....	....	....	....	....	....	776	10,639	62,639	150,721	194,690	259,402	437,674	Claims on General Government	22a
	....	....	....	....	....	....	....	....	—	—	722	2,790	18,692	24,446	19,870	*of which:* Claims on Local Govts	22ab
	....	....	....	....	....	....	....	....	15,639	48,173	62,460	69,371	33,217	33,079	46,901	Claims on Nonfin.Pub.Enterprises	22c
	....	....	....	....	....	....	....	....	20,208	74,017	133,786	157,337	236,439	345,963	521,645	Claims on Private Sector	22d
	....	....	....	....	....	....	....	....	—	—	525	242	8,076	7,271	13,060	Claims on Other Financial Insts	22f
	....	....	....	....	....	....	....	....	12,519	32,589	69,332	87,303	162,532	149,471	249,673	Demand Deposits	24
	....	....	....	....	....	....	....	....	17,101	61,183	124,497	164,899	158,716	283,997	456,528	Time, Savings,& Fgn.Currency Dep.	25
	....	....	....	....	....	....	....	....	12,086	37,309	55,256	69,448	80,455	190,873	290,213	*of which: Fgn. Currency Deposits*	25b
	....	....	....	....	....	....	....	....	211	3,516	11,858	30,372	42,436	43,311	107,817	Money Market Instruments	26aa
	....	....	....	....	....	....	....	....	—	—	—	—	6,270	22,595	10,224	Restricted Deposits	26b
	....	....	....	....	....	....	....	....	4,705	14,473	29,970	58,892	104,197	203,137	222,627	Foreign Liabilities	26c
	....	....	....	....	....	....	....	....	2,117	6,914	9,741	11,557	18,237	20,676	28,672	General Government Deposits	26d
	....	....	....	....	....	....	....	....	919	2,246	4,252	4,211	9,140	10,148	15,627	*of which:* Local Govt. Deposits	26db
	....	....	....	....	....	....	....	....	8,464	17,181	8,006	6,799	8,780	71,894	200,122	Credit from Monetary Authorities	26g
	....	....	....	....	....	....	....	....	12,031	26,211	66,688	123,818	143,909	157,595	293,199	Capital Accounts	27a
	....	....	....	....	....	....	....	....	3,187	44,229	22,180	14,030	–26,963	–19,605	–18,913	Other Items (Net)	27r
End of Period																**Monetary Survey**	
	....	....	....	....	....	....	....	....	28,576	59,387	66,040	45,572	12,120	–98,770	107,183	Foreign Assets (Net)	31n
	....	....	....	....	....	....	....	....	44,449	193,640	363,671	539,297	659,248	1,109,112	1,487,197	Domestic Credit	32
	....	....	....	....	....	....	....	....	8,458	71,127	166,578	311,467	381,189	722,237	905,161	Claims on General Govt. (Net)	32an
	....	....	....	....	....	....	....	....	15,762	48,424	62,545	69,438	33,263	33,229	47,015	Claims on Nonfin.Pub.Enterprises	32c
	....	....	....	....	....	....	....	....	20,229	74,089	134,023	158,150	236,720	346,375	521,961	Claims on Private Sector	32d
	....	....	....	....	....	....	....	....	—	—	525	242	8,076	7,271	13,060	Claims on Other Financial Insts	32f
	....	....	....	....	....	....	....	....	23,881	68,544	151,267	192,402	298,289	342,817	526,771	Money	34
	....	....	....	....	....	....	....	....	17,102	61,187	124,514	164,922	158,956	285,825	458,103	Quasi-Money	35
	....	....	....	....	....	....	....	....	211	3,516	11,858	30,372	42,436	43,311	107,817	Money Market Instruments	36aa
	....	....	....	....	....	....	....	....	—	—	—	—	6,270	22,595	10,224	Restricted Deposits	36b
	....	....	....	....	....	....	....	....	12,669	43,225	94,218	177,997	213,461	275,708	445,043	Capital Accounts	37a
	....	....	....	....	....	....	....	....	19,162	76,555	47,854	19,176	–48,044	40,086	46,422	Other Items (Net)	37r
	....	....	....	....	....	....	....	....	40,983	129,731	275,781	357,324	457,245	628,642	984,874	Money plus Quasi-Money	35l
Percent Per Annum																**Interest Rates**	
	....	....	....	....	....	....	....	....	....	....	160.0	48.0	28.0	60.0	55.0	Refinancing Rate *(End of Period)*	60
	....	....	....	....	....	....	....	....	....	....	190.4	47.7	21.0	50.6	14.8	Money Market Rate	60b
	....	....	....	....	....	....	....	....	....	....	168.0	86.1	23.4	....	....	Treasury Bill Rate	60c
	....	....	....	....	....	....	....	....	....	....	102.0	55.1	I 16.8	17.1	13.7	Deposit Rate	60l
	....	....	....	....	....	....	....	....	....	....	320.3	146.8	I 32.0	41.8	39.7	Lending Rate	60p
Previous Period																**Prices, Production, Labor**	
	....	....	....	....	....	....	....	....	943.76	337.00	236.46	50.81	17.20	5.05	58.90	Producer Prices	63.x *x*
	....	....	....	....	....	....	....	....	874.62	307.63	197.47	47.73	14.74	27.67	85.68	Consumer Prices	64.x *x*
	....	....	....	....	....	....	....	....	822.1	255.9	142.2	64.8	23.7	15.3	....	Wages	65.x *x*
Period Averages																	
	....	....					....	131.4	120.9	107.1	100.0	91.8	84.0	80.7	81.4	Industrial Employment	67
Period Averages																	
	....	....	....	....	....	....	....	73,008	....	....	69,469	68,264	....	66,736	....	Labor Force	67d
	....	....	....	....	....	....	....	71,068	68,642	64,785	64,149	62,928	60,021	57,860	....	Employment	67e
	....	....	....	....	....	....	62	578	I 836	1,637	2,327	2,506	1,990	1,929	....	Unemployment	67c
	....	....	....	....	....	....	....	.8	5.3	I 7.0	8.3	9.3	10.8	11.9	....	Unemployment Rate (%)	67r
Millions of US Dollars																**International Transactions**	
	....	....	....	....	....	....	....	42,039	44,297	I 67,542	81,096	88,599	88,288	74,888	74,663	Exports	70.. *d*
	....	....	....	....	....	....	....	36,984	32,806	I 50,518	60,945	68,828	73,660	60,476	40,429	Imports, c.i.f.	71.. *d*

Russia

		1970	1971	1972	1973	1974	1975	1976	1977	1978	1979	1980	1981	1982	1983	1984
Balance of Payments																*Millions of US Dollars:*
Current Account, n.i.e.	78ald	....	....	....	....	....	....	....	....	....	....	....	....	....	....	....
Goods: Exports f.o.b.	78aad	....	....	....	....	....	....	....	....	....	....	....	....	....	....	....
Goods: Imports f.o.b.	78abd	....	....	....	....	....	....	....	....	....	....	....	....	....	....	....
Trade Balance	78acd	....	....	....	....	....	....	....	....	....	....	....	....	....	....	....
Services: Credit	78add	....	....	....	....	....	....	....	....	....	....	....	....	....	....	....
Services: Debit	78aed	....	....	....	....	....	....	....	....	....	....	....	....	....	....	....
Balance on Goods & Services	78afd	....	....	....	....	....	....	....	....	....	....	....	....	....	....	....
Income: Credit	78agd	....	....	....	....	....	....	....	....	....	....	....	....	....	....	....
Income: Debit	78ahd	....	....	....	....	....	....	....	....	....	....	....	....	....	....	....
Balance on Gds, Serv. & Inc.	78aid	....	....	....	....	....	....	....	....	....	....	....	....	....	....	....
Current Transfers, n.i.e.: Credit	78ajd	....	....	....	....	....	....	....	....	....	....	....	....	....	....	....
Current Transfers: Debit	78akd	....	....	....	....	....	....	....	....	....	....	....	....	....	....	....
Capital Account, n.i.e.	78bcd	....	....	....	....	....	....	....	....	....	....	....	....	....	....	....
Capital Account, n.i.e.: Credit	78bad	....	....	....	....	....	....	....	....	....	....	....	....	....	....	....
Capital Account: Debit	78bbd	....	....	....	....	....	....	....	....	....	....	....	....	....	....	....
Financial Account, n.i.e.	78bjd	....	....	....	....	....	....	....	....	....	....	....	....	....	....	....
Direct Investment Abroad	78bdd	....	....	....	....	....	....	....	....	....	....	....	....	....	....	....
Dir. Invest. in Rep. Econ., n.i.e.	78bed	....	....	....	....	....	....	....	....	....	....	....	....	....	....	....
Portfolio Investment Assets	78bfd	....	....	....	....	....	....	....	....	....	....	....	....	....	....	....
Equity Securities	78bkd	....	....	....	....	....	....	....	....	....	....	....	....	....	....	....
Debt Securities	78bld	....	....	....	....	....	....	....	....	....	....	....	....	....	....	....
Portfolio Investment Liab., n.i.e.	78bgd	....	....	....	....	....	....	....	....	....	....	....	....	....	....	....
Equity Securities	78bmd	....	....	....	....	....	....	....	....	....	....	....	....	....	....	....
Debt Securities	78bnd	....	....	....	....	....	....	....	....	....	....	....	....	....	....	....
Financial Derivatives Assets	78bwd	....	....	....	....	....	....	....	....	....	....	....	....	....	....	....
Financial Derivatives Liabilities	78bxd	....	....	....	....	....	....	....	....	....	....	....	....	....	....	....
Other Investment Assets	78bhd	....	....	....	....	....	....	....	....	....	....	....	....	....	....	....
Monetary Authorities	78bod	....	....	....	....	....	....	....	....	....	....	....	....	....	....	....
General Government	78bpd	....	....	....	....	....	....	....	....	....	....	....	....	....	....	....
Banks	78bqd	....	....	....	....	....	....	....	....	....	....	....	....	....	....	....
Other Sectors	78brd	....	....	....	....	....	....	....	....	....	....	....	....	....	....	....
Other Investment Liab., n.i.e.	78bid	....	....	....	....	....	....	....	....	....	....	....	....	....	....	....
Monetary Authorities	78bsd	....	....	....	....	....	....	....	....	....	....	....	....	....	....	....
General Government	78btd	....	....	....	....	....	....	....	....	....	....	....	....	....	....	....
Banks	78bud	....	....	....	....	....	....	....	....	....	....	....	....	....	....	....
Other Sectors	78bvd	....	....	....	....	....	....	....	....	....	....	....	....	....	....	....
Net Errors and Omissions	78cad	....	....	....	....	....	....	....	....	....	....	....	....	....	....	....
Overall Balance	78cbd	....	....	....	....	....	....	....	....	....	....	....	....	....	....	....
Reserves and Related Items	79dad	....	....	....	....	....	....	....	....	....	....	....	....	....	....	....
Reserve Assets	79dbd	....	....	....	....	....	....	....	....	....	....	....	....	....	....	....
Use of Fund Credit and Loans	79dcd	....	....	....	....	....	....	....	....	....	....	....	....	....	....	....
Exceptional Financing	79ded	....	....	....	....	....	....	....	....	....	....	....	....	....	....	....
International Investment Position																*Millions of US Dollars*
Assets	79aad	....	....	....	....	....	....	....	....	....	....	....	....	....	....	....
Direct Investment Abroad	79abd	....	....	....	....	....	....	....	....	....	....	....	....	....	....	....
Portfolio Investment	79acd	....	....	....	....	....	....	....	....	....	....	....	....	....	....	....
Equity Securities	79add	....	....	....	....	....	....	....	....	....	....	....	....	....	....	....
Debt Securities	79aed	....	....	....	....	....	....	....	....	....	....	....	....	....	....	....
Financial Derivatives	79ald	....	....	....	....	....	....	....	....	....	....	....	....	....	....	....
Other Investment	79afd	....	....	....	....	....	....	....	....	....	....	....	....	....	....	....
Monetary Authorities	79agd	....	....	....	....	....	....	....	....	....	....	....	....	....	....	....
General Government	79ahd	....	....	....	....	....	....	....	....	....	....	....	....	....	....	....
Banks	79aid	....	....	....	....	....	....	....	....	....	....	....	....	....	....	....
Other Sectors	79ajd	....	....	....	....	....	....	....	....	....	....	....	....	....	....	....
Reserve Assets	79akd	....	....	....	....	....	....	....	....	....	....	....	....	....	....	....
Liabilities	79lad	....	....	....	....	....	....	....	....	....	....	....	....	....	....	....
Dir. Invest. in Rep. Economy	79lbd	....	....	....	....	....	....	....	....	....	....	....	....	....	....	....
Portfolio Investment	79lcd	....	....	....	....	....	....	....	....	....	....	....	....	....	....	....
Equity Securities	79ldd	....	....	....	....	....	....	....	....	....	....	....	....	....	....	....
Debt Securities	79led	....	....	....	....	....	....	....	....	....	....	....	....	....	....	....
Financial Derivatives	79lld	....	....	....	....	....	....	....	....	....	....	....	....	....	....	....
Other investment	79lfd	....	....	....	....	....	....	....	....	....	....	....	....	....	....	....
Monetary Authorities	79lgd	....	....	....	....	....	....	....	....	....	....	....	....	....	....	....
General Government	79lhd	....	....	....	....	....	....	....	....	....	....	....	....	....	....	....
Banks	79lid	....	....	....	....	....	....	....	....	....	....	....	....	....	....	....
Other Sectors	79ljd	....	....	....	....	....	....	....	....	....	....	....	....	....	....	....

1985	1986	1987	1988	1989	1990	1991	1992	1993	1994	1995	1996	1997	1998	1999	Balance of Payments

Minus Sign Indicates Debit

1985	1986	1987	1988	1989	1990	1991	1992	1993	1994	1995	1996	1997	1998	1999	
....	....	....	....	....	....	....	....	....	8,848	8,026	12,450	2,548	1,034	24,995	Current Account, n.i.e. .... 78al *d*
....	....	....	....	....	....	....	....	....	67,826	82,913	90,564	89,008	74,888	74,663	Goods: Exports f.o.b. .... 78aa *d*
....	....	....	....	....	....	....	....	....	-50,149	-62,188	-67,630	-71,645	-57,791	-39,362	Goods: Imports f.o.b. .... 78ab *d*
....	....	....	....	....	....	....	....	....	17,677	20,725	22,934	17,363	17,097	35,301	*Trade Balance* .... 78ac *d*
....	....	....	....	....	....	....	....	....	8,425	10,568	13,283	14,079	12,373	9,087	Services: Credit .... 78ad *d*
....	....	....	....	....	....	....	....	....	-15,140	-19,971	-18,405	-19,830	-16,219	-12,427	Services: Debit .... 78ae *d*
....	....	....	....	....	....	....	....	....	10,962	11,322	17,812	11,612	13,251	31,961	*Balance on Goods & Services* .... 78af *d*
....	....	....	....	....	....	....	....	....	3,499	4,281	4,336	4,367	4,299	3,834	Income: Credit .... 78ag *d*
....	....	....	....	....	....	....	....	....	-5,308	-7,650	-9,768	-13,071	-16,106	-11,336	Income: Debit .... 78ah *d*
....	....	....	....	....	....	....	....	....	9,153	7,953	12,380	2,908	1,444	24,459	*Balance on Gds, Serv. & Inc.* .... 78ai *d*
....	....	....	....	....	....	....	....	....	238	811	771	411	269	1,028	Current Transfers, n.i.e.: Credit .... 78aj *d*
....	....	....	....	....	....	....	....	....	-543	-738	-701	-771	-679	-492	Current Transfers: Debit .... 78ak *d*
....	....	....	....	....	....	....	....	....	2,408	-348	-463	-796	-382	-332	Capital Account, n.i.e. .... 78bc *d*
....	....	....	....	....	....	....	....	....	5,882	3,122	3,066	2,138	1,705	883	Capital Account, n.i.e.: Credit .... 78ba *d*
....	....	....	....	....	....	....	....	....	-3,474	-3,470	-3,529	-2,934	-2,087	-1,215	Capital Account: Debit .... 78bb *d*
....	....	....	....	....	....	....	....	....	-29,952	-7,200	-23,436	-286	-13,010	-19,487	Financial Account, n.i.e. .... 78bj *d*
....	....	....	....	....	....	....	....	....	-101	-357	-770	-2,603	-1,025	-2,143	Direct Investment Abroad .... 78bd *d*
....	....	....	....	....	....	....	....	....	638	2,016	2,478	6,638	2,764	2,890	Dir. Invest. in Rep. Econ., n.i.e. .... 78be *d*
....	....	....	....	....	....	....	....	....	114	-1,704	-173	-157	-257	254	Portfolio Investment Assets .... 78bf *d*
....	....	....	....	....	....	....	....	....	-19	-42	-117	32	-11	5	Equity Securities .... 78bk *d*
....	....	....	....	....	....	....	....	....	133	-1,662	-56	-189	-246	249	Debt Securities .... 78bl *d*
....	....	....	....	....	....	....	....	....	-78	-739	4,584	17,765	6,294	-815	Portfolio Investment Liab., n.i.e. .... 78bg *d*
....	....	....	....	....	....	....	....	....	44	46	2,154	1,266	714	212	Equity Securities .... 78bm *d*
....	....	....	....	....	....	....	....	....	-122	-785	2,430	16,499	5,580	-1,027	Debt Securities .... 78bn *d*
....	....	....	....	....	....	....	....	....	....	....	....	....	....	....	Financial Derivatives Assets .... 78bw *d*
....	....	....	....	....	....	....	....	....	....	....	....	....	....	....	Financial Derivatives Liabilities .... 78bx *d*
....	....	....	....	....	....	....	....	....	-19,380	6,290	-30,492	-26,638	-16,184	-15,293	Other Investment Assets .... 78bh *d*
....	....	....	....	....	....	....	....	....							Monetary Authorities .... 78bo *d*
....	....	....	....	....	....	....	....	....	-3,009	-1,081	-276	7,167	-1,480	-1,288	General Government .... 78bp *d*
....	....	....	....	....	....	....	....	....	-1,881	4,350	-1,933	-1,292	705	-3,843	Banks .... 78bq *d*
....	....	....	....	....	....	....	....	....	-14,490	3,021	-28,283	-32,513	-15,409	-10,162	Other Sectors .... 78br *d*
....	....	....	....	....	....	....	....	....	-11,145	-12,706	937	4,709	-4,602	-4,380	Other Investment Liab., n.i.e. .... 78bi *d*
....	....	....	....	....	....	....	....	....	-308	392	-236	-37	84	-78	Monetary Authorities .... 78bs *d*
....	....	....	....	....	....	....	....	....	-11,745	-9,176	-5,790	-10,767	-3,277	-2,790	General Government .... 78bt *d*
....	....	....	....	....	....	....	....	....	1,288	2,446	4,264	8,646	-6,380	-1,179	Banks .... 78bu *d*
....	....	....	....	....	....	....	....	....	-380	-6,368	2,699	6,867	4,971	-333	Other Sectors .... 78bv *d*
....	....	....	....	....	....	....	....	....	-273	-8,776	-5,741	-8,021	-8,965	-6,989	Net Errors and Omissions .... 78ca *d*
....	....	....	....	....	....	....	....	....	-18,969	-8,298	-17,190	-6,555	-21,323	-1,813	*Overall Balance* .... 78cb *d*
....	....	....	....	....	....	....	....	....	18,969	8,298	17,190	6,555	21,323	1,813	Reserves and Related Items .... 79da *d*
....	....	....	....	....	....	....	....	....	1,935	-10,382	2,840	-1,930	5,306	-1,772	Reserve Assets .... 79db *d*
....	....	....	....	....	....	....	....	....	1,514	5,473	3,237	1,526	5,206	-3,603	Use of Fund Credit and Loans .... 79dc *d*
....	....	....	....	....	....	....	....	....	15,520	13,207	11,113	6,959	10,811	7,187	Exceptional Financing .... 79de *d*

Millions of US Dollars

1985	1986	1987	1988	1989	1990	1991	1992	1993	1994	1995	1996	1997	1998	1999	International Investment Position
....	....	....	....	....	....	....	....	....	22,276	28,590	28,988	33,378	25,407	28,886	Assets .... 79aa *d*
....	....	....	....	....	....	....	....	....	2,272	2,420	2,685	2,789	2,703	1,715	Direct Investment Abroad .... 79ab *d*
....	....	....	....	....	....	....	....	....	486	764	1,230	1,382	1,308	861	Portfolio Investment .... 79ac *d*
....	....	....	....	....	....	....	....	....	7	27	43	11	18	6	Equity Securities .... 79ad *d*
....	....	....	....	....	....	....	....	....	479	737	1,187	1,371	1,290	855	Debt Securities .... 79ae *d*
....	....	....	....	....	....	....	....	....	—	—	—	—	—	—	Financial Derivatives .... 79al *d*
....	....	....	....	....	....	....	....	....	13,013	8,199	9,749	11,423	9,173	13,855	Other Investment .... 79af *d*
....	....	....	....	....	....	....	....	....	—	—	—	—	—	—	Monetary Authorities .... 79ag *d*
....	....	....	....	....	....	....	....	....	—	—	—	—	—	—	General Government .... 79ah *d*
....	....	....	....	....	....	....	....	....	13,013	8,199	9,749	11,423	9,173	13,855	Banks .... 79ai *d*
....	....	....	....	....	....	....	....	....	—	—	—	—	—	—	Other Sectors .... 79aj *d*
....	....	....	....	....	....	....	....	....	6,505	17,207	15,324	17,784	12,223	12,455	Reserve Assets .... 79ak *d*
....	....	....	....	....	....	....	....	....	7,380	15,492	22,162	32,827	29,926	23,676	Liabilities .... 79la *d*
....	....	....	....	....	....	....	....	....	332	345	426	970	373	731	Dir. Invest. in Rep. Economy .... 79lb *d*
....	....	....	....	....	....	....	....	....	369	437	567	1,032	495	346	Portfolio Investment .... 79lc *d*
....	....	....	....	....	....	....	....	....	79	132	122	241	36	40	Equity Securities .... 79ld *d*
....	....	....	....	....	....	....	....	....	290	305	445	791	459	306	Debt Securities .... 79le *d*
....	....	....	....	....	....	....	....	....	—	—	—	—	—	—	Financial Derivatives .... 79ll *d*
....	....	....	....	....	....	....	....	....	6,679	14,710	21,169	30,825	29,058	22,599	Other investment .... 79lf *d*
....	....	....	....	....	....	....	....	....	4,198	9,617	12,508	13,231	19,335	15,238	Monetary Authorities .... 79lg *d*
....	....	....	....	....	....	....	....	....	—	—	—	—	—	—	General Government .... 79lh *d*
....	....	....	....	....	....	....	....	....	2,481	5,093	8,661	17,594	9,723	7,361	Banks .... 79li *d*
....	....	....	....	....	....	....	....	....	—	—	—	—	—	—	Other Sectors .... 79lj *d*

Russia

		1970	1971	1972	1973	1974	1975	1976	1977	1978	1979	1980	1981	1982	1983	1984
Government Finance																*Millions of Rubles:*
Deficit (-) or Surplus	80	...	...	...	...	...	...	...	...	...	...	...	...	...	...	...
Total Revenue and Grants	81y	...	...	...	...	...	...	...	...	...	...	...	...	...	...	...
Revenue	81	...	...	...	...	...	...	...	...	...	...	...	...	...	...	...
Grants	81z	...	...	...	...	...	...	...	...	...	...	...	...	...	...	...
Exp. & Lending Minus Repay.	82z	...	...	...	...	...	...	...	...	...	...	...	...	...	...	...
Expenditure	82	...	...	...	...	...	...	...	...	...	...	...	...	...	...	...
Lending Minus Repayments	83	...	...	...	...	...	...	...	...	...	...	...	...	...	...	...
Total Financing	80h	...	...	...	...	...	...	...	...	...	...	...	...	...	...	...
Total Net Borrowing	84	...	...	...	...	...	...	...	...	...	...	...	...	...	...	...
Net Domestic	84a	...	...	...	...	...	...	...	...	...	...	...	...	...	...	...
Net Foreign	85a	...	...	...	...	...	...	...	...	...	...	...	...	...	...	...
Use of Cash Balances	87	...	...	...	...	...	...	...	...	...	...	...	...	...	...	...
Total Debt by Currency	88z	...	...	...	...	...	...	...	...	...	...	...	...	...	...	...
Debt: Rubles	88b	...	...	...	...	...	...	...	...	...	...	...	...	...	...	...
Foreign Currency	89b	...	...	...	...	...	...	...	...	...	...	...	...	...	...	...
National Accounts																*Millions of Rubles*
Househ.Cons.Expend.,incl.NPISHs	96f	...	...	...	...	...	...	...	...	...	...	...	...	...	...	...
Government Consumption Expend.	91f	...	...	...	...	...	...	...	...	...	...	...	...	...	...	...
Gross Fixed Capital Formation	93e	...	...	...	...	...	...	...	...	...	...	...	...	...	...	...
Changes in Inventories	93i	...	...	...	...	...	...	...	...	...	...	...	...	...	...	...
Exports of Goods and Services	90c	...	...	...	...	...	...	...	...	...	...	...	...	...	...	...
Imports of Goods and Services	98c	...	...	...	...	...	...	...	...	...	...	...	...	...	...	...
GDP, Production Based	99bp	...	...	...	...	...	...	...	...	...	...	...	...	...	...	...
Statistical Discrepancy	99bs	...	...	...	...	...	...	...	...	...	...	...	...	...	...	...
																Millions:
Population	99z	...	...	...	...	...	...	...	...	...	...	...	...	...	...	...

	1985	1986	1987	1988	1989	1990	1991	1992	1993	1994	1995	1996	1997	1998	1999		
Government Finance																	
Year Ending December 31																	
Deficit (-) or Surplus	....	....	....	....	....	....	....	....	....	....	−69,508	−147,607	−150,415	−126,958	−56,641	Deficit (-) or Surplus	80
Total Revenue and Grants	....	....	....	....	....	....	....	....	....	....	226,071	281,770	322,690	299,403	608,033	Total Revenue and Grants	81y
Revenue	....	....	....	....	....	....	....	....	....	....	....	....	....	....	....	Revenue	81
Grants	....	....	....	....	....	....	....	....	....	....	....	....	....	....	....	Grants	81z
Exp. & Lending Minus Repay.	....	....	....	....	....	....	....	....	....	....	295,579	429,377	473,105	426,361	664,674	Exp. & Lending Minus Repay.	82z
Expenditure	....	....	....	....	....	....	....	....	....	....	277,744	409,792	454,768	416,872	655,391	Expenditure	82
Lending Minus Repayments	....	....	....	....	....	....	....	....	....	....	17,835	19,585	18,337	9,489	9,283	Lending Minus Repayments	83
Total Financing	....	....	....	....	....	....	....	....	....	....	69,508	147,607	150,415	126,958	56,641	Total Financing	80h
Total Net Borrowing	....	....	....	....	....	....	....	....	....	....	72,248	137,224	159,722	154,733	101,063	Total Net Borrowing	84
Net Domestic	....	....	....	....	....	....	....	....	....	....	48,814	103,968	106,253	64,545	53,644	Net Domestic	84a
Net Foreign	....	....	....	....	....	....	....	....	....	....	23,434	33,256	53,469	90,188	47,419	Net Foreign	85a
Use of Cash Balances	....	....	....	....	....	....	....	....	....	....	−2,740	10,383	−9,307	−27,775	−44,422	Use of Cash Balances	87
Total Debt by Currency	....	....	....	....	....	....	....	....	....	....	787,689	1,122,323	1,302,052	3,786,106	....	Total Debt by Currency	88z
Debt: Rubles	....	....	....	....	....	....	....	....	....	....	226,505	427,323	565,992	750,556	....	Debt: Rubles	88b
Foreign Currency	....	....	....	....	....	....	....	....	....	....	561,184	695,000	736,060	3,035,550	....	Foreign Currency	89b
National Accounts																	
Millions of Rubles																	
Househ.Cons.Expend.,incl.NPISHs	....	....	....	....	....	....	....	6,550	76,997	285,371	796,430	1,107,891	1,352,744	1,587,754	2,489,276	Househ.Cons.Expend.,incl.NPISHs	96f
Government Consumption Expend.	....	....	....	....	....	....	....	2,634	29,758	136,682	299,391	436,738	539,103	527,493	720,505	Government Consumption Expend.	91f
Gross Fixed Capital Formation	....	....	....	....	....	....	....	4,550	34,965	133,209	327,941	454,369	482,451	472,916	741,125	Gross Fixed Capital Formation	93e
Changes in Inventories	....	....	....	....	....	....	....	2,031	11,352	22,763	63,648	74,326	81,793	−50,650	−36,804	Changes in Inventories	93i
Exports of Goods and Services	....	....	....	....	....	....	....	11,848	65,525	169,535	426,735	532,239	592,333	839,457	2,019,074	Exports of Goods and Services	90c
Imports of Goods and Services	....	....	....	....	....	....	....	−9,173	−52,300	−141,666	−373,593	−442,815	−518,881	−636,570	1,257,317	Imports of Goods and Services	98c
GDP, Production Based	....	....	....	....	....	....	....	19,006	171,510	610,745	1,540,493	2,145,656	2,478,594	2,696,355	4,545,490	GDP, Production Based	99bp
Statistical Discrepancy	....	....	....	....	....	....	....	566	5,213	4,852	−59	−17,122	−50,949	−44,045	−130,369	Statistical Discrepancy	99bs
Midyear Estimates																	
Population	....	....	....	....	....	....	....	148.31	148.15	147.97	148.14	147.74	147.10	146.54	147.20	Population	99z

(See notes in the back of the book.)

Rwanda

		1970	1971	1972	1973	1974	1975	1976	1977	1978	1979	1980	1981	1982	1983	1984
Exchange Rates														*Francs per SDR:*		
Official Rate	aa	100.00	100.00	100.00	100.00	113.67	108.68	107.86	112.77	120.95	122.30	118.41	108.06	102.41	102.71	102.71
														Francs per US Dollar:		
Official Rate	ae	100.00	92.11	92.11	82.90	92.84	92.84	92.84	92.84	92.84	92.84	92.84	92.84	92.84	98.54	104.36
Official Rate	rf	100.00	99.74	92.11	84.05	92.84	92.84	92.84	92.84	92.84	92.84	92.84	92.84	92.84	94.34	100.17
Fund Position														*Millions of SDRs:*		
Quota	2f. s	19.00	19.00	19.00	19.00	19.00	19.00	19.00	19.00	23.00	23.00	34.50	34.50	34.50	43.80	43.80
SDRs	1b. s	.50	1.43	.39	2.43	2.48	2.39	2.39	2.35	2.39	4.58	7.72	9.83	10.83	8.40	8.29
Reserve Position in the Fund	1c. s	—	.07	—	—	—	—	2.07	2.07	2.93	5.47	8.36	7.28	7.30	9.64	9.66
Total Fund Cred.&Loans Outstg.	2tl	2.93	—	—	—	—	—	—	—	—	5.76	10.62	10.69	10.69	10.69	10.69
International Liquidity										*Millions of US Dollars Unless Otherwise Indicated:*						
Total Reserves minus Gold	1l. d	7.70	5.78	6.37	15.18	12.96	25.59	64.29	82.87	87.60	152.31	186.57	173.10	128.40	110.89	106.86
SDRs	1b. d	.50	1.55	.42	2.93	3.04	2.80	2.78	2.85	3.11	6.03	9.85	11.44	11.95	8.79	8.13
Reserve Position in the Fund	1c. d	—	.08	—	—	—	—	2.40	2.51	3.82	7.21	10.66	8.47	8.05	10.09	9.47
Foreign Exchange	1d. d	7.20	4.15	5.95	12.25	9.92	22.79	59.10	77.51	80.67	139.07	166.06	153.18	108.40	92.00	89.26
Monetary Authorities: Other Liab.	4.. d	2.14	1.89	2.87	4.63	5.53	5.65	15.52	18.85	19.25	24.63	37.37	34.50	25.42	31.18	28.84
Deposit Money Banks: Assets	7a. d	.89	1.97	.31	1.18	1.36	2.89	3.34	13.92	12.41	25.28	21.29	26.11	28.00	20.90	31.57
Liabilities	7b. d	.31	2.93	.48	.86	.01	2.03	3.17	6.67	4.75	7.27	8.41	13.63	25.10	17.90	15.78
Other Banking Insts.: Liabilities	7f. d	....	....	....	....	....	1.11	1.19	1.85	3.67	5.99	5.10	6.42	6.20	8.81	7.66
Monetary Authorities														*Millions of Francs:*		
Foreign Assets	11	770	532	586	1,259	1,203	2,376	5,968	7,710	8,133	14,141	17,321	16,071	11,921	10,927	11,151
Claims on Central Government	12a	985	1,146	1,623	2,105	2,199	1,604	1,583	1,211	1,399	1,205	1,232	1,219	2,483	3,887	3,937
Claims on Official Entities	12bx	21	81	68	147	116	194	166	100	78	51	25	7	14	2	2
Claims on Private Sector	12d	—	10	10	39	59	18	334	295	301	456	517	635	285	264	248
Claims on Deposit Money Banks	12e	58	204	31	73	721	531	51	562	671	249	504	417	730	1,027	1,643
Claims on Other Financial Insts	12f	69	123	162	130	121	160	87	67	40	38	36	93	356	601	532
Reserve Money	14	2,073	2,021	2,258	2,921	3,842	3,905	5,109	5,803	5,930	8,532	7,978	6,964	7,237	8,065	8,559
of which: Currency Outside DMBs	14a	1,238	1,409	1,446	2,003	2,553	2,722	3,070	3,948	4,443	5,242	5,689	6,086	6,260	6,662	7,030
Time Deposits	15	....	....	....	....	110	153	224	131	88	94	135	972	623	453	395
Foreign Liabilities	16c	507	174	265	384	513	525	1,441	1,750	1,787	2,991	4,727	4,359	3,455	4,175	4,103
Central Government Deposits	16d	87	130	218	490	217	600	783	1,364	1,786	1,850	4,542	3,973	3,488	2,825	2,872
Counterpart Funds	16e	86	64	41	39	22	8	117	108	73	46	21	99	61	118	86
Capital Accounts	17a	299	506	710	799	806	951	1,309	1,409	1,708	3,030	3,357	3,917	4,494	4,659	4,727
Other Items (Net)	17r	−982	−646	−586	−509	−528	−513	−793	−620	−750	−402	−1,126	−1,842	−3,570	−3,587	−3,230
Deposit Money Banks														*Millions of Francs:*		
Reserves	20	275	345	245	483	328	200	1,345	1,087	673	2,328	999	315	585	874	966
Foreign Assets	21	89	182	29	98	127	269	310	1,292	1,152	2,347	1,976	‡2,424	2,600	2,060	3,294
Claims on Central Government	22a	437	576	775	779	1,123	1,430	784	600	504	596	426	653	1,220	1,982	2,757
Claims on Official Entities	22bx	—	10	10	—	—	194	237	121	148	183	194	269	400	852	701
Claims on Private Sector	22d	529	636	453	855	1,717	1,640	1,782	3,662	4,478	3,793	5,689	6,837	7,742	8,085	10,021
Demand Deposits	24	828	949	936	1,449	1,518	1,869	2,702	3,429	4,016	4,745	5,020	‡5,191	4,777	5,056	5,743
Time and Savings Deposits	25	404	449	453	464	953	994	1,306	1,973	2,132	2,738	3,065	‡3,237	4,090	5,306	6,154
Foreign Liabilities	26c	31	270	44	72	1	188	294	619	441	675	781	‡1,265	2,330	1,764	1,647
Central Government Deposits	26d	—	6	15	53	5	5	28	137	143	1,423	166	‡714	837	917	1,824
Credit from Monetary Authorities	26g	16	5	3	9	578	494	56	529	350	137	572	490	742	1,113	1,810
Capital Accounts	27a	115	134	148	164	190	170	230	314	369	447	500	541	1,015	1,330	2,096
Other Items (Net)	27r	−64	−65	−86	5	391	519	557	714	−495	−920	−818	1,228	−1,244	−1,635	−1,533
Monetary Survey														*Millions of Francs:*		
Foreign Assets (Net)	31n	321	270	306	902	816	1,932	4,544	6,633	7,057	12,822	13,790	‡12,871	8,735	7,047	8,695
Domestic Credit	32	1,977	2,465	2,888	3,555	5,169	4,729	4,334	4,677	5,134	3,114	3,481	‡5,080	8,229	12,015	13,586
Claims on Central Govt. (Net)	32an	1,348	1,595	2,176	2,359	3,127	2,464	1,605	327	—	−1,449	−3,034	‡−2,815	−622	2,128	1,998
Claims on Official Entities	32bx	21	91	78	147	116	387	403	221	225	234	219	276	414	853	703
Claims on Private Sector	32d	529	646	462	893	1,775	1,658	2,115	3,957	4,779	4,249	6,207	7,472	8,027	8,348	10,269
Claims on Other Financial Insts	32f	79	133	172	156	151	220	212	173	130	81	90	147	410	685	616
Money	34	2,165	2,472	2,520	3,565	4,288	4,850	6,516	8,035	8,961	11,255	12,026	‡11,729	11,442	12,294	13,332
Quasi-Money	35	404	449	453	464	1,063	1,147	1,530	2,104	2,220	2,831	3,200	‡4,209	4,712	5,759	6,549
Other Items (Net)	37r	−564	−188	221	433	809	1,170	1,548	2,124	1,010	2,555	3,302	3,416	1,904	2,106	3,498
Money plus Quasi-Money	35l	2,568	2,921	2,973	4,029	5,350	5,997	8,047	10,138	11,181	14,086	15,226	‡15,938	16,154	18,054	19,881
Other Banking Institutions														*Millions of Francs:*		
Cash	40.. k	10	2	59	36	109	92	53	45	45	73	80	263	187	396	183
Claims on Official Entities	42bx k	55	55	—	—	—	—	77	28	26	125	191	188	214	195	154
Claims on Private Sector	42d. k	27	90	159	216	239	449	455	545	670	955	1,019	1,166	1,436	1,863	2,088
Long Term Foreign Liabilities	46cl k	....	....	....	....	....	103	110	172	340	556	474	596	575	868	800
Credit from Monetary Authorities	46g. k	69	121	162	130	117	157	85	63	40	38	36	93	356	601	532
Cred. from Deposit Money Banks	46h. k	....	....	....	....	....	20	70	45	20	80					
Capital Accounts	47a. k	50	51	63	169	215	221	286	318	450	469	1,080	956	1,001	1,240	1,444
Other Items (Net)	47r. k	−25	−26	−7	−47	16	40	34	20	−109	10	−300	−29	−95	−256	−350

1985	1986	1987	1988	1989	1990	1991	1992	1993	1994	1995	1996	1997	1998	1999		
															Exchange Rates	
End of Period																
102.71	102.71	102.71	102.71	102.71	171.18	171.18	201.39	201.39	201.94	445.67	437.37	411.31	450.75	479.24	Official Rate	aa
End of Period (ae) Period Average (rf)																
93.49	84.18	73.02	76.71	77.62	121.12	119.79	146.27	146.37	138.33	299.81	304.16	304.67	320.34	349.53	Official Rate	ae
101.26	87.64	79.67	76.45	79.98	82.60	125.14	133.35	144.31	....	262.20	306.82	301.53	312.31	333.94	Official Rate	rf
															Fund Position	
End of Period																
43.80	43.80	43.80	43.80	43.80	43.80	43.80	59.50	59.50	59.50	59.50	59.50	59.50	59.50	80.10	Quota	2f.s
8.19	8.10	8.01	7.85	7.54	7.15	6.73	2.43	2.11	1.75	13.65	12.71	19.64	17.36	10.54	SDRs	1b.s
9.32	9.32	9.33	7.08	7.10	6.44	6.46	10.40	9.79	9.79	—	—			—	Reserve Position in the Fund	1c.s
9.15	7.02	4.90	2.77	.65	.07	8.76	8.76	8.76	8.76	17.69	16.81	29.93	40.08	55.29	Total Fund Cred.&Loans Outstg.	2tl
															International Liquidity	
End of Period																
113.33	162.30	164.19	118.33	70.37	44.35	110.12	78.72	47.46	51.25	99.10	106.74	153.34	168.75	174.18	Total Reserves minus Gold	1l.d
9.00	9.91	11.36	10.56	9.91	10.17	9.63	3.34	2.90	2.55	20.29	18.28	26.50	24.44	14.46	SDRs	1b.d
10.24	11.40	13.24	9.53	9.33	9.16	9.24	14.30	13.45	14.29						Reserve Position in the Fund	1c.d
94.09	141.00	139.59	98.24	51.13	25.01	91.25	61.08	31.11	34.40	78.80	88.47	126.84	144.31	159.72	Foreign Exchange	1d.d
19.33	20.03	24.02	24.22	15.24	46.51	32.75	29.15	28.52	40.45	28.36	20.62	21.89	50.05	21.13	Monetary Authorities: Other Liab.	4..d
28.90	21.12	28.99	35.03	29.80	32.44	45.27	41.66	31.68	26.63	51.92	66.27	73.17	75.22	56.62	Deposit Money Banks: Assets	7a.d
24.79	9.89	9.23	12.88	6.77	7.45	8.60	8.76	6.07	5.61	4.09	4.53	12.63	11.91	5.36	Liabilities	7b.d
9.36	8.78	18.70	22.30	25.99	17.56	17.92	15.59	14.73	8.67	7.96	7.41	4.70	2.99	2.92	Other Banking Insts.: Liabilities	7f.d
															Monetary Authorities	
End of Period																
10,595	13,663	11,989	9,077	5,462	5,372	13,191	11,514	6,946	7,089	29,710	32,469	46,720	54,058	60,882	Foreign Assets	11
3,519	4,375	7,151	6,348	9,667	18,608	20,611	29,127	34,915	32,834	34,359	35,125	42,125	44,447	50,716	Claims on Central Government	12a
2	2	—	—	—	—	—	—	—	680	762	730	729	729	219	Claims on Official Entities	12bx
267	240	223	191	178	144	128	115	123	151	157	253	220	342	561	Claims on Private Sector	12d
2,830	928	872	3,095	3,050	1,327	655	917	1,321	846	1,725	153	301	908	1,793	Claims on Deposit Money Banks	12e
598	548	321	631	816	555	378	32	20	11	9	9	9	426	431	Claims on Other Financial Insts	12f
9,584	10,877	12,051	10,822	9,261	10,129	14,588	14,097	18,024	19,708	27,340	33,507	37,314	34,016	39,051	Reserve Money	14
7,161	7,686	8,203	8,439	7,744	8,593	8,822	10,321	11,522	11,924	17,257	19,908	20,635	22,865	21,501	*of which: Currency Outside DMBs*	14a
547	633	663	688	544	1,216	601	913	346	291	207	201	181	142	855	Time Deposits	15
2,747	2,409	2,262	2,144	1,249	5,645	5,425	6,026	5,935	7,365	16,383	13,624	18,974	34,112	33,907	Foreign Liabilities	16c
3,082	3,048	3,076	2,320	1,243	2,452	5,911	7,527	4,492	4,430	19,156	15,753	15,032	16,276	20,929	Central Government Deposits	16d
62	50	42	33	766	732	1,083	4,098	4,157	4,596	2,304	3,231	4,174	3,408	1,620	Counterpart Funds	16e
4,923	4,965	4,965	5,139	5,486	6,526	8,024	8,631	12,310	13,989	20,240	13,150	11,681	12,590	15,615	Capital Accounts	17a
-3,134	-2,227	-2,502	-1,802	625	-695	-670	414	-1,939	-8,770	-18,906	-10,727	2,748	365	2,625	Other Items (Net)	17r
															Deposit Money Banks	
End of Period																
1,391	1,870	2,277	966	701	1,040	5,097	3,117	5,778	6,618	8,590	13,816	16,035	11,835	15,851	Reserves	20
2,702	1,778	2,117	2,687	2,313	3,929	5,423	6,093	4,637	3,683	15,566	20,157	22,293	24,095	19,792	Foreign Assets	21
3,068	3,698	4,851	7,100	6,348	5,421	5,448	6,667	4,495	4,311	4,528	4,968	5,573	6,995	7,747	Claims on Central Government	22a
677	641	688	853	1,533	2,533	810	298	679	581	354	205	15	421	687	Claims on Official Entities	22bx
13,140	13,198	13,356	16,302	17,597	14,629	12,122	15,308	17,875	16,234	28,381	28,615	44,948	54,079	59,573	Claims on Private Sector	22d
6,306	8,234	7,922	8,228	7,305	7,346	8,587	11,571	12,876	16,165	22,586	24,979	34,523	31,509	37,009	Demand Deposits	24
8,184	8,641	10,885	12,471	13,588	13,804	14,879	14,249	13,356	8,084	22,181	22,851	32,445	36,051	38,778	Time and Savings Deposits	25
2,317	832	674	988	525	903	1,030	1,281	889	776	1,226	1,378	3,847	3,816	1,872	Foreign Liabilities	26c
1,711	2,256	2,103	2,621	3,457	3,220	2,800	2,953	2,854	3,370	5,482	10,944	9,072	12,322	9,705	Central Government Deposits	26d
2,729	1,634	610	2,829	2,820	1,399	600	469	719	287	1,624	63	63	61	1,550	Credit from Monetary Authorities	26g
2,458	2,595	2,681	3,001	3,348	3,469	2,876	3,535	3,778	3,745	6,908	7,683	11,832	16,749	19,926	Capital Accounts	27a
-2,728	-3,007	-1,586	-2,230	-2,552	-2,589	-1,873	-2,575	-1,007	-998	-2,589	-136	-2,919	-3,083	-5,167	Other Items (Net)	27r
															Monetary Survey	
End of Period																
8,233	12,200	11,170	8,633	6,001	2,752	12,159	10,300	4,760	2,632	27,666	37,624	46,191	40,225	44,895	Foreign Assets (Net)	31n
16,561	17,489	21,504	26,576	31,531	36,447	31,088	41,349	50,926	47,175	44,016	43,307	69,621	78,951	89,470	Domestic Credit	32
1,793	2,768	6,823	8,508	11,315	18,358	17,347	25,314	32,064	29,346	14,249	13,396	23,594	22,844	27,829	Claims on Central Govt. (Net)	32an
678	643	688	853	1,533	2,533	810	298	679	1,261	1,116	935	744	1,150	906	Claims on Official Entities	32bx
13,407	13,438	13,580	16,493	17,776	14,773	12,250	15,423	17,998	16,385	28,538	28,868	45,168	54,421	60,134	Claims on Private Sector	32d
682	640	413	723	908	783	682	314	185	184	113	108	115	536	600	Claims on Other Financial Insts	32f
14,577	17,212	17,669	18,210	15,931	16,724	18,023	22,509	24,919	28,810	40,658	45,423	55,746	55,291	59,237	Money	34
8,731	9,274	11,549	13,159	14,132	15,020	15,480	15,162	13,701	8,375	22,388	23,052	32,626	36,193	39,633	Quasi-Money	35
2,426	3,924	3,960	4,125	7,536	7,467	9,743	13,981	17,069	12,620	8,637	12,457	27,440	27,692	35,517	Other Items (Net)	37r
23,308	26,486	29,217	31,369	30,062	31,744	33,503	37,671	38,621	37,185	63,046	68,475	88,372	91,484	98,869	Money plus Quasi-Money	35l
															Other Banking Institutions	
End of Period																
292	200	292	191	127	134	584	887	1,332	1,340	1,363	1,559	1,495	862	1,445	Cash	40..k
106	98	70	45	119	143	131	108	83	—	52	491	21	316	298	Claims on Official Entities	42bx k
2,258	2,456	2,961	4,184	4,264	4,362	3,162	3,038	2,732	3,024	3,835	3,126	4,152	5,161	5,807	Claims on Private Sector	42d.k
875	740	1,366	1,711	2,017	2,127	2,147	2,281	2,155	1,199	2,386	2,253	1,433	957	1,021	Long Term Foreign Liabilities	46cl k
598	548	321	631	816	555	354	10	9	9	9	9	9	9	431	Credit from Monetary Authorities	46g.k
															Cred.from Deposit Money Banks	46h.k
1,542	1,970	2,077	2,160	2,108	2,502	1,932	2,208	2,310	3,996	3,736	4,228	4,067	4,986	6,074	Capital Accounts	47a.k
-359	-503	-441[e]	-82[e]	-431[e]	-545[e]	-555[e]	-466	-327	-763	-881	-1,314	159	386	25	Other Items (Net)	47r.k

Rwanda

		1970	1971	1972	1973	1974	1975	1976	1977	1978	1979	1980	1981	1982	1983	1984
Interest Rates															*Percent Per Annum*	
Discount Rate *(End of Period)*	60	5.00	5.00	5.00	5.00	5.00	5.00	5.00	5.00	5.00	9.00	9.00	9.00	9.00	9.00	9.00
Deposit Rate	60l	....	....	....	....	....	....	....	....	2.00	2.71	6.25	6.25	6.25	6.25	6.25
Lending Rate	60p	....	....	....	....	....	....	....	....	12.50	13.04	13.50	13.50	13.50	13.50	13.50
Prices															*Index Numbers (1995=100):*	
Consumer Prices	64	6.7	6.8	7.0	7.6	10.0	Ɪ13.0	14.0	15.9	18.0	20.8	22.3	23.8	26.8	28.5	30.1
International Transactions															*Millions of Francs*	
Exports	70	2,481	2,233	1,795	2,787	3,372	3,872	7,471	8,511	6,655	10,961	10,354	10,199	9,550	11,405	14,496
Imports, c.i.f.	71	2,910	3,305	3,183	2,819	5,416	9,167	9,858	11,406	17,447	17,856	22,568	23,775	25,666	25,453	27,872
															1995=100	
Volume of Exports	72	124	130	107	271	291	371	442	288	253	524	289	411	377	384	439
Export Prices	74	15	12	12	14	17	15	28	48	35	32	27	34	Ɪ36	44	50
Balance of Payments															*Millions of US Dollars:*	
Current Account, n.i.e.	78ald	....	....	....	....	....	....	18.8	22.1	−46.0	45.8	−48.3	−74.0	−90.5	−48.6	−41.5
Goods: Exports f.o.b.	78aad	....	....	....	....	....	....	114.2	126.5	111.7	203.0	133.6	113.3	108.5	124.1	142.6
Goods: Imports f.o.b.	78abd	....	....	....	....	....	....	−104.5	−102.3	−144.9	−159.5	−195.8	−207.1	−214.7	−197.6	−197.5
Trade Balance	78acd	....	....	....	....	....	....	9.7	24.2	−33.3	43.5	−62.2	−93.8	−106.2	−73.6	−54.9
Services: Credit	78add	....	....	....	....	....	....	8.0	11.0	14.2	23.7	31.8	37.3	33.3	27.9	31.9
Services: Debit	78aed	....	....	....	....	....	....	−49.5	−74.7	−116.4	−147.6	−123.4	−121.7	−120.9	−113.0	−113.2
Balance on Goods & Services	78afd	....	....	....	....	....	....	−31.8	−39.5	−135.6	−80.4	−153.9	−178.2	−193.8	−158.7	−136.2
Income: Credit	78agd	....	....	....	....	....	....	1.2	3.4	4.5	8.4	17.1	25.2	16.1	8.6	8.2
Income: Debit	78ahd	....	....	....	....	....	....	−5.1	−7.9	−9.5	−11.9	−15.4	−16.7	−18.8	−16.5	−14.6
Balance on Gds, Serv. & Inc.	78aid	....	....	....	....	....	....	−35.7	−44.0	−140.6	−83.9	−152.2	−169.6	−196.5	−166.5	−142.7
Current Transfers, n.i.e.: Credit	78ajd	....	....	....	....	....	....	68.8	85.0	113.7	150.8	126.9	119.2	129.7	141.3	122.5
Current Transfers: Debit	78akd	....	....	....	....	....	....	−14.3	−18.9	−19.1	−21.1	−23.1	−23.5	−23.7	−23.4	−21.4
Capital Account, n.i.e.	78bcd	....	....	....	....	....	....	−.7	−1.3	−.6	.3	.4	.4	3.9	—	−.1
Capital Account, n.i.e.: Credit	78bad	....	....	....	....	....	....	—	—	—	1.7	1.8	1.8	5.5	1.7	1.6
Capital Account: Debit	78bbd	....	....	....	....	....	....	−.7	−1.3	−.6	−1.4	−1.4	−1.4	−1.6	−1.7	−1.7
Financial Account, n.i.e.	78bjd	....	....	....	....	....	....	16.6	18.8	47.1	15.1	72.8	51.9	52.5	31.4	53.0
Direct Investment Abroad	78bdd	....	....	....	....	....	....	—	—	—	—	—	—	—	—	—
Dir. Invest. in Rep. Econ., n.i.e.	78bed	....	....	....	....	....	....	5.9	5.0	4.7	12.6	16.4	18.0	20.7	11.1	15.1
Portfolio Investment Assets	78bfd	....	....	....	....	....	....	—	—	—	—	—	—	—	—	—
Equity Securities	78bkd	....	....	....	....	....	....	—	—	—	—	—	—	—	—	—
Debt Securities	78bld	....	....	....	....	....	....	—	—	—	—	—	—	—	—	—
Portfolio Investment Liab., n.i.e.	78bgd	....	....	....	....	....	....	—	.1	—	—	.6	.6	—	—	.1
Equity Securities	78bmd	....	....	....	....	....	....	—	—	—	—	.6	.6	—	—	.1
Debt Securities	78bnd	....	....	....	....	....	....	—	.1	—	—	—	—	—	—	—
Financial Derivatives Assets	78bwd	....	....	....	....	....	....									
Financial Derivatives Liabilities	78bxd	....	....	....	....	....	....									
Other Investment Assets	78bhd	....	....	....	....	....	....	−2.8	−17.5	11.3	−12.3	16.2	9.9	15.4	2.9	.4
Monetary Authorities	78bod	....	....	....	....	....	....	....	....	....	....	....	....	....	....	....
General Government	78bpd	....	....	....	....	....	....	—	—	—	—	—	—	—	—	—
Banks	78bqd	....	....	....	....	....	....	—	—	—	—	—	—	—	—	—
Other Sectors	78brd	....	....	....	....	....	....	−2.8	−17.5	11.3	−12.3	16.2	9.9	15.4	2.9	.4
Other Investment Liab., n.i.e.	78bid	....	....	....	....	....	....	13.5	31.3	31.2	14.9	39.6	23.4	16.4	17.3	37.5
Monetary Authorities	78bsd	....	....	....	....	....	....	3.5	8.4	.8	1.9	6.8	−2.0	−9.1	6.8	−1.5
General Government	78btd	....	....	....	....	....	....	17.5	26.7	20.9	10.1	25.3	24.8	20.8	25.4	35.9
Banks	78bud	....	....	....	....	....	....	−.8	3.2	.3	2.2	.1	−4.0	11.5	−6.0	−1.2
Other Sectors	78bvd	....	....	....	....	....	....	−6.8	−7.0	9.2	.7	7.4	4.6	−6.8	−8.9	4.3
Net Errors and Omissions	78cad	....	....	....	....	....	....	−2.0	−5.2	.1	.5	−1.9	14.9	−2.5	−1.1	−3.6
Overall Balance	78cbd	....	....	....	....	....	....	32.6	34.5	.7	61.7	23.0	−6.7	−36.6	−18.4	7.8
Reserves and Related Items	79dad	....	....	....	....	....	....	−32.6	−34.5	−.7	−61.7	−23.0	6.7	36.6	18.4	−7.8
Reserve Assets	79dbd	....	....	....	....	....	....	−32.6	−34.5	−.7	−70.0	−29.3	.1	36.6	18.4	−7.8
Use of Fund Credit and Loans	79dcd	....	....	....	....	....	....	—	—	—	7.5	6.3	.1	—	—	—
Exceptional Financing	79ded	....	....	....	....	....	....	—	—	—	.8	—	6.6			
Government Finance															*Millions of Francs:*	
Deficit (-) or Surplus	80	57	−466	−818	Ɪ−653	−728	−727	−1,225	−1,026	−1,291	−1,618	−1,875	....	....	....	....
Total Revenue and Grants	81y	1,946	1,856	1,880	2,419	3,369	5,010	6,750	8,703	9,180	12,478	13,805	....	....	....	....
Revenue	81	1,946	1,856	1,880	2,419	3,369	4,539	6,749	8,703	9,180	12,478	13,805	....	....	....	....
Grants	81z	—	—	—	—	—	471	1	—	—	—	—	....	....	....	....
Exp. & Lending Minus Repay.	82z	....	....	....	3,072	4,097	5,737	7,975	9,729	10,471	14,096	15,680	....	....	....	....
Expenditure	82	1,888	2,319	2,696	3,069	4,060	5,651	7,881	9,610	10,370	13,790	15,458	....	....	....	....
Lending Minus Repayments	83	1	3	2	Ɪ3	37	86	94	119	101	306	222	....	....	....	....
Statistical Discrepancy	80xx	....	....	....	....	....	....	....	....	....	....	....				
Total Financing																
Total Net Borrowing	84	−236	361	690	653	728	727	1,225	1,026	1,291	1,618	1,875	....	....	....	....
Net Domestic	84a	−192	297	674	521	246	140	−687	−426	−766	−487	1,139	....	....	....	....
Net Foreign	85a	−18	−3	32	235	377	1,321	2,117	2,213	1,567	2,664	2,858	....	....	....	....
Use of Cash Balances	87	−27	66	−16	−103	105	−734	−205	−761	490	−559	−2,122	....	....	....	....
Total Debt by Residence	88	....	....	....	....	....	....	....	....	6,099	9,788	11,547	16,919	....	....	....
Domestic	88a	....	....	....	374	392	470	506	853	824	832	940	....	....	....	....
Foreign	89a	....	....	....	....	....	....	....	5,246	8,964	10,715	15,979	....	....	....	....
National Accounts															*Billions of Francs:*	
Exports of Goods & Services	90c	2.5	2.3	1.9	2.8	3.5	4.8	9.0	10.2	12.0	20.2	15.6	12.1	15.1	16.1	20.0
Government Consumption	91f	1.9	2.2	2.4	2.8	3.4	8.8	10.2	12.1	12.8	13.0	13.5	24.6	16.9	16.7	16.2
Gross Fixed Capital Formation	93e	1.6	2.0	2.2	2.3	3.0	7.0	8.0	9.1	11.3	14.3	13.2	16.0	18.7	20.7	24.6
Increase/Decrease(-) in Stocks	93i	15.7	15.7	16.2	17.4	20.5	.3	.6	1.7	2.1	−2.7	4.2	.3	4.5	−1.5	.5
Private Consumption	96f	19.3	19.5	19.9	19.8	24.9	41.2	46.1	51.2	62.1	74.5	90.0	96.4	107.2	119.2	128.9
Imports of Goods & Services	98c	−3.4	−3.8	−3.7	−3.3	−6.1	−9.3	−12.0	−12.7	−19.3	−21.9	−28.5	−26.7	−31.6	−29.5	−31.2
Gross Domestic Product (GDP)	99b	37.7	38.1	38.9	41.7	49.2	52.8	61.9	71.6	81.1	97.4	108.0	122.6	130.9	142.1	159.1
GDP Volume 1980 Prices	99b.p	80.8	81.8	82.0	84.8	85.4	87.1	88.7	93.3	102.4	112.0	108.0	110.7	115.2	....	....
GDP Volume 1985 Prices	99b.p	....	....	....	....	....	....	....	....	....	....	....	....	163.9	173.7	166.3
GDP Volume 1995 Prices	99b.p	....	....	....	....	....	....	....	....	....	....	....	....	....	....	....
GDP Volume (1995=100)	99bvp	92.4	93.5	93.7	96.9	97.6	99.6	101.4	106.6	117.1	128.0	123.4	126.5	131.7	139.6	133.6
GDP Deflator (1990=100)	99bip	12.1	12.1	12.3	12.8	15.0	15.7	18.1	19.9	20.6	22.6	26.0	28.8	29.5	30.2	35.3
															Millions:	
Population	99z	3.68	3.79	3.90	4.01	4.12	4.20	4.29	4.36	4.80	4.98	5.16	5.35	5.55	5.76	5.87

Percent Per Annum

Interest Rates

	1985	1986	1987	1988	1989	1990	1991	1992	1993	1994	1995	1996	1997	1998	1999	Code
Discount Rate (End of Period)	9.00	9.00	9.00	9.00	9.00	14.00	14.00	11.00	11.00	11.00	16.00	16.00	10.75	11.38	11.19	60
Deposit Rate	6.25	6.25	6.25	6.25	6.31	6.88	8.75	7.73	5.00	....	....	10.92	9.46	8.50	7.95	60l
Lending Rate	13.88	14.00	13.00	12.00	12.00	13.17	19.00	16.67	15.00	....	....	....	....	....	....	60p

Period Averages

Prices

	1985	1986	1987	1988	1989	1990	1991	1992	1993	1994	1995	1996	1997	1998	1999	Code
Consumer Prices	30.6	30.2	31.5	32.4	32.8	34.1	40.8	44.7	50.3	....	100.0	107.4	120.3	127.8	124.7	64

Millions of Francs

International Transactions

	1985	1986	1987	1988	1989	1990	1991	1992	1993	1994	1995	1996	1997	1998	1999	Code
Exports	13,221	16,466	8,949	8,291	7,635	9,224	11,598	8,917	9,427	4,056	14,731	18,569	26,190	18,696	20,388	70
Imports, c.i.f.	30,244	30,624	28,018	28,280	26,642	23,059	38,454	38,263	47,907	17,270	62,193	78,837	89,694	89,218	84,508	71

1995=100

	1985	1986	1987	1988	1989	1990	1991	1992	1993	1994	1995	1996	1997	1998	1999	Code
Volume of Exports	438	544	617	467	441	625	541	484	432	190	100	98	238	255	....	72
Export Prices	45	48	23	....	25	23	32	25	31	31	100	93	140	93	....	74

Balance of Payments

Minus Sign Indicates Debit

	1985	1986	1987	1988	1989	1990	1991	1992	1993	1994	1995	1996	1997	1998	1999	Code
Current Account, n.i.e.	-63.7	-69.2	-134.8	-144.9	-123.0	-108.1	-33.8	-83.3	-129.0	-46.2	57.5	-8.5	-62.2	-143.0	....	78al d
Goods: Exports f.o.b.	126.1	184.1	121.4	117.9	104.7	102.6	95.6	68.5	67.7	32.2	56.7	61.7	93.2	64.5		78aa d
Goods: Imports f.o.b.	-219.3	-259.2	-267.0	-278.6	-254.1	-227.7	-228.1	-240.5	-267.8	-367.4	-219.1	-218.5	-278.2	-262.6		78ab d
Trade Balance	-93.2	-75.1	-145.5	-160.7	-149.4	-125.0	-132.5	-171.9	-200.1	-335.2	-162.5	-156.8	-185.0	-198.1		78ac d
Services: Credit	34.9	43.3	46.2	48.2	43.0	42.2	43.0	31.4	34.3	....	17.9	21.5	51.2	47.2		78ad d
Services: Debit	-114.2	-148.4	-147.0	-134.3	-118.6	-131.1	-111.6	-114.6	-136.4	-109.6	-154.7	-149.7	-198.3	-219.3		78ae d
Balance on Goods & Services	-172.6	-180.2	-246.4	-246.8	-225.0	-213.9	-201.1	-255.1	-302.2	-444.8	-299.2	-284.9	-332.1	-370.2		78af d
Income: Credit	9.2	9.3	10.3	8.7	9.3	4.4	3.5	4.7	3.0	—	24.3	5.4	8.0	8.8		78ag d
Income: Debit	-17.0	-22.4	-24.2	-30.7	-23.4	-20.9	-17.2	-16.1	-18.2	—	-17.5	-18.8	-24.8	-17.3		78ah d
Balance on Gds, Serv. & Inc.	-180.5	-193.2	-260.4	-268.9	-239.1	-230.4	-214.8	-266.5	-317.4	-444.8	-292.5	-298.3	-348.9	-378.7		78ai d
Current Transfers, n.i.e.: Credit	136.7	151.6	155.0	153.0	141.6	147.4	209.3	213.6	208.5	398.6	354.9	293.9	311.6	252.6		78aj d
Current Transfers: Debit	-20.0	-27.6	-29.4	-29.0	-25.5	-25.1	-28.3	-30.4	-20.1	—	-4.9	-4.1	-24.9	-16.9		78ak d
Capital Account, n.i.e.	-.3	—	.4	.4	.5	-.6	-.3	.1	-1.3	—	—	—	—		78bc d
Capital Account, n.i.e.: Credit	1.3	2.0	2.3	2.4	2.7	1.7	2.6	1.9	1.0	—	—	—	—		78ba d
Capital Account: Debit	-1.7	-2.0	-1.9	-2.0	-2.2	-2.4	-2.9	-1.7	-2.4	—	—	—	—		78bb d
Financial Account, n.i.e.	69.3	103.9	122.3	93.7	53.9	55.7	99.1	62.4	88.5	-12.5	-10.7	24.8	46.8	-15.2		78bj d
Direct Investment Abroad																78bd d
Dir. Invest. in Rep. Econ., n.i.e.	14.6	17.6	17.5	21.0	15.5	7.7	4.6	2.2	5.8	—	2.2	2.2	2.6	7.1		78be d
Portfolio Investment Assets	—	—	—	—	—	-.3	-.1	—	—	—	—	-.1	—		78bf d
Equity Securities	—	—	—	—	—	-.3	-.1	—	—	—	—	-.1	—		78bk d
Debt Securities																78bl d
Portfolio Investment Liab., n.i.e.																78bg d
Equity Securities																78bm d
Debt Securities																78bn d
Financial Derivatives Assets																78bw d
Financial Derivatives Liabilities																78bx d
Other Investment Assets	-6.7	-1.6	12.8	17.7	8.8	8.3	23.8	19.2	—	—	-52.0	-13.6	1.2	.8		78bh d
Monetary Authorities																78bo d
General Government	—	—	—	—	—	-.6	-.2	—	—	—	—	—	—		78bp d
Banks	—	—	—	—	—	—	—	—	—	—	-38.6	-13.6	1.2	.8		78bq d
Other Sectors	-6.7	-1.6	12.8	17.7	8.8	8.9	24.0	19.2	—	—	-13.4	—	—		78br d
Other Investment Liab., n.i.e.	61.4	87.9	91.9	55.0	29.6	40.0	70.8	41.0	82.7	-12.5	39.1	36.3	43.0	-23.1		78bi d
Monetary Authorities	-7.0	-1.5	3.6	4.2	-5.7	27.9	-13.6	4.5	3.9	—	—	—	—		78bs d
General Government	59.5	68.2	93.3	66.6	44.7	39.3	75.3	34.6	61.8	-12.5	39.1	37.2	43.0	-22.6		78bt d
Banks	6.6	.3	-2.0	4.1	-5.8	.5	1.0	1.9	7.4	—	—	-.9	—	-.5		78bu d
Other Sectors	2.2	20.9	-3.1	-19.9	-3.5	-27.6	8.0	.2	9.6	—	—	—	—		78bv d
Net Errors and Omissions	-3.6	-4.5	1.5	.4	1.9	30.3	-.2	16.7	-8.1	62.4	5.8	4.1	45.9	29.7		78ca d
Overall Balance	1.7	30.2	-10.6	-50.4	-66.7	-22.9	65.2	-4.0	-49.9	3.7	52.6	20.3	30.5	-128.4		78cb d
Reserves and Related Items	-1.7	-30.2	10.6	50.4	66.7	22.9	-65.2	4.0	49.9	-3.7	-52.6	-20.3	-30.5	128.4		79da d
Reserve Assets	-.1	-27.7	13.3	27.8	48.9	1.2	-77.0	4.0	25.4	-3.7	-66.0	-19.1	-48.4	27.4		79db d
Use of Fund Credit and Loans	-1.6	-2.5	-2.8	-2.9	-2.7	-.8	11.7	—	—	—	13.3	-1.3	17.9	13.5		79dc d
Exceptional Financing				25.5	20.5	22.4	—	—	24.5	—	—	—	—	87.6		79de d

Government Finance

Year Ending December 31

	1985	1986	1987	1988	1989	1990	1991	1992	1993	1994	1995	1996	1997	1998	1999	Code
Deficit (-) or Surplus	....	....	....		-6,317[P]	-11,280[P]	-7,551[P]	-21,211	-25,218	-18,983	-10,694	-27,046	-14,921	-32,137	-40,334	80
Total Revenue and Grants					31,278[P]	29,015[P]	39,738[P]	44,289	44,005	7,547	60,033	70,935	98,398	87,930	129,466	81y
Revenue					25,987[P]	23,144[P]	26,056[P]	27,563	25,865	6,032	23,128	39,534	57,677	65,986	65,866	81
Grants					5,291[P]	5,871[P]	13,682[P]	16,726	18,140	1,515	36,905	31,401	40,721	21,944	63,600	81z
Exp. & Lending Minus Repay.					37,595[P]	40,295[P]	47,289[P]	65,500	69,223	26,530	70,727	97,981	113,319	120,067	169,800	82z
Expenditure					37,706[P]	40,436[P]	47,658[P]	65,635	67,189	26,560	70,727	97,981	113,908	120,228	168,200	82
Lending Minus Repayments					-111[P]	-141[P]	-369[P]	-135	2,034	-30	—	—	-589	-161	1,600	83
Statistical Discrepancy								4,081	12,006	15,569	13,094	10,511	991	-6,816	-5,116	80xx

Total Financing

	1985	1986	1987	1988	1989	1990	1991	1992	1993	1994	1995	1996	1997	1998	1999	Code
Total Net Borrowing					6,317	11,280[P]	7,551[P]	17,130	13,212	3,414	-2,400	16,535	13,930	38,953	45,450	84
Net Domestic					2,216	5,910[P]	767[P]	6,608	4,643	5,856	-14,192	3,600	200	4,287	9,750	84a
Net Foreign					4,101[P]	5,370[P]	6,784[P]	10,522	8,569	-2,442	11,792	12,935	13,730	34,666	35,700	85a
Use of Cash Balances					241[P]	-1,138[P]	-3,039[P]	....	....	....	....	....	....	....	....	87
Total Debt by Residence					66,595[P]	106,297[P]	114,512[P]	....	....	....	....	....	....	485,908	535,065	88
Domestic					17,179[P]	23,773[P]	25,500[P]	....	....	....	....	....	....	85,338	91,190	88a
Foreign					49,416[P]	82,524[P]	89,012[P]	....	....	....	....	....	....	400,570	443,875	89a

National Accounts

Billions of Francs

	1985	1986	1987	1988	1989	1990	1991	1992	1993	1994	1995	1996	1997	1998	1999	Code
Exports of Goods & Services	18.7	21.4	16.9	16.1	16.4	12.3	17.9	15.7	15.2	10.0	20.0	26.0	44.0	35.0	36.5	90c
Government Consumption	19.5	20.1	23.2	17.0	17.0	22.0	28.9	35.2	32.9	13.6	30.9	44.0	49.9	54.5	61.2	91f
Gross Fixed Capital Formation	27.0	26.8	26.9	25.5	25.7	31.3	33.5	45.8	51.5	19.0	51.3	66.8	84.5	99.5	114.3	93e
Increase/Decrease(-) in Stocks	3.0	.2	—	1.0	.1	-1.1	-2.9	-.1	-1.9	-2.0	-1.3	—	—	....	....	93i
Private Consumption	139.8	134.7	137.9	149.4	159.5	178.6	202.5	222.0	241.0	230.0	334.0	408.0	529.0	590.0	540.8	96f
Imports of Goods & Services	-34.5	-34.3	-36.1	-34.5	-34.9	-30.0	-43.1	-50.0	-58.0	-107.1	-98.0	-113.0	-143.0	-147.0	-117.1	98c
Gross Domestic Product (GDP)	173.7	170.2	171.2	175.9	190.1	213.5	237.9	269.0	282.0	166.0	337.0	431.0	561.6	632.0	635.7	99b
GDP Volume 1980 Prices	173.6	183.2	182.1	191.2	192.1	195.9	....	....	....	....	....	....	....	....	....	99b.p
GDP Volume 1995 Prices						527.6	507.5	542.6	497.2	250.4	335.2	387.6	438.9	480.6	508.7	99b.p
GDP Volume (1995=100)	139.5	147.2	146.3	153.6	154.3	157.4	151.4	161.8	148.3	74.7	100.0	115.6	130.9	143.4	151.7	99bv p
GDP Deflator (1990=100)	37.0	34.3	34.7	34.0	36.5	40.3	46.6	49.3	56.4	65.9	100.0	110.6	127.3	130.8	124.3	99bi p

Midyear Estimates

	1985	1986	1987	1988	1989	1990	1991	1992	1993	1994	1995	1996	1997	1998	1999	Code
Population	6.06	6.24	6.42	6.87	7.03	7.18	6.71	6.25	5.74	5.37	5.26	5.48	5.96	6.60	7.24	99z

(See notes in the back of the book.)

St. Kitts and Nevis

		1970	1971	1972	1973	1974	1975	1976	1977	1978	1979	1980	1981	1982	1983	1984
Exchange Rates													*E. Caribbean Dollars per SDR:*			
Official Rate	aa	2.0053	2.0417	2.2194	2.4925	2.5024	2.7770	3.1369	3.2797	3.5175	3.5568	3.4436	3.1427	2.9784	2.8268	2.6466
													E. Caribbean Dollars per US Dollar			
Official Rate	ae	2.0053	1.8805	2.0442	2.0661	2.0439	2.3721	2.7000	2.7000	2.7000	2.7000	2.7000	2.7000	2.7000	2.7000	2.7000
													Index Numbers (1995=100):			
Nominal Effective Exchange Rate	ne c	...	...	...	...	...	...	...	...	...	85.33	83.18	86.69	90.74	94.70	99.72
Real Effective Exchange Rate	re c	...	...	...	...	...	...	...	...	...	112.91	112.37	116.08	119.23	120.52	122.83
Fund Position													*Millions of SDRs:*			
Quota	2f. s	...	...	...	...	...	...	...	...	...	...	...	...	...	...	4.50
SDRs	1b. s	...	...	...	...	...	...	...	...	...	...	...	...	...	...	—
Reserve Position in the Fund	1c. s	...	...	...	...	...	...	...	...	...	...	...	...	...	...	—
Total Fund Cred.&Loans Outstg.	2tl	...	...	...	...	...	...	...	...	...	...	...	...	...	...	—
International Liquidity													*Millions of US Dollars Unless Otherwise Indicated:*			
Total Reserves minus Gold	1l. d	...	...	...	...	...	...	...	...	...	...	...	4.02	3.33	3.15	5.65
SDRs	1b. d	...	...	...	...	...	...	...	...	...	...	...	—	—	—	—
Reserve Position in the Fund	1c. d	...	...	...	...	...	...	...	...	...	...	...	—	—	—	—
Foreign Exchange	1d. d	...	...	...	...	...	...	...	...	...	...	...	4.02	3.33	3.15	5.65
Deposit Money Banks: Assets	7a. d	...	...	...	...	...	...	...	...	...	22.18	33.13	15.48	12.37	24.81	21.86
Liabilities	7b. d	...	...	...	...	...	...	...	...	...	11.25	13.71	14.91	10.65	24.34	17.47
Monetary Authorities													*Millions of E. Caribbean Dollars:*			
Foreign Assets	11	...	...	...	...	...	...	...	...	...	3.65	—	20.27	11.01	14.44	15.26
Claims on Central Government	12a	...	...	...	...	...	...	...	...	...	3.36	3.36	3.36	5.91	6.40	14.10
Claims on Deposit Money Banks	12e	...	...	...	...	...	...	...	...	...	—	—	—	—	—	1.03
Reserve Money	14	...	...	...	...	...	...	...	...	...	7.01	3.36	23.63	16.92	20.84	30.39
of which: Currency Outside DMBs	14a	...	...	...	...	...	...	...	...	...	...	...	10.33	11.10	11.59	12.61
Foreign Liabilities	16c	...	...	...	...	...	...	...	...	...	—	—	—	—	—	—
Central Government Deposits	16d	...	...	...	...	...	...	...	...	...	—	—	—	—	—	—
Other Items (Net)	17r	...	...	...	...	...	...	...	...	...	—	—	—	—	—	—
Deposit Money Banks													*Millions of E. Caribbean Dollars:*			
Reserves	20	...	...	...	...	...	...	...	...	...	8.56	4.20	13.29	5.82	9.25	17.33
Foreign Assets	21	...	...	...	...	...	...	...	...	...	59.89	89.45	41.78	33.40	66.99	59.01
Claims on Central Government	22a	...	...	...	...	...	...	...	...	...	6.94	5.00	6.68	15.26	21.97	26.76
Claims on Local Government	22b	...	...	...	...	...	...	...	...	...	—	—	—	—	—	—
Claims on Nonfin.Pub.Enterprises	22c	...	...	...	...	...	...	...	...	...	8.19	21.48	32.57	35.78	43.60	45.51
Claims on Private Sector	22d	...	...	...	...	...	...	...	...	...	43.24	52.77	67.40	75.71	84.80	96.58
Claims on Nonbank Financial Insts	22g	...	...	...	...	...	...	...	...	...	3.36	.36	.31	.31	.30	.29
Demand Deposits	24	...	...	...	...	...	...	...	...	...	10.81	9.34	16.09	14.39	15.99	16.64
Time, Savings,& Fgn.Currency Dep.	25	...	...	...	...	...	...	...	...	...	74.73	87.31	90.41	105.43	123.11	141.64
Foreign Liabilities	26c	...	...	...	...	...	...	...	...	...	30.37	37.02	40.26	28.74	65.71	47.18
Central Government Deposits	26d	...	...	...	...	...	...	...	...	...	15.62	21.87	18.10	22.56	24.29	33.87
Credit from Monetary Authorities	26g	...	...	...	...	...	...	...	...	...	5.70	5.44	3.65	2.81	3.16	.58
Capital Accounts	27a	...	...	...	...	...	...	...	...	...	7.29	10.02	13.35	12.30	13.80	13.70
Other Items (Net)	27r	...	...	...	...	...	...	...	...	...	−14.32	2.25	−19.82	−19.94	−19.15	−8.12
Monetary Survey													*Millions of E. Caribbean Dollars:*			
Foreign Assets (Net)	31n	...	...	...	...	...	...	...	...	...	33.17	52.43	21.79	15.66	15.71	27.10
Domestic Credit	32	...	...	...	...	...	...	...	...	...	49.48	61.08	92.22	110.42	132.78	149.38
Claims on Central Govt. (Net)	32an	...	...	...	...	...	...	...	...	...	−5.32	−13.52	−8.06	−1.39	4.08	7.00
Claims on Local Government	32b	...	...	...	...	...	...	...	...	...	—	—	—	—	—	—
Claims on Nonfin.Pub.Enterprises	32c	...	...	...	...	...	...	...	...	...	8.19	21.48	32.57	35.78	43.60	45.51
Claims on Private Sector	32d	...	...	...	...	...	...	...	...	...	43.24	52.77	67.40	75.71	84.80	96.58
Claims on Nonbank Financial Inst	32g	...	...	...	...	...	...	...	...	...	3.36	.36	.31	.31	.30	.29
Money	34	...	...	...	...	...	...	...	...	...	9.25	8.02	26.42	25.49	27.58	29.26
Quasi-Money	35	...	...	...	...	...	...	...	...	...	74.73	87.31	90.41	105.43	123.11	141.64
Capital Accounts	37a	...	...	...	...	...	...	...	...	...	7.29	10.02	13.35	12.30	13.80	13.70
Other Items (Net)	37r	...	...	...	...	...	...	...	...	...	−8.62	8.17	−16.17	−17.14	−15.99	−8.12
Money plus Quasi-Money	35l	...	...	...	...	...	...	...	...	...	83.98	95.32	116.84	130.92	150.69	170.90
Interest Rates													*Percent Per Annum*			
Treasury Bill Rate	60c	...	...	...	...	...	...	...	...	...	...	6.5	6.5	6.5	6.5	6.5
Deposit Rate	60l	...	...	...	...	...	...	...	...	...	...	6.0	6.0	6.0	6.0	6.0
Lending Rate	60p	...	...	...	...	...	...	...	...	...	...	...	9.0	9.0	9.0	10.0
Prices													*Index Numbers (1995=100):*			
Consumer Prices	64	...	...	...	...	...	...	...	...	...	53.3	62.8	69.3	73.4	75.1	77.2

	1985	1986	1987	1988	1989	1990	1991	1992	1993	1994	1995	1996	1997	1998	1999		
End of Period																**Exchange Rates**	
	2.9657	3.3026	3.8304	3.6334	3.5482	3.8412	3.8622	3.7125	3.7086	3.9416	4.0135	3.8825	3.6430	3.8017	3.7058	Official Rate.................................	**aa**
End of Period (ae)																	
	2.7000	2.7000	2.7000	2.7000	2.7000	2.7000	2.7000	2.7000	2.7000	2.7000	2.7000	2.7000	2.7000	2.7000	2.7000	Official Rate.................................	**ae**
Period Averages																	
	101.84	101.75	99.12	96.97	100.86	99.22	99.27	98.51	102.47	102.38	100.00	101.34	103.74	104.73	105.01	Nominal Effective Exchange Rate .... **ne c**	
	122.37	118.12	110.85	103.67	106.12	102.39	101.99	100.65	103.49	102.26	100.00	100.80	109.54	112.51	115.38	Real Effective Exchange Rate .... **re c**	
End of Period																**Fund Position**	
	4.50	4.50	4.50	4.50	4.50	4.50	4.50	6.50	6.50	6.50	6.50	6.50	6.50	6.50	8.90	Quota	**2f. s**
	—	—	—	—	—	—	—	—	—	—	—	—	—	—	—	SDRs	**1b. s**
	—	.01	.01	.01	.01	.01	.01	.01	.02	.01	.01	.01	.01	.01	.07	Reserve Position in the Fund	**1c. s**
															1.63	1.63	Total Fund Cred.&Loans Outstg.	**2tl**
End of Period																**International Liquidity**	
	7.41	10.23	10.57	10.32	16.39	16.28	16.63	26.24	29.42	31.82	33.47	32.73	36.07	46.80	49.58	Total Reserves minus Gold.....................	**1l. d**
	—	.01	.01	.01	.01	.01	.01	.01	.02	.02	.02	.02	.02	.02	.10	SDRs	**1b. d**
																Reserve Position in the Fund	**1c. d**
	7.41	10.22	10.56	10.31	16.38	16.27	16.62	26.23	29.40	31.80	33.45	32.71	36.05	46.78	49.48	Foreign Exchange	**1d. d**
	27.92	27.22	46.98	43.06	31.40	32.62	33.68	45.57	59.65	70.62	76.69	88.78	121.88	123.28	112.59	Deposit Money Banks: Assets	**7a. d**
	24.21	20.99	33.53	29.20	22.35	22.52	27.24	45.10	58.96	73.35	77.53	90.28	106.08	105.06	125.20	Liabilities...........	**7b. d**
End of Period																**Monetary Authorities**	
	20.02	27.63	28.56	27.86	44.27	43.97	44.96	70.93	79.54	85.80	90.37	88.38	97.38	119.22	132.86	Foreign Assets	**11**
	16.07	16.04	16.03	14.91	10.71	14.63	14.15	7.80	8.34	4.95	4.42	4.01	3.20	8.73	8.56	Claims on Central Government	**12a**
	.21	.10	1.68	1.61	.06	.05	.05	.03	.01	3.52	.01		.01			Claims on Deposit Money Banks	**12e**
	36.30	43.77	46.27	44.39	55.04	58.65	59.10	78.70	87.89	94.27	92.80	89.87	95.75	114.65	129.44	Reserve Money	**14**
	9.39	12.22	13.00	16.08	22.65	21.43	23.86	23.04	28.08	28.28	30.29	32.38	31.85	35.84	41.45	*of which: Currency Outside DMBs*	**14a**
	—	—	—	—	—	—	—	—	—	—	—	—	—	6.18	6.02	Foreign Liabilities...........................	**16c**
	—	—	—	—	—	—	.06	.06	—	—	2.00	2.52	4.84	7.12	5.96	Central Government Deposits	**16d**
	—	—	—	—	—	—	—	—	—	—	—	—	—	—	—	Other Items (Net)	**17r**
End of Period																**Deposit Money Banks**	
	26.81	30.54	33.22	30.10	32.62	34.68	38.69	57.09	63.95	65.79	65.14	58.01	65.65	78.64	89.69	Reserves	**20**
	75.39	73.49	126.85	116.25	84.79	88.07	90.93	123.05	161.06	190.68	207.07	239.71	329.07	332.85	303.98	Foreign Assets	**21**
	35.65	41.21	39.37	48.48	53.56	65.95	71.31	70.63	57.69	63.70	84.07	118.44	89.62	128.11	154.16	Claims on Central Government	**22a**
				5.49	5.69	6.33	6.88	6.57	7.52	6.97	8.50	7.34	6.41	12.29	18.18	Claims on Local Government	**22b**
	56.20	58.20	2.31	8.52	19.75	34.55	31.64	30.17	32.46	41.50	87.13	105.10	117.67	134.96	160.45	Claims on Nonfin.Pub.Enterprises...........	**22c**
	104.76	102.64	122.81	170.08	223.98	231.91	262.49	334.56	375.78	416.36	440.86	465.57	521.06	563.67	610.17	Claims on Private Sector	**22d**
	.25	.25	.25	.25	.25	.25	1.00	1.00	1.18	.03	.50	1.10	1.69	3.70	5.77	Claims on Nonbank Financial Insts	**22g**
	23.51	37.59	42.25	32.40	38.58	38.56	36.49	42.07	47.83	44.54	52.86	56.38	55.80	71.88	72.52	Demand Deposits	**24**
	171.31	182.75	156.98	182.42	218.54	241.44	258.69	302.55	332.09	339.43	390.56	395.15	465.57	506.96	524.01	Time, Savings,& Fgn.Currency Dep........	**25**
	65.36	56.68	90.52	78.85	60.36	60.81	73.55	121.76	159.18	198.05	209.32	243.75	286.42	283.67	338.05	Foreign Liabilities	**26c**
	28.88	11.92	12.14	45.43	61.47	70.68	81.52	100.42	112.65	141.51	169.22	194.81	202.28	225.67	256.83	Central Government Deposits	**26d**
	1.02	2.90	.65	—	1.88	—	.03	—	3.50	3.50	4.87	11.71	4.65	10.60	7.67	Credit from Monetary Authorities	**26g**
	14.25	16.88	22.00	24.22	33.96	42.13	51.90	55.82	58.70	63.12	73.89	90.49	108.25	121.57	120.19	Capital Accounts	**27a**
	−5.28	−2.39	.27	15.85	5.85	8.10	.75	.46	−14.32	−5.12	−7.45	2.99	8.20	33.87	23.15	Other Items (Net)	**27r**
End of Period																**Monetary Survey**	
	30.05	44.45	64.88	65.26	68.70	71.22	62.34	72.22	81.42	78.44	88.12	84.34	140.04	162.22	92.77	Foreign Assets (Net)	**31n**
	184.04	206.41	168.64	202.31	252.47	282.93	305.88	350.24	370.31	391.99	454.26	504.23	532.52	618.67	694.52	Domestic Credit	**32**
	22.84	45.32	43.26	17.97	2.80	9.90	3.88	−22.06	−46.62	−72.86	−82.74	−74.88	−114.30	−95.95	−100.06	Claims on Central Govt. (Net)	**32an**
	—	—	—	5.49	5.69	6.33	6.88	6.57	7.52	6.97	8.50	7.34	6.41	12.29	18.18	Claims on Local Government	**32b**
	56.20	58.20	2.31	8.52	19.75	34.55	31.64	30.17	32.46	41.50	87.13	105.10	117.67	134.96	160.45	Claims on Nonfin.Pub.Enterprises	**32c**
	104.76	102.64	122.81	170.08	223.98	231.91	262.49	334.56	375.78	416.36	440.86	465.57	521.06	563.67	610.17	Claims on Private Sector	**32d**
	.25	.25	.25	.25	.25	.25	1.00	1.00	1.18	.03	.50	1.10	1.69	3.70	5.77	Claims on Nonbank Financial Inst	**32g**
	32.90	49.81	55.26	48.48	61.23	59.99	60.35	65.12	75.92	72.84	83.17	88.79	87.88	107.74	114.08	Money	**34**
	171.31	182.75	156.98	182.42	218.54	241.44	258.69	302.55	332.09	339.43	390.56	395.15	465.57	506.96	524.01	Quasi-Money.................................	**35**
	14.25	16.88	22.00	24.22	33.96	42.13	51.90	55.82	58.70	63.12	73.89	90.49	108.25	121.57	120.19	Capital Accounts	**37a**
	−4.37	1.42	−.71	12.44	7.43	10.59	−2.72	−1.02	−14.98	−4.95	−5.24	14.14	10.86	44.62	29.01	Other Items (Net)	**37r**
	204.21	232.56	212.24	230.90	279.78	301.44	319.04	367.66	408.01	412.26	473.73	483.94	553.45	614.70	638.09	Money plus Quasi-Money	**35l**
Percent Per Annum																**Interest Rates**	
	6.5	6.5	6.5	6.5	6.5	6.5	6.5	6.5	6.5	6.5	6.5	6.5	6.5	6.5	6.5	Treasury Bill Rate.........................	**60c**
	6.3	6.0	5.3	7.0	7.0	7.0	7.0	7.0	5.5	5.5	5.5	5.5	5.5	5.5	5.5	Deposit Rate.................................	**60l**
	10.2	10.2	12.0	12.0	12.0	12.0	12.0	12.7	13.0	13.0	12.6	12.3	13.0	13.0	11.5	Lending Rate.................................	**60p**
Period Averages																**Prices**	
	79.2	79.2	79.9	80.1	84.3	87.7	91.4	94.1	95.7	97.1	100.0	102.1	111.2	115.0	119.5	Consumer Prices...........................	**64**

St. Kitts and Nevis

		1970	1971	1972	1973	1974	1975	1976	1977	1978	1979	1980	1981	1982	1983	1984
International Transactions														*Millions of E. Caribbean Dollars*		
Exports	70	8	8	12	17	24	47	46	41	45	45	64	66	51	50	54
Imports, c.i.f.	71	23	31	31	36	39	51	58	59	65	87	121	129	118	139	140
Balance of Payments															*Millions of US Dollars*	
Current Account, n.i.e.	78al d	...	...	...	...	...	...	...	...	...	...	−2.66	−4.70	−8.72	−14.74	−4.34
Goods: Exports f.o.b.	78aa d	...	...	...	...	...	...	...	...	...	...	24.12	24.26	18.84	18.43	20.15
Goods: Imports f.o.b.	78ab d	...	...	...	...	...	...	...	...	...	...	−40.80	−43.42	−39.82	−46.74	−47.23
Trade Balance	78ac d	...	...	...	...	...	...	...	...	...	...	−16.68	−19.16	−20.99	−28.32	−27.09
Services: Credit	78ad d	...	...	...	...	...	...	...	...	...	...	8.10	10.00	13.20	13.00	20.32
Services: Debit	78ae d	...	...	...	...	...	...	...	...	...	...	−5.84	−7.19	−12.64	−10.82	−9.17
Balance on Goods & Services	78af d	...	...	...	...	...	...	...	...	...	...	−14.42	−16.35	−20.42	−26.14	−15.94
Income: Credit	78ag d	...	...	...	...	...	...	...	...	...	...	.70	1.20	1.30	1.80	.90
Income: Debit	78ah d	...	...	...	...	...	...	...	...	...	...	−1.94	−2.24	−.70	−.70	−.80
Balance on Gds, Serv. & Inc.	78ai d	...	...	...	...	...	...	...	...	...	...	−15.66	−17.40	−19.82	−25.04	−15.84
Current Transfers, n.i.e.: Credit	78aj d	...	...	...	...	...	...	...	...	...	...	13.00	12.70	13.10	13.20	14.80
Current Transfers: Debit	78ak d	...	...	...	...	...	...	...	...	...	...	—	—	−2.00	−2.90	−3.30
Capital Account, n.i.e.	78bc d	...	...	...	...	...	...	...	...	...	...	—	—	—	—	—
Capital Account, n.i.e.: Credit	78ba d	...	...	...	...	...	...	...	...	...	...	—	—	—	—	—
Capital Account: Debit	78bb d	...	...	...	...	...	...	...	...	...	...	—	—	—	—	—
Financial Account, n.i.e.	78bj d	...	...	...	...	...	...	...	...	...	...	4.94	5.70	1.74	15.55	7.35
Direct Investment Abroad	78bd d	...	...	...	...	...	...	...	...	...	...	—	—	—	—	—
Dir. Invest. in Rep. Econ., n.i.e.	78be d	...	...	...	...	...	...	...	...	...	...	1.00	.90	2.20	13.50	6.00
Portfolio Investment Assets	78bf d	...	...	...	...	...	...	...	...	...	...	—	—	—	—	—
Equity Securities	78bk d	...	...	...	...	...	...	...	...	...	...	—	—	—	—	—
Debt Securities	78bl d	...	...	...	...	...	...	...	...	...	...	—	—	—	—	—
Portfolio Investment Liab., n.i.e.	78bg d	...	...	...	...	...	...	...	...	...	...	—	—	—	—	—
Equity Securities	78bm d	...	...	...	...	...	...	...	...	...	...	—	—	—	—	—
Debt Securities	78bn d	...	...	...	...	...	...	...	...	...	...	—	—	—	—	—
Financial Derivatives Assets	78bw d	...	...	...	...	...	...	...	...	...	...	...	...	...	...	...
Financial Derivatives Liabilities	78bx d	...	...	...	...	...	...	...	...	...	...	...	...	...	...	...
Other Investment Assets	78bh d	...	...	...	...	...	...	...	...	...	...	—	—	3.10	−12.44	2.95
Monetary Authorities	78bo d	...	...	...	...	...	...	...	...	...	...	—	—	—	—	...
General Government	78bp d	...	...	...	...	...	...	...	...	...	...	—	—	—	—	...
Banks	78bq d	...	...	...	...	...	...	...	...	...	...	—	—	3.10	−12.44	2.95
Other Sectors	78br d	...	...	...	...	...	...	...	...	...	...	—	—	—	—	...
Other Investment Liab., n.i.e.	78bi d	...	...	...	...	...	...	...	...	...	...	3.94	4.80	−3.57	14.49	−1.60
Monetary Authorities	78bs d	...	...	...	...	...	...	...	...	...	...	...	...	...	...	...
General Government	78bt d	...	...	...	...	...	...	...	...	...	...	.59	.58	.20	.10	3.70
Banks	78bu d	...	...	...	...	...	...	...	...	...	...	—	3.50	−4.27	13.69	−7.00
Other Sectors	78bv d	...	...	...	...	...	...	...	...	...	...	3.36	.72	.50	.70	1.70
Net Errors and Omissions	78ca d	...	...	...	...	...	...	...	...	...	...	−3.88	−.90	3.19	.39	−1.21
Overall Balance	78cb d	...	...	...	...	...	...	...	...	...	...	−1.60	.10	−3.80	1.20	1.80
Reserves and Related Items	79da d	...	...	...	...	...	...	...	...	...	...	1.60	−.10	3.80	−1.20	−1.80
Reserve Assets	79db d	...	...	...	...	...	...	...	...	...	...	1.60	−.10	3.80	−1.20	−1.80
Use of Fund Credit and Loans	79dc d	...	...	...	...	...	...	...	...	...	...	—	—	—	—	—
Exceptional Financing	79de d	...	...	...	...	...	...	...	...	...	...	—	—	—	—	—
Government Finance														*Millions of E. Caribbean Dollars*		
Deficit (-) or Surplus	80	...	...	...	...	...	...	...	...	...	...	...	...	...	...	...
Revenue	81	...	...	...	...	...	...	...	...	...	...	...	...	...	...	...
Grants Received	81z	...	...	...	...	...	...	...	...	...	...	...	...	...	...	...
Expenditure	82	...	...	...	...	...	...	...	...	...	...	...	...	...	...	...
Lending Minus Repayments	83	...	...	...	...	...	...	...	...	...	...	...	...	...	...	...
Financing																
Domestic	84a	...	...	...	...	...	...	...	...	...	...	...	...	...	...	...
Foreign	85a	...	...	...	...	...	...	...	...	...	...	...	...	...	...	...
National Accounts														*Millions of E. Caribbean Dollars*		
Exports of Goods & Services	90c	...	...	...	16.6	...	46.8	...	51.5	58.6	64.3	86.7	92.2	80.6	78.8	104.1
Government Consumption	91f	...	...	...	10.5	...	12.1	...	16.1	20.6	22.9	27.1	39.7	36.5	36.8	45.4
Gross Fixed Capital Formation	93e	...	...	...	7.1	...	7.7	...	30.8	25.1	37.3	49.4	46.1	55.0	59.9	57.1
Private Consumption	96f	...	...	...	47.4	...	57.1	...	47.2	57.3	73.5	92.3	108.9	120.0	133.1	139.6
Imports of Goods & Services	98c	...	...	...	−35.6	...	−51.4	...	−64.8	−69.1	−90.2	−125.9	−136.6	−130.4	−150.4	−157.1
Gross Domestic Product (GDP)	99b	...	...	...	48.6	...	74.1	75.5	80.7	92.5	107.7	129.7	152.8	161.8	161.2	189.1
GDP Volume (1995=100)	99bv p	...	...	...	...	...	...	...	45.9	49.3	53.8	58.2	58.9	58.0	57.4	63.4
GDP Deflator (1995=100)	99bi p	...	...	...	...	...	...	...	28.2	30.1	32.1	35.8	41.6	44.8	45.1	47.9
																Millions:
Population	99z	.04	.04	.04	.04	.04	.04	.04	.04	.04	.04	.04	.04	.04	.05	.04

	1985	1986	1987	1988	1989	1990	1991	1992	1993	1994	1995	1996	1997	1998	1999		
International Transactions																	
Millions of E. Caribbean Dollars																	
Exports	55	68	76	74	77	75	74	71	73	61	51	59	....	....	....	70
Imports, c.i.f.	139	170	215	252	277	298	297	257	319	345	359	403	....	....	....	71
Balance of Payments																	
Minus Sign Indicates Debit																	
Current Account, n.i.e.	-6.68	-8.90	-16.11	-27.53	-38.37	-46.97	-34.90	-15.76	-30.07	-26.44	....	....				78al d
Goods: Exports f.o.b.	20.37	26.12	28.72	28.41	29.20	28.32	28.58	33.00	31.93	29.29	....	....				78aa d
Goods: Imports f.o.b.	-46.70	-55.35	-69.96	-81.96	-90.19	-97.44	-97.05	-84.15	-94.57	-98.27	....	....				78ab d
Trade Balance	-26.33	-29.23	-41.23	-53.56	-60.98	-69.12	-68.47	-51.16	-62.64	-68.98	....	....				78ac d
Services: Credit	22.80	31.72	40.41	46.75	50.00	54.06	68.39	79.11	83.72	91.67	....	....				78ad d
Services: Debit	-10.32	-17.17	-21.40	-24.90	-29.22	-34.93	-35.35	-41.26	-46.46	-45.57	....	....				78ae d
Balance on Goods & Services	-13.84	-14.68	-22.22	-31.70	-40.20	-49.98	-35.43	-13.31	-25.38	-22.89	....	....				78af d
Income: Credit	.30	2.27	3.21	4.51	3.54	3.31	2.65	2.51	2.14	2.86	....	....				78ag d
Income: Debit	-1.60	-3.96	-4.98	-8.63	-12.71	-7.77	-9.87	-12.98	-14.81	-15.90	....	....				78ah d
Balance on Gds, Serv. & Inc.	-15.14	-16.37	-23.99	-35.83	-49.36	-54.44	-42.66	-23.79	-38.05	-35.92	....	....				78ai d
Current Transfers, n.i.e.: Credit	12.62	9.56	10.58	11.80	17.68	17.17	13.94	13.74	14.16	15.15	....	....				78aj d
Current Transfers: Debit	-4.15	-2.09	-2.71	-3.50	-6.69	-9.70	-6.18	-5.72	-6.18	-5.67	....	....				78ak d
Capital Account, n.i.e.	—	5.19	6.90	7.60	5.14	2.43	3.84	3.67	3.33	1.73	....	....				78bc d
Capital Account, n.i.e.: Credit	—	5.37	7.10	7.80	5.34	3.05	3.84	3.83	3.53	2.61	....	....				78ba d
Capital Account: Debit	—	-.19	-.20	-.20	-.20	-.62	—	-.17	-.20	-.88	....	....				78bb d
Financial Account, n.i.e.	9.15	5.83	13.70	18.78	51.16	51.06	25.23	23.56	15.22	26.05	....	....				78bj d
Direct Investment Abroad	—	—	—	—	—	—	—	—	—	—	....	....				78bd d
Dir. Invest. in Rep. Econ., n.i.e.	8.00	9.20	16.65	13.13	40.80	48.79	21.44	12.51	13.71	15.34	....	....				78be d
Portfolio Investment Assets	—	—	—	—	—	—	-.07	—	2.22	—	....	....				78bf d
Equity Securities	—	—	—	—	—	—	-.07	—	2.22	—	....	....				78bk d
Debt Securities	—	—	—	—	—	—	—	—	—	—	....	....				78bl d
Portfolio Investment Liab., n.i.e.	—	—	—	—	—	—	—	—	2.22	—	....	....				78bg d
Equity Securities	—	—	—	—	—	—	—	—	2.22	—	....	....				78bm d
Debt Securities	—	—	—	—	—	—	—	—	—	—	....	....				78bn d
Financial Derivatives Assets	....	....	....	—	—	—	—	—	—	—	....	....				78bw d
Financial Derivatives Liabilities	....	....	....	—	—	—	—	—	—	—	....	....				78bx d
Other Investment Assets	-5.90	-1.76	-7.44	-.40	4.80	-1.05	3.66	5.95	-.20	3.43	....	....				78bh d
Monetary Authorities	—	—	—	—	—	—	—	—	—	—	....	....				78bo d
General Government	—	—	—	—	—	—	—	—	—	—	....	....				78bp d
Banks	-5.90	-1.76	-7.44	-.40	4.80	-1.05	3.66	5.95	-.20	3.43	....	....				78bq d
Other Sectors	—	—	—	—	—	—	—	—	—	—	....	....				78br d
Other Investment Liab., n.i.e.	7.05	-1.61	4.49	6.04	5.56	3.33	.20	5.10	-2.73	7.28	....	....				78bi d
Monetary Authorities	—	—	—	—	—	—	—	—	—	—	....	....				78bs d
General Government	.40	-1.56	4.62	5.85	5.99	3.38	.41	1.28	2.02	3.65	....	....				78bt d
Banks	5.65	—	—	—	—	—	—	—	—	—	....	....				78bu d
Other Sectors	1.00	-.05	-.13	.19	-.43	-.05	-.21	3.82	-4.75	3.63	....	....				78bv d
Net Errors and Omissions	-.53	.89	-3.94	1.07	-11.59	-6.43	6.48	-1.65	14.89	.98	....	....				78ca d
Overall Balance	1.94	3.01	.54	-.08	6.33	.09	.65	9.81	3.37	2.32	....	....				78cb d
Reserves and Related Items	-1.94	-3.01	-.54	.08	-6.33	-.09	-.65	-9.81	-3.37	-2.32	....	....				79da d
Reserve Assets	-1.94	-3.01	-.54	.08	-6.33	-.09	-.65	-9.81	-3.37	-2.32	....	....				79db d
Use of Fund Credit and Loans	—	—	—	—	—	—	—	—	—	—	....	....				79dc d
Exceptional Financing	—	—	—	—	—	—	—	—	—	—	....	....				79de d
Government Finance																	
Year Ending December 31																	
Deficit (-) or Surplus	-13.12	2.85	-47.46	I -23.95	-3.77	-.05	-1.28	6.61	9.90	6.77 P	....	....				80
Revenue	59.95	71.71	82.26	I 93.57	111.60	122.87	121.43	137.42	165.33	181.84 P	....	....				81
Grants Received	4.07	5.45	7.99	11.81	7.52	3.45	4.97	2.79	.59	1.64 P	....	....				81z
Expenditure	74.57	71.75	80.90	I 124.79	122.13	123.69	126.51	134.97	155.98	176.49 P	....	....				82
Lending Minus Repayments	2.57	2.56	56.81	4.54	.76	2.68	1.17	-1.37	.04	.22 P	....	....				83
Financing																	
Domestic	....	....	....	I 3.83	-9.06	-1.58	-.39	-5.37	-14.20	-10.88 P	....	....				84a
Foreign	....	....	....	I 20.12	12.83	1.63	1.67	-1.24	4.30	4.11 P	....	....				85a
National Accounts																	
Millions of E. Caribbean Dollars																	
Exports of Goods & Services	116.6	156.2	186.7	202.9	215.8	224.3	263.9	287.9	312.3	324.6	300.1	321.3	....		....	90c
Government Consumption	47.4	50.3	56.7	60.2	68.7	79.2	79.9	82.9	92.2	111.1	126.5	132.7	....		....	91f
Gross Fixed Capital Formation	63.9	69.4	98.0	191.3	224.8	238.1	190.8	191.6	242.8	227.9	228.4	175.6	....		....	93e
Private Consumption	146.7	177.0	199.9	179.7	204.9	254.6	263.7	264.1	332.5	403.6	393.3	555.7	....		....	96f
Imports of Goods & Services	-164.0	-198.6	-249.3	-292.2	-327.8	-365.3	-351.7	-348.8	-380.7	-388.3	-457.8	-455.9	....		....	98c
Gross Domestic Product (GDP)	210.6	254.2	292.0	342.0	386.5	429.8	444.2	490.9	535.5	598.7	622.7	663.5	724.1		....	99b
GDP Volume (1995=100)	67.4	75.3	81.8	89.3	96.1	98.3	98.6	101.9	91.7	96.7	100.0	105.9	112.5		....	99bv p
GDP Deflator (1995=100)	50.2	54.2	57.3	61.5	64.6	70.3	72.3	77.4	93.8	99.5	100.0	100.6	103.3		....	99bi p
Midyear Estimates																	
Population	.04	.04	.04	.04	.04	.04	.04	.04	.04	.04	.04	.04	.04	.04	.04	99z

(See notes in the back of the book.)

St. Lucia

	1970	1971	1972	1973	1974	1975	1976	1977	1978	1979	1980	1981	1982	1983	1984
Exchange Rates										*E.Caribbean Dollars per SDR: End of Period (aa)*					
Official Rate .... aa	2.0053	2.0417	2.2194	2.4925	2.5024	2.7770	3.1369	3.2797	3.5175	3.5568	3.4436	3.1427	2.9784	2.8268	2.6466
Official Rate .... ae	2.0053	1.8805	2.0442	2.0661	2.0439	2.3721	2.7000	2.7000	2.7000	2.7000	2.7000	2.7000	2.7000	2.7000	2.7000
												Index Numbers (1995=100):			
Official Rate .... ah x	134.8	137.3	140.7	137.9	131.6	125.0	103.5	100.0	100.0	100.0	100.0	100.0	100.0	100.0	100.0
Nominal Effective Exchange Rate .... ne c	....	....	....	....	....	....	....	....	....	....	72.6	70.8	75.0	79.2	83.4	90.1
Real Effective Exchange Rate .... re c	....	....	....	....	....	....	....	....	....	....	95.6	97.2	106.7	109.4	111.2	116.4
Fund Position												*Millions of SDRs:*			
Quota .... 2f. s	....	....	....	....	....	....	....	....	....	3.60	5.40	5.40	5.40	7.50	7.50
SDRs .... 1b. s	....	....	....	....	....	....	....	....	....	—	.07	.23	.01	.01	—
Reserve Position in the Fund .... 1c. s	....	....	....	....	....	....	....	....	....	—	—	—	—	—	—
Total Fund Cred.&Loans Outstg. 2tl	....	....	....	....	....	....	....	....	....		1.35	4.05	2.55	2.55	2.02
International Liquidity										*Millions of US Dollars Unless Otherwise Indicated:*					
Total Reserves minus Gold .... 1l. d	....	....	....	....	....	3.24	5.19	5.65	6.76	8.12	8.29	7.61	8.21	8.87	12.38
SDRs .... 1b. d	....	....	....	....	....	....	....	....	....	—	.09	.27	.01	.01	—
Reserve Position in the Fund .... 1c. d	....	....	....	....	....	....	....	....	....	—	—	—	—	—	—
Foreign Exchange .... 1d. d	....	....	....	....	....	3.24	5.19	5.65	6.76	8.12	8.20	7.34	8.20	8.86	12.38
Deposit Money Banks: Assets .... 7a. d	....	....	....	....	....	5.06	5.32	4.70	5.60	7.44	10.07	7.09	8.71	15.00	12.37
Liabilities .... 7b. d	....	....	....	....	....	8.94	9.12	7.82	9.82	15.05	18.62	14.79	15.48	14.94	15.25
Monetary Authorities										*Millions of E. Caribbean Dollars:*					
Foreign Assets 11	....	....	....	....	....	7.69	14.02	15.26	18.24	21.94	22.38	20.55	22.44	23.94	25.97
Claims on Central Government 12a	....	....	....	....	....	3.87	3.87	3.87	5.87	9.13	15.81	24.40	20.03	20.06	37.45
Claims on Deposit Money Banks 12e	....	....	....	....	....	—	—	—	—	—	—	—	—	—	.34
Reserve Money 14	....	....	....	....	....	11.56	17.89	19.14	24.12	31.06	33.54	32.22	34.87	36.80	58.41
of which: Currency Outside DMBs 14a	....	....	....	....	....	9.56	12.07	15.04	17.67	22.05	24.61	27.69	28.04	30.26	30.08
Foreign Liabilities 16c	....	....	....	....	....	—	—	—	—	—	4.65	12.73	7.59	7.21	5.35
Central Government Deposits 16d	....	....	....	....	....	—	—	—	—	—	—	—	—	—	—
Other Items (Net) 17r	....	....	....	....	....	—	—	—	—	—	—	—	—	—	—
Deposit Money Banks										*Millions of E. Caribbean Dollars:*					
Reserves 20	....	....	....	....	....	2.00	5.82	4.10	6.45	9.01	8.93	4.53	6.82	6.54	29.08
Foreign Assets 21	....	....	....	....	....	12.01	14.35	12.68	15.12	20.10	27.18	19.14	23.53	40.49	33.41
Claims on Central Government 22a	....	....	....	....	....	19.66	16.23	15.86	10.86	19.30	14.97	12.68	17.41	19.22	20.96
Claims on Local Government 22b	....	....	....	....	....	—	—	—	—	—	—	—	—	—	—
Claims on Nonfin.Pub.Enterprises 22c	....	....	....	....	....	2.60	3.00	3.90	4.70	5.21	2.17	5.88	4.81	2.47	3.44
Claims on Private Sector 22d	....	....	....	....	....	61.14	70.01	90.53	110.75	128.40	163.53	184.98	196.95	208.06	237.22
Claims on Nonbank Financial Insts 22g	....	....	....	....	....	—	—	—	—	—	.80	.32	.65	.93	1.27	1.56
Demand Deposits 24	....	....	....	....	....	11.07	16.98	17.97	20.72	23.16	28.06	25.84	29.52	28.13	32.98
Time, Savings,& Fgn.Currency Dep. 25	....	....	....	....	....	61.46	71.46	73.47	88.99	104.41	114.56	142.91	157.06	187.39	210.97
Foreign Liabilities 26c	....	....	....	....	....	21.20	24.64	21.11	26.52	40.62	50.28	39.92	41.79	40.33	41.18
Central Government Deposits 26d	....	....	....	....	....	—	—	—	1.70	3.13	5.81	6.31	7.70	3.37	.62
Credit from Monetary Authorities 26g	....	....	....	....	....	.30	.90	.50	1.20	.61	.80	—	.40	—	—
Capital Accounts 27a	....	....	....	....	....	2.00	2.00	2.00	2.00	2.22	3.46	6.23	7.12	8.01	9.16
Other Items (Net) 27r	....	....	....	....	....	1.39	−6.56	12.02	6.75	8.68	14.11	6.66	6.86	10.82	30.75
Monetary Survey										*Millions of E. Caribbean Dollars:*					
Foreign Assets (Net) 31n	....	....	....	....	....	−1.50	3.74	6.83	6.84	1.41	−5.38	−12.96	−3.42	16.89	12.85
Domestic Credit 32	....	....	....	....	....	87.27	93.11	114.17	130.48	159.72	190.99	222.28	232.42	247.72	300.01
Claims on Central Govt. (Net) 32an	....	....	....	....	....	23.53	20.10	19.73	15.03	25.31	24.97	30.77	29.73	35.92	57.79
Claims on Local Government 32b	....	....	....	....	....	—	—	—	—	—	—	—	—	—	—
Claims on Nonfin.Pub.Enterprises 32c	....	....	....	....	....	2.60	3.00	3.90	4.70	5.21	2.17	5.88	4.81	2.47	3.44
Claims on Private Sector 32d	....	....	....	....	....	61.14	70.01	90.53	110.75	128.40	163.53	184.98	196.95	208.06	237.22
Claims on Nonbank Financial Inst 32g	....	....	....	....	....	—	—	—	—	—	.80	.32	.65	.93	1.27	1.56
Money 34	....	....	....	....	....	20.63	29.05	33.01	38.39	45.22	52.67	53.53	57.57	58.39	63.06
Quasi-Money 35	....	....	....	....	....	61.46	71.46	73.47	88.99	104.41	114.56	142.91	157.06	187.39	210.97
Capital Accounts 37a	....	....	....	....	....	2.00	2.00	2.00	2.00	2.22	4.74	8.55	9.32	10.11	11.12
Other Items (Net) 37r	....	....	....	....	....	1.69	−5.66	12.52	7.95	9.29	13.64	4.33	5.05	8.73	27.71
Money plus Quasi-Money 35l	....	....	....	....	....	82.09	100.50	106.48	127.37	149.63	167.24	196.44	214.62	245.78	274.03
Interest Rates												*Percent Per Annum*			
Treasury Bill Rate 60c	....	....	....	....	....	....	....	....	....	....	6.5	6.5	6.5	6.5	6.5
Deposit Rate 60l	....	....	....	....	....	....	....	....	....	....	5.5	8.0	8.0	8.0	8.6
Lending Rate 60p	....	....	....	....	....	....	....	....	7.5	7.5	11.0	13.0	13.0	13.0	13.3
Prices												*Index Numbers (1995=100):*			
Consumer Prices 64	15.0	16.2	17.5	19.9	26.7	31.4	34.4	37.5	41.6	45.5	54.3	62.6	65.4	66.4	67.2
International Transactions												*Millions of E. Caribbean Dollars*			
Exports 70	18.73	12.23	15.11	19.23	32.91	36.81	54.19	66.29	77.68	96.63	157.41	124.36	122.83	149.63	132.40
Imports, c.i.f. 71	54.59	69.00	68.69	74.17	91.12	100.43	125.71	160.23	223.50	273.20	334.20	348.90	318.70	388.40	320.00
														1980=100	
Unit Value of Exports 74	....	....	....	....	....	62.7	60.3	I 71.7	74.7	87.0	100.0	107.4	116.6	123.3	....

St. Lucia

362

	1985	1986	1987	1988	1989	1990	1991	1992	1993	1994	1995	1996	1997	1998	1999		
E.Caribbean Dollars per US Dollar: End of Period (ae)																**Exchange Rates**	
	2.9657	3.3026	3.8304	3.6334	3.5482	3.8412	3.8622	3.7125	3.7086	3.9416	4.0135	3.8825	3.6430	3.8017	3.7058	Official Rate	aa
	2.7000	2.7000	2.7000	2.7000	2.7000	2.7000	2.7000	2.7000	2.7000	2.7000	2.7000	2.7000	2.7000	2.7000	2.7000	Official Rate	ae
Period Averages																	
	100.0	100.0	100.0	100.0	100.0	100.0	100.0	100.0	100.0	100.0	100.0	100.0	100.0	100.0	100.0	Official Rate	ah x
	93.1	88.6	84.5	82.0	85.0	84.5	87.3	89.1	98.6	103.2	100.0	102.1	107.0	109.1	110.4	Nominal Effective Exchange Rate	ne c
	115.0	108.1	106.1	99.3	101.2	95.5	97.7	98.4	102.3	101.3	100.0	101.3	103.7	106.2	111.4	Real Effective Exchange Rate	re c
End of Period																**Fund Position**	
	7.50	7.50	7.50	7.50	7.50	7.50	7.50	11.00	11.00	11.00	11.00	11.00	11.00	11.00	15.30	Quota	2f. s
	—	—	—	—	—	1.23	1.27	1.31	1.34	1.36	1.39	1.42	1.45	1.48	1.50	SDRs	1b. s
	—	—	—	—	—	—	—	—	—	—	—	—	—	—	—	Reserve Position in the Fund	1c. s
	.30	—	—	—	—	—	—	—	—	—	—	—	—	—	—	Total Fund Cred.&Loans Outstg.	2tl
End of Period																**International Liquidity**	
	12.65	25.11	30.80	32.65	38.21	44.59	48.75	55.46	60.04	57.79	63.09	56.14	60.98	70.61	74.52	Total Reserves minus Gold	1l. d
	—	—	—	—	—	1.75	1.82	1.80	1.84	1.99	2.07	2.04	1.95	2.08	2.06	SDRs	1b. d
	—	—	—	—	—	—	—	—	—	—	—	—	—	—	—	Reserve Position in the Fund	1c. d
	12.65	25.11	30.80	32.65	38.21	42.84	46.93	53.66	58.20	55.80	61.02	54.10	59.03	68.54	72.45	Foreign Exchange	1d. d
	19.45	30.42	41.77	53.12	39.67	43.66	46.84	48.60	35.08	25.22	30.03	30.28	32.55	53.05	54.27	Deposit Money Banks: Assets	7a. d
	15.78	15.02	18.74	19.44	24.14	30.12	32.81	36.37	39.84	53.33	56.32	80.02	94.18	87.29	96.58	Liabilities	7b. d
End of Period																**Monetary Authorities**	
	39.17	67.81	83.12	88.16	105.62	128.65	141.52	149.75	162.21	156.62	170.34	151.58	164.65	190.67	201.19	Foreign Assets	11
	34.91	36.05	34.26	30.70	31.60	29.91	30.43	13.82	11.85	9.71	12.94	23.74	13.78	12.76	12.63	Claims on Central Government	12a
	—	—	1.45	1.68	1.10	.48	.04	.81	.02	.02	.02	.02	.03	.09	.08	Claims on Deposit Money Banks	12e
	73.20	103.87	118.84	120.52	135.87	150.78	162.31	160.48	168.11	160.29	178.60	170.67	173.37	197.37	203.61	Reserve Money	14
	33.01	39.05	52.06	56.28	67.28	64.23	68.09	64.26	67.88	66.85	75.13	70.30	69.61	77.52	84.06	*of which: Currency Outside DMBs*	14a
	.89	—	—	—	—	—	—	—	—	—	—	—	—	—	—	Foreign Liabilities	16c
	—	—	—	.01	2.45	8.25	9.68	3.90	5.97	6.06	4.70	4.67	5.08	6.15	10.29	Central Government Deposits	16d
	—	—	—	—	—	—	—	—	—	—	—	—	—	—	—	Other Items (Net)	17r
End of Period																**Deposit Money Banks**	
	36.01	63.19	65.96	61.67	69.15	84.98	93.01	97.73	102.30	103.66	97.02	101.94	105.33	108.52	129.00	Reserves	20
	52.52	82.13	112.77	143.42	107.11	117.88	126.46	131.23	94.72	68.09	81.07	81.77	87.89	143.24	146.52	Foreign Assets	21
	31.01	41.91	43.53	38.42	36.92	34.80	32.63	47.91	52.12	47.49	43.65	48.13	63.06	109.65	119.95	Claims on Central Government	22a
	—	—	—	.24	.24	.64	3.91	6.44	1.84	2.09	1.57	1.47	2.31	2.19	1.76	Claims on Local Government	22b
	2.84	1.99	2.75	2.96	10.61	14.61	11.44	31.27	49.25	57.48	72.67	67.82	64.61	46.72	47.09	Claims on Nonfin.Pub.Enterprises	22c
	251.61	275.15	310.21	401.52	519.42	578.48	623.78	683.36	751.43	860.41	946.42	1,071.26	1,171.82	1,258.19	1,394.19	Claims on Private Sector	22d
	1.62	1.66	4.72	10.18	7.88	11.12	10.64	9.59	2.84	8.72	8.28	13.60	14.50	14.11	30.47	Claims on Nonbank Financial Insts	22g
	38.04	58.58	70.53	84.00	90.27	103.26	99.84	147.62	157.78	166.37	187.93	174.83	189.68	197.29	227.41	Demand Deposits	24
	257.59	314.58	356.75	375.16	444.02	509.31	561.49	546.91	547.77	618.95	673.13	731.81	756.03	848.10	912.16	Time, Savings,& Fgn.Currency Dep.	25
	42.59	40.56	50.59	52.50	65.17	81.32	88.60	98.20	107.57	143.99	152.07	216.05	254.30	235.68	260.77	Foreign Liabilities	26c
	1.63	6.20	8.30	88.53	97.49	117.86	123.47	158.49	174.24	170.92	195.35	213.77	235.09	318.57	354.53	Central Government Deposits	26d
	—	—	—	.16	—	—	2.20	.70	9.03	9.60	2.00	.09	2.10	—	.45	Credit from Monetary Authorities	26g
	9.40	9.79	11.06	17.73	26.97	26.36	47.44	64.46	65.08	71.81	91.47	92.24	101.87	121.80	168.89	Capital Accounts	27a
	26.36	36.33	42.71	40.33	27.41	4.40	-21.18	-8.85	-6.97	-33.70	-51.27	-42.80	-29.57	-38.81	-55.23	Other Items (Net)	27r
End of Period																**Monetary Survey**	
	48.21	109.38	145.30	179.08	147.56	165.21	179.39	182.78	149.35	80.73	99.35	17.29	-1.76	98.23	86.95	Foreign Assets (Net)	31n
	320.36	350.58	387.17	395.49	506.72	543.45	579.67	630.00	689.13	808.91	885.49	1,007.58	1,089.90	1,118.89	1,241.25	Domestic Credit	32
	64.29	71.77	69.50	-19.41	-31.42	-61.41	-70.09	-100.66	-116.24	-119.78	-143.45	-146.57	-163.33	-202.31	-232.25	Claims on Central Govt. (Net)	32an
	—	—	—	.24	.24	.64	3.91	6.44	1.84	2.09	1.57	1.47	2.31	2.19	1.76	Claims on Local Government	32b
	2.84	1.99	2.75	2.96	10.61	14.61	11.44	31.27	49.25	57.48	72.67	67.82	64.61	46.72	47.09	Claims on Nonfin.Pub.Enterprises	32c
	251.61	275.15	310.21	401.52	519.42	578.48	623.78	683.36	751.43	860.41	946.42	1,071.26	1,171.82	1,258.19	1,394.19	Claims on Private Sector	32d
	1.62	1.66	4.72	10.18	7.88	11.12	10.64	9.59	2.84	8.72	8.28	13.60	14.50	14.11	30.47	Claims on Nonbank Financial Inst	32g
	71.05	97.62	122.58	140.28	157.54	167.50	168.13	212.47	226.02	233.85	263.98	245.65	259.67	276.12	313.48	Money	34
	257.59	314.58	356.75	375.16	444.02	509.31	561.49	546.91	547.77	618.95	673.13	731.81	756.03	848.10	912.16	Quasi-Money	35
	11.60	12.23	13.89	20.42	29.59	29.21	50.30	67.21	67.83	74.73	94.44	95.12	104.57	124.61	171.63	Capital Accounts	37a
	28.34	35.52	39.24	38.71	23.13	2.65	-20.87	-13.82	-3.14	-37.88	-46.72	-47.69	-32.13	-31.70	-69.06	Other Items (Net)	37r
	328.64	412.21	479.34	515.44	601.56	676.80	729.63	759.39	773.79	852.80	937.11	977.45	1,015.70	1,124.22	1,225.64	Money plus Quasi-Money	35l
Percent Per Annum																**Interest Rates**	
	7.0	7.0	7.0	7.0	7.0	7.0	7.0	7.0	7.0	7.0	7.0	7.0	7.0	7.0	7.0	Treasury Bill Rate	60c
	9.1	7.5	5.0	5.0	5.0	5.6	6.1	5.5	5.0	4.5	6.3	7.0	6.3	7.1	9.3	Deposit Rate	60l
	14.0	14.0	11.6	10.6	10.0	10.5	10.5	10.5	10.2	10.1	10.0	10.3	10.5	10.5	10.5	Lending Rate	60p
Period Averages																**Prices**	
	68.2	69.5	74.8	75.4	78.4	82.1	86.8	91.2	92.3	94.6	100.0	101.8	102.0	104.2	109.7	Consumer Prices	64
Millions of E. Caribbean Dollars																**International Transactions**	
	152.73	234.59	214.80	312.00	294.70	343.70	297.80	331.50	322.98	287.12	335.26	220.94	177.84	....	....	Exports	70
	337.50	417.90	483.90	595.00	739.10	731.60	797.00	845.00	810.50	814.78	826.30	820.25	896.86	905.09	....	Imports, c.i.f.	71
1980=100																	
	....	....	....	....	....	....	....	....	....	....	....	....	....	....	....	Unit Value of Exports	74

St. Lucia

	1970	1971	1972	1973	1974	1975	1976	1977	1978	1979	1980	1981	1982	1983	1984
Balance of Payments													*Millions of US Dollars:*		
Current Account, n.i.e. .... 78al d	....	....	....	....	....	....	−5.40	−10.90	−23.00	−28.10	−33.30	−39.80	−30.80	−4.91	−13.40
Goods: Exports f.o.b. .... 78aa d	....	....	....	....	....	....	19.10	22.60	26.80	31.90	46.00	41.60	41.60	47.50	47.80
Goods: Imports f.o.b. .... 78ab d	....	....	....	....	....	....	−43.63	−53.90	−75.27	−91.99	−112.55	−117.17	−107.35	−97.08	−107.71
Trade Balance .... 78ac d							−24.53	−31.30	−48.47	−60.09	−66.55	−75.57	−65.75	−49.58	−59.91
Services: Credit .... 78ad d	....	....	....	....	....	....	12.50	17.80	27.70	33.80	40.50	38.50	44.70	54.20	64.00
Services: Debit .... 78ae d	....	....	....	....	....	....	−6.46	−8.40	−12.83	−13.41	−22.15	−23.63	−27.75	−30.02	−38.29
Balance on Goods & Services .... 78af d							−18.50	−21.90	−33.60	−39.70	−48.20	−60.70	−48.80	−25.40	−34.20
Income: Credit .... 78ag d	....	....	....	....	....	....	.50	.90	1.30	1.00	1.00	1.50	—	.69	—
Income: Debit .... 78ah d	....	....	....	....	....	....	−.30	—	−.50	−.60	−.70	−.90	−1.20	−1.50	−3.20
Balance on Gds, Serv. & Inc. .... 78ai d							−18.30	−21.00	−32.80	−39.30	−47.90	−60.10	−50.00	−26.21	−37.40
Current Transfers, n.i.e.: Credit .... 78aj d	....	....	....	....	....	....	12.90	10.10	9.80	11.20	14.60	20.30	24.00	27.50	30.40
Current Transfers: Debit .... 78ak d													−4.80	−6.20	−6.40
Capital Account, n.i.e. .... 78bc d	....	....	....	....	....	....									
Capital Account, n.i.e.: Credit .... 78ba d							—	—	—	—	—	—	—	—	—
Capital Account: Debit .... 78bb d							—	—	—	—	—	—	—	—	—
Financial Account, n.i.e. .... 78bj d	....	....	....	....	....	....	−2.02	15.70	23.06	27.20	29.24	43.76	30.58	7.20	13.86
Direct Investment Abroad .... 78bd d															
Dir. Invest. in Rep. Econ., n.i.e. .... 78be d							3.00	13.00	20.60	26.00	30.90	38.20	26.50	10.00	12.00
Portfolio Investment Assets .... 78bf d							—	—	—	—	—	—	—	—	—
Equity Securities .... 78bk d							—	—	—	—	—	—	—	—	—
Debt Securities .... 78bl d							—	—	—	—	—	—	—	—	—
Portfolio Investment Liab., n.i.e. .... 78bg d							—	—	—	—	—	—	—	—	—
Equity Securities .... 78bm d							—	—	—	—	—	—	—	—	—
Debt Securities .... 78bn d							—	—	—	—	—	—	—	—	—
Financial Derivatives Assets .... 78bw d							....	....	....	....	....	....	....	....	....
Financial Derivatives Liabilities .... 78bx d							....	....	....	....	....	....	....	....	....
Other Investment Assets .... 78bh d							−7.65	.80	−.24	−1.69	−3.27	2.75	−1.42	−5.00	1.29
Monetary Authorities .... 78bo d							....	....	....	....	....	....	....	....	....
General Government .... 78bp d							—	—	—	—	—	—	—	—	—
Banks .... 78bq d							−7.65	.80	−.24	−1.69	−3.27	2.75	−1.42	−5.00	1.29
Other Sectors .... 78br d							—	—	—	—	—	—	—	—	—
Other Investment Liab., n.i.e. .... 78bi d							2.64	1.90	2.70	2.89	1.61	2.80	5.50	2.20	.57
Monetary Authorities .... 78bs d							—	—	—	—	—	—	—	—	—
General Government .... 78bt d							2.64	.80	1.40	.15	.30	2.50	6.00	1.30	−.23
Banks .... 78bu d							—	—	—	—	—	—	—	—	—
Other Sectors .... 78bv d							—	1.10	1.30	2.74	1.31	.30	−.50	.90	.80
Net Errors and Omissions .... 78ca d	....	....	....	....	....	....	9.94	−4.24	.94	2.47	2.11	−8.72	2.58	−1.99	−.26
Overall Balance .... 78cb d							2.52	.56	1.00	1.57	−1.95	−4.77	2.36	.30	.20
Reserves and Related Items .... 79da d	....	....	....	....	....	....	−2.52	−.56	−1.00	−1.57	1.95	4.77	−2.36	−.30	−.20
Reserve Assets .... 79db d							−2.52	−.56	−1.00	−1.57	.21	1.50	−.75	−.80	−1.19
Use of Fund Credit and Loans .... 79dc d							—	—	—	—	1.74	3.27	−1.60	—	−.54
Exceptional Financing .... 79de d							—	—	—	—	—	—	—	.50	1.53
Government Finance													*Millions of E. Caribbean Dollars:*		
Deficit (-) or Surplus 80							....	−1.48	4.73	−12.85	−7.84	−15.81	14.30	....	
Revenue 81							....	60.03	83.14	91.79	103.45	116.19	122.28	⅟ 119.26	
Grants Received 81z							....	5.71	13.12	8.95	16.57	21.09	31.81	....	
Expenditure 82							....	66.58	90.73	112.71	126.95	152.19	138.67	....	
Lending Minus Repayments 83							....	.64	.80	.88	.91	.90	1.12	....	
Financing															
Domestic 84a	....	....	....	....	....	....	....	−2.72	−8.35	1.32	−5.25	....	....		
Foreign 85a								4.20	3.62	11.53	13.09	....	....		
National Accounts													*Millions of E. Caribbean Dollars*		
Exports of Goods & Services 90c	....	....	....	....	....	51.5	82.8	107.1	147.2	176.3	233.6	216.3	224.1	248.4	261.4[e]
Government Consumption 91f						23.2	26.5	37.0	44.7	44.8	63.7	71.1	92.1	90.8	102.7[e]
Gross Capital Formation 93						56.8	65.6	87.7	124.8	155.8	181.2	198.8	144.7	116.5	126.0
Private Consumption 96f						96.5	108.9	110.5	145.2	194.3	176.6	221.8	244.4	238.2	266.7[e]
Imports of Goods & Services 98c						−104.8	−131.3	−166.2	−237.9	−284.6	−351.5	−369.1	−344.3	−316.4	−348.4[e]
Gross Domestic Product (GDP) 99b	....	....	....	....	....	123.2	152.5	219.5	257.0	311.7	365.8	418.9	453.0	491.1	541.6
GDP Volume 1990 Prices .... 99b, p	....					....		493.0	548.9	571.9	560.0	583.1	596.1	628.4	670.6
GDP Volume (1995=100) .... 99bv p						....		40.4	45.0	46.9	45.9	47.8	48.9	51.5	55.0
GDP Deflator (1995=100) .... 99bi p	....					....		36.3	38.2	44.4	53.2	58.5	61.9	63.7	65.8
													Millions:		
Population 99z	.10	....	....	.11	.12	.11	.11	.11	.11	.12	.12	.13	.13	.13	.13

	1985	1986	1987	1988	1989	1990	1991	1992	1993	1994	1995	1996	1997	1998	1999		
Minus Sign Indicates Debit																**Balance of Payments**	
	−12.50	−6.68	−14.31	−17.91	−63.26	−57.04	−71.85	−54.83	−49.34	−48.53	−33.17	−80.34	....	....	....	Current Account, n.i.e.	**78al** *d*
	52.00	84.41	81.70	122.26	116.04	130.95	113.89	127.16	123.52	99.90	114.63	86.31	....	....	....	Goods: Exports f.o.b.	**78aa** *d*
	−113.63	−136.22	−156.70	−194.48	−240.89	−238.77	−261.39	−270.84	−264.00	−265.62	−269.38	−270.67	....	....	....	Goods: Imports f.o.b.	**78ab** *d*
	−61.63	−51.81	−75.00	−72.22	−124.85	−107.82	−147.51	−143.67	−140.48	−165.72	−154.74	−184.35	....	....	....	*Trade Balance*	**78ac** *d*
	69.50	82.07	98.44	117.19	136.43	150.60	172.19	194.94	204.67	237.71	265.87	269.64	....	....	....	Services: Credit	**78ad** *d*
	−37.97	−43.34	−46.52	−59.64	−71.32	−81.22	−80.55	−86.34	−89.01	−104.99	−124.51	−142.65	....	....	....	Services: Debit	**78ae** *d*
	−30.10	−13.08	−23.08	−14.68	−59.74	−38.44	−55.87	−35.07	−24.83	−33.00	−13.38	−57.37	....	....	....	*Balance on Goods & Services*	**78af** *d*
	—	3.30	4.11	6.41	5.85	5.94	4.63	5.46	4.36	4.97	5.75	3.39	....	....	....	Income: Credit	**78ag** *d*
	−3.30	−8.11	−9.15	−17.22	−16.44	−32.13	−34.28	−34.23	−38.11	−38.33	−44.71	−40.27	....	....	....	Income: Debit	**78ah** *d*
	−33.40	−17.89	−28.11	−25.50	−70.33	−64.63	−85.52	−63.85	−58.58	−66.37	−52.34	−94.25	....	....	....	*Balance on Gds, Serv. & Inc.*	**78ai** *d*
	27.60	15.87	17.90	12.73	12.30	13.86	16.90	16.38	21.87	26.13	28.70	26.45	....	....	....	Current Transfers, n.i.e.: Credit	**78aj** *d*
	−6.70	−4.66	−4.10	−5.15	−5.23	−6.28	−3.23	−7.36	−12.63	−8.30	−9.53	−12.54	....	....	....	Current Transfers: Debit	**78ak** *d*
	—	10.50	12.03	7.86	8.48	3.85	6.57	8.95	3.84	10.71	13.21	8.73	....	....	....	Capital Account, n.i.e.	**78bc** *d*
	—	10.50	12.03	7.86	8.48	3.85	6.57	9.13	4.18	11.83	13.58	9.47	....	....	....	Capital Account, n.i.e.: Credit	**78ba** *d*
	—	—	—	—	—	—	—	−.19	−.34	−1.12	−.37	−.74	....	....	....	Capital Account: Debit	**78bb** *d*
	11.66	6.21	12.13	7.60	52.20	51.54	59.20	59.77	56.08	41.70	28.06	61.24	....	....	....	Financial Account, n.i.e.	**78bj** *d*
													....	....	....	Direct Investment Abroad	**78bd** *d*
	17.00	14.52	15.00	16.44	26.63	44.79	57.74	40.89	34.09	32.41	30.31	23.03	....	....	....	Dir. Invest. in Rep. Econ., n.i.e.	**78be** *d*
	—	—	—	—	—	—	−.14	—	—	—	—	—	....	....	....	Portfolio Investment Assets	**78bf** *d*
	—	—	—	—	—	—	−.14	—	—	—	—	—	....	....	....	Equity Securities	**78bk** *d*
	—	—	—	—	—	—	—	—	—	—	—	—	....	....	....	Debt Securities	**78bl** *d*
	—	—	—	—	—	.18	—	−.51	—	−.47	−.47	−.99	....	....	....	Portfolio Investment Liab., n.i.e.	**78bg** *d*
	—	—	—	—	—	.18	—	−.51	—	−.47	−.47	−.06	....	....	....	Equity Securities	**78bm** *d*
	....	—	—	—	—	—	—	—	—	—	—	−.93	....	....	....	Debt Securities	**78bn** *d*
													....	....	....	Financial Derivatives Assets	**78bw** *d*
	....	....	....	....	....	....	....	....	....	....	....	....	....	....	....	Financial Derivatives Liabilities	**78bx** *d*
	−7.15	−11.63	−7.15	−11.52	18.15	1.96	−.48	.79	17.00	12.49	−1.81	23.44	....	....	....	Other Investment Assets	**78bh** *d*
	....	....	....	....	....	....	....	....	....	....	....	....	....	....	....	Monetary Authorities	**78bo** *d*
	....	....	....	....	....	....	....	....	....	....	....	....	....	....	....	General Government	**78bp** *d*
	−7.15	−11.63	−7.15	−11.52	18.15	1.96	−.48	.79	17.00	12.49	−1.81	23.44	....	....	....	Banks	**78bq** *d*
	....	....	....	....	....	....	....	....	....	....	....	....	....	....	....	Other Sectors	**78br** *d*
	1.81	3.32	4.28	2.68	7.42	4.61	2.07	18.60	4.99	−2.72	.04	15.76	....	....	....	Other Investment Liab., n.i.e.	**78bi** *d*
	—	—	—	—	—	—	—	—	—	—	—	—	....	....	....	Monetary Authorities	**78bs** *d*
	−1.89	2.61	5.29	7.41	11.74	4.38	3.12	21.03	5.81	3.62	5.48	10.90	....	....	....	General Government	**78bt** *d*
	—	—	—	—	—	—	—	—	—	—	—	—	....	....	....	Banks	**78bu** *d*
	3.70	.71	−1.01	−4.73	−4.32	.23	−1.05	−2.43	−.81	−6.34	−5.44	4.86	....	....	....	Other Sectors	**78bv** *d*
	2.00	1.42	−.73	4.30	8.18	7.95	13.82	−7.11	−6.09	−6.29	−2.84	3.49	....	....	....	Net Errors and Omissions	**78ca** *d*
	1.16	11.45	9.11	1.85	5.59	6.30	7.74	6.78	4.49	−2.41	5.27	−6.88	....	....	....	*Overall Balance*	**78cb** *d*
	−1.16	−11.45	−9.11	−1.85	−5.59	−6.30	−7.74	−6.78	−4.49	2.41	−5.27	6.88	....	....	....	Reserves and Related Items	**79da** *d*
	−3.00	−11.11	−9.11	−1.85	−5.59	−6.30	−7.74	−6.78	−4.49	2.41	−5.27	6.88	....	....	....	Reserve Assets	**79db** *d*
	−1.75	−.34	—	—	—	—	—	—	—	—	—	—	....	....	....	Use of Fund Credit and Loans........	**79dc** *d*
	3.59	—	—	—	—	—	—	—	—	—	—	—	....	....	....	Exceptional Financing	**79de** *d*
Year Beginning April 1																**Government Finance**	
	−11.10	−11.40	8.10	19.10	10.90	−1.10	....	....	....	....	....	....	....	....	....	Deficit (-) or Surplus	**80**
	145.80	169.50	193.90	229.90	268.00	265.00	299.80ᴾ	....	....	....	....	....	....	....	....	Revenue	**81**
	16.30	16.60	27.90	16.70	11.80	3.90	3.30ᴾ	....	....	....	....	....	....	....	....	Grants Received......................	**81z**
	173.20	197.50	211.60	224.20	267.70	257.70	280.20ᴾ	....	....	....	....	....	....	....	....	Expenditure	**82**
	—	—	2.10	3.30	1.20	12.30	....	....	....	....	....	....	....	....	....	Lending Minus Repayments	**83**
																Financing	
	....	....	....	....	....	....	....	....	....	....	....	....	....	....	....	Domestic	**84a**
	....	....	....	....	....	....	....	....	....	....	....	....	....	....	....	Foreign......................	**85a**
Millions of E. Caribbean Dollars																**National Accounts**	
	....	....	....	....	....	....	....	....	....	....	....	....	....	....	....	Exports of Goods & Services	**90c**
	....	....	....	....	....	....	....	....	....	....	....	....	....	....	....	Government Consumption......................	**91f**
	....	....	....	....	....	....	....	....	....	....	....	....	....	....	....	Gross Capital Formation	**93**
	....	....	....	....	....	....	....	....	....	....	....	....	....	....	....	Private Consumption	**96f**
	....	....	....	....	....	....	....	....	....	....	....	....	....	....	....	Imports of Goods & Services	**98c**
	601.8	729.7	799.0	910.5	1,030.7	1,122.5	1,208.9	1,340.2	1,338.6	1,400.0	1,495.8	1,542.9	1,565.7	1,698.2	....	Gross Domestic Product (GDP)	**99b**
	723.0	843.4	875.8	1,003.5	1,085.2	1,122.5	1,116.8	1,189.9	1,188.6	1,212.8	1,219.2	1,229.3	1,235.5	....	....	GDP Volume 1990 Prices	**99b.***p*
	59.3	69.2	71.8	82.3	89.0	92.1	91.6	97.6	97.5	99.5	100.0	100.8	101.3	....	....	GDP Volume (1995=100)	**99bv** *p*
	67.8	70.5	74.4	74.0	77.4	81.5	88.2	91.8	91.8	94.1	100.0	102.3	103.3	....	....	GDP Deflator (1995=100)	**99bi** *p*
Midyear Estimates																	
	.14	.14	.14	.15	.13	.13	.14	.14	.14	.14	.15	.15	.15	.15	.15	**Population**......................	**99z**

(See notes in the back of the book.)

St. Vincent & Grens.

		1970	1971	1972	1973	1974	1975	1976	1977	1978	1979	1980	1981	1982	1983	1984
Exchange Rates											*E. Caribbean Dollars per SDR: End of Period (aa)*					
Official Rate	aa	2.0053	2.0417	2.2194	2.4925	2.5024	2.7770	3.1369	3.2797	3.5175	3.5568	3.4436	3.1427	2.9784	2.8268	2.6466
Official Rate	ae	2.0053	1.8805	2.0442	2.0661	2.0439	2.3721	2.7000	2.7000	2.7000	2.7000	2.7000	2.7000	2.7000	2.7000	2.7000
											Index Numbers (1995=100):					
Official Rate	ahx	134.8	137.3	140.7	137.9	131.6	125.0	103.5	100.0	100.0	100.0	100.0	100.0	100.0	100.0	100.0
Nominal Effective Exchange Rate	nec	....	....	....	....	....	....	....	....	....	68.3	66.6	69.8	73.2	76.4	80.4
Real Effective Exchange Rate	rec	....	....	....	....	....	....	....	....	....	102.1	101.3	107.1	110.9	114.9	116.8
Fund Position											*Millions of SDRs:*					
Quota	2f. s	...	...								1.70	2.60	2.60	2.60	4.00	4.00
SDRs	1b. s	...	...								—	.05	.15	.03	.01	—
Reserve Position in the Fund	1c. s	...	...								—	—	—	—	.35	—
Total Fund Cred.&Loans Outstg.	2tl	...	...								—	.20	1.50	1.50	1.50	1.01
International Liquidity											*Millions of US Dollars Unless Otherwise Indicated:*					
Total Reserves minus Gold	1l. d	...	...					4.66	4.81	5.26	8.90	7.27	9.00	4.78	5.70	12.82
SDRs	1b. d	...	...					....	....	....	—	.06	.17	.03	.01	—
Reserve Position in the Fund	1c. d	...	...					....	....	....	—	—	—	—	.37	—
Foreign Exchange	1d. d	...	...					4.66	4.81	5.26	8.90	7.21	8.83	4.75	5.32	12.82
Deposit Money Banks: Assets	7a. d	...	...				6.02	7.91	7.90	9.03	7.08	8.84	11.21	10.70	9.81	8.49
Liabilities	7b. d	...	...				5.67	6.34	8.87	9.21	10.29	12.15	12.02	14.26	12.19	13.25
Monetary Authorities											*Millions of E. Caribbean Dollars:*					
Foreign Assets	11	...	...				7.21	12.58	12.99	14.19	24.04	19.63	24.31	18.58	17.31	25.45
Claims on Central Government	12a	...	...				1.69	2.94	4.09	4.09	4.09	5.10	8.93	11.48	11.03	19.71
Claims on Deposit Money Banks	12e	...	...				—	—	—	—	—	—	—	—	—	2.45
Reserve Money	14	...	...				8.90	15.52	17.07	18.28	28.12	24.04	28.53	25.59	24.10	44.93
of which: Currency Outside DMBs	14a	...	...				8.00	9.52	9.50	11.07	12.94	12.85	15.36	17.61	20.14	22.53
Foreign Liabilities	16c	...	...				—	—	—	—	—	.69	4.71	4.47	4.24	2.67
Central Government Deposits	16d	...	...				—	—	—	—	—	—	—	—	—	—
Other Items (Net)	17r	...	...				—	—	—	—	—	—	—	—	—	—
Deposit Money Banks											*Millions of E. Caribbean Dollars:*					
Reserves	20	...	...				.90	6.00	7.57	7.21	15.18	11.18	13.17	7.98	3.95	27.05
Foreign Assets	21	...	...				14.29	21.35	21.32	24.37	19.11	23.87	30.25	28.89	26.48	22.93
Claims on Central Government	22a	...	...				4.80	3.40	6.10	7.00	9.58	4.77	6.16	12.36	12.68	10.67
Claims on Local Government	22b	...	...				—	—	—	—	—	—	—	—	—	—
Claims on Nonfin.Pub.Enterprises	22c	...	...				2.70	2.50	3.30	4.70	9.52	11.65	4.57	30.45	35.37	43.96
Claims on Private Sector	22d	...	...				26.34	26.55	35.88	48.00	54.35	68.03	87.88	83.97	97.54	104.56
Claims on Nonbank Financial Insts	22g	...	...				.06	.06	.06	.06	.34	.39	.62	.86	.67	.78
Demand Deposits	24	...	...				5.34	6.55	7.10	11.55	14.78	15.21	17.93	17.27	20.42	25.27
Time, Savings,& Fgn.Currency Dep.	25	...	...				33.76	39.72	44.71	55.58	68.71	73.03	86.70	100.24	111.49	123.58
Foreign Liabilities	26c	...	...				13.46	17.13	23.94	24.88	27.77	32.81	32.44	38.49	32.93	35.79
Central Government Deposits	26d	...	...				—	1.50	1.50	1.70	.28	.14	.19	.23	5.84	3.78
Credit from Monetary Authorities	26g	...	...				—	.70	.80	1.00	—	—	1.34	5.66	1.92	2.07
Capital Accounts	27a	...	...				.40	.40	.40	.40	.45	1.57	3.47	5.73	8.41	10.51
Other Items (Net)	27r	...	...				-3.87	-6.14	-4.22	-3.77	-3.90	-2.88	.60	-3.11	-4.31	8.94
Monetary Survey											*Millions of E. Caribbean Dollars:*					
Foreign Assets (Net)	31n	...	...				8.04	16.80	10.37	13.68	15.38	10.00	17.41	4.51	6.62	9.92
Domestic Credit	32	...	...				35.60	33.96	47.92	62.15	77.60	89.79	107.97	138.89	151.45	175.88
Claims on Central Govt. (Net)	32an	...	...				6.49	4.84	8.69	9.39	13.39	9.72	14.89	23.61	17.87	26.59
Claims on Local Government	32b	...	...				—	—	—	—	—	—	—	—	—	—
Claims on Nonfin.Pub.Enterprises	32c	...	...				2.70	2.50	3.30	4.70	9.52	11.65	4.57	30.45	35.37	43.96
Claims on Private Sector	32d	...	...				26.34	26.55	35.88	48.00	54.35	68.03	87.88	83.97	97.54	104.56
Claims on Nonbank Financial Inst	32g	...	...				.06	.06	.06	.06	.34	.39	.62	.86	.67	.78
Money	34	...	...				13.35	16.08	16.61	22.62	27.72	28.06	33.28	34.88	40.56	47.79
Quasi-Money	35	...	...				33.76	39.72	44.71	55.58	68.71	73.03	86.70	100.24	111.49	123.58
Capital Accounts	37a	...	...				.40	.40	.40	.40	.45	2.19	4.56	6.77	9.40	11.44
Other Items (Net)	37r	...	...				-3.87	-5.44	-3.42	-2.77	-3.90	-3.49	.84	1.51	-3.38	3.00
Money plus Quasi-Money	35l	...	...				47.11	55.79	61.31	78.20	96.43	101.10	119.98	135.12	152.05	171.37
Interest Rates											*Percent Per Annum*					
Treasury Bill Rate	60c	....	....				....	....	....	....	....	6.5	6.5	6.5	6.5	6.5
Deposit Rate	60l	....	....				....	....	....	....	....	4.5	4.5	5.5	5.5	5.8
Lending Rate	60p	....	....				....	....	8.5	8.5	8.5	10.0	10.0	10.0	10.7	12.0
Prices											*Index Numbers (1995=100):*					
Consumer Prices	64					28.7	30.7	34.1	37.6	40.8	47.1	55.2	62.3	66.8	70.4	72.3
International Transactions											*Millions of E. Caribbean Dollars*					
Exports	70	7.1	5.9	6.6	10.1	14.6	16.4	24.5	26.8	44.0	39.3	41.7	64.9	87.0	110.8	144.6
Imports, c.i.f.	71	30.5	36.0	35.2	38.1	52.3	53.9	62.0	81.9	97.7	125.8	154.2	157.1	175.8	190.0	206.8

1985	1986	1987	1988	1989	1990	1991	1992	1993	1994	1995	1996	1997	1998	1999		
E.Caribbean Dollars per US Dollar: End of Period (ae)															**Exchange Rates**	
2.9657	3.3026	3.8304	3.6334	3.5482	3.8412	3.8622	3.7125	3.7086	3.9416	4.0135	3.8825	3.6430	3.8017	3.7058	Official Rate	**aa**
2.7000	2.7000	2.7000	2.7000	2.7000	2.7000	2.7000	2.7000	2.7000	2.7000	2.7000	2.7000	2.7000	2.7000	2.7000	Official Rate	**ae**
Period Averages																
100.0	100.0	100.0	100.0	100.0	100.0	100.0	100.0	100.0	100.0	100.0	100.0	100.0	100.0	100.0	Official Rate	**ah** *x*
82.1	82.8	80.6	79.1	82.7	82.7	86.0	88.1	98.1	103.4	100.0	102.7	108.7	112.4	113.6	Nominal Effective Exchange Rate	**ne** *c*
115.6	113.7	108.5	101.9	102.8	100.3	102.5	101.0	108.0	105.0	100.0	104.2	107.9	111.7	111.2	Real Effective Exchange Rate	**re** *c*
End of Period															**Fund Position**	
4.00	4.00	4.00	4.00	4.00	4.00	4.00	6.00	6.00	6.00	6.00	6.00	6.00	6.00	6.00	Quota	**2f.** *s*
—	.01	—	—	—	—	.01	.09	.09	.09	.08	.07	.07	.07	.06	SDRs	**1b.** *s*
—	—	—	—	—	—	—	.50	.50	.50	.50	.50	.50	.50	.50	Reserve Position in the Fund	**1c.** *s*
.33	—	—	—	—	—	—	—	—	—	—	—	—	—	—	Total Fund Cred.&Loans Outstg.	**2tl**
End of Period															**International Liquidity**	
13.80	25.83	20.22	21.82	22.77	26.49	22.68	33.38	31.51	31.25	29.83	30.19	31.19	38.77	42.58	Total Reserves minus Gold	**1l.** *d*
—	.01	—	—	—	—	.01	.12	.12	.12	.12	.11	.09	.09	.09	SDRs	**1b.** *d*
—	—	—	—	—	—	—	.69	.69	.73	.74	.72	.67	.70	.69	Reserve Position in the Fund	**1c.** *d*
13.80	25.82	20.22	21.82	22.77	26.49	22.67	32.57	30.70	30.40	28.97	29.36	30.42	37.97	41.81	Foreign Exchange	**1d.** *d*
12.69	19.66	25.23	34.31	37.29	48.65	43.82	41.84	47.01	49.54	45.76	45.09	47.82	53.50	89.92	Deposit Money Banks: Assets	**7a.** *d*
14.18	16.14	17.46	14.49	19.40	19.99	21.76	28.80	29.45	26.77	32.13	35.35	29.73	24.98	51.95	Liabilities	**7b.** *d*
End of Period															**Monetary Authorities**	
41.93	69.76	54.99	60.05	63.90	75.35	65.85	96.75	84.95	84.45	80.56	81.50	84.22	104.67	114.98	Foreign Assets	**11**
16.37	15.45	17.46	10.57	12.79	11.93	15.02	9.04	9.94	9.25	8.68	8.94	9.05	7.61	16.11	Claims on Central Government	**12a**
.95	—	—	—	—	1.32	.01	.01	.01	.01	.01	—	.01	.01	.01	Claims on Deposit Money Banks	**12e**
58.28	85.21	72.06	69.49	74.27	84.79	76.27	99.19	94.58	91.52	86.59	84.41	92.05	111.17	129.90	Reserve Money	**14**
32.03	41.42	23.27	25.15	32.12	23.96	19.09	30.30	28.22	32.02	28.59	27.01	33.49	36.43	57.49	*of which: Currency Outside DMBs*	**14a**
.98	—	—	—	—	—	—	—	—	—	—	—	—	—	—	Foreign Liabilities	**16c**
—	—	.39	1.13	2.43	3.81	4.61	6.62	.32	2.19	2.65	6.03	1.23	1.12	1.20	Central Government Deposits	**16d**
—	—	—	—	—	—	—	—	—	—	—	—	—	—	—	Other Items (Net)	**17r**
End of Period															**Deposit Money Banks**	
26.81	41.81	45.10	40.92	40.11	60.56	55.40	65.36	73.06	60.14	54.30	50.67	60.73	87.28	73.08	Reserves	**20**
34.27	53.07	68.12	92.64	100.69	131.35	118.31	112.97	126.94	133.75	123.56	121.75	129.13	144.44	242.78	Foreign Assets	**21**
9.59	31.96	37.92	35.94	44.38	31.27	29.34	39.80	42.34	44.25	75.60	74.22	79.23	84.23	95.93	Claims on Central Government	**22a**
—	—	—	2.39	—	—	3.29	3.29	—	.26	.11	.06	.18	.16	—	Claims on Local Government	**22b**
45.03	21.86	22.58	25.37	23.67	24.88	25.14	32.16	38.39	47.55	22.03	24.94	21.04	18.71	19.98	Claims on Nonfin.Pub.Enterprises	**22c**
107.35	108.18	130.05	159.41	189.83	204.33	238.67	258.45	265.98	285.12	347.02	398.83	447.16	486.42	545.63	Claims on Private Sector	**22d**
.47	1.23	1.33	.72	1.14	3.10	2.91	1.11	2.65	5.85	6.12	13.50	14.45	14.80	14.69	Claims on Nonbank Financial Insts	**22g**
20.52	21.74	29.89	37.50	37.73	49.37	41.41	61.10	62.86	76.54	79.60	87.43	112.29	131.73	148.38	Demand Deposits	**24**
143.68	163.97	190.87	184.16	209.67	245.33	254.37	249.83	279.28	282.14	303.39	321.29	344.21	397.65	453.14	Time, Savings,& Fgn.Currency Dep.	**25**
38.29	43.58	47.15	39.13	52.37	53.96	58.76	77.76	79.51	72.28	86.75	95.43	80.28	67.44	140.26	Foreign Liabilities	**26c**
3.18	10.42	18.18	76.90	75.67	80.55	95.03	95.88	101.95	110.64	124.38	141.22	165.25	196.62	203.79	Central Government Deposits	**26d**
—	—	—	—	.94	—	—	—	—	—	—	.01	.63	.50	.01	Credit from Monetary Authorities	**26g**
10.97	13.91	15.18	24.18	20.72	24.26	36.65	31.99	35.65	47.87	51.83	58.98	78.74	81.82	93.54	Capital Accounts	**27a**
6.88	4.50	3.82	−4.48	2.71	5.31	−13.15	−6.71	−9.89	−12.57	−17.22	−20.39	−29.49	−29.72	−47.03	Other Items (Net)	**27r**
End of Period															**Monetary Survey**	
36.93	79.25	75.96	113.55	112.22	152.73	125.40	131.96	132.38	145.92	117.37	107.81	133.07	181.67	217.49	Foreign Assets (Net)	**31n**
175.64	168.27	190.77	156.36	193.70	194.44	214.74	238.06	257.04	279.43	332.52	373.23	404.63	414.18	487.35	Domestic Credit	**32**
22.79	36.99	36.80	−31.53	−20.93	−41.16	−55.28	−53.66	−49.98	−59.34	−42.75	−64.09	−78.20	−105.90	−92.95	Claims on Central Govt. (Net)	**32an**
—	—	—	2.39	—	—	3.29	3.29	—	.26	.11	.06	.18	.16	—	Claims on Local Government	**32b**
45.03	21.86	22.58	25.37	23.67	24.88	25.14	32.16	38.39	47.55	22.03	24.94	21.04	18.71	19.98	Claims on Nonfin.Pub.Enterprises	**32c**
107.35	108.18	130.05	159.41	189.83	204.33	238.67	258.45	265.98	285.12	347.02	398.83	447.16	486.42	545.63	Claims on Private Sector	**32d**
.47	1.23	1.33	.72	1.14	3.10	2.91	1.11	2.65	5.85	6.12	13.50	14.45	14.80	14.69	Claims on Nonbank Financial Inst	**32g**
52.55	63.16	53.16	62.64	69.85	73.33	60.51	91.40	91.10	108.57	108.46	115.03	146.29	168.23	205.90	Money	**34**
143.68	163.97	190.87	184.16	209.67	245.33	254.37	249.83	279.28	282.14	303.39	321.29	344.21	397.65	453.14	Quasi-Money	**35**
12.01	15.06	16.52	25.45	21.96	25.60	38.00	33.29	36.95	49.25	53.23	60.34	80.02	73.15	94.84	Capital Accounts	**37a**
4.33	5.33	6.17	−2.33	4.44	2.92	−12.73	−4.49	−17.90	−14.61	−15.19	−15.62	−32.82	−43.17	−49.03	Other Items (Net)	**37r**
196.23	227.13	244.03	246.80	279.52	318.66	314.87	341.23	370.37	390.71	411.85	436.32	490.50	565.88	659.04	Money plus Quasi-Money	**35l**
Percent Per Annum															**Interest Rates**	
6.5	6.5	6.5	6.5	6.5	6.5	6.5	6.5	6.5	6.5	6.5	6.5	6.5	6.5	6.5	Treasury Bill Rate	**60c**
5.9	6.0	5.3	4.8	4.3	4.3	4.4	5.0	4.3	4.0	5.0	4.5	5.3	5.5	5.5	Deposit Rate	**60l**
12.1	12.5	12.5	12.1	12.4	12.5	13.5	11.4	11.2	11.0	11.0	11.0	12.0	12.5	12.5	Lending Rate	**60p**
Period Averages															**Prices**	
73.9	74.6	77.1	77.3	79.4	85.5	90.2	93.3	97.3	98.3	100.0	104.4	104.9	107.1	108.2	Consumer Prices	**64**
Millions of E. Caribbean Dollars															**International Transactions**	
170.8	172.3	141.3	230.2	201.4	223.4	181.2	210.9	156.1	136.1	115.2	125.2	124.5	134.0	131.4	Exports	**70**
213.9	235.7	266.4	330.1	344.2	367.4	377.1	356.6	362.7	351.0	366.7	356.0	490.7	520.2	542.6	Imports, c.i.f.	**71**

		1970	1971	1972	1973	1974	1975	1976	1977	1978	1979	1980	1981	1982	1983	1984
Balance of Payments														*Millions of US Dollars:*		
Current Account, n.i.e.	78al d	....	....	....	....	....	....	....	....	2.70	−3.60	−9.30	−.80	−10.81	−2.60	−1.00
Goods: Exports f.o.b.	78aa d	....	....	....	....	....	....	....	....	18.10	19.10	21.10	29.80	32.19	41.10	53.60
Goods: Imports f.o.b.	78ab d	....	....	....	....	....	....	....	....	−32.91	−42.09	−51.91	−52.91	−58.59	−63.36	−68.94
Trade Balance	78ac d	....	....	....	....	....	....	....	....	−14.81	−22.99	−30.81	−23.11	−26.40	−22.26	−15.34
Services: Credit	78ad d	....	....	....	....	....	....	....	....	11.10	13.70	17.70	18.90	15.70	17.80	19.10
Services: Debit	78ae d	....	....	....	....	....	....	....	....	−5.59	−9.81	−11.39	−13.29	−15.01	−15.24	−17.26
Balance on Goods & Services	78af d	....	....	....	....	....	....	....	....	−9.30	−19.10	−24.50	−17.50	−25.71	−19.70	−13.50
Income: Credit	78ag d	....	....	....	....	....	....	....	....	.20	.60	.80	1.40	.20	.20	—
Income: Debit	78ah d	....	....	....	....	....	....	....	....	−.20	−1.20	−1.70	−2.10	−2.90	−2.50	−3.00
Balance on Gds, Serv. & Inc.	78ai d	....	....	....	....	....	....	....	....	−9.30	−19.70	−25.40	−18.20	−28.41	−22.00	−16.50
Current Transfers, n.i.e.: Credit	78aj d	....	....	....	....	....	....	....	....	12.00	21.40	23.90	26.50	26.20	27.10	22.80
Current Transfers: Debit	78ak d	....	....	....	....	....	....	....	....	—	−5.30	−7.80	−9.10	−8.60	−7.70	−7.30
Capital Account, n.i.e.	78bc d	....	....	....	....	....	....	....	....	—	—	—	—	—	—	—
Capital Account, n.i.e.: Credit	78ba d	....	....	....	....	....	....	....	....	—	—	—	—	—	—	—
Capital Account: Debit	78bb d	....	....	....	....	....	....	....	....	—	—	—	—	—	—	—
Financial Account, n.i.e.	78bj d	....	....	....	....	....	....	....	....	−.18	5.82	5.65	.87	6.64	3.53	5.47
Direct Investment Abroad	78bd d	....	....	....	....	....	....	....	....							
Dir. Invest. in Rep. Econ., n.i.e.	78be d	....	....	....	....	....	....	....	....	−.50	.60	1.10	.50	1.50	2.10	1.40
Portfolio Investment Assets	78bf d	....	....	....	....	....	....	....	....	—	—	—	—	—	—	—
Equity Securities	78bk d	....	....	....	....	....	....	....	....	—	—	—	—	—	—	—
Debt Securities	78bl d	....	....	....	....	....	....	....	....	—	—	—	—	—	—	—
Portfolio Investment Liab., n.i.e.	78bg d	....	....	....	....	....	....	....	....	—	—	—	—	—	—	—
Equity Securities	78bm d	....	....	....	....	....	....	....	....	—	—	—	—	—	—	—
Debt Securities	78bn d	....	....	....	....	....	....	....	....	—	—	—	—	—	—	—
Financial Derivatives Assets	78bw d	....	....	....	....	....	....	....	....	....	....	....	....	....	....	....
Financial Derivatives Liabilities	78bx d	....	....	....	....	....	....	....	....	....	....	....	....	....	....	....
Other Investment Assets	78bh d	....	....	....	....	....	....	....	....	−1.13	1.95	−1.72	−2.20	.50	.89	1.31
Monetary Authorities	78bo d	....	....	....	....	....	....	....	....							
General Government	78bp d	....	....	....	....	....	....	....	....							
Banks	78bq d	....	....	....	....	....	....	....	....	−1.13	1.95	−1.72	−2.20	.50	.89	1.31
Other Sectors	78br d	....	....	....	....	....	....	....	....	—	—	—	—	—	—	—
Other Investment Liab., n.i.e.	78bi d	....	....	....	....	....	....	....	....	1.45	3.27	6.27	2.56	4.64	.54	2.76
Monetary Authorities	78bs d	....	....	....	....	....	....	....	....	—	—	—	—	—	—	—
General Government	78bt d	....	....	....	....	....	....	....	....	—	—	.60	.80	1.60	.60	−.10
Banks	78bu d	....	....	....	....	....	....	....	....	.35	1.07	1.87	−.14	2.24	−2.06	1.06
Other Sectors	78bv d	....	....	....	....	....	....	....	....	1.10	2.20	3.80	1.90	.80	2.00	1.80
Net Errors and Omissions	78ca d	....	....	....	....	....	....	....	....	−2.37	1.63	1.73	.08	.46	−.64	.04
Overall Balance	78cb d	....	....	....	....	....	....	....	....	.15	3.84	−1.92	.14	−3.70	.30	4.52
Reserves and Related Items	79da d	....	....	....	....	....	....	....	....	−.15	−3.84	1.92	−.14	3.70	−.30	−4.52
Reserve Assets	79db d	....	....	....	....	....	....	....	....	−.15	−3.84	1.66	−1.74	3.70	−.30	−4.02
Use of Fund Credit and Loans	79dc d	....	....	....	....	....	....	....	....	—	—	.26	1.60	—	—	−.49
Exceptional Financing	79de d	....	....	....	....	....	....	....	....	....	....	....	....	....	....	....
Government Finance										*Millions of E. Caribbean Dollars: Year Ending June 30 through 1990*						
Deficit (-) or Surplus	80	....	....	....	....	....	....	....	....	....	....	−.3	1.6	−7.1	−.4	−8.3
Revenue	81	....	....	....	....	....	....	....	....	24.5	31.8	43.2	45.9	62.9	74.9	78.6
Grants Received	81z	....	....	....	....	....	....	....	....	6.4	7.4	3.8	12.9	5.3	4.7	4.7
Expenditure	82	....	....	....	....	....	....	....	....	30.3	41.1	47.3	57.2	75.3	80.0	91.6
Lending Minus Repayments	83	....	....	....	....	....	....	....	....	....	....	....	....	....	....	....
Debt: Domestic	88a	....	....	....	....	....	....	....	....	....	....	....	....	....	....	....
Foreign	89a	....	....	....	....	....	....	....	....	....	....	....	....	....	....	....
National Accounts														*Millions of E. Caribbean Dollars*		
Exports of Goods & Services	90c	....	....	....	....	....	....	....	....	74.0	76.3	89.5	116.0	135.9	155.7	193.0
Government Consumption	91f	....	....	....	....	....	17.0	17.9	21.9	27.6	34.0	37.4	46.8	54.0	58.3	62.9
Gross Fixed Capital Formation	93e	....	....	....	....	....	18.4	17.1	33.9	34.4	48.6	62.8	64.2	64.7	62.9	70.5
Increase/Decrease(-) in Stocks	93i	....	....	....	....	....	.3	.7	2.6	—	—	—	—	—	—	6.9
Private Consumption	96f	....	....	....	....	....	56.0	66.1	84.4	90.6	123.8	140.9	147.9	177.4	195.4	175.6
Imports of Goods & Services	98c	....	....	....	....	....	—	—	−86.0	−103.9	−140.2	−170.9	−178.8	−204.7	−217.5	−231.6
Gross Domestic Product (GDP)	99b	....	....	....	....	....	70.4	83.7	97.3	122.6	142.6	159.7	196.1	227.4	254.9	277.2
GDP Volume 1977 prices	99b.p	....	....	....	....	....	83.1	91.7	97.0	91.4	95.7	99.3	105.9	112.0	117.8	124.0
GDP Volume 1990 prices	99b.p	....	....	....	....	....	....	....	....	....	....	....	....	....	....	....
GDP Volume (1995=100)	99bv p	....	....	....	....	....	39.5	43.6	46.1	43.5	45.5	47.2	50.4	53.3	56.0	59.0
GDP Deflator (1995=100)	99bi p	....	....	....	....	....	25.0	26.9	29.6	39.6	43.9	47.4	54.6	59.9	63.8	65.9
																Millions:
Population	99z	....	....	....	....	....	....	.11	.11	.12	.12	.10	.10	.11	.11	.11

Minus Sign Indicates Debit

Balance of Payments

	1985	1986	1987	1988	1989	1990	1991	1992	1993	1994	1995	1996	1997	1998	1999	
Current Account, n.i.e.	3.70	-10.20	-20.24	-16.79	-29.66	-23.56	-43.91	-20.94	-43.83	-57.99	-41.17	-35.22	....	....	....	78al *d*
Goods: Exports f.o.b.	63.20	66.11	54.37	87.41	77.37	85.41	67.41	79.01	57.11	48.90	61.94	52.33	....	....	....	78aa *d*
Goods: Imports f.o.b.	-71.28	-77.19	-86.33	-107.59	-112.56	-120.41	-120.35	-116.90	-118.11	-115.43	-119.37	-127.48	....	....	....	78ab *d*
Trade Balance	-8.08	-11.07	-31.96	-20.19	-35.19	-35.00	-52.94	-37.89	-61.01	-66.54	-57.43	-75.15	....	....	....	78ac *d*
Services: Credit	19.20	26.78	36.73	37.10	38.14	44.76	45.27	59.31	62.28	63.66	74.37	94.23	....	....	....	78ad *d*
Services: Debit	-17.92	-25.19	-27.47	-28.69	-34.05	-31.86	-32.88	-42.49	-43.89	-55.59	-55.14	-56.14	....	....	....	78ae *d*
Balance on Goods & Services	-6.80	-9.49	-22.71	-11.78	-31.10	-22.10	-40.55	-21.07	-42.61	-58.47	-38.20	-37.05	....	....	....	78af *d*
Income: Credit	.20	2.26	3.96	4.48	4.63	4.62	5.10	4.82	2.89	3.70	3.84	3.99	....	....	....	78ag *d*
Income: Debit	-3.10	-10.70	-8.22	-15.74	-11.48	-15.67	-16.30	-12.51	-11.11	-15.04	-15.67	-13.51	....	....	....	78ah *d*
Balance on Gds, Serv. & Inc.	-9.70	-17.93	-26.97	-23.04	-37.95	-33.14	-51.75	-28.76	-50.83	-69.80	-50.04	-46.57	....	....	....	78ai *d*
Current Transfers, n.i.e.: Credit	22.10	11.67	12.40	12.33	13.00	14.46	14.46	16.20	15.59	19.42	16.81	18.53	....	....	....	78aj *d*
Current Transfers: Debit	-8.70	-3.93	-5.67	-6.08	-4.71	-4.87	-6.62	-8.39	-8.59	-7.61	-7.94	-7.18	....	....	....	78ak *d*
Capital Account, n.i.e.	—	8.81	6.80	8.56	10.70	18.64	21.40	13.71	6.31	4.01	6.18	4.11	....	....	....	78bc *d*
Capital Account, n.i.e.: Credit	—	9.00	7.12	10.15	12.15	18.88	21.64	14.33	7.00	5.37	6.92	5.23	....	....	....	78ba *d*
Capital Account: Debit	—	-.19	-.32	-1.59	-1.44	-.23	-.25	-.62	-.69	-1.36	-.74	-1.11	....	....	....	78bb *d*
Financial Account, n.i.e.	.83	6.57	17.15	3.51	17.52	1.99	20.63	17.86	32.78	50.91	35.80	18.31	....	....	....	78bj *d*
Direct Investment Abroad																78bd *d*
Dir. Invest. in Rep. Econ., n.i.e.	1.80	7.37	4.96	9.11	10.59	7.67	8.83	14.81	31.36	47.28	30.64	18.20	....	....	....	78be *d*
Portfolio Investment Assets	—	—	—	—	—	—	—	—	.03	.45	—	—	....	....	....	78bf *d*
Equity Securities	—	—	—	—	—	—	—	—	.03	.45	—	—	....	....	....	78bk *d*
Debt Securities																78bl *d*
Portfolio Investment Liab., n.i.e.	—	—	—	—	—	—	—	—	—	-.21	—	-3.44	....	....	....	78bg *d*
Equity Securities	—	—	—	—	—	—	—	—	—	-.21	—	-.40	....	....	....	78bm *d*
Debt Securities	—				—	—	—	—	—	—	—	-3.04	....	....	....	78bn *d*
Financial Derivatives Assets																78bw *d*
Financial Derivatives Liabilities																78bx *d*
Other Investment Assets	-4.20	-5.30	-3.78	-12.04	1.96	-10.78	5.68	2.96	-4.53	3.70	9.13	3.89	....	....	....	78bh *d*
Monetary Authorities	....															78bo *d*
General Government																78bp *d*
Banks	-4.20	-5.30	-3.78	-12.04	1.96	-10.78	5.68	2.96	-4.53	3.70	9.13	3.89	....	....	....	78bq *d*
Other Sectors																78br *d*
Other Investment Liab., n.i.e.	3.23	4.50	15.96	6.44	4.96	5.10	6.12	.10	5.91	-.31	-3.97	-.34	....	....	....	78bi *d*
Monetary Authorities	—	—	—	—	—	—	—	—	—		—		....	....	....	78bs *d*
General Government	-.30	5.41	15.19	6.59	4.93	6.44	6.33	3.43	3.67	1.65	-3.02	.20	....	....	....	78bt *d*
Banks	.93															78bu *d*
Other Sectors	2.60	-.91	.78	-.15	.04	-1.34	-.20	-3.33	2.25	-1.96	-.96	-.54	....	....	....	78bv *d*
Net Errors and Omissions	1.86	6.67	-8.93	6.64	2.87	8.35	-1.63	-1.08	3.44	3.54	-1.11	13.18	....	....	....	78ca *d*
Overall Balance	6.38	11.86	-5.22	1.93	1.43	5.44	-3.51	9.55	-1.29	.47	-.30	.38	....	....	....	78cb *d*
Reserves and Related Items	-6.38	-11.86	5.22	-1.93	-1.43	-5.44	3.51	-9.55	1.29	-.47	.30	-.38	....	....	....	79da *d*
Reserve Assets	-5.70	-11.49	5.22	-1.93	-1.43	-5.44	3.51	-9.55	1.29	-.47	.30	-.38	....	....	....	79db *d*
Use of Fund Credit and Loans	-.68	-.37	—	—	—	—	—	—	—	—	—	—	....	....	....	79dc *d*
Exceptional Financing	....	....	....	....	....	....	....	....	....	....	....	....	....	....	....	79de *d*

Government Finance

Year Ending December 31 Beginning 1991

	1985	1986	1987	1988	1989	1990	1991	1992	1993	1994	1995	1996	1997	1998	1999	
Deficit (-) or Surplus	6.1	4.4	5.2	-5.7	-8.7	-12.7	I.3	-27.2	-22.3	-6.7	-2.2	-15.4	-83.7	-70.3 P	....	80
Revenue	90.8	100.8	107.5	116.4	126.9	137.2	I170.0	175.9	185.1	195.6	204.1	220.1	240.5	258.7 P	....	81
Grants Received	6.1	5.0	5.9	3.9	35.5	32.4	I32.3	14.5	.9	2.1	1.5	1.4	12.8	32.6 P	....	81z
Expenditure	90.8	101.4	108.2	126.0	171.1	182.3	I201.9	217.6	208.3	204.4	207.8	236.9	337.0	361.6 P	....	82
Lending Minus Repayments							I								—P	83
Debt: Domestic		59.0	68.4	68.3	57.2	59.3	I60.5	70.9	117.4	124.5	133.7	139.4	144.0	147.1 P	....	88a
Foreign	74.7	84.4	100.2	118.0	145.3	I156.8	181.5	197.3	213.6	236.2	233.0	225.8	256.8 P	....		89a

National Accounts

Millions of E. Caribbean Dollars

	1985	1986	1987	1988	1989	1990	1991	1992	1993	1994	1995	1996	1997	1998	1999	
Exports of Goods & Services	222.5	246.0	240.0	332.0	306.0	352.0	303.0	373.0	322.0	304.0	368.0	393.0	379.0	404.0	....	90c
Government Consumption	60.2	67.8	76.6	80.3	92.0	93.6	117.6	149.8	129.0	139.0	144.0	152.0	150.0	161.0	....	91f
Gross Fixed Capital Formation	76.2	102.0	125.0	135.0	138.0	159.0	169.0	153.0	165.0	165.0	215.0	213.0	235.0	272.0	....	93e
Increase/Decrease(-) in Stocks	9.9	2.8	9.9	13.6	12.5	7.1	7.7	13.9	18.0	19.0	20.0	21.9	....		....	93i
Private Consumption	175.7	197.5	244.0	260.0	332.0	341.0	442.0	384.0	465.0	490.0	456.0	475.0	587.0	632.0	....	96f
Imports of Goods & Services	-239.9	-275.0	-306.0	-368.0	-395.0	-411.0	-458.0	-430.0	-437.0	-462.0	-471.0	-481.0	-558.0	-615.0	....	98c
Gross Domestic Product (GDP)	304.6	346.0	383.7	444.0	479.0	535.0	574.0	630.0	645.0	657.0	713.0	752.0	793.0	854.0	....	99b
GDP Volume 1977 prices	130.7	140.2	....	....	....	....	....	....	....	....	....	....	....	....	....	99b.*p*
GDP Volume 1990 prices	....	414.0	433.0	496.0	509.0	535.0	543.0	575.0	589.0	577.0	621.0	630.0	653.0	687.0	....	99b.*p*
GDP Volume (1995=100)	62.1	66.7	69.7	79.9	82.0	86.2	87.4	92.6	94.8	92.9	100.0	101.4	105.2	110.6	....	99bv *p*
GDP Deflator (1995=100)	68.7	72.8	77.2	78.0	82.0	87.1	92.1	95.4	95.4	99.2	100.0	104.0	105.8	108.3	....	99bi *p*

Midyear Estimates

	1985	1986	1987	1988	1989	1990	1991	1992	1993	1994	1995	1996	1997	1998	1999	
Population	.11	.11	.11	.11	.10	.11	.11	.11	.11	.11	.11	.11	.11	.11	.11	99z

(See notes in the back of the book.)

Samoa

		1970	1971	1972	1973	1974	1975	1976	1977	1978	1979	1980	1981	1982	1983	1984
Exchange Rates																*SDRs per Tala:*
Official Rate	ac	1.3868	1.3631	1.3674	1.3666	1.3465	1.1133	1.0759	1.0998	1.0743	.8332	.8438	.7816	.7328	.5895	.4673
																US Dollars per Tala:
Official Rate	ag	1.3868	1.4799	1.4847	1.6486	1.6486	1.3033	1.2500	1.3359	1.3996	1.0976	1.0762	.9098	.8083	.6172	.4581
Official Rate	rh	1.3868	1.3910	1.4806[e]	1.6281[e]	1.6486[e]	1.5920	1.2547	1.2706	1.3586	1.2205	1.0876	.9649	.8297	.6496	.5441
															Index Numbers (1995=100):	
Official Rate	ahx	342.9[e]	312.1	366.0[e]	402.5[e]	407.6[e]	393.6	310.2	314.1	335.9	301.7	268.9	238.5	205.1	160.6	134.5
Nominal Effective Exchange Rate	ne c	....	....	....	....	....	....	....	....	....	224.7	201.6	191.4	180.2	149.7	134.6
Real Effective Exchange Rate	re c	....	....	....	....	....	....	....	....	....	136.6	145.1	150.0	153.7	141.0	135.0
Fund Position																*Millions of SDRs:*
Quota	2f. s	....	2.00	2.00	2.00	2.00	2.00	2.00	2.00	3.00	3.00	4.50	4.50	4.50	6.00	6.00
SDRs	1b. s	....	—	.21	.21	.21	.04	—	.03	.04	—	—	.01	.01	.41	.15
Reserve Position in the Fund	1c. s	....	.36	.36	.36	.36										
Total Fund Cred.&Loans Outstg.	2tl	....					1.26	1.92	1.84	3.49	4.75	4.51	6.41	5.70	7.56	9.97
International Liquidity												*Millions of US Dollars Unless Otherwise Indicated:*					
Total Reserves minus Gold	1l. d	5.22	6.41	4.53	5.08	5.96	6.39	5.24	9.13	4.78	4.82	2.77	3.28	3.48	7.23	10.56
SDRs	1b. d	....	—	.23	.25	.26	.05	—	.04	.05	—	—	.01	.01	.43	.15
Reserve Position in the Fund	1c. d	....	.39	.39	.43	.44	—	—	—	—	—	—	—	—	—	—
Foreign Exchange	1d. d	5.22	6.02	3.91	4.39	5.26	6.34	5.24	9.09	4.73	4.82	2.77	3.27	3.47	6.80	10.41
Other Official Insts.: Assets	3b. d	4.42	4.85	4.58	3.09	2.30	.91	.69	.74	1.34	.84	.56	.51	.50	.34	.22
Deposit Money Banks: Assets	7a. d	4.36	5.04	3.45	4.08	5.39	5.42	4.72	7.35	3.89	4.16	2.31	3.01	3.14	6.02	6.89
Liabilities	7b. d	—		.41	.01					.05	.65	3.07	.81	1.13	.23	.24
Monetary Authorities																*Millions of Tala:*
Foreign Assets	11	.69	.91	.71	.60	.77	.74	.42	1.18	.64	.61	.43	.29	.52	2.01	8.00
Claims on Central Government	12a	−.59	−.80	.13	.15	.18	.39	.48	.66	.67	.84	2.71	4.79	6.75	6.78	6.66
Claims on Deposit Money Banks	12e	—	—	—	—	—	—	—	—	—	—	2.73	2.57	1.75	2.03	1.28
Reserve Money	14	.10	.12	.13	.15	.18	.38	.48	.66	.67	.84	5.44	7.35	8.41	9.41	10.94
of which: Currency Outside DMBs	14a	.09	.10	.12	.14	.17	.19	.22	.23	.25	.17	3.56	5.28	6.05	6.02	7.08
Liabs. of Central Bank: Securities	16ac															
Foreign Liabilities	16c	—	—	—	—	—	1.13	1.78	1.67	3.25	5.70	5.34	8.21	7.87	12.84	21.36
Central Government Deposits	16d	—	—	.56	.44	.61	−.58	−1.56	−.69	−2.81	−5.72	−5.91	−9.37	−8.82	−12.75	−18.65
Capital Accounts	17a	—	—	.15	.15	.16	.19	.20	.19	.20	.62	1.01	1.46	1.57	1.93	2.70
Other Items (Net)	17r	—	—	—	—	—	—	—	—	—	—	−.01	−.01	−.01	−.61	−.40
Deposit Money Banks																*Millions of Tala:*
Reserves	20	.01	.01	.01	.01	.01	.20	.26	.43	.41	.66	1.89	2.07	2.37	3.39	3.86
Other Claims on Monetary Author.	20c	—														
Foreign Assets	21	3.15	3.35	2.29	2.43	3.27	4.16	3.78	5.50	2.78	3.79	2.14	3.31	3.88	9.76	15.05
Claims on Central Government	22a	.30	.48	.65	1.03	1.03	1.20	1.35	2.67	3.39	4.59	6.08	10.86	15.17	8.30	4.42
Claims on Nonfin.Pub.Enterprises	22c	—	—	—	.41	.34	.36	.58	.55	1.93	4.78	6.65	10.51	12.77	10.57	10.11
Claims on Private Sector	22d	1.58	1.99	3.17	2.85	4.06	3.91	5.91	7.15	9.78	10.73	11.33	11.99	14.17	15.94	19.04
Demand Deposits	24	1.19	1.83	2.19	2.62	3.04	3.29	3.83	4.52	4.97	5.60	5.58	8.83	11.37	10.91	12.28
Time and Savings Deposits	25	1.40	1.52	1.57	2.12	2.56	2.80	3.59	4.53	5.11	9.01	10.46	18.67	26.89	21.95	24.15
Foreign Liabilities	26c	—	—	.27	.01	—	—	—	—	.03	.60	2.86	.89	1.39	.37	.52
Central Government Deposits	26d	1.07	.94	.59	.28	.42	.67	.55	1.72	1.01	1.18	.60	.98	1.64	1.71	6.16
Credit from Monetary Authorities	26g	1.06	1.21	—	—	—	—	—	—	—	—	2.73	2.57	1.75	2.03	1.28
Capital Accounts	27a	—	—	.50	.50	.75	1.00	1.00	1.50	1.47	1.68	1.77	2.23	2.00	3.00	8.73
Other Items (Net)	27r	.31	.33	1.00	1.22	1.95	2.05	2.91	4.02	5.70	6.50	4.09	4.58	3.32	7.97	−.64
Monetary Survey																*Millions of Tala:*
Foreign Assets (Net)	31n	3.84	4.26	2.74	3.02	I4.04	3.77	2.41	5.00	.13	−1.89	−5.63	−5.49	−4.86	−1.45	1.17
Domestic Credit	32	.21	.73	2.79	3.72	4.58	5.75	9.33	9.99	17.57	25.48	32.08	46.53	56.04	52.63	52.73
Claims on Central Govt. (Net)	32an	−1.37	−1.25	−.38	.46	.18	1.49	2.84	2.29	5.86	9.97	14.10	24.03	29.10	26.12	23.57
Claims on Nonfin.Pub.Enterprises	32c	—	—	—	.41	.34	.36	.58	.55	1.93	4.78	6.65	10.51	12.77	10.57	10.11
Claims on Private Sector	32d	1.58	1.99	3.17	2.85	4.06	3.91	5.91	7.15	9.78	10.73	11.33	11.99	15.94	19.04	
Money	34	1.28	1.94	2.31	2.76	I3.21	3.48	4.04	4.76	5.23	5.77	9.14	14.11	17.42	16.93	19.36
Quasi-Money	35	1.40	1.52	1.57	2.12	2.56	2.80	3.59	4.53	5.11	9.01	10.46	18.67	26.89	21.95	24.15
Capital Accounts	37a	—	—	.65	.65	.91	1.19	1.20	1.69	1.67	2.30	2.78	3.69	3.57	4.93	11.43
Other Items (Net)	37r	1.36	1.54	1.00	1.22	1.95	2.06	2.92	4.01	5.71	6.50	4.08	4.58	3.30	7.36	−1.04
Money plus Quasi-Money	35l	2.68	3.46	3.88	4.88	I5.77	6.28	7.64	9.28	10.33	14.78	19.60	32.77	44.31	38.88	43.51
Other Banking Institutions																*Millions of Tala:*
Deposits	45	.56	.59	.66	.70	.87	.83	.88	.85	.81	.85	.88	.81	1.01	1.15	1.27
Liquid Liabilities	55l	3.24	4.05	4.54	5.58	I6.64	7.11	8.52	10.13	11.14	15.63	20.48	33.58	45.32	40.03	44.78
Interest Rates																*Percent Per Annum*
Deposit Rate	60l	....	....	....	....	....	....	....	....	....	6.5	6.5	6.5	9.0	11.8	12.0
Lending Rate	60p	....	....	....	....	....	....	....	....	....	....	....	....	....	20.0	20.0
Government Bond Yield	61	....	....	....	....	....	....	....	....	....	8.0	8.0	11.5	12.3	14.9	17.5

	1985	1986	1987	1988	1989	1990	1991	1992	1993	1994	1995	1996	1997	1998	1999		
																Exchange Rates	
End of Period																	
	.3947	.3720	.3505	.3459	.3323	.3013	.2855	.2844	.2792	.2794	.2662	.2857	.2679	.2359	.2414	Official Rate	**ac**
End of Period (ag) Period Average (rh)																	
	.4336	.4550	.4973	.4655	.4367	.4286	.4084	.3910	.3835	.4079	.3957	.4108	.3615	.3322	.3313	Official Rate	**ag**
	.4457	.4474	.4716	.4810	.4408	.4330	.4171	.4056	.3894	.3945	.4045	.4062	.3912	.3398	.3320	Official Rate	**rh**
Period Averages																	
	110.2	110.6	116.6	118.9	109.0	107.1	103.1	100.3	96.3	97.5	100.0	100.4	96.7	84.0	82.1	Official Rate	**ahx**
	119.6	110.1	106.9	103.1	98.4	96.7	96.2	96.9	100.0	102.5	100.0	102.2	104.3	100.0	97.2	Nominal Effective Exchange Rate	**nec**
	122.7	114.1	109.2	109.7	106.2	110.8	101.7	105.2	103.1	109.8	100.0	105.0	112.5	108.4	104.7	Real Effective Exchange Rate	**rec**
End of Period																**Fund Position**	
	6.00	6.00	6.00	6.00	6.00	6.00	6.00	8.50	8.50	8.50	8.50	8.50	8.50	8.50	11.60	Quota	**2f. s**
	.01	.79	1.31	2.44	.69	2.94	2.59	1.89	1.95	1.99	2.04	2.10	2.14	2.19	2.24	SDRs	**1b. s**
	—	—	—	.03	.03	.03	.03	.66	.66	.66	.67	.67	.68	.68	.68	Reserve Position in the Fund	**1c. s**
	9.95	8.28	5.79	2.85	1.23	.59	.16	—	—	—	—	—	—	—	—	Total Fund Cred.&Loans Outstg.	**2tl**
End of Period																**International Liquidity**	
	14.02	23.75	37.20	49.20	55.07	69.05	67.81	61.16	50.71	50.80	55.31	60.80	64.21	61.42	68.20	Total Reserves minus Gold	**1l. d**
	.01	.97	1.86	3.28	.91	4.18	3.70	2.60	2.68	2.91	3.03	3.02	2.89	3.09	3.07	SDRs	**1b. d**
	—	—	—	.01	.04	.04	.04	.04	.91	.91	.97	1.00	.97	.92	.96	.94	Reserve Position in the Fund	**1c. d**
	14.01	22.78	35.34	45.90	54.12	64.82	64.06	57.65	47.11	46.92	51.28	56.82	60.39	57.37	64.19	Foreign Exchange	**1d. d**
	.27	.23	.33	....	....	....	....	....	....	....	....	....	....	....	....	Other Official Insts.: Assets	**3b. d**
	2.03	3.49	5.14	5.40	5.03	5.50	2.79	3.76	3.11	6.26	4.66	5.38	6.98	8.00	11.41	Deposit Money Banks: Assets	**7a. d**
	.29	.02	.66	.85	.43	.57	1.21	.22	.50	2.86	1.67	3.41	3.97	3.11	11.07	Liabilities	**7b. d**
End of Period																**Monetary Authorities**	
	27.66	44.68	64.47	86.51	117.15	148.25	159.24	135.99	112.38	109.39	119.13	134.91	158.30	166.00	171.41	Foreign Assets	**11**
	6.87	1.96	1.88	2.51	2.51	4.23	1.94	1.69	1.69	.07	.07	—	—	—	—	Claims on Central Government	**12a**
	4.99	5.05	11.05	5.35	7.81	29.34	16.89	5.85	6.00	6.23	.06	.03	.06	.09	.06	Claims on Deposit Money Banks	**12e**
	25.09	35.14	40.37	41.81	58.01	88.33	79.77	63.29	58.25	60.11	62.73	75.57	90.03	48.86	59.31	Reserve Money	**14**
	8.44	9.18	10.53	10.72	12.48	12.94	13.96	12.31	13.95	16.82	21.60	20.96	30.39	24.82	29.09	*of which: Currency Outside DMBs*	**14a**
														25.51	27.39	Liabs. of Central Bank: Securities	**16ac**
	25.22	22.26	16.75	8.24	3.70	1.96	.56	—	—	—	—	—	.03	.14	.10	Foreign Liabilities	**16c**
	-15.97	-11.90	13.93	33.59	49.97	66.37	79.40	79.89	64.54	49.07	48.37	56.79	69.61	90.22	83.38	Central Government Deposits	**16d**
	5.41	5.68	6.12	10.45	12.59	22.26	27.86	24.94	26.58	28.29	27.60	27.51	28.46	30.29	30.29	Capital Accounts	**17a**
	-.23	.51	.23	.29	3.19	2.90	-9.53	-24.59	-29.31	-21.78	-19.44	-24.93	-29.78	-28.93	-29.00	Other Items (Net)	**17r**
End of Period																**Deposit Money Banks**	
	16.65	25.96	29.84	31.09	45.53	75.39	65.80	50.98	44.30	43.29	41.13	54.41	59.64	24.04	30.22	Reserves	**20**
														25.51	27.39	Other Claims on Monetary Author.	**20c**
	4.68	7.67	10.33	11.60	11.52	12.83	6.84	9.61	8.10	15.34	11.78	13.09	19.30	24.09	34.45	Foreign Assets	**21**
	1.39	2.40	4.21	4.42	4.29	3.79	3.45	2.99	3.62	3.67	1.30	.66	—	—	9.41	Claims on Central Government	**22a**
	12.08	12.25	10.48	6.24	4.07	2.57	2.35	2.37	.56	3.16	3.70	4.08	3.24	3.26	13.61	Claims on Nonfin.Pub.Enterprises	**22c**
	22.39	26.61	32.63	39.95	42.32	58.81	63.19	70.91	81.29	75.49	97.38	115.15	137.69	163.84	192.91	Claims on Private Sector	**22d**
	11.52	12.45	18.16	19.47	20.68	34.35	28.97	25.73	29.70	30.38	39.34	39.86	44.14	41.71	51.23	Demand Deposits	**24**
	32.44	41.52	51.96	56.73	68.29	73.69	75.78	81.52	77.63	90.88	107.30	115.69	131.17	143.67	156.05	Time and Savings Deposits	**25**
	.67	.04	1.32	1.83	.98	1.34	2.97	.57	1.30	7.00	4.23	8.29	10.97	9.37	33.40	Foreign Liabilities	**26c**
	1.00	6.79	1.95	4.65	5.52	3.01	2.35	1.96	3.01	2.32	3.36	8.31	16.56	14.09	23.79	Central Government Deposits	**26d**
	4.99	5.05	11.02	5.35	7.82	29.34	17.64	5.85	5.99	6.23	.06	.03	.10	.09	.05	Credit from Monetary Authorities	**26g**
	11.12	12.63	14.68	18.29	19.21	25.97	26.75	22.72	27.26	21.72	22.48	34.61	31.97	37.34	56.52	Capital Accounts	**27a**
	-4.55	-3.59	-11.60	-13.02	-14.77	-14.31	-12.83	-1.49	-7.02	-17.58	-21.48	-19.40	-15.04	-5.53	-13.05	Other Items (Net)	**27r**
End of Period																**Monetary Survey**	
	6.45	30.05	56.73	88.04	123.99	157.78	162.55	145.03	119.18	Ⅰ117.73	126.68	139.71	166.60	180.58	172.36	Foreign Assets (Net)	**31n**
	57.70	48.33	33.32	14.88	-2.30	.02	-10.82	-3.89	19.61	31.00	50.72	54.79	54.76	62.79	108.76	Domestic Credit	**32**
	23.23	9.47	-9.79	-31.31	-48.69	-61.36	-76.36	-77.17	-62.24	-47.65	-50.36	-64.44	-86.17	-104.31	-97.76	Claims on Central Govt. (Net)	**32an**
	12.08	12.25	10.48	6.24	4.07	2.57	2.35	2.37	.56	3.16	3.70	4.08	3.24	3.26	13.61	Claims on Nonfin.Pub.Enterprises	**32c**
	22.39	26.61	32.63	39.95	42.32	58.81	63.19	70.91	81.29	75.49	97.38	115.15	137.69	163.84	192.91	Claims on Private Sector	**32d**
	19.96	21.63	28.69	30.19	33.16	47.29	42.93	38.04	43.65	Ⅰ47.20	60.94	60.82	74.53	66.53	80.32	Money	**34**
	32.44	41.52	51.96	56.73	68.29	73.69	75.78	81.52	77.63	90.88	107.30	115.69	131.17	143.67	156.05	Quasi-Money	**35**
	16.53	18.31	20.80	28.74	31.80	48.23	54.61	47.66	53.84	50.01	50.08	62.12	60.43	67.63	86.81	Capital Accounts	**37a**
	-4.78	-3.08	-11.40	-12.73	-11.57	-11.41	-21.60	-26.08	-36.34	-39.36	-40.92	-44.13	-44.78	-34.46	-42.06	Other Items (Net)	**37r**
	52.40	63.15	80.65	86.92	101.45	120.98	118.71	119.56	121.28	Ⅰ138.08	168.24	176.51	205.70	210.20	236.37	Money plus Quasi-Money	**35l**
End of Period																**Other Banking Institutions**	
	1.54	1.59	1.72	1.94	3.50	3.86	8.44	6.60	2.56	2.63	....	....	....	....	....	Deposits	**45**
	53.94	64.74	82.37	88.86	104.95	124.84	127.15	126.16	123.84	140.71	....	....	....	....	....	Liquid Liabilities	**55l**
Percent Per Annum																**Interest Rates**	
	12.0	13.5	12.0	12.0	12.0	8.3	8.3	6.4	5.5	5.5	5.5	5.5	5.5	6.5	6.5	Deposit Rate	**60l**
	19.0	18.8	17.5	17.5	17.0	13.3	14.8	12.9	12.0	12.0	12.0	12.0	12.0	11.5	11.5	Lending Rate	**60p**
	15.0	14.2	13.5	13.5	13.5	13.5	13.5	13.5	13.5	13.5	13.5	13.5	13.5	13.5	13.5	Government Bond Yield	**61**

Samoa

		1970	1971	1972	1973	1974	1975	1976	1977	1978	1979	1980	1981	1982	1983	1984
Prices and Production														*Index Numbers (1995=100):*		
Consumer Prices	64	9.1	9.5	ꟷ10.3	11.5	14.3	15.6	16.4	18.8	19.1	21.3	ꟷ28.3	34.1	40.3	47.0	52.6
Manufacturing Production	66ey	....	....	....	....	....	....	....	....	....	....	....	....	....	....	....
International Transactions														*Thousands of Tala*		
Exports	70	....	....	....	....	....	....	5,447	11,584	8,169	14,981	15,828	11,150	16,248	27,410	36,781
Imports, c.i.f.	71	9,791	9,614	13,044	14,433	15,909	23,160	23,627	ꟷ32,254	38,567	60,946	57,438	58,396	60,115	75,100	93,285
Balance of Payments														*Millions of US Dollars:*		
Current Account, n.i.e.	78al d	....	....	....	....	....	....	....	−11.19	−18.10	−22.04	−12.91	−15.12	−6.62	3.51	.66
Goods: Exports f.o.b.	78aa d	....	....	....	....	....	....	....	14.73	9.74	18.13	17.22	10.78	13.46	17.69	18.34
Goods: Imports f.o.b.	78ab d	....	....	....	....	....	....	....	−37.34	−47.66	−67.15	−56.86	−51.38	−45.31	−44.12	−45.55
Trade Balance	78ac d	....	....	....	....	....	....	....	−22.61	−37.92	−49.02	−39.64	−40.60	−31.86	−26.42	−27.21
Services: Credit	78ad d	....	....	....	....	....	....	....	2.42	3.91	3.63	8.43	7.48	8.24	9.13	8.53
Services: Debit	78ae d	....	....	....	....	....	....	....	−5.09	−6.76	−9.89	−14.86	−11.59	−12.61	−12.45	−12.18
Balance on Goods & Services	78af d	....	....	....	....	....	....	....	−25.28	−40.77	−55.28	−46.07	−44.71	−36.22	−29.73	−30.86
Income: Credit	78ag d	....	....	....	....	....	....	....	—	—	—	.02	.13	.08	.14	.34
Income: Debit	78ah d	....	....	....	....	....	....	....	−.11	−1.49	−1.62	−2.56	−2.79	−2.24	−2.83	−2.33
Balance on Gds, Serv. & Inc.	78ai d	....	....	....	....	....	....	....	−25.39	−42.26	−56.90	−48.60	−47.37	−38.37	−32.43	−32.85
Current Transfers, n.i.e.: Credit	78aj d	....	....	....	....	....	....	....	14.20	24.16	34.86	36.17	32.49	32.29	36.67	33.86
Current Transfers: Debit	78ak d	....	....	....	....	....	....	....	—	—	—	−.48	−.25	−.54	−.72	−.35
Capital Account, n.i.e.	78bc d	....	....	....	....	....	....	....	—	—	—	—	—	—	—	—
Capital Account, n.i.e.: Credit	78ba d	....	....	....	....	....	....	....	—	—	—	—	—	—	—	—
Capital Account: Debit	78bb d	....	....	....	....	....	....	....	—	—	—	—	—	—	—	—
Financial Account, n.i.e.	78bj d	....	....	....	....	....	....	....	8.87	7.80	19.47	8.19	2.63	−.08	2.58	4.56
Direct Investment Abroad	78bd d	....	....	....	....	....	....	....	—	—	—	—	—	—	—	—
Dir. Invest. in Rep. Econ., n.i.e.	78be d	....	....	....	....	....	....	....	—	—	—	—	—	—	—	—
Portfolio Investment Assets	78bf d	....	....	....	....	....	....	....	—	—	—	—	—	—	—	—
Equity Securities	78bk d	....	....	....	....	....	....	....	—	—	—	—	—	—	—	—
Debt Securities	78bl d	....	....	....	....	....	....	....	—	—	—	—	—	—	—	—
Portfolio Investment Liab., n.i.e.	78bg d	....	....	....	....	....	....	....	—	—	—	—	—	—	—	—
Equity Securities	78bm d	....	....	....	....	....	....	....	—	—	—	—	—	—	—	—
Debt Securities	78bn d	....	....	....	....	....	....	....	—	—	—	—	—	—	—	—
Financial Derivatives Assets	78bw d	....	....	....	....	....	....	....						....	....	....
Financial Derivatives Liabilities	78bx d	....	....	....	....	....	....	....						....	....	....
Other Investment Assets	78bh d	....	....	....	....	....	....	....	—	—	—	—	—	−.05	.08	.02
Monetary Authorities	78bo d	....	....	....	....	....	....	....	—	—	—	—	—			
General Government	78bp d	....	....	....	....	....	....	....	—	—	—	—	—			
Banks	78bq d	....	....	....	....	....	....	....	—	—	—	—	—			
Other Sectors	78br d	....	....	....	....	....	....	....	—	—	—	—	—	−.05	.08	.02
Other Investment Liab., n.i.e.	78bi d	....	....	....	....	....	....	....	8.87	7.80	19.47	8.19	2.63	−.03	2.50	4.54
Monetary Authorities	78bs d	....	....	....	....	....	....	....						.07	−.05	.01
General Government	78bt d	....	....	....	....	....	....	....	3.99	10.88	6.99	6.51	5.56	3.22	3.28	5.73
Banks	78bu d	....	....	....	....	....	....	....	—	.04	2.46	−.77	−1.91	.41	−.66	.08
Other Sectors	78bv d	....	....	....	....	....	....	....	4.87	−3.12	11.79	−.78	−1.03	−3.74	−.07	−1.28
Net Errors and Omissions	78ca d	....	....	....	....	....	....	....	4.31	3.56	1.67	2.27	6.80	3.52	1.10	2.00
Overall Balance	78cb d	....	....	....	....	....	....	....	1.98	−6.75	−.90	−2.45	−5.70	−3.18	7.20	7.22
Reserves and Related Items	79da d	....	....	....	....	....	....	....	−1.98	6.75	.90	2.45	5.70	3.18	−7.20	−7.22
Reserve Assets	79db d	....	....	....	....	....	....	....	−3.35	4.65	−.77	2.28	−.63	−.65	−4.78	−5.90
Use of Fund Credit and Loans	79dc d	....	....	....	....	....	....	....	−.09	2.10	1.63	−.31	2.32	−.78	1.97	2.48
Exceptional Financing	79de d	....	....	....	....	....	....	....	1.46	—	.05	.48	4.01	4.61	−4.39	−3.80
National Accounts														*Millions of Tala*		
GDP Volume 1980 prices	99b. p	79.2	89.6	91.2	97.9	87.5	84.0	92.0	91.1	96.8	109.8	103.0	93.7	92.8	....	....
GDP Volume 1984 prices	99b. p	....	....	....	....	....	....	....	....	....	....	....	....	176.6	178.8	181.2
GDP Volume 1994 prices	99b. p	....	....	....	....	....	....	....	....	....	....	....	....	....	....	....
GDP Volume (1995=100)	99bv p	111.3	126.0	128.2	137.6	123.0	118.1	129.3	128.0	136.2	154.3	144.9	131.7	130.4	132.0	133.8
Population	99z	.14	.15	.15	.15	.15	ꟷ.15	.15	.15	.15	.15	.16	.16	.16	.16	.16

Millions: (Population row units)

Samoa

	1985	1986	1987	1988	1989	1990	1991	1992	1993	1994	1995	1996	1997	1998	1999	
Prices and Production																
Period Averages																
Consumer Prices	57.3	60.6	63.4	68.8	73.2	84.4	82.9	90.3	91.9	103.0	100.0	105.4	112.6	115.1	....	64
Manufacturing Production	....	....	....	....	....	....	....	....	....	80.4	100.0	111.5	101.8	98.1	....	66ey
International Transactions																
Thousands of Tala																
Exports	36,180	23,495	24,968	31,397	29,206	20,494	15,515	14,349	16,522	9,121	21,859	24,868	38,531	43,243	61,695	70
Imports, c.i.f.	115,074	105,375	131,010	157,296	171,220	186,120	225,337	271,325	269,079	206,347	235,353	247,126	247,377	285,652	346,765	71
Balance of Payments																
Minus Sign Indicates Debit																
Current Account, n.i.e.	1.78	7.22	7.29	7.95	12.81	7.28	-28.64	-52.50	-38.69	5.76	9.33	12.28	9.13	20.09	....	78al d
Goods: Exports f.o.b.	16.12	10.51	11.77	15.09	12.87	8.88	6.47	5.82	6.44	3.52	8.76	10.08	14.63	20.40	....	78aa d
Goods: Imports f.o.b.	-46.60	-42.84	-55.79	-66.57	-66.99	-70.16	-77.58	-89.90	-87.41	-68.81	-80.29	-90.76	-100.11	-96.91	....	78ab d
Trade Balance	-30.48	-32.34	-44.02	-51.47	-54.12	-61.29	-71.11	-84.07	-80.98	-65.29	-71.53	-80.67	-85.48	-76.51	....	78ac d
Services: Credit	10.33	13.34	16.43	26.89	30.90	35.66	30.73	36.65	35.80	43.00	55.70	65.15	65.24	62.56	....	78ad d
Services: Debit	-11.09	-12.38	-14.94	-18.25	-18.80	-24.78	-34.62	-43.43	-38.24	-28.17	-35.19	-34.33	-40.08	-29.09	....	78ae d
Balance on Goods & Services	-31.23	-31.38	-42.53	-42.83	-42.02	-50.41	-75.00	-90.85	-83.42	-50.46	-51.02	-49.85	-60.32	-43.04	....	78af d
Income: Credit	.68	1.26	2.75	2.89	4.48	6.70	7.21	6.15	4.33	4.03	4.66	5.45	5.52	5.97	....	78ag d
Income: Debit	-2.58	-2.33	-2.22	-2.12	-2.39	-1.53	-2.39	-2.55	-4.42	-4.45	-4.42	-2.43	-4.14	-2.39	....	78ah d
Balance on Gds, Serv. & Inc.	-33.13	-32.45	-42.00	-42.07	-39.94	-45.24	-70.19	-87.25	-83.51	-50.88	-50.79	-46.84	-58.94	-39.47	....	78ai d
Current Transfers, n.i.e.: Credit	35.48	40.74	50.35	52.95	56.29	56.67	44.64	39.07	49.93	62.75	66.74	66.89	73.71	64.12	....	78aj d
Current Transfers: Debit	-.57	-1.06	-1.07	-2.93	-3.54	-4.16	-3.09	-4.32	-5.11	-6.11	-6.62	-7.77	-5.65	-4.56	....	78ak d
Capital Account, n.i.e.	—	—	—	—	—	—	—	—	—	—	—	—	—	—	....	78bc d
Capital Account, n.i.e.: Credit	—	—	—	—	—	—	—	—	—	—	—	—	—	—	....	78ba d
Capital Account: Debit	—	—	—	—	—	—	—	—	—	—	—	—	—	—	....	78bb d
Financial Account, n.i.e.	-.47	-.74	3.15	.49	.48	9.42	21.67	15.94	15.55	-5.46	-5.60	-3.60	-5.93	-4.99	....	78bj d
Direct Investment Abroad	—	—	—	—	—	—	—	—	—	—	—	—	—	—	....	78bd d
Dir. Invest. in Rep. Econ., n.i.e.	—	—	—	—	—	—	—	—	—	—	—	—	—	—	....	78be d
Portfolio Investment Assets	—	—	—	—	—	—	—	—	—	—	—	—	—	—	....	78bf d
Equity Securities	—	—	—	—	—	—	—	—	—	—	—	—	—	—	....	78bk d
Debt Securities	—	—	—	—	—	—	—	—	—	—	—	—	—	—	....	78bl d
Portfolio Investment Liab., n.i.e.	—	—	—	—	—	—	—	—	....	....	....	....	....	....	....	78bg d
Equity Securities	—	—	—	—	—	—	—	—	....	....	....	....	....	....	....	78bm d
Debt Securities	—	—	—	—	—	—	—	—	....	....	....	....	....	....	....	78bn d
Financial Derivatives Assets																78bw d
Financial Derivatives Liabilities																78bx d
Other Investment Assets	-.05	.04	-.13	-.31	-.08	-.03	-.22	—							....	78bh d
Monetary Authorities																78bo d
General Government																78bp d
Banks	—	—	—	—	—	—	—	—	—	—	—	—	—	—	....	78bq d
Other Sectors	-.05	.04	-.13	-.31	-.08	-.03	-.22	—							....	78br d
Other Investment Liab., n.i.e.	-.42	-.78	3.28	.80	.56	9.45	21.90	15.94	15.55	-5.46	-5.60	-3.60	-5.93	-4.99	....	78bi d
Monetary Authorities	-.01	.13	-.04	-.04	—	—	—	—	—	-.13	.01	-.01	-.01	.16	....	78bs d
General Government	.73	.51	3.29	1.12	1.54	9.73	21.55	16.54	15.26	6.82	3.80	.20	-1.48	-1.04	....	78bt d
Banks	.07	-.28	.60	.25	-.37	.16	.68	-.24	.56	.03	-1.12	1.65	1.05	-.54	....	78bu d
Other Sectors	-1.20	-1.14	-.58	-.53	-.61	-.44	-.33	-.36	-.27	-12.18	-8.29	-5.44	-5.49	-3.57	....	78bv d
Net Errors and Omissions	3.92	.90	-1.85	1.67	-2.61	-5.68	4.89	23.83	13.83	-4.17	-1.70	-1.30	7.89	-9.59	....	78ca d
Overall Balance	5.23	7.38	8.59	10.10	10.68	11.02	-2.08	-12.72	-9.31	-3.86	2.04	7.38	11.09	5.51	....	78cb d
Reserves and Related Items	-5.23	-7.38	-8.59	-10.10	-10.68	-11.02	2.08	12.72	9.31	3.86	-2.04	-7.38	-11.09	-5.51	....	79da d
Reserve Assets	-4.09	-9.38	-9.28	-8.42	-10.66	-11.51	-.42	12.95	8.30	3.86	-2.04	-7.38	-11.09	-5.51	....	79db d
Use of Fund Credit and Loans	-.07	-1.94	-3.22	-3.96	-2.09	-.86	-.59	-.22	—	—	—	—	—	—	....	79dc d
Exceptional Financing	-1.07	3.94	3.91	2.28	2.07	1.34	3.08	—	1.01	—	—	—	—	—	....	79de d
National Accounts																
Millions of Tala																
GDP Volume 1980 prices	....	....	....	....	....	....	....	....	....	....	....	....	....	....	....	99b. p
GDP Volume 1984 prices	192.0	193.2	195.1	194.8	197.3	182.6	131.6	128.6	131.7	126.8	....	....	....	....	....	99b. p
GDP Volume 1994 prices	....	....	....	....	....	....	....	....	....	468.8	500.7	531.4	539.9	....	....	99b. p
GDP Volume (1995=100)	141.8	142.7	144.1	143.8	145.7	134.8	97.2	95.0	97.2	93.6	100.0	106.1	107.8	....	....	99bv p
Midyear Estimates																
Population	.16	.16	.16	.16	.16	.16	.16	.16	.16	.16	.17	.17	.17	.17	.17	99z

(See notes in the back of the book.)

São Tomé & Príncipe

		1970	1971	1972	1973	1974	1975	1976	1977	1978	1979	1980	1981	1982	1983	1984
Exchange Rates															*Dobras per SDR:*	
Market Rate	aa	28.7	29.9	29.3	31.2	30.1	32.2	36.7	45.3	45.3	45.3	45.3	45.3	45.3	45.3	45.3
													Dobras per US Dollar: End of Period (ae)			
Market Rate	ae	28.8	27.6	27.0	25.8	24.6	27.5	31.5	37.3	34.7	34.3	35.5	38.9	41.0	43.2	46.2
Market Rate	rf	28.8	28.4	27.1	24.5	25.4	25.5	30.2	37.6	36.2	35.0	34.8	38.4	41.0	42.3	44.2
Fund Position															*Millions of SDRs:*	
Quota	2f. s	....	....	....	....	....	....	....	1.60	2.00	2.00	3.00	3.00	3.00	3.00	4.00
SDRs	1b. s	....	....	....	....	....	....	....	—	—	.21	.17	.37	.37	.36	.08
Reserve Position in the Fund	1c. s	....	....	....	....	....	....	....		.40	.40	.65	.65	.65	.65	—
Total Fund Cred.&Loans Outstg.	2tl			....						—	—	—	—	—	—	—
International Liquidity												*Millions of US Dollars Unless Otherwise Indicated:*				
Total Reserves minus Gold	1l. d	....	....	....	....	....	....	....								
SDRs	1b. d	....	....	....	....	....	....	....			.28	.22	.43	.41	.38	.08
Reserve Position in the Fund	1c. d	....	....	....	....	....	....	....	—	—						
Foreign Exchange	1d. d	....	....	....	....	....	....	....	—	.52	.53	.83	.76	.72	.68	—
Monetary Authorities: Other Liab.	4.. d	....	....	....	....	....	....	....	....	....	....	....	....	....	....	....
Banking Institutions: Assets	7a. d	....	....	....	....	....	....	....	....	....	....	....	....	....	....	....
Liabilities	7b. d	....	....	....	....	....	....	....	....	....	....	....	....	....	....	....
Monetary Authorities															*Millions of Dobras:*	
Foreign Assets	11	....	....	....	....	....	....	....								
Claims on Central Government	12a	....	....	....	....	....	....	....								
Claims on Nonfin.Pub.Enterprises	12c	....	....	....	....	....	....	....								
Claims on Private Sector	12d	....	....	....	....	....	....	....								
Claims on Banking Institutions	12e	....	....	....	....	....	....	....								
Reserve Money	14	....	....	....	....	....	....	....								
of which: Currency Outside Banks	14a	....	....	....	....	....	....	....								
Foreign Liabilities	16c	....	....	....	....	....	....	....								
Central Government Deposits	16d	....	....	....	....	....	....	....								
Counterpart Funds	16e	....	....	....	....	....	....	....								
Capital Accounts	17a	....	....	....	....	....	....	....								
of which: Valuation Adjustment	17rv	....	....	....	....	....	....	....								
Other Items (Net)	17r	....	....	....	....	....	....	....								
Banking Institutions															*Millions of Dobras:*	
Reserves	20	....	....	....	....	....	....	....								
Foreign Assets	21	....	....	....	....	....	....	....								
Claims on Private Sector	22d	....	....	....	....	....	....	....								
Demand Deposits	24	....	....	....	....	....	....	....								
Time, Savings,& Fgn.Currency Dep.	25	....	....	....	....	....	....	....								
of which: Fgn. Currency Deposits	25b	....	....	....	....	....	....	....								
Foreign Liabilities	26c	....	....	....	....	....	....	....								
Central Government Deposits	26d	....	....	....	....	....	....	....								
Counterpart Funds	26e	....	....	....	....	....	....	....								
Credit from Monetary Authorities	26g	....	....	....	....	....	....	....								
Capital Accounts	27a	....	....	....	....	....	....	....								
Other Items (Net)	27r	....	....	....	....	....	....	....								
Banking Survey															*Millions of Dobras:*	
Foreign Assets (Net)	31n	....	....	....	....	....	....	....								
Domestic Credit	32	....	....	....	....	....	....	....								
Claims on Central Govt.(Net)	32an	....	....	....	....	....	....	....								
Claims on Nonfin.Pub.Enterprises	32c	....	....	....	....	....	....	....								
Claims on Private Sector	32d	....	....	....	....	....	....	....								
Money	34	....	....	....	....	....	....	....								
Quasi-Money	35	....	....	....	....	....	....	....								
Counterpart Funds	36e	....	....	....	....	....	....	....								
Capital Accounts	37a	....	....	....	....	....	....	....								
Other Items (Net)	37r	....	....	....	....	....	....	....								
Money plus Quasi-Money	35l	....	....	....	....	....	....	....								
Interest Rates															*Percent Per Annum*	
Discount Rate *(End of Period)*	60	....	....	....	....	....	....	....								
Deposit Rate	60l	....	....	....	....	....	....	....							....	....
Lending Rate	60p	....	....	....	....	....	....	....							....	....
International Transactions															*Millions of US Dollars*	
Exports	70.. d	8.329	6.624	7.336	13.169	17.318	7.064	8.230	22.999	21.090	26.588	16.984	8.532	....	....	12.229
Imports, c.i.f.	71.. d	9.062	7.798	7.944	10.086	9.855	11.295	8.780	14.103	17.898	19.881	18.879	16.637	....	....	
																Millions:	
Population	99z	.07	.07	.07	.08	.08	.08	.08	.08	.08	.08	.09	.10	.10	.10	.10

1985	1986	1987	1988	1989	1990	1991	1992	1993	1994	1995	1996	1997	1998	1999		
															Exchange Rates	
End of Period																
45.3	45.3	103.3	132.1	184.5	200.6	400.6	516.4	709.7	1,730.4	2,611.6	4,074.0	9,403.9	9,694.3	10,019.3	Market Rate	**aa**
Period Average (rf)																
41.2	37.0	72.8	98.2	140.4	141.0	280.0	375.5	516.7	1,185.3	1,756.9	2,833.2	6,969.7	6,885.0	7,300.0	Market Rate	**ae**
44.6	38.6	54.2	86.3	124.7	143.3	201.8	321.3	429.9	732.6	1,420.3	2,203.2	4,552.5	6,883.2	7,119.0	Market Rate	**rf**
															Fund Position	
End of Period																
4.00	4.00	4.00	4.00	4.00	4.00	4.00	5.50	5.50	5.50	5.50	5.50	5.50	5.50	7.40	Quota	**2f.** *s*
.04	—	—	—	.01	—	—	—	.01	.01	.03	.01	—	—	—	SDRs	**1b.** *s*
—	.01	—	—	—	—	—	—	—	—	—	—	—	—	—	Reserve Position in the Fund	**1c.** *s*
—	—	—	—	.80	.80	.80	.80	.80	.72	.56	.40	.24	.08	—	Total Fund Cred.&Loans Outstg.	**2tl**
															International Liquidity	
End of Period																
....	....	....	....	....	....	....	....	....	....	5.14	5.03	12.43	9.68	10.88	Total Reserves minus Gold	**1l.** *d*
.04	—	—	—	.01	—	—	—	.01	.01	.04	.02	—	—	—	SDRs	**1b.** *d*
—	.01	—	—	—	—	—	—	—	—	—	—	—	—	—	Reserve Position in the Fund	**1c.** *d*
....	....	....	....	....	....	....	....	....	....	5.09	5.01	12.43	9.68	10.88	Foreign Exchange	**1d.** *d*
....										5.05	4.94	5.31	—	—	Monetary Authorities: Other Liab.	**4..** *d*
....										7.11	8.08	8.03	6.85	6.28	Banking Institutions: Assets	**7a.** *d*
....										1.49	.77	.37	1.34	1.47	Liabilities	**7b.** *d*
															Monetary Authorities	
End of Period																
....										9,026	14,252	86,611	101,965	114,071	Foreign Assets	**11**
....										10,290	28,743	28,939	28,831	28,831	Claims on Central Government	**12a**
....										7,837	—	—	—	—	Claims on Nonfin.Pub.Enterprises	**12c**
....										80	204	50	44	38	Claims on Private Sector	**12d**
....										2,375	1,757	1,839	1,839	1,839	Claims on Banking Institutions	**12e**
....										10,462	18,945	46,401	51,085	45,800	Reserve Money	**14**
....										4,794	6,845	14,818	18,652	20,920	*of which: Currency Outside Banks*	**14a**
....										10,331	15,614	39,258	795	10	Foreign Liabilities	**16c**
....										—	6,868	41,985	30,994	41,664	Central Government Deposits	**16d**
....										10,333	9,091	11,197	24,271	26,168	Counterpart Funds	**16e**
....										1,887	-2,356	-13,966	46,025	54,715	Capital Accounts	**17a**
....										-2,018	-5,432	-21,841	29,394	34,652	*of which: Valuation Adjustment*	**17rv**
....										-3,405	-3,207	-7,436	-20,491	-23,578	Other Items (Net)	**17r**
															Banking Institutions	
End of Period																
....										5,488	12,730	30,646	30,485	26,776	Reserves	**20**
....										12,491	22,880	55,935	47,139	45,855	Foreign Assets	**21**
....										6,614	8,599	11,897	22,429	27,751	Claims on Private Sector	**22d**
....										9,431	16,837	34,384	27,731	27,187	Demand Deposits	**24**
....										6,110	13,830	31,992	35,892	32,168	Time, Savings,& Fgn.Currency Dep.	**25**
....										6,011	13,086	30,803	32,763	27,340	*of which: Fgn. Currency Deposits*	**25b**
....										2,626	2,173	2,562	9,205	10,704	Foreign Liabilities	**26c**
....										2,462	3,313	1,516	2,447	2,447	Central Government Deposits	**26d**
....										609	105	105	105	105	Counterpart Funds	**26e**
....										250	1,150	3,700	1,200	1,200	Credit from Monetary Authorities	**26g**
....										3,687	11,828	30,722	36,555	38,547	Capital Accounts	**27a**
....										-582	-5,028	-6,503	-13,082	-11,977	Other Items (Net)	**27r**
															Banking Survey	
End of Period																
....										8,559	19,345	100,726	139,104	149,212	Foreign Assets (Net)	**31n**
....										22,359	27,365	-2,615	17,863	12,509	Domestic Credit	**32**
....										7,829	18,562	-14,561	-4,610	-15,280	Claims on Central Govt.(Net)	**32an**
....										7,837	—	—	—	—	Claims on Nonfin.Pub.Enterprises	**32c**
....										6,694	8,803	11,947	22,473	27,789	Claims on Private Sector	**32d**
....										14,225	23,683	49,202	47,584	49,441	Money	**34**
....										6,110	13,830	31,992	35,892	32,168	Quasi-Money	**35**
....										10,942	9,196	11,302	24,375	26,273	Counterpart Funds	**36e**
....										5,574	9,473	16,757	82,580	93,262	Capital Accounts	**37a**
....										-5,932	-9,472	-11,142	-33,464	-39,424	Other Items (Net)	**37r**
....										20,335	37,513	81,195	83,476	81,610	Money plus Quasi-Money	**35l**
															Interest Rates	
Percent Per Annum																
....	....	....	....	25.0	25.0	45.0	45.0	30.0	32.0	50.0	35.0	55.0	29.5	17.0	Discount Rate *(End of Period)*	**60**
....	....	....	....	16.0	16.0	35.0	35.0	35.0	35.0	35.0	31.0	36.8	38.3	27.0	Deposit Rate	**60l**
....	....	....	....	20.0	20.0	37.0	37.0	37.0	30.0	52.0	38.0	51.5	55.6	40.3	Lending Rate	**60p**
															International Transactions	
Millions of US Dollars																
5.826	9.887	6.520	9.510	4.914	4.400	6.013	5.480	5.200	5.900	5.100	4.900	5.300	....	....	Exports	**70..** *d*
9.878	17.020	13.550	14.132	18.115	21.300	30.604	29.224	32.000	30.400	29.300	22.400	16.100	....	....	Imports, c.i.f.	**71..** *d*
Midyear Estimates																
.11	.11	.11	.11	.12	.12	.12	.12	.12	.12	.13	.14	.14	.14	.14	Population	**99z**

Saudi Arabia

		1970	1971	1972	1973	1974	1975	1976	1977	1978	1979	1980	1981	1982	1983	1984
Exchange Rates																*Riyals per SDR:*
Official Rate	aa	4.5000	4.5057	4.5057	4.2825	4.3464	4.1324	4.1013	4.2576	4.3187	4.4328	4.2407	3.9749	3.7892	3.6591	3.5043
																Riyals per US Dollar:
Official Rate	ae	4.5000	4.1500	4.1500	3.5500	3.5500	3.5300	3.5300	3.5050	3.3150	3.3650	3.3250	3.4150	3.4350	3.4950	3.5750
Official Rate	rf	4.5000	4.4868	4.1448	3.7066	3.5500	3.5176	3.5300	3.5251	3.3996	3.3608	3.3267	3.3825	3.4282	3.4548	3.5238
														Index Numbers (1995=100):		
Official Rate	ah x	83.2	80.7	90.2	101.0	105.5	106.5	106.1	106.2	110.2	111.4	112.6	110.7	109.3	108.4	106.3
Nominal Effective Exchange Rate	ne c	....	....	....	....	....	....	....	....	....	121.0	123.7	134.2	144.9	149.6	155.4
Real Effective Exchange Rate	re c	....	....	....	....	....	....	....	....	....	....	207.9	210.5	214.8	212.7	208.4
Fund Position																*Millions of SDRs:*
Quota	2f. s	90	134	134	134	134	134	134	134	600	600	1,040	2,100	2,100	3,202	3,202
SDRs	1b. s	—	—	—	—	—	—	—	—	—	149	213	213	579	487	586
Reserve Position in the Fund	1c. s	23	34	34	34	595	1,570	2,206	2,215	1,896	1,290	1,896	3,428	4,621	8,903	10,188
of which: Outstg.Fund Borrowing	2c	—	—	—	—	562	1,515	2,150	2,124	1,658	970	1,352	2,439	3,212	6,913	8,104
International Liquidity											*Millions of US Dollars Unless Otherwise Indicated:*					
Total Reserves minus Gold	1l. d	542	1,327	2,383	3,747	14,153	23,193	26,900	29,903	‡19,200	19,273	23,437	32,236	29,549	27,287	24,748
SDRs	1b. d	—	—	—	—	—	—	—	—	—	196	271	248	638	510	574
Reserve Position in the Fund	1c. d	22	36	36	40	729	1,838	2,563	2,691	2,470	1,699	2,418	3,990	5,098	9,321	9,986
Foreign Exchange	1d. d	520	1,291	2,347	3,707	13,424	21,355	24,337	27,212	‡16,730	17,378	20,747	27,998	23,813	17,457	14,188
Gold (Million Fine Troy Ounces)	1ad	3.400	3.086	3.086	3.086	3.081	3.081	3.081	3.081	4.539	4.567	4.567	4.567	4.596	4.596	4.596
Gold (National Valuation)	1an d	119	117	117	130	130	126	125	131	207	211	204	186	177	168	158
Monetary Authorities: Other Assets	3.. d	....	....	....	....	....	15,385	22,564	....	....	....					
Deposit Money Banks: Assets	7a. d	.10	.15	.32	.39	.46	1.02	2.35	3.22	3.48	5.39	9.69	15.63	17.76	17.85	18.81
Liabilities	7b. d	.04	.07	.05	.09	.24	.51	1.32	1.24	1.83	2.22	2.75	2.66	1.74	1.94	2.23
Other Banking Insts.: Assets	7e. d	....	....	....	....	....	....	.17	.25	.29	.29	.30	.38	.39	.42	.41
Monetary Authorities																*Billions of Riyals:*
Foreign Assets	11	3.96	6.88	11.93	16.94	78.13	136.40	180.69	207.96	197.99	206.11	288.52	431.85	472.93	437.98	392.21
Reserve Money	14	1.82	2.19	2.87	4.34	5.85	11.84	19.13	31.13	43.40	38.72	34.46	39.20	44.65	43.73	43.00
of which: Currency Outside DMBs	14a	1.63	1.67	2.42	3.05	4.14	6.68	10.59	16.25	19.18	23.71	25.68	29.49	34.44	35.42	35.11
Central Government Deposits	16d	1.32	3.58	8.20	11.83	44.86	89.40	124.99	133.43	112.02	109.01	182.86	321.01	332.73	303.35	258.81
Other Items (Net)	17r	.82	1.11	.86	.78	27.42	35.17	36.57	43.39	42.57	58.38	71.19	71.64	95.55	90.90	90.40
Deposit Money Banks																*Billions of Riyals:*
Reserves	20	.22	.53	.46	1.23	1.61	4.85	7.11	13.03	22.12	13.59	8.19	8.27	10.81	‡8.26	11.04
Foreign Assets	21	.45	.64	1.32	1.37	1.63	3.62	8.29	11.28	11.55	18.14	32.23	53.36	61.00	‡62.38	67.24
Claims on Central Government	22a	—	—	—	—	—	.01	.10	.08	.23	.21	.24	1.97	‡—		
Claims on Public Enterprises	22c	....	....	....	....											
Claims on Private Sector	22d	1.71	1.82	1.82	2.36	4.43	6.72	9.88	10.68	14.40	26.73	37.25	43.25	50.16	‡58.54	62.18
Demand Deposits	24	.77	.98	1.36	2.23	3.19	7.50	13.68	22.16	30.03	31.00	33.28	43.49	49.34	‡49.51	47.86
Quasi-Monetary Deposits	25a	.70	.90	1.21	1.42	1.94	3.13	4.31	5.85	7.63	9.38	13.83	21.93	29.68	‡34.13	41.79
Foreign Currency Deposits	25b	.04	.03	.06	.10	.50	.47	1.03	1.30	1.20	1.90	4.65	8.08	10.33	‡18.02	20.58
Foreign Liabilities	26c	.16	.28	.23	.32	.87	1.79	4.67	4.34	6.07	7.47	9.15	9.07	5.97	‡6.80	7.97
Credit from Monetary Authorities	26g	—	—	—	—	—	—	—	—	1.32	.03	—	.02	.05	‡2.06	1.63
Capital Accounts	27a	.17	.19	.20	.24	.33	.68	.94	1.25	1.85	2.54	4.15	5.56	7.82	‡14.47	18.16
Other Items (Net)	27r	.44	.48	.43	.53	.66	1.35	.24	−.19	−.69	5.60	9.25	10.16	12.54	‡2.70	.76
Monetary Survey																*Billions of Riyals:*
Foreign Assets (Net)	31n	4.25	7.24	13.03	17.99	78.89	138.23	184.31	214.90	203.47	216.78	311.59	476.14	527.96	‡493.56	451.48
Domestic Credit	32	.39	−1.76	−6.37	−9.46	−40.42	−82.67	−115.10	−122.65	−97.54	−82.05	−145.40	−277.52	−280.60	‡−246.51	−199.18
Claims on Central Govt. (Net)	32an	−1.32	−3.58	−8.20	−11.83	−44.86	−89.39	−124.98	−133.33	−111.93	−108.78	−182.65	−320.77	−330.76	‡−303.35	−258.81
Claims on Public Enterprises	32c	....	....	....	....											
Claims on Private Sector	32d	1.71	1.82	1.82	2.36	4.43	6.72	9.88	10.68	14.40	26.73	37.25	43.25	50.16	56.84	59.63
Money	34	2.40	2.65	3.78	5.29	7.33	14.18	24.27	38.41	49.21	54.70	58.96	72.98	83.78	‡84.93	82.98
Quasi-Money	35	.74	.94	1.26	1.52	2.44	3.60	5.34	7.14	8.82	11.28	18.48	30.01	40.01	‡52.16	62.37
Other Items (Net)	37r	1.40	1.77	1.48	1.60	28.51	37.51	39.19	46.31	47.15	67.96	85.19	88.83	115.19	‡108.48	105.24
Money plus Quasi-Money	35l	3.14	3.59	5.04	6.81	9.78	17.78	29.61	45.56	58.03	65.98	77.44	102.99	123.79	‡137.09	145.35
Other Banking Institutions																*Billions of Riyals:*
Cash	40	.01	.01	.02	.02	.02	.01	‡3.73	2.06	3.97	3.57	8.04	7.35	6.33	4.29	3.91
Foreign Assets	41	....	....	....	....	....	....	.59	.87	.95	.99	1.01	1.29	1.34	1.46	1.45
Claims on Private Sector	42d	.04	.04	.04	.05	.05	.13	‡12.14	33.31	47.12	63.59	81.20	103.46	132.66	152.83	168.45
Capital Accounts	47a	.05	.05	.06	.06	.07	.17	‡15.10	32.69	42.83	69.52	91.44	113.75	142.24	160.26	176.73
Other Items (Net)	47r	.02	—				−.03	‡1.36	3.55	9.21	−1.36	−1.19	−1.65	−1.92	−1.67	−2.92
Interest Rates																*Percent per Annum*
Deposit Rate	601	....	....									....	....			
Prices, Production, Labor																*Index Numbers (1995=100):*
Share Prices (1985=100)	62	....	....	....	....	....	....	....	....	....	....	....	....	....	....	....
Wholesale Prices	63	....	....	....	....	....	....	....	....	....	....	....	....	....	....	....
Consumer Prices	64	‡28.7	30.0	31.3	36.5	44.3	59.7	78.5	87.4	‡86.0	‡87.6	‡90.9	93.5	94.4	94.6	93.2
Crude Petroleum	66aa	47.3	59.4	75.2	94.7	105.7	88.2	107.2	114.7	104.0	118.8	123.7	122.5	80.8	63.6	58.1
Employment	67e	....	....	....	....	....	....	....	....	....	....	....	....	....	*Number in Thousands:*	

1985	1986	1987	1988	1989	1990	1991	1992	1993	1994	1995	1996	1997	1998	1999		
															Exchange Rates	
End of Period																
4.0037	4.5808	5.3129	5.0396	4.9215	5.3279	5.3570	5.1494	5.1440	5.4671	5.5669	5.3852	5.0529	5.2731	5.1400	Official Rate	aa
End of Period (ae) Period Average (rf)																
3.6450	3.7450	3.7450	3.7450	3.7450	3.7450	3.7450	3.7450	3.7450	3.7450	3.7450	3.7450	3.7450	3.7450	3.7450	Official Rate	ae
3.6221	3.7033	3.7450	3.7450	3.7450	3.7450	3.7450	3.7450	3.7450	3.7450	3.7450	3.7450	3.7450	3.7450	3.7450	Official Rate	rf
Period Averages																
103.4	101.1	100.0	100.0	100.0	100.0	100.0	100.0	100.0	100.0	100.0	100.0	100.0	100.0	100.0	Official Rate	ah x
154.9	124.9	110.4	105.0	109.6	103.9	104.2	102.0	107.4	105.4	100.0	103.6	111.0	118.0	116.0	Nominal Effective Exchange Rate	ne c
194.3	148.6	126.4	118.0	119.3	109.8	110.4	104.3	107.7	103.3	100.0	102.4	107.5	111.3	106.4	Real Effective Exchange Rate	re c
															Fund Position	
End of Period																
3,202	3,202	3,202	3,202	3,202	3,202	3,202	3,202	5,131	5,131	5,131	5,131	5,131	5,131	6,986	Quota	2f. s
529	336	371	396	467	70	62	202	403	416	448	481	512	546	110	SDRs	1b. s
9,707	8,838	8,016	6,540	3,688	2,099	1,292	797	869	604	575	561	532	524	987	Reserve Position in the Fund	1c. s
7,837	7,748	7,352	6,051	3,224	1,712	950	525	175	—	—	—	—	—	—	*of which:* Outstg.Fund Borrowing	2c
															International Liquidity	
Approximately End of Period																
25,004	18,324	22,684	20,553	16,748	11,668	11,673	5,935	7,428	7,378	8,622	I14,321	14,876	14,220	16,997	Total Reserves minus Gold	1l. d
581	411	526	532	614	99	89	278	553	607	666	692	691	769	152	SDRs	1b. d
10,662	10,811	11,372	8,801	4,847	2,986	1,848	1,096	1,193	882	854	807	718	737	1,355	Reserve Position in the Fund	1c. d
13,761	7,102	10,786	11,219	11,287	8,582	9,737	4,561	5,682	5,888	7,101	I12,822	13,467	12,714	15,490	Foreign Exchange	1d. d
4.596	4.596	4.596	4.596	4.596	4.596	4.596	4.596	4.596	4.596	4.596	4.596	4.596	4.596	4.596	Gold (Million Fine Troy Ounces)	1ad
177	197	228	216	211	229	230	221	221	235	239	231	217	226	221	Gold (National Valuation)	1an d
....	....	....	....	....	....	....	....	....	....	....	....	....	....	....	Monetary Authorities: Other Assets	3.. d
19.38	23.14	27.29	30.64	31.73	32.97	31.76	27.15	29.80	26.21	26.16	28.35	26.57	22.95	24.43	Deposit Money Banks: Assets	7a. d
2.85	3.82	6.54	7.67	9.24	8.06	7.45	7.66	9.96	10.45	10.59	10.32	12.29	11.51	13.66	Liabilities	7b. d
.40	.42	1.11	1.12	1.12	1.20	1.14	1.15	1.15	1.15	1.02	1.02	1.04	1.04	1.04	Other Banking Insts.: Assets	7e. d
															Monetary Authorities	
Approximately End of Period																
319.53	276.17	256.54	232.81	226.64	212.22	208.95	214.89	193.08	185.56	174.04	196.07	219.03	175.60	....	Foreign Assets	11
42.12	45.83	46.34	43.44	41.83	52.48	54.53	53.89	53.79	56.23	54.93	54.15	58.24	57.53	....	Reserve Money	14
35.77	38.81	38.84	35.95	33.88	44.78	44.62	43.77	42.62	44.97	43.89	43.04	45.82	45.02	55.06	*of which:* Currency Outside DMBs	14a
232.34	118.51	55.01	44.64	26.82	22.32	30.45	41.97	42.48	35.53	34.63	45.52	48.51	48.74	....	Central Government Deposits	16d
45.06	111.83	155.19	144.72	157.99	137.42	123.97	119.04	96.81	93.80	84.48	96.40	112.28	69.33	....	Other Items (Net)	17r
															Deposit Money Banks	
Approximately End of Period																
12.56	13.92	18.59	10.69	11.75	11.64	12.68	10.65	11.53	11.65	11.18	11.21	12.55	12.57	16.55	Reserves	20
70.65	86.67	102.20	114.74	118.84	123.46	118.95	I101.67	111.59	98.15	97.97	106.17	99.52	85.94	91.49	Foreign Assets	21
—	.08	.12	7.76	10.29	13.33	31.71	I37.92	43.46	50.03	52.28	65.27	83.21	89.37	102.27	Claims on Central Government	22a
....	....	....	....	....	....	....	24.67	22.60	26.93	24.45	16.70	20.86	23.60	14.35	Claims on Public Enterprises	22c
63.49	62.64	62.14	74.01	78.23	70.99	82.65	I86.04	101.93	113.19	121.15	123.55	133.68	160.66	162.19	Claims on Private Sector	22d
46.06	47.47	51.70	57.48	57.51	57.17	75.38	I79.69	78.89	80.73	81.52	90.08	95.47	95.39	101.76	Demand Deposits	24
44.09	44.92	45.25	44.23	48.30	42.82	48.69	I53.72	56.89	60.60	69.70	81.73	86.27	91.31	95.09	Quasi-Monetary Deposits	25a
21.09	29.36	31.37	40.23	39.76	42.90	46.29	I42.22	48.41	47.29	46.32	44.10	44.88	50.61	49.72	Foreign Currency Deposits	25b
10.38	14.29	24.49	28.73	34.60	30.17	27.91	I28.69	37.29	39.15	39.68	38.65	46.04	43.11	51.15	Foreign Liabilities	26c
5.78	7.43	8.81	10.95	14.11	15.91	16.02	13.37	19.80	21.42	18.63	13.57	18.33	29.44	20.58	Credit from Monetary Authorities	26g
19.09	20.92	22.96	26.76	29.82	31.94	34.50	I28.17	34.48	36.96	39.25	42.65	44.87	47.60	48.69	Capital Accounts	27a
-1.15	-1.63	-2.98	-2.04	-6.08	-2.79	-4.30	I15.10	15.34	13.80	11.94	12.11	13.96	14.68	19.84	Other Items (Net)	27r
															Monetary Survey	
Approximately End of Period																
379.80	348.55	334.26	318.82	310.88	305.51	299.98	I287.87	267.37	244.55	232.33	263.59	272.50	218.44	....	Foreign Assets (Net)	31n
-172.53	-59.16	3.91	33.65	56.74	56.30	74.90	I106.66	125.52	154.62	163.26	160.00	189.24	224.88	....	Domestic Credit	32
-232.34	-118.43	-54.89	-36.88	-16.54	-8.99	1.26	I-4.05	.98	14.50	17.66	19.75	34.69	40.63	....	Claims on Central Govt. (Net)	32an
....	....	....	....	....	....	....	24.67	22.60	26.93	24.45	16.70	20.86	23.60	14.35	Claims on Public Enterprises	32c
59.81	59.26	58.80	70.52	73.28	65.30	73.64	I86.04	101.93	113.19	121.15	123.55	133.68	160.66	162.19	Claims on Private Sector	32d
81.83	86.28	90.54	93.43	91.38	101.94	120.00	I123.46	121.51	125.69	125.41	133.11	141.29	140.41	156.82	Money	34
65.18	74.28	76.62	84.46	88.06	85.72	94.97	I95.94	105.30	107.89	116.02	125.83	131.15	141.92	144.81	Quasi-Money	35
58.89	128.28	169.55	173.71	187.09	172.85	158.35	I175.13	166.08	165.59	154.17	164.64	189.30	160.99	....	Other Items (Net)	37r
147.01	160.56	167.16	177.89	179.44	187.67	214.98	I219.40	226.81	233.58	241.43	258.95	272.44	282.33	301.62	Money plus Quasi-Money	35l
															Other Banking Institutions	
Approximately End of Period																
5.28	6.96	11.77	14.67	14.89	12.66	12.78	18.60	21.88	17.21	14.34	21.92	28.20	21.62	13.00	Cash	40
1.47	1.58	4.14	4.20	4.21	4.48	4.26	4.30	4.32	4.31	3.81	3.84	3.90	3.90	3.90	Foreign Assets	41
173.01	176.49	176.85	175.08	175.78	173.99	172.17	171.36	168.81	172.90	178.07	181.43	178.96	188.18	199.56	Claims on Private Sector	42d
182.37	185.01	190.59	190.66	188.16	190.91	191.42	190.66	190.66	190.46	190.46	190.46	190.46	190.46	191.33	Capital Accounts	47a
-2.61	.03	2.17	3.29	6.72	.21	-2.21	3.61	4.35	3.95	5.76	16.73	20.61	23.25	25.13	Other Items (Net)	47r
															Interest Rates	
Percent per Annum																
....	....	6.680	8.029	9.036	8.014	5.829	3.649	3.521	5.100	6.178	5.469	5.790	6.211	6.137	Deposit Rate	601
															Prices, Production, Labor	
Period Averages																
....	....	78.1	89.2	108.7	98.0	176.5	188.9	179.3	128.3	136.8	153.1	195.8	141.3	202.9	Share Prices (1985=100)	62
67.3	69.8	74.8	84.8	85.8	87.3	89.9	91.1	91.6	93.3	100.0	99.7	99.7	97.9	98.3	Wholesale Prices	63
90.3	87.4	86.1	86.8	87.7	89.6	93.9	93.8	94.8	95.4	100.0	101.2	101.3	100.7	99.3	Consumer Prices	64
42.2	62.9	52.4	64.7	64.2	80.1	101.9	104.1	100.3	100.3	100.0	101.3	99.9	103.2	97.6	Crude Petroleum	66aa
Period Averages																
....	....	3,933	3,966	3,518	3,267	3,109	3,140	2,495	2,496	2,495	....	....	....	....	Employment	67e

		1970	1971	1972	1973	1974	1975	1976	1977	1978	1979	1980	1981	1982	1983	1984
International Transactions															*Billions of Riyals*	
Exports	70	10.67	17.27	19.78	28.92	126.22	104.41	135.15	153.21	138.24	213.18	362.89	405.48	271.09	158.44	132.30
Petroleum	70a	10.88	16.66	22.71	28.92	126.46	104.05	135.91	153.47	127.11	197.02	337.40	377.30	251.16	147.89	120.73
Crude Petroleum	70aa	8.27	13.09	16.90	26.55	118.93	97.26	127.73	146.00	120.16	186.03	320.45	359.56	235.21	142.15	114.57
Refined Petroleum	70ab	1.81	1.93	2.09	2.47	7.53	6.79	8.18	7.47	6.95	10.99	16.95	17.75	15.95	5.74	6.16
Imports, c.i.f.	71	3.12	3.63	4.71	7.31	10.15	14.82	30.69	51.66	69.18	82.22	100.35	119.30	139.34	135.42	118.74
Volume of Exports															*1995=100*	
Petroleum	72a	49.7	146.5	78.5	98.9	110.6	92.2	112.1	118.6	106.5	121.0	126.7	124.3	80.6	56.5	47.9
Crude Petroleum	72aa	51.1	66.6	86.6	111.4	125.8	104.8	127.8	136.6	122.3	140.0	146.9	143.4	89.7	63.2	50.8
Refined Petroleum	72ab	43.1	40.2	42.9	44.0	43.6	36.3	42.7	39.1	36.9	37.0	37.5	40.4	40.6	30.8	34.9
Export Prices															*1995=100:*	
Crude Petroleum	76aa *d*	....	....	....	....	....	....	....	....	....	104.0	173.4	195.6	199.8	173.4	169.1
Balance of Payments															*Millions of US Dollars:*	
Current Account, n.i.e.	78al *d*	....	972	2,089	2,520	23,025	14,385	14,360	11,991	−2,212	10,206	41,503	39,627	7,575	−16,852	−18,401
Goods: Exports f.o.b.	78aa *d*	....	2,706	4,058	7,702	30,870	27,888	36,314	41,052	37,534	58,771	101,574	112,422	74,203	45,864	37,545
Goods: Imports f.o.b.	78ab *d*	....	−805	−1,197	−1,853	−3,569	−6,004	−10,385	−14,698	−20,020	−20,911	−25,563	−29,889	−34,444	−33,218	−28,557
Trade Balance	78ac *d*	....	1,901	2,861	5,849	27,301	21,884	25,929	26,354	17,514	37,860	76,011	82,533	39,759	12,646	8,987
Services: Credit	78ad *d*	....	154	217	356	645	841	1,074	1,407	1,627	4,079	5,191	7,021	4,565	4,151	4,112
Services: Debit	78ae *d*	....	−374	−509	−955	−2,163	−4,375	−7,935	−10,272	−14,396	−27,318	−30,231	−40,236	−34,852	−37,259	−32,856
Balance on Goods & Services	78af *d*	....	1,680	2,570	5,250	25,783	18,351	19,068	17,489	4,745	14,621	50,972	49,318	9,472	−20,462	−19,757
Income: Credit	78ag *d*	....	67	106	205	1,220	1,839	2,884	3,989	4,301	4,915	7,443	10,956	14,060	15,868	13,366
Income: Debit	78ah *d*	....	−421	−162	−2,048	−2,445	−2,124	−3,280	−4,079	−4,512	−2,065	−6,917	−9,599	−6,210	−3,022	−3,127
Balance on Gds, Serv. & Inc.	78ai *d*	....	1,326	2,514	3,407	24,558	18,066	18,671	17,398	4,533	17,472	51,498	50,675	17,321	−7,616	−9,518
Current Transfers, n.i.e.: Credit	78aj *d*	....	—	—	—	—	—	—	—	—	—	—	—	—	—	—
Current Transfers: Debit	78ak *d*	....	−354	−425	−888	−1,532	−3,681	−4,312	−5,407	−6,745	−7,266	−9,995	−11,048	−9,746	−9,237	−8,882
Capital Account, n.i.e.	78bc *d*	....	—	—	—	—	—	—	—	—	—	—	—	—	—	—
Capital Account, n.i.e.: Credit	78ba *d*	....	—	—	—	—	—	—	—	—	—	—	—	—	—	—
Capital Account: Debit	78bb *d*	....	—	—	—	—	—	—	—	—	—	—	—	—	—	—
Financial Account, n.i.e.	78bj *d*	....	−299	−1,033	−1,603	−12,637	−5,327	−10,633	−9,295	−4,488	−9,972	−37,566	−30,059	−9,883	15,343	16,921
Direct Investment Abroad	78bd *d*	....														
Dir. Invest. in Rep. Econ., n.i.e.	78be *d*	....	−111	34	−626	−3,732	1,865	−397	783	556	−1,271	−3,192	6,498	11,128	4,944	4,850
Portfolio Investment Assets	78bf *d*	....	−7	−31	−283	−5,101	−9,923	−9,457	−8,260	2,248	−1,021	−22,007	−32,808	−11,487	7,531	13,413
Equity Securities	78bk *d*	....														
Debt Securities	78bl *d*	....	−7	−31	−283	−5,101	−9,923	−9,457	−8,260	2,248	−1,021	−22,007	−32,808	−11,487	7,531	13,413
Portfolio Investment Liab., n.i.e.	78bg *d*	....														
Equity Securities	78bm *d*	....														
Debt Securities	78bn *d*	....														
Financial Derivatives Assets	78bw *d*	....	....	....	....	....	....	....							....	....
Financial Derivatives Liabilities	78bx *d*	....	....	....	....	....	....	....							....	....
Other Investment Assets	78bh *d*	....	−198	−1,047	−715	−3,918	3,551	−292	−1,696	−7,801	−8,096	−12,871	−3,725	−8,620	2,628	−1,674
Monetary Authorities	78bo *d*	....								−1,032	−1,149	−595	−1,419			
General Government	78bp *d*	....	−116	−99	−456	−2,389	2,650	1,159	417	−6,536	1,678	1,975	1,419			
Banks	78bq *d*	....	−42	−166	−11	−73	−566	−1,323	−848	−79	−1,976	−4,220	−6,250	−2,229	−2,119	−2,282
Other Sectors	78br *d*	....	−40	−782	−248	−1,456	1,467	−127	−1,265	−153	−6,650	−10,031	2,525	−6,391	4,747	607
Other Investment Liab., n.i.e.	78bi *d*	....	18	12	22	115	−819	−487	−122	509	417	505	−24	−904	240	332
Monetary Authorities	78bs *d*	....	—	—	—	—	—	—	—	—	—	—	—	—	—	—
General Government	78bt *d*	....	—	—	—	—	—	—	—	—	—	—	—	—	—	—
Banks	78bu *d*	....	27	−12	24	155	262	816	−94	509	417	505	−24	−904	240	332
Other Sectors	78bv *d*	....	−9	24	−3	−39	−1,080	−1,303	−28	—	—	—	—	—	—	—
Net Errors and Omissions	78ca *d*	....	—	—	—	—	—	—	—	—	—	—	—	—	—	—
Overall Balance	78cb *d*	....	673	1,057	917	10,388	9,058	3,727	2,696	−6,700	234	3,937	9,568	−2,308	−1,509	−1,480
Reserves and Related Items	79da *d*	....	−673	−1,057	−917	−10,388	−9,058	−3,727	−2,696	6,700	−234	−3,937	−9,568	2,308	1,509	1,480
Reserve Assets	79db *d*	....	−673	−1,057	−917	−10,388	−9,058	−3,727	−2,696	6,700	−234	−3,937	−9,568	2,308	1,509	1,480
Use of Fund Credit and Loans	79dc *d*	....														
Exceptional Financing	79de *d*	....	....	....	....	....	....	....	....	....	....	....	....	....	....	....
National Accounts															*Billions of Riyals*	
Exports of Goods & Services	90c	10.30	19.86	30.01	85.68	114.46	120.28	140.32	140.76	147.24	258.49	368.43	354.92	219.45	167.18	145.53
Government Consumption	91f	3.42	4.29	5.34	9.86	15.91	28.88	41.03	47.03	71.90	77.56	81.92	128.53	126.85	121.33	121.06
Gross Fixed Capital Formation	93e	2.60	3.40	5.69	8.40	17.70	33.54	51.19	66.89	76.65	97.07	106.38	122.31	115.45	103.23	96.49
Increase/Decrease(-) in Stocks	93i	.21	.10	−.11	.84	.75	.78	.84	7.61	−7.38	−17.35	6.43	−19.80	−2.56	9.33	19.60
Private Consumption	96f	5.86	6.92	7.90	9.83	18.04	23.90	34.37	54.61	68.61	102.39	114.91	126.51	151.29	157.37	159.35
Imports of Goods & Services	98c	−4.99	−6.30	−8.27	−15.29	−27.26	−42.86	−62.70	−91.51	−107.48	−132.35	−157.46	−187.76	−195.26	−186.41	−190.64
Gross Domestic Product (GDP)	99b	17.40	28.26	40.55	99.32	139.60	164.53	205.06	225.40	249.54	385.81	520.59	524.72	415.23	372.02	351.40
Net Factor Inc/Pmts(-) Abroad	98.n	−3.83	−7.67	−10.46	−16.97	−14.20	.87	2.67	−1.78	−6.64	−4.75	−12.16	−1.82	18.16	20.44	20.94
Gross National Income (GNI)	99a	13.57	20.59	30.15	82.35	125.40	165.39	207.72	223.62	242.90	381.06	508.42	522.90	433.39	392.46	372.34
GDP Volume 1970 Prices	99b. *p*	17.40	22.96	27.50	31.64	31.72	34.46	39.67	42.03	44.84	49.37	53.28	54.16	48.34	48.29	47.22
GDP Volume (1995=100)	99bv *p*	27.7	36.5	43.7	50.3	50.5	54.8	63.1	66.8	71.3	78.5	84.7	86.1	76.9	76.8	75.1
GDP Deflator (1995=100)	99bi *p*	13.1	16.2	19.4	41.2	57.8	62.7	67.9	70.5	73.1	102.7	128.3	127.3	112.8	101.2	97.8
Population	99z	6.20	6.38	6.57	6.76	6.97	7.25	7.62	8.06	8.49	8.93	9.37	9.81	10.25	11.17	*Millions:* 11.98

	1985	1986	1987	1988	1989	1990	1991	1992	1993	1994	1995	1996	1997	1998	1999		
Billions of Riyals																**International Transactions**	
Exports	99.54	74.75	86.88	91.29	106.29	166.34	179.00	188.32	158.77	159.59	187.40	227.43	233.62 ^{P}	148.96 ^{P}	....	Exports	70
	....	66.88	76.50	75.67	90.24	150.28	163.49	174.24	144.64	142.83	163.08	203.25	199.77	121.97	....	Petroleum	70a
	....	54.26	55.17	55.05	70.62	123.28	139.83	148.31	119.91	117.20	132.99	163.28	163.02	98.84	....	Crude Petroleum	70aa
	....	12.62	21.33	20.62	19.61	27.00	23.66	25.93	24.73	25.63	30.09	39.97	36.76	23.13	....	Refined Petroleum	70ab
	85.56	70.78	75.31	81.58	79.22	90.14	108.90	124.60	105.60	87.40	105.20	103.98	106.96	112.40	....	Imports, c.i.f.	71
1995=100																Volume of Exports	
	35.2	52.6	43.5	55.4	56.1	70.3	96.6	103.7	101.3	99.9	100.0	100.3	99.6	102.0	....	Petroleum	72
	33.0	51.9	35.8	48.3	50.2	66.7	98.9	104.9	100.0	99.1	100.0	97.4	98.3	101.6	....	Crude Petroleum	72aa
	44.9	55.4	77.3	86.6	82.1	86.2	86.3	98.2	107.0	103.3	100.0	113.2	105.4	103.6	....	Refined Petroleum	72ab
Index of Prices in US Dollars																Export Prices	
	165.7	118.3	103.9	83.9	96.3	121.9	98.9	103.6	89.9	90.4	100.0	118.1	111.8	72.1	104.6	Crude Petroleum	76aa *d*
Minus Sign Indicates Debit																Balance of Payments	
	−12,932	−11,795	−9,773	−7,340	−9,538	−4,152	−27,546	−17,740	−17,268	−10,487	−5,325	681	305	−13,150	−1,701	Current Account, n.i.e.	78al *d*
	27,478	20,185	23,199	24,377	28,385	44,414	47,789	50,287	42,395	42,614	50,041	60,729	60,731	38,822	48,482	Goods: Exports f.o.b.	78aa *d*
	−20,364	−17,066	−18,283	−19,805	−19,231	−21,525	−25,971	−30,248	−25,873	−21,325	−25,650	−25,358	−26,370	−27,535	−25,717	Goods: Imports f.o.b.	78ab *d*
	7,115	3,119	4,916	4,571	9,154	22,889	21,818	20,039	16,522	21,289	24,390	35,370	34,362	11,287	22,765	*Trade Balance*	78ac *d*
	3,561	2,606	2,515	2,294	2,510	3,031	2,908	3,466	3,283	3,347	3,480	2,772	4,257	4,730	5,156	Services: Credit	78ad *d*
	−25,822	−20,336	−18,830	−14,935	−19,874	−22,414	−38,804	−32,282	−24,464	−17,893	−19,083	−24,295	−25,963	−16,882	−18,858	Services: Debit	78ae *d*
	−15,146	−14,611	−11,399	−8,069	−8,211	3,506	−14,077	−8,777	−4,659	6,743	8,787	13,848	12,655	−865	9,063	*Balance on Goods & Services*	78af *d*
	12,418	11,279	10,537	10,454	10,433	9,199	8,700	7,378	6,208	4,032	4,987	5,127	5,756	5,810	5,881	Income: Credit	78ag *d*
	−1,756	−659	−676	−716	−1,017	−1,220	−1,933	−1,944	−2,300	−2,560	−2,184	−2,681	−2,971	−3,041	−2,570	Income: Debit	78ah *d*
	−4,484	−3,991	−1,538	1,669	1,204	11,485	−7,311	−3,343	−751	8,215	11,591	16,294	15,440	1,903	12,374	*Balance on Gds, Serv. & Inc.*	78ai *d*
																Current Transfers, n.i.e.: Credit	78aj *d*
	−8,448	−7,804	−8,235	−9,009	−10,742	−15,637	−20,235	−14,397	−16,517	−18,702	−16,916	−15,613	−15,134	−15,053	−14,076	Current Transfers: Debit	78ak *d*
	—	—	—	—	—	—	—	—	—	—	—	—	—	—	—	Capital Account, n.i.e.	78bc *d*
	—	—	—	—	—	—	—	—	—	—	—	—	—	—	—	Capital Account, n.i.e.: Credit	78ba *d*
	—	—	—	—	—	—	—	—	—	—	—	—	—	—	—	Capital Account: Debit	78bb *d*
	12,222	4,176	12,413	5,821	6,030	−1,224	27,595	12,075	18,763	10,341	6,542	5,069	343	12,431	4,516	Financial Account, n.i.e.	78bj *d*
																Direct Investment Abroad	78bd *d*
	491	967	−1,175	−328	−654	1,864	160	−79	1,369	350	−1,877	−1,129	3,044	4,289	−2,163	Dir. Invest. in Rep. Econ., n.i.e.	78be *d*
	8,415	3,463	6,151	3,060	−1,786	−3,342	471	−6,500	8,213	−2,527	4,057	−2,642	−7,362	6,941	11,712	Portfolio Investment Assets	78bf *d*
																Equity Securities	78bk *d*
	8,415	3,463	6,151	3,060	−1,786	−3,342	471	−6,500	8,213	−2,527	4,057	−2,642	−7,362	6,941	11,712	Debt Securities	78bl *d*
	—	—	—	—	—	—	—	—	—	—	—	—	—	—	—	Portfolio Investment Liab., n.i.e.	78bg *d*
	—	—	—	—	—	—	—	—	—	—	—	—	—	—	—	Equity Securities	78bm *d*
	—	—	—	—	—	—	—	—	—	—	—	—	—	—	—	Debt Securities	78bn *d*
	....	....	....	....	....	....	....	....	....	....	....	....	....	....	....	Financial Derivatives Assets	78bw *d*
	....	....	....	....	....	....	....	....	....	....	....	....	....	....	....	Financial Derivatives Liabilities	78bx *d*
	2,653	−1,310	4,713	1,957	6,903	1,437	27,562	18,446	6,885	12,022	4,221	9,115	2,688	1,983	−7,180	Other Investment Assets	78bh *d*
	—	—	—	—	—	—	—	—	—	—	—	—	—	—	—	Monetary Authorities	78bo *d*
	—	—	—	—	—	—	—	—	—	—	—	—	—	—	—	General Government	78bp *d*
	−4,263	−5,617	−4,147	−3,348	−1,095	−1,234	1,207	4,621	−2,661	3,588	46	−2,188	1,777	3,621	−1,478	Banks	78bq *d*
	6,916	4,307	8,860	5,306	7,997	2,670	26,355	13,825	9,545	8,434	4,175	11,303	911	−1,639	−5,702	Other Sectors	78br *d*
	663	1,056	2,724	1,132	1,567	−1,183	−598	208	2,296	497	142	−275	1,973	−782	2,147	Other Investment Liab., n.i.e.	78bi *d*
	—	—	—	—	—	—	—	—	—	—	—	—	—	—	—	Monetary Authorities	78bs *d*
	—	—	—	—	—	—	—	—	—	—	—	—	—	—	—	General Government	78bt *d*
	663	1,056	2,724	1,132	1,567	−1,183	−598	208	2,296	497	142	−275	1,973	−782	2,147	Banks	78bu *d*
	—	—	—	—	—	—	—	—	—	—	—	—	—	—	—	Other Sectors	78bv *d*
															—	Net Errors and Omissions	78ca *d*
	−709	−7,619	2,640	−1,519	−3,508	−5,376	49	−5,664	1,495	−146	1,217	5,749	648	−719	2,815	*Overall Balance*	78cb *d*
	709	7,619	−2,640	1,519	3,508	5,376	−49	5,664	−1,495	146	−1,217	−5,749	−648	719	−2,815	Reserves and Related Items	79da *d*
	709	7,619	−2,640	1,519	3,508	5,376	−49	5,664	−1,495	146	−1,217	−5,749	−648	719	−2,815	Reserve Assets	79db *d*
	—	—	—	—	—	—	—	—	—	—	—	—	—	—	—	Use of Fund Credit and Loans	79dc *d*
	....	....	....	....	....	....	....	....	....	....	....	....	....	....	....	Exceptional Financing	79de *d*
Billions of Riyals																**National Accounts**	
	113.16	85.99	99.05	103.08	118.21	181.13	197.28	207.87	179.40	181.89	209.37	246.11	251.19	170.79	207.95	Exports of Goods & Services	90c
	114.39	106.37	107.71	97.42	96.56	120.13	165.00	148.97	127.78	119.56	122.85	140.28	151.65	156.65	156.01	Government Consumption	91f
	76.31	66.14	65.20	56.92	60.41	73.80	86.51	93.98	98.45	84.21	93.56	90.75	102.39	97.03	95.57	Gross Fixed Capital Formation	93e
	−10.62	−12.32	−12.87	2.73	6.76	2.75	7.34	8.51	9.17	6.19	5.54	4.46	5.66	5.40	5.34	Increase/Decrease(-) in Stocks	93i
	158.59	140.15	135.54	139.40	145.03	155.87	168.75	183.92	193.91	185.83	193.52	206.34	206.18	198.57	202.66	Private Consumption	96f
	−137.89	−115.24	−119.17	−114.40	−116.15	−141.69	−182.84	−181.83	−164.87	−127.66	−146.18	−158.68	−168.45	−147.68	−145.54	Imports of Goods & Services	98c
	313.94	271.09	275.45	285.15	310.82	391.99	442.04	461.40	443.84	450.03	478.65	529.25	548.62	480.77	521.99	Gross Domestic Product (GDP)	99b
	13.59	18.58	17.38	19.94	18.70	6.52	−4.88	−8.61	−7.18	−16.54	−8.91	−11.94	−9.64	....	....	Net Factor Inc/Pmts(-) Abroad	98.n
	327.53	289.67	292.84	305.08	329.52	398.52	437.16	452.78	436.66	433.49	469.74	517.32	538.98	....	....	Gross National Income (GNI)	99a
	45.30	47.82	47.17	50.73	50.83	56.24	60.96	62.66	62.26	62.58	62.88	63.75	65.46	66.49	66.75	GDP Volume 1970 Prices	99b.*p*
	72.1	76.1	75.0	80.7	80.8	89.4	97.0	99.7	99.0	99.5	100.0	101.4	104.1	105.7	106.2	GDP Volume (1995=100)	99bv *p*
	91.0	74.5	76.7	73.8	80.3	91.6	95.3	96.7	93.6	94.5	100.0	109.1	110.1	95.0	102.7	GDP Deflator (1995=100)	99bi *p*
Midyear Estimates																	
	12.65	13.36	13.61	14.02	14.43	14.87	I 16.54	16.96	17.35	17.71	18.25	18.83	19.48	20.18	19.90	**Population**	99z

(See notes in the back of the book.)

Senegal

		1970	1971	1972	1973	1974	1975	1976	1977	1978	1979	1980	1981	1982	1983	1984
Exchange Rates														*Francs per SDR:*		
Official Rate	aa	276.02	283.61	278.00	284.00	272.08	262.55	288.70	285.76	272.28	264.78	287.99	334.52	370.92	436.97	470.11
														Francs per US Dollar:		
Official Rate	ae	276.02	261.22	256.05	235.42	222.22	224.27	248.49	235.25	209.00	201.00	225.80	287.40	336.25	417.37	479.60
Official Rate	rf	276.40	275.59	252.03	222.89	240.70	214.31	238.95	245.68	225.66	212.72	211.28	271.73	328.61	381.07	436.96
Fund Position														*Millions of SDRs:*		
Quota	2f. s	34.0	34.0	34.0	34.0	34.0	34.0	34.0	34.0	42.0	42.0	63.0	63.0	63.0	85.1	85.1
SDRs	1b. s	1.2	2.5	5.7	5.3	4.6	3.3	1.2	1.7	9.7	11.5	—	3.7	4.9	3.8	.1
Reserve Position in the Fund	1c. s	3.3	3.6	3.9	4.2	—	—	—	—	2.1				.9	.9	1.0
Total Fund Cred.&Loans Outstg.	2tl	—	—	—	—	—	25.4	25.4	25.4	57.0	70.5	109.9	160.2	200.0	220.5	234.7
International Liquidity												*Millions of US Dollars Unless Otherwise Indicated:*				
Total Reserves minus Gold	1l. d	22.1	24.6	38.5	12.1	6.3	31.1	25.2	33.7	18.8	19.1	8.1	8.7	11.4	12.2	3.7
SDRs	1b. d	1.2	2.7	6.2	6.4	5.7	3.9	1.3	2.1	12.7	15.1	—	4.4	5.4	3.9	.1
Reserve Position in the Fund	1c. d	3.3	3.9	4.2	5.0	—	—	—	—	2.8	—	—	—	1.0	1.0	.9
Foreign Exchange	1d. d	17.6	18.1	28.1	.6	.6	27.3	23.9	31.6	3.4	4.0	8.1	4.3	5.0	7.3	2.6
Gold (Million Fine Troy Ounces)	1ad	....	....	....	....	....	....	—	.015	.022	.029	.029	.029	.029	.029	.029
Gold (National Valuation)	1and	....	....	....	....	....	....		.6	1.0	1.3	1.3	12.2	12.4	11.2	9.6
Monetary Authorities: Other Liab.	4.. d	.4	1.1	1.0	11.6	11.9	.5	14.4	19.3	36.0	117.6	158.9	210.8	255.5	241.0	196.2
Deposit Money Banks: Assets	7a. d	8.9	8.4	10.9	15.5	19.0	22.8	37.2	46.0	46.6	53.2	57.7	43.1	55.4	45.1	40.4
Liabilities	7b. d	23.6	30.8	41.3	47.2	57.7	85.8	77.5	101.0	144.2	228.6	211.4	173.9	159.5	115.2	133.2
Monetary Authorities														*Billions of Francs:*		
Foreign Assets	11	6.1	7.5	9.8	2.8	1.4	7.0	6.3	7.9	3.9	3.8	1.8	2.5	3.8	5.1	1.8
Claims on Central Government	12a	—	—	—	—	—	.4	3.4	8.1	8.2	16.5	36.8	59.6	116.2	132.3	145.3
Claims on Deposit Money Banks	12e	13.5	13.6	12.9	25.2	38.5	39.5	42.8	44.3	71.2	79.2	108.1	146.7	168.6	173.8	157.9
Claims on Other Financial Insts	12f	—	—	—	—	—		1.1	1.4	1.2	1.2	.5	1.4	1.7	2.4	2.6
Reserve Money	14	16.1	16.9	17.7	21.5	32.2	34.6	38.7	44.6	55.8	51.1	62.0	85.8	106.7	103.1	102.1
of which: Currency Outside DMBs	14a	15.2	15.9	16.5	19.5	29.0	29.5	33.7	39.5	46.2	42.9	51.4	73.6	84.5	78.3	77.3
Foreign Liabilities	16c	.1	.3	.3	2.7	2.6	6.8	10.9	11.8	27.0	49.1	76.7	123.4	169.3	206.0	212.7
Central Government Deposits	16d	2.2	1.7	1.6	.7	2.0	2.6	1.0	1.4	1.9	1.4	12.9	6.2	20.5	15.9	13.5
Other Items (Net)	17r	1.2	2.2	3.2	3.2	3.2	3.0	2.9	4.0	-.2	-.9	-4.4	-5.3	-6.2	-11.5	-20.7
Deposit Money Banks														*Billions of Francs:*		
Reserves	20	.8	1.5	1.3	2.2	2.3	4.7	5.2	5.4	9.1	6.6	10.1	11.7	21.9	21.2	24.2
Foreign Assets	21	2.5	2.1	2.8	3.6	4.2	5.1	9.2	10.8	9.7	10.7	13.0	12.4	18.6	18.8	19.4
Claims on Central Government	22a	3.4	3.6	5.3	6.3	8.0	10.6	14.4	12.6	12.3	‖14.1	15.6	14.5	13.5	13.5	14.9
Claims on Private Sector	22d	36.6	38.6	46.0	62.7	88.8	106.2	121.1	143.3	194.3	‖230.6	268.3	322.8	353.8	366.7	372.2
Claims on Other Financial Insts	22f	....	....	....	....	....	....	....	....	....	‖6.7	2.9	2.4	2.1	2.3	2.5
Demand Deposits	24	17.3	17.4	21.0	23.0	36.9	42.9	58.6	66.7	76.5	‖74.3	82.0	85.1	98.7	106.1	109.6
Time Deposits	25	2.8	2.8	3.7	8.2	9.5	10.9	18.8	21.9	32.3	‖39.9	39.8	53.7	73.3	83.8	95.5
Foreign Liabilities	26c	3.3	5.0	6.6	7.1	8.9	15.4	15.3	19.9	26.3	35.2	34.8	35.8	38.3	30.9	47.7
Long-Term Foreign Liabilities	26cl	3.3	2.9	4.0	3.8	3.9	3.8	4.0	3.9	3.8	10.8	12.9	14.2	15.3	16.0	16.2
Central Government Deposits	26d	2.2	2.5	4.2	4.3	6.1	8.2	4.4	4.2	4.5	‖12.3	13.6	19.0	15.1	16.4	18.8
Credit from Monetary Authorities	26g	13.5	13.6	12.9	25.2	38.5	39.5	42.8	44.3	71.2	78.2	107.6	146.9	169.6	175.3	156.0
Other Items (Net)	27r	.9	1.6	3.0	3.2	-.4	6.0	6.0	11.3	10.9	18.1	19.2	9.2	-.5	-6.1	-10.6
Treasury Claims: Private Sector	22d. i	1.0	1.2	1.3	.7	.8	.8	.8	1.3	1.8	1.8	1.4	1.3	1.1	1.9	1.5
Post Office: Checking Deposits	24.. i	2.0	1.9	1.6	1.7	1.9	2.3	2.5	2.9	3.7	3.6	4.1	4.0	5.3	4.8	4.7
Monetary Survey														*Billions of Francs:*		
Foreign Assets (Net)	31n	5.2	4.4	5.8	-3.4	-5.9	-10.1	-10.7	-12.9	-39.6	-69.8	-96.7	-144.3	-185.2	-213.0	-239.2
Domestic Credit	32	37.5	39.9	47.2	65.7	90.7	108.8	137.0	162.7	213.3	‖259.0	301.7	379.5	456.9	489.6	509.9
Claims on Central Govt. (Net)	32an	—	—	—	2.2	1.0	1.9	14.0	16.7	16.0	‖18.8	28.7	51.6	98.3	116.3	131.1
Claims on Private Sector	32d	37.6	39.8	47.3	63.5	89.7	106.9	121.9	144.6	196.1	‖232.4	269.7	324.1	354.9	368.6	373.7
Claims on Other Financial Insts	32f							1.1	1.4	1.2	‖7.9	3.4	3.8	3.8	4.7	5.2
Money	34	34.5	35.2	39.1	44.2	67.8	75.2	94.9	109.1	126.5	‖121.2	137.9	163.2	189.0	189.2	191.6
Quasi-Money	35	2.8	2.8	3.7	8.2	9.5	10.9	18.8	21.9	32.3	‖39.9	39.8	53.7	73.3	83.8	95.5
Long-Term Foreign Liabilities	36cl	3.3	2.9	4.0	3.8	3.9	3.8	4.0	3.9	3.8	10.8	12.9	14.2	15.3	16.0	16.2
Other Items (Net)	37r	2.2	3.3	6.2	6.1	3.6	8.8	8.7	14.9	11.0	17.4	14.4	4.1	-5.9	-12.5	-32.6
Money plus Quasi-Money	35l	37.3	38.0	42.8	52.4	77.3	86.1	113.6	131.0	158.8	‖161.1	177.7	216.9	262.3	273.0	287.1
Other Banking Institutions														*Billions of Francs:*		
Savings Deposits	45	.5	.6	.7	.7	.9	....	....	....	....	1.6	1.7	1.7	1.9	1.9	1.9
Liquid Liabilities	55l	37.8	38.6	43.5	53.1	78.1	....	....	....	....	‖162.7	179.4	218.7	264.2	274.9	289.0
Interest Rates														*Percent Per Annum:*		
Discount Rate (*End of Period*)	60	3.50	3.50	3.50	5.50	5.50	8.00	8.00	8.00	8.00	8.00	10.50	10.50	12.50	10.50	10.50
Money Market Rate	60b	....	....	....	....	....	....	7.28	7.40	7.40	7.80	10.00	13.67	14.66	12.23	11.84
Deposit Rate	60l	3.00	3.00	3.00	5.75	5.75	5.88	6.00	6.00	6.00	6.00	6.19	6.25	7.75	7.50	7.25
Lending Rate	60p	....	....	....	....	....	....		12.00	12.00	12.00	14.50	14.50	16.00	14.50	14.50
Prices, Production, Labor														*Index Numbers (1995=100):*		
Consumer Prices	64	15.6	16.2	17.2	19.1	22.3	29.3	29.6	33.0	34.1	37.4	40.7	43.1	50.6	56.5	63.1
Industrial Production	66	65.4	64.7	80.8	73.6	78.2	91.0	93.5	‖98.6	88.5	99.5	82.0	89.8	93.1	96.6	94.7
														Number in Thousands:		
Labor Force	67d	....	....	....	....	....	....	....	....	....	....	....	....	....	....	....
Employment	67e	....	....	....	....	....	....	....	....	....	....	....	....	....	....	....
Unemployment	67c	....	....	....	....	....	....	....	....	....	....	....	....	....	....	....
International Transactions														*Billions of Francs:*		
Exports	70	42.18	34.71	54.41	43.24	93.98	99.10	115.93	152.92	101.40	113.86	100.77	135.88	180.04	235.48	277.02
Imports, c.i.f.	71	53.86	60.60	70.55	80.17	119.38	124.62	153.89	187.55	170.31	197.98	222.26	292.34	325.94	390.72	428.60
														1985=100		
Unit Value of Exports	74	19.4	21.6	21.1	25.0	47.5	‖40.2	39.2	47.1	50.8	54.4	53.2	73.0	‖70.7	78.7	100.3
Unit Value of Imports	75	19.5	22.8	23.6	26.9	38.5	‖40.8	42.9	46.7	46.1	51.8	67.4	75.6	‖85.3	93.3	102.4

1985	1986	1987	1988	1989	1990	1991	1992	1993	1994	1995	1996	1997	1998	1999		
															Exchange Rates	
End of Period																
415.26	394.78	378.78	407.68	380.32	364.84	370.48	378.57	404.89	I780.44	728.38	753.06	807.94	791.61	I896.19	Official Rate	aa
End of Period (ae) Period Average (rf)																
378.05	322.75	267.00	302.95	289.40	256.45	259.00	275.32	294.77	I534.60	490.00	523.70	598.81	562.21	I652.95	Official Rate	ae
449.26	346.31	300.54	297.85	319.01	272.26	282.11	264.69	283.16	I555.20	499.15	511.55	583.67	589.95	I615.70	Official Rate	rf
															Fund Position	
End of Period																
85.1	85.1	85.1	85.1	85.1	85.1	85.1	118.9	118.9	118.9	118.9	118.9	118.9	118.9	161.8	Quota	2f.s
.1	2.5	—	—	3.6	.2	.3	—	.3	.7	2.6	1.2	.3	.4	1.8	SDRs	1b.s
1.0	1.0	1.0	1.0	1.0	1.0	1.0	1.1	1.1	1.1	1.2	1.3	1.3	1.4	1.4	Reserve Position in the Fund	1c.s
243.7	236.3	241.6	236.5	240.4	221.0	228.9	197.4	177.8	205.4	233.3	226.5	216.5	207.8	198.2	Total Fund Cred.&Loans Outstg.	2tl
															International Liquidity	
End of Period																
5.1	9.4	9.2	10.5	19.0	11.0	13.2	12.4	3.4	179.6	271.8	288.3	386.2	430.8	402.9	Total Reserves minus Gold	1l.d
.1	3.0	—	—	4.7	.2	.4	—	.4	1.1	3.8	1.7	.5	.5	2.5	SDRs	1b.d
1.1	1.2	1.4	1.3	1.3	1.4	1.5	1.4	1.5	1.7	1.8	1.8	1.8	1.9	1.9	Reserve Position in the Fund	1c.d
3.9	5.2	7.8	9.1	13.0	9.3	11.3	10.9	1.5	176.9	266.2	284.8	383.9	428.4	398.5	Foreign Exchange	1d.d
.029	.029	.029	.029	.029	.029	.029	.029	.029	.029	.029	.029	.029	.029	.029	Gold (Million Fine Troy Ounces)	1ad
9.4	11.7	13.7	12.0	11.3	11.0	10.3	10.1	10.8	10.8	11.2	10.9	8.9	8.5	8.6	Gold (National Valuation)	1and
334.8	289.8	317.8	407.1	303.7	330.0	282.2	298.2	408.2	144.4	122.8	116.9	101.6	109.2	96.6	Monetary Authorities: Other Liab.	4..d
41.9	40.0	39.7	58.3	84.8	51.2	66.7	72.8	68.6	131.4	159.9	146.7	151.3	220.4	258.2	Deposit Money Banks: Assets	7a.d
167.1	150.9	204.3	226.9	259.7	183.1	192.2	171.8	154.7	134.0	131.7	105.0	94.0	117.5	119.9	Liabilities	7b.d
															Monetary Authorities	
End of Period																
1.9	3.0	2.5	3.2	5.5	2.8	3.4	3.4	1.0	96.0	133.2	151.0	231.3	242.2	263.1	Foreign Assets	11
158.1	164.5	170.1	172.9	174.0	163.9	165.5	163.6	158.4	265.5	271.4	229.7	293.7	296.4	279.1	Claims on Central Government	12a
179.7	160.6	156.4	194.5	190.0	183.9	179.8	189.0	172.3	11.5	—	2.6	31.7	26.9	12.6	Claims on Deposit Money Banks	12e
3.1	3.6	3.6	3.6	.5	.5	.6	.6	.6	.6	.7	.5	.5	.4	—	Claims on Other Financial Insts	12f
108.2	125.8	132.6	131.8	164.4	158.5	169.6	181.7	126.6	188.9	196.6	168.7	174.2	186.0	215.7	Reserve Money	14
86.2	104.3	100.7	92.8	102.7	95.2	97.5	107.2	93.0	145.6	152.1	141.9	142.3	158.5	179.4	of which: Currency Outside DMBs	14a
234.5	194.0	180.7	221.7	179.8	165.3	157.9	156.8	192.3	237.5	230.1	231.7	235.7	225.9	240.6	Foreign Liabilities	16c
6.0	6.0	9.3	9.9	7.6	5.8	6.0	4.0	5.7	13.8	19.2	26.8	142.1	137.4	105.0	Central Government Deposits	16d
-5.8	6.1	10.0	10.8	18.1	21.5	15.8	14.0	7.6	-66.5	-40.7	-43.5	5.0	16.6	-6.6	Other Items (Net)	17r
															Deposit Money Banks	
End of Period																
22.4	28.3	32.1	39.6	67.6	62.3	71.3	74.1	34.1	31.8	31.1	24.9	32.4	27.1	35.7	Reserves	20
15.8	12.9	10.6	17.7	24.6	13.1	17.3	20.1	20.2	70.2	78.4	76.8	90.6	123.9	168.6	Foreign Assets	21
14.5	15.4	15.7	24.8	21.7	15.5	32.7	22.8	28.6	57.9	61.5	120.0	109.6	122.4	110.6	Claims on Central Government	22a
394.5	389.7	401.5	431.4	441.5	410.3	396.1	417.5	424.3	349.9	355.6	411.0	428.3	437.1	483.0	Claims on Private Sector	22d
3.6	4.2	4.2	5.3	2.7	2.0	1.9	2.1	1.6	1.3	.2	—	—	—	—	Claims on Other Financial Insts	22f
103.4	117.1	109.7	117.0	124.5	104.7	112.3	106.6	101.4	155.3	160.2	198.5	196.3	234.0	255.9	Demand Deposits	24
106.6	106.7	118.4	119.6	138.1	147.0	158.4	167.6	138.8	161.4	184.6	216.4	237.7	233.2	273.2	Time Deposits	25
52.1	37.1	43.1	57.0	63.7	38.6	41.9	38.3	36.4	58.3	51.4	42.4	50.0	62.5	72.5	Foreign Liabilities	26c
11.1	11.6	11.4	11.7	11.5	8.4	7.9	9.0	9.2	13.4	13.2	12.6	6.3	3.5	5.8	Long-Term Foreign Liabilities	26cl
17.5	23.8	32.1	38.0	61.4	66.7	83.1	100.8	118.1	136.4	136.3	161.7	109.5	101.5	97.6	Central Government Deposits	26d
182.1	167.5	159.0	196.8	194.8	184.3	181.4	190.2	176.8	11.5	—	3.6	31.7	26.9	12.6	Credit from Monetary Authorities	26g
-22.0	-13.4	-9.6	-21.3	-35.9	-46.3	-65.7	-75.8	-71.9	-25.1	-18.9	-2.5	29.4	48.9	80.5	Other Items (Net)	27r
2.2	2.1	2.2	.7	.9	1.2	.5	2.4	2.3	2.3	2.2	3.0	2.8	2.9	3.2	Treasury Claims: Private Sector	22d.i
3.8	5.5	3.8	4.9	3.5	3.9	3.0	3.4	3.0	3.9	4.3	2.8	4.0	4.1	3.9	Post Office: Checking Deposits	24..i
															Monetary Survey	
End of Period																
-268.8	-215.2	-210.7	-257.9	-213.4	-188.0	-179.0	-171.6	-207.4	-129.5	-69.9	-46.3	36.1	77.7	118.7	Foreign Assets (Net)	31n
554.2	553.1	557.5	595.0	574.8	523.7	510.6	505.2	492.7	529.0	538.1	575.5	584.5	621.5	674.1	Domestic Credit	32
150.7	153.5	146.0	154.0	129.3	109.7	111.6	82.6	63.9	174.9	179.5	161.0	152.9	181.1	187.8	Claims on Central Govt. (Net)	32an
396.8	391.7	403.7	432.1	442.4	411.5	396.6	419.9	426.6	352.2	357.8	414.1	431.1	439.9	486.2	Claims on Private Sector	32d
6.7	7.8	7.8	9.0	3.2	2.5	2.5	2.7	2.2	1.9	.8	.5	.5	.4	—	Claims on Other Financial Insts	32f
193.5	227.0	214.4	214.9	230.8	204.2	213.2	217.4	197.7	305.3	316.8	343.6	343.2	397.0	439.8	Money	34
106.6	106.7	118.4	119.6	138.1	147.0	158.4	167.6	138.8	161.4	184.6	216.4	237.7	233.2	273.2	Quasi-Money	35
11.1	11.6	11.4	11.7	11.5	8.4	7.9	9.0	9.2	13.4	13.2	12.6	6.3	3.5	5.8	Long-Term Foreign Liabilities	36cl
-25.8	-7.4	2.6	-9.1	-19.1	-23.8	-47.9	-60.4	-60.5	-80.7	-46.4	-43.4	33.4	65.5	73.9	Other Items (Net)	37r
300.1	333.7	332.8	334.5	368.9	351.2	371.6	385.0	336.5	466.7	501.4	560.0	580.9	630.2	713.0	Money plus Quasi-Money	35l
															Other Banking Institutions	
End of Period																
1.9	2.4	2.4	3.5	3.8	4.2	....	....	....	....	....	—		—	—	Savings Deposits	45
302.0	336.0	335.2	338.0	372.7	355.4	....	....	....	....	....	560.0	580.9	630.2	713.0	Liquid Liabilities	55l
															Interest Rates	
Percent Per Annum																
10.50	8.50	8.50	9.50	11.00	11.00	11.00	12.50	10.50	10.00	7.50	6.50	6.00	6.25	5.75	Discount Rate (End of Period)	60
10.66	8.58	8.37	8.72	10.07	10.98	10.94	11.44	....	....	....	....	....	4.81	4.95	Money Market Rate	60b
7.25	6.08	5.25	5.25	6.42	7.00	7.00	7.75	....	....	....	....	....	3.50	3.50	Deposit Rate	60l
14.50	13.50	13.50	13.58	15.13	16.00	16.00	16.75	....	....	....	....	....	....	....	Lending Rate	60p
															Prices, Production, Labor	
Period Averages																
71.3	75.7	72.6	71.3	71.6	71.8	70.6	70.5	70.1	92.7	100.0	102.8	I104.6	105.8	106.6	Consumer Prices	64
97.0	103.8	104.5	89.0	84.8	100.1	92.2	90.8	85.0	93.2	100.0	96.5	98.2	118.2	....	Industrial Production	66
Period Averages																
....	....	....	1,897	....	....	....	....	....	....	....	....	....	....	....	Labor Force	67d
85	86	....	....	....	....	130	....	....	....	....	....	....	....	....	Employment	67e
11	10	8	17	8	10	14	12	10	....	....	....	....	....	....	Unemployment	67c
															International Transactions	
Billions of Francs																
252.49	216.58	182.25	176.08	221.10	207.38	197.71	178.08	200.20	439.10	483.50	504.50	528.00	570.90	....	Exports	70
370.97	332.93	307.60	321.57	389.54	332.12	330.94	273.72	307.70	567.40	704.90	734.60	780.00	848.00	....	Imports, c.i.f.	71
1985=100																
100.0	70.0	66.6	....	....	....	....	....	....	....	....	....	....	....	....	Unit Value of Exports	74
100.0	72.4	68.9	....	....	....	....	....	....	....	....	....	....	....	....	Unit Value of Imports	75

Senegal

722

Millions of US Dollars (Balance of Payments); *Millions of US Dollars* (International Investment Position); *Billions of Francs* (Government Finance, National Accounts); *Millions* (Population)

	Code	1970	1971	1972	1973	1974	1975	1976	1977	1978	1979	1980	1981	1982	1983	1984
Balance of Payments																
Current Account, n.i.e.	78ald	...	...	...	...	-65.6	-85.6	-92.8	-67.5	-235.8	-264.2	-386.5	-462.3	-266.6	-306.1	-274.1
Goods: Exports f.o.b.	78aa d	...	...	...	...	472.6	542.6	536.5	685.3	434.7	517.6	470.2	603.4	564.5	642.1	632.5
Goods: Imports f.o.b.	78ab d	...	...	...	...	-552.5	-611.5	-659.6	-772.5	-744.2	-813.3	-875.1	-1,020.3	-815.1	-917.2	-818.9
Trade Balance	78ac d					-79.9	-69.0	-123.1	-87.2	-309.5	-295.7	-404.9	-416.8	-250.5	-275.1	-186.4
Services: Credit	78ad d					127.3	145.6	159.5	169.9	240.4	298.6	336.7	379.6	319.7	306.0	268.4
Services: Debit	78ae d					-126.6	-170.4	-174.6	-202.7	-210.8	-287.9	-339.9	-494.7	-414.6	-391.9	-370.0
Balance on Goods & Services	78af d					-79.2	-93.7	-138.2	-120.0	-279.9	-285.1	-408.1	-531.9	-345.4	-361.0	-288.0
Income: Credit	78ag d					8.8	8.0	7.7	9.7	11.7	16.5	23.6	19.1	19.3	24.5	14.9
Income: Debit	78ah d					-58.6	-83.8	-68.6	-63.9	-87.6	-95.6	-122.0	-115.8	-117.0	-123.9	-138.3
Balance on Gds, Serv. & Inc.	78ai d					-129.0	-169.6	-199.2	-174.3	-355.8	-364.2	-506.5	-628.6	-443.2	-460.5	-411.4
Current Transfers, n.i.e.: Credit	78aj d					102.0	134.1	152.5	158.1	208.2	223.4	245.4	275.5	274.4	238.9	212.4
Current Transfers: Debit	78ak d					-38.6	-50.2	-46.1	-51.3	-88.2	-123.4	-125.4	-109.1	-97.8	-84.6	-75.2
Capital Account, n.i.e.	78bc d					—	—	—	—	—	—	—	—	—	—	—
Capital Account, n.i.e.: Credit	78ba d					—	—	—	—	—	—	—	—	—	—	—
Capital Account: Debit	78bb d					—	—	—	—	—	—	—	—	—	—	—
Financial Account, n.i.e.	78bj d					45.4	92.2	80.0	70.3	189.9	277.6	356.0	315.8	134.9	189.7	189.9
Direct Investment Abroad	78bd d					-3.2	6.9	.4	-2.9	-.5	-3.9	-1.6	-14.8	-18.0	1.6	-1.9
Dir. Invest. in Rep. Econ., n.i.e.	78be d					10.3	22.5	35.9	28.0	-5.0	8.9	14.5	34.4	28.1	-34.7	29.1
Portfolio Investment Assets	78bf d					.2	—	—	—	.7	—	-.4	-1.8	-.3	-1.0	-.1
Equity Securities	78bk d					.2	—	—	—	.7	—	-.4	-1.8	-.3	-1.0	-.1
Debt Securities	78bl d															
Portfolio Investment Liab., n.i.e.	78bg d					2.9	2.9	9.2	.6	8.3	-2.6	3.2	1.1	.9	-.8	1.7
Equity Securities	78bm d					2.7	2.4	11.3	2.3	7.5	—	.1	.6	1.0	-.8	1.2
Debt Securities	78bn d					.2	.6	-2.1	-1.7	.8	-2.6	3.0	.5	-.2	-.1	.6
Financial Derivatives Assets	78bw d					...	...	...	...	...	...	...	...	...	...	...
Financial Derivatives Liabilities	78bx d					...	...	...	...	...	...	...	...	...	...	...
Other Investment Assets	78bh d					-42.7	2.3	-22.4	-14.2	-4.0	-57.8	-25.8	-59.3	-63.1	-22.4	20.3
Monetary Authorities	78bo d															
General Government	78bp d					-.5	-3.0	-.8	—	—	-1.8	-1.6	-.1	-.2	.1	.1
Banks	78bq d					-17.3	-8.6	-10.1	-2.5	-9.8	-5.7	-12.7	-5.5	-18.8	-2.1	-14.5
Other Sectors	78br d					-24.9	14.0	-11.6	-11.7	5.8	-50.3	-11.6	-53.7	-44.1	-20.4	34.8
Other Investment Liab., n.i.e.	78bi d					78.0	57.6	57.0	58.7	190.4	333.1	366.1	356.2	187.4	247.0	140.7
Monetary Authorities	78bs d					.6	-12.3	14.4	3.9	13.3	75.7	58.2	90.8	77.0	38.6	-14.7
General Government	78bt d					50.0	33.3	46.9	27.1	109.1	112.2	256.2	144.4	59.6	141.5	64.2
Banks	78bu d					14.3	25.2	-.1	16.9	34.0	78.2	3.2	20.9	15.6	-12.2	37.9
Other Sectors	78bv d					13.0	11.4	-4.1	10.8	34.0	67.0	48.6	100.1	35.2	79.1	53.2
Net Errors and Omissions	78ca d					14.3	-11.2	6.2	.5	-14.7	-40.6	-36.6	13.6	-4.7	6.6	-14.2
Overall Balance	78cb d					-5.9	-4.5	-6.5	3.2	-60.5	-27.1	-67.2	-132.9	-136.4	-109.9	-98.4
Reserves and Related Items	79da d					5.9	4.5	6.5	-3.2	60.5	27.1	67.2	132.9	136.4	109.9	98.4
Reserve Assets	79db d					5.9	-26.3	6.2	-3.7	20.1	8.9	15.2	2.9	-3.5	-2.2	7.8
Use of Fund Credit and Loans	79dc d					—	30.8	—	—	39.9	17.7	50.9	57.4	43.8	21.1	15.7
Exceptional Financing	79de d					—	—	.3	.5	.5	.5	.5	72.6	96.1	91.0	74.9
International Investment Position																
Assets	79aa d					...	...	...	...	...	...	...	...	...	...	...
Direct Investment Abroad	79ab d					...	...	...	...	...	...	...	...	...	...	...
Portfolio Investment	79ac d					...	...	...	...	...	...	...	...	...	...	...
Equity Securities	79ad d					...	...	...	...	...	...	...	...	...	...	...
Debt Securities	79ae d					...	...	...	...	...	...	...	...	...	...	...
Financial Derivatives	79al d					...	...	...	...	...	...	...	...	...	...	...
Other Investment	79af d					...	...	...	...	...	...	...	...	...	...	...
Monetary Authorities	79ag d					...	...	...	...	...	...	...	...	...	...	...
General Government	79ah d					...	...	...	...	...	...	...	...	...	...	...
Banks	79ai d					...	...	...	...	...	...	...	...	...	...	...
Other Sectors	79aj d					...	...	...	...	...	...	...	...	...	...	...
Reserve Assets	79ak d					...	...	...	...	...	...	...	...	...	...	...
Liabilities	79la d					...	...	...	...	...	...	...	...	...	...	...
Dir. Invest. in Rep. Economy	79lb d					...	...	...	...	...	...	...	...	...	...	...
Portfolio Investment	79lc d					...	...	...	...	...	...	...	...	...	...	...
Equity Securities	79ld d					...	...	...	...	...	...	...	...	...	...	...
Debt Securities	79le d					...	...	...	...	...	...	...	...	...	...	...
Financial Derivatives	79ll d					...	...	...	...	...	...	...	...	...	...	...
Other Investment	79lf d					...	...	...	...	...	...	...	...	...	...	...
Monetary Authorities	79lg d					...	...	...	...	...	...	...	...	...	...	...
General Government	79lh d					...	...	...	...	...	...	...	...	...	...	...
Banks	79li d					...	...	...	...	...	...	...	...	...	...	...
Other Sectors	79lj d					...	...	...	...	...	...	...	...	...	...	...
Government Finance																
Deficit (-) or Surplus	80	1.24	-1.20	...	-7.51	...	-2.15	...	-15.09	1.49	-4.26	‡5.44	-22.63	‡-52.30	-55.47	-82.44
Revenue	81	39.98	41.43	...	47.70	...	77.03	...	86.22	98.14	107.55	‡153.67	150.89	‡170.63	182.71	192.46
Grants Received	81z	.01	.01	...	—	...	.02	.17	.05	.04	.26	‡.36	1.18	‡9.89	13.59	24.77
Expenditure	82	38.20	42.31	...	51.00	...	75.64	90.80	96.96	96.80	111.50	‡147.18	171.89	‡231.01	250.04	298.46
Lending Minus Repayments	83	.55	.33	...	4.21	...	3.56	.62	4.40	-.11	.57	‡1.41	2.81	‡1.81	1.73	1.21
Financing																
Net Borrowing: Domestic	84a	...	...	...	...	...	2.31	...	...	...	...	‡10.60	23.51	‡49.64	15.91	23.86
Foreign	85a	...	...	...	...	...	-.16	...	...	...	...	‡-16.90	6.47	‡26.08	41.78	40.60
Use of Cash Balances	87											‡1.86	-7.35	‡-23.42	-2.22	17.98
Debt: Domestic	88a													‡123.59	147.28	172.58
Foreign	89a													‡313.96	423.84	520.68
National Accounts																
Exports of Goods & Services	90c	63.8	62.5	81.9	77.4	141.3	144.5	162.8	204.4	146.4	181.0	169.7	208.5	279.9	299.8	373.3
Government Consumption	91f	32.6	35.4	37.2	40.0	45.6	56.4	65.5	71.1	83.2	101.3	128.1	137.6	154.5	170.3	188.8
Gross Fixed Capital Formation	93e	24.9	25.8	31.1	32.9	43.0	47.0	51.0	51.7	55.8	68.6	83.2	85.1	103.4	123.2	126.1
Increase/Decrease(-) in Stocks	93i	7.2	8.2	8.9	12.1	23.2	14.9	12.0	18.8	15.6	-1.7	-9.2	1.0	.5	-2.5	5.1
Private Consumption	96f	185.7	194.9	207.6	220.4	246.6	308.8	365.5	381.4	404.9	470.3	534.2	597.3	715.6	792.4	824.8
Imports of Goods & Services	98c	-72.5	-78.1	-91.4	-102.7	-158.6	-162.6	-194.6	-240.6	-208.0	-233.9	-275.0	-355.8	-405.1	-438.2	-496.9
Gross Domestic Product (GDP)	99b	241.5	248.4	275.1	279.7	340.3	408.5	461.8	486.1	498.5	585.2	631.0	673.6	848.9	944.9	1,021.2
Net Primary Income from Abroad	98.n	7.0	11.8	8.2	5.3	4.9	3.0	12.2	13.9	12.6	9.3	9.8	29.4	37.8	22.1	15.8
Gross National Income (GNI)	99a	248.5	260.2	283.3	285.0	345.2	411.5	474.0	500.1	511.0	594.4	640.8	702.9	886.6	966.9	1,037.1
GDP Volume 1987 Prices	99b.p	925.6	924.3	983.3	928.4	967.4	1,040.1	1,133.1	1,102.7	1,059.1	1,133.1	1,095.8	1,082.8	1,249.0	1,276.1	1,225.0
GDP Volume (1995=100)	99bv p	57.8	57.7	61.4	57.9	60.4	64.9	70.7	66.1	70.7	68.4	67.6	78.0	79.6	76.5	
GDP Deflator (1995=100)	99bi p	18.7	19.3	20.1	21.6	25.2	28.2	29.2	31.6	33.8	37.0	41.3	44.6	48.7	53.1	59.8
Population	99z	4.27	4.40	4.55	4.70	4.84	4.98	5.12	5.25	5.40	5.55	5.70	5.86	6.03	6.20	6.37

	Code	1985	1986	1987	1988	1989	1990	1991	1992	1993	1994	1995	1996	1997	1998	1999
Balance of Payments		*Minus Sign Indicates Debit*														
Current Account, n.i.e.	78al*d*	-361.1	-369.8	-430.2	-405.1	-348.1	-363.3	-371.7	-401.3	-433.0	-187.5	-244.5	-199.5	-184.9	....	....
Goods: Exports f.o.b.	78aa*d*	548.1	694.5	707.5	713.2	804.1	937.9	848.5	860.6	736.8	818.8	993.3	988.0	904.6	....	....
Goods: Imports f.o.b.	78ab*d*	-795.8	-883.3	-955.8	-956.0	-1,004.1	-1,164.3	-1,114.0	-1,191.8	-1,086.7	-1,022.0	-1,242.9	-1,264.0	-1,176.0	....	....
Trade Balance	78ac*d*	-247.7	-188.7	-248.3	-242.8	-199.9	-226.4	-265.5	-331.1	-349.9	-203.2	-249.6	-275.9	-271.5	....	....
Services: Credit	78ad*d*	276.3	334.5	363.6	398.1	397.7	514.8	448.6	481.4	413.9	412.3	512.5	378.6	371.7	....	....
Services: Debit	78ae*d*	-366.7	-484.7	-503.8	-519.3	-514.4	-675.6	-622.6	-654.2	-581.3	-492.7	-578.2	-395.8	-391.7	....	....
Balance on Goods & Services	78af*d*	-338.2	-339.0	-388.5	-364.0	-316.6	-387.2	-439.5	-503.9	-517.3	-283.6	-315.3	-293.1	-291.5	....	....
Income: Credit	78ag*d*	30.8	47.8	53.1	50.5	57.0	84.3	85.3	96.5	82.8	63.3	87.2	81.3	67.9	....	....
Income: Debit	78ah*d*	-133.9	-173.6	-205.1	-222.3	-219.5	-213.3	-175.9	-173.0	-162.3	-164.5	-211.5	-154.1	-139.8	....	....
Balance on Gds, Serv. & Inc.	78ai*d*	-441.2	-464.9	-540.5	-535.8	-479.1	-516.3	-530.1	-580.5	-596.8	-384.7	-439.6	-366.0	-363.4	....	....
Current Transfers, n.i.e.: Credit	78aj*d*	142.3	169.4	195.4	218.0	215.2	257.1	269.4	290.8	267.0	267.0	284.7	244.3	258.8	....	....
Current Transfers: Debit	78ak*d*	-62.2	-74.3	-85.0	-87.2	-84.1	-104.1	-111.1	-111.6	-103.2	-69.7	-89.6	-77.8	-80.3	....	....
Capital Account, n.i.e.	78bc*d*	88.0	101.7	123.7	147.6	148.3	171.6	171.7	182.8	153.7	190.6	187.0	169.2	96.0	....	....
Capital Account, n.i.e.: Credit	78ba*d*	106.2	121.3	149.5	170.0	169.9	197.4	193.3	198.3	165.9	200.5	201.2	169.3	96.3	....	....
Capital Account: Debit	78bb*d*	-18.2	-19.6	-25.8	-22.4	-21.6	-25.8	-21.6	-15.5	-12.2	-9.9	-14.2	-.1	-.3	....	....
Financial Account, n.i.e.	78bj*d*	179.2	203.2	210.6	173.0	14.4	55.4	16.8	113.2	129.4	48.5	44.2	-4.4	204.3	....	....
Direct Investment Abroad	78bd*d*	-3.1	4.6	1.9	-13.8	-8.6	9.5	19.1	-51.3	-.3	-17.4	3.3	-3.0	.5	....	....
Dir. Invest. in Rep. Econ., n.i.e.	78be*d*	-15.8	-8.4	-4.0	14.9	26.8	56.9	-7.6	21.4	-.8	66.9	31.7	8.4	176.4	....	....
Portfolio Investment Assets	78bf*d*	—	—	—	-.1	—	-1.0	—	—	—	-1.5	-.4	-25.8	-18.9	....	....
Equity Securities	78bk*d*	—	—	—	-.1	—	-1.0	—	—	—	-1.5	-.4	-2.4	.9	....	....
Debt Securities	78bl*d*	—	—	—	—	—	—	—	—	—	—	—	-23.4	-19.9	....	....
Portfolio Investment Liab., n.i.e.	78bg*d*	.6	2.1	.7	1.2	.1	1.6	6.5	.7	5.8	.5	4.0	-4.8	-8.1	....	....
Equity Securities	78bm*d*	-.2	—	.7	1.2	-.7	1.3	-.2	.9	6.1	.5	4.1	—	8.4	....	....
Debt Securities	78bn*d*	.8	2.1	—	—	.8	.3	6.7	-.2	-.3	—	-.1	-4.8	-16.4	....	....
Financial Derivatives Assets	78bw*d*	....	—	—	—	—	—	—	—	—	—	—	—	-.7	....	....
Financial Derivatives Liabilities	78bx*d*	—	—	—	—	—	—	—	—	—	—	—	—	—	....	....
Other Investment Assets	78bh*d*	6.3	-.6	7.9	-41.8	-15.1	57.8	-34.2	-24.9	4.1	-92.5	-6.2	-70.8	-22.1	....	....
Monetary Authorities	78bo*d*	....	....	....	....	....	....	....	....	....	....	....	....	....	....	....
General Government	78bp*d*	—	—	-.2	.1	—	.3	—	-.7	-.6	—	—	-3.1	-.9	....	....
Banks	78bq*d*	10.4	.5	3.4	-28.9	-15.4	56.7	-31.1	-24.4	-2.6	-108.8	10.9	30.9	-24.4	....	....
Other Sectors	78br*d*	-4.0	-1.1	4.8	-13.1	.3	.8	-3.1	.2	7.4	16.3	-17.1	-98.6	3.3	....	....
Other Investment Liab., n.i.e.	78bi*d*	191.2	205.5	204.1	212.6	11.1	-69.5	33.0	167.4	120.7	92.6	11.8	91.6	77.1	....	....
Monetary Authorities	78bs*d*	72.2	-95.6	-29.0	130.5	-110.4	-12.3	-42.6	34.3	135.3	-76.2	-35.7	1.5	.3	....	....
General Government	78bt*d*	127.8	245.1	265.9	96.9	106.8	82.9	87.3	173.0	69.0	90.7	83.9	22.0	39.5	....	....
Banks	78bu*d*	-9.9	-36.7	17.3	47.2	32.4	-94.9	13.4	-23.4	-6.6	9.8	-27.1	-1.5	24.6	....	....
Other Sectors	78bv*d*	1.0	92.6	-50.1	-61.9	-17.6	-45.2	-25.1	-16.5	-77.0	68.3	-9.3	69.6	12.8	....	....
Net Errors and Omissions	78ca*d*	2.7	29.9	-.3	-21.0	12.3	-1.2	3.1	-19.6	8.4	-28.9	-19.6	8.0	-9.2	....	....
Overall Balance	78cb*d*	-91.2	-35.0	-96.2	-105.5	-173.1	-137.5	-180.1	-124.9	-141.5	22.8	-32.9	-26.8	106.1	....	....
Reserves and Related Items	79da*d*	91.2	35.0	96.2	105.5	173.1	137.5	180.1	124.9	141.5	-22.8	32.9	26.8	-106.1	....	....
Reserve Assets	79db*d*	-.2	-3.3	1.9	-2.3	-7.8	9.8	-2.1	.1	8.5	-170.1	-74.8	-34.8	-137.4	....	....
Use of Fund Credit and Loans	79dc*d*	8.5	-8.4	6.8	-6.5	6.2	-27.7	10.6	-44.2	-27.4	38.9	42.9	-9.8	-12.8	....	....
Exceptional Financing	79de*d*	83.0	46.7	87.5	114.3	174.8	155.4	171.6	169.0	160.3	108.4	64.9	71.4	44.0	....	....
International Investment Position		*Millions of US Dollars*														
Assets	79aa*d*	....	108.1	124.7	140.7	172.3	123.8	158.8	172.8	155.7	376.6	561.4	640.7	711.4	....	....
Direct Investment Abroad	79ab*d*	....	—	—	—	—	—	—	—	—	—	9.9	10.2	2.7	....	....
Portfolio Investment	79ac*d*	....	—	—	—	—	—	—	—	—	—	8.6	33.2	52.2	....	....
Equity Securities	79ad*d*	....	....	....	....	....	....	....	....	....	....	.9	3.2	.7	....	....
Debt Securities	79ae*d*	....	....	....	....	....	....	....	....	....	....	7.6	30.0	51.5	....	....
Financial Derivatives	79al*d*	....	....	....	....	....	....	....	....	....	....	.1	.1	.8	....	....
Other Investment	79af*d*	84.7	98.7	115.5	130.2	153.3	112.8	145.6	160.4	152.3	197.0	271.0	308.9	269.5	....	....
Monetary Authorities	79ag*d*	—	—	—	—	—	—	—	—	—	—	—	—	—	....	....
General Government	79ah*d*	....	....	....	....	....	....	....	....	....	....	....	....	....	....	....
Banks	79ai*d*	84.7	98.7	115.5	130.2	153.3	112.8	145.6	160.4	152.3	197.0	144.4	104.9	115.6	....	....
Other Sectors	79aj*d*	....	....	....	....	....	....	....	....	....	....	....	....	....	....	....
Reserve Assets	79ak*d*	1.7	9.4	9.2	10.5	19.0	11.0	13.2	12.4	3.4	179.6	271.8	288.3	386.3	....	....
Liabilities	79la*d*	....	3,085.5	3,869.6	3,933.6	3,429.1	3,564.8	3,607.3	3,951.1	3,643.7	3,443.6	4,261.8	4,100.6	4,072.1	....	....
Dir. Invest. in Rep. Economy	79lb*d*	....	—	—	—	—	—	—	—	—	—	78.6	76.4	256.2	....	....
Portfolio Investment	79lc*d*	....	—	—	—	—	—	—	—	—	—	83.3	73.0	56.8	....	....
Equity Securities	79ld*d*	....	....	....	....	....	....	....	....	....	....	10.3	9.4	17.2	....	....
Debt Securities	79le*d*	....	....	....	....	....	....	....	....	....	....	73.0	63.6	39.6	....	....
Financial Derivatives	79ll*d*	....	—	—	—	—	—	—	—	—	—	—	—	—	....	....
Other Investment	79lf*d*	2,438.5	3,085.5	3,869.6	3,933.6	3,429.1	3,564.8	3,607.3	3,951.1	3,643.7	3,443.6	4,099.9	3,951.3	3,759.1	....	....
Monetary Authorities	79lg*d*	356.1	578.9	660.6	726.6	621.6	646.2	609.6	569.8	652.9	446.1	470.1	442.5	394.6	....	....
General Government	79lh*d*	1,904.0	2,337.1	2,984.6	2,962.9	2,514.2	2,690.2	2,754.8	3,171.5	2,801.1	2,882.7	3,323.6	3,199.0	....	....	....
Banks	79li*d*	178.4	169.5	224.4	244.1	293.3	228.4	242.8	209.8	189.7	114.8	184.9	171.3	176.4	....	....
Other Sectors	79lj*d*	—	—	—	—	—	—	—	—	—	—	121.3	138.5	163.7	....	....
Government Finance		*Year Ending June 30*														
Deficit (-) or Surplus	80	....	....	....	....	....	....	....	....	....	....	....	....	....	....	....
Revenue	81	....	....	....	....	....	....	....	....	....	....	....	....	....	....	....
Grants Received	81z	....	....	....	....	....	....	....	....	....	....	....	....	....	....	....
Expenditure	82	....	....	....	....	....	....	....	....	....	....	....	....	....	....	....
Lending Minus Repayments	83	....	....	....	....	....	....	....	....	....	....	....	....	....	....	....
Financing																
Net Borrowing: Domestic	84a	....	....	....	....	....	....	....	....	....	....	....	....	....	....	....
Foreign	85a	....	....	....	....	....	....	....	....	....	....	....	....	....	....	....
Use of Cash Balances	87	....	....	....	....	....	....	....	....	....	....	....	....	....	....	....
Debt: Domestic	88a	....	....	....	....	....	....	....	....	....	....	....	....	....	....	....
Foreign	89a	....	....	....	....	....	....	....	....	....	....	....	....	....	....	....
National Accounts		*Billions of Francs*														
Exports of Goods & Services	90c	331.3	333.0	332.9	337.5	393.6	394.7	397.2	357.5	341.2	652.0	718.2	727.7	868.4	901.9	....
Government Consumption	91f	194.5	200.8	215.6	218.1	229.7	222.3	222.3	239.9	227.7	258.4	276.1	286.4	289.0	307.2	....
Gross Fixed Capital Formation	93e	134.0	156.8	172.1	188.6	195.8	200.3	209.3	222.9	207.1	295.1	327.7	387.0	460.4	556.2	....
Increase/Decrease(-) in Stocks	93i	-12.7	-8.2	.3	—	-20.9	13.8	-15.1	6.9	3.0	49.0	45.7	52.5	....	....	....
Private Consumption	96f	998.1	1,048.2	1,099.6	1,171.0	1,151.5	1,185.1	1,187.0	1,220.4	1,191.5	1,450.6	1,763.9	1,878.6	1,951.9	2,060.0	....
Imports of Goods & Services	98c	-486.7	-427.2	-434.3	-431.9	-473.9	-470.5	-449.4	-452.2	-432.9	-683.1	-897.6	-952.7	-1,014.0	-1,064.3	....
Gross Domestic Product (GDP)	99b	1,158.5	1,303.3	1,382.3	1,483.3	1,475.9	1,551.5	1,551.5	1,595.4	1,537.8	2,022.3	2,234.0	2,379.6	2,555.7	2,761.0	....
Net Primary Income from Abroad	98.n	35.0	30.0	34.2	46.3	51.4	62.7	78.2	86.3	79.3	179.2	86.2	111.4	112.9	119.2	....
Gross National Income (GNI)	99a	1,193.5	1,333.3	1,416.6	1,529.7	1,527.3	1,614.1	1,629.7	1,681.7	1,617.1	2,201.4	2,320.3	2,491.0	2,668.8	2,880.2	....
GDP Volume 1987 Prices	99b.*p*	1,271.3	1,329.3	1,382.3	1,452.4	1,432.1	1,487.7	1,481.8	1,514.6	1,481.0	1,523.5	1,602.2	1,684.7	1,769.7	1,869.8	....
GDP Volume (1995=100)	99bv*p*	79.3	83.0	86.3	90.7	89.4	92.9	92.5	94.5	92.4	95.1	100.0	105.1	110.5	116.7	....
GDP Deflator (1995=100)	99bi*p*	65.4	70.3	71.7	73.2	73.9	74.8	75.1	75.5	74.5	95.2	100.0	101.3	103.6	105.9	....
		Midyear Estimates														
Population	99z	6.55	6.72	6.91	6.91	7.10	7.30	7.50	7.70	7.91	8.13	8.57	8.80	9.04	9.28	9.28

(See notes in the back of the book.)

Seychelles

		1970	1971	1972	1973	1974	1975	1976	1977	1978	1979	1980	1981	1982	1983	1984
Exchange Rates															*Rupees per SDR:*	
Official Rate	aa	5.5702	5.6713	‡6.1650	6.9235	6.9511	7.7137	9.0995	8.4974	8.5380	8.3197	8.3197	7.2345	7.2345	7.2345	7.2345
														Rupees per US Dollar:		
Official Rate	ae	5.5702	5.2236	‡5.6783	5.7392	5.6774	6.5892	7.8321	6.9954	6.5536	6.3156	6.5184	6.2273	6.5475	6.9227	7.3578
Official Rate	rf	5.5555	5.4858	5.3385	5.4423	5.7031	6.0268	7.4189	7.6434	6.9525	6.3327	6.3920	6.3149	6.5525	6.7676	7.0589
Fund Position															*Millions of SDRs:*	
Quota	2f. s	....	....	....	....	....	....	....	1.00	1.30	1.30	2.00	2.00	2.00	3.00	3.00
SDRs	1b. s	....	....	....	....	....	....	....	—	—	.09	.04	.17	.16	.05	.02
Reserve Position in the Fund	1c. s	....	....	....	....	....	....	....	—	—	—	—	—	—	—	—
Total Fund Cred.&Loans Outstg.	2tl	....	....	....	....	....	....	....	.10	.10	.25	.43	.44	.44	—	—
International Liquidity												*Millions of US Dollars Unless Otherwise Indicated:*				
Total Reserves minus Gold	1l. d	....	....	....	4.27	5.04	6.34	6.49	11.51	9.26	12.15	18.44	13.80	13.07	9.97	5.40
SDRs	1b. d	....	....	....	....	....	....	....	—	—	.12	.05	.20	.18	.05	.02
Reserve Position in the Fund	1c. d	....	....	....	....	....	....	....	.12	.13	.33	.55	.51	.49	—	—
Foreign Exchange	1d. d	....	....	....	4.27	5.04	6.34	6.49	11.39	9.13	11.70	17.84	13.09	12.41	9.92	5.38
Deposit Money Banks: Assets	7a. d	....	2.27	2.79	.10	—	1.81	4.09	3.40	6.32	5.57	7.49	7.19	2.93	3.08	3.67
Liabilities	7b. d	....								1.24	1.08	1.20	3.65	3.88	3.58	2.43
Monetary Authorities															*Millions of Rupees:*	
Foreign Assets	11	....	13.4	17.1	17.8	18.9	26.7	31.8	48.0	45.5	70.7	122.5	88.3	87.7	71.5	62.4
Claims on Central Government	12a	....	1.8	1.8	1.5	1.5	1.5	1.5	1.5	9.3	4.4	1.5	18.6	33.3	58.0	69.7
Claims on Deposit Money Banks	12e	....	—	—	—	—	—	—	—	—	—	—	10.5	13.8	13.7	9.6
Reserve Money	14	....	13.0	17.8	20.1	21.1	24.9	33.2	42.3	48.7	64.3	108.7	98.3	93.2	99.6	96.1
of which: Currency Outside DMBs	14a	....	12.4	17.0	18.9	20.1	22.7	31.1	40.1	43.9	52.9	61.7	65.3	62.6	64.3	69.9
Central Government Deposits	16d	....	—	—	—	—	—	—	—	—	—	—	1.0	1.0	2.0	13.7
Capital Accounts	17a	....	—	—	—	—	—	—	—	4.0	9.6	13.2	13.9	13.9	13.9	13.9
Other Items (Net)	17r	....	2.2	1.1	-.8	-.7	3.3	.1	7.2	2.1	1.2	2.1	4.2	26.7	27.7	18.0
Deposit Money Banks															*Millions of Rupees:*	
Reserves	20	....	.6	.8	1.2	1.0	2.2	2.1	2.2	4.8	5.8	27.3	18.6	15.4	21.9	16.5
Foreign Assets	21	....	11.6	14.3	.6	4.0	11.9	32.0	23.8	41.4	35.2	44.8	44.8	19.2	21.3	27.0
Claims on Central Government	22a	....	2.0	1.4	5.2	5.9	7.0	10.2	8.4	6.8	17.7	26.2	39.2	36.2	48.3	69.6
Claims on Nonfin.Pub.Enterprises	22c	....	—	—	—	—	—	—	—	1.0	1.0	10.4	32.8	53.7	87.1	106.0
Claims on Private Sector	22d	....	19.0	33.7	48.1	50.7	54.8	83.5	117.0	137.1	155.4	160.1	155.3	143.7	137.4	120.4
Demand Deposits	24	....	13.0	20.7	21.4	21.8	25.1	36.5	43.7	51.1	56.2	77.3	78.2	65.5	53.6	55.1
Time and Savings Deposits	25	....	19.9	27.1	31.7	32.6	48.6	70.7	78.3	89.4	110.9	141.7	135.9	127.2	146.8	183.5
Restricted Deposits	26b	....	—	—	—	—	—	—	—	—	—	—	—	—	—	—
Foreign Liabilities	26c	....	—	—	—	—	—	—	—	8.1	6.8	7.8	22.7	25.4	24.8	17.9
Central Government Deposits	26d	....	—	—	2.8	1.8	2.9	8.8	14.6	14.1	9.6	8.7	11.4	14.8	17.2	19.6
Credit from Monetary Authorities	26g	....	—	—	—	—	—	—	—	—	—	—	10.5	13.8	13.7	9.6
Capital Accounts	27a	....	—	—	—	—	—	16.0	16.0	28.8	24.0	24.0	24.0	24.0	24.0	24.0
Other Items (Net)	27r	....	.3	2.4	-.8	5.4	-.7	-4.2	-1.2	-.4	7.6	13.3	8.0	12.9	12.7	10.9
Monetary Survey															*Millions of Rupees:*	
Foreign Assets (Net)	31n	....	25.0	31.4	18.4	22.9	38.6	63.8	71.8	78.8	99.1	163.5	110.4	81.5	68.0	71.5
Domestic Credit	32	....	22.8	36.9	52.0	56.3	60.4	86.4	112.3	141.1	169.9	190.5	234.5	267.5	289.4	314.5
Claims on Central Govt. (Net)	32an	....	3.8	3.2	3.9	5.6	5.6	2.9	-4.7	2.0	12.5	19.0	45.4	53.7	87.1	106.0
Claims on Nonfin.Pub.Enterprises	32c	....	—	—	—	—	—	—	—	1.0	1.0	10.4	32.8	69.1	63.9	87.1
Claims on Private Sector	32d	....	19.0	33.7	48.1	50.7	54.8	83.5	117.0	137.1	155.4	160.1	155.3	143.7	137.4	120.4
Money	34	....	25.4	37.7	40.3	41.9	47.8	67.6	83.8	95.0	114.7	158.7	157.9	143.3	131.3	134.7
Quasi-Money	35	....	19.9	27.1	31.7	32.6	48.6	70.7	78.3	89.4	110.9	141.7	135.9	127.2	146.8	183.5
Restricted Deposits	36b	....	—	—	—	—	—	—	—	—	—	—	—	—	—	—
Capital Accounts	37a	....	—	—	—	—	—	16.0	16.0	32.8	33.6	37.2	37.9	37.9	37.9	37.9
Other Items (Net)	37r	....	2.5	3.5	-1.6	4.7	2.6	-4.1	6.0	2.7	9.8	16.4	13.2	40.6	41.4	29.9
Money plus Quasi-Money	35l	....	45.3	64.8	72.0	74.5	96.4	138.3	162.1	184.4	225.6	300.4	293.8	270.5	278.1	318.2
Other Banking Institutions															*Millions of Rupees:*	
Reserves	40	....	....	....	....	....	....	....	....	....	....	—	—	—	—	—
Claims on Central Government	42a	....	....	....	....	....	....	....	....	....	....	7.2	7.8	7.8	5.5	.6
Claims on Nonfin.Pub.Enterprises	42c	....	....	....	....	....	....	....	....	....	....	—	1.0	2.3	16.7	23.8
Claims on Private Sector	42d	....	....	....	....	....	....	....	....	....	....	.3	6.0	9.1	7.6	7.4
Claims on Deposit Money Banks	42e	....	....	....	....	....	....	....	....	....	....	—	9.6	14.9	18.9	22.4
Time and Savings Deposits	45	....	....	....	....	....	....	....	....	....	....	—	14.8	12.7	11.4	4.4
Capital Accounts	47a	....	....	....	....	....	....	....	....	....	....	3.0	6.5	10.6	22.2	23.1
Other Items (Net)	47r	....	....	....	....	....	....	....	....	....	....	4.6	31.9	33.3	33.6	40.5
												-.1	.8	2.9	4.3	-5.0
Banking Survey															*Millions of Rupees:*	
Foreign Assets (Net)	51n	....	....	....	....	....	....	....	....	....	....	163.5	110.4	81.5	68.0	71.5
Domestic Credit	52	....	....	....	....	....	....	....	....	....	....	189.8	250.1	292.8	331.6	367.1
Claims on Central Govt. (Net)	52an	....	....	....	....	....	....	....	....	....	....	19.0	46.4	56.0	103.8	129.8
Claims on Nonfin.Pub.Enterprises	52c	....	....	....	....	....	....	....	....	....	....	10.7	38.8	78.2	71.5	94.5
Claims on Private Sector	52d	....	....	....	....	....	....	....	....	....	....	160.1	164.9	158.6	156.3	142.8
Liquid Liabilities	55l	....	....	....	....	....	....	....	....	....	....	296.2	292.5	273.3	294.8	340.7
Restricted Deposits	56b	....	....	....	....	....	....	....	....	....	....	—	—	—	—	—
Capital Accounts	57a	....	....	....	....	....	....	....	....	....	....	41.8	69.8	71.2	71.5	78.4
Other Items (Net)	57r	....	....	....	....	....	....	....	....	....	....	15.3	-1.8	29.8	33.3	19.5
Interest Rates															*Percent Per Annum:*	
Discount Rate (*End of Period*)	60	....	....	....	....	....	....	....	....	....	....	....	6.00	6.00	6.00	6.00
Treasury Bill Rate	60c	....	....	....	....	....	....	....	....	....	....	....	6.00	6.00	6.00	6.00
Deposit Rate	60l	....	....	....	....	....	....	....	....	....	....	9.56	9.15	10.10	12.07	12.61
Lending Rate	60p	....	....	....	....	....	....	....	....	....	....	....	9.00	9.00	9.08	9.50
Prices and Labor															*Index Numbers (1995=100):*	
Consumer Prices	64	15.0	17.2	20.8	24.6	30.6	36.3	41.7	‡47.9	53.6	60.3	68.5	‡75.7	75.0	79.6	82.8
Employment	67e	....	....	....	....	....	....	....	....	....	....	....	....	*Number in Thousands:*		

	1985	1986	1987	1988	1989	1990	1991	1992	1993	1994	1995	1996	1997	1998	1999	
Exchange Rates																
End of Period																
Official Rate	7.2345	7.2345	7.2345	7.2345	7.2345	7.2345	7.2345	7.2345	7.2345	7.2345	7.2345	7.2345	6.9218	7.6699	7.3671	aa
End of Period (ae) Period Average (rf)																
Official Rate	6.6018	5.9290	5.1435	5.3966	5.4672	5.1188	5.0627	5.2545	5.2579	4.9695	4.8639	4.9946	5.1249	5.4521	5.3676	ae
Official Rate	7.1343	6.1768	5.6000	5.3836	5.6457	5.3369	5.2893	5.1220	5.1815	5.0559	4.7620	4.9700	5.0263	5.2622	5.3426	rf
Fund Position																
End of Period																
Quota	3.00	3.00	3.00	3.00	3.00	3.00	3.00	6.00	6.00	6.00	6.00	6.00	6.00	6.00	8.80	2f. s
SDRs	.01	.02	—	.01	.01	.01	.04	.01	.01	.02	.02	.02	.03	.03	.03	1b. s
Reserve Position in the Fund	—	.02	.03	.04	.05	.05	.05	.80	.80	.80	.80	.80	.80	—	—	1c. s
Total Fund Cred.&Loans Outstg.	—	—	—	—	—	—	—	—	—	—	—	—	—	—	—	2tl
International Liquidity																
End of Period																
Total Reserves minus Gold	8.50	7.75	13.71	8.71	12.11	16.64	27.65	31.26	35.65	30.15	27.10	21.76	26.32	21.59	30.35	1l. d
SDRs	.01	.02	—	.01	.01	.01	.06	.01	.02	.02	.03	.03	.04	.04	.04	1b. d
Reserve Position in the Fund	—	.02	.03	.04	.05	.07	.07	.07	1.10	1.10	1.17	1.20	1.16	1.09	—	1c. d
Foreign Exchange	8.49	7.70	13.67	8.64	12.04	16.55	27.52	30.14	34.53	28.96	25.87	20.57	25.20	21.55	30.31	1d. d
Deposit Money Banks: Assets	4.85	5.48	5.99	6.58	4.99	11.23	17.88	9.44	7.66	5.03	9.91	19.28	30.97	29.36	43.73	7a. d
Liabilities	3.57	3.41	4.94	4.65	7.85	11.55	13.95	6.76	7.32	6.42	10.36	17.96	33.41	34.72	47.06	7b. d
Monetary Authorities																
End of Period																
Foreign Assets	59.9	49.6	72.7	46.5	65.6	84.4	138.4	157.6	180.5	142.8	126.9	99.1	127.2	115.1	160.2	11
Claims on Central Government	106.3	101.5	139.3	165.7	103.3	105.4	110.9	241.4	302.0	529.2	663.3	790.5	926.8	575.1	640.2	12a
Claims on Deposit Money Banks	6.5	20.7	13.7	21.4	30.7	18.5	13.0	4.0	21.5	7.0	1.8	—	—	10.0	—	12e
Reserve Money	107.7	106.1	105.6	134.0	140.0	164.0	206.3	311.8	383.8	566.7	684.8	778.7	924.0	468.7	512.8	14
of which: Currency Outside DMBs	75.8	78.1	82.4	95.6	99.5	104.5	113.6	122.5	134.5	141.6	148.1	165.7	192.2	206.4	248.0	14a
Central Government Deposits	24.4	28.6	93.8	91.3	26.8	21.4	30.3	64.3	58.8	30.9	21.4	15.4	18.1	18.2	49.0	16d
Capital Accounts	13.9	13.9	13.9	13.9	13.9	15.8	13.9	13.9	13.9	13.9	13.9	13.9	13.9	14.1	25.9	17a
Other Items (Net)	26.7	23.2	12.4	-5.6	18.9	7.1	11.8	13.0	47.5	67.5	71.9	81.6	98.1	199.2	212.7	17r
Deposit Money Banks																
End of Period																
Reserves	31.2	27.3	22.5	38.0	39.8	58.8	91.9	188.5	248.7	424.5	536.0	612.3	731.1	261.6	264.1	20
Foreign Assets	32.0	32.5	30.8	35.5	27.3	57.5	90.5	49.6	40.3	25.0	48.2	96.3	158.7	160.1	234.7	21
Claims on Central Government	184.2	270.0	335.8	411.8	526.1	547.2	633.6	632.9	779.0	692.3	747.8	843.1	1,096.9	2,106.7	905.1	22a
Claims on Nonfin.Pub.Enterprises	24.9	21.9	23.3	35.7	40.3	41.4	58.4	54.1	80.9	118.9	92.4	68.7	51.8	55.9	42.6	22c
Claims on Private Sector	104.6	90.8	88.6	96.2	127.0	137.2	150.2	157.8	172.8	209.0	245.1	269.6	397.5	460.0	503.5	22d
Demand Deposits	78.8	76.2	72.1	91.8	119.4	111.6	151.8	170.0	200.7	184.4	186.2	284.0	456.5	574.2	823.3	24
Time and Savings Deposits	208.1	250.3	285.9	351.7	412.9	507.3	541.4	620.3	768.5	768.7	875.1	939.0	1,339.2	1,608.8	1,837.7	25
Restricted Deposits	—	—	—	—	—	—	—	—	—	198.2	301.4	317.1	218.0	178.3	148.0	26b
Foreign Liabilities	23.6	20.2	25.4	25.1	42.9	59.1	70.6	35.5	38.5	31.9	50.4	89.7	171.2	189.3	252.6	26c
Central Government Deposits	21.2	34.0	48.3	60.1	84.3	46.0	80.1	83.9	107.7	118.8	112.8	88.5	163.2	180.9	203.5	26d
Credit from Monetary Authorities	6.5	9.7	13.7	21.4	30.7	18.5	13.0	4.0	21.5	7.0	1.8	—	—	10.0	—	26g
Capital Accounts	24.7	24.8	24.8	25.8	26.3	27.7	75.5	71.8	74.7	76.0	76.0	80.8	96.5	103.9	110.8	27a
Other Items (Net)	14.0	27.3	30.8	41.3	44.0	71.9	92.2	97.4	110.1	84.7	65.8	90.9	-8.6	198.9	-1,425.9	27r
Monetary Survey																
End of Period																
Foreign Assets (Net)	68.3	61.9	78.1	56.9	50.0	82.8	158.3	171.7	182.3	135.9	124.7	105.7	114.7	85.9	142.3	31n
Domestic Credit	375.4	422.6	445.9	559.0	686.6	764.8	843.7	939.0	1,169.2	1,400.7	1,615.4	1,869.0	2,292.7	2,999.6	1,839.9	32
Claims on Central Govt. (Net)	244.9	308.9	333.0	426.1	518.3	585.2	634.1	726.1	914.5	1,071.8	1,276.9	1,529.7	1,842.4	2,482.7	1,292.8	32an
Claims on Nonfin.Pub.Enterprises	24.9	21.9	23.3	35.7	40.3	41.4	58.4	54.1	80.9	118.9	92.4	68.7	51.8	55.9	42.6	32c
Claims on Private Sector	104.6	90.8	88.6	96.2	127.0	137.2	150.2	157.8	172.8	209.0	245.1	269.6	397.5	460.0	503.5	32d
Money	155.3	155.0	155.2	187.8	219.6	216.8	266.2	293.3	335.8	326.6	335.0	450.4	649.4	781.3	1,072.0	34
Quasi-Money	208.1	250.3	285.9	351.7	412.9	507.3	541.4	620.3	768.5	768.7	875.1	939.0	1,339.2	1,608.8	1,837.7	35
Restricted Deposits	—	—	—	—	—	—	—	—	—	198.2	301.4	317.1	218.0	178.3	148.0	36b
Capital Accounts	38.6	38.7	38.7	39.7	40.2	43.5	89.4	85.7	88.6	89.9	89.9	94.7	110.3	118.0	136.7	37a
Other Items (Net)	41.7	40.5	44.2	36.7	63.9	80.0	105.0	111.4	158.6	153.2	138.7	173.5	90.5	399.1	-1,212.2	37r
Money plus Quasi-Money	363.4	405.3	441.1	539.5	632.5	724.1	807.6	913.6	1,104.3	1,095.3	1,210.1	1,389.4	1,988.6	2,390.1	2,909.7	35l
Other Banking Institutions																
End of Period																
Reserves	1.7	3.0	2.0	2.3	3.6	2.0	3.6	4.0	3.5	2.4	3.6	1.9	—	—	—	40
Claims on Central Government	29.1	33.0	41.3	53.6	57.6	61.6	68.0	86.9	121.9	121.3	93.2	115.8	—	—	—	42a
Claims on Nonfin.Pub.Enterprises	17.7	30.3	44.3	53.0	65.0	76.2	83.2	77.5	65.1	78.1	55.1	49.1	34.5	28.0	20.7	42c
Claims on Private Sector	24.3	27.4	34.2	40.6	45.2	58.7	61.4	76.3	99.3	124.9	152.4	186.6	163.8	176.2	189.8	42d
Claims on Deposit Money Banks	3.3	3.8	2.2	1.5	4.7	1.5	1.8	1.7	4.3	4.1	12.1	10.0	9.9	17.8	24.5	42e
Time and Savings Deposits	27.8	35.3	41.7	50.0	60.1	61.0	69.9	92.7	138.2	182.8	176.1	197.0	—	—	—	45
Capital Accounts	41.4	46.2	56.4	60.3	63.2	69.2	72.3	77.0	85.6	92.9	93.9	100.6	115.0	129.2	147.7	47a
Other Items (Net)	6.9	16.0	25.9	40.7	52.8	69.8	75.8	76.7	70.1	55.1	46.5	65.8	93.2	92.8	87.3	47r
Banking Survey																
End of Period																
Foreign Assets (Net)	68.3	61.9	78.1	56.9	50.0	82.8	158.3	171.7	182.3	135.9	124.7	105.7	114.7	85.9	142.3	51n
Domestic Credit	445.5	512.3	564.7	705.2	853.4	960.3	1,055.3	1,178.7	1,454.5	1,724.0	1,915.1	2,219.5	2,490.0	3,202.8	2,049.4	52
Claims on Cental Govt. (Net)	274.0	341.9	374.3	479.7	575.9	646.8	702.1	813.0	1,036.4	1,193.1	1,370.1	1,645.5	1,842.4	2,482.7	1,292.8	52an
Claims on Nonfin.Pub.Enterprises	42.6	52.2	67.6	88.7	105.3	117.6	141.6	131.6	146.0	197.0	147.5	117.8	86.3	83.9	63.3	52c
Claims on Private Sector	128.9	118.2	122.8	136.8	172.2	195.9	211.6	234.1	272.1	333.9	397.5	456.2	561.3	636.2	693.3	52d
Liquid Liabilities	389.5	437.6	480.8	587.2	689.0	783.1	873.9	1,002.3	1,239.0	1,275.7	1,382.5	1,584.4	1,988.6	2,390.1	2,909.7	55l
Restricted Deposits	—	—	—	—	—	—	—	—	—	198.2	301.4	317.1	218.0	178.3	148.0	56b
Capital Accounts	80.0	84.9	95.1	100.0	103.4	112.7	161.7	162.7	174.2	182.8	183.8	195.3	225.3	247.2	284.4	57a
Other Items (Net)	44.3	51.7	66.9	74.9	111.0	147.3	178.0	185.4	223.4	203.2	172.0	228.4	172.8	473.1	-1,150.4	57r
Interest Rates																
Percent Per Annum																
Discount Rate *(End of Period)*	6.00	6.00	6.00	6.00	6.00	11.00	1.00	1.00	1.00	1.00	1.00	1.00	1.00	1.00	1.00	60
Treasury Bill Rate	12.48	12.90	15.15	13.90	13.41	13.00	13.00	13.00	12.91	12.36	12.15	11.47	10.50	7.96	4.50	60c
Deposit Rate	9.60	10.00	10.00	10.00	9.59	9.53	9.55	9.60	9.51	8.92	9.22	9.90	9.20	7.53	5.13	60l
Lending Rate	....	....	....	....	15.52	15.65	15.57	15.58	15.66	15.70	15.76	16.22	14.88	14.39	12.01	60p
Prices and Labor																
Period Averages																
Consumer Prices	83.5	83.7	85.9	87.5	88.8	92.3	94.2	97.2	98.5	100.3	100.0	98.9	99.5	102.1	....	64
Period Averages																
Employment	18	19	19	21	22	24	24	24	25	25	26	26	28	....	....	67e

Seychelles

		1970	1971	1972	1973	1974	1975	1976	1977	1978	1979	1980	1981	1982	1983	1984
International Transactions																*Millions of Rupees*
Exports	70	11.90	10.16	13.99	19.68	41.56	38.27	64.34	84.76	105.43	138.63	135.21	108.34	100.09	137.25	181.47
Imports, c.i.f.	71	55.92	84.00	111.67	135.12	160.46	191.35	290.62	349.74	402.05	534.78	631.44	589.01	641.32	594.08	618.73
Balance of Payments																*Millions of US Dollars:*
Current Account, n.i.e.	78al d	...	...	...	...	...	...	−3.90	−1.87	−3.98	−12.26	−15.62	−18.79	−40.64	−26.05	−13.29
Goods: Exports f.o.b.	78aa d	...	...	...	...	...	...	3.05	4.83	6.63	6.22	5.65	4.64	3.84	4.99	4.98
Goods: Imports f.o.b.	78ab d	...	...	...	...	...	...	−33.19	−38.63	−51.82	−71.58	−83.66	−79.19	−83.00	−74.50	−73.94
Trade Balance	78ac d	...	...	...	...	...	...	−30.14	−33.81	−45.19	−65.35	−78.01	−74.55	−79.16	−69.51	−68.97
Services: Credit	78ad d	...	...	...	...	...	...	33.89	48.24	63.80	83.62	91.22	88.69	77.76	76.80	95.07
Services: Debit	78ae d	...	...	...	...	...	...	−10.80	−21.72	−27.87	−35.74	−40.10	−40.50	−41.83	−40.08	−46.36
Balance on Goods & Services	78af d	...	...	...	...	...	...	−7.05	−7.29	−9.26	−17.47	−26.89	−26.35	−43.23	−32.78	−20.26
Income: Credit	78ag d	...	...	...	...	...	...	.80	1.58	2.29	4.91	5.90	4.29	2.79	2.37	2.09
Income: Debit	78ah d	...	...	...	...	...	...	−2.87	−4.97	−6.04	−7.64	−7.68	−6.88	−6.72	−7.12	−7.82
Balance on Gds, Serv. & Inc.	78ai d	...	...	...	...	...	...	−9.13	−10.68	−13.02	−20.19	−28.67	−28.95	−47.17	−37.54	−25.98
Current Transfers, n.i.e.: Credit	78aj d	...	...	...	...	...	...	6.17	10.24	11.26	10.45	16.18	14.78	12.80	17.63	18.30
Current Transfers: Debit	78ak d	...	...	...	...	...	...	−.94	−1.44	−2.23	−2.52	−3.13	−4.62	−6.28	−6.15	−5.60
Capital Account, n.i.e.	78bc d	...	...	...	...	...	...	—	—	—	—	—	—	—	—	—
Capital Account, n.i.e.: Credit	78ba d	...	...	...	...	...	...	—	—	—	—	—	—	—	—	—
Capital Account: Debit	78bb d	...	...	...	...	...	...	—	—	—	—	—	—	—	—	—
Financial Account, n.i.e.	78bj d	...	...	...	...	...	...	2.95	3.99	8.37	16.65	18.35	13.85	34.02	15.85	16.00
Direct Investment Abroad	78bd d	...	...	...	...	...	...	−2.02	−2.26	−2.68	−3.13	−3.81	−7.23	−4.94	−3.24	−3.92
Dir. Invest. in Rep. Econ., n.i.e.	78be d	...	...	...	...	...	...	6.34	7.06	6.33	7.51	9.52	10.07	10.01	9.12	9.77
Portfolio Investment Assets	78bf d	...	...	...	...	...	...	—	—	—	—	—	—	—	—	—
Equity Securities	78bk d	...	...	...	...	...	...	—	—	—	—	—	—	—	—	—
Debt Securities	78bl d	...	...	...	...	...	...	—	—	—	—	—	—	—	—	—
Portfolio Investment Liab., n.i.e.	78bg d	...	...	...	...	...	...	—	—	—	—	—	—	—	—	—
Equity Securities	78bm d	...	...	...	...	...	...	—	—	—	—	—	—	—	—	—
Debt Securities	78bn d	...	...	...	...	...	...	—	—	—	—	—	—	—	—	—
Financial Derivatives Assets	78bw d	...	...	...	...	...	...	...	...	...	...	...	...	...	...	...
Financial Derivatives Liabilities	78bx d	...	...	...	...	...	...	...	...	...	...	...	...	...	...	...
Other Investment Assets	78bh d	...	...	...	...	...	...	−3.48	−1.27	.60	4.56	.81	3.21	4.73	−.42	−1.78
Monetary Authorities	78bo d	...	...	...	...	...	...	—	—	—	—	—	—	—	—	—
General Government	78bp d	...	...	...	...	...	...	−.77	−2.34	1.97	3.75	2.79	.25	.32	.03	.03
Banks	78bq d	...	...	...	...	...	...	−2.71	1.07	−1.37	.82	−1.98	2.96	4.41	−.45	−1.80
Other Sectors	78br d	...	...	...	...	...	...	—	—	—	—	—	—	—	—	—
Other Investment Liab., n.i.e.	78bi d	...	...	...	...	...	...	2.12	.46	4.11	7.71	11.84	7.79	24.21	10.38	11.92
Monetary Authorities	78bs d	...	...	...	...	...	...	—	—	—	—	—	—	—	—	—
General Government	78bt d	...	...	...	...	...	...	−.04	.46	2.63	8.06	11.84	7.79	24.21	10.38	11.92
Banks	78bu d	...	...	...	...	...	...	2.16	—	1.48	−.35	—	—	—	—	—
Other Sectors	78bv d	...	...	...	...	...	...	—	—	—	—	—	—	—	—	—
Net Errors and Omissions	78ca d	...	...	...	...	...	...	1.63	.12	−5.26	−.76	5.23	−.38	6.41	7.71	−4.25
Overall Balance	78cb d	...	...	...	...	...	...	.69	2.24	−.88	3.63	7.96	−5.33	−.21	−2.50	−1.54
Reserves and Related Items	79da d	...	...	...	...	...	...	−.69	−2.24	.88	−3.63	−7.96	5.33	.21	2.50	1.54
Reserve Assets	79db d	...	...	...	...	...	...	−.69	−2.24	.88	−3.63	−7.96	5.33	.21	2.50	1.54
Use of Fund Credit and Loans	79dc d	...	...	...	...	...	...	—	—	—	—	—	—	—	—	—
Exceptional Financing	79de d	...	...	...	...	...	...	—	—	—	—	—	—	—	—	—
Government Finance																*Millions of Rupees:*
Deficit (-) or Surplus	80	...	...	5.5	−11.0	−.8	−.7	−3.1	20.1	−28.8	...	...	...	...		
Total Revenue and Grants	81y	...	...	80.2	67.7	90.9	96.6	126.4	184.5	196.5	...	...	...	...		
Revenue	81	...	...	35.7	44.6	52.3	58.7	90.3	133.9	165.5	...	...	...	...		
Grants	81z	...	...	44.5	23.1	38.6	37.9	36.1	50.6	31.0	...	...	...	...		
Exp. & Lending Minus Repay.	82z	...	...	74.7	78.7	91.7	97.3	129.5	164.4	225.3	...	...	...	...		
Expenditure	82	...	...	74.1	76.0	81.8	94.2	126.4	156.0	218.2	...	...	...	...		
Lending Minus Repayments	83	...	...	.6	2.7	9.9	3.1	3.1	8.4	7.1	...	...	...	...		
Total Financing	80h	...	...	−5.5	11.0	.8	.7	3.1	−20.1	28.8	...	...	...	...		
Domestic	84a	...	...	−4.8	11.0	3.1	3.2	5.7	−20.0	12.0	...	...	...	...		
Foreign	85a	...	...	−.7	—	−2.3	−2.5	−2.6	−.1	16.8	...	...	...	...		
Total Debt by Residence	88	...	...	10.6	10.4	12.1	17.0	16.4	24.4	...	...	...	...	...		
Domestic	88a	...	...	4.1	4.3	6.3	11.5	11.5	15.8	...	...	...	...	...		
Foreign	89a	...	...	6.5	6.1	5.8	5.5	4.9	8.6	...	...	...	...	...		
National Accounts																*Millions of Rupees*
Exports of Goods & Services	90c	...	...	...	...	...	...	271.9	386.3	488.4	582.6	640.1	467.0	404.4	415.0	539.7
Government Consumption	91f	...	...	...	...	...	...	81.5	117.1	149.5	211.4	270.0	308.5	338.0	326.0	327.7
Gross Fixed Capital Formation	93e	...	...	...	...	...	...	134.5	190.5	253.5	256.6	344.2	329.7	302.9	219.9	226.9
Increase/Decrease(-) in Stocks	93i	...	...	...	...	...	...	8	7	4	9	17	−13	10	−10	5
Private Consumption	96f	...	...	...	...	...	...	200.3	198.5	195.3	377.6	416.3	515.5	598.6	673.3	653.0
Imports of Goods & Services	98c	...	...	...	...	...	...	−330.4	−406.2	−495.8	−630.8	−745.4	−636.2	−686.0	−635.3	−684.0
Gross Domestic Product (GDP)	99b	...	...	138.0	168.0	194.0	235.0	365.6	493.0	595.0	806.3	941.9	971.9	968.2	989.4	1,067.9
Net Factor Inc/Pmts(-) Abroad	98.n	...	...	...	...	...	...	−15.8	−29.6	−38.3	−56.3	−34.1	−16.3	−26.2	−32.6	−41.2
Gross National Income (GNI)	99a	...	...	...	...	...	...	349.8	463.4	556.7	750.0	907.8	955.6	942.0	956.8	1,026.7
GDP Volume 1976 Prices	99b.p	...	...	...	...	...	...	365.6	394.4	421.0	490.4	477.9	458.7	449.2	446.4	460.3
GDP Volume 1986 Prices	99b.p	...	...	...	...	...	...	...	...	1,062.5	1,221.4	1,183.4	1,104.8	1,088.2	1,069.6	1,155.3
GDP Volume (1995=100)	99bv p	...	...	...	...	...	...	47.6	51.4	54.8	63.0	61.1	57.0	56.2	55.2	59.6
Population	99z	.05	.05	.06	.06	.06	.06	.06	.06	.06	.06	.06	.06	.06	.06	*Millions:* .06

	1985	1986	1987	1988	1989	1990	1991	1992	1993	1994	1995	1996	1997	1998	1999		
																International Transactions	
Millions of Rupees																	
	199.69	113.66	124.07	171.33	193.52	301.50	258.27	245.66	265.02	262.15	252.00	495.80	....	....	....	Exports	70
	704.72	651.96	633.90	856.63	930.15	993.78	910.42	980.87	1,234.86	1,042.38	1,109.20	1,362.81	1,710.99	2,120.86	....	Imports, c.i.f.	71
																Balance of Payments	
Minus Sign Indicates Debit																	
	−19.20	−33.29	−21.11	−28.41	−39.65	−12.98	−8.17	−6.90	−38.82	−25.88	−53.92	−56.51	−63.24	....	....	Current Account, n.i.e.	78ald
	4.64	4.41	8.09	17.26	34.36	57.15	49.33	48.07	51.30	52.14	53.14	77.97	115.21	....	....	Goods: Exports f.o.b.	78aad
	−84.14	−89.34	−96.25	−134.96	−154.16	−166.38	−162.84	−180.50	−216.30	−188.64	−214.14	−262.72	−302.71	....	....	Goods: Imports f.o.b.	78abd
	−79.50	−84.93	−88.16	−117.70	−119.80	−109.23	−113.51	−132.42	−165.00	−136.50	−161.00	−184.75	−187.51	....	....	*Trade Balance*	78acd
	111.99	123.27	144.85	164.42	144.22	171.78	167.49	194.07	213.41	198.53	218.02	235.72	241.22	....	....	Services: Credit	78add
	−59.27	−74.53	−85.06	−81.61	−65.55	−80.48	−67.80	−76.59	−93.03	−84.76	−100.88	−107.99	−119.34	....	....	Services: Debit	78aed
	−26.79	−36.19	−28.37	−34.89	−41.12	−17.94	−13.82	−14.94	−44.62	−22.73	−43.87	−57.02	−65.62	....	....	*Balance on Goods & Services*	78afd
	2.16	2.06	2.70	3.09	3.91	4.50	5.03	5.24	5.04	3.17	5.90	6.16	6.31	....	....	Income: Credit	78agd
	−8.09	−10.55	−16.67	−20.53	−14.86	−17.77	−15.84	−14.46	−15.96	−14.27	−24.25	−21.14	−17.96	....	....	Income: Debit	78ahd
	−32.71	−44.68	−42.35	−52.33	−52.07	−31.20	−24.62	−24.16	−55.54	−33.83	−62.22	−72.00	−77.28	....	....	*Balance on Gds, Serv. & Inc.*	78aid
	17.02	19.85	27.62	34.00	22.16	28.55	26.31	31.10	31.83	21.32	19.55	27.57	27.13	....	....	Current Transfers: n.i.e.: Credit	78ajd
	−3.51	−8.46	−6.39	−10.08	−9.74	−10.32	−9.86	−13.84	−15.11	−13.37	−11.25	−12.08	−13.09	....	....	Current Transfers: Debit	78akd
																Capital Account, n.i.e.	78bcd
	—	—	—	....	....	....	....	....	....	....	....	....	....	....	....	Capital Account, n.i.e.: Credit	78bad
	—	—	—	....	....	....	....	....	....	....	....	....	....	....	....	Capital Account: Debit	78bbd
	16.45	33.57	18.88	21.33	44.30	22.94	30.72	−2.49	25.59	7.42	16.73	22.90	49.57	....	....	Financial Account, n.i.e.	78bjd
	−10.56	−5.78	−5.39	−4.29	−.92	−1.13	−1.14	−1.17	−1.16	−12.82	−15.71	−13.12	−9.95	....	....	Direct Investment Abroad	78bdd
	11.65	14.20	19.40	23.20	22.43	20.24	19.58	9.01	18.64	29.51	40.31	29.78	54.41	....	....	Dir. Invest. in Rep. Econ., n.i.e.	78bed
	—	—	—	—	.80	1.53	−.42	−.14	−.34	−.88	−2.67	3.70	.08	....	....	Portfolio Investment Assets	78bfd
																Equity Securities	78bkd
	—	—	—	—	.80	1.53	−.42	−.14	−.34	−.88	−2.67	3.70	.08	....	....	Debt Securities	78bld
								−.02	.04	.16	−.18	−.02	−.04	....	....	Portfolio Investment Liab., n.i.e.	78bgd
	—	—	—	—	—	—	—	−.02	.04	.16	−.18	−.02	−.04	....	....	Equity Securities	78bmd
	—	—	—	—	—	—	—	−.02	.04	.16	−.18	−.02	−.04	....	....	Debt Securities	78bnd
																Financial Derivatives Assets	78bwd
																Financial Derivatives Liabilities	78bxd
	.03	−.61	1.13	−.93	.45	−2.84	−6.24	.13	−1.56	.15	−2.84	−8.18	−16.83	....	....	Other Investment Assets	78bhd
																Monetary Authorities	78bod
	−.02	.05	−.10	.04												General Government	78bpd
	.05	−.66	1.23	−.97	.45	−.96	−4.35	2.09	1.34	1.73	−1.16	−6.17	−12.69	....	....	Banks	78bqd
						−1.88	−1.89	−1.95	−2.89	−1.58	−1.68	−2.01	−4.14	....	....	Other Sectors	78brd
	15.33	25.76	3.73	3.35	21.55	5.14	18.93	−10.31	9.97	−8.69	−2.17	10.73	21.89	....	....	Other Investment Liab., n.i.e.	78bid
						4.37	.09	−1.05	−.86	.82	−1.89	−2.86	10.13	....	....	Monetary Authorities	78bsd
	15.33	25.76	3.73	3.35	8.95	−4.40	14.49	−6.48	4.28	−3.77	−10.81	−1.31	2.77	....	....	General Government	78btd
	—	—	—	—	3.19	3.20	2.32	−7.10	.53	−1.52	5.75	9.91	8.09	....	....	Banks	78bud
					5.04	6.25	3.17	4.13	4.34	−1.52	5.75	5.28	.90	....	....	Other Sectors	78bvd
	2.70	−1.64	6.19	2.82	−5.53	−5.71	−20.75	5.44	3.17	6.76	23.15	20.58	8.44	....	....	Net Errors and Omissions	78cad
	−.06	−1.36	3.96	−4.26	−.88	4.26	1.81	−3.95	−10.06	−11.70	−14.03	−13.03	−5.23	....	....	*Overall Balance*	78cbd
	.06	1.36	−3.96	4.26	.88	−4.26	−1.81	3.95	10.06	11.70	14.03	13.03	5.23	....	....	Reserves and Related Items	79dad
	.06	1.36	−3.96	4.26	.88	−4.26	−11.65	−5.43	−3.45	6.08	1.43	3.93	5.23	....	....	Reserve Assets	79dbd
	—	—	—	—	—	—	9.84	9.38	13.51	5.62	12.60	9.09	—	....	....	Use of Fund Credit and Loans	79dcd
	....	....	....	....	....	....	9.84	9.38	13.51	5.62	12.60	9.09	....	....	....	Exceptional Financing	79ded
																Government Finance	
Year Ending December 31																	
	1−179.8	−251.8	−53.0	−61.1	−155.5	−.9	−104.6	−98.6	−181.9	18.2	−54.5	−311.6	−453.0	−602.4	....	Deficit (-) or Surplus	80
	1507.5	547.3	681.9	787.4	930.7	1,035.9	1,003.4	1,136.8	1,247.7	1,338.1	1,200.5	1,095.9	1,185.7	1,339.9	....	Total Revenue and Grants	81y
	1476.4	515.6	639.3	763.4	896.8	989.1	961.4	1,097.6	1,209.6	1,319.5	1,187.8	1,082.1	1,176.2	1,312.1	....	Revenue	81
	131.1	31.7	42.6	24.0	33.9	46.8	42.0	39.2	38.1	18.6	12.8	13.8	9.5	27.8	....	Grants	81z
	687.3	799.1	734.9	848.5	1,086.2	1,036.8	1,108.0	1,235.4	1,429.6	1,319.9	1,255.1	1,407.5	1,638.7	1,942.3	....	Exp. & Lending Minus Repay.	82z
	1685.8	767.3	701.9	768.8	971.9	958.7	1,079.6	1,203.8	1,393.6	1,297.4	1,206.6	1,382.2	1,543.0	1,792.1	....	Expenditure	82
	11.5	31.8	33.0	79.7	114.3	78.1	28.4	31.6	36.0	22.5	48.4	25.3	95.7	150.2	....	Lending Minus Repayments	83
	1179.7	251.8	53.0	61.1	155.5	.9	104.6	98.6	182.0	−18.3	54.5	311.6	453.0	602.4	....	Total Financing	80h
	1134.0	106.4	73.5	105.2	123.0	36.2	43.6	131.6	161.8	16.3	102.1	279.8	464.7	629.4	....	Domestic	84a
	145.7	145.4	−20.5	−44.1	32.5	−35.3	61.0	−33.0	20.2	−34.6	−47.6	31.9	−11.7	−27.0	....	Foreign	85a
	....	....	....	....	....	....	....	....	....	....	....	....	....	....	....	Total Debt by Residence	88
	....	....	....	....	....	....	....	....	....	....	....	....	....	....	....	Domestic	88a
	....	....	....	....	....	....	....	....	....	....	....	....	....	....	....	Foreign	89a
																National Accounts	
Millions of Rupees																	
	596.5	496.9	541.7	737.3	989.9	1,128.3	1,115.4	1,207.4	1,319.2	1,250.5	1,292.0	1,592.9	1,896.9	2,045.5	....	Exports of Goods & Services	90c
	417.4	497.6	406.6	415.6	471.7	544.4	558.4	674.6	714.7	722.2	669.1	736.0	733.0	847.0	....	Government Consumption	91f
	273.5	309.6	260.1	357.3	418.0	451.9	422.1	465.4	651.2	648.5	733.9	822.6	863.1	1,100.0	....	Gross Fixed Capital Formation	93e
	—	6	16	33	55	32	20	6	46	17	—	−19	109	56	....	Increase/Decrease(-) in Stocks	93i
	700.7	700.3	870.5	909.9	1,025.4	1,125.0	1,115.4	1,207.4	1,241.6	1,129.8	1,179.4	1,191.0	1,465.8	1,603.9	....	Private Consumption	96f
	−783.2	−720.0	−698.8	−925.2	−1,241.6	−1,314.0	−1,218.4	−1,315.4	−1,544.2	−1,326.0	−1,454.8	−1,841.4	−2,159.7	−2,525.8	....	Imports of Goods & Services	98c
	1,204.9	1,290.0	1,395.9	1,527.9	1,720.9	1,967.1	1,980.1	2,221.1	2,431.5	2,440.4	2,419.8	2,482.1	2,910.2	3,126.7	....	Gross Domestic Product (GDP)	99b
	−42.2	−52.4	−78.2	−59.2	−45.3	−70.1	−56.8	−47.3	−31.6	−23.4	−88.2	−74.4	−48.9	−84.0	....	Net Factor Inc/Pmts(-) Abroad	98.n
	1,162.7	1,237.6	1,317.7	1,434.3	1,675.2	1,915.4	1,944.5	2,173.6	2,399.9	2,417.0	2,331.6	2,407.7	2,861.3	3,042.7	....	Gross National Income (GNI)	99a
	505.4	511.0	533.3	....	....	....	....	....	....	....	....	....	....	....	....	GDP Volume 1976 Prices	99b.p
	1,274.2	1,290.0	1,346.5	1,418.2	1,564.1	1,680.7	1,726.8	1,851.4	1,965.9	1,950.0	1,937.9	1,974.3	2,425.3	2,605.7	....	GDP Volume 1986 Prices	99b.p
	65.8	66.6	69.5	73.2	80.7	86.7	89.1	95.5	101.4	100.6	100.0	101.9	125.2	134.5	....	GDP Volume (1995=100)	99bv p
Midyear Estimates																	
	.07	.07	.07	.07	.07	.07	.07	.07	.07	.07	.07	.08	.08	.08	.08	**Population**	99z

(See notes in the back of the book.)

Sierra Leone

		1970	1971	1972	1973	1974	1975	1976	1977	1978	1979	1980	1981	1982	1983	1984
Exchange Rates															*Leones per SDR:*	
Market Rate	aa	.84	.85	.92	1.04	1.04	1.16	1.36	1.27	1.37	1.37	1.37	1.37	1.36	2.63	2.46
															Leones per US Dollar:	
Market Rate	ae	.84	.78	.85	.86	.85	.99	1.17	1.05	1.05	1.04	1.06	1.17	1.23	2.51	2.51
Market Rate	rf	.83	.83	.80	.82	.86	.90	1.11	1.15	1.05[e]	1.06	1.05	1.16	1.24	1.89	2.51
															Index Numbers (1995=100):	
Market Rate	ahx	88,036.5	577.2	91,925.8	90,100.8	85,944.6	81,637.0	66,365.9	64,136.8	70,264.3[e]	69,534.4	70,018.8	63,485.2	59,362.6	43,786.5	29,277.1
Nominal Effective Exchange Rate	ne c	....	....	....	....	....	....	....	....	....	33,617.6	33,653.5	35,249.3	37,405.6	30,331.4	23,077.8
Real Effective Exchange Rate	re c	....	....	....	....	....	....	....	....	....						
Fund Position															*Millions of SDRs:*	
Quota	2f. s	25.0	25.0	25.0	25.0	25.0	25.0	25.0	25.0	31.0	31.0	46.5	46.5	46.5	57.9	57.9
SDRs	1b. s	.5	3.1	5.7	5.7	4.4	3.9	2.9	1.4	.2	—	—	.1	.5	.1	—
Reserve Position in the Fund	1c. s	4.9	4.9	4.9	4.9								1.1			
Total Fund Cred.&Loans Outstg.	2tl					4.3	4.9	22.4	32.1	35.6	43.8	46.6	72.2	70.9	88.9	97.5
International Liquidity												*Millions of US Dollars Unless Otherwise Indicated:*				
Total Reserves minus Gold	1l. d	39.4	38.4	46.5	51.8	54.6	28.4	25.2	33.4	34.8	46.7	30.6	16.0	8.4	16.2	7.7
SDRs	1b. d	.5	3.4	6.2	6.9	5.4	4.6	3.4	1.7	.3	—	—	.1	.5	.1	—
Reserve Position in the Fund	1c. d	4.9	5.3	5.3	5.9								1.2			
Foreign Exchange	1d. d	34.0	29.7	34.9	39.0	49.2	23.8	21.8	31.7	34.5	46.7	30.6	14.6	7.9	16.1	7.7
Monetary Authorities: Other Liab.	4.. d	—	—	—	1.4	5.2	8.3	6.3	-3.3	-.1	1.8	102.4	152.0	157.4	208.5	216.9
Deposit Money Banks: Assets	7a. d	.1	1.0	.5	2.7	4.2	2.4	3.5	7.7	11.6	11.0	14.0	5.3	7.4	7.6	16.0
Liabilities	7b. d	1.9	5.8	.1	3.0	5.6	2.5	.5	.9	.3	.2	—	—	.1	.3	3.9
Monetary Authorities															*Millions of Leones:*	
Foreign Assets	11	29	29	36	43	47	28	29	36	37	48	32	19	7	33	9
Claims on Central Government	12a	6	8	7	14	16	42	60	69	117	214	296	425	583	719	924
Claims on Nonfin.Pub.Enterprises	12c	....														
Claims on Private Sector	12d	—	—	—	—	5	2			2	3	8	4	3	3	4
Claims on Deposit Money Banks	12e															
Claims on Other Banking Insts	12f	....														
Claims on Nonbank Financial Insts	12g	....														
Reserve Money	14	23	25	28	35	39	43	50	58	94	144	133	134	253	317	450
of which: Currency Outside DMBs	14a	19	21	25	30	31	37	41	52	63	72	86	86	121	197	260
Time, Savings,& Fgn.Currency Dep.	15	....														
Restricted Deposits	16b															
Foreign Liabilities	16c	—	—	—	1	9	14	38	41	63	86	205	310	324	790	813
Long-Term Foreign Liabilities	16cl	....														
Central Government Deposits	16d	5	2	2	6	5	—	5	6	7	36	26	28	20	52	32
Capital Accounts	17a	4	7	10	10	11	12	12	17	14	20	25	29	32	32	33
of which: Valuation Adjustment	17rv	4	4	4	5	4	4	—	-4	-17	-26	-29	-34	-33	-355	-230
Other Items (Net)	17r	3	3	3	6	4	3	-15	-16	-22	-20	-53	-54	-35	-435	-392
Deposit Money Banks															*Millions of Leones:*	
Reserves	20	3	3	3	4	6	4	8	5	29	71	121	158	261	297	365
Foreign Assets	21	—	1	—	2	4	2	4	8	12	11	15	6	9	19	40
Claims on Central Government	22a	5	7	8	13	16	19	31	38	51	54	51	53	62	121	169
Claims on Nonfin.Pub.Enterprises	22c	—	—	—	—	3	1	1	3	6	4	4	4	4	4	6
Claims on Private Sector	22d	19	20	22	28	35	40	43	46	63	68	83	96	110	129	108
Claims on Nonbank Financial Insts	22g	....														
Demand Deposits	24	10	11	13	17	22	22	30	32	43	55	65	63	128	156	222
Time, Savings,& Fgn.Currency Dep.	25	14	16	18	23	30	31	40	52	72	87	108	116	166	193	223
Foreign Liabilities	26c	2	4	—	2	5	3	1	1	—	—	—	—	—	1	10
Central Government Deposits	26d	—	—	—	—	—	—	1	1	1	—	2	2	4	6	6
Credit from Monetary Authorities	26g	—	—	—	—	—	—	—	—	—	—	—	—	—	—	—
Capital Accounts	27a	4	3	3	4	4	5	5	7	8	10	11	12	17	18	21
Other Items (Net)	27r	-2	-4	-1	1	3	5	11	9	37	57	88	124	131	197	207
Monetary Survey															*Millions of Leones:*	
Foreign Assets (Net)	31n	27	26	36	42	37	14	-5	2	-14	-27	-157	-285	-308	-739	-774
Domestic Credit	32	26	32	35	49	70	102	130	151	231	307	413	551	738	919	1,172
Claims on Central Govt. (Net)	32an	7	12	14	20	27	61	86	101	160	232	318	448	621	783	1,055
Claims on Nonfin.Pub.Enterprises	32c	—	—	—	—	3	1	1	3	6	4	4	4	4	4	6
Claims on Private Sector	32d	19	20	22	28	40	41	44	47	65	71	91	99	114	132	111
Claims on Other Banking Insts	32f	....														
Claims on Nonbank Financial Inst	32g	....														
Money	34	29	32	39	48	55	60	72	84	107	128	153	152	253	359	486
Quasi-Money	35	14	16	18	23	30	31	40	52	72	87	108	116	166	193	223
Restricted Deposits	36b	....														
Long-Term Foreign Liabilities	36cl	....														
Capital Accounts	37a	8	10	13	14	16	17	18	24	23	30	36	41	48	50	54
Other Items (Net)	37r	2	—	2	7	7	8	-4	-7	15	36	-40	-42	-37	-422	-365
Money plus Quasi-Money	35l	43	48	57	71	85	92	112	136	179	215	261	268	420	552	709
Interest Rates															*Percent Per Annum*	
Treasury Bill Rate	60c	5.50	5.50	5.50	5.50	5.50	5.50	5.50	5.50	5.50	6.25	9.38	10.00	10.00	11.00	12.00
Deposit Rate	60l	....							7.00	7.00	7.25	9.17	10.00	10.00	11.00	12.00
Lending Rate	60p	8.00	8.00	8.00	8.00	8.00	8.50	9.00	11.00	11.00	11.00	11.00	15.00	15.00	17.25	18.00
Prices															*Index Numbers (1995=100):*	
Wholesale Prices (1985=100)	63	4.0	4.3	4.7	6.0	7.6	8.8	10.8	12.8	14.9	18.1	22.1	27.0	32.3	46.3	67.0
Consumer Prices (1995=100,000)	64.a	300.6	296.8	313.1	330.9	378.6	453.9	532.0	576.3	639.1	774.9	875.0	1,079.4	1,369.7	2,308.3	3,845.0
Consumer Prices	64	—	—	—	—	—	—	.1	.1	.1	1.1	.1	.1	.2	.2	.4
															Number in Thousands:	
Employment	67e	....														

Exchange Rates

1985	1986	1987	1988	1989	1990	1991	1992	1993	1994	1995	1996	1997	1998	1999		
End of Period																
5.74	43.53	32.69	52.57	85.89	268.43	621.93	723.68	793.41	894.90	1,402.35	1,307.24	1,799.00	2,239.84	3,123.90	Market Rate	aa
End of Period (ae) Period Average (rf)																
5.21	35.59	23.04	39.06	65.36	188.68	434.78	526.32	577.63	613.01	943.40	909.09	1,333.33	1,590.76	2,276.05	Market Rate	ae
5.09	16.09	34.04	32.51	59.81	151.45	295.34	499.44	567.46	586.74	755.22	920.73	981.48	1,563.62	1,804.20	Market Rate	rf
Period Averages																
15,537.5	8,752.9	2,385.3	2,354.0	1,263.4	508.9	267.6	147.9	129.6	125.3	100.0	80.0	77.0	47.0	41.2	Market Rate	ahx
13,070.4	6,314.8	1,538.3	1,501.3	896.8	373.8	208.4	121.6	124.6	131.3	100.0	82.7	86.1	54.5	48.5	Nominal Effective Exchange Rate	nec
....	....	124.6	145.4	126.2	94.1	95.3	86.8	96.7	110.6	100.0	101.0	116.0	99.6	117.1	Real Effective Exchange Rate	rec

Fund Position

1985	1986	1987	1988	1989	1990	1991	1992	1993	1994	1995	1996	1997	1998	1999		
End of Period																
57.9	57.9	57.9	57.9	57.9	57.9	57.9	57.9	57.9	77.2	77.2	77.2	77.2	77.2	103.7	Quota	2f. s
—	.3	—	—	—	—	—	1.2	2.8	6.2	11.5	5.3	8.3	7.4	15.2	SDRs	1b. s
														—	Reserve Position in the Fund	1c. s
92.0	82.9	81.5	80.8	79.5	76.2	70.7	67.0	61.0	100.2	110.9	118.8	123.9	135.4	142.0	Total Fund Cred.&Loans Outstg.	2tl

International Liquidity

1985	1986	1987	1988	1989	1990	1991	1992	1993	1994	1995	1996	1997	1998	1999		
End of Period																
10.8	13.7	6.3	7.4	3.7	5.4	9.6	18.9	29.0	40.6	34.6	26.6	38.5	44.1	39.5	Total Reserves minus Gold	1l. d
—	.3	—	—	—	—	—	1.7	3.8	9.0	17.1	7.6	11.2	10.4	20.8	SDRs	1b. d
														—	Reserve Position in the Fund	1c. d
10.8	13.3	6.3	7.4	3.7	5.4	9.6	17.2	25.1	31.6	17.5	18.9	27.3	33.7	18.6	Foreign Exchange	1d. d
247.8	176.4	276.7	263.9	254.5	243.6	248.4	302.4	322.1	470.2	326.2	53.5	14.8	19.2	7.7	Monetary Authorities: Other Liab.	4.. d
10.0	13.8	12.5	11.4	12.7	8.7	7.5	16.1	22.5	16.9	22.5	19.9	15.6	19.2	17.9	Deposit Money Banks: Assets	7a. d
2.1	4.7	1.4	1.0	.1	—	—	—	2.7	2.9	3.1	—	—	—	—	Liabilities	7b. d

Monetary Authorities

1985	1986	1987	1988	1989	1990	1991	1992	1993	1994	1995	1996	1997	1998	1999		
End of Period																
7	232	514	791	2,067	1,016	4,169	11,143	18,943	30,443	48,695	ɪ27,262	53,008	83,128	98,035	Foreign Assets	11
2,037	2,810	4,394	5,518	8,365	31,922	35,265	30,009	25,328	462,872	408,928	ɪ415,564	470,930	475,265	524,834	Claims on Central Government	12a
											203	203	13	66	Claims on Nonfin.Pub.Enterprises	12c
2	57	12	95	102	103	107	112	126	160	324	ɪ1,031	2,577	1,749	788	Claims on Private Sector	12d
											ɪ1,173	495	1,049	1,736	Claims on Deposit Money Banks	12e
											33	34		4	Claims on Other Banking Insts	12f
											302	85	6	26	Claims on Nonbank Financial Insts	12g
691	1,423	2,404	4,274	7,449	12,395	20,258	24,095	24,995	31,352	35,148	ɪ43,548	91,008	72,415	100,627	Reserve Money	14
442	1,006	1,364	2,255	4,058	8,337	15,650	18,270	21,882	23,604	30,023	ɪ36,186	57,260	61,492	82,815	*of which: Currency Outside DMBs*	14a
											812	5,397	259	1,394	Time, Savings,& Fgn.Currency Dep.	15
											3	213	24	34	Restricted Deposits	16b
1,845	9,910	9,069	14,585	23,494	66,428	152,002	207,647	234,495	377,912	463,327	ɪ203,964	242,632	334,003	460,925	Foreign Liabilities	16c
											19,421	22,120	31,180	44,973	Long-Term Foreign Liabilities	16cl
5	13	299	-27	297	713	828	1,974	6,598	5,936	10,955	ɪ2,042	4,528	4,615	5,472	Central Government Deposits	16d
35	41	42	44	45	59	146	147	149	24,151	24,156	ɪ190,158	227,935	153,387	156,255	Capital Accounts	17a
-527	-7,161	-4,103	-5,439	-7,535	-21,574	-66,072	-47,145	-90,274	-108,690	-111,158	ɪ832	-40,714	-57,997	-135,494	*of which: Valuation Adjustment*	17rv
-530	-8,288	-6,894	-12,471	-20,751	-46,554	-133,693	-192,599	-221,840	54,124	-75,639	ɪ-14,379	-66,500	-34,672	-144,194	Other Items (Net)	17r

Deposit Money Banks

1985	1986	1987	1988	1989	1990	1991	1992	1993	1994	1995	1996	1997	1998	1999		
End of Period																
418	570	1,515	1,968	3,287	3,963	4,498	5,707	2,855	7,523	4,701	ɪ5,926	26,240	8,088	23,229	Reserves	20
52	493	288	445	830	1,644	3,255	8,462	12,986	10,378	21,232	ɪ18,079	20,852	30,555	40,852	Foreign Assets	21
406	556	811	988	1,193	1,379	1,819	2,795	8,589	9,921	12,763	ɪ18,470	10,311	41,161	72,209	Claims on Central Government	22a
15	21	—	51	53	67	50	50	26	81	21	ɪ30	335	63	68	Claims on Nonfin.Pub.Enterprises	22c
133	370	605	1,105	2,592	3,092	8,008	10,257	14,847	16,576	17,276	ɪ20,705	24,506	26,895	24,234	Claims on Private Sector	22d
											598	594	2,094	2,165	Claims on Nonbank Financial Insts	22g
454	833	1,494	2,332	4,513	5,820	9,338	13,005	12,753	14,719	19,462	ɪ15,616	24,494	25,875	47,800	Demand Deposits	24
313	433	859	1,241	1,565	3,565	6,306	10,446	15,951	16,955	16,481	ɪ32,044	37,625	50,896	58,686	Time, Savings,& Fgn.Currency Dep.	25
11	169	33	40	5	3	13	11	1,551	1,761	2,896	ɪ—	—	—	—	Foreign Liabilities	26c
5	9	243	97	251	167	239	634	1,356	1,916	2,172	ɪ2,102	3,190	5,059	14,107	Central Government Deposits	26d
											ɪ174	74	42	21	Credit from Monetary Authorities	26g
24	28	82	118	155	627	850	1,025	1,292	5,483	8,961	ɪ20,564	18,607	22,994	34,664	Capital Accounts	27a
218	537	509	729	1,466	-38	885	2,150	6,399	3,645	6,021	ɪ-6,591	-1,153	3,990	7,480	Other Items (Net)	27r

Monetary Survey

1985	1986	1987	1988	1989	1990	1991	1992	1993	1994	1995	1996	1997	1998	1999		
End of Period																
-1,797	-9,354	-8,299	-13,389	-20,601	-63,771	-144,591	-188,052	-204,117	-338,852	-396,296	ɪ-158623	-168,771	-220,319	-322,038	Foreign Assets (Net)	31n
2,583	3,792	5,280	7,687	11,757	35,682	44,182	40,615	40,961	481,758	426,184	ɪ452,793	501,856	537,572	604,813	Domestic Credit	32
2,432	3,344	4,663	6,436	9,010	32,420	36,017	30,196	25,963	464,940	408,563	ɪ429,891	473,523	506,752	577,463	Claims on Central Govt. (Net)	32an
15	21	—	51	53	67	50	50	26	81	21	ɪ233	538	76	134	Claims on Nonfin.Pub.Enterprises	32c
135	427	617	1,199	2,694	3,195	8,115	10,369	14,973	16,736	17,600	ɪ21,736	27,083	28,644	25,022	Claims on Private Sector	32d
											33	34		4	Claims on Other Banking Insts	32f
											900	679	2,100	2,190	Claims on Nonbank Financial Inst	32g
900	1,852	2,889	4,637	8,675	14,253	25,092	31,387	35,053	38,542	49,902	ɪ53,208	83,611	89,744	134,078	Money	34
313	433	859	1,241	1,565	3,565	6,306	10,446	15,951	16,955	16,481	ɪ32,856	43,022	51,155	60,080	Quasi-Money	35
											3	213	24	34	Restricted Deposits	36b
											19,421	22,120	31,180	44,973	Long-Term Foreign Liabilities	36cl
58	69	124	162	200	686	995	1,172	1,441	29,633	33,116	ɪ210,721	246,542	176,381	190,919	Capital Accounts	37a
-485	-7,916	-6,890	-11,742	-19,285	-46,593	-132,802	-190,442	-215,601	57,775	-69,611	ɪ-22,040	-62,423	-31,232	-147,310	Other Items (Net)	37r
1,213	2,285	3,747	5,879	10,240	17,818	31,397	41,834	51,004	55,497	66,383	ɪ86,064	126,633	140,899	194,159	Money plus Quasi-Money	35l

Interest Rates

1985	1986	1987	1988	1989	1990	1991	1992	1993	1994	1995	1996	1997	1998	1999		
Percent Per Annum																
12.00	14.50	16.50	18.00	22.00	47.50	50.67	78.63	28.64	12.19	14.73	29.25	12.71	22.10	32.42	Treasury Bill Rate	60c
11.33	14.17	12.67	16.33	20.00	40.50	47.80	54.67	27.00	11.63	7.03	13.96	9.91	7.12	9.50	Deposit Rate	60l
17.00	17.19	28.54	28.00	29.67	52.50	56.25	62.83	50.46	27.33	28.83	32.12	23.87	23.83	26.83	Lending Rate	60p

Prices

1985	1986	1987	1988	1989	1990	1991	1992	1993	1994	1995	1996	1997	1998	1999		
Period Averages																
100.0	....	....	....											...	Wholesale Prices (1985=100)	63
6,789.3	12,279.7	34,223.4	45,957.5	73,899.9	155,888.6	315,977.8	522,943.8	639,086.6	793,726.3	....	....	....	....	...	Consumer Prices (1995=100,000)	64,a
.7	1.2	3.4	4.6	7.4	15.6	31.6	52.3	ɪ63.9	79.4	100.0	123.1	141.5	191.8	257.2	Consumer Prices	64
Period Averages																
69	74	69	70	....	....	....	....	....	....	....	....	....	....	....	Employment	67e

Sierra Leone

		1970	1971	1972	1973	1974	1975	1976	1977	1978	1979	1980	1981	1982	1983	1984
International Transactions																*Millions of Leones*
Exports	70	84	81	92	107	123	105	109	155	178	211	234	173	137	198	335
Imports, c.i.f.	71	97	94	95	127	189	168	171	206	291	334	447	378	368	287	394
Balance of Payments																*Millions of US Dollars*
Current Account, n.i.e.	78al d	...	...	...	...	...	...	...	−49.6	−112.0	−179.1	−165.2	−132.1	−169.9	−17.6	−23.0
Goods: Exports f.o.b.	78aa d	...	...	...	...	...	...	...	150.3	193.6	211.6	226.6	165.9	122.6	115.1	139.2
Goods: Imports f.o.b.	78ab d	...	...	...	...	...	...	...	−165.0	−253.0	−336.3	−385.9	−282.0	−260.3	−133.0	−149.7
Trade Balance	78ac d	...	...	...	...	...	...	...	−14.7	−59.4	−124.7	−159.3	−116.1	−137.7	−17.9	−10.5
Services: Credit	78ad d	...	...	...	...	...	...	...	10.7	17.7	31.2	48.9	37.2	25.3	26.7	34.5
Services: Debit	78ae d	...	...	...	...	...	...	...	−50.7	−56.2	−72.6	−85.3	−59.6	−72.7	−42.1	−47.6
Balance on Goods & Services	78af d	...	...	...	...	...	...	...	−54.7	−97.9	−166.0	−195.8	−138.6	−185.1	−33.3	−23.6
Income: Credit	78ag d	...	...	...	...	...	...	...	1.8	.4	.3	.6	.5	.2	.3	.2
Income: Debit	78ah d	...	...	...	...	...	...	...	−16.7	−33.9	−42.3	−22.5	−37.4	−35.2	−21.2	−32.6
Balance on Gds, Serv. & Inc.	78ai d	...	...	...	...	...	...	...	−69.6	−131.4	−208.0	−217.6	−175.5	−220.2	−54.2	−56.0
Current Transfers, n.i.e.: Credit	78aj d	...	...	...	...	...	...	...	22.1	21.8	31.7	56.7	44.4	54.3	39.0	34.6
Current Transfers: Debit	78ak d	...	...	...	...	...	...	...	−2.1	−2.4	−2.7	−4.2	−1.0	−4.0	−2.4	−1.6
Capital Account, n.i.e.	78bc d	...	...	...	...	...	...	...	—	—	—	.1	—	.1	.1	.1
Capital Account, n.i.e.: Credit	78ba d	...	...	...	...	...	...	...	—	—	—	.1	—	.1	.1	.1
Capital Account: Debit	78bb d	...	...	...	...	...	...	...	—	—	—	—	—	.1	.1	.1
Financial Account, n.i.e.	78bj d	...	...	...	...	...	...	...	17.3	76.1	106.1	111.5	71.4	21.8	−78.1	−60.8
Direct Investment Abroad	78bd d	...	...	...	...	...	...	...								
Dir. Invest. in Rep. Econ., n.i.e.	78be d	...	...	...	...	...	...	...	5.1	24.3	16.1	−18.7	7.5	4.7	1.7	5.9
Portfolio Investment Assets	78bf d	...	...	...	...	...	...	...	—	2.4	2.4	—	—	—	—	—
Equity Securities	78bk d	...	...	...	...	...	...	...	—	—	—	—	—	—	—	—
Debt Securities	78bl d	...	...	...	...	...	...	...	—	2.4	2.4	—	—	—	—	—
Portfolio Investment Liab., n.i.e.	78bg d	...	...	...	...	...	...	...	—	—	—	−1.4	—	—	—	—
Equity Securities	78bm d	...	...	...	...	...	...	...	—	—	—	—	—	—	—	—
Debt Securities	78bn d	...	...	...	...	...	...	...	—	—	—	−1.4	—	—	—	—
Financial Derivatives Assets	78bw d	...	...	...	...	...	...	...	...	...	...	...	...	...	...	...
Financial Derivatives Liabilities	78bx d	...	...	...	...	...	...	...	...	...	...	...	...	...	...	...
Other Investment Assets	78bh d	...	...	...	...	...	...	...	−3.1	2.0	4.9	2.0	9.6	16.1	−38.6	−16.2
Monetary Authorities	78bo d	...	...	...	...	...	...	...								
General Government	78bp d	...	...	...	...	...	...	...	−1.8	—	.1	.1	—	.1	.1	—
Banks	78bq d	...	...	...	...	...	...	...	−3.4	−3.9	.8	−3.3	7.4	−2.3	−5.2	−8.4
Other Sectors	78br d	...	...	...	...	...	...	...	2.1	5.9	4.1	5.2	2.2	18.4	−33.5	−7.8
Other Investment Liab., n.i.e.	78bi d	...	...	...	...	...	...	...	15.4	47.5	82.7	129.6	54.3	1.0	−41.2	−50.4
Monetary Authorities	78bs d	...	...	...	...	...	...	...	−7.3	14.4	10.6	2.6	22.1	−11.3	−1.0	16.6
General Government	78bt d	...	...	...	...	...	...	...	16.4	29.3	41.5	91.3	4.7	16.5	−56.7	−55.0
Banks	78bu d	...	...	...	...	...	...	...	.3	−.6	−.1	−.2	—	.2	.3	3.6
Other Sectors	78bv d	...	...	...	...	...	...	...	5.9	4.3	30.7	35.9	27.4	−4.4	16.2	−15.6
Net Errors and Omissions	78ca d	...	...	...	...	...	...	...	11.9	27.0	17.9	−22.3	−46.2	68.3	2.9	−12.4
Overall Balance	78cb d	...	...	...	...	...	...	...	−20.4	−8.9	−55.2	−75.9	−107.0	−79.7	−92.8	−96.1
Reserves and Related Items	79da d	...	...	...	...	...	...	...	20.4	8.9	55.2	75.9	107.0	79.7	92.8	96.1
Reserve Assets	79db d	...	...	...	...	...	...	...	−5.0	−1.6	−3.9	19.3	15.4	9.8	−13.6	9.6
Use of Fund Credit and Loans	79dc d	...	...	...	...	...	...	...	11.3	4.3	10.6	3.8	30.7	−1.4	19.7	9.4
Exceptional Financing	79de d	...	...	...	...	...	...	...	14.1	6.2	48.5	52.7	60.9	71.3	86.7	77.2
Government Finance																*Millions of Leones:*
Deficit (-) or Surplus	80	...	I−4	−8	−12	I−21	−60	−48	−51	−79	−119	−148	−121	−167	−271	−206
Revenue	81	...	I54	60	64	I92	97	95	119	157	174	190	221	182	156	229
Grants Received	81z	...				I—	—	—	—	12	19	7	16	10	15	37
Expenditure	82	...	I58	68	76	I113	157	144	170	249	311	334	358	353	416	451
Lending Minus Repayments	83	...	...	...	...	I—	—	—	—	—	1	12	—	6	26	21
Financing																
Domestic	84a	...	5	—	11	I8	27	30	36	39	81	105	105	134	229	206
Foreign	85a	...	−1	8	1	I13	33	19	15	41	38	44	16	34	43	—
Debt: Domestic	88a	...	...	...	...	I45	69	109	143	196	292	391	487	648	878	1,078
Foreign	89a	...	...	...	...	I71	118	136	153	229	290	366	396	485	518	870
National Accounts																*Millions of Leones:*
Exports of Goods & Services	90c	112	I109	104	116	134	154	143	156	199	233	264	297	253	208	290
Government Consumption	91f	25	I32	32	42	49	64	59	71	77	96	97	90	138	167	189
Gross Fixed Capital Formation	93e	53	I47	43	44	57	76	72	81	100	128	172	236	205	235	332
Increase/Decrease(-) in Stocks	93i	2	I6	−1	2	19	14	−2	17	−4	10	16	11	10	33	15
Private Consumption	96f	269	I268	287	300	364	477	534	631	719	880	1,048	1,172	1,416	1,647	2,242
Imports of Goods & Services	98c	−106	I−113	−108	−110	−145	−212	−192	−212	−242	−318	−442	−514	−416	−413	−339
Gross Domestic Product (GDP)	99b	355	I349	356	393	478	573	614	744	850	1,029	1,156	1,292	1,605	1,876	2,730
Net Factor Inc/Pmts(-) Abroad	98.n	−7	I−3	−8	−6	−7	−7	−10	−11	−17	−41	−45	−23	−43	−43	−40
Gross National Income (GNI)	99a	349	I345	348	388	471	566	604	733	833	989	1,111	1,269	1,562	1,833	2,690
Net National Income	99e	315	I314	317	355	433	521	554	675	764	907	1,008	1,145	1,409	1,650	2,410
GDP Volume 1973 Prices	99b.p	...	386	382	393	409	421	409	415	416	447	460	489	497	...	...
GDP Volume 1980/81 Prices	99b.p	...	...	...	...	...	...	...	...	...	...	...	...	1,314	1,295	1,313
GDP Volume 1984/85 Prices	99b.p	...	...	...	...	...	...	...	...	...	...	...	...	...	...	...
GDP Volume 1989/90 Prices	99b.p	...	...	...	...	...	...	...	...	...	...	...	...	...	...	...
GDP Volume (1995=100)	99bv p	...	107.2	106.0	109.3	113.7	117.1	113.6	115.2	115.6	124.1	127.9	135.8	138.0	136.0	137.9
GDP Deflator (1995=100)	99bi p	...	I—	—	.1	.1	.1	.1	.1	.1	.1	.1	.1	.2	.2	.3
																Millions:
Population	99z	2.69	2.76	2.83	2.90	2.97	3.05	3.09	3.14	3.19	3.19	3.26	3.34	3.41	3.49	3.51

1985	1986	1987	1988	1989	1990	1991	1992	1993	1994	1995	1996	1997	1998	1999		
															International Transactions	
Millions of Leones																
649	1,978	4,689	3,330	8,248	21,023	43,946	74,918	67,094	68,010	30,148	43,004	15,412	10,482	11,347	Exports	70
789	2,021	4,424	5,215	10,902	22,572	45,488	72,776	83,460	88,492	102,488	193,628	80,010	148,226	153,856	Imports, c.i.f.	71
															Balance of Payments	
Minus Sign Indicates Debit																
2.8	140.7	-30.3	-2.8	-59.7	-69.4	15.3	-5.5	-57.8	-89.1	-126.5	....	....	....	....	Current Account, n.i.e.	78al *d*
135.8	131.7	142.0	107.9	142.0	148.5	149.5	150.4	118.3	116.0	41.5	....				Goods: Exports f.o.b.	78aa *d*
-141.2	-111.4	-114.8	-138.2	-160.4	-140.4	-138.6	-139.0	-187.1	-188.7	-168.1					Goods: Imports f.o.b.	78ab *d*
-5.4	20.3	27.1	-30.3	-18.3	8.1	11.0	11.4	-68.8	-72.7	-126.7					*Trade Balance*	78ac *d*
24.0	20.8	40.9	48.6	35.8	61.1	67.6	47.0	58.5	100.2	86.8					Services: Credit	78ad *d*
-42.9	-33.9	-42.0	-34.6	-44.8	-74.4	-63.8	-62.9	-61.5	-107.6	-91.8					Services: Debit	78ae *d*
-24.2	7.2	26.0	-16.3	-27.3	-5.2	14.7	-4.5	-71.9	-80.1	-131.7					*Balance on Goods & Services*	78af *d*
.2	.1	.2	.2	.2	.7	7.9	6.8	2.3	1.5	.7					Income: Credit	78ag *d*
7.6	127.3	-63.2	4.6	-39.9	-71.8	-17.1	-15.1	-5.6	-57.0	-21.4					Income: Debit	78ah *d*
-16.4	134.6	-37.0	-11.5	-67.0	-76.3	5.5	-12.8	-75.2	-135.7	-152.3					*Balance on Gds, Serv. & Inc.*	78ai *d*
21.2	6.5	7.3	9.3	7.9	7.1	10.0	8.2	19.1	47.5	35.3					Current Transfers, n.i.e.: Credit	78aj *d*
-2.0	-.3	-.6	-.6	-.7	-.2	-.2	-.8	-1.7	-.9	-9.5					Current Transfers: Debit	78ak *d*
—	—	.1	.1	.1			.1	.1	.1	—					Capital Account, n.i.e.	78bc *d*
—	—	.1	.1	.1			.1	.1	.1	—					Capital Account, n.i.e.: Credit	78ba *d*
—	—	—	—	—			—	—	—	—					Capital Account: Debit	78bb *d*
-67.6	-279.4	-1.2	-6.7	-17.9	-.8	-1.4	-18.2	49.1	-25.5	61.6	....				Financial Account, n.i.e.	78bj *d*
—	—	—	—	—	—	—	—	—	—	—					Direct Investment Abroad	78bd *d*
-31.0	-140.3	39.4	-23.1	22.4	32.4	7.5	-5.6	-7.5	-2.9	-1.7					Dir. Invest. in Rep. Econ., n.i.e.	78be *d*
—	—	—	—	—	—	—	—	—	—	—					Portfolio Investment Assets	78bf *d*
—	—	—	—	—	—	—	—	—	—	—					Equity Securities	78bk *d*
—	—	—	—	—	—	—	—	—	—	—					Debt Securities	78bl *d*
—	—	—	—	—	—	—	—	—	—	—					Portfolio Investment Liab., n.i.e.	78bg *d*
—	—	—	—	—	—	—	—	—	—	—					Equity Securities	78bm *d*
—	—	—	—	—	—	—	—	—	—	—					Debt Securities	78bn *d*
....	....	....	....	....	....	....	....	....	....	....					Financial Derivatives Assets	78bw *d*
....	....	....	....	....	....	....	....	....	....	....					Financial Derivatives Liabilities	78bx *d*
-10.5	-48.4	7.3	32.0	23.4	-20.1	-9.5	-31.2	-14.6	-.8	15.6					Other Investment Assets	78bh *d*
....	....	....	....	....	....	....	....	....	....	....					Monetary Authorities	78bo *d*
—	—	—	—	—	—	—	—	—	—	—					General Government	78bp *d*
-2.4	-27.4	5.9	-4.8	-6.3	-5.1	-5.6	-7.8	-10.0	4.4	15.9					Banks	78bq *d*
-8.1	-21.0	1.4	36.8	29.7	-15.0	-3.9	-23.4	-4.6	-5.2	-.4					Other Sectors	78br *d*
-26.2	-90.7	-47.9	-15.6	-63.7	-13.1	.7	18.6	71.2	-21.8	47.8					Other Investment Liab., n.i.e.	78bi *d*
10.9	6.0	-15.3	26.9	5.6	19.8	19.4		44.5	—	—					Monetary Authorities	78bs *d*
-46.3	-171.7	-6.1	-36.2	-68.3	-33.3	-25.3	16.6	31.1	-15.2	41.9					General Government	78bt *d*
.2	9.8	-4.0	.2	-.6			3.1	-2.6	2.8	-1.5					Banks	78bu *d*
9.0	65.3	-22.4	-6.5	-.4	.3	6.5	-1.1	-1.8	-9.5	7.4					Other Sectors	78bv *d*
-9.3	42.0	-21.9	-62.5	29.2	49.2	-28.9	39.8	16.1	55.1	19.3					Net Errors and Omissions	78ca *d*
-74.1	-96.6	-53.4	-71.9	-48.4	-20.9	-14.9	16.2	7.5	-59.5	-45.6					*Overall Balance*	78cb *d*
74.1	96.6	53.4	71.9	48.4	20.9	14.9	-16.2	-7.5	59.5	45.6					Reserves and Related Items	79da *d*
.6	-13.6	-.7	-6.7	9.3	-5.1	-10.7	-14.0	-13.6	-18.6	2.4					Reserve Assets	79db *d*
-5.4	-11.2	-1.7	-1.0	-1.6	-4.5	-7.5	-5.2	-8.4	55.1	15.9					Use of Fund Credit and Loans	79dc *d*
78.8	121.4	55.8	79.6	40.7	30.6	33.0	3.0	14.4	22.9	27.3					Exceptional Financing	79de *d*
															Government Finance	
Year Ending December 31																
-376	-184	-3,337	-2,157	-2,865	-2,413	‡-10,477	-16,502	-17,099	-26,123	-39,835	-49,925	-48,300	‡-66,092	....	Deficit (-) or Surplus	80
286	490	1,264	2,333	3,693	5,499	‡17,902	35,384	54,294	67,414	61,743	69,713	85,498	77,199	....	Revenue	81
41	105	838	305	532	322	2,522	5,107	7,302	11,117	5,734	8,529	9,495	22,456	....	Grants Received	81z
578	778	5,412	4,656	7,090	8,191	‡30,901	56,993	78,695	104,654	107,312	128,167	143,293	165,420	....	Expenditure	82
124	—	27	139	—	43	‡—	—	—	—	—	—	—	327	....	Lending Minus Repayments	83
															Financing	
322	147	2,406	1,290	2,952	1,929	5,127	356	61	-1,681	2,431	25,270	7,488	....	....	Domestic	84a
54	36	931	867	-87	484	5,350	16,146	17,037	27,804	37,404	24,655	40,812	....	....	Foreign	85a
1,402	2,124	4,353	5,986	7,304	10,642	16,140	16,508	18,164	24,311	26,007	41,613	52,368	126,083	....	Debt: Domestic	88a
1,995	4,961	17,138	17,431	32,821	87,566	156,136	367,739	408,626	444,894	656,205	966,326	941,853	1,840,991	....	Foreign	89a
															National Accounts	
Year Ending June 30 through 1997; December 31 Thereafter																
647	940	7,183	9,854	13,347	25,299	56,540	113,833	154,686	167,652	203,126	142,692	114,154	148,400	308,235	Exports of Goods & Services	90c
345	498	2,106	2,300	4,064	7,525	18,538	27,810	47,119	58,384	62,837	81,249	853,121	109,577	121,441	Government Consumption	91f
424	730	2,270	1,837	4,745	8,722	14,868	25,346	26,943	42,066	40,970	43,841	13,152	40,772	64,643	Gross Fixed Capital Formation	93e
53	109	19	185	-99	461	1,541	8,505	-3,947	2,548	-988	-638	-2,414	361	-11,010	Increase/Decrease(-) in Stocks	93i
4,002	6,238	16,105	25,067	43,608	76,988	146,449	231,440	341,641	382,914	538,422	699,785	671,197	839,100	976,431	Private Consumption	96f
-725	-1,184	-5,211	-4,937	-9,861	-22,862	-45,508	-79,674	-99,254	-109,853	-133,978	-92,198	-64,505	-103,207	-233,068	Imports of Goods & Services	98c
4,365	7,888	22,472	34,305	55,804	96,133	192,428	327,259	467,188	543,711	710,389	874,731	816,995	1,035,003	1,226,672	Gross Domestic Product (GDP)	99b
-12	954	-1,775	-6,265	-6,448	-10,166	-18,055	-41,693	-66,915	-70,238	-84,216	-100,977	-91,315	-217,935	-97,805	Net Factor Inc/Pmts(-) Abroad	98.n
4,704	7,542	20,697	28,040	49,356	85,967	174,373	285,566	400,273	473,474	626,173	773,754	725,680	817,068	1,128,867	Gross National Income (GNI)	99a
4,056	8,366	19,635	26,292	46,427	75,404	163,932	265,180	370,175	438,369	584,266	743,879	665,049	853,670	989,003	Net National Income	99e
....	....	....	....	....	....	....	....	....	....	....	....	....	....	....	GDP Volume 1973 Prices	99b.*p*
1,277	....	....	....	....	....	....	....	....	....	....					GDP Volume 1980/81 Prices	99b.*p*
4,785	4,668	4,923	....	....	....	....	....	....	....	....					GDP Volume 1984/85 Prices	99b.*p*
....	....	101,702	94,503	95,191	96,133	93,405	80,679	75,716	75,831	73,708	71,894	67,139	67,224	59,407	GDP Volume 1989/90 Prices	99b.*p*
134.1	130.9	138.0	128.2	129.1	130.4	126.7	109.5	102.7	102.9	100.0	97.5	91.1	91.2	80.6	GDP Volume (1995=100)	99bv *p*
.5	.8	2.3	3.8	6.1	10.4	21.4	42.1	64.0	74.4	100.0	126.2	126.3	159.7	214.2	GDP Deflator (1995=100)	99bi *p*
Midyear Estimates																
3.58	3.66	3.74	3.82	3.91	3.99	4.04	4.06	4.08	4.12	4.19	4.29	4.42	4.57	4.72	**Population**	99z

(See notes in the back of the book.)

Singepore

		1970	1971	1972	1973	1974	1975	1976	1977	1978	1979	1980	1981	1982	1983	1984
Exchange Rates													*Singapore Dollars per SDR:*			
Market Rate	aa	3.0800	3.1486	3.0617	‡2.9991	2.8307	2.9144	2.8529	2.8406	2.8186	2.8441	2.6701	2.3836	2.3259	2.2269	2.1349
													Singapore Dollars per US Dollar:			
Market Rate	ae	3.0800	2.9000	2.8200	‡2.4861	2.3120	2.4895	2.4555	2.3385	2.1635	2.1590	2.0935	2.0478	2.1085	2.1270	2.1780
Market Rate	rf	3.0612	3.0507[e]	2.8125[e]	2.4574	2.4369	2.3713	2.4708	2.4394	2.2740	2.1746	2.1412	2.1127	2.1400	2.1131	2.1331
													Index Numbers (1995=100):			
Market Rate	ah x	45.8[e]	46.7[e]	50.4[e]	57.9	58.2	59.9	57.4	58.1	62.4	65.2	66.2	67.2	66.3	67.1	66.5
Nominal Effective Exchange Rate	ne c	....	....	....	....	....	....	....	....	....	70.9	72.6	77.5	82.6	85.8	88.2
Real Effective Exchange Rate	re c	....	....	....	....	....	....	....	....	....	92.8	92.4	97.6	102.3	103.5	105.2
Fund Position													*Millions of SDRs:*			
Quota	2f. s	30.0	37.0	37.0	37.0	37.0	37.0	37.0	37.0	49.0	49.0	92.4	92.4	92.4	92.4	92.4
SDRs	1b. s	—	—	—	—	—	—	—	—	—	12.2	15.1	27.5	49.4	59.7	58.0
Reserve Position in the Fund	1c. s	7.5	9.3	9.3	9.3	9.3	9.3	9.4	9.4	13.1	21.5	44.3	63.4	67.7	68.5	69.1
of which: Outstg.Fund Borrowing	2c	—	—	—	—	—	—	—	—	—	—	—	—	—	—	—
Total Fund Cred.&Loans Outstg.	2tl	—	—	—	—	—	—	—	—	—	—	—	—	—	—	—
International Liquidity												*Millions of US Dollars Unless Otherwise Indicated:*				
Total Reserves (see notes)	1l. d	1,012	1,452	1,748	2,286	2,812	3,007	3,364	3,858	5,303	5,818	6,567	7,549	8,480	9,264	10,416
SDRs	1b. d	—	—	—	—	—	—	—	—	—	16	19	32	54	57	57
Reserve Position in the Fund	1c. d	8	10	10	11	11	11	11	11	17	28	57	74	75	72	68
Foreign Exchange	1d. d	1,005	1,442	1,738	2,275	2,801	2,996	3,353	3,846	5,286	5,774	6,491	7,443	8,351	9,130	10,291
Deposit Money Banks: Assets	7a. d	214	307	383	603	828	956	1,317	1,681	2,190	3,233	3,706	5,630	5,073	5,824	7,869
Liabilities	7b. d	171	400	604	1,083	1,173	1,191	1,696	2,186	3,053	3,866	4,513	6,942	6,686	8,751	11,463
Other Banking Insts.: Assets	7e. d	10	12	15	11	10	8	9	8	6	7	8	9	38	58	103
Liabilities	7f. d	4	4	3	4	4	2	4	4	3	4	7	3	4	10	7
ACU: Foreign Assets	7k. d	315	888	2,229	4,202	7,721	9,590	13,292	16,381	21,621	29,478	40,914	64,608	76,218	82,350	93,400
Foreign Liabilities	7m. d	323	880	2,201	4,056	7,325	9,406	13,273	16,142	20,425	27,315	38,942	62,685	76,130	83,878	96,901
Monetary Authorities													*Millions of Singapore Dollars:*			
Foreign Assets	11	3,102	4,095	4,930	5,800	6,503	7,486	8,262	9,023	11,474	12,562	13,758	15,491	17,918	19,755	22,748
Reserve Money	14	891	996	1,296	1,779	1,850	2,197	2,563	2,904	3,369	3,838	4,340	4,809	5,690	6,220	6,656
of which: Currency Outside DMBs	14a	727	806	1,005	1,114	1,306	1,638	1,947	2,243	2,583	2,941	3,137	3,382	3,996	4,335	4,619
Central Government Deposits	16d	2,201	2,897	3,444	3,816	4,191	4,676	4,755	5,423	6,123	7,019	7,026	2,442	6,771	3,943	2,806
Other Items (Net)	17r	10	202	190	205	462	613	944	696	1,982	1,705	2,392	8,240	5,457	9,592	13,286
Deposit Money Banks													*Millions of Singapore Dollars:*			
Reserves	20	168	190	291	664	541	560	616	661	787	898	1,192	1,428	1,720	1,900	2,060
Foreign Assets	21	656	‡866	1,079	1,529	1,915	2,379	3,234	3,932	4,739	6,979	7,758	11,530	10,697	12,387	17,139
Claims on Central Government	22a	686	971	1,202	967	1,021	1,179	1,477	1,640	1,761	1,803	2,214	2,587	2,946	3,505	3,753
Claims on Private Sector	22d	2,664	3,110	4,172	6,141	6,840	7,688	8,601	9,511	11,035	13,652	17,823	22,867	27,222	32,578	35,602
Demand Deposits	24	904	‡954	1,380	1,518	1,552	1,834	2,053	2,169	2,343	2,765	2,998	3,860	4,161	4,272	4,247
Time and Savings Deposits	25	2,217	‡2,445	2,897	3,470	4,066	4,692	5,202	5,394	5,936	7,193	9,930	12,429	14,647	16,918	18,254
Foreign Liabilities	26c	523	‡1,129	1,704	2,747	2,712	2,964	4,164	5,111	6,606	8,347	9,448	14,216	14,098	18,614	24,966
Central Government Deposits	26d	82	107	293	715	1,052	1,144	1,119	1,092	1,209	1,488	2,360	2,818	3,212	3,354	3,526
Other Items (Net)	27r	448	‡502	470	851	935	1,172	1,390	1,978	2,228	3,539	4,251	5,089	6,467	7,212	7,561
Monetary Survey													*Millions of Singapore Dollars:*			
Foreign Assets (Net)	31n	3,235	‡3,829	4,303	4,578	5,702	6,896	7,326	7,837	9,597	11,179	11,901	12,691	14,429	13,439	14,833
Domestic Credit	32	1,163	1,090	1,637	2,578	2,619	3,048	4,206	4,638	5,467	6,951	10,654	20,195	20,189	28,789	33,029
Claims on Central Govt. (Net)	32an	-1,501	-2,020	-2,535	-3,564	-4,222	-4,641	-4,397	-4,875	-5,571	-6,704	-7,172	-2,673	-7,037	-3,792	-2,579
Claims on Private Sector	32d	2,664	3,110	4,172	6,142	6,841	7,689	8,603	9,513	11,038	13,655	17,826	22,868	27,226	32,581	35,608
Money	34	1,631	‡1,760	2,385	2,632	2,858	3,472	4,000	4,412	4,926	5,706	6,135	7,242	8,157	8,607	8,866
Quasi-Money	35	2,217	‡2,445	2,897	3,470	4,066	4,692	5,202	5,394	5,936	7,193	9,930	12,429	14,647	16,918	18,254
Other Items (Net)	37r	550	‡714	658	1,054	1,397	1,780	2,330	2,669	4,202	5,231	6,490	13,215	11,814	16,703	20,742
Money plus Quasi-Money	35l	3,848	‡4,205	5,282	6,102	6,924	8,164	9,202	9,806	10,862	12,899	16,065	19,671	22,804	25,525	27,120
Other Banking Institutions																
Finance Companies													*Millions of Singapore Dollars:*			
Cash	40	184	240	279	318	395	366	398	384	380	393	441	677	662	608	724
Foreign Assets	41	31	33	42	28	24	21	22	20	13	15	18	19	81	122	225
Claims on Private Sector	42d	278	372	479	738	888	947	1,082	1,229	1,486	1,936	2,509	3,422	4,421	5,593	6,027
Time and Savings Deposits	45	389	542	675	843	1,021	1,043	1,183	1,295	1,503	1,806	2,108	2,937	3,707	4,544	5,265
Foreign Liabilities	46c	12	11	9	11	10	5	9	10	7	9	15	6	9	22	15
Capital Accounts	47a	89	102	119	181	227	242	268	286	308	363	476	672	816	1,043	1,117
Other Items (Net)	47r	3	-11	-2	49	48	43	43	42	61	166	368	502	632	714	580
Post Office: Savings Deposits	45.. i	73	91	125	171	269	548	957	1,589	2,029	2,525	2,757	3,266	5,058	5,917	7,287
Nonbank Financial Institutions													*Millions of Singapore Dollars:*			
Cash	40.. s	18	21	32	17	25	45	52	56	67	74	106	146	180	235	298
Foreign Assets	41.. s	23	25	23	22	20	78	78	78	78	78	78	78	78	78	78
Claims on Central Government	42a. s	42	46	55	62	70	79	97	127	135	156	152	171	211	241	238
Claims on Private Sector	42d. s	59	69	80	119	129	732	732	732	732	732	732	732	732	732	732
Fixed Assets	42h. s	14	16	19	19	27	30	31	32	34	35	37	41	58	63	70
Incr.in Total Assets(Within Per.)	49z. s	15	21	37	28	33	51	50	57	68	74	126	142	154	193	189
Liquid Liabilities	55l	4,125	‡4,599	5,803	6,797	7,819	9,390	10,944	12,306	14,014	16,837	20,489	25,198	30,908	35,378	38,948
Interest Rates													*Percent Per Annum*			
Money Market Rate	60b	....	....	3.57	11.69	8.90	4.39	4.15	4.76	5.93	7.76	10.98	11.54	7.92	7.11	7.67
Eurodollar Rate in Singapore	60d	....	....	....	....	6.44	5.12	7.31	11.88	15.06	18.25	14.38	9.56	9.94	8.75	
Deposit Rate	60l	....	....	....	....	....	4.06	4.75	6.20	9.37	10.71	7.22	6.31	6.98		
Lending Rate	60p	....	....	....	....	....	....	7.17	8.50	11.72	13.65	10.23	9.05	9.72		
Prices, Production, Labor													*Index Numbers (1995=100):*			
Wholesale Prices	63	....	....	....	....	86.1	84.8	90.5	94.6	96.1	109.9	131.4	136.5	130.8	126.0	125.2
Consumer Prices	64	37.7	38.4	39.2	46.9	57.3	58.8	57.7	59.5	62.4	65.0	70.5	76.3	79.3	80.2	82.3
Manufacturing Production	66ey	11.5	13.7	16.2	19.0	19.7	19.6	21.9	23.9	26.7	30.8	34.5	37.9	‡35.8	36.5	39.8
													Number in Thousands:			
Labor Force	67d	....	....	....	....	....	....	....	....	....	....	....	....	....	....	
Employment	67e	....	....	....	....	....	....	....	....	....	....	....	....	....	....	
Unemployment	67c	....	....	....	....	....	....	....	....	....	....	....	....	....	....	
Unemployment Rate (%)	67r	....	....	....	....	....	....	....	....	....	....	....	....	....	....	2.7

1985	1986	1987	1988	1989	1990	1991	1992	1993	1994	1995	1996	1997	1998	1999		
															Exchange Rates	
End of Period																
2.3122	2.6604	2.8352	2.6190	2.4895	2.4818	2.3323	2.2617	2.2087	2.1324	2.1023	2.0129	2.2607	2.3380	2.2866	Market Rate	aa
End of Period (ae)	*Period Average (rf)*															
2.1050	2.1750	1.9985	1.9462	1.8944	1.7445	1.6305	1.6449	1.6080	1.4607	1.4143	1.3998	1.6755	1.6605	1.6660	Market Rate	ae
2.2002	2.1774	2.1060	2.0124	1.9503	1.8125	1.7276	1.6290	1.6158	1.5274	1.4174	1.4100	1.4848	1.6736	1.6950	Market Rate	rf
Period Averages																
64.5	65.1	67.3	70.4	72.7	78.3	82.1	87.0	87.7	92.9	100.0	100.5	95.7	84.8	83.6	Market Rate	ah x
88.3	77.7	74.3	74.7	79.7	84.9	88.8	91.7	93.4	97.1	100.0	104.7	107.3	106.7	101.2	Nominal Effective Exchange Rate	ne c
102.6	87.5	82.1	81.0	84.6	89.1	92.2	94.0	94.8	98.4	100.0	103.5	105.7	101.8	95.8	Real Effective Exchange Rate	re c
End of Period															**Fund Position**	
92.4	92.4	92.4	92.4	92.4	92.4	92.4	357.6	357.6	357.6	357.6	357.6	357.6	357.6	862.5	Quota	2f. s
66.0	73.8	81.2	79.0	79.4	81.4	81.3	49.4	56.9	24.1	33.1	42.5	52.2	64.9	89.2	SDRs	1b. s
80.6	79.9	79.1	77.9	80.1	68.9	60.1	113.4	157.4	172.8	199.8	204.7	248.4	297.6	303.4	Reserve Position in the Fund	1c. s
—	—	—	—	—	—	—	—	—	—	—	—	—	31.3	—	*of which:* Outstg.Fund Borrowing	2c
—	—	—	—	—	—	—	—	—	—	—	—	—	—	—	Total Fund Cred.&Loans Outstg.	2tl
End of Period															**International Liquidity**	
12,847	12,939	15,227	17,073	20,345	27,748	34,133	39,885	48,361	58,177	68,695	76,847	71,289	74,928	76,843	Total Reserves (see notes)	1l. d
72	90	115	106	104	116	116	68	78	35	49	61	70	91	122	SDRs	1b. d
89	98	112	105	105	98	86	156	216	252	297	294	335	419	416	Reserve Position in the Fund	1c. d
12,686	12,751	15,000	16,861	20,136	27,535	33,931	39,661	48,066	57,890	68,349	76,491	70,883	74,418	76,304	Foreign Exchange	1d. d
9,595	12,052	14,761	17,763	25,744	25,142	25,814	31,396	31,345	38,992	39,115	43,079	46,963	45,153	55,854	Deposit Money Banks: Assets	7a. d
12,829	13,441	15,367	17,360	23,947	24,937	24,569	29,450	32,085	40,976	46,753	55,327	62,784	50,466	53,565	Liabilities	7b. d
115	101	113	89	97	139	120	129	124	163	168	12	124	107	80	Other Banking Insts.: Assets	7e. d
5	2	5	11	6	3	3	6	10	27	19	12	11	5	8	Liabilities	7f. d
110,763	149,821	194,968	230,252	280,224	321,451	296,259	292,475	306,703	326,698	373,774	396,655	425,242	395,279	367,891	ACU: Foreign Assets	7k. d
116,881	157,710	201,466	235,012	284,414	329,919	304,431	298,497	321,390	340,295	391,907	419,343	447,032	417,074	384,960	Foreign Liabilities	7m. d
End of Period															**Monetary Authorities**	
27,080	28,158	30,442	33,277	38,607	48,521	55,803	65,788	77,867	85,166	97,337	107,751	119,617	124,584	128,457	Foreign Assets	11
6,944	7,319	7,910	8,932	10,316	11,056	12,232	13,531	14,669	15,577	17,040	18,189	19,200	16,641	21,395	Reserve Money	14
4,739	5,034	5,440	5,997	6,610	7,109	7,497	8,279	8,942	9,420	9,907	10,293	10,704	10,146	11,315	*of which:* Currency Outside DMBs	14a
6,159	5,491	6,247	7,676	13,465	17,678	20,177	25,077	30,080	35,669	44,471	51,554	57,520	57,484	58,994	Central Government Deposits	16d
13,977	15,348	16,285	16,669	14,826	19,787	23,394	27,180	33,118	33,920	35,826	38,008	42,897	50,459	48,068	Other Items (Net)	17r
End of Period															**Deposit Money Banks**	
2,219	2,318	2,476	2,932	3,709	3,951	4,750	5,301	5,770	6,150	7,152	7,900	8,498	6,423	10,076	Reserves	20
20,197	26,214	29,499	34,570	48,769	43,860	42,089	51,644	50,402	56,956	55,321	60,302	78,687	74,976	93,053	Foreign Assets	21
4,020	3,976	5,287	5,412	6,826	7,923	9,765	11,587	12,758	13,568	15,754	17,538	18,883	26,477	30,949	Claims on Central Government	22a
35,790	34,484	36,693	40,789	48,757	55,798	62,725	68,851	79,282	91,375	109,885	127,272	143,409	154,844	150,199	Claims on Private Sector	22d
4,046	4,788	5,591	5,961	7,135	8,152	8,933	10,236	13,940	13,991	15,443	16,747	16,807	17,093	19,794	Demand Deposits	24
19,363	21,134	26,059	30,130	37,801	46,584	53,112	57,213	59,248	70,569	76,618	84,911	95,933	133,545	143,365	Time and Savings Deposits	25
27,006	29,235	30,710	33,786	45,366	43,502	40,060	48,443	51,592	59,854	66,123	77,447	105,194	83,799	89,240	Foreign Liabilities	26c
3,525	2,507	2,212	3,560	5,344	4,733	5,268	5,744	6,385	6,584	7,538	6,896	1,529	1,766	1,632	Central Government Deposits	26d
8,286	9,328	9,383	10,266	12,415	8,561	11,956	15,747	17,047	17,051	22,390	27,011	30,014	26,517	30,246	Other Items (Net)	27r
End of Period															**Monetary Survey**	
19,930	25,002	29,137	33,979	41,933	48,780	57,718	68,397	76,196	81,833	86,164	90,260	92,836	115,512	130,951	Foreign Assets (Net)	31n
30,134	30,471	33,530	34,973	36,782	41,317	47,053	49,624	55,583	62,699	73,638	86,368	103,251	122,081	120,535	Domestic Credit	32
−5,664	−4,022	−3,172	−5,824	−11,983	−14,488	−15,680	−19,234	−23,707	−28,685	−36,255	−40,912	−40,166	−32,773	−29,677	Claims on Central Govt. (Net)	32an
35,790	34,493	36,702	40,797	48,765	55,805	62,733	68,858	79,290	91,384	109,893	127,280	143,417	154,854	150,212	Claims on Private Sector	32d
8,785	9,822	11,031	11,958	13,745	15,261	16,430	18,515	22,882	23,411	25,350	27,040	27,511	27,239	31,109	Money	34
19,363	21,134	26,059	30,130	37,801	46,584	53,112	57,213	59,248	70,569	76,618	84,911	95,933	133,545	143,365	Quasi-Money	35
21,916	24,517	25,577	26,864	27,169	28,252	35,229	42,293	49,649	50,552	57,834	64,677	72,643	76,809	77,012	Other Items (Net)	37r
28,148	30,956	37,090	42,088	51,546	61,845	69,542	75,728	82,130	93,980	101,968	111,951	123,444	160,784	174,474	Money plus Quasi-Money	35l
															Other Banking Institutions	
															Finance Companies	
End of Period																
875	1,085	1,136	1,010	1,117	1,557	1,996	1,953	1,788	2,574	2,848	2,561	2,513	2,822	3,046	Cash	40
242	221	225	173	183	243	196	212	200	238	237	215	208	179	133	Foreign Assets	41
5,549	5,338	5,759	6,684	8,196	8,958	9,555	10,251	12,047	15,110	16,717	17,073	18,034	16,891	15,751	Claims on Private Sector	42d
5,004	4,886	5,372	5,821	7,422	8,520	9,097	9,552	10,558	13,753	15,435	15,058	15,734	15,421	14,387	Time and Savings Deposits	45
11	4	10	22	12	6	6	10	17	39	26	16	18	9	14	Foreign Liabilities	46c
1,132	1,148	1,177	1,250	1,333	1,416	1,510	1,679	1,850	2,203	2,621	3,015	3,269	3,371	3,408	Capital Accounts	47a
519	607	562	774	728	815	1,133	1,176	1,611	1,927	1,720	1,760	1,734	1,091	1,121	Other Items (Net)	47r
9,129	10,559	11,165	12,140	13,050	13,240	15,531	18,007	20,085	20,127	22,188	24,734	25,130	....	....	Post Office: Savings Deposits	45.. i
End of Period															**Nonbank Financial Institutions**	
420	353	384	478	697	974	954	761	1,160	1,772	2,269	2,657	3,041	3,809	4,036	Cash	40.. s
78	171	250	175	200	205	246	830	1,160	1,090	1,546	2,082	2,055	2,696	3,574	Foreign Assets	41.. s
232	217	232	300	422	440	567	1,337	1,190	918	901	746	815	933	2,417	Claims on Central Government	42a. s
732	980	1,215	1,524	1,766	2,198	2,854	2,919	4,270	5,488	6,715	8,261	10,095	10,392	16,333	Claims on Private Sector	42d. s
66	71	85	95	105	116	131	237	313	335	657	1,173	1,377	1,861	1,874	Fixed Assets	42h. s
198	269	391	422	644	785	830	1,375	1,944	1,682	2,481	2,996	2,379	2,564	8,170	Incr.in Total Assets(Within Per.)	49z. s
41,407	45,315	52,492	59,040	70,901	82,048	92,174	101,333	110,985	125,286	136,743	149,182	161,795	....	....	Liquid Liabilities	55l
Percent Per Annum															**Interest Rates**	
5.38	4.27	3.89	4.30	5.34	6.61	4.76	2.74	2.50	3.68	2.56	2.93	4.35	5.00	2.04	Money Market Rate	60b
8.13	6.75	8.00	9.31	8.38	7.75	4.38	3.50	3.38	6.50	5.63	5.63	5.91	5.13	6.06	Eurodollar Rate in Singapore	60d
4.99	3.91	2.89	2.74	3.21	4.67	4.63	2.86	2.30	3.00	3.50	3.41	3.47	4.60	1.68	Deposit Rate	60l
7.93	6.82	6.10	5.96	6.21	7.36	7.58	5.95	5.39	5.88	6.37	6.26	6.32	7.44	5.80	Lending Rate	60p
Period Averages															**Prices, Production, Labor**	
122.4	103.9	111.8	109.7	⌶112.5	114.5	109.8	105.0	100.4	100.0	100.0	100.1	99.0	⌶96.0	98.0	Wholesale Prices	63
82.7	81.6	82.0	83.2	85.2	88.1	91.2	93.2	95.4	98.3	100.0	101.4	103.4	⌶103.1	103.2	Consumer Prices	64
⌶36.9	40.1	47.1	55.7	61.3	67.4	71.1	72.8	80.2	90.6	⌶100.0	103.3	108.0	107.6	122.5	Manufacturing Production	66ey
Period Averages																
....	....	....	....	....	....	....	1,620	1,636	1,693	1,748	1,801	1,876	1,932	....	Labor Force	67d
1,234	1,214	1,267	1,332	1,394	1,537	1,524	1,576	1,592	1,649	1,702	1,748	1,831	1,870	....	Employment	67e
....	....	84	62	46	31	26	30	43	44	44	47	54	46	62	Unemployment	67c
4.1	6.5	4.7	3.3	2.2	1.7	1.9	2.7	2.7	2.6	2.7	3.0	2.4	3.2	....	Unemployment Rate (%)	67r

Singapore

		1970	1971	1972	1973	1974	1975	1976	1977	1978	1979	1980	1981	1982	1983	1984
International Transactions																*Millions of Singapore Dollars*
Exports	70	4,756	5,371	6,149	8,907	14,155	12,758	16,266	20,091	22,986	30,940	41,452	44,291	44,473	46,155	51,340
Imports, c.i.f.	71	7,535	8,658	9,539	12,513	20,406	19,269	22,406	25,522	29,630	38,352	51,355	58,249	60,244	59,504	61,134
																1995=100
Volume of Exports	72	....	....	6	8	9	8	9	11	12	Ɪ15	16	16	17	19	21
Volume of Imports	73	....	....	11	12	Ɪ14	14	14	16	17	20	23	26	28	28	29
Exports (Direct Prices)	76	....	....	....	....	....	....	....	....	....	125.8	155.1	160.9	156.0	148.6	142.8
Imports (Direct Prices)	76.x	....	....	....	....	82.3	80.9	88.2	92.7	96.2	108.7	126.9	129.0	123.3	120.1	119.3
Balance of Payments																*Millions of US Dollars*
Current Account, n.i.e.	78ald	....	....	−495	−519	−1,021	−584	−567	−295	−453	−736	−1,563	−1,470	−1,296	−610	−385
Goods: Exports f.o.b.	78aad			2,170	3,599	5,906	5,481	6,654	8,245	10,123	14,248	19,430	21,090	21,016	21,894	24,091
Goods: Imports f.o.b.	78abd			−3,127	−4,735	−7,764	−7,511	−8,442	−9,729	−12,090	−16,450	−22,400	−25,785	−26,196	−26,252	−26,734
Trade Balance	78acd			−958	−1,137	−1,859	−2,030	−1,788	−1,484	−1,967	−2,202	−2,971	−4,695	−5,181	−4,358	−2,643
Services: Credit	78add			961	1,377	1,931	2,416	2,364	2,594	3,127	3,595	4,856	7,184	8,128	7,834	6,153
Services: Debit	78aed			−484	−655	−900	−966	−1,054	−1,277	−1,547	−2,050	−2,912	−3,254	−3,613	−3,782	−4,024
Balance on Goods & Services	78afd			−481	−414	−828	−580	−478	−167	−388	−657	−1,027	−765	−665	−306	−513
Income: Credit	78agd			113	167	225	380	370	391	528	806	953	1,092	1,243	1,300	1,603
Income: Debit	78ahd			−129	−268	−380	−345	−410	−475	−554	−849	−1,382	−1,644	−1,668	−1,390	−1,252
Balance on Gds, Serv. & Inc.	78aid			−497	−515	−982	−545	−518	−251	−414	−701	−1,456	−1,317	−1,091	−396	−162
Current Transfers, n.i.e.: Credit	78ajd			79	103	70	65	49	48	64	86	87	130	98	121	121
Current Transfers: Debit	78akd			−76	−107	−109	−104	−98	−93	−102	−121	−194	−283	−303	−336	−344
Capital Account, n.i.e.	78bcd	....	....	—	—	—	—	—	—	—	—	—	—	—	—	—
Capital Account, n.i.e.: Credit	78bad			—	—	—	—	—	—	—	—	—	—	—	—	—
Capital Account: Debit	78bbd			—	—	—	—	—	—	—	—	—	—	—	—	—
Financial Account, n.i.e.	78bjd	....	....	395	722	500	580	849	607	1,013	998	1,582	2,167	2,309	2,463	1,580
Direct Investment Abroad	78bdd			−20	−26	−30	−38	−45	−85	−113	−167	−98	15	−304	−49	−92
Dir. Invest. in Rep. Econ., n.i.e.	78bed			161	353	340	292	231	291	300	836	1,236	1,660	1,602	1,134	1,302
Portfolio Investment Assets	78bfd			−13	−17	−20	−29	−32	−40	−139	−108	−121	−193	−106	−160	−161
Equity Securities	78bkd			−7	−9	−9	−12	−15	−23	−36	−63	−25	−171	−140	−218	−64
Debt Securities	78bld			−6	−9	−10	−17	−17	−17	−102	−45	−96	−22	34	58	−97
Portfolio Investment Liab., n.i.e.	78bgd			77	50	35	27	82	136	12	30	134	145	78	111	10
Equity Securities	78bmd			26	50	35	27	47	14	18	43	146	157	98	201	18
Debt Securities	78bnd			51	—	—	—	36	121	−6	−12	−13	−12	−20	−89	−8
Financial Derivatives Assets	78bwd			....	....	....	....	....	....	....	....	....	....	....	....	....
Financial Derivatives Liabilities	78bxd			....	....	....	....	....	....	....	....	....	....	....	....	....
Other Investment Assets	78bhd			−98	−212	−195	−235	−399	−347	−545	−1,112	−741	−2,645	184	−824	−3,071
Monetary Authorities	78bod			....	....	....	....	....	....	....	....	....	....	....	....	....
General Government	78bpd			—	−8	−6	−1	−2	−4	−6	—	—	—	—	—	—
Banks	78bqd			−76	−183	−158	−196	−346	−261	−355	−974	−363	−1,785	390	−800	−2,228
Other Sectors	78brd			−22	−22	−30	−38	−51	−82	−184	−138	−377	−860	−206	−24	−843
Other Investment Liab., n.i.e.	78bid			289	575	370	563	1,012	651	1,499	1,519	1,173	3,186	856	2,251	3,593
Monetary Authorities	78bsd			....	....	....	....	....	....	....	....	....	....	....	....	....
General Government	78btd			16	18	7	10	7	5	18	−4	−2	−3	5	5	−3
Banks	78bud			205	424	−14	106	429	347	650	790	500	2,257	−55	2,137	2,978
Other Sectors	78bvd			69	132	377	446	576	299	832	733	675	932	906	109	618
Net Errors and Omissions	78cad			435	210	816	412	17	1	104	254	643	212	165	−793	329
Overall Balance	78cbd			335	413	295	407	298	313	665	516	663	909	1,177	1,059	1,524
Reserves and Related Items	79dad			−335	−413	−295	−407	−298	−313	−665	−516	−663	−909	−1,177	−1,059	−1,524
Reserve Assets	79dbd			−335	−413	−295	−407	−298	−313	−665	−516	−663	−909	−1,177	−1,059	−1,524
Use of Fund Credit and Loans	79dcd			—	—	—	—	—	—	—	—	—	—	—	—	—
Exceptional Financing	79ded			....	....	....	....	....	....	....	....	....	....	....	....	....
Government Finance																*Millions of Singapore Dollars:*
Deficit (-) or Surplus	80	201	45	213	133	109	284	53	102	42	77	99	754	1,013	922	2,088
Total Revenue and Grants	81y	1,328	1,520	1,872	2,158	2,691	3,370	3,450	3,702	4,126	4,710	6,149	7,663	9,905	11,462	11,471
Revenue	81	1,328	1,520	1,872	2,158	2,691	3,370	3,450	3,702	4,126	4,710	6,149	7,663	9,905	11,462	11,471
Grants	81z															
Exp. & Lending Minus Repay.	82z	1,127	1,475	1,659	2,025	2,582	3,086	3,397	3,600	4,084	4,633	6,050	6,909	8,892	10,540	9,383
Expenditure	82	1,014	1,237	1,320	1,520	1,839	2,287	2,673	3,093	3,581	3,918	4,944	5,712	6,724	7,812	8,396
Lending Minus Repayments	83	113	238	339	505	743	799	724	507	503	715	1,106	1,197	2,168	2,728	987
Total Financing	80h	−201	−45	−213	−133	−109	−284	−53	−102	−42	−77	−99	−754	−1,013	−922	−2,088
Total Net Borrowing	84	590	839	527	390	755	1,243	1,579	1,963	1,548	1,724	2,187	2,351	3,835	5,116	3,869
Use of Cash Balances	87	−791	−884	−740	−523	−864	−1,527	−1,632	−2,065	−1,590	−1,801	−2,286	−3,105	−4,848	−6,038	−5,957
Total Debt by Currency	88z	2,017	2,734	3,483	3,758	4,522	5,698	7,318	9,133	10,695	12,402	14,675	17,138	20,730	25,032	28,078
National	88b	....	....	....	....	....	....	....	....	....	....	....	....	....	....	....
Foreign	89b	....	....	....	....	....	....	....	....	....	....	....	....	....	....	....
National Accounts																*Millions of Singapore Dollars*
Exports (Net)	90n	−1,179	−1,484	−1,378	−1,041	−2,133	−1,508	−1,199	−424	−898	−1,445	−2,216	−1,634	−1,441	−664	−1,113
Government Consumption	91f	693	861	990	1,118	1,298	1,423	1,542	1,716	1,965	2,034	2,447	2,789	3,570	3,995	4,333
Gross Fixed Capital Formation	93e	1,889	2,473	3,054	3,561	4,695	4,698	5,288	5,458	6,365	7,520	10,203	12,785	15,506	17,464	19,122
Increase/Decrease(-) in Stocks	93i	356	271	300	439	897	336	694	341	592	1,380	1,425	802	153	132	295
Private Consumption	96f	3,920	4,532	5,071	6,340	7,658	8,121	8,606	9,269	10,149	11,245	12,911	14,329	15,283	16,202	17,570
Gross Domestic Product (GDP)	99b	5,805	6,823	8,156	10,205	12,543	13,373	14,651	16,039	17,830	20,523	25,091	29,339	32,670	36,733	40,048
Net Factor Inc/Pmts(-) Abroad	98.n	56	−10	−21	−224	−288	−28	−81	−187	−43	−79	−902	−1,148	−894	−172	767
Gross National Income (GNI)	99a	5,861	6,813	8,135	9,981	12,255	13,345	14,570	15,852	17,787	20,444	24,189	28,191	31,776	36,561	40,815
GDP Volume 1968 prices	99b.p	5,579	6,277	7,120	7,941	8,445	8,790	9,447	....	....	....	....	....	....	....	....
GDP Volume 1985 prices	99b.p	....	....	....	....	....	....	20,549	22,143	24,046	26,285	28,833	31,603	33,772	36,537	39,573
GDP Volume 1990 Prices	99b.p	....	....	....	....	....	....	....	....	....	....	....	....	....	....	46,092
GDP Volume (1995=100)	99bvp	13.7	15.5	17.5	19.6	20.8	21.7	23.3	25.1	27.2	29.8	32.7	35.8	38.3	41.4	44.8
GDP Deflator (1995=100)	99bip	35.7	37.3	39.3	44.1	51.0	52.2	53.2	54.1	55.4	58.3	65.0	69.3	72.2	75.1	75.6
																Millions:
Population	99z	2.07	2.11	2.15	2.19	2.23	2.26	2.29	2.33	2.35	2.38	2.41	2.44	2.47	2.41	2.44

	1985	1986	1987	1988	1989	1990	1991	1992	1993	1994	1995	1996	1997	1998	1999		
International Transactions																	
Millions of Singapore Dollars																	
Exports	50,179	48,986	60,266	79,051	87,117	95,206	101,880	103,351	119,475	147,327	167,515	176,271	185,613	183,763	194,305		70
Imports, c.i.f.	57,819	55,543	68,416	88,228	96,864	109,806	114,195	117,530	137,602	156,397	176,317	185,183	196,606	174,867	188,143		71
1995=100																	
Volume of Exports	21	24	29	38	43	46	52	57	67	86	100	106	114	115	121		72
Volume of Imports	28	31	35	45	49	56	61	65	77	89	100	106	115	104	110		73
Exports (Direct Prices)	140.0	120.3	124.4	122.7	I122.1	122.7	116.1	108.5	106.1	101.8	100.0	99.1	97.6	I95.7	95.9		76
Imports (Direct Prices)	116.1	102.5	111.0	111.4	I111.4	110.4	106.8	103.2	101.1	100.1	100.0	98.8	97.4	I95.5	97.1		76.x
Balance of Payments																	
Minus Sign Indicates Debit																	
Current Account, n.i.e.	-4	319	-109	1,937	2,964	3,122	4,880	5,915	4,211	11,400	14,436	13,898	16,912	21,025	21,254		78al d
Goods: Exports f.o.b.	23,187	22,738	29,096	40,703	45,700	54,679	61,333	66,565	77,858	97,919	118,456	126,010	125,746	110,591	115,639		78aa d
Goods: Imports f.o.b.	-24,705	-23,679	-30,239	-40,675	-46,012	-56,311	-61,443	-68,387	-80,582	-96,565	-117,479	-123,786	-124,628	-95,780	-104,337		78ab d
Trade Balance	-1,518	-940	-1,143	28	-313	-1,633	-110	-1,821	-2,724	1,354	977	2,224	1,118	14,811	11,303		78ac d
Services: Credit	4,688	4,806	5,795	7,563	9,658	12,811	13,823	16,200	18,597	23,044	29,817	29,670	30,217	18,926	23,693		78ad d
Services: Debit	-3,554	-3,808	-4,612	-5,797	-6,849	-8,642	-9,124	-9,537	-11,321	-13,898	-17,761	-19,732	-19,107	-17,490	-18,879		78ae d
Balance on Goods & Services	-385	58	40	1,794	2,497	2,537	4,589	4,842	4,552	10,500	13,033	12,162	12,228	16,246	16,117		78af d
Income: Credit	1,854	2,230	2,921	3,882	4,752	6,508	7,558	8,214	8,075	9,783	12,717	14,668	15,702	14,471	15,422		78ag d
Income: Debit	-1,260	-1,786	-2,884	-3,495	-3,959	-5,502	-6,801	-6,666	-7,880	-8,222	-10,429	-11,859	-9,831	-8,509	-9,122		78ah d
Balance on Gds, Serv. & Inc.	210	502	76	2,181	3,289	3,543	5,346	6,390	4,747	12,061	15,321	14,971	18,099	22,209	22,417		78ai d
Current Transfers, n.i.e.: Credit	113	120	108	111	114	123	129	172	140	145	156	157	150	136	134		78aj d
Current Transfers: Debit	-326	-303	-293	-356	-440	-544	-595	-647	-676	-806	-1,042	-1,229	-1,338	-1,320	-1,297		78ak d
Capital Account, n.i.e.	—	—	-49	-55	-41	-22	-34	-38	-71	-84	-71	-139	-173	-226	-191		78bc d
Capital Account, n.i.e.: Credit	—	—	—	—	—	—	—	—	—	—	—	—	—	—	—		78ba d
Capital Account: Debit	—	—	-49	-55	-41	-22	-34	-38	-71	-84	-71	-139	-173	-226	-191		78bb d
Financial Account, n.i.e.	698	-445	470	987	1,251	3,947	2,346	1,793	-1,212	-8,841	-4,734	-5,198	-13,234	-21,313	-17,367		78bj d
Direct Investment Abroad	-238	-181	-206	-118	-882	-2,034	-526	-1,317	-2,152	-4,577	-6,281	-6,935	-8,858	1,525	-3,943		78bd d
Dir. Invest. in Rep. Econ., n.i.e.	1,047	1,710	2,836	3,655	2,887	5,575	4,887	2,204	4,686	8,550	7,206	8,984	8,085	5,493	6,984		78be d
Portfolio Investment Assets	-347	-287	-67	-329	-451	-1,610	-665	1,091	-7,833	-7,840	-7,769	-11,955	-12,859	-8,741	-9,229		78bf d
Equity Securities	-259	-121	-104	-260	-358	-468	-524	165	-7,555	-7,414	-7,972	-10,364	-12,942	-8,459	-8,859		78bk d
Debt Securities	-88	-167	37	-69	-93	-1,142	-141	926	-278	-426	203	-1,591	83	-282	-369		78bl d
Portfolio Investment Liab., n.i.e.	521	-261	320	36	375	573	-242	1,398	2,867	114	410	940	-50	897	2,144		78bg d
Equity Securities	531	-194	321	36	400	573	-242	1,398	2,759	169	462	962	-62	905	2,146		78bm f
Debt Securities	-10	-68	-2	—	-25	—	—	—	108	-55	-52	-21	12	-8	-2		78bn d
Financial Derivatives Assets	....	....	....	....	....	....	....	....	....	....	....	....	....	....	....		78bw d
Financial Derivatives Liabilities	....	....	....	....	....	....	....	....	....	....	....	....	....	....	....		78bx d
Other Investment Assets	-2,250	-3,197	-2,272	-2,589	-8,091	-220	1,831	-6,685	-7,104	-10,999	-10,281	-12,079	-35,644	-4,644	-17,935		78bh d
Monetary Authorities																	78bo d
General Government	—	—	—	—	—	—	-1	—	—	—	—	—	-1	—	-661		78bp d
Banks	-1,390	-2,763	-1,560	-2,520	-7,280	2,708	1,025	-5,866	769	-4,291	1,154	-3,533	-12,382	2,218	-10,705		78bq d
Other Sectors	-860	-434	-711	-68	-811	-2,928	806	-819	-7,872	-6,708	-11,435	-8,547	-23,261	-6,862	-6,569		78br d
Other Investment Liab., n.i.e.	1,964	1,772	-141	332	7,413	1,664	-2,940	5,101	8,324	5,911	11,981	15,846	36,092	-15,842	4,611		78bi d
Monetary Authorities																	78bs d
General Government	-9	-13	-18	-20	-17	-37	-15	-9	-9	-4	-3	—	—	—	—		78bt d
Banks	927	1,023	700	1,529	5,937	-1,028	-1,992	5,146	1,949	5,409	4,423	8,031	18,687	-12,787	3,267		78bu d
Other Sectors	1,046	762	-823	-1,177	1,493	2,729	-933	-36	6,384	506	7,562	7,814	17,405	-3,055	1,344		78bv d
Net Errors and Omissions	643	664	782	-1,210	-1,436	-1,616	-2,995	-1,570	4,650	2,261	-1,031	-1,165	4,435	3,479	498		78ca d
Overall Balance	1,337	538	1,095	1,659	2,738	5,431	4,197	6,100	7,578	4,736	8,599	7,396	7,940	2,966	4,194		78cb d
Reserves and Related Items	-1,337	-538	-1,095	-1,659	-2,738	-5,431	-4,197	-6,100	-7,578	-4,736	-8,599	-7,396	-7,940	-2,966	-4,194		79da d
Reserve Assets	-1,337	-538	-1,095	-1,659	-2,738	-5,431	-4,197	-6,100	-7,578	-4,736	-8,599	-7,396	-7,940	-2,966	-4,194		79db d
Use of Fund Credit and Loans	—	—	—	—	—	—	—	—	—	—	—	—	—	—	—		79dc d
Exceptional Financing	....	....	....	....	....	....	....	....	....	....	....	....	....	....	....		79de d
Government Finance																	
Year Ending December 31																	
Deficit (-) or Surplus	595	707	-2,040	3,139	689	6,495	7,591	9,537	12,998	13,086	15,870	18,868	13,612	23,163	14,577		80
Total Revenue and Grants	10,854	17,262	12,076	14,117	15,915	19,021	22,001	25,355	29,488	33,094	40,026	47,617	57,048	59,724	49,950		81y
Revenue	10,854	17,262	12,076	14,117	15,915	19,021	22,001	25,355	29,488	33,094	40,026	47,617	57,048	59,724	49,950		81
Grants																	81z
Exp. & Lending Minus Repay.	10,259	16,555	14,116	10,978	15,226	12,526	14,410	15,818	16,490	20,008	24,156	28,749	43,436	36,561	35,373		82z
Expenditure	10,597	9,949	14,550	11,914	10,543	13,256	13,893	14,804	14,339	15,670	17,419	20,681	29,222	25,586	26,665		82
Lending Minus Repayments	-338	6,606	-434	-936	4,683	-730	517	1,014	2,151	4,338	6,737	8,068	14,214	10,975	8,708		83
Total Financing	-595	-707	2,040	-3,139	-689	-6,495	-7,591	-9,537	-12,998	-13,086	-15,870	-18,868	-13,612	-23,163	-14,577		80h
Total Net Borrowing	4,978	4,118	5,933	33,617	5,779	7,370	10,518	-7,731	5,309	12,552	16,402	10,159	12,215	22,540	17,148		84
Use of Cash Balances	-5,573	-4,825	-3,893	-36,756	-6,468	-13,865	-18,109	-1,806	-18,307	-25,638	-32,272	-29,027	-25,827	-45,703	-31,725		87
Total Debt by Currency	32,173	33,905	38,353	41,936	46,339	51,565	59,163	67,376	69,944	75,467	86,630	94,831	102,372	115,183	125,777		88z
National	....	....	....	....	....	....	....	....	....	....		94,831	102,372	115,183	125,777		88b
Foreign												—	—	—	—		89b
National Accounts																	
Millions of Singapore Dollars																	
Exports (Net)	-946	143	83	3,609	4,869	4,598	7,928	7,887	7,356	16,039	18,473	17,596	18,134	25,117	....		90n
Government Consumption	5,549	5,270	5,315	5,337	6,013	6,780	7,351	7,459	8,723	9,008	10,124	12,207	13,395	14,080	....		91f
Gross Fixed Capital Formation	16,425	14,132	14,405	15,667	18,906	21,578	25,095	28,806	32,753	36,202	39,973	49,549	54,382	52,260	....		93e
Increase/Decrease(-) in Stocks	126	585	1,893	1,663	1,459	2,771	656	269	2,505	-500	894	-1,771	242	-4,904	....		93i
Private Consumption	17,553	18,405	20,697	24,390	27,664	30,847	33,536	36,415	42,232	47,183	49,283	52,737	56,749	55,674	....		96f
Gross Domestic Product (GDP)	38,924	39,264	42,973	50,714	58,190	66,464	73,947	79,960	93,102	106,677	118,195	128,727	140,466	138,529	143,981		99b
Net Factor Inc/Pmts(-) Abroad	1,406	949	78	781	1,546	1,824	1,308	2,522	315	2,384	3,244	4,375	5,949	6,332	....		98.n
Gross National Income (GNI)	40,330	40,213	43,051	51,495	59,736	68,288	75,255	82,482	93,417	109,061	121,846	133,398	148,400	147,660	....		99a
GDP Volume 1968 prices	....	....	....	....	....	....	....	....	....	....	....	....	....	....	....		99b.p
GDP Volume 1985 prices	....	....	....	....	....	....	....	....	....	....	....	....	....	....	....		99b.p
GDP Volume 1990 Prices	45,345	46,388	49,838	55,636	60,991	66,464	71,207	75,844	85,485	95,230	102,808	110,558	119,835	120,316	126,756		99b.p
GDP Volume (1995=100)	44.1	45.1	48.5	54.1	59.3	64.6	69.3	73.8	83.1	92.6	100.0	107.5	116.6	117.0	123.3		99bv p
GDP Deflator (1995=100)	74.7	73.6	75.0	79.3	83.0	87.0	90.3	91.7	94.7	97.4	100.0	101.3	102.0	100.1	98.8		99bi p
Midyear Estimates																	
Population	2.48	2.52	2.55	2.85	2.93	3.02	3.09	3.18	3.26	3.36	3.47	3.61	3.74	3.87	3.89		99z

(See notes in the back of the book.)

Slovak Republic

936

	1970	1971	1972	1973	1974	1975	1976	1977	1978	1979	1980	1981	1982	1983	1984
Exchange Rates												*Koruny per SDR:*			
Official Rate .... aa	....	....	....	....	....	....	....	....	....	....	....	....	....	....	....
												Koruny per US Dollar:			
Official Rate .... ae	....	....	....	....	....	....	....	....	....	....	....	....	....	....	....
Official Rate .... rf	....	....	....	....	....	....	....	....	....	....	....	....	....	....	....
												Index Numbers (1995=100):			
Nominal Effective Exchange Rate .... ne *c*	....	....	....	....	....	....	....	....	....	....	....	....	....	....	....
Real Effective Exchange Rate .... re *c*	....	....	....	....	....	....	....	....	....	....	....	....	....	....	....
Fund Position												*Millions of SDRs:*			
Quota .... 2f. *s*	....	....	....	....	....	....	....	....	....	....	....	....	....	....	....
SDRs .... 1b. *s*	....	....	....	....	....	....	....	....	....	....	....	....	....	....	....
Reserve Position in the Fund .... 1c. *s*	....	....	....	....	....	....	....	....	....	....	....	....	....	....	....
Total Fund Cred.&Loans Outstg. 2tl	....	....	....	....	....	....	....	....	....	....	....	....	....	....	....
International Liquidity										*Millions of US Dollars Unless Otherwise Indicated:*					
Total Reserves minus Gold 1l.*d*	....	....	....	....	....	....	....	....	....	....	....	....	....	....	....
SDRs 1b.*d*	....	....	....	....	....	....	....	....	....	....	....	....	....	....	....
Reserve Position in the Fund 1c.*d*	....	....	....	....	....	....	....	....	....	....	....	....	....	....	....
Foreign Exchange 1d.*d*	....	....	....	....	....	....	....	....	....	....	....	....	....	....	....
Gold (Million Fine Troy Ounces) 1ad	....	....	....	....	....	....	....	....	....	....	....	....	....	....	....
Gold (National Valuation) 1an*d*	....	....	....	....	....	....	....	....	....	....	....	....	....	....	....
Monetary Authorities: Other Assets ...... 3..*d*	....	....	....	....	....	....	....	....	....	....	....	....	....	....	....
Other Liab. .... 4..*d*	....	....	....	....	....	....	....	....	....	....	....	....	....	....	....
Deposit Money Banks: Assets 7a.*d*	....	....	....	....	....	....	....	....	....	....	....	....	....	....	....
Liabilities 7b.*d*	....	....	....	....	....	....	....	....	....	....	....	....	....	....	....
Monetary Authorities												*Millions of Koruny:*			
Foreign Assets 11	....	....	....	....	....	....	....	....	....	....	....	....	....	....	....
Claims on Central Government 12a	....	....	....	....	....	....	....	....	....	....	....	....	....	....	....
Claims on Nonfin.Pub.Enterprises 12c	....	....	....	....	....	....	....	....	....	....	....	....	....	....	....
Claims on Deposit Money Banks 12e	....	....	....	....	....	....	....	....	....	....	....	....	....	....	....
Reserve Money 14	....	....	....	....	....	....	....	....	....	....	....	....	....	....	....
of which: Currency Outside DMBs 14a	....	....	....	....	....	....	....	....	....	....	....	....	....	....	....
Time & Foreign Currency Deposits 15	....	....	....	....	....	....	....	....	....	....	....	....	....	....	....
Foreign Liabilities 16c	....	....	....	....	....	....	....	....	....	....	....	....	....	....	....
Long-Term Foreign Liabilities 16cl	....	....	....	....	....	....	....	....	....	....	....	....	....	....	....
Central Government Deposits 16d	....	....	....	....	....	....	....	....	....	....	....	....	....	....	....
Capital Accounts 17a	....	....	....	....	....	....	....	....	....	....	....	....	....	....	....
Other Items (Net) 17r	....	....	....	....	....	....	....	....	....	....	....	....	....	....	....
Deposit Money Banks												*Millions of Koruny:*			
Reserves 20	....	....	....	....	....	....	....	....	....	....	....	....	....	....	....
Foreign Assets 21	....	....	....	....	....	....	....	....	....	....	....	....	....	....	....
Claims on General Government 22a	....	....	....	....	....	....	....	....	....	....	....	....	....	....	....
of which: Cl. on Natl.Property Fd 22ae	....	....	....	....	....	....	....	....	....	....	....	....	....	....	....
Claims on Nonfin.Pub.Enterprises 22c	....	....	....	....	....	....	....	....	....	....	....	....	....	....	....
Claims on Private Sector 22d	....	....	....	....	....	....	....	....	....	....	....	....	....	....	....
Claims on Other Financial Insts 22f	....	....	....	....	....	....	....	....	....	....	....	....	....	....	....
Demand Deposits 24	....	....	....	....	....	....	....	....	....	....	....	....	....	....	....
Time & Foreign Currency Deposits 25	....	....	....	....	....	....	....	....	....	....	....	....	....	....	....
of which: Fgn. Currency Deposits 25b	....	....	....	....	....	....	....	....	....	....	....	....	....	....	....
Bonds 26ab	....	....	....	....	....	....	....	....	....	....	....	....	....	....	....
Foreign Liabilities 26c	....	....	....	....	....	....	....	....	....	....	....	....	....	....	....
Long-Term Foreign Liabilities 26cl	....	....	....	....	....	....	....	....	....	....	....	....	....	....	....
General Government Deposits 26d	....	....	....	....	....	....	....	....	....	....	....	....	....	....	....
of which: Natl.Property Fd.Deps. 26de	....	....	....	....	....	....	....	....	....	....	....	....	....	....	....
Credit from Monetary Authorities 26g	....	....	....	....	....	....	....	....	....	....	....	....	....	....	....
Liabilities to Other Financ. Insts 26i	....	....	....	....	....	....	....	....	....	....	....	....	....	....	....
Capital Accounts 27a	....	....	....	....	....	....	....	....	....	....	....	....	....	....	....
Other Items (Net) 27r	....	....	....	....	....	....	....	....	....	....	....	....	....	....	....
Monetary Survey												*Millions of Koruny:*			
Foreign Assets (Net) 31n	....	....	....	....	....	....	....	....	....	....	....	....	....	....	....
Domestic Credit 32	....	....	....	....	....	....	....	....	....	....	....	....	....	....	....
Claims on General Govt. (Net) 32an	....	....	....	....	....	....	....	....	....	....	....	....	....	....	....
Claims on Nonfin.Pub.Enterprises 32c	....	....	....	....	....	....	....	....	....	....	....	....	....	....	....
Claims on Private Sector 32d	....	....	....	....	....	....	....	....	....	....	....	....	....	....	....
Claims on Other Financial Insts 32f	....	....	....	....	....	....	....	....	....	....	....	....	....	....	....
Money 34	....	....	....	....	....	....	....	....	....	....	....	....	....	....	....
Quasi-Money 35	....	....	....	....	....	....	....	....	....	....	....	....	....	....	....
Bonds 36ab	....	....	....	....	....	....	....	....	....	....	....	....	....	....	....
Long-Term Foreign Liabilities 36cl	....	....	....	....	....	....	....	....	....	....	....	....	....	....	....
Capital Accounts 37a	....	....	....	....	....	....	....	....	....	....	....	....	....	....	....
Other Items (Net) 37r	....	....	....	....	....	....	....	....	....	....	....	....	....	....	....
Money plus Quasi-Money 35l	....	....	....	....	....	....	....	....	....	....	....	....	....	....	....
Interest Rates												*Percent Per Annum*			
Discount Rate *(End of Period)* 60	....	....	....	....	....	....	....	....	....	....	....	....	....	....	....
Deposit Rate 60l	....	....	....	....	....	....	....	....	....	....	....	....	....	....	....
Lending Rate 60p	....	....	....	....	....	....	....	....	....	....	....	....	....	....	....
Prices, Production, Labor												*Index Numbers (1995=100):*			
Producer Prices 63										....	31.6	32.9	35.4	35.7	38.6
Consumer Prices 64	....	....	....	....	....	....	....	....	....	....	....	....	....	....	....
Wages 65	....	....	....	....	....	....	....	....	....	....	....	....	....	....	....
Industrial Production 66	....	....	....	....	....	....	....	....	....	....	....	....	....	....	....
Industrial Employment 67	....	....	....	....	....	....	....	....	....	....	....	....	....	....	....
												Number in Thousands:			
Labor Force 67d	....	....	....	....	....	....	....	....	....	....	....	....	....	....	....
Employment 67e	....	....	....	....	....	....	....	....	....	....	....	....	....	....	....
Unemployment 67c	....	....	....	....	....	....	....	....	....	....	....	....	....	....	....
Unemployment Rate (%) 67r	....	....	....	....	....	....	....	....	....	....	....	....	....	....	....
International Transactions												*Millions of Koruny*			
Exports 70	....	....	....	....	....	....	....	....	....	....	....	....	....	....	....
Imports, c.i.f. 71	....	....	....	....	....	....	....	....	....	....	....	....	....	....	....
Imports, f.o.b. 71.v	....	....	....	....	....	....	....	....	....	....	....	....	....	....	....

1985	1986	1987	1988	1989	1990	1991	1992	1993	1994	1995	1996	1997	1998	1999		
End of Period															**Exchange Rates**	
....	....	....	....	....	....	....	....	45.605	45.660	43.954	45.864	46.930	51.975	58.011	Official Rate	**aa**
End of Period (ae) Period Average (rf)																
....	....	....	....	....	....	....	....	33.202	31.277	29.569	31.895	34.782	36.913	42.266	Official Rate	**ae**
....	....	....	....	....	....	....	....	30.770	32.045	29.713	30.654	33.616	35.233	41.363	Official Rate	**rf**
Period Averages																
....	....	....	....	....	131.94	104.19	105.70	103.54	99.33	100.00	100.66	105.75	103.55	93.34	Nominal Effective Exchange Rate	**ne c**
....	....	....	....	....	92.41	89.77	91.32	96.32	97.25	100.00	99.67	104.61	102.31	99.93	Real Effective Exchange Rate	**re c**
End of Period															**Fund Position**	
....	....	....	....	....	....	....	....	257.4	257.4	257.4	257.4	257.4	257.4	357.5	Quota	**2f.s**
....	....	....	....	....	....	....	....	.3	58.9	39.0	11.2	19.6	1.2	.6	SDRs	**1b.s**
....	....	....	....	....	....	....	....	—	—	—	—	—	—	—	Reserve Position in the Fund	**1c.s**
....	....	....	....	....	....	....	....	405.2	439.8	307.5	222.0	184.4	134.6	96.5	Total Fund Cred.&Loans Outstg.	**2tl**
End of Period															**International Liquidity**	
....	....	....	....	....	....	....	....	416	1,691	3,364	3,419	3,230	2,869	3,371	Total Reserves minus Gold	**1l.d**
....	....	....	....	....	....	....	....	—	86	58	16	26	2	1	SDRs	**1b.d**
....	....	....	....	....	....	....	....	—	—	—	—	—	—	—	Reserve Position in the Fund	**1c.d**
....	....	....	....	....	....	....	....	415	1,605	3,306	3,403	3,204	2,867	3,370	Foreign Exchange	**1d.d**
....	....	....	....	....	....	....	....	1.290	1.290	1.290	1.290	1.290	1.290	1.290	Gold (Million Fine Troy Ounces)	**1ad**
....	....	....	....	....	....	....	....	76	80	85	79	72	68	59	Gold (National Valuation)	**1and**
....	....	....	....	....	....	....	....	98	153	171	129	202	609	564	Monetary Authorities: Other Assets	**3..d**
....	....	....	....	....	....	....	....	1,040	1,355	1,428	1,351	659	1,578	760	Other Liab.	**4..d**
....	....	....	....	....	....	....	....	987	1,427	1,823	2,514	3,618	3,794	1,618	Deposit Money Banks: Assets	**7a.d**
....	....	....	....	....	....	....	....	425	499	979	2,160	2,851	2,628	643	Liabilities	**7b.d**
End of Period															**Monetary Authorities**	
....	....	....	....	....	....	....	....	19,557	60,184	107,032	115,665	121,904	130,881	168,820	Foreign Assets	**11**
....	....	....	....	....	....	....	....	46,476	46,456	25,743	30,068	5,495	9,067	1,778	Claims on Central Government	**12a**
....	....	....	....	....	....	....	....	352	294	133	238	272	336	288	Claims on Nonfin.Pub.Enterprises	**12c**
....	....	....	....	....	....	....	....	40,654	36,143	36,485	36,585	41,340	55,242	40,225	Claims on Deposit Money Banks	**12e**
....	....	....	....	....	....	....	....	39,494	48,544	76,532	83,172	98,816	94,137	124,116	Reserve Money	**14**
....	....	....	....	....	....	....	....	25,122	28,101	34,536	43,505	48,740	49,759	57,472	*of which: Currency Outside DMBs*	**14a**
....	....	....	....	....	....	....	....	9	25	60	131	117	86	364	Time & Foreign Currency Deposits	**15**
....	....	....	....	....	....	....	....	43,064	46,342	40,915	39,124	18,112	54,023	33,579	Foreign Liabilities	**16c**
....	....	....	....	....	....	....	....	9,933	16,112	14,821	14,135	13,447	11,221	4,148	Long-Term Foreign Liabilities	**16cl**
....	....	....	....	....	....	....	....	6,458	11,726	16,152	18,060	16,558	11,650	25,526	Central Government Deposits	**16d**
....	....	....	....	....	....	....	....	4,151	7,977	8,239	9,244	9,316	10,322	10,580	Capital Accounts	**17a**
....	....	....	....	....	....	....	....	3,930	12,351	12,674	18,690	12,647	14,088	12,798	Other Items (Net)	**17r**
End of Period															**Deposit Money Banks**	
....	....	....	....	....	....	....	....	13,961	19,656	29,040	39,628	50,105	42,741	53,650	Reserves	**20**
....	....	....	....	....	....	....	....	32,773	44,634	53,916	80,189	125,842	140,045	68,402	Foreign Assets	**21**
....	....	....	....	....	....	....	....	28,798	50,693	74,653	89,709	112,716	93,002	76,936	Claims on General Government	**22a**
....	....	....	....	....	....	....	....	12,083	7,803	5,282	3,465	1,273	1,033	1,472	*of which: Cl. on Natl.Property Fd*	**22ae**
....	....	....	....	....	....	....	....	114,419	93,158	59,919	83,467	I 95,465	91,193	156,476	Claims on Nonfin.Pub.Enterprises	**22c**
....	....	....	....	....	....	....	....	118,563	107,195	143,386	184,312	I 288,963	329,084	303,524	Claims on Private Sector	**22d**
....	....	....	....	....	....	....	....	1,310	1,290	8,534	12,528	14,814	709	428	Claims on Other Financial Insts	**22f**
....	....	....	....	....	....	....	....	90,742	94,931	113,179	129,528	116,651	96,863	95,586	Demand Deposits	**24**
....	....	....	....	....	....	....	....	137,344	174,427	203,328	236,632	I 279,996	320,891	368,800	Time & Foreign Currency Deposits	**25**
....	....	....	....	....	....	....	....	28,509	38,395	39,896	41,690	46,964	68,548	75,851	*of which: Fgn. Currency Deposits*	**25b**
....	....	....	....	....	....	....	....	564	952	4,414	12,046	13,257	11,971	8,664	Bonds	**26ab**
....	....	....	....	....	....	....	....	13,762	14,909	28,342	68,212	98,410	95,367	25,815	Foreign Liabilities	**26c**
....	....	....	....	....	....	....	....	341	686	615	690	755	1,650	1,383	Long-Term Foreign Liabilities	**26cl**
....	....	....	....	....	....	....	....	9,458	12,151	25,436	33,197	31,917	28,018	23,248	General Government Deposits	**26d**
....	....	....	....	....	....	....	....	5,151	1,506	2,119	2,914	2,926	2,175	1,600	*of which: Natl.Property Fd.Deps.*	**26de**
....	....	....	....	....	....	....	....	41,204	37,705	38,406	40,224	51,606	61,528	40,741	Credit from Monetary Authorities	**26g**
....	....	....	....	....	....	....	....	—	—	—	—	—	—	—	Liabilities to Other Financ. Insts	**26i**
....	....	....	....	....	....	....	....	48,722	63,813	66,953	76,526	82,642	95,243	93,704	Capital Accounts	**27a**
....	....	....	....	....	....	....	....	-32,313	-82,948	-111,225	-107,221	I 12,670	-14,756	1,478	Other Items (Net)	**27r**
End of Period															**Monetary Survey**	
....	....	....	....	....	....	....	....	-4,496	43,567	91,691	88,518	131,225	121,536	177,827	Foreign Assets (Net)	**31n**
....	....	....	....	....	....	....	....	294,005	275,220	270,836	349,154	I 469,394	483,896	490,849	Domestic Credit	**32**
....	....	....	....	....	....	....	....	59,358	73,272	58,808	68,520	69,736	62,401	29,940	Claims on General Govt. (Net)	**32an**
....	....	....	....	....	....	....	....	114,771	93,452	60,052	83,705	I 95,737	91,529	156,764	Claims on Nonfin.Pub.Enterprises	**32c**
....	....	....	....	....	....	....	....	118,566	107,206	143,442	184,401	I 289,107	329,257	303,717	Claims on Private Sector	**32d**
....	....	....	....	....	....	....	....	1,310	1,290	8,534	12,528	14,814	709	428	Claims on Other Financial Insts	**32f**
....	....	....	....	....	....	....	....	116,615	123,820	149,657	173,350	165,658	146,833	153,058	Money	**34**
....	....	....	....	....	....	....	....	137,353	174,452	203,388	236,763	I 280,113	320,977	369,164	Quasi-Money	**35**
....	....	....	....	....	....	....	....	564	952	4,414	12,046	13,257	11,971	8,664	Bonds	**36ab**
....	....	....	....	....	....	....	....	10,274	16,798	15,436	14,825	14,202	12,871	5,531	Long-Term Foreign Liabilities	**36cl**
....	....	....	....	....	....	....	....	52,873	71,790	75,192	85,770	91,958	105,565	104,284	Capital Accounts	**37a**
....	....	....	....	....	....	....	....	-28,170	-69,025	-85,560	-85,081	I 35,431	7,217	27,979	Other Items (Net)	**37r**
....	....	....	....	....	....	....	....	253,968	298,272	353,045	410,113	I 559,144	641,168	737,324	Money plus Quasi-Money	**35l**
Percent Per Annum															**Interest Rates**	
....	....	....	....	....	....	....	....	12.00	12.00	9.75	8.80	8.80	8.80	8.80	Discount Rate *(End of Period)*	**60**
....	....	....	....	....	....	....	....	8.02	9.32	9.01	9.30	13.44	16.25	14.37	Deposit Rate	**60l**
....	....	....	....	....	....	....	....	14.41	14.56	16.85	13.92	18.65	21.17	21.07	Lending Rate	**60p**
Period Averages															**Prices, Production, Labor**	
39.3	39.3	39.3	39.3	38.2	40.0	I 67.6	71.2	83.4	91.7	100.0	I 104.1	108.8	112.3	116.6	Producer Prices	**63**
....	....	....	....	....	36.7	59.2	65.1	80.2	91.0	100.0	I 105.8	112.3	119.8	132.5	Consumer Prices	**64**
....	....	....	....	....	....	....	....	70.5	83.6	100.0	114.6	127.2	136.1	148.3	Wages	**65**
....	....	....	....	....	....	....	....	88.1	92.4	100.0	102.6	103.9	109.1	....	Industrial Production	**66**
....	....	....	....	....	....	....	....	99.5	97.9	100.0	100.8	100.5	100.6	98.4	Industrial Employment	**67**
Period Averages																
....	....	....	....	....	....	....	....	2,509	2,511	2,481	....	2,473	....	....	Labor Force	**67d**
....	....	....	....	....	....	....	....	2,196	2,103	2,147	2,218	2,194	2,167	....	Employment	**67e**
....	....	....	....	....	....	....	....	369	334	325	278	287	297	....	Unemployment	**67c**
....	....	....	....	....	....	....	....	....	13.7	13.2	11.1	11.6	11.9	....	Unemployment Rate (%)	**67r**
Millions of Koruny															**International Transactions**	
....	....	....	....	....	....	....	....	168,114	214,375	255,096	270,643	277,434	377,807	422,344	Exports	**70**
....	....	....	....	....	....	....	....	204,786	218,638	273,831	350,847	361,833	479,549	....	Imports, c.i.f.	**71**
....	....	....	....	....	....	....	....	195,034	211,811	260,791	340,903	345,006	460,736	468,031	Imports, f.o.b.	**71.v**

Slovak Republic

	1970	1971	1972	1973	1974	1975	1976	1977	1978	1979	1980	1981	1982	1983	1984

Balance of Payments *Millions of US Dollars:*

Item	Code
Current Account, n.i.e.	78al d
Goods: Exports f.o.b.	78aa d
Goods: Imports f.o.b.	78ab d
Trade Balance	78ac d
Services: Credit	78ad d
Services: Debit	78ae d
Balance on Goods & Services	78af d
Income: Credit	78ag d
Income: Debit	78ah d
Balance on Gds, Serv. & Inc.	78ai d
Current Transfers, n.i.e.: Credit	78aj d
Current Transfers: Debit	78ak d
Capital Account, n.i.e.	78bc d
Capital Account, n.i.e.: Credit	78ba d
Capital Account: Debit	78bb d
Financial Account, n.i.e.	78bj d
Direct Investment Abroad	78bd d
Dir. Invest. in Rep. Econ., n.i.e.	78be d
Portfolio Investment Assets	78bf d
Equity Securities	78bk d
Debt Securities	78bl d
Portfolio Investment Liab., n.i.e.	78bg d
Equity Securities	78bm d
Debt Securities	78bn d
Financial Derivatives Assets	78bw d
Financial Derivatives Liabilities	78bx d
Other Investment Assets	78bh d
Monetary Authorities	78bo d
General Government	78bp d
Banks	78bq d
Other Sectors	78br d
Other Investment Liab., n.i.e.	78bi d
Monetary Authorities	78bs d
General Government	78bt d
Banks	78bu d
Other Sectors	78bv d
Net Errors and Omissions	78ca d
Overall Balance	78cb d
Reserves and Related Items	79da d
Reserve Assets	79db d
Use of Fund Credit and Loans	79dc d
Exceptional Financing	79de d

International Investment Position *Millions of US Dollars*

Item	Code
Assets	79aa d
Direct Investment Abroad	79ab d
Portfolio Investment	79ac d
Equity Securities	79ad d
Debt Securities	79ae d
Financial Derivatives	79al d
Other Investment	79af d
Monetary Authorities	79ag d
General Government	79ah d
Banks	79ai d
Other Sectors	79aj d
Reserve Assets	79ak d
Liabilities	79la d
Dir. Invest. in Rep. Economy	79lb d
Portfolio Investment	79lc d
Equity Securities	79ld d
Debt Securities	79le d
Financial Derivatives	79ll d
Other investment	79lf d
Monetary Authorities	79lg d
General Government	79lh d
Banks	79li d
Other Sectors	79lj d

Government Finance *Millions of Koruny:*

Item	Code
Deficit (-) or Surplus	80
Total Revenue and Grants	81y
Revenue	81
Grants	81z
Exp. & Lending Minus Repay.	82z
Expenditure	82
Lending Minus Repayments	83
Total Financing	80h
Domestic	84a
Foreign	85a
Total Debt by Residence	88
Domestic	88a
Foreign	89a

National Accounts *Millions of Koruny*

Item	Code
Exports of Goods & Services	90c
Government Consumption	91f
Gross Fixed Capital Formation	93e
Increase/Decrease(-) in Stocks	93i
Private Consumption	96f
Imports of Goods & Services	98c
Gross Domestic Product (GDP)	99b
GDP Volume 1995 Prices	99b.p
GDP Volume (1995=100)	99bv p
GDP Deflator (1995=100)	99bi p

Millions:

Item	Code
Population	99z

1985	1986	1987	1988	1989	1990	1991	1992	1993	1994	1995	1996	1997	1998	1999		
Minus Sign Indicates Debit															Balance of Payments	
....	....	....	....	....	....	....	....	-580	671	390	-2,090	-1,961	-2,126	-1,155	Current Account, n.i.e.	**78al *d***
....	....	....	....	....	....	....	....	5,452	6,706	8,591	8,824	9,641	10,720	10,201	Goods: Exports f.o.b.	**78aa *d***
....	....	....	....	....	....	....	....	-6,365	-6,645	-8,820	-11,106	-11,725	-13,071	-11,310	Goods: Imports f.o.b.	**78ab *d***
....	....	....	....	....	....	....	....	-912	61	-229	-2,283	-2,084	-2,351	-1,109	*Trade Balance*	**78ac *d***
....	....	....	....	....	....	....	....	1,939	2,261	2,378	2,066	2,167	2,292	1,899	Services: Credit	**78ad *d***
....	....	....	....	....	....	....	....	-1,666	-1,600	-1,838	-2,028	-2,094	-2,276	-1,844	Services: Debit	**78ae *d***
....	....	....	....	....	....	....	....	-640	722	311	-2,245	-2,011	-2,334	-1,054	*Balance on Goods & Services*	**78af *d***
....	....	....	....	....	....	....	....	185	155	250	224	315	437	268	Income: Credit	**78ag *d***
....	....	....	....	....	....	....	....	-224	-275	-263	-270	-438	-595	-568	Income: Debit	**78ah *d***
....	....	....	....	....	....	....	....	-678	602	297	-2,291	-2,135	-2,492	-1,353	*Balance on Gds, Serv. & Inc.*	**78ai *d***
....	....	....	....	....	....	....	....	216	166	243	483	540	645	466	Current Transfers, n.i.e.: Credit	**78aj *d***
....	....	....	....	....	....	....	....	-118	-98	-150	-282	-367	-279	-268	Current Transfers: Debit	**78ak *d***
....	....	....	....	....	....	....	....	564	84	46	30	—	70	158	Capital Account, n.i.e.	**78bc *d***
....	....	....	....	....	....	....	....	771	84	46	30	—	83	171	Capital Account, n.i.e.: Credit	**78ba *d***
....	....	....	....	....	....	....	....	-208	—	—	—	—	-12	-13	Capital Account: Debit	**78bb *d***
....	....	....	....	....	....	....	....	-153	71	1,211	2,268	1,780	1,912	1,789	Financial Account, n.i.e.	**78bj *d***
....	....	....	....	....	....	....	....	-61	-14	-10	-48	-95	-145	376	Direct Investment Abroad	**78bd *d***
....	....	....	....	....	....	....	....	199	270	236	351	174	562	354	Dir. Invest. in Rep. Econ., n.i.e.	**78be *d***
....	....	....	....	....	....	....	....	-774	-26	157	-12	-81	-57	247	Portfolio Investment Assets	**78bf *d***
....	....	....	....	....	....	....	....	-774	-26	174	69	86	33	2	Equity Securities	**78bk *d***
....	....	....	....	....	....	....	....	....	—	-17	-81	-167	-91	246	Debt Securities	**78bl *d***
....	....	....	....	....	....	....	....	465	304	53	29	93	841	405	Portfolio Investment Liab., n.i.e.	**78bg *d***
....	....	....	....	....	....	....	....	465	111	-16	28	102	-35	47	Equity Securities	**78bm *d***
....	....	....	....	....	....	....	....	....	193	69	1	-10	876	358	Debt Securities	**78bn *d***
....	....	....	....	....	....	....	....	....	—	—	—	—	—	....	Financial Derivatives Assets	**78bw *d***
....	....	....	....	....	....	....	....	....	—	—	—	—	—	....	Financial Derivatives Liabilities	**78bx *d***
....	....	....	....	....	....	....	....	-412	-548	-116	-334	-1,028	190	1,713	Other Investment Assets	**78bh *d***
....	....	....	....	....	....	....	....	....	....	....	....	....	—	....	Monetary Authorities	**78bo *d***
....	....	....	....	....	....	....	....	232	-211	140	337	61	117	9	General Government	**78bp *d***
....	....	....	....	....	....	....	....	-530	-344	-248	-662	-1,122	110	1,878	Banks	**78bq *d***
....	....	....	....	....	....	....	....	-114	7	-8	-10	33	-37	-174	Other Sectors	**78br *d***
....	....	....	....	....	....	....	....	430	84	891	2,282	2,718	520	-1,307	Other Investment Liab., n.i.e.	**78bi *d***
....	....	....	....	....	....	....	....	—	38	42	52	153	55	14	Monetary Authorities	**78bs *d***
....	....	....	....	....	....	....	....	145	-52	-173	-124	184	-321	55	General Government	**78bt *d***
....	....	....	....	....	....	....	....	99	38	463	1,440	1,084	-138	-1,882	Banks	**78bu *d***
....	....	....	....	....	....	....	....	186	60	559	914	1,298	924	506	Other Sectors	**78bv *d***
....	....	....	....	....	....	....	....	183	380	144	162	280	-333	-14	Net Errors and Omissions	**78ca *d***
....	....	....	....	....	....	....	....	14	1,205	1,791	370	99	-478	777	*Overall Balance*	**78cb *d***
....	....	....	....	....	....	....	....	-14	-1,205	-1,791	-370	-99	478	-777	Reserves and Related Items	**79da *d***
....	....	....	....	....	....	....	....	-104	-1,256	-1,590	-245	-47	545	-725	Reserve Assets	**79db *d***
....	....	....	....	....	....	....	....	89	51	-201	-125	-52	-67	-52	Use of Fund Credit and Loans	**79dc *d***
....	....	....	....	....	....	....	....	....	....	....	....	....	....	....	Exceptional Financing	**79de *d***
Millions of US Dollars															International Investment Position	
....	....	....	....	....	....	....	....	....	8,421	10,155	10,309	10,646	10,320	8,253	Assets	**79aa *d***
....	....	....	....	....	....	....	....	....	166	138	181	233	403	340	Direct Investment Abroad	**79ab *d***
....	....	....	....	....	....	....	....	....	429	259	282	330	406	145	Portfolio Investment	**79ac *d***
....	....	....	....	....	....	....	....	....	424	234	171	71	35	27	Equity Securities	**79ad *d***
....	....	....	....	....	....	....	....	....	5	25	111	259	371	118	Debt Securities	**79ae *d***
....	....	....	....	....	....	....	....	....	—	—	—	—	—	—	Financial Derivatives	**79al *d***
....	....	....	....	....	....	....	....	....	5,633	5,896	5,948	6,461	6,267	4,025	Other Investment	**79af *d***
....	....	....	....	....	....	....	....	....	—	—	—	—	—	....	Monetary Authorities	**79ag *d***
....	....	....	....	....	....	....	....	....	2,947	2,928	2,393	2,135	1,897	1,659	General Government	**79ah *d***
....	....	....	....	....	....	....	....	....	1,451	1,676	2,276	3,141	3,203	1,176	Banks	**79ai *d***
....	....	....	....	....	....	....	....	....	1,234	1,291	1,280	1,185	1,167	1,190	Other Sectors	**79aj *d***
....	....	....	....	....	....	....	....	....	2,192	3,863	3,898	3,623	3,244	3,743	Reserve Assets	**79ak *d***
....	....	....	....	....	....	....	....	....	6,137	7,287	9,723	11,790	14,553	12,871	Liabilities	**79la *d***
....	....	....	....	....	....	....	....	....	897	1,268	2,000	2,025	2,787	2,817	Dir. Invest. in Rep. Economy	**79lb *d***
....	....	....	....	....	....	....	....	....	582	608	563	595	1,549	1,843	Portfolio Investment	**79lc *d***
....	....	....	....	....	....	....	....	....	56	43	62	157	102	135	Equity Securities	**79ld *d***
....	....	....	....	....	....	....	....	....	527	565	500	438	1,447	1,709	Debt Securities	**79le *d***
....	....	....	....	....	....	....	....	....	—	—	—	—	—	—	Financial Derivatives	**79ll *d***
....	....	....	....	....	....	....	....	....	4,657	5,411	7,161	9,170	10,217	8,211	Other investment	**79lf *d***
....	....	....	....	....	....	....	....	....	682	537	442	507	536	522	Monetary Authorities	**79lg *d***
....	....	....	....	....	....	....	....	....	1,101	958	786	912	621	671	General Government	**79lh *d***
....	....	....	....	....	....	....	....	....	537	901	2,290	3,109	2,950	947	Banks	**79li *d***
....	....	....	....	....	....	....	....	....	2,338	3,015	3,642	4,642	6,109	....	Other Sectors	**79lj *d***
Year Ending December 31															**Government Finance**	
....	....	....	....	....	....	....	....	....	....	....	....	....	-35,088	....	Deficit (-) or Surplus	**80**
....	....	....	....	....	....	....	....	....	....	....	....	....	265,241	....	Total Revenue and Grants	**81y**
....	....	....	....	....	....	....	....	....	....	....	....	....	262,966	....	Revenue	**81**
....	....	....	....	....	....	....	....	....	....	....	....	....	2,275	....	Grants	**81z**
....	....	....	....	....	....	....	....	....	....	....	....	....	300,329	....	Exp. & Lending Minus Repay.	**82z**
....	....	....	....	....	....	....	....	....	....	....	....	....	299,593	....	Expenditure	**82**
....	....	....	....	....	....	....	....	....	....	....	....	....	736	....	Lending Minus Repayments	**83**
....	....	....	....	....	....	....	....	....	....	....	....	....	35,088	....	Total Financing	**80h**
....	....	....	....	....	....	....	....	....	....	....	....	....	—	....	Domestic	**84a**
....	....	....	....	....	....	....	....	....	....	....	....	....	35,088	....	Foreign	**85a**
....	....	....	....	....	....	....	....	....	....	....	....	....	....	....	Total Debt by Residence	**88**
....	....	....	....	....	....	....	....	....	....	....	....	....	....	....	Domestic	**88a**
....	....	....	....	....	....	....	....	....	....	....	....	....	....	....	Foreign	**89a**
Millions of Koruny															**National Accounts**	
....	....	....	....	....	....	....	....	227,800	286,600	325,800	334,000	396,900	456,800	....	Exports of Goods & Services	**90c**
....	....	....	....	....	....	....	....	92,300	93,900	108,100	132,100	146,200	154,700	....	Government Consumption	**91f**
....	....	....	....	....	....	....	....	120,700	129,400	141,500	212,700	252,700	292,400	....	Gross Fixed Capital Formation	**93e**
....	....	....	....	....	....	....	....	-19,700	-27,600	5,100	14,000	200	-9,700	....	Increase/Decrease(-) in Stocks	**93i**
....	....	....	....	....	....	....	....	196,200	221,900	252,700	286,100	322,300	360,100	....	Private Consumption	**96f**
....	....	....	....	....	....	....	....	-248,200	-263,700	-316,400	-403,200	-464,400	-536,900	....	Imports of Goods & Services	**98c**
....	....	....	....	....	....	....	....	369,100	440,500	516,800	575,700	653,900	717,400	....	Gross Domestic Product (GDP)	**99b**
....	....	....	....	....	....	....	....	460,800	483,400	516,800	550,800	586,800	612,700	....	GDP Volume 1995 Prices	**99b.*p***
....	....	....	....	....	....	....	....	89.2	93.5	100.0	106.6	113.5	118.6	....	GDP Volume (1995=100)	**99bv *p***
....	....	....	....	....	....	....	....	80.1	91.1	100.0	104.5	111.4	117.1	....	GDP Deflator (1995=100)	**99bi *p***
Midyear Estimates																
....	....	....	....	....	....	....	....	5.32	5.35	5.36	5.37	5.38	5.39	5.40	**Population**	**99z**

(See notes in the back of the book.)

Slovenia

	1970	1971	1972	1973	1974	1975	1976	1977	1978	1979	1980	1981	1982	1983	1984
Exchange Rates															*Tolars per SDR:*
Official Rate .... **aa**	....	....	....	....	....	....	....	....	....	....	....	....	....	....	....
															Tolars per US Dollar:
Official Rate .... **ae**	....	....	....	....	....	....	....	....	....	....	....	....	....	....	....
Official Rate .... **rf**	....	....	....	....	....	....	....	....	....	....	....	....	....	....	....
Fund Position															*Millions of SDRs:*
Quota .... **2f. s**	....	....	....	....	....	....	....	....	....	....	....	....	....	....	....
SDRs .... **1b. s**	....	....	....	....	....	....	....	....	....	....	....	....	....	....	....
Reserve Position in the Fund .... **1c. s**	....	....	....	....	....	....	....	....	....	....	....	....	....	....	....
Total Fund Cred.&Loans Outstg. **2tl**	....	....	....	....	....	....	....	....	....	....	....	....	....	....	....
International Liquidity												*Millions of US Dollars Unless Otherwise Indicated:*			
Total Reserves minus Gold .... **1l. d**	....	....	....	....	....	....	....	....	....	....	....	....	....	....	....
SDRs .... **1b. d**	....	....	....	....	....	....	....	....	....	....	....	....	....	....	....
Reserve Position in the Fund .... **1c. d**	....	....	....	....	....	....	....	....	....	....	....	....	....	....	....
Foreign Exchange .... **1d. d**	....	....	....	....	....	....	....	....	....	....	....	....	....	....	....
Gold (Million Fine Troy Ounces) **1ad**	....	....	....	....	....	....	....	....	....	....	....	....	....	....	....
Gold (National Valuation) .... **1an d**	....	....	....	....	....	....	....	....	....	....	....	....	....	....	....
Monetary Authorities: Other Assets .... **3.. d**	....	....	....	....	....	....	....	....	....	....	....	....	....	....	....
Other Liab. .... **4.. d**	....	....	....	....	....	....	....	....	....	....	....	....	....	....	....
Deposit Money Banks: Assets .... **7a. d**	....	....	....	....	....	....	....	....	....	....	....	....	....	....	....
Liabilities .... **7b. d**	....	....	....	....	....	....	....	....	....	....	....	....	....	....	....
Monetary Authorities															*Billions of Tolars:*
Foreign Assets **11**	....	....	....	....	....	....	....	....	....	....	....	....	....	....	....
Claims on Central Government **12a**	....	....	....	....	....	....	....	....	....	....	....	....	....	....	....
Claims on Private Sector **12d**	....	....	....	....	....	....	....	....	....	....	....	....	....	....	....
Claims on Deposit Money Banks **12e**	....	....	....	....	....	....	....	....	....	....	....	....	....	....	....
Reserve Money **14**	....	....	....	....	....	....	....	....	....	....	....	....	....	....	....
of which: Currency Outside DMBs **14a**	....	....	....	....	....	....	....	....	....	....	....	....	....	....	....
Bonds **16ab**	....	....	....	....	....	....	....	....	....	....	....	....	....	....	....
Restricted Deposits **16b**	....	....	....	....	....	....	....	....	....	....	....	....	....	....	....
Foreign Liabilities **16c**	....	....	....	....	....	....	....	....	....	....	....	....	....	....	....
Central Government Deposits **16d**	....	....	....	....	....	....	....	....	....	....	....	....	....	....	....
Capital Accounts **17a**	....	....	....	....	....	....	....	....	....	....	....	....	....	....	....
Other Items (Net) **17r**	....	....	....	....	....	....	....	....	....	....	....	....	....	....	....
Deposit Money Banks															*Billions of Tolars:*
Reserves **20**	....	....	....	....	....	....	....	....	....	....	....	....	....	....	....
Other Claims on Monetary Author. **20n**	....	....	....	....	....	....	....	....	....	....	....	....	....	....	....
Foreign Assets **21**	....	....	....	....	....	....	....	....	....	....	....	....	....	....	....
Claims on General Government **22a**	....	....	....	....	....	....	....	....	....	....	....	....	....	....	....
Claims on Private Sector **22d**	....	....	....	....	....	....	....	....	....	....	....	....	....	....	....
Claims on Other Financial Insts **22f**	....	....	....	....	....	....	....	....	....	....	....	....	....	....	....
Demand Deposits **24**	....	....	....	....	....	....	....	....	....	....	....	....	....	....	....
Time, Savings,& Fgn.Currency Dep. **25**	....	....	....	....	....	....	....	....	....	....	....	....	....	....	....
Money Market Instruments **26aa**	....	....	....	....	....	....	....	....	....	....	....	....	....	....	....
Bonds **26ab**	....	....	....	....	....	....	....	....	....	....	....	....	....	....	....
Restricted Deposits **26b**	....	....	....	....	....	....	....	....	....	....	....	....	....	....	....
Foreign Liabilities **26c**	....	....	....	....	....	....	....	....	....	....	....	....	....	....	....
General Government Deposits **26d**	....	....	....	....	....	....	....	....	....	....	....	....	....	....	....
of which: Local Govt. Deposits **26db**	....	....	....	....	....	....	....	....	....	....	....	....	....	....	....
Central Govt. Lending Funds **26f**	....	....	....	....	....	....	....	....	....	....	....	....	....	....	....
Credit from Monetary Authorities **26g**	....	....	....	....	....	....	....	....	....	....	....	....	....	....	....
Liabilities to Other Financ. Insts **26i**	....	....	....	....	....	....	....	....	....	....	....	....	....	....	....
Capital Accounts **27a**	....	....	....	....	....	....	....	....	....	....	....	....	....	....	....
Other Items (Net) **27r**	....	....	....	....	....	....	....	....	....	....	....	....	....	....	....
Monetary Survey															*Billions of Tolars:*
Foreign Assets (Net) **31n**	....	....	....	....	....	....	....	....	....	....	....	....	....	....	....
Domestic Credit **32**	....	....	....	....	....	....	....	....	....	....	....	....	....	....	....
Claims on General Govt. (Net) **32an**	....	....	....	....	....	....	....	....	....	....	....	....	....	....	....
Claims on Private Sector **32d**	....	....	....	....	....	....	....	....	....	....	....	....	....	....	....
Claims on Other Financial Insts **32f**	....	....	....	....	....	....	....	....	....	....	....	....	....	....	....
Money **34**	....	....	....	....	....	....	....	....	....	....	....	....	....	....	....
Quasi-Money **35**	....	....	....	....	....	....	....	....	....	....	....	....	....	....	....
Money Market Instruments **36aa**	....	....	....	....	....	....	....	....	....	....	....	....	....	....	....
Bonds **36ab**	....	....	....	....	....	....	....	....	....	....	....	....	....	....	....
Restricted Deposits **36b**	....	....	....	....	....	....	....	....	....	....	....	....	....	....	....
Central Govt. Lending Funds **36f**	....	....	....	....	....	....	....	....	....	....	....	....	....	....	....
Liabilities to Other Financ. Insts **36i**	....	....	....	....	....	....	....	....	....	....	....	....	....	....	....
Capital Accounts **37a**	....	....	....	....	....	....	....	....	....	....	....	....	....	....	....
Other Items (Net) **37r**	....	....	....	....	....	....	....	....	....	....	....	....	....	....	....
Money plus Quasi-Money **35l**	....	....	....	....	....	....	....	....	....	....	....	....	....	....	....

1985	1986	1987	1988	1989	1990	1991	1992	1993	1994	1995	1996	1997	1998	1999		
End of Period															**Exchange Rates**	
....	....	....	....	....	....	81.09	135.71	181.09	184.61	187.28	203.44	228.27	226.97	270.07	Official Rate	**aa**
End of Period (ae) Period Average (rf)																
....	....	....	....	....	....	56.69	98.70	131.84	126.46	125.99	141.48	169.18	161.20	196.77	Official Rate	**ae**
....	....	....	....	....	....	27.57	81.29	113.24	128.81	118.52	135.36	159.69	166.13	181.77	Official Rate	**rf**
End of Period															**Fund Position**	
....	....	....	....	....	....	....	....	150.50	150.50	150.50	150.50	150.50	150.50	231.70	Quota	**2f. s**
....	....	....	....	....	....	....	....	.03	.04	.04	.09	.05	.17	1.17	SDRs	**1b. s**
....	....	....	....	....	....	....	....	12.88	12.87	12.88	12.88	12.88	46.46	78.40	Reserve Position in the Fund	**1c. s**
....	....	....	....	....	....	....	....	8.53	4.94	2.69	.90	—	—	—	Total Fund Cred.&Loans Outstg.	**2tl**
End of Period															**International Liquidity**	
....	....	....	....	....	....	112.14	715.54	787.80	1,498.98	1,820.79	2,297.36	3,314.67	3,638.52	3,168.00	Total Reserves minus Gold	**1l. d**
....	....	....	....	....	....	....	....	.05	.06	.13	.07	.24	1.60	SDRs	**1b. d**
....	....	....	....	....	....	....	....	17.68	18.80	19.14	18.51	17.37	65.41	107.61	Reserve Position in the Fund	**1c. d**
....	....	....	....	....	....	112.14	715.54	770.07	1,480.12	1,801.59	2,278.71	3,297.22	3,572.87	3,058.79	Foreign Exchange	**1d. d**
....	....	....	....	....	....	.0003	.0003	.0003	.0003	.0003	.0003	.0003	.0003	.0003	Gold (Million Fine Troy Ounces)	**1ad**
....	....	....	....	....	....	.11	.11	.13	.12	.13	.12	.09	.09	.09	Gold (National Valuation)	**1an d**
....	....	....	....	....	....	2.39	1.35	1.08	103.28	170.14	33.70	41.27	46.83	51.95	Monetary Authorities: Other Assets	**3.. d**
....	....	....	....	....	....	....	....	.06	.09	.14	.42	.34	1.05	.63	Other Liab.	**4.. d**
....	....	....	....	....	....	1,989.68	2,065.82	1,431.92	2,301.70	2,395.17	2,581.52	1,869.71	2,003.17	1,768.94	Deposit Money Banks: Assets	**7a. d**
....	....	....	....	....	....	1,282.22	1,183.47	1,058.95	1,258.55	1,483.20	1,458.57	1,219.38	1,333.58	1,354.25	Liabilities	**7b. d**
End of Period															**Monetary Authorities**	
....	....	....	....	....	....	6.50	70.77	104.02	190.06	250.85	329.81	559.27	594.10	629.76	Foreign Assets	**11**
....	....	....	....	....	....	8.65	8.88	18.78	15.65	15.28	15.52	15.67	16.01	16.61	Claims on Central Government	**12a**
....	....	....	....	....	....	.02	.05	.08	.10	.11	.15	.19	.21	.22	Claims on Private Sector	**12d**
....	....	....	....	....	....	3.82	16.29	16.00	29.90	43.06	15.72	18.08	3.91	25.82	Claims on Deposit Money Banks	**12e**
....	....	....	....	....	....	15.92	37.11	51.29	80.49	100.79	116.55	143.36	171.63	208.23	Reserve Money	**14**
....	....	....	....	....	....	9.18	24.18	32.72	47.28	59.96	66.84	78.12	93.65	125.01	*of which: Currency Outside DMBs*	**14a**
....	....	....	....	....	....	—	40.76	50.39	99.77	126.67	178.45	364.97	362.48	337.76	Bonds	**16ab**
....	....	....	....	....	....	.05	.04	.37	1.82	1.91	.86	2.29	4.30	4.30	Restricted Deposits	**16b**
....	....	....	....	....	....	—	—	1.55	.92	.52	.24	.06	.17	.12	Foreign Liabilities	**16c**
....	....	....	....	....	....	1.64	5.78	5.99	27.41	47.51	22.30	23.12	18.50	26.25	Central Government Deposits	**16d**
....	....	....	....	....	....	1.50	12.40	29.33	27.17	31.82	43.31	58.65	55.45	96.59	Capital Accounts	**17a**
....	....	....	....	....	....	-.13	-.10	-.03	-1.88	.08	-.51	.77	1.69	-.83	Other Items (Net)	**17r**
End of Period															**Deposit Money Banks**	
....	....	....	....	....	....	6.77	7.76	12.67	31.07	38.13	48.11	63.09	74.44	79.37	Reserves	**20**
....	....	....	....	....	....	—	36.17	42.74	83.47	108.46	160.92	345.08	344.49	327.91	Other Claims on Monetary Author.	**20n**
....	....	....	....	....	....	112.80	203.90	188.79	291.07	301.77	365.23	316.32	322.91	348.01	Foreign Assets	**21**
....	....	....	....	....	....	11.32	24.18	208.08	257.88	315.96	319.59	372.50	407.79	428.40	Claims on General Government	**22a**
....	....	....	....	....	....	122.01	236.86	316.45	427.04	609.72	736.01	829.98	1,066.35	1,304.35	Claims on Private Sector	**22d**
....	....	....	....	....	....	.50	.91	2.03	5.53	12.75	9.38	12.36	20.36	37.79	Claims on Other Financial Insts	**22f**
....	....	....	....	....	....	20.21	44.48	64.36	84.15	104.10	127.42	151.36	191.99	237.01	Demand Deposits	**24**
....	....	....	....	....	....	90.06	197.72	334.95	494.13	647.77	807.04	1,005.28	1,188.44	1,333.69	Time, Savings,& Fgn.Currency Dep.	**25**
....	....	....	....	....	....	2.55	10.00	16.44	12.51	26.97	13.24	18.47	21.37	13.56	Money Market Instruments	**26aa**
....	....	....	....	....	....	.13	.66	2.57	8.27	18.09	23.84	33.95	36.28	40.80	Bonds	**26ab**
....	....	....	....	....	....	3.48	6.04	9.51	10.28	10.98	17.04	17.63	14.93	10.80	Restricted Deposits	**26b**
....	....	....	....	....	....	72.69	116.81	139.61	159.15	186.87	206.36	206.29	214.97	266.48	Foreign Liabilities	**26c**
....	....	....	....	....	....	12.20	33.55	57.93	87.22	94.87	140.69	167.98	191.06	190.12	General Government Deposits	**26d**
....	....	....	....	....	....	1.12	5.31	7.59	8.04	11.43	6.53	6.53	6.91	10.88	*of which:* Local Govt. Deposits	**26db**
....	....	....	....	....	....	.74	.91	2.43	4.87	8.29	12.34	14.04	24.35	27.88	Central Govt. Lending Funds	**26f**
....	....	....	....	....	....	1.40	15.61	15.48	29.64	41.66	15.28	17.83	3.53	25.47	Credit from Monetary Authorities	**26g**
....	....	....	....	....	....	3.01	6.00	9.92	5.53	10.39	15.43	23.33	33.20	41.83	Liabilities to Other Financ. Insts	**26i**
....	....	....	....	....	....	65.04	104.77	151.07	209.53	248.29	273.20	303.74	335.79	373.42	Capital Accounts	**27a**
....	....	....	....	....	....	-18.10	-26.77	-33.54	-9.24	-11.50	-12.64	-20.58	-19.57	-35.16	Other Items (Net)	**27r**
End of Period															**Monetary Survey**	
....	....	....	....	....	....	46.61	157.86	151.64	321.05	365.23	488.45	669.24	701.86	711.24	Foreign Assets (Net)	**31n**
....	....	....	....	....	....	128.66	231.54	481.50	591.57	811.45	917.66	1,039.61	1,301.17	1,570.99	Domestic Credit	**32**
....	....	....	....	....	....	6.13	-6.27	162.93	158.89	188.87	172.13	197.08	214.24	228.64	Claims on General Govt. (Net)	**32an**
....	....	....	....	....	....	122.04	236.91	316.53	427.14	609.83	736.16	830.17	1,066.56	1,304.56	Claims on Private Sector	**32d**
....	....	....	....	....	....	.50	.91	2.03	5.53	12.75	9.38	12.36	20.36	37.79	Claims on Other Financial Insts	**32f**
....	....	....	....	....	....	29.43	68.77	97.28	131.44	164.06	194.29	229.48	287.26	363.70	Money	**34**
....	....	....	....	....	....	90.06	197.72	334.95	494.13	647.77	807.04	1,005.28	1,188.44	1,333.69	Quasi-Money	**35**
....	....	....	....	....	....	2.55	10.00	16.44	12.51	26.97	13.24	18.47	21.37	13.56	Money Market Instruments	**36aa**
....	....	....	....	....	....	.13	41.42	52.96	108.04	144.76	202.29	398.92	398.76	378.56	Bonds	**36ab**
....	....	....	....	....	....	3.53	6.08	9.88	12.10	12.90	17.90	19.92	19.23	15.10	Restricted Deposits	**36b**
....	....	....	....	....	....	.74	.91	2.43	4.87	8.29	12.34	14.04	24.35	27.88	Central Govt. Lending Funds	**36f**
....	....	....	....	....	....	3.01	6.00	9.92	5.53	10.39	15.43	23.33	33.20	41.83	Liabilities to Other Financ. Insts	**36i**
....	....	....	....	....	....	66.54	117.17	180.40	236.70	280.11	316.51	362.39	391.24	470.01	Capital Accounts	**37a**
....	....	....	....	....	....	-20.72	-58.68	-71.12	-92.71	-118.58	-172.94	-362.99	-360.83	-362.09	Other Items (Net)	**37r**
....	....	....	....	....	....	119.49	266.50	432.23	625.56	811.83	1,001.33	1,234.76	1,475.70	1,697.39	Money plus Quasi-Money	**35l**

Slovenia

		1970	1971	1972	1973	1974	1975	1976	1977	1978	1979	1980	1981	1982	1983	1984

Interest Rates — *Percent Per Annum*

Central Bank Rate *(End of Per.)*	60	....	....	....	....	....	....	....	....	....	....	....		....	....	....
Money Market Rate	60b	....	....	....	....	....	....	....	....	....	....	....		....	....	....
Treasury Bill Rate	60c	....	....	....	....	....	....	....	....	....	....	....		....	....	....
Deposit Rate	60l	....	....	....	....	....	....	....	....	....	....	....		....	....	....
Lending Rate	60p	....	....	....	....	....	....	....	....	....	....	....		....	....	....

Prices, Production, Labor — *Index Numbers (1995=100):*

Producer Prices	63	....	....	....	....	....	....	....	....	....	....	....		....	....	....
Consumer Prices	64	....	....	....	....	....	....	....	....	....	....	....		....	....	....
Wages	65	....	....	....	....	....	....	....	....	....	....	....		....	....	....
Industrial Production	66..c	....	....	....	....	....	....	....	....	....	....	....		....	....	....
Employment	67	....	....	....	....	....	....	....	....	....	....	....		....	....	....

Number in Thousands:

Labor Force	67d	....	....	....	....	....	....	....	....	....	....	....		....	....	....
Employment	67e	....	....	....	....	....	....	....	....	....	....	....		....	....	....
Unemployment	67c	....	....	....	....	....	....	....	....	....	....	....		....	....	....
Unemployment Rate (%)	67r	....	....	....	....	....	....	....	....	....	....	....		....	....	....

International Transactions — *Millions of US Dollars*

Exports	70..d	....	....	....	....	....	....	....	....	....	....	....		....	....	....
Imports, c.i.f.	71..d	....	....	....	....	....	....	....	....	....	....	....		....	....	....

Balance of Payments — *Millions of US Dollars:*

Current Account, n.i.e.	78al d	....	....	....	....	....	....	....	....	....	....	....	....	....	....	....
Goods: Exports f.o.b.	78aa d	....	....	....	....	....	....	....	....	....	....	....		....	....	....
Goods: Imports f.o.b.	78ab d	....	....	....	....	....	....	....	....	....	....	....		....	....	....
Trade Balance	78ac d	....	....	....	....	....	....	....	....	....	....	....		....	....	....
Services: Credit	78ad d	....	....	....	....	....	....	....	....	....	....	....		....	....	....
Services: Debit	78ae d	....	....	....	....	....	....	....	....	....	....	....		....	....	....
Balance on Goods & Services	78af d	....	....	....	....	....	....	....	....	....	....	....		....	....	....
Income: Credit	78ag d	....	....	....	....	....	....	....	....	....	....	....		....	....	....
Income: Debit	78ah d	....	....	....	....	....	....	....	....	....	....	....		....	....	....
Balance on Gds, Serv. & Inc.	78ai d	....	....	....	....	....	....	....	....	....	....	....		....	....	....
Current Transfers, n.i.e.: Credit	78aj d	....	....	....	....	....	....	....	....	....	....	....		....	....	....
Current Transfers: Debit	78ak d	....	....	....	....	....	....	....	....	....	....	....		....	....	....
Capital Account, n.i.e.	78bc d	....	....	....	....	....	....	....	....	....	....	....		....	....	....
Capital Account, n.i.e.: Credit	78ba d	....	....	....	....	....	....	....	....	....	....	....		....	....	....
Capital Account: Debit	78bb d	....	....	....	....	....	....	....	....	....	....	....		....	....	....
Financial Account, n.i.e.	78bj d	....	....	....	....	....	....	....	....	....	....	....		....	....	....
Direct Investment Abroad	78bd d	....	....	....	....	....	....	....	....	....	....	....		....	....	....
Dir. Invest. in Rep. Econ., n.i.e.	78be d	....	....	....	....	....	....	....	....	....	....	....		....	....	....
Portfolio Investment Assets	78bf d	....	....	....	....	....	....	....	....	....	....	....		....	....	....
Equity Securities	78bk d	....	....	....	....	....	....	....	....	....	....	....		....	....	....
Debt Securities	78bl d	....	....	....	....	....	....	....	....	....	....	....		....	....	....
Portfolio Investment Liab., n.i.e.	78bg d	....	....	....	....	....	....	....	....	....	....	....		....	....	....
Equity Securities	78bm d	....	....	....	....	....	....	....	....	....	....	....		....	....	....
Debt Securities	78bn d	....	....	....	....	....	....	....	....	....	....	....		....	....	....
Financial Derivatives Assets	78bw d	....	....	....	....	....	....	....	....	....	....	....		....	....	....
Financial Derivatives Liabilities	78bx d	....	....	....	....	....	....	....	....	....	....	....		....	....	....
Other Investment Assets	78bh d	....	....	....	....	....	....	....	....	....	....	....		....	....	....
Monetary Authorities	78bo d	....	....	....	....	....	....	....	....	....	....	....		....	....	....
General Government	78bp d	....	....	....	....	....	....	....	....	....	....	....		....	....	....
Banks	78bq d	....	....	....	....	....	....	....	....	....	....	....		....	....	....
Other Sectors	78br d	....	....	....	....	....	....	....	....	....	....	....		....	....	....
Other Investment Liab., n.i.e.	78bi d	....	....	....	....	....	....	....	....	....	....	....		....	....	....
Monetary Authorities	78bs d	....	....	....	....	....	....	....	....	....	....	....		....	....	....
General Government	78bt d	....	....	....	....	....	....	....	....	....	....	....		....	....	....
Banks	78bu d	....	....	....	....	....	....	....	....	....	....	....		....	....	....
Other Sectors	78bv d	....	....	....	....	....	....	....	....	....	....	....		....	....	....
Net Errors and Omissions	78ca d	....	....	....	....	....	....	....	....	....	....	....		....	....	....
Overall Balance	78cb d	....	....	....	....	....	....	....	....	....	....	....		....	....	....
Reserves and Related Items	79da d	....	....	....	....	....	....	....	....	....	....	....		....	....	....
Reserve Assets	79db d	....	....	....	....	....	....	....	....	....	....	....		....	....	....
Use of Fund Credit and Loans	79dc d	....	....	....	....	....	....	....	....	....	....	....		....	....	....
Exceptional Financing	79de d	....	....	....	....	....	....	....	....	....	....	....		....	....	....

	1985	1986	1987	1988	1989	1990	1991	1992	1993	1994	1995	1996	1997	1998	1999		
Percent Per Annum																**Interest Rates**	
	....	....	....	....	....	....	....	....	....	....	14.62	11.42	13.78	8.55	8.35	Central Bank Rate *(End of Per.)*	60
	....	....	....	....	....	....	....	67.58	39.15	29.08	12.18	13.98	9.71	7.45	6.87	Money Market Rate	60b
	....	....	....	....	....	....	....	....	....	....	....	....	....	....	8.63	Treasury Bill Rate	60c
	....	....	....	....	....	....	682.53	153.02	33.04	28.10	15.38	15.08	13.19	10.54	7.24	Deposit Rate	60l
	....	....	....	....	....	....	824.56	195.11	48.61	38.87	23.36	22.60	20.02	16.09	12.38	Lending Rate	60p
Period Averages																**Prices, Production, Labor**	
	....	....	....	....	....	....	....	62.0	75.3	88.7	100.0	106.8	113.3	120.1	122.6	Producer Prices	63
	....	....	....	....	....	....	....	56.2	74.1	88.8	100.0	109.7	119.7	129.9	138.5	Consumer Prices	64
	....	....	....	....	....	....	....	43.4	65.8	84.3	100.0	114.8	127.9	140.1	153.2	Wages	65
	....	....	....	....	....	....	....	92.8	90.8	98.0	100.0	99.3	101.4	105.4	103.9	Industrial Production	66..c
	....	....	....	....	....	....	....	Ɩ105.2	101.4	100.1	100.0	99.6	99.8	100.0	101.7	Employment	67
Period Averages																	
	....	....	....	....	....	....	....	....	....	934	952	946	967	983	....	Labor Force	67d
	....	....	....	....	....	....	....	....	845	851	882	878	898	907	....	Employment	67e
	....	....	....	....	....	....	....	103	Ɩ85	85	70	69	69	75	....	Unemployment	67c
	....	....	....	....	....	....	....	11.5	Ɩ9.1	9.0	7.4	7.3	7.1	7.9	....	Unemployment Rate (%)	67r
Millions of US Dollars																**International Transactions**	
	....	....	....	....	....	....	3,852	Ɩ6,681	6,083	6,828	8,316	8,312	8,372	9,048	8,604	Exports	70..d
	....	....	....	....	....	....	4,147	Ɩ6,142	6,499	7,304	9,492	9,423	9,357	10,110	9,952	Imports, c.i.f.	71..d
Minus Sign Indicates Debit																**Balance of Payments**	
	....	....	....	....	....	....	....	978.3	191.0	600.1	−23.0	39.0	36.5	−3.8	−581.1	Current Account, n.i.e.	78al d
	....	....	....	....	....	....	....	6,680.9	6,082.9	6,830.3	8,350.3	8,370.0	8,407.1	9,095.5	8,608.5	Goods: Exports f.o.b.	78aa d
	....	....	....	....	....	....	....	−5,891.8	−6,237.1	−7,168.0	−9,304.7	−9,251.6	−9,178.7	−9,870.4	−9,765.2	Goods: Imports f.o.b.	78ab d
	....	....	....	....	....	....	....	789.1	−154.2	−337.7	−954.4	−881.6	−771.6	−774.9	−1,156.7	*Trade Balance*	78ac d
	....	....	....	....	....	....	....	1,219.3	1,392.1	1,804.8	2,023.2	2,127.4	2,042.6	2,047.9	1,950.2	Services: Credit	78ad d
	....	....	....	....	....	....	....	−1,037.8	−1,017.4	−1,128.7	−1,392.0	−1,422.9	−1,452.7	−1,534.8	−1,584.1	Services: Debit	78ae d
	....	....	....	....	....	....	....	970.6	220.5	338.4	−323.2	−177.1	−181.7	−261.8	−790.6	*Balance on Goods & Services*	78af d
	....	....	....	....	....	....	....	111.7	114.5	334.4	439.1	419.4	416.7	460.4	425.4	Income: Credit	78ag d
	....	....	....	....	....	....	....	−150.1	−166.0	−164.9	−229.6	−264.9	−286.1	−314.4	−335.4	Income: Debit	78ah d
	....	....	....	....	....	....	....	932.2	169.0	507.9	−113.7	−22.6	−51.1	−115.8	−700.6	*Balance on Gds, Serv. & Inc.*	78ai d
	....	....	....	....	....	....	....	93.0	154.9	238.6	250.1	206.8	217.0	268.9	330.0	Current Transfers, n.i.e.: Credit	78aj d
	....	....	....	....	....	....	....	−46.9	−132.9	−146.4	−159.4	−145.2	−129.4	−156.9	−210.5	Current Transfers: Debit	78ak d
	....	....	....	....	....	....	....	—	4.1	−4.3	−18.2	−5.2	−4.2	−4.0	−.8	Capital Account, n.i.e.	78bc d
	....	....	....	....	....	....	....	—	6.7	2.7	3.0	5.6	5.0	3.6	3.3	Capital Account, n.i.e.: Credit	78ba d
	....	....	....	....	....	....	....	—	−2.6	−7.0	−21.2	−10.8	−9.2	−7.6	−4.1	Capital Account: Debit	78bb d
	....	....	....	....	....	....	....	−13.3	−80.9	130.6	424.9	547.9	1,189.7	−4.8	443.7	Financial Account, n.i.e.	78bj d
	....	....	....	....	....	....	....	1.8	−1.3	2.9	−5.5	−7.6	−25.5	−10.9	−43.8	Direct Investment Abroad	78bd d
	....	....	....	....	....	....	....	111.0	112.6	128.1	175.9	185.4	320.8	165.4	83.4	Dir. Invest. in Rep. Econ., n.i.e.	78be d
	....	....	....	....	....	....	....	−8.9	−1.5	−32.5	−28.9	6.6	−2.0	−30.2	−9.1	Portfolio Investment Assets	78bf d
	....	....	....	....	....	....	....	—	—	....	....	....	....	....	−1.6	Equity Securities	78bk d
	....	....	....	....	....	....	....	−8.9	−1.5	−32.5	−28.9	6.6	−2.0	−30.2	−7.5	Debt Securities	78bl d
	....	....	....	....	....	....	....	—	4.5	....	15.5	630.5	237.6	119.9	374.0	Portfolio Investment Liab., n.i.e.	78bg d
	....	....	....	....	....	....	....	—	—	....	....	....	51.7	7.2	−3.2	Equity Securities	78bm d
	....	....	....	....	....	....	....	—	4.5	....	15.5	630.5	185.9	112.7	377.2	Debt Securities	78bn d
	....	....	....	....	....	....	....	....	....	....	....	....	....	....	....	Financial Derivatives Assets	78bw d
	....	....	....	....	....	....	....	....	....	....	....	....	....	....	....	Financial Derivatives Liabilities	78bx d
	....	....	....	....	....	....	....	−157.6	−313.5	−306.6	−350.9	−425.5	288.2	−591.3	−687.2	Other Investment Assets	78bh d
	....	....	....	....	....	....	....	.5	—	−98.3	−66.8	131.5	−7.6	−5.3	−5.6	Monetary Authorities	78bo d
	....	....	....	....	....	....	....	−.1	−.3	−.4	−2.2	−1.3	−1.3	−1.9	−1.5	General Government	78bp d
	....	....	....	....	....	....	....	−173.8	−473.6	−358.8	−293.6	−317.7	476.5	−51.5	−9.6	Banks	78bq d
	....	....	....	....	....	....	....	15.8	160.4	150.9	11.7	−238.0	−179.5	−532.6	−670.5	Other Sectors	78br d
	....	....	....	....	....	....	....	40.4	118.3	338.7	618.8	158.5	370.7	342.3	726.4	Other Investment Liab., n.i.e.	78bi d
	....	....	....	....	....	....	....	—	—	—	—	.2	—	.1	—	Monetary Authorities	78bs d
	....	....	....	....	....	....	....	−18.3	80.2	79.3	127.4	−73.5	−4.5	−17.9	13.8	General Government	78bt d
	....	....	....	....	....	....	....	11.3	−41.9	112.5	259.5	−29.5	23.9	88.6	239.0	Banks	78bu d
	....	....	....	....	....	....	....	47.4	80.0	146.9	231.9	261.3	351.3	271.5	473.6	Other Sectors	78bv d
	....	....	....	....	....	....	....	−332.4	10.7	−76.3	−144.9	7.9	66.4	170.3	56.9	Net Errors and Omissions	78ca d
	....	....	....	....	....	....	....	632.6	124.9	650.1	238.8	589.6	1,288.4	157.7	−81.3	*Overall Balance*	78cb d
	....	....	....	....	....	....	....	−632.6	−124.9	−650.1	−238.8	−589.6	−1,288.4	−157.7	81.3	Reserves and Related Items	79da d
	....	....	....	....	....	....	....	−632.6	−111.0	−644.9	−235.3	−587.0	−1,287.2	−157.7	81.3	Reserve Assets	79db d
	....	....	....	....	....	....	....	—	−13.8	−5.2	−3.4	−2.6	−1.2	—	—	Use of Fund Credit and Loans	79dc d
	....	....	....	....	....	....	....	....	....	....	....	....	....	....	....	Exceptional Financing	79de d

Slovenia

	1970	1971	1972	1973	1974	1975	1976	1977	1978	1979	1980	1981	1982	1983	1984

International Investment Position — *Millions of US Dollars*

Assets .... 79aa d	...	...	...	...	...	...	...	...	...	...	...	...	...	...	...
Direct Investment Abroad .... 79ab d	...	...	...	...	...	...	...	...	...	...	...	...	...	...	...
Portfolio Investment .... 79ac d	...	...	...	...	...	...	...	...	...	...	...	...	...	...	...
Equity Securities............................ 79ad d	...	...	...	...	...	...	...	...	...	...	...	...	...	...	...
Debt Securities .... 79ae d	...	...	...	...	...	...	...	...	...	...	...	...	...	...	...
Financial Derivatives........................ 79al d	...	...	...	...	...	...	...	...	...	...	...	...	...	...	...
Other Investment .... 79af d	...	...	...	...	...	...	...	...	...	...	...	...	...	...	...
Monetary Authorities...................... 79ag d	...	...	...	...	...	...	...	...	...	...	...	...	...	...	...
General Government...................... 79ah d	...	...	...	...	...	...	...	...	...	...	...	...	...	...	...
Banks .... 79ai d	...	...	...	...	...	...	...	...	...	...	...	...	...	...	...
Other Sectors .... 79aj d	...	...	...	...	...	...	...	...	...	...	...	...	...	...	...
Reserve Assets .... 79ak d	...	...	...	...	...	...	...	...	...	...	...	...	...	...	...
Liabilities .... 79la d	...	...	...	...	...	...	...	...	...	...	...	...	...	...	...
Dir. Invest. in Rep. Economy........... 79lb d	...	...	...	...	...	...	...	...	...	...	...	...	...	...	...
Portfolio Investment .... 79lc d	...	...	...	...	...	...	...	...	...	...	...	...	...	...	...
Equity Securities .... 79ld d	...	...	...	...	...	...	...	...	...	...	...	...	...	...	...
Debt Securities .... 79le d	...	...	...	...	...	...	...	...	...	...	...	...	...	...	...
Financial Derivatives........................ 79ll d	...	...	...	...	...	...	...	...	...	...	...	...	...	...	...
Other investment................................ 79lf d	...	...	...	...	...	...	...	...	...	...	...	...	...	...	...
Monetary Authorities...................... 79lg d	...	...	...	...	...	...	...	...	...	...	...	...	...	...	...
General Government...................... 79lh d	...	...	...	...	...	...	...	...	...	...	...	...	...	...	...
Banks .... 79li d	...	...	...	...	...	...	...	...	...	...	...	...	...	...	...
Other Sectors .... 79lj d	...	...	...	...	...	...	...	...	...	...	...	...	...	...	...

Government Finance — *Billions of Tolars:*

Deficit (-) or Surplus.............................. 80	...	...	...	...	...	...	...	...	...	...	...	...	...	...	...
Revenue 81	...	...	...	...	...	...	...	...	...	...	...	...	...	...	...
Grants Received 81z	...	...	...	...	...	...	...	...	...	...	...	...	...	...	...
Expenditure 82	...	...	...	...	...	...	...	...	...	...	...	...	...	...	...
Lending Minus Repayments 83	...	...	...	...	...	...	...	...	...	...	...	...	...	...	...
Financing															
Net Borrowing: Domestic 84a	...	...	...	...	...	...	...	...	...	...	...	...	...	...	...
Foreign........................ 85a	...	...	...	...	...	...	...	...	...	...	...	...	...	...	...
Use of Cash Balances 87	...	...	...	...	...	...	...	...	...	...	...	...	...	...	...

National Accounts — *Billions of Tolars*

Househ.Cons.Expend.,incl.NPISHs 96f	...	...	...	...	...	...	...	...	...	...	...	...	...	...	...
Government Consumption Expend......... 91f	...	...	...	...	...	...	...	...	...	...	...	...	...	...	...
Gross Fixed Capital Formation 93e	...	...	...	...	...	...	...	...	...	...	...	...	...	...	...
Changes in Inventories 93i	...	...	...	...	...	...	...	...	...	...	...	...	...	...	...
Exports of Goods and Services 90c	...	...	...	...	...	...	...	...	...	...	...	...	...	...	...
Imports of Goods and Services................ 98c	...	...	...	...	...	...	...	...	...	...	...	...	...	...	...
Gross Domestic Product (GDP) 99b	...	...	...	...	...	...	...	...	...	...	...	...	...	...	...
GDP Volume 1992 Prices.................... 99b.p	...	...	...	...	...	...	...	...	...	...	...	...	...	...	...
GDP Volume 1995 Prices.................... 99b.p	...	...	...	...	...	...	...	...	...	...	...	...	...	...	...
GDP Volume (1995=100) .... 99bv p	...	...	...	...	...	...	...	...	...	...	...	...	...	...	...
GDP Deflator (1995=100).................... 99bi p	...	...	...	...	...	...	...	...	...	...	...	...	...	...	...

Millions:

Population.. 99z	...	...	...	...	...	...	...	...	...	...	...	...	...	...	...

1985	1986	1987	1988	1989	1990	1991	1992	1993	1994	1995	1996	1997	1998	1999		

Millions of US Dollars — International Investment Position

1993	1994	1995	1996	1997	1998	1999	Item	Code
....	5,899.1	6,798.1	7,128.0	7,714.5	8,447.7	7,834.4	Assets	79aa d
....	354.1	490.0	478.5	452.4	599.8	621.0	Direct Investment Abroad	79ab d
....	62.0	106.4	93.9	55.1	48.0	62.7	Portfolio Investment	79ac d
....	15.0	17.1	15.8	14.7	25.1	32.4	Equity Securities	79ad d
....	47.0	89.3	78.1	40.4	22.9	30.3	Debt Securities	79ae d
....	—	—	—	—	—	—	Financial Derivatives	79al d
....	3,983.9	4,380.8	4,258.2	3,892.3	4,161.3	3,982.6	Other Investment	79af d
....	103.3	170.1	33.3	40.7	46.3	51.8	Monetary Authorities	79ag d
....	—	—	—	—	—	—	General Government	79ah d
....	1,709.1	1,909.3	2,066.3	1,397.7	1,511.2	1,330.3	Banks	79ai d
....	2,171.5	2,301.4	2,158.6	2,453.9	2,603.8	2,600.5	Other Sectors	79aj d
....	1,499.1	1,820.9	2,297.4	3,314.7	3,638.6	3,168.1	Reserve Assets	79ak d
....	5,122.1	6,300.6	7,687.3	8,304.1	9,564.3	9,860.0	Liabilities	79la d
....	1,326.0	1,763.3	2,062.9	2,447.7	2,903.5	2,683.5	Dir. Invest. in Rep. Economy	79lb d
....	88.9	104.1	1,167.7	1,329.1	1,463.5	1,733.5	Portfolio Investment	79lc d
....	45.9	62.7	133.8	155.7	137.0	147.7	Equity Securities	79ld d
....	43.0	41.4	1,033.9	1,173.4	1,326.5	1,585.8	Debt Securities	79le d
....	—	—	—	—	—	—	Financial Derivatives	79ll d
....	3,707.2	4,433.2	4,456.7	4,527.3	5,197.3	5,443.0	Other investment	79lf d
....	7.3	4.1	1.6	.2	.4	.3	Monetary Authorities	79lg d
....	418.3	579.3	593.4	503.1	573.9	480.8	General Government	79lh d
....	706.3	880.2	1,176.5	1,151.3	1,249.1	1,411.9	Banks	79li d
....	2,575.3	2,969.6	2,685.2	2,872.7	3,373.9	3,550.0	Other Sectors	79lj d

Year Ending December 31 — Government Finance

1993	1994	1995	1996	1997	1998	1999	Item	Code
5.35	−5.06	−6.46	1.61	−43.20	−20.34	−29.63	Deficit (-) or Surplus	80
611.45	768.50	926.42	1,041.65	1,163.40	1,330.58	1,445.54	Revenue	81
—	—	.49	.96	1.76	2.45	3.18	Grants Received	81z
606.09	773.56	933.36	1,041.00	1,208.36	1,363.54	1,477.07	Expenditure	82
					−10.17	1.28	Lending Minus Repayments	83
							Financing	
−3.09	−5.41	−10.53	−11.65	12.32	22.95	−19.80	Net Borrowing: Domestic	84a
6.82	3.82	6.27	23.08	20.10	11.32	61.04	Foreign	85a
−9.08	6.65	10.70	−13.05	10.78	−7.90	−11.61	Use of Cash Balances	87

Billions of Tolars — National Accounts

1992	1993	1994	1995	1996	1997	1998	Item	Code
	839.2	1,050.2	1,290.4	1,463.3	1,641.5	1,806.6	Househ.Cons.Expend.,incl.NPISHs	96f
	302.6	374.3	448.2	516.9	595.1	666.7	Government Consumption Expend.	91f
	270.2	372.7	475.0	576.7	684.1	785.2	Gross Fixed Capital Formation	93e
	7.4	15.3	44.0	23.7	20.5	32.0	Changes in Inventories	93i
	843.1	1,111.3	1,225.7	1,419.9	1,660.3	1,838.7	Exports of Goods and Services	90c
	−827.5	−1,070.8	−1,262.1	−1,445.0	−1,694.6	−1,885.7	Imports of Goods and Services	98c
	1,435.1	1,853.0	2,221.5	2,555.4	2,907.3	3,243.5	Gross Domestic Product (GDP)	99b
1,018.0	1,046.9	1,102.7	1,148.0	....	....	....	GDP Volume 1992 Prices	99b. p
....	....	....	2,221.5	2,294.4	2,382.1	....	GDP Volume 1995 Prices	99b. p
88.7	91.2	96.1	100.0	103.3	107.2	....	GDP Volume (1995=100)	99bv p
....	70.8	86.8	100.0	111.4	122.0	....	GDP Deflator (1995=100)	99bi p

Midyear Estimates

1992	1993	1994	1995	1996	1997	1998	1999	Item	Code
2.00	1.99	1.99	1.99	1.99	1.99	1.98	1.99	Population	99z

Solomon Islands

		1970	1971	1972	1973	1974	1975	1976	1977	1978	1979	1980	1981	1982	1983	1984
Exchange Rates																*Solomon Islands Dollars per SDR:*
Official Rate	aa	.8969	.9116	.8515	.8107	.9226	.9312	1.0694	1.0642	1.1324	1.1306	1.0172	1.0346	1.1527	1.2788	1.3170
													Solomon Islands Dollars per US Dollar:			
Official Rate	ae	.8969	.8396	.7843	.6720	.7536	.7955	.9205	.8761	.8692	.8582	.7975	.8889	1.0449	1.2214	1.3435
Official Rate	rf	.8929	.8816	.8373[e]	.7041	.6981[e]	.7639	.8183	.9018	.8737	.8660	.8298	.8702	.9711	1.1486	1.2737
															Index Numbers (1995=100):	
Official Rate	ah x	380.1[e]	168.6	406.8[e]	483.6[e]	489.4[e]	446.1	417.2	377.7	389.8	393.4	410.7	391.9	352.5	297.0	267.7
Nominal Effective Exchange Rate	ne c	....	....	....	....	....	....	....	....	....	330.7	345.6	347.7	339.6	302.3	289.0
Real Effective Exchange Rate	re c	....	....	....	....	....	....	....	....	....	140.3	148.6	158.5	163.2	147.9	149.3
Fund Position																*Millions of SDRs:*
Quota	2f. s	....	....	....	....	....	....	....	....	2.10	2.10	3.20	3.20	3.20	5.00	5.00
SDRs	1b. s	....	....	....	....	....	....	....	....	—	.04	.97	1.22	1.24	1.65	1.34
Reserve Position in the Fund	1c. s	....	....	....	....	....	....	....	....	—	.43	.72	.01	.02	.47	.48
Total Fund Cred.&Loans Outstg.	2tl	....	....	....	....	....	....	....	....	—	—	—	.80	2.40	3.36	3.16
International Liquidity													*Millions of US Dollars Unless Otherwise Indicated:*			
Total Reserves minus Gold	1l. d	....	....	....	....	....	....	....	2.87	29.19	36.96	29.60	21.59	37.23	47.33	44.70[e]
SDRs	1b. d	....	....	....	....	....	....	....	....	—	.05	1.24	1.42	1.37	1.73	1.31
Reserve Position in the Fund	1c. d	....	....	....	....	....	....	....	....	—	.57	.92	.01	.02	.49	.47
Foreign Exchange	1d. d	....	....	....	....	....	....	....	2.87	29.19	36.34	27.45	20.16	35.84	45.11	42.92[e]
Deposit Money Banks: Assets	7a. d	....	....	....	....	....	....	....	....	.73	1.13	1.02	.96	.81	1.67	1.57
Liabilities	7b. d	....	....	....	....	....	....	....	....	1.85	1.20	2.12	3.07	2.48	2.74	1.44
Monetary Authorities														*Millions of Solomon Islands Dollars:*		
Foreign Assets	11	....	....	....	....	....	....	....	....	25.37	31.72	23.61	19.19	38.91	55.57	59.04
Claims on Central Government	12a	....	....	....	....	....	....	....	....	—	—	.13	.42	3.23	3.27	3.35
Claims on Nonfin.Pub.Enterprises	12c	....	....	....	....	....	....	....	....	—	—	—	—	—	—	.50
Claims on Deposit Money Banks	12e	....	....	....	....	....	....	....	....	.21	.16	—	.20	.70	—	—
Reserve Money	14	....	....	....	....	....	....	....	....	24.20	26.91	17.36	9.69	15.58	20.73	28.79
of which: Currency Outside DMBs	14a	....	....	....	....	....	....	....	....	3.85	4.84	5.66	6.42	7.15	9.30	12.75
Restricted Deposits	16b	....	....	....	....	....	....	....	....	—	—	—	—	—	—	5.44
Foreign Liabilities	16c	....	....	....	....	....	....	....	....	.16	.58	.42	5.64	19.09	28.97	18.32
Central Government Deposits	16d	....	....	....	....	....	....	....	....	.65	1.81	3.13	.43	2.19	6.38	3.57
Capital Accounts	17a	....	....	....	....	....	....	....	....	.75	3.03	2.88	5.48	8.54	12.11	18.16
Other Items (Net)	17r	....	....	....	....	....	....	....	....	−.18	−.45	−.06	−1.43	−2.56	−9.35	−11.38
Deposit Money Banks														*Millions of Solomon Islands Dollars:*		
Reserves	20	....	....	....	....	....	....	....	....	19.18	24.24	11.59	2.20	7.41	9.42	16.01
Foreign Assets	21	....	....	....	....	....	....	....	....	.64	.97	.82	.85	.85	2.04	2.12
Claims on Central Government	22a	....	....	....	....	....	....	....	....	.09	.53	1.24	1.68	3.05	5.83	4.62
Claims on Local Government	22b	....	....	....	....	....	....	....	....	—	—	—	—	—	—	—
Claims on Nonfin.Pub.Enterprises	22c	....	....	....	....	....	....	....	....	—	—	5.15	5.78	5.26	5.13	5.90
Claims on Private Sector	22d	....	....	....	....	....	....	....	....	5.70	13.14	17.34	21.39	22.45	20.56	29.88
Claims on Other Banking Insts	22f	....	....	....	....	....	....	....	....	—	—	—	—	—	—	—
Demand Deposits	24	....	....	....	....	....	....	....	....	3.97	6.15	9.48	7.81	8.63	9.13	15.57
Time and Savings Deposits	25	....	....	....	....	....	....	....	....	19.48	28.57	23.87	17.92	23.90	29.16	35.91
Money Market Instruments	26aa	....	....	....	....	....	....	....	....	—	—	.03	.04	.10	.31	.41
Foreign Liabilities	26c	....	....	....	....	....	....	....	....	1.61	1.03	1.69	2.73	2.59	3.34	1.93
Central Government Deposits	26d	....	....	....	....	....	....	....	....	1.29	3.03	2.54	3.08	1.76	1.05	1.53
Credit from Monetary Authorities	26g	....	....	....	....	....	....	....	....	.20	.16	—	.20	.70	—	—
Capital Accounts	27a	....	....	....	....	....	....	....	....	—	—	—	—	—	2.97	5.68
Other Items (Net)	27r	....	....	....	....	....	....	....	....	−.94	−.05	−1.47	.12	−1.63	−.03	−2.51
Monetary Survey														*Millions of Solomon Islands Dollars:*		
Foreign Assets (Net)	31n	....	....	....	....	....	....	....	....	24.24	31.08	22.31	11.67	18.07	25.29	40.91
Domestic Credit	32	....	....	....	....	....	....	....	....	3.85	8.83	18.19	25.75	30.04	27.36	39.15
Claims on Central Govt. (Net)	32an	....	....	....	....	....	....	....	....	−1.85	−4.31	−4.29	−1.42	2.33	1.67	2.87
Claims on Local Government	32b	....	....	....	....	....	....	....	....	—	—	—	—	—	—	—
Claims on Nonfin.Pub.Enterprises	32c	....	....	....	....	....	....	....	....	—	—	5.15	5.78	5.26	5.13	6.40
Claims on Private Sector	32d	....	....	....	....	....	....	....	....	5.70	13.14	17.34	21.39	22.45	20.56	29.88
Claims on Other Banking Insts	32f	....	....	....	....	....	....	....	....	—	—	—	—	—	—	—
Money	34	....	....	....	....	....	....	....	....	7.82	10.99	15.14	14.23	15.78	18.43	28.32
Quasi-Money	35	....	....	....	....	....	....	....	....	19.48	28.57	23.87	17.92	23.90	29.16	35.91
Money Market Instruments	36aa	....	....	....	....	....	....	....	....	—	—	.03	.04	.10	.31	.41
Restricted Deposits	36b	....	....	....	....	....	....	....	....	—	—	—	—	—	—	5.44
Capital Accounts	37a	....	....	....	....	....	....	....	....	.75	3.03	2.88	5.48	11.51	12.11	23.84
Other Items (Net)	37r	....	....	....	....	....	....	....	....	.04	−2.67	−1.42	−.24	−3.17	−7.36	−13.86
Money plus Quasi-Money	35l	....	....	....	....	....	....	....	....	27.29	39.56	39.01	32.15	39.68	47.59	64.23
Other Banking Institutions														*Millions of Solomon Islands Dollars:*		
Reserves	40	....	....	....	....	....	....	....	.90	.81	3.61	4.00	3.47	5.78	8.22	8.36
Claims on Private Sector	42d	....	....	....	....	....	....	....	1.22	4.76	7.79	12.32	17.00	18.06	24.35	26.17
Quasi-Monetary Liabilities	45	....	....	....	....	....	....	....	....	....	....	....	....	....	....	....
Central Govt. Lending Funds	46f	....	....	....	....	....	....	....	1.48	5.27	7.19	11.92	15.26	20.73	24.68	25.75
Credit from Monetary Authorities	46g	....	....	....	....	....	....	....	—	—	—	—	.18	.25	.01	.06
Credit from Deposit Money Banks	46h	....	....	....	....	....	....	....	—	—	2.84	2.93	2.70	3.25	5.43	.51
Liabs. to Nonbank Financial Insts	46j	....	....	....	....	....	....	....	—	—	.50	.50	1.52	1.51	1.95	5.70
Capital Accounts	47a	....	....	....	....	....	....	....	.73	2.20	3.40	4.16	4.91	3.38	6.28	8.56
Other Items (Net)	47r	....	....	....	....	....	....	....	−.09	−1.90	−2.52	−3.18	−4.10	−5.29	−5.78	−6.06

1985	1986	1987	1988	1989	1990	1991	1992	1993	1994	1995	1996	1997	1998	1999		
End of Period															**Exchange Rates**	
1.7714	2.4299	2.8009	2.8505	3.1500	3.7184	3.9978	4.2622	4.4611	4.8597	5.1668	5.2081	6.4067	6.8417	6.9671	Official Rate	**aa**
End of Period (ae) Period Average (rf)																
1.6126	1.9865	1.9743	2.1182	2.3969	2.6137	2.7949	3.0998	3.2478	3.3289	3.4758	3.6219	4.7483	4.8591	5.0761	Official Rate	**ae**
1.4808	1.7415	2.0033	2.0825	2.2932	2.5288	2.7148	2.9281	3.1877	3.2914	3.4059	3.5664	3.7169	4.8156	4.8381	Official Rate	**rf**
Period Averages																
229.8	196.5	170.0	163.6	148.7	134.7	125.6	116.2	106.8	103.5	100.0	95.5	91.2	70.7	69.1	Official Rate	**ah** x
264.8	203.2	163.5	149.0	139.6	126.6	120.0	113.1	111.1	108.4	100.0	97.9	100.5	84.6	81.2	Nominal Effective Exchange Rate	**ne** c
136.3	115.2	99.8	102.5	105.8	96.8	99.4	98.3	99.2	102.4	100.0	106.9	116.6	108.8	111.7	Real Effective Exchange Rate	**re** c
End of Period															**Fund Position**	
5.00	5.00	5.00	5.00	5.00	5.00	5.00	7.50	7.50	7.50	7.50	7.50	7.50	7.50	10.40	Quota	**2f.** s
.77	1.29	.17	—	.05	.25	.07	.04	.03	.01	.01	.01	—	—	.01	SDRs	**1b.** s
.51	.51	.52	.52	.53	.53	.54	.54	.54	.54	.54	.54	.54	.54	.54	Reserve Position in the Fund	**1c.** s
2.76	2.83	1.55	1.25	1.09	.47	—	—	—	—	—	—	—	—	—	Total Fund Cred.&Loans Outstg.	**2tl**
End of Period															**International Liquidity**	
35.61 e	29.57	36.75	39.62	26.16	17.60	8.54	23.50	20.07	17.42	15.91	32.58	36.34	49.04	51.14	Total Reserves minus Gold	**1l.** d
.85	1.58	.24	—	.07	.36	.10	.06	.04	.01	.01	.01	—	—	.01	SDRs	**1b.** d
.56	.62	.74	.70	.70	.75	.77	.74	.74	.79	.80	.77	.73	.76	.74	Reserve Position in the Fund	**1c.** d
34.20 e	27.37	35.77	38.92	25.40	16.49	7.67	22.70	19.29	16.62	15.10	31.80	35.61	48.28	50.39	Foreign Exchange	**1d.** d
2.46	1.92	3.39	2.46	.52	1.20	2.33	2.13	2.13	3.57	1.30	3.27	3.94	1.29	6.06	Deposit Money Banks: Assets	**7a.** d
2.10	1.67	2.79	1.20	1.31	3.81	2.88	1.71	1.75	4.82	1.82	4.00	2.56	2.58	5.56	Liabilities	**7b.** d
Approximately End of Period															**Monetary Authorities**	
46.07	58.79	71.07	82.95	62.47	44.85	23.59	73.45	65.07	58.21	55.39	117.71	153.90	237.15	261.57	Foreign Assets	**11**
10.00	5.90	10.14	11.94	21.00	31.70	58.01	37.92	45.39	64.47	77.98	73.06	76.36	76.15	46.56	Claims on Central Government	**12a**
.50	.68	7.32	11.96	11.65	10.59	9.65	11.92	4.22	4.20	4.20	4.20	4.20	4.20	4.01	Claims on Nonfin.Pub.Enterprises	**12c**
7.80	6.55	.10	.15	6.76	.06	.03	—	—	—	—	—	—	—	—	Claims on Deposit Money Banks	**12e**
22.39	22.98	23.83	32.21	27.01	31.02	42.11	42.06	46.97	61.48	75.63	98.60	92.47	134.96	134.61	Reserve Money	**14**
13.89	13.58	16.84	20.21	22.65	25.22	27.80	30.83	42.11	50.23	54.93	59.67	70.79	81.28	100.07	of which: Currency Outside DMBs	**14a**
.07	.09	.10	.86	.03	2.70	.34	.14	1.02	.83	1.10	1.71	1.28	3.51	1.46	Restricted Deposits	**16b**
22.29	18.44	8.92	5.90	10.40	3.56	1.16	1.67	5.70	1.39	1.24	2.28	.59	2.13	1.64	Foreign Liabilities	**16c**
4.82	5.88	25.82	23.24	8.56	1.80	4.88	5.98	11.11	4.28	3.84	6.55	59.78	56.00		Central Government Deposits	**16d**
19.62	29.12	35.70	42.51	46.94	49.13	52.16	50.99	52.31	57.39	59.41	68.82	103.81	108.23	109.93	Capital Accounts	**17a**
−4.81	−4.59	−5.75	−5.33	−5.75	−7.78	−6.29	23.56	2.70	−5.32	−4.10	19.71	29.77	8.89	8.51	Other Items (Net)	**17r**
Approximately End of Period															**Deposit Money Banks**	
7.70	9.40	7.16	12.28	4.41	5.78	14.06	6.64	4.86	12.50	22.04	39.90	21.64	51.50	52.34	Reserves	**20**
3.96	3.81	6.70	5.20	1.25	3.13	6.50	6.61	6.91	11.88	4.51	11.85	18.69	6.29	30.78	Foreign Assets	**21**
8.10	11.60	25.79	32.64	31.97	39.36	69.94	105.47	130.86	152.14	159.00	160.33	162.70	165.53	180.30	Claims on Central Government	**22a**
.35	.13		.01	.06	.64	.28	.48	.41	1.24	.22	.60	.31	.21	.22	Claims on Local Government	**22b**
1.05	.23	.06	.86	1.58	6.89	6.13	1.46	2.71	.91	1.22	2.71	.75	.78	2.58	Claims on Nonfin.Pub.Enterprises	**22c**
47.10	51.62	55.02	69.52	92.23	82.31	75.64	72.22	84.22	107.06	121.96	128.20	141.27	176.99	191.74	Claims on Private Sector	**22d**
.64	1.12	.82		.73	1.57	.41	.32	—	—	—	—	—	—	—	Claims on Other Banking Insts	**22f**
14.45	16.80	20.39	28.82	28.25	39.23	51.74	74.08	81.82	112.65	116.02	138.08	141.66	130.82	166.48	Demand Deposits	**24**
37.59	41.65	59.76	79.04	76.68	75.65	94.02	111.12	125.88	149.70	170.41	195.89	207.49	218.50	194.08	Time and Savings Deposits	**25**
.43	.64	.61	.49	.56	.26	.16	.13	.49	.54	—	—	.31	—	.61	Money Market Instruments	**26aa**
3.38	3.33	5.51	2.54	3.14	9.97	8.05	5.32	5.67	16.05	6.33	14.49	12.16	12.54	28.21	Foreign Liabilities	**26c**
.33	2.03	2.03	4.08	6.01	2.21	7.94	4.31	5.17	5.24	9.32	7.83	8.22	4.35	12.88	Central Government Deposits	**26d**
6.40	6.55	.10	.15	5.76	.06	.03	—	—	—	—	—	—	—	—	Credit from Monetary Authorities	**26g**
8.83	9.26	10.04	10.29	13.62	16.57	18.39	22.72	32.30	30.87	28.80	32.54	38.35	62.39	72.19	Capital Accounts	**27a**
−2.51	−2.34	−2.88	−4.90	−1.80	−4.28	−7.37	−24.50	−21.36	−29.31	−21.93	−45.25	−62.82	−27.31	−16.49	Other Items (Net)	**27r**
Approximately End of Period															**Monetary Survey**	
24.36	40.83	63.34	79.72	50.18	34.45	20.88	73.08	60.61	52.64	52.33	112.79	159.84	228.77	262.50	Foreign Assets (Net)	**31n**
62.59	63.37	71.29	91.99	129.95	162.28	210.32	220.60	256.67	313.68	350.97	357.41	370.82	359.72	356.53	Domestic Credit	**32**
12.95	9.59	8.08	9.65	23.71	60.29	118.21	134.20	165.10	200.27	223.37	221.72	224.29	177.55	157.98	Claims on Central Govt. (Net)	**32an**
.35	.13		.01	.06	.64	.28	.48	.41	1.24	.22	.60	.31	.21	.22	Claims on Local Government	**32b**
1.55	.91	7.38	12.82	13.23	17.47	15.78	13.38	6.94	5.11	5.42	6.90	4.95	4.98	6.60	Claims on Nonfin.Pub.Enterprises	**32c**
47.10	51.62	55.02	69.52	92.23	82.31	75.64	72.22	84.22	107.06	121.96	128.20	141.27	176.99	191.74	Claims on Private Sector	**32d**
.64	1.12	.82		.73	1.57	.41	.32	—	—	—	—	—	—	—	Claims on Other Banking Insts	**32f**
28.33	30.38	37.23	49.03	50.90	64.46	79.54	104.91	123.93	162.88	170.96	197.75	212.45	212.10	266.54	Money	**34**
37.59	41.65	59.76	79.04	76.68	75.65	94.02	111.12	125.88	149.70	170.41	195.89	207.49	218.50	194.08	Quasi-Money	**35**
.43	.64	.61	.49	.56	.26	.16	.13	.49	.54	—	—	.31	—	.61	Money Market Instruments	**36aa**
.07	.09	.10	.86	.03	2.70	.34	.14	1.02	.83	1.10	1.71	1.28	3.51	1.46	Restricted Deposits	**36b**
28.45	38.38	45.75	52.80	60.56	65.70	70.54	73.71	84.61	88.26	88.21	101.36	142.16	170.63	182.11	Capital Accounts	**37a**
−7.92	−6.93	−8.81	−10.52	−8.60	−12.04	−13.40	3.66	−18.65	−35.88	−27.37	−26.51	−33.02	−16.25	−25.78	Other Items (Net)	**37r**
65.92	72.03	96.98	128.07	127.58	140.11	173.56	216.03	249.81	312.58	341.37	393.64	419.93	430.60	460.62	Money plus Quasi-Money	**35l**
End of Period															**Other Banking Institutions**	
7.59	8.17	‖12.62	....	....	9.77	14.57	17.05	11.35	....	....	68.17	71.50	18.56	14.56	Reserves	**40**
31.28	33.12	‖40.81	13.27	16.95	18.17	20.42	54.50	65.65	....	....	113.32	125.99	139.13	126.38	Claims on Private Sector	**42d**
....	....	.36	.97	2.57	2.94	3.34	5.96	9.12	10.00	11.76	13.90	16.48	17.18	19.31	Quasi-Monetary Liabilities	**45**
25.79	26.11	‖28.65	5.00	4.74	6.71	6.50	6.47	12.22	7.44	2.43	1.88	1.35	1.32	1.32	Central Govt. Lending Funds	**46f**
.19	.67	‖6.76	....	....	6.21	9.87	9.26	6.81	....	....	11.77	11.35	6.13	6.44	Credit from Monetary Authorities	**46g**
.45	.45	‖.40	....	....	.55	.12	.12	.04	....	....	—	—	—	—	Credit from Deposit Money Banks	**46h**
9.91	13.61	‖13.15	....	....	10.38	10.13	9.22	8.31	....	....	3.47	1.67	7.40	7.33	Liabs. to Nonbank Financial Insts	**46j**
8.84	9.95	‖7.44	....	....	4.11	7.79	13.79	16.58	....	....	18.03	26.77	34.82	15.83	Capital Accounts	**47a**
−6.31	−9.50	‖−3.33	....	....	−2.95	−2.75	26.74	23.93	....	....	132.44	139.88	90.84	90.70	Other Items (Net)	**47r**

Solomon Islands

	1970	1971	1972	1973	1974	1975	1976	1977	1978	1979	1980	1981	1982	1983	1984
Banking Survey													*Millions of Solomon Islands Dollars:*		
Foreign Assets (Net) **51n**	....	....	....	....	....	....	....	....	24.24	31.08	22.31	11.67	18.07	25.29	40.91
Domestic Credit **52**	....	....	....	....	....	....	....	....	8.61	16.63	30.52	42.75	48.10	51.71	65.32
Claims on Central Govt. (Net) ... **52an**	....	....	....	....	....	....	....	....	−1.85	−4.31	−4.29	−1.42	2.33	1.67	2.87
Claims on Local Government ... **52b**															
Claims on Nonfin.Pub.Enterprises ... **52c**									—	—	5.15	5.78	5.26	5.13	6.40
Claims on Private Sector ... **52d**									10.46	20.93	29.66	38.39	40.51	44.90	56.05
Liquid Liabilities **55l**	....	....	....	....	....	....	....	....	26.49	35.95	35.01	28.68	33.90	39.38	55.87
Money Market Instruments ... **56aa**									—	—	.03	.04	.10	.31	.41
Restricted Deposits ... **56b**									—	—	—	—	—	—	5.44
Central Govt. Lending Funds ... **56f**									5.27	7.19	11.92	15.26	20.73	24.68	25.75
Liabs. to Nonbank Financial Insts ... **56j**									—	.50	.50	1.52	1.51	1.95	5.70
Capital Accounts **57a**									2.95	6.43	7.05	10.39	14.89	18.40	32.40
Other Items (Net) **57r**									−1.86	−2.36	−1.67	−1.47	−4.96	−7.70	−19.34
Nonbank Financial Institutions													*Millions of Solomon Islands Dollars:*		
Reserves **40.m**	....	....	....	....	....	....	....	....	....	....	5.75	4.62	8.03	9.42	7.93
Claims on Central Government ... **42a.m**	....										1.25	2.68	4.88	7.41	12.66
Claims on Nonfin.Pub.Enterprises ... **42c.m**											1.00	1.25	.99	.97	1.96
Claims on Private Sector ... **42d.m**											.69	.67	.73	.31	.42
Claims on Other Banking Insts ... **42f.m**											—	1.50	1.49	1.92	5.52
Capital Accounts **47a.m**											8.88	11.54	16.73	22.37	30.79
Other Items (Net) **47r.m**	....										−.19	−.82	−.61	−2.34	−2.29
Interest Rates													*Percent Per Annum*		
Treasury Bill Rate **60c**	....	....	....	....	....	....	....	....	....	....	....	5.83	7.50	8.92	9.00
Deposit Rate **60l**	....											6.23	6.92	8.38	8.00
Lending Rate **60p**	....											9.00	10.58	11.50	12.00
Government Bond Yield **61**	....											10.00	11.00	11.00	11.00
Prices, Production, Labor													*Index Numbers (1990=100):*		
Consumer Prices (1995=100) ... **64**	....	8.7	9.3	9.6	11.4	I 12.6	13.1	14.3	15.2	16.4	18.5	21.6	24.4	25.9	28.7
Copra Production **66ag**	78.1	82.7	67.2	51.1	90.6	84.0	75.6	92.7	87.4	106.7	92.6	106.9	102.1	90.2	135.2
Fish Catch **66al**	....	14.5	28.0	22.7	32.1	24.9	55.0	42.0	60.8	83.1	79.8	88.8	71.8	120.9	125.1
													Number in Thousands:		
Employment **67e**	....														
International Transactions													*Millions of Solomon Islands Dollars*		
Exports **70**	7.13	9.08	9.14	9.55	18.25	11.82	19.95	29.61	32.95	59.97	61.28	57.56	56.56	71.20	118.56
Imports, c.i.f. **71**	11.52	13.25	13.86	12.94	18.82	25.04	24.25	29.62	37.05	60.43	73.85	79.17	68.99	84.76	100.60
Volume of Exports **72**	40.9	48.1	48.5	40.4	44.4	43.0	48.2	49.3	57.9	73.8	76.1	83.1	79.2	95.5	105.6
Unit Value of Exports **74**	21.5	23.4	I 19.2	23.3	43.4	28.3	44.2	64.6	61.2	87.8	94.5	75.8	77.4	79.1	118.4
Balance of Payments													*Millions of US Dollars*		
Current Account, n.i.e. .... **78al d**	....	....	....	....	....	−12.57	1.71	5.77	3.32	10.28	−12.17	−26.55	−25.02	−14.63	.16
Goods: Exports f.o.b. .... **78aa d**						15.45	24.32	32.82	35.03	68.48	73.27	66.19	58.28	61.99	93.11
Goods: Imports f.o.b. .... **78ab d**						−28.54	−25.79	−28.61	−35.37	−58.43	−74.11	−75.85	−59.11	−61.47	−67.60
Trade Balance .... **78ac d**						−13.09	−1.47	4.21	−.34	10.05	−.84	−9.65	−.82	.52	25.52
Services: Credit .... **78ad d**						2.49	3.06	3.33	5.27	5.77	11.69	12.99	13.70	15.15	9.50
Services: Debit .... **78ae d**						−9.82	−9.04	−10.65	−17.40	−20.79	−27.96	−37.69	−36.97	−34.13	−38.63
Balance on Goods & Services ... **78af d**						−20.42	−7.45	−3.10	−12.48	−4.97	−17.11	−34.36	−24.10	−18.46	−3.61
Income: Credit .... **78ag d**						—	—	—	—	—	—	2.37	1.83	5.02	
Income: Debit .... **78ah d**						−1.96	−3.91	−4.10	−3.43	−4.62	−14.94	−3.91	−11.22	−10.19	−13.82
Balance on Gds, Serv. & Inc. ... **78ai d**						−22.39	−11.37	−7.21	−15.91	−9.58	−32.05	−38.27	−32.95	−26.82	−12.40
Current Transfers, n.i.e.: Credit ... **78aj d**						9.82	13.08	12.97	19.23	19.86	19.88	17.47	15.34	17.24	17.12
Current Transfers: Debit .... **78ak d**												−5.75	−7.41	−5.05	−4.55
Capital Account, n.i.e. .... **78bc d**	....					—	—	—	—	—	—	—	−1.03	−.96	−.86
Capital Account, n.i.e.: Credit ... **78ba d**						—	—	—	—	—	—	—	—	—	—
Capital Account: Debit .... **78bb d**						—	—	—	—	—	—	—	−1.03	−.96	−.86
Financial Account, n.i.e. .... **78bj d**	....					7.85	4.89	7.32	6.18	6.35	3.13	6.78	14.42	13.23	−11.15
Direct Investment Abroad .... **78bd d**						—	—	—	—	—	—	—	—	—	—
Dir. Invest. in Rep. Econ., n.i.e. ... **78be d**						7.85	4.89	4.44	4.58	3.46	2.41	.23	1.03	.44	1.96
Portfolio Investment Assets .... **78bf d**						—	—	—	—	—	—	—	—	—	—
Equity Securities .... **78bk d**						—	—	—	—	—	—	—	—	—	—
Debt Securities .... **78bl d**						—	—	—	—	—	—	—	—	—	—
Portfolio Investment Liab., n.i.e. ... **78bg d**						—	—	—	—	—	—	—	—	—	—
Equity Securities .... **78bm d**						—	—	—	—	—	—	—	—	—	—
Debt Securities .... **78bn d**						—	—	—	—	—	—	—	—	—	—
Financial Derivatives Assets .... **78bw d**															
Financial Derivatives Liabilities ... **78bx d**															
Other Investment Assets .... **78bh d**						—	—	—	—	.58	−3.25	2.64	—	−1.04	−.16
Monetary Authorities .... **78bo d**						—	—	—	—	—	—	—	—	—	—
General Government .... **78bp d**						—	—	—	—	—	—	—	—	—	—
Banks .... **78bq d**						—	—	—	—	.58	−3.25	2.64	—	−1.04	−.16
Other Sectors .... **78br d**						—	—	—	—	—	—	—	—	—	—
Other Investment Liab., n.i.e. .... **78bi d**						—	—	2.88	1.60	2.31	3.98	3.91	13.39	13.84	−12.95
Monetary Authorities .... **78bs d**						—	—	—	—	—	—	—	—	—	—
General Government .... **78bt d**						—	—	2.88	1.60	2.31	3.98	3.91	6.59	6.70	−16.49
Banks .... **78bu d**						—	—	—	—	—	—	—	—	.44	.47
Other Sectors .... **78bv d**						—	—	—	—	—	—	—	6.80	6.70	3.06
Net Errors and Omissions .... **78ca d**	....					6.02	−4.77	−6.21	5.72	−9.05	—	13.13	16.86	5.99	1.31
Overall Balance .... **78cb d**						1.31	1.83	6.88	15.22	7.57	−9.04	−6.64	5.22	3.64	−10.54
Reserves and Related Items .... **79da d**						−1.31	−1.83	−6.88	−15.22	−7.57	9.04	6.64	−5.22	−3.64	10.54
Reserve Assets .... **79db d**						−1.31	−1.83	−6.88	−15.22	−7.54	9.04	5.71	−16.41	−10.58	−.72
Use of Fund Credit and Loans ... **79dc d**									—	−.04	—	.93	1.71	1.02	−.20
Exceptional Financing .... **79de d**	....												9.47	5.92	11.46

Item	Code	1985	1986	1987	1988	1989	1990	1991	1992	1993	1994	1995	1996	1997	1998	1999
Banking Survey		*Approximately End of Period*														
Foreign Assets (Net)	51n	24.36	40.83	63.34	....	....	34.45	20.88	73.08	60.61	....	....	112.79	159.84	228.77	262.50
Domestic Credit	52	93.87	96.49	I112.10	....	....	180.44	230.74	275.10	322.32	....	....	470.73	496.81	498.85	482.90
Claims on Central Govt. (Net)	52an	12.95	9.59	8.08	....	....	60.29	118.21	134.20	165.10	....	....	221.72	224.29	177.55	157.98
Claims on Local Government	52b	.35	.13	—	....	....	.64	.28	.48	.41	....	....	.60	.31	.21	.22
Claims on Nonfin.Pub.Enterprises	52c	1.55	.91	7.38	....	....	17.47	15.78	13.38	6.94	....	....	6.90	4.95	4.98	6.60
Claims on Private Sector	52d	78.38	84.74	I95.83	....	....	100.47	96.06	126.72	149.88	....	....	241.52	267.26	316.12	318.11
Liquid Liabilities	55l	58.34	63.86	I84.72	....	....	133.28	162.33	204.95	247.58	....	....	339.37	364.91	429.22	465.37
Money Market Instruments	56aa	.43	.64	.61	....	....	.26	.16	.13	.49	....	....	—	.31	—	.61
Restricted Deposits	56b	.07	.09	.10	....	....	2.70	.34	.14	1.02	....	....	1.71	1.28	3.51	1.46
Central Govt. Lending Funds	56f	25.79	26.11	28.65	....	....	6.71	6.50	6.47	12.22	....	....	1.88	1.35	1.32	1.32
Liabs. to Nonbank Financial Insts	56j	9.91	13.61	I13.15	....	....	10.38	10.13	9.22	8.31	....	....	3.47	1.67	7.40	7.33
Capital Accounts	57a	37.29	48.33	I53.19	....	....	69.81	78.33	87.49	101.19	....	....	119.39	168.92	205.45	197.94
Other Items (Net)	57r	-13.59	-15.31	I-4.98	....	....	-8.24	-6.17	39.77	12.13	....	....	117.70	118.21	80.72	71.36
Nonbank Financial Institutions		*End of Period*														
Reserves	40.*m*	4.21	5.44	9.92	11.90	13.95	15.31	24.64	22.79	21.61	26.98	....	....	38.85	47.24	45.73
Claims on Central Government	42a.*m*	18.24	21.47	25.04	28.66	31.81	29.51	38.61	49.14	68.00	73.98	....	....	83.78	125.30	118.73
Claims on Nonfin.Pub.Enterprises	42c.*m*	2.76	2.43	5.46	5.74	8.40	12.20	11.14	17.75	23.72	39.95	....	....	44.44	49.24	44.70
Claims on Private Sector	42d.*m*	.20	.27	.41	2.98	4.23	12.25	16.72	15.24	24.69	31.83	....	....	53.47	59.76	61.66
Claims on Other Banking Insts	42f.*m*	9.65	13.55	13.36	12.59	11.27	10.92	10.68	8.07	8.43	7.37	....	....	25.10	7.62	3.09
Capital Accounts	47a.*m*	39.28	50.12	62.42	74.05	90.20	105.71	129.45	153.64	187.03	223.57	....	....	317.28	359.00	384.31
Other Items (Net)	47r.*m*	-4.23	-6.98	-8.23	-12.17	-20.55	-25.53	-27.66	-40.65	-40.58	-43.46	....	....	-71.64	-69.84	-110.39
Interest Rates		*Percent Per Annum*														
Treasury Bill Rate	60c	9.58	12.00	11.33	11.00	11.00	11.00	13.71	13.50	12.15	11.25	12.50	12.75	12.88	6.00	6.00
Deposit Rate	60l	8.73	10.50	10.67	10.23	10.46	10.50	10.50	12.00	9.77	9.00	8.38	6.46	2.42	2.33	2.88
Lending Rate	60p	12.83	15.13	17.33	18.00	18.00	18.00	19.46	19.75	17.80	15.72	16.59	17.78	15.71	14.84	14.50
Government Bond Yield	61	12.00	13.00	12.33	12.00	12.44	12.75	12.92	13.00	13.00	13.00	13.00	11.50	11.75	12.50	12.88
Prices, Production, Labor		*Period Averages*														
Consumer Prices (1995=100)	64	31.5	35.8	39.7	46.3	53.2	I57.9	66.6	73.8	80.5	91.2	100.0	111.8	120.8	135.7	146.9
Copra Production	66ag	133.0	100.5	86.2	92.9	110.7	100.0	68.5	72.3	70.5	65.8	86.3	91.2	114.7	....	....
Fish Catch	66al	108.3	154.0	112.9	146.0	128.7	100.0	132.3	149.0	111.4	135.8	195.0	142.8	142.8	170.6	....
		Period Averages														
Employment	67e	24	24	25	22	25	26	27	27	30	33	33	34	....	....	....
International Transactions		*Millions of Solomon Islands Dollars*														
Exports	70	103.81	114.90	128.30	170.57	171.26	178.11	228.71	301.18	411.44	467.88	573.15	576.65	648.70	608.30	....
Imports, c.i.f.	71	123.20	125.34	161.93	203.30	259.82	231.04	305.71	326.61	436.29	459.51	526.27	536.87	....	....	....
Volume of Exports	72	96.4	118.5	86.9	92.6	94.4	100.0	122.2	136.3	....	....	....	....	....	....	....
Unit Value of Exports	74	112.1	78.9	84.8	93.9	92.5	100.0	105.9	102.8	....	....	....	....	....	....	....
Balance of Payments		*Minus Sign Indicates Debit*														
Current Account, n.i.e.	78al*d*	-27.82	-11.94	-16.81	-37.65	-33.23	-27.76	-35.84	-1.43	-7.65	-3.43	8.34	14.58	-37.91	8.12	....
Goods: Exports f.o.b.	78aa*d*	70.98	63.85	63.20	81.92	74.70	70.11	83.43	101.74	129.06	142.16	168.30	161.51	156.45	141.83	....
Goods: Imports f.o.b.	78ab*d*	-71.85	-67.41	-69.49	-104.63	-94.28	-77.35	-91.98	-87.43	-136.87	-142.22	-154.53	-150.55	-184.53	-159.90	....
Trade Balance	78ac*d*	-.88	-3.56	-6.29	-22.71	-19.58	-7.24	-8.55	14.31	-7.81	-.06	13.77	10.96	-28.09	-18.07	....
Services: Credit	78ad*d*	9.39	16.65	21.03	21.99	26.51	25.35	31.61	36.03	42.44	49.95	41.81	53.14	70.35	55.07	....
Services: Debit	78ae*d*	-43.15	-49.90	-49.77	-66.22	-75.26	-78.69	-88.26	-78.04	-80.68	-105.94	-76.93	-85.47	-107.18	-54.53	....
Balance on Goods & Services	78af*d*	-34.64	-36.81	-35.03	-66.94	-68.33	-60.58	-65.20	-27.70	-46.05	-56.06	-21.35	-21.37	-64.92	-17.53	....
Income: Credit	78ag*d*	3.58	3.33	3.29	3.55	3.88	2.33	1.36	.99	.69	1.52	1.20	2.36	2.69	2.12	....
Income: Debit	78ah*d*	-8.64	-9.24	-11.03	-12.10	-11.77	-7.59	-10.39	-10.89	-4.61	-4.44	-7.96	-9.42	-11.17	-10.01	....
Balance on Gds, Serv. & Inc.	78ai*d*	-39.71	-42.72	-42.77	-75.49	-76.22	-65.84	-74.22	-37.60	-49.97	-58.97	-28.10	-28.43	-73.39	-25.42	....
Current Transfers, n.i.e.: Credit	78aj*d*	16.01	34.34	29.45	42.93	47.14	43.66	46.82	43.78	47.84	66.60	53.17	57.48	52.57	56.44	....
Current Transfers: Debit	78ak*d*	-4.12	-3.56	-3.49	-5.09	-4.14	-5.58	-8.44	-7.62	-5.52	-11.06	-16.74	-14.47	-17.08	-22.90	....
Capital Account, n.i.e.	78bc*d*	-.95	-.52	-.35	-.38	-.17	-.16	-.26	-.44	.85	2.70	.65	-2.19	-1.00	6.65	....
Capital Account, n.i.e.: Credit	78ba*d*	—	—	—	—	—	—	—	—	.94	2.86	1.50	.50	.30	6.91	....
Capital Account: Debit	78bb*d*	-.95	-.52	-.35	-.38	-.17	-.16	-.26	-.44	-.09	-.15	-.85	-2.69	-1.29	-.27	....
Financial Account, n.i.e.	78bj*d*	14.38	2.64	7.74	43.79	25.12	22.86	15.10	22.44	8.22	1.49	-8.31	-1.37	45.68	16.88	....
Direct Investment Abroad	78bd*d*	—	—	—	—	—	—	—	—	—	—	—	—	—	—	....
Dir. Invest. in Rep. Econ., n.i.e.	78be*d*	.68	3.10	10.48	1.68	11.60	10.44	14.51	14.17	23.37	2.10	2.03	5.94	33.85	8.80	....
Portfolio Investment Assets	78bf*d*	—	—	—	—	—	—	—	—	—	—	—	—	—	—	....
Equity Securities	78bk*d*	—	—	—	—	—	—	—	—	—	—	—	—	—	—	....
Debt Securities	78bl*d*	—	—	—	—	—	—	—	—	—	—	—	—	—	—	....
Portfolio Investment Liab., n.i.e.	78bg*d*	—	—	—	—	—	—	—	—	—	—	—	—	—	—	....
Equity Securities	78bm*d*	—	—	—	—	—	—	—	—	—	—	—	—	—	—	....
Debt Securities	78bn*d*	—	—	—	—	—	—	—	—	—	—	—	—	—	—	....
Financial Derivatives Assets	78bw*d*	....	....	....	....	....	....	....	....	—	—	—	—	—	—	....
Financial Derivatives Liabilities	78bx*d*	....	....	....	....	....	....	....	....	—	—	—	—	—	—	....
Other Investment Assets	78bh*d*	-.27	-5.05	-11.28	18.82	-.74	-.75	-1.25	-.07	—	—	—	—	—	—	....
Monetary Authorities	78bo*d*	....	....	....	....	....	....	....	....	—	—	—	—	—	—	....
General Government	78bp*d*	—	-4.48	-10.53	19.74	—	—	—	—	—	—	—	—	—	—	....
Banks	78bq*d*	-.27	-.57	-.75	-.91	-.74	-.75	-1.25	-.07	—	—	—	—	—	—	....
Other Sectors	78br*d*	—	—	—	—	—	—	—	—	—	—	—	—	—	—	....
Other Investment Liab., n.i.e.	78bi*d*	13.98	4.59	8.54	23.29	14.26	13.17	1.84	8.33	-15.15	-.61	-10.34	-7.32	11.84	8.08	....
Monetary Authorities	78bs*d*	.47	—	1.50	—	2.22	1.07	—	.41	1.32	-1.25	.03	.08	-.62	-.37	....
General Government	78bt*d*	6.08	-.98	12.43	8.50	-1.74	-5.97	-5.01	1.57	.94	-1.34	6.20	5.72	5.17	8.60	....
Banks	78bu*d*	1.42	-1.03	1.95	.05	-1.35	2.77	-.85	-.82	.03	3.31	-2.85	2.30	-.62	-1.23	....
Other Sectors	78bv*d*	6.01	6.60	-7.34	14.74	15.13	15.30	7.70	7.17	-17.44	-1.34	-13.71	-15.42	7.91	1.08	....
Net Errors and Omissions	78ca*d*	-.41	-8.47	2.82	-10.87	-5.21	-8.60	8.36	-6.16	-3.16	-2.79	-1.45	6.96	2.31	-14.41	....
Overall Balance	78cb*d*	-14.80	-18.29	-6.61	-5.10	-13.49	-13.67	-12.64	14.40	-1.74	-2.03	-.77	17.98	9.09	17.24	....
Reserves and Related Items	79da*d*	14.80	18.29	6.61	5.10	13.49	13.67	12.64	-14.40	1.74	2.03	.77	-17.98	-9.09	-17.24	....
Reserve Assets	79db*d*	9.74	8.57	-4.28	-4.28	11.61	8.58	8.34	-17.14	1.74	2.03	.77	-17.98	-9.09	-17.24	....
Use of Fund Credit and Loans	79dc*d*	-.41	.13	-1.64	-.41	-.21	-.84	-.64	—	—	—	—	—	—	—	....
Exceptional Financing	79de*d*	5.47	9.59	12.53	9.80	2.09	5.93	4.94	2.73	—	—	—	—	—	—	....

Solomon Islands

	1970	1971	1972	1973	1974	1975	1976	1977	1978	1979	1980	1981	1982	1983	1984
Government Finance												*Millions of Solomon Islands Dollars:*			
Deficit (-) or Surplus 80	...	...	...	...	...	.04	.03	-.63	.72	-2.94	-3.60	-9.21	-13.04	-13.38	-6.53
Revenue 81	...	...	...	...	...	6.82	8.28	11.05	13.45	20.93	23.38	29.92	33.25	34.36	47.71
Grants Received 81z	...	...	...	...	...	6.23	8.51	8.90	14.68	11.39	13.47	7.33	5.51	6.04	4.70
Expenditure 82	...	...	...	...	...	12.87	16.29	19.48	27.61	31.91	36.17	41.83	46.38	49.94	56.24
Lending Minus Repayments 83	...	...	...	...	...	.14	.47	1.10	-.20	3.35	4.28	4.63	5.42	3.84	2.70
Financing															
Net Borrowing: Domestic 84a	...	...	...	...	...	.01	-.04	-.01	-.01	2.11	3.13	2.97	4.69	6.44	...
Foreign 85a	...	...	...	...	...	.13	.06	.17	.69	2.03	3.42	3.24	5.01	7.64	...
Use of Cash Balances 87	...	...	...	...	...	-.18	-.05	.47	-1.40	-1.20	-2.95	3.00	3.34	-.70	...
Debt: Domestic 88a	...	...	...	...	...	.09	.08	.07	.06	...	9.44	12.05	17.37	21.24	25.32
Foreign 89a	...	...	...	...	...	.59	.64	.79	1.51	...	6.36	9.90	11.94	24.20	29.60
National Accounts												*Millions of Solomon Islands Dollars*			
Exports of Goods & Services 90c	7.1	9.1	9.1	9.6	18.3	11.8	20.0	29.6	30.6	60.2	60.8	...	...	...	135.2
Government Consumption 91f	5.5	5.1	5.5	...	...	...	...	...	...	...	...	...	...	...	52.1
Gross Fixed Capital Formation 93e	4.2	7.2	7.4	...	...	...	...	...	...	...	...	...	...	...	43.0
Increase/Decrease(-) in Stocks 93i	...	...	...	...	...	...	...	...	...	...	...	...	...	...	7.9
Private Consumption 96f	23.3	24.5	23.6	...	...	...	...	...	85.0	103.0	118.1	...	...	...	122.0
Imports of Goods & Services 98c	-10.0	-11.5	-12.1	-11.3	-16.4	-21.8	-21.1	-25.8	-30.9	-50.5	-61.5	...	...	...	-138.5
Gross Domestic Product (GDP) 99b	28.6	30.5	31.7	35.6	50.9	49.5	59.0	73.5	85.8	112.7	119.1	140.6	158.5	141.4	221.7
GDP Volume 1984 Prices..................... 99b.p	...	...	...	...	...	...	...	...	...	...	186.8	199.3	197.1	204.8	221.7
GDP Volume (1985=100) .... 99bv p	...	...	...	...	...	...	...	...	...	...	82.1	87.6	86.7	90.1	97.5
GDP Deflator (1985=100).................. 99bi p	...	...	...	...	...	...	...	...	...	...	61.2	67.7	77.2	66.3	96.0
															Millions:
Population.................................... 99z	.16	.17	.18	.18	.19	.19	.20	.20	.21	.22	.23	.23	.24	.25	.26

	1985	1986	1987	1988	1989	1990	1991	1992	1993	1994	1995	1996	1997	1998	1999		
Year Ending December 31																**Government Finance**	
	−19.33ᴾ	−15.06ᴾ	−34.05ᴾ	−32.96ᴾ	....	....	....	....	....	....	....	....	....	....	....	Deficit (-) or Surplus	80
	53.19ᴾ	57.10ᴾ	69.45ᴾ	82.44ᴾ	114.31ᴾ	122.80ᴾ	132.38ᶠ	....	....	....	....	....	....	....	....	Revenue	81
	2.05ᴾ	25.39ᴾ	30.20ᴾ	37.56ᴾ	....	....	....	....	....	....	....	....	....	....	....	Grants Received	81z
	73.29ᴾ	96.22ᴾ	125.73ᴾ	138.26ᴾ	145.05ᴾ	167.57ᴾ	231.67ᶠ	....	....	....	....	....	....	....	....	Expenditure	82
	1.28ᴾ	1.33ᴾ	7.97ᴾ	14.70ᴾ	2.35ᴾ	4.89ᴾ	6.46ᶠ	....	....	....	....	....	....	....	....	Lending Minus Repayments	83
																Financing	
	....	....	14.01ᴾ	15.03ᴾ	....	....	....	....	....	....	....	....	....	....	....	Net Borrowing: Domestic	84a
	....	....	35.14ᴾ	20.36ᴾ	....	....	....	....	....	....	....	....	....	....	....	Foreign	85a
	....	....	−15.10ᴾ	−2.43ᴾ	....	....	....	....	....	....	....	....	....	....	....	Use of Cash Balances	87
	....	....	....	....	....	....	....	....	....	....	....	....	....	....	....	Debt: Domestic	88a
	....	....	....	....	....	....	....	....	....	....	....	....	....	....	....	Foreign	89a
Millions of Solomon Islands Dollars																**National Accounts**	
	121.1	132.9	163.6	227.0	249.0	....	....	....	....	....	....	....	....	....	....	Exports of Goods & Services	90c
	66.6	84.1	106.3	123.8	133.4	....	....	....	....	....	....	....	....	....	....	Government Consumption	91f
	49.9	63.6	59.6	122.1	....	....	....	....	....	....	....	....	....	....	....	Gross Fixed Capital Formation	93e
	12.2	2.5	7.9	10.0	....	....	....	....	....	....	....	....	....	....	....	Increase/Decrease(-) in Stocks	93i
	152.0	159.3	184.9	253.6	300.0	....	....	....	....	....	....	....	....	....	....	Private Consumption	96f
	−164.9	−189.8	−229.6	−380.1	−405.9	....	....	....	....	....	....	....	....	....	....	Imports of Goods & Services	98c
	236.9	252.5	292.7	356.4	384.4	526.3	598.3	763.1	901.2	1,052.5	....	....	....	....	....	Gross Domestic Product (GDP)	99b
	227.4	222.4	211.0	....	....	....	....	....	....	....	....	....	....	....	....	GDP Volume 1984 Prices	99b.p
	100.0	97.8	92.8	....	....	....	....	....	....	....	....	....	....	....	....	GDP Volume (1985=100)	99bv p
	100.0	109.0	133.2	....	....	....	....	....	....	....	....	....	....	....	....	GDP Deflator (1985=100)	99bi p
Midyear Estimates																	
	.27	.28	.29	.30	.31	.32	.33	.34	.35	.37	.38	.39	.40	.42	.43	**Population**	99z

(See notes in the back of the book.)

South Africa

199		1970	1971	1972	1973	1974	1975	1976	1977	1978	1979	1980	1981	1982	1983	1984
Exchange Rates																*Rand per SDR:*
Principal Rate..................aa=	**wa**	.71723	.83085	.85000	.80966	.84435	1.01797	1.01029	1.05627	1.13286	1.08924	.95066	1.11341	1.18729	1.27926	1.94563
																Rand per US Dollar:
Principal Rate..................ae=	**we**	.71723	.76526	.78290	.67116	.68963	.86957	.86957	.86957	.86957	.82686	.74538	.95657	1.07631	1.22190	1.98491
Principal Rate..................rf=	**wf**	.71429	.71522	.76873	.69396	.67948	.73951	.86957	.86957	.86957	.84202	.77883	.87758	1.08582	1.11410	1.47528
																Index Numbers (1995=100):
Principal Rate	**ahx**	506.2	306.4	469.7	523.6	533.9	495.5	417.1	417.1	417.1	430.8	466.2	416.7	335.3	326.1	252.2
Nominal Effective Exchange Rate...........	**nec**	....	....	....	....	....	....	....	....	....	384.2	411.2	411.2	363.4	372.0	307.9
Real Effective Exchange Rate	**rec**	....	....	....	....	....	....	....	....	....	124.2	136.1	143.0	135.5	149.3	131.8
Fund Position																*Millions of SDRs:*
Quota	**2f.s**	200	320	320	320	320	320	320	320	424	424	636	636	636	916	916
SDRs	**1b.s**	39	—	38	1	40	43	42	40	39	25	37	115	99	27	2
Reserve Position in the Fund	**1c.s**	50	81	81	81	81	—	—	—	—	—	128	107	—	70	70
Total Fund Cred.&Loans Outstg.	**2tl**	—	—	—	—	—	—	315	392	314	77	—	—	795	745	745
International Liquidity																*Millions of US Dollars Unless Otherwise Indicated:*
Total Reserves minus Gold	**1l.d**	346	266	609	449	377	489	425	416	423	434	726	666	485	823	242
SDRs	**1b.d**	39	1	41	2	48	51	48	48	51	33	47	134	109	29	2
Reserve Position in the Fund	**1c.d**	50	87	87	97	100	—	—	—	—	—	164	125	—	73	69
Foreign Exchange	**1d.d**	256	178	480	350	229	438	377	368	372	401	515	407	376	721	171
Gold (Million Fine Troy Ounces)	**1ad**	19.03	11.72	17.93	18.99	18.25	17.75	12.67	9.72	9.79	10.03	12.15	9.29	7.57	7.79	7.36
Gold (National Valuation)	**1and**	658	433	677	836	782	603	431	330	1,931	4,451	6,512	3,339	3,075	2,660	2,039
Monetary Authorities: Other Assets	**3..d**	52	70	93	109	181	208	274	270	388	490	506	515	488	427	281
Other Liab.	**4..d**	94	162	66	3	45	699	805	599	186	16	—	1,204	539	1,187	1,228
Banking Institutions: Assets	**7a.d**	121	163	106	161	162	181	165	158	224	316	542	465	482	613	473
Liabilities	**7b.d**	164	215	261	347	513	495	823	753	791	815	804	1,476	1,481	1,623	1,275
Monetary Authorities																*Millions of Rand:*
Foreign Assets	**11**	784	585	1,112	939	959	1,168	1,017	917	2,429	4,472	5,811	4,453	4,472	4,812	5,089
Claims on Central Government	**12a**	633	615	620	1,086	1,122	1,598	1,232	962	954	1,163	2,679	3,508	2,917	2,246	499
Claims on Private Sector	**12d**	7	15	4	13	10	18	27	16	42	211	403	327	491	913	819
Claims on Banking Institutions	**12e**	226	264	44	135	108	286	299	551	230	195	127	105	434	1,393	1,902
Reserve Money	**14**	833	874	943	1,124	1,309	1,503	1,588	1,703	1,906	2,188	3,560	4,159	3,687	4,204	4,860
of which: Currency Outside Banks	**14a**	513	570	627	747	880	1,026	1,106	1,149	1,285	1,460	1,861	2,273	2,491	2,763	3,190
Foreign Liabilities	**16c**	67	122	52	2	31	608	1,018	935	518	97	—	1,152	1,523	2,404	3,887
Central Government Deposits	**16d**	477	294	545	867	745	1,065	1,113	1,218	1,416	1,409	2,391	1,649	3,708	3,369	1,277
Capital Accounts	**17a**	39	60	92	93	94	112	112	118	127	173	199	278	297	317	468
Other Items (Net)	**17r**	234	130	149	86	20	–218	–1,258	–1,529	–311	2,174	2,871	1,154	–901	–930	–2,182
Banking Institutions																*Millions of Rand:*
Reserves	**20**	536	502	590	732	823	1,028	954	869	1,016	1,268	2,582	2,955	2,661	2,673	2,754
Foreign Assets	**21**	86	122	83	114	112	158	144	138	195	261	404	445	518	750	938
Claims on Central Government	**22a**	1,170	1,235	1,617	1,631	1,800	2,530	3,193	4,232	4,732	5,478	5,052	4,125	4,778	4,845	4,185
Claims on Private Sector	**22d**	6,447	7,121	7,983	10,185	11,919	14,038	15,292	16,481	18,580	21,351	26,849	34,429	40,221	48,050	59,814
Demand Deposits	**24**	1,735	1,863	2,170	2,622	3,114	3,229	3,305	3,470	3,819	4,701	6,472	8,892	10,553	13,721	20,110
Time and Savings Deposits	**25**	5,543	6,013	7,137	8,810	10,203	12,682	14,034	15,693	18,465	21,363	25,444	28,388	31,885	34,634	37,930
Foreign Liabilities	**26c**	117	161	204	244	354	431	716	655	688	674	600	1,412	1,594	1,983	2,531
Central Government Deposits	**26d**	27	31	31	76	40	47	75	297	378	188	280	329	496	594	614
Capital Accounts	**27a**	412	442	471	573	659	804	871	943	1,060	1,194	1,429	1,715	1,872	2,202	2,438
Other Items (Net)	**27r**	405	470	261	336	285	561	583	662	113	238	663	1,217	1,779	3,184	4,067
Banking Survey																*Millions of Rand:*
Foreign Assets (Net)	**31n**	686	424	940	806	686	287	–574	–536	1,419	3,963	5,615	2,333	1,873	1,175	–390
Domestic Credit	**32**	7,753	8,662	9,648	11,972	14,067	17,072	18,556	20,177	22,515	26,606	32,312	40,410	44,202	52,091	63,424
Claims on Central Govt. (Net)	**32an**	1,299	1,526	1,661	1,774	2,138	3,015	3,237	3,679	3,892	5,044	5,061	5,654	3,491	3,128	2,792
Claims on Private Sector	**32d**	6,453	7,135	7,987	10,198	11,929	14,057	15,319	16,498	18,622	21,562	27,252	34,755	40,711	48,963	60,632
Money	**34**	2,259	2,446	2,808	3,382	4,011	4,286	4,437	4,648	5,133	6,198	8,398	11,273	13,124	16,586	23,413
Quasi-Money	**35**	5,543	6,013	7,137	8,810	10,203	12,682	14,034	15,693	18,465	21,363	25,444	28,388	31,885	34,634	37,930
Capital Accounts	**37a**	451	502	563	666	754	916	983	1,061	1,187	1,367	1,627	1,993	2,169	2,519	2,905
Other Items (Net)	**37r**	186	125	80	–80	–215	–525	–1,471	–1,761	–851	1,641	2,457	1,089	–1,103	–474	–1,214
Money plus Quasi-Money	**35l**	7,802	8,459	9,944	12,192	14,214	16,968	18,471	20,341	23,597	27,561	33,842	39,661	45,010	51,220	61,343
Nonbank Financial Institutions																*Millions of Rand:*
Cash	**40..s**	343	335	372	463	625	686	798	752	790	1,472	2,398	3,531	3,268	3,258	5,625
Claims on Central Government	**42a.s**	462	575	827	986	1,129	1,396	1,835	2,273	2,767	3,180	3,678	5,020	7,252	8,851	10,752
Claims on Official Entities	**42b.s**	1,126	1,255	1,367	1,497	1,594	1,822	2,099	2,715	3,280	4,313	4,716	5,511	6,989	8,211	9,296
Claims on Private Sector	**42d.s**	2,296	2,611	2,809	3,193	3,561	3,951	4,288	4,762	5,370	6,102	7,653	9,347	10,891	14,127	16,695
Real Estate	**42h.s**	308	355	400	552	688	951	1,217	1,462	1,635	1,807	2,294	2,766	3,875	5,018	6,348
Incr.in Total Assets(Within Per.)	**49z.s**	477	596	644	916	906	1,209	1,431	1,727	1,878	3,032	3,865	5,436	6,100	7,190	9,251
Financial Survey																*Millions of Rand:*
Foreign Assets (Net)	**51n**	686	424	940	806	686	287	–574	–536	1,419	3,963	5,615	2,333	1,873	1,175	–390
Domestic Credit	**52**	11,637	13,103	14,651	17,648	20,351	24,241	26,778	29,927	33,932	40,201	48,359	60,288	69,334	83,280	100,167
Claims on Central Govt. (Net)	**52an**	1,761	2,101	2,488	2,760	3,267	4,411	5,072	5,952	6,659	8,224	8,739	10,674	10,743	11,979	13,544
Claims on Official Entities	**52b**	1,126	1,255	1,367	1,497	1,594	1,822	2,099	2,715	3,280	4,313	4,716	5,511	6,989	8,211	9,296
Claims on Private Sector	**52d**	8,749	9,746	10,796	13,391	15,490	18,008	19,607	21,260	23,992	27,664	34,905	44,102	51,602	63,090	77,327
Liquid Liabilities	**55l**	7,459	8,124	9,572	11,729	13,589	16,282	17,673	19,589	22,807	26,089	31,444	36,130	41,742	47,962	55,718
Other Items (Net)	**57r**	4,864	5,403	6,018	6,725	7,447	8,246	8,532	9,802	12,543	18,075	22,530	26,491	29,466	36,493	44,060
Interest Rates																*Percent Per Annum*
Discount Rate *(End of Period)*	**60**	5.50	6.50	6.00	3.78	6.48	7.42	8.28	8.41	7.87	4.70	6.54	14.54	14.35	17.75	20.75
Money Market Rate	**60b**	4.55	5.61	5.37	4.12	6.13	6.24	I 8.50	8.29	7.99	5.39	4.40	10.25	16.90	13.98	20.31
Treasury Bill Rate	**60c**	4.39	5.38	5.30	3.18	5.43	6.12	7.44	7.87	7.81	5.26	4.65	9.80	15.59	13.45	19.33
Deposit Rate	**60l**	....	....	....	....	....	....	....	8.00	7.67	6.00	5.54	8.19	13.00	13.71	18.29
Lending Rate	**60p**	8.17	8.83	8.79	8.00	10.17	11.79	12.25	12.50	12.13	10.00	9.50	14.00	19.33	16.67	22.33
Government Bond Yield	**61**	7.15	8.38	8.35	7.83	8.96	9.71	10.44	11.01	10.40	9.26	10.09	12.99	13.51	12.67	15.23

1985	1986	1987	1988	1989	1990	1991	1992	1993	1994	1995	1996	1997	1998	1999		
															Exchange Rates	
End of Period																
2.80926	2.67072	2.73793	3.19971	3.33272	3.64560	3.92372	4.19788	4.66667	5.17298	5.42197	6.73325	6.56747	8.25106	8.44711	Principal Rate...aa= ...wa	
End of Period (we) Period Average (wf)																
2.55754	2.18341	1.92994	2.37773	2.53601	2.56253	2.74303	3.05300	3.39750	3.54350	3.64750	4.68250	4.86750	5.86000	6.15450	Principal Rate...ae= ...we	
2.22868	2.28503	2.03603	2.27347	2.62268	2.58732	2.76132	2.85201	3.26774	3.55080	3.62709	4.29935	4.60796	5.52828	6.10948	Principal Rate...rf= ...wf	
Period Averages																
165.5	159.9	178.2	160.4	138.6	140.2	131.6	127.3	111.1	102.2	100.0	84.9	78.8	66.2	59.4	Principal Rate	ahx
209.5	165.4	164.0	141.4	128.9	125.2	121.4	118.1	113.9	108.0	100.0	88.0	88.4	76.2	69.0	Nominal Effective Exchange Rate	ne c
100.0	92.4	104.2	98.4	98.7	101.4	106.0	109.6	107.5	103.0	100.0	92.2	98.6	89.4	84.6	Real Effective Exchange Rate	re c
															Fund Position	
End of Period																
916	916	916	916	916	916	916	1,365	1,365	1,365	1,365	1,365	1,365	1,365	1,869	Quota	2f. s
1	—	1	1	1	2	1	—	9	1	3	1	7	132	210	SDRs	1b. s
—	—	—	—	—	—	—	—	—	—	—	—	—	—	—	Reserve Position in the Fund	1c. s
745	398	—	—	—	—	—	—	614	614	614	614	307	—	—	Total Fund Cred.&Loans Outstg.	2tl
															International Liquidity	
End of Period																
315	370	641	780	960	1,008	899	992	1,020	1,685	2,820	942	4,799	4,357	6,353	Total Reserves minus Gold	1l. d
1	—	2	1	2	2	2	—	12	1	5	1	9	185	288	SDRs	1b. d
—	—	—	—	—	—	—	—	—	—	—	—	—	—	—	Reserve Position in the Fund	1c. d
314	370	639	779	958	1,006	897	991	1,008	1,684	2,815	940	4,790	4,171	6,065	Foreign Exchange	1d. d
4.84	4.82	5.83	3.47	3.08	4.09	6.47	6.65	4.76	4.20	4.25	3.79	3.99	4.00	3.94	Gold (Million Fine Troy Ounces)	1ad
1,420	1,698	2,541	1,295	1,137	1,415	2,074	1,992	1,658	1,445	1,481	1,261	1,048	1,034	1,020	Gold (National Valuation)	1and
251	335	374	271	271	365	252	478	453	392	306	227	24	19	12	Monetary Authorities: Other Assets	3..d
1,201	511	499	545	570	I324	126	385	1,812	1,633	225	93	2,161	3,177	3,254	Other Liab.	4..d
734	835	1,089	757	679	465	....	I873	811	1,042	799	1,412	1,603	2,874	4,909	Banking Institutions: Assets	7a. d
1,750	2,141	2,262	2,060	2,372	2,613	....	I7,418	6,135	7,854	9,184	9,489	9,676	10,483	9,029	Liabilities	7b. d
															Monetary Authorities	
End of Period																
5,093	5,247	6,865	5,579	6,008	I7,144	8,847	10,570	10,637	12,479	16,801	11,375	28,579	31,701	45,450	Foreign Assets	11
774	1,255	494	1,304	1,519	I6,739	7,547	4,935	8,844	13,531	10,274	16,254	13,067	12,578	10,942	Claims on Central Government	12a
945	543	1,171	1,780	2,240	I1,809	1,707	2,414	2,978	4,296	3,003	2,055	2,502	720	3,922	Claims on Private Sector	12d
857	658	988	1,633	2,513	I3,620	3,774	4,901	6,219	5,995	6,513	11,975	10,939	6,346	3,253	Claims on Banking Institutions	12e
5,426	5,800	6,819	9,398	12,077	I14,588	17,912	17,952	16,428	19,347	25,091	28,517	31,771	33,453	40,466	Reserve Money	14
3,552	4,181	5,025	6,128	7,314	I8,064	8,836	9,536	10,490	12,237	14,332	15,954	17,327	18,510	22,663	of which: Currency Outside Banks	14a
5,165	2,177	963	1,296	1,445	I832	347	1,176	9,023	8,966	4,151	4,572	12,535	18,617	20,028	Foreign Liabilities	16c
197	2,368	2,474	5,239	9,863	I10,701	13,737	9,419	12,180	10,962	10,963	9,770	8,334	6,623	5,084	Central Government Deposits	16d
663	633	651	755	790	I873	944	1,021	1,148	1,270	1,339	1,637	1,646	2,059	2,157	Capital Accounts	17a
−3,782	−3,275	−1,388	−6,392	−11,896	I−7,680	−11,064	−6,749	−10,101	−4,245	−4,953	−2,837	802	−9,407	−4,167	Other Items (Net)	17r
															Banking Institutions	
End of Period																
3,171	3,895	4,364	4,265	5,566	5,407	....	I6,112	4,773	6,586	10,356	11,702	13,514	14,726	17,969	Reserves	20
1,876	1,822	2,101	1,801	1,721	1,192	....	I2,666	2,757	3,693	2,913	6,610	7,805	16,844	30,213	Foreign Assets	21
5,680	7,872	9,215	11,486	14,775	13,087	....	I13,515	20,788	21,501	24,813	27,437	37,011	46,206	50,100	Claims on Central Government	22a
69,119	75,433	86,742	110,584	132,320	151,879	....	I211,881	235,544	278,079	324,111	380,493	434,884	506,140	555,251	Claims on Private Sector	22d
17,689	18,898	26,893	33,375	35,559	41,031	....	I58,977	63,902	81,736	97,050	130,858	155,065	194,873	237,085	Demand Deposits	24
48,960	53,259	59,359	76,097	96,625	105,579	....	I117,031	124,142	141,757	162,301	165,626	195,762	205,958	205,656	Time and Savings Deposits	25
4,476	4,675	4,365	4,898	6,016	6,695	....	I22,648	20,843	27,829	33,497	44,431	47,097	61,431	55,568	Foreign Liabilities	26c
641	563	764	1,223	1,466	1,645	....	I4,039	9,937	8,173	17,748	22,387	21,137	21,158	27,027	Central Government Deposits	26d
2,909	3,578	3,932	4,890	6,094	7,747	....	I16,021	20,065	23,998	29,302	34,470	41,664	51,920	63,626	Capital Accounts	27a
5,172	8,050	7,109	7,652	8,622	8,868	....	I15,458	24,972	26,366	22,295	28,470	32,489	48,576	64,571	Other Items (Net)	27r
															Banking Survey	
End of Period																
−2,671	218	3,638	1,186	268	I810	....	I−10,588	−16,472	−20,624	−17,934	−31,018	−23,247	−31,503	67	Foreign Assets (Net)	31n
75,679	82,172	94,385	118,691	139,524	I161,168	....	I219,287	246,036	298,272	333,490	394,082	457,993	537,863	588,104	Domestic Credit	32
5,616	6,196	6,471	6,327	4,965	I7,480	....	I4,992	7,514	15,897	6,376	11,534	20,607	31,003	28,931	Claims on Central Govt. (Net)	32an
70,063	75,977	87,914	112,364	134,560	I153,688	....	I214,295	238,522	282,375	327,114	382,548	437,386	506,860	559,173	Claims on Private Sector	32d
21,332	23,207	32,026	39,934	43,343	I50,354	....	I70,809	75,550	94,511	111,844	147,664	173,335	194,873	259,937	Money	34
48,960	53,259	59,359	76,097	96,625	105,579	....	I117,031	124,142	141,757	162,301	165,626	195,762	205,958	205,656	Quasi-Money	35
3,572	4,211	4,583	5,645	6,884	8,622	....	I17,042	21,213	25,268	30,641	36,107	43,310	53,979	65,783	Capital Accounts	37a
−857	1,713	2,056	−1,799	−7,060	I−2,577	....	I3,816	8,659	16,112	10,770	13,667	22,339	32,891	56,796	Other Items (Net)	37r
70,293	76,466	91,384	116,031	139,969	I155,933	....	I187,840	199,692	236,268	274,145	313,290	369,097	419,490	465,593	Money plus Quasi-Money	35l
															Nonbank Financial Institutions	
End of Period																
6,125	9,793	15,217	23,615	26,848	26,774	28,578	32,026	35,931	43,655	60,144	59,890	70,311	82,378	102,034	Cash	40.. s
12,462	13,177	14,371	18,236	19,813	24,612	30,665	41,076	59,428	66,880	84,992	93,588	106,149	103,428	97,810	Claims on Central Government	42a. s
12,422	14,046	14,618	15,992	15,357	16,745	15,921	18,473	24,813	22,889	22,765	20,969	24,130	21,204	21,048	Claims on Official Entities	42b. s
23,599	32,736	40,287	45,433	61,382	80,922	153,356	167,034	222,407	268,488	326,976	358,163	359,677	370,342	537,494	Claims on Private Sector	42d. s
8,271	9,050	11,300	12,695	15,538	19,158	27,127	32,354	35,735	38,868	44,064	47,464	53,414	52,273	65,397	Real Estate	42h. s
14,163	15,923	16,991	20,178	22,967	29,273	87,436	35,316	87,351	62,466	98,161	41,133	33,607	15,944	194,158	Incr.in Total Assets(Within Per.)	49z. s
															Financial Survey	
End of Period																
−2,671	218	3,638	1,186	268	I810	....	I−10,588	−16,472	−20,624	−17,934	−31,018	−23,247	−31,503	67	Foreign Assets (Net)	51n
124,162	142,131	163,661	198,352	236,076	I283,447	....	I445,870	552,684	656,529	768,223	866,802	947,949	1,032,837	1,244,456	Domestic Credit	52
18,078	19,373	20,842	24,563	24,778	I32,092	....	I46,068	66,942	82,777	91,368	105,122	126,756	134,431	126,741	Claims on Central Govt. (Net)	52an
12,422	14,046	14,618	15,992	15,357	16,745	....	18,473	24,813	22,889	22,765	20,969	24,130	21,204	21,048	Claims on Official Entities	52b
93,662	108,713	128,201	157,797	195,942	I234,610	....	I381,329	460,929	550,863	654,090	740,711	797,063	877,202	1,096,667	Claims on Private Sector	52d
64,168	66,673	76,167	92,416	113,121	I129,159	....	I155,814	163,761	192,613	214,001	253,400	298,786	337,112	363,559	Liquid Liabilities	55l
57,323	75,677	91,131	107,122	123,224	I155,098	....	I279,468	372,451	443,292	536,288	582,384	625,916	664,222	880,965	Other Items (Net)	57r
															Interest Rates	
Percent Per Annum																
13.00	9.50	9.50	14.50	18.00	18.00	17.00	14.00	12.00	13.00	15.00	17.00	16.00	I19.32	12.00	Discount Rate (End of Period)	60
18.21	10.92	9.50	13.90	18.77	19.46	17.02	14.11	10.83	10.24	13.07	15.54	15.59	17.11	13.06	Money Market Rate	60b
17.56	10.43	8.71	12.03	16.84	17.80	16.68	13.77	11.31	10.93	13.53	15.04	15.26	16.53	12.85	Treasury Bill Rate	60c
17.02	10.98	8.70	13.54	18.13	18.86	17.30	13.78	11.50	11.11	13.54	14.91	15.38	16.50	12.24	Deposit Rate	60l
21.50	14.33	12.50	15.33	19.83	21.00	20.31	18.91	16.16	15.58	17.90	19.52	20.00	21.79	18.00	Lending Rate	60p
16.79	16.37	15.30	16.37	16.90	16.15	16.34	15.44	13.97	14.83	16.11	15.48	14.70	15.12	14.90	Government Bond Yield	61

South Africa

		1970	1971	1972	1973	1974	1975	1976	1977	1978	1979	1980	1981	1982	1983	1984
Prices, Production, Labor																*Index Numbers (1995=100):*
Share Prices: Industry & Comm.	62a	19.5	16.6	20.0	24.3	19.8	19.2	19.3	17.9	20.8	27.8	40.9	40.4	35.4	44.8	I43.9
Gold Mining	62b	10.8	11.5	16.4	27.0	57.6	43.2	27.7	26.7	35.2	50.7	106.0	83.9	67.4	104.8	I118.6
Prices: Home & Import Goods	63	5.3	5.6	6.1	6.9	8.1	9.5	10.9	12.4	13.6	15.7	18.2	20.7	23.6	26.1	28.2
Home Goods	63a	5.5	5.8	6.2	7.0	8.2	9.3	10.8	12.3	13.5	15.4	17.7	20.3	23.0	25.5	27.6
Consumer Prices	64	I5.4	5.8	6.1	6.7	7.5	8.5	9.5	10.5	11.6	13.1	15.0	17.2	19.7	22.2	24.8
Manufacturing Production	66ey c	49.4	52.7	54.7	59.6	63.4	65.9	67.5	65.0	73.0	78.1	86.8	94.3	90.5	87.8	92.1
Mining Production	66zx c	116.8	113.9	107.3	110.3	102.9	98.6	99.6	101.2	102.2	105.6	104.2	104.1	103.3	103.7	108.4
Gold Production	66kr c															
Manufacturing Employment	67ey c	I71.8	74.1	76.0	79.9	84.4	87.6	89.7	88.0	88.3	90.4	94.2	I96.5	97.6	93.9	94.0
Mining Employment	67zx c	I120.4	118.7	114.9	123.4	121.9	114.2	120.1	127.4	129.3	134.8	139.1	140.2	134.9	132.1	I137.1
																Number in Thousands:
Unemployment	67c	....	....	....	....	....	....	....	....	....	....	....	....	....	....	....
Unemployment Rate (%)	67r	....	....	....	....	....	....	....	....	....	....	....	....	....	....	....
International Transactions																*Millions of Rand*
Exports	70	2,389	2,491	3,160	I4,187	5,908	6,448	6,826	8,612	11,106	15,345	I19,880	18,129	19,189	20,620	25,320
Gold Output (Net)	70kr	837	922	1,161	1,769	2,565	2,540	2,346	2,795	3,907	6,003	10,140	8,338	8,641	9,929	11,684
Imports, c.i.f.	71	2,745	3,121	3,031	I3,564	5,344	6,084	6,335	5,452	6,622	7,562	I15,264	20,118	19,987	17,617	23,538
Imports, f.o.b.	71.v	2,547	2,887	2,813	I3,275	4,909	5,545	5,859	5,118	6,263	7,027	I14,363	18,439	18,374	16,204	21,636
																1995=100
Volume of Exports	72	36	37	I44	45	47	46	50	60	65	74	I71	65	65	58	64
Volume of Imports	73	69	74	I63	72	89	83	71	55	62	61	I80	91	76	76	76
Unit Value of Exports	74	6	6	I6	7	9	11	12	13	14	16	I19	21	22	25	28
Unit Value of Imports	75	4	4	I5	5	7	8	10	11	13	16	I19	22	26	28	31
Import Prices (1985=100)	76.x	13.3	13.9	15.6	17.4	21.3	26.1	30.8	33.8	37.2	44.5	53.4	59.1	68.0	74.8	80.9
Balance of Payments																*Millions of US Dollars:*
Current Account, n.i.e.	78al d	....	....	....	....	....	....	-1,908	609	1,582	3,445	3,508	-4,489	-3,178	9	-1,589
Goods: Exports f.o.b.	78aa d							8,296	10,443	13,041	17,696	25,698	20,632	17,328	18,241	16,948
Goods: Imports f.o.b.	78ab d							-8,559	-7,913	-9,222	-11,589	-18,268	-20,622	-16,683	-14,202	-14,774
Trade Balance	78ac d							-263	2,530	3,819	6,107	7,430	10	645	4,039	2,174
Services: Credit	78ad d							1,400	1,598	1,863	2,226	2,929	3,005	2,790	2,676	2,484
Services: Debit	78ae d							-1,662	-1,919	-2,290	-2,700	-3,805	-4,202	-3,689	-3,407	-3,209
Balance on Goods & Services	78af d							-526	2,209	3,392	5,633	6,554	-1,187	-254	3,308	1,449
Income: Credit	78ag d							329	247	378	550	631	525	446	524	565
Income: Debit	78ah d							-1,815	-1,976	-2,318	-2,880	-3,916	-4,168	-3,627	-4,018	-3,701
Balance on Gds, Serv. & Inc.	78ai d							-2,011	481	1,452	3,302	3,269	-4,831	-3,435	-186	-1,687
Current Transfers, n.i.e.: Credit	78aj d							210	220	251	336	526	582	448	459	369
Current Transfers: Debit	78ak d							-107	-91	-121	-194	-287	-240	-190	-264	-272
Capital Account, n.i.e.	78bc d							31	-76	-49	-27	—	-23	-6	1	2
Capital Account, n.i.e.: Credit	78ba d							92	38	43	46	64	45	42	45	37
Capital Account: Debit	78bb d							-61	-114	-92	-74	-64	-67	-48	-44	-36
Financial Account, n.i.e.	78bj d							1,381	-197	-527	-2,267	-1,242	1,932	3,213	694	2,156
Direct Investment Abroad	78bd d							-32	-68	-238	-11	-746	-700	43	-157	-184
Dir. Invest. in Rep. Econ., n.i.e.	78be d							18	-122	-109	-488	-19	121	338	69	435
Portfolio Investment Assets	78bf d							-2	7	3	-238	-18	6	6	66	—
Equity Securities	78bk d							-6	7	3	-238	-18	6	6	66	—
Debt Securities	78bl d							3	—	—	—	—	—	—	—	—
Portfolio Investment Liab., n.i.e.	78bg d							-29	1	125	-244	-372	-294	-196	-600	1,115
Equity Securities	78bm d							-44	5	11	-149	-65	-237	-245	-1,051	661
Debt Securities	78bn d							15	-3	114	-96	-307	-57	49	451	454
Financial Derivatives Assets	78bw d							....	....	....	....	....	....	....	....	....
Financial Derivatives Liabilities	78bx d							....	....	....	....	....	....	....	....	....
Other Investment Assets	78bh d							-250	-215	-213	-601	-250	-528	-144	-387	-360
Monetary Authorities	78bo d							....	....	....	....	....	....	....	....	....
General Government	78bp d							-167	5	—	-61	-2	-211	-78	22	-66
Banks	78bq d							1	—	-2	-19	2	-1	-11	-49	58
Other Sectors	78br d							-84	-220	-210	-520	-250	-316	-54	-360	-353
Other Investment Liab., n.i.e.	78bi d							1,676	200	-95	-686	163	3,327	3,166	1,704	1,150
Monetary Authorities	78bs d							198	-23	-204	-49	22	7	35	72	45
General Government	78bt d							213	-94	-362	12	-199	317	987	25	98
Banks	78bu d							328	-70	23	3	124	1,300	174	379	334
Other Sectors	78bv d							937	388	447	-652	215	1,702	1,969	1,227	673
Net Errors and Omissions	78ca d							-201	-661	-520	-685	-1,451	388	-276	-403	-1,149
Overall Balance	78cb d							-697	-324	487	466	815	-2,191	-247	301	-581
Reserves and Related Items	79da d							697	324	-487	-466	-815	2,191	247	-301	581
Reserve Assets	79db d							311	415	-40	3	-690	1,046	49	-942	525
Use of Fund Credit and Loans	79dc d							365	89	-97	-308	-101	—	848	-52	—
Exceptional Financing	79de d							21	-181	-350	-161	-24	1,145	-650	694	56
International Investment Position																*Millions of US Dollars*
Assets	79aa d											17,159	13,543	13,599	13,254	11,873
Direct Investment Abroad	79ab d											5,543	5,626	6,289	6,065	6,461
Portfolio Investment	79ac d											394	427	442	412	640
Equity Securities	79ad d											272	326	340	300	487
Debt Securities	79ae d											122	100	102	112	153
Financial Derivatives	79al d															
Other Investment	79af d											3,469	3,046	2,858	2,710	2,069
Monetary Authorities	79ag d															
General Government	79ah d															
Banks	79ai d											13	14	18	4	2
Other Sectors	79aj d															
Reserve Assets	79ak d											7,752	4,444	4,010	4,067	2,703
Liabilities	79la d															
Dir. Invest. in Rep. Economy	79lb d											16,465	15,234	15,879	15,386	12,840
Portfolio Investment	79lc d											5,234	4,210	4,110	4,005	3,464
Equity Securities	79ld d											4,002	3,277	3,101	2,715	1,877
Debt Securities	79le d											1,232	932	1,009	1,291	1,586
Financial Derivatives	79ll d											—	—	—	—	—
Other investment	79lf d															
Monetary Authorities	79lg d											78	68	979	896	842
General Government	79lh d															
Banks	79li d											1,152	1,642	1,698	2,191	2,078
Other Sectors	79lj d															

1985	1986	1987	1988	1989	1990	1991	1992	1993	1994	1995	1996	1997	1998	1999	
Period Averages															**Prices, Production, Labor**
46.9	24.2	35.4	27.9	39.0	40.9	54.4	61.1	66.5	91.8	I100.0	116.1	120.1	107.1	103.8	Share Prices: Industry & Comm. **62a**
126.0	99.1	138.1	84.9	101.3	105.9	72.8	61.9	95.4	137.1	I100.0	119.9	85.7	69.8	72.7	Gold Mining **62b**
33.0	39.5	45.0	50.9	58.6	I65.6	73.1	79.1	84.4	91.3	100.0	107.0	114.5	118.6	125.5	Prices: Home & Import Goods **63**
31.8	37.7	43.5	49.4	56.8	I63.8	71.6	78.2	83.6	91.0	100.0	107.5	115.8	119.9	....	Home Goods **63a**
28.8	34.1	39.6	44.7	51.3	58.7	67.6	77.0	84.5	92.1	100.0	107.4	116.5	124.6	131.0	Consumer Prices.. **64**
92.3	90.8	93.1	99.4	100.7	98.3	94.7	91.9	I91.7	94.0	100.0	101.5	104.3	101.1	101.4	Manufacturing Production .... **66ey *c***
109.2	105.9	101.3	103.1	101.7	99.8	98.9	99.3	I102.3	100.8	100.0	98.4	100.3	99.5	98.0	Mining Production.................................. **66zx *c***
....	....	117.8	120.7	117.8	116.4	115.6	117.9	119.1	111.4	100.0	95.8	I95.3	90.8	86.6	Gold Production.................................. **66kr *c***
91.4	I90.6	91.3	97.5	97.5	97.1	I94.5	99.4	98.7	I99.4	100.0	96.3	92.3	89.0	....	Manufacturing Employment................. **67ey *c***
142.5	I147.8	147.8	144.5	142.5	137.1	I127.0	112.3	103.7	I102.2	100.0	95.3	92.1	70.3	....	Mining Employment............................ **67zx *c***
Period Averages															
....	....	....	122	116	111	248	288	313	271	273	296	310	....	....	Unemployment... **67c**
....	....	....	....	....	....	....	....	....	4.4	4.5	5.1	5.4	....	....	Unemployment Rate (%)......................... **67r**
Millions of Rand															**International Transactions**
36,312	42,011	43,202	49,724	58,199	60,929	64,355	66,774	79,279	89,907	101,051	126,101	142,937	145,518	163,182	Exports.. **70**
15,461	16,727	17,768	19,280	19,095	18,070	19,648	19,391	22,449	23,671	22,537	26,300	25,818	25,907	23,289	Gold Output (Net)............................... **70kr**
25,226	29,688	31,105	42,566	48,515	47,605	52,006	56,358	65,411	83,042	110,826	129,522	151,779	161,802	163,092	Imports, c.i.f. **71**
22,691	26,864	28,673	39,484	44,741	44,212	48,209	52,857	58,779	76,154	98,039	115,524	129,735	143,326	147,091	Imports, f.o.b. **71.v**
1995=100															
76	79	77	I82	89	84	84	90	91	96	100	142	....	....	....	Volume of Exports **72**
65	63	65	I80	80	74	74	76	79	92	100	114	....	....	....	Volume of Imports **73**
36	41	43	I49	59	62	657	69	76	85	100	110	....	....	....	Unit Value of Exports................................ **74**
40	46	48	I53	59	64	70	74	80	88	100	106	....	....	....	Unit Value of Imports................................ **75**
100.0	122.6	134.5	....	....	....	....	....	....	....	....	....	....	....	....	Import Prices (1985=100)....................... **76.x**
Minus Sign Indicates Debit															Balance of Payments
2,622	3,163	2,934	1,204	1,564	2,065	2,260	1,967	1,502	114	-2,204	-1,881	-2,273	-1,936	-464	Current Account, n.i.e. .... **78al *d***
16,244	18,330	21,088	22,432	22,399	23,560	23,794	24,527	24,717	26,333	30,071	30,263	31,171	29,234	28,361	Goods: Exports f.o.b......................... **78aa *d***
-10,402	-11,130	-13,925	-17,210	-16,810	-16,778	-17,184	-18,248	-18,485	-21,852	-27,404	-27,569	-28,848	-27,216	-24,611	Goods: Imports f.o.b. .... **78ab *d***
5,842	7,200	7,163	5,222	5,589	6,783	6,610	6,279	6,232	4,481	2,667	2,695	2,324	2,018	3,751	*Trade Balance*................................ **78ac *d***
1,995	2,048	2,469	2,585	2,729	3,559	3,190	3,352	3,276	3,750	4,618	5,028	5,334	5,292	4,959	Services: Credit .... **78ad *d***
-2,488	-2,899	-3,367	-3,484	-3,655	-4,239	-3,816	-4,357	-4,707	-5,087	-5,969	-5,732	-6,003	-5,471	-5,395	Services: Debit .... **78ae *d***
5,349	6,348	6,265	4,323	4,664	6,102	5,983	5,274	4,802	3,145	1,316	1,991	1,655	1,839	3,314	*Balance on Goods & Services* .... **78af *d***
610	678	641	659	815	833	875	930	696	972	1,136	1,076	1,298	1,319	1,412	Income: Credit .... **78ag *d***
-3,410	-3,962	-4,183	-3,940	-4,101	-4,929	-4,084	-3,872	-3,352	-3,394	-4,011	-4,195	-4,502	-4,348	-4,264	Income: Debit .... **78ah *d***
2,549	3,064	2,723	1,043	1,378	2,006	2,774	2,332	2,145	723	-1,558	-1,127	-1,549	-1,190	462	*Balance on Gds, Serv. & Inc.*............ **78ai *d***
299	324	367	309	325	298	126	123	127	143	196	54	138	60	66	Current Transfers, n.i.e.: Credit .... **78aj *d***
-226	-226	-157	-148	-139	-238	-640	-488	-769	-752	-841	-808	-862	-806	-993	Current Transfers: Debit.................. **78ak *d***
—	-11	2	14	15	12	-35	-42	-57	-67	-40	-47	-192	-56	-43	Capital Account, n.i.e......................... **78bc *d***
27	19	21	29	23	23	—	—	—	—	—	—	—	—	25	Capital Account, n.i.e.: Credit .... **78ba *d***
-26	-30	-19	-15	-8	-12	-35	-42	-57	-67	-40	-47	-192	-56	-68	Capital Account: Debit .... **78bb *d***
-1,992	-2,515	-1,509	-1,636	-1,464	243	-1,285	-243	-344	1,087	4,003	3,018	8,131	4,896	4,098	Financial Account, n.i.e. .... **78bj *d***
-47	-71	-112	-65	-163	-28	-206	-1,939	-292	-1,261	-2,494	-1,048	-2,324	-1,590	-1,118	Direct Investment Abroad .... **78bd *d***
-449	-50	-192	158	-201	-89	254	3	11	374	1,248	816	3,811	550	1,376	Dir. Invest. in Rep. Econ., n.i.e. .... **78be *d***
12	-3	—	—	—	—	-394	-98	-3	-82	-447	-2,000	-4,587	-5,575	-5,082	Portfolio Investment Assets .... **78bf *d***
12	-3	—	—	—	—	-263	-32	-15	-29	-387	-1,698	-3,891	-4,768	-4,018	Equity Securities............................ **78bk *d***
—	—	—	—	—	—	-131	-66	11	-53	-61	-302	-696	-807	-1,064	Debt Securities................................ **78bl *d***
297	-708	-181	-54	-138	-50	630	1,841	751	2,918	2,937	4,446	11,274	9,869	13,557	Portfolio Investment Liab., n.i.e. ...... **78bg *d***
-121	-586	—	—	—	—	-1,446	-188	895	88	2,914	2,318	5,473	8,632	8,528	Equity Securities........................... **78bm *d***
418	-122	-181	-54	-138	-50	2,076	2,029	-145	2,830	23	2,127	5,802	1,237	5,029	Debt Securities............................... **78bn *d***
....	....	....	....	....	....	....	....	....	....	....	....	....	....	-46	Financial Derivatives Assets............ **78bw *d***
....	....	....	....	....	....	....	....	....	....	....	....	53	97	-76	Financial Derivatives Liabilities........ **78bx *d***
-802	-905	-38	-175	-742	-97	-82	-321	-269	-298	-525	-599	-1,983	-694	-1,343	Other Investment Assets .... **78bh *d***
....	....	—	34	—	-99	-17	-266	-24	44	75	12	206	—	6	Monetary Authorities..................... **78bo *d***
6	-32	1	-31	-44	-26	-82	-2	—	-1	1	—	2	1	—	General Government...................... **78bp *d***
-159	-114	139	-2	-10	113	-17	-23	15	-85	62	-127	-122	-135	-76	Banks.. **78bq *d***
-648	-759	-178	-176	-687	-85	34	-30	-259	-255	-663	-484	-2,069	-560	-1,273	Other Sectors..................................... **78br *d***
-1,003	-778	-987	-1,500	-221	506	-1,487	271	-542	-565	3,284	1,403	1,887	2,237	-3,171	Other Investment Liab., n.i.e. .... **78bi *d***
-25	-21	-12	4	86	43	-330	279	1,495	-105	-1,414	-89	2,186	1,172	105	Monetary Authorities..................... **78bs *d***
-267	-39	-150	-169	-141	-193	185	266	-617	-467	118	469	-22	4	-270	General Government...................... **78bt *d***
862	100	-234	233	488	258	-510	-11	-359	360	2,945	1,044	-283	784	-882	Banks .... **78bu *d***
-1,574	-817	-592	-1,568	-654	399	-831	-263	-1,061	-353	1,635	-21	6	277	-2,124	Other Sectors..................................... **78bv *d***
-1,145	-129	-80	-961	-201	-904	208	-1,179	-2,442	-451	-852	-2,362	-1,070	-1,984	364	Net Errors and Omissions .... **78ca *d***
-514	508	1,347	-1,379	-86	1,416	1,147	503	-1,341	683	906	-1,272	4,596	920	3,955	*Overall Balance*............................... **78cb *d***
514	-508	-1,347	1,379	86	-1,416	-1,147	-503	1,341	-683	-906	1,272	-4,596	-920	-3,955	Reserves and Related Items .... **79da *d***
526	570	-906	766	-527	-356	-1,147	-503	491	-683	-906	1,272	-4,175	-502	-3,955	Reserve Assets .... **79db *d***
—	-409	-515	—	—	—	—	—	850	—	—	—	-421	-418	—	Use of Fund Credit and Loans.......... **79dc *d***
-12	-669	75	612	613	-1,060	—	—	—	—	—	—	—	—	....	Exceptional Financing .... **79de *d***
Millions of US Dollars															International Investment Position
11,161	13,694	16,876	13,893	20,172	21,432	23,376	25,834	25,743	27,559	33,893	35,056	47,869	56,809	....	Assets .... **79aa *d***
6,446	7,587	8,958	7,630	13,143	15,010	16,103	17,795	17,960	19,105	23,301	24,349	27,492	29,009	....	Direct Investment Abroad............... **79ab *d***
507	658	577	699	297	84	269	216	145	98	632	2,605	7,818	16,033	....	Portfolio Investment .... **79ac *d***
389	519	419	570	263	50	222	177	109	61	569	2,237	6,653	13,635	....	Equity Securities.......................... **79ad *d***
118	138	158	128	34	34	47	39	36	38	63	368	1,164	2,398	....	Debt Securities .... **79ae *d***
—	—	—	—	—	—	—	—	—	—	—	—	—	—	....	Financial Derivatives .... **79al *d***
1,910	2,948	3,441	2,927	4,133	3,680	3,401	4,005	4,171	4,349	4,985	4,657	5,297	4,565	....	Other Investment............................. **79af *d***
—	—	—	—	—	—	252	475	453	392	306	227	24	19	....	Monetary Authorities................... **79ag *d***
372	509	571	448	1,373	1,431	1,331	1,839	1,838	2,040	2,371	2,148	1,839	1,596	....	General Government.................... **79ah *d***
4	1	19	11	285	279	17	37	19	104	39	150	258	300	....	Banks .... **79ai *d***
1,535	2,437	2,851	2,467	2,475	1,970	1,800	1,653	1,862	1,813	2,269	2,132	3,176	2,650	....	Other Sectors................................ **79aj *d***
2,298	2,502	3,901	2,638	2,599	2,658	3,603	3,818	3,467	4,008	4,975	3,445	7,262	7,201	....	Reserve Assets .... **79ak *d***
....	31,735	33,385	28,352	34,078	34,959	36,841	40,898	44,022	52,197	62,610	60,449	68,546	70,604	....	Liabilities.. **79la *d***
10,546	12,257	13,331	11,057	8,067	9,198	10,209	10,662	10,694	12,615	15,014	13,236	16,736	15,676	....	Dir. Invest. in Rep. Economy........... **79lb *d***
4,498	5,286	5,432	4,667	6,778	8,524	10,292	12,549	13,470	18,998	23,446	23,804	28,143	31,579	....	Portfolio Investment .... **79lc *d***
1,938	2,164	2,034	1,750	2,788	3,366	4,854	5,359	6,027	9,246	12,492	13,366	13,144	16,904	....	Equity Securities.......................... **79ld *d***
2,560	3,122	3,398	2,917	3,990	5,158	5,438	7,190	7,443	9,752	10,953	10,439	14,999	14,675	....	Debt Securities .... **79le *d***
—	—	—	—	—	—	—	5	2	4	10	14	66	119	....	Financial Derivatives....................... **79ll *d***
....	14,192	14,622	12,628	19,232	17,237	16,340	17,683	19,855	20,580	24,140	23,395	23,601	23,230	....	Other investment .... **79lf *d***
880	541	45	41	1,500	328	129	390	2,660	2,534	1,142	979	2,578	3,181	....	Monetary Authorities................... **79lg *d***
....	2,617	2,580	2,340	9,733	8,364	3,125	3,920	3,512	3,108	3,072	3,244	2,776	2,537	....	General Government.................... **79lh *d***
1,994	2,051	2,248	1,979	1,312	5,342	5,008	5,131	4,968	5,944	9,038	9,310	8,861	9,154	....	Banks .... **79li *d***
....	8,983	9,748	8,268	6,688	3,203	8,077	8,242	8,715	8,993	10,889	9,861	9,386	8,358	....	Other Sectors................................ **79lj *d***

South Africa

	1970	1971	1972	1973	1974	1975	1976	1977	1978	1979	1980	1981	1982	1983	1984
Government Finance														Millions of Rand:	
Deficit (-) or Surplus 80	−401	−853	−769	−212	−598	−1,680	−2,011	−1,735	−2,048	−2,112	−1,320	−1,775	−2,307	−3,578	−5,677
Total Revenue and Grants 81y	2,160	2,488	2,882	3,797	4,715	5,316	6,232	6,918	7,966	9,781	12,953	14,823	17,321	19,736	23,545
Revenue 81	....	....	....	....	....	....	....	....	....	....	....	....	....	....	....
Grants 81z	....	....	....	....	....	....	....	....	....	....	....	....	....	....	....
Exp. & Lending Minus Repay. 82z	....	....	....	....	....	....	....	....	....	....	....	....	....	....	....
Expenditure 82	2,561	3,341	3,651	4,009	5,313	6,996	8,243	8,653	10,014	11,893	14,273	16,598	19,628	23,314	29,222
Lending Minus Repayments 83	....	....	....	....	....	....	....	....	....	....	....	....	....	....	....
Total Financing 80h	401	853	769	212	598	1,680	2,011	1,735	2,048	2,112	1,320	1,775	2,307	3,578	5,677
Total Net Borrowing 84	279	585	995	531	463	1,877	2,138	1,811	2,215	2,056	2,050	1,237	4,153	3,502	3,670
Net Domestic 84a	156	457	911	653	345	1,628	1,688	1,835	2,456	2,192	2,155	1,077	3,632	3,622	3,363
Net Foreign 85a	123	128	84	−122	118	249	450	−24	−241	−136	−105	160	521	−120	307
Use of Cash Balances 87	122	268	−226	−319	135	−197	−127	−76	−167	56	−730	538	−1,846	76	2,007
Total Debt by Currency 88z	5,374	6,016	7,052	7,524	7,986	10,094	12,106	13,971	16,249	18,185	19,983	21,726	25,775	29,704	35,161
National 88b	5,146	5,600	6,550	7,164	7,476	9,208	10,781	12,615	15,065	17,251	19,380	20,832	24,447	28,342	32,834
Foreign 89b	228	416	502	360	510	886	1,325	1,356	1,184	934	603	894	1,328	1,362	2,327
National Accounts														Millions of Rand	
Exports of Goods & Services .... 90c. c	2,747	3,054	3,987	4,953	6,716	7,480	8,504	10,339	12,681	16,470	22,022	20,688	21,863	22,985	28,015
Government Consumption .... 91f. c	1,516	1,828	1,937	2,219	2,802	3,687	4,465	5,034	5,526	6,329	8,158	9,877	12,361	14,115	17,927
Gross Fixed Capital Formation .... 93e. c	3,085	3,605	4,176	4,885	5,945	7,846	9,046	9,312	10,087	12,015	16,040	19,738	22,459	24,498	26,209
Increase/Decrease(-) in Stocks ...... 93i. c	403	575	−184	110	1,066	681	−490	−370	−434	238	2,569	3,807	−2,167	−893	485
Private Consumption .... 96f. c	7,613	8,536	9,503	11,134	13,106	15,167	17,116	18,914	21,086	24,427	30,797	38,086	44,564	51,596	59,705
Imports of Goods & Services .... 98c. c	−3,189	−3,629	−3,568	−4,406	−6,838	−8,128	−8,795	−8,491	−9,931	−11,969	−17,034	−21,881	−21,953	−19,594	−25,931
Gross Domestic Product (GDP) .... 99b. c	12,473	13,767	15,535	19,218	23,690	26,646	30,020	33,263	38,247	45,772	60,328	71,080	80,531	91,457	107,221
Net Factor Inc/Pmts(-) Abroad 98.n	−523	−524	−605	−724	−938	−1,249	−1,443	−1,659	−1,877	−2,144	−2,739	−3,314	−3,583	−3,958	−4,655
Gross National Income (GNI) 99a	10,621	11,710	13,122	16,382	20,183	22,087	24,433	26,811	30,697	36,884	58,589	67,766	76,938	87,499	102,566
Net National Income 99e	10,974	12,148	13,513	17,042	20,931	22,862	25,403	27,825	31,637	37,683	50,566	58,078	64,939	73,283	86,445
GDP Volume 1985 Prices .... 99b. r	82,637	86,173	87,599	91,604	97,202	98,850	101,074	100,979	104,023	‡107,966	115,114	121,285	120,820	118,589	124,636
GDP Volume 1995 Prices .... 99b. r	....	....	....	....	....	....	....	....	....	....	....	....	....	....	....
GDP Volume (1995=100) .... 99bv r	59.2	61.7	62.8	65.6	69.6	70.8	72.4	72.3	74.5	‡77.3	82.5	86.9	86.6	85.0	89.3
GDP Deflator (1995=100) .... 99bi r	3.8	4.1	4.5	5.3	6.2	6.9	7.6	8.4	9.4	‡10.8	13.3	14.9	17.0	19.6	21.9
															Millions:
Population 99z	22.47	23.03	23.67	24.30	24.92	25.47	26.13	26.68	27.30	27.67	28.28	28.90	29.54	31.93	32.25

Year Ending December 31

Government Finance

	1985	1986	1987	1988	1989	1990	1991	1992	1993	1994	1995	1996	1997	1998	1999		
Deficit (-) or Surplus	-3,546	-5,879	-8,593	-6,483	-5,710	-10,457	I-13,987	-26,423	-28,342	-38,690	-23,465	-28,563	-28,129	-19,464	-14,774	80	
Total Revenue and Grants	29,667	35,030	40,048	48,824	65,524	72,614	I77,701	83,464	95,710	111,916	125,470	147,738	162,983	181,749	203,401	81y	
Revenue	....	....	....	....	....	....	....	....	....	....	....	....	....	....	....	81	
Grants	....	....	....	....	....	....	....	....	....	....	....	....	....	....	....	81z	
Exp. & Lending Minus Repay.	....	....	....	....	....	....	....	....	....	....	....	....	....	....	....	82z	
Expenditure	33,213	40,909	48,641	55,307	71,234	83,071	I91,688	109,887	124,052	150,606	148,935	176,301	191,112	201,213	218,175	82	
Lending Minus Repayments	....	....	....	....	....	....	....	....	....	....	....	....	....	....	....	83	
Total Financing	3,546	5,879	8,593	6,483	5,710	10,457	I13,987	26,423	28,342	38,690	23,465	28,563	28,129	19,465	14,776	80h	
Total Net Borrowing	2,467	8,081	8,446	9,208	10,292	7,511	I19,466	21,223	31,469	37,928	25,504	24,224	26,507	21,647	13,271	84	
Net Domestic	2,605	8,096	8,536	9,256	10,479	7,586	I18,996	20,649	31,632	35,317	24,323	21,596	23,553	21,591	7,653	84a	
Net Foreign	-138	-15	-90	-48	-187	-75	I470	574	-163	2,611	1,181	2,628	2,954	56	5,618	85a	
Use of Cash Balances	1,079	-2,202	147	-2,725	-4,582	2,946	I-5,479	5,200	-3,127	762	-2,039	4,339	1,622	-2,182	1,505	87	
Total Debt by Currency	40,620	48,360	58,924	69,684	91,282	102,360	124,920	147,327	185,538	I239,714	275,489	302,608	I336,133	361,401	391,420	88z	
National	37,866	45,830	56,657	67,285	89,249	100,404	122,821	144,960	180,542	I231,656	265,879	288,349	I320,981	345,559	371,395	88b	
Foreign	2,754	2,530	2,267	2,399	2,033	1,956	2,099	2,367	4,996	8,058	9,610	14,259	15,152	15,842	20,025	89b	

Millions of Rand

National Accounts

	1985	1986	1987	1988	1989	1990	1991	1992	1993	1994	1995	1996	1997	1998	1999		
Exports of Goods & Services	I39,698	45,508	48,627	57,890	66,021	70,558	74,537	79,399	91,578	106,844	125,867	151,795	168,415	190,088	203,571	90c. c	
Government Consumption	I21,297	25,672	30,516	35,865	44,713	56,991	65,667	75,257	85,551	96,503	100,424	120,139	135,599	146,800	154,066	91f. c	
Gross Fixed Capital Formation	I28,715	28,992	30,850	39,717	49,585	55,485	56,954	58,255	62,603	73,047	87,042	99,381	111,279	122,088	119,698	93e. c	
Increase/Decrease(-) in Stocks	I-3,734	-1,609	28	2,311	1,249	-5,566	-1,530	-3,319	2,603	8,013	11,517	6,477	-1,464	-2,406	1,983	93i. c	
Private Consumption	I66,167	78,211	93,277	113,151	133,955	181,872	210,316	237,190	265,392	299,541	343,037	385,280	431,072	464,760	501,334	96f. c	
Imports of Goods & Services	I-28,546	-32,239	-35,187	-47,027	-53,449	-54,377	-58,018	-64,404	-75,917	-95,747	-121,091	-143,340	-160,719	-180,959	-183,339	98c. c	
Gross Domestic Product (GDP)	I123,126	143,255	167,098	200,448	240,639	289,816	331,980	372,227	426,133	482,120	548,100	618,417	683,666	740,581	801,115	99b. c	
Net Factor Inc/Pmts(-) Abroad	I-5,986	-7,010	-6,693	-7,572	-9,310	-11,529	-8,859	-8,401	-8,700	-8,600	-10,427	-13,379	-14,795	-16,680	-17,422	98.n	
Gross National Income (GNI)	I117,140	136,245	160,405	192,876	231,329	278,287	323,121	363,826	417,433	473,520	537,673	605,038	668,871	723,901	783,693	99a	
Net National Income	I97,495	111,548	132,407	160,492	192,955	232,297	272,870	309,599	358,858	409,020	465,846	526,115	581,716	629,215	680,176	99e	
GDP Volume 1985 Prices	123,126	....	....	....	....	....	....	....	....	....	....	....	....	....	....	99b. r	
GDP Volume 1995 Prices	I254,175	254,221	259,561	270,463	276,940	276,060	273,249	267,257	270,702	278,143	287,506	296,827	301,802	302,075	....	99b. r	
GDP Volume (1995=100)	I88.2	88.2	90.1	93.9	96.1	I95.8	94.8	92.8	93.9	97.0	100.0	104.2	106.8	107.5	108.8	99bv r	
GDP Deflator (1995=100)	I25.5	29.6	33.8	39.0	45.7	55.2	63.9	73.2	82.8	90.7	100.0	108.3	116.8	125.7	134.4	99bi r	

Midyear Estimates

	1985	1986	1987	1988	1989	1990	1991	1992	1993	1994	1995	1996	1997	1998	1999		
Population	33.04	33.83	34.63	35.42	36.24	34.01	36.20	36.99	37.80	38.63	39.48	40.34	41.23	42.13	43.05	99z	

(See notes in the back of the book.)

Spain

		1970	1971	1972	1973	1974	1975	1976	1977	1978	1979	1980	1981	1982	1983	1984
Exchange Rates															*Pesetas per SDR through 1998,*	
Market Rate	aa	69.72	71.68	69.02	68.70	ʃ68.70	69.98	79.34	98.28	91.34	87.14	101.08	113.43	138.55	164.06	169.97
															Pesetas per US Dollar through 1998,	
Market Rate	ae	69.72	66.02	63.57	56.95	ʃ56.11	59.77	68.29	80.91	70.11	66.15	79.25	97.45	125.60	156.70	173.40
Market Rate	rf	70.00	69.47	64.27	58.26	57.69	57.41	66.90	75.96	76.67	67.13	71.70	92.32	109.86	143.43	160.76
															Pesetas per ECU:	
ECU Rate	ea	....	....	....	....	....	....	....	....	....	....	99.6098	102.6777	107.4669	127.3924	126.5083
ECU Rate	eb	....	....	....	....	....	....	....	....	....	....					
															Index Numbers (1995=100):	
Market Rate	ahx	178.7	180.0	193.9	214.1	216.0	216.8	186.5	165.6	163.0	185.7	174.2	135.5	114.0	87.3	77.7
Nominal Effective Exchange Rate	neu	208.3	205.5	206.3	206.9	215.5	207.5	196.6	173.7	155.5	168.2	156.5	148.0	141.8	119.8	119.8
Real Effective Exchange Rate	reu	....	....	....	....	....	78.9	84.9	89.9	97.7	113.8	ʃ106.0	103.2	102.4	88.3	91.0
Fund Position															*Millions of SDRs:*	
Quota	2f.s	395	395	395	395	395	395	395	395	557	557	836	836	836	1,286	1,286
SDRs	1b.s	43	87	129	129	134	121	91	48	103	206	231	319	186	65	155
Reserve Position in the Fund	1c.s	45	104	104	104	121	—	—	—	136	133	206	206	206	322	363
of which: Outstg.Fund Borrowing	2c	—	—	—	—	—	—	—	—	—	—	—	—	—	—	—
Total Fund Cred.&Loans Outstg.	2tl						496	572	572	615	205	205	142	5	—	—
International Liquidity														*Millions of US Dollars Unless Otherwise Indicated:*		
Total Res.Min.Gold (Eurosys.Def)	1l.d	1,319	2,727	4,473	6,170	5,874	5,506	4,704	5,977	10,112	13,224	11,863	10,805	7,655	7,402	11,955
SDRs	1b.d	43	94	140	155	164	142	105	59	134	272	294	371	205	68	151
Reserve Position in the Fund	1c.d	45	113	113	125	148	—	—	—	178	176	262	239	227	337	356
Foreign Exchange	1d.d	1,231	2,520	4,221	5,889	5,562	5,364	4,599	5,918	9,801	12,777	11,307	10,195	7,223	6,997	11,448
o/w: Fin.Deriv.Rel.to Reserves	1dd d	....	....	....	....	....	....	....	....	....	....	....	....	....	....	....
Other Reserve Assets	1e.d	....	....	....	....	....	....	....	....	....	....	....	....	....	....	....
Gold (Million Fine Troy Ounces)	1ad d	14.23	14.23	14.23	14.27	14.27	14.27	14.27	14.44	14.52	14.61	14.61	14.61	14.61	14.61	14.63
Gold (National Valuation)	1an d	498	498	541	602	602	602	602	609	613	617	617	4,353	3,666	3,827	3,832
Memo: Euro Cl. on Non-EA Res.	1dg d	....	....	....	....	....	....	....	....	....	....	....	....	....	....	....
Non-Euro Cl. on EA Res.	1dh d	....	....	....	....	....	....	....	....	....	....	....	....	....	....	....
Mon. Auth.: Other Foreign Assets	3..d	....	....	....	....	....	....	....	....	....	....	....	....	....	....	....
Foreign Liabilities	4..d	87	18	9	4	8	14	37	9	8	7	6	11	12	4	7
Banking Insts.: Foreign Assets	7a.d	1,004	1,569	2,514	3,774	3,033	3,242	3,644	4,583	7,228	10,535	12,790	14,824	ʃ17,362	15,712	17,524
Foreign Liab.	7b.d	1,284	2,124	3,197	4,766	5,352	6,366	8,300	10,842	14,813	20,568	24,499	27,871	ʃ21,534	19,417	21,209
Monetary Authorities														*Billions of Pesetas through 1998;*		
Fgn. Assets (Cl.on Non-EA Ctys)	11	127	227	320	399	359	354	329	486	777	939	906	1,182	930	ʃ1,245	2,096
Claims on General Government	12a.u	....	....	....	....	....	....	....	....	....	....	....	....	....	....	....
o/w: Claims on Gen.Govt.in Cty	12a	134	117	97	120	202	296	321	458	570	833	1,227	1,821	2,687	ʃ3,616	2,723
Claims on Banking Institutions	12e.u	....	....	....	....	....	....	....	....	....	....	....	....	....	....	....
o/w: Claims on Bank.Inst.in Cty	12e	104	61	72	73	154	180	367	360	230	325	315	384	531	ʃ752	1,053
Claims on Other Resident Sectors	12d.u	....	....	....	....	....	....	....	....	....	....	....	....	....	....	....
o/w: Cl. on Oth.Res.Sect.in Cty	12d	108	91	36	13	79	70	108	149	202	238	242	254	300	320	313
Claims on ECB	12u	....	....	....	....	....	....	....	....	....	....	....	....	....	....	....
Currency in Circulation	14a	269	301	338	398	461	542	636	806	987	1,095	1,256	1,413	1,625	ʃ1,688	1,867
Liabilities to Banking Insts	14c.u	....	....	....	....	....	....	....	....	....	....	....	....	....	....	....
o/w: Liabs to Bank.Inst.in Cty	14c	45	91	118	143	202	239	261	286	377	736	851	953	1,241	ʃ3,638	3,673
Demand Dep. of Other Res.Sect.	14d.u	....	....	....	....	....	....	....	....	....	....	....	....	....	....	....
o/w: D.Dep.of Oth.Res.Sect.in Cty	14d	....	....	....	....	....	....	....	....	....	....	....	....	....	87	87
Other Dep. of Other Res.Sect.	15..u	....	....	....	....	....	....	....	....	....	....	....	....	....	....	....
o/w: O.Dep.of Oth.Res.Sect.in Cty	15	....	....	....	....	....	....	....	....	....	....	....	....	....	....	....
Money Market Instruments	16m.u	....	....	....	....	....	....	....	....	....	....	....	....	....	....	....
o/w: MMI Held by Resid.of Cty	16m	....	....	....	....	....	....	....	....	....	....	....	....	....	....	....
Bonds (Debt Securities)	16n.u	....	....	....	....	....	....	....	....	....	....	....	....	....	....	....
o/w: Bonds Held by Resid.of Cty	16n	....	....	....	....	....	....	....	....	....	....	....	....	....	....	....
Foreign Liab. (to Non-EA Ctys)	16c	45	9	4	2	3	262	353	420	418	135	156	126	16	4	9
Central Government Deposits	16d.u	....	....	....	....	....	....	....	....	....	....	....	....	....	....	....
o/w: Cent.Govt.Dep. in Cty	16d	26	34	34	44	52	45	45	90	74	109	98	118	203	ʃ273	338
Liabilities to ECB	16u	....	....	....	....	....	....	....	....	....	....	....	....	....	....	....
Capital Accounts	17a	....	....	....	....	....	....	....	....	....	....	....	....	....	441	527
Other Items (Net)	17r	87	61	31	18	74	−188	−170	−149	−77	259	328	1,031	1,363	ʃ−199	−317
Banking Institutions														*Billions of Pesetas through 1998;*		
Claims on Monetary Authorities	20	43	89	101	121	178	201	226	244	289	532	629	694	893	ʃ3,699	3,853
Claims on Bk.Inst.in Oth.EA Ctys	20b.u	....	....	....	....	....	....	....	....	....	....	....	....	....	....	....
Fgn. Assets (Cl.on Non-EA Ctys)	21	70	101	162	219	170	194	249	371	507	697	1,014	1,445	2,103	ʃ2,462	3,039
Claims on General Government	22a.u	....	....	....	....	....	....	....	....	....	....	....	....	....	....	....
o/w: Claims on Gen.Govt.in Cty	22a	406	485	549	605	638	720	897	968	1,251	1,560	1,854	2,492	3,163	ʃ2,602	6,084
Claims on Other Resident Sectors	22d.u	....	....	....	....	....	....	....	....	....	....	....	....	....	....	....
o/w: Cl. on Oth.Res.Sect.in Cty	22d	1,759	2,081	2,571	3,270	4,107	5,055	6,240	7,609	8,682	10,054	11,891	13,979	16,121	ʃ17,481	18,120
Demand Deposits	24..u	....	....	....	....	....	....	....	....	....	....	....	....	....	....	....
o/w: D.Dep.of Oth.Res.Sect.in Cty	24	480	643	801	985	1,163	1,398	1,690	1,996	2,205	2,438	2,739	3,086	3,460	ʃ3,428	3,718
Other Deposits	25..u	....	....	....	....	....	....	....	....	....	....	....	....	....	....	....
o/w: O.Dep.of Oth.Res.Sect.in Cty	25	1,212	1,508	1,847	2,305	2,771	3,301	3,889	4,620	5,641	6,954	8,234	9,650	11,425	ʃ10,806	11,137
Money Market Instruments	26m.u	....	....	....	....	....	....	....	....	....	....	....	....	....	....	....
o/w: MMI Held by Resid.of Cty	26m	....	....	....	....	....	....	....	....	....	....	....	....	....	....	....
Bonds (Debt Securities)	26n.u	....	....	....	....	....	....	....	....	....	....	....	....	....	....	....
o/w: Bonds Held by Resid.of Cty	26n	56	60	81	135	187	241	285	315	329	336	390	453	550	ʃ3,601	5,738
Foreign Liab. (to Non-EA Ctys)	26c	90	137	206	277	300	381	567	877	1,039	1,361	1,942	2,716	3,775	ʃ3,352	3,986
Central Government Deposits	26d.u	....	....	....	....	....	....	....	....	....	....	....	....	....	....	....
o/w: Cent.Govt.Dep. in Cty	26d	27	35	36	45	53	69	75	95	92	121	166	209	344	ʃ764	983
Credit from Monetary Authorities	26g	104	61	72	73	148	180	368	359	236	301	306	392	554	ʃ758	1,058
Liab. to Bk.Inst.in Oth. EA Ctys	26h.u	....	....	....	....	....	....	....	....	....	....	....	....	....	....	....
Capital Accounts	27a	166	193	236	305	392	490	589	669	800	1,085	1,230	1,531	1,628	ʃ2,140	2,623
Other Items (Net)	27r	141	118	103	91	80	111	149	260	387	247	381	573	601	ʃ1,431	1,868

1985	1986	1987	1988	1989	1990	1991	1992	1993	1994	1995	1996	1997	1998	1999	
															Exchange Rates
Euros per SDR Thereafter: End of Period															
169.32	161.94	154.63	152.67	144.19	137.87	138.31	157.61	195.34	192.32	180.47	188.77	204.68	200.79	1.3662	Market Rate ... aa
Euros per US Dollar Thereafter: End of Period (ae) Period Average (rf)															
154.15	132.40	109.00	113.45	109.72	96.91	96.69	114.62	142.21	131.74	121.41	131.28	151.70	142.61	.9954	Market Rate ... ae
170.04	140.05	123.48	116.49	118.38	101.93	103.91	102.38	127.26	133.96	124.69	126.66	146.41	149.40	.9386	Market Rate ... rf
End of Period (ea) Period Average (eb)															
....	....	140.6100	132.0000	130.3000	131.0000	129.3690	138.3730	159.2800	161.5520	155.5610	162.6500	167.3270	166.3860	....	ECU Rate ... ea
129.3040	137.4546	142.2559	137.5998	130.3166	129.6826	128.5632	132.2572	148.6617	158.4871	161.1758	158.6182	165.3915	167.4876	....	ECU Rate ... eb
Period Averages															
73.4	89.2	101.2	107.1	105.4	122.6	120.3	122.1	98.4	93.1	100.0	98.4	85.2	83.5	....	Market Rate ... ah x
117.7	113.0	111.4	115.2	120.9	124.3	124.6	121.7	108.0	100.8	100.0	100.6	96.3	95.8	94.4	Nominal Effective Exchange Rate ... ne u
90.5	88.0	89.4	93.8	102.0	108.4	112.5	116.3	108.0	101.4	100.0	103.4	101.8	105.2	....	Real Effective Exchange Rate ... re u
															Fund Position
End of Period															
1,286	1,286	1,286	1,286	1,286	1,286	1,286	1,935	1,935	1,935	1,935	1,935	1,935	1,935	3,049	Quota ... 2f, s
254	353	420	457	523	489	319	134	157	174	277	314	351	408	190	SDRs ... 1b. s
369	423	554	786	930	797	749	832	751	760	1,065	1,110	1,409	1,558	1,111	Reserve Position in the Fund ... 1c. s
—	—	—	—	—	—	—	—	—	—	—	—	—	62	—	of which: Outstg.Fund Borrowing ... 2c
—	—	—	—	—	—	—	—	—	—	—	—	—	—	—	Total Fund Cred.&Loans Outstg. ... 2tl
															International Liquidity
End of Period															
11,175	14,755	30,669	37,074	41,467	51,228	65,822	45,504	41,045	41,546	34,485	57,927	68,398	55,258	I33,115	Total Res.Min.Gold (Eurosys.Def) ... 1l.d
280	432	596	615	687	696	456	184	216	255	411	451	474	575	260	SDRs ... 1b.d
405	518	785	1,058	1,222	1,134	1,071	1,144	1,031	1,109	1,583	1,597	1,902	2,193	1,525	Reserve Position in the Fund ... 1c.d
10,490	13,805	29,287	35,401	39,558	49,398	64,295	44,176	39,798	40,182	32,491	55,879	66,023	52,490	31,329	Foreign Exchange ... 1d.d
....	....	....	....	....	....	....	....	....	....	....	....	....	....	....	o/w: Fin.Deriv.Rel.to Reserves ... 1ddd
														—	Other Reserve Assets ... 1e.d
14.65	14.82	11.92	14.04	15.72	15.61	15.62	15.62	15.62	15.62	15.63	15.63	15.63	19.54	16.83	Gold (Million Fine Troy Ounces) ... 1ad
3,722	3,785	3,767	4,766	5,419	4,777	4,498	4,217	4,217	4,217	4,221	4,221	4,139	5,617	4,895	Gold (National Valuation) ... 1and
....	....	....	....	....	....	....	....	....	....	....	....	....	....	4,134	Memo: Euro Cl. on Non-EA Res. ... 1dgd
														—	Non-Euro Cl. on EA Res. ... 1dhd
....	....	....	....	....	....	....	....	....	....	....	....	....	....		Mon. Auth.: Other Foreign Assets ... 3..d
19	418	450	817	798	523	483	457	462	515	551	983	454	480	I1,004	Foreign Liabilities ... 4..d
20,039	23,817	25,728	24,571	27,511	39,107	46,642	68,542	117,311	110,693	146,061	129,727	111,176	126,792	I66,435	Banking Insts.: Foreign Assets ... 7a.d
20,939	25,409	33,186	36,998	43,627	63,986	73,724	81,501	87,093	100,658	109,245	123,359	135,020	179,175	I125,417	Foreign Liab. ... 7b.d
															Monetary Authorities
Billions of Euros Beginning 1999: End of Period															
1,696	I1,996	3,643	4,609	4,938	5,348	6,731	5,604	6,152	5,796	4,566	7,960	10,708	8,751	41.50	Fgn. Assets (Cl.on Non-EA Ctys) ... 11
														15.17	Claims on General Government ... 12a.u
3,295	I2,498	2,865	2,917	2,740	2,459	3,011	1,881	-219	2,981	3,074	3,056	2,984	3,023	15.17	o/w: Claims on Gen.Govt.in Cty ... 12a
														53.93	Claims on Banking Institutions ... 12e.u
975	I1,426	1,384	958	2,128	1,595	1,545	4,296	6,525	5,949	6,641	4,439	2,267	4,471	24.18	o/w: Claims on Bank.Inst.in Cty ... 12e
														—	Claims on Other Resident Sectors ... 12d.u
309	I309	322	343	74	56	47	36	22	21	20	21	21	22	—	o/w: Cl. on Oth.Res.Sect.in Cty ... 12d
														6.08	Claims on ECB ... 12u
2,083	I2,402	2,736	3,241	3,836	4,534	5,608	6,025	6,509	7,165	7,535	7,942	8,378	8,437	61.35	Currency in Circulation ... 14a
														15.94	Liabilities to Banking Insts ... 14c.u
2,645	I3,804	4,219	4,324	5,500	1,792	2,110	1,728	1,283	1,430	1,394	1,310	1,484	1,788	12.49	o/w: Liabs to Bank.Inst.in Cty ... 14c
														5.22	Demand Dep. of Other Res.Sect. ... 14d.u
131	I158	183	174	135	128	102	106	131	132	193	175	207	190	5.22	o/w: D.Dep.of Oth.Res.Sect.in Cty ... 14d
														—	Other Dep. of Other Res.Sect. ... 15..u
															o/w: O.Dep.of Oth.Res.Sect.in Cty ... 15
														3.30	Money Market Instruments ... 16m.u
....	49	1,054	1,007	654	3,388	3,867	3,314	3,067	2,860	2,334	1,947	1,613	1,219	....	o/w: MMI Held by Resid.of Cty ... 16m
														—	Bonds (Debt Securities) ... 16n.u
															o/w: Bonds Held by Resid.of Cty ... 16n
21	I55	49	93	88	51	47	52	66	68	67	129	69	69	1.00	Foreign Liab. (to Non-EA Ctys) ... 16c
														16.87	Central Government Deposits ... 16d.u
216	I101	151	187	186	149	139	95	193	2,058	1,752	2,742	1,890	2,120	16.87	o/w: Cent.Govt.Dep. in Cty ... 16d
														—	Liabilities to ECB ... 16u
469	I334	478	452	417	392	690	1,506	2,207	1,166	1,267	1,594	2,752	2,870	16.01	Capital Accounts ... 17a
-291	I-673	-656	-645	-976	-1,229	-1,010	-975	-132	-243	-363	-412	-426		-3.00	Other Items (Net) ... 17r
															Banking Institutions
Billions of Euros Beginning 1999: End of Period															
3,916	I3,844	5,243	5,294	6,047	5,163	5,912	5,043	4,348	4,328	3,725	3,262	3,093	2,992	15.79	Claims on Monetary Authorities ... 20
														50.08	Claims on Bk.Inst.in Oth.EA Ctys ... 20b.u
3,089	I3,152	2,804	2,800	3,019	3,800	4,517	7,868	16,690	14,565	17,737	17,057	16,909	18,155	66.13	Fgn. Assets (Cl.on Non-EA Ctys) ... 21
														146.00	Claims on General Government ... 22a.u
7,797	I9,858	10,738	10,870	11,979	14,159	13,061	14,585	16,114	20,853	22,358	24,083	22,400	21,258	136.21	o/w: Claims on Gen.Govt.in Cty ... 22a
														529.64	Claims on Other Resident Sectors ... 22d.u
19,568	I22,245	26,088	31,863	37,839	41,647	46,568	49,059	49,600	50,345	53,764	57,682	65,592	76,417	519.57	o/w: Cl. on Oth.Res.Sect.in Cty ... 22d
														127.47	Demand Deposits ... 24..u
4,262	I5,001	5,864	7,037	7,980	9,595	10,270	9,584	9,657	10,159	10,291	11,144	13,391	16,768	125.54	o/w: D.Dep.of Oth.Res.Sect.in Cty ... 24
														319.89	Other Deposits ... 25..u
12,279	I16,466	17,267	18,575	20,451	23,000	26,219	28,416	32,208	34,492	37,397	37,579	35,679	36,346	310.68	o/w: O.Dep.of Oth.Res.Sect.in Cty ... 25
														42.59	Money Market Instruments ... 26m.u
....	....	....	....	....	....	....	....	....	....	....	....	....	....	....	o/w: MMI Held by Resid.of Cty ... 26m
														53.63	Bonds (Debt Securities) ... 26n.u
6,675	I1,796	1,547	1,511	1,223	1,113	1,422	1,449	1,906	2,214	2,316	2,394	2,693	3,025	....	o/w: Bonds Held by Resid.of Cty ... 26n
3,487	I3,378	3,634	4,258	4,904	6,468	7,419	9,497	12,459	13,303	13,316	16,436	20,741	25,889	124.84	Foreign Liab. (to Non-EA Ctys) ... 26c
														5.65	Central Government Deposits ... 26d.u
1,139	I1,169	1,268	1,581	2,611	2,544	2,749	2,890	2,866	2,706	2,954	3,063	3,352	3,882	5.62	o/w: Cent.Govt.Dep. in Cty ... 26d
984	I1,426	1,384	957	2,112	1,590	1,572	4,282	6,525	6,063	6,643	4,447	2,265	4,450	24.18	Credit from Monetary Authorities ... 26g
														54.22	Liab. to Bk.Inst.in Oth. EA Ctys ... 26h.u
3,161	I3,959	4,789	6,020	6,963	7,851	9,472	9,424	10,234	10,709	10,807	11,261	12,026	12,668	80.53	Capital Accounts ... 27a
2,359	I5,905	9,119	10,888	12,641	12,608	10,935	11,015	10,897	10,445	13,860	15,761	17,847	15,794	-25.36	Other Items (Net) ... 27r

Spain

	1970	1971	1972	1973	1974	1975	1976	1977	1978	1979	1980	1981	1982	1983	1984
Banking Survey (Nat'l Residency)														*Billions of Pesetas through 1998;*	
Foreign Assets (Net) **31n**	62	183	272	340	226	–94	–342	–440	–173	140	–177	–215	–755	I426	1,240
Domestic Credit **32**	2,354	2,705	3,183	3,919	4,920	6,026	7,446	9,000	10,539	12,455	14,949	18,220	21,724	I22,981	25,919
Claims on General Govt. (Net) **32an**	487	532	576	636	734	901	1,098	1,242	1,655	2,163	2,816	3,986	5,303	I5,180	7,486
Claims on Other Resident Sectors **32d**	1,867	2,172	2,607	3,283	4,186	5,125	6,348	7,758	8,884	10,292	12,133	14,233	16,421	I17,801	18,433
Currency in Circulation **34a.n**	269	301	338	398	461	542	636	806	987	1,095	1,256	1,413	1,625	I1,688	1,867
Demand Deposits **34b.n**	480	643	801	985	1,163	1,398	1,690	1,996	2,205	2,438	2,739	3,086	3,460	I3,515	3,805
Other Deposits .... **35..n**	1,212	1,508	1,847	2,304	2,770	3,301	3,889	4,620	5,641	6,954	8,234	9,651	11,425	I10,845	11,222
Money Market Instruments **36m**	....	....	....	....	....	....	....	....	....	....	....	....	....	....	....
Bonds (Debt Securities) **36n**	57	60	81	136	187	242	285	316	329	336	390	453	496	I3,601	5,738
o/w: Bonds Over Two Years **36na**	....	....	....	....	....	....	....	....	....	....	....	....	....	....	....
Capital Accounts **37a**	166	193	236	305	392	490	589	669	800	1,085	1,230	1,531	1,628	I2,582	3,150
Other Items (Net) **37r**	231	182	152	131	172	–40	15	153	404	686	922	1,871	2,335	I1,177	1,377
Banking Survey (EA-Wide Residency)														*Billions of Euros*	
Foreign Assets (Net) **31n.u**	....	....	....	....	....	....	....	....	....	....	....	....	....	....	....
Domestic Credit .... **32..u**	....	....	....	....	....	....	....	....	....	....	....	....	....	....	....
Claims on General Govt. (Net) **32an.u**	....	....	....	....	....	....	....	....	....	....	....	....	....	....	....
Claims on Other Resident Sect. **32d.u**	....	....	....	....	....	....	....	....	....	....	....	....	....	....	....
Currency in Circulation **34a.u**	....	....	....	....	....	....	....	....	....	....	....	....	....	....	....
Demand Deposits **34b.u**	....	....	....	....	....	....	....	....	....	....	....	....	....	....	....
Other Deposits .... **35..u**	....	....	....	....	....	....	....	....	....	....	....	....	....	....	....
o/w: Other Dep. Over Two Yrs **35ab.u**	....	....	....	....	....	....	....	....	....	....	....	....	....	....	....
Money Market Instruments **36m.u**	....	....	....	....	....	....	....	....	....	....	....	....	....	....	....
Bonds (Debt Securities) **36n.u**	....	....	....	....	....	....	....	....	....	....	....	....	....	....	....
o/w: Bonds Over Two Years **36na.u**	....	....	....	....	....	....	....	....	....	....	....	....	....	....	....
Capital Accounts **37a**	....	....	....	....	....	....	....	....	....	....	....	....	....	....	....
Other Items (Net) **37r.u**	....	....	....	....	....	....	....	....	....	....	....	....	....	....	....
Money (National Definitions)														*Billions of Pesetas:*	
M1 .... **59ma**	757.0	944.4	1,171.6	1,444.6	1,696.5	2,019.7	2,407.7	2,864.6	3,326.7	3,655.4	4,103.2	4,626.0	5,003.4	5,347.5	5,788.4
M2 .... **59mb**	1,423.6	1,732.3	2,146.8	2,595.2	2,996.6	3,575.9	4,320.2	5,118.9	5,989.6	6,672.3	7,438.2	8,307.5	9,034.8	9,830.7	10,565.7
M3 .... **59mc**	2,049.6	2,540.8	3,120.4	3,895.0	4,669.3	5,554.0	6,607.7	7,857.8	9,377.7	11,105.3	12,933.4	15,012.5	17,304.1	19,794.6	22,801.6
ALP **59md**	2,049.6	2,540.9	3,120.4	3,895.0	4,669.3	5,554.0	6,607.8	7,857.9	9,389.3	11,130.1	13,014.2	15,210.5	17,794.9	20,535.2	23,619.1
Interest Rates														*Percent Per Annum*	
Bank of Spain Rate*(End of Period)* **60**	6.50	5.00	5.00	6.00	7.00	7.00	7.00	I8.03	9.02	7.98	10.90	10.51	18.40	21.40	12.50
Money Market Rate **60b**	....	....	....	....	9.61	6.70	9.97	13.12	20.77	13.13	15.46	15.89	17.17	19.45	12.60
Treasury Bill Rate **60c**	....	....	....	....	....	....	....	....	14.41	15.70	15.70	15.80	15.70	19.80	13.43
Deposit Rate **60l**	....	....	....	....	....	....	....	....	....	9.61	13.05	11.41	12.26	12.31	12.30
Lending Rate **60p**	....	....	....	....	....	....	....	....	14.96	15.77	16.85	15.26	14.98	15.00	16.58
Government Bond Yield **61**	....	....	....	....	....	....	....	....	....	13.31	15.96	15.81	15.99	16.91	16.52
Prices, Production, Labor														*Index Numbers (1995=100):*	
Share Prices **62**	25.1	I25.5	33.4	42.2	42.8	36.7	31.7	21.8	17.6	15.1	14.1	18.0	16.5	16.7	22.8
Industrial Prices **63**	12.5	13.2	14.1	15.5	I18.3	I20.0	22.7	27.3	31.7	36.3	42.7	49.4	55.5	63.3	71.0
Consumer Prices **64**	7.7	8.3	9.0	10.1	11.6	13.6	16.0	19.9	23.9	27.6	31.9	36.6	41.8	46.9	52.2
Harmonized CPI **64h**															
Wages **65**	I3.3	3.8	4.4	5.3	6.7	8.6	11.2	14.6	18.4	I22.6	26.8	I30.2	35.1	40.3	45.1
Industrial Production .... **66..c**	49.6	52.9	61.3	68.2	73.3	I70.0	73.4	77.4	79.2	80.5	80.5	79.9	78.9	81.1	81.8
Total Employment **67**	102.9	103.6	104.9	103.9	105.4	103.9	I104.2	103.2	101.2	98.8	I94.7	91.5	90.4	89.6	88.6
														Number in Thousands:	
Labor Force **67d**	....	....	....	....	....	....	....	....	....	....	....	....	....	....	....
Employment **67e**	....	....	....	....	....	....	....	....	....	....	....	....	....	....	....
Unemployment **67c**	....	....	....	....	....	....	....	....	....	....	....	....	....	....	2,475
Unemployment Rate (%) **67r**	....	....	....	....	....	....	....	....	....	....	....	....	....	....	18.4
International Transactions														*Billions of Pesetas through 1998;*	
Exports **70**	167.2	205.7	245.3	302.5	408.6	441.5	583.5	775.3	1,001.4	1,221.2	1,493.2	1,888.4	2,258.0	2,838.6	3,778.1
Imports, c.i.f. **71**	332.3	347.9	438.8	561.6	889.0	932.2	1,170.4	1,350.6	1,431.5	1,704.1	2,450.7	2,970.4	3,465.6	4,176.5	4,629.0
														1995=100	
Volume of Exports (1990=100) **72**	37.3	44.9	50.9	58.7	62.8	64.8	I74.4	83.8	93.7	104.2	109.9	I52.8	57.2	62.3	74.1
Volume of Imports (1990=100) **73**	34.0	33.9	42.2	47.6	49.1	48.7	I53.8	50.3	48.5	54.2	58.2	I41.5	41.8	41.6	40.9
Unit Value of Exports **74**	I16.6	16.4	17.0	19.3	23.7	I25.5	26.9	31.7	35.5	38.9	46.3	51.2	57.2	66.8	75.2
Unit Value of Imports **75**	I15.6	16.4	16.4	18.7	26.7	I28.6	31.6	37.5	41.1	42.2	57.4	77.2	86.5	105.9	118.4
Export Prices (1975=100) **76**	57.9	60.2	66.6	78.3	85.9	100.0	116.5	135.9	156.1	179.6	....	....	....	....	....

	1985	1986	1987	1988	1989	1990	1991	1992	1993	1994	1995	1996	1997	1998	1999	
Billions of Euros Beginning 1999: End of Period																**Banking Survey (Nat'l Residency)**
	1,383	I 1,715	2,764	3,059	2,965	2,628	3,782	3,923	10,317	6,990	8,921	8,452	6,808	949	22.24	Foreign Assets (Net) 31n
	29,614	I 33,640	38,593	44,225	49,835	55,628	59,799	62,576	62,460	69,435	74,510	79,037	85,755	94,718	648.46	Domestic Credit 32
	9,737	I 11,086	12,183	12,019	11,921	13,925	13,184	13,481	12,837	19,069	20,726	21,334	20,142	18,279	128.89	Claims on General Govt. (Net)........... 32an
	19,877	I 22,554	26,409	32,206	37,913	41,703	46,615	49,095	49,622	50,366	53,784	57,703	65,613	76,439	519.57	Claims on Other Resident Sectors 32d
	2,083	I 2,402	2,736	3,241	3,836	4,534	5,608	6,025	6,509	7,165	7,535	7,942	8,378	8,437	61.35	Currency in Circulation 34a.n
	4,394	I 5,158	6,048	7,210	8,115	9,723	10,372	9,690	9,788	10,291	10,484	11,319	13,598	16,959	130.76	Demand Deposits 34b.n
	12,407	I 16,466	17,267	18,575	20,451	23,000	26,219	28,416	32,208	34,492	37,397	37,579	35,679	36,344	310.68	Other Deposits .... 35..n
	....	49	1,054	1,007	654	3,388	3,867	3,314	3,067	2,860	2,334	1,947	1,613	1,219	45.89	Money Market Instruments 36m
	6,676	I 1,796	1,547	1,511	1,223	1,113	1,422	1,449	1,906	2,214	2,316	2,394	2,693	3,025	53.63	Bonds (Debt Securities)........................ 36n
	....	....	....	....	....	....	....	....	....	....	....	....	....	....	37.49	o/w: Bonds Over Two Years............. 36na
	3,630	I 4,293	5,267	6,472	7,380	8,243	10,162	10,930	12,441	11,875	12,074	12,855	14,778	15,538	96.54	Capital Accounts 37a
	1,806	I 5,191	7,438	9,272	11,143	8,257	5,931	6,675	6,857	7,529	11,289	13,454	15,824	14,143	-28.14	Other Items (Net) 37r
End of Period																**Banking Survey (EA-Wide Residency)**
	....	....	....	....	....	....	....	....	....	....	....	....	....	....	-18.21	Foreign Assets (Net) 31n.u
	....	....	....	....	....	....	....	....	....	....	....	....	....	....	668.28	Domestic Credit .... 32..u
	....	....	....	....	....	....	....	....	....	....	....	....	....	....	138.64	Claims on General Govt. (Net)........... 32an u
	....	....	....	....	....	....	....	....	....	....	....	....	....	....	529.64	Claims on Other Resident Sect. 32d.u
	....	....	....	....	....	....	....	....	....	....	....	....	....	....	61.35	Currency in Circulation 34a.u
	....	....	....	....	....	....	....	....	....	....	....	....	....	....	132.68	Demand Deposits 34b.u
	....	....	....	....	....	....	....	....	....	....	....	....	....	....	319.89	Other Deposits...................................... 35..u
	....	....	....	....	....	....	....	....	....	....	....	....	....	....	32.17	o/w: Other Dep. Over Two Yrs....... 35ab u
	....	....	....	....	....	....	....	....	....	....	....	....	....	....	45.89	Money Market Instruments 36m.u
	....	....	....	....	....	....	....	....	....	....	....	....	....	....	53.63	Bonds (Debt Securities)........................ 36n.u
	....	....	....	....	....	....	....	....	....	....	....	....	....	....	37.49	o/w: Bonds Over Two Years............. 36na u
	....	....	....	....	....	....	....	....	....	....	....	....	....	....	96.54	Capital Accounts 37a
	....	....	....	....	....	....	....	....	....	....	....	....	....	....	-59.90	Other Items (Net) 37r.u
End of Period																**Money (National Definitions)**
	6,535.5	7,450.2	8,650.8	10,319.7	11,859.6	14,163.1	15,898.8	15,631.3	16,180.5	17,337.6	17,887.8	19,116.1	21,834.9	25,270.6	....	M1 .... 59ma
	11,835.6	13,425.5	15,078.3	17,563.4	19,611.5	23,037.3	25,797.5	25,690.3	26,966.7	28,753.4	29,637.5	31,717.5	35,483.7	40,616.5	....	M2 .... 59mb
	25,558.1	28,381.5	31,837.5	35,992.9	41,134.9	46,686.1	51,777.9	54,237.5	59,260.7	63,675.8	70,439.4	73,819.5	77,136.6	78,665.1	....	M3 .... 59mc
	26,733.7	30,345.2	34,877.6	39,562.2	45,450.9	50,792.7	56,546.9	59,449.7	65,429.1	70,045.8	76,479.0	82,118.8	85,674.3	86,588.1	....	ALP 59md
Percent Per Annum																**Interest Rates**
	10.50	11.84	13.50	12.40	14.52	14.71	12.50	13.25	9.00	7.38	9.00	6.25	4.75	3.00	....	Bank of Spain Rate(End of Period) 60
	11.61	11.49	16.06	11.29	14.39	14.76	13.20	13.01	12.33	7.81	8.98	7.65	5.49	4.34	2.72	Money Market Rate 60b
	10.90	8.63	I 11.38	10.79	13.57	14.17	12.45	12.44	10.53	8.11	9.79	7.23	5.02	3.79	3.01	Treasury Bill Rate 60c
	10.53	9.05	8.97	9.06	9.55	10.65	10.47	10.43	9.63	6.70	7.68	6.12	3.96	2.92	1.85	Deposit Rate 60l
	13.52	12.19	16.36	12.43	15.84	16.01	14.38	14.23	12.78	8.95	10.05	8.50	6.08	5.01	3.95	Lending Rate 60p
	13.37	11.36	12.81	11.74	13.70	14.68	12.43	12.17	10.16	9.69	11.04	8.18	5.84	4.55	4.30	Government Bond Yield 61
Period Averages																**Prices, Production, Labor**
	28.8	I 58.7	84.4	93.6	101.7	87.4	89.7	77.8	91.4	106.2	100.0	124.0	187.8	276.1	302.0	Share Prices 62
	76.6	77.3	78.0	80.3	83.7	85.5	86.8	87.9	90.1	94.0	100.0	101.7	102.7	102.0	102.7	Industrial Prices 63
	56.8	61.8	65.1	68.2	72.9	77.7	82.4	87.2	91.2	95.5	100.0	103.6	105.6	107.5	110.0	Consumer Prices 64
	....	....	....	....	....	....	....	....	....	....	100.0	103.6	105.5	107.4	109.8	Harmonized CPI 64h
	49.6	55.0	59.1	62.9	67.5	73.4	79.4	85.5	91.3	95.4	100.0	105.3	109.6	....	115.5	Wages 65
	83.4	86.0	90.0	92.7	96.9	96.2	93.5	89.0	95.6	100.0	99.3	106.1	111.8	114.9	Industrial Production .... 66..c
	87.8	92.3	95.1	97.8	101.8	104.5	104.7	102.7	98.3	97.4	100.0	102.9	106.0	109.7	114.7	Total Employment 67
Period Averages																
	....	....	....	....	....	....	....	....	15,319	....	15,625	15,936	16,121	16,265	....	Labor Force 67d
	11,026	10,881	11,369	11,773	12,258	12,579	12,609	12,366	11,838	11,730	12,042	12,396	12,765	13,205	....	Employment.. 67e
	2,642	2,933	2,938	2,848	2,561	2,441	2,464	2,789	3,481	3,738	3,584	3,540	3,356	3,060	....	Unemployment.. 67c
	19.5	21.2	20.5	19.5	17.3	16.3	16.4	18.4	22.7	24.2	22.9	22.2	20.8	18.8	....	Unemployment Rate (%) 67r
Millions of Euros Beginning 1999																**International Transactions**
	4,099.2	3,801.8	4,195.6	4,686.4	5,134.5	5,630.6	6,064.7	6,657.6	7,754.6	9,746.6	11,339.6	12,931.2	15,266.9	16,290.8	I 103343.2	Exports... 70
	5,073.2	4,890.8	6,029.9	7,039.5	8,396.4	8,898.4	9,636.8	10,204.5	10,131.0	12,306.3	14,106.7	15,435.7	17,966.0	19,837.9	I 135866.3	Imports, c.i.f. 71
1995=100																
	76.0	74.0	79.5	85.0	89.0	100.0	111.5	117.0	135.4	160.4	....	....	....	....	....	Volume of Exports (1990=100) 72
	44.1	52.5	65.8	78.1	91.0	100.0	111.7	121.5	117.8	130.5	....	....	....	....	....	Volume of Imports (1990=100) 73
	80.4	77.3	79.3	83.5	87.4	85.7	84.9	85.8	89.9	93.9	100.0	101.0	104.3	104.4	103.5	Unit Value of Exports 74
	120.1	95.5	92.8	90.8	92.7	89.5	87.1	86.0	90.5	95.8	100.0	100.3	103.9	101.5	101.5	Unit Value of Imports............................. 75
	....	....	....	....	....	....	....	....	....	....	....	....	....	....	....	Export Prices (1975=100) 76

Spain

		1970	1971	1972	1973	1974	1975	1976	1977	1978	1979	1980	1981	1982	1983	1984
Balance of Payments																*Millions of US Dollars:*
Current Account, n.i.e.	78al d	....	....	....	....	....	−3,893	−4,622	−2,455	1,251	757	−5,580	−5,363	−4,548	−3,013	1,778
Goods: Exports f.o.b.	78aa d	....	....	....	....	....	7,821	9,015	10,601	13,491	18,357	20,547	20,974	21,288	20,794	23,737
Goods: Imports f.o.b.	78ab d	....	....	....	....	....	−15,207	−16,299	−16,736	−17,555	−24,041	−32,272	−31,086	−30,542	−28,601	−28,380
Trade Balance	78ac d	....	....	....	....	....	−7,386	−7,284	−6,135	−4,064	−5,684	−11,725	−10,113	−9,254	−7,806	−4,643
Services: Credit	78ad d	....	....	....	....	....	5,434	5,105	6,152	8,195	10,285	11,593	11,331	11,542	11,365	12,325
Services: Debit	78ae d	....	....	....	....	....	−2,539	−2,807	−2,895	−3,184	−4,284	−5,732	−5,714	−5,953	−5,136	−4,502
Balance on Goods & Services	78af d	....	....	....	....	....	−4,491	−4,986	−2,879	947	317	−5,864	−4,496	−3,665	−1,577	3,180
Income: Credit	78ag d	....	....	....	....	....	597	425	449	758	1,348	1,723	2,027	1,936	1,325	1,489
Income: Debit	78ah d	....	....	....	....	....	−769	−875	−1,111	−1,730	−2,324	−3,085	−4,210	−4,095	−3,658	−3,746
Balance on Gds, Serv. & Inc.	78ai d	....	....	....	....	....	−4,662	−5,437	−3,541	−25	−658	−7,226	−6,680	−5,825	−3,910	923
Current Transfers, n.i.e.: Credit	78aj d	....	....	....	....	....	1,068	1,145	1,228	1,487	1,745	1,956	1,596	1,503	1,324	1,281
Current Transfers: Debit	78ak d	....	....	....	....	....	−299	−330	−142	−211	−330	−310	−279	−226	−427	−426
Capital Account, n.i.e.	78bc d	....	....	....	....	....	379	331	323	383	371	407	374	303	268	240
Capital Account, n.i.e.: Credit	78ba d	....	....	....	....	....	379	331	323	383	373	411	382	312	278	253
Capital Account: Debit	78bb d	....	....	....	....	....	—	—	—	—	−1	−4	−8	−9	−10	−13
Financial Account, n.i.e.	78bj d	....	....	....	....	....	2,638	2,732	4,432	2,144	4,672	5,247	5,996	2,334	4,005	4,922
Direct Investment Abroad	78bd d	....	....	....	....	....	−170	−193	−115	−102	−133	−311	−271	−511	−243	−248
Dir. Invest. in Rep. Econ., n.i.e.	78be d	....	....	....	....	....	683	478	608	1,178	1,397	1,493	1,707	1,783	1,622	1,772
Portfolio Investment Assets	78bf d	....	....	....	....	....	−17	−13	−1	−4	−16	−14	−12	−81	−6	−175
Equity Securities	78bk d	....	....	....	....	....	−17	−13	−1	−4	−16	−14	−12	−81	−6	−175
Debt Securities	78bl d	....	....	....	....	....	—	—	—	—	—	—	—	—	—	—
Portfolio Investment Liab., n.i.e.	78bg d	....	....	....	....	....	−70	−85	9	77	102	14	115	13	48	229
Equity Securities	78bm d	....	....	....	....	....	−70	−85	9	44	99	14	115	13	48	229
Debt Securities	78bn d	....	....	....	....	....	—	—	—	33	3	—	—	—	—	—
Financial Derivatives Assets	78bw d	....	....	....	....	....	....	....	....	....	....	....	....	....	....	....
Financial Derivatives Liabilities	78bx d	....	....	....	....	....	....	....	....	....	....	....	....	....	....	....
Other Investment Assets	78bh d	....	....	....	....	....	−341	−553	−363	−1,046	−832	−765	−787	−2,151	−388	−616
Monetary Authorities	78bo d	....	....	....	....	....	−22	−17	70	−25	9	−39	46	63	—	—
General Government	78bp d	....	....	....	....	....	−15	−66	−5	−195	36	26	−25	−162	−76	−152
Banks	78bq d	....	....	....	....	....	−5	1	−60	19	−116	95	−24	−430	−134	−87
Other Sectors	78br d	....	....	....	....	....	−300	−471	−368	−846	−761	−847	−784	−1,622	−177	−377
Other Investment Liab., n.i.e.	78bi d	....	....	....	....	....	2,554	3,099	4,295	2,041	4,154	4,830	5,244	3,281	2,972	3,961
Monetary Authorities	78bs d	....	....	....	....	....	—	—	—	—	—	—	—	—	—	—
General Government	78bt d	....	....	....	....	....	28	626	1,278	−235	337	141	678	1,178	1,096	680
Banks	78bu d	....	....	....	....	....	743	770	829	96	1,446	612	567	212	649	1,226
Other Sectors	78bv d	....	....	....	....	....	1,783	1,703	2,188	2,180	2,371	4,078	3,999	1,891	1,228	2,054
Net Errors and Omissions	78ca d	....	....	....	....	....	47	469	−1,154	−19	−2,350	−869	−1,734	−1,194	−1,525	−2,123
Overall Balance	78cb d	....	....	....	....	....	−829	−1,090	1,146	3,759	3,450	−795	−727	−3,104	−265	4,817
Reserves and Related Items	79da d	....	....	....	....	....	829	1,090	−1,146	−3,759	−3,450	795	727	3,104	265	−4,817
Reserve Assets	79db d	....	....	....	....	....	223	1,001	−1,146	−3,809	−2,925	795	802	3,256	270	−4,817
Use of Fund Credit and Loans	79dc d	....	....	....	....	....	606	89	—	50	−525	—	−75	−151	−5	—
Exceptional Financing	79de d	....	....	....	....	....	—	—	—	—	—	—	—	—	—	—
International Investment Position																*Millions of US Dollars*
Assets	79aa d	....	....	....	....	....	....	....	....	....	....	....	42,332	34,042	32,539	39,451
Direct Investment Abroad	79ab d	....	....	....	....	....	....	....	....	....	....	1,931	2,326	2,954	3,273	3,536
Portfolio Investment	79ac d	....	....	....	....	....	....	....	....	....	....	149	207	580	586	874
Equity Securities	79ad d	....	....	....	....	....	....	....	....	....	....	114	126	209	216	235
Debt Securities	79ae d	....	....	....	....	....	....	....	....	....	....	35	81	371	371	639
Financial Derivatives	79al d	....	....	....	....	....	....	....	....	....	....	—	—	—	—	—
Other Investment	79af d	....	....	....	....	....	....	....	....	....	....	....	27,761	23,075	20,712	22,864
Monetary Authorities	79ag d	....	....	....	....	....	....	....	....	....	....	....	....	....	....	....
General Government	79ah d	....	....	....	....	....	....	....	....	....	....	....	....	....	....	....
Banks	79ai d	....	....	....	....	....	....	....	....	....	....	....	21,147	16,929	15,272	16,783
Other Sectors	79aj d	....	....	....	....	....	....	....	....	....	....	....	....	....	....	....
Reserve Assets	79ak d	....	....	....	....	....	....	....	....	....	....	11,257	12,037	7,434	7,967	12,177
Liabilities	79la d	....	....	....	....	....	....	....	....	....	....	....	58,840	54,289	52,687	56,029
Dir. Invest. in Rep. Economy	79lb d	....	....	....	....	....	....	....	....	....	....	....	5,289	5,220	5,160	5,473
Portfolio Investment	79lc d	....	....	....	....	....	....	....	....	....	....	463	483	382	354	533
Equity Securities	79ld d	....	....	....	....	....	....	....	....	....	....	420	450	359	332	475
Debt Securities	79le d	....	....	....	....	....	....	....	....	....	....	43	33	23	22	59
Financial Derivatives	79ll d	....	....	....	....	....	....	....	....	....	....	—	—	—	—	—
Other investment	79lf d	....	....	....	....	....	....	....	....	....	....	....	53,068	48,687	47,174	50,022
Monetary Authorities	79lg d	....	....	....	....	....	....	....	....	....	....	....	175	20	8	10
General Government	79lh d	....	....	....	....	....	....	....	....	....	....	....	....	....	....	....
Banks	79li d	....	....	....	....	....	....	....	....	....	....	....	26,821	21,533	19,421	21,209
Other Sectors	79lj d	....	....	....	....	....	....	....	....	....	....	....	....	....	....	....

Minus Sign Indicates Debit

1985	1986	1987	1988	1989	1990	1991	1992	1993	1994	1995	1996	1997	1998	1999	Balance of Payments	
2,785	3,914	−263	−3,795	−10,924	−18,009	−19,798	−21,537	−5,804	−6,389	792	407	2,512	−3,135	−12,621	Current Account, n.i.e.	78ald
24,851	27,755	34,753	40,692	44,945	55,658	60,167	65,826	62,021	73,925	93,439	102,735	106,926	111,986	111,005	Goods: Exports f.o.b.	78aa d
−29,611	−34,953	−48,495	−59,396	−70,351	−84,815	−90,501	−96,247	−77,020	−88,817	−111,854	−119,017	−120,333	−132,744	−140,213	Goods: Imports f.o.b.	78ab d
−4,759	−7,197	−13,742	−18,703	−25,406	−29,158	−30,335	−30,420	−14,999	−14,892	−18,415	−16,283	−13,407	−20,758	−29,208	*Trade Balance*	78ac d
12,723	17,836	21,705	24,457	24,618	27,937	29,171	33,921	30,446	33,859	40,209	44,387	44,161	49,308	53,350	Services: Credit	78ad d
−4,551	−5,983	−8,255	−10,732	−11,983	−16,054	−17,263	−21,314	−18,902	−18,865	−21,509	−23,979	−24,315	−27,421	−30,427	Services: Debit	78ae d
3,412	4,655	−291	−4,979	−12,772	−17,275	−18,426	−17,813	−3,454	102	284	4,126	6,439	1,129	−6,285	*Balance on Goods & Services*	78af d
1,817	1,666	1,862	2,690	3,775	7,817	10,923	14,084	11,845	8,687	13,689	14,095	13,162	14,621	12,483	Income: Credit	78ag d
−3,505	−3,488	−4,438	−5,999	−6,544	−11,350	−15,193	−19,874	−15,456	−16,457	−17,817	−20,207	−19,911	−22,134	−21,991	Income: Debit	78ah d
1,724	2,833	−2,868	−8,287	−15,540	−20,808	−22,695	−23,603	−7,066	−7,668	−3,843	−1,986	−310	−6,385	−15,793	*Balance on Gds, Serv. & Inc.*	78ai d
1,722	2,783	4,584	7,478	8,496	7,849	9,767	10,771	8,821	9,171	12,055	11,112	11,738	12,690	13,462	Current Transfers, n.i.e.: Credit	78aj d
−660	−1,702	−1,979	−2,986	−3,880	−5,050	−6,870	−8,705	−7,558	−7,893	−7,420	−8,718	−8,916	−9,441	−10,290	Current Transfers: Debit	78ak d
65	51	31	11	−9	1,451	3,166	3,726	2,872	2,305	6,004	6,589	6,437	6,330	7,043	Capital Account, n.i.e.	78bc d
78	71	50	48	50	1,753	3,535	4,219	3,997	3,571	7,374	7,713	7,275	7,160	8,063	Capital Account, n.i.e.: Credit	78ba d
−13	−20	−19	−37	−59	−302	−370	−493	−1,125	−1,266	−1,370	−1,124	−837	−830	−1,019	Capital Account: Debit	78bb d
−3,217	−1,641	14,229	14,615	18,342	22,970	32,015	5,959	−434	4,491	−7,951	20,138	8,547	−14,156	−11,214	Financial Account, n.i.e.	78bj d
−250	−378	−745	−1,235	−1,473	−3,522	−4,442	−2,192	−3,188	−4,051	−4,206	−5,577	−12,423	−19,065	−35,248	Direct Investment Abroad	78bd d
1,968	3,451	4,571	7,021	8,428	13,984	12,493	13,276	9,681	9,216	6,297	6,796	6,384	11,905	9,321	Dir. Invest. in Rep. Econ., n.i.e.	78be d
−259	−469	29	−136	−166	−1,357	−2,359	−2,829	−6,567	−1,492	−490	−3,653	−16,450	−44,193	−47,342	Portfolio Investment Assets	78bf d
−259	−469	29	−136	−166	−329	−327	−145	−728	−1,039	−534	−776	−5,272	−10,120	−17,292	Equity Securities	78bk d
—	—	—	—	—	−1,028	−2,033	−2,684	−5,839	−453	44	−2,877	−11,178	−34,073	−30,050	Debt Securities	78bl d
491	1,697	3,770	2,427	8,155	10,382	22,517	12,098	55,314	−20,856	21,653	3,128	11,772	16,736	46,293	Portfolio Investment Liab., n.i.e.	78bg d
488	1,682	3,434	2,100	6,387	4,309	2,772	3,648	6,600	1,154	4,215	147	−294	10,072	9,867	Equity Securities	78bm d
3	15	336	327	1,768	6,073	19,745	8,450	48,714	−22,010	17,438	2,981	12,066	6,664	36,427	Debt Securities	78bn d
....	....	....	....	....	−10	−50	18								Financial Derivatives Assets	78bw d
....	....	....	....	....	3	−28	71	−2,791	158	−557	−875	41	−2,776	112	Financial Derivatives Liabilities	78bx d
−1,391	−322	793	−596	−108	−13,175	−7,740	−40,441	−71,940	9,152	−36,816	2,469	−1,415	−21,604	−26,345	Other Investment Assets	78bh d
....	....	....	....	....	....	....	....	−3	3	−71	−4	8	−422	−39,310	Monetary Authorities	78bo d
−263	−326	−271	−785	−737	−951	−676	−897	−663	−620	−402	−502	−377	−427	−229	General Government	78bp d
−495	−179	1,140	1,315	1,336	−7,520	−3,215	−28,758	−63,178	14,437	−26,899	9,969	13,175	−1,960	4,113	Banks	78bq d
−633	184	−76	−1,127	−708	−4,704	−3,849	−10,786	−8,097	−4,668	−9,446	−6,993	−14,220	−13,795	9,081	Other Sectors	78br d
−3,776	−5,620	5,812	7,134	3,506	16,665	11,624	25,958	19,058	12,363	6,168	17,849	20,638	44,841	41,995	Other Investment Liab., n.i.e.	78bi d
—	—	195	−303	643	—	—	—	−121	27	23	461	−466	−2	−11	Monetary Authorities	78bs d
71	−2,028	648	670	1,364	1,274	−271	3,418	938	3,007	1,493	−226	4	1,043	−295	General Government	78bt d
−1,353	−82	1,641	2,643	1,547	14,402	8,169	13,609	13,242	10,572	4,049	18,646	20,490	38,957	26,476	Banks	78bu d
−2,493	−3,510	3,328	4,125	−47	988	3,725	8,932	4,999	−1,242	604	−1,032	611	4,843	15,825	Other Sectors	78bv d
−1,908	20	−1,291	−2,414	−2,693	777	−1,075	−5,957	−1,838	−371	−5,260	−2,856	−5,741	−3,395	−6,001	Net Errors and Omissions	78ca d
−2,275	2,344	12,706	8,416	4,716	7,188	14,307	−17,809	−5,203	36	−6,414	24,279	11,756	−14,355	−22,794	*Overall Balance*	78cb d
2,275	−2,344	−12,706	−8,416	−4,716	−7,188	−14,307	17,809	5,203	−36	6,414	−24,279	−11,756	14,355	22,794	Reserves and Related Items	79da d
2,275	−2,344	−12,706	−8,416	−4,716	−7,188	−14,307	17,809	5,203	−36	6,414	−24,279	−11,756	14,355	22,794	Reserve Assets	79db d
—	—	—	—	—	—	—	—	—	—	—	—	—	—	—	Use of Fund Credit and Loans	79dc d
—	—	—	—	—	—	—	—	—	—	—	—	—	—	....	Exceptional Financing	79de d

Millions of US Dollars

1985	1986	1987	1988	1989	1990	1991	1992	1993	1994	1995	1996	1997	1998	1999	International Investment Position	
43,313	53,588	78,156	86,418	102,968	133,538	161,700	165,640	213,765	222,968	270,475	289,368	308,285	399,088	438,351	Assets	79aa d
4,455	5,938	8,421	9,434	11,372	15,652	20,528	22,010	23,943	30,173	36,661	40,091	47,877	69,176	97,553	Direct Investment Abroad	79ab d
1,221	2,507	2,511	2,848	3,860	5,654	8,206	9,710	14,781	17,550	18,821	21,451	34,871	82,198	117,341	Portfolio Investment	79ac d
319	493	798	987	1,267	1,879	2,255	1,972	2,264	3,484	3,847	4,464	9,136	20,104	34,408	Equity Securities	79ad d
902	2,014	1,713	1,861	2,593	3,775	5,952	7,738	12,516	14,066	14,974	16,987	25,735	62,094	82,934	Debt Securities	79ae d
															Financial Derivatives	79al d
26,472	30,411	34,063	33,572	42,794	57,223	63,519	85,198	131,942	131,411	177,631	167,412	155,153	186,926	185,995	Other Investment	79af d
—	—	—	—	—	—	—	—	—	—	—	—	—	—	36,314	Monetary Authorities	79ag d
....	1,299	1,923	2,331	2,761	—	—	—	4,669	5,473	6,029	6,330	6,335	6,914	6,750	General Government	79ah d
19,111	22,032	23,707	22,526	24,546	36,343	41,259	62,880	104,751	96,577	129,900	115,102	93,697	100,879	85,402	Banks	79ai d
....	7,080	8,433	8,715	15,488	20,879	22,260	22,317	22,522	29,361	41,702	45,980	55,121	79,134	57,528	Other Sectors	79aj d
11,165	14,733	33,161	40,565	44,942	55,010	69,447	48,722	43,100	43,834	37,362	60,414	70,384	60,788	37,462	Reserve Assets	79ak d
59,201	68,848	94,874	109,765	138,975	195,398	246,259	258,566	308,359	323,518	383,472	399,147	410,120	525,346	556,049	Liabilities	79la d
7,290	10,658	16,667	21,427	28,893	65,916	79,570	86,230	80,203	96,259	111,474	109,320	100,361	118,921	112,579	Dir. Invest. in Rep. Economy	79lb d
1,136	3,211	8,435	10,757	20,350	36,370	59,077	54,163	103,794	84,060	115,436	123,314	134,613	178,259	196,156	Portfolio Investment	79lc d
1,066	2,959	6,820	7,893	14,067	20,974	22,529	18,577	22,818	24,146	29,800	36,153	44,416	70,431	77,634	Equity Securities	79ld d
70	252	1,615	2,864	6,283	15,396	36,548	35,585	80,977	59,914	85,636	87,161	90,197	107,828	118,522	Debt Securities	79le d
															Financial Derivatives	79ll d
50,775	54,979	69,772	77,580	89,732	93,112	107,612	118,173	124,362	143,200	156,562	166,513	175,146	228,166	247,313	Other investment	79lf d
20	60	30	415	406	—	—	—	—	—	—	—	—	—	—	Monetary Authorities	79lg d
....	4,910	5,460	5,713	7,062	2,497	2,462	4,491	6,448	9,807	12,083	11,244	9,875	11,409	9,874	General Government	79lh d
20,939	25,365	33,189	37,001	43,627	70,157	80,820	88,167	92,234	106,005	115,304	129,179	139,715	185,026	192,253	Banks	79li d
....	24,644	31,094	34,451	38,637	20,457	24,331	25,515	25,680	27,387	29,174	26,090	25,557	31,731	45,186	Other Sectors	79lj d

Spain

		1970	1971	1972	1973	1974	1975	1976	1977	1978	1979	1980	1981	1982	1983	1984
Government Finance																*Billions of Pesetas through 1998;*
Central Government																
Deficit (-) or Surplus	80	−19.7	−63.5	−36.1	−23.4	−82.3	−111.2	−128.3	−248.6	−254.4	−400.9	ⅉ−555.8	−780.2	−1,450.2	−1,714.9	−2,501.1
Total Revenue and Grants	81y	327.3	377.3	443.7	531.2	629.8	758.4	899.7	1,159.2	1,479.4	1,762.4	ⅉ2,179.1	2,574.7	3,002.8	3,631.4	4,218.5
Revenue	81	327.3	377.3	443.7	531.2	629.8	758.4	899.7	1,159.2	1,479.4	1,762.4	ⅉ2,179.1	2,574.7	3,002.8	3,631.4	4,218.5
Grants	81z															
Exp. & Lending Minus Repay.	82z	346.9	440.8	479.8	554.6	712.1	869.6	1,028.1	1,407.8	1,733.8	2,163.3	ⅉ2,734.9	3,355.0	4,453.0	5,346.3	6,720.6
Expenditure	82	326.5	414.6	456.8	526.2	659.2	766.2	905.7	1,249.4	1,571.8	1,994.5	ⅉ2,552.7	3,097.2	4,058.5	4,809.9	5,909.3
Lending Minus Repayments	83	20.5	26.2	23.0	28.4	52.9	103.4	122.3	158.4	162.0	168.8	182.2	257.8	394.5	536.4	811.3
Total Financing	80h	19.5	63.4	36.1	23.4	82.2	111.2	128.2	248.5	254.2	401.1	ⅉ555.8	780.2	1,450.3	1,714.9	2,502.1
Total Net Borrowing	84	18.5	61.2	58.3	9.0	27.9	53.8	181.7	190.6	113.4	242.3	579.2	785.2	1,423.1	1,785.8	2,541.7
Net Domestic	84a	17.9	61.9	58.8	8.7	22.3	52.0	148.0	103.5	151.3	237.1	579.2	742.2	1,345.9	1,661.8	2,421.1
Net Foreign	85a	.6	−.7	−.5	.4	5.6	1.8	33.7	87.1	−37.9	5.2	—	43.0	77.2	124.0	120.7
Use of Cash Balances	87	1.0	2.2	−22.2	14.4	54.3	57.4	−53.5	57.9	140.8	158.8	—	−6.9	−51.7	−21.0	−40.7
Total Debt by Residence	88	365.7	443.6	483.1	505.7	588.2	699.6	822.6	1,112.8	1,358.2	1,748.8	ⅉ2,316.7	3,135.5	4,781.7	6,763.4	9,395.9
Domestic	88a	344.1	421.3	458.2	481.6	558.0	666.2	757.9	934.7	1,220.4	1,619.4	ⅉ2,183.1	2,930.8	4,428.8	6,198.1	8,657.9
Foreign	89a	21.6	22.3	24.9	24.1	30.2	33.4	64.7	178.1	137.8	129.4	ⅉ133.6	204.7	352.9	565.3	738.0
General Government																*As Percent of*
Deficit (-) or Surplus	80g	....	....	....	....	....	....	....	....	....	....	....	....	....	....	....
Debt	88g	....	....	....	....	....	....	....	....	....	....	....	....	....	....	....
National Accounts																*Billions of Pesetas: through 1998;*
Househ.Cons.Expend.,incl.NPISHs	96f. c	1,701	1,926	2,245	2,694	3,333	3,920	4,817	6,050	7,272	8,582	9,992	11,301	12,939	14,604	16,305
Government Consumption Expend	91f. c	249	286	331	399	509	631	820	1,059	1,344	1,639	2,008	2,370	2,784	3,280	3,647
Gross Fixed Capital Formation	93e. c	684	706	868	1,108	1,436	1,593	1,808	2,201	2,551	2,843	3,368	3,729	4,264	4,686	4,779
Changes in Inventories	93i. c	21	26	32	31	113	127	145	97	28	99	157	−1	116	155	254
Exports of Goods and Services	90c. c	348	422	507	611	740	816	997	1,334	1,710	1,975	2,387	3,042	3,631	4,667	5,865
Imports of Goods & Services	98c. c	−373	−397	−500	−644	−988	−1,047	−1,320	−1,522	−1,621	−1,936	−2,743	−3,397	−4,011	−4,860	−5,329
Gross Domestic Product (GDP)	99b. c	2,630	2,968	3,483	4,199	5,143	6,039	7,267	9,220	11,285	13,201	15,168	17,045	19,723	22,532	25,520
Net Factor Inc/Pmts(-) Abroad	98.n	−17	−16	−16	−12	−1	−19	−40	−62	−87	−78	−130	−238	−285	−358	−397
Gross National Income (GNI)	99a	2,559	2,904	3,416	4,128	5,101	6,000	7,194	9,116	11,143	13,052	15,079	16,751	19,283	21,877	24,715
Net National Income	99e	2,324	2,641	3,124	3,786	4,667	5,470	6,558	8,312	10,166	11,858	13,464	14,820	17,029	19,239	21,685
GDP Volume 1970 Prices	99b. r	2,630	2,704	2,924	3,154	3,334	3,371	3,472	3,587	3,651	3,658	3,714	3,726	3,764	3,856	3,945
GDP Volume 1986 Prices	99b. r	....	....	....	....	....	....	....	....	....	....	....	....	....	....	30,527
GDP Volume 1995 Prices	99b. r	....	....	....	....	....	....	....	....	....	....	....	....	....	....	....
GDP Volume (1995=100)	99bv r	49.2	51.5	55.7	60.0	63.4	63.7	65.8	67.7	68.7	68.7	69.6	69.5	70.6	72.1	73.2
GDP Deflator (1995=100)	99bi r	7.7	8.3	9.0	10.0	11.6	13.6	15.8	19.5	23.5	27.5	31.2	35.2	40.1	44.8	50.0
																Millions:
Population	99z	33.78	34.13	34.49	34.86	35.22	35.60	35.97	36.35	36.67	36.99	37.54	37.75	37.97	38.16	38.33

Millions of Euros Beginning 1999; Year Ending December 31

	1985	1986	1987	1988	1989	1990	1991	1992	1993	1994	1995	1996	1997	1998	1999	Government Finance — Central Government	
	‡-1719.5	-1,521.2	-1,422.5	193.9	-898.8	-1,273.9	-1,405.4	-2,100.5	-3,738.0	-4,147.6	-3,382.2	-3,951.0	-1,975.7	-1,047.5	-5,911	Deficit (-) or Surplus	80
	‡4,440.1	5,752.8	7,029.4	7,908.4	9,543.4	10,203.1	11,242.7	12,286.5	12,683.7	12,960.3	14,077.2	14,629.5	16,636.5	17,518.9	110,370	Total Revenue and Grants	81y
	‡4,440.1	5,752.8	7,029.4	7,908.4	9,543.4	10,203.1	11,242.7	12,286.5	12,683.7	12,960.3	14,077.2	14,629.5	16,636.5	17,518.9	110,370	Revenue	81
	‡—														—	Grants	81z
	‡6,159.6	7,274.0	8,451.9	7,714.5	10,442.2	11,477.0	12,648.1	14,387.0	16,421.7	17,107.9	17,459.4	18,580.5	18,612.2	18,566.4	116,281	Exp. & Lending Minus Repay.	82z
	‡5,925.8	7,192.9	8,369.4	9,084.5	10,316.6	11,375.1	12,611.6	14,160.0	16,465.8	16,438.3	17,241.5	18,313.1	18,685.6	18,633.4	116,724	Expenditure	82
	‡233.8	81.1	82.5	-1,370.0	125.6	101.9	36.5	227.0	-44.1	669.6	217.9	267.4	-73.4	-67.0	-443	Lending Minus Repayments	83
	‡1,719.2	1,521.1	1,423.1	-194.5	899.8	1,274.3	1,405.5	2,100.5	3,737.5	4,147.2	3,381.4	3,950.5	1,975.0	....	....	Total Financing	80h
	‡1,726.5	1,516.7	1,415.0	-164.9	998.4	2,648.8	1,710.9	2,177.0	6,238.6	2,317.7	3,100.2	4,986.8	1,039.6	....	....	Total Net Borrowing	84
	2,332.0	2,118.1	1,727.4	-96.8	1,395.0	....	....	....	....	....	....	....	....	....	....	Net Domestic	84a
	32.9	-174.4	58.0	163.6	305.0	....	....	....	....	....	....	....	....	....	....	Net Foreign	85a
	‡7.3	-4.4	-8.1	29.6	98.6	1,374.5	305.4	76.5	2,501.1	-1,829.5	-281.2	1,036.3	-935.4	110.5	....	Use of Cash Balances	87
	‡11390.5	13,269.1	15,058.2	15,086.0	16,687.2	19,490.5	21,190.5	23,911.0	31,236.7	34,266.0	38,539.3	43,748.1	45,417.3	47,019.1	....	Total Debt by Residence	88
	‡10676.0	12,795.3	14,515.3	14,429.1	15,806.9	18,269.3	18,183.8	20,371.5	21,751.8	27,389.8	29,995.0	34,760.5	34,922.3	35,531.8	....	Domestic	88a
	‡714.5	473.8	542.9	656.9	880.3	1,221.2	3,006.7	3,539.5	9,484.9	6,876.2	8,544.3	8,987.6	10,495.0	11,487.3	....	Foreign	89a

Gross Domestic Product — General Government

	1985	1986	1987	1988	1989	1990	1991	1992	1993	1994	1995	1996	1997	1998	1999		
	....	....	....	....	....	-4.3	-4.5	-4.1	-7.0	-6.3	-7.1	-5.0	-3.2	-2.6	-1.1	Deficit (-) or Surplus	80g
						44.8	45.5	48.0	60.0	62.6	64.2	68.0	66.7	64.9	63.5	Debt	88g

Billions of Euros Beginning 1999 — National Accounts

	1985	1986	1987	1988	1989	1990	1991	1992	1993	1994	1995	1996	1997	1998	1999		
	18,080	20,438	22,860	25,180	28,367	31,303	34,269	37,277	38,482	40,724	43,332	45,668	48,277	51,116	‡329	Househ.Cons.Expend.,incl.NPISHs	96f.c
	4,152	4,740	5,452	5,924	6,831	7,815	8,882	10,093	10,701	10,963	11,650	12,256	12,585	15,092	‡99	Government Consumption Expend	91f.c
	5,409	6,297	7,518	9,083	10,868	12,261	13,067	12,889	12,100	12,860	14,494	14,976	16,029	19,800	‡134	Gross Fixed Capital Formation	93e.c
	14	162	258	419	449	461	438	488	10	154	251	248	73	258	‡2	Changes in Inventories	93i.c
	6,407	6,417	6,996	7,575	8,150	8,555	9,409	10,420	11,841	14,443	16,732	18,761	22,106	23,605	‡155	Exports of Goods and Services	90c.c
	-5,860	-5,730	-6,935	-8,023	-9,621	-10,251	-11,137	-12,063	-12,180	-14,331	-16,660	-18,165	-21,172	-23,311	‡-159	Imports of Goods & Services	98c.c
	28,201	32,324	36,144	40,159	45,044	50,145	54,927	59,105	60,953	64,812	69,780	73,743	77,897	82,650	‡559	Gross Domestic Product (GDP)	99b.c
	-331	-296	-304	-411	-384	-452	-554	-708	-526	-1,182	-607	-890	-1,135	....	....	Net Factor Inc/Pmts(-) Abroad	98.n
	27,870	32,028	35,840	39,748	44,660	49,693	54,373	58,397	60,426	63,630	69,173	72,854	76,762	....	....	Gross National Income (GNI)	99a
	24,521	28,170	31,662	35,148	39,627	44,148	48,349	51,945	53,446	56,201	61,222	64,491	67,911	....	....	Net National Income	99e
	....	....	....	....	....	....	....	....	....	....	....	....	....	....		GDP Volume 1970 Prices	99b.r
	31,322	32,324	34,148	35,880	37,609	39,018	39,903	40,177	39,710	40,604	41,707	42,715	44,224	45,901		GDP Volume 1986 Prices	99b.r
	....	....	....	....	....	....	....	....	....	....	....	....	....	80,468	‡501.7	GDP Volume 1995 Prices	99b.r
	75.1	77.5	81.9	86.0	90.2	93.6	95.7	96.3	95.2	97.4	100.0	102.4	106.0	110.1	114.2	GDP Volume (1995=100)	99bv r
	53.8	59.8	63.3	66.9	71.6	76.8	82.3	87.9	91.7	95.4	100.0	103.2	105.3	107.6	‡116.8	GDP Deflator (1995=100)	99bi r

Midyear Estimates

	1985	1986	1987	1988	1989	1990	1991	1992	1993	1994	1995	1996	1997	1998	1999		
	38.41	38.52	38.61	38.72	38.79	38.85	38.92	39.01	39.09	39.15	39.21	39.27	39.32	39.37	39.42	Population	99z

(See notes in the back of the book.)

Sri Lanka

		1970	1971	1972	1973	1974	1975	1976	1977	1978	1979	1980	1981	1982	1983	1984
Exchange Rates															*Rupees per SDR:*	
Market Rate	aa	5.958	6.469	7.272	8.140	8.195	9.029	10.257	18.901	20.200	20.346	22.957	23.919	23.518	26.174	25.760
															Rupees per US Dollar:	
Market Rate	ae	5.958	5.958	6.698	6.748	6.693	7.713	8.828	15.560	15.505	15.445	18.000	20.550	21.320	25.000	26.280
Market Rate	rf	5.952	5.935	5.970e	6.403e	6.651e	7.007e	8.412e	8.873e	15.611e	15.572e	16.534	19.246	20.812	23.529	25.438
Fund Position															*Millions of SDRs:*	
Quota	2f.s	98	98	98	98	98	98	98	98	119	119	179	179	179	223	223
SDRs	1b.s	—	—	13	13	14	11	12	20	26	22	—	20	6	1	—
Reserve Position in the Fund	1c.s	—	—	—	—	—	—	—	—	—	—	—	1	6	17	6
Total Fund Cred.&Loans Outstg.	2tl	79	72	75	74	102	125	134	170	227	305	307	443	437	425	413
International Liquidity												*Millions of US Dollars Unless Otherwise Indicated:*				
Total Reserves minus Gold	1l.d	43	50	59	87	78	57	92	293	398	517	246	327	351	297	511
SDRs	1b.d	—	—	14	16	18	13	14	24	34	29	—	23	7	1	—
Reserve Position in the Fund	1c.d	—	—	—	—	—	—	—	—	—	—	—	1	6	18	6
Foreign Exchange	1d.d	43	50	46	70	60	45	78	269	363	488	246	304	338	278	505
Gold (Million Fine Troy Ounces)	1ad	....	....	....	....	....	....	....	....	.042	.063	.063	.063	.063	.063	.063
Gold (National Valuation)	1and	....	....	....	....	....	....	....	—	9	18	16	14	13	11	11
Monetary Authorities: Other Liab.	4..d	75	59	55	40	48	45	63	44	20	39	42	8	89	76	1
Deposit Money Banks: Assets	7a.d	25	34	48	44	59	51	65	80	85	109	130	114	168	205	199
Liabilities	7b.d	10	12	22	11	11	11	12	9	14	22	26	30	75	114	120
FCBU: Assets	7k.d	....	....	....	....	....	....	....	....	....	29	114	205	379	545	463
Liabilities	7m.d	....	....	....	....	....	....	....	....	....	14	131	231	428	640	498
Monetary Authorities															*Millions of Rupees:*	
Foreign Assets	11	194	238	302	510	453	442	829	4,534	6,170	7,972	‡4,706	6,929	7,494	7,760	13,725
Claims on Central Government	12a	2,197	2,286	2,368	2,353	2,447	2,537	3,760	4,978	5,868	7,768	‡16,081	19,334	23,142	25,331	20,732
Claims on Deposit Money Banks	12e	204	229	125	239	679	594	401	894	1,091	693	‡1,070	1,278	1,159	2,662	2,041
Reserve Money	14	1,381	1,575	1,856	2,179	2,357	2,202	2,769	4,028	4,535	5,538	6,629	7,822	9,679	12,240	14,296
of which: Currency Outside DMBs	14a	935	1,115	1,202	1,437	1,539	1,610	2,081	2,792	3,016	3,774	4,181	4,823	5,988	7,200	8,561
Foreign Liabilities	16c	916	749	912	872	1,156	1,472	1,932	3,897	4,892	6,810	‡7,790	10,760	12,183	13,025	10,678
Central Government Deposits	16d	145	104	91	94	120	15	31	....	1,049	740	1,364	1,450	1,286	1,772	2,337
Capital Accounts	17a											5,763	7,140	8,256	8,475	8,450
Other Items (Net)	17r	365	511	113	73	168	−42	359	2,669	3,976	4,324	‡310	368	391	241	737
Deposit Money Banks															*Millions of Rupees:*	
Reserves	20	406	404	606	802	789	562	652	1,145	1,342	1,742	2,049	2,730	3,069	4,678	5,670
Foreign Assets	21	151	185	320	297	394	395	573	1,243	1,316	‡1,681	2,347	2,342	3,585	5,126	5,233
Claims on Central Government	22a	639	692	745	499	386	‡415	782	914	801	864	939	1,563	1,719	1,579	2,878
Claims on Nonfin.Pub.Enterprises	22ca	....	....	....	....	....	....	....	....	....	3,347	4,123	4,488	4,677	4,385	4,148
Claims on Cooperatives	22cb	....	....	....	....	....	....	....	....	....	....	....	1,368	1,294	1,188	1,823	1,568
Claims on Private Sector	22d	1,599	1,736	2,117	2,134	3,188	3,363	3,919	5,714	8,666	11,853	‡11,344	15,396	19,379	25,552	29,656
Demand Deposits	24	1,005	1,009	1,241	1,312	1,377	1,443	2,038	2,526	2,863	3,857	5,139	5,111	5,665	7,334	8,002
Time and Savings Deposits	25	1,112	1,251	1,456	1,337	1,582	1,648	2,117	3,303	5,425	8,668	11,624	15,269	19,779	23,523	27,674
Foreign Liabilities	26c	60	68	145	75	75	86	103	135	224	337	472	613	1,606	2,857	3,141
Central Government Deposits	26d	221	199	514	446	530	452	714	871	‡990	1,073	1,642	1,503	1,568	1,763	2,299
Credit from Monetary Authorities	26g	....	....	....	....	....	....	....	....	....	609	1,180	1,436	1,413	2,875	2,401
Capital Accounts	27a	130	154	162	171	214	239	281	374	520	906	1,272	2,268	2,602	2,705	2,932
Other Items (Net)	27r	83	143	60	85	310	206	132	685	2,534	2,271	‡841	1,612	984	2,085	2,703
Monetary Survey															*Millions of Rupees:*	
Foreign Assets (Net)	31n	−630	−394	−435	−140	−384	−721	−633	1,744	2,371	2,506	‡−1,210	−2,102	−2,709	−2,996	5,138
Domestic Credit	32	4,126	4,473	4,696	4,519	5,435	5,823	7,644	10,547	13,184	18,556	‡31,088	31,088	47,695	55,604	54,748
Claims on Central Govt. (Net)	32an	2,527	2,737	2,579	2,386	2,247	2,460	3,725	4,834	4,518	6,703	‡14,014	17,944	22,008	23,375	18,974
Claims on Nonfin.Pub.Enterprises	32ca	....	....	....	....	....	....	....	....	....	3,347	4,123	4,488	4,677	4,385	4,148
Claims on Cooperatives	32cb	....	....	....	....	....	....	....	....	....	....	....	1,368	1,294	1,188	1,823	1,568
Claims on Private Sector	32d	1,599	1,736	2,117	2,134	3,188	3,363	3,919	5,714	8,666	11,853	‡11,420	15,417	19,475	25,629	29,677
Money	34	1,949	2,128	2,461	2,755	2,923	3,064	4,133	5,332	5,895	7,643	9,333	9,949	11,672	14,589	16,647
Quasi-Money	35	1,179	1,333	1,541	1,361	1,685	1,706	2,186	3,492	5,698	8,908	11,970	15,587	20,342	24,123	28,265
Other Items (Net)	37r	435	701	345	286	546	390	761	3,655	4,752	6,106	‡8,576	11,745	12,972	13,896	14,974
Money plus Quasi-Money	35l	3,128	3,461	4,002	4,116	4,608	4,770	6,319	8,824	11,593	16,551	21,303	25,536	32,014	38,712	44,912
Liquid Liabilities	55l	3,129	3,462	4,969	5,263	5,950	6,351	8,207	11,204	14,619	20,701	26,256	30,975	39,668	48,221	56,145
Interest Rates															*Percent Per Annum*	
Bank Rate *(End of Period)*	60	6.50	6.50	6.50	6.50	6.50	6.50	6.50	10.00	10.00	10.00	12.00	14.00	14.00	13.00	13.00
Money Market Rate	60b	....	....	....	....	....	....	....	9.50	11.00	21.06	19.00	16.88	23.88	21.42
Treasury Bill Rate	60c	....	....	....	....	....	....	....	....	....	....	15.60	12.28	12.38	13.08
Deposit Rate	60l	....	....	....	....	....	....	....	8.50	8.50	14.50	17.88	17.50	18.25	19.79
Lending Rate	60p	....	....	....	....	....	....	....	18.00	18.00	19.00	19.00	17.75	13.25	13.15
Government Bond Yield	61	....	....	....	....	....	....	....	....	....	....	....	....	....	14.67
Prices and Labor															*Index Numbers (1995=100):*	
Wholesale Prices	63	....	....	....	....	10.5	10.9	11.8	14.2	16.5	18.1	24.2	28.3	29.8	37.3	46.8
Consumer Prices	64	8.4	8.6	9.2	10.1	11.3	12.0	12.2	12.4	13.9	15.3	19.4	22.8	25.3	28.8	33.6
Wages: Agr. Minimum Rates	65	3.7	3.8	4.0	4.4	5.6	6.4	6.6	8.3	‡12.0	14.8	18.5	18.5	21.8	23.9	30.1
															Number in Thousands:	
Labor Force	67d	....	....	....	....	....	....	....	....	....	....	....	....	....	....	....
Employment	67e	....	....	....	....	....	....	....	....	....	....	....	....	....	....	....
Unemployment	67c	....	....	....	....	....	....	....	....	....	....	....	....	....	....	....
Unemployment Rate (%)	67r	....	....	....	....	....	....	....	....	....	....	....	....	....	....	....
International Transactions															*Millions of Rupees*	
Exports	70	2,033	2,039	2,016	2,630	3,503	3,969	4,840	6,570	13,193	15,282	17,595	21,043	21,454	25,096	37,347
Tea	70s	1,119	1,144	1,162	1,261	1,360	1,932	2,100	3,503	6,401	5,722	6,170	6,444	6,342	8,295	15,764
Imports, c.i.f.	71	2,295	2,100	2,199	2,763	4,770	5,196	4,902	6,061	15,100	22,603	33,942	36,583	41,946	45,558	47,541
															1995=100	
Volume of Exports	72	37.5	36.5	35.8	36.1	31.2	37.5	35.8	33.0	35.1	‡35.4	37.8	39.8	41.8	39.4	46.2
Tea	72s	86.5	86.2	79.0	85.4	72.9	88.3	83.0	77.1	80.0	77.9	76.7	76.1	75.2	65.6	84.8
Volume of Imports	73	24.5	21.7	21.4	19.1	13.4	16.6	18.2	23.3	31.9	‡39.2	46.3	41.7	41.7	45.9	47.5
Unit Value of Exports	74	2.5	2.5	2.5	3.0	4.6	4.3	5.1	8.2	15.0	‡16.3	18.2	19.8	19.3	24.8	31.6
Tea	74s	5.2	5.4	6.0	6.0	7.6	8.9	10.3	18.4	32.5	29.8	32.6	34.3	34.2	51.3	75.5
Unit Value of Imports	75	2.1	2.2	2.4	3.2	5.5	6.4	5.8	7.1	13.1	‡20.0	25.3	29.4	30.6	31.9	33.4

1985	1986	1987	1988	1989	1990	1991	1992	1993	1994	1995	1996	1997	1998	1999		
End of Period															**Exchange Rates**	
30.105	34.885	43.642	44.453	52.566	57.248	60.908	63.250	68.076	72.963	80.341	81.540	82.689	95.436	98.979	Market Rate	aa
End of Period (ae) Period Average (rf)																
27.408	28.520	30.763	33.033	40.000	40.240	42.580	46.000	49.562	49.980	54.048	56.705	61.285	67.780	72.115	Market Rate	ae
27.163	28.017	29.445	31.807	36.047	40.063	41.372	43.830	48.322	49.415	51.252	55.271	58.995	64.593	70.402	Market Rate	rf
End of Period															**Fund Position**	
223	223	223	223	223	223	223	304	304	304	304	304	304	304	413	Quota	2f.*s*
—	—	—	—	10	—	—	—	—	—	1	1	—	1	1	SDRs	1b.*s*
6	—	—	—	—	—	—	20	20	20	20	20	20	20	48	Reserve Position in the Fund	1c.*s*
361	284	195	267	278	288	280	338	376	423	400	369	321	261	188	Total Fund Cred.&Loans Outstg.	2tl
End of Period															**International Liquidity**	
451	353	279	222	244	423	685	927	1,629	2,046	2,088	1,962	2,024	1,980	1,636	Total Reserves minus Gold	1l.*d*
—	—	—	—	13	—	—	—	—	—	1	2	—	1	1	SDRs	1b.*d*
7	—	—	—	—	—	—	28	28	30	30	29	27	29	65	Reserve Position in the Fund	1c.*d*
445	353	279	222	231	422	685	899	1,601	2,016	2,057	1,931	1,996	1,950	1,569	Foreign Exchange	1d.*d*
.063	.063	.063	.063	.063	.063	.111	.160	.063	.063	.063	.063	.063	.063	.063	Gold (Million Fine Troy Ounces)	1ad
10	10	10	10	10	10	10	37	6	6	6	5	5	....	....	Gold (National Valuation)	1an*d*
10	8	67	11	I207	291	363	420	625	713	754	691	624	530	515	Monetary Authorities: Other Liab.	4..*d*
209	239	301	298	294	422	438	504	516	639	508	503	793	871	1,058	Deposit Money Banks: Assets	7a.*d*
149	185	251	229	249	303	394	464	547	615	652	714	803	989	1,133	Liabilities	7b.*d*
458	430	382	422	492	524	432	539	456	540	574	504	682	479	439	FCBU: Assets	7k.*d*
489	447	408	371	400	448	428	635	601	665	682	615	702	438	306	Liabilities	7m.*d*
End of Period															**Monetary Authorities**	
12,650	10,341	8,871	7,620	I10,056	17,304	30,581	41,868	78,290	96,807	106,838	104,541	120,189	132,549	113,519	Foreign Assets	11
29,524	32,386	34,178	46,570	I51,466	55,023	61,318	50,072	35,515	38,275	45,276	53,191	39,664	39,832	57,450	Claims on Central Government	12a
1,824	2,811	3,136	3,480	I4,312	5,570	5,344	5,506	4,900	3,376	2,812	2,259	1,692	1,122	748	Claims on Deposit Money Banks	12e
18,084	18,695	20,626	25,941	I27,482	33,141	42,374	45,972	57,539	68,518	79,535	85,824	84,037	92,904	97,675	Reserve Money	14
9,816	11,570	13,495	18,484	I19,644	22,120	24,852	27,280	32,133	38,906	42,198	42,565	45,680	51,767	58,481	*of which: Currency Outside DMBs*	14a
11,157	10,124	10,571	12,241	I22,912	28,215	29,121	30,077	41,297	46,076	50,427	46,457	43,048	38,906	38,037	Foreign Liabilities	16c
3,161	2,514	1,587	3,528	I2,776	3,604	9,027	2,666	1,801	2,813	3,040	3,510	6,476	3,108	2,463	Central Government Deposits	16d
10,612	11,654	13,334	14,675	I14,853	13,324	14,550	18,156	17,251	19,873	25,344	25,564	32,307	42,686	40,584	Capital Accounts	17a
983	2,552	67	1,285	I–2,189	–387	2,172	575	817	1,178	–3,420	–1,364	–4,322	–4,102	–7,043	Other Items (Net)	17r
End of Period															**Deposit Money Banks**	
8,228	8,040	5,728	6,802	I7,611	9,406	15,421	16,289	20,562	25,389	35,449	41,188	36,500	39,667	40,110	Reserves	20
5,726	6,803	9,265	9,875	I11,753	16,967	18,634	23,162	25,567	31,918	27,452	28,549	48,596	59,043	76,317	Foreign Assets	21
2,897	2,753	5,362	7,862	I8,382	14,701	13,861	13,886	18,782	21,039	20,581	26,470	40,090	44,626	52,130	Claims on Central Government	22a
4,438	4,739	7,366	10,787	I13,862	15,636	14,077	15,032	7,775	5,163	8,527	9,938	10,338	9,485	13,376	Claims on Nonfin.Pub.Enterprises	22ca
1,304	1,425	1,123	1,319	I1,178	1,416	1,238	1,739	1,903	2,541	3,939	1,465	1,661	1,812	1,608	Claims on Cooperatives	22cb
32,793	35,400	39,653	48,322	I50,781	63,052	76,734	93,826	113,544	140,820	175,905	193,062	214,079	241,454	272,979	Claims on Private Sector	22d
8,761	9,358	11,243	13,511	I15,375	17,256	21,641	22,741	27,169	31,415	32,970	35,516	40,108	44,470	50,059	Demand Deposits	24
30,803	31,085	34,697	37,469	I40,078	50,668	63,519	79,741	100,780	121,210	153,319	174,998	202,406	219,906	249,522	Time and Savings Deposits	25
4,078	5,290	7,714	9,122	I9,962	12,191	16,793	21,356	27,119	30,746	35,215	40,474	49,240	67,063	81,712	Foreign Liabilities	26c
3,687	3,863	3,357	5,011	I5,851	9,723	8,639	9,075	6,304	9,290	9,483	12,902	13,728	11,646	12,667	Central Government Deposits	26d
2,165	3,140	3,479	3,906	I4,046	6,625	5,614	5,603	5,843	4,054	3,625	4,050	4,775	4,813	5,171	Credit from Monetary Authorities	26g
3,164	3,410	3,954	4,774	I5,395	6,690	8,960	9,868	21,851	28,278	33,460	39,238	44,368	50,220	51,571	Capital Accounts	27a
2,729	3,013	4,053	11,172	I12,860	18,027	14,799	15,552	–932	1,877	3,780	–6,505	–3,361	–2,030	5,819	Other Items (Net)	27r
End of Period															**Monetary Survey**	
3,140	1,730	–149	–3,868	I–11,065	–6,135	3,301	13,598	35,442	51,902	48,649	46,159	76,497	85,623	70,087	Foreign Assets (Net)	31n
65,707	72,280	83,743	107,368	I117,313	138,704	150,156	163,657	170,050	197,073	242,938	268,921	286,942	323,438	383,181	Domestic Credit	32
25,573	28,763	34,596	45,893	I51,220	56,397	57,514	52,218	46,192	47,211	53,334	63,249	59,550	69,704	94,450	Claims on Central Govt. (Net)	32an
4,438	4,739	7,366	10,787	I13,862	15,636	14,077	15,032	7,775	5,163	8,527	9,938	10,338	9,485	13,376	Claims on Nonfin.Pub.Enterprises	32ca
1,304	1,425	1,123	1,319	I1,178	1,416	1,238	1,739	1,903	2,541	3,939	1,465	1,661	1,812	1,608	Claims on Cooperatives	32cb
33,585	36,533	39,722	48,391	I50,833	63,122	76,819	93,872	113,616	141,597	176,578	193,709	214,833	241,877	273,185	Claims on Private Sector	32d
18,662	21,051	24,901	32,155	I35,088	39,596	46,600	50,057	59,355	70,462	75,217	78,202	85,851	96,269	108,554	Money	34
31,994	31,750	36,052	37,857	I40,780	52,241	65,847	80,867	101,852	121,674	154,269	175,313	202,708	219,944	246,753	Quasi-Money	35
18,192	21,209	22,641	33,488	I30,380	40,733	41,009	46,330	44,285	56,839	62,101	61,565	74,880	92,849	97,960	Other Items (Net)	37r
50,656	52,801	60,953	70,012	75,867	91,838	112,447	130,923	161,206	192,136	229,486	253,515	288,560	316,213	355,307	Money plus Quasi-Money	35l
63,884	67,002	77,332	88,077	95,818	113,332	138,892	163,746	203,364	245,462	287,242	320,350	366,425	400,492	448,591	Liquid Liabilities	55l
Percent Per Annum															**Interest Rates**	
11.00	11.00	10.00	10.00	14.00	15.00	17.00	17.00	17.00	17.00	17.00	17.00	17.00	17.00	16.00	Bank Rate *(End of Period)*	60
14.56	12.95	13.14	18.65	22.19	21.56	25.42	21.63	25.65	18.54	41.87	24.33	18.42	15.74	16.69	Money Market Rate	60b
13.39	10.48	7.30	13.59	14.81	14.08	13.75	16.19	16.52	12.68	16.81	I17.40	....	12.59	12.51	Treasury Bill Rate	60c
17.33	12.21	11.50	13.23	16.43	19.42	18.54	18.33	18.42	15.33	16.13	16.03	14.17	13.00	11.75	Deposit Rate	60l
13.40	11.57	9.80	12.42	13.17	13.00	13.83	13.00	16.43	12.96	14.68	16.27	12.00	6.00	7.00	Lending Rate	60p
15.33	12.00	12.00	11.49	11.71	12.20	15.68	16.00	16.25	....	....	....	....	....	....	Government Bond Yield	61
Period Averages															**Prices and Labor**	
39.7	38.5	43.7	51.4	56.1	68.5	74.8	81.3	87.5	91.9	100.0	120.5	128.8	136.9	136.3	Wholesale Prices	63
34.1	36.8	39.7	45.2	50.5	61.3	68.8	76.6	85.6	92.9	100.0	115.9	127.0	138.9	145.4	Consumer Prices	64
32.9	34.7	36.4	45.5	52.5	62.2	69.5	79.9	96.7	98.9	100.0	109.3	117.0	132.1	134.3	Wages: Agr. Minimum Rates	65
Period Averages																
....	....	....	....	....	....	....	5,922	6,016	6,134	6,102	6,209	6,213	6,693	....	Labor Force	67d
5,132	....	....	....	....	5,964	5,136	4,986	5,072	5,148	5,316	5,587	5,569	5,946	....	Employment	67e
840	....	....	....	....	1,005	843	818	874	813	759	710	....	701	....	Unemployment	67c
....	....	....	....	....	14.4	14.1	14.1	14.7	13.6	12.5	11.3	....	10.6	....	Unemployment Rate (%)	67r
Millions of Rupees															**International Transactions**	
36,207	34,072	41,133	46,928	56,175	76,624	82,225	107,855	138,175	158,554	195,117	226,801	273,836	310,397	324,453	Exports	70
12,003	9,253	10,654	12,299	13,664	19,823	17,867	14,893	19,911	20,964	24,638	34,068	42,533	50,280	43,728	Tea	70s
54,049	54,559	60,528	71,200	80,225	107,729	126,643	153,555	193,550	235,576	272,201	301,076	345,285	380,138	415,873	Imports, c.i.f.	71
1995=100																
47.8	51.0	I51.8	50.3	51.3	59.7	I62.2	64.7	74.0	81.0	I86.8	90.4	100.0	98.5	104.5	Volume of Exports	72
82.2	86.3	83.5	91.3	84.8	89.7	88.2	75.4	90.7	95.3	100.0	101.4	111.5	113.0	111.7	Tea	72s
45.5	51.7	I53.0	50.3	47.2	49.8	I56.6	65.6	76.7	86.2	I88.7	89.0	100.0	108.5	107.0	Volume of Imports	73
28.1	25.0	I29.0	33.9	40.0	48.5	I49.4	62.0	68.1	71.4	I82.0	91.5	100.0	115.6	113.8	Unit Value of Exports	74
59.3	43.5	51.8	54.7	65.4	89.7	82.2	80.1	89.1	89.2	100.0	136.4	154.8	180.7	158.9	Tea	74s
36.2	33.5	I37.8	46.9	56.2	71.3	I74.1	77.6	81.7	86.5	100.0	110.5	114.7	....	....	Unit Value of Imports	75

	1970	1971	1972	1973	1974	1975	1976	1977	1978	1979	1980	1981	1982	1983	1984
Balance of Payments													*Millions of US Dollars:*		
Current Account, n.i.e. .... 78al *d*	....	....	....	....	....	−110.0	−6.5	140.3	−67.7	−228.5	−657.2	−445.6	−548.9	−466.2	.9
Goods: Exports f.o.b. .... 78aa *d*	....	....	....	....	....	558.4	559.6	761.6	845.7	981.1	1,061.6	1,062.5	1,013.9	1,061.2	1,461.6
Goods: Imports f.o.b. .... 78ab *d*	....	....	....	....	....	−686.2	−579.5	−655.1	−898.7	−1,304.3	−1,845.1	−1,694.5	−1,794.3	−1,725.6	−1,698.7
Trade Balance .... 78ac *d*	....	....	....	....	....	−127.7	−20.0	106.5	−52.9	−323.2	−783.5	−632.0	−780.4	−664.4	−237.1
Services: Credit .... 78ad *d*	....	....	....	....	....	73.5	72.5	93.5	104.4	152.9	231.1	279.4	290.6	297.9	276.2
Services: Debit .... 78ae *d*	....	....	....	....	....	−117.5	−103.4	−113.7	−181.5	−232.8	−351.4	−359.2	−390.6	−407.3	−383.5
Balance on Goods & Services .. 78af *d*	....	....	....	....	....	−171.7	−50.9	86.3	−130.1	−403.1	−903.8	−711.8	−880.5	−773.7	−344.4
Income: Credit .... 78ag *d*	....	....	....	....	....	7.1	3.9	11.8	20.2	39.5	47.2	33.0	43.8	44.7	58.1
Income: Debit .... 78ah *d*	....	....	....	....	....	−25.5	−24.1	−27.5	−35.2	−54.8	−72.8	−128.8	−137.8	−181.8	−191.9
Balance on Gds, Serv. & Inc. .. 78ai *d*	....	....	....	....	....	−190.1	−71.1	70.5	−145.1	−418.4	−929.4	−807.6	−974.4	−910.8	−478.3
Current Transfers, n.i.e.: Credit .. 78aj *d*	....	....	....	....	....	85.9	70.9	77.6	94.6	201.6	287.8	388.7	451.0	464.6	503.6
Current Transfers: Debit .... 78ak *d*	....	....	....	....	....	−5.9	−6.3	−7.8	−17.1	−11.7	−15.5	−26.6	−25.5	−20.0	−24.4
Capital Account, n.i.e. .... 78bc *d*	....	....	....	....	....	—	—	—	—	—	—	—	—	—	—
Capital Account, n.i.e.: Credit .. 78ba *d*	....	....	....	....	....	—	—	—	—	—	—	—	—	—	—
Capital Account: Debit .... 78bb *d*	....	....	....	....	....	—	—	—	—	—	—	—	—	—	—
Financial Account, n.i.e. ...... 78bj *d*	....	....	....	....	....	86.5	45.3	−7.8	92.0	177.9	345.4	371.9	579.7	448.4	285.8
Direct Investment Abroad ...... 78bd *d*	....	....	....	....	....										
Dir. Invest. in Rep. Econ., n.i.e. .. 78be *d*	....	....	....	....	....	.1	—	−1.2	1.5	46.9	43.0	49.3	63.6	37.8	32.6
Portfolio Investment Assets ...... 78bf *d*	....	....	....	....	....	10.6	—	—	—	—	—	—	—	—	—
Equity Securities .... 78bk *d*	....	....	....	....	....										
Debt Securities .... 78bl *d*	....	....	....	....	....	10.6	—	—	—	—	—	—	—	—	—
Portfolio Investment Liab., n.i.e. .. 78bg *d*	....	....	....	....	....	—	.5	—	.5	—	—	—	—	—	—
Equity Securities .... 78bm *d*	....	....	....	....	....	—	.5	—	.5	—	—	—	—	—	—
Debt Securities .... 78bn *d*	....	....	....	....	....										
Financial Derivatives Assets ...... 78bw *d*	....	....	....	....	....	....	....	....	....	....	....	....	....	....	....
Financial Derivatives Liabilities .. 78bx *d*	....	....	....	....	....	....	....	....	....	....	....	....	....	....	....
Other Investment Assets .... 78bh *d*	....	....	....	....	....	−2.1	−18.8	−62.6	−6.4	−22.3	−40.0	−7.2	−72.8	−57.3	−35.2
Monetary Authorities .... 78bo *d*	....	....	....	....	....										
General Government .... 78bp *d*	....	....	....	....	....	−2.0	2.4	4.2	−1.6	1.1	−.3	−6.1	−13.3	8.7	−31.5
Banks .... 78bq *d*	....	....	....	....	....	−.1	−21.2	−66.7	−4.8	−23.4	−39.7	−1.1	−59.4	−66.0	−3.7
Other Sectors .... 78br *d*	....	....	....	....	....										
Other Investment Liab., n.i.e. .. 78bi *d*	....	....	....	....	....	77.9	63.6	56.0	96.4	153.3	342.4	329.9	588.9	467.9	288.4
Monetary Authorities .... 78bs *d*	....	....	....	....	....	12.0	−8.1	−9.3	1.7	19.2	13.6	−25.4	79.3	2.0	−73.3
General Government .... 78bt *d*	....	....	....	....	....	102.5	81.8	75.1	81.7	117.6	124.8	260.9	260.9	278.7	351.3
Banks .... 78bu *d*	....	....	....	....	....	1.6	2.0	3.7	5.7	7.3	7.8	7.9	47.7	53.3	41.2
Other Sectors .... 78bv *d*	....	....	....	....	....	−38.1	−12.1	−13.6	7.3	9.3	196.2	86.5	201.0	134.0	−30.8
Net Errors and Omissions ...... 78ca *d*	....	....	....	....	....	−2.4	.1	20.7	−17.7	49.4	16.2	24.0	.6	14.8	−39.7
Overall Balance .... 78cb *d*	....	....	....	....	....	−25.9	38.8	153.2	6.7	−1.3	−295.5	−49.7	31.4	−2.9	247.0
Reserves and Related Items ...... 79da *d*	....	....	....	....	....	25.9	−38.8	−153.2	−6.7	1.3	295.5	49.7	−31.4	2.9	−247.0
Reserve Assets .... 79db *d*	....	....	....	....	....	−1.1	−50.4	−198.6	−80.5	−102.7	290.4	−108.0	−25.7	16.9	−235.1
Use of Fund Credit and Loans .. 79dc *d*	....	....	....	....	....	27.0	11.0	43.5	71.7	101.8	3.3	156.6	−6.3	−14.1	−11.9
Exceptional Financing .... 79de *d*	....	....	....	....	....	—	.6	1.9	2.1	2.2	1.9	1.2	.6	.2	—
Government Finance													*Millions of Rupees:*		
Deficit (-) or Surplus 80	−898	−1,153	−1,168	I −960	−767	−1,704	−2,518	−1,671	−5,290	−6,300	−12,157	−10,518	−13,927	−12,846	−10,482
Revenue 81	2,698	2,997	3,322	I 3,670	4,360	4,668	5,340	6,277	11,245	12,158	13,444	14,775	16,209	23,318	34,062
Grants Received 81z				I 49	253	405	381	500	661	1,390	2,620	2,721	3,376	3,473	3,293
Expenditure 82	3,594	4,146	4,493	I 4,637	5,332	6,715	8,072	8,364	16,626	19,426	27,515	25,901	33,768	37,865	44,546
Lending Minus Repayments 83	3	3	−3	I 42	48	62	167	84	570	422	706	2,113	−256	1,772	3,291
Financing (by Residence of Lender)															
Domestic 84a	....	....	....	I 828	641	1,395	1,927	917	1,998	3,953	9,162	5,638	9,183	6,534	3,989
Foreign 85a	....	....	....	I 132	126	309	591	754	3,292	2,347	2,995	4,880	4,744	6,312	6,493
Debt: Domestic 88a	....	....	....	I 8,585	9,444	10,859	12,692	14,159	17,145	21,011	29,379	35,828	45,575	52,355	52,237
Foreign 89a	....	....	....	I 2,989	3,302	4,288	5,406	11,498	14,247	15,031	22,774	30,050	35,376	46,729	54,192
Debt (by Currency)															
Net Borrowing: Rupees 84b	696	727	701	....	....	....	....	....	....	....	....	....	....	....	....
Foreign Currency 85b	168	278	248	....	....	....	....	....	....	....	....	....	....	....	....
Finance from Foreign Aid 86a	53	—	—	....	....	....	....	....	....	....	....	....	....	....	....
Treasury Depository Functions 86c	156	−10	231	....	....	....	....	....	....	....	....	....	....	....	....
Use of Cash Balances 87	−175	157	−12	....	....	....	....	....	....	....	....	....	....	....	....
Debt: Rupees 88b	5,808	6,444	7,096	....	....	....	....	....	....	....	....	....	....	....	....
Intragovernmental Debt 88s	528	718	870	....	....	....	....	....	....	....	....	....	....	....	....
Debt: Foreign Currency 89b	1,567	1,887	2,352	....	....	....	....	....	....	....	....	....	....	....	....
National Accounts													*Millions of Rupees:*		
Exports of Goods & Services 90c	3,478	3,458	3,404	4,481	6,283	7,306	8,773	12,311	14,835	17,660	21,434	25,892	27,148	32,016	44,285
Government Consumption 91f	1,623	1,764	1,897	2,016	2,743	2,480	3,021	3,118	4,043	4,798	5,685	6,310	8,242	9,889	11,935
Gross Fixed Capital Formation 93e	2,359	2,140	2,206	2,493	2,972	3,699	4,595	5,035	8,521	13,246	20,845	23,279	30,279	35,342	39,558
Increase/Decrease(-) in Stocks 93i	230	258	432	35	763	441	301	224	33	281	1,620	331	248	−210	150
Private Consumption 96f	9,882	10,169	10,952	14,083	19,068	21,942	22,991	26,698	32,105	40,371	53,399	68,751	79,226	94,945	111,235
Imports of Goods & Services 98c	−3,908	−3,739	−3,644	−4,704	−8,058	−9,291	−9,478	−10,979	−16,872	−23,969	−36,456	−39,558	−45,905	−50,381	−53,417
Gross Domestic Product (GDP) 99b	13,664	14,050	15,247	18,404	23,771	26,577	30,203	36,407	42,665	52,387	66,527	85,005	99,238	121,601	153,746
Net Factor Inc/Pmts(-) Abroad 98.n	−220	−188	−178	−183	−183	−213	−282	−252	−237	−240	−432	−1,868	−1,959	−3,214	−3,401
GDP at Factor Cost 99ba	13,187	13,674	14,720	17,920	23,302	25,691	28,032	34,684	40,479	49,782	62,246	79,337	94,679	113,878	140,039
Gross National Income (GNI) 99a	12,746	12,798	14,042	16,784	21,482	23,619	25,704	31,256	42,428	52,147	67,906	82,659	97,279	118,387	149,293
Net National Income 99e	12,237	12,426	13,576	15,869	20,489	22,439	24,212	29,707	37,110	49,700	63,457	77,868	89,983	109,671	137,091
GDP Vol.at Fact.Cost,'70 Prices .. 99ba *p*	13,187	13,209	13,631	14,138	14,585	14,987	15,431	16,078	17,401	18,501	19,575	20,706	21,756	....	....
GDP Vol.at Fact.Cost,'82 Prices .. 99ba *p*	....	....	....	....	....	....	....	....	....	....	....	....	94,679	99,375	104,395
GDP Vol.at Fact.Cost,'96 Prices .. 99ba *p*	....	....	....	....	....	....	....	....	....	....	....	....			
GDP Volume (1995=100) .... 99bv *p*	34.2	34.2	35.3	36.6	37.8	38.8	40.0	41.7	45.1	47.9	50.7	53.7	56.4	59.2	62.2
GDP Deflator (1995=100) .... 99bi *p*	6.5	6.7	7.0	8.2	10.3	11.1	11.7	13.9	15.0	17.4	20.5	24.7	28.1	32.2	37.7
													Millions:		
Population 99z	12.52	12.61	12.86	13.09	13.28	13.50	13.72	13.94	14.19	14.47	14.75	15.01	15.19	15.42	15.60

1985	1986	1987	1988	1989	1990	1991	1992	1993	1994	1995	1996	1997	1998	1999		
Minus Sign Indicates Debit															Balance of Payments	
–418.5	–417.1	–326.1	–394.5	–413.7	–298.3	–594.8	–450.7	–382.2	–757.4	–769.9	–682.7	–394.7	–288.4	....	Current Account, n.i.e.	**78al*d***
1,315.8	1,208.5	1,393.9	1,477.1	1,505.1	1,853.0	2,003.3	2,301.4	2,785.7	3,208.3	3,797.9	4,095.2	4,638.7	4,734.9	....	Goods: Exports f.o.b.	**78aa*d***
–1,838.5	–1,764.3	–1,866.0	–2,017.5	–2,055.1	–2,325.6	–2,808.0	–3,016.5	–3,527.8	–4,293.4	–4,782.6	–4,895.0	–5,278.3	–5,302.4	....	Goods: Imports f.o.b.	**78ab*d***
–522.6	–555.7	–472.2	–540.5	–550.1	–472.5	–804.7	–715.1	–742.1	–1,085.0	–984.7	–799.7	–639.6	–567.5	....	*Trade Balance*	**78ac*d***
245.4	305.3	328.2	339.2	345.6	439.6	546.6	621.4	634.4	753.9	819.2	765.5	875.3	913.0	....	Services: Credit	**78ad*d***
–457.1	–499.7	–533.2	–547.1	–565.8	–639.2	–762.5	–823.2	–874.3	–1,052.3	–1,199.1	–1,204.3	–1,302.6	–1,358.8	....	Services: Debit	**78ae*d***
–734.4	–750.2	–677.2	–748.4	–770.3	–672.0	–1,020.6	–916.9	–982.1	–1,383.4	–1,364.6	–1,238.6	–1,066.9	–1,013.2	....	*Balance on Goods & Services*	**78af*d***
83.3	68.0	69.3	68.7	58.6	93.0	54.5	68.1	111.4	143.9	223.3	175.1	233.3	213.9	....	Income: Credit	**78ag*d***
–210.1	–206.0	–210.8	–240.8	–221.3	–259.8	–232.5	–246.2	–234.3	–312.0	–360.6	–378.2	–392.9	–392.2	....	Income: Debit	**78ah*d***
–861.2	–888.1	–818.7	–920.5	–933.0	–838.8	–1,198.5	–1,094.9	–1,105.0	–1,551.6	–1,501.9	–1,441.6	–1,226.5	–1,191.6	....	*Balance on Gds, Serv. & Inc.*	**78ai*d***
468.9	502.9	530.0	563.7	546.6	578.8	644.5	730.4	795.4	882.3	846.7	881.4	966.5	1,054.2	....	Current Transfers, n.i.e.: Credit	**78aj*d***
–26.1	–31.8	–37.3	–37.7	–27.3	–38.3	–40.8	–86.1	–72.6	–88.1	–114.7	–122.4	–134.7	–151.0	....	Current Transfers: Debit	**78ak*d***
—	—	—	—	—	—	—	—	—	—	120.6	95.9	87.1	60.7	....	Capital Account, n.i.e.	**78bc*d***
—	—	—	—	—	—	—	—	—	—	124.2	99.7	91.3	65.4	....	Capital Account, n.i.e.: Credit	**78ba*d***
—	—	—	—	—	—	—	—	—	—	–3.5	–3.8	–4.2	–4.7	....	Capital Account: Debit	**78bb*d***
373.3	359.4	395.3	253.3	580.3	529.1	692.9	479.0	1,022.1	958.8	730.1	452.2	466.7	342.7	....	Financial Account, n.i.e.	**78bj*d***
–1.4	–.5	–1.3	–2.1	–2.0	–.8	–4.5	–1.6	–6.9	–8.3	—	—	—	—	....	Direct Investment Abroad	**78bd*d***
26.2	29.7	59.5	45.7	19.7	43.4	48.4	122.6	194.5	166.4	56.0	119.9	430.1	193.2	....	Dir. Invest. in Rep. Econ., n.i.e.	**78be*d***
—	—	—	—	—	—	32.1	25.7	200.1	292.9	105.3	76.8	139.9	88.6	....	Portfolio Investment Assets	**78bf*d***
—	—	—	—	—	—	—	—	....	....	....	—	—	—	....	Equity Securities	**78bk*d***
—	—	—	—	—	—	32.1	25.7	200.1	292.9	105.3	76.8	139.9	88.6	....	Debt Securities	**78bl*d***
—	—	—	—	—	—	—	—	–132.9	–265.9	–107.3	–70.2	–126.8	–112.4	....	Portfolio Investment Liab., n.i.e.	**78bg*d***
—	—	—	—	—	—	—	—	....	....	....	....	—	—	....	Equity Securities	**78bm*d***
—	—	—	—	—	—	—	—	–132.9	–265.9	–107.3	–70.2	–126.8	–112.4	....	Debt Securities	**78bn*d***
....	....	....	....	....	....	....	....	....	....	....	—	....	....	....	Financial Derivatives Assets	**78bw*d***
....	....	....	....	....	....	....	....	....	....	....	....	....	....	....	Financial Derivatives Liabilities	**78bx*d***
–20.9	–30.0	–56.9	–15.8	–11.3	–115.8	–51.6	–100.3	16.4	–134.0	41.7	–27.9	–392.9	73.3	....	Other Investment Assets	**78bh*d***
....	....	....	....	....	....	....	....	—	—	—	....	—	—	....	Monetary Authorities	**78bo*d***
–1.9	8.5	25.2	.7	–27.5	14.8	–13.0	3.3	–2.4	9.4	3.6	–6.4	1.7	–2.9	....	General Government	**78bp*d***
–19.0	–38.4	–82.1	–16.6	16.2	–130.6	–38.6	–103.6	18.8	–143.4	38.1	–21.5	–394.6	76.2	....	Banks	**78bq*d***
—	—	—	—	—	—	—	—	—	—	—	....	—	—	....	Other Sectors	**78br*d***
369.4	360.2	394.0	225.5	573.8	602.4	668.6	432.7	750.9	907.6	634.4	353.6	416.5	99.9	....	Other Investment Liab., n.i.e.	**78bi*d***
10.3	–2.3	62.0	–43.0	251.1	116.8	3.8	–22.2	25.9	9.6	14.4	11.6	30.3	16.7	....	Monetary Authorities	**78bs*d***
289.1	314.6	223.7	277.2	217.2	408.9	532.5	233.3	262.6	246.9	448.4	218.0	144.5	198.2	....	General Government	**78bt*d***
34.4	43.1	81.4	28.9	63.1	55.5	106.2	108.3	128.2	73.4	86.7	95.8	209.4	–129.8	....	Banks	**78bu*d***
35.5	4.8	27.0	–37.7	42.4	21.2	26.1	113.3	334.3	577.7	85.0	28.2	32.3	14.9	....	Other Sectors	**78bv*d***
–43.0	–34.4	–122.5	37.3	–115.0	–115.1	225.6	173.3	128.0	106.3	157.9	143.6	148.0	109.1	....	Net Errors and Omissions	**78ca*d***
–88.2	–92.0	–53.2	–103.9	51.5	115.7	323.7	201.7	767.9	307.7	238.7	9.0	307.2	224.2	....	*Overall Balance*	**78cb*d***
88.2	92.0	53.2	103.9	–51.5	–115.7	–323.7	–201.7	–767.9	–307.7	–238.7	–9.0	–307.2	–224.2	....	Reserves and Related Items	**79da*d***
141.4	182.7	167.9	3.2	–65.1	–132.3	–312.5	–284.6	–820.7	–373.5	–204.7	36.3	–241.4	–141.6	....	Reserve Assets	**79db*d***
–53.2	–90.7	–114.6	100.7	13.6	16.5	–11.2	82.9	52.8	65.9	–34.1	–45.2	–65.7	–82.6	....	Use of Fund Credit and Loans	**79dc*d***
—	—	—	—	—	—	—	—	—	—	—	....	—	—	....	Exceptional Financing	**79de*d***
Year Ending December 31															**Government Finance**	
–15,678	–18,202	–17,073	–28,195	–21,778	–25,153	–35,197	–22,912	–32,084	I –49,474	–55,196	–59,913	–40,234	–81,559 P	....	Deficit (-) or Surplus	**80**
36,248	37,238	42,144	41,749	53,979	67,964	76,460	85,780	98,495	110,038	136,257	146,280	165,036	175,032 P	....	Revenue	**81**
3,307	3,753	4,677	6,588	6,407	6,697	7,870	8,280	8,025	8,257	9,028	7,739	7,329	7,200 P	....	Grants Received	**81z**
54,174	57,202	62,376	69,010	77,634	91,300	109,060	114,586	134,728	157,476	195,880	212,787	228,732	253,808 P	....	Expenditure	**82**
1,059	1,991	1,518	7,522	4,530	8,514	10,467	2,386	3,876	I 10,293	4,601	1,145	–16,133	9,983 P	....	Lending Minus Repayments	**83**
															Financing (by Residence of Lender)	
8,569	9,141	11,357	21,067	15,852	13,509	15,868	15,551	22,229	I 37,696	33,972	49,753	30,276	71,363 P	....	Domestic	**84a**
7,109	9,061	5,716	7,128	5,926	11,644	19,329	7,361	9,855	11,778	21,224	10,160	9,958	10,196 P	....	Foreign	**85a**
63,197	70,085	80,133	98,596	117,561	133,898	152,119	170,020	213,685	249,118	285,759	349,007	382,962	446,547 P	....	Debt: Domestic	**88a**
68,196	86,723	92,857	125,997	156,298	176,883	214,579	235,538	269,883	300,174	346,286	360,313	383,615	461,454 P	....	Foreign	**89a**
															Debt (by Currency)	
....	....	....	....	....	....	....	....	....	....	....	....	....	....	....	Net Borrowing: Rupees	**84b**
....	....	....	....	....	....	....	....	....	....	....	....	....	....	....	Foreign Currency	**85b**
....	....	....	....	....	....	....	....	....	....	....	....	....	....	....	Finance from Foreign Aid	**86a**
....	....	....	....	....	....	....	....	....	....	....	....	....	....	....	Treasury Depository Functions	**86c**
....	....	....	....	....	....	....	....	....	....	....	....	....	....	....	Use of Cash Balances	**87**
....	....	....	....	....	....	....	....	....	....	....	....	....	....	....	Debt: Rupees	**88b**
....	....	....	....	....	....	....	....	....	....	....	....	....	....	....	Intragovernmental Debt	**88s**
....	....	....	....	....	....	....	....	....	....	....	....	....	....	....	Debt: Foreign Currency	**89b**
Millions of Rupees															**National Accounts**	
42,237	42,568	49,559	57,885	68,666	97,117	107,016	135,114	168,858	195,805	237,711	268,640	325,289	364,785	....	Exports of Goods & Services	**90c**
16,599	18,480	19,538	21,849	26,410	31,405	36,633	40,972	45,791	56,002	76,604	81,021	92,196	99,109	....	Government Consumption	**91f**
38,457	42,326	45,752	49,961	54,249	70,417	84,206	100,039	125,875	154,260	170,875	183,509	216,873	257,163	....	Gross Fixed Capital Formation	**93e**
225	137	148	601	473	1,038	950	3,200	1,800	2,250	950	2,755	230	175	....	Increase/Decrease(-) in Stocks	**93i**
126,503	139,370	151,949	173,457	194,680	244,288	288,214	320,466	373,785	434,933	489,057	569,416	643,839	723,506	....	Private Consumption	**96f**
–61,646	–63,407	–70,223	–81,771	–92,587	–122,481	–144,674	–174,508	–216,544	–264,166	–307,425	–337,213	–388,154	–430,234	....	Imports of Goods & Services	**98c**
162,375	179,474	196,723	221,982	251,891	321,784	372,345	425,283	499,565	579,084	667,772	768,128	890,272	1,014,504	....	Gross Domestic Product (GDP)	**99b**
–3,400	–3,861	–4,336	–5,266	–5,739	–6,685	–7,367	–7,820	–5,979	–8,310	–6,958	–11,258	–9,409	–11,529	....	Net Factor Inc/Pmts(-) Abroad	**98.n**
148,321	163,713	177,731	203,516	228,138	290,615	337,399	386,999	453,092	523,300	598,327	695,934	739,763	774,796	....	GDP at Factor Cost	**99ba**
158,975	175,613	192,387	216,716	246,152	315,099	364,978	417,463	493,586	570,774	660,814	756,875	880,828	1,002,968	....	Gross National Income (GNI)	**99a**
146,788	160,870	175,333	203,938	232,298	298,256	345,111	....	....	....	....	....	....	....	....	Net National Income	**99e**
....	....	....	....	....	....	....	....	....	....	....	....	....	....	....	GDP Vol.at Fact.Cost,'70 Prices	**99ba*p***
109,570	114,261	115,922	119,050	121,729	129,244	135,204	140,990	150,783	159,269	167,953	174,261	....	....	....	GDP Vol.at Fact.Cost,'82 Prices	**99ba*p***
....	....	....	....	....	....	....	....	....	....	....	695,934	739,763	774,796	....	GDP Vol.at Fact.Cost,'96 Prices	**99ba*p***
65.2	68.0	69.0	70.9	72.5	77.0	80.5	83.9	89.8	94.8	100.0	103.8	110.3	115.5	....	GDP Volume (1995=100)	**99bv*p***
38.0	40.2	43.0	48.0	52.6	63.1	70.0	77.0	84.3	92.2	100.0	112.1	112.1	112.1	....	GDP Deflator (1995=100)	**99bi*p***
Midyear Estimates																
15.84	16.13	16.36	16.60	16.83	17.02	17.27	17.43	17.65	17.89	18.14	18.32	18.55	18.77	18.64	**Population**	**99z**

(See notes in the back of the book.)

Sudan

		1970	1971	1972	1973	1974	1975	1976	1977	1978	1979	1980	1981	1982	1983	1984
Exchange Rates															*Dinars per SDR:*	
Market Rate	aa	.03	.04	.04	.04	.04	.04	.04	.04	.05	.07	.06	.10	.14	.14	.13
															Dinars per US Dollar:	
Market Rate	ae	.03	.03	.03	.03	.03	.03	.03	.03	.04	.05	.05	.09	.13	.13	.13
Market Rate	rf	.03	.03	.03	.03	.03	.03	.03	.03	.04	.04	.05	.06	.10	.13	.13
Fund Position															*Millions of SDRs:*	
Quota	2f. s	72.0	72.0	72.0	72.0	72.0	72.0	72.0	72.0	88.0	88.0	132.0	132.0	132.0	169.7	169.7
SDRs	1b. s	.1	—	4.9	13.6	21.5	7.3	—	—	6.0	10.0	—	.5	—	.1	—
Reserve Position in the Fund	1c. s	—	—	—	—	—	—	—	—	—	—	—	—	—	—	—
Total Fund Cred.&Loans Outstg.	2tl	30.9	15.2	28.1	29.0	71.7	113.4	119.1	99.5	150.6	222.4	338.0	484.8	524.6	666.7	677.6
International Liquidity													*Millions of US Dollars Unless Otherwise Indicated:*			
Total Reserves minus Gold	1l. d	21.7	27.9	35.6	61.3	124.3	36.4	23.6	23.1	28.4	67.4	48.7	17.0	20.5	16.6	17.2
SDRs	1b. d	.1	—	5.3	16.4	26.4	8.6	—	—	7.9	13.2	—	.6	—	.1	—
Reserve Position in the Fund	1c. d	—	—	—	—	—	—	—	—	—	—	—	—	—	—	—
Foreign Exchange	1d. d	21.6	27.9	30.3	44.9	97.9	27.8	23.6	23.1	20.5	54.2	48.7	16.4	20.5	16.5	17.2
Monetary Authorities: Other Liab.	4. d	34.1	106.6	127.5	136.5	144.0	362.1	483.6	536.1	501.8	559.8	682.6	898.3	873.9	1,520.2	1,614.7
Deposit Money Banks: Assets	7a. d	1.4	1.2	2.7	13.4	17.4	18.1	67.8	172.6	168.1	193.7	435.0	309.5	289.2	409.4	512.7
Liabilities	7b. d	14.0	14.0	21.9	45.4	34.9	57.2	72.1	145.3	106.9	73.2	144.1	146.8	122.0	117.2	136.7
Monetary Authorities													*Millions of Dinars through 1991;*			
Foreign Assets	11	.9	1.0	1.3	2.3	3.9	1.2	.8	.9	1.3	3.4	2.0	1.5	2.7	2.2	2.2
Claims on Central Government	12a														163.1	198.5
Claims on Nonfin.Pub.Enterprises	12c	2.5	3.8	5.0	4.9	8.4	16.0	18.2	18.1	22.7	28.4	37.7	53.4	79.6	147.3	58.2
Claims on Deposit Money Banks	12e	2.3	2.2	2.1	2.4	2.7	3.2	2.7	3.6	5.5	6.6	7.3	9.7	12.2	16.8	20.3
Reserve Money	14	7.8	8.5	9.3	11.9	16.3	19.3	23.5	38.0	50.2	66.7	75.1	121.1	158.2	174.0	244.4
of which: Currency Outside DMBs	14a	6.7	7.0	7.5	9.3	11.9	12.9	15.3	19.9	27.9	38.0	50.8	63.0	82.0	102.2	124.7
Quasi-Monetary Deposits	15	....	....	....	....	....	....	....	....	....	....	....	....	....	1.3	10.3
Cent. Bk. Liab.: Musharaka Certif.	16ac															
Foreign Liabilities	16c	2.3	3.9	5.1	5.0	8.1	17.2	21.7	22.9	26.4	39.2	51.2	124.4	178.8	278.8	287.7
Central Government Deposits	16d	.2	.3	.7	.5	4.1	3.5	4.6	3.2	5.4	30.6	46.9	47.9	70.9	....	....
Capital Accounts	17a	.8	1.1	1.4	1.4	1.4	1.4	1.7	2.4	2.8	12.8	2.8	1.8	1.9	4.5	4.2
Valuation Adjustment	17rv	....	....	....	....	....	....	....	....	....	....	....	....	....	−153.2	−153.2
Other Items (Net)	17r	−5.4	−6.8	−8.1	−9.1	−14.8	−21.1	−29.7	−44.0	−55.4	−101.0	−129.1	−230.7	−315.2	−86.0	−114.1
Deposit Money Banks													*Millions of Dinars through 1991;*			
Reserves	20	.5	.5	1.1	1.9	2.4	3.4	4.4	11.5	17.6	24.0	19.6	39.1	40.8	82.6	93.7
Other Claims on Monetary Author.	20c	....	....	....	....	....	....	....	....	....	....	....	....	....	....	....
Foreign Assets	21	.1	—	.1	.4	.6	.6	2.4	6.0	6.7	9.7	21.7	27.9	37.6	53.2	66.7
Claims on Central Government	22a	2.1	2.3	2.9	3.7	5.4	6.0	7.6	10.6	13.3	15.9	16.8	28.5	46.6	9.4	9.6
Claims on Private Sector	22d	7.1	7.0	8.5	9.9	12.3	18.6	22.8	26.5	34.3	46.1	59.3	77.8	114.3	137.7	160.9
Claims on Nonbank Financial Insts	22f	....	....	....	....	....	....	....	....	....	....	....	....	....	....	....
Demand Deposits	24	4.3	4.5	6.2	7.4	9.9	12.1	15.5	22.6	29.2	39.2	54.0	65.3	88.4	116.5	132.6
Time and Savings Deposits	25	2.1	2.3	2.9	3.7	5.4	6.0	6.6	10.8	12.6	15.9	18.2	28.8	46.5	76.1	85.2
Foreign Liabilities	26c	.5	.4	.7	1.3	1.2	2.0	2.5	5.1	4.3	3.7	7.2	13.2	15.9	15.2	17.8
Central Government Deposits	26d	.1	.1	.3	.2	.2	.3	.8	1.5	1.9	1.5	1.3	2.5	1.2	4.6	5.7
Credit from Monetary Authorities	26g	1.5	.8	.6	.9	.9	1.3	.9	1.4	3.3	4.0	5.3	7.1	9.3	14.8	12.7
Capital Accounts	27a	.6	.6	.6	.6	.6	.6	1.0	1.6	1.9	2.1	2.9	4.5	9.4	24.7	32.6
Valuation Adjustment	27rv	....	....	....	....	....	....	....	....	....	....	....	....	....	....	....
Other Items (Net)	27r	.6	1.0	1.1	1.6	2.5	6.4	9.9	11.7	18.7	29.3	30.4	51.7	68.5	31.1	44.3
Monetary Survey													*Millions of Dinars through 1991;*			
Foreign Assets (Net)	31n	−1.8	−3.3	−4.4	−3.6	−4.8	−17.4	−21.0	−21.0	−22.7	−29.8	−34.7	−108.2	−154.3	−238.6	−236.6
Domestic Credit	32	17.6	20.6	24.6	27.5	35.7	56.7	72.6	95.6	118.6	145.5	177.0	237.8	276.1	357.4	427.2
Claims on Central Govt. (Net)	32an	7.2	8.4	9.8	11.2	13.2	20.0	29.4	48.8	59.3	68.7	77.7	103.7	79.1	167.9	202.5
Claims on Nonfin.Pub.Enterprises	32c	2.5	3.8	5.0	4.9	8.4	16.0	18.2	18.1	22.7	28.4	37.7	53.4	79.6	147.3	58.2
Claims on Private Sector	32d	7.1	7.0	8.5	9.9	12.3	18.6	22.8	26.5	34.3	46.1	59.3	77.8	114.3	137.7	160.9
Claims on Nonbank Financial Inst	32f	....	....	....	....	....	....	....	....	....	....	....	....	....	4.5	5.7
Money	34	11.6	12.4	14.4	17.6	23.7	28.1	35.0	49.7	63.4	83.7	109.7	153.1	209.1	233.6	276.4
Quasi-Money	35	1.4	1.6	2.2	3.0	4.1	4.9	6.2	9.2	11.7	14.1	16.7	26.4	44.3	77.4	95.5
Valuation Adjustment	37rv	....	....	....	....	....	....	....	....	....	....	....	....	....	−153.2	−153.2
Other Items (Net)	37r	2.8	3.2	3.6	3.4	3.2	6.3	10.4	15.7	20.8	18.0	15.9	−49.9	−131.7	18.5	29.6
Money plus Quasi-Money	35l	13.0	14.0	16.6	20.5	27.8	33.0	41.2	58.9	75.1	97.7	126.4	179.5	253.4	311.0	371.9
Other Banking Institutions															*Millions of Dinars:*	
Savings Deposits	45	.7	.7	.7	.7	1.4	1.2	1.4	1.4	1.6	1.9	2.0	2.1	2.3	2.5	2.7
Liquid Liabilities	55l	13.7	14.7	17.3	21.3	29.2	34.2	42.6	60.3	76.6	99.6	128.4	181.6	255.7	313.5	374.6
Interest Rates															*Percent Per Annum*	
Deposit Rate	60l	....	....	....	....	....	....	....	....	6.0	6.0	6.0	8.6	10.5	13.5	13.5
Prices														*Index Numbers (1995=100):*		
Consumer Prices	64	—	—	—	—	—	—	—	.1	.1	.1	.1	.1	.2	.2	.3

	1985	1986	1987	1988	1989	1990	1991	1992	1993	1994	1995	1996	1997	1998	1999		
End of Period																**Exchange Rates**	
	.27	.31	.64	.61	.59	.64	2.14	18.58	29.86	58.39	78.24	208.40	232.34	334.83	353.70	Market Rate.............	**aa**
End of Period (ae) Period Average (rf)																	
	.25	.25	.45	.45	.45	1.50	13.51	21.74	40.00	52.63	144.93	172.20	237.80	257.70		Market Rate.............	**ae**
	.23	.25	.30	.45	.45	.45	.70	9.74	15.93	28.96	58.09	125.08	157.57	200.80	252.55	Market Rate.............	**rf**
End of Period																**Fund Position**	
	169.7	169.7	169.7	169.7	169.7	169.7	169.7	169.7	169.7	169.7	169.7	169.7	169.7	169.7	169.7	Quota........	**2f. s**
	—	—	—	—	—	—	—	—	—	—	—	—	—	—	—	SDRs........	**1b. s**
	—	—	—	—	—	—	—	—	—	—	—	—	—	—	—	Reserve Position in the Fund	**1c. s**
	672.7	672.7	672.7	672.7	672.7	671.6	671.6	671.6	671.6	671.6	645.7	621.2	590.5	548.4	520.8	Total Fund Cred.&Loans Outstg.	**2tl**
End of Period																**International Liquidity**	
	12.2	58.5	11.7	12.1	15.9	11.4	7.6	27.5	37.4	78.2	163.4	106.8	81.6	90.6	188.7	Total Reserves minus Gold..........	**1l. d**
	—	—	—	—	—	—	—	—	—	—	—	—	—	—	—	SDRs........	**1b. d**
	—	—	—	—	—	—	—	—	—	—	—	—	—	—	—	Reserve Position in the Fund	**1c. d**
	12.2	58.5	11.7	12.1	15.9	11.4	7.6	27.5	37.4	78.1	163.3	106.8	81.6	90.6	188.7	Foreign Exchange	**1d. d**
	1,180.0	1,308.7	1,016.3	1,703.6	1,809.5	2,400.6	1,340.4	2,165.8	2,288.0	2,471.8	3,407.1	2,549.9	2,464.4	2,538.9	2,618.8	Monetary Authorities: Other Liab.	**4.. d**
	618.1	493.9	354.5	500.2	539.8	616.9	599.5	32.2	44.8	27.0	32.1	20.7	258.4	268.8	266.1	Deposit Money Banks: Assets	**7a. d**
	215.5	165.9	137.5	136.2	134.4	154.6	106.6	7.0	6.9	3.8	5.3	3.0	25.6	19.9	13.4	Liabilities..........	**7b. d**
Billions of Dinars Beginning 1992: End of Period																**Monetary Authorities**	
	3.4	15.6	6.7	8.9	8.0	44.6	72.0	ⅼ.4	.8	3.1	8.6	15.5	14.0	21.6	48.6	Foreign Assets	**11**
	289.4	428.5	617.4	872.6	1,590.7	2,231.4	3,593.2	ⅼ10.8	16.5	22.0	32.9	76.0	84.8	101.8	134.8	Claims on Central Government	**12a**
	114.7	165.6	228.3	272.4	356.8	388.8	269.8	ⅼ.2	.2	.2	.2	.2	.2	.2	3.5	Claims on Nonfin.Pub.Enterprises........	**12c**
	22.2	22.4	24.8	29.3	35.5	44.0	34.8	ⅼ.1	.5	.4	.4	.4	2.4	6.1	7.2	Claims on Deposit Money Banks	**12e**
	395.0	561.5	716.0	944.7	1,751.5	2,333.8	3,460.8	ⅼ8.8	14.4	20.2	35.7	64.9	87.2	112.8	152.4	Reserve Money	**14**
	193.0	276.0	362.5	560.1	924.0	1,311.3	2,166.3	ⅼ4.4	9.5	14.8	24.9	44.4	58.5	82.1	108.1	*of which: Currency Outside DMBs*	**14a**
	10.2	8.9	17.5	19.0	22.4	26.8	38.9	ⅼ.6	.6	2.1	3.2	3.2	3.1	3.3	3.2	Quasi-Monetary Deposits........	**15**
															4.9	Cent. Bk. Liab.: Musharaka Certif.	**16ac**
	461.2	512.3	843.8	1,133.3	1,172.3	1,467.3	3,305.5	ⅼ40.5	67.8	134.2	224.8	485.6	547.8	767.5	838.1	Foreign Liabilities	**16c**
	....	....	....	....	....	....	....	ⅼ1.2	.9	.9	1.2	10.8	9.2	3.7	5.1	Central Government Deposits	**16d**
	4.2	5.9	12.8	21.2	34.8	37.4	39.4	ⅼ—	.1	.2	.4	1.2	1.2	2.0	2.6	Capital Accounts	**17a**
	−320.9	−341.8	−592.5	−836.4	−894.9	−1,060.6	−2,946.4	ⅼ−39.2	−63.1	−124.9	−206.6	−444.8	−515.0	−724.2	−772.0	Valuation Adjustment	**17rv**
	−120.0	−114.7	−120.5	−98.5	−95.1	−96.0	71.5	ⅼ−.4	−2.7	−6.9	−16.8	−28.9	−32.0	−40.4	−39.5	Other Items (Net)	**17r**
Billions of Dinars Beginning 1992: End of Period																**Deposit Money Banks**	
	ⅼ200.9	269.5	328.3	320.3	725.8	831.5	1,008.5	ⅼ3.7	4.6	5.6	8.0	14.3	28.1	30.6	37.9	Reserves	**20**
	....	....	....	....	....	....	....	....	....	....	....	....	....	4.9	4.2	Other Claims on Monetary Author.	**20c**
	ⅼ154.5	123.5	159.5	225.1	242.9	277.6	898.8	ⅼ4.4	9.7	10.8	16.9	30.0	44.5	63.9	68.6	Foreign Assets	**21**
	10.0	11.2	6.0	6.0	24.3	1.0	—	ⅼ—	.5	.2	.2	.1		.1	.2	Claims on Central Government	**22a**
	ⅼ188.2	263.8	379.3	450.9	494.1	766.7	1,404.9	ⅼ2.7	4.5	8.8	13.1	31.9	39.4	44.3	43.6	Claims on Private Sector........	**22d**
	....	....	....	....	....	....	....	ⅼ—	.1	.1	.1	.2	.4	.4	.4	Claims on Nonbank Financial Insts	**22f**
	ⅼ192.5	263.6	363.3	474.4	847.0	1,144.3	1,871.4	ⅼ4.6	6.2	9.5	15.6	30.9	41.4	46.9	56.9	Demand Deposits	**24**
	ⅼ86.2	187.5	272.0	275.6	259.3	437.5	942.8	ⅼ3.4	10.1	13.7	25.7	36.1	55.0	72.7	85.1	Time and Savings Deposits	**25**
	ⅼ53.9	41.5	61.9	61.3	60.5	69.6	159.9	ⅼ.9	1.5	1.5	2.8	4.3	4.4	4.7	3.4	Foreign Liabilities	**26c**
	26.5	66.4	112.1	107.9	110.9	121.6	171.7	ⅼ.2	.3	.2	.3	.8	.4	.4	3.5	Central Government Deposits	**26d**
	3.1	1.2	1.0	1.2	1.4	1.5	8.4	ⅼ—	.1	.1	.8	.1	.1	.3	3.0	Credit from Monetary Authorities	**26g**
	ⅼ65.2	77.3	76.4	115.7	141.4	160.7	242.2	ⅼ.6	1.7	3.9	5.5	11.1	14.8	20.3	24.5	Capital Accounts	**27a**
	30.0	30.0	30.0	30.0	30.0	49.6	300.0	ⅼ1.2	1.1	.7	1.1	1.4	2.8	2.4	−.4	Valuation Adjustment	**27rv**
	ⅼ−3.6	.6	−43.4	−63.8	36.7	−108.0	−384.1	ⅼ−.2	−1.6	−4.1	−13.5	−8.2	−6.5	−3.6	−21.3	Other Items (Net)	**27r**
Billions of Dinars Beginning 1992: End of Period																**Monetary Survey**	
	ⅼ−357.2	−414.6	−739.5	−960.6	−981.9	−1,214.7	−2,494.6	ⅼ−36.7	−58.7	−121.7	−202.1	−444.4	−493.7	−686.8	−724.3	Foreign Assets (Net)	**31n**
	ⅼ583.0	811.1	1,127.4	1,502.4	2,368.9	3,283.1	5,113.1	ⅼ12.9	21.4	31.5	46.2	98.8	117.0	145.3	178.5	Domestic Credit	**32**
	272.9	373.3	511.4	770.7	1,504.1	2,110.8	3,421.6	ⅼ9.4	15.8	21.1	31.5	64.6	75.2	97.7	126.3	Claims on Central Govt. (Net)	**32an**
	114.7	165.6	228.3	272.4	356.8	388.8	269.8	ⅼ.8	.9	1.4	1.4	1.9	1.9	2.8	8.2	Claims on Nonfin.Pub.Enterprises	**32c**
	ⅼ188.2	263.8	379.3	450.9	494.1	766.7	1,404.9	ⅼ2.7	4.5	8.8	13.1	31.9	39.4	44.3	43.6	Claims on Private Sector	**32d**
	7.2	8.4	8.4	8.4	13.9	16.9	16.9	ⅼ—	.1	.1	.1	.2	.4	.4	.4	Claims on Nonbank Financial Inst	**32f**
	ⅼ414.5	584.9	776.8	1,121.8	1,889.9	2,765.9	4,430.5	ⅼ8.9	15.7	24.3	40.5	75.4	99.8	129.1	165.0	Money	**34**
	ⅼ196.4	196.4	289.5	294.6	281.7	464.3	981.7	ⅼ4.1	10.8	15.8	28.9	39.3	58.1	76.1	88.3	Quasi-Money	**35**
	−290.9	−311.8	−562.5	−806.4	−864.9	−1,011.0	−2,646.4	ⅼ−38.0	−62.0	−124.3	−205.5	−443.4	−512.2	−721.9	−772.4	Valuation Adjustment	**37rv**
	ⅼ−19.8	1.3	−41.6	7.7	100.2	−76.5	−73.0	ⅼ1.2	−1.8	−6.0	−19.8	−16.9	−22.4	−24.7	−26.7	Other Items (Net)	**37r**
	ⅼ610.8	781.3	1,066.4	1,416.4	2,171.6	3,230.2	5,412.2	ⅼ13.0	26.5	40.0	69.4	114.7	157.9	205.2	253.3	Money plus Quasi-Money	**35l**
End of Period																**Other Banking Institutions**	
	3.0	....	....	....	....	....	....	....	....	....	....	....	....	....	....	Savings Deposits	**45**
	571.3	....	....	....	....	....	....	....	....	....	....	....	....	....	....	Liquid Liabilities	**55l**
Percent Per Annum																**Interest Rates**	
	....	....	....	....	....	....	....	....	....	....	....	....	....	....	....	Deposit Rate........	**601**
Period Averages																**Prices**	
	ⅼ.4	.5	....	ⅼ1.0	1.7	2.8	6.3	13.7	27.6	59.4	100.0	232.8	341.4	399.8	463.8	Consumer Prices........	**64**

Sudan

732

		1970	1971	1972	1973	1974	1975	1976	1977	1978	1979	1980	1981	1982	1983	1984
International Transactions														*Millions of US Dollars: Year Ending June 30 through 1994,*			
Exports	70..d	298.4	328.5	357.2	434.2	350.4	437.9	554.3	661.0	517.6	534.5	542.7	656.8	498.1	623.5	628.7
Imports, c.i.f.	71..d	287.5	331.4	320.1	436.1	642.1	887.2	980.4	1,081.2	1,194.3	1,109.2	1,576.4	1,552.9	1,282.4	1,354.4	1,146.7
Balance of Payments														*Millions of US Dollars:*		
Current Account, n.i.e.	78al d	....	....	....	....	....	....	....	–89.6	–110.0	–257.6	–317.0	–648.3	–249.1	–219.2	36.5
Goods: Exports f.o.b.	78aa d	....	....	....	....	....	....	....	658.2	563.0	514.1	689.4	792.7	400.9	514.2	519.0
Goods: Imports f.o.b.	78ab d	....	....	....	....	....	....	....	–644.2	–623.9	–735.8	–1,127.4	–1,633.6	–750.3	–703.2	–599.8
Trade Balance	78ac d	....	....	....	....	....	....	....	14.1	–60.9	–221.7	–438.0	–840.9	–349.4	–188.9	–80.8
Services: Credit	78ad d	....	....	....	....	....	....	....	120.9	162.4	202.9	292.4	425.5	471.7	269.2	258.5
Services: Debit	78ae d	....	....	....	....	....	....	....	–199.3	–229.9	–269.4	–353.0	–466.1	–328.7	–343.7	–284.6
Balance on Goods & Services	78af d	....	....	....	....	....	....	....	–64.3	–128.5	–288.3	–498.6	–881.4	–206.4	–263.4	–107.0
Income: Credit	78ag d	....	....	....	....	....	....	....	5.2	14.5	3.8	48.8	44.0	44.1	25.8	9.8
Income: Debit	78ah d	....	....	....	....	....	....	....	–87.6	–74.9	–78.9	–96.0	–146.5	–193.3	–227.8	–163.4
Balance on Gds, Serv. & Inc.	78ai d	....	....	....	....	....	....	....	–146.7	–188.8	–363.4	–545.8	–983.9	–355.6	–465.3	–260.6
Current Transfers, n.i.e.: Credit	78aj d	....	....	....	....	....	....	....	60.0	81.7	118.0	272.2	403.7	131.9	274.5	306.5
Current Transfers: Debit	78ak d	....	....	....	....	....	....	....	–2.9	–2.9	–12.2	–43.4	–68.1	–25.4	–28.3	–9.5
Capital Account, n.i.e.	78bc d	....	....	....	....	....	....	....	–.3	1.3	9.9	–3.2	8.3	.6	–.3	—
Capital Account, n.i.e.: Credit	78ba d	....	....	....	....	....	....	....	.3	1.3	9.9	6.6	14.7	1.2	—	—
Capital Account: Debit	78bb d	....	....	....	....	....	....	....	–.6	—	—	–9.8	–6.3	–.6	–.3	—
Financial Account, n.i.e.	78bj d	....	....	....	....	....	....	....	–63.2	–7.7	175.4	–263.7	228.8	34.0	–148.8	–153.0
Direct Investment Abroad	78bd d	....	....	....	....	....	....	....	—	—	—	—	—	—	—	—
Dir. Invest. in Rep. Econ., n.i.e.	78be d	....	....	....	....	....	....	....	—	—	—	—	—	—	—	9.1
Portfolio Investment Assets	78bf d	....	....	....	....	....	....	....	—	—	—	—	—	—	—	—
Equity Securities	78bk d	....	....	....	....	....	....	....	—	—	—	—	—	—	—	—
Debt Securities	78bl d	....	....	....	....	....	....	....	—	—	—	—	—	—	—	—
Portfolio Investment Liab., n.i.e.	78bg d	....	....	....	....	....	....	....	—	—	—	—	—	—	—	—
Equity Securities	78bm d	....	....	....	....	....	....	....	—	—	—	—	—	—	—	—
Debt Securities	78bn d	....	....	....	....	....	....	....	—	—	—	—	—	—	—	—
Financial Derivatives Assets	78bw d	....	....	....	....	....	....	....	....	....	....	....	....	....	....	....
Financial Derivatives Liabilities	78bx d	....	....	....	....	....	....	....	....	....	....	....	....	....	....	....
Other Investment Assets	78bh d	....	....	....	....	....	....	....	–104.8	–13.2	–26.1	–241.0	105.2	20.3	–120.2	–41.9
Monetary Authorities	78bo d	....	....	....	....	....	....	....								
General Government	78bp d	....	....	....	....	....	....	....								
Banks	78bq d	....	....	....	....	....	....	....	–104.8	–13.2	–26.1	–241.0	105.2	20.3	–120.2	–41.9
Other Sectors	78br d	....	....	....	....	....	....	....	—	—	—	—	—	—	—	—
Other Investment Liab., n.i.e.	78bi d	....	....	....	....	....	....	....	41.6	5.5	201.5	–22.7	123.6	13.7	–28.6	–120.2
Monetary Authorities	78bs d	....	....	....	....	....	....	....	14.6	–3.4	15.2	25.0	23.2	–17.9	–15.2	–52.6
General Government	78bt d	....	....	....	....	....	....	....	–64.6	28.3	237.1	–83.7	85.4	57.5	–8.5	–73.3
Banks	78bu d	....	....	....	....	....	....	....	79.8	–11.5	–35.3	70.8	15.0	–25.9	–4.8	5.7
Other Sectors	78bv d	....	....	....	....	....	....	....	11.8	–7.9	–15.6	–34.8	—			
Net Errors and Omissions	78ca d	....	....	....	....	....	....	....	–15.1	14.5	–35.0	58.0	14.7	12.6	145.5	–1.4
Overall Balance	78cb d	....	....	....	....	....	....	....	–168.2	–101.9	–107.3	–525.9	–396.4	–201.9	–222.8	–118.0
Reserves and Related Items	79da d	....	....	....	....	....	....	....	168.2	101.9	107.3	525.9	396.4	201.9	222.8	118.0
Reserve Assets	79db d	....	....	....	....	....	....	....	–3.2	–7.8	–55.4	35.4	–199.2	–136.5	34.4	–.6
Use of Fund Credit and Loans	79dc d	....	....	....	....	....	....	....	–22.9	64.5	93.1	147.5	172.3	45.6	152.7	11.4
Exceptional Financing	79de d	....	....	....	....	....	....	....	194.3	45.2	69.6	342.9	423.2	292.8	35.7	107.1
Government Finance									*Millions of Dinars through 1991; Billions of Dinars beginning 1992:*							
Deficit (-) or Surplus	80	....	....	⌐–.6	–1.6	–1.0	–7.5	–5.9	–16.8	–15.2	–13.6	–13.0	....	–32.6	....	....
Revenue	81	....	....	⌐15.0	15.4	18.9	25.4	29.8	32.7	40.4	54.7	55.9	....	84.0	....	....
Grants Received	81z	....	....	⌐.6	.3	.4	.5	.1	2.4	—		10.7	....	19.4	....	....
Expenditure	82	....	....	⌐15.9	17.2	19.7	33.4	35.8	51.7	55.4	68.3	78.0	....	119.8	....	....
Lending Minus Repayments	83	....	....	⌐.3	.1	.6	—	—	.3	.1	.1	1.6	....	16.2	....	....
Financing																
Domestic	84a	....	....	⌐–.3	.3	–1.4	3.4	–4.7	12.7	17.2	12.7	1.8	....	19.8	....	....
Foreign	85a	....	....	⌐.9	1.3	2.4	4.1	10.6	4.1	–2.0	.9	11.2	....	12.9	....	....
Debt: Domestic	88a	....	....	⌐8.9	9.1	12.6	....	....	....	....	....	....	....	....	....	....
Foreign	89a	....	....	⌐10.1	11.4	13.8	....	....	....	....	....	....	....	....	....	....
National Accounts									*Millions of Dinars through 1991; Billions of Dinars beginning 1992:*							
Gross Domestic Product (GDP)	99b	76.1	83.2	89.7	124.6	151.1	184.8	234.0	288.3	325.4	397.2	495.1	639.8	672.0	917.8	1,131.1
																Millions:
Population	99z	14.09	14.44	14.81	14.96	15.34	15.73	16.13	16.95	17.56	18.11	18.68	19.28	19.90	20.53	21.43

	1985	1986	1987	1988	1989	1990	1991	1992	1993	1994	1995	1996	1997	1998	1999	International Transactions	
Year Ending December 31 Thereafter																	
Exports	373.9	333.3	503.9	509.1	671.8	374.1	305.0	319.3	417.3	502.6	Ɪ 555.6	620.3	594.2	595.8	....	Exports	70..*d*
Imports, c.i.f.	770.7	960.9	871.0	1,060.5	....	618.5	890.3	820.9	944.9	1,227.4	Ɪ 1,218.8	1,547.5	1,579.6	1,914.7	....	Imports, c.i.f.	71..*d*
																Balance of Payments	
Minus Sign Indicates Debit																	
	148.9	−26.3	−232.4	−358.0	−150.3	−372.2	−954.7	−506.2	−202.2	−601.7	−499.9	−826.8	−828.1	−956.5	−465.2	Current Account, n.i.e.	78al *d*
	444.2	326.8	265.0	427.0	544.4	326.5	302.5	213.4	306.3	523.9	555.7	620.3	594.2	595.7	780.1	Goods: Exports f.o.b.	78aa *d*
	−579.0	−633.7	−694.8	−948.5	−1,051.0	−648.8	−1,138.2	−810.2	−532.8	−1,045.4	−1,066.0	−1,339.5	−1,421.9	−1,732.2	−1,256.0	Goods: Imports f.o.b.	78ab *d*
	−134.8	−306.9	−429.7	−521.5	−506.6	−322.3	−835.7	−596.8	−226.5	−521.5	−510.3	−719.2	−827.7	−1,136.5	−475.9	*Trade Balance*	78ac *d*
	374.2	220.5	184.7	161.7	272.6	172.5	77.0	155.5	69.4	76.2	125.3	50.7	31.5	15.8	81.6	Services: Credit	78ad *d*
	−346.4	−188.0	−228.6	−244.6	−378.2	−228.0	−197.3	−204.1	−109.8	−223.7	−172.3	−200.8	−172.8	−204.0	−275.3	Services: Debit	78ae *d*
	−107.0	−274.4	−473.7	−604.4	−612.2	−377.8	−956.0	−645.4	−266.9	−669.0	−557.3	−869.3	−969.0	−1,324.7	−669.6	*Balance on Goods & Services*	78af *d*
	12.1	8.3	7.5	9.9	7.0	12.4	2.7	—	.7	1.6	1.9	6.3	16.9	13.7	19.1	Income: Credit	78ag *d*
	−113.5	−93.6	−94.4	−96.7	−117.5	−148.0	−129.1	−93.5	−20.9	−15.9	−4.9	−.7	−5.3	−10.6	−123.2	Income: Debit	78ah *d*
	−208.3	−359.8	−560.6	−691.2	−722.6	−513.4	−1,082.4	−738.9	−287.1	−683.3	−560.3	−863.7	−957.4	−1,321.6	−773.7	*Balance on Gds, Serv. & Inc.*	78ai *d*
	369.5	357.6	332.4	334.4	576.7	143.3	127.9	232.7	84.9	120.1	346.2	236.3	439.1	731.8	702.2	Current Transfers, n.i.e.: Credit	78aj *d*
	−12.2	−24.1	−4.1	−1.1	−4.4	−2.1	−.2	—	....	−38.5	−285.8	−199.4	−309.8	−366.7	−393.7	Current Transfers: Debit	78ak *d*
	—	—	—	—	—	—	—	—	....	....	....	....	....	−54.2	−22.9	Capital Account, n.i.e.	78bc *d*
	—	—	—	—	—	—	—	—	....	....	....	....	....	13.0	45.8	Capital Account, n.i.e.: Credit	78ba *d*
	—	—	—	—	—	—	—	—	....	....	....	....	....	−67.2	−68.7	Capital Account: Debit	78bb *d*
	−443.9	−86.2	85.8	67.5	117.8	116.9	584.1	316.4	326.6	276.0	473.7	136.8	195.0	333.4	435.3	Financial Account, n.i.e.	78bj *d*
									....	....	....	....	....			Direct Investment Abroad	78bd *d*
	−3.0	—	—	—	3.5	—	—	—	....	....	—	.4	97.9	370.7	370.8	Dir. Invest. in Rep. Econ., n.i.e.	78be *d*
	—	—	—	—	—	—	—	—	....	....	....	....	....	....	....	Portfolio Investment Assets	78bf *d*
	—	—	—	—	—	—	—	—	....	....	....	....	....	....	....	Equity Securities	78bk *d*
	—	—	—	—	—	—	—	—	....	....	....	....	....	....	....	Debt Securities	78bl *d*
	—	—	—	—	—	—	—	—	....	....	....	....	....	....	....	Portfolio Investment Liab., n.i.e.	78bg *d*
	—	—	—	—	—	—	—	—	....	....	....	....	....	....	....	Equity Securities	78bm *d*
	—	—	—	—	—	—	—	—	....	....	....	....	....	....	....	Debt Securities	78bn *d*
	....	....	....	....	....	....	....	....	....	....	....	....	....	....	....	Financial Derivatives Assets	78bw *d*
	....	....	....	....	....	....	....	....	....	....	....	....	....	....	....	Financial Derivatives Liabilities	78bx *d*
	−497.4	90.6	116.6	−65.3	−39.6	−28.5	−74.0	−82.8	....	....	....	....	....	−78.5	−38.4	Other Investment Assets	78bh *d*
	—	—	—	—	—	—	—	—	....	....	....	....	....			Monetary Authorities	78bo *d*
	−134.7	−33.4	179.8	80.5	—	—	—	—	....	....	....	....	....			General Government	78bp *d*
	−362.6	124.0	−63.1	−145.8	−39.6	−28.5	−74.0	−82.8	....	....	....	....	....	−78.5	−38.4	Banks	78bq *d*
	—	—	—	—	—	—	—	—	....	....	....	....	....			Other Sectors	78br *d*
	56.5	−176.8	−30.8	132.8	153.9	145.4	658.1	399.2	326.6	276.0	473.7	136.4	97.1	41.2	102.9	Other Investment Liab., n.i.e.	78bi *d*
	16.5	−16.4	169.4	75.9	44.8	30.6	155.6	110.4	163.3	28.3	73.6	62.4	20.1	8.0	−3.7	Monetary Authorities	78bs *d*
	−108.0	−109.6	−235.7	63.1	111.4	102.7	486.3	268.5	200.8	−3.1	9.8	−22.5	−45.1	−1.0	—	General Government	78bt *d*
	147.5	−49.6	35.5	−6.3	−2.3	12.1	16.1	20.3	−37.5	250.8	390.3	96.2	119.3	34.2	106.6	Banks	78bu *d*
	.4	−1.2	—	—	—	—	—	—	....	....	—	.3	2.8			Other Sectors	78bv *d*
	−126.0	−88.5	−196.5	3.1	−160.3	10.9	97.9	31.0	−82.6	344.8	89.3	727.5	651.2	750.5	167.6	Net Errors and Omissions	78ca *d*
	−420.9	−201.0	−343.0	−287.4	−192.8	−244.4	−272.8	−158.8	41.8	19.1	63.1	37.5	18.1	73.2	114.8	*Overall Balance*	78cb *d*
	420.9	201.0	343.0	287.4	192.8	244.4	272.8	158.8	−41.8	−19.1	−63.1	−37.5	−18.1	−73.2	−114.8	Reserves and Related Items	79da *d*
	5.0	−46.3	46.8	−.4	−3.8	4.5	3.8	29.3	−41.8	−19.1	−23.6	−2.0	24.0	−16.0	−110.0	Reserve Assets	79db *d*
	−4.9	—	—	—	—	—	−1.4	—	—	—	−39.5	−35.5	−42.1	−57.2	−37.8	Use of Fund Credit and Loans	79dc *d*
	420.8	247.3	296.2	287.8	196.6	241.3	269.0	129.5	—	—	—	—	—		33.0	Exceptional Financing	79de *d*
Year Ending June 30 through 1994; December 31 Thereafter																**Government Finance**	
	....	....	....	....	....	Ɪ−16000.0	Ɪ−48.0	−68.0	−93.0	Ɪ−13.5	−34.6	−13.4	....	....		Deficit (-) or Surplus	80
	....	....	....	....	....	Ɪ15000.0	Ɪ35.0	78.0	131.0	Ɪ36.5	62.9	107.3	....	....		Revenue	81
	....	....	....	....	....	Ɪ—	Ɪ—	—	—	Ɪ—	—	—	....	....		Grants Received	81z
	....	....	....	....	....	Ɪ31000.0	Ɪ83.0	146.0	224.0	Ɪ50.0	97.5	120.7	....	....		Expenditure	82
	....	....	....	....	....	Ɪ—	Ɪ—	—	—	Ɪ—	—	—	....	....		Lending Minus Repayments	83
																Financing	
	....	....	....	....	....	Ɪ9,000.0	Ɪ34.0	38.0	72.0	Ɪ9.3	32.4	10.8	....	....		Domestic	84a
	....	....	....	....	....	Ɪ7,000.0	Ɪ14.0	30.0	21.0	Ɪ4.2	2.2	2.6	....	....		Foreign	85a
	....	....	....	....	....	....	....	....	....	....	....	....	....	....		Debt: Domestic	88a
	....	....	....	....	....	....	....	....	....	....	....	....	....	....		Foreign	89a
Year Ending June 30 through 1994; December 31 Thereafter																**National Accounts**	
	1,391.3	2,014.1	3,647.1	4,679.1	8,256.2	11,011.1	19,029.3	Ɪ40.8	83.5	168.0	Ɪ483.2	1,021.7	1,601.2	....	....	Gross Domestic Product (GDP)	99b
Midyear Estimates																	
	22.11	22.80	23.52	24.24	24.99	25.75	26.53	27.32	28.13	28.95	Ɪ26.62	27.16	27.72	28.29	28.88	**Population**	99z

(See notes in the back of the book.)

Suriname

		1970	1971	1972	1973	1974	1975	1976	1977	1978	1979	1980	1981	1982	1983	1984
Exchange Rates														*Guilders per SDR:*		
Market Rate	aa	1.88	1.94	1.94	2.15	2.19	2.09	2.07	2.17	2.33	2.35	2.28	2.08	1.97	1.87	1.75
														Guilders per US Dollar:		
Market Rate	ae	1.88	1.78	1.78	1.78	1.78	1.78	1.78	1.78	1.78	1.78	1.78	1.78	1.78	1.78	1.78
Market Rate	rf	1.89	1.88	1.78	1.78	1.78	1.78	1.78	1.78	1.78	1.78	1.78	1.78	1.78	1.78	1.78
Fund Position														*Millions of SDRs:*		
Quota	2f. s	....	....	....	....	....	....	....	....	25.00	25.00	37.50	37.50	37.50	49.30	49.30
SDRs	1b. s	....	....	....	....	....	....	....	....	—	2.60	2.07	5.40	8.48	1.74	1.28
Reserve Position in the Fund	1c. s	....	....	....	....	....	....	....	....	4.75	4.75	7.87	7.87	7.88	2.95	—
Total Fund Cred.&Loans Outstg.	2tl	....	....	....	....	....	....	....	....							
International Liquidity											*Millions of US Dollars Unless Otherwise Indicated:*					
Total Reserves minus Gold	1l. d	27.83	33.09	37.59	56.44	67.55	91.41	110.22	94.03	132.42	169.53	189.25	207.09	175.76	59.15	24.87
SDRs	1b. d	....	....	....	....	....	....	....	....		3.43	2.64	6.29	9.35	1.82	1.25
Reserve Position in the Fund	1c. d									6.19	6.26	10.04	9.16	8.69	3.09	
Foreign Exchange	1d. d	27.83	33.09	37.59	56.44	67.55	91.41	110.22	94.03	126.24	159.84	176.57	191.64	157.71	54.24	23.62
Gold (Million Fine Troy Ounces)	1ad	.248	.248	.248	.148	.148	.148	.148	.148	.054	.054	.054	.054	.054	.054	.054
Gold (National Valuation)	1an d	8.57	9.83	9.29e	....	6.16	6.16	6.16	6.16	2.26	2.26	2.26	2.26	2.26	19.60	14.89
Monetary Authorities: Other Liab.	4. d	.13	.02	.01	.03	.08	.07	.11	.05	4.24	5.60	.22	.23	.22	.22	.32
Deposit Money Banks: Assets	7a. d	12.69	10.10	13.50	15.54	10.04	22.08	28.55	28.90	41.65	37.36	51.94	52.25	49.12	31.03	16.81
Liabilities	7b. d	5.58	7.54	6.32	6.80	6.83	7.99	13.15	13.47	16.07	18.89	22.78	25.67	27.96	21.85	28.04
Monetary Authorities														*Millions of Guilders:*		
Foreign Assets	11	69	75	79	111	131	173	206	177	237	304	339	371	315	140	71
Claims on Central Government	12a	6	6	8	13	23	53	124	187	62	55	37	81	182	461	717
Claims on Private Sector	12d	1		1	1	1	1	1	1	1	—	—	—	—	—	—
Claims on Deposit Money Banks	12e	—	—	—	—	—	—	—	—	—	—	—	—	—	—	—
Reserve Money	14	61	67	70	99	99	124	159	197	199	241	242	298	327	423	627
of which: Currency Outside DMBs	14a	49	53	58	73	79	89	110	125	145	156	178	197	268	265	305
Time & Fgn. Currency Deposits	15	—	—	—	—	—	—	—	—	—	—	—	—	—	—	—
Foreign Liabilities	16c	—	—	—	—	—	—	—	—	8	10	—	—	—	—	1
Central Government Deposits	16d	5	6	10	—	19	52	117	116	19	25	29	24	32	25	16
Capital Accounts	17a	8	8	7	7	7	15	22	22	22	28	39	48	50	49	48
Other Items (Net)	17r	3	—	3	18	30	35	33	29	54	56	67	82	88	104	96
Deposit Money Banks														*Millions of Guilders:*		
Reserves	20	11	13	11	24	19	33	49	70	52	80	53	79	54	153	316
Foreign Assets	21	24	17	24	28	18	39	51	52	74	67	93	93	88	55	30
Claims on Central Government	22a	2	6	5	13	15	15	24	18	18	18	17	28	30	73	110
Claims on Private Sector	22d	91	105	118	121	149	157	230	284	360	421	460	546	615	620	627
Demand Deposits	24	37	44	44	58	60	78	88	92	99	112	106	139	148	185	267
Quasi-Monetary Liabilities	25	59	67	83	96	105	122	199	252	302	339	365	430	455	516	591
Bonds	26ab	2	2	3	2	2	2	2	2	7	7	7	7	7	7	7
Foreign Liabilities	26c	6	7	4	6	5	7	15	18	22	27	34	39	43	32	43
Long-Term Foreign Liabilities	26cl	5	6	7	7	7	7	9	6	6	7	7	7	7	7	7
Central Government Deposits	26d	2	—	3	—	1	2	13	7	1	9	6	5	3	7	7
Credit from Monetary Authorities	26g	—	—	—	—	—	—	—	—	—	—	—	—	—	—	—
Capital Accounts	27a	13	13	14	16	18	24	29	44	56	66	75	84	96	103	108
Other Items (Net)	27r	4	1	–1	2	3	3	–1	2	11	19	24	34	27	43	54
Monetary Survey														*Millions of Guilders:*		
Foreign Assets (Net)	31n	87	86	99	133	144	205	242	211	282	334	398	424	360	163	57
Domestic Credit	32	93	111	120	147	168	172	249	366	421	461	480	626	792	1,121	1,431
Claims on Central Govt. (Net)	32an	1	6	1	25	19	14	18	82	61	40	20	79	176	501	804
Claims on Private Sector	32d	92	106	119	122	150	157	230	284	361	421	461	546	615	620	627
Money	34	86	98	103	133	140	169	198	220	246	273	294	358	421	455	577
Quasi-Money	35	59	67	83	96	105	122	199	252	302	339	365	430	455	516	591
Bonds	36ab	2	2	3	2	2	2	2	2	7	7	7	7	7	7	7
Long-Term Foreign Liabilities	36cl	5	6	7	7	7	7	9	6	6	7	7	7	7	7	7
Capital Accounts	37a	20	21	21	23	25	38	51	66	78	95	114	132	146	152	156
Other Items (Net)	37r	7	2	2	20	32	38	31	31	64	75	91	116	116	146	150
Money plus Quasi-Money	35l	145	165	187	229	245	291	397	472	548	612	660	788	876	971	1,169
Interest Rates														*Percent per Annum*		
Money Market Rate	60b	....	....	....	....	....	....	....	....	....	....	....	....	....	....	....
Deposit Rate	60l	....	....	....	....	....	....	....	....	....	....	....	....	....	....	....
Lending Rate	60p	....	....	....	....	....	....	....	....	....	....	....	....	....	....	....
Prices and Labor														*Index Numbers (1995=100):*		
Consumer Prices	64	.2	.2	.2	.2	.2	.2	.3	.3	.3	.4	I.4	.5	.5	.5	.5
														Number in Thousands:		
Labor Force	67d	....	....	....	....	....	....	....	....	....	....	....	....	....	....	....
Employment	67e	....	....	....	....	....	....	....	....	....	....	....	....	....	....	....
Unemployment	67c	....	....	....	....	....	....	....	....	....	....	....	....	....	....	....
Unemployment Rate (%)	67r	....	....	....	....	....	....	....	....	....	....	....	....	....	....	....
International Transactions														*Millions of Guilders*		
Exports	70	272.0	296.0	306.0	320.0	481.0	495.0	492.0	553.0	658.0	I793.0	918.0	846.0	765.0	655.0	635.0
Imports, c.i.f.	71	217.7	237.8	258.2	280.1	410.5	449.8	525.1	709.9	724.5	I733.5	900.3	1,013.6	912.8	808.5	617.3

	1985	1986	1987	1988	1989	1990	1991	1992	1993	1994	1995	1996	1997	1998	1999		
End of Period																**Exchange Rates**	
Market Rate	1.96	2.18	2.53	2.40	2.35	2.54	2.55	2.45	2.45	†597.81	605.00	576.62	541.05	564.62	1,355.35		**aa**
End of Period (ae) Period Average (rf)																	
Market Rate	1.78	1.78	1.78	1.78	1.78	1.78	1.78	1.78	1.78	†409.50	407.00	401.00	401.00	401.00	987.50		**ae**
Market Rate	1.78	1.78	1.78	1.78	1.78	1.78	1.78	1.78	1.78	134.12	442.23	401.26	401.00	401.00	....		**rf**
End of Period																**Fund Position**	
Quota	49.30	49.30	49.30	49.30	49.30	49.30	49.30	49.30	67.60	67.60	67.60	67.60	67.60	67.60	92.10		**2f. s**
SDRs	.76	.28	—	—	—	—	—	—	—	—	7.75	8.22	8.23	8.25	2.00		**1b. s**
Reserve Position in the Fund	—	—	—	—	—	—	—	—	—	—	—	—	—	—	6.13		**1c. s**
Total Fund Cred.&Loans Outstg.	—	—	—	—	—	—	—	—	—	—	—	—	—	—	—		**2tl**
End of Period																**International Liquidity**	
Total Reserves minus Gold	23.42	20.89	15.10	12.56	9.25	21.07	1.10	17.30	17.70	39.70	132.92	96.32	109.11	106.14	....		**1l. d**
SDRs	.83	.34	—	—	—	—	—	—	—	—	11.52	11.82	11.11	11.62	2.75		**1b. d**
Reserve Position in the Fund															8.41		**1c. d**
Foreign Exchange	22.59	20.55	15.10	12.56	9.25	21.07	1.10	17.30	17.70	39.70	121.40	84.50	98.00	94.52	....		**1d. d**
Gold (Million Fine Troy Ounces)	.054	.054	.054	.054	.054	.054	.054	.054	.054	.054	.093	.134	.193	.128			**1ad**
Gold (National Valuation)	15.83	18.75	23.84	20.44	19.79	18.66	17.71	16.21	841.67	14.32	41.34	58.18	54.53	59.25	73.59		**1and**
Monetary Authorities: Other Liab.	.40	13.05	14.55	33.07	39.79	36.13	55.47	46.80	1,316.25	18.08	3.25	3.03	74.80	93.28	107.38		**4.. d**
Deposit Money Banks: Assets	11.52	5.20	11.59	9.89	17.55	21.98	21.63	20.20	1,093.54	49.67	68.84	116.40	128.94	122.43	180.59		**7a. d**
Liabilities	31.70	49.41	57.28	61.50	69.19	82.39	90.01	93.38	379.49	28.67	45.76	75.15	86.06	96.35	160.55		**7b. d**
End of Period																**Monetary Authorities**	
Foreign Assets	70	72	69	59	52	71	45	65	3,277	23,546	65,538	56,984	60,615	64,237	126,179		**11**
Claims on Central Government	1,062	1,494	1,998	2,479	2,853	2,627	3,261	3,512	5,224	5,307	4,909	6,768	6,376	17,015	27,953		**12a**
Claims on Private Sector	—	—	15	15	15	15	1	2	9	31	69	246	387	724			**12d**
Claims on Deposit Money Banks	—	19	2	3	2	—	—	2	4	13	—	26	13,414	15,726	34,190		**12e**
Reserve Money	957	1,303	1,564	1,903	2,195	2,322	2,946	3,317	5,640	17,361	56,775	50,953	50,738	83,725	119,548		**14**
of which: Currency Outside DMBs	405	451	638	788	874	958	1,143	1,347	2,638	10,486	25,199	27,404	32,255	50,702	81,853		**14a**
Time & Fgn. Currency Deposits	—	30	249	363	432	120	63	2	—								**15**
Foreign Liabilities	1	23	26	59	71	64	99	84	2,349	7,403	1,321	1,214	29,996	37,404	106,036		**16c**
Central Government Deposits	22	14	14	11	12	13	13	15	29	844	9,900	9,076	3,021	3,161	8,138		**16d**
Capital Accounts	50	51	54	53	53	54	54	54		4,668	4,723	4,589	4,420	5,938	12,094		**17a**
Other Items (Net)	103	165	162	167	161	139	146	108	434	-1,401	-2,240	-1,985	-7,526	-32,862	-56,770		**17r**
End of Period																**Deposit Money Banks**	
Reserves	544	828	912	1,098	1,299	1,339	1,768	1,914	2,873	6,242	29,584	19,142	18,531	31,462	32,392		**20**
Foreign Assets	21	9	21	18	31	39	39	36	1,952	20,341	28,016	46,675	51,705	49,095	178,333		**21**
Claims on Central Government	124	142	123	129	140	207	225	225	266	392	567	913	8,639	20,814	23,659		**22a**
Claims on Private Sector	690	728	773	924	1,145	1,454	1,809	2,464	3,133	6,645	20,120	45,486	63,382	79,103	106,638		**22d**
Demand Deposits	467	754	910	1,140	1,269	1,268	1,708	1,818	3,276	9,763	30,912	25,156	35,476	39,929	51,357		**24**
Quasi-Monetary Liabilities	664	676	665	753	1,021	1,401	1,712	2,344	3,179	7,218	20,995	52,609	61,973	87,578	108,132		**25**
Bonds	7	5	5	5	5	5	6	23	104	153	357	256	226	28	30		**26ab**
Foreign Liabilities	50	81	95	103	117	140	153	159	669	11,721	18,603	30,113	34,486	38,612	158,517		**26c**
Long-Term Foreign Liabilities	7	7	7	7	7	7	7	8	9	18	20	22	24	24	24		**26cl**
Central Government Deposits	13	15	11	9	23	23	40	25	103	956	1,273	371	885	167	542		**26d**
Credit from Monetary Authorities	—	19	2	3	2	—	—	2	4	13	—	26	14,197	15,726	34,190		**26g**
Capital Accounts	125	134	137	156	176	245	296	369	602	2,834	5,242	8,710	11,656	12,492	20,909		**27a**
Other Items (Net)	45	16	-2	-8	-4	-51	-81	-108	279	945	885	-5,048	-16,667	-14,082	-32,678		**27r**
End of Period																**Monetary Survey**	
Foreign Assets (Net)	40	-23	-32	-85	-105	-94	-168	-141	2,210	24,763	73,630	72,332	47,838	37,316	39,960		**31n**
Domestic Credit	1,840	2,335	2,868	3,526	4,120	4,266	5,259	6,162	8,493	10,554	14,456	43,789	74,736	113,991	150,294		**32**
Claims on Central Govt. (Net)	1,150	1,608	2,095	2,587	2,959	2,797	3,434	3,696	5,358	3,900	-5,696	-1,767	11,109	34,501	42,932		**32an**
Claims on Private Sector	690	728	773	939	1,161	1,469	1,825	2,465	3,135	6,654	20,152	45,556	63,627	79,490	107,362		**32d**
Money	880	1,229	1,562	1,945	2,165	2,251	2,886	3,221	6,043	20,883	58,103	56,967	68,467	92,191	138,512		**34**
Quasi-Money	664	705	913	1,115	1,453	1,521	1,776	2,346	3,179	7,218	20,995	52,609	61,973	87,578	108,132		**35**
Bonds	7	5	5	5	5	5	6	23	104	153	357	256	226	28	30		**36ab**
Long-Term Foreign Liabilities	7	7	7	7	7	7	7	8	9	18	20	22	24	24	24		**36cl**
Capital Accounts	174	185	191	209	229	300	350	423	656	7,501	9,966	13,299	16,076	18,429	33,003		**37a**
Other Items (Net)	148	181	159	159	157	88	65	—	712	-456	-1,355	-7,033	-24,193	-46,944	-89,448		**37r**
Money plus Quasi-Money	1,544	1,934	2,475	3,060	3,618	3,772	4,662	5,567	9,222	28,101	79,098	109,576	130,440	179,770	246,644		**35l**
Percent per Annum																**Interest Rates**	
Money Market Rate	....	....	....	....	....	....	....	....	....	....	....	....	....	....	....		**60b**
Deposit Rate	....	....	....	....	....	4.6	4.5	4.8	7.5	21.0	17.8	....	18.0	16.3			**60l**
Lending Rate	....	....	....	....	....	8.9	8.9	9.4	15.4	40.2	35.8	....	29.0	27.8			**60p**
Period Averages																**Prices and Labor**	
Consumer Prices	.6	.7	1.1	1.2	1.2	1.4	1.8	2.6	6.4	29.8	100.0	99.3	106.4	126.6	251.8		**64**
Period Averages																	
Labor Force	....	....	....	....	....	97	....	107	92	90	90	....	....	....	....		**67d**
Employment	....	....	....	....	....	82	....	89	83	78	82	87	....	....	....		**67e**
Unemployment	....	15	19	20	15	15	....	18	14	11	8	11	....	....	....		**67c**
Unemployment Rate (%)	....	....	....	....	....	15.8	....	17.2	14.7	12.7	8.4	11.0	....	....	....		**67r**
Millions of Guilders																**International Transactions**	
Exports	587.0	598.0	546.0	731.0	967.0	843.0	641.0	698.0	2,124.0	60,182.0	211,021.0	173,806.0	281,197.0	174,868.0	....		**70**
Imports, c.i.f.	532.9	584.4	525.4	626.4	790.6	842.5	909.0	966.6	1,760.3	56,745.9	258,916.7	200,951.0	263,902.1	221,388.1	....		**71**

Suriname

	1970	1971	1972	1973	1974	1975	1976	1977	1978	1979	1980	1981	1982	1983	1984
Balance of Payments														*Millions of US Dollars:*	
Current Account, n.i.e. 78ald	....	....	....	....	....	....	....	-2.7	51.7	78.6	31.5	-48.5	-97.6	-282.3	-137.6
Goods: Exports f.o.b. 78aad	....	....	....	....	....	....	....	617.9	733.9	792.7	918.2	845.7	765.1	654.7	667.8
Goods: Imports f.o.b. 78abd	....	....	....	....	....	....	....	-578.5	-613.2	-660.2	-810.4	-904.0	-821.7	-716.9	-699.0
Trade Balance 78acd	....	....	....	....	....	....	....	39.4	120.7	132.5	107.8	-58.3	-56.6	-62.2	-31.2
Services: Credit 78add	....	....	....	....	....	....	....	89.6	111.2	124.0	176.0	164.1	144.4	120.8	98.6
Services: Debit 78aed	....	....	....	....	....	....	....	-205.6	-222.5	-254.8	-364.1	-351.8	-369.1	-316.0	-201.8
Balance on Goods & Services 78afd	....	....	....	....	....	....	....	-76.6	9.4	1.7	-80.3	-246.0	-281.3	-257.4	-134.4
Income: Credit 78agd	....	....	....	....	....	....	....	12.9	14.9	25.2	45.7	64.7	63.9	29.5	8.9
Income: Debit 78ahd	....	....	....	....	....	....	....	-84.6	-81.2	-105.5	-81.1	-43.9	-51.8	-49.4	-6.4
Balance on Gds, Serv. & Inc. 78aid	....	....	....	....	....	....	....	-148.3	-56.9	-78.6	-115.7	-225.2	-269.2	-277.3	-131.9
Current Transfers, n.i.e.: Credit 78ajd	....	....	....	....	....	....	....	155.6	118.5	168.9	162.5	192.0	190.2	17.4	10.5
Current Transfers: Debit 78akd	....	....	....	....	....	....	....	-10.0	-9.9	-11.7	-15.3	-15.3	-18.6	-22.4	-16.2
Capital Account, n.i.e. 78bcd	....	....	....	....	....	....	....	-3.4	-2.6	-.6	-3.9	-1.1	-3.4	-4.8	-2.9
Capital Account, n.i.e.: Credit 78bad	....	....	....	....	....	....	....	2.0	3.4	3.5	3.4	3.8	3.3	4.6	5.7
Capital Account: Debit 78bbd	....	....	....	....	....	....	....	-5.4	-6.0	-4.1	-7.3	-4.9	-6.7	-9.4	-8.6
Financial Account, n.i.e. 78bjd	....	....	....	....	....	....	....	-26.1	24.5	-30.0	17.4	50.9	22.4	88.8	-18.6
Direct Investment Abroad 78bdd	....	....	....	....	....	....	....	....	....	....	....	—	—	—	—
Dir. Invest. in Rep. Econ., n.i.e. 78bed	....	....	....	....	....	....	....	-22.6	-13.5	-27.4	18.1	61.7	-11.1	81.5	-70.9
Portfolio Investment Assets 78bfd	....	....	....	....	....	....	....	—	—	—	—	-1.0	-1.4	—	—
Equity Securities 78bkd	....	....	....	....	....	....	....					-1.0	-1.4		
Debt Securities 78bld	....	....	....	....	....	....	....	—	—	—	—	—	—	—	—
Portfolio Investment Liab., n.i.e. 78bgd	....	....	....	....	....	....	....	-.2	-.5	—	—	-.6	-.7	—	—
Equity Securities 78bmd	....	....	....	....	....	....	....	-.3	.3	—	—	-.6	-.7	—	—
Debt Securities 78bnd	....	....	....	....	....	....	....	.1	-.8	—	—	—	—	—	—
Financial Derivatives Assets 78bwd	....	....	....	....	....	....	....	....	....	....	....	....	....	....	....
Financial Derivatives Liabilities 78bxd	....	....	....	....	....	....	....	....	....	....	....	....	....	....	....
Other Investment Assets 78bhd	....	....	....	....	....	....	....	-1.4	-8.5	—	-16.9	-26.5	-13.2	33.6	-.9
Monetary Authorities 78bod	....	....	....	....	....	....	....	....	....	....	....	....	....	....	....
General Government 78bpd	....	....	....	....	....	....	....	—	—	—	—	—	—	—	—
Banks 78bqd	....	....	....	....	....	....	....	-1.2	-8.1	3.0	-16.8	-26.9	-13.2	33.6	-.9
Other Sectors 78brd	....	....	....	....	....	....	....	-.2	-.4	-3.0	-.1	.4			
Other Investment Liab., n.i.e. 78bid	....	....	....	....	....	....	....	-1.9	47.0	-2.6	16.2	17.3	48.8	-26.3	53.2
Monetary Authorities 78bsd	....	....	....	....	....	....	....	-2.1	-.8	2.1	-1.2	4.7	2.6	1.3	-2.3
General Government 78btd	....	....	....	....	....	....	....	-2.3	37.6	-2.9	-2.9	-4.4	-2.2	-2.7	.7
Banks 78bud	....	....	....	....	....	....	....	1.2	3.7	-1.2	4.6	6.1	1.7	-7.7	5.3
Other Sectors 78bvd	....	....	....	....	....	....	....	1.3	6.5	-.6	15.7	10.9	46.7	-17.2	49.5
Net Errors and Omissions 78cad	....	....	....	....	....	....	....	.4	-4.1	-.3	1.3	21.4	-.4	13.3	68.2
Overall Balance 78cbd	....	....	....	....	....	....	....	-31.8	69.5	47.7	46.3	22.7	-79.0	-185.0	-90.9
Reserves and Related Items 79dad	....	....	....	....	....	....	....	31.8	-69.5	-47.7	-46.3	-22.7	79.0	185.0	90.9
Reserve Assets 79dbd	....	....	....	....	....	....	....	31.8	-69.5	-47.7	-46.3	-22.7	79.0	185.0	90.9
Use of Fund Credit and Loans 79dcd	....	....	....	....	....	....	....	—	—	—	—	—	—	—	—
Exceptional Financing 79ded	....	....	....	....	....	....	....	....	....	....	....	....	....	....	....
Government Finance														*Millions of Guilders:*	
Deficit (-) or Surplus 80	....	-2.05	-1.76	-19.12	-8.80	-2.15	-21.85	-63.10	-22.72	20.01	24.40	-56.53	-98.85	-309.59	-263.19
Revenue 81	....	146.72	158.10	166.14	186.59	297.37	286.38	335.46	413.02	418.24	477.82	488.26	516.64	486.78	515.38
Grants Received 81z	....	18.34	37.83	33.78	41.86	20.76	116.72	138.45	99.03	144.08	131.56	168.89	172.96	4.46	3.60
Expenditure 82	....	166.61	196.26	217.53	237.27	318.48	424.21	540.54	536.78	542.32	580.81	713.56	788.15	801.26	768.12
Lending Minus Repayments 83	....	.50	1.43	1.51	-.02	1.80	.74	-3.53	-2.01	-.01	4.17	.12	.30	-.43	14.05
Financing															
Domestic 84a	....	5.91	1.76	9.12	8.80	2.15	21.85	66.35	-15.86	-22.81	-20.30	56.29	98.33	310.10	263.31
Foreign 85a	....	-3.86	—	10.00	—	—	—	-3.25	38.58	2.80	-4.10	.24	.52	-.51	-.12
Debt: Domestic 88a	....	17.60	21.30	31.20	43.11	41.52	58.93	43.22	....	....	....	....	....	....	782.40
Foreign 89a	....	156.90	187.50	197.30	194.71	10.99	8.77	7.83	....	....	....	....	....	....	55.50
National Accounts														*Millions of Guilders*	
Exports of Goods & Services 90c	....	....	351	369	543	578	618	707	814	917	1,094	1,009	910	776	749
Government Consumption 91f	128	138	136	116	133	137	123	282	335	343	339	431	520	437	499
Gross Capital Formation 93	101	105	135	156	245	353	304	479	477	357	421	555	507	276	204
Private Consumption 96f	293	309	316	386	434	503	604	609	693	870	916	1,041	1,084	1,314	1,119
Imports of Goods & Services 98c	....	....	-317	-349	-536	-634	-620	-795	-848	-922	-1,179	-1,258	-1,191	-1,035	-843
Gross Domestic Product (GDP) 99b	550	600	619	680	820	930	1,030	1,283	1,471	1,565	1,590	1,778	1,830	1,767	1,728
Net Factor Inc/Pmts(-) Abroad 98.n	-75	-85	-84	-71	-45	-25	-67	-61	-55	-74	-30	23	13	-20	3
Gross National Income (GNI) 99a	475	514	535	609	774	905	963	1,221	1,416	1,492	1,559	1,801	1,843	1,747	1,731
Net National Income 99e	....	....	476	530	674	797	862	1,091	1,262	1,323	1,388	1,615	1,661	1,565	1,558
GDP Volume 1980 Prices 99b.p	....	....	....	1,332	1,367	1,231	1,342	1,479	1,560	1,468	1,342	1,437	1,377	1,323	1,298
GDP Volume (1990=100) 99bvp	....	....	....	94.7	97.2	87.5	95.4	105.1	110.9	104.3	95.4	102.2	97.9	94.0	92.3
GDP Deflator (1990=100) 99bip	....	....	....	23.7	27.8	35.1	35.6	40.3	43.8	49.5	55.0	57.4	61.7	62.0	61.8
														Millions:	
Population 99z	.37	.37	1.38	.38	.38	.36	.35	.36	.37	.37	.35	.36	.36	.37	.37

	1985	1986	1987	1988	1989	1990	1991	1992	1993	1994	1995	1996	1997	1998	1999	
Minus Sign Indicates Debit																**Balance of Payments**
	-18.3	-36.9	135.6	114.3	293.5	66.8	-133.4	25.4	44.0	58.6	72.9	....	....	....	....	Current Account, n.i.e. .... 78al *d*
	599.9	601.7	604.7	639.7	980.3	831.6	617.5	608.6	298.3	293.6	415.6	....	....	....	....	Goods: Exports f.o.b. .... 78aa *d*
	-552.5	-542.8	-489.6	-427.4	-590.6	-668.3	-619.5	-486.5	-213.9	-194.3	-292.6	....	....	....	....	Goods: Imports f.o.b. .... 78ab *d*
	47.4	58.9	115.1	212.3	389.7	163.3	-2.0	122.1	84.4	99.3	123.0					*Trade Balance* .... 78ac *d*
	79.0	45.8	144.4	40.5	42.3	37.0	39.8	40.4	46.5	72.6	103.7					Services: Credit .... 78ad *d*
	-141.4	-137.4	-121.3	-136.2	-161.9	-171.3	-174.4	-176.1	-101.6	-113.5	-161.5					Services: Debit .... 78ae *d*
	-15.0	-32.7	138.2	116.6	270.1	29.0	-136.6	-13.6	29.3	58.4	65.2					*Balance on Goods & Services* .... 78af *d*
	4.9	2.9	2.2	2.4	1.7	4.0	2.5	1.3	.2	.9	2.7					Income: Credit .... 78ag *d*
	-5.8	-8.3	-10.4	-17.5	-13.0	-19.2	-22.5	-14.6	-6.4	-4.7	-5.3					Income: Debit .... 78ah *d*
	-15.9	-38.1	130.0	101.5	258.8	13.8	-156.6	-26.9	23.1	54.6	62.6					*Balance on Gds, Serv. & Inc.* .... 78ai *d*
	7.4	9.2	11.9	20.2	43.0	63.4	36.5	67.7	26.7	6.2	12.6					Current Transfers, n.i.e.: Credit .... 78aj *d*
	-9.8	-8.0	-6.3	-7.4	-8.3	-10.4	-13.3	-15.4	-5.8	-2.2	-2.3					Current Transfers: Debit .... 78ak *d*
	-2.4	-3.0	-2.1	-2.7	-2.8	-5.0	-1.9	-5.7	.5	-.2	....					Capital Account, n.i.e. .... 78bc *d*
	3.5	1.6	2.0	2.7	2.0	.5	4.1	4.6	3.5	.2	....					Capital Account, n.i.e.: Credit .... 78ba *d*
	-5.9	-4.6	-4.1	-5.4	-4.8	-5.5	-6.0	-10.3	-3.0	-.4	....					Capital Account: Debit .... 78bb *d*
	25.9	1.9	-90.3	-117.6	-308.6	-26.7	57.9	-86.6	-73.1	-84.1	-30.2					Financial Account, n.i.e. .... 78bj *d*
																Direct Investment Abroad .... 78bd *d*
	21.3	-60.4	-129.6	-171.0	-299.7	-76.8	18.5	-54.3	-46.6	-30.2	-21.3					Dir. Invest. in Rep. Econ., n.i.e. .... 78be *d*
																Portfolio Investment Assets .... 78bf *d*
	—	—	—	—	—	—	—	—	—	—	—					Equity Securities .... 78bk *d*
	—	—	—	—	—	—	—	—	—	—	—					Debt Securities .... 78bl *d*
	-.4	-.3	-.1	—	—	.9	-4.1	2.6	—	—	....					Portfolio Investment Liab., n.i.e. ...... 78bg *d*
	-.4	-.2	-.1	—	—	—	—	—	—	—	....					Equity Securities .... 78bm *d*
	—	-.1	—	—	—	.9	-4.1	2.6	—	—	....					Debt Securities .... 78bn *d*
	....	....														Financial Derivatives Assets .... 78bw *d*
																Financial Derivatives Liabilities .... 78bx *d*
	3.4	3.2	1.3	-.9	-23.8	27.8	4.9	-.1	-4.4	-19.1	3.2					Other Investment Assets .... 78bh *d*
	....	....														Monetary Authorities .... 78bo *d*
																General Government .... 78bp *d*
	3.4	4.3	.2	—	1.7	.1	-.4	-6.6	-14.5	-31.3	-10.0					Banks .... 78bq *d*
	—	-1.1	1.1	-.9	-25.5	27.7	5.3	6.5	10.1	12.2	13.2					Other Sectors .... 78br *d*
	1.6	59.4	38.1	54.3	14.9	21.4	38.6	-34.8	-22.1	-34.8	-12.1					Other Investment Liab., n.i.e. .... 78bi *d*
	1.9	2.1	2.9	.7	.2	.1	.2	.6								Monetary Authorities .... 78bs *d*
	-1.2	.8	1.8	12.7	11.5	-3.3	9.0	10.6	2.0	2.1	4.2					General Government .... 78bt *d*
	4.2	16.4	5.4	37.1	19.7	9.2	.1	-41.8	-23.7	-29.6	-10.1					Banks .... 78bu *d*
	-3.3	40.1	28.0	3.8	-16.5	15.4	29.3	-4.2	-.4	-7.3	-6.2					Other Sectors .... 78bv *d*
	-19.9	-33.0	-59.7	-3.2	17.7	-16.8	-.9	45.4	41.3	60.0	53.9					Net Errors and Omissions .... 78ca *d*
	-14.7	-71.0	-16.5	-9.2	-.2	18.3	-78.3	-21.5	12.7	34.3	96.6					*Overall Balance* .... 78cb *d*
	14.7	71.0	16.5	9.2	.2	-18.3	78.3	21.5	-12.7	-34.3	-96.6					Reserves and Related Items .... 79da *d*
	14.7	71.0	16.5	9.2	.2	-18.3	78.3	21.5	-12.7	-34.3	-96.6					Reserve Assets .... 79db *d*
																Use of Fund Credit and Loans........... 79dc *d*
																Exceptional Financing .... 79de *d*
Year Ending December 31																**Government Finance**
	-349.18	-445.74	....	....	....	....	....	....	....	....	....	....	....	....	....	Deficit (-) or Surplus 80
	490.38	494.88	....	....	....	....	....	....	....							Revenue 81
	1.40	2.78	....													Grants Received........... 81z
	803.35	925.69	....													Expenditure 82
	37.61	17.71	....													Lending Minus Repayments 83
																Financing
	349.18	421.59	....													Domestic 84a
	—	24.15	....													Foreign 85a
	1,137.08	1,582.01	....													Debt: Domestic 88a
	38.37	124.24	....													Foreign 89a
Millions of Guilders																**National Accounts**
	642	581	609	681	1,023	869	657	649	14,960	....						Exports of Goods & Services 90c
	589	656	737	848	815	777	1,085	1,239	1,752	....						Government Consumption........... 91f
	252	391	509	387	565	660	829	1,164	2,627	....						Gross Capital Formation 93
	961	737	608	972	1,065	1,624	1,982	2,619	2,769	....						Private Consumption 96f
	-697	-583	-502	-566	-755	-844	-794	-668	-11,619	....						Imports of Goods & Services 98c
	1,747	1,782	1,960	2,322	2,690	3,030	3,620	5,020	11,120	64,890	191,960	231,390	266,530	328,080	....	Gross Domestic Product (GDP) 99b
	-1	-5	-8	-15	-11	-15	-20	-13	-254	....						Net Factor Inc/Pmts(-) Abroad 98.n
	1,746	1,777	1,952	2,307	2,702	3,070	3,739	4,990	10,135	....						Gross National Income (GNI) 99a
	1,551	1,585	1,716	2,063	2,414	2,730	3,272	4,354	8,714	....						Net National Income 99e
	1,324	1,334	1,251	1,349	1,406	1,407	1,456	1,540	1,471	1,459	....					GDP Volume 1980 Prices 99b.*p*
	94.1	94.8	88.9	95.9	100.0	100.0	103.5	109.5	104.5	103.7	....					GDP Volume (1990=100) .... 99bv *p*
	61.2	62.0	72.7	79.9	88.8	100.0	115.4	151.3	351.0	2,065.0	....					GDP Deflator (1990=100) .... 99bi *p*
Midyear Estimates																
	.38	.38	.39	.39	.40	.40	.40	.40	.40	.40	.41	.41	.42	.41	.42	**Population** 99z

(See notes in the back of the book.)

Swaziland

		1970	1971	1972	1973	1974	1975	1976	1977	1978	1979	1980	1981	1982	1983	1984
Exchange Rates															SDRs per Lilangeni:	
Official Rate	ac	1.39425	1.20359	1.17647	1.23509	1.18434	.98235	.98982	.94673	.88272	.91807	1.05190	.89814	.84226	.78170	.51397
															US Dollars per Lilangeni:	
Official Rate	ag	1.39425	1.30675	1.27731	1.48995	1.45005	1.15000	1.15000	1.15000	1.15000	1.20940	1.34160	1.04540	.92910	.81840	.50380
Official Rate	rh	1.40000	1.39820	1.30181	1.44408	1.47216	1.36629	1.15000	1.15000	1.15000	1.18785	1.28543	1.14914	.92451	.89909	.69536
Fund Position															Millions of SDRs:	
Quota	2f. s	8.00	8.00	8.00	8.00	8.00	8.00	8.00	8.00	12.00	12.00	18.00	18.00	18.00	24.70	24.70
SDRs	1b. s	.01	.01	.75	.82	.87	1.01	.94	.87	.96	2.16	1.82	5.92	4.98	1.47	2.29
Reserve Position in the Fund	1c. s	.11	.20	.29	.20	.39	1.05	2.00	2.00	2.80	2.74	4.26	4.28	.01	1.70	1.73
Total Fund Cred.&Loans Outstg.	2tl	—	—	—	—	—	—	—	—	—	2.43	4.47	4.50	4.50	14.48	14.48
International Liquidity													Millions of US Dollars Unless Otherwise Indicated:			
Total Reserves minus Gold	1l. d	....	....	....	....	13.47	45.61	73.39	94.71	113.61	113.70	158.74	96.36	76.12	92.50	80.10
SDRs	1b. d	.01	.01	.81	.99	1.07	1.18	1.09	1.06	1.25	2.85	2.32	6.89	5.49	1.54	2.24
Reserve Position in the Fund	1c. d	.11	.22	.31	.24	.48	1.23	2.32	2.43	3.65	3.61	5.43	4.98	.01	1.78	1.70
Foreign Exchange	1d. d					11.93	43.20	69.97	91.22	108.71	107.25	150.99	84.49	70.62	89.18	76.16
Monetary Authorities: Other Liab.	4.. d					.18	.19	.04	.40	3.80	3.81	1.15	1.43	1.11	.95	3.89
Deposit Money Banks: Assets	7a. d	8.74	.17	14.66	7.18	17.36	22.25	9.63	13.70	8.22	5.73	4.18	7.17	9.03	11.50	4.93
Liabilities	7b. d	8.10	16.77	2.06	.01	—	.03	.07	.03	.24	1.11	4.66	5.52	6.71	10.97	4.38
Monetary Authorities															Millions of Emalangeni:	
Foreign Assets	11	....	....	....	....	10.19	39.97	64.48	83.45	97.98	92.19	114.35	88.00	83.95	117.64	163.05
Claims on Central Government	12a					.67	.75	.88	.66	10.51	3.52	5.12	5.96	7.29	6.63	19.82
Claims on Deposit Money Banks	12e					.02	4.20	—	—	—	2.70	—	4.00	—	1.17	1.17
Reserve Money	14	....				6.34	13.51	33.60	46.53	44.40	46.20	57.24	49.20	54.97	79.52	106.10
of which: Currency Outside DMBs	14a					3.33	5.11	6.52	7.31	8.90	9.59	11.90	14.41	15.03	15.23	16.77
Time Deposits	15					—	—	—	—	—	—	1.88	2.54	3.60	3.77	9.71
Foreign Liabilities	16c					.13	.17	.04	.35	3.30	5.79	5.11	6.38	6.54	19.68	35.89
Central Government Deposits	16d					3.14	29.20	27.51	31.44	54.84	42.28	52.64	33.26	17.51	13.20	18.13
Capital Accounts	17a					.50	1.01	1.33	1.74	5.39	7.34	8.91	11.11	12.12	12.73	15.63
Other Items (Net)	17r					.78	1.03	2.88	4.06	.55	−3.21	−6.31	−4.53	−3.48	−3.47	−1.41
Deposit Money Banks															Millions of Emalangeni:	
Reserves	20	1.02	1.26	1.36	1.57	2.58	8.51	25.97	32.72	34.48	34.30	45.23	32.51	42.09	59.34	86.47
Foreign Assets	21	6.24	.12	11.48	5.06	11.97	19.34	8.37	11.91	7.15	4.74	3.12	6.86	9.72	14.05	9.79
Claims on Central Government	22a	1.41	2.13	2.49	9.07	8.05	13.09	2.68	2.00	9.54	7.00	4.00	5.92	8.44	14.26	7.12
Claims on Private Sector	22d	16.49	24.20	17.40	22.60	29.25	43.43	46.32	48.38	74.78	84.69	97.11	130.04	138.13	143.26	152.54
Demand Deposits	24	6.43	10.06	13.01	11.70	13.59	18.23	22.17	20.67	27.72	30.58	37.93	36.59	42.11	44.21	48.74
Time and Savings Deposits	25	10.78	14.13	13.96	22.32	23.72	38.08	48.31	55.33	77.37	76.69	81.97	87.70	99.70	133.53	161.15
Foreign Liabilities	26c	5.79	12.58	1.61	.01	—	.03	.06	.03	.21	.92	3.47	5.28	7.22	13.40	8.70
Central Government Deposits	26d	2.49	2.68	4.48	.29	10.78	16.96	5.69	6.74	9.56	16.77	17.93	25.71	23.85	18.36	13.60
Capital Accounts	27a	—	—	—	3.19	4.63	4.63	7.15	8.27	14.12	14.34	17.53	19.53	22.13	26.40	26.65
Other Items (Net)	27r	−.33	−11.73	−.34	.80	−.87	6.44	−.03	3.97	−3.02	−8.58	−9.37	.51	3.37	−4.99	−2.93
Monetary Survey															Millions of Emalangeni:	
Foreign Assets (Net)	31n	....	....	....	....	22.04	59.12	72.76	94.99	101.62	90.22	108.89	83.20	79.92	98.60	128.26
Domestic Credit	32	....	....	....	....	24.07	11.27	16.93	13.27	31.03	37.03	36.85	85.33	114.86	135.82	151.22
Claims on Central Govt. (Net)	32an	....	....	....	....	−5.20	−32.33	−29.63	−35.53	−44.36	−48.54	−61.45	−47.09	−25.62	−10.67	−4.79
Claims on Private Sector	32d	....	....	....	....	29.26	43.59	46.56	48.80	75.39	85.57	98.30	132.42	140.48	146.49	156.01
Money	34	....	....	....	....	16.93	23.42	28.79	34.16	37.21	40.91	49.86	51.08	58.09	60.84	67.81
Quasi-Money	35	....	....	....	....	23.72	38.08	48.31	55.33	77.37	76.69	83.85	90.23	103.30	137.30	170.86
Other Items (Net)	37r	....	....	....	....	5.46	8.89	12.58	18.78	18.06	9.64	12.04	27.21	33.39	36.28	40.81
Money plus Quasi-Money	35l	....	....	....	....	40.65	61.50	77.11	89.48	114.58	117.60	133.70	141.32	161.38	198.14	238.67
Interest Rates															Percent Per Annum	
Discount Rate (End of Period)	60	....	....	....	....	....	....	....	9.00	9.00	8.50	7.00	7.00	10.50	16.00	13.50	19.00
Money Market Rate	60b	....	....	....	....	....	....									
Treasury Bill Rate	60c	....	....	....	....		6.00	6.00	6.00	7.71	7.71	7.71	12.00	14.60	13.04	17.74
Deposit Rate	60l	....	....	....	5.50	8.25	7.75	7.75	7.75	7.25	4.50	4.50	9.00	12.00	12.50	16.50
Lending Rate	60p	....	9.00	8.50	8.00	11.00	10.50	10.50	10.50	10.25	9.50	9.50	13.50	18.00	18.00	22.00
Prices and Labor															Index Numbers (1995=100):	
Consumer Prices	64	5.1	5.3	5.4	6.0	7.2	8.0	8.5	10.3	11.2	Ɪ13.0	15.5	18.6	20.6	Ɪ23.0	Ɪ25.9
															Number in Thousands:	
Labor Force	67d	....														
Employment	67e	....													....	....
International Transactions															Millions of Emalangeni	
Exports	70	50.9	55.7	63.0	74.2	121.5	145.7	159.1	143.1	170.6	194.8	286.9	340.3	351.8	338.5	345.6
Imports, c.i.f.	71	42.8	47.8	53.3	66.6	93.4	131.6	174.1	158.3	270.8	365.7	484.7	516.8	569.3	612.8	642.7

1985	1986	1987	1988	1989	1990	1991	1992	1993	1994	1995	1996	1997	1998	1999		
End of Period															**Exchange Rates**	
.35597	.37443	.36524	.31253	.30005	.27430	.25486	.23822	.21429	.19331	.18443	.14852	.15227	.12120	.11838	Official Rate	**ac**
End of Period (ag) Period Average (rh)																
.39100	.45800	.51815	.42057	.39432	.39024	.36456	.32755	.29433	.28221	.27416	.21356	.20544	.17065	.16248	Official Rate	**ag**
.45783	.44082	.49141	.44227	.38218	.38665	.36280	.35092	.30641	.28177	.27574	.23416	.21724	.18246	.16370	Official Rate	**rh**
End of Period															**Fund Position**	
24.70	24.70	24.70	24.70	24.70	24.70	24.70	36.50	36.50	36.50	36.50	36.50	36.50	36.50	50.70	Quota	**2f. s**
.26	2.24	2.79	1.23	.80	8.49	8.65	5.84	5.88	5.89	5.90	5.93	5.94	5.96	2.42	SDRs	**1b. s**
1.76	.03	.03	.01	.01	.02	.02	3.00	3.00	3.00	3.00	3.00	3.00	3.00	6.55	Reserve Position in the Fund	**1c. s**
12.85	8.57	4.30	1.16	.26	.03	—	—	—	—	—	—	—	—	—	Total Fund Cred.&Loans Outstg.	**2tl**
End of Period															**International Liquidity**	
83.42	96.45	127.16	140.01	180.61	216.47	171.93	309.06	264.29	296.97	298.20	254.00	294.84	358.61	375.93	Total Reserves minus Gold	**1l. d**
.29	2.74	3.96	1.66	1.05	12.08	12.37	8.03	8.08	8.60	8.77	8.52	8.02	8.39	3.33	SDRs	**1b. d**
1.93	.04	.04	.01	.01	.03	.03	4.13	4.12	4.38	4.46	4.32	4.05	4.23	8.99	Reserve Position in the Fund	**1c. d**
81.20	93.67	123.16	138.34	179.55	204.36	159.53	296.90	252.09	283.99	284.96	241.16	282.77	345.99	363.61	Foreign Exchange	**1d. d**
1.05	1.60	2.39	3.98	2.59	2.65	2.81	1.55	1.48	32.02	21.34	20.14	1.24	21.98	49.16	Monetary Authorities: Other Liab.	**4.. d**
7.31	6.33	17.82	64.40	63.90	58.16	41.13	52.01	52.43	43.59	47.52	107.45	91.79	99.16	135.46	Deposit Money Banks: Assets	**7a. d**
3.31	6.58	6.21	16.40	14.43	12.33	10.68	20.83	19.69	17.83	17.61	50.70	20.92	6.13	9.43	Liabilities	**7b. d**
End of Period															**Monetary Authorities**	
213.14	214.25	244.39	328.23	466.85	537.75	I 806.91	929.80	875.03	872.21	1,023.66	1,335.33	1,427.69	2,083.56	2,329.22	Foreign Assets	**11**
25.97	31.70	11.51	3.71	.87	.13	—	—	—	40.00	20.63	.06	—	—	—	Claims on Central Government	**12a**
—	1.10	.10	.60	2.93	11.41	12.81	9.60	6.82	5.65	30.00	36.76	43.19	42.55	44.31	Claims on Deposit Money Banks	**12e**
118.35	188.97	189.47	157.29	204.60	200.79	181.98	287.97	255.34	300.24	307.81	284.95	300.47	275.33	307.27	Reserve Money	**14**
17.45	25.21	27.19	32.20	37.20	48.19	52.99	56.09	75.19	69.59	80.33	90.85	109.00	107.23	136.95	*of which: Currency Outside DMBs*	**14a**
49.50	8.21	5.88	48.00	36.56	21.98	23.72	25.11	43.92	36.90	52.57	53.45	77.68	48.33	50.14	Time Deposits	**15**
38.78	26.39	16.38	13.18	7.43	6.90	7.70	4.74	5.02	113.47	77.82	94.32	6.04	128.81	302.53	Foreign Liabilities	**16c**
10.94	12.09	33.73	87.07	192.08	211.47	I 515.06	500.48	508.49	386.14	555.97	771.74	995.41	1,471.42	1,577.12	Central Government Deposits	**16d**
22.57	21.81	21.95	25.05	26.69	30.10	31.88	33.48	32.55	40.09	42.02	50.49	50.67	62.45	87.31	Capital Accounts	**17a**
−1.01	−10.41	−11.41	1.95	3.29	78.06	59.37	87.61	32.55	41.02	38.10	117.21	40.61	139.76	49.18	Other Items (Net)	**17r**
End of Period															**Deposit Money Banks**	
93.38	159.65	163.60	138.62	165.74	132.53	125.94	217.80	185.65	227.46	232.42	199.22	193.84	151.48	176.57	Reserves	**20**
18.68	13.82	34.39	153.13	162.05	149.04	112.82	158.78	178.14	154.45	173.32	503.13	446.80	581.07	833.68	Foreign Assets	**21**
11.67	25.08	5.50	11.25	9.75				30.00	38.00	49.79	68.35	52.17	52.73	50.21	Claims on Central Government	**22a**
151.94	161.24	202.62	260.87	335.83	465.99	654.58	673.59	739.14	902.68	915.60	971.81	1,095.03	1,159.43	1,223.39	Claims on Private Sector	**22d**
56.55	86.80	94.94	110.42	131.64	144.21	158.41	197.76	215.06	241.75	282.57	331.99	382.76	393.64	525.72	Demand Deposits	**24**
166.84	202.55	240.46	319.26	435.38	430.19	539.03	659.16	731.45	833.28	811.70	951.43	1,135.61	1,375.32	1,512.47	Time and Savings Deposits	**25**
8.46	14.37	11.99	39.01	36.60	31.60	29.29	63.58	66.89	63.17	64.22	237.41	101.82	35.92	58.04	Foreign Liabilities	**26c**
17.83	14.02	6.23	15.37	35.72	90.12	92.96	89.16	73.71	90.88	114.57	101.22	10.17	14.25	14.70	Central Government Deposits	**26d**
26.83	31.28	44.78	67.08	46.99	61.85	67.69	74.36	96.20	92.33	97.61	75.09	127.53	114.39	139.44	Capital Accounts	**27a**
−.83	10.76	7.72	12.74	−12.96	−10.40	5.96	−33.83	−50.37	1.17	.47	45.37	29.97	11.19	33.48	Other Items (Net)	**27r**
End of Period															**Monetary Survey**	
184.59	187.31	250.42	429.17	584.87	648.30	I 882.74	1,020.26	981.26	850.02	1,054.94	1,506.73	1,766.63	2,499.89	2,802.34	Foreign Assets (Net)	**31n**
168.03	196.02	183.89	178.09	124.15	171.53	I 55.80	93.58	195.81	514.28	328.00	181.28	154.69	−261.20	−303.00	Domestic Credit	**32**
8.87	30.69	−22.93	−87.44	−217.16	−301.46	I −608.02	−589.64	−552.19	−399.02	−600.12	−804.55	−953.40	−1,432.94	−1,541.61	Claims on Central Govt. (Net)	**32an**
159.15	165.33	206.82	265.53	341.30	472.99	663.83	683.22	748.00	913.30	928.12	985.83	1,108.09	1,171.74	1,238.62	Claims on Private Sector	**32d**
76.92	115.14	125.42	142.77	168.98	192.58	211.54	254.29	290.50	311.59	363.16	423.03	491.75	500.87	662.69	Money	**34**
216.34	210.76	246.33	367.26	471.93	452.17	562.75	684.27	775.37	870.18	864.27	1,004.88	1,213.29	1,423.66	1,562.61	Quasi-Money	**35**
59.36	57.41	62.53	97.21	68.07	175.08	164.23	175.28	111.21	182.54	155.52	260.10	216.28	314.16	274.04	Other Items (Net)	**37r**
293.26	325.90	371.75	510.02	640.92	644.74	774.29	938.56	1,065.87	1,181.76	1,227.43	1,427.91	1,705.04	1,924.52	2,225.30	Money plus Quasi-Money	**35l**
Percent Per Annum															**Interest Rates**	
12.50	9.50	9.00	11.00	12.00	12.00	13.00	12.00	11.00	12.00	15.00	16.75	15.75	18.00	12.00	Discount Rate *(End of Period)*	**60**
....	....	....	....	8.39	10.50	10.61	10.25	9.73	7.01	8.52	9.77	10.35	10.63	8.86	Money Market Rate	**60b**
16.47	9.76	5.96	7.28	10.16	11.14	12.67	12.34	8.25	8.35	10.87	13.68	14.37	13.09	11.19	Treasury Bill Rate	**60c**
10.19	5.75	4.81	9.23	8.92	8.85	10.85	9.00	7.38	8.00	10.25	12.25	11.25	13.43	7.53	Deposit Rate	**60l**
17.00	12.50	11.88	15.00	14.50	14.50	16.25	15.00	14.00	15.00	18.00	19.75	18.75	21.00	15.00	Lending Rate	**60p**
Period Averages															**Prices and Labor**	
31.2	35.5	40.3	I 49.0	52.7	59.6	65.0	69.9	78.3	89.1	100.0	106.4	114.0	123.3	130.8	Consumer Prices	**64**
Period Averages																
....	157	....	....	....	....	....	....	....	....	....	....	....	....	....	Labor Force	**67d**
73	76	....	83	86	91	92	92	92	93	87	87	90	....	....	Employment	**67e**
Millions of Emalangeni															**International Transactions**	
392.9	635.5	862.4	1,059.9	1,313.9	1,439.9	1,639.0	1,820.2	2,236.5	2,779.8	3,472.2	3,812.7	....	....	....	Exports	**70**
707.1	798.9	885.8	1,167.6	1,524.5	1,714.1	1,979.0	2,468.0	2,852.3	3,291.9	4,005.8	5,015.7	5,486.6	....	....	Imports, c.i.f.	**71**

Swaziland

		1970	1971	1972	1973	1974	1975	1976	1977	1978	1979	1980	1981	1982	1983	1984
Balance of Payments																*Millions of US Dollars:*
Current Account, n.i.e.	78al d	....	....	....	....	42.5	51.5	30.4	11.6	–70.7	–119.3	–129.7	–81.4	–113.8	–107.0	–77.5
Goods: Exports f.o.b.	78aa d	....	....	....	....	178.8	197.0	193.4	183.9	198.7	241.6	368.3	388.3	324.0	303.8	230.8
Goods: Imports f.o.b.	78ab d	....	....	....	....	–111.9	–139.7	–155.9	–171.2	–247.7	–363.3	–538.1	–504.0	–439.0	–464.8	–372.1
Trade Balance	78ac d	....	....	....	....	67.0	57.3	37.5	12.6	–49.0	–121.6	–169.9	–115.7	–115.0	–160.9	–141.3
Services: Credit	78ad d	....	....	....	....	23.0	25.0	25.8	29.2	20.1	31.4	36.1	41.4	32.9	41.2	43.7
Services: Debit	78ae d	....	....	....	....	–28.8	–39.5	–42.1	–46.0	–63.7	–83.3	–80.0	–100.9	–107.4	–93.0	–86.5
Balance on Goods & Services	78af d	....	....	....	....	61.1	42.9	21.2	–4.1	–92.6	–173.6	–213.8	–175.1	–189.5	–212.7	–184.2
Income: Credit	78ag d	....	....	....	....	4.4	13.3	15.8	20.7	25.4	27.4	46.4	68.6	54.6	66.9	70.9
Income: Debit	78ah d	....	....	....	....	–38.3	–23.1	–15.2	–17.8	–29.9	–20.0	–41.1	–48.4	–40.2	–27.5	–31.4
Balance on Gds, Serv. & Inc.	78ai d	....	....	....	....	27.2	33.0	21.7	–1.3	–97.1	–166.1	–208.5	–154.9	–175.1	–173.3	–144.7
Current Transfers, n.i.e.: Credit	78aj d	....	....	....	....	28.6	37.2	44.0	50.4	70.5	95.0	143.7	131.7	123.6	128.1	113.0
Current Transfers: Debit	78ak d	....	....	....	....	–13.2	–18.7	–35.4	–37.5	–44.2	–48.2	–64.8	–58.1	–62.3	–61.8	–45.8
Capital Account, n.i.e.	78bc d	....	....	....	....	—	—	—	—	–1.5	–1.4	–2.1	–1.9	–.6	–1.7	–1.9
Capital Account, n.i.e.: Credit	78ba d	....	....	....	....	—	—	—	—	—	—	—	—	—	—	—
Capital Account: Debit	78bb d	....	....	....	....	—	—	—	—	–1.5	–1.4	–2.1	–1.9	–.6	–1.7	–1.9
Financial Account, n.i.e.	78bj d	....	....	....	....	–14.7	11.9	20.6	24.6	80.4	100.3	36.5	21.7	32.1	66.5	29.4
Direct Investment Abroad	78bd d	....	....	....	....	—	—	—	—	—	—	–9.0	–5.4	2.9	.1	–4.9
Dir. Invest. in Rep. Econ., n.i.e.	78be d	....	....	....	....	3.5	14.5	7.4	20.0	21.7	55.5	26.5	37.1	–13.6	–5.7	5.0
Portfolio Investment Assets	78bf d	....	....	....	....	—	—	—	—	—	—	—	—	–.1	–.7	.1
Equity Securities	78bk d	....	....	....	....	—	—	—	—	—	—	—	—	—	–.1	—
Debt Securities	78bl d	....	....	....	....	—	—	—	—	—	—	—	—	–.1	–.6	.1
Portfolio Investment Liab., n.i.e.	78bg d	....	....	....	....	—	—	—	—	—	—	—	—	–.2	.4	–.1
Equity Securities	78bm d	....	....	....	....	—	—	—	—	—	—	—	—	–.2	.4	–.1
Debt Securities	78bn d	....	....	....	....	—	—	—	—	—	—	—	—	—	—	—
Financial Derivatives Assets	78bw d	....	....	....	....	....	....	....	....	....	....	....	....	....	....	....
Financial Derivatives Liabilities	78bx d	....	....	....	....	....	....	....	....	....	....	....	....	....	....	....
Other Investment Assets	78bh d	....	....	....	....	–25.0	–9.1	–.7	–3.3	11.2	9.9	—	–24.8	–19.9	7.6	–4.2
Monetary Authorities	78bo d	....	....	....	....	....	....	....	....	....	....	....	....	....	....	....
General Government	78bp d	....	....	....	....	1.0	–6.6	–9.5	.6	7.0	6.4	–2.4	–20.0	–9.8	13.6	11.5
Banks	78bq d	....	....	....	....	–11.5	–9.2	12.3	–3.9	4.1	3.4	2.4	–4.8	–2.8	–4.0	2.7
Other Sectors	78br d	....	....	....	....	–14.6	6.8	–3.5	—	—	—	—	—	–7.4	–2.0	–18.4
Other Investment Liab., n.i.e.	78bi d	....	....	....	....	6.8	6.5	13.9	7.9	47.5	34.9	19.0	14.7	63.1	64.8	33.6
Monetary Authorities	78bs d	....	....	....	....	.1	—	.1	—	—	–.5	–2.1	.6	.1	—	4.5
General Government	78bt d	....	....	....	....	3.8	5.5	7.9	7.9	47.3	34.6	17.7	12.1	19.1	27.5	13.4
Banks	78bu d	....	....	....	....	—	—	—	—	.2	.8	3.3	2.1	1.7	5.6	–2.8
Other Sectors	78bv d	....	....	....	....	2.8	.9	5.9	—	—	—	—	—	42.2	31.8	18.5
Net Errors and Omissions	78ca d	....	....	....	....	–17.7	–24.2	–23.1	–14.5	7.7	12.0	129.4	13.3	73.1	53.8	41.7
Overall Balance	78cb d	....	....	....	....	10.2	39.2	27.8	21.8	15.9	–8.4	34.1	–48.3	–9.1	11.6	–8.3
Reserves and Related Items	79da d	....	....	....	....	–10.2	–39.2	–27.8	–21.8	–15.9	8.4	–34.1	48.3	9.1	–11.6	8.3
Reserve Assets	79db d	....	....	....	....	–10.2	–39.2	–27.8	–21.8	–15.9	5.3	–36.8	48.3	9.1	–22.3	8.3
Use of Fund Credit and Loans	79dc d	....	....	....	....	—	—	—	—	—	3.2	2.6	—	—	10.7	—
Exceptional Financing	79de d	....	....	....	....	....	....	....	....	....	....	....	....	....	....	....
International Investment Position																*Millions of US Dollars*
Assets	79aa d	....	....	....	....	....	....	....	....	....	....	....	169.6	156.7	172.2	154.0
Direct Investment Abroad	79ab d	....	....	....	....	....	....	....	....	....	....	....	24.4	18.3	15.3	11.8
Portfolio Investment	79ac d	....	....	....	....	....	....	....	....	....	....	....	1.9	.9	1.4	.8
Equity Securities	79ad d	....	....	....	....	....	....	....	....	....	....	....	—	—	—	—
Debt Securities	79ae d	....	....	....	....	....	....	....	....	....	....	....	1.9	.9	1.4	.8
Financial Derivatives	79al d	....	....	....	....	....	....	....	....	....	....	....	—	—	—	—
Other Investment	79af d	....	....	....	....	....	....	....	....	....	....	....	51.5	59.8	60.0	59.9
Monetary Authorities	79ag d	....	....	....	....	....	....	....	....	....	....	....	—	—	—	—
General Government	79ah d	....	....	....	....	....	....	....	....	....	....	....	1.5	2.2	2.5	1.1
Banks	79ai d	....	....	....	....	....	....	....	....	....	....	....	8.0	9.9	12.4	5.6
Other Sectors	79aj d	....	....	....	....	....	....	....	....	....	....	....	42.0	47.7	45.1	53.1
Reserve Assets	79ak d	....	....	....	....	....	....	....	....	....	....	....	91.8	77.6	95.5	81.5
Liabilities	79la d	....	....	....	....	....	....	....	....	....	....	....	536.8	525.1	529.4	401.5
Dir. Invest. in Rep. Economy	79lb d	....	....	....	....	....	....	....	....	....	....	....	280.5	228.7	199.0	126.5
Portfolio Investment	79lc d	....	....	....	....	....	....	....	....	....	....	....	.5	.3	.3	.2
Equity Securities	79ld d	....	....	....	....	....	....	....	....	....	....	....	.5	.3	.3	.2
Debt Securities	79le d	....	....	....	....	....	....	....	....	....	....	....	—	—	—	—
Financial Derivatives	79ll d	....	....	....	....	....	....	....	....	....	....	....	—	—	—	—
Other Investment	79lf d	....	....	....	....	....	....	....	....	....	....	....	255.8	296.1	330.0	274.8
Monetary Authorities	79lg d	....	....	....	....	....	....	....	....	....	....	....	6.3	6.0	16.1	18.1
General Government	79lh d	....	....	....	....	....	....	....	....	....	....	....	156.5	163.0	167.9	155.2
Banks	79li d	....	....	....	....	....	....	....	....	....	....	....	5.5	6.7	11.0	4.6
Other Sectors	79lj d	....	....	....	....	....	....	....	....	....	....	....	87.5	120.4	135.0	96.9
Government Finance																*Millions of Emalangeni:*
Deficit (-) or Surplus	80	....	–2.0	–4.6	–10.8	1.7	17.4	–8.5	–8.6	–40.0	3.9	27.6	–48.9	–31.9	–19.6	–3.6
Revenue	81	....	17.4	21.2	28.5	45.6	69.9	54.6	80.8	98.7	126.0	148.8	131.1	178.6	179.6	210.8
Grants Received	81z	....	.1	.1	.1	.7	.1	.1	.4	6.6	8.0	7.7	5.0	5.4	5.9	10.7
Expenditure	82	....	19.1	23.3	38.3	39.5	46.8	57.6	75.2	119.0	97.5	117.3	166.1	183.2	190.5	209.7
Lending Minus Repayments	83	....	.4	2.7	1.0	5.1	5.8	5.5	14.5	26.2	32.7	11.6	19.0	17.7	14.6	15.4
Financing																
Domestic	84a	....	1.1	–.8	3.7	–11.0	–20.9	9.0	2.9	–5.7	–10.5	–27.7	42.5	14.9	18.1	9.2
Foreign	85a	....	.9	5.4	7.1	9.3	3.5	–.5	5.6	45.6	6.6	.1	6.4	17.0	1.4	–5.6
Debt: Domestic	88a	2.0	3.2	4.1	10.8	12.0	12.8	9.2	10.3	15.3	15.0	12.0	17.0	22.0	26.6	27.3
Foreign	89a	....	....	....	....	....	4.1	....	....	94.4	116.4	116.5	127.0	166.4	198.6	371.5
National Accounts																*Millions of Emalangeni:*
Exports of Goods & Services	90c	48.9	56.0	65.3	108.4	146.4	155.4	179.4	172.4	186.4	221.1	325.7	388.0	416.8	400.6	509.5
Government Consumption	91f	10.4	10.9	13.6	20.2	26.4	36.1	43.3	54.1	70.2	74.9	103.9	133.8	141.0	135.8	182.1
Gross Fixed Capital Formation	93e	9.5	16.1	20.0	24.9	35.7	41.6	50.6	68.1	144.8	142.1	147.8	140.2	152.8	208.5	208.5
Increase/Decrease(-) in Stocks	93i	2.8	2.4	2.7	6.1	7.1	–2.0	2.0	3.0	–3.0	6.0	23.8	15.3	23.4	–5.7	.9
Private Consumption	96f	45.3	44.0	59.2	60.7	50.6	102.8	120.2	146.8	153.5	249.2	286.9	360.2	394.9	450.4	510.8
Imports of Goods & Services	98c	–40.8	–48.4	–63.2	–86.5	–106.4	–121.3	–160.2	–181.4	–256.7	–344.6	–465.9	–536.6	–582.2	–610.0	–722.9
Gross Domestic Product (GDP)	99b	76.1	81.0	97.6	133.8	159.8	213.3	235.3	263.0	295.2	348.7	422.1	500.9	546.7	579.6	662.3
Net Factor Inc/Pmts(-) Abroad	98.n	–9.6	–9.4	–9.4	–19.3	–3.7	50.4	46.1	–2.3	–14.6	–22.2	–5.7	5.7	15.5	30.6	53.1
Gross National Income (GNI)	99a	66.5	71.6	88.2	114.5	156.1	263.7	281.4	260.7	280.6	326.5	416.4	506.6	562.2	610.2	715.4
Net National Income	99e	59.7	63.9	79.7	104.7	144.7	251.2	267.6	245.5	263.9	308.1	390.3	476.5	524.9	563.6	668.2
GDP Volume 1980 prices	99b.*p*	....	....	....	....	....	....	....	351.0	385.7	441.6	422.1	451.1	....	....	....
GDP Volume 1985 Prices	99b.*p*	....	....	....	....	....	....	....	....	....	....	....	711.5	719.7	728.0	773.4
GDP Volume (1995=100)	99bv*p*	....	....	....	....	....	....	....	37.0	40.7	46.6	44.5	47.6	48.1	48.7	51.7
GDP Deflator (1995=100)	99bi*p*	....	....	....	....	....	....	....	15.5	15.8	16.3	20.6	22.9	24.7	25.9	27.9
																Millions:
Population	99z	.42	.44	.45	.46	.48	.49	.50	.51	.53	.53	.55	.57	.59	.60	.63

1985	1986	1987	1988	1989	1990	1991	1992	1993	1994	1995	1996	1997	1998	1999		
Minus Sign Indicates Debit															Balance of Payments	
-38.4	10.8	65.6	95.1	77.1	50.7	47.2	-40.6	-63.7	1.9	-29.7	-53.1	9.0	-16.8	17.2	Current Account, n.i.e.	78al*d*
176.7	278.4	423.9	466.6	494.1	550.3	593.8	638.5	684.7	790.9	867.8	849.4	960.1	966.1	941.3	Goods: Exports f.o.b.	78aa*d*
-272.7	-296.7	-381.1	-449.0	-515.6	-589.2	-635.0	-779.6	-788.6	-841.0	-1,064.4	-1,054.4	-1,088.6	-1,082.6	-1,052.1	Goods: Imports f.o.b.	78ab*d*
-95.9	-18.2	42.8	17.6	-21.5	-38.8	-41.2	-141.1	-103.9	-50.1	-196.6	-205.0	-128.5	-116.5	-110.8	*Trade Balance*	78ac*d*
27.8	30.5	54.1	65.4	92.0	107.6	91.3	98.4	92.8	112.8	151.8	100.8	124.5	107.0	71.8	Services: Credit	78ad*d*
-62.5	-61.6	-98.5	-106.4	-89.9	-178.6	-181.6	-208.4	-256.4	-201.8	-209.5	-240.8	-244.5	-190.5	-173.2	Services: Debit	78ae*d*
-130.6	-49.4	-1.6	-23.4	-19.4	-109.8	-131.5	-251.1	-267.5	-139.1	-254.2	-345.0	-248.5	-200.0	-212.2	*Balance on Goods & Services*	78af*d*
71.8	73.0	95.1	120.8	146.1	161.6	173.5	196.8	155.2	138.5	162.6	200.8	182.7	159.3	173.6	Income: Credit	78ag*d*
-32.8	-57.4	-86.1	-77.2	-143.3	-102.7	-103.7	-113.7	-107.3	-155.0	-82.0	-68.7	-43.6	-108.9	-78.7	Income: Debit	78ah*d*
-91.6	-33.8	7.4	20.2	-16.6	-50.9	-61.7	-168.0	-219.5	-155.6	-173.7	-212.9	-109.5	-149.6	-117.3	*Balance on Gds, Serv. & Inc.*	78ai*d*
88.4	85.4	108.8	127.8	151.3	175.4	189.0	222.4	248.1	252.6	257.2	268.7	231.2	243.4	239.6	Current Transfers, n.i.e.: Credit	78aj*d*
-35.3	-40.8	-50.7	-53.0	-57.7	-73.7	-80.0	-95.0	-92.3	-95.1	-113.3	-108.9	-112.7	-110.6	-105.0	Current Transfers: Debit	78ak*d*
-.9	-.8	-.4	—	.6	2.2	-.1	-.1	—	-.2	—	.1	—	.1	—	Capital Account, n.i.e.	78bc*d*
—	—	.3	.3	.7	2.3	.3	.4	.3	.1	.3	.1	.1	.1	—	Capital Account, n.i.e.: Credit	78ba*d*
-.9	-.8	-.7	-.2	-.1	-.1	-.5	-.5	-.3	-.3	-.4	—	—	—	—	Capital Account: Debit	78bb*d*
21.1	20.9	-19.7	-58.1	-10.9	-38.9	23.5	38.3	-2.4	-63.1	-74.5	-4.6	-2.9	41.6	-34.9	Financial Account, n.i.e.	78bj*d*
-2.7	-2.3	-6.7	-12.3	-15.6	-7.6	-25.0	-33.2	-27.8	-64.7	-20.6	6.4	12.0	-30.2	-.2	Direct Investment Abroad	78bd*d*
11.7	31.1	56.3	50.6	67.2	30.1	82.1	87.3	71.9	63.3	51.7	21.7	-15.3	124.0	32.6	Dir. Invest. in Rep. Econ., n.i.e.	78be*d*
-.1	—	-1.2	-.2	-.5	-.5	-.6	-1.0	-.1	-3.9	-9.5	-2.0	-2.0	-3.0	-.4	Portfolio Investment Assets	78bf*d*
—	—	....	—	—	—	—	-.9	—	—	-1.9	-.2	-2.0	-1.2	-.2	Equity Securities	78bk*d*
-.1	—	-1.2	-.2	-.5	-.5	-.5	-.1	-.1	-3.9	-7.6	-1.7	—	-1.8	-.2	Debt Securities	78bl*d*
2.0	-.4	2.4	6.3	7.4	-2.2	-.1	-.1	-.9	.1	.8	.4	-.1	.1	-.9	Portfolio Investment Liab., n.i.e.	78bg*d*
2.0	-.4	2.4	6.3	7.4	-2.2	-.1	-.1	-.9	.1	.8	.4	-.1	.1	-.9	Equity Securities	78bm*d*
—	—	....	....	....	....	....	....	....	....	....	....	....	....	....	Debt Securities	78bn*d*
....	—	....	....	....	....	....	....	....	....	....	....	....	....	....	Financial Derivatives Assets	78bw*d*
....	—	....	....	....	....	....	....	....	....	....	....	....	....	....	Financial Derivatives Liabilities	78bx*d*
-16.5	-7.0	-61.1	-110.3	-80.8	-39.0	-41.1	-40.8	-78.2	-80.5	-86.2	-154.9	-16.7	-27.7	-89.4	Other Investment Assets	78bh*d*
....	.4	.9	....	....	....	....	....	....	....	....	....	....	....	....	Monetary Authorities	78bo*d*
-1.5	-4.6	-13.4	-24.6	-35.3	-14.7	.4	-.6	-25.3	-17.9	-6.7	-2.7	9.0	-5.4	58.2	General Government	78bp*d*
-3.9	2.1	-10.2	-52.9	-3.9	4.3	12.8	-15.4	-6.9	5.7	-5.3	-77.0	11.1	-22.9	-41.7	Banks	78bq*d*
-11.1	-4.9	-38.5	-32.8	-41.6	-28.5	-54.2	-24.8	-46.0	-68.3	-74.2	-75.2	-36.7	.5	-105.9	Other Sectors	78br*d*
26.7	-.5	-9.4	7.8	11.4	-19.8	8.1	26.1	32.7	22.7	-10.7	123.6	19.1	-21.7	23.4	Other Investment Liab., n.i.e.	78bi*d*
-2.3	.4	.5	2.2	-1.1	.1	.3	-1.1	.1	30.6	-9.8	3.8	-19.2	22.2	28.4	Monetary Authorities	78bs*d*
-1.4	20.1	-16.9	-4.7	-1.9	-20.8	-8.4	-10.7	-10.8	-14.8	-7.1	3.2	-.6	-1.2	-4.6	General Government	78bt*d*
3.6	-1.2	-.7	14.1	-1.1	.5	-1.3	12.5	-.3	.7	.4	41.5	-25.9	-13.8	.3	Banks	78bu*d*
26.8	-19.8	7.7	-3.8	15.5	.5	17.5	25.3	43.8	6.2	5.9	75.1	64.8	-28.9	-.8	Other Sectors	78bv*d*
13.7	-23.2	-24.2	-25.0	-15.6	-3.0	-56.8	94.3	2.3	48.8	134.1	72.9	19.2	25.6	39.2	Net Errors and Omissions	78ca*d*
-4.5	7.6	21.2	12.0	51.1	11.1	13.7	91.9	-63.7	-12.5	29.8	15.4	25.3	50.5	21.5	*Overall Balance*	78cb*d*
4.5	-7.6	-21.2	-12.0	-51.1	-11.1	-13.7	-91.9	63.7	12.5	-29.8	-15.4	-25.3	-50.5	-21.5	Reserves and Related Items	79da*d*
6.1	-2.5	-15.6	-7.7	-50.0	-10.8	-13.7	-91.9	63.7	12.5	-29.8	-15.4	-25.3	-50.5	-21.5	Reserve Assets	79db*d*
-1.6	-5.0	-5.6	-4.2	-1.2	-.3	—	—	—	—	—	—	—	—	—	Use of Fund Credit and Loans	79dc*d*
....	....	....	....	....	....	....	....	....	....	....	....	....	....	....	Exceptional Financing	79de*d*
Millions of US Dollars															International Investment Position	
167.7	167.0	1,026.6	964.1	1,058.5	1,111.1	605.7	688.5	662.4	781.8	928.1	922.4	910.4	922.6	1,062.2	Assets	79aa*d*
8.8	9.4	20.3	22.5	35.4	38.3	51.6	49.2	52.6	108.8	135.5	95.4	79.4	88.4	83.6	Direct Investment Abroad	79ab*d*
.7	.9	2.3	2.0	2.4	2.9	3.4	3.9	3.6	7.3	16.6	14.8	16.1	16.2	15.8	Portfolio Investment	79ac*d*
—	—	—	—	—	—	.1	.9	.8	.8	2.7	2.3	4.0	4.5	4.5	Equity Securities	79ad*d*
.7	.9	2.3	2.0	2.4	2.9	3.3	3.0	2.8	6.6	14.0	12.5	12.0	11.6	11.3	Debt Securities	79ae*d*
—	—	—	—	—	—	—	—	—	—	—	—	—	—	—	Financial Derivatives	79al*d*
73.5	59.1	875.6	806.1	838.1	862.4	327.7	332.5	366.9	422.7	498.5	529.8	525.4	462.7	586.1	Other Investment	79af*d*
—	—	—	—	—	—	—	—	—	—	—	—	—	—	—	Monetary Authorities	79ag*d*
6.9	9.0	784.1	657.1	650.2	643.5	81.5	73.6	83.4	88.2	69.8	56.1	45.4	42.8	39.9	General Government	79ah*d*
7.7	6.9	13.8	55.4	57.0	60.5	43.7	53.7	54.8	46.9	50.8	110.3	95.6	101.0	137.5	Banks	79ai*d*
58.9	43.2	77.7	93.6	131.0	158.4	202.5	205.2	228.7	287.7	377.9	363.5	384.4	318.9	408.7	Other Sectors	79aj*d*
84.7	97.5	128.5	133.5	182.5	207.5	223.0	302.9	239.2	242.9	277.4	282.4	289.5	355.3	376.7	Reserve Assets	79ak*d*
390.2	469.9	350.5	575.9	638.9	647.2	720.8	762.0	822.0	881.0	925.3	894.6	834.5	858.8	917.9	Liabilities	79la*d*
104.2	154.7	240.4	249.4	309.1	335.8	399.6	437.7	462.5	506.8	535.6	437.2	406.0	452.6	473.0	Dir. Invest. in Rep. Economy	79lb*d*
7.4	8.3	2.7	3.2	4.5	2.2	1.9	1.7	.6	.7	1.4	1.5	1.4	1.3	.3	Portfolio Investment	79lc*d*
7.4	8.3	2.7	3.2	4.5	2.2	1.9	1.7	.6	.7	1.4	1.5	1.4	1.3	.3	Equity Securities	79ld*d*
—	—	—	—	—	—	—	—	—	—	—	—	—	—	—	Debt Securities	79le*d*
—	—	—	—	—	—	—	—	—	—	—	—	—	—	—	Financial Derivatives	79ll*d*
278.5	306.9	107.3	323.2	325.2	309.2	319.3	322.7	358.9	373.6	388.3	456.0	427.1	404.9	444.6	Other Investment	79lf*d*
15.1	12.0	8.5	5.3	2.9	2.7	2.8	1.5	1.5	32.0	21.3	20.1	1.2	22.0	49.2	Monetary Authorities	79lg*d*
158.2	207.1	—	227.9	223.1	206.7	205.5	184.7	192.1	175.3	194.5	194.4	177.4	216.8	237.8	General Government	79lh*d*
6.7	6.6	6.7	18.9	16.6	16.9	14.5	24.7	21.9	21.7	21.5	54.9	28.2	10.4	10.3	Banks	79li*d*
98.5	81.2	92.2	71.1	82.5	82.8	96.5	111.7	143.5	144.5	150.9	186.5	220.2	155.6	147.4	Other Sectors	79lj*d*
Year Beginning April 1															**Government Finance**	
-27.6	-48.9	21.6	59.2	95.9	†165.6	121.2	-42.3	-171.2	-197.5	68.3	-216.9	216.5	-7.1	-193.6	Deficit (-) or Surplus	80
232.3	243.9	330.7	422.6	570.5	†745.6	795.5	844.0	953.0	1,185.7	1,447.7	1,610.6	2,020.5	2,230.3	2,401.9	Revenue	81
10.2	11.8	6.6	5.6	14.2	†10.8	20.6	46.3	28.7	31.4	7.5	38.0	18.3	44.7	84.6	Grants Received	81z
257.9	291.0	301.3	354.8	427.3	†581.9	704.1	1,025.5	1,138.4	1,415.6	1,382.1	1,861.1	1,826.6	2,214.8	2,630.7	Expenditure	82
12.2	13.5	14.4	14.2	61.6	†8.9	-9.2	-92.9	14.4	-1.1	4.8	4.4	-4.3	67.3	49.4	Lending Minus Repayments	83
															Financing	
24.8	21.1	-27.1	-52.0	-92.8	†-160.0	-105.4	50.4	196.5	235.5	-80.6	192.2	-258.5	-191.2	143.1	Domestic	84a
2.8	27.8	5.5	-7.2	-3.1	†-5.6	-15.8	-8.2	-25.3	-38.0	12.3	24.7	42.0	198.3	50.5	Foreign	85a
40.9	50.0	53.9	51.6	36.2	†26.0	24.6	24.6	53.1	72.5	102.5	97.6	77.6	77.6	70.0	Debt: Domestic	88a
245.6	299.4	344.6	398.9	434.0	†447.0	459.5	515.9	630.2	699.0	697.9	792.6	820.0	908.3	1,317.9	Foreign	89a
Year Ending June 30 through 1997; December 31 Thereafter															**National Accounts**	
454.8	706.0	967.2	1,198.6	1,521.6	1,707.6	1,953.3	2,169.4	2,733.6	2,970.6	3,814.6	4,265.2	4,947.3	....	....	Exports of Goods & Services	90c
182.9	226.3	208.3	262.9	296.5	412.3	474.7	490.1	781.0	874.0	951.0	1,185.8	1,639.2	....	....	Government Consumption	91f
197.6	163.6	196.2	350.5	416.0	419.6	477.1	697.6	829.4	1,176.6	1,530.8	1,530.0	1,997.0	....	....	Gross Fixed Capital Formation	93e
12.8	41.2	-19.5	20.0	21.4	16.3	22.5	24.9	29.0	33.9	37.4	47.2	54.4	....	....	Increase/Decrease(-) in Stocks	93i
635.6	672.6	723.9	956.7	1,106.6	1,357.4	1,511.7	1,760.4	1,595.1	1,914.5	2,313.9	3,072.6	3,228.6	....	....	Private Consumption	96f
-681.2	-783.4	-886.7	-1,215.4	-1,534.3	-1,689.2	-2,011.8	-2,377.3	-2,742.7	-3,199.1	-4,051.5	-4,858.4	-5,821.1	....	....	Imports of Goods & Services	98c
802.5	1,026.3	1,189.4	1,573.3	1,827.8	2,224.0	2,427.5	2,765.1	3,225.4	3,770.5	4,596.2	5,242.5	6,045.4	....	....	Gross Domestic Product (GDP)	99b
76.5	62.5	23.4	89.5	-40.1	152.7	192.6	237.2	156.6	-58.9	295.7	455.6	617.7	....	....	Net Factor Inc/Pmts(-) Abroad	98.n
879.0	1,088.8	1,212.8	1,662.8	1,787.7	2,376.7	2,620.1	3,002.3	3,382.0	3,711.6	4,891.9	5,698.1	6,663.1	....	....	Gross National Income (GNI)	99a
823.7	1,020.4	1,137.3	1,564.6	1,669.9	2,234.2	2,467.6	2,831.5	3,192.4	3,497.4	4,656.1	5,439.7	6,365.9	....	....	Net National Income	99e
....	....	....	....	....	....	....	....	....	....	....	....	....	....	....	GDP Volume 1980 prices	99b.*p*
802.5	901.6	1,033.5	1,101.7	1,202.4	1,309.6	1,341.7	1,358.8	1,403.1	1,451.6	1,495.7	1,549.3	1,606.9	....	....	GDP Volume 1985 Prices	99b.*p*
53.7	60.3	69.1	73.7	80.4	87.6	89.7	90.8	93.8	97.1	100.0	103.6	107.4	....	....	GDP Volume (1995=100)	99bv*p*
32.5	37.0	37.5	46.5	49.5	55.3	58.9	66.2	74.8	84.5	100.0	110.1	122.4	....	....	GDP Deflator (1995=100)	99bi*p*
Midyear Estimates																
.65	.67	.69	.72	.74	.77	.80	.83	.85	.88	.91	.94	†.93	.95	.98	**Population**	99z

(See notes in the back of the book.)

Sweden

144

INTERNATIONAL FINANCIAL STATISTICS YEARBOOK 2000

		1970	1971	1972	1973	1974	1975	1976	1977	1978	1979	1980	1981	1982	1983	1984
Exchange Rates															*Kronor per SDR:*	
Official Rate	aa	5.1700	5.2820	‡5.1495	5.5341	4.9960	5.1339	4.7943	5.6721	5.5961	5.4623	5.5771	6.4844	8.0466	8.3766	8.8116
															Kronor per US Dollar:	
Official Rate	ae	5.1700	4.8650	‡4.7430	4.5875	4.0805	4.3855	4.1265	4.6695	4.2955	4.1465	4.3728	5.5710	7.2945	8.0010	8.9895
Official Rate	rf	5.1732	5.1259	4.7624	4.3673	4.4394	4.1522	4.3559	4.4816	4.5185	4.1847	4.2296	5.0634	6.2826	7.6671	8.2718
										Kronor per ECU through 1998; Kronor per Euro Beginning 1999:						
Euro Rate	ea	....	....	....	....	....	....	....	....	....	5.9729	5.7329	6.0037	7.0809	6.6260	6.3699
Euro Rate	eb	....	....	....	....	....	....	....	....	....	5.8729	5.8797	5.6327	6.1417	6.8243	6.5113
													Index Numbers (1995=100):			
Official Rate	ahx	137.3	167.4	149.5	163.4	160.6	171.9	163.6	159.3	157.7	166.2	168.5	141.5	114.5	93.0	86.2
Nominal Effective Exchange Rate	neu	178.2	177.0	178.8	177.3	176.0	182.8	186.9	179.5	162.6	162.3	163.0	161.4	145.3	128.8	131.7
Real Effective Exchange Rate	reu	....	....	....	....	....	116.9	122.9	117.0	146.7	145.1	‡145.1	143.7	126.9	118.8	121.1
Fund Position															*Millions of SDRs:*	
Quota	2f.s	325	325	325	325	325	325	325	325	450	450	675	675	675	1,064	1,064
SDRs	1b.s	38	73	107	107	107	107	107	107	112	173	174	225	233	123	181
Reserve Position in the Fund	1c.s	126	84	90	88	89	95	232	225	191	181	194	166	149	241	258
of which: Outstg.Fund Borrowing	2c	45	—	—	—	—	—	50	64	55	43	31	18	6		
International Liquidity												*Millions of US Dollars Unless Otherwise Indicated:*				
Total Reserves minus Gold	1l.d	561	893	1,358	2,284	1,487	2,839	2,255	3,415	4,124	3,514	3,418	3,601	3,513	4,034	3,845
SDRs	1b.d	38	79	116	129	131	125	124	130	146	228	222	261	257	129	178
Reserve Position in the Fund	1c.d	126	91	98	106	109	111	269	274	249	238	247	193	164	252	253
Foreign Exchange	1d.d	397	723	1,144	2,049	1,247	2,602	1,862	3,011	3,729	3,048	2,949	3,147	3,091	3,653	3,414
Gold (Million Fine Troy Ounces)	1ad	5.715	5.778	5.782	5.790	5.790	5.790	5.790	5.929	5.999	6.069	6.069	6.069	6.069	6.069	6.069
Gold (National Valuation)	1and	200	220	220	244	248	237	235	252	274	280	271	247	234	222	208
Deposit Money Banks: Assets	7a.d	985	1,187	1,418	2,214	3,177	3,629	4,145	4,609	4,902	5,948	8,036	7,515	6,725	7,122	6,741
Liabilities	7b.d	769	940	1,019	1,393	1,782	2,478	3,236	4,414	5,811	9,070	12,518	14,100	13,157	13,980	13,098
Other Banking Insts.: Assets	7e.d	—	—	—	—	—	—	—	—	—	—	947	1,215	1,542	1,964	1,944
Liabilities	7f.d											1,045	1,609	2,337	3,189	3,855
Monetary Authorities															*Billions of Kronor:*	
Foreign Assets	11	3.62	5.07	7.33	11.24	7.62	12.82	11.37	17.66	19.79	16.27	15.73	20.87	25.99	32.64	33.91
Claims on Central Government	12a	10.17	11.33	10.85	8.89	16.67	16.40	17.88	15.65	20.96	34.68	33.19	43.16	50.46	37.73	67.20
Claims on Deposit Money Banks	12e	1.11	.01			2.96	.25	2.75	3.61	—	6.01	6.23	1.23		13.06	.55
Claims on Other Financial Insts.	12f	....	....	....	....											
Reserve Money	14	12.56	14.07	15.44	16.92	22.83	22.68	25.10	27.62	31.41	43.13	38.98	43.55	46.46	47.44	50.54
of which: Currency Outside DMBs	14a	11.40	12.81	14.14	15.38	17.32	20.13	22.16	24.41	27.57	30.94	33.58	36.06	38.06	41.93	45.11
Restricted Deposits	16b	1.25	1.05	1.05	1.24	2.28	4.47	3.32	2.86	2.39	5.57	5.72	4.17	3.89	14.92	12.95
Foreign Liabilities	16c	—	—	—	—	—	—	.91	1.98	1.87	1.80	1.47	1.57	1.90	1.15	.44
Central Government Deposits	16d	.04	.05	.39	.34	.26	.22	.19	.04	.15	.18	.07	.06	.08	.02	.14
Other Items (Net)	17r	1.05	1.25	1.31	1.63	1.88	2.10	2.48	4.42	4.93	6.27	8.91	15.92	24.12	19.91	37.59
Deposit Money Banks															*Billions of Kronor:*	
Reserves	20	1.30	1.33	1.42	1.55	5.73	2.74	3.13	3.33	3.96	12.30	5.65	8.49	8.41	‡4.77	5.26
Foreign Assets	21	5.10	5.72	6.83	10.10	12.96	15.91	17.10	21.52	21.06	24.66	35.14	41.87	51.31	‡59.59	63.82
Claims on Central Government	22a	6.41	7.56	11.50	15.11	13.83	20.38	15.62	17.88	34.41	36.10	54.27	79.56	77.70	‡99.93	100.16
Claims on Local Government	22b														10.15	10.47
Claims on Private Sector	22d	72.45	78.40	87.49	97.72	108.14	120.72	136.27	154.87	171.81	197.84	219.18	241.98	273.39	‡289.03	323.52
Claims on Other Financial Insts	22f	19.36	20.08	22.54	23.50	25.15	28.47	30.60	34.89	39.95	47.02	51.39	61.15	71.44	‡86.30	102.64
Demand,Time,Savings,Fgn.Cur.Dep.	25l	87.47	96.12	108.87	124.55	136.17	151.24	157.85	171.97	202.96	239.04	269.34	307.13	332.30	‡354.68	385.47
Bonds	26ab	....	....	....	....	....	....	....	....	....	....	....	....		2.19	2.16
Foreign Liabilities	26c	3.98	4.53	4.91	6.35	7.27	10.87	13.36	20.61	24.96	37.61	54.74	78.55	102.74	‡120.44	139.57
Central Government Deposits	26d	—	.01	—	.01	.01	.01	.02	.05	.08	.12	.13	.15	.17	‡.95	1.41
Credit from Monetary Authorities	26g	1.11	.01	—	—	2.96	.25	2.75	3.77	.09	6.32	6.51	1.82	.19	‡13.07	.62
Credit from Other Financial Insts	26i	1.37	2.21	2.27	4.22	4.22	4.52	6.15	7.63	9.18	10.25	9.39	16.77	16.82	‡16.30	23.05
Capital Accounts	27a	35.59	36.45	36.66	37.90	41.39	48.23	51.36	53.95	55.51	58.07	60.27	63.76	70.90	‡83.32	83.15
Other Items (Net)	27r	10.69	10.21	13.72	12.84	15.18	21.36	22.62	28.51	34.01	24.70	25.64	27.87	30.13	‡-41.17	-29.55
Monetary Survey															*Billions of Kronor:*	
Foreign Assets (Net)	31n	4.74	6.26	9.25	14.99	13.31	17.86	14.21	16.59	14.02	1.53	-5.34	-17.38	-27.34	‡-29.36	-42.27
Domestic Credit	32	108.87	117.85	132.53	145.47	164.11	186.38	200.90	223.97	267.71	316.30	358.81	425.52	473.38	‡523.67	604.50
Claims on Central Govt. (Net)	32an	16.54	18.84	21.96	23.65	30.23	36.54	33.29	33.44	55.13	70.47	87.26	122.51	127.90	‡136.69	165.81
Claims on Local Government	32b														10.15	10.47
Claims on Private Sector	32d	72.65	78.55	87.64	97.90	108.38	121.03	136.67	155.30	172.25	198.46	219.83	241.52	273.72	‡289.66	324.33
Claims on Other Financial Insts	32f	19.68	20.46	22.93	23.92	25.50	28.81	30.94	35.23	40.32	47.37	51.72	61.49	71.76	‡86.61	102.91
Money plus Quasi-Money	35l	98.88	108.94	123.02	139.94	153.50	171.39	180.03	196.40	230.54	270.00	302.95	343.24	370.76	‡397.51	431.23
Bonds	36ab	....	....	....	....	....	....	....	....	....	....	....	....		2.19	2.16
Restricted Deposits	36b	1.25	1.05	1.05	1.24	2.28	4.47	3.32	2.86	2.39	5.57	5.72	4.17	3.89	14.92	12.95
Liabilities to Other Banking Inst.	36i	1.37	2.21	2.27	4.22	4.22	4.52	6.15	7.63	9.18	10.25	9.39	16.77	16.82	‡16.30	23.05
Capital Accounts	37a	5.02	5.47	5.71	5.76	6.36	7.09	7.72	8.69	10.36	11.65	13.38	16.29	22.86	‡104.15	110.44
Other Items (Net)	37r	13.49	14.12	17.71	19.26	21.65	28.39	31.76	41.30	48.79	42.25	44.79	60.74	71.31	‡-40.76	-17.60
Money plus Quasi-Money	35l	98.88	108.94	123.02	139.94	153.50	171.39	180.03	196.40	230.54	270.00	302.95	343.24	370.76	‡397.51	431.23
Unused Bank Credits	39b	6.29	8.61	9.69	10.40	11.89	14.78	15.70	16.09	19.89	18.94	29.16	25.64	28.12	‡44.30	45.78
Money (National Definitions)															*Billions of Kronor:*	
Broad Money	39m	103.32	113.58	126.95	143.24	155.99	175.76	184.70	202.04	238.45	277.53	307.44	349.22	376.21	402.52	431.52
Other Banking Institutions															*Billions of Kronor:*	
Cash	40	.74	.59	.74	1.19	.81	1.18	.93	1.15	2.46	2.31	2.52	‡4.87	6.86	4.90	8.33
Foreign Assets	41											4.14	‡6.77	11.25	15.72	17.48
Claims on Central Government	42a	.02	—	—	.50	.35	.30	.16	.04	.08	.08	.08	‡.43	1.69	3.10	4.89
Claims on Local Government	42b															
Claims on Private Sector	42d	53.81	63.01	71.61	81.08	93.09	108.05	121.96	137.45	155.48	174.09	194.19	‡248.70	282.39	331.48	379.14
Claims on Deposit Money Banks	42e	....	....	....	....	....	....	....	....	....	....	....	....	....	....	....
Time, Savings,& Fgn. Currency Dep.	45	—	—	—	—	—	—	—	—	—	—	—	‡—		—	.22
Bonds	46ab	46.91	1.85	2.59	4.80	6.71	10.14	14.27	15.81	18.17	21.43	28.66	‡176.20	186.36	208.35	232.85
Foreign Liabilities	46c											4.57	‡8.96	21.19	25.52	34.66
Central Govt. Lending Funds	46f	22.22	27.81	31.83	37.16	43.04	48.18	54.05	60.52	67.30	73.18	79.70	86.87	93.31	99.65	110.99
Credit from Deposit Money Banks	46h	19.36	20.08	22.54	23.50	25.15	28.47	30.60	34.89	39.95	47.02	51.39	‡61.15	71.44	86.30	102.64
Capital Accounts	47a												7.36	8.19	9.21	10.11
Other Items (Net)	47r	-19.93	-25.04	-29.18	-34.04	-39.86	-44.28	-50.61	-56.75	-62.14	-69.17	-75.19	-79.77	-78.30	-73.83	-81.63

1985	1986	1987	1988	1989	1990	1991	1992	1993	1994	1995	1996	1997	1998	1999		
															Exchange Rates	
End of Period																
8.3650	8.3409	8.2963	8.2855	8.1833	8.1063	7.9096	9.6841	11.4054	10.8927	9.8973	9.8802	10.6280	11.3501	11.7006	Official Rate	aa
End of Period (ae) Period Average (rf)																
7.6155	6.8190	5.8480	6.1570	6.2270	5.6980	5.5295	7.0430	8.3035	7.4615	6.6582	6.8710	7.8770	8.0610	8.5250	Official Rate	ae
8.6039	7.1236	6.3404	6.1272	6.4469	5.9188	6.0475	5.8238	7.7834	7.7160	7.1333	6.7060	7.6349	7.9499	8.2624	Official Rate	rf
End of Period (ea) Period Average (eb)																
6.7172	7.2518	7.5529	7.1762	7.4106	7.6754	7.4502	8.5490	9.2963	9.1779	8.6973	8.6280	8.7323	9.4880	1.0046	Euro Rate	ea
6.5198	6.9944	7.3096	7.2439	7.1013	7.5200	7.4798	7.5299	9.1146	9.1579	9.3337	8.5156	8.6551	8.9085	1.0668	Euro Rate	eb
Period Averages																
83.1	100.1	112.4	116.3	110.5	120.5	118.1	122.9	91.7	92.4	100.0	106.2	93.4	89.6	86.2	Official Rate	ahx
131.0	127.5	125.4	125.6	126.4	123.6	123.4	125.0	102.1	100.7	100.0	109.6	105.5	103.2	101.8	Nominal Effective Exchange Rate	neu
122.5	124.0	123.5	128.1	137.5	137.5	136.8	137.2	104.7	101.7	100.0	110.7	104.8	101.7	....	Real Effective Exchange Rate	reu
															Fund Position	
End of Period																
1,064	1,064	1,064	1,064	1,064	1,064	1,064	1,614	1,614	1,614	1,614	1,614	1,614	1,614	2,396	Quota	2f.s
224	261	208	299	260	204	290	33	42	46	297	199	277	292	228	SDRs	1b.s
250	253	277	251	254	234	308	451	451	451	451	451	589	900	863	Reserve Position in the Fund	1c.s
—	—	—	—	—	—	—	—	—	—	—	—	—	112	—	*of which:* Outstg.Fund Borrowing	2c
															International Liquidity	
End of Period																
5,793	6,551	8,174	8,492	9,559	17,988	18,331	22,624	19,050	23,254	24,051	19,107	10,824	14,098	15,019	Total Reserves minus Gold	1l.d
246	320	296	402	341	290	414	45	58	68	441	286	373	412	313	SDRs	1b.d
274	310	394	337	333	333	441	621	620	659	671	649	795	1,267	1,184	Reserve Position in the Fund	1c.d
5,273	5,921	7,485	7,752	8,885	17,365	17,476	21,959	18,372	22,527	22,939	18,172	9,656	12,420	13,522	Foreign Exchange	1d.d
6.069	6.069	6.069	6.069	6.069	6.069	6.069	6.069	6.069	6.069	4.702	4.702	4.722	4.722	5.961	Gold (Million Fine Troy Ounces)	1ad
233	260	301	286	279	302	304	292	292	310	245	237	223	233	286	Gold (National Valuation)	1and
8,943	10,787	15,023	14,905	30,505	I 34,919	34,247	32,056	26,261	24,727	36,158	44,707	44,943	50,853	53,087	Deposit Money Banks: Assets	7a.d
17,199	23,621	35,051	43,924	72,015	I 99,361	93,185	62,745	50,253	50,925	55,100	56,670	60,376	86,846	76,769	Liabilities	7b.d
2,394	3,465	4,519	5,107	7,629	I 6,027	5,513	4,395	3,743	4,661	5,734	8,834	11,116	12,171	13,226	Other Banking Insts.: Assets	7e.d
4,343	5,556	7,430	9,401	10,829	I 5,269	6,623	22,534	20,605	22,196	16,597	14,535	13,686	29,960	34,387	Liabilities	7f.d
															Monetary Authorities	
End of Period																
44.41	45.74	50.29	53.74	60.69	103.77	99.85	163.29	175.69	177.95	171.96	140.21	93.41	136.22	152.55	Foreign Assets	11
68.14	88.93	96.14	93.35	89.50	53.24	132.31	145.98	98.99	87.52	71.03	59.05	53.09	32.84	I 27.69	Claims on Central Government	12a
5.86	4.15	2.40	17.40	27.87	19.68	23.55	61.02	1.26	.01	2.61	9.64	40.33	43.85	I 45.63	Claims on Deposit Money Banks	12e
....	....	....	....	....	....	....	....	....	....	....	....	....	....	1.31	Claims on Other Financial Insts.	12f
52.04	65.28	68.37	80.91	89.56	96.86	89.36	110.95	163.84	200.59	170.74	114.30	84.76	87.95	102.91	Reserve Money	14
46.12	50.38	52.22	55.14	60.66	62.00	64.80	64.30	67.05	68.81	68.55	70.71	72.97	74.63	78.64	*of which: Currency Outside DMBs*	14a
28.20	36.22	28.01	23.51	26.53	12.96	6.07	2.39	1.46	.92	.59	.12	.03	.02	....	Restricted Deposits	16b
.29	1.40	.04	—	.09	.05	—	12.47	.08	.22	3.48	4.14	3.98	4.10	I 5.26	Foreign Liabilities	16c
.09	.03	.01	.01	—	—	88.89	159.57	21.79	—	—	—	—	—	I 2.17	Central Government Deposits	16d
37.77	35.90	52.40	60.06	61.88	66.82	71.40	84.92	88.78	63.75	70.78	90.34	98.05	120.85	116.85	Other Items (Net)	17r
															Deposit Money Banks	
End of Period																
7.71	13.85	15.38	18.81	19.88	24.91	15.50	35.40	21.25	8.75	9.42	11.13	10.17	13.52	30.67	Reserves	20
67.80	71.09	97.46	131.34	186.70	242.68	272.46	328.95	329.24	281.57	408.71	I 572.15	682.15	698.05	741.63	Foreign Assets	21
87.50	86.87	104.81	110.62	134.54	86.39	89.11	65.32	149.50	162.35	143.46	122.00	109.15	167.93	86.99	Claims on Central Government	22a
8.93	9.86	12.11	11.49	14.53	21.39	23.59	19.68	14.58	17.54	24.99	31.05	36.85	37.58	42.74	Claims on Local Government	22b
340.62	398.71	453.89	581.82	705.26	791.16	785.40	784.30	631.41	605.08	596.72	I 623.21	711.06	771.67	848.41	Claims on Private Sector	22d
120.94	135.27	131.61	137.07	164.33	225.84	235.30	169.86	182.54	247.87	267.14	I 310.92	359.86	448.69	467.02	Claims on Other Financial Insts	22f
398.35	454.49	481.59	518.29	574.27	574.29	597.36	618.55	643.01	644.16	664.37	746.37	753.29	748.02	814.05	Demand,Time,Savings,Fgn.Cur.Dep.	25l
2.37	5.31	7.37	14.00	17.93	25.86	25.78	28.91	27.77	27.00	22.83	11.25	25.12	30.81	31.96	Bonds	26ab
144.66	160.50	214.66	311.77	420.48	616.56	615.87	545.64	532.70	504.20	568.22	I 639.64	788.10	985.59	924.94	Foreign Liabilities	26c
1.22	1.72	1.99	.37	1.10	.89	.53	.38	.34	.43	1.61	2.38	.86	12.24	31.02	Central Government Deposits	26d
6.74	5.76	3.02	19.50	27.51	20.25	31.14	82.15	.74	.02	.01	10.53	31.65	29.26	34.44	Credit from Monetary Authorities	26g
22.42	21.31	38.44	45.57	47.23	38.69	38.80	49.57	40.96	40.16	48.80	66.23	88.88	110.27	119.72	Credit from Other Financial Insts	26i
99.45	104.28	111.03	128.91	168.98	54.09	70.17	57.71	78.31	83.63	100.76	61.74	74.37	82.99	88.53	Capital Accounts	27a
-41.72	-37.71	-42.84	-47.26	-32.28	61.73	41.70	20.60	4.68	23.55	43.85	I 132.33	146.98	138.26	172.80	Other Items (Net)	27r
															Monetary Survey	
End of Period																
-32.75	-45.07	-66.95	-126.70	-173.18	-270.16	-243.56	-65.87	-27.85	-44.90	8.97	I 68.58	-16.52	-155.42	I -36.02	Foreign Assets (Net)	31n
626.63	718.54	796.90	934.12	1,107.09	1,177.11	1,176.29	1,025.20	1,054.89	1,119.92	1,101.73	I 1143.85	1,269.15	1,446.47	I 1440.97	Domestic Credit	32
154.32	174.06	198.95	203.60	222.93	138.73	132.00	51.35	226.37	249.43	212.88	178.67	161.37	188.54	I 81.49	Claims on Central Govt. (Net)	32an
8.93	9.86	12.11	11.49	14.53	21.39	23.59	19.68	14.58	17.54	24.99	31.05	36.85	37.58	42.74	Claims on Local Government	32b
341.38	399.35	454.23	581.96	705.30	791.16	785.40	784.30	631.41	605.08	596.72	I 623.21	711.06	771.67	848.41	Claims on Private Sector	32d
120.94	135.27	131.61	137.07	164.33	225.84	235.30	169.86	182.54	247.87	267.14	I 310.92	359.86	448.69	468.33	Claims on Other Financial Insts	32f
445.43	506.20	536.39	577.06	640.31	645.27	672.07	694.10	723.03	728.05	750.56	817.08	826.26	822.65	892.69	Money plus Quasi-Money	35l
2.37	5.31	7.37	14.00	17.93	25.86	25.78	28.91	27.77	27.00	22.83	11.25	25.12	30.81	31.96	Bonds	36ab
28.20	36.22	28.01	23.51	26.53	12.96	6.07	2.39	1.46	.92	.59	.12	.03	.02	....	Restricted Deposits	36b
22.42	21.31	38.44	45.57	47.23	38.69	38.80	49.57	40.96	40.16	48.80	66.23	88.88	110.27	119.72	Liabilities to Other Banking Inst.	36i
133.03	139.00	143.53	177.53	220.44	106.10	127.08	120.77	137.90	160.25	175.22	137.45	156.62	183.06	202.95	Capital Accounts	37a
-37.55	-34.57	-23.79	-30.25	-18.54	78.08	62.93	63.60	95.92	118.65	112.70	I 180.30	155.72	144.25	I 157.64	Other Items (Net)	37r
445.43	506.20	536.39	577.06	640.31	645.27	672.07	694.10	723.03	728.05	750.56	817.08	826.26	822.65	892.69	Money plus Quasi-Money	35l
46.65	63.28	87.93	120.22	134.76	152.30	154.42	166.20	173.66	184.13	197.97	....	....	....	....	*Unused Bank Credits*	39b
															Money (National Definitions)	
End of Period																
428.82	474.26	494.05	519.65	571.68	636.46	661.79	682.85	710.06	712.33	731.81	815.53	826.24	843.42	926.98	*Broad Money*	39m
															Other Banking Institutions	
End of Period																
9.99	2.65	4.94	7.56	7.37	I 4.30	.34	.08	.03	.64	.02	—	—	—	—	Cash	40
18.54	26.19	26.43	36.87	43.90	I 48.90	43.70	46.54	37.45	46.15	38.26	I 60.70	87.56	98.11	112.75	Foreign Assets	41
8.06	7.94	9.67	12.19	10.22	I 6.99	17.49	18.01	17.40	28.84	23.98	16.02	16.26	18.53	18.67	Claims on Central Government	42a
—	—	.70	.08	—	I —	.19	.02	—	.02	.01	I 35.70	39.04	40.72	42.16	Claims on Local Government	42b
436.34	555.81	437.97	524.09	604.80	I 1020.15	1,113.06	1,133.15	1,124.98	1,133.60	1,162.92	I 1154.15	1,161.62	1,200.06	1,249.53	Claims on Private Sector	42d
....	....	....	....	....	31.24	31.02	36.98	31.36	25.92	I 28.69	39.90	46.18	59.23	54.60	Claims on Deposit Money Banks	42e
.76	7.76	21.14	30.15	49.08	I 92.12	98.53	96.86	66.01	92.34	134.44	167.26	173.49	2.43	.52	Time, Savings,& Fgn. Currency Dep.	45
279.36	356.16	409.46	485.56	567.35	I 693.97	765.21	849.44	960.64	915.53	856.98	804.90	736.65	720.90	648.43	Bonds	46ab
33.60	38.58	34.59	46.86	57.03	I 37.78	43.07	42.10	26.57	41.49	24.08	I 99.87	107.80	241.51	293.15	Foreign Liabilities	46c
127.30	155.06	168.26	194.40	225.27	239.54	262.71	279.70	278.12	247.18	230.97	I 189.15	184.74	211.22	171.99	Central Govt. Lending Funds	46f
120.94	135.27	131.61	137.07	164.33	I 116.31	150.85	93.48	51.38	66.74	81.61	96.58	170.02	222.74	250.19	Credit from Deposit Money Banks	46h
11.36	12.73	14.46	17.74	19.38	21.34	23.12	47.15	66.72	73.35	82.26	60.74	65.24	68.36	73.71	Capital Accounts	47a
-100.38	-112.98	-299.81	-331.01	-416.16	I -89.49	-137.69	-173.97	-238.24	-201.50	-156.47	-112.04	-87.29	-50.51	39.73	Other Items (Net)	47r

		1970	1971	1972	1973	1974	1975	1976	1977	1978	1979	1980	1981	1982	1983	1984
Banking Survey															*Billions of Kronor:*	
Foreign Assets (Net)	51n	4.74	6.26	9.25	14.99	13.31	17.86	14.21	16.59	14.02	1.53	−5.77	−19.57	−37.29	−39.16	−59.45
Domestic Credit	52	....	....	....	....	....	....	....	....	....	....	....	....	....	771.41	885.11
Claims on Central Govt. (Net)	52an	16.56	18.84	21.96	24.15	30.58	36.84	33.45	33.47	55.21	70.55	87.34	122.94	129.59	Ⅰ139.56	170.19
Claims on Local Government	52b	....	....	....	....	....	....	....	....	....	....	....	....	....	10.15	10.47
Claims on Private Sector	52d	126.46	141.56	159.25	178.97	201.47	229.08	258.63	292.75	327.74	372.55	414.02	490.22	556.11	621.14	703.47
Liquid Liabilities	55l	98.88	108.94	123.02	139.94	153.50	171.39	180.03	196.40	230.54	270.00	302.95	343.24	370.76	Ⅰ397.51	431.45
Bonds	56ab	....	....	....	....	....	....	....	....	....	....	....	....	....	210.54	235.01
Central Govt. Lending Funds	56f	24.66	30.55	34.90	40.63	47.30	53.00	59.61	67.28	75.40	82.53	90.54	98.46	106.07	112.16	121.59
Capital Accounts	57a	....	....	....	....	....	....	....	....	....	....	....	23.65	31.05	113.36	120.56
Other Items (Net)	57r	....	....	....	....	....	....	....	....	....	....	....	....	....	−101.32	−82.95
Nonbank Financial Institutions															*Billions of Kronor:*	
Cash	40.. l	.78	1.02	1.10	1.20	1.49	1.22	1.28	1.70	1.81	2.70	2.59	3.91	3.21	3.11	6.17
Foreign Assets	41.. l	....	....	....	....	....	....	....	....	....	....	....	1.38	2.19	2.88	2.96
Claims on Central Government	42a. l	3.20	3.01	3.57	4.27	5.49	6.13	7.49	9.04	12.24	15.82	19.59	24.35	34.57	46.20	57.50
Claims on Private Sector	42d. l	15.98	17.00	18.01	19.42	21.66	24.14	27.31	30.93	34.81	39.29	44.92	35.72	37.91	41.60	43.99
Claims on Other Banking Insts	42f. l	8.99	10.69	12.35	13.76	15.81	18.51	20.34	23.30	27.08	30.49	33.55	52.28	55.97	63.71	73.49
Interest Rates															*Percent Per Annum*	
Discount Rate *(End of Period)*	60	7.00	5.00	5.00	5.00	7.00	6.00	8.00	8.00	6.50	9.00	10.00	11.00	10.00	8.50	9.50
Repurchase Rate *(End of Period)*	60a	....	....	3.34	3.83	9.00	7.83	7.93	9.96	7.16	8.19	12.17	14.35	13.29	10.85	11.77
Money Market Rate	60b	9.83	5.79	3.06	3.27	7.33	7.83	7.93	9.96	7.16	8.19	12.17	14.35	13.29	10.85	11.77
Treasury Bill Rate	60c	8.44	5.85	3.75	2.79	6.85	7.29	6.50	9.42	6.63	6.79	11.58	12.54	13.22	12.34	11.93
Deposit Rate *(End of Period)*	60l	7.50	5.50	5.50	5.50	7.50	6.50	8.50	8.50	7.00	9.50	11.25	11.75	11.25	9.75	10.75
Lending Rate *(End of Period)*	60p	9.39	9.39	8.93	8.93	11.19	10.25	12.91	12.79	11.16	13.67	15.18	16.73	16.52	14.91	16.00
Government Bond Yield	61	7.39	7.23	7.29	7.39	7.79	8.79	9.28	9.74	10.09	10.47	11.74	13.49	13.04	12.30	12.28
Prices, Production, Labor															*Index Numbers (1995=100):*	
Share Prices	62	4	4	5	5	5	6	7	6	6	6	7	10	12	24	26
Forest Industries	62a	3	3	4	4	6	6	9	7	6	6	7	11	12	28	33
Engineering Industries	62b	4	5	5	5	5	6	6	5	5	4	4	7	9	20	21
Prices: Domestic Supply	63	17	17	18	20	25	27	29	32	35	39	44	49	56	62	67
Consumer Prices	64	16	17	19	20	22	24	26	29	32	35	Ⅰ39	44	48	52	56
Harmonized CPI	64h	....	....	....	....	....	....	....	....	....	....	....	....	....	....	....
Wages: Hourly Earnings	65	15	15	16	18	20	23	27	28	31	33	36	40	43	46	50
Industrial Production	66.. c	68	Ⅰ69	70	75	79	78	76	72	71	75	74	74	72	75	81
Industrial Employment	67	138	137	136	138	146	148	Ⅰ142	137	132	133	133	128	124	123	125
															Number in Thousands:	
Labor Force	67d	....	....	....	....	....	....	....	....	....	....	....	....	....	....	....
Employment	67e	....	....	....	....	....	....	....	....	....	....	....	....	....	....	....
Unemployment	67c	....	....	....	....	....	....	....	....	....	....	....	....	....	....	....
Unemployment Rate (%)	67r	....	....	....	....	....	....	....	....	....	....	....	....	....	....	....
International Transactions															*Millions of Kronor*	
Exports	70	35,150	38,224	41,749	53,153	70,514	72,012	80,195	Ⅰ85,677	98,206	118,210	130,747	144,876	168,134	210,516	242,809
Imports, c.i.f.	71	36,251	36,192	38,618	47,500	73,850	72,390	85,300	Ⅰ90,221	92,751	122,962	141,329	146,040	173,933	200,368	218,570
															1995=100	
Volume of Exports	72	40	42	45	53	56	Ⅰ51	53	54	58	62	61	62	64	Ⅰ71	77
Volume of Imports	73	42	40	42	46	53	Ⅰ54	57	56	52	60	62	58	61	Ⅰ63	66
Export Prices	76	17	17	18	20	27	29	30	32	34	38	43	46	52	58	63
Import Prices	76.x	16	16	17	19	27	28	30	34	36	43	50	55	63	71	75
Balance of Payments															*Millions of US Dollars:*	
Current Account, n.i.e.	78ald	−253	365	586	1,452	−529	−308	−1,602	−2,120	−191	−2,349	−4,331	−2,778	−3,285	−725	736
Goods: Exports f.o.b.	78aa d	6,750	7,402	8,697	12,097	15,797	17,259	18,287	18,930	21,598	27,377	30,662	28,389	26,575	27,204	29,123
Goods: Imports f.o.b.	78ab d	−6,447	−6,508	−7,479	−10,066	−15,405	−16,181	−18,124	−18,654	−19,023	−28,072	−32,860	−28,226	−26,797	−25,303	−25,701
Trade Balance	78ac d	303	894	1,218	2,031	392	1,078	162	275	2,574	−695	−2,198	163	−222	1,901	3,422
Services: Credit	78ad d	1,353	1,615	1,917	2,482	3,041	3,431	3,624	3,909	4,654	6,619	7,489	7,035	6,521	6,292	6,293
Services: Debit	78ae d	−1,776	−1,957	−2,285	−2,775	−3,555	−4,144	−4,517	−5,037	−5,610	−6,471	−7,018	−6,863	−6,909	−6,224	−6,334
Balance on Goods & Services	78af d	−120	552	850	1,738	−122	365	−730	−852	1,619	−546	−1,727	336	−610	1,968	3,381
Income: Credit	78ag d	153	133	153	261	306	351	492	511	831	1,008	1,238	1,682	2,431	2,125	2,312
Income: Debit	78ah d	−145	−156	−183	−259	−318	−404	−665	−962	−1,490	−1,755	−2,617	−3,790	−4,159	−3,962	−4,201
Balance on Gds, Serv. & Inc.	78ai d	−112	529	821	1,740	−133	312	−902	−1,303	959	−1,293	−3,107	−1,773	−2,338	131	1,492
Current Transfers, n.i.e.: Credit	78aj d	15	14	17	16	29	26	44	40	49	148	92	92	81	124	100
Current Transfers: Debit	78ak d	−157	−178	−252	−305	−426	−647	−744	−857	−1,199	−1,204	−1,317	−1,097	−1,028	−980	−856
Capital Account, n.i.e.	78bc d	−12	−14	−19	−23	−23	−34	−46	−60	−60	−65	−73	−69	−80	−81	−171
Capital Account, n.i.e.: Credit	78ba d	—	—	—	—	—	—	—	—	—	—	—	—	—	1	—
Capital Account: Debit	78bb d	−12	−14	−19	−23	−23	−34	−46	−60	−60	−65	−73	−69	−80	−82	−171
Financial Account, n.i.e.	78bj d	143	125	166	−294	99	1,660	971	805	80	−320	454	652	−1,333	−4,722	−5,812
Direct Investment Abroad	78bd d	−213	−176	−265	−293	−430	−434	−596	−737	−415	−618	−625	−825	−1,212	−1,458	−1,497
Dir. Invest. in Rep. Econ., n.i.e.	78be d	108	84	65	84	77	80	5	81	70	112	251	181	355	226	290
Portfolio Investment Assets	78bf d	−6	12	—	−23	−11	−4	5	9	17	−23	−35	14	−34	−60	3
Equity Securities	78bk d	—	−4	2	5	—	−5	5	11	9	5	−5	−6	−15	−8	17
Debt Securities	78bl d	−6	16	−2	−27	−11	—	—	−2	8	−28	−31	19	−19	−52	−14
Portfolio Investment Liab., n.i.e.	78bg d	54	62	176	103	47	599	712	573	129	−265	−231	473	180	749	219
Equity Securities	78bm d	−6	−10	−31	−16	−32	−21	−25	−30	−33	−26	−54	77	201	804	172
Debt Securities	78bn d	60	72	208	119	79	620	737	603	162	−239	−176	396	−21	−55	47
Financial Derivatives Assets	78bw d	....	....	....	....	....	....	....	....	....	....	....	....	....	....	....
Financial Derivatives Liabilities	78bx d	....	....	....	....	....	....	....	....	....	....	....	....	....	....	....
Other Investment Assets	78bh d	−178	−84	−254	−607	−795	−733	−1,049	−1,253	221	−366	−183	−1,130	−1,744	−1,903	−939
Monetary Authorities	78bo d	....	....	....	....	....	....	....	....	....	....	....	....	....	....	....
General Government	78bp d	−35	−68	−23	−82	−133	−304	−133	−193	9	−35	62	−101	−305	−173	−110
Banks	78bq d	−143	76	−239	−675	−683	−308	−604	−664	121	−92	35	−295	−332	−190	−2
Other Sectors	78br d	—	−92	8	151	20	−122	−312	−396	92	−240	−281	−734	−1,107	−1,541	−827
Other Investment Liab., n.i.e.	78bi d	377	226	443	442	1,212	2,153	1,894	2,132	59	839	1,277	1,940	1,123	−2,276	−3,888
Monetary Authorities	78bs d	—	—	—	—	—	—	—	—	−31	−16	−5	−69	−44	−108	−15
General Government	78bt d	−8	33	31	34	32	76	97	91	−880	72	−334	−1,653	−1,312	−3,512	−5,524
Banks	78bu d	64	−70	97	305	288	555	874	1,328	898	1,833	1,738	2,527	1,068	1,040	966
Other Sectors	78bv d	321	263	315	103	892	1,522	923	714	72	−1,049	−122	1,135	1,409	304	684
Net Errors and Omissions	78ca d	151	−228	−382	−265	−301	−122	153	300	−523	−133	−1,447	−596	408	47	−586
Overall Balance	78cb d	29	248	351	870	−753	1,196	−524	−1,075	−693	−2,868	−5,398	−2,790	−4,291	−5,481	−5,834
Reserves and Related Items	79da d	−29	−248	−351	−870	753	−1,196	524	1,075	693	2,868	5,398	2,790	4,291	5,481	5,834
Reserve Assets	79db d	−29	−248	−351	−870	753	−1,404	513	−1,101	−654	676	105	−203	41	−686	43
Use of Fund Credit and Loans	79dc d	—	—	—	—	—	—	—	—	—	—	—	—	—	—	—
Exceptional Financing	79de d	—	—	—	—	—	208	12	2,176	1,347	2,191	5,292	2,994	4,249	6,167	5,790

1985	1986	1987	1988	1989	1990	1991	1992	1993	1994	1995	1996	1997	1998	1999		
End of Period															**Banking Survey**	
-47.81	-57.46	-75.10	-136.69	-186.32	I -259.04	-242.93	-61.44	-16.98	-40.24	23.15	I 29.41	-36.77	-298.81	I -216.41	Foreign Assets (Net)	51n
949.89	1,146.09	1,113.63	1,333.40	1,557.78	I 1978.41	2,071.73	2,006.51	2,014.73	2,034.50	2,021.48	I 2038.79	2,126.20	2,257.10	2,283.00	Domestic Credit	52
162.17	181.07	208.63	215.79	233.16	I 145.71	149.49	69.36	243.76	278.27	236.86	194.68	177.63	207.06	100.16	Claims on Central Govt. (Net)	52an
8.93	9.86	12.81	11.56	14.53	21.39	23.78	19.70	14.58	17.55	25.00	I 66.75	75.89	78.30	84.90	Claims on Local Government	52b
777.72	955.16	892.20	1,106.05	1,310.09	I 1811.31	1,898.46	1,917.45	1,756.39	1,738.68	1,759.64	I 1777.36	1,872.68	1,971.73	2,097.94	Claims on Private Sector	52d
446.19	513.96	557.53	607.21	689.40	737.39	770.61	790.96	789.03	820.39	885.00	984.34	999.74	825.08	893.21	Liquid Liabilities	55l
281.73	361.47	416.83	499.56	585.28	I 719.83	790.98	878.35	988.42	942.53	879.81	816.16	761.77	751.71	680.39	Bonds	56ab
135.75	159.35	170.61	195.72	226.08	239.54	262.71	279.70	278.12	247.18	230.97	I 189.15	184.74	211.22	171.99	Central Govt. Lending Funds	56f
144.38	151.73	158.00	195.27	239.82	127.44	150.20	167.92	204.63	233.60	257.48	198.19	221.86	251.42	276.66	Capital Accounts	57a
-105.97	-97.88	-264.44	-301.05	-369.12	-104.83	-145.69	-171.86	-262.45	-249.45	-208.62	I -119.63	-78.68	-81.15	I 44.34	Other Items (Net)	57r
End of Period															**Nonbank Financial Institutions**	
5.83	7.57	4.54	9.32	7.53	6.94	7.74	9.67	9.08	8.63	7.21	8.25	22.52	14.14	22.70	Cash	40.. *l*
3.49	3.71	4.98	6.70	18.98	55.96	74.17	77.98	100.48	102.79	131.88	203.66	288.09	394.10	509.62	Foreign Assets	41.. *l*
59.67	56.93	48.58	47.51	52.82	50.52	73.97	77.43	130.95	161.20	254.55	253.97	259.93	290.98	341.92	Claims on Central Government	42a. *l*
51.15	53.83	122.25	150.81	176.69	153.11	155.86	160.00	201.46	215.18	239.53	296.04	363.62	410.38	587.06	Claims on Private Sector	42d. *l*
88.59	113.52	125.84	159.04	183.06	175.10	204.02	231.03	242.55	188.15	159.25	205.46	216.78	241.47	216.25	Claims on Other Banking Insts	42f. *l*
Percent Per Annum															**Interest Rates**	
10.50	7.50	7.50	8.50	10.50	11.50	8.00	I 10.00	5.00	7.00	7.00	3.50	2.50	2.00	1.50	Discount Rate *(End of Period)*	60
13.94	10.02	9.04	9.70	11.09	12.60	11.28	16.62	8.83	I 7.51	8.91	4.27	4.19	3.50	3.25	Repurchase Rate *(End of Period)*	60a
13.85	10.15	9.16	10.08	11.52	13.45	11.81	18.42	9.08	7.36	8.54	6.28	4.21	4.24	3.14	Money Market Rate	60b
14.17	9.83	9.39	10.08	11.50	13.66	11.59	12.85	8.35	7.40	8.75	5.79	4.11	4.19	3.12	Treasury Bill Rate	60c
12.00	9.00	8.75	9.50	I 9.16	9.93	7.96	I 7.80	5.10	4.91	6.16	2.47	2.50	1.91	1.65	Deposit Rate *(End of Period)*	60l
16.89	I 12.57	12.65	13.29	14.81	16.69	16.05	I 15.20	11.40	10.64	11.11	7.38	7.01	5.94	5.53	Lending Rate *(End of Period)*	60p
13.09	10.26	I 11.68	11.35	11.18	13.08	10.69	10.02	8.54	I 9.41	....	....	....	....	....	Government Bond Yield	61
Period Averages															**Prices, Production, Labor**	
24	40	47	53	73	67	64	54	71	90	100	....	177	205	242	Share Prices	62
29	51	66	77	90	68	74	64	78	95	100	....	129	125	133	Forest Industries	62a
20	32	31	33	51	51	49	46	67	88	100	....	182	203	268	Engineering Industries	62b
70	68	70	74	79	83	I 84	83	89	93	100	98	99	99	100	Prices: Domestic Supply	63
60	63	66	69	74	82	89	91	95	98	100	100	101	101	101	Consumer Prices	64
....	....	....	....	....	....	....	....	....	....	100	101	103	104	104	Harmonized CPI	64h
54	58	62	67	74	81	85	89	92	95	100	107	111	115	118	Wages: Hourly Earnings	65
83	84	86	87	90	I 88	83	82	83	91	I 100	101	108	114	116	Industrial Production	66.. c
127	128	126	127	128	125	I 115	105	96	95	100	101	100	100	99	Industrial Employment	67
Period Averages																
....	....	....	....	....	....	....	....	4,320	....	4,319	4,310	4,264	4,255	....	Labor Force	67d
4,299	I 4,299	4,316	4,375	4,442	4,485	4,396	4,209	I 3,964	3,928	3,986	3,963	3,922	3,979	4,067	Employment	67e
85	98	94	77	66	75	134	233	I 356	340	332	346	342	278	241	Unemployment	67c
2.5	2.2	2.1	1.7	1.5	1.6	3.2	5.9	I 8.2	8.0	7.7	8.0	8.0	6.5	5.6	Unemployment Rate (%)	67r
Millions of Kronor															**International Transactions**	
260,500	265,104	281,333	304,190	332,220	340,040	332,800	326,040	388,300	471,600	567,700	569,200	632,800	673,600	700,800	Exports	70
244,609	232,479	257,386	279,261	315,620	320,380	301,260	290,510	332,490	397,410	460,500	488,700	501,100	542,200	565,600	Imports, c.i.f.	71
1995=100																
80	81	84	87	89	89	I 88	90	98	104	100	95	98	96	94	Volume of Exports	72
72	75	81	85	91	92	I 85	91	94	105	100	94	101	100	95	Volume of Imports	73
65	66	68	72	77	I 79	80	78	85	90	100	95	96	95	94	Export Prices	76
77	69	71	73	78	I 80	81	79	90	94	100	96	98	97	100	Import Prices	76.x
Minus Sign Indicates Debit															Balance of Payments	
-1,010	32	-21	-534	-3,101	-6,339	-4,653	-8,827	-4,159	743	4,940	5,892	7,406	4,639	....	Current Account, n.i.e.	78al *d*
30,173	36,845	44,013	49,367	51,071	56,835	54,542	55,363	49,348	60,199	79,903	84,690	83,194	85,179	....	Goods: Exports f.o.b.	78aa *d*
-27,788	-31,811	-39,528	-44,487	-47,054	-53,433	-48,185	-48,642	-41,801	-50,641	-63,926	-66,053	-65,195	-67,547	....	Goods: Imports f.o.b.	78ab *d*
2,385	5,035	4,485	4,880	4,017	3,402	6,357	6,720	7,548	9,558	15,978	18,636	17,999	17,632	....	*Trade Balance*	78ac *d*
6,121	6,664	8,946	10,420	11,355	13,725	14,725	16,195	12,589	13,674	15,622	16,930	17,769	17,952	....	Services: Credit	78ad *d*
-6,681	-8,463	-10,634	-12,662	-14,389	-17,058	-17,352	-19,090	-13,355	-14,690	-17,216	-18,755	-19,524	-21,721	....	Services: Debit	78ae *d*
1,824	3,236	2,798	2,637	983	70	3,730	3,826	6,782	8,542	14,384	16,811	16,245	13,862	....	*Balance on Goods & Services*	78af *d*
2,584	3,142	4,372	5,277	6,968	9,691	9,435	8,142	7,127	9,611	14,906	14,338	14,404	16,564	....	Income: Credit	78ag *d*
-4,561	-5,187	-5,935	-7,070	-9,302	-14,164	-15,833	-18,181	-16,261	-15,530	-21,379	-22,641	-20,513	-22,349	....	Income: Debit	78ah *d*
-153	1,191	1,234	844	-1,350	-4,403	-2,669	-6,213	-2,352	2,623	7,910	8,508	10,135	8,077	....	*Balance on Gds, Serv. & Inc.*	78ai *d*
117	111	267	382	298	386	393	405	456	544	1,555	2,524	2,319	2,266	....	Current Transfers, n.i.e.: Credit	78aj *d*
-975	-1,269	-1,523	-1,760	-2,049	-2,321	-2,378	-3,019	-2,263	-2,424	-4,525	-5,140	-5,048	-5,704	....	Current Transfers: Debit	78ak *d*
-221	-182	-139	-234	-296	-353	-63	6	23	23	14	9	-228	868	....	Capital Account, n.i.e.	78bc *d*
—	—	38	29	38	38	38	37	37	37	32	31	211	1,502	....	Capital Account, n.i.e.: Credit	78ba *d*
-221	-182	-177	-263	-334	-391	-101	-31	-15	-14	-18	-22	-439	-634	....	Capital Account: Debit	78bb *d*
-2,893	259	770	2,897	9,837	19,278	-1,336	10,214	11,518	6,078	-5,052	-10,046	-10,121	5,961	....	Financial Account, n.i.e.	78bj *d*
-1,805	-3,963	-4,780	-7,471	-10,296	-14,629	-7,262	-419	-1,471	-6,685	-11,399	-5,112	-12,119	-22,671	....	Direct Investment Abroad	78bd *d*
393	1,083	639	1,673	1,812	1,982	6,351	-5	3,705	6,269	14,939	5,492	10,271	19,413	....	Dir. Invest. in Rep. Econ., n.i.e.	78be *d*
-47	-153	-327	-686	-4,475	-3,644	-2,313	-1,578	-94	-2,459	-10,765	-13,136	-13,818	-17,615	....	Portfolio Investment Assets	78bf *d*
2	-26	21	-509	-4,324	-3,271	-2,350	-505	-76	-2,509	-9,378	-7,518	-10,179	-7,427	....	Equity Securities	78bk *d*
-49	-127	-348	-177	-150	-373	37	-1,073	-18	51	-1,386	-5,618	-3,640	-10,188	....	Debt Securities	78bl *d*
609	—	-738	-673	3,227	6,112	8,859	2,563	1,472	721	8,201	1,661	-2,384	2,023	....	Portfolio Investment Liab., n.i.e.	78bg *d*
557	306	-667	-446	-290	192	1,817	2,257	4,212	6,795	1,853	4,047	-1,687	-328	....	Equity Securities	78bm *d*
52	-306	-71	-227	3,517	5,920	7,042	306	-2,741	-6,074	6,348	-2,386	-697	2,351	....	Debt Securities	78bn *d*
....	....	....	....	....	....	....	....	....	....	20,264	24,800	31,244	30,125	....	Financial Derivatives Assets	78bw *d*
....	....	....	....	....	....	....	....	....	....	-21,096	-23,243	-29,280	-31,428	....	Financial Derivatives Liabilities	78bx *d*
-219	-875	-2,274	-2,133	-5,074	-9,618	-946	1,633	1,159	-3,400	-12,197	-10,828	-9,670	-5,901	....	Other Investment Assets	78bh *d*
....	....	....	....	....	....	....	....	....	....	....	....	—	—	....	Monetary Authorities	78bo *d*
-134	-196	-259	-160	-384	-559	-350	-337	-144	-290	-483	-303	-322	-244	....	General Government	78bp *d*
54	-1	-220	-479	-2,010	-6,597	342	1,083	4,682	2,902	-8,037	-10,239	-4,971	-1,135	....	Banks	78bq *d*
-140	-678	-1,795	-1,494	-2,681	-2,462	-938	887	-3,379	-6,012	-3,677	-287	-4,377	-4,522	....	Other Sectors	78br *d*
-1,823	4,168	8,251	12,187	24,643	39,074	-6,025	8,020	6,748	11,633	6,999	10,320	15,635	32,015	....	Other Investment Liab., n.i.e.	78bi *d*
-21	—	—	—	—	—	—	—	—	—	—	—	-39	88	....	Monetary Authorities	78bs *d*
-4,939	-935	-268	-1,924	-1,933	-2,216	-2,780	28,567	11,723	5,075	8,842	1,817	-1,583	578	....	General Government	78bt *d*
1,477	2,129	4,829	8,171	16,626	27,867	-8,276	-26,461	-10,851	-1,957	-1,055	2,935	9,269	20,205	....	Banks	78bu *d*
1,660	2,973	3,689	5,940	9,950	13,423	5,031	5,914	5,876	8,515	-788	5,569	7,988	11,144	....	Other Sectors	78bv *d*
-526	68	153	-1,190	-5,185	-5,034	5,989	5,560	-4,852	-4,462	-1,566	-2,241	-3,769	-8,214	....	Net Errors and Omissions	78ca *d*
-4,651	177	762	938	1,254	7,552	-63	6,953	2,530	2,381	-1,664	-6,386	-6,712	3,254	....	*Overall Balance*	78cb *d*
4,651	-177	-762	-938	-1,254	-7,552	63	-6,953	-2,530	-2,381	1,664	6,386	6,712	-3,254	....	Reserves and Related Items	79da *d*
-1,551	-177	-762	-938	-1,254	-7,552	63	-6,953	-2,530	-2,381	1,664	6,386	6,712	-3,254	....	Reserve Assets	79db *d*
—	—	—	—	—	—	—	—	—	—	—	—	—	—	....	Use of Fund Credit and Loans	79dc *d*
6,201	—	—	—	—	—	—	—	—	—	—	—	—	—	....	Exceptional Financing	79de *d*

		1970	1971	1972	1973	1974	1975	1976	1977	1978	1979	1980	1981	1982	1983	1984
International Investment Position														*Millions of US Dollars*		
Assets	79aa d	....	....	....	....	....	....	....	....	....	....	....	....	26,595	30,371	30,591
Direct Investment Abroad	79ab d	...	...	...	...	...	...	...	...	...	...	...	...	5,758	6,624	7,342
Portfolio Investment	79ac d	...	...	...	...	...	...	...	...	...	...	...	...	685	750	667
Equity Securities	79ad d													411	500	445
Debt Securities	79ae d													274	250	222
Financial Derivatives	79al d															
Other Investment	79af d													16,725	18,998	18,800
Monetary Authorities	79ag d													—	—	—
General Government	79ah d													1,234	1,500	1,446
Banks	79ai d													6,992	7,499	7,231
Other Sectors	79aj d													8,500	9,999	10,123
Reserve Assets	79ak d													3,427	4,000	3,782
Liabilities	79la d													45,651	50,369	49,391
Dir. Invest. in Rep. Economy	79lb d													3,427	3,375	3,337
Portfolio Investment	79lc d													1,645	2,250	1,669
Equity Securities	79ld d													1,645	2,250	1,669
Debt Securities	79le d													—	—	—
Financial Derivatives	79ll d															
Other investment	79lf d													40,579	44,744	44,385
Monetary Authorities	79lg d													—	—	—
General Government	79lh d													14,257	16,373	15,796
Banks	79li d													14,120	15,123	15,574
Other Sectors	79lj d													12,201	13,248	13,015
Government Finance														*Billions of Kronor:*		
Deficit (-) or Surplus	80	I-3.10	-2.44	-2.47	-3.21	-7.98	-7.55	-1.17	-6.06	-20.45	-33.22	-43.03	-51.52	-52.59	-68.68	-62.88
Revenue	81	I51.05	58.37	66.10	70.08	78.77	93.35	122.49	140.24	153.85	165.53	185.75	212.65	240.08	272.38	309.76
Grants Received	81z	I.24	.27	.37	.42	.38	.37	.39	.53	.80	1.04	1.00	1.11	1.33	—	—
Expenditure	82	I43.86	49.10	56.93	63.39	74.78	88.57	108.79	131.66	156.38	182.76	208.79	245.39	273.44	320.73	348.76
Lending Minus Repayments	83	I10.53	11.98	12.01	10.32	12.35	12.70	15.26	15.17	18.72	17.03	20.99	19.89	20.56	20.33	23.88
Financing																
Domestic	84a	I3.17	2.44	2.47	3.21	7.95	7.47	1.09	1.19	14.31	29.55	25.81	36.90	36.77	49.79	41.36
Foreign	85a	I-.07	—	—	—	.03	.08	.08	4.87	6.14	3.67	17.22	14.62	15.82	18.89	21.52
Total Debt	88	I27.85	29.92	32.39	36.00	44.09	52.50	54.58	65.00	83.31	112.20	159.57	213.21	272.80	352.52	414.48
Debt: Domestic	88a	I27.85	29.92	32.39	36.00	44.05	52.39	54.39	59.93	72.11	97.32	127.47	166.49	210.26	271.09	311.53
Other Levels of Government	88aa	....	....	....	....	....	2.48	3.17	3.80	3.73	4.51	4.51	5.63	7.10	17.79	15.03
Monetary Authorities	88ab	....	....	....	....	....	18.46	11.55	13.15	12.69	15.16	26.05	36.64	58.00	39.52	45.78
Deposit Money Banks	88ac						13.71	17.91	16.49	24.44	37.28	44.54	61.39	72.79	96.69	92.37
Other Domestic	88ad						17.74	21.76	26.49	31.25	40.37	52.37	62.83	72.37	117.09	158.35
Debt: Foreign	89a	I—	—	—	—	.04	.11	.19	5.07	11.20	14.88	32.10	46.72	62.54	81.43	102.95
Intragovernmental Debt	88s	I3.11	3.49	4.83	7.20	8.59	11.18	14.17	17.35	21.92	26.89	32.52	39.76	46.89	54.80	68.16
Total Debt	88	I27.85	29.92	32.39	36.00	44.09	52.50	54.58	65.00	83.31	112.20	159.57	213.21	272.80	352.52	414.48
Debt: Kronor	88b	....	....	....	....	....	....	....	....	....	....	....	....	....	....	....
Held By: Bank of Sweden	88ba	....	....	....	....	....	....	....	....	....	....	....	....	....	....	....
Commercial Banks	88bb	....	....	....	....	....	....	....	....	....	....	....	....	....	....	....
Other Financial Inst.	88bc	....	....	....	....	....	....	....	....	....	....	....	....	....	....	....
Local Governments	88bd	....	....	....	....	....	....	....	....	....	....	....	....	....	....	....
Bus. & Individuals	88be	....	....	....	....	....	....	....	....	....	....	....	....	....	....	....
Nonresidents	88bf	....	....	....	....	....	....	....	....	....	....	....	....	....	....	....
Intragovernmental Debt	88s	I3.11	3.49	4.83	7.20	8.59	11.18	14.17	17.35	21.92	26.89	32.52	39.76	46.89	54.80	68.16
Debt: Foreign Currency	89b	....	....	....	....	....	....	....	....	....	....	....	....	....	....	....
National Accounts														*Billions of Kronor*		
Househ.Cons.Expend.,incl.NPISHs	96f	91.99	98.96	108.82	119.92	136.86	156.07	180.49	197.75	219.26	242.31	273.33	305.55	340.04	369.44	403.78
Government Consumption Expend	91f	36.47	41.21	45.50	50.98	59.01	70.69	83.19	101.14	116.89	132.72	153.76	170.16	185.67	203.51	221.06
Gross Fixed Capital Formation	93e	38.11	39.72	44.44	48.22	55.24	59.99	67.22	76.78	78.52	89.76	106.43	109.40	118.09	132.30	148.79
Changes in Inventories	93i	5.27	1.98	-.18	-1.19	6.07	10.01	7.87	-2.40	-7.42	.96	5.92	-6.29	-10.26	-7.76	
Exports of Goods and Services	90c	41.52	45.32	49.28	62.13	82.49	84.68	94.07	101.33	116.40	140.57	156.47	174.11	204.76	253.26	289.82
Imports of Goods and Services	98c	-42.48	-43.17	-46.21	-55.88	-84.45	-85.26	-99.77	-107.51	-112.17	-145.20	-166.55	-175.30	-208.23	-238.14	-260.70
Gross Domestic Product (GDP)	99b	172.23	186.22	203.76	226.74	256.13	300.79	340.20	370.02	412.45	462.31	528.26	578.91	633.68	709.85	794.30
Net Factor Inc/Pmts(-) Abroad	98.n	-.06	.18	.36	.77	.71	.81	.46	-.69	-1.38	-1.27	-4.02	-8.65	-13.29	-16.59	-19.81
Gross National Income (GNI)	99a	172.17	186.40	204.12	227.51	256.84	301.59	340.66	369.33	413.55	463.82	524.23	570.26	620.40	693.26	774.49
Net National Income	99e	154.76	165.17	178.86	204.80	230.40	271.10	305.50	328.80	367.60	412.04	464.81	503.79	545.72	608.93	682.74
GDP Volume 1975 prices	99b.p	262.90	264.95	270.67	281.19	293.36	299.82	303.34	297.35	301.31	314.22	320.36				
GDP Volume 1985 prices	99b.p	....	....	....	....	....	....	....	....	....	....		791.00	791.26	800.05	814.54	846.98
GDP Volume 1991 Prices	99b.p	....	....	....	....	....	....	....	....	....	....	....	....	....	....	....
GDP Volume 1995 Prices	99b.p	....	....	....	....	....	....	....	....	....	....	....	....	....	....	....
GDP Volume (1995=100)	99bv p	65.9	66.4	67.8	70.5	73.5	75.1	76.0	74.5	75.5	78.7	80.3	80.3	81.2	82.7	86.0
GDP Deflator (1995=100)	99bi p	15.3	16.4	17.5	18.8	20.3	23.4	26.1	29.0	31.9	34.3	38.4	42.1	45.6	50.1	53.9
														Millions:		
Population	99z	8.04	8.10	8.12	8.14	8.16	8.19	8.22	8.25	8.28	8.29	8.31	8.32	8.33	8.33	8.34

	1985	1986	1987	1988	1989	1990	1991	1992	1993	1994	1995	1996	1997	1998	1999	
Millions of US Dollars																**International Investment Position**
Assets	39,656	49,567	68,400	74,388	101,013	141,102	150,827	148,658	135,124	165,515	227,989	248,580	241,838	295,255	....	79aa *d*
Direct Investment Abroad	10,768	16,131	23,940	28,423	38,221	49,491	53,531	47,707	44,560	59,237	69,088	71,751	79,099	94,674	....	79ab *d*
Portfolio Investment	1,182	1,466	2,052	2,924	8,833	12,110	17,000	14,057	17,583	22,114	36,947	50,357	69,478	100,589	....	79ac *d*
Equity Securities	788	1,027	1,026	1,787	7,548	10,355	14,830	11,217	15,054	18,227	29,738	38,859	51,248	71,207	....	79ad *d*
Debt Securities	394	440	1,026	1,137	1,285	1,755	2,170	2,840	2,529	3,887	7,209	11,498	18,230	29,382	....	79ae *d*
Financial Derivatives											15,920	16,446	16,450	15,579	....	79al *d*
Other Investment	21,798	25,224	33,858	34,270	44,163	61,250	62,212	63,609	51,785	60,310	80,352	89,652	65,265	67,529	....	79af *d*
Monetary Authorities																79ag *d*
General Government	1,838	2,200	2,907	3,086	4,015	4,914	5,245	12,921	4,456	5,227	6,158	6,258	6,174	6,517	....	79ah *d*
Banks	8,929	10,705	15,048	14,780	21,037	34,925	34,180	32,231	26,254	24,660	36,346	44,681	46,599	46,143	....	79ai *d*
Other Sectors	11,030	12,319	15,903	16,404	19,110	21,411	22,787	18,458	21,075	30,423	37,848	38,713	12,492	14,869	....	79aj *d*
Reserve Assets	5,909	6,746	8,550	8,771	9,798	18,252	18,085	23,285	21,196	23,855	25,682	20,375	11,546	16,884	....	79ak *d*
Liabilities	60,666	74,498	96,272	108,332	141,802	202,176	219,007	208,434	215,813	261,074	324,863	352,787	339,476	389,867	....	79la *d*
Dir. Invest. in Rep. Economy	4,333	6,013	9,234	9,907	10,920	12,461	17,904	13,773	12,886	23,454	33,042	34,056	42,399	53,792	....	79lb *d*
Portfolio Investment	2,758	5,133	3,591	5,035	10,760	18,252	28,755	30,953	47,089	57,897	77,348	99,549	207,565	225,711	....	79lc *d*
Equity Securities	2,758	4,839	3,933	5,685	6,905	6,669	10,489	13,063	21,798	35,918	48,061	70,295	79,472	94,033	....	79ld *d*
Debt Securities	—	293	-342	-650	3,854	11,583	18,266	17,890	25,291	21,979	29,287	29,253	128,093	131,678	....	79le *d*
Financial Derivatives											16,821	17,610	16,420	15,936	....	79ll *d*
Other investment	53,575	63,352	83,447	93,390	120,122	171,464	172,348	163,709	155,838	179,723	197,651	201,572	73,091	94,427	....	79lf *d*
Monetary Authorities									1,704			146				79lg *d*
General Government	18,515	19,504	21,375	18,678	16,380	15,269	13,202	37,200	47,089	57,227	65,934	64,328	1,836	2,238	....	79lh *d*
Banks	18,909	23,611	35,055	43,853	63,112	99,509	92,775	62,757	50,340	50,928	55,270	56,615	51,247	68,238	....	79li *d*
Other Sectors	16,151	20,238	27,018	30,859	40,630	56,687	66,371	62,047	58,409	71,567	76,447	80,483	20,009	23,951	....	79lj *d*
Year Ending December 31																**Government Finance**
Deficit (-) or Surplus	-61.51	-57.17	-3.93	5.76	22.61	13.61	-36.53	-74.07	-231.41	I-133.63	-153.18	-58.02	I-16.66	6.84	64.02	80
Revenue	351.83	377.72	440.30	476.09	532.23	601.67	610.35	610.94	544.63	I419.06	459.93	590.08	640.06	696.46	714.73	81
Grants Received											I5.66	10.40	8.88	9.87	9.22	81z
Expenditure	388.32	406.96	423.32	445.98	484.45	554.83	615.52	665.96	747.15	I552.69	618.77	658.50	I665.60	699.49	659.93	82
Lending Minus Repayments	25.02	27.93	20.91	24.35	25.17	33.23	31.36	19.05	28.89	....	....	....	....	....	....	83
Financing																
Domestic	25.39	75.75	-3.84	12.38	-16.09	-9.74	15.71	50.27	66.36	I129.85	135.42	27.07	-11.34	-20.25	47.11	84a
Foreign	36.12	-18.58	7.77	-18.14	-6.52	-3.87	20.82	23.80	165.05	I3.78	17.76	30.95	28.01	13.43	-111.14	85a
Total Debt	480.48	529.89	532.53	510.33	516.75	504.06	530.58	606.26	828.02	I1098.92	1,169.48	1,189.53	1,208.36	1,217.64	1,142.23	88
Debt: Domestic	341.41	409.40	404.27	400.21	413.15	404.33	410.02	461.90	518.61	I585.96	638.76	627.85	618.69	614.53	650.28	88a
Other Levels of Government	14.38	10.99	8.41	8.90	13.32	28.35	29.75	15.39	8.38	I—	—	—	—	—	—	88aa
Monetary Authorities	45.52	90.29	86.45	68.65	81.95	79.13	53.71	32.98	103.09	I78.47	57.96	46.21	58.12	49.14	50.50	88ab
Deposit Money Banks	88.74	60.65	58.49	45.45	41.02	46.86	48.80	52.23	61.27	I96.77	94.77	90.86	88.08	143.74	58.93	88ac
Other Domestic	192.77	247.47	250.92	277.21	276.86	249.99	277.76	361.30	345.87	I410.72	486.03	490.78	472.49	421.65	540.85	88ad
Debt: Foreign	139.07	120.49	128.26	110.12	103.60	99.73	120.56	144.36	309.41	I512.96	530.72	561.68	589.67	603.11	491.95	89a
Intragovernmental Debt	71.98	66.11	76.72	87.29	72.96	76.30	93.79	103.66	132.59	I187.67	216.67	221.67	223.72	231.23	231.94	88s
Total Debt	480.48	529.89	532.53	510.33	516.75	504.06	530.58	606.26	828.02	I1098.92	1,169.48	1,189.53	1,208.36	1,217.64	1,142.23	88
Debt: Kronor																88b
Held By: Bank of Sweden	....	....	....	....	....	....	....	....	....	....	....	....	....	....	....	88ba
Commercial Banks	....	....	....	....	....	....	....	....	....	....	....	....	....	....	....	88bb
Other Financial Inst.	....	....	....	....	....	....	....	....	....	....	....	....	....	....	....	88bc
Local Governments	....	....	....	....	....	....	....	....	....	....	....	....	....	....	....	88bd
Bus. & Individuals	....	....	....	....	....	....	....	....	....	....	....	....	....	....	....	88be
Nonresidents	....	....	....	....	....	....	....	....	....	....	....	....	....	....	....	88bf
Intragovernmental Debt	71.98	66.11	76.72	87.29	72.96	76.30	93.79	103.66	132.59	I187.67	216.67	221.67	223.72	231.23	231.94	88s
Debt: Foreign Currency	....	....	....	....	....	....	....	....	....	....	....	....	....	....	....	89b
Billions of Kronor																**National Accounts**
Househ.Cons.Expend.,incl.NPISHs	443.67	487.33	537.87	584.35	632.74	692.67	771.31	777.32	796.40	I830.86	859.85	884.15	919.17	950.50	996.79	96f
Government Consumption Expend	239.16	257.25	269.88	286.81	322.63	372.13	394.39	402.50	406.00	I436.92	451.41	476.07	484.64	504.97	532.77	91f
Gross Fixed Capital Formation	166.98	175.50	197.95	225.11	271.00	292.53	280.37	244.60	205.70	I240.46	265.17	276.27	269.60	298.96	326.94	93e
Changes in Inventories	-.48	-5.84	-4.76	-3.56	-.49	-2.48	-21.17	-6.66	-13.70	I13.42	18.97	2.66	11.02	16.85	6.41	93i
Exports of Goods and Services	305.87	311.13	332.48	359.69	394.47	406.83	404.18	401.59	473.30	I583.02	693.98	685.93	773.59	828.20	863.29	90c
Imports of Goods and Services	-291.19	-281.03	-313.31	-341.35	-387.75	-401.80	-381.76	-377.64	-421.50	-493.70	I-576.06	-568.70	-644.88	-709.30	-754.11	98c
Gross Domestic Product (GDP)	866.60	947.26	1,023.60	1,114.50	1,232.60	1,359.88	1,447.33	1,441.72	1,446.20	I1596.36	1,713.32	1,756.36	1,813.13	1,890.20	1,972.09	99b
Net Factor Inc/Pmts(-) Abroad	-21.09	-20.02	-16.47	-21.08	-28.86	-40.62	-41.44	-53.04	-57.01	-62.03	....	....	....	....	....	98.n
Gross National Income (GNI)	844.70	925.57	1,003.08	1,089.39	1,198.49	1,310.55	1,393.64	1,391.30	1,400.49	....	....	....	....	....	....	99a
Net National Income	745.23	818.35	886.61	961.56	1,203.75	1,319.26	1,405.89	1,388.69	1,385.17	1,454.92	....	....	....	....	....	99e
GDP Volume 1975 prices	865.79	884.99	910.20	934.95	957.17	970.21	954.06	....	....	....	....	....	....	....	....	99b.*p*
GDP Volume 1985 prices	....	....	....	....	....	....	1,447.33	1,426.75	1,395.07	1,441.64	....	....	....	....	....	99b.*p*
GDP Volume 1991 Prices	....	....	....	....	....	....	....	....	....	....	....	....	....	....	....	99b.*p*
GDP Volume 1995 Prices	....	....	....	....	....	....	....	....	....	I1652.33	1,713.32	1,731.79	1,766.09	1,818.22	1,887.00	99b.*p*
GDP Volume (1995=100)	87.9	89.8	92.4	94.9	97.1	98.5	96.8	95.4	93.3	96.4	100.0	101.1	103.1	106.1	110.1	99bv.*p*
GDP Deflator (1995=100)	57.6	61.6	64.7	68.6	74.1	80.6	87.2	88.2	90.4	I96.6	100.0	101.4	102.7	104.0	104.5	99bi.*p*
Midyear Estimates																
Population	8.36	8.37	8.40	8.44	8.49	8.56	8.62	8.67	8.72	8.78	8.83	8.84	8.85	8.85	8.86	99z

(See notes in the back of the book.)

Switzerland

146

		1970	1971	1972	1973	1974	1975	1976	1977	1978	1979	1980	1981	1982	1983	1984
Exchange Rates																*Francs per SDR:*
Market Rate	aa	4.3160	4.2506	4.0975	3.9134	3.1098	3.0671	2.8459	2.4294	2.1105	2.0814	2.2492	2.0934	2.2002	2.2818	2.5338
																Francs per US Dollar:
Market Rate	ae	4.3160	3.9150	3.7740	3.2440	2.5400	2.6200	2.4495	2.0000	1.6200	1.5800	1.7635	1.7985	1.9945	2.1795	2.5850
Market Rate	rf	4.3730	4.1339	3.8193	3.1648	2.9793	2.5813	2.4996	2.4035	1.7880	1.6627	1.6757	1.9642	2.0303	2.0991	2.3497
																Index Numbers (1995=100):
Market Rate	ahx	27.4	28.7	30.9	37.5	39.8	45.8	47.2	49.3	66.5	71.0	70.5	60.3	58.3	56.3	50.4
Nominal Effective Exchange Rate	neu	37.4	38.3	38.3	41.8	45.3	50.4	56.3	57.3	69.9	70.6	69.7	71.6	77.4	81.0	80.2
Real Effective Exchange Rate	reu	....	....	....	....	....	97.0	99.1	93.1	71.3	68.7	ɪ67.1	68.1	72.1	75.0	73.0
Fund Position																*Millions of SDRs:*
Quota	2f. s	—	—	—	—	—	—	—	—	—	—	—	—	—	—	—
SDRs	1b. s	—	—	—	—	—	—	—	—	—	—	5	—	4	13	9
Reserve Position in the Fund	1c. s	—	—	—	—	—	81	250	391	308	207	252	397	467	636	593
of which: Outstg.Fund Borrowing	2c	—	—	—	—	—	81	250	391	308	207	252	397	467	636	593
International Liquidity													*Millions of US Dollars Unless Otherwise Indicated:*			
Total Reserves minus Gold	1l. d	2,401	3,808	4,399	5,007	5,446	7,019	9,606	10,289	17,763	16,435	15,656	13,979	15,460	15,034	15,296
SDRs	1b. d	—	—	—	—	—	—	—	—	—	—	6	—	13	9
Reserve Position in the Fund	1c. d	—	—	—	—	—	95	290	475	402	273	322	462	515	666	581
Foreign Exchange	1d. d	2,401	3,808	4,399	5,007	5,446	6,924	9,316	9,814	17,361	16,162	15,328	13,517	14,941	14,355	14,706
Gold (Million Fine Troy Ounces)	1ad	78.03	83.11	83.11	83.20	83.20	83.20	83.28	83.28	83.28	83.28	83.28	83.28	83.28	83.28	83.28
Gold (National Valuation)	1and	2,703	3,093	3,094	3,666	4,682	4,539	4,860	5,952	7,348	7,534	6,750	6,619	5,968	5,462	4,605
Monetary Authorities: Other Liab.	4..d	14	34	91	115	78	62	111	90	240	1,409	1,298	915	456	84	49
Deposit Money Banks: Assets	7a. d	16,199	23,924	25,521	29,992	ɪ23,778	27,533	32,072	40,986	54,407	64,946	66,452	70,672	ɪ69,446	68,374	ɪ62,091
Liabilities	7b. d	13,890	20,189	20,987	24,958	ɪ19,954	19,513	23,396	28,249	38,779	44,009	47,949	58,606	ɪ56,124	54,517	ɪ49,078
Trustee Accounts: Assets	7k. d	....	9,375	8,203	12,238	18,156	20,107	23,404	29,749	37,120	53,326	73,238	92,778	92,950	94,011	ɪ99,738
Liabilities	7m. d	....	8,516	7,422	9,988	14,600	17,103	20,330	25,952	32,014	44,226	60,635	76,195	85,074	82,968	ɪ85,513
Monetary Authorities																*Billions of Francs:*
Foreign Assets	11	22.14	26.50	28.51	29.03	28.87	32.00	37.55	36.37	42.92	38.29	39.27	37.40	43.79	44.61	50.80
Claims on Central Government	12a	1.67	1.30	1.34	.98	1.48	1.23	1.49	1.91	1.49	2.21	2.70	2.67	2.88	3.26	3.46
Claims on Deposit Money Banks	12e	.63	.18	1.35	1.74	3.08	2.05	1.24	1.62	.47	2.75	3.54	5.67	3.95	5.28	5.63
Reserve Money	14	22.92	27.16	29.31	30.42	31.45	32.20	34.67	35.92	42.16	38.89	39.42	37.75	40.27	40.60	42.19
of which: Currency Outside DMBs	14a	14.54	15.60	17.82	19.08	20.33	20.12	20.78	21.49	23.64	24.99	25.44	24.74	25.98	26.31	27.88
Central Government Deposits	16d	.57	.99	1.33	.39	.63	1.61	3.69	2.48	4.04	2.24	.37	.80	.76	.76	1.11
Other Items (Net)	17r	.95	–.17	.55	.90	1.34	1.49	1.93	1.50	–1.33	2.12	5.72	7.19	9.58	11.80	16.61
Deposit Money Banks																*Billions of Francs:*
Reserves	20	10.70	13.61	11.92	10.94	ɪ11.26	12.98	14.34	15.53	17.04	15.80	16.50	15.35	ɪ17.89	18.62	ɪ15.75
Foreign Assets	21	70.84	91.87	98.00	97.29	ɪ60.40	72.14	78.56	81.97	88.14	102.61	117.19	127.10	ɪ138.51	149.02	ɪ160.51
Claims on Central Government	22a	13.71	17.16	19.96	21.89	ɪ14.53	15.40	17.22	15.90	17.08	20.24	20.34	21.40	ɪ22.25	11.81	29.74
Claims on Private Sector	22d	98.72	106.93	116.48	126.30	ɪ118.05	126.25	137.41	148.41	164.12	175.47	195.78	213.66	ɪ262.06	281.61	ɪ305.10
Demand Deposits	24	21.35	26.78	28.55	28.84	ɪ25.39	27.58	32.49	32.24	42.70	40.13	39.61	40.14	ɪ45.11	49.45	ɪ47.86
Time and Savings Deposits	25	64.05	68.08	78.02	85.43	ɪ71.69	78.61	84.56	93.37	97.30	114.15	115.10	130.44	ɪ160.54	164.86	ɪ197.99
Bonds	26ab	30.00	34.32	36.01	36.23	ɪ21.87	28.07	31.23	33.62	35.23	34.05	39.63	44.93	ɪ60.22	61.44	ɪ103.97
Foreign Liabilities	26c	60.74	77.53	80.59	80.96	ɪ50.68	51.12	57.31	56.50	62.82	69.54	84.56	105.40	ɪ111.94	118.82	ɪ126.87
Other Items (Net)	27r	17.83	22.87	23.21	24.97	ɪ34.60	41.38	41.95	46.08	48.33	56.27	70.91	56.60	ɪ62.90	66.50	ɪ34.41
Monetary Survey																*Billions of Francs:*
Foreign Assets (Net)	31n	32.17	40.71	45.57	44.98	ɪ38.38	52.85	58.53	61.66	67.84	69.15	69.61	57.46	ɪ69.45	74.63	ɪ84.32
Domestic Credit	32	113.52	124.41	136.45	148.77	ɪ133.42	141.26	152.44	163.73	178.65	195.68	218.45	236.94	ɪ286.42	295.93	337.20
Claims on Central Govt. (Net)	32an	14.81	17.47	19.97	22.48	ɪ15.37	15.01	15.02	15.33	14.53	20.21	22.67	23.27	ɪ24.36	14.32	32.10
Claims on Private Sector	32d	98.72	106.93	116.48	126.30	ɪ118.05	126.25	137.41	148.41	164.12	175.47	195.78	213.66	ɪ262.06	281.61	ɪ305.10
Money	34	36.02	42.50	46.51	48.10	ɪ45.95	47.88	53.33	53.83	66.52	65.26	65.16	64.93	ɪ71.14	75.82	ɪ75.82
Quasi-Money	35	64.05	68.08	78.02	85.43	ɪ71.69	78.61	84.56	93.37	97.30	114.15	115.10	114.15	ɪ160.54	164.86	ɪ197.99
Bonds	36ab	30.00	34.32	36.01	36.23	ɪ21.87	28.07	31.23	33.62	35.23	34.05	39.63	44.93	ɪ60.22	61.44	ɪ103.97
Other Items (Net)	37r	15.64	20.24	21.50	23.98	ɪ32.29	39.55	41.85	44.57	47.45	51.38	68.17	54.09	ɪ63.98	68.44	ɪ43.73
Money plus Quasi-Money	35l	100.07	110.57	124.52	133.52	ɪ117.64	126.49	137.89	147.20	163.81	179.40	180.27	195.37	ɪ231.67	240.68	ɪ273.81
Other Banking Institutions																*Billions of Francs:*
Foreign Assets	41..x	35.94	36.00	31.50	39.70	46.12	52.68	57.33	59.50	60.13	84.26	129.16	166.86	185.39	204.90	257.82
Domestic Liabilities	45..x	10.31	3.30	3.00	7.30	9.03	7.87	7.53	7.59	8.27	14.38	22.23	29.83	15.71	24.07	36.77
Foreign Liabilities	46c.x	25.63	32.70	28.50	32.40	37.09	44.81	49.80	51.90	51.86	69.88	106.93	137.04	169.68	180.83	221.05
Nonbank Financial Institutions																*Billions of Francs:*
Claims on Central Government	42a. s	.43	.40	.40	.38	.41	.46	.66	.67	.68	.67	.63	....	.73	.74	....
Claims on Priv.Sec.& Local Govt.	42d. s	12.86	13.98	15.39	16.73	17.79	19.74	22.06	24.23	26.60	29.73	35.94	39.36	43.10	47.23	52.71
Real Estate	42h. s	3.56	4.04	4.52	5.03	5.38	5.69	5.94	6.28	6.88	7.60	8.32	9.03	9.85	10.68	11.62
Incr.in Total Assets(Within Per.)	49z. s	1.53	1.75	1.97	1.93	1.63	2.42	2.84	2.58	3.21	4.13	4.17	3.13	5.57	4.95	6.42
Liquid Liabilities	55l	110.38	113.87	127.52	140.82	149.19	158.53	170.95	182.33	201.29	226.77	242.96	265.72	ɪ309.00	264.75	ɪ310.58
Interest Rates																*Percent Per Annum*
Bank Rate (End of Period)	60	3.75	3.75	3.75	4.50	5.50	3.00	2.00	1.50	1.00	2.00	3.00	6.00	4.50	4.00	4.00
Money Market Rate	60b	6.75	1.15	2.69	3.64	5.97	2.75	1.51	2.47	.66	ɪ1.00	2.29	2.93	1.32	1.84	ɪ57.81
Treasury Bill Rate	60c	....	....	....	....	....	....	....	....	....	....	5.15	7.82	3.87	3.04	3.58
Deposit Rate	60l	....	....	....	....	....	....	....	....	....	....	....	8.75	4.40	3.31	3.77
Lending Rate	60p	....	....	....	....	....	....	....	....	....	....	....	5.56	5.98	5.49	5.49
Government Bond Yield	61	5.82	5.27	4.97	5.60	7.15	6.44	4.99	4.05	3.33	3.45	4.77	5.57	4.83	4.52	4.70

	1985	1986	1987	1988	1989	1990	1991	1992	1993	1994	1995	1996	1997	1998	1999	
Exchange Rates																
End of Period																
Market Rate	2.2809	1.9858	1.8130	2.0239	2.0323	1.8431	1.9389	2.0020	2.0322	1.9146	1.7102	1.9361	1.9636	1.9382	2.1955	**aa**
End of Period (ae) Period Average (rf)																
Market Rate	2.0765	1.6235	1.2780	1.5040	1.5465	1.2955	1.3555	1.4560	1.4795	1.3115	1.1505	1.3464	1.4553	1.3765	1.5996	**ae**
Market Rate	2.4571	1.7989	1.4912	1.4633	1.6359	1.3892	1.4340	1.4062	1.4776	1.3677	1.1825	1.2360	1.4513	1.4498	1.5022	**rf**
Period Averages																
Market Rate	48.5	66.0	79.3	80.9	72.2	85.4	82.7	84.2	79.9	86.5	100.0	95.6	81.4	81.6	78.7	**ah x**
Nominal Effective Exchange Rate	79.6	85.5	89.2	88.4	83.9	88.2	86.9	85.2	88.0	93.8	100.0	98.4	92.7	94.5	93.5	**ne u**
Real Effective Exchange Rate	72.5	80.5	84.1	85.7	82.1	87.3	89.6	85.6	86.8	94.3	100.0	99.7	95.4	99.7	....	**re u**
Fund Position																
End of Period																
Quota	—	—	—	—	—	—	—	2,470	2,470	2,470	2,470	2,470	2,470	2,470	3,459	**2f. s**
SDRs	3	—	10	15	4	1	2	12	113	162	181	88	170	192	345	**1b. s**
Reserve Position in the Fund	501	370	212	102	32	—	—	581	605	643	981	1,065	1,407	1,828	1,218	**1c. s**
of which: Outstg.Fund Borrowing	501	370	212	102	32	—	—	—	—	—	—	—	—	230	—	**2c**
International Liquidity																
End of Period																
Total Reserves minus Gold	18,016	21,786	27,476	24,203	25,276	29,223	29,004	33,255	32,635	34,729	36,413	38,433	39,028	41,191	36,321	**1l. d**
SDRs	3	—	14	20	5	2	2	16	155	236	269	126	230	271	473	**1b. d**
Reserve Position in the Fund	550	452	300	137	42	—	—	799	830	939	1,459	1,531	1,899	2,574	1,672	**1c. d**
Foreign Exchange	17,463	21,334	27,162	24,045	25,230	29,221	29,002	32,440	31,650	33,554	34,685	36,775	36,899	38,346	34,176	**1d. d**
Gold (Million Fine Troy Ounces)	83.28	83.28	83.28	83.28	83.28	83.28	83.28	83.28	83.28	83.28	83.28	83.28	83.28	83.28	83.28	**1ad**
Gold (National Valuation)	5,733	7,332	9,315	7,915	7,697	9,189	8,782	8,176	8,046	9,077	10,347	8,841	8,182	8,667	7,464	**1an d**
Monetary Authorities: Other Liab.	54	79	101	123	123	—	—	—	—	—	—	—	33	119	134	**4..d**
Deposit Money Banks: Assets	85,244	116,102	158,534	140,737	132,779	153,254	147,565	143,589	154,224	187,875	212,374	I263,362	314,438	369,712	463,670	**7a. d**
Liabilities	63,396	82,400	109,973	102,794	110,325	133,572	131,765	125,791	129,333	171,093	184,869	I223,836	268,969	300,777	395,023	**7b. d**
Trustee Accounts: Assets	120,219	137,338	173,415	178,320	222,824	290,797	281,023	268,344	235,558	271,584	288,831	I294,323	293,492	311,232	292,460	**7k. d**
Liabilities	100,398	111,322	137,912	140,664	170,156	219,395	213,727	204,428	182,470	213,280	232,765	I239,280	241,593	255,032	243,663	**7m. d**
Monetary Authorities																
End of Period																
Foreign Assets	50.04	48.17	49.38	47.91	51.74	49.23	52.35	59.22	60.94	59.98	56.30	63.13	69.04	69.34	71.05	**11**
Claims on Central Government	3.74	3.90	3.83	4.08	4.31	4.62	4.95	4.99	5.02	5.13	5.19	5.26	7.12	7.22	7.14	**12a**
Claims on Deposit Money Banks	5.97	6.18	5.83	3.35	1.71	1.44	1.18	1.34	1.36	1.36	1.30	1.87	2.86	1.09	28.53	**12e**
Reserve Money	41.51	43.54	46.06	37.42	35.94	36.92	35.96	39.60	39.10	39.33	38.40	40.35	39.43	42.47	49.67	**14**
of which: Currency Outside DMBs	27.31	28.54	28.92	30.64	30.90	31.45	31.28	31.37	31.38	32.64	33.02	34.61	34.33	35.43	39.44	**14a**
Central Government Deposits	2.57	.98	1.38	2.51	2.50	.69	.22	.42	.49	.75	1.12	1.08	I2.69	15.36	17.16	**16d**
Other Items (Net)	15.67	13.72	11.60	15.41	19.32	17.69	22.31	25.53	27.73	26.33	23.84	29.83	35.15	36.46	39.87	**17r**
Deposit Money Banks																
End of Period																
Reserves	15.78	17.15	18.74	9.29	8.59	8.27	7.90	7.82	8.01	7.64	8.27	I9.61	9.83	10.95	17.17	**20**
Foreign Assets	177.01	188.49	202.61	211.67	205.34	198.54	200.02	209.07	228.17	246.40	244.34	I354.59	457.60	508.91	741.69	**21**
Claims on Central Government	27.46	25.61	28.26	26.14	29.60	31.26	33.51	36.17	47.40	49.57	I50.70	I52.66	52.44	51.68	53.46	**22a**
Claims on Private Sector	335.25	355.19	388.23	431.83	490.01	532.78	552.02	563.92	574.31	594.37	611.70	I608.17	625.65	635.67	676.49	**22d**
Demand Deposits	46.52	46.91	56.97	57.27	54.66	52.76	51.61	54.86	59.86	62.22	67.63	I93.57	105.45	113.88	124.00	**24**
Time and Savings Deposits	211.30	219.20	239.91	255.57	279.51	283.91	293.89	300.34	329.73	343.60	358.01	I374.36	396.05	413.84	474.49	**25**
Bonds	116.63	125.64	135.43	145.67	157.12	172.43	181.45	183.49	173.22	164.72	161.13	I149.66	137.25	127.55	123.04	**26ab**
Foreign Liabilities	131.64	133.78	140.55	154.60	170.62	173.04	178.61	183.15	191.35	224.39	212.69	I301.37	391.43	414.02	631.88	**26c**
Other Items (Net)	49.41	60.92	64.98	65.82	71.64	88.72	87.89	95.13	103.74	103.04	115.54	I106.06	115.34	137.93	135.39	**27r**
Monetary Survey																
End of Period																
Foreign Assets (Net)	95.30	102.75	111.31	104.79	86.28	74.73	73.77	85.13	97.76	81.99	87.94	I116.35	135.17	164.06	180.64	**31n**
Domestic Credit	363.88	383.71	418.94	459.54	521.42	567.97	590.26	604.67	626.24	648.31	I666.47	I665.01	I682.53	679.22	719.93	**32**
Claims on Central Govt. (Net)	28.63	28.52	30.71	27.71	31.41	35.19	38.23	40.75	51.93	53.94	I54.77	I56.84	I56.88	43.54	43.44	**32an**
Claims on Private Sector	335.25	355.19	388.23	431.83	490.01	532.78	552.02	563.92	574.31	594.37	611.70	I608.17	625.65	635.67	676.49	**32d**
Money	73.93	75.54	85.98	88.00	85.65	84.30	82.89	86.23	91.24	94.86	100.65	I128.18	139.78	149.31	163.44	**34**
Quasi-Money	211.30	219.20	239.91	255.57	279.51	283.91	293.89	300.34	329.73	343.60	358.01	I374.36	396.05	413.84	474.49	**35**
Bonds	116.63	125.64	135.43	145.67	157.12	172.43	181.45	183.49	173.22	164.72	161.13	I149.66	137.25	127.55	123.04	**36ab**
Other Items (Net)	57.33	66.09	68.93	75.10	85.42	102.07	105.79	119.74	129.82	127.11	134.62	I129.16	144.62	152.58	139.59	**37r**
Money plus Quasi-Money	285.23	294.74	325.89	343.57	365.16	368.20	376.79	386.57	420.97	438.46	458.66	I502.54	535.83	563.15	637.93	**35l**
Other Banking Institutions																
End of Period																
Foreign Assets	249.63	222.97	221.63	268.19	344.60	376.73	380.93	390.71	348.51	356.18	332.30	I396.28	427.12	428.41	467.82	**41..x**
Domestic Liabilities	41.16	42.24	45.37	56.64	81.45	92.50	91.22	93.06	78.54	76.47	64.50	I74.11	75.53	77.36	78.06	**45..x**
Foreign Liabilities	208.48	180.73	176.25	211.56	263.15	284.23	289.71	297.65	269.96	279.72	267.80	I322.17	351.59	351.05	389.76	**46c.x**
Nonbank Financial Institutions																
End of Period																
Claims on Central Government	....	....	....	....	....	....	....	....	....	....	....	....	....	....	....	**42a. s**
Claims on Priv.Sec.& Local Govt.	59.09	66.26	73.75	84.75	96.37	102.44	114.79	127.21	139.24	152.91	163.99	180.80	200.00	227.30	....	**42d. s**
Real Estate	12.46	13.49	14.41	15.45	16.77	17.64	18.65	19.75	20.82	21.79	22.50	23.40	24.30	25.00	....	**42h. s**
Incr.in Total Assets(Within Per.)	7.23	8.19	8.41	12.04	12.95	6.93	13.35	13.54	13.09	14.64	11.79	24.11	20.50	28.10	....	**49z. s**
Liquid Liabilities	326.40	337.35	371.26	400.20	446.61	460.71	468.01	479.63	499.51	514.93	523.16	576.65	....	....	....	**55l**
Interest Rates																
Percent Per Annum																
Bank Rate (End of Period)	4.00	4.00	2.50	3.50	6.00	6.00	7.00	6.00	4.00	3.50	1.50	1.00	1.00	1.00	.50	**60**
Money Market Rate	....	40.63	25.42	3.56	9.69	8.75	7.56	6.38	4.13	3.50	1.75	1.50	1.00	.88	1.09	**60b**
Treasury Bill Rate	4.15	3.54	3.18	3.01	6.60	8.32	7.74	7.76	4.75	3.97	2.78	1.72	1.45	1.32	1.17	**60c**
Deposit Rate	4.36	3.51	3.08	4.50	8.08	8.28	7.63	5.50	3.50	3.63	1.28	1.34	1.00	.69	1.24	**60l**
Lending Rate	5.43	5.46	5.24	5.07	5.85	7.42	7.83	7.80	6.40	5.51	5.48	4.97	4.47	4.07	3.90	**60p**
Government Bond Yield	4.78	4.29	4.12	4.15	5.20	I6.68	6.35	5.48	4.05	5.23	3.73	3.63	3.08	2.39	I3.51	**61**

Switzerland

		1970	1971	1972	1973	1974	1975	1976	1977	1978	1979	1980	1981	1982	1983	1984
Prices, Production, Labor															*Index Numbers (1995=100):*	
Share Prices	62	....	....	....	....	....	....	....	....	....	....	....	....	....	....	....
Producer Prices	63	56.7	59.0	61.4	66.6	75.9	76.9	76.1	76.0	75.0	76.4	79.8	84.3	87.4	88.4	91.0
Prices: Home & Imported Goods	63s	60.8	62.1	64.4	71.2	82.7	80.9	80.3	80.5	77.8	80.8	84.9	89.8	92.2	92.6	95.6
Consumer Prices	64	37.7	40.2	42.9	46.6	51.2	54.6	55.6	56.3	56.9	58.9	61.3	65.3	71.0	73.1	
Wages: Hourly Earn. (1990=100)	65	ɪ35.6	ɪ39.0	ɪ42.5	46.3	ɪ51.1	54.8	55.5	ɪ58.2	59.7	61.8	65.1	69.2	74.2	77.1	79.1
Industrial Production	66	72	73	75	79	80	70	70	74	74	75	80	79	76	76	78
Manufacturing Employment	67ey	149.2	147.2	143.4	142.1	141.7	128.8	ɪ119.9	119.5	120.0	119.9	121.9	122.0	118.2	114.1	113.4
															Number in Thousands:	
Labor Force	67d	....	....	....	....	....	....	....	....	....	....	....	....	....	....	....
Employment	67e	....	....	....	....	....	....	....	....	....	....	....	....	....	....	....
Unemployment	67c	....	....	....	....	....	....	....	....	....	....	....	....	....	....	....
Unemployment Rate (%)	67r	....	....	....	....	....	....	....	....	....	....	....	....	....	....	....
International Transactions															*Millions of Francs*	
Exports	70	22,140	23,631	26,114	29,943	35,353	33,418	37,015	42,011	41,779	ɪ44,080	49,645	52,857	52,687	53,764	60,630
Imports, c.i.f.	71	27,874	29,649	32,332	36,574	42,929	34,271	36,874	42,932	42,300	ɪ48,739	60,883	60,093	58,115	61,276	69,150
															1995=100	
Volume of Exports(1985=100)	72	52.1	53.6	56.8	63.0	65.6	60.4	67.7	75.5	79.2	80.7	82.3	85.9	82.8	82.8	88.5
Volume of Exports	72.a	....	....	....	....	....	....	....	....	....	....	....	....	....	....	....
Volume of Imports(1985=100)	73	....	....	....	....	....	....	....	70.3	76.7	82.1	88.0	86.6	84.8	89.0	89.6
Volume of Imports	73.a	....	....	....	....	....	....	....	....	....	....	....	....	....	....	....
Unit Value of Exp.(1985=100)	74	61.6	64.1	67.2	69.0	78.3	80.1	79.5	81.4	78.3	80.7	89.4	91.8	94.9	96.8	101.7
Unit Value of Exports	74.a	....	....	....	....	....	....	....	....	....	....	....	....	....	....	....
Unit Value of Imp.(1985=100)	75	66.1	66.8	68.1	72.7	87.3	83.3	79.3	84.0	74.7	79.3	95.9	93.2	91.9	92.6	96.5
Unit Value of Imports	75.a	....	....	....	....	....	....	....	....	....	....	....	....	....	....	....
Import Prices	76.x	72.7	71.3	73.2	84.8	102.8	92.8	93.1	94.1	86.2	93.6	100.0	106.1	106.2	104.9	109.1
Balance of Payments															*Millions of US Dollars:*	
Current Account, n.i.e.	78al d	....	....	....	....	....	....	....	1,924	2,075	−245	−201	3,427	2,534	1,212	6,142
Goods: Exports f.o.b.	78aa d	....	....	....	....	....	....	....	20,992	28,837	33,827	41,708	40,104	36,073	34,167	36,896
Goods: Imports f.o.b.	78ab d	....	....	....	....	....	....	....	−22,710	−31,014	−38,727	−46,958	−42,488	−39,987	−39,987	−38,509
Trade Balance	78ac d	....	....	....	....	....	....	....	−1,718	−2,178	−4,900	−5,250	−2,384	−3,219	−5,820	−1,613
Services: Credit	78ad d	....	....	....	....	....	....	....	4,289	5,436	5,957	6,888	6,816	6,979	8,230	8,152
Services: Debit	78ae d	....	....	....	....	....	....	....	−2,524	−3,516	−4,237	−4,885	−4,696	−4,733	−4,625	−4,527
Balance on Goods & Services	78af d	....	....	....	....	....	....	....	47	−257	−3,180	−3,248	−264	−973	−2,216	2,012
Income: Credit	78ag d	....	....	....	....	....	....	....	4,953	7,075	8,805	10,867	12,330	11,959	10,521	11,105
Income: Debit	78ah d	....	....	....	....	....	....	....	−2,411	−3,820	−4,808	−6,681	−7,637	−7,432	−6,180	−6,141
Balance on Gds, Serv. & Inc.	78ai d	....	....	....	....	....	....	....	2,590	2,998	816	939	4,430	3,554	2,126	6,976
Current Transfers, n.i.e.: Credit	78aj d	....	....	....	....	....	....	....	304	425	490	522	733	823	946	929
Current Transfers: Debit	78ak d	....	....	....	....	....	....	....	−969	−1,348	−1,552	−1,662	−1,736	−1,842	−1,860	−1,763
Capital Account, n.i.e.	78bc d	....	....	....	....	....	....	....	—	—	—	—	—	—	....	....
Capital Account, n.i.e.: Credit	78ba d	....	....	....	....	....	....	....	—	—	—	—	—	—	....	....
Capital Account: Debit	78bb d	....	....	....	....	....	....	....	—	—	—	—	—	—	....	....
Financial Account, n.i.e.	78bj d	....	....	....	....	....	....	....	−6,523	−5,940	−14,701	−11,341	−7,807	−12,212	−6,268	−5,816
Direct Investment Abroad	78bd d	....	....	....	....	....	....	....							−492	−1,139
Dir. Invest. in Rep. Econ.	78be d	....	....	....	....	....	....	....							643	777
Portfolio Investment Assets	78bf d	....	....	....	....	....	....	....	−4,761	−6,210	−7,113	−7,068	−8,488	−12,480	−5,754	−4,660
Equity Securities	78bk d	....	....	....	....	....	....	....							−600	−782
Debt Securities	78bl d	....	....	....	....	....	....	....	−4,761	−6,210	−7,113	−7,068	−8,488	−12,480	−5,154	−3,878
Portfolio Investment Liab., n.i.e.	78bg d	....	....	....	....	....	....	....	—	—	—	—	—	—	1,766	1,784
Equity Securities	78bm d	....	....	....	....	....	....	....	—	—	—	—	—	—	1,775	1,599
Debt Securities	78bn d	....	....	....	....	....	....	....	—	—	—	—	—	—	−9	185
Financial Derivatives Assets	78bw d	....	....	....	....	....	....	....	....	....	....	....	....	....	....	....
Financial Derivatives Liabilities	78bx d	....	....	....	....	....	....	....	....	....	....	....	....	....	....	....
Other Investment Assets	78bh d	....	....	....	....	....	....	....	−1,440	−3,807	−12,383	−13,145	−9,502	−2,689	−1,605	−3,965
Monetary Authorities	78bo d	....	....	....	....	....	....	....								
General Government	78bp d	....	....	....	....	....	....	....							−177	169
Banks	78bq d	....	....	....	....	....	....	....	−1,440	−3,431	−8,659	−8,551	−5,700	−5,523	−1,708	−1,733
Other Sectors	78br d	....	....	....	....	....	....	....	—	−376	−3,724	−4,594	−3,801	2,834	280	−2,401
Other Investment Liab., n.i.e.	78bi d	....	....	....	....	....	....	....	−323	4,077	4,795	8,872	10,183	2,957	−826	1,387
Monetary Authorities	78bs d	....	....	....	....	....	....	....	14	539	759	1	−431	−133	−465	2
General Government	78bt d	....	....	....	....	....	....	....	—	—	—	—	—	—	—	—
Banks	78bu d	....	....	....	....	....	....	....	−337	3,538	4,036	8,871	10,614	3,090	−196	255
Other Sectors	78bv d	....	....	....	....	....	....	....							−164	1,130
Net Errors and Omissions	78ca d	....	....	....	....	....	....	....	5,644	11,044	11,772	11,880	3,429	13,044	4,857	1,165
Overall Balance	78cb d	....	....	....	....	....	....	....	1,045	7,179	−3,175	337	−951	3,366	−199	1,491
Reserves and Related Items	79da d	....	....	....	....	....	....	....	−1,045	−7,179	3,175	−337	951	−3,366	199	−1,491
Reserve Assets	79db d	....	....	....	....	....	....	....	−1,045	−7,179	3,175	−337	951	−3,366	199	−1,491
Use of Fund Credit and Loans	79dc d	....	....	....	....	....	....	....	—	—	—	—	—	—	—	—
Exceptional Financing	79de d	....	....	....	....	....	....	....	....	....	....	....	....	....	....	....

1985	1986	1987	1988	1989	1990	1991	1992	1993	1994	1995	1996	1997	1998	1999		
Period Averages															**Prices, Production, Labor**	
. . .	. . .	. . .	. . .	60.5	57.6	59.0	64.7	83.2	95.7	100.0	125.0	177.4	236.3	240.4	Share Prices	62
92.8	91.6	91.0	92.9	95.9	98.1	99.4	100.1	100.5	100.1	100.0	98.2	97.5	96.3	95.4	Producer Prices	63
97.8	93.9	92.0	94.1	98.2	99.6	100.0	100.1	100.3	100.0	100.0	97.7	97.7	96.3	95.0	Prices: Home & Imported Goods	63s
75.6	76.2	77.3	78.7	81.2	85.6	90.6	Ɪ94.3	97.4	98.2	100.0	100.8	101.3	101.3	102.2	Consumer Prices	64
82.1	85.4	87.5	90.7	94.3	100.0	107.5	113.4	116.2	. . .	. . .	. . .	. . .	. . .	. . .	Wages: Hourly Earn. (1990=100)	65
82	85	86	93	95	Ɪ97	97	96	94	98	100	100	105	108	112	Industrial Production	66
114.4	Ɪ116.0	115.8	115.8	117.0	118.7	116.6	Ɪ110.7	105.0	101.0	100.0	98.5	95.7	95.9	95.9	Manufacturing Employment	67ey
Period Averages																
. . .	. . .	. . .	. . .	. . .	. . .	. . .	. . .	3,873	. . .	3,860	3,925	3,928	3,974	. . .	Labor Force	67d
3,354	3,430	3,515	3,607	3,704	3,821	Ɪ3,755	3,742	3,729	3,705	3,742	3,789	3,803	. . .	. . .	Employment	67e
30	26	25	22	17	18	39	92	163	171	153	169	188	140	99	Unemployment	67c
1.0	.8	.8	.7	.6	.5	1.1	2.5	4.5	4.7	4.2	4.7	5.2	3.9	2.7	Unemployment Rate (%)	67r
Millions of Francs															**International Transactions**	
66,624	67,004	67,477	74,064	84,268	88,257	87,947	Ɪ86,148	86,659	90,213	92,012	94,174	105,133	109,113	114,446	Exports	70
74,750	73,513	75,171	82,399	95,209	96,611	95,032	Ɪ86,739	83,767	87,279	90,775	91,967	103,088	106,866	113,416	Imports, c.i.f.	71
1995=100																
100.0	102.1	102.6	. . .	. . .	. . .	. . .	. . .	. . .	. . .	. . .	. . .	. . .	. . .	. . .	Volume of Exports(1985=100)	72
. . .	. . .	. . .	Ɪ80.0	84.2	88.0	86.8	90.9	91.5	96.0	100.0	101.3	109.1	114.3	118.3	Volume of Exports	72.a
100.0	108.3	115.3	. . .	. . .	. . .	. . .	. . .	. . .	. . .	. . .	. . .	. . .	. . .	. . .	Volume of Imports(1985=100)	73
. . .	. . .	. . .	Ɪ85.2	89.8	92.2	90.9	86.9	85.9	93.9	100.0	101.4	107.8	116.6	126.1	Volume of Imports	73.a
100.0	98.0	101.7	. . .	. . .	. . .	. . .	. . .	. . .	. . .	. . .	. . .	. . .	. . .	. . .	Unit Value of Exp.(1985=100)	74
. . .	. . .	. . .	Ɪ92.9	98.9	99.9	102.7	103.0	102.9	102.2	100.0	101.0	104.7	103.7	105.1	Unit Value of Exports	74.a
100.0	89.9	86.6	. . .	. . .	. . .	. . .	. . .	. . .	. . .	. . .	. . .	. . .	. . .	. . .	Unit Value of Imp.(1985=100)	75
. . .	. . .	. . .	Ɪ99.8	108.2	107.4	107.5	109.9	107.5	102.4	100.0	100.0	105.3	101.0	99.1	Unit Value of Imports	75.a
112.3	100.5	95.1	97.7	105.0	104.1	101.9	100.1	99.8	99.7	100.0	96.3	98.2	96.0	94.0	Import Prices	76.x
Minus Sign Indicates Debit															**Balance of Payments**	
6,039	4,654	6,288	8,846	8,043	6,941	10,374	14,235	17,908	17,372	21,562	21,219	26,960	24,547	. . .	Current Account, n.i.e.	78al *d*
37,303	48,800	55,604	63,164	65,811	78,033	74,256	79,870	75,424	82,625	97,139	95,536	95,039	93,859	. . .	Goods: Exports f.o.b.	78aa *d*
−39,387	−54,295	−61,621	−68,359	−70,769	−85,207	−78,853	−80,155	−73,853	−79,295	−93,916	−93,286	−92,247	−92,871	. . .	Goods: Imports f.o.b.	78ab *d*
−2,083	−5,495	−6,017	−5,194	−4,958	−7,174	−4,597	−285	1,571	3,330	3,223	2,250	2,793	988	. . .	*Trade Balance*	78ac *d*
8,817	12,029	15,218	16,114	15,811	18,893	19,785	21,065	21,476	22,618	26,027	26,250	25,303	26,683	. . .	Services: Credit	78ad *d*
−4,842	−6,547	−8,183	−9,226	−9,183	−11,195	−11,096	−11,928	−11,544	−12,969	−15,244	−15,905	−14,294	−15,406	. . .	Services: Debit	78ae *d*
1,892	−12	1,019	1,693	1,669	524	4,092	8,852	11,503	12,980	14,005	12,595	13,801	12,264	. . .	*Balance on Goods & Services*	78af *d*
10,906	14,013	17,533	20,057	22,697	28,686	27,518	26,238	25,152	26,747	31,575	32,997	35,065	43,720	. . .	Income: Credit	78ag *d*
−5,952	−8,256	−10,759	−11,191	−14,640	−19,939	−18,663	−17,902	−16,007	−18,932	−19,778	−20,384	−18,505	−27,702	. . .	Income: Debit	78ah *d*
6,845	5,745	7,792	10,559	9,726	9,270	12,946	17,189	20,648	20,795	25,802	25,208	30,361	28,282	. . .	*Balance on Gds, Serv. & Inc.*	78ai *d*
1,017	1,548	1,911	2,054	1,919	2,357	2,367	2,531	2,484	2,526	2,996	2,960	2,626	2,787	. . .	Current Transfers, n.i.e.: Credit	78aj *d*
−1,823	−2,638	−3,415	−3,768	−3,602	−4,686	−4,939	−5,484	−5,225	−5,949	−7,237	−6,949	−6,027	−6,523	. . .	Current Transfers: Debit	78ak *d*
. . .	. . .	. . .	. . .	. . .	. . .	−48	−43	−133	−146	−132	−123	−79	−301	. . .	Capital Account, n.i.e.	78bc *d*
. . .	. . .	. . .	. . .	. . .	. . .	. . .	. . .	. . .	. . .	. . .	. . .	. . .	. . .	. . .	Capital Account, n.i.e.: Credit	78ba *d*
. . .	. . .	. . .	. . .	. . .	. . .	−48	−43	−133	−146	−132	−123	−79	−301	. . .	Capital Account: Debit	78bb *d*
−7,272	−3,162	−8,057	−14,698	−7,668	−11,462	−11,656	−15,778	−18,985	−16,600	−13,041	−27,409	−26,688	−29,698	. . .	Financial Account, n.i.e.	78bj *d*
−4,573	−1,460	−1,273	−8,695	−7,850	−6,370	−6,541	−6,057	−8,764	−10,793	−12,210	−16,152	−18,005	−14,226	. . .	Direct Investment Abroad	78bd *d*
1,267	2,122	2,320	405	2,827	4,961	3,178	1,249	899	4,104	3,599	4,373	5,693	5,488	. . .	Dir. Invest. in Rep. Econ., n.i.e.	78be *d*
−6,535	−7,538	−6,371	−13,837	−9,394	−577	−17,549	−9,698	−30,337	−19,058	−8,855	−22,402	−20,959	−14,807	. . .	Portfolio Investment Assets	78bf *d*
−1,425	−2,105	−2,006	3,358	958	679	−4,531	−6,464	−16,650	−8,073	−4,064	−14,686	−9,159	−2,529	. . .	Equity Securities	78bk *d*
−5,110	−5,433	−4,366	−17,195	−10,352	−1,255	−13,018	−3,234	−13,687	−10,986	−4,792	−7,716	−11,800	−12,277	. . .	Debt Securities	78bl *d*
5,431	8,940	4,639	6,421	6,371	−551	5,570	3,571	12,501	912	4,960	12,895	9,033	10,248	. . .	Portfolio Investment Liab., n.i.e.	78bg *d*
5,049	8,437	3,453	4,255	5,310	−1,579	2,951	1,810	7,923	−1,572	5,851	11,677	6,945	8,633	. . .	Equity Securities	78bm *d*
382	503	1,186	2,166	1,062	1,028	2,619	1,761	4,578	2,484	−891	1,218	2,088	1,615	. . .	Debt Securities	78bn *d*
. . .	. . .	. . .	. . .	. . .	. . .	. . .	. . .	. . .	. . .	. . .	. . .	. . .	. . .	. . .	Financial Derivatives Assets	78bw *d*
. . .	. . .	. . .	. . .	. . .	. . .	. . .	. . .	. . .	. . .	. . .	. . .	. . .	. . .	. . .	Financial Derivatives Liabilities	78bx *d*
−10,158	−13,459	−24,089	−7,641	−14,202	−28,846	2,828	−8,495	7,405	−31,086	−737	−70,795	−54,168	−59,724	. . .	Other Investment Assets	78bh *d*
−105	−212	323	−215	−156	−184	−246	−250	−173	−115	−67	−7	192	201	. . .	Monetary Authorities	78bo *d*
. . .	. . .	. . .	. . .	. . .	. . .	. . .	. . .	. . .	. . .	. . .	. . .	. . .	. . .	. . .	General Government	78bp *d*
−7,361	−10,840	−17,184	−297	6,832	−6,008	1,778	−4,811	−2,449	−19,220	−9,451	−60,244	−51,163	−45,756	. . .	Banks	78bq *d*
−2,692	−2,408	−7,228	−7,129	−20,879	−22,654	1,296	−3,434	10,027	−11,751	8,781	−10,544	−3,196	−14,169	. . .	Other Sectors	78br *d*
7,296	8,234	16,719	8,648	14,580	19,921	858	3,652	−688	39,322	202	64,672	51,718	43,324	. . .	Other Investment Liab., n.i.e.	78bi *d*
−1	−23	51	3	−30	−42	38	−43	91	−104	−3	−9	10	80	. . .	Monetary Authorities	78bs *d*
. . .	. . .	. . .	−42	−185	−53	−1	84	79	40	266	32	121	−4	. . .	General Government	78bt *d*
4,973	5,174	13,417	3,314	8,285	12,056	1,896	−732	4,074	30,262	1,609	49,120	51,563	34,000	. . .	Banks	78bu *d*
2,323	3,083	3,251	5,372	6,509	7,962	−1,075	4,344	−4,932	9,123	−1,670	15,529	24	9,249	. . .	Other Sectors	78bv *d*
2,461	−402	4,982	3,470	995	5,686	2,325	5,946	1,693	437	−8,336	9,060	1,965	6,349	. . .	Net Errors and Omissions	78ca *d*
1,228	1,091	3,213	−2,382	1,369	1,165	995	4,360	483	1,062	53	2,747	2,159	897	. . .	*Overall Balance*	78cb *d*
−1,228	−1,091	−3,213	2,382	−1,369	−1,165	−995	−4,360	−483	−1,062	−53	−2,747	−2,159	−897	. . .	Reserves and Related Items	79da *d*
−1,228	−1,091	−3,213	2,382	−1,369	−1,165	−995	−4,360	−483	−1,062	−53	−2,747	−2,159	−897	. . .	Reserve Assets	79db *d*
—	—	—	—	—	—	—	—	—	—	—	—	—	—	. . .	Use of Fund Credit and Loans	79dc *d*
. . .	. . .	. . .	. . .	. . .	. . .	. . .	. . .	. . .	. . .	. . .	. . .	. . .	. . .	. . .	Exceptional Financing	79de *d*

Switzerland

	1970	1971	1972	1973	1974	1975	1976	1977	1978	1979	1980	1981	1982	1983	1984
International Investment Position															*Millions of US Dollars*
Assets .... 79aa *d*	...	...	...	...	...	...	...	...	...	...	...	...	...	...	183,033
Direct Investment Abroad .... 79ab *d*	...	...	...	...	...	...	...	...	...	...	...	...	...	...	17,850
Portfolio Investment .... 79ac *d*	...	...	...	...	...	...	...	...	...	...	...	...	...	...	62,879
Equity Securities .... 79ad *d*	...	...	...	...	...	...	...	...	...	...	...	...	...	...	13,663
Debt Securities .... 79ae *d*	...	...	...	...	...	...	...	...	...	...	...	...	...	...	49,216
Financial Derivatives .... 79al *d*	...	...	...	...	...	...	...	...	...	...	...	...	...	...	
Other Investment .... 79af *d*	...	...	...	...	...	...	...	...	...	...	...	...	...	...	82,651
Monetary Authorities .... 79ag *d*	...	...	...	...	...	...	...	...	...	...	...	...	...	...	—
General Government .... 79ah *d*	...	...	...	...	...	...	...	...	...	...	...	...	...	...	464
Banks .... 79ai *d*	...	...	...	...	...	...	...	...	...	...	...	...	...	...	56,697
Other Sectors .... 79aj *d*	...	...	...	...	...	...	...	...	...	...	...	...	...	...	25,490
Reserve Assets .... 79ak *d*	...	...	...	...	...	...	...	...	...	...	...	...	...	...	19,654
Liabilities .... 79la *d*	...	...	...	...	...	...	...	...	...	...	...	...	...	...	100,621
Dir. Invest. in Rep. Economy .... 79lb *d*	...	...	...	...	...	...	...	...	...	...	...	...	...	...	11,070
Portfolio Investment .... 79lc *d*	...	...	...	...	...	...	...	...	...	...	...	...	...	...	22,579
Equity Securities .... 79ld *d*	...	...	...	...	...	...	...	...	...	...	...	...	...	...	20,740
Debt Securities .... 79le *d*	...	...	...	...	...	...	...	...	...	...	...	...	...	...	1,840
Financial Derivatives .... 79ll *d*	...	...	...	...	...	...	...	...	...	...	...	...	...	...	
Other investment .... 79lf *d*	...	...	...	...	...	...	...	...	...	...	...	...	...	...	66,971
Monetary Authorities .... 79lg *d*	...	...	...	...	...	...	...	...	...	...	...	...	...	...	50
General Government .... 79lh *d*	...	...	...	...	...	...	...	...	...	...	...	...	...	...	—
Banks .... 79li *d*	...	...	...	...	...	...	...	...	...	...	...	...	...	...	48,943
Other Sectors .... 79lj *d*	...	...	...	...	...	...	...	...	...	...	...	...	...	...	17,978
Government Finance															*Millions of Francs:*
Deficit (-) or Surplus 80	295	−869	−54	−1,425	−884	−1,766	−1,377	−1,291	−64	−2,352	−76	−1,491	901	−1,446	⅃ −241
Revenue 81	7,661	8,003	10,060	10,111	11,835	11,599	13,781	12,959	15,079	13,655	16,456	15,939	18,857	17,752	⅃ 20,282
Expenditure 82	7,169	8,374	9,426	10,786	11,905	12,662	15,185	14,211	15,428	15,951	16,474	17,140	18,001	18,897	⅃ 20,160
Lending Minus Repayments 83	197	498	688	750	814	703	−27	39	−285	56	58	290	−45	301	⅃ 363
Financing															
Net Domestic Borrowing 84a	−320	1,085	601	88	1,472	1,880	4,623	888	751	1,070	1,217	465	−369	547	⅃ 1,870
Other Financing 86c	−103	426	−105	91	242	94	−901	133	509	392	116	92	98	62	⅃ −417
Use of Cash Balances 87	128	−642	−442	1,246	−830	−208	−2,345	270	−1,196	890	−1,257	934	−630	837	⅃ −1,212
Total Debt 88	7,496	8,606	9,572	10,014	11,760	14,405	18,390	19,372	20,549	22,405	⅃ 31,680	31,612	33,111	33,340	36,610
National Accounts															*Billions of Francs:*
Exports of Goods & Services .... 90c. *c*	29.7	32.1	35.8	40.2	45.9	44.0	47.7	53.4	53.2	56.0	62.6	69.1	69.6	71.8	80.6
Government Consumption .... 91f. *c*	9.6	11.4	12.9	14.8	16.6	17.9	18.9	19.2	19.8	20.8	23.5	25.6	27.7	29.6	30.8
Gross Fixed Capital Formation .... 93e. *c*	25.0	30.1	34.6	38.2	38.9	33.7	29.2	30.2	32.5	34.6	44.4	48.4	48.7	51.4	54.5
Increase/Decrease(-) in Stocks .... 93i. *c*	4.3	3.3	2.5	2.5	5.2	−1.5	.2	—	.4	3.3	7.0	2.7	.4	−2.1	2.3
Private Consumption .... 96f. *c*	53.3	59.7	67.8	75.9	83.1	86.0	88.9	92.6	95.3	100.7	111.2	118.6	125.9	131.3	137.0
Imports of Goods & Services .... 98c. *c*	−31.3	−33.6	−36.8	−41.7	−48.7	−40.0	−43.0	−49.7	−49.5	−56.8	−68.6	−70.9	−68.7	−71.9	−81.2
Gross Domestic Product (GDP) .... 99b. *c*	90.7	103.0	116.7	130.1	141.1	140.2	142.0	145.8	151.7	158.5	180.1	193.5	203.6	210.1	224.1
Net Factor Inc/Pmts(-) Abroad 98.n	3.3	3.5	3.8	4.5	5.4	4.5	5.2	6.1	5.8	6.6	7.0	9.2	9.2	10.1	12.8
Gross National Income (GNI) 99a	93.9	106.5	120.5	134.5	146.5	144.6	147.2	151.9	157.5	165.2	177.3	194.0	205.2	214.0	226.1
Net National Income 99e	83.2	94.2	106.4	119.3	130.3	129.4	132.3	135.9	141.1	148.5	159.4	174.4	184.8	193.1	204.4
GDP Volume 1980 Prices .... 99b. *r*	148.5	154.9	160.2	165.3	167.2	156.0	154.7	158.4	159.3	163.2	170.4	....	....	....	....
GDP Volume 1990 Prices .... 99b. *r*	....	....	....	....	....	....	....	....	....	....	259.0	263.1	259.3	260.6	268.5
GDP Volume (1995=100) .... 99bv *r*	71.4	74.5	77.1	79.5	80.4	75.0	74.4	76.2	76.6	78.5	81.9	83.2	82.0	82.4	84.9
GDP Deflator (1995=100) .... 99bi *r*	34.9	38.1	41.7	45.0	48.3	51.4	52.5	52.7	54.5	55.6	60.5	64.0	68.3	70.1	72.6
															Millions:
Population 99z	6.19	6.23	6.39	6.43	6.44	6.41	6.35	6.33	6.34	6.36	6.32	6.35	6.39	6.42	6.44

1985	1986	1987	1988	1989	1990	1991	1992	1993	1994	1995	1996	1997	1998	1999		
Millions of US Dollars															International Investment Position	
253,356	341,122	450,027	439,407	477,797	565,776	589,550	586,857	647,256	745,894	860,302	924,354	1,009,556	1,191,694	....	Assets	79aa *d*
25,093	34,226	45,276	48,907	54,629	66,087	75,884	74,413	91,571	112,586	142,479	141,591	165,365	181,536	....	Direct Investment Abroad	79ab *d*
95,723	135,215	172,000	176,666	186,541	191,525	214,903	219,559	271,003	293,846	347,040	359,820	382,782	465,951	....	Portfolio Investment	79ac *d*
23,244	33,141	36,440	36,888	46,083	41,552	51,635	56,416	89,414	100,797	120,544	138,922	165,437	207,857	....	Equity Securities	79ad *d*
72,479	102,073	135,560	139,778	140,458	149,973	163,268	163,144	181,589	193,049	226,496	220,898	217,344	258,094	....	Debt Securities	79ae *d*
														....	Financial Derivatives	79al *d*
108,431	142,017	194,129	181,996	203,250	270,166	260,142	252,214	243,644	293,976	322,130	375,575	414,210	493,794	....	Other Investment	79af *d*
678	1,099	1,016	971	976	1,243	1,086	889	884	1,037	1,250	1,052	946	943	....	Monetary Authorities	79ag *d*
74,827	99,794	136,437	122,510	113,698	132,993	128,507	127,784	133,536	163,586	183,010	231,511	276,738	335,011	....	General Government	79ah *d*
32,927	41,123	56,677	58,515	88,576	135,930	130,550	123,541	109,224	129,353	137,870	143,012	136,526	157,840	....	Banks	79ai *d*
24,108	29,665	38,622	31,838	33,378	37,999	38,620	40,671	41,038	45,487	48,653	47,368	47,200	50,413	....	Other Sectors	79aj *d*
143,578	209,309	259,255	250,664	290,706	347,890	354,059	351,455	404,168	472,873	556,487	587,560	700,953	837,885	....	Reserve Assets	79ak *d*
14,604	24,756	34,444	32,497	33,344	43,944	45,618	42,986	49,532	61,690	73,324	69,002	74,142	85,889	....	Liabilities	79la *d*
47,899	73,876	76,840	76,228	93,655	93,784	103,124	109,190	162,151	162,400	208,583	203,380	272,805	353,573	....	Dir. Invest. in Rep. Economy	79lb *d*
42,414	67,107	67,138	65,761	81,930	78,971	85,946	90,876	139,056	134,721	179,290	176,566	246,515	323,810	....	Portfolio Investment	79lc *d*
5,485	6,769	9,701	10,467	11,725	14,813	17,177	18,314	23,095	27,679	29,293	26,814	26,289	29,763	....	Equity Securities	79ld *d*
														....	Debt Securities	79le *d*
														....	Financial Derivatives	79ll *d*
81,075	110,677	147,971	141,939	163,708	210,162	205,318	199,279	192,485	248,783	274,580	315,178	354,006	398,423	....	Other investment	79lf *d*
62	54	128	112	77	46	85	38	128	36	37	24	33	119	....	Monetary Authorities	79lg *d*
—	—	383	284	81	39	36	114	192	258	568	514	596	625	....	General Government	79lh *d*
59,464	81,470	109,509	102,230	109,793	132,940	131,141	124,595	127,430	168,268	180,343	217,172	257,602	292,031	....	Banks	79li *d*
21,549	29,153	37,951	39,313	53,757	77,136	74,055	74,532	64,735	80,222	93,631	97,468	95,775	105,648	....	Other Sectors	79lj *d*
Year Ending December 31															Government Finance	
−1,183	2,372	670	1,980	157	1,276	−3,297	−2,437	−8,351	−4,443	−5,141	−4,404	−4,917	363	−2,399	Deficit (-) or Surplus	80
20,702	24,347	23,296	27,066	26,427	30,385	30,247	32,355	29,559	33,752	32,202	35,279	34,695	39,359	37,742	Revenue	81
21,534	21,671	22,219	24,099	25,964	28,764	32,422	34,354	35,443	36,759	37,474	39,417	38,151	41,634	40,839	Expenditure	82
351	304	407	987	306	345	1,122	438	2,467	1,436	−131	266	1,461	−2,638	−698	Lending Minus Repayments	83
															Financing	
3,509	−1,603	1,145	−1,676	1,321	−203	5,408	8,801	14,923	7,399	6,472	5,706	8,486	13,860	−6,817	Net Domestic Borrowing	84a
−1,124	59	−1,329	299	−2,884	−26	−1,812	−1,810	−1,131	−1,598	−1,050	1,202	−596	−4,245	−10,960	Other Financing	86c
−1,202	−828	−486	−603	1,406	−1,047	−299	−4,554	−5,441	−1,358	−281	−2,504	−2,973	−9,978	20,176	Use of Cash Balances	87
39,161	38,782	38,597	39,289	38,287	38,509	43,915	55,297	67,513	75,714	82,152	88,418	97,050	109,620	102,254	Total Debt	88
Billions of Francs															National Accounts	
89.0	89.1	90.5	98.0	110.5	115.0	116.7	122.2	125.3	127.0	127.5	131.5	147.7	152.9	161.3	Exports of Goods & Services	90c. *c*
32.9	34.6	35.5	38.2	41.8	46.4	50.9	53.4	53.5	54.8	55.0	56.6	56.2	56.5	57.0	Government Consumption	91f. *c*
57.9	62.0	65.1	73.0	80.5	85.9	85.0	78.6	75.4	78.7	77.6	73.9	72.9	75.5	78.6	Gross Fixed Capital Formation	93e. *c*
1.6	.1	−.1	.1	2.9	3.8	−.2	−3.5	−3.1	−3.3	—	.5	2.3	5.1	1.2	Increase/Decrease(-) in Stocks	93i. *c*
143.8	149.1	154.6	160.3	168.8	179.6	193.4	201.9	206.8	211.2	216.1	219.8	223.9	228.5	234.6	Private Consumption	96f. *c*
−88.1	−86.4	−88.4	−96.8	−111.1	−113.4	−112.1	−110.2	−108.1	−111.0	−112.9	−116.4	−131.5	−138.4	−143.5	Imports of Goods & Services	98c. *c*
237.2	248.5	257.2	272.7	293.3	317.3	333.7	342.4	349.8	357.5	363.3	365.8	371.6	380.0	389.3	Gross Domestic Product (GDP)	99b. *c*
13.4	11.6	11.4	14.5	14.8	13.6	14.3	13.4	15.6	12.7	15.6	....	....	....	....	Net Factor Inc/Pmts(-) Abroad	98.n
241.4	254.9	266.1	283.0	305.2	327.6	345.4	352.2	358.4	365.6	377.6	....	....	....	....	Gross National Income (GNI)	99a
218.0	230.5	240.5	255.2	274.7	294.8	311.1	316.7	322.2	328.8	339.8	....	....	....	....	Net National Income	99e
															GDP Volume 1980 Prices	99b. *r*
277.7	282.2	284.3	293.1	305.9	317.3	314.8	314.4	312.9	314.5	316.1	317.1	322.4	329.1	334.6	GDP Volume 1990 Prices	99b. *r*
87.8	89.3	89.9	92.7	96.8	100.4	99.6	99.5	99.0	99.5	100.0	100.3	102.0	104.1	105.9	GDP Volume (1995=100)	99bv *r*
74.3	76.6	78.7	80.9	83.4	87.0	92.2	94.8	97.3	98.9	100.0	100.4	100.3	100.5	101.2	GDP Deflator (1995=100)	99bi *r*
Midyear Estimates																
6.47	6.50	6.55	6.59	6.65	6.71	6.80	6.88	6.94	6.99	7.04	7.07	7.09	7.11	7.13	Population	99z

(See notes in the back of the book.)

Syrian Arab Republic

	1970	1971	1972	1973	1974	1975	1976	1977	1978	1979	1980	1981	1982	1983	1984
Exchange Rates												*Pounds per SDR: End of Period (aa)*			
Principal Rate.................... **aa**	3.820	4.147	4.147	4.584	4.530	4.331	4.560	4.768	5.113	5.171	5.006	4.569	4.330	4.109	3.847
Principal Rate.................... **ae**	3.820	3.820	3.820	3.800	3.700	3.700	3.925	3.925	3.925	3.925	3.925	3.925	3.925	3.925	3.925
Fund Position													*Millions of SDRs:*		
Quota.................................. **2f.** *s*	50	50	50	50	50	50	50	50	63	63	95	95	95	95	139
SDRs.................................. **1b.** *s*	—	—	4	8	8	7	7	6	6	12	10	15	12	9	5
Reserve Position in the Fund.......... **1c.** *s*	—	—	—	—	—	7	13	—	—	—	—	7	7	—	—
Total Fund Cred.&Loans Outstg. **2tl**	10	5	23	18	5	—	—	—	—	1	—	—	—	—	—
International Liquidity										*Millions of US Dollars Unless Otherwise Indicated:*					
SDRs.................................. **1b.** *d*	—	—	4	10	10	9	8	8	8	16	12	17	13	9	5
Reserve Position in the Fund.......... **1c.** *d*	—	—	—	—	—	8	15	—	—	—	—	9	8	—	—
Gold (Million Fine Troy Ounces) **1ad**	.800	.800	.800	.800	.789	.789	.789	.811	.811	.833	.833	.833	.833	.833	.833
Gold (National Valuation) .... **1an** *d*	27	27	27	28	28	28	27	28	27	29e	29	29	29	29	29
Monetary Authorities: Other Assets .... **3..** *d*	15	10	16	16	34	28	32	74	41	409	15	124	92	149	195
Other Liab. .... **4..** *d*	85	104	134	101	56	287	347	296	352	409	530	672	929	904	1,641
Deposit Money Banks: Assets .... **7a.** *d*	12	10	22	33	62	88	125	65	73	188	109	69	292	244	141
Liabilities .... **7b.** *d*	16	39	49	61	88	42	155	210	126	139	377	637	722	990	928
Monetary Authorities													*Millions of Pounds:*		
Foreign Assets........................ **11**	264	362	571	1,605	1,956	2,808	1,382	2,297	1,766	2,485	1,499	1,749	1,253	902	1,916
Claims on Central Government.......... **12a**	2,275	2,711	3,208	2,588	3,486	4,445	7,175	7,932	11,934	12,447	18,228	22,560	35,248	41,519	55,165
Claims on Official Entities.......... **12bx**	132	115	81	78	40	28	23	13	12	9	62	59	57	56	56
Claims on Deposit Money Banks **12e**	330	234	346	432	629	756	1,306	1,191	842	1,532	1,493	1,496	1,429	2,246	1,179
Reserve Money........................ **14**	2,093	2,264	2,684	3,301	4,300	5,142	6,431	8,026	10,463	11,905	15,896	17,250	25,700	32,548	43,095
of which: Currency Outside DMBs.......... **14a**	1,795	1,846	2,245	2,757	3,413	3,945	5,259	6,797	8,459	9,903	13,422	14,046	17,348	20,500	25,155
Foreign Liabilities.................. **16c**	359	418	606	464	230	1,061	1,363	1,163	1,382	1,609	2,080	2,637	3,645	3,546	6,441
Central Government Deposits **16d**	419	536	586	715	995	1,611	1,745	1,782	2,008	2,459	3,011	4,986	7,351	7,391	7,255
Capital Accounts.................... **17a**	47	68	93	100	100	96	100	100	110	141	176	195	185	185	185
Other Items (Net).................. **17r**	61	115	216	100	464	107	226	340	569	351	117	790	1,105	1,054	1,340
Deposit Money Banks													*Millions of Pounds:*		
Reserves.............................. **20**	194	291	296	390	468	603	817	736	1,411	938	1,622	1,994	6,466	9,816	14,935
Foreign Assets...................... **21**	48	40	83	126	229	327	490	255	287	737	426	272	1,144	957	555
Claims on Central Government.......... **22a**	84	101	136	173	230	295	405	485	612	782	918	1,383	1,700	2,136	2,849
Claims on Official Entities.......... **22bx**	840	965	1,347	1,744	3,027	4,647	6,746	8,148	8,089	9,819	14,176	21,672	20,802	22,468	19,556
Claims on Private Sector **22d**	551	570	578	653	694	861	1,146	1,339	1,651	2,437	2,944	3,489	4,472	5,938	6,580
Demand Deposits.................... **24**	441	566	786	957	1,784	2,640	3,091	3,676	4,883	5,552	7,611	9,917	10,895	15,174	17,872
Time and Savings Deposits.......... **25**	144	180	235	277	398	514	665	957	1,249	1,535	1,873	2,655	3,590	4,739	6,645
Restricted Deposits **26b**	152	272	267	436	537	444	1,090	1,258	1,106	1,586	2,505	5,162	7,783	7,887	7,616
Foreign Liabilities.................. **26c**	60	147	186	231	327	155	610	824	495	545	1,479	2,500	2,833	3,884	3,644
Central Government Deposits **26d**	133	154	169	181	259	1,128	1,485	1,569	1,669	1,839	2,211	3,226	4,132	3,826	4,008
Credit from Monetary Authorities **26g**	326	234	345	421	629	756	1,298	1,190	842	1,232	1,493	1,495	1,421	2,246	1,179
Capital Accounts.................... **27a**	174	181	186	190	227	248	338	384	445	532	607	914	1,032	1,139	1,301
Other Items (Net).................. **27r**	250	202	224	354	428	743	866	952	1,184	1,643	2,005	2,585	2,495	1,954	1,688
Monetary Survey													*Millions of Pounds:*		
Foreign Assets (Net)................ **31n**	−108	−163	−138	1,036	1,627	1,919	−102	565	175	1,068	−1,634	−3,117	−4,081	−5,572	−7,614
Domestic Credit **32**	3,330	3,773	4,595	4,339	6,222	7,538	12,264	14,566	18,621	21,196	31,105	40,950	50,795	60,900	72,942
Claims on Central Govt. (Net).......... **32an**	1,807	2,122	2,589	1,864	2,462	2,001	4,350	5,065	8,869	8,931	13,924	15,730	25,465	32,438	46,751
Claims on Official Entities.......... **32bx**	972	1,080	1,428	1,822	3,066	4,675	6,768	8,162	8,101	9,828	14,238	21,731	20,858	22,524	19,612
Claims on Private Sector.......... **32d**	551	570	578	653	694	861	1,146	1,339	1,651	2,437	2,944	3,489	4,472	5,938	6,580
Money................................ **34**	2,341	2,502	3,151	3,797	5,540	6,966	8,561	10,924	13,866	16,119	21,854	24,832	29,518	36,978	45,607
Quasi-Money........................ **35**	144	180	235	277	398	514	665	957	1,249	1,535	1,873	2,655	3,590	4,739	6,645
Restricted Deposits **36b**	152	272	267	436	537	444	1,090	1,258	1,106	1,586	2,505	5,162	7,783	7,887	7,616
Other Items (Net).................. **37r**	527	601	741	804	1,295	1,407	1,665	1,818	2,377	2,767	2,934	4,824	5,420	5,259	4,939
Money plus Quasi-Money.......... **35l**	2,484	2,682	3,386	4,074	5,939	7,480	9,226	11,881	15,115	17,654	23,727	27,487	33,109	41,717	52,251
Interest Rates													*Percent Per Annum*		
Discount Rate *(End of Period)* **60**	5.00	5.00	5.00	5.00	5.00	5.00	5.00	5.00	5.00	5.00	5.00	5.00	5.00	5.00	5.00
Prices and Production													*Index Numbers (1995=100):*		
Wholesale Prices **63**	3.2	3.5	3.4	4.5	5.1	5.5	6.1	6.7	7.5	8.2	I 9.4	11.2	12.4	12.8	13.9
Consumer Prices **64**	3.0	3.2	3.2	3.9	I 4.5	5.0	5.6	6.3	6.6	6.9	8.2	9.7	11.1	11.8	12.9
Industrial Production **66**	I 19.7	21.3	23.5	25.1	29.4	I 34.2	37.3	36.4	39.5	39.5	44.4	50.1	52.8	61.7	I 61.7
													Number in Thousands:		
Labor Force.......................... **67d**	....	....	....	....	....	....	....	....	....	....	....	....	....	....	....
Employment **67e**	....	....	....	....	....	....	....	....	....	....	....	....	....	....	....
Unemployment **67c**	....	....	....	....	....	....	....	....	....	....	....	....	....	....	....
Unemployment Rate (%)............ **67r**	....	....	....	....	....	....	....	....	....	....	....	....	....	....	....

1985	1986	1987	1988	1989	1990	1991	1992	1993	1994	1995	1996	1997	1998	1999		
Pounds per US Dollar: End of Period (ae)															**Exchange Rates**	
4.311	4.801	5.568	15.105	14.751	15.969	16.057	15.434	15.418	16.387	16.686	16.141	15.145	15.805	15.406	Principal Rate	aa
3.925	3.925	3.925	11.225	11.225	11.225	11.225	11.225	11.225	11.225	11.225	11.225	11.225	11.225	11.225	Principal Rate	ae
End of Period															**Fund Position**	
139	139	139	139	139	139	139	139	210	210	210	210	210	210	294	Quota	2f. s
3	—	—	—	—	—	—	—	—	—	—	—	—	—	—	SDRs	1b. s
—	—	—	—	—	—	—	—	—	—	—	—	—	—	—	Reserve Position in the Fund	1c. s
—	—	—	—	—	—	—	—	—	—	—	—	—	—	—	Total Fund Cred.&Loans Outstg.	2tl
End of Period															**International Liquidity**	
3	—	—	—	—	—	—	—	—	—	—	—	—	—	—	SDRs	1b. d
—	—	—	—	—	—	—	—	—	—	—	—	—	—	—	Reserve Position in the Fund	1c. d
.833	.833	.833	.833	.833	.833	.833	.833	.833	.833	.833	.833	.833	.833	.833	Gold (Million Fine Troy Ounces)	1ad
29	29	29	29	29	29	29	29	29	29	29	29	29	29	29	Gold (National Valuation)	1and
194	430	942	1,140	....	....	....	....	....	....	....	....	....	....	....	Monetary Authorities: Other Assets	3..d
2,362	2,858	3,629	3,578	3,680	4,019	1,433	1,169	1,037	1,041	1,124	1,041	1,084	1,137	....	Other Liab.	4..d
152	223	241	302	500	992	1,730	2,326	2,667	3,017	3,573	16,084	19,819	22,780	....	Deposit Money Banks: Assets	7a.d
1,166	1,263	1,311	1,126	1,062	919	742	587	493	343	226	471	248	325	....	Liabilities	7b.d
End of Period															**Monetary Authorities**	
1,193	2,352	4,653	15,265	25,868	37,540	18,657	23,544	24,368	28,568	37,206	49,156	52,376	55,216	....	Foreign Assets	11
74,003	79,407	83,159	83,334	88,713	104,776	114,399	136,064	153,089	178,802	203,998	241,730	265,783	270,370	....	Claims on Central Government	12a
56	56	106	106	106	106	106	106	106	106	106	106	106	106	....	Claims on Official Entities	12bx
1,825	1,197	915	3,126	8,356	18,697	32,730	51,499	71,006	90,674	104,602	112,460	126,599	135,455	....	Claims on Deposit Money Banks	12e
58,516	62,753	68,590	64,983	78,421	100,745	108,332	132,508	151,867	164,996	172,711	185,864	194,799	204,513	....	Reserve Money	14
29,562	36,262	41,852	52,171	59,962	76,202	92,450	107,602	126,116	135,021	143,800	153,715	159,808	178,191	....	*of which: Currency Outside DMBs*	14a
9,273	11,218	14,244	40,160	41,304	45,112	16,085	13,117	11,640	11,683	12,614	11,686	12,168	12,768	....	Foreign Liabilities	16c
8,305	9,098	8,839	17,593	24,711	35,276	56,417	76,633	93,898	126,027	156,479	213,995	256,253	272,085	....	Central Government Deposits	16d
185	185	185	185	185	558	9,245	11,186	14,242	18,755	23,902	23,902	33,839	38,195	....	Capital Accounts	17a
797	−242	−3,024	−21,090	−21,578	−20,571	−24,190	−22,230	−23,078	−23,311	−19,795	−31,995	−52,193	−66,416	....	Other Items (Net)	17r
End of Period															**Deposit Money Banks**	
25,334	23,729	23,309	9,467	11,939	17,503	20,149	23,773	24,814	31,503	29,294	41,393	25,837	24,608	....	Reserves	20
597	876	947	3,389	5,610	11,132	19,423	26,105	29,932	33,870	40,104	180,547	222,465	255,707	....	Foreign Assets	21
3,532	3,772	5,004	5,566	5,873	6,915	16,502	20,179	21,827	24,791	26,683	13,784	20,601	21,214	....	Claims on Central Government	22a
16,279	18,918	22,035	47,162	52,579	59,134	72,383	89,540	120,043	119,980	138,591	147,546	164,580	160,445	....	Claims on Official Entities	22bx
6,825	7,601	8,971	12,068	16,073	20,009	26,787	35,556	44,067	51,695	62,844	67,099	74,239	73,659	....	Claims on Private Sector	22d
22,222	22,962	23,438	24,595	28,987	35,888	41,973	53,341	63,918	72,215	81,113	84,360	93,665	97,739	....	Demand Deposits	24
8,018	9,236	10,781	16,068	21,341	28,054	45,303	54,929	64,386	74,007	80,567	86,917	95,713	108,094	....	Time and Savings Deposits	25
9,841	11,587	17,535	11,262	10,156	11,039	13,022	15,121	16,051	10,087	9,769	27,181	33,234	22,788	....	Restricted Deposits	26b
4,575	4,959	5,147	12,642	11,918	10,316	8,327	6,593	5,538	3,847	2,535	5,290	2,782	3,652	....	Foreign Liabilities	26c
3,561	3,555	3,912	3,880	4,114	3,919	4,781	5,973	6,668	6,875	8,425	8,202	12,863	13,702	....	Central Government Deposits	26d
1,825	1,199	924	3,138	8,724	18,770	27,890	51,671	71,340	91,012	104,983	123,085	137,828	138,660	....	Credit from Monetary Authorities	26g
1,423	1,505	1,831	2,228	2,647	3,148	7,318	10,344	13,234	17,189	22,652	29,335	34,056	39,028	....	Capital Accounts	27a
604	−779	−4,051	2,864	4,187	3,558	6,675	−2,775	−410	−13,163	−12,528	85,999	97,580	111,973	....	Other Items (Net)	27r
End of Period															**Monetary Survey**	
−12,057	−12,948	−13,791	−34,148	−21,744	−6,756	13,668	29,940	37,123	46,908	62,161	212,727	259,891	294,503	....	Foreign Assets (Net)	31n
88,828	97,101	106,523	126,763	134,518	151,744	168,980	198,840	238,565	242,472	267,318	248,067	256,193	240,007	....	Domestic Credit	32
65,669	70,527	75,412	67,427	65,761	72,495	69,703	73,638	74,350	70,691	65,777	33,317	17,269	5,797	....	Claims on Central Govt. (Net)	32an
16,335	18,974	22,141	47,268	52,685	59,240	72,489	89,646	120,149	120,086	138,697	147,652	164,686	160,551	....	Claims on Official Entities	32bx
6,825	7,601	8,971	12,068	16,073	20,009	26,787	35,556	44,067	51,695	62,844	67,099	74,239	73,659	....	Claims on Private Sector	32d
54,976	61,214	67,821	79,814	95,030	118,717	135,609	161,449	194,589	210,436	228,123	244,170	260,927	281,981	....	Money	34
8,018	9,236	10,781	16,068	21,341	28,054	45,303	54,929	64,386	74,007	80,567	86,917	95,713	108,094	....	Quasi-Money	35
9,841	11,587	17,535	11,262	10,156	11,039	13,022	15,121	16,051	10,087	9,769	27,181	33,234	22,788	....	Restricted Deposits	36b
3,437	1,444	−4,151	−15,504	−13,752	−12,823	−11,289	−2,719	661	−5,151	11,019	102,526	126,209	121,648	....	Other Items (Net)	37r
62,994	70,450	78,601	95,882	116,370	146,772	180,912	216,378	258,975	284,443	308,690	331,087	356,640	390,076	....	Money plus Quasi-Money	35l
Percent Per Annum															**Interest Rates**	
5.00	5.00	5.00	5.00	5.00	5.00	5.00	5.00	5.00	5.00	....	....	....	....	....	Discount Rate *(End of Period)*	60
Period Averages															**Prices and Production**	
15.3	21.5	⟨31.6	46.5	52.9	64.5	73.5	75.5	81.9	93.5	100.0	103.2	105.8	105.2	....	Wholesale Prices	63
15.1	20.5	32.7	44.1	49.1	⟨58.6	63.9	70.9	80.3	92.6	100.0	108.2	110.8	110.2	....	Consumer Prices	64
58.7	61.1	⟨62.8	61.3	70.6	77.6	83.0	88.4	⟨90.0	97.0	100.0	101.0	107.0	109.0	....	Industrial Production	66
Period Averages																
....	....	....	....	....	3,485	....	....	....	....	....	....	....	4,411	....	Labor Force	67d
....	....	....	2,883	....	3,250	....	....	....	....	....	....	....	....	....	Employment	67e
....	....	....	177	....	235	....	....	....	....	....	....	....	....	....	Unemployment	67c
....	....	....	5.8	....	6.8	....	....	....	....	....	....	....	....	....	Unemployment Rate (%)	67r

Syrian Arab Republic

		1970	1971	1972	1973	1974	1975	1976	1977	1978	1979	1980	1981	1982	1983	1984
International Transactions																*Millions of Pounds*
Exports	70	775	743	1,098	1,341	2,914	3,441	4,141	4,199	4,160	6,453	8,273	8,254	7,954	7,548	7,275
Imports, c.i.f.	71	1,377	1,677	2,061	2,341	4,572	6,236	9,203	10,605	9,650	13,067	16,187	20,302	15,808	17,829	16,155
																1995=100
Volume of Exports	72	34.5	28.3	34.5	32.1	‡31.1	37.9	39.9	38.9	41.2	37.9	32.7	29.8	31.7	31.1	29.1
Volume of Imports	73	16.9	17.7	‡17.7	20.9	26.3	41.3	41.8	52.0	46.7	52.6	53.6	70.3	60.6	66.0	61.7
Unit Value of Exports	74	16.6	20.0	‡23.3	29.1	54.7	46.6	59.4	64.0	68.7	89.6	116.4	129.2	112.9	105.9	108.3
Unit Value of Imports	75	9.9	11.4	‡13.7	16.9	23.7	26.4	33.2	30.6	32.7	40.6	52.8	68.6	64.4	74.4	69.6
Balance of Payments																*Millions of US Dollars:*
Current Account, n.i.e.	78ald	....	....	....	....	....	....	....	−167	−64	896	251	−308	−250	−844	−794
Goods: Exports f.o.b.	78aad								1,070	1,061	1,648	2,112	2,212	2,002	1,918	1,834
Goods: Imports f.o.b.	78abd								−2,402	−2,204	−3,055	−4,010	−4,404	−3,636	−4,024	−3,687
Trade Balance	78acd								−1,332	−1,142	−1,407	−1,898	−2,193	−1,633	−2,106	−1,853
Services: Credit	78add								330	259	376	365	431	483	560	512
Services: Debit	78aed								−418	−579	−590	−521	−814	−757	−854	−906
Balance on Goods & Services	78afd								−1,421	−1,463	−1,621	−2,054	−2,575	−1,907	−2,400	−2,247
Income: Credit	78agd								146	638	905	864	530	436	402	351
Income: Debit	78ahd								−35	−22	−15	−79	−111	−177	−148	−128
Balance on Gds, Serv. & Inc.	78aid								−1,310	−846	−731	−1,269	−2,156	−1,648	−2,146	−2,023
Current Transfers, n.i.e.: Credit	78ajd								1,143	782	1,629	1,522	1,851	1,400	1,304	1,232
Current Transfers: Debit	78akd								—	—	−2	−2	−3	−2	−3	−3
Capital Account, n.i.e.	78bcd								—	—	—	—	—	—	—	—
Capital Account, n.i.e.: Credit	78bad								—	—	—	—	—	—	—	—
Capital Account: Debit	78bbd								—	—	—	—	—	—	—	—
Financial Account, n.i.e.	78bjd								337	385	124	196	287	175	714	1,035
Direct Investment Abroad	78bdd								—	—	—	—	—	—	—	—
Dir. Invest. in Rep. Econ., n.i.e.	78bec								—	—	—	—	—	—	—	—
Portfolio Investment Assets	78bfd								—	—	—	—	—	—	—	—
Equity Securities	78bkd								—	—	—	—	—	—	—	—
Debt Securities	78bld								—	—	—	—	—	—	—	—
Portfolio Investment Liab., n.i.e.	78bgd								—	—	—	—	—	—	—	—
Equity Securities	78bmd								—	—	—	—	—	—	—	—
Debt Securities	78bnd								—	—	—	—	—	—	—	—
Financial Derivatives Assets	78bwd								....	....	....	....	....	....	....	....
Financial Derivatives Liabilities	78bxd								....	....	....	....	....	....	....	....
Other Investment Assets	78bhd								18	25	−148	47	−64	−172	−3	83
Monetary Authorities	78bod								—	—	—	—	—	—	—	—
General Government	78bpd								−42	33	−33	−32	−104	52	−51	−20
Banks	78bqd								60	−8	−115	79	39	−224	48	103
Other Sectors	78brd								—	—	—	—	—	—	—	—
Other Investment Liab., n.i.e.	78bid								318	360	272	149	351	346	716	952
Monetary Authorities	78bsd								−51	56	68	121	143	258	284	744
General Government	78btd								228	359	127	9	−151	−179	189	290
Banks	78bud								54	−84	13	24	262	91	269	−62
Other Sectors	78bvd								87	29	64	−5	97	176	−27	−19
Net Errors and Omissions	78cad								22	−424	−825	−701	−30	−17	−15	−25
Overall Balance	78cbd								192	−103	195	−254	−51	−92	−145	216
Reserves and Related Items	79dad								−192	103	−195	254	51	92	145	−216
Reserve Assets	79dbd								−192	103	−196	255	51	92	145	−216
Use of Fund Credit and Loans	79dcd								—	—	1	−1	—	—	—	—
Exceptional Financing	79ded								—	—	—	—	—	—	—	—
Government Finance																*Millions of Pounds:*
Deficit (-) or Surplus	80	....	....	−327	−574	−740	−992	−2,332	−2,928	−2,935	303	−4,976	−4,157	....	....	....
Revenue	81	....	....	2,346	2,766	4,285	8,698	9,058	10,320	7,341	9,201	13,759	14,844	....	....	....
Grants Received	81z	....	....	—	—	550	—	665	100	3,070	6,384	5,967	6,359	....	....	....
Expenditure	82	....	....	2,673	3,340	5,575	9,690	12,055	13,348	13,346	15,282	24,702	25,360	....	....	....
Financing																
Total Financing	84	....	....	....	....	....	....	2,332	2,928	2,935	−303	4,976	4,157	....	....	....
Domestic	84a	....	....	....	....	....	....	1,564	2,034	....	....	5,032	1,765	....	....	....
Foreign	85a	....	....	....	....	....	....	768	894	....	....	−99	1,598	....	....	....
Unallocable Financing	87c	....	....	....	....	....	....	—	—	....	....	43	794	....	....	....
National Accounts																*Millions of Pounds*
Exports of Goods & Services	90c	1,190	1,390	1,674	2,175	3,816	4,409	4,828	4,908	4,808	7,458	9,345	10,290	9,572	9,714	9,360
Government Consumption	91f	1,192	1,432	1,638	2,125	2,815	4,343	4,960	5,293	6,470	8,424	11,870	13,656	15,103	16,154	17,070
Gross Capital Formation	93	806	1,162	1,624	1,793	3,102	5,241	7,891	9,218	9,015	10,383	14,355	15,482	16,513	17,508	18,082
Private Consumption	96f	4,944	5,819	6,479	6,309	11,459	13,599	15,523	18,078	22,210	26,742	33,858	48,051	44,992	48,904	47,535
Imports of Goods & Services	98c	−1,432	−1,790	−2,187	−2,541	−5,347	−6,996	−8,479	−10,984	−10,114	−14,033	−18,168	−21,687	−17,149	−19,549	−18,083
Gross Domestic Product (GDP)	99b	6,800	8,013	9,228	9,861	15,845	20,597	24,725	27,013	32,389	38,974	51,270	65,777	68,788	73,291	75,342
GDP Volume 1985 prices	99b.p	27,965	30,738	38,431	35,147	43,627	52,145	57,861	57,124	‡62,109	64,365	72,078	78,931	80,606	81,758	78,429
GDP Volume 1995 Prices	99b.p	....	....	....	....	....	....	....	....	....	....	....	....	....	....	....
GDP Volume (1995=100)	99bvp	21.9	24.1	30.1	27.6	34.2	40.9	45.4	44.8	‡48.7	50.5	56.5	61.9	63.2	64.1	61.5
GDP Deflator (1995=100)	99bip	5.4	5.8	5.4	6.3	8.1	8.8	9.5	10.6	‡11.6	13.5	15.9	18.6	19.1	20.0	21.4
																Millions:
Population	99z	6.26	6.48	6.71	6.94	7.19	7.44	7.72	8.02	‡8.15	8.42	8.70	9.00	9.30	9.61	9.93

1985	1986	1987	1988	1989	1990	1991	1992	1993	1994	1995	1996	1997	1998	1999		
Millions of Pounds															**International Transactions**	
6,427	5,199	15,192	15,093	33,740	47,280	38,500	34,720	35,319	34,200	40,000	44,890	43,960	32,440	38,880	Exports	70
15,570	10,709	27,915	25,040	23,544	26,940	31,070	39,178	46,468	61,370	52,860	60,390	45,210	43,720	43,010	Imports, c.i.f.	71
1995=100																
27.1	I26.2	I27.5	30.5	46.7	59.9	65.3	62.9	94.6	102.4	100.0	98.2	109.6	....	....	Volume of Exports	72
64.9	I61.1	I46.0	39.5	37.1	40.3	43.1	57.7	90.7	111.3	100.0	100.8	87.9	....	....	Volume of Imports	73
105.9	I78.0	I72.2	68.9	85.6	111.1	90.0	75.6	74.4	80.0	100.0	105.6	83.3	....	....	Unit Value of Exports	74
58.6	I69.6	I70.3	86.4	83.9	84.7	97.5	83.1	78.8	89.0	100.0	105.9	90.7	....	....	Unit Value of Imports	75
Minus Sign Indicates Debit															**Balance of Payments**	
–958	–504	–298	–151	1,222	1,762	699	55	–203	–791	367	81	483	59	....	Current Account, n.i.e.	78al *d*
1,856	1,037	1,357	1,348	3,013	4,156	3,438	3,100	3,253	3,329	3,858	4,178	4,057	3,135	....	Goods: Exports f.o.b.	78aa *d*
–3,946	–2,363	–2,226	–1,986	–1,821	–2,062	–2,354	–2,941	–3,512	–4,604	–4,001	–4,516	–3,603	–3,307	....	Goods: Imports f.o.b.	78ab *d*
–2,090	–1,326	–869	–639	1,192	2,094	1,084	159	–259	–1,275	–143	–338	454	–172	....	*Trade Balance*	78ac *d*
656	566	600	667	893	874	1,065	1,281	1,595	1,863	1,979	1,833	1,604	1,795	....	Services: Credit	78ad *d*
–975	–699	–690	–636	–792	–892	–1,002	–1,102	–1,442	–1,611	–1,537	–1,555	–1,489	–1,481	....	Services: Debit	78ae *d*
–2,409	–1,459	–958	–608	1,293	2,075	1,146	338	–106	–1,023	299	–60	569	142	....	*Balance on Goods & Services*	78af *d*
379	333	359	382	452	430	415	619	432	638	444	534	421	389	....	Income: Credit	78ag *d*
–139	–137	–459	–461	–745	–831	–1,096	–1,214	–1,064	–997	–983	–1,017	–1,006	–995	....	Income: Debit	78ah *d*
–2,169	–1,263	–1,058	–687	1,000	1,674	465	–258	–738	–1,382	–240	–543	–16	–464	....	*Balance on Gds, Serv. & Inc.*	78ai *d*
1,214	759	761	537	227	91	238	321	543	597	610	630	504	525	....	Current Transfers, n.i.e.: Credit	78aj *d*
–2	—	–1	–1	–5	–3	–4	–8	–8	–6	–3	–6	–5	–2	....	Current Transfers: Debit	78ak *d*
—	—	—	—	—	—	—	—	28	102	20	26	18	20	....	Capital Account, n.i.e.	78bc *d*
—	—	—	—	—	—	—	—	28	102	20	26	18	20	....	Capital Account, n.i.e.: Credit	78ba *d*
—	—	—	—	—	—	—	—	—	—	—	—	—	—	....	Capital Account: Debit	78bb *d*
789	591	399	85	–1,708	–1,836	–515	–50	598	1,159	467	674	70	437	....	Financial Account, n.i.e.	78bj *d*
—	—	—	—	—	—	—	—	—	—	—	—	—	—	....	Direct Investment Abroad	78bd *d*
—	—	—	—	—	—	—	—	109	251	100	89	80	80	....	Dir. Invest. in Rep. Econ., n.i.e.	78be *d*
—	—	—	—	—	—	—	—	—	—	—	—	—	—	....	Portfolio Investment Assets	78bf *d*
—	—	—	—	—	—	—	—	—	—	—	—	—	—	....	Equity Securities	78bk *d*
—	—	—	—	—	—	—	—	—	—	—	—	—	—	....	Debt Securities	78bl *d*
—	—	—	—	—	—	—	—	—	—	—	—	—	—	....	Portfolio Investment Liab., n.i.e.	78bg *d*
—	—	—	—	—	—	—	—	—	—	—	—	—	—	....	Equity Securities	78bm *d*
—	—	—	—	—	—	—	—	—	—	—	—	—	—	....	Debt Securities	78bn *d*
....	....	....	....	....	....	....	....	....	....	....	....	....	....	....	Financial Derivatives Assets	78bw *d*
....	....	....	....	....	....	....	....	....	....	....	....	....	....	....	Financial Derivatives Liabilities	78bx *d*
–50	–307	–530	–256	–1,580	–2,008	–1,294	–1,175	–815	–718	–787	–762	–997	–1,049	....	Other Investment Assets	78bh *d*
—	—	—	—	—	—	—	—	—	—	—	—	—	—	....	Monetary Authorities	78bo *d*
–38	–236	–511	–196	–977	–831	–194	–74	—	—	—	—	—	—	....	General Government	78bp *d*
–12	–71	–18	–60	–198	–493	–313	–241	—	—	—	—	—	—	....	Banks	78bq *d*
—	—	—	—	–405	–684	–787	–860	–815	–718	–787	–762	–997	–1,049	....	Other Sectors	78br *d*
839	898	929	341	–128	172	779	1,126	1,304	1,626	1,154	1,347	987	1,406	....	Other Investment Liab., n.i.e.	78bi *d*
463	499	776	–69	103	154	7	28	11	20	58	–99	73	66	....	Monetary Authorities	78bs *d*
–120	144	207	297	–757	–731	–35	173	–121	339	33	200	–134	180	....	General Government	78bt *d*
260	99	48	45	–64	–143	–190	–226	–128	–147	–112	–9	–68	5	....	Banks	78bu *d*
236	157	–102	68	590	892	997	1,151	1,542	1,414	1,175	1,255	1,116	1,155	....	Other Sectors	78bv *d*
–17	–26	–23	34	420	110	–112	70	–119	96	–69	98	–117	–115	....	Net Errors and Omissions	78ca *d*
–186	61	79	–32	–66	36	72	76	304	566	785	879	454	401	....	*Overall Balance*	78cb *d*
186	–61	–79	32	66	–36	–72	–76	–304	–566	–785	–879	–454	–401	....	Reserves and Related Items	79da *d*
186	–61	–79	32	66	–36	–72	–76	–304	–566	–785	–879	–454	–401	....	Reserve Assets	79db *d*
—	—	—	—	—	—	—	—	—	—	—	—	—	—	....	Use of Fund Credit and Loans	79dc *d*
—	—	—	—	—	—	—	—	—	—	—	—	—	—	....	Exceptional Financing	79de *d*
Year Ending December 31															**Government Finance**	
....	–8,267	–3,355	2,319	–1,267	921	4,184	6,273	115	–18,860	–10,059	–1,577	–1,723	....	....	Deficit (-) or Surplus	80
....	24,128	28,276	38,181	48,374	58,639	70,965	85,788	92,619	111,892	131,002	152,231	179,202	....	....	Revenue	81
....	2,061	3,812	6,156	3,426	763	9,995	6,250	2,864	1,264	896	1,788	798	....	....	Grants Received	81z
....	34,456	35,443	42,018	53,067	58,481	76,776	85,765	95,368	132,016	141,957	155,596	181,723	....	....	Expenditure	82
															Financing	
....	....	....	....	....	....	....	....	....	....	....	....	....	....	....	Total Financing	84
....	....	....	....	....	....	....	....	....	....	....	....	....	....	....	Domestic	84a
....	....	....	....	....	....	....	....	....	....	....	....	....	....	....	Foreign	85a
....	....	....	....	....	....	....	....	....	....	....	....	....	....	....	Unallocable Financing	87c
Millions of Pounds															**National Accounts**	
9,949	11,256	20,003	31,212	62,811	76,042	76,038	97,577	115,294	167,327	177,229	219,872	241,719	241,316	....	Exports of Goods & Services	90c
19,785	21,440	22,945	24,529	33,433	38,502	47,582	53,588	56,239	68,019	76,709	81,316	84,994	89,853	....	Government Consumption	91f
20,016	22,443	23,223	25,992	33,808	44,395	55,992	86,120	107,466	151,622	155,504	163,076	155,464	162,572	....	Gross Capital Formation	93
54,650	67,026	98,496	152,683	141,717	184,389	231,883	274,195	303,988	348,865	378,143	489,728	515,411	546,198	....	Private Consumption	96f
–21,175	–22,232	–36,955	–48,369	–62,877	–75,000	–99,931	–139,850	–169,242	–229,732	–216,610	–263,135	–252,019	–244,213	....	Imports of Goods & Services	98c
83,225	99,933	127,712	186,047	208,892	268,328	311,564	371,630	413,755	506,101	570,975	674,817	731,471	775,786	....	Gross Domestic Product (GDP)	99b
83,225	79,109	80,618	91,313	83,133	....	....	....	....	....	....	....	....	....	....	GDP Volume 1985 prices	99b.*p*
....	....	....	....	372,387	389,469	420,242	476,850	501,546	539,929	570,975	612,896	628,148	677,173	....	GDP Volume 1995 Prices	99b.*p*
65.3	62.1	63.2	71.6	65.2	68.2	73.6	83.5	87.8	94.6	100.0	107.3	110.0	118.6	....	GDP Volume (1995=100)	99bv *p*
22.3	28.2	35.4	45.5	56.1	68.9	74.1	77.9	82.5	93.7	100.0	110.1	116.4	114.6	....	GDP Deflator (1995=100)	99bi *p*
Midyear Estimates																
10.27	10.61	10.97	11.34	11.72	12.12	12.53	12.96	13.39	13.84	14.15	14.62	15.10	15.60	16.11	**Population**	99z

Tanzania

		1970	1971	1972	1973	1974	1975	1976	1977	1978	1979	1980	1981	1982	1983	1984
Exchange Rates															*Shillings per SDR:*	
Official Rate	aa	7.14	7.76	7.76	8.32	8.75	9.66	9.66	9.66	9.66	10.83	10.44	9.69	10.55	13.04	17.75
															Shillings per US Dollar:	
Official Rate	ae	7.14	7.14	7.14	6.90	7.14	8.26	8.32	7.96	7.41	8.22	8.18	8.32	9.57	12.46	18.11
Official Rate	rf	7.14	7.14	7.14	7.02	7.13	7.37[e]	8.38[e]	8.29[e]	7.71[e]	8.22[e]	8.20[e]	8.28[e]	9.28[e]	11.14[e]	15.29
Fund Position															*Millions of SDRs:*	
Quota	2f. s	42.0	42.0	42.0	42.0	42.0	42.0	42.0	42.0	55.0	55.0	82.5	82.5	82.5	107.0	107.0
SDRs	1b. s	1.9	6.3	6.7	6.6	1.7	1.2	5.1	5.6	6.1	2.8	—	.3	—	.1	.1
Reserve Position in the Fund	1c. s	6.9	6.9	6.9	10.5								1.7			
Total Fund Cred.&Loans Outstg.	2tl	—	—	—	—	38.9	62.6	83.6	91.2	81.5	115.5	134.3	125.7	114.4	88.1	60.2
International Liquidity												*Millions of US Dollars Unless Otherwise Indicated:*					
Total Reserves minus Gold	1l. d	65.0	60.3	119.6	144.6	50.2	65.4	112.3	281.8	99.9	68.0	20.3	18.8	4.8	19.4	26.9
SDRs	1b. d	1.9	6.9	7.3	8.0	2.0	1.3	5.9	6.8	7.9	3.7	—	.4	—	.1	.1
Reserve Position in the Fund	1c. d	6.9	7.5	7.5	12.7	—	—	—	—	—	—	—	1.9	—	—	—
Foreign Exchange	1d. d	56.2	45.9	104.8	124.0	48.2	64.1	106.4	275.0	91.9	64.3	20.3	16.5	4.8	19.3	26.8
Monetary Authorities: Other Liab.	4.. d	1.2	1.4	6.2	3.7	21.6	26.4	2.4	42.3	57.3	34.4	19.6	-5.2	6.8	18.9	36.5
Deposit Money Banks: Assets	7a. d	53.6	85.6	97.1	100.1	113.1	91.9	82.9	91.8	84.5	122.5	172.1	127.5	170.0	206.0	86.8
Liabilities	7b. d	9.8	18.0	14.2	14.3	18.1	15.0	28.4	37.0	92.9	45.3	23.0	23.0	65.0	26.0	376.2
Monetary Authorities															*Billions of Shillings:*	
Foreign Assets	11	.46	.43	.83	1.04	.40	.55	.94	2.30	.76	.72	.38	.35	.27	.34	.51
Claims on Central Government	12a	.42	.64	.55	.51	1.06	1.37	1.60	1.31	2.87	5.04	6.55	7.99	9.48	10.02	13.26
Claims on Deposit Money Banks	12e	.07	.16	.14	—	.90	1.01	.73	.38	.84	.23	.29	.47	.50	.34	.47
Reserve Money	14	.86	1.05	1.28	1.29	1.62	1.88	2.23	2.60	3.16	4.39	5.56	7.14	8.63	8.89	11.57
of which: Currency Outside DMBs	14a	.82	.99	1.20	1.20	1.52	1.76	2.07	2.38	2.92	4.06	5.25	6.61	7.99	8.19	10.47
Foreign Liabilities	16c	.01	.01	.04	.03	.49	.82	.83	1.22	1.21	1.53	1.56	1.17	1.27	1.38	1.73
Central Government Deposits	16d	.01	.01	—	.01	.03	.01	.01	.01	—	—	—	—	—	.08	.02
Capital Accounts	17a	.08	.15	.18	.20	.22	.25	.19	.20	.17	.17	.22	.45	.30	.45	-.20
Other Items (Net)	17r	-.02	.01	.02	.02	—	-.04	.01	-.04	-.06	-.10	-.12	.04	.05	-.10	1.12
Deposit Money Banks															*Billions of Shillings:*	
Reserves	20	.05	.06	.08	.09	.11	.13	.16	.21	.29	.30	.32	.53	.62	.81	1.30
Foreign Assets	21	.38	.61	.69	.69	.81	.76	.69	.73	.63	1.01	1.41	1.06	1.63	2.57	1.57
Claims on Central Government	22a	.15	.29	.46	.61	.90	1.51	2.16	1.87	2.13	3.39	4.87	6.65	9.49	11.58	12.74
Claims on Official Entities	22bx	.69	.91	.85	1.26	2.21	2.63	3.08	3.69	5.01	5.67	6.20	7.19	7.77	8.68	12.01
Claims on Private Sector	22d	.63	.52	.63	.50	.61	.64	.54	.68	.98	1.03	1.14	1.22	1.71	1.89	1.39
Demand Deposits	24	.86	1.07	1.13	1.55	1.94	2.53	3.26	4.00	3.91	6.38	8.10	8.79	10.33	12.37	10.14
Time, Savings,& Fgn.Currency Dep.	25	.54	.57	.76	.88	1.01	1.27	1.62	1.96	2.57	3.37	4.17	5.29	6.41	8.56	9.59
Foreign Liabilities	26c	.07	.13	.10	.10	.13	.12	.24	.29	.69	.37	.19	.19	.62	.32	6.81
Central Government Deposits	26d	.38	.52	.54	.53	.49	.65	.52	.29	.40	.47	.52	.79	1.44	.81	.85
Credit from Monetary Authorities	26g	.07	.16	.14	—	.90	1.02	.74	.38	.90	.26	.32	.28	.41	.40	.43
Capital Accounts	27a	.08	.12	.14	.17	.21	.27	.34	.41	.52	.81	1.05	1.15	1.41	1.58	1.70
Other Items (Net)	27r	-.10	-.17	-.09	-.07	-.05	-.19	-.09	-.15	.05	-.26	-.41	.16	.59	1.48	-.51
Monetary Survey															*Billions of Shillings:*	
Foreign Assets (Net)	31n	.77	.90	1.38	1.61	.58	.36	.56	1.51	-.51	-.17	.04	.05	—	1.20	-6.46
Domestic Credit	32	1.54	1.92	2.04	2.42	4.35	5.62	6.95	7.32	10.66	14.76	18.31	22.33	27.07	31.32	38.53
Claims on Central Govt. (Net)	32an	.18	.41	.47	.58	1.44	2.22	3.22	2.89	4.60	7.96	10.90	13.84	17.54	20.72	25.13
Claims on Official Entities	32bx	.69	.92	.87	1.26	2.22	2.67	3.13	3.69	5.01	5.67	6.20	7.19	7.77	8.68	12.01
Claims on Private Sector	32d	.63	.52	.63	.50	.61	.64	.54	.68	.98	1.03	1.14	1.22	1.71	1.89	1.39
Money	34	1.68	2.06	2.33	2.75	3.46	4.28	5.33	6.38	6.83	10.44	13.35	15.40	18.32	20.56	20.61
Quasi-Money	35	.54	.57	.76	.88	1.01	1.27	1.62	1.96	2.57	3.37	4.17	5.29	6.41	8.56	9.59
Capital Accounts	37a	.16	.27	.32	.37	.43	.53	.53	.61	.68	.98	1.26	1.60	1.72	2.03	1.50
Other Items (Net)	37r	-.08	-.07	.01	.04	.05	-.10	.03	-.12	.06	-.21	-.44	.08	.63	1.36	.37
Money plus Quasi-Money	35l	2.22	2.62	3.09	3.62	4.46	5.55	6.95	8.35	9.40	13.81	17.52	20.69	24.73	29.13	30.20
Other Banking Institutions															*Billions of Shillings:*	
Deposits	45	.05	.05	.05	.06	.08	.09	.09	.11	.16	.18	.21	.25	.29	.36	.44
Liquid Liabilities	55l	2.27	2.67	3.14	3.69	4.54	5.64	7.04	8.46	9.56	13.99	17.73	20.94	25.02	29.48	30.64
Interest Rates															*Percent Per Annum*	
Discount Rate (End of Period)	60	....	....	4.27	4.27	4.77	4.77	4.77	4.77	4.77	4.77	4.77	4.00	4.00	4.00	4.00
Treasury Bill Rate	60c	....	....	....	....	....	....	....	....	....	....	....	....	....	....	....
Deposit Rate	60l	....	....	....	....	4.00	4.00	4.00	4.00	4.00	4.00	4.00	4.00	4.00	4.00	4.00
Lending Rate	60p	....	....	....	....	....	....	....	....	6.54	11.50	11.50	12.00	12.00	13.00	13.00
Prices and Production															*Index Numbers (1995=100):*	
Consumer Prices	64	.6	.6	.7	.7	.9	1.1	1.2	1.3	1.4	1.6	2.1	2.6	3.3	4.3	5.8
Manufacturing Production	66ey	....	....	....	....	....	....	....	....	....	....	....	....	....	....	....

	1985	1986	1987	1988	1989	1990	1991	1992	1993	1994	1995	1996	1997	1998	1999		
Exchange Rates																	
End of Period																	
	18.12	63.26	118.77	168.21	252.71	279.69	334.58	460.63	659.13	764.16	818.10	856.51	842.70	958.87	1,094.34	Official Rate	aa
End of Period (ae) Period Average (rf)																	
	16.50	51.72	83.72	125.00	192.30	196.60	233.90	335.00	479.87	523.45	550.36	595.64	624.57	681.00	797.33	Official Rate	ae
	17.47	32.70	64.26	99.29	143.38	195.06	219.16	297.71	405.27	509.63	574.76	579.98	612.12	664.67	744.76	Official Rate	rf
Fund Position																	
End of Period																	
	107.0	107.0	107.0	107.0	107.0	107.0	107.0	146.9	146.9	146.9	146.9	146.9	146.9	146.9	198.9	Quota	2f. s
	—	4.6	.1	—	—	—	—	—	—	—	.1	.1	.1	.3	.2	SDRs	1b. s
								10.0	10.0	10.0	10.0	10.0	10.0	10.0	10.0	Reserve Position in the Fund	1c. s
	52.6	58.2	80.0	105.1	97.8	98.4	100.2	160.5	156.2	145.5	132.7	143.4	182.4	190.2	227.6	Total Fund Cred.&Loans Outstg.	2tl
International Liquidity																	
End of Period																	
	16.0	61.1	31.8	77.7	54.2	192.8	203.9	327.3	203.3	332.1	270.2	440.1	622.1	599.2	775.5	Total Reserves minus Gold	1l. d
	—	5.6	.1	—	—	—	—	—	—	—	.1	.1	.1	.4	.3	SDRs	1b. d
								13.7	13.7	14.6	14.8	14.3	13.5	14.0	13.7	Reserve Position in the Fund	1c. d
	16.0	55.5	31.7	77.7	54.2	192.8	203.9	313.6	189.6	317.5	255.3	425.6	608.5	584.8	761.5	Foreign Exchange	1d. d
	181.4	148.1	336.4	537.8	497.8	759.7	796.5	991.9	957.8	900.7	836.9	808.7	574.9	574.5	678.5	Monetary Authorities: Other Liab.	4.. d
	52.5	39.7	19.0	1.0	36.0	61.0	53.0	103.0	145.4	146.6	309.2	304.8	373.9	392.4	377.6	Deposit Money Banks: Assets	7a. d
	511.3	150.1	553.0	640.0	9.0	21.0	28.0	307.0	93.6	20.9	51.4	8.1	7.8	3.6	2.2	Liabilities	7b. d
Monetary Authorities																	
End of Period																	
	.26	2.54	2.66	9.71	10.43	37.90	47.70	139.86	‡97.56	173.82	150.65	264.72	390.09	407.27	618.45	Foreign Assets	11
	25.17	32.53	35.26	33.78	44.47	129.35	130.37	179.07	‡262.10	270.60	326.37	299.38	269.69	234.08	302.79	Claims on Central Government	12a
	.01	1.73	19.78	43.98	55.56	60.09	58.32	2.30	‡2.07	—	5.46	5.46	4.61	5.36	4.16	Claims on Deposit Money Banks	12e
	14.03	19.72	27.88	36.65	43.76	62.28	70.35	112.75	‡152.32	226.44	314.89	335.77	364.94	418.73	508.67	Reserve Money	14
	12.67	18.31	24.55	31.70	41.09	57.92	63.60	95.45	‡122.17	176.31	244.31	257.66	287.88	307.80	384.86	of which: Currency Outside DMBs	14a
	3.95	11.34	37.66	84.90	120.44	176.87	212.67	366.80	‡506.18	517.26	499.09	509.17	373.50	397.37	543.32	Foreign Liabilities	16c
	.08	1.61	2.23	.29	-1.12	.25	13.46	-16.18	‡25.35	29.56	39.67	82.66	87.32	83.03	84.01	Central Government Deposits	16d
	-.18	-.53	-15.01	-34.10	-40.52	-87.46	-105.77	-184.66	‡-278.34	-242.89	-266.81	-238.07	-16.35	-2.23	45.80	Capital Accounts	17a
	7.57	4.64	4.93	-.29	-12.11	75.39	45.69	42.54	‡-43.78	-85.94	-104.36	-119.97	-145.01	-250.20	-256.41	Other Items (Net)	17r
Deposit Money Banks																	
End of Period																	
	1.62	1.22	3.09	4.95	‡4.83	6.89	10.29	14.38	‡30.13	49.91	66.03	72.80	59.71	113.20	123.20	Reserves	20
	.87	2.05	1.57	2.23	‡6.96	12.00	12.39	34.39	‡69.78	76.74	170.16	181.55	233.56	267.26	301.08	Foreign Assets	21
	8.50	3.76	3.64	17.30	‡3.59	3.59	3.49	33.14	‡93.39	124.41	181.09	261.94	247.39	312.75	331.26	Claims on Central Government	22a
	16.20	19.73	46.62	62.34	‡30.49	41.42	56.47	44.71	‡49.26	57.18	46.83	17.34	16.22	3.06	4.72	Claims on Official Entities	22bx
	2.40	2.94	5.85	8.02	‡89.10	115.48	152.41	133.49	‡186.31	222.98	201.02	116.56	166.75	239.86	302.17	Claims on Private Sector	22d
	12.80	17.50	22.58	32.90	‡42.62	55.08	75.20	90.66	‡125.16	153.32	183.97	191.55	205.99	237.72	247.72	Demand Deposits	24
	13.88	14.50	19.31	23.65	‡32.83	52.33	76.26	116.24	‡173.62	240.12	329.52	372.28	433.20	481.47	584.95	Time, Savings,& Fgn.Currency Dep.	25
	11.72	38.58	46.32	79.97	‡1.70	4.07	6.61	102.75	‡44.94	10.92	28.26	4.83	4.88	2.46	1.77	Foreign Liabilities	26c
	.79	.73	1.65	1.23	‡1.74	2.24	3.49	5.00	‡4.82	22.52	21.75	20.96	28.43	25.33	21.56	Central Government Deposits	26d
	.50	1.24	18.09	43.98	‡51.45	62.68	60.69	73.99	‡147.40	1.34	7.59	.16	12.76	—	5.43	Credit from Monetary Authorities	26g
	1.99	2.57	3.84	3.81	‡8.30	8.67	10.99	-12.45	‡48.62	139.91	-29.91	75.62	43.11	61.64	27.26	Capital Accounts	27a
	-12.10	-45.43	-51.01	-90.71	‡-3.66	-5.69	1.81	-116.10	‡-115.69	-36.90	123.95	-15.21	-4.74	127.52	173.73	Other Items (Net)	27r
Monetary Survey																	
End of Period																	
	-14.54	-45.33	-79.75	-152.93	‡-104.76	-131.05	-159.19	-295.30	‡-383.77	-277.62	-206.54	-67.72	245.27	274.70	374.44	Foreign Assets (Net)	31n
	51.40	56.66	87.51	119.94	‡167.04	287.36	325.80	401.60	‡560.89	623.10	693.88	591.60	584.31	681.39	835.36	Domestic Credit	32
	32.80	33.95	35.01	49.56	‡47.44	130.45	116.92	223.39	‡325.32	342.94	446.03	457.70	401.34	438.47	528.48	Claims on Central Govt. (Net)	32an
	16.20	19.73	46.62	62.34	‡30.49	41.42	56.47	44.71	‡49.26	57.18	46.83	17.34	16.22	3.06	4.72	Claims on Official Entities	32bx
	2.40	2.94	5.85	8.02	‡89.10	115.48	152.41	133.49	‡186.31	222.98	201.02	116.56	166.75	239.86	302.17	Claims on Private Sector	32d
	25.47	35.81	47.13	64.60	‡83.72	113.00	138.80	186.12	‡247.33	329.63	428.28	449.21	493.87	545.52	632.58	Money	34
	13.88	14.50	19.31	23.65	‡32.83	52.33	76.26	116.24	‡173.62	240.12	329.52	372.28	433.20	481.47	584.95	Quasi-Money	35
	1.81	2.04	-11.18	-30.28	‡-32.23	-78.79	-94.78	-197.11	‡-229.73	-102.98	-296.73	-162.45	26.76	59.41	73.07	Capital Accounts	37a
	-4.30	-41.02	-47.50	-90.97	‡-22.03	69.76	46.32	1.05	‡-14.11	-121.28	26.26	-135.17	-124.24	-130.30	-80.80	Other Items (Net)	37r
	39.34	50.31	66.44	88.25	‡116.54	165.33	215.06	302.36	‡420.95	569.74	757.81	821.50	927.07	1,026.98	1,217.53	Money plus Quasi-Money	35l
Other Banking Institutions																	
End of Period																	
	.55	.68	.87	.11	.16	.26	1.86	.80	‡1.12	1.67	2.28	2.10	2.50	3.26	5.31	Deposits	45
	39.89	50.99	67.31	88.36	‡116.70	165.60	216.92	303.16	‡422.07	571.42	760.08	823.60	929.57	1,030.25	1,222.84	Liquid Liabilities	55l
Interest Rates																	
Percent Per Annum																	
	5.00	8.00	12.50	14.50	15.50	....	....	14.50	14.50	67.50	47.90	19.00	16.20	17.60	20.20	Discount Rate (End of Period)	60
									34.00	35.09	40.33	15.30	9.59	11.83	10.05	Treasury Bill Rate	60c
	4.50	8.50	15.75	17.46	17.00	....	....	....	....	....	24.63	13.59	7.83	7.75	7.75	Deposit Rate	60l
	12.29	18.50	27.50	29.63	31.00	....	....	....	31.00	39.00	42.83	37.21	29.23	26.67	29.83	Lending Rate	60p
Prices and Production																	
Period Averages																	
	7.7	10.2	13.3	17.4	‡21.9	29.8	38.3	46.7	58.5	77.9	100.0	121.0	140.4	158.4	170.9	Consumer Prices	64
	95	92	102	110	111	109	111	105	105	95	100	120	....	....	....	Manufacturing Production	66ey

Tanzania

		1970	1971	1972	1973	1974	1975	1976	1977	1978	1979	1980	1981	1982	1983	1984
International Transactions														*Millions of Shillings*		
Exports	70	1,797	1,913	2,313	2,581	2,878	2,764	3,683	4,198	3,669	4,096	4,192	4,706	4,144	4,138	4,388
Imports, c.i.f.	71	2,274	2,726	2,883	3,479	5,377	5,710	5,350	6,161	8,798	9,073	10,308	9,739	10,499	8,877	9,653
Balance of Payments														*Millions of US Dollars:*		
Current Account, n.i.e.	78al d	…	…	…	…	…	…	−27.8	−66.1	−467.3	−346.5	−522.2	−407.6	−524.1	−305.2	−359.5
Goods: Exports f.o.b.	78aa d	…	…	…	…	…	…	490.4	538.5	476.0	545.7	582.7	613.0	412.9	383.2	398.5
Goods: Imports f.o.b.	78ab d	…	…	…	…	…	…	−555.7	−646.7	−992.5	−960.7	−1,089.1	−1,061.3	−952.0	−708.4	−760.3
Trade Balance	78ac d	…	…	…	…	…	…	−65.3	−108.2	−516.5	−415.0	−506.4	−448.2	−539.1	−325.2	−361.8
Services: Credit	78ad d	…	…	…	…	…	…	135.4	106.8	130.2	140.0	165.1	184.8	114.5	106.3	105.8
Services: Debit	78ae d	…	…	…	…	…	…	−141.0	−163.9	−245.3	−237.6	−295.0	−252.1	−193.0	−161.5	−174.8
Balance on Goods & Services	78af d	…	…	…	…	…	…	−70.9	−165.4	−631.6	−512.6	−636.4	−515.5	−617.6	−380.4	−430.7
Income: Credit	78ag d	…	…	…	…	…	…	7.4	11.1	19.1	11.6	14.0	10.9	2.8	1.7	1.6
Income: Debit	78ah d	…	…	…	…	…	…	−25.7	−31.8	−24.8	−20.2	−27.6	−32.2	−27.7	−29.2	−89.4
Balance on Gds, Serv. & Inc.	78ai d	…	…	…	…	…	…	−89.2	−186.1	−637.3	−521.3	−649.9	−536.8	−642.5	−407.9	−518.5
Current Transfers, n.i.e.: Credit	78aj d	…	…	…	…	…	…	105.5	144.9	194.8	200.3	153.2	152.5	136.5	127.6	180.4
Current Transfers: Debit	78ak d	…	…	…	…	…	…	−44.2	−24.9	−24.8	−25.6	−25.5	−23.2	−18.1	−24.9	−21.4
Capital Account, n.i.e.	78bc d	…	…	…	…	…	…	−6.8	−5.3	−6.0	—	—	—	—	—	—
Capital Account, n.i.e.: Credit	78ba d	…	…	…	…	…	…	—	—	.1	—	—	—	—	—	—
Capital Account: Debit	78bb d	…	…	…	…	…	…	−6.8	−5.3	−6.1	—	—	—	—	—	—
Financial Account, n.i.e.	78bj d	…	…	…	…	…	…	60.4	111.0	214.2	150.3	218.7	242.5	193.4	278.5	11.3
Direct Investment Abroad	78bd d	…	…	…	…	…	…	—	—	—	—	—	—	—	—	—
Dir. Invest. in Rep. Econ., n.i.e.	78be d	…	…	…	…	…	…	—	—	—	—	—	—	—	—	—
Portfolio Investment Assets	78bf d	…	…	…	…	…	…	—	—	—	—	—	—	—	—	—
Equity Securities	78bk d	…	…	…	…	…	…	—	—	—	—	—	—	—	—	—
Debt Securities	78bl d	…	…	…	…	…	…	—	—	—	—	—	—	—	—	—
Portfolio Investment Liab., n.i.e.	78bg d	…	…	…	…	…	…	—	—	—	—	—	—	—	—	—
Equity Securities	78bm d	…	…	…	…	…	…	—	—	—	—	—	—	—	—	—
Debt Securities	78bn d	…	…	…	…	…	…	—	—	—	—	—	—	—	—	—
Financial Derivatives Assets	78bw d	…	…	…	…	…	…	…	…	…	…	…	…	…	…	…
Financial Derivatives Liabilities	78bx d	…	…	…	…	…	…	…	…	…	…	…	…	…	…	…
Other Investment Assets	78bh d	…	…	…	…	…	…	8.2	−4.9	14.1	−47.2	—	—	—	—	—
Monetary Authorities	78bo d	…	…	…	…	…	…	—	—	—	—	—	—	—	—	—
General Government	78bp d	…	…	…	…	…	…	—	—	—	—	—	—	—	—	—
Banks	78bq d	…	…	…	…	…	…	8.2	−4.9	14.1	−47.2	—	—	—	—	—
Other Sectors	78br d	…	…	…	…	…	…	—	—	—	—	—	—	—	—	—
Other Investment Liab., n.i.e.	78bi d	…	…	…	…	…	…	52.2	116.0	200.1	197.5	218.7	242.5	193.4	278.5	11.3
Monetary Authorities	78bs d	…	…	…	…	…	…	−25.3	38.4	17.5	—	−8.1	−16.3	−.1	−1.0	−3.0
General Government	78bt d	…	…	…	…	…	…	95.9	53.6	94.5	138.1	130.1	167.2	134.3	177.7	−95.4
Banks	78bu d	…	…	…	…	…	…	13.4	7.0	51.1	−38.9	—	—	—	—	—
Other Sectors	78bv d	…	…	…	…	…	…	−31.8	17.0	37.0	98.3	96.7	91.6	59.1	101.8	109.8
Net Errors and Omissions	78ca d	…	…	…	…	…	…	−4.3	69.1	8.4	23.8	−46.6	78.7	58.2	−61.7	126.9
Overall Balance	78cb d	…	…	…	…	…	…	21.5	108.7	−250.7	−172.4	−350.1	−86.3	−272.5	−88.4	−221.2
Reserves and Related Items	79da d	…	…	…	…	…	…	−21.5	−108.7	250.7	172.4	350.1	86.3	272.5	88.4	221.2
Reserve Assets	79db d	…	…	…	…	…	…	−46.5	−163.7	199.2	30.2	54.9	8.4	13.9	−14.6	−7.5
Use of Fund Credit and Loans	79dc d	…	…	…	…	…	…	24.2	8.8	−12.0	43.4	25.0	−11.3	−12.4	−28.1	−28.4
Exceptional Financing	79de d	…	…	…	…	…	…	.8	46.2	63.5	98.9	270.1	89.1	271.0	131.1	257.1
Government Finance														*Millions of Shillings:*		
Deficit (-) or Surplus	80	−369	−688	−555	−360	−851	−1,865	−1,805	−855	−1,936	−4,134	−4,046	−5,026	−7,024	−5,383	−5,669
Total Revenue and Grants	81y	1,606	1,695	1,893	2,579	3,399	4,321	4,531	5,522	7,805	7,947	9,963	9,729	10,363	13,610	14,740
Revenue	81	1,595	1,683	1,855	2,295	3,000	3,944	4,062	4,896	7,096	6,833	8,963	8,571	9,406	12,581	13,506
Grants	81z	12	12	38	284	399	377	469	626	709	1,114	1,000	1,158	957	1,029	1,234
Exp. & Lending Minus Repay.	82z	1,976	2,383	2,448	2,938	4,249	6,186	6,336	6,377	9,741	12,081	14,008	14,755	17,387	18,993	20,409
Expenditure	82	1,918	2,405	2,376	2,995	4,230	6,163	6,326	6,270	9,622	11,921	13,943	14,755	17,387	18,993	20,409
Lending Minus Repayments	83	58	−23	72	−57	20	24	11	108	119	160	65	—	—	—	—
Financing																
Overall Adjustment	80x	…	…	…	…	…	…	…	…	…	…	…	…	…	…	…
Total Financing	80h	369	688	555	360	851	1,865	1,805	855	1,936	4,134	4,046	…	7,024	5,384	5,669
Domestic	84a	264	452	312	151	629	1,269	1,357	116	1,153	3,407	3,291	…	6,227	4,736	5,630
Foreign	85a	105	236	243	209	222	597	448	739	783	727	755	612	797	648	39
National Accounts														*Billions of Shillings:*		
Exports of Goods & Services	90c	2.20	2.37	2.75	2.94	3.40	3.46	5.30	5.63	4.69	5.13	5.54	5.99	5.29	5.46	7.71
Government Consumption	91f	1.21	1.37	1.49	1.97	2.60	3.26	3.99	4.31	5.59	5.96	5.49	6.11	9.53	9.44	13.84
Gross Fixed Capital Formation	93e	1.88	2.37	2.36	2.60	3.03	3.54	5.16	6.66	7.33	8.59	8.63	10.62	14.62	11.90	15.06
Increase/Decrease(-) in Stocks	93i	.19	.22	.08	.16	.48	.46	.44	.86	.76	.87	1.06	1.50	−.19	−.56	−.98
Private Consumption	96f	6.40	6.73	7.82	9.28	12.04	14.17	15.38	17.98	23.36	25.50	32.49	35.04	43.66	52.97	64.06
Imports of Goods & Services	98c	−2.61	−3.23	−3.33	−3.84	−5.57	−5.89	−5.84	−6.57	−9.57	−9.76	−11.09	−10.16	−10.99	−9.69	−14.30
GDP, Production Based	99bp	9.17	9.81	11.17	13.10	15.99	19.01	24.42	28.87	32.17	36.28	42.12	49.10	61.93	68.52	85.39
Net Factor Inc/Pmts(-) Abroad	98.n	−.02	−.05	−.04	−.05	−.04	−.05	−.10	−.09	−.05	−.07	−.11	−.18	−.23	−.31	−1.34
Gross National Income (GNI)	99a	9.15	9.77	11.13	13.05	15.96	18.96	24.32	28.78	32.12	36.21	42.01	48.93	61.70	69.22	84.05
Net National Income	99e	8.64	9.21	10.52	12.18	15.12	18.05	23.41	27.77	30.99	34.94	40.47	47.38	60.13	67.60	82.17
GDP, Prod. Based, 1992 Prices	99bp p	…	…	…	…	…	…	…	…	…	…	…	…	…	…	…
GDP Volume (1995=100)	99bv p	…	…	…	…	…	…	…	…	…	…	…	…	…	…	…
GDP Deflator (1995=100)	99bi p	…	…	…	…	…	…	…	…	…	…	…	…	…	…	…
																Millions:
Population	99z	13.27	13.63	14.00	14.37	14.76	15.31	Ɪ16.41	16.92	17.44	17.98	18.58	19.17	19.78	20.41	21.06

Millions of Shillings

	1985	1986	1987	1988	1989	1990	1991	1992	1993	1994	1995	1996	1997	1998	1999	Code
International Transactions																
Exports	4,265	11,285	18,512	27,041	51,463	64,571	74,708	123,966	181,147	265,177	390,378	441,344	438,798	449,301	410,627	70
Imports, c.i.f.	14,959	30,577	59,340	80,828	146,705	265,984	338,990	449,480	615,990	765,757	968,910	804,949	818,703	967,080	1,220,072	71

Minus Sign Indicates Debit

	1985	1986	1987	1988	1989	1990	1991	1992	1993	1994	1995	1996	1997	1998	1999	Code
Balance of Payments																
Current Account, n.i.e.	−375.1	−322.0	−407.4	−356.6	−335.1	−558.9	−737.5	−714.2	−1,048.0	−710.9	−646.3	−510.9	−629.8	−956.5	....	78ald
Goods: Exports f.o.b.	328.5	335.9	287.9	386.5	415.1	407.8	363.0	406.4	446.9	519.4	682.5	764.1	715.3	589.5	....	78aad
Goods: Imports f.o.b.	−869.2	−913.3	−1,000.5	−1,033.0	−1,070.1	−1,186.3	−1,229.9	−1,335.2	−1,304.0	−1,309.3	−1,340.0	−1,213.1	−1,164.4	−1,365.3	....	78abd
Trade Balance	−540.7	−577.5	−712.6	−646.5	−655.0	−778.5	−866.9	−928.8	−857.1	−789.9	−657.5	−449.0	−449.1	−775.9	....	78acd
Services: Credit	105.6	100.7	105.3	117.4	117.3	130.6	142.3	169.9	317.9	418.2	582.6	608.1	494.1	555.0	....	78add
Services: Debit	−208.7	−219.0	−224.4	−263.4	−272.5	−287.7	−300.1	−341.3	−717.0	−503.3	−799.4	−953.4	−797.3	−988.1	....	78aed
Balance on Goods & Services	−643.8	−695.7	−831.7	−792.5	−810.2	−935.6	−1,024.7	−1,100.2	−1,256.2	−875.0	−874.2	−794.3	−752.4	−1,209.0	....	78afd
Income: Credit	2.5	9.5	5.9	3.2	5.4	5.9	7.9	8.2	21.9	30.9	31.8	50.3	44.9	35.1	....	78agd
Income: Debit	−100.4	−108.9	−164.7	−188.4	−182.5	−190.9	−192.5	−236.8	−172.9	−153.4	−142.0	−105.4	−168.2	−173.7	....	78ahd
Balance on Gds, Serv. & Inc.	−741.7	−795.1	−990.4	−977.8	−987.3	−1,120.7	−1,209.3	−1,328.9	−1,407.2	−997.5	−984.5	−849.4	−875.7	−1,347.7	....	78aid
Current Transfers, n.i.e.: Credit	394.2	501.2	609.9	642.9	682.0	592.8	504.5	650.1	389.8	311.5	370.5	370.9	313.6	426.6	....	78ajd
Current Transfers: Debit	−27.6	−28.0	−27.0	−21.7	−29.8	−31.0	−32.7	−35.5	−30.7	−25.0	−32.3	−32.3	−67.7	−35.5	....	78akd
Capital Account, n.i.e.	—	—	—	—	—	327.2	353.7	302.4	205.2	262.6	190.9	191.0	360.6	422.9	....	78bcd
Capital Account, n.i.e.: Credit	—	—	—	—	—	327.2	353.7	302.4	205.2	262.6	190.9	191.0	360.6	422.9	....	78bad
Capital Account: Debit																78bbd
Financial Account, n.i.e.	−72.3	9.5	60.4	33.9	21.8	68.1	120.0	70.2	130.5	−91.7	66.7	−92.8	3.6	77.6	....	78bjd
Direct Investment Abroad	—	—	—	—	—	—	—	—	—	—	—	—	—	—	....	78bdd
Dir. Invest. in Rep. Econ., n.i.e.	—	—	—	—	—	—	—	12.2	20.5	50.0	119.9	150.1	157.9	172.3	....	78bed
Portfolio Investment Assets	—	—	—	—	—	—	—	—	—	—	—	—	—	—		78bfd
Equity Securities	—	—	—	—	—	—	—	—	—	—	—	—	—	—		78bkd
Debt Securities	—	—	—	—	—	—	—	—	—	—	—	—	—	—		78bld
Portfolio Investment Liab., n.i.e.	—	—	—	—	—	—	—	—	—	—	—	—	—	—		78bgd
Equity Securities	—	—	—	—	—	—	—	—	—	—	—	—	—	—		78bmd
Debt Securities	—	—	—	—	—	—	—	—	—	—	—	—	—	—		78bnd
Financial Derivatives Assets	....	....	....	....	....											78bwd
Financial Derivatives Liabilities	....	....	....	....	....											78bxd
Other Investment Assets	....	....	....	....	—	—	—	—	56.7	11.9	−75.1	20.1	−85.0	−50.7	....	78bhd
Monetary Authorities	....	....	....	....	—	—	—	—	—	—	—	—	—	—	....	78bod
General Government	....	....	....	....	—	—	—	—	—	—	—	—	—	—	....	78bpd
Banks	....	....	....	....	—	—	—	—	−68.6	−75.6	−162.5	−19.6	−85.0	−50.7	....	78bqd
Other Sectors	....	....	....	....	—	—	—	—	125.3	87.5	87.4	39.7	—	—	....	78brd
Other Investment Liab., n.i.e.	−72.3	9.5	60.4	33.9	21.8	68.1	120.0	58.1	53.3	−153.6	21.8	−262.9	−69.3	−44.0	....	78bid
Monetary Authorities	−.9	89.6	64.9	−1.6	−3.1	4.4	−5.5	8.8	.2	11.9	5.9	14.9	24.6	−48.7	....	78bsd
General Government	−39.4	−24.6	−9.5	30.7	26.2	54.7	115.0	31.3	−56.5	−202.0	−71.2	−225.9	−32.4	—	....	78btd
Banks	—	—	—	—	—	1.9	1.4	.2	−1.4	6.7	22.9	−23.5	−67.6	−17.6	....	78bud
Other Sectors	−32.0	−55.5	5.0	4.8	−1.3	7.2	9.1	17.7	111.0	29.8	64.2	−28.5	6.2	22.4	....	78bvd
Net Errors and Omissions	−39.6	−40.1	55.5	−61.3	−13.5	37.7	1.6	137.7	137.3	121.4	30.0	158.6	−31.9	−53.5	....	78cad
Overall Balance	−487.0	−352.5	−291.5	−383.9	−326.8	−126.0	−262.1	−203.9	−575.1	−418.6	−358.7	−254.0	−297.5	−509.4	....	78cbd
Reserves and Related Items	487.0	352.5	291.5	383.9	326.8	126.0	262.1	203.9	575.1	418.6	358.7	254.0	297.5	509.4	....	79dad
Reserve Assets	10.9	−45.0	30.7	−45.9	23.5	−140.8	−85.3	−255.4	60.5	−122.8	43.3	−195.4	−206.9	22.3	....	79dbd
Use of Fund Credit and Loans	−7.5	7.3	28.4	34.2	−9.3	—	2.1	83.7	−6.0	−15.4	−19.6	15.7	53.2	9.6	....	79dcd
Exceptional Financing	483.7	390.3	232.4	395.6	312.6	266.7	345.4	375.6	520.7	556.8	335.1	433.8	451.2	477.5	....	79ded

Year Ending June 30

	1985	1986	1987	1988	1989	1990	1991	1992	1993	1994	1995	1996	1997	1998	1999	Code
Government Finance																
Deficit (−) or Surplus	−8,408	−8,643	−15,406	−11,908	−14,698	−15,340	−47,324	9,601	−72,141	−104,515	−64,559	−21,269	77,143	−68,139	24,422	80
Total Revenue and Grants	20,101	23,067	32,465	63,389	91,400	125,531	159,968	206,364	222,422	349,234	389,743	495,255	653,446	738,442	859,269	81y
Revenue	18,639	22,032	29,321	47,480	70,415	97,867	137,093	173,566	164,109	242,444	331,238	448,373	572,030	619,083	689,324	81
Grants	1,462	1,035	3,144	15,909	20,985	27,664	22,875	32,798	58,313	106,790	58,505	46,882	81,416	119,359	169,944	81z
Exp. & Lending Minus Repay.	28,509	31,710	47,871	75,297	106,098	140,871	207,292	161,474	263,413	374,962	398,024	420,522	515,390	730,338	816,706	82z
Expenditure	28,509	31,710	47,871	75,297	106,098	140,871	207,292	161,474	263,413	374,962	398,024	420,522	515,390	730,338	816,706	82
Lending Minus Repayments	—	—	—	—	—	—	—	—	—	—	—	—	—	—	—	83
Financing																
Overall Adjustment	....	....	....	....	....	....	....	−35,289	−31,150	−78,787	−56,278	−96,002	−60,913	−76,243	−18,141	80x
Total Financing	8,408	8,643	15,406	11,908	14,698	15,340	47,324	−9,601	72,141	104,515	64,559	21,269	−77,142	68,138	−24,423	80h
Domestic	7,988	8,638	12,315	−2,728	21,188	12,361	29,608	−32,277	44,144	40,557	61,603	56,169	−28,074	3,669	−5,739	84a
Foreign	420	5	3,091	14,636	−6,490	2,979	17,716	22,676	27,997	63,958	2,956	−34,900	−49,068	64,469	−18,684	85a

Billions of Shillings

	1985	1986	1987	1988	1989	1990	1991	1992	1993	1994	1995	1996	1997	1998	1999	Code
National Accounts																
Exports of Goods & Services	7.59	14.28	ɪ29.56	48.81	71.93	104.84	111.47	170.44	310.31	473.89	727.18	751.16	741.44	748.97	888.98	90c
Government Consumption	18.56	23.62	ɪ55.60	84.54	101.41	147.65	205.73	269.02	334.52	393.50	462.32	435.33	413.56	433.79	451.14	91f
Gross Fixed Capital Formation	18.97	35.35	ɪ71.06	81.45	112.21	213.98	282.43	369.37	429.55	561.82	591.94	620.60	692.40	892.70	989.34	93e
Increase/Decrease(−) in Stocks	1.90	−5.87	ɪ1.70	2.05	2.36	2.93	3.65	3.68	4.00	4.84	5.86	6.64	8.40	9.91	10.31	93i
Private Consumption	84.04	118.04	ɪ269.31	416.01	523.19	687.71	887.12	1,133.19	1,445.37	1,931.98	2,532.84	3,130.07	3,968.07	4,909.25	5,667.44	96f
Imports of Goods & Services	−18.83	−37.02	ɪ−86.52	−141.34	−208.54	−311.13	−365.41	−539.10	−823.21	−1,002.88	−1,253.74	−1,203.52	−1,208.30	−1,565.33	−1,698.68	98c
GDP, Production Based	112.21	148.39	ɪ329.49	506.43	633.75	830.69	1,086.27	1,369.87	1,725.54	2,298.87	3,020.50	3,767.64	4,708.63	5,571.64	6,431.55	99bp
Net Factor Inc/Pmts(−) Abroad	−1.66	−3.39	ɪ−12.68	−20.31	−30.01	−37.67	−40.61	−67.08	−61.19	−69.43	−63.38	−36.92	−75.78	−104.67	....	98.n
Gross National Income (GNI)	110.56	145.01	ɪ316.81	486.11	603.74	793.02	1,045.67	1,302.79	1,664.35	2,236.44	2,957.12	3,730.72	4,632.85	5,466.47	....	99a
Net National Income	108.08	141.24	ɪ311.47	479.22	589.79	778.66	1,026.04	1,264.03	1,619.70	2,175.83	2,876.16	3,640.05	4,520.41	5,333.21	....	99e
GDP, Prod. Based, 1992 Prices	....	....	ɪ1154.33	1,201.24	1,246.46	1,334.28	1,361.92	1,369.87	1,386.40	1,408.12	1,458.40	1,524.68	1,578.30	1,505.83	1,577.33	99bp p
GDP Volume (1995=100)	....	....	ɪ79.2	82.4	85.5	91.5	93.4	93.9	95.1	96.6	100.0	104.5	108.2	103.3	108.2	99bv p
GDP Deflator (1995=100)	....	....	ɪ13.8	20.4	24.5	30.1	38.5	48.3	60.1	78.8	100.0	119.3	144.0	178.7	196.9	99bi p

Midyear Estimates

	1985	1986	1987	1988	1989	1990	1991	1992	1993	1994	1995	1996	1997	1998	1999	Code
Population	21.73	22.46	23.22	24.00	23.89	24.57	25.27	25.99	26.73	27.49	28.28	29.09	29.98	ɪ32.10	32.79	99z

(See notes in the back of the book.)

Thailand

		1970	1971	1972	1973	1974	1975	1976	1977	1978	1979	1980	1981	1982	1983	1984
Exchange Rates															*Baht per SDR:*	
Official Rate	aa	20.927	ⅠΙ22.721	22.721	24.579	24.946	23.881	23.701	24.780	26.564	26.906	26.312	26.771	25.372	24.080	26.613
															Baht per US Dollar:	
Official Rate	ae	20.928	Ι20.928	20.928	20.375	20.375	20.400	20.400	20.400	20.390	20.425	20.630	23.000	23.000	23.000	27.150
Official Rate	rf	20.800	20.800	20.800	20.620	20.375	20.379	20.400	20.400	20.336	20.419	20.476	21.820	23.000	23.000	23.639
Fund Position															*Millions of SDRs:*	
Quota	2f. s	134	134	134	134	134	134	134	134	181	181	272	272	272	387	387
SDRs	1b. s	—	14	29	29	30	30	29	30	27	37	6	52	22	15	2
Reserve Position in the Fund	1c. s	34	34	34	34	34	34	34	34	—	—	—	—	—	29	29
of which: Outstg.Fund Borrowing	2c	—	—	—	—	—	—	—	—	—	—	—	—	—	—	—
Total Fund Cred.&Loans Outstg.	2tl	—	—	—	—	—	—	67	81	191	278	273	737	767	994	922
International Liquidity												*Millions of US Dollars Unless Otherwise Indicated:*					
Total Reserves minus Gold	1l. d	824	788	963	1,207	1,758	1,679	1,798	1,813	2,009	1,843	1,560	1,732	1,538	1,607	1,921
SDRs	1b. d	—	16	31	34	36	35	34	37	35	49	8	61	25	16	2
Reserve Position in the Fund	1c. d	34	36	36	40	41	39	39	41	—	—	—	—	—	30	28
Foreign Exchange	1d. d	790	736	896	1,132	1,681	1,605	1,725	1,735	1,974	1,794	1,552	1,671	1,513	1,561	1,890
Gold (Million Fine Troy Ounces)	1ad	2.342	2.340	2.340	2.340	2.340	2.340	2.340	2.397	2.426	2.455	2.487	2.487	2.487	2.487	2.487
Gold (National Valuation)	1an d	82	82	89	99	100	96	95	102	548	1,286	1,466	995	1,114	949	768
Monetary Authorities: Other Liab.	4.. d	—	—	—	—	—	—	—	—	—	—	—	—	—	—	—
Deposit Money Banks: Assets	7a. d	128	178	226	298	299	290	384	446	565	771	919	1,118	1,318	1,069	1,134
Liabilities	7b. d	176	184	198	366	421	466	528	868	1,453	1,846	1,379	1,462	1,276	1,865	1,875
Other Banking Insts.: Assets	7e. d	—	—	—	—	—	—	—	—	—	—	—	—	—	—	—
Liabilities	7f. d	8	11	11	10	14	28	181	235	289	378	394	473	458	571	803
Monetary Authorities															*Billions of Baht:*	
Foreign Assets	11	19.5	19.2	23.3	27.6	39.4	37.7	37.9	38.3	51.8	63.9	62.4	62.7	61.0	58.8	72.9
Claims on Central Government	12a	11.7	13.4	15.6	17.0	14.1	13.8	19.6	26.1	35.3	44.0	59.9	71.3	87.7	100.7	96.0
Claims on Nonfin.Pub.Enterprises	12c	—	—	—	—	—	—	.1	.1	—	—	—	—	—	—	—
Claims on Deposit Money Banks	12e	.8	1.3	1.3	2.9	3.9	7.2	5.4	5.9	8.0	16.5	16.5	19.8	20.7	22.9	23.8
Claims on Other Financial Insts.	12f	.2	.1	.3	.4	.7	.9	1.3	1.1	2.1	3.0	5.4	4.8	5.3	5.0	8.3
Reserve Money	14	15.4	17.0	20.1	23.7	26.8	29.7	33.5	36.6	42.9	50.3	57.3	61.1	68.4	75.6	79.8
of which: Currency Outside DMBs	14a	11.9	13.1	15.3	18.7	20.5	22.3	25.8	28.7	33.2	40.8	45.9	47.8	54.0	59.6	63.5
Money Market Instruments	16aa	—	—	—	—	—	—	—	—	—	—	—	—	—	—	—
Foreign Liabilities	16c	—	—	—	—	—	—	1.6	2.0	5.1	7.5	7.2	19.7	19.5	23.9	24.5
Central Government Deposits	16d	6.4	4.9	6.5	8.0	10.5	7.2	5.4	4.6	5.9	5.8	6.7	5.9	6.5	5.8	5.7
Capital Accounts	17a	10.3	11.9	14.0	16.4	20.8	22.5	23.0	27.6	43.6	63.7	72.5	75.0	79.6	81.6	93.4
Other Items (Net)	17r	.1	.1	-.2	-.1	—	.1	.8	.6	-.2	.2	.7	-3.1	.7	.4	-2.3
Deposit Money Banks															*Billions of Baht:*	
Reserves	20	2.4	3.0	3.4	3.6	5.2	6.5	6.3	6.8	8.4	7.6	10.4	11.8	12.8	15.0	14.6
Other Claims on Monetary Author.	20c	—	—	—	—	—	—	Ι—	—	—	—	—	—	—	—	—
Foreign Assets	21	2.7	3.7	4.7	6.1	6.1	5.9	Ι7.8	9.1	11.5	15.7	19.0	25.7	30.3	24.6	30.8
Claims on Central Government	22a	5.9	8.3	13.9	15.0	15.9	17.7	Ι21.0	22.5	24.5	26.1	29.1	38.7	53.7	53.1	80.6
Claims on Nonfin.Pub.Enterprises	22c	.3	.5	.5	.9	1.2	1.4	Ι1.8	2.5	3.8	4.5	5.4	6.4	6.2	12.0	13.0
Claims on Private Sector	22d	26.6	29.3	33.0	47.1	63.6	77.3	Ι89.4	114.3	146.8	179.3	201.3	237.3	281.6	371.7	433.5
Claims on Other Financial Insts.	22f	1.9	1.9	1.6	2.0	3.7	6.6	Ι5.4	8.3	11.0	12.1	15.4	14.9	15.7	25.1	34.0
Demand Deposits	24	6.7	7.5	8.7	10.5	11.7	12.0	Ι15.1	16.4	21.1	22.2	25.1	25.0	23.5	21.3	24.5
Time, Savings,& Fgn.Currency Dep.	25	22.3	27.3	35.4	43.7	55.9	68.5	Ι84.3	105.4	125.7	142.1	180.3	219.1	284.6	365.6	449.1
Foreign Liabilities	26c	3.7	3.8	4.1	7.5	8.6	9.5	Ι10.8	17.7	29.6	37.7	28.4	33.6	29.3	42.9	50.9
Central Government Deposits	26d	2.0	2.0	2.6	3.0	3.4	3.3	Ι4.7	5.0	5.6	7.5	7.7	11.8	11.6	15.8	16.5
Credit from Monetary Authorities	26g	.8	1.3	1.3	2.9	4.0	7.3	5.5	6.0	8.1	16.7	16.7	20.2	20.9	23.4	24.3
Liabilities to Other Banking Insts	26i	—	—	—	—	—	—	1.6	.4	.2	.8	1.1	1.6	2.7	2.7	2.1
Capital Accounts	27a	3.4	4.0	4.4	5.7	8.0	9.8	Ι10.2	12.1	15.0	18.2	19.5	21.5	24.6	28.1	36.3
Other Items (Net)	27r	.9	.8	.6	1.4	3.9	4.9	Ι.5	.5	.5	.1	1.6	2.0	3.0	1.8	2.6
Monetary Survey															*Billions of Baht:*	
Foreign Assets (Net)	31n	18.5	19.1	23.9	26.2	36.9	34.1	Ι33.4	27.7	28.6	34.4	45.7	35.1	42.5	16.5	28.3
Domestic Credit	32	38.0	46.6	55.8	71.5	85.2	107.1	Ι128.6	165.4	212.3	256.0	302.5	356.1	432.7	546.6	643.9
Claims on Central Govt. (Net)	32an	9.0	14.7	20.3	20.9	16.0	20.9	Ι30.5	39.0	48.2	56.8	74.6	92.3	123.3	132.2	154.4
Claims on Nonfin.Pub.Enterprises	32c	.3	.5	.5	.9	1.2	1.4	Ι1.9	2.6	3.8	4.6	5.4	6.4	6.2	12.0	13.0
Claims on Private Sector	32d	26.6	29.3	33.1	47.2	63.6	77.4	Ι89.6	114.5	147.0	179.6	201.7	237.8	282.2	372.3	434.2
Claims on Other Financial Insts	32f	2.1	2.0	1.9	2.4	4.4	7.4	Ι6.7	9.3	13.1	15.1	20.8	19.7	21.0	30.1	42.3
Money	34	19.4	21.3	24.8	30.0	32.7	34.7	Ι41.4	45.4	54.5	63.5	71.4	73.3	78.3	81.8	88.8
Quasi-Money	35	22.3	27.3	35.4	43.7	55.9	68.5	Ι84.3	105.4	125.7	142.1	180.3	219.1	284.6	365.6	449.1
Money Market Instruments	36aa	—	—	—	—	—	—	Ι—	—	—	—	—	—	—	—	—
Liabilities to Other Banking Insts	36i	—	—	—	—	—	—	Ι.6	.4	.2	.8	1.1	1.6	2.7	2.7	2.1
Capital Accounts	37a	13.8	15.8	18.4	22.2	28.9	32.3	Ι33.2	39.7	58.7	81.9	91.9	96.5	104.2	109.6	129.6
Other Items (Net)	37r	1.1	1.2	1.1	1.9	4.6	5.7	Ι2.5	2.2	1.7	2.0	3.4	.7	5.3	3.4	2.4
Money plus Quasi-Money	35l	41.7	48.6	60.2	73.6	88.7	103.2	Ι125.7	150.8	180.3	205.7	251.8	292.4	362.9	447.4	537.9
Other Banking Institutions																
Development Institutions																*Billions of Baht:*
Cash	40	.1	.2	.2	.3	Ι.5	.8	1.9	2.7	4.4	4.6	4.1	5.6	3.4	2.9	4.3
Other Claims on Monetary Author.	40c	—	—	—	—	Ι—	—	—	—	—	—	—	—	—	—	—
Foreign Assets	41	....	....	....	....	—	—	—	—	—	—	—	—	—	—	—
Claims on Central Government	42a	—	—	—	—	—	—	—	—	—	—	.7	1.5	—	.2	.3
Claims on Nonfin.Pub.Enterprises	42c	—	—	—	—	—	—	—	—	—	—	—	—	—	—	—
Claims on Private Sector	42d	1.6	1.9	2.3	2.6	Ι3.7	6.2	9.0	11.5	14.0	18.2	24.0	28.1	30.4	32.4	38.3
Demand Deposits	44	—	—	—	—	Ι—	—	.4	.4	.3	.4	.5	.6	1.0	1.7	4.1
Time and Savings Deposits	45	.2	.2	.3	.4	Ι.8	1.4	1.4	1.9	2.3	2.4	3.1	3.8	3.8	4.3	5.5
Bonds	46ab	.1	.2	.2	.2	.2	.2	.4	.2	.2	.2	.9	2.0	2.1	2.6	2.9
Long-Term Foreign Liabilities	46cl	.2	.2	.2	.2	Ι.3	.6	.9	1.4	2.7	4.8	5.9	7.6	8.3	9.3	13.5
Central Govt. Lending Funds	46f	.1	.1	.1	.1	Ι.5	.5	.6	.6	.8	.6	.7	.8	.6	.5	.8
Credit from Monetary Authorities	46g	.2	.1	.3	.4	Ι.7	.8	1.3	1.2	2.1	2.6	4.6	4.2	4.7	4.2	4.1
Credit from Deposit Money Banks	46h	.1	—	—	—	Ι.2	2.0	4.4	6.3	7.8	9.3	9.5	9.7	10.0	9.3	9.8
Capital Accounts	47a	.9	1.3	1.3	1.5	Ι1.6	1.7	1.9	2.3	2.8	3.2	3.2	3.7	4.7	5.1	6.2
Other Items (Net)	47r	—	—	—	—	Ι-.1	-.2	-.3	-.1	-.5	—	1.1	1.1	-1.2	-1.4	-4.4

1985	1986	1987	1988	1989	1990	1991	1992	1993	1994	1995	1996	1997	1998	1999		
End of Period															**Exchange Rates**	
29.273	31.962	35.566	33.965	33.761	35.979	36.161	35.090	35.081	36.628	37.445	36.826	I63.748	51.662	51.428	Official Rate	aa
End of Period (ae) Period Average (rf)																
26.650	26.130	25.070	25.240	25.690	25.290	25.280	25.520	25.540	25.090	25.190	25.610	I47.247	36.691	37.470	Official Rate	ae
27.159	26.299	25.723	25.294	25.702	25.585	25.517	25.400	25.320	25.150	24.915	25.343	31.364	41.359	38.150	Official Rate	rf
End of Period															**Fund Position**	
387	387	387	387	387	387	387	574	574	574	574	574	574	574	1,082	Quota	2f.s
1	27	42	45	13	9	6	9	16	22	30	41	358	278	188	SDRs	1b.s
29	29	29	29	29	32	155	243	272	285	319	333	—	—	—	Reserve Position in the Fund	1c.s
—	—	—	—	—	—	—	—	—	—	—	—	—	—	—	*of which:* Outstg.Fund Borrowing	2c
1,021	874	686	492	207	1	—	—	—	—	—	—	1,800	2,300	2,500	Total Fund Cred.&Loans Outstg.	2tl
End of Period															**International Liquidity**	
2,190	2,804	4,007	6,097	9,515	13,305	17,517	20,359	24,473	29,332	35,982	37,731	26,179	28,825	34,063	Total Reserves minus Gold	1l.d
1	33	60	61	16	13	8	12	22	32	45	60	482	391	258	SDRs	1b.d
32	35	41	39	38	45	222	335	373	416	474	480	—	—	—	Reserve Position in the Fund	1c.d
2,157	2,736	3,906	5,997	9,461	13,247	17,287	20,012	24,078	28,884	35,463	37,192	25,697	28,434	33,805	Foreign Exchange	1d.d
2.487	2.487	2.476	2.476	2.476	2.476	2.476	2.474	2.474	2.474	2.474	2.474	2.474	2.474	2.474	Gold (Million Fine Troy Ounces)	1ad
813	972	1,204	1,015	993	968	899	823	967	947	963	914	713	711	718	Gold (National Valuation)	1and
—	—	1	—	4	3	4	5	6	6	5	4	4,733	7,967	9,390	Monetary Authorities: Other Liab.	4..d
1,263	1,606	1,538	1,782	2,733	2,229	2,872	3,046	6,165	6,739	9,365	7,028	8,665	12,605	15,158	Deposit Money Banks: Assets	7a.d
1,722	1,215	1,482	2,444	3,319	4,340	4,902	6,567	13,799	31,086	46,214	48,781	40,307	29,058	19,165	Liabilities	7b.d
—	—	—	—	—	—	—	—	—	27	34	72	100	407	403	Other Banking Insts.: Assets	7e.d
776	860	857	869	1,021	1,557	1,894	2,518	3,323	4,035	5,939	8,748	6,973	5,550	4,437	Liabilities	7f.d
End of Period															**Monetary Authorities**	
80.0	98.6	130.5	179.3	269.7	360.6	465.1	539.1	649.1	759.0	929.7	988.8	1,270.7	1,083.4	1,303.3	Foreign Assets	11
106.9	98.9	92.5	47.2	36.2	57.9	54.9	60.6	50.7	32.5	29.7	33.5	31.8	170.7	139.7	Claims on Central Government	12a
—	—	—	—	—	—	—	—	—	—	8.4	17.9	71.5	75.0	64.0	Claims on Nonfin.Pub.Enterprises	12c
25.5	34.8	42.0	57.8	41.6	42.7	38.0	37.1	21.2	26.4	37.8	55.9	309.4	158.6	85.9	Claims on Deposit Money Banks	12e
12.8	14.1	13.6	15.0	16.1	17.4	18.6	22.4	25.2	39.9	47.5	76.6	438.7	511.3	393.9	Claims on Other Financial Insts.	12f
86.5	95.3	116.7	134.0	156.7	185.8	210.5	248.0	288.1	329.9	404.3	458.9	531.4	507.6	785.8	Reserve Money	14
64.0	71.1	86.7	99.0	119.0	137.5	149.3	180.2	208.6	241.9	284.1	304.3	334.0	318.3	472.4	*of which: Currency Outside DMBs*	14a
—	—	—	—	—	—	—	—	—	18.1	16.9	28.5	330.5	541.6	172.9	Money Market Instruments	16aa
29.9	27.9	24.4	16.7	7.1	.1	.1	.1	.2	.1	.1	.1	338.4	411.1	480.4	Foreign Liabilities	16c
8.0	10.3	9.0	15.0	58.2	115.5	173.9	201.6	213.7	235.8	328.5	341.7	283.3	96.6	81.5	Central Government Deposits	16d
103.3	117.3	136.0	138.4	148.6	172.0	202.2	231.8	263.1	306.8	337.8	377.8	803.2	814.0	1,013.2	Capital Accounts	17a
–2.6	–4.6	–7.4	–4.8	–7.0	5.3	–10.1	–22.5	–18.9	–33.0	–34.4	–34.4	–164.6	–371.9	–547.1	Other Items (Net)	17r
End of Period															**Deposit Money Banks**	
21.2	22.1	25.7	32.4	33.8	51.6	60.4	60.9	73.5	79.7	117.8	165.8	203.6	145.7	143.0	Reserves	20
—	—	—	—	—	—	—	—	—	5.5	5.9	17.5	262.2	356.4	94.8	Other Claims on Monetary Author.	20c
33.7	42.0	38.6	45.0	70.2	56.4	72.6	77.7	157.5	169.1	235.9	180.0	409.4	462.5	568.0	Foreign Assets	21
77.7	104.8	115.6	124.3	123.3	110.7	82.9	69.7	50.3	41.8	40.7	20.2	15.6	154.7	249.2	Claims on Central Government	22a
13.6	14.6	14.9	14.5	15.9	18.1	47.7	53.2	76.5	94.2	108.4	112.7	99.9	108.5	135.1	Claims on Nonfin.Pub.Enterprises	22c
481.2	501.5	614.8	796.1	1,045.4	1,408.8	1,696.9	2,045.1	2,536.5	3,304.1	4,089.2	4,688.3	5,729.6	5,299.6	5,014.5	Claims on Private Sector	22d
32.5	36.3	51.7	52.8	60.4	69.0	91.2	113.1	126.6	158.0	213.4	213.9	331.3	173.1	233.8	Claims on Other Financial Insts.	22f
21.1	30.5	44.5	48.1	53.9	55.0	70.0	66.1	82.4	96.4	94.3	106.1	86.6	93.9	94.9	Demand Deposits	24
507.6	569.3	676.2	807.6	1,032.4	1,333.7	1,610.0	1,868.1	2,210.9	2,482.9	2,922.3	3,303.0	3,910.6	4,311.6	4,279.1	Time, Savings,& Fgn.Currency Dep.	25
45.9	31.8	37.2	61.7	85.3	109.8	123.9	167.6	352.4	780.0	1,164.1	1,249.3	1,904.4	1,066.2	718.1	Foreign Liabilities	26c
19.7	20.9	23.6	28.4	32.7	35.6	50.5	76.5	92.7	122.5	135.5	178.1	190.5	229.8	242.3	Central Government Deposits	26d
26.1	33.6	42.0	57.6	41.2	42.3	37.6	36.3	21.2	24.9	36.2	53.8	313.1	154.5	48.3	Credit from Monetary Authorities	26g
4.8	3.2	1.8	7.3	14.9	15.4	10.4	14.9	20.0	55.9	86.3	85.7	118.2	56.9	152.8	Liabilities to Other Banking Insts	26i
42.4	44.1	57.5	68.3	83.1	111.3	143.5	170.2	222.4	369.8	471.3	600.2	690.8	1,067.7	1,162.3	Capital Accounts	27a
–7.7	–12.2	–21.5	–13.9	5.6	11.5	5.7	19.9	18.8	–80.2	–98.7	–177.6	–162.6	–280.0	–259.5	Other Items (Net)	27r
End of Period															**Monetary Survey**	
37.8	80.8	107.5	145.9	247.5	307.1	413.7	449.1	454.0	148.0	1.4	–80.7	–562.6	68.6	672.7	Foreign Assets (Net)	31n
697.9	739.7	871.2	1,007.4	1,207.2	1,530.9	1,767.6	2,085.9	2,559.3	3,312.1	4,073.4	4,643.4	6,244.6	6,166.5	5,906.3	Domestic Credit	32
156.9	172.4	175.5	128.1	68.6	17.5	–86.7	–147.8	–205.5	–284.1	–393.6	–466.1	–426.4	–1.0	65.1	Claims on Central Govt. (Net)	32an
13.6	14.6	14.9	14.5	15.9	18.1	47.7	53.2	76.5	94.2	116.8	130.7	171.3	183.5	199.1	Claims on Nonfin.Pub.Enterprises	32c
482.0	502.3	615.6	796.9	1,046.2	1,408.8	1,696.9	2,045.1	2,536.5	3,304.1	4,089.2	4,688.3	5,729.6	5,299.6	5,014.5	Claims on Private Sector	32d
45.4	50.4	65.3	67.9	76.6	86.4	109.8	135.5	151.8	197.9	261.0	290.5	770.1	684.4	627.6	Claims on Other Financial Insts	32f
85.8	102.4	132.4	148.5	174.7	195.4	222.4	249.7	296.2	346.4	388.3	423.7	430.1	451.0	739.7	Money	34
507.6	569.3	676.2	807.6	1,032.4	1,333.7	1,610.0	1,868.1	2,210.9	2,482.9	2,922.3	3,303.0	3,910.6	4,311.6	4,279.1	Quasi-Money	35
—	—	—	—	—	—	—	—	—	12.7	11.0	11.1	68.4	185.2	78.1	Money Market Instruments	36aa
4.8	3.2	1.8	7.3	14.9	15.4	10.4	14.9	20.0	55.9	86.3	85.7	118.2	56.9	152.8	Liabilities to Other Banking Insts	36i
145.7	161.4	193.5	206.7	231.7	283.3	345.7	402.1	485.5	676.6	809.1	977.9	1,493.9	1,881.7	2,175.5	Capital Accounts	37a
–8.3	–15.8	–25.1	–16.9	1.0	10.2	–7.1	.2	.6	–114.4	–142.3	–238.6	–339.2	–651.3	–846.1	Other Items (Net)	37r
593.5	671.8	808.6	956.1	1,207.1	1,529.1	1,832.4	2,117.8	2,507.1	2,829.4	3,310.6	3,726.7	4,340.7	4,762.6	5,018.8	Money plus Quasi-Money	35l
															Other Banking Institutions	
End of Period															Development Institutions	
4.9	4.2	5.0	6.1	13.9	15.7	16.0	8.1	12.5	19.8	18.3	39.8	51.0	46.9	23.3	Cash	40
—	—	—	—	—	—	—	—	—	—	—	—	17.4	43.0	17.3	Other Claims on Monetary Author	40c
—	—	—	—	—	—	—	—	—	—	—	1.0	4.0	14.4	15.0	Foreign Assets	41
.3	.1	—	—	.8	—	.1	.1	—	—	.3	.2	—	30.4	23.7	Claims on Central Government	42a
—	.1	—	—	—	—	—	—	—	—	—	.6	.1	.5	.4	Claims on Nonfin.Pub.Enterprises	42c
43.3	45.5	49.0	55.3	69.7	94.0	121.2	159.3	209.1	270.5	365.7	498.2	674.6	678.6	686.1	Claims on Private Sector	42d
6.5	8.0	8.6	12.4	20.7	26.7	36.7	43.8	46.4	60.9	54.3	40.8	52.3	69.3	80.1	Demand Deposits	44
5.2	6.1	6.6	8.1	11.6	16.7	21.9	28.0	44.9	56.1	100.7	88.3	189.8	233.7	190.9	Time and Savings Deposits	45
2.5	1.7	3.0	5.5	10.3	15.0	25.7	37.0	65.7	94.6	144.7	151.3	167.0	183.7	188.8	Bonds	46ab
16.3	18.2	19.1	19.3	19.9	21.7	20.2	23.1	26.0	29.9	33.1	91.4	206.1	160.6	139.6	Long-Term Foreign Liabilities	46cl
.7	.7	.7	.4	.5	1.4	1.4	1.4	3.0	1.7	4.2	100.9	56.4	89.6	88.0	Central Govt. Lending Funds	46f
4.6	3.6	4.0	4.1	4.8	6.0	6.9	8.6	9.2	9.0	8.5	32.2	32.0	19.8	18.3	Credit from Monetary Authorities	46g
10.7	11.1	12.3	14.1	14.5	15.3	17.1	12.5	7.6	11.6	7.1	5.2	6.2	4.8	2.0	Credit from Deposit Money Banks	46h
7.0	6.7	7.3	7.7	11.8	12.3	15.4	17.0	25.7	35.3	41.7	49.9	60.6	79.0	110.3	Capital Accounts	47a
–5.0	–6.1	–7.6	–10.1	–9.7	–5.3	–8.0	–3.9	–6.8	–8.8	–9.9	–20.2	–23.4	–26.7	–52.3	Other Items (Net)	47r

	1970	1971	1972	1973	1974	1975	1976	1977	1978	1979	1980	1981	1982	1983	1984
Finance and Securities Companies														*Billions of Baht:*	
Reserves .... 40.. f	....	....	....	....	....	....	1.2	1.2	1.4	2.0	2.0	3.9	5.8	4.1	3.6
Other Claims on Monetary Author ......40c. f	....	....	....	....	....	....	—	—	—	—	—	—	—	—	—
Claims on Central Government ....42a. f	....	....	....	....	....	....	—	—	—	—	—	3.5	5.5	5.3	9.5
Claims on Nonfin.Pub.Enterprises ....42c. f	....	....	....	....	....	....	.9	1.5	2.3	2.6	3.0	.2	.5	.7	.5
Claims on Private Sector ....42d. f	....	....	....	....	....	....	22.5	30.7	44.0	45.0	50.3	59.1	71.5	83.3	88.0
Bonds ....46ab f							15.3	21.3	32.1	33.8	41.3	53.2	66.6	70.1	66.3
Foreign Liabilities ....46c. f	....	....	....	....	....	....	2.8	3.4	3.2	2.9	2.3	3.3	2.3	3.8	8.3
Credit from Monetary Authorities ....46g. f	....	....	....	....	....	....	—	—	—	.3	1.1	.2	.2	.7	3.9
Cred. from Deposit Money Banks ......46h. f	....	....	....	....	....	....	3.1	4.1	5.0	5.3	5.2	4.1	6.0	10.0	15.1
Capital Accounts ....47a. f	....	....	....	....	....	....	2.8	4.2	6.3	8.2	7.9	8.0	8.8	10.3	9.0
Other Items (Net) ....47r. f	....	....	....	....	....	....	.6	.5	1.0	-.8	-2.3	-2.1	-.6	-1.6	-1.1
Government Savings Bank														*Billions of Baht:*	
Cash ....40.. g	.2	.1	.1	.2	.7	.7	.3	.3	.4	.8	.8	.8	.8	1.6	4.6
Other Claims on Monetary Auth. ......40c. g	....	....	....	....	....	....	—	—	—	—	—	—	—	—	—
Claims on Central Government ....42a. g	5.9	6.8	8.4	10.8	11.9	12.7	14.1	16.3	17.5	20.3	24.7	26.2	31.1	38.8	46.6
Claims on Nonfin.Pub.Enterprises ....42c. g	.2	.1	.1	.1	.1	.1	.4	.6	.5	.6	.4	.9	.8	.2	.1
Claims on Private Sector ....42d. g	.2	.3	.3	.3	.3	.3	.3	.3	.3	.3	.4	.3	.4	.6	.8
Demand Deposits ....44.. g	.2	.2	.1	.1	.3	.2	2.7	3.3	4.0	4.7	5.7	6.3	7.7	9.0	10.1
Time and Savings Deposits ....45.. g	4.4	5.0	6.4	8.3	9.5	10.2	8.9	10.7	11.4	14.4	16.7	18.8	21.9	27.1	32.5
Bonds ....46ab g	1.3	1.3	1.4	1.6	1.6	1.6	1.5	1.6	1.7	1.8	1.7	1.8	2.2	2.8	3.2
Central Government Deposits ....46d. g	—	—	—	—	—	.1	.1	.2	.1	.2	.1	.1	.2	.2	1.1
Capital Accounts ....47a. g	.5	.6	.7	.9	1.1	1.2	1.4	1.4	1.8	2.0	2.1	2.3	2.3	2.9	2.9
Other Items (Net) ....47r. g	.2	.1	.2	.4	.5	.5	.5	.4	-.3	-1.0	-.2	-1.2	-1.2	-.8	2.4
Banking Survey														*Billions of Baht:*	
Foreign Assets (Net) 51n	18.5	19.1	23.9	26.2	36.9	34.1	Ɪ30.6	24.3	25.4	31.5	43.5	31.8	40.2	12.7	20.0
Domestic Credit 52	43.9	53.7	65.0	82.7	Ɪ96.6	118.7	Ɪ169.1	216.7	277.5	328.5	385.7	454.6	551.9	677.8	784.2
Claims on Central Govt. (Net) 52an	14.9	21.5	28.7	31.7	27.8	33.5	Ɪ44.4	55.1	65.6	77.6	100.7	121.8	159.8	176.4	209.3
Claims on Nonfin.Pub.Enterprises........ 52c	.5	.7	.6	.9	1.3	1.4	Ɪ3.2	4.7	6.6	7.8	8.8	7.5	7.5	12.8	13.7
Claims on Private Sector 52d	28.4	31.5	35.7	50.0	67.5	83.8	Ɪ121.4	156.9	205.3	243.1	276.3	325.3	384.7	488.6	561.3
Liquid Liabilities 55l	46.5	54.0	67.0	82.4	Ɪ99.1	114.7	Ɪ135.7	162.9	192.0	220.3	271.0	311.6	387.3	480.9	577.4
Bonds 56ab	1.3	1.5	1.6	1.8	1.7	1.7	Ɪ17.2	23.1	34.0	35.7	44.0	57.0	71.0	75.6	72.3
Long-Term Foreign Liabilities................ 56cl	.2	.2	.2	.2	Ɪ.3	.6	.9	1.4	2.7	4.8	5.9	7.6	8.3	9.3	13.5
Capital Accounts 57a	14.6	17.1	19.8	23.6	30.4	33.9	Ɪ39.2	47.6	69.6	95.2	105.2	110.5	120.1	127.9	147.8
Other Items (Net) 57r	-.2	-.2	.2	.9	2.0	1.9	Ɪ6.6	6.1	4.7	4.0	3.3	-.4	5.6	-3.2	-6.9
Interest Rates														*Percent Per Annum*	
Discount Rate *(End of Period)* 60	....	....	....	....	....	....	7.70	9.00	12.50	12.50	13.50	14.50	12.50	13.00	12.00
Money Market Rate................................ 60b								8.27	10.40	13.28	14.66	17.25	14.95	12.15	13.58
Treasury Bill Rate.................................. 60c								6.32	7.04	7.40	9.16	11.57	11.64	9.35	10.00
Deposit Rate 60l								8.00	8.00	8.25	12.00	12.50	13.00	13.00	13.00
Lending Rate 60p							11.04	10.90	10.98	12.96	16.15	17.21	16.96	15.21	16.79
Government Bond Yield 61							8.50	8.90	9.25	13.25	13.00	13.06	13.85	11.13	12.41
Prices and Labor														*Index Numbers (1995=100):*	
Wholesale Prices 63	21.6	21.7	23.4	28.8	37.1	38.4	39.9	43.1	46.3	51.5	61.8	67.7	68.3	Ɪ69.7	67.5
Consumer Prices 64	20.3	20.4	21.4	24.7	30.7	Ɪ32.3	33.7	36.2	39.1	43.0	51.5	58.0	61.0	63.3	63.8
														Number in Thousands:	
Labor Force.. 67d	....	....	....	....	....	....	....	....	....	....	....	....	....	....	....
Employment 67e	....	....	....	....	....	....	....	....	....	....	....	....	....	....	....
Unemployment 67c	....	....	....	....	....	....	....	....	....	....	....	....	....	....	....
Unemployment Rate (%)........................ 67r	....	....	....	....	....	....	....	....	....	....	....	....	....	....	....
International Transactions														*Billions of Baht:*	
Exports 70	14.8	17.3	22.5	32.2	49.8	45.0	60.8	71.2	83.1	108.2	133.2	153.0	159.7	146.5	175.2
Rice 70n	2.5	2.9	4.4	3.6	9.8	5.9	8.6	13.4	10.4	15.6	19.5	26.4	22.5	20.2	25.9
Rubber 70l	2.2	1.9	1.9	4.6	5.0	3.5	5.3	6.2	8.0	12.4	12.4	10.8	9.5	11.8	13.0
Maize 70j	2.0	2.3	2.1	3.0	6.1	5.7	5.7	3.3	4.0	5.6	7.3	8.3	8.3	8.5	10.1
Tin 70q	1.6	1.6	1.7	2.0	3.1	2.2	3.0	4.5	7.2	9.3	11.3	9.1	7.8	5.3	5.3
Imports, c.i.f. 71	27.0	26.8	30.9	42.2	64.0	66.8	72.9	94.2	108.9	146.2	188.7	216.7	196.6	236.6	245.2
														1995=100	
Volume of Exports 72	3.8	5.0	5.9	5.5	6.2	5.9	8.2	9.4	10.2	Ɪ11.1	11.5	12.9	14.4	13.1	15.8
Rice 72n	17.2	25.4	34.1	13.7	16.6	15.3	31.8	47.5	25.9	45.1	45.2	48.9	61.0	56.0	74.5
Rubber 72l	15.8	17.6	18.2	22.3	20.7	19.0	21.4	23.0	25.3	29.8	26.0	27.0	31.1	31.8	33.9
Maize 72j	1,328.4	1,718.8	1,691.4	1,271.9	2,047.9	1,930.9	2,219.4	1,414.7	1,809.5	1,847.1	2,020.6	2,362.0	2,597.0	2,439.2	2,885.0
Tin 72q	831.6	817.7	816.4	847.5	776.3	622.9	749.5	801.4	1,082.0	1,170.4	1,269.3	1,124.3	930.4	662.6	689.9
Volume of Imports 73	11.7	9.9	11.5	14.2	13.1	12.9	13.5	16.0	17.2	Ɪ20.0	20.7	20.2	17.9	22.8	23.4
Unit Value of Exports.............................. 74	22.0	21.2	22.0	34.6	51.2	Ɪ45.2	43.9	44.9	48.5	Ɪ57.9	68.5	70.5	65.6	66.5	65.9
Rice (Unit Value)................................ 74n	30.2	23.5	26.8	54.0	121.1	78.4	55.6	57.9	82.7	71.1	88.8	110.9	75.8	74.0	71.6
Rice (Wholesale Price)........................ 76n	37.2	33.9	39.0	76.5	138.0	92.6	64.8	69.5	93.8	85.4	111.1	131.8	84.4	79.7	74.6
Rubber (Unit Value) 74l	23.1	17.7	16.7	33.4	39.6	29.8	40.5	43.8	51.8	67.6	77.5	65.5	49.7	60.6	62.7
Rubber (Wholesale Price) 76l	21.5	17.6	17.5	35.5	38.9	29.0	40.1	42.2	50.9	65.4	74.1	62.2	50.1	62.2	57.5
Maize (Unit Value) 74j	27.0	24.2	22.5	42.5	54.1	53.8	46.6	43.1	40.0	55.6	65.8	64.4	58.4	63.4	64.1
Tin (Unit Value).................................... 74q	47.9	47.3	50.2	59.1	98.3	88.9	97.7	139.6	164.6	194.7	220.2	199.2	205.8	195.7	188.5
Unit Value of Imports 75	12.9	13.5	14.3	16.7	27.0	Ɪ30.1	31.8	34.1	36.8	Ɪ42.6	52.8	62.5	64.1	60.5	60.9

1985	1986	1987	1988	1989	1990	1991	1992	1993	1994	1995	1996	1997	1998	1999		
End of Period															**Finance and Securities Companies**	
4.8	3.8	4.9	6.1	9.7	9.2	12.3	22.7	31.2	40.2	51.8	51.5	37.4	79.6	195.1	Reserves	**40.. f**
—	—	—	—	—	—	—	—	—	2.9	3.2	7.6	35.0	65.2	39.3	Other Claims on Monetary Author	**40c. f**
14.7	16.7	20.2	20.3	23.0	26.2	30.8	28.3	40.0	9.7	5.6	4.0	1.6	29.7	23.2	Claims on Central Government	**42a. f**
.9	1.1	.9	1.3	1.4	3.8	6.9	4.4	10.6	36.3	32.8	45.0	26.5	8.0	2.7	Claims on Nonfin.Pub.Enterprises	**42c. f**
90.1	95.5	107.5	145.7	217.1	311.3	408.2	568.5	761.1	1,035.1	1,363.1	1,554.7	1,373.8	1,165.5	347.6	Claims on Private Sector	**42d. f**
76.9	80.0	85.0	116.9	173.2	230.3	301.2	415.4	559.0	763.2	931.8	1,081.1	549.8	499.8	388.0	Bonds	**46ab f**
4.4	4.3	2.3	2.6	6.4	17.6	27.7	41.2	58.8	71.3	116.5	132.6	123.3	43.1	26.6	Foreign Liabilities	**46c. f**
7.8	10.4	9.4	10.3	9.6	9.0	8.5	3.8	3.5	8.5	9.1	30.1	449.3	561.9	439.8	Credit from Monetary Authorities	**46g. f**
15.2	17.2	31.2	25.1	28.4	27.7	39.2	52.7	68.5	98.6	146.6	148.1	144.2	103.7	98.4	Cred. from Deposit Money Banks	**46h. f**
9.0	9.7	10.9	15.6	21.0	31.6	44.8	76.6	101.0	145.6	196.7	226.2	197.4	158.6	-353.2	Capital Accounts	**47a. f**
-2.7	-4.4	-5.3	2.7	12.6	34.3	36.9	34.2	52.2	36.9	55.7	44.7	10.2	-19.0	8.3	Other Items (Net)	**47r. f**
End of Period															**Government Savings Bank**	
3.4	7.6	15.2	13.2	7.6	8.7	20.2	25.0	29.6	52.9	77.8	82.4	62.6	62.4	51.3	Cash	**40.. g**
—	—	—	—	—	—	—	—	—	9.4	8.1	2.1	31.5	71.7	18.4	Other Claims on Monetary Auth.	**40c. g**
57.7	81.1	85.7	95.9	100.0	93.0	80.7	69.0	60.4	40.7	30.3	26.2	18.0	43.9	137.8	Claims on Central Government	**42a. g**
.1	.4	2.1	3.7	5.4	9.7	12.5	18.9	31.5	26.8	29.6	47.2	67.4	87.6	121.1	Claims on Nonfin.Pub.Enterprises	**42c. g**
1.0	1.2	1.6	2.1	2.9	6.3	7.0	14.7	18.1	26.8	35.4	45.5	64.9	68.8	69.2	Claims on Private Sector	**42d. g**
12.1	15.1	19.1	23.1	27.4	31.7	30.7	36.0	41.4	47.1	49.7	54.5	55.0	54.3	51.0	Demand Deposits	**44.. g**
40.3	45.3	50.6	53.5	62.4	65.6	70.9	75.6	100.7	109.8	131.3	153.0	188.4	276.4	310.2	Time and Savings Deposits	**45.. g**
3.5	20.4	26.8	28.8	16.7	13.7	16.6	16.4	—	—	—	—	—	—	—	Bonds	**46ab g**
.4	2.5	2.2	2.8	.4	.6	.7	.8	1.5	1.2	1.1	1.2	3.5	3.3	16.3	Central Government Deposits	**46d. g**
4.3	5.7	5.6	6.1	9.2	8.9	9.9	11.1	13.1	15.9	18.6	21.4	19.7	25.0	38.5	Capital Accounts	**47a. g**
1.6	1.3	.4	.6	-.1	-3.0	-8.4	-12.3	-16.9	-17.3	-19.4	-26.8	-22.1	-24.5	-18.4	Other Items (Net)	**47r. g**
End of Period															**Banking Survey**	
33.4	76.6	105.2	143.3	241.2	289.5	386.0	407.9	395.1	77.3	-114.3	-211.4	-681.3	40.5	661.2	Foreign Assets (Net)	**51n**
860.3	928.5	1,070.8	1,260.9	1,550.6	1,988.2	2,324.5	2,812.8	3,537.0	4,558.9	5,674.1	6,573.2	7,697.8	7,591.8	6,674.1	Domestic Credit	**52**
229.2	267.8	279.2	241.5	192.0	136.1	24.1	-51.3	-106.5	-234.9	-358.6	-437.0	-410.4	99.7	233.4	Claims on Central Govt. (Net)	**52an**
14.6	16.2	18.0	19.4	22.7	31.7	67.1	76.5	118.6	157.3	179.2	223.4	265.4	279.6	323.3	Claims on Nonfin.Pub.Enterprises	**52c**
616.4	644.5	773.6	1,000.0	1,335.9	1,820.4	2,233.3	2,787.6	3,524.8	4,636.4	5,853.5	6,786.8	7,842.8	7,212.5	6,117.4	Claims on Private Sector	**52d**
644.5	730.6	868.2	1,027.9	1,298.1	1,636.2	1,944.0	2,245.4	2,667.1	2,990.2	3,498.5	3,889.6	4,675.0	5,207.4	5,381.1	Liquid Liabilities	**55l**
82.8	102.0	114.9	151.2	200.2	259.0	343.5	468.8	624.7	857.8	1,076.5	1,232.4	716.8	683.5	576.8	Bonds	**56ab**
16.3	18.2	19.1	19.3	19.9	21.7	20.2	23.1	26.0	29.9	33.1	91.4	206.1	160.6	139.6	Long-Term Foreign Liabilities	**56cl**
166.0	183.5	217.2	236.2	273.7	336.1	415.8	506.8	625.3	873.4	1,066.2	1,275.4	1,771.7	2,144.2	1,971.2	Capital Accounts	**57a**
-16.0	-29.3	-43.4	-30.4	—	24.6	-12.9	-23.3	-10.9	-115.2	-114.5	-127.0	-353.0	-563.4	-733.6	Other Items (Net)	**57r**
Percent Per Annum															**Interest Rates**	
11.00	8.00	8.00	8.00	8.00	12.00	11.00	11.00	9.00	9.50	10.50	10.50	12.50	12.50	4.00	Discount Rate (End of Period)	**60**
13.48	8.07	5.91	8.66	‡10.60	12.87	11.15	6.93	6.54	7.25	10.96	9.23	14.59	13.02	1.77	Money Market Rate	**60b**
11.02	6.76	3.63	5.08	....	....	....	....	....	....	....	....	....	....	....	Treasury Bill Rate	**60c**
13.00	9.75	9.50	9.50	9.50	12.25	13.67	8.88	8.63	8.46	11.58	10.33	10.52	10.65	4.73	Deposit Rate	**60l**
16.08	13.38	10.71	11.58	12.25	14.42	15.40	12.17	11.17	10.90	13.25	13.40	13.65	14.42	8.98	Lending Rate	**60p**
12.11	9.11	7.48	7.50	8.09	10.60	10.75	10.75	10.75	10.75	10.75	10.75	10.75	10.25	6.69	Government Bond Yield	**61**
Period Averages															**Prices and Labor**	
67.5	67.2	71.2	77.1	80.6	83.4	89.1	89.3	88.9	92.4	100.0	104.7	108.8	123.8	115.8	Wholesale Prices	**63**
65.4	‡66.6	68.3	70.9	74.6	‡79.1	83.6	87.1	90.0	94.5	100.0	105.8	111.8	120.8	121.1	Consumer Prices	**64**
Period Averages																
....	....	28,380	....	31,209	....	....	....	....	30,729	....	32,543	33,339	33,352	....	Labor Force	**67d**
25,853	26,691	27,639	29,464	‡30,669	30,842	31,137	32,383	32,150	32,093	32,512	32,232	33,162	32,138	....	Employment	**67e**
995	969	1,722	929	‡433	710	869	456	494	423	375	354	293	1,138	....	Unemployment	**67c**
3.7	3.5	5.9	3.1	‡1.4	2.2	2.7	1.4	1.5	1.3	1.1	1.1	.9	3.4	....	Unemployment Rate (%)	**67r**
Billions of Baht															**International Transactions**	
193.4	233.4	301.5	403.6	516.3	589.8	725.6	824.6	935.9	1,137.6	1,406.3	1,412.1	1,807.1	2,247.5	2,214.0	Exports	**70**
22.5	20.3	22.7	34.7	45.5	27.8	30.5	36.2	32.6	59.3	48.6	50.7	65.1	86.9	68.3	Rice	**70n**
13.6	15.1	20.5	27.2	26.4	23.6	25.0	28.9	30.4	41.8	61.3	63.4	57.5	55.4	40.3	Rubber	**70l**
7.7	9.3	3.9	3.8	4.1	4.1	3.9	.5	.7	.6	.5	.4	.5	.9	.4	Maize	**70j**
5.6	3.1	2.3	2.2	2.5	1.9	.9	1.1	.4	.4	.4	.8	1.4	2.6	2.5	Tin	**70q**
251.2	241.4	334.2	513.1	662.7	844.4	958.8	1,033.2	1,166.6	1,369.0	1,763.6	1,832.8	1,924.3	1,774.1	1,574.4	Imports, c.i.f.	**71**
1995=100																
‡16.9	19.9	24.0	29.6	36.8	41.2	49.2	55.1	61.6	72.9	‡100.0	90.1	97.0	104.6	117.1	Volume of Exports	**72**
65.5	73.0	71.7	82.1	99.1	64.8	67.2	79.0	80.9	78.4	100.0	88.1	154.3	105.5	110.3	Rice	**72n**
39.5	43.5	50.7	53.6	63.6	66.6	72.1	83.8	88.8	97.9	100.0	109.9	109.8	114.4	116.2	Rubber	**72l**
2,552.3	3,681.8	1,513.0	1,114.2	1,084.2	1,133.4	1,132.1	133.9	181.7	132.1	100.0	....	56.0	125.7	74.0	Maize	**72j**
671.6	705.4	513.0	489.1	432.3	444.1	233.8	274.8	131.1	102.8	100.0	....	....	....	....	Tin	**72q**
‡21.9	22.6	29.0	40.3	48.6	59.0	64.1	69.0	76.7	89.0	‡100.0	90.6	81.0	59.0	72.9	Volume of Imports	**73**
‡67.7	69.6	74.5	80.7	83.1	84.8	87.6	89.1	89.9	92.4	‡100.0	110.8	132.0	151.4	133.1	Unit Value of Exports	**74**
70.7	57.2	65.1	86.9	94.4	88.1	93.4	94.2	83.0	155.5	100.0	118.5	86.7	169.3	127.3	Rice (Unit Value)	**74n**
73.9	64.4	69.0	87.7	96.4	86.6	93.8	85.1	75.2	84.8	100.0	107.2	118.7	158.0	117.9	Rice (Wholesale Price)	**76n**
56.1	56.7	66.2	82.7	67.8	57.8	56.5	56.4	55.9	69.7	100.0	94.1	85.4	79.1	56.6	Rubber (Unit Value)	**74l**
52.3	53.9	64.3	76.1	63.3	56.2	53.5	55.6	53.5	71.9	100.0	90.2	81.1	75.8	61.1	Rubber (Wholesale Price)	**76l**
55.0	45.8	47.3	62.6	68.8	66.6	63.2	73.0	67.5	81.2	100.0	....	174.5	127.0	108.0	Maize (Unit Value)	**74j**
207.1	108.1	112.6	112.3	142.3	104.3	92.4	96.5	85.5	90.8	100.0	....	....	....	....	Tin (Unit Value)	**74q**
‡66.7	61.9	67.0	73.9	79.1	83.2	86.9	87.4	87.4	89.4	‡100.0	113.0	134.0	162.5	141.2	Unit Value of Imports	**75**

Thailand

Balance of Payments		1970	1971	1972	1973	1974	1975	1976	1977	1978	1979	1980	1981	1982	1983	1984
														Millions of US Dollars:		
Current Account, n.i.e.	78al *d*	...	...	...	...	...	−606	−440	−1,097	−1,153	−2,087	−2,076	−2,571	−1,003	−2,873	−2,109
Goods: Exports f.o.b.	78aa *d*	...	...	...	...	...	2,177	2,959	3,454	4,045	5,234	6,449	6,902	6,835	6,308	7,338
Goods: Imports f.o.b.	78ab *d*	...	...	...	...	...	−2,850	−3,152	−4,238	−4,904	−6,785	−8,352	−8,930	−7,565	−9,169	−9,236
Trade Balance	78ac *d*	...	...	...	...	...	−673	−193	−784	−858	−1,550	−1,902	−2,029	−731	−2,861	−1,898
Services: Credit	78ad *d*	...	...	...	...	...	603	508	531	819	1,034	1,490	1,612	1,717	1,846	1,964
Services: Debit	78ae *d*	...	...	...	...	...	−628	−748	−845	−1,005	−1,352	−1,644	−1,819	−1,658	−1,909	−1,910
Balance on Goods & Services	78af *d*	...	...	...	...	...	−698	−433	−1,099	−1,045	−1,868	−2,057	−2,236	−672	−2,924	−1,843
Income: Credit	78ag *d*	...	...	...	...	...	209	154	194	269	394	636	740	864	1,073	1,113
Income: Debit	78ah *d*	...	...	...	...	...	−198	−208	−232	−418	−672	−865	−1,243	−1,378	−1,300	−1,554
Balance on Gds, Serv. & Inc.	78ai *d*	...	...	...	...	...	−687	−487	−1,137	−1,193	−2,146	−2,286	−2,739	−1,186	−3,151	−2,284
Current Transfers, n.i.e.: Credit	78aj *d*	...	...	...	...	...	91	59	52	52	71	229	181	198	296	194
Current Transfers: Debit	78ak *d*	...	...	...	...	...	−10	−12	−13	−12	−12	−19	−14	−15	−19	−19
Capital Account, n.i.e.	78bc *d*	...	...	...	...	...	−1	—	—	—	1	6	2	—	−1	−1
Capital Account, n.i.e.: Credit	78ba *d*	...	...	...	...	...	—	—	—	—	1	7	2	—	—	—
Capital Account: Debit	78bb *d*	...	...	...	...	...	−1	−1	−1	−1	—	−1	−1	−1	−1	−1
Financial Account, n.i.e.	78bj *d*	...	...	...	...	...	469	539	1,046	1,360	1,977	2,044	2,479	1,293	1,966	2,567
Direct Investment Abroad	78bd *d*	...	...	...	...	...	—	—	—	−6	−4	−3	−2	−2	−1	−1
Dir. Invest. in Rep. Econ., n.i.e.	78be *d*	...	...	...	...	...	86	79	106	56	55	190	291	191	350	401
Portfolio Investment Assets	78bf *d*	...	...	...	...	...	—	—	—	—	—	—	—	—	—	—
Equity Securities	78bk *d*	...	...	...	...	...	—	—	—	—	—	—	—	—	—	—
Debt Securities	78bl *d*	...	...	...	...	...	—	—	—	—	—	—	—	—	—	—
Portfolio Investment Liab., n.i.e.	78bg *d*	...	...	...	...	...	1	−1	—	76	180	96	44	68	108	155
Equity Securities	78bm *d*	...	...	...	...	...	1	−1	—	6	4	51	11	27	15	34
Debt Securities	78bn *d*	...	...	...	...	...	—	—	—	70	176	45	33	42	93	121
Financial Derivatives Assets	78bw *d*	...	...	...	...	...	....	....	....	....	....	....	....	....	....	....
Financial Derivatives Liabilities	78bx *d*	...	...	...	...	...	....	....	....	....	....	....	....	....	....	....
Other Investment Assets	78bh *d*	...	...	...	...	...	−1	10	4	−12	−43	−21	−42	−84	−108	−79
Monetary Authorities	78bo *d*	...	...	...	...	...	...	....	....	....	....	....	....	....	....	....
General Government	78bp *d*	...	...	...	...	...	—	11	3	1	−18	6	4	−33	−63	−67
Banks	78bq *d*	...	...	...	...	...	—									
Other Sectors	78br *d*	...	...	...	...	...	−1	−1	—	−13	−25	−26	−46	−50	−45	−12
Other Investment Liab., n.i.e.	78bi *d*	...	...	...	...	...	383	451	936	1,246	1,789	1,782	2,188	1,120	1,618	2,091
Monetary Authorities	78bs *d*	...	...	...	...	...	−1	—	—	1	1	1				
General Government	78bt *d*	...	...	...	...	...	−6	106	38	228	359	251	313	211	147	212
Banks	78bu *d*	...	...	...	...	...	89	85	361	630	324	−438	−9	−225	630	97
Other Sectors	78bv *d*	...	...	...	...	...	301	261	537	387	1,104	1,968	1,884	1,134	841	1,782
Net Errors and Omissions	78ca *d*	...	...	...	...	...	86	−19	44	−231	20	−180	133	−521	587	71
Overall Balance	78cb *d*	...	...	...	...	...	−51	81	−8	−25	−88	−206	42	−231	−320	529
Reserves and Related Items	79da *d*	...	...	...	...	...	51	−81	8	25	88	206	−42	231	320	−529
Reserve Assets	79db *d*	...	...	...	...	...	51	−158	−9	−112	−24	212	−574	50	−84	−457
Use of Fund Credit and Loans	79dc *d*	...	...	...	...	...	—	77	17	137	112	−6	532	31	240	−72
Exceptional Financing	79de *d*	...	...	...	...	...	—	—	—	—	—	—	—	150	164	—

International Investment Position																
														Millions of US Dollars		
Assets	79aa *d*	...	...	...	...	...	....	....	....	....	....	....	....	....	....	....
Direct Investment Abroad	79ab *d*	...	...	...	...	...	....	....	....	....	....	....	....	....	....	....
Portfolio Investment	79ac *d*	...	...	...	...	...	....	....	....	....	....	....	....	....	....	....
Equity Securities	79ad *d*	...	...	...	...	...	....	....	....	....	....	....	....	....	....	....
Debt Securities	79ae *d*	...	...	...	...	...	....	....	....	....	....	....	....	....	....	....
Financial Derivatives	79al *d*	...	...	...	...	...	....	....	....	....	....	....	....	....	....	....
Other Investment	79af *d*	...	...	...	...	...	....	....	....	....	....	....	....	....	....	....
Monetary Authorities	79ag *d*	...	...	...	...	...	....	....	....	....	....	....	....	....	....	....
General Government	79ah *d*	...	...	...	...	...	....	....	....	....	....	....	....	....	....	....
Banks	79ai *d*	...	...	...	...	...	....	....	....	....	....	....	....	....	....	....
Other Sectors	79aj *d*	...	...	...	...	...	....	....	....	....	....	....	....	....	....	....
Reserve Assets	79ak *d*	...	...	...	...	...	....	....	....	....	....	....	....	....	....	....
Liabilities	79la *d*	...	...	...	...	...	....	....	....	....	....	....	....	....	....	....
Dir. Invest. in Rep. Economy	79lb *d*	...	...	...	...	...	....	....	....	....	....	....	....	....	....	....
Portfolio Investment	79lc *d*	...	...	...	...	...	....	....	....	....	....	....	....	....	....	....
Equity Securities	79ld *d*	...	...	...	...	...	....	....	....	....	....	....	....	....	....	....
Debt Securities	79le *d*	...	...	...	...	...	....	....	....	....	....	....	....	....	....	....
Financial Derivatives	79ll *d*	...	...	...	...	...	....	....	....	....	....	....	....	....	....	....
Other investment	79lf *d*	...	...	...	...	...	....	....	....	....	....	....	....	....	....	....
Monetary Authorities	79lg *d*	...	...	...	...	...	....	....	....	....	....	....	....	....	....	....
General Government	79lh *d*	...	...	...	...	...	....	....	....	....	....	....	....	....	....	....
Banks	79li *d*	...	...	...	...	...	....	....	....	....	....	....	....	....	....	....
Other Sectors	79lj *d*	...	...	...	...	...	....	....	....	....	....	....	....	....	....	....

Minus Sign Indicates Debit

	1985	1986	1987	1988	1989	1990	1991	1992	1993	1994	1995	1996	1997	1998	1999	Balance of Payments	
	-1,537	247	-366	-1,654	-2,498	-7,281	-7,571	-6,303	-6,364	-8,085	-13,554	-14,691	-3,024	14,048	11,050	Current Account, n.i.e.	78al *d*
	7,059	8,803	11,595	15,781	19,834	22,810	28,232	32,099	36,398	44,478	55,447	54,408	56,652	52,747	56,722	Goods: Exports f.o.b.	78aa *d*
	-8,391	-8,415	-12,019	-17,856	-22,750	-29,561	-34,221	-36,260	-40,694	-48,204	-63,415	-63,897	-55,100	-36,706	-43,245	Goods: Imports f.o.b.	78ab *d*
	-1,332	388	-424	-2,074	-2,916	-6,751	-5,989	-4,161	-4,297	-3,726	-7,968	-9,488	1,551	16,041	13,477	*Trade Balance*	78ac *d*
	2,041	2,302	3,070	4,647	5,457	6,419	7,272	9,288	11,059	11,640	14,845	17,007	15,763	13,156	14,243	Services: Credit	78ad *d*
	-1,815	-1,852	-2,406	-3,569	-4,505	-6,309	-8,040	-10,368	-12,469	-15,396	-18,804	-19,585	-17,337	-11,998	-14,096	Services: Debit	78ae *d*
	-1,105	839	239	-996	-1,964	-6,641	-6,757	-5,241	-5,707	-7,482	-11,927	-12,066	-22	17,199	13,624	*Balance on Goods & Services*	78af *d*
	1,122	1,031	1,098	1,297	1,589	2,059	2,254	1,532	2,140	2,562	3,801	3,969	3,742	3,324	3,133	Income: Credit	78ag *d*
	-1,719	-1,848	-1,928	-2,191	-2,369	-2,913	-3,329	-3,240	-3,546	-4,292	-5,915	-7,354	-7,223	-6,889	-6,079	Income: Debit	78ah *d*
	-1,703	22	-590	-1,891	-2,744	-7,494	-7,832	-6,949	-7,113	-9,213	-14,040	-15,451	-3,502	13,633	10,678	*Balance on Gds, Serv. & Inc.*	78ai *d*
	190	250	247	268	281	278	411	1,000	1,222	1,901	1,190	1,651	1,392	820	853	Current Transfers, n.i.e.: Credit	78aj *d*
	-25	-25	-23	-31	-34	-65	-150	-355	-473	-774	-704	-891	-913	-405	-481	Current Transfers: Debit	78ak *d*
	—	—	2	—	—	-1	—	—	—	—	—	....	....	....	....	Capital Account, n.i.e.	78bc *d*
	1	1	2	—	—	—	—	—	—	—	—	....	....	....	....	Capital Account, n.i.e.: Credit	78ba *d*
	-1	—	—	—	—	-1	—	—	—	—	—	....	....	....	....	Capital Account: Debit	78bb *d*
	1,538	-131	1,062	3,839	6,599	9,098	11,759	9,475	10,500	12,167	21,909	19,486	-16,877	-14,454	-9,360	Financial Account, n.i.e.	78bj *d*
	-1	-1	-170	-24	-50	-140	-167	-147	-233	-493	-886	-931	-390	-130	-374	Direct Investment Abroad	78bd *d*
	163	263	352	1,105	1,775	2,444	2,014	2,113	1,804	1,366	2,068	2,336	3,746	6,941	5,718	Dir. Invest. in Rep. Econ., n.i.e.	78be *d*
	—	—	—	—	—	—	....	....	—	-5	-2	-41	-446	-201	80	Portfolio Investment Assets	78bf *d*
	—	—	—	—	—	—	....	....	—	-5	-2	-41	-446	-201	80	Equity Securities	78bk *d*
																Debt Securities	78bl *d*
	895	-29	346	530	1,486	-38	-81	924	5,455	2,486	4,083	3,585	4,798	159	735	Portfolio Investment Liab., n.i.e.	78bg *d*
	41	96	499	444	1,424	440	37	455	2,679	-389	2,123	1,164	3,899	355	879	Equity Securities	78bm *d*
	854	-126	-153	86	63	-478	-118	469	2,776	2,875	1,960	2,421	899	-196	-144	Debt Securities	78bn *d*
	....	....	....	....	....	....	....	....	....	....	....	....	....	....	....	Financial Derivatives Assets	78bw *d*
																Financial Derivatives Liabilities	78bx *d*
	-242	-150	141	269	-313	-164	352	104	-3,265	-1,027	-2,738	2,661	-2,404	-3,824	-1,459	Other Investment Assets	78bh *d*
	....	....	....	....	....	....	....	....	....	....	....	....	....	....	....	Monetary Authorities	78bo *d*
	-196	-150	153	250	-337	-220	247	—	—	—	....	....	....	....	....	General Government	78bp *d*
	—	—	—	—	—	—	—	104	-3,265	-1,027	-2,737	2,741	-2,457	-3,876	-1,412	Banks	78bq *d*
	-46	—	-12	19	23	57	105	—	—	—	-1	-80	53	52	-46	Other Sectors	78br *d*
	722	-213	393	1,960	3,700	6,996	9,642	6,479	6,739	9,839	19,383	11,876	-22,181	-17,399	-14,061	Other Investment Liab., n.i.e.	78bi *d*
	—	—	—	—	—	—	—	—	—	—	—	—	-9,483	702	2,741	Monetary Authorities	78bs *d*
	507	25	434	-51	-206	-999	9	-611	-464	-705	46	-58	524	100	-62	General Government	78bt *d*
	-359	-563	243	984	700	1,027	213	1,758	6,589	14,295	13,218	2,909	-3,522	-11,382	-11,884	Banks	78bu *d*
	574	325	-285	1,027	3,207	6,969	9,420	5,333	614	-3,751	6,118	9,025	-9,700	-6,820	-4,857	Other Sectors	78bv *d*
	103	598	248	411	928	1,419	431	-142	-230	87	-1,196	-2,627	1,651	-2,815	-423	Net Errors and Omissions	78ca *d*
	105	714	945	2,596	5,029	3,235	4,618	3,029	3,907	4,169	7,159	2,167	-18,250	-3,222	1,266	*Overall Balance*	78cb *d*
	-105	-714	-945	-2,596	-5,029	-3,235	-4,618	-3,029	-3,907	-4,169	-7,159	-2,167	18,250	3,222	-1,266	Reserves and Related Items	79da *d*
	-205	-545	-700	-2,336	-4,667	-2,961	-4,618	-3,029	-3,907	-4,169	-7,159	-2,167	9,900	-1,433	-4,553	Reserve Assets	79db *d*
	100	-168	-245	-260	-363	-274	-1	—	—	—	—	—	2,437	679	269	Use of Fund Credit and Loans	79dc *d*
	—	—	—	—	—	—	....	....	—	—	—	—	5,913	3,976	3,017	Exceptional Financing	79de *d*

Millions of US Dollars

	1985	1986	1987	1988	1989	1990	1991	1992	1993	1994	1995	1996	1997	1998	1999	International Investment Position	
	....	....	....	....	....	....	....	....	....	....	....	....	35,781	42,453	....	Assets	79aa *d*
	....	....	....	....	....	....	....	....	....	....	....	....	401	411	....	Direct Investment Abroad	79ab *d*
	....	....	....	....	....	....	....	....	....	....	....	....	445	667	....	Portfolio Investment	79ac *d*
	....	....	....	....	....	....	....	....	....	....	....	....	—	—	....	Equity Securities	79ad *d*
	....	....	....	....	....	....	....	....	....	....	....	....	445	667	....	Debt Securities	79ae *d*
	....	....	....	....	....	....	....	....	....	....	....	....			....	Financial Derivatives	79al *d*
	....	....	....	....	....	....	....	....	....	....	....	....	8,043	11,839	....	Other Investment	79af *d*
	....	....	....	....	....	....	....	....	....	....	....	....	—	—	....	Monetary Authorities	79ag *d*
	....	....	....	....	....	....	....	....	....	....	....	....			....	General Government	79ah *d*
	....	....	....	....	....	....	....	....	....	....	....	....	8,043	11,839	....	Banks	79ai *d*
	....	....	....	....	....	....	....	....	....	....	....	....	—	—	....	Other Sectors	79aj *d*
	....	....	....	....	....	....	....	....	....	....	....	....	26,892	29,536	....	Reserve Assets	79ak *d*
	....	....	....	....	....	....	....	....	....	....	....	....	64,498	63,270	....	Liabilities	79la *d*
	....	....	....	....	....	....	....	....	....	....	....	....	555	2,829	....	Dir. Invest. in Rep. Economy	79lb *d*
	....	....	....	....	....	....	....	....	....	....	....	....	4,331	4,024	....	Portfolio Investment	79lc *d*
	....	....	....	....	....	....	....	....	....	....	....	....	—	—	....	Equity Securities	79ld *d*
	....	....	....	....	....	....	....	....	....	....	....	....	4,331	4,024	....	Debt Securities	79le *d*
	....	....	....	....	....	....	....	....	....	....	....	....			....	Financial Derivatives	79ll *d*
	....	....	....	....	....	....	....	....	....	....	....	....	59,612	56,417	....	Other investment	79lf *d*
	....	....	....	....	....	....	....	....	....	....	....	....	7,157	11,203	....	Monetary Authorities	79lg *d*
	....	....	....	....	....	....	....	....	....	....	....	....	13,356	16,263	....	General Government	79lh *d*
	....	....	....	....	....	....	....	....	....	....	....	....	38,873	28,722	....	Banks	79li *d*
	....	....	....	....	....	....	....	....	....	....	....	....	....	....	....	Other Sectors	79lj *d*

Thailand

	1970	1971	1972	1973	1974	1975	1976	1977	1978	1979	1980	1981	1982	1983	1984
Government Finance															*Millions of Baht:*
Deficit (-) or Surplus 80	−5,403	−7,176	I−7,263	−5,170	2,170	−7,401	−16,081	−12,095	−13,064	−13,160	−25,658	−21,360	−41,120	−22,824	−33,183
Total Revenue and Grants 81y	....	....	....	....	....	....	....	....	....	....	....	....	....	....	....
Revenue 81	18,886	19,992	I21,561	27,311	38,352	39,083	43,584	53,917	65,190	78,666	95,556	111,963	116,058	143,635	148,080
Grants 81z	....	....	....	....	....	....	....	....	....	....	....	....	....	....	....
Exp. & Lending Minus Repay. 82z															
Expenditure 82	24,289	27,168	I28,824	32,481	36,182	46,484	59,665	66,012	78,254	91,826	121,214	133,323	157,178	166,459	181,263
Lending Minus Repayments 83	....	....	....	....	....	....	....	....	....	....	....	....	....	....	....
Extrabudgetary Deficits/Surpluses 80xz															
Total Financing 80h	5,403	7,176	I7,265	5,169	−2,169	7,402	16,079	12,095	13,064	13,160	25,658	21,360	41,120	22,824	33,183
Total Net Borrowing 84	4,206	6,221	I8,700	6,430	35	4,970	14,247	11,395	14,028	12,167	26,468	21,214	41,659	22,404	32,802
Net Domestic 84a	....	....	....	....	....	....	....	....	....	....	....	....	....	....	....
Net Foreign 85a															
Use of Cash Balances 87	1,197	955	I−1,435	−1,261	−2,204	2,432	1,832	700	−964	993	−810	146	−539	420	381
Total Debt by Currency 88z	27,315	32,990	I42,427	47,340	45,861	48,031	60,696	72,597	92,078	113,380	140,036	168,839	209,504	242,532	292,922
National 88b	23,644	29,012	I38,058	42,461	40,875	43,212	53,575	64,372	77,181	90,166	109,781	127,456	160,372	185,815	219,143
Foreign 89b	3,671	3,978	I4,369	4,879	4,986	4,819	7,121	8,225	14,897	23,214	30,255	41,383	49,132	56,717	73,779
National Accounts															*Billions of Baht*
Exports of Goods & Services 90c	22.1	24.5	30.9	41.3	60.3	55.7	70.1	80.5	97.1	126.2	159.7	181.3	192.9	185.2	216.4
Government Consumption 91f	16.6	17.7	18.6	21.6	26.1	31.3	38.0	42.9	54.6	66.8	81.4	97.0	110.2	118.6	130.1
Gross Fixed Capital Formation 93e	35.0	35.8	38.6	49.9	65.0	69.4	79.4	104.6	123.3	142.9	184.0	212.8	226.7	262.1	282.6
Increase/Decrease(-) in Stocks 93i	2.7	1.4	−1.8	10.0	9.3	11.8	3.7	3.9	14.3	9.2	9.1	12.8	−3.6	13.9	8.6
Private Consumption 96f	103.2	104.8	117.6	149.0	190.1	211.3	237.7	271.9	315.0	364.0	433.6	496.4	535.0	599.6	628.9
Imports of Goods & Services 98c	−28.6	−28.9	−32.6	−44.5	−66.9	−69.7	−78.7	−102.4	−117.7	−163.7	−201.2	−229.0	−207.3	−251.2	−258.6
Gross Domestic Product (GDP) 99b	147.4	153.4	170.1	222.1	279.2	303.3	346.5	403.5	488.2	558.9	662.5	760.4	841.6	921.0	988.1
Net Factor Inc/Pmts(-) Abroad 98.n	.2	−1.1	−.6	−.9	−.1	—	−.9	−1.3	−3.6	−6.2	−5.4	−12.0	−12.9	−6.7	−11.5
Gross National Income (GNI) 99a	147.6	153.3	169.5	221.2	279.1	303.3	345.6	402.3	484.6	552.6	657.1	748.3	828.6	914.3	976.6
Net National Income 99e	137.4	141.7	156.5	206.5	261.9	283.1	322.2	375.2	453.0	515.4	610.4	693.7	765.5	841.8	894.1
GDP Volume 1972 prices 99b.p	155.7	163.4	170.1	186.9	195.0	204.4	223.6	245.7	271.4	285.8	299.5	....	....	....	....
GDP Volume 1988 Prices..................... 99b.p	....	....	....	....	....	....	....	....	....	....	913.7	967.7	1,019.5	1,076.4	1,138.4
GDP Volume (1995=100) .... 99bv p	16.2	17.0	17.7	19.4	20.3	21.3	23.3	25.6	28.2	29.7	31.2	33.0	34.8	36.7	38.8
GDP Deflator (1995=100)................. 99bi p	22.2	22.0	23.5	27.9	33.6	34.8	36.4	38.6	42.2	45.9	51.9	56.3	59.1	61.3	62.2
															Millions:
Population.. 99z	36.37	37.49	38.59	39.69	40.78	41.87	42.96	44.04	45.10	46.14	46.72	47.74	48.71	49.68	50.64

Year Ending December 31

Item	Code	1985	1986	1987	1988	1989	1990	1991	1992	1993	1994	1995	1996	1997	1998	1999
Government Finance																
Deficit (-) or Surplus	80	-38,979	-34,132	-8,860	36,099	65,335	107,049	100,455	71,793	55,618	101,239	134,965	I43,303	-15,061	-128,951	-154,193
Total Revenue and Grants	81y	....	....	....	....	....	....	....	....	....	....	....	....	....	....	....
Revenue	81	160,569	169,829	202,365	258,231	328,248	411,747	462,539	511,835	575,100	680,455	777,286	853,201	847,689	717,779	713,066
Grants	81z	....	....	....	....	....	....	....	....	....	....	....	....	....	....	....
Exp. & Lending Minus Repay.	82z	199,548	203,961	211,225	222,132	262,913	304,698	362,084	440,042	519,482	579,216	642,321	819,083	875,714	842,581	833,042
Expenditure	82	....	....	....	....	....	....	....	....	....	....	....	....	....	....	....
Lending Minus Repayments	83	....	....	....	....	....	....	....	....	....	....	....	....	....	....	....
Extrabudgetary Deficits/Surpluses	80xz	....	....	....	....	....	....	....	....	....	....	....	I9,185	12,964	-4,149	-34,217
Total Financing	80h	38,979	34,132	8,860	-36,099	-65,335	-107,049	-100,455	-71,793	-55,618	-101,239	-134,965	I-43,303	15,061	128,951	154,192
Total Net Borrowing	84	39,672	35,586	7,032	-32,887	-21,952	-52,626	-43,400	-44,468	-44,605	-80,051	-44,147	I-28,788	-76,109	-7,764	135,204
Net Domestic	84a												-25,123	-72,348	-3,361	84,566
Net Foreign	85a												-3,665	-3,761	-4,403	50,638
Use of Cash Balances	87	-693	-1,454	1,828	-3,212	-43,383	-54,423	-57,055	-27,325	-11,013	-21,188	-90,818	-14,515	91,170	136,715	18,988
Total Debt by Currency	88z	351,136	413,596	450,842	437,942	420,040	371,839	325,692	300,261	271,406	219,829	193,630	175,594	299,547	674,032	....
National	88b	249,253	301,235	322,121	304,878	291,225	278,346	230,109	202,694	161,071	103,200	72,696	44,254	31,755	426,928	642,371
Foreign	89b	101,883	112,361	128,721	133,064	128,815	93,493	95,583	97,567	110,335	116,629	120,934	131,340	267,792	247,104	....

Billions of Baht

Item	Code	1985	1986	1987	1988	1989	1990	1991	1992	1993	1994	1995	1996	1997	1998	1999
National Accounts																
Exports of Goods & Services	90c	245.3	290.2	375.6	514.9	648.5	745.3	901.5	1,046.7	1,198.9	1,408.7	1,749.3	1,807.3	2,565.9	2,717.5	2,683.1
Government Consumption	91f	142.9	144.6	147.2	156.7	176.8	205.4	231.1	280.2	316.0	354.4	413.0	467.6	471.3	506.1	540.6
Gross Fixed Capital Formation	93e	287.0	292.2	359.3	478.5	642.9	881.8	1,043.6	1,111.3	1,252.9	1,450.2	1,716.0	1,893.7	1,595.5	1,352.3	1,279.4
Increase/Decrease(-) in Stocks	93i	11.4	1.0	3.1	29.8	8.3	21.2	30.3	20.1	13.3	10.0	17.7	28.0	-26.5	-140.2	-111.5
Private Consumption	96f	657.4	695.8	781.1	885.0	1,030.6	1,235.0	1,378.1	1,550.5	1,732.3	1,959.7	2,229.3	2,510.3	2,646.8	2,596.1	2,693.5
Imports of Goods & Services	98c	-274.1	-267.1	-368.3	-536.6	-696.1	-909.5	-1,065.5	-1,160.2	-1,317.6	-1,584.5	-2,030.8	-2,096.6	-2,200.2	-1,977.7	-2,144.3
Gross Domestic Product (GDP)	99b	1,056.5	1,133.4	1,299.9	1,559.8	1,857.0	2,183.5	2,506.6	2,830.9	3,195.8	3,598.6	4,094.5	4,610.3	4,752.7	5,054.0	4,940.8
Net Factor Inc/Pmts(-) Abroad	98.n	-17.6	-22.4	-22.4	-24.8	-23.7	-27.4	-36.9	-63.0	-63.0	-75.0	-85.6	-117.9	-145.9	....	....
Gross National Income (GNI)	99a	1,038.9	1,111.0	1,277.5	1,535.0	1,833.3	2,156.1	2,469.7	2,768.0	3,116.5	3,559.8	4,109.0	4,571.7	4,681.3	....	....
Net National Income	99e	945.9	1,006.9	1,161.0	1,401.6	1,676.2	1,965.1	2,235.2	2,485.3	2,773.1	3,161.7	3,629.9	3,918.7	4,082.2	....	....
GDP Volume 1972 prices	99b.p															
GDP Volume 1988 Prices	99b.p	1,191.3	1,257.2	1,376.8	1,559.8	1,750.0	1,945.4	2,111.9	2,282.6	2,481.3	2,695.1	2,933.2	3,095.0	3,081.8	2,768.2	2,860.3
GDP Volume (1995=100)	99bv p	40.6	42.9	46.9	53.2	59.7	66.3	72.0	77.8	84.6	91.9	100.0	105.5	105.1	94.4	97.5
GDP Deflator (1995=100)	99bi p	63.5	64.6	67.6	71.6	76.0	80.4	85.0	88.8	92.3	95.7	100.0	106.7	110.5	130.8	123.7

Midyear Estimates

Item	Code	1985	1986	1987	1988	1989	1990	1991	1992	1993	1994	1995	1996	1997	1998	1999
Population	99z	51.58	52.51	53.43	54.33	55.21	55.84	56.57	57.29	58.01	58.71	59.40	60.00	60.60	61.20	61.81

(See notes in the back of the book.)

Togo

		1970	1971	1972	1973	1974	1975	1976	1977	1978	1979	1980	1981	1982	1983	1984
Exchange Rates																*Francs per SDR:*
Official Rate	aa	276.02	283.61	278.00	284.00	272.08	262.55	288.70	285.76	272.28	264.78	287.99	334.52	370.92	436.97	470.11
																Francs per US Dollar:
Official Rate	ae	276.02	261.22	256.05	235.42	222.22	224.27	248.49	235.25	209.00	201.00	225.80	287.40	336.25	417.37	479.60
Official Rate	rf	276.40	275.59	252.03	222.89	240.70	214.31	238.95	245.68	225.66	212.72	211.28	271.73	328.61	381.07	436.96
														Index Numbers (1995=100):		
Official Rate	ah x	180.5	98.6	197.9	224.6	207.2	233.0	209.0	203.0	221.4	234.6	236.4	184.6	152.6	131.5	114.5
Nominal Effective Exchange Rate	ne c	....	....	....	....	....	....	....	....	....	107.9	110.5	103.9	99.2	98.9	100.3
Real Effective Exchange Rate	re c	....	....	....	....	....	....	....	....	....	....	....	173.1	171.4	164.4	163.8	146.7
Fund Position																*Millions of SDRs:*
Quota	2f. s	15.0	15.0	15.0	15.0	15.0	15.0	15.0	15.0	19.0	19.0	28.5	28.5	28.5	38.4	38.4
SDRs	1b. s	1.9	3.5	5.1	5.1	5.1	5.1	5.0	4.8	4.4	6.3	5.8	6.5	3.9	1.2	2.1
Reserve Position in the Fund	1c. s	2.1	2.1	2.1	2.1	2.1	2.1	2.1	2.1	2.0	3.3	—	—	.2	.2	.2
Total Fund Cred.&Loans Outstg.	2tl	—	—	—	—	—	—	7.5	7.5	6.2	10.8	25.5	32.8	32.8	51.9	63.5
International Liquidity												*Millions of US Dollars Unless Otherwise Indicated:*				
Total Reserves minus Gold	1l. d	35.4	40.5	36.5	37.9	54.5	41.2	66.6	46.1	70.0	65.5	77.6	151.5	167.7	172.8	203.3
SDRs	1b. d	1.9	3.8	5.5	6.1	6.2	5.9	5.8	5.8	5.7	8.3	7.4	7.6	4.3	1.3	2.0
Reserve Position in the Fund	1c. d	2.1	2.2	2.2	2.5	2.5	2.4	2.4	2.5	2.6	4.4	—	—	.2	.2	.2
Foreign Exchange	1d. d	31.4	34.5	28.7	29.3	45.7	32.8	58.4	37.9	61.7	52.8	70.2	143.9	163.2	171.4	201.1
Gold (Million Fine Troy Ounces)	1ad	....	....	....	....	....	....	—	.006	.010	.013	.013	.013	.013	.013	.013
Gold (National Valuation)	1an d	....	....	....	....	....	....	....	.3	.4	.6	.6	5.3	5.3	4.8	4.2
Monetary Authorities: Other Liab.	4.. d	.3	.8	1.4	.1	1.4	3.9	2.2	1.4	4.3	20.7	6.6	1.7	2.2	3.7	2.3
Deposit Money Banks: Assets	7a. d	10.9	10.8	8.1	7.2	63.0	13.9	21.5	27.3	63.7	69.0	49.4	69.7	64.8	46.5	46.7
Liabilities	7b. d	8.9	11.0	12.0	18.4	22.7	32.7	32.8	51.5	81.5	61.0	77.6	79.4	64.2	46.2	52.9
Monetary Authorities																*Billions of Francs:*
Foreign Assets	11	9.8	10.4	9.3	8.7	12.1	9.2	16.6	10.9	14.6	13.2	17.5	43.5	56.4	72.1	97.5
Claims on Central Government	12a	—	—	—	—	—	2.4	2.5	6.3	10.3	13.1	12.8	21.9	22.6	32.0	33.7
Claims on Deposit Money Banks	12e	—	.1	.2	.7	.6	2.6	4.2	6.8	5.1	9.8	13.2	7.1	7.2	6.3	6.6
Claims on Other Financial Insts	12f	—	—	—	—	—	—	.2	.4	.6	.6	.5	.5	.4	.5	.6
Reserve Money	14	4.8	5.9	5.7	6.5	9.1	11.6	18.9	19.9	25.8	27.0	31.7	57.9	71.0	78.4	99.1
of which: Currency Outside DMBs	14a	4.6	5.6	5.4	6.0	8.4	9.9	14.2	16.0	20.8	21.5	27.8	50.7	54.3	45.5	37.0
Foreign Liabilities	16c	.1	.2	.3	—	.3	.9	2.7	2.5	4.4	10.0	12.9	15.5	17.0	28.2	34.6
Central Government Deposits	16d	4.4	3.3	2.0	1.5	2.0	.4	.3	.5	.8	.7	.7	1.1	.7	7.6	10.6
Other Items (Net)	17r	.5	1.0	1.4	1.5	1.4	1.4	1.5	1.5	−.3	−1.0	−1.3	−1.6	−2.0	−3.2	−5.9
Deposit Money Banks																*Billions of Francs:*
Reserves	20	.2	.4	.3	.4	.6	1.6	4.2	3.9	4.9	4.9	4.4	7.6	16.5	33.0	63.1
Foreign Assets	21	3.0	2.8	2.1	1.7	14.0	3.1	5.3	6.4	13.3	13.9	11.2	20.0	21.8	19.4	22.4
Claims on Central Government	22a	—	—	—	—	—	—	—	.6	1.3	₹14.1	4.6	3.8	3.4	3.2	2.3
Claims on Private Sector	22d	7.8	8.9	9.7	13.1	16.0	24.3	31.7	43.1	49.2	₹56.2	64.1	62.0	69.2	67.3	70.8
Claims on Other Financial Insts	22f										₹.7	.6	.5	.7	.6	.5
Demand Deposits	24	5.3	6.0	6.1	5.2	16.3	11.1	18.2	19.9	26.6	₹30.4	26.8	28.5	34.9	36.6	52.7
Time Deposits	25	2.5	2.2	2.1	4.4	5.4	6.7	8.3	11.6	16.8	₹13.9	17.2	20.6	27.1	34.7	45.4
Foreign Liabilities	26c	1.8	2.1	2.0	2.9	3.4	5.7	6.5	10.5	15.4	10.3	15.3	20.8	19.3	17.4	23.5
Long-Term Foreign Liabilities	26cl	.7	.7	1.1	1.4	1.7	1.7	1.7	1.6	1.7	1.9	2.2	2.0	2.3	1.9	1.9
Central Government Deposits	26d	.1	.1	.1	.5	.7	.9	1.3	4.0	3.6	₹11.2	11.2	9.5	11.4	16.6	24.1
Credit from Monetary Authorities	26g	—	.1	.2	.7	.6	2.6	4.2	6.8	5.1	9.8	12.9	6.7	7.3	6.4	6.7
Other Items (Net)	27r	.6	.9	.5	.2	2.5	.5	1.2	−.5	−.4	2.2	−.7	5.8	9.4	9.9	4.8
Treasury Claims: Private Sector	22d. i	.6	.5	.4	.2	.3	.4	.3	1.1	1.8	2.0	1.8	1.5	2.0	2.0	1.5
Post Office: Checking Deposits	24.. i	.3	.3	.3	.3	.4	.5	.6	.6	.7	.7	.8	.7	.9	1.0	1.0
Monetary Survey																*Billions of Francs:*
Foreign Assets (Net)	31n	11.0	10.8	9.1	7.5	22.4	5.8	12.7	4.3	8.2	6.6	.5	27.2	41.9	45.9	61.8
Domestic Credit	32	3.6	5.8	7.9	11.5	13.8	26.0	33.4	46.4	57.7	₹63.5	71.5	78.7	85.1	80.4	74.1
Claims on Central Govt. (Net)	32an	−4.7	−3.6	−2.3	−1.9	−2.5	1.4	1.2	1.9	6.2	₹14.0	4.5	14.3	12.8	10.0	.7
Claims on Private Sector	32d	8.4	9.4	10.2	13.3	16.3	24.6	32.1	44.2	51.0	₹58.2	65.9	63.5	71.2	69.3	72.3
Claims on Other Financial Insts	32f	—	—	—	—	—	—	.2	.4	.6	₹1.3	1.1	.9	1.1	1.1	1.0
Money	34	10.2	11.9	11.8	11.6	25.1	21.6	32.9	36.5	48.1	₹52.7	55.3	80.0	90.1	83.1	90.7
Quasi-Money	35	2.5	2.2	2.1	4.4	5.4	6.7	8.3	11.6	16.8	₹13.9	17.2	20.6	27.1	34.7	45.4
Long-Term Foreign Liabilities	36cl	.7	.7	1.1	1.4	1.7	1.7	1.7	1.6	1.7	1.9	2.2	2.0	2.3	1.9	1.9
Other Items (Net)	37r	1.3	1.8	2.0	1.7	4.0	1.9	3.2	1.0	−.6	1.7	−2.8	3.4	7.5	6.6	−2.1
Money plus Quasi-Money	35l	12.7	14.1	13.9	15.9	30.5	28.3	41.2	48.1	64.9	₹66.5	72.6	100.6	117.2	117.8	136.1
Other Banking Institutions																*Billions of Francs:*
Savings Deposits	45	.7	.9	1.0	1.1	1.3	1.6	1.9	2.2	2.4	2.6	2.6	3.5	3.8	3.9	4.2
Liquid Liabilities	55l	13.4	15.0	14.9	17.0	31.7	29.6	43.1	50.3	67.3	₹69.1	75.2	104.1	121.0	121.6	140.3
Interest Rates																*Percent Per Annum:*
Discount Rate (End of Period)	60	3.50	3.50	3.50	5.50	5.50	8.00	8.00	8.00	8.00	8.00	10.50	10.50	10.50	10.50	10.50
Money Market Rate	60b	....	....	....	....	....	....	7.28	7.38	7.42	7.72	10.13	13.35	14.66	12.23	11.84
Deposit Rate	60l	3.00	3.00	3.00	5.75	5.75	5.88	6.00	6.00	6.00	6.00	6.19	6.25	7.75	7.50	7.25
Lending Rate	60p	....	....	....	....	....	....		12.00	12.00	12.00	14.50	14.50	16.00	14.50	14.50
Prices and Labor															*Index Numbers (1995=100):*	
Consumer Prices	64	16.2	17.3	18.6	₹19.3	21.8	25.7	28.7	35.2	35.3	38.0	42.7	51.1	56.7	62.1	59.9
															Number in Thousands:	
Employment	67e	....	....	....	....	....	....	....	....	....	....	....	....	....	....	....
International Transactions																*Millions of Francs:*
Exports	70	15,176	13,626	12,659	13,755	45,174	26,962	24,914	39,115	54,238	46,432	71,285	57,469	58,173	61,921	83,588
Imports, c.i.f.	71	17,928	19,455	21,381	22,388	28,612	37,270	44,420	69,834	100,898	110,208	116,357	117,769	128,354	108,141	118,460
																1985=100
Export Prices	74	17	16	15	17	43	₹44	33	45	47	52	49	51	54	61	84
Unit Value of Imports	75	24	24	26	28	36	₹40	47	53	59	66	71	80	83	100	100

1985	1986	1987	1988	1989	1990	1991	1992	1993	1994	1995	1996	1997	1998	1999		
															Exchange Rates	
End of Period																
415.26	394.78	378.78	407.68	380.32	364.84	370.48	378.57	404.89	‡780.44	728.38	753.06	807.94	791.61	‡896.19	Official Rate	aa
End of Period (ae) Period Average (rf)																
378.05	322.75	267.00	302.95	289.40	256.45	259.00	275.32	294.77	‡534.60	490.00	523.70	598.81	562.21	‡652.95	Official Rate	ae
449.26	346.31	300.54	297.85	319.01	272.26	282.11	264.69	283.16	‡555.20	499.15	511.55	583.67	589.95	‡615.70	Official Rate	rf
Period Averages																
111.9	144.3	166.1	167.8	156.5	183.7	177.4	188.9	176.3	90.0	100.0	97.5	85.6	84.7	81.1	Official Rate	ahx
105.6	115.7	122.1	126.5	132.9	154.1	156.4	168.4	176.5	95.5	100.0	100.6	97.1	100.5	97.7	Nominal Effective Exchange Rate	ne c
140.3	151.2	150.2	142.7	132.5	137.1	130.3	132.4	127.9	86.7	100.0	101.9	101.0	109.4	105.3	Real Effective Exchange Rate	re c
															Fund Position	
End of Period																
38.4	38.4	38.4	38.4	38.4	38.4	38.4	54.3	54.3	54.3	54.3	54.3	54.3	54.3	73.4	Quota	2f. s
.1	.5	.1	.1	1.3	.1	.3	.2	.1	—	.3	.2	—	.1	.2	SDRs	1b. s
.2	.2	.2	.2	.2	.2	.3	.3	.2	.3	.3	.3	.3	.3	.3	Reserve Position in the Fund	1c. s
67.6	73.8	60.1	57.9	57.4	61.1	55.3	55.8	49.9	56.0	70.4	62.5	64.9	67.4	60.4	Total Fund Cred.&Loans Outstg.	2tl
															International Liquidity	
End of Period																
296.6	342.0	354.9	232.1	285.3	353.2	364.9	272.5	156.3	94.4	130.4	88.5	118.6	117.7	122.0	Total Reserves minus Gold	1l. d
.1	.6	.1	.1	1.7	.2	.4	.3	.1	.1	.4	.4	—	.1	.2	SDRs	1b. d
.2	.3	.3	.3	.3	.3	.4	.3	.3	.4	.4	.4	.3	.3	.3	Reserve Position in the Fund	1c. d
296.3	341.1	354.5	231.7	283.3	352.7	364.1	271.9	155.9	94.0	129.6	87.8	118.3	117.3	121.4	Foreign Exchange	1d. d
.013	.013	.013	.013	.013	.013	.013	.013	.013	.013	.013	.013	.013	.013	.013	Gold (Million Fine Troy Ounces)	1ad
4.1	5.0	5.9	5.2	4.9	4.7	4.4	4.3	4.7	4.7	4.8	4.7	3.8	3.7	3.7	Gold (National Valuation)	1and
3.8	16.5	-3.2	10.4	6.1	4.6	12.1	-.1	10.3	5.5	1.1	2.8	2.7	8.9	3.1	Monetary Authorities: Other Liab.	4..d
50.1	43.3	64.3	78.4	117.9	84.4	93.6	87.9	58.4	109.7	111.1	100.6	66.3	69.1	60.0	Deposit Money Banks: Assets	7a. d
67.7	88.2	104.7	88.0	93.0	83.0	92.0	95.1	64.8	40.6	76.1	77.8	71.8	71.5	64.1	Liabilities	7b. d
															Monetary Authorities	
End of Period																
112.1	110.4	94.8	70.3	82.6	90.6	94.5	75.0	46.1	50.5	63.9	46.3	71.0	66.2	79.7	Foreign Assets	11
40.7	42.8	42.7	42.5	39.6	41.9	39.5	40.0	40.4	49.8	71.1	70.2	66.0	76.5	67.8	Claims on Central Government	12a
4.0	6.0	5.2	3.8	4.8	4.5	6.4	6.4	6.4	6.4	7.2	2.0	7.5	4.2	5.0	Claims on Deposit Money Banks	12e
.8	1.1	1.6	1.5	1.6	.5	1.6	1.6	1.5	1.3	.3	.2	.3	.3	.3	Claims on Other Financial Insts	12f
116.3	118.8	115.2	86.1	93.9	104.4	110.1	90.4	61.3	62.8	80.9	70.7	71.2	79.0	90.3	Reserve Money	14
39.2	46.0	48.3	23.2	21.3	32.1	36.3	22.1	10.3	44.8	73.5	59.7	60.3	65.3	79.5	of which: Currency Outside DMBs	14a
32.5	37.7	23.8	27.6	23.8	23.5	23.6	21.1	23.2	46.7	51.8	48.6	54.1	58.3	56.2	Foreign Liabilities	16c
10.8	2.5	.5	1.3	6.6	3.8	2.6	6.5	6.6	9.6	8.1	8.4	9.9	5.8	3.8	Central Government Deposits	16d
-2.0	1.4	4.7	3.2	4.3	5.8	5.7	5.1	3.3	-10.3	-3.6	-3.4	6.3	8.3	2.6	Other Items (Net)	17r
															Deposit Money Banks	
End of Period																
77.6	72.9	67.2	62.7	70.5	72.6	73.7	69.0	54.1	15.1	12.5	14.9	17.7	7.9	9.0	Reserves	20
18.9	14.0	17.2	23.8	34.1	21.7	24.2	24.2	17.2	58.6	54.4	52.7	39.7	38.8	39.2	Foreign Assets	21
.7	.9	.8	1.2	1.7	1.6	1.4	2.1	1.9	12.4	12.3	16.5	17.4	16.7	14.1	Claims on Central Government	22a
69.7	89.3	96.4	99.7	95.3	99.1	112.0	110.6	101.9	101.8	130.4	140.2	154.8	161.9	146.6	Claims on Private Sector	22d
.6	.6	.7	.7	.9	.9	.7	.5	.6	.5	—				—	Claims on Other Financial Insts	22f
42.2	42.8	41.8	40.3	40.8	42.2	41.2	34.1	35.1	49.3	56.4	59.9	60.6	63.5	61.1	Demand Deposits	24
60.5	75.8	72.8	79.9	82.8	84.6	86.4	78.1	66.7	68.2	68.7	66.2	73.8	65.4	68.9	Time Deposits	25
23.8	26.0	24.8	23.7	25.0	18.9	21.6	24.3	17.2	19.9	33.7	37.3	42.5	39.1	40.1	Foreign Liabilities	26c
1.8	2.4	3.2	3.0	2.0	2.3	2.3	1.9	1.9	1.7	3.5	3.4	.5	1.2	1.7	Long-Term Foreign Liabilities	26cl
35.2	32.1	40.8	38.3	50.6	46.6	49.8	53.2	43.1	39.1	37.4	32.8	29.8	28.9	20.6	Central Government Deposits	26d
4.1	8.0	5.3	3.9	2.8	3.4	6.4	6.4	7.1	7.4	2.0	7.6	4.7	8.5	5.0	Credit from Monetary Authorities	26g
—	-9.4	-6.4	-1.2	-1.4	-2.2	4.4	8.4	4.5	2.7	7.9	16.9	17.7	18.8	11.4	Other Items (Net)	27r
1.6	2.1	—	.4	2.2	1.0	.4	1.5	1.4	.6	.9	.7	.7	.5	.3	Treasury Claims: Private Sector	22d. i
1.3	.8	1.0	.9	1.0	1.0	1.0	.9	1.0	1.0	1.3	1.2	1.7	1.2	1.9	Post Office: Checking Deposits	24.. i
															Monetary Survey	
End of Period																
74.8	60.6	63.4	42.8	67.9	69.8	73.6	53.8	22.8	42.5	32.7	13.2	14.0	7.7	22.6	Foreign Assets (Net)	31n
67.8	101.0	101.8	106.8	83.0	94.6	103.8	96.0	97.6	118.1	169.8	187.1	200.4	221.8	206.2	Domestic Credit	32
-4.9	7.8	3.2	4.5	-17.0	-6.9	-10.9	-18.2	-7.8	13.8	38.3	46.0	44.7	59.1	59.1	Claims on Central Govt. (Net)	32an
71.3	91.4	96.4	100.1	97.5	100.1	112.4	112.1	103.3	102.5	131.2	140.9	155.5	162.4	146.8	Claims on Private Sector	32d
1.4	1.8	2.2	2.2	2.6	1.4	2.3	2.1	2.1	1.8	.3	.2	.3	.3	.3	Claims on Other Financial Insts	32f
82.7	89.7	91.0	64.4	63.2	75.3	78.5	57.1	46.6	95.3	131.2	121.0	123.3	131.8	144.8	Money	34
60.5	75.8	72.8	79.9	82.8	84.6	86.4	78.1	66.7	68.2	68.7	66.2	73.8	65.4	68.9	Quasi-Money	35
1.8	2.4	3.2	3.0	2.0	2.3	2.3	1.9	1.9	1.7	3.5	3.4	.5	1.2	1.7	Long-Term Foreign Liabilities	36cl
-2.4	-6.3	-1.8	2.3	3.1	2.2	10.2	12.8	5.3	-4.6	-.9	9.6	16.9	31.1	13.4	Other Items (Net)	37r
143.2	165.5	163.8	144.3	145.9	159.8	164.9	135.2	113.3	163.5	199.9	187.2	197.0	197.2	213.7	Money plus Quasi-Money	35l
															Other Banking Institutions	
End of Period																
5.5	6.2	6.4	6.2	9.9	....	....	....	....	....	....	—	—	—	—	Savings Deposits	45
148.7	171.7	170.2	150.5	155.8	....	....	....	....	....	....	187.2	197.0	197.2	213.7	Liquid Liabilities	55l
															Interest Rates	
Percent Per Annum																
10.50	8.50	8.50	9.50	11.00	11.00	11.00	12.50	10.50	10.00	7.50	6.50	6.00	6.25	5.75	Discount Rate (End of Period)	60
10.66	8.58	8.37	8.72	10.07	10.98	10.94	11.44	....	....	....	....	....	4.81	4.95	Money Market Rate	60b
7.25	6.08	5.25	5.25	6.42	7.00	7.00	7.75	....	....	....	....	....	3.50	3.50	Deposit Rate	60l
14.50	13.50	13.50	14.50	16.00	16.00	16.00	17.50	....	....	....	....	....	....		Lending Rate	60p
															Prices and Labor	
Period Averages																
58.8	61.2	61.2	61.1	60.6	61.2	61.5	62.3	‡61.7	85.9	100.0	104.7	‡113.3	114.4	114.3	Consumer Prices	64
Period Averages																
61	62	64	64	58	57	59	61	60	56	54	50	49	....	....	Employment	67e
															International Transactions	
Millions of Francs																
85,380	70,551	73,212	72,209	78,188	72,942	71,433	72,779	38,512	182,300	188,400	225,400	246,600	242,400	....	Exports	70
129,406	107,983	127,308	145,170	150,533	158,287	125,220	104,461	50,810	123,265	295,700	339,900	376,400	372,100	....	Imports, c.i.f.	71
1985=100																
100	....	....	....	....	....	....	....	....	....	....	....	....	....	....	Export Prices	74
100	....	....	....	....	....	....	....	....	....	....	....	....	....	....	Unit Value of Imports	75

Togo

		1970	1971	1972	1973	1974	1975	1976	1977	1978	1979	1980	1981	1982	1983	1984
Balance of Payments																*Millions of US Dollars:*
Current Account, n.i.e.	78ald	....	....	....	....	131.8	−75.5	−27.6	−87.3	−217.4	−212.7	−95.0	−44.2	−86.8	−47.9	16.3
Goods: Exports f.o.b.	78aad					215.1	141.0	158.9	199.3	262.0	290.6	475.8	377.7	344.8	273.5	291.0
Goods: Imports f.o.b.	78abd					−98.0	−211.5	−180.6	−252.7	−410.9	−464.3	−524.1	−413.9	−408.2	−291.8	−263.2
Trade Balance	78acd					117.0	−70.6	−21.8	−53.4	−148.9	−173.8	−48.3	−36.2	−63.3	−18.3	27.8
Services: Credit	78add					14.5	27.9	23.8	27.6	36.0	45.2	73.9	97.1	88.3	70.6	76.8
Services: Debit	78aed					−38.2	−69.1	−60.0	−90.3	−134.2	−145.4	−166.8	−146.0	−136.0	−117.7	−112.6
Balance on Goods & Services	78afd					93.3	−111.7	−58.0	−116.1	−247.1	−273.9	−141.2	−85.1	−111.1	−65.4	−8.1
Income: Credit	78agd					6.4	6.5	6.5	7.0	7.3	10.2	20.7	15.6	16.7	16.1	17.2
Income: Debit	78ahd					−6.0	−11.3	−10.4	−20.2	−27.7	−32.0	−60.6	−43.4	−59.0	−59.2	−56.0
Balance on Gds, Serv. & Inc.	78aid					93.7	−116.6	−61.9	−129.3	−267.6	−295.8	−181.2	−112.9	−153.4	−108.5	−46.9
Current Transfers, n.i.e.: Credit	78ajd					44.6	49.9	43.2	53.9	66.0	99.9	101.4	83.3	80.1	73.6	75.5
Current Transfers: Debit	78akd					−6.5	−8.8	−8.8	−11.8	−15.8	−16.9	−15.2	−14.5	−13.6	−13.0	−12.3
Capital Account, n.i.e.	78bcd	....	....	....	....	—	—	—	—	—	—	—	—	—	—	—
Capital Account, n.i.e.: Credit	78bad	....	....	....	....	—	—	—	—	—	—	—	—	—	—	—
Capital Account: Debit	78bbd	....	....	....	....	—	—	—	—	—	—	—	—	—	—	—
Financial Account, n.i.e.	78bjd	....	....	....	....	−81.5	92.5	24.1	70.4	236.6	207.5	62.8	.4	11.8	2.3	−37.0
Direct Investment Abroad	78bdd					—	—	—	—	—	—	—	—	—	—	—
Dir. Invest. in Rep. Econ., n.i.e.	78bed					−44.3	5.2	5.6	11.3	92.9	52.6	42.7	10.2	16.1	1.4	−9.9
Portfolio Investment Assets	78bfd					—	—	—	—	—	—	−.3	−.2	−.2	−.9	−.3
Equity Securities	78bkd					—	—	—	—	—	—	−.3	−.2		—	—
Debt Securities	78bld					—	—	—	—	—	—			−.2	−.9	−.3
Portfolio Investment Liab., n.i.e.	78bgd					.8	.6	21.0	1.5	—	2.5	2.2	—	—	.7	.1
Equity Securities	78bmd					.8	.6	21.0	1.5	—	2.5	2.2	—	—	.7	.1
Debt Securities	78bnd					—	—	—	—	—	—	—	—	—	—	—
Financial Derivatives Assets	78bwd					....	....	....	....	....	....	....	....	....	....	....
Financial Derivatives Liabilities	78bxd					....	....	....	....	....	....	....	....	....	....	....
Other Investment Assets	78bhd					−65.6	51.2	−26.0	−12.9	−42.3	5.4	4.9	−60.3	−31.5	16.9	−15.4
Monetary Authorities	78bod															
General Government	78bpd					−1.5	−.3	−.5	−1.2	−1.0	−2.2	−1.9	−2.9	−1.8	−1.3	−1.6
Banks	78bqd					−55.5	42.8	−16.9	−13.0	−43.7	−8.0	18.7	−23.9	−15.1	9.4	−5.4
Other Sectors	78brd					−8.7	8.7	−8.6	1.3	2.4	15.6	−12.0	−33.6	−14.6	8.9	−8.5
Other Investment Liab., n.i.e.	78bid					27.7	35.4	23.5	70.6	186.1	147.1	13.3	50.8	27.4	−15.9	−11.5
Monetary Authorities	78bsd															
General Government	78btd					24.9	26.5	16.6	15.9	104.0	124.5	−12.7	−88.8	−47.3	−10.4	−26.5
Banks	78bud					3.2	11.6	5.6	48.1	24.9	−18.9	19.6	19.6	−.3	−6.6	14.2
Other Sectors	78bvd					−.5	−2.7	1.2	6.7	57.1	41.5	6.4	120.0	75.1	1.2	.9
Net Errors and Omissions	78cad					−16.0	−6.1	.2	−15.4	.5	−10.3	−.6	−2.6	−3.2	7.5	−.1
Overall Balance	78cbd					34.3	10.9	−3.3	−32.2	19.7	−15.6	−32.8	−46.3	−78.2	−38.1	−20.8
Reserves and Related Items	79dad					−34.3	−10.9	3.3	32.2	−19.7	15.6	32.8	46.3	78.2	38.1	20.8
Reserve Assets	79dbd					−34.3	−10.9	−8.3	32.2	−18.2	9.7	−12.6	−92.5	−38.4	−40.9	−57.8
Use of Fund Credit and Loans	79dcd					—	—	8.6	—	−1.5	5.9	19.3	9.0	—	20.1	11.7
Exceptional Financing	79ded					—	—	3.0	—	—	—	26.1	129.9	116.6	58.8	66.9
Government Finance																*Millions of Francs:*
Deficit (-) or Surplus	80	....	....		....	....			−39,363	−58,836	−17,942	−4,689	−14,821	−4,794	−5,607	−7,862
Revenue	81								46,861	56,549	69,674	72,833	66,660	76,771	79,406	91,987
Grants Received	81z								20	97	334	63	4,231	4,878	6,515	10,717
Expenditure	82								72,677	84,667	68,297	73,943	85,137	86,410	91,863	110,567
Lending Minus Repayments	83								13,567	30,815	19,653	3,642	575	33	−335	−1
Financing																
Total Financing	84								39,363	58,836	17,942	4,689	14,821	4,794	5,607	7,862
Net Borrowing: Domestic	84a								8,869	5,746	−1,312	−53	7,362	5,351	17,266	....
Foreign	85a								31,438	55,411	23,196	4,247	6,597	3,103	5,562	....
Use of Cash Balances	87								−944	−2,321	−3,942	495	862	−3,660	−17,221	....
Debt: Domestic	88a								....	....	....	....	....	....	16,282	4,277
Debt: Foreign	89a								....	....	....	....	209,964	231,683	292,270	320,487
National Accounts																*Billions of Francs*
Exports of Goods & Services	90c	21.5	22.8	20.2	18.3	55.2	35.6	43.4	45.0	66.8	71.6	114.9	103.4	110.7	131.1	160.7
Government Consumption	91f	5.2	6.4	7.3	8.2	10.8	19.2	22.2	28.6	29.2	32.3	35.4	38.7	41.8	48.3	49.4
Gross Fixed Capital Formation	93e	9.2	13.3	16.2	18.9	20.0	29.2	33.7	58.7	88.5	101.4	82.3	67.7	63.6	66.6	55.7
Increase/Decrease(-) in Stocks	93i	1.4	1.6	1.4	2.4	2.1	7.4	3.1	6.9	4.6	6.4	.6	11.4	7.3	−1.6	−8.5
Private Consumption	96f	59.6	63.4	69.5	70.0	72.8	95.6	90.8	106.1	123.1	131.0	151.6	180.6	194.9	208.6	219.6
Imports of Goods & Services	98c	−23.5	−27.6	−27.9	−26.0	−32.2	−58.7	−56.9	−76.6	−123.2	−129.9	−146.4	−143.8	−148.6	−155.0	−163.1
Gross Domestic Product (GDP)	99b	73.7	81.8	87.6	90.4	130.6	128.3	136.3	168.8	189.0	212.8	238.4	258.0	269.7	298.0	313.8
Net National Income	99e	67.8	76.8	80.7	82.9	121.8	121.7	129.2	159.1	173.3	194.0	212.2	224.3	230.0	247.4	266.3
GDP Volume 1970 prices	99b.p	73.7	78.2	81.1	77.8	81.1	80.6	80.2	84.6	93.2	....					
GDP Volume 1978 Prices	99b.p	....	....	....	....	....	....	....	....	189.0	199.2	202.9	195.8	188.3	189.7	192.2
GDP Volume (1995=100)	99bvp	66.9	71.0	73.6	70.6	73.6	73.1	72.8	76.8	84.6	89.1	90.8	87.6	84.3	84.9	86.0
GDP Deflator (1995=100)	99bip	16.9	17.7	18.2	19.6	27.2	26.9	28.7	33.7	34.3	36.6	40.2	45.1	49.1	53.8	55.9
																Millions:
Population	99z	1.96	2.01	2.07	2.12	2.17	2.23	2.29	2.35	2.41	2.47	2.55	2.69	2.70	2.85	2.94

1985	1986	1987	1988	1989	1990	1991	1992	1993	1994	1995	1996	1997	1998	1999		
Minus Sign Indicates Debit															**Balance of Payments**	
−33.5	−65.6	−60.5	−87.2	−50.8	−99.8	−146.9	−140.6	−82.4	−56.3	−122.0	−153.9	−116.9	−140.1	....	Current Account, n.i.e.	78al *d*
282.0	362.4	397.5	435.3	411.7	513.8	514.4	419.7	264.0	328.4	377.4	440.6	422.5	420.3	....	Goods: Exports f.o.b.	78aa *d*
−303.7	−418.6	−437.1	−504.5	−470.1	−602.7	−567.0	−547.4	−375.3	−365.5	−506.5	−567.8	−530.6	−553.5	....	Goods: Imports f.o.b.	78ab *d*
−21.7	−56.2	−39.6	−69.1	−58.4	−88.9	−52.6	−127.7	−111.3	−37.1	−129.1	−127.2	−108.1	−133.2	....	*Trade Balance*	78ac *d*
87.0	103.7	118.8	105.1	128.0	149.1	116.4	129.2	84.6	70.9	87.3	116.2	88.5	76.0	....	Services: Credit	78ad *d*
−131.8	−172.3	−196.6	−200.2	−195.8	−244.1	−286.3	−203.3	−128.2	−125.3	−164.3	−201.4	−167.8	−149.2	....	Services: Debit	78ae *d*
−66.6	−124.8	−117.4	−164.1	−126.2	−183.9	−222.4	−201.8	−154.9	−91.6	−206.0	−212.3	−187.4	−206.4	....	*Balance on Goods & Services*	78af *d*
23.5	27.5	18.9	20.8	24.0	32.8	29.7	31.4	26.8	9.1	8.8	45.6	35.0	44.4	....	Income: Credit	78ag *d*
−61.5	−69.5	−66.1	−70.5	−63.8	−65.3	−58.7	−58.6	−17.7	−54.0	−42.4	−72.0	−63.9	−67.7	....	Income: Debit	78ah *d*
−104.6	−166.8	−164.6	−213.8	−166.0	−216.4	−251.4	−229.0	−145.7	−136.5	−239.6	−238.8	−216.3	−229.7	....	*Balance on Gds, Serv. & Inc.*	78ai *d*
90.5	120.4	125.2	148.4	134.0	145.6	128.7	111.1	82.6	91.3	129.7	106.8	120.2	101.8	....	Current Transfers, n.i.e.: Credit	78aj *d*
−19.4	−19.1	−21.2	−21.8	−18.8	−29.1	−24.2	−22.7	−19.3	−11.2	−12.1	−21.9	−20.8	−12.2	....	Current Transfers: Debit	78ak *d*
—	—	—	—	—	—	—	—	—	—	—	5.6	5.8	6.1	....	Capital Account, n.i.e.	78bc *d*
—	—	—	—	—	—	—	—	—	—	—	5.6	5.8	6.1	....	Capital Account, n.i.e.: Credit	78ba *d*
—	—	—	—	—	—	—	—	—	—	....	....	....	....	....	Capital Account: Debit	78bb *d*
31.1	23.5	−44.8	29.9	−2.8	75.2	67.8	−23.8	−105.1	−40.5	−52.8	151.3	126.9	114.1	....	Financial Account, n.i.e.	78bj *d*
										5.8	−2.8	−2.5	−10.6	....	Direct Investment Abroad	78bd *d*
16.3	6.1	7.2	13.0	9.2	18.2	6.5	—	−11.9	15.4	26.2	17.3	21.0	30.2	....	Dir. Invest. in Rep. Econ., n.i.e.	78be *d*
−.3	−4.0	.7	−.3	−1.1	−1.8	1.1	—	−.7	.7	5.0	−16.1	6.7	−5.2	....	Portfolio Investment Assets	78bf *d*
—	−2.7	1.3	.4	−.4	−1.0	1.1	—	.3	1.1	5.0	−.3	7.0	−4.4	....	Equity Securities	78bk *d*
−.3	−1.3	−.7	−.7	−.6	−.7	—	—	−.9	−.4	—	−15.8	−.3	−.7	....	Debt Securities	78bl *d*
.7	1.4	.7	1.0	1.3	4.4	2.6	—	.1	—	....	20.1	9.4	11.4	....	Portfolio Investment Liab., n.i.e.	78bg *d*
.7	1.4	.7	1.0	1.3	4.4	2.6	—	—	—	....	18.8	10.6	11.6	....	Equity Securities	78bm *d*
								.1	—	....	1.3	−1.2	−.2	....	Debt Securities	78bn *d*
....	....	....	....	....	....	....	....	....	....	20.6	.3	2.1	−.1	....	Financial Derivatives Assets	78bw *d*
											1.6	−7.0	−.2	....	Financial Derivatives Liabilities	78bx *d*
−16.1	−4.5	−42.2	−15.6	−72.3	25.2	7.5	.2	−3.2	−1.5	12.1	−19.2	−1.6	16.2	....	Other Investment Assets	78bh *d*
....	....	....	....	....	....	....	....	....	....	....	....	....	....	....	Monetary Authorities	78bo *d*
−9.4	−.1	−.1	−.5	−.3	−.2	−.1	—	—	—	....	−3.7	12.2	5.3	....	General Government	78bp *d*
2.9	11.1	−11.1	−20.4	−49.9	38.6	11.8	.2	—	—	....	4.6	....	−.7	....	Banks	78bq *d*
−9.6	−15.5	−30.9	5.3	−22.1	−13.2	−4.1	—	−3.2	−1.5	12.1	−20.1	−13.8	11.6	....	Other Sectors	78br *d*
30.5	24.5	−11.2	31.8	60.1	29.1	50.1	−24.0	−89.5	−55.2	−122.4	150.1	98.9	72.3	....	Other Investment Liab., n.i.e.	78bi *d*
											3.8	4.8	5.8	....	Monetary Authorities	78bs *d*
−22.2	4.6	−69.5	8.5	.2	−28.4	21.3	−53.3	−44.8	−19.3	−133.5	67.8	62.0	45.0	....	General Government	78bt *d*
5.2	7.2	8.7	−.3	−2.8	−11.3	2.4	10.4	−.7	−66.2	....	13.1	....	−6.4	....	Banks	78bu *d*
47.5	12.7	49.7	23.6	62.7	68.8	26.5	18.9	−44.0	30.3	11.0	65.4	32.0	28.0	....	Other Sectors	78bv *d*
−.7	−1.0	−25.1	9.4	26.1	−19.3	31.0	4.0	−2.1	−.2	−19.3	−27.9	−2.7	2.7	....	Net Errors and Omissions	78ca *d*
−3.1	−43.1	−130.4	−47.9	−27.6	−43.9	−48.1	−160.3	−189.6	−97.1	−194.0	−24.9	13.1	−17.2	....	*Overall Balance*	78cb *d*
3.1	43.1	130.4	47.9	27.6	43.9	48.1	160.3	189.6	97.1	194.0	24.9	−13.1	17.2	....	Reserves and Related Items	79da *d*
−32.6	10.9	52.0	3.5	−38.6	−29.5	−13.9	73.6	102.2	−7.7	−26.9	34.3	−26.2	8.8	....	Reserve Assets	79db *d*
4.5	7.4	−17.7	−2.8	−.7	5.3	−7.9	.6	−8.3	9.3	22.0	−11.4	3.4	3.0	....	Use of Fund Credit and Loans	79dc *d*
31.2	24.8	96.2	47.1	66.9	68.1	69.9	86.1	95.7	95.5	199.0	2.0	9.7	5.4	....	Exceptional Financing	79de *d*
Year Ending December 31															**Government Finance**	
−6,104	−16,644	−9,380	....	....	....	....	....	....	....	....	....	....	....		Deficit (-) or Surplus	80
107,212	104,880	99,492	....	....	....	....	....	....	....	....	....	....	....		Revenue	81
9,386	15,600	8,382	....	....	....	....	....	....	....	....	....	....	....		Grants Received	81z
122,702	137,121	117,144	....	....	....	....	....	....	....	....	....	....	....		Expenditure	82
—	3	110	....	....	....	....	....	....	....	....	....	....	....		Lending Minus Repayments	83
															Financing	
6,104	16,644	....	....	....	....	....	....	....	....	....	....	....	....		Total Financing	84
3,264	13	....	....	....	....	....	....	....	....	....	....	....	....		Net Borrowing: Domestic	84a
2,840	11,691	....	....	....	....	....	....	....	....	....	....	....	....		Foreign	85a
	4,940	....	....	....	....	....	....	....	....	....	....	....	....		Use of Cash Balances	87
6,412	4,213	....	....	....	....	....	....	....	....	....	....	....	....		Debt: Domestic	88a
293,683	283,430	280,615	308,066	....	....	....	....	....	....	....	....	....	....		Debt: Foreign	89a
Billions of Francs															**National Accounts**	
165.8	133.2	128.6	149.1	137.5	99.0	108.0	119.5	83.5	221.7	232.0	237.2	254.8	....	....	Exports of Goods & Services	90c
44.7	44.6	53.4	51.3	52.3	53.8	54.6	55.7	54.0	77.1	79.2	99.7	91.8	....	....	Government Consumption	91f
91.8	101.7	92.8	102.3	99.3	94.8	88.0	100.8	30.2	63.1	97.2	99.2	106.8	....	....	Gross Fixed Capital Formation	93e
−5.7	4.5	1.2	.1	.2	.3	2.0	4.8	1.8	17.6	14.9	5.0	7.0	....	....	Increase/Decrease(-) in Stocks	93i
235.4	258.8	262.5	266.8	288.0	298.6	283.9	330.8	298.3	438.1	564.0	606.8	685.7	....	....	Private Consumption	96f
−193.8	−177.5	−166.6	−168.0	−162.5	−118.9	−122.0	−168.1	−115.4	−272.5	−334.8	−305.9	−328.9	....	....	Imports of Goods & Services	98c
338.2	365.3	372.4	410.7	414.8	427.6	414.5	443.5	352.3	545.0	652.5	742.0	817.2	....	....	Gross Domestic Product (GDP)	99b
287.7	313.5	320.4	356.9	377.6	394.2	405.0	398.6	321.5	444.7	526.2	....	....		....	Net National Income	99e
....	....	....	....	....	....	....	....	....	....	....	....	....	....	....	GDP Volume 1970 prices	99b. *p*
192.3	199.7	203.5	216.7	226.7	227.8	226.5	214.5	175.0	209.0	223.5	245.2	255.6	252.3		GDP Volume 1978 Prices	99b. *p*
86.0	89.4	91.1	97.0	101.4	101.9	101.3	96.0	78.3	93.5	100.0	109.7	114.4	112.9	....	GDP Volume (1995=100)	99bv *p*
60.2	62.7	62.7	64.9	62.7	64.3	62.7	70.8	69.0	89.3	100.0	103.7	109.5	....	....	GDP Deflator (1995=100)	99bi *p*
Midyear Estimates																
3.03	3.12	3.22	3.32	3.41	3.51	3.62	3.73	3.84	3.93	4.06	4.17	4.28	4.40	4.51	**Population**	99z

(See notes in the back of the book.)

Tonga

		1970	1971	1972	1973	1974	1975	1976	1977	1978	1979	1980	1981	1982	1983	1984
Exchange Rates														*Pa'anga per SDR:*		
Official Rate	aa	.8969	.9116	.8515	.8107	.9226	.9312	1.0694	1.0642	1.1324	1.1916	1.0802	1.0320	1.1249	1.1607	1.1841
														Pa'anga per US Dollar:		
Official Rate	ae	.8969	.8396	.7843	.6720	.7536	.7955	.9205	.8761	.8692	.9046	.8470	.8866	1.0198	1.1086	1.2080
Official Rate	rf	.8929	.8806	.8192	.7041	.6958	.7639	.8183	.9018	.8737	.8946	.8782	.8702	.9859	1.1100	1.1395
Fund Position														*Millions of SDRs:*		
Quota	2f. s	...	...	...	...	...	...	...	...	...	...	...	...	...	...	...
SDRs	1b. s	...	...	...	...	...	...	...	...	...	...	...	...	...	...	...
Reserve Position in the Fund	1c. s	...	...	...	...	...	...	...	...	...	...	...	...	...	...	...
Total Fund Cred.&Loans Outstg.	2tl	...	...	...	...	...	...	...	...	...	...	...	...	...	...	...
International Liquidity													*Millions of US Dollars Unless Otherwise Indicated:*			
Total Reserves minus Gold	1l. d	...	...	...	...	...	...	...	9.00	10.12	12.56	13.75	13.98	15.56	20.95	26.02
SDRs	1b. d	...	...	...	...	...	...	...	...	...	...	...	...	...	...	...
Reserve Position in the Fund	1c. d	...	...	...	...	...	...	...	...	...	...	...	...	...	...	...
Foreign Exchange	1d. d	...	...	...	...	...	...	...	9.00	10.12	12.56	13.75	13.98	15.56	20.95	26.02
Monetary Authorities: Other Liab.	4.. d	...	...	...	...	...	...	...	...	...	...	...	...	...	...	...
Deposit Money Banks: Assets	7a. d	...	...	...	...	.09	.12	.15	.05	.05	.06	.11	.14	.22	.29	.35
Liabilities	7b. d	...	...	...	...	.01	.13	.07	.03	.23	.40	.33	.94	.46	.24	.22
Other Banking Insts.: Liabilities	7f. d	...	...	...	...	—	—	—	—	—	—	.04	.15	.41	.38	.55
Monetary Authorities														*Thousands of Pa'anga:*		
Foreign Assets	11	...	...	...	...	...	...	...	...	...	...	...	...	15,554	20,874	25,928
Claims on Central Government	12a	...	...	...	...	...	...	...	...	...	...	...	...	2,734	3,379	3,095
Claims on Other Banking Insts	12f	...	...	...	...	...	...	...	...	...	...	...	...			
Reserve Money	14	...	...	...	...	...	...	...	...	...	...	...	...	17,860	23,715	28,421
of which: Currency Outside DMBs	14a	...	...	...	...	...	...	...	...	...	...	...	...	2,505	3,168	3,404
Liabs. of Central Bank: Securities	16ac	...	...	...	...	—	—	—	—	—	—	—	—	—	—	—
Foreign Liabilities	16c	...	...	...	...											
Central Government Deposits	16d	...	...	...	...	377	367	335	430	382	435	427	357	409	469	513
Capital Accounts	17a	...	...	...	...	794	1,313	—	—	—	—	—	—	—	—	—
Other Items (Net)	17r	...	...	...	...	-451	-606	-574	-851	-1,050	-1,183	-74	-1,466	19	69	89
Deposit Money Banks														*Thousands of Pa'anga:*		
Reserves	20	...	...	...	...	5,710	2,894	4,039	8,373	7,685	10,064	11,576	12,309	13,849	19,493	23,963
Foreign Assets	21	...	...	...	...	71	97	136	44	43	52	93	122	221	322	425
Claims on Central Government	22a	...	...	...	...	—	518	—	—	—	200	200	431	431	431	431
Claims on Nonfin.Pub.Enterprises	22c	...	...	...	...											
Claims on Private Sector	22d	...	...	...	...	40	668	2,088	3,012	3,088	4,090	5,170	6,921	9,555	9,600	9,849
Claims on Other Banking Insts	22f	...	...	...	...	—	—	—	50	50	100	150	150	233	274	311
Demand Deposits	24	...	...	...	...	1,190	1,382	1,445	2,224	2,651	2,705	3,200	3,505	4,912	6,451	6,650
Time, Savings,& Fgn.Currency Dep.	25	...	...	...	...	2,324	2,381	3,497	5,860	6,038	7,084	8,140	8,226	8,928	10,035	11,870
Foreign Liabilities	26c	...	...	...	...	11	101	62	25	204	366	280	833	471	263	260
Central Government Deposits	26d	...	...	...	...	1,500	1,573	1,142	1,482	1,309	2,237	2,550	2,795	4,054	5,930	7,375
Capital Accounts	27a	...	...	...	...	794	1,313	1,861	2,223	3,065	4,457	5,487	6,526	7,964	8,993	10,333
Other Items (Net)	27r	...	...	...	...	2	-2,573	-1,744	-335	-2,401	-2,343	-2,468	-1,952	-2,040	-1,552	-1,509
Monetary Survey														*Thousands of Pa'anga:*		
Foreign Assets (Net)	31n	...	...	...	...	...	...	...	...	...	...	...	...	15,304	20,933	26,093
Domestic Credit	32	...	...	...	...	...	...	...	...	...	...	...	...	8,490	7,285	5,798
Claims on Central Govt. (Net)	32an	...	...	...	...	...	...	...	...	...	...	...	...	-1,298	-2,589	-4,362
Claims on Nonfin.Pub.Enterprises	32c	...	...	...	...											
Claims on Private Sector	32d	...	...	...	...	40	668	2,088	3,012	3,088	4,090	5,170	6,921	9,555	9,600	9,849
Claims on Other Banking Insts	32f	...	...	...	...	—	—	—	—	—	—	—	—	233	274	311
Money	34	...	...	...	...	1,190	1,382	1,445	2,224	2,651	2,705	3,200	3,505	7,417	9,619	10,054
Quasi-Money	35	...	...	...	...	2,324	2,381	3,497	5,860	6,038	7,084	8,140	8,226	8,928	10,035	11,870
Capital Accounts	37a	...	...	...	...	1,588	2,626	1,861	2,223	3,065	4,457	5,487	6,526	7,964	8,993	10,333
Other Items (Net)	37r	...	...	...	...	...	...	...	...	...	...	...	...	-515	-429	-366
Money plus Quasi-Money	35l	...	...	...	...	3,514	3,763	4,942	8,084	8,689	9,789	11,340	11,731	16,345	19,654	21,924
Other Banking Institutions														*Thousands of Pa'anga:*		
Reserves	40	...	...	...	...	...	...	...	—	46	497	555	—	1	422	341
Claims on Central Government	42a	...	...	...	...	...	...	...	—	—	—	—	—	—	—	—
Claims on Nonfin.Pub.Enterprises	42c	...	...	...	...	...	...	...	—	—	—	—	—	—	—	—
Claims on Private Sector	42d	...	...	...	...	...	...	...	196	706	1,398	2,135	3,043	4,031	4,391	5,880
Claims on Deposit Money Banks	42e	...	...	...	...	...	...	...	175	75	650	675	725	925	525	500
Bonds	46ab	...	...	...	...	...	...	...	—	—	—	—	—	—	—	—
Long-Term Foreign Liabilities	46cl	...	...	...	...	...	...	...	—	—	—	36	133	419	419	668
Central Government Deposits	46d	...	...	...	...	...	...	...	—	—	—	—	—	—	—	—
Central Govt. Lending Funds	46f	...	...	...	...	...	...	...	—	—	1,054	1,593	1,917	2,065	2,041	2,150
Credit from Monetary Authorities	46g	...	...	...	...	...	...	...	33	—	—	—	41	—	34	125
Credit from Deposit Money Banks	46h	...	...	...	...	...	...	...	—	—	—	—	—	—	250	225
Capital Accounts	47a	...	...	...	...	...	...	...	332	796	1,490	1,736	1,811	2,874	3,162	3,653
Other Items (Net)	47r	...	...	...	...	...	...	...	6	31	1	—	-134	-401	-568	-100
Banking Survey														*Thousands of Pa'anga:*		
Foreign Assets (Net)	51n	...	...	...	...	...	...	...	...	...	...	...	...	15,304	20,933	26,093
Domestic Credit	52	...	...	...	...	...	...	...	...	...	...	...	...	12,288	11,402	11,367
Claims on Central Govt. (Net)	52an	...	...	...	...	...	...	...	...	...	...	...	...	-1,298	-2,589	-4,362
Claims on Nonfin.Pub.Enterprises	52c	...	...	...	...	...	...	...	...	...	...	...	...	—	—	—
Claims on Private Sector	52d	...	...	...	...	...	...	...	3,208	3,794	5,488	7,305	9,964	13,586	13,991	15,729
Liquid Liabilities	55l	...	...	...	...	...	...	...	8,084	8,643	9,292	10,785	11,731	16,344	19,232	21,583
Bonds	56ab	...	...	...	...	...	...	...	—	—	—	—	—	—	—	—
Long-Term Foreign Liabilities	56cl	...	...	...	...	...	...	...	—	—	—	36	133	419	419	668
Central Govt. Lending Funds	56f	...	...	...	...	...	...	...	—	—	1,054	1,593	1,917	2,065	2,041	2,150
Capital Accounts	57a	...	...	...	...	...	...	...	2,555	3,861	5,947	7,223	8,337	10,838	12,155	13,986
Other Items (Net)	57r	...	...	...	...	...	...	...	1,364	2,252	5,302	...	8,010	-2,074	-1,512	-927
Interest Rates														*Percent Per Annum*		
Deposit Rate	60l	...	...	...	...	...	...	...	...	...	...	6.25	6.25	6.25	6.25	6.25
Lending Rate	60p	...	...	...	...	...	...	...	...	...	...	10.00	10.00	10.00	10.00	10.00

1985	1986	1987	1988	1989	1990	1991	1992	1993	1994	1995	1996	1997	1998	1999	
End of Period															**Exchange Rates**
1.6132	1.8399	1.9635	1.5748	1.6539	1.8435	1.9050	1.9116	1.8946	1.8371	1.8883	1.7438	1.8377	2.2749	2.2107	Official Rate ... **aa**
End of Period (ae) Period Average (rf)															
1.4686	1.5042	1.3841	1.1703	1.2585	1.2958	1.3317	1.3902	1.3793	1.2584	1.2703	1.2127	1.3620	1.6156	1.6107	Official Rate ... **ae**
1.4319	1.4960	1.4282	1.2750	1.2612	1.2800	1.2961	1.3471	1.3841	1.3202	1.2709	1.2323	1.2635	1.4921	1.5994	Official Rate ... **rf**
End of Period															**Fund Position**
3.25	3.25	3.25	3.25	3.25	3.25	3.25	5.00	5.00	5.00	5.00	5.00	5.00	5.00	6.90	Quota ... **2f.s**
—	.03	.05	.08	.12	.17	.74	.38	.44	.49	.04	.08	.11	.15	.03	SDRs ... **1b.s**
.74	.74	.74	.74	.74	.74	.74	1.18	1.19	1.20	1.21	1.21	1.21	1.22	1.70	Reserve Position in the Fund ... **1c.s**
—	—	—	—	—	—	—	—	—	—	—	—	—	—	—	Total Fund Cred.&Loans Outstg. ... **2tl**
End of Period															**International Liquidity**
27.51	22.48	28.88	30.51	24.85	31.34	32.28	31.77	37.06	35.54	28.71	30.62	27.49	28.66	26.15	Total Reserves minus Gold ... **1l.d**
—	.04	.07	.11	.16	.24	1.06	.52	.60	.71	.06	.11	.14	.21	.05	SDRs ... **1b.d**
.81	.91	1.05	1.00	.97	1.05	1.06	1.62	1.64	1.76	1.80	1.74	1.63	1.72	2.33	Reserve Position in the Fund ... **1c.d**
26.70	21.54	27.76	29.41	23.72	30.04	30.17	29.62	34.82	33.07	26.85	28.77	25.72	26.73	23.77	Foreign Exchange ... **1d.d**
—	—	—	—	—	.50	.35	.13	.58	.36	.24	.10	.11	.39	.18	Monetary Authorities: Other Liab. ... **4..d**
.29	.12	.12	.21	.26	1.69	.42	.33	1.54	1.84	1.96	1.39	1.61	4.27	2.88	Deposit Money Banks: Assets ... **7a.d**
.62	.74	.45	.54	.36	.48	.37	.47	.64	.94	1.22	.63	4.34	4.86	4.35	Liabilities ... **7b.d**
.67	.82	1.55	2.67	2.52	2.36	2.64	2.86	3.65	4.33	3.83	3.51	2.94	2.46	2.31	Other Banking Insts.: Liabilities ... **7f.d**
End of Period															**Monetary Authorities**
27,772	34,726	40,491	35,775	26,902	38,340	42,219	44,165	49,994	41,812	31,493	33,157	32,798	36,311	34,576	Foreign Assets ... **11**
2,730	3,374	3,760	4,184	5,336	13,121	10,407	10,432	11,236	9,516	5,493	5,439	5,439	5,456	5,404	Claims on Central Government ... **12a**
—	—	—	—	—	—	650	—	—	—	—	—	—	—	—	Claims on Other Banking Insts ... **12f**
29,986	37,127	42,879	38,532	28,419	47,067	48,418	51,698	19,226	18,368	15,125	21,629	24,300	26,805	28,804	Reserve Money ... **14**
3,569	4,474	4,892	5,503	5,971	6,767	7,165	7,127	7,894	7,346	7,321	6,850	6,471	8,076	9,443	*of which: Currency Outside DMBs* ... **14a**
—	—	—	—	—	—	—	—	42,590	39,200	29,367	24,893	21,818	15,963	13,471	Liabs. of Central Bank: Securities ... **16ac**
—	—	—	—	—	648	460	184	803	455	306	122	155	623	295	Foreign Liabilities ... **16c**
400	771	873	1,002	1,432	488	488	1,091	3,432	2,142	1,814	1,577	1,366	6,358	7,126	Central Government Deposits ... **16d**
—	—	—	—	1,001	2,786	3,659	2,725	2,789	2,922	3,000	2,459	1,676	1,146	1,039	Capital Accounts ... **17a**
116	202	499	425	1,386	472	251	-1,101	-7,610	-11,759	-12,626	-12,084	-11,078	-9,128	-10,757	Other Items (Net) ... **17r**
End of Period															**Deposit Money Banks**
25,417	31,653	37,987	33,029	39,635	40,300	41,253	42,000	48,582	46,688	35,000	39,252	38,006	33,857	33,572	Reserves ... **20**
420	178	168	242	326	2,194	557	457	2,125	2,314	2,491	1,682	2,189	6,893	4,644	Foreign Assets ... **21**
431	200	200	2,213	2,305	2,203	5,974	6,898	6,816	6,262	9,057	8,970	10,616	10,039	9,632	Claims on Central Government ... **22a**
—	—	—	832	2,092	1,437	1,188	413	55	152	103	497	164	1,551	1,392	Claims on Nonfin.Pub.Enterprises ... **22c**
15,330	16,783	23,957	28,756	33,555	33,271	32,730	31,051	31,351	47,273	57,191	59,114	68,094	79,720	87,420	Claims on Private Sector ... **22d**
311	350	350	350	350	350	350	350	350	3,850	2,450	1,550	2,375	2,000	3,000	Claims on Other Banking Insts ... **22f**
7,360	8,817	10,306	10,182	11,200	15,529	18,509	15,285	18,969	18,612	17,288	16,089	17,330	17,305	21,525	Demand Deposits ... **24**
16,632	19,489	23,959	22,523	23,725	27,017	29,557	30,173	34,715	44,862	46,652	54,702	59,488	69,484	75,511	Time, Savings,& Fgn.Currency Dep. ... **25**
909	1,118	620	632	450	628	493	654	879	1,181	1,545	760	5,909	7,850	7,007	Foreign Liabilities ... **26c**
6,427	7,339	11,543	13,584	12,415	16,413	10,931	10,382	12,324	15,335	13,599	11,171	9,215	8,135	8,530	Central Government Deposits ... **26d**
12,200	15,342	19,515	21,290	22,843	26,731	27,627	32,559	30,758	36,560	38,275	38,264	37,889	39,919	36,738	Capital Accounts ... **27a**
-1,619	-2,941	-3,281	-2,789	7,630	-6,563	-5,065	-7,884	-8,366	-10,011	-11,067	-9,921	-8,387	-8,633	-9,651	Other Items (Net) ... **27r**
End of Period															**Monetary Survey**
27,283	33,786	40,039	35,385	26,778	39,258	41,823	43,784	50,437	42,490	32,133	33,957	28,923	34,731	31,917	Foreign Assets (Net) ... **31n**
11,975	12,597	15,851	21,749	29,791	33,481	39,880	37,671	34,052	49,576	58,881	62,822	76,107	84,273	91,192	Domestic Credit ... **32**
-3,666	-4,536	-8,456	-8,189	-6,206	-1,577	4,962	5,857	2,296	-1,699	-863	1,661	5,474	1,002	-620	Claims on Central Govt. (Net) ... **32an**
—	—	—	832	2,092	1,437	1,188	413	55	152	103	497	164	1,551	1,392	Claims on Nonfin.Pub.Enterprises ... **32c**
15,330	16,783	23,957	28,756	33,555	33,271	32,730	31,051	31,351	47,273	57,191	59,114	68,094	79,720	87,420	Claims on Private Sector ... **32d**
311	350	350	350	350	350	1,000	350	350	3,850	2,450	1,550	2,375	2,000	3,000	Claims on Other Banking Insts ... **32f**
10,929	13,291	15,198	15,685	17,171	22,296	25,674	22,412	27,016	27,510	24,609	23,214	23,801	25,381	30,968	Money ... **34**
16,632	19,489	23,959	22,523	23,725	27,017	29,557	30,173	34,715	44,862	46,652	54,702	59,488	69,484	75,511	Quasi-Money ... **35**
12,200	15,342	19,515	21,290	23,844	29,517	31,286	35,284	33,547	39,482	41,275	40,723	39,565	41,065	37,777	Capital Accounts ... **37a**
-503	-1,739	-2,782	-2,364	-8,171	-6,091	-4,814	-6,414	-10,789	-19,788	-21,522	-21,860	-17,824	-16,926	-21,147	Other Items (Net) ... **37r**
27,561	32,780	39,157	38,208	40,896	49,313	55,231	52,585	61,731	72,372	71,261	77,916	83,289	94,865	106,479	Money plus Quasi-Money ... **35l**
End of Period															**Other Banking Institutions**
338	360	292	157	100	2,141	4,302	2,997	4,277	6,695	4,290	834	475	1,247	1,734	Reserves ... **40**
—	—	—	—	100	100	1,164	1,553	1,651	2,000	2,000	1,700	1,700	1,700	2,000	Claims on Central Government ... **42a**
—	—	—	—	—	—	636	574	926	3,647	2,937	2,940	1,452	987	834	Claims on Nonfin.Pub.Enterprises ... **42c**
6,551	8,441	10,370	16,474	18,749	22,187	22,278	24,569	29,380	31,176	37,063	38,270	41,669	41,055	31,939	Claims on Private Sector ... **42d**
950	790	2,100	500	200	800	450	100	—	3,200	100	3,578	3,600	2,800	4,100	Claims on Deposit Money Banks ... **42e**
—	—	—	—	—	—	—	—	2,476	9,189	1,823	2,005	3,908	4,604	5,022	Bonds ... **46ab**
977	1,235	2,144	3,125	3,169	3,052	3,516	3,973	5,040	5,444	4,863	4,256	4,008	3,976	3,728	Long-Term Foreign Liabilities ... **46cl**
6	—	—	—	—	—	—	—	—	—	3,600	3,600	3,600	3,600	2,000	Central Government Deposits ... **46d**
2,362	2,957	3,536	6,092	7,825	11,219	12,485	14,029	14,597	15,761	16,155	17,411	16,743	15,950	14,552	Central Govt. Lending Funds ... **46f**
—	3	—	—	59	—	650	—	—	—	—	—	—	—	—	Credit from Monetary Authorities ... **46g**
200	175	347	307	269	226	169	—	—	—	2,100	1,200	2,200	2,000	2,000	Credit from Deposit Money Banks ... **46h**
4,149	4,825	6,218	7,235	8,936	10,681	12,980	15,514	16,643	17,703	19,828	21,356	22,074	22,391	19,874	Capital Accounts ... **47a**
145	396	517	372	-1,109	50	-970	-3,723	-2,522	-1,379	-1,979	-2,506	-3,637	-4,732	-6,569	Other Items (Net) ... **47r**
End of Period															**Banking Survey**
27,283	33,786	40,039	35,385	26,778	39,258	41,823	43,784	50,437	42,490	32,133	33,957	28,923	34,731	31,917	Foreign Assets (Net) ... **51n**
18,209	20,688	25,871	37,873	48,290	55,418	62,958	64,017	65,659	82,549	94,831	100,582	114,953	122,415	120,965	Domestic Credit ... **52**
-3,672	-4,536	-8,456	-8,189	-6,106	-1,477	6,126	7,410	3,947	301	-2,463	-239	3,574	-898	-620	Claims on Central Govt. (Net) ... **52an**
—	—	—	832	2,092	1,437	1,824	987	981	3,799	3,040	3,437	1,616	2,538	2,226	Claims on Nonfin.Pub.Enterprises ... **52c**
21,881	25,224	34,327	45,230	52,304	55,458	55,008	55,620	60,731	78,449	94,254	97,384	109,763	120,775	119,359	Claims on Private Sector ... **52d**
27,223	32,420	38,865	38,051	40,796	47,172	50,929	49,588	57,454	65,677	66,971	77,082	82,814	93,618	104,745	Liquid Liabilities ... **55l**
—	—	—	—	—	—	—	—	2,476	9,189	1,823	2,005	3,908	4,604	5,022	Bonds ... **56ab**
977	1,235	2,144	3,125	3,169	3,052	3,516	3,973	5,040	5,444	4,863	4,256	4,008	3,976	3,728	Long-Term Foreign Liabilities ... **56cl**
2,362	2,957	3,536	6,092	7,825	11,219	12,485	14,029	14,597	15,761	16,155	17,411	16,743	15,950	14,552	Central Govt. Lending Funds ... **56f**
16,349	20,167	25,733	28,525	32,780	40,198	44,266	50,798	50,190	57,185	61,103	62,079	61,639	63,456	57,651	Capital Accounts ... **57a**
-1,419	-2,305	-4,368	-2,535	-9,502	-6,965	-6,415	-10,587	-13,661	-28,217	-23,951	-28,294	-25,236	-24,458	-32,816	Other Items (Net) ... **57r**
Percent Per Annum															**Interest Rates**
6.25	6.25	6.25	6.25	7.25	7.25	7.25	4.25	4.25	4.67	4.75	5.58	5.50	5.50	5.42	Deposit Rate ... **60l**
10.00	10.00	10.00	10.00	13.50	13.50	13.50	13.50	9.94	9.39	9.71	10.49	10.10	10.46	10.32	Lending Rate ... **60p**

Tonga

866

Prices — *Index Numbers (1995=100):*

		1970	1971	1972	1973	1974	1975	1976	1977	1978	1979	1980	1981	1982	1983	1984
Consumer Prices	64	....	....	....	....	....	17.4	18.6	21.9	24.0	25.3	31.0	35.6	39.5	43.3	¥43.4
International Transactions														*Thousands of Pa'anga*		
Exports	70	2,745	2,299	2,140	3,277	4,754	4,629	3,358	6,505	5,078	6,879	6,659	7,706	4,301	6,455	10,439
Imports, c.i.f.	71	5,539	6,305	7,456	7,997	11,819	12,972	11,655	17,698	22,317	26,210	33,134	35,002	41,198	41,664	46,315
Balance of Payments														*Thousands of US Dollars:*		
Current Account, n.i.e.	78al d	....	−623	−1,522	−1,355	785	234	−2,027	−1,983	−2,663	−1,539	−6,796	−5,921	7,091	526	−4,833
Goods: Exports f.o.b.	78aa d		2,699	2,961	3,543	4,863	7,434	4,382	4,123	5,974	6,254	7,781	8,878	4,785	5,799	8,318
Goods: Imports f.o.b.	78ab d		−5,225	−6,820	−8,243	−10,801	−18,277	−15,699	−14,840	−21,465	−24,562	−33,486	−41,541	−35,498	−33,577	−34,959
Trade Balance	78ac d		−2,526	−3,859	−4,700	−5,938	−10,842	−11,316	−10,717	−15,491	−18,308	−25,705	−32,663	−30,713	−27,778	−26,641
Services: Credit	78ad d		1,023	1,440	1,970	3,461	7,603	4,661	5,367	6,531	5,686	9,159	9,831	9,488	10,352	13,547
Services: Debit	78ae d		−925	−1,403	−1,493	−1,926	−3,952	−2,926	−3,665	−4,783	−2,899	−5,584	−6,032	−7,594	−9,474	−12,813
Balance on Goods & Services	78af d		−2,428	−3,821	−4,222	−4,403	−7,191	−9,581	−9,015	−13,743	−15,522	−22,131	−28,864	−28,819	−26,900	−25,908
Income: Credit	78ag d		268	455	266	332	353	655	676	1,609	2,883	2,029	4,517	5,219	3,211	2,389
Income: Debit	78ah d		−19	−32	−72	−145	−60	−219	−340	−224	−392	−478	−556	−908	−118	−139
Balance on Gds, Serv. & Inc.	78ai d		−2,179	−3,397	−4,029	−4,216	−6,898	−9,145	−8,679	−12,358	−13,032	−20,580	−24,903	−24,509	−23,807	−23,658
Current Transfers, n.i.e.: Credit	78aj d		1,852	2,129	3,126	5,402	7,613	8,100	8,138	10,347	12,410	15,465	21,638	35,209	30,431	21,995
Current Transfers: Debit	78ak d		−296	−254	−452	−401	−480	−983	−1,442	−652	−918	−1,681	−2,656	−3,610	−6,098	−3,170
Capital Account, n.i.e.	78bc d		82	95	570	147	98	79	61	—	—	—	—	−453	−137	1,114
Capital Account, n.i.e.: Credit	78ba d		101	120	642	203	149	134	135	—	—	—	—	151	848	1,624
Capital Account: Debit	78bb d		−19	−24	−72	−56	−51	−55	−74	—	—	—	—	−604	−986	−510
Financial Account, n.i.e.	78bj d	....	1,297	801	1,193	251	2,262	2,034	1,467	3,815	4,260	8,281	6,758	93	3,239	8,570
Direct Investment Abroad	78bd d	....	—	—	—	—	—	—	—	—	—	—	—	—	—	—
Dir. Invest. in Rep. Econ., n.i.e.	78be d	....	—	—	—	—	—	—	—	—	—	—	—	—	—	21
Portfolio Investment Assets	78bf d	....	—	—	—	—	—	—	—	—	—	—	—	—	—	—
Equity Securities	78bk d	....	—	—	—	—	—	—	—	—	—	—	—	—	—	—
Debt Securities	78bl d	....	—	—	—	—	—	—	—	—	—	—	—	—	—	—
Portfolio Investment Liab., n.i.e.	78bg d	....	—	—	—	—	—	—	—	—	—	—	—	—	—	—
Equity Securities	78bm d	....	—	—	—	—	—	—	—	—	—	—	—	—	—	—
Debt Securities	78bn d	....	—	—	—	—	—	—	—	—	—	—	—	—	—	—
Financial Derivatives Assets	78bw d	....	....	....	....	....	....	....	....	....	....	....	....	....	....	....
Financial Derivatives Liabilities	78bx d	....	....	....	....	....	....	....	....	....	....	....	....	....	....	....
Other Investment Assets	78bh d	....	....	....	....	....	....	....	....	....	....	....	....	....	....	....
Monetary Authorities	78bo d	....	....	....	....	....	....	....	....	....	....	....	....	....	....	....
General Government	78bp d	....	....	....	....	....	....	....	....	....	....	....	....	....	....	....
Banks	78bq d	....	....	....	....	....	....	....	....	....	....	....	....	....	....	....
Other Sectors	78br d	....	....	....	....	....	....	....	....	....	....	....	....	....	....	....
Other Investment Liab., n.i.e.	78bi d	....	1,297	801	1,193	251	2,262	2,034	1,467	3,815	4,260	8,281	6,758	93	3,239	8,549
Monetary Authorities	78bs d		—	—	—	—	—	—	—	—	—	—	—	—	—	166
General Government	78bt d		1,297	801	1,193	251	2,262	2,034	1,467	2,107	2,298	1,395	4,812	3,221	−132	216
Banks	78bu d		—	—	—	—	—	—	—	1,398	1,825	6,012	821	533	3,367	7,904
Other Sectors	78bv d		—	—	—	—	—	—	—	311	137	874	1,124	−3,661	4	264
Net Errors and Omissions	78ca d	....	−727	367	−445	550	−613	−2,409	2,798	−36	−278	−291	−610	−5,151	1,765	212
Overall Balance	78cb d	....	28	−259	−37	1,733	1,982	−2,323	2,343	1,116	2,443	1,194	226	1,580	5,393	5,064
Reserves and Related Items	79da d	....	−28	259	37	−1,733	−1,982	2,323	−2,343	−1,116	−2,443	−1,194	−226	−1,580	−5,393	−5,064
Reserve Assets	79db d	....	−28	259	37	−1,733	−1,982	2,323	−2,343	−1,116	−2,443	−1,194	−226	−1,580	−5,393	−5,064
Use of Fund Credit and Loans	79dc d	....	—	—	—	—	—	—	—	—	—	—	—	—	—	—
Exceptional Financing	79de d	....	....	....	....	....	....	....	....	....	....	....	....	....	—	....
Government Finance														*Thousands of Pa'anga*		
Deficit (-) or Surplus	80	....	....	....	....	....	....	....	....	....	....	....	....	−1,524	1,061	324
Revenue	81	....	....	....	....	....	....	....	....	....	....	....	....	15,529	18,054	17,786
Grants Received	81z	....	....	....	....	....	....	....	....	....	....	....	....	10,658	7,422	9,616
Expenditure	82	....	....	....	....	....	....	....	....	....	....	....	....	26,178	23,698	26,239
Lending Minus Repayments	83	....	....	....	....	....	....	....	....	....	....	....	....	1,533	717	839
Financing																
Domestic	84a	....	....	....	....	....	....	....	....	....	....	....	—	1,026	−1,824	−757
Foreign	85a	....	....	....	....	....	....	....	....	....	....	....	—	498	763	433
National Accounts														*Millions of Pa'anga:*		
Gross Domestic Product (GDP)	99b	....	....	....	....	....	24.83	24.58	30.79	36.32	39.94	52.88	66.39	79.69	86.28	74.48
GDP Volume (1990=100)	99bv p	....	....	....	....	....	33.1	33.3	34.9	35.6	36.3	42.0	47.9	55.0	58.2	83.8
GDP Deflator (1990=100)	99bi p	....	....	....	....	....	47.4	46.5	55.6	64.4	69.5	79.5	87.5	91.6	93.7	56.1
																Millions:
Population	99z	.08	.08	.08	.09	.09	.09	.09	.09	.09	.09	.09	.09	.09	.10	.10

	1985	1986	1987	1988	1989	1990	1991	1992	1993	1994	1995	1996	1997	1998	1999		
Period Averages																**Prices**	
	50.6	61.6	64.5	70.9	73.8	81.0	89.5	96.7	97.6	98.6	‡100.0	103.0	105.2	108.6	113.5	Consumer Prices	64
																International Transactions	
Thousands of Pa'anga																	
	7,785	9,484	9,552	10,555	12,298	15,299	17,988	17,402	23,430	18,367	18,443	13,573	....	....	....	Exports	70
	58,928	60,823	68,459	70,689	68,336	78,991	76,817	84,294	84,933	91,210	98,034	91,807	....	....	....	Imports, c.i.f.	71
Minus Sign Indicates Debit																Balance of Payments	
	1,609	2,441	1,544	−12,743	7,435	5,795	−74	−468	−5,928	....	....	....			....	Current Account, n.i.e.	78al *d*
	5,554	6,323	6,883	8,722	9,395	11,912	13,437	12,306	16,082	....	....	....			....	Goods: Exports f.o.b.	78aa *d*
	−30,488	−32,579	−38,749	−48,592	−49,728	−50,769	−49,452	−51,301	−56,606	....	....	....			....	Goods: Imports f.o.b.	78ab *d*
	−24,934	−26,256	−31,865	−39,870	−40,333	−38,857	−36,015	−38,995	−40,524							*Trade Balance*	78ac *d*
	15,654	15,309	19,772	17,192	27,067	26,363	20,370	16,623	15,953							Services: Credit	78ad *d*
	−15,594	−16,627	−18,542	−25,719	−21,037	−23,351	−22,445	−22,246	−21,145							Services: Debit	78ae *d*
	−24,874	−27,573	−30,636	−48,397	−34,304	−35,845	−38,089	−44,619	−45,716							*Balance on Goods & Services*	78af *d*
	2,953	3,987	5,388	4,876	3,911	5,180	3,560	4,244	5,557							Income: Credit	78ag *d*
	−416	−122	−1,571	−1,275	−1,145	−893	−1,059	−1,211	−2,383							Income: Debit	78ah *d*
	−22,337	−23,707	−26,819	−44,795	−31,538	−31,558	−35,588	−41,586	−42,542							*Balance on Gds, Serv. & Inc.*	78ai *d*
	26,403	28,743	33,489	36,930	44,063	43,528	41,774	50,552	49,740							Current Transfers, n.i.e.: Credit	78aj *d*
	−2,458	−2,594	−5,126	−4,877	−5,089	−6,176	−6,259	−9,434	−13,125							Current Transfers: Debit	78ak *d*
	289	1,030	−89	34	−238	−115	127	557	605	....	....	....			....	Capital Account, n.i.e.	78bc *d*
	578	1,677	520	124	138	241	485	732	1,340							Capital Account, n.i.e.: Credit	78ba *d*
	−290	−647	−610	−90	−376	−356	−358	−176	−735							Capital Account: Debit	78bb *d*
	−1,066	−1,585	1,659	4,405	−8,203	−1,733	2,984	4,421	3,189	....	....	....			....	Financial Account, n.i.e.	78bj *d*
	—	—	—	—	—	−1	−24	−2	−1							Direct Investment Abroad	78bd *d*
	130	178	49	29	174	198	359	1,224	2,178							Dir. Invest. in Rep. Econ., n.i.e.	78be *d*
	—	—	—	—	1	32	128	—	—							Portfolio Investment Assets	78bk *d*
	—	—	—	—	1	32	128	—	—							Equity Securities	78bl *d*
	—	—	—	—	—	—	—	—	—							Debt Securities	78bl *d*
	22	4	—	−82	−9,392	−8,162	−2,381	−141	−64							Portfolio Investment Liab., n.i.e.	78bg *d*
	—	4	—	−82	−8	−89	−19	−33	—							Equity Securities	78bm *d*
	22	—	—	—	−9,384	−8,073	−2,361	−109	−64							Debt Securities	78bn *d*
																Financial Derivatives Assets	78bw *d*
	....	....	....	....	....	....	....	....		....	....	....			....	Financial Derivatives Liabilities	78bx *d*
	−2	−22	−222	755	727	4,787	4,768	815	—							Other Investment Assets	78bh *d*
																Monetary Authorities	78bo *d*
	−2	−22	−222	755	723	3,611	1,235	812	—							General Government	78bp *d*
	—	—	—	—	—	—	62	—	—							Banks	78bq *d*
	—	—	—	—	4	1,176	3,471	4	—							Other Sectors	78br *d*
	−1,216	−1,745	1,832	3,703	287	1,412	134	2,525	1,076							Other Investment Liab., n.i.e.	78bi *d*
	—	—	—	−285	—	−363	−80	−68	−14							Monetary Authorities	78bs *d*
	678	208	634	2,625	1,612	248	−725	3,095	1,095							General Government	78bt *d*
	−3,489	−856	515	511	411	1,750	134	−208	—							Banks	78bu *d*
	1,595	−1,096	683	851	−1,735	−222	805	−294	−4							Other Sectors	78bv *d*
	655	−7,008	3,133	9,992	−4,628	2,443	−2,144	−3,437	−260	....	....	....			....	Net Errors and Omissions	78ca *d*
	1,486	−5,121	6,246	1,688	−5,634	6,390	893	1,072	−2,393							*Overall Balance*	78cb *d*
	−1,486	5,121	−6,246	−1,688	5,634	−6,390	−893	−1,072	2,393	....	....	....			....	Reserves and Related Items	79da *d*
	−1,486	5,121	−6,246	−1,688	5,634	−6,390	−893	−1,072	2,393							Reserve Assets	79db *d*
	—	—	—	—	—	—	—	—	—							Use of Fund Credit and Loans	79dc *d*
	....	....	....	....	....	....	....	....	—	....	....	....			....	Exceptional Financing	79de *d*
Year Ending June 30																**Government Finance**	
	−2,104	−4,781	−6,693	622	−64	−1,893 [P]	−10,051 [f]	....	....						....	Deficit (−) or Surplus	80
	22,204	26,218	29,210	33,750	32,740	39,806 [P]	51,686 [f]	....							....	Revenue	81
	18,668	8,431	15,585	16,278	23,778	29,384 [P]	51,530 [f]	....							....	Grants Received	81z
	37,983	37,923	42,425	43,985	54,150	68,862 [P]	99,175 [f]	....							....	Expenditure	82
	4,993	1,507	9,063	5,421	2,432	2,221 [P]	14,092 [f]	....							....	Lending Minus Repayments	83
																Financing	
	979	3,301	−805	−622	64	293 [P]	2,717 [f]	....							....	Domestic	84a
	1,125	1,480	7,498	—	—	1,600 [P]	7,334 [f]	....							....	Foreign	85a
Year Ending June 30																**National Accounts**	
	80.01	100.03	114.84	141.30	146.00	158.40	193.20	198.20	201.00	214.80					....	Gross Domestic Product (GDP)	99b
	88.5	96.3	97.9	94.5	95.5	100.0	105.9	101.9	101.8	106.7	....	....			....	GDP Volume (1990=100)	99bv *p*
	57.1	65.6	74.1	94.4	96.5	100.0	115.1	122.8	124.6	127.1	....	....			....	GDP Deflator (1990=100)	99bi *p*
Midyear Estimates																	
	.10	.09	.09	.09	.10	.10	.10	.10	.10	.10	.10	.10	.10	.10	.10	**Population**	99z

(See notes in the back of the book.)

Trinidad and Tobago

		1970	1971	1972	1973	1974	1975	1976	1977	1978	1979	1980	1981	1982	1983	1984
Exchange Rates														*TT Dollars per SDR:*		
Market Rate	aa	2.0053	2.0417	2.2194	2.4924	2.5024	2.7769	2.7884	2.9153	3.1267	3.1616	3.0610	2.7935	2.6475	2.5127	2.3525
														TT Dollars per US Dollar:		
Market Rate	ae	2.0053	1.8805	2.0442	2.0661	2.0439	2.3721	2.4000	2.4000	2.4000	2.4000	2.4000	2.4000	2.4000	2.4000	2.4000
Market Rate	rf	2.0000	1.9749	1.9213	1.9592	2.0532	2.1698	2.4358	2.4000	2.4000	2.4000	2.4000	2.4000	2.4000	2.4000	2.4000
														Index Numbers (1995=100):		
Nominal Effective Exchange Rate	ne c	....	....	....						....	162.87	161.07	170.82	181.48	188.34	200.29
Real Effective Exchange Rate	re c	....	....	....						....	114.02	116.94	128.64	142.57	163.32	187.54
Fund Position														*Millions of SDRs:*		
Quota	2f. s	63.0	63.0	63.0	63.0	63.0	63.0	63.0	63.0	82.0	82.0	123.0	123.0	123.0	170.1	170.1
SDRs	1b. s	.5	7.2	7.3	7.1	7.9	7.6	7.6	12.2	16.9	31.2	35.8	51.3	73.5	94.4	103.1
Reserve Position in the Fund	1c. s	6.6	6.6	6.6	—	4.8	18.7	27.8	27.6	29.8	37.8	63.0	78.3	96.7	118.6	126.8
of which: Outstg.Fund Borrowing	2c	—	—	—	—	—	2.9	10.0	10.0	10.0	7.9	5.4	2.9	.4	—	—
Total Fund Cred.&Loans Outstg.	2tl	—	—	—	—	—									—	—
International Liquidity											*Millions of US Dollars Unless Otherwise Indicated:*					
Total Reserves minus Gold	1l. d	43.0	69.4	58.3	47.0	390.3	751.0	1,013.5	1,481.7	1,804.8	2,140.0	2,780.8	3,347.5	3,080.5	2,104.5	1,356.7
SDRs	1b. d	.5	7.8	7.9	8.6	9.6	8.9	8.8	14.8	22.0	41.1	45.7	59.7	81.0	98.9	101.1
Reserve Position in the Fund	1c. d	6.6	7.1	7.1	—	5.8	21.9	32.2	33.5	38.8	49.7	80.3	91.1	106.7	124.2	124.3
Foreign Exchange	1d. d	35.9	54.4	43.2	38.4	374.9	720.2	972.5	1,433.4	1,744.0	2,049.2	2,654.8	3,196.7	2,892.8	1,881.5	1,131.3
Gold (Million Fine Troy Ounces)	1ad	....	....	....	....	....	....	.027	.040	.054	.054	.054	.054	.054	.054	.054
Gold (National Valuation)	1an d	....	....	....	....	....	....	1.1	1.7	2.3	2.3	2.3	2.3	2.3	2.3	2.3
Monetary Authorities: Other Liab.	4.. d															
Deposit Money Banks: Assets	7a. d	3.9	11.9	3.4	3.8	3.4	3.6	5.9	12.9	19.1	41.1	48.0	49.6	63.8	50.3	56.3
Liabilities	7b. d	7.7	13.6	15.3	25.0	19.3	23.2	21.3	34.6	57.5	47.9	76.1	86.9	104.5	119.1	141.1
Other Banking Insts.: Assets	7e. d	.7	.8	.8	.8	1.0	3.3	2.3	2.8	2.4	2.5	2.4	2.4	2.4	2.2	3.8
Liabilities	7f. d	....	....	....	....	....	4.8	5.1	5.5	4.7	10.2	10.6	14.3	15.9	17.8	28.4
Monetary Authorities														*Millions of TT Dollars:*		
Foreign Assets	11	85.8	136.5	106.7	97.5	796.2	1,778.8	2,461.8	3,586.7	4,363.5	5,163.5	6,694.7	8,064.1	7,410.4	5,087.1	3,322.5
Claims on Central Government	12a	20.7	—	38.9	58.0	.8	.5	.2				45.0	24.6	26.5	31.9	131.5
Claims on Nonfin.Pub.Enterprises	12c	22.8	23.2	13.4	19.2	19.8	11.1	11.0	24.6	33.5	17.6	40.7	20.8	12.3	45.1	42.1
Claims on Private Sector	12d															
Claims on Deposit Money Banks	12e	—	....	1.7	3.0	.1					....	....	....	....	—	53.8
Claims on Other Banking Insts	12f	—	—	—	—	—									—	
Claims on Nonbank Financial Insts	12g	....	....													
Reserve Money	14	91.6	119.7	131.4	151.8	303.2	478.8	639.2	664.4	695.6	1,225.6	1,335.8	1,637.4	2,631.9	2,488.1	2,291.2
of which: Currency Outside DMBs	14a	56.5	68.4	81.2	79.7	98.5	138.2	177.2	230.9	295.5	412.1	467.2	532.2	725.9	758.1	709.7
Foreign Liabilities	16c															
Central Government Deposits	16d	24.8	16.4	−3.4	−15.2	460.1	1,202.7	1,694.8	2,891.1	3,436.6	3,609.7	5,020.6	5,748.5	3,786.3	2,137.7	1,101.1
Capital Accounts	17a	29.8	43.7	55.0	64.7	88.3	283.1	263.9	257.7	433.5	747.6	884.3	1,320.9	1,629.9	1,708.5	824.0
Other Items (Net)	17r	−16.8	−20.1	−22.3	−23.6	−34.6	−174.1	−124.9	−201.9	−168.7	−401.7	−460.3	−597.3	−598.8	−1,170.2	−666.3
Deposit Money Banks														*Millions of TT Dollars:*		
Reserves	20	35.1	51.3	50.2	72.1	204.7	340.6	462.0	433.6	400.1	813.7	868.6	1,070.0	1,856.8	1,629.2	1,497.2
Foreign Assets	21	7.8	21.9	6.3	7.9	7.0	8.5	14.1	31.0	45.8	98.7	115.2	119.0	153.1	120.8	135.2
Claims on Central Government	22a	61.9	119.6	115.0	147.0	168.8	158.7	157.3	172.9	213.8	276.3	399.9	491.0	707.2	1,072.4	570.6
Claims on Local Government	22b	.1	.1	—	1.3	.6	1.4	5.1	7.2	12.0	8.0	5.7	5.1	33.5	3.5	32.2
Claims on Nonfin.Pub.Enterprises	22c	—		10.5	9.0	8.4	5.0	1.7				44.9	235.7	340.6	520.8	596.7
Claims on Private Sector	22d	330.4	361.5	502.7	585.5	665.7	888.1	1,247.6	1,761.7	2,341.0	2,745.5	3,310.3	4,058.4	4,893.8	5,671.5	6,075.2
Claims on Other Banking Insts	22f	....	....	....	....	....	....							....	....	
Claims on Nonbank Financial Insts	22g	....	....											....		
Demand Deposits	24	94.9	108.4	129.9	132.9	171.4	254.2	394.6	494.4	640.8	734.6	869.8	1,287.4	1,772.2	1,575.6	1,500.3
Time, Savings,& Fgn.Currency Dep.	25	337.2	429.1	511.8	610.2	802.7	995.9	1,291.5	1,634.5	2,004.9	2,669.0	2,960.9	3,637.4	4,847.7	5,499.3	6,048.1
Foreign Liabilities	26c	15.4	25.1	28.2	51.7	39.5	55.1	51.1	83.0	138.0	114.9	182.7	208.5	250.9	285.9	338.7
Central Government Deposits	26d	12.1	13.5	19.1	19.0	35.5	58.8	66.2	79.1	86.3	194.8	281.5	374.3	452.2	507.2	233.3
Credit from Monetary Authorities	26g	—	—	1.7	3.0	—	—	—	—	—	—	—	—	—	—	19.0
Liabilities to Other Banking Insts	26i	....	....											....		
Capital Accounts	27a	5.1	6.4	30.0	41.8	51.5	74.2	110.0	139.3	192.0	262.0	361.4	411.7	531.2	636.6	781.4
Other Items (Net)	27r	−29.4	−28.1	−36.0	−35.8	−45.4	−35.9	−25.6	−23.9	−49.3	−33.1	88.3	59.9	130.8	513.6	−13.7
Monetary Survey														*Millions of TT Dollars:*		
Foreign Assets (Net)	31n	78.2	133.3	84.8	53.7	763.7	1,732.2	2,424.8	3,534.7	4,271.3	5,147.3	6,627.2	7,974.6	7,312.6	4,922.0	3,119.0
Domestic Credit	32	399.0	474.5	664.8	816.2	368.5	−196.7	−338.1	−1,003.8	−922.6	−757.1	−1,455.6	−1,287.2	1,775.4	4,700.3	6,113.9
Claims on Central Govt. (Net)	32an	45.7	89.7	138.2	201.2	−326.0	−1,102.3	−1,603.5	−2,797.3	−3,309.1	−3,528.2	−4,857.2	−5,607.2	−3,504.8	−1,540.6	−632.3
Claims on Local Government	32b	.1	.1	—	1.3	.6	1.4	5.1	7.2	12.0	8.0	5.7	5.1	33.5	3.5	32.2
Claims on Nonfin.Pub.Enterprises	32c	22.8	23.2	23.9	28.2	28.2	16.1	12.7	24.6	33.5	17.6	85.6	256.5	352.9	565.9	638.8
Claims on Private Sector	32d	330.4	361.5	502.7	585.5	665.7	888.1	1,247.6	1,761.7	2,341.0	2,745.5	3,310.3	4,058.4	4,893.8	5,671.5	6,075.2
Claims on Other Banking Insts	32f	....	....	....	....	....	....							....	....	
Claims on Nonbank Financial Inst	32g	....	....	....	....	....								....		
Money	34	151.4	176.8	211.1	212.6	269.9	392.4	571.8	725.3	936.3	1,146.7	1,337.0	1,854.7	2,547.2	2,434.5	2,294.0
Quasi-Money	35	337.2	429.1	511.8	610.2	802.7	995.9	1,291.5	1,634.5	2,004.9	2,669.0	2,960.9	3,637.4	4,847.7	5,499.3	6,048.1
Liabilities to Other Banking Insts	36i	....	....	....	....	....								....		
Capital Accounts	37a	34.9	50.1	85.0	106.5	139.8	357.3	373.9	397.0	625.5	1,009.6	1,245.7	1,732.6	2,161.1	2,345.1	1,605.4
Other Items (Net)	37r	−46.2	−48.2	−58.3	−59.4	−80.1	−210.0	−150.5	−225.9	−218.0	−435.0	−372.0	−537.3	−467.9	−656.6	−714.5
Money plus Quasi-Money	35l	488.6	605.9	722.9	822.8	1,072.6	1,388.3	1,863.3	2,359.8	2,941.2	3,815.7	4,297.9	5,492.1	7,394.9	7,933.8	8,342.1

1985	1986	1987	1988	1989	1990	1991	1992	1993	1994	1995	1996	1997	1998	1999		
End of Period															**Exchange Rates**	
3.9543	4.4035	5.1072	5.7192	5.5852	6.0463	6.0793	5.8438	7.9860	8.6616	8.9146	8.9074	8.5001	9.2881	8.6467	Market Rate	aa
End of Period (ae) Period Average (rf)																
3.6000	3.6000	3.6000	4.2500	4.2500	4.2500	4.2500	4.2500	5.8141	5.9332	5.9971	6.1945	6.2999	6.5965	6.2999	Market Rate	ae
2.4500	3.6000	3.6000	3.8438	4.2500	4.2500	4.2500	4.2500	5.3511	5.9249	5.9478	6.0051	6.2517	6.2983	6.2989	Market Rate	rf
Period Averages																
203.62	134.06	115.67	104.47	96.99	99.47	106.59	114.37	104.55	101.63	100.00	103.82	104.37	106.44	108.08	Nominal Effective Exchange Rate	ne c
196.07	135.64	125.71	117.92	116.32	118.80	119.23	121.79	109.99	102.52	100.00	101.80	100.94	105.95	110.30	Real Effective Exchange Rate	re c
End of Period															**Fund Position**	
170.1	170.1	170.1	170.1	170.1	170.1	170.1	246.8	246.8	246.8	246.8	246.8	246.8	246.8	335.6	Quota	2f. s
107.8	112.0	—	—	6.9	.8	1.5	.2	.2	.1	.1	—	.1	.1	—	SDRs	1b. s
124.4	77.2	53.0	—	—	—	—	—	—	—	—	—	—	—	—	Reserve Position in the Fund	1c. s
—	—	—	—	—	—	—	—	—	—	—	—	—	—	—	*of which:* Outstg.Fund Borrowing	2c
—	—	—	85.1	155.8	231.6	269.1	205.3	112.8	62.4	33.8	16.5	3.1	—	—	Total Fund Cred.&Loans Outstg.	2tl
End of Period															**International Liquidity**	
1,128.5	474.1	187.8	127.1	246.5	492.0	338.6	172.2	206.3	352.4	358.2	543.9	706.4	783.1	945.4	Total Reserves minus Gold	1l. d
118.4	136.9	—	—	9.0	1.1	2.1	.3	.3	.1	.2	—	.1	.1	—	SDRs	1b. d
136.6	94.4	75.2	—	—	—	—	—	—	—	—	—	—	—	—	Reserve Position in the Fund	1c. d
873.5	242.8	112.6	127.1	237.5	490.9	336.5	171.9	206.0	352.3	358.0	543.8	706.2	783.0	945.4	Foreign Exchange	1d. d
.054	.054	.054	.054	.054	.054	.054	.054	.054	.056	.054	.054	.058	.058	.058	Gold (Million Fine Troy Ounces)	1ad
1.5	1.5	2.3	2.0	2.0	2.0	2.0	2.0	1.4	1.4	1.4	1.3	1.3	....	....	Gold (National Valuation)	1an d
—	67.6	50.9	50.7	74.0	116.2	113.9	86.9	99.8	55.0	33.7	32.2	29.3	31.8	37.7	Monetary Authorities: Other Liab.	4.. d
56.3	81.8	77.2	112.1	131.4	114.8	97.9	99.3	208.4	294.1	216.4	287.3	265.2	298.4	381.7	Deposit Money Banks: Assets	7a. d
85.7	70.8	91.4	56.4	48.2	49.7	39.9	60.8	66.5	50.5	98.7	137.6	154.1	182.2	239.8	Liabilities	7b. d
2.4	3.8	2.5	3.9	4.0	24.1	4.6	5.2	3.0	8.5	11.7	29.2	76.7	73.4	79.8	Other Banking Insts.: Assets	7e. d
14.1	16.9	16.8	15.6	23.6	23.7	35.5	53.5	53.2	62.4	62.2	58.2	30.2	41.2	37.6	Liabilities	7f. d
End of Period															**Monetary Authorities**	
4,096.4	1,748.2	1,481.0	1,509.2	2,274.6	3,321.6	2,825.1	2,180.4	3,610.2	4,602.3	4,577.1	ⅈ4,764.4	5,641.3	6,210.7	7,457.7	Foreign Assets	11
188.1	1,350.7	1,573.8	2,123.0	2,404.4	2,457.6	2,777.6	3,220.3	2,122.3	1,514.0	724.1	ⅈ93.6	752.4	709.8	899.8	Claims on Central Government	12a
31.9	5.6	5.6	5.6	36.4	22.6	28.6	29.3	28.5	28.5	361.3	ⅈ346.6	345.0	336.0	334.0	Claims on Nonfin.Pub.Enterprises	12c
....	....	....	....	....	....	....	....	....	....	....	52.7	48.4	44.9	41.0	Claims on Private Sector	12d
125.4	360.7	535.0	542.1	258.2	109.5	644.1	260.1	250.0	507.2	384.7	ⅈ807.2	802.6	807.2	803.4	Claims on Deposit Money Banks	12e
—	—	1.5	15.9	15.9	15.9	23.5	23.5	21.7	18.7	18.7	ⅈ.5	.5	2.7	.6	Claims on Other Banking Insts	12f
....	....	....	....	....	....	....	....	....	....	....	56.9	48.1	36.7	31.8	Claims on Nonbank Financial Insts	12g
2,452.6	2,069.8	1,619.0	1,650.2	1,869.4	2,068.1	2,421.0	2,185.9	2,083.4	3,269.7	3,247.8	ⅈ3,538.0	4,106.4	4,963.7	5,146.5	Reserve Money	14
684.7	723.1	702.6	671.8	693.3	735.3	747.8	698.2	707.4	744.6	832.8	ⅈ909.8	1,063.0	1,046.8	1,292.4	*of which:* Currency Outside DMBs	14a
—	243.3	183.4	702.0	1,184.5	1,893.8	2,119.7	1,568.9	1,480.8	867.3	503.1	ⅈ346.3	211.2	209.9	237.6	Foreign Liabilities	16c
995.5	750.6	747.2	876.9	782.3	760.5	872.4	927.1	526.8	780.1	579.3	ⅈ1,377.1	2,516.0	1,484.6	2,491.6	Central Government Deposits	16d
1,070.6	1,126.9	1,329.3	1,389.5	1,483.1	1,699.3	1,721.3	1,564.3	2,513.8	2,651.5	2,648.5	ⅈ1,510.1	1,594.5	1,861.6	1,962.1	Capital Accounts	17a
-76.9	-725.3	-282.0	-422.9	-329.8	-494.6	-835.6	-532.6	-572.1	-897.8	-912.8	ⅈ-649.6	-789.8	-371.8	-269.7	Other Items (Net)	17r
End of Period															**Deposit Money Banks**	
1,673.2	1,241.9	805.4	857.0	1,065.1	1,195.8	1,540.1	1,348.8	1,221.2	2,320.3	2,245.4	ⅈ2,370.0	2,772.7	3,058.6	3,021.7	Reserves	20
202.6	294.3	278.0	476.5	558.5	487.8	416.0	421.9	1,211.6	1,745.0	1,297.7	ⅈ1,779.4	1,671.0	1,968.2	2,404.5	Foreign Assets	21
569.5	575.6	1,221.3	978.2	834.1	913.5	559.3	568.6	774.9	899.4	1,729.1	ⅈ2,084.6	3,823.1	2,293.1	2,728.1	Claims on Central Government	22a
37.9	12.7	11.5	9.2	—	—	—	—	.7	1.9	1.9	ⅈ—	54.4	2.1	16.4	Claims on Local Government	22b
752.5	861.1	1,050.0	1,376.0	1,240.3	1,002.2	969.6	689.8	747.7	377.9	801.3	ⅈ779.5	773.8	904.0	562.1	Claims on Nonfin.Pub.Enterprises	22c
5,843.6	5,917.4	6,130.8	5,900.5	6,181.9	6,428.3	7,608.5	7,710.0	7,995.1	7,625.6	8,739.4	ⅈ9,741.0	11,835.3	13,433.3	14,498.6	Claims on Private Sector	22d
....	....	....	....	....	....	....	....	....	....	....	252.1	238.0	231.0	207.7	Claims on Other Banking Insts	22f
....	....	....	....	....	....	....	....	....	....	....	1,711.1	616.6	111.2	128.0	Claims on Nonbank Financial Insts	22g
1,483.0	1,260.3	1,357.0	1,082.3	1,327.6	1,703.6	2,040.7	1,858.9	2,274.3	2,798.8	2,921.0	ⅈ2,524.6	3,130.4	2,819.7	3,182.0	Demand Deposits	24
6,183.3	6,124.7	6,327.2	6,673.6	6,960.6	7,085.7	6,984.4	6,525.9	7,492.1	8,651.1	8,966.8	ⅈ12194.9	13,215.0	15,516.0	15,790.9	Time, Savings,& Fgn.Currency Dep.	25
308.4	254.7	329.0	239.9	204.8	211.1	169.5	258.4	386.6	299.8	591.7	ⅈ852.3	970.5	1,201.9	1,510.5	Foreign Liabilities	26c
208.8	134.1	147.3	111.6	131.0	201.8	162.4	135.2	143.2	102.1	267.8	ⅈ364.6	204.9	203.2	281.9	Central Government Deposits	26d
47.5	355.3	476.4	542.1	258.2	109.5	641.7	260.1	288.7	507.1	384.9	ⅈ395.3	388.4	386.9	385.1	Credit from Monetary Authorities	26g
....	....	....	....	....	....	....	....	....	....	....	455.7	312.8	681.7	410.6	Liabilities to Other Banking Insts	26i
890.9	668.1	1,163.5	1,284.4	1,443.9	1,358.4	1,450.1	1,525.6	1,669.4	1,748.2	1,771.6	ⅈ2,513.5	3,093.9	3,443.9	4,017.6	Capital Accounts	27a
-42.6	105.8	-303.4	-336.5	-446.2	-642.5	-355.3	175.0	-303.1	-1,137.0	-89.0	ⅈ-583.3	469.0	-2,251.8	-2,011.6	Other Items (Net)	27r
End of Period															**Monetary Survey**	
3,990.6	1,544.5	1,246.6	1,043.7	1,443.8	1,704.5	951.9	774.9	2,954.4	5,180.3	4,780.0	ⅈ5,345.2	6,130.6	6,767.1	8,114.0	Foreign Assets (Net)	31n
6,219.2	7,838.4	9,100.0	9,419.9	9,799.7	9,877.8	10,932.3	11,179.2	11,020.9	9,583.8	11,528.7	ⅈ13376.9	15,814.6	16,417.0	16,674.6	Domestic Credit	32
-446.7	1,041.6	1,900.6	2,112.7	2,325.2	2,408.8	2,302.1	2,726.6	2,227.2	1,531.2	1,606.1	ⅈ436.5	1,854.5	1,315.1	854.3	Claims on Central Govt. (Net)	32an
37.9	12.7	11.5	9.2	—	—	—	—	.7	1.9	1.9	ⅈ—	54.4	2.1	16.4	Claims on Local Government	32b
784.4	866.7	1,055.6	1,381.6	1,276.7	1,024.8	998.2	719.1	776.2	406.4	1,162.6	ⅈ1,126.1	1,118.9	1,240.0	896.1	Claims on Nonfin.Pub.Enterprises	32c
5,843.6	5,917.4	6,130.8	5,900.5	6,181.9	6,428.3	7,608.5	7,710.0	7,995.1	7,625.6	8,739.4	ⅈ9,793.7	11,883.6	13,478.2	14,539.6	Claims on Private Sector	32d
....	....	....	1.5	15.9	15.9	15.9	23.5	23.5	21.7	18.7	ⅈ252.6	238.5	233.7	208.4	Claims on Other Banking Insts	32f
....	....	....	....	....	....	....	....	....	....	....	1,768.0	664.8	147.9	159.8	Claims on Nonbank Financial Inst	32g
2,260.5	2,088.2	2,170.3	1,875.5	2,133.1	2,575.9	2,921.6	2,696.0	3,136.5	3,748.2	3,923.4	ⅈ3,685.0	4,464.1	4,724.8	5,306.8	Money	34
6,183.3	6,124.7	6,327.2	6,673.6	6,960.6	7,085.7	6,984.4	6,525.9	7,492.1	8,651.1	8,966.8	ⅈ12194.9	13,215.0	15,516.0	15,790.9	Quasi-Money	35
....	....	....	....	....	....	....	....	....	....	....	455.7	312.8	681.7	410.6	Liabilities to Other Banking Insts	36i
1,961.5	1,795.0	2,492.8	2,673.9	2,927.0	3,057.7	3,171.4	3,089.9	4,183.2	4,399.7	4,420.1	ⅈ4,023.6	4,688.3	5,305.5	5,979.8	Capital Accounts	37a
-195.5	-624.9	-643.7	-759.4	-777.2	-1,137.1	-1,193.3	-357.6	-836.5	-2,034.9	-1,001.6	ⅈ-1637.1	-735.0	-3,043.9	-2,699.5	Other Items (Net)	37r
8,443.8	8,212.9	8,497.5	8,549.1	9,093.7	9,661.6	9,906.0	9,221.9	10,628.6	12,399.3	12,890.2	ⅈ15880.0	17,679.0	20,240.8	21,097.8	Money plus Quasi-Money	35l

Trinidad and Tobago

		1970	1971	1972	1973	1974	1975	1976	1977	1978	1979	1980	1981	1982	1983	1984
Other Banking Institutions																
Other Banklike Institutions															*Millions of TT Dollars:*		
Reserves	40	.4	.8	.4	.8	1.2	1.0	1.8	2.6	3.9	4.4	5.9	19.1	28.3	51.1	49.0
Foreign Assets	41	1.3	1.4	1.6	1.7	2.1	7.8	5.6	6.8	5.9	5.9	5.8	5.7	5.7	5.2	9.1
Claims on Central Government	42a	8.3	7.8	8.2	8.3	7.8	16.4	3.8	5.0	4.1	6.2	3.7	4.1	.7	22.3	13.7
Claims on Local Government	42b	....	....	—	—	—	—	—	—	—	—	—	—	—	—	—
Claims on Nonfin.Pub.Enterprises	42c	—	—	—	—	—	.1	—	—	.1	—	—	—	3.4	—	....
Claims on Private Sector	42d	25.5	26.6	37.5	39.5	33.5	134.7	192.6	276.1	447.7	521.3	723.4	970.5	1,390.2	1,721.5	2,333.9
Claims on Deposit Money Banks	42e	—	—	—	—	—	24.9	16.4	11.8	41.0	14.6	33.2	45.8	98.6	81.8	185.2
Claims on Nonbank Financial Insts	42g	....	....	....	....	....	....	....	....	....	....	....	....	....	....	....
Time, Savings,& Fgn.Currency Dep.	45	⁑16.0	15.2	19.5	21.6	29.0	133.0	175.8	238.7	376.9	431.3	608.0	883.1	1,335.0	1,685.1	2,228.2
Foreign Liabilities	46c	.1	.1	—	—	—	.3	.2	.5	.5	—	.5	.7	5.5	8.5	30.9
Central Government Deposits	46d	....	....	....	....	....	....	....	....	....	....	....	....	....	....	....
Credit from Monetary Authorities	46g	....	....	....	....	....	....	....	....	....	....	....	....	....	....	....
Credit from Deposit Money Banks	46h	10.3	10.5	15.5	14.0	1.7	3.0	8.7	18.4	46.1	52.3	39.5	49.2	30.7	59.2	125.2
Capital Accounts	47a	—	—	—	—	—	14.6	15.7	17.7	23.1	30.4	51.8	71.1	191.5	210.3	297.3
Other Items (Net)	47r	9.2	10.9	12.8	14.6	13.9	34.0	19.9	26.9	56.1	38.4	72.4	41.2	−35.8	−81.3	−90.7
Other Banking Institutions (cont.)																
Development Banks															*Millions of TT Dollars:*		
Reserves	40..n	....	....	....	....	....	.1	.3	.2	.2	.4	.4	−.3	3.0	9.5	5.0
Claims on Central Government	42a.n	....	....	....	....	....	—	—	—	—	2.4	—	—	—	2.0	2.5
Claims on Private Sector	42d.n	....	....	....	....	....	58.0	65.2	97.1	129.8	197.6	265.1	368.1	638.7	763.7	836.8
Claims on Deposit Money Banks	42e.n	....	....	....	....	....	15.4	18.5	20.5	26.6	12.4	14.0	19.4	66.2	52.5	50.6
Foreign Liabilities	46c.n	....	....	....	....	....	11.1	12.0	12.7	10.8	24.4	24.8	33.7	32.7	34.2	37.3
Central Government Deposits	46d.n	....	....	....	....	....	35.4	50.0	76.0	124.4	156.9	220.4	308.1	363.3	582.4	604.3
Credit from Dep. Money Banks	46h.n	....	....	....	....	....	....	....	....	....	....	....	....	....	....	....
Capital Accounts	47a.n	....	....	....	....	....	22.3	19.6	21.8	27.3	38.7	48.0	60.3	315.9	102.2	127.7
Other Items (Net)	47r.n	....	....	....	....	....	4.6	2.5	7.3	−6.0	−7.2	−13.7	−14.9	−4.0	108.9	125.7
Banking Survey															*Millions of TT Dollars:*		
Foreign Assets (Net)	51n	....	....	....	....	....	1,728.7	2,418.3	3,528.3	4,265.8	5,128.8	6,607.7	7,945.9	7,280.2	4,884.5	3,059.9
Domestic Credit	52	....	....	....	....	....	−22.9	−126.4	−701.6	−186.1	−252.3	3,445.4	6,627.6	8,696.9		
Claims on Central Govt. (Net)	52an	....	....	....	....	....	−1,121.2	−1,649.6	−2,868.3	−3,429.4	−3,676.4	−5,073.9	−5,911.2	−3,867.4	−2,098.8	−1,220.4
Claims on Local Government	52b	....	....	....	....	....	1.4	5.1	7.2	12.0	8.0	5.7	5.1	33.5	3.5	32.2
Claims on Nonfin.Pub.Enterprises	52c	....	....	....	....	....	16.2	12.7	24.6	33.6	17.9	85.9	256.8	356.6	566.2	639.1
Claims on Private Sector	52d	....	....	....	....	....	1,080.8	1,505.4	2,134.9	2,918.5	3,464.4	4,298.9	5,397.0	6,922.7	8,156.7	9,245.9
Claims on Nonbank Financial Inst	52g	....	....	....	....	....	....	....	....	....	....	....	....	....	....	....
Liquid Liabilities	55l	....	....	....	....	....	1,520.2	2,037.0	2,595.7	3,314.1	4,242.2	4,899.5	6,356.4	8,698.6	9,558.4	10,516.3
Capital Accounts	57a	....	....	....	....	....	394.3	409.2	436.5	675.9	1,078.7	1,345.5	1,864.1	2,668.4	2,657.6	2,030.4
Other Items (Net)	57r	....	....	....	....	....	−208.7	−154.4	−205.5	−189.5	−378.3	−320.8	−526.8	−641.4	−703.9	−789.8
Nonbank Financial Institutions															*Millions of TT Dollars:*		
Reserves	40..s	....	....	....	....	16.8	34.9	48.4	54.3	74.7	85.7	23.8	63.8	44.3	98.0	132.4
Foreign Assets	41..s	....	....	....	....	65.6	63.7	55.8	75.2	58.9	75.0	52.0	25.6	43.1	83.5	126.8
Claims on Central Government	42a.s	....	....	....	....	88.9	82.1	90.6	93.3	139.7	130.2	121.6	132.5	133.8	140.7	106.3
Claims on Private Sector	42d.s	....	....	....	....	164.2	162.3	229.1	263.3	310.7	339.9	567.7	751.9	818.4	913.5	1,138.5
Fixed Assets	42h.s	....	....	....	....	11.2	19.1	20.5	25.2	45.0	35.1	41.0	53.1	87.9	131.0	157.4
Incr.in Total Assets(Within Per.)	49z.s	....	....	....	....	....	15.4	82.2	67.0	117.7	36.8	140.3	220.7	100.6	239.3	294.6
Interest Rates															*Percent Per Annum*		
Bank Rate *(End of Period)*	60	6.00	5.00	5.00	6.00	6.00	6.00	6.00	6.00	6.00	6.00	6.00	6.00	6.00	7.50	7.50
Treasury Bill Rate	60c	5.32	5.11	3.74	4.37	5.57	3.99	3.98	3.94	3.60	3.16	3.07	3.06	3.05	3.08	3.39
Deposit Rate	60l	....	....	....	....	....	....	....	....	....	....	....	....	....	....	....
Deposit Rate (Foreign Currency)	60l.f	....	....	....	....	....	....	....	....	....	....	....	6.57	6.25	6.40	6.76
Lending Rate	60p	....	....	....	....	....	....	....	....	....	....	10.00	11.38	11.50	11.71	12.75
Government Bond Yield	61	8.16	8.27	7.83	7.99	8.31	8.25	8.18	8.07	8.07	8.12	8.61	8.84	9.84	9.88	9.89
Prices, Production, Labor															*Index Numbers (1995=100):*		
Share Prices	62	....	....	....	....	....	....	....	....	....	....	....	....	....	....	....
Producer Prices	63	....	....	....	....	....	....	....	....	....	33.7	40.3	47.1	53.6	60.3	63.3
Consumer Prices	64	7.3	7.6	8.3	9.5	11.6	⁑13.6	15.1	16.8	18.6	21.3	25.0	28.6	⁑31.9	36.8	41.7
Wages: Avg Weekly Earn.('90=100)	65	....	....	....	....	....	....	....	23.7	27.6	34.1	41.9	50.5	59.2	70.6	80.8
Industrial Production	66	....	....	....	....	....	....	....	....	53.2	54.5	57.7	51.3	53.3	48.7	59.6
Crude Petroleum Production	66aa	107.0	98.9	107.4	127.1	142.9	164.8	162.9	175.3	175.7	164.1	162.8	144.9	135.5	122.3	130.2
Total Employment	67	....	137.5	....	155.2	151.3	153.4	161.0	⁑162.4	165.7	165.6	166.7	163.4	157.9	160.5	152.2
															Number in Thousands:		
Labor Force	67d	....	....	....	....	....	....	....	....	....	....	....	....	....	....	....
Employment	67e	....	....	....	....	....	....	....	....	....	....	....	....	....	....	....
Unemployment	67c	....	....	....	....	....	....	....	....	....	....	....	....	....	....	....
Unemployment Rate (%)	67r	....	....	....	....	....	....	....	....	....	....	....	....	....	....	....
International Transactions															*Millions of TT Dollars*		
Exports	70	963.1	1,040.2	1,068.4	1,371.4	4,162.8	3,875.2	5,391.8	5,231.5	4,895.1	6,265.0	9,784.8	9,026.0	7,372.4	5,646.3	5,216.2
Imports, c.i.f.	71	1,087.0	1,314.2	1,467.6	1,560.1	3,774.9	3,239.2	4,904.3	4,365.2	4,721.0	5,051.0	7,626.4	7,498.9	8,873.1	6,196.7	4,605.9
																1995=100	
Volume of Exports	72	118.9	114.8	117.6	116.9	⁑125.6	108.2	126.5	118.5	107.5	104.7	101.0	90.0	92.1	90.2	103.4
Volume of Imports	73	72.7	82.6	81.1	89.3	⁑111.2	81.2	111.9	92.2	95.6	107.2	121.9	113.7	111.6	126.0	⁑142.4
Unit Value of Exports	74	5.6	6.3	6.4	8.3	⁑22.3	25.8	29.8	32.5	32.5	42.9	68.6	75.6	72.4	71.9	⁑71.4
Unit Value of Imports	75	4.9	5.4	5.9	6.9	⁑15.7	18.1	21.3	21.9	22.9	26.0	39.0	44.0	49.8	50.2	⁑50.3

1985	1986	1987	1988	1989	1990	1991	1992	1993	1994	1995	1996	1997	1998	1999		

Other Banking Institutions
Other Banklike Institutions

End of Period

35.6	22.0	111.9	117.8	104.9	114.8	118.4	128.7	143.7	148.0	171.5	ℐ241.5	272.7	409.8	485.3	Reserves	40
8.7	13.6	9.1	16.6	17.0	102.5	19.6	22.3	17.5	50.3	70.4	ℐ181.1	483.1	484.4	502.7	Foreign Assets	41
15.1	10.6	.8	.3	87.8	151.2	165.0	181.3	505.7	588.7	965.4	ℐ1,190.0	1,437.1	1,075.4	1,098.9	Claims on Central Government	42a
....	....	....	....	....	....	....	....	....	....	....	—	4.1	4.7	5.1	Claims on Local Government	42b
.9	—	....	....	....	9.6	85.6	12.4	9.2	65.5	33.0	ℐ147.5	137.0	80.3	196.2	Claims on Nonfin.Pub.Enterprises	42c
2,594.9	2,053.1	2,197.6	2,234.4	1,965.4	2,184.2	2,436.0	2,749.3	2,852.1	3,341.6	3,982.3	ℐ2,770.0	3,141.9	3,358.5	3,903.7	Claims on Private Sector	42d
153.8	102.3	161.6	199.8	301.2	222.7	216.5	356.7	381.8	325.2	335.6	ℐ786.2	645.4	1,195.6	1,418.3	Claims on Deposit Money Banks	42e
....	....	....	....	....	....	....	....	....	....	....	47.4	37.8	201.3	526.1	Claims on Nonbank Financial Insts	42g
2,399.9	1,964.1	2,071.2	2,189.2	2,096.1	2,221.2	2,272.5	2,471.7	2,805.5	2,894.1	3,138.9	ℐ2,993.9	3,180.3	4,017.2	4,792.5	Time, Savings,& Fgn.Currency Dep.	45
18.1	10.3	—	—	—	1.6	.4	.3	.3	1.4	.3	ℐ169.5	152.5	238.0	207.3	Foreign Liabilities	46c
....	....	....	....	....	....	....	....	....	....	....	47.8	100.7	33.6	34.8	Central Government Deposits	46d
....	....	....	....	....	....	....	....	....	....	....	25.3	44.6	52.7	49.9	Credit from Monetary Authorities	46g
200.3	76.3	209.8	251.4	96.2	213.1	165.0	147.0	138.9	30.3	48.5	ℐ92.1	249.0	70.0	670.2	Credit from Deposit Money Banks	46h
245.6	261.2	302.3	300.8	322.2	341.6	428.0	464.4	470.6	512.2	690.3	ℐ762.5	885.4	1,188.8	1,474.7	Capital Accounts	47a
−55.0	−110.3	−102.3	−172.3	−38.2	7.5	174.7	367.3	494.7	1,081.3	1,680.2	ℐ1,272.7	1,546.5	1,209.6	906.9	Other Items (Net)	47r

Other Banking Institutions (cont.)
Development Banks

End of Period

4.4	3.3	—	—	4.8	.9	.5	—	—	—	—	—	—	—	—	Reserves	40..n
.8	—	—	—	—	—	—	—	—	27.8	33.7	—	—	—	—	Claims on Central Government	42a.n
883.5	922.7	965.3	919.4	940.6	1,007.9	987.2	1,126.5	1,165.7	1,011.9	1,031.3	845.5	852.8	927.5	998.6	Claims on Private Sector	42d.n
37.5	35.9	2.5	3.9	1.5	.9	32.9	72.5	99.4	110.6	88.6	48.0	78.2	101.3	37.6	Claims on Deposit Money Banks	42e.n
32.7	50.6	60.6	66.5	100.1	99.0	150.5	226.9	309.1	368.9	373.0	190.9	37.9	33.6	29.4	Foreign Liabilities	46c.n
591.3	610.0	720.4	598.1	416.3	614.8	427.3	419.2	401.6	517.4	500.8	446.8	440.3	430.7	426.9	Central Government Deposits	46d.n
—	—	17.0	19.6	26.2	26.4	21.7	33.6	27.3	28.0	40.2	16.0	30.0	17.3	18.4	Credit from Dep. Money Banks	46h.n
153.6	160.8	150.9	193.4	345.5	194.9	346.2	389.9	389.2	282.4	275.0	204.4	356.0	377.7	404.0	Capital Accounts	47a.n
148.5	140.6	19.0	45.9	58.7	74.5	75.0	129.4	137.9	−46.4	−35.4	35.4	66.8	169.5	157.5	Other Items (Net)	47r.n

Banking Survey

End of Period

3,948.5	1,497.3	1,195.1	993.9	1,360.8	1,706.4	820.5	570.0	2,662.5	4,860.3	4,477.1	ℐ5,165.9	6,423.3	6,979.9	8,380.0	Foreign Assets (Net)	51n
9,130.7	10,214.9	11,541.9	11,960.1	12,361.2	12,599.9	14,155.3	14,806.1	15,130.3	14,083.2	17,054.9	ℐ17630.1	20,645.8	21,366.6	22,733.1	Domestic Credit	52
−1,022.2	442.2	1,181.1	1,514.9	1,996.6	1,945.1	2,039.8	2,488.7	2,331.3	1,630.3	2,104.4	ℐ1,131.9	2,750.6	1,926.2	1,491.5	Claims on Central Govt. (Net)	52an
37.9	12.7	11.5	9.2	—	—	—	—	.7	1.9	1.9	ℐ—	58.6	6.8	21.5	Claims on Local Government	52b
793.0	866.7	1,055.6	1,381.6	1,276.7	1,034.4	1,083.8	731.5	785.4	471.9	1,195.6	ℐ1,273.7	1,255.8	1,320.3	1,092.3	Claims on Nonfin.Pub.Enterprises	52c
9,322.0	8,893.3	9,293.7	9,054.4	9,087.9	9,620.4	11,031.7	11,585.8	12,012.9	11,979.1	13,753.0	ℐ13409.1	15,878.3	17,764.2	19,441.9	Claims on Private Sector	52d
....	....	....	....	....	....	....	....	....	....	....	1,815.4	702.6	349.2	685.9	Claims on Nonbank Financial Inst	52g
10,803.8	10,151.7	10,456.8	10,620.4	11,080.1	11,767.1	12,059.6	11,564.9	13,290.4	15,145.4	15,857.6	ℐ18632.3	20,586.7	23,848.2	25,404.9	Liquid Liabilities	55l
2,360.8	2,217.0	2,946.1	3,168.0	3,594.7	3,594.3	3,945.6	3,944.2	5,043.0	5,194.3	5,385.4	ℐ4,990.5	5,929.7	6,872.0	7,858.5	Capital Accounts	57a
−85.4	−656.6	−665.9	−834.5	−952.8	−1,055.1	−1,029.3	−133.0	−540.6	−1,396.2	289.0	ℐ−826.8	552.7	−2,373.7	−2,150.3	Other Items (Net)	57r

Nonbank Financial Institutions

End of Period

62.0	24.5	75.0	135.7	20.0	23.6	....	....	....	....	....	....	....	....	....	Reserves	40..s
163.0	171.2	550.0	432.9	235.3	347.5	....	....	....	....	....	....	....	....	....	Foreign Assets	41..s
200.3	295.8	322.6	447.0	452.3	619.3	....	....	....	....	....	....	....	....	....	Claims on Central Government	42a.s
1,438.6	1,679.2	1,245.8	1,653.9	1,625.6	2,406.2	....	....	....	....	....	....	....	....	....	Claims on Private Sector	42d.s
169.8	205.5	209.7	204.9	243.2	289.2	....	....	....	....	....	....	....	....	....	Fixed Assets	42h.s
372.2	342.7	26.9	471.2	−297.9	1,109.4	....	....	....	....	....	....	....	....	....	*Incr.in Total Assets(Within Per.)*	49z.s

Interest Rates

Percent Per Annum

7.50	5.97	7.50	9.50	9.50	9.50	11.50	13.00	13.00	13.00	13.00	13.00	13.00	13.00	13.00	Bank Rate *(End of Period)*	60
3.47	3.99	4.63	4.88	7.13	7.50	7.67	9.26	9.45	10.00	8.41	10.44	9.83	11.93	10.40	Treasury Bill Rate	60c
5.31	6.04	6.03	6.01	6.28	5.96	5.79	6.99	7.06	6.91	....	....	6.91	7.95	8.51	Deposit Rate	60l
....	....	....	....	....	....	....	....	....	....	....	....	6.35	6.69	6.41	Deposit Rate (Foreign Currency)	60l.f
12.69	12.00	11.50	12.58	13.31	12.87	13.17	15.33	15.50	15.98	15.17	15.79	15.33	17.33	17.04	Lending Rate	60p
9.89	9.62	9.54	9.76	10.77	10.73	10.85	13.30	....	....	....	....	....	....	....	Government Bond Yield	61

Prices, Production, Labor

Period Averages

....	....	....	....	....	....	....	....	....	71.8	100.0	133.8	202.8	350.6	334.3	Share Prices	62
66.4	70.6	73.6	78.0	84.9	86.1	86.3	86.9	91.6	96.5	100.0	102.9	104.9	106.4	....	Producer Prices	63
44.9	48.3	53.5	57.7	ℐ64.3	71.4	74.1	78.8	87.4	95.1	100.0	103.4	107.2	113.2	117.1	Consumer Prices	64
86.8	88.4	92.2	93.7	94.5	100.0	100.1	103.0	104.6	109.9	....	....	....	....	....	Wages: Avg Weekly Earn.('90=100)	65
57.3	69.6	72.3	ℐ69.4	69.5	71.2	79.4	87.0	81.5	93.0	100.0	97.7	105.3	109.8	....	Industrial Production	66
134.8	129.3	119.5	115.8	114.3	115.7	110.3	103.9	94.8	100.3	100.0	98.9	94.8	94.1	....	Crude Petroleum Production	66aa
134.1	126.4	120.1	113.0	113.0	105.0	105.9	104.5	102.5	107.1	ℐ100.0	102.9	106.5	111.1	....	Total Employment	67

Period Averages

....	....	....	....	....	....	492	....	504	....	521	530	....	....	....	Labor Force	67d
400	391	372	372	366	374	401	406	405	416	432	444	....	....	....	Employment	67e
73	81	107	105	103	94	91	99	100	94	89	86	81	79	....	Unemployment	67c
15.5	17.5	22.3	22.0	22.0	20.0	18.5	19.6	19.8	18.4	17.2	16.3	15.0	14.2	....	Unemployment Rate (%)	67r

International Transactions

Millions of TT Dollars

5,247.1	4,988.6	5,264.6	5,424.2	6,706.9	8,330.7	8,436.4	7,188.3	8,800.9	11,055.2	14,608.6	15,014.4	15,887.6	14,220.5	....	Exports	70
3,739.0	4,860.2	4,387.5	4,310.3	5,190.4	4,712.3	7,084.8	4,693.5	7,495.3	6,700.9	10,191.1	12,866.8	18,705.9	18,886.8	....	Imports, c.i.f.	71

1995=100

ℐ95.0	93.7	92.1	95.0	93.1	100.0	....	....	....	....	....	....	....	....	....	Volume of Exports	72
125.6	128.4	101.5	85.4	104.1	100.0	....	....	....	....	....	....	....	....	....	Volume of Imports	73
68.2	66.4	69.6	66.1	83.6	100.0	....	....	....	....	....	....	....	....	....	Unit Value of Exports	74
49.8	67.6	77.4	85.7	98.6	100.0	....	....	....	....	....	....	....	....	....	Unit Value of Imports	75

Trinidad and Tobago

	1970	1971	1972	1973	1974	1975	1976	1977	1978	1979	1980	1981	1982	1983	1984
Balance of Payments														*Millions of US Dollars:*	
Current Account, n.i.e. .... 78al d	....	....	....	....	....	340.3	260.9	182.8	54.4	−19.2	357.0	414.6	−599.5	−946.6	−466.7
Goods: Exports f.o.b. .... 78aa d	....	....	....	....	....	1,072.5	1,153.3	1,284.7	1,301.0	1,759.1	2,728.3	2,725.6	2,317.3	2,102.7	2,173.4
Goods: Imports f.o.b. .... 78ab d	....	....	....	....	....	−658.1	−766.0	−867.8	−1,057.5	−1,334.1	−1,789.1	−1,763.5	−2,486.8	−2,233.3	−1,704.9
Trade Balance .... 78ac d	....	....	....	....	....	414.4	387.3	416.8	243.5	425.0	939.2	962.1	−169.4	−130.6	468.5
Services: Credit .... 78ad d	....	....	....	....	....	217.3	237.4	263.8	263.8	308.5	410.6	418.0	471.9	242.9	266.3
Services: Debit .... 78ae d	....	....	....	....	....	−197.3	−235.8	−289.2	−355.3	−474.2	−645.3	−714.8	−882.4	−897.4	−849.4
Balance on Goods & Services .... 78af d	....	....	....	....	....	434.5	388.9	391.5	151.9	259.4	704.5	665.3	−580.0	−785.1	−114.5
Income: Credit .... 78ag d	....	....	....	....	....	43.3	60.3	77.0	125.0	159.9	232.3	344.7	357.0	230.3	141.5
Income: Debit .... 78ah d	....	....	....	....	....	−124.8	−163.7	−263.2	−196.3	−407.5	−537.9	−543.1	−281.9	−367.5	−466.2
Balance on Gds, Serv. & Inc. ... 78ai d	....	....	....	....	....	352.9	285.5	205.3	80.6	11.7	398.9	466.9	−504.8	−922.3	−439.3
Current Transfers, n.i.e.: Credit .... 78aj d	....	....	....	....	....	2.8	1.9	1.7	1.8	1.8	1.8	1.9	2.0	5.9	13.2
Current Transfers: Debit .... 78ak d	....	....	....	....	....	−15.4	−26.4	−24.1	−28.0	−32.6	−43.8	−54.2	−96.6	−30.2	−40.6
Capital Account, n.i.e. .... 78bc d	....	....	....	....	....	−8.5	−5.5	−8.7	−11.8	−14.8	−22.3	−40.1	−45.4	−56.3	−55.8
Capital Account, n.i.e.: Credit .... 78ba d	....	....	....	....	....						4.6	2.8	3.5	3.5	3.4
Capital Account: Debit .... 78bb d	....	....	....	....	....	−8.5	−5.5	−8.7	−11.8	−14.8	−26.8	−42.9	−49.0	−59.8	−59.2
Financial Account, n.i.e. .... 78bj d	....	....	....	....	....	37.2	−16.1	282.4	287.5	372.3	226.8	303.1	439.0	380.8	−122.8
Direct Investment Abroad .... 78bd d	....	....	....	....	....									−3.6	−3.5
Dir. Invest. in Rep. Econ., n.i.e. .... 78be d	....	....	....	....	....	93.0	132.2	83.5	128.8	93.8	184.5	258.1	203.5	117.7	113.2
Portfolio Investment Assets .... 78bf d	....	....	....	....	....	—	—	—	−7.9	−2.7	−12.7	1.8	.3	.1	
Equity Securities .... 78bk d	....	....	....	....	....	—	—	—							
Debt Securities .... 78bl d	....	....	....	....	....	—	—	—	−7.9	−2.7	−12.7	1.8	.3	.1	
Portfolio Investment Liab., n.i.e. .... 78bg d	....	....	....	....	....	−1.1	−9.4	−1.1	107.5	−1.1	−6.5	−.5	—	—	
Equity Securities .... 78bm d	....	....	....	....	....										
Debt Securities .... 78bn d	....	....	....	....	....	−1.1	−9.4	−1.1	107.5	−1.1	−6.5	−.5	—	—	
Financial Derivatives Assets .... 78bw d	....	....	....	....	....	....	....	....	....	....	....	....	....	....	....
Financial Derivatives Liabilities ...... 78bx d	....	....	....	....	....	....	....	....	....	....	....	....	....	....	....
Other Investment Assets .... 78bh d	....	....	....	....	....	−35.6	−100.5	−1.0	−27.3	−87.6	−87.4	−100.4	−49.5	−79.6	−166.0
Monetary Authorities .... 78bo d	....	....	....	....	....										
General Government .... 78bp d	....	....	....	....	....	−35.1	−76.7	−21.3	−12.0	−7.0	−17.1	−140.3	−2.5	−40.8	−87.7
Banks .... 78bq d	....	....	....	....	....	−.5	−2.4	−7.3	−7.2	−20.3	−7.5	−2.6	−14.8	13.3	−5.4
Other Sectors .... 78br d	....	....	....	....	....	—	−21.3	27.6	−8.2	−60.3	−62.8	42.6	−32.3	−52.1	−73.0
Other Investment Liab., n.i.e. .... 78bi d	....	....	....	....	....	−19.0	−38.3	201.0	86.5	370.0	148.8	144.1	284.8	346.2	−66.5
Monetary Authorities .... 78bs d	....	....	....	....	....	−4.8	.9	1.8	.7	−3.2	6.1	.5			
General Government .... 78bt d	....	....	....	....	....	−7.6	−25.6	152.8	−.5	56.2	67.9	15.3	122.0	99.4	168.9
Banks .... 78bu d	....	....	....	....	....	7.6	−1.4	14.0	26.5	−8.1	38.8	16.0	17.7	14.6	24.5
Other Sectors .... 78bv d	....	....	....	....	....	−14.2	−12.2	32.3	59.8	325.0	35.9	112.3	145.0	232.2	−260.0
Net Errors and Omissions .... 78ca d	....	....	....	....	....	89.1	−38.9	−12.6	7.3	5.4	86.8	−109.0	−1.1	−250.7	−47.6
Overall Balance .... 78cb d	....	....	....	....	....	458.1	200.5	443.9	337.5	343.8	648.3	568.6	−206.9	−872.8	−692.9
Reserves and Related Items .... 79da d	....	....	....	....	....	−458.1	−200.5	−443.9	−337.5	−343.8	−648.3	−568.6	206.9	872.8	692.9
Reserve Assets .... 79db d	....	....	....	....	....	−458.1	−200.5	−443.9	−337.5	−343.8	−648.3	−568.6	206.9	872.8	692.9
Use of Fund Credit and Loans .... 79dc d	....	....	....	....	....	—	—	—	—	—	—	—	—	—	—
Exceptional Financing .... 79de d	....	....	....	....	....	—	—	—	—	—	—	—	—	—	—
Government Finance														*Millions of TT Dollars:*	
Deficit (-) or Surplus 80	32.8	−57.7	−39.2	....	....	Ɪ499.9	799.7	301.6	−61.0	1,105.6	545.8	Ɪ−2346.7	−2,216.0	−1,655.7
Revenue 81	313.2	346.6	528.9	....	....	Ɪ2,340.8	3,043.9	3,155.5	4,118.8	6,487.8	7,232.8	Ɪ7,066.9	6,552.0	6,612.8
Grants Received 81z						Ɪ—						Ɪ—		
Expenditure 82	280.4	404.3	568.1	....	....	Ɪ1,599.7	1,913.4	2,680.5	3,654.7	4,621.7	5,061.5	Ɪ9,464.4	8,779.6	8,276.0
Lending Minus Repayments 83	....	....	....	....	....	Ɪ241.2	330.8	173.4	525.1	760.5	1,625.5	Ɪ−50.8	−11.6	−7.5
Financing															
Domestic 84a	....	....	....	....	....	Ɪ49.7	62.8	42.1	40.9	14.3	−12.4	....	....	....
Foreign 85a	....	....	....	....	....	Ɪ−80.2	360.2	259.3	132.3	162.1	25.9	....	....	....
Use of Cash Balances 87	3.1	15.8	−57.0	3.5	−417.8	−465.3	Ɪ−469.4	−1,222.7	−603.0	−112.2	−1,282.0	−559.3			
Financing (by Currency)															
Net Borrowing: TT Dollars 84b	−22.8	39.8	56.6	36.6	16.6	24.3	....	....	....	....	....	....	....	....	....
Foreign Currency 85b	−13.1	2.1	39.6	49.2	−17.9	−22.7	....	....	....	....	....	....	....	....	....
Use of Cash Balances 87	3.1	15.8	−57.0	3.5	−417.8	−465.3	Ɪ−469.4	−1,222.7	−603.0	−112.2	−1,282.0	−559.3			
Debt: TT Dollars 88b	234.4	275.9	333.9	370.2	387.3	411.7	....	....	....	....	....	....	....	....	....
Foreign Currency 89b	158.2	163.7	199.2	255.7	241.4	215.7	....	....	....	....	....	....	....	....	....
National Accounts														*Millions of TT Dollars*	
Exports of Goods & Services 90c	703	757	824	1,132	2,378	2,808	3,401	3,733	3,766	4,979	7,550	7,542	6,694	5,756	5,981
Government Consumption 91f	215	280	334	366	475	652	743	967	1,148	1,536	1,805	2,110	4,032	3,907	4,179
Gross Fixed Capital Formation 93e	344	581	615	579	651	1,085	1,398	1,735	2,323	2,952	4,204	4,342	5,189	4,770	3,954
Increase/Decrease(-) in Stocks 93i	81	21	37	86	264	364	98	272	261	261	376	199	228	199	165
Private Consumption 96f	986	980	1,234	1,385	1,774	2,257	2,896	3,605	4,443	5,663	6,865	8,197	11,103	11,594	10,224
Imports of Goods & Services 98c	−685	−848	−963	−984	−1,350	−1,866	−2,445	−2,779	−3,391	−4,345	−5,834	−5,952	−8,070	−7,606	−6,283
Gross Domestic Product (GDP) 99b	1,644	1,771	2,082	2,564	4,193	5,300	6,091	7,533	8,550	11,046	14,966	16,438	19,176	18,719	18,615
Net Factor Inc/Pmts(-) Abroad 98.n	−130	−132	−136	−180	−586	−181	−265	−464	−611	−756	−481	−154	−295	−339	−765
Gross National Income (GNI) 99a	1,514	1,639	1,946	2,384	3,607	4,749	5,255	6,340	7,938	10,290	14,485	16,284	18,881	18,381	17,850
Net National Income 99e	1,367	1,472	1,705	2,166	3,316	4,795	5,328	6,414	7,314	9,592	13,637	15,354	17,739	16,923	16,231
GDP Volume 1970 prices 99b.p	1,644	1,661	1,757	1,786	1,854	1,881	2,002	2,184	2,403	2,490	2,748	2,874	2,990	....	....
GDP Volume 1985 Prices 99b.p	....	....	....	....	....	....	....	....	....	....	....	....	....	20,104	18,850
GDP Volume (1995=100) .... 99bv p	70.4	71.1	75.2	76.5	79.4	80.6	85.7	93.6	102.9	106.6	117.7	123.1	128.1	116.3	109.0
GDP Deflator (1995=100) .... 99bi p	7.4	7.9	8.7	10.6	16.7	20.8	22.4	25.4	26.2	32.7	40.1	42.1	47.2	50.8	53.9
														Millions:	
Population 99z	1.03	1.03	1.05	1.06	1.07	Ɪ1.01	1.02	1.04	1.06	1.06	1.08	1.09	1.12	1.14	1.17

Balance of Payments

Minus Sign Indicates Debit

1985	1986	1987	1988	1989	1990	1991	1992	1993	1994	1995	1996	1997	1998	1999		
-47.9	-411.9	-225.0	-88.6	-38.5	459.0	-4.7	138.9	113.1	217.8	293.8	105.1	-613.6	-643.5	....	Current Account, n.i.e.	78al d
2,141.7	1,378.4	1,414.3	1,469.5	1,550.8	1,960.1	1,774.5	1,691.4	1,500.1	1,777.6	2,456.1	2,354.1	2,448.0	2,258.0	....	Goods: Exports f.o.b.	78aa d
-1,354.6	-1,209.4	-1,057.6	-1,064.2	-1,045.2	-947.6	-1,210.3	-995.6	-952.9	-1,036.6	-1,868.5	-1,971.6	-2,976.6	-2,998.9	....	Goods: Imports f.o.b.	78ab d
787.1	168.9	356.7	405.3	505.5	1,012.5	564.2	695.7	547.2	741.1	587.7	382.4	-528.6	-740.8		*Trade Balance*	78ac d
264.1	271.7	209.3	271.3	280.8	328.5	405.3	452.7	353.4	326.6	342.6	461.2	546.5	671.7		Services: Credit	78ad d
-725.5	-613.6	-493.5	-453.9	-439.8	-479.2	-534.4	-561.9	-466.4	-438.1	-241.9	-217.5	-254.1	-255.4		Services: Debit	78ae d
325.7	-172.9	72.5	222.6	346.6	861.9	435.1	586.6	434.2	629.5	688.4	626.2	-236.2	-324.5		*Balance on Goods & Services*	78af d
195.8	96.8	16.8	20.3	32.4	39.6	48.6	29.8	40.2	56.7	76.6	39.1	63.8	64.0		Income: Credit	78ag d
-545.2	-307.4	-291.7	-322.3	-410.1	-436.4	-490.7	-477.9	-366.0	-468.7	-466.7	-553.1	-445.0	-405.3		Income: Debit	78ah d
-23.7	-383.5	-202.4	-79.4	-31.1	465.2	-7.0	138.5	108.4	217.5	298.3	112.2	-617.4	-665.8		*Balance on Gds, Serv. & Inc.*	78ai d
10.1	.8	6.3	3.5	5.2	7.8	15.6	11.1	23.7	28.3	34.0	34.2	37.0	58.4		Current Transfers, n.i.e.: Credit	78aj d
-34.3	-29.2	-28.9	-12.7	-12.7	-13.9	-13.3	-10.7	-19.0	-27.9	-38.5	-41.3	-33.2	-36.2		Current Transfers: Debit	78ak d
-35.2	-21.5	-14.2	-20.4	-17.2	-19.2	-16.1	-16.5	-11.5	-6.4	-11.9	....	....	....		Capital Account, n.i.e.	78bc d
3.1	....	1.8	—	.4	.4	.4	.4	1.3	1.1	1.1	....	....	....		Capital Account, n.i.e.: Credit	78ba d
-38.3	-21.5	-16.0	-20.4	-17.5	-19.6	-16.5	-16.9	-12.8	-7.5	-13.0	....	....	....		Capital Account: Debit	78bb d
20.4	-196.4	78.4	-141.5	-166.5	-506.3	-226.8	-154.2	98.8	-32.2	-214.7	43.0	697.2	471.5		Financial Account, n.i.e.	78bj d
-8.2	-7.3	1.9	—	—	—	—	—	—	—	....	....	....	....		Direct Investment Abroad	78bd d
1.2	-14.5	33.1	62.9	148.9	109.4	169.3	177.9	379.2	516.2	298.9	355.4	999.3	729.8		Dir. Invest. in Rep. Econ., n.i.e.	78be d
—	—	—	—	—	—	—	—	—	—	-7.9	—	—	-.4		Portfolio Investment Assets	78bf d
—	—	—	—	—	—	—	—	—	—	-7.9	—	—	-.4		Equity Securities	78bk d
—	—	—	—	—	—	—	—	—	—	....					Debt Securities	78bl d
—	—	—	—	—	—	—	—	—	—	16.7					Portfolio Investment Liab., n.i.e.	78bg d
—	—	—	—	—	—	—	—	—	—	16.7					Equity Securities	78bm d
—	—	—	—	—	—	—	—	—	—	....					Debt Securities	78bn d
															Financial Derivatives Assets	78bw d
															Financial Derivatives Liabilities	78bx d
-73.2	-12.2	58.8	60.9	44.5	63.0	4.4	-31.3	-76.2	-233.5	-57.3	3.0	32.6	1.0		Other Investment Assets	78bh d
															Monetary Authorities	78bo d
-72.9	7.2	32.1	88.2	8.1	.9	-5.2	—	—	-56.1	32.4	3.0	32.6	1.0		General Government	78bp d
-27.7	-25.1	4.3	-51.9	-20.3	17.1	16.2	-5.3	-105.6	-109.3	-23.7	....	....	....		Banks	78bq d
27.4	5.7	22.4	24.6	56.7	45.0	-6.6	-26.0	29.3	-68.2	-66.0	....	....	....		Other Sectors	78br d
100.6	-162.3	-15.5	-265.4	-359.8	-678.8	-400.5	-300.8	-204.2	-314.9	-465.1	-315.4	-334.7	-258.8		Other Investment Liab., n.i.e.	78bi d
—	—	—	—	-47.3	—	—	—	—	—	—	—	—	-1.4		Monetary Authorities	78bs d
149.6	-73.1	-1.8	3.8	-153.8	-244.5	-166.1	-101.9	19.9	-7.2	-116.8	47.3	-245.4	-104.7		General Government	78bt d
-12.4	-15.0	17.4	-24.7	-2.3	-2.8	-6.4	16.5	20.4	-10.2	-51.3	-27.3	-21.9	-49.6		Banks	78bu d
-36.5	-74.3	-31.1	-244.4	-156.4	-431.4	-228.1	-215.4	-244.9	-297.4	-297.0	-335.4	-67.4	-103.2		Other Sectors	78bv d
-238.6	-91.8	-94.8	21.1	45.4	-112.0	-29.0	-72.6	-41.8	6.3	16.5	90.0	110.0	252.2		Net Errors and Omissions	78ca d
-301.3	-721.6	-255.6	-229.4	-176.8	-178.5	-276.5	-104.4	158.6	185.5	83.7	238.1	193.6	80.2		*Overall Balance*	78cb d
301.3	721.6	255.6	229.4	176.8	178.5	276.5	104.4	-158.6	-185.5	-83.7	-238.1	-193.6	-80.2		Reserves and Related Items	79da d
301.3	721.6	255.6	27.4	-158.5	-197.7	102.7	124.4	-29.4	-113.6	-40.1	-213.0	-175.3	-76.0		Reserve Assets	79db d
—	—	—	115.4	91.4	100.9	50.7	-89.8	-129.2	-71.9	-43.6	-25.1	-18.4	-4.2		Use of Fund Credit and Loans	79dc d
—	—	—	86.6	243.8	275.3	123.1	69.8	—	—	—	....	....	....		Exceptional Financing	79de d

Government Finance

Year Ending December 31

1985	1986	1987	1988	1989	1990	1991	1992	1993	1994	1995	1996	1997	1998	1999		
-917.4	-1,012.3	-1,012.0	-983.7	-709.6	....	....	....	15.9	117.5	62.5	....	....	....		Deficit (-) or Surplus	80
6,664.0	5,455.8	5,300.0	4,947.6	4,965.2	....	....	....	7,116.1	7,905.1	8,847.3	....	....	....		Revenue	81
.8	....	....	....	12.3	....	....	....	17.8	36.0	51.6	....	....	....		Grants Received	81z
7,684.1	6,569.7	6,386.8	6,060.6	5,854.9	....	....	....	7,193.6	7,826.9	8,917.9	....	....	....		Expenditure	82
-101.9	-101.6	-74.8	-129.3	-167.8	....	....	....	-75.6	-3.3	-81.5	....	....	....		Lending Minus Repayments	83
															Financing	
....	....	....	....	....	....	....	....	582.8	218.1	-878.7	....	....	....		Domestic	84a
....	....	....	....	....	....	....	....	-598.7	-335.6	816.2	....	....	....		Foreign	85a
....	....	....	....	....	....	....	....	—	—	—	....	....	....		Use of Cash Balances	87
															Financing (by Currency)	
....	....	....	....	....	....	....	....				....	....	....		Net Borrowing: TT Dollars	84b
....	....	....	....	....	....	....	....				....	....	....		Foreign Currency	85b
....	....	....	....	....	....	....	....	—	—	—	....	....	....		Use of Cash Balances	87
....	....	....	....	....	....	....	....				....	....	....		Debt: TT Dollars	88b
....	....	....	....	....	....	....	....				....	....	....		Foreign Currency	89b

National Accounts

Millions of TT Dollars

1985	1986	1987	1988	1989	1990	1991	1992	1993	1994	1995	1996	1997	1998	1999		
5,883	5,740	5,854	6,727	7,834	10,276	10,159	9,867	10,765	13,504	17,042	17,778	19,306	18,453	....	Exports of Goods & Services	90c
4,109	4,042	3,730	3,424	3,099	3,487	3,835	4,117	4,171	4,432	5,029	5,473	5,579	6,281	....	Government Consumption	91f
3,656	3,593	3,200	2,185	2,714	2,970	3,565	3,152	3,421	5,962	4,809	5,717	9,582	9,839	....	Gross Fixed Capital Formation	93e
-265	135	139	70	331	5	115	37	95	-41	229	129	225	232	....	Increase/Decrease(-) in Stocks	93i
9,824	10,717	9,959	10,768	10,773	11,576	13,364	13,674	15,491	15,027	17,020	19,536	22,302	23,862	....	Private Consumption	96f
-5,136	-6,967	-5,610	-5,889	-6,378	-6,776	-8,479	-7,730	-9,453	-9,573	-12,444	-14,184	-20,441	-20,470	....	Imports of Goods & Services	98c
18,071	17,260	17,272	17,285	18,373	21,539	22,559	23,118	24,491	29,312	31,697	34,448	36,552	38,197	....	Gross Domestic Product (GDP)	99b
-859	-911	-1,003	-1,176	-1,635	-1,710	-1,906	-1,931	-1,852	-2,596	-2,923	-3,144	-2,507	-2,175	....	Net Factor Inc/Pmts(-) Abroad	98.n
16,942	16,349	16,269	16,109	16,738	19,830	20,653	21,186	22,639	26,716	28,748	31,305	34,046	36,022	....	Gross National Income (GNI)	99a
15,309	14,552	14,398	14,165	14,708	17,697	18,199	18,573	19,996	23,670	25,934	27,534	29,817	31,410	....	Net National Income	99e
....	....	....	....	....	....	....	....	....	....	....	....	....	....	....	GDP Volume 1970 prices	99b, p
18,071	17,478	16,681	16,027	15,895	16,134	16,567	16,294	16,058	16,630	17,288	17,950	18,507	19,327	....	GDP Volume 1985 Prices	99b, p
104.5	101.1	96.5	92.7	91.9	93.3	95.8	94.3	92.9	96.2	100.0	103.8	107.1	111.8	....	GDP Volume (1995=100)	99bv p
54.5	53.9	56.5	58.8	63.0	72.8	74.3	77.4	83.2	96.1	100.0	104.7	107.7	107.8	....	GDP Deflator (1995=100)	99bi p

Midyear Estimates

1985	1986	1987	1988	1989	1990	1991	1992	1993	1994	1995	1996	1997	1998	1999		
1.18	1.20	1.21	1.21	1.21	1.22	1.24	1.24	1.25	1.25	1.26	1.26	1.28	1.28	1.29	**Population**	99z

(See notes in the back of the book.)

Tunisia

		1970	1971	1972	1973	1974	1975	1976	1977	1978	1979	1980	1981	1982	1983	1984
Exchange Rates															*Dinars per SDR:*	
Market Rate	aa	.5200	.5211	ᴵ.5255	.5369	.4978	.4979	.5007	.5005	.5255	.5215	.5340	.6002	.6792	.7612	.8494
														Dinars per US Dollar:		
Market Rate	ae	.5200	.4800	ᴵ.4840	.4451	.4066	.4253	.4310	.4121	.4034	.3959	.4187	.5157	.6158	.7271	.8666
Market Rate	rf	.5250	.5229ᵉ	.4771ᵉ	.4216ᵉ	.4365	.4023	.4288	.4290	.4162	.4065	.4050	.4938	.5907	.6788	.7768
														Index Numbers (1995=100):		
Nominal Effective Exchange Rate	ne c	....	....	....	....	....	....	....	....	....	176.71	178.68	182.81	176.62	172.74	170.46
Real Effective Exchange Rate	re c	....	....	....	....	....	....	....	....	....	147.39	145.22	144.19	143.11	140.69	140.44
Fund Position															*Millions of SDRs:*	
Quota	2f. s	35.0	48.0	48.0	48.0	48.0	48.0	48.0	48.0	63.0	63.0	94.5	94.5	94.5	138.2	138.2
SDRs	1b. s	—	2.0	7.9	7.6	8.5	8.2	10.0	9.6	8.5	14.6	11.8	17.4	16.0	3.6	1.9
Reserve Position in the Fund	1c. s	—	—	5.9	12.0	12.0	12.0	12.0	12.0	11.7	11.3	19.2	19.2	19.2	30.1	29.4
Total Fund Cred.&Loans Outstg.	2tl	13.3	2.6	—	—	—	—	—	24.0	24.0	24.0					
International Liquidity												*Millions of US Dollars Unless Otherwise Indicated:*				
Total Reserves minus Gold	1l. d	55.2	142.9	217.8	301.8	412.8	379.9	365.8	351.2	443.0	579.3	590.1	536.1	606.5	567.3	406.3
SDRs	1b. d	—	2.2	8.6	9.2	10.4	9.6	11.6	11.6	11.1	19.3	15.1	20.3	17.7	3.7	1.9
Reserve Position in the Fund	1c. d	—	—	6.4	14.5	14.7	14.1	14.0	14.6	15.2	14.9	24.5	22.3	21.2	31.5	28.8
Foreign Exchange	1d. d	55.2	140.7	202.8	278.1	387.7	356.2	340.3	325.0	416.7	545.1	550.6	493.5	567.6	532.0	375.6
Gold (Million Fine Troy Ounces)	1ad	.126	.129	.129	.129	.129	.129	.129	.150	.160	.170	.187	.187	.187	.187	.187
Gold (National Valuation)	1an d	4.4	....	....	....	5.8	5.6	5.5	6.7	7.3	7.9	8.2	6.6	5.6	4.7	4.0
Deposit Money Banks: Assets	7a. d	9.8	15.4	19.1	25.5	47.8	45.1	36.7	44.9	61.7	104.7	125.4	162.0	195.7	233.6	225.5
Liabilities	7b. d	62.8	88.6	105.4	140.2	198.6	212.1	233.3	254.4	316.4	352.8	410.1	402.9	391.2	397.9	410.0
Other Banking Insts.: Liabilities	7f. d	14.1	18.8	26.0	30.3	56.7	58.4	121.3	152.5	197.5	257.0	266.6	252.4	259.5	292.3	
Monetary Authorities															*Millions of Dinars:*	
Foreign Assets	11	32	74	110	144	176	169	159	144	166	200	220	260	265	381	331
Claims on Central Government	12a	50	50	50	49	48	47	48	46	52	46	47	48	73	59	56
Claims on Deposit Money Banks	12e	31	12	24	36	55	106	111	151	167	153	199	304	446	549	697
Reserve Money	14	80	104	119	140	182	209	223	234	274	301	338	426	525	617	680
of which: Currency Outside DMBs	14a	67	80	94	112	140	163	185	214	250	265	300	343	440	533	573
Foreign Liabilities	16c	14	9	4	2	3	1	2	15	22	18	5	8	10	—	44
Central Government Deposits	16d	5	11	39	53	44	42	17	28	35	29	63	80	103	108	92
Capital Accounts	17a	7	10	13	17	31	42	48	53	59	63	77	90	128	150	204
Other Items (Net)	17r	7	3	9	16	18	28	27	11	−6	−13	−17	7	19	113	63
Deposit Money Banks															*Millions of Dinars:*	
Reserves	20	11	20	24	26	41	46	36	25	32	48	40	52	36	51	68
Foreign Assets	21	5	7	9	11	19	19	16	18	25	41	53	84	120	170	195
Claims on Central Government	22a	32	30	41	49	49	49	71	102	136	173	204	245	284	335	405
Claims on Private Sector	22d	255	285	332	396	518	673	757	872	987	1,088	1,334	1,756	2,207	2,675	3,024
Demand Deposits	24	118	153	175	202	251	296	305	337	412	493	619	729	886	1,050	1,107
Quasi-Monetary Liabilities	25	58	63	76	103	142	192	258	300	362	434	495	609	672	776	950
Foreign Liabilities	26c	15	18	24	26	35	41	43	46	55	58	77	98	120	159	191
Long-Term Foreign Liabilities	26cl	18	25	27	35	46	50	57	58	73	81	95	110	121	130	164
Counterpart Funds	26e	10	10	10	10	10	9	9	9	9	9	9	9	10	10	10
Central Govt. Lending Funds	26f	17	19	28	30	38	41	43	50	60	72	80	96	111	136	159
Credit from Monetary Authorities	26g	30	9	24	35	56	106	114	169	153	125	180	366	563	743	929
Capital Accounts	27a	29	32	34	39	44	50	60	69	77	86	96	134	158	192	228
Other Items (Net)	27r	8	14	9	3	7	2	−9	−21	−20	−8	−21	−14	8	36	−45
Post Office: Checking Deposits	24.. i	7	7	9	10	13	15	23	25	26	26	31	42	52	67	82
Monetary Survey															*Millions of Dinars:*	
Foreign Assets (Net)	31n	8	55	91	126	157	146	130	101	114	165	191	237	255	391	290
Domestic Credit	32	340	362	394	452	585	744	888	1,033	1,184	1,321	1,573	2,040	2,561	3,101	3,592
Claims on Central Govt. (Net)	32an	85	77	61	55	66	70	125	145	178	214	219	255	307	354	451
Claims on Private Sector	32d	256	286	333	397	520	675	763	888	1,005	1,107	1,354	1,784	2,255	2,747	3,142
Money	34	193	241	278	323	404	475	514	576	688	786	951	1,165	1,455	1,699	1,814
Quasi-Money	35	58	63	76	103	142	192	258	300	362	434	495	609	672	776	950
Long-Term Foreign Liabilities	36cl	18	25	27	35	46	50	57	58	73	81	95	110	121	130	164
Counterpart Funds	36e	17	12	13	15	15	17	13	13	12	11	11	14	29	27	28
Central Govt. Lending Funds	36f	17	19	28	30	38	41	43	50	60	72	80	96	111	136	159
Other Items (Net)	37r	46	58	63	72	97	114	133	137	104	102	132	284	429	725	767
Money plus Quasi-Money	35l	251	304	355	426	546	668	772	876	1,050	1,219	1,445	1,774	2,127	2,475	2,764
Other Banking Institutions															*Millions of Dinars:*	
Foreign Assets (Net)	41n	—	—	ᴵ—	—	—	—	—	—	—	—	—	—	—	—	—
Claims on Central Govt. (Net)	42an	....	....	12	17	21	28	33	37	45	54	62	80	97	116	121
Claims on Private Sector	42d	15	20	ᴵ27	37	59	81	124	157	205	255	291	351	450	662	867
Monetary Deposits	44	....	....	4	6	10	9	9	10	15	15	16	21	22	37	55
Time and Savings Deposits	45	9	11	ᴵ15	20	34	64	80	92	113	138	149	184	230	274	303
Long-Term Foreign Liabilities	46cl	7	9	13	13	23	25	52	63	80	102	112	130	160	213	—
Central Govt. Lending Funds	46f	3	3	ᴵ5	5	6	6	6	6	6	10	19	35	46	78	347
Capital Accounts	47a	6	9	9	13	13	18	20	23	29	31	33	85	154	211	302
Other Items (Net)	47r	−11	−12	ᴵ−6	−3	−7	−12	−10	−1	8	13	25	−23	−65	−33	−18
Banking Survey															*Millions of Dinars*	
Foreign Assets (Net)	51n	8	55	ᴵ91	126	157	146	130	101	114	165	191	237	255	391	290
Domestic Credit	52	366	395	ᴵ433	506	665	854	1,045	1,227	1,434	1,630	1,926	2,471	3,108	3,879	4,581
Claims on Government (Net)	52an	....	....	74	71	86	98	158	182	224	268	282	336	403	470	572
Claims on Private Sector	52d	271	306	ᴵ360	434	578	756	887	1,045	1,211	1,362	1,645	2,135	2,705	3,409	4,009
Liquid Liabilities	55l	260	315	ᴵ373	453	591	740	860	978	1,178	1,373	1,610	1,979	2,379	2,786	3,122
Long Term Foreign Liabilities	56cl	25	34	40	48	69	75	109	121	153	183	206	240	280	343	164
Other Items (Net)	57r	89	101	ᴵ112	131	162	185	205	228	218	239	301	489	705	1,142	1,585
Interest Rates															*Percent Per Annum*	
Discount Rate *(End of Period)*	60	5.00	5.00	5.00	5.00	5.00	5.00	5.00	5.75	5.75	5.75	5.75	7.00	7.00	7.00	7.00
Money Market Rate	60b	....	....	....	....	....	....	....	....	....	....	....	8.50	8.25	8.38	8.89
Deposit Rate	60l	....	....	....	....	....	....	....	2.50	2.50	2.50	2.50	4.00	4.50	4.50	4.50
Lending Rate	60p	....	....	....	....	....	....	....	7.25	7.25	7.25	7.25	8.10	8.50	8.50	8.50

1985	1986	1987	1988	1989	1990	1991	1992	1993	1994	1995	1996	1997	1998	1999		
End of Period															**Exchange Rates**	
.8314	1.0277	1.1035	1.2090	1.1888	1.1904	1.2366	1.3071	1.4376	1.4470	1.4134	1.4358	1.5483	1.5502	1.7191	Market Rate	aa
End of Period (ae) Period Average (rf)																
.7570	.8402	.7779	.8985	.9046	.8368	.8645	.9507	1.0466	.9912	.9508	.9985	1.1475	1.1010	1.2525	Market Rate	ae
.8345	.7940	.8287	.8578	.9493	.8783	.9246	.8844	1.0037	1.0116	.9458	.9734	1.1059	1.1387	1.1862	Market Rate	rf
Period Averages																
166.08	139.16	115.28	109.69	105.10	100.82	100.70	102.35	99.15	99.66	100.00	100.67	99.91	99.21	99.05	Nominal Effective Exchange Rate	ne c
139.47	119.33	102.41	100.46	99.11	96.39	98.79	100.86	97.08	97.82	100.00	100.64	100.54	100.45	100.96	Real Effective Exchange Rate	re c
End of Period															**Fund Position**	
138.2	138.2	138.2	138.2	138.2	138.2	138.2	206.0	206.0	206.0	206.0	206.0	206.0	206.0	286.5	Quota	2f. s
.5	22.6	38.1	21.0	6.4	1.7	23.0	8.8	1.3	1.8	4.7	11.1	12.1	2.1	19.3	SDRs	1b. s
26.4	—	—	—	—	—	—	—	—	—	—	—	—	—	20.2	Reserve Position in the Fund	1c. s
—	149.7	190.7	205.7	205.7	123.7	180.1	211.1	207.3	207.3	197.1	165.0	128.4	91.8	55.2	Total Fund Cred.&Loans Outstg.	2tl
End of Period															**International Liquidity**	
232.7	305.3	525.5	899.3	961.9	794.8	789.9	852.0	853.8	1,461.5	1,605.3	1,897.6	1,978.1	1,850.1	2,261.5	Total Reserves minus Gold	1l. d
.5	27.6	54.1	28.3	8.5	2.5	32.9	12.1	1.8	2.7	7.0	15.9	16.3	2.9	26.5	SDRs	1b. d
29.0	—	—	—	—	—	—	—	—	.1	.1	.1	.1	.1	27.7	Reserve Position in the Fund	1c. d
203.2	277.7	471.4	871.0	953.4	792.3	757.0	839.9	852.0	1,458.8	1,598.2	1,881.7	1,961.7	1,847.1	2,207.3	Foreign Exchange	1d. d
.187	.187	.187	.187	.187	.187	.215	.215	.215	.216	.217	.217	.217	.217	.217	Gold (Million Fine Troy Ounces)	1ad
4.5	4.5	4.8	4.2	4.2	5.2	5.0	4.6	4.2	4.4	4.8	4.4	3.8	4.0	3.5	Gold (National Valuation)	1and
223.7	218.3	365.5	392.2	453.9	610.0	603.7	570.6	545.2	536.9	451.6	569.5	607.8	663.2	639.6	Deposit Money Banks: Assets	7a. d
471.6	425.0	....	578.3	584.9	753.9	1,342.7	1,461.9	1,374.3	1,729.3	1,740.8	1,938.4	1,845.2	1,979.9	2,091.4	Liabilities	7b. d
—	—	—	....	....	....	....	—	—	—	—	—	—	—	—	Other Banking Insts.: Liabilities	7f. d
End of Period															**Monetary Authorities**	
210	187	386	762	843	629	671	868	930	1,462	1,536	1,913	2,277	2,053	2,868	Foreign Assets	11
50	62	71	49	54	64	95	117	122	93	85	103	58	78	79	Claims on Central Government	12a
819	980	840	557	603	911	1,134	1,079	1,177	835	829	178	115	114	116	Claims on Deposit Money Banks	12e
740	747	806	858	991	1,129	1,264	1,355	1,420	1,523	1,667	2,264	2,448	2,159	2,818	Reserve Money	14
633	651	705	801	875	1,005	1,104	1,156	1,179	1,196	1,315	1,473	1,594	1,695	1,994	*of which: Currency Outside DMBs*	14a
1	155	226	251	246	165	234	296	324	326	304	251	244	173	166	Foreign Liabilities	16c
81	87	72	119	139	119	164	71	128	198	137	254	231	241	244	Central Government Deposits	16d
232	266	264	58	60	68	92	99	108	119	128	134	142	151	103	Capital Accounts	17a
25	–25	–71	83	64	122	146	243	248	224	214	–709	–615	–478	–268	Other Items (Net)	17r
End of Period															**Deposit Money Banks**	
67	47	55	86	89	118	130	129	181	294	275	760	816	356	853	Reserves	20
169	183	284	352	411	510	522	542	571	532	429	569	697	730	801	Foreign Assets	21
501	575	631	652	715	762	793	535	536	544	341	291	682	556	942	Claims on Central Government	22a
3,481	3,736	4,017	4,449	5,648	5,957	6,466	7,402	7,907	8,510	9,274	9,373	10,540	11,542	12,654	Claims on Private Sector	22d
1,261	1,322	1,253	1,595	1,561	1,565	1,437	1,555	1,676	1,957	2,092	2,371	2,847	3,091	3,435	Demand Deposits	24
1,103	1,206	1,687	1,986	2,650	2,892	3,196	3,490	3,777	4,003	4,166	4,736	5,660	5,871	7,120	Quasi-Monetary Liabilities	25
178	167	253	314	328	378	424	605	614	780	817	1,076	1,214	1,260	1,684	Foreign Liabilities	26c
179	190	....	206	201	253	736	785	824	934	839	859	904	919	936	Long-Term Foreign Liabilities	26cl
10	10	....	16	3	3	—	—	—	—	—	—	—	—	—	Counterpart Funds	26e
194	214	....	236	367	412	—	—	—	—	—	—	—	—	—	Central Govt. Lending Funds	26f
1,059	1,239	1,152	840	1,308	1,356	1,536	1,485	1,494	1,175	1,119	206	153	148	136	Credit from Monetary Authorities	26g
270	321	368	419	530	592	710	885	1,053	1,246	1,672	1,914	2,150	2,361	2,578	Capital Accounts	27a
–36	–128	–154	–72	–86	–104	–128	–196	–244	–214	–384	–171	–192	–467	–638	Other Items (Net)	27r
84	77	91	95	....	100	128	157	110	122	184	230	162	164	321	Post Office: Checking Deposits	24.. i
End of Period															**Monetary Survey**	
201	49	192	550	679	596	535	509	562	888	846	1,154	1,516	1,350	1,819	Foreign Assets (Net)	31n
4,175	4,521	4,917	5,131	6,367	6,765	7,319	8,141	8,546	9,072	9,746	9,743	11,212	12,100	13,753	Domestic Credit	32
554	627	721	677	715	808	853	739	639	562	473	371	672	557	1,099	Claims on Central Govt. (Net)	32an
3,621	3,894	4,196	4,454	5,653	5,957	6,466	7,402	7,907	8,510	9,274	9,373	10,540	11,542	12,654	Claims on Private Sector	32d
2,059	2,112	2,126	2,494	2,524	2,678	2,697	2,894	2,998	3,319	3,637	4,109	4,645	4,994	5,794	Money	34
1,103	1,206	1,687	1,986	2,650	2,892	3,196	3,490	3,777	4,003	4,166	4,736	5,660	5,871	7,120	Quasi-Money	35
179	190	....	206	201	253	736	785	824	934	839	859	904	919	936	Long-Term Foreign Liabilities	36cl
32	57	....	95	97	69	70	64	78	49	39	47	67	80	81	Counterpart Funds	36e
194	214	....	236	367	412	—	—	—	—	—	—	—	—	—	Central Govt. Lending Funds	36f
808	792	795	663	1,208	1,058	1,155	1,417	1,430	1,655	1,912	1,146	1,453	1,584	1,641	Other Items (Net)	37r
3,162	3,318	3,813	4,481	5,174	5,570	5,893	6,384	6,775	7,322	7,803	8,845	10,304	10,865	12,914	Money plus Quasi-Money	35l
End of Period															**Other Banking Institutions**	
3	5	....	....	....	....	....	21	25	29	18	7	37	28	41	Foreign Assets (Net)	41n
131	148	....	....	....	....	....	—	—	1	—	9	7	7	37	Claims on Central Govt. (Net)	42an
1,068	1,203	....	....	....	....	....	1,667	1,943	2,171	2,395	2,684	2,984	3,311	3,510	Claims on Private Sector	42d
43	62	....	....	....	....	....	5	8	7	11	8	7	11	11	Monetary Deposits	44
336	402	....	....	....	....	....	327	393	418	443	489	507	674	791	Time and Savings Deposits	45
—	—	....	....	....	....	....	—	—	—	—	—	—	—	—	Long-Term Foreign Liabilities	46cl
460	457	....	....	....	....	....	535	688	843	918	985	1,061	1,012	1,005	Central Govt. Lending Funds	46f
397	462	....	....	....	....	....	846	906	952	1,049	1,115	1,192	1,246	1,296	Capital Accounts	47a
–35	–27	....	....	....	....	....	–25	–27	–18	–7	104	260	402	486	Other Items (Net)	47r
End of Period															**Banking Survey**	
204	54	....	....	....	....	....	529	587	917	864	1,161	1,553	1,378	1,860	Foreign Assets (Net)	51n
5,373	5,872	....	....	....	....	....	9,808	10,490	11,244	12,142	12,437	14,203	15,417	17,300	Domestic Credit	52
685	775	....	....	....	....	....	739	639	563	473	380	679	564	1,136	Claims on Government (Net)	52an
4,688	5,097	....	....	....	....	....	9,069	9,851	10,681	11,669	12,057	13,524	14,853	16,163	Claims on Private Sector	52d
3,542	3,781	....	....	....	....	....	6,716	7,176	7,746	8,256	9,341	10,819	11,551	13,715	Liquid Liabilities	55l
179	190	....	....	....	....	....	785	824	934	839	859	904	919	936	Long Term Foreign Liabilities	56cl
1,856	1,955	....	....	....	....	....	2,837	3,076	3,482	3,911	3,397	4,033	4,325	4,509	Other Items (Net)	57r
Percent Per Annum															**Interest Rates**	
9.25	9.25	9.25	9.25	11.37	11.88	11.88	11.38	8.88	8.88	8.88	7.88	....	....	....	Discount Rate *(End of Period)*	60
10.28	9.95	10.00	9.15	9.40	11.53	11.79	11.73	10.48	8.81	8.81	8.64	6.88	6.89	5.99	Money Market Rate	60b
5.35	6.75	7.22	7.37	....	....	....	....	....	....	....	....	....	....	....	Deposit Rate	60l
9.63	9.17	11.08	9.87	4.82	....	....	....	....	....	....	....	....	....	....	Lending Rate	60p

Tunisia

		1970	1971	1972	1973	1974	1975	1976	1977	1978	1979	1980	1981	1982	1983	1984
Prices, Production, Labor																*Index Numbers (1995=100):*
Producer Prices	63	I16.8	18.0	18.3	19.3	23.4	25.6	25.9	27.1	28.0	30.0	33.3	37.4	43.8	I46.6	50.7
Home Goods	63a	I31.0	33.9	34.4	36.1	41.3	45.0	46.4	49.4	51.2	54.9	60.2	65.7	80.6	86.9	93.1
Consumer Prices	64	....	....	....	....	....	....	....	....	....	....	....	....	....	45.7	49.8
Industrial Production	66	I34.6	37.2	40.0	41.7	45.2	46.4	47.5	I52.1	57.7	64.3	68.9	71.5	70.7	I76.8	77.0
Mining Production	66zx	I51.9	52.1	52.2	53.1	56.9	59.3	51.6	I57.0	64.4	66.7	74.3	73.4	70.7	I84.6	76.6
Crude Petroleum Production	66aa	98.0	96.7	93.9	91.6	97.7	108.8	87.6	100.7	115.7	131.5	132.0	127.5	120.5	130.6	129.4
																Number in Thousands:
Labor Force	67d	....	....	....	....	....	....	....	....	....	....	....	....	....	....	....
Employment	67e	....	....	....	....	....	....	....	....	....	....	....	....	....	....	....
Unemployment	67c	....	....	....	....	....	....	....	....	....	....	....	....	....	....	....
International Transactions																*Millions of Dinars*
Exports	70	95.8	113.3	150.3	178.8	397.7	345.6	338.3	398.3	468.4	726.7	904.8	1,233.0	1,164.7	1,263.9	1,399.1
Imports, c.i.f.	71	160.4	180.0	222.2	286.1	488.7	572.8	656.7	782.5	889.7	1,156.8	1,427.4	1,866.0	2,008.5	2,109.8	2,508.9
																1990=100
Volume of Exports	72	75	81	105	92	95	87	92	88	102	108	102	I100	100	92	91
Volume of Imports	73	27	33	38	38	50	49	56	73	77	96	91	I92	96	91	99
Unit Value of Exports	74	9	10	10	13	27	27	24	25	27	37	48	I61	66	69	75
Balance of Payments																*Millions of US Dollars:*
Current Account, n.i.e.	78ald	....	....	....	....	....	....	–396	–566	–459	–300	–353	–454	–662	–570	–765
Goods: Exports f.o.b.	78aad	....	....	....	....	....	....	788	788	942	1,557	2,195	2,491	2,004	1,862	1,782
Goods: Imports f.o.b.	78abd	....	....	....	....	....	....	–1,434	–1,613	–1,788	–2,487	–3,166	–3,453	–3,167	–2,947	–2,948
Trade Balance	78acd	....	....	....	....	....	....	–646	–825	–846	–930	–970	–962	–1,163	–1,084	–1,166
Services: Credit	78add	....	....	....	....	....	....	515	539	711	999	1,067	994	997	1,003	915
Services: Debit	78aed	....	....	....	....	....	....	–296	–315	–365	–445	–600	–579	–611	–616	–611
Balance on Goods & Services	78afd	....	....	....	....	....	....	–427	–601	–500	–376	–504	–547	–777	–697	–862
Income: Credit	78agd	....	....	....	....	....	....	26	16	19	52	94	99	105	88	99
Income: Debit	78ahd	....	....	....	....	....	....	–191	–196	–231	–312	–353	–401	–400	–357	–353
Balance on Gds, Serv. & Inc.	78aid	....	....	....	....	....	....	–592	–781	–711	–637	–763	–849	–1,072	–965	–1,116
Current Transfers, n.i.e.: Credit	78ajd	....	....	....	....	....	....	208	231	274	359	430	415	430	414	368
Current Transfers: Debit	78akd	....	....	....	....	....	....	–12	–16	–22	–22	–20	–20	–20	–19	–17
Capital Account, n.i.e.	78bcd	....	....	....	....	....	....	–12	–12	–14	–7	–7	–10	–5	–7	–5
Capital Account, n.i.e.: Credit	78bad	....	....	....	....	....	....	—	—	—	—	—	—	—	—	—
Capital Account: Debit	78bbd	....	....	....	....	....	....	–12	–12	–14	–7	–7	–10	–5	–7	–5
Financial Account, n.i.e.	78bjd	....	....	....	....	....	....	448	539	517	332	358	516	714	385	622
Direct Investment Abroad	78bdd	....	....	....	....	....	....	—	—	2	—	—	–2	–2	1	1
Dir. Invest. in Rep. Econ., n.i.e.	78bed	....	....	....	....	....	....	110	93	91	49	235	296	340	184	113
Portfolio Investment Assets	78bfd	....	....	....	....	....	....	—	—	—	—	—	–8	–7	–22	–8
Equity Securities	78bkd	....	....	....	....	....	....	—	—	—	—	—	–8	–7	–22	–8
Debt Securities	78bld	....	....	....	....	....	....	—	—	—	—	—	—	—	—	—
Portfolio Investment Liab., n.i.e.	78bgd	....	....	....	....	....	....	–5	2	–2	–2	15	79	69	60	99
Equity Securities	78bmd	....	....	....	....	....	....	—	—	—	—	17	77	69	62	103
Debt Securities	78bnd	....	....	....	....	....	....	–5	2	–2	–2	–2	2	—	–1	–4
Financial Derivatives Assets	78bwd	....	....	....	....	....	....	....	....	....	....	....	....	....	....	....
Financial Derivatives Liabilities	78bxd	....	....	....	....	....	....	....	....	....	....	....	....	....	....	....
Other Investment Assets	78bhd	....	....	....	....	....	....	–9	–7	–144	–209	–119	–288	–125	–301	–49
Monetary Authorities	78bod	....	....	....	....	....	....	....	....	....	....	....	....	....	....	....
General Government	78bpd	....	....	....	....	....	....	9	23	–74	–96	–67	–111	–39	–199	—
Banks	78bqd	....	....	....	....	....	....	14	—	–10	–47	–32	–65	–63	–72	–32
Other Sectors	78brd	....	....	....	....	....	....	–33	–30	–60	–66	–20	–111	–24	–29	–17
Other Investment Liab., n.i.e.	78bid	....	....	....	....	....	....	352	450	569	495	227	439	438	461	465
Monetary Authorities	78bsd	....	....	....	....	....	....	2	2	14	—	–42	10	—	–15	57
General Government	78btd	....	....	....	....	....	....	51	161	207	66	86	61	59	116	130
Banks	78bud	....	....	....	....	....	....	7	7	19	10	44	45	37	57	41
Other Sectors	78bvd	....	....	....	....	....	....	292	280	329	418	138	324	342	302	237
Net Errors and Omissions	78cad	....	....	....	....	....	....	–49	–19	39	92	69	–3	112	228	46
Overall Balance	78cbd	....	....	....	....	....	....	–10	–59	82	117	67	50	159	35	–102
Reserves and Related Items	79dad	....	....	....	....	....	....	10	59	–82	–117	–67	–50	–159	–35	102
Reserve Assets	79dbd	....	....	....	....	....	....	10	31	–82	–117	–35	–50	–159	–35	102
Use of Fund Credit and Loans	79dcd	....	....	....	....	....	....	—	28	—	—	–32	—	—	—	—
Exceptional Financing	79ded	....	....	....	....	....	....	....	....	....	....	....	....	....	....	....
Government Finance																*Millions of Dinars:*
Deficit (-) or Surplus	80	....	....	–9.5	–17.1	–15.4	–25.2	–62.4	–132.2	–101.2	–139.6	–98.9	–105.5	–277.4	–458.8	–307.3
Revenue	81	....	....	246.3	279.1	388.1	486.8	526.9	626.4	779.8	941.2	1,109.2	1,328.7	1,649.3	1,848.0	2,276.1
Grants Received	81z	....	....	16.5	14.9	18.4	18.9	15.4	13.4	7.7	10.8	22.0	5.4	8.4	6.5	9.3
Expenditure	82	....	....	241.1	291.1	396.1	506.0	577.2	729.8	845.5	993.6	1,117.4	1,353.4	1,814.5	2,142.0	2,438.0
Lending Minus Repayments	83	....	....	31.2	20.0	25.8	24.9	27.5	42.2	43.2	98.0	112.7	86.2	120.6	171.3	154.7
Financing																
Domestic	84a	....	....	7.4	1.8	9.0	7.6	42.2	36.4	25.7	2.8	18.5	–3.2	81.2	174.7	160.5
Foreign	85a	....	....	2.1	15.3	6.4	17.6	20.2	95.8	75.5	136.8	80.4	108.7	196.2	284.1	146.8
Debt: Domestic	88a	....	110.7	123.2	146.9	140.5	147.1	175.5	230.8	293.1	267.8	313.3	358.4	405.8	485.0	601.8
Foreign	89a	....	251.0	276.9	287.4	318.3	353.0	441.9	550.1	676.9	804.5	897.1	1,102.6	1,430.5	1,867.2	2,108.7
National Accounts																*Millions of Dinars*
Exports of Goods & Services	90c	166	212	271	300	547	546	562	649	769	1,139	1,425	1,722	1,773	1,948	2,114
Government Consumption	91f	127	134	151	169	199	250	293	355	405	444	510	616	794	927	1,030
Gross Fixed Capital Formation	93e	151	168	214	248	315	461	558	665	765	894	982	1,290	1,635	1,750	1,920
Increase/Decrease(-) in Stocks	93i	–1	10	19	–5	36	85	20	–5	–7	–27	37	56	–116	–140	75
Private Consumption	96f	517	596	707	790	971	1,032	1,205	1,409	1,563	1,775	2,171	2,553	2,997	3,434	3,944
Imports of Goods & Services	98c	–200	–230	–283	–328	–542	–630	–716	–873	–1,008	–1,285	–1,615	–2,074	–2,279	–2,421	–2,843
Gross Domestic Product (GDP)	99b	756	881	1,068	1,151	1,548	1,741	1,933	2,192	2,484	2,922	3,541	4,162	4,804	5,668	6,412
Net Primary Inc/Pmts(-) Abroad	98.n	–15	–3	–8	–12	–8	–2	–25	–19	–4	–6	–22	32	53	64	49
Gross National Income (GNI)	99a	....	....	....	....	....	....	....	....	....	....	....	....	....	....	....
Net Current Transf.from Abroad	98t	....	....	....	....	....	....	....	....	....	....	....	....	....	....	....
Gross Nat'l Disposable Income	99i	756	902	1,088	1,181	1,533	1,775	1,928	2,254	2,532	2,983	3,546	4,263	4,938	5,654	6,393
Nat'l Disposable Income, Net	99k	707	842	1,018	1,106	1,442	1,647	1,752	2,040	2,276	2,674	3,163	3,814	4,393	4,994	5,617
GDP Volume 1972 prices	99b.p	824	907	1,068	1,061	1,146	1,228	1,325	....	....	....	....	....	....	....	....
GDP Volume 1980 prices	99b.p	....	....	....	....	....	....	2,810	2,906	3,093	3,296	3,541	3,736	3,718	3,892	....
GDP Volume 1990 Prices	99b.p	....	....	....	....	....	....	....	....	....	....	....	....	....	8,528	9,058
GDP Volume (1995=100)	99bvp	29.3	32.2	37.9	37.7	40.7	43.6	47.1	48.7	51.8	55.2	59.3	62.6	62.3	65.2	69.3
GDP Deflator (1995=100)	99bip	15.1	16.0	16.5	17.9	22.3	23.4	24.1	26.4	28.1	31.0	35.0	39.0	45.2	51.0	54.3
																Millions:
Population	99z	5.13	5.20	5.28	I5.33	5.46	5.61	5.77	5.93	6.08	6.22	6.39	6.57	6.70	6.84	7.03

1985	1986	1987	1988	1989	1990	1991	1992	1993	1994	1995	1996	1997	1998	1999	744	
Period Averages															**Prices, Production, Labor**	
56.4	62.0	67.7	73.6	77.8	I 80.0	84.3	87.4	91.5	94.6	100.0	103.7	105.9	109.6	111.1	Producer Prices	63
100.0	106.4	109.5	....	....	....	....	....	....	....	....	....	....	....	....	Home Goods	63a
53.4	56.7	61.3	I 65.8	70.9	75.5	81.7	86.4	89.9	94.1	100.0	103.7	107.5	110.9	113.9	Consumer Prices	64
77.9	78.1	78.2	81.1	82.7	I 82.4	88.8	92.2	92.4	97.0	100.0	102.7	107.2	114.7	120.1	Industrial Production	66
66.0	80.8	86.8	87.9	95.8	I 88.7	89.1	85.2	73.5	79.1	100.0	105.5	93.2	113.7	121.8	Mining Production	66zx
127.7	124.0	117.8	115.9	116.3	106.3	122.7	122.8	109.7	103.4	100.0	99.0	89.9	92.0	93.0	Crude Petroleum Production	66aa
Period Averages																
....	....	....	....	2,360	....	....	....	....	2,772	....	....	....	....	....	Labor Force	67d
....	1,874	....	....	1,979	....	....	....	....	2,321	....	....	....	....	....	Employment	67e
84	80	84	92	106	152	133	137	142	160	190	181	....	....	....	Unemployment	67c
Millions of Dinars															**International Transactions**	
1,443.0	1,403.7	1,770.7	2,055.4	2,782.0	3,087.4	3,417.1	3,549.7	3,818.1	4,696.6	5,172.9	5,372.0	6,147.9	6,531.6	6,966.9	Exports	70
2,287.0	2,295.1	2,509.2	3,167.0	4,163.6	4,826.4	4,789.0	5,688.8	6,237.2	6,647.3	7,464.1	7,498.8	8,756.0	9,476.1	10,060.5	Imports, c.i.f.	71
1990=100																
82	92	95	96	116	I 100	110	111	121	137	....	....	....	....	....	Volume of Exports	72
76	76	67	83	99	I 100	107	104	116	120	....	....	....	....	....	Volume of Imports	73
76	68	77	83	94	I 100	98	95	96	101	....	....	....	....	....	Unit Value of Exports	74
Minus Sign Indicates Debit															Balance of Payments	
–581	–605	–54	210	–218	–463	–469	–1,104	–1,323	–537	–774	–478	–595	–735	–503	Current Account, n.i.e.	78al *d*
1,708	1,763	2,101	2,399	2,931	3,515	3,696	4,041	3,746	4,643	5,470	5,519	5,559	5,724	5,873	Goods: Exports f.o.b.	78aa *d*
–2,593	–2,698	–2,829	–3,496	–4,138	–5,193	–4,895	–6,078	–5,810	–6,210	–7,459	–7,280	–7,514	–7,875	–8,014	Goods: Imports f.o.b.	78ab *d*
–886	–934	–728	–1,097	–1,207	–1,678	–1,199	–2,037	–2,064	–1,567	–1,989	–1,761	–1,955	–2,152	–2,141	*Trade Balance*	78ac *d*
965	960	1,241	1,854	1,446	1,688	1,410	1,972	2,040	2,267	2,509	2,632	2,613	2,757	2,920	Services: Credit	78ad *d*
–612	–670	–664	–750	–716	–846	–841	–1,158	–1,356	–1,361	–1,352	–1,244	–1,182	–1,257	–1,234	Services: Debit	78ae *d*
–533	–645	–151	7	–477	–836	–631	–1,223	–1,380	–661	–832	–373	–524	–651	–455	*Balance on Goods & Services*	78af *d*
40	20	21	48	70	97	56	101	73	71	119	66	77	90	89	Income: Credit	78ag *d*
–400	–384	–448	–513	–518	–552	–609	–646	–629	–745	–835	–1,030	–939	–947	–978	Income: Debit	78ah *d*
–894	–1,009	–578	–458	–926	–1,291	–1,183	–1,768	–1,936	–1,336	–1,548	–1,338	–1,386	–1,507	–1,345	*Balance on Gds, Serv. & Inc.*	78ai *d*
328	418	537	678	719	847	728	682	629	816	805	879	821	792	859	Current Transfers, n.i.e.: Credit	78aj *d*
–16	–14	–13	–10	–12	–19	–14	–17	–16	–17	–31	–20	–30	–20	–18	Current Transfers: Debit	78ak *d*
–6	–4	–6	–3	–7	–7	–5	–5	–2	–3	32	37	77	61	59	Capital Account, n.i.e.	78bc *d*
—	—	—	—	—	—	—	—	5	5	47	46	95	83	72	Capital Account, n.i.e.: Credit	78ba *d*
–6	–4	–6	–3	–7	–7	–5	–5	–7	–8	–15	–9	–18	–22	–13	Capital Account: Debit	78bb *d*
381	375	180	323	132	326	401	957	1,272	1,144	958	816	699	515	1,082	Financial Account, n.i.e.	78bj *d*
6	–1	–1	–1	–4	1	–3	–5	—	–6	5	–1	–6	1	–3	Direct Investment Abroad	78bd *d*
108	64	92	61	78	76	125	526	562	432	264	238	339	651	350	Dir. Invest. in Rep. Econ., n.i.e.	78be *d*
–5	–6	–7	–5	–1	–1	–2	–3	–6	–1	2	–5	–1	—	—	Portfolio Investment Assets	78bf *d*
—	—	—	–2	—	–3	–1	–3	—	1	—	—	–1	—	—	Equity Securities	78bk *d*
–5	–6	–7	–2	–1	2	–1	—	–6	–2	2	–5	—	—	—	Debt Securities	78bl *d*
35	38	16	8	19	3	36	50	24	16	23	67	109	58	17	Portfolio Investment Liab., n.i.e.	78bg *d*
36	39	17	9	16	5	34	47	20	6	12	29	55	58	–3	Equity Securities	78bm *d*
–1	–1	–1	–1	3	–1	2	2	4	10	12	38	54	—	19	Debt Securities	78bn *d*
....	....	....	....	....	....	....	....	....	....	....	....	....	....	....	Financial Derivatives Assets	78bw *d*
....	....	....	....	....	....	....	....	....	....	....	....	....	....	....	Financial Derivatives Liabilities	78bx *d*
2	–137	–154	59	–124	–343	–261	–369	–143	–326	–327	–705	–729	–508	–228	Other Investment Assets	78bh *d*
....	–45	–62	–44	–4	–82	–43	35	15	86	88	95	14	—	—	Monetary Authorities	78bo *d*
—	—	—	—	—	—	—	—	—	—	—	—	—	....	....	General Government	78bp *d*
31	–69	–60	166	–90	–17	61	–320	–12	67	150	–305	–250	10	8	Banks	78bq *d*
–29	–23	–33	–62	–31	–244	–278	–84	–146	–479	–565	–494	–493	–517	–236	Other Sectors	78br *d*
235	418	235	201	164	589	506	758	836	1,029	990	1,221	987	313	947	Other Investment Liab., n.i.e.	78bi *d*
–53	—	—	–1	–1	–2	11	11	5	—	–1	–11	28	—	—	Monetary Authorities	78bs *d*
91	186	81	169	218	57	294	166	234	411	546	517	324	–49	338	General Government	78bt *d*
–16	91	93	30	27	57	34	122	75	168	44	189	90	—	....	Banks	78bu *d*
212	141	62	2	–80	477	168	458	522	450	401	527	544	362	609	Other Sectors	78bv *d*
–20	18	66	–113	195	477	55	343	119	–77	–119	67	206	–13	46	Net Errors and Omissions	78ca *d*
–226	–215	186	417	101	333	–18	191	67	527	97	442	386	–173	684	*Overall Balance*	78cb *d*
226	215	–186	–417	–101	–333	18	–191	–67	–527	–97	–442	–386	173	–684	Reserves and Related Items	79da *d*
226	35	–239	–437	–101	–220	–56	–237	–61	–527	–82	–395	–336	187	–688	Reserve Assets	79db *d*
—	179	53	21	—	–112	74	45	–5	—	–15	–47	–51	–50	–50	Use of Fund Credit and Loans	79dc *d*
....	....	....	....	....	....	....	....	....	....	....	....	....	35	54	Exceptional Financing	79de *d*
Year Ending December 31															**Government Finance**	
I –354.2	–510.9	–372.1	–326.9	–411.6	–585.5	–704.9	–419.4	–475.4	–219.2	–543.6	–599.0	....	....	....	Deficit (-) or Surplus	80
I 2,328.3	2,400.2	2,497.2	2,728.2	2,927.9	3,325.8	3,496.1	4,037.8	4,442.1	4,958.7	5,121.9	5,670.1	....	....	....	Revenue	81
I 3.4	4.1	23.6	30.3	143.2	70.5	32.5	56.7	53.3	63.4	44.6	42.3	....	....	....	Grants Received	81z
I 2,559.0	2,697.4	2,800.1	3,004.0	3,424.6	3,742.6	4,092.0	4,393.6	4,850.6	5,101.2	5,584.2	6,208.3	....	....	....	Expenditure	82
I 126.9	217.8	92.8	81.4	58.1	239.2	141.5	120.3	120.2	140.1	125.9	103.1	....	....	....	Lending Minus Repayments	83
															Financing	
I 155.6	273.8	285.5	157.5	294.1	393.8	419.2	278.5	300.3	1.2	53.8	72.6	....	....	....	Domestic	84a
I 198.6	237.1	86.6	169.4	117.5	191.7	285.7	140.9	175.1	218.0	489.8	526.4	....	....	....	Foreign	85a
I 750.6	867.1	949.1	1,062.3	1,275.7	1,614.4	2,428.6	2,648.8	2,986.3	3,165.7	3,251.4	3,574.0	....	....	....	Debt: Domestic	88a
I 2,441.8	3,178.4	3,190.9	3,750.5	3,847.5	4,309.4	4,869.6	4,957.8	5,710.3	6,169.9	6,556.5	6,969.0	....	....	....	Foreign	89a
Millions of Dinars															**National Accounts**	
2,253	2,161	2,799	3,639	4,352	4,711	4,856	5,419	5,931	7,106	7,657	8,030	9,183	9,638	10,467	Exports of Goods & Services	90c
1,142	1,217	1,305	1,387	1,656	1,769	1,993	2,193	2,385	2,582	2,777	2,976	3,274	3,586	3,901	Government Consumption	91f
1,850	1,685	1,620	1,680	2,157	2,635	2,892	3,729	4,122	4,279	4,121	4,422	5,153	5,592	6,450	Gross Fixed Capital Formation	93e
–15	–36	27	5	136	293	235	273	165	–382	92	354	423	643	484	Increase/Decrease(-) in Stocks	93i
4,356	4,665	5,124	5,582	6,042	6,881	7,504	8,461	9,093	9,799	10,728	11,610	12,567	13,610	14,821	Private Consumption	96f
–2,676	–2,671	–2,878	–3,608	–4,752	–5,473	–5,452	–6,368	–7,033	–7,570	–8,323	–8,326	–9,699	–10,366	–11,184	Imports of Goods & Services	98c
7,018	7,160	8,035	8,661	I 9,590	10,816	12,029	13,706	14,663	15,814	17,052	19,066	20,901	22,701	24,939	Gross Domestic Product (GDP)	99b
–68	–50	–2	52	I –387	–359	–512	–628	–874	–918	–811	–1,004	–998	–988	–1,042	Net Primary Inc/Pmts(-) Abroad	98.n
....	....	....	....	I 9,203	10,457	11,517	13,078	13,789	14,896	16,241	18,062	19,903	21,714	23,897	Gross National Income (GNI)	99a
....	....	....	....	I 547	595	514	499	594	673	712	801	834	942	1,030	Net Current Transf.from Abroad	98t
6,955	7,087	8,128	8,882	I 9,750	11,052	12,031	13,577	14,383	15,569	16,953	18,863	20,737	22,656	24,928	Gross Nat'l Disposable Income	99i
6,058	6,093	7,024	7,691	....	....	....	....	....	....	....	....	....	....	....	Nat'l Disposable Income, Net	99k
....	....	....	....	....	....	....	....	....	....	....	....	....	....	....	GDP Volume 1972 prices	99b. *p*
....	....	....	....	....	....	....	....	....	....	....	....	....	....	....	GDP Volume 1980 prices	99b. *p*
9,345	9,158	9,607	9,763	10,101	10,816	11,238	12,115	12,381	12,774	13,074	14,009	14,768	15,500	16,462	GDP Volume 1990 Prices	99b. *p*
71.5	70.0	73.5	74.7	77.3	82.7	86.0	92.7	94.7	97.7	100.0	107.1	113.0	118.6	125.9	GDP Volume (1995=100)	99bv *p*
57.6	60.0	64.1	68.0	I 72.8	76.7	82.1	86.7	90.8	94.9	100.0	104.4	108.5	112.3	116.2	GDP Deflator (1995=100)	99bi *p*
Midyear Estimates																
7.26	7.46	7.68	7.82	7.97	8.15	8.32	8.48	8.66	8.81	8.96	9.09	9.21	9.33	9.46	**Population**	99z

(See notes in the back of the book.)

Turkey

		1970	1971	1972	1973	1974	1975	1976	1977	1978	1979	1980	1981	1982	1983	1984
Exchange Rates															*Liras per SDR:*	
Market Rate	aa	15	15	15	17	17	18	19	24	33	47	115	156	206	296	436
															Liras per US Dollar:	
Market Rate	ae	15	14	14	14	14	15	17	19	25	35	90	134	187	283	445
Market Rate	rf	12	15	14	14	14	14	16	18	24	31	76	111	163	225	367
Fund Position															*Millions of SDRs:*	
Quota	2f. s	151	151	151	151	151	151	151	151	200	200	300	300	300	429	429
SDRs	1b. s	—	5	38	28	35	27	18	—	—	—	—	—	—	1	—
Reserve Position in the Fund	1c. s	—	—	28	38	38	—	—	—	—	—	—	—	—	32	32
Total Fund Cred.&Loans Outstg.	2tl	74	62	—	—	—	208	337	337	478	480	827	1,136	1,319	1,497	1,455
International Liquidity												*Millions of US Dollars Unless Otherwise Indicated:*				
Total Reserves minus Gold	1l. d	304	631	1,262	1,986	1,562	944	990	638	801	658	1,077	928	1,080	1,288	1,271
SDRs	1b. d	—	5	42	34	42	32	21	—	—	—	—	—	—	1	—
Reserve Position in the Fund	1c. d	—	—	31	46	46	—	—	—	—	—	—	—	—	34	32
Foreign Exchange	1d. d	304	626	1,190	1,906	1,473	912	969	638	801	658	1,077	928	1,080	1,253	1,239
Gold (Million Fine Troy Ounces)	1ad	3.629	3.429	3.571	3.571	3.569	3.570	3.570	3.634	3.667	3.765	3.768	3.768	3.769	3.775	3.800
Gold (National Valuation)	1and	127	130	136	151	151	151	151	153	155	155	155	155	155	155	823
Monetary Authorities: Other Liab.	4.. d	461	440	989	1,249	1,445	2,233	4,258	4,188	5,166	5,544	7,086	6,160	6,047	7,084	7,440
Deposit Money Banks: Assets	7a. d	25	38	50	74	58	309	191	137	215	258	547	794	950	992	2,076
Liabilities	7b. d	34	50	101	104	100	73	135	58	58	80	82	46	343	446	1,693
Other Banking Insts.: Assets	7e. d	....	....	....	....	....	....	....	....	....	....	....	....	....	....	....
Liabilities	7f. d	115	135	147	201	238	288	526	580	656	853	619	529	504	439	492
Monetary Authorities									*Millions of Liras through 1977; Billions from 1978 to 1995;*							
Foreign Assets	11	Ɪ8,162	12,895	21,680	31,893	25,306	17,968	23,591	16,252	Ɪ42	59	270	496	808	1,404	1,662
Claims on Central Government	12a	Ɪ10,532	12,987	13,985	14,331	18,857	41,966	51,767	90,297	Ɪ144	262	631	993	1,349	1,803	4,441
of which: Revaluation Account	12ag e															
Claims on Official Entities	12bx	Ɪ3,584	5,459	5,809	5,688	9,946	9,551	25,528	46,510	Ɪ68	124	180	236	261	256	41
Claims on Nonfin.Pub.Enterprises	12c															
Claims on Deposit Money Banks	12e	Ɪ8,969	7,624	13,702	18,319	26,192	41,770	71,843	100,138	Ɪ151	214	317	420	377	629	307
Claims on Other Banking Insts	12f	Ɪ—	—	14	78	6,245	13,514	22,281	35,840	Ɪ42	47	49	54	67	76	37
Claims on Nonbank Financial Insts	12g															
Reserve Money	14	Ɪ19,790	26,312	35,877	45,364	58,413	76,906	93,045	136,680	Ɪ199	309	458	717	1,011	1,397	2,101
of which: Currency Outside DMBs	14a	Ɪ11,851	13,918	15,980	20,703	26,154	32,909	42,471	62,961	Ɪ94	144	218	280	412	548	736
Time and Savings Deposits	15	37	75	211	787	859	680	909	769	Ɪ2	1	1	64	3	4	2
Foreign Currency Deposits	15.a															
Restricted Deposits	16b	2,189	1,819	1,558	1,922	1,958	3,000	13,249	50,385	Ɪ96	150	142	94	73	61	90
Foreign Liabilities	16c	Ɪ8,025	7,098	13,847	17,481	20,210	37,504	77,487	89,390	Ɪ146	218	734	1,000	1,401	2,447	3,943
Central Government Deposits	16d	Ɪ675	789	1,150	1,279	972	1,460	2,072	2,571	Ɪ2	5	49	269	301	191	37
Central Govt. Lending Funds	16f	104	990	696	578	1,180	1,068	1,858	3,050	Ɪ4	9	26	38	11	16	10
Capital Accounts	17a	Ɪ854	1,345	1,691	1,905	2,380	3,122	3,970	5,101	Ɪ7	9	17	26	39	55	75
Other Items (Net)	17r	Ɪ−427	536	160	994	574	1,028	2,419	1,091	Ɪ−9	3	20	−10	23	−3	230
Deposit Money Banks									*Millions of Liras through 1977; Billions from 1978 to 1995:*							
Reserves	20	Ɪ7,710	12,087	19,095	23,539	30,303	42,688	49,355	72,040	Ɪ100	151	220	429	592	827	1,299
Nonreserve Claims on Mon. Auths	20n															
Central Bank Bonds	20r	2,189	1,819	1,558	1,922	1,958	3,000	13,249	50,385	Ɪ96	150	142	94	73	61	90
Foreign Assets	21	376	529	700	1,038	815	4,677	3,175	2,668	Ɪ5	9	49	106	177	281	923
Claims on Central Government	22a	Ɪ3,735	6,189	7,551	7,242	7,450	9,878	16,056	23,756	Ɪ32	42	68	159	384	376	915
Claims on Local Government	22b															
Claims on Official Entities	22bx	Ɪ6,069	7,669	9,881	14,641	19,131	25,699	33,568	36,194	Ɪ40	78	159	161	156	199	174
Claims on Nonfin.Pub.Enterprises	22c															
Claims on Private Sector	22d	Ɪ32,536	37,196	49,420	64,989	84,172	121,233	161,596	205,772	Ɪ261	381	660	1,231	1,814	2,708	3,625
Claims on Other Banking Insts	22f	2,062	2,125	2,255	2,330	2,427	2,481	2,795	1,843	Ɪ2	2	2	3	12	17	26
Claims on Nonbank Financial Insts	22g															
Demand Deposits	24	Ɪ23,542	29,766	36,943	49,239	62,559	84,725	108,073	145,642	Ɪ190	298	Ɪ520	736	994	1,520	1,686
Time and Savings Deposits	25	Ɪ8,894	13,020	18,008	20,542	24,577	29,002	30,776	34,403	Ɪ44	84	Ɪ186	690	1,272	1,393	3,045
Foreign Currency Deposits	25.a															
Money Market Instruments	26aa															
Bonds	26ab	418	402	360	375	386	767	833	1,302	Ɪ1	2	2	2	7	12	9
Restricted Deposits	26b	Ɪ21	21	20	20	404	2,993	7,634	27,859	Ɪ28	25	38	101	181	379	512
Foreign Liabilities	26c	504	701	1,419	1,454	1,398	1,103	2,248	1,130	Ɪ1	3	7	6	64	126	753
Central Government Deposits	26d	Ɪ3,933	5,780	7,908	10,493	11,607	17,100	20,032	26,048	Ɪ35	51	Ɪ42	85	94	173	255
Central Govt. Lending Funds	26f	Ɪ440	439	369	374	551	1,145	2,084	3,135	Ɪ5	2	7	67	218	268	376
Credit from Monetary Authorities	26g	6,300	4,434	5,993	14,119	23,178	22,226	34,927	55,796	Ɪ151	214	317	420	377	629	307
Credit from Other Financial Insts.	26i	2,502	2,535	2,894	3,814	4,919	6,159	9,440	12,852	Ɪ9	10	7	—	2	1	2
Capital Accounts	27a	Ɪ7,494	9,410	11,418	12,507	13,972	17,057	19,658	22,498	Ɪ27	52	81	80	174	291	455
Other Items (Net)	27r	Ɪ636	1,109	5,121	2,778	2,779	27,398	44,110	62,046	Ɪ44	72	93	−5	−175	−323	−347
Monetary Survey									*Millions of Liras through 1977; Billions from 1978 to 1995:*							
Foreign Assets (Net)	31n	Ɪ9	5,625	7,114	13,996	4,513	−15,962	−52,969	−71,600	Ɪ−100	−153	−422	−404	−480	−889	−2,111
Domestic Credit	32	Ɪ53,910	65,056	79,857	97,527	135,649	205,762	291,487	411,593	Ɪ551	880	1,659	2,482	3,648	5,071	8,965
Claims on Central Govt. (Net)	32an	Ɪ9,659	12,607	12,478	9,801	13,728	33,284	45,719	85,434	Ɪ139	248	609	798	1,339	1,815	5,062
Claims on Local Government	32b															
Claims on Official Entities	32bx	Ɪ9,653	13,128	15,690	20,329	29,077	35,250	59,096	82,704	Ɪ108	202	339	397	417	456	215
Claims on Nonfin.Pub.Enterprises	32c															
Claims on Private Sector	32d	Ɪ32,536	37,196	49,420	64,989	84,172	121,233	161,596	205,772	Ɪ261	381	660	1,231	1,814	2,708	3,625
Claims on Other Banking Insts	32f	Ɪ2,062	2,125	2,269	2,408	8,672	15,995	25,076	37,683	Ɪ44	50	51	56	79	93	62
Claims on Nonbank Financial Inst	32g															
Money	34	Ɪ35,622	43,991	53,725	71,063	90,668	118,943	151,763	210,282	Ɪ289	456	758	1,024	1,413	2,090	2,487
Quasi-Money	35	Ɪ8,931	13,095	18,219	21,329	25,436	29,682	31,685	35,172	Ɪ46	85	187	755	1,275	1,397	3,047
Money Market Instruments	36aa															
Bonds	36ab															
Restricted Deposits	36b															
Central Govt. Lending Funds	36f	Ɪ544	1,429	1,065	952	1,731	2,213	3,942	6,185	Ɪ9	11	33	105	229	284	386
Other Items (Net)	37r	Ɪ8,829	12,168	13,955	18,194	22,401	38,980	51,148	88,407	Ɪ107	173	259	195	251	412	935
Money plus Quasi-Money	35l	Ɪ44,553	57,086	71,944	92,392	116,104	148,625	183,448	245,454	Ɪ335	542	945	1,779	2,688	3,487	5,534
Other Banking Institutions									*Millions of Liras through 1977; Billions from 1978 to 1995;*							
Reserves	40	211	218	264	333	360	513	608	383	Ɪ1	1	2	3	3	4	10
Foreign Assets	41	—	—	—	—	—	74	299	3	Ɪ—	—	—	1	2	3	4
Claims on Central Government	42a	102	102	335	185	343	305	764	1,842	Ɪ2	2	2	5	4	4	35
Claims on Local Government	42b															
Claims on Official Entities	42bx	10,398	10,636	10,421	12,688	22,312	33,437	55,401	77,766	Ɪ95	115	127	173	251	304	333
Claims on Nonfin.Pub.Enterprises	42c															
Claims on Private Sector	42d	2,861	2,737	3,092	4,066	4,751	5,931	7,709	9,692	Ɪ15	27	50	84	126	179	301
Claims on Deposit Money Banks	42e	2,502	2,535	2,894	3,814	4,919	6,159	9,440	12,852	Ɪ9	10	7	—	2	1	2
Claims on Nonbank Financial Insts	42g															

1985	1986	1987	1988	1989	1990	1991	1992	1993	1994	1995	1996	1997	1998	1999		
End of Period															**Exchange Rates**	
634	927	1,448	2,442	3,041	4,168	7,266	11,776	19,879	56,534	88,669	154,976	277,413	442,775	743,077	Market Rate	aa
End of Period (ae) Period Average (rf)																
577	758	1,021	1,815	2,314	2,930	5,080	8,564	14,473	38,726	59,650	107,775	205,605	314,464	541,400	Market Rate	ae
522	675	857	1,422	2,122	2,609	4,172	6,872	10,985	29,609	45,845	81,405	151,865	260,724	418,783	Market Rate	rf
End of Period															**Fund Position**	
429	429	429	429	429	429	429	642	642	642	642	642	642	642	964	Quota	2f.s
—	—	—	—	—	—	—	—	—	1	2	1	1	1	—	SDRs	1b.s
32	32	32	32	32	32	32	32	32	32	32	32	32	32	113	Reserve Position in the Fund	1c.s
1,208	887	543	222	36	—	—	—	—	236	461	461	440	276	649	Total Fund Cred.&Loans Outstg.	2tl
End of Period															**International Liquidity**	
1,056	1,412	1,776	2,344	4,780	6,050	5,144	6,159	6,272	7,169	12,442	16,436	18,658	19,489	23,340	Total Reserves minus Gold	1l.d
—	—	—	—	—	1	—	—	—	1	3	1	1	1	—	SDRs	1b.d
35	39	46	43	42	46	46	44	44	47	48	46	44	45	155	Reserve Position in the Fund	1c.d
1,020	1,372	1,730	2,301	4,738	6,003	5,098	6,115	6,227	7,121	12,391	16,388	18,614	19,442	23,185	Foreign Exchange	1d.d
3.858	3.840	3.831	3.822	3.785	4.095	4.163	4.047	4.031	3.820	3.747	3.747	3.748	3.748	3.744	Gold (Million Fine Troy Ounces)	1ad
1,069	1,237	1,535	1,368	1,354	1,512	1,536	1,494	1,488	1,410	1,383	1,372	1,384	1,125	1,011	Gold (National Valuation)	1and
9,507	I 8,118	10,583	9,911	8,993	8,725	7,399	6,985	7,490	9,939	12,212	12,284	11,605	12,816	11,036	Monetary Authorities: Other Liab.	4..d
1,994	I 2,728	3,075	4,892	4,222	4,973	5,486	8,540	10,708	8,655	9,951	9,400	10,474	11,616	14,896	Deposit Money Banks: Assets	7a.d
2,507	I 1,563	1,885	1,712	1,957	3,796	3,688	6,379	9,369	3,245	5,293	8,089	11,394	14,647	I 18,078	Liabilities	7b.d
....	13	786	148	467	540	620	555	612	478	1,015	942	1,062	1,084	1,146	Other Banking Insts.: Assets	7e.d
551	I 210	334	382	451	594	998	928	937	799	816	839	765	864	I 2,026	Liabilities	7f.d
Trillions of Liras Beginning 1996: End of Period															**Monetary Authorities**	
2,241	I 2,681	3,738	9,643	16,939	24,249	37,875	73,521	124,914	372,848	888,772	I 2,029	4,260	6,896	13,864	Foreign Assets	11
6,668	I 9,500	14,352	22,672	26,947	31,654	50,033	87,974	141,746	349,901	598,000	I 868	806	470	—	Claims on Central Government	12a
....	4	8	16	21	26	32	35	32	133	26	-50	-291	-500	-1,510	*of which:* Revaluation Account	12ag e
122	....	....	....	....	....	....	....	....	....	....	....	....	....	....	Claims on Official Entities	12bx
....	57	91	466	553	902	4,728	11,601	12,515	25,930	1,203	I 2	2	2	3	Claims on Nonfin.Pub.Enterprises	12c
369	I 711	1,646	3,165	3,140	4,511	4,477	8,655	16,866	20,503	28,677	I 73	831	2,103	3,137	Claims on Deposit Money Banks	12e
50	I 78	835	628	1,137	1,519	1,332	1,517	1,996	71	29	I—	—	10	—	Claims on Other Banking Insts	12f
....	27	30	25	21	—	—	—	—	—	—	I—	—	—	—	Claims on Nonbank Financial Insts	12g
2,900	I 4,588	6,759	12,084	20,780	28,746	43,077	76,773	128,902	282,973	507,819	I 972	1,943	3,506	6,923	Reserve Money	14
1,011	I 1,300	2,208	3,424	6,833	11,343	16,834	30,244	51,364	101,401	188,506	I 316	599	1,031	1,887	*of which: Currency Outside DMBs*	14a
5	I 373	110	190	207	365	667	1,982	2,942	6,773	12,425	I 33	56	112	232	Time and Savings Deposits	15
....	151	115	531	611	743	1,052	1,843	3,827	3,130	12,147	I 39	111	135	23	Foreign Currency Deposits	15.a
72	I 148	213	341	221	39	15	14	11	12	15	I—	—	—	—	Restricted Deposits	16b
6,249	I 6,974	11,590	18,529	20,916	25,564	37,587	59,826	108,401	398,227	769,307	I 1,395	2,508	4,152	6,457	Foreign Liabilities	16c
120	I 1,012	1,842	3,850	4,578	5,057	6,366	14,309	16,541	22,482	103,109	I 225	875	833	1,945	Central Government Deposits	16d
30	....	....	....	....	....	....	....	....	....	....	....	....	....	....	Central Govt. Lending Funds	16f
103	I 135	209	348	486	1,246	1,327	3,468	8,784	13,753	19,192	I 114	204	436	1,327	Capital Accounts	17a
-30	I -328	-145	726	938	1,075	8,355	25,054	28,630	41,901	92,667	I 193	201	305	97	Other Items (Net)	17r
Trillions of Liras Beginning 1996: End of Period															**Deposit Money Banks**	
1,834	I 3,400	5,103	9,134	13,603	16,967	25,834	44,839	74,625	172,477	314,480	I 641	1,298	2,433	4,544	Reserves	20
....	-169	514	-138	28	6	3,660	14,213	14,396	8,449	19,497	I 46	—	—	5	Nonreserve Claims on Mon. Auths	20n
72	153	394	848	549	132	1,191	....	....	....	....	....	....	....	....	Central Bank Bonds	20r
1,150	I 2,067	3,139	8,878	9,769	14,571	27,867	73,144	154,976	335,160	593,596	I 1,016	2,161	3,662	8,078	Foreign Assets	21
2,030	I 2,644	4,512	7,413	14,702	20,064	35,090	56,219	100,523	224,793	413,347	I 1,406	2,892	8,291	21,178	Claims on Central Government	22a
....	149	383	545	563	753	—	—	—	2,756	4,746	I 6	8	20	22	Claims on Local Government	22b
439	....	....	....	....	....	....	....	....	....	....	....	....	....	....	Claims on Official Entities	22bx
....	1,371	2,249	3,401	3,221	6,814	9,095	7,120	24,052	44,629	40,289	I 49	217	290	625	Claims on Nonfin.Pub.Enterprises	22c
5,725	I 9,454	14,484	20,617	34,828	61,060	98,780	182,233	336,615	571,521	1,356,669	I 3,203	7,252	11,493	16,565	Claims on Private Sector	22d
32	I 29	40	49	579	568	1,030	2,489	4,856	17,848	28,032	I 58	129	204	585	Claims on Other Banking Insts	22f
....	22	79	233	284	397	660	992	1,893	2,192	4,827	I 13	58	119	499	Claims on Nonbank Financial Insts	22g
2,402	I 3,710	6,175	7,480	12,082	18,671	27,114	45,590	73,402	125,850	193,429	I 562	887	1,387	2,400	Demand Deposits	24
5,120	I 6,698	8,023	15,516	27,779	41,408	75,477	124,654	183,910	434,518	959,241	I 2,098	4,237	9,138	17,904	Time and Savings Deposits	25
....	2,285	5,241	8,981	13,524	21,051	49,889	101,391	186,790	561,875	1,145,819	I 2,410	4,894	8,654	18,138	Foreign Currency Deposits	25.a
....	787	1,367	1,251	1,979	2,382	3,397	3,709	3,064	4,633	6,919	I 11	—	—	—	Money Market Instruments	26aa
7	I 7	7	54	389	413	704	6,192	24,524	15,757	36,690	I 6	81	123	I—	Bonds	26ab
550	....	....	....	....	....	....	....	....	....	....	....	....	....	....	Restricted Deposits	26b
1,446	I 1,184	1,924	3,107	4,528	11,122	18,736	54,629	135,596	125,647	315,755	I 872	2,343	4,606	I 9,787	Foreign Liabilities	26c
491	I 2,747	5,115	8,124	12,542	20,329	26,333	38,069	65,803	91,715	143,856	I 393	838	1,495	3,371	Central Government Deposits	26d
576	....	....	....	....	....	....	....	....	....	....	....	....	....	....	Central Govt. Lending Funds	26f
369	I 806	2,226	2,813	3,205	3,516	4,450	8,652	17,903	12,661	12,586	I 14	62	168	365	Credit from Monetary Authorities	26g
4	....	....	....	....	....	....	....	....	....	....	....	....	....	....	Credit from Other Financial Insts.	26i
676	I 1,624	3,039	6,816	9,341	16,680	28,044	50,209	99,670	182,053	383,839	I 869	1,864	3,944	6,645	Capital Accounts	27a
-359	I -880	-2,613	-4,013	-7,793	-14,371	-32,126	-51,846	-78,726	-174,883	-422,650	I -796	-1,192	-3,003	-6,509	Other Items (Net)	27r
Trillions of Liras Beginning 1996: End of Period															**Monetary Survey**	
-4,304	I -3,410	-6,637	-3,116	1,264	2,134	9,419	32,211	35,893	184,134	397,307	I 778	1,570	1,800	I 5,697	Foreign Assets (Net)	31n
14,456	I 19,572	30,100	44,074	65,713	98,346	168,049	297,767	541,851	1,125,444	2,200,176	I 4,988	9,650	18,569	34,160	Domestic Credit	32
8,088	I 8,385	11,908	18,111	24,529	26,332	52,424	91,815	159,925	460,497	764,382	I 1,656	1,984	6,432	15,863	Claims on Central Govt. (Net)	32an
....	149	383	545	563	753	—	—	—	2,756	4,746	I 6	8	20	22	Claims on Local Government	32b
561	....	....	....	....	....	....	....	....	....	....	....	....	....	....	Claims on Official Entities	32bx
....	1,428	2,340	3,866	3,774	7,716	13,823	18,721	36,567	70,559	41,492	I 51	219	291	627	Claims on Nonfin.Pub.Enterprises	32c
5,725	I 9,454	14,484	20,617	34,828	61,060	98,780	182,233	336,615	571,521	1,356,669	I 3,203	7,252	11,493	16,565	Claims on Private Sector	32d
82	I 107	875	677	1,716	2,087	2,362	4,007	6,852	17,918	28,061	I 58	129	214	585	Claims on Other Banking Insts	32f
....	49	109	258	305	397	660	992	1,893	2,192	4,827	I 13	58	119	499	Claims on Nonbank Financial Inst	32g
3,468	I 5,062	8,438	11,020	19,092	30,237	44,279	76,373	125,868	228,413	384,391	I 882	1,492	2,433	4,307	Money	34
5,125	I 9,507	13,489	25,219	42,121	63,566	127,085	229,870	377,469	1,006,296	2,129,632	I 4,580	9,298	18,040	36,297	Quasi-Money	35
....	787	1,367	1,251	1,979	2,382	3,397	3,709	3,064	4,633	6,919	I 11	—	—	—	Money Market Instruments	36aa
....	7	7	54	389	413	704	6,192	24,524	15,757	36,690	I 6	81	123	I—	Bonds	36ab
....	148	213	341	221	39	15	14	11	12	15	I—	—	—	—	Restricted Deposits	36b
606	....	....	....	....	....	....	....	....	....	....	....	....	....	....	Central Govt. Lending Funds	36f
953	I 651	-51	3,073	3,176	3,843	1,990	13,821	46,809	54,467	39,836	I 286	349	-227	-747	Other Items (Net)	37r
8,593	I 14,568	21,926	36,239	61,213	93,803	171,363	306,242	503,336	1,234,709	2,514,022	I 5,462	10,790	20,473	40,604	Money plus Quasi-Money	35l
Trillions of Liras Beginning 1996: End of Period															**Other Banking Institutions**	
14	I 88	294	663	1,746	2,400	5,938	10,381	19,738	52,327	84,106	I 147	257	457	894	Reserves	40
9	I 10	802	269	1,081	1,582	3,152	4,757	8,859	18,513	60,545	I 101	218	341	620	Foreign Assets	41
32	I 42	44	119	323	330	449	461	2,623	4,579	7,079	I 17	43	86	334	Claims on Central Government	42a
....	—	—	—	—	—	1,158	2,292	5,717	5,942	10,131	I 24	45	93	387	Claims on Local Government	42b
418	....	....	....	....	....	....	....	....	....	....	....	....	....	....	Claims on Official Entities	42bx
....	512	613	1,206	1,108	1,614	1,453	1,320	1,713	1,272	9,222	I 7	17	11	42	Claims on Nonfin.Pub.Enterprises	42c
390	I 585	895	1,778	2,989	4,480	9,406	13,931	22,562	45,137	78,314	I 170	332	573	825	Claims on Private Sector	42d
4	....	....	....	....	....	....	....	....	....	....	....	....	....	....	Claims on Deposit Money Banks	42e
....	—	—	—	18	21	10	119	710	230	136	I 1	5	7	35	Claims on Nonbank Financial Insts	42g

Turkey

186	1970	1971	1972	1973	1974	1975	1976	1977	1978	1979	1980	1981	1982	1983	1984
Other Banking Institutions (cont.)									*Millions of Liras through 1977; Billions from 1978 to 1995;*						
Time and Savings Deposits **45**	....	....	....	....	....	....	....	....	....	....	....	....	....	....	....
Bonds **46ab**	7,973	7,927	8,563	11,583	14,930	19,312	30,410	38,526	I 45	50	57	70	71	121	103
Foreign Liabilities **46c**	....	....	....	....	....	....	....	....	....	....	....	....	....	....	....
Long-Term Foreign Liabilities **46cl**	1,729	1,897	2,061	2,815	3,326	4,358	8,759	11,275	I 17	30	56	71	94	124	219
Central Government Deposits **46d**	....	....	....	....	....	....	....	....	....	....	....	....	....	....	....
Central Govt. Lending Funds **46f**	2,974	2,602	1,949	1,631	2,275	2,110	4,466	4,557	I 6	5	9	46	75	70	99
Credit from Monetary Authorities **46g**	—	—	14	78	6,245	13,514	22,281	35,840	I 42	47	49	54	67	76	37
Credit from Deposit Money Banks **46h**	1,869	1,932	2,028	2,103	2,200	2,157	2,471	1,452	I 2	2	1	1	7	9	18
Capital Accounts **47a**	1,588	1,647	2,075	2,388	2,664	3,060	3,787	6,405	I 7	11	14	17	64	79	189
Other Items (Net) **47r**	–59	223	316	488	1,045	1,908	2,047	4,483	I 4	9	3	7	10	16	22
Banking Survey									*Millions of Liras through 1977; Billions from 1978 to 1995;*						
Foreign Assets (Net) **51n**	9	5,625	7,114	13,996	4,513	–15,888	–52,670	–71,597	I –100	–153	–421	–403	–478	–885	–2,106
Domestic Credit **52**	65,209	76,406	91,436	112,058	154,383	229,440	330,285	463,210	I 620	974	1,787	2,688	3,950	5,466	9,571
Claims on Central Govt. (Net) **52an**	9,761	12,709	12,813	9,986	14,071	33,589	46,483	87,276	I 141	250	610	803	1,343	1,819	5,098
Claims on Local Government **52b**	....	....	....	....	....	....	....	....	....	....	....	....	....	....	....
Claims on Official Entities **52bx**	20,051	23,764	26,111	33,017	51,389	68,687	114,497	160,470	I 203	316	466	570	668	760	548
Claims on Nonfin.Pub.Enterprises **52c**	....	....	....	....	....	....	....	....	....	....	....	....	....	....	....
Claims on Private Sector **52d**	35,397	39,933	52,512	69,055	88,923	127,164	169,305	215,464	I 276	408	711	1,315	1,939	2,887	3,926
Claims on Nonbank Financial Inst **52g**	....	....	....	....	....	....	....	....	....	....	....	....	....	....	....
Liquid Liabilities **55l**	44,342	56,868	71,680	92,059	115,744	148,112	182,840	245,071	I 334	541	943	1,776	2,685	3,483	5,524
Bonds **56ab**	8,391	8,329	8,923	11,958	15,316	20,079	31,243	39,828	I 46	51	60	73	78	133	112
Long-Term Foreign Liabilities **56cl**	1,729	1,897	2,061	2,815	3,326	4,358	8,759	11,275	I 17	30	56	71	94	124	219
Central Govt. Lending Funds **56f**	3,518	4,031	3,014	2,583	4,006	4,323	8,408	10,742	I 15	17	42	151	304	354	484
Other Items (Net) **57r**	7,245	10,908	12,865	16,654	20,578	36,698	46,385	84,750	I 108	181	265	214	311	486	1,127
Interest Rates													*Percent Per Annum*		
Discount Rate *(End of Period)* **60**	9.00	9.00	9.00	8.75	9.00	9.00	9.00	9.00	10.00	10.75	26.00	31.50	31.50	48.50	52.00
Interbank Money Market Rate **60b**	....	....	....	....	....	....	....	....	....	....	....	....	....	....	....
Treasury Bill Rate **60c**	....	....	....	....	....	....	....	....	....	....	....	....	....	....	....
Deposit Rate **60l**	....	....	....	4.00	6.00	6.00	6.00	6.00	6.00	7.33	8.00	26.50	45.00	45.33	51.42
Prices, Production, Labor												*Index Numbers (1995=100):*			
Wholesale Prices **63**	....	....	....	....	....	....	....	....	....	....	....	.2	.3	.4	.6
Consumer Prices (1995=100,000) **64.a**	8.6	10.0	11.1	12.8	14.9	17.7	20.8	26.4	38.4	61.0	128.1	175.0	228.9	300.8	446.3
Consumer Prices **64**	—	—	—	—	—	—	—	—	—	.1	.1	.2	I .2	.3	.4
Industrial Production **66**	....	....	....	....	....	....	....	....	....	....	....	....	....	....	....
													Number in Thousands:		
Labor Force **67d**	....	....	....	....	....	....	....	....	....	....	....	....	....	....	....
Employment **67e**	....	....	....	....	....	....	....	....	....	....	....	....	....	....	....
Unemployment **67c**	....	....	....	....	....	....	....	....	....	....	....	....	....	....	....
Unemployment Rate (%) **67r**	....	....	....	....	....	....	....	....	....	....	....	....	....	....	....
International Transactions													*Millions of US Dollars*		
Exports .... **70..*d***	588	677	885	1,317	1,532	1,401	1,960	1,753	2,288	2,261	2,910	4,703	5,746	5,728	7,134
Imports, c.i.f. .... **71..*d***	948	1,171	1,563	2,086	3,778	4,739	5,129	5,796	4,599	5,070	7,910	8,933	8,843	9,235	10,757
Imports, f.o.b. **71.v*d***	844	1,042	1,391	1,857	3,589	4,502	4,872	5,506	4,369	4,816	7,514	8,567	8,406	8,761	10,137
															1995=100
Volume of Exports **72**	....	....	....	....	....	....	....	....	....	....	....	....	....	....	....
Volume of Imports **73**	....	....	....	....	....	....	....	....	....	....	....	....	....	....	....
Unit Value of Exports **74**	....	....	....	....	....	....	....	....	....	....	....	....	....	....	....
Unit Value of Imports **75**	....	....	....	....	....	....	....	....	....	....	....	....	....	....	....
Balance of Payments													*Millions of US Dollars:*		
Current Account, n.i.e. **78al*d***	....	....	....	....	–561	–1,648	–2,029	–3,140	–1,265	–1,413	–3,408	–1,936	–952	–1,923	–1,439
Goods: Exports f.o.b. **78aa*d***	....	....	....	....	1,532	1,401	1,960	1,753	2,288	2,261	2,910	4,703	5,890	5,905	7,389
Goods: Imports f.o.b. **78ab*d***	....	....	....	....	–3,589	–4,502	–4,872	–5,506	–4,369	–4,815	–7,513	–8,567	–8,518	–8,895	-10,331
Trade Balance **78ac*d***	....	....	....	....	–2,057	–3,101	–2,912	–3,753	–2,081	–2,554	–4,603	–3,864	–2,628	–2,990	–2,942
Services: Credit **78ad*d***	....	....	....	....	549	616	580	534	467	674	711	1,264	1,918	1,939	2,220
Services: Debit **78ae*d***	....	....	....	....	–366	–436	–517	–687	–310	–367	–569	–468	–1,031	–1,166	–1,296
Balance on Goods & Services **78af*d***	....	....	....	....	–1,874	–2,921	–2,849	–3,906	–1,924	–2,247	–4,461	–3,068	–1,741	–2,217	–2,018
Income: Credit **78ag*d***	....	....	....	....	1	1	1	6	66	34	51	52	120	102	146
Income: Debit **78ah*d***	....	....	....	....	–178	–165	–301	–347	–506	–1,010	–1,169	–1,478	–1,608	–1,568	–1,649
Balance on Gds, Serv. & Inc. **78ai*d***	....	....	....	....	–2,051	–3,085	–3,149	–4,247	–2,364	–3,223	–5,579	–4,494	–3,229	–3,683	–3,521
Current Transfers, n.i.e.: Credit **78aj*d***	....	....	....	....	1,508	1,449	1,134	1,123	1,116	1,829	2,184	2,575	2,295	1,806	2,131
Current Transfers: Debit **78ak*d***	....	....	....	....	–18	–12	–14	–16	–17	–19	–13	–17	–18	–46	–49
Capital Account, n.i.e. **78bc*d***	....	....	....	....	—	—	—	—	—	—	—	—	—	—	—
Capital Account, n.i.e.: Credit **78ba*d***	....	....	....	....	—	—	—	—	—	—	—	—	—	—	—
Capital Account: Debit **78bb*d***	....	....	....	....	—	—	—	—	—	—	—	—	—	—	—
Financial Account, n.i.e. **78bj*d***	....	....	....	....	178	327	1,132	1,645	802	–396	645	899	280	883	–507
Direct Investment Abroad **78bd*d***	....	....	....	....	—	—	—	—	—	—	—	—	—	—	....
Dir. Invest. in Rep. Econ., n.i.e. **78be*d***	....	....	....	....	64	114	10	27	34	75	18	95	55	46	113
Portfolio Investment Assets **78bf*d***	....	....	....	....	—	—	—	—	—	—	—	—	—	—	....
Equity Securities **78bk*d***	....	....	....	....	—	—	—	—	—	—	—	—	—	—	....
Debt Securities **78bl*d***	....	....	....	....	—	—	—	—	—	—	—	—	—	—	....
Portfolio Investment Liab., n.i.e. **78bg*d***	....	....	....	....	—	—	—	—	—	—	—	—	—	—	....
Equity Securities **78bm*d***	....	....	....	....	—	—	—	—	—	—	—	—	—	—	....
Debt Securities **78bn*d***	....	....	....	....	—	—	—	—	—	—	—	—	—	—	....
Financial Derivatives Assets **78bw*d***	....	....	....	....	....	....	....	....	....	....	....	....	....	....	....
Financial Derivatives Liabilities **78bx*d***	....	....	....	....	....	....	....	....	....	....	....	....	....	....	....
Other Investment Assets **78bh*d***	....	....	....	....	—	—	—	149	–17	–109	85	360	–181	177	–1,625
Monetary Authorities **78bo*d***	....	....	....	....	....	....	....	....	....	....	....	....	....	....	–551
General Government **78bp*d***	....	....	....	....	—	—	—	149	–17	–109	85	360	–181	177	....
Banks **78bq*d***	....	....	....	....	—	—	—	—	—	—	—	—	—	—	–1,074
Other Sectors **78br*d***	....	....	....	....	—	—	—	—	—	—	—	—	—	—	....
Other Investment Liab., n.i.e. **78bi*d***	....	....	....	....	114	213	1,122	1,469	785	–362	542	444	406	660	1,005
Monetary Authorities **78bs*d***	....	....	....	....	–2	40	73	173	307	63	141	–46	496	300	173
General Government **78bt*d***	....	....	....	....	–126	–118	–119	164	–280	1,986	154	100	–972	–365	–379
Banks **78bu*d***	....	....	....	....	–26	–91	–558	–77	–45	–2,220	–70	–105	114	175	648
Other Sectors **78bv*d***	....	....	....	....	268	382	1,726	1,209	803	–191	317	495	768	550	563
Net Errors and Omissions **78ca*d***	....	....	....	....	–170	–351	–831	–634	–874	651	1,435	650	–76	408	469
Overall Balance **78cb*d***	....	....	....	....	–553	–1,672	–1,728	–2,129	–1,337	–1,158	–1,328	–387	–748	–632	–1,477
Reserves and Related Items **79da*d***	....	....	....	....	553	1,672	1,728	2,129	1,337	1,158	1,328	387	748	632	1,477
Reserve Assets **79db*d***	....	....	....	....	551	383	79	366	–153	148	–529	–293	–358	–186	–63
Use of Fund Credit and Loans **79dc*d***	....	....	....	....	—	254	149	—	175	4	456	365	204	196	–43
Exceptional Financing **79de*d***	....	....	....	....	2	1,035	1,500	1,763	1,315	1,006	1,400	315	902	622	1,582

Other Banking Institutions (cont.)

Trillions of Liras Beginning 1996: End of Period

	1985	1986	1987	1988	1989	1990	1991	1992	1993	1994	1995	1996	1997	1998	1999	Code
Time and Savings Deposits	....	97	140	321	387	718	793	1,255	1,664	1,827	2,897	ℐ2	3	3	332	45
Bonds	147	ℐ226	510	1,228	2,205	3,102	5,075	8,856	16,545	39,255	50,758	ℐ70	130	104	ℐ—	46ab
Foreign Liabilities	....	159	341	693	1,044	1,741	5,071	7,946	13,558	30,961	48,672	ℐ90	157	272	ℐ1,097	46c
Long-Term Foreign Liabilities	318	....	....													46cl
Central Government Deposits	....	185	240	311	263	794	4,643	5,309	13,202	23,550	44,215	ℐ67	142	214	181	46d
Central Govt. Lending Funds	127															46f
Credit from Monetary Authorities	50	ℐ84	891	711	1,435	1,514	1,121	775	1,364	71	30	ℐ15	30	47	82	46g
Credit from Deposit Money Banks	16	ℐ281	309	1,166	1,121	1,760	3,348	5,900	11,252	42,689	88,224	ℐ160	284	502	690	46h
Capital Accounts	227	ℐ333	461	603	1,148	2,457	4,825	7,495	12,058	13,174	33,010	ℐ86	194	384	763	47a
Other Items (Net)	−18	ℐ−128	−243	−997	−337	−1,657	−3,311	−4,278	−7,720	−23,527	−18,274	ℐ−24	−23	42	−8	47r

Banking Survey

Trillions of Liras Beginning 1996: End of Period

	1985	1986	1987	1988	1989	1990	1991	1992	1993	1994	1995	1996	1997	1998	1999	Code
Foreign Assets (Net)	−4,295	ℐ−3,559	−6,175	−3,540	1,301	1,976	7,500	29,021	31,194	171,686	409,180	ℐ789	1,631	1,869	ℐ5,221	51n
Domestic Credit	15,215	ℐ20,418	30,537	46,189	68,172	101,911	173,519	306,573	555,122	1,141,136	2,232,782	ℐ5,080	9,821	18,911	35,018	52
Claims on Central Govt. (Net)	8,120	ℐ8,241	11,712	17,919	24,589	25,869	48,230	86,966	149,346	441,527	727,245	ℐ1,606	1,885	6,304	16,016	52an
Claims on Local Government	....	149	383	545	563	753	1,158	2,292	5,717	8,698	14,876	ℐ30	54	113	409	52b
Claims on Official Entities	980															52bx
Claims on Nonfin.Pub.Enterprises	....	1,940	2,954	5,072	4,881	9,330	15,276	20,041	38,279	71,831	50,714	ℐ58	236	303	670	52c
Claims on Private Sector	6,116	ℐ10,039	15,379	22,395	37,817	65,540	108,186	196,164	359,178	616,658	1,434,983	ℐ3,372	7,584	12,066	17,389	52d
Claims on Nonbank Financial Inst	....	49	109	258	323	419	670	1,110	2,602	2,422	4,963	ℐ14	62	126	534	52g
Liquid Liabilities	8,579	ℐ15,420	23,325	37,595	62,168	94,611	169,760	300,968	488,455	1,189,694	2,440,215	ℐ5,330	10,541	20,026	40,053	55l
Bonds	154	ℐ233	517	1,283	2,594	3,515	5,779	15,048	41,069	55,012	87,448	ℐ76	212	227	ℐ—	56ab
Long-Term Foreign Liabilities	318															56cl
Central Govt. Lending Funds	734															56f
Other Items (Net)	1,135	ℐ1,206	520	3,772	4,711	5,761	5,481	19,579	56,791	68,116	114,298	ℐ464	700	527	186	57r

Interest Rates

Percent Per Annum

	1985	1986	1987	1988	1989	1990	1991	1992	1993	1994	1995	1996	1997	1998	1999	Code
Discount Rate (End of Period)	52.00	48.00	45.00	54.00	54.00	45.00	48.00	48.00	48.00	55.00	50.00	....	....	....	....	60
Interbank Money Market Rate			39.82	60.62	40.66	51.91	72.75	65.35	62.83	136.47	72.30	76.24	70.32	74.60	73.53	60b
Treasury Bill Rate			41.92	54.56	48.01	43.46	67.01	72.17								60c
Deposit Rate	49.25	40.58	35.00	49.08	53.45	47.50	62.67	68.74	64.58	87.79	76.02	80.74	79.49	80.11	78.43	60l

Prices, Production, Labor

Period Averages

	1985	1986	1987	1988	1989	1990	1991	1992	1993	1994	1995	1996	1997	1998	1999	Code
Wholesale Prices	.8	1.1	ℐ1.4	2.4	4.0	6.1	9.5	15.4	24.3	ℐ53.8	100.0	175.9	319.9	549.6	841.2	63
Consumer Prices (1995=100,000)	647.0	871.0	1,209.3	2,100.2	3,429.1	5,497.3	9,123.8	15,517.1	25,773.5	53,161.0	100,000.0	180,346.9	334,964.1	618,482.3		64.a
Consumer Prices	.6	.9	ℐ1.2	2.1	3.4	5.5	9.1	15.5	25.8	ℐ53.2	100.0	180.3	335.0	618.5	1,019.7	64
Industrial Production	....	65.5	72.4	73.6	76.3	83.5	88.1	ℐ92.8	98.2	92.1	100.0	105.9	ℐ117.3	118.3	....	66

Period Averages

	1985	1986	1987	1988	1989	1990	1991	1992	1993	1994	1995	1996	1997	1998	1999	Code
Labor Force									20,384	....	22,078	22,259	21,818	23,415	....	67d
Employment	16,162	....	....	ℐ18,445	18,856	19,946	19,452	19,959	19,905	20,396	21,378	21,698	20,815	21,958	....	67e
Unemployment	....	....	....	1,748	1,821	1,615	1,787	1,745	1,722	1,740	1,522	1,332	1,545	1,547	....	67c
Unemployment Rate (%)	....	....	....	8.7	8.8	7.5	8.4	8.0	8.0	7.6	6.6	5.8	6.9	6.2	....	67r

International Transactions

Millions of US Dollars

	1985	1986	1987	1988	1989	1990	1991	1992	1993	1994	1995	1996	1997	1998	1999	Code
Exports	7,958	7,457	10,190	11,662	11,625	12,959	13,594	14,715	15,345	18,106	21,637	23,224	26,261	26,974	26,588	70..d
Imports, c.i.f.	11,343	11,105	14,158	14,335	15,792	22,302	21,047	22,871	29,428	23,270	35,709	43,627	48,559	45,921	40,692	71..d
Imports, f.o.b.	10,732	10,506	13,394	13,562	14,940	21,003	19,782	21,291	27,661	21,875	33,564	39,916	46,226	....		71.vd

1995=100

	1985	1986	1987	1988	1989	1990	1991	1992	1993	1994	1995	1996	1997	1998	1999	Code
Volume of Exports	....	....	....	....	66.2	ℐ69.9	74.6	76.9	81.8	93.9	100.0	109.7	124.4	131.9	....	72
Volume of Imports	....	....	....	....	67.9	ℐ78.0	75.0	76.1	104.4	73.3	100.0	129.3	159.9	150.9	....	73
Unit Value of Exports	....	....	....	....	85.0	ℐ93.7	92.9	94.1	91.5	88.8	100.0	95.6	91.0	87.5	....	74
Unit Value of Imports	....	....	....	....	85.2	ℐ89.8	87.0	85.3	80.0	85.6	100.0	94.0	85.8	82.8	....	75

Balance of Payments

Minus Sign Indicates Debit

	1985	1986	1987	1988	1989	1990	1991	1992	1993	1994	1995	1996	1997	1998	1999	Code
Current Account, n.i.e.	−1,013	−1,465	−806	1,596	938	−2,625	250	−974	−6,433	2,631	−2,338	−2,437	−2,679	1,871	....	78ald
Goods: Exports f.o.b.	8,255	7,583	10,322	11,929	11,780	13,026	13,667	14,891	15,611	18,390	21,975	32,446	32,631	31,220	....	78aad
Goods: Imports f.o.b.	−11,230	−10,664	−13,551	−13,706	−15,999	−22,581	−21,007	−23,081	−29,771	−22,606	−35,187	−43,028	−48,029	−45,552	....	78abd
Trade Balance	−2,975	−3,081	−3,229	−1,777	−4,219	−9,555	−7,340	−8,190	−14,160	−4,216	−13,212	−10,582	−15,398	−14,332	....	78acd
Services: Credit	2,864	2,997	3,813	5,652	6,414	8,016	8,372	9,407	10,652	10,801	14,606	13,051	19,373	23,321	....	78add
Services: Debit	−1,333	−1,428	−1,695	−1,925	−2,465	−3,071	−3,218	−3,625	−3,948	−3,782	−5,024	−6,426	−8,507	−9,860	....	78aed
Balance on Goods & Services	−1,444	−1,512	−1,111	1,950	−270	−4,610	−2,186	−2,408	−7,456	2,803	−3,630	−3,957	−4,532	−871	....	78afd
Income: Credit	298	341	382	374	684	917	935	1,012	1,135	890	1,489	1,577	1,900	2,481	....	78agd
Income: Debit	−1,851	−2,218	−2,467	−2,887	−3,011	−3,425	−3,598	−3,637	−3,880	−4,154	−4,693	−4,504	−4,913	−5,466	....	78ahd
Balance on Gds, Serv. & Inc.	−2,997	−3,389	−3,196	−563	−2,597	−7,118	−4,849	−5,033	−10,201	−461	−6,834	−6,884	−7,545	−3,856	....	78aid
Current Transfers, n.i.e.: Credit	2,022	2,030	2,456	2,220	3,574	4,525	5,131	4,075	3,800	3,113	4,512	4,466	4,909	5,860	....	78ajd
Current Transfers: Debit	−38	−106	−66	−61	−39	−32	−32	−16	−32	−21	−16	−19	−43	−133	....	78akd
Capital Account, n.i.e.	—	—	—	23	—	—	—	—	—	—	—	—	—	—	....	78bcd
Capital Account, n.i.e.: Credit	—	—	—	23	—	—	—	—	—	—	—	—	—	—	....	78bad
Capital Account: Debit	—	—	—	—	—	—	—	—	—	—	—	—	—	—	....	78bbd
Financial Account, n.i.e.	1,065	2,124	1,891	−958	780	4,037	−2,397	3,648	8,963	−4,194	4,643	8,763	8,616	773	....	78bjd
Direct Investment Abroad	....	....	−9	....	....	16	−27	−65	−14	−49	−113	−110	−251	−367	....	78bdd
Dir. Invest. in Rep. Econ., n.i.e.	99	125	115	354	663	684	810	844	636	608	885	722	805	940	....	78bed
Portfolio Investment Assets	....	....	−25	−6	−59	−134	−91	−754	−563	35	−466	−1,380	−710	−1,297	....	78bfd
Equity Securities	....	....	−25	−6	−59	−134	−91	−50	−139	5	−75	−7	−50	171	....	78bkd
Debt Securities								−704	−424	30	−391	−1,387	−660	−1,468	....	78bld
Portfolio Investment Liab., n.i.e.	....	146	307	1,184	1,445	681	714	3,165	4,480	1,123	703	1,950	2,344	−5,089	....	78bgd
Equity Securities			—	17	89	147	350	570	989	195	191	8	−518		....	78bmd
Debt Securities	....	146	307	1,184	1,428	592	567	2,815	3,910	134	508	1,759	2,336	−4,571	....	78bnd
Financial Derivatives Assets															....	78bwd
Financial Derivatives Liabilities															....	78bxd
Other Investment Assets	127	−313	−945	−1,428	371	−409	−2,563	−2,438	−3,291	2,423	−383	331	−1,750	−1,464	....	78bhd
Monetary Authorities	−255	−220	−511	−381	712	361	29	36	−61	−18	−102	−117	−98	−95	....	78bod
General Government												—	—		....	78bpd
Banks	382	−93	−434	−1,046	−370	−769	−2,595	−2,474	−3,230	2,441	−281	1,448	−976	−942	....	78bqd
Other Sectors	....	....	....	−1	29	−1	3	....	....	....	....	−1,000	−676	−427	....	78brd
Other Investment Liab., n.i.e.	839	2,166	2,448	−1,062	−1,640	3,199	−1,240	2,896	7,715	−8,334	4,017	7,250	8,178	8,050	....	78bid
Monetary Authorities	35	67	967	−697	−13	−419	−1,089	300	1,085	1,415	1,734	1,456	1,195	760	....	78bsd
General Government	49	1,341	1,403	610	−1,089	503	330	−1,310	−1,953	−2,516	−1,991	−2,232	−1,406	−1,655	....	78btd
Banks	326	755	1,006	−144	240	2,279	396	2,100	4,495	−7,053	1,973	3,046	2,232	3,195	....	78bud
Other Sectors	429	3	−928	−831	−778	836	−877	1,806	4,088	−180	2,301	4,980	6,157	5,750	....	78bvd
Net Errors and Omissions	−836	−119	−505	515	969	−469	948	−1,190	−2,222	1,766	2,355	−1,782	−2,594	−2,203	....	78cad
Overall Balance	−784	540	580	1,153	2,710	943	−1,199	1,484	308	203	4,660	4,544	3,343	441	....	78cbd
Reserves and Related Items	784	−540	−580	−1,153	−2,710	−943	1,199	−1,484	−308	−203	−4,660	−4,544	−3,343	−441	....	79dad
Reserve Assets	360	−162	−137	−721	−2,471	−895	1,199	−1,484	−308	−547	−5,007	−4,544	−3,316	−217	....	79dbd
Use of Fund Credit and Loans	−251	−378	−443	−432	−239	−48	—	—	—	344	347	....	−27	−224	....	79dcd
Exceptional Financing	676	—	—	—	—	—	—	—	—	—	—	....	....	....	....	79ded

Turkey

		1970	1971	1972	1973	1974	1975	1976	1977	1978	1979	1980	1981	1982	1983	1984
International Investment Position															*Millions of US Dollars*	
Assets	79aa d	....	....	....	....	....	....	....	....	....	....	....	....	....	2,288	3,931
Direct Investment Abroad	79ab d	....	....	....	....	....	....	....	....	....	....	....	....	....	....	....
Portfolio Investment	79ac d	....	....	....	....	....	....	....	....	....	....	....	....	....	—	—
Equity Securities	79ad d	....	....	....	....	....	....	....	....	....	....	....	....	....	—	—
Debt Securities	79ae d	....	....	....	....	....	....	....	....	....	....	....	....	....	....	....
Financial Derivatives	79al d	....	....	....	....	....	....	....	....	....	....	....	....	....	....	....
Other Investment	79af d	....	....	....	....	....	....	....	....	....	....	....	....	793	845	1,860
Monetary Authorities	79ag d	....	....	....	....	....	....	....	....	....	....	....	....	....	....	....
General Government	79ah d	....	....	....	....	....	....	....	....	....	....	....	....	....	....	....
Banks	79ai d	....	....	....	....	....	....	....	....	....	....	....	....	....	845	1,860
Other Sectors	79aj d	....	....	....	....	....	....	....	....	....	....	....	....	....	—	—
Reserve Assets	79ak d	....	....	....	....	....	....	....	....	....	....	1,236	1,730	1,235	1,443	2,071
Liabilities	79la d	....	....	....	....	....	....	....	....	....	....	....	....	....	19,554	20,471
Dir. Invest. in Rep. Economy	79lb d	....	....	....	....	....	....	....	....	....	....	....	....	....	—	—
Portfolio Investment	79lc d	....	....	....	....	....	....	....	....	....	....	....	....	....	5	5
Equity Securities	79ld d	....	....	....	....	....	....	....	....	....	....	....	....	....	—	—
Debt Securities	79le d	....	....	....	....	....	....	....	....	....	....	....	....	....	5	5
Financial Derivatives	79ll d	....	....	....	....	....	....	....	....	....	....	....	....	....	....	....
Other investment	79lf d	....	....	....	....	....	....	....	....	....	....	....	....	18,833	19,549	20,466
Monetary Authorities	79lg d	....	....	....	....	....	....	....	....	....	....	....	....	2,603	5,552	5,215
General Government	79lh d	....	....	....	....	....	....	....	....	....	....	....	....	....	10,630	10,845
Banks	79li d	....	....	....	....	....	....	....	....	....	....	....	....	906	83	544
Other Sectors	79lj d	....	....	....	....	....	....	....	....	....	....	....	....	....	3,284	3,862
Government Finance											*Millions of Liras through 1977; Billions 1978-1995; Trillions beg.*						
Deficit (-) or Surplus	80	⊥–3,620	–6,457	–5,105	–5,499	–7,451	–6,998	–13,235	–52,839	⊥–55	–137	–161	–117	....	⊥–483	–1,815
Revenue	81	⊥28,820	38,481	47,500	59,384	71,710	109,003	143,732	186,900	⊥291	497	957	1,446	....	⊥2,309	2,721
Grants Received	81z	⊥—	—	—	—	10	—	—	—	⊥—	—	—	—	....	⊥1	....
Expenditure	82	⊥31,640	44,330	52,393	64,403	77,098	112,931	154,209	229,414	⊥328	610	1,117	1,526	....	⊥2,791	4,535
Lending Minus Repayments	83	⊥800	608	212	480	2,073	3,070	2,758	10,325	⊥18	23	1	37	....	⊥2	2
Financing																
Domestic	84a	⊥3,200	5,900	4,360	4,940	7,240	6,920	13,300	52,180	⊥53	133	137	29	....	....	....
Foreign	85a	⊥370	484	742	560	206	82	25	567	⊥2	3	24	88	....	....	....
Total Debt	88	⊥45,040	58,030	64,490	68,000	78,050	101,040	135,220	207,170	⊥324	508	968	2,052	....	....	5,033
Domestic	88a	⊥24,330	32,890	36,990	41,560	46,960	70,080	100,280	164,480	⊥244	405	621	1,131	....	....	....
Foreign	89a	⊥20,710	25,140	27,500	26,440	31,090	30,960	34,940	42,690	⊥80	103	347	922	....	⊥2,567	....
National Accounts											*Billions of Liras through 1995;*						
Exports of Goods & Services	90c	....	....	....	....	....	....	....	....	....	....	....	....	....	....	....
Government Consumption	91f	....	....	....	....	....	....	....	....	....	....	....	....	....	....	....
Gross Fixed Capital Formation	93e	....	....	....	....	....	....	....	....	....	....	....	....	....	....	....
Increase/Decrease(-) in Stocks	93i	....	....	....	....	....	....	....	....	....	....	....	....	....	....	....
Private Consumption	96f	....	....	....	....	....	....	....	....	....	....	....	....	....	....	....
Imports of Goods & Services	98c	....	....	....	....	....	....	....	....	....	....	....	....	....	....	....
Gross Domestic Product (GDP)	99b	....	....	....	....	....	....	....	....	....	....	....	....	....	....	....
GDP Vol. 1987 Prices(trillions)	99b.p	33.8	35.6	38.3	39.5	41.8	44.7	49.5	51.1	51.9	51.6	50.3	52.7	54.6	57.3	61.2
GDP Volume (1995=100)	99bv p	34.5	36.4	39.1	40.4	42.7	45.7	50.6	52.2	53.0	52.7	51.4	53.9	55.8	58.6	62.5
GDP Deflator (1995=100)	99bi p	....	....	....	....	....	....	....	....	....	....	....	....	....	....	....
																Millions:
Population	99z	35.32	36.22	37.13	38.07	39.04	40.09	40.92	41.77	42.64	43.53	44.47	45.47	46.69	47.86	49.07

	1985	1986	1987	1988	1989	1990	1991	1992	1993	1994	1995	1996	1997	1998	1999		
Millions of US Dollars																**International Investment Position**	
	3,724	4,696	6,294	9,466	11,688	13,686	15,319	18,555	21,291	20,194	27,396	27,613	30,035	31,343	....	Assets	79aa *d*
	—	—	—	—	—	—	—	—	—	—	—	—	—	—	....	Direct Investment Abroad	79ab *d*
	....	....	....	....	....	....	....	....	....	....	....	....	....	—	....	Portfolio Investment	79ac *d*
	....	....	....	....	....	....	....	....	....	....	....	....	....	—	....	Equity Securities	79ad *d*
	—	—	—	—	—	—	—	—	—	—	—	—	—	—	....	Debt Securities	79ae *d*
	1,628	2,051	2,994	5,748	5,461	6,199	8,862	10,901	13,545	11,624	13,571	9,909	10,448	10,563	....	Financial Derivatives	79al *d*
	—	157	152	2,201	1,489	1,130	1,101	1,088	1,034	1,061	1,103	1,160	1,211	1,265	....	Other Investment	79af *d*
															....	Monetary Authorities	79ag *d*
	1,628	1,894	2,842	3,547	3,972	5,069	7,761	9,813	12,511	10,563	12,468	8,749	9,237	9,298	....	General Government	79ah *d*
															....	Banks	79ai *d*
	2,096	2,645	3,300	3,718	6,227	7,487	6,457	7,654	7,746	8,570	13,825	17,704	19,587	20,780	....	Other Sectors	79aj *d*
	24,308	29,492	35,656	39,939	42,064	50,285	50,578	55,736	67,452	66,027	74,015	83,942	91,029	102,652	....	Reserve Assets	79ak *d*
															....	Liabilities	79la *d*
	48	217	712	3,321	5,226	5,877	6,683	9,316	12,623	13,788	14,186	13,081	13,721	14,024	....	Dir. Invest. in Rep. Economy	79lb *d*
	—	—	—	—	—	—	—	—	—	—	—	—	—	—	....	Portfolio Investment	79lc *d*
	48	217	712	3,321	5,226	5,877	6,683	9,316	12,623	13,788	14,186	13,081	13,721	14,024	....	Equity Securities	79ld *d*
	—	—	—	—	—	—	—	—	—	—	—	—	—	—	....	Debt Securities	79le *d*
	24,260	29,275	34,944	36,618	36,838	44,408	43,895	46,420	54,829	52,239	59,829	70,861	77,308	88,628	....	Financial Derivatives	79ll *d*
	5,330	4,903	4,755	7,240	7,718	8,010	6,765	6,680	7,208	9,658	12,216	12,374	11,756	12,978	....	Other investment	79lf *d*
	12,584	15,814	20,393	20,122	19,322	21,407	22,393	20,635	19,733	21,660	21,428	23,239	21,986	22,204	....	Monetary Authorities	79lg *d*
	1,122	2,141	3,223	3,775	3,419	5,869	6,620	8,262	12,461	5,814	8,025	10,386	12,131	15,616	....	General Government	79lh *d*
	5,224	6,417	6,573	5,481	6,379	9,122	8,117	10,843	15,427	15,107	18,160	24,862	31,435	37,830	....	Banks	79li *d*
															....	Other Sectors	79lj *d*
1996: Year Ending Feb.28/29 through 1981, December 31 thereafter																**Government Finance**	
	−2,050	−1,259	−2,346	−3,859	−7,502	−11,781	−33,317	−47,328	−133,105	−150,838	−316,621	Ɪ−1,238	....	....	....	Deficit (-) or Surplus	80
	4,836	7,052	10,430	17,547	31,254	54,937	90,650	176,370	355,736	750,673	1,401,847	Ɪ2,726	....	....	....	Revenue	81
	—	—	15	40	115	1,636	8,434	1,700	1,597	942	7,404	Ɪ2	....	....	....	Grants Received	81z
	6,884	8,294	12,773	21,424	38,840	68,316	132,350	225,256	490,129	902,077	1,725,514	Ɪ3,966	....	....	....	Expenditure	82
	1	18	18	22	32	38	51	142	309	376	358	Ɪ—	....	....	....	Lending Minus Repayments	83
																Financing	
	....	1,158	....	3,683	7,907	11,913	31,596	43,395	112,795	219,353	396,181	Ɪ1,373	2,685 [p]		....	Domestic	84a
	....	101	....	176	−404	−131	1,721	3,933	20,310	−68,515	−79,560	Ɪ−134	−453 [p]		....	Foreign	85a
	7,101	10,801	....	57,937	86,925	118,883	202,456	371,934	667,854	1,702,786	2,782,173	Ɪ5,602	12,876 [p]		....	Total Debt	88
	3,671	6,417	....	28,458	41,934	57,180	97,647	194,237	356,555	799,309	1,361,007	Ɪ3,149	6,283 [p]		....	Domestic	88a
	3,431	4,384	....	29,479	44,991	61,703	104,809	177,697	311,299	903,477	1,421,166	Ɪ2,453	6,593 [p]		....	Foreign	89a
Trillions of Liras Beginning 1996																**National Accounts**	
	....	....	11,642	24,106	36,833	52,533	87,215	157,360	270,997	826,379	1,544,078	Ɪ3,182	7,088	12,781	....	Exports of Goods & Services	90c
	....	....	5,845	9,837	21,240	43,083	78,256	140,584	258,084	450,605	837,243	Ɪ1,709	3,535	6,499	....	Government Consumption	91f
	....	....	18,491	33,738	51,837	89,892	149,272	258,406	525,506	952,322	1,850,288	Ɪ3,706	7,618	12,794	....	Gross Fixed Capital Formation	93e
	....	....	687	−1,247	1,522	6,601	−6,160	2,454	21,619	−121,416	127,149	Ɪ−80	−377	−103	....	Increase/Decrease(-) in Stocks	93i
	....	....	51,017	82,050	149,140	269,564	434,365	760,256	1,369,339	2,706,262	5,457,903	Ɪ9,938	19,619	35,316	....	Private Consumption	96f
	....	....	−13,269	−22,683	−40,420	−69,092	−104,819	−189,646	−383,358	−788,530	1,890,237	Ɪ−4,111	−8,763	−14,573	....	Imports of Goods & Services	98c
	....	....	74,416	125,801	220,152	392,580	638,130	1,129,413	2,062,187	3,868,430	7,762,456	Ɪ14,772	28,836	51,625	....	Gross Domestic Product (GDP)	99b
	63.8	68.2	74.7	76.3	76.5	83.6	84.4	89.4	96.6	91.3	97.9	104.7	112.6	115.8	....	GDP Vol. 1987 Prices(trillions)	99b. *p*
	65.2	69.7	76.3	78.0	78.1	85.4	86.2	91.3	98.7	93.3	100.0	107.0	115.1	118.3	....	GDP Volume (1995=100)	99bv *p*
	....	....	1.3	2.1	3.6	5.9	9.5	15.9	26.9	53.4	100.0	177.8	322.9	562.3	....	GDP Deflator (1995=100)	99bi *p*
Midyear Estimates																	
	50.31	51.43	52.56	53.71	54.89	56.10	57.06	57.93	58.51	59.71	60.61	61.53	62.47	63.45	64.39	**Population**	99z

(See notes in the back of the book.)

Uganda

	1970	1971	1972	1973	1974	1975	1976	1977	1978	1979	1980	1981	1982	1983	1984
Exchange Rates												*Shillings per Thousand SDRs through 1984*			
Principal Rate .... aa	71.4	77.6	77.6	83.2	87.5	96.6	96.6	96.6	96.6	96.6	96.6	991.1	1,167.3	2,512.7	5,097.1
												Shillings per Thousand US Dollars 1984			
Principal Rate .... ae	71.4	71.4	71.4	69.0	71.4	82.6	83.1	79.5	74.2	73.3	75.7	851.5	1,058.2	2,400.0	5,200.0
Principal Rate .... rf	71.4	71.4	71.4	70.2	71.4	74.2	82.7	82.6	77.4	74.8	74.2	500.5	940.5	1,538.6	3,597.0
												Index Numbers (1995=100):			
Principal Rate .... ahx	....	....	....	....	....	....	....	....	....	....	....	582,555.4	103,416.6	66,766.7	28,897.5
Nominal Effective Exchange Rate ... nec	....	....	....	....	....	....	....	....	....	160,644.8	170,348.4	86,880.4	18,298.0	13,390.9	7,829.6
Real Effective Exchange Rate .... rec	....	....	....	....	....	....	....	....	....	....	1,024.0	728.0	252.4	199.3	135.9
Fund Position															*Millions of SDRs:*
Quota .... 2f. s	40.0	40.0	40.0	40.0	40.0	40.0	40.0	40.0	50.0	50.0	75.0	75.0	75.0	99.6	99.6
SDRs .... 1b. s	5.4	9.6	13.7	13.4	5.0	3.2	.9	4.5	8.1	8.4	—	2.6	10.1	.9	.2
Reserve Position in the Fund .... 1c. s	6.5	—	—	—	—	—	—	—	5.9	—	—	—	3.5	3.5	3.5
Total Fund Cred.&Loans Outstg. 2tl	—	10.0	10.0	10.0	15.0	24.1	32.7	32.7	29.2	26.2	70.1	182.5	265.9	360.6	343.8
International Liquidity												*Millions of US Dollars Unless Otherwise Indicated:*			
Total Reserves minus Gold 1l.d	56.6	26.9	36.0	29.1	16.8	31.0	44.5	47.2	52.7	22.8	3.0	30.0	78.3	106.5	₤67.9
SDRs 1b.d	5.4	10.4	14.9	16.2	6.2	3.7	1.0	5.4	10.5	11.0	—	3.0	11.1	.9	.2
Reserve Position in the Fund 1c.d	6.5	—	—	—	—	—	—	—	7.7	—	—	—	3.9	3.7	3.5
Foreign Exchange 1d.d	44.8	16.5	21.1	12.9	10.6	27.3	43.5	41.8	34.5	11.8	3.0	27.0	63.3	101.9	₤64.3
Monetary Authorities: Other Liab. .... 4..d	—	—	5.2	5.8	5.8	3.4	3.6	6.3	5.4	20.5	13.3	42.4	38.3	3.7	9.6
Deposit Money Banks: Assets 7a.d	9.9	8.7	9.0	5.5	9.9	12.2	17.7	32.2	31.5	33.3	18.5	11.7	25.1	29.6	26.8
Liabilities 7b.d	2.2	5.6	8.4	3.3	7.1	2.7	7.4	12.0	5.6	18.8	4.2	1.0	6.3	9.8	7.2
Monetary Authorities												*Thousands of Shillings through 1978;*			
Foreign Assets 11	4,079	1,923	2,568	2,009	1,197	2,561	3,703	3,755	3,909	₤2	—	36	83	256	353
Claims on Central Government 12a	3,369	6,951	7,952	12,383	16,702	23,547	31,912	38,662	54,424	₤73	127	232	328	₤1,715	2,972
Claims on Nonfin.Pub.Enterprises 12c	600	600	600	600	600	600	693	1,062	1,466	₤1	1	2	3	62	22
Claims on Private Sector 12d	—	—	—	—	—	—	—	—	—	₤—	—	—	—	—	—
Claims on Deposit Money Banks 12e	277	30	—	—	—	—	—	—	—	₤—	—	2	20	45	89
Reserve Money 14	6,961	6,996	7,869	10,009	13,311	20,957	30,029	34,367	51,094	₤84	115	148	176	282	610
of which: Currency Outside DMBs 14a	5,901	5,934	6,157	7,959	10,920	13,672	22,052	28,891	35,312	₤58	73	114	128	189	487
Liabs. of Central Bank: Securities 16ac															
Restricted Deposits 16b	10	23	87	111	42	47	48	7	15	₤1	1	4	4	11	39
Foreign Liabilities 16c	—	775	1,147	1,232	1,724	2,610	3,461	3,662	3,222	₤4	8	217	351	915	1,802
Central Government Deposits 16d	7	13	12	16	8	3	6	6	1	₤—	—	7	11	₤445	576
Capital Accounts 17a	938	1,214	1,563	1,675	1,721	1,876	1,897	2,440	2,446	₤2	2	32	33	76	176
Other Items (Net) 17r	409	483	442	1,949	1,693	1,215	867	2,997	3,021	₤-16	2	-135	-141	349	233
of which: Valuation Adjustment 17rv	-519	-427	-429	-514	-458	-671	-673	-631	-26	₤—	1	153	117	508	1,483
Deposit Money Banks												*Thousands of Shillings through 1978;*			
Reserves 20	988	1,083	1,550	2,058	2,995	8,754	8,599	5,233	14,844	₤31	46	41	26	60	246
Other Claims on Monetary Author. 20c	—	—	—	—	—	—	—	—	—	₤—	—	—	—	—	—
Foreign Assets 21	706	620	640	380	710	1,010	1,468	2,565	2,336	₤2	1	10	27	71	140
Claims on Central Government 22a	2,642	2,760	6,800	10,880	14,500	12,510	16,881	17,345	19,731	₤23	26	92	51	41	26
Claims on State and Local Govts. 22b	—	78	—	18	260	61	73	196	204	₤—	—	—	1	—	1
Claims on Nonfin.Pub.Enterprises 22c	—	—	—	—	—	—	1,000	4,000	5,000	₤6	9	5	82	66	123
Claims on Private Sector 22d	8,493	8,740	9,390	11,470	14,840	16,290	17,312	23,155	24,978	₤26	49	107	129	214	222
Demand Deposits 24	5,175	5,283	9,081	13,070	19,013	18,672	22,372	28,826	34,453	₤47	66	166	165	235	460
Time and Savings Deposits 25	5,617	5,283	6,025	7,700	8,533	14,256	17,428	16,126	22,937	₤31	45	62	87	109	176
Foreign Liabilities 26c	159	400	600	230	510	220	613	953	418	₤1	—	1	7	24	37
Central Government Deposits 26d	217	321	304	344	171	421	176	327	708	₤1	1	1	1	1	1
Central Government Lending Funds 26f	—	—	—	—	—	—	—	—	—	₤—	—	—	—	—	—
Credit from Monetary Authorities 26g	229	30	—	—	—	—	—	—	—	₤—	—	3	3	—	—
Capital Accounts 27a	1,459	1,480	1,310	1,520	1,770	1,800	4,635	5,878	7,293	₤9	10	14	58	247	221
Other Items (Net) 27r	-27	484	1,060	1,942	3,308	3,256	109	384	1,284	₤—	9	9	-6	-164	-139
Monetary Survey												*Thousands of Shillings through 1978;*			
Foreign Assets (Net) 31n	4,625	1,368	1,461	927	-327	741	1,097	1,705	2,605	₤-1	-6	-171	-248	-612	-1,347
Domestic Credit 32	14,881	18,795	24,426	34,991	46,723	52,584	67,689	84,087	105,094	₤129	211	430	582	1,652	2,789
Claims on Central Govt. (Net) 32an	5,787	9,377	14,436	22,903	31,023	35,633	48,611	55,674	73,446	₤95	151	316	367	1,310	2,421
Claims on State and Local Govts. 32b	—	78	—	18	260	61	73	196	204	₤—	—	—	1	—	1
Claims on Nonfin.Pub.Enterprises 32c	600	600	600	600	600	600	1,693	5,062	6,466	₤7	10	7	85	128	145
Claims on Private Sector 32d	8,493	8,740	9,390	11,470	14,840	16,290	17,312	23,155	24,978	₤26	49	107	129	214	222
Money 34	11,076	11,217	15,238	21,029	29,933	32,344	44,424	57,717	69,765	₤105	139	279	294	424	948
Quasi-Money 35	5,617	5,283	6,025	7,700	8,533	14,256	17,428	16,126	22,937	₤31	45	62	87	109	176
Liabs. of Central Bank: Securities 36ac	—	—	—	—	—	—	—	—	—	₤—	—	—	—	—	—
Restricted Deposits 36b	10	23	87	111	42	47	48	7	15	₤1	1	4	4	11	39
Central Government Lending Funds 36f	—	—	—	—	—	—	—	—	—	₤—	—	—	—	—	—
Capital Accounts 37a	2,397	2,694	2,873	3,195	3,491	3,676	6,532	8,318	9,739	₤11	12	46	91	323	397
Other Items (Net) 37r	405	946	1,664	3,883	4,397	3,002	354	3,624	5,243	₤-21	7	-133	-142	173	-117
Money plus Quasi-Money 35l	16,693	16,500	21,263	28,729	38,466	46,600	61,852	73,843	92,702	₤136	184	342	381	533	1,124
Interest Rates												*Percent Per Annum*			
Bank Rate (End of Period) 60	....	....	....	....	....	....	....	....	....	....	8.00	10.00	11.00	15.50	24.00
Treasury Bill Rate 60c	....	....	....	....	....	....	....	....	....	....	5.08	6.08	9.50	11.17	18.00
Deposit Rate 60l	....	....	....	....	....	....	....	....	....	....	6.80	7.23	9.00	10.67	16.00
Lending Rate 60p	....	....	....	....	....	....	....	....	....	....	10.80	12.50	14.50	16.17	21.92
Government Bond Yield 61	....	....	....	....	....	....	....	....	....	....	....	10.00	12.00	12.63	18.00
Prices															*Index Numbers (1995=100):*
Consumer Prices 64	....	....	....	....	....	....	....	....	....	....	—	—	—	—	₤—

1985	1986	1987	1988	1989	1990	1991	1992	1993	1994	1995	1996	1997	1998	1999		
and per SDR thereafter: End of Period															**Exchange Rates**	
Ɪ15.4	17.1	85.1	222.0	486.2	768.2	1,308.8	1,673.6	1,552.3	1,352.9	1,500.5	1,480.5	1,538.3	1,918.7	2,067.1	Principal Rate	**aa**
and per US Dollar thereafter: End of Period (ae) Period Average (rf)																
Ɪ14.0	14.0	60.0	165.0	370.0	540.0	915.0	1,217.2	1,130.2	926.8	1,009.5	1,029.6	1,140.1	1,362.7	1,506.0	Principal Rate	**ae**
Ɪ6.7	14.0	42.8	106.1	223.1	428.9	734.0	1,133.8	1,195.0	979.4	968.9	1,046.1	1,083.0	1,240.3	1,454.8	Principal Rate	**rf**
Period Averages																
15,233.2	6,908.5	3,454.8	1,123.9	460.2	228.7	135.5	85.8	81.0	99.2	100.0	92.4	89.5	78.3	66.6	Principal Rate	**ah**x
5,049.1	2,219.6	1,110.6	418.4	229.1	134.2	88.5	61.9	75.4	102.9	100.0	97.2	100.5	91.4	81.9	Nominal Effective Exchange Rate	**ne** c
177.5	186.5	238.0	217.0	183.1	112.4	82.9	76.9	82.2	102.2	100.0	99.7	107.0	94.6	88.1	Real Effective Exchange Rate	**re** c
End of Period															**Fund Position**	
99.6	99.6	99.6	99.6	99.6	99.6	99.6	133.9	133.9	133.9	133.9	133.9	133.9	133.9	180.5	Quota	**2f.** s
—	—	—	—	—	4.8	7.2	6.6	—	2.1	.3	.7	4.0	3.5	1.7	SDRs	**1b.** s
3.5	3.5	—	—	—	—	—	—	—	—	—	—	—	—	—	Reserve Position in the Fund	**1c.** s
277.6	203.4	192.8	187.6	171.2	198.2	230.9	250.1	243.0	262.6	280.6	290.1	291.7	282.7	270.8	Total Fund Cred.&Loans Outstg.	**2tl**
End of Period															**International Liquidity**	
27.3	29.2	54.6	49.3	14.1	44.0	58.9	94.4	146.4	321.4	458.9	528.4	633.5	725.4	763.1	Total Reserves minus Gold	**1l.** d
—	—	—	—	—	6.8	10.3	9.0	.1	3.1	.5	1.1	5.4	5.0	2.3	SDRs	**1b.** d
3.9	4.3	—	—	—	—	—	—	—	—	—	—	—	—	—	Reserve Position in the Fund	**1c.** d
23.4	24.9	54.6	49.3	14.1	37.2	48.6	85.4	146.3	318.3	458.4	527.3	628.1	720.4	760.8	Foreign Exchange	**1d.** d
3.3	7.6	....	....	....	....	....	2.6	1.8	7.7	2.7	3.0	1.4	7.5	2.0	Monetary Authorities: Other Liab.	**4..**d
11.5	21.4	29.5	15.5	15.7	27.3	43.0	72.2	91.4	145.2	132.5	142.6	160.8	190.2	199.8	Deposit Money Banks: Assets	**7a.** d
3.4	7.3	5.2	6.4	6.6	14.5	13.2	21.6	.7	8.0	.1	—	2.0	2.1	25.5	Liabilities	**7b.** d
Millions of Shillings Beginning 1979: End of Period															**Monetary Authorities**	
382	409	....	....	....	....	Ɪ117,077	172,280	299,209	466,801	538,084	660,961	951,073	1,090,382		Foreign Assets	**11**
6,768	7,945	....	....	....	....	Ɪ792,165	791,083	963,065	1,152,678	1,227,762	1,348,131	1,591,129	1,801,563		Claims on Central Government	**12a**
108	39	....	....	....	....	Ɪ24,257	20,753	23,188	24,180	24,471	25,129	25,559	3,501		Claims on Nonfin.Pub.Enterprises	**12c**
—	—	....	....	....	....	Ɪ4,768	4,357	1,468	543	543	453	453	27,355		Claims on Private Sector	**12d**
—	22	....	....	....	....	Ɪ10,126	6,272	3,861	1,879	7,718	13,062	31,823	61,838		Claims on Deposit Money Banks	**12e**
1,750	4,614	....	....	....	....	Ɪ138,594	170,973	253,143	287,894	321,373	350,611	420,770	484,136		Reserve Money	**14**
1,050	3,509	....	....	....	....	Ɪ98,335	132,638	176,522	204,519	221,094	240,456	285,878	330,759		of which: Currency Outside DMBs	**14a**
—	—	....	....	....	....	Ɪ—	—	—	—	—	—	7,000	6,697	52,423	Liabs. of Central Bank: Securities	**16ac**
66	103	....	....	....	....	Ɪ8,452	10,550	9,332	10,450	9,961	13,430	26,583	123,493		Restricted Deposits	**16b**
4,314	3,591	....	....	....	....	Ɪ421,730	379,305	362,368	423,836	432,552	450,428	552,698	562,726		Foreign Liabilities	**16c**
1,106	2,452	....	....	....	....	Ɪ464,830	550,278	830,115	1,247,927	1,319,140	1,457,689	1,688,728	1,925,470		Central Government Deposits	**16d**
204	217	....	....	....	....	Ɪ80,792	61,501	20,493	56,716	140,814	215,895	408,857	492,398		Capital Accounts	**17a**
-183	-2,563	....	....	....	....	Ɪ-166006	-177,863	-184,660	-380,742	-425,262	-447,227	-504,296	-656,007		Other Items (Net)	**17r**
4,586	7,429													....	of which: Valuation Adjustment	**17rv**
Millions of Shillings Beginning 1979: End of Period															**Deposit Money Banks**	
715	968	2,481	2,750	4,829	11,989	27,386	34,640	37,060	75,123	79,600	109,620	104,216	129,412	121,020	Reserves	**20**
—	—	—	—	—	—	—	—	—	—	—	—	7,000	6,697	52,423	Other Claims on Monetary Author.	**20c**
161	299	1,773	2,550	5,802	14,742	39,334	87,883	103,303	134,547	133,770	146,797	183,340	259,234	300,949	Foreign Assets	**21**
30	46	38	338	126	2,740	986	5,846	14,273	34,744	41,750	65,669	182,640	199,239	286,115	Claims on Central Government	**22a**
—	—	1	11	6	306	—	215	300	—	—	—	—	—	1,410	Claims on State and Local Govts.	**22b**
424	1,699	3,423	4,370	6,343	12,120	23,713	27,909	32,533	51,210	56,629	65,852	65,829	63,586	70,658	Claims on Nonfin.Pub.Enterprises	**22c**
608	1,236	3,496	10,866	29,633	49,364	64,572	105,081	166,945	190,691	245,818	323,181	319,964	424,824	491,896	Claims on Private Sector	**22d**
1,140	2,449	7,465	15,948	32,871	47,660	78,626	107,676	126,758	177,498	204,182	229,742	272,076	326,559	363,063	Demand Deposits	**24**
366	1,056	2,014	3,227	8,480	19,400	30,837	57,880	155,490	209,414	233,302	315,372	402,455	512,419	589,826	Time and Savings Deposits	**25**
48	102	314	1,052	2,427	7,834	12,115	26,272	749	7,437	77	—	2,230	2,924	38,426	Foreign Liabilities	**26c**
2	5	154	485	1,174	1,762	2,153	8,152	11,194	28,002	38,677	73,013	49,032	46,290	99,810	Central Government Deposits	**26d**
—	—	—	—	—	—	—	—	14,520	18,814	15,394	7,990	11,166	10,980	17,026	Central Government Lending Funds	**26f**
—	—	—	492	1,303	4,809	9,617	7,582	10,471	6,714	8,452	150	7,244	23,400	112,206	Credit from Monetary Authorities	**26g**
415	533	1,723	4,848	8,942	39,704	48,947	51,137	37,654	35,998	50,065	73,334	145,901	169,815	172,642	Capital Accounts	**27a**
-32	103	-449	-5,172	-8,157	-30,214	-26,090	2,960	-2,722	2,439	7,419	11,518	-27,115	-9,396	-68,528	Other Items (Net)	**27r**
Millions of Shillings Beginning 1979: End of Period															**Monetary Survey**	
-3,819	-2,985	....	....	....	....	Ɪ-243043	-104,471	63,951	176,658	252,329	391,643	654,685	790,178		Foreign Assets (Net)	**31n**
6,830	8,509	....	....	....	....	Ɪ487,344	468,472	406,249	234,994	315,325	435,515	569,771	657,218		Domestic Credit	**32**
5,690	5,534	....	....	....	....	Ɪ325,030	243,884	139,692	-92,176	-98,722	24,050	55,349	62,398		Claims on Central Govt. (Net)	**32an**
—	1	....	....	....	....	300	—	—	—	—	—	—	1,410		Claims on State and Local Govts.	**32b**
532	1,738	....	....	....	....	Ɪ52,166	53,286	74,398	80,809	90,323	90,958	89,145	74,159		Claims on Nonfin.Pub. Enterprises	**32c**
608	1,236	....	....	....	....	Ɪ109,849	171,302	192,159	246,361	323,724	320,507	425,277	519,251		Claims on Private Sector	**32d**
2,190	5,959	....	....	....	....	Ɪ206,011	259,396	354,020	408,701	450,836	512,532	612,437	693,823		Money	**34**
366	1,056	....	....	....	....	57,880	155,490	209,414	233,302	315,372	402,455	512,419	589,826		Quasi-Money	**35**
—	—	....	....	....	....	Ɪ—	—	—	—	—	—	—	—		Liabs. of Central Bank: Securities	**36ac**
66	103	....	....	....	....	Ɪ8,452	10,550	9,332	10,450	9,961	13,430	26,583	123,493		Restricted Deposits	**36b**
—	—	....	....	....	....	—	14,520	18,814	15,394	7,990	11,166	10,980	17,026		Central Government Lending Funds	**36f**
619	750	....	....	....	....	Ɪ131,929	99,155	56,490	106,781	214,148	361,796	578,672	665,040		Capital Accounts	**37a**
-230	-2,344	....	....	....	....	Ɪ-159970	-175,110	-177,869	-362,976	-430,653	-474,221	-516,635	-641,811		Other Items (Net)	**37r**
2,556	7,015	....	....	....	....	Ɪ263,890	414,886	563,434	642,002	766,208	914,987	1,124,856	1,283,648		Money plus Quasi-Money	**35l**
Percent Per Annum															**Interest Rates**	
24.00	36.00	31.00	45.00	55.00	50.00	46.00	41.00	24.00	15.00	13.30	15.85	14.08	9.10	15.75	Bank Rate (End of Period)	**60**
22.00	30.67	30.50	33.00	42.17	41.00	34.17	....	Ɪ21.30	12.52	8.75	11.71	10.59	7.77	7.43	Treasury Bill Rate	**60c**
Ɪ20.00	23.33	20.00	21.50	32.17	31.25	31.17	35.83	16.26	9.99	7.61	10.62	11.84	11.36	8.73	Deposit Rate	**60l**
24.00	33.33	34.67	35.00	40.00	38.67	34.42	....	....	....	20.16	20.29	21.37	20.86	21.55	Lending Rate	**60p**
24.00	38.33	40.00	38.50	45.33	44.50	42.00	43.50	....	....	....	....	....	....	....	Government Bond Yield	**61**
Period Averages															**Prices**	
1	2	6	19	30	41	52	79	84	92	100	107	115	115	122	Consumer Prices	**64**

Uganda

		1970	1971	1972	1973	1974	1975	1976	1977	1978	1979	1980	1981	1982	1983	1984
International Transactions														*Thousands of Shillings through 1978;*		
Exports	70	2,013	1,857	2,019	2,043	2,250	1,902	3,006	4,859	2,682	I 32	26	122	328	593	1,388
Imports, c.i.f. (Cash Basis)	71	12,290	17,830	11,570	11,380	15,220	15,270	14,240	19,920	19,630	I 15	22	....	....	....	....
Balance of Payments														*Millions of US Dollars:*		
Current Account, n.i.e.	78al d	....	....								....	−82.7	1.2	−69.9	−72.2	103.5
Goods: Exports f.o.b.	78aa d	....	....								....	319.4	228.8	347.1	367.7	407.3
Goods: Imports f.o.b.	78ab d	....	....								....	−317.6	−284.3	−337.6	−342.5	−286.8
Trade Balance	78ac d	....	....								....	1.8	−55.5	9.5	25.2	120.5
Services: Credit	78ad d	....	....								....	9.9	44.3	—	—	16.8
Services: Debit	78ae d	....	....								....	−123.4	−100.4	−160.4	−150.0	−82.3
Balance on Goods & Services	78af d	....	....								....	−111.7	−111.6	−150.9	−124.8	55.0
Income: Credit	78ag d	....	....								....	1.4	.8	—	—	—
Income: Debit	78ah d	....	....								....	−8.8	−13.2	−26.3	−50.9	−36.9
Balance on Gds, Serv. & Inc.	78ai d	....	....								....	−119.1	−124.0	−177.2	−175.7	18.1
Current Transfers, n.i.e.: Credit	78aj d	....	....								....	40.0	125.7	107.3	103.5	85.4
Current Transfers: Debit	78ak d	....	....								....	−3.6	−.5	—	—	—
Capital Account, n.i.e.	78bc d	....	....								....	−.5	—	—	—	—
Capital Account, n.i.e.: Credit	78ba d	....	....								....	—	—	—	—	—
Capital Account: Debit	78bb d	....	....								....	−.5	—	—	—	—
Financial Account, n.i.e.	78bj d	....	....								....	−66.5	−96.3	14.8	27.7	−58.2
Direct Investment Abroad	78bd d	....	....								....	—	—	—	—	—
Dir. Invest. in Rep. Econ., n.i.e.	78be d	....	....								....	—	—	—	—	—
Portfolio Investment Assets	78bf d	....	....								....	—	—	—	—	—
Equity Securities	78bk d	....	....								....	—	—	—	—	—
Debt Securities	78bl d	....	....								....	—	—	—	—	—
Portfolio Investment Liab., n.i.e.	78bg d	....	....								....	—	—	—	—	—
Equity Securities	78bm d	....	....								....	—	—	—	—	—
Debt Securities	78bn d	....	....								....	—	—	—	—	—
Financial Derivatives Assets	78bw d	....	....								....	....	....	....	....	....
Financial Derivatives Liabilities	78bx d	....	....								....	....	....	....	....	....
Other Investment Assets	78bh d	....	....								....	14.7	6.8	−13.4	−4.5	30.1
Monetary Authorities	78bo d	....	....								....	—	—	—	—	—
General Government	78bp d	....	....								....	—	—	—	—	24.0
Banks	78bq d	....	....								....	14.7	6.8	−13.4	−4.5	2.8
Other Sectors	78br d	....	....								....	—	—	—	—	3.3
Other Investment Liab., n.i.e.	78bi d	....	....								....	−81.2	−103.1	28.2	32.2	−88.3
Monetary Authorities	78bs d	....	....								....	−7.3	27.5	−3.3	4.8	−97.2
General Government	78bt d	....	....								....	−59.3	−109.4	26.2	23.9	32.1
Banks	78bu d	....	....								....	−14.6	−3.2	5.3	3.5	−23.2
Other Sectors	78bv d	....	....								....	—	−18.0	—	—	—
Net Errors and Omissions	78ca d	....	....								....	−64.6	−31.7	−24.7	−36.6	21.6
Overall Balance	78cb d	....	....								....	−214.3	−126.8	−79.8	−81.1	66.9
Reserves and Related Items	79da d	....	....								....	214.3	126.8	79.8	81.1	−66.9
Reserve Assets	79db d	....	....								....	26.1	−34.6	−34.5	−28.6	26.5
Use of Fund Credit and Loans	79dc d	....	....								....	58.4	129.5	92.0	101.4	−16.1
Exceptional Financing	79de d	....	....								....	129.8	31.9	22.4	8.3	−77.3
Government Finance														*Thousands of Shillings through 1978;*		
Deficit (-) or Surplus	80	−4,134	−7,519	I −8,990	−8,610	−15,260	−12,370	−13,180	−12,780	−1,600	I −35	−39	−100	−146	−134	−221
Revenue	81	10,838	12,880	I 15,320	12,400	11,400	20,890	23,510	34,200	57,930	I 26	39	28	247	527	903
Grants Received	81z	....	....	60	30	390	20	1,060	190	—	I —	1	3	30	10	35
Expenditure	82	14,972	20,399	I 24,370	21,040	27,050	33,280	37,750	47,170	59,530	I 61	77	128	417	664	1,151
Lending Minus Repayments	83	....	....	—	—	—	—	—	—	—	I —	2	4	6	6	8
Financing																
Total Financing	84											39	100	146	134	221
Net Borrowing: Domestic	84a	2,770	3,819	....								39	100	148	120	229
Foreign	85a	1,663	3,642	....	....	....	4,430	3,120	2,620	1,100	I 5	—	1	−1	15	−8
Use of Cash Balances	87	−299	58	....							I —	—	—	—	—	—
Adj. to Total Financing	84x	....	....								....	—	—	−1	−1	—
Debt: Domestic	88a	....	....								I 84	123	223	371	491	720
Foreign	89a											....	....	....	....	....
National Accounts														*Thousands of Shillings through 1978;*		
Exports of Goods & Services	90c	21,000	20,000	21,000	20,000	22,000	18,000	28,000	46,000	26,000	....	....	....	....	645	1,528
Government Consumption	91f														660	1,581
Gross Fixed Capital Formation	93e	12,000	17,000	13,000	10,000	16,000	15,000	12,000	18,000	19,000					553	906
Increase/Decrease(-) in Stocks	93i	1,000	—	−1,000	1,000	1,000	2,000	3,000	5,000	6,000					−30	44
Private Consumption	96f	79,000	91,000	98,000	115,000	144,000	213,000	245,000	456,000	628,000					5,802	8,367
Imports of Goods & Services	98c	−18,000	−24,000	−18,000	−16,000	−22,000	−23,000	−24,000	−39,000	−35,000	....	....	....	....	−1,015	−1,548
Gross Domestic Product (GDP)	99b	94,500	103,700	113,900	129,500	160,300	225,000	264,500	485,700	643,000	I 996	1,352	2,665	3,953	6,142	9,598
GDP Volume 1991 Prices	99b, p	....	....								....	....	....	....	1,599.5	1,523.5
GDP Volume (1995=100)	99bv p														53.0	50.5
GDP Deflator (1995=100)	99bi p	—	—	—	—	—	—	—	—	.1	.1	.1	.2	.3	.2	.3
																Millions:
Population	99z	9.81	10.13	10.46	10.81	11.17	11.55	11.94	12.35	12.78	13.22	13.12	13.58	14.01	14.23	14.66

Item	1985	1986	1987	1988	1989	1990	1991	1992	1993	1994	1995	1996	1997	1998	1999	Code
International Transactions																
Millions of Shillings Beginning 1979																
Exports	2,600	6,100	13,684	29,070	55,674	64,653	146,661	159,387	213,846	393,960	446,086	613,598	594,804	624,509	748,862	70
Imports, c.i.f. (Cash Basis)	....	4,300	36,336	94,112	87,851	125,059	137,250	580,685	....	850,411	1,024,317	1,247,379	1,425,904	1,753,335	1,955,849	71
Balance of Payments																
Minus Sign Indicates Debit																
Current Account, n.i.e.	4.6	-43.3	-112.0	-195.2	-259.5	-263.3	-169.8	-99.6	-224.3	-207.5	-338.9	-252.3	-387.8	....	....	78al d
Goods: Exports f.o.b.	347.8	406.8	333.6	266.3	277.7	177.8	173.2	151.2	200.0	463.0	560.3	639.3	575.6	....	....	78aa d
Goods: Imports f.o.b.	-238.3	-360.9	-475.6	-523.5	-588.3	-491.0	-377.1	-421.9	-478.3	-714.2	-926.8	-986.9	-1,042.5	....	....	78ab d
Trade Balance	109.5	45.9	-142.0	-257.2	-310.6	-313.2	-203.9	-270.7	-278.3	-251.2	-366.5	-347.6	-466.9	....	....	78ac d
Services: Credit	23.1	11.8	—	—	—	—	20.8	34.5	93.6	64.1	104.0	144.7	164.6	....	....	78ad d
Services: Debit	-129.9	-130.5	-218.2	-235.2	-237.2	-195.3	-241.8	-247.7	-293.1	-436.3	-562.7	-674.6	-693.1	....	....	78ae d
Balance on Goods & Services	2.7	-72.8	-360.2	-492.4	-547.8	-508.5	-424.9	-483.9	-477.8	-623.4	-825.2	-877.5	-995.4	....	....	78af d
Income: Credit	1.5	2.9	—	—	—	—	2.8	4.1	6.4	13.8	17.7	29.7	40.5	....	....	78ag d
Income: Debit	-21.0	-38.9	-18.0	-25.2	-23.3	-47.8	-76.7	-88.3	-65.3	-71.0	-113.3	-79.2	-52.5	....	....	78ah d
Balance on Gds, Serv. & Inc.	-16.8	-108.8	-378.2	-517.6	-571.1	-556.3	-498.8	-568.1	-536.7	-680.6	-920.8	-927.0	-1,007.5	....	....	78ai d
Current Transfers, n.i.e.: Credit	21.7	66.6	266.2	322.4	311.6	293.0	329.0	468.5	312.4	473.1	581.9	674.7	619.6	....	....	78aj d
Current Transfers: Debit	-.3	-1.1	—	—	—	—	—	—	—	—	—	—	—	....	....	78ak d
Capital Account, n.i.e.	—	—	—	—	—	—	—	—	42.4	36.1	48.3	61.4	31.9	....	....	78bc d
Capital Account, n.i.e.: Credit	—	—	—	—	—	—	—	—	42.4	36.1	48.3	61.4	31.9	....	....	78ba d
Capital Account: Debit	—	—	—	—	—	—	—	—	—	—	—	—	—	....	....	78bb d
Financial Account, n.i.e.	80.8	17.1	31.2	3.6	213.0	211.8	137.6	114.8	56.6	76.8	210.7	140.5	300.2	....	....	78bj d
Direct Investment Abroad	—	—	—	—	—	—	—	—	—	—	—	—	—	....	....	78bd d
Dir. Invest. in Rep. Econ., n.i.e.	—	—	—	—	—	—	1.0	3.0	54.6	88.2	121.2	121.0	175.0	....	....	78be d
Portfolio Investment Assets	—	—	—	—	—	—	—	—	—	—	—	—	—	....	....	78bf d
Equity Securities	—	—	—	—	—	—	—	—	—	—	—	—	—	....	....	78bk d
Debt Securities	—	—	—	—	—	—	—	—	—	—	—	—	—	....	....	78bl d
Portfolio Investment Liab., n.i.e.	—	—	—	—	—	—	—	—	—	—	—	—	—	....	....	78bg d
Equity Securities	—	—	—	—	—	—	—	—	—	—	—	—	—	....	....	78bm d
Debt Securities	—	—	—	—	—	—	—	—	—	—	—	—	—	....	....	78bn d
Financial Derivatives Assets	....	....	....	....	....	....	....	....	....	....	....	....	....	....	....	78bw d
Financial Derivatives Liabilities	....	....	....	....	....	....	....	....	....	....	....	....	....	....	....	78bx d
Other Investment Assets	69.3	131.8	—	—	—	—	.4	1.8	-5.0	-40.3	-9.9	-37.2	-14.0	....	....	78bh d
Monetary Authorities	....	....	....	....	....	....	....	....	....	....	....	....	....	....	....	78bo d
General Government	13.7	36.0	—	—	—	—	—	—	—	—	—	—	—	....	....	78bp d
Banks	15.3	-9.9	—	—	—	—	—	—	-8.7	-53.0	12.7	-10.1	-18.2	....	....	78bq d
Other Sectors	40.3	105.7	—	—	—	—	.4	1.8	3.7	12.7	-22.6	-27.1	4.2	....	....	78br d
Other Investment Liab., n.i.e.	11.5	-114.7	31.2	3.6	213.0	211.8	136.2	110.0	7.0	28.9	99.4	56.7	139.2	....	....	78bi d
Monetary Authorities	—	-18.5	-66.2	-42.1	-19.5	-.3	-.2	-6.6	2.2	.9	1.7	1.1	.2	....	....	78bs d
General Government	-16.9	-112.0	145.8	75.6	233.3	257.9	167.8	150.7	56.3	50.8	111.7	114.4	159.5	....	....	78bt d
Banks	-3.8	3.9	—	—	40.6	-26.3	-9.6	-22.8	—	—	—	—	—	....	....	78bu d
Other Sectors	32.2	11.9	-48.4	-29.9	-41.4	-19.5	-21.8	-11.3	-51.5	-22.8	-14.0	-58.8	-20.5	....	....	78bv d
Net Errors and Omissions	-52.2	-.6	26.4	154.9	-38.0	9.5	.6	9.0	-.1	32.5	28.8	41.3	20.9	....	....	78ca d
Overall Balance	33.2	-26.8	-54.4	-36.7	-84.5	-41.9	-31.7	24.2	-125.4	-62.1	-51.2	-9.1	-34.8	....	....	78cb d
Reserves and Related Items	-33.2	26.8	54.4	36.7	84.5	41.9	31.7	-24.2	125.4	62.1	51.2	9.1	34.8	....	....	79da d
Reserve Assets	17.3	-36.4	-20.3	2.4	1.8	5.2	-12.7	-50.6	-49.4	-166.9	-140.7	-68.9	-105.2	....	....	79db d
Use of Fund Credit and Loans	-67.8	-87.2	-15.1	-7.8	-20.7	36.5	44.4	26.4	-9.8	27.1	27.5	13.3	2.5	....	....	79dc d
Exceptional Financing	17.3	77.8	89.8	42.1	103.4	.3	—	—	184.7	201.9	164.3	64.8	137.6	....	....	79de d
Government Finance																
Millions of Shillings Beginning 1979: Year Ending June 30																
Deficit (-) or Surplus	-630	I-1,639	-5,557	-5,499	-29,582	-62,394	-60,316	-263,572	-113,513	-169,806	-131,554	-112,872	-120,191[f]	....	....	80
Revenue	1,621	I2,844	5,005	22,262	47,854	94,526	136,808	185,381	291,075	399,152	531,194	622,790	744,344[f]	....	....	81
Grants Received	78	I384	853	5,640	14,160	20,295	70,184	94,635	313,754	282,487	253,876	325,023	351,091[f]	....	....	81z
Expenditure	2,329	I4,867	11,415	33,401	89,670	174,928	262,808	535,088	717,142	848,645	905,277	1,057,885	1,213,626[f]	....	....	82
Lending Minus Repayments	—	I—	—	1,926	2,287	—	4,500	8,500	1,200	2,800	11,347	2,800	2,000[f]	....	....	83
Financing																
Total Financing	631	I1,638	5,557	5,499	29,582	—	60,316	263,572	113,513	169,806	131,554	112,872	120,191[f]	....	....	84
Net Borrowing: Domestic	496	I1,164	4,195	4,943	13,400	-22,268	9,372	56,027	-23,826	-26,962	-86,701	-60,262	-51,990[f]	....	....	84a
Foreign	135	I474	1,362	556	19,404	91,816	63,229	140,433	200,816	243,227	211,719	209,432	231,400[f]	....	....	85a
Use of Cash Balances	—	I—	—	—	-3,222	-9,441	-12,285	2,490	-72,868	-51,017	-22,182	-34,200	-30,001[f]	....	....	87
Adj. to Total Financing	—	I—	—	—	—	—	—	64,622	9,391	4,558	28,718	-2,098	-29,218[f]	....	....	84x
Debt: Domestic	1,251	I2,016	4,775	5,233	11,612	....	....	....	....	....	....	....	....	....	....	88a
Foreign	....	....	....	....	....	....	....	....	....	....	....	....	....	4,473	....	89a
National Accounts																
Millions of Shillings Beginning 1979																
Exports of Goods & Services	3,010	I7,708	19,242	48,494	87,833	111,544	186,573	253,431	310,187	555,517	648,754	791,972	....	....	....	90c
Government Consumption	3,193	I5,747	16,934	44,319	79,095	128,254	206,111	321,603	424,897	476,591	577,183	660,574	....	....	....	91f
Gross Fixed Capital Formation	2,124	I5,911	26,581	69,030	128,343	228,129	362,871	547,106	647,912	738,346	984,963	1,012,671	....	....	....	93e
Increase/Decrease(-) in Stocks	-48	I—	—	—	—	—	1,099	-5,460	3,107	-27,115	-5,190	-7,539	....	....	....	93i
Private Consumption	23,215	I58,551	206,195	585,818	1,127,445	1,465,718	1,995,117	3,338,716	3,521,432	4,356,600	4,997,984	5,434,499	....	....	....	96f
Imports of Goods & Services	-3,780	I-11,921	-45,241	-108,394	-218,105	-321,285	-511,646	-754,349	-803,611	-945,341	1,240,509	1,374,620	....	....	....	98c
Gross Domestic Product (GDP)	25,622	I65,444	224,041	634,634	1,178,185	1,602,094	2,222,861	3,687,704	4,024,186	5,171,744	5,977,762	6,636,521	....	....	....	99b
GDP Volume 1991 Prices	1,526.4	1,618.1	1,721.6	1,856.1	1,984.2	2,106.9	2,222.9	2,325.8	2,489.9	2,753.3	3,018.1	3,195.1	....	....	....	99b.p
GDP Volume (1995=100)	50.6	53.6	57.0	61.5	65.7	69.8	73.6	77.1	82.5	91.2	100.0	105.9	....	....	....	99bv p
GDP Deflator (1995=100)	.8	I2.0	6.6	17.3	30.0	38.4	50.5	80.1	81.6	94.8	100.0	104.9	....	....	....	99bi p
Midyear Estimates																
Population	15.11	15.61	16.15	15.78	16.18	16.46	16.90	17.34	17.88	18.41	19.26	19.85	20.44	21.03	21.62	99z

(See notes in the back of the book.)

		1970	1971	1972	1973	1974	1975	1976	1977	1978	1979	1980	1981	1982	1983	1984

Exchange Rates

Hryvnias per SDR:

Official Rate	aa	...	...	...	...	...	...	...	...	...	...	...	...	...	...	...

Hryvnias per US Dollar:

Official Rate	ae	...	...	...	...	...	...	...	...	...	...	...	...	...	...	...
Official Rate	rf	...	...	...	...	...	...	...	...	...	...	...	...	...	...	...

Index Numbers (1995=100):

Nominal Effective Exchange Rate	ne c	...	...	...	...	...	...	...	...	...	...	...	...	...	...	...
Real Effective Exchange Rate	re c	...	...	...	...	...	...	...	...	...	...	...	...	...	...	...

Fund Position

Millions of SDRs:

Quota	2f. s	...	...	...	...	...	...	...	...	...	...	...	...	...	...	...
SDRs	1b. s	...	...	...	...	...	...	...	...	...	...	...	...	...	...	...
Reserve Position in the Fund	1c. s	...	...	...	...	...	...	...	...	...	...	...	...	...	...	...
Total Fund Cred.&Loans Outstg.	2tl	...	...	...	...	...	...	...	...	...	...	...	...	...	...	...

International Liquidity

Millions of US Dollars Unless Otherwise Indicated:

Total Reserves minus Gold	1l. d	...	...	...	...	...	...	...	...	...	...	...	...	...	...	...
SDRs	1b. d	...	...	...	...	...	...	...	...	...	...	...	...	...	...	...
Reserve Position in the Fund	1c. d	...	...	...	...	...	...	...	...	...	...	...	...	...	...	...
Foreign Exchange	1d. d	...	...	...	...	...	...	...	...	...	...	...	...	...	...	...
Gold (Million Fine Troy Ounces)	1ad	...	...	...	...	...	...	...	...	...	...	...	...	...	...	...
Gold (National Valuation)	1an d	...	...	...	...	...	...	...	...	...	...	...	...	...	...	...
Monetary Authorities: Other Assets	3.. d	...	...	...	...	...	...	...	...	...	...	...	...	...	...	...
Other Liab.	4.. d	...	...	...	...	...	...	...	...	...	...	...	...	...	...	...
Deposit Money Banks: Assets	7a. d	...	...	...	...	...	...	...	...	...	...	...	...	...	...	...
Liabilities	7b. d	...	...	...	...	...	...	...	...	...	...	...	...	...	...	...

Monetary Authorities

Millions of Hryvnias:

Foreign Assets	11	...	...	...	...	...	...	...	...	...	...	...	...	...	...	...
Claims on General Government	12a	...	...	...	...	...	...	...	...	...	...	...	...	...	...	...
Claims on Nonfin.Pub.Enterprises	12c	...	...	...	...	...	...	...	...	...	...	...	...	...	...	...
Claims on Private Sector	12d	...	...	...	...	...	...	...	...	...	...	...	...	...	...	...
Claims on Banks	12e	...	...	...	...	...	...	...	...	...	...	...	...	...	...	...
Reserve Money	14	...	...	...	...	...	...	...	...	...	...	...	...	...	...	...
of which: Currency Outside Banks	14a	...	...	...	...	...	...	...	...	...	...	...	...	...	...	...
Time, Savings,& Fgn.Currency Dep.	15	...	...	...	...	...	...	...	...	...	...	...	...	...	...	...
Foreign Liabilities	16c	...	...	...	...	...	...	...	...	...	...	...	...	...	...	...
General Government Deposits	16d	...	...	...	...	...	...	...	...	...	...	...	...	...	...	...
Capital Accounts	17a	...	...	...	...	...	...	...	...	...	...	...	...	...	...	...
Other Items (Net)	17r	...	...	...	...	...	...	...	...	...	...	...	...	...	...	...

Banking Institutions

Millions of Hryvnias:

Reserves	20	...	...	...	...	...	...	...	...	...	...	...	...	...	...	...
Foreign Assets	21	...	...	...	...	...	...	...	...	...	...	...	...	...	...	...
Claims on General Government	22a	...	...	...	...	...	...	...	...	...	...	...	...	...	...	...
Claims on Nonfin.Pub.Enterprises	22c	...	...	...	...	...	...	...	...	...	...	...	...	...	...	...
Claims on Private Sector	22d	...	...	...	...	...	...	...	...	...	...	...	...	...	...	...
Claims on Nonbank Financial Insts	22g	...	...	...	...	...	...	...	...	...	...	...	...	...	...	...
Demand Deposits	24	...	...	...	...	...	...	...	...	...	...	...	...	...	...	...
Time, Savings,& Fgn.Currency Dep.	25	...	...	...	...	...	...	...	...	...	...	...	...	...	...	...
of which: Fgn. Currency Deposits	25b	...	...	...	...	...	...	...	...	...	...	...	...	...	...	...
Bonds	26ab	...	...	...	...	...	...	...	...	...	...	...	...	...	...	...
Foreign Liabilities	26c	...	...	...	...	...	...	...	...	...	...	...	...	...	...	...
General Government Deposits	26d	...	...	...	...	...	...	...	...	...	...	...	...	...	...	...
Credit from Monetary Authorities	26g	...	...	...	...	...	...	...	...	...	...	...	...	...	...	...
Liab. to Nonbank Financial Insts	26j	...	...	...	...	...	...	...	...	...	...	...	...	...	...	...
Capital Accounts	27a	...	...	...	...	...	...	...	...	...	...	...	...	...	...	...
Other Items (Net)	27r	...	...	...	...	...	...	...	...	...	...	...	...	...	...	...

Banking Survey

Millions of Hryvnias:

Foreign Assets (Net)	31n	...	...	...	...	...	...	...	...	...	...	...	...	...	...	...
Domestic Credit	32	...	...	...	...	...	...	...	...	...	...	...	...	...	...	...
Claims on General Govt. (Net)	32an	...	...	...	...	...	...	...	...	...	...	...	...	...	...	...
Claims on Nonfin.Pub.Enterprises	32c	...	...	...	...	...	...	...	...	...	...	...	...	...	...	...
Claims on Private Sector	32d	...	...	...	...	...	...	...	...	...	...	...	...	...	...	...
Claims on Nonbank Financial Inst	32g	...	...	...	...	...	...	...	...	...	...	...	...	...	...	...
Money	34	...	...	...	...	...	...	...	...	...	...	...	...	...	...	...
Quasi-Money	35	...	...	...	...	...	...	...	...	...	...	...	...	...	...	...
Bonds	36ab	...	...	...	...	...	...	...	...	...	...	...	...	...	...	...
Liab. to Nonbank Financial Insts	36j	...	...	...	...	...	...	...	...	...	...	...	...	...	...	...
Capital Accounts	37a	...	...	...	...	...	...	...	...	...	...	...	...	...	...	...
Other Items (Net)	37r	...	...	...	...	...	...	...	...	...	...	...	...	...	...	...
Money plus Quasi-Money	35l	...	...	...	...	...	...	...	...	...	...	...	...	...	...	...

Interest Rates

Percent Per Annum

Refinancing Rate (End of Period)	60	...	...	...	...	...	...	...	...	...	...	...	...	...	...	...
Money Market Rate	60b	...	...	...	...	...	...	...	...	...	...	...	...	...	...	...
Deposit Rate	60l	...	...	...	...	...	...	...	...	...	...	...	...	...	...	...
Lending Rate	60p	...	...	...	...	...	...	...	...	...	...	...	...	...	...	...

Prices and Labor

Percent Change over

Wholesale Prices	63.x x	...	...	...	...	...	...	...	...	...	...	...	...	...	...	...
Consumer Prices	64.x x	...	...	...	...	...	...	...	...	...	...	...	...	...	...	...
Wages: Average Earnings	65.x x	...	...	...	...	...	...	...	...	...	...	...	...	...	...	...

Index Numbers (1995=100):

Industrial Employment	67	...	...	...	...	...	...	...	...	...	...	...	...	...	...	...

Number in Thousands:

Labor Force	67d	...	...	...	...	...	...	...	...	...	...	...	...	...	...	...
Employment	67e	...	...	...	...	...	...	...	...	...	...	...	...	...	...	...
Unemployment	67c	...	...	...	...	...	...	...	...	...	...	...	...	...	...	...
Unemployment Rate (%)	67r	...	...	...	...	...	...	...	...	...	...	...	...	...	...	...

1985	1986	1987	1988	1989	1990	1991	1992	1993	1994	1995	1996	1997	1998	1999		Code
															Exchange Rates	
															End of Period	
....	....	....	....	....	....	....	.0088	.1732	1.5212	2.6668	I2.7163	2.5622	4.8253	7.1594	Official Rate	aa
															End of Period (ae) Period Average (rf)	
....	....	....	....	....	....	....	.0064	.1261	1.0420	1.7940	I1.8890	1.8990	3.4270	5.2163	Official Rate	ae
....	....	....	....	....	....	....		.0453	.3275	1.4731	1.8295	1.8617	2.4495	4.1304	Official Rate	rf
															Period Averages	
							8,268.73	1,115.92	188.10	100.00	88.20	100.63	107.28	136.27	Nominal Effective Exchange Rate	ne c
							134.54	58.92	83.55	100.00	117.87	133.55	130.36	126.63	Real Effective Exchange Rate	re c
															Fund Position	
															End of Period	
							997.30	997.30	997.30	997.30	997.30	997.30	997.30	1,372.00	Quota	2f. s
							—	—	123.73	97.06	46.72	52.70	129.53	47.86	SDRs	1b. s
							.01	.01	.01	—	—	.01	.01	—	Reserve Position in the Fund	1c. s
							—	—	249.33	1,037.30	1,573.30	1,780.56	1,985.05	2,044.62	Total Fund Cred.&Loans Outstg.	2tl
															International Liquidity	
															End of Period	
							468.8	161.6	650.7	1,050.6	1,960.0	2,341.1	761.3	1,046.4	Total Reserves minus Gold	1l. d
							—	—	180.6	144.3	67.2	71.1	182.4	65.7	SDRs	1b. d
							—	—	—	—	—	—	—	—	Reserve Position in the Fund	1c. d
							468.8	161.6	470.1	906.3	1,892.8	2,270.0	578.9	980.7	Foreign Exchange	1d. d
							.0003	.0115	.0360	.0470	.0316	.0613	.1100	.1624	Gold (Million Fine Troy Ounces)	1ad
							.1	4.4	13.7	18.3	11.6	17.7	31.6	47.2	Gold (National Valuation)	1an d
							981.4	88.1	4.3	2.5	2.3	—	235.9	104.9	Monetary Authorities: Other Assets	3.. d
							2,398.5	279.9	7.3	22.1	36.6	67.6	175.6	172.4	Other Liab.	4.. d
							863.5	1,264.5	1,406.3	1,044.3	942.1	963.1	906.8	849.2	Deposit Money Banks: Assets	7a. d
							896.3	570.4	724.8	302.0	334.4	949.9	507.2	338.7	Liabilities	7b. d
															Monetary Authorities	
															End of Period	
							9.2	32.0	696.8	2,027.1	3,729.0	4,479.4	I3,525.4	6,251.8	Foreign Assets	11
							17.5	131.2	1,410.7	4,393.1	6,211.3	7,430.1	I15075.2	19,712.8	Claims on General Government	12a
							—	.5	4.8				I		Claims on Nonfin.Pub.Enterprises	12c
							—	.2	.3	.1	1.2	35.0	I104.8	154.0	Claims on Private Sector	12d
							18.7	147.7	336.3	665.2	859.6	1,555.0	I1,365.1	1,687.8	Claims on Banks	12e
							18.1	301.2	1,528.2	3,557.1	4,974.9	7,410.5	I8,639.6	12,209.2	Reserve Money	14
							4.8	127.7	793.1	2,623.3	4,040.6	6,132.3	I7,157.3	9,583.3	of which: Currency Outside Banks	14a
							—	2.5	2.1	158.4	21.8		I31.1	23.1	Time, Savings,& Fgn.Currency Dep.	15
							15.3	35.3	386.9	2,805.9	4,342.8	4,690.6	I10180.1	15,537.6	Foreign Liabilities	16c
							—	18.6	166.7	97.7	216.0	334.0	I455.1	592.1	General Government Deposits	16d
							.5	12.2	75.8	231.3	420.8	914.5	I2,230.7	1,185.4	Capital Accounts	17a
							11.5	−58.1	289.2	390.3	688.1	128.0	I−1,466.1	−1,741.0	Other Items (Net)	17r
															Banking Institutions	
															End of Period	
							16.5	182.4	762.9	960.3	848.6	925.5	I1,454.6	2,613.3	Reserves	20
							5.5	159.5	1,465.3	1,873.4	1,779.7	1,829.0	I3,107.6	4,429.7	Foreign Assets	21
							1.3	17.1	—	207.6	774.5	1,815.4	I1,530.5	1,133.3	Claims on General Government	22a
							25.5	389.5	1,426.7	3,662.8	4,932.0	5,549.0	I1,440.9	1,782.4	Claims on Nonfin.Pub.Enterprises	22c
							1.3	20.9	556.5	804.2	1,128.2	2,259.1	I7,922.1	11,046.0	Claims on Private Sector	22d
							—	—	—	4.1	5.5	—	I129.4	153.5	Claims on Nonbank Financial Insts	22g
							15.8	213.6	1,061.9	2,041.9	2,253.9	2,887.3	I3,145.5	4,489.3	Demand Deposits	24
							4.5	137.1	1,353.7	2,228.3	2,887.1	3,462.8	I4,971.4	7,552.2	Time, Savings,& Fgn.Currency Dep.	25
							2.1	87.6	1,019.5	1,560.2	1,558.6	1,635.8	I3,181.9	5,306.7	of which: Fgn. Currency Deposits	25b
							—	—	—	—	—	—	I220.2	305.0	Bonds	26ab
							5.7	71.9	755.2	541.8	631.6	1,803.8	I1,738.2	1,766.6	Foreign Liabilities	26c
							3.7	87.0	323.7	514.4	795.5	805.0	I544.2	487.7	General Government Deposits	26d
							14.4	158.2	169.4	632.0	699.7	979.8	I1,237.2	1,569.4	Credit from Monetary Authorities	26g
							—	—	—	16.6	3.4	5.8	I227.3	211.4	Liab. to Nonbank Financial Insts	26j
							1.3	66.1	396.9	1,406.2	3,018.1	4,261.4	I5,462.2	7,497.7	Capital Accounts	27a
							4.6	35.3	150.7	131.1	−820.9	−1,827.9	I−1,961.1	−2,721.1	Other Items (Net)	27r
															Banking Survey	
															End of Period	
							−6.3	84.3	1,020.0	552.8	534.3	−186.0	I−5285.3	−6,622.6	Foreign Assets (Net)	31n
							41.9	453.7	2,908.6	8,459.8	12,041.1	15,949.6	I25203.5	32,902.1	Domestic Credit	32
							15.0	42.6	920.3	3,988.6	5,974.2	8,106.5	I15606.3	19,766.2	Claims on General Govt. (Net)	32an
							25.5	390.0	1,431.5	3,662.8	4,932.0	5,549.0	I1,440.9	1,782.4	Claims on Nonfin.Pub.Enterprises	32c
							1.3	21.1	556.7	804.3	1,129.4	2,294.1	I8,026.8	11,200.0	Claims on Private Sector	32d
							—	—	—	4.1	5.5	—	I129.4	153.5	Claims on Nonbank Financial Inst	32g
							20.7	341.9	1,860.0	4,681.9	6,315.5	9,050.4	I10326.4	14,082.2	Money	34
							4.5	139.5	1,355.7	2,231.5	3,045.5	3,484.6	I5,002.4	7,575.2	Quasi-Money	35
							—	—	—	—	—	—	I220.2	305.0	Bonds	36ab
							—	—	—	16.6	3.4	5.8	I227.3	211.4	Liab. to Nonbank Financial Insts	36j
							1.8	78.4	472.7	1,637.5	3,438.9	5,176.0	I7,692.8	8,683.1	Capital Accounts	37a
							8.5	−21.9	240.1	445.1	−228.0	−1,953.1	I−3551.1	−4,577.4	Other Items (Net)	37r
							25.2	481.5	3,215.7	6,913.3	9,361.0	12,535.0	I15328.9	21,657.4	Money plus Quasi-Money	35l
															Interest Rates	
															Percent Per Annum	
							80.00	240.00	252.00	110.00	40.00	35.00	60.00	45.00	Refinancing Rate (End of Period)	60
							....	....	....	....	....	22.05	40.41	44.98	Money Market Rate	60b
							....	148.63	208.63	70.29	33.63	18.21	22.25	20.70	Deposit Rate	60l
							....	184.25	250.28	122.70	79.88	49.12	54.50	54.95	Lending Rate	60p
															Prices and Labor	
															Previous Period	
								4,619.3	1,143.8	487.9	51.9	7.7	....	....	Wholesale Prices	63.xx
								4,734.9	891.2	376.7	80.3	15.9	....	....	Consumer Prices	64.xx
								2,331.9	786.6	I434.2	....	....	....	....	Wages: Average Earnings	65.xx
															Period Averages	
							129.4	119.4	108.8	100.0	92.2	90.9	....	....	Industrial Employment	67
															Period Averages	
....	....	....	....	....	....	....				25,562	....	....	25,936	....	Labor Force	67d
....	....	....	....	....	....	....				24,125	24,114	23,756	22,998	....	Employment	67e
....	....	....	....	....	....	....				1,437	1,998	2,330	2,937	....	Unemployment	67c
....	....	....	....	....	....	....				5.6	7.6	8.9	11.3	....	Unemployment Rate (%)	67r

Ukraine

926

	1970	1971	1972	1973	1974	1975	1976	1977	1978	1979	1980	1981	1982	1983	1984
International Transactions														*Millions of US Dollars*	
Exports .... 70..*d*	....	....	....	....	....	....	....	....	....	....	....	....	....	....	....
Imports, c.i.f. .... 71..*d*	....	....	....	....	....	....	....	....	....	....	....	....	....	....	....
Imports, f.o.b. 71.v*d*	....	....	....	....	....	....	....	....	....	....	....	....	....	....	....
Balance of Payments														*Millions of US Dollars:*	
Current Account, n.i.e. 78al*d*	....	....	....	....	....	....	....	....	....	....	....	....	....	....	....
Goods: Exports f.o.b. 78aa*d*	....	....	....	....	....	....	....	....	....	....	....	....	....	....	....
Goods: Imports f.o.b. 78ab*d*	....	....	....	....	....	....	....	....	....	....	....	....	....	....	....
Trade Balance............................ 78ac*d*	....	....	....	....	....	....	....	....	....	....	....	....	....	....	....
Services: Credit................................. 78ad*d*	....	....	....	....	....	....	....	....	....	....	....	....	....	....	....
Services: Debit 78ae*d*	....	....	....	....	....	....	....	....	....	....	....	....	....	....	....
Balance on Goods & Services 78af*d*	....	....	....	....	....	....	....	....	....	....	....	....	....	....	....
Income: Credit 78ag*d*	....	....	....	....	....	....	....	....	....	....	....	....	....	....	....
Income: Debit 78ah*d*	....	....	....	....	....	....	....	....	....	....	....	....	....	....	....
Balance on Gds, Serv. & Inc. 78ai*d*	....	....	....	....	....	....	....	....	....	....	....	....	....	....	....
Current Transfers, n.i.e.: Credit 78aj*d*	....	....	....	....	....	....	....	....	....	....	....	....	....	....	....
Current Transfers: Debit 78ak*d*	....	....	....	....	....	....	....	....	....	....	....	....	....	....	....
Capital Account, n.i.e. 78bc*d*	....	....	....	....	....	....	....	....	....	....	....	....	....	....	....
Capital Account, n.i.e.: Credit.......... 78ba*d*	....	....	....	....	....	....	....	....	....	....	....	....	....	....	....
Capital Account: Debit 78bb*d*	....	....	....	....	....	....	....	....	....	....	....	....	....	....	....
Financial Account, n.i.e. 78bj*d*	....	....	....	....	....	....	....	....	....	....	....	....	....	....	....
Direct Investment Abroad 78bd*d*	....	....	....	....	....	....	....	....	....	....	....	....	....	....	....
Dir. Invest. in Rep. Econ., n.i.e. ... 78be*d*	....	....	....	....	....	....	....	....	....	....	....	....	....	....	....
Portfolio Investment Assets 78bf*d*	....	....	....	....	....	....	....	....	....	....	....	....	....	....	....
Equity Securities.............................. 78bk*d*	....	....	....	....	....	....	....	....	....	....	....	....	....	....	....
Debt Securities 78bl*d*	....	....	....	....	....	....	....	....	....	....	....	....	....	....	....
Portfolio Investment Liab., n.i.e. 78bg*d*	....	....	....	....	....	....	....	....	....	....	....	....	....	....	....
Equity Securities.............................. 78bm*d*	....	....	....	....	....	....	....	....	....	....	....	....	....	....	....
Debt Securities 78bn*d*	....	....	....	....	....	....	....	....	....	....	....	....	....	....	....
Financial Derivatives Assets 78bw*d*	....	....	....	....	....	....	....	....	....	....	....	....	....	....	....
Financial Derivatives Liabilities 78bx*d*	....	....	....	....	....	....	....	....	....	....	....	....	....	....	....
Other Investment Assets 78bh*d*	....	....	....	....	....	....	....	....	....	....	....	....	....	....	....
Monetary Authorities 78bo*d*	....	....	....	....	....	....	....	....	....	....	....	....	....	....	....
General Government 78bp*d*	....	....	....	....	....	....	....	....	....	....	....	....	....	....	....
Banks 78bq*d*	....	....	....	....	....	....	....	....	....	....	....	....	....	....	....
Other Sectors 78br*d*	....	....	....	....	....	....	....	....	....	....	....	....	....	....	....
Other Investment Liab., n.i.e. 78bi*d*	....	....	....	....	....	....	....	....	....	....	....	....	....	....	....
Monetary Authorities 78bs*d*	....	....	....	....	....	....	....	....	....	....	....	....	....	....	....
General Government 78bt*d*	....	....	....	....	....	....	....	....	....	....	....	....	....	....	....
Banks 78bu*d*	....	....	....	....	....	....	....	....	....	....	....	....	....	....	....
Other Sectors 78bv*d*	....	....	....	....	....	....	....	....	....	....	....	....	....	....	....
Net Errors and Omissions................... 78ca*d*	....	....	....	....	....	....	....	....	....	....	....	....	....	....	....
Overall Balance 78cb*d*	....	....	....	....	....	....	....	....	....	....	....	....	....	....	....
Reserves and Related Items 79da*d*	....	....	....	....	....	....	....	....	....	....	....	....	....	....	....
Reserve Assets 79db*d*	....	....	....	....	....	....	....	....	....	....	....	....	....	....	....
Use of Fund Credit and Loans 79dc*d*	....	....	....	....	....	....	....	....	....	....	....	....	....	....	....
Exceptional Financing 79de*d*	....	....	....	....	....	....	....	....	....	....	....	....	....	....	....
National Accounts														*Millions of Hryvnias through 1993;*	
Househ.Cons.Expend.,Incl.NPISHs 96f	....	....	....	....	....	....	....	....	....	....	....	....	....	....	....
Government Consumption Expend. 91f	....	....	....	....	....	....	....	....	....	....	....	....	....	....	....
Gross Fixed Capital Formation 93e	....	....	....	....	....	....	....	....	....	....	....	....	....	....	....
Changes in Inventories 93i	....	....	....	....	....	....	....	....	....	....	....	....	....	....	....
Exports of Goods and Services 90c	....	....	....	....	....	....	....	....	....	....	....	....	....	....	....
Imports of Goods and Services................ 98c	....	....	....	....	....	....	....	....	....	....	....	....	....	....	....
Gross Domestic Product (GDP) 99b	....	....	....	....	....	....	....	....	....	....	....	....	....	....	....
Net Primary Income from Abroad 98.n	....	....	....	....	....	....	....	....	....	....	....	....	....	....	....
Gross National Income (GNI) 99a	....	....	....	....	....	....	....	....	....	....	....	....	....	....	....
															Millions:
Population... 99z	....	....	....	....	....	....	....	....	....	....	....	....	....	....	....

Millions of US Dollars

International Transactions

1985	1986	1987	1988	1989	1990	1991	1992	1993	1994	1995	1996	1997	1998	1999		
...	...	...	...	...	...	...	8,045	7,817	10,305	13,317	14,441	14,232	12,637	11,582	Exports	70..d
...	...	...	...	...	...	...	7,099	9,533	10,748	16,052	18,639	17,114	14,676	11,846	Imports, c.i.f.	71..d
...	...	...	...	...	...	...	7,099	9,533	10,589	11,328	....	....	....	....	Imports, f.o.b.	71.v d

Minus Sign Indicates Debit

Balance of Payments

1985	1986	1987	1988	1989	1990	1991	1992	1993	1994	1995	1996	1997	1998	1999		
....	....	....	....	....	....	....	....	....	−1,163	−1,152	−1,184	−1,335	−1,296	834	Current Account, n.i.e.	78al d
....	....	....	....	....	....	....	....	....	13,894	14,244	15,547	15,418	13,699	12,463	Goods: Exports f.o.b.	78aa d
....	....	....	....	....	....	....	....	....	−16,469	−16,946	−19,843	−19,623	−16,283	−12,945	Goods: Imports f.o.b.	78ab d
....	....	....	....	....	....	....	....	....	−2,575	−2,702	−4,296	−4,205	−2,584	−482	*Trade Balance*	78ac d
....	....	....	....	....	....	....	....	....	2,747	2,846	4,799	4,937	3,922	3,771	Services: Credit	78ad d
....	....	....	....	....	....	....	....	....	−1,538	−1,334	−1,625	−2,268	−2,545	−2,292	Services: Debit	78ae d
....	....	....	....	....	....	....	....	....	−1,366	−1,190	−1,122	−1,536	−1,207	997	*Balance on Goods & Services*	78af d
....	....	....	....	....	....	....	....	....	56	247	102	158	122	98	Income: Credit	78ag d
....	....	....	....	....	....	....	....	....	−400	−681	−673	−802	−993	−967	Income: Debit	78ah d
....	....	....	....	....	....	....	....	....	−1,710	−1,624	−1,693	−2,180	−2,078	128	*Balance on Gds, Serv. & Inc.*	78ai d
....	....	....	....	....	....	....	....	....	583	557	619	942	868	754	Current Transfers, n.i.e.: Credit	78aj d
....	....	....	....	....	....	....	....	....	−36	−85	−110	−97	−86	−48	Current Transfers: Debit	78ak d
....	....	....	....	....	....	....	....	....	97	6	5	—	−3	−10	Capital Account, n.i.e.	78bc d
....	....	....	....	....	....	....	....	....	106	6	5	—	—	—	Capital Account, n.i.e.: Credit	78ba d
....	....	....	....	....	....	....	....	....	−9	—	—	—	−3	−10	Capital Account: Debit	78bb d
....	....	....	....	....	....	....	....	....	−557	−726	317	1,413	−1,340	−55	Financial Account, n.i.e.	78bj d
....	....	....	....	....	....	....	....	....	−8	−10	5	−42	4	−7	Direct Investment Abroad	78bd d
....	....	....	....	....	....	....	....	....	159	267	521	623	743	496	Dir. Invest. in Rep. Econ., n.i.e.	78be d
....	....	....	....	....	....	....	....	....	—	−12	−1	−2	−2	−11	Portfolio Investment Assets	78bf d
....	....	....	....	....	....	....	....	....	....	....	−11	−14	−3	−5	Equity Securities	78bk d
....	....	....	....	....	....	....	....	....	....	−12	10	12	1	−6	Debt Securities	78bl d
....	....	....	....	....	....	....	....	....	—	16	199	1,605	−1,379	73	Portfolio Investment Liab., n.i.e.	78bg d
....	....	....	....	....	....	....	....	....	....	....	46	248	227	129	Equity Securities	78bm d
....	....	....	....	....	....	....	....	....	—	16	153	1,357	−1,606	−56	Debt Securities	78bn d
....	....	....	....	....	....	....	....	....	....	....	....	....	....	....	Financial Derivatives Assets	78bw d
....	....	....	....	....	....	....	....	....	....	....	....	....	....	....	Financial Derivatives Liabilities	78bx d
....	....	....	....	....	....	....	....	....	−3,026	−1,574	−821	−1,583	−1,321	−1,440	Other Investment Assets	78bh d
....	....	....	....	....	....	....	....	....	....	....	....	....	....	....	Monetary Authorities	78bo d
....	....	....	....	....	....	....	....	....	....	....	....	....	....	....	General Government	78bp d
....	....	....	....	....	....	....	....	....	−779	−328	83	−536	−46	51	Banks	78bq d
....	....	....	....	....	....	....	....	....	−2,247	−1,246	−904	−1,047	−1,275	−1,491	Other Sectors	78br d
....	....	....	....	....	....	....	....	....	2,318	587	414	812	615	834	Other Investment Liab., n.i.e.	78bi d
....	....	....	....	....	....	....	....	....	—	—	—	—	—	—	Monetary Authorities	78bs d
....	....	....	....	....	....	....	....	....	−1,097	−783	−477	−267	−857	−379	General Government	78bt d
....	....	....	....	....	....	....	....	....	577	724	565	−51	−264	−16	Banks	78bu d
....	....	....	....	....	....	....	....	....	2,838	646	326	1,130	1,736	1,229	Other Sectors	78bv d
....	....	....	....	....	....	....	....	....	423	248	259	−781	−818	−953	Net Errors and Omissions	78ca d
....	....	....	....	....	....	....	....	....	−1,200	−1,624	−603	−703	−3,457	−184	*Overall Balance*	78cb d
....	....	....	....	....	....	....	....	....	1,200	1,624	603	703	3,457	184	Reserves and Related Items	79da d
....	....	....	....	....	....	....	....	....	−549	−469	−894	−385	1,328	−281	Reserve Assets	79db d
....	....	....	....	....	....	....	....	....	368	1,221	776	283	279	75	Use of Fund Credit and Loans	79dc d
....	....	....	....	....	....	....	....	....	1,380	871	721	805	1,850	390	Exceptional Financing	79de d

Billions of Hryvnias Beginning 1994

National Accounts

1985	1986	1987	1988	1989	1990	1991	1992	1993	1994	1995	1996	1997	1998	1999		
....	....	....	....	....	....	....	28.30	840.56	‡7.07	37.19	57.98	68.97	....	....	Househ.Cons.Expend.,Incl.NPISHs	96f
....	....	....	....	....	....	....	3.70	108.69	‡1.09	4.46	7.14	8.42	....	....	Government Consumption Expend.	91f
....	....	....	....	....	....	....	13.80	363.49	‡2.86	12.76	17.01	17.03	....	....	Gross Fixed Capital Formation	93e
....	....	....	....	....	....	....	3.50	174.63	‡1.39	1.79	1.47	1.57	....	....	Changes in Inventories	93i
....	....	....	....	....	....	....	12.10	383.70	‡4.26	25.66	37.22	37.47	....	....	Exports of Goods and Services	90c
....	....	....	....	....	....	....	−11.10	−388.34	‡−4.64	−27.34	−39.30	−40.98	....	....	Imports of Goods and Services	98c
....	....	....	....	....	....	....	50.30	1,482.73	‡12.04	54.52	81.52	92.48	....	....	Gross Domestic Product (GDP)	99b
....	....	....	....	....	....	....	−.10	−35.81	‡−.08	−.88	−1.05	....	....	....	Net Primary Income from Abroad	98.n
....	....	....	....	....	....	....	50.30	1,446.92	‡11.96	53.64	....	....	....	....	Gross National Income (GNI)	99a

Midyear Estimates

1985	1986	1987	1988	1989	1990	1991	1992	1993	1994	1995	1996	1997	1998	1999		
....	....	....	....	....	....	....	52.06	52.24	52.11	51.73	51.33	50.89	50.50	50.66	**Population**	99z

(See notes in the back of the book.)

United Arab Emirates

	1970	1971	1972	1973	1974	1975	1976	1977	1978	1979	1980	1981	1982	1983	1984
Exchange Rates													*Dirhams per SDR:*		
Official Rate .... aa	4.7619	4.7619	4.7619	4.8344	4.8735	4.6791	4.6206	4.7349	5.0001	4.9611	4.6820	4.2729	4.0495	3.8434	3.5984
													Dirhams per US Dollar:		
Official Rate .... ae	4.7619	4.3860	4.3860	4.0075	3.9805	3.9970	3.9770	3.8980	3.8380	3.7660	3.6710	3.6710	3.6710	3.6710	3.6710
Official Rate .... rf	4.7619	4.7480	4.3860	3.9963	3.9590	3.9613	3.9531	3.9032	3.8712	3.8157	3.7074	3.6710	3.6710	3.6710	3.6710
												Index Numbers (1995=100):			
Official Rate .... ahx	77.1	77.3	83.7	91.7	92.5	92.7	92.9	93.8	94.8	96.2	99.0	100.0	100.0	100.0	100.0
Nominal Effective Exchange Rate ...... nec	....	....	....	....	....	....	....	....	....	99.2	102.1	114.2	126.5	132.4	141.7
Fund Position													*Millions of SDRs:*		
Quota .... 2f. s	—	—	15.0	15.0	15.0	15.0	15.0	15.0	120.0	120.0	202.6	202.6	202.6	202.6	202.6
SDRs .... 1b. s	—	—	—	—	—	—	—	—	—	15.4	8.0	29.5	50.3	61.5	66.0
Reserve Position in the Fund ...... 1c. s	—	—	3.8	3.8	69.6	114.8	114.1	96.5	71.7	62.1	93.1	147.9	201.4	214.6	222.3
of which: Outstg.Fund Borrowing 2c	—	—	—	—	63.8	100.0	100.0	84.0	57.9	46.5	44.7	75.4	105.0	102.9	93.9
International Liquidity											*Millions of US Dollars Unless Otherwise Indicated:*				
Total Reserves minus Gold 1l.d	....	....	....	91.7	452.9	987.9	1,906.5	800.3	811.8	1,432.3	2,014.7	3,202.2	2,215.5	2,072.4	2,286.9
SDRs 1b.d	—	—	—	—	—	—	—	—	—	20.2	10.2	34.4	55.5	64.4	64.7
Reserve Position in the Fund 1c.d	—	—	4.1	4.5	85.2	134.4	132.6	117.2	93.4	81.7	118.8	172.1	222.2	224.7	217.9
Foreign Exchange 1d.d	....	....	....	87.2	367.7	853.5	1,773.9	683.1	718.4	1,330.3	1,885.8	2,995.7	1,937.8	1,783.3	2,004.3
Gold (Million Fine Troy Ounces) 1ad	....	....	....	....	....	....	....	.545	.569	.576	.577	.577	.678	.817	.817	.817
Gold (National Valuation) 1and	—	—	—	—	—	—	—	67.8	72.7	75.3	76.8	78.8	184.6	184.6	184.6	184.6
Monetary Authorities: Other Assets ...... 3..d													1,132.7		
Deposit Money Banks: Assets 7a.d	....	....	....	402.2	1,106.4	1,794.3	2,574.7	2,077.4	2,584.2	3,556.7	5,286.4	7,914.3	9,548.5	9,538.0	12,100.6
Liabilities 7b.d	....	....	....	108.6	225.7	436.5	892.7	2,262.8	2,761.1	4,028.3	4,571.2	6,142.9	7,229.5	6,719.6	5,666.5
RLB: Foreign Assets 7k.d	....	....	....	....	....	....	....	85.8	268.0	313.3	378.8	332.9	490.5	601.1	459.5
Foreign Liabilities 7m.d	....	....	....	....	....	....	....	115.3	316.1	376.2	424.9	419.9	343.4	515.9	332.7
Monetary Authorities													*Millions of Dirhams:*		
Foreign Assets 11	....	....	....	365	1,976	4,189	9,001	3,419	3,405	5,721	7,726	12,629	13,271	10,204	11,029
Claims on Central Government 12a	....	....	....	45	120	459	1,307	1,712	1,540	1,538	1,544	1,484	1,486	1,488	1,491
Claims on Official Entities 12bx	....	....	....	—	—	—	100	12	12	11	5	—	12	12	5
Claims on Deposit Money Banks 12e	....	....	....	16	172	527	1,013	1,199	1,391	1,042	689	335	239	1,469	1,081
Claims on Other Financial Insts 12f	....	....	....	—	—	2	18	31	16	22	18	14	7	4	—
Reserve Money 14	....	....	....	411	1,051	1,526	2,776	3,796	4,259	5,475	4,451	5,321	6,044	5,992	6,529
of which: Currency Outside DMBs 14a	....	....	....	265	429	628	1,077	1,392	1,704	1,965	2,143	2,771	2,990	2,879	2,929
Quasi-Monetary Deposits 15	....	....	....	—	293	60	52	34	10	—	—	—	—	—	—
Foreign Liabilities 16c	....	....	....	—	—	1	824	616	487	513	390	233	8	6	5
Central Government Deposits 16d	....	....	....	18	919	3,578	7,631	2,041	1,776	2,173	4,508	6,938	6,078	3,527	3,340
Capital Accounts 17a	....	....	....	9	10	20	30	30	30	237	711	2,074	3,084	3,758	3,816
Other Items (Net) 17r	....	....	....	−12	−4	9	140	−161	−194	−70	−83	−111	−203	−112	−85
Deposit Money Banks													*Millions of Dirhams:*		
Reserves 20	....	....	....	146	594	898	1,699	2,404	2,553	3,507	2,295	2,543	3,043	3,099	3,590
Foreign Assets 21	....	....	....	1,588	4,404	7,172	10,240	8,098	9,918	13,395	19,406	29,054	35,052	35,014	44,421
Claims on Central Government 22a	....	....	....	137	273	358	737	1,498	1,907	2,958	2,305	2,418	3,641	4,177	4,330
Claims on Official Entities 22bx	....	....	....	—	9	91	299	713	584	892	840	1,015	916	798	659
Claims on Private Sector 22d	....	....	....	1,627	3,362	5,691	10,472	15,819	19,357	21,212	25,173	29,902	31,713	33,467	33,385
Claims on Other Financial Insts 22f	....	....	....	14	37	125	146	170	210	283	606	537	924	1,236	2,349
Demand Deposits 24	....	....	....	705	1,107	1,975	3,648	3,822	4,072	4,303	5,212	6,198	6,749	6,245	5,963
Time and Savings Deposits 25	....	....	....	1,287	4,207	6,157	11,977	10,291	11,790	11,954	16,172	20,125	23,907	27,217	37,978
Foreign Liabilities 26c	....	....	....	429	898	1,745	3,550	8,821	10,597	15,171	16,781	22,551	26,540	24,668	20,802
Central Government Deposits 26d	....	....	....	979	2,159	3,578	2,949	2,324	2,503	4,358	3,675	3,737	3,791	3,326	4,108
Central Govt. Lending Funds 26f	....	....	....	7	6	5	5	290	658	925	1,569	2,054	907	736	526
Credit from Monetary Authorities 26g	....	....	....	16	172	527	1,013	1,192	1,391	1,039	689	335	239	1,469	1,031
Capital Accounts 27a	....	....	....	125	175	392	609	1,867	3,548	4,553	5,523	8,397	10,756	11,583	12,027
Other Items (Net) 27r	....	....	....	−34	−46	−45	−119	95	−31	−56	1,005	2,071	2,399	2,547	6,301
Monetary Survey													*Millions of Dirhams:*		
Foreign Assets (Net) 31n	....	....	....	1,524	5,481	9,615	14,866	2,080	2,239	3,432	9,962	18,898	21,776	20,544	34,643
Domestic Credit 32	....	....	....	826	724	−412	2,555	15,582	19,359	20,385	22,310	24,692	28,831	34,330	34,777
Claims on Central Govt. (Net) 32an	....	....	....	−815	−2,685	−6,339	−8,536	−1,155	−832	−2,035	−4,335	−6,773	−4,742	−1,188	−1,627
Claims on Official Entities 32bx	....	....	....	—	9	91	399	725	596	903	846	1,015	928	810	664
Claims on Private Sector 32d	....	....	....	1,627	3,362	5,693	10,475	15,826	19,363	21,218	25,179	29,907	31,718	33,471	33,390
Claims on Other Financial Insts 32f	....	....	....	14	39	142	217	186	232	300	620	543	928	1,236	2,349
Money 34	....	....	....	970	1,536	2,603	4,725	5,215	5,776	6,269	7,355	8,969	9,739	9,124	8,892
Quasi-Money 35	....	....	....	1,287	4,499	6,217	12,029	10,325	11,800	11,954	16,172	20,125	23,907	27,218	37,978
Other Items (Net) 37r	....	....	....	94	170	383	667	2,122	4,022	5,595	8,745	14,496	16,961	18,531	22,550
Money plus Quasi-Money 35l	....	....	....	2,257	6,036	8,820	16,754	15,540	17,576	18,222	23,527	29,094	33,646	36,342	46,870
Production													*Index Numbers (1995=100):*		
Crude Petroleum 66aa	35.5	48.3	54.9	69.4	76.4	77.3	88.6	91.1	83.5	83.4	78.2	68.5	57.8	53.8	51.2

	1985	1986	1987	1988	1989	1990	1991	1992	1993	1994	1995	1996	1997	1998	1999		
																Exchange Rates	
End of Period																	
	4.0323	4.4903	5.2079	4.9401	4.8243	5.2226	5.2511	5.0476	5.0423	5.3591	5.4569	5.2788	4.9551	5.1710	5.0405	Official Rate	**aa**
End of Period (ae) Period Average (rf)																	
	3.6710	3.6710	3.6710	3.6710	3.6710	3.6710	3.6710	3.6710	3.6710	3.6710	3.6710	3.6710	3.6725	3.6725	3.6725	Official Rate	**ae**
	3.6710	3.6710	3.6710	3.6710	3.6710	3.6710	3.6710	3.6710	3.6710	3.6710	3.6710	3.6710	3.6711	3.6725	3.6725	Official Rate	**rf**
Period Averages																	
	100.0	100.0	100.0	100.0	100.0	100.0	100.0	100.0	100.0	100.0	100.0	100.0	100.0	100.0	100.0	Official Rate	**ah** x
	145.8	119.7	106.8	101.6	106.8	102.4	103.5	102.1	107.2	105.3	100.0	103.9	112.3	121.1	119.0	Nominal Effective Exchange Rate	**ne** c
																Fund Position	
End of Period																	
	202.6	202.6	202.6	202.6	202.6	202.6	202.6	392.1	392.1	392.1	392.1	392.1	392.1	392.1	611.7	Quota	**2f.** s
	68.3	76.5	79.8	82.3	85.9	90.8	95.5	52.4	54.1	55.0	55.9	57.6	58.4	59.2	4.5	SDRs	**1b.** s
	201.7	181.0	159.1	135.3	138.4	126.3	126.1	158.3	162.8	149.1	185.8	204.4	197.4	233.9	212.6	Reserve Position in the Fund	**1c.** s
	72.6	46.4	22.5	3.2	.1	—	—	—	—	—	—	—	—	—	—	*of which:* Outstg.Fund Borrowing	**2c**
																International Liquidity	
End of Period																	
	3,204.3	3,369.9	4,725.3	4,433.5	4,456.6	4,583.9	5,365.4	5,711.8	6,103.7	6,658.8	7,470.9	8,055.5	8,372.3	9,077.1	10,675.1	Total Reserves minus Gold	**1l.** d
	75.0	93.5	113.2	110.8	112.9	129.1	136.6	72.1	74.4	80.3	83.1	82.8	78.7	83.3	6.2	SDRs	**1b.** d
	221.5	221.4	225.6	182.0	181.9	179.7	180.4	217.6	223.6	217.7	276.2	293.9	266.3	329.3	291.7	Reserve Position in the Fund	**1c.** d
	2,907.8	3,054.9	4,386.5	4,140.7	4,161.8	4,275.1	5,048.4	5,422.1	5,805.7	6,360.8	7,111.6	7,678.8	8,027.3	8,664.4	10,377.1	Foreign Exchange	**1d.** d
	.817	.817	.817	.817	.797	.797	.796	.796	.798	.795	.795	.798	.795	.795	.397	Gold (Million Fine Troy Ounces)	**1ad**
	184.6	184.6	184.6	184.6	182.0	181.7	181.7	182.0	182.5	181.7	181.7	182.8	181.3	181.3	90.7	Gold (National Valuation)	**1an** d
	....	....	....	....	....	....	....	....	....	....	....	....	....	....	....	Monetary Authorities: Other Assets	**3..** d
	12,070.1	13,475.9	13,188.7	15,505.7	16,378.1	17,134.0	18,931.9	18,496.6	17,997.8	17,737.4	17,377.8	19,086.9	20,735.7	22,108.9	22,010.3	Deposit Money Banks: Assets	**7a.** d
	5,422.6	4,594.9	4,789.9	6,153.1	5,603.4	6,779.1	7,042.0	7,157.7	7,221.7	8,997.8	7,653.5	10,053.4	12,351.5	14,446.6	14,577.8	Liabilities	**7b.** d
	540.6	498.4	448.1	475.8	433.4	386.0	210.3	162.9	118.8	106.0	134.0	134.6	154.7	200.7	265.5	RLB: Foreign Assets	**7k.** d
	308.7	239.4	259.2	300.5	186.6	94.5	113.6	79.0	60.2	35.4	59.1	112.8	101.3	75.4	281.0	Foreign Liabilities	**7m.** d
																Monetary Authorities	
End of Period																	
	14,543	13,805	18,322	17,225	17,211	17,734	20,654	21,804	23,357	25,812	28,408	30,567	31,692	34,512	40,185	Foreign Assets	**11**
	1,493	2,226	—	—	13	364	—	425	—	—	—	—	—	—	—	Claims on Central Government	**12a**
	5	5	—	—	—	—	—	—	—	—	—	—	—	—	—	Claims on Official Entities	**12bx**
	190	1,076	1,080	1,076	555	50	50	50	50	50	50	50	50	50	50	Claims on Deposit Money Banks	**12e**
	—	—	—	—	—	—	—	—	—	—	—	—	—	—	—	Claims on Other Financial Insts	**12f**
	7,562	7,756	11,864	10,902	9,600	9,663	11,192	13,576	13,124	16,501	18,667	20,188	20,294	20,326	26,530	Reserve Money	**14**
	3,161	3,246	3,511	3,600	3,612	4,392	4,676	5,108	5,667	6,031	6,404	6,767	7,366	8,195	10,272	*of which:* Currency Outside DMBs	**14a**
	—	—	—	—	—	—	—	—	—	—	—	—	—	—	—	Quasi-Monetary Deposits	**15**
	6	5	5	7	10	202	252	336	313	380	175	75	52	11	403	Foreign Liabilities	**16c**
	3,308	1,985	4,815	4,615	4,621	5,069	7,057	6,166	6,788	7,178	7,930	8,591	9,692	10,692	11,518	Central Government Deposits	**16d**
	5,405	7,367	2,628	2,631	2,649	2,664	1,738	1,696	1,695	1,708	1,711	1,704	1,692	1,700	1,755	Capital Accounts	**17a**
	−49	−2	88	146	899	549	464	505	1,486	96	−25	54	12	1,832	29	Other Items (Net)	**17r**
																Deposit Money Banks	
End of Period																	
	4,394	4,514	8,286	7,264	5,963	5,247	6,525	8,466	7,452	10,465	12,258	13,416	12,923	12,127	16,256	Reserves	**20**
	44,309	49,470	48,416	56,922	60,124	62,899	69,499	67,901	66,070	65,114	63,794	70,068	76,152	81,195	80,833	Foreign Assets	**21**
	9,491	5,892	7,491	6,856	7,250	8,251	10,040	10,806	12,334	12,558	12,787	10,394	9,105	12,719	15,725	Claims on Central Government	**22a**
	636	612	704	1,058	785	1,187	1,323	1,421	2,791	5,869	5,840	5,064	5,511	5,236	5,581	Claims on Official Entities	**22bx**
	33,628	36,232	38,975	42,493	46,086	46,897	50,618	53,713	57,691	63,836	71,759	78,927	89,925	102,416	110,276	Claims on Private Sector	**22d**
	2,064	1,961	1,634	1,721	1,637	2,482	1,477	2,193	3,014	2,656	2,526	2,330	2,689	3,443	3,075	Claims on Other Financial Insts	**22f**
	6,344	5,956	6,585	7,154	7,444	6,370	8,336	9,873	12,507	13,152	14,420	15,499	18,002	19,589	19,980	Demand Deposits	**24**
	40,381	42,875	44,844	47,403	52,132	47,246	53,432	54,530	50,241	54,635	60,537	64,676	69,437	71,000	79,847	Time and Savings Deposits	**25**
	19,906	16,868	17,584	22,588	20,570	24,886	25,851	26,276	26,511	33,031	28,096	36,906	45,361	53,055	53,537	Foreign Liabilities	**26c**
	3,882	4,335	5,158	5,907	6,292	10,662	10,619	11,008	14,830	12,550	15,156	9,962	6,948	10,920	11,671	Central Government Deposits	**26d**
	559	482	434	385	353	332	307	282	243	184	113	95	92	77	62	Central Govt. Lending Funds	**26f**
	190	1,076	1,080	1,076	555	605	911	51	50	51	54	55	50	51	54	Credit from Monetary Authorities	**26g**
	14,286	12,659	13,138	13,378	14,395	15,254	16,063	16,838	17,516	19,563	21,616	23,273	25,435	29,883	31,910	Capital Accounts	**27a**
	8,973	14,431	16,684	18,422	20,104	21,607	23,963	25,642	27,455	27,331	28,971	29,733	30,980	32,560	34,685	Other Items (Net)	**27r**
																Monetary Survey	
End of Period																	
	38,940	46,401	49,148	51,552	56,755	55,545	64,050	63,093	62,603	57,515	63,931	63,654	62,431	62,641	67,078	Foreign Assets (Net)	**31n**
	40,134	40,614	38,839	41,617	44,872	43,466	45,800	51,400	54,229	65,207	69,841	78,178	90,607	102,221	111,489	Domestic Credit	**32**
	3,795	1,797	−2,482	−3,666	−3,650	−7,116	−7,636	−5,943	−9,284	−7,170	−10,299	−8,159	−7,535	−8,893	−7,464	Claims on Central Govt. (Net)	**32an**
	641	617	704	1,058	785	1,187	1,323	1,421	2,791	5,869	5,840	5,064	5,511	5,236	5,581	Claims on Official Entities	**32bx**
	33,635	36,238	38,983	42,504	46,100	46,913	50,636	53,729	57,708	63,852	71,774	78,943	89,942	102,435	110,297	Claims on Private Sector	**32d**
	2,064	1,961	1,634	1,721	1,637	2,482	1,477	2,193	3,014	2,656	2,526	2,330	2,689	3,443	3,075	Claims on Other Financial Insts	**32f**
	9,505	9,201	10,096	10,753	11,056	10,762	13,012	14,981	18,174	19,183	20,824	22,266	25,368	27,784	30,252	Money	**34**
	40,382	42,875	44,844	47,403	52,132	47,246	53,432	54,530	50,241	54,635	60,537	64,676	69,437	71,000	79,847	Quasi-Money	**35**
	29,188	34,939	33,047	35,013	38,439	41,001	43,405	44,982	48,417	48,904	52,410	54,885	58,233	66,076	68,468	Other Items (Net)	**37r**
	49,887	52,076	54,940	58,156	63,188	58,008	66,444	69,511	68,415	73,818	81,361	86,942	94,805	98,784	110,099	Money plus Quasi-Money	**35l**
																Production	
Period Averages																	
	51.0	63.6	65.4	68.5	85.6	94.3	109.2	104.0	99.8	99.4	100.0	100.4	102.4	100.8	103.6	Crude Petroleum	**66aa**

United Arab Emirates

	1970	1971	1972	1973	1974	1975	1976	1977	1978	1979	1980	1981	1982	1983	1984
International Transactions														*Millions of US Dollars*	
Exports .... 70..*d*	523	871	1,157	1,807	6,414	7,262	9,535	9,636	9,126	13,652	20,676	21,238	16,837	14,672	14,192
Imports, c.i.f. .... 71..*d*	267	309	482	821	1,705	2,685	3,337	5,055	5,371	6,966	8,746	9,646	9,440	8,294	6,936
Volume of Exports														*1985=100*	
Crude Petroleum 72aa	69.7	9.4	10.8	135.4	149.9	151.7	173.9	178.8	163.7	163.7	153.4	134.4	113.3	ɪ105.6	100.4
Export Prices														*1985=100:*	
Crude Petroleum *(Murban)* .... 76aa *d*	11.2	13.7	15.4	17.7	ɪ68.1	64.7	72.1	77.9	80.1	184.9	222.3	212.6	196.9	176.5	ɪ170.6
Government Finance														*Millions of Dirhams:*	
Deficit (-) or Surplus 80	....	....	37	30	62	590	596	−211	−503	202	2,302	2,355	....	....	....
Revenue 81	....	....	5	17	21	51	96	259	204	252	269	201	....	....	....
Grants Received 81z	....	....	196	403	780	1,722	3,006	5,736	6,780	8,610	17,339	22,259			
Expenditure 82	....	....	164	390	734	1,157	2,144	5,068	6,815	8,132	13,332	18,666	19,980	16,310	15,669
Lending Minus Repayments 83	....	....	—	—	4	26	361	1,138	672	528	1,974	1,439	....	....	....
Financing															
Domestic 84a	....	....	−37	−30	−62	−590	−596	211	503	−202	−2,302	−2,355	....	....	....
Foreign 85a	....	....	—	—	—	—	—	—	—	—	—	—			
National Accounts														*Billions of Dirhams:*	
Exports of Goods & Services 90c	....	....	5.5	9.4	29.4	29.5	36.6	41.8	40.2	57.2	85.6	83.7	71.6	60.9	59.8
Government Consumption 91f	....	....	.9	1.3	2.7	3.3	4.6	7.4	8.2	9.6	12.0	21.5	22.0	19.0	17.7
Gross Fixed Capital Formation 93e	....	....	1.8	2.1	4.1	12.1	16.6	22.7	25.8	28.4	30.1	30.6	31.7	31.7	29.1
Increase/Decrease(-) in Stocks 93i	....	....	—	.8	.7	—	.4	2.1	−2.3	−.8	1.0	1.2	.5	.5	.3
Private Consumption 96f	....	....	.9	1.5	2.2	6.2	7.7	11.6	12.5	15.2	19.0	24.9	26.8	27.5	27.5
Imports of Goods & Services 98c	....	....	−2.5	−3.7	−8.0	−11.6	−14.8	−22.3	−23.9	−29.7	−37.9	−40.8	−40.2	−36.7	−32.7
Gross Domestic Product (GDP) 99b	....	....	6.6	11.4	31.1	39.5	51.1	63.3	60.5	79.9	109.8	121.1	112.4	102.9	101.7
GDP Volume 1980 Prices.................... 99b.*p*	....	....	....	43.4	49.6	52.7	60.7	71.2	69.6	86.9	109.8	113.0	103.6	100.9	105.4
GDP Volume (1990=100) .... 99bv *p*	....	....	....	38.2	43.8	46.5	53.5	62.8	61.3	76.6	96.9	99.6	91.4	89.0	92.9
GDP Deflator (1990=100) ....99bi *p*	....	....	....	24.1	57.5	68.8	77.3	81.6	79.8	84.4	91.8	98.4	99.6	93.6	88.6
														Millions:	
Population... 99z	.23	.28	.34	.42	.49	.51	.59	.69	.79	.92	1.01	1.10	1.17	1.21	ɪ1.31

	1985	1986	1987	1988	1989	1990	1991	1992	1993	1994	1995	1996	1997	1998	1999		
Millions of US Dollars																**International Transactions**	
	14,043	12,387	14,165	13,934	17,596	23,544	24,436	24,756	....	....	....	....	....	....	....	Exports	70..d
	6,549	6,422	7,226	8,522	10,010	11,199	13,746	17,414	19,520	21,024	20,984	22,638	29,952	24,728	....	Imports, c.i.f.	71..d
1985=100																Volume of Exports	
	100.0	124.8	128.4	134.5	....	....	....	....	....	....	....	....	....	....	....	Crude Petroleum	72aa
Index of Prices in US Dollars																Export Prices	
	164.4	81.0	105.2	82.8	97.9	128.5	103.0	106.3	92.4	92.0	100.0	114.9	112.2	75.0	106.4	Crude Petroleum *(Murban)*	76aa d
Year Ending December 31																**Government Finance**	
	....	....	−624	−314	−780	456	−625	1,050	−323	290 [P]	....	....	897	−538	....	Deficit (-) or Surplus	80
	....	....	2,769	1,921	1,355	1,971	1,626	4,110	2,975	3,294 [P]	....	....	5,609	5,918	....	Revenue	81
	....	....	9,865	10,950	11,332	12,927	12,997	12,511	12,273	12,689 [P]	....	....	13,403	13,318	....	Grants Received	81z
	....	....	13,258	13,185	13,467	14,442	15,248	15,571	15,571	15,693 [P]	....	....	18,050	19,156	....	Expenditure	82
	....	....	—	—	—	—	—	—	—	— [P]	....	....	65	618	....	Lending Minus Repayments	83
																Financing	
	....	....	624	314	780	−456	625	−1,050	323	−290 [P]	....	....	−897	538	....	Domestic	84a
	....	....	—	—	—	—	—	—	—	— [P]	....	....	—	—	....	Foreign	85a
Billions of Dirhams																**National Accounts**	
	57.7	37.9	48.5	46.8	59.4	82.0	84.2	92.0	98.4	104.8	109.4	125.8	128.6	115.0	....	Exports of Goods & Services	90c
	19.5	17.5	17.8	18.5	20.1	20.1	21.1	22.8	23.4	24.2	25.4	26.2	28.1	28.6	....	Government Consumption	91f
	24.5	23.4	20.3	20.8	22.4	24.1	25.8	29.8	36.4	37.5	39.8	40.9	48.8	49.2	....	Gross Fixed Capital Formation	93e
	.5	.5	.6	.9	1.2	1.3	1.4	1.6	1.9	2.0	2.1	2.3	2.2	2.2	....	Increase/Decrease(-) in Stocks	93i
	28.3	31.6	33.8	38.7	41.9	46.7	51.4	57.9	57.7	60.7	69.3	74.4	86.2	90.7	....	Private Consumption	96f
	−31.3	−31.7	−34.0	−38.8	−44.9	−50.6	−59.4	−74.1	−87.3	−94.6	−99.0	−105.9	−112.7	−115.0	....	Imports of Goods & Services	98c
	99.2	79.2	87.0	86.9	100.1	123.5	124.5	130.0	130.4	134.6	147.0	163.8	181.2	170.7	....	Gross Domestic Product (GDP)	99b
	102.8	81.0	83.9	83.7	96.5	113.4	114.3	117.4	....	....	....	....	....	....	....	GDP Volume 1980 Prices	99b. p
	90.7	71.4	74.0	73.8	85.1	100.0	100.8	103.5	....	....	....	....	....	....	....	GDP Volume (1990=100)	99bv p
	88.6	89.8	95.2	95.3	95.2	100.0	100.0	101.6	....	....	....	....	....	....	....	GDP Deflator (1990=100)	99bi p
Midyear Estimates																	
	1.38	1.44	1.50	1.79	1.86	1.92	1.98	2.04	2.10	2.16	2.31	2.44	2.58	2.72	2.40	**Population**	99z

		1970	1971	1972	1973	1974	1975	1976	1977	1978	1979	1980	1981	1982	1983	1984
Exchange Rates														*SDRs per Pound:*		
Market Rate	ac	2.3937	2.3510	ɪ2.1627	1.9258	1.9182	1.7285	1.4653	1.5691	1.5616	1.6883	1.8700	1.6392	1.4636	1.3855	1.1798
														US Dollars per Pound:		
Market Rate	ag	2.3937	2.5525	ɪ2.3481	2.3232	2.3485	2.0235	1.7024	1.9060	2.0345	2.2240	2.3850	1.9080	1.6145	1.4506	1.1565
Market Rate	rh	2.4000	2.4344	2.5018	2.4522	2.3390	2.2218	1.8062	1.7455	1.9195	2.1216	2.3263	2.0279	1.7505	1.5170	1.3363
														ECUs per Pound:		
ECU Rate	ec	....	....	....	....	....	....	....	....	....	1.5445	1.8062	1.7652	1.6659	1.7525	1.6398
ECU Rate	ed	....	....	....	....	....	....	....	....	....	....	....	1.8136	1.7846	1.7072	1.6932
														Index Numbers (1995=100):		
Market Rate	ahx	151.8	154.8	158.5	155.4	148.2	140.8	114.4	110.6	121.6	134.4	147.4	128.5	110.9	96.1	84.7
Nominal Effective Exchange Rate	neu	204.5	204.5	195.3	173.3	167.6	153.0	132.5	125.8	126.4	133.3	146.7	130.8	145.3	136.3	131.3
Real Effective Exchange Rate	reu	....	....	....	....	....	84.5	77.7	76.4	88.9	102.7	ɪ123.1	131.8	125.5	116.4	111.9
Fund Position														*Millions of SDRs:*		
Quota	2f. s	2,800	2,800	2,800	2,800	2,800	2,800	2,800	2,800	2,925	2,925	4,388	4,388	4,388	6,194	6,194
SDRs	1b. s	266	591	604	600	688	696	603	501	415	965	447	852	1,061	494	507
Reserve Position in the Fund	1c. s	—	—	116	117	206	304	—	—	—	—	1,045	1,236	1,408	2,010	2,012
of which: Outstg.Fund Borrowing	2c	—	—	—	—	—	—	—	—	—	—	—	—	—	—	—
Total Fund Cred.&Loans Outstg.	2tl	1,829	497	—	—	—	—	1,700	3,340	1,805	813	563	313	52	—	—
International Liquidity											*Billions of US Dollars Unless Otherwise Indicated:*					
Total Reserves minus Gold	1l. d	1.48	7.99	4.85	5.59	6.04	4.60	3.37	20.11	16.03	19.74	20.65	15.24	12.40	11.34	9.44
SDRs	1b. d	.27	.64	.66	.72	.84	.82	.70	.61	.54	1.27	.57	.99	1.17	.52	.50
Reserve Position in the Fund	1c. d	—	—	.13	.14	.25	.36	—	—	—	—	1.33	1.44	1.55	2.10	1.97
Foreign Exchange	1d. d	1.21	7.35	4.06	4.72	4.94	3.43	2.67	19.50	15.49	18.47	18.75	12.81	9.67	8.72	6.97
Gold (Million Fine Troy Ounces)	1ad	38.52	22.18	21.08	21.01	21.03	21.03	21.03	22.23	22.83	18.25	18.84	19.03	19.01	19.01	19.03
Gold (National Valuation)	1and	1.35	.84	.80	.89	.89	.89	.89	.94	.96	3.26	6.99	7.33	4.56	5.91	5.48
Deposit Money Banks: Assets	7a. d	37.03	45.49	60.14	88.59	108.55	125.74	145.61	ɪ171.53	217.69	285.49	356.32	432.71	462.82	485.21	489.71
Liabilities	7b. d	39.95	51.07	64.81	96.23	119.03	135.62	154.52	ɪ183.66	226.89	304.43	377.71	ɪ451.40	489.64	519.63	538.22
Monetary Authorities														*Billions of Pounds:*		
Foreign Assets	11	1.37	3.82	2.66	2.64	2.51	1.95	ɪ2.43	10.72	7.69	10.13	11.49	12.22	10.51	12.27	13.55
Claims on Central Govt. (Net)	12an	8.97	5.60	7.98	9.18	11.03	11.41	ɪ9.33	2.05	6.52	5.41	4.66	4.40	7.23	6.35	3.98
Claims on Deposit Money Banks	12e	—	.08	—	—	—	—	.45	.47	—	.05	—	—	.10	.05	.10
Reserve Money	14	4.71	4.47	5.42	7.13	7.41	8.16	9.78	10.30	11.30	12.41	12.05	12.51	13.05	13.41	11.95
of which: Currency Outside DMBs	14a	3.32	3.59	4.08	4.38	5.09	5.81	6.58	7.56	8.73	9.51	10.24	ɪ10.69	11.22	ɪ11.01	9.16
Foreign Liabilities	16c	5.33	4.51	4.59	4.21	5.39	4.73	ɪ1.92	2.15	2.19	2.40	3.28	3.25	3.77	4.04	4.31
Other Items (Net)	17r	.29	.51	.63	.48	.74	.47	.50	.79	.71	.78	.82	.85	1.02	1.22	1.37
Deposit Money Banks														*Billions of Pounds:*		
Reserves	20	1.57	1.08	1.56	3.00	2.61	2.68	3.56	3.15	3.04	3.44	2.39	2.38	2.56	2.41	2.79
Foreign Assets	21	15.47	17.82	25.61	38.13	46.22	ɪ62.14	85.53	88.13	105.93	128.68	150.86	225.02	285.59	339.91	435.15
Claims on Central Govt. (Net)	22an	2.98	4.39	2.65	2.52	3.35	5.91	5.60	7.42	6.36	6.17	7.19	ɪ8.05	7.15	7.15	7.27
Claims on Official Entities	22bx	2.75	3.55	3.74	4.52	4.62	5.82	6.41	6.74	6.73	7.45	8.83	ɪ13.13	11.81	9.94	10.84
Claims on Private Sector	22d	10.79	12.63	19.43	26.38	31.04	ɪ30.94	35.42	39.34	44.84	53.61	63.73	ɪ83.04	100.38	119.74	146.54
Demand,Time,Savings,Fgn.Cur.Dep.	25l	14.63	16.73	21.91	28.77	32.34	ɪ34.20	38.02	41.42	47.39	53.62	64.55	ɪ84.79	95.18	106.31	121.65
Foreign Liabilities	26c	16.69	20.01	27.60	41.42	50.69	67.00	90.77	95.17	110.52	135.82e	157.16	232.32	295.38	350.71	453.62
Other Items (Net)	27r	2.24	2.73	3.48	4.36	4.82	ɪ6.27	7.72	8.18	9.01	9.90	11.27	ɪ14.52	16.91	22.13	27.32
Banking Survey														*Billions of Pounds:*		
Foreign Assets (Net)	31n	−5.18	−2.88	−3.92	−4.86	−7.34	ɪ−7.65	ɪ−4.73	1.52	.91	.59	1.91	1.67	−3.06	−2.56	−9.23
Domestic Credit	32	25.48	26.16	33.79	42.60	50.04	ɪ54.07	56.76	55.56	64.45	72.63	84.40	ɪ108.62	126.55	143.18	168.63
Claims on Central Govt. (Net)	32an	11.95	9.99	10.62	11.71	14.38	17.31	14.93	9.48	12.88	11.58	11.85	ɪ12.45	14.37	13.50	11.25
Claims on Official Entities	32bx	2.75	3.55	3.74	4.52	4.62	5.82	6.41	6.74	6.73	ɪ7.45	8.83	ɪ13.13	11.81	9.94	10.84
Claims on Private Sector	32d	10.79	12.63	19.43	26.38	31.04	ɪ30.94	35.42	39.34	44.84	53.61	63.73	ɪ83.04	100.38	ɪ119.74	146.54
Other Items (Net)	37r	2.36	2.96	3.89	4.59	5.28	ɪ6.32	7.28	8.09	9.24	10.09	11.53	ɪ14.73	17.10	23.30	28.59
Money plus Quasi-Money	35l	17.95	20.32	25.99	33.14	37.43	ɪ40.10	44.74	48.99	56.12	63.13	74.79	ɪ93.62	106.40	117.32	130.81
Money (National Definitions)														*Billions of Pounds:*		
M0	59mc	4.21	4.43	5.05	5.59	6.45	7.19	7.99	9.12	10.36	11.62	12.24	12.56	12.95	13.85	14.62
M4	59md	....	....	....	....	....	....	....	....	....	....	....	....	154.91	175.30	198.93
														Millions of Pounds:		
M0, Seasonally Adjusted	59mc c	180	191	555	494	819	689	762	1,017	1,190	1,188	650	589	376	755	708
M4, Seasonally Adjusted	59md c	....	....	....	....	....	....	....	....	....	....	....	....	....	20,146	23,072
Interest Rates														*Percent Per Annum*		
Money Market Rate	60b	2.00	1.42	3.45	1.92	4.63	6.08	5.54	2.13	7.99	11.55	15.62	13.12	11.77	10.01	9.51
Treasury Bill Rate	60c	7.02	5.58	5.51	9.29	11.37	10.16	11.12	7.69	8.50	12.98	15.11	12.99	11.41	9.04	9.30
Treas. Bill Rate(Bond Equivalent)	60cs	....	....	....	....	....	10.56	11.62	8.06	8.74	13.40	15.77	13.43	11.96	9.93	9.61
Eurodollar Rate in London	60d	8.51	6.57	5.46	9.16	11.01	6.99	5.58	6.05	8.78	12.01	14.06	16.83	13.13	9.61	10.78
Deposit Rate	60l	5.21	3.83	4.15	8.02	9.50	7.08	7.54	4.90	6.08	11.71	14.13	10.67	12.42	11.19	7.27
Lending Rate	60p	7.25	7.50	7.50	8.00	9.00	9.00	9.00	9.75	9.25	13.92	16.17	13.25	11.84	9.85	9.75
Govt. Bond Yield: Short-Term	61a	7.92	6.69	7.55	10.41	12.51	11.48	12.06	10.08	11.32	12.64	13.84	14.65	12.79	10.81	11.29
Long-Term	61	9.22	8.90	8.90	10.71	14.77	14.39	14.43	12.73	12.47	12.99	13.79	14.74	12.88	10.81	10.42
Prices, Production, Labor														*Index Numbers (1995=100):*		
Industrial Share Prices	62	8.1	9.5	12.1	10.5	6.2	7.7	9.2	11.8	13.3	15.1	16.2	18.2	21.1	26.7	31.8
Prices: Manufacturing Output	63	15.8	17.2	18.1	19.5	19.8	24.3	28.4	33.7	36.8	41.1	47.7	52.8	57.3	61.0	64.6
Consumer Prices	64	12.4	13.6	14.6	15.9	ɪ18.5	22.9	26.7	31.0	33.5	38.0	44.8	50.2	54.5	57.0	59.8
Harmonized CPI	64h	....	....	....	....	....	....	....	....	....	....	....	....	....	....	....
Wages: Avg. Monthly Earnings	65.. c	8.4	9.0	10.1	11.5	13.5	17.1	19.9	21.7	24.5	28.3	34.1	38.5	42.1	45.6	48.4
Industrial Production	66.. c	69.2	68.8	70.0	76.3	74.8	70.7	73.0	76.8	79.0	82.1	76.7	74.2	75.7	78.4	78.5
Employment	67.. c	97.4	97.9	97.9	100.3	100.9	100.6	99.8	97.9	100.8	104.7	101.0	97.3	95.2	95.5	96.4
														Number in Thousands:		
Labor Force	67d	....	....	....	....	....	....	....	....	....	....	....	....	....	....	....
Employment	67e	....	....	....	....	....	....	....	....	....	....	....	....	....	....	....
Unemployment	67c	....	....	....	....	....	....	....	....	....	....	....	....	....	....	....
Unemployment Rate (%)	67r	....	....	....	....	....	....	....	....	....	....	....	....	....	....	....

		1985	1986	1987	1988	1989	1990	1991	1992	1993	1994	1995	1996	1997	1998	1999
Exchange Rates		*End of Period*														
Market Rate	ac	1.3151	1.2055	1.3192	1.3447	1.2217	1.3552	1.3078	1.0996	1.0784	1.0703	1.0427	1.1808	1.2257	1.1814	1.1777
		End of Period (ag) Period Average (rh)														
Market Rate	ag	1.4445	1.4745	1.8715	1.8095	1.6055	1.9280	1.8707	1.5120	1.4812	1.5625	1.5500	1.6980	1.6538	1.6635	1.6164
Market Rate	rh	1.2963	1.4670	1.6389	1.7814	1.6397	1.7847	1.7694	1.7655	1.5020	1.5316	1.5785	1.5617	1.6377	1.6564	1.6182
		End of Period (ec) Period Average (ed)														
ECU Rate	ec	1.6251	1.3794	1.4351	1.5419	1.3463	1.4126	1.3964	1.2528	1.3225	1.2705	1.1832	1.3564	1.5011	1.4175	....
ECU Rate	ed	1.6989	1.4948	1.4138	1.5057	1.4872	1.4011	1.4265	1.3607	1.2822	1.2897	1.2070	1.2304	1.4452	1.4796	....
		Period Averages														
Market Rate	ahx	82.1	92.9	103.8	112.9	103.9	113.1	112.1	111.9	95.2	97.0	100.0	98.9	103.8	104.9	102.5
Nominal Effective Exchange Rate	neu	131.2	119.6	117.1	124.2	120.6	117.8	118.8	114.3	104.8	105.2	100.0	101.7	118.5	122.5	122.3
Real Effective Exchange Rate	reu	111.6	103.5	107.4	112.4	109.4	109.3	113.6	113.7	104.4	105.2	100.0	102.4	124.5	137.2	....
Fund Position		*End of Period*														
Quota	2f.s	6,194	6,194	6,194	6,194	6,194	6,194	6,194	7,415	7,415	7,415	7,415	7,415	7,415	7,415	10,739
SDRs	1b.s	1,030	1,270	974	981	870	878	919	393	210	335	279	239	350	332	374
Reserve Position in the Fund	1c.s	1,810	1,621	1,253	1,239	1,246	1,179	1,293	1,464	1,354	1,366	1,630	1,689	2,198	3,111	3,847
of which: Outstg.Fund Borrowing	2c	—	—	—	—	—	—	—	—	—	—	—	—	—	382	—
Total Fund Cred.&Loans Outstg.	2tl	—	—	—	—	—	—	—	—	—	—	—	—	—	—	—
International Liquidity		*End of Period*														
Total Reserves minus Gold	1l.d	12.86	18.42	41.72	44.10	34.77	35.85	41.89	36.64	36.78	41.01	42.02	39.90	32.32	32.21	29.83
SDRs	1b.d	1.13	1.55	1.38	1.32	1.14	1.25	1.31	.54	.29	.49	.41	.34	.47	.47	.51
Reserve Position in the Fund	1c.d	1.99	1.98	1.78	1.67	1.64	1.68	1.85	2.01	1.86	1.99	2.42	2.43	2.97	4.38	5.28
Foreign Exchange	1d.d	9.74	14.89	38.56	41.12	31.99	32.93	38.73	34.09	34.63	38.53	39.18	37.12	28.88	27.36	24.04
Gold (Million Fine Troy Ounces)	1ad	19.03	19.01	19.01	19.00	18.99	18.94	18.89	18.61	18.45	18.44	18.43	18.43	18.42	23.00	20.55
Gold (National Valuation)	1and	4.31	4.90	5.79	6.47	5.46	5.24	5.04	4.77	4.56	5.31	5.24	5.48	4.81	5.08	4.31
Deposit Money Banks: Assets	7a.d	I 590.07	715.54	875.31	883.08	922.94	1,068.97	I 992.21	1,019.46	1,053.63	1,200.67	1,350.86	1,460.35	1,685.14	1,870.41	1,798.37
Liabilities	7b.d	625.74	758.98	926.53	960.09	1,024.56	1,201.03	I 1122.63	1,115.27	1,129.07	1,274.82	1,429.20	1,533.44	1,748.76	1,894.34	1,873.65
Monetary Authorities		*End of Period*														
Foreign Assets	11	10.75	I 16.74	24.36	29.26	24.27	20.43	24.35	28.84	30.22	28.33	31.89	27.40	22.92	23.35	22.18
Claims on Central Govt. (Net)	12an	9.16	I 8.67	4.00	1.79	10.22	15.60	14.22	15.90	14.97	28.53	25.07	29.86	27.63	29.94	....
Claims on Deposit Money Banks	12e	.20	I —	.05	.04	.11	.04	—	—	.18	—	—	—	—	—	—
Reserve Money	14	12.72	I 17.03	18.26	20.04	21.74	22.01	22.24	23.58	25.19	26.53	28.37	29.36	31.43	32.47	38.00
of which: Currency Outside DMBs	14a	9.84	I 13.39	14.18	15.34	16.20	16.35	16.71	17.76	18.87	19.94	21.21	22.10	23.43	24.32	27.13
Foreign Liabilities	16c	5.98	I 7.92	9.41	10.39	12.13	13.10	15.46	20.22	25.99	31.86	31.16	28.36	23.61	21.24	....
Other Items (Net)	17r	1.41	I .46	.74	.65	.73	.96	.86	.94	-5.80	-1.52	-2.57	-.46	-4.49	-.42	-.79
Deposit Money Banks		*End of Period*														
Reserves	20	2.88	3.55	I 4.26	5.01	5.83	5.97	5.88	6.28	6.78	7.04	7.56	7.71	8.26	8.39	11.54
Foreign Assets	21	403.28	479.73	I 460.81	484.11	566.13	545.18	516.71	I 649.72	686.90	741.28	845.36	835.98	1,041.03	1,143.91	1,133.95
Claims on Central Govt. (Net)	22an	7.89	7.18	I 16.16	15.28	12.07	11.37	11.14	I 1.55	2.66	11.80	19.72	14.92	10.59	10.74	2.43
Claims on Official Entities	22bx	8.40	5.98	I 6.09	4.58	3.20	3.26	3.14	4.27	5.68	6.10	5.74	4.80	4.34	3.75	2.70
Claims on Private Sector	22d	167.39	206.32	I 377.41	468.57	583.11	645.26	663.09	I 684.06	707.29	745.72	829.53	912.27	973.37	1,016.75	1,094.06
Demand,Time,Savings,Fgn.Cur.Dep.	25l	135.69	167.94	I 323.70	378.96	457.37	507.04	515.40	I 558.19	583.02	623.09	707.05	784.34	813.96	875.83	906.77
Foreign Liabilities	26c	416.01	493.40	I 473.34	510.86	608.30	590.45	563.99	I 688.74	713.08	764.98	867.36	844.81	1,051.56	1,120.83	1,129.87
Other Items (Net)	27r	38.15	41.42	I 67.68	87.73	104.66	113.56	120.56	I 98.95	113.20	123.88	133.51	146.54	172.06	186.88	208.03
Banking Survey		*End of Period*														
Foreign Assets (Net)	31n	-7.97	-4.91	I 2.42	-7.88	-30.04	-37.94	-38.39	I -30.40	-21.96	-27.22	-21.27	-9.79	-11.22	25.19	....
Domestic Credit	32	192.84	225.22	I 403.65	490.22	608.60	675.49	691.59	I 705.78	730.60	792.16	880.06	961.86	1,015.92	1,061.17	....
Claims on Central Govt. (Net)	32an	17.05	12.93	I 20.16	17.07	22.29	26.97	25.36	I 17.45	17.64	40.34	44.79	44.78	38.22	40.67	....
Claims on Official Entities	32bx	8.40	I 7.73	6.09	4.58	3.20	3.26	3.14	4.27	5.68	6.10	5.74	4.80	4.34	3.75	2.70
Claims on Private Sector	32d	167.39	206.32	I 377.41	468.57	583.11	645.26	663.09	I 684.06	707.29	745.72	829.53	912.27	973.37	1,016.75	1,094.06
Other Items (Net)	37r	39.35	41.96	I 68.38	88.35	105.28	114.48	121.43	I 99.43	106.76	121.91	130.54	145.62	167.31	186.22	206.57
Money plus Quasi-Money	35l	145.52	178.36	I 337.69	393.99	473.28	523.08	531.77	I 575.95	601.89	643.03	728.26	806.45	837.38	900.15	933.91
Money (National Definitions)		*End of Period*														
M0	59mc	15.16	15.95	16.63	18.04	19.01	19.49	20.09	20.58	21.73	23.32	24.54	26.15	27.80	29.35	32.74
M4	59md	224.79	257.89	304.37	358.37	426.19	478.10	504.72	517.92	544.10	567.20	623.54	683.00	722.20	782.85	812.86
		Period Change														
M0, Seasonally Adjusted	59mc c	531	749	638	1,203	1,005	476	557	535	1,168	1,390	1,222	1,556	1,593	1,462	3,280
M4, Seasonally Adjusted	59md c	26,291	35,131	43,135	53,042	64,830	51,768	28,292	18,614	23,990	25,642	55,839	59,977	79,909	59,726	30,538
Interest Rates		*Percent Per Annum*														
Money Market Rate	60b	12.41	10.80	9.47	9.72	13.62	14.64	11.77	9.39	5.46	4.76	5.98	5.89	6.56	7.09	5.11
Treasury Bill Rate	60c	11.55	10.34	9.25	9.87	13.28	14.09	10.85	8.94	5.25	5.15	6.33	5.77	6.48	6.82	5.04
Treas. Bill Rate(Bond Equivalent)	60cs	12.00	10.77	9.54	10.05	13.74	14.64	11.22	9.21	5.35	5.18	6.40	5.89	6.62	7.23	5.07
Eurodollar Rate in London	60d	8.33	6.76	7.12	7.90	9.25	8.25	5.95	3.77	3.24	4.68	5.97	5.44	5.66	5.50	5.36
Deposit Rate	60l	11.79	9.85	8.57	8.55	11.51	12.54	10.28	7.46	3.97	3.66	4.11	3.05	3.63	4.48	....
Lending Rate	60p	12.33	10.83	9.64	10.29	13.92	14.75	11.54	9.42	5.92	5.48	6.69	5.96	6.58	7.21	5.33
Govt. Bond Yield: Short-Term	61a	11.13	10.01	9.36	9.66	10.73	12.08	10.18	8.94	6.65	7.83	7.93	7.28	6.98	5.77	5.38
Long-Term	61	10.50	9.86	9.47	9.36	9.58	11.08	9.92	9.12	7.87	8.05	8.26	8.10	7.09	5.45	4.70
Prices, Production, Labor		*Period Averages*														
Industrial Share Prices	62	39.2	48.6	64.2	57.7	69.2	67.9	74.5	77.9	89.4	96.1	100.0	113.3	128.3	150.5	....
Prices: Manufacturing Output	63	68.6	69.5	71.9	74.6	78.1	83.0	87.5	90.2	93.8	96.1	100.0	102.6	103.6	104.2	105.4
Consumer Prices	64	63.4	65.6	68.3	71.7	77.3	84.6	89.6	92.9	94.4	96.7	100.0	102.4	105.7	109.3	111.0
Harmonized CPI	64h	....	....	....	73.8	77.7	83.1	89.4	93.2	95.5	97.4	100.0	102.5	104.3	106.0	107.4
Wages: Avg. Monthly Earnings	65..c	52.4	56.6	61.0	66.3	72.4	79.4	85.6	90.7	93.6	97.0	100.0	103.5	108.0	113.5	119.0
Industrial Production	66..c	82.8	84.8	88.2	92.5	94.4	94.1	91.0	91.3	93.3	98.3	100.0	101.1	102.1	102.7	103.2
Employment	67..c	96.6	96.5	99.1	101.5	103.1	102.5	99.3	97.1	97.8	98.7	100.0	101.3	104.3	106.1	107.4
		Period Averages														
Labor Force	67d	....	....	....	....	....	....	28,768	....	28,271	....	....	28,552	28,716	28,713	....
Employment	67e	24,539	24,568	24,930	25,860	26,689	26,935	26,400	I 25,812	25,511	25,697	25,972	26,219	26,682	26,947	....
Unemployment	67c	3,076	3,293	2,953	I 2,370	I 1,799	1,665	2,292	2,779	2,919	2,636	2,326	2,122	1,602	1,362	1,263
Unemployment Rate (%)	67r	11.2	11.8	10.6	I 8.4	I 6.3	5.9	8.1	9.9	10.4	9.4	8.3	7.5	5.7	4.7	....

United Kingdom

		1970	1971	1972	1973	1974	1975	1976	1977	1978	1979	1980	1981	1982	1983	1984
International Transactions																*Millions of Pounds*
Exports	70	8,096	9,070	9,602	12,087	16,309	19,607	25,277	31,990	35,380	40,637	47,357	50,998	55,558	60,684	70,488
Imports, c.i.f.	71	9,113	9,799	11,073	15,723	23,139	24,046	31,084	36,219	39,533	46,925	49,773	51,169	56,978	66,101	78,967
Imports, f.o.b. (on a BOP basis)	71.v	8,141	8,820	10,155	14,449	21,511	22,441	29,041	34,005	36,573	43,814	45,792	47,416	53,421	62,237	75,601
																1995=100
Volume of Exports	72	32.4	34.6	35.1	39.1	40.9	40.1	43.6	47.9	49.2	51.1	51.7	51.1	52.7	53.7	58.3
Volume of Imports	73	42.1	43.3	45.7	50.8	50.3	45.8	48.3	48.3	49.9	53.9	50.8	48.3	50.8	53.8	59.8
Export Prices	76	14.6	15.4	16.3	18.3	23.3	28.5	34.2	40.4	44.4	49.2	56.6	61.6	65.9	70.5	76.1
Import Prices	76.x	13.3	13.9	14.5	18.5	27.1	30.9	37.8	43.7	45.4	48.3	53.2	57.8	62.7	68.3	74.5
Balance of Payments																*Billions of US Dollars:*
Current Account, n.i.e.	78al d	1.97	2.72	.53	−2.41	−7.45	−3.47	−1.38	.15	2.16	−.78	6.86	14.13	7.98	5.29	1.83
Goods: Exports f.o.b.	78aa d	19.51	21.99	23.51	29.11	38.11	42.47	45.03	55.32	67.12	86.02	109.62	102.16	96.66	91.96	93.49
Goods: Imports f.o.b.	78ab d	−19.54	−21.47	−25.35	−35.36	−50.35	−49.75	−52.10	−59.32	−70.18	−92.99	−106.27	−95.20	−93.49	−94.34	−100.60
Trade Balance	78ac d	−.03	.52	−1.84	−6.26	−12.24	−7.27	−7.07	−4.00	−3.06	−6.97	3.35	6.96	3.17	−2.38	−7.11
Services: Credit	78ad d	8.12	9.47	10.51	12.71	15.44	16.97	17.93	20.28	24.00	30.74	36.45	34.01	30.86	29.07	28.43
Services: Debit	78ae d	−7.11	−8.13	−8.95	−11.03	−13.19	−14.06	−13.60	−14.62	−16.87	−22.43	−27.93	−26.31	−25.55	−23.27	−22.83
Balance on Goods & Services	78af d	.98	1.86	−.29	−4.58	−9.99	−4.37	−2.74	1.65	4.06	1.33	11.87	14.66	8.47	3.42	−1.51
Income: Credit	78ag d	3.59	3.74	8.51	12.07	14.52	14.56	15.09	15.40	21.47	37.25	55.07	74.88	77.59	64.36	68.52
Income: Debit	78ah d	−2.16	−2.40	−7.02	−8.81	−10.99	−12.60	−12.29	−14.94	−19.93	−34.69	−55.48	−72.34	−75.06	−60.07	−62.79
Balance on Gds, Serv. & Inc.	78ai d	2.41	3.19	1.21	−1.32	−6.46	−2.41	.05	2.11	5.61	3.89	11.45	17.20	11.00	7.71	4.21
Current Transfers, n.i.e.: Credit	78aj d	.55	.60	.66	.95	1.14	1.68	1.42	1.59	2.33	2.98	4.41	5.75	6.00	5.70	5.34
Current Transfers: Debit	78ak d	−.99	−1.08	−1.34	−2.04	−2.13	−2.74	−2.85	−3.56	−5.77	−7.65	−9.01	−8.83	−9.01	−8.12	−7.72
Capital Account, n.i.e.	78bc d	—	—	—	—	—	—	—	—	—	—	—	—	—	—	....
Capital Account, n.i.e.: Credit	78ba d	—	—	—	—	—	—	—	—	—	—	—	—	—	—	—
Capital Account: Debit	78bb d	—	—	—	—	—	—	—	—	—	—	—	—	—	—	—
Financial Account, n.i.e.	78bj d	−1.51	1.24	.50	.20	3.26	.10	−6.15	6.01	−8.19	1.04	−7.49	−19.51	−6.85	−8.58	−12.49
Direct Investment Abroad	78bd d	−1.68	−1.99	−2.02	−4.98	−4.38	−3.00	−4.34	−4.17	−6.82	−12.54	−11.23	−12.15	−7.16	−8.18	−7.98
Dir. Invest. in Rep. Econ., n.i.e.	78be d	1.49	1.77	1.21	2.72	4.37	3.32	3.01	4.43	3.79	6.47	10.12	5.88	5.41	5.18	−.35
Portfolio Investment Assets	78bf d	−.32	−.11	−1.51	.68	1.70	−.12	.13	.02	−2.06	−1.90	−7.79	−9.20	−13.21	−11.17	−14.70
Equity Securities	78bk d	−.32	−.11	−1.51	.68	1.70	−.12	.13	.02	−2.06	−1.90	−7.79	−6.66	−7.46	−5.40	−.05
Debt Securities	78bl d	—	—	—	—	—	—	—	—	—	—	—	−2.53	−5.75	−5.77	−14.65
Portfolio Investment Liab., n.i.e.	78bg d	.33	1.64	1.25	.27	2.88	−1.00	−.35	2.97	−.40	3.03	2.88	.15	.01	2.55	.46
Equity Securities	78bm d	.22	.44	.44	.56	.34	.01	.47	.73	.01	.75	.46	.56	.09	1.45	1.38
Debt Securities	78bn d	.11	1.20	.82	−.29	2.55	−1.02	−.82	2.24	−.42	2.28	2.43	−.41	−.08	1.10	−.92
Financial Derivatives Assets	78bw d	....	....	....	....	....	....	....	....	....	....	....	....	....	....	....
Financial Derivatives Liabilities	78bx d	....	....	....	....	....	....	....	....	....	....	....	....	....	....	....
Other Investment Assets	78bh d	−1.16	−3.48	−.63	−2.49	−3.68	−1.99	−4.62	−3.26	−4.07	−69.84	−81.22	−86.31	−37.57	−27.36	−22.50
Monetary Authorities	78bo d	....	....	....	....	....	....	....	....	....	....	....	....	....	....	....
General Government	78bp d	−.58	−2.96	1.14	−.90	−1.28	−1.37	−1.20	−.68	−.35	−.28	.82	.20	−.28	−.72	−1.00
Banks	78bq d	−.32	−.40	−.98	−.36	−.47	−.46	−1.25	−.68	−2.27	−65.10	−76.38	−80.65	−35.26	−28.05	−18.10
Other Sectors	78br d	−.26	−.11	−.79	−1.23	−1.93	−.15	−2.17	−1.90	−1.45	−4.46	−5.67	−5.86	−2.03	1.41	−3.40
Other Investment Liab., n.i.e.	78bi d	−.18	3.40	2.19	4.00	2.36	2.90	.02	6.04	1.38	75.82	79.74	82.13	45.67	30.40	32.57
Monetary Authorities	78bs d	−2.88	−.85	.49	.22	−.43	.18	−.27	−.22	.03	−.06	.01	.04	−.03	−.03	—
General Government	78bt d	−.21	−.19	−.17	−.09	−.18	−.08	.12	.16	.41	.49	−.66	−.16	.65	−.97	−.24
Banks	78bu d	2.17	3.47	.66	1.91	1.04	1.34	−.90	3.51	−.93	73.27	79.38	80.35	43.67	32.91	35.09
Other Sectors	78bv d	.75	.99	1.22	1.96	1.92	1.45	1.07	2.59	1.86	2.11	1.00	1.89	1.38	−1.51	−2.28
Net Errors and Omissions	78ca d	−.07	.65	−2.46	.31	.33	—	.74	6.65	3.43	1.89	1.93	1.79	−3.79	1.52	9.65
Overall Balance	78cb d	.39	4.61	−1.43	−1.90	−3.86	−3.36	−6.79	12.80	−2.59	2.14	1.30	−3.59	−2.65	−1.76	−1.01
Reserves and Related Items	79da d	−.39	−4.61	1.43	1.90	3.86	3.36	6.79	−12.80	2.59	−2.14	−1.30	3.59	2.65	1.76	1.01
Reserve Assets	79b d	.02	−3.47	1.97	−.58	−.26	1.42	1.41	−16.71	4.32	−1.76	−.22	5.03	2.42	.91	1.01
Use of Fund Credit and Loans	79dc d	−.41	−1.33	−.54	—	—	—	1.98	1.90	−1.96	−1.27	−.33	−.30	−.29	−.06	—
Exceptional Financing	79de d	—	.20	—	2.48	4.11	1.95	3.40	2.00	.23	.89	−.75	−1.13	.52	.91	—
International Investment Position																*Billions of US Dollars*
Assets	79aa d	....	....	....	....	....	....	....	....	....	....	550.82	630.33	671.78	705.65	721.39
Direct Investment Abroad	79ab d	....	....	....	....	....	....	....	....	....	....	79.21	85.72	84.02	83.88	86.88
Portfolio Investment	79ac d	....	....	....	....	....	....	....	....	....	....	45.55	49.18	66.06	86.60	106.09
Equity Securities	79ad d	....	....	....	....	....	....	....	....	....	....	32.03	34.71	43.08	57.87	55.47
Debt Securities	79ae d	....	....	....	....	....	....	....	....	....	....	13.52	14.47	22.98	28.72	50.62
Financial Derivatives	79al d	....	....	....	....	....	....	....	....	....	....	....	....	....	....	....
Other Investment	79af d	....	....	....	....	....	....	....	....	....	....	394.41	472.60	500.80	516.60	513.13
Monetary Authorities	79ag d	....	....	....	....	....	....	....	....	....	....	....	....	....	....	....
General Government	79ah d	....	....	....	....	....	....	....	....	....	....	11.21	9.82	10.13	9.79	6.75
Banks	79ai d	....	....	....	....	....	....	....	....	....	....	352.32	429.54	459.08	482.33	450.34
Other Sectors	79aj d	....	....	....	....	....	....	....	....	....	....	30.87	33.24	31.59	24.48	56.04
Reserve Assets	79ak d	....	....	....	....	....	....	....	....	....	....	31.66	22.83	20.90	18.57	15.29
Liabilities	79la d	....	....	....	....	....	....	....	....	....	....	507.67	568.04	601.55	625.05	630.83
Dir. Invest. in Rep. Economy	79lb d	....	....	....	....	....	....	....	....	....	....	63.01	57.26	52.15	54.01	46.38
Portfolio Investment	79lc d	....	....	....	....	....	....	....	....	....	....	28.15	23.52	24.61	26.51	112.05
Equity Securities	79ld d	....	....	....	....	....	....	....	....	....	....	11.46	8.49	8.86	11.31	12.74
Debt Securities	79le d	....	....	....	....	....	....	....	....	....	....	16.69	15.03	15.75	15.20	99.31
Financial Derivatives	79ll d	....	....	....	....	....	....	....	....	....	....	....	....	....	....	....
Other investment	79lf d	....	....	....	....	....	....	....	....	....	....	416.51	487.25	524.79	544.54	472.40
Monetary Authorities	79lg d	....	....	....	....	....	....	....	....	....	....	3.75	3.16	3.40	2.31	....
General Government	79lh d	....	....	....	....	....	....	....	....	....	....	4.13	3.59	3.51	3.45	4.14
Banks	79li d	....	....	....	....	....	....	....	....	....	....	374.19	447.76	485.96	514.87	439.25
Other Sectors	79lj d	....	....	....	....	....	....	....	....	....	....	34.43	32.74	31.93	23.90	29.01

Millions of Pounds

International Transactions

	1985	1986	1987	1988	1989	1990	1991	1992	1993	1994	1995	1996	1997	1998	1999	
Exports	78,392	72,988	79,849	81,655	93,771	103,692	104,877	108,508	120,936	133,030	153,353	167,764	171,595	164,066	165,739	70
Imports, c.i.f.	85,027	86,176	94,026	106,571	121,699	126,086	118,786	125,867	137,404	147,564	168,055	184,113	187,135	189,532	196,504	71
Imports, f.o.b. (on a BOP basis)	81,336	82,186	90,735	101,826	116,837	120,527	113,697	120,447	134,858	145,793	164,659	179,578	183,124	....	....	71.v

1995=100

	1985	1986	1987	1988	1989	1990	1991	1992	1993	1994	1995	1996	1997	1998	1999	
Volume of Exports	61.7	64.2	67.7	69.4	73.1	77.8	78.2	80.0	80.1	90.5	100.0	108.2	116.5	118.1	120.7	72
Volume of Imports	62.1	66.6	71.2	81.0	87.4	87.8	83.3	88.4	88.8	94.3	100.0	109.8	119.4	130.7	139.0	73
Export Prices	80.1	72.2	74.7	75.5	78.9	81.7	82.8	84.5	95.0	96.9	100.0	100.9	95.2	90.5	90.6	76
Import Prices	78.2	74.6	76.8	76.1	79.3	81.2	82.2	82.9	91.2	94.3	100.0	100.1	93.8	88.0	86.8	76.x

Minus Sign Indicates Debit

Balance of Payments

	1985	1986	1987	1988	1989	1990	1991	1992	1993	1994	1995	1996	1997	1998	1999	
Current Account, n.i.e.	3.31	-1.32	-9.39	-31.23	-38.48	-33.86	-14.97	-18.20	-16.01	-2.04	-5.97	-.72	10.83	-1.10	-20.64	78ald
Goods: Exports f.o.b.	100.86	106.43	130.47	143.73	151.44	182.80	183.51	189.37	183.03	207.37	242.55	261.57	281.31	271.78	267.32	78aa d
Goods: Imports f.o.b.	-104.82	-120.49	-149.68	-182.02	-192.06	-215.35	-201.67	-212.70	-203.06	-224.26	-261.09	-281.80	-300.80	-305.80	-310.39	78ab d
Trade Balance	-3.96	-14.06	-19.21	-38.29	-40.62	-32.55	-18.17	-23.33	-20.03	-16.89	-18.53	-20.23	-19.49	-34.01	-43.07	78ac d
Services: Credit	31.31	37.07	44.05	47.46	47.84	55.76	55.28	62.64	60.07	66.70	76.82	82.65	94.19	100.81	103.22	78ad d
Services: Debit	-22.96	-27.97	-33.14	-39.73	-41.40	-48.63	-47.35	-52.73	-50.19	-56.69	-62.77	-68.69	-73.86	-80.73	-85.22	78ae d
Balance on Goods & Services	4.39	-4.96	-8.30	-30.56	-34.17	-25.42	-10.24	-13.43	-10.14	-6.89	-4.48	-6.27	.84	-13.93	-25.07	78af d
Income: Credit	66.82	69.40	86.95	110.94	134.56	158.64	150.24	132.11	119.11	127.72	154.58	160.21	176.67	180.89	173.37	78ag d
Income: Debit	-63.93	-62.59	-84.61	-108.68	-134.60	-159.46	-153.81	-128.27	-118.07	-115.80	-145.18	-147.62	-158.42	-157.30	-162.30	78ah d
Balance on Gds, Serv. & Inc.	7.28	1.85	-5.97	-28.30	-34.21	-26.23	-13.81	-9.59	-9.11	5.03	4.92	6.32	19.09	9.65	-14.00	78ai d
Current Transfers, n.i.e.: Credit	4.57	5.68	13.91	17.19	16.54	18.33	25.22	20.50	19.91	19.59	21.09	33.35	25.05	25.35	29.09	78aj d
Current Transfers: Debit	-8.54	-8.85	-17.34	-20.12	-20.81	-25.95	-26.38	-29.11	-26.81	-26.66	-31.99	-40.39	-33.31	-36.10	-35.73	78ak d
Capital Account, n.i.e.	....	....	.55	.42	.45	.89	.50	.75	.46	.05	.84	1.14	1.32	.79	1.27	78bc d
Capital Account, n.i.e.: Credit	....	....	1.49	1.55	1.59	2.07	1.91	2.16	1.67	1.93	1.84	2.18	2.77	2.44	2.52	78ba d
Capital Account: Debit	....	....	-.94	-1.13	-1.13	-1.18	-1.40	-1.42	-1.21	-1.88	-.99	-1.04	-1.45	-1.65	-1.25	78bb d
Financial Account, n.i.e.	-1.79	-1.18	27.95	32.09	24.17	30.98	23.08	2.47	19.93	-7.67	1.18	2.42	-25.49	-9.78	11.52	78bj d
Direct Investment Abroad	-10.61	-17.02	-31.40	-37.34	-35.43	-19.51	-16.31	-19.36	-26.81	-34.15	-44.46	-35.16	-63.50	-119.62	-198.67	78bd d
Dir. Invest. in Rep. Econ., n.i.e.	5.48	8.57	15.73	21.46	30.58	32.52	16.26	16.19	15.59	9.21	20.32	25.78	37.00	63.70	82.30	78be d
Portfolio Investment Assets	-20.35	-33.79	9.26	-21.17	-63.01	-29.93	-56.94	-49.34	-133.56	31.46	-61.72	-93.45	-84.99	-57.38	-31.30	78bf d
Equity Securities	-5.61	-8.83	4.80	-9.66	-25.65	-1.08	-24.50	7.36	-11.93	-1.49	-13.17	-16.61	7.04	-4.74	-26.18	78bk d
Debt Securities	-14.74	-24.97	4.47	-11.50	-37.37	-28.86	-32.44	-56.70	-121.63	32.95	-48.55	-76.84	-92.03	-52.64	-5.12	78bl d
Portfolio Investment Liab., n.i.e.	2.80	37.19	59.31	53.77	30.14	24.73	20.29	15.81	43.08	50.91	58.56	69.88	44.31	29.17	197.66	78bg d
Equity Securities	3.73	7.81	19.22	9.62	11.13	3.44	4.68	18.26	26.12	7.42	8.09	9.46	7.85	61.78	119.43	78bm d
Debt Securities	-.93	29.37	40.08	44.15	19.01	21.29	15.61	-2.45	16.97	43.50	50.47	60.43	36.46	-32.61	78.23	78bn d
Financial Derivatives Assets	....	....	....	....	....	....	....	....	....	....	....	....	....	—	—	78bw d
Financial Derivatives Liabilities	....	....	....	....	....	....	....	....	....	....	....	....	....	—	—	78bx d
Other Investment Assets	-31.88	-79.90	-89.24	-38.17	-59.27	-94.37	35.93	-58.45	-68.92	-44.11	-75.79	-215.66	-276.14	-24.65	-79.09	78bh d
Monetary Authorities	....	....	....	....	....	....	....	....	....	....	....	....	....	....	....	78bo d
General Government	-.94	-.75	-1.31	-1.58	-1.43	-1.83	-1.58	-1.19	-.91	-.95	-1.01	-1.02	-.30	-.15	-.46	78bp d
Banks	-30.76	-78.70	-83.94	-32.06	-49.58	-67.69	53.71	-33.86	6.20	-75.22	-35.54	-103.18	-239.95	-28.37	30.74	78bq d
Other Sectors	-.19	-.45	-3.99	-4.53	-8.26	-24.84	-16.20	-23.40	-74.21	32.06	-39.24	-111.46	-35.89	3.88	-109.37	78br d
Other Investment Liab., n.i.e.	52.77	83.77	64.29	53.53	121.17	117.54	23.85	97.64	190.55	-20.99	104.27	251.02	317.82	99.00	40.63	78bi d
Monetary Authorities	....	....	....	....	....	....	....	....	....	....	....	....	....	....	....	78bs d
General Government	.01	.04	.62	.16	.05	-.46	-1.36	-.51	.33	.86	.59	-1.06	-1.74	.42	.54	78bt d
Banks	48.20	77.92	68.14	49.90	81.71	94.11	-16.92	55.74	58.79	76.64	41.95	111.45	242.90	78.01	18.59	78bu d
Other Sectors	4.57	5.82	-4.47	3.47	39.42	23.88	42.13	42.41	131.43	-98.49	61.73	140.63	76.66	20.57	21.50	78bv d
Net Errors and Omissions	1.04	6.16	.02	3.32	6.43	2.03	-3.91	8.31	1.06	11.16	3.10	-3.50	9.45	9.83	6.81	78ca d
Overall Balance	2.57	3.65	19.13	4.59	-7.42	.04	4.70	-6.67	5.44	1.50	-.85	-.65	-3.90	-.26	-1.03	78cb d
Reserves and Related Items	-2.57	-3.65	-19.13	-4.59	7.42	-.04	-4.70	6.67	-5.44	-1.50	.85	.65	3.90	.26	1.03	79da d
Reserve Assets	-2.57	-3.65	-20.10	-4.45	8.41	-.13	-4.66	2.43	-1.26	-1.48	.90	.65	3.90	.26	1.03	79db d
Use of Fund Credit and Loans	—	—	—	—	—	—	—	—	—	—	—	—	—	—	—	79dc d
Exceptional Financing	—	—	.97	-.14	-.99	.09	-.05	4.24	-4.17	-.02	-.04	—	—	—	—	79de d

Billions of US Dollars

International Investment Position

	1985	1986	1987	1988	1989	1990	1991	1992	1993	1994	1995	1996	1997	1998	1999	
Assets	857.50	1,062.88	1,279.47	1,379.58	1,513.72	1,728.21	1,756.30	1,731.03	2,001.37	2,090.41	2,385.97	2,775.20	3,212.04	3,508.68	3,825.17	79aa d
Direct Investment Abroad	100.31	118.95	160.83	188.77	197.76	232.74	236.17	226.27	252.26	271.65	311.45	352.86	374.56	498.72	664.10	79ab d
Portfolio Investment	153.64	216.67	227.73	278.19	364.98	380.34	473.28	479.20	676.02	647.46	755.13	908.62	1,036.46	1,136.74	1,300.01	79ac d
Equity Securities	81.89	120.36	125.19	165.29	220.78	195.33	239.47	209.94	287.40	291.92	336.30	404.67	466.94	504.96	679.26	79ad d
Debt Securities	71.75	96.31	102.54	112.90	144.21	185.01	233.80	269.27	388.62	355.54	418.83	503.94	569.52	631.79	620.76	79ae d
Financial Derivatives	—	—	—	—	—	—	—	—	—	—	—	—	—	—	—	79al d
Other Investment	584.48	701.55	840.34	860.67	908.77	1,071.85	998.24	982.78	1,029.05	1,123.37	1,270.24	1,467.33	1,763.23	1,834.37	1,825.19	79af d
Monetary Authorities	—	—	—	—	—	—	—	—	—	—	—	—	—	—	—	79ag d
General Government	9.48	10.38	14.64	15.60	15.14	20.02	21.02	18.07	18.61	20.59	21.42	24.57	24.24	24.53	24.30	79ah d
Banks	512.30	625.20	749.35	765.05	794.57	912.99	815.75	799.32	777.87	887.99	991.94	1,070.68	1,353.60	1,443.49	1,350.68	79ai d
Other Sectors	62.69	65.96	76.36	80.01	99.07	138.84	161.47	165.39	232.57	214.78	256.89	372.08	385.39	366.35	450.21	79aj d
Reserve Assets	19.07	25.72	50.57	51.95	42.21	43.28	48.61	42.78	44.04	47.93	49.15	46.39	37.79	38.84	35.86	79ak d
Liabilities	755.01	915.87	1,185.35	1,287.37	1,431.77	1,744.12	1,750.44	1,696.97	1,947.50	2,055.67	2,374.29	2,778.41	3,348.68	3,709.78	4,039.18	79lb d
Dir. Invest. in Rep. Economy	64.03	76.29	117.57	139.39	160.74	218.85	226.44	186.10	189.93	191.54	213.80	250.61	276.41	323.14	394.56	79la d
Portfolio Investment	124.78	157.57	240.54	287.55	311.70	364.69	390.53	373.54	454.60	499.98	598.92	729.53	973.15	1,142.30	1,434.82	79lc d
Equity Securities	22.89	36.97	67.51	79.35	103.48	114.05	131.80	140.33	198.06	197.10	237.05	296.29	506.21	685.85	930.88	79ld d
Debt Securities	101.89	120.60	173.04	208.21	208.22	250.63	258.73	233.20	256.54	302.89	361.87	433.25	466.94	456.45	503.94	79le d
Financial Derivatives	—	—	—	—	—	—	—	—	—	—	—	—	—	—	—	79ll d
Other investment	566.20	682.00	827.24	860.42	959.33	1,160.58	1,133.47	1,137.33	1,302.97	1,364.15	1,561.57	1,798.27	2,099.11	2,244.34	2,209.80	79lf d
Monetary Authorities	—	—	—	—	—	—	—	—	—	—	—	—	—	—	—	79lg d
General Government	4.45	5.30	6.89	6.96	7.65	8.24	6.67	9.54	5.59	6.68	7.29	6.68	4.78	5.20	5.63	79lh d
Banks	525.76	632.47	776.50	804.70	865.24	1,035.79	962.90	948.64	982.44	1,114.41	1,242.42	1,327.39	1,577.99	1,729.51	1,669.13	79li d
Other Sectors	35.99	44.24	43.85	48.76	86.44	116.55	163.90	179.15	314.93	243.05	311.86	464.20	516.34	509.63	535.04	79lj d

United Kingdom

		1970	1971	1972	1973	1974	1975	1976	1977	1978	1979	1980	1981	1982	1983	1984
Government Finance															*Millions of Pounds*	
Deficit (-) or Surplus	80	ꟷ923	−384	−1,742	−2,524	−3,828	−7,796	−7,251	−4,934	−8,808	−11,164	−10,733	−12,141	−9,514	−13,372	−10,282
Revenue	81	ꟷ19,088	20,170	21,311	23,158	29,442	37,683	44,145	50,125	55,042	64,369	81,640	91,806	106,415	112,590	120,665
Grants Received	81z	ꟷ—	—	—	7	23	27	46	117	110	179	408	992	1,363	1,153	1,039
Expenditure	82	ꟷ16,301	18,231	20,781	23,503	30,335	41,190	48,634	53,513	61,884	72,188	88,475	103,089	113,728	122,347	130,718
Lending Minus Repayments	83	ꟷ1,864	2,323	2,272	2,186	2,958	4,316	2,808	1,663	2,076	3,524	4,306	1,850	3,564	4,768	1,268
Overall Adjustment	80x	....	....	....	....	....	....	....	....	....	....	....	....	....	....	....
Financing																
Domestic Borrowing	84a	ꟷ389	2,725	96	3,263	2,917	8,426	7,468	11,556	6,451	10,376	9,419	8,040	6,083	14,189	10,044
Bank of England, Banking Dept	84aa	....	....	....	....	....	....	....	....	....	....	....	....	....	....	....
Notes and Coin	84ab	....	....	....	....	....	....	....	....	....	....	....	....	....	....	....
Dep Money Bks: Bills & Bonds	84ac	....	....	....	....	....	....	....	....	....	....	....	....	....	....	....
National Savings	84ad	....	....	....	....	....	....	....	....	....	....	....	....	....	....	....
Tax Certificates	84ae	....	....	....	....	....	....	....	....	....	....	....	....	....	....	....
Other Dom. Hold. Bills & Bonds	84af	....	....	....	....	....	....	....	....	....	....	....	....	....	....	....
Other Transactions (Net)	84ag	....	....	....	....	....	....	....	....	....	....	....	....	....	....	....
Foreign Borrowing	85a	ꟷ−965	51	213	−319	1,084	−465	−527	1,345	130	1,389	1,425	154	286	871	668
EEA External Currency Flow	85aa	....	....	....	....	....	....	....	....	....	....	....	....	....	....	....
of which: Treasury IMF Acct.	85ab	....	....	....	....	....	....	....	....	....	....	....	....	....	....	....
Fgn Hold.of Treas.Bills &Bonds	85ac	....	....	....	....	....	....	....	....	....	....	....	....	....	....	....
Other Fgn. Hold. of Govt. Debt	85ad	....	....	....	....	....	....	....	....	....	....	....	....	....	....	....
Use of Cash Balances	87	ꟷ−318	−2,416	1,438	−329	−359	263	−169	−8,544	2,058	−1,477	−286	2,862	1,546	−616	−427
Adj. to Total Financing	84x	ꟷ−29	24	−5	−91	186	−428	479	577	169	876	175	1,085	1,599	−1,072	−3
															Millions of Pounds	
Debt: Domestic	88a	ꟷ25,921	28,168	29,017	31,988	36,045	46,699	57,219	66,817	75,327	80,496	96,606	100,629	112,609	126,680	139,899
Foreign	89a	ꟷ5,158	5,289	5,613	5,528	6,825	6,675	6,414	6,873	6,505	8,632	10,142	10,462	10,799	12,354	12,990
National Accounts															*Billions of Pounds*	
Househ.Cons.Expend.,incl.NPISHs	96f. c	31.14	34.92	39.53	45.24	52.18	64.21	74.68	85.27	98.33	116.69	135.45	150.39	164.69	181.05	193.94
Government Consumption Expend	91f. c	9.08	10.35	11.79	13.46	16.81	23.27	27.27	29.76	33.70	39.09	49.19	55.67	60.60	65.93	69.83
Gross Fixed Capital Formation	93e. c	10.04	11.24	12.35	15.23	18.13	21.86	25.52	28.20	32.21	38.21	43.24	43.33	47.39	51.49	58.70
Changes in Inventories	93i. c	.38	.11	.03	1.53	1.05	−1.35	.90	1.82	1.80	2.16	−2.57	−2.77	−1.19	1.47	1.30
Exports of Goods and Services	90c. c	11.49	12.89	13.59	17.03	22.83	26.80	35.02	43.21	47.38	54.80	62.50	67.32	72.58	79.75	91.51
Imports of Goods and Services	98c. c	−11.05	−12.10	−13.66	−18.84	−27.01	−28.66	−36.48	−42.26	−45.23	−54.17	−57.45	−60.24	−67.63	−77.43	−92.58
Gross Domestic Product (GDP)	99b. c	51.17	57.08	63.94	73.56	83.18	105.00	124.33	144.84	167.10	196.59	229.58	252.24	275.85	301.52	323.10
GDP Volume 1995 Ref., Chained	99b. r	416.79	425.20	440.44	472.70	464.84	461.61	474.51	485.67	502.20	516.08	504.75	498.31	507.29	526.29	539.01
GDP Volume (1995=100)	99bv r	58.5	59.7	61.8	66.3	65.2	64.8	66.6	68.2	70.5	72.4	70.8	69.9	71.2	73.9	75.6
GDP Deflator (1995=100)	99bi r	12.3	13.4	14.5	15.6	17.9	22.7	26.2	29.8	33.3	38.1	45.5	50.6	54.4	57.3	59.9
																Millions:
Population	99z	55.42	55.61	55.78	55.91	55.92	55.90	55.89	55.85	55.84	55.88	56.33	56.35	56.31	56.35	56.51

	1985	1986	1987	1988	1989	1990	1991	1992	1993	1994	1995	1996	1997	1998	1999		
Year Ending December 31																**Government Finance**	
	−10,268	−9,112	−2,880	7,284	4,959	3,566	−7,050	−29,218	−46,447	−39,868	−38,922	−27,440	−16,136	4,876	....	Deficit (-) or Surplus	80
	133,839	139,836	151,367	169,355	179,438	201,410	214,505	218,613	217,062	236,083	253,918	270,360	288,223	315,091	....	Revenue	81
	667	753	937	736	1,199	1,752	4,616	1,907	2,558	1,752	1,233	2,424	1,739	1,384	....	Grants Received	81z
	141,102	147,419	155,882	162,909	174,464	208,761	234,249	261,542	272,600	284,051	295,172	307,310	306,579	310,880	....	Expenditure	82
	3,672	2,282	−698	−102	1,214	−9,165	−8,078	−11,804	−6,533	−6,348	−1,099	−7,086	−481	719	....	Lending Minus Repayments	83
	....	....	....	....	....	....	....	....	....	....	....	....	....	....	....	Overall Adjustment	80x
																Financing	
	8,615	7,831	11,525	−4,245	−11,166	−4,493	4,725	20,397	32,798	34,931	38,275	20,446	18,064	−4,665	....	Domestic Borrowing	84a
	....	....	....	....	....	....	....	....	....	....	....	....	....	....	....	Bank of England, Banking Dept	84aa
	....	....	....	....	....	....	....	....	....	....	....	....	....	....	....	Notes and Coin	84ab
	....	....	....	....	....	....	....	....	....	....	....	....	....	....	....	Dep Money Bks: Bills & Bonds	84ac
	....	....	....	....	....	....	....	....	....	....	....	....	....	....	....	National Savings	84ad
	....	....	....	....	....	....	....	....	....	....	....	....	....	....	....	Tax Certificates	84ae
	....	....	....	....	....	....	....	....	....	....	....	....	....	....	....	Other Dom. Hold. Bills & Bonds	84af
	....	....	....	....	....	....	....	....	....	....	....	....	....	....	....	Other Transactions (Net)	84ag
	3,490	3,413	4,530	2,243	6,207	927	2,325	8,821	13,649	4,937	647	6,994	−1,928	−211	....	Foreign Borrowing	85a
	....	....	....	....	....	....	....	....	....	....	....	....	....	....	....	EEA External Currency Flow	85aa
	....	....	....	....	....	....	....	....	....	....	....	....	....	....	....	*of which: Treasury IMF Acct.*	85ab
	....	....	....	....	....	....	....	....	....	....	....	....	....	....	....	Fgn Hold.of Treas.Bills &Bonds	85ac
	....	....	....	....	....	....	....	....	....	....	....	....	....	....	....	Other Fgn. Hold. of Govt. Debt	85ad
	−166	−2,780	−12,360	−2,801	....	....	....	....	....	....	....	....	....	....	....	Use of Cash Balances	87
	−1,671	648	−815	−2,481	−3,002	490	−1,216	875	....	....	....	....	....	....	....	Adj. to Total Financing	84x
Year Beginning April 1																	
	151,448	161,726	169,590	178,613	164,616	158,374	160,638	169,660	201,928	243,394	277,476	314,021	341,171	....	....	Debt: Domestic	88a
	15,113	18,452	22,008	24,164	27,747	27,580	28,535	34,678	47,998	58,262	56,234	58,691	60,213	....	....	Foreign	89a
Billions of Pounds																**National Accounts**	
	211.95	235.07	258.14	291.63	320.00	347.25	368.23	387.31	412.40	433.83	454.17	485.42	517.03	546.93	582.01	Househ.Cons.Expend.,incl.NPISHs	96f. *c*
	73.79	79.26	85.08	91.66	98.98	109.54	120.80	128.27	130.57	135.54	140.41	146.11	147.77	154.11	162.85	Government Consumption Expend	91f. *c*
	64.46	68.69	78.79	96.13	111.04	114.20	104.59	100.31	101.22	107.53	116.27	125.49	134.19	149.74	160.50	Gross Fixed Capital Formation	93e. *c*
	.82	.68	1.23	4.33	2.68	−1.80	−4.93	−1.94	.33	3.71	4.51	1.77	4.39	3.46	−1.89	Changes in Inventories	93i. *c*
	101.93	97.78	106.44	107.43	121.88	133.50	135.37	143.29	162.08	178.77	202.41	220.30	229.33	224.96	229.03	Exports of Goods and Services	90c. *c*
	−98.72	−100.89	−111.45	−124.66	−142.69	−148.20	−141.12	−150.67	−168.77	−183.33	−205.22	−224.49	−228.82	−233.37	−244.53	Imports of Goods and Services	98c. *c*
	354.23	380.60	418.22	466.52	511.89	554.49	582.95	606.58	637.82	676.04	712.55	754.60	803.89	847.16	889.87	Gross Domestic Product (GDP)	99b. *c*
	559.53	583.15	609.02	640.59	654.32	658.48	648.64	648.98	664.02	693.18	712.55	730.77	756.43	772.78	788.73	GDP Volume 1995 Ref., Chained	99b. *r*
	78.5	81.8	85.5	89.9	91.8	92.4	91.0	91.1	93.2	97.3	100.0	102.6	106.2	108.5	110.7	GDP Volume (1995=100)	99bv *r*
	63.3	65.3	68.7	72.8	78.2	84.2	89.9	93.5	96.1	97.5	100.0	103.3	106.3	109.6	112.8	GDP Deflator (1995=100)	99bi *r*
Midyear Estimates																	
	56.68	56.85	57.01	57.16	57.36	57.56	57.81	58.01	58.19	58.39	58.61	58.80	59.01	Ɪ 58.85	58.74	Population	99z

(See notes in the back of the book.)

United States

111		1970	1971	1972	1973	1974	1975	1976	1977	1978	1979	1980	1981	1982	1983	1984
Exchange Rates												*End of Period (sa and sc) Period Averages (sb and sd)*				
US Dollar/SDR Rate..............aa=	sa	1.0000	1.0857	1.0857	1.2064	1.2244	1.1707	1.1618	1.2147	1.3028	1.3173	1.2754	1.1640	1.1031	1.0470	.9802
US Dollar/SDR Rate	sb	1.0000	1.0030	1.0857	1.1921	1.2026	1.2142	1.1545	1.1675	1.2520	1.2920	1.3015	1.1792	1.1040	1.0690	1.0250
SDR/US Dollar Rate..............ac=	sc	1.0000	.9211	.9211	.8290	.8168	.8542	.8607	.8232	.7676	.7591	.7841	.8591	.9065	.9552	1.0202
SDR/US Dollar Rate	sd	1.0000	.9970	.9211	.8388	.8315	.8236	.8662	.8565	.7987	.7740	.7683	.8481	.9058	.9355	.9756
										Dollars per ECU through 1998; Dollars per Euro Beginning 1999:						
Euro Rate	ea	....	....	....	....	....	....	....	....	....	1.4419	1.3096	1.0852	.9677	.8274	.7089
Euro Rate	eb	....	....	....	....	....	....	....	....	1.2740	1.3706	1.3910	1.1176	.9812	.8913	.7890
													Index Numbers (1995=100):			
Nominal Effective Exchange Rate	neu	149.8	145.9	134.9	125.3	128.5	128.5	133.6	131.7	119.0	117.4	117.7	128.9	142.7	147.9	158.1
Real Effective Exchange Rate	reu	....	....	....	....	....	117.6	120.6	118.6	128.2	128.7	I 132.0	144.6	161.4	162.2	170.4
Fund Position															*Billions of SDRs:*	
Quota	2f.s	6.70	6.70	6.70	6.70	6.70	6.70	6.70	6.70	8.41	8.41	12.61	12.61	12.61	17.92	17.92
SDRs	1b.s	.85	1.10	1.80	1.80	1.94	1.99	2.06	2.16	1.20	2.07	2.05	3.52	4.76	4.80	5.75
Reserve Position in the Fund	1c.s	1.94	.58	.43	.46	1.51	1.89	3.82	4.07	.80	.95	2.24	4.34	6.66	10.81	11.77
of which: Outstg.Fund Borrowing	2c	—	—	—	—	—	—	—	.58	—	—	.30	.75	1.14	1.43	1.32
International Liquidity											*Billions of US Dollars Unless Otherwise Indicated:*					
Total Reserves minus Gold	1l.d	3.41	2.11	2.66	2.73	4.23	4.63	7.15	7.59	6.98	7.78	15.60	18.92	22.81	22.63	23.84
SDRs	1b.d	.85	1.19	1.96	2.17	2.37	2.33	2.39	2.63	1.56	2.72	2.61	4.10	5.25	5.03	5.64
Reserve Position in the Fund	1c.d	1.94	.63	.46	.55	1.85	2.21	4.43	4.95	1.05	1.25	2.85	5.05	7.35	11.31	11.54
Foreign Exchange	1d.d	.63	.28	.24	.01	.01	.08	.32	.02	4.37	3.81	10.13	9.77	10.21	6.29	6.66
Gold (Million Fine Troy Ounces)	1ad	316.34	291.60	275.97	275.97	275.97	274.71	274.68	277.55	276.41	264.60	264.32	264.11	264.03	263.39	262.79
Gold (National Valuation)	1and	11.07	10.21	10.49	11.65	11.65	11.60	11.60	11.72	11.67	11.17	11.16	11.15	11.15	11.12	11.10
Deposit Money Banks: Assets	7a.d	11.80	13.61	17.99	23.89	42.47	54.70	72.68	88.05	I 118.58	136.03	176.91	254.62	360.54	397.17	409.88
Liabilities	7b.d	31.27	26.91	34.43	40.02	64.05	62.72	71.15	87.33	I 101.08	141.00	151.45	189.92	254.55	305.78	338.12
Monetary Authorities															*Billions of US Dollars:*	
Foreign Assets	11	13.9	11.8	13.0	14.2	15.9	16.2	18.7	19.3	18.7	18.9	26.8	30.1	33.9	33.7	34.9
Claims on Central Government	12a	66.8	76.4	78.1	86.7	87.5	95.2	100.9	108.6	121.6	129.8	132.4	139.7	146.7	157.7	168.7
Federal Reserve Float	13a	4.3	4.3	4.0	3.1	2.0	10.1	2.5	3.6	6.5	6.8	4.5	1.8	2.7	1.6	.8
Reserve Money	14	81.2	88.8	92.2	99.6	105.6	112.6	118.8	130.5	145.3	155.0	164.3	170.0	181.4	191.5	205.6
of which: Currency Outside Banks	14a	50.0	53.5	57.8	61.9	69.1	74.2	79.7	88.0	97.4	107.6	116.8	122.8	131.9	146.6	160.5
Foreign Liabilities	16c	.1	.3	.3	.3	.4	.4	.4	.4	.4	.4	.4	.5	.3	.2	.3
Central Government Deposits	16d	1.5	1.7	1.4	1.9	2.7	6.9	10.3	7.0	5.5	3.9	5.5	7.3	9.3	6.2	9.2
Other Items (Net)	17r	2.0	1.9	1.1	2.2	–3.3	1.7	–7.3	–6.3	–4.5	–3.9	–6.6	–6.3	–7.7	–4.8	–10.6
Banking Institutions																
Commercial Banks															*Billions of US Dollars:*	
Reserves	20	31.2	35.3	34.3	37.8	37.5	38.3	37.3	40.8	46.7	48.3	47.3	43.7	45.6	41.1	43.9
Foreign Assets	21	10.8	12.6	15.2	21.9	38.9	52.1	66.6	79.0	93.1	114.5	160.8	197.6	176.9	183.5	179.0
Claims on Central Government	22a	62.5	65.6	68.1	59.2	55.1	85.0	103.8	102.0	95.3	95.6	111.5	113.8	134.0	179.5	181.5
Claims on State and Local Govts	22b	70.2	82.8	90.0	95.7	101.2	102.9	106.0	115.2	126.2	135.6	148.8	154.0	158.3	162.1	174.6
Claims on Private Sector	22d	328.0	362.7	426.3	510.7	574.8	572.6	618.1	702.2	813.0	921.0	989.4	1,081.1	1,159.9	1,252.0	1,419.7
Demand Deposits	24	192.4	205.9	225.9	239.0	238.9	247.2	260.9	285.2	310.6	338.0	347.8	356.5	375.8	390.8	419.5
Time and Savings Deposits	25	180.6	209.3	234.0	246.8	265.0	305.3	359.9	388.7	403.4	433.9	479.9	522.1	620.1	750.9	826.0
Money Market Instruments	26aa	56.8	69.6	84.0	123.4	168.1	157.1	146.8	177.1	230.6	255.5	314.7	383.1	394.6	356.1	399.1
Bonds	26ab	3.2	5.2	8.3	9.2	10.4	14.5	18.0	21.1	22.1	21.9	23.2	26.1	32.4	42.0	55.5
Foreign Liabilities	26c	27.0	22.8	30.3	35.6	53.0	55.0	60.8	72.8	84.4	121.2	131.2	113.3	108.0	124.6	132.2
Central Government Deposits	26d	7.9	10.2	10.9	9.9	4.8	3.1	3.0	7.3	14.1	14.5	11.9	10.8	16.9	11.5	15.6
Credit from Monetary Authorities	26g	8.9	8.7	9.9	7.5	4.3	7.6	5.2	7.9	14.2	15.0	10.8	5.1	6.2	4.0	5.3
Other Items (Net)	27r	25.9	27.4	30.5	53.8	63.0	61.3	77.2	79.0	94.9	115.0	138.3	173.2	120.9	138.2	145.5
Credit Unions and Savings Insts															*Billions of US Dollars:*	
Reserves	20..t	5.9	8.5	10.8	10.0	11.5	16.9	15.5	16.5	17.0	16.0	22.7	24.4	42.3	47.2	40.6
Claims on Central Government	22a.t	10.1	9.8	9.2	7.8	6.7	11.4	15.3	16.9	14.1	12.3	14.1	14.3	17.9	34.6	43.4
Claims on State and Local Govts	22b.t	.3	.5	1.0	1.1	1.4	3.1	3.6	4.0	4.6	4.1	3.6	3.6	3.3	3.1	2.8
Claims on Private Sector	22d.t	244.3	282.1	328.8	367.0	391.7	436.9	501.3	577.6	652.5	713.9	762.2	789.1	796.1	915.6	1,061.6
Demand Deposits	24..t	.4	.5	.6	.8	.9	1.3	2.1	3.1	4.2	5.4	8.3	16.7	25.0	36.5	44.4
Time and Savings Deposits	25..t	232.3	272.0	317.1	343.6	363.1	421.2	488.1	554.5	606.1	636.3	674.2	681.9	722.8	808.6	884.8
Money Market Instruments	26aa t	.7	1.5	2.7	3.8	7.2	8.2	9.5	13.8	22.8	39.9	54.7	69.7	79.5	127.8	193.7
Bonds	26ab t	—	—	—	—	—	.1	.1	1.3	2.0	3.4	3.7	3.2	3.7	4.0	5.9
Other Items (Net)	27r.t	27.2	26.9	29.5	37.7	40.1	37.6	36.0	42.3	53.1	61.4	61.7	59.9	28.6	23.6	19.6
Money Market Funds															*Billions of US Dollars:*	
Foreign Assets	21.m	—	—	—	—	—	—	—	—	.5	5.1	6.8	18.9	23.8	21.9	21.1
Claims on Central Government	22a.m	—	—	—	—	.1	.9	1.2	.9	.9	1.6	3.5	21.5	42.7	22.8	25.2
Claims on Local Government	22b.m	—	—	—	—	—	—	—	—	—	—	2.0	4.4	13.3	16.9	24.0
Claims on Private Sector	22d.m	—	—	—	—	.7	.5	.9	1.1	4.3	23.3	36.6	81.6	81.6	79.9	114.9
Claims on Banks	22e.m	—	—	—	—	1.6	2.2	1.5	1.8	4.5	12.1	21.4	43.8	41.4	24.0	22.7
Time Deposits	25.m	—	—	—	—	2.4	3.7	3.7	3.9	10.8	45.2	76.4	186.3	219.9	179.5	232.2
Other Items (Net)	27r.m	—	—	—	—	—	–.1	–.1	–.1	–.7	–3.1	–6.2	–16.2	–17.2	–13.9	–24.3
Banking Survey															*Billions of US Dollars:*	
Foreign Assets (Net)	31n	–2.5	1.4	–2.5	.2	1.3	13.0	24.2	25.1	27.5	16.8	62.7	132.7	126.2	114.4	102.6
Domestic Credit	32	772.7	868.7	990.5	1,118.2	1,216.3	1,304.6	1,444.6	1,622.1	1,820.7	2,027.0	2,195.3	2,394.1	2,536.6	2,815.2	3,200.1
Claims on Central Govt. (Net)	32an	129.9	140.0	143.1	141.8	142.0	182.5	207.8	214.0	212.2	220.9	244.1	271.1	315.1	376.9	394.1
Claims on State and Local Govts	32b	70.5	83.4	91.0	96.8	102.6	106.0	109.6	119.2	130.8	139.7	154.3	162.0	175.0	182.1	201.3
Claims on Private Sector	32d	572.3	645.3	756.4	879.6	971.8	1,016.2	1,127.2	1,288.9	1,477.6	1,666.4	1,796.9	1,960.9	2,046.5	2,256.2	2,604.6
Money	34	242.8	259.9	284.3	301.7	308.9	322.7	342.7	376.3	412.1	451.0	472.9	496.0	532.7	573.9	624.4
Quasi-Money	35	413.0	481.3	551.0	590.4	630.4	730.2	851.6	947.1	1,020.4	1,115.4	1,230.5	1,390.3	1,562.9	1,739.0	1,943.0
Money Market Instruments	36aa	57.5	71.1	86.7	127.2	175.3	165.2	156.2	191.0	253.5	295.4	369.4	452.8	474.0	483.9	592.8
Bonds	36ab	3.2	5.2	8.3	9.2	10.4	14.5	18.1	22.4	24.1	25.3	26.9	29.3	36.0	46.0	61.4
Other Items (Net)	37r	53.8	52.5	57.7	90.0	92.6	85.0	100.2	110.5	138.1	156.9	158.3	158.4	57.2	86.7	81.0
Money plus Quasi-Money	35l	655.8	741.2	835.3	892.0	939.4	1,052.9	1,194.3	1,323.4	1,432.5	1,566.4	1,703.4	1,886.3	2,095.6	2,312.9	2,567.4

1985	1986	1987	1988	1989	1990	1991	1992	1993	1994	1995	1996	1997	1998	1999	Item	Code
End of Period (sa and sc) Period Averages (sb and sd)															**Exchange Rates**	
1.0984	1.2232	1.4187	1.3457	1.3142	1.4227	1.4304	1.3750	1.3736	1.4599	1.4865	1.4380	1.3493	1.4080	1.3725	US Dollar/SDR Rate ... aa=	sa
1.0153	1.1732	1.2931	1.3439	1.2818	1.3568	1.3682	1.4084	1.3963	1.4317	1.5170	1.4518	1.3760	1.3565	1.3673	US Dollar/SDR Rate	sb
.9104	.8175	.7049	.7431	.7609	.7029	.6991	.7273	.7280	.6850	.6727	.6954	.7412	.7102	.7286	SDR/US Dollar Rate ... ac=	sc
.9849	.8524	.7734	.7441	.7802	.7371	.7309	.7100	.7162	.6985	.6592	.6888	.7267	.7372	.7314	SDR/US Dollar Rate	sd
End of Period (ea) Period Average (eb)																
.8879	1.0704	1.3034	1.1726	1.1970	1.3633	1.3409	1.2109	1.1200	1.2300	1.3142	1.2530	1.1042	1.1668	1.0046	Euro Rate	ea
.7622	.9812	1.1543	1.1839	1.1024	1.2730	1.2405	1.2968	1.1723	1.1886	1.3081	1.2680	1.1341	1.1200	1.0668	Euro Rate	eb
Period Averages																
163.4	133.0	117.5	109.5	114.3	109.0	107.3	105.2	108.4	106.4	100.0	105.2	113.8	119.3	116.4	Nominal Effective Exchange Rate	ne*u*
174.8	141.5	123.3	116.5	119.0	110.9	108.0	104.9	108.0	106.9	100.0	106.0	115.4	123.2	....	Real Effective Exchange Rate	re*u*
End of Period															**Fund Position**	
17.92	17.92	17.92	17.92	17.92	17.92	17.92	26.53	26.53	26.53	26.53	26.53	26.53	26.53	37.15	Quota	2f.*s*
6.64	6.86	7.25	7.16	7.57	7.72	7.86	6.18	6.57	6.88	7.42	7.17	7.43	7.53	7.54	SDRs	1b.*s*
10.88	9.59	8.00	7.24	6.88	6.38	6.63	8.55	8.59	8.24	9.85	10.73	13.39	17.12	13.09	Reserve Position in the Fund	1c.*s*
1.10	.77	.42	.19	.04	—	—	—	—	—	—	—	—	.98	—	*of which:* Outstg.Fund Borrowing	2c
End of Period															**International Liquidity**	
32.10	37.45	34.72	36.74	63.55	72.26	66.66	60.27	62.35	63.28	74.78	64.04	58.91	70.71	60.50	Total Reserves minus Gold	1l.*d*
7.29	8.39	10.28	9.64	9.95	10.99	11.24	8.50	9.02	10.04	11.04	10.31	10.03	10.60	10.35	SDRs	1b.*d*
11.95	11.73	11.35	9.75	9.05	9.08	9.49	11.76	11.80	12.03	14.65	15.43	18.07	24.11	17.97	Reserve Position in the Fund	1c.*d*
12.86	17.33	13.09	17.36	44.55	52.19	45.93	40.01	41.53	41.22	49.10	38.29	30.81	36.00	32.18	Foreign Exchange	1d.*d*
262.65	262.04	262.38	261.87	261.93	261.91	261.91	261.84	261.79	261.73	261.70	261.66	261.64	261.61	261.67	Gold (Million Fine Troy Ounces)	1ad
11.09	11.06	11.08	11.06	11.06	11.06	11.06	11.06	11.05	11.05	11.05	11.05	11.05	11.05	11.05	Gold (National Valuation)	1an*d*
417.32	470.29	511.25	560.15	599.62	578.44	587.53	562.24	552.33	546.14	606.46	665.94	791.26	813.16	872.58	Deposit Money Banks: Assets	7a.*d*
381.26	477.22	572.95	645.26	713.61	733.40	720.46	755.41	828.19	941.32	1,011.91	1,028.68	1,207.31	1,265.47	1,324.50	Liabilities	7b.*d*
End of Period															**Monetary Authorities**	
43.2	48.4	45.8	47.8	75.5	85.2	75.9	72.0	73.4	74.3	85.8	75.1	70.0	81.8	71.5	Foreign Assets	11
187.6	208.5	230.8	247.7	245.7	256.0	288.4	312.4	350.3	383.5	397.7	410.2	447.5	463.5	494.2	Claims on Central Government	12a
1.0	1.3	.8	1.3	1.0	2.2	.7	3.3	.9	–.7	.1	4.3	.7	1.6	–.2	Federal Reserve Float	13a
226.1	260.1	272.0	287.0	298.8	325.6	337.2	366.8	400.2	434.6	453.8	475.2	513.2	543.8	652.4	Reserve Money	14
175.3	186.3	201.8	217.3	228.9	254.8	277.0	298.5	327.5	363.5	381.9	406.1	437.6	473.2	567.9	*of which:* Currency Outside Banks	14a
.5	.3	.2	.3	.6	.4	1.0	.2	.4	.3	.4	.2	.5	.2	.1	Foreign Liabilities	16c
17.1	17.8	14.0	19.9	23.7	34.0	38.8	28.0	36.3	29.2	37.7	30.0	22.6	26.0	48.1	Central Government Deposits	16d
–11.9	–20.0	–8.8	–10.5	–.9	–16.6	–11.9	–7.4	–12.3	–7.0	–8.3	–15.8	–18.2	–23.1	–135.0	Other Items (Net)	17r
															Banking Institutions	
End of Period															Commercial Banks	
50.3	68.1	61.7	61.6	59.7	67.9	60.1	60.9	64.2	67.3	67.5	67.5	74.1	66.5	89.3	Reserves	20
170.1	161.8	143.5	150.5	126.8	121.0	147.5	125.4	78.9	38.9	34.1	102.0	151.0	237.2	306.3	Foreign Assets	21
189.4	197.7	194.4	185.3	165.3	172.1	232.5	294.4	322.2	290.4	278.7	261.8	270.1	214.0	226.6	Claims on Central Government	22a
231.8	203.4	174.3	151.6	133.8	117.4	103.2	97.5	99.2	97.6	93.4	94.2	96.7	104.9	110.7	Claims on State and Local Govts	22b
1,564.0	1,783.8	1,946.0	2,138.0	2,361.0	2,494.3	2,545.3	2,624.0	2,754.3	2,940.9	3,223.1	3,422.5	3,750.4	4,125.2	4,399.7	Claims on Private Sector	22d
473.7	568.3	548.5	565.6	562.3	584.0	621.6	714.3	788.4	756.7	710.8	676.3	656.4	623.0	626.2	Demand Deposits	24
907.9	982.1	1,010.0	1,084.0	1,184.7	1,307.7	1,386.5	1,389.2	1,377.2	1,376.2	1,490.1	1,613.2	1,761.5	1,945.2	2,016.2	Time and Savings Deposits	25
399.7	394.5	442.1	477.6	501.9	456.6	412.7	339.2	308.9	331.7	390.9	488.2	585.8	643.7	750.0	Money Market Instruments	26aa
74.4	90.5	104.0	109.1	113.7	108.9	113.2	127.7	134.9	142.6	161.1	168.9	192.7	220.2	240.6	Bonds	26ab
153.4	168.6	194.0	213.9	193.5	216.0	225.8	247.3	256.3	311.2	305.2	327.2	380.7	448.4	532.1	Foreign Liabilities	26c
25.8	27.5	21.6	29.0	25.6	30.9	36.4	30.6	42.6	23.8	19.0	28.7	27.8	13.2	49.6	Central Government Deposits	26d
5.0	4.1	5.4	4.8	2.7	4.6	1.7	7.2	1.9	—	.4	8.7	3.5	3.3	—	Credit from Monetary Authorities	26g
165.6	179.2	194.2	203.1	262.3	264.1	290.7	346.8	408.5	492.8	619.2	636.9	733.7	850.9	917.9	Other Items (Net)	27r
End of Period															Credit Unions and Savings Insts	
51.1	65.0	53.9	52.9	47.2	46.1	52.9	52.7	54.0	41.2	43.8	41.7	43.1	54.3	66.5	Reserves	20.. *t*
40.7	46.0	58.7	49.3	38.9	34.4	39.0	53.9	50.8	49.2	36.7	34.8	30.2	23.3	19.8	Claims on Central Government	22a. *t*
3.4	3.1	3.1	2.8	2.6	3.0	2.4	2.1	2.1	2.0	2.0	2.1	2.1	2.5	3.0	Claims on State and Local Govts	22b. *t*
1,157.3	1,262.9	1,386.9	1,514.5	1,441.5	1,314.4	1,161.4	1,089.7	1,092.5	1,126.8	1,151.9	1,202.6	1,224.8	1,287.7	1,386.2	Claims on Private Sector	22d. *t*
57.4	74.9	81.9	89.5	89.7	86.3	105.9	109.0	115.1	111.8	128.0	154.9	186.1	228.6	268.1	Demand Deposits	24.. *t*
945.6	996.5	1,038.5	1,103.8	1,100.8	1,041.4	964.2	904.2	845.9	807.0	789.6	763.8	712.6	681.3	654.7	Time and Savings Deposits	25.. *t*
196.9	216.1	252.6	282.3	225.0	165.7	108.4	101.0	106.1	122.8	133.6	141.5	154.2	183.5	216.5	Money Market Instruments	26aa *t*
10.5	15.4	19.8	21.7	18.3	12.7	8.6	5.5	3.9	3.1	3.1	2.7	2.8	2.6	2.7	Bonds	26ab *t*
42.0	73.9	109.7	122.3	96.4	91.8	68.7	78.6	128.5	174.5	180.1	218.3	244.4	271.7	333.4	Other Items (Net)	27r. *t*
End of Period															Money Market Funds	
18.9	22.0	21.4	29.3	26.1	26.7	21.5	20.3	10.0	15.7	19.7	23.1	23.2	30.6	42.9	Foreign Assets	21.*m*
24.4	27.8	14.2	11.4	14.6	44.9	78.3	78.4	79.4	66.1	70.0	90.2	86.2	103.6	103.8	Claims on Central Government	22a*m*
36.5	64.1	61.8	66.1	70.1	84.0	90.6	96.0	105.6	113.4	127.7	144.5	167.0	193.0	210.5	Claims on Local Government	22b*m*
117.3	121.2	139.0	148.0	209.0	242.4	235.1	234.2	243.9	279.5	347.9	399.7	468.7	669.3	833.6	Claims on Private Sector	22d*m*
17.5	20.0	34.2	34.4	43.2	33.2	34.9	32.0	30.7	28.9	48.9	81.6	112.8	126.0	158.1	Claims on Banks	22e*m*
242.4	290.6	313.8	335.0	424.7	493.3	535.0	539.5	559.7	603.0	745.3	891.1	1,048.7	1,334.2	1,584.8	Time Deposits	25.*m*
–27.9	–35.5	–43.2	–45.8	–61.8	–62.2	–74.7	–78.7	–90.1	–99.4	–131.2	–152.0	–190.9	–211.7	–235.9	Other Items (Net)	27r*m*
End of Period															**Banking Survey**	
78.3	63.4	16.4	13.4	34.3	16.5	18.0	–29.9	–94.4	–182.6	–166.0	–127.2	–137.1	–99.0	–111.5	Foreign Assets (Net)	31n
3,517.6	3,880.9	4,181.0	4,472.6	4,639.8	4,704.4	4,707.0	4,829.3	5,026.0	5,300.1	5,674.8	6,006.1	6,493.7	7,148.1	7,690.6	Domestic Credit	32
399.2	434.7	462.4	444.8	415.2	442.5	563.0	680.5	723.7	736.3	726.3	738.3	783.5	765.3	746.7	Claims on Central Govt. (Net)	32an
271.6	270.5	239.1	220.5	206.5	204.5	196.2	195.6	206.9	213.0	223.1	240.8	265.7	300.3	324.2	Claims on State and Local Govts	32b
2,846.8	3,175.6	3,479.4	3,807.3	4,018.1	4,057.4	3,947.8	3,953.2	4,095.4	4,350.8	4,725.4	5,027.0	5,444.5	6,082.5	6,619.7	Claims on Private Sector	32d
706.4	829.5	832.2	872.4	880.8	925.1	1,004.4	1,121.9	1,231.0	1,232.0	1,220.7	1,237.3	1,280.2	1,324.8	1,462.1	Money	34
2,095.8	2,269.2	2,362.3	2,522.8	2,710.3	2,842.3	2,885.6	2,832.9	2,782.7	2,786.1	3,025.0	3,268.1	3,522.8	3,960.7	4,255.7	Quasi-Money	35
596.6	610.6	694.7	759.8	727.0	622.3	521.1	440.2	414.9	454.5	524.6	629.7	740.1	827.2	966.6	Money Market Instruments	36aa
84.9	105.9	123.8	130.7	132.0	121.6	121.8	133.1	138.8	145.7	164.2	171.6	195.5	222.8	243.4	Bonds	36ab
112.2	129.0	184.3	200.2	224.1	209.6	192.2	271.4	364.1	499.1	574.3	572.2	618.2	713.7	651.3	Other Items (Net)	37r
2,802.2	3,098.7	3,194.5	3,395.2	3,591.0	3,767.4	3,890.0	3,954.7	4,013.7	4,018.1	4,245.7	4,505.4	4,803.0	5,285.5	5,717.8	Money plus Quasi-Money	35l

United States

		1970	1971	1972	1973	1974	1975	1976	1977	1978	1979	1980	1981	1982	1983	1984
Other Financial Institutions														*Billions of US Dollars:*		
Claims on Central Government	42a	10.2	8.0	8.3	9.2	10.7	10.8	15.9	12.3	10.8	6.5	11.6	22.4	31.3	23.7	46.3
Claims on State and Local Govts	42b	12.7	15.1	16.2	17.2	15.7	17.5	22.6	26.8	28.8	33.9	33.0	37.7	43.8	55.6	70.0
Claims on Private Sector	42d	218.4	256.8	293.7	285.4	245.6	260.8	288.6	295.4	323.2	350.5	377.5	345.4	396.8	501.8	517.6
Claims on Banks	42e	7.6	9.0	10.1	10.3	10.8	10.7	12.3	13.1	13.6	14.7	15.8	16.2	18.3	18.3	19.6
Claims on Other Financial Insts	42f	4.1	4.9	5.8	5.0	3.6	4.3	5.5	5.2	5.9	7.1	9.2	13.7	17.1	18.9	24.1
Credit Market Instruments	46aa	59.8	71.4	76.1	59.3	41.5	54.0	62.5	65.4	61.4	71.4	73.5	69.3	85.5	139.7	161.5
Bonds	46ab	20.2	23.0	27.3	31.8	37.6	41.5	44.9	52.9	57.8	60.2	66.1	69.6	77.7	85.3	115.2
Liabilities to Banks	46h	153.9	180.6	211.0	205.7	179.1	187.9	212.5	212.6	227.9	255.9	291.3	299.5	319.0	350.8	367.0
Other Items (Net)	47r	19.1	18.8	19.8	30.4	28.3	20.6	25.1	21.9	35.2	25.2	16.1	−3.1	25.1	42.6	34.0
Insurance Companies & Pension Funds														*Billions of US Dollars:*		
Claims on Central Government	42a.s	14.7	13.0	13.7	14.2	16.4	24.4	34.8	43.2	47.9	56.3	71.2	95.9	142.7	188.3	240.8
Claims on State and Local Govts	42b.s	22.4	26.0	30.2	33.6	35.3	39.7	47.6	59.0	73.3	83.2	91.3	94.9	99.7	99.2	95.9
Claims on Private Sector	42d.s	364.0	411.6	469.1	474.1	469.7	555.3	622.6	668.0	762.4	863.4	1,006.6	1,071.5	1,229.2	1,404.4	1,509.1
Claims on Banks	42e.s	11.2	12.6	14.8	17.4	20.7	23.9	26.5	30.5	36.6	42.5	46.4	51.6	66.3	80.4	93.0
Claims on Other Financial Insts	42f.s	1.7	1.8	1.8	2.2	2.5	3.4	4.1	4.6	5.1	8.1	12.7	17.7	20.0	20.3	24.9
Insurance and Pension Reserves	47a.s	349.6	392.8	452.3	466.5	479.8	583.4	654.9	713.0	818.4	930.6	1,092.0	1,185.1	1,404.9	1,644.1	1,799.8
Other Items (Net)	47r.s	64.4	72.2	77.3	74.9	64.8	63.4	80.7	92.2	106.9	122.9	136.3	146.5	153.0	148.4	163.9
Financial Survey														*Billions of US Dollars:*		
Foreign Assets (Net)	51n	−2.5	1.4	−2.5	.2	1.3	13.0	24.2	25.1	27.5	16.8	62.7	132.7	126.2	114.4	102.6
Domestic Credit	52	1,014.0	1,148.5	1,308.8	1,430.1	1,488.4	1,593.7	1,771.8	1,956.6	2,183.5	2,417.9	2,617.4	2,799.5	3,008.4	3,396.3	3,834.0
Claims on Central Govt. (Net)	52an	140.1	147.9	151.4	151.0	152.7	193.3	223.8	226.3	223.0	227.5	255.6	293.5	346.4	400.7	440.4
Claims on State and Local Govts	52b	83.2	98.5	107.2	114.0	118.3	123.5	132.2	146.0	159.6	173.6	187.3	199.7	218.8	237.7	271.3
Claims on Private Sector	52d	790.7	902.1	1,050.2	1,165.1	1,217.4	1,276.9	1,415.8	1,584.3	1,800.8	2,016.9	2,174.5	2,306.3	2,443.3	2,758.0	3,122.3
Liquid Liabilities	55l	655.8	741.2	835.3	892.0	939.4	1,052.9	1,194.3	1,323.4	1,432.5	1,566.4	1,703.4	1,886.3	2,095.6	2,312.9	2,567.4
Credit Market Instruments	56aa	117.3	142.5	162.8	186.6	216.8	219.3	218.7	256.4	314.9	366.7	442.9	522.0	559.5	623.6	754.3
Bonds	56ab	23.5	28.2	35.6	41.0	47.9	56.1	63.0	75.3	81.9	85.4	93.0	98.9	113.7	131.3	176.6
Other Items (Net)	57r	215.1	238.0	272.5	310.7	285.6	278.5	319.9	326.8	381.7	416.2	440.8	425.0	365.9	442.9	438.3
Money Stock, Liquid Assets, and Debt Measures (National Definitions)														*Billions of US Dollars:*		
M1	59ma	220.1	234.5	256.1	270.2	281.8	295.3	314.5	340.0	367.9	393.2	419.5	447.0	485.8	533.3	564.6
M1, Seasonally Adjusted	59ma c	214.3	228.2	249.1	262.7	274.0	286.8	305.9	330.5	356.9	381.4	408.1	436.2	474.3	520.8	551.2
M2	59mb	627.8	711.2	803.1	856.5	903.8	1,018.3	1,154.1	1,273.8	1,371.8	1,480.2	1,606.2	1,761.8	1,919.8	2,139.1	2,324.4
M2, Seasonally Adjusted	59mb c	626.4	710.1	802.1	855.3	902.2	1,016.4	1,152.3	1,270.7	1,366.5	1,474.3	1,600.4	1,756.1	1,911.2	2,127.8	2,311.8
M3	59mc	678.2	776.6	886.2	985.2	1,071.1	1,173.8	1,314.2	1,477.0	1,653.5	1,816.4	2,002.2	2,260.1	2,470.0	2,710.9	3,007.2
M3, Seasonally Adjusted	59mc c	677.0	775.9	885.8	984.9	1,070.0	1,171.7	1,311.9	1,472.5	1,646.1	1,809.7	1,996.5	2,254.9	2,460.9	2,699.2	2,992.8
L	59md	815.7	903.0	1,023.1	1,141.7	1,248.9	1,368.0	1,518.5	1,709.0	1,915.9	2,124.0	2,331.8	2,602.6	2,850.5	3,157.9	3,529.9
L, Seasonally Adjusted	59md c	814.8	902.6	1,022.9	1,141.5	1,248.5	1,366.5	1,516.7	1,705.4	1,911.3	2,121.2	2,330.0	2,601.8	2,846.0	3,150.7	3,518.9
Debt	59me	1,413.4	1,547.1	1,703.5	1,889.5	2,062.4	2,250.2	2,495.3	2,811.4	3,199.9	3,588.2	3,929.9	4,340.5	4,775.7	5,354.4	6,140.6
Debt, Seasonally Adjusted	59me c	1,416.8	1,550.5	1,706.8	1,892.0	2,065.0	2,252.4	2,497.2	2,814.1	3,202.8	3,591.9	3,934.2	4,345.9	4,782.2	5,351.8	6,148.8
Treasury Securities by Holders														*Billions of US Dollars:*		
Total	59t	289.9	315.9	330.1	336.7	348.8	434.9	503.7	561.0	614.9	652.1	730.0	815.9	978.1	1,163.4	1,360.8
Nonresidents	59ta	19.8	46.3	54.8	55.2	60.1	68.0	80.8	108.7	132.9	116.0	127.5	135.5	150.7	163.6	200.3
Residents	59tb	270.1	269.6	275.4	281.5	288.8	366.9	422.9	452.3	482.0	536.1	602.6	680.4	827.4	999.9	1,160.5
Monetary Authorities	59tb a	62.1	69.0	69.8	78.5	80.1	86.7	93.3	100.9	109.5	116.3	119.3	127.7	135.6	150.6	159.2
Commercial Banks	59tb b	62.5	65.6	68.1	59.2	55.1	85.0	103.8	102.0	95.3	95.6	111.5	113.8	134.0	179.5	181.5
Govt. Sponsored Enterprises	59tb c	3.1	2.5	1.3	1.2	1.4	2.9	4.4	1.0	1.4	1.2	1.7	1.9	3.4	1.8	2.7
Other Financial Institutions	59tb d	41.3	39.8	38.1	33.6	36.6	61.7	88.7	89.8	88.7	90.2	114.1	172.7	255.5	299.6	392.2
Nonfinancial Sectors	59tb e	101.2	92.7	98.2	109.1	115.6	130.5	132.8	158.7	187.0	232.8	255.9	264.3	298.9	368.4	424.9
Interest Rates														*Percent Per Annum*		
Discount Rate (End of Period)	60	5.50	4.50	4.50	7.50	7.75	6.00	5.25	6.00	9.50	12.00	13.00	12.00	8.50	8.50	8.00
Federal Funds Rate	60b	7.18	4.66	4.43	8.73	10.50	5.82	5.05	5.54	7.93	11.20	13.36	16.38	12.26	9.09	10.23
Commercial Paper Rate	60bc	....	....	....	....	....	....	5.24	5.54	7.94	10.97	12.66	15.32	11.89	8.87	10.10
Treasury Bill Rate	60c	6.44	4.34	4.07	7.03	7.87	5.82	4.99	5.27	7.22	10.04	11.62	14.08	10.73	8.62	9.39
Treas. Bill Rate(Bond Equivalent)	60cs	....	....	....	....	....	5.78	4.99	5.29	7.19	10.07	10.61	13.35	11.34	8.83	9.98
Certificates of Deposit Rate	60lc	....	....	....	....	....	....	5.26	5.58	8.20	11.22	13.07	15.91	12.27	9.07	10.37
Lending Rate (Prime Rate)	60p	7.91	5.72	5.25	8.02	10.80	7.86	6.84	6.82	9.06	12.67	15.27	18.87	14.86	10.79	12.04
Govt. Bond Yield: Med.-Term	61a	7.29	5.66	5.72	6.95	7.82	7.49	6.77	6.69	8.29	9.71	11.55	14.44	12.92	10.45	11.89
Long-Term	61	7.35	6.16	6.21	6.84	7.56	7.99	7.61	7.42	8.41	9.44	11.46	13.91	13.00	11.11	12.44
Prices, Production, Labor														*Index Numbers (1995=100):*		
Industrial Share Prices	62	14.2	16.9	19.0	18.8	14.5	15.0	17.8	16.9	16.5	17.9	21.0	22.5	20.8	28.1	28.3
Producer Prices	63	29.6	30.5	31.9	36.1	42.9	46.8	49.0	52.0	56.0	63.1	72.0	78.6	80.1	81.1	83.1
Industrial Goods	63a	28.1	29.1	30.1	32.1	39.3	43.8	46.6	49.8	53.4	60.3	70.1	77.6	79.7	80.6	82.3
Finished Goods	63b	30.7	31.7	32.7	35.6	41.1	45.5	47.5	50.6	54.6	60.6	68.8	75.2	78.2	79.4	81.1
Consumer Goods	63ba	31.1	32.0	33.0	36.6	42.3	46.4	48.1	51.2	55.2	61.8	70.6	76.9	79.6	80.7	82.3
Capital Equipment	63bb	29.3	30.5	31.3	32.3	36.9	42.6	45.4	48.3	52.2	56.7	62.8	69.2	73.2	75.2	77.0
Consumer Prices	64	25.5	26.6	27.4	29.2	32.4	35.3	37.4	39.8	42.8	47.6	54.1	59.7	63.3	65.4	68.2
Wages: Hourly Earnings(Mfg)	65ey	27.1	28.9	30.9	33.0	35.8	39.0	42.2	45.9	49.9	54.1	58.8	64.6	68.7	71.4	74.3
Industrial Production	66..c	51.3	52.0	57.1	61.7	60.8	55.5	60.6	65.5	69.3	71.6	69.7	70.8	67.0	69.5	75.7
Crude Petroleum Production	66aa	147.6	145.0	145.1	141.1	134.5	128.3	125.0	126.3	133.4	131.1	132.1	131.4	132.5	133.1	136.4
Nonagr. Employment	67..c	60.5	60.8	62.9	65.5	66.8	65.7	67.7	70.4	74.0	76.7	77.2	77.8	76.4	76.9	80.6
														Number in Thousands:		
Labor Force	67d	....	....	....	....	....	....	....	....	....	....	....	....	....	....	....
Employment	67e	....	....	....	....	....	....	....	....	....	....	....	....	....	....	....
Unemployment	67c	....	....	....	....	....	....	....	....	....	....	....	....	....	....	....
Unemployment Rate (%)	67r	....	....	....	....	....	....	....	....	....	....	....	....	....	....	....

1985	1986	1987	1988	1989	1990	1991	1992	1993	1994	1995	1996	1997	1998	1999		
End of Period															**Other Financial Institutions**	
72.8	125.7	118.2	91.2	166.2	164.5	190.1	213.7	226.7	204.0	273.5	252.2	263.7	286.2	228.2	Claims on Central Government	**42a**
104.0	142.5	149.5	163.9	190.9	215.4	264.6	315.4	389.1	390.0	390.8	389.8	384.4	406.9	407.6	Claims on State and Local Govts	**42b**
732.0	873.8	968.5	1,077.6	1,250.6	1,286.5	1,538.7	1,809.5	2,135.9	2,235.2	2,803.1	3,480.6	4,382.7	5,206.2	6,548.0	Claims on Private Sector	**42d**
23.7	29.6	31.5	36.9	39.0	40.9	37.5	33.6	35.9	38.4	41.4	46.1	56.3	60.4	67.4	Claims on Banks	**42e**
39.1	73.8	78.8	80.2	102.1	126.7	178.2	237.2	303.0	350.7	410.2	485.1	540.2	662.8	804.4	Claims on Other Financial Insts	**42f**
297.3	499.2	559.4	617.8	748.9	826.2	1,014.9	1,257.8	1,629.6	1,763.9	2,189.4	2,744.0	3,538.6	4,280.2	5,328.6	Credit Market Instruments	**46aa**
148.2	219.4	280.2	325.4	393.5	460.5	547.2	630.8	748.2	863.0	1,040.5	1,206.8	1,360.4	1,630.0	1,831.3	Bonds	**46ab**
418.0	475.8	481.0	511.8	597.1	610.9	706.6	728.6	745.4	738.9	839.8	919.7	1,000.3	1,078.5	1,195.5	Liabilities to Banks	**46h**
108.1	50.8	25.9	−5.3	9.2	−63.6	−59.7	−7.7	−32.7	−147.6	−150.7	−216.7	−272.0	−366.2	−299.8	Other Items (Net)	**47r**
End of Period															**Insurance Companies & Pension Funds**	
291.9	317.3	344.8	361.8	384.0	419.8	461.3	505.1	557.7	590.1	609.8	606.8	597.7	580.3	585.5	Claims on Central Government	**42a. s**
100.7	117.0	137.2	144.2	144.6	150.2	138.2	146.7	162.8	168.4	175.6	190.1	210.4	232.7	231.9	Claims on State and Local Govts	**42b. s**
1,807.3	1,996.0	2,161.6	2,356.0	2,771.6	2,914.2	3,371.1	3,647.0	4,074.9	4,298.5	5,055.0	5,831.1	7,025.3	8,189.0	9,181.4	Claims on Private Sector	**42d. s**
105.0	113.3	98.4	112.0	135.8	126.5	126.1	104.4	95.4	88.1	78.2	63.2	52.0	53.6	54.5	Claims on Banks	**42e. s**
32.7	47.6	51.7	62.4	69.9	95.8	97.2	137.9	199.6	207.8	308.7	461.3	616.9	756.1	1,030.7	Claims on Other Financial Insts	**42f. s**
2,160.9	2,389.9	2,550.7	2,787.1	3,242.4	3,495.8	3,885.9	4,212.8	4,683.0	4,953.6	5,796.9	6,661.4	7,926.8	9,139.4	10,447.1	Insurance and Pension Reserves	**47a. s**
176.8	201.3	243.0	249.2	263.4	210.7	307.9	328.3	407.3	399.3	430.5	491.1	575.4	672.2	636.9	Other Items (Net)	**47r. s**
End of Period															**Financial Survey**	
78.3	63.4	16.4	13.4	34.3	16.5	18.0	−29.9	−94.4	−182.6	−166.0	−127.2	−137.1	−99.0	−111.5	Foreign Assets (Net)	**51n**
4,426.4	5,022.8	5,417.2	5,805.3	6,247.4	6,370.6	6,700.4	7,167.9	7,777.7	8,129.3	9,142.1	10,128.7	11,524.6	13,047.3	14,874.4	Domestic Credit	**52**
472.0	560.4	580.7	536.0	581.4	606.9	753.1	894.2	950.5	940.2	999.8	990.5	1,047.2	1,051.5	974.9	Claims on Central Govt. (Net)	**52an**
375.6	413.0	388.6	384.4	397.4	419.8	460.8	511.0	596.0	603.0	613.8	630.6	650.2	707.2	731.8	Claims on State and Local Govts	**52b**
3,578.8	4,049.5	4,447.9	4,884.9	5,268.6	5,343.9	5,486.5	5,762.8	6,231.3	6,586.0	7,528.5	8,507.6	9,827.2	11,288.7	13,167.7	Claims on Private Sector	**52d**
2,802.2	3,098.7	3,194.5	3,395.2	3,591.0	3,767.4	3,890.0	3,954.7	4,013.7	4,018.1	4,245.7	4,505.4	4,803.0	5,285.5	5,717.8	Liquid Liabilities	**55l**
893.9	1,109.8	1,254.1	1,377.6	1,475.9	1,448.4	1,536.0	1,698.0	2,044.6	2,218.5	2,714.0	3,373.6	4,278.7	5,107.3	6,295.2	Credit Market Instruments	**56aa**
233.1	325.4	404.0	456.1	525.5	582.1	669.0	763.9	887.0	1,008.8	1,204.7	1,378.4	1,555.9	1,852.8	2,074.6	Bonds	**56ab**
575.5	552.3	581.0	589.7	689.3	589.2	623.4	721.5	738.0	701.3	811.8	744.1	749.9	702.7	675.3	Other Items (Net)	**57r**
															Money Stock, Liquid Assets, and Debt Measures (National Definitions)	
633.4	740.0	765.5	803.3	810.9	843.2	916.0	1,046.0	1,153.8	1,174.6	1,152.6	1,105.1	1,097.7	1,121.3	1,147.4	*M1*	**59ma**
619.3	724.2	749.6	786.3	792.5	824.4	896.3	1,024.3	1,129.7	1,150.1	1,126.8	1,081.1	1,073.9	1,097.4	1,122.9	*M1, Seasonally Adjusted*	**59ma c**
2,510.3	2,747.9	2,846.1	3,010.0	3,175.1	3,294.9	3,396.6	3,453.7	3,511.5	3,527.0	3,673.8	3,845.2	4,065.0	4,422.0	4,683.7	*M2*	**59mb**
2,497.6	2,734.5	2,833.4	2,996.9	3,161.3	3,281.0	3,381.0	3,435.7	3,490.8	3,505.4	3,650.1	3,822.9	4,041.9	4,396.8	4,655.4	*M2, Seasonally Adjusted*	**59mb c**
3,224.0	3,516.2	3,705.2	3,948.5	4,104.5	4,167.8	4,222.8	4,236.1	4,299.3	4,373.1	4,638.8	4,973.4	5,427.2	6,026.3	6,512.0	*M3*	**59mc**
3,209.7	3,501.2	3,692.2	3,935.5	4,091.4	4,155.8	4,208.2	4,219.2	4,280.0	4,354.1	4,617.5	4,952.4	5,403.2	5,996.7	6,477.0	*M3, Seasonally Adjusted*	**59mc c**
3,841.1	4,140.2	4,358.0	4,683.6	4,915.3	5,001.0	5,032.7	5,108.3	5,201.9	5,344.6	5,732.8	6,111.6	6,636.7	....	....	*L*	**59md**
3,827.1	4,122.4	4,340.0	4,663.7	4,893.2	4,977.5	5,008.0	5,081.4	5,173.3	5,315.8	5,702.3	6,083.6	6,611.3	....	....	*L, Seasonally Adjusted*	**59md c**
7,065.7	7,929.1	8,669.4	9,462.3	10,158.1	10,824.8	11,301.3	11,826.8	12,411.0	12,999.2	13,705.4	14,440.5	15,231.8	16,279.8	17,380.1	*Debt*	**59me**
7,068.4	7,933.6	8,677.1	9,466.6	10,160.1	10,825.0	11,300.0	11,824.0	12,409.1	12,997.9	13,705.9	14,443.9	15,234.7	16,282.9	17,381.1	*Debt, Seasonally Adjusted*	**59me c**
End of Period															**Treasury Securities by Holders**	
1,586.6	1,802.2	1,944.6	2,082.3	2,227.0	2,465.8	2,757.8	3,061.6	3,309.9	3,465.6	3,608.5	3,755.1	3,778.3	3,723.7	3,652.8	Total	**59t**
226.4	269.4	296.3	353.8	423.7	438.4	476.3	520.3	594.6	632.6	841.3	1,093.3	1,252.0	1,316.3	1,306.7	Nonresidents	**59ta**
1,360.2	1,532.8	1,648.3	1,728.5	1,803.3	2,027.4	2,281.5	2,541.2	2,715.3	2,833.0	2,767.2	2,661.9	2,526.3	2,407.4	2,346.1	Residents	**59tb**
177.8	197.6	222.6	233.7	226.8	235.1	266.5	295.0	332.0	364.5	378.2	390.9	430.7	452.1	478.0	Monetary Authorities	**59tb a**
189.4	197.7	194.4	185.3	165.3	172.1	232.5	294.4	322.2	290.4	278.7	261.8	270.1	214.0	226.6	Commercial Banks	**59tb b**
6.8	16.3	21.0	26.3	13.0	34.3	40.8	58.7	51.6	51.9	58.0	18.8	25.9	25.2	30.9	Govt. Sponsored Enterprises	**59tb c**
470.9	557.0	567.7	541.6	655.2	701.2	812.1	911.7	963.4	960.2	1,047.1	1,031.1	1,004.5	1,018.1	958.2	Other Financial Institutions	**59tb d**
515.4	564.2	642.6	741.7	743.1	884.7	929.7	981.4	1,046.1	1,166.0	1,005.3	959.3	795.1	698.1	652.5	Nonfinancial Sectors	**59tb e**
Percent Per Annum															**Interest Rates**	
7.50	5.50	6.00	6.50	7.00	6.50	3.50	3.00	3.00	4.75	5.25	5.00	5.00	4.50	5.00	Discount Rate *(End of Period)*	**60**
8.10	6.81	6.66	7.57	9.22	8.10	5.69	3.52	3.02	4.20	5.84	5.30	5.46	5.35	4.97	Federal Funds Rate	**60b**
7.95	6.50	6.81	7.66	8.99	8.06	5.87	3.75	3.22	4.66	5.93	5.41	5.57	5.34	5.18	Commercial Paper Rate	**60bc**
7.49	5.97	5.83	6.67	8.12	7.51	5.41	3.46	3.02	4.27	5.51	5.02	5.07	4.82	4.66	Treasury Bill Rate	**60c**
7.79	6.12	6.29	7.13	7.95	7.36	5.53	3.76	3.32	4.99	5.71	5.22	5.34	4.83	4.81	Treas. Bill Rate(Bond Equivalent)	**60cs**
8.05	6.52	6.86	7.73	9.09	8.15	5.84	3.68	3.17	4.63	5.92	5.39	5.62	5.47	5.33	Certificates of Deposit Rate	**60lc**
9.93	8.33	8.20	9.32	10.87	10.01	8.46	6.25	6.00	7.14	8.83	8.27	8.44	8.35	7.99	Lending Rate (Prime Rate)	**60p**
9.64	7.06	7.67	8.26	8.56	8.25	6.81	5.31	4.44	6.26	6.26	5.99	6.10	5.14	5.49	Govt. Bond Yield: Med.-Term	**61a**
10.62	7.68	8.38	8.85	8.50	8.55	7.86	7.01	5.87	7.08	6.58	6.44	6.35	5.26	5.64	Long-Term	**61**
Period Averages															**Prices, Production, Labor**	
32.4	40.9	51.6	47.8	57.7	60.9	69.5	76.5	80.6	84.1	100.0	123.5	159.3	198.7	251.3	Industrial Share Prices	**62**
I 82.7	80.3	82.4	85.7	90.0	93.2	93.4	93.9	95.3	96.5	100.0	102.3	102.3	99.7	100.6	Producer Prices	**63**
82.7	79.7	81.8	84.7	88.9	92.2	92.8	93.6	94.9	96.1	100.0	101.5	101.8	99.5	100.8	Industrial Goods	**63a**
81.8	80.7	82.4	84.4	88.8	93.1	95.1	96.2	97.5	98.2	100.0	102.7	103.1	102.2	104.0	Finished Goods	**63b**
82.7	80.8	82.5	84.6	89.3	94.1	96.0	96.9	97.9	98.1	100.0	103.2	103.7	102.7	105.1	Consumer Goods	**63ba**
78.7	80.2	81.7	83.6	86.9	89.8	92.6	94.3	96.1	98.2	100.0	101.2	101.1	100.6	100.7	Capital Equipment	**63bb**
70.6	71.9	74.6	77.6	81.4	85.7	89.4	92.1	94.8	97.3	100.0	102.9	105.3	107.0	109.3	Consumer Prices	**64**
77.1	78.7	80.1	82.4	84.8	87.5	90.4	92.6	95.0	97.5	100.0	103.3	106.4	109.1	112.5	Wages: Hourly Earnings(Mfg)	**65ey**
77.0	77.8	81.4	85.1	86.6	86.5	84.7	87.4	90.4	95.4	100.0	104.4	111.0	115.7	119.7	Industrial Production	**66.. c**
137.5	133.0	127.9	125.0	117.4	111.9	113.1	109.9	104.8	102.2	100.0	99.3	98.8	97.1	90.0	Crude Petroleum Production	**66aa**
83.1	84.8	87.0	89.8	92.1	93.4	92.4	92.7	94.5	97.4	100.0	102.1	104.7	107.4	109.7	Nonagr. Employment	**67.. c**
Period Averages																
115,462	117,834	119,865	121,669	123,870	I124,961	125,505	I127,211	128,040	I131,057	132,304	133,945	I136,297	137,673	139,368	Labor Force	**67d**
107,150	109,597	112,440	114,968	117,342	117,914	116,877	I117,598	119,306	I123,060	124,900	126,709	I129,558	131,464	133,488	Employment	**67e**
8,312	8,237	7,425	6,701	6,528	I7,047	8,628	9,613	8,734	I7,997	7,404	7,236	I6,739	6,210	5,880	Unemployment	**67c**
7.2	7.0	6.2	5.5	5.3	I5.6	6.8	7.5	6.8	I6.1	5.6	5.4	I5.0	4.6	4.2	Unemployment Rate (%)	**67r**

United States

		1970	1971	1972	1973	1974	1975	1976	1977	1978	1979	1980	1981	1982	1983	1984
International Transactions															*Billions of US Dollars*	
Exports	70	42.66	43.55	49.20	70.82	99.44	Ɪ108.86	116.79	123.18	145.85	186.36	225.57	238.72	216.44	205.64	223.98
Imports, c.i.f.	71	42.39	48.34	58.86	73.20	110.88	Ɪ105.88	132.50	160.41	186.05	222.23	256.98	273.35	254.88	269.88	346.36
Imports, f.o.b.	71.v	39.95	45.56	55.58	69.48	103.32	Ɪ99.31	124.61	151.53	176.05	210.29	245.26	260.98	243.95	258.05	330.68
															1995=100	
Volume of Exports	72	26.6	26.3	28.7	35.6	39.1	Ɪ38.3	39.7	40.4	44.8	50.3	53.6	52.0	46.6	43.8	47.1
Volume of Imports	73	26.0	28.2	32.0	33.5	34.3	Ɪ30.0	36.5	40.8	43.8	43.9	40.5	40.8	38.7	42.7	53.9
Export Prices	76	27.4	28.3	29.3	34.1	43.5	48.6	50.3	52.1	55.7	63.3	71.9	78.5	79.4	80.3	81.4
Import Prices	76.x	21.1	22.2	23.8	28.3	41.9	45.7	47.1	51.0	55.1	65.7	82.3	86.9	85.5	81.9	83.4
Balance of Payments															*Billions of US Dollars:*	
Current Account, n.i.e.	78ald	2.62	−.98	−5.26	7.58	1.70	17.88	3.84	−15.10	−15.77	−.13	2.15	4.84	−11.60	−44.22	−99.01
Goods: Exports f.o.b.	78aad	42.45	43.31	49.38	71.41	98.31	107.09	114.74	120.81	142.05	184.47	224.25	237.05	211.17	201.80	219.93
Goods: Imports f.o.b.	78abd	−39.86	−45.58	−55.80	−70.50	−103.82	−98.18	−124.23	−151.91	−176.00	−212.01	−249.76	−265.07	−247.65	−268.89	−332.41
Trade Balance	78acd	2.59	−2.27	−6.42	.91	−5.51	8.91	−9.49	−31.10	−33.95	−27.54	−25.51	−28.02	−36.48	−67.09	−112.48
Services: Credit	78add	11.45	12.80	13.35	17.04	20.77	23.33	27.58	31.09	35.45	38.83	47.55	57.25	63.99	64.22	71.11
Services: Debit	78aed	−14.65	−15.57	−17.05	−19.09	−21.66	−22.27	−24.91	−27.63	−31.69	−36.23	−40.97	−44.88	−51.04	−54.26	−66.91
Balance on Goods & Services	78afd	−.61	−5.04	−10.12	−1.14	−6.40	9.97	−6.82	−27.64	−30.19	−24.94	−18.93	−15.65	−23.53	−57.13	−108.28
Income: Credit	78agd	11.75	12.71	14.77	21.78	27.63	25.37	29.29	32.40	42.47	64.37	72.67	86.65	86.32	85.26	104.86
Income: Debit	78ahd	−5.07	−4.81	−5.85	−8.95	−12.11	−12.58	−13.32	−14.67	−22.16	−33.43	−43.09	−54.26	−57.14	−54.45	−74.86
Balance on Gds, Serv. & Inc.	78aid	6.07	2.86	−1.20	11.69	9.12	22.76	9.15	−9.91	−9.88	6.00	10.65	16.74	5.65	−26.32	−78.28
Current Transfers, n.i.e.: Credit	78ajd	.38	.40	.61	.70	.72	.72	.76	.70	.81	1.14	1.32	1.23	2.04	2.01	2.16
Current Transfers: Debit	78akd	−3.83	−4.24	−4.67	−4.81	−8.14	−5.60	−6.07	−5.89	−6.70	−7.27	−9.82	−13.13	−19.29	−19.91	−22.89
Capital Account, n.i.e.	78bcd	—	—	—	—	—	—	—	.20	.30	.15	.14	.19	.18	.16	.16
Capital Account, n.i.e.: Credit	78bad	—	—	—	—	—	—	—	.26	.40	.25	.26	.19	.18	.16	.16
Capital Account: Debit	78bbd	—	—	—	—	—	—	—	−.06	−.10	−.10	−.12				
Financial Account, n.i.e.	78bjd	−4.64	10.56	7.71	−3.51	3.87	−22.93	−12.96	16.73	1.60	−27.80	−20.71	−25.97	−25.01	23.01	80.80
Direct Investment Abroad	78bdd	−6.53	−5.72	−7.41	−9.53	−4.95	−13.98	−11.66	−11.26	−14.72	−25.37	−19.23	−9.62	.98	−7.74	−12.35
Dir. Invest. in Rep. Econ., n.i.e.	78bed	1.26	.87	1.35	2.12	3.33	2.56	3.25	2.90	5.85	8.70	16.93	25.19	12.47	10.47	24.76
Portfolio Investment Assets	78bfd	−1.08	−1.10	−.62	−.67	−1.82	−6.23	−8.87	−5.45	−3.63	−4.70	−3.57	−5.70	−7.98	−6.78	−4.77
Equity Securities	78bkd	−.09	−.22	.41	.21	.26	−.02	−.32	−.41	.52	−.87	−2.45	−.19	−1.37	−3.69	−.95
Debt Securities	78bld	−.99	−.88	−1.03	−.88	−2.08	−6.21	−8.55	−5.04	−4.15	−3.83	−1.12	−5.51	−6.61	−3.09	−3.82
Portfolio Investment Liab., n.i.e.	78bgd	2.25	9.93	14.07	4.82	1.71	11.13	12.84	29.49	10.73	5.37	14.15	21.15	17.49	8.53	29.73
Equity Securities	78bmd	.70	.84	2.43	2.76	.25	3.05	.86	1.32	1.31	1.05	4.24	4.82	3.31	5.99	−1.28
Debt Securities	78bnd	1.55	9.09	11.64	2.06	1.46	8.08	11.98	28.17	9.42	4.32	9.91	16.33	14.18	2.54	31.01
Financial Derivatives Assets	78bwd	....	....	....	....	....	....	....	....	....	....	....	....	....	....	....
Financial Derivatives Liabilities	78bxd	....	....	....	....	....	....	....	....	....	....	....	....	....	....	....
Other Investment Assets	78bhd	−3.27	−5.89	−6.72	−10.69	−22.60	−18.51	−27.90	−17.64	−43.01	−32.79	−57.12	−93.13	−111.85	−46.19	−15.96
Monetary Authorities	78bod															
General Government	78bpd	−1.71	−1.69	−2.17	−2.30	.13	−3.63	−4.24	−4.25	−5.49	−3.27	−6.24	−4.60	−7.60	−5.30	−5.38
Banks	78bqd	−.96	−2.97	−3.50	−5.99	−19.49	−13.53	−21.38	−11.45	−33.67	−17.15	−40.43	−75.29	−107.03	−34.95	−13.61
Other Sectors	78brd	−.60	−1.23	−1.05	−2.40	−3.24	−1.35	−2.28	−1.94	−3.85	−12.37	−10.45	−13.24	2.78	−5.94	3.03
Other Investment Liab., n.i.e.	78bid	2.73	12.47	7.04	10.44	28.20	2.10	19.38	18.69	46.38	20.99	28.13	36.14	63.87	64.72	59.39
Monetary Authorities	78bsd	9.51	18.69	−.48	−.35	4.20	1.77	3.36	8.70	20.33	−20.39	10.08	−2.84	1.78	13.33	7.59
General Government	78btd	−.46	−.51	.18	.94	.30	1.53	4.64	1.41	2.47	−.04	.61	−.34	.61	.60	.75
Banks	78bud	−8.33	−6.07	6.53	8.83	21.84	−1.52	11.97	7.50	21.10	38.02	9.43	38.52	64.30	53.40	32.22
Other Sectors	78bvd	2.01	.36	.81	1.02	1.86	.32	−.59	1.08	2.48	3.40	8.01	.80	−2.82	−2.61	18.83
Net Errors and Omissions	78cad	−.54	−11.75	−2.67	−4.19	−4.09	5.82	11.68	−1.46	13.18	27.78	25.41	25.00	41.41	22.25	21.17
Overall Balance	78cbd	−2.56	−2.17	−.22	−.12	1.48	.77	2.56	.37	−.69	—	6.99	4.06	4.98	1.20	3.13
Reserves and Related Items	79dad	2.56	2.17	.22	.12	−1.48	−.77	−2.56	−.37	.69	—	−6.99	−4.06	−4.98	−1.20	−3.13
Reserve Assets	79dbd	2.56	2.17	.22	.12	−1.48	−.77	−2.56	−.37	.69	—	−6.99	−4.06	−4.98	−1.20	−3.13
Use of Fund Credit and Loans	79dcd	—	—	—	—	—	—	—	—	—	—	—	—	—	—	—
Exceptional Financing	79ded	....	....	....	....	....	....	....	....	....	....					
International Investment Position															*Billions of US Dollars*	
Assets	79aad	....	....	....	....	....	....	....	....	....	....	755.41	820.09	958.79	1,127.64	1,125.16
Direct Investment Abroad	79abd											215.38	228.35	226.64	274.34	270.57
Portfolio Investment	79acd											62.45	62.15	74.05	84.72	88.80
Equity Securities	79add											18.93	16.47	17.44	26.15	25.99
Debt Securities	79aed											43.52	45.68	56.60	58.57	62.81
Financial Derivatives	79ald															
Other Investment	79afd											306.17	405.03	514.67	645.46	660.74
Monetary Authorities	79agd											—	—	—	—	—
General Government	79ahd													74.68	79.63	84.97
Banks	79aid											203.87	293.51	404.58	434.51	445.63
Other Sectors	79ajd													35.41	131.33	130.14
Reserve Assets	79akd											171.41	124.56	143.44	123.11	105.04
Liabilities	79lad											500.84	583.37	725.08	872.28	993.04
Dir. Invest. in Rep. Economy	79lbd											83.05	113.38	130.43	153.32	172.38
Portfolio Investment	79lcd											175.54	184.05	269.23	302.36	349.22
Equity Securities	79ldd											64.57	64.63	88.32	109.56	104.85
Debt Securities	79led											110.97	119.42	180.91	192.80	244.37
Financial Derivatives	79lld															
Other investment	79lfd											242.25	285.94	325.42	416.61	471.44
Monetary Authorities	79lgd											47.00	50.20	31.27	36.78	40.80
General Government	79lhd													13.64	14.23	14.96
Banks	79lid											151.45	192.10	252.98	303.86	338.27
Other Sectors	79ljd													27.53	61.73	77.42

1985	1986	1987	1988	1989	1990	1991	1992	1993	1994	1995	1996	1997	1998	1999		
Billions of US Dollars															**International Transactions**	
218.82	227.16	254.12	322.43	363.81	393.59	421.73	448.16	464.77	512.63	584.74	625.07	688.70	682.14	702.10	Exports	70
352.46	382.30	424.44	459.54	492.92	516.99	508.36	553.92	603.44	689.22	770.85	822.02	899.02	944.35	1,059.43	Imports, c.i.f.	71
336.53	365.44	406.24	440.95	473.21	495.31	488.45	532.67	580.51	663.83	743.54	795.29	870.57	911.90	1,024.62	Imports, f.o.b.	71.v
1995=100																
46.3	47.7	52.4	62.1	68.3	73.2	77.8	82.6	85.2	92.1	100.0	106.3	118.9	121.6	126.8	Volume of Exports	72
56.2	63.1	65.3	67.5	70.2	71.4	70.2	75.9	83.2	93.4	100.0	105.6	118.4	132.3	147.2	Volume of Imports	73
80.7	81.5	82.9	ɪ88.8	91.1	ɪ91.9	92.7	92.8	93.2	ɪ95.2	100.0	100.6	99.0	95.9	94.7	Export Prices	76
81.3	78.6	84.3	ɪ88.4	91.0	ɪ94.0	94.0	94.7	94.1	ɪ95.7	100.0	101.0	98.5	92.6	93.4	Import Prices	76.x
Minus Sign Indicates Debit															Balance of Payments	
−124.47	−149.24	−162.64	−123.06	−98.90	−79.32	4.29	−50.61	−85.29	−121.69	−113.57	−129.29	−143.85	−220.56	−338.92	Current Account, n.i.e.	78ald
215.91	224.11	250.94	321.09	363.47	390.71	418.58	442.13	458.73	504.45	577.69	613.96	681.66	672.21	685.34	Goods: Exports f.o.b.	78aa d
−338.09	−368.75	−410.18	−447.70	−478.00	−498.95	−491.40	−536.45	−589.44	−668.59	−749.57	−803.33	−876.37	−917.18	−1,030.16	Goods: Imports f.o.b.	78ab d
−122.18	−144.64	−159.24	−126.61	−114.53	−108.25	−72.82	−94.32	−130.72	−164.14	−171.88	−189.37	−194.71	−244.97	−344.82	*Trade Balance*	78ac d
73.09	84.69	96.86	109.17	124.87	145.35	161.38	173.78	183.06	197.62	215.79	235.85	256.88	261.70	274.76	Services: Credit	78ad d
−72.03	−79.83	−90.37	−98.01	−101.85	−117.04	−118.04	−116.48	−122.29	−131.88	−141.45	−150.79	−166.91	−181.00	−197.49	Services: Debit	78ae d
−121.12	−139.78	−152.75	−115.45	−91.51	−79.93	−29.49	−37.02	−69.95	−98.40	−97.54	−104.32	−104.73	−164.28	−267.55	*Balance on Goods & Services*	78af d
93.73	97.27	108.43	137.00	161.57	172.08	149.56	132.52	134.62	165.97	212.23	224.62	258.66	258.32	273.88	Income: Credit	78ag d
−73.94	−81.92	−94.27	−118.46	−141.84	−143.65	−125.61	−110.24	−111.45	−150.06	−192.82	−207.41	−255.43	−270.53	−298.65	Income: Debit	78ah d
−101.33	−124.43	−138.60	−96.92	−71.78	−51.50	−5.54	−14.74	−46.77	−82.49	−78.13	−87.11	−101.50	−176.48	−292.33	*Balance on Gds, Serv. & Inc.*	78ai d
2.50	2.72	3.09	3.76	4.14	8.87	46.91	6.70	5.04	5.55	6.30	6.72	6.34	7.50	8.27	Current Transfers, n.i.e.: Credit	78aj d
−25.64	−27.53	−27.13	−29.90	−31.25	−36.69	−37.09	−42.57	−43.57	−44.74	−41.74	−48.91	−48.69	−51.57	−54.86	Current Transfers: Debit	78ak d
.16	.30	.36	.50	.43	−6.45	−4.29	.61	−.03	−.30	.50	.67	.12	.60	−.17	Capital Account, n.i.e.	78bc d
.16	.30	.36	.50	.49	.45	.44	.61	.49	.54	.80	.67	.30	.62	.52	Capital Account, n.i.e.: Credit	78ba d
—	—	—	—	−.06	−6.90	−4.73	—	−.52	−.84	−.30	—	−.18	−.02	−.69	Capital Account: Debit	78bb d
105.20	118.13	160.36	144.00	74.93	63.92	40.83	93.07	83.60	125.37	146.50	187.42	287.38	216.60	369.49	Financial Account, n.i.e.	78bj d
−14.06	−24.21	−35.28	−22.81	−43.72	−37.52	−38.23	−48.73	−84.41	−80.70	−99.48	−92.69	−109.95	−132.83	−152.16	Direct Investment Abroad	78bd d
20.01	35.76	58.85	58.16	68.65	48.95	23.70	20.98	52.55	47.44	59.64	88.98	109.26	193.37	282.51	Dir. Invest. in Rep. Econ., n.i.e.	78be c
−7.50	−4.27	−5.25	−7.98	−22.07	−28.77	−45.67	−49.17	−146.25	−60.31	−100.07	−115.86	−89.17	−102.82	−97.88	Portfolio Investment Assets	78bf d
−3.70	−1.15	2.13	−1.10	−17.21	−7.40	−30.66	−32.40	−63.38	−48.10	−50.42	−60.04	−41.97	−77.75	−97.77	Equity Securities	78bk d
−3.80	−3.12	−7.38	−6.88	−4.86	−21.36	−15.02	−16.77	−82.88	−12.21	−49.65	−55.82	−47.20	−25.06	−.11	Debt Securities	78bl d
76.04	85.78	66.93	73.85	95.70	22.02	57.54	71.98	110.98	139.40	237.48	367.72	383.96	266.83	335.31	Portfolio Investment Liab., n.i.e.	78bg d
4.33	17.90	15.03	−2.88	8.99	−15.95	10.42	−5.61	20.93	.89	16.56	11.13	66.76	43.81	94.26	Equity Securities	78bm d
71.71	67.88	51.90	76.73	86.71	37.97	47.12	77.59	90.05	138.51	220.91	356.59	317.20	223.02	241.05	Debt Securities	78bn d
....	....	....	....	....	....	....	....	....	....	....	....	....	....	—	Financial Derivatives Assets	78bw d
....	....	....	....	....	....	....	....	....	....	....	....	....	....	—	Financial Derivatives Liabilities	78bx d
−13.37	−83.77	−48.16	−72.15	−84.58	−13.13	13.41	19.12	31.03	−40.91	−121.38	−178.88	−265.16	−50.39	−131.28	Other Investment Assets	78bh d
....	....	....	....	....	....	....	....	....	....	....	....	....	....	....	Monetary Authorities	78bo d
−1.73	−2.02	1.01	2.97	1.23	2.32	2.92	−1.67	−.35	−.37	−.98	−.99	.07	−.43	−.36	General Government	78bp d
−5.33	−59.98	−42.12	−53.93	−58.16	12.38	−.61	21.18	30.62	−4.20	−75.11	−91.56	−144.82	−24.92	−61.43	Banks	78bq d
−6.31	−21.77	−7.05	−21.19	−27.65	−27.82	11.10	−.39	.77	−36.34	−45.29	−86.33	−120.40	−25.04	−69.49	Other Sectors	78br d
44.08	108.84	123.26	114.93	60.95	72.36	30.09	78.89	119.70	120.44	170.31	118.15	258.44	42.43	132.98	Other Investment Liab., n.i.e.	78bi d
−8.29	25.37	16.75	19.08	−18.06	24.50	29.34	30.31	68.00	9.60	46.72	56.88	−18.85	6.87	24.60	Monetary Authorities	78bs d
.85	2.20	−2.33	−.47	.16	1.87	1.37	2.19	1.31	1.56	−.11	−.32	−1.80	−3.11	−3.70	General Government	78bt d
40.42	77.92	90.46	63.43	56.76	−.44	2.51	32.79	39.90	108.00	64.18	22.18	171.31	29.26	82.66	Banks	78bu d
11.10	3.36	18.39	32.89	22.09	46.44	−3.13	13.60	10.49	1.28	59.52	39.40	107.78	9.41	29.42	Other Sectors	78bv d
22.94	30.50	−7.22	−17.53	48.82	24.09	−46.58	−46.99	3.10	−8.73	−23.68	−65.46	−142.63	10.09	−39.12	Net Errors and Omissions	78ca d
3.84	−.31	−9.15	3.92	25.29	2.23	−5.76	−3.93	1.38	−5.35	9.75	−6.67	1.01	6.73	−8.72	*Overall Balance*	78cb d
−3.84	.31	9.15	−3.92	−25.29	−2.23	5.76	3.93	−1.38	5.35	−9.75	6.67	−1.01	−6.73	8.72	Reserves and Related Items	79da d
−3.84	.31	9.15	−3.92	−25.29	−2.23	5.76	3.93	−1.38	5.35	−9.75	6.67	−1.01	−6.73	8.72	Reserve Assets	79db d
—	—	—	—	—	—	—	—	—	—	—	—	—	—	—	Use of Fund Credit and Loans	79dc d
....	....	....	....	....	....	....	....	....	....	....	....	....	....	—	Exceptional Financing	79de d
Billions of US Dollars															**International Investment Position**	
1,300.67	1,592.44	1,756.91	2,006.59	2,348.08	2,291.73	2,468.35	2,464.16	3,055.30	3,276.09	3,869.68	4,544.51	5,288.89	5,947.98	....	Assets	79aa d
386.35	530.07	590.25	692.46	832.46	731.76	827.54	798.63	1,027.55	1,067.80	1,307.16	1,526.24	1,784.49	2,140.53	....	Direct Investment Abroad	79ab d
119.40	158.12	188.59	232.85	314.29	342.31	455.75	515.04	853.53	948.67	1,169.64	1,467.99	1,739.40	1,968.96	....	Portfolio Investment	79ac d
44.38	72.40	94.70	128.66	197.35	197.60	278.98	314.23	543.86	627.46	776.81	1,002.93	1,201.00	1,407.13	....	Equity Securities	79ad d
75.02	85.72	93.89	104.19	116.95	144.72	176.77	200.82	309.67	321.21	392.83	465.06	538.40	561.83	....	Debt Securities	79ae d
—	—	—	—	—	—	—	—	—	—	—	—	—	—		Financial Derivatives	79al d
676.99	764.37	815.71	937.10	1,032.61	1,043.00	1,025.84	1,003.05	1,009.31	1,096.22	1,216.81	1,389.54	1,630.16	1,692.49	....	Other Investment	79af d
—	—	—	—	—	—	—	—	—	—	—	—	—	—		Monetary Authorities	79ag d
87.75	89.64	88.88	86.12	84.49	81.99	79.14	80.72	81.03	80.12	81.10	82.05	81.96	82.38	....	General Government	79ah d
447.36	507.34	549.46	653.23	713.82	695.69	690.40	668.02	686.25	693.12	768.15	857.51	985.81	1,013.89	....	Banks	79ai d
141.87	167.39	177.37	197.76	234.31	265.32	256.30	254.30	242.03	322.98	367.56	449.98	562.39	596.22	....	Other Sectors	79aj d
117.93	139.87	162.37	144.18	168.71	174.66	159.22	147.44	164.91	163.40	176.07	160.74	134.84	146.00	....	Reserve Assets	79ak d
1,205.82	1,493.87	1,708.18	1,997.90	2,397.23	2,458.58	2,731.45	2,918.79	3,235.68	3,450.39	4,292.28	5,092.01	6,355.15	7,485.45	....	Liabilities	79la d
220.00	272.97	316.20	391.53	534.73	539.60	669.14	696.18	768.40	757.85	1,005.73	1,229.12	1,642.36	2,194.10	....	Dir. Invest. in Rep. Economy	79lb d
455.76	601.20	659.88	768.48	939.28	929.27	1,057.84	1,158.68	1,335.53	1,413.55	1,870.64	2,364.70	2,919.78	3,442.95	....	Portfolio Investment	79lc d
136.79	183.17	189.01	213.81	276.10	243.79	298.96	328.99	373.52	397.72	527.62	656.75	919.52	1,185.89	....	Equity Securities	79ld d
318.97	418.03	470.87	554.67	663.18	685.48	758.88	829.69	962.01	1,015.83	1,343.02	1,707.95	2,000.26	2,257.06	....	Debt Securities	79le d
—	—	—	—	—	—	—	—	—	—	—	—	—	—		Financial Derivatives	79ll d
530.07	619.71	732.10	837.89	923.22	989.71	1,004.48	1,063.94	1,131.75	1,278.99	1,415.91	1,498.19	1,793.01	1,848.40	....	Other investment	79lf d
46.04	50.12	55.58	61.26	67.12	85.93	101.32	114.80	133.73	157.18	169.48	186.85	211.63	228.25	....	Monetary Authorities	79lg d
15.80	17.99	15.67	15.20	15.37	17.24	18.61	20.80	22.11	23.68	23.57	23.26	21.46	18.35	....	General Government	79lh d
381.23	460.89	550.67	616.88	673.63	673.13	675.64	707.67	746.87	858.31	922.44	941.35	1,106.36	1,141.01	....	Banks	79li d
86.99	90.70	110.19	144.55	167.09	213.41	208.91	220.67	229.04	239.82	300.42	346.73	453.56	460.79	....	Other Sectors	79lj d

United States

		1970	1971	1972	1973	1974	1975	1976	1977	1978	1979	1980	1981	1982	1983	1984
Government Finance															*Billions of US Dollars:*		
Deficit (-) or Surplus	80	−11.4	−24.8	−17.4	−8.0	−10.9	−75.4	−56.6	−51.1	−44.2	−27.9	−68.8	−76.1	−145.6	−200.8	−194.4
Total Revenue and Grants	81y	190.5	194.0	221.5	250.4	280.3	280.7	317.6	366.1	416.9	480.5	533.0	622.3	608.8	612.9	683.2
Revenue	81	190.5	194.0	221.5	250.4	280.3	280.7	317.6	366.1	416.9	480.5	533.0	622.3	608.8	612.9	683.2
Grants	81z	—	—	—	—	—	—	—	—	—	—	—	—	—	—	—
Exp. & Lending Minus Repay.	82z	201.9	218.8	238.9	258.4	291.2	356.1	374.2	417.2	461.1	508.5	601.8	698.4	754.4	813.7	877.6
Expenditure	82	....	....	....	....	....	....	....	....	....	....	....	....	....	....	....
Lending Minus Repayments	83	....	....	....	....	....	....	....	....	....	....	....	....	....	....	....
Total Financing	80h	11.4	24.8	17.4	8.0	10.9	75.4	56.6	51.0	44.2	27.9	68.8	76.1	145.6	200.8	194.4
Total Net Borrowing	84	12.9	26.5	18.1	12.6	4.2	79.3	53.6	51.4	45.9	33.7	75.5	74.4	155.1	194.1	201.8
Net Domestic	84a	....	....	....	....	....	....	....	....	....	....	....	....	....	....	....
Net Foreign	85a	....	....	....	....	....	....	....	....	....	....	....	....	....	....	....
Use of Cash Balances	87	−1.5	−1.7	−.8	−4.6	6.7	−3.9	3.0	−.4	−1.7	−5.8	−6.7	1.8	−9.5	6.6	−7.4
Total Debt by Residence	88	291.2	317.3	331.6	339.4	351.5	437.3	506.5	563.8	618.2	658.0	737.7	825.4	987.7	1,174.5	1,373.4
Domestic	88a	271.4	271.2	277.1	284.7	292.7	370.8	428.4	454.2	485.1	539.0	608.0	688.8	838.2	1,008.2	1,167.5
Foreign	89a	19.8	46.1	54.5	54.7	58.8	66.5	78.1	109.6	133.1	119.0	129.7	136.6	149.5	166.3	205.9
National Accounts															*Billions of US Dollars*		
Exports of Goods & Services	90c. c	57.0	59.3	66.2	91.8	124.3	136.3	148.9	158.8	186.1	228.7	278.9	302.8	282.6	277.0	303.1
Gov't Consumption & Investment	91ff c	237.1	251.0	270.1	287.9	322.4	361.1	384.5	415.3	455.6	503.5	569.7	631.4	684.4	735.9	800.8
of which: Gross Capital Form	93gf c	28.6	30.1	I 34.3	37.0	44.0	48.3	48.7	49.2	54.5	62.8	72.7	74.6	75.7	79.1	81.5
Priv. Gross Fixed Capital Form	93ee c	150.4	169.9	198.5	228.6	235.4	236.5	274.8	339.0	410.2	472.7	484.2	541.0	531.0	570.0	670.1
Increase/Decrease(-) in Stocks	93i. c	2.0	8.3	9.1	15.9	14.0	−6.3	17.1	22.3	25.8	18.0	−6.3	29.8	−14.9	−5.8	65.4
Private Consumption	96f. c	684.9	702.4	770.7	852.5	932.4	1,030.3	1,149.8	1,278.4	1,430.4	1,596.3	1,762.9	1,944.2	2,079.3	2,286.4	2,498.4
Imports of Goods & Services	98c. c	−55.8	−62.3	−74.2	−91.2	−127.5	−122.7	−151.1	−182.4	−212.3	−252.7	−293.8	−317.8	−303.2	−328.6	−405.1
Gross Domestic Product (GDP)	99b. c	1,039.7	1,128.6	1,240.4	1,385.5	1,501.0	1,635.2	1,823.9	2,031.4	2,295.9	2,566.4	2,795.6	3,131.3	3,259.2	3,534.9	3,932.7
Net Factor Inc/Pmts(-) Abroad	98.n c	6.4	7.7	8.7	12.7	15.7	13.3	17.2	20.7	22.1	32.9	35.3	34.7	36.5	36.9	35.3
Gross National Income (GNI)	99a. c	1,046.1	1,136.2	1,249.1	1,398.2	1,516.7	1,648.4	1,841.0	2,052.1	2,318.0	2,599.3	2,830.8	3,166.1	3,295.7	3,571.8	3,968.1
Net National Income	99e. c	936.7	1,017.0	1,117.8	1,254.9	1,351.5	1,457.0	1,631.6	1,820.1	2,056.1	2,298.3	2,484.8	2,770.2	2,858.1	3,114.6	3,484.6
GDP Volume 1996 Ref., Chained	99b. r	3,578.0	3,697.7	3,898.4	4,123.4	4,099.0	4,084.4	4,311.7	4,511.8	4,760.6	4,912.1	4,900.9	5,021.0	4,919.3	5,132.3	5,505.2
GDP Volume (1995=100)	99bv r	47.4	49.0	51.7	54.7	54.3	54.1	57.2	59.8	63.1	65.1	65.0	66.6	65.2	68.0	73.0
GDP Deflator (1995=100)	99bi r	29.6	31.1	32.4	34.3	37.3	40.8	43.1	45.9	49.2	53.3	58.1	63.6	67.5	70.2	72.8
																Millions:
Population	99z	205.05	207.66	209.90	211.91	213.85	215.97	218.04	220.24	222.59	225.06	227.76	229.94	232.17	234.30	236.37

Year Ending December 31

1985	1986	1987	1988	1989	1990	1991	1992	1993	1994	1995	1996	1997	1998	1999		
															Government Finance	
−215.6	−209.2	−166.6	−140.5	−155.0	−236.0	−265.6	−326.8	−226.5	−184.6	−146.2	−110.8	−2.4	54.4	158.3	Deficit (-) or Surplus	80
745.1	781.9	869.0	925.7	997.9	1,052.1	1,059.8	1,101.4	1,175.2	1,277.5	1,367.2	1,474.7	1,619.3	1,747.7	1,858.3	Total Revenue and Grants	81y
745.1	781.9	869.0	925.7	997.9	1,052.1	....	....	....	1,277.5	1,367.2	1,474.7	1,619.3	1,747.7	1,858.3	Revenue	81
—	—	—	—												Grants	81z
960.7	991.1	1,035.6	1,066.2	1,152.9	1,288.1	1,325.4	1,428.3	1,401.8	1,462.1	1,513.4	1,585.4	1,621.8	1,693.3	1,700.0	Exp. & Lending Minus Repay.	82z
....	....	....	....	....	....	....	....	....	....	....	....	....	....	....	Expenditure	82
															Lending Minus Repayments	83
215.6	209.2	166.6	140.5	155.0	236.0	265.6	326.8	226.5	184.6	146.2	110.8	2.4	−54.4	−158.3	Total Financing	80h
232.5	210.7	157.0	149.5	149.2	242.1	290.7	308.8	248.2	161.3	151.1	119.9	4.3	−62.2	−93.8	Total Net Borrowing	84
....	....	....	....	....	....	....	....	....	....	....	....	....	....	....	Net Domestic	84a
															Net Foreign	85a
−16.9	−1.5	9.6	−9.0	5.8	−6.1	−25.1	18.1	−21.7	23.3	−4.9	−9.1	−1.9	7.9	−64.4	Use of Cash Balances	87
1,598.5	1,813.3	1,953.9	2,096.9	2,245.8	2,565.1	2,860.3	3,149.8	3,403.8	3,551.7	3,698.7	3,842.1	3,866.5	3,805.7	3,711.9 [p]	Total Debt by Residence	88
1,373.7	1,549.9	1,654.2	1,734.7	1,819.7	2,078.0	2,339.4	2,573.1	2,753.5	2,884.4	2,863.5	2,740.0	2,624.9	2,527.0	2,443.2 [p]	Domestic	88a
224.8	263.4	299.7	362.2	426.1	487.1	520.9	576.7	650.3	667.3	835.2	1,102.1	1,241.6	1,278.7	1,268.7 [p]	Foreign	89a

Billions of US Dollars

1985	1986	1987	1988	1989	1990	1991	1992	1993	1994	1995	1996	1997	1998	1999		
															National Accounts	
303.0	320.3	365.6	446.9	509.0	557.2	601.6	636.8	658.0	725.1	818.6	874.2	968.0	966.3	998.3	Exports of Goods & Services	90c. c
878.3	942.3	997.9	1,036.9	1,100.2	1,181.4	1,235.5	1,270.5	1,293.0	1,327.9	1,372.0	1,421.9	1,481.0	1,529.7	1,630.1	Gov't Consumption & Investment	91ff c
95.2	109.4	161.3	149.3	172.8	183.8	194.7	200.1	202.5	205.9	213.5	219.3	230.8	238.0	257.4	of which: Gross Capital Form	93gf c
714.5	740.7	754.3	802.7	845.2	847.2	800.4	851.6	934.0	1,034.6	1,110.7	1,212.1	1,315.4	1,460.0	1,578.0	Priv. Gross Fixed Capital Form	93ee c
21.8	6.6	27.1	18.5	27.7	14.5	−.2	15.0	21.1	62.6	33.0	30.0	68.3	71.2	44.6	Increase/Decrease(-) in Stocks	93i. c
2,712.6	2,895.2	3,105.3	3,356.6	3,596.7	3,831.5	3,971.2	4,209.7	4,454.7	4,716.4	4,969.0	5,237.5	5,524.4	5,848.6	6,257.3	Private Consumption	96f. c
−417.2	−452.2	−507.9	−553.2	−589.7	−628.6	−622.3	−664.6	−718.5	−812.1	−902.8	−963.1	−1,056.3	−1,115.9	−1,252.2	Imports of Goods & Services	98c. c
4,213.0	4,452.9	4,742.5	5,108.3	5,489.1	5,803.2	5,986.2	6,318.9	6,642.3	7,054.3	7,400.5	7,813.2	8,300.8	8,759.9	9,256.1	Gross Domestic Product (GDP)	99b. c
25.3	15.5	13.7	18.4	20.4	29.0	24.7	23.5	24.3	16.8	20.4	18.1	4.2	−9.9	−20.0	Net Factor Inc/Pmts(-) Abroad	98.n c
4,238.4	4,468.3	4,756.2	5,126.8	5,509.4	5,832.2	6,010.9	6,342.3	6,666.7	7,071.1	7,420.9	7,831.2	8,305.0	8,750.0	9,236.2	Gross National Income (GNI)	99a. c
3,720.7	3,915.5	4,168.8	4,497.9	4,830.8	5,119.7	5,261.0	5,553.7	5,853.1	6,195.5	6,508.6	6,874.9	7,295.3	7,683.1	8,100.5	Net National Income	99e. c
5,717.1	5,912.4	6,113.3	6,368.4	6,591.8	6,707.9	6,676.4	6,880.0	7,062.6	7,347.7	7,543.8	7,813.2	8,144.8	8,495.7	8,848.2	GDP Volume 1996 Ref., Chained	99b. r
75.8	78.4	81.0	84.4	87.4	88.9	88.5	91.2	93.6	97.4	100.0	103.6	108.0	112.6	117.3	GDP Volume (1995=100)	99bv r
75.1	76.8	79.1	81.8	84.9	88.2	91.4	93.6	95.9	97.9	100.0	101.9	103.9	105.1	106.6	GDP Deflator (1995=100)	99bi r

Midyear Estimates

1985	1986	1987	1988	1989	1990	1991	1992	1993	1994	1995	1996	1997	1998	1999		
238.49	240.68	242.84	245.06	247.34	249.95	252.64	255.37	258.08	260.60	263.04	265.46	268.01	270.56	273.13	Population	99z

(See notes in the back of the book.)

Uruguay

		1970	1971	1972	1973	1974	1975	1976	1977	1978	1979	1980	1981	1982	1983	1984
Exchange Rates																*Pesos per Thousand SDRs through 1978*
Market Rate	aa	.2480	.2693	.7871	1.1195	2.0079	3.1608	4.6008	6.5594	9.1664	I.0111	.0128	.0135	.0370	.0450	.0725
												Pesos per Thousand US Dollars through 1978				
Market Rate	ae	.2480	.2480	.7250	.9280	1.6400	2.7000	3.9600	5.4000	7.0360	I.0084	.0100	.0116	.0335	.0430	.0740
Market Rate	rf	.2480	.2480	.5308	.8572	1.0983	2.2358ᵉ	3.3025	4.6467	6.0233	I.0078	.0091	.0108	.0139	.0344	.0559
													Index Numbers (1995=100):			
Market Rate	ahx	....	....	....	740,043.8	972,809.6	286,832.3	193,828.7	137,293.5	105,941.1	80,879.7	69,861.9	58,665.2	48,196.6	18,572.6	11,493.7
Nominal Effective Exchange Rate	nec	....	....	....	....	....	....	....	....	....	....	162.7	165.0	182.4	211.4	124.6	121.0
Real Effective Exchange Rate	rec	....	....	....	....	....	....	....	....	....	....	103.4	117.1	122.0	76.0	74.2
Fund Position															*Millions of SDRs:*		
Quota	2f. s	69	69	69	69	69	69	69	69	84	84	126	126	126	164	164
SDRs	1b. s	—	—	8	11	12	2	4	8	11	26	26	37	2	4	5
Reserve Position in the Fund	1c. s										17	16	27	28		9	
Total Fund Cred.&Loans Outstg.	2tl	18	17	37	32	64	100	125	98	—	—	—	—	87	227	227
International Liquidity													*Millions of US Dollars Unless Otherwise Indicated:*			
Total Reserves minus Gold	11. d	14	20	69	101	81	59	176	322	352	I323	384	430	116	207	134
SDRs	1b. d	—	—	8	13	15	2	4	10	15	34	33	43	2	4	5
Reserve Position in the Fund	1c. d									22	21	34	33		10	
Foreign Exchange	1d. d	14	20	61	88	66	57	172	312	316	I267	317	354	114	193	129
Gold (Million Fine Troy Ounces)	1ad	4.614	4.229	3.536	3.536	3.536	3.539	3.544	3.576	3.640	I3.310	3.422	3.392	2.858	2.602	2.618
Gold (National Valuation)	1and	....	161	135	149	152	319	319	435	562	I513	530	526	443	403	647
Monetary Authorities: Other Assets	3..d	5	5	61	20	19	8	10	19	74	....	....	....			
Monetary Authorities: Other Liab.	4..d	138	171	209	126	190	197	175	167	152	199	147	149	622	1,548	1,578
Banking Institutions: Assets	7a. d	15	12	18	21	25	77	126	160	268	366	376	633	737	635	584
Liabilities	7b. d	89	51	49	41	39	72	37	103	52	161	245	273	1,406	1,197	1,219
Monetary Authorities											*Pesos through 1971; Thousands of Pesos from 1972 to 1985;*					
Foreign Assets	11	43,276	46,051	I190	242	412	I469	1,004	1,815	2,503	4,031	5,454	6,609	I21,194	34,765	64,336
Claims on Central Government	12a	36,637	70,328	I116	172	351	I531	942	1,157	1,382	2,231	3,963	4,440	I12,496	31,917	88,011
Claims on Local Government	12b	4,908	6,062	I12	28	35	I29	25	47	89	32	50	174	I—	—	—
Claims on Nonfin.Pub.Enterprises	12c	—	—	I—	—	—	I—	—	—	—	—	—	—	I1,486	12,979	19,803
Claims on Private Sector	12d	34,043	61,844	I124	207	470	I12	16	22	29	33	32	30	I3,212	17,815	30,322
Claims on Banking Institutions	12e	7,100	18,679	I33	55	109	I575	745	910	1,058	1,543	1,637	2,142	I16,855	31,924	50,133
Reserve Money	14	78,799	121,247	I181	320	517	I613	1,186	1,727	3,180	4,508	7,040	8,222	I14,458	25,137	48,033
of which: Currency Outside Banks	14a	56,959	84,408	I121	202	316	I469	781	1,114	1,814	3,186	5,103	6,145	I7,879	8,405	12,106
Time, Savings,& Fgn.Currency Dep.	15	10,231	19,379	I33	69	107	I70	64	175	211	247	655	740	I2,392	1,193	3,152
Liabs. of Central Bank: Securities	16ac	—	—	I—	—	—	I—	—	—	—	—	—	—	I—	261	2,036
Foreign Liabilities	16c	35,314	43,338	I170	137	407	I807	1,436	1,426	917	1,445	1,171	1,370	I12,025	15,211	23,585
Long-Term Foreign Liabilities	16cl	3,320	3,541	I10	16	32	I28	86	120	155	232	297	354	I12,030	61,579	109,673
Central Government Deposits	16d	16,630	26,129	I48	101	189	I35	167	192	171	634	2,286	2,467	I2,588	13,767	63,418
Capital Accounts	17a	....	....	....	....	....	76	135	141	203	199	41	278	I8,368	4,182	17,200
Other Items (Net)	17r	−18,330	−10,670	I33	61	125	I−13	−342	170	224	605	−354	−37	I3,383	8,070	−14,492
Banking Institutions											*Pesos through 1971; Thousands of Pesos from 1972 to 1985;*					
Reserves	20	10,304	22,950	I58	69	134	I370	811	1,650	1,864	1,520	2,374	3,328	I10,896	30,233	39,805
Other Claims on Monetary Author.	20c			I—			I—							I—		
Foreign Assets	21	3,632	3,040	I13	19	40	I209	499	862	1,885	3,094	3,762	7,318	I24,701	27,301	43,203
Claims on Central Government	22a	2,949	5,467	I12	23	35	I260	379	585	722	533	1,141	1,933	I8,400	12,813	40,842
Claims on Local Government	22b	—	38	I—	—	—	I156	149	157	389	683	870	1,040	I917	1,065	1,756
Claims on Nonfin.Pub.Enterprises	22c	—	—	I—	—	—	I—	—	—	—	—	—	—	I4,183	2,666	5,395
Claims on Private Sector	22d	49,321	61,590	I128	207	372	I1,531	2,635	4,881	8,659	19,076	34,301	48,175	I88,827	83,847	112,894
Demand Deposits	24	17,399	29,423	I57	106	174	I489	785	1,052	1,718	3,351	4,734	4,385	I5,028	5,403	8,934
Time, Savings,& Fgn.Currency Dep.	25	31,616	42,519	I85	117	225	I733	1,816	3,809	7,540	14,631	26,697	43,662	I67,958	77,998	137,181
Money Market Instruments	26aa													I—		
Foreign Liabilities	26c	22,098	12,723	I36	38	64	I167	97	483	284	1,271	2,356	3,081	I19,727	21,739	50,235
Long-Term Foreign Liabilities	26cl	—	—	I—	—	—	I27	51	71	85	89	89	72	I27,387	29,716	39,950
Central Government Deposits	26d	—	—	I—	—	—	I134	199	300	470	799	1,327	1,045	I2,573	3,437	4,014
Credit from Monetary Authorities	26g	6,500	15,000	I34	53	98	I534	667	1,064	907	1,343	1,524	2,065	I7,887	10,873	16,215
Liab. to Nonbank Financial Insts	26j			I—			I—							I—		
Capital Accounts	27a	....	....	....	....	....	23	—	—	—	—	—	—	I10,880	11,174	15,358
Other Items (Net)	27r	−11,407	−6,580	I1	4	20	I419	858	1,356	2,515	3,422	5,721	7,483	I−3,516	−2,415	−27,991
Banking Survey											*Pesos through 1971; Thousands of Pesos from 1972 to 1985;*					
Foreign Assets (Net)	31n	−10,504	−6,970	I−3	86	−19	I−309	225	768	3,188	4,409	5,689	9,475	I14,144	25,116	33,720
Domestic Credit	32	111,228	178,370	I346	535	1,073	I2,403	3,835	6,374	10,619	21,155	36,744	52,280	I114,360	145,898	231,591
Claims on Central Govt. (Net)	32an	22,956	49,666	I81	94	197	I622	955	1,250	1,463	1,331	1,491	2,861	I15,735	27,526	61,421
Claims on Local Government	32b	4,908	5,270	I12	28	35	I185	174	204	478	715	920	1,214	I917	1,065	1,756
Claims on Nonfin.Pub.Enterprises	32c	—	—	I—	—	—	I—	—	—	—	—	—	—	I5,669	15,645	25,198
Claims on Private Sector	32d	83,364	123,434	I253	414	841	I1,596	2,706	4,920	8,678	19,109	34,333	48,205	I92,039	101,662	143,216
Money	34	74,358	113,831	I178	308	490	I834	1,380	1,938	3,588	6,160	9,082	9,838	I13,276	14,090	21,190
Quasi-Money	35	41,847	61,898	I118	186	332	I803	1,880	3,984	7,751	14,878	27,352	44,402	I70,350	79,191	140,333
Money Market Instruments	36aa			I—			I—							I—		
Liabs. of Central Bank: Securities	36ac	—	—	I—	—	—	I—	—	—	—	—	—	—	I—	261	2,036
Long-Term Foreign Liabilities	36cl	3,320	3,541	I10	16	32	I55	137	191	240	321	386	426	I39,417	91,295	149,623
Liabs. to Nonbank Financial Insts	36j			I—			I—							I—		
Capital Accounts	37a	....	....	....	....	....	99	135	141	203	199	41	278	I19,248	15,356	32,558
Other Items (Net)	37r	−18,801	−7,870	I37	112	201	I303	529	888	2,025	4,006	5,572	6,810	I−13,787	−29,179	−80,429
Money plus Quasi-Money	35l	116,205	175,729	I295	493	822	I1,637	3,260	5,922	11,339	21,038	36,434	54,240	I83,626	93,281	161,523

1985	1986	1987	1988	1989	1990	1991	1992	1993	1994	1995	1996	1997	1998	1999		
															Exchange Rates	
and per SDR thereafter: End of Period																
.1370	.2202	.3965	.6056	1.0566	2.2663	3.5589	4.7850	6.0656	8.1766	10.5704	12.5289	13.5465	15.2307	15.9417	Market Rate	aa
and per US Dollar thereafter: End of Period (ae) Period Average (rf)																
.1248	.1800	.2795	.4500	.8040	1.5930	2.4880	3.4800	4.4160	5.6010	7.1110	8.7130	10.0400	10.8170	11.6150	Market Rate	ae
.1012	.1514	.2255	.3585	.6212	1.1695	2.0177	3.0248	3.9411	5.0439	6.3490	7.9718	9.4418	10.4719	11.3393	Market Rate	rf
Period Averages																
6,375.9	4,219.0	2,846.2	1,796.3	1,062.6	560.7	318.4	211.0	161.1	126.1	100.0	79.6	67.1	60.4	55.8	Market Rate	ah x
109.4	79.7	63.6	62.2	79.0	93.4	76.8	72.9	91.8	119.7	100.0	82.6	74.5	69.8	69.4	Nominal Effective Exchange Rate	ne c
71.5	70.3	68.3	65.2	67.2	61.3	70.0	75.2	89.5	96.7	100.0	101.4	106.7	108.8	112.5	Real Effective Exchange Rate	re c
End of Period															**Fund Position**	
164	164	164	164	164	164	164	225	225	225	225	225	225	225	307	Quota	2f. s
13	10	48	22	17	8	3	—	—	—	2	3	—	1	1	SDRs	1b. s
							15	15	15	15	15	15	15	36	Reserve Position in the Fund	1c. s
319	323	277	230	153	71	40	38	28	20	14	6	—	114	114	Total Fund Cred.&Loans Outstg.	2tl
End of Period															**International Liquidity**	
174	482	530	532	501	524	336	509	758	969	1,150	1,251	1,556	2,073	2,080	Total Reserves minus Gold	1l. d
15	12	68	30	23	11	5	—	—	—	4	4	—	1	1	SDRs	1b. d
—	—	—	—	—	—	—	21	21	22	23	22	21	22	49	Reserve Position in the Fund	1c. d
160	470	462	502	478	512	331	488	737	946	1,124	1,225	1,536	2,051	2,030	Foreign Exchange	1d. d
2.619	2.605	2.609	2.609	2.609	2.395	2.263	2.028	1.700	1.704	1.715	1.736	1.760	1.783	1.800	Gold (Million Fine Troy Ounces)	1ad
648	678	817	970	855	737	640	541	454	497	525	672	651	517	518	Gold (National Valuation)	1an d
....	....	....	....	....	....	....	....	....	....	....	....	....	....	....	Monetary Authorities: Other Assets	3.. d
1,611	1,873	2,050	2,065	1,983	2,014	1,300	1,107	1,062	1,030	976	941	911	884	730	Monetary Authorities: Other Liab.	4.. d
667	776	947	1,280	1,895	2,470	3,184	3,797	3,790	3,499	3,479	4,179	4,758	5,015	5,803	Banking Institutions: Assets	7a. d
1,066	1,134	1,216	1,713	2,263	2,601	2,830	3,337	3,393	3,335	3,364	3,966	4,697	5,315	6,076	Liabilities	7b. d
Millions of Pesos Beginning 1986: End of Period															**Monetary Authorities**	
113,942	I 229	451	735	1,201	2,353	3,352	4,525	6,453	9,847	14,663	18,855	23,437	I 30,927	33,135	Foreign Assets	11
119,097	I 315	681	998	1,161	1,749	1,969	4,036	6,080	8,306	11,544	13,985	16,586	I 22,044	25,926	Claims on Central Government	12a
	I														Claims on Local Government	12b
36,478	I 89	144	289	549	1,165	1,806	2,538	2,568	3,227	3,985	4,694	5,335	I 5,253	4,998	Claims on Nonfin.Pub.Enterprises	12c
47,923	I 57	77	85	15	145	108	62	145	130	150	115	163	I 434	458	Claims on Private Sector	12d
81,124	I 123	219	269	479	1,048	1,610	2,372	3,272	4,071	5,386	6,770	8,928	I 10,258	10,803	Claims on Banking Institutions	12e
89,225	I 158	280	500	968	2,329	4,132	5,989	8,543	11,314	14,761	19,564	24,455	I 27,602	33,455	Reserve Money	14
23,309	I 43	76	125	219	420	851	1,426	2,313	3,314	4,327	5,269	6,498	I 7,084	7,639	*of which: Currency Outside Banks*	14a
2,561	I 8	16	37	83	241	311	408	716	997	2,083	3,927	4,873	I 6,299	7,247	Time, Savings,& Fgn.Currency Dep.	15
4,259	I 19	29	62	98	184	126	192	—	—	1,342	533	803	I 1,368	1,883	Liabs. of Central Bank: Securities	16ac
53,830	I 88	136	188	250	463	645	370	372	471	399	295	25	I 1,756	1,849	Foreign Liabilities	16c
190,829	I 321	547	880	1,506	2,906	2,732	3,664	4,486	5,465	6,691	7,980	9,122	I 9,549	8,454	Long-Term Foreign Liabilities	16cl
88,099	I 297	650	927	1,092	1,811	2,627	4,290	5,691	8,342	11,089	14,208	18,471	I 26,238	26,301	Central Government Deposits	16d
-61,295	I -130	-167	-320	-808	-1,898	-3,093	-3,490	-2,149	-2,491	683	363	-780	I 1,318	1,386	Capital Accounts	17a
31,056	I 54	80	101	217	425	1,365	2,109	858	1,483	-1,319	-2,451	-2,521	I -5,214	-5,254	Other Items (Net)	17r
Millions of Pesos Beginning 1986: End of Period															**Banking Institutions**	
76,370	I 165	268	518	1,043	2,534	3,583	4,873	6,439	7,651	9,420	12,932	15,781	I 17,772	21,389	Reserves	20
	I 10	11	18	35	60	40	182	—	593	525	397		I 911	1,735	Other Claims on Monetary Author.	20c
83,235	I 140	265	576	1,523	3,935	7,922	13,215	16,738	19,600	24,742	36,410	47,774	I 54,249	67,403	Foreign Assets	21
48,338	I 56	66	146	287	731	1,161	1,580	2,055	3,918	3,944	4,980	7,368	I 9,240	6,207	Claims on Central Government	22a
3,109	I 5	6	13	21	30	44	58	71	116	194	249	303	I 3,707	3,994	Claims on Local Government	22b
5,348	I 8	12	23	30	64	65	97	161	285	535	713	820	I 949	1,238	Claims on Nonfin.Pub.Enterprises	22c
216,717	I 359	538	1,043	1,890	3,382	5,660	9,801	14,556	20,896	32,242	43,728	58,466	I 107,288	118,105	Claims on Private Sector	22d
20,388	I 36	52	76	136	294	555	975	1,466	2,012	2,659	3,474	3,738	I 7,314	7,217	Demand Deposits	24
205,957	I 403	628	1,175	2,442	5,356	9,636	14,211	18,886	26,921	37,094	50,401	65,892	I 82,058	94,100	Time, Savings,& Fgn.Currency Dep.	25
	I												I 3,531	4,640	Money Market Instruments	26aa
67,106	I 83	137	259	557	1,145	2,166	3,881	5,569	6,192	9,127	13,370	19,378	I 53,737	66,428	Foreign Liabilities	26c
65,888	I 122	203	511	1,262	2,998	4,874	7,732	9,417	12,485	14,792	21,184	27,778	I 3,752	4,148	Long-Term Foreign Liabilities	26cl
9,399	I 17	55	96	147	382	553	1,014	1,093	1,570	1,845	2,655	4,523	I 7,538	4,803	Central Government Deposits	26d
22,049	I 37	46	101	123	274	391	660	996	818	1,042	1,476	2,073	I 10,135	10,162	Credit from Monetary Authorities	26g
	I											86	I 215	183	Liab. to Nonbank Financial Insts	26j
	I 37	65	117	235	558	848	1,614	2,414	3,250	5,631	8,054	10,034	I 45,520	49,476	Capital Accounts	27a
42,330	I 9	-20	—	-73	-271	-547	-282	180	-783	-519	-1,078	-2,591	I -19,685	-21,086	Other Items (Net)	27r
Millions of Pesos Beginning 1986: End of Period															**Banking Survey**	
76,241	I 198	443	864	1,918	4,679	8,462	13,488	17,249	22,784	29,879	41,600	51,807	I 29,683	32,261	Foreign Assets (Net)	31n
379,512	I 577	819	1,573	2,715	5,075	7,634	12,867	18,852	26,966	39,661	51,602	66,048	I 115,139	129,824	Domestic Credit	32
69,937	I 58	42	121	210	288	-49	312	1,351	2,312	2,555	2,102	961	I -2,492	1,030	Claims on Central Govt. (Net)	32an
3,109	I 5	6	13	21	30	44	58	71	116	194	249	303	I 3,707	3,995	Claims on Local Government	32b
41,826	I 97	155	311	579	1,229	1,871	2,634	2,729	3,512	4,520	5,407	6,155	I 6,202	6,236	Claims on Nonfin.Pub.Enterprises	32c
264,640	I 417	616	1,128	1,904	3,528	5,768	9,863	14,700	21,027	32,392	43,843	58,630	I 107,721	118,564	Claims on Private Sector	32d
44,152	I 81	130	204	365	717	1,408	2,410	3,805	5,341	7,066	8,819	10,295	I 14,420	14,874	Money	34
208,518	I 410	644	1,213	2,525	5,597	9,946	14,619	19,602	27,918	39,177	54,328	70,764	I 88,357	101,347	Quasi-Money	35
	I												I 3,531	4,640	Money Market Instruments	36aa
4,259	I 9	18	44	62	125	86	11	—	—	749	9	406	I 456	147	Liabs. of Central Bank: Securities	36ac
256,717	I 442	750	1,391	2,769	5,904	7,606	11,395	13,903	17,950	21,483	29,165	36,900	I 13,302	12,603	Long-Term Foreign Liabilities	36cl
	I											86	I 215	183	Liabs. to Nonbank Financial Insts	36j
-61,295	I -93	-102	-202	-574	-1,340	-2,245	-1,876	265	759	6,314	8,417	9,254	I 46,838	50,863	Capital Accounts	37a
3,402	I -75	-178	-213	-515	-1,248	-704	-204	-1,473	-2,219	-5,248	-7,536	-9,849	I -22,297	-22,572	Other Items (Net)	37r
252,670	I 492	773	1,417	2,890	6,314	11,354	17,030	23,407	33,259	46,243	63,147	81,059	I 102,777	116,221	Money plus Quasi-Money	35l

Uruguay

		1970	1971	1972	1973	1974	1975	1976	1977	1978	1979	1980	1981	1982	1983	1984
Money (National Definitions)												*Thousands of Pesos through 1985:*				
Reserve Money	19ma	....	....	170	314	447	726	1,302	1,832	3,211	5,468	7,873	8,221	10,695	15,673	26,003
M1	59ma	....	....	195	346	564	893	1,458	2,015	3,270	6,129	9,340	10,324	13,166	14,047	21,062
M2	59mb	....	....	278	496	842	1,402	2,375	3,355	6,488	13,190	24,220	30,625	34,132	40,946	60,725
Interest Rates												*Percent Per Annum*				
Discount Rate *(End of Period)*	60	....	....	....	....	....	....	....	....	....	....	....	72.10	83.70	112.70	133.20
Discount Rate (Fgn.Cur.)*(End Per)*	60.. f	....	....	....	....	....	....	....	....	....	....	....	....	....	19.90	24.70
Money Market Rate	60b	....	....	....	....	....	....	....	....	....	....	....	....	....	....	....
Treasury Bill Rate	60c	....	....	....	....	....	....	....	....	....	....	....	....	....	....	....
Treasury Bill Rate (Fgn.Currency)	60c. f	....	....	....	....	....	....	....	....	....	....	....	....	....	....	....
Savings Rate	60k	....	....	....	....	....	....	....	22.36	25.18	22.17	25.70	25.20	23.35	31.48	34.15
Savings Rate (Fgn.Currency)	60k. f	....	....	....	....	....	....	....	....	....	....	6.00	5.69	5.43	5.18	5.14
Deposit Rate	60l	....	....	....	....	....	....	....	30.20	35.62	47.61	42.01	50.06	46.09	50.13	71.40	68.39
Deposit Rate (Fgn.Currency)	60l. f	....	....	....	....	....	....	....	....	7.11	7.71	9.27	13.08	14.76	12.33	10.01	10.19
Lending Rate	60p	....	....	....	....	....	....	....	62.00	64.13	74.20	65.56	66.62	60.40	58.54	93.64	83.23
Lending Rate (Fgn.Currency)	60p. f	....	....	....	....	....	....	....	....	12.29	14.49	15.39	17.43	19.51	18.81	17.12	17.45
Prices, Production, Labor												*Index Numbers (1995=100):*				
Wholesale Prices (1995=1,000,000)	63.a	9.0	10.8	20.5	44.1	78.7	135.7	204.4	307.2	456.5	823.6	1,167.5	1,441.1	1,627.1	2,822.7	5,006.8
Wholesale Prices	63	....	....	....	....	....	....	....	....	....	....	....	....	....	....	....
Consumer Prices (1995=1,000,000)	64.a	6.2	7.7	13.6	26.9	47.6	86.3	130.0	205.7	297.4	496.1	811.0	1,087.2	1,293.6	1,930.1	2,997.5
Consumer Prices	64	....	....	....	....	....	....	....	....	....	....	....	....	....	....	....
Manufacturing Production	66ey	87	88	89	88	90	96	98	104	109	117	120	115	95	88	91
												Number in Thousands:				
Labor Force	67d	....	....	....	....	....	....	....	....	....	....	....	....	....	....	....
Employment	67e	....	....	....	....	....	....	....	....	....	....	....	....	....	....	....
Unemployment	67c	....	....	....	....	....	....	....	....	....	....	....	....	....	....	145
Unemployment Rate (%)	67r	....	....	....	....	....	....	....	....	....	....	....	....	....	....	....
International Transactions												*Millions of US Dollars*				
Exports	70..d	232.7	205.7	214.1	321.5	382.2	383.9	546.5	607.5	686.1	788.1	1,058.6	1,215.4	1,022.9	1,045.1	933.8
Imports, c.i.f.	71..d	230.9	228.9	211.6	284.8	486.7	556.5	587.2	729.9	757.3	1,206.3	1,680.3	1,641.1	1,110.0	787.5	776.7
Balance of Payments												*Millions of US Dollars:*				
Current Account, n.i.e.	78ald	....	....	....	....	....	....	....	....	−127.0	−357.1	−709.1	−461.4	−234.6	−62.6	−129.1
Goods: Exports f.o.b.	78aa d	....	....	....	....	....	....	....	....	686.1	788.1	1,058.5	1,229.7	1,256.4	1,156.4	924.6
Goods: Imports f.o.b.	78ab d	....	....	....	....	....	....	....	....	−709.8	−1,166.2	−1,668.2	−1,592.1	−1,038.4	−739.7	−732.2
Trade Balance	78ac d	....	....	....	....	....	....	....	....	−23.7	−378.1	−609.7	−362.4	218.0	416.7	192.4
Services: Credit	78ad d	....	....	....	....	....	....	....	....	226.8	406.1	467.5	471.0	280.9	278.2	364.8
Services: Debit	78ae d	....	....	....	....	....	....	....	....	−260.4	−337.3	−475.5	−547.1	−472.5	−334.7
Balance on Goods & Services	78af d	....	....	....	....	....	....	....	....	−57.3	−309.3	−617.7	−397.3	−48.2	222.4	222.5
Income: Credit	78ag d	....	....	....	....	....	....	....	....	18.4	54.2	67.7	145.8	147.2	62.5	87.2
Income: Debit	78ah d	....	....	....	....	....	....	....	....	−95.2	−109.1	−167.8	−219.6	−344.0	−358.5	−448.8
Balance on Gds, Serv. & Inc.	78ai d	....	....	....	....	....	....	....	....	−134.1	−364.2	−717.8	−471.1	−245.0	−73.6	−139.1
Current Transfers, n.i.e.: Credit	78aj d	....	....	....	....	....	....	....	....	8.8	9.2	11.2	12.5	13.4	14.1	13.0
Current Transfers: Debit	78ak d	....	....	....	....	....	....	....	....	−1.7	−2.1	−2.5	−2.8	−3.0	−3.1	−3.0
Capital Account, n.i.e.	78bc d	....	....	....	....	....	....	....	....	—	—	—	—	—	—	—
Capital Account, n.i.e.: Credit	78ba d	....	....	....	....	....	....	....	....	—	—	—	—	—	—	—
Capital Account: Debit	78bb d	....	....	....	....	....	....	....	....	—	—	—	—	—	—	—
Financial Account, n.i.e.	78bj d	....	....	....	....	....	....	....	....	97.1	453.0	715.0	648.4	1,082.0	249.7	164.7
Direct Investment Abroad	78bd d	....	....	....	....	....	....	....	....	—	—	—	—	−13.7	5.6	3.4
Dir. Invest. in Rep. Econ., n.i.e.	78be d	....	....	....	....	....	....	....	....	128.8	215.5	289.5	48.6	—	—	—
Portfolio Investment Assets	78bf d	....	....	....	....	....	....	....	....	—	—	—	—	—	—	—
Equity Securities	78bk d	....	....	....	....	....	....	....	....	—	—	—	—	—	—	—
Debt Securities	78bl d	....	....	....	....	....	....	....	....	—	—	—	—	—	—	—
Portfolio Investment Liab., n.i.e.	78bg d	....	....	....	....	....	....	....	....	−11.6	−35.7	−11.8	3.1	77.6	28.3	62.5
Equity Securities	78bm d	....	....	....	....	....	....	....	....	—	—	—	—	—	—	—
Debt Securities	78bn d	....	....	....	....	....	....	....	....	−11.6	−35.7	−11.8	3.1	77.6	28.3	62.5
Financial Derivatives Assets	78bw d	....	....	....	....	....	....	....	....	....	....	....	....	....	....	....
Financial Derivatives Liabilities	78bx d	....	....	....	....	....	....	....	....	....	....	....	....	....	....	....
Other Investment Assets	78bh d	....	....	....	....	....	....	....	....	−45.8	−99.2	−26.9	−389.1	54.6	98.0	38.1
Monetary Authorities	78bo d	....	....	....	....	....	....	....	....	—	—	—	—	—	—	—
General Government	78bp d	....	....	....	....	....	....	....	....	−6.7	−1.2	−7.0	−3.7	−4.2	−4.0	—
Banks	78bq d	....	....	....	....	....	....	....	....	−98.9	−98.0	−19.9	−385.4	58.8	102.0	38.1
Other Sectors	78br d	....	....	....	....	....	....	....	....	59.8	—	—	—	—	—	—
Other Investment Liab., n.i.e.	78bi d	....	....	....	....	....	....	....	....	25.7	372.4	464.2	985.8	963.5	117.8	60.7
Monetary Authorities	78bs d	....	....	....	....	....	....	....	....	−25.8	32.8	−31.6	23.0	403.3	339.5	15.2
General Government	78bt d	....	....	....	....	....	....	....	....	65.0	135.6	128.3	85.3	22.0	−9.3	29.7
Banks	78bu d	....	....	....	....	....	....	....	....	56.7	223.1	332.0	469.4	176.0	−131.8	−2.6
Other Sectors	78bv d	....	....	....	....	....	....	....	....	−70.2	−19.1	35.5	408.1	362.2	−80.6	18.4
Net Errors and Omissions	78ca d	....	....	....	....	....	....	....	....	160.8	−10.8	89.5	−161.5	−1,264.5	−252.5	−121.2
Overall Balance	78cb d	....	....	....	....	....	....	....	....	130.9	85.1	95.4	25.5	−417.1	−65.4	−85.6
Reserves and Related Items	79da d	....	....	....	....	....	....	....	....	−130.9	−85.1	−95.4	−25.5	417.1	65.4	85.6
Reserve Assets	79db d	....	....	....	....	....	....	....	....	−5.5	−85.1	−95.4	−25.5	322.6	−82.7	85.6
Use of Fund Credit and Loans	79dc d	....	....	....	....	....	....	....	....	−125.5	—	—	—	94.5	148.2	—
Exceptional Financing	79de d	....	....	....	....	....	....	....	....	—	—	—	—	—	—	—

Money (National Definitions)

Millions of Pesos Beginning 1986: End of Period

	1985	1986	1987	1988	1989	1990	1991	1992	1993	1994	1995	1996	1997	1998	1999	
Reserve Money	54,217	I91	172	292	341	651	1,175	2,055	2,892	4,594	5,928	7,650	9,571	12,910	9,879	19ma
M1	43,735	I79	127	207	363	739	1,460	2,453	4,399	6,226	8,273	10,713	12,577	14,501	15,001	59ma
M2	115,099	I193	306	512	846	1,604	3,099	4,942	7,598	10,031	14,352	17,991	21,392	24,763	26,095	59mb

Interest Rates

Percent Per Annum

	1985	1986	1987	1988	1989	1990	1991	1992	1993	1994	1995	1996	1997	1998	1999	
Discount Rate (End of Period)	145.10	138.40	143.40	154.50	219.60	251.60	219.00	162.40	164.30	182.30	178.70	160.30	95.50	73.70	66.39	60
Discount Rate (Fgn.Cur.)(End Per)	19.80	14.40	16.80	17.90	21.60	19.80	17.40	14.40	14.30	17.40	17.60	17.50	17.30	15.30	15.68	60.. f
Money Market Rate	....	....	....	....	....	....	....	....	....	39.82	36.81	28.47	23.43	20.48	13.96	60b
Treasury Bill Rate										44.60	39.40	29.20	23.18	....	....	60c
Treasury Bill Rate (Fgn.Currency)										4.91	6.11	5.36	5.18	....	....	60c. f
Savings Rate	34.30	32.03	27.83	27.62	27.62	31.01	30.05	24.52	17.18	16.12	15.98	15.00	11.50	7.15	5.40	60k
Savings Rate (Fgn.Currency)	4.68	4.11	3.89	3.91	4.08	3.97	2.98	1.89	1.65	1.54	1.80	1.73	1.71	1.51	1.13	60k. f
Deposit Rate	81.90	61.70	60.83	67.82	84.70	97.83	75.23	54.47	39.38	36.98	38.24	28.13	19.61	15.09	14.25	60l
Deposit Rate (Fgn.Currency)	8.68	6.15	5.61	6.00	6.93	6.53	4.92	3.42	3.09	3.45	4.56	4.84	4.85	4.92	4.99	60l. f
Lending Rate	94.58	94.73	95.80	101.52	127.58	174.45	152.88	117.77	97.33	95.08	99.10	91.52	71.55	57.93	53.28	60p
Lending Rate (Fgn.Currency)	16.43	14.37	12.22	12.67	14.14	14.04	12.24	11.80	11.17	11.68	13.83	13.14	12.67	12.42	12.63	60p. f

Prices, Production, Labor

Period Averages

	1985	1986	1987	1988	1989	1990	1991	1992	1993	1994	1995	1996	1997	1998	1999	
Wholesale Prices (1995=1,000,000)	8,840.7	14,778.8	24,122.3	37,977.8	65,771.4											63.a
Wholesale Prices					6.6	13.7	25.6	40.6	I54.1	72.6	100.0	125.0	145.5	159.0	157.6	63
Consumer Prices (1995=1,000,000)																64.a
Consumer Prices					4.4	9.3	18.7	31.5	48.6	70.3	100.0	128.3	153.8	170.4	180.0	64
Manufacturing Production	90	I100	110	109	98	106	107	109	99	103	100	104	110	113	....	66ey

Period Averages

	1985	1986	1987	1988	1989	1990	1991	1992	1993	1994	1995	1996	1997	1998	1999	
Labor Force							1,239	1,259	1,261					1,239	....	67d
Employment	....	1,021	1,091	1,103	1,134	1,136	1,128	1,146	1,156	1,188	1,206			1,114	....	67e
Unemployment	79	122	109	104	98	106	111	113	105	120	138			125	....	67c
Unemployment Rate (%)	....	10.7	9.1	8.6	8.0	8.5	9.0	9.0	8.3	9.2	10.2			10.1	....	67r

International Transactions

Millions of US Dollars

	1985	1986	1987	1988	1989	1990	1991	1992	1993	1994	1995	1996	1997	1998	1999	
Exports	909.0	1,087.8	1,189.2	1,404.5	1,598.8	1,692.9	1,604.7	1,702.5	1,645.3	1,913.4	2,106.0	2,397.2	2,725.7	2,768.7	2,232.2	70..d
Imports, c.i.f.	707.7	870.0	1,141.9	1,157.2	1,202.8	1,342.9	1,636.5	2,045.1	2,325.7	2,786.1	2,866.9	3,322.8	3,726.8	3,810.5	3,356.8	71..d

Balance of Payments

Minus Sign Indicates Debit

	1985	1986	1987	1988	1989	1990	1991	1992	1993	1994	1995	1996	1997	1998	1999	
Current Account, n.i.e.	−98.0	41.9	−140.7	22.1	133.5	185.9	42.4	−8.8	−243.8	−438.3	−212.5	−233.4	−287.4	−475.5	−605.0	78al d
Goods: Exports f.o.b.	853.6	1,087.8	1,182.3	1,404.5	1,599.0	1,692.9	1,604.7	1,801.4	1,731.6	1,917.6	2,147.6	2,448.5	2,793.1	2,829.3	2,304.5	78aa d
Goods: Imports f.o.b.	−675.4	−814.5	−1,079.9	−1,112.2	−1,136.2	−1,266.9	−1,543.7	−1,923.2	−2,118.3	−2,623.6	−2,710.6	−3,135.4	−3,497.5	−3,601.4	−3,172.9	78ab d
Trade Balance	178.2	273.3	102.4	292.3	462.8	426.0	61.0	−121.8	−386.7	−706.0	−563.0	−686.9	−704.4	−772.1	−868.4	78ac d
Services: Credit	403.5	422.1	406.9	348.3	433.3	465.6	596.2	830.3	1,028.4	1,330.7	1,359.2	1,398.7	1,424.1	1,319.1	1,281.5	78ad d
Services: Debit	−339.6	−387.1	−356.3	−315.4	−421.7	−392.5	−422.5	−558.8	−746.5	−861.6	−857.7	−839.0	−888.6	−883.6	−896.6	78ae d
Balance on Goods & Services	242.1	308.3	153.1	325.1	474.4	499.1	234.7	149.7	−104.8	−236.9	−61.5	−127.2	−168.9	−336.6	−483.5	78af d
Income: Credit	77.4	92.7	103.5	114.7	203.2	258.3	234.7	225.0	250.1	282.5	404.3	460.5	547.3	608.0	647.6	78ag d
Income: Debit	−428.3	−384.4	−405.3	−439.0	−552.1	−579.6	−467.1	−412.1	−442.5	−525.1	−631.3	−649.2	−740.0	−805.9	−839.1	78ah d
Balance on Gds, Serv. & Inc.	−108.8	16.6	−148.7	.8	125.5	177.8	2.3	−37.4	−297.2	−479.5	−288.5	−315.9	−361.6	−534.5	−675.0	78ai d
Current Transfers, n.i.e.: Credit	15.2	29.6	14.5	26.0	15.0	15.8	50.1	36.0	61.2	49.2	84.0	90.7	83.0	75.0	78.4	78aj d
Current Transfers: Debit	−4.4	−4.3	−6.5	−4.7	−7.0	−7.7	−10.0	−7.4	−7.8	−8.0	−8.0	−8.2	−8.8	−16.0	−8.4	78ak d
Capital Account, n.i.e.	—	—	—	—	—	—	—	—	—	—	—	—	—	....	....	78bc d
Capital Account, n.i.e.: Credit	—	—	—	—	—	—	—	—	—	—	—	—	—	....	....	78ba d
Capital Account: Debit	—	—	—	—	—	—	—	—	—	—	—	—	—	....	....	78bb d
Financial Account, n.i.e.	−74.6	18.4	293.4	201.4	−11.1	−89.7	−431.4	−91.5	228.0	537.2	421.7	233.6	608.7	125.7	478.4	78bj d
Direct Investment Abroad	−7.9	−4.5	4.9	−2.3	—	—	—	—	—	—	—	—	−13.2	−9.3	....	78bd d
Dir. Invest. in Rep. Econ., n.i.e.	—	37.0	50.1	46.8	—	—	—	—	101.5	154.5	156.6	136.8	126.4	164.1	228.8	78be d
Portfolio Investment Assets	—	—	—	−60.1	—	—	—	—	—	—	—	—	—	—	....	78bf d
Equity Securities	—	—	—	−24.9	—	—	—	—	—	—	—	—	—	—	....	78bk d
Debt Securities	—	—	—	−35.2	—	—	—	—	—	—	—	—	—	—	....	78bl d
Portfolio Investment Liab., n.i.e.	221.4	91.9	183.0	224.3	129.8	107.8	47.4	83.4	29.3	158.1	288.8	179.9	209.6	—	—	78bg d
Equity Securities	....	....	....	....	....	....	....	....	....	....	....	....	....	....	....	78bm d
Debt Securities	221.4	91.9	183.0	224.3	129.8	107.8	47.4	83.4	29.3	158.1	288.8	179.9	209.6	—	—	78bn d
Financial Derivatives Assets															....	78bw d
Financial Derivatives Liabilities															....	78bx d
Other Investment Assets	−126.2	−190.9	−245.7	−390.4	−764.3	−632.0	−399.0	−589.8	−19.3	−71.8	−961.9	−1,238.5	−626.6	−428.0	140.2	78bh d
Monetary Authorities	....	....	....	....	....	....	....	....	....	−10.1	....	....	....	....	....	78bo d
General Government	.1	—	−1.1	−.6	—	—	—	—	—	—	—	—	—	—	....	78bp d
Banks	−61.1	−105.1	−164.8	−290.1	−586.6	−441.5	−387.2	−589.8	−18.6	−44.0	−961.3	−1,232.4	−636.4	−428.0	140.2	78bq d
Other Sectors	−65.2	−85.8	−79.8	−99.7	−177.7	−190.5	−11.8	—	−.7	−17.7	−.6	−6.1	9.8	—	—	78br d
Other Investment Liab., n.i.e.	−161.9	84.9	301.1	383.1	623.4	434.5	−79.8	414.9	116.5	296.4	938.2	1,155.4	912.5	398.9	109.4	78bi d
Monetary Authorities	−20.9	7.0	2.6	−52.1	−81.4	−21.6	−281.4	−139.2	−23.7	5.7	−62.5	−10.3	−31.3	−242.2	42.7	78bs d
General Government	−2.3	37.0	11.6	−12.2	11.0	15.6	111.1	104.9	120.3	134.0	18.6	20.3	96.8	169.1	244.4	78bt d
Banks	−92.0	35.5	156.7	464.7	641.2	393.0	234.7	434.2	16.0	99.8	1,017.9	1,112.9	778.9	477.9	−121.7	78bu d
Other Sectors	−46.7	5.4	130.2	−17.3	52.6	47.5	−144.2	15.0	3.9	56.9	−35.8	32.5	68.1	−5.9	−56.0	78bv d
Net Errors and Omissions	238.7	221.3	−104.7	−247.0	−62.6	35.7	468.8	238.3	208.7	10.2	18.6	152.2	78.8	285.5	96.8	78ca d
Overall Balance	66.1	281.6	48.0	−23.5	59.8	131.9	79.8	138.0	192.9	109.1	227.8	152.4	400.1	−64.3	−29.8	78cb d
Reserves and Related Items	−66.1	−281.6	−48.0	23.5	−59.8	−131.9	−79.8	−138.0	−192.9	−109.1	−227.8	−152.4	−400.1	64.3	29.8	79da d
Reserve Assets	−164.0	−287.0	−26.9	46.8	3.2	−40.2	−113.5	−186.2	−178.6	−98.5	−218.0	−140.8	−391.7	−515.2	6.6	79db d
Use of Fund Credit and Loans	97.9	5.5	−61.1	−63.3	−98.0	−111.5	−41.3	−2.5	−14.4	−10.6	−9.8	−11.6	−8.3	160.1	—	79dc d
Exceptional Financing	—	—	40.0	40.0	35.0	19.8	75.0	50.7	—	—	—	—	....	419.4	23.2	79de d

Uruguay

		1970	1971	1972	1973	1974	1975	1976	1977	1978	1979	1980	1981	1982	1983	1984
International Investment Position																*Millions of US Dollars*
Assets	79aa d	....	....	....	....	....	....	....	....	....	....	....	....	....	....	....
Direct Investment Abroad	79ab d	....	....	....	....	....	....	....	....	....	....	....	....	....	24.0	22.3
Portfolio Investment	79ac d	....	....	....	....	....	....	....	....	....	....	....	....	....	....	....
Equity Securities	79ad d	....	....	....	....	....	....	....	....	....	....	....	—	....	....	—
Debt Securities	79ae d	....	....	....	....	....	....	....	....	....	....	....	....	....	....	....
Financial Derivatives	79al d	....	....	....	....	....	....	....	....	....	....	....	....	....	....	....
Other Investment	79af d	....	....	....	....	....	....	....	....	....	....	....	....	....	....	....
Monetary Authorities	79ag d	....	....	....	....	....	....	....	....	....	....	....	....	....	....	....
General Government	79ah d	....	....	....	....	....	....	....	....	....	....	....	....	....	....	....
Banks	79ai d	....	....	....	....	....	....	....	....	....	....	....	....	....	....	....
Other Sectors	79aj d	....	....	....	....	....	....	....	....	....	....	....	....	....	....	....
Reserve Assets	79ak d	....	....	....	....	....	....	....	....	....	....	1,157.1	1,177.2	767.9	940.0	1,007.8
Liabilities	79la d	....	....	....	....	....	....	....	....	....	....	....	....	....	....	....
Dir. Invest. in Rep. Economy	79lb d	....	....	....	....	....	....	....	....	....	....	....	....	....	....	....
Portfolio Investment	79lc d	....	....	....	....	....	....	....	....	....	....	....	....	312.7	322.1	383.1
Equity Securities	79ld d	....	....	....	....	....	....	....	....	....	....	....	—	—	—	—
Debt Securities	79le d	....	....	....	....	....	....	....	....	....	....	....	....	312.7	322.1	383.1
Financial Derivatives	79ll d	....	....	....	....	....	....	....	....	....	....	....	—	....	....	....
Other Investment	79lf d	....	....	....	....	....	....	....	....	....	....	....	2,896.6	3,942.2	4,249.8	4,274.6
Monetary Authorities	79lg d	....	....	....	....	....	....	....	....	....	....	....	162.2	672.7	1,176.8	1,177.5
General Government	79lh d	....	....	....	....	....	....	....	....	....	....	....	....	....	....	....
Banks	79li d	....	....	....	....	....	....	....	....	....	....	....	1,258.3	1,434.1	1,304.7	1,307.0
Other Sectors	79lj d	....	....	....	....	....	....	....	....	....	....	....	....	....	....	....
Government Finance												*Pesos through 1971; Thousands of Pesos from 1972 to 1985;*				
Deficit (-) or Surplus	80	−8,300	−42,200	‡−31	−31	−174	−359	−262	−264	−280	−1	30	−1,835	−11,654	−7,273	−15,308
Revenue	81	82,900	103,100	‡278	552	914	1,519	2,800	4,539	6,923	12,188	20,525	29,077	27,454	40,139	55,513
Expenditure	82	91,200	145,300	‡306	580	1,084	1,877	3,054	4,677	7,068	11,615	20,136	30,487	38,107	46,305	69,373
Lending Minus Repayments	83			‡3	3	4	1	8	126	135	574	359	425	1,001	1,107	1,448
Financing																
Net Borrowing	84	7,600	42,500	‡7	12	201	482	558	329	490	923	1,846	1,305	9,570	5,388	28,063
Domestic	84a			‡4	−5	104	220	349	246	423	512	1,030	289	8,402	5,588	21,767
Foreign	85a	....	....	‡3	17	97	262	209	83	67	411	816	1,016	1,168	−200	6,296
Use of Cash Balances	87			‡24	19	−27	−123	−296	−65	−210	−922	−1,876	530	2,084	1,885	−12,755
Debt: Domestic	88a			‡112	138	404	429	1,135	1,450	1,790	2,462	3,964	4,305	16,904	23,860	51,376
Foreign	89a	....	....	‡129	179	419	968	1,622	2,187	3,514	4,743	4,278	5,897	18,547	34,411	58,344
National Accounts												*Pesos through 1971; Thousands of Pesos from 1972 to 1985;*				
Exports of Goods & Services	90c	72,500	70,800	‡178	354	641	1,317	2,350	3,774	5,530	9,400	13,861	17,987	18,072	45,100	72,065
Government Consumption	91f	92,100	118,600	‡153	364	680	1,116	1,755	2,451	3,821	6,789	11,482	17,336	20,100	25,500	36,851
Gross Fixed Capital Formation	93e	68,500	82,800	‡121	229	465	1,090	1,952	3,030	4,943	9,312	15,422	19,205	19,382	24,000	29,600
Increase/Decrease(-) in Stocks	93i	1,000	8,400	‡26	93	60	12	−81	−2	8	663	572	−403	−827	1,000	3,200
Private Consumption	96f	448,000	522,000	‡938	1,844	3,463	6,244	9,107	15,018	22,919	43,441	69,890	91,147	94,076	121,300	187,300
Imports of Goods & Services	98c	−80,900	−80,100	‡−174	−323	−763	−1,613	−2,445	−4,356	−6,291	−11,980	−19,023	−22,819	−22,107	−41,400	−57,950
Gross Domestic Product (GDP)	99b	601,000	722,000	‡1,242	2,561	4,546	8,166	12,638	19,915	30,930	57,625	92,204	122,453	128,696	175,400	271,000
Net Factor Inc/Pmts(-) Abroad	98.n	−6,000	−6,000	‡−15	−22	−54	−168	−244	−317	−465	−454	−912	−797	−2,729	−9,950	−20,310
Gross National Income (GNI)	99a	595,000	716,000	‡1,227	2,539	4,492	7,998	12,394	19,598	30,465	57,171	91,292	121,656	125,967	165,460	250,720
GDP Volume 1978 Prices (Millions)	99b. p	26	26	25	26	26	28	29	29	31	33	35	35	32	30	....
GDP Volume 1983 Prices (Millions)	99b. p	....	....	....	....	....	....	....	....	....	....	....	....	....	175	174
GDP Volume (1995=100)	99bv p	58	58	57	57	59	63	65	66	69	74	78	78	80	72	67
GDP Deflator (1995=10 millions)	99bi p	84.5	101.4	177.1	363.9	626.2	1,062.6	1,581.5	2,463.2	3,634.4	6,377.7	9,627.3	12,547.4	....	....	....
GDP Deflator (1995=100)	99bi p	....	....	....	....	....	....	....	....	....	....	....	.1	.1	.2	.3
																Millions:
Population	99z	2.73	2.74	2.75	2.76	2.77	‡2.83	2.85	2.86	2.88	2.89	2.91	2.93	2.95	2.97	2.99

Millions of US Dollars

1985	1986	1987	1988	1989	1990	1991	1992	1993	1994	1995	1996	1997	1998	1999	Code	International Investment Position
…	…	…	…	…	4,441.8	4,729.1	5,271.3	5,519.6	6,235.9	7,348.5	8,718.0	9,556.8	10,664.4	…	79aa *d*	Assets
31.7	30.8	27.3	…	…	—	—	—	—	—	—	—	—	—	…	79ab *d*	Direct Investment Abroad
…	…	…	…	…	—	70.5	48.1	48.1	50.4	52.4	56.9	61.7	66.9	…	79ac *d*	Portfolio Investment
…	…	…	…	…										…	79ad *d*	Equity Securities
—	—	—	—	—	—	70.5	48.1	48.1	50.4	52.4	56.9	61.7	66.9	…	79ae *d*	Debt Securities
															79al *d*	Financial Derivatives
…	…	…	…	…	2,198.8	2,627.2	3,232.4	3,270.3	3,892.6	4,805.5	6,060.9	6,718.3	7,276.9	…	79af *d*	Other Investment
…	…	…	…	…	25.8	55.9	73.6	72.6	80.2	83.3	49.1	111.8	113.1	…	79ag *d*	Monetary Authorities
															79ah *d*	General Government
…	…	…	…	…	2,145.5	2,539.6	3,119.2	3,161.4	3,758.3	4,667.5	5,951.0	6,555.5	7,108.0	…	79ai *d*	Banks
…	…	…	…	…	27.5	31.7	39.6	36.3	54.1	54.7	60.8	51.0	55.8	…	79aj *d*	Other Sectors
1,219.1	1,673.1	1,893.9	1,707.9	1,615.3	2,243.0	2,031.4	1,990.8	2,201.2	2,292.9	2,490.6	2,600.2	2,776.8	3,320.6	…	79ak *d*	Reserve Assets
…	…	…	…	…	7,483.3	7,224.3	7,749.5	7,953.1	9,170.3	10,391.8	11,604.0	12,484.5	13,662.4	…	79la *d*	Liabilities
															79lb *d*	Dir. Invest. in Rep. Economy
610.2	702.1	885.1	…	…	1,341.4	1,388.9	1,472.4	1,512.6	1,668.6	1,954.9	2,136.7	2,187.3	2,606.7	…	79lc *d*	Portfolio Investment
															79ld *d*	Equity Securities
610.2	702.1	885.1	…	…	1,341.4	1,388.9	1,472.4	1,512.6	1,668.6	1,954.9	2,136.7	2,187.3	2,606.7	…	79le *d*	Debt Securities
															79ll *d*	Financial Derivatives
4,290.8	4,537.7	5,002.4	…	…	6,141.9	5,835.4	6,277.1	6,440.5	7,501.7	8,436.9	9,467.3	10,297.2	11,055.7	…	79lf *d*	Other Investment
1,292.9	1,355.7	1,398.3	…												79lg *d*	Monetary Authorities
															79lh *d*	General Government
1,216.0	1,296.0	1,454.9	…	…	2,893.7	3,157.9	3,607.1	3,644.8	4,150.3	5,182.4	6,275.2	7,152.8	7,628.9	…	79li *d*	Banks
…															79lj *d*	Other Sectors

Millions of Pesos Beginning 1986: Year Ending December 31

1985	1986	1987	1988	1989	1990	1991	1992	1993	1994	1995	1996	1997	1998	1999	Code	Government Finance
−11,651	†−6	−14	−46	−146	36	184	222	−304	−2,308	−1,467	−2,379	−2,435	−1,817	…	80	Deficit (-) or Surplus
109,323	†220	395	668	1,157	2,598	5,768	10,421	17,799	26,409	33,923	45,535	60,165	70,664	…	81	Revenue
118,413	†223	406	708	1,292	2,539	5,550	10,165	18,103	28,717	35,390	47,914	62,363	72,673	…	82	Expenditure
2,561	†4	3	5	11	23	34	34	—	—	—	—	237	−192	…	83	Lending Minus Repayments
																Financing
35,368	†26	375	46	146	−36	−184	−222	304	2,308	…	…	…	…	…	84	Net Borrowing
18,318	†15	334	−33	53	−187	−300	−451	322	1,378	…	…	…	…	…	84a	Domestic
17,050	†11	42	79	93	151	116	229	−18	930	…	…	…	…	…	85a	Foreign
−23,717	†−20	−361	—	—	—	—	—	—	—	…	…	…	…	…	87	Use of Cash Balances
75,227	†102	153	245	483	802	1,176	2,058	3,608	7,728	…	…	…	…	…	88a	Debt: Domestic
120,712	†176	330	626	1,231	2,634	4,384	7,137	9,328	13,893	…	…	…	…	…	89a	Foreign

Millions of Pesos Beginning 1986

1985	1986	1987	1988	1989	1990	1991	1992	1993	1994	1995	1996	1997	1998	1999	Code	National Accounts
128,100	†233	360	650	1,232	2,559	4,679	7,965	11,308	17,423	23,275	32,169	42,580	47,829	…	90c	Exports of Goods & Services
69,154	†128	220	359	647	1,362	2,731	4,478	7,199	10,363	14,506	20,952	25,748	29,899	…	91f	Government Consumption
46,100	†88	189	325	560	1,055	2,418	4,469	7,543	10,512	13,192	17,940	22,581	27,761	…	93e	Gross Fixed Capital Formation
8,400	†12	48	34	−14	18	318	300	401	811	1,628	1,332	1,479	6,673	…	93i	Increase/Decrease(-) in Stocks
327,970	†610	1,164	1,880	3,343	6,758	14,164	26,300	39,627	60,968	85,374	112,531	139,217	154,960	…	96f	Private Consumption
−101,050	†−181	−319	−522	−928	−1,968	−4,039	−7,645	−11,564	−17,965	−23,403	−32,475	−43,076	−48,977	…	98c	Imports of Goods & Services
478,600	†891	1,662	2,726	4,839	9,784	20,271	35,868	54,514	88,111	114,572	152,449	188,529	218,145	…	99b	Gross Domestic Product (GDP)
−35,630	†−44	−68	−113	−212	−377	−478	−583	−747	−1,258	−1,444	−1,506	−1,859	−2,067	…	98.n	Net Factor Inc/Pmts(-) Abroad
443,010	†846	1,593	2,613	4,628	9,407	19,793	35,285	53,766	80,853	113,128	150,943	186,669	216,078	…	99a	Gross National Income (GNI)
176	192	207	210	212	213	220	238	244	262	258	273	286	299	289	99b.*p*	GDP Volume 1978 Prices (Millions)
															99b.*p*	GDP Volume 1983 Prices (Millions)
68	74	80	81	82	82	85	92	95	101	100	105	111	116	112	99bv *p*	GDP Volume (1995=100)
	.6	1.0	1.7	3.0	5.2	10.8	21.6	34.5	51.0	70.9	100.0	126.4	151.3	166.0	99bi *p*	GDP Deflator (1995=10 millions)
														174.1	99bi *p*	GDP Deflator (1995=100)

Midyear Estimates

1985	1986	1987	1988	1989	1990	1991	1992	1993	1994	1995	1996	1997	1998	1999	Code	
3.01	3.03	3.04	3.06	3.09	3.11	3.13	3.15	3.17	3.20	3.22	3.24	3.27	3.29	3.31	99z	**Population**

(See notes in the back of the book.)

Vanuatu

		1970	1971	1972	1973	1974	1975	1976	1977	1978	1979	1980	1981	1982	1983	1984
Exchange Rates																*Vatu per SDR:*
Official Rate	aa	84.44	91.67	89.86	91.80	87.95	84.86	93.32	92.37	88.01	85.59	93.09	106.19	106.06	106.55	100.55
															Vatu per US Dollar:	
Official Rate	ae	84.44	84.44	82.76	76.10	71.83	72.49	80.32	76.04	67.56	64.97	72.99	91.23	96.15	101.77	102.58
Official Rate	rf	100.99	100.69	81.61	72.04	77.80	69.27	77.24	79.41	72.94	68.76	68.29	87.83	96.21	99.37	99.23
Fund Position																*Millions of SDRs:*
Quota	2f. s	....	....	....	....	....	....	....	....	....	....	....	6.90	6.90	9.00	9.00
SDRs	1b. s	....	....	....	....	....	....	....	....	....	....	....	—	—	.02	.09
Reserve Position in the Fund	1c. s	....	....	....	....	....	....	....	....	....	....	....	—	1.04	1.57	1.58
Total Fund Cred.&Loans Outstg.	2tl	....	....	....	....	....	....	....	....	....	....	....	—	—	—	—
International Liquidity														*Millions of US Dollars Unless Otherwise Indicated:*		
Total Reserves minus Gold	1l. d	....	....	....	....	....	....	....	....	....	....	....	8.46	5.67	6.59	8.09
SDRs	1b. d	....	....	....	....	....	....	....	....	....	....	....	—	—	.02	.09
Reserve Position in the Fund	1c. d	....	....	....	....	....	....	....	....	....	....	....	—	1.15	1.64	1.55
Foreign Exchange	1d. d	....	....	....	....	....	....	....	....	....	....	....	8.46	4.52	4.93	6.45
Monetary Authorities	1da d	....	....	....	....	....	....	....	....	....	....	....	7.13	4.27	4.75	6.20
Government	1db d	....	....	....	....	....	....	....	....	....	....	....	1.33	.25	.18	.25
Deposit Money Banks: Assets	7a. d	....	....	3.61	7.49	2.75	5.52	29.26	42.49	45.31	52.59	34.98	137.26	195.93	170.31	196.57
Liabilities	7b. d	....	....	....	....	....	....	6.31	8.02	5.06	7.11	5.80	117.09	146.14	111.74	114.17
Monetary Authorities																*Millions of Vatu:*
Foreign Assets	11	....	....	....	....	....	....	594	682	836	1,079	1,158	772	671	674	829
Claims on Central Government	12a	....	....	....	....	....	....	....	....	....	....	....	10	23	39	39
Claims on Nonfin.Pub.Enterprises	12c	....	....	....	....	....	....	....	....	....	....	....	....	....	....	....
Claims on Private Sector	12d	....	....	....	....	....	....	....	....	....	....	....	....	....	....	....
Claims on Deposit Money Banks	12e	....	....	....	....	....	....	....	....	....	....	....	49	194	183	167
of which: Fgn.Currency Claims	12ex	....	....	....	....	....	....	....	....	....	....	....	—	180	121	60
Reserve Money	14	....	....	....	....	....	....	567	670	776	965	849	642	678	796	981
of which: Currency Outside DMBs	14a	....	....	....	....	....	....	494	564	699	846	720	597	634	748	922
Liabs. of Central Bank: Securities	16ac	....	....	....	....	....	....	....	....	....	....	....	....	....	....	....
Foreign Liabilities	16c	....	....	....	....	....	....	....	....	....	....	....	1	46	23	12
Central Government Deposits	16d	....	....	....	....	....	....	26	9	62	104	309	122	152	21	30
Capital Accounts	17a	....	....	....	....	....	....	....	....	....	....	....	106	132	155	182
Valuation Adjustment	17rv	....	....	....	....	....	....	....	....	....	....	....	....	....	....	....
Other Items (Net)	17r	....	....	....	....	....	....	1	3	-2	10	—	-40	-120	-100	-170
Deposit Money Banks																*Millions of Vatu:*
Reserves	20	....	....	....	....	....	....	26	48	51	83	105	42	42	47	58
Other Claims on Monetary Author.	20c	....	....	....	....	....	....	....	....	....	....	....	....	....	....	....
Foreign Assets	21	....	....	....	....	....	....	2,350	3,231	3,061	3,417	2,553	12,523	18,838	17,332	20,164
Claims on Central Government	22a	....	....	....	....	....	....	305	272	225	121	102	103	85	67	194
Claims on Nonfin.Pub.Enterprises	22c	....	....	....	....	....	....	....	....	....	....	....	....	....	68	30
Claims on Private Sector	22d	....	....	....	....	....	....	2,123	2,169	2,747	2,480	2,646	3,135	3,252	3,492	3,497
Claims on Other Financial Insts	22f	....	....	....	....	....	....	....	....	....	....	....	1,310	714	30	482
Demand Deposits	24	....	....	....	....	....	....	1,135	1,206	1,189	1,248	1,162	851	1,110	1,525	2,104
Time, Savings,& Fgn.Currency Dep.	25	....	....	....	....	....	....	3,763	4,046	3,981	3,949	3,379	3,874	6,192	6,353	7,926
of which: Nonreporting Bks' Deps	25e	....	....	....	....	....	....	....	....	....	....	....	1,562	2,073	813	395
Foreign Liabilities	26c	....	....	....	....	....	....	507	610	342	462	423	10,682	14,052	11,372	11,712
Central Government Deposits	26d	....	....	....	....	....	....	53	286	594	686	347	1,314	840	780	1,465
Credit from Monetary Authorities	26g	....	....	....	....	....	....	....	....	....	....	....	—	246	202	176
Capital Accounts	27a	....	....	....	....	....	....	276	342	346	259	370	586	720	1,188	1,476
Other Items (Net)	27r	....	....	....	....	....	....	-930	-770	-368	-503	-275	-193	-227	-383	-434
Monetary Survey																*Millions of Vatu:*
Foreign Assets (Net)	31n	....	....	....	....	....	....	2,437	3,303	3,555	4,034	3,288	2,611	5,412	6,611	9,270
Domestic Credit	32	....	....	....	....	....	....	2,349	2,146	2,316	1,811	2,092	3,123	3,082	2,895	2,746
Claims on Central Govt. (Net)	32an	....	....	....	....	....	....	226	-23	-431	-669	-554	-1,322	-885	-695	-1,263
Claims on Nonfin.Pub.Enterprises	32c	....	....	....	....	....	....	....	....	....	....	....	....	....	68	30
Claims on Private Sector	32d	....	....	....	....	....	....	2,123	2,169	2,747	2,480	2,646	3,135	3,252	3,492	3,497
Claims on Other Financial Insts	32f	....	....	....	....	....	....	....	....	....	....	....	1,310	714	30	482
Money	34	....	....	....	....	....	....	1,629	1,770	1,888	2,094	1,882	1,451	1,746	2,274	3,027
Quasi-Money	35	....	....	....	....	....	....	3,763	4,046	3,981	3,949	3,379	3,874	6,192	6,353	7,926
Capital Accounts	37a	....	....	....	....	....	....	....	....	....	....	....	692	852	1,342	1,658
Other Items (Net)	37r	....	....	....	....	....	....	-606	-367	2	-198	119	-282	-295	-463	-595
Money plus Quasi-Money	35l	....	....	....	....	....	....	5,392	5,816	5,869	6,043	5,261	5,325	7,938	8,627	10,953
Other Banking Institutions																*Millions of Vatu:*
Cash	40	....	....	....	....	....	....	....	....	....	....	....	....	....	....	129
Foreign Assets	41	....	....	....	....	....	....	....	....	....	....	....	....	....	....	18
Claims on Central Government	42a	....	....	....	....	....	....	....	....	....	....	....	....	....	....	—
Claims on Private Sector	42d	....	....	....	....	....	....	....	....	....	....	....	....	....	....	530
Claims on Deposit Money Banks	42e	....	....	....	....	....	....	....	....	....	....	....	....	....	....	231
Time and Savings Deposits	45	....	....	....	....	....	....	....	....	....	....	....	....	....	....	228
Foreign Liabilities	46c	....	....	....	....	....	....	....	....	....	....	....	....	....	....	159
Capital Accounts	47a	....	....	....	....	....	....	....	....	....	....	....	....	....	....	298
Other Items (Net)	47r	....	....	....	....	....	....	....	....	....	....	....	....	....	....	223
Banking Survey																*Millions of Vatu:*
Foreign Assets (Net)	51n	....	....	....	....	....	....	....	....	....	....	....	....	....	....	9,129
Domestic Credit	52	....	....	....	....	....	....	....	....	....	....	....	....	....	....	2,794
Claims on Central Govt. (Net)	52an	....	....	....	....	....	....	....	....	....	....	....	....	....	....	-1,263
Claims on Nonfin.Pub.Enterprises	52c	....	....	....	....	....	....	....	....	....	....	....	....	....	....	30
Claims on Private Sector	52d	....	....	....	....	....	....	....	....	....	....	....	....	....	....	4,027
Liquid Liabilities	55l	....	....	....	....	....	....	....	....	....	....	....	....	....	....	11,053
Other Items (Net)	57r	....	....	....	....	....	....	....	....	....	....	....	....	....	....	871
Interest Rates																*Percent Per Annum:*
Money Market Rate	60b	....	....	....	....	....	....	....	....	....	....	....	....	....	....	....
Deposit Rate	60l	....	....	....	....	....	....	....	....	....	....	....	10.75	10.42	9.44	8.75
Lending Rate	60p	....	....	....	....	....	....	....	....	....	....	....	17.00	17.17	17.50	16.83
Government Bond Yield	61	....	....	....	....	....	....	....	....	....	....	....	....	....	....	....
Prices																*Index Numbers (1995=100):*
Consumer Prices	64	....	....	....	....	....	....	29.2	30.9	32.9	34.2	38.1	48.3	51.5	52.4	55.2

1985	1986	1987	1988	1989	1990	1991	1992	1993	1994	1995	1996	1997	1998	1999	
End of Period															**Exchange Rates**
110.12	142.18	142.00	141.37	145.48	155.43	158.48	163.63	165.93	163.62	169.07	159.28	167.73	182.73	176.90	Official Rate ... aa
End of Period (ae) Period Average (rf)															
100.25	116.24	100.56	105.05	110.70	109.25	110.79	119.00	120.80	112.08	113.74	110.77	124.31	129.78	128.89	Official Rate ... ae
106.03	106.08	109.85	104.43	116.04	117.06	111.68	113.39	121.58	116.41	112.11	111.72	115.87	127.52	129.08	Official Rate ... rf
End of Period															**Fund Position**
9.00	9.00	9.00	9.00	9.00	9.00	9.00	9.00	12.50	12.50	12.50	12.50	12.50	12.50	17.00	Quota ... 2f. s
.15	.20	.26	.31	.40	.50	.59	.68	.15	.22	.29	.36	.44	.53	.60	SDRs ... 1b. s
1.58	1.59	1.59	1.60	1.61	1.61	1.61	1.61	2.49	2.49	2.49	2.49	2.50	2.50	2.50	Reserve Position in the Fund ... 1c. s
—	—	—	—	—	—	—	—	—	—	—	—	—	—	—	Total Fund Cred.&Loans Outstg. ... 2tl
End of Period															**International Liquidity**
10.61	21.42	40.17	40.67	35.08	37.69	39.84	42.46	45.59	43.58	48.29	43.92	37.30	44.67	41.35	Total Reserves minus Gold ... 1l. d
.16	.24	.37	.42	.53	.71	.84	.94	.21	.31	.43	.52	.60	.74	.83	SDRs ... 1b. d
1.74	1.94	2.26	2.15	2.12	2.29	2.30	2.21	3.42	3.63	3.70	3.58	3.37	3.51	3.43	Reserve Position in the Fund ... 1c. d
8.71	19.23	37.55	38.10	32.44	34.69	36.69	39.31	41.96	39.63	44.16	39.82	33.34	40.41	37.10	Foreign Exchange ... 1d. d
8.48	18.89	36.93	37.54	31.91	34.25	35.97	39.00	41.95	39.62	44.16	39.82	33.34	40.41	37.10	Monetary Authorities ... 1da d
.23	.34[e]	.62	.56	.53	.44	.72	.31	.01	.01	—	—	—	—	—	Government ... 1db d
288.38	274.75	284.51	139.14	209.94	235.09	183.03	150.93	157.83	158.73	183.94	205.28	204.83	189.99	164.26	Deposit Money Banks: Assets ... 7a. d
190.45	177.57	190.14	38.75	51.98	64.10	22.54	20.07	29.48	26.54	32.05	28.42	47.97	25.01	33.92	Liabilities ... 7b. d
End of Period															**Monetary Authorities**
1,063	2,496	4,040	4,272	4,012	4,120	4,413	4,978	5,519	4,883	5,491	4,865	4,638	5,796	5,331	Foreign Assets ... 11
12	—	—	—	—	—	—	—	—	307	420	408	898	1,221	1,401	Claims on Central Government ... 12a
....	....	....	....	....	....	....	....	....	310	327	353	260	36	32	Claims on Nonfin.Pub.Enterprises ... 12c
—	—	44	81	88	81	78	63	73	76	95	108	124	130	148	Claims on Private Sector ... 12d
395	363	—	4	2	8	8	—	4	1	3	98	257	—	316	Claims on Deposit Money Banks ... 12e
395	363	—	4	2	8	8	—	4	1	3	2	1	—	—	*of which: Fgn.Currency Claims* ... 12ex
1,228	1,371	1,233	1,380	1,823	1,570	2,008	1,956	3,005	2,801	3,654	3,500	3,493	3,674	4,493	Reserve Money ... 14
963	906	1,000	954	1,037	934	1,148	901	1,224	1,351	1,566	1,571	1,662	2,042	1,936	*of which: Currency Outside DMBs* ... 14a
—	—	—	—	—	—	—	—	—	—	—	—	—	1,233	297	Liabs. of Central Bank: Securities ... 16ac
24	35	5	25	4	45	42	1	21	25	5	18	4	17	23	Foreign Liabilities ... 16c
32	795	2,199	2,286	1,737	1,633	2,039	2,594	2,315	2,102	1,962	1,739	2,104	1,679	1,902	Central Government Deposits ... 16d
253	359	508	624	538	814	589	780	748	740	641	654	672	686	698	Capital Accounts ... 17a
18	436	409	364	295	584	330	319	248	134	236	87	64	61	49	Valuation Adjustment ... 17rv
-85	-137	-270	-322	-297	-437	-509	-610	-741	I -224	-162	-166	-161	-169	-233	Other Items (Net) ... 17r
End of Period															**Deposit Money Banks**
236	357	276	349	826	546	972	1,070	1,821	1,397	2,033	1,829	1,742	1,238	2,215	Reserves ... 20
—	—	—	—	—	—	—	—	—	—	—	—	—	1,001	297	Other Claims on Monetary Author. ... 20c
28,910	31,937	28,611	14,617	23,241	25,684	20,278	17,960	19,065	17,790	20,921	22,738	25,462	24,657	21,171	Foreign Assets ... 21
187	210	384	553	591	583	560	833	937	527	506	492	496	1,131	930	Claims on Central Government ... 22a
32	90	82	19	27	15	11	20	6	105	62	30	134	108	53	Claims on Nonfin.Pub.Enterprises ... 22c
3,287	3,485	4,079	4,365	4,799	5,966	6,226	7,914	7,944	8,540	9,075	9,796	9,580	10,605	12,158	Claims on Private Sector ... 22d
324	348	—	2	3	3	4	6	100	38	21	—	2	—	—	Claims on Other Financial Insts ... 22f
1,679	1,904	3,219	2,441	3,270	2,918	3,209	4,119	4,448	4,339	4,690	4,880	4,941	5,368	5,296	Demand Deposits ... 24
9,749	12,828	10,386	11,953	18,460	20,203	19,560	18,248	18,778	19,443	22,225	24,879	24,645	27,626	24,377	Time, Savings,& Fgn.Currency Dep. ... 25
1,260	3,140	1,676	3,469	6,650	6,099	1,683	1,487	80	—	—	—	—	—	—	*of which:* Nonreporting Bks' Deps ... 25e
19,093	20,641	19,121	4,070	5,754	7,003	2,497	2,388	3,561	2,975	3,645	3,148	5,963	3,246	4,372	Foreign Liabilities ... 26c
1,544	276	359	322	394	396	629	376	709	296	161	10	52	140	141	Central Government Deposits ... 26d
398	364	—	4	2	8	1	—	3	1	3	1	3	—	316	Credit from Monetary Authorities ... 26g
1,188	1,354	1,130	1,449	2,083	1,034	2,557	3,124	2,297	1,726	1,698	2,142	1,350	2,468	2,734	Capital Accounts ... 27a
-676	-939	-784	-335	-475	1,234	-402	-452	76	-381	197	-176	460	-108	-413	Other Items (Net) ... 27r
End of Period															**Monetary Survey**
10,856	13,757	13,525	14,794	21,494	22,755	22,152	20,549	21,003	19,674	22,763	24,438	24,132	27,189	22,107	Foreign Assets (Net) ... 31n
2,265	3,062	2,030	2,412	3,377	4,619	4,211	5,865	6,036	I 7,514	8,383	9,437	9,337	11,412	12,679	Domestic Credit ... 32
-1,377	-861	-2,175	-2,055	-1,541	-1,446	-2,108	-2,137	-2,087	-1,564	-1,197	-849	-762	533	288	Claims on Central Govt. (Net) ... 32an
32	90	82	19	27	15	11	20	6	I 416	389	382	394	144	85	Claims on Nonfin.Pub.Enterprises ... 32c
3,287	3,485	4,122	4,446	4,887	6,047	6,304	7,976	8,017	8,616	9,170	9,904	9,703	10,735	12,306	Claims on Private Sector ... 32d
324	348	—	2	3	3	4	6	100	I 46	21	—	2	—	—	Claims on Other Financial Insts ... 32f
2,643	2,811	4,219	3,516	4,369	3,894	4,377	5,056	5,679	5,728	6,306	6,528	6,642	7,600	7,616	Money ... 34
9,749	12,828	10,386	11,953	18,460	20,203	19,560	18,248	18,778	19,443	22,225	24,879	24,645	27,626	24,377	Quasi-Money ... 35
1,441	1,713	1,638	2,073	2,621	1,848	3,146	3,904	3,045	2,466	2,339	2,797	2,022	3,155	3,432	Capital Accounts ... 37a
-712	-533	-689	-336	-578	1,429	-719	-793	-463	I -449	275	-329	159	221	-639	Other Items (Net) ... 37r
12,392	15,639	14,606	15,469	22,829	24,097	23,936	23,303	24,457	25,171	28,531	31,407	31,287	35,226	31,994	Money plus Quasi-Money ... 35l
End of Period															**Other Banking Institutions**
97	187	125	61	69	76	111	30	43	15	5	572	36	....	....	Cash ... 40
23	24	145	147	—	—	56	41	42	45	51	—	—	....	....	Foreign Assets ... 41
—	30	210	245	245	250	358	50	60	10	10	10	10	....	....	Claims on Central Government ... 42a
545	562	510	611	606	612	495	507	608	598	691	40	548	....	....	Claims on Private Sector ... 42d
278	292	25	9	17	129	87	—	—	—	—	—	—	....	....	Claims on Deposit Money Banks ... 42e
294	315	341	370	395	403	445	—	—	—	—	—	—	....	....	Time and Savings Deposits ... 45
230	291	323	188	362	430	296	238	183	625	495	492	491	....	....	Foreign Liabilities ... 46c
259	390	384	517	356	266	503	450	450	450	535	535	535	....	....	Capital Accounts ... 47a
161	99	-33	-2	-176	-32	-137	-60	120	-407	-273	-405	-432	....	....	Other Items (Net) ... 47r
End of Period															**Banking Survey**
10,649	13,490	13,346	14,752	21,133	22,325	21,912	20,352	20,862	19,094	22,318	23,946	23,641	....	....	Foreign Assets (Net) ... 51n
2,487	3,306	2,750	3,266	4,224	5,478	5,060	6,417	6,604	I 8,076	9,063	9,487	9,893	....	....	Domestic Credit ... 52
-1,377	-831	-1,965	-1,810	-1,296	-1,196	-1,750	-2,087	-2,027	-1,554	-1,187	-839	-752	....	....	Claims on Central Govt. (Net) ... 52an
32	90	82	19	27	15	11	20	6	I 416	389	382	394	....	....	Claims on Nonfin.Pub.Enterprises ... 52c
3,832	4,047	4,632	5,057	5,492	6,659	6,798	8,484	8,625	9,214	9,861	9,944	10,251	....	....	Claims on Private Sector ... 52d
12,589	15,767	14,822	15,778	23,155	24,424	24,271	23,273	24,414	25,156	28,526	30,835	31,251	....	....	Liquid Liabilities ... 55l
546	1,028	1,274	2,241	2,202	3,379	2,702	3,495	3,052	I 2,014	2,855	2,597	2,283	....	....	Other Items (Net) ... 57r
Percent Per Annum															**Interest Rates**
7.00	6.96	6.50	7.50	7.08	7.00	7.00	5.92	6.00	6.00	6.00	6.00	6.00	8.65	6.99	Money Market Rate ... 60b
7.34	6.81	5.48	6.94	6.58	7.00	7.00	4.69	5.00	5.06	3.00	4.50	3.73	3.29	1.60	Deposit Rate ... 60l
15.75	16.00	15.42	17.04	17.00	17.33	18.00	16.25	16.00	16.00	10.50	10.50	10.50	10.96	10.29	Lending Rate ... 60p
9.50	9.50	9.50	9.50	I 8.00	8.00	8.00	8.00	8.00	8.00	8.00	8.00	8.00	8.00	8.00	Government Bond Yield ... 61
Period Averages															**Prices**
55.8	I 58.5	67.9	73.8	79.5	83.3	88.7	92.3	95.6	97.8	100.0	100.9	103.8	107.2	....	Consumer Prices ... 64

Vanuatu

	1970	1971	1972	1973	1974	1975	1976	1977	1978	1979	1980	1981	1982	1983	1984
International Transactions															*Millions of Vatu*
Exports 70	1,162	1,285	1,206	1,498	2,380	800	1,309	2,536	2,682	2,851	2,449	2,833	2,201	2,941	4,395
Imports, c.i.f. 71	1,311	1,844	2,373	2,552	3,860	2,754	2,628	3,146	3,739	4,232	4,993	5,116	5,819	6,356	6,881
Balance of Payments															*Millions of US Dollars:*
Current Account, n.i.e. .... 78al d	....	....	....	....	....	....	....	....	....	....	....	....	−7.66	−8.29	3.12
Goods: Exports f.o.b. .... 78aa d	....	....	....	....	....	....	....	....	....	....	....	....	10.67	17.92	32.54
Goods: Imports f.o.b. .... 78ab d	....	....	....	....	....	....	....	....	....	....	....	....	−43.27	−45.82	−51.48
Trade Balance........................ 78ac d	....	....	....	....	....	....	....	....	....	....	....	....	−32.60	−27.90	−18.94
Services: Credit .... 78ad d	....	....	....	....	....	....	....	....	....	....	....	....	36.99	38.11	42.43
Services: Debit .... 78ae d	....	....	....	....	....	....	....	....	....	....	....	....	−14.35	−16.82	−20.07
Balance on Goods & Services .... 78af d	....	....	....	....	....	....	....	....	....	....	....	....	−9.96	−6.60	3.42
Income: Credit .... 78ag d	....	....	....	....	....	....	....	....	....	....	....	....	5.59	6.50	8.78
Income: Debit .... 78ah d	....	....	....	....	....	....	....	....	....	....	....	....	−26.70	−23.71	−27.90
Balance on Gds, Serv. & Inc. .... 78ai d	....	....	....	....	....	....	....	....	....	....	....	....	−31.07	−23.81	−15.70
Current Transfers, n.i.e.: Credit ... 78aj d	....	....	....	....	....	....	....	....	....	....	....	....	24.78	17.17	20.84
Current Transfers: Debit .... 78ak d	....	....	....	....	....	....	....	....	....	....	....	....	−1.37	−1.65	−2.02
Capital Account, n.i.e. .... 78bc d	....	....	....	....	....	....	....	....	....	....	....	....	19.50	16.66	16.10
Capital Account, n.i.e.: Credit .... 78ba d	....	....	....	....	....	....	....	....	....	....	....	....	19.96	17.11	16.57
Capital Account: Debit .... 78bb d	....	....	....	....	....	....	....	....	....	....	....	....	−.46	−.45	−.47
Financial Account, n.i.e. .... 78bj d	....	....	....	....	....	....	....	....	....	....	....	....	−15.29	−11.18	−27.51
Direct Investment Abroad .... 78bd d	....	....	....	....	....	....	....	....	....	....	....	....	—	—	—
Dir. Invest. in Rep. Econ., n.i.e. ... 78be d	....	....	....	....	....	....	....	....	....	....	....	....	6.93	5.87	7.44
Portfolio Investment Assets .... 78bf d	....	....	....	....	....	....	....	....	....	....	....	....	—	—	—
Equity Securities...................... 78bk d	....	....	....	....	....	....	....	....	....	....	....	....	—	—	—
Debt Securities....................... 78bl d	....	....	....	....	....	....	....	....	....	....	....	....	—	—	—
Portfolio Investment Liab., n.i.e. ... 78bg d	....	....	....	....	....	....	....	....	....	....	....	....	—	—	—
Equity Securities...................... 78bm d	....	....	....	....	....	....	....	....	....	....	....	....	—	—	—
Debt Securities....................... 78bn d	....	....	....	....	....	....	....	....	....	....	....	....	—	—	—
Financial Derivatives Assets .... 78bw d	....	....	....	....	....	....	....	....	....	....	....	....			
Financial Derivatives Liabilities ...... 78bx d	....	....	....	....	....	....	....	....	....	....	....	....			
Other Investment Assets .... 78bh d	....	....	....	....	....	....	....	....	....	....	....	....	−60.81	22.19	−35.57
Monetary Authorities .... 78bo d	....	....	....	....	....	....	....	....	....	....	....	....	...	...	...
General Government .... 78bp d	....	....	....	....	....	....	....	....	....	....	....	....	−.77	.16	.12
Banks .... 78bq d	....	....	....	....	....	....	....	....	....	....	....	....	−60.04	22.03	−35.70
Other Sectors .... 78br d	....	....	....	....	....	....	....	....	....	....	....	....	—	—	—
Other Investment Liab., n.i.e. .... 78bi d	....	....	....	....	....	....	....	....	....	....	....	....	38.58	−39.24	.62
Monetary Authorities .... 78bs d	....	....	....	....	....	....	....	....	....	....	....	....	.74	−.21	−.12
General Government .... 78bt d	....	....	....	....	....	....	....	....	....	....	....	....	−.30	.39	.85
Banks .... 78bu d	....	....	....	....	....	....	....	....	....	....	....	....	38.12	−39.49	−.19
Other Sectors .... 78bv d	....	....	....	....	....	....	....	....	....	....	....	....	.03	.07	.08
Net Errors and Omissions.................. 78ca d	....	....	....	....	....	....	....	....	....	....	....	....	6.37	3.79	2.13
Overall Balance .... 78cb d	....	....	....	....	....	....	....	....	....	....	....	....	2.91	.98	−6.17
Reserves and Related Items .... 79da d	....	....	....	....	....	....	....	....	....	....	....	....	−2.91	−.98	6.17
Reserve Assets .... 79db d	....	....	....	....	....	....	....	....	....	....	....	....	−3.25	−.98	2.55
Use of Fund Credit and Loans .... 79dc d	....	....	....	....	....	....	....	....	....	....	....	....	—	—	—
Exceptional Financing .... 79de d	....	....	....	....	....	....	....	....	....	....	....	....	.33	—	3.62
Government Finance															
Deficit (-) or Surplus.................. 80	....	....	....	....	....	....	....	....	....	....	....	650.7	−338.3	−57.2	432.5
Revenue 81	....	....	....	....	....	....	....	....	....	....	....	1,366.1	1,607.4	1,897.7	2,503.4
Grants Received 81z	....	....	....	....	....	....	....	....	....	....	....	1,756.4	1,204.7	1,007.0	1,376.5
Expenditure 82	....	....	....	....	....	....	....	....	....	....	....	2,456.8	2,750.4	2,961.9	3,215.5
Lending Minus Repayments 83	....	....	....	....	....	....	....	....	....	....	....	15.0	400.0	—	231.9
Financing															
Domestic 84a	....	....	....	....	....	....	....	....	....	....	....	−627.7	364.3	78.2	−413.8
Foreign 85a	....	....	....	....	....	....	....	....	....	....	....	−23.0	−26.0	−21.0	−18.7
Debt: Domestic 88a	....	....	....	....	....	....	....	....	....	....	....	....	....	....	252.5
Foreign 89a	....	....	....	....	....	....	....	....	....	....	....	....	....	....	325.2
National Accounts															*Millions of Vatu*
Exports of Goods & Services 90c	....	....	....	....	....	....	....	....	....	....	....	....	....	5,934	5,934
Government Consumption 91f	....	....	....	....	....	....	....	....	....	....	....	....	....	3,660	3,660
Gross Fixed Capital Formation 93e	....	....	....	....	....	....	....	....	....	....	....	....	....	2,142	2,142
Increase/Decrease(-) in Stocks 93i	....	....	....	....	....	....	....	....	....	....	....	....	....	463	463
Private Consumption 96f	....	....	....	....	....	....	....	....	....	....	....	....	....	5,450	5,450
Imports of Goods & Services................. 98c	....	....	....	....	....	....	....	....	....	....	....	....	....	−7,326	−7,326
Gross Domestic Product (GDP) 99b	....	....	....	....	....	....	....	....	....	....	....	....	9,442	10,150	10,150
Net Factor Inc/Pmts(-) Abroad 98.n	....	....	....	....	....	....	....	....	....	....	....	....	....	−497	−497
Gross National Income (GNI) 99a	....	....	....	....	....	....	....	....	....	....	....	....	....	9,653	9,653
GDP Volume 1983 Prices.................... 99b. p	....	....	....	....	....	....	....	....	....	....	....	....	....	10,150	10,846
GDP Volume (1995=100) .... 99bv p	....	....	....	....	....	....	....	....	....	....	....	....	....	70.1	75.0
GDP Deflator (1995=100)................. 99bi p	....	....	....	....	....	....	....	....	....	....	....	....	....	54.3	50.8
															Millions:
Population........................... 99z	.08	.08	.09	.09	.09	.10	.10	.10	.10	1.11	.12	.12	.12	.13	.13

Millions of Vatu

1985	1986	1987	1988	1989	1990	1991	1992	1993	1994	1995	1996	1997	1998	1999	International Transactions	
3,252	1,841	1,943	2,066	2,560	2,202	2,035	2,677	2,758	2,911	3,173	3,368	4,087	4,323	....	Exports	70
7,378	6,105	7,638	7,361	8,250	11,211	9,216	9,276	9,581	10,404	10,659	10,888	10,888	11,257	....	Imports, c.i.f.	71

Minus Sign Indicates Debit

1985	1986	1987	1988	1989	1990	1991	1992	1993	1994	1995	1996	1997	1998	1999	Balance of Payments	
-10.37	-11.70	-24.37	-15.19	-12.25	-6.18	-13.71	-13.07	-14.93	-19.78	-18.25	-26.94	-19.34	4.54	....	Current Account, n.i.e.	78al d
18.67	8.81	13.73	15.39	13.74	13.73	14.86	17.80	17.43	25.11	28.28	30.20	35.32	33.78	....	Goods: Exports f.o.b.	78aa d
-52.29	-46.81	-57.09	-57.89	-57.92	-79.34	-74.01	-66.79	-64.71	-74.68	-79.44	-81.11	-78.99	-76.23	....	Goods: Imports f.o.b.	78ab d
-33.62	-37.99	-43.36	-42.50	-44.18	-65.61	-59.15	-48.99	-47.28	-49.58	-51.16	-50.91	-43.67	-42.45	....	*Trade Balance*	78ac d
38.16	30.58	36.15	39.97	40.29	60.17	66.09	69.93	68.88	78.14	81.65	92.75	87.79	116.36	....	Services: Credit	78ad d
-20.37	-15.80	-15.59	-17.79	-19.11	-23.86	-26.95	-26.79	-29.97	-33.44	-35.27	-36.50	-35.95	-45.48	....	Services: Debit	78ae d
-15.83	-23.21	-22.80	-20.32	-23.01	-29.30	-20.01	-5.85	-8.36	-4.88	-4.78	5.34	8.16	28.42	....	*Balance on Goods & Services*	78af d
26.73	40.82	31.14	23.38	23.42	31.92	24.88	17.60	14.95	9.94	13.07	15.82	15.41	20.29	....	Income: Credit	78ag d
-40.22	-48.96	-51.86	-40.99	-29.18	-33.32	-49.18	-47.55	-43.48	-47.36	-49.79	-47.55	-45.68	-36.59	....	Income: Debit	78ah d
-29.31	-31.35	-43.52	-37.93	-28.76	-30.70	-44.31	-35.80	-36.89	-42.30	-41.49	-26.39	-22.11	12.12	....	*Balance on Gds, Serv. & Inc.*	78ai d
20.97	20.94	24.61	26.28	20.42	25.01	31.10	23.28	22.54	23.24	23.81	22.39	21.77	24.43	....	Current Transfers, n.i.e.: Credit	78aj d
-2.02	-1.28	-5.46	-3.54	-3.90	-.50	-.50	-.55	-.58	-.72	-.56	-22.94	-19.00	-32.01	....	Current Transfers: Debit	78ak d
11.65	8.90	19.04	17.87	8.78	16.47	19.14	17.22	26.30	37.28	31.62	4.90	-5.46	-9.09	....	Capital Account, n.i.e.	78bc d
12.32	9.30	19.54	17.96	8.91	16.51	19.34	26.59	32.04	41.45	38.33	43.38	23.75	25.36	....	Capital Account, n.i.e.: Credit	78ba d
-.67	-.41	-.50	-.10	-.13	-.04	-.20	-9.37	-5.74	-4.17	-6.71	-38.48	-29.21	-34.45	....	Capital Account: Debit	78bb d
5.07	12.92	19.35	9.95	24.19	13.79	-27.79	23.71	14.53	-13.41	25.30	20.88	-16.73	-.55	....	Financial Account, n.i.e.	78bj d
—	—	—	—	—	—	—	—	—	—	—					Direct Investment Abroad	78bd d
4.63	2.02	12.89	10.81	9.17	13.11	25.47	26.45	25.97	29.79	31.04	32.73	30.23	26.94	....	Dir. Invest. in Rep. Econ., n.i.e.	78be d
—	—	—	—	—	—	—	—	—	—	—	....	....	-.55		Portfolio Investment Assets	78bf d
—	—	—	—	—	—	—	—	—	—	—	....				Equity Securities	78bk d
—	—	—	—	—	—	—	—	—	—	—	....	....	-.55		Debt Securities	78bl d
—	—	—	—	—	—	—	—	—	—	—	....				Portfolio Investment Liab., n.i.e.	78bg d
—	—	—	—	—	—	—	—	—	—	—	....				Equity Securities	78bm d
—	—	—	—	—	—	—	—	—	—	—	....				Debt Securities	78bn d
										....	....	....	....		Financial Derivatives Assets	78bw d
										....	....	....	....		Financial Derivatives Liabilities	78bx d
-81.72	-20.11	18.59	145.38	-.79	-.93	15.28	-8.57	-27.50	-45.47	-1.59	-16.63	-23.53	5.89	....	Other Investment Assets	78bh d
															Monetary Authorities	78bo d
-.13	-.10	.36	-.22	-.13	-.34	-.39	-.38	-.43	-.45	-.30	-.39	-.46			General Government	78bp d
-81.60	-20.00	18.23	145.60	-.66	3.88	52.40	21.22	-10.76	10.60	-2.18	-16.25	-23.07	5.89	....	Banks	78bq d
—	—	—	—	—	-4.46	-36.74	-29.42	-16.31	-55.62	.89	....				Other Sectors	78br d
82.17	31.02	-12.14	-146.25	15.81	1.60	-68.55	5.83	16.05	2.27	-4.15	4.78	-23.43	-32.84	....	Other Investment Liab., n.i.e.	78bi d
.12	.12	-.26	.18	-.14	.34	—	-.36	.16	-.05	-.18	-.12	.12	-.11	....	Monetary Authorities	78bs d
.80	.74	1.00	.87	1.51	7.56	12.48	7.03	6.60	2.17	2.21	.45	.68	10.30	....	General Government	78bt d
81.17	30.15	-12.92	-147.29	14.44	-6.30	-81.03	-.84	9.29	.16	-6.54	4.46	-24.23	-41.68	....	Banks	78bu d
.08		.04											-1.35		Other Sectors	78bv d
-6.62	-5.34	-15.12	-17.30	-12.96	-19.38	19.31	-27.10	-22.44	-10.21	-33.38	-4.14	39.37	13.17	....	Net Errors and Omissions	78ca d
-.26	4.78	-1.10	-4.67	7.77	4.69	-3.05	.75	3.45	-6.12	5.30	-5.30	-2.16	8.06	....	*Overall Balance*	78cb d
.26	-4.78	1.10	4.67	-7.77	-4.69	3.05	-.75	-3.45	6.12	-5.30	5.30	2.16	-8.06	....	Reserves and Related Items	79da d
.26	-4.78	-12.93	-.68	-7.77	-4.69	-.40	-4.16	-6.70	4.86	-5.30	5.30	2.16	-8.06	....	Reserve Assets	79db d
															Use of Fund Credit and Loans	79dc d
—	—	14.04	5.36	—	—	3.45	3.41	3.26	1.26	....	....	....	....		Exceptional Financing	79de d

1985	1986	1987	1988	1989	1990	1991	1992	1993	1994	1995	1996	1997	1998	1999	Government Finance	
-62.3	-855.2	511.6	-629.5	....	....	....	....	....	....	....	....	....	....	....	Deficit (-) or Surplus	80
2,851.2	2,778.1	3,367.3	3,850.2	....	....	....	....	....	....	....	....	....	....	....	Revenue	81
843.4	543.5	2,385.0	1,806.0	....	....	....	....	....	....	....	....	....	....	....	Grants Received	81z
3,696.9	4,131.8	5,214.0	6,236.2	....	....	....	....	....	....	....	....	....	....	....	Expenditure	82
60.0	45.0	26.7	49.5	....	....	....	....	....	....	....	....	....	....	....	Lending Minus Repayments	83
															Financing	
19.1	798.7	-816.9	336.7	....	....	....	....	....	....	....	....	....	....	....	Domestic	84a
43.2	56.5	305.3	292.8	....	....	....	....	....	....	....	....	....	....	....	Foreign	85a
194.5	250.7	702.2	885.5	....	....	....	....	....	....	....	....	....	....	....	Debt: Domestic	88a
600.2	757.1	900.4	1,117.8	....	....	....	....	....	....	....	....	....	....	....	Foreign	89a

1985	1986	1987	1988	1989	1990	1991	1992	1993	1994	1995	1996	1997	1998	1999	National Accounts	
5,652	5,001	4,421	4,232	6,099	8,301	9,488	10,471	10,772	11,796	12,041	....	....	....	....	Exports of Goods & Services	90c
4,237	4,123	3,814	3,817	4,881	5,054	5,868	5,988	6,765	6,903	6,916	....	....	....	....	Government Consumption	91f
2,619	3,183	3,321	2,847	5,470	7,241	5,258	5,645	6,075	6,618	8,128	....	....	....	....	Gross Fixed Capital Formation	93e
634	559	267	350	606	488	500	520	540	580	570	....	....	....	....	Increase/Decrease(-) in Stocks	93i
6,079	6,118	6,051	6,330	10,545	11,267	11,301	11,662	11,701	12,286	12,777	....	....	....	....	Private Consumption	96f
-8,737	-7,754	-7,696	-7,362	-10,670	-13,714	-12,863	-12,270	-12,789	-14,278	-14,603	....	....	....	....	Imports of Goods & Services	98c
10,966	10,743	10,789	10,850	16,367	17,899	20,339	21,541	23,779	24,962	26,633	....	....	....	....	Gross Domestic Product (GDP)	99b
378	460	-690	-287	553	1,283	-1,409	-2,133	-2,696	-3,021	-2,792	....	....	....	....	Net Factor Inc/Pmts(-) Abroad	98.n
11,344	11,203	10,099	10,563	16,920	19,182	18,930	19,408	21,083	21,941	23,841	....	....	....	....	Gross National Income (GNI)	99a
10,966	10,743	10,789	10,850	11,343	11,938	13,183	13,088	13,676	14,024	14,469	....	....	....	....	GDP Volume 1983 Prices	99b.p
75.8	74.2	74.6	75.0	78.4	82.5	91.1	90.5	94.5	96.9	100.0	....	....	....	....	GDP Volume (1995=100)	99bv.p
54.3	54.3	54.3	54.3	78.4	81.5	83.8	89.4	94.5	96.7	100.0	....	....	....	....	GDP Deflator (1995=100)	99bi.p

Midyear Estimates

1985	1986	1987	1988	1989	1990	1991	1992	1993	1994	1995	1996	1997	1998	1999		
.14	.14	.14	.15	.14	.14	.15	.15	.16	.16	.17	.17	.18	.18	.19	Population	99z

(See notes in the back of the book.)

Venezuela, Rep. Bol.

		1970	1971	1972	1973	1974	1975	1976	1977	1978	1979	1980	1981	1982	1983	1984
Exchange Rates															*Bolivares per SDR:*	
Official Rate	aa	4.450	4.723	4.723	5.169	5.246	5.016	4.987	5.214	5.592	5.655	5.475	4.996	4.735	4.502	7.352
															Bolivares per US Dollar:	
Official Rate	ae	4.450	4.350	4.350	4.285	4.285	4.285	4.293	4.293	4.293	4.293	4.293	4.293	4.293	4.300	7.500
Official Rate	rf	4.450	4.447	4.400	4.305	4.285	4.285	4.290	4.293	4.293	4.293	4.293	4.293	4.293	4.297	7.017
Secondary Rate	xe	....	....	....	....	....	....	....	....	....	....	....	....	....	6.0000	6.0000
Tertiary Rate	yf	....	....	....	....	....	....	....	....	....	....	....	....	....		12.655
														Index Numbers (1995=100):		
Market Rate	ahx	3,928.3	3,931.2	4,018.6	4,071.4	4,079.5	4,079.5	4,075.3	4,072.3	4,072.3	4,072.3	4,072.3	4,072.3	4,072.3	4,067.7	2,592.3
Nominal Effective Exchange Rate	ne c	....	....	....	....	....	....	....	....	....	1,474.5	1,522.7	1,664.5	1,810.8	1,682.2	1,395.9
Real Effective Exchange Rate	re c	....	....	....	....	....	....	....	....	....	....	156.6	175.5	189.7	173.2	146.9
Fund Position															*Millions of SDRs:*	
Quota	2f. s	330	330	330	330	330	330	330	330	660	660	990	990	990	1,372	1,372
SDRs	1b. s	48	83	118	118	120	124	126	136	167	268	270	382	399	337	382
Reserve Position in the Fund	1c. s	117	111	111	111	401	805	926	833	588	408	490	549	682	877	827
of which: Outstg.Fund Borrowing	2c	—	—	—	—	252	602	610	559	361	185	206	276	348	361	330
Total Fund Cred.&Loans Outstg.	2tl	—	—	—	—	—	—	—	—	—	—	—	—	—	—	—
International Liquidity													*Millions of US Dollars Unless Otherwise Indicated:*			
Total Reserves minus Gold	1l. d	637	1,097	1,307	1,940	6,034	8,403	8,124	7,735	6,035	7,320	6,604	8,164	6,579	7,643	8,901
SDRs	1b. d	47	90	128	143	147	145	146	166	218	353	344	445	440	353	375
Reserve Position in the Fund	1c. d	117	121	121	134	491	942	1,075	1,011	766	538	625	639	752	918	811
Foreign Exchange	1d. d	472	886	1,058	1,663	5,396	7,316	6,902	6,558	5,051	6,430	5,635	7,081	5,386	6,372	7,716
Gold (Million Fine Troy Ounces)	1ad	10.97	11.17	11.17	11.17	11.18	11.18	11.18	11.32	11.39	11.46	11.46	11.46	11.46	11.46	11.46
Gold (National Valuation)	1and	384	425	425	472	472	472	472	478	481	484	484	484	3,439	3,439	3,439
Monetary Authorities: Other Liab.	4..d	20	38	61	87	102	218	119	260	98	104	229	188	125	121	91
Deposit Money Banks: Assets	7a. d	30	43	112	62	130	221	214	329	614	765	770	719	525	1,296	1,118
Liabilities	7b. d	79	70	102	168	171	216	370	691	1,002	778	837	1,189	2,035	1,974	1,455
Other Banking Insts.: Assets	7e. d	6	2	67	70	48	17	47	47	99	161	212	168	130	120	75
Liabilities	7f. d	122	146	249	307	253	59	157	402	729	1,770	1,862	2,044	2,510	2,460	1,362
Monetary Authorities															*Billions of Bolivares:*	
Foreign Assets	11	4.00	6.01	6.84	10.22	27.39	37.89	36.76	35.17	27.93	33.45	30.38	37.06	41.59	47.90	71.89
Claims on Central Government	12a	.50	.35	.37	.41	.50	.89	.89	1.33	1.37	2.61	2.04	1.79	4.69	2.57	5.57
Claims on Nonfin.Pub.Enterprises	12c	.05	.04	.02	.01	.01	—	—	—	—	—	—	—	—	—	.23
Claims on Nonbank Pub. Fin. Inst	12cg	.01	—	—	—	—	—	—	—	—	—	—	—	—	—	—
Claims on Deposit Money Banks	12e	.05	.04	.06	.06	.16	.25	.20	1.02	2.21	2.12	2.28	.92	4.71	1.52	3.07
Claims on Other Banking Insts	12f	.15	.01	.01	.11	.22	.09	—	.64	2.45	2.63	4.06	6.43	8.05	9.04	11.34
Reserve Money	14	3.96	4.87	5.46	6.77	9.62	13.54	16.12	19.73	21.82	24.63	26.30	30.79	36.04	46.22	58.05
of which: Currency Outside DMBs	14a	2.12	2.29	2.53	2.81	3.74	4.65	5.74	7.28	-7.66	9.87	12.21	13.35	12.93	14.54	14.97
Time, Savings,& Fgn.Currency Dep.	15	.01	.01	.01	.01	.01	.41	.16	.05	.06	.05	.07	.11	.22	.21	.29
Liabs. of Central Bank: Securities	16ac	—	.13	.05												
Foreign Liabilities	16c	.02	.05	.05	.04	.07	.09	.12	.24	.18	.13	.16	.21	.15	.13	.13
Long-Term Foreign Liabilities	16cl	.07	.11	.22	.34	.37	.85	.39	.88	.24	.32	.83	.60	.39	.39	.55
Central Government Deposits	16d	.39	.66	.68	1.86	4.29	5.28	6.68	6.62	5.34	9.48	5.30	8.74	4.94	3.39	7.50
Liab. to Nonbank Pub. Fin. Insts	16dg	—	—	—	—	11.79	16.36	11.66	7.50	2.14	1.37	.33	.39	.60	.32	.65
Capital Accounts	17a	.69	.93	1.15	2.24	2.50	2.83	3.15	3.54	4.24	5.46	7.01	8.94	6.04	11.99	22.10
Other Items (Net)	17r	-.39	-.30	-.31	-.45	-.36	-.24	-.42	-.39	-.06	-.64	-1.24	-3.57	10.66	-1.61	2.83
Deposit Money Banks															*Billions of Bolivares:*	
Reserves	20	1.73	2.45	2.85	3.80	4.90	5.87	8.71	10.66	10.97	12.09	11.61	15.39	13.73	23.24	19.87
Other Claims on Monetary Author.	20c	—	—	.05	—	—	—	—	—	—	—	—	—	—	—	—
Foreign Assets	21	.13	.19	.49	.27	.56	.95	.92	1.41	2.63	3.28	3.30	3.09	2.25	5.57	8.39
Claims on Central Government	22a	.28	—	.36	.42	.65	.90	.90	1.97	1.63	1.50	1.38	7.12	4.10	5.95	7.88
Claims on State and Local Govts	22b	—	—	—	—	—	—	—	—	—	.03	.12	.12	.11	.17	.07
Claims on Nonfin.Pub.Enterprises	22c	.07	.46	.27	.50	.53	.56	.50	.56	.71	.77	.78	.86	1.13	1.30	.77
Claims on Nonbank Pub. Fin. Inst	22cg	....	....	....	....	....	....	....	....	....	....	....	....	....	....	....
Claims on Private Sector	22d	8.68	9.58	11.20	14.20	18.97	28.70	39.29	46.46	56.52	59.04	69.33	75.65	85.15	89.04	103.64
Claims on Other Banking Insts	22f	....	....	.03	.06	.07	.03	.07	.13	.12	.33	.60	.52	.51	.47	.50
Claims on Nonbank Financial Insts	22g	....	....	....	....	....	....	....	....	....	....	....	....	....	....	....
Demand Deposits	24	4.82	5.73	6.92	8.44	12.12	17.85	21.21	27.58	33.25	33.75	39.44	42.58	38.22	52.24	57.45
Time, Savings,& Fgn.Currency Dep.	25	4.71	5.56	6.80	8.20	9.75	14.89	21.48	26.22	29.02	32.01	37.64	46.21	52.60	63.82	69.00
Money Market Instruments	26aa	....	....	....	....	....	....	....	....	....	....	....	....	....	....	....
Bonds	26ab	....	....	....	....	....	....	....	....	....	....	....	....	....	....	....
Restricted Deposits	26b	....	....	....	....	....	....	....	....	....	....	....	....	....	....	....
Foreign Liabilities	26c	.10	.10	.12	.22	.29	.31	.46	1.00	.92	1.33	1.17	1.10	1.87	1.79	2.45
Long-Term Foreign Liabilities	26cl	.25	.20	.33	.51	.45	.61	1.13	1.97	3.38	2.00	2.42	4.00	6.87	6.70	8.47
Central Government Deposits	26d	.43	.42	.40	.55	1.46	1.36	2.99	4.40	6.93	5.34	6.45	5.89	3.91	3.42	4.96
Liab. to Nonbank Pub. Fin. Insts	26dg	—	—	—	—	—	—	—	—	—	—	—	—	—	—	1.64
Credit from Monetary Authorities	26g	.03	.02	.02	—	.13	—	.15	.97	2.14	2.65	2.35	.56	5.04	2.50	4.75
Liabilities to Other Banking Insts	26i	.12	.17	.49	.56	.78	.84	1.09	1.09	1.28	1.55	1.57	2.53	2.17	2.62	2.11
Liab. to Nonbank Financial Insts	26j	....	....	....	....	....	....	....	....	....	....	....	....	....	....	....
Capital Accounts	27a	1.66	1.83	1.95	2.21	2.58	3.17	3.67	4.51	5.12	5.77	6.55	7.35	8.56	9.09	6.96
Other Items (Net)	27r	-1.23	-1.35	-1.76	-1.43	-1.89	-2.04	-1.79	-6.54	-9.46	-7.38	-10.47	-7.47	-12.25	-16.46	-16.67
Monetary Survey															*Billions of Bolivares:*	
Foreign Assets (Net)	31n	4.01	6.04	7.17	10.23	27.60	38.43	37.09	35.34	29.46	35.27	32.36	38.84	41.82	51.56	77.69
Domestic Credit	32	8.93	9.38	11.19	13.30	15.21	24.53	32.09	40.32	50.57	52.19	67.16	78.48	95.04	101.85	117.76
Claims on Central Govt. (Net)	32an	-.04	-.73	-.35	-1.58	-4.60	-4.85	-7.89	-7.72	-9.27	-10.72	-8.33	-5.72	-.06	1.70	.98
Claims on State and Local Govts	32b	—	—	—	—	—	—	—	—	—	.03	.23	.25	.24	.27	.29
Claims on Nonfin.Pub.Enterprises	32c	.12	.50	.29	.51	.53	.56	.51	.56	.71	.77	.78	.86	1.13	1.30	1.00
Claims on Nonbank Pub.Fin.Inst	32cg	.01	—	—	—	—	—	—	—	—	—	—	—	—	—	—
Claims on Private Sector	32d	8.70	9.60	11.21	14.20	18.98	28.70	39.39	46.71	56.57	59.16	69.82	76.14	85.17	89.07	103.64
Claims on Other Banking Insts	32f	.15	.01	.04	.16	.29	.12	.07	.77	2.57	2.96	4.66	6.95	8.56	9.51	11.84
Claims on Nonbank Financial Inst	32g	—	—	—	—	—	—	—	—	—	—	—	—	—	—	—

1985	1986	1987	1988	1989	1990	1991	1992	1993	1994	1995	1996	1997	1998	1999		
End of Period															**Exchange Rates**	
8.238	17.736	20.571	19.513	56.612	71.673	88.048	109.244	145.102	I248.175	431.082	685.188	680.359	794.833	889.730	Official Rate	aa
End of Period (ae) Period Average (rf)																
7.500	14.500	14.500	14.500	43.079	50.380	61.554	79.450	105.640	I170.000	290.000	476.500	504.250	564.500	648.250	Official Rate	ae
7.500	8.083	14.500	14.500	34.681	46.900	56.816	68.376	90.826	148.503	I176.843	417.333	488.635	547.556	605.717	Official Rate	rf
6.0000	7.5000	7.5000	39.1820	....	....	....	....	....	....	....	....	....	....	....	Secondary Rate	xe
13.758	5.783	27.533	33.555	....	....	....	....	....	....	....	....	....	....	....	Tertiary Rate	yf
Period Averages																
2,330.7	2,236.9	1,205.6	1,205.6	578.6	374.0	308.6	257.0	193.7	122.7	100.0	43.8	35.8	32.0	28.9	Market Rate	ah x
1,307.3	1,042.7	628.7	600.8	335.5	242.9	217.7	195.4	171.8	122.9	100.0	45.2	39.0	36.1	33.4	Nominal Effective Exchange Rate	ne c
140.9	117.7	84.2	94.2	80.1	70.9	76.2	79.2	83.2	79.9	100.0	84.3	110.5	135.5	152.3	Real Effective Exchange Rate	re c
End of Period															**Fund Position**	
1,372	1,372	1,372	1,372	1,372	1,372	1,372	1,951	1,951	1,951	1,951	1,951	1,951	1,951	2,659	Quota	2f. s
451	498	534	56	36	7	188	55	354	317	255	317	135	74	93	SDRs	1b. s
745	656	473	30	3	—	—	145	145	145	145	145	145	145	322	Reserve Position in the Fund	1c. s
265	176	91	30	3	—	—	—	—	—	—	—	—	—	—	of which: Outstg.Fund Borrowing	2c
—	—	—	—	759	2,117	2,271	2,143	1,951	1,810	1,506	1,527	1,199	870	540	Total Fund Cred.&Loans Outstg.	2tl
End of Period															**International Liquidity**	
10,251	6,437	5,963	3,092	4,106	8,321	10,666	9,562	9,216	8,067	6,283	11,788	14,378	11,920	12,277	Total Reserves minus Gold	1l. d
496	609	757	76	47	10	269	75	486	463	380	456	183	104	127	SDRs	1b. d
818	802	671	41	4	—	—	199	199	212	215	208	196	204	442	Reserve Position in the Fund	1c. d
8,937	5,026	4,535	2,975	4,055	8,311	10,397	9,288	8,531	7,393	5,688	11,124	14,000	11,612	11,708	Foreign Exchange	1d. d
11.46	11.46	11.46	11.46	11.46	11.46	11.46	11.46	11.46	11.46	11.46	11.46	11.46	9.76	9.76	Gold (Million Fine Troy Ounces)	1ad
3,439	3,439	3,439	3,439	3,439	3,439	3,439	3,439	3,440	3,440	3,440	3,440	3,440	2,929	2,887	Gold (National Valuation)	1an d
117	78	362	1,232	1,174	1,557	1,101	1,461	2,180	2,142	1,784	1,322	722	156	121	Monetary Authorities: Other Liab.	4..d
927	636	1,061	1,311	1,003	1,268	1,380	1,425	1,495	1,133	647	787	767	859	1,192	Deposit Money Banks: Assets	7a. d
1,956	2,066	3,068	4,421	1,059	839	950	613	634	261	181	238	209	170	131	Liabilities	7b. d
73	40	57	51	28	17	11	6	28	32	23	39	36	66	7	Other Banking Insts.: Assets	7e. d
1,352	1,042	1,025	988	321	214	—	4	1	1						Liabilities	7f. d
End of Period															**Monetary Authorities**	
80.99	86.22	I109.44	95.16	324.04	593.78	866.81	1,032.97	1,340.04	1,951.31	2,813.96	7,254.35	9,045.05	8,466.61	9,853.71	Foreign Assets	11
3.77	1.46	I7.44	11.30	45.87	265.20	245.49	276.47	359.09	632.06	1,038.12	1,649.37	1,664.38	1,391.04	1,066.64	Claims on Central Government	12a
.09	.38	I.14	.10	4.92	10.72	8.73	10.35	10.05	10.05	22.18	10.00	.57	.55	.55	Claims on Nonfin.Pub.Enterprises	12c
8.68	12.07	I11.70	37.11	42.64	44.50	15.09	15.12	15.47	813.15	1,355.13	1,372.56	1,384.14	1,386.24	1,385.64	Claims on Nonbank Pub. Fin. Inst	12cg
1.00	3.72	I4.39	19.34	13.42	14.95	12.57	15.53	33.90	18.59	26.42	10.90	10.17	.80	.90	Claims on Deposit Money Banks	12e
5.93	6.23	I7.73	11.98	7.55	7.91	3.63	2.21	1.43	1.05	1.00	.46	.39	.77	.77	Claims on Other Banking Insts	12f
59.75	48.96	I62.70	67.27	109.32	251.01	364.66	394.49	432.66	714.10	954.74	2,439.92	3,843.35	3,782.68	5,080.81	Reserve Money	14
15.99	18.51	I24.83	31.20	40.29	56.42	76.46	108.63	136.55	278.53	355.23	I574.35	987.34	1,235.05	1,816.79	of which: Currency Outside DMBs	14a
.40	.41	I.15	.23	6.11	9.60	9.85	8.74	8.71	16.24	21.91	32.67	61.32	40.20	43.43	Time, Savings,& Fgn.Currency Dep.	15
—	—	I—	—	15.89	119.12	60.73	54.89	70.88	744.71	609.34	1,659.38	1,803.07	1,579.69	895.74	Liabs. of Central Bank: Securities	16ac
.15	.41	I4.28	11.84	92.79	219.48	235.53	299.93	455.52	718.66	1,026.71	1,534.47	1,093.96	709.82	491.25	Foreign Liabilities	16c
.72	.72	I.96	6.02	11.23	32.41	50.45	59.11	92.72	139.77	140.25	92.69	82.69	68.39	66.82	Long-Term Foreign Liabilities	16cl
15.72	13.36	I25.85	10.72	38.39	88.36	134.37	75.58	119.69	222.88	192.32	991.37	1,681.87	727.60	674.80	Central Government Deposits	16d
.81	1.80	I3.94	9.80	21.61	27.05	101.87	96.30	21.96	59.60	70.09	98.00	15.85	10.59	3.32	Liab. to Nonbank Pub. Fin. Insts	16dg
15.13	29.75	I31.28	67.98	171.48	77.79	93.13	103.29	117.36	311.91	325.79	2,252.13	3,334.23	4,321.60	4,931.54	Capital Accounts	17a
7.77	14.66	I11.68	1.13	-17.78	133.44	119.77	268.97	474.09	545.38	1,916.14	1,149.43	188.36	5.46	120.52	Other Items (Net)	17r
End of Period															**Deposit Money Banks**	
22.04	23.62	I25.15	32.62	41.67	108.25	250.50	279.85	291.61	400.34	483.54	I1054.36	1,874.69	2,392.37	2,921.31	Reserves	20
				11.03	64.47	55.09	15.80	13.92	354.06	252.27	I990.29	783.22	802.00	390.76	Other Claims on Monetary Author.	20c
6.95	9.22	I15.39	19.02	43.19	63.89	84.93	113.19	157.92	192.57	187.51	I374.27	385.99	484.14	771.76	Foreign Assets	21
13.59	16.55	I22.75	24.27	31.96	48.89	25.76	39.83	139.48	440.70	839.70	I711.46	765.19	777.96	1,220.47	Claims on Central Government	22a
.09	.07	.05	.06	.22	.04	.02	.53	—	1.20	4.92	I1.19	.12	.15	13.51	Claims on State and Local Govts	22b
1.07	1.20	1.33	1.06	3.95	2.28	31.73	26.71	79.64	136.68	179.52	I8.06	8.44	10.01	23.75	Claims on Nonfin.Pub.Enterprises	22c
											286.40	56.41	32.21	45.43	Claims on Nonbank Pub. Fin. Inst	22cg
115.39	149.75	I201.25	261.92	300.88	376.47	559.31	767.97	859.81	797.97	1,184.61	I2359.04	5,287.72	6,021.81	6,655.06	Claims on Private Sector	22d
.48	.60	I1.78	1.78	2.34	2.94	3.18	.99	.80	.72	.18	I32.87	30.41	99.51	138.57	Claims on Other Banking Insts	22f
									10.75	12.79	I38.23	61.52	70.42	186.70	Claims on Nonbank Financial Insts	22g
66.62	83.48	I82.88	105.84	109.37	150.91	241.61	245.24	256.54	666.18	902.56	I1968.61	3,641.96	3,715.03	4,260.83	Demand Deposits	24
76.43	95.27	I131.27	149.95	256.09	460.70	673.39	817.46	1,077.76	1,532.33	2,079.16	I2482.82	3,643.52	4,679.50	5,430.40	Time, Savings,& Fgn.Currency Dep.	25
											25.52	61.12	15.43	34.07	Money Market Instruments	26aa
											18.41	.51	3.48	8.96	Bonds	26ab
											43.27	63.17	68.21	94.91	Restricted Deposits	26b
1.86	3.17	5.56	11.44	6.87	8.21	22.54	22.04	32.29	11.25	17.07	I78.01	95.33	69.11	76.59	Foreign Liabilities	26c
12.81	26.79	I38.93	52.66	38.76	34.06	35.97	26.68	34.71	33.16	35.54	I35.02	9.68	26.54	7.98	Long-Term Foreign Liabilities	26cl
7.76	8.09	9.39	6.20	7.62	13.88	23.74	24.68	27.81	47.20	57.95	I262.77	464.51	492.97	865.93	Central Government Deposits	26d
5.86	6.09	6.07	2.90	3.78	4.42	6.53	9.70	16.17	106.12	13.42	I38.11	51.53	52.57	109.29	Liab. to Nonbank Pub. Fin. Insts	26dg
1.96	3.75	I4.83	20.49	8.98	14.31	14.70	14.82	33.04	17.73	25.57	I5.87	2.64		29.75	Credit from Monetary Authorities	26g
2.56	2.83	I3.75	5.98	8.52	16.45	27.80	32.90	37.02	31.05	21.87	I58.11	62.51	120.14	143.83	Liabilities to Other Banking Insts	26i
											38.53	105.51	195.18	160.53	Liab. to Nonbank Financial Insts	26j
4.31	6.76	I8.80	23.71	31.17	44.32	68.14	100.37	146.86	90.55	330.50	I1222.07	1,700.82	2,455.45	2,524.29	Capital Accounts	27a
-20.57	-35.22	I-23.78	-38.46	-35.91	-80.03	-103.89	-49.05	-119.04	-200.58	-338.59	I-420.96	-649.10	-1,203.03	-1,380.04	Other Items (Net)	27r
End of Period															**Monetary Survey**	
85.93	91.85	I114.99	90.90	267.56	429.99	693.68	824.19	1,010.14	1,413.97	1,957.69	I6016.14	8,241.76	8,171.82	10,057.63	Foreign Assets (Net)	31n
125.97	166.84	I218.99	332.69	398.34	658.37	734.88	1,039.91	1,318.27	2,574.26	4,387.89	I5215.51	7,112.92	8,570.11	9,196.37	Domestic Credit	32
-6.13	-3.44	I-5.05	18.64	31.83	211.85	113.14	216.04	351.07	802.68	1,627.54	I1106.69	283.19	948.44	746.39	Claims on Central Govt. (Net)	32an
.22	.07	I.10	.11	.24	.08	.06	.53	—	1.20	4.92	I1.19	.12	.15	13.51	Claims on State and Local Govts	32b
1.16	1.58	I1.47	1.16	8.86	13.00	40.47	37.06	89.69	146.73	201.71	I18.06	9.01	10.56	24.30	Claims on Nonfin.Pub.Enterprises	32c
8.68	12.07	I11.70	37.11	42.64	44.50	15.09	15.12	15.47	813.15	1,355.13	I1658.96	1,440.54	1,418.45	1,431.07	Claims on Nonbank Pub.Fin.Inst	32cg
115.63	149.75	I201.25	261.92	304.88	378.08	559.32	767.97	859.82	797.98	1,184.62	I2359.05	5,287.73	6,021.82	6,655.07	Claims on Private Sector	32d
6.41	6.82	I9.51	13.76	9.90	10.85	6.80	3.20	2.23	1.78	1.18	I33.33	30.80	100.28	139.34	Claims on Other Banking Insts	32f
—	—	I—	—	—	—	—	—	—	10.75	12.79	I38.23	61.52	70.42	186.70	Claims on Nonbank Financial Inst	32g

		1970	1971	1972	1973	1974	1975	1976	1977	1978	1979	1980	1981	1982	1983	1984
Monetary Survey (cont.)																*Billions of Bolivares:*
Money	34	7.03	8.14	9.60	11.43	16.87	25.52	28.70	36.98	27.32	46.35	54.26	58.02	60.44	75.96	96.25
Quasi-Money	35	4.72	5.57	6.80	8.21	9.76	15.30	21.64	26.27	29.09	32.06	37.71	46.32	52.82	64.03	69.29
Money Market Instruments	36aa	....	....	....	....	....	....	....	....	....	....	....	....	....	....	....
Bonds	36ab	....	....	....	....	....	....	....	....	....	....	....	....	....	....	....
Liabs. of Central Bank: Securities	36ac	—	.13	.05	—	....	....	—	—	—	—	—	—	....	....	....
Restricted Deposits	36b	....	....	....	....	....	....	....	....	....	....	....	....	....	....	....
Long-Term Foreign Liabilities	36cl	.32	.31	.54	.84	.82	1.46	1.52	2.84	3.62	2.32	3.25	4.60	7.26	7.09	9.02
Liab. to Central Pub. Insts	36dg	—	—	—	—	11.79	16.36	11.66	7.50	2.14	1.37	.33	.39	.60	.32	2.29
Liabilities to Other Banking Insts	36i	.12	.17	.49	.56	.78	.84	1.09	1.09	1.28	1.55	1.57	2.53	2.17	2.62	2.11
Liab. to Nonbank Financial Insts	36j	....	....	....	....	....	....	....	....	....	....	....	....	....	....	....
Capital Accounts	37a	2.35	2.76	3.10	4.44	5.09	6.00	6.81	8.05	9.36	11.23	13.55	16.29	14.60	21.08	29.05
Other Items (Net)	37r	−1.59	−1.66	−2.23	−1.95	−2.30	−2.53	−2.24	−7.07	7.23	−7.42	−11.16	−10.83	−1.02	−17.70	−12.57
Money plus Quasi-Money	35l	11.74	13.71	16.41	19.63	26.63	40.82	50.34	63.24	56.41	78.41	91.97	104.34	113.26	139.99	165.55
Other Banking Institutions																*Billions of Bolivares:*
Reserves	40	.05	.09	.09	.18	.52	.28	.65	1.00	.71	1.35	1.65	1.68	.98	.78	1.43
Other Claims on Monetary Author.	40c	....	....	....	....	....	....	....	....	....	....	....	....	....	....	....
Foreign Assets	41	.03	.01	.29	.30	.20	.07	.20	.20	.43	.69	.91	.72	.56	.52	.56
Claims on Central Government	42a	.81	1.13	1.18	1.07	1.08	.43	.63	.71	1.01	.91	.73	4.98	1.52	.92	2.37
Claims on Nonfin.Pub.Enterprises	42c	—	.01	.02	.02	.01	.02	.02	.46	.01	.01	.01	.01	.01	.22	—
Claims on Nonbank Pub. Fin. Inst	42cg	....	....	....	....	....	....	....	....	....	....	....	....	....	....	....
Claims on Private Sector	42d	5.89	7.54	8.79	13.30	16.69	18.39	24.97	34.06	43.59	56.28	73.86	87.55	101.14	105.46	109.28
Claims on Deposit Money Banks	42e	.13	.22	.58	.74	1.12	1.13	1.43	1.50	2.09	2.22	2.40	3.50	2.88	3.53	3.25
Claims on Nonbank Financial Insts	42g	....	....	....	....	....	....	....	....	....	....	....	....	....	....	....
Demand Deposits	44	.07	.10	.15	.26	.57	.70	1.01	1.63	2.79	3.19	3.33	3.26	4.20	4.23	5.63
Time, Savings,& Fgn.Currency Dep.	45	3.32	4.92	6.44	9.56	12.33	15.20	20.30	25.56	29.82	36.40	45.34	56.84	64.28	76.43	82.81
Money Market Instruments	46aa	....	....	....	....	....	....	....	....	....	....	....	....	....	....	....
Bonds	46ab	.48	.56	.52	.65	.79	.83	1.03	1.66	3.21	5.11	9.78	11.92	15.53	9.78	7.62
Restricted Deposits	46b	....	....	....	....	....	....	....	....	....	....	....	....	....	....	....
Foreign Liabilities	46c	....	....	....	....	....	....	....	.02	.05	1.01	.74	1.15	1.62	.89	.74
Long-Term Foreign Liabilities	46cl	.54	.64	1.08	1.32	1.08	.25	.67	1.71	3.08	6.59	7.25	7.62	9.15	9.69	9.48
Central Government Deposits	46d	.94	1.06	.77	.92	1.26	.63	1.41	1.74	1.49	2.10	4.60	4.69	3.53	7.91	8.64
Liab. to Nonbank Pub. Fin. Insts	46dg	....	....	....	....	....	....	....	....	....	....	....	....	....	....	....
Credit from Monetary Authorities	46g	.18	.04	.01	.11	.22	.09	—	.64	1.97	1.98	3.41	6.18	8.34	7.80	9.19
Credit from Deposit Money Banks	46h	.14	.24	.31	1.19	1.48	1.66	2.23	3.21	2.98	3.09	3.03	3.01	2.22	2.74	3.11
Liab. to Nonbank Financial Insts	46j	....	....	....	....	....	....	....	....	....	....	....	....	....	....	....
Capital Accounts	47a	4.97	4.69	5.04	6.09	7.49	1.87	2.37	3.15	3.90	4.32	5.15	6.01	6.47	6.59	7.90
Other Items (Net)	47r	−3.73	−3.24	−3.38	−4.49	−5.60	−.91	−1.14	−1.38	−1.47	−2.32	−3.07	−2.23	−8.26	−14.62	−18.22
Banking Survey																*Billions of Bolivares:*
Foreign Assets (Net)	51n	4.03	6.05	7.46	10.53	27.80	38.50	37.29	35.53	29.84	34.95	32.53	38.42	40.76	51.19	77.51
Domestic Credit	52	14.55	16.97	20.35	26.59	31.43	42.61	56.21	73.03	91.12	104.34	132.49	159.38	185.61	191.03	208.94
Claims on Central Govt. (Net)	52an	−.17	−.66	.05	−1.44	−4.78	−5.06	−8.67	−8.76	−9.76	−11.90	−12.21	−5.43	−2.07	−5.28	−5.29
Claims on State and Local Govts	52b	—	—	—	—	—	—	—	—	—	.03	.23	.25	.24	.27	.29
Claims on Nonfin.Pub.Enterprises	52c	.12	.51	.30	.52	.54	.58	.52	1.03	.71	.77	.78	.87	1.14	1.52	1.00
Claims on Nonbank Pub.Fin.Insts	52cg	.01														
Claims on Private Sector	52d	14.59	17.13	20.00	27.50	35.67	47.09	64.36	80.76	100.16	115.44	143.68	163.69	186.31	194.52	212.93
Claims on Nonbank Financial Inst	52g	....	....	....	....	....	....	....	....	....	....	....	....	....	....	....
Liquid Liabilities	55l	15.09	18.63	22.91	29.27	39.00	56.43	71.00	89.42	88.31	116.65	138.99	162.76	180.77	219.86	252.56
Money Market Instruments	56aa	....	....	....	....	....	....	....	....	....	....	....	....	....	....	....
Bonds	56ab	.48	.56	.52	.65	.79	.83	1.03	1.66	3.21	5.11	9.78	11.92	15.53	9.78	7.62
Liabs. of Central Bank: Securities	56ac	—	.13	.05	—	....	....	—	—	—	—	—	—	....	....	....
Restricted Deposits	56b	....	....	....	....	....	....	....	....	....	....	....	....	....	....	....
Long-Term Foreign Liabilities	56cl	.86	.95	1.63	2.16	1.90	1.71	2.19	4.55	6.70	8.91	10.50	12.23	16.41	16.78	18.49
Liab. to Nonbank Pub. Fin. Insts	56dg	—	—	—	—	11.79	16.36	11.66	7.50	2.14	1.37	.33	.39	.60	.32	2.29
Liab. to Nonbank Financial Insts	56j	....	....	....	....	....	....	....	....	....	....	....	....	....	....	....
Capital Accounts	57a	7.32	7.45	8.14	10.53	12.58	7.87	9.18	11.21	13.26	15.55	18.70	22.30	21.07	27.67	36.95
Other Items (Net)	57r	−5.16	−4.69	−5.43	−5.49	−6.83	−2.10	−1.56	−5.78	7.33	−8.30	−13.27	−11.80	−8.00	−32.20	−31.46
Interest Rates																*Percent Per Annum*
Discount Rate *(End of Period)*	60	5.00	5.00	5.00	5.00	5.00	7.00	7.00	7.00	7.50	11.00	13.00	14.00	13.00	11.00	11.00
Money Market Rate	60b															
Savings Rate	60k															
Deposit Rate	60l															
Lending Rate	60p															12.29
Government Bond Yield	61															9.57
																13.15
Prices, Production, Labor																*Index Numbers (1995=100):*
Industrial Share Prices	62	13.6	14.3	15.7	19.1	24.2	27.4	32.1	33.5	23.3	18.9	15.4	13.4	10.0	9.9	12.9
Prices: Home & Import Goods	63	.8	.8	.8	.9	1.0	1.2	1.2	1.4	1.5	1.6	1.9	2.2	2.4	2.5	13.0
Home Goods	63a	.7	.7	.7	.8	.9	1.0	1.1	1.2	1.3	1.5	1.8	2.1	2.3	2.4	12.9
Consumer Prices	64	.9	.9	.9	1.0	1.1	1.2	1.3	1.4	1.4	1.6	2.0	2.3	2.5	2.7	3.0
Crude Petroleum Production	66aa	128	123	112	116	103	81	80	77	75	82	75	75	68	62	62
Labor Force	67d	....	....	....	....	....	....	....	....	....	....	....	....	....	....	*Number in Thousands:*
Employment	67e	....	....	....	....	....	....	....	....	....	....	....	....	....	....	....
Unemployment	67c	....	....	....	....	....	....	....	....	....	....	....	....	....	....	....
Unemployment Rate (%)	67r	....	....	....	....	....	....	....	....	....	....	....	....	....	....	....
International Transactions																*Billions of Bolivares:*
Exports	70	11.7	13.5	13.8	21.0	47.4	37.7	39.9	41.0	39.4	61.5	82.5	86.4	70.8	64.7	97.2
Petroleum	70a	10.6	12.8	12.6	18.6	45.2	35.7	37.6	39.1	37.5	58.5	78.3	81.7	67.1	59.5	85.2
Crude Petroleum	70aa	6.9	8.4	8.1	11.6	27.9	24.8	24.0	25.6	23.8	36.6	53.2	58.4	44.7	36.6	53.7
Imports, c.i.f.	71	8.3	9.2	10.6	12.1	17.9	25.7	29.2	47.0	50.5	45.8	50.8	56.3	55.6	37.5	52.8
Imports, f.o.b.	71.v	7.5	8.3	9.5	10.9	16.2	22.8	25.9	41.9	45.5	41.3	45.8	50.7	50.1	33.7	47.6
																Millions of US Dollars:
Exports	70..d	3,169	3,124	3,166	3,298	11,153	8,800	9,299	9,551	9,187	14,317	19,221	20,980	16,590	13,937	15,997
Petroleum	70a.d	2,371	2,882	2,857	4,328	10,548	8,324	8,763	9,110	8,740	13,633	17,562	18,609	15,633	13,857	14,824
Imports, f.o.b.	71.vd	1,684	1,878	2,207	2,534	3,757	5,324	6,787	9,766	10,601	9,613	10,655	11,808	11,661	5,783	7,004
Volume of Exports																*1995=100*
Petroleum	72a	135.2	127.9	120.0	121.0	110.9	81.2	84.4	77.1	77.7	82.5	73.0	68.3	60.8	59.1	59.9
Crude Petroleum	72aa	131.8	125.2	115.7	114.9	95.7	79.7	74.4	71.5	67.4	75.9	69.6	68.6	57.5	53.3	54.7
Refined Pretroleum	72ab	142.4	133.2	128.6	133.4	142.1	84.5	105.1	88.5	98.7	95.9	79.9	67.8	67.7	70.9	70.5
Import Prices (Wholesale)	76.x	.9	1.0	1.0	1.1	1.3	1.4	1.5	1.6	1.7	1.9	2.1	2.4	2.6	2.7	13.2

	1985	1986	1987	1988	1989	1990	1991	1992	1993	1994	1995	1996	1997	1998	1999		
End of Period																**Monetary Survey (cont.)**	
	104.71	109.32	I 122.46	145.31	167.98	266.00	341.49	367.36	408.60	981.09	1,367.35	I 3349.35	5,590.96	5,181.04	6,496.66	Money	34
	76.83	95.68	I 131.42	150.18	262.20	470.30	683.24	826.20	1,086.46	1,548.58	2,101.07	I 2515.49	3,704.84	4,719.69	5,473.82	Quasi-Money	35
	....	....	....	....	....	....	....	....	....	....	....	25.52	61.12	15.43	34.07	Money Market Instruments	36aa
	....	....	....	....	....	....	....	....	....	....	....	18.41	.51	3.48	8.96	Bonds	36ab
	—	—	I—	—	4.86	54.65	5.64	39.09	56.96	390.65	357.06	I 669.09	1,019.85	777.68	504.98	Liabs. of Central Bank: Securities	36ac
	....	....	....	....	....	....	....	....	....	....	....	43.27	63.17	68.21	94.91	Restricted Deposits	36b
	13.54	27.51	I 39.89	58.68	39.38	45.29	68.38	77.14	93.83	125.89	175.32	I 175.28	92.37	94.93	74.79	Long-Term Foreign Liabilities	36cl
	6.67	7.89	I 10.02	12.70	25.39	31.47	108.40	106.00	38.13	165.72	83.52	I 136.11	67.39	63.16	112.62	Liab. to Nonbank Pub. Fin. Insts	36dg
	2.56	2.83	I 3.75	5.98	8.52	16.45	27.80	32.90	37.02	31.05	21.87	I 58.11	62.51	120.14	143.83	Liabilities to Other Banking Insts	36i
	....	....	....	....	....	....	....	....	....	....	....	38.53	105.51	195.18	160.53	Liab. to Nonbank Financial Insts	36j
	19.44	36.51	I 40.08	91.69	202.65	122.11	161.27	203.66	264.22	402.46	656.29	I 3474.20	5,035.06	6,777.05	7,455.83	Capital Accounts	37a
	-11.84	-21.05	I -13.63	-40.95	-45.07	82.08	32.33	211.75	343.19	342.80	1,583.11	I 728.28	-448.61	-1,274.06	-1,306.99	Other Items (Net)	37r
	181.54	205.00	I 253.88	295.49	430.19	736.30	1,024.73	1,193.56	1,495.06	2,529.67	3,468.42	I 5864.84	9,295.80	9,900.74	11,970.48	Money plus Quasi-Money	35l
End of Period																**Other Banking Institutions**	
	1.08	.73	I 1.11	.95	2.36	4.56	4.98	7.87	12.34	22.69	27.57	I 33.82	73.37	86.69	205.61	Reserves	40
	....	....	—	—	.10	.25	.01	.12	.07	1.39	2.06	I 37.18	38.38	22.66	8.50	Other Claims on Monetary Author.	40c
	.55	.58	I .82	.74	1.21	.85	.68	.50	2.99	5.42	6.55	I 18.68	18.17	37.28	4.43	Foreign Assets	41
	2.64	2.88	I 3.01	4.52	5.06	13.60	19.46	40.74	32.00	103.93	88.07	I 21.33	17.73	18.22	96.70	Claims on Central Government	42a
	—	—	I .04	.03	.31	2.15	3.63	1.13	.81	1.71	.02	I 27.89	5.02	3.08	—	Claims on Nonfin.Pub.Enterprises	42c
	....	....	....	....	....	....	....	....	....	....	....	15.35	10.48	4.47	5.26	Claims on Nonbank Pub. Fin. Inst	42cg
	116.82	126.02	I 143.56	157.61	172.95	200.02	265.93	341.90	361.62	326.46	430.61	I 349.22	811.01	950.54	1,386.86	Claims on Private Sector	42d
	4.06	4.20	I 5.63	8.55	11.65	20.99	34.35	44.89	81.30	47.11	44.77	I 97.97	92.94	119.34	153.42	Claims on Deposit Money Banks	42e
	....	....	....	....	....	....	....	....	....	....	....	8.26	10.52	15.39	26.54	Claims on Nonbank Financial Insts	42g
	5.13	5.39	I 7.30	7.28	6.91	7.90	6.95	8.11	11.15	13.43	16.13	I 28.99	46.25	109.46	156.73	Demand Deposits	44
	84.19	80.63	I 79.97	81.60	143.17	196.35	286.56	387.14	452.53	460.63	558.42	I 403.18	741.66	846.22	1,254.94	Time, Savings,& Fgn.Currency Dep.	45
	....	....	....	....	....	....	....	....	....	....	....	—	—	—	—	Money Market Instruments	46aa
	17.79	25.10	I 34.26	45.51	15.24	16.88	11.06	8.86	11.03	8.49	7.04	I .77	.76	18.89	50.31	Bonds	46ab
	....	....	....	....	....	....	....	....	....	....	....	.28	1.19	1.27	2.40	Restricted Deposits	46b
	.73	.69	I .68	1.16	1.12	.39	—	—	—	—	—	I .06	—	—	—	Foreign Liabilities	46c
	9.41	14.43	I 14.19	13.17	12.69	10.37	.02	.29	.07	.12	—	I—	—	—	—	Long-Term Foreign Liabilities	46cl
	12.05	18.11	I 17.45	13.30	14.95	10.36	20.82	19.76	5.27	1.03	.76	I 13.37	40.80	30.89	191.78	Central Government Deposits	46d
	—	—	.50	1.81	1.81	1.68	1.65	1.36	.79	.64	.14	I 2.18	2.71	.58	3.82	Liab. to Nonbank Pub. Fin. Insts	46dg
	4.21	5.78	I 9.44	14.60	8.64	3.55	3.19	1.90	.56	.50	.18	I 4.86	.02	.01	.05	Credit from Monetary Authorities	46g
	3.29	3.45	I 4.96	6.56	5.36	4.10	6.85	6.08	8.40	8.17	7.36	I 38.68	110.74	115.62	107.08	Credit from Deposit Money Banks	46h
	....	....	....	....	....	....	....	....	....	....	....	7.24	17.44	6.62	38.47	Liab. to Nonbank Financial Insts	46j
	8.13	7.99	I 9.44	11.18	12.65	19.31	30.01	40.17	60.63	63.72	77.47	I 157.45	208.94	270.41	370.71	Capital Accounts	47a
	-19.78	-27.15	I -24.01	-23.77	-28.90	-28.45	-38.06	-36.52	-59.30	-48.02	-67.82	I -47.36	-92.90	-142.32	-288.97	Other Items (Net)	47r
End of Period																**Banking Survey**	
	85.75	91.75	I 115.13	90.47	267.65	430.45	694.36	824.69	1,013.13	1,419.39	1,964.24	I 6034.76	8,259.93	8,209.11	10,062.06	Foreign Assets (Net)	51n
	226.98	270.80	I 338.64	467.80	551.81	852.92	996.28	1,400.72	1,705.20	3,003.55	4,904.65	I 5590.86	7,896.09	9,430.63	10,380.60	Domestic Credit	52
	-15.54	-18.68	I -19.49	9.87	21.93	215.09	111.78	237.02	377.80	905.58	1,714.85	I 1114.66	260.13	935.76	651.30	Claims on Central Govt. (Net)	52an
	.22	.07	I .11	.11	.24	.08	.06	.53	—	1.20	4.92	I 1.19	.12	.15	13.51	Claims on State and Local Govts	52b
	1.16	1.58	I 1.51	1.19	9.17	15.15	44.10	38.18	90.49	148.44	201.73	I 45.95	14.03	13.63	24.30	Claims on Nonfin.Pub.Enterprises	52c
	8.68	12.07	I 11.70	37.11	42.64	44.50	15.09	15.12	15.47	813.15	1,355.13	I 1674.31	1,451.02	1,422.92	1,436.33	Claims on Nonbank Pub.Fin.Insts	52cg
	232.45	275.77	I 344.81	419.53	477.83	578.10	825.25	1,109.88	1,221.44	1,124.44	1,615.24	I 2708.27	6,098.74	6,972.35	8,041.93	Claims on Private Sector	52d
	—	—	I—	—	—	—	—	—	—	10.75	12.79	I 46.49	72.05	85.81	213.23	Claims on Nonbank Financial Inst	52g
	269.78	290.28	I 340.04	383.42	577.90	935.98	1,313.25	1,580.94	1,946.40	2,981.03	4,015.39	I 6263.18	10,010.34	10,769.73	13,176.54	Liquid Liabilities	55l
	....	....	....	....	....	....	....	....	....	....	....	25.53	61.13	15.43	34.07	Money Market Instruments	56aa
	17.79	25.10	I 34.26	45.51	15.24	16.88	11.06	8.86	11.03	8.49	7.04	I 19.19	1.27	22.37	59.27	Bonds	56ab
	—	—	I—	—	4.76	54.40	5.63	38.97	56.89	389.27	355.00	I 631.91	981.47	755.03	496.47	Liabs. of Central Bank: Securities	56ac
	....	....	....	....	....	....	....	....	....	....	....	43.55	64.36	69.49	97.31	Restricted Deposits	56b
	22.95	41.94	I 54.08	71.85	52.07	55.66	68.39	77.43	93.90	126.00	175.32	I 175.28	92.37	94.93	74.79	Long-Term Foreign Liabilities	56cl
	6.67	7.89	I 10.52	14.51	27.19	33.15	110.05	107.36	38.92	166.36	83.65	I 138.30	70.10	63.75	116.44	Liab. to Nonbank Pub. Fin. Insts	56dg
	....	....	....	....	....	....	....	....	....	....	....	45.78	122.95	201.80	199.00	Liab. to Nonbank Financial Insts	56j
	27.57	44.50	I 49.51	102.87	215.30	141.42	191.28	243.83	324.86	466.18	733.76	I 3631.65	5,244.00	7,047.45	7,826.55	Capital Accounts	57a
	-32.03	-47.16	I -34.63	-59.88	-73.00	45.89	-9.04	168.02	246.34	285.61	1,498.74	I 651.27	-491.97	-1,400.23	-1,637.77	Other Items (Net)	57r
Percent Per Annum																**Interest Rates**	
	8.00	8.00	8.00	8.00	45.00	43.00	43.00	52.20	71.25	48.00	49.00	45.00	45.00	60.00	38.00	Discount Rate *(End of Period)*	60
	....	....	....	....	....	....	....	....	....	....	....	16.70	12.47	18.58	7.48	Money Market Rate	60b
	....	....	....	....	....	....	....	28.76	38.59	29.11	22.17	19.53	7.59	12.34	8.15	Savings Rate	60k
	10.52	8.93	8.94	8.95	28.91	27.82	31.10	35.43	53.75	39.02	24.72	27.58	14.70	34.84	21.28	Deposit Rate	60l
	9.33	8.49	8.47	8.50	22.50	I 35.53	37.16	41.33	59.90	54.66	39.74	39.41	23.69	46.35	32.13	Lending Rate	60p
	12.55	12.07	13.49	14.86	17.32	20.06	27.14	31.66	41.03	54.73	53.38	49.09	25.41	47.88	37.05	Government Bond Yield	61
Period Averages																**Prices, Production, Labor**	
	14.4	22.7	50.5	43.8	23.2	I 24.4	56.4	65.2	52.4	I 93.8	100.0	300.0	533.2	322.9	311.7	Industrial Share Prices	62
	3.4	4.0	5.8	6.9	13.7	17.5	21.3	26.4	35.6	63.4	100.0	203.2	263.7	322.2	374.4	Prices: Home & Import Goods	63
	3.3	3.9	5.3	6.4	12.9	16.8	20.7	26.0	35.4	62.4	100.0	199.6	264.8	329.4	387.6	Home Goods	63a
	3.3	3.7	4.8	6.2	11.3	16.0	21.4	28.2	38.9	62.5	100.0	199.9	299.9	407.2	I 503.2	Consumer Prices	64
	58	62	59	66	67	75	83	82	85	90	100	103	112	113	102	Crude Petroleum Production	66aa
Period Averages																	
	....	....	....	....	....	....	7,418	7,538	7,546	8,027	8,545	....	9,507	....	....	Labor Force	67d
	5,106	5,396	5,694	6,035	6,113	6,405	6,701	6,986	7,103	7,626	7,667	7,819	8,287	....	....	Employment	67e
	767	667	575	478	672	743	702	582	503	687	875	1,043	1,061	....	....	Unemployment	67c
	13.1	11.0	9.2	7.3	9.9	10.4	9.5	7.7	6.7	8.7	10.3	11.8	11.4	....	....	Unemployment Rate (%)	67r
Billions of Bolivares																**International Transactions**	
	94.0	77.8	I 123.4	154.7	470.5	831.2	863.0	975.4	1,311.8	2,409.8	3,332.6	9,803.1	10,295.6	9,393.5	12,316.8	Exports	70
	77.6	53.8	I 100.9	118.2	347.5	665.4	700.2	770.9	979.9	1,751.6	2,444.8	7,844.8	8,853.1	6,557.6	9,954.5	Petroleum	70a
	44.7	29.9	I 64.5	68.9	201.6	415.1	432.9	492.4	637.6	1,197.8	1,641.7	5,346.6	5,934.9	4,220.1	6,592.4	Crude Petroleum	70aa
	61.8	75.1	I 127.8	236.4	266.4	347.9	637.7	961.9	1,107.2	1,324.0	2,202.0	4,179.9	7,145.5	8,604.0	8,800.5	Imports, c.i.f.	71
	55.6	67.6	I 115.1	213.0	240.0	313.4	574.5	866.6	997.4	1,192.8	1,983.8	3,765.7	6,437.3	7,751.3	7,928.3	Imports, f.o.b.	71.v
Millions of US Dollars																	
	14,438	8,660	10,577	10,244	13,286	17,497	15,155	14,185	14,686	16,089	18,457	23,060	21,624	17,193	19,852	Exports	70..*d*
	12,956	7,178	9,054	8,158	10,001	13,953	12,302	11,208	11,030	11,473	13,739	18,520	18,186	12,021	16,295	Petroleum	70a.*d*
	7,303	7,661	8,702	11,465	7,030	6,608	10,042	12,672	11,271	8,277	11,396	8,901	13,159	14,250	13,323	Imports, f.o.b.	71.v*d*
																Volume of Exports	
1995=100																	
	54.7	61.0	59.6	65.8	64.7	74.0	83.5	80.4	84.4	90.8	100.0	107.2	118.4	118.7	737.6	Petroleum	72a
	44.9	51.3	55.6	55.0	53.4	67.2	74.8	77.6	83.3	91.6	100.0	107.3	119.6	119.3	....	Crude Petroleum	72aa
	74.6	80.7	67.8	87.8	87.8	87.9	101.3	86.2	86.7	89.3	100.0	106.9	115.8	117.3	117.6	Refined Pretroleum	72ab
	3.7	4.4	7.3	8.5	16.2	19.5	23.2	27.3	36.7	66.3	100.0	213.8	260.6	301.3	335.8	Import Prices (Wholesale)	76.x

Venezuela, Rep. Bol.

		1970	1971	1972	1973	1974	1975	1976	1977	1978	1979	1980	1981	1982	1983	1984
Balance of Payments															*Millions of US Dollars:*	
Current Account, n.i.e.	78al d	−104	−11	−101	877	5,760	2,171	254	−3,179	−5,735	350	4,728	4,000	−4,246	4,427	4,651
Goods: Exports f.o.b.	78aa d	2,640	3,152	3,202	4,803	11,290	8,982	9,342	9,661	9,174	14,360	19,275	20,181	16,516	14,759	16,075
Goods: Imports f.o.b.	78ab d	−1,713	−1,896	−2,222	−2,626	−3,876	−5,462	−7,337	−10,194	−11,234	−10,004	−10,877	−12,123	−13,584	−6,409	−7,246
Trade Balance	78ac d	927	1,256	980	2,177	7,414	3,520	2,005	−533	−2,060	4,356	8,398	8,058	2,932	8,350	8,829
Services: Credit	78ad d	139	148	159	247	325	370	341	504	629	599	693	757	1,041	1,082	688
Services: Debit	78ae d	−525	−594	−665	−748	−1,143	−1,646	−2,068	−2,955	−3,935	−4,195	−4,253	−4,980	−6,050	−2,681	−2,632
Balance on Goods & Services	78af d	541	810	474	1,676	6,596	2,244	278	−2,984	−5,366	760	4,838	3,835	−2,077	6,751	6,885
Income: Credit	78ag d	54	39	57	229	356	740	693	782	1,052	1,346	2,264	3,581	2,565	1,500	2,097
Income: Debit	78ah d	−607	−777	−537	−917	−993	−640	−485	−694	−1,014	−1,349	−1,935	−3,007	−4,095	−3,613	−4,159
Balance on Gds, Serv. & Inc.	78ai d	−12	72	−6	988	5,959	2,344	486	−2,896	−5,328	757	5,167	4,409	−3,607	4,638	4,823
Current Transfers, n.i.e.: Credit	78aj d	2	2	2	2	2	2	2	1	1	1	—	—	—	—	61
Current Transfers: Debit	78ak d	−94	−85	−97	−113	−201	−175	−234	−284	−408	−408	−439	−409	−639	−211	−233
Capital Account, n.i.e.	78bc d	—	—	—	—	—	—	—	—	—	—	—	—	—	—	—
Capital Account, n.i.e.: Credit	78ba d	—	—	—	—	—	—	—	—	—	—	—	—	—	—	—
Capital Account: Debit	78bb d	—	—	—	—	—	—	—	—	—	—	—	—	—	—	—
Financial Account, n.i.e.	78bj d	81	504	−226	208	−875	164	65	1,702	3,182	3,251	164	−1,882	−1,528	−3,716	−2,019
Direct Investment Abroad	78bd d	—	—	—	—	—	—	—	—	—	—	—	—	−4		−21
Dir. Invest. in Rep. Econ., n.i.e.	78be d	−23	211	−376	−84	−430	418	−889	−3	67	88	55	184	257	86	18
Portfolio Investment Assets	78bf d	−11	−9	1	−11	−14	−63	−191	−108	−239	6	−264	−118	−10	−7	—
Equity Securities	78bk d	—	—	—	2	−3	−2	−16	−20	−10	24	2	−5	−10	−7	—
Debt Securities	78bl d	−11	−9	1	−13	−11	−61	−175	−88	−229	−18	−266	−113			—
Portfolio Investment Liab., n.i.e.	78bg d	−1	−1	14	−1	−5	−6	914	67	363	−80	1,574	201	1,592	208	—
Equity Securities	78bm d	—	—	—	—	—	—	—	—	—	—	—	—	—	—	—
Debt Securities	78bn d	−1	−1	14	−1	−5	−6	914	67	363	−80	1,574	201	1,592	208	—
Financial Derivatives Assets	78bw d	....	....	....	....	....	....	....	....	....	....	....	....	....	....	....
Financial Derivatives Liabilities	78bx d	....	....	....	....	....	....	....	....	....	....	....	....	....	....	....
Other Investment Assets	78bh d	−67	80	−108	14	−483	−760	−1,182	−722	−991	−988	−1,807	−2,963	−5,000	−1,059	−1,469
Monetary Authorities	78bo d	....	....	....	....	....	....	....	....	....	....	....	....	....	....	....
General Government	78bp d	—	−1	−22	−42	−135	−112	−50	−62	−166	−44	−212	−141	53	−93	−22
Banks	78bq d	−1	−12	−62	43	−24	−83	−12	−119	−200	−158	12	52	95	−233	−292
Other Sectors	78br d	−66	93	−24	13	−324	−565	−1,120	−541	−625	−786	−1,607	−2,874	−5,148	−733	−1,155
Other Investment Liab., n.i.e.	78bi d	183	223	243	290	57	575	1,413	2,468	3,982	4,225	606	814	1,637	−2,944	−547
Monetary Authorities	78bs d	2	8	−3	−2	8	4	8	24	−8	−13	4	11	−14	−7	−2
General Government	78bt d	128	182	120	127	−143	−12	944	1,332	2,020	1,080	21	−99	1,236	412	−765
Banks	78bu d	2	—	3	25	−12	59	287	535	677	−562	181	538	842	−113	101
Other Sectors	78bv d	51	33	123	140	204	524	174	577	1,293	3,720	400	364	−427	−3,236	119
Net Errors and Omissions	78ca d	69	−75	497	−474	−417	380	2,024	2,276	1,488	497	−1,129	−2,139	−2,386	−265	−996
Overall Balance	78cb d	46	418	170	611	4,468	2,715	2,343	799	−1,065	4,098	3,763	−21	−8,160	446	1,636
Reserves and Related Items	79da d	−46	−418	−170	−611	−4,468	−2,715	−2,343	−799	1,065	−4,098	−3,763	21	8,160	−446	−1,636
Reserve Assets	79db d	−46	−418	−170	−611	−4,468	−2,715	−2,343	−799	1,065	−4,098	−3,763	21	8,160	−446	−1,636
Use of Fund Credit and Loans	79dc d	—	—	—	—	—	—	—	—	—	—	—	—	—	—	—
Exceptional Financing	79de d	—	—	—	—	—	—	—	—	—	—	—	—	—	—	—
International Investment Position															*Millions of US Dollars*	
Assets	79aa d	....	....	....	....	....	....	....	....	....	....	....	....	....	28,179	31,017
Direct Investment Abroad	79ab d	....	....	....	....	....	....	....	....	....	....	....	....	....	133	154
Portfolio Investment	79ac d	....	....	....	....	....	....	....	....	....	....	....	....	....	—	—
Equity Securities	79ad d	....	....	....	....	....	....	....	....	....	....	....	....	....	—	—
Debt Securities	79ae d	....	....	....	....	....	....	....	....	....	....	....	....	....	—	—
Financial Derivatives	79al d	....	....	....	....	....	....	....	....	....	....	....	....	....	—	—
Other Investment	79af d	....	....	....	....	....	....	....	....	....	....	....	....	....	16,016	17,269
Monetary Authorities	79ag d	....	....	....	....	....	....	....	....	....	....	....	....	....	—	—
General Government	79ah d	....	....	....	....	....	....	....	....	....	....	....	....	....	401	423
Banks	79ai d	....	....	....	....	....	....	....	....	....	....	....	....	....	1,230	1,522
Other Sectors	79aj d	....	....	....	....	....	....	....	....	....	....	....	....	....	14,385	15,324
Reserve Assets	79ak d	....	....	....	....	....	....	....	....	....	....	19,881	19,869	14,610	12,030	13,594
Liabilities	79la d	....	....	....	....	....	....	....	....	....	....	....	....	....	37,545	37,016
Dir. Invest. in Rep. Economy	79lb d	....	....	....	....	....	....	....	....	....	....	....	....	....	1,266	1,284
Portfolio Investment	79lc d	....	....	....	....	....	....	....	....	....	....	....	....	....	—	—
Equity Securities	79ld d	....	....	....	....	....	....	....	....	....	....	....	....	....	....	....
Debt Securities	79le d	....	....	....	....	....	....	....	....	....	....	....	....	....	....	....
Financial Derivatives	79ll d	....	....	....	....	....	....	....	....	....	....	....	....	....	....	....
Other Investment	79lf d	....	....	....	....	....	....	....	....	....	....	....	....	....	36,279	35,732
Monetary Authorities	79lg d	....	....	....	....	....	....	....	....	....	....	....	....	....	162	185
General Government	79lh d	....	....	....	....	....	....	....	....	....	....	....	....	....	29,189	28,399
Banks	79li d	....	....	....	....	....	....	....	....	....	....	....	....	....	770	871
Other Sectors	79lj d	....	....	....	....	....	....	....	....	....	....	....	....	....	6,158	6,277

Balance of Payments

Minus Sign Indicates Debit

Description	Code	1985	1986	1987	1988	1989	1990	1991	1992	1993	1994	1995	1996	1997	1998	1999
Current Account, n.i.e.	78al d	3,327	-2,245	-1,390	-5,809	2,161	8,279	1,736	-3,749	-1,993	2,541	2,014	8,914	3,467	-2,562	....
Goods: Exports f.o.b.	78aa d	14,478	8,664	10,564	10,217	13,059	17,623	15,159	14,202	14,779	16,105	19,082	23,707	23,703	17,564	....
Goods: Imports f.o.b.	78ab d	-7,501	-7,866	-8,870	-12,080	-7,365	-6,917	-10,259	-12,880	-11,504	-8,480	-12,069	-9,937	-13,678	-14,816	....
Trade Balance	78ac d	6,977	798	1,694	-1,863	5,694	10,706	4,900	1,322	3,275	7,625	7,013	13,770	10,025	2,748	....
Services: Credit	78ad d	797	828	864	835	929	1,183	1,229	1,312	1,340	1,576	1,671	1,573	1,489	1,457	....
Services: Debit	78ae d	-2,043	-2,148	-2,238	-2,863	-1,911	-2,534	-3,431	-4,263	-4,525	-4,672	-4,836	-4,842	-5,495	-5,054	....
Balance on Goods & Services	78af d	5,731	-522	320	-3,891	4,712	9,355	2,698	-1,629	90	4,529	3,848	10,501	6,019	-849	....
Income: Credit	78ag d	1,914	1,761	1,455	1,653	1,582	2,658	2,168	1,607	1,599	1,626	1,867	1,579	2,139	2,428	....
Income: Debit	78ah d	-4,147	-3,363	-3,074	-3,424	-3,950	-3,432	-2,766	-3,353	-3,314	-3,530	-3,810	-3,304	-4,547	-3,987	....
Balance on Gds, Serv. & Inc.	78ai d	3,498	-2,124	-1,299	-5,662	2,344	8,581	2,100	-3,375	-1,625	2,625	1,905	8,776	3,611	-2,408	....
Current Transfers, n.i.e.: Credit	78aj d	68	80	137	87	237	444	370	533	452	606	413	526	221	229	....
Current Transfers: Debit	78ak d	-239	-201	-228	-234	-420	-746	-734	-907	-820	-690	-304	-388	-365	-383	....
Capital Account, n.i.e.	78bc d	—	—	—	—	—	—	—	—	—	—	—	—	—	—	....
Capital Account, n.i.e.: Credit	78ba d	—	—	—	—	—	—	—	—	—	—	—	—	—	—	....
Capital Account: Debit	78bb d	—	—	—	—	—	—	—	—	—	—	—	—	—	—	....
Financial Account, n.i.e.	78bj d	-629	-707	960	-1,180	-3,650	-4,061	2,204	3,386	2,656	-3,204	-2,964	-1,784	1,067	844	....
Direct Investment Abroad	78bd d	-11	-460	-37	-68	-179	-375	-188	-156	-886	-358	-91	-507	-500	-267	....
Dir. Invest. in Rep. Econ., n.i.e.	78be d	68	16	21	89	213	451	1,916	629	372	813	985	2,183	5,536	4,435	....
Portfolio Investment Assets	78bf d	—	—	—	—	-8	-1,952	17	2	79	-22	-14	-41	-600	806	....
Equity Securities	78bk d	—	—	—	—	-8	-2	-8	-44	-1	10	-3	-11	-18	-62	....
Debt Securities	78bl d	—	—	—	—	—	-1,950	25	46	80	-32	-11	-30	-582	868	....
Portfolio Investment Liab., n.i.e.	78bg d	—	—	—	—	-526	17,928	334	1,001	542	275	-787	780	1,106	239	....
Equity Securities	78bm d	—	—	—	—	—	—	—	165	48	585	270	1,318	1,445	190	....
Debt Securities	78bn d	—	—	—	—	-526	17,928	334	836	494	-310	-1,057	-538	-339	49	....
Financial Derivatives Assets	78bw d					—	—	—	—	—	—	—	—	—	—	....
Financial Derivatives Liabilities	78bx d	....	....	....	....	—	—	—	—	—	—	—	—	—	—	....
Other Investment Assets	78bh d	-314	-16	-789	-1,595	-369	-2,305	-925	-590	615	-4,173	-661	-1,592	-3,385	-3,630	....
Monetary Authorities	78bo d	....	....	....	....											....
General Government	78bp d	-30	-43	-88	-51	-58	-46	-12	-45	-16	-27	240	57	-273	262	....
Banks	78bq d	303	123	-104	-379	767	-899	-147	-58	-538	-932	216	-53	-25	-140	....
Other Sectors	78br d	-587	-96	-597	-1,165	-1,078	-1,360	-766	-487	1,169	-3,214	-1,117	-1,596	-3,087	-3,752	....
Other Investment Liab., n.i.e.	78bi d	-372	-247	1,765	394	-2,781	-17,808	1,050	2,500	1,934	261	-2,396	-2,607	-1,090	-739	....
Monetary Authorities	78bs d	21	35	253	831	11	146	-758	282	778	-51	-317	-289	-454	-17	....
General Government	78bt d	-794	-910	-657	227	890	-18,171	586	593	-210	128	-262	-543	-194	197	....
Banks	78bu d	-122	134	967	-726	-411	16	308	86	113	-77	52	153	31	-74	....
Other Sectors	78bv d	523	494	1,202	62	-3,271	201	914	1,539	1,253	261	-1,869	-1,928	-473	-845	....
Net Errors and Omissions	78ca d	-999	-930	-505	3,117	1,603	-1,742	-1,516	-299	-539	-281	-494	-892	-1,459	-1,226	....
Overall Balance	78cb d	1,699	-3,882	-935	-3,872	114	2,476	2,424	-662	124	-944	-1,444	6,238	3,075	-2,944	....
Reserves and Related Items	79da d	-1,699	3,882	935	3,872	-114	-2,476	-2,424	662	-124	944	1,444	-6,238	-3,075	2,944	....
Reserve Assets	79db d	-1,699	3,882	935	3,872	-1,077	-4,376	-2,645	845	144	1,145	1,907	-6,271	-2,624	3,392	....
Use of Fund Credit and Loans	79dc d	—	—	—	—	964	1,900	221	-183	-268	-201	-463	33	-452	-448	....
Exceptional Financing	79de d	—	—	—	—	—	—	—	—	—	—	—	—	—	—	....

International Investment Position

Millions of US Dollars

Description	Code	1985	1986	1987	1988	1989	1990	1991	1992	1993	1994	1995	1996	1997	1998	1999
Assets	79aa d	33,186	29,927	30,080	27,731	29,488	38,443	42,227	41,806	43,156	46,634	45,944	25,364	27,660	....	....
Direct Investment Abroad	79ab d	165	625	662	730	866	1,221	1,368	1,568	2,447	3,124	3,427	4,427	4,903	....	....
Portfolio Investment	79ac d	—	—	—	—	—	1,950	1,925	1,879	1,799	1,796	1,530	85	781	....	....
Equity Securities	79ad d	—	—	—	—	—	—	—	—	—	—	—	25	18	....	....
Debt Securities	79ae d	—	—	—	—	—	1,950	1,925	1,879	1,799	1,796	1,530	60	763	....	....
Financial Derivatives	79al d															
Other Investment	79af d	17,583	17,599	18,388	19,983	20,529	22,806	23,773	24,363	25,106	28,955	30,391	4,036	2,937	....	....
Monetary Authorities	79ag d	—	—													
General Government	79ah d	453	496	584	635	693	739	751	796	812	812	874	....	....	....	....
Banks	79ai d	1,219	1,096	1,200	1,579	1,111	1,978	2,123	2,181	2,719	3,774	3,586	....	....	....	....
Other Sectors	79aj d	15,911	16,007	16,604	17,769	18,725	20,089	20,899	21,386	21,575	24,369	25,931	....	....	....	....
Reserve Assets	79ak d	15,438	11,703	11,030	7,018	8,093	12,466	15,161	13,996	13,804	12,759	10,596	16,816	19,039	....	....
Liabilities	79la d	36,691	36,460	38,246	38,729	37,102	39,689	42,988	47,046	50,713	51,730	49,250	10,763	11,494	....	....
Dir. Invest. in Rep. Economy	79lb d	1,352	1,368	1,389	1,478	1,691	2,142	4,058	4,687	5,059	5,872	6,772	....	....	....	....
Portfolio Investment	79lc d	—	—	—	—	—	18,483	18,945	20,241	22,816	22,844	22,555	4,188	6,212	....	....
Equity Securities	79ld d	—	—	—	—	—	—	—	—	917	1,184	1,060	2,391	3,801	....	....
Debt Securities	79le d	—	—	—	—	—	18,483	18,945	20,241	21,899	21,660	21,495	1,797	2,411	....	....
Financial Derivatives	79ll d															
Other Investment	79lf d	35,339	35,092	36,857	37,251	35,411	19,064	19,985	22,118	22,838	23,014	19,923	6,575	5,282	....	....
Monetary Authorities	79lg d	208	58	311	1,142	2,151	4,363	3,841	3,821	4,376	4,246	3,525	3,183	2,152	....	....
General Government	79lh d	27,582	26,857	26,200	26,427	26,949	8,358	8,642	8,975	8,459	8,454	8,009	....	....	....	....
Banks	79li d	749	883	1,850	1,124	981	940	1,248	1,335	1,447	1,394	1,451	295	324	....	....
Other Sectors	79lj d	6,800	7,294	8,496	8,558	5,330	5,403	6,254	7,987	8,556	8,920	6,938	3,097	2,806	....	....

Venezuela, Rep. Bol.

		1970	1971	1972	1973	1974	1975	1976	1977	1978	1979	1980	1981	1982	1983	1984
Government Finance															*Billions of Bolivares:*	
Deficit (-) or Surplus	80	I−.7	.2	−.2	1.2	5.0	1.9	−4.0	−6.7	−6.9	4.0	.1	−3.9	−12.7	I−4.4	13.5
Revenue	81	I10.1	12.4	13.3	17.0	44.3	42.4	39.9	42.9	42.7	50.9	66.5	97.5	83.7	I77.4	104.5
Grants Received	81z	I.2	.1	.2	—	.7	.1	.1	.1	.2	.2	.3	.3	.3	I.1	.1
Expenditure	82	I9.8	11.1	12.7	14.2	22.8	27.5	32.7	42.2	46.3	44.8	55.8	84.5	84.5	I73.4	82.6
Lending Minus Repayments	83	I1.2	1.2	1.0	1.7	17.3	13.0	11.3	7.5	3.5	2.3	10.9	17.2	12.2	I8.4	8.5
Financing																
Net Borrowing	84	I.8	—	.2	.5	−1.2	−1.3	8.0	6.8	8.6	−2.7	3.6	6.8	6.3	....	....
Domestic	84a	I.4	.2	.2	.5	−.9	−1.3	−.7	.6	−1.5	−1.6	−1.9	8.2	−1.6	....	....
Foreign	85a	I.4	−.2	—	—	−.3	—	8.7	6.2	10.2	−1.1	5.5	−1.4	7.9	....	....
Use of Cash Balances	87	I−.1	−.2	−.1	−1.7	−3.8	−.6	−4.0	−.1	−1.7	−1.3	−3.7	−2.9	6.4	....	....
															Billions of Bolivares:	
Debt	88	I2.3	2.1	2.2	2.2	2.1	3.7	12.8	21.4	32.5	32.0	35.6	46.5	55.3	I57.8	85.5
Domestic	88a	I.8	.8	.9	1.1	1.2	1.4	1.7	3.8	4.0	4.1	3.2	16.3	19.3	I18.1	23.5
Foreign	89a	I1.5	1.3	1.3	1.1	.9	2.3	11.2	17.5	28.4	27.9	32.4	30.3	36.0	I39.7	62.0
National Accounts															*Billions of Bolivares*	
Exports of Goods & Services	90c	12.4	14.7	14.5	21.2	48.8	39.3	41.1	43.5	42.0	64.0	85.5	89.6	75.2	74.1	108.8
Government Consumption	91f	6.9	7.8	8.5	9.6	12.8	15.9	19.8	23.0	24.1	27.8	35.1	42.6	42.6	41.3	43.3
Gross Fixed Capital Formation	93e	11.5	13.3	15.8	18.6	21.0	30.6	42.8	60.5	71.8	65.6	64.1	69.8	70.2	55.4	67.3
Increase/Decrease(-) in Stocks	93i	3.9	3.8	3.4	2.8	5.9	5.8	3.7	4.2	.6	.1	−1.4	−4.4	5.2	−21.2	6.2
Private Consumption	96f	27.6	29.0	31.8	35.2	44.9	56.3	66.9	80.1	94.8	110.3	135.4	160.5	182.2	183.4	256.3
Imports of Goods & Services	98c	−10.0	−11.1	−12.4	−14.2	−21.1	−29.9	−39.2	−55.5	−64.1	−60.0	−64.6	−73.0	−84.1	−42.5	−76.2
Gross Domestic Product (GDP)	99b	52.3	57.4	61.5	73.3	112.2	118.1	135.1	155.7	169.1	207.7	254.2	285.2	291.3	290.5	405.8
Net Factor Inc/Pmts(-) Abroad	98.n	−2.4	−3.3	−2.1	−3.0	−2.7	.3	.2	−.4	−.6	−.6	−.8	1.2	−6.6	−9.9	6.8
Gross National Income (GNI)	99a	49.9	54.2	59.4	70.3	109.5	118.4	135.3	155.3	168.4	207.0	255.4	287.5	284.7	280.6	412.6
Net National Income	99e	45.0	48.9	53.9	64.4	103.0	110.9	126.8	144.8	155.9	192.1	238.3	267.6	263.1	256.6	379.8
GDP Volume 1968 Prices	99b.p	50.92	52.46	53.89	57.26	60.73	64.42	70.07	74.78	76.38	77.40	75.86	75.63	76.14	71.87	70.89
GDP Volume 1984 Prices	99b.p	....	....	....	....	....	....	....	....	....	....	....	....	....	....	405.75
GDP Volume (1995=100)	99bv p	51.4	53.0	54.4	57.8	61.3	65.1	70.8	75.5	77.2	78.2	76.6	76.4	76.9	72.6	71.6
GDP Deflator (1995=100)	99bi p	.7	.8	.8	.9	1.3	1.3	1.4	1.5	1.6	1.9	2.4	2.7	2.8	2.9	4.1
																Millions:
Population	99z	10.28	10.61	10.94	11.28	11.63	I12.67	13.12	13.59	14.07	14.55	15.02	15.48	15.94	16.39	16.85

	1985	1986	1987	1988	1989	1990	1991	1992	1993	1994	1995	1996	1997	1998	1999		
Government Finance																		
Year Ending December 31																		
	23.6	−10.0	ɪ−31.5	ɪ−41.8	−1.3	.9	60.3	−128.2	−125.1	−485.8	−493.9	456.5	955.5	−1,442.7	....	Deficit (-) or Surplus	80
	126.5	108.7	ɪ123.1	ɪ167.9	288.4	539.5	718.8	749.1	946.0	1,575.1	2,242.6	5,767.8	10,241.0	9,017.5	....	Revenue	81
	.1	—	ɪ—	ɪ	—	—	—	—	—	—	—	—	—	—	....	Grants Received	81z
	94.6	105.2	ɪ139.1	ɪ189.4	263.9	472.5	607.4	824.7	1,013.8	1,666.3	2,541.5	4,964.2	8,894.3	10,281.0	....	Expenditure	82
	8.4	13.4	ɪ15.5	ɪ20.3	25.8	66.1	51.1	52.6	57.3	394.6	195.0	347.1	391.2	179.2	....	Lending Minus Repayments	83
																Financing	
	....	....	....	....	....	−.9	−60.4	128.1	125.0	485.8	493.9	−456.5	−955.5	1,442.7	....	Net Borrowing	84
	....	....	....	....	....	−23.2	−47.6	79.0	131.8	530.6	476.2	−301.7	−1,360.0	1,132.7	....	Domestic	84a
	....	....	....	....	....	22.3	−12.8	49.1	−6.8	−44.8	17.7	−154.8	404.5	310.0	....	Foreign	85a
	....	....	....	....	....	....	....	....	....	....	....	....	....	....	....	Use of Cash Balances	87
Year Ending December 31																		
	98.4	....	....	....	....	....	....	....	....	....	98.4	....	....	....	....	Debt	88
	38.7	67.7	....	....	....	....	....	....	....	....	....	....	....	....	....	Domestic	88a
	59.7															Foreign	89a
Billions of Bolivares																**National Accounts**	
	108.3	97.5	145.7	180.1	503.0	899.2	952.4	1,088.8	1,470.3	2,677.5	3,709.8	10,748.9	12,251.0	10,419.9	....	Exports of Goods & Services	90c
	48.6	54.7	71.1	91.9	144.4	191.8	293.2	379.4	466.0	627.0	974.8	1,475.6	2,782.7	3,928.0	....	Government Consumption	91f
	80.6	99.8	147.9	199.3	255.0	322.1	552.0	886.4	1,091.1	1,528.4	2,255.6	4,645.8	7,775.8	9,484.6	....	Gross Fixed Capital Formation	93e
	5.4	2.6	23.2	44.8	−63.2	−89.2	15.4	93.6	−68.5	−300.3	223.4	227.6	674.1	721.2	....	Increase/Decrease(-) in Stocks	93i
	287.3	337.1	450.4	597.7	977.3	1,415.4	2,021.2	2,877.6	3,977.4	6,077.1	9,507.7	18,618.0	28,705.3	37,925.6	....	Private Consumption	96f
	−81.1	−99.6	−158.8	−238.4	−330.9	−460.1	−796.6	−1,194.4	−1,482.4	−1,934.5	−2,985.7	−6,278.3	−8,977.0	−10,448.9	....	Imports of Goods & Services	98c
	449.0	492.1	679.4	875.5	1,485.5	2,279.3	3,037.5	4,131.5	5,453.9	8,675.2	13,685.7	29,437.7	43,211.9	52,030.3	....	Gross Domestic Product (GDP)	99b
	−10.6	−3.0	−.2	−2.2	−62.4	−67.7	−57.3	−123.8	−162.4	−274.6	−322.9	−665.7	−991.2	−922.6	....	Net Factor Inc/Pmts(-) Abroad	98.n
	438.4	489.2	679.2	873.4	1,423.1	2,211.6	2,980.2	4,007.7	5,291.5	8,400.6	13,362.8	28,772.0	42,220.8	51,107.7	....	Gross National Income (GNI)	99a
	401.9	446.0	623.0	801.7	1,315.8	2,057.3	2,759.7	3,698.4	4,869.1	7,774.8	12,435.1	26,887.6	39,376.4	47,462.6	....	Net National Income	99e
	....	....	....	....	....	....	....	....	....	....	....	....	....	....	....	GDP Volume 1968 Prices	99b.p
	411.53	437.61	457.35	485.58	447.55	478.32	524.86	556.67	558.20	545.09	566.63	565.51	601.53	600.86	557.78	GDP Volume 1984 Prices	99b.p
	72.6	77.2	80.7	85.7	79.0	84.4	92.6	98.2	98.5	96.2	100.0	99.8	106.2	106.0	98.4	GDP Volume (1995=100)	99bv p
	4.5	4.7	6.2	7.5	13.7	19.7	24.0	30.7	40.5	65.9	100.0	215.5	297.4	358.5	....	GDP Deflator (1995=100)	99bi p
Midyear Estimates																		
	17.32	17.53	17.97	18.16	18.87	19.50	19.97	20.44	20.91	21.38	21.84	22.31	22.78	23.44	23.71	**Population**	99z

(See notes in the back of the book.)

Yemen, Republic of

			1970	1971	1972	1973	1974	1975	1976	1977	1978	1979	1980	1981	1982	1983	1984

Exchange Rates — *Rials per SDR:*

Principal Rate	aa	....

Rials per US Dollar:

Principal Rate	ae	....
Principal Rate	rf	....

Fund Position — *Millions of SDRs:*

Quota	2f. s	— — — — — — — — — — — — — — —
SDRs	1b. s	— — — — — — — — — — — — — — —
Reserve Position in the Fund	1c. s	— — — — — — — — — — — — — — —
Total Fund Cred.&Loans Outstg.	2tl	— — — — — — — — — — — — — — —

International Liquidity — *Millions of US Dollars Unless Otherwise Indicated:*

Total Reserves minus Gold	1l. d	....
SDRs	1b. d	— — — — — — — — — — — — — — —
Reserve Position in the Fund	1c. d	— — — — — — — — — — — — — — —
Foreign Exchange	1d. d	....
Gold (Million Fine Troy Ounces)	1ad	....
Gold (National Valuation)	1an d	....
Deposit Money Banks: Assets	7a. d	....
Liabilities	7b. d	....

Monetary Authorities — *Millions of Rials:*

Foreign Assets	11	....
Claims on Central Government	12a	....
Claims on Nonfin.Pub.Enterprises	12c	....
Reserve Money	14	....
of which: Currency Outside Banks	14a	....
Time, Savings,& Fgn.Currency Dep.	15	....
Foreign Liabilities	16c	....
Central Government Deposits	16d	....
Capital Accounts	17a	....
Other Items (Net)	17r	....

Deposit Money Banks — *Millions of Rials:*

Reserves	20	....
Foreign Assets	21	....
Claims on Central Government	22a	....
Claims on Nonfin.Pub.Enterprises	22c	....
Claims on Private Sector	22d	....
Demand Deposits	24	....
Time, Savings,& Fgn.Currency Dep.	25	....
Restricted Deposits	26b	....
Foreign Liabilities	26c	....
Central Government Deposits	26d	....
Capital Accounts	27a	....
Other Items (Net)	27r	....

Monetary Survey — *Millions of Rials:*

Foreign Assets (Net)	31n	....
Domestic Credit	32	....
Claims on Central Govt. (Net)	32an	....
Claims on Nonfin.Pub.Enterprises	32c	....
Claims on Private Sector	32d	....
Money	34	....
Quasi-Money	35	....
Restricted Deposits	36b	....
Capital Accounts	37a	....
Other Items (Net)	37r	....
Money plus Quasi-Money	35l	....

Prices — *Index Numbers (1995=100):*

Consumer Prices	64	....

International Transactions — *Millions of Rials*

Exports	70	....
Imports, c.i.f.	71	....

1985	1986	1987	1988	1989	1990	1991	1992	1993	1994	1995	1996	1997	1998	1999		
															Exchange Rates	
End of Period																
....	....	....	....	....	17.086	17.179	16.514	16.496	17.533	‡74.384	182.492	176.023	199.447	....	Principal Rate	aa
End of Period (ae) Period Average (rf)																
....	....	....	....	....	12.010	12.010	12.010	12.010	12.010	‡50.040	126.910	130.460	141.650	....	Principal Rate	ae
....	....	....	....	....	....	12.010	12.010	12.010	12.010	40.839	‡94.157	129.281	135.882	....	Principal Rate	rf
															Fund Position	
End of Period																
—	—	—	—	—	120.5	120.5	176.5	176.5	176.5	176.5	176.5	176.5	176.5	243.5	Quota	2f. *s*
—	—	—	—	—	9.4	11.7	2.9	.5	33.5	37.0	33.3	124.1	131.6	128.5	SDRs	1b. *s*
—	—	—	—	—	—	—	—	—	—	—	—	—	—	—	Reserve Position in the Fund	1c. *s*
—	—	—	—	—	.1	—	—	—	—	—	84.0	185.4	238.4	297.6	Total Fund Cred.&Loans Outstg.	2tl
															International Liquidity	
End of Period																
....	....	....	....	....	422.2	679.3	320.5	145.3	254.8	619.0	1,017.2	1,203.1	995.5		Total Reserves minus Gold	1l. *d*
—	—	—	—	—	13.4	16.8	4.0	.6	48.9	55.0	47.9	167.4	185.2	176.3	SDRs	1b. *d*
—	—	—	—	—	—	—	—	—	—	—	—	—	—		Reserve Position in the Fund	1c. *d*
....	....	....	....	....	408.8	662.5	316.5	144.6	205.9	564.0	969.3	1,035.7	810.3	....	Foreign Exchange	1d. *d*
....	....	....	....	....	.050	.050	.050	.050	.050	.050	.050	.050	.050	....	Gold (Million Fine Troy Ounces)	1ad
....	....	....	....	....	2.2	2.5	2.4	2.4	2.6	2.6	18.6	18.5	15.3	....	Gold (National Valuation)	1an *d*
....	....	....	....	....	520.2	565.6	543.7	547.7	477.2	861.1	334.5	455.9	457.9	....	Deposit Money Banks: Assets	7a. *d*
....	....	....	....	....	404.9	564.2	590.4	549.4	548.1	479.1	209.8	60.8	50.2	....	Liabilities	7b. *d*
															Monetary Authorities	
End of Period																
....	....	....	....	....	5,165	8,442	3,896	1,777	4,562	32,448	134,124	167,520	153,964	....	Foreign Assets	11
....	....	....	....	....	74,914	82,253	104,818	135,664	180,586	209,342	199,058	171,234	196,702	....	Claims on Central Government	12a
....	....	....	....	....	162	318	352	76	57	—	10	50	1,108	....	Claims on Nonfin.Pub.Enterprises	12c
....	....	....	....	....	63,315	69,148	83,927	108,933	147,585	176,756	189,030	165,443	184,002	....	Reserve Money	14
....	....	....	....	....	39,895	45,161	55,531	79,019	111,006	129,114	120,477	126,904	139,668	....	*of which: Currency Outside Banks*	14a
....	....	....	....	....	423	289	316	2,352	3,881	9,440	19,966	22,193	18,978	....	Time, Savings,& Fgn.Currency Dep.	15
....	....	....	....	....	2,041	2,149	2,136	1,913	2,053	11,323	43,931	66,613	84,138	....	Foreign Liabilities	16c
....	....	....	....	....	6,880	8,803	14,063	16,326	18,294	27,011	41,003	46,106	18,171	....	Central Government Deposits	16d
....	....	....	....	....	716	1,094	1,075	1,077	1,100	2,738	5,835	5,673	6,323	....	Capital Accounts	17a
....	....	....	....	....	6,865	9,532	7,289	6,919	12,293	14,522	33,428	32,474	40,165	....	Other Items (Net)	17r
															Deposit Money Banks	
End of Period																
....	....	....	....	....	20,533	20,097	24,120	25,987	32,879	44,055	59,903	28,052	35,714	....	Reserves	20
....	....	....	....	....	6,248	6,792	6,530	6,578	5,731	43,088	42,453	59,472	64,857	....	Foreign Assets	21
....	....	....	....	....	155	239	352	281	336	1,295	6,963	34,873	36,267	....	Claims on Central Government	22a
....	....	....	....	....	2,813	3,968	3,793	3,395	3,401	11,011	2,237	1,641	317	....	Claims on Nonfin.Pub.Enterprises	22c
....	....	....	....	....	7,723	8,708	10,040	12,653	14,143	23,865	22,358	34,380	45,957	....	Claims on Private Sector	22d
....	....	....	....	....	12,640	14,097	18,237	21,489	25,390	22,985	27,353	28,875	31,490	....	Demand Deposits	24
....	....	....	....	....	12,782	14,271	15,096	17,251	19,359	71,956	88,640	106,272	130,753	....	Time, Savings,& Fgn.Currency Dep.	25
....	....	....	....	....	2,834	1,786	1,329	1,240	1,210	1,977	3,661	3,540	3,684	....	Restricted Deposits	26b
....	....	....	....	....	4,863	6,776	7,091	6,599	6,582	23,973	26,624	7,932	7,114	....	Foreign Liabilities	26c
....	....	....	....	....	2,182	1,880	1,272	1,543	1,863	1,127	171	474	52	....	Central Government Deposits	26d
....	....	....	....	....	1,237	1,443	1,564	1,997	2,829	4,601	6,669	10,762	17,615	....	Capital Accounts	27a
....	....	....	....	....	934	-449	247	-1,224	-745	-3,305	-19,203	564	-7,597	....	Other Items (Net)	27r
															Monetary Survey	
End of Period																
....	....	....	....	....	4,508	6,310	1,199	-157	1,658	40,240	106,023	152,447	127,569	....	Foreign Assets (Net)	31n
....	....	....	....	....	76,704	84,803	103,762	134,201	178,365	217,375	189,453	195,598	262,128	....	Domestic Credit	32
....	....	....	....	....	66,007	71,809	89,836	118,076	160,765	182,499	164,848	159,527	214,746	....	Claims on Central Govt. (Net)	32an
....	....	....	....	....	2,974	4,286	3,886	3,472	3,457	11,011	2,247	1,691	1,425	....	Claims on Nonfin.Pub.Enterprises	32c
....	....	....	....	....	7,723	8,708	10,040	12,653	14,143	23,865	22,358	34,380	45,957	....	Claims on Private Sector	32d
....	....	....	....	....	56,498	62,995	78,314	103,306	139,590	164,019	156,579	166,384	179,927	....	Money	34
....	....	....	....	....	13,205	14,560	15,412	19,604	23,239	81,396	108,605	128,465	149,731	....	Quasi-Money	35
....	....	....	....	....	2,834	1,786	1,329	1,240	1,210	1,977	3,661	3,540	3,684	....	Restricted Deposits	36b
....	....	....	....	....	1,953	2,536	2,640	3,073	3,929	7,339	12,504	16,434	23,938	....	Capital Accounts	37a
....	....	....	....	....	6,722	9,236	7,266	6,824	12,054	2,884	14,126	32,920	32,419	....	Other Items (Net)	37r
....	....	....	....	....	69,703	77,555	93,726	122,909	162,829	245,415	265,184	294,849	329,658	....	Money plus Quasi-Money	35l
															Prices	
Period Averages																
....	....	....	....	....	19	25	33	44	64	100	130	137	148	....	Consumer Prices	64
															International Transactions	
Millions of Rials																
....	....	....	....	....	8,316	7,918	7,435	7,333	11,216	79,434	251,830	323,716	203,480	380,010	Exports	70
....	....	....	....	....	18,867	24,314	31,076	33,883	25,070	64,591	191,862	260,331	294,510	312,749	Imports, c.i.f.	71

Yemen, Republic of

		1970	1971	1972	1973	1974	1975	1976	1977	1978	1979	1980	1981	1982	1983	1984
Balance of Payments															*Millions of US Dollars:*	
Current Account, n.i.e.	78al *d*	....	....	....	....	....	....	....	....	....	....	....	....	....	....	....
Goods: Exports f.o.b.	78aa *d*	....	....	....	....	....	....	....	....	....	....	....	....	....	....	....
Goods: Imports f.o.b.	78ab *d*	....	....	....	....	....	....	....	....	....	....	....	....	....	....	....
Trade Balance	78ac *d*	....	....	....	....	....	....	....	....	....	....	....	....	....	....	....
Services: Credit	78ad *d*	....	....	....	....	....	....	....	....	....	....	....	....	....	....	....
Services: Debit	78ae *d*	....	....	....	....	....	....	....	....	....	....	....	....	....	....	....
Balance on Goods & Services	78af *d*	....	....	....	....	....	....	....	....	....	....	....	....	....	....	....
Income: Credit	78ag *d*	....	....	....	....	....	....	....	....	....	....	....	....	....	....	....
Income: Debit	78ah *d*	....	....	....	....	....	....	....	....	....	....	....	....	....	....	....
Balance on Gds, Serv. & Inc.	78ai *d*	....	....	....	....	....	....	....	....	....	....	....	....	....	....	....
Current Transfers, n.i.e.: Credit	78aj *d*	....	....	....	....	....	....	....	....	....	....	....	....	....	....	....
Current Transfers: Debit	78ak *d*	....	....	....	....	....	....	....	....	....	....	....	....	....	....	....
Capital Account, n.i.e.	78bc *d*	....	....	....	....	....	....	....	....	....	....	....	....	....	....	....
Capital Account, n.i.e.: Credit	78ba *d*	....	....	....	....	....	....	....	....	....	....	....	....	....	....	....
Capital Account: Debit	78bb *d*	....	....	....	....	....	....	....	....	....	....	....	....	....	....	....
Financial Account, n.i.e.	78bj *d*	....	....	....	....	....	....	....	....	....	....	....	....	....	....	....
Direct Investment Abroad	78bd *d*	....	....	....	....	....	....	....	....	....	....	....	....	....	....	....
Dir. Invest. in Rep. Econ., n.i.e.	78be *d*	....	....	....	....	....	....	....	....	....	....	....	....	....	....	....
Portfolio Investment Assets	78bf *d*	....	....	....	....	....	....	....	....	....	....	....	....	....	....	....
Equity Securities	78bk *d*	....	....	....	....	....	....	....	....	....	....	....	....	....	....	....
Debt Securities	78bl *d*	....	....	....	....	....	....	....	....	....	....	....	....	....	....	....
Portfolio Investment Liab., n.i.e.	78bg *d*	....	....	....	....	....	....	....	....	....	....	....	....	....	....	....
Equity Securities	78bm *d*	....	....	....	....	....	....	....	....	....	....	....	....	....	....	....
Debt Securities	78bn *d*	....	....	....	....	....	....	....	....	....	....	....	....	....	....	....
Financial Derivatives Assets	78bw *d*	....	....	....	....	....	....	....	....	....	....	....	....	....	....	....
Financial Derivatives Liabilities	78bx *d*	....	....	....	....	....	....	....	....	....	....	....	....	....	....	....
Other Investment Assets	78bh *d*	....	....	....	....	....	....	....	....	....	....	....	....	....	....	....
Monetary Authorities	78bo *d*	....	....	....	....	....	....	....	....	....	....	....	....	....	....	....
General Government	78bp *d*	....	....	....	....	....	....	....	....	....	....	....	....	....	....	....
Banks	78bq *d*	....	....	....	....	....	....	....	....	....	....	....	....	....	....	....
Other Sectors	78br *d*	....	....	....	....	....	....	....	....	....	....	....	....	....	....	....
Other Investment Liab., n.i.e.	78bi *d*	....	....	....	....	....	....	....	....	....	....	....	....	....	....	....
Monetary Authorities	78bs *d*	....	....	....	....	....	....	....	....	....	....	....	....	....	....	....
General Government	78bt *d*	....	....	....	....	....	....	....	....	....	....	....	....	....	....	....
Banks	78bu *d*	....	....	....	....	....	....	....	....	....	....	....	....	....	....	....
Other Sectors	78bv *d*	....	....	....	....	....	....	....	....	....	....	....	....	....	....	....
Net Errors and Omissions	78ca *d*	....	....	....	....	....	....	....	....	....	....	....	....	....	....	....
Overall Balance	78cb *d*	....	....	....	....	....	....	....	....	....	....	....	....	....	....	....
Reserves and Related Items	79da *d*	....	....	....	....	....	....	....	....	....	....	....	....	....	....	....
Reserve Assets	79db *d*	....	....	....	....	....	....	....	....	....	....	....	....	....	....	....
Use of Fund Credit and Loans	79dc *d*	....	....	....	....	....	....	....	....	....	....	....	....	....	....	....
Exceptional Financing	79de *d*	....	....	....	....	....	....	....	....	....	....	....	....	....	....	....
Government Finance															*Millions of Rials:*	
Deficit (-) or Surplus	80	....	....	....	....	....	....	....	....	....	....	....	....	....	....	....
Revenue	81	....	....	....	....	....	....	....	....	....	....	....	....	....	....	....
Grants Received	81z	....	....	....	....	....	....	....	....	....	....	....	....	....	....	....
Expenditure	82	....	....	....	....	....	....	....	....	....	....	....	....	....	....	....
Lending Minus Repayments	83	....	....	....	....	....	....	....	....	....	....	....	....	....	....	....
Financing																
Domestic	84a	....	....	....	....	....	....	....	....	....	....	....	....	....	....	....
Foreign	85a	....	....	....	....	....	....	....	....	....	....	....	....	....	....	....
National Accounts															*Millions of Rials*	
Exports of Goods & Services	90c	....	....	....	....	....	....	....	....	....	....	....	....	....	....	....
Government Consumption	91f	....	....	....	....	....	....	....	....	....	....	....	....	....	....	....
Gross Fixed Capital Formation	93e	....	....	....	....	....	....	....	....	....	....	....	....	....	....	....
Increase/Decrease(-) in Stocks	93i	....	....	....	....	....	....	....	....	....	....	....	....	....	....	....
Private Consumption	96f	....	....	....	....	....	....	....	....	....	....	....	....	....	....	....
Imports of Goods & Services	98c	....	....	....	....	....	....	....	....	....	....	....	....	....	....	....
Gross Domestic Product (GDP)	99b	....	....	....	....	....	....	....	....	....	....	....	....	....	....	....
Net Factor Inc/Pmts(-) Abroad	98.n	....	....	....	....	....	....	....	....	....	....	....	....	....	....	....
Gross National Income (GNI)	99a	....	....	....	....	....	....	....	....	....	....	....	....	....	....	....
GDP Volume 1990 Prices	99b. *p*	....	....	....	....	....	....	....	....	....	....	....	....	....	....	....
GDP Volume (1995=100)	99bv *p*	....	....	....	....	....	....	....	....	....	....	....	....	....	....	....
															Millions:	
Population	99z	....	....	....	....	....	....	....	....	....	....	....	....	....	9.10	9.42

	1985	1986	1987	1988	1989	1990	1991	1992	1993	1994	1995	1996	1997	1998	1999		
Minus Sign Indicates Debit																**Balance of Payments**	
	....	....	....	....	....	738.7	−663.2	−1,091.3	−1,247.6	365.9	182.7	106.3	51.6	−228.1	....	Current Account, n.i.e.	**78al** *d*
	....	....	....	....	....	1,384.4	1,196.6	1,094.9	1,166.9	1,824.0	1,937.2	2,262.8	2,264.0	1,500.7	....	Goods: Exports f.o.b.	**78aa** *d*
	....	....	....	....	....	−1,475.6	−1,896.8	−1,891.1	−2,086.9	−1,521.9	−1,948.2	−2,293.5	−2,406.5	−2,201.2	....	Goods: Imports f.o.b.	**78ab** *d*
	....	....	....	....	....	−91.2	−700.2	−796.2	−920.0	302.1	−11.0	−30.7	−142.5	−700.5	....	*Trade Balance*	**78ac** *d*
	....	....	....	....	....	105.6	114.0	161.9	177.2	148.0	179.4	185.7	207.6	207.5	....	Services: Credit	**78ad** *d*
	....	....	....	....	....	−694.4	−775.0	−1,013.8	−1,094.6	−622.6	−590.5	−555.4	−633.9	−569.5	....	Services: Debit	**78ae** *d*
	....	....	....	....	....	−680.0	−1,361.2	−1,648.1	−1,837.4	−172.5	−422.1	−400.4	−568.8	−1,062.5	....	*Balance on Goods & Services*	**78af** *d*
	....	....	....	....	....	37.9	43.3	38.1	22.0	22.0	37.4	46.8	69.6	65.5	....	Income: Credit	**78ag** *d*
	....	....	....	....	....	−491.6	−609.5	−552.5	−499.5	−600.6	−536.5	−728.5	−704.5	−487.4	....	Income: Debit	**78ah** *d*
	....	....	....	....	....	−1,133.7	−1,927.4	−2,162.5	−2,314.9	−751.1	−921.2	−1,082.1	−1,203.7	−1,484.4	....	*Balance on Gds, Serv. & Inc.*	**78ai** *d*
	....	....	....	....	....	1,896.8	1,309.1	1,100.2	1,092.8	1,133.6	1,120.5	1,207.6	1,268.7	1,273.0	....	Current Transfers, n.i.e.: Credit	**78aj** *d*
	....	....	....	....	....	−24.4	−44.9	−29.0	−25.5	−16.6	−16.6	−19.2	−13.4	−16.7	....	Current Transfers: Debit	**78ak** *d*
	....	....	....	....	....	....	....	....	....	....	....	....	....	....	....	Capital Account, n.i.e.	**78bc** *d*
	....	....	....	....	....	....	....	....	....	....	....	....	....	....	....	Capital Account, n.i.e.: Credit	**78ba** *d*
	....	....	....	....	....	....	....	....	....	....	....	....	....	....	....	Capital Account: Debit	**78bb** *d*
	....	....	....	....	....	−284.2	237.7	91.8	−87.9	−837.5	−819.0	−252.0	−76.5	−164.4	....	Financial Account, n.i.e.	**78bj** *d*
	....	....	....	....	....	....	....	....	....	....	....	....	....	....	....	Direct Investment Abroad	**78bd** *d*
	....	....	....	....	....	−130.9	582.5	713.6	897.1	10.5	−217.7	−60.1	−138.5	−209.7	....	Dir. Invest. in Rep. Econ., n.i.e.	**78be** *d*
	....	....	....	....	....	....	....	....	....	....	....	....	....	....	....	Portfolio Investment Assets	**78bf** *d*
	....	....	....	....	....	....	....	....	....	....	....	....	....	....	....	Equity Securities	**78bk** *d*
	....	....	....	....	....	....	....	....	....	....	....	....	....	....	....	Debt Securities	**78bl** *d*
	....	....	....	....	....	....	....	....	....	....	....	....	....	....	....	Portfolio Investment Liab., n.i.e.	**78bg** *d*
	....	....	....	....	....	....	....	....	....	....	....	....	....	....	....	Equity Securities	**78bm** *d*
	....	....	....	....	....	....	....	....	....	....	....	....	....	....	....	Debt Securities	**78bn** *d*
	....	....	....	....	....	....	....	....	....	....	....	....	....	....	....	Financial Derivatives Assets	**78bw** *d*
	....	....	....	....	....	....	....	....	....	....	....	....	....	....	....	Financial Derivatives Liabilities	**78bx** *d*
	....	....	....	....	....	−348.5	−57.1	32.3	−53.7	71.8	105.7	106.9	−136.5	−118.9	....	Other Investment Assets	**78bh** *d*
	....	....	....	....	....	....	....	....	....	....	....	....	....	....	....	Monetary Authorities	**78bo** *d*
	....	....	....	....	....	....	....	....	....	....	....	....	....	....	....	General Government	**78bp** *d*
	....	....	....	....	....	−348.5	−45.0	20.2	−2.4	70.5	138.2	3.2	−120.7	−2.4	....	Banks	**78bq** *d*
	....	....	....	....	....		−12.1	12.1	−51.3	1.3	−32.5	103.7	−15.8	−116.5	....	Other Sectors	**78br** *d*
	....	....	....	....	....	195.2	−287.7	−654.1	−931.3	−919.8	−707.0	−298.8	198.5	164.2	....	Other Investment Liab., n.i.e.	**78bi** *d*
	....	....	....	....	....	46.1	13.6	−43.2	−31.0	57.0	3.4	119.9	159.2	88.3	....	Monetary Authorities	**78bs** *d*
	....	....	....	....	....	83.8	−660.2	−737.6	−774.5	−682.3	−678.9	−520.6	−66.4	−63.7	....	General Government	**78bt** *d*
	....	....	....	....	....	65.3	158.9	26.7	−225.8	−94.5	−81.5	21.9	−149.1	−10.5	....	Banks	**78bu** *d*
	....	....	....	....	....		200.0	100.0	100.0	−200.0	50.0	80.0	254.8	150.1	....	Other Sectors	**78bv** *d*
	....	....	....	....	....	−711.4	−268.0	−248.5	222.4	−181.0	161.8	−222.6	−103.8	−43.7	....	Net Errors and Omissions	**78ca** *d*
	....	....	....	....	....	−256.9	−693.5	−1,248.0	−1,113.1	−652.6	−474.5	−368.3	−128.7	−436.2	....	*Overall Balance*	**78cb** *d*
	....	....	....	....	....	256.9	693.5	1,248.0	1,113.1	652.6	474.5	368.3	128.7	436.2	....	Reserves and Related Items	**79da** *d*
	....	....	....	....	....	−14.0	−254.6	343.8	174.8	−204.2	−263.2	−415.9	−190.9	217.9	....	Reserve Assets	**79db** *d*
	....	....	....	....	....	.1	−.2	—	—	—	—	122.5	139.4	72.3	....	Use of Fund Credit and Loans..........	**79dc** *d*
	....	....	....	....	....	270.8	948.3	904.2	938.3	856.8	737.7	661.8	180.2	146.0	....	Exceptional Financing	**79de** *d*
Year Ending December 31																**Government Finance**	
	....	....	....	....	....	−11,167	−7,120	−23,428	−29,297	−44,788	−24,907	−17,428	−9,085	−19,116[f]	−40,278[f]	Deficit (-) or Surplus	**80**
	....	....	....	....	....	23,941	37,982	32,911	36,720	41,384	89,646	216,053	287,347	300,791[f]	279,418[f]	Revenue	**81**
	....	....	....	....	....	1,397	300	—	1,201	856	1,620	1,870	4,639[p]	5,480[f]	4,219[f]	Grants Received	**81z**
	....	....	....	....	....	35,193	44,067	54,848	65,247	85,875	111,128	215,738	285,910	309,942[f]	310,702[f]	Expenditure.....................................	**82**
	....	....	....	....	....	1,312	1,335	1,491	1,971	1,153	5,045	19,613	12,460	15,445[f]	13,213[f]	Lending Minus Repayments	**83**
																Financing	
	....	....	....	....	....	7,145	5,803	23,055	28,804	43,838	25,976	11,860	5,051	−7,750[f]	25,283[f]	Domestic	**84a**
	....	....	....	....	....	4,022	1,317	373	493	950	−1,069	5,568	4,034	26,866[f]	14,995[f]	Foreign	**85a**
Millions of Rials																**National Accounts**	
	....	....	....	....	....	18,060	20,760	23,100	33,160	43,537	111,821	284,059	318,088	234,175	389,095	Exports of Goods & Services	**90c**
	....	....	....	....	....	22,115	28,800	37,187	45,483	57,585	74,017	97,458	120,106	124,473	161,215	Government Consumption......................	**91f**
	....	....	....	....	....	14,980	20,548	37,487	40,772	56,773	99,025	143,207	149,654	223,163	210,249	Gross Fixed Capital Formation	**93e**
	....	....	....	....	....	3,332	3,379	4,869	6,622	6,123	6,486	12,863	29,549	10,810	9,935	Increase/Decrease(-) in Stocks	**93i**
	....	....	....	....	....	88,998	125,037	146,822	203,024	230,912	413,081	463,969	574,584	556,931	750,546	Private Consumption	**96f**
	....	....	....	....	....	−25,390	−53,710	−65,540	−101,370	−102,651	−215,921	−299,444	−339,084	−351,871	−474,574	Imports of Goods & Services	**98c**
	....	....	....	....	....	122,095	144,814	183,925	227,691	292,279	488,509	702,112	852,897	797,681	1,046,466	Gross Domestic Product (GDP)	**99b**
	....	....	....	....	....	−940	−2,970	−4,606	−4,160	−5,035	−16,173	−71,468	−76,040	−49,515	−97,936	Net Factor Inc/Pmts(-) Abroad	**98.n**
	....	....	....	....	....	121,155	141,844	179,319	223,531	287,244	472,336	630,644	776,857	748,166	948,530	Gross National Income (GNI)	**99a**
	....	....	....	....	....	122,095	119,542	125,327	125,829	121,273	130,912	134,754	145,652	153,342	159,160	GDP Volume 1990 Prices	**99b.p**
	....	....	....	....	....	93.3	91.3	95.7	96.1	92.6	100.0	102.9	111.3	117.1	121.6	GDP Volume (1995=100)	**99bv p**
Midyear Estimates																**Population**	
	9.60	9.88	10.16	10.61	10.95	11.28	11.61	11.95	12.30	Ɪ14.86	15.37	15.92	16.48	17.07	17.68	Population	**99z**

(See notes in the back of the book.)

Zambia

	1970	1971	1972	1973	1974	1975	1976	1977	1978	1979	1980	1981	1982	1983	1984
Exchange Rates														*Kwacha per SDR:*	
Official Rate .... aa	.71	.78	.78	.78	.79	.75	.92	.92	ɪ1.02	1.02	1.02	1.02	1.02	1.28	2.16
														Kwacha per US Dollar:	
Official Rate .... ae	.71	.71	.71	.64	.64	.64	.79	.76	.79	.78	.80	.88	.93	1.51	2.20
Official Rate .... rf	.71	.71	.71	.65ᵉ	.64ᵉ	.64ᵉ	.70	.79ᵉ	.80	.79	.79	.87	.93	1.26	1.81
												Index Numbers (1995=100):			
Official Rate .... ahx	119,875.8ᵉ	379.9	119,871.2ᵉ	131,406.6	133,069.9ᵉ	133,069.9ᵉ	121,112.3	108,428.7ᵉ	107,049.7	107,938.9	108,589.0	98,607.6	92,247.2	68,468.6	47,719.5
Nominal Effective Exchange Rate .... nec	....	....	....	....	....	....	....	....	....	32,799.6	33,774.7	35,316.7	39,236.2	34,733.2	28,212.8
Real Effective Exchange Rate .... rec	....	....	....	....	....	....	....	....	....	....	141.2	144.6	161.0	149.6	129.0
Fund Position														*Millions of SDRs:*	
Quota 2f.s	76.0	76.0	76.0	76.0	76.0	76.0	76.0	76.0	141.0	141.0	211.5	211.5	211.5	270.3	270.3
SDRs 1b.s	8.9	18.9	.2	—	11.7	15.7	19.2	11.4	12.1	4.2	—	7.7	14.5	—	—
Reserve Position in the Fund 1c.s	19.0	19.0	—	—	—	—	—	—	—	—	—	7.5	—	—	—
Total Fund Cred.&Loans Outstg. 2tl	—	19.0	38.0	57.0	57.0	75.9	95.2	95.2	245.1	343.0	350.8	670.6	618.3	678.5	753.8
International Liquidity											*Millions of US Dollars Unless Otherwise Indicated:*				
Total Reserves minus Gold 1l.d	508.0	277.1	158.4	185.5	164.4	142.0	92.7	66.3	51.1	80.0	78.2	56.2	58.2	54.5	54.2
SDRs 1b.d	8.9	20.6	.2	—	14.3	18.4	22.3	13.8	15.8	5.6	—	8.9	16.0	—	—
Reserve Position in the Fund 1c.d	19.0	20.6	—	—	—	—	—	—	—	—	—	8.7	—	—	—
Foreign Exchange 1d.d	480.1	235.9	158.2	185.5	150.1	123.6	70.4	52.5	35.3	74.4	78.2	38.5	42.2	54.5	54.2
Gold (Million Fine Troy Ounces) 1ad	.183	.200	.200	.200	.168	.168	.168	.168	.201	.217	.217	.217	.217	.217	.002
Gold (National Valuation) 1and	5.8	....	....	....	7.1	7.1	6.8	7.1	9.1	10.7	10.4	9.5	83.5	70.9	.7
Monetary Authorities: Other Liab. .... 4..d							122.4	77.5	98.0	666.5	471.3	650.6	938.8	699.5	506.7
Deposit Money Banks: Assets 7a.d	24.8	13.8	10.7	9.0	18.6	7.6	12.5	10.7	33.4	96.6	56.1	93.7	33.1	37.7	29.3
Liabilities 7b.d	4.2	14.0	25.1	26.8	36.8	37.3	36.6	55.6	59.5	48.2	77.7	64.8	108.2	46.4	54.6
Monetary Authorities											*Millions of Kwacha through 1985;*				
Foreign Assets 11	367.0	197.0	114.9	123.8	132.0	95.5	79.3	55.8	47.4	70.7	71.3	53.2	129.9	174.0	123.7
Claims on Central Government 12a	—	17.7	57.4	103.6	61.6	215.1	276.4	255.9	908.5	853.7	1,114.4	1,392.0	1,663.6	1,850.2	1,941.5
Claims on Nonfin.Pub.Enterprises 12c															
Claims on Private Sector 12d	2.0	2.0	—	.5	.5	47.7	53.1	123.6	114.5	80.9	61.9	61.9	160.5	165.5	165.5
Claims on Deposit Money Banks 12e	1.0		—	—	16.0	2.6	4.2	8.2	8.2	3.8	6.6	74.2	101.8	103.5	100.7
Reserve Money 14	137.1	89.2	105.8	138.8	128.2	183.2	231.9	228.7	240.6	252.2	287.2	334.5	386.7	440.7	518.5
of which: Currency Outside DMBs 14a	42.8	58.3	61.4	69.4	79.6	102.4	121.1	118.4	130.9	126.2	151.1	190.1	209.5	238.8	285.6
Time, Savings,& Fgn.Currency Dep. 15	....														
Foreign Liabilities 16c	.2	15.0	29.6	44.9	45.4	60.8	90.4	89.4	726.1	690.4	810.3	1,175.4	1,295.1	1,711.3	2,358.2
Central Government Deposits 16d	202.6	32.4	4.6	20.7	23.7	18.0	19.0	22.9	9.2	1.7	2.5	1.3	1.1	1.5	.5
Capital Accounts 17a	17.2	23.0	36.3	37.3	39.1	45.1	50.9	52.9	55.4	70.4	85.4	100.2	100.2	118.8	154.0
Other Items (Net) 17r	79.0	57.1	−3.9	2.2	−26.3	62.4	44.5	55.9	52.4	−2.2	78.3	−27.7	280.0	29.6	−697.4
Deposit Money Banks											*Millions of Kwacha through 1985;*				
Reserves 20	27.7	34.0	44.5	56.7	56.5	57.8	87.2	99.9	583.2	461.2	567.5	618.5	814.0	824.0	972.8
Foreign Assets 21	17.7	ɪ9.9	7.6	5.8	12.0	4.9	9.9	8.1	26.3	75.2	45.1	82.7	30.8	56.9	64.5
Claims on Central Government 22a	55.2	ɪ39.4	82.3	115.0	38.8	134.2	288.8	544.8	146.6	282.3	275.1	123.6	352.7	310.6	430.8
Claims on Local Government 22b															
Claims on Nonfin.Pub.Enterprises 22c	—	30.9	8.3	9.1	11.1	13.6	22.4	10.6	16.4	34.0	13.4	88.2	50.8	84.1	498.2
Claims on Private Sector 22d	140.9	ɪ150.3	157.0	167.2	325.7	333.1	325.7	337.8	295.1	370.6	433.4	623.2	708.9	802.4	556.5
Claims on Other Banking Insts. 22f	....	....	....	....	....	....	....	....	....	....	....	....	....	....	....
Claims on Nonbank Financial Insts. 22g	....	....	....	....	....	....	....	....	....	....	....	....	....	....	....
Demand Deposits 24	143.1	ɪ140.3	140.0	173.5	186.0	219.7	255.7	268.0	260.8	387.1	358.3	371.3	472.7	547.7	581.5
Time, Savings,& Fgn.Currency Dep. 25	103.5	ɪ119.9	139.7	151.9	175.0	163.2	223.1	305.9	242.6	315.5	388.1	415.1	619.8	658.9	833.9
Money Market Instruments 26aa	11.7	17.5	15.6	9.7	9.0	14.5	14.6	11.9	9.4	17.9	17.5	27.9	36.9	53.3	46.0
Foreign Liabilities 26c	3.0	ɪ10.0	17.9	17.3	23.7	24.0	29.1	42.2	46.8	37.5	62.5	57.2	100.6	70.1	120.1
Central Government Deposits 26d	16.2	ɪ15.2	13.2	26.8	27.8	28.6	20.2	31.9	27.5	30.3	32.5	21.0	25.4	30.6	38.0
Credit from Monetary Authorities 26g	1.0	—	—	—	42.2	42.5	39.9	39.9	8.2	6.8	3.8	73.5	20.7	18.5	15.7
Liabs. to Other Banking Insts. 26i	....														
Capital Accounts 27a		ɪ10.3	12.3	15.4	20.0	22.8	26.7	38.6	47.2	58.3	72.1	100.1	124.4	157.4	194.0
Other Items (Net) 27r	−42.5	−49.0	−39.0	−40.7	−39.6	28.3	124.9	262.9	425.1	369.8	399.8	470.2	556.7	541.7	693.6
Monetary Survey											*Millions of Kwacha through 1985;*				
Foreign Assets (Net) 31n	381.7	ɪ181.9	75.1	67.4	74.9	15.6	−30.2	−67.7	−699.3	−582.0	−756.4	−1,096.7	−1,235.0	−1,550.4	−2,290.6
Domestic Credit 32	−26.7	ɪ191.9	287.0	347.9	386.1	697.0	918.9	1,204.3	1,440.0	1,588.6	1,863.2	2,260.8	2,910.0	3,180.3	3,553.9
Claims on Central Govt. (Net) 32an	−163.7	ɪ9.5	121.8	171.1	48.9	302.7	526.1	745.9	1,018.3	1,104.1	1,354.5	1,493.4	1,989.9	2,128.7	2,333.8
Claims on Local Government 32b															
Claims on Nonfin.Pub.Enterprises 32c	—	30.9	8.3	9.1	11.1	13.6	22.4	10.6	16.4	34.0	13.4	88.2	50.8	84.1	498.2
Claims on Private Sector 32d	142.9	ɪ152.3	157.0	167.7	326.2	380.8	378.8	461.4	409.6	451.5	495.3	685.1	869.4	967.9	722.0
Claims on Other Banking Insts. 32f	....	....	....	....	....	....	....	....	....	....	....	....	....	....	....
Claims on Nonbank Financial Inst. 32g	....	....	....	....	....	....	....	....	....	....	....	....	....	....	....
Money 34	186.0	ɪ198.6	201.3	258.9	265.7	330.6	400.4	392.8	396.8	516.6	519.0	563.7	689.5	795.3	869.9
Quasi-Money 35	169.6	ɪ119.9	139.7	151.9	175.0	163.2	223.1	305.9	242.6	315.5	388.1	415.1	619.8	658.9	833.9
Money Market Instruments 36aa	11.7	17.5	15.6	9.7	9.0	14.5	14.6	11.9	9.4	17.9	17.5	27.9	36.9	53.3	46.0
Liabs. to Other Banking Insts. 36i															
Capital Accounts 37a	17.2	ɪ33.3	48.5	52.7	59.0	67.8	77.6	91.4	102.6	128.7	157.5	200.2	224.5	276.2	348.0
Other Items (Net) 37r	−29.5	27.5	−6.9	−20.6	−8.6	181.6	223.9	387.4	44.7	98.2	110.2	57.4	204.5	−34.9	−680.4
Money plus Quasi-Money 35l	355.6	ɪ318.5	341.1	410.8	440.7	493.7	623.5	698.7	639.4	832.2	907.1	978.7	1,309.3	1,454.2	1,703.8
Liquid Liabilities 55l	422.8	ɪ388.8	413.5	492.1	526.9	588.8	724.1	804.7	750.6	949.8	1,049.1	1,123.4	1,457.9	1,618.0	1,893.3

1985	1986	1987	1988	1989	1990	1991	1992	1993	1994	1995	1996	1997	1998	1999		
															Exchange Rates	
End of Period																
6.26	15.55	11.35	13.46	28.45	60.82	127.26	494.60	686.78	993.10	1,421.28	1,844.46	1,908.97	3,236.95	3,612.71	Official Rate	aa
End of Period (ae) Period Average (rf)																
5.70	12.71	8.00	10.00	21.65	42.75	88.97	359.71	500.00	680.27	956.13	1,282.69	1,414.84	2,298.92	2,632.19	Official Rate	ae
3.14	7.79	9.52	8.27	13.81	30.29	64.64	172.21	452.76	669.37	864.12	1,207.90	1,314.50	1,862.07	2,388.02	Official Rate	rf
Period Averages																
31,551.6	11,724.1	9,632.6	10,407.9	6,637.3	2,953.7	1,384.7	547.8	193.7	114.0	100.0	71.5	65.2	46.7	35.9	Official Rate	ahx
22,549.9	7,699.3	6,186.2	7,428.0	5,972.1	2,820.9	1,388.5	548.7	209.8	135.9	100.0	75.0	73.7	55.9	43.9	Nominal Effective Exchange Rate	nec
125.1	61.3	66.9	101.5	129.3	106.9	99.8	95.7	108.6	104.5	100.0	104.6	125.3	114.5	111.9	Real Effective Exchange Rate	rec
End of Period															**Fund Position**	
270.3	270.3	270.3	270.3	270.3	270.3	270.3	270.3	270.3	270.3	363.5	363.5	363.5	363.5	489.1	Quota	2f. s
—	—	—	—	—	—	—	—	—	—	8.2	1.4	.8	.6	.1	SDRs	1b. s
—	—	—	—	—	—	—	—	—	—	—	—	—	—	—	Reserve Position in the Fund	1c. s
728.9	701.6	698.8	698.8	685.0	666.7	641.6	615.6	565.8	551.2	833.4	833.4	843.4	843.4	853.4	Total Fund Cred.&Loans Outstg.	2tl
End of Period															**International Liquidity**	
200.1	70.3	108.8	134.0	116.2	193.1	184.6	....	192.3	268.1	222.7	222.7	239.1	69.4	45.4	Total Reserves minus Gold	1l. d
—	—	—	—	—	—	—	—	—	—	12.1	2.0	1.1	.8	.1	SDRs	1b. d
—	—	—	—	—	—	—	—	—	—	—	—	—	—	—	Reserve Position in the Fund	1c. d
200.1	70.3	108.8	134.0	116.2	193.1	184.6	....	192.3	268.1	210.5	220.7	238.0	68.6	45.3	Foreign Exchange	1d. d
.003	.003	.004	.013	.017	.021	.022	....	....	....	....	....	....	....	....	Gold (Million Fine Troy Ounces)	1ad
.9	1.0	1.8	4.1	....	....	....	....	....	....	....	....	....	....	....	Gold (National Valuation)	1and
478.2	343.6	408.2	471.4	523.6	578.4	483.3	....	678.7	736.0	1,128.8	1,088.8	1,007.1	1,001.4	974.3	Monetary Authorities: Other Liab.	4.. d
48.2	60.7	111.8	141.4	169.6	165.7	134.9	120.7	205.5	84.3	116.5	148.7	155.0	198.9	201.4	Deposit Money Banks: Assets	7a. d
90.5	44.0	61.8	50.3	55.0	49.3	34.1	20.0	16.8	15.6	9.3	11.2	13.2	29.2	34.9	Liabilities	7b. d
Billions of Kwacha Beginning 1986: End of Period															**Monetary Authorities**	
1,145.7	↓.9	.7	↓1.4	2.5	9.2	13.9	....	137.7	213.7	208.1	268.4	338.4	103.0	211.2	Foreign Assets	11
2,149.3	↓2.6	2.3	↓12.1	26.0	59.0	118.6	....	611.9	1,114.7	2,017.5	2,636.7	2,659.5	4,670.2	5,584.5	Claims on Central Government	12a
									20.2	9.1	1.2	1.3	1.3	5.3	7.9	Claims on Nonfin.Pub.Enterprises	12c
160.5	↓.2	.2	↓.1	.1	.9	.4	....	2.1	4.4	14.0	23.6	25.1	30.7	31.4	Claims on Private Sector	12d
173.7	↓.1	.1	↓—	—	2.1	4.2	....	7.8	—	121.8	157.2	164.9	161.4	120.9	Claims on Deposit Money Banks	12e
634.4	↓1.7	2.4	↓3.8	6.3	11.3	22.7	....	102.3	151.4	129.2	175.0	259.3	303.0	389.2	Reserve Money	14
342.5	↓.6	1.0	1.8	2.2	4.6	9.2	....	40.4	56.3	77.8	106.3	136.7	↓169.7	212.2	*of which: Currency Outside DMBs*	14a
										5.4		1.5	2.3	.7	.8	1.6	Time, Savings,& Fgn.Currency Dep.	15
5,548.0	↓12.1	9.6	↓14.1	30.8	65.3	124.7	....	727.9	1,048.1	1,337.6	1,731.8	1,771.9	2,890.4	3,221.2	Foreign Liabilities	16c
8.1	↓—		↓-1.6	-2.6	-.5	-29.3	....	267.8	173.6	545.4	895.6	955.0	1,351.6	2,011.9	Central Government Deposits	16d
198.5	↓11.1	1.1	↓1.0	1.2	4.4	1.2	....	-411.6	-52.7	286.0	329.8	421.6	444.8	493.0	Capital Accounts	17a
-2,757.1	↓-11.2	-9.9	↓-3.7	-7.1	-9.3	17.8	....	87.9	21.6	62.9	-47.3	-219.2	-20.0	-160.9	Other Items (Net)	17r
Billions of Kwacha Beginning 1986: End of Period															**Deposit Money Banks**	
1,095.7	↓1.8	1.9	3.8	4.9	8.3	14.7	20.8	49.8	96.1	34.6	62.8	87.8	↓134.7	175.6	Reserves	20
274.7	↓.8	.9	1.4	3.7	7.1	12.0	43.4	102.8	57.4	116.5	190.7	224.6	↓457.3	530.2	Foreign Assets	21
787.7	↓1.4	2.5	2.7	3.6	4.2	14.2	38.3	71.4	84.7	202.8	216.4	222.7	↓153.0	231.6	Claims on Central Government	22a
															2.6	.4	Claims on Local Government	22b
577.4	↓.7	.7	1.5	2.7	4.3	7.0	13.4	29.1	16.8	35.6	49.7	40.9	↓119.1	248.9	Claims on Nonfin.Pub.Enterprises	22c
612.9	↓1.1	1.6	2.8	6.2	9.1	15.5	29.2	68.9	136.0	240.0	350.2	386.1	↓392.7	522.0	Claims on Private Sector	22d
....	....	....	....	....	....	....	....	....	....	....	....	....	.4	.4	Claims on Other Banking Insts.	22f
....	....	....	....	....	....	....	....	....	....	....	....	....	2.7	1.4	Claims on Nonbank Financial Insts.	22g
886.3	↓1.7	2.2	3.5	5.7	8.1	13.5	33.0	56.8	83.8	140.2	163.1	217.2	↓243.7	299.0	Demand Deposits	24
870.4	↓1.8	3.0	4.9	8.8	12.0	26.1	45.1	105.8	191.0	287.6	423.4	515.6	↓679.0	883.3	Time, Savings,& Fgn.Currency Dep.	25
46.4	↓.1	.1	.2	1.0	2.3	5.4	10.7	15.0	14.9	23.3	31.1	29.8	↓11.8	9.9	Money Market Instruments	26aa
515.9	↓.6	.5	.5	1.2	2.1	3.0	7.2	8.4	10.6	9.3	14.4	19.1	↓67.1	91.8	Foreign Liabilities	26c
56.2	↓.1	.2	.4	.8	1.2	3.2	5.7	5.8	12.4	44.6	57.7	63.6	↓61.3	125.2	Central Government Deposits	26d
88.7	↓—	—	—	—	1.5	.3	....	.2	2.7	60.2	86.6	82.5	↓21.4	78.5	Credit from Monetary Authorities	26g
														.1	1.3	Liabs. to Other Banking Insts.	26i
245.4	↓.4	.8	1.1	2.0	3.8	7.9	17.8	44.2	58.5	74.5	112.7	138.1	↓227.8	297.2	Capital Accounts	27a
639.2	↓1.0	.8	1.6	1.7	2.1	4.0	25.5	85.7	17.0	-10.1	-19.2	-103.8	↓-49.7	-75.6	Other Items (Net)	27r
Billions of Kwacha Beginning 1986: End of Period															**Monetary Survey**	
-4,643.5	↓-11.0	-8.5	↓-11.9	-25.8	-51.2	-101.7	....	-495.9	-787.6	-1,022.4	-1,287.1	-1,228.0	↓-2397.2	-2,571.6	Foreign Assets (Net)	31n
4,223.4	↓5.8	7.0	↓20.5	40.4	76.8	181.8	....	530.0	1,179.7	1,921.1	2,324.6	2,316.9	↓3,963.7	4,491.7	Domestic Credit	32
2,872.6	↓3.9	4.5	↓16.1	31.5	62.5	159.0	....	409.7	1,013.4	1,630.3	1,899.7	1,863.6	↓3,410.2	3,679.1	Claims on Central Govt. (Net)	32an
														2.6	.4	Claims on Local Government	32b
577.4	↓.7	.7	↓1.5	2.7	4.3	7.0	....	49.3	25.9	36.9	51.0	42.2	↓124.4	256.9	Claims on Nonfin.Pub.Enterprises	32c
773.4	↓1.3	1.8	↓2.9	6.3	10.1	15.8	....	71.0	140.4	254.0	373.8	411.1	↓423.5	553.5	Claims on Private Sector	32d
....	....	....	....	....	....	....	....	....	....	....	....	....	.4	.4	Claims on Other Banking Insts.	32f
....	....	....	....	....	....	....	....	....	....	....	....	—	↓2.7	1.4	Claims on Nonbank Financial Inst	32g
1,231.5	↓2.3	3.2	↓5.2	7.9	12.8	22.7	....	97.3	141.0	227.1	271.1	355.2	↓414.9	513.0	Money	34
870.4	↓1.8	3.0	↓4.9	8.8	12.0	26.1	....	111.2	191.0	289.1	425.7	516.3	↓679.8	884.9	Quasi-Money	35
46.4	↓.1	.1	.2	1.0	2.3	5.4	....	15.0	14.9	23.3	31.1	29.8	↓11.8	9.9	Money Market Instruments	36aa
														.1	1.3	Liabs. to Other Banking Insts.	36i
443.9	↓1.5	1.9	↓2.0	3.1	8.2	9.1	....	-367.4	5.8	360.5	442.5	559.7	↓672.6	790.2	Capital Accounts	37a
-2,813.7	↓-9.7	-8.6	↓-3.8	-6.3	-9.5	16.8	....	177.9	39.4	-1.1	-133.0	-372.1	↓-212.8	-279.2	Other Items (Net)	37r
2,101.8	↓4.1	6.3	↓10.1	16.7	24.7	48.8	....	208.6	332.0	516.2	696.9	871.5	↓1,094.7	1,397.9	Money plus Quasi-Money	35l
....	....	....	....	....	....	....	....	....	....	....	....	....	....	....	Liquid Liabilities	55l

Zambia

	1970	1971	1972	1973	1974	1975	1976	1977	1978	1979	1980	1981	1982	1983	1984
Interest Rates														Percent Per Annum	
Discount Rate *(End of Period)* 60	5.00	5.00	5.00	5.00	5.00	5.00	5.00	6.00	6.00	6.50	6.50	7.50	7.50	10.00	14.50
Treasury Bill Rate 60c	....	3.34	4.34	3.94	3.96	4.00	4.15	4.38	4.38	4.44	4.50	5.75	6.00	7.50	7.67
Deposit Rate 60l	....	3.50	3.75	4.00	4.00	4.00	5.31	6.25	6.25	6.75	7.00	6.17	6.00	7.00	7.71
Lending Rate 60p	....	7.00	7.25	7.50	7.50	7.50	8.13	8.25	8.25	9.08	9.50	9.50	9.50	13.00	14.54
Prices and Production												Index Numbers (1995=100):			
Wholesale Prices 63	—	—	—	—	—	—	—	—	.1	.1	.1	.1	.1	.1	.1
Home & Import Goods 63a	.6	.6	.6	.7	.8	.9	1.1	1.3	1.6	1.8	2.2	2.3	2.6	3.2	4.0
Consumer Prices 64	....	....	....	....	....	....	....	....	....	....	....	....	....	....	....
Cons.Prices (Low Inc.Households) 64a	.02	Ⅰ.03	.03	.03	.03	.03	.04	.05	.06	.06	.07	.08	.09	.11	.13
Industrial Production 66	129.1	125.2	139.1	139.2	151.0	139.8	148.7	142.0	142.2	133.4	Ⅰ137.6	132.2	128.3	138.1	135.1
Mining Production (1999=100) 66zx	139.4	130.4	143.0	140.2	146.3	132.7	144.5	135.0	135.5	115.7	Ⅰ125.2	114.1	118.1	116.0	111.8
														Number in Thousands:	
Employment 67e	....	....	....	....	....	....	....	....	....	....		....	....		
International Transactions												Millions of Kwacha through 1985;			
Exports 70	715.0	875.8	541.8	742.1	905.1	521.2	749.1	708.0	686.7	1,090.0	1,029.0	976.6	950.5	1,047.5	1,199.4
Imports, c.i.f. 71	340.9	396.9	403.8	346.9	506.6	597.6	468.6	530.0	492.8	593.8	859.0	923.0	930.0	693.0	1,086.0
Balance of Payments												Millions of US Dollars:			
Current Account, n.i.e. .... 78al *d*	....	....	....	....	....	....	....	....	−281	78	−516	−729	−562	−263	−147
Goods: Exports f.o.b. .... 78aa *d*	....	....	....	....	....	....	....	....	831	1,408	1,457	996	942	923	893
Goods: Imports f.o.b. .... 78ab *d*	....	....	....	....	....	....	....	....	−618	−756	−1,114	−1,065	−1,003	−711	−612
Trade Balance .... 78ac *d*	....	....	....	....	....	....	....	....	213	652	343	−69	−61	212	280
Services: Credit .... 78ad *d*	....	....	....	....	....	....	....	....	113	116	152	153	122	99	75
Services: Debit .... 78ae *d*	....	....	....	....	....	....	....	....	−408	−456	−651	−584	−409	−334	−291
Balance on Goods & Services ...... 78af *d*	....	....	....	....	....	....	....	....	−82	311	−157	−501	−348	−23	65
Income: Credit .... 78ag *d*	....	....	....	....	....	....	....	....	8	11	16	20	15	3	5
Income: Debit .... 78ah *d*	....	....	....	....	....	....	....	....	−162	−181	−221	−130	−203	−241	−187
Balance on Gds, Serv. & Inc. .... 78ai *d*	....	....	....	....	....	....	....	....	−236	142	−362	−610	−537	−261	−117
Current Transfers, n.i.e.: Credit ... 78aj *d*	....	....	....	....	....	....	....	....	27	38	35	30	32	44	14
Current Transfers: Debit .... 78ak *d*	....	....	....	....	....	....	....	....	−72	−101	−190	−148	−57	−46	−44
Capital Account, n.i.e. .... 78bc *d*	....	....	....	....	....	....	....	....	−17	−41	−21	−13	−4	−8	−6
Capital Account, n.i.e.: Credit ...... 78ba *d*	....	....	....	....	....	....	....	....							
Capital Account: Debit .... 78bb *d*	....	....	....	....	....	....	....	....	−17	−41	−21	−13	−4	−8	−6
Financial Account, n.i.e. .... 78bj *d*	....	....	....	....	....	....	....	....	30	119	287	459	253	38	151
Direct Investment Abroad .... 78bd *d*	....	....	....	....	....	....	....	....	—	—	—	—	—	—	—
Dir. Invest. in Rep. Econ., n.i.e. .... 78be *d*	....	....	....	....	....	....	....	....	39	35	62	−38	39	26	17
Portfolio Investment Assets .... 78bf *d*	....	....	....	....	....	....	....	....	—	—	—	—	—	—	—
Equity Securities .... 78bk *d*	....	....	....	....	....	....	....	....	—	—	—	—	—	—	—
Debt Securities .... 78bl *d*	....	....	....	....	....	....	....	....	—	—	—	—	—	—	—
Portfolio Investment Liab., n.i.e. ...... 78bg *d*	....	....	....	....	....	....	....	....	—	—	—	—	—	—	—
Equity Securities .... 78bm *d*	....	....	....	....	....	....	....	....	—	—	—	—	—	—	—
Debt Securities .... 78bn *d*	....	....	....	....	....	....	....	....	—	—	—	—	—	—	—
Financial Derivatives Assets ...... 78bw *d*	....	....	....	....	....	....	....	....	....	....	....	....	....	....	....
Financial Derivatives Liabilities ...... 78bx *d*	....	....	....	....	....	....	....	....	....	....	....	....	....	....	....
Other Investment Assets .... 78bh *d*	....	....	....	....	....	....	....	....	17	−25	56	−64	30	−19	−7
Monetary Authorities .... 78bo *d*	....	....	....	....	....	....	....	....	....	....	....	....	....	....	....
General Government .... 78bp *d*	....	....	....	....	....	....	....	....	−4	−6	−8	2	−10	−5	−5
Banks .... 78bq *d*	....	....	....	....	....	....	....	....	−23	−61	38	−43	56	−5	8
Other Sectors .... 78br *d*	....	....	....	....	....	....	....	....	43	42	26	−22	−16	−10	−10
Other Investment Liab., n.i.e. ...... 78bi *d*	....	....	....	....	....	....	....	....	−25	109	170	561	184	32	141
Monetary Authorities .... 78bs *d*	....	....	....	....	....	....	....	....	9	−3	2	1	−26	−4	−2
General Government .... 78bt *d*	....	....	....	....	....	....	....	....	8	136	301	285	98	86	47
Banks .... 78bu *d*	....	....	....	....	....	....	....	....	6	−12	32	−6	47	−61	8
Other Sectors .... 78bv *d*	....	....	....	....	....	....	....	....	−48	−12	−165	281	65	11	88
Net Errors and Omissions .... 78ca *d*	....	....	....	....	....	....	....	....	−75	−88	26	−181	−77	211	−87
Overall Balance .... 78cb *d*	....	....	....	....	....	....	....	....	−342	68	−225	−464	−390	−21	−89
Reserves and Related Items .... 79da *d*	....	....	....	....	....	....	....	....	342	−68	225	464	390	21	89
Reserve Assets .... 79db *d*	....	....	....	....	....	....	....	....	5	13	22	39	−6	4	59
Use of Fund Credit and Loans ...... 79dc *d*	....	....	....	....	....	....	....	....	185	126	9	373	−57	65	76
Exceptional Financing .... 79de *d*	....	....	....	....	....	....	....	....	152	−207	194	52	453	−47	−46
Government Finance												Millions of Kwacha through 1985;			
Deficit (-) or Surplus............... 80	23.4	−194.1	Ⅰ−175.6	−266.4	64.4	−340.8	−269.9	−261.4	−324.5	−241.1	−567.5	−449.6	−668.2	−327.3	−413.7
Revenue 81	457.2	312.5	Ⅰ296.8	469.4	649.1	447.8	453.0	498.3	555.7	594.2	765.1	807.1	839.9	1,013.5	1,090.5
Grants Received 81z	....	....	Ⅰ1.3	1.4	.9	14.5	8.9	33.8	19.5	25.8	25.6	24.0	29.1	53.7	23.0
Expenditure 82	360.3	482.4	Ⅰ432.7	469.1	531.3	678.2	685.2	706.2	668.8	809.5	1,135.2	1,277.7	1,409.1	1,346.3	1,441.2
Lending Minus Repayments 83	73.5	24.2	Ⅰ41.0	268.1	54.3	124.9	46.6	87.3	230.9	51.6	223.0	3.0	128.1	48.2	86.0
Financing															
Net Borrowing: Domestic 84a	3.0	8.1	Ⅰ128.5	118.8	....	266.6	239.7	243.1	298.4	....	....	160.6	531.6	215.3	289.5
Foreign 85a	13.4	35.9	Ⅰ15.2	147.0	36.7	58.9	30.2	19.0	21.1	137.5	269.6	247.4	111.6	119.9	129.3
Use of Cash Balances 87	−39.8	150.2	Ⅰ31.9	.6	....	15.3	....	−.7	5.0	....	....	41.6	25.0	−7.9	−5.1
Debt: Domestic 88a	....	....	239.1	Ⅰ335.0	468.9	344.8	573.9	817.9	1,146.3	1,455.9	....	2,011.2	2,746.4	2,919.7	3,229.1
Foreign 89a	....	163.2	....	....	....	....	....	....	556.8	633.8	,....	1,285.4	1,846.0	2,666.0	3,545.0
National Accounts												Millions of Kwacha through 1985;			
Exports of Goods & Services 90c	685.4	500.6	586.1	780.4	943.9	575.0	832.3	781.5	755.3	1,208.3	1,268.0	998.0	993.1	1,280.7	1,806.9
Government Consumption 91f	198.5	272.6	314.5	344.8	357.8	435.7	501.0	525.0	537.8	633.0	781.6	986.0	995.9	1,008.8	1,240.1
Gross Fixed Capital Formation 93e	372.3	393.4	445.0	422.9	502.0	602.0	445.0	483.0	437.0	450.0	558.3	610.0	618.0	615.0	622.6
Increase/Decrease(-) in Stocks 93i	Ⅰ−11.5	47.4	31.4	42.0	185.3	40.0	6.5	7.0	100.0	−74.0	155.0	63.3	−15.1	−40.0	101.4
Private Consumption 96f	Ⅰ494.3	492.6	535.7	530.2	664.4	814.5	847.0	1,022.8	1,251.5	1,412.6	1,691.9	2,262.2	2,314.9	2,645.5	2,779.4
Imports of Goods & Services 98c	Ⅰ−470.5	−525.7	−564.7	−529.0	−765.5	−883.8	−736.0	−832.9	−830.9	−969.5	−1,391.2	−1,434.1	−1,311.5	−1,328.8	−1,619.4
Gross Domestic Product (GDP) 99b	1,219.5	1,180.9	1,348.0	1,591.3	1,887.9	1,583.4	1,895.8	1,986.4	2,250.7	2,660.4	3,063.6	3,485.4	3,595.3	4,181.2	4,931.0
Net Factor Inc/Pmts(-) Abroad 98.n	Ⅰ33.4	43.6	74.1	−90.5	−81.2	−81.8	−79.7	−68.6	49.5	−83.4	−138.5	−114.5	−36.4	−3.8	−64.1
Gross National Income (GNI) 99a	Ⅰ1,186.1	1,137.3	1,273.9	1,681.8	1,969.1	1,665.2	1,975.5	2,055.0	2,201.2	2,743.8	3,202.1	3,599.9	3,631.7	4,177.4	4,866.9
Net National Income 99e	Ⅰ1,098.7	974.1	1,069.1	1,293.5	1,582.4	1,268.8	1,522.0	1,607.4	1,809.1	2,124.3	2,495.9	3,004.1	2,870.3	3,508.4	3,925.7
GDP Volume 1977 Prices (Billions) 99b.*p*	1.778	1.776	1.939	1.921	2.050	2.000	2.087	1.986	1.998	1.937	1.996	2.119	2.059	2.019	2.012
GDP Volume (1995=100) .... 99bv *p*	81.2	81.1	88.6	87.7	93.6	91.3	95.3	90.7	91.2	88.5	91.1	96.8	94.0	92.2	91.9
GDP Deflator (1995=100) .... 99bi *p*	.1	—	.1	.1	.1	.1	.1	.1	.1	.1	.1	.1	.1	.2	.2
														Millions:	
Population................................. 99z	4.25	4.39	4.53	4.68	4.83	4.98	5.14	5.30	5.47	5.52	5.56	5.87	6.05	6.24	6.44

1985	1986	1987	1988	1989	1990	1991	1992	1993	1994	1995	1996	1997	1998	1999		
Percent Per Annum															**Interest Rates**	
25.00	30.00	15.00	15.00	....	....	....	47.00	72.50	20.50	40.20	47.00	17.70	....	....	Discount Rate (End of Period)	60
13.21	24.25	16.50	15.17	18.50	25.92	....	....	124.03	74.21	39.81	52.78	29.48	24.94	36.19	Treasury Bill Rate	60c
15.33	17.74	13.23	11.44	11.44	25.65	....	48.50	....	46.14	30.24	42.13	34.48	13.08	20.27	Deposit Rate	60l
18.60	27.40	21.20	18.39	18.39	35.10	....	54.57	113.31	70.56	45.53	53.78	46.69	31.80	40.52	Lending Rate	60p
Period Averages															**Prices and Production**	
.2	.4	.8	.8	1.5	3.3	6.4	14.1	34.1	58.1	100.0	....	....	....	....	Wholesale Prices	63
5.5	11.4	22.9	24.0	46.1	100.0	193.0	447.2	....	....	....	....	....	....	....	Home & Import Goods	63a
.20	.32	.46	.70	1.56	3.24	6.26	16.84	48.51	74.52	100.00	146.27	182.56	....	....	Consumer Prices	64
I.17	.26	.38	.59	1.34	2.92	5.62	I16.72	48.15	73.96	100.00	145.19	....	....	....	Cons.Prices (Low Inc.Households)	64a
136.9	133.7	130.9	136.1	132.8	128.2	123.8	133.0	122.0	107.0	100.0	....	....	....	....	Industrial Production	66
108.6	107.1	104.6	100.9	102.5	100.0	90.1	100.8	92.0	76.8	....	....	....	....	....	Mining Production (1999=100)	66zx
Period Averages																
362	361	362	361	360	....	....									Employment	67e
Billions of Kwacha Beginning 1986															**International Transactions**	
1,508.2	I5.4	8.1	9.8	18.4	39.1	69.6	129.5	374.1	620.5	898.6	1,252.7	1,203.0	....	....	Exports	70
2,133.0	I4.4	6.6	6.9	12.6	36.6	51.8	144.1	366.3	397.7	604.8	1,004.3	1,077.0	....	....	Imports, c.i.f.	71
Minus Sign Indicates Debit															**Balance of Payments**	
-395	-348	-245	-293	-219	-594	-306	....	....	....	....	....	....	....	....	Current Account, n.i.e.	78al d
797	692	852	1,189	1,340	1,254	1,172	....	....	....	....	....	....	....	....	Goods: Exports f.o.b.	78aa d
-571	-518	-585	-687	-774	-1,511	-752	....	....	....	....	....	....	....	....	Goods: Imports f.o.b.	78ab d
226	175	267	502	566	-257	420	....	....	....	....	....	....	....	....	*Trade Balance*	78ac d
68	47	48	58	85	107	83	....	....	....	....	....	....	....	....	Services: Credit	78ad d
-254	-199	-223	-289	-444	-386	-363	....	....	....	....	....	....	....	....	Services: Debit	78ae d
39	23	91	271	208	-537	140	....	....	....	....	....	....	....	....	*Balance on Goods & Services*	78af d
2	1	1	3	1	2	10	....	....	....	....	....	....	....	....	Income: Credit	78ag d
-413	-354	-329	-604	-509	-439	-696	....	....	....	....	....	....	....	....	Income: Debit	78ah d
-371	-330	-236	-330	-300	-974	-546	....	....	....	....	....	....	....	....	*Balance on Gds, Serv. & Inc.*	78ai d
8	23	10	64	114	398	262	....	....	....	....	....	....	....	....	Current Transfers, n.i.e.: Credit	78aj d
-32	-41	-19	-27	-32	-18	-22	....	....	....	....	....	....	....	....	Current Transfers: Debit	78ak d
-3	-3	-2	-2	-3	-3	-1	....	....	....	....	....	....	....	....	Capital Account, n.i.e.	78bc d
—	—	—	—	—	—	—	....	....	....	....	....	....	....	....	Capital Account, n.i.e.: Credit	78ba d
-3	-3	-2	-2	-3	-3	-1	....	....	....	....	....	....	....	....	Capital Account: Debit	78bb d
363	-99	-147	23	1,827	497	18	....	....	....	....	....	....	....	....	Financial Account, n.i.e.	78bj d
—	—	—	—	—	—	—	....	....	....	....	....	....	....	....	Direct Investment Abroad	78bd d
52	28	75	93	164	203	34	....	....	....	....	....	....	....	....	Dir. Invest. in Rep. Econ., n.i.e.	78be d
—	—	—	—	—	—	—	....	....	....	....	....	....	....	....	Portfolio Investment Assets	78bf d
—	—	—	—	—	—	—	....	....	....	....	....	....	....	....	Equity Securities	78bk d
—	—	—	—	—	—	—	....	....	....	....	....	....	....	....	Debt Securities	78bl d
—	—	—	—	—	—	—	....	....	....	....	....	....	....	....	Portfolio Investment Liab., n.i.e.	78bg d
—	—	—	—	—	—	—	....	....	....	....	....	....	....	....	Equity Securities	78bm d
—	—	—	—	—	—	—	....	....	....	....	....	....	....	....	Debt Securities	78bn d
....	....	....	....	....	....	....	....	....	....	....	....	....	....	....	Financial Derivatives Assets	78bw d
....	....	....	....	....	....	....	....	....	....	....	....	....	....	....	Financial Derivatives Liabilities	78bx d
-26	-38	-57	-347	26	-275	-125	....	....	....	....	....	....	....	....	Other Investment Assets	78bh d
....	....	....	....	....	....	....	....	....	....	....	....	....	....	....	Monetary Authorities	78bo d
—	1	—	1	—	-7	-54	....	....	....	....	....	....	....	....	General Government	78bp d
-16	-12	-19	-56	-172	-109	-76	....	....	....	....	....	....	....	....	Banks	78bq d
-9	-27	-39	-292	197	-159	6	....	....	....	....	....	....	....	....	Other Sectors	78br d
337	-90	-165	277	1,637	569	108	....	....	....	....	....	....	....	....	Other Investment Liab., n.i.e.	78bi d
-20	-35	-4	-4	-3	23	5	....	....	....	....	....	....	....	....	Monetary Authorities	78bs d
221	-218	-77	24	-241	11	38	....	....	....	....	....	....	....	....	General Government	78bt d
31	-44	-7	1	50	30	14	....	....	....	....	....	....	....	....	Banks	78bu d
105	207	-76	256	1,831	504	51	....	....	....	....	....	....	....	....	Other Sectors	78bv d
-145	315	153	40	-1,712	322	110	....	....	....	....	....	....	....	....	Net Errors and Omissions	78ca d
-181	-134	-242	-232	-106	222	-179	....	....	....	....	....	....	....	....	*Overall Balance*	78cb d
181	134	242	232	106	-222	179	....	....	....	....	....	....	....	....	Reserves and Related Items	79da d
-127	121	71	-51	-82	-119	-26	....	....	....	....	....	....	....	....	Reserve Assets	79db d
-25	-31	-4	—	-17	-25	-35	....	....	....	....	....	....	....	....	Use of Fund Credit and Loans	79dc d
332	44	175	284	205	-77	241	....	....	....	....	....	....	....	....	Exceptional Financing	79de d
Billions of Kwacha Beginning 1986: Year Ending December 31															**Government Finance**	
-1,072.6	I-2.8	-2.5	-3.5	I-5.9	-9.8	-98.4	-37.3	-115.6	-27.4	-136.9	-96.2	-488.5	-330.4P	-275.4f	Deficit (-) or Surplus	80
1,555.5	I3.0	4.3	5.1	I9.9	23.4	41.5	113.5	266.4	502.8	600.8	745.3	957.0	1,097.6P	1,430.4f	Revenue	81
19.6	I.2	.1	.5	I1.1	.3	2.7	....	....	.6	5.6	25.4	4.7	432.7P	414.2f	Grants Received	81z
2,484.1	I5.4	6.8	8.6	I13.6	30.9	127.6	171.2	391.1	492.2	727.5	842.7	1,313.6	1,717.1P	1,874.3f	Expenditure	82
163.6	I.6	.1	.5	I2.3	2.6	15.0	9.4	26.6	38.6	15.7	24.2	136.6	143.6P	245.7f	Lending Minus Repayments	83
															Financing	
457.0	I1.6	1.1	2.1	I2.0	8.6	50.4	37.3	38.0	-46.5	-351.4	-91.2	-283.9	50.2P	....	Net Borrowing: Domestic	84a
599.7	I1.2	1.4	1.1	I2.5	-2.5	23.3	-25.0	36.4	-35.7	-560.0	129.4	775.6	253.8P	....	Foreign	85a
15.9	I—	.1	.2	I1.3	-37.2	-24.7	-25.1	-41.2	-109.6	-1,048.3	-58.0	3.2	-26.4	....	Use of Cash Balances	87
4,076.8	I5.8	7.1	9.3	I.9	.8	.8	.8	1.6	149.9	238.8	265.8	303.2	212.8P	....	Debt: Domestic	88a
9,542.1	I33.1	20.5	....	I101.8	276.1	605.0	937.3	2,396.3	3,502.4	4,869.4	7,378.7	8,185.9	10,408.4P	....	Foreign	89a
Billions of Kwacha Beginning 1986															**National Accounts**	
2,740.2	I5.9	8.5	10.3	14.8	42.3	75.0	147.1	420.9	806.5	1,082.3	1,237.4	1,552.0	....	....	Exports of Goods & Services	90c
1,686.7	I3.5	4.4	4.6	7.6	21.6	69.5	85.5	273.2	293.6	464.0	676.5	792.3	....	....	Government Consumption	91f
724.5	I1.4	1.9	2.4	3.6	15.3	24.8	60.2	170.0	512.1	799.4	1,719.6	1,928.6	....	....	Gross Fixed Capital Formation	93e
328.5	I1.7	.9	1.0	2.3	4.3	-.8	7.5	52.9	-69.1	104.8	63.1	73.9	....	....	Increase/Decrease(-) in Stocks	93i
4,294.6	I6.6	11.8	19.8	45.5	71.6	117.1	447.6	1,015.7	1,602.7	1,775.9	2,033.2	3,006.0	....	....	Private Consumption	96f
-2,702.6	I-5.9	-7.7	-8.1	-18.7	-41.7	-67.3	-178.4	-450.6	-905.2	-1,228.2	-1,710.4	-2,196.0	....	....	Imports of Goods & Services	98c
7,071.9	I13.1	19.8	30.0	55.2	113.3	218.3	569.6	1,482.1	2,240.7	2,998.3	3,969.5	5,155.8	....	....	Gross Domestic Product (GDP)	99b
-86.2	I-1.0	-1.7	-1.9	-6.5	-12.7	-44.0	-87.0	-377.2	69.0	-104.9	-13.2	-72.9	....	....	Net Factor Inc/Pmts(-) Abroad	98.n
6,985.7	I12.1	18.1	28.1	48.7	100.6	174.3	482.6	1,104.9	2,309.7	2,893.4	3,956.3	5,082.9	....	....	Gross National Income (GNI)	99a
5,430.0	I8.4	14.4	15.5	43.4	89.6	151.9	425.2	866.0	1,518.0	2,227.4	3,394.4	....	....	....	Net National Income	99e
2.045	2.059	2.114	2.247	2.224	2.214	2.213	2.174	2.322	2.241	2.190	2.332	2.414	....	....	GDP Volume 1977 Prices (Billions)	99b.p
93.4	94.0	96.6	102.6	101.6	101.1	101.0	99.3	106.0	102.3	100.0	106.5	110.2	....	....	GDP Volume (1995=100)	99bv p
.3	I.5	.7	1.0	1.8	3.7	7.2	19.1	46.6	73.0	100.0	124.3	156.0	....	....	GDP Deflator (1995=100)	99bi p
Midyear Estimates																
6.73	7.11	7.37	7.53	7.80	8.07	7.96	8.19	8.46	8.76	9.11	9.45	9.78	10.10	10.41	**Population**	99z

(See notes in the back of the book.)

Zimbabwe

698		1970	1971	1972	1973	1974	1975	1976	1977	1978	1979	1980	1981	1982	1983	1984
Exchange Rates																*SDRs per Zimbabwe Dollar:*
Official Rate	ac	1.3963	1.3724	1.4127	1.3678	1.4885	1.3672	1.3904	1.2728	1.1369	1.1259	1.2434	1.1980	.9859	.8640	.6790
																US Dollars per Zimbabwe Dollar:
Official Rate	ag	1.3963	1.4900	1.5338	1.6500	1.8225	1.6005	1.6154	1.5461	1.4811	1.4832	1.5858	1.3944	1.0876	.9046	.6656
Official Rate	rh	1.4000	1.4042	1.5161	1.7070	1.6949	1.7603	1.5984	1.5919	1.4764	1.4709	1.5561	1.4518	1.3205	.9895	.8037
Fund Position																*Millions of SDRs:*
Quota	2f. *s*	....	....	....	....	....	....	....	....	....	....	150.0	150.0	150.0	150.0	191.0
SDRs	1b. *s*	....	....	....	....	....	....	....	....	....	....	—	8.8	6.3	6.1	2.3
Reserve Position in the Fund	1c. *s*	....	....	....	....	....	....	....	....	....	....	—	—	—	—	—
Total Fund Cred.&Loans Outstg.	2tl	....	....	....	....	....	....	....	....	....	....	—	37.5	37.5	191.1	261.3
International Liquidity																*Millions of US Dollars Unless Otherwise Indicated:*
Total Reserves minus Gold	1l. *d*	20.3	6.1	61.3	124.7	70.8	80.0	76.6	72.6	148.0	298.9	213.5	169.5	140.4	75.4	45.4
SDRs	1b. *d*	....	....	....	....	....	....	....	....	....	....	—	10.3	6.9	6.4	2.3
Reserve Position in the Fund	1c. *d*	....	....	....	....	....	....	....	....	....	....	—	—	—	—	—
Foreign Exchange	1d. *d*	20.3	6.1	61.3	124.7	70.8	80.0	76.6	72.6	148.0	298.9	213.5	159.2	133.5	68.9	43.1
Gold (Million Fine Troy Ounces)	1ad	1.05	.82	.55	.75	.50	.35	.27	.15	.16	.26	.35	.47	.39	.59	.70
Gold (National Valuation)	1an *d*	36.5	30.4	21.2	30.9	22.9	14.0	10.7	5.9	6.0	9.6	112.9	99.1	83.6	111.6	110.5
Monetary Authorities: Other Liab.	4.. *d*	....	....	....	....	....	47.9	100.0	110.1	23.8	12.0	—	173.5	232.2	334.0	95.2
Deposit Money Banks: Assets	7a. *d*	....	....	....	....	....	9.6	19.5	15.9	18.7	44.8	60.7	21.5	32.4	24.0	15.6
Liabilities	7b. *d*	....	....	....	....	....	—	—	—	—	30.7	56.6	27.6	26.8	23.9	30.2
Monetary Authorities																*Millions of Zimbabwe Dollars:*
Foreign Assets	11	....	....	....	....	....	59	54	51	104	139	170	165	206	207	421
Claims on Central Government	12a	....	....	....	....	....	81	89	104	77	78	122	201	347	347	303
Claims on Nonfin.Pub.Enterprises	12c	....	....	....	....	....	—	—	—	—	1	—	96	1	189	157
Claims on Private Sector	12d	....	....	....	....	....	—	—	—	56	63	50	131	59	350	7
Claims on Deposit Money Banks	12e	....	....	....	....	....	5	9	7	—	—	—	5	—	24	—
Reserve Money	14	....	....	....	....	....	120	148	165	156	182	245	325	389	407	449
of which: Currency Outside DMBs	14a	....	....	....	....	....	67	79	84	95	108	157	199	238	227	259
Central Bank Bills Outstanding	16ad	....	....	....	....	....	—	—	—	—	10	—	—	—	—	65
Foreign Liabilities	16c	....	....	....	....	....	30	62	71	16	8	—	156	252	590	528
Central Government Deposits	16d	....	....	....	....	....	17	8	—	26	76	66	94	—	—	—
Capital Accounts	17a	....	....	....	....	....	6	6	7	8	8	8	8	8	8	8
Other Items (Net)	17r	....	....	....	....	....	–27	–72	–81	31	–2	24	15	–36	111	–161
Deposit Money Banks																*Millions of Zimbabwe Dollars:*
Reserves	20	....	....	....	....	....	42	47	56	55	60	82	115	143	161	169
Other Claims on Monetary Author.	20c	....	....	....	....	....	—	—	—	—	10	—	—	—	—	65
Foreign Assets	21	....	....	....	....	....	6	12	10	13	30	38	15	30	27	23
Claims on Central Government	22a	....	....	....	....	....	....	....	....	....	249	315	203	228	219	313
Claims on Local Government	22b	....	....	....	....	....	—	—	—	—	1	1	2	1	—	—
Claims on Nonfin.Pub.Enterprises	22c	....	....	....	....	....	....	....	....	....	135	171	292	423	349	477
Claims on Private Sector	22d	....	....	....	....	....	....	....	....	....	455	561	721	868	935	I 659
Claims on Other Banking Insts	22f	....	....	....	....	....	—	—	—	—	—	—	—	3	6	3
Claims on Nonbank Financial Insts	22g	....	....	....	....	....	—	—	—	—	—	—	—	—	—	—
Demand Deposits	24	....	....	....	....	....	250	269	288	317	354	473	478	588	512	608
Time and Savings Deposits	25	....	....	....	....	....	....	....	....	....	469	578	714	916	942	971
Money Market Instruments	26aa	....	....	....	....	....	—	—	—	—	—	—	—	—	—	124
Foreign Liabilities	26c	....	....	....	....	....	—	—	—	—	21	36	20	25	26	45
Central Government Deposits	26d	....	....	....	....	....	....	....	....	....	4	4	23	24	20	50
Credit from Monetary Authorities	26g	....	....	....	....	....	5	9	7	—	—	—	5	—	24	—
Capital Accounts	27a	....	....	....	....	....	33	48	69	75	88	102	121	143	150	194
Other Items (Net)	27r	....	....	....	....	....	....	....	....	....	3	–25	–12	1	23	I –285
Monetary Survey																*Millions of Zimbabwe Dollars:*
Foreign Assets (Net)	31n	....	....	....	....	....	35	4	–10	101	140	173	5	–40	–384	–129
Domestic Credit	32	....	....	....	....	....	....	....	....	....	901	1,150	1,528	1,905	2,375	I 1,870
Claims on Central Govt. (Net)	32an	....	....	....	....	....	....	....	....	....	247	367	287	551	546	566
Claims on Local Government	32b	....	....	....	....	....	—	—	—	—	1	1	2	1	—	—
Claims on Nonfin.Pub.Enterprises	32c	....	....	....	....	....	....	....	....	....	135	171	388	423	538	634
Claims on Private Sector	32d	....	....	....	....	....	....	....	....	....	518	611	851	927	1,285	I 666
Claims on Other Banking Insts	32f	....	....	....	....	....	—	—	—	—	—	—	—	3	6	3
Claims on Nonbank Financial Inst	32g	....	....	....	....	....	—	—	—	—	—	—	—	—	—	—
Money	34	....	....	....	....	....	324	352	375	415	463	633	679	827	751	874
Quasi-Money	35	....	....	....	....	....	....	....	....	....	472	580	721	921	939	971
Money Market Instruments	36aa	....	....	....	....	....	—	—	—	—	—	—	—	—	—	124
Capital Accounts	37a	....	....	....	....	....	39	55	76	82	96	110	129	151	158	202
Other Items (Net)	37r	....	....	....	....	....	....	....	....	....	10	—	5	–34	143	I –431
Money plus Quasi-Money	35l	....	....	....	....	....	....	....	....	....	935	1,213	1,399	1,748	1,691	1,845
Other Banking Institutions																*Millions of Zimbabwe Dollars:*
Reserves	40	....	....	....	....	....	26	24	27	40	34	30	69	71	116	108
Foreign Assets	41	....	....	....	....	....	—	—	—	—	—	3	—	—	—	—
Claims on Central Government	42a	....	....	....	....	....	....	....	....	....	317	361	349	437	451	566
Claims on Local Government	42b	....	....	....	....	....	....	....	....	....	19	21	26	26	26	26
Claims on Nonfin.Pub.Enterprises	42c	....	....	....	....	....	15	16	22	23	22	29	29	31	24	39
Claims on Private Sector	42d	....	....	....	....	....	380	393	402	426	461	533	576	580	628	661
Claims on Nonbank Financial Insts	42g	....	....	....	....	....	—	—	—	—	—	—	—	—	—	—
Time and Savings Deposits	45	....	....	....	....	....	480	524	581	644	766	865	934	1,019	1,082	1,266
Money Market Instruments	46aa	....	....	....	....	....	63	47	41	30	28	44	68	73	82	65
Foreign Liabilities	46c	....	....	....	....	....	....	....	....	....	4	5	8	10	16	4
Credit from Deposit Money Banks	46h	....	....	....	....	....	—	—	—	—	3	3	2	3	2	7
Capital Accounts	47a	....	....	....	....	....	41	45	49	55	64	76	88	91	99	106
Other Items (Net)	47r	....	....	....	....	....	....	....	....	....	–12	–18	–51	–50	–35	–49
Banking Survey																*Millions of Zimbabwe Dollars:*
Foreign Assets (Net)	51n	....	....	....	....	....	....	....	....	....	137	170	–3	–50	–399	–132
Domestic Credit	52	....	....	....	....	....	....	....	....	....	1,720	2,093	2,508	2,975	3,499	I 3,158
Claims on Central Govt. (Net)	52an	....	....	....	....	....	....	....	....	....	565	728	637	988	997	1,131
Claims on Local Government	52b	....	....	....	....	....	....	....	....	....	20	22	27	26	26	27
Claims on Nonfin.Pub.Enterprises	52c	....	....	....	....	....	15	16	22	23	157	200	417	454	562	673
Claims on Private Sector	52d	....	....	....	....	....	....	....	....	....	979	1,143	1,428	1,507	1,913	I 1,327
Claims on Nonbank Financial Inst	52g	....	....	....	....	....	—	—	—	—	—	—	—	—	—	—
Liquid Liabilities	55l	....	....	....	....	....	....	....	....	....	1,668	2,048	2,265	2,695	2,657	3,003
Money Market Instruments	56aa	....	....	....	....	....	63	47	41	30	28	44	68	73	82	190
Capital Accounts	57a	....	....	....	....	....	80	100	125	138	160	187	217	242	257	308
Other Items (Net)	57r	....	....	....	....	....	....	....	....	....	1	–15	–44	–85	103	I –476

Zimbabwe

1985	1986	1987	1988	1989	1990	1991	1992	1993	1994	1995	1996	1997	1998	1999		698
End of Period															**Exchange Rates**	
.5547	.4872	.4239	.3825	.3352	.2666	.1384	.1327	.1050	.0817	.0723	.0642	.0398	.0190	.0191	Official Rate	ac
End of Period (ag) Period Average (rh)																
.6093	.5959	.6013	.5147	.4405	.3793	.1980	.1824	.1442	.1192	.1074	.0923	.0537	.0268	.0262	Official Rate	ag
.6204	.6006	.6020	.5550	.4732	.4085	.2917	.1963	.1545	.1227	.1155	.1008	.0841	.0467	.0261	Official Rate	rh
End of Period															**Fund Position**	
191.0	191.0	191.0	191.0	191.0	191.0	191.0	261.3	261.3	261.3	261.3	261.3	261.3	261.3	353.4	Quota	2f.s
13.2	5.0	16.3	.5	.5	.2	.1	.3	.6	—	.5	6.8	.2	.3	.8	SDRs	1b.s
—	—	—	—	—	—	.1	.1	.1	.1	.1	.1	.1	.2	.3	Reserve Position in the Fund	1c.s
240.5	191.1	110.3	52.2	22.2	4.8	—	157.2	205.0	257.5	310.0	304.1	285.5	289.2	268.8	Total Fund Cred.&Loans Outstg.	2tl
End of Period															**International Liquidity**	
93.4	106.4	166.1	178.6	94.6	149.2	149.7	222.2	432.0	405.3	595.5	598.8	160.1	130.8	268.0	Total Reserves minus Gold	1l.d
14.5	6.2	23.1	.6	.7	.3	.1	.4	.9	.1	.8	9.8	.3	.4	1.1	SDRs	1b.d
—	—	.1	.1	.1	.1	.1	.1	.1	.1	.1	.2	.2	.3	.4	Reserve Position in the Fund	1c.d
78.8	100.2	143.0	178.0	93.8	148.9	149.5	221.7	431.1	405.1	594.6	588.9	159.6	130.1	266.5	Foreign Exchange	1d.d
.77	.54	.42	.40	.45	.38	.41	.55	.50	.47	.76	.64	.77	.62	.73	Gold (Million Fine Troy Ounces)	1ad
127.8	110.0	98.5	79.1	82.2	69.6	67.9	88.1	79.1	89.7	139.7	117.2	56.0	82.6	105.4	Gold (National Valuation)	1and
47.6	52.7	36.6	29.7	28.4	163.1	479.6	435.2	291.1	76.1	36.5	28.5	224.6	335.6	229.9	Monetary Authorities: Other Liab.	4..d
13.4	25.4	26.1	28.2	32.8	40.2	49.1	95.5	79.6	321.3	275.0	299.8	314.7	179.3	156.9	Deposit Money Banks: Assets	7a.d
43.9	62.2	61.3	62.4	66.0	96.8	186.0	220.6	518.6	579.3	814.4	827.8	623.8	458.3	245.0	Liabilities	7b.d
End of Period															**Monetary Authorities**	
522	524	459	519	425	611	1,512	1,656	3,545	4,152	6,701	7,710	3,991	7,937	14,241	Foreign Assets	11
244	356	566	399	355	830	963	2,034	2,760	7,102	13,640	22,828	30,545	47,543	58,734	Claims on Central Government	12a
237	188	158	124	182	305	263	177	99	134	131	160	188	674	653	Claims on Nonfin.Pub.Enterprises	12c
4	6	26	29	90	158	285	466	207	182	216	285	361	808	1,095	Claims on Private Sector	12d
1	147	—	—	—	—	618	266	311	448	1,330	1,337	1,403	4,373	3,232	Claims on Deposit Money Banks	12e
541	626	669	843	1,027	1,290	1,705	1,933	2,938	3,632	3,722	6,174	8,509	11,052	17,786	Reserve Money	14
321	380	389	503	618	770	889	861	1,191	1,467	1,823	2,440	3,558	4,468	7,256	*of which: Currency Outside DMBs*	14a
55	—	50	200	—	—	—	—	—	2,050	917	—	—	—	—	Central Bank Bills Outstanding	16ad
512	481	321	194	131	448	2,422	3,571	3,971	3,791	4,631	5,048	11,349	27,758	22,839	Foreign Liabilities	16c
4	1	1	—	1	12	1	2	1	3,311	14,737	22,833	18,043	26,064	43,773	Central Government Deposits	16d
8	8	8	8	8	8	8	8	392	670	872	804	842	1,015	1,965	Capital Accounts	17a
–112	105	160	–176	–115	146	–495	–916	–380	–1,436	–2,860	–2,541	–2,255	–4,553	–8,409	Other Items (Net)	17r
End of Period															**Deposit Money Banks**	
208	217	239	313	385	472	766	1,046	1,188	2,019	1,819	3,598	4,279	6,045	10,109	Reserves	20
55	—	50	99	—	—	—	—	—	2,052	579	—	—	—	—	Other Claims on Monetary Author.	20c
22	43	43	55	75	106	248	524	552	2,695	2,561	3,250	5,856	6,699	5,985	Foreign Assets	21
355	334	481	519	698	597	464	489	1,456	968	6,031	7,149	7,103	6,737	11,234	Claims on Central Government	22a
1	2	—	—	—	—	2	3	11	28	25	32	95	240	267	Claims on Local Government	22b
659	794	659	721	861	637	502	406	1,120	732	630	957	1,084	1,834	2,645	Claims on Nonfin.Pub.Enterprises	22c
672	749	1,033	1,489	1,988	2,503	4,241	5,967	9,056	11,736	15,060	18,147	27,098	36,811	41,357	Claims on Private Sector	22d
17	7	13	10	32	24	152	44	63	28	186	306	915	141	1,481	Claims on Other Banking Insts	22f
—	—	—	—	—	—	—	—	31	58	8	56	40	186	95	Claims on Nonbank Financial Insts	22g
688	727	835	1,104	1,292	1,651	2,094	2,294	4,550	5,791	9,352	11,290	17,102	21,424	27,804	Demand Deposits	24
1,152	1,138	1,620	1,860	2,387	2,506	2,009	2,470	3,473	5,753	5,238	8,136	9,757	8,251	11,512	Time and Savings Deposits	25
166	205	—	92	4	38	96	30	592	691	479	314	891	1,274	2,548	Money Market Instruments	26aa
72	104	102	121	150	255	940	1,209	3,597	4,859	7,583	8,972	11,608	17,126	9,345	Foreign Liabilities	26c
44	68	92	119	134	179	588	695	509	440	694	1,078	1,753	1,702	1,995	Central Government Deposits	26d
—	—	—	—	30	—	124	122	249	429	1,329	1,331	951	3,798	2,615	Credit from Monetary Authorities	26g
206	243	282	343	425	587	791	1,017	1,435	1,920	2,054	2,515	4,412	6,445	9,510	Capital Accounts	27a
–339	–338	–412	–433	–384	–878	–265	644	–929	433	171	–142	–3	–1,326	7,847	Other Items (Net)	27r
End of Period															**Monetary Survey**	
–39	–18	80	259	219	14	–1,602	–2,601	–3,471	–1,803	–2,952	–3,061	–13,110	–30,247	–11,959	Foreign Assets (Net)	31n
2,140	2,367	2,843	3,171	4,070	4,863	6,284	9,013	14,342	17,242	20,496	26,008	47,633	67,209	71,793	Domestic Credit	32
551	622	954	798	918	1,237	838	1,826	3,705	4,320	4,240	6,066	17,852	26,515	24,201	Claims on Central Govt. (Net)	32an
1	2	—	—	—	—	2	3	11	28	25	32	95	240	267	Claims on Local Government	32b
896	982	817	845	1,042	942	765	583	1,219	866	761	1,117	1,272	2,509	3,298	Claims on Nonfin.Pub.Enterprises	32c
676	755	1,059	1,518	2,078	2,661	4,527	6,432	9,263	11,918	15,276	18,431	27,459	37,618	42,452	Claims on Private Sector	32d
17	7	13	10	32	24	152	44	63	28	186	306	915	141	1,481	Claims on Other Banking Insts	32f
—	—	—	—	—	—	—	125	81	83	8	56	40	186	95	Claims on Nonbank Financial Inst	32g
1,021	1,127	1,259	1,617	1,933	2,467	3,036	3,211	6,259	7,396	11,270	13,874	21,320	26,332	35,473	Money	34
1,152	1,138	1,620	1,860	2,387	2,506	2,009	2,470	3,473	5,753	5,238	8,136	9,757	8,251	11,512	Quasi-Money	35
166	205	—	193	4	38	96	30	592	689	817	314	891	1,274	2,548	Money Market Instruments	36aa
214	251	290	351	433	595	799	1,025	1,827	2,589	2,926	3,319	5,253	7,459	11,475	Capital Accounts	37a
–451	–371	–245	–591	–468	–730	–1,257	–323	–1,280	–990	–2,706	–2,697	–2,698	–6,354	–1,173	Other Items (Net)	37r
2,173	2,265	2,879	3,477	4,321	4,973	5,045	5,681	9,731	13,149	16,507	22,011	31,077	34,583	46,985	Money plus Quasi-Money	35l
End of Period															**Other Banking Institutions**	
101	180	171	925	134	231	259	175	679	914	3,634	4,453	7,510	4,691	5,058	Reserves	40
—	1	—	—	4	—	2	2	10	8	36	70	25	24	55	Foreign Assets	41
765	908	1,120	1,256	1,652	1,746	2,159	2,187	2,348	2,795	3,962	4,410	3,723	4,050	9,233	Claims on Central Government	42a
31	27	28	29	31	38	41	43	42	43	64	266	432	438	443	Claims on Local Government	42b
54	53	53	59	36	52	82	126	182	404	2,147	590	857	1,075	1,468	Claims on Nonfin.Pub.Enterprises	42c
704	801	960	500	1,599	2,292	3,225	3,463	3,414	4,036	5,575	8,289	12,412	14,998	16,091	Claims on Private Sector	42d
—	—	—	—	—	—	—	—	—	—	5	2,486	741	30	3	Claims on Nonbank Financial Insts	42g
1,551	1,856	2,170	2,628	3,297	4,248	5,284	5,359	6,705	9,348	14,894	20,685	26,024	23,959	28,522	Time and Savings Deposits	45
33	40	59	76	69	133	226	192	208	386	481	459	1,356	2,742	1,878	Money Market Instruments	46aa
2	2	1	—	—	—	—	—	—	1	158	167	127	90	101	Foreign Liabilities	46c
2	2	3	1	5	6	20	20	157	25	113	70	423	322	907	Credit from Deposit Money Banks	46h
120	138	163	200	268	373	521	591	639	691	1,047	1,499	2,143	2,045	4,044	Capital Accounts	47a
–54	–69	–65	–136	–185	–401	–282	–166	–1,033	–2,251	–1,271	–2,316	–4,374	–3,851	–3,099	Other Items (Net)	47r
End of Period															**Banking Survey**	
–41	–19	79	258	222	14	–1,600	–2,598	–3,461	–1,796	–3,074	–3,158	–13,212	–30,313	–12,004	Foreign Assets (Net)	51n
3,678	4,149	4,991	5,005	7,356	8,968	11,640	14,787	20,265	24,492	32,064	41,743	64,883	87,659	97,551	Domestic Credit	52
1,316	1,530	2,075	2,054	2,571	2,982	2,997	4,012	6,053	7,115	8,201	10,476	21,575	30,565	33,434	Claims on Central Govt. (Net)	52an
32	29	28	29	31	39	44	46	53	70	89	298	527	678	710	Claims on Local Government	52b
950	1,035	870	904	1,078	994	847	709	1,402	1,270	2,908	1,707	2,129	3,584	4,766	Claims on Nonfin.Pub.Enterprises	52c
1,380	1,555	2,019	2,018	3,676	4,952	7,751	9,895	12,677	15,954	20,852	26,720	39,871	52,617	58,543	Claims on Private Sector	52d
—	—	—	—	—	—	—	125	81	83	13	2,542	781	215	98	Claims on Nonbank Financial Inst	52g
3,623	3,941	4,878	5,180	7,483	8,991	10,070	10,865	15,758	21,583	27,768	38,243	49,591	53,850	70,449	Liquid Liabilities	55l
199	245	59	269	74	171	322	222	800	1,075	1,297	773	2,248	4,016	4,425	Money Market Instruments	56aa
333	389	453	551	701	968	1,320	1,616	2,466	3,280	3,974	4,819	7,396	9,504	15,519	Capital Accounts	57a
–519	–445	–319	–737	–680	–1,148	–1,672	–513	–2,219	–3,243	–4,050	–5,249	–7,564	–10,024	–4,846	Other Items (Net)	57r

Zimbabwe

		1970	1971	1972	1973	1974	1975	1976	1977	1978	1979	1980	1981	1982	1983	1984
Interest Rates															*Percent Per Annum*		
Bank Rate *(End of Period)*	60	4.50	4.50	4.50	4.50	4.50	4.50	4.50	4.50	4.50	4.50	4.50	9.00	9.00	9.00	9.00
Money Market Rate	60b	....	....	....	....	....	4.25	4.25	4.25	4.25	4.25	4.15	6.83	9.50	9.09	8.90
Treasury Bill Rate	60c	....	....	....	....	....			....	3.55	3.54	3.39	5.70	8.50	8.52	8.49
Deposit Rate	60l	....	....	....	....	....	4.00	3.75	3.50	3.25	3.25	3.52	7.46	14.46	12.80	10.30
Lending Rate	60p	....	....	....	....	....			....	17.54	17.54	17.54	20.19	23.00	23.08	23.00
Government Bond Yield	61	6.50	6.50	6.50	6.50	6.50	6.50	6.54	7.63	8.75	8.75	8.94	11.54	13.00	13.08	13.29
Prices, Production, Labor															*Index Numbers (1995=100):*		
Consumer Prices	64	3.9	4.1	4.2	4.3	4.6	I 5.0	5.6	6.2	6.5	7.7	8.1	9.2	10.2	12.5	15.0
Manufacturing Production	66ey	57.1	61.6	70.8	76.6	81.9	I 81.2	76.2	72.0	70.2	77.3	88.6	96.9	96.3	93.7	89.5
															Number in Thousands:		
Labor Force	67d	....	....	....	....	....	....	....	....	....	....	....	....	....	....	....
Employment	67e	....	....	....	....	....	....	....	....	....	....	....	....	....	....	....
International Transactions															*Millions of Zimbabwe Dollars*		
Exports	70	264.6	287.7	340.6	402.7	503.1	531.3	557.4	550.9	599.1	715.6	909.3	875.0	968.4	1,150.2	1,451.6
Imports, c.i.f.	71	270.2	324.9	315.9	354.9	504.0	531.2	440.1	446.3	464.3	631.7	930.8	1,170.4	1,244.1	1,220.8	1,380.8
Imports, f.o.b.	71.v	235.0	282.5	274.7	308.6	438.3	461.9	382.7	388.1	403.7	549.3	809.4	1,017.7	1,081.8	1,061.6	1,200.7
															1985=100		
Volume of Exports	72	85.3	94.1	112.7	115.1	119.9	I 112.2	112.8	107.1	111.4	109.8	104.6	99.6	102.5	106.2	104.8
Volume of Imports	73	102.3	115.5	114.7	123.7	128.9	I 122.9	89.8	82.7	75.6	74.6	102.8	126.9	136.7	114.6	114.2
Unit Value of Exports	74	19.3	19.6	19.7	21.5	28.2	I 30.1	31.5	32.7	34.9	40.1	53.1	58.7	56.9	64.4	84.0
Unit Value of Imports	75	19.2	20.5	20.0	20.9	28.5	I 31.4	35.6	39.3	44.7	61.1	65.5	65.2	64.9	76.2	85.9
Balance of Payments															*Millions of US Dollars:*		
Current Account, n.i.e.	78al d	....	....	....	....	....	....	....	1.1	54.0	−56.5	−149.4	−546.1	−632.1	−397.9	−42.9
Goods: Exports f.o.b.	78aa d	....	....	....	....	....	....	....	900.8	927.7	1,079.8	1,441.1	1,451.4	1,312.1	1,153.7	1,173.6
Goods: Imports f.o.b.	78ab d	....	....	....	....	....	....	....	−671.1	−657.4	−875.2	−1,335.0	−1,534.0	−1,472.0	−1,069.6	−989.3
Trade Balance	78ac d	....	....	....	....	....	....	....	229.6	270.3	204.6	106.1	−82.6	−159.9	84.1	184.3
Services: Credit	78ad d	....	....	....	....	....	....	....	65.3	69.9	88.3	169.1	134.2	181.5	145.1	139.4
Services: Debit	78ae d	....	....	....	....	....	....	....	−226.8	−231.1	−276.4	−394.5	−535.9	−437.4	−430.9	−357.5
Balance on Goods & Services	78af d	....	....	....	....	....	....	....	68.1	109.0	16.5	−119.3	−484.3	−415.8	−201.7	−33.9
Income: Credit	78ag d	....	....	....	....	....	....	....	39.0	36.3	62.7	103.9	94.0	80.4	69.6	55.2
Income: Debit	78ah d	....	....	....	....	....	....	....	−105.8	−90.5	−132.0	−165.1	−211.9	−290.9	−254.8	−170.9
Balance on Gds, Serv. & Inc.	78ai d	....	....	....	....	....	....	....	1.3	54.9	−52.8	−180.4	−602.2	−626.4	−387.0	−149.7
Current Transfers, n.i.e.: Credit	78aj d	....	....	....	....	....	....	....	28.2	26.1	36.0	105.0	141.9	87.3	95.4	193.3
Current Transfers: Debit	78ak d	....	....	....	....	....	....	....	−28.3	−27.0	−39.7	−74.0	−85.8	−93.1	−106.3	−86.6
Capital Account, n.i.e.	78bc d	....	....	....	....	....	....	....	−15.1	−16.6	−52.2	−93.7	−89.8	−77.0	−62.3	−57.1
Capital Account, n.i.e.: Credit	78ba d	....	....	....	....	....	....	....	5.3	5.6	7.7	3.7	27.3	30.1	18.9	3.3
Capital Account: Debit	78bb d	....	....	....	....	....	....	....	−20.4	−22.3	−59.9	−97.4	−117.1	−107.1	−81.2	−60.4
Financial Account, n.i.e.	78bj d	....	....	....	....	....	....	....	−14.6	64.7	109.2	−29.8	499.4	594.5	251.8	8.7
Direct Investment Abroad	78bd d	....	....	....	....	....	....	....								
Dir. Invest. in Rep. Econ., n.i.e.	78be d	....	....	....	....	....	....	....	−3.8	2.5	.1	1.6	3.6	−.8	−2.1	−2.5
Portfolio Investment Assets	78bf d	....	....	....	....	....	....	....	.2	—	.6	.5	2.3	.7	—	39.4
Equity Securities	78bk d	....	....	....	....	....	....	....	—	—	—	—	—	—	—	—
Debt Securities	78bl d	....	....	....	....	....	....	....	.2	—	.6	.5	2.3	.7	—	39.4
Portfolio Investment Liab., n.i.e.	78bg d	....	....	....	....	....	....	....	−8.4	−8.3	−9.4	−27.9	−32.3	−47.5	−42.7	−36.6
Equity Securities	78bm d	....	....	....	....	....	....	....								
Debt Securities	78bn d	....	....	....	....	....	....	....	−8.4	−8.3	−9.4	−27.9	−32.3	−47.5	−42.7	−36.6
Financial Derivatives Assets	78bw d	....	....	....	....	....	....	....								
Financial Derivatives Liabilities	78bx d	....	....	....	....	....	....	....								
Other Investment Assets	78bh d	....	....	....	....	....	....	....	3.2	−3.1	−30.0	6.5	−5.4	62.3	36.7	43.2
Monetary Authorities	78bo d	....	....	....	....	....	....	....								
General Government	78bp d	....	....	....	....	....	....	....								
Banks	78bq d	....	....	....	....	....	....	....	3.2	−3.1	−30.0	6.5	−5.4	62.3	36.7	43.2
Other Sectors	78br d	....	....	....	....	....	....	....								
Other Investment Liab., n.i.e.	78bi d	....	....	....	....	....	....	....	−5.7	73.6	147.9	−10.4	531.3	579.9	259.8	−34.8
Monetary Authorities	78bs d	....	....	....	....	....	....	....								
General Government	78bt d	....	....	....	....	....	....	....	14.2	106.7	170.7	−18.6	367.9	503.1	303.5	6.4
Banks	78bu d	....	....	....	....	....	....	....	−2.9	−3.0	3.2	28.9	−.9	−40.0	−51.1	−31.5
Other Sectors	78bv d	....	....	....	....	....	....	....	−17.0	−30.1	−26.0	−20.6	164.3	116.8	7.4	−9.7
Net Errors and Omissions	78ca d	....	....	....	....	....	....	....	20.5	−26.7	119.5	186.6	128.4	92.3	34.5	44.9
Overall Balance	78cb d	....	....	....	....	....	....	....	−8.1	75.4	119.9	−86.3	−8.1	−22.4	−174.0	−46.3
Reserves and Related Items	79da d	....	....	....	....	....	....	....	8.1	−75.4	−119.9	86.3	8.1	22.4	174.0	46.3
Reserve Assets	79db d	....	....	....	....	....	....	....	8.1	−75.4	−119.9	86.3	−37.3	22.4	7.3	−26.7
Use of Fund Credit and Loans	79dc d	....	....	....	....	....	....	....	—	—	—	—	45.4	—	166.6	73.0
Exceptional Financing	79de d	....	....	....	....	....	....	....	....	....	....	....	....	....	....	....

	1985	1986	1987	1988	1989	1990	1991	1992	1993	1994	1995	1996	1997	1998	1999		
Interest Rates																	
Percent Per Annum																	
	9.00	9.00	9.00	9.00	9.00	10.25	20.00	29.50	28.50	29.50	29.50	27.00	31.50	I 39.50	74.41	Bank Rate (*End of Period*)	60
	8.80	9.10	9.30	9.08	8.73	8.68	17.49	34.77	34.18	30.90	29.64	26.18	25.15	37.22	53.13	Money Market Rate	60b
	8.48	8.71	8.73	8.38	8.35	8.39	14.44	26.16	33.04	29.22	27.98	24.53	22.07	32.78	50.48	Treasury Bill Rate	60c
	10.04	10.28	9.58	9.68	8.85	8.80	14.20	28.63	29.45	26.75	25.92	21.58	18.60	29.06	38.51	Deposit Rate	60l
	17.17	13.00	13.00	13.00	13.00	11.71	15.50	19.77	36.33	34.86	34.73	34.23	32.55	42.06	55.39	Lending Rate	60p
	13.26	13.20	13.87	14.00	14.00	15.24	17.27	17.40	....	....	....	....	....	....	....	Government Bond Yield	61
Prices, Production, Labor																	
Period Averages																	
	16.3	18.6	21.0	22.5	25.4	I 29.8	36.8	52.3	66.7	81.6	100.0	121.4	144.2	190.1	....	Consumer Prices	64
	98.4	101.9	104.7	109.8	115.9	122.3	128.5	115.1	105.7	115.8	100.0	103.6	106.9	....	....	Manufacturing Production	66ey
Period Averages																	
	....	....	3,260	....	....	....	....	3,502	....	....	....	....	4,921	....	....	Labor Force	67d
	1,055	1,081	1,085	1,131	1,167	1,192	1,244	1,236	1,239	1,264	1,240	1,273	1,323	....	....	Employment	67e
International Transactions																	
Millions of Zimbabwe Dollars																	
	1,795.5	2,170.3	2,371.4	2,966.4	3,267.3	4,231.4	5,546.5	7,365.7	10,164.2	15,364.7	18,359.1	24,209.3	....	....	....	Exports	70
	1,446.5	1,640.4	1,741.7	2,043.2	3,438.1	4,528.2	7,443.1	11,232.3	11,798.4	18,270.6	23,048.1	28,095.1	....	....	....	Imports, c.i.f.	71
	1,446.5	1,640.4	1,741.7	2,043.2	2,989.7	3,937.6	6,472.3	9,767.2	10,259.5	15,887.5	20,043.0	....	....	....	....	Imports, f.o.b.	71.v
1985=100																	
	100.0	124.9	....	....	....	....	....	....	....	....	....	....	....	....	....	Volume of Exports	72
	100.0	121.0	....	....	....	....	....	....	....	....	....	....	....	....	....	Volume of Imports	73
	100.0	101.9	....	....	....	....	....	....	....	....	....	....	....	....	....	Unit Value of Exports	74
	100.0	104.6	....	....	....	....	....	....	....	....	....	....	....	....	....	Unit Value of Imports	75
Balance of Payments																	
Minus Sign Indicates Debit																	
	-64.2	16.8	58.0	125.3	17.0	-139.8	-457.0	-603.7	-115.7	-424.9	....	....	....	....	....	Current Account, n.i.e.	78al d
	1,119.6	1,322.7	1,452.0	1,664.9	1,693.5	1,747.9	1,693.8	1,527.6	1,609.1	1,961.1						Goods: Exports f.o.b.	78aa d
	-918.9	-1,011.6	-1,071.0	-1,163.6	-1,318.3	-1,505.2	-1,645.7	-1,782.1	-1,487.0	-1,803.5						Goods: Imports f.o.b.	78ab d
	200.6	311.2	381.0	501.3	375.2	242.7	48.1	-254.5	122.1	157.6						*Trade Balance*	78ac d
	295.5	169.0	164.6	190.3	241.8	264.2	273.5	305.1	372.1	383.2						Services: Credit	78ad d
	-462.3	-316.0	-349.8	-410.9	-457.0	-495.5	-627.4	-660.9	-563.8	-711.7						Services: Debit	78ae d
	33.8	164.2	195.7	280.7	160.0	11.3	-305.9	-610.3	-69.6	-170.9						*Balance on Goods & Services*	78af d
	37.8	36.4	33.0	17.4	26.0	22.9	26.1	26.0	35.0	27.5						Income: Credit	78ag d
	-166.9	-225.5	-228.4	-234.0	-236.1	-286.3	-278.0	-302.3	-287.1	-321.2						Income: Debit	78ah d
	-95.3	-24.9	.4	64.1	-50.0	-252.0	-557.8	-886.6	-321.6	-464.5						*Balance on Gds, Serv. & Inc.*	78ai d
	171.7	169.7	220.8	211.2	211.4	204.0	191.7	347.3	270.6	69.4						Current Transfers, n.i.e.: Credit	78aj d
	-140.6	-128.0	-163.2	-150.1	-144.3	-91.8	-90.9	-64.4	-64.7	-29.8						Current Transfers: Debit	78ak d
	-11.5	-10.0	-10.0	-8.6	-7.6	-7.0	-2.8	-1.4	-.4	284.4						Capital Account, n.i.e.	78bc d
	.1	.2	.2	.3	.2	.4	.1	.2	.6	285.4						Capital Account, n.i.e.: Credit	78ba d
	-11.7	-10.2	-10.2	-9.0	-7.9	-7.4	-2.9	-1.6	-1.0	-1.0						Capital Account: Debit	78bb d
	120.7	118.1	59.8	48.0	47.8	242.6	536.5	373.4	327.2	-25.5						Financial Account, n.i.e.	78bj d
	—	—	—	22.2	—	—	—	—	—	-4.7						Direct Investment Abroad	78bd d
	2.9	7.5	-30.5	-18.1	-10.2	-12.2	2.8	15.0	28.0	34.7						Dir. Invest. in Rep. Econ., n.i.e.	78be d
	45.9	38.2	56.8	—	—	10.4	41.8	27.6	—	—						Portfolio Investment Assets	78bf d
	—	—	—	—	—	—	—	—	—	—						Equity Securities	78bk d
	45.9	38.2	56.8	—	—	10.4	41.8	27.6	—	—						Debt Securities	78bl d
	-36.8	-37.0	-55.9	-60.9	-36.7	-32.1	-34.6	-37.1	-5.1	50.2						Portfolio Investment Liab., n.i.e.	78bg d
	—	—	—	—	—	—	—	—	—	56.9						Equity Securities	78bm d
	-36.8	-37.0	-55.9	-60.9	-36.7	-32.1	-34.6	-37.1	-5.1	-6.7						Debt Securities	78bn d
	....	....	....	....	....	....	....	....	....	....						Financial Derivatives Assets	78bw d
	....	....	....	....	....	....	....	....	....	....						Financial Derivatives Liabilities	78bx d
	24.6	34.4	19.8	4.9	—	—	38.0	15.9	99.9	-260.3						Other Investment Assets	78bh d
	....	....	....	....	....	....	....	....	....	....						Monetary Authorities	78bo d
	24.6	34.4	19.8	4.9	—	—	38.0	15.9	99.9	-260.3						General Government	78bp d
	....	....	....	....	....	....	....	....	....	....						Banks	78bq d
	....	....	....	....	....	....	....	....	....	....						Other Sectors	78br d
	84.2	75.0	69.6	99.9	94.7	276.5	488.4	352.0	204.4	154.7						Other Investment Liab., n.i.e.	78bi d
	—	—	—	—	3.0	97.6	128.7	-78.2	-7.8	-109.9						Monetary Authorities	78bs d
	49.7	98.4	82.1	70.4	67.6	88.6	275.0	407.9	191.0	62.0						General Government	78bt d
	-7.0	-26.5	-18.0	—	3.1	14.6	—	—	—	—						Banks	78bu d
	41.5	3.1	5.6	29.4	21.0	75.8	84.7	22.3	21.2	202.6						Other Sectors	78bv d
	37.2	-69.4	16.6	-63.0	-103.8	-9.9	-31.4	37.2	14.9	80.2	....	....	....	....	....	Net Errors and Omissions	78ca d
	82.2	55.5	124.5	101.6	-46.8	85.8	45.2	-194.6	225.9	-85.8	....	....	....	....	....	*Overall Balance*	78cb d
	-82.2	-55.5	-124.5	-101.6	46.8	-85.8	-45.2	194.6	-225.9	85.8	....	....	....	....	....	Reserves and Related Items	79da d
	-61.2	3.0	-19.5	-23.0	85.5	-62.8	-38.4	-31.1	-293.6	12.9	....	....	....	....	....	Reserve Assets	79db d
	-21.0	-58.5	-104.9	-78.6	-38.8	-23.0	-6.9	225.7	67.7	72.8	....	....	....	....	....	Use of Fund Credit and Loans	79dc d
	....	....	....	....	....	....	....	....	....	....	....	....	....	....	....	Exceptional Financing	79de d

Zimbabwe

		1970	1971	1972	1973	1974	1975	1976	1977	1978	1979	1980	1981	1982	1983	1984
Government Finance															*Millions of Zimbabwe Dollars:*	
Deficit (-) or Surplus	80	....	....	....	....	....	....	−118	−95	−254	−293	−376	−262	−545	−394	−647
Total Revenue and Grants	81y	....	....	....	....	....	....	492	576	573	611	830	1,131	1,532	1,890	2,110
Revenue	81	....	....	....	....	....	....	492	576	573	611	830	1,130	1,514	1,866	2,034
Grants	81z	....	....	....	....	....	....	—	—	—	—	—	2	18	23	77
Exp. & Lending Minus Repay.	82z	....	....	....	....	....	....	611	671	827	905	1,206	1,393	2,077	2,283	2,758
Expenditure	82	....	....	....	....	....	....	539	674	802	881	1,198	1,301	1,882	2,079	2,546
Lending Minus Repayments	83	....	....	....	....	....	....	72	−2	24	24	7	91	195	205	212
Total Financing	80h	....	....	....	....	....	....	118	95	254	293	376	262	545	394	647
Domestic	84a	....	....	....	....	....	....	119	98	130	172	297	116	414	350	325
Foreign	85a	....	....	....	....	....	....	−1	−3	124	121	79	146	132	44	322
Total Debt by Residence	88	....	....	....	....	....	....	785	864	1,146	1,479	1,828	2,081	2,464	2,846	3,744
Domestic	88a	....	....	....	....	....	....	693	764	914	1,117	1,393	1,507	1,622	1,860	2,306
Foreign	89a	....	....	....	....	....	....	92	100	233	361	435	574	841	987	1,438
National Accounts															*Millions of Zimbabwe Dollars*	
Exports of Goods & Services	90c	324	355	417	....	577	590	617	610	675	798	1,043	1,117	1,141	1,345	1,708
Government Consumption	91f	126	143	157	180	221	256	319	382	451	537	677	763	1,027	1,159	1,364
Gross Fixed Capital Formation	93e	175	221	256	330	421	468	427	379	341	395	528	830	1,039	1,238	1,185
Increase/Decrease(-) in Stocks	93i	47	56	40	51	91	72	−18	40	−60	−37	120	196	62	−235	28
Private Consumption	96f	715	849	936	988	1,166	1,254	1,354	1,344	1,546	1,933	2,219	2,969	3,378	4,341	3,792
Imports of Goods & Services	98c	−315	−379	−376	....	−587	−613	−533	−558	−593	−803	−1,146	−1,442	−1,450	−1,542	−1,673
Gross Domestic Product (GDP)	99b	1,086	1,262	1,429	1,538	1,832	1,995	2,166	2,198	2,359	2,822	3,441	4,430	5,220	5,994	6,403
Net Factor Inc/Pmts(-) Abroad	98.n	−21	−30	−35	−39	−40	−45	−58	−48	−42	−53	−47	−115	−194	−248	−195
Gross National Income (GNI)	99a	1,065	1,232	1,394	1,499	1,792	1,950	2,108	2,150	2,317	2,769	3,394	4,318	5,023	5,742	6,212
GDP Volume 1980 Prices	99b.p	....	....	....	2,889	3,389	3,266	3,230	3,064	2,998	3,112	3,441	3,872	3,974	4,037	3,960
GDP Volume 1990 Prices	99b.p	....	....	....	....	....	....	....	....	....	....	....	....	....	....	....
GDP Volume (1995=100)	99bv p	....	....	52.3	53.1	62.3	60.1	59.4	56.3	55.1	57.2	63.3	71.2	73.1	74.2	72.8
GDP Deflator (1995=100)	99bi p	....	....	4.5	4.7	4.8	5.4	5.9	6.4	7.0	8.0	8.9	10.1	11.6	13.2	14.3
																Millions:
Population	99z	5.31	5.50	5.69	5.89	6.08	16.14	6.33	6.52	6.72	6.93	7.10	7.36	7.48	7.74	7.98

Government Finance

Year Ending June 30

Item	1985	1986	1987	1988	1989	1990	1991	1992	1993	1994	1995	1996	1997	1998	1999	Code
Deficit (-) or Surplus	‡ -513	-638	-977	-1,005	-1,111	-1,138ᵖ	-2,107	-3,861	-2,645	-2,092	-5,791	-5,147	-5,077	....	....	80
Total Revenue and Grants	‡ 2,305	2,608	3,034	3,644	4,356	5,307ᵖ	6,759	8,634	11,752	13,699	18,687	23,811	31,126	....	....	81y
Revenue	‡ 2,132	2,500	2,954	3,526	4,267	5,193ᵖ	6,527	8,285	11,152	12,776	16,998	22,808	30,670	....	....	81
Grants	‡ 173	108	80	118	90	114ᵖ	232	349	600	923	1,690	1,003	456	....	....	81z
Exp. & Lending Minus Repay.	‡ 2,818	3,246	4,011	4,649	5,467	6,445ᵖ	8,866	12,495	14,396	15,790	24,479	28,958	36,202	....	....	82z
Expenditure	‡ 2,617	3,077	3,783	4,264	4,960	5,872ᵖ	8,132	11,217	12,390	14,538	22,000	29,691	36,454	....	....	82
Lending Minus Repayments	‡ 200	169	228	385	507	573ᵖ	734	1,278	2,006	1,252	2,479	-733	-252	....	....	83
Total Financing	‡ 513	638	977	1,005	1,111	1,138ᵖ	2,108	3,860	2,645	2,092	5,791	5,147	5,077	....	....	80h
Domestic	‡ 25	378	765	830	982	937ᵖ	1,503	1,321	1,279	1,733	4,802	3,973	5,168	....	....	84a
Foreign	‡ 488	260	212	175	129	201ᵖ	605	2,539	1,366	359	990	1,175	-91	....	....	85a
Total Debt by Residence	‡ 4,118	5,197	6,137	7,295	8,633	10,412ᵖ	16,264	20,400	25,054	31,131	47,503	53,201	59,303	....	....	88
Domestic	‡ 2,422	2,977	3,622	4,470	5,397	6,375ᵖ	7,849	7,993	9,071	12,875	24,671	31,407	30,371	....	....	88a
Foreign	‡ 1,696	2,221	2,515	2,825	3,236	4,037ᵖ	8,415	12,407	15,983	18,257	22,832	21,793	28,932	....	....	89a

National Accounts

Millions of Zimbabwe Dollars

Item	1985	1986	1987	1988	1989	1990	1991	1992	1993	1994	1995	1996	1997	1998	1999	Code
Exports of Goods & Services	2,020	2,492	2,690	3,350	4,087	4,915	7,075	9,364	13,050	19,431	23,562	30,910	....	....	....	90c
Government Consumption	1,838	2,140	2,617	3,879	3,273	4,180	4,775	8,308	6,350	9,375	11,100	14,492	17,057	....	....	91f
Gross Fixed Capital Formation	1,299	1,559	1,804	2,197	2,452	3,913	6,097	7,690	10,021	11,879	14,996	19,245	20,509	....	....	93e
Increase/Decrease(-) in Stocks	322	310	-131	441	180	-179	-439	-732	-347	1,324	-3,031	429	156	....	....	93i
Private Consumption	5,619	6,091	6,603	7,116	11,320	13,565	20,163	22,309	27,190	34,659	40,351	50,438	66,112	....	....	96f
Imports of Goods & Services	-2,002	-2,230	-2,383	-2,873	-3,803	-4,899	-8,048	-12,548	-13,784	-20,509	-25,216	-30,747	....	....	....	98c
Gross Domestic Product (GDP)	9,168	10,368	11,252	14,039	17,310	21,494	29,623	34,296	42,481	55,780	61,393	84,786	....	....	....	99b
Net Factor Inc/Pmts(-) Abroad	-221	-317	-324	-391	-446	-707	-979	-1,407	-1,604	-2,405	-2,794	-2,931	-3,908	....	....	98.n
Gross National Income (GNI)	8,944	10,053	10,927	13,648	16,863	20,687	28,644	32,889	40,877	53,375	58,599	81,855	....	....	....	99a
GDP Volume 1980 Prices	4,213	....	....	....	....	....	....	....	....	....	....	....	....	....	....	99b.*p*
GDP Volume 1990 Prices	17,193	17,553	17,754	19,095	20,091	21,494	22,682	20,634	20,908	22,338	22,192	23,884	24,915	....	....	99b.*p*
GDP Volume (1995=100)	77.5	79.1	80.0	86.0	90.5	96.9	102.2	93.0	94.2	100.7	100.0	107.6	112.3	....	....	99bv *p*
GDP Deflator (1995=100)	19.3	21.4	22.9	26.6	31.1	36.0	47.2	60.1	73.4	90.3	100.0	128.3	....	....	....	99bi *p*

Midyear Estimates

Item	1985	1986	1987	1988	1989	1990	1991	1992	1993	1994	1995	1996	1997	1998	1999	Code
Population	8.38	8.41	8.64	8.88	9.12	9.37	10.14	10.41	10.78	11.15	11.53	11.91	12.29	12.68	13.08	99z

(See notes in the back of the book.)

COUNTRY
NOTES

Total Fund Credit & Loans Outstanding

Includes outstanding use of Fund's credits within GRA, and SAF, PRGF, and Trust Fund loans.

Real Effective Exchange Rate Indices

The indicators of real effective exchange rates based on *relative unit labor costs (line 65um)* and *relative normalized unit labor costs (line reu)* in manufacturing represent the product of the index of the ratio of the relevant indicator (in national currency) for the country listed to a weighted geometric average of the corresponding indicators for 20 other industrial countries (again in national currency, and including in addition to the other 16 countries listed on this table, Australia, New Zealand, Greece, and Portugal) and the index of the nominal effective exchange rate, which is calculated by weighting the exchange rates for the countries listed in the same manner as the other indicators. This index for the nominal effective exchange rate is presented as *line* neu in the country pages of the 17 countries in the table and Greece. Indicators of real effective exchange rates based on *relative value-added deflators (line 99by), relative wholesale prices (line 63ey),* and *relative export unit values (line 74ey)* in manufacturing are calculated in the same fashion, but using only the 16 other countries listed on this table for weighting the index concerned and the nominal effective exchange rate. The reference base is 1995_100 in accordance with all indices published in *IFS*.

Several of the measures of real effective exchange rates are subject to frequent and sometimes substantial revision. To an important extent, these revisions stem from the procedures used to estimate several of the indicators. Thus, the national data underlying the two labor cost series and the value-added deflator series are calculated by benchmarking the best available monthly or quarterly series on reasonably comprehensive and comparable, but periodically revised, annual data from the national accounts. While such benchmarking makes these series particularly susceptible to revision, it also permits the calculation of up-to-date quarterly series which, on an annual basis, are also reasonably comprehensive and comparable.

The total trade weights used to construct the associated nominal effective exchange rates for the five indices are designed to make them particularly relevant with respect to movements in costs and prices affecting exports and imports of manufactured goods. The weights, which are built up from aggregate trade flows for manufactured goods (SITC 5–8) averaged over the period 1989–91, take into account the relative importance of a country's trading partners in its direct bilateral relations with them, in both the home and foreign markets; of the competitive relations with third countries in particular markets; and of the differences among countries in the importance of foreign trade to the manufacturing sector.

Estimates shown for the Euro Area for relative unit labor costs and relative normalized unit labor costs are generated using a subset of the trade weights described in the paragraph above, where the weights for the Euro Area relate to the trade of the Euro Area as a whole with its partners in the system. A synthetic euro has been constructed for the period before the introduction of the euro using trade weights drawn from the same weighting scheme, Euro Area member exchange rates, and the official lock-in rates, which were used to determine the initial value of the euro. This method

(national currency series times lock-in rates times Euro Area member trade weights specific to this system) has also been used to estimate the Euro Area unit labor cost and normalized unit labor cost series denominated in euros.

The nature and scope of the various national indicators entering into the indices are briefly described below. While mention is made of specific deficiencies in some of the selected measures of costs and prices, the emphasis is on what they purport to measure. Because these measures of costs and prices contain a considerable amount of staff estimation, they are not published in *IFS*.

Unit labor costs are defined as compensation of employees per unit of real output (or value added) in the manufacturing sector. Account is taken of employer-paid social insurance premia and other employment taxes, as well as wages and salaries. For the most recent quarters, however, indices typically refer more narrowly to wages or wages and salaries per unit of total output of manufactured goods (rather than that of value added in the manufacturing sector).

Normalized unit labor costs in manufacturing are calculated by dividing an index of actual hourly compensation per worker by the normalized index of output per man-hour in local currency. The data printed are the product of this variable after weighting (to obtain the relative measure) and the nominal effective exchange rate **(neu).** The purpose of normalizing output per man-hour is to remove distortions arising from cyclical movements, which occur largely because changes in hours worked do not correspond closely to changes in the effective inputs of labor. The Hodrick-Prescott filter, which smoothes a time series by removing short-run fluctuations while retaining changes of larger amplitude, is the method used to normalize output per man-hour. The monthly series are estimated by extrapolating the quarterly local currency series for the period needed, interpolating these estimates from quarterly into monthly series and reweighting the interpolated monthly series to obtain the monthly relative series. **Where the monthly data are extrapolated, data for the corresponding quarters are not shown.** Monthly nominal effective exchange rates are computed using monthly exchange rates and the same weights as are used for quarterly nominal effective exchange rates, and real effective rates are calculated using the nominal effective rates and interpolated relative monthly normalized unit labor costs. The extrapolation and interpolation of the quarterly series is acceptable because the quarterly series have been smoothed, and the trend of these series is retained in the extrapolation. The interpolated monthly trend series is used to adjust the more current nominal effective exchange rate. The annual series (for both relative, and relative normalized, unit labor costs) may not correspond with the average of the quarterly series because only the annual series include Switzerland.

Value-added deflators represent the quotient of the current and constant price estimates of value added in the manufacturing sector, adjusted for changes in indirect taxes. Such indicators, which share the properties of the corresponding GDP deflator series for the overall economy, are best viewed in this context as composite indicators of the cost (per unit of real value added) of all factors of production. They differ from final product prices in that they abstract from the costs of intermediate inputs obtained by the manufacturing sector from other sectors. Extrapolation beyond the most recent benchmark year is based on wholesale prices for manufacturers adjusted to exclude the influence of changes in raw material prices.

Wholesale prices are intended to measure final product prices (excluding indirect taxes, which are not generally imposed on exported goods). However, the various national indices tend to lack comparability in both concept and commodity composition. Wherever possible, use is made of indices that approximate final product prices (e.g., industry selling prices or finished goods prices).

Export unit values serve as proxies for data on final product prices for traded goods but suffer from some of the same compositional drawbacks as wholesale prices. In addition, because of the less-than-complete homogeneity of the commodity classes upon which the unit values are calculated, the national series are often somewhat erratic. On the other hand, the unit value relatives (each computed as the ratio of one country's index to that of its competitors) tend to be much less variable than relatives derived from other price or cost indicators. This is because of the degree of competition that is characteristic of international trade and the resultant selectivity in the composition of a country's exports. International competition often places severe limits on how far an exporter's prices may diverge from those charged by competitors, so that goods not competitively priced tend to disappear from the trade flows for which unit values are computed. Consequently, export unit values imperfectly reflect underlying cost developments.

An indicator of real effective exchange rates based on relative consumer prices is also shown (*line* rec) to afford comparison with a wider group of partner—or competitor—countries. The weighting scheme is based on disaggregated trade data for manufactured goods and primary products covering the three-year period 1988–90 and is derived according to the same methodology as that followed for other countries discussed in the Introduction (section 1). The consumer price index that is used as a cost indicator is that shown on the country pages *(line 64)*. However, it should be borne in mind that, especially for the industrial countries, consumer price indices are in a number of respects conceptually inferior to the other measures of domestic costs and prices discussed above for the purpose of compiling indices of real effective exchange rates, owing to the inclusion of various factors which may differ across countries, for example, indirect taxes.

Estimates shown for the Euro Area for relative consumer prices are generated using a subset of the trade weights described in the paragraph above, where the weights for the Euro Area relate to the trade of the Euro Area as a whole with its partners in the system. A synthetic euro has been constructed for the period before the introduction of the euro using trade weights drawn from the same weighting scheme, Euro Area member exchange rates, and the official lock-in rates, which were used to determine the initial value of the euro. The Euro area consumer price series from January 1995 onward is the Harmonized Index of Consumer Prices, provided by the ECB, and prior to this period, it is the trade-weighted average of the individual member countries' consumer price indices. Trade weights used in the construction are specific to this system and are the same as those used in the construction of the synthetic euro.

As indicated in the Introduction, movements in these indices need to be interpreted with considerable caution. While every effort is made to use national data that are as internationally comparable as possible, the degree to which it is practicable to ensure comparability is limited by the character of the available data. For this reason, the table provides a wide array of available indicators.

Wholesale Prices

There is significant diversity in the methodology used by countries to compile these indices.

Exports and Imports

ɪ Prior to 1998, data for South Africa refer to the South African Common Customs Area (SACCA), which includes Botswana, Lesotho, Namibia, South Africa, and Swaziland. Beginning in 1998, data refer to South Africa only, excluding intra-trade of the SACCA. Data for SACCA excluding South Africa amount to 1.987 billion U.S. dollars in 1998 for Exports and .703 billion U.S. dollars in 1998 for Imports.

Export Unit Value/Export Prices and Import Unit Value/Import Prices

The country indices are unit value indices, except for a few, which are components of wholesale price indices or based on specific price quotations. The exceptions are marked 'w' in the guide to the coverage of *IFS* on page viii.

Commodity Price Index

ɪ Prior to 1982, the World index and all components (food, beverages, agricultural raw materials, and metals), except fertilizer, were calculated by backward recursion of percent changes based on the previously published indices. (00176axd)

Albania

Interest Rates

Deposit Rate: ɪ The minimum rate on commercial banks' 12-month deposits (set by the central bank) was replaced by a guideline rate in 1993. ɪ Beginning in 1995, data refer to the weighted average rate on new 12-month deposits of the three commercial banks with the highest level of outstanding deposits.

Lending Rate: ɪ Data beginning in 1995 refer to the weighted average rate on new 12-month loans of the three commercial banks with the highest level of outstanding loans.

Algeria

Monetary Authorities

ɪ Beginning in 1992, data reflect the introduction of a new reporting system.

Deposit Money Banks

ɪ Beginning in 1992, data reflect improved classification including the separate identification of claims on nonfinancial public enterprises, which were previously included with claims on private sector.

Monetary Survey

✗See notes on monetary authorities and deposit money banks.

Argentina

Monetary Authorities

✗Beginning in 1990, data may not be comparable with data for earlier periods because of a change in the valuation system and adjustments to the accounts of the Central Bank of the Republic of Argentina. ✗Beginning in 1994, data are based on more detailed sectorization of the accounts.

Deposit Money Banks

✗ Beginning in 1990, data are based on an improved reporting system. ✗ See note on monetary authorities.

Monetary Survey

✗ See notes on monetary authorities and deposit money banks.

Other Banking Institutions

✗ See notes on monetary authorities and deposit money banks.

Banking Survey

✗ See notes on monetary authorities and deposit money banks.

Government Finance

✗ Beginning in 1995, data cover the operations of the consolidated central government.

Armenia

Interest Rates

Refinancing Rate (End of Period): ✗ Beginning in 1999, repo rate at which the Central Bank of Armenia conducts repurchase agreements with resident banks.

National Accounts

✗ Beginning in 1994, data at previous year's prices are used to construct *line 99bvp.*

Aruba

International Transactions

✗ Data for *Exports* and *Imports, c.i.f.* are based on customs records and include imports into, and exports from, the Free Zone.

Australia

Monetary Authorities

✗ Beginning in 1989, data are based on an improved sectorization of the accounts.

Deposit Money Banks

✗Before 1971, data relate to net foreign assets. ✗ Beginning in 1984, foreign assets and liabilities are compiled under a new, more comprehensive statistical collection. ✗ Starting in 1989, the coverage of accounts has been expanded to include domestic assets and liabilities denominated in foreign currencies as well as foreign assets and foreign liabilities denominated in Australian dollars.

Monetary Survey

✗ See notes on monetary authorities and deposit money banks.

Interest Rates

Money Market Rate: ✗ Beginning in 1995, rate paid on unsecured overnight loans of cash as calculated by the Australian Financial Markets Association and published on Reuters page at 11 a.m. ✗ Beginning in 1999, weighted average rate of the interest rates at which banks have borrowed and lent exchange settlement funds during the day. The rate is weighted by loan amounts.

Treasury Bill Rate: ✗ Beginning in 1995, estimated closing yield in the secondary market on thirteen-week treasury notes.

Deposit Rate: ✗ From 1991 onward, weighted average yield on certificates of deposit.

Lending Rate: ✗ Beginning in 1977, rate charged by banks on loans to small and large businesses.

Government Bond Yield: ✗ From 1970 onward, the long-term government bond yield *(line 61)* comprises assessed secondary market yields on non-rebate bonds with maturity of ten years. ✗ From 1982 onward, the short-term government bond yield *(line 61a)* comprises assessed secondary market yields on non-rebate bonds with maturity of two years. ✗ Beginning in 1994, the short-term yield refers to bonds with maturity of three years.

Government Finance

✗ Beginning in 1970, annual data are as reported in the *Government Finance Statistics Yearbook* and cover consolidated central government. Also beginning in 1970, data relate to a fiscal year different from calendar year. ✗ From 1988 onward, purchases and sales of stocks, land, and intangible assets are recorded on a net basis.

National Accounts

✗ From midquarter 1959 onwards, data have been revised following the implementation of improved compilation methods and the *1993 SNA.*

Austria

International Liquidity

✗ Beginning in 1999, *Total Reserves minus Gold (line 1l.d)* is defined in accordance with the Eurosystem's statistical definition of international reserves. Data on *lines 3..d, 4..d, 7a.d,* and *7b.d* are based on a Euro Area-wide definition of residency.

Banking Institutions

✗ From 1974 onward, banks' external accounts are based on the foreign exchange record, which provides an improved resident/nonresident distinction. ✗ Beginning in 1984, data are based on improved classification. ✗ Beginning in 1995, data on claims on government were revised to reflect the institutional classification of the government sector in the *European System of Accounts 1995 (1995 ESA)*.

Banking Survey (National Residency)

✗ See notes on banking institutions.

Interest Rates

Deposit Rate (line 60l): ✗ Rate on deposits up to one year in maturity; prior to 1998, rate on savings deposits due at call.

Prices, Production, Labor

Industrial Production:✗ Prior to 1995, the index excludes energy. Beginning in 1995, the index covers mining, manufacturing, and energy.

Government Finance

✗ Beginning in 1970, annual data are as reported in the *Government Finance Statistics Yearbook* and cover consolidated central government.

National Accounts

✗ From 1995 onwards, data have revised following the implementaion of the *1995 ESA*.

Bahamas, The

International Liquidity

✗ Prior to 1977, data for *line 1d.d* included small foreign exchange holdings by the government, which were transferred to the Central Bank of The Bahamas at this date.

Government Finance

✗ From 1988 onward, data cover the budgetary central government and no longer cover operations of the National Insurance Board, which is a social security fund. ✗From 1993 onward, fiscal years begin on July 1, rather than on January 1.

National Accounts

✗ Beginning in 1989, data have been revised following the implementation of the *1993 SNA*.

Bahrain

International Liquidity

✗ Prior to 1991, data for *lines 7a.d* and *7b.d* include positions with offshore banking units, which were classified as nonresident institutions.

Monetary Authorities

✗See note on deposit money banks.

Deposit Money Banks

✗ Beginning in 1991, data are compiled from a new set of statistical returns, and the institutional coverage is extended to include all kinds of resident banks, that is, full commercial banks (FCUs), offshore banking units (OBUs), and investment banks

(IBs). Deposit money banks' claims on and liabilities to nonresidents therefore exclude positions with OBUs (previously treated as nonresidents), and their claims on and liabilities to resident banks include positions with OBUs.

Monetary Survey

✗See note on deposit money banks.

Interest Rates

Deposit Rate: ✗ Prior to 1990, data refer to the maximum recommended rate on Bahrain dinar time deposits with maturities of at least three months and under six months. The rate was prescribed by the Bahrain Monetary Agency; however, banks could exceed the recommended rate. Beginning in 1990, data refer to the weighted average of interest rates on time deposits with maturities of at least three months and under six months. ✗ Beginning in 1998, data refer to time deposits between BD 10,000 and 50,000 with maturities of three to twelve months.

Lending Rate: ✗ Prior to 1988, data refer to the minimum recommended rate on consumer loans with maturities of at least three months and under six months. From 1988–94, data refer to the maximum recommended rate on consumer loans with maturities of at least 12 months and under 15 months. Beginning in 1994, data refer to the weighted average of interest rates on consumer loans with maturities of at least 12 months and under 15 months. ✗ Beginning in 1998, data refer to the weighted average rate on all personal loans extended in the last month of the quarter.

Bangladesh

Monetary Authorities

✗ The sectorization and classification of accounts have been revised from 1982 and again from 1987.

Deposit Money Banks

✗ See note on monetary authorities.

Monetary Survey

✗ See note on monetary authorities.

Barbados

International Liquidity

✗ Beginning in 1972, *line 1dbd* includes sinking funds held against domestic government debt.

Belarus

Deposit Money Banks

✗ Beginning in 1996, data are based on an improved reporting system.

Monetary Survey

✗ See note on deposit money banks.

Belgium

International Liquidity

✗ Beginning in 1980, data on gold and foreign exchange holdings exclude the deposits made with the European Monetary Institute (EMI)—which became the European Central Bank (ECB) in 1998—of the gold and gross U.S. dollar holdings; the holdings of European currency units (ECUs) issued by the EMI against these deposits are included in *line 1d.d. Gold (National Valuation) (line 1and):* ✗ Prior to 1990, 20 percent of official gold was valued at market prices. Beginning in 1990, official gold is revalued at market prices. ✗ For data on *lines 7a.d* and *7b.d* beginning in 1992, see note on banking institutions. ✗ Beginning in 1999, *Total Reserves minus Gold (line 1l.d)* is defined in accordance with the Eurosystem's statistical definition of international reserves. Data on *lines 3..d, 4..d, 7a.d,* and *7b.d* are based on a Euro Area-wide definition of residency.

Monetary Authorities

✗ Beginning in 1980, foreign currencies participating in the exchange rate mechanism of the EMS were valued at their midpoint rates, while gold and other foreign currencies were valued at historical prices. ✗ Beginning in 1990, foreign-currency-denominated assets and liabilities and gold are valued at exchange rates and prices that are derived from market rates, rather than from historical exchange rates and costs. The effects of valuation changes are shown in *line 17r.*

Banking Institutions

✗ Beginning in 1992, data exclude the Rediscount and Guarantee Institute. Certain breaks in the series may occur in 1992 owing to the radical reform of the reporting procedure of the credit institutions that was introduced at that time. First, the contents of the report forms were revised, and second, all types of institutions had to report according to the same scheme. Formerly, there were distinct report forms for deposit banks, savings banks, and public credit institutions. Now they are legally considered as equals.

Banking Survey (National Residency)

✗See notes on monetary authorities and banking institutions.

Interest Rates

Money Market Rate: ✗ Prior to 1991, the call money rate. Beginning in 1991, the averages of borrowing and lending rates for three-month interbank transactions.

Deposit Rate: ✗ Prior to 1993, the indicative rates published by the banks. Thereafter, the rate on three-month time deposits weighted by volume.

International Transactions

Import Prices: ✗ Source B index, base 1975, refers to the import component of the industrial products group of the general wholesale price index of Belgium (country code 124).

Government Finance

✗ Beginning in 1970, annual data are as reported in the *Government Finance Statistics Yearbook* and cover consolidated central government. ✗ From 1996 onward, data are compiled on the basis of *1995 ESA* rules and are not comparable with data for previous years.

National Accounts

✗ From 1985 onwards, data have been revised following the implementation of the *1995 ESA*.

Belize

Government Finance

✗ Beginning in 1979, data relate to a fiscal year different from calendar year. Data for 1979 cover 15 months.

Benin

Exchange Rates

Official Rate (End of Period and *Period Average):* ✗ From 1999 onward, the CFA franc is pegged to the euro at a rate of CFA franc 655.957 per euro. Prior to 1999, the official rate was pegged to the French franc. ✗ In 1994 the CFA franc was devalued to CFAF 100 per French franc from CFAF 50, at which it had been fixed since 1948.

Deposit Money Banks

✗ Beginning in 1979, *Central Government Deposits (line 26d)* include the deposits of public establishments of an administrative or social nature (EPAS) and exclude those of the savings bank; *Demand* and *Time Deposits (lines 24* and *25)* include deposits of the savings bank and exclude deposits of EPAS; and *Claims on Private Sector (line 22d)* exclude claims on other financial institutions.

Monetary Survey

✗ Beginning in 1979, *Claims on Other Financial Institutions (line 32f)* includes claims of deposit money banks on other financial institutions; see deposit money bank notes for explanation of other break symbols.

Other Banking Institutions

Liquid Liabilities (line 55l): ✗See notes on deposit money banks and monetary survey.

Bhutan

International Liquidity

✗ Prior to 1995, data for *line 1dxd* include convertible currency foreign assets, held on behalf of the government by the Bank of Bhutan and the Royal Insurance Corporation of Bhutan, and foreign exchange held by the government of Bhutan.

Monetary Authorities

✗ The sectorization and classification of accounts were revised in 1993, following the introduction of a more detailed reporting of accounts. Data on *Claims on Deposit Money Banks,* which previously had been included in *Claims on Other Financial Institutions,* are shown separately beginning that date.

Deposit Money Banks

✗ The sectorization and classification of accounts were revised in 1993, following the introduction of a more detailed reporting of accounts. *Claims on Private Sector (line 22d):*✗ Prior to 1993, claims on state enterprises were included in *Claims on Nonfinancial Public Enterprises (line 22c).* Beginning in this year, data include claims on such enterprises that were privatized.

Monetary Survey

✗ See notes on monetary authorities and deposit money banks.

Prices, Production, and Tourism

Electricity Production: The large increase in 1986–87 is due to the beginning of production of the Chukha hydroelectric facility. From July 1988 onwards, the data refer to Chukha production only.

Government Finance

✗ Through 1986, fiscal year begins April 1; from 1988 onward, fiscal year ends June 30. Data for 1988 fiscal year cover 15 months. ✗ From 1989 onward, data on grants include grants received in kind. Also, data on expenditure include the value of grants in kind.

Bolivia

Monetary Authorities

✗ Beginning in 1987, data reflect the introduction of improved sectorization and classification of domestic and foreign accounts. ✗ Starting in 1996, data are based on an improved sectorization of the accounts.

Deposit Money Banks

✗ See note on monetary authorities. ✗ Beginning in 1996, comprises commercial banks, the State Bank, and specialized banks (previously classified as other banking institutions). See note on monetary authorities.

Monetary Survey

✗ See notes on monetary authorities and deposit money banks.

Other Banking Institutions

✗ See note on monetary authorities. ✗ Beginning in 1996, comprises savings and loans associations, savings and credit cooperatives, and financial funds. See note on monetary authorities.

Banking Survey

✗ See notes on monetary authorities, deposit money banks, and other banking institutions.

Interest Rates

Deposit Rate: ✗ Beginning in 1986, weighted average rate, including surcharges and commissions, offered by commercial banks on time deposits in national currency. The rate is weighted by deposit amounts.

Lending Rate: ✗ Beginning in 1986, weighted average rate, including surcharges and commissions, charged by commercial banks on loans in national currency. The rate is weighted by loan amounts.

Prices, Production, Labor

Consumer Prices: ✗ Prior to 1970, the index covers prices in La Paz, reference base 1966; beginning in 1970, the index covers prices in La Paz and El Alto, reference base 1980; and beginning in 1992, the index covers prices in La Paz, Santa Cruz, Cochabamba, and El Alto, reference base 1991.

Government Finance

✗ Beginning in 1993, data cover the operations of the general government.

Brazil

Monetary Authorities

✗ Beginning in 1971, in 1978, and again in 1988, data are based on improved sectorization of the accounts. ✗ Consolidates the accounts of the Central Bank of Brazil and Bank of Brazil through 1985. Beginning in 1986, comprises the Central Bank of Brazil only.

Deposit Money Banks

✗ See note on monetary authorities. ✗ Comprises only commercial banks through 1985. Beginning in 1986, consolidates the accounts of the commercial banks and the Bank of Brazil. ✗ Beginning in 1988, comprises commercial banks, Bank of Brazil, multiple banks, Federal Savings Bank, and state savings banks. Data reflect the introduction of a new accounting system, which provides an improved sectorization of the accounts.

Monetary Survey

✗ See notes on monetary authorities and deposit money banks.

Other Banking Institutions

✗ See note on monetary authorities. ✗ Beginning in 1978, the accounts of the National Bank of Cooperative Credit are also consolidated in this category. ✗ Beginning in 1988, comprises investment banks, National Bank for Economic and Social Development, state development banks, finance and investment companies, and housing credit companies. Beginning in 1996, includes mortgage companies. See note on deposit money banks.

Banking Survey

✗ See notes on monetary authorities, deposit money banks, and other banking institutions.

Interest Rates

Money Market Rate: ✗ Beginning in 1980, Special Settlement and Custody System (SELIC) overnight rate, which is a weighted average rate on loans between financial institutions involving firm sales of or repurchase agreements based on federal securities in the SELIC. The rate is weighted by loan amounts.

Deposit Rate: ✗ Beginning in 1989, average rate offered by banks on certificates of deposit of 30 days or longer.

International Transactions

Volume of Exports and Imports: ✗ Data on total volume are based on quantities in metric tons. Prior to 1985, volume data are Laspeyres indices, base 1977.

Unit Value of Exports and Imports: ✗ Indices are calculated from value and volume indices except for unit value of export data prior to 1985, which are from source A, base 1977.

Government Finance

✗ Beginning in 1970, data are as reported in the *Government Finance Statistics Yearbook* and cover consolidated central government.

Bulgaria

Monetary Authorities

✗ Beginning in 1997, data are based on improved accounting procedures.

Deposit Money Banks

✗ Beginning in 1995, data are based on a new accounting system.

Monetary Survey

✗ See notes on monetary authorities and deposit money banks.

Prices

Consumer Prices: ✗ Until the end of 1992, the weights referred to retail turnover data of 1990. For the period 1993–95, the weights were based on the household budget survey of 1992. ✗ Beginning in 1996, the weights are revised annually. From 1998 onwards, the basket includes 900 items of goods and services.

Government Finance

✗ Prior to 1994, data are as reported in the *Government Finance Statistics Yearbook.* Thereafter, data are as reported by the Bulgarian National Bank and are taken from the *Report on the Execution of the State Budget* and unpublished reports on the operations of the consolidated central government.

Burkina Faso

Exchange Rates

Official Rate (End of Period and *Period Average):* ✗ From 1999 onward, the CFA franc is pegged to the euro at a rate of CFA franc 655.957 per euro. Prior to 1999, the official rate was pegged to the French franc. ✗ In 1994 the CFA franc was devalued to CFAF 100 per French franc from CFAF 50, at which it had been fixed since 1948.

Deposit Money Banks

✗ Beginning in 1979, *Central Government Deposits (line 26d)* include the deposits of public establishments of an administrative or social nature (EPAS) and exclude those of the savings bank; *Demand* and *Time Deposits (lines 24* and *25)* include deposits of the savings bank and exclude deposits of EPAS; and *Claims on Private Sector (line 22d)* exclude claims on other financial institutions.

Monetary Survey

✗ Beginning in 1979, *Claims on Other Financial Institutions (line 32f)* includes claims of deposit money banks on other financial institutions; see deposit money bank notes for explanation of other break symbols.

Other Banking Institutions

Liquid Liabilities (line 55l): ✗ See notes on deposit money banks and monetary survey.

Government Finance

✗ Beginning in 1977, annual data cover social security funds in addition to budgetary accounts. ✗ Beginning in 1985, data also cover extrabudgetary accounts.

Burundi

Deposit Money Banks

✗ Beginning in 1980, data are based on an improved sectorization of the accounts. ✗ Beginning in 1991, data reflect changes in the coverage of the other monetary institutions.

Monetary Survey

✗ See note on deposit money banks.

Other Banking Institutions

✗ Beginning in 1997, includes the Fonds de Promotion de l'Habitat Urbain (FPHU).

Prices and Labor

Consumer Prices: ✗ Prior to 1980, data refer to the index of consumer prices of civil servants in Bujumbura, base 1970. From 1980 through 1992, data refer to prices paid by unskilled and clerical workers and small traders in Bujumbura, base January 1980=100. Beginning in 1993, source base is January 1991=100. The weights are derived from a household budget survey conducted in 1979.

Government Finance

✗ Beginning in 1997, data are presented in a new format and are not directly comparable with data for earlier periods. Debt data cover the outstanding debt of the nonfinancial public sector, comprising direct government debt, onlent government debt, and debt guaranteed by the government.

Cambodia

International Liquidity

✗ Prior to 1994, *Foreign Exchange (line 1d.d)* excludes portion of official reserves that was held by the Foreign Trade Bank. Beginning in 1994, official foreign reserves were centralized at the National Bank of Cambodia (central bank).

Cameroon

Exchange Rates

Official Rate (End of Period and *Period Average):* ✗ From 1999 onward, the CFA franc is pegged to the euro at a rate of CFA franc 655.957 per euro. Prior to 1999, the official rate was pegged to the French franc. ✗ In 1994, the CFA franc was devalued to CFAF 100 per French franc from CFAF 50, at which it had been fixed since 1948.

Monetary Authorities

✗ Beginning in 1988, the sectorization and classification of accounts have been revised. ✗ Beginning in 1991, *Claims on Central Government* include government assumption of certain nonperforming bank loans.

Deposit Money Banks

✗ Beginning in 1977, data are based on improved sectorization of the accounts. ✗ Beginning in 1991, the counterpart of government assumption of certain nonperforming bank loans was reclassified from *Credit from Monetary Authorities* to *Capital Accounts*. ✗ Beginning in 1992, the coverage of the banking system has been revised. Claims and deposits of nonactive banks or banks in the process of liquidation have been excluded from the monetary accounts.

Monetary Survey

✗ See notes on monetary authorities and deposit money banks.

Interest Rates

Discount Rate (End of Period): ✗Beginning in 1994, rate charged by the BEAC to financial institutions on refinancing operations.

Deposit Rate: ✗ Beginning in 1990, minimum rate offered by deposit money banks on savings accounts.

Lending Rate: ✗ Beginning in 1990, maximum rate charged by deposit money banks on all loans, excluding charges and fees.

Government Finance

✗ Data prior to 1990 cover budgetary, extrabudgetary, and social security accounts. Data for 1990 and 1991 cover the general budget units, *Caisse nationale de prevoyance sociale* (National Social Security Fund), and *Caisse autonome d'amortissement* (Autonomous Amortization Fund). ✗ Beginning in 1992, data cover the general budget units and *Caisse autonome d'amortissement* only. ✗ Data for 1995 cover budgetary central government only.

Canada

Deposit Money Banks

✗ Beginning in 1981, all wholly- and majority-owned subsidiaries of the chartered banks (including mortgage loan subsidiaries and foreign banking subsidiaries) are consolidated in accordance with Canadian banking law. Unconsolidated data are not available on a monthly basis. In addition, data for *lines 24 and 25,* which were previously calculated from monthly averages of Wednesday figures, in the absence of an adequate classification of month ends, are now calculated mostly from month-end figures.

Monetary Survey

✗ See note on deposit money banks.

Other Banking Institutions

✗ Prior to 1973, data relate to savings institutions. After this date, other banklike institutions are included in the consolidation of the banking survey. ✗ Prior to 1981, other banking institutions comprised all trust and mortgage loan companies, local credit unions, *caisses populaires,* Quebec savings banks, and sales finance and consumer loan companies. From 1981, mortgage loan companies affiliated with chartered banks have been excluded from this group, as they have been consolidated with the accounts of chartered banks in their reporting to the Bank of Canada.

Banking Survey

✗ See notes on deposit money banks and other banking institutions.

Government Finance

✗ Beginning in 1974, annual data are as reported in the *Government Finance Statistics Yearbook* and cover consolidated central government. ✗ Data classification changes may have been introduced between 1987 and 1988, as a result of revisions applied from 1988 through 1995.

National Accounts

✗ Beginning in 1995, data have been revised following the implementation of the *1993 SNA.*

Cape Verde

Monetary Authorities

✗ Beginning in 1995, data are based on an improved sectorization of the accounts.

Deposit Money Banks

✗ See note on monetary authorities.

Monetary Survey

✗ See note on monetary authorities.

Interest Rates

Deposit Rate: ✗ Beginning in 1995, maximum rate offered by the Bank of Cape Verde on 61- to 90-day time deposits.

Central African Republic

Exchange Rates

Official Rate (End of Period and *Period Average):* ✗ From 1999 onward, the CFA franc is pegged to the euro at a rate of CFA franc 655.957 per euro. Prior to 1999, the official rate was pegged to the French franc. ✗ In 1994 the CFA franc was devalued to CFAF 100 per French franc from CFAF 50, at which it had been fixed since 1948.

Monetary Authorities

✗ Beginning in 1988, the sectorization and classification of accounts have been revised. ✗ Beginning in 1991, *Claims on Central Government* include government assumption of certain nonperforming bank loans.

Deposit Money Banks

✗ Beginning in 1977, data are based on improved sectorization of the accounts. ✗ Beginning in 1991, the counterpart of government assumption of certain nonperforming bank loans was reclassified from *Credit from Monetary Authorities* to *Capital Accounts*. ✗ Beginning in 1992, the coverage of the banking system has been revised. Claims and deposits of nonactive banks or banks in the process of liquidation have been excluded from the monetary accounts.

Monetary Survey

✗ See notes on monetary authorities and deposit money banks.

Interest Rates

Discount Rate (End of Period): ✗ Beginning in 1994, rate charged by the BEAC to financial institutions on refinancing operations.

Deposit Rate: ✗ Beginning in 1990, minimum rate offered by deposit money banks on savings accounts.

Lending Rate: Beginning in 1990, maximum rate charged by deposit money banks on all loans, excluding charges and fees.

Chad

Exchange Rates

Official Rate (End of Period and *Period Average):* From 1999 onward, the CFA franc is pegged to the euro at a rate of CFA franc 655.957 per euro. Prior to 1999, the official rate was pegged to the French franc. In 1994 the CFA franc was devalued to CFAF 100 per French franc from CFAF 50, at which it had been fixed since 1948.

Monetary Authorities

Beginning in 1988, the sectorization and classification of accounts have been revised. Beginning in 1991, *Claims on Central Government* include government assumption of certain nonperforming bank loans.

Deposit Money Banks

Beginning in 1991, the counterpart of government assumption of certain nonperforming bank loans was reclassified from *Credit from Monetary Authorities* to *Capital Accounts.* See note on monetary authorities.

Monetary Survey

See notes on monetary authorities and deposit money banks.

Interest Rates

Discount Rate (End of Period): Beginning in 1994, rate charged by the BEAC to financial institutions on refinancing operations.

Deposit Rate: Beginning in 1990, minimum rate offered by deposit money banks on savings accounts.

Lending Rate: Beginning in 1990, maximum rate charged by deposit money banks on all loans, excluding charges and fees.

Government Finance

Prior to 1986, data cover budgetary central government only. Beginning in 1986, data are as reported for the *Government Finance Statistics Yearbook* and cover budgetary central government and the Autonomous Amortization Fund. Beginning in 1991, data are as reported by the Banque des Etats de l'Afrique Centrale.

Chile

Monetary Authorities

Beginning in 1976, data are based on improved sectorization of the accounts.

Deposit Money Banks

See note on monetary authorities.

Monetary Survey

See note on monetary authorities.

Prices, Production, and Labor

Industrial Share Prices: Beginning in 1978, index of industrial share prices, base December 29, 1978. Beginning in 1980, index of industrial share prices, base December 30, 1980.

International Transactions

Trade data, which are derived from customs returns, have been updated with central bank payments data for current periods.

Government Finance

Beginning in 1972, annual data are as reported in the *Government Finance Statistics Yearbook* and cover consolidated central government (including all extrabudgetary and social security funds). Data for 1984–86 also cover accounts of some nonfinancial public enterprises and one public financial institution included in national sources. Beginning in 1987, data exclude the operations of nonfinancial public enterprises.

China, People's Republic: Mainland

The data refer to the People's Republic of China, excluding the Hong Kong Special Administrative Region. Data on transactions and assets and liabilities vis-à-vis Hong Kong are treated as international transactions and external positions respectively.

International Liquidity

Beginning in 1984, *Foreign Exchange (line 1d.d)* includes foreign government securities. Prior to 1992, *Foreign Exchange* included foreign exchange holdings of the Bank of China. Starting in that year, it includes foreign exchange holdings of the People's Bank of China only.

Monetary Authorities

Data classification from 1993 onwards has been revised. For the period 1993–96, data on *Foreign Assets (line 11)* refer to net foreign assets. Prior to 1997, *Central Government Deposits (line 16d)* also include some deposits of provincial and local government units.

Banking Institutions

Prior to 1993, the data comprise the accounts of the deposit money banks. Subsequently, the data also include the accounts of the other banking institutions.

Banking Survey

Data prior to 1985 exclude the rural credit cooperatives and the People's Construction Bank of China.

Interest Rates

Lending Rate (End of Period): Prior to 1989, rate on working capital loans to state industrial enterprises. Thereafter, rate on working capital loans of one-year maturity.

International Transactions

Prior to 1980, the data are provided by the Ministry of Foreign Trade and exclude exports of complete plants in the form of foreign aid. Thereafter, more comprehensive data are provided by the Customs Office.

China, People's Republic: Hong Kong

The data refer to the Hong Kong Special Administrative Region (HKSAR). Data on transactions and assets and liabilities vis-à-vis

The Mainland of China are treated as international transactions and external positions respectively.

International Liquidity

Foreign Exchange (line 1d.d): ✗ Beginning in 1997, data include the foreign exchange reserves of the Land Fund of the Hong Kong Special Administrative Region government.

Monetary Authorities

✗ Beginning in 1999, *Reserve Money (line 14)* also includes Exchange Fund bills and notes.

Prices, Production, Labor

Consumer Prices: ✗ Beginning in 1995, the CPI is based on a wider range of households with an average monthly expenditure of HK$ 4,000–59,999.

Colombia

Monetary Authorities

✗ Beginning in 1978, the financial funds (for the financing of agriculture, industry, housing, etc.) are considered as part of the Bank of the Republic in the treatment of the accounts of these funds with commercial and specialized banks. ✗ Beginning in 1989, data reflect the introduction of a new system of accounts, which provides an improved sectorization of the accounts.

Deposit Money Banks

✗ See note on monetary authorities. Beginning in 1978, data exclude the accounts of the Agricultural Bank (Caja de Crédito Agrario, Industrial y Minero). ✗ Beginning in 1990, includes the Agricultural Bank and Social Savings Bank. Data reflect the introduction of a new system of accounts, which provides an improved sectorization of the accounts. Beginning in 1994, includes the Central Mortgage Bank.

Monetary Survey

✗ See notes on monetary authorities and deposit money banks.

Other Banking Institutions

✗ Beginning in 1974, data cover a wider range of institutions. ✗ Beginning in 1990, includes commercial financing companies and financial cooperative institutions and excludes the Agricultural Bank and Social Savings Bank. Data reflect the introduction of a new system of accounts, which provides an improved sectorization of the accounts. Beginning in 1991, includes the Banco de Comercio Exterior (BANCOLDEX), Fondo para el Financiamiento del Sector Agropecuario (FINAGRO), and Financiera de Desarrollo Territorial (FINDETER). Beginning in 1993, includes the Fondo Nacional de Desarrollo (FONADE). Beginning in 1994, excludes the Central Mortgage Bank. Beginning in 1998, includes the Fondo de Garantías de Instituciones Financieras (FOGAFIN).

Banking Survey

✗ See notes on monetary authorities, deposit money banks, and other banking institutions.

Interest Rates

Discount Rate (End of Period): ✗ Beginning in 1986, corresponds to DTF (see note for deposit rate in monthly issue of *IFS*) plus two points. ✗ Beginning in 1990, corresponds to DTF plus eight points. Beginning in 1992, corresponds to DTF plus seven points.

Prices, Production, Labor

Share Prices: ✗ Beginning in 1991, index of prices on the Bogotá Stock Exchange, base January 2, 1991.

National Accounts

✗ Beginning in 1970, data are compiled by the National Department of Statistics (DANE). ✗ Beginning in 1994, data are compiled according to the *1993 SNA*.

Comoros

Exchange Rates

Official Rate (End of Period and *Period Average):* ✗ From 1999 onward, the Comorian franc is pegged to the euro at a rate of Comorian francs 491.9677 per euro. Prior to 1999, the official rate was pegged to the French franc. ✗ In 1994 the Comorian franc was devalued to CF 75 per French franc from CF 50, at which it had been fixed since 1948.

International Liquidity

✗ Beginning in 1998, data are based on an improved reporting and classification of accounts.

Monetary Authorities

✗ See note to international liquidity.

Deposit Money Banks

✗ See note to international liquidity.

Monetary Survey

✗ See note to international liquidity.

Other Banking Institutions

✗ See note to international liquidity.

Banking Survey

✗ See note to international liquidity.

Congo, Democratic Republic of

Exchange Rates

✗ In 1991, a new system was introduced, with the external value of the zaïre determined on the basis of demand and supply conditions prevailing in the foreign exchange market. ✗ In 1993, the new zaïre, equal to three million old zaïres, was introduced.

Government Finance

✗ Beginning in 1971, data are as reported in the *Government Finance Statistics Yearbook (GFSY)* and cover consolidated central government. ✗ Beginning in 1994, *GFSY* data exclude social security.

Congo, Republic of

Exchange Rates

Official Rate (End of Period and *Period Average):* ✗ From 1999 onward, the CFA franc is pegged to the euro at a rate of CFA franc 655.957 per euro. Prior to 1999, the official rate was pegged to the French franc. ✗ In 1994 the CFA franc was devalued to CFAF 100 per French franc from CFAF 50, at which it had been fixed since 1948.

Monetary Authorities

✗ Beginning in 1988, the sectorization and classification of accounts have been revised. ✗ Beginning in 1991, *Claims on Central Government* include government assumption of certain nonperforming bank loans.

Deposit Money Banks

✗ Beginning in 1977, data are based on improved sectorization of the accounts. ✗ Beginning in 1991, the counterpart of government assumption of certain nonperforming bank loans was reclassified from *Credit from Monetary Authorities* to *Capital Accounts*. ✗ Beginning in 1992, the coverage of the banking system has been revised. Claims and deposits of nonactive banks or banks in the process of liquidation have been excluded from the monetary accounts.

Monetary Survey

✗ See notes on monetary authorities and deposit money banks.

Interest Rates

Discount Rate (End of Period): ✗ From 1994 onward, rate charged by the BEAC to financial institutions on refinancing operations.

Deposit Rate: ✗ From 1990 onward, minimum rate offered by deposit money banks on savings accounts.

Lending Rate ✗ From 1990 onward, maximum rate charged by deposit money banks on all loans, excluding charges and fees.

Government Finance

✗ Prior to 1980, data cover budgetary central government only. Beginning in 1980, data cover consolidated central government, including all extrabudgetary and social security funds.

Costa Rica

Monetary Authorities

✗ Beginning in 1997, data are based on an improved sectorization of the accounts.

Deposit Money Banks

✗ See note on monetary authorities.

Monetary Survey

✗ See note on monetary authorities.

Prices and Labor

Producer Prices: ✗ Source B, modified laspeyres index, reference year December 1999=100. Weights were derived from a 1997 industrial survey. Index covers manufacturing industry with production for domestic market.

Government Finance

✗ From 1987 onwards, data were revised to have the same presentation as the Treasury cash flow.

Côte d'Ivoire

Exchange Rates

Official Rate (End of Period and *Period Average):* ✗ From 1999 onward, the CFA franc is pegged to the euro at a rate of CFA franc 655.957 per euro. Prior to 1999, the official rate was pegged to the French franc. ✗ In 1994 the CFA franc was devalued to CFAF 100 per French franc from CFAF 50, at which it had been fixed since 1948.

Deposit Money Banks

✗ Beginning in 1979, *Central Government Deposits (line 26d)* include the deposits of public establishments of an administrative or social nature (EPAS) and exclude those of the savings bank; *Demand* and *Time Deposits (lines 24* and *25)* include deposits of the savings bank and exclude deposits of EPAS; and *Claims on Private Sector (line 22d)* exclude claims on other financial institutions.

Monetary Survey

✗ Beginning in 1979, *Claims on Other Financial Institutions (line 32f)* includes claims of deposit money banks on other financial institutions; see deposit money bank notes for explanation of other break symbols.

Croatia

Deposit Money Banks

✗ Beginning in 1999, deposit money banks comprise commercial banks and savings banks; prior to 1999, savings banks were classified as other banking institutions.

International Transactions

✗ Beginning in 1992, the data include foreign trade with countries of the Former Socialist Federal Republic of Yugoslavia.

Cyprus

Monetary Authorities

✗ Beginning in 1988, the data reflect improved classification in the report forms.

Deposit Money Banks

✗ See note on monetary authorities.

Monetary Survey

✗ See note on monetary authorities.

Other Banking Institutions

✗ Prior to 1988, only specialized credit institutions were included. Beginning in 1988, comprises specialized credit institutions, cooperative credit institutions, and offshore banks.

Banking Survey

✗See notes on monetary authorities and other banking institutions.

Interest Rates

Discount Rate: ✗In 1996, the central bank rate applicable for the discount of treasury bills was replaced with the rate applicable for the central bank's Lombard-type overnight facility with treasury bills as collateral.

Czech Republic

Monetary Authorities

✗ Beginning in 1997, data are based on an improved classification of accounts.

Deposit Money Banks

✗ See note on monetary authorities.

Monetary Survey

✗ See note on monetary authorities.

Denmark

International Liquidity

Gold (National Valuation) (line 1and): ✗ From 1980, official gold is revalued on the basis of the London market prices.

Monetary Authorities

✗ From 1987–90, the accounts of the monetary authorities include the postal giro system. From 1991 onward, comprises Danmarks Nationalbank.

Deposit Money Banks

✗ Beginning in 1987, the accounts of commercial banks and other monetary institutions were consolidated. ✗The accounts of the deposit money banks were completely restructured from 1991. The accounts of the postal giro system are included in the deposit money banks sector from 1991.

Monetary Survey

✗ See notes on monetary authorities and deposit money banks.

Interest Rates

Money Market Rate: ✗ Prior to 1982, arithmetic average of overnight interbank rates. From 1982 to 1992, weighted average of three-month interbank rates. ✗ From 1993 onwards, arithmetic average of offered interbank rates.

Deposit Rate: ✗ Prior to 1990, weighted average of rates on time deposits for one to less than twelve months. From 1990 to 1993, calculated from interest accrued on both krone- and foreign currency-denominated deposit accounts (including deposits under capital pension schemes) divided by average deposit balance in a quarter. ✗From 1994 onwards, calculated from interest accrued on krone-denominated deposit accounts (excluding deposits under capital pension schemes) divided by average deposit balance in a quarter.

Lending Rate: ✗ Prior to 1990, weighted average of rates on overdrafts. From 1990 to 1993, calculated from interest accrued on both krone- and foreign currency-denominated loan accounts divided by average loan balance (including nonperforming loans from 1991) in a quarter. ✗ From 1994 onwards, calculated from interest accrued on krone-denominated loan accounts divided by average loan balance in a quarter.

Government Bond Yield: ✗ Prior to 1984, yield of perpetual bond. From 1984, yield on five-year government bonds.

Mortgage Bond Yield: ✗ Before 1981, data relate to the 5 percent bonds with a remaining period to maturity of about 40 years. From 1981, yield on 20-year mortgage credit bonds.

Prices, Production, Labor

Wages, Hourly Earnings: Data are in kroner from source S and represent mainly male workers in manufacturing industries, including construction, employing 20 or more persons. ✗ Prior to 1988, enterprises employing 6 or more persons were sampled. Annual data are calculated independently and are not an average of quarterly data.

Government Finance

✗Beginning in 1970, annual data are as reported in the *Government Finance Statistics Yearbook* and cover consolidated central government. Data are derived from Statsregnskabet (central government accounts), accounts of government agencies, parish funds accounts, and social security funds accounts. Data through 1975 relate to a fiscal year different from calendar year.

National Accounts

✗ From 1988 to 1995, data have been revised following the implementation of the *1993 SNA*. From 1996 onwards, data have been revised following the implementation of the *1995 ESA*.

Djibouti

Government Finance

✗ Data for 1979 cover budgetary central government and social security funds. ✗ Data for 1980 and 1986 cover budgetary central government and operations of other Treasury accounts. ✗ Data for 1981–85 and for 1988 cover budgetary central government only.

Dominican Republic

Prices

✗ Prior to 1978, data refer only to consumer prices in Santo Domingo.

Ecuador

Monetary Authorities

✗Beginning in 1990 and in 1998, data are based on an improved sectorization and classification of the accounts.

Deposit Money Banks

✗ Beginning in 1990, comprises private banks and the National Development Bank. ✗ See note on monetary authorities.

Monetary Survey

✗ See note on monetary authorities.

Other Banking Institutions

✗ Beginning in 1990, comprises private finance companies, National Financial Corporation, Housing Bank of Ecuador, and savings and loans associations. See note on monetary authorities.

Banking Survey

✗ See note on monetary authorities.

International Transactions

✗ Trade data, which are derived from customs returns, have been updated with central bank payments data for current periods.

Government Finance

✗ Beginning in 1973, annual data are identical to data reported in the *Government Finance Statistics Yearbook* and cover budgetary central government. ✗ Beginning in 1986, annual data are derived from monthly data.

Egypt

Monetary Authorities

✗ Beginning in 1980, data are based on improved classification and sectorization.

Deposit Money Banks

✗ See note on monetary authorities.

Monetary Survey

✗ See note on monetary authorities.

Other Banking Institutions

✗ See note on monetary authorities.

Government Finance

✗ Beginning in 1980, data relate to a fiscal year different from calendar year. ✗ Prior to 1996, data include the operations of the Public Authority for Insurance and Pensions and the Public Authority for Social Insurance, which were incorrectly included as social security funds. Prior to 1996, data also exclude the operations of the General Authority for Supply of Commodities (GASC).

National Accounts

✗ Compilation procedures were revised in 1970. Data for 1970 to 1979 relate to calendar year. Beginning in 1980, data relate to a fiscal year ending June 30.

El Salvador

Monetary Authorities

✗ Prior to 1982, credit to certain institutions (mainly INCAFE and INAZUCAR) was included in *line 12d*. Beginning in 1982, data

have been separately identified in *lines 12c* and *12f*. Also beginning in 1982, *line 17r* reflects the transfer of several accounts from it, mainly to *lines 16e* and *16f*.

Deposit Money Banks

✗ Beginning in 1982, data are based on an improved sectorization of the accounts.

Monetary Survey

✗ See notes on monetary authorities and deposit money banks.

Government Finance

✗ Beginning in 1994, data are derived from the Quarterly Review of the Central Reserve Bank of El Salvador and cover all central government operations of the budget and special funds.

Equatorial Guinea

Exchange Rates

Official Rate (End of Period and *Period Average):* ✗ From 1999 onward, the CFA franc is pegged to the euro at a rate of CFA franc 655.957 per euro. Prior to 1999, the official rate was pegged to the French franc. ✗ In 1994, the CFA franc was devalued to CFAF 100 per French franc from CFAF 50, at which it had been fixed since 1948.

Monetary Authorities

✗ Beginning in 1988, the sectorization and classification of accounts have been revised. ✗ Beginning in 1991, *Claims on Central Government* include government assumption of certain nonperforming bank loans.

Deposit Money Banks

✗ Beginning in 1991, the counterpart of government assumption of certain nonperforming bank loans was reclassified from *Credit from Monetary Authorities* to *Capital Accounts*.

Monetary Survey

✗ See notes on monetary authorities and deposit money banks.

Interest Rates

Discount Rate (End of Period): ✗ From 1994 onward, rate charged by the BEAC to financial institutions on refinancing operations.

Deposit Rate: ✗ From 1990 onward, minimum rate offered by deposit money banks on savings accounts.

Lending Rate: ✗ From 1990 onward, maximum rate charged by deposit money banks on all loans, excluding charges and fees.

Estonia

Monetary Authorities

✗ Beginning in 1993, data are based on an improved sectorization and classification of the accounts.

Banking Survey

✗ See note on monetary authorities.

International Transactions

✗ Beginning in 1994, foreign trade statistics exclude re-exports.

Ethiopia

Deposit Money Banks

✗ Prior to 1979, loans and advances of the commercial banks were included in *Claims on Private Sector (line 22d)*. Beginning in 1979, these loans and advances are separated into *line 22d* and *Claims on Other Financial Institutions (line 22f)*. ✗ Beginning in 1983, data exclude the Djibouti branch of the Commercial Bank of Ethiopia.

Monetary Survey

✗ See note on deposit money banks.

Government Finance

✗ Beginning in 1972, data are as reported in the *Government Finance Statistics Yearbook* and cover budgetary central government and some extrabudgetary accounts. ✗ Starting in 1982, data cover budgetary central government only. ✗ Beginning in 1992, data are as reported by the National Bank of Ethiopia, cover the operations of the budgetary central government, and include grants in kind operations. Revenue data include loan repayments, and expenditure data include lending operations.

National Accounts

✗ Beginning in 1992, data exclude Eritrea. Also starting in 1992, *line 96f* includes a statistical discrepancy.

Euro Area

International Transactions

Balance of Payments: ✗ Statistics for 1998 for the Euro Area, compiled by the European Central Bank (ECB), provide only a summary presentation of the key aggregates. Statistics are compiled by aggregating gross cross-border transactions of Euro Area residents vis-à-vis non-Euro Area residents as reported by the 11 participating counties. Transactions between residents of the participating member states are not included. The concepts and definitions used are based on current international and European standards, notably the fifth edition of the IMF's *Balance of Payments Manual* and the operational methodological rules adopted by the ECB (ECB Guideline of December 1, 1998 [ECB/1998/17]).

The data for 1998 are not fully comparable with those that will be published for 1999. An improved methodology will be implemented starting in 1999 for the various components of the financial accounts n.i.e., providing better measures of transactions between residents and nonresidents of the Euro Area. Also, Euro Area reserve assets flows for 1998 are aggregates of national data and include transactions in instruments issued by other residents of the Euro Area; they do not correspond to the 1999 Eurosystem's definition of reserve assets.

Fiji

Monetary Authorities

✗ Data refer to the Currency Board through 1973, to the Central Monetary Authority until 1983, and to the Reserve Bank of Fiji thereafter. Prior to 1990, monetary data refer to the last Wednesday of the period.

Monetary Survey

✗ See note on monetary authorities.

Government Finance

✗ Fiscal data from 1990 onward are as reported by the Reserve Bank of Fiji, rather than from the *Government Finance Statistics Yearbook*.

Finland

International Liquidity

✗ Beginning in 1999, *Total Reserves minus Gold (line 1l.d)* is defined in accordance with the Eurosystem's statistical definition of international reserves. Data on lines *3..d, 4..d, 7a.d,* and *7b.d* are based on a Euro Area-wide definition of residency.

Banking Institutions

✗ Beginning in 1991, data are based on an improved sectorization of the accounts.

Banking Survey (National Residency)

✗ See note on banking institutions.

Prices, Production, Labor

Share Prices: ✗ Beginning in 1987, index, base 1990, refers to the average of daily buying quotations.

Wages: Hourly Earnings: ✗ Beginning in 1985, the series covers only manufacturing. Prior to 1985, series covers manufacturing, mining, and quarrying.

Government Finance

✗ Beginning in 1972 (1971 for debt data), annual data are as reported in the *Government Finance Statistics Yearbook* and cover consolidated central government.

National Accounts

✗ From 1988 onwards, data have been revised following the implementation of the *1995 ESA*.

France

International Liquidity

✗ Beginning in 1977, *line 7a.d* includes buyers' credits. ✗ For data on lines *7a.b* and *7b.d,* beginning in 1978, see note on banking institutions. ✗ Beginning in 1979, data on gold (*line 1ad*) and foreign exchange holdings exclude the deposits of the gold and gross U.S. dollar holdings made with the European Monetary Cooperation Fund (EMCF), which became the European Monetary Institute (EMI), and then the European Central Bank (ECB) in 1998;

the holdings of ECUs issued by the EMCF against these deposits are included in *line 1d.d.* ✗ Beginning in 1999, *Total Reserves minus Gold (line 1l.d)* is defined in accordance with the Eurosystem's statistical definition of international reserves. Data on *lines 3..d, 4..d, 7a.d,* and *7b.d* are based on a Euro Area-wide definition of residency.

Monetary Authorities

✗Beginning in 1975, gold holdings in *line 11* are revalued at market price; the contra-entry of the valuation difference is included in *line 17r.* ✗Beginning in 1979, the ECU counterpart of the U.S. dollar and gold deposits with the EMCF is included in *line 11*; the contra-entry is recorded in *line 17a,* and the difference in valuation of gold between the Bank of France method and that of the EMCF is included in *line 17r.* ✗Between 1996 and 1998, gold receivables from EMI, and ECUs payable to the EMI were treated as off-balance-sheet items in accordance with the revised accounting system of the Bank of France.

Banking Institutions

✗Beginning in 1977, data reflect institutional changes and an extension in coverage to include "finance companies" specializing in granting credits to households and private companies. ✗Beginning in 1978, data reflect other institutional changes in the banking sector, including the development of new financial assets.

Banking Survey (National Residency)

✗See notes on monetary authorities and banking institutions.

Prices, Production, Labor

Share Prices: ✗ Prior to 1987, the index was calculated from a sample of 180 shares on the Paris exchange. Beginning in 1987, the index covers the common shares of 40 enterprises having the largest capitalization.

International Transactions

Unit Value data: ✗From January 1994 onwards, the methodology was changed to broaden the geographical coverage and to improve the validation procedures and the representativeness of the products selected.

Government Finance

✗Beginning in 1972, data are as reported in the *Government Finance Statistics Yearbook* and cover consolidated central government (including extrabudgetary and social security accounts). Debt data are as reported by the Banque de France.

National Accounts

✗ From 1995 onwards, data have been revised following the implementation of the *1995 ESA.*

Gabon

Exchange Rates

Official Rate (End of Period and *Period Average):* ✗ From 1999 onward, the CFA franc is pegged to the euro at a rate of CFA franc 655.957 per euro. Prior to 1999, the official rate was pegged to the French franc. ✗ In 1994, the CFA franc was devalued to CFAF 100 per French franc from CFAF 50, at which it had been fixed since 1948.

Monetary Authorities

✗ Beginning in 1988, the sectorization and classification of accounts have been revised. ✗Starting in 1991, *Claims on Central Government* include government assumption of certain nonperforming bank loans.

Deposit Money Banks

✗ Beginning in 1977, data are based on improved sectorization of the accounts. ✗ Starting in 1991, the counterpart of government assumption of certain nonperforming bank loans was reclassified from *Credit from Monetary Authorities* to *Capital Accounts.* ✗ Beginning in 1992, the coverage of the banking system was revised. Claims and deposits of nonactive banks or banks in the process of liquidation have been excluded from the monetary accounts. See note on monetary authorities.

Monetary Survey

✗ See notes on monetary authorities and deposit money banks.

Interest Rates

Discount Rate (End of Period): ✗ From 1994 onward, rate charged by the BEAC to financial institutions on refinancing operations.

Deposit Rate: ✗ From 1990 onward, minimum rate offered by deposit money banks on savings accounts.

Lending Rate: ✗ From 1990 onward, maximum rate charged by deposit money banks on all loans, excluding charges and fees.

Government Finance

✗ Prior to 1976, data cover Treasury accounts and the National Social Security Fund only. Beginning in 1976, data also cover operations of the Autonomous Amortization Fund, which is responsible for most foreign borrowing and related investment expenditures. ✗ Starting in 1979, data cover the operations of the Treasury only. ✗ Beginning in 1989, data are based on a revised budgetary nomenclature.

Gambia, The

Monetary Authorities

✗ Beginning in 1978, data are based on an improved sectorization of the domestic accounts. ✗ Beginning in 1984, domestic currency deposits made by the government in lieu of external debt service payments (i.e., special accounts) have been placed in *line 16b,* with a contra-entry in *line 16c.* From the same date onward, deposit money bank deposits with the central bank, arising from the receipt from the customers of domestic currency payments on account of external debt service (i.e., commercial arrears), have been treated similarly. In addition, *line 16b* includes the contra-entry of The Gambia Produce Marketing Board export proceeds, because access to that account is limited.

Deposit Money Banks

✗ See note on monetary authorities. ✗ Beginning in 1984, a contra-entry to domestic currency payments received from customers to meet external debt service obligations (i.e., commercial arrears) is shown in *line 26b.*

Monetary Survey

✗ See notes on monetary authorities and deposit money banks.

Government Finance

✗ Beginning in 1972, data are as reported in the *Government Finance Statistics Yearbook* and cover budgetary central government. ✗ In 1990, data also include selected extrabudgetary accounts.

Germany

With the coming into effect on July 1, 1990 of the treaty on German Economic, Monetary, and Social Union (GEMSU) between the former Federal Republic of Germany (FRG) and the former German Democratic Republic (GDR), the deutsche mark became the sole currency of the GEMSU area, and customs borders between the two states were abolished. On October 3, 1990, the former GDR became part of the FRG under international law. The membership of the FRG in the Fund, under the designation Germany, remains unchanged. The presentation of exchange rates and Fund accounts shown for Germany in *IFS* is unaffected by the unification of the former FRG and the former GDR.

Data on international liquidity, money and banking, and international transactions cover the former FRG and the former GDR beginning with end-June (second quarter) 1990 for stock data and July 1990 for flow data. Data on prices, production, labor market, and national accounts cover the former FRG and the former GDR from 1991 onward. Data on industrial employment and wages refer only to the former FRG.

International Liquidity

✗ Beginning in 1999, *Total Reserves minus Gold (line 1l.d)* is defined in accordance with the Eurosystem's statistical definition of international reserves. Data on lines *3..d*, *4..d*, *7a.d*, and *7b.d* are based on a Euro Area-wide definition of residency.

Banking Institutions

✗ Beginning in 1985, coverage of financial institutions was broadened to include all cooperative banks.

Banking Survey (National Residency)

✗ See note on banking institutions.

Government Finance

✗ Beginning in 1970, data are as reported in the *Government Finance Statistics Yearbook* and cover consolidated central government, including extrabudgetary and social security accounts. ✗ Data for social security funds and the European Recovery Program are on a cash basis only beginning in 1974 and 1975, respectively. ✗ Beginning in 1990, central government extrabudgetary operations include operations of the German Unity Fund. ✗ Prior to 1992, data cover government operations on the territory of the former Federal Republic of Germany; beginning in 1992, data refer to government operations on the territory of unified Germany;

Ghana

Monetary Authorities

✗ Beginning in 1991, data reflect the introduction of a new reporting system.

Deposit Money Banks

✗ Beginning in 1973, the classification of claims on the private sector and claims on the public enterprises is revised. ✗ See note on monetary authorities.

Monetary Survey

✗ See notes on monetary authorities and deposit money banks.

Government Finance

✗ For the period 1972–82, data relate to a fiscal year different from calendar year (ends June 30).

Greece

International Liquidity

✗ Prior to 1975, data on *Foreign Exchange (line 1d.d)* exclude import documentary credit at the time of opening of the account. Beginning in 1975, data exclude such credit at time of payment. ✗ Beginning in 1986, data on *Gold* and *Foreign Exchange* exclude the deposits made with the European Monetary Institute (EMI) of gold and gross U.S. dollar holdings; the holdings of European currency units (ECUs) issued by the EMI against these deposits are included in *line 1d.d. Gold (National Valuation) (line 1and):* ✗ Before 1985, gold was valued at SDR 35 per fine troy ounce. Beginning in 1985, gold is revalued each December at 65 percent of the average buying market price of gold during that month.

Monetary Authorities

✗ Beginning in 1987, the data reflect improved classification in the report forms.

Deposit Money Banks

✗ See note on monetary authorities.

Monetary Survey

✗ See note on monetary authorities.

Other Banking Institutions

✗ Beginning in 1978, data are based on improved classification and sectorization.

Interest Rates

Deposit Rate: ✗ Prior to1988, maximum rate offered by deposit money banks on three- to six-month drachma deposits by individuals and enterprises. Beginning in 1988, data refer to deposits with a maturity of three to twelve months.

Lending Rate: ✗ Prior to 1999, rate on short-term loans to enterprises and households and, thereafter, rate on short-term loans to enterprises only.

Central Bank Rate: ✗ Prior to 1998, discount rate offered by the Bank of Greece and, thereafter, rate on deposits of 14-day maturity placed with the Bank of Greece.

National Accounts

✗ Beginning in 1988, a statistical discrepancy is included in *line 93i* but, prior to 1988, is in *lines 99a* and *99b*. ✗ Beginning in 1995, concepts and definitions are in accordance with the *1995 ESA*.

Grenada

Monetary Authorities

✗ For the period 1975 through 1978 *lines 11* and *14* include net local interbank claims of commercial banks as a proxy for banks' deposits with Eastern Caribbean Central Bank (ECCB).

Deposit Money Banks

✗ For the period 1975 through 1978, *lines 20, 21,* and *26c* include net local interbank claims of commercial banks as a proxy for banks' deposits with ECCB. Beginning in 1979, the data reflect improved reporting of commercial bank accounts with the ECCB (*line 20*) and with branches in other member countries (*lines 20, 21,* and *26c*).

Monetary Survey

✗ See note on deposit money banks.

Government Finance

✗ Prior to 1978 and from 1991 onward, data are as reported in the *Government Finance Statistics Yearbook*. From 1978 through 1980, data are as reported by the Ministry of Finance for publication in *IFS*.

Guatemala

Monetary Authorities

✗ Beginning in 1997, data are based on an improved sectorization of the accounts.

Deposit Money Banks

✗ See note on monetary authorities.

Monetary Survey

✗ See note on monetary authorities.

Other Banking Institutions

✗ Beginning in 1990, comprises Financiera Industrial y Agropecuaria S. A. (FIASA), Financiera Guatemalteca S. A. (FIGSA), Financiera Industrial S. A. (FISA), Financiera de Inversion S. A. (FIVSA), Financiera del Pais S. A. (FIPASA), and Corporacion Financiera Nacional (CORFINA). ✗ See note on monetary authorities.

Banking Survey

✗ See notes on monetary authorities and other banking institutions.

Interest Rates

Deposit Rate: ✗ Beginning in 1997, weighted average rate offered by commercial banks on time and savings deposits. The rate is weighted by deposit amounts.

Lending Rate: ✗ Beginning in 1997, weighted average rate charged by commercial banks on loans. The rate is weighted by loan amounts.

Government Finance

✗ Prior to 1994, revenue data included grants, and expenditure data included lending minus repayments. Expenditure is not adjusted for changes in floating debt.

Guinea

Monetary Authorities

✗ Beginning in 1996, *Claims on Other Banking Institutions (line 12f)* excludes the Caisse Nationale de Sécurité Sociale (CNSS), which is included under *Claims on Central Government (line 12a)*.

Guinea-Bissau

Exchange Rates

Official Rate (End of Period and *Period Average):*✗ Beginning in 1999, the CFAF is pegged to the euro at a rate of CFA franc 655.957 per euro. Prior to 1999, the official rate was pegged to the French franc at the rate of CFAF 100 per French franc.

Monetary Authorities

✗ Beginning in 1997, data reflect Guinea-Bissau's entry into the West African Monetary Union and the compilation of the data on the Central Bank of West African States' (BCEAO's) basis.

Deposit Money Banks

✗ See note on monetary authorities.

Monetary Survey

✗ See note on monetary authorities.

Government Finance

✗ Prior to 1987, data are as reported in the *Government Finance Statistics Yearbook (GFSY)* and cover budgetary central government. Beginning in 1987, data are derived from Ministry of Finance sources and cover budgetary central government.

Guyana

Monetary Authorities

✗ Beginning in 1993, data are based on an improved reporting system.

Monetary Survey

✗ See note on monetary authorities.

Banking Survey

✗ See note on monetary authorities.

Government Finance

✗ Beginning in 1970, data as reported by the Central Bank of Guyana cover budgetary central government. ✗Prior to 1986, foreign debt comprises central government debt; beginning in 1986, foreign debt also includes debt of the Bank of Guyana and public guaranteed debt.

Haiti

Monetary Authorities

✗ Beginning in 1997, data are based on an improved sectorization of the accounts.

Deposit Money Banks

✗ See note on monetary authorities.

Monetary Survey

✗ See note on monetary authorities.

Honduras

Monetary Authorities

✗ Beginning in 1997, data are based on an improved sectorization of the accounts.

Deposit Money Banks

✗ See note on monetary authorities.

Monetary Survey

✗ See note on monetary authorities.

Other Banking Institutions

✗ Beginning in 1997, comprises development banks, savings and loans associations, and finance companies. See note on monetary authorities.

Banking Survey

✗ See note on monetary authorities.

Government Finance

✗ Prior to 1991, data on capital revenue and expenditure are not included.

Hungary

Monetary Authorities

✗ Beginning in 1990, *Claims on Central Government* include debt of the central budget, owing to valuation differences previously recorded in *Valuation Changes (line 17rv)*. *Time and Foreign Currency Deposits* include foreign currency deposits of banking institutions.

Banking Institutions

✗ Beginning in 1990, *Demand Deposits (line 24)* include sight forint deposits of households, previously shown in *Time, Savings, and Foreign Currency Deposits (line 25)*. Prior to 1990, demand deposits included only current accounts of domestic nonbanks.

Banking Survey

✗ See notes on monetary authorities and banking institutions.

Interest Rates

Deposit Rate: ✗ Beginning in 1990, weighted average rate offered by banking institutions on deposits from entrepreneurs with original maturity of more than one month but less than one year.

Prices, Production, Labor

Consumer Prices: ✗ Prior to 1985, the consumer price index compares current month item prices with their levels in the same month of the base year. From 1985 forward, the index compares current item prices with their average level in 1985.

Government Finance

✗ Beginning in 1991, annual data are as reported by the Ministry of Finance and cover the consolidated operations of the central government, namely, the central budget, social security funds, and extrabudgetary funds. Lending minus repayments data do not include privatization receipts.

Iceland

Interest Rates

Discount Rate (End of Period): ✗Data prior to 1992 refer to central bank rates on overdrafts to deposit money banks. Beginning in 1992, data refer to central bank's discount rate on loans within quota.

Treasury Bill Rate: ✗ Prior to 1992, data refer to yields set by the government in the primary market. Beginning in 1992, data refer to annualized secondary market yield on 90-day treasury bills.

Deposit Rate:✗ Prior to 1988, data refer to interest rate on 3-month deposits. ✗ From 1989 to 1994, data refer to interest rate on 12- to 18-month deposits. ✗ Starting in 1995, data refer to interest rate on 12-month deposits.

India

Deposit Money Banks

✗ Since 1978, a new classification of *Demand* and *Time Deposits* has reduced *lines 24* and *34* and increased *lines 25* and *35*.

Interest Rates

Government Bond Yield: ✗ Beginning in 1971, this rate is the average yield on government 5!/2 percent bonds maturing in the years 1999 and 2000.

Government Finance

✗ Beginning in 1974, data are as reported in the *Government Finance Statistics Yearbook* and cover consolidated central government. Data are reported by the Ministry of Finance.

National Accounts

✗ From 1987 onwards, data have been revised following the implementation of the *1993 SNA*.

Indonesia

International Liquidity

✗ Beginning in 1971, *line 1d.d* includes the foreign exchange holdings of the West Irian branch of Bank Indonesia and excludes foreign currency accounts of residents.

Monetary Authorities

✗ Beginning in 1992, data are based on improved classification and reporting of accounts.

Deposit Money Banks

✗ See note on monetary authorities.

Monetary Survey

✗ See note on monetary authorities.

Interest Rates

Deposit Rate: ✗ Beginning in 1990, weighted average rate paid by commercial banks on three-month deposits.

Prices, Production, Labor

✗ Prior to 1979, the CPI series is based on an index that covered Djakarta only. Between 1979 and 1990, the CPI series is based on a survey of 17 capital cities. ✗Beginning in 1990, index covers 27 provincial capital cities.

Government Finance

✗ Prior to 1972, data are as reported for *IFS*. Beginning in 1972, data are as reported in the *Government Finance Statistics Yearbook* and cover consolidated central government.

Iran, Islamic Republic of

International Transactions

✗ Beginning in 1980, data on the value and volume of oil exports and on the value of total exports are rough estimates based on information published in various petroleum industry journals.

Balance of Payments: ✗Prior to 1976, year ending December 31.

Government Finance

✗ Prior to 1988, the consolidated central government data exclude the operations of the Organization for Protection of Consumers and Producers.

Ireland

International Liquidity

✗ Beginning in 1999, *Total Reserves minus Gold (line 1l.d)* is defined in accordance with the Eurosystem's statistical definition of international reserves. Data on lines *3..d*, *4..d*, *7a.d*, and *7b.d* are based on a Euro Area-wide definition of residency.

Banking Institutions

✗ Beginning in 1982, data reflect the introduction of an improved call report form, which for the first time records data of resident offices on a residency-of-customer basis. From that date, the activities of nonresident offices are, therefore, excluded from the data, and accounts of nonresidents at resident offices are classified under *Foreign Assets (line 21)* and *Foreign Liabilities (line 26c)*.

Banking Survey (National Residency)

✗ See notes on banking institutions. ✗Beginning in 1982, *line 34* reflects changes affecting the data on banking institutions, including improved sectorization, the exclusion of nonresident accounts, and a change in the method of allocating items in transit.

Nonbank Financial Institutions:

✗ Prior to 1995, consolidated the accounts of building societies, state-sponsored financial institutions, trustees' savings banks, hire-purchase finance companies, national installment savings, and the post office savings bank.

Interest Rates

Discount Rate (End of Period): ✗ Prior to 1979, data refer to the discount rate. Afterward, data refer to short-term facility rate charged by the Bank of Ireland on funds, up to a specified quota, lent to banks experiencing day-to-day liquidity shortages.

Lending Rate: ✗ Prior to 1992, data refer to the rate charged to AAA customers in the primary, manufacturing, and service sectors.

National Accounts

✗ Source S. Data are based on the *1995 ESA*. Prior to 1990, data are based on the *1979 ESA*.

Israel

Deposit Money Banks

✗ Beginning in 1992, other deposits, which were previously included in *Time and Savings Deposits (line 25)*, are included in *Demand Deposits (line 24)*. Earmarked government deposits, which were previously included in *Restricted Deposits (line 26b)*, are included in *Central Government Deposits (line 26d)*. A new reporting procedure was also introduced, which resulted in other changes in the classification of accounts.

Monetary Survey

✗ See note on deposit money banks.

Prices, Production, Labor

✗ As of 1979, the indices for wages, industrial production, and industrial employment exclude the diamond sector. *Wages: Daily Earnings:* ✗ Prior to 1978, the series covered workers only. As of that date, it is based on all employees.

International Transactions

Export and *Import Unit Value* indices: ✗ Prior to 1976, indices are Paasche indices; beginning in 1976, they are Laspeyres indices; from 1984 onwards they are compiled using Fischer's ideal formula. The weights are revised every two years. For example, for 1981 the weights are calculated on the basis of Israel's trade in 1979.

Government Finance

✗ Beginning in 1972, data are as reported in the *Government Finance Statistics Yearbook* and cover budgetary central government. ✗ Beginning in 1974, data also include social security funds. ✗ Through 1991, fiscal years begin April 1; from 1992 onward, fiscal years end December 31. ✗ Break symbols in 1991 data indicate that data refer to the nine-month period April 1 through December 31.

National Accounts

✗ Source S. From 1995 onward, data are compiled according to the *1993 SNA*, and *line 99b.p* data are annually chained using the prices of the previous year.

Italy

International Liquidity

✗ Beginning in 1999, *Total Reserves minus Gold (line 1l.d)* is defined in accordance with the Eurosystem's statistical definition of

international reserves. Data on lines *3..d*, *4..d*, *7a.d*, and *7b.d* are based on a Euro Area-wide definition of residency.

Banking Institutions

✗Beginning in 1989, data are based on improved classification following the adoption by the Bank of Italy of the sectoral classification and definitions based on the *1995 ESA*.

Banking Survey (National Residency)

✗See note on banking institutions.

Interest Rates

Money Market Rate: ✗ Beginning in 1991, data represent arithmetic averages of daily rates, which are weighted averages of rates (based on the volume of transactions for the day).

Lending Rate: ✗ Beginning in 1990, data refer to the average rate charged by banking institutions and specialized credit institutions on short-term lira loans.

Government Bond Yield: Long-Term Rate: ✗ Prior to 1991, the data are average yields to maturity on bonds with original maturities of 15 to 20 years, issued on behalf of the Treasury by the Consortium of Credit for Public Works. *Medium-Term Rate:* ✗ Prior to 1991, the data are average yields to maturity on treasury bonds with maximum original maturities of 9 years.

Government Finance

✗ Beginning in 1993, data exclude all autonomous government agencies except the State Roads Agency. However, debt data include the debts of the above-mentioned agencies assumed by the government, and expenditure data include the corresponding interest payments. Revenue data include privatization proceeds.

National Accounts

✗ Data from 1998 onwards are in accordance with the *1995 ESA*.

Jamaica

Deposit Money Banks

✗ Prior to 1973, *Demand Deposits* and *Time and Savings Deposits* include nonresident deposits. Beginning in that year, nonresident deposits are included in *Foreign Liabilities*.

Monetary Survey

✗ See note on deposit money banks.

Banking Survey

✗ See note on deposit money banks.

Japan

International Liquidity

✗ Beginning in 1973, data for *lines 7a.d* and *7b.d* include long-term foreign accounts and therefore are not the U.S. dollar equivalents of *lines 21* and *26c,* which comprise only short-term accounts; data are from the Bank for International Settlement's *Annual Report* and *Quarterly Press Release*.

Monetary Authorities

✗ Beginning in 1970, data are based on an improved sectorization of accounts. ✗ Prior to 1978, *line 11* was reported on a gross basis with foreign liabilities being included in *line 17r*. Beginning in 1978, data for *line 11* are provided net of foreign liabilities.

Monetary Survey

✗ See note on monetary authorities.

Interest Rates

Money Market Rate: ✗ Beginning in 1990, lending rate for collateral and overnight loans in the Tokyo Call Money Market.

Private Bill Rate: ✗ Beginning in 1991, rate on newly issued certificates of three-month deposits.

Deposit Rate: ✗ Beginning in 1992, average interest rate for the last week of the month on unregulated three-month time deposits, ranging in size from three million yen to under ten million yen.

Lending Rate: ✗ Before 1993, the lending rate excluded overdrafts. Beginning in 1993, the rate is the weighted average of contracted interest rates charged by all banks on short- and long-term loans, discounts, and overdrafts.

Government Bond Yield: ✗Prior to 1999, arithmetic average yield to maturity of all ordinary government bonds. Beginning in 1999, arithmetic average yield on newly issued government bonds with 10-year maturity.

International Transactions

Balance of Payments: ✗Balance of payments data prior to 1991 were converted to the format of the fifth edition of the *Balance of Payments Manual* using a set of conversion keys developed by the Fund.

Government Finance

✗Beginning in 1975, data are as reported in the *Government Finance Statistics Yearbook*. ✗ Prior to 1991, data cover budgetary central government only. From 1991 onwards, data (excluding debt data) cover consolidated central government. Also beginning in 1991, data for financing abroad and foreign debt are included in domestic financing and domestic debt, respectively.

Jordan

International Liquidity

✗During 1991–93, reported holdings of foreign currency are net of foreign currency deposits of licensed banks at the Central Bank of Jordan.

Monetary Authorities

✗ Beginning in 1993, *lines 11* and *14* reflect foreign currency deposits of licensed banks.

Deposit Money Banks

✗ Beginning in 1993, *line 26d* includes deposits of the Social Security Corporation, which previously were included in *lines 24* and *25*.

Monetary Survey

✗ See notes on monetary authorities and deposit money banks.

Other Banking Institutions

✗ Prior to 1993, comprises the Industrial Development Bank, the Agricultural Credit Corporation, and the Municipal Loan Fund. Beginning in 1993, comprises Cities and Villages Development Bank, Agricultural Credit Corporation, Industrial Development Bank, the Housing Corporation, and Jordan Cooperative Organization.

Kazakhstan

Monetary Authorities

✗ Beginning in 1997, the monetary authorities comprise the National Bank of Kazakhstan (NBK) only, and the data are compiled according to the new chart of accounts for the NBK.

Deposit Money Banks

✗ Prior to 1997, *Demand Deposits (line 24)* includes all deposit liabilities. Subsequently, the data for the commercial banks include data for the Republican Budget Bank. *Other Deposits (line 25)* includes restricted deposits.

Monetary Survey

✗ See notes on monetary authorities and deposit money banks.

Interest Rates

Refinancing Rate (End of Period): ✗ Annualized interest rate until 1995; thereafter, compound annual rate, which is established as the minimum interest rate for NBK auctions of credit to commercial banks.

Kenya

Government Finance

✗ Through 1996, expenditure data are on a commitment basis. Beginning in 1997, expenditure data are on a cash basis. Domestic financing data through 1996 include privatization proceeds, the adjustment of expenditure data to a cash basis, as well as the statistical discrepancy. Beginning in 1997, revenue data include privatization proceeds, and the statistical discrepancy is identified separately.

Korea

International Liquidity

✗ Beginning in 1988, *line 7a.d* includes claims of foreign banks' branches on nonresidents.

Interest Rates

Deposit Rate: ✗ From 1996 onward, the rate is an average, weighted by the amount of deposits for periods of one year or more but less than two years at the nationwide commercial banks.

Lending Rate: ✗ From 1996 onward, the rate is an average, weighted by new loans extended during the period by nationwide commerical banks.

Government Finance

✗ Beginning in 1970, data are as reported in the *Government Finance Statistics Yearbook* and cover consolidated central government.

Kuwait

Monetary Authorities

✗ The Central Bank began operations in 1969. Beginning in that year, data are based on fully sectored and consolidated accounts.

Deposit Money Banks

✗ See note on monetary authorities. ✗ Prior to 1981, consolidates commercial banks only. Beginning in 1981, consolidates commercial banks, specialized banks, and Kuwait Finance House.

Monetary Survey

✗ See notes on monetary authorities and deposit money banks.

Government Finance

✗ Beginning in 1972, data include year-end adjustments that were not available for earlier years and also adjustments resulting from the treatment on a net basis of nonfinancial public enterprises. ✗ Fiscal year ends March 31 through 1971; ends June 30 thereafter. ✗ Beginning in 1974, data cover the operations of the budgetary central government and are presented on a calendar year basis to allow comparison with other Kuwaiti macroeconomic data.

Kyrgyz Republic

National Accounts

GDP by major expenditure category at current prices is estimated using the *1993 SNA* framework. From 1993 onward, estimates have been made for unrecorded production, trade, and household consumption.

Lao People's Democratic Republic

Exchange Rates

✗ Data prior to 1991 refer to the midpoint between the buying and selling rates quoted by state-owned commercial banks. Beginning in 1991, data refer to the midpoint between the buying and selling rates quoted by the Bank of Lao P.D.R. (central bank). ✗ In 1995, a floating exchange rate policy was adopted, and the commercial banks were allowed to set their rates. Data beginning in 1995 refer to the simple average of midpoint rates reported by the commercial banks on a daily basis, covering their transactions for the previous day.

Interest Rates

Deposit Rate: ✗ Prior to 1991, the rate set by the Bank of Lao P.D.R. on commercial banks' three-month domestic-currency time deposits. Beginning in 1991, minimum rate fixed by the Bank of

Lao P.D.R. on commercial banks' three-month domestic-currency time deposits.

Lending Rate: ✗ Prior to 1993, data refer to the rate set by the Bank of Lao P.D.R. on commercial banks' short-term loans to the commerce and services sectors. From 1993 to 1995, data refer to the maximum rate set by the Bank of Lao P.D.R. for commercial banks' nonagricultural loans. ✗ The lending rate was liberalized in 1995; data beginning then refer to the highest rate quoted by the commercial banks on nonagricultural loans.

Latvia

Banking Institutions

✗ Prior to 1994, data for *Claims on Central Government* and *Central Government Deposits* comprise accounts that were maintained on a cumulative flow basis. Thereafter, these data are on a stock basis. Beginning in 1994, data are based on an improved sectorization and classification of the accounts.

Banking Survey

✗ See note on banking institutions.

Government Finance

✗ Data prior to 1996 cover the budgetary central government only. From January through March 1996, data cover the budgetary central government and the Social Security Fund. From April 1996 onward, data cover the budgetary central government, the Social Security Fund, and the special budgets. ✗ From 1997 onwards, expenditure on education and health functions was shifted within components of central government and between local governments and central government. ✗ Prior to 1998, data are not consolidated. Beginning in 1998, data are presented on a consolidated basis.

Lebanon

Interest Rates

Treasury Bill Rate: ✗ Beginning in 1986, secondary market yield on three-month treasury bills determined by the Central Bank of Lebanon.

Lesotho

Interest Rates

Treasury Bill Rate: ✗ Beginning in 1994, average rate of three issues of 91-day treasury bills. The rate is determined through securities auctions conducted by the Central Bank of Lesotho.

Liberia

Monetary Authorities

✗ Beginning in 1980, data are based on an improved sectorization of the accounts.

Monetary Survey

✗ See note on monetary authorities.

Interest Rates

Lending Rate: ✗ Beginning in 1998, average rate offered by commercial banks on all loans.

Government Finance

✗ During the period 1977–87, data relate to a fiscal year different from calendar year (fiscal year ends June 30).

Libya

Exchange Rates

In 1971 the Libyan dinar, equal to the Libyan pound, was introduced.

Monetary Authorities

✗ Beginning in 1997, date are based on improved reporting and classification of accounts.

Deposit Money Banks

✗ Prior to 1999, some central government time deposits are included in *Time and Foreign Currency Deposits (line 25)*.

Monetary Survey

✗ See notes on monetary authorities and deposit money banks.

Lithuania

Banking Institutions

✗ Beginning in 1994, overdrafts, which were previously included in *Claims on the Private Sector,* are properly sectorized.

Banking Survey

✗ See note on banking institutions.

Government Finance

✗ In 1997, expenditure on health functions and their financing were shifted from local to central government.

Luxembourg

International Liquidity

✗ Beginning in 1989, data on gold holdings exclude the gold deposits made with the European Monetary Institute (EMI), which became the European Central Bank (ECB) in 1998; the holdings of European currency units (ECUs) issued by the EMI against these gold deposits are included in *line 1d.d.* ✗ Beginning in 1999, *Total Reserves minus Gold (line 1l.d)* is defined in accordance with the Eurosystem's statistical definition of international reserves. Data on lines *3..d, 4..d, 7a.d,* and *7b.d* are based on a Euro Area-wide definition of residency.

Banking Institutions

✗ Reflect significant changes in the reporting by the commercial banks to the Institut Monétaire Luxembourgeois that commenced at the end of 1992.

Banking Survey (National Residency)

✗See note on banking institutions.

Interest Rates

Government Bond Yield: ✗ Weighted average yield to final maturity of all government bonds quoted in the Luxembourg Stock Exchange. Before 1978, data referred to the average weighted yield to average maturity as then calculated by the Luxembourg stock exchange.

Macedonia

Monetary Authorities

✗ Prior to 1995, local governments were included in central government, and nonfinancial public enterprises and some government units were included in the private sector.

Monetary Survey

✗ See note on monetary authorities.

International Transactions

International Investment Position: ✗Data are incomplete. Banking and official sector data are included. Private sector transactions are partially covered.

Madagascar

Monetary Authorities

✗ Beginning in 1979, claims on public enterprises are separately identified.

Deposit Money Banks

✗ Beginning in 1979, data are based on an improved classification; as a result, bonds, central government lending funds, and credit from the central bank are separately identified.

Monetary Survey

✗ See notes on monetary authorities and deposit money banks.

Government Finance

✗ Prior to 1972, data are as reported by the Central Bank of the Republic of Madagascar for publication in *IFS*. Beginning in 1972, data are as reported in the *Government Finance Statistics Yearbook (GFSY)* and cover the general budget, the *Caisse nationale de prevoyance sociale* (National Social Security Fund), and the *Office des anciens combattants* (Veterans' Office). ✗ Beginning in 1988, *GFSY* data cover the general budget and extrabudgetary units excluding social security.

Malawi

Other Banking Institutions

✗ Beginning in 1988, data exclude the accounts for the Post Office Savings Bank.

Prices, Production, and Labor

Consumer Prices: ✗ Beginning in 1991, the index covers the cities of Blantyre, Lilongwe, Mzuzu, and Zomba, base 1990. *Industrial Production:* ✗ Prior to 1988, manufacturing production, base 1970.

Government Finance

✗ Prior to 1971, data are as reported by the Reserve Bank of Malawi for publication in *IFS*. Beginning in 1971, data are as reported in the *Government Finance Statistics Yearbook* and cover budgetary central government.

Malaysia

Monetary Authorities

✗ Beginning in 1992, comprises the Bank Negara Malaysia only. ✗ Beginning in 1996, data are based on an improved sectorization of the accounts.

Deposit Money Banks

✗ Beginning in 1980, claims on other banking institutions (*line 22f*), which were previously included in *line 27r*, are shown separately. ✗Beginning in 1992, data are based on an improved sectorization of the accounts. ✗See note on monetary authorities.

Monetary Survey

✗ See notes on monetary authorities and deposit money banks.

Other Banking Institutions

✗ Beginning in 1971, includes the Employees Provident Fund. ✗ Beginning in 1974, includes merchant banks. ✗ Starting in 1992, comprises finance companies, merchant banks, and discount houses and excludes National Savings Bank and the Employees Provident Fund. ✗ See note on monetary authorities.

Banking Survey

✗ See notes on monetary authorities, deposit money banks, and other banking institutions.

Interest Rates

Money Market Rate: ✗ Beginning in 1996, average overnight interbank rate.

Deposit Rate: ✗ Beginning in 1996, weighted average rate offered by commercial banks on new three-month time deposits. The rate is weighted by deposit amounts.

Lending Rate: ✗ Beginning in 1996, weighted average base lending rate charged by commercial banks. The rate is weighted by loan amounts.

Government Finance

✗ Prior to 1970, quarterly and annual data differ from source B in that, in *IFS*, special receipts (foreign grants) are included in

Revenue (line 81) instead of being considered as a financing item; lending minus repayments comprise repayment of lending made through the Development Fund; and the gold subscription to the Fund (made by the government) is excluded from *Expenditure (line 82)* and *Use of Cash Balances (line 87)*.⌘ Beginning in 1997, special receipts are included in *Use of Cash Balances (line 87)*.

Maldives

Monetary Authorities

⌘ Before 1981, the data relate to the monetary authority functions of the Department of Finance (Treasury) and the State Trading Organization, which managed a large part of the official foreign exchange holdings. Beginning in 1981, comprises the Maldives Monetary Authority only, which was established in that year. *Claims on Central Government (line 12a):* ⌘ Prior to 1985, data include claims on nonfinancial public enterprises. *Foreign Liabilities (line 16c):* ⌘ Prior to 1985, data include amounts of government foreign borrowing, with a contra-entry in *Claims on Central Government (line 12a)*.

Deposit Money Banks

⌘ Beginning in 1981, data are based on an improved sectorization of the accounts. *Foreign Liabilities (line 26c):* ⌘Prior to 1985, data exclude nonresident deposits with domestic banks.

Monetary Survey

⌘ See notes on monetary authorities and deposit money banks.

Mali

Exchange Rates

Official Rate (End of Period and *Period Average):* ⌘ From 1999 onward, the CFA franc is pegged to the euro at a rate of CFA franc 655.957 per euro. Prior to 1999, the official rate was pegged to the French franc. ⌘ In 1994 the CFA franc was devalued to CFAF 100 per French franc from CFAF 50, at which it had been fixed since 1948.

Monetary Authorities

⌘ Beginning in 1975, data are based on an improved sectorization of the accounts. ⌘ At the end of 1983, data reflect the consolidation and transfer to the government of the central bank's liabilities under the operations account and the cancellation of certain loans to the government and to state enterprises. Beginning in 1984, data reflect Mali's re-entry into the West African Monetary Union and the compilation of the data on the Central Bank of West African States' (BCEAO's) basis.

Deposit Money Banks

⌘ Beginning in 1979, data are based on an improved sectorization of the accounts. ⌘ See note on monetary authorities.

Monetary Survey

⌘ See notes on monetary authorities and deposit money banks.

Prices

Consumer Prices: ⌘ Beginning in 1997, BCEAO harmonized index.

Government Finance

⌘ Beginning in 1980, data also cover extrabudgetary foreign grants and loans not recorded in the treasury accounts. ⌘ Data for 1980 and 1981 do not cover social security operations. ⌘ From 1989 to 1997, net lending and privatization receipts are included in revenue.

Malta

Deposit Money Banks

⌘ Beginning in 1995, data for offshore banks (international banking institutions) have been included in the consolidation.

Monetary Survey

⌘ See note on deposit money banks.

Banking Survey

⌘ See note on deposit money banks.

Government Finance

⌘ Prior to 1979, data relate to a fiscal year different from calendar year (fiscal year ends April 1 through 1978).

Mauritania

Monetary Authorities

⌘ The sectorization and classification of accounts have been revised from 1989 onward.

Deposit Money Banks

⌘ See note on monetary authorities.

Monetary Survey

⌘ See note on monetary authorities.

Government Finance

⌘ Prior to 1978, data cover budgetary and social security operations. Beginning in 1978, data also cover extrabudgetary operations. ⌘ Beginning in 1990, data cover the consolidated operations of the treasury and operations financed with foreign resources not recorded in the treasury accounts.

Mauritius

Government Finance

⌘Prior to 1973, data are as reported by the Bank of Mauritius for publication in *IFS*. Beginning in 1973, data are as published in the *Government Finance Statistics Yearbook (GFSY)* and cover budgetary central government. ⌘Changes in the coverage of the consolidated central government in 1983, 1988, 1989, 1992, 1993, and 1994 are as specified in the *GFSY*.

Mexico

Monetary Authorities

✗Beginning in 1977, data are based on an improved sectorization of the accounts. ✗Beginning in 1997, data reflect methodological changes in compilation.

Deposit Money Banks

✗Comprises only commercial banks through 1976. Beginning in 1977, comprises commercial banks and national credit corporations. See note on monetary authorities. ✗ Beginning in 1982, data reflect the introduction of a new plan of accounts, which provides an improved sectorization of domestic and foreign accounts. ✗ Beginning in 1997, data reflect changes in the chart of accounts, accounting criteria, and the methodology for compiling monetary accounts, which identify positions with nonresidents and the various domestic sectors by financial instrument.

Monetary Survey

✗See notes on monetary authorities and deposit money banks.

Other Banking Institutions

✗Prior to 1977, national credit institutions other than commercial banks were also included, and rediscount operations were not included, since they were classified under contingency or memorandum accounts. Beginning in 1977, comprises development banks. See note on monetary authorities. ✗ See note on deposit money banks.

Banking Survey

✗ See notes on monetary authorities, deposit money banks, and other banking institutions.

Interest Rates

Money Market Rate: ✗ Beginning in 1989, average of rates quoted by deposit money banks on three-month bankers' acceptances. ✗ Beginning in 1995, weighted average rate on loans between financial institutions (TIIE). The rate is weighted by daily loan amounts..

Treasury Bill Rate: ✗ Beginning in 1988, average yield on 28-day treasury bills, calculated from the weighted average rate of discount on daily transactions among dealers on the Mexican Securities Exchange.

Prices, Production, Labor

Industrial Production: ✗ From 1975 onwards, annual data have been adjusted to include production of petroleum and gas and petroleum refining. ✗ Monthly data have been adjusted from 1979 onwards.

National Accounts

✗ Data revisions on total GDP extend further back than that of its components. Hence, components do not add up to GDP for some years. ✗ Beginning in 1993, data have been revised significantly following the implementation of the *1993 SNA*.

Moldova

Monetary Authorities

✗ Beginning in 1996, data are based on an improved sectorization of the accounts.

Deposit Money Banks

✗ Beginning in 1998, data reflect the introduction of a new accounting system.

Monetary Survey

✗ See notes on monetary authorities and deposit money banks.

Mongolia

Exchange Rates

✗ From 1993 onward, the midpoint of the average buying and selling rates that are freely determined on the basis of market transactions between commercial banks and the nonbank public. Also beginning in 1993, all exchange rates were unified in the context of the floating exchange rate system.

Government Finance

✗ Beginning in 1992, annual data are as reported in the *Government Finance Statistics Yearbook (GFSY)* and cover consolidated central government. ✗ From 1997 onward, the data cover the expenditures of the Reserve Funds.

Morocco

International liquidity

✗ Beginning in 1997, data are based on a broader coverage of institutions and a reclassification of institutions previously classified as other banking institutions.

Monetary Authorities

✗ Beginning in 1980, *Claims on Central Government (line 12a)* include the Fund drawings that have been transferred to the Treasury, and *Claims on Private Sector (line 12d)* exclude *Claims on Other Financial Institutions (line 12f)*. ✗Beginning in 1990, data are based on a more detailed classification of accounts. ✗ For data beginning in 1997, see note on international liquidity.

Deposit Money Banks

✗ Beginning in 1982, data are based on improved classification. ✗ For data beginning in 1990 and 1997, see notes on international liquidity and monetary authorities.

Monetary Survey

✗ See notes on international liquidity, monetary authorities, and deposit money banks.

Other Banking Institutions

For data beginning in 1982, 1990, and 1997, see notes on international liquidity, monetary authorities, and deposit money banks.

Government Finance

✗ Prior to 1970, data are as reported for publication in *IFS*. Beginning in 1970, data are as reported in the *Government Finance Statistics Yearbook* and cover budgetary central government, the Moroccan Pension Fund, and the National Social Security Fund.

Mozambique

Monetary Authorities

✗ Beginning in 1989, data are based on an improved sectorization of the accounts. ✗ Prior to 1991, comprises the former Banco de Moçambique, which performed central and commercial banking functions. Data are based on an improved classification of the accounts.

Banking Institutions

✗ Beginning in 1991, comprises the Banco Popular de Desenvolvimento, Banco Standard Totta de Moçambique, and Banco Comercial de Moçambique, which was the commercial department of the former Banco de Moçambique. Beginning in 1994, includes the Banco Fomento Exterior and Banco Português do Atlântico. See note on monetary authorities.

Banking Survey

✗ See notes on monetary authorities and banking institutions.

National Accounts

✗ Source S. From 1991 onward, data are compiled according to the *1993 SNA*.

Myanmar

International Liquidity

✗ In 1970 the Union of Myanmar Bank assumed the foreign assets of all banks and the small holdings of the insurance board. Data for other banks were formerly reported separately in *line 7a.d.*

Monetary Authorities

Comprises accounts of the Central Bank of Myanmar (prior to 1989, the Union of Myanmar Bank) and the short-term foreign assets of Myanmar Foreign Trade Bank, which are included in *Foreign Assets (line 11)* with a contra-entry in *Reserve Money (line 14)* prior to 1991 and *Other Liabilities to DMBs (line 14n)* since January 1991. ✗ For data beginning in 1970 and in 1989, see notes on international liquidity and deposit money banks. ✗ Prior to 1991, *Claims on Central Government (line 12a)* refer to claims on central government net of small amounts of central government deposits at the central bank; since 1989, central government deposits are maintained at the commercial banks. ✗ Beginning in 1991, data are based on an improved reporting and classification of accounts.

Deposit Money Banks

✗ The 1970 consolidation of all financial institutions into a Union of Myanmar Bank resulted in substantial changes in the structure of banking statistics. ✗ Beginning in 1989, claims on government and on nonfinancial public enterprises have been settled through budgetary operations. ✗ Beginning in 1991, data are based on an improved reporting and classification of accounts.

Monetary Survey

✗ The 1970 consolidation of all financial institutions into a Union of Myanmar Bank resulted in substantial changes in the structure of monetary statistics. Postal deposits, which were reported in *line 34* since 1966, are now included in *line 35*. *Line 31n* is net of foreign liabilities, which were not identified before 1970. In addition, accounts of public enterprises now reported in *line 32c* were previously reported partly in *line 32an* and partly in *line 32d*. See notes on monetary authorities and deposits money banks.

Government Finance

✗ Fiscal year ends September 30 through 1973; ends March 31 thereafter. ✗ Prior to 1992, data include operations of city and township development committees. ✗ Prior to 1996, data are as reported in the *Government Finance Statistics Yearbook*; beginning in 1996, data are as reported by the central bank.

National Accounts

✗ Data prior to 1974 refer to fiscal years ending September 30. Data from 1974 onward relate to the new fiscal year, ending March 31. For the year ending September 1974, that is, based on the old fiscal year, GDP at current market prices was estimated to be 14,852 million kyats.

Namibia

Government Finance

✗ Data are as reported in the *Government Finance Statistics Yearbook* and cover, prior to 1990, budgetary central government and one extrabudgetary fund (the University of Namibia). Beginning in 1990, data cover budgetary central government only.

Nepal

Monetary Authorities

✗ Prior to 1970, *line 14d* includes foreign liabilities. Hence, *lines 14, 31n*, and *34* are overstated before this date.

Interest Rates

Government Bond Yield: ✗ Prior to 1984, *line 61* included government development bonds. Beginning in 1984, annual coupon rate on national savings certificates with five years maturity issued by the government to mobilize funds from nonbank sources.

Government Finance

✗ Prior to 1972 (1971 for debt data), data are as reported by Nepal Rastra Bank for publication in *IFS*. Also prior to 1972, foreign grants received for budgetary support are reported as deficit finance. *Use of Cash Balances* includes the residual, which reflects mainly unspent balances of foreign grants and timing differences. Beginning in 1972 (1971 for debt data), data are as reported in the *Government Finance Statistics Yearbook* and cover consolidated central government. ✗ Beginning in 1979, data for foreign grants and borrowing have been adjusted to eliminate receivable items. Data relate to a fiscal year different from calendar year. ✗ Beginning in 1991, data are as reported by the Nepal Rastra Bank for publication in *IFS*.

Netherlands

International Liquidity

✗ Beginning in 1999, *Total Reserves minus Gold (line 1l.d)* is defined in accordance with the Eurosystem's statistical definition of

international reserves. Data on lines *3..d*, *4..d*, *7a.d*, and *7b.d* are based on a Euro Area-wide definition of residency.

Banking Institutions

✗ Beginning in 1982, the data reflect improved classifications on the report forms used to collect these data from the banks.

Banking Survey (National Residency)

✗ See note on banking institutions.

Money (National Definitions)

✗ Prior to 1982, the concept of domestic liquidity (also referred to as M2, *line 38n*) comprised certain liquid liabilities of the central and local governments. From 1982, new monetary aggregates, which are denoted as *M3H* and *M3H seasonally adjusted*, have been introduced. In comparison with M2, the broader M3H includes savings with an original maturity of less than two years but excludes liquid liabilities of the central and local governments.

Nonbank Financial Institutions

✗ Prior to 1985, data for insurance companies relate only to life insurance. Beginning in 1985, the data for insurance companies are based on a new and extended survey of the largest seven insurance companies, covering about 85 to 90 percent of the balance sheet total of all insurance companies.

Interest Rates

Discount Rate (End of Period): Effective 1994, the discount facility was discontinued.

Money Market Rate: ✗ Prior to 1971, data refer to the short-term lending rate to local authorities.

Deposit Rate (line 60l): ✗ Prior to 1994, interest rate offered by banks on time deposits with three months' notice. Beginning in 1994, interest rate on savings deposits with minimum balance of f. 10,000.

Lending Rate (line 60p): ✗ Prior to 1999, referred to the midpoint of the minimum and maximum interest rate charged on current account advances. Beginning in 1999, represents base rate charged by commercial banks on advances.

International Transactions

✗ Beginning in 1986, data exclude an estimate of trade with BLEU.

Government Finance

✗ Prior to 1978, lending minus repayments data do not include repayments on domestic lending.

Netherlands Antilles

Prices and Labor

Consumer Prices: ✗ Source S index covering Aruba, Curaçao, and from 1975 also Bonaire. ✗ As of 1986, data cover only Curaçao and Bonaire, base December 1984. ✗ Beginning in 1990, data cover only Curaçao, base year February 1996.

International Transactions

✗ As of 1986, data exclude Aruba.

Government Finance

✗ Beginning in 1980, data also cover social security operations. ✗ Beginning in 1986, the island government of Aruba became independent of the Netherlands Antilles. ✗ Provisional data for 1995 do not include social security operations.

New Zealand

Monetary Authorities

✗ Beginning in 1988, data are based on an improved sectorization of the accounts.

Banking Institutions

✗ Comprises four trading banks through 1987. Beginning in 1988, comprises registered banks and 'other M3 institutions' (certain corporations and savings institutions). See note on monetary authorities.

Banking Survey

✗ See notes on monetary authorities and banking institutions.

Interest Rates

Deposit Rate: ✗ Beginning in 1988, data refer to the quarterly weighted averages for registered banks' total New Zealand dollar deposits. ✗ Beginning in 1990, weighted average rate offered by New Zealand's six largest banks on six-month deposits of NZ$10,000 or more, each bank's rate being weighted according to its share of the group's total N.Z. dollar deposits.

Lending Rate: ✗ Beginning in 1987, weighted average base business rate charged by New Zealand's six largest banks, each bank's rate being weighted according to its share of the group's private sector claims.

Government Bond Yield: ✗ Beginning in 1987, rate on the five-year "benchmark" bond, a specific bond selected by the Reserve Bank of New Zealand to provide a representative five-year bond rate.

Prices, Production, Labor

Share Prices: ✗ Beginning in 1987, gross index calculated by the New Zealand Stock Exchange, base June 30, 1986.

International Transactions

✗ Prior to 1978, data exclude veal. *Balance of Payments:* Annual balance of payments data for years prior to 1980 are compiled on the basis of fiscal years commencing April 1. From 1980 onwards, the data are on a calendar year basis.

Government Finance

✗ Prior to 1970, the data are as reported by the Department of Statistics for publication in *IFS*. Beginning in 1970, data are as reported in the *Government Finance Statistics Yearbook*. The data cover budgetary central government only. ✗ Beginning in 1986, data for *lines 84a* and *85a* cover domestic and foreign financing respectively. ✗ Through 1988, fiscal year begins April 1; beginning in 1990, ends June 30.

Nicaragua

Monetary Authorities

✗ Beginning in 1983, data are based on a new reporting system.
✗ Beginning in 1996, data are based on an improved sectorization of the accounts.

Deposit Money Banks

✗ See note on monetary authorities.

Monetary Survey

✗ See note on monetary authorities.

Nonbank Financial Institutions

✗ See note on monetary authorities.

Financial Survey

✗ See note on monetary authorities.

Niger

Exchange Rates

Official Rate (End of Period and *Period Average):* ✗ From 1999 onward, the CFA franc is pegged to the euro at a rate of CFA franc 655.957 per euro. Prior to 1999, the official rate was pegged to the French franc. ✗ In 1994 the CFA franc was devalued to CFAF 100 per French franc from CFAF 50, at which it had been fixed since 1948.

Prices and Labor

Consumer Prices: ✗ Beginning in 1997, BCEAO harmonized index.

Nigeria

Monetary Authorities

✗ Beginning in 1992, data are based on an improved sectorization of the accounts.

Deposit Money Banks

✗ Prior to 1973, central government deposits with commercial banks were included in *Demand Deposits* and *Time and Savings Deposits.* ✗ See note on monetary authorities.

Monetary Survey

✗ See notes on monetary authorities and deposit money banks.

Norway

Monetary Survey

✗ Beginning in 1976, data for the Bank of Norway and deposit money banks are based upon improved sectorization in national source data.

Other Banking Institutions

✗ Beginning in 1977, data for state banks are based upon improved sectorization in national source data.

Government Finance

✗ Beginning in 1972 (except for debt data beginning in 1971), data are as reported in the *Government Finance Statistics Yearbook* and cover the consolidated central government.

National Accounts

✗ From 1988 onwards, data have been revised significantly, following the implementation of improved compilation methods and the *1993 SNA.*

Oman

Deposit Money Banks

✗ Prior to 1979, some components of foreign assets and foreign liabilities were reported on a net basis.

Monetary Survey

✗ See note on deposit money banks.

Pakistan

Exchange Rates

✗ Prior to 1998, the State Bank of Pakistan buying rate. During 1998, the rate established by the State Bank of Pakistan. ✗ From 1999 onward, Free Interbank Exchange rate, as determined in the interbank foreign exchange market.

Interest Rates

Discount Rate (End of Period): ✗ Prior to 1994, rate at which the State Bank of Pakistan made advances to scheduled banks against acceptable securities. Beginning in 1994, data refer to the State Bank of Pakistan discount rate for its three-day repo facility.

Treasury Bill Rate: ✗ Prior to 1997, rate on six-month federal treasury bill. Beginning in 1997, rate on six-month federal treasury bond (STFB).

Prices, Production, Labor

Wholesale Prices: ✗ Source S. Beginning in July 1991, base 1990–91, index numbers of wholesale prices including food, raw material, fuel, lighting, lubricants, and manufactures.

International Transactions

✗ All trade data are from source S. *Value of Exports and Imports*: Exports data include re-exports. Trade in military goods and silver bullions are excluded.

Government Finance

✗ Prior to 1973, data are as reported by the State Bank of Pakistan for publication in *IFS*. Beginning in 1973, data are as reported in the *Government Finance Statistics Yearbook* and are not comparable with previous years, which included the former East Pakistan. ✗ Beginning in 1978, data on uses of cash balances are not available.

Panama

Interest Rates

Deposit Rate: ✗ Beginning in 1992, weighted average rate offered by domestic deposit money banks on six-month time deposits. The rate is weighted by deposit amounts.

Lending Rate: ✗ Beginning in 1990, weighted average rate charged by domestic deposit money banks on one- to five-year loans for trading activities. The rate is weighted by loan amounts.

International Transactions

Balance of Payments: ✗ Through 1979 the transactions of international license banks have been wholly excluded from the balance of payments. In addition, through 1979 the enterprises operating in the Colón Free Zone have been treated as nonresidents of Panama. Beginning in 1980, data cover all transactions of Panama, including the Colón Free Zone; transactions of international license banks and of enterprises operating in the Colón Free Zone are both covered.

Government Finance

✗ Through 1972, data for floating debt have been excluded from *Expenditure (line 82)* and *Net Borrowing (line 84)*. Beginning in 1973, data are as reported in the *Government Finance Statistics Yearbook*.

Papua New Guinea

Interest Rates

Discount Rate (line 60): ✗ Beginning in 1993, maximum average rate charged by the Bank of Papua New Guinea on loans to deposit money banks against acceptable commercial paper.

Government Finance

✗ Prior to 1978, data relate to a fiscal year ending June 30. ✗ Data for 1985–87 cover the operations of the consolidated central government. ✗ Data through 1984 and from 1988 onward cover budgetary central government only. ✗ From 1998 onward, the data exclude the operations of extrabudgetary accounts.

National Accounts

✗ Prior to 1977, data relate to fiscal years ending June 30. Since this date, data refer to calendar years.

Paraguay

Monetary Authorities

✗ Beginning in 1988, data are based on an improved sectorization of the accounts.

Deposit Money Banks

✗ Beginning in 1988, comprises commercial banks and the National Development Bank. See note on monetary authorities.

Monetary Survey

✗ See notes on monetary authorities and deposit money banks.

Other Banking Institutions

✗ Beginning in 1988, comprises savings and loans associations for housing, National Housing Bank, Cattle Fund, Credit Agency for Farm Equipment, Bank Employees Retirement and Pension Fund, finance companies, and Paraguayan Institute for Housing and Urbanization, which was abolished in 1992.

Banking Survey

✗ See notes on monetary authorities, deposit money banks, and other banking institutions.

Interest Rates

Discount Rate (End of Period): ✗ Beginning in 1990, rate charged by the Central Bank of Paraguay on short-term liquidity loans to commercial banks.

Savings Rate: ✗ Beginning in 1994, weighted average rate offered by commercial banks on savings deposits in national currency. The rate is weighted by deposit amounts.

Deposit Rate: ✗ Beginning in 1999, weighted average rate offered by commercial banks on 90- to 180-day time deposits in national currency. The rate is weighted by deposit amounts.

Lending Rate: ✗ Beginning in 1994, weighted average rate charged by commercial banks on commercial, developmental, personal, and various loans in national currency. The rate is weighted by loan amounts.

Government Finance

✗ Beginning in 1972, data are as reported in the *Government Finance Statistics Yearbook* and relate to the consolidated central government. ✗ Beginning in 1989, data cover budgetary central government only. However, data on outstanding debt relate to the budgetary central government for all years.

Peru

International Liquidity

✗ In 1970 essentially all foreign exchange reserves of banks were transferred to the Central Reserve Bank.

International Transactions

✗ Prior to 1975, data on exports and imports in U.S. dollars were derived by conversion of national currency data into U.S. dollars. Annual figures include grants and other adjustments.

Government Finance

✗ Beginning in 1984, data are as reported in the *Government Finance Statistics Yearbook (GFSY)*. Through 1989, data relate to the budgetary central government only; beginning in 1990, data cover consolidated central government. Expenditure data include interest arrears. ✗ Beginning in 1992, changes in the coverage are as specified in the *GFSY*.

Philippines

Monetary Authorities

✗ Beginning in 1983, data are based on an improved sectorization of the accounts. ✗ Beginning in 1993, data reflect the financial restructuring of the Central Bank of the Philippines. The Bangko Sentral ng Pilipinas (BSP) was created to take over the monetary authority functions of the former Central Bank of the Philippines. At the same time, the Central Bank-Board of Liquidators (CB-BOL), an agency of the central government, was created to liquidate the nonperforming assets of the former Central Bank of the Philippines. *Line 12a* includes claims on the CB-BOL. *Line 16c* includes foreign liabilities assumed by the BSP which, prior to 1993, were included in *lines 16b* and *16d*.

Deposit Money Banks

x Before 1976, *line 21* included, and *line 22d* excluded, certain claims on residents. Beginning in 1976, the sectorization of foreign accounts was improved. x See note on monetary authorities.

Monetary Survey

x See notes on monetary authorities and deposit money banks.

Interest Rates

Discount Rate (End of Period): x Prior to 1985, data refer to the rediscount rate for loans for traditional exports, which account for a large part of total rediscount credits. Beginning in 1985, the rediscount facility was unified, and data refer to the single rate charged on all rediscount loans.

Government Finance

x Beginning in 1972, data are derived from *Cash Operations Statements,* Bureau of Treasury. x During the period 1972–75, data relate to a fiscal year different from calendar year (fiscal year ends June 30).

Poland

Monetary Authorities

x Beginning in 1981, data are based on an improved reporting system. x Beginning in 1991, data are based on a new system of accounts and an improved reporting system.

Deposit Money Banks

x See note on monetary authorities.

Monetary Survey

x See note on monetary authorities.

Interest Rates

Discount Rate (End of Period): x Beginning in 1989, rate at which the National Bank of Poland rediscounts bills of exchange to commercial banks.

Money Market Rate: x Starting in 1992, weighted average rate on outstanding deposits of one month or less in the interbank market.

Deposit Rate: x Beginning in 1991, lowest rate offered by main commercial banks on 12-month deposits in domestic currency. x From 1994 onward, weighted average rate offered by commercial banks on households' deposits in domestic currency.

Lending Rate: x Beginning in 1995, weighted average rate charged by commercial banks on minimum risk loans.

Prices, Production, Labor

Consumer Prices: x Through 1990, monthly indices were based on the value of sales of the preceding year. From 1991 onward, monthly price indices are based on the value of household expenditure in the first ten months of the preceding year from the household budget survey. Annual values are computed from the monthly data.

Industrial Production: x Before 1991, the data covered only the socialized sector. Since 1991, covers both private and socialized units engaged in industrial production, where the number of employed persons exceeds five (annual data) or 50 (monthly and quarterly data).

Industrial Employment: x Before 1991, the data covered only the socialized sector. Since 1991, covers both private and socialized units where the number of employed persons exceeds five.

International Transactions

Exports and *Imports:* x Data in zlotys since 1982 are not comparable to previous yearly data, which are in foreign exchange zlotys. x Since 1991, data include import and export invoices as well as customs declarations. Annual data are obtained on the basis of direct surveys of price changes.

National Accounts

x Beginning in 1990, data have been revised following the implementation of the *1993 SNA.* x Beginning in 1994, data at the previous year's prices are used to construct *line 99bvpyf*.

Portugal

International Liquidity

x For data on *line 4..d* for 1976, see note on banking institutions. x Beginning in 1999, *Total Reserves minus Gold (line 11.d)* is defined in accordance with the Eurosystem's statistical definition of international reserves. Data on lines *3..d, 4..d, 7a.d,* and *7b.d* are based on a Euro Area-wide definition of residency.

Monetary Authorities

x See note on banking institutions.

Banking Institutions

x In 1976, the statistical reporting of data was changed (the "residency"criterion was adopted to identify the "external sector," instead of the "foreign currency" or "domestic currency" criterion formerly used; also the split between the general government and the rest of the economy was implemented).

Banking Survey (National Residency)

x See note on banking institutions.

Interest Rates

Banco de Portugal Rate (End of Period): x Prior to 1987, end-of-year rate on first tranche rate at which the Banco de Portugal rediscounted the financial claims held by the banking system. From 1987 until 1991, corresponds to the Banco de Portugal discount rate. x Beginning in 1992, interest rate on regular provision of liquidity announced by the Banco de Portugal.

Money Market Rate: ✗ Prior to 1986, weighted average rate for interbank deposits up to three days. From 1986 to 1991, weighted average rate for interbank deposits up to five days. ✗Beginning in 1992, weighted average rate for interbank overnight transactions.

Treasury Bill Rate: ✗ Prior to 1986, average rate of all treasury bills issued. Beginning in 1986, weighted average rate of three-month treasury bills in the primary market, excluding underwriting by the Banco de Portugal.

Lending Rate: ✗Prior to 1988, administrative end-of-year maximum rate on 91- to 180-day loans. ✗Beginning in 1991, weighted average rate charged by monetary financial institutions (excluding savings banks and mutual agricultural credit banks) on 91-to 180-day loans and advances to nonfinancial private enterprises (excluding anomalous observations).

Prices, Production, Labor

✗ *Consumer Prices*: Source S, Laspeyres index, reference base 1997. The weights are derived from a household expenditure survey conducted from October 1994 to September 1995. The index covers 700 items.

International Transactions

All trade data are from source S. *Import Prices:* ✗ Data refer to the wholesale price index of imported goods, base first quarter 1991.

Government Finance

✗Beginning in 1975, data are as reported in the *Government Finance Statistics Yearbook* and relate to the consolidated central government. However, data on outstanding debt are derived from the *Annual Report* of the Finance Ministry.

Qatar

International Liquidity

✗ See note on deposit money banks.

Monetary Authorities

✗Beginning in 1993, revised data are based on the availability of additional classification detail.

Deposit Money Banks

✗ Prior to 1993, claims on the central government and nonfinancial public enterprises were included indistinguishably in claims on the private sector; borrowing from banks abroad was included in other liabilities, and deposits of nonfinancial public enterprises were included in government deposits. Revisions to capital accounts are based on the availability of additional classification detail.

Monetary Survey

✗ See notes on monetary authorities and deposit money banks.

Romania

Monetary Authorities

✗ Beginning in 1981, data are based on improved classification. ✗ Starting in 1990, data reflect significant classification changes resulting from the reform of the banking system, by which com-

mercial operations of the National Bank of Romania were transferred to the newly created Commercial Bank, and the former specialized banks were authorized to engage in any type of regular banking activity. ✗Beginning in 1993, substantial revisions were made to the classification of accounts and the compilation of data.

Deposit Money Banks

✗ See note on monetary authorities. ✗ Beginning in 1996, commercial banks' claims on the nonbank sector were reclassified into claims on nonfinancial public enterprises, private sector, and nonbank financial institutions.

Monetary Survey

✗ See note on monetary authorities.

Russia

Interest Rates

Deposit Rate: ✗ Beginning in 1997, weighted average rate offered by commercial banks on time deposits of households in national currency with remaining maturity of up to one year. The rate is weighted by deposit amounts.

Lending Rate: ✗Beginning in 1997, weighted average rate charged by commercial banks on loans of up to one year in national currency to legal entities (companies and organizations). The rate is weighted by loan amounts.

International Transactions

✗ Data prior to 1994 exclude trade with the Baltic countries and the other countries of the former Soviet Union.

International Investment Position:✗ Data cover only the banking sector.

Rwanda

Deposit Money Banks

✗ Beginning in 1981, the classification of external and government accounts has been improved.

Monetary Survey

✗ See note on deposit money banks.

Government Finance

✗ Through 1993, data are as reported in the *Government Finance Statistics Yearbook*. From 1994 onward, data are as reported by the National Bank of Rwanda and cover consolidated central government.

St. Kitts and Nevis

Government Finance

✗ Data prior to 1988 cover operations of the budgetary central government and the Social Security Fund. Beginning in 1988, data also cover operations of the trust funds.

St. Lucia

Government Finance

✗ Prior to 1984, data refer to the consolidated central government. Beginning in 1984, data cover budgetary operations only.

St. Vincent and the Grenadines

Government Finance

✗ Prior to 1991, operations of the national insurance scheme were not included.

Samoa

Monetary Survey

✗ Prior to 1974, nonresident deposits were reported in *line 34*. Subsequently, *line 31n* includes these deposits.

International Transactions

✗ Prior to 1977, data are based on customs clearances; diplomatic imports are included in total imports. Afterward, data refer to actual imports landed in Samoa.

Saudi Arabia

International Liquidity

✗ Up until 1978, *line 1d.d* included the foreign exchange cover against the note issue, which as of March 1978 amounted to about US$5.3 billion. Beginning in 1978, *line 1d.d* excludes this foreign exchange cover, which together with *line 3..d* is included in *line 11*. ✗ The authorities reviewed their methodology for classifying foreign assets and provided revised data on *Foreign Exchange (line 1d.d)* for 1996 onward.

Deposit Money Banks

✗ Beginning in 1983, data are based on an improved classification. ✗ Beginning in 1992, claims on public enterprises *(line 22c)* include claims on financial and nonfinancial public enterprises and may include a small amount of loans and advances to central government. Demand deposits *(line 24),* quasi-monetary deposits *(line 25a),* and foreign currency deposits *(line 25b)* may include some central government deposits.

Monetary Survey

✗ See note on deposit money banks.

Other Banking Institutions

✗ Prior to 1976, data refer to the Saudi Agricultural Bank. Beginning in 1976, consolidates the Saudi Agricultural Bank, the Saudi Industrial Development Fund, the Public Investment Fund, the Real Estate Development Fund, and the Saudi Credit Bank.

Prices, Production, and Labor

✗ Prior to 1979, the index is based on 1970 weights and covers Riyadh only. Thereafter, the index covers middle-income population of ten cities, base 1988.

Senegal

Exchange Rates

Official Rate (End of Period and *Period Average):* ✗ From 1999 onward, the CFA franc is pegged to the euro at a rate of CFA franc 655.957 per euro. Prior to 1999, the official rate was pegged to the French franc. ✗ In 1994 the CFA franc was devalued to CFAF 100 per French franc from CFAF 50, at which it had been fixed since 1948.

Deposit Money Banks

✗ Beginning in 1979, *Central Government Deposits (line 26d)* include the deposits of public establishments of an administrative or social nature (EPAS) and exclude those of the savings bank; *Demand* and *Time Deposits (lines 24* and *25)* include deposits of the savings bank and exclude deposits of EPAS; and *Claims on Private Sector (line 22d)* exclude claims on other financial institutions.

Monetary Survey

✗ Beginning in 1979, *Claims on Other Financial Institutions (line 32f)* includes claims of deposit money banks on other financial institutions. See note on deposit money banks.

Other Banking Institutions

Liquid Liabilities (line 55l): ✗ See notes on deposit money banks and monetary survey.

Government Finance

✗ Beginning in 1980, data include social security operations. ✗ Beginning in 1982, data also cover extrabudgetary foreign grants and loans for capital expenditure not recorded in the treasury accounts.

Seychelles

Interest Rates

Discount Rate (End of Period): ✗ Beginning in 1990, rate on concessionary loans of the Central Bank of Seychelles for selected industries.

Government Finance

✗ Prior to 1985, data are as reported by the Ministry of Finance for the *Government Finance Statistics Yearbook*. Subsequently, data are as reported by the Central Bank of Seychelles and cover budgetary central government.

Sierra Leone

Monetary Authorities

✗ Beginning in 1996, data are based on an improved sectorization of the accounts.

Deposit Money Banks

✗ See note on monetary authorities.

Monetary Survey

✗ See note on monetary authorities.

Government Finance

✗ Prior to 1974, data are a consolidation of central government current, capital, and extrabudgetary accounts, given separately in Sierra Leone's *Government Financial Reports.* Subsequently, data are as reported in the *Government Finance Statistics Yearbook* and cover transactions of the recurrent and development budgets of the central government. ✗ From 1991 onward, revenue data include loan repayments, and expenditure data include lending operations. These data should be included in the lending minus repayments aggregates but are not disaggregated in the source data.

Singapore

Deposit Money Banks

✗ Beginning in 1971, data are based on an improved sectorization of resident and nonresident accounts.

Monetary Survey

✗ See note on deposit money banks.

Slovak Republic

Deposit Money Banks

✗ Beginning in 1997, data are based on an improved classification of accounts.

Monetary Survey

✗ See note to deposit money banks.

Solomon Islands

Other Banking Institutions

✗ Beginning in 1987, includes credit unions.

Banking Survey

✗ See note on other banking institutions.

International Transactions

✗ Trade indices are provided by the national authorities.

South Africa

Monetary Authorities

✗ Beginning in 1990, accounts of the Corporation for Public Deposits—a full subsidiary of the South African Reserve Bank—have been included in the compilation of the monetary authorities' accounts.

Banking Institutions

✗ Beginning in 1992, data reflect the implementation of South Africa's Banks Act (Act No. 94 of 1990), which expanded the coverage of the banking sector and resulted in changes in the reporting and presentation of monetary accounts. The accounts of financial institutions, previously published under the sections for deposit money banks and other banking institutions, have been consolidated.

Banking Survey

✗ See notes on monetary authorities and banking institutions.

Financial Survey

✗ See notes on monetary authorities and banking institutions.

Interest Rates

Discount Rate (End of Period): ✗ Beginning in 1998, data refer to the rate on repurchase agreements between the South African Reserve Bank and commercial banks.

Money Market Rate: ✗ Beginning in 1976, lower margin of interbank deposits at call.

Prices, Production, Labor

Consumer Prices: ✗ Source S index of consumer prices of goods and services, 1985 weights, base 1995. *Share Prices*: ✗ Beginning in 1995, index of average prices of ordinary shares quoted on the Johannesburg Stock Exchange, base 1995.

International Transactions

✗ Beginning in 1998, foreign trade data refer to South Africa only. Excludes intra-trade of the South African Common Custom Area. Prior to 1998, trade data refer to the South African Common Custom Area, which includes Botswana, Lesotho, Swaziland, Namibia, and South Africa. *Exports:* Source S, value of exports, f.o.b., including gold exports. ✗ Beginning in 1973, export data exclude certain mineral oils. *Imports c.i.f.* and *f.o.b.:* Data are from source S. ✗ Prior to 1980, petroleum products and defense equipment were excluded. ✗ Beginning in 1981, strategic materials are included in the calculation of the export and import unit values.

Government Finance

✗ From 1991 onward, data include the revenue, expenditure, and financing of the former Transkei, Bophuthatswana, Venda and Ciskei (TBVC), and self-governing states. ✗ From 1994 onward, outstanding debt data include debt of former TBVC countries and self-governing states. This debt was assumed by the national government in terms of section 239 of the Second Amendment Bill of the Constitution of the Republic of South Africa. ✗ From 1997 onward, outstanding debt data include part of Namibia's debt, guaranteed by South Africa before Namibia's independence and subsequently assumed by South Africa. Data are presented on a calendar year basis to allow comparisons with other South African macroeconomic data. For South Africa, the fiscal year ends March 31.

National Accounts

✗ Since 1985, national accounts data correspond to the new set of national accounts estimates first published in 1994 by the Reserve Bank.

Spain

International Liquidity

✗ Beginning in 1999, *Total Reserves minus Gold (line 1l.d)* is defined in accordance with the Eurosystem's statistical definition of

international reserves. Data on *lines 3..d*, *4..d*, *7a.d*, and *7b.d* are based on a Euro Area-wide definition of residency.

Monetary Authorities

✗ Beginning in 1983, data are based on a new system of accounts with a revised transactor breakdown. ✗ From 1986, data reflect an introduction of a new reporting system. ✗ In accordance with provisions of the Treaty of European Union, beginning in 1994 overdrafts or loans from the Banco de España to the government were prohibited. Accordingly, *Credit to Central Government (line 12a)* shows net Treasury indebtedness through 1993 and gross indebtedness (without deducting the Treasury's current account) from 1994 onward.

Banking Institutions

✗Through 1982, the coverage of *line 24* is confined to the commercial and savings banks. Beginning in 1983, cooperative banks and money market intermediary companies are included. From 1983, data are based on the new bank returns, which are aimed at a uniform reporting system for all financial institutions. ✗ From 1986 onward, data reflect an introduction of a new reporting system.

Banking Survey (National Residency)

✗See notes on monetary authorities and banking institutions.

Interest Rates

Banco de España Rate: ✗ Until 1977, rate at which the Banco de España discounted financial paper for commercial and savings banks. From 1977 to 1989, weighted average of the interest rate on loans granted to the banking system, through auction, by the Banco de España. Beginning in 1990, average weighted rate of the ten-day securities repurchase tender (Banco de España certificates, government debt, and other book-entry debt). Data are for the last day of the month on which a tender took place.

Treasury Bill Rate: ✗ Prior to 1987, discount rate on three-month monetary regulation certificates, issued by the Banco de España. Beginning in 1987, data refer to the discount rate on one-year treasury bills.

Prices, Production, Labor

Employment: ✗ Beginning with the third quarter of 1976, coverage of data includes a stricter definition of 'marginally employed.' Prior to this period, a wider definition of marginally employed permitted the inclusion in total employment of persons who were not part of the economically active population. From the second quarter of 1980 onwards, data no longer include 14- and 15-year-old employees.

Government Finance

✗ Beginning in 1980, data reflect the separation from central government of the autonomous communities and reflect the adoption of altered accounting classifications. Also beginning in 1980, data on *Use of Cash Balances (line 87)* reflect only the variation in the deposits with the Banco de España, whereas in previous years, data corresponded to the net position of the state with the Banco de España. Data on *Net Foreign Borrowing (line 85a)* are now classified on a pure residence criterion, whereas in previous years, data contained proceeds from domestic borrowing issued in foreign currency. ✗ Beginning in 1985, the methodology followed in the compilation of the fiscal accounts was harmonized with the methodology used to compile the annual data presented in the *Financial Accounts of the Spanish Economy.*

National Accounts

✗ From 1998 onwards, data have been revised following the implementation of the *1995 ESA.*

Sri Lanka

Monetary Authorities

✗ Beginning in 1975, data are based on improved classification and sectorization. ✗ Beginning in 1989, data are compiled from a new report form.

Deposit Money Banks

✗ ee note on monetary authorities.

Monetary Survey

✗ See note on monetary authorities.

Interest Rates

Treasury Bill Rate: ✗ Beginning in 1996, discount rate in the primary market.

Government Finance

✗ Beginning in 1973, data are as reported in the *Government Finance Statistics Yearbook* and relate to the consolidated central government. ✗ From 1994 onward, privatization proceeds have been included in domestic financing.

Sudan

Exchange Rates

Market Rate (End of Period and *Period Average):* ✗ Effective 1992, a unified exchange rate system was introduced. Under the new system, the exchange rate is determined by a committee of local bankers, without official intervention, and is quoted uniformly by all commercial banks. Since 1992, all restrictions on foreign currency transactions have been lifted.

Monetary Authorities

✗ Beginning in 1983 and again in 1992, data reflect improvements in classification. Prior to 1992, *Claims on Central Government (line 12a)* was net of central government deposits.

Deposit Money Banks

✗ Beginning in 1985, data are based on a new bank reporting system. ✗Beginning in 1992, data reflect improvements in classification.

Monetary Survey

✗ See notes on monetary authorities and deposit money banks.

Government Finance

✗ Data for 1972–90 are as reported in the *Government Finance Statistics Yearbook* and cover budgetary central government. ✗ Beginning in 1991, data, also relating to the budgetary central government, are as reported by the Ministry of Finance and Economy.

Suriname

International Transactions

✗ Trade data, which are compiled by the Central Bureau of Statistics, have been updated with the Bank of Suriname balance of payments data on a cash basis for current periods.

Swaziland

Monetary Authorities

✗ Beginning in 1991, the Capital Investment Fund of the central government is included in *line 11*, with a contra-entry in *line 16d*.

Monetary Survey

✗ See note on monetary authorities.

Government Finance

✗ Prior to 1990, data are as reported in the *Government Finance Statistics Yearbook* and cover budgetary central government. Beginning in 1990, data are as reported by the Bank of Swaziland and cover budgetary central government.

Sweden

International Liquidity

✗ *Lines 7a.d, 7b.d, 7e.d,* and *7f.d:* The banks' positions with their branches abroad are included from 1990.

Monetary Authorities

✗ Beginning in 1999, data are based on a revised reporting of accounts.

Deposit Money Banks

✗ Beginning in 1983, data reflect improved classification of accounts. ✗ Beginning in 1996, data on accounts of deposit money banks are not strictly comparable with earlier figures, owing to the adoption of the 1995 European System of Accounts.

Monetary Survey

✗ See notes on monetary authorities and deposit money banks.

Other Banking Institutions

✗ Beginning in 1990 and in 1996, data are based on a revised reporting of accounts.

Banking Survey

✗ See notes on deposit money banks and other banking institutions.

Interest Rates

Discount Rate (End of Period): ✗ Before 1992, rate charged by the Riksbank to commercial banks on short-term loans. Beginning in 1992, the official discount rate is calculated on a quarterly basis as a rounded value of the average of long-term bond rates minus 2.5 percent.

Deposit Rate: ✗ Before 1992, average quarterly rate on savings deposits with the deposit money banks. Beginning in 1992, average deposit rate of the six largest banks, at quarter end.

Lending Rate: ✗ Before 1992, deposit money banks' average lending rate to households at quarter end. Beginning in 1992, average rate of the six largest banks' loans to households, at quarter end.

Prices, Production, Labor

Industrial Employment: ✗ Prior to 1976, series on employed labor force, 16–71 years of age. From 1976, series relates to 16–64 years of age.

International Transactions

✗ Prior to 1977, data refer to exports and imports for which customs documents were processed by the Customs Office during the period. Beginning in 1977, data refer to actual imports and exports of the period.

Government Finance

✗ From 1970 through 1993, data are as reported in the *Government Finance Statistics Yearbook* and refer to a fiscal year ending June 30. ✗ Beginning in 1994, data cover the operations of budgetary central government and are reported by the Central Bureau of Statistics. ✗ From 1994 through 1996, expenditure data are not adjusted to a cash basis.

National Accounts

✗ From 1994 onwards, concepts and definitions are in accordance with the *1995 ESA.*

Switzerland

International Liquidity

✗ Prior to 1974, practices with regard to trustee accounts varied from bank to bank and from time to time, and some accounts that were not recorded in the balance sheets of individual banks are excluded. Banks were required to separate all trustee accounts from their balance sheets by the end of 1974. As a result, the proportion of trustee accounts included in banks' balance sheets declined from about 50 percent at the end of 1971 to 40 percent at the end of 1972 and to 17 percent at the end of 1973. Beginning in 1974, *line 7a.d* includes all foreign investments on behalf of trustee accounts *(line 7k.d)*, and *line 7b.d* includes all funds deposited in trustee accounts by nonresidents *(line 7m.d)*. ✗See note on deposit money banks.

Monetary Authorities

✗Beginning in 1997, *Central Government Deposits (line 16d)* includes deposits of the Swiss Confederation.

Deposit Money Banks

✗ Before 1974, data relate to all banks in Switzerland, with nonresident branches of Swiss banks being consolidated. Beginning in 1974, data relate to resident banks which are subject to minimum reserves on external liabilities. ✗Before 1982, data relate to a similar sample of banks as shown in present data. From 1982, data relate to all banks. ✗ Beginning in 1984, data relate to those banks that are subject to minimum reserves on foreign liabilities only. ✗ From 1996 onward, data reflect a new reporting format.

Monetary Survey

✗ See notes on monetary authorities and deposit money banks.

Other Banking Institutions

✗ From 1996 onward, data reflect a new reporting format.

Interest Rates

Government Bond Yield: ✗ Prior to 1999, data cover government bonds with a maturity of up to 20 years. Beginning in 1999, data refer to the unweighted average yield on government bonds with a maturity of up to 29 years.

International Transactions

✗ Since 1979, trade value data for the volume and unit value of imports include trade of gems, semi-precious stones, and antiques. ✗ Since 1992, trade value data for exports and imports exclude diamonds and precious metals.

Government Finance

✗ Beginning in 1980, debt data were redefined. ✗ Beginning in 1984, federal accounts are harmonized with the cantonal accounting model.

Tanzania

Monetary Authorities

✗ In 1993 substantial revisions were made to the classification of accounts and the compilation of data.

Deposit Money Banks

✗ Beginning in 1989, data are based on an improved sectorization of the accounts. ✗See note on monetary authorities.

Monetary Survey

✗ See notes on monetary authorities and deposit money banks.

Other Banking Institutions

✗ See note on monetary authorities.

Thailand

Deposit Money Banks

✗ In 1976 a new system of bank returns was introduced that led to changes in the coverage of commercial bank data.

Monetary Survey

✗ See note on deposit money banks.

Other Banking Institutions

✗ Beginning in 1974, data are based on a new reporting system, providing an improved sectorization of the accounts.

Banking Survey

✗ See note on other banking institutions. ✗ See note on deposit money banks.

Interest Rates

Money Market Rate: ✗ Beginning in 1989, daily average of commercial banks' overnight rates for interbank lending.

Prices and Labor

Wholesale Prices: ✗ Prior to 1991, the index is computed with 1976 weights. Thereafter, it is computed with 1985 weights. The index is a base-weighted arithmetic average of price relatives and covers 500 items.

Consumer Prices: ✗ For data prior to 1990, the weights (and included items) are derived from a survey conducted in 1986 among families of two to seven persons, residing in urban areas, with monthly family incomes in the range of Baht 2,500–4,000. From 1990 onwards, data and weights are derived from a socioeconomic survey conducted only in urban areas in 1994 among families of two to seven persons with monthly incomes ranging from 6,000 Baht to 36,000 Baht.

Government Finance

✗ Beginning in 1972, data are as reported in the *Government Finance Statistics Yearbook*, cover consolidated central government, and relate to a fiscal year different from calendar year. ✗ Through 1995, extrabudgetary deficits and surpluses are included in domestic borrowing. From 1996 onward, extrabudgetary deficits and surpluses are shown separately above the line and are included in the overall deficit/surplus.

Togo

Exchange Rates

Official Rate (End of Period and *Period Average):* ✗ From 1999 onward, the CFA franc is pegged to the euro at a rate of CFA franc 655.957 per euro. Prior to 1999, the official rate was pegged to the French franc. ✗ In 1994 the CFA franc was devalued to CFAF 100 per French franc from CFAF 50, at which it had been fixed since 1948.

Deposit Money Banks

✗ Beginning in 1979, *Central Government Deposits (line 26d)* include the deposits of public establishments of an administrative or social nature (EPAS) and exclude those of the savings bank; *Demand* and *Time Deposits (lines 24* and *25)* include deposits of the savings bank and exclude deposits of EPAS; and *Claims on Private Sector (line 22d)* exclude claims on other financial institutions.

Monetary Survey

✗ Beginning in 1979, *Claims on Other Financial Institutions (line 32f)* includes claims of deposit money banks on other financial institutions. See note on deposit money banks.

Other Banking Institutions

Liquid Liabilities (line 55l): ✗ See notes on deposit money banks and monetary survey.

Tonga

Interest Rates

Lending Rate: ✗ Beginning in 1993, data refer to the average rate, which is the total interest received and accrued on all performing loans and overdrafts, as of the last business day of the quarter, divided by the average size of the portfolio during the quarter.

Trinidad and Tobago

Monetary Authorities

✗ Beginning in 1996, data are based on an improved sectorization of the accounts.

Deposit Money Banks

✗ See note on monetary authorities.

Monetary Survey

✗ See note on monetary authorities.

Other Banking Institutions

✗ Prior to 1970, data relate to post office savings deposits only. ✗ See note on monetary authorities.

Banking Survey

✗ See note on monetary authorities.

Government Finance

✗ Prior to 1976, data are as reported by the Central Bank for Trinidad and Tobago for publication in *IFS*. Beginning in 1976, data are as reported in the *Government Finance Statistics Yearbook* and cover budgetary central government, statutory bodies, and the National Insurance Board. ✗ Beginning in 1982, data cover budgetary central government only.

Tunisia

Prices, Production, Labor

Producer Prices: ✗ Source B index (as supplied by the National Institute of Statistics), base 1990, covering sections C, D, and E of the International Standard Industrial Classification (ISIC). Prior to 1983, data relate to the wholesale price index.

Government Finance

✗ Beginning in 1985, data for budgetary central government are based on a revised budgetary nomenclature.

Turkey

International Liquidity

✗ See notes on monetary authorities and deposit money banks.

Monetary Authorities

✗ Beginning in 1970, data are based on a more detailed classification of accounts and therefore are not strictly comparable with data for earlier periods. ✗Beginning in 1986, data reflect improved sectoral classification.

Deposit Money Banks

✗ See note on monetary authorities. ✗Beginning in 1996, *Foreign Assets (line 21)* include foreign currency checks received, which were previously recorded in *Other Items (Net) (line 27r)*.

Monetary Survey

✗ See notes on monetary authorities and deposit money banks.

Other Banking Institutions

✗ See note on monetary authorities. ✗Beginning in 1996, *Foreign Assets (line 41)* includes foreign currency checks received, which were previously recorded among *Other Items (Net) (line 47r)*.

Banking Survey

✗ See notes on deposit money banks and other banking institutions.

Prices, Production, Labor

Consumer Prices: ✗ Prior to 1994, source S, general index of cost of living for Turkish urban areas of more than 10,000 persons, base 1987, for households with consumption of 5,000–29,999 liras, developed on the basis of the 1987 Household Income and Consumption Expenditure Survey. Beginning in 1994, the source S CPI is a Laspeyres index, base 1994, covering all cities with a population greater than 20,000. The items and the weights are derived from the 1994 Household Income and Expenditure Survey. The index includes 410 items, which are priced twice monthly (four times each month for vegetables and fruits) from the 35 cities covered. *Industrial Production:* ✗ Beginning in 1992, source S industrial production index base 1992, calculated by main economic activities according to ISIC Rev. 2, using a Laspeyres formula. The index covers mining, manufacturing, electricity, gas, and water. The 122 selected goods represent 60 percent of the value of industrial production. Prior to 1992, source S, index of industrial production, base 1986. The series covers mining, manufacturing, and energy.

Government Finance

✗ Beginning in 1970, data are as reported in the *Government Finance Statistics Yearbook* and cover budgetary central government.

Uganda

International Liquidity

✗ Before 1984, data for *Foreign Exchange (line 1d.d)* were obtained by converting the shilling value of the Bank of Uganda's foreign exchange holdings, as maintained by the Accounts Department of the Bank of Uganda, using the prevailing exchange rate given in *line ae*. Beginning in 1984, data are based on the U.S. dollar value of these assets, as reported by the Foreign Exchange Operations Department of the Bank of Uganda.

Monetary Authorities

✗ Prior to 1983, the main government accounts were shown on a net basis in *Claims on Central Government (line 12a)*. Beginning in 1983, *line 12a* and *Central Government Deposits (line 16d)* are presented on a gross basis. ✗ Data for 1987 onwards are not comparable with prior periods, owing to a reclassification of accounts. For 1987 through 1991, data are available only as of June each year, which is the end of the financial year for the Bank of Uganda.

Monetary Survey

✗ See note on monetary authorities.

Interest Rates

Treasury Bill Rate: ✗ Prior to 1993, rates were determined by the Bank of Uganda. Subsequently, rates are determined at auctions held every two weeks.

Deposit Rate: ✗ Beginning in 1985, rate offered by commercial banks on time deposits of less than 12 months.

Prices

Consumer Prices: ✗ Data for years prior to 1987 are from the consumer price index (CPI) for middle-income households in Kampala (April 1981=100). CPI data for 1987–88 are estimates based on 1989–90 expenditure weights for all households in Kampala and price data gathered by the Statistics Department and Bank of Uganda. Beginning in 1989, consumer prices refer to the CPI for all households in Kampala (with expenditure weights drawn from the Household Budget Survey of 1989–90).

International Transactions

✗ Total exports and imports are compiled by Customs up to 1980 and since then are based on the Marketing Board data.

Government Finance

✗ Beginning in 1972, data are as reported in the *Government Finance Statistics Yearbook* and cover budgetary central government. ✗ Beginning in 1986, data are as reported by the Bank of Uganda for inclusion in *IFS* and continue to cover budgetary central government.

Ukraine

Monetary Authorities

✗ Beginning in 1998, data reflect the introduction of a new accounting system.

Banking Institutions

✗ See note on monetary authorities.

Banking Survey

✗ See note on monetary authorities.

United Kingdom

International Liquidity

✗ From 1985 onwards, deposit money banks' assets *(line 7a.d)* and their claims on nonbanks *(line 7add)* include holdings of bonds issued by nonresidents.

Monetary Authorities

✗ The breaks in the series reflect changes in the coverage of the banking sector referred to in the notes for deposit money banks.

Deposit Money Banks

✗ A new system of bank returns was introduced in 1975. As a result of this change, (1) money at call and money placed overnight are now reported in *line 24* rather than in *line 25*—a shift of approximately 700 million pounds sterling—and (2) *line 21* is estimated to have increased by about 1,300 million pounds sterling. ✗ Beginning in 1981, they comprise the U.K. monetary sector as described in the December 1981 issue of the Bank of England's *Monetary and Financial Statistics,* subject to the same exclusions as the banking sector. ✗ Prior to 1987, building societies are treated as part of the private sector. Beginning in 1987,

comprises U.K. banks authorized under the Banking Act of 1987, the Banking Department of the Bank of England, certain institutions in the Channel Islands and the Isle of Man, and building societies as defined by the Building Societies Act of 1986. ✗ In 1992, a new balance sheet report was introduced for the building society sector within the U.K., resulting in discontinuity for most of the building society data.

Banking Survey

✗ Breaks in series occur as a result of changes in coverage referred to in the notes for deposit money banks.

International Transactions

✗ Prior to 1970, trade indices refer to total unadjusted series. From 1970, trade indices refer to total seasonally adjusted series, base 1995, source S.

Government Finance

✗ Beginning in 1970, data are as reported in the *Government Finance Statistics Yearbook* and cover consolidated central government.

United States

Prices, Production, Labor

Producer Prices: ✗ For data through 1986, the index used implicit quantity weights representing the net selling value of commodities in 1972. The weights were derived from the 1982 shipment values as reported in the Census of Manufactures and other sources for January 1987-December 1991 data. Weights for most traditional commodity groups currently reflect 1987 values of shipments.

Consumer Prices: ✗ Beginning in 1983, the cost of shelter to the homeowner is measured by a rental equivalence, and since 1987, an enhanced housing survey represents optimally both owners and renters in the estimation of shelter costs. ✗ Beginning in 1998, the weights are compiled from the Consumer Expenditure Survey carried out from 1993 through 1995. Reference base 1982–84=100.

International Transactions

✗ Beginning in 1975, data include exports and imports of nonmonetary gold.

Uruguay

Monetary Authorities

✗ Beginning in 1975, data include only the Central Bank accounts which have been generated from the end-of-month issue of provisional balance sheets produced every ten days by the Central Bank of Uruguay. ✗ Beginning in 1982, data for *Long-Term Foreign Liabilities (line 16cl)* include long-term foreign financing and, beginning in 1983, include liabilities relating to external debt refinancing. ✗ Prior to 1982, gold holdings are valued at the historical price of gold, and the gold component of *line 11* is not comparable with *line 1and* converted into national currency. Beginning in 1982, however, the national currency value of gold holdings is based on the national valuation. ✗ Beginning in 1998, data are based on an improved sectorization and classification of the accounts.

Banking Institutions

☓ Beginning in 1975, includes the Bank of the Republic of Uruguay (BROU). ☓ Beginning in 1982, data are based on improved sectorization, which properly distinguishes between resident and nonresident transactions; in addition, data are based on actual, rather than preliminary, information. ☓ Beginning in 1998, comprises private banks, BROU, and the Mortgage Bank of Uruguay (BHU). See note to monetary authorities.

Banking Survey

☓ See notes on monetary authorities and banking institutions.

Government Finance

☓ Beginning in 1972, data are as reported in the *Government Finance Statistics Yearbook* and cover consolidated central government, including extrabudgetary and social security accounts. Data show the transactions of nonfinancial public enterprises on a net basis.

Vanuatu

Monetary Authorities

☓ Prior to 1994, separate data for claims on nonfinancial public enterprises and claims on the private sector were unavailable, and these data were indistinguishably included in *Other Items, Net (line 17r)*.

Monetary Survey

☓ See note on monetary authorities.

Banking Survey

☓ See note on monetary authorities.

Interest Rates

Government Bond Yield: ☓ Prior to 1989, data refer to the yield on three-year maturities. Subsequently, data refer to the yield on ten-year maturities.

Venezuela, Republica Bolivariana de

Monetary Authorities

☓ Beginning in 1987, data are based on an improved reporting system.

Deposit Money Banks

☓ See note on monetary authorities. ☓ Beginning in 1996, data reflect the introduction of a new accounting system, which provides an improved sectorization of the accounts.

Monetary Survey

☓ See notes on monetary authorities and deposit money banks.

Other Banking Institutions

☓ See notes on monetary authorities and deposit money banks.

Banking Survey

☓ See notes on monetary authorities and deposit money banks.

Interest Rates

Lending Rate: ☓ Beginning in 1990, weighted average rate charged by commercial and universal banks on industrial, agricultural, commercial, and car loans in national currency. The rate is weighted by loan amounts.

Prices, Production, Labor

Industrial Share Prices: ☓ Beginning in 1990, the index, base January 1, 1971, refers to the average of daily quotations on the Caracas Stock Exchange. ☓ Beginning in 1994, the index, base December 1993, refers to the average of daily quotations on the Caracas Stock Exchange.

Government Finance

☓ Beginning in 1970, data are as reported in the *Government Finance Statistics Yearbook* and cover, in addition to budgetary central government, some extrabudgetary and social security accounts. ☓ However, operations of social security funds other than the Venezuelan Social Security Institute are covered only beginning in 1983. ☓ For 1987, data cover the budgetary central government only. ☓ Beginning in 1988, data cover the budgetary central government and the Venezuelan Social Security Institute.

Yemen, Republic of

Exchange Rates

Principal Rate (End of Period and *Period Average):* ☓ Effective March 29, 1995, the official rate was changed from YRls 12.01 to YRls 50.04 per U.S. dollar. In addition, a market-determined exchange rate prevails in the money bazaar, which applies to most private transactions.

Zambia

Monetary Authorities

☓ Beginning in 1988, data reflect the introduction of a new accounting system.

Deposit Money Banks

☓ Beginning in 1971, data are based on a new reporting system, which resulted mainly in improved sector classification distinguishing between resident and nonresident accounts and the government and private sectors. ☓ Beginning in 1998, data are based on an improved sectorization of the accounts.

Monetary Survey

☓ See notes on monetary authorities and deposit money banks.

Government Finance

☓ Prior to 1972, data are as reported by the Bank of Zambia for publication in *IFS*. Subsequently, data are as reported in the *Government Finance Statistics Yearbook* ☓ From 1972–85 and from 1989 onwards, data cover budgetary central government only. ☓ From 1986–88, data include certain extrabudgetary accounts.

Zimbabwe

Deposit Money Banks

✗ Prior to 1984, *line 22d* includes claims on state and local governments and claims on public financial enterprises. Subsequently, these claims have been identified and omitted from the series.

Monetary Survey

✗ See note on deposit money banks.

Banking Survey

✗ See note on deposit money banks.

Interest Rates

Bank Rate (End of Period): ✗ Beginning in 1998, rate charged on rediscounted loans and repurchase agreements.

Government Finance

✗ Beginning in 1985, data cover budgetary and extrabudgetary accounts of the central government. Also beginning in 1985, data relate to a fiscal year different from calendar year.